APPLETON'S
REVISED CUYAS DICTIONARY
ENGLISH–SPANISH
SPANISH–ENGLISH

APPLETON'S REVISED

English-Spanish AND *Spanish-English*

DICTIONARY

CONTAINING MORE THAN ONE HUNDRED AND TWENTY
THOUSAND PRINCIPAL AND SUBSIDIARY TERMS,
WITH IDIOMS AND TECHNICAL USAGES;
NEW PRONOUNCING KEYS AND THE
FUNDAMENTAL FORMS OF THE
IRREGULAR VERBS

By

ARTURO CUYAS

Revised and enlarged by

Lewis E. Brett (Part I)

and

**Helen S. Eaton, with the assistance of
Walter Beveraggi-Allende (Part II)**

FOURTH EDITION

A P P L E T O N - C E N T U R Y - C R O F T S , I N C .

NEW YORK

1953

DICCIONARIO REVISADO

Inglés-Español Y *Español-Inglés*

DE APPLETON

CONTIENE MAS DE CIENTO VEINTE MIL VOCABLOS
PRINCIPALES Y SECUNDARIOS, CON MODISMOS Y
VOCES TECNICAS; CLAVES NUEVAS DE PRONUN-
CIACION, Y LAS FORMAS FUNDAMENTALES
DE LOS VERBOS IRREGULARES

por

ARTURO CUYAS

Corregido y aumentado

por

Lewis E. Brett (Parte I)

y

**Helen S. Eaton, con la colaboración de
Walter Beveraggi-Allende (Parte II)**

CUARTA EDICION

APPLETON-CENTURY-CROFTS, INC.

NEW YORK

1953

PARTE I

PART II

PART I

ENGLISH–SPANISH

PARTE I

INGLES–ESPAÑOL

PREFACIO DE LA PRIMERA EDICION

Los prodigiosos descubrimientos e invenciones que marcan el progreso realizado de medio siglo a esta parte en todos los ramos de la actividad humana, y sus múltiples aplicaciones a los usos de la vida, han enriquecido de tal modo el vocabulario de las lenguas modernas, y muy particularmente de la inglesa, que cada día se hace sentir más la necesidad de un diccionario que responda a las exigencias del creciente intercambio de ideas y productos entre los pueblos de la raza anglosajona y los que hablan la armoniosa lengua castellana.

A mediados del siglo XIX vió la luz el diccionario bilingüe de Velázquez, basado sobre el antiguo de Seoane, Neuman y Baretti, y aumentado con multitud de vocablos que lo ponían a la altura de aquella época.

Cuantos diccionarios se han publicado posteriormente, tanto en Europa como en América, han sido meras copias del famoso léxico de Velázquez, o, a lo sumo, revisiones más o menos concienzudas, con aditamento de algunas palabras modernas. Pero, por muy meritorias que sean algunas de esas revisiones, resultan deficientes en la práctica para los que tienen ocasión de consultar con frecuencia el diccionario.

Esa experiencia ha evidenciado la necesidad de compilar un diccionario bilingüe enteramente nuevo, trazado sobre un patrón más moderno y más exacto que el que ha servido para los publicados hasta hoy día.

El propósito a que se ha ajustado la presente obra ha sido reunir en un volumen manuable el más nutrido, completo y correcto vocabulario de los idiomas inglés y español que pueda hallarse en un diccionario bilingüe, descartando un sinnúmero de arcaísmos, vocablos desusados, provincialismos y palabras de incorrecta ortografía de que suelen estar plagados otros diccionarios y que sólo contribuyen a engrosar su tamaño.

Con este fin, y para que el diccionario resulte enteramente nuevo y contenga los más recientes y autorizados neologismos de uno y otro idioma, el autor ha adoptado como base y punto de partida, para la parte española-inglesa, la reciente edición del Diccionario de la Academia, transcribiendo palabra por palabra cuantos vocablos contiene aquel léxico, así como todos los más usuales modismos, con la sola excepción de las voces anticuadas y de las que han caído totalmente en desuso, y anotando los equivalentes ingleses de las diversas acepciones de cada palabra. Igual procedimiento se ha seguido para la parte inglesa-española, sirviendo de base el admirable *Standard Dictionary*, también de reciente publicación, cuyos vocablos, acepciones y modismos se han transcrito con sus equivalencias castellanas.

El convencimiento de que el oficio y la verdadera utilidad de todo diccionario bilingüe consisten en dar equivalencias en lugar de definiciones, que en nada auxilian al traductor y que éste puede buscar en el diccionario de su propio idioma, ha hecho necesaria una cuidadosa y ardua labor de investigación para hallar los equivalentes exactos en una y otra lengua, especialmente de las voces de tecnología científica y de los tecnicismos mercantiles e industriales que en gran número se han incluído en esta obra, por considerarlos de suma utilidad, dado el creciente desarrollo de las relaciones entre los Estados Unidos y los países hispanoamericanos.

Para tener una idea de lo nutrida que va esta obra en punto a tecnicismos, bastará cotejar las voces cuyas raíces son *electr-*, *hydr-*, *micro-*, *photo-*, con las de otros diccionarios bilingües, sin contar los innumerables términos que figuran entre las acepciones de muchos vocablos y cuyo carácter técnico se indica por medio de una abreviatura entre paréntesis, lo cual, sobre economizar espacio y hacer inútiles otras explicaciones, es de gran auxilio para el traductor.

En otro punto esencial difiere esta obra de todos los diccionarios bilingües publicados hasta la fecha, y es en el sistema de anotación fonética adoptado para representar la pronunciación inglesa. Tras un estudio detenido de este importantísimo punto y después de examinar cuidadosamente los sistemas adoptados en otros diccionarios, el autor ha formulado uno enteramente nuevo que se expone a continuación, en el cual ha procurado simplificar las dificultades que presenta la pronunciación inglesa, reduciéndolas a una clave breve, sencilla y de fácil aplicación.*

Multum in parvo ha sido el ideal que ha perseguido el autor en la compilación de esta obra, y al logro de este empeño han coadyuvado eficazmente los editores produciendo un libro que contiene, en forma compacta y de esmerada tipografía, mayor suma de información que otros voluminosos diccionarios.

Arturo Cuyás.

* Nueva York, *julio de 1903.*

PREFACIO DE LA NUEVA EDICION

Esta edición (la cuarta) del diccionario de Cuyás, en su parte primera, "Inglés-Español", es fruto de varios años de esfuerzo asiduo y representa, en el sentido más estricto de la palabra, una revisión completa de las anteriores. Con el fin de modernizar todos los aspectos de la misma, se ha revisado escrupulosamente cada uno de los términos que lo componen, de acuerdo con las autoridades máximas para las dos lenguas.

Con respecto a las autoridades inglesas, puede recordarse aquí que Cuyás basaba su obra en el *Standard Dictionary*, en tanto que Antonio Llano, en su revisión de ella, adoptó el *New International Dictionary* de Webster, aunque consultó también obras como el *Century* y el *Oxford*. La presente edición, necesariamente teniendo muy en cuenta el material ya existente, ha sacado provecho también de su referencia continua al *New Century Dictionary* y a otros de reciente publicación. Para la parte española se han consultado la última edición del *Diccionario* de la Academia, así como el de José Alemany, el *Pequeño Larousse ilustrado*, la grande *Enciclopedia Espasa-Calpe*, el *Diccionario general de americanismos*, de Santamaría, y especialmente la muy moderna y completa obra Sapiens, *Enciclopedia ilustrada de la lengua castellana*. También se han estudiado con provecho numerosas obras técnicas, revistas y diccionarios que tratan de materias más especializadas (derecho, medicina, química, comercio, arte, pedagogía, etc.), tomando de allí neologismos que se usan corrientemente en sus respectivos campos, aunque no se encuentran todavía en los diccionarios usuales.

Por otra parte, la experiencia de muchos años de cátedra, de publicaciones y de viajes y estudios en el extranjero me han sugerido la inclusión de multitud de vocablos, modismos y otras expresiones de gran utilidad no ya sólo para el estudiante o lector ocasional sino también para el investigador serio o traductor escrupuloso que busca, y a menudo necesita, matices precisos en el sentido y el uso de las expresiones. En suma, se han tenido en cuenta constantemente las necesidades de cuantos buscan una guía en una de las tareas más difíciles y delicadas: la de verter una lengua en otra; y se ha hecho todo lo posible para ayudarles a evitar muchos de los escollos encontrados en su labor.   Para ello no sólo se han añadido miles de expresiones nuevas, sino que muy a menudo se ha dado a los términos existentes un orden más lógico; se ha tenido gran esmero en hacer resaltar los grupos que guardan relación entre sí mediante una puntuación clara e inequívoca; en lo posible se han indicado las preposiciones adecuadas, y para facilitar la rápida identificación de los usos especiales de un vocablo se han puesto entre paréntesis las palabras explicatorias. Asimismo se verá que para muchos vocablos se ha encontrado y dado por primera vez aquí el equivalente exacto en español, sustituyendo la antigua circunlocución o palabra sinónima.

Todavía otros cambios pueden mencionarse brevemente.   En esta revisión se ha incorporado en el cuerpo de la obra la masa considerable de materias que antes figuraba en el *Suplemento*.   Asimismo se ha aumentado notablemente el número de abreviaturas que figuran en el texto mismo para denotar las partes de la oración y la función gramatical de ciertas voces, o para indicar el uso técnico y especializado de otras.   Este sistema utilísimo que ya se inició en el Cuyás original se ha extendido hasta abarcar muchos centenares de casos adicionales, contribuyendo así a precisar la acepción o función exacta de un vocablo determinado.   Y se han extendido además las materias presentadas en el *Apéndice*, v. gr., la lista de nombres geográficos, la de nombres propios ordinarios de personas y nombres de personajes notables, y la de abreviaturas más usuales.

Otra innovación de la presente edición, de gran utilidad, es el método sencillísimo que se ha ideado para indicar el género de los substantivos—indicación punto menos que indispensable para la correcta versión del inglés al español.   Los detalles de esta innovación se hallan en la ADVERTENCIA (pág. xxviii).

Finalmente, uno de los aspectos en que se ha mejorado más la presente edición es un sistema completamente nuevo de anotación fonética que permite una pronunciación mucho más exacta del inglés de lo que ha sido posible hasta ahora en cualquier diccionario inglés-español.   Después de varias tentativas de adaptación del sistema Cuyás y de las modificaciones introducidas en ediciones posteriores parecía aconsejable formular un sistema virtualmente nuevo.   En esta tarea han colaborado valiosamente ciertos miembros del *Department of Speech*, de Queens College, particularmente las profesoras Dr. Beatrice Jacoby y Dr. Lois Rossignol Mayper, quienes además de contribuir a la elaboración del sistema fonético usado en esta edición han efectuado gran parte de la labor necesaria para las nuevas transcripciones fonéticas de cada uno de los vocablos incluídos en este diccionario. Para una explicación detallada del nuevo sistema, véase la sección *Pronunciación inglesa* y su *clave* correspondiente (páginas xiv-xv).

Al terminar este prefacio el autor desea expresar su profundo agradecimiento a cuantos de un modo u otro han contribuído generosamente en la preparación de esta revisión. Entre ellos figuran sus colegas los doctores y profesores Isabel Brugada, Zenia Da Silva, Frederick Fales, Angel Flores, Francisco García-Lorca, Helena Percas y Juan Sesplugues.

LEWIS E. BRETT.

Queens College, New York.

PRONUNCIACION INGLESA

El alfabeto inglés consta de 26 letras, de las cuales cinco son vocales, veinte consonantes y una—la *y*—puede, como en español, hacer ambos oficios.

Pero, al paso que el alfabeto español tiene 28 letras para expresar los 25 sonidos que constituyen la fonética del idioma, las 26 letras del alfabeto inglés no bastan para representar los numerosos sonidos que se emplean en la complicada pronunciación de esa lengua. Ni siquiera están acordes los ortólogos ingleses respecto del número de sonidos de su fonética, ascendiendo éstos, según ciertos peritos, a 43 o 46 sonidos distintos, casi la mitad de ellos asignados a las solas vocales. Hasta en la pronunciación de numerosas palabras están en desacuerdo lexicógrafos ingleses de reconocida autoridad, por no haber reglas generales que determinen la recta pronunciación de los vocablos. Agrávase la confusión y auméntanse las dificultades por ser tan caprichosa a menudo la ortografía inglesa.

Son tantas, en efecto, las dificultades prosódicas que presenta el idioma, que los lexicógrafos ingleses se ven en la necesidad de representar en sus diccionarios la correcta pronunciación de cada vocablo por medio de una clave fonética. Pero tampoco en esto se encuentra concordancia en los varios léxicos, porque cada uno de ellos ha adoptado un sistema de representación fonética distinto que exige larga y detallada explicación. Y si esto es así tratándose de diccionarios destinados a personas para quienes el inglés es idioma vernáculo, resulta doblemente necesaria alguna explicación gráfica de los sonidos ingleses a personas de habla distinta, para quienes muchos de esos sonidos son desconocidos y de difícil pronunciación.

Por eso presentamos aquí un nuevo sistema de representación fonética destinado a indicar la pronunciación casi exacta de todas las palabras inglesas que figuran en este diccionario. Con el doble fin de evitar los extremos de una simplificación peligrosa y de un refinamiento excesivo, hemos procurado usar símbolos fonéticos (entre los cuales entran bastantes letras del alfabeto ordinario, de inmediata comprensión por parte del lector de habla española) sacados en su mayor parte del alfabeto fonético de la Asociación Fonética Internacional, de aceptación universal. Sólo unos pocos fueron tomados de otros sistemas, *cada*, pero más interdental, fuerte y largo, y por lo tanto menos relajado. Ejemplos: **this, that, them, there, although.**

(2) El signo fonético [θ] representa un sonido parecido al de la *c* o *z* castellana en *vecino*, *zorra*, pero menos interdental y menos enérgico: lo tiene en la mayoría de los casos. Ejemplos: **theatre, thick, throat, both, truth, worth, youth.**

§ 13. *wh* = [h] *o* [hw]

(1) El signo fonético [h] representa un sonido que es una aspiración laríngea bastante más suave que la de la *j* española: lo tienen pocas palabras, en que es verdaderamente muda la *w*. Ejemplos: **who, whole, whoop.**

(2) El signo fonético [hw] representa un sonido que combina el de la *h* con el de la *w* (o sea, la *u* española en *cuatro* o la *ou* francesa de *oui*): lo tiene la *wh* en la mayoría de los casos. Ejemplos: **what, when, white, whopper, why.** En el habla corriente se pierde a veces el elemento de *h*, quedando tan sólo la *w*.

§ 14. *n* = [ŋ]

El signo fonético [ŋ] representa un sonido parecido al de la *n* española en *banco*, *lengua*: lo tiene la *n* cuando va seguida del sonido de la *k* o de una *g* velar, que a veces se pierden en la pronunciación. Ejemplos: **anchor, anxious, drink, think; angle, English, gong, sing, tongue.**

ALFABETO INGLES

No obstante lo expuesto, sería incompleta nuestra labor si no apuntásemos a continuación, siquiera someramente y por vía de inventario, los diversos sonidos que tienen cada letra del alfabeto inglés, los diptongos y triptongos, y algunas otras combinaciones. Entiéndase que lo dicho en cuanto a los casos en que las letras tienen los sonidos expresados son sólo generalidades, no *reglas*. En inglés no hay reglas de pronunciación.

I. LETRAS

Letra	Nombre fonético	Signo fonético	Sonidos	Ejemplos
a	eį		tiene ocho sonidos, prescindiendo de ciertas gradaciones difíciles de distinguir; a saber:	
"	"	[a]	(1) sonido parecido al de la *a* española en *caso*, que a veces se acerca a la *a* velar de *bajo*. Es de notar que en muchas palabras como **quality, wander, watch,** etc., la vocal acentuada suele o puede pronunciarse también con el sonido representado por [ɔ] (véase § 4), o con un sonido que fluctúa entre la [a] y la [ɔ].	car, art, army, calm, gargle, father; quality, quantity, squat, wander, wash, watch.
"	"	[æ]	(2) sonido descrito en § 1.	has, man, that, balcony.

Letra	Nombre fonético	Signo fonético	Sonidos	Ejemplos
”	”	[ε]	(3) sonido descrito en § 2.	any, many; bare, daring.
”	”	[ei]	(4) sonido de la *ei* española en *seis*. Se oye como diptongo sobre todo cuando la vocal es tónica.	baby, bale, case, fame, say, table, (fe)male.
”	”	[ɔ]	(5) sonido descrito en § 4.	all, almighty, call, quart, war, ward.
”	”	[a̯]	(6) sonido algo parecido al descrito arriba (4), más breve y atenuado, pero sin pérdida completa de su calidad distintiva: ocurre sólo en sílabas inacentuadas.	centenary, certain, legitimacy, militarism.
”	”	[a̯]	(7) sonido vago e impreciso de la vocal mencionada arriba (2): se encuentra sólo en posición átona.	attire, errant, final, fiscal.
”	”	[ä̯]	(8) sonido que representa una articulación muy relajada de la vocal descrita arriba (1): se encuentra las más veces al final de sílaba inacentuada o delante de *r*.	forward, opera, sofa, cellar.
b	bi	[b]	(1) sonido de la *b* española en *lumbre*.	babble, baby, bobbin.
”	”		(2) es muda cuando va seguida de *t* o precedida de *m* en la misma sílaba.	debt, doubt(ful); comb(er), lamb(kin).
c	si	[k]	(1) sonido de la *c* española en *casa*: lo tiene cuando va seguida de *a, o, u* o una consonante, excepto a veces en la combinación *ch*. (Véase § 8, y la parte IV de este ALFABETO INGLES).	car, corn, cut, clam, crib, fact, chaos, ache, acme.
”	”	[s]	(2) sonido de la *s* española en *sala*: lo tiene generalmente delante de *e, i, y*, o *e* muda.	cent, city, society, fancy, place, benefice.
”	”	[ŝ]	(3) sonido descrito en § 8. Lo tiene delante de *e* o *i* en ciertos casos.	ocean, social, beneficial, precious.
”	”		(4) la *c* es muda cuando va precedida de *s* y va seguida de *e, i*, o *y*.	abscess, scent, science, scion, scythe.
d	di	[d]	(1) sonido de la *d* española en *onda*: lo tiene en la mayoría de los casos.	den, did, dude, cadet, add, meddle.

Letra	Nombre fonético	Signo fonético	Sonidos	Ejemplos
"	"	[t]	(2) sonido de la *t* española en *tus* más una aspiración laríngea: lo tiene en los tiempos pretéritos y los participios terminados en *ed*, cuando precede una consonante sorda.	fixed, advanced, bare-faced, beached, disliked.
"	"	[dž]	(3) sonido descrito en § 11.	arduous, grandeur.
e	i		tiene siete sonidos, prescindiendo de ciertas gradaciones difíciles de distinguir; a saber:	
"	"	[ɛ]	(1) sonido descrito en § 2.	bell, let, mend, epidemic.
"	"	[ei]	(2) sonido de la *ei* española en *seis*; ocurre en muy pocas palabras, generalmente de origen francés.	crochet, café, éclair, éclat, étude, eight(een).
"	"	[œ]	(3) sonido descrito en § 3.	her, discern, person, term.
"	"	[i]	(4) sonido descrito en § 6.	be, she, adhesion, deem, peep.
"	"	[i̯]	(5) sonido descrito en § 6.	been, blanket, affected; mere, deer.
"	"	[ē]	(6) sonido algo parecido al mencionado arriba (4), muy breve y atenuado, pero sin pérdida completa de su calidad distintiva: ocurre sólo en sílabas inacentuadas.	adequate, courtesy, disintegrate, senility.
"	"	[e̜]	(7) sonido vago e impreciso de la vocal mencionada arriba (1): ocurre sólo en sílaba inacentuada.	ardent, accident, gravel, lacerate.
"	"		(8) la *e* es muda al final de dicción o sílaba en muchas palabras sin regla fija.	face, lie, rue, sense, ladle, here(after), table(spoon).
f	ɛf	[f]	sonido parecido al de la *f* española en *fama*, pero labiodental en vez de bilabial: lo tiene siempre.	far, fell, fib, fulfill, roof.
g	dži	[g]	(1) sonido semejante al de la *g* española en *tengo*: lo tiene en la mayoría de los casos.	agnostic, anger, begin, get, gone, gun, glass, grit.
"	"	[dž]	(2) sonido descrito en § 11.	gem, gin, gymnast.
"	"	[ž]	(3) sonido descrito en § 10.	mirage, rouge.
"	"		(4) la *g* es muda cuando va seguida de *m* o *n* en la misma sílaba.	paradigm; gnat, gnome, design, malign.

Letra	Nombre fonético	Signo fonético	Sonidos	Ejemplos
h	eįch	[h]	(1) sonido que es una aspiración laríngea, bastante más suave que la j española: lo tiene cuando forma principio de dicción o de sílaba.	here, hum, abhor, behave.
"	"		(2) la h es muda en algunas palabras sin regla fija. (Para las combinaciones ch, gh, ph, rh, sh, th, y wh, véanse §§ 12, 13 y la parte IV de este ALFABETO INGLES.)	chaos, ghost, rhetoric, myrrh, messiah, John, Thomas.
i	aį		tiene cuatro sonidos, prescindiendo de ciertas gradaciones difíciles de distinguir; a saber:	
"	"	[i]	(1) sonido descrito en § 6.	machine, police, valise.
"	"	[į]	(2) sonido descrito en § 6.	bridge, pin, finish, mirror.
"	"	[aį]	(3) sonido de la a española en caso más el de la i de sin.	high, life, time; fire, admire, wire, wiry.
"	"	[œ]	(4) sonido descrito en § 3.	fir, bird, first, stir, third, virgin, flirt(atious).
j	dżeį	[dż]	sonido descrito en § 11.	join, judge, juice, major.
k	keį	[k]	(1) sonido igual al de la c española en casa: lo tiene en todos los casos menos cuando es muda.	joke, kill, oak.
"	"		(2) la k es muda cuando precede a una n.	knight, knew, knot.
l	ɛl	[l]	(1) sonido semejante al de la l española en lado, pero más velar: lo tiene en la mayoría de los casos.	lard, ale, cold, salad, molten, talc, almoner, call, small.
"	"		(2) la l es muda cuando va seguida de f, k, m o v, y en otros casos sin regla fija.	calf, calves, caulk, chalk, talk, becalm, palm, alms; could, should, would.
m	ɛm	[m]	sonido igual al de la m española en mano: lo tiene en todos los casos, excepto en mnemonics, donde es muda.	amount, cameo, ham, man.
n	ɛn	[n]	(1) sonido igual al de la n española en nota: lo tiene en la mayoría de los casos.	any, can, done, no, nun.
"	"	[ŋ]	(2) sonido descrito en § 14.	anchor, angle, singing, sink.

Letra	Nombre fonético	Signo fonético	Sonidos	Ejemplos
,,	,,		(3) la *n* es muda al final de dicción cuando va precedida de *m* en la misma sílaba. Como caso aislado la palabra **kiln** se pronuncia a discreción *kil* o *kiln*.	condemn, limn.
o	oụ		tiene diez sonidos, prescindiendo de ciertas gradaciones difíciles de distinguir; a saber:	
,,	,,	[o]	(1) sonido de la *o* española en *sola* pero más breve: suele tenerlo en posición átona.	obey, obese, notation, nobility, polemic.
,,	,,	[oụ]	(2) sonido que combina el de la *o* española de *sola* con el de la *u* española en *burro*: lo tiene en posición tónica, y a menudo al final de dicción aun en posición átona.	alone, dole, bold, colt, mode, note, poll, motive; Negro, tango, tempo.
,,	,,	[ɔ]	(3) sonido descrito en § 4.	cost, loft, song; for, horse; fore, four, floor.
,,	,,	[œ]	(4) sonido descrito en § 3. Lo tiene delante de una *r*, en palabras o sílabas que principian con *w*.	word, worm, worship, figwort.
,,	,,	[u]	(5) sonido descrito en § 7.	do, to, too, two, food, hoop, fool, cool, tomb.
,,	,,	[ụ]	(6) sonido descrito en § 7.	cook, foot, good, wood, would, wolf, woman.
,,	,,	[ʌ]	(7) sonido descrito en § 5.	come, done, ton, won, blood, flood, mother, oven.
,,	,,	[a]	(8) sonido parecido al de la *a* española en *caso*, pero más breve: lo tiene sin regla fija en muchas palabras, todas las cuales pueden o suelen pronunciarse también con un sonido que fluctúa entre la [a] y la [ɔ].	cobble, dock, got, hot, modern.
,,	,,	[aụ]	(9) sonido que combina el de la *a* española en *caso* con el de la *u* española en *burro*. Forma un verdadero diptongo y se pronuncia así en muchas palabras sin regla fija, donde la *o* va seguida de una *u* o *w* muda.	house, mouth, hour; cow, how, now, powder.

Letra	Nombre fonético	Signo fonético	Sonidos	Ejemplos
"	"	[ǫ]	(10) denota una articulación relajada de los sonidos representados por los signos fonéticos [o], [ɔ], [ʌ] y [a] descritos arriba (1, 3, 7, 8): se encuentra sólo en posición átona.	succotash; factor, flavor; abbot, atom, mission, station; obscure, occur, connect.
p	pi	[p]	(1) sonido parecido al de la p española en *pan*, añadiendo una aspiración laríngea: lo tiene en todos los casos menos cuando es muda.	apart, map, people, pepper, sop, top.
"	"		(2) la p es muda cuando precede a una n, s, t al principio de dicción o sílaba.	pneumonia; psalm, pseudo, pshaw, psychology; ptomaine.
q	kịu	[kw]	(1) sonido igual al de la cu española en *cual*: lo tiene en todos los casos cuando va seguida de una u que se pronuncia.	acquire, inquire, quality, queen, quit, quote, request.
"	"	[k]	(2) sonido de la qu española en *que*: lo tiene cuando va seguida de una u muda.	antique, coquette, masquerade, piquant, lacquer, Basque.
r	ar	[r]	sonido fricativo, distinto no sólo de la simple r vibrante del español sino también de su variante fricativa. Se pronuncia sin vibración alguna, y la rr inglesa es igual a la r simple excepto en las combinaciones como **earring, far-reaching**, etc. Suele perderse en muchísimos casos en el habla corriente; v. gr., en palabras aisladas como **iron, irony** (pero no en **ironical**); delante de una o más consonantes (**hark, north, sparks**); delante de e muda (**fire, bare, core, pure**); y especialmente en la sílaba final de palabras que terminan en vocal inacentuada más r (**dollar, pitcher, color, satyr**). Pero se oye la r siempre que va eslabonada con una vocal siguiente que se pronuncia (**coloring, bearable, purify, laborer, mother and child**, etc.). Por eso la transcripción fonética que damos en este diccionario indica entre paréntesis la r final que se pronuncia o no según las circunstancias; por ej., **color**, kʌ́lǫ(r).	rat, rose, berate; arrogant, marriage, merry; car, far; care, mire, fear, poor; barter, suitor.

Letra	Nombre fonético	Signo fonético	Sonidos	Ejemplos
s	es	[s]	(1) sonido de la s española en *sala*, pero más tenso y más largo: lo tiene siempre al principio de dicción; generalmente cuando se escribe *ss*, y en muchas palabras sin regla fija.	satire, settle, sin, son, sun; lass, missive; us, yes, also, ask, castle.
"	"	[z]	(2) sonido descrito en § 9.	has, noise, dregs.
"	"	[ŝ]	(3) sonido descrito en § 8.	mission, fissure.
"	"	[ẑ]	(4) sonido descrito en § 10.	pleasure, vision.
"	"		(5) la s es muda en algunas palabras sin regla fija.	demesne, island, viscount.
t	ti	[t]	(1) sonido parecido al de la t española en *tal*, pero la punta de la lengua se retira hacia los alvéolos y se añade una aspiración laríngea: lo tiene en la mayoría de los casos.	amount, cat, grotto, master, tea, title, total, tub.
"	"	[ch]	(2) sonido de la ch española en *mucho*: lo tiene en la terminación *ture*, y en otros casos sin regla fija.	furniture, picture; actual, christian, virtuous, natural, catch.
"	"	[ŝ]	(3) sonido descrito en § 8.	action, partial.
"	"		(4) la t es muda en ciertas palabras sin regla fija.	often, soften; hasten, listen; castle, bustle.
u	yu, ịu		tiene ocho sonidos, prescindiendo de ciertas gradaciones difíciles de distinguir; a saber:	
"	"	[u]	(1) sonido de la u española en *suyo*. Conviene notar que existen muchas palabras para las cuales no hay regla determinada que indique cuándo se pronuncia la [u] pura, o bien un sonido representado por [ịu] o [yu] (véase el número 2 a continuación). En ciertos casos son igualmente correctas o aceptables las tres pronunciaciones; por ej., **duty** = dútị, dịútị, dyútị. Pero hay casos en que nunca se oye la [u] pura; v. gr., **music, mute, muse, accuse.**	ruby, rude, rumor, rule, ruse, tuna.

Letra	Nombre fonético	Signo fonético	Sonidos	Ejemplos
"	"	[iu] [iu̯] o [yu][yu̯]	(2) sonidos que corresponden respectivamente a los de *ciudad* y *yugo* en español, la [i̯] teniendo articulación semivocal y la [y] siendo de articulación semiconsonante. Debe observarse que en posición átona o delante de una *r*, la [u] de este diptongo adquiere a menudo el valor abierto de la [u̯]. En la práctica, sin embargo, tan escasa resulta la diferencia entre estos sonidos que se pueden usar casi indiferentemente, excepto que para las palabras que comienzan con la vocal *u* en inglés se usará siempre aquí el signo fonético [yu] o [yu̯].	accuse, confusion, music, mute, pupil; united, use; cure, curious, fury, furious, pure, purify.
"	"	[u̯]	(3) sonido descrito en § 7.	bull, bush, pull, pulpit, put, plural, sure, umlaut.
"	"	[œ]	(4) sonido descrito en § 3.	burn, current, fur, hurt.
"	"	[ʌ]	(5) sonido descrito en § 5.	crush, just, public, rumble, supper, under.
"	"	[ɛ]	(6) sonido descrito en § 2. Ocurre en pocos casos.	bury, burial, burier.
"	"	[ū]	(7) sonido parecido al descrito arriba (2), muy breve y atenuado, pero sin pérdida completa de su calidad distintiva: ocurre sólo en sílabas inacentuadas.	commensurate, corduroy, secular, tabular.
"	"	[ṳ]	(8) sonido semejante al descrito anteriormente (7), pero más relajado.	censure, natural, transfigure.
"	"		(9) la *u* es muda en muchas palabras cuando va precedida de *g* o *q*, sin regla fija, o cuando va seguida de *y*.	guard, guess, guide; antique, coquette, masquerade; buy, guy.
v	vi	[v]	sonido parecido al de la *v* española en *ave*, pero labiodental en vez de bilabial: lo tiene siempre.	advice, over, velvet, vivid.
w	dʌblyu o dʌb(l)iu̯	[w]	(1) sonido igual al de la *u* española en *cuatro*, o al de la *ou* francesa en *oui*: lo tiene en la mayoría de los casos.	we, win, worm, awake, swoon, backward.
"	"		(2) la *w* es muda cuando va seguida de *r* a principio de dicción o de sílaba, y en ciertas palabras sin regla fija.	write, wrong, unwritten; answer, sword, who, whole, follow, elbow, owe.

Letra	Nombre fonético	Signo fonético	Sonidos	Ejemplos
"	"		(3) para el sonido de *wh* en ciertas palabras, véase § 13.	
x	ɛks	[ks]	(1) sonido parecido al de la *x* española en *flexión* o *examen*, en dicción fuerte o enfática: lo tiene cuando precede a una consonante; cuando es final de dicción, y generalmente cuando precede a una vocal inacentuada.	next, sexton, excuse, extoll; box, ox, tax; execution, exegesis.
"	"	[gz]	(2) sonido que combina el de la *g* fricativa con el de la *z* (véase § 9): lo tiene generalmente cuando precede a una vocal tónica.	exact, examine, example, exist.
"	"	[ŝ]	(3) sonido descrito en § 8.	anxious.
"	"	[z]	(4) sonido descrito en § 9.	xylophone, xanthic, anxiety.
y	waį		tiene cuatro sonidos, tres como vocal y uno como consonante; a saber:	
"	"	[į]	(1) sonido descrito en § 6.	lyric, pyramid, fancy, very.
"	"	[aį]	(2) sonido que combina el de la *a* española en *caso* con el de la *i* española en *sin*.	by, sky, dye, style, type, nylon, typhoon, lyre.
"	"	[œ]	(3) sonido descrito en § 3.	myrrh, myrtle.
"	"	[y]	(4) sonido semejante al de la *y* española en *ayer*, pero más relajado: lo tiene como consonante, o sea, cuando empieza una palabra o sílaba.	year, yard, yes; halyard.
"	"		(5) la *y* es muda cuando es final de dicción o de sílaba y va precedida de una vocal pronunciada.	day, say, whey; saying, daytime.
z	zi	[z]	(1) sonido descrito en § 9.	prize, size, zeal.
"	"	[ż]	(2) sonido descrito en § 10.	azure, seizure.

II. DIPTONGOS

ae	tiene a veces el sonido de	[ei]	. . . . .	maelstrom
"	"	"	"	[ɛ]	. . . . .	anæsthesia
"	"	"	"	[i]	. . . . .	Caesarism
ai	"	"	"	[eį]	. . . . .	train, claim
"	"	"	"	[æ]	. . . . .	plaid
"	"	"	"	[ɛ]	. . . . .	said, again, chair

II. DIPTONGOS (*continuación*)

"	tiene a veces el sonido de	[ai̯]	. . . . .	aisle
ao	" " "	[ei̯]	. . . . .	gaol
au	" " "	[ɔ]	. . . . .	fraud, fault, launch
"	" " "	[ei̯]	. . . . .	gauge
"	" " "	[ou̯]	. . . . .	hautboy, hauteur
aw	" " "	[ɔ]	. . . . .	law, awl, raw
ay	" " "	[ei̯]	. . . . .	ray, say
"	" " "	[ɛ]	. . . . .	says [sɛz], prayer
"	" " "	[ai̯]	. . . . .	aye
ea	" " "	[a]	. . . . .	heart, hearth
"	" " "	[ei̯]	. . . . .	break, great
"	" " "	[ɛ]	. . . . .	bread, instead, pear
"	" " "	[i]	. . . . .	leaf, clean
"	" " "	[i̯ o i]	. . . . .	fear, near, rear
"	" " "	[œ]	. . . . .	earth, hearse
ee	" " "	[i]	. . . . .	feel, need
"	" " "	[i̯ o i]	. . . . .	been; cheer, career
ei	" " "	[ai̯]	. . . . .	height
"	" " "	[ɛ]	. . . . .	heifer, heir, their
"	" " "	[ei̯]	. . . . .	reign, eight
"	" " "	[i]	. . . . .	seize, deceive
"	" " "	[i]	. . . . .	mullein
eo	" " "	[ɛ]	. . . . .	leopard
"	" " "	[i]	. . . . .	people
"	" " "	[ou̯]	. . . . .	yeoman
"	" " "	[ə]	. . . . .	surgeon, dungeon
eu	" " "	[i̯u]	. . . . .	feud, deuce
"	" " "	[u]	. . . . .	maneuver
ew	" " "	[i̯u o u]	. . . . .	blew, flew, dew
"	" " "	[i̯u]	. . . . .	few
"	" " "	[yu]	. . . . .	ewe
"	" " "	[ou̯]	. . . . .	sew
ey	" " "	[ai̯]	. . . . .	eye, geyser
"	" " "	[ei̯]	. . . . .	whey, they, obey
"	" " "	[ɛ o i̯]	. . . . .	eyrie
"	" " "	[i]	. . . . .	key
ie	" " "	[ai̯]	. . . . .	tie, pie, die
"	" " "	[e]	. . . . .	friend
"	" " "	[i]	. . . . .	fiend, mien
"	" " "	[i̯ o i]	. . . . .	sieve; gonfalonier, cashier
io	" " "	[ə]	. . . . .	question, million
oa	" " "	[ɔ]	. . . . .	broad
"	" " "	[ou̯]	. . . . .	road, load
oe	" " "	[i]	. . . . .	foetus, amoeba
"	" " "	[ou̯]	. . . . .	doe, foe, hoe, toe
"	" " "	[ʌ]	. . . . .	does (*verb*)
"	" " "	[u]	. . . . .	shoe, canoe
oi	" " "	[ɔi̯]	. . . . .	oil
"	" " "	[wai̯]	. . . . .	choir
"	" " "	[ʌ]	. . . . .	porpoise
oo	" " "	[ɔ u o̤u̯]	. . . . .	floor, door
"	" " "	[o̤u̯ o u]	. . . . .	brooch
"	" " "	[u]	. . . . .	doom, noon, broom
"	" " "	[ṳ]	. . . . .	crook, look, poor
"	" " "	[ʌ]	. . . . .	blood, flood
ou	" " "	[au̯]	. . . . .	loud, count
"	" " "	[ɔ u o̤u̯]	. . . . .	court, course
"	" " "	[ɔ]	. . . . .	fought, bought
"	" " "	[ʌ]	. . . . .	touch, young

II. DIPTONGOS (*continuación*)

,,	tiene a veces el sonido de [u]	.	.	.	.	.	coupé, coup, troupe
,,	,, ,, ,, ,,	[ų]					could, should
,,	,, ,, ,, ,,	[œ]					courage
,,	,, ,, ,, ,,	[ǫ]					labour
ow	,, ,, ,, ,,	[aų]	.	.	.	.	cow, down
,,	,, ,, ,, ,,	[oų]	.	.	.	.	low, crow, know
,,	,, ,, ,, ,,	[ɔ o a]	.	.	.	.	knowledge
oy	,, ,, ,, ,,	[ɔį]	.	.	.	.	toy, boy
ua	,, ,, ,, ,,	[weį]	.	.	.	.	suasion, persuade
,,	,, ,, ,, ,,	[wa o weį]	.	.	.	suave
ue	,, ,, ,, ,,	[įu]	.	.	.	.	cue
,,	,, ,, ,, ,,	[įu o u]	.	.	.	due, pursue
,,	,, ,, ,, ,,	[u]	.	.	.	.	true, rue, flue
ui	,, ,, ,, ,,	[i]	.	.	.	.	build, guilt
,,	,, ,, ,, ,,	[u o įu]	.	.	.	juice, suit, fruit
uy	,, ,, ,, ,,	[aį]	.	.	.	.	buy, guy
ye	,, ,, ,, ,,	[aį]	.	.	.	.	lye, bye

III. TRIPTONGOS

eau	tiene a veces el sonido de [oų]	.	.	.	.	.	beau
,,	,, ,, ,, ,,	[įu]	.	.	.	.	beautiful
eue	,, ,, ,, ,,	[įu]	.	.	.	.	queue
ieu	,, ,, ,, ,,	[įu o u]	.	.	.	.	adieu
iew	,, ,, ,, ,,	[įu]	.	.	.	.	view
uay	,, ,, ,, ,,	[i]	.	.	.	.	quay
,,	,, ,, ,, ,,	[weį o waį]	.	.	.	Paraguay

IV. OTRAS COMBINACIONES

ch	tiene a veces el sonido de *ch* en *mucho*	. . .	church, child
,,	,, ,, ,, ,, [k] (o sea, la *c* en *casa*)		ache, chaos, scheme
,,	,, ,, ,, ,, [ŝ] (véase § 8) . .		crochet, chagrin
,,	,, ,, un ,, entre [k] y la *j* de *juro*		loch, pibroch
,,	es muda en pocas palabras		schism
ck	tiene siempre el sonido de [k]		back, lock, sick
gh	tiene a veces el sonido de [f]		rough, tough
,,	,, ,, ,, ,, *g* en *tengo* . . .		ghastly, ghost
,,	es a veces muda		high, dough, might
gu	tiene generalmente el sonido de *gu* en *guitarra*	.	guitar, guest
,,	tiene a veces el sonido de *gu* en *lengua* . .		guano, guava, Guelph
ph	tiene generalmente el sonido de [f]		philosophy, zephyr
,,	es a veces muda		phthisis
qu	tiene a veces el sonido de [kw] (véase *q* en el alfabeto)		quantity, quote
,,	tiene a veces el sonido de [k] (véase *q* en el alfabeto)		antique, Basque
rh	tiene el sonido de [r] sólo cuando ocurre en una misma sílaba		rhetoric, myrrh
sh	tiene siempre el sonido de [ŝ] (véase § 8) . .		fish, ship
th	tiene a veces el sonido de [ð] (véase § 12) . .		this, that, there
,,	,, ,, ,, ,, [θ] (,, § 12) . .		theatre, thick
,,	tiene en pocas palabras un sonido parecido a la *t* en *tal*		thaler, thyme
wh	tiene generalmente el sonido de [hw] (véase § 13)		what, when, white
,,	tiene en pocas palabras el sonido de [h] (véase § 13)		who, whole

ADVERTENCIA

PARA LA MEJOR COMPRENSION DEL PLAN DE LA OBRA

La tendencia a simplificar la ortografía ha hecho que en los Estados Unidos se elimine alguna letra innecesaria en ciertas palabras, como **clamor, honor,** que en Inglaterra continúan escribiéndose en su integridad (**clamour, honour**). En tales casos hemos suprimido completamente la *u*, con poquísimas excepciones (v. gr.: **glamour, labor** *o* **labour**). Estas y otras supresiones parecidas, autorizadas por el uso y por los lexicógrafos, se indican encerrando entre paréntesis la letra que suele o puede suprimirse, v. gr.: **glamo(u)r, jewel(l)er, jewel(le)ry, judg(e)ment, rat(t)an, gast(e)ropod.**

Asimismo, para economizar espacio, se marcan con un paréntesis algunos substantivos y los numerosos adjetivos que tienen dos terminaciones, v. gr.: **gelatin(e, knur(l, labiate(d, comic(al,** que pueden escribirse íntegramente o bien **gelatin, knur, labiate, comic.**

En la representación fonética de los vocablos que tienen dos terminaciones, se suprimen las sílabas idénticas que ya sabrá suplir el buen sentido del lector, v. gr.: **abstinence, abstinency** [ǽbstɪnẹns, -ɪ], pronúnciese [ǽbstɪnẹns, ǽbstɪnẹnsɪ].

Análogamente, al dar palabras que tienen una misma parte común que se pronuncia de igual manera en todas ellas, la pronunciación completa no siempre se indica sino en la primera, y con las otras se da únicamente la de la parte no común precedida de un guión. Así, **censorial** [sɛnsóɾɪạl], **censorious** [-ʌs], **censoriously** [-lɪ], **censoriousness** [-nɪs], indica que las tres últimas deben pronunciarse [sɛnsóɾɪʌs], [sɛnsóɾɪʌslɪ], [sɛnsóɾɪʌsnɪs].

En cuanto a palabras compuestas, debe observarse que existe en inglés la mayor variedad y confusión respecto de su ortografía y orden de presentación, que en el uso pueden cambiar rápida y a veces caprichosamente. Por ejemplo, muchas palabras como **classroom, class-room** o **class room** siguen encontrándose en las tres formas indicadas, aunque el uso actual puede favorecer una de ellas (en este caso es la primera). Por consiguiente, lo importante es atenerse a esta regla general, en que seguimos el atinado ejemplo dado en la edición anterior: se debe buscar toda frase en que entran dos o más términos, sea que éstos formen o no una palabra compuesta con sus elementos divididos por un guión, en el artículo correspondiente al *primer* elemento, con el cual principia la frase o palabra respectiva, haciendo caso omiso de cuál de dichos elementos sea el más importante—problema a veces imposible de resolver. Por ejemplo, **cast iron** se da en el artículo **cast,** y no en **iron; carbon steel,** en **carbon,** y no en **steel; broad-faced,** en **broad; folding bed,** en **folding; easy chair,** en **easy.** Si el lector tiene presente esta regla fija, no perderá tiempo buscando frases donde no están. Hay unas pocas excepciones, como el substantivo **close-up,** provenientes de la dificultad de clasificación gramatical; mas ellas no causarán dificultad alguna, si el lector observa la regla adicional, también muy útil, de buscar toda expresión compuesta de dos palabras separadas primero como frase, bajo el primer elemento, y luego como voz independiente. Otras excepciones se deben a que el segundo elemento es el que casi seguramente buscará el lector. Recíprocamente, si no encontrare como voz independiente una palabra compuesta que se le presente, puede hallarla como frase bajo el primer elemento. Si, por ejemplo, viere en alguna parte **waterwheel**, y no hallare esta voz en el lugar que le corresponde como palabra indivisa, puede buscar la frase **water wheel** en el artículo **water**.

A propósito de frases, inclusas las formadas por verbos modificados por partículas, se ha adoptado el orden alfabético para los elementos que siguen a la palabra principal. Después de las frases que principian con la palabra principal, se dan, también en orden alfabético, los idiotismos en que ella entra, si los hay, que no empiecen con ella. Para ahorrar espacio, la palabra que encabeza el artículo no se repite en cada frase, poniendo solamente su inicial. Véanse, por ejemplo, los artículos **back** y **cat**.

En las frases formadas por un verbo seguido de una partícula modificante, se han separado las correspondientes al verbo usado transitivamente de las correspondientes al verbo usado intransitivamente, cuando el verbo se usa de ambos modos. Esto también ahorra mucho tiempo.

Cuando en un mismo párrafo se dan los equivalentes de una palabra que pertenece a dos o más partes de la oración, los correspondientes a cada una de éstas van encabezados por un número romano impreso en letra gruesa, que se destaca claramente, facilitando así el trabajo de buscar los equivalentes en la división del caso.

Indicación del género: En un diccionario de este tamaño hay millares de nombres substantivos españoles (muchos de los cuales aparecen repetidas veces en el curso de la obra) cuyo género gramatical puede ofrecer dificultades y suscitar dudas a quien no domine a la perfección ese idioma. Pero querer indicar para todos estos substantivos su género gramatical sería tarea interminable y además ociosa, porque afortunadamente es posible establecer ciertas reglas y clasificaciones que permiten *suprimir* toda indicación de género en la gran mayoría de los casos. Como nuestro propósito es facilitar la tarea del lector y no confundirle con una serie de clasificaciones ingeniosas pero complicadas e inútiles, nos limitamos aquí a establecer casi al desnudo las sencillas reglas siguientes:

(1) si no hay indicación contraria, debe considerarse como *femenino* todo nombre que termine en -*a*, -*d* (especialmente -*dad*, -*tad*, -*tud*), -*ión* (especialmente -*ción*), -*ie*, -*is*, -*umbre* y -*z*. Ejemplos: **cara; bondad, libertad, virtud; lección; serie; crisis; muchedumbre; cruz.** Sólo las excepciones van indicadas con la abreviatura *m.* Ejemplos: **clima, mapa, planeta; abad; avión, gorrión; pie, balompié; paréntesis; alumbre; juez.**

(2) salvo contadas excepciones y categorías que se mencionan a continuación, todos los otros vocablos, sea cual fuere su desinencia, deben considerarse como *masculinos* si no hay contraria indicación. Ejemplos: **remo; accidente; papel; rey; orador.** Las excepciones van indicadas con la abreviatura *f.* Ejemplos: **mano; clase; cárcel; ley; flor.**

(3) también son masculinos, y usados comúnmente en forma singular a pesar de su apariencia, muchos vocablos que reúnen en sí un elemento verbal con otro substantivo. Ejemplos: **cortabolsas, cortacircuitos, limpiabotas, paracaídas, rascacielos.**

(4) ciertas palabras suelen o pueden usarse casi indiferentemente en ambos géneros, y por lo tanto van indicadas con la abreviatura *mf.* Ejemplos: **análisis, arte, azúcar, calor, camarada, colega, dote, mar, mártir, puente, radio, reo, testigo.**

(5) no llevan ni necesitan indicación de género los vocablos que terminan en *-ante*, *-iente*, *-ista*, porque refiriéndose a personas son de ambos géneros.   Ejemplos: **acompañante, visitante, pariente, periodista.**

(6) otras palabras se usan en los dos géneros, pero con cambio completo de sentido; éstas llevan una indicación del género en los casos o usos que violan las reglas ya indicadas (1 y 2) o que se prestan a equívocos.   Ejemplos: **capital, clave, cólera, corte, cura, haz, orden, parte, pez.**

(7) las letras del alfabeto son todas femeninas; las notas musicales son masculinas.

ABREVIATURAS DE LA PARTE
INGLESA–ESPAÑOLA

Fuera de estas abreviaturas, se usan las bien conocidas del sistema métrico. A propósito de éstas bueno es advertir que, cuando se refieren a un número decimal, se escriben siempre después del número completo, y no hacia arriba de los enteros; así: 4,75 m., y no 4ᵐ,75.

a.	adjetivo.
abrev.	abreviatura.
adv.	adverbio.
aer.	aeronáutica.
agr.	agricultura.
alb.	albañilería.
alem.	alemán.
álg.	álgebra.
Am.	América.
Am. C.	América Central.
anat.	anatomía.
ant.	anticuado.
Ant.	Antillas (Cuba, etc.).
antig. gr. o rom. . .	antigüedad griega o romana.
api.	apicultura.
apl.	aplícase.
Arg.	Argentina.
arit.	aritmética.
arm.	armadura; armas de fuego.
arq.	arquitectura.
arqueol.	arqueología.
art.	artículo.
art(i).	artillería, armas de fuego.
ast(r).	astronomía, astrología.
aut.	automovilismo.
aux.	auxiliar.
azú.	industria azucarera.
b. a.	bellas artes.
bact.	bacteriología.
bib.	bíblico, Biblia.
biol.	biología.
bioquím.	bioquímica.
blas.	blasón.
bot.	botánica.
cant.	cantería.
carp.	carpintería.
carr.	carruajería.
caz.	caza.
cer(á).	cerámica.
cerr.	cerrajería.
cetr.	cetrería.
cir.	cirugía.
coc.	cocina.
com.	comercio.
comp.	comparativo.
conj.	conjunción.
const(r). . . .	construcciones.
contr.	contracción.
cost.	costura.
crist.	cristalografía.
Ch.	Chile.
danz.	danza.
def.	definido.
defect.	defectivo.
dem.	demostrativo.
dent.	dentistería.
dep.	deportes.

der.	derecho.
desp(ec). . . .	despectivo.
dib.	dibujo.
dim.	diminutivo.
dipl.	diplomacia.
elec.	electricidad.
embr.	embriología.
enc.	encuadernación.
ent.	entomología.
e. p.	economía política.
equit.	equitación.
esc.	escultura.
Esco.	Escocia.
esgr.	esgrima.
esp.	especialmente.
E. U.	Estados Unidos.
f.	femenino.
fam.	familiar.
farm.	farmacia.
f. c.	ferrocarriles.
fig.	figurado.
Fil.	Filipinas.
filol.	filología.
fil(os).	filosofía.
fís.	física.
fisiol.	fisiología.
fon.	fonética.
for.	voz forense.
fort.	fortificación.
fot(o).	fotografía.
fr.	francés.
frec.	frecuentemente.
fund.	fundición.
gal.	galicismo.
gen.	generalmente.
geog.	geografía.
geol.	geología.
geom.	geometría.
ger.	gerundio.
gram.	gramática.
herr.	herrería.
hidr.	hidráulica.
hist.	historia.
hist. n.	historia natural.
hort.	horticultura.
ict.	ictiología.
igl.	iglesia.
imp.	imperfecto.
impers.	impersonal.
imp(r).	imprenta.
impv.	imperativo.
ind.	industria.
indef.	indefinido.
indic.	indicativo.
inf.	infinitivo.
ing.	ingeniería.
Ing(l).	Inglaterra.
interj.	interjección.
int(ern). . . .	internacional.
irón.	irónico.

irr.	irregular.
ital.	italiano.
joy.	joyería.
lat.	latín.
leng. ord.	lenguaje ordinario.
locom.	locomotora.
lóg.	lógica.
ll.	llámase, llamado.
m.	masculino.
magn.	magnetismo.
m. comb. int.	máquinas de combustión interna.
maq.	maquinaria.
mar.	marina.
mat.	matemáticas.
mec.	mecánica.
med.	medicina.
met(al).	metalurgia.
meteor.	meteorología.
Méx.	México.
mf.	masculino y femenino.
mil.	milicia.
min(er).	minería, minerología.
mit.	mitología.
mol.	molinería.
mús.	música.
m. v.	máquinas de vapor.
N. A.	Norte América.
naveg.	navegación.
obst.	obstetricia.
ópt.	óptica.
orn.	ornitología.
pa.	participio activo.
pal.	paleontología.
pap.	fabricación del papel.
pat.	patología.
p. ej.	por ejemplo.
period.	periodismo.
pers.	personal.
pert.	perteneciente (a).
petr.	petrografía.
pint.	pintura.
piro.	pirotecnia.
pl.	plural.
poét.	poética.
pol.	política.
pos.	posesivo.
pp.	participio pasado.
prep.	preposición.
pret.	pretérito.
P. Rico	Puerto Rico.

pron.	pronombre.
pros.	prosodia.
psic.	psicología.
quím.	química.
rad.	radiocomunicación.
radtlf.	radiotelefonía.
radtlg.	radiotelegrafía.
refl.	reflejo o reflexivo.
rel.	relativo (gram.).
rel.	relativo (a).
relig.	religión.
reloj.	relojería.
ret.	retórica.
s.	substantivo.
S. A.	Sud América.
sast.	sastrería.
sing.	singular.
sociol.	sociología.
somb.	sombrerería.
subj.	subjuntivo.
super.	superlativo.
t.	también.
tal.	talabartería.
teat.	teatro.
tec(n).	tecnología.
tej.	tejidos.
ten.	tenería.
teo(l).	teología.
teos.	teosofía.
term.	terminación.
tint.	tintorería.
tlf.	telefonía.
tlg.	telegrafía.
ton.	tonelería.
top.	topografía.
trig.	trigonometría.
Ú., ú.	Úsase, úsase.
u. refl.	usado reflexivamente.
V., v.	Véa(n)se, véa(n)se.
va.	verbo activo.
Venez.	Venezuela.
vet.	veterinaria.
vg., v.g., v.gr.	*verbi gratia*
vid.	vidriería.
vn.	verbo neutro.
vr.	verbo reflexivo o recíproco.
vulg.	vulgarismo.
zap.	zapatería.
zool.	zoología.

NUEVO DICCIONARIO BILINGÜE

DE LAS

LENGUAS INGLESA Y ESPAÑOLA

PARTE INGLESA–ESPAÑOLA

Las abreviaturas y los nombres propios van al final.

<table>
<tr><td>A</td><td>ABD</td></tr>
</table>

a [ei], s. a; (mús., A) la.—A I, A number I, de primera calidad o categoría, de lo mejor.—from A to Z, desde el alfa hasta la omega, de pe a pa.

a [a o, si es enfático, ei]. I. art. indef. un, una (antes de sonido consonante; v.g. a man, un hombre; a woman, una mujer; a unit, una unidad); por, cada; v.g. ten dollars a pound, diez dólares por libra. Se pospone a los adjetivos many, such, what, y a adjetivos precedidos de as, how, so, too; v.g. many a man, muchos hombres (v. MANY); such a man, un hombre tal, semejante hombre; what a man! ¡qué hombre! as old a man, un hombre tan viejo; too old a man, un hombre demasiado viejo. Interpuesto entre el adjetivo half y un substantivo, no se traduce (half a pound, media libra; half a month, medio mes). II. prep. Se usaba, y aún se usa a veces, antes del gerundio para indicar acción o proceso, en casos en que hoy se emplea el gerundio solo o el infinitivo; v.g. he went a hunting, él fué a cazar.—a.-maying (v. MAY).

A [ei], a. en A, en forma de A.

aardvark [árdvark], s. oricteropo del Cabo, especie de mamífero hormiguero sudafricano.

aardwolf [árdwulf], s. prótel, hiena sudafricana.

Aaronic(al [erάnik(al], a. aarónico, aaronita; levítico pontifical.

Aaron's-beard [érɒnz bírd], s. (bot.) barba de Aarón; zumillo; saxífraga de China; también se da este nombre a varias otras plantas.

abaca [abaká], s. (bot.) abacá; cáñamo de Manila.

aback [abǽk], adv. detrás, atrás; hacia atrás; (mar.) en facha.—to take a., turbar, desconcertar, coger de improviso.

abacist [ǽbasist], s. abacista.

abacus [ǽbakʌs], s. (arit.) ábaco; (arq.) loseta rectangular; aparador; báculo.

abaft [abǽft]. I. adv. (mar.) hacia la popa, a popa, en popa; atrás. II. prep. detrás de.

abalone [æbalóuni], s. (zool.) oreja marina.

abandon [abǽndɒn]. I. va. abandonar, dejar, desertar, desamparar; renunciar, dar de mano a; entregar, ceder; desmantelar.—to a. oneself, entregarse (al vicio, gozo, etc.). II. s. indiferencia, naturalidad, desenfado, desenfreno, abandono, abandonamiento.

abandoned [-d], a. abandonado; encenagado (en los vicios); malvado.

abandonment [-mɛnt], s. abandono, abandonamiento, desamparo, deserción, desvalimiento, dejación; (for.) deserción (de una apelación).

abase [abéis], va. abatir, humillar, degradar, envilecer.

abasement [-mɛnt], s. abatimiento, humillación, degradación, envilecimiento.

abash [abǽʃ], va. avergonzar, correr, confundir, cortar, sonrojar.

abashment [-mɛnt], s. confusión, vergüenza, embarazo, sonrojo.

abate [abéit]. I. va. disminuir, reducir, rebajar; (for.) suprimir, impedir; suspender; condonar; anular; (metal.) reducir el temple. II. vn. menguar, moderarse, apaciguarse, calmarse; (for.) frustrarse, no surtir efecto, fallar; ocupar sin derecho fincas tras la muerte de su último dueño.

abatement [-mɛnt], s. extenuación, rebaja, disminución o supresión; (for.) anulación; cesación; cantidad rebajada o condonada; usurpación u ocupación, sin derecho, de una finca tras la muerte de su último dueño.

abater [-œ(r)], s. (for.) el que suprime o mitiga (un estorbo, impedimento, etc.); intruso, usurpador.

abatis [ǽbatis], s. (mil.) tala, valla defensiva de árboles enteros cortados.

abattoir [æbætwár], s. matadero, desolladero.

abb [æb], s. urdimbre; lana para la urdimbre; lana en borra.

abbacy [ǽbasi], s. abadía, dignidad de abad.

abbatial [æbéiʃal], a. abacial, abadengo.

abbé [ǽbei], s. abate.

abbess [ǽbis], s. abadesa, prelada, superiora.

abbey [ǽbi], s. abadía, monasterio, convento.

abbot [ǽbɒt], s. abad, superior.

abbotship [ǽbɒtʃip], s. abadía (dignidad), abadiato.

abbreviate [abrívieit], va. abreviar, reducir, compendiar.

abbreviation [-éiʃɒn], s. abreviación; abreviatura; cifra, compendio, epítome.

abbreviator [-eitɒ(r)], s. abreviador, compendiador; (igl.) abreviador.

abbreviatory [-átɔri], a. abreviativo, abreviador.—abbreviature [-achu(r)], s. abreviatura, compendio, epítome.

A B C, a-b-c [éi bí sí], s. alfabeto; abecedario, abecé; cartilla; rudimentos.

abdicant [ǽbdikant], s. y a. abdicante, que abdica o renuncia.

abdicate [-keit]. I. va., vn. abdicar, renunciar, dimitir. II. va. (for.) desheredar.

abdication [-kéjṣǫn], s. abdicación, renuncia; dimisión; dejamiento, dejación.

abdicative [ǽbdikǎtiv], a. abdicativo, renunciativo, que implica abdicación.

abdomen [ǽbdomen], s. abdomen, vientre.

abdominal [æbdámǐnǎl]. I. a. abdominal. II. s. y a. (zool.), abdominal, malacopterigio.

abdominous [æbdámǐnʌs], a. barrigón.

abduce [æbdjús], va. (fisiol.) abducir.

abducent [-ẹnt], s. y a. (anat.) abductor.

abduct [æbdʌ́kt], va. secuestrar, raptar, arrebatar, robar (a alguien); plagiar; (anat.) abducir.

abduction [æbdʌ́kṣǫn], s. robo, rapto, secuestro (de una persona); plagio; (anat. y lóg.) abducción.

abductor [æbdʌ́ktǫ(r)]. I. s. raptor, secuestrador. II. a. (anat.) abductor (músculo).

abeam [ǎbím], adv. (mar.) por el través; en ángulo recto con la quilla.

abecedarian [eibisidérǐǎn], s. y a. que aprende o enseña el alfabeto; novicio, bisoño.

abed [ǎbéd], adv. en cama, acostado.

abele [ǎbíl], s. (bot.) álamo blanco.

abelmosk [éibẹlmask], s. (bot.) abelmosco.

aberrance, aberrancy [æbérǎns, -i̧], s. error, desvío, extravío.

aberrant [æbérǎnt], a. extraviado; anormal, anómalo.

aberration [æbẹréiṣǫn], s. error; extravío; desliz, desviación; (astr. y ópt.) aberración.

abet [ǎbét], va. instigar, excitar, inducir, apoyar, favorecer.

abetment [-mẹnt], s. instigación, excitación, apoyo.

abetter, abettor [-œ(r)], s. (for.) fautor, instigador; cómplice.

abeyance [ǎbéiǎns], s. inacción transitoria, suspensión; estado latente; (for.) expectativa, espera.—in a., en suspenso; latente; (for.) en espera de su dueño o reclamante legítimo (dícese de bienes mostrencos, cargos vacantes, etc.).

abeyant [-ǎnt], a. yacente, vacante, mostrenco, expectante.

abhor [æbhór], va. aborrecer, derrenegar, repugnar, detestar, abominar, odiar.

abhorrence [-ẹns], s. aborrecimiento, detestación, aversión, execración, repugnancia.

abhorrent [-ẹnt], a. aborrecible, repugnante, detestable, odioso; contrario, opuesto; que detesta.

abhorrently [-li̧], adv. aborreciblemente, odiosamente.

abhorrer [-œ(r)], s. aborrecedor.

abidance [ǎbáidǎns], s. permanencia, residencia. —a. by, adhesión a.

abide [ǎbáid] (pret. y pp. ABODE). I. va. esperar; soportar, sufrir. II. vn. habitar, morar; permanecer; perdurar.—to a. by, sostenerse en; estar con; sujetarse a, obrar de acuerdo con, cumplir con, acatar, atenerse a.

abiding [-iŋ]. I. s. permanencia; residencia, morada. II. a. durable, perdurable, permanente.

Abietineæ [æbjetínji], f. pl. (bot.) abietíneas.

abigail [ǽbigeil], s. doncella (criada), camarera.

ability [ǎbíliti], s. poder, facultad, habilidad, capacidad, talento, ingenio, aptitud, disposición.—to the best of one's a., lo mejor que se pueda, a más y mejor.

abintestate [æbintésteit], s. y a. abintestato.

abiogenesis [æbioudźénisis], s. abiogénesis, generación espontánea.

abiological [-ládźikǎl], a. abiológico, inorgánico.

abiology [eibaiálodźi], s. abiología, ciencia de los seres inorgánicos.

abiosis [æbióusis], s. abiosis, ausencia de vida.

abirritant [æbiritǎnt], s. y a. contrairritante.

abject [ǽbdźekt], a. abyecto, servil, bajo; desanimado, abatido.

abjection [æbdźékṣǫn], s. abyección, servilismo, bajeza.

abjectly [æbdźéktli], adv. abyectamente.

abjectness [-nis], s. = ABJECTION.

abjuration [æbdźuréiṣǫn], s. abjuración, retractación; renuncia.

abjure [æbdźúr]. I. va. abjurar, retractarse de; renunciar solemnemente a. II. vn. retractarse; hacer renuncia solemne (del reino, etc.).

ablactation [æblæktéiṣǫn], s. ablactación, destete; manera de injertar los árboles por aproximación.

ablation [æbléiṣǫn], s. (cir.) ablación, extirpación; (geol.) erosión, desgaste (de una roca); merma, reducción (de un helero por derretimiento).

ablative [éblǎtiv], s. y a. (gram.) ablativo.

ablaut [áblaut], s. variación de la raíz de una palabra.

ablaze [ǎbléiz], a. en llamas, ardiendo.

able [éibl], a. capaz, apto, hábil, competente, idóneo, diestro, poderoso; (for.) capaz, competente, legalmente habilitado o capacitado.—a.-bodied, robusto, sano, físicamente capaz.—able-bodied seaman, marinero capaz de ejecutar todas las maniobras del oficio.—a.-minded, de gran talento.—to be a., poder, saber.

ablegate [éblẹgeit], s. (igl.) ablegado, nuncio.

ablepsia [eiblépsiǎ], s. (med.) ablepsia, ceguera.

abloom [ǎblúm], a. en flor; floreciente.

abluent [ébluẹnt], s. y a. (med.) abluente, detersivo, detergente.

ablush [ǎblʌ́š], a. y adv. avergonzado, ruborizado.

ablution [æblúṣǫn], s. ablución; lavamiento.

ably [éibli], adv. hábilmente.

abnegate [ǽbnẹgeit], va. renunciar a; abjurar, negar, repudiar.

abnegation [-géiṣǫn], s. abnegación; renuncia, repudiación.

abnormal [æbnórmǎl], a. anormal, irregular, disforme, heteróclito.

abnormality [-mǽliti], s. irregularidad, anomalía, anormalidad, deformidad, monstruosidad.

abnormally [-mǎli], adv. anormalmente.

abnormity [-mi̧ti], s. = ABNORMALITY.

aboard [ǎbórd], adv. (mar.) a bordo.—to fall a., abordar, chocar.—to go a., ir a bordo, embarcarse.—to take a., embarcar.—all a!, ¡viajeros al tren!, (Méx.) ¡vámonos!

abode [ǎbóǒd], s. domicilio, residencia, habitación, mansión, morada; estancia, permanencia.

abode, pret. y pp. de TO ABIDE.

abolish [ǎbáliš], va. abolir, suprimir, derogar, anular, revocar.

abolishable [-ǎbl], a. abolible, derogable.

abolisher [-œ(r)], s. derogador, anulador, revocador, destructor.

abolishment [-mẹnt], s. abolición.

abolition [æbolíṣǫn], s. abolición, derogación, extinción.

abolitionist [-i̧st], s. abolicionista; (E. U.) abolicionista, enemigo de la esclavitud.

abomasum [æboméisʌm], s. (anat.) abomaso.

abominable [ǎbáminǎbl], a. abominable, execrable, detestable; nefando, aborrecible.

abominableness [-nis], s. calidad de abominable, execrabilidad, odiosidad.

abominably [-ǎbli], adv. abominablemente.

abominate [ǎbámineit], va. abominar, detestar, aborrecer, execrar.

abomination [-néiṣǫn], s. abominación, odio, detestación; enormidad, maldad.

aboriginal [æboridźinǎl], a. aborigen, primitivo, originario.

aborigines [æborídźiniz], s. pl. aborígenes.

abort [ǎbórt], vn. abortar, malparir; (biol.) atrofiarse o cesar prematuramente de crecer; (med.) acortar o impedir el desarrollo de una enfermedad; (fig.) fracasarse.

aborted [-id], a. nacido prematuramente; (biol.) de desarrollo incompleto; fracasado.

aborticide [-ịsạịd], *s.* aborticidio, destrucción del feto; lo que destruye el feto y causa aborto.

abortifacient [-ịféịẹnt], *s.* y *a.* abortifaciente, abortivo, que causa aborto.

abortion [ạbórṣọn], *s.* aborto, malparto; abortón, muévedo; fiasco, fracaso.

abortionist [-ịst], *s.* abortista o malpartista.

abortive [ạbórtịv]. I. *s.* y *a.* abortivo. II. *a.* infructuoso, malogrado; (biol.) imperfectamente desarrollado; estéril; (med.) que acorta la duración (de una enfermedad).

abortively [-lị], *adv.* abortivamente; a destiempo; prematuramente.

abortiveness [-nịs], *s.* abortamiento; fracaso, mal éxito, malogro.

abound [ạbáụnd], *vn.* abundar, verbenear, manar, rodar.—**to a. with**, abundar en, rebosar de.—**abounding in or with**, abundante en, nutrido de.

about [ạbáụt]. I. *adv.* casi; poco más o menos, como (*about six hours*, como seis horas); alrededor, por todos lados, a la redonda; acá y acullá, de Ceca en Meca; por aquí, por ahí (en el lugar, edificio, etc.); en la dirección opuesta; por turnos, en rotación.—**a. face**, (mil.) media vuelta (voz de mando).—**all a.**, por todas partes.—**to be a.**, estar levantado y andando (dícese de un enfermo). II. *prep.* de, cerca de, sobre; con respecto a; alrededor de, en torno de; por, en (*to walk about town*, andar o pasear por el pueblo; *to quarrel about*, reñir por; *to think about*, pensar en); cerca de, cosa de, unos, unas (*about two miles*, cosa de dos millas); como de, poco más o menos de (*the book is about this size*, el libro es como de este tamaño); ocupado en, atendiendo a; con (*I have no money about me*, no tengo dinero conmigo, o aquí).—**to be a. to**, estar para, al punto de, o al (hacer algo).—**what a.?** *V.* WHAT.

about-face [-féịs]. I. *s.* media vuelta; (fig.) cambio de opinión o de conducta, cambio al partido contrario (*to do an about-face*, pasarse al partido opuesto, decir o hacer lo contrario, desdecirse). II. *vn.* dar media vuelta.

above [ạbÁv]. I. *a.* dicho, susodicho, supradicho, precitado; superior, anterior, precedente.—**the above (-mentioned) figures**, dichas cifras, las cifras precedentes o susodichas. II. *s.* lo dicho, lo antedicho, etc., lo precedente, lo anterior. III. *adv.* y *prep.* sobre, arriba (de), (por) encima (de), superior (a), fuera de, más que o de, anteriormente.—**from a.**, de lo alto, del cielo.—**a. my reach**, fuera de mi alcance.—**a. my strength**, superior a mis fuerzas.—**a. all (else)**, sobre todo, más que todo.—**a. ten members**, más de diez socios.—**six degrees a. zero**, seis grados sobre cero.—**to be a. something**, ser incapaz de, estar por encima de algo.

aboveboard [-bọrd], *a.* y *adv.* franco, sincero; sin dolo, a vista de todos, a las claras, al descubierto.

aboveground [-grạụnd]. I. *a.* y *adv.* sobre la superficie de la tierra o arriba de ella. II. *a.* vivo, con vida.

abovestairs [-stẹrz], *adv.* = UPSTAIRS.

abracadabra [æbrạkạdǽbrạ], *s.* abracadabra; palabra altisonante y misteriosa.

abradant [ạbréịdạnt], *s.* y *a.* = ABRASIVE.

abrade [ạbréịd], *va.* raer, desgastar por rozamiento, raspar, descarnar, desmoronar.

abrader [-œ(r)], *s.* material rayente.

abrasion [ạbréịẓọn], *s.* desgaste (esp. por rozamiento); rozadura, raspadura; (geol. y med.) abrasión.

abrasive [ạbréịsịv]. I. *a.* rayente, raspante. II. *s.* abrasivo, substancia raspante.

abreast [ạbrést], *adv.* de frente, en fila, al lado (uno de otro); (mar.) por el través.—**four a.**, cuatro de frente, de cuatro en cuatro.—**to keep a. of something**, estar al tanto (al día, al corriente o al nivel) de algo.

abridge [ạbrídẓ], *va.* abreviar, compendiar, sincopar, resumir, reducir, recopilar; privar, despojar.

abridgment [-mẹnt], *s.* compendio, recopilación, epítome, resumen; abreviación, diminución, contracción.

abroad [ạbród], *adv.* en el extranjero, fuera del país; fuera de su morada ordinaria (como los animales); en grande espacio; entre el público, del dominio público, en público. (A veces no se traduce, o se emplea otra forma; *there is a rumor abroad*, hay un rumor, se dice; *to set abroad*, hacer público, divulgar.)—**to go a.**, ir al extranjero.—**to be all a.**, estar errado, extraviado o perplejo.

abrogate [ǽbrogeịt], *va.* abrogar, abolir, anular, revocar.

abrogation [-éịṣọn], *s.* abrogación, abolición, anulación, revocación, rescisión.

abrogative [ǽbrogǽtịv], *a.* revocatorio.

abrotanum [ạbrátạnʌm], *s.* (bot.) abrótano.

abrupt [ạbrÁpt], *a.* brusco, repentino, súbito; quebrado, áspero, precipitoso, desigual; grosero, bronco.

abruption [ạbrÁpṣọn], *s.* separación violenta; (cir.) abrupción.

abruptly [ạbrÁptlị], *adv.* precipitadamente; de rondón; repentinamente, bruscamente, ex abrupto.

abruptness [-nịs], *s.* precipitación, inconsideración; prontitud; brusquedad.

abscess [ǽbsẹs], *s.* absceso, (a)postema.

abscissa [æbsịsậ], *s.* (mat.) abscisa.

abscission [æbsịṣọn], *s.* corte, abscisión.

abscond [æbskánd], *vn.* esconderse, evadirse, fugarse; substraerse a la justicia.

absconder [æbskándœ(r)], *s.* desaparecido, prófugo, contumaz.

absence [ǽbsẹns], *s.* ausencia; falta; distracción de ánimo.—**in the a. of**, a falta de.

absent [ǽbsẹnt], *a.* ausente; no existente; distraído, abstraído.—**to be a.**, faltar.—**a.-minded**, distraído, absorto, encantado, abstraído, (estar) en Babia.—**a.-mindedness**, distracción, enajenamiento, desatención.

absent [æbsént], *vr.* ausentarse, retirarse (de), dejar de concurrir.

absentee [æbsẹntí], *s.* y *a.* absentista; ausente; el que permanece o está ausente de su tierra, empleo, etc.

absenteeism [-ịzm], *s.* absentismo.

absinthe [ǽbsịnθ], *s.* absenta, licor de ajenjo, absintio.—**absinthian** [æbsịnθịạn], *a.* perteneciente al ajenjo.

absinthiate [-ịeịt], *va.* impregnar con ajenjo.

absinthin [-ịn], *s.* (quím.) absintina.

absinthism [ǽbsịnθịzm], *s.* (med.) absintismo, enfermedad debida al abuso del ajenjo.

absinthium [æbsịnθịʌm], *s.* (bot.) ajenjo.

absolute [ǽbsolụt], *a.* absoluto; completo, positivo; categórico, perentorio; (for.) absoluto, sin restricción; (quím.) puro.—**the a.**, lo absoluto.—**a. alcohol**, alcohol absoluto, alcohol puro.—**a. ceiling**, (aer.) techo, altura máxima que un avión puede alcanzar en una atmósfera tipo.—**a. electrometer**, (elec.) electrómetro absoluto.—**a. pressure**, (fís.) presión absoluta, en que cero corresponde al vacío.—**a. scale**, (fís.) escala termométrica absoluta, o de temperaturas absolutas.—**a. temperature**, (fís.) temperatura absoluta.—**a. term**, (mat.) término absoluto o independiente (que no contiene la incógnita).—**a. unit**, (fís.) unidad absoluta.—**a. value**, (mat.) valor absoluto.—**a. weed**, (agr.) maleza perjudicial y sin valor intrínseco.—**a. zero**, (fís.) cero absoluto.

absolutely [-lị], *adv.* absolutamente; de todo punto, positivamente, sin reserva; terminante o categóricamente.

absoluteness [æbsolutnịs], s. absolutismo; calidad de absoluto.

absolution [æbsolúṣọn], s. absolución.

absolutism [æbsolutizm], s. absolutismo, despotismo, poder absoluto y autocrático, autocracia.

absolutist [-ịst], s. y a. absolutista, autócrata.

absolutory [æbsályụtọrị], **absolvatory** [-vạtọrị], a. absolutorio.

absolve [æbsálv], va. absolver, justificar, dispensar, remitir los pecados; desligar, exentar.

absolved [-d], pp. absuelto.

absolver [-œ(r)], s. absolvedor, dispensador.

absolving [-ịŋ], a. absolutorio.

absonant [æbsonạnt], a. discordante, contrario, disonante.

absorb [æbsórb]. I. va. absorber; empapar, embeber, chupar; ocupar (el ánimo) intensamente, preocupar; incorporar; amortiguar. II. vr. abstraerse, enfrascarse, ensimismarse.

absorbability [-ạbịlịtị], s. absorbibilidad, propiedad o capacidad de ser absorbido o empapado.

absorbable [-ạbl], a. absorbible.

absorbed [-d], a. absorbido; absorto.

absorbefacient [-ịféịṣẹnt], s. y a. que causa absorción.

absorbency [-ẹnsị], s. absorbencia.

absorbent [-ẹnt], a. absorbente.—**a. cotton,** (med.) algodón hidrófilo.—**a. gland,** glándula linfática.

absorber [-œ(r)], s. absorbente; (mec.) amortiguador; economizador (de energía).

absorbing [-ịŋ], a. absorbente; interesante; (fig.) cautivante.

absorption [æbsórpṣọn], s. absorción, absorbimiento, absorbencia, sorbo; concentración, preocupación.—**a. lines,** (fís.) rayas oscuras (del espectro), rayas de Fraunhofer.—**a. spectrum,** (fís.) espectro de absorción o de rayas oscuras.

absorptive [-tịv], a. absorbente.

abstain [æbstéịn], vn. abstenerse, privarse.

abstainer [-œ(r)], s. abstemio, abstencionista, el que se abstiene.

abstemious [æbstímịʌs], a. sobrio, abstemio, templado, abstinente, continente.

abstemiously [-lị], adv. sobriamente.

abstemiousness [-nịs], s. sobriedad, templanza.

abstention [æbsténṣọn], s. abstención, abstinencia.

absterge [æbstœ́rdʑ], va. (med.) absterger; enjugar, limpiar.

abstergent [-ẹnt], s. y a. abstergente.

abstersion [æbstœ́rṣọn], s. abstersión.

abstersive [-sịv], s. y a. abstersivo, abstergente.

abstinence, abstinency [æbstịnẹns, -ị], s. abstinencia, ayuno, inedia, sobriedad.—**day of a., día** (m.) de ayuno.—**total a.,** abstinencia absoluta de bebidas alcohólicas.

abstinent [æbstịnẹnt], a. abstinente, sobrio.

abstinently [-lị], adv. abstinentemente.

abstract [æbstrækt]. I. a. sumario, resumen, compendio, extracto, epítome, término abstracto; abstracción.—**in the a.,** en abstracto. II. a. abstracto; distraído.—**a. number,** número abstracto.

abstract [æbstrǽkt], va. abstraer (t. vn.); compendiar, resumir, extractar, epitomar, trasuntar; quitar, sustraer, hurtar; separar, alejar; distraer; (quím.) extraer.

abstracted [-ịd], a. distraído, olvidadizo (= ABSENT-MINDED); separado, desligado.

abstractedly [-lị], adv. abstractivamente.

abstractedness [-nịs], s. abstracción; calidad de abstracto; distracción, absorción.

abstracter, abstractor [-œ(r)], s. compendiador, extractador; ratero, ladrón.

abstraction [æbstrǽkṣọn], s. abstracción; separación; retraimiento, recogimiento; distrac-

ción, desatención, descuido; ratería, hurto; extracción.

abstractive [æbstrǽktịv], a. abstractivo.

abstractly, abstractively [-lị, -ịvlị], adv. en abstracto, abstractivamente.

abstractness [-nịs], s. abstracción; calidad de abstracto.

abstruse [æbstrús], a. abstruso, recóndito.

abstrusely [-lị], adv. abstrusamente.

abstruseness [-nịs], s. obscuridad, dificultad, reconditez; calidad de abstruso.

absurd [æbsœ́rd], a. absurdo, irracional, ridículo, disparatado, descabellado, prepóstero.

absurdity [-ịtị], s. absurdo, despropósito, disparate, dislate, absurdidad, contrasentido.

absurdly [-lị], adv. absurdamente, disparatadamente.—**to act a.,** disparatar.

absurdness [-nịs], s. = ABSURDITY.

abulia [æbịúlịạ], s. (med.) abulia, falta de voluntad.

abundance [ạbʌ́ndạns], s. abundancia, copia, acopio, plenitud, exuberancia, afluencia; caudal.

abundant [ạbʌ́ndạnt], a. abundante, abundoso, copioso, rico.

abundantly [-lị], adv. abundante, abundosa o copiosamente; (fam.) a chorros; asaz.

abuse [ạbịúz]. I. va. abusar de; engañar; profanar, violar; denostar, insultar, injuriar; ultrajar, seducir, maltratar. II. [ạbịús], s. abuso; corruptela; seducción, engaño; injuria, contumelia, denuesto; ultraje, maltrato; violación, estupro.

abuser [ạbịúzœ(r)], s. abusador; ultrajador; denostador, insultador; embaucador, engañador.

abusive [ạbịúsịv], a. abusivo, ofensivo, insultante, injurioso.

abusively [-lị], adv. abusivamente, ofensivamente.

abusiveness [-nịs], s. vituperación; vituperio, injuria, ofensa, insulto; abuso, uso impropio.

abut [ạbʌ́t], vn. terminar, confinar, (co)lindar, parar, rematar, comarcar, descabezar.—**to a. upon, on, against,** terminar en, confinar con, (co)lindar con, empalmar con; (mar.) topar.

abutilon [ạbịútịḷọn], s. (bot.) abutilón, malvavisco.

abutment [ạbʌ́tmẹnt], s. contigüidad; remate; refuerzo; confín, linde, lindero; (constr.) estribo, pilar, contrafuerte, macho, botarel.

abuttal [ạbʌ́tạl], s. límite, linde; contigüidad, contacto.—pl. partes (f. pl.) salientes de tierras.

abutter [-œ(r)], s. tierra o persona colindante.

abutting [-ịŋ], a. confín, confinante, (co)lindante.

abysm [ạbịzm], **abyss** [ạbịs], s. abismo; sima; báratro, infierno; las profundidades del mar.

abysmal [ạbịzmạl], a. abismal, insondable; de las profundidades del mar.

abyssal [ạbịsạl], a. abismal, insondable.—**a. zone,** la región profunda del mar.

Abyssinian [ạbịsịnịạn], s. y a. abisinio.

acacia [ạkéịṣạ], s. (bot.) acacia; guacia.

acacin(e) [ạkạsịn], s. acacina, guacia.

academic [ạkạdémịk], s. académico; estudiante, colegial.

academic(al [-(ạl], a. académico, colegial, de colegio, universitario; convencional, tradicional, de usanza; teórico; (A.) platónico.

academically [-ạlị], adv. académicamente.

academician [ạkạdẹmịṣạn], s. académico, miembro de una academia.

academist [ạkǽdẹmịst], s. academista.

academy [ạkǽdẹmị], s. academia, colegio, liceo; gimnasio.—**a. figure,** (b. a.) dibujo del natural.

Acadian [ạkéịdịạn], s. y a. acadiense, de Acadia.

acaleph [ǽkạlẹf], s. (zool.) acalefo, medusa.

acanaceous [ạkạnéịṣạs], a. (bot.) espinoso.

acantha [ạkǽnθạ], s. (bot.) espina, pincho; (zool.) aleta; (anat.) columna vertebral.

acanthaceous [ækænθéiŝʌs], *a.* (bot.) acantáceo.
acanthine [ækǽnθin], *a.* acantino, espinoso.
acanthocarpous [ækænθokárpʌs], *a.* (bot.) acantocarpo.
acanthocephalan [-séfǎlǎn], *s.* y *a.* (zool.) acantocéfalo.
acanthopterygian [ækænθaptęrídżiǎn], *s.* y *a.* (zool.) acantopterigio.
acanthus [ækǽnθʌs], *s.* (bot. y arq.) acanto.
acardia [eikárdiǎ], *s.* (med.) acardia, falta congénita del corazón.
acariasis [ækǎráiǎsis], *s.* (med.) acariasis, sarna, comezón.
Acarida [ǎkǽridǎ], *s. pl.* (zool.) acáridos, ácaros.
acarpous [eikárpʌs], *a.* (bot.) acarpo; que no da fruto.
acarus [ǽkǎrʌs], *s.* (ent.) ácaro, arador.
acatalectic [eikætǎléktik], *s.* y *a.* (pros.) acataléctico.
acatalepsia [-lépsiǎ], *s.* (med.) acatalepsia; deficiencia mental; inferioridad mental.
acatalepsy [eikǽtǎlepsi], *s.* (fil.) acatalepsia; escepticismo; duda filosófica.
acataleptic [-léptik], *s.* y *a.* (med. y fil.) acataléptico.
acaudal [eikódǎl], *a.* acáudeo, sin cola.
acaulescent [ækolésənt], *a.* (bot.) acaule.
accede [æksíd], *vn.* acceder; asentir, consentir, convenir en; llegar a, subir, ascender (al trono, etc.).
accelerant [æksélęrǎnt], *s.* acelerador; (quím.) catalizador.
accelerate [æksélęreit], **I.** *va.* acelerar, apresurar. **II.** *vn.* apresurarse, darse prisa.
accelerating [-iŋ], *a.* acelerador, aceleratriz.
acceleration [-éiŝǒn], *s.* aceleración; prisa, aumento de velocidad.—**poor a.**, (aut.) pique pobre.
accelerative [-iv], *a.* acelerador.—**a. force**, fuerza aceleratriz.
accelerator [-ǫ(r)], *s.* acelerador; cualquier cosa que sirve para acelerar; (aut.) acelerador.
accelerograph [-ogræf], *s.* (fís.) acelerógrafo.
accelerometer [-ámętœ(r)], *s.* (aer.) acelerómetro.
accent [ǽksənt], *s.* acento, inflexión, dejo.—**a. mark, written a., graphic a.**, acento ortográfico.
accent [æksént], *va.* acentuar, recalcar.
accented [-id], *a.* acentuado; (gram.) tónico.
accentual [æksénchuǎl], *a.* rítmico, relativo al acento.
accentuate [æksénchueit], *va.* acentuar; cargar (una sílaba); hacer más patente; dar mayor fuerza a.
accentuation [-éiŝǒn], *s.* acentuación.
accept [æksépt], *va.* aceptar, recibir, admitir, creer en; abrazar, acoger bien; reconocer; entender, interpretar; (com.) aceptar (un giro, etc.); (for.) adir (la herencia).
acceptable [-ǎbl], *a.* aceptable, acepto, grato, admisible; bien recibido, de recibo.
acceptableness, acceptability [-nis, -ǎbiliti], *s.* aceptabilidad; agrado, gracia.
acceptably [-ǎbli], *adv.* aceptablemente, gustosamente, agradablemente.
acceptance [-ǎns], *s.* aceptación; buena acogida; admisión; (com.) giro aceptado.—**a. house**, casa de aceptación de giros.
acceptation [-éiŝǒn], *s.* acepción, significado; aceptación, recepción, recibimiento.
acceptor [-ǫ(r)], *s.* (com.) aceptante, aceptador.
access [ǽkses], *s.* acceso, entrada; aumento, acrecentamiento, añadidura; (med.) accesión, acceso, ataque, paroxismo.
accessary [æksésǎri], *s.* y *a.* = ACCESSORY.
accessibility [-ibiliti], *s.* accesibilidad, asequibilidad.
accessible [æksésibl], *a.* accesible, conquistable, asequible, alcanzadizo.

accession [ækséŝǒn], **I.** *s.* aumento, acrecentamiento; advenimiento, ascenso (al trono); accesión; asentimiento, consentimiento; adquisición nueva (de libros en una biblioteca, etc.); (med.) acceso.—**a. book**, registro. **II.** *va.* registrar, catalogar.
accessorial [æksęsórial], *a.* accesorio.
accessorily [æksęsǫrili], *adv.* accesoriamente.
accessory [æksésǫri]. **I.** *a.* accesorio; concomitante, contribuyente, secundario; adicional, adjunto. **II.** *s.* dependencia; accesorio; adminículo; (for.) cómplice, fautor, instigador.—**a. after (before) the fact**, encubridor (instigador) de un delito.—*pl.* accesorios, repuestos, arreos, enseres, dependencias, guarniciones.—**a. store**, casa de venta de repuestos o accesorios.
accidence [ǽksidęns], *s.* libro de rudimentos de la gramática; (gram.) accidente.
accident [ǽksidęnt], *s.* accidente, casualidad; accidente, contratiempo, lance, paso, incidente, peripecia, percance; cosa o suceso insubstancial; (mar. y com.) siniestro; (gram.) accidente, inflexión.—**a. insurance**, seguro contra accidentes.—**by a.**, accidentalmente, por casualidad.—**traffic a.**, accidente de circulación o tránsito.
accidental [æksidéntǎl]. **I.** *a.* accidental, casual, contingente, fortuito.—**a. color**, (fís.) color accidental (el de la imagen que persiste tras retirar la vista de un objeto brillante).—**a. image**, (fís.) imagen accidental. **II.** *s.* (mús.) accidente.
accidentally [-i], *adv.* accidentalmente, casualmente.
accipiter [æksípitœ(r)], *s.* (orn.) accípitre, ave (f.) de rapiña.—**accipitral** [æksípitrǎl], *a.* accipitrino.
acclaim [ækléim], *va.* y *vn.* aclamar, aplaudir, proclamar, vitorear, vocear.
acclamation, acclaim [æklǎméiŝǒn], *s.* aclamación, aplauso, celebración, proclamación.
acclamatory [æklémǎtǫri], *a.* aclamatorio.
acclimate [ækláimit], *va.* aclimatar, connaturalizar.
acclimated [-id], *pp.* y *a.* aclimatado.
acclimation, o acclimatization [ækliméiŝǒn, æklǎimǎtizéiŝǒn] *s.* aclimatación, connaturalización.
acclimatize [ækláimǎtaiz]. **I.** *va.* aclimatar, acostumbrar a otro clima. **II.** *vn.* aclimatarse, connaturalizarse.
acclivity [æklíviti], *s.* subida, cuesta ascendiente.
acclivous [ækláivʌs], *a.* inclinado hacia arriba, empinado.
accolade [ækoléid], *s.* acolada; espaldarazo dado al caballero al armarlo; (mús.) corchete, barra; (arq.) moldura de dos curvas unidas en forma de corchete.
accoladed [-id], *a.* armado caballero; caballero titulado (que tiene el título de *Sir*).
accommodate [ǎkámodeit]. **I.** *va.* acomodar, ajustar, adecuar; componer, arreglar (una disputa, etc.); servir, complacer; hacer un favor a; hospedar; tener espacio o capacidad para; (com.) prestar dinero a. **II.** *vn.* conformarse, adaptarse, avenirse.
accommodating [-iŋ], *a.* bondadoso, servicial, complaciente, acomodadizo, acomodaticio, oficioso.
accommodation [-éiŝǒn], *s.* acomodación, acomodamiento; servicio, favor; adaptación, adecuación; ajuste, arreglo, componenda, acuerdo; aplicación o interpretación errónea (de un escrito, pasaje, etc.); cuarto, localidad, habitación.—*pl.* facilidades, comodidades, alojamiento.—**a. and board**, alojamiento y manutención.—**a. bill, draft, note**, (com.) giro, pagaré de favor.—**a. ladder**, (mar.) escalera real.—**a. train**, tren de escala, tren

ómnibus, tren carreta.—**sleeping car a.**, localidad en coche dormitorio.

accommodator [-ǫ(r)], *s.* acomodador, arreglador, etc.; aparato para adaptar.

accompaniment [ǝkámpǝnimǝnt], *s.* acompañamiento, concomitancia.

accompanist [-ist], *s.* (mús.) acompañador, acompañante.

accompany [ǝkámpǝni], *va.* acompañar, concomitar, conducir, ir con; (mús.) acompañar.

accomplice [ǝkámplis], *s.* cómplice, correo.

accomplish [ǝkámpliʃ], *va.* efectuar, cumplir, verificar, llevar a cabo; completar; lograr, realizar.

accomplished [-t], *a.* perfecto, acabado, cabal, cumplido, consumado; culto.

accomplisher [-œ(r)], *s.* el que realiza, ejecuta o cumple algo.

accomplishment [-mǝnt], *s.* consumación, realización, ejecución, logro, efectuación, cumplimiento.—*pl.* conocimientos, prendas, habilidades.

accord [ǝkórd]. I. *va.* conceder, otorgar, tributar; ajustar, conciliar, concordar, acordar, poner de acuerdo. II. *vn.* concordar; convenir, avenirse, concertar, acordar, estar de acuerdo.

accord, *s.* acuerdo, convenio; concierto, buena inteligencia; armonía; (mús.) diapasón, acorde. —**in a.**, de consuno.—**in a. with**, de acuerdo con, acorde con.—**of one's own a.**, espontáneamente.—**with one a.**, unánimemente, de consuno.

accordance, accordancy [-ǝns, -i], *s.* conformidad, buena inteligencia, armonía, acuerdo, concesión.—**in a. with**, de acuerdo o de conformidad con.

accordant [-ǝnt], *a.* acorde, conforme, propio, en armonía, conveniente, en consonancia con.

accordantly [-li], *adv.* acordemente.

according [-iŋ], *a.* conforme; acorde.—**a. as**, *conj.* según que, a medida que, como.—**a. to**, según, conforme a, con arreglo a.—*p.a.* que concede.

accordingly [-li], *adv.* en conformidad; en efecto, de consiguiente; por lo tanto; por ende, pues.

accordion [ǝkórdiǫn], *s.* (mús.) acordeón.—**a.-pleated**, afollado, acordonado.

accordionist [-ist], *s.* acordeonista.

accost [ǝkóst], *va.* dirigirse a, hablar a, abordar, emprender a o con.

accosted [-id], *a.* (blas.) acostado.

accouchement [ǝkúʃmǝnt], *s.* parto, alumbramiento.

accoucheur [ǝkuʃǽr], *s.* comadrón, partero.

accoucheuse [ǝkuʃǽz], *s.* partera, comadre, *f.*

account [ǝkáǫnt]. I. *va.* tener por, considerar, estimar, juzgar. II. *vn.* dar cuenta y razón.— **to a. for,** dar razón de; responder de; explicar, dar cuenta de. III. *s.* narración, relato, informe, relación; importancia, mérito, valor, monta, posición; explicación, cuenta, razón. motivo; cómputo, cálculo, manera de contar o de medir (el tiempo, etc.); consideración, aprecio; (com.) cuenta.—**a. book,** libro de cuentas. —**a. current,** cuenta corriente.—**a. payable,** cuenta a pagar.—**a. receivable,** cuenta a cobrar.—**a. rendered,** cuenta girada o enviada.—**a. sales,** cuenta de ventas, estado de ventas (hechas por un comerciante por cuenta de otro).—**a. settled,** cuenta convenida.—**charge a.,** cuenta abierta o corriente. —**by all accounts,** según el decir o la opinión general.—**for a. of,** en favor de; por cuenta de. —**in a. with,** en cuenta con.—**of a.,** de nota, de importancia; imaginaria (se dice de la moneda).—**of no a.,** de poco más o menos, de poca monta *(people of no account,* gente de poca monta, gentuza).—**on a.,** a cuenta.—**on a. of,** a causa de; con motivo de; por amor de *(on your account,* por amor de usted, por usted); por cuenta de.—**on my own a.,** por mi propio

bien; por mi cuenta, por mi cuenta y riesgo. —**on no a.,** de ninguna manera; por ningún motivo.—**to keep an a.,** llevar cuenta, tener cuenta abierta.—**to take into a.,** tener en cuenta, contar con.—**to turn to a.,** aprovechar, sacar provecho de.

accountability, accountableness [-ǝbíliti, -ǝblnis], *s.* contabilidad; responsabilidad.

accountable [-ǝbl], *a.* responsable; explicable.

accountant [-ǝnt], *s.* contador, contabilista, tenedor de libros.—**a. general,** jefe de contabilidad.

accounting [-iŋ], *s.* contabilidad, contaduría; estado de cuentas; explicación.—**a. machine,** máquina de contabilidad.—**to ask an a.,** pedir rendición de cuentas.

accouter accoutre [ǝkútœ(r)], *va.* aviar, equipar, vestir, ataviar.

accouterment, accoutrement [-mǝnt], *s.* avío, equipo, apresto, atavío, pertrechos, *m. pl.*

accredit [ǝkrédit], *va.* acreditar; dar credenciales; autorizar; dar crédito, creer, confiar en; atribuir a.

accredited [-id], *a.* acreditado; autorizado; (dipl.) provisto de credenciales.

accrescent [ǝkrésǝnt], *a.* creciente, acrescente, que aumenta; (bot.) que sigue creciendo después de florecer.

accrete [ǝkrít]. I. *va. y vn.* acrecer(se), aumentar(se), adherirse. II. *a.* acrecido, aumentado, adherido.

accretion [ǝkríʃǫn], *s.* acrecentamiento, aumento; (for.) acrecencia (derecho de); (min.) acreción; (med.) adherencia de órganos normalmente separados.

accretive [ǝkrítiv], *a.* aumentativo, creciente, que aumenta (otra cosa) agregándose.

accrual [ǝkrúǝl], *s.* aumento, incremento; rédito. —*pl.* acumulaciones (de intereses).

accrue [ǝkrú], *vn.* crecer, aumentar, tomar incremento; agregarse; acumularse; redituarse (interés); resultar, provenir, originarse; (for.) ser otorgado.

accruer [-œ(r)], *s.* (for.) acrecencia, derecho de acrecer.

accubation [ækyụbéiʃǫn], *s.* reclinación; parto.

accumbent [ækámbǝnt], *a.* reclinado; (bot.) acumbente.

accumulate [ǝkyúmiuleit]. I. *va.* acumular, amontonar, atesorar, hacinar, reunir, recoger. II. *vn.* crecer, acumularse, amontonarse. III. *a.* juntado, acumulado, amontonado.

accumulation [-léiʃǫn], *s.* acumulación, amontonamiento, hacinamiento.

accumulative [-iv], *a.* acumulativo, acumulado, añadido.

accumulatively [-li], *adv.* acumulativamente.

accumulator [-ǫ(r)], *s.* acumulador, amontonador; (mec. y elec.) acumulador.

accuracy [ǽkyụrǝsi], *s.* exactitud, precisión, esmero, puntualidad.—**minute a.,** menudencia, impertinencia.

accurate [ǽkyụrit], *a.* exacto, preciso, puntual; certero (en el tiro); exacto, afinado o seguro (en los cálculos).

accurately [-li], *adv.* con exactitud, con esmero, correctamente.

accurateness [-nis], *s.* = ACCURACY.

accursed, accurst [ǝkǽrst], *a.* maldito, maldecido; detestable, execrable; desventurado; perverso; infausto, fatal; anatematizado, excomulgado.—**a. be,** mal haya, maldito sea.

accusant [ǝkyúzǝnt], *s.* acusador.

accusation [ækyuzéiʃǫn], *s.* acusación, imputación, cargo, inculpación, delación, denuncia.

accusative [ǝkyúzǝtiv], *a. y s.* acusativo.

accusatory [ǝkyúzǝtǫri], *a.* acusatorio, acusador.

accuse [ǝkyúz], *va.* acusar, delatar, denunciar, (in)culpar, tachar, sindicar, tildar (de), levantar cargo.

accused [-d], *s. y a.* acusado, procesado.

accuser [-œ(r)], *s.* acusador, delatante, delator, denunciador, denunciante.

accustom [ɐkʌstɔm], *va.* y *vn.* acostumbrar(se), avezar(se), habituar(se), hacer(se).

accustomed [-d], *a.* acostumbrado; de costumbre, habitual, sólito, hecho, cursado.—**to be a.**, acostumbrar, soler.—**to become a.**, acostumbrarse, etc.

ace [ejs]. I. *s.* as (de naipe o dado); migaja, partícula; (en tenis, etc.) un solo tanto; mala suerte; lo peor; lo mejor; (aer.) as, aviador militar que ha puesto cinco enemigos fuera de combate; aviador sobresaliente.—**within an a. of**, muy cerca de, por poco, en un tris, a dos dedos de. II. *a.* sobresaliente.—**a.-high**, (tenido) en grandísima estima, muy favorecido, de primera.

acedia [æsídjɐ], *s.* acidia, desidia, flojedad, pereza; [asɪdiɐ], (ict.) acedía, especie de platija.

acentric [ejséntrɪk], *a.* sin centro; fuera del centro, excéntrico; (med.) acéntrico, que no se origina en un centro nervioso.

acephalia [æsɛféjliɐ], *s.* acefalía, falta de cabeza.

acephalism [ejséfalɪzm], *s.* acefalismo.

acephalous [-ʌs], *a.* acéfalo.

acerate, acerated [æsɐrejt, -ɪd], *a.* puntiagudo.

acerb [ɐsœrb], *a.* acerbo, ácido, agrio, áspero.

acerbate [æsœrbejt], *va.* agriar, exasperar.

acerbity [ɐsœrbɪti], *s.* acerbidad, amargura, agrura, aspereza, dureza.

acerose [æsɛrous], *a.* (bot.) aciculado.

acerous [æsɛrʌs], *a.* sin antenas; sin astas.

acescency [æséssensi], *s.* acescencia, acedía.

acescent [æsésɐnt], *a.* acescente, repuntado, agriado, agrete.

acetabulum [æsɛtæbyʊlʌm], *s.* (anat.) acetábulo en que encaja la cabeza del fémur.

acetal [æsɛtal], *s.* (quím.) acetal.

acetamide [æsɛtæmajd], *s.* (quím.) acetamida.

acetanilid(e [æsɛtænilajd], *s.* (quím.) acetanilida, antifebrina.

acetate [æsɛtejt], *s.* (quím.) acetato.

acetic [æsítɪk], *a.* acético.

acetify [æsétɪfaj], *va.* acetificar.

acetimeter [æsɛtímitœ(r)], *s.* (quím.) acetímetro.

acetimetry [-trɪ], *s.* (quím.) acetimetría.

acetin [æsɛtɪn], *s.* (quím.) acetina.

acetol [æsɛtoʊl], *s.* (quím.) acetol.

acetone [æsɛtoʊn], *s.* (quím.) acetona.

acetous, acetose [æsɛtʌs, -toʊs], *a.* acetoso.

acetyl [æsɛtɪl]. I. *s.* (quím.) acetilo. II. *a.* de acetilo.

acetylene [æsétilin]. I. *a.* acetilénico. II. *s.* (quím.) acetileno.—**a. torch**, pico de acetileno.

acetylic [-ɪk], *a.* acetílico.

ache [ejk]. I. *s.* dolor, dolencia, mal; aflicción, pena, pesar.—*pl.* agujetas. II. *vn.* doler (*my head aches*, me duele la cabeza).

Achean, Achæan [ɐkíɐn], *a.* y *s.* aqueo.

achievable [ɐchívɐbl], *a.* acabable, ejecutable, hacedero, factible.

achieve [ɐchív], *va.* acabar, realizar, ejecutar, llevar a cabo; lograr, alcanzar; obtener, ganar.

achievement [-mɛnt], *s.* realización, ejecución, logro; hecho muy notable o meritorio, proeza, hazaña; (blas.) timbre.

aching [éjkɪŋ]. I. *a.* doliente, dolorido, que duele. II. *s.* dolencia, mal continuo.

achor [éjkɔr], *s.* (med.) acores.

achroma, achromia [ejkróʊmɐ, -mjɐ], *s.* acromia.

achromatic [ækromǽtɪk], *a.* (ópt.) acromático.

achromatism [ækróʊmɐtɪzm], *s.* (ópt.) acromatismo.

achromatize [-tajz], *va.* acromatizar.

achromatopsia [-tápsjɐ], *s.* acromatopsia.

achromic [ejkróʊmjk], *a.* acrómico, descolorido.

achy [éjkɪ], *a.* (a)dolorido, con dolor.

acicular [æsíkjulɐ(r)], *a.* acicular.

aciculate [æsíkjulejt], *a.* acicular.

acid [æsɪd], *s.* y *a.* ácido.

acid, *s.*—**a.-forming**, acidógeno, que produce gas.—**a. proof**, a prueba de ácidos, resistente a los ácidos.—**a. steel**, acero (hecho por el procedimiento) ácido.—**a. test**, prueba rigurosa decisiva.

acidification [æsɪdɪfɪkéjʂɔn], *s.* acidificación.

acidify [æsɪdɪfaj], *va.* acidificar, acidular.

acidimeter [æsɪdímetœ(r)], *s.* (quím.) acidímetro.

acidimetry [-trɪ], *s.* (quím.) acidimetría.

acidity, acidness [æsídɪtɪ, æsɪdnɪs], *s.* acidez, agrura, acedía.

acidosis [æsɪdóʊsɪs], *s.* (med.) asescencia, acidismo, exceso de acidez en la sangre.

acidulate [æsídʒʊlejt], *va.* acidular; agriar, avinagrar.

acidulous [-ʌs], *a.* agrio, acídulo.

acierage [æsjɛrɪdʒ], *s.* (met.) aceración.

acierate [-ejt], *va.* (met.) acerar.

aciform [æsɪfɔrm], *a.* (bot.) aciforme, de forma de aguja.

Acineta [æsɪnítɐ], *s.* (bot. y zool.) acineta.

aciniform [æsínɪfɔrm], *a.* (bot.) aciniforme.

acinose [æsɪnoʊs], **acinous** [-ʌs], *a.* (bot.) acinoso.

acinus [æsɪnʌs], *s.* (anat. y bot.) acino.

ack-ack [ǽkæk], *s.* (mil.) fuego concentrado de baterías antiaéreas.

acknowledge [æknálɪdʒ], *va.* reconocer; confesar, admitir; (for.) certificar, testificar, confirmar.—**to a. receipt**, acusar recibo.

acknowledgment [-mɛnt], *s.* reconocimiento; confesión, admisión; acuse de recibo; confirmación; (for.) testificación, testificata.

aclastic [ejklǽstɪk], *a.* (ópt.) aclasto.

aclinic [ejklínɪk], *a.* (fís.) aclínico.

acme [ækmɪ], *s.* cima, pináculo, cumbre; (fig.) apogeo, auge, culminación, colmo; (med.) acmé o acme.

acne [æknɪ], *s.* (med. y vet.) acné o acne, *mf.*, barros, pústulas.

acock [ɐkák], *a.* ladeado (el sombrero, etc.); avisado.

acologic [ækolódʒɪk], *a.* acológico.

acology [ækalodʒɪ], *s.* (med.) acología.

acolyte [ækolajt], *s.* acólito; monacillo, misario, monaguillo.

aconite [ækonajt], **aconitum** [ækonájtʌm], *s.* (med. y bot.) acónito.

aconitic [ækonítɪk], *a.* (quím.) aconítico.

aconitine [ækánɪtɪn], *s.* (quím.) aconitina.

acorn [éjkɔrn], *s.* (bot.) bellota.—**a. barnacle** o **shell**, lapa.

acosmism [ejkázmjzm], *s.* (fil.) acosmismo.

acotyledon [ejkatɪlídɔn], *s.* acotiledón.

acotyledonous [-ʌs], *a.* acotiledóneo.

acoustic [ɐkústɪk], *a.* acústico.

acoustician [ækustíʂɐn], *s.* acústico, versado en acústica.

acoustics [ɐkústɪks], *s.* acústica.

acquaint [ɐkwéjnt], *va.* instruir, familiarizar; enterar, informar, hacer saber a, imponer, advertir.—**to a. oneself with**, familiarizarse con, ponerse al corriente de, informarse de.

acquaintance [-ɐns], *s.* conocimiento (**a. with**, conocimiento de); familiaridad, relaciones, relacionado; conocimiento mutuo (de dos personas), hecho de conocerse entre sí; conocido (persona a quien se conoce).

acquainted [-id], *a.* conocido (*are you two acquainted?* ¿se conocen Vds. dos?); impuesto, enterado.—**a. with**, impuesto o enterado (de algo).—**to be a. with**, conocer (algo o a una persona).—**to make a. with**, relacionar con; enterar de.

acquest [ɐkwést], *s.* (for.) adquisición; propiedad no heredada.

acquiesce [ækwiɛ́s], *vn.* asentir; consentir, conformarse.

acquiescence [-ɛns], *s.* aquiescencia, asenso,

consentimiento, conformidad; sumisión, resignación.

acquiescent [-ęnt], *a*. condescendiente, acomodadizo, conforme, sumiso.

acquirable [ąkwáįrąbl], *a*. adquirible, asequible.

acquire [ąkwáįr], *va*. adquirir, obtener, aquisitar, alcanzar, ganar, contraer (hábitos, etc.).

acquirement [-męnt], *s*. adquisición.—*pl*. conocimientos, saber.

acquirer [-œ(r)], *s*. adquiridor.

acquiring [-įŋ], *a*. adquiridor, adquir(i)ente.

acquisition [ækwįzíśǫn], *s*. adquisición, consecución.

acquisitive [ækwízįtįv], *a*. capaz de adquirir; dispuesto a adquirir; adquisitivo.—**a. prescription**, (for.) prescripción adquisitiva.

acquisitively [-lį], *adv*. por adquisición.

acquisitiveness [-nįs], *s*. adquisividad; calidad de adquisitivo; tendencia a adquirir.

acquit [ąkwįt], *va*. absolver, exculpar, dispensar, libertar; exonerar, descargar, relevar; pagar.—**to a. oneself**, portarse, conducirse, desempeñar su trabajo, salir, hacerlo (bien, mal).

acquittal [-ąl], **acquitment** [-męnt], *s*. absolución; descargo; pago.

acquittance [-ąns], *s*. descargo de una deuda; recibo, quita, carta de pago.

acquitted [-įd], *pp*. absuelto.

acre [éįkœr], *s*. acre (medida de superficie-40,47 áreas).—**a. foot**, (ing.) acrepié, cantidad de agua suficiente para cubrir un acre hasta una altura de 1 pie.—**a. inch**, acrepulgada.—**God's a.**, camposanto.

acreage [éįkœrįdž], *s*. número de acres; extensión de tierra o de terreno; superficie medida en acres.

acred [éįkœrd], *a*. de acres, hacendado, afincado, que posee tierras (*large-acred man*, terrateniente, hombre de muchos terrenos).

acrid [ǽkrįd], *a*. acre, mordaz, picante, agrio, mordicante.

acridity, acridness [ækrídįtį, ǽkrįdnįs], *s*. acritud, acrimonia.

acrimonious [ækrįmóųnįʌs], *a*. acrimonioso, sarcástico, mordaz, picante.

acrimoniously [-lį], *adv*. con acrimonia, con aspereza, mordazmente.

acrimoniousness [-nįs], **acrimony** [ǽkrįmoųnį], *s*. acrimonia, acritud, amargura, aspereza, mordacidad, virulencia.

acritical [eįkrítįkąl], *a*. (med.) acrítico, que no tiene crisis.

acroamatic [ækroąmǽtįk], *a*. acroamático, oral.

acrobat [ǽkrobæt], *s*. acróbata, volatín, volteador, (Méx.) cirquero.

acrobatic [ækrobǽtįk], *a*. acrobático.—**a. feat**, volatín.

acrobatics [-s], **acrobatism** [ǽkrobætįzm], *s*. acrobatismo, acrobacia.

acrocarpous [ækrokárpʌs], *a*. (bot.) acrocárpeo.

acrocephalous [-séfąlʌs], *a*. (med.) acrocéfalo.

acrogen [ǽkrodžįn], *s*. acrógena.

acrolein [ąkróųlįįn], *s*. (quím.) acroleína, acrol.

acrolith [ǽkrolįθ], *s*. (arqueol.) acrólito.

acromegaly [ækromégąlį], *s*. (med.) acromegalia.

acromial [ækróųmįąl], *a*. (anat.) acromiano, acromial.

acromion [ækróųmįąn], *s*. (anat.) acromio(n).

acronycal [ækránįkąl], *a*. (astr.) acrónico.

acropolis [ækrápolįs], *s*. acrópolis, ciudadela griega.

acrosporous [ækrospóųrʌs], *a*. (bot.) acrósporo.

across [ąkrós]. **I.** *adv*. de través, a través, transversalmente; de una parte a otra; al otro lado; en cruz. **II.** *prep*. a través de; al otro lado de; por.—**a. the way**, frente.—**to come o run a.**, encontrarse (algo); encontrarse con, topar o tropezar con.—**to lay o place a.**, cruzar.

acrostic [ąkróstįk], *s*. y *a*. acróstico.

acroterium [ækrotírįʌm], *s*. (arq.) acrotera.

acrylic [ækrílįk], *a*. (quím.) acrílico (ácido).

act [ækt]. **I.** *vn*. obrar, actuar, funcionar, oficiar de, operar; representar (en el teatro); fingir, simular; conducirse, portarse, andar.—**to a. for someone**, representar a uno.—**to a. against**, oponerse a.—**to a. as** (a notary), hacer de (notario).—**to a. as if**, hacer como que, o como si.—**to a. to no purpose**, hacer por hacer.—**to a. up**, jaranear, travesear. **II.** *va*. hacer o desempeñar el papel de (vg.: *to act the buffoon*, hacer de bufón).—**to a. on**, o **upon**, influir en, obrar sobre.—**to a. out**, representar dramática o teatralmente.—**to a. the part of**, hacer el papel de, hacer las veces de, reemplazar.

act [ækt], *s*. acción, acto, hecho, obra; (teat.) acto o jornada; (for.) ley, *f*., disposición, decreto, acta; instrumento, documento.—**a. of God**, (for.) caso fortuito, fuerza mayor.—**a. of grace**, acto de clemencia.—**a. of honor**, (com.) acto o protesta de intervención.—**a. of indemnity**, bi.l de indemnidad.—**a. of settlement**, (Ing.) ley que ha fijado la sucesión en la casa de Hánover.—**Acts, Acts of the Apostles**, (bib.) Actos o Hechos de los Apóstoles.—**in the (very) a.**, en flagrante.

acting [ǽktįŋ]. **I.** *s*. acción, efecto; (teat.) representación, desempeño. **II.** *a*. interino, suplente, obrante.

actinia [æktínįą], *s*. (zool.) actinia, estrellamar, *f*., anemone (*f*.) de mar, ortiga de mar.

actinic(al [æktínįk(ąl], *a*. actínico.

actinism [ǽktįnįzm], *s*. actinismo.

actinium [æktínįąm], *s*. (quím.) actinio.

actinograph [æktínogrœf], *s*. actinógrafo.

actinolite [-lajt], *s*. (min.) actinota.

actinometer [æktįnámetœ(r)], *s*. actinómetro.

actinometric [æktįnomét̯rįk], *a*. actinométrico.

actinometry [æktįnámetrį], *s*. actinometría.

actinomorphic [æktįnomórfįk], **actinomorphous** [-ʌs], *a*. (bot.) actinomorfo.

actinomycosis [-maįkóųsįs], *s*. (med. y vet.) actinomicosis.

action [ǽkśǫn], *s*. acción, acto, obra, hecho; operación, golpe, funcionamiento, accionamiento; actividad; actuación; movimiento; gesto; (teat.) argumento, acción; (mil.) acción, batalla; (mec.) marcha, mecanismo; (for.) acción, demanda, proceso, expediente, proceder; (b. a.) actitud, ademán.—**to bring an a.**, (for.) entablar un pleito.—**to put in a.**, actuar.—**to take a.**, proceder (contra).—**to take a. on**, dar curso a, tomar medidas acerca de.

actionable [-ąbl], *a*. (for.) punible, justiciable, procesable.

actionably [-ąblį], *adv*. de un modo procesario.

activate [ǽktįvejt], *va*. activar, hacer activo; tratar (aguas inmundas) por aeración prolongada. —**activated sludge**, residuo lodoso de la aeración prolongada.

activation [-éįśǫn], *s*. activación.

activator [-ǫ(r)], *s*. (quím.) activador.

active [ǽktįv], *a*. activo, ejecutivo, agencioso, diligente, ágil, ligero, enérgico, eficaz.—**a. bond**, bono que devenga interés fijo desde que se emite.—**a. list**, lista de oficiales militares en servicio.—**to make a.**, activar, agilitar.

actively [-lį], *adv*. activamente, acuciosamente.

activity [æktívįtį], *s*. actividad, diligencia, vigor, agilidad, vida.—*pl*. ocupaciones, actividades.

actor [ǽktǫ(r)], *s*. agente; (teat.) cómico, actor, comediante, histrión, *m*., representante; (for.) actor, demandante; apoderado.

actress [ǽktrįs], *s*. (teat.) actriz, cómica, comediante, histrionisa; (for.) actora, etc.

actual [ǽkchuąl], *a*. real, verdadero, existente, efectivo; propiamente dicho; actual. (Hoy apenas si se usa en este último sentido.)—**a. sin**, (teol.) pecado actual.

actuality [ækchuǽlįtį], **actualness** [ǽkchuąlnįs], *s*. realidad; actualidad.

actualize [ǽkchuąlajz], *va*. realizar, dar realidad

a, llevar a cabo; (for.) actuar, proceder judicialmente.

actually [ǽkchu̱ali̱], *adv.* realmente, en realidad, verdaderamente, de hecho; en o con efecto, efectivamente.

actuarial [ækchu̱ériạl], *a.* rel. al actuario de seguros; (for.) actuario.

actuary [ǽkchu̱eri̱], *s.* actuario (especialista en cálculos de seguros); (for.) actuario, escribano, registrador.

actuate [ǽkchu̱eit]. **I.** *va.* mover, impulsar, excitar, animar, poner en acción. **II.** *vn.* obrar,—**actuated** [-i̱d], *a.* movido, animado.—**actuation** [-éi̱şon], *s.* actuación, operación; impulsión; puesta en acción.

acuity [aki̱úiti̱], *s.* acuidad, agudeza.

aculeate [aki̱úlieit]. **I.** *a.* (zool.) aculeado, acúleo; (bot.) espinoso, provisto de púas. **II.** *s.* (zool.) aculeado, aculeata, *m.*

aculeiform [aki̱úlii̱form], *a.* aculeiforme.

acumen [aki̱úmi̱n], *s.* cacumen; agudeza, sutileza, perspicacia, penetración; (fam.) caletre, pesquis; (bot.) punta aguda.

acuminate [-eit]. **I.** *a.* (bot.) acuminado, que termina en punta. **II.** *va.* aguzar, afilar. **III.** *vn.* rematar en punta.

acumination [-éi̱şon], *s.* punta aguda.

acuminous [-as], *a.* = ACUMINATE.

acupressure [ǽki̱upreşu̱(r)], *s.* (cir.) acupresión.

acupuncture [ǽki̱upaɲkchu̱r], *s.* (cir.) acupuntura.

acute [aki̱út]. **I.** *a.* agudo; ingenioso, perspicaz, vivo, fino, delgado, sutil, penetrante; crítico; (med.) agudo.—**a. angle**, (geom.) ángulo agudo.—**a.-angled**, (geom.) acutángulo, oxigonio. **II.** *s.* (gram.) acento agudo.

acutely [-li̱], *adv.* agudamente; despiertamente; vivamente.

acuteness [-ni̱s], *s.* agudeza; delgadez, sutileza; perspicacia, viveza, penetración; discreción; violencia de una enfermedad.

acyclic [eisáikli̱k], *a.* (elec.) acíclico (se aplica a dínamos); (bot.) acíclico o no verticilado.

ad [æd], *s.* anuncio, aviso.

adactylous [eidǽkti̱las], *a.* (zool.) adácti·lo.

adage [ǽdi̱dź], *s.* adagio, refrán, proverbio.

adagio [adádźou̱], *s.* (mús.) adagio.

Adam [ǽdạm], *s.* Adán; pecado original, depravación humana.—**A.'s ale**, (fam.) agua.—**A.'s apple**, nuez de la garganta, manzana de Adán; una variedad de plátano.—**A.'s needle and thread**, una especie de yuca.—**not to know from A.**, (fam.) no conocer absolutamente.

adamant [ǽdạmænt]. **I.** *s.* (ant.) adamante. substancia sumamente dura; diamante; (poét.) dureza. **II.** *a.* firme, inexorable.

adamantine [ædạmǽnti̱n], *a.* diamantino, adiamantado, adamantino; indisoluble; inflexible, impregnable.—**a. spar**, corindón de la India.

Adamite [ǽdạmait], *s.* adamita, *mf.*

adapt [adǽpt], *va.* adaptar, acomodar, ajustar, proporcionar, amoldar; tomar y compendiar (un escrito); (teat.) refundir, arreglar.

adaptable [-abl], **adaptive** [-iv], *a.* adaptable, aplicable, acomodable.

adaptability [-abi̱li̱ti̱], *s.* adaptabilidad.

adaptation [ædæptéi̱şon], **adaption** [adǽpşon], *s.* adaptación; ajuste; (teat.) arreglo, refundición.

adapter [adǽptœ(r)], *s.* el o lo que adapta; (tec.) adaptador; (quím.) alargadera, tubo que comunica una retorta con otra vasija; (mec.) ajustador, manguito de reducción.

add [æd]. **I.** *va.* sumar, adicionar, totalizar; agregar, añadir.—**to a. up**, sumar. **II.** *vn.* sumar.—**to a. to**, aumentar.

addax [ǽdæks], *s.* (zool.) variedad de antílope.

addend [ǽdend], *s.* (arit.) sumando.

addenda [ædéndạ], *s.* (pl. de ADDENDUM) aditamentos; apéndice.

addendum [-am], *s.* adición, apéndice; (mec.)

cabeza de un diente de engranaje.—**a. circle**, **a. line** o **a.** simplemente, (mec.) periferia de una rueda dentada.

adder [ǽdœ(r)], *s.* víbora; serpiente.—**puff a.**, víbora sudafricana.—**a.'s grass** o **a.'s tongue**, (bot.) lengua de sierpe.—**a.'s wort**, (bot.) escorzonera.

addict [adi̱kt]. **I.** *va.* dedicar, consagrar, aplicar. **II.** *vn.* entregarse, dedicarse, darse, abandonarse (al vicio, placer, etc.). **III.** [ǽdi̱kt], *s.* adicto, aficionado; enviciado, morfinómano.

addicted [-i̱d], *a.* adicto, dado, entregado o afecto a, apasionado por, partidario de.

addictedness [-ni̱s], **addiction** [adi̱kşon], *s.* inclinación, propensión, afición, apego; entrega, dedicación a.

adding machine [ǽdi̱ŋ mạşín], *s.* sumadora, máquina de sumar.

additament [ædi̱tạment], *s.* aditamento.

addition [ædi̱şon], *s.* adición, añadidura, agregación; aditamento, adjunto; (arit.) adición, suma.—**in a.**, por añadidura, además, fuera de esto.—**in a. to**, además de, fuera de.

additional [-al], *a.* adicional.

additionally [-i̱], *adv.* adicionalmente, en adición.

additive [ǽdi̱ti̱v], *a.* aditivo, que debe agregarse.

addle [ǽdl]. **I.** *a.* huero, gárgol, podrido (esp. de huevos); estéril, infecundo, vacío. **II.** *va.* y *vn.* enhuerar(se), engorar; esterilizar, hacer estéril, echar(se) a perder; confundir, embrollar.—**a.-brain(ed)**, **a.-head(ed)**, **a.-pate(d)**, *s.* y *a.*, (fam.) estúpido, mentecato, chalado, atontado.

address [adrés]. **I.** *va.* dirigir la palabra, arengar o hablar a uno; emprender (a o con uno); enderezar; dirigir, sobrescribir o poner el sobrescrito (a una carta); obsequiar, requebrar (a uno); (com.) consignar. **II.** *vn.* dirigirse a uno (de palabra o por escrito); aplicarse, consagrarse, dedicarse (a algo).

address [adrés o ǽdres], *s.* dirección, señas, *f. pl.*; sobrescrito; membrete; discurso, alocución, plática; petición, solicitud, memorial; trato, tratamiento; tono, talante, gracia; manera de hablar o conversar; habilidad, destreza, maña. —**Address to the Crown**, contestación al discurso de la Corona.—*pl.* galanteo, requiebros, obsequios amorosos.

addressee [adresí], *s.* destinatario (de una carta, mercancías, etc.).

addresser [adrésœ(r)], *s.* expedidor, remitente; peticionario, suplicante, exponente.

addressing machine, *s.* = ADDRESSOGRAPH.

addressograph [adrésográf], *s.* máquina para imprimir sobrescritos (es nombre de fábrica).

adduce [adi̱ús], *va.* aducir, alegar, traer (razones o pruebas).

adducent [-ent], *a.* (anat.) aductor.

adduct [adi̱kt], *va.* (fisiol.) causar aducción.

adduction [adi̱kşon], *s.* presentación, exposición, alegación (de hechos, etc.); (anat.) aducción.

adductor [adi̱kto(r)], *s.* (anat.) músculo aductor.

adeem [adím], *va.* (for.) anular un legado, en vida del testador, por otra disposición de lo legado, o por entrega anticipada de lo mismo o su equivalente al legatario.

ademption [adémpşon], *s.* (for.) anulación de un legado, o enajenación, en vida, de bienes testados.

adenia [adínia̱], *s.* (med.) adenia, adenopatía.

adenitis [ædenáitis], *s.* (med.) adenitis.

adenography [ædenágrạfi̱], *s.* (anat.) adenografía.

adenoid, adenoidal [ǽdenoid, ædenóidal], *a.* adenoideo, glandiforme.

adenoid, *s.* (anat. y med.) vegetación o tumor adenoideo.—*pl.* (med.) hipertrofia del tejido adenoideo de la faringe nasal.

adenology [ædenálodźi̱], *s.* (anat.) adenología.

adenoma [ædenóuma̱], *s.* (med.) adenoma, *m.*

adenopathy [ædɛnápɐθḭ], s. adenopatía.
adenose [ǽdḭnoṵs], a. adenoso, glandular.
adephagia [ædɛfḗịdżịɐ̣], s. adefagia, voracidad.
adephagous [ædḗfɐgʌs], a. adéfago, voraz.
adept [ɐdépt], s. y a. adepto, perito.
adequacy [ǽdɛkwɐṣḭ], s. calidad de adecuado, suficiencia, adecuación.
adequate [ǽdɛkwịt], a. adecuado, proporcionado, suficiente, a propósito, idóneo, competente.
adequately [-lḭ], adv. adecuadamente.
adequateness [-nḭs], s. adecuación.
adhere [ædhír], vn. adherirse, unirse; allegarse; (a)pegarse; aficionarse.
adherence [-ɛns], **adherency** [-ḭ], s. adhesión, apego, adherencia.
adherent [-ɛnt], a. adherente, adicto; adhesivo, pegajoso.
adherent, adherer [-œ(r)], s. adherente, secuaz, partidario, parcial, sectario.
adherently [-ɛntlị], adv. con adhesión, parcialmente.
adhesion [ædhíṣɔn], s. adhesión, adherencia.
adhesive [ædhíṣịv]. I. s. adhesivo, substancia adhesiva. II. a. adhesivo, adherente, pegadizo, conglutinante; tenaz; engomado (sello).—a. tape, o **plaster**, esparadrapo, tafetán inglés, cinta adherente. V. FRICTION TAPE.
adhesively [-lị], adv. tenazmente, en unión estrecha.
adhesiveness [-nịs], s. calidad de adhesivo; adhesividad, adherencia; tenacidad; propensidad a la amistad y a la sociabilidad.
adhibit [ædhíbịt], va. dejar entrar, admitir; aplicar, dar; unir, agregar.
adiabatic [ædịɐbǽtịk], a. (fís.) adiabático.
adiantum [ædịéntʌm], s. (bot.) adianto, culantrillo.
adiaphoresis [ædịæforísịs], s. (med.) adiaforesis.
adieu [ɐdịú]. I. interj. adiós. II. s. despedida; adiós.—to bid a., despedirse (de).
adipocere [ǽdịposịr], s. adipocira.
adipose [ǽdịpoṵs]. I. a. adiposo, seboso. II. s. grasa, sebo, unto, gordura.
adiposis [ædịpóṵsịs], s. gordura; (med.) adiposis.
adiposity [ædịpásịtị], s. adiposidad, obesidad.
adit [ǽdịt], s. acceso o entrada (esp. de una mina); (min.) socavón.
adjacence [ædżéịsɛns], **adjacency** [-ḭ] s. adyacencia, contigüidad, proximidad, vecindad.
adjacent [ædżéịsɛnt], a. adyacente, contiguo, colindante; limítrofe.
adjectival [ædżɛktáịvɐl], a. (gram.) adjetival.
adjective [ǽdżɛktịv], s. (gram.) adjetivo, adjunto.
adjectively [-lị], adv. adjetivadamente.
adjoin [ɐdżóịn]. I. va. juntar, unir, asociar. II. vn. (co)lindar (con), estar contiguo (a) o en proximidad (a).
adjoining [-ịŋ], a. contiguo; inmediato.
adjourn [ɐdżǿrn]. I. va. diferir, aplazar, clausurar, trasladar, suspender o levantar la sesión (de un cuerpo deliberante). II. vn. levantarse o suspenderse (una sesión); terminarse las sesiones (de un cuerpo deliberante); retirarse o trasladarse (a otro sitio).
adjournment [-mɛnt], s. aplazamiento, traslación, suspensión, clausura; (for.) espera.
adjudge [ɐdżʌ́dż]. I. va. adjudicar; aplicar, conceder (premio); decidir, juzgar, sentenciar, condenar; decretar. II. vn. dictar sentencia.
adjudger [-œ(r)], s. adjudicador.
adjudgment [-mɛnt], **adjudication** [ɐdżudịkéịṣɔn], s. adjudicación; (naut.) enjagüe.
adjudicate [ɐdżúdịkeịt]. I. va. determinar judicialmente; adjudicar. V. ADJUDGE. II. vn. ejercer las funciones de juez.
adjudicative [-ịv], a. adjudicativo.
adjudicator [-ọ(r)], s. adjudicador.
adjunct [ǽdżʌŋkt]. I. s. aditamento, adjunto; ayudante, coadjutor; subalterno; (gram.) modificante, modificativo, atributo. II. a. adjunto, auxiliar, subordinado.
adjunction [ædżʌ́ŋkṣɔn], s. unión, adición; (for.) adjunción.
adjunctive [ædżʌ́ŋktịv], s. y a. que junta o une; adjunto; agregado.
adjunctively [-lị], adv. juntamente.
adjunctly [-lị], adv. de un modo auxiliar.
adjuration [ædżuréịṣɔn], s. conjuro, ruego encarecido, impetración; orden (f.) solemne.
adjure [ɐdżúr], va. conjurar, implorar, impetrar, suplicar; mandar, ordenar solemnemente.
adjust [ɐdżʌ́st], va. ajustar, acomodar, adaptar, concertar, igualar; ajustar, arreglar, componer, dirimir (disputas, etc.); finiquitar, ajustar (cuentas); regular, graduar; verificar, corregir (un instrumento).
adjustable [-ɐbl], a. ajustable, arreglable, componible; regulable, graduable, adaptable.
adjuster [-œ(r)], s. ajustador, mediador, concertador, componedor, tasador; (mec.) armador; mecanismo regulador.
adjustment [-mɛnt], s. arreglo, adaptación; arreglo, ajuste, ajustamiento, composición (de disputas, etc.); (com.) finiquito (de cuentas); prorrateo (de pérdidas, ganancias, etc.); regulación; corrección, verificación (de un instrumento).
adjutancy [ǽdżutɐnsị], s. (mil.) ayudantía.
adjutant [ǽdżutɐnt], s. (mil.) ayudante.—a. bird, (orn.) marabú, grulla de la India.
adjuvant [ǽdżuvɐnt], a. y s. adjutor.
admeasurement [ædmɛ́żụrmɛnt], s. repartimiento; medición justa.
adminicle [ædmínịkl], s. adminículo, ayuda; (for.) prueba corroborante.
administer [ædmínịstœ(r)]. I. va. administrar, manejar; desempeñar o ejercer (un cargo); suministrar, proveer, surtir; dar, aplicar (remedios, un golpe, un castigo, etc.).—to a. an oath, tomar juramento. II. vn. servir, auxiliar (=MINISTER); contribuir; obrar en calidad de administrador.
administerial [-tírịɐl], a. administrativo.
administrable [ædmínịstrɐbl], a. que se puede administrar.
administrant [-trɐnt], a. y s. director, jefe ejecutivo; administrador, ra.
administration [-tréịṣɔn], s. administración; ministerio, gobierno, dirección; intendencia, mayordomía; manejo; distribución.
administrative [ædmínịstreịtịv], a. administrativo; gubernativo.
administrator [-treịtọ(r)], s. administrador, curador; albacea, mf., testamentario; gobernante.—public a., fideicomisario abintestato.
administratorship [-šịp], s. administración, empleo o dignidad de administrador.
administratrix [-tréịtrịks], s. administradora; curadora, albacea; fideicomisaria abintestato.
admirable [ǽdmịrɐbl], a. admirable, admirativo.
admirableness [-nịs], **admirability** [-bílịtị], s. excelencia, prestancia.
admirably [-blị], adv. admirablemente.
admiral [ǽdmịrɐl], s. almirante; almiranta o capitana (nave); jefe de una flota mercante.
admiralship [-šịp], s. almirantazgo (título o grado).
admiralty [-tị], s. almirantazgo (tribunal); departamento o ministerio de marina.—a. alloy, brass, o metal, latón estañoso (contiene como 1% de estaño, y en el comercio se llama latón "admiralty").—a. law, derecho marítimo; código marítimo.
admiration [ædmịréịṣɔn], s. admiración.—a. mark, a. point, o note of a., punto de admiración (!).
admirative [ædmáịrɐtịv], a. admirativo.
admire [ædmáịr]. I. va. admirar; estimar en alto grado; contemplar con placer, sorpresa y apro-

bación. **II.** *vn.* admirarse de; sentir admiración por.

admirer [-œ(r)], *s.* admirador; enamorado, pretendiente; apasionado, gran aficionado.

admiring [-iŋ], *a.* admirativo; admirado.

admiringly [-lį], *adv.* admirativamente.

admissibility [ædmįsįbḯlįtį], *s.* admisibilidad.

admissible [ædmĺsįbl], *a.* admisible, aceptable; permitido, lícito.

admissibly [-blį], *adv.* admisiblemente.

admission [ædmĺşọn], *s.* admisión, entrada; recepción, acceso; precio de entrada; concesión, reconocimiento.—**a. ticket,** billete o boleto de entrada, boletín, póliza.—**no a.,** se prohibe la entrada (t. a veces, entrada libre).—**a. port,** (m.v.) lumbrera de admisión.

admissive [ædmĺşįv], **admissory** [-orį], *a.* que implica admisión; concesivo.

admit [ædmĺt], *va.* admitir; recibir, dar entrada; permitir; conceder, confesar, reconocer; (mec.) introducir.

admittable [-ạbl], *a.* admisible.

admittance [-ạns], *s.* admisión; entrada; derecho de entrada; (elec.) admitancia.—**no a.,** se prohibe la entrada.

admitted [-įd], *a.* aceptado, concedido, de validez reconocida.

admittedly [-lį], *adv.* reconocidamente, concedidamente.

admitter [-œ(r)], *s.* el que admite, concede, etc.

admix [ædmĺks], *va.* mezclar, incorporar (con algo).

admixtion [-chọn], **admixture** [-chü(r)], *s.* admixtión, mixtura, mezcla; ingrediente agregado a algo.

admonish [ædmánįş], *va.* amonestar; advertir, prevenir; exhortar; reprender sin dureza.

admonisher [-œ(r)], *s.* amonestador.

admonishment [-mẹnt], **admonition** [ædmonĺşọn], *s.* admonición, amonestación; advertencia, prevención; exhortación, parénesis; represión suave.

admonitor [ædmánįtọ(r)], *s.* admonitor, censor.

admonitory, admonitive [-torį, -tįv], *a.* exhortatorio, parenético.

adnascence [ædnǽşẹns], *s.* (bot. y zool.) adhesión de partes entre sí por toda su superficie.

adnascent [-ẹnt], **adnate** [ǽdneįt], *a.* (bot. y zool.) adnato; adherente a otra cosa.

ado [ạdú], *s.* alharaca, bulla, bullicio; pena, trabajo, dificultad.—**much a. about nothing,** nada entre dos platos, más es el ruido que las nueces.—**without more a.,** sin más ni menos, sin más rodeos.

adobe [ạdóųbį], *s.* adobe.—**a. wall,** tapia.

adolescence [ædoléşẹns] o **adolescency** [-į], *s.* adolescencia.

adolescent [-ẹnt], *a.* y *s.* adolescente.

Adonic [ạdánįk], *a.* y *s.* adónico; verso adónico.

adopt [ạdápt], *va.* adoptar, prohijar, ahijar; (for.) arrogar; asumir; aceptar, tomar.

adoptable [-ạbl], *a.* adoptable.

adopted [-įd], *a.* adoptivo, adoptado.

adoptedly [-lį], *adv.* adoptivamente.

adopter [-œ(r)], *s.* adoptador, adoptante, prohijador.

adopting [-įŋ], *a.* adoptante, adoptador.

adoption [ạdápşọn], *s.* adopción, prohijamiento, arrogación; aceptación.

adoptive [ạdáptįv], *a.* adoptivo.

adorable [ạdórạbl], *a.* adorable.

adorableness [-nįs], *s.* cualidad de adorable.

adorably [-blį], *adv.* adorablemente.

adoration [ædoréışọn], *s.* adoración; idolatría.

adore [ạdór], *va.* adorar; idolatrar; glorificar.

adorer [-œ(r)], *s.* adorador, adorante; amante.

adorn [ạdórn], *va.* adornar, (ex)ornar, ornamentar, embellecer, hermosear, ataviar, acicalar, aderezar, pulir.

adornment [-mẹnt], *s.* adorno, atavío, ornamento, aderezo, aciclamiento.—*pl.* arrequives.

adrenal [ædrínạl], *s.* y *a.* (anat.) cápsula suprarrenal; situado cerca o sobre el riñón.

adrenalin (e [ædrénạlįn], *s.* adrenalina.

Adriatic [eįdrįǽtįk], *a.* adriático, del mar Adriático.

adrift [ạdrĺft], *adv.* (mar.) al garete; a la deriva; sin amarras; flotando a merced de las olas; (fig.) abandonado, a la ventura.

adrip [ạdrĺp], *a.* goteando.

adroit [ạdróįt], *a.* diestro, hábil, listo, mañoso.

adroitly [-lį], *adv.* hábilmente, diestramente.

adroitness [-nįs], *s.* destreza, habilidad, maña, prontitud, (fam.) ten con ten.

adscititious [ædsįtĺşạs], *a.* completivo, adicional, añadido; adventicio; extrínseco.

adscript [ǽdskrįpt]. **I.** *a.* y *pp.* adscrito; escrito después. **II.** *s.* siervo de la gleba.

adscription [ædskrĺpşọn], *s.* adscripción.

adsorb [ædsórb], *va.* adsorber.

adsorption [ædsórpşọn], *s.* adsorción.

adsorptive [-tįv], *a.* adsorbente.

adulate [ǽdżuleįt], *va.* adular, lisonjear.

adulation [-éįşọn], *s.* adulación, lisonja.

adulator [ǽdżuleįtọ(r)], *s.* adulador.

adulatory [ǽdżulạtorį], *a.* adulatorio.

adult [ạdÁlt], *a.* y *s.* adulto; persona mayor.

adulterant [ạdÁltœrạnt], *s.* y *a.* adulterante.

adulterate [-eįt]. **I.** *va.* adulterar, impurificar, falsear, falsificar, viciar. **II.** *a.* adulterado, falso, impuro, espurio; adúltero.

adulteration [-éįşọn], *s.* adulteración, corrupción, impureza, falsificación.

adulterator [-eįtọ(r)], *s.* adulterador.

adulterer [-œ(r)], *s.* adúltero.

adulteress [-įs], *s.* adúltera.

adulterine [-įn]. **I.** *a.* espurio. **II.** *s.* hijo adulterino.

adulterize [-aįz], *vn.* cometer adulterio.

adulterous [-Ás], *a.* adúltero; adulterino, espurio.

adultery [-į], *s.* adulterio.

adulthood [ạdÁlthụd], **adultness** [-nįs], *s.* edad adulta.

adumbrant [ædÁmbrạnt], *a.* (pint.) bosquejado; ligeramente sombreado.

adumbrate [-breįt], *va.* esquiciar, bosquejar, sombrear; presagiar, anunciar.

adumbration [-bréįşọn], *s.* esquicio, bosquejo, esbozo; presagio; (pint.) adumbración.

aduncate [ædÁ̇ŋkeįt]. **I.** *vn.* encorvarse como un garfio, engarabatarse. **II.** *a.* adunco, combo, encorvado.

aduncity [ædÁ̇nsįtį], *s.* corvadura, comba.

aduncous [ædÁŋkạs], *a.* adunco, encorvado.

adust [ạdÁst], *a.* cálido; adusto; tostado, requemado, moreno.

advance [ædvǽns]. **I.** *va.* avanzar, poner más adelante; adelantar, promover, ascender; mejorar, aventajar; acelerar, apresurar; (com.) anticipar dinero, pagar adelantado; proponer, ofrecer, insinuar; encarecer, subir el precio de. **II.** *vn.* avanzar, adelantarse; adelantar, progresar; subir de valor o precio. **III.** *s.* avance; delantera; mejora, adelanto, progreso; (*pl.*) propuestas, solicitudes, insinuaciones; requerimientos amorosos; (com.) adelanto, anticipo, préstamo; alza; recargo de precio, precio adicional (= EXTRA); (mec.) avance a la admisión. **IV.** *a.* previo, anticipado.—**a. base,** (mil.) base de vanguardia.—**a. guard,** (mil.) avanzada.—**a. payment,** (com.) adelanto, anticipo.—**a. sale,** venta anticipada.—**a. sheet,** (impr.) capilla; *pl.* pliegos sueltos impresos anticipados de un libro que se envían a los críticos, revistas, etc., antes de la publicación.—**a day in a.,** con un día de anticipación.—**in a.,** anticipadamente; antes; al frente; adelante; de antemano; (com.) por adelantado, anticipado.—**sent in a.,** premiso.

advanced [-t], *a.* avanzado, adelantado, desarrollado; anticipado.—**a. in years**, entrado en años, de edad madura.—**a. studies**, estudios superiores.

advancement [-mént], *s.* adelantamiento, progreso; promoción, ascenso; elevación, subida, prosperidad.

advancer [-œ(r)], *s.* adelantador; promotor, impulsor.

advantage [ædváentidź]. **I.** *s.* ventaja, superioridad, delantera; facilidad, comodidad, conveniencia; ganancia, provecho, partido, beneficio, pro, *mf.*, (Col.) gabela.—**a. ground**, puesto ventajoso, situación favorable.—**to have the a. over**, llevar la ventaja a.—**to show to a.**, lucirse, salir airoso.—**to take a. of**, aprovechar(se de), valerse de, sacar partido de; engañar, embaucar.—**to a.**, ventajosamente, con provecho; en circunstancias o condiciones ventajosas.—**to one's a.**, con ventaja o provecho para uno. **II.** *va.* adelantar, mejorar, beneficiar, favorecer; remunerar; promover. **III.** *vn.* medrar, sacar ventaja.

advantageous [ædvantéidźas], *a.* provechoso, ventajoso, conveniente, aventajado, útil.

advantageously [-lį], *adv.* ventajosamente.

advantageousness [-njs], *s.* ventaja, conveniencia, calidad de ventajoso, utilidad.

advent [ædvent], *s.* venida, advenimiento, llegada; (A.) adviento.

Adventism, Adventist [-jzm, -jst]. *V.* SECOND.

adventitious [ædventíšas], *a.* adventicio, extraño, accidental, espontáneo.

adventitiously [-lį], *adv.* accidentalmente.

adventive [ædvéntįv], *a.* (biol.) advenedizo; accidental, casual.

adventure [ædvénchų(r)]. **I.** *s.* aventura; casualidad, contingencia; lance; (com.) ancheta, pacotilla. **II.** *va.* aventurar, arriesgar. **III.** *vn.* aventurarse (a), osar, atreverse, arriesgarse.

adventurer [-œ(r)], *s.* aventurero.

adventuresome [-sAm], **adventurous** [-As], *a.* aventurero, audaz, emprendedor, arrojado, intrépido; arriesgado, aventurado, peligroso.

adventuress [-js], *s.* aventurera.

adventurously [-Aslį], *adv.* aventureramente, arriesgadamente, arrojadamente.

adventurousness, adventuresomeness [-njs, -sAmnjs], *s.* intrepidez, arrojo, temeridad, osadía.

adverb [ædvœrb], *s.* (gram.) adverbio.

adverbial [ædvœrbįal], *a.* adverbial.

adverbially [-į], *adv.* adverbialmente.

adversary [ædvœrserį], *s.* adversario, enemigo, antagonista, contrario.—**the A.**, Satanás, el diablo.

adversative [ædvœrsątįv], *a.* (gram.) adversativo.

adverse [ædvœrs], *a.* adverso, contrario, opuesto; hostil, enemigo; funesto, aciago, desgraciado.

adversely [-lį], *adv.* adversamente.

adverseness [-njs], *s.* oposición, contrariedad, resistencia.

adversity [-itį], *s.* adversidad, desgracia, calamidad, infortunio.

advert [ædvœrt], *vn.* y *va.* (con **to**) referirse a, hacer referencia a, llamar o dirigir la atención a; (hacer) notar, advertir, reparar.

advertence, advertency [-ęns], [-į], *s.* advertencia; aviso, observación; atención, cuidado, vigilancia.

advertent [-ęnt], *a.* avisado, atento.

advertise [ædvœrtajz], *va.* avisar, anunciar, poner anuncios, hacer propaganda o publicidad.

advertisement [ædvœrtįzmęnt], *s.* aviso, anuncio, notificación, reclamo.

advertiser [ædvœrtajzœ(r)], *s.* anunciante, avisador.

advertising [-įŋ], *s.* propaganda, publicidad.

advice [ædvájs], *s.* consejo; aviso, noticia, informe, notificación, dictamen, parecer, adver-

tencia, admonición.—**a. boat**, (mar.) aviso.—**to take a.**, pedir o seguir consejo.

advisability [ædvajzạbílįtį], **advisableness** [ædvájzạblnįs], *s.* prudencia, cordura; conveniencia, propiedad; ventaja.

advisable [ædvájzạbl], *a.* aconsejable, prudente; deseable, conveniente.—**to be a.**, convenir.

advise [ædvájz]. **I.** *va.* aconsejar; avisar, informar, notificar, advertir, amonestar, denunciar, comunicar; asesorar. **II.** *vn.* consultar, aconsejarse, pedir o tomar consejo; aconsejar.

advised [-d], *a.* premeditado, deliberado; avisado, aconsejado, advertido, orejeado.—**to keep a.**, tener al corriente.

advisedly [-įdlį], *adv.* deliberadamente, advertidamente, avisadamente, prudentemente; adrede, aposta.—**advisedness** [-įdnįs], *s.* juicio, cordura; reflexión, deliberación.

advisement [-męnt], *s.* deliberación, consideración.—**to take under a.**, someter a consideración, estudio o deliberación.—**under a.**, en tela de juicio.

adviser [-œ(r)], *s.* consejero, aconsejador, consultor, monitor; informante.—**legal a.**, abogado, asesor.

advisory [-orį], *a.* aconsejador, de carácter de consejo; consultivo, asesor.—**a. board**, consejo, junta consultiva.

advocacy [ædvokạsį], *s.* abogacía; defensa (de una doctrina, de un reo); vindicación, apología, intercesión.

advocate [ædvokejt]. **I.** *va.* defender, abogar por, propugnar, apoyar, vindicar, interceder. **II.** *s.* abogado, letrado; defensor, intercesor, medianero, partidario.

advocateship [-šįp], *s.* abogacía.

advowee [ædvauį], *s.* (igl.) colador; patrono.

advowson [ædváuzǫn], *s.* (igl.) colación; patronato.

adynamia [ædįnémįạ], *s.* adinamia.

adynamic [ædįnæmįk], *a.* débil, adinámico.

adytum [ædįtʌm], *s.* ádito. *V.* SANCTUM.

adz, adze [ædz]. **I.** *s.* azuela.—**cooper's a.**, doladera. **II.** *va.* azolar, desbastar.

æ *s.* diptongo de origen latino, equivalente al griego *ai*; en muchos derivados se reemplaza æ por la *e* sola; por ej. *ædile* o *edile*.

ædile [ídaįl], *s.* edil.—**ædileship** [-šįp], *s.* edilidad.

ædilian [idílįan], **ædilitian** [idilíźạn], *a.* edilicio.

Ægean [idźíạn], *a.* del mar Egeo.

ægis [ídźįs], *s.* escudo, broquel, égida, amparo.

Æolian [ióųlįan], **Æolic** [-įk], *a.* eolio, eólico.—**Æ. harp**, arpa eolia.

æolipile [iálįpaįl], *s.* (fís.) eolípila.

æon [íǫn], *s.* evo, eón.

aerate [éięrejt], *va.* airear, ventilar, orear; cargar de aire, o de ácido carbónico (como el pan, aguas gaseosas, etc.); producir aeración en el agua potable; (med.) arterializar la sangre; (fig.) hacer etéreo.—**aerated waters**, aguas gaseosas.

aeration [eięréišǫn], *s.* aeración; ventilación, oreo; arterialización de la sangre.

aerator [éięrejtǫ(r)], *s.* aparato para la aeración.

aerial [eiríạl]. **I.** *a.* aéreo, elevado; etéreo.—**a. camera**, aparato de fotografía aérea.—**a. ladder**, escalera alargable del servicio de bomberos.—**a. torpedo**, torpedo aéreo. **II.** *s.* (aer.) antena.

aerie [éri], *s.* nido de águila.

aeriferous [eięríferạs], *a.* aerífero.

aeriform [éięrįform], *a.* aeriforme; gaseiforme.

aerify [-faį], *va.* aerificar; gasificar.

aerobatics [eięrobǽtįks], *s.* acrobacia aérea.

aerobe [éięroųb], *s.* (biol.) aerobio.

aerobic [eięróųbįk], *a.* (biol.) aerobio.

aerobiosis [eięrobaįóųsįs], *s.* (biol.) aerobiosis.

aeroboat [éięroboųt], *s.* hidroaeroplano.

aerobus [-bʌs], *s.* aeroplano de viajeros, aerobús.

aerocraft [-kræft], *s.* = AIRCRAFT.

aerocyst [-sįst], *s.* (bot.) aerocisto.

aerodrome [-droqm], s. aeródromo.
aerodynamic [-dajnǽmjk], a. aerodinámico.
aerodynamics [-s], s. aerodinámica.
aerofoil [-fɔjl], s. (aer.) superficie de sustentación.
aerogram [-græm], s. radiotelegrama, aerograma.
aerography [ejɛrǽgrafj], s. aerografía.
aerogun [éjɛrogʌn], s. cañón antiaéreo.
aerolite [-lajt], s. aerolito.
aerology [ejɛrǽlodźj], s. aerología.
aeromancy [éjɛromænsj], s. aeromancia.
aeromechanics [-mɛkǽnjks], s. aeromecánica.
aerometer [ejɛrǽmɛtɔ(r)], s. aerómetro.
aerometric [ejɛromɛ́trjk], a. aerométrico.
aerometry [ejɛrǽmɛtrj], s. aerometría.
aeromotor [éjɛromoutɔ(r)], s. motor de aeroplano; aeroplano impulsado por motor.
aeronaut [-nɔt], s. aeronauta, m. y f.
aeronautic [-nɔ́tjk], a. aeronáutico, aéreo.
aeronautics [-s], s. aeronáutica, aerostación.
aeronef [-nɛf], s. aeronave, f.
aerophobia [-fóubjạ], s. aerofobia.
aerophotography [-fotǽgrafj], s. aerofotografía.
aeroplane [-plejn], s. aeroplano, avión, m.
aeroscope [-skoup], s. aeroscopio, aeróscopo.
aeroscopy [ejɛráskopj], s. aeroscopia.
aerostat [éjɛrostæt], s. aeróstato, globo dirigible; globo aerostático.—**aerostatic** [-stǽtjk], a. aerostático.—**aerostatics**, s. aerostática.—
aerostation [-stéjʂ̣ɔn], s. aerostación, navegación aérea en globos dirigibles.
aerotherapeutics [-θɛrapjútjks], s. (med.) aeroterapia.
aeroview [-vju], s. vista aérea, vista tomada desde un avión.
æruginous, V. ERUGINOUS.
Æsculapian [eskjuléjpjạn]. I. s. Esculapio, médico. II. a. esculapiano, de Esculapio; médico; medicinal.
Æsopian, Æsopic [isápjạn, -jk], a. esópico.
æsthesia, æsthete, etc., æstival, æther, ætiology, V. ESTHESIA, ESTHETE, etc.
afar [afár], adv. lejos, distante, a gran distancia.—**from a.**, de lejos, desde lejos, a distancia.—**a. off**, muy distante, remoto.
afebrile [ejfébrjl], a. sin fiebre; apirético.
Afer [éjfœ(r)], s. ábrego, áfrico; viento sudoeste.
affability [æfabjlítj], **affableness** [ǽfablnjs], s. afabilidad, agrado, dulzura, amabilidad.
affable [ǽfabl], a. afable, amable, atento.
affably [-blj], adv. afablemente.
affair [afǽr], s. asunto, negocio, cuestión, lance; cosa; diligencia; (mil.) acción, encuentro.—**a. of honor**, lance de honor, duelo.—**a. of the heart**, amorío, intriga amorosa.—**to be one's a.**, correr por cuenta de uno.
affect [afékt], va. afectar, influir en, hacer efecto o mella en; afectar, conmover, impresionar; imitar, remedar, tomar la forma o el carácter de; afectar, fingir; frecuentar; gustar de, tener afición a; (com.) hipotecar.
affectation [æfɛktéjʂ̣ɔn], s. afectación; dengue, melindre, remilgo; (lit.) culteranismo; (Am.) mitote.
affected [aféktjd], a. emocionado, conmovido, enternecido; afectado, artificioso, remilgado, relamido, denguero; inclinado, afecto; afectado, alterado; atacado (de enfermedad).—**a. quadratic**, (mat.) ecuación completa de segundo grado.
affectedly [-lj], adv. afectadamente.
affectedness [-njs], s. V. AFFECTATION.
affecter [aféktœ(r)], s. afectador, fingidor.
affecting [aféktjŋ], a. conmovedor, patético, lastimero.
affectingly [-lj], adv. conmovedoramente.
affection [aféksɔn], s. afecto, cariño, (bien)querencia, afición, amor, terneza, devoción; emoción, sentimiento; inclinación, propensidad; impresión, afección; estado transitorio; cualidad, propiedad; (med.) afección.
affectionate [-jt], a. afectuoso, cariñoso, amoroso.

affectionately [-lj], adv. afectuosamente.
affectionateness [-njs], s. cualidad de afectuoso.
affective [aféktjv], a. afectivo; conmovedor; emotivo.
afferent [áfɛrɛnt], a. (fisiol.) aferente.
affiance [afájạns]. I. s. palabra de casamiento, esponsales; confianza. II. va. dar palabra de casamiento; dar prenda.—**affianced bride**, novia desposada, prometida.—**to become affianced**, comprometerse.
affiant [afájạnt], s. (for.) deponente, declarante.
affidavit [æfjdéjvjt], s. (for.) declaración o deposición jurada, af(f)idávit; atestación, testimonio, certificación, acta.
affiliate [afíljejt]. I. va. afiliar; prohijar, ahijar, adoptar; asociar; aclarar la filiación de; (for.) legitimar. II. vn. y vr. afiliarse, asociarse, unirse (a un partido, etc.). III. s. afiliado; afiliada (sociedad o compañía).
affiliate(d [-jd], a. prohijado, afiliado.
affiliation [-éjʂ̣ɔn], s. afiliación; adopción (de un hijo); asociación; (for.) legitimación de un hijo.
affined [afájnd], a. afín, pariente por afinidad.
affinity [afínjtj], s. afinidad, atracción; conformidad, semejanza o analogía; amor; persona que inspira enamoramiento; conexión, enlace; parentezco por matrimonio; (biol. y filol.) analogía que indica origen común; (quím.) afinidad.
affirm [afœ́rm]. I. va. afirmar, aseverar; confirmar. II. vn. afirmarse en alguna cosa; declarar formalmente ante un juez.
affirmable [-abl], a. que se puede afirmar.
affirmably [-ablj], adv. afirmativamente.
affirmance [-ạns], s. afirmación; confirmación, ratificación.
affirmant [-ạnt], s. afirmante.
affirmation [æfœrméjʂ̣ɔn], s. afirmación, aserto, aserción; palabra que se da solemnemente en vez de juramento; confirmación, ratificación.
affirmative [afœ́rmạtjv]. I. a. afirmativo. II. s. aserción; afirmativa.
affirmatively [-lj], adv. afirmativamente, aseveradamente, asertivamente.
affirmatory [-ạtorj], a. asertorio, afirmativo.
affirmer [-œ(r)], s. afirmante, afirmador.
affix [afíks], va. anexar, fijar, añadir, pegar, unir; poner (firma, sello).
affix [ǽfjks], s. añadidura; (gram.) afijo, prefijo, sufijo.
afflation [æfléjʂ̣ɔn], s. resuello, inspiración.
afflatus [æfléjtạs], s. (poét.) estro, aflato, inspiración divina; (med.) golpe de aire; eructo.
afflict [aflíkt], va. afligir, angustiar, a(con)gojar, acuitar, atribular, desconsolar, causar dolor o pena a; castigar.—**to be afflicted with**, sufrir de.
afflicting [-jŋ], a. aflictivo, penoso.
afflictingly [-lj], **afflictively** [aflíktjvlj], adv. aflictivamente.
affliction [aflíksɔn], s. aflicción; cuita, angustia, duelo, pena, tribulación; desgracia, calamidad, plaga; (med.) mal, achaque; afección.
afflictive [aflíktjv], a. aflictivo, congojoso.
affluence [ǽfluɛns], s. abundancia, copia, opulencia, riqueza; afluencia, aflujo.
affluent [ǽfluɛnt]. I. a. opulento, afluente, abundante, copioso. II. s. afluente, tributario.
affluently [-lj], adv. copiosamente.
afflux [ǽflʌks], **affluxion** [æflʌ́ksɔn], s. aflujo, afluencia; (med.) aflujo.
afforce [afórs], va. (for.) reforzar (un jurado, etc.).
afforcement [-mɛnt], s. (for.) refuerzo.
afford [afórd], va. producir, proporcionar, proveer, facilitar, brindar, deparar; tener medios o recursos para una cosa, permitirse el lujo de. [Con **can**, indica capacidad—generalmente financiera—de hacer algo sin perjuicio propio, v.g., *I cannot afford to buy that*, no me conviene (o no tengo con que) comprar eso.]
afforestation [æfarjstéjʂ̣ɔn], s. plantación de un bosque.

affranchise, affranchisement, *V.* ENFRANCHISE, ENFRANCHISEMENT.

affray [əfréi], *s.* riña, pendencia, refriega.

affreight [əfréit], *va.* fletar.

affreightment [-mənt], *s.* (com.) fletamento.

affricate [ǽfrikit], *s.* (fon.) africada.—**affricative** [əfríkətiv]. **I.** *a.* africado. **II.** *s.* africada.

affright [əfráit]. **I.** *va.* (poét.) aterrar, espantar, asustar. **II.** *s.* terror repentino, susto.

affrighted [-id], *a.* aterrorizado, asustado.

affrightedly [-li], *adv.* con espanto.

affront [əfrʌnt]. **I.** *va.* afrentar, insultar, ultrajar. **II.** *s.* afrenta, insulto, ultraje, agravio.

affronté [æfrôntéi], *a.* (blas.) afrontado, frente a frente.

affronter [əfrʌntœ(r)], *s.* agresor, provocador.

affronting, affrontive [-iŋ, -iv], *a.* insultante, injurioso.

affusion [æfiúʒən], *s.* afusión.

afghan [ǽfgən], *s.* cubrecama de punto; (A-) *s.* y *a.* afgano, de Afganistán.

afield [əfíld], *adv.* en el campo; al campo; lejos de casa; lejos del camino, descarriado; lejos del asunto.

afire [əfáir], *adv.* ardiendo.

aflame [əfléim], *adv.* en llamas; (fig.) inflamado.—**to be a. with,** arder de, o en, (ira, amor, etc.).

afloat [əflóut], *a.* y *adv.* (mar.) a flote, flotante, a nado; a bordo; sin rumbo; inundado; en circulación (apl. a rumores, etc.).—**to keep a.,** mantenerse a flote.

afoot [əfút], *a.* y *adv.* a pie; en movimiento; en preparación.

afore [əfóur]. **I.** *prep.* antes de; delante. **II.** *adv.* (poco u.) en otro tiempo; (mar.) a proa.

aforegoing [-gouiŋ], *a.* antedicho, precedente, anterior.

aforehand [-hænd], *adv.* de antemano; con preparación.

aforementioned [-menchənd], **aforenamed** [-neimd], **aforesaid** [-sed], *a.* dicho, susodicho, mencionado, consabido, referido, el tal.

aforethought [-θɔt]. **I.** *a.* premeditado. **II.** *s.* premeditación.—**with malice a.,** con premeditación.

aforetime [-taim], *adv.* en otro tiempo, antiguamente.

afoul [əfául], *adv.* y *a.* (mar.) en colisión; enredado.

afraid [əfréid], *a.* amedrentado, atemorizado, temeroso, tímido, miedoso.—**to be a.,** tener miedo, temer, acoquinarse.—**to become a.,** amedrentarse, sobrecogerse.

afresh [əfréś], *adv.* de nuevo, otra vez.

African [ǽfrikən], *s.* y *a.* africano; negro.

Africander, Afrikander [æfríkændœ(r)], *s.* africánder, el nacido en el África del Sur de raza europea.

Afro-American [ǽfroəmérikən], *s.* y *a.* afroamericano, negro americano.

Afro-Cuban [-kiúbən], *a.* y *s.* afrocubano.

afront [əfrʌnt], *adv.* enfrente, al frente, de cara.

aft [æft], *adv.* (mar.) a popa o en popa.—**a. deck,** cubierta de popa.

after [ǽftœ(r)]. **I.** *prep.* después de; detrás de, tras (de); al cabo de; en pos de, en seguimiento de; por (= en busca de); respecto de; según, a la manera de. **II.** *adv.* después, en seguida, seguidamente. **III.** *conj.* después (de) que, así que; una vez que. **IV.** *a.* posterior, siguiente; consiguiente, subsiguiente, resultante; (mar.) de popa.—**a. all,** después de todo.—**a. the example of,** a ejemplo de.—**a. the manner of,** a la manera de.—**a. the Spanish fashion,** a la española.—**day a. day,** día (*m.*) tras día.—**day a. tomorrow,** pasado mañana.—**the day a.,** el día siguiente; al otro día.—**soon** (o **shortly**) **a.,** poco después.—**to be a. something,** buscar algo. NOTA. **After** entra en la composición de muchas palabras y significa después de, nuevo, posterior, subsiguiente; los

principales compuestos, fuera de los que se dan después como voces separadas, son: **a.-acceptation,** aceptación tardía.—**a.-account,** cuenta nueva.—**a.-act,** acto subsiguiente.—**a.-age,** posteridad.—**a.-attack,** (mil.) segundo ataque.—**a.-blossom,** o **fruit,** redrojo.—**a.-clap,** golpe inesperado, revés.—**a.-comer,** sucesor.—**a.-cost,** gasto extraordinario.—**a.-crop,** segunda cosecha.—**a.-damp,** mofeta.—**a.-deck,** (mar.) cubierta de popa.—**a.-dinner,** sobremesa (**a.-dinner speech,** brindis, *m.*, discurso de sobremesa).—**a.-game,** desquite.—**a.-gathering,** espigueo.—**a.-glow,** resplandor crepuscular.—**a.-hope,** esperanza renovada.—**a.-hours,** deshora, tarde.—**a.-image,** imagen (*f.*) accidental (que persiste como estado psicológico).—**a.-life,** vida futura.—**a.-love,** segunda pasión, nuevos amores.—**a.-pains,** (obst.) entuertos.—**a.-reckoning,** nueva cuenta.—**a.-repentance,** arrepentimiento tardío.—**a.-state,** estado o vida futura.—**a.-swarm,** (api.) escamocho.—**a.-taste,** resabio, dejo.—**a.-times,** tiempos venideros, porvenir.—**a.-tossing,** marejada.—**a.-touch,** (pint.) retoque.—**a.-wit,** entendimiento tardío.

afterbirth [-bœrθ], *s.* secundinas, pares, *f. pl.*, placenta, que se expelen en el alumbramiento.

aftermath [-mæθ], *s.* segunda siega; otoño; resultados, consecuencias.

aftermost [-moust], *a.* postrero, último, trasero; (naut.) popel.

afternoon [-nún], *s.* tarde, *f.*

afterpeak [-pik], *s.* (mar.) racel o delgado de popa.

afterpiece [-pis], *s.* (teat.) sainete, entremés, fin de fiesta; (mar.) talón del timón.

afterthought [-θɔt], *s.* idea tardía; algo que se ocurrió más tarde.

afterward o **afterwards** [-wərd, -z], *adv.* después.—**long a.,** mucho tiempo después.

afterwise [-waiz], *a.* discreto pasada la ocasión, o después de tiempo.

aga, agha [ága], *s.* agá, *m.*, oficial turco.

again [əgén], *adv.* otra vez, segunda vez, aun, nuevamente, de nuevo; por otra parte, además; asimismo.—**a. and a.,** muchas veces.—**as much a.,** otro tanto más.—**now and a., a** veces, de vez en cuando.—**once and a.,** repetidas veces.—**never a.,** nunca más.—**come a.,** vuelva Vd.—**to do a.,** hacer de nuevo, volver a hacer o rehacer (algo).

against [əgénst], *prep.* contra; enfrente de; junto a (una pared, etc.); en contraste con, comparado con; listo para.—**a. time,** dentro de tiempo limitado (apl. a carreras); (hacer algo) tratando de terminar (llegar, etc.) antes de cierto tiempo, o a tiempo.—**a. the grain,** a contrapelo, al redopelo; de mal grado.

agalloch(um) [əgǽlok(ʌm), *s.* (bot.) agáloco.

agama [ǽgəmə], *s.* (zool.) ágama, *m.*

agami [ǽgəmi], *s.* (orn.) agamí, ave zancuda.

agamic [əgǽmik], **agamous** [ǽgəməs], *a.* (biol.) ágamo, asexual; (bot.) criptógamo.

agape [əgéip], *adv.* con la boca abierta.

agape [ǽgəpi], *s.* ágapi, convite de fraternidad y caridad de los primeros cristianos.

agar-agar [ágar-ágar], *s.* agar-agar, *mf.*

agaric [ǽgərik], *s.* agárico, garzo.

agasp [əgǽsp], *adv.* y *a.* jadeante; anhelante, ansioso.

agate [ǽgit], *s.* ágata; (imp.) tipo de 5½ puntos.—**a.-ware,** utensilios de imitación de ágata.

agaty [ǽgəti], *a.* agatídeo, agatino.

agave [əgéivi], *s.* (bot.) agave, *f.*, maguey, cabuya, pita, piñuela.

agaze [əgéiz], *a.* y *adv.* en el acto de mirar.

age [éidʒ]. **I.** *s.* edad; época, período, era, siglo; vejez, ancianidad, senectud, envejecimiento.—**ages,** (fam.) larguísimo tiempo, una eternidad.—**a.-old,** secular, centenario, milenario.—**full a.,** mayoría, mayor edad.—**golden a.,** edad de oro; siglo de oro.—**of a.**, mayor (de edad).—**under a.**, menor (de edad); menoría.—**to become of a.**, llegar a mayor edad. **II.** *vn.* envejecerse; deteriorar (a veces mejorar) por envejecimiento. **III.** *va.* (tec.) acelerar artificialmente el desarrollo de ciertas propiedades; curar; dar su punto a, sazonar, perfeccionar (a veces dejando en reposo por algún tiempo, como el vino y ciertas substancias químicas).

aged [-(i̯)d], *a.* anciano, viejo, añejo, envejecido.
—**a. ten years**, de la edad de (o que tiene) diez años.

ageing [-iŋ] **I.** *ger.* de TO AGE. **II.** *s.* envejecimiento; cambio debido a la acción del tiempo; acción de sazonarse o llegar a su punto.

ageless [-li̯s], *a.* sempiterno; que no tiene edad.

agelong [-lɒŋ], *a.* que dura mucho tiempo.

agency [éi̯dźɛnsi̯], *s.* acción, operación, obra; instrumento; agencia; diligencia, gestión, influencia, medio, mediación, órgano, fuerza; factoraje.—**a. office**, oficina de negocios.—**authorized a.**, agencia oficial o autorizada.—**free a.**, libre albedrío.

agenda [adźéndạ], **agendum** [adźéndʌm], *s.* agenda, memorándum; orden (*m.*) del día; programa, *m.* (de deliberaciones, etc.); (igl.) ritual. (La primera palabra, que es el plural de la segunda, es más usada.)

agent [éi̯dźɛnt]. **I.** *a.* activo, operativo. **II.** *s.* agente, el que o lo que obra y tiene facultad para hacer algo; representante, comisionado, factor, gestor; solicitador. (fís.) agente; (for.) mandatario, apoderado.—**a. provocateur** (se pronuncia como en francés), agente provocador, agente que secreta y fingidamente instiga a la ejecución de actos punibles, a fin de obtener pruebas de culpabilidad.

agentship [-ši̯p], *s.* agencia, factoría.

ageratum [ædźɛ́ri̯ei̯tʌm], *s.* (bot.) variedad de ágerato.

agglomerate [aglómɛrei̯t], *va.* y *vn.* aglomerar(se), amontonar(se).

agglomerate, agglomeration [-éi̯šɒn], *s.* aglomeración, amontonamiento.

agglutinant [aglútinạnt], *a.* y *s.* aglutinante.

agglutinate [-ei̯t], *va.* aglutinar, pegar, encolar.

agglutination [-éi̯šɒn], *s.* aglutinación.

agglutinative [-éi̯ti̯v], *a.* aglutinativo, adhesivo, pegante.—**a. language**, lengua aglutinante.

aggrandize [ǽgrændai̯z], *va.* agrandar, engrandecer; elevar, exaltar, relevar, ensalzar.

aggrandizement [agréndi̯zmɛnt], *s.* engrandecimiento; elevación, exaltación.

aggrandizer [ǽgrændai̯zœ(r)], *s.* ensalzador.

aggravate [ǽgrạvei̯t], *va.* aumentar, agravar; empeorar; (fam.) irritar, exasperar.

aggravating [-iŋ], *a.* agravante; irritante, provocativo.

aggravatingly [-li̯], *adv.* agravantemente.

aggravation [-éi̯šɒn], *s.* agravación, agravamiento; empeoramiento; (for.) circunstancia agravante; (fam.) provocación, vejación; irritación.

aggregate [ǽgrigei̯t]. **I.** *a.* agregado, juntado, unido; aglomerado; mezclado. **II.** *s.* agregado, suma, conjunto, totalidad; mezcla, materias mezcladas; (ing.) agregado, material duro (apl. al hormigón).—**in the a.**, en conjunto. **III.** *va.* y *vn.* agregar, sumar, juntar; ascender a.

aggregately [-li̯], *adv.* colectivamente, en junto.

aggregation [-éi̯šɒn], *s.* agregación; agregado, colección; masa, conjunto, total.

aggregative [-i̯v], *a.* colectivo.

aggregator [-ọ(r)], *s.* colector, agregador.

aggress [agrés], *vn.* ser el agresor; cometer una agresión o invasión; acometer, agredir; invadir.

aggression [agréšɒn], *s.* agresión, ataque u ofensa sin provocación; acometida; intrusión.

aggressive [agrési̯v], *a.* agresivo, acometedor.

aggressively [-li̯], *adv.* agresivamente.

aggressiveness [-ni̯s], *s.* agresividad, acometividad, carácter agresivo.

aggressor [agrésọ(r)], *s.* agresor, atacador, acometedor.

aggrieve [agrív], *va.* afligir, apenar, apesadumbrar; vejar, oprimir, perjudicar, dañar, agraviar.—**to be, o feel one's self, aggrieved**, agraviarse.

aghast [agǽst], *a.* horrorizado, despavorido, estupefacto.

agile [ǽdźi̯l], *a.* ágil, pronto, listo.

agility [adźíli̯ti̯], *s.* agilidad, ligereza, expedición, soltura, prontitud.

aging [éi̯dźiŋ] = AGEING.

agio [ǽdźi̯ou̯], *s.* (com.) agio; agiotaje.

agiotage [-ti̯dź], *s.* (com.) agiotaje.

agitable [ǽdźi̯tạbl], *a.* agitable.

agitate [ǽdźi̯tei̯t]. **I.** *va.* agitar, revolver, menear; inquietar, perturbar, solevantar, conmover, alborotar; discutir o debatir con ahinco; tramar, urdir, maquinar. **II.** *vn.* excitar la opinión pública; alborotar, encresparse.

agitation [-éi̯šɒn], *s.* agitación; discusión, ventilación; perturbación, ajetreo, conmoción.

agitator [-ọ(r)], *s.* agitador, revolvedor; perturbador, alborotador; demagogo, incitador.

agleam [aglím], *a.* (poét.) fulguroso, centelleante.

aglet [ǽgli̯t], *s.* herrete de agujeta o cordón.—*pl.* (mil.) cordones.

aglow [aglóu̯], *adv.* y *a.* fulgurante, en fulguración, encendido.

aglutition [æglutíšɒn], *s.* (med.) aglutición, incapacidad de tragar.

agnail [ǽgnei̯l], *s.* panadizo, uñero.

agnate, agnatic [ǽgnei̯t, ægnǽti̯k], *a.* agnado, agnaticio.

agnate, *s.* (for.) agnado.

agnation [ægnéi̯šɒn], *s.* agnación; parentesco.

agnomen [ægnóu̯mi̯n], *s.* sobrenombre.

agnomination [ægnaminéi̯šɒn], *s.* (ret.) agnominación, paronomasia; aliteración.

agnostic [ægnásti̯k], *a.* y *s.* agnóstico.

agnosticism [-ti̯si̯zm], *s.* agnosticismo.

agnus [ǽgnʌs], **Agnus Dei**, [-déji̯], *s.* agnusdéi.—**A. bell**, toque (*s.* de campana) de agnusdéi.—**a. castus**, (bot.) agnocasto o sauzgatillo.

ago [agóu̯], *adv.* (contr. de AGONE) hace, ha; *a long time ago*, hace mucho tiempo; *long ago*, tiempo ha; *how long ago?* ¿cuánto ha?

agog [agág], *adv.* y *a.* ansioso, anhelante; ansiosamente, con viva curiosidad; (Cuba) con embullo.

agoing [agóu̯iŋ], *adv.* en acción, en movimiento.—**to set a.**, poner en marcha.

agometer [agámɛtœ(r)], *s.* (elec.) agómetro, una especie de reóstato.

agon [ǽgon], *s.* fiesta agonal.

agonic [agáni̯k], *a.* (geom.) ágono.

agonist [ǽgoni̯st], *s.* atleta o combatiente.

agonistic(al [ægoni̯stik(ạl], *a.* agonístico, agonal.

agonistics [-s], *s.* agonística.

agonize [ǽgonai̯z]. **I.** *va.* angustiar; causar gran pena, atormentar. **II.** *vn.* agonizar; penar, sufrir intensamente, retorcerse de dolor; luchar; hacer grandes esfuerzos.

agonizing [-iŋ], *a.* angustioso, agonizante.

agonizingly [-li̯], *adv.* en agonías.

agony [ǽgoni̯], *s.* agonía; angustia, zozobra; intensa emoción.—**a. column**, (fam.) columna o sección (de un periódico) de anuncios personales, sobre todo los relativos a personas desaparecidas.

agora [ǽgorạ], *s.* (hist. griega) ágora.

agoraphobia [-fóu̯bi̯ạ], *s.* (pat.) agorafobia.

agouti [agúti̯], *s.* (zool.) agutí, acutí, acure.

agraffe [agrǽf], *s.* broche; grapita que sujeta cada cuerda del piano.

agraphia [ægrǽfi̯ạ], *s.* (pat.) agrafia.

agrarian [agréri̯an]. **I.** *a.* y *s.* agrario. **II.** *s.* agrarista.—**agrarianism** [-i̯zm], *s.* agrarismo; (pol.) división y reparto igual de tierras.

agree [əgrí], *vn.* concordar, acordar, coincidir, estar conforme o de acuerdo; entenderse, conformarse, concertarse, avenirse, ponerse de acuerdo; consentir; quedar o convenir (en) (*we agreed to go*, convinimos en ir; *we agreed on the price*, convinimos en el precio); sentar, probar, venir (bien o mal), hacer provecho (*this climate agrees with me*, este clima me sienta bien; *wine does not agree with me*, el vino me hace daño, o no me prueba); dar la razón a (*I agree with you*, te doy la razón, soy de tu parecer); (gram.) concordar.

agreeability [-əbíliti], *s. V.* AGREEABLENESS.

agreeable [-əbl], *a.* agradable, ameno; satisfactorio, aceptable; afable, simpático; condescendiente, complaciente.—**a. to**, de acuerdo con.

agreeableness [-nịs], *s.* agrado, amenidad, afabilidad; placibilidad, deleite.

agreeably [-əbli], *adv.* agradablemente; complacientemente; conformemente.

agreed [-d], *a.* convenido, concedido; reconocido; ajustado, acordado; de acuerdo, conforme.

agreement [-mẹnt], *s.* acuerdo, convenio, pacto, ajuste, concierto, avenencia; consentimiento; armonía; conformidad, acomodamiento; (gram.) concordancia.—**a. of opinion**, consenso.—**in a. (with)**, de acuerdo, acorde con.—**to reach an a.**, ponerse de acuerdo.

agrestic [əgréstịk], *a.* agreste, rústico, tosco, campestre.

agricultural [ægrịkÁlchụrạl], *a.* agrícola, agrario, geopónico.—**a. engineer**, ingeniero agrónomo.

agriculture [ǽgrịkÁlchụr(r)], *s.* agricultura; agronomía; geoponía o geopónica.

agricultur(al)ist [ægrịkÁlchụr(ạl)ịst], *s.* agricultor, agrónomo, agrícola, *mf.*

agrimony [ǽgrịmonị], *s.* (bot.) agrimonia.

agriology [ægrịálodʒị], *s.* estudio de los pueblos no civilizados.

agrology [ægrálodʒị], *s.* agrología.

agronomic(al [ægronámịk(ạl)], *a.* agrónomo, agronómico.

agronomics [-s], *s.* agronomía (considerada como parte de la economía política).

agronomist [ægránomịst], *s.* agrónomo.

agronomy [ægránomị], *s.* agronomía.

aground [əgráụnd], *adv.* (mar.) varado, encallado.—**to run a.**, encallar, vararse, enarenarse.

ague [éịgịu], *s.* (med.) fiebre palúdica, calentura intermitente; calofrío, escalofrío.—**a. tree**, (bot.) sasafrás.

aguish [-ịš], *a.* palúdico, escalofriado.

aguishness [-nịs], *s.* (med.) paludismo.

agynous [ǽdʒịnʌs], *a.* (bot.) agínico, ágino.

ah! [a], *interj.* ¡ah! ¡ay!

aha! [ahá], *interj.* ¡ajá!

ahead [əhéd], *adv.* delante, al frente, a la cabeza; adelante; hacia delante; (mar.) por la proa, avante.—**to be a.**, ir a la cabeza, ir delante.—**to get a.**, adelantarse, ganar la delantera; empujarse.—**to go a.**, avanzar.—**go a.!**, ¡adelante! ¡avance!—**a. of time**, por anticipado, con anticipación.

ahem! [əhém], *interj.* ¡oiga! ¡hola!

ahoy [əhóị], *interj.* ¡ah del barco! ¡ha!

aid [eịd]. **I.** *va.* y *vn.* ayudar, socorrer, auxiliar, coadyuvar, apoyar. **II.** *s.* ayuda, auxilio, concurso, socorro, apoyo, amparo; subsidio; auxiliador; (mil.) ayudante.—**first a.**, primeros auxilios (en accidentes).

aide-de-camp [éịddẹkǽmp], *s.* (mil.) edecán, ayudante de campo.

aider [éịdœ(r)], *s.* auxiliador, auxiliante, socorredor.

aidless [éịdlịs], *a.* desvalido, desamparado.

aigret(te [éịgret], *s.* (orn.) garzota; airón, garzota, cresta, copete, penacho; plumero.

aiguillette [eịgwịlét], *s.* (mil.) herrete, agujeta.—*pl.* cordones.

ail [eịl]. **I.** *va.* afligir, molestar, inquietar.—**what**

ails you? ¿qué tiene Vd? ¿qué le pasa a Vd? **II.** *vn.* sufrir, estar enfermo, indispuesto.

ailanthus [eịlǽnθʌs], *s.* (bot.) ailanto.

aileron [éịleran], *s.* (aer.) alerón.

ailing [éịliŋ], *a.* doliente, achacoso, enfermizo.

ailment [éịlmẹnt], *s.* dolencia, achaque, padecimiento, indisposición.

aim [eịm]. **I.** *va.* apuntar (un arma); dirigir, largar, asestar, encarar. **II.** *vn.* (con *at*) hacer puntería; aspirar a, pretender, tratar de, proponerse, tender a, tirar a.—**to a. high**, picar alto. **III.** *s.* puntería, encaro; blanco; designio, mira, propósito, fin, finalidad.—**accurate a.**, tino.—**to miss one's a.**, errar el tiro.—**to take one's a. well**, tomar bien sus medidas.

aimless [éịmlịs], *a.* sin objeto, sin designio, sin rumbo, a la ventura.

ain't [eịnt], *contr. vulg.* de *am not, is not, are not, has not, have not.*

air [er]. **I.** *va.* airear, ventilar, orear, aventar, ventear; secar (al aire o por calor); ostentar; sacar a lucir, pregonar, divulgar (opiniones propias). **II.** *s.* aire; atmósfera; brisa; semblante, ademán, talante; (mús.) aire, tonada; *pl.* ínfulas (*to put on airs*, darse tono o ínfulas).—**in the a.**, en vilo, en volandas; incierto, indeciso.—**in the open a.**, al aire libre, al raso, a la intemperie, al fresco.—**to be on the a.**, estar (hablando) en la radio; estar(se) transmitiendo por radio.—**to go on the a.**, hablar o dedicarse a hablar por radio para el público.—**up in the a.**, indeciso; perplejo; muy enojado o agitado. **III.** *a.* de aire; neumático; para aire; aéreo; aeronáutico, de aviación.—**a. arm** = A. FORCE.—**a. balloon**, globo aerostático.—**a. base**, base (*f.*) de (operaciones de) aviación.—**a. bladder**, (ict.) vejiga natatoria; (bot.) = A. VESICLE.—**a. blast**, chorro de aire.—**a.-borne**, transmitido, o llevado por el aire (gérmenes, etc.); transportado por avión o por aplanaderas (tropas, etc.).—**a. brake**, freno neumático.—**a. brush**, pulverizador de aire comprimido, aerógrafo.—**a. bubble**, burbuja de aire.—**a.-built**, quimérico, vano, sin fundamento.—**a. cannon**, cañón aéreo.—**a. casing**, cámara de aire aisladora.—**a. castle**, castillo de naipes, castillo en el aire.—**a. chamber**, cámara de aire.—**a. cleaner**, depurador del aire.—**a. cock**, llave (*f.*) de escape de aire.—**a. compressor**, compresor de aire.—**a. condenser**, condensador de enfriamiento por aire.—**a.-condition**, proveer de aire acondicionado.—**a.-conditioned**, de (con) aire acondicionado.—**a. conditioning**, acondicionamiento del aire.—**a.-cooled**, enfriado por aire.—**a. cooling**, enfriamiento por aire.—**A. Corps**, Cuerpo de Aviación.—**a. cushion**, almohada neumática, cojín de viento.—**a. drain**, conducto de ventilación; conducto de escape de gases.—**a.-dried**, secado al aire.—**a. drill**, taladro neumático.—**a. duct**, canal de aire.—**a. fleet**, flotilla de aeroplanos, fuerzas militares aeronáuticas.—**a. force**, o **service**, fuerzas aéreas militares; ejército aéreo; servicio militar de aviación.—**a. furnace**, horno de tiro natural; horno de calentar aire.—**a. gun**, escopeta de aire comprimido.—**a. hole**, respirador, registro, resolladero, ventosa; (fund.) sopladura; (aer.) vacío, región de extrema rarefacción del aire.—**a. intake**, entrada de aire.—**a. jacket**, camisa de natación, chaqueta salvavidas.—**a. lane**, (aer.) vía aérea.—**a. level**, nivel de burbuja.—**a. lift**, bomba de aire comprimido.—**a. line**, línea recta; (aer.) línea de aviones, línea (empresa) aérea o de transporte aéreo.—**a. liner**, avión (*m.*) de una empresa de transporte aéreo.—**a. lock**, acumulación de aire, e interrupción que causa; cámara bajo presión (de un cajón sumergido).—**a. mail**, correo aéreo.—**a.-mail service**, servicio aeropostal.—**by a. mail**, por vía aérea, por avión.—

a. meter, contador de aire o de gas.—**a.-minded,** interesado en aeronáutica.—**A. Ministry,** (Ingl.) Ministerio de Aviación.—**a. motor,** motor de aire comprimido.—**a. pilot,** piloto aviador.—**a. pipe,** tubo de llamada de aire o de ventilación; tubo para dar aire a los buzos.—**a. plant,** planta aerícola o epífita (que se alimenta de aire).—**a. pocket,** (aer.) bache o bolsa de aire; depresión. *V.* A. HOLE. **a. pressure,** presión atmosférica.—**a. proof,** hermético.—**a. pump,** (fís.) máquina neumática; (m.v.) bomba de aire, bomba de aspiración del condensador.—**a. raid,** ataque aéreo, incursión aérea.—**a. raid alarm o warning,** aviso de ataque aéreo.—**a. raid defense,** protección antiaérea.—**a. raid drill,** ejercicio antiaéreo.—**a. raid shelter,** refugio contra aeroplanos.—**a. raid warden,** jefe de manzana.—**a. sac,** saco aéreo (de las aves).—**a. screw,** hélice (*f.*) de avión.—**a. shaft,** respiradero; pozo de ventilación.—**a.-slaked,** apagada al aire (apl. a la cal).—**a. sleeve o sock,** (aer.) indicador de la dirección del viento.—**a. speed,** (aer.) velocidad de un avión con respecto al aire.—**a. speed indicator,** (aer.) indicador de velocidad.—**a. squadron,** escuadrilla aérea.—**a. tight,** hermético, a prueba de aire.—**a. trap,** sifón obturador, tubo en U.—**a. tube** = A. PIPE.—**a. valve,** válvula (de admisión o de salida) de aire.—**a. vesicle,** (anat.) vesícula aérea; (bot.) ampolla o vesícula de aire.—**a. view** = AEROVIEW.

aircraft [érkræft], *s.* máquina(s) de volar (aeroplanos, dirigibles, etc.).—**a. carrier,** (buque) portaaviones.—**a. fabric,** tela de aviación.—**a. plant,** talleres de aviación.

airdrome [érdroụm], *s.* aeródromo, aeropuerto, campo de aviación; cobertizo o hangar.

Airedale [érdeịl], *s.* variedad de perro terrier de origen inglés.

airfield [érfild], *s. V.* AIRPORT.

airfoil [érfoịl], *s.* (aer.) superficie de sustentación; plano aerodinámico; ala.

airily [érịlị], *adv.* airosamente, ligeramente, vivamente, alegremente; (fam.) pomposamente, con ínfulas.

airiness [érịnịs], *s.* ventilación, oreo; airosidad, vivacidad, viveza; ligereza, actividad.

airing [érịŋ], *s.* ventilación, oreo; caminata, paseata, paseo para tomar el aire.—**to take an a.,** dar una vuelta; orearse.

airless [érlịs], *a.* falto de ventilación.

airlike [érlaịk], *a.* tenue o ligero como el aire.

airline [érlaịn], *a.* aeroviario, aéreo.

airman [érmæn], *s.* aviador, aeronauta.

airometer [erámeteœ(r)], *s.* aerómetro; gasómetro.

airplane [érpleịn], *s.* aeroplano, avión, *m.*—**a. carrier,** (buque) portaaviones.

airport [érpɔrt], *s.* aeropuerto; puerto aéreo; paradero o estación para aeroplanos.

airship [érṣịp], *s.* aeronave, *f.,* dirigible.

airsick [érsịk], *a.* atacado, o que sufre, de mal de altura, especialmente en viajes aéreos.

airsickness [-nịs], *s.* mareo en viaje aéreo.

airway [érweị], *s.* conducto para aire; pozo o galería de ventilación; (aer.) ruta de aviación, vía aérea.—*pl.* red aérea.

airwoman [érwụman], *s.* aviadora.

airworthy [érwœrðị], *a.* (aer.) apto o seguro para el servicio (apl. a aeroplanos y dirigibles).

airy [érị], *a.* aéreo, airoso; bien ventilado; aeriforme, etéreo, vaporoso; tenue; ligero, trivial; vivaz, alegre; visionario; vanidoso, estirado.

aisle [áịl], *s.* pasillo, pasadizo, corredor; (arq.) nave, *f.* (lateral), ala.

aisled [-d], *a.* provisto de pasillos.

ait [eịt], *s.* mejana, isleta (en un río).

aitch [eịch] *s.* hache, *f.* (letra).

ajar [aḍżár], *adv.* y *a.* entreabierto, entornado; en pugna.—**to set a.,** entornar, entreabrir.

akimbo [akímboụ], *a.* en jarras.

akin [akín], *a.* consanguíneo, emparentado, afín; análogo, semejante.

akinesia [ækínísịạ], *s.* (med.) acinesia.

alabaster [ǽlabæstœ(r)], *s.* alabastro.

alabastrine [ælạbǽstrịn], *a.* alabastrino.

a la carte [alakárt], según la lista (de comidas), según se pida. (En casi todas partes se dice *a la carta,* aunque esta expresión se tacha de galicismo.)

alack! alackaday! [ạlǽk, -ạdéị], *interj.* ¡ay! ¡ay de mí! ¡guay!

alacrity [ạlǽkrịtị], *s.* alacridad, presteza, oficiosidad, vivacidad.

a la king [alakíŋ], (coc.) con salsa de hongos y pimientos.

a la mode [alamóụd], *adv.* (fam.) a la moda.

alanin(e [ǽlạnịn], *s.* (quím.) alanina.

alar [éịlạ(r)], *a.* alado, alígero; (bot., anat.) axilar.

alarm [ạlárm]. I. *s.* alarma; despertador; mecanismo de alarma; señal de alarma; rebato.—**a. bell,** campana o timbre de alarma.—**a. clock,** (reloj) despertador.—**to sound the a.,** dar la alarma, tocar a rebato. II. *va.* alarmar; dar la alarma a; asustar, turbar, inquietar. III. *vn.* dar la alarma; asustarse, alebrarse.

alarming [-ịŋ], *a.* alarmante.

alarmingly [-lị], *adv.* alarmantemente.

alarmist [-ịst], *s.* alarmista.

alarum [ạlǽrʌm], *s.* rebato; despertador.

alas! [ạlǽs], *interj.* ¡ay! ¡guay!—**a. for,** guay de, pobre de.

Alaskan [ạlǽskạn], *a.* y *s.* alaskense, de Alaska.

alate, alated [éịleịt, -ịd], *a.* (bot.) alado.

alaternus [ælạtœrnʌs], *s.* (bot.) aladierna, alaterno, ladierno.

alb [ælb], *s.* (igl.) alba.

albacore [ǽlbạkoụr], *s.* (ict.) albacora, bonito.

Albanian [ælbéịnịạn], *s.* y *a.* albanés, albano.

albata [ælbéịtạ], *s.* plata blanca de Alemania.

albatross [ǽlbạtros], *s.* (orn.) albatros.

albeit [olbíịt], *adv.* aunque, bien que, si bien.

albescent [ælbésẹnt], *a.* blanquecino, emblanqueciéndose, albicante.

Albian [ǽlbịạn], *a.* y *s.* (geol.) alb(i)ense.

Albigenses [ælbịdźénsịz], *s. pl.* albigenses.

Albigensian [-sịạn], *s.* y *a.* albigense.

albinism [ǽlbịnịzm], *s.* albinismo.

albino [ælbáịnoụ], *s.* albino; (Am.) bebeco.

Albion [ǽlbịọn], *s.* Albión, Inglaterra.

albite [ǽlbaịt], *s.* (min.) albatita.

albuginea [ælbịudźínịạ], *s.* (anat.) albugínea.

albugineous [ælbịudźínịʌs], *a.* albugíneo.

albugo [ælbịúgoụ], *s.* (med.) albugo.

album [ǽlbʌm], *s.* álbum.

albumen [ælbịúmẹn], *s.* (bot.) albumen.

albumenize [-aịz], *va.* albuminar; impregnar con albumen.

albumin [ǽlbịumịn], *s.* (bioquím.) albúmina.

albuminate [-eịt], *s.* albuminato.

albuminin [-ịn], *s.* (bioquím.) albuminina.

albuminize [-aịz], *va.* = ALBUMENIZE.

albuminoid [-oịd]. I. *a.* albuminoideo, albuminoide. II. *s.* albuminoide.

albuminous [-ʌs], *a.* albuminoso.

albuminuria [-iúrịạ], *s.* (med.) albuminuria.

albumose [ǽlbịumoụs], *s.* (bioquím.) albumosa.

albumosuria [-iúrịạ], *s.* (med.) albumosuria.

alburnum [ælbœrnʌm], *s.* (bot.) albura, alburno o alborno; madera albúrente.—*V.* SAPWOOD.

Alcaic [ælkéịịk]. I. *s.* verso alcaico. II. *a.* alcaico.

alchemic(al [ælkémịk(ạl], *a.* alquímico.

alchemically [-lị], *adv.* alquímicamente.

alchemist [ǽlkemịst], *s.* alquimista.

alchemistic(al [ælkemístịk(ạl], *a.* alquímico.

alchemy [ǽlkemị], *s.* alquimia.

alcohol [ǽlkohol], *s.* alcohol.—**absolute a.,** alcohol absoluto o puro.—**denatured a.,** alcohol desnaturalizado, alcohol de arder.—**wood a.,** alcohol metílico.

alcoholate [-eịt], *s.* (med.) alcoholato.

alcoholic [ælkohóljk]. **I.** *a.* alcohólico. **II.** *s.* (en *pl.*) líquidos alcohólicos.

alcoholism [ǽlkoholjzm], *s.* alcoholismo.

alcoholization [-jzéjṣọn], *s.* (quím.) alcoholización.

alcoholize [-ajz], *va.* alcoholar o alcoholizar.

alcoholometer [-ámetœ(r)], *s.* alcoholímetro.

alcoholometry [-trj], *s.* alcoholimetría.

Alcoran [ælkorán], *s.* Alcorán, Corán.

Alcoranic [-jk], *a.* alcoránico.

Alcoranist [-jst], *s.* alcoranista.

alcove [ǽlkoụv], *s.* alcoba, retrete; (Am.) dormida.

alcyon [ǽlsjọn], *a.* y *s.* *V.* HALCYON.

Aldebaran [ældébaṛạn], *s.* (ast.) Aldebarán.

aldehyde [ǽldẹhajd], *s.* (quím.) aldehido.

alder [óldœ(r)], *s.* (bot.) aliso, arraclán, frángula.

alderman [óldœrmạn], *s.* regidor, concejal.

aldermanship [-šjp], *s.* regiduría, concejalía.

aldermanic [-mǽnjk], *a.* perteneciente al regidor.

Aldine [óldajn], *a.* aldino.

ale [ejl], *s.* ale, *f.*, cerveza inglesa muy fuerte.— **a. conner**, inspector de cervecerías.

aleak [ạlík], *adv.* y *a.* que se sale o deja fugar (el agua, etc.); saliéndose, goteando.

aleatory [éjljạtorj], *a.* (for.) aleatorio; de azar.

aleberry [éjlberj], *s.* bebida de cerveza hervida con pan y especias.

alecost [éjlkast], *s.* (bot.) atanasia.

alee [ạlí], *adv.* (mar.) a sotavento.

alegar [ǽlēgạ(r)], *s.* cerveza agria.

alehoof [éjlhụf], *s.* (bot.) hiedra terrestre.

alehouse [éjlhaụs], *s.* taberna, cervezería.—**a. keeper**, tabernero.

alembic [ạlémbjk], *s.* alambique, retorta, destiladera, destilador.

alert [ạlǽrt]. **I.** *a.* alerto, vigilante; vivo, activo. —**on the a.**, sobre aviso, en guardia. **II.** *s.* alarma; (mil.) sorpresa. **III.** *va.* poner sobre aviso.

alertness [-njs], *s.* vigilancia, cuidado; viveza, actividad, prontitud.

alette [ạlét], *s.* (arq.) aleta.

aleurone [ælúroụn], *s.* (bot., bioquím.) aleurona.

aleurometer [ạlurámetœ(r)], *s.* aleurómetro.

alewife [éjlwajf], *s.* tabernera; (ict.) especie de sábalo o arenque norteamericano.

Alexandrian [ælegzǽndrjạn], *s.* y *a.* alejandrino.

Alexandrine [-drjn], *s.* verso alejandrino.

alexipharmic, alexiteric(al [ǽleksjfármjk, -térjk(ạl], *a.* alexifármaco.

alfalfa [ælfǽlfạ], *s.* alfalfa, mielga.—**a. field**, alfalfal, alfalfar.

alga [ǽlgạ], *pl.* **algae** [ǽldžj], *s.* (bot.) alga.

algal [ǽlgạl], *a.* algáceo.

algebra [ǽldžebrạ], *s.* álgebra.

algebraic(al [ǽldžebréjjk(ạl], *a.* algebraico.

algebraist [ǽldžebrejjst], *s.* algebrista.

Algerian [ældžírjạn], **Algerine** [ældžerín], *a.* y *s.* argelino.

algesia [ældžízjạ], *s.* algesia, gran sensibilidad al dolor.—**algesic** [-zjk], *a.* algésico.

algid [ǽldžjd], *a.* álgido.

algidity [ældžjdítj], *s.* (med.) algidez.

algoid [ǽlgojd], *a.* algáceo, semejante a las algas.

algology [ælgólodžj], *s.* algología, ficología.

Algonkin [ælgánkjn], **Algonquian** [-k(w)jạn], **Algonquin** [-k(w)jn], *s.* y *a.* algonquino.

algor [ǽlgọr], *s.* (med.) algidez.

algorism [ǽlgorjzm], *s.* (mat.) algoritmia.

algorithm [ǽlgorjðm], *s.* (mat.) algoritmo.

algorithmic [ælgorjðmjk], *a.* algorítmico.

algous [ǽlgẠs], *a.* algoso; algoide.

alguazil [ælgwạzíl], *s.* alguacil, corchete, esbirro.

alias [éjljạs]. **I.** *adv.* alias, por otro nombre. **II.** *s.* alias, nombre ficticio.

alibi [ǽljbaj], *s.* prueba de ausencia; disculpa, excusa; (for.) coartada.—**to prove an a.**, probar la coartada.

alible [ǽljbl], *a.* alible, nutritivo.

alidade [ǽljdejd], *s.* alidada.

alien [éjljẹn]. **I.** *a.* ajeno, no pertinente, extraño; extranjero, forastero; de extranjeros; discorde, contrario. **II.** *s.* extranjero, forastero.—**a. laws**, leyes (*f. pl.*) de extranjería.

alienable [-ạbl], *a.* enajenable, traspasable.

alienage [-jdž], **alienship** [-šjp], *s.* extranjía, extranjería.

alienate [-ejt], *va.* enajenar, traspasar; quitar, indisponer, robar (el amor, etc.); alejar, hacer indiferente.

alienation [-éjṣọn], *s.* enajenamiento, enajenación, desapropio, traspaso de dominio; extrañación, desapego, alejamiento, desunión, desvío; alienación, enajenación mental.

alienee [-í], *s.* (for.) aquel a quien pasa la propiedad de una cosa.

alienism [-jzm], *s.* = ALIENAGE; (med.) frenopatía, frenopatología.

alienist [-jst], *s.* alienista, frenópata, *mf.*

alienor [-ọ(r)], *s.* (for.) enajenante; enajenador.

aliferous [ǽljfẹras], *a.* alífero; (poét.) alígero.

aliform [ǽljform], *a.* aliforme.

alight [ạlájt]. **I.** *vn.* descender, bajar, apearse, desmontar(se); (con **on**) posarse (sobre); dar (con), tropezar con; (aer.) aterrizar; acuatizar, amarar (un hidroavión). **II.** *a.* y *adv.* ardiendo; encendido; iluminado.

alighting [-jŋ], *s.* descenso, bajada; (aer.) aterrizaje; acuatizaje, amaraje.

align [ạlájn], *va.* alinear(se); poner en línea recta.

alignment [-mẹnt], *s.* alineación, alineamiento.

alike [ạlájk]. **I.** *adv.* igualmente, del mismo modo; a la par. **II.** *a.* semejante; igual, conforme.

aliment [ǽljmẹnt]. **I.** *s.* alimento, nutrimento; sustento. **II.** *va.* alimentar; sustentar.

alimental [æljmẹ́ntạl], *a.* nutritivo, alimenticio.

alimentally [-jl], *adv.* nutritivamente.

alimentary [æljmẹ́ntạrj], *a.* de nutrición, de alimentación. *V.* ALIMENTAL.—**a. tract** o **canal**, tubo digestivo, conducto alimenticio.

alimentation [-éjṣọn], *s.* alimentación.

alimentiveness [æljmẹ́ntjvnjs], *s.* instinto de la alimentación; apetito.

alimony [ǽljmonj], *s.* (for.) alimentos, asistencias de divorcio o separación.

aline [ạlájn], *va.* y *vn.* alinear(se). *V.* ALIGN.

alinement [-mẹnt] = ALIGNEMENT.

aliped [ǽljped], *a.* y *s.* alípedo, quiróptero.

aliquant [ǽljkwạnt], *a.* alicuanta.

aliquot [ǽljkwọt], *a.* alícuota.—**a. parts**, (arit.) partes alícuotas.

alive [ạlájv], *a.* vivo, viviente; vivo, no apagado; activo, animado, concurrido, en vivo; sensible. —**a. with**, lleno de, pululante o plagado de.— **man a.!** ¡hombre!—**while a.**, en vida.

alizarine [ǽljzarjn], *s.* alizarina.

alkalescence [ǽlkạlḗsẹns], *s.* alcalescencia.

alkalescent [-ẹnt], *a.* alcalescente.

alkali [ǽlkạlaj], *s.* (quím.) álcali o cali.—**a. soil**, (agr.) suelo con gran cantidad de sales solubles eflorescentes.

alkalify [-ljfaj], *va.* alcalizar.

alkaligenous [-ljdžẹnas], *a.* alcalígeno.

alkalimeter [-límetœ(r)], *s.* alcalímetro.

alkalimetry [-límetrj], *s.* alcalimetría.

alkaline [-lajn], *a.* alcalino.

alkalinity [-línjtj], *s.* alcalinidad.

alkalization [-ljzéjṣọn], *s.* alcalización.

alkalize [-lajz], *va.* alcalizar.

alkaloid [-lojd], *s.* alcaloide, base orgánica.

alkaloid(al [-lójd(ạl], *a.* alcaloideo.

alkanet [ǽlkạnet], *s.* (bot.) orcaneta, buglosa, onoquiles, melera; ancusa.

alkermes [ælkœ́rmjz], *s.* (farm.) alquermes.

all [ọl]. **I.** *a.* todo, todos; todo, lleno de (*he was all promises*, era todo promesas). **II.** *s.* y *pron.* todo, totalidad, conjunto; todos, todo el mundo; todo lo. **III.** *adv.* completamente, enteramente; muy, -ísimo; exclusivamente, sólo, no más. NOTA.—**All** entra en la composición de numerosos vocablos, unas veces como adverbio en el sentido de "enteramente," y otras como nombre o adjetivo en el sentido de "todo" o "todos." En unos pocos compuestos, como **almighty,** todopoderoso, pierde una **l**; en los demás suele escribirse con un guión entre los dos elementos, como se ve en **all-powerful,** omnipotente, todopoderoso, poderosísimo, **allsteel,** todo de acero, **all-day task,** tarea de todo el día, y en otros ejemplos dados a continuación.—a. **abroad,** (fam.) defectuoso, equivocado; confundido, perplejo.—a. **along,** siempre, constantemente, sin cesar; de un extremo a otro de, por todo (el camino, tiempo, etc.).—a. **and singular, a. and sundry,** (for.) todos y cada uno, colectiva e individualmente.—a. **around,** por todas partes; en todo respecto. V. A. ROUND.—a. **at once,** repentinamente, de repente; de un golpe; a un tiempo.—a. **but,** todo(s) menos, o sino; casi, poco menos que, por poco (*I fell and all but killed myself,* caí y por poco me mato).—a.-**consuming,** que todo lo consume.—a. **day** (**night,** etc.), todo el día (toda la noche, etc.).—a.-**embracing,** omnímodo, que lo abraza y comprende todo.—**A. Fools' Day,** día (*m.*) de engañabobos (el primero de abril en varios países). V. APRIL.—a. **fours,** las cuatro patas; cierto juego de naipes.—**to go on a. fours,** gatear, andar a gatas.—a. **hail!** ¡salud! ¡bienvenido!—a. **in,** (fam.) agotado, molido, muerto o rendido de cansancio.—a. **in a.,** en (con)junto, en todo; completamente.—a.-**inclusive,** omnímodo; todo incluído o comprendido.—a.-**knowing,** omnisciente.—a. **of,** todo(s); por lo menos (*all of them,* todos ellos; *all of two miles,* por lo menos dos millas).—a. **of a sudden** = A. AT ONCE.—a. **off,** abandonado, frustrado (viaje, plan, etc.); completamente erróneo.—a. **one,** del mismo tenor; una misma cosa; igual, indiferente, que no importa (*it is all one (to me),* (me) es igual; lo mismo da).—a. **others,** los demás, todos los otros.—a. **out,** (fam.) completamente; apagado (el fuego, un incendio); agotado, rendido; equivocado, confundido; resueltamente, con toda energía (*an all-out effort,* un esfuerzo supremo o total).—a. **out!** ¡salgan todos!—a. **out of,** sin, desprovisto de, etc. (*I am all out of tobacco, patience,* etc., se me ha acabado o agotado el tabaco, la paciencia, etc.).—a. **over,** terminado, acabado (*it is all over,* ha acabado, se acabó, o ha pasado, etc.); por todas partes; (fam.) exactamente, como, copia de.—a.-**possessed,** (fam.) maniático, destornillado, loco (fig.).—a. **right,** sano y salvo; sin duda, ciertamente; está bien, corriente, bueno; (con **to be**) satisfactorio, apropiado, aceptable, bueno (buen sujeto, buena persona), competente.—a.-**round,** completo; acabado, consumado; de idoneidad general; por todas partes.—a.-**seeing,** omnividente, que todo lo ve.—a. **set,** (fam.) listo, dispuesto.—A. **Souls' Day,** día (*m.*) de (los) difuntos (dos de noviembre).—a. **that,** todo el (o lo) que, todos los que, cuanto(s).—a. **the better** (**worse**), tanto mejor (peor).—a. **the same,** a pesar de eso, o de todo; sin embargo; todo igual. V. SAME.—a. **the way,** por el, o en, todo el camino (o viaje, marcha, travesía, etc.); en todo, enteramente.—a. **the way** (**up o down**) **to,** hasta (*he went all the way up to the roof,* subió hasta el tejado).—a. **there,** (fam.) (afirmativamente), listo, alerta, despierto; (**not to be a. there,** no estar en su juicio cabal, estar un poco chiflado).—a. **told,** en (con)junto, por todo; teniéndolo(s) todo(s) en cuenta.—a. **too,** demasiado; muy; perfectamente, evidentemente; desgraciadamente (*it is all too true that my son did it,* desgraciadamente es verdad que mi hijo lo hizo).—a.-**wise,** sapientísimo, que lo sabe todo.—**above a.,** sobre todo, ante todo.—**after a.,**

después de todo, al fin y al cabo.—**and a.** (**that**), y demás, y otras cosas por el estilo, etcétera.—**at a.,** absolutamente; de alguna (o ninguna) manera, en absoluto; siquiera algo, siquiera un poco (a menudo empleado enfática o expletivamente, y puede dejarse sin traducir; *v. g. has he any money at all?* ¿él tiene dinero? o, más explícitamente, ¿él tiene siquiera algún dinero? *was he there at all?* ¿él (siquiera) estuvo allí?).—**at a. hours,** a toda(s) hora(s); a altas horas de la noche, tarde por la noche.—**for a.,** a pesar de.—**for a. I know,** quizá, posiblemente, eso no es imposible.—**for a. that,** con todo, a pesar de eso.—**for good and a.,** una vez por todas; definitivamente; para siempre.—**in a.,** por todo, en (con)junto.—**not at a.,** de ninguna manera, nada de eso; no por cierto, no tal; no hay de qué.—**of a.** (**people, things,** etc.). Esta frase se usa a menudo para expresar sorpresa, o sorpresa y desprecio, y puede traducirse, cambiando un poco el giro, por medio de ¡qué cosa! ¡quién lo creyera! ¿habráse visto? no faltaba más, etc. (*they appointed John, of all people!* nombraron a Juan, ¡quién lo hubiera creído! o ¡qué cosa! *he asked me to marry him, of all things!* me propuso casamiento, ¿habráse visto? o no faltaba más).—**once for a.,** una vez por todas; por última vez.—**that's a. there is to it,** no es, o no hay, más que eso; no hay más que hablar, (fam.) sanseacabó.—**the A.,** el gran todo, el universo.—**to be a. up with,** haber fracasado enteramente; estar de baja (fig.), haberlo perdido todo, estar caído por completo; estar desahuciado.—**to lose** (**stake,** etc.) **one's a.,** perder (arriesgar, etc.) todo lo que se tiene.

Allah [ǽlǎ], *s.* Alá.
allantois [ælǽntoįs], *s.* (zool.) alantoides.
allay [ǝléį], *va.* aliviar, aquietar; apaciguar, calmar, mitigar, templar.
allayer [-œ(r)], *s.* aliviador, apaciguador; calmante, mitigante, sedante.
allayment [-męnt], *s.* alivio, desahogo.
allegation [ælęǧéįšǫn], *s.* alegación, argumento; (for.) alegato.
allege [ǝlédž], *va.* alegar; declarar o afirmar; sostener; pretender; (for.) deducir.
allegeable [-ǝbl], *a.* que se puede alegar.
alleged [-d], *a.* alegado; supuesto, pretendido.
allegedly [-ǐdlį], *adv.* según se afirma, según se pretende (gen. insinuando que sin razón).
alleger [-œ(r)], *s.* alegador, afirmante, declarante.
allegiance [ǝlídžǝns], *s.* lealtad, homenaje, fidelidad, obediencia (a un país o gobierno).—**to swear a.,** hacer pleito homenaje, jurar obediencia, etc.
allegiant [ǝlídžǝnt]. I. *a.* leal. II. *s.* súbdito.
allegoric(al [ælęǧórįk(ǎl], *a.* alegórico.
allegorically [-į], *adv.* alegóricamente.
allegoricalness [-nįs], *s.* calidad de alegórico.
allegorist [ælęǧorįst], **allegorizer** [ælęǧoráįzœ(r)], *s.* alegorista, el que alegoriza.
allegorization [-įzéįšǫn], *s.* alegorización.
allegorize [ælęǧoraįz]. I. *va.* alegorizar. II. *vn.* usar alegorías.
allegory [ælęǧorį], *s.* alegoría.
allegretto [alęgrétou], *s.* (mús.) alegreto.
allegro [ǝléįgrou], *s.* (mús.) alegro.
allelujah [ǝlįlúlyǎ], *s.* e *interj.* aleluya.
allemande [ǽlmǎnd], *s.* (danz.) aleman(d)a.
allergic [ǝlœ́rdžįk], *a.* alérgico.—**allergist** [ǽlœrdžįst], *s.* alergista, especialista en alergia. —**allergy** [ǽlœrdžį], *s.* alergia, susceptibilidad anormal a ciertas substancias.
alleviate [ǝlívįeįt], *va.* aliviar, aligerar, mitigar, calmar, desahogar.—**alleviation** [-éįšǫn], *s.* alivio, paliativo, calmante, aligeramiento, mitigación; relevación.
alleviative [ǝlívįǝtįv], *a.* y *s.* paliativo.
alley [ǽlį], **alley-way** [-weį], *s.* calle estrecha, callejuela, callejón; paseo arbolado (de jardín o

alliaceous [æliéi̯ʃi̯ʌs], *a.* aliáceo.

Allhallowmass [ɔlhǽloumʌs], *s.* festividad de Todos los Santos.—**Allhallows** [ɔlhǽlouz], *s.* día (*m.*) de Todos los Santos (primero de noviembre).—**Allhallowstide** [-tai̯d], *s.* época de Todos los Santos.

alliance [ǝláiǝns], *s.* alianza, unión, fusión, liga, asociación; conexión o parentesco.

allied [ǝláid], *a.* aliado, unido; relacionado.

allies [ǝlai̯z o ǝláiz], *s.* (*pl.* de ALLY) aliados.

alligation [æligéiʃǝn], *s.* (arit.) aligación.

alligator [ǽligeitǝ(r)], *s.* (zool.) caimán; (Am.) lagarto (de Indias), (Arg.) yacaré.—**a. apple,** anona de los pantanos.—**a. pear,** aguacate, palta.—**a.-tree,** ocozol, árbol que da el liquidámbar.

alliteration [ǝlitǝréiʃǝn], *s.* aliteración.

alliterative [ǝlítǝrǝtiv], *a.* aliterado.

allocate [ǽlokeit], *va.* colocar; señalar, asignar.

allocation [ælokéiʃǝn], *s.* colocación; asignación, distribución.

allocatur [æloké̯itǝ(r)], *s.* (for.) "cúmplase."

allochroite [ǝlákroai̯t], *s.* (min.) alocroíta.

allocution [ǝlokiúʃǝn], *s.* alocución.

allod [ǽlad], *s. V.* ALLODIUM.

allodial [ǝlóu̯dial], *a.* (for.) alodial.

allodium [ǝlóu̯diʌm], *s.* (for.) alodio.

allogamy [ǽlágǝmi], *s.* (bot.) alogamia (= CROSS-FERTILIZATION).

allopath [ǽlopæθ], **allopathist** [ǝlápǝθi̯st], *s.* (med.) alópata, *mf.*

allopathic [ǝlopǽθi̯k], *a.* alopático, alópata.

allopathy [ǝlápǝθi], *s.* (med.) alopatía.

allophane [ǽlofein], *s.* (min.) alófana.

allot [ǝlát], *va.* distribuir por suerte, destinar, adjudicar, repartir, asignar.

allotment [-mǝnt], *s.* lote, parte, *f.*, porción; asignación, repartimiento, adjudicación.

allotropic [ǝlotrápik], *a.* alotrópico.

allotropism [ǝlátropizm], **allotropy** [ǝlátropi], *s.* (quím.) alotropía.

allottable [ǝlátǝbl], *a.* repartible, asignable.

allow [ǝláu̯]. **I.** *va.* permitir, consentir, dejar, conceder; dar, ceder; confesar, admitir; aprobar; (com.) rebajar, descontar, deducir. **II.** *vn.* (con **for**) tener en cuenta; dejar (espacio, etc.) para.

allowable [-ǝbl], *a.* admisible, permisible.

allowableness [-nis], *s.* calidad de permisible; licitud, legitimidad; propiedad.

allowably [-ǝbli], *adv.* permisivamente.

allowance [-ǝns], *s.* concesión; asignación; ración, gajes, pensión, abono, alimentos, mesada; permiso; indulgencia; (com.) descuento, rebaja, bonificación, refacción; (tecn.) tolerancia, discrepancia permitida.—**to make a. for,** hacerse cargo de; tener en cuenta.—**annual a.,** anualidad.—**baggage a.,** concesión de equipaje.—**monthly a.,** mensualidad.—**retirement a.,** jubilación; pensión de retiro.

alloy [ælói̯]. **I.** *s.* mezcla; impureza; (fund.) aleación; liga.—**a. steel,** acero de aleación. **II.** *va.* desvirtuar con elementos impuros o de inferior calidad (literal y figuradamente); (fund.) alear, ligar (los metales).

alloyage [-id̮ʒ], *s.* (fund.) aleación.

allspice [ɔ́lspai̯s], *s.* pimienta de Jamaica; (bot.) calicanto.

allude [ǝliúd], *vn.* aludir, referirse a (indirecta o casualmente, o con insinuación).

allure [ǝliúr]. **I.** *va.* halagar, atraer, tentar, seducir; cebar. **II.** *s.* porte, continente, talante. *V.* ALLUREMENT.

allurement [-mǝnt], *s.* tentación, seducción; atractivo, halago; aliciente, cebo, añagaza.

allurer [-œ(r)], *s.* seductor, engañador.

alluring [-iŋ], *a.* seductivo, tentador.

alluringly [-li], *adv.* halagüeñamente, seductoramente.

alluringness [-nis], *s.* calidad de atractivo o tentador; incentivo, halago, seducción.

allusion [ǝliúʒǝn], *s.* alusión; insinuación indirecta.

allusive [ǝliúsiv], *a.* alusivo.

allusively [-li], *adv.* alusivamente.

allusiveness [-nis], *s.* calidad de alusivo.

alluvial [ǝliúvi̯ǝl], *a.* aluvial.—**a. cone,** o **fan,** abanico aluvial (apl. al formado por un arroyo al entrar en un valle).

alluvion [ǝliúvi̯ǝn], *s.* avenida, inundación; (geol.) aluvión, *m.;* (for.) derrubio.

alluvium [ǝliúvi̯ǝm], *s.* (geol.) aluvión, *m.;* terrero, derrubio.

ally [ǝlái̯]. **I.** *va.* unir. **II.** *vn.* aliarse, coligarse, confederarse. **III.** *s.* aliado; pariente, allegado, confederado, compañero; auxiliador; cuerpo u organismo análogo.

alma mater [ǽlmǝ méitœ(r)], *s.* la universidad o colegio donde uno se ha educado.

almanac [ɔ́lmǝnæk], *s.* almanaque, calendario.—**a. pad,** taco.—**ecclesiastical a.,** añalejo.

almandite [ǽlmǝndait], *s.* (min.) almandina.

almightiness [ɔlmáitinis], *s.* omnipotencia.

almighty [ɔlmáiti]. **I.** *a.* todopoderoso, omnipotente. **II.** *s.* **-the A.,** Dios.

almond [ámǝnd], *s.* (bot.) almendra, alloza; almendro, allozo; (anat.) amígdala.—**a. brittle,** crocante, guirlache.—**a.-like,** o **a.-shaped,** almendrado, amigdáleo.—**a. milk,** almendrada.—**a. paste,** turrón.

almoner [ǽlmonœ(r)], *s.* limosnero.

almonry [-ri], *s.* lugar donde se reparten limosnas.

almost [ɔ́lmoust], *adv.* casi, cerca de, por poco.

alms [ámz], *s.* limosna.—**a. basket, box,** etc., limosnera, cepillo o cepo, bacinilla, plato o cesto para limosna; (Am.) alcancía, macuto.

almsdeed [-did], *s.* obra de caridad.

almsgiver [-givœ(r)], *s.* limosnero; el que da limosna.

almsgiving [-giviŋ], *s.* acto de dar limosna.

almshouse [-haus], *s.* hospicio, casa de caridad.

alnage [ǽlnid̮ʒ], *s.* aneaje, medida por anas.

alod(ial), **alodium.** *V.* ALLODIAL, etc.

aloe [ǽlou̯], *s.* (bot.) áloe, lináloe, azabara, zabida o zabila.—**aloes,** (*sing.* o *pl.*) áloe o acíbar.—**a. wood,** palo (de) áloe, agáloco o calambac.—**American a.,** *V.* CENTURY PLANT.

aloetic(al [ǝloétik(ǝl], *a.* aloético.

aloft [ǝlɔ́ft], *adv.* arriba, en alto, en los aires; (mar.) arriba; en la arboladura superior.—**to be a.,** (aer.) estar en vuelo, o volando.—**to set a.,** elevar, subir.

aloin [ǽloin], *s.* (quím.) aloína.

alone [ǝlóu̯n], *a.* y *adv.* solo, solitario, señero, sin compañía, a solas; único; solamente, tan sólo.—**to let a.,** dejar en paz, no molestar, no tocar, etc.

aloneness [-nis], *s.* soledad; el estado de ser solo, sin compañía, o sin igual.

along [ǝlɔ́ŋ]. **I.** *prep.* a lo largo de; en todo el largo de; al lado de. **II.** *adv.* a lo largo; adelante.—**a. with,** con, junto con.—**to get a.,** adelantar, ir tirando o pasando; llevarse (bien o mal).—**to go a. with,** acompañar, ir con; estar conforme con.—**a. about ten,** a eso de las diez.—**a. about Christmas,** por Navidad.—**a. these lines,** en este sentido.—**come a.,** venga Vd. conmigo.—**move a.,** váyase, ¡largo de aquí!—**go a. this street,** siga Vd. por esta calle.—**he fooled us all a.,** nos engañó desde el principio.

alongshore [-ʃor], *adv.* a lo largo de la costa, a la orilla.

alongside [-said], *adv.* y *prep.* a lo largo de, al lado, costado con costado, junto a (*alongside a ship,* al bordo, al costado de un buque).—**to bring a.,** (mar.) abarloar.

aloof [ǝlúf], *adv.* lejos, de lejos, apartado, a distancia.—**to stand** o **keep a.,** mantenerse apartado, no mezclarse, no tomar parte, retraerse, aislarse.

aloofness [-nis], *s.* alejamiento, aislamiento, retraimiento; no participación; indiferencia, huraña.

alopecia [ælopísiä], *s.* (med.) alopecia, peladera.

aloud [aláud], *adv.* alto, en voz alta, recio.

alpaca [ælpǽkä], *s.* alpaca, paco; (tej.) alpaca.

alpenglow [ǽlpinglou], *s.* resplandor rojizo que se ve en las montañas al amanecer o a la puesta del sol.

alpenhorn [-horn], *s.* (alem.) corneta alpestre.

alpenstock [-stak], *s.* (alem.) bastón de pincho, palo con punta de hierro que se emplea en la ascensión de los Alpes u otras montañas.

alpestrine [ælpéstrin], *a.* alpestre, alpino.

alpha [ǽlfä], *s.* alfa (letra griega); (fig.) principio. —**a. and omega**, el primero y el último, el principio y el fin.—**a. rays**, (fís.) rayos alfa.

alphabet [ǽlfabet], *s.* alfabeto, abecedario, abecé.

alphabet, alphabetize [-aiz], *va.* alfabetizar, ordenar alfabéticamente.

alphabetarian [-éirian], *s.* el que aprende el alfabeto.

alphabetic(al [ælfabétik(al], *a.* alfabético.

alphabetically [-i], *adv.* alfabéticamente.

alphenic [ælfénik], *s.* alfeñique; azúcar candi.

alpine [ǽlpain], *a.* alpino, alpestre; de las grandes alturas.

alpinist [ǽlpinist], *s.* alpinista, aficionado a excursiones en las montañas.

alpist [ǽlpist], *s.* (bot.) alpiste.

alquifou [ælkifú], *s.* (min.) alquifol.

already [olrédi], *adv.* ya, antes de ahora.

Alsatian [ælséiñan], *s.* y *a.* alsaciano.

alsike [ǽlsik], *s.* (bot.) trébol sueco.

also [ólsou], *adv.* también, igualmente, además, asimismo; (for.) ítem (más); otrosí.

alt [ælt]. **I.** *s.* la parte más alta de la gama musical. **II.** *a.* (mús.) alto; agudo.

Altaic [æltéiïk], *s.* y *a.* altaico.

Altar [óltä(r], *s.* (astr.) el Altar, Ara.

altar [óltä(r], *s.* altar; ara; árula.—**a. boy**, acólito.—**a. bread**, pan eucarístico; hostia.—**a. cloth**, sabanilla, mantel, palia.—**a.-piece**, retablo.—**a. screen**, contrarretablo.—**a. slab**, ara.—**a. table**, mesa del altar.

altarage [-idʒ], *s.* (igl.) pie (*m.*) de altar.

alter [óltœr], **I.** *va.* alterar, cambiar, modificar, mudar, inmutar, variar; (E. U.) castrar.—**to a. one's condition**, tomar estado, casarse. **II.** *vn.* alterarse, cambiar, variar.

alterability [-abíliti], *s.* alterabilidad.

alterable [-abl], *a.* alterable; mudable.

alterableness [-nis], *s.* alterabilidad.

alterably [-abli], *adv.* mudablemente.

alterant [-ant], *a.* alterante.

alteration [-éiñon], *s.* alteración, cambio, muda, inmutación, reforma, corrección.

alterative [-ątiv]. **I.** *a.* alterativo. **II.** *s.* alterante.

altercate [ǽltœrkeit], *vn.* altercar, controvertir.

altercation [-éiñon], *s.* altercación, altercado, controversia, disputa; (fam.) agarrada.

alterer [óltœrœr], *s.* alterador.

altern [ǽltœrn], *a.* alterno.

alternant [æltœrnant], *a.* alternante.

alternate [æltœrneit]. **I.** *va.* alternar; revezar. **II.** *vn.* alternar, turnar; (elec.) alternar. **III.** [-it], *a.* alterno o alternativo.—**a. angles**, (geom.) ángulos alternos. **IV.** *s.* suplente, substituto.

alternately [æltœrnitli], *adv.* alternadamente, por turno.

alternating [æltœrneitin], *a.* alternante, alternativo.—**a. current**, (elec.) corriente alterna.

alternation [-éiñon], **alternateness** [æltœrnątnis], *s.* alternación; turno, revezo.

alternative [æltœrnątiv]. **I.** *s.* alternativa. **II.** *a.* alternativo.—**a. conjunction**, (gram.) conjunción disyuntiva.

alternatively [-li], *adv.* alternativamente, por turno.

alternativeness [-nis], *s.* alternativa.

alternator [ǽltœrneito(r], *s.* (elec.) alternador.

althea [ælθíä], *s.* (bot.) malvavisco; rosa de Siria; malva rósea.

altho, although [olðóu], *conj.* aunque, si (bien), bien que, no obstante, aun cuando.

althorn [ǽlthorn], *s.* (mús.) alto (ll. t. **alto horn**).

altigraph [ǽltigræf], *s.* altímetro registrador, aneroide registrador.

altimeter [æltímetœr], *s.* altímetro.

altimetry [-tri], *s.* altimetría.

altiscope [ǽltiskoup], *s.* (ópt.) altiscopio.

altisonant [æltísonant], **altisonous** [-ʌs], *a.* altisonante, pomposo, retumbante; altísono.

altitude [ǽltitiud], *s.* altura, altitud, elevación; cumbre, cima.

alto [ǽltou], *a.* y *s.* (mús.) contralto; viola.

altogether [oltugéðœr]. **I.** *adv.* en (con)junto; enteramente, totalmente, del todo; para siempre. **II.** *s.* conjunto, totalidad.—**in the a.**, (fam.) enteramente desnudo, en cueros.

alto-relievo [æltorilívoü], *s.* (b. a.) alto relieve.

altruism [ǽltruizm], *s.* altruísmo.

altruist [-ist], *s.* altruísta.

altruistic [-ístik], *a.* altruísta, perteneciente al altruísmo; benévolo, desinteresado.

aludel [ǽliudel], *s.* (quím.) aludel.

alum [ǽlʌm]. **I.** *s.* alumbre, *m.*, (en)jebe.—**a. flower**, alumbre calcinado en polvo.—**a. mine**, **a. works**, alumbrera.—**a. stone**, alunita.—**concentrated a.**, sulfato de aluminio. **II.** *va.* (tint.) alumbrar.

alumina [æliúminä], *s.* (quím.) alúmina.

aluminate [-eit], *s.* aluminato.

aluminiferous [-ífɛras], *a.* aluminífero.

aluminite [-ait], *s.* (min.) aluminita.

aluminium [æliumíniʌm], **aluminum** [æliúminʌm], *s.* (quím.) aluminio.—**a. bronze**, **a. gold**, bronce de aluminio (aleación de cobre y aluminio).

aluminous [-ʌs], *a.* aluminoso, alumínico, arciloso; alumbroso, alumbrado.

alumish [ǽlamiʃ], *a.* alumbroso, alumbrado.

alumna [alámnä], *s.* (*pl.* **alumnae**) alumna, estudiante; esp. la graduada de una universidad o escuela.

alumnus [-ʌs], *s.* (*pl.* **alumni**) alumno, estudiante; esp. el graduado de una universidad o escuela.

alunite [ǽliunait], *s.* (min.) alunita.

alveary [ælvíeri], *s.* colmena; (anat.) alveario.

alveolar [ælvíolä(r], *a.* alveolar.

alveolate [ælvíoleit], *a.* alveolado.

alveolus [ælvíolʌs], *s.* alvéolo; celdilla, cavidad.

alvine [ǽlvin], *a.* (anat.) alvino.

alway (poét.) [ólwei], **always** [-z], *adv.* siempre.

alyssum [alísʌm], *s.* (bot.) alhelí.

am [æm], *1a. pers. pres. ind.* de TO BE.

amadou [ǽmadu], *s.* yesca, hupe, *f.*

amain [améin], *adv.* con vehemencia, vigorosamente, con todas sus fuerzas; sin demora.

amalgam [ǽmælgam], *s.* amalgama; mezcla.—**a. arc**, (elec.) arco formado en un tubo de vacío con electrodos de amalgama.

amalgamate [-eit], *va.* y *vn.* amalgamar; unir, incorporar.

amalgamation [-éiñon], *s.* amalgamación; mezcla.—**a. works**, azoguería.

amalgamator [-eito(r], *s.* amalgamador; azoguero.

amanita [æmanáitä], *s.* (bot.) amanita.

amanous [ǽmanas], *a.* sin manos.

amanuensis [amænyuénsis], *s.* amanuense, escribiente, memorialista, notario.

amaranth [ǽmarænθ], *s.* (bot.) amaranto, moco de pavo; color carmesí o purpúreo.

amaranthine [æmaræneθin], *a.* de amaranto; encarnado, purpurino; inmarcesible.

Amaryllis [æmərílis], s. (bot.) familia de las amarilídeas; (a-) planta amarilídea; amarilis.

amass [əmǽs], va. acumular, amontonar, amasar.

amassment [-mɛnt], s. cúmulo, montón.

amateur [ǽmətiur], s. y a. aficionado; de afición.

amateurish [æmətiúriʃ], a. como de aficionado; superficial; torpe, desmañado; novicio.

amateurishly [-li], adv. chapuceramente.

amateurism [æmətiúrizm], s. estado o carácter de aficionado, no profesional.

amative [ǽmətiv], a. amatorio.

amativeness [-nis], s. amatividad.

amatorial [æmətóriəl], **amatory** [ǽmətori], a. amatorio, erótico.

amaurosis [æmoróusis], s. (med.) amaurosis, gota serena.

amaurotic [æmorátik], a. amaurótico.

amaze [əmǽiz], va. asombrar, aturdir, helar, pasmar, dejar atónito, admirado o maravillado.

amazed [-d], a. atónito, pasmado, absorto, asombrado.

amazedly [-idli], adv. pasmadamente.

amazedness [-nis], **amazement** [-mɛnt], s. asombro, pasmo, aturdimiento.

amazing [-iŋ], a. pasmoso, asombroso, admirable.

amazingly [-li], adv. pasmosamente, asombrosamente.

Amazon [ǽməzan], s. amazona; (a-) marimacho; (orn.) papagayo del Amazonas.—**A. stone**, (min.) amazonita.

Amazonian [æməzóunian], a. amazónico, amazonio.

amazonite [ǽməzanait], s. (min.) amazonita.

ambage [ǽmbidʒ], s. ambages, m. pl.; camino tortuoso.

ambagious [æmbéidʒʌs], a. ambagioso, ambiguo.

ambary [æmbári], s. cáñamo de la India (ll. t. gambo, bangue).

ambassador [æmbǽsədo(r)], s. embajador.

ambassadorship [-ʃip], s. embajada (cargo).

ambassadress [-dris], s. embajadora.

amber [ǽmbœ(r)]. I. s. ámbar, electro, cárabe; color de ámbar.—**a. seed**, semilla del abelmosco o de la algalia.—**a. varnish**, barniz de succino.—**black a.**, azabache.—**yellow a.**, succino. II. a. ambarino. III. va. cubrir con ámbar; ambarar.

ambergris [-gris], s. ámbar gris.

amberoid [-ojd], s. ámbar prensado.

ambidexter [æmbidǽkstœ(r)], s. persona ambidextra; (fig.) el que obra con doblez o come a dos carrillos.

ambidexterity [-stériti], **ambidextrousness** [æmbidǽkstrasnis], s. igual manejo de ambas manos; doblez, simulación.

ambidextrous [-stras], a. ambidextro; falso, hipócrita.

ambient [ǽmbiɛnt], a. y s. ambiente.

ambiguity [æmbigiúiti], **ambiguousness** [æmbígiuasnis], s. ambigüedad, dilogía.

ambiguous [æmbígiuas], a. ambiguo, equívoco, ambagioso, enigmático.

ambiguously [-li], adv. ambiguamente.

ambit [ǽmbit], s. ámbito, recinto, contorno.

ambition [æmbíʃɔn], s. ambición, codicia; aspiración; energía, determinación.

ambitious [æmbíʃʌs], a. ambicioso, codicioso; de aspiraciones; enérgico, emprendedor.

ambitiously [-li], adv. ambiciosamente; anhelosamente.

ambitiousness [-nis], s. calidad de ambicioso; energía.

ambitus [ǽmbitʌs], s. borde; ámbito; extensión.

amble [ǽmbl]. I. vn. amblar. II. s. (paso de) andadura, ambladura.

ambler [ǽmblœ(r)], s. caballo que ambla.

amblingly [ǽmbliŋli], adv. a paso de andadura.

amblyopia [æmblióupiə], s. (med.) ambliopía.

ambo [ǽmbou], s. (igl.) ambón.

ambroid [ǽmbrojd], s. ámbar prensado.

ambrosia [æmbróuʒiə], s. ambrosía.

ambrosial [-l], a. ambrosíaco, delicioso, deleitable; celestial, divino.

Ambrosian [-ʒiən], a. ambrosiano.

ambry [ǽmbri], s. despensa; aparador; armario; alacena.

ambulacrum [æmbiuléikrʌm], s. (zool.) ambulacro.

ambulance [ǽmbiulans], s. hospital de sangre; ambulancia.

ambulant [-ant], a. ambulante.

ambulation [-éiʃɔn], s. ambulación, paseo.

ambulative [-ātiv], a. ambulante, ambulativo, mudable.

ambulatory [-ātori]. I. s. (arq.) paseo, galería, corredor; ambulatorio, ambulante, que puede andar. II. a. (for.) alterable.

ambuscade [æmbʌskéid]. I. s. emboscada, asechanza, asecho. II. va. atacar desde una emboscada. III. vn. estar en o preparar una emboscada, emboscarse.

ambush [ǽmbuʃ]. I. va. acechar, poner celada; asechar, insidiar. II. s. (mil.) emboscada, celada, zalagarda; insidia. V. AMBUSCADE.—**to lie in a.**, asechar, estar emboscado o en asecho.

ameba [emíbə], s. = AMŒBA.

ameer, amir [əmír], s. amir, emir.

ameliorate [əmílyoreit], va., vn. mejorar(se), adelantar(se).

amelioration [-éiʃɔn], s. mejora, adelanto; mejoría, alivio, mejoramiento.

ameliorator [-eito(r)], s. mejorador.

amen [eimen o amén], interj., adv. y s. amén.—**to say a. to**, sancionar, aprobar; terminar.

amenability [əminəbíliti], s. responsabilidad; docilidad, sumisión.

amenable [əmínəbl], a. responsable; sujeto a; tratable, dócil.

amenableness [-nis], s. V. AMENABILITY.

amend [əménd]. I. va. enmendar, rectificar, modificar, corregir, reformar. II. vn. enmendarse, reformarse, restablecerse.

amendable [-əbl], a. enmendable, reparable, reformable, corregible.

amendatory [-ətori], a. correctivo, reformatorio.—**a. deed**, (for.) escritura de modificación.

amender [-œ(r)], s. enmendador, reformador, corrector.

amending [-iŋ], s. la acción de enmendar.

amendment [-mɛnt], s. enmienda, reforma; cambio, modificación; remedio, remiendo; (agr.) substancia que mejora el suelo cambiando sus propiedades físicas no nutritivas.

amends [əméndz], s. compensación, satisfacción, reparación.—**to make a.**, dar cumplida satisfacción; compensar, reparar, expiar, resarcir.

amenity [əméniti], s. amenidad; afabilidad.

amenorrhea [eimenoríə], s. (med.) amenorrea; menostasia, opilación.

ament [éimɛnt], s. idiota, mf., imbécil.

ament [ǽment], **amentum** [əméntʌm], s. (bot.) amento.

amentaceous [æmentéiʃʌs], a. (bot.) amentáceo.

amental [eiméntal], a. no mental; sin mente.

amentia [eiménʃiə], s. demencia, locura.

amerce [əmœrs], va. multar; castigar; despojar.

amerceable [-əbl], a. digno de ser multado.—**amercement** [-mɛnt], s. multa a discreción del juez.—**amercer** [-œ(r)], s. multador.

American [əmérikən], s. y a. americano; norteamericano, estad(o)unidense.—**A. plan**, plan americano (en los hoteles); habitación con pensión.—**A. Union**, Unión Norteamericana, Estados Unidos.

Americana [əmerikéinə], s. pl. colección de objetos o escritos americanos.

Americanism [əmérikənizm], s. americanismo; instituciones norteamericanas; fidelidad a estas instituciones.

Americanist [-ist], s. americanista.

Americanization [-izéiṣọn], s. americanización.
Americanize [-aiẓ], va. y vn. americanizar(se).
Amerind [ǽmẹrịnd], s. amerind(i)o, indígena americano.
Amerindian [æmẹríndiạn], a. y s. amerind(i)o, relativo a los indígenas americanos.
amethyst [ǽmẹθịst], s. (min.) amatista; color de amatista.—**amethystine** [æmẹθístịn], a. parecido a la amatista.
amiability [eimiạbílịti], **amiableness** [éimiạblnịṣ], s. amabilidad, afabilidad.
amiable [-bl], a. amable, afable.
amiably [-bli], adv. amablemente.
amianthus [æmiǽnθʌs], s. (min.) amianto.
amicable [ǽmịkạbl], a. amigable, amistoso.
amicability [-bílịti], **amicableness** [-blnịṣ], s. afecto, cariño, amistad, amigabilidad.
amicably [-bli], adv. amigablemente.
amice [ǽmịṣ], s. (igl.) amito.
amid [ạmíd], **amidst** [ạmídst], prep. entre, en medio de; mezclado con; rodeado por.
amid(e [ǽmaid], s. (quím.) amida.
amidin(e [ǽmịdịn], s. (quím.) amidina.
amidogen [ǽmídodẓen], s. (quím.) amidógeno.
amidol [ǽmịdọl], s. (quím.) amidol.
amidships [ạmídṣịps], adv. (mar.) en medio del navío.
amin(e [ạmín], s. (quím.) amina.
aminic [ạmínịk], a. amínico.—**amino acid** [æmíno ǽsịd], s. (bioquím.) aminoácido.
amir [ạmír], s. = AMEER.
amiss [ạmís]. I. adv. fuera de lugar o de sazón, mal, impropiamente, fuera del caso, de más.—**to take a.**, llevar o tomar a mal. II. a. inoportuno; impropio; malo, errado.—**to be a.**, venir mal; estar de más (hacer algo).
amity [ǽmịti], s. amistad, bienquerencia, concordia, armonía.
ammeter [ǽmitœ(r], s. (elec.) amperímetro.
ammonia [ạmóunịạ], s. (quím.) amoníaco.—**a. water**, agua amoniacal.
ammoniac [ạmóuniæk], s. amoníaco (goma.).
ammoniac(al [æmonáiæk(ạl], a. amoniacal.
ammonic [ạmóuṇịk], a. amónico.
ammonification [-fịkéiṣọn], s. (agr.) saturar de amoníaco o sales amoniacales; formación de amoníaco por acción microbiana.
ammonify [-ifai], va. tratar con amoníaco o sales amoniacales.
Ammonite [ǽmọnait], s. y a. (hist.) amonita, descendiente de Amón.
ammonite, s. (pal.) amonita (molusco fósil); (quím.) amonita (explosivo); (agr.) abono obtenido de residuos animales.
ammonium [æmóuṇiạm], s. (quím.) amonio.
ammunition [æmyuníṣọn]. I. s. (mil.) munición, municiones, pertrechos.—**a. belt**, banda de cartuchos.—**a. dump**, depósito de municiones. II. va. (a)municionar.
amnesia [æmníẓịạ], s. (med.) amnesia.
amnesty [ǽmnẹsti]. I. s. amnistía, indulto.—**to receive a.**, amnistiarse. II. va. amnistiar, indultar.
amnion [ǽmniọn], s. (anat.) amnios, f.
amniotic [æmniátịk], a. amniótico.
amock, amok(e, a. y adv. V. AMUCK.
amœba [ạmíbạ], s. (zool.) amiba, amibo.
amœboid [ạmíbọid], a. (biol.) amiboideo.
amomum [ạmóumʌm], s. (bot.) amomo.
among [ạmʌ́ɳ], **amongst** [ạmʌ́ɳst], prep. entre, mezclado con, en medio de.
amoral [eimárạl], a. amoral, sin moralidad.
amoralism [-iẓm], s. amoralismo.
amorality [eimorélịti], s. amoralidad.
amorist [ǽmorịst], s. amante, galán.
Amorite [ǽmorait], s. y a. amorreo, amorita, mf.
amorous [ǽmoras], a. enamorado, amoroso, tierno, apasionado, cariñoso, enamoradizo.
amorously [-li], adv. amorosamente.
amorousness [-nịṣ], s. calidad de amoroso; enamoramiento.

amorphism [ạmórfịẓm], s. amorfía, amorfismo; nihilismo; anarquismo.
amorphous [ạmórfʌs], a. amorfo, informe; anómalo, heterogéneo; (quím.) amorfo.
amortizable [ạmórtaiẓạbl], a. amortizable.
amortization [ạmórtaiẓéiṣọn], **amortizement** [ạmórtiẓmẹnt], s. (for. y com.) amortización.
amortize [ạmórtaiẓ], va. (for. y com.) amortizar.
amount [ạmáunt]. I. s. cantidad, monta(nte), valor, importe, suma; monto (capital más intereses). II. vn. (con **to**) montar, subir ascender (a), valer, importar.
amour [ạmúr], s. amores, m. pl., amorío, lío.—**a.-propre**, amor propio.
amourette [æmụrét], s. amorcillo.
amperage [æmpírịdẓ], s. (elec.) amperaje, amperios.
ampere [ǽmpir], s. (elec.) amperio.—**a. centimeter**, amperio-centímetro.—**a. foot**, amperio-pie.—**a. hour**, amperio-hora.—**a. turn**, amperio-vuelta.—**back a. turn**, contra-amperio-vuelta.
amperemeter [-mitœ(r], s. (elec.) amperímetro.
ampersand [ǽmpœrsænd], s. el signo &, y.
Amphibia [æmfíbiạ], s. pl. anfibios.
amphibian [-ạn]. I. s. y a. anfibio. II. s. (aer.) anfibio, aeroplano de tierra y agua.—**a. tank**, (mil.) tanque anfibio.
amphibion [-ọn], s. (aer.) = AMPHIBIAN.
amphibious [æmfíbiạs], a. anfibio.
amphibiousness [-nịṣ], s. calidad de anfibio.
amphibole [ǽmfịboul], s. (min.) anfíbol.
amphibolite [æmfíbolait], s. (petr.) anfibolita.
amphibological [æmfịbọládẓịkạl], **amphibolic** [æmfịbálịk], a. (min.) anfibólico; ambiguo; (med.) de pronóstico incierto, anfibológico, dudoso, obscuro.
amphibologically [-i], adv. anfibológicamente.
amphibology [æmfịbálọdẓi], s. anfibología, doble sentido, ambigüedad.
amphibolous [æmfíbolas], a. (lóg.) de doble sentido.
amphiboly [æmfíboli], s. ambigüedad, equívoco.
amphibrach [ǽmfịbræk], s. (pros.) anfíbraco.
amphictyon [æmfíktiọn], s. anfiction, m.
amphictyonic [-ánịk], a. anfictiónico.
amphictyony [æmfíktiọni], s. anfictionía.
amphimacer [æmfímạsœ(r], s. (pros.) anfímacro.
amphioxus [æmfiáksʌs], s. (zool.) anfioxo.
amphipod [ǽmfipad], s. y a. (zool.) anfípodo.—**amphipodal** [æmfípodạl], a. anfípodo.
amphiprostyle [æmfíprostail], s. (arq.) anfipróstilo.
amphisbæna [æmfịsbínạ], s. (zool.) anfis(i)bena.
amphiscii [æmfíṣiai], s. pl. anfiscios.
amphitheater, amphitheatre [æmfịθiạtœ(r], s. anfiteatro, circo.—**amphitheatric(al** [-θiạtrík(ạl], a. anfiteatral, de forma de anfiteatro.
Amphitryon [æmfítriọn], s. anfitrión, m.
amphora [ǽmforạ], s. ánfora.
amphoric [æmfárịk], a. anfóreo; (med.) anfórico.
ample [ǽmpl], a. amplio; anchuroso, extensivo, lato, bastante, suficiente, abundante; capaz, cumplido.
ampleness [-nịṣ], s. amplitud, anchura, capacidad, holgura, abundancia, profusión.
amplexicaul [æmpléksikɔl], a. (bot.) amplexicaulo.
ampliation [æmpliéiṣọn], s. ampliación; (for.) aplazamiento de fallo, demora, prórroga.
ampliative [ǽmplieitiv], a. ampliativo.
amplification [-fịkéiṣọn], s. amplificación, ampliación; (ópt.) aumento (del microscopio, etc.)
amplificative [ǽmplifịkeitiv], **amplificatory** [æmplífịkạtori], a. amplificativo, amplificador.
amplificator [æmplifíkeitọ(r], s. amplificador.
amplifier [ǽmplifaiœ(r], s. amplificador, ampliador, aumentador; (elec.) amplificador; (rad.) altavoz, altoparlante.—**a. tube**, válvula o lámpara amplificadora.

amplify [-faj], *va.* amplificar; ampliar, extender, dilatar, agrandar, aumentar.

amplitude [-tjud], *s.* amplitud, extensión, dilatación; (ffs., astr.) amplitud.

amply [áempli], *adv.* ampliamente; latamente; suficientemente; abundantemente; con creces.

ampoule [æmpúl], **ampule** [áempul], *s.* ampolleta o tubo de jeringa hipodérmica.

ampulla [æmpálä], *s.* (anat.) ampolla; (igl.) ampolla, vinajera.

ampullaceous [æmpaléjšas], *a.* ampollar.

amputate [áempjutejt], *va.* amputar, desmembrar.

amputation [-téjšon], *s.* (cir.) amputación, ablación; desmembración.

amputator [-tejto(r)], *s.* amputador, operador de una amputación.—**amputee** [-tí], *s.* persona a quien se ha hecho amputación.

amuck [amák]. **I.** *a.* frenético. **II.** *adv.* furiosamente.—**to run a.,** correr amok, atacar a ciegas, a troche y moche.

amulet [áemjuljt], *s.* amuleto, talismán, dije.

amuse [amjúz], *va.* entretener, distraer, divertir, hacer gracia (a); embobar.—**to a. oneself,** distraerse, divertirse, holgarse, recrearse.

amusement [-ment], *s.* diversión, pasatiempo, distracción, divertimiento, entretenimiento.—**a. place** o **spot,** recreo, lugar de diversión.

amuser [-œ(r)], *s.* entretenedor.

amusing [-iŋ], *a.* divertido, recreativo, entretenido; risible, gracioso.—**to be a.,** tener gracia.

amusingly [-li], *adv.* divertidamente, entretenidamente.

amygdala [amígdalä], *s.* (anat.) amígdala.

amygdalaceous [-léjšas], *a.* (bot.) amigdaláceo.

amygdalate [-lejt], *a.* almendrado; amigdáleo; hecho de, o semejante a, almendras.

amygdalin [-lin], *s.* (quím.) amigdalina.

amygdaline, amigdaloid [-lojd], *a.* almendrado; amigdaloide.

amygdaloid, *s.* (geol.) roca amigdaloide.

amyl [áemjl]. **I.** *s.* (quím.) amilo. **II.** *a.* amílico.—**a. alcohol,** alcohol amílico.

amylaceous [-éjšas], *a.* amiláceo.

amylene [áemjlin], *s.* (quím.) amileno.

amylic [æmíljk], *a.* amílico.

an [æn], *art. indef.* un, uno, una (antes de *sonido* vocal, excepto la *u* de **unit, eulogy,** etc.; v.g. *an enemy,* un enemigo; *an hour,* una hora). **V.** A.

ana [áenä], *adv.* (med.) ana.

ana [éjnä], *s.* (colección de) apuntes curiosos.

Anabaptism [ænäbáeptjzm], *s.* anabaptismo.

Anabaptist [-tjst], *s.* anabaptista.

anabasis [ænáebasjs], *s.* (med.) anábasis; (mil.) invasión (a).—(hist.) Anábasis.

anabatic [ænäbáetjk], *a.* ascendente (viento, etc.); anabático.

anabolism [ænábolizm], *s.* (biol.) anabolismo, metabolismo constructivo.

anacamptic [ænäkáemptjk], *a.* (fís.) anacámptico, referente a la reflexión de la luz o del sonido.

anacanth [áenäkænθ], *s.* (ict.) anacant(in)o.

anacardiaceous [ænäkardjéjšas], *a.* (bot.) anacardiáceo.

anacardic [ænäkárdjk], *a.* anacardino.

anacardium [-djam], *s.* (bot.) anacardo.

anachronism [ænáekronjzm], *s.* anacronismo.

anachronistic [-tjstjk], *a.* anacronístico.

anachronous [ænáekronas], *a.* anacrónico.

anaclastics, *s.* V. DIOPTRICS.

anacoluthon [ænäkolúθan], *s.* (gram.) anacoluto.

anaconda [ænäkándä], *s.* (zool.) anaconda, boa.

Anacreontic [anäkrjántjk], *a.* anacreóntico.

anæmia [ænímjä], *s.* (med.) anemia.

anæmic [-jk], *a.* anémico.

anaerobe [ænéjeroub], *s.*, **anaerobic** [-óubjk], *a.* (biol.) anaerobio.

anæsthesia [ænesθíäjä], *s.* (med.) anestesia.

anæsthetic [ænesθétjk], *a.* y *s.* anestésico.

anæsthetize [ænésθetajz], *va.* anestesiar.

anaglyph [áenaglif], *s.* (b.a., arq., fot.) anáglifo.

anagoge [ænagóudžj], *s.* anagoge.

anagogic(al [ænagádžjk(al], *a.* anagógico, místico.

anagogics [-s], *s.* anagogía.

anagram [áenagræm], *s.* anagrama, *m.*

anagrammatical [ænagrammétjkal], *a.* anagramático, que forma anagrama.

anagrammatist [ænagrámatjst], *s.* anagramatista, el que hace anagramas.

anagrammatize [-tajz], *va.* y *vn.* anagramatizar, componer anagramas.

anal [éjnal], *a.* (anat.) anal, relativo al ano.

analecta [ænaléktä], **analects** [áenalekts], *s. pl.* analectas.—**analectic** [-léktjk], *a.* analéctico.

analeptic [ænaléptjk], *a.* (med.) analéptico, restaurativo.

analgesia [ænaldžízjä], *s.* (med.) analgesia.

analgesic [-džizjk], *a.* y *s.* analgésico, anodino.

analogical [ænaládžjkal], *a.* analógico.

analogically [-i], *adv.* analógicamente.

analogicalness [-njs], *s.* calidad de analógico.

analogize [ænélodžajz], *va.* explicar por analogía.

analogous [ænélogas], *a.* análogo, semejante, parecido; congenial.

analogously [-li], *adv.* análogamente.

analogue [áenalag], *s.* término análogo.

analogy [ænélodžj], *s.* analogía, semejanza, correlación, afinidad, conformidad.

analysis [ænélisjs], *s.* análisis, *mf.*

analyst [áenaljst], *s.* analizador; (mat.) analista.

analytic(al [ænaljtjk(al], *a.* analítico, resolutivo.—**a. geometry,** geometría analítica.

analytically [-i], *adv.* analíticamente.

analytics [-s], *s.* ciencia del análisis; (filos.) analítica; (mat.) geometría analítica.

analyze [áenalajz], *va.* analizar, resolver.

analyzer [-œ(r)], *s.* analizador.

Anamese, V. ANNAMESE.

anamnesis [ænemnísjs], *s.* anamnesis; recuerdo; (med.) antecedentes de una enfermedad.

anamorphosis [ænamórfosjs], *s.* anamorfosis.

anandrous [ænéndras], *a.* (bot.) anandro, que carece de estambres.

ananthous [ænénθas], *a.* (bot.) ananto, que carece de flores.

anap(a)est [áenapest], *s.* (pros.) anapesto (◡ ◡ −).

anap(a)estic [ænapéstjk], *a.* y *s.* (verso) anapéstico.

anaphora [ænéforä], *s.* (ret.) anáfora.

anaphrodisia [ænæfrodízjä], *s.* anafrodisia.

anaphrodisiac [-zjak], *a.* y *a.* (med.) anafrodisíaco, antiafrodisíaco.

anaphylaxis [ænafjléksjs], *s.* (med.) anafilaxis.

anaplastic [ænaplæstjk], *a.* anaplástico, relativo a la anaplastia.

anaplasty [ænaplæstj], *s.* (cir.) anaplastia.

anarchic(al [ænárkjk(al], *a.* anárquico.

anarchism [ænárkjzm], *s.* anarquismo; anarquía.

anarchist [-kjst], *s.*, **anarchistic** [-kjstjk], *a.* anarquista.

anarchy [ænárkj], *s.* anarquía.

anasarca [ænasárkä], *s.* (med.) anasarca.

anasarcous [-as], *a.* hidrópico.

anastasis [ænéstasjs], *s.* (med.) convalescencia.

anastatic [ænastétjk], *a.* grabado en relieve.

anastigmatic [ænæstigmétjk], *a.* anastigmático, sin astigmatismo.

anastomose [ænéstomous], *vn.* (anat., bot.) anastomosarse, anastomizarse.

anastomosis [-móusjs], *s.* anastomosis.

anastomotic [-mátjk], *a.* anastomótico.

anastrophe [ænéstrofj], *s.* (ret.) anástrofe.

anathema [ænéθemä], *s.* anatema, *mf.*; excomunión; maldición, imprecación.

anathematic(al [-métjk(al], *a.* perteneciente al

anatema.—**anathematically** [-i̱], *adv.* a modo de anatema.

anathematization [-ma̱ti̱zéi̱ṣo̱n], *s.* anatema, *mf.*, anatematismo.

anathematize [-ma̱ta̱i̱z], *va.* anatematizar; excomulgar; maldecir.

anathematizer [-œ(r)], *s.* anatematizador.

Anatolian [æna̱tóulia̱n], *s. y a.* anatolio.

anatomical [æna̱támi̱ka̱l], *a.* anatómico.

anatomically [-i̱], *adv.* anatómicamente.

anatomist [a̱nǽtomi̱st], *s.* anatomista; disector.

anatomize [-ma̱iz], *va.* anatomizar; disecar, analizar minuciosamente.

anatomy [-mi̱], *s.* anatomía; disección; disecación; esqueleto.

ancestor [ǽnsɛsto̱(r)], *s.* progenitor, antecesor, antepasado, ascendiente.—*pl.* padres, mayores.

ancestral [ænsɛ́stra̱l], *a.* de los antepasados; hereditario.—**a. mansion,** solar, casa solariega.

ancestry [ǽnsɛstri̱], *s.* linaje, prosapia, abolengo, alcurnia, ascendencia, estirpe, *f.*

anchor [ǽŋko̱(r)]. **I.** *va.* (mar.) sujetar con el ancla, poner (el barco) sobre el ancla, aferrar; (tec.) sujetar; asegurar, atirantar, empotrar. **II.** *vn.* (mar.) anclar, fondear, surtir. **III.** *s.* (mar.) ancla, ancora, ferro; (constr.) riostra, tirante, soporte; (tec.) artificio de sujeción o amarre (áncora, perno, tornillo, etc.); áncora (de escape de reloj); (fig.) áncora, amparo.—**a. arms,** brazos del ancla.—**a. back,** galga del ancla.—**a. beam,** serviola.—**a. bill,** pico del ancla.—**a. bolt,** tornillo o perno de anclaje o de cimiento.—**a. chocks,** calzos de ancla.—**a. crown,** cruz del ancla.—**a. drag,** rastra.—**a. escapement,** escape de áncora (de reloj).—**a. flukes,** uñas del ancla.—**a. forge,** ancorería.—**a. ground,** fondeadero, tenedero.—**a. ice,** hielo esponjoso formado en el fondo del agua.—**a. light,** linterna de un buque anclado.—**a. mast,** (aer.) = **MOORING MAST.**—**a. ring,** arganeo.—**a. shank,** caña del ancla.—**a. stock,** cepo del ancla.—**a. stopper,** capón.—**a. tripper,** disparador.—**a. watch,** guardia de cubierta de un barco anclado.—**at a.,** al ancla, anclado.—**best bower a.,** ancla de ajuste.—**bower a.,** ancla de proa.—**drag a.,** ancla de arrastre.—**foul a.,** ancla enredada.—**kedge a.,** anclote.—**sheet a.,** ancla mayor.—**small bower a.,** ancla sencilla.—**stream a.,** anclote.—**to drop o cast a.,** dar fondo, anclar, echar anclas.—**to ride at a.,** estar fondeado o anclado.—**to stock the a.,** encepar el ancla.—**to weigh a.,** zarpar, levar anclas.

anchorable [-a̱bl], *a.* fondable, propio para anclaje.

anchorage [-i̱dẓ], *s.* (mar.) ancladero, agarradero, fondeadero; anclaje, ancoraje.—**a. fees,** (derechos de) anclaje.

anchored [-d], *a.* anclado, surto; asegurado, sobre las anclas; de forma de ancla.

anchoress [ǽŋko̱ri̱s], *s.* ermitaña.

anchoret [ǽŋko̱ret], **anchorite** [-a̱it], *s.* ermitaño, anacoreta, *mf.*

anchoritic(al [-ĭti̱k(a̱l], *a.* anacorético.

anchorless [ǽŋko̱rli̱s], *a.* sin ancla; inseguro.

anchorsmith [-smi̱θ], *s.* ancorero.

anchovy [ǽnchou̯vi̱], *s.* (ict.) ancho(v)a, boquerón, haleche, lacha.

anchusin [æŋkúsi̱n], *s.* (quím.) ancusina.

ancient [éi̱nṣent]. **I.** *a.* antiguo, vetusto. **II.** *s.* (en *pl.*) antepasados, mayores; la antigüedad.

anciently [-li̱], *adv.* antiguamente.

ancientness [-ni̱s], *s.* antigüedad.

ancillary [ǽnsi̱leri̱], *a.* ancilario; subordinado, subsidario, dependiente, auxiliar; sucursal.

ancipital, ancipitous [ænsípi̱ta̱l, -tʌs], *a.* de dos caras; de doble filo.

ancon [ǽŋkan], *s.* (anat.) codo; (arq.) ancón, ménsula.

ancoral [ǽŋko̱ra̱l], *a.* perteneciente o semejante a una áncora; (zool.) encorvado.

and [ænd], *conj.* y, e.—**and so forth,** o **and so on,** etcétera; y así sucesivamente.—**ifs and ands,** dimes y diretes. Se emplea a veces antes del infinitivo, sobre todo después de *to go, to come, to try,* para indicar acción o propósito, vg. *I must go and see,* debo ir a ver; *I shall try and speak to him,* trataré de hablarle.

Andalusian [ænda̱ljúẓa̱n], *a. y s.* andaluz.

andalusite [ænda̱ljúsa̱it], *s.* (min.) andalucita.

andante [ændǽnti̱], *a., adv. y s.* (mús.) andante.

andantino [-tínou̯], *a., adv. y s.* (mús.) andantino.

Andean [ændía̱n], *a. y s.* andino; (Am.) colla, *mf.*

andesite [ǽndi̱za̱it], *s.* (min.) andesita.

andiron [ǽnda̱io̱rn], *s.* morillo.

androecium [ændrĭṣi̱ʌm], *s.* (bot.) androceo.

androgen [ǽndrodẓen], *s.*, **androgenous** [ændrádẓɛnʌs], *a.* (bioquím.) andrógeno.

androgyne [ǽndrodẓi̱n], *s.* hermafrodita; hombre afeminado; mujer ahombrada; eunuco.

androgynous [ændrádẓi̱nʌs], *a.* (bot., zool.) andrógino, hermafrodita.

androgyny [ændrádẓi̱ni̱], *s.* androginia, hermafroditismo.

android [ǽndro̱i̱d], *s.* androide, autómata de forma humana.

anecdotal [ǽni̱kdou̯ta̱l], **anecdotic(al** [æni̱kdáti̱k(a̱l], *a.* anecdótico.

anecdote [ǽni̱kdou̯t], *s.* anécdota.

anecdotist [-i̱st], *s.* anecdotista.

anemia [æními̱a̱], *s.* (med.) anemia.

anemic [æními̱k], *a.* anémico.

anemograph [ænémogræf], *s.* (meteorol.) anemógrafo, anemómetro registrador.

anemographic [-grǽfi̱k], *a.* anemográfico.

anemography [ænemágrafi̱], *s.* anemografía.

anemometer [ænemámeto̱(r)], *s.* anemómetro.

anemometrograph [ænemométrogræf], *s.* anemometrógrafo.

anemometry [ænemámetri̱], *s.* anemometría.

anemone [ǽnémoni̱], *s.* (bot.) anemone, *f.*, anémona.—**sea a.,** (zool.) actinia, anémona de mar.

anemoscope [ænémoskou̯p], *s.* anemoscopio.

anent [ænént], *prep.* tocante a, concerniente a.

aneroid [ǽnero̱i̱d], *a.* aneroide.—**a. barometer,** barómetro aneroide.

anesthesia, etc. *V.* ANÆSTHESIA, etc.

aneurism [ǽnjuri̱zm], *s.* (med.) aneurisma, *mf.*

aneurismal [ænjurízma̱l], *a.* aneurismal.

anew [a̱njú], *adv.* de nuevo, otra vez; nuevamente, de un modo nuevo, de refresco.

anfractuous [ænfrǽkchuas], **anfractuose** [-ou̯s], *a.* anfractuoso, sinuoso, tortuoso.

anfractuosity [-ási̱ti̱], *s.* anfractuosidad, sinuosidad.

angel [éi̱ndẓel]. **I.** *s.* ángel, serafín, etc.; antigua moneda inglesa; (fam.) caballo blanco.—**a. fish,** (ict.) angelote o peje ángel; cierto pez (*m.*) tropical.—**a. shot,** (arti.) bala encadenada. **II.** *a.* angelical.

angelhood [-hu̯d], *s.* condición de ángel.

angelic(al [ændẓéli̱k(a̱l], *a.* angelical, angélico, seráfico.

angelica [-ă], *s.* (bot.) angélica; (A.) vino dulce de California.

angelically [-li̱], *adv.* angélica o angelicalmente.

Angelus [ǽndẓelʌs], *s.* (igl.) ángelus.

anger [ǽŋgœ(r)]. **I.** *s.* ira, cólera, enojo.—**to provoke to a.,** encolerizar, causar ira. **II.** *va.* enfadar, provocar, enfurecer, enojar, airar.

Angevin(e [ǽndẓevi̱n], *s. y a.* angevino.

angina [ændẓái̱na̱ o éndẓi̱na̱], *s.* (med.) angina.—**a. pectoris,** angina de pecho.

angiology [ændẓi̱álodẓi̱], *s.* (anat.) angiología.

angiosperm(ous [ændẓi̱o̱spœ́rm(ʌs], *s. y a.* (bot.) angiospermo.

angle [ǽŋgl]. **I.** *vn.* pescar con caña; intrigar, insinuarse, buscar solapadamente. **II.** *s.* ángulo; esconce; esquina, rincón, recodo; (arq.) encuentro; (tec.) codo; hierro en ángulo; avíos (*m. pl.*) de pescar; (fig.) punto de vista.—**a.**

bar, = A. IRON.—**a. block,** (carp.) coda; bloque o zapata en la unión de dos piezas; polea de cambio de dirección.—**a. brace,** (constr.) cuadral; escuadra; (mec.) berbiquí de manivela para esquinas.—**a. bracket,** consola o soporte angular, escuadra saliente de esquina; escuadra de unión.—**a. brick,** ladrillo de aristas oblicuas. —**a. bulb,** hierro en ángulo con un borde ensanchado.—**a. float,** (alb.) palustrillo.—**a. gauge,** goniómetro.—**a. iron,** esquinal, hierro angular, escuadra, cantonera.—**a. line,** (top.) poligonal, línea quebrada.—**a. plate,** plancha en ángulo, o angular.—**a. rafter,** (arq.) lima, par o alfarda (de un tejado).—**a. tie,** (constr.) cuadral.—**a. valve,** válvula de conductos en ángulo recto.—**a. of advance,** (m. v.) ángulo de avance (de la excéntrica).—**a. of attack,** (aer.) ángulo de ataque.—**a. of bank,** (aer.) ángulo de balance o de escora lateral.—**a. of contact,** (mec.) ángulo o arco de contacto (de una correa).—**a. of deflection,** (arti.) ángulo de elevación.—**a. of depression,** ángulo de depresión.—**a. of draft** = ANGLE OF TRACTION. —**a. of elevation,** ángulo de elevación, ángulo con el horizonte.—**a. of entrance,** (m. v.. hidr.) ángulo de entrada.—**a. of friction,** ángulo de rozamiento.—**a. of incidence,** ángulo de incidencia.—**a. of intersection,** (f. c.) ángulo de contingencia.—**a. of lag,** (elec.) ángulo de retraso.—**a. of lead,** (elec.) ángulo de avance.—**a. of pitch,** (aer.) ángulo de cabeceo.—**a. of reflection,** (fís.) ángulo de reflexión.—**a. of refraction,** (fís.) ángulo de refracción.—**a. of repose** = ANGLE OF FRICTION.—**a. of roll,** (aer.) = A. OF BANK.—**a. of torsion,** ángulo de torsión.—**a. of traction,** ángulo de tracción, ángulo entre la fuerza de tracción y la superficie de arrastre.—**a. of twist,** ángulo de torsión.—**a. of yaw,** (aer.) ángulo de derrape.—**a. of zero lift,** (aer.) ángulo de resistencia nula.—**at an a.,** en ángulo, inclinado.—**at right angles,** en ángulo recto.

Angle, s. y a. anglo.

angled [ǽngld], a. anguloso, esquinado.

angler [ǽnglœ(r)], s. pescador (de caña); (ict.) pejesapo, pescador, rape.

anglesite [ǽnglɘsait], s. (min.) anglesita.

angleworm [ǽnglwœrm], s. lombriz de tierra.

Anglican [ǽngliḳạn], a. y s. anglicano.

Anglicanism [-izm], s. anglicanismo.

Anglicism [ǽnglisizm], s. anglicismo, inglesismo.

Anglicize [-aiz], va. inglesar.

angling [ǽngliŋ], s. pesca (gen. con caña).

Anglo-American [ǽnglo-ạmériḳạn], a. y s. angloamericano.

Anglomania [-méiniạ], s. anglomanía.

Anglomaniac [-méinịæk], a. y s. anglómano.

Anglo-Norman [-nórmạn], s. y a. anglonormando.

Anglophile [-fail], s. y a. anglófilo.

Anglophobe [-foub], s. y a. anglófobo.

Anglophobia [-fóubịạ], s. anglofobia.

Anglo-Saxon [-sǽksọn], s. y a. anglosajón.

Angola cat, etc., s. = ANGORA CAT, etc.

Angora [ængóụrạ], s. angora, mf.—**A. cat, goat,** gato, cabra de Angora o Angola (Ankara).

angostura (bark) [æŋgọstịúrạ(bark)], s. (bot. y farm.) corteza de angostura.

angrily [ǽngrịli], adv. colérica o airadamente.

angriness [-nịs], s. V. ANGER.

angry [ǽngri], a. enojado, encolerizado, bravo, airado; (med.) irritado, inflamado.—**to be- (come) a.,** enfadarse, airarse, quemarse, atufarse, sulfurarse.

anguilliform [æŋgwíḷịform], a. anguiliforme, en forma de anguila.

anguish [ǽngwiš], s. ansia, angustia, zozobra.

anguished [-t], a. atormentado, angustiado, afligido, acongojado.

angular [ǽngiulạ(r)], a. angular, anguloso.—**a.**

advance, a. lead, (m. v.) ángulo de avance, o de calado (de la excéntrica).

angularity [-lǽrịti], **angularness** [ǽngiulạrnịs], s. cualidad de angular o anguloso; esquinadura.

angularly [-li], adv. angularmente.

angulate, angulated [ǽngiuleit, -id], a. (bot.) anguloso, angular.

angulation [-léišọn], s. formación angular.

anhelation [ænhịléišọn], s. (med.) anhélito.

anhydride [ænháidrịd], s. (quím.) anhídrido.

anhydrite [-drait], s. (min.) anhidrita.

anhydrous [-drʌs], a. (quím.) anhidro.

ani [aní], s. (Am.) (orn.) aní, ave trepadora.

anil [ǽnil], s. (bot.) añil, índigo.

anile [ǽnail], a. chocha; como una vieja que chochea.

anilin(e [ǽnilin], s. (quím.) anilina.—**a. dye,** tinte de anilina.—**a. poisoning,** anilismo.

anility [anílịti], s. chochera, chochez.

animadversion [ænimædvœ́ršọn], s. animadversión, censura, reproche, reprensión.

animadvert [-vœ́rt], vn. censurar, reprochar, criticar.

animadverter [-œ(r)], s. censurador, criticastro.

animal [ǽnimạl], s. y a. animal; bruto, bestia.— **a. black o charcoal,** carbón o negro animal.— **a. magnetism,** mesmerismo.—**a. spirits,** vivacidad, ardor, exuberancia vital.

animalcule [ænimǽlkiul], s. animálculo.

animalism [ǽnimạlizm], s. animalismo; estado o actividad animal; sensualidad.—**animality** [ænimǽlịti], s. animalidad.

animalization [-izéišọn], s. animalización.

animalize [-aiz], va. animalizar.

animate [ǽnimeit], va. animar; infundir ánimo o valor, excitar, alentar; vivificar.

animate [ǽnimịt], a. viviente, animado.

animated [ǽnimeitịd], a. vivo, vivaz, animado.

animating [-iŋ], a. animante, vivificante, excitante; alegre, divertido.

animation [-éišọn], s. animación; (fig.) movimiento, calor, fuego; viveza, espíritu.

animative [ǽnimeitiv], a. animador, inspirador.

animator [-ọ(r)], s. animador, alentador.

animé [ǽnimei], s. anime (resina del curbaril).

animism [ǽnimizm], s. animismo.—**animist** [-ịst], s. animista, que profesa el animismo.

animosity [ænimásịti], s. animosidad, rencor.

animus [ǽnimạs], s. ánimo, intención; animosidad, tema, mala voluntad, inquina, odio.

anion [ǽnaiọn], s. (quím. física) anión, m.

anise [ǽnis], s. (bot.) anís, matalahuva.

aniseed [ǽnisid], s. anís, grano de anís.

anisette [ænisét], s. (Fr.) anisete, (aguardiente) anisado.

anisomerous [ænaisámerʌs], a. (bot.) anisómero.

anisometric [-sométrịk], a. anisométrico.

anisopetalous [-sopétạlʌs], a. (bot.) anisopétalo.

anisophyllous [-sofíḷʌs], a. (bot.) anisófilo.

anisyl [ǽnisịl], s. (quím.) anisilo.

ankle [ǽŋkl], s. (anat.) tob:llo.—**a. bone,** astrálago.—**a. strap,** correílla de zapato que cruza el pie un poco arriba del empeine.

anklet [ǽŋklịt], s. (joy.) ajorca, carcax; calcetín corto, tobillera; (cir.) vendaje para el tobillo; calceta o grillo(s).

ankylose [ǽŋkilous], va. y vn. anquilosar(se).

ankylosis [-lóusịs], s. (med., anat.) anquilosis.

annalist [ǽnạlist], s. analista, cronista, cronógrafo.

annals [ǽnạlz], s. pl. anales, crónicas, fastos.

Annamese [ænạmíz], s. y a., **Annamite** [ǽnạmait], s. y a. anamita (pueblo, raza, lengua).

annates [ǽneits], **annats** [ǽnæts], s. pl. (igl.) anata.

annatto [ænǽtou], s. (bot.) achiote, bija (ll.t. **annotto** y **arnotto**).

anneal [ænîl], va. (fund.) recocer; templar; fijar (colores, esmalte) por calor; (fig.) fortalecer.

annealing [-iŋ], s. recocción, recocido, temple;

esmaltación.—a. furnace, carquesa, horno de recocido.—a. pot, crisol de templar.

annelid [ǽnelid], a. y s. anillado; anélido.

Annelida [ænélidạ], s. pl. (zool.) anélidos.

annex [ạnéks]. I. va. anexar, anexionar, adjuntar, agregar, unir. II. [ǽnɛks], s. aditamento, anexo, adición, apéndice; dependencia, edificio anexo. —pl. anexidades.

annexation [ænekséiṣọn], annexment [ạnéksmẹnt], s. anexión, adición, unión.

annexationist [ænekséiṣọnịst], s. anexionista.

annexed [ạnékst], a. adjunto, anexo, anejo.

annihilable [ạnáiịlạbl], a. aniquilable.

annihilate [-léịt], va. aniquilar, anonadar, demoler o destruir por completo.

annihilation [-léiṣọn], s. aniquilación, anonadamiento.

annihilator [-léịtọ(r)], s. aniquilador.—annihilative [-léịtịv], a. aniquilador.

anniversary [ænịvǿersạrị]. I. s. aniversario. II. a. anual, añal.—a. funeral, añal, cabo de año.

annonaceous [ænọnéiṣạs], a. (bot.) anonáceo.

annotate [ǽnoteịt], va. anotar, comentar, acotar, apostillar, glosar.

annotation [-éiṣọn], s. nota, notación; anotación, apunte, acotación, apostilla.

annotator [ǽnoteịtọ(r)], s. anotador, comentador, postillador, glosador.

announce [ạnáụns], va. anunciar, notificar, declarar, avisar, dar parte de; pregonar.

announcement [-mẹnt], s. aviso o anuncio; declaración, proclama; prospecto.

announcer [-œ(r)], s. anunciador, publicador, avisador; (rad.) anunciador o anunciante, noticiador, locutor o prologuista de radio.

annoy [ạnóị], va. molestar, incomodar, vejar, fastidiar, cargar, aburrir, encocorar.

annoyance [-ạns], s. molestia, pena, incomodidad; disgusto, fastidio, aburrimiento; lata, engorro, pejiguera, chinchorrería.

annoyer [-œ(r)], s. molestador, persona enojosa, chinchorrero.

annoying [-iŋ], a. fastidioso, molesto, incómodo, importuno, engorroso.

annual [ǽnyuạl]. I. a. anual, añal, cadañal. II. s. (igl.) añal, aniversario.

annually [-ị], adv. anualmente.

annuitant [ạnịúịtạnt], s. rentista, censualista, vitalicista.

annuity [ạnịúịtị], s. anualidad, juro, renta vitalicia, pensión, censual.

annul [ạnál], va. anular, invalidar, rescindir, derogar, irritar, revocar, abolir; anonadar.

annular [ǽnyulạ(r)], annulary [-lerị], a. anular.

annulate(d [-leịt(ịd], a. anuloso, anillado.

annulet [-lịt], s. anillejo, sortijilla; (arq.) anillo, filete o listel.

annulment [ạnálmẹnt], s. anulación, rescisión, cancelación, revocación, derogación.

annulose [ǽnyuloụs], a. anuloso, anillado.

annulus [ǽnyulạs], s. (bot., zool., astr., etc.) anillo; (geom.) corona circular; (arq.) = ANNULET.

annunciate [ạnánṣịeịt], va. V. ANNOUNCE.

annunciation [-ṣịéiṣọn], s. anunciación, proclamación; promulgación; (A., igl.) Anunciación.

annunciator [ạnánṣịeịtọ(r)], s. anunciador, avisador; proclamador; (elec.) anunciador o indicador de timbres (en los hoteles, etc.).

anodal [ænóụdạl], anodic [ænádịk], a. anódico.

anode [ǽnoụd], s. (elec.) ánodo.—a. battery, (rad.) batería de la lámpara termiónica.—a. rays, rayos anódicos de un tubo de vacío.

anodyne [ǽnodaịn], a. y s. (med.) anodino, calmante.

anodynia [-dínịạ], s. (med.) anodinia, falta de dolor.

anoint [ạnóịnt], va. untar, pringar; (igl.) ungir, olear; signar con óleo.—to a. a dying person, administrar la extremaunción.—to a. the palm, (fam.) untar la mano, sobornar.

anointer [-œ(r)], s. untador; el que unge.

anointing [-iŋ], anointment [-mẹnt], s. unción; untadura, untamiento, óleo.

anomalism [ạnámạlịzm], anomalousness [-ʌsnịs], anomaly [-ị], s. anomalía, anormalidad, irregularidad.

anomalistic(al [-ịstịk(ạl], a. anomalístico.—anomalistic year, año anomalístico.

anomalous [-ʌs], a. anómalo, irregular.

anomalously [-lị], adv. anómalamente.

anon [ạnán], adv. pronto, a poco, luego, en seguida, inmediatamente.—ever and a., una y otra vez, a menudo.

anonym [ǽnonịm], s. persona o escritor anónimo; seudónimo.

anonymity [ænonímịtị], s. (carácter de) anónimo.

anonymous [ạnánịmạs], a. anónimo.

anonymously [-lị], adv. anónimamente.

anopheles [ænáfẹlịz], s. (zool.) anofeles, género de mosquitos que transmiten la malaria.

anorthite [ænórθaịt], s. (min.) anortita.

another [ạnáðœr(r)]. I. a. otro, distinto, diferente.—a. time, otra vez. II. pron. otro, uno más.—a. 's, ajeno, de otro.—a. such, (fam.) otro que tal.—one a., uno(s) a otro(s), etc.—give me a., déme otro, o uno más.

ansate(d [ǽnseịt(ịd], a. con asas.

Anser [ǽnsœ(r)], s. (zool.) género de los ánsares.

anserine [-ạịn], a. (zool.) ansarino; como ganso; tonto, necio, mentecato.

answer [ǽnsœ(r)], va. y vn. responder, contestar, reponer; refutar; corresponder, satisfacer; obedecer; llenar el objeto, servir, convenir; (for.) replicar; comparecer.—to a. back, replicar, refunfuñar.—to a. for, abonar, acreditar, fiar, salir fiador de, respaldar, responder de; ser responsable de; hacer oficio de.—to a. to the name of, tener por nombre, llamarse; reconocer como nombre suyo.

answer, s. respuesta, contestación; refutación; (for.) réplica, dúplica; defensa; (mat.) solución, resultado.

answerable [-ạbl], a. responsable; correspondiente; equivalente; conforme; discutible, refutable.

answerably [-ạblị], adv. correspondientemente; responsablemente.

answerableness [-nịs], s. responsabilidad; cuenta; correspondencia, correlación.

answerer [-œ(r)], s. fiador; respondedor.

ant [ænt], s. (ent.) hormiga.—a. bear, (zool.) oso hormiguero.—a. bird, (orn.) pájaro hormiguero.—a. cow, (ent.) pulgón.—a. hill, hormiguero en forma de montículo.—a. lion, (ent.) hormiga león.—white a., hormiga blanca, termes.

anta [ǽntạ], s. (arq.) anta, pilastra, parástade.

antacid [æntǽsịd], a. y s. antiácido.

antagonism [æntǽgọnịzm], s. antagonismo, contienda, oposición.

antagonist [-ịst], s. antagonista, contrario, contendor, adversario.

antagonistic [-ịstịk], a. antagónico, contrario, opuesto, hostil.

antagonize [-aịz]. I. va. contender con, oponerse a; contrariar. II. vn. ser antagónico.

antalgic [æntǽldʒịk], a. antálgico, anodino.

antaphrodisiac [æntæfrodízịæk], s. y a. (med.) antiafrodisíaco.

antapoplectic [æntæpopléktịk], a. (med.) antiapopléctico.

antarctic [æntárktịk], a. antártico.

antarthritic [-arθrítịk], a. (med.) antiartrítico.

antasthmatic [-æzmǽtịk], a. antiasmático.

ante [ǽntị]. I. prefijo, ante, antes, antes de.—a. bellum, antes de la guerra.—a. meridiem (A. M.), antes del mediodía.—a. mortem, antes de morir. II. vn. (generalmente con up) poner su tanto o apuesta (en el juego); pagar la apuesta. **III.** *s.* tanto, suma que se apuesta y se pone sobre la mesa.

anteater [ǽntitœ(r)], *s.* (zool.) mamífero hormiguero; oso hormiguero; (Am.) tamanduá.

antecede [æntisíd], *vn.* anteceder, preceder.

antecedence [-éns], **antecedency** [-i], *s.* antecedencia, precedencia.

antecedent [-ent], *a.* y *s.* antecedente, precedente.

antecedently [-li], *adv.* anteriormente.

antecessor [æntiséso(r)], *s.* antecesor, predecesor.

antechamber [ǽntichejmbœ(r)], *s.* antecámara, antesala.

antechapel [-chæpęl], *s.* (arq.) antecapilla.

antechoir [-kwair], *s.* (arq.) antecoro.

antechurch [-chœrch], *s.* (arq.) anteiglesia.

antedate [-déit]. **I.** *va.* antedatar; (for.) retrotraer. **II.** [ǽntideit], *s.* anticipación; antedata.

antedating [-déitiŋ], *s.* (for.) retrotracción.

antediluvian [-dilúviąn], *a.* y *s.* antediluviano.

antelope [ǽntęloup], *s.* antílope; gacela, gamuza.

antemeridian [æntimęrídiąn], *a.* antemeridiano.

antemetic [-métik], *s.* y *a.* (med.) antiemético.

antemundane [-mÁndein], *a.* antemundano, que antecedió a la creación del mundo.

antenatal [-néital], *a.* antenatal.

antenna [æntǽną], *s.* (zool. y rad.) antena.—**a. (grounding) switch,** (rad.), interruptor de conexión de la antena con tierra.—**a. resistance,** (rad.) resistencia del circuito de la antena.

antennae [æntǽni], *s. pl.* (zool.) antenas.

antenuptial [æntinÁpšąl], *a.* antenupcial.

antepaschal [-péskąl], *a.* antepascual.

antepenult [-pínʌlt] *o* **antepenultimate** [-pinÁltimit], *a.* y *s.* (gram.) antepenúltimo.

antepileptic [æntepiléptik], *a.* (med.) antiepiléptico.

anteprandial [-prǽndiąl], *a.* de antes de comer.

anterior [æntíriǫ(r)], *a.* anterior, delantero, de adelante, precedente.

anteriority [æntiriáriti], *s.* anterioridad, precedencia, antelación.

anteriorly [æntíriǫrli], *adv.* anteriormente.

anteroom [ǽntirum], *s.* antecámara.

anteversion [-vœ́ršǫn], *s.* (med.) anteroversión.

antevert [-vœ́rt], *va.* volver hacia adelante.

anthelmintic [ænθelmíntik], *a.* y *s.* antihelmíntico.

anthem [ǽnθem], *s.* antífona, motete, himno.

anther [ǽnθœ(r)], *s.* (bot.) antera, borlilla.

antheral [ǽnθœrąl], *a.* referente a anteras.

antheridium [ænθęrídiąm], *s.* (bot.) anteridio.

anthological [ænθǫládžikąl], *a.* antológico.

anthology [ænθálǫdži], *s.* antología, florilegio.

anthophagous [ænθáfagąs], *a.* antófago.

Anthozoa [ænθozóuą̃], *s. pl.* (zool.) antozoarios.

anthracene [ǽnθrasin], *s.* (quím.) antraceno.

anthracic [ænθrǽsik], *a.* (med.) antrácico.

anthracite [ǽnθrasait], *s.* antracita.

anthracnose [ænθrǽknous], *s.* antracnosis.

anthrax [ǽnθræks], *s.* (med.) ántrax, carbunclo, avispero; fiebre esplénica; (vet.) bacera, lobado.

anthropocentric [ænθroposéntrik], *a.* antropocéntrico.

anthropogeny [-pádženi], *s.* antropogenia.

anthropography [-págrafi], *s.* antropografía.

anthropoid [ǽnθropoid], *s.* y *a.* antropoide(o).

anthropologic(al [-poládžik(ąl], *a.* antropológico.

anthropologist [-pálǫdžist], *s.* antropólogo.

anthropology [-pálǫdži], *s.* antropología.

anthropometric [-pométrik], *a.* antropométrico.

anthropometrist [-pámetrist], *s.* antropómetra, *m.*

anthropometry [-pámetri], *s.* antropometría.

anthropomorphism [-pomórfizm], *s.* antropomorfismo.

anthropomorphite [-pomórfait], *s.* antropomorfita.

anthropomorphous [-pomórfʌs], *a.* antropomorfo.

anthropophagi [-páfodžai], *s. pl.* antropófagos.

anthropophagous [-páfagʌs], *a.* antropófago.

anthropophagy [-páfadži], *s.* antropofagia.

anthroposophy [-pásofi], *s.* antroposofía.

anthropozoic [-pozóuik], *a.* (geol.) antropozoico.

anti [ǽnti], *afijo,* contra o contrario a.—NOTA. Con este afijo se forman muchos compuestos, cuyo significado es lo contrario de lo que expresa el segundo elemento.

antiaircraft [-érkræft], *a.* (mil.) de defensa contra fuerzas aéreas, antiaéreo.

antialcoholic [-ælkohólik], *a.* antialcohólico.

antibacchius [-bǽkias], *s.* (pros.) antibaquio.

antibilious [-bíliʌs], *a.* (med.) antibilioso.

antibiotic [-baiátik], *a.* (biol.) antibiótico.

antibody [-badi], *s.* (fisiol.) anticuerpo.

antic [ǽntik]. **I.** *a.* extraño, ridículo, grotesco. **II.** *s.* zapateta, cabriola; (gen. *pl.*) travesuras, adefesios, extravagancias; bufón, gracioso. **III.** *vn.* hacer travesuras, etc.; cabriolar.

anticathode [-kǽθoud], *s.* (fís.) anticátodo.

antichresis [-krísis], *s.* (for.) anticresis.

Antichrist [-kraist], *s.* anticristo, anticristo.

antichristian [-kríschąn], *s.* y *a.* anticristiano.

anticipate [æntísipeit], *va.* esperar, prever; prevenir, anticipar(se), adelantar(se) a; impedir.

anticipation [-éišǫn], *s.* anticipación, adelantamiento, previsión; expectación.

anticipator [-ǫ(r)], *s.* anticipador.

anticipatory [æntísipątǫri], *a.* anticipante.

anticlerical [æntiklérikąl], *a.* anticlerical.

anticlericalism [-izm], *s.* anticlericalismo.

anticlimax [-klǽimæks], *s.* (ret.) anticlímax.

anticlinal [-klǽinąl], *a.* y *s.* (geol.) anticlinal.

anticoherer [-kohírœ(r)], *s.* (radtlg.) anticohesor.

anticonstitutional [-kanstitiúšǫnąl], *a.* anticonstitucional.

anticyclone [-sáikloun], *s.* anticiclón.

antidiphtheritic [-difθęrítik], *s.* y *a.* (med.) antidiftérico.

antidotal [-doutąl], *a.* alexifármaco.

antidote [-dout], *s.* antídoto, contraveneno.

antidynastic(al [-dainǽstik(ąl], *a.* antidinástico.

antidysenteric [-disęntérik], *a.* antidisentérico.

antifebrile [-fíbril], *a.* (med.) antifebril.

antiforeignism [-fárinizm], *s.* xenofobia, odio o aversión a los extranjeros.

antifreeze [-fríz], *s.* y *a.* anticongelante.

antifriction [-fríkšǫn], *a.* contra el rozamiento. —**a. compound,** lubricante.—**a. metal,** metal antifricción.—**a. wheels,** rodillos de fricción.

antigen [ǽntidžen], *s.* (fisiol.) antígeno.

antiherpetic [-hœrpétik], *a.* y *s.* (med.) antiherpético.

antihydrophobic [-haidrofóubik], *a.* antirrábico.

antihysteric [-histérik], *a.* y *s.* (med.) antihistérico.

anti-imperialism [-impíriąlizm], *s.* antiimperialismo.

anti-imperialist(ic [-ist(ik], *s.* y *a.* antiimperialista.

antiknock [-nák], *a.* antidetonante (gasolina).

anti-Leaguer [-lígœ(r)], *s.* opuesto a la Sociedad de las Naciones.

Antillean [æntilíąn], *s.* y *a.* antillano.

antilogarithm [-lágąriðm], *s.* (mat.) antilogaritmo, número correspondiente a un logaritmo.

antilogy [æntílǫdži], *s.* antilogía.

antimacassar [ǽntimąkǽsą̃(r)], *s.* antimacasar, cubierta del respaldo de un sofá o sillón.

antimalarial [-mąlériąl], *a.* (med.) antipalúdico.

antimask *o* **antimasque** [-mæsk], *s.* (teat.) especie de entremés.

antimilitarist(ic [-mílitąrist(ik], *s.* y *a.* antimilitarista.

antimonarchic(al [-monárkik(ąl], *a.,* **antimonarchist** [-mánąrkist], *s.* antimonárquico.

antimonial [-móuniąl], *a.* (quím.) antimonial.

antimon(i)ate [-(i)eįt], *s.* (quím.) antimoniato.
antimonic [-mánįk], *a.* (quím.) antimónico.
antimonious [-móunįas], *a.* (quím.) antimonioso.
antimony [ǽntįmounį], *s.* antimonio.
antinephritic [-nįfrítįk], *a.* (med.) antinefrítico.
antinode [-noųd], *s.* (fís.) sección ventral, o de entre nodos (de una cuerda que vibra).
antinomy [æntínomį], *s.* antinomia; paradoja.
Antiochian [æntíóukįan], *s.* y *a.* antioqueno.
antipapist [-péipįst], *a.* y *s.* antipapista.
antipathetic(al [-paθétįk(al], *a.* antipático; contrario, opuesto; adverso.
antipathy [æntípaθį], *s.* antipatía, antagonismo, tirria, repugnancia.
antiperistaltic [-perįstǽltįk], *a.* antiperistáltico.
antipharmic [-fármįk], *a.* (med.) alexifármaco.
antiphlogistic [-flodžístįk], *s.* y *a.* antiflogístico.
antiphon [ǽntįfon], **antiphony** [æntífonį], *s.* (igl.) antífona.
antiphonal [æntífonal], **antiphonary** [-nerį], *s.* y *a.* (libro) antifonal o antifonario.
antiphrasis [æntífrasįs], *s.* (ret.) antifrasis.
antipodal [æntípodal], **antipodean** [-dían], *a.* antípoda; contrario; opuesto.
antipode [ǽntįpoųd], *s.* antípoda, *m.*
antipodes [æntípodįz], *s. pl.* antípodas.
antipoison [ǽntįpoįzon], *s.* antídoto, contraveneno.
antipope [-poųp], *s.* antipapa, *m.*
antiputrefactive [-pįutręfǽktįv], *a.* y *s.* (med.) antipútrido, antiséptico.
antipyretic [-paįrétįk], *a.* y *s.* (med.) antipirético, febrífugo.
antipyrine [-páįrįn], *s.* (farm.) antipirina; analgesina.
antiquarian [-kwérįan], *s.* y *a.* anticuario.
antiquarianism [-įzm], *s.* afición a las antigüedades.
antiquary [ǽntįkwerį], *s.* anticuario.
antiquate [ǽntįkweįt], *va.* anticuar.
antiquated [-įd], *a.* anticuado.
antique [æntík]. **I.** *a.* antiguo. **II.** *s.* antigüedad, antigualla.—**a. shop,** tienda de antigüedades.
antiquity [æntíkwįtį], *s.* antigüedad; ancianidad, vejez, vetustez.
antirevolutionary [æntįrevolúšǫnąrį], **antirevolutionist** [-įst], *a.* y *s.* antirrevolucionario.
antirheumatic [-rumǽtįk], *a.* y *s.* antirreumático.
antirrhinum [-ráįnʌm], *s.* (bot.) antirrino.
anti-saloon [-sạlún], *a.* enemigo de las tabernas y de la venta de licores; prohibicionista.—**A. League,** Liga antialcohólico.
antiscians [æntíšạnz] *o* **antiscii** [æntíšįąį], *s. pl.* (geog.) antiscios.
antiscorbutic(al [-æntįskorbįútįk(ạl], *a.* y *s.* (med.) antiescorbútico.
antiscrofulous [-skráfyǫlʌs], *a.* antiescrofuloso.
anti-Semite [-sémaįt], *s.* antisemita.
anti-Semitic [-sémįtįk], *a.* antisemítico.
anti-Semitism [-sémįtįzm], *s.* antisemitismo.
antisepsis [-sépsįs], *s.* (med.) antisepsia.
antiseptic [-séptįk], *a.* y *s.* antiséptico, antipútrido, desinfectante.
antiserum [-sírʌm], *s.* antisuero.
antiskid [-skįd], *a.* antideslizante (llantas, etc.).
antislavery [-sléįvœrį]. **I.** *s.* antiesclavismo, oposición a la esclavitud. **II.** *a.* antiesclavista.
antisocial [-sóųšạl], *a.* antisocial.
antispasmodic [-spæzmádįk], *a.* y *s.* antiespasmódico.
antispastic [-spǽstįk], *a.* y *s.* (med.) antispástico.
antistrophe [æntístrofį], *s.* antistrofa.
antisubmarine [-sʌbmạrin], *a.* (mil.) (de defensa) contra submarinos.
antisyphilitic [-sįfįlítįk], *a.* y *s.* (med.) antisifilítico.
antitank [-tǽŋk], *a.* (mil.) antitanque.
antitetanic [-tįtánįk], *a.* (med.) antitétano.
antithesis [æntíθesįs], *s.* (ret.) antítesis; retruécano; oposición, contraste.

antithetical [-θétįkạl], *a.* antitético.
antitoxic [-táksįk], *a.* antitóxico, antivenenoso.
antitoxin [-táksįn], *s.* (med.) antitoxina.
antitrade [-treįd], *a.* y *s.* (viento) contraalisio.
antitragus [ǽntįtragʌs], *s.* (anat.) antitrago.
anti-Trinitarian [-trįnįtérįạn], *s.* antitrinitario.
antitrust [æntįtrʌst], *s.* antimonopolio; contra u opuesto a los trusts.
antitype [-taįp], *s.* antitipo.
antivenereal [-vęnírįạl], *s.* (med.) antivenéreo.
antler [ǽntlœ(r)], *s.* asta, cuerna o cornamenta del ciervo.
antlered [-d], *a.* que tiene astas, astado.
antoeci [æntísaį], *s. pl.* (geog.) antecos.
antonomasia [æntonoméįžįą], *s.* (ret.) antonomasia.
antonomastic [-mǽstįk], *a.* antonomástico.
antonym [ǽntonįm], *s.* antónimo, vocablo de significación opuesta a otro.
antrum [ǽntrʌm], *s.* antro, cueva; (anat.) antro.
Anura [ænįúrą], *s. pl.* (zool.) anuros.
anuran [-ạn], *a.* y *s.* (zool.) anuro (sin cola).
anuria [ạnįúrįą], *s.* (med.) anuria.
anus [éįnʌs], *s.* (anat.) ano, sieso, orificio.
anvil [ǽnvįl]. **I.** *s.* yunque; (anat.) yunque.— **double-beak a.,** bigornia.—**to be on the a.,** estar sobre el tapete (en discusión o preparación). **II.** *va.* formar o trabajar sobre el yunque; martillar.
anxiety [æŋzáįętį], *s.* ansia, ansiedad, inquietud, afán, desasosiego, cuidado; anhelo.
anxious [ǽŋkšʌs], *a.* inquieto, impaciente, ansioso; anheloso, deseoso; angustioso, aflictivo. —**to be a.,** no tenerlas todas consigo.
anxiously [-lį], *adv.* ansiosa o impacientemente.
anxiousness [-nįs], *s.* ansiedad, solicitud; anhelo.
any [énį]. **I.** *a.* y *pron.* cualquier(a), cualesquier(a); algún, alguno; todo (*any child knows that,* todo, o cualquier, niño sabe eso).—**a. way (at all),** de cualquier modo, no importa cómo; así como así.—**at a. rate, o in a. case,** de todos modos, sea como fuere.—**not a.,** ninguno (más enfático, alguno, después del sustantivo: v.g. *I haven't any money (at all),* no tengo dinero alguno).—[Cuando *any* se usa partitiva o negativamente, por lo común no se traduce: v.g. *have you any money?* ¿tiene Vd. dinero? *I have not any money,* no tengo dinero.] **II.** *adv.* Como adverbio, *any* es a menudo expletivo o enfático, y no se traduce: v.g. *any farther,* más lejos.—**a. longer,** más tiempo, todavía; más. —**a. more,** más, aún; todavía.—**not a. longer, not a. more,** ya no, no más.—**not a.,** no . . . nada (*he didn't work a.,* no trabajó nada).—**not a. too** (seguido de *a.* o *adv.*), no . . . ni con mucho, no . . . ni mucho menos (*that is not any too easy,* eso no es fácil, ni con mucho, *o,* eso no es tan fácil); no más de lo absolutamente necesario (*I did not come any too early,* no vine más temprano de lo absolutamente necesario, *o,* apenas tuve tiempo para llegar, *o,* llegué precisamente a tiempo); no más de lo que conviene, o de lo debido. (Gen., al traducir esta locución, es mejor cambiar el giro.)—**to be a. good,** servir para algo o en algo, valer algo (*nada* en oración negativa).
anybody [énįbadį], *pron.* alguno, alguien, cualquiera; todo el mundo, toda persona.—**not a.,** nadie, ninguno.
anyhow [énįhaụ], *adv.* de cualquier modo, a todas luces; en cualquier caso; sin embargo, con todo, como quiera que sea; de todos modos; salga lo que saliere, sea lo que (se) fuere.
anyone [énįwʌn], *s.* = ANYBODY.
anything [énįθįŋ], *pron.* algo, alguna cosa, cualquier cosa; todo, todo lo que; (con negación) nada.—**a. else,** otra cosa.—**like a.** (*V.* LIKE).— **to be a. but,** ser todo menos, no ser absolutamente, o de ninguna manera, o ni con mucho (*he is anything but rich,* no es rico, ni con mucho).

anyway [éniwei]. V. ANYHOW.
anywhere [énihwer], *adv.* donde quiera, en todas partes; (con negación) en ninguna parte.—a. **near**, siquiera aproximadamente.
anywise [éniwaiz], *adv.* de cualquier manera.
Anzac [ǽnzæk], *s.* ejército expedicionario de Australia y Nueva Zelandia en la guerra mundial de 1914; soldado de este ejército.
aorist [éiorist], *s.* (gram.) aoristo.
aorta [eiórtǝ], *s.* (anat.) aorta.
aortic [eiórtik], *a.* aórtico.
apace [apéis], *adv.* aprisa, aceleradamente.
Apache [apǽchi], *s.* y *a.* apache.
apart [apárt], *adv.* aparte, a un lado; separadamente, de por sí; además; dejando a un lado, prescindiendo de; en pedazos, en partes.
apartment [apártment], *s.* aposento; piso, cuarto, apartam(i)ento, departamento.—a. **building** = A. HOUSE.—a. **hotel**, casa de apartamentos donde se sirven comidas.—a. **house**, casa de apartamentos, de departamentos o de pisos.—rear **a.**, trascuarto.
apathetic [æpǝθétik], *a.* apático, indiferente.
apathy [ǽpǝθi], *s.* apatía, flema, indiferencia, insensibilidad, dejadez.
apatite [ǽpataít], *s.* (min.) apatita.
ape [eip]. I. *s.* (zool.) mono, simio; imitador.—a.-like, simiesco, símico. II. *va.* imitar, remedar.
apeak [apík], *adv.* (mar.) en posición vertical.
Apennine [ǽpenain], *a.* de los Apeninos.
apepsy [eipépsi], **apepsia** [-siǝ], *s.* (med.) apepsia.
aperient [apírient], **aperitive** [apéritiv], *a.* y *s.* (med.) aperitivo, laxante.
aperiodic [eipiriádik], *a.* aperiódico.
apéritif [æpéritif], *s.* aperitivo.
aperture [ǽpœrchǝr], *s.* abertura, paso, rendija, buco, portillo, vacío, orificio.
apetalous [eipétalʌs], *a.* (bot.) apétalo.
apex [éipeks], *s.* (*pl.* -XES o APICES) ápice, cúspide, *f.*, punta, vértice; fastigio, cima.
aphaeresis [æféresis], *s.* (gram.) aféresis.
aphasia [æféiʒiǝ], *s.* (med.) afasia.
aphasic [æféizik], *a.* afásico.
aphelion [æfílion], *s.* (astr.) afelio.
aphesis [ǽfesis], *s.* (gram.) afesis.
aphid [éifid], **aphis** [éifis], *s.* (ent.) áfido, afídido, pulgón.
aphodian [afóudian], *a.* y *s.* (zool.) afodino; *s.* afodio.
aphonia [eifóuniǝ], *s.* afonía, ronquera crónica.
aphonic [eifánik], *a.* sin sonido; afónico, afono; mudo.—a. **letter**, letra muda.
aphorism [ǽforizm], *s.* aforismo.
aphoristical [æforístikǝl], *a.* aforístico.
aphoristically [-i], *adv.* sentenciosamente.
aphrodisia [æfrodíziǝ], *s.* (pat.) afrodisia.
aphrodisiac [-dzíæk], *a.* y *s.* afrodisíaco; lascivo, lujurioso.
aphtha [ǽfθǝ], *s.* (med.) afta.
aphthous [ǽfθʌs], *a.* (med.) aftoso.
aphyllous [ǽfílʌs], *a.* (bot.) áfilo, sin hojas.
apiarian [eipiérian], *a.* apiario; apícola.—apiarist [éipiarist], *s.* apicultor.—apiary [éipieri], *s.* apiario, colmenar, abejar, abejera.
apical [ǽpikǝl], *a.* apical, cimero.
apiculate [æpíkyuleit], *a.* (bot.) apiculado.
apiculture [éipikʌlchǝr], *s.* apicultura.
apiculturist [-kálchǝrist], *s.* apicultor.
apiculus [æpíkyulʌs], *s.* (bot.) apículo.
apiece [apís], *adv.* por persona, por cabeza o barba; cada uno; sendos (*they had a lance* *apiece*, tenían sendas lanzas).
apiology [eipiálodʒi], *s.* estudio de las abejas.
apish [éipiʃ], *a.* monesco, simiesco, símico.
apishly [-li], *adv.* de modo servilmente imitativo; afectadamente, frívolamente.
apishness [-nis], *s.* monería, monada.
aplanatic [æplanǽtik], *a.* (ópt.) aplanático.
aplenty [aplénti], *a.* y *adv.* en abundancia; mucho; muy.

aplomb [aplóm], *s.* aplomo, seguridad; posición vertical; verticalidad.
apnea, apnoea [æpníǝ], *s.* (med.) apnea.
Apocalypse [apákalips], *s.* Apocalipsis.
apocalyptic(al [-líptik(ǝl], *a.* apocalíptico.
apochromatic [æpakromǽtik], *a.* apocromático.
apocopate [apákopeit], *va.* (gram.) apocopar.
apocopation [-éiʃon], *s.* apócope, *f.*
apocope [æpákopi], *s.* (gram.) apócope, *f.*
apocrypha [apákrifǝ], *s. pl.* libros apócrifos.
apocryphal [-l], *a.* apócrifo.
apod(al [ǽpad(ǝl], **apodous** [-ʌs], *a.* (zool.) ápodo.
Apoda [ǽpodǝ], **Apodes** [-diz], *s. pl.* (zool.) ápodos.
apodictic(al [æpodíktik(ǝl], *a.* apodíctico.
apodosis [æpádosis], *s.* (ret.) apódosis.
apogee [ǽpodʒi], *s.* (astr.) apogeo; auge.
apograph [ǽpogræf], *s.* apógrafo.
Apollinarian [apalinérian], *s.* y *a.* (igl.) apolinarista.
Apollonian [æpalóunian], *a.* apolíneo, de Apolo.
apologetic(al [apalodʒétik(ǝl], *a.* apologético.
apologetically [-i], *adv.* apologéticamente.
apologetics [-iks], *s.* (teo.) apologética.
apologia [æpolóudʒiǝ], *s.* justificación o defensa.
apologist [apálodʒist], *s.* apologista.
apologize [-aiz]. I. *va.* excusar, disculpar. II. *vn.* disculparse, excusarse, dar satisfacción.
apologizer [-œ(r)], *s.* defensor, apologista.
apologue [ǽpolag], *s.* apólogo, fábula.
apology [apálodʒi], *s.* apología, defensa; excusa, disculpa, justificación; satisfacción.
apomorphin(e [æpomórfin], *s.* (quím.) apomorfina.
aponeurosis [-njuróusis], *s.* (anat.) aponeurosis.
aponeurotic [-njurátik], *a.* aponeurótico.
apophasis [æpáfasis], *s.* (ret.) insinuación por pretendida omisión.
apophyge [æpáfidʒi], *s.* (arq.) apófige, *f.*, imoscapo.
apophysis [æpáfisis], *s.* (anat.) apófisis.
apoplectic(al [æpopléktik(ǝl], *a.* apopléctico.
apoplexy [ǽpopleksi], *s.* (med.) apoplejía.
aport [apórt], *adv.* (mar.) a babor (el timón).
aposiopesis [æposaiopésis], *s.* (ret.) reticencia.
apostasy [apástasi], *s.* apostasía.
apostate [apásteit]. I. *s.* apóstata, *mf.*, elche. II. *a.* falso, pérfido.
apostatical [æpostǽtikǝl], *a.* apostático.
apostatize [apástǝtaiz], *vn.* apostatar, renegar.
apostem [ǽpastem], o **aposteme** [-im], *s.* (med.) apostema, absceso.
apostematous [-témǝtʌs], *a.* apostemoso.
apostle [apásl], *s.* apóstol.
apostleship [-ʃip], **apostolate** [apástoleit], *s.* apostolado.
apostolic(al [æpostálik(ǝl], *a.* apostólico.—A. **See**, (igl.) sede apostólica, la Santa Sede.
apostolically [-i], *adv.* apostólicamente.
apostolicalness [-nis], *s.* calidad de apostólico.
apostolicity [apastolísiti], *s.* apostolicidad.
apostrophe [apástrofi], *s.* (ret.) apóstrofe, *mf.*; (gram.) apóstrofo, virgulilla.
apostrophic(al [æpostráfik(ǝl], *a.* perteneciente al apóstrofe.
apostrophize [apástrofaiz]. I. *va.* y *vn.* apostrofar. II. *vn.* (gram.) hacer una elisión; usar el apóstrofo.
apothecary [apáθekeri], *s.* boticario, farmacéutico.—a.'s **file**, recetario.—a.'s **measure**, sistema de medidas para líquidos usado en farmacia.—a.'s **shop**, botica, farmacia.—a.'s **weight**, sistema de pesos usado en farmacia.
apothecium [æpoθísiam], *s.* (bot.) apotecia.
apothegm [ǽpoθem], *s.* apotegma, *m.*, proloquio.
apothegmatical [æpoθegmǽtikǝl], *a.* sentencioso.
apothem [ǽpoθem], *s.* (geom.) apotema; (farm.) sedimento de una pócima.
apotheosis [æpaθióusis], *s.* apoteosis.

apotheosize [æpáθjosaįz], _va._ deificar.

apozem [ǽpozem], _s._ (farm.) (a)pócima, apócema.

Appalachian [æpąléjchįan], _a._ apalache, de los montes Apalaches o Alleghanys de los E. U.

appal(l [apɔ́l], _va._ espantar, aterrar; consternar, desmayar, desanimar.

appalling [-įŋ], _a._ espantoso, aterrador.

appanage [ǽpąnįdž], _s._ dependencia; infantado; don o condición natural o concomitante.

apparatus [æpąréįtąs], _s._ instrumento, dispositivo, aparejo, aparato.

apparel [apǽręl]. **I.** _s._ ropa; vestiduras; (mar.) aparejo y demás accesorios (de un barco).— **wearing a.**, ropa, ropaje, traje, indumentaria, vestidos, _m. pl._ **II.** _va._ vestir, trajear; adornar; proveer.

apparency [apéręnsį], _s._ calidad de evidente, lo evidente; calidad de heredero forzoso.

apparent [apǽręnt], _a._ aparente; claro, manifiesto; especioso.— **a. horizon**, horizonte sensible.— **a. time**, tiempo solar verdadero.— **heir a.**, heredero forzoso.

apparently [-lį], _adv._ evidentemente, claramente; al parecer, aparentemente.

apparition [æpąríšǫn], _s._ aparición, aparecimiento; visión, fantasma, _m._, espectro.

apparitor [apǽrįtǫ(r)], _s._ ministril, esbirro, muñidor; bedel.

appeal [apíl]. **I.** _vn._ (seguido de **to**) mover, despertar, excitar, hacer llamamiento a; interesar a; llamar la atención de; atraer a; apelar o recurrir a; pedir a, suplicar a; poner por testigo a; exhortar a; (for.) apelar, acudir en apelación; alzarse; suplicar de la sentencia.— **to a. from the chair**, apelar de la resolución o del fallo del presidente (o de quien preside).— **to a. to the country**, (pol.) apelar al pueblo disolviendo el parlamento para hacer nuevas elecciones. **II.** _va._ apelar de, llevar a un tribunal superior. **III.** _s._ simpatía, atracción; halago, incentivo, estímulo; súplica, instancia; llamamiento; exhortación; recurso a decisión ajena; (for.) apelación, recurso (de alzada).— **without a.**, (for.) sin recurso, inapelable.

appealable [-ąbl], _a._ apelable.— **appealer** [-œ(r)], _s._ apelante.— **appealing** [-įŋ], _a._ suplicante; atrayente, que despierta simpatía o aprobación.

appear [apír], _vn._ aparecer(se), mostrarse, (a)personarse, presentarse; brotar, surgir; parecer, semejar; (for.) comparecer; (a)personarse.— **to a. to be**, aparentar, representar.

appearance [-ąns], _s._ apariencia, cosa que parece; apariencia, aspecto, (fam.) pergeño, facha; aparición; surgimiento; (for.) comparecencia. —_pl._ **to all a.**, al parecer, a lo que parece, según todas las apariencias.— **to save a.**, por el bien parecer.

appearer [-œ(r)], _s._ el que aparece; compareciente.

appeasable [apíząbl], _a._ aplacable, mitigable.

appeasableness [-nįs], _s._ aplacabilidad.

appease [apíz]. _va._ aplacar, apaciguar, desenojar, pacificar; calmar, mitigar.

appeasement [-męnt], _s._ apaciguamiento, aplacación, desenojo, pacificación; alivio.

appeaser [-œ(r)], _s._ apaciguador, reconciliador, pacificador, aplacador.

appeasive [-įv], _a._ **appeasing** [-įŋ], _a._ apaciguador, pacificador, aplacador; calmante.

appellable [apéląbl], _a._ apelable.

appellancy [apélansį], _s._ apelación.

appellant [apélant]. **I.** _s._ apelante, recurrente; demandante. **II.** _a._ perteneciente al apelante o a la apelación.

appellate [apélįt], _a._ (for.) de apelación; que tiene jurisdicción en las apelaciones.— **a. court**, tribunal de apelaciones o de casación.

appellation [æpεléįšǫn], _s._ nombre (apelativo), denominación; título, tratamiento.

appellative [apélątįv]. **I.** _s._ apelativo; sobrenombre; apellido; (gram.) apelativo. **II.** _a._ apelativo, común.

appellatively [-lį], _adv._ apelativamente.

appellee [æpεlí], _s._ (for.) apelado, demandado.

append [apénd], _va._ añadir, anexar; atar; colgar.

appendage [-įdž], _s._ pertenencia, dependencia, accesorio; colgajo; apéndice.

appendant [-ant]. **I.** _a._ pendiente, colgante; anexo, adjunto; puesto, pegado; accesorio. **II.** _s._ accesorio; dependencia.

appendectomy [æpεndéktomį], **appendicectomy** [-dįséktomį], _s._ (cir.) apend(ic)ectomía, operación para extraer el apéndice vermiforme.

appendices [apéndįsiz], _s. pl._ de APPENDIX.

appendicitis [apεndįsáįtįs], _s._ (med.) apendicitis.

appendicular [æpεndįkįulą(r)], _a._ apendicular; relativo al apéndice vermiforme.

appendiculate [-lįt], _a._ apendiculado.

appendix [apéndįks], _s._ apéndice, anexo, suplemento; aditamento; (bot. y zool.) apéndice; (anat.) apéndice vermiforme; (aer.) apéndice (de un dirigible).

apperceive [æpœrsív], _va._ (psic.) percibir y reconocer las relaciones del objeto percibido con percepciones o ideas anteriores, conocer por apercepción.

apperception [-sépšǫn], _s._ (psic.) apercepción, conciencia.

appertain [æpœrtéįn], _vn._ pertenecer, tocar, relacionarse (con), atañer, concernir.

appetence [ǽpįtεns], **appetency** [-į], _s._ anhelo, avidez; apetencia, inclinación, propensión.

appetite [ǽpętaįt], _s._ apetito, hambre, apetencia, gana; deseo, anhelo.— **inordinate a.**, caninez. —**lack of a.**, desgana, inapetencia.— **without a.**, desganado.

appetitive [-įv], _a._ apetitivo; apetecedor.

appetize [ǽpętaįz], _va._ abrir o excitar el apetito.

appetizer [-œ(r)], _s._ aperitivo; apetite.

appetizing [-įŋ], _a._ apetitivo; apetitoso, aperitivo; tentador, excitante.

Appian Way [ǽpįan wéį], _s._ Vía Apia.

applaud [aplɔ́d], _va._ y _vn._ aplaudir, palm(ot)ear, vitorear, aclamar, alabar; dar palmadas.

applauder [-œ(r)], _s._ aplaudidor, aclamador.

applause [aplɔ́z], _s._ aplauso, palmada, palmoteo; alabanza, aclamación.

applausive [aplósįv], _a._ laudatorio.

apple [ǽpl], _s._ (bot.) manzana, poma.— **a. butter**, mermelada de manzanas.— **a. green** (color), verde manzana.— **a. of discord**, manzana de la discordia.— **a. of love**, tomate.— **a. of the eye**, niña del ojo.— **a. orchard**, manzanal, pomar.— **a. pie** o **tart**, (coc.) pastel(illo) de manzanas. —**a.-pie order**, (fam.) orden perfecto.— **a. tree**, manzano.

applejack [-džæk], _s._ aguardiente de manzana.

applesauce [-sɔs], _s._ compota de manzana; (fam.) tonterías.

appliance [apláįans], _s._ herramienta, instrumento, utensilio, aparato, adminículo, artificio; artefacto; accesorio, dispositivo; aplicación.

applicability [æplįkąbílįtį], **applicableness** [ǽplįkąblnįs], _s._ aplicabilidad.

applicable [ǽplįkąbl], _a._ aplicable; pertinente.

applicably [-blį], _adv._ aplicablemente.

applicant [ǽplįkąnt], _s._ suplicante, peticionario, solicitante, aspirante, pretendiente, candidato.

application [-éįšǫn], _s._ aplicación; uso, empleo; consagración; medicamento aplicado; súplica; petición, solicitud, memorial, (Méx.) ocurso.— **a. blank**, o **form**, formulario.— **to fill out an a.**, llenar un formulario.— **to make a.**, formular solicitud.— **to make a. to**, recurrir a; dirigirse a.

applicative [ǽplįkeįtįv], **applicatory** [ǽplįkątorį], _a._ aplicable, aplicativo.

applied [apláįd], _a._ aplicado; adaptado, utilizado. —**a. for**, pedido, encargado.— **patent a. for**, se ha solicitado patente.—a. **mathematics**, matemáticas aplicadas.

applier [əplái̯œ(r)], *s.* el que aplica, adapta o solicita algo.

appliqué [æplįkéį], *s.* (cost.) aplicación.

apply [əplái]. I. *va.* aplicar; dar, administrar; poner; fijar; apropiar; (refl.) darse, aplicarse o consagrarse; ponerse a.—**to a. the brake(s to)**, frenar. II. *vn.* dirigirse, acudir, ir; ser aplicable o pertinente.—**to a. for**, solicitar, pedir.

appogiatura [apadžatúra], *s.* (mús.) apoyatura.

appoint [əpóįnt], *va.* nombrar, designar, elegir, comisionar, destinar, adscribir; señalar, asignar; (for.) discernir (tutor); ordenar, prescribir, resolver; amueblar, equipar, proveer de lo necesario o de accesorios (en este sentido generalmente no se usa sino el participio **appointed**, v.g., *a well-appointed room*, un cuarto bien amueblado y provisto); establecer, sentar.—**appointed day**, día (a)diado.

appointee [-í], *s.* persona nombrada o electa; (for.) aquel a quien se asigna el derecho de disponer de bienes ajenos total o parcialmente.

appointer [-œ(r)], *s.* el que nombra, ordena, designa; nominador, etc.

appointment [-mənt], *s.* nombramiento, señalamiento; puesto, empleo, destino; cita, compromiso; acuerdo, convenio; orden, mandato, decreto; *pl.* equipo; mobiliario; accesorios.

apportion [əpóršən], *va.* (pror)ratear, repartir; adjudicar; derramar (tributos).

apportionment [-mənt], *s.* (pror)rateo; prorrata; repartimiento, distribución.

appose [æpóųz], *va.* poner o fijar lado a lado, aplicar; yuxtaponer.

apposite [ǽpozįt], *a.* adaptado, propio, oportuno, a propósito; yuxtapuesto.

appositely [-lį], *adv.* convenientemente, a propósito.

appositeness [-nįs], *s.* adaptación; propiedad.

apposition [æpozįšən], *s.* (gram.) aposición; adición, añadidura, yuxtaposición.

appositive [əpázįtįv], *a.* (gram.) apositivo.

appraisable [əpréįząbl], *a.* tasable, apreciable.

appraise [əpréįz], *va.* (a)valuar, valorar, justipreciar, aforar, tasar; estimar, apreciar.

appraisal [-ąl], **appraisement** [-męnt], *s.* tasa (-ción), avalúo, valuación, aprecio, aforo.

appraiser [-œ(r)], *s.* tasador, avaluador, apreciador.

appraisingly [-įŋlį], *adv.* tasativamente.

appreciable [əprįšįąbl], *a.* apreciable, estimable; perceptible, sensible, notable.

appreciate [əprįšįeįt]. I. *va.* apreciar, estimar; valuar, tasar; encarecer. II. *vn.* subir en valor.

appreciation [-éįšən], *s.* valuación, tasa, avalúo; alza, aumento de precio; aprecio, apreciación; sensibilidad, estimativa.

appreciative, appreciatory [əprįšįątįv, -torį], *a.* apreciativo, comprensivo.

appreciator [əprįšįeįto(r)], *s.* avaluador, tasador; el que reconoce los méritos de algo.

apprehend [æprįhénd], *va.* y *vn.* comprender, entender, percibir; temer, sospechar, maliciar, recelar; aprehender, asir; prender, capturar.

apprehender [-œ(r)], *s.* aprehensor.

apprehensible [æprįhénsįbl], *a.* comprensible.

apprehension [-šən], *s.* aprensión, recelo, cuidado, malicia; comprensión; aprehensión, estimación, idea; presa, prisión, captura.—**to be dull of a.**, tener la cabeza dura.

apprehensive [-sįv], *a.* aprensivo, receloso, tímido, sobrecogido; aprehensivo, agudo, penetrante, perspicaz; consciente.

apprehensively [-lį], *adv.* aprehensivamente.

apprehensiveness [-nįs], *s.* aprensión, recelo.

apprentice [əpréntįs]. I. *s.* aprendiz, *m.*, novicio, principiante; meritorio.—**a. seaman**, grumete, aprendiz de marinero. II. *va.* alquilar o contratar como aprendiz.

apprenticeship [-šįp], *s.* aprendizaje, noviciado.

apprise, apprize [əpráįz], *va.* informar, avisar, comunicar, dar parte (de algo); valuar, tasar.

apprizement [-męnt], *s.* aviso, notificación.

apprizer [-œ(r)], *s.* el que informa, avisa, etc.; (raro) valuador, tasador.

approach [əpróųch]. I. *va.* y *vn.* aproximar(se), acercar(se); allegar(se); hacer propuestas, insinuaciones a uno. II. *s.* acercamiento; acceso; proximidad; *pl.* (fort.) aproches, ataques; *pl.* (const.) accesos, vía de entrada o de acceso.

approachable [-ąbl], *a.* accesible, atracable; abordable, comunicativo.

approaching [-įŋ]. I. *a.* próximo, cercano, venidero. II. *s.* acercamiento, apropincuación.

approbate [ǽprobeįt], *va.* (E. U.) aprobar; licenciar, autorizar.

approbation [-éįšən], *s.* aprobación, aplauso, aceptación, beneplácito.

approbative [ǽprobątįv], **approbatory** [-torį], *a.* aprobatorio.

appropriable [əpróųprįąbl], *a.* apropiable.

appropriate [əpróųprįeįt]. I. *va.* apropiar(se), destinar, consignar; posesionarse, incautarse, adjudicarse; votar, asignar (una partida). II. [-prįįt], *a.* apropiado, apto, a propósito, pertinente.—**to be a.**, caer bien, venir al pelo.

appropriately [-lį], *adv.* apropiadamente, propiamente, aptamente.

appropriateness [-nįs], *s.* aptitud; propiedad.

appropriation [-éįšən], *s.* apropiación, consignación; suma votada o consignada para algún objeto; (for.) enajenación de un beneficio.

appropriator [əpróųprįeįto(r)], *s.* apropiador.

approvable [əprúvąbl], *a.* aprobable.

approval [-ąl], *s.* aprobación; beneplácito, visto bueno; consentimiento.—**on a.**, (com.) a prueba.

approve [əprúv]. I. *va.* aprobar, sancionar, confirmar, ratificar; dar el visto bueno a; probar, demostrar; (for.) apropiarse.—**to a. one's self worthy**, demostrar que uno es digno. II. *vn.* (seguido de **of**), aprobar, sancionar.

approver [-œ(r)], *s.* aprobador, aprobante.

approximate [əprǽksįmęt]. I. *a.* próximo, inmediato, cercano; aproximado. II. [-eįt], *va.* y *vn.* aproximar(se), acercar(se).

approximately [-mįtlį], *adv.* aproximadamente.

approximation [-éįšən], *s.* aproximación, acercamiento; cálculo aproximado o prudencial.

approximative [-ątįv], *a.* aproximativo, aproximado.

approximatively [-lį], *adv.* aproximadamente.

appulse [əpáls], *s.* choque, encuentro; aproximación; (astr.) apulso.

appurtenance [əpœrtęnąns], *s.* (for.) adjunto; pertenencia, dependencia.—*pl.* (com.) incidentes; arreos; anexidades.

appurtenant [-ąnt], *s.* a. perteneciente, anejo, accesorio. II. *s.* = APPURTENANCE.

apricot [éįprįkąt], *s.* (bot.) albar(i)coque, damasco.—**a. tree**, albar(i)coquero.

April [éįprįl], *s.* abril.—**A. Fools' Day**, primer día de abril.—**A. fool**, el que es burlado en ese día.

apriorism [eįprąįóųrįzm], *s.* (filos.) apriorismo.—**apriorist** [-įst], *s.* apriorista.

aprioristic [-įstįk], *a.* apriorístico.

apron [éįprən], *s.* delantal, devantal, excusalí; mandil, plastrón; batiente de un dique; plancha de protección; plancha de guía; cubierta, manta; (art.) planchada o plomada de cañón; (mec.) cubierta protectora de palastro; portaherramienta; correa sin fin; plancha delantera de un torno; (hidr.) entablado, empedrado u otra obra de protección al pie de una presa, muro de defensa, etc.—**a. conveyor**, transportador de cadena sin fin.—**a. of the stem**, (mar.) albitana, contrabranque.—**a. stage**, (teat.) primer plano.—**a. strings**, cintas del delantal.—**tied to the a. strings**, dominado por la mujer o madre.

aproned [-d], *a.* vestido con delantal.

apropos [æpropóu], *adv.* y *a.* a propósito, oportunamente, oportuno, pertinente.

apse, apsis [æps, ǽpsįs], *s.* (arq.) ábside, *mf.;* (astr.) ápside.—**a. aisle**, girola.—**western a.**, contraábside.

apsidal [ǽpsįdąl], *a.* del ábside.

apt [æpt], *a.* apto, idóneo, capaz; propio, pertinente; propenso, listo, inclinado; fácil, dispuesto, pronto, vivo.

Aptera [ǽptęrą], *s. pl.* (zool.) ápteros.

apteral [-ąl], *a.* (arq.) áptero; (zool.) = APTEROUS.

apterous [-ʌs], *a.* (zool.) áptero, sin alas.

apteryx [-įks], *s.* (zool.) ápterix o aptérix, ave (*f.*) de Nueva Zelandia de alas rudimentarias.

aptitude [ǽptįtįud], **aptness** [ǽptnįs], *s.* aptitud, capacidad, idoneidad; tendencia, disposición, facilidad.

aptly [ǽptlį], *adv.* aptamente; prontamente.

Apulian [ąpiúlįąn], *s.* y *a.* pullés, de la Pulla (Apulia).

apyretic [eįpaįrétįk], *a.* (med.) apirético, sin fiebre.

apyrexia [-réksįą], *s.* apirexia, período sin fiebre.

aqua [ǽkwą], *s.* agua.—**a. ammoniæ**, agua amoniacal.—**a. fontana**, agua de manantial.—**a. fortis**, agua fuerte.—**a. pura**, agua destilada.—**a. regia**, agua regia.—**a. tofana**, tofana.—**a. vitæ**, alcohol, licor.

aquafortist [-fórtįst], *s.* (b.a.) aguafuertista, acuafortista.

aquamarine [-marín], *s.* (min.) aguamarina.

aquapuncture [-pʌŋkchų(r)], *s.* (med.) acuapuntura.

aquarelle [ækwąrél], *s.* (pint.) acuarela.

aquarellist [-įst], *s.* acuarelista.

aquarium [ąkwérįʌm], *s.* acuario, pecera.

Aquarius [ąkwérįʌs], *s.* (astr.) Acuario.

aquatic(al [ąkwǽtįk(ąl], *a.* acuático, acuátil.

aquatint [ǽkwątįnt], *s.* acuatinta, aguatinta, grabado al agua tinta.

aqueduct [ǽkwįdʌkt], *s.* acueducto.

aqueous [éįkwįʌs], **aquose** [éįkwoųs], *a.* ácueo, acuoso, aguoso, aguazoso.—**a. humor**, humor ácueo, aguaza.

aqueousness [-nįs], **aquosity** [eįkwásįtį], *s.* acuosidad.

aquiferous [ækwíferʌs], *a.* que conduce o surte agua o flúido acuoso; (anat.) acuífero.

aquiline [ǽkwįlįn], *a.* aguileño, aquilino.

Aquitanian [ækwįtéįnįąn], *a.* y *s.* aquitano, aquitánico.

Ara [éįrą], *s.* (astr.) Ara, el Altar.

Arab [ǽrąb], **Arabian** [ąréįbįąn], *s.* y *a.* árabe, arábigo.—**street A.**, pillete de calle, golfo.—**The Arabian Nights**, las Mil y una Noches.

arabesque [ærąbésk], *s.* y *a.* (b.a.) arabesco.—**a. work**, aceituní.

Arabic [ǽrąbįk]. I. *s.* árabe, lengua arábiga. II. *a.* arábigo.—**A. numeral**, cifra arábiga, número arábigo.

Arabism [-įzm], *s.* arabismo.

Arabist [-įst], *s.* arabista.

arable [ǽrąbl], *a.* labrantío, cultivable.

Arachnida [æréknįdą], *s. pl.* arácnidos.

arachnoid [-nɔįd]. I. *a.* semejante a una telaraña; (zool.) aracnoideo, aracnoideo; (anat.) aracnoideo; (bot.) aracnoide. II. *s.* (zool.) arácnido, aracnoideo; (anat.) aracnoides, *f.* (ll. t. **a. membrane**).

arachnoiditis [-aįtįs], **arachnitis** [æræknáįtįs], *s.* (med.) aracnoiditis.

arachnology [æræknálodžį], *s.* aracnología.

Aragonese [ærągoníz], *a.* y *s.* aragonés.

aragonite [ærǽgonaįt], *s.* (min.) aragonito.

Aramaic [ærąméįįk], **Aramean** [ærąmíąn], *a.* y *s.* arameo.

-raneous [æréįnįʌs], *a.* semejante a la telaraña.

Araucanian [ærɔkéįnįąn], *a.* y *s.* araucano.

rbalest, arbalist [árbąlįst], *s.* ballesta.

arbalester, arbalister [-œ(r)], *s.* ballestero.

arbiter [árbįtœ(r)], *s.* arbitrador, árbitro.

arbitrable [-trąbl], *a.* arbitrable.

arbitrage [-trįdž], *s.* (com., etc.) arbitraje.

arbitral [-trąl], *a.* arbitral; arbitrable.

arbitrament [arbítrąmęnt], *s.* arbitraje; arbitramento; arbitrio.

arbitrarily [árbįtrerįlį], *adv.* arbitrariamente.

arbitrariness [-įnįs], *s.* arbitrariedad.

arbitrary [-į], *a.* arbitrario, despótico, absoluto; (for.) discrecional.

arbitrate [árbįtreįt], *va.* y *vn.* arbitrar, terciar, componer; decidir como árbitro.

arbitration [-éįšǫn], *s.* arbitramento, arbitraje, arbitración, componenda, tercería.—**a. of exchange**, (com.) arbitraje de cambio.

arbitrator [-tǫ(r)], *s.* arbitrador, árbitro; tercero, componedor; ponente.

arbitratrix [-trįks], **arbitress** [árbįtrįs], *s.* arbitradora.

arbor [árbǫ(r)], *s.* (mec.) árbol, eje; tambor; (bot.) árbol; emparrado, bacelar; glorieta, cenador.—**a. shaft** = CARDAN JOINT.—**a. vitæ**, (bot.) tuya, árbol conífero, árbol de la vida; (anat.) aspecto ramoso de la sección vertical del cerebelo, centro medular, árbol de la vida.

arboreal, arboreous [arbórįąl, -įʌs], **arborous** [árbǫrʌs], *a.* arbóreo.

arbored [árbǫrd], *a.* arbolado.

arborescence [arbǫrésęns], *s.* arborescencia.

arborescent [-ęnt], *a.* arborescente.

arboretum [arbǫrítʌm], *s.* plantel, almáciga, criadero de árboles; jardín botánico.

arboriculture [árbǫrįkalchų(r)], *s.* arboricultura.

arboriculturist [-įst], *s.* arboricultor.

arborist [árbǫrįst], *s.* arbolista, arborista.

arbuscle [árbąsl], *s.* arbustillo.

arbutus [arbįútʌs], *s.* (bot.) madroño, gayuba.—**trailing a.**, epigea.

arc [ark]. I. *s.* (geom., elec., astr.) arco.—**a. lamp**, o **light**, lámpara o luz de arco voltaico.—**a. lighting**, alumbrado de arco.—**a. process**, (quím.) fijación del nitrógeno del aire combinándolo con el oxígeno por medio del arco eléctrico.—**a. welding**, soldadura de arco. II. *vn.* (elec.) formar arco.

arcade [arkéįd], *s.* arcada; arquería, porche, soportales, *m. pl.*, galería.

Arcadian [arkéįdįąn], *a.* y *s.* arcadio, árcade, arcádico; simple, pastoral.

arcane [arkéįn], *a.* arcano, misterioso.

arcanum [-ʌm], *s.* arcano, misterio, secreto.—*pl.* arcana, arcanos.

arch [arch]. I. *va.* (arq.) arquear, encorvar, enarcar, voltear, montear; abovedar. II. *vn.* formar bóveda. III. *s.* (geom. y arq.) arco; bóveda.—**the a. of heaven**, la bóveda celeste.—**a. of the aorta**, (anat.) la curvatura de la aorta.—**Gothic a., pointed a.**, arco ojival, arco gótico.—**horseshoe a.**, arco de herradura.—**round** o **semicircular a.**, arco de medio punto. IV. *a.* travieso; picaresco, socarrón, astuto; principal, insigne, de primer orden, grande.

Arch(a)ean [arkíąn], *a.* (geol.) arqueano.

archæologic(al [arkįoládžįk(ąl], *a.* arqueológico.

archæologist [arkįálodžįst], *s.* arqueólogo.

archæology [arkįálodžį], *s.* arqueología.

archaic [arkéįįk], *a.* arcaico, anticuado, desusado.

archaism [árk(e)įįzm], *s.* arcaísmo.

archaist [-įst], *s.* arcaísta.

archaistic [-ístįk], *a.* arcaizante.

archaize [-aįz], *vn.* y *va.* arcaizar.

archangel [árkéįndžęl], *s.* arcángel.

archangelic [arkændžélįk], *a.* arcangélico.

archbishop [árchbįšǫp], *s.* arzobispo, metropolitano.—**archbishopric** [-rįk], *s.* arzobispado.

archdeacon [árchdíkǫn], *s.* arcediano; archidiácono.

archdeaconry [-rį], **archdeaconship** [-šįp], *s.* arcedianato.

archdiocese [-dájosiz], *s.* archidiócesis, arquidiócesis.

archducal [-djúkạl], *a.* archiducal.

archduchess [-dáchịs], *s.* archiduquesa.

archduchy [-dáchị], *s.* archiducado.

archduke [-djúk], *s.* archiduque.

archdukedom [-dọm], *s.* archiducado.

arched [archt], *a.* arqueado, abovedado, corvo.

archenemy [árchénịmị], *s.* el enemigo malo, el demonio, satanás.

archeologist, etc. *V.* ARCHÆOLOGIST, etc.

Archeozoic [arkjozóụịk], *a.* (geol.) arqueozoico.

archer [árchœ(r)], *s.* arquero, ballestero, flechero.

archeress [-ịs], *s.* ballestera, flechadora.

archery [-ị], *s.* ballestería.

archetypal [árkịtaipạl], *a.* arquetípico, perteneciente al arquetipo.

archetype [árkịtaip], *s.* arquetipo, prototipo.

archfiend [árchfínd], *s.* el demonio, el diablo.

archidiaconal [arkịdajǽkonạl], *a.* perteneciente al arcediano.

archiepiscopacy [arkịịpịskopạsị], **archiepiscopate** [-pejt], *s.* arzobispado.

archiepiscopal [-pạl], *a.* arquiepiscopal o arzobispal.—**a. diocese,** arquidiócesis.—**a. church,** metrópoli, *f.*

archil [árkịl], *s.* (bot.) orchilla, urchilla.

archimandrite [arkịmǽndrajt], *s.* archimandrita, *m.*

Archimedean [arkịmídịạn], *a.* arquimédico, de Arquimedes.

arching [árchịŋ], **I.** *a.* arqueado. **II.** *s.* arqueo, curvatura.

archipelago [arkịpélạgọụ], *s.* archipiélago.

architect [árkịtekt], *s.* arquitecto; (fig.) artífice.

architectonic [-tektánịk], *a.* arquitectónico.

architectonics [-s], *s.* arquitectura, arte arquitectónico; (filos.) arquitectónica (término kantiano).

architectural [-tékchụrạl], *a.* arquitectural, arquitectónico.

architecture [árkịtekchụ(r)], *s.* arquitectura.

architrave [árkịtrejv], *s.* (arq.) arquitrabe.

archive [árkạjv], *s.* archivo; documento archivado.—*pl.* estaneo.

archivist [árkịvịst], *s.* archivero, archivista.

archivolt [árkịvoụlt], *s.* (arq.) archivolta, arquivolta.

archlike [árchlajk], *a.* en forma de arco.

archly [árchlị], *adv.* jocosamente, sutilmente.

archness [árchnịs], *s.* travesura, astucia, sutileza de ingenio.

archon [árkan], *s.* aconte.

archontate [-tejt], *s.* arcontato.

archpriest [árchpríst], *s.* gran sacerdote; arcipreste.

archpriesthood [-hụd], *s.* arciprestazgo.

archvillain [archvílạn], *s.* bellaconazo, picarón.

archvillainy [-ị], *s.* gran bellaquería.

archway [árchwej], *s.* arcada; pasadizo bajo un arco; pasaje abovedado.

archwise [árchwajz], *a.* en figura de arco.

arciform [ársiform], *a.* en forma de arco.

arcing [árkịŋ]. **I.** *s.* (elect.) formación de arco. **II.** *a.* (elec.) que forma arco.

arcograph [árkogrœf], *s.* arcógrafo.

arctic [árktịk]. **I.** *a.* ártico, septentrional; frígido.—**a. fox,** (zool.) zorro azul. **II.** *s.* región ártica, círculo ártico.—*pl.* zapato(ne)s de goma o de abrigo.

Arcturus [arktjúrạs], *s.* (astr.) Arturo.

arcuate [árkjujt], *a.* arqueado.

arcuation [arkjuéjšọn], *s.* arqueo, encorvamiento, curvatura; (agr.) acodadura.

arcubalist [árkjubạlịst], *s.* ballesta.

arcubalister [-bǽljstœ(r)], *s.* ballestero.

ardency [árdẹnsị], **ardentness** [árdẹntnịs], *s.* ardor, vehemencia, anhelo, calor, ansia.

ardent [árdẹnt], *a.* ardiente; vehemente, apasionado, vivo.—**a. spirits,** licores espirituosos.

ardently [-lị], *adv.* apasionadamente, ardientemente, calurosamente, fogosamente.

ardor [árdọ(r)], *s.* ardor, calor, fuego; pasión ahinco, vehemencia, fervor; acaloramiento.

arduous [árdẑụẠs], *a.* arduo, difícil, laborioso alto, escabroso, enhiesto.

arduously [-lị], *adv.* arduamente.

arduousness [-nịs], *s.* arduidad.

are [ar]. 2*a. pers. sing.,* 1 *a.,* 2 *a.* y 3 *a. pers. pl pres. ind.* de TO BE.

are [er], *s.* área (medida de cien metros cuadrados)

area [érịạ], *s.* área; extensión, superficie; región zona; comarca; terreno, tierra; (geom.) área superficie.

areca [érịkạ], *s.* (bot.) areca y su fruto; bonga

arena [ạrínạ], *s.* arena, liza, redondel, ruedo.

arenaceous [ærịnéjšịẠs], **arenose** [érịnoụs], *a* arenisco, arenoso, arenáceo.

areola [æríolạ], *s.* (anat.) aréola.

areolar [-(r)], *a.* areolar.

areometer [ærịámetœ(r)], *s.* areómetro, pesalị cores.

Areopagite [ærịápạdẑajt], *s.* areopagita, *m.*

Areopagus [ærịápạgạs], *s.* Areópago.

argal, argali [árgạl, -ị], *s.* (zool.) argalí, carnere salvaje de Siberia y de las Montañas Rocosas

argala [-ạ̈], *s.* (orn.) marabú; garza carroñera de la India.

Argand lamp [árgœnd læmp], *s.* quinqué.

argent [árdẑẹnt]. **I.** *a.* argénteo, argentino. **II.** *s* (poét.) plata; blancura; (blas.) argén.

argentation [-éišọn], *s.* plateadura, baño de plata.

argenteous [ardẑéntịẠs], *a.* argénteo, argentino

argentiferous [ardẑẹntífẹrạs], *a.* argentífero.

argentine [árdẑẹntịn]. **I.** *a.* argentino. **II.** *s* metal blanco plateado; precipitado de estañ y cinc; materia plateada de las escamas de lo peces.

Argentine, Argentinean [-tin, -tịnịạn], *s.* y *a* argentino, de la Argentina.

argentite [-tajt], *s.* (mín.) argirosa.

argil [árdẑịl], *s.* argil(l)a, arcilla; alumunita.

argillaceous [-éịšịẠs], **argillous** [ardẑílẠs], *a* arcilloso.

argol [árgạl], *s.* tártaro, rasuras, *f. pl.;* estiércc seco.

argon [árgan], *s.* (quím.) argón, argo.

Argonaut [árgonọt], *s.* (mit.) argonauta, *m.;* (a. (zool.) argonauta, *m.*

Argonautic [argonótịk], *a.* (mit.) argonáutico.

argosy [árgosị], *s.* bajel con cargamento valiosc

argot [árgọt], *s.* jerga, jerigonza; germanía; len guaje vulgar, caló.

argue [árgju]. **I.** *va.* debatir, disputar, discuti argüir, razonar; sostener; demostrar, indica: **II.** *vn.* disputar, argüir, argumentar.

arguer [-œ(r)], *s.* argumentador, arguyente, ra zonador, opinante; discutidor, ergotista.

arguing [-ịŋ], *s.* razonamiento, argumentación.

argument [-mẹnt], *s.* argumento, tema, *m.,* asunto debate, controversia, disputa; prueba, demo: tración; (for.) alegación, alegato.

argumentation [-mẹntéịšọn], *s.* argumentació raciocinio.

argumentative [-mḝntẠtịv], *a.* demostrativ argumentador, argumentativo.

Argus [árgạs], *s.* (mit.) Argos; (fig.) persona mu vigilante; (orn.) faisán de Oceanía.—**A.-eyec** lince, de vista penetrante.

argute [argjút], *a.* agudo, sutil; astuto, perspica: penetrante (sonido); (bot.) dentado.

arguteness [-nịs], *s.* argucia, agudeza, sutilez: perspicacia.

aria [árịạ], *s.* (mús.) aria.

Arian [érịạn], *a.* y *s.* arriano. *V.* ARYAN.—**Arianism** [-ịzm], *s.* arrianismo (herejía).

arid [érịd], *a.* árido, seco.

aridity [ạrídịtị], o **aridness** [érịdnịs], *s.* aride: sequedad, enjutez.

Aries [érịiz], *s.* (astr.) Aries.

arietta [arjétā], s. (mús.) arieta.

aright [arájt], adv. acertadamente, rectamente, justamente.—**to set a.**, rectificar.

aril [ǽrjl], s. (bot.) arilo.

arillate(d [-ejt(jd], a. arilado, que tiene arilo.

arise [arájz], vn. (pret. AROSE, pp. ARISEN) subir, elevarse; surgir, aparecer; levantarse, ponerse en pie; proceder, provenir o emanar (de); presentarse, ofrecerse; suscitarse; originarse, producirse, sobrevenir; resucitar.

arista [arjstā], s. (bot.) arista.

aristocracy [ærjstákrasj], s. aristocracia.

aristocrat [ærjstokræt], s. aristócrata, mf.

aristocratic(al [-krǽtjk(al], a. aristocrático.

aristocratically [-j], adv. aristocráticamente.

aristolochiaceous [-lokjéjŝAs], a. (bot.) aristoloquiáceo.

Aristophanic [ærjstofǽnjk], a. aristofánico.

Aristotelian [-tíljan], **Aristotelic** [-tíljk], a. y s. aristotélico.

Aristotelianism [-jzm], s. aristotelismo.

arithmetic [arjθmetjk], s. aritmética.

arithmetical [ærjθmétjkal], a. aritmético.

arithmetician [arjθmetíŝan], s. aritmético.

arithmometer [ærjθmámetœr], s. aritmómetro.

ark [ark], s. arca; (mar.) lanchón; (E. U.) bote de fondo plano para transporte interior.—**A. of the Covenant**, arca de la alianza.

arm [arm]. I. s. brazo (del cuerpo, de una silla, de mar); pata delantera; rama; canal; arma (instrumento e instituto); (fig.) brazo, mano (de la ley, etc.); (mar.) cabo de una verga; brazo de ancla; (mec.) brazo, palanca; brazo de palanca.—pl. armas, servicio militar; ramos del servicio militar; ciencia o profesión de las armas; blasones.—**a. band**, brazal, faja que ciñe la manga, en señal de luto, dignidad, etc.—**a. bone**, (anat.) canilla o caña del brazo.—**in a.**, de bracero, de bracete, del brazo.—**a.'s reach**, alcance del brazo.—**at a.'s length**, a una brazada; a distancia prudente.—**call to arms**, rebato.—**fire arms**, armas de fuego.—**in arms**, en hostilidad armada; en fuerte oposición; de pecho, de teta (niño).—**side arms**, armas de cinto, armas de oficiales.—**to arms!** ¡a las armas!—**under arms**, sobre las armas. II. va. armar; fortalecer; proveer de medios o elementos. III. vn. armarse.

armada [armádā], s. armada, flota.

armadillo [armadjloq], s. (zool.) armadillo, tatú, vergonzoso.—**giant a.**, prio(no)donte.

armament [ármament], s. armamento; equipo.

armature [ármachur], s. (elec.) armadura (de un imán); inducido (de una dínamo); (mil.) armadura; armamento, equipo; (hist. nat.) armas naturales, medios de defensa (de los animales y plantas).

armchair [ármcher], s. sillón, butaca, silla de brazos, silla poltrona.

armed [armd], pp. y a. armado, provisto de armas.

Armenian [armínjan], a. y s. armenio.

armful [ármfql], s. brazada, brazado.

armhole [ármhoql], s. (sast.) sobaquera.

armiger [ármjdźœ(r], s. armígero, caballero; escudero que llevaba las armas de su señor.

armillary [ármjlerj], a. armilar, anular.—**a. sphere**, (astr.) esfera armilar.

arming [ármjn], s. acto de armar(se) o de proveer(se) de armas; armamento; (elec.) armadura (de imán).—pl. (mar.) empavesadas.

armipotent [armípotent], a. armipotente.

armistice [ármjstjs], s. armisticio.

armless [ármljs], a. desarmado; manco.

armlet [ármljt], s. brazuelo; brazal o brazalete, avambrazo (del arnés); ensenada pequeña (del mar).

armor [ármo(r]. I. s. armadura, arnés; acorazamiento; coraza, blindaje.—**a. bearer**, escudero.—**a. belt**, cintura acorazada.—**a.-clad**, a. provisto de blindaje; s. (buque de guerra) acorazado.—**a.-piercing**, taladrante; que atraviesa una armadura o coraza.—**a. plate**, coraza, plancha de blindaje. II. va. acorazar, blindar.

armored [-d], pp. y a. armado, blindado, acorazado.—**a. car** o **train**, automóvil, camión o tren blindado.—**a. concrete**, hormigón o cemento armado.—**a. cruiser**, crucero acorazado.

armorer [ármgrœ(r], s. armero; mallero.

armorial [armórjal], a. heráldico.—**a. ensigns**, blasón, armas.

armoring [ármgrjn], s. acorazamiento, blindaje; armadura.

armory [ármgrj], s. armería; (E. U.) arsenal; maestranza; cuartel; armadura, armas; blasón, heráldica; escudo de armas.

armpit [ármpjt], s. (anat.) sobaco, axila.

armscye [ármsaj], s. (sast.) sobaquera.

army [ármj], s. ejército, tropas; multitud, muchedumbre.—**a. chaplain**, capellán castrense.—**a. corps**, cuerpo de ejército.—**a. register**, escalafón.—**a. worm**, (ent.) larva o gusano de la esciara, noctua, etc.

arnatto [arnǽtou], **arnotto** [arnátou], (bot.) bija, achiote. V. ANNATTO.

arnica [árnjkā], s. (bot., farm.) árnica.

aroma [aróumā], s. aroma, m.; fragancia.

aromatic(al [ærómǽtjk(al], a. aromático.

aromatics [-s], s. pl. aromas, especias.

aromatization [-zéjŝon], s. aromatización.

aromatize [aróumatajz], va. aromatizar, aromar.

aromatizer [-œ(r], s. aromatizador.

arose [aróuz], pret. de TO ARISE.

around [aráund]. I. adv. alrededor o en derredor, a la redonda; a la vuelta; por todos lados; de un lado para otro.—**the other way a.**, al contrario, viceversa, al revés. II. prep. al volver de, alrededor de, cerca de, en torno de.—**a. the corner**, (fam.) a la vuelta de la esquina.—**a. Christmas**, (fam.) por Navidad.—**all a. the town**, (fam.) por toda la ciudad.

arousal [aráuzal], s. despertamiento.

arouse [aráuz], va. despertar; mover, excitar, alborotar; suscitar (interés, etc.).

arow [aróu], adv. (poét.) en fila, en línea.

arpeggio [arpédźjou], s. (mús.) arpegio.

arquebus [árkwjbas], s. arcabuz, m.

arquebusier [-ír], s. arcabucero.

arrack [ǽrak], s. arac o raque, licor espiritoso.

arraign [aréjn], va. (for.) procesar criminalmente, instruir de cargos; acusar, denunciar.

arraignment [-ment], s. (for.) proceso, instrucción de cargos, procesamiento, causa criminal; acusación, denuncia.

arrange [aréjndź]. I. va. arreglar, acomodar, preparar, aprestar; hacer arreglos para; colocar, ordenar; disponer, convenir, concertar; (mús.) arreglar, adaptar. II. vn. prevenir, hacer arreglos; concertarse, convenir.

arrangement [-ment], s. colocación; orden, ordenación, arreglo, distribución; preparativo, medida, providencia, disposición, convenio.

arranger [-œ(r], s. arreglador, ordenador.

arrant [ǽrant], a. notorio, redomado, insigne, consumado, de siete suelas.—**a. fool**, (fam.) tonto de marca.

arrantly [-lj], adv. redomadamente.

arras [ǽras], s. tapicería de Arras.

array [aréj]. I. s. orden de batalla, formación, ordenación; pompa, aparato; galería, gala, atavío; conjunto, colección.—**to challenge the a.**, (for.) recusar todo el jurado. II. va. poner en orden de batalla; formar las tropas; guarnecer, ataviar, adornar; (for.) colocar los jurados.

arrear [arír], s. (ú. más en pl.) atrasos, caídos; cantidades vencidas y no pagadas.

arrearage [-jdź], s. atrasos, caídos.

arrest [arést], s. prisión, arresto, reclusión; detención; aprehensión; (mec.) parada, interrupción.

arrest, va. impedir, detener, retener, atajar.

reprimir; arrestar, prender, recluir, capturar; atraer y fijar (la atención).

arrester [-œ(r)], *s.* detenedor, aprehensor.

arresting [-ɪŋ], *a.* impresionante, llamativo.

arrhizous [ǽrɑ́ɪʌs], **arrhizal** [-ɑ̱l], *a.* sin raíces.

arrhythmic [ɑrɪ́ðmɪk], *a.* (med.) arrítmico.

arris [ǽrɪs], *s.* (arq.) esquina, ángulo externo; filo; lima tesa, lima hoya.

arrival [ǽrɑ́ɪvɑ̱l], *s.* arribo, llegada; entrada; logro, consecución; advenimiento; persona que llega. —**a new a.**, un recién venido; advenedizo.

arrive [ǽrɑ́ɪv], *vn.* llegar, arribar; advenir.—**to a. at**, llegar a (un resultado, etc.).—**to a. at, o in,** llegar a (un pueblo, un punto).

arrogance [ǽrogɑ̱ns], **arrogancy** [-ɪ], *s.* arrogancia, soberbia, altivez(a).

arrogant [ǽrogɑ̱nt], *a.* arrogante, soberbio.

arrogantly [-lɪ], *adv.* arrogantemente.

arrogate [ǽrogeɪt], *va.* arrogarse, usurpar.

arrogation [-éɪʂ̱ɑ̱n], *s.* arrogación.

arrow [ǽrou], *s.* flecha, saeta, vira, virote.—**a. grass,** trigloquín, planta acuática.—**a.-headed** o **-shaped,** aflechado, sagital; cuneiforme (ú. de ciertos caracteres).—**a. wood,** (bot.) especie de viburno.—**a. wound,** flechazo.

arrowhead [-hed], *s.* punta de flecha, casquillo (de hierro); (bot.) sagitaria.

arrowroot [-rut], *s.* (bot.) arrurruz, *m.*

arrowy [ǽrouwɪ], *a.* en forma de flecha o saeta; rápido como la flecha.

arroyo [ǽrɔ́jou], *s.* arroyo; barranco, torrentera.

arsenal [ǽrsɪnɑ̱l], *s.* arsenal; maestranza, atarazana, armería.

arsenate [ǽrsɪneɪt], *s.* (quím.) arseniato.

arsenic [ǽrsɪnɪk], *s.* (quím.) arsénico.

arsenic(al [ɑrsénɪk(ɑ̱l], *a.* (quím.) arsénico, arsenical.

arsenid(e [ǽrsɪnɑɪd], *s.* (quím.) arseniuro.

arsenious [ɑrsínjʌs], *a.* (quím.) arsenioso.

arsenite [ǽrsɪnɑɪt], *s.* (quím.) arsenito.

arseniuret [ɑrsényȗret], *s.* (quím.) arseniuro.

arsenopyrite [ɑrsɪnopáɪrɑɪt], *s.* arsenopirita, piritas arsenicales.

arsis [ǽrsɪs], *s.* sílaba acentuada; inflexión de voz; (mús.) parte no acentuada de un compás.

arson [ǽrsɑn], *s.* incendio premeditado.

art [ɑrt], 2 *a. pers. pres. ind.* de TO BE.

art, *s.* arte, *mf.,* habilidad, maña, destreza; astucia, artificio; oficio, gremio.—**a. gallery,** pinacoteca, galería o salón de pintura(s).—**arts and crafts,** artes y oficios.

arterial [ɑrtírɪɑ̱l], *a.* arterial, arterioso.

arterialize [-ɑɪz], *va.* arterializar.

arterialization [-ɪzéɪʂɑ̱n], *s.* arterialización.

arteriography [-ʌ́grɑfɪ], *s.* arteriografía.

arteriole [ɑrtírɪol], *s.* arteriola, arteria pequeña.

arteriology [-ʌ́lodʑɪ], *s.* arteriología.

arteriosclerosis [-osklɛróʉsɪs], *s.* arteriosclerosis.

arteriotomy [-átomɪ], *s.* (cir.) arteriotomía.

arteritis [ɑrterɑ́ɪtɪs], *s.* arteritis.

artery [ǽrterɪ], *s.* arteria.

artesian [ɑrtíʐɑn], *a.* artesiano.—**a. well,** pozo artesiano.

artful [ǽrtful], *a.* artificial, artificioso; artero, mañero, ladino, astuto; diestro, ingenioso.

artfully [-ɪ], *adv.* artificiosamente, diestramente, con arte; insidiosa, socarronamente.

artfulness [-nɪs], *s.* artería, astucia, amaño; habilidad, industria, alicantina; socarronería.

arthralgia [ɑrθrǽldʑɪ], *s.* (med.) artralgia.

arthritic(al [ɑrθrítɪk(ɑ̱l], *a.* artrítico; artético.

arthritis [ɑrθrɑ́ɪtɪs], *s.* (med.) artritis, *m.*

arthritism [ǽrθrɪtɪzm], *s.* (med.) artritismo.

arthrography [ɑrθrǽgrɑfɪ], *s.* (anat.) artrografía.

arthrology [ɑrθrʌ́lodʑɪ], *s.* (anat.) artrología.

arthropod [ǽrθropɑd], *s. y a.* (zool.) artrópodo.

arthropodal [ɑrθrʌ́pɑdɑ̱l], **arthropodous** [-dʌs], *a.* artrópodo, relativo a los artrópodos.

arthrosis [ɑrθróʉsɪs], *s.* (anat.) articulación.

arthrotomy [ɑrθrátomɪ], *s.* (cir.) artrotomía.

artichoke [ǽrtɪchouk], *s.* (bot.) alcachofa, cardo alcachofero, alcaucil cultivado.—**Jerusalem a.,** (bot.) especie de girasol tuberoso; aguaturma, cotufa, pataca.—**wild a.,** (bot.) alcaucil, arcacil.

article [ǽrtɪkl]. **I.** *s.* artículo (literario, definido, indefinido, de una ley, de doctrina, de comercio); escrito; pacto, convenio; cosa, objeto; parte, *f.*— *pl.* escritura, cédula; constitución; reglamento, ordenanza.—**articles of marriage,** capítulos matrimoniales, carta de dote.—**articles of partnership,** (for.) escritura de sociedad.— **articles of religion,** reglas o constitución (de una iglesia o secta); declaración de fe.—**articles of war,** código militar.—**small articles,** menudencias.—**to be under articles,** estar contratado.—**to sign articles,** escriturarse.—**to surrender under articles,** capitular. **II.** *va.* formular en artículos; escriturar; contratar, dividir o colocar en artículos; acusar por escrito; comprometer (a un abogado, aprendiz, etc.) por contrato. **III.** *vn.* pactar, capitular.

articular [ɑrtɪkjulɑ̱(r)], *a.* articular.—**articularly** [-lɪ], *adv.* articuladamente.

Articulata [-léɪtɑ̱]. *s. pl.* (zool.) articulados.

articulate [ɑrtɪkjuleɪt]. **I.** *va.* articular, enunciar, pronunciar; unir, atar. **II.** *vn.* articular, enunciar; estar unido por articulación. **III.** [-lɪt], *s.* (zool.) articulado. **IV.** *a.* articulado; claro, distinto.

articulately [-lɪ], *adv.* articuladamente.

articulateness [-nɪs], *s.* la calidad de ser articulado.

articulation [-léɪʂɑn], *s.* (anat.) articulación, coyuntura; (bot.) nudo; (pros.) articulación, pronunciación.

artifact [ǽrtɪfækt], *s.* artefacto.

artifice [ǽrtɪfɪs], *s.* artificio; ardid, maña, artería.

artificer [ɑrtɪfɪsœ(r)], *s.* artífice; inventor, autor; artesano hábil, oficial, mecánico.

artificial [ɑrtɪfɪʂɑ̱l], *a.* artificial, fabricado; imitado, falso; ficticio, fingido; postizo; afectado, artificioso.—**a. fertilizer,** abono químico.—**a. light,** luz artificial.—**a. person,** (for.) persona jurídica.

artificiality [-iǽlɪtɪ], **artificialness** [ɑrtɪfɪʂɑlnɪs] *s.* calidad de artificial o artificioso; apariencia afectación.

artificially [ɑrtɪfɪʂɑlɪ], *adv.* artificialmente.

artillerist [ɑrtɪlerɪst], *s.* artillero.

artillery [ɑrtɪlerɪ], *s.* artillería.—**a. park,** parque de artillería.

artilleryman [-mɑn], *s.* artillero.

artiodactyl [ɑrtɪodǽktɪl], *a. y s.* (zool.) artiodáctilo.

artisan [ǽrtɪzɑn], *s.* artesano, artífice, oficial.

artist [ǽrtɪst], *s.* artista; artífice; actor, músico

artistic [ɑrtɪ́stɪk], *a.* artístico.

artistically [-ɑlɪ], *adv.* artísticamente.

artistry [ǽrtɪstrɪ], *s.* arte, *mf.,* habilidad artística.

artless [ǽrtlɪs], *a.* natural, sin arte, sencillo cándido, ingenuo, sin dolo; (fam.) chabacano

artlessly [-lɪ], *adv.* sencillamente, cándidamente chabacanamente, sin arte.

artlessness [-nɪs], *s.* sencillez, candidez, naturali dad.

artocarpeous [ɑrtokɑ́rpɪʌs], *a.* (bot.) artocárpeo

arum [ǽrʌm], *a.* (bot.) aro, yaro, tragontina malanga; especie de cala.

arundinaceous [ɑrʌndɪnéɪʂʌs], **arundineou** [ɑrʌndɪ́nɪʌs], *a.* (bot.) arundíneo; pertenecient o semejante a las cañas.

aruspex [ǽrʌspeks], **aruspice** [-pɪs], *s.* arúspice

Aryan [ɛ́rjɑn], *s. y a.* ario (pueblo, idioma).

as [æs], *s.* as, primitiva moneda romana; pes romano de una libra.

as [æz]. **I.** *adv., conj. y pron. rel.* como; a medid que, mientras (que); según, conforme; cuand en el momento en que, al (+ inf.), vg. *as h entered the room,* al entrar en la sala, o entrand en la sala; como, ya que, porque, por (+ inf. vg. *as it was the first time,* por ser la primera ve

—a. . . . a., tan . . . como; a pesar de lo . . . que, vg. *as large as this one,* tan grande como éste; *as weak as he was, he got up,* a pesar de lo débil que estaba, se levantó, o débil y todo, se levantó.—a. . . . **again** a., dos veces más . . . que, vg. *as large again as this room,* dos veces más grande (o mayor) que este cuarto.—a. **against,** for, comparado con.—a. . . . a. **anything,** a. . . . a. **can be,** muy . . . , sumamente . . . , vg. *as pretty as can be,* sumamente bonita.—a. **a friend,** como (a guisa de, a fuer de, en son de, o en calidad de) amigo.—a. **best he can,** como mejor pueda.—a. **early** a. (antes de una expresión de tiempo), ya en, allá, remontando hasta (la época designada).— a. **far** a., hasta.—a. **far** a. I know, que yo sepa, hasta donde yo puedo juzgar, según se me alcanza.—a. **far** a. **it goes,** hasta donde va, en lo que contiene, etc. (subentendiéndose que hay alguna deficiencia).—a. **far back** a. (antes de una expresión de tiempo) = A. EARLY A.— a. **for,** en cuanto a, por lo que toca o respecta a, referente a.—a. **from** (antes de una expresión de tiempo), a partir de.—a. **good** a., expresión que se usa para indicar que algo puede darse por hecho o seguro, vg. *that is as good as lost,* eso puede darse por perdido.—a. **if,** como, como si, vg. *as if jesting,* como bromeando; *as if it were true,* como si fuera verdad. —a. **if to,** como para, como tratando de.—a. **is,** (com. fam.) como está.—a. **it is,** como está, como están las cosas; así como así.—a. **it were,** por decirlo así.—a. **late** a. (antes de una expresión de tiempo), tan recientemente como, apenas, no más, no hace más que, etc., vg. *I saw her as late as last Friday,* no hace más que el viernes pasado que la vi.—a. **many** a., tantos como, cuantos; hasta, vg. *I have as many as you,* tengo tantos como Vd.; *as many as arrived,* cuantos llegaron; *as many as 10 men,* hasta diez hombres.—a. **much,** tan; tanto; otro tanto; eso en substancia.—a. **much** a., tanto como, tanto cuanto, cuanto; hasta, vg. *you're worth as much as you have,* tanto vales cuanto tienes; *as much as you want,* cuanto Vd. quiera.—a. **much** a. **to say,** como quien dice. —a. **of,** con fecha de.—a. **per,** según, de acuerdo con.—a. **regards** = A. FOR.—a. **soon** a., así que, luego que, tan pronto como, en cuanto.—a. **soon** a. **possible,** cuanto antes.— a. **such,** como tal.—a. **the case may be,** según el caso.—a. **though** = A. IF.—a. **to** = A. FOR.—a. **well,** también, además, vg. *pretty and useful as well,* bonito y útil también.—a. **well** a., tan bien como; lo mismo que; así como, vg. *the men as well as the women,* tanto los hombres como las mujeres, los hombres lo mismo que las mujeres.—**you might,** o **may, as well** (+ inf.), lo mismo da que, es mejor que, vg. *you might as well say you did it,* lo mismo da que Vd. diga que lo hizo.—a. **yet,** aún. todavía, hasta ahora.—**strange** a. **it seems,** o **may appear,** etc., aunque parece extraño, por extraño que parezca.

asaf(o)etida [æsịfétịdẫ], *s.* asafétida.

asarabacca [æsẫrabǽkẫ], **asarum** [æsẫrʌm], *s.* (bot.) ásaro, asarabácara.

asbestic [æsbéstịk], **asbestine** [-tịn], *a.* asbestino; incombustible.

asbestos [-tọs], *s.* asbesto, amianto.

ascarid [ǽskẫrịd], *s.* (zool.) ascáride, *f.,* lombriz intestinal.

ascend [ạsénd], *va.* y *vn.* ascender, subir; adelantar; elevar(se), encumbrar(se); subir de grado.

ascendable [-ạbl], *a.* accesible, que se puede subir.

ascendant [-ạnt], **ascendent** [-ẹnt]. I. *s.* altura, elevación; ascendiente, influjo, poder; predominio; padre, antepasado; (astr.) ascensión. II. *a.* ascendente; superior, predominante.

ascendancy [-ạnsị], **ascendency** [-ẹnsị], *s.* ascendiente, influjo, poder.

ascending [-ịŋ], *a.* ascendente.

ascension [ạsénṣọn], *s.* ascensión, subida; (igl.) la Ascensión de Jesucristo.

ascensional [-ạl], *a.* (astr.) ascensional.

ascent [ạsént], *s.* subida, elevación, ascensión; asunción, ascenso, promoción; cuesta, pendiente.

ascertain [æscœrtéịn]. I. *va.* averiguar, descubrir, determinar, indagar. II. *vr.* cerciorarse (de).

ascertainable [-ạbl], *a.* averiguable, descubrible.

ascertainer [-œ(r)], *s.* averiguador, indagador.

ascertainment [-mẹnt], *s.* averiguación, indagación, determinación.

ascetic [ạsétịk]. I. *a.* ascético. II. *s.* asceta, *mf.*

asceticism [ạsétịsịzm], *s.* ascetismo, ascética.

ascians [ǽ꜀(i)ạnz], **ascii** [ǽ꜀ịi], *s. pl.* (geog.) ascios.

ascidian [ạsídịạn], *s.* (zool.) ascidia.

ascidium [ạsídịʌm], *s.* (bot.) ascidia.

ascites [ạsáịtiz], *s.* (med.) ascitis.

ascitic(al [ạsítịk(ạl], *a.* ascítico, hidrópico.

ascribable [ạskráịbạbl], *a.* atribuíble, imputable.

ascribe [ạskráịb], *va.* atribuir, imputar, achacar.

ascription [ạskrípṣọn], *s.* atribución.

ascus [ǽskʌs], *s.* (bot.) teca, asco.

asea [ạsíí], *adv.* en el mar, al mar.

asepsis [ạsépsịs], *s.* (med.) asepsia.

aseptic [ạséptịk], *a.* aséptico.

asepticism [-tịsịzm], *s.* tratamiento aséptico.

asepticize [-aịz], *va.* (med.) aseptizar, hacer aséptico.

asexual [ạséksʉạl], *a.* asexual; sin sexo.

ash [æ꜀], (sing. de ASHES), *s.* ceniza, cenizas.—a.-colored, cenizo, ceniciento.—a. **fire,** fuego lento cubierto con cenizas.—a. **hole,** a. **pan,** a. **pit,** cenicero.—a. **tray,** cenicero.—a. **tub,** coladero, cubeta de lejía.—A. **Wednesday,** miércoles de ceniza.

ash, *s.* (bot.) fresno.

ashamed [ạ꜀éịmd], *a.* avergonzado, corrido.—**to be** a., avergonzarse, sonrojarse, correrse, tener vergüenza.

ashen [æ꜀ẹn], *a.* de fresno; ceniciento; pálido.

ashery [æ꜀œrị], *s.* fábrica de potasa.

ashes [æ꜀ịz], *s. pl.* ceniza(s); restos mortales.

ashlar, ashler [æ꜀lẫ(r)], *s.* (const.) sillar, canto o carretal, piedra de talla; sillería.

ashlaring, ashlering [-ịŋ], *s.* (carp.) ligazones de los cabrios del techo; (const.) sillería, cantería.

ashore [ạ꜀ór], *adv.* en tierra, a tierra.—**to get** o **put** a., desembarcar.—**to go** a., desembarcar(se).—**to run** a., encallar, varar; irse a la costa.

ashy [æ꜀ị], *a.* cenizoso, ceniciento.—a.-pale, pálido, lívido.

Asian [éịẓạn], **Asiatic** [eịẓịǽtịk], *a.* y *s.* asiático. —A. **cholera,** (med.) cólera(-morbo) o tifo asiático.

Asiaticism [eịẓịǽtịsịzm], *s.* imitación de las costumbres asiáticas o algo rel. a éstas.

aside [ạsáịd]. I. *adv.* a un lado, al lado; aparte.— a. **from,** aparte de, además de. II. *s.* (teat.) aparte.

asinine [ǽsịnaịn], *a.* as(i)nino, asnal, borriqueño.

ask [æsk]. I. *va.* preguntar; pedir, solicitar, suplicar; invitar, convidar.—**to** a. **a question,** hacer una pregunta. II. *vn.* preguntar; pedir.— **to** a. **for,** preguntar por; pedir.—**to** a. **one down, in, up,** rogar a uno que baje, entre, suba.

askance [ạskǽns], *adv.* al sesgo, de soslayo, de reojo, de refilón; con desdén; con recelo.

asker [æskœ(r)], *s.* inquiridor; suplicante.

askew [ạskjú], *a.* y *adv.* sesgado, oblicuo, desviado; sesgadamente, de soslayo.

asking [æskịŋ], *s.* súplica, ruego; publicación (de amonestaciones).—**for the** a., sin más que pedirlo.—**third time of** a., tercera amonestación.

aslant [əslǽnt]. **I.** adv. y a. oblicuamente, inclinado, sesgo, al soslayo. **II.** prep. al través de.

asleep [əslíp], adv. y a. dormido, durmiendo; entumecido.—**to fall a.**, dormirse, quedarse dormido.

aslope [əslóup], adv. en declive, en pendiente.

asp [æsp], s. (zool.) áspid(e); (bot.) V. ASPEN.

aspalathus [æspǽləθʌs], s. (bot.) aspálato.

asparagin(e [æspǽrəd̮in], s. (quím.) aspar(a)-gina.

asparagus [æspǽrəgʌs], s. (bot.) espárrago.

aspect [ǽspekt], s. aspecto, semblante, traza, (fam.) pergeño; apariencia; fase, f., faceta, faz, ver.

aspen [ǽspin]. **I.** s. (bot.) tiemblo. **II.** a. perteneciente al álamo temblón; tembloroso.

asper [ǽspœr], s. aspro, moneda turca.

asperate [ǽspəreit], va. hacer áspera alguna cosa.

asperges [æspœrd̮iz], s. (igl.) hisopo; (A.) asperges.

aspergill(um [ǽspœrd̮il, -d̮iʌm], s. (igl.) hisopo.

asperity [æspériti], s. aspereza; rudeza, acrimonia.

aspermatous, aspermous [eispœrmətʌs, -mʌs], a. (bot.) aspermo, sin semilla.

asperse [æspœrs], va. difamar, calumniar, denigrar, infamar; rociar; asperjar, hisopear.

asperser [-œr], s. infamador; rociador; hisopo.

aspersion [æspœrẑən], s. difamación, calumnia; rociad(ur)a, aspersión; (igl.) asperges; (fam.) rociada, reprensión.

aspersive [æspœrsiv], a. calumnioso, defamatorio.

aspersorium [æspœrsóuriʌm], s. (igl.) acetre; hisopo.

asphalt [ǽsfolt], va. asfaltar.

asphalt o asphaltum [æsfǽltʌm], s. asfalto, betún judaico; (Cuba) chapapote.

asphaltic [æsfóltik], a. asfáltico, bituminoso.

asphodel [ǽsfodel], s. (bot.) asfódelo o gamón.

asphyxia [æsfíksiə] (med.), **asphyxiation** [-éi-ẑən], s. asfixia, sofocación.

asphyxial [æsfíksiəl], a. asfíctico, asfíxico.

asphyxiant [-ənt], a. y s. asfixiante.

asphyxiate [-eit], va. asfixiar, sofocar.

asphyxiating [-iŋ], a. asfixiante.

aspic [ǽspik], s. (bot.) espliego; (zool.) áspid(e); (coc.) especie de gelatina con tomate, carne, etc.

aspirant [əspáirənt]. **I.** s. aspirante, pretendiente, candidato. **II.** a. aspirante.

aspirate [ǽspireit]. **I.** va. aspirar, pronunciar con aspiración; (fisiol.) aspirar. **II.** [-it], a. aspirado.

aspiration [-éiẑən], s. aspiración, anhelo, deseo, ambición; (gram., fisiol.) aspiración.

aspirator [-ọr)], s. (fís.) aspirador.

aspiratory [əspáirətori], a. aspiratorio.

aspire [əspáir], vn. (gen. con to) aspirar, ambicionar, pretender; subir, ascender.

aspirer [-œr], s. aspirante.

aspirin [ǽspirin], s. (quím., farm.) aspirina.

aspiring [əspáiriŋ], a. ambicioso; aspirante.

asquint [əskwint], adv. al soslayo, de través.

ass [æs], s. (zool.) asno, burro, borrico, jumento; (fig.) asno, bestia, porro.—**a.-like**, asinino.

assagai, assegai [ǽsəgai], s. azagaya, venablo sudafricano; (bot.) árbol de azagayas, de que éstas se hacen.

assail [əséil], va. asaltar, atacar, arremeter, acometer, embestir, sobresaltar.

assailable [-əbl], a. que puede ser asaltado.

assailant [-ənt], **assailer** [-œr)], s. y a. asaltador, asaltante, acometedor, embestidor, agresor.

assailment [-mənt], s. asalto, agresión.

assart [əsárt]. **I.** s. (agr.) roza. **II.** va. rozar.

assassin [əsǽsin], s. asesino.

assassinate [-eit]. **I.** va. asesinar. **II.** vn. ser asesino, cometer asesinato.

assassination [-éiẑən], s. asesinato.

assassinator [-eitọr)], s. asesino.

assault [əsólt]. **I.** s. asalto, ataque, acometida, agresión, embestid(ur)a; violación; salte-

---

(amient)o; atraco. **II.** va. asaltar, atacar; violar o tratar de violar (a una mujer); atracar. V. TO ASSAIL.

assaulter [-œr], s. asaltador, agresor; atracador.

assay [əséi]. **I.** va. probar, examinar, investigar; tratar de; verificar, contrastar (moneda, pesas); (metal.) ensayar, (a)quilatar; (quím.) analizar. **II.** s. prueba, determinación, verificación; contraste (de pesas, moneda, etc.); (metal., quím.) ensaye, ensayo, aquilatación; substancia que se ensaya; muestra de ensaye, resultado de un ensaye.—**a. master**, ensayador, contraste, marcador.

assayer [-œr], s. (met.) ensayador, contraste, (a)quilatador, (Am.) ensayista.

assaying [-iŋ], s. (met.) ensaye; docimasia.

assemblage [əsémbld̮], s. reunión, asamblea junta; grupo; asociación; arreglo (de partes, datos, etc.); (mec.) montaje.

assemble [əsémbl]. **I.** va. juntar; allegar; convocar, congregar, aunar; (mec.) montar, armar. **II.** vn. reunirse, juntarse, convenir, afluir.

assembler [-blœr)], s. el que junta o reúne; miembro de una junta o asamblea; (mec.) montador de máquinas, etc.).

assembling [-bliŋ], s. acción de juntar(se) o de reunir; (mec.) montaje, montadura.

assembly [-bli], s. reunión, asamblea, junta, convención, congreso; (mec.) grupo, juego, conjunto de piezas; asamblea, cuerpo legislativo de un estado, departamento, etc.; (mil.) asamblea (llamada).—**a. line**, (mec.) montaje, tren de ensemblaje.—**a.-line production**, producción en gran serie, trabajo en cadena.—**a. plant o shop**, taller de montaje.—**a. room**, sala de sesiones, conferencias, juntas, diversiones, etc.; salón de actos; paraninfo (de una universidad).

assemblyman [-mən], s. individuo de un congreso o asamblea; asambleísta; concejal de ayuntamiento.

assent [əsént]. **I.** vn. asentir, convenir. **II.** s. asenso, asentimiento, aquiescencia; beneplácito.

assentation [æsəntéiẑən], s. condescendencia o complacencia servil.

assentient [æsénʃənt]. **I.** a. que conviene o asiente. **II.** s. consentidor.—**assentingly** [əséntiŋli], adv. con asenso, mostrando asentimiento.

assentor [əséntọr)], s. (for. Ingl.) sancionador, confirmante (de un nombramiento, etc.).

assert [əsœrt], va. afirmar, asegurar, aseverar; mantener, defender; hacer valer.—**to a. oneself**, hacerse sentir, hacer valer sus derechos.

asserter, assertor [-œr)], s. afirmador, defensor.

assertion [əsœrʃən], s. aserción, aseveración, aserto, afirmación, deposición, fe, f.

assertive [əsœrtiv], a. asertivo; dogmático.

assertory [əsœrtori], a. afirmativo; declaratorio.

assess [əsés], va. amillarar, gravar con impuesto, imponer contribución; fijar o determinar (un impuesto, una indemnización); tasar, avaluar.

assessable [-əbl], a. gravable, sujeto a contribución o impuesto.

assessment [-mənt], s. imposición o distribución de contribuciones, etc., avalúo; impuesto o contribución, amillaramiento, tasa de tributación; (com.) dividendo pasivo.

assessor [-ọr)], s. imponedor o repartidor de contribuciones; (for.) asesor.

assessorship [-ọrʃip], s. asesoría.

asset [ǽset], s. (com.) cada partida del activo; (fig.) posesión, ventaja, elemento de buen éxito.—pl. **assets**, (com.) activo; haber; capital; (for.) haberes disponibles que deja una persona.—**active**, o **current a.**, activo corriente.—**fixed a.**, activo fijo.—**(in)tangible a.**, activo (in)tangible.—**personal a.**, bienes muebles y personales.—**real a.**, bienes raíces.

asseverate [əséverejt], va. aseverar, afirmar.

asseveration [-éiẑən], s. aseveración, fe, f.

assibilate [əsíbjleit], va. (fon.) asibilar.

assibilation [-éiẑən], s. (fon.) asibilación.

---

assiduity [æsịdịúịtị], *s.* asiduidad, diligencia, laboriosidad, aplicación, constancia.

assiduous [æsịdẓџʌs], *a.* asiduo, constante, aplicado, hacendoso, diligente, laborioso.

assiduously [-lị], *adv.* asidua o diligentemente.

assiduousness [-nịs], *s. V.* ASSIDUITY.

assign [ạsáịn]. I. *va.* asignar, fijar, señalar, destinar, adjudicar, transferir; adscribir (a un cargo); (for.) consignar, ceder, traspasar. II. *vn.* hacer traspaso o cesión de bienes. III. *s.* (for.) cesionario; apoderado; (Am.) asignatario.

assignable [-ạbl], *a.* asignable, transferible, negociable, cesible.

assignat [ǽsịgnæt], *s.* asignado.

assignation [-éịṣọn], *s.* asignación, consignación; cesión, traspaso; cita, señalamiento de hora y lugar (ú. esp. de amor ilícito).

assignee [ạsáịni *o* ạsainị], *s.* cesionario; poderhabiente, apoderado; síndico. *V.* ASSIGN.

assigner [ạsáịnœ(r)], **assignor** [æsịnór], *s.* cesionista, cedente, asignante, transferidor.

assignment [ạsáịnmẹnt], *s.* asignación, señalamiento, cesión; encargo (periodístico, etc.); (for.) escritura de cesión de bienes, dejación, traspaso, renuncia, o traslación de dominio.

assimilable [ạsịmịlạbl], *a.* asimilable; semejable.

assimilate [-leịt]. I. *va.* asimilar; asemejar, comparar. II. *vn.* (fisiol.) asimilarse.

assimilation [-léịṣọn], *s.* asimilación; semejanza.

assimilative [ạsịmịleịtịv], *a.* asimilativo.

assist [ạsịst]. I. *va.* asistir, socorrer; auxiliar, ayudar. II. *vn.* ayudar; asistir, concurrir.

assistance [-ạns], *s.* auxilio, socorro, ayuda, asistencia; concurso; acudimiento.

assistant [-ạnt]. I. *s.* ayudante, auxiliar, agregado, adjunto, asistente, adjutor, portanveces; (igl.) acólito. II. *a.* ayudador, auxiliar; segundo; sub- (vg. *a. cashier,* cajero auxiliar; *a. engineer,* segundo maquinista; *a. editor,* subredactor o subdirector; *a. secretary,* subsecretario).

assize [ạsáịz], *s.* tasa.—*pl.* sesión de un tribunal.

associable [ạsóụṣạbl], *a.* asociable.

associate [ạsóụṣịeịt]. I. *va.* asociar, juntar, unir. II. *vn.* asociarse, juntarse, mancomunarse.

associate [-ịt]. I. *a.* asociado; confederado. II. *s.* compañero, (con)socio, aparcero, coadjutor; miembro, individuo de una sociedad; cómplice; (filos.) imagen asociada.

association [-éịṣọn], *s.* asociación; unión; conjunción; (com.) sociedad, compañía.—**A. football,** balompié, *m.,* juego del fútbol.—**a. of ideas,** asociación de ideas.—**Bar a.,** colegio de abogados.

associationism [-ịzm], *s.* (psic.) asociacionismo.

associative [ạsóụṣịeịtịv], *a.* asociativo.

assonance [ǽsonạns], *s.* asonancia.

assonant [-ạnt], *a.* y *s.* asonante.

assonate [-eịt], *vn.* asonar, asonantar.

assort [ạsórt]. I. *va.* ordenar, clasificar, separar, surtir con variedad. II. *vn.* asociarse; conformarse, concordar.

assorted [-ịd], *a.* variado, mezclado, surtido.

assortment [-mẹnt], *s.* clasificación, distribución; surtido variado, acopio.

assuage [ạswéịdẓ], *va.* mitigar, calmar, ablandar, aliviar, acallar, atemperar, apaciguar.

assuagement [-mẹnt], *s.* mitigación, alivio.

assuasive [ạswéịsịv], *a.* mitigativo, calmante.

assume [ạsúm]. I. *va.* tomar, asumir, arrogar; apropiar, usurpar; presumir, suponer, dar por sentado, poner por caso. II. *vn.* arrogarse, atribuirse, apropiarse.

assumed [-d], *a.* supuesto, dado por sentado; falso, fingido, pretendido, supositicio.

assuming [-ịŋ], *a.* arrogante, altivo, presuntuoso.—**a. that,** dado o supuesto que.

assumpsit [ạsʌmpsịt], *s.* (for.) promesa o pacto verbal; reclamación judicial.

assumption [-ṣọn], *s.* suposición, supuesto; toma, asunción, arrogación; arrogancia; (A., igl.)

asunción; fiesta de la asunción de la Virgen.—**a. of office,** toma de posesión.

assumptive [-tịv], *a.* supuesto; que puede asumirse; arrogante, presuntuoso.

assurance [ạṣúrạns], *s.* declaración, manifestación; seguridad, certeza, confianza, convicción; audacia, arrojo, resolución; descoco, descaro, desvergüenza; (com.) seguro. *V.* INSURANCE.

assure [ạṣúr], *va.* asegurar, afirmar; cerciorar, protestar; infundir confianza; confirmar; (com.) asegurar contra algún riesgo.—**to a. of,** asegurar, manifestar.

assured [-d]. I. *a.* seguro, cierto; descarado, atrevido, audaz. II. *s.* y *a.* (com.) asegurado (contra algún riesgo).

assuredly [-ịdlị], *adv.* cierta o indubitablemente, sin duda; con toda seguridad, de fijo.

assuredness [-ịdnịs], *s.* certeza, seguridad.

assurer [ạṣúrœ(r)], *s.* asegurador.

Assyrian [ạsịrịạn], *a.* y *s.* asirio; de Asiria.

Assyriologist [-álodẓist], *s.* asiriólogo.

Assyriology [-dẓị], *s.* asiriología.

astasia [ạstéịẓịạ], *s.* (med.) astasia.

astatic [eịstǽtịk], *a.* (fís.) astático.—**a. pair,** par de agujas astáticas.

astatize [ǽstạtạịz], *va.* hacer astático.

aster [ǽstœ(r)], *s.* (bot.) aster, planta asteroidea; (biol.) aster.—**a. ray** (biol.), estría radial que parte de la esfera atractiva.

Asterias [ǽstírịạs], *s. pl.* (zool.) astéridos, asterídeos; clase (*f.*) de estrellamares.

asteriated [ǽstírịeịtịd], *a.* (min.) que tiene la propiedad del asterismo.—**a. sapphire,** zafiro que tiene esta propiedad.

asterisk [ǽstẹrịsk], *s.* asterisco.

asterism [ǽstẹrịzm], *s.* (astr.) asterismo, constelación; grupo de estrellas; (impr.) grupo triangular de tres asteriscos; (min.) asterismo, reflexión de la luz en forma de estrella.

astern [ạstέrn], *adv.* (mar.) por la popa, a popa.

asteroid [ǽstẹrọịd], *s.* (astr.) asteroide; (zool.) asteroideo, estrellamar.

asteroidean [ǽstẹróịdịạn], *a.* y *s.* (zool.) asteroideo, estelárido.

asthenia [æsθínịạ̈], *s.* (med.) astenia, debilidad general.

asthenic [æsθénịk], *a.* asténico, flaco, débil.

asthma [ǽzmạ̈], *s.* (med.) asma.—**a. paper,** papel impregnado de salitre.

asthmatic(al [æzmǽtịk(ạl)], *a.* y *s.* asmático.

astigmatic [æstịgmǽtịk], *a.* astigmático.

astigmatism [æstígmạtịzm], *s.* (ópt. y med.) astigmatismo.

astigmometer [æstịgmámẹtœ(r)], *s.* astigmómetro.

astir [ạstέr], *adv.* activo, en movimiento.

astomatous [ạstámạtʌs], *a.* (biol., zool.) sin boca ni poros respiratorios.

astonish [ạstánịs], *va.* asombrar, pasmar, helar.

astonished [-t], *pp.* y *a.* asombrado, atónito, pasmado, estupefacto, helado.

astonishing [-ịŋ], *a.* sorprendente, asombroso, pasmoso.—**astonishingly** [-lị], *adv.* pasmosamente, asombrosamente.

astonishment [-mẹnt], *s.* pasmo, asombro, espanto, sorpresa.

astound [ạstáụnd], *va.* y *vn.* pasmar, sorprender; aturdir, confundir, helar, sacar de tino.

astounding [-ịŋ], *a.* asombroso, pasmoso, sorprendente; (fam.) despampanante.

astraddle [ạstrǽdl], *adv.* a horcajadas.

astragal [ǽstrạgạl], *s.* (arq. y arti.) astrágalo, tondino, anillo; (anat.) astrágalo.—*pl.* dados.

astragalus [ǽstrǽgạlʌs], *s.* (anat.) astrágalo, talón, empeine, taba, chita; (bot.) astrágalo, tragacanto, alquitira.

astrakhan [ǽstrạkạn], *s.* astracán (piel); tela astracán (imitación de la piel).

astral [ǽstrạl]. I. *a.* astral, estelar, sidéreo, sideral.—**a. body,** (teos.) cuerpo astral; fantasma.—a. lamp, lámpara astral (que no arroja sombras). II. s. lámpara astral.

astrand [ǽstrænd], a. (mar.) encallado, varado.

astray [ǽstréi], adv. y a. desviada o descarriadamente; por el mal camino; desviado, errado.— **to go a.**, extraviarse, perderse, errar el camino.

astrict [æstríkt], va. astringir, apretar.

astriction [æstríkʃon], s. astricción.

astrictive [-tiv], a. astrictivo, constrictivo.

astride [æstráid], adv. a horcajadas.

astringe [æstríndʒ], va. astringir; apretar, comprimir; restringir.

astringency [-ɛnsi], s. astricción, astringencia; aspereza de carácter.

astringent [-ɛnt], a. y s. astringente, estíptico; austero; áspero, agrio.

astrochemistry [æstrokémistri], s. astroquímica.

astrography [æstrágrafi], s. astrografía.

astrolabe [ǽstroleib], s. astrolabio.

astrolater [æstrálætœ(r)], s. astrólatra, mf.

astrolatry [-tri], s. astrolatría.

astrologer [æstrálodʒœ(r)], s. astrólogo, judiciario.

astrologic(al [æstroládʒik(al)], a. astrológico, judiciario.—**astrologically** [-i], adv. astrológicamente.

astrology [æstrálodʒi], s. astrología.

astrometer [æstrámɛtœ(r)], s. astrómetro.

astrometry [-tri], s. astrometría.

astronomer [æstránomœ(r)], s. astrónomo.

astronomic(al [æstronámik(al)], a. astronómico. —**astronomically** [-i], adv. astronómicamente.

astronomy [æstránomi], s. astronomía.

astrophotography [æstrofotágrafi], s. astrofotografía, fotografía de los astros.

astrophotometry [-fotámetri], s. astrofotometría.

astrophysical [-fízikal], a. astrofísico.

astrophysicist [-fízisist], s. astrofísico.

astrophysics [-fíziks], s. astrofísica.

astrosphere [ǽstrosfir], s. (biol.) esfera atractiva del aster.

astrut [æstrát], adv. hinchadamente, pomposamente, con ínfulas.

astute [æstiút], a. astuto, agudo, sagaz.

astuteness [-nis], s. astucia, sagacidad.

asunder [æsándœ(r)], adv. separadamente; en dos, a pedazos.—**to part a.**, separar.

aswim [æswím], adv. y a. flotante, flotando; a nado, nadando.

asyllabic [eisilǽbik], a. no silábico.

asylum [æsáilam], s. asilo, refugio, amparo; acogida, sagrado; casa de beneficencia.

asymmetric(al [eisimétrik(al)], a. asimétrico.

asymmetry [eisímitri], s. asimetría.

asymptote [ǽsimptout], s. (geom.) asíntota.

asymptotic [æsimptátik], a. asintótico.

asynchronism [eisínkronizm], s. asincronismo.

asynchronous [-nas], a. asincrónico.

asyndeton [æsíndetan], s. (ret.) asíndeton.

at [æt], prep. a; con; de; por; de acuerdo con; vg. at the door, a, o en, la puerta; at six dollars, a seis dólares; at your disposal, a su disposición; at nine o'clock, a las nueve; angry at me, enfadado conmigo; surprised at his conduct, sorprendido de su conducta; at one stroke, de un golpe; at Rome, en Roma; at that time, en ese tiempo; at war, en guerra; enter at this gate, entre por esta puerta; I did it at his command, lo hice por orden suya, o según sus órdenes. Con un substantivo de acción, at forma frases adverbiales que se traducen por el gerundio; vg. at play, jugando; at work, trabajando. En lenguaje fam., se usa por sí solo después de where y to be para indicar confusión, atolondramiento, o simplemente lugar (como en una narración); vg. I didn't know where I was at, yo estaba perplejo, o confundido; no sabía por dónde andaba: where were we at in the story? ¿por dónde íbamos en el cuento? Antes de nombres propios en el caso posesivo forma expresiones elípticas en que se sobrentiende casa, tienda, etc.; vg. I bought this at Johnson's, compré esto en la tienda de Johnson; we were at Porter's, estábamos en la casa (o restaurante, hotel, tienda, etc.) de Porter.

atabal [ǽtabæl], s. atabal, timbal moro.

atacamite [atékamait], s. (min.) atacamita.

ataghan [ǽtagæn], s. yatagán.

ataman [ǽtamæn], s. atamán, jefe cosaco.

ataunt [atónt], adv. (mar.) enteramante aparejado.

atavism [ǽtavizm], s. atavismo.

atavistic [ætavístik], atavic [ætǽvik], a. atávico.

ataxia [atǽksia], s. (med.) ataxia.

ataxic [atǽksik], a. atáxico.

ate [eit], pret. de TO EAT.

atelier [ætœlyei], s. taller, estudio.

athanasia [æθanéiʒiä], s. inmortalidad.

atheism [éiθiizm], s. ateísmo.

atheist [éiθiist], s. ateísta, ateo.

atheistic(al [eiθiístik(al)], a. ateo, ateísta, ateístico, impío.

atheneum [æθeníam], s. ateneo.

Athenian [æθíniạn], a. y s. ateniense.

athermancy [eiθérmansi], s. atermancia, impermeabilidad al calor radiante.—**athermanous** [-manạs], a. atérmano, atérmico.

athirst [aθérst], adv. sediento.

athlete [ǽθlit], s. atleta, m.; gimnasta, m.; deportista.—**a.'s foot**, (med.) tricotifosis de los pies.—**a.'s heart**, (med.) corazón atlético, hipertrofia del corazón.

athletic [æθlétik], a. atlético; fornido, lacertoso. —**a. contest**, concurso atlético.—**a. event**, prueba de atletismo.—**a. field**, campo atlético o de deporte.

athletics [-s], s. pl. deportes, deportismo, atletismo; agonística, gimnasia.

athwart [aθwórt]. I. prep. al o a través de, por el través de; contra.—**a. ship(s)**, (mar.) de babor a estribor. II. adv. contrariamente, a tuertas.

atilt [atílt], adv. en postura inclinada; en ristre.

Atlantean [ætlæntiạn], a. atlántico.

atlantes [ætlǽntiz], s. pl. (arq.) atlantes. V. ATLAS.

Atlantic [ætlǽntik]. I. a. atlántico.—**A. Charter**, (pol.) carta del Atlántico (1941). II. s. el mar Atlántico.

atlas [ǽtlạs], s. atlas; (arq.) atlante o telamón; (anat.) atlas.

atmometer [ætmámetœ(r)], s. atmómetro.

atmosphere [ǽtmosfir], s. atmósfera, aire, medio ambiente; alcance, esfera de influencia; (fís.) atmósfera, unidad de presión.

atmospheric(al [-férik(al)], a. atmosférico.

atmospherics [-fériks], s. (rad.) perturbaciones eléctricas atmosféricas (= STATIC).

atoll [ǽtal], s. atolón, isla madrepórica.

atom [ǽtọm], s. (fís., quím.) átomo, corpúsculo; (fig.) átomo, pizca, jota.—**a. bomb**, bomba atómica.—**a. smasher**, (fís.) ciclotrón, aparato para desagregar los átomos.—**a. splitting**, fisión del átomo.

atomic(al [ætámik(al)], a. atómico; diminuto.— **a. heat**, calor atómico.—**a. number**, número de cargas eléctricas positivas de un átomo.—**a. theory**, teoría atómica.—**a. weight**, peso atómico.

atomicity [ætọmísiti], s. (quím.) atomicidad.

atomism [ǽtọmizm], s. atomismo.

atomist [ǽtọmist], s. atomista.

atomistic [ætọmístik], a. atómico; atomístico.

atomization [ætọmaizéiʃọn], s. atomización, pulverización.

atomize [ǽtọmaiz], va. atomizar, pulverizar, rociar.—**atomizer** [-œ(r)], s. pulverizador, vaporizador; aromatizador, perfumador.

atomy [ǽtọmi], s. átomo; motita; (ant.) esqueleto; enano, pigmeo.

atone [atóụn], va. y vn. (gen. con for) expiar.

purgar; reparar, compensar, dar reparación, satisfacer; propiciar, aplacar.

atonement [-mẹnt], s. expiación, reparación; compensación, satisfacción; propiciación, sacrificio.

atonic [ætánịk]. **I.** a. (med.) atónico, débil, falto de vigor; (gram.) átono, sin acento prosódico; (fon.) sordo. **II.** s. (med.) calmante; (gram.) sílaba inacentuada; (fon.) consonante sorda.

atony [ǽtọnị], s. (med.) atonía.

atop [ɐtáp], adv. y prep. encima (de).

atrabilarian [ætrɐbịléịrịɐn], a. y s., **atrabilarious** [-ʌs], a. atrabiliario, atrabilioso; melancólico, hipocondríaco.

atrabilious [ætrɐbíịlyʌs], a. V. ATRABILARIAN.

atrichia [ɐtríkịɐ], **atrichosis** [ætrịkóụsịs], s. pérdida o ausencia de pelo; calvicie; alopecia.

atrium [éịtrịʌm], s. atrio.

atrocious [ɐtróụsʌs], a. atroz, nefando, execrable. —**atrociously** [-lị], adv. atrozmente.—**atrociousness** [-nịs], **atrocity** [ɐtrásịtị], s. atrocidad, enormidad, maldad horrible.

atrophic [ɐtráfịk], a. atrófico, descaecido.

atrophied [ǽtrofịd], a. atrofiado; enflaquecido.

atrophy [ǽtrofị]. **I.** s. (med.) atrofia. **II.** va. atrofiar. **III.** vn. atrofiarse.

atropin(e [ǽtropịn], s. (quím., farm.) atropina.

attach [ɐtǽch]. **I.** va. pegar, juntar, atar, vincular, fijar, conectar; enganchar; prender, coger; asignar; dar, atribuir (importancia, etc.); ganar, granjearse; acompañar, adjuntar; (elec.) enchufar; (for.) embargar, secuestrar, decomisar, incautarse (de bienes, etc.). **II.** vr. pegarse, adherirse.

attachable [-ɐbl], a. pegadizo; secuestrable.

attaché [atašéị], s. (dipl.) agregado.

attached [ɐtǽcht], pp. y a. fijo; anejo o anexo; contiguo; adicto, devoto.

attachment [ɐtǽchmẹnt], s. unión, enlace, vinculación, fijación; adminículo, accesorio; afecto, cariño; adhesión, apego, devoción, ley, f., fidelidad; (elec.) enchufe; (for.) secuestro, embargo, incautación.

attack [ɐtǽk]. **I.** va. y vn. atacar, acometer, arremeter, asaltar, atentar, embestir; abordar (un asunto). **II.** s. ataque, agresión, asalto, atentado, arremetida, embestid(ur)a; (med.) acceso.

attain [ɐtéịn], va., vn lograr, alcanzar, obtener.

attainable [-ɐbl], a. asequible, accesible, realizable.—**attainableness** [-nịs], s. accesibilidad; calidad de alcanzable o realizable.

attainder [ɐtéịndœ(r)], s. (for.) proscripción o muerte civil.—**bill of a.,** decreto de proscripción y confiscación.

attainment [ɐtéịnmẹnt], s. logro, consecución, obtención, adquisición.—pl. dotes, prendas.

attaint [ɐtéịnt]. **I.** va. deshonrar, infamar; corromper, viciar; (for.) condenar, proscribir. **II.** s. mancha, baldón; (for.) muerte civil.

attar [ǽtɐ(r)], s. aceite esencial (de rosas, etc.).

attemper [ɐtémpœ(r)], va. atemperar, diluir, mollficar; acomodar; harmonizar. V. TEMPER.

attempt [ɐtémpt]. **I.** va. intentar, atentar; aventurar; tentar; probar, ensayar; procurar o querer (hacer algo). **II.** vn. probar, pretender. **III.** s. prueba, ensayo, esfuerzo, tentativa, atentado, conato (de rebelión, etc.).—**attemptability** [-ɐbịlịtị], s. la calidad de poderse intentar.—**attemptable** [-ɐbl], a. intentable.

attend [ɐténd]. **I.** va. atender, cuidar; servir; acompañar, asistir o concurrir a, presenciar; oír(misa); auxiliar (a un moribundo); cortejar (a una dama); seguir (como efecto o consecuencia). **II.** vn. atender; acudir; prestar atención, oír; asistir, concurrir.—**to a. on,** o **upon,** servir a.—**to a. to,** despachar; entender u ocuparse en.—**well attended,** muy concurrido (espectáculo, etc.).

attendance [-ɐns], s. presencia, asistencia; (for.) comparecencia; corte, f., obsequio; tren, séquito,

comitiva, acompañamiento; público, concurrencia, auditorio; servidumbre, asistencia, servicio.—**to dance a. on,** servir obsequiosamente.

attendant [-ɐnt]. **I.** s. sirviente, servidor; encargado; cortesano; seguidor, concomitante, acompañante; cortejo, galán, obsequiante.—pl. subalternos, tren, séquito, servidumbre. **II.** a. concomitante, acompañante, concurrente.—**attending physician,** médico de cabecera.

attention [ɐténšọn], s. atención, miramiento, esmero, cuidado, ojo; (med.) asistencia; (mil.) voz de mando ¡atención!—pl. cortejo; galanteo, agasajo, obsequio.

attentive [ɐténtịv], a. atento, solícito, aplicado; galante, obsequioso, cortés.—**attentively** [-lị], adv. atentamente, con atención y cuidado.—**attentiveness** [-nịs], s. cuidado; miramiento; cortesía, finura.

attenuant [ɐtényuɐnt], a. y s. atenuante.

attenuate [ɐtényueịt]. **I.** va. atenuar, adelgazar, diluir, disminuir; extenuar. **II.** vn. atenuarse, adelgazarse, etc. **III.** a. atenuado, delgado.

attenuating [-ịŋ], a. extenuativo.

attenuation [-eịšọn], s. atenuación, adelgazamiento, flaqueza; extenuación; dilución.

attest [ɐtést], va. atestiguar, atestar, deponer, declarar, certificar; garantizar; autenticar, confirmar; dar testimonio (de); (for.) dar fe.

attest, attestation [ætéstéịšọn], s. atestación, deposición, testimonio, confirmación, auténtica, certificado, certificación.

attestor [ætéstọ(r)], s. testigo; certificador.

attic [ǽtịk], s. desván, guardilla, sotabanco, buhardilla, camaranchón; (arq.) ático.

Attic, a. ático, clásico.—**A. salt** o **wit,** sal ática.

Atticism [ǽtịsịzm], s. aticismo.

attire [ɐtáị(r)]. **I.** va. vestir, ataviar, adornar. **II.** s. atavío, adorno, traje, ropa; astas (f. pl.) de ciervo.

attitude [ǽtịtjud], s. actitud, ademán, postura; (aer.) posición.—**attitudinal** [ætịtjúdịnɐl], a. referente a la actitud.

attitudinarian [-nérịɐn], **attitudinizer** [ætịtjúdịnaịzœ(r)], s. el que se coloca en posturas afectadas.—**attitudinize** [-naịz], vn. entonarse, pavonearse, tomar posturas afectadas.

attorney [ɐtórnị], s. (for.) abogado, apoderado, poderhabiente.—**a. at law,** procurador público, procurador de oficio en los tribunales.—**a. general,** (Ingl.) fiscal de la corona; (E. U.) fiscal del estado, ministro de justicia, que actúa como consejero y apoderado o abogado de la nación.—**a. in fact** = PRIVATE ATTORNEY.—**district a.,** fiscal de un distrito judicial.—**private a.,** apoderado, agente, encargado por otro de asuntos extrajudiciales.—**public a.** = A. AT LAW.—**by a.,** por poder (P. P.).—**to act as a.,** procurar.

attorneyship [-šịp], s. procuraduría.

attract [ɐtrǽkt], va. y vn. atraer; captar; cautivar, seducir.—**to a. attention,** llamar la atención.

attractability [-ɐbịlịtị], s. calidad de atraíble.

attractable [-ɐbl], a. atraíble.

attracter, attractor [-œ(r)], s. el que atrae.

attraction [ɐtrǽkšọn], s. atracción; atractivo, aliciente, interés.

attractive [ɐtrǽktịv], a. atractivo, atrayente, interesante; agradable, simpático.—**attractively** [-lị], adv. atractivamente.—**attractiveness** [-nịs], s. atracción, calidad de atractivo; gracia; hechizos.

attributable [ɐtríbịutɐbl], a. atribuible, imputable.

attribute [ɐtríbịut], va. atribuir, imputar, achacar.

attribute [ǽtrịbịut], s. atributo; característica, distintivo; (gram.) atributo.

attribution [ætrịbịúšọn], s. atribución, atributo.

attributive [ɐtríbịutịv]. **I.** a. atributivo; (b.a.) atribuído. **II.** s. (gram.) calificativo.

attrite [ətráit], *a.* (teol.) pesaroso, atrito.

attrition [ætríʃən], *s.* roce, rozadura, frotación, frote, refregón, desgaste; (teol.) atrición.

attune [ətiún], *va.* armonizar, acordar, afinar.

atwain [ətwéin], *adv.* (ant.) en dos, separadamente.

atwirl [ətwǿrl], *a.* y *adv.* en rotación, girando, dando vueltas.—**atwist** [ətwíst], *adv.* y *a.* torcidamente, al través, sesgado.

aubade [oubád], *s.* (mús. y poét.) alborada, albada.

auburn [ǿbœrn], *a.* castaño rojizo.

auction [ǿkʃən]. I. *s.* almoneda, subasta, remate; (Am.) venduta.—**a. room,** martillo.—**to put up at a.,** poner en pública subasta. II. *va.* almonedar, subastar, rematar.

auctioneer [ɔ̀kʃɔnír]. I. *s.* subastador, pregonero, rematador; (Am.) martillero, vendutero. II. *va.* vender en pública subasta.

audacious [ɔdéiʃʌs], *a.* audaz, osado; descarado.

audaciously [-li], *adv.* audaz, osada, arrojada o atrevidamente; descaradamente.

audaciousness [-nis], **audacity** [ɔdǽsiti], *s.* audacia, osadía, arrojo; impudencia, descaro.

audibility [ɔ̀dibíliti], **audibleness** [ǿdiblnis], *s.* audibilidad, perceptibilidad.

audible [ǿdibl], *a.* audible, oíble, perceptible.

audibly [ǿdibli], *adv.* audiblemente.

audience [ǿdiens], *s.* auditorio, concurso, concurrencia, público; los oyentes o circunstantes; audición; audiencia o entrevista.—**a. chamber,** sala o cámara de recepción; (for.) audiencia.

audient [ǿdient], *a.* oyente; que escucha.

audio-frequency [ǿdiou fríkwensi], *s.* (rad.) audio-frecuencia; frecuencia auditiva.

audiometer [ɔdiámetœ(r)], *s.* audiómetro, instrumento para probar la audición.

audion [ǿdiɔn], *s.* (rad.) audión, *m.* (marca de fábrica).

audiphone [ǿdifoun], *s.* audífono, aparato para transmitir el sonido a los sordos por los dientes.

audit [ǿdit]. I. *s.* intervención y ajuste de cuentas. II. *va.* intervenir, revisar o glosar una cuenta.—**auditing of accounts,** intervención de cuentas.

audition [ɔdíʃən], *s.* audición; prueba de idoneidad, examen de prueba (a menudo en concurso) a que se somete a quien solicita un puesto como músico, etc.

auditive [ǿditiv], *a.* auditivo, auditorio.

auditor [ǿditɔ(r)], *s.* interventor, revisor o glosador de cuentas; contador, perito contabilista; ordenador de pagos; oyente, oidor, auditor.

auditorium [ɔ̀ditórjʌm], *s.* auditorio; salón de actos; sala de espectáculos; cualquier sala, teatro o edificio destinado a reuniones y funciones públicas.

auditorship [ǿditɔrʃip], *s.* oficio de interventor; intervención; contaduría.

auditory [ǿditori]. I. *s.* auditorio, público; sala, teatro. II. *a.* auditorio, auditivo.

Augean [ɔdʒían], *a.* referente a Augías; sucísimo; corrompidísimo.—**the A. stables,** los establos de Augías (apl. a lugares muy sucios y a gente o asociaciones corrompidas o desmoralizadas).

auger [ǿgœ(r)], *s.* barrena; taladro; sonda de taladrar.—**a. bit,** (carp.) gusanillo de taladro. —**a. worm,** (ent.) gusano horadador.

aught [ɔt]. I. *s.* algo; cero; (con negación) nada. II. *adv.* absolutamente; en cualquier respecto; en cualquier, o algún, grado.

augite [ǿdʒait], *s.* (min.) augita.

augment [ɔgmént], *va.* y *vn.* aumentar; crecer.

augmentable [-abl], *a.* aumentable.

augmentation [-éiʃən], *s.* aumentación, aumento, acrecentamiento; creces, *f. pl.*

augmentative [-ativ], *a.* aumentativo.

augur [ǿgœ(r)], *s.* augur, agorero, adivino, arúspice.

augur, *va.* y *vn.* augurar, pronosticar, predecir,
agorar, ominar.—**to a. ill** (o **well**), ser de mal (o buen) agüero.

augural [ǿgyʊ̀ral], **augurial** [ɔgyúrial], *a.* augural.

augury [ǿgyʊ̀ri], *s.* augurio, agüero, pronóstico.

august [ɔgʌ́st], *a.* augusto, majestuoso.

August [ǿgʌst], *s.* agosto (mes).

Augustan [ɔgʌ́stan], *a.* augustal, de Augusto.

Augustinian [ɔgʌstíniən], *a.* y *s.* agustiniano; agustino (monje, orden).

augustness [ɔgʌ́stnis], *s.* majest(uosid)ad.

auk [ɔk], *s.* (orn.) alca, ave marítima relacionada a los pingüinos.

auld [ɔld], *a.* (Esco.) viejo, antiguo.—**a. lang syne** [-læŋ sáin], antaño, tiempos que fueron.

aulic [ǿlik], *a.* áulico, palaciego.

aunt [ænt *o* ant], *s.* tía.—**aunty, auntie** [ǽnti], *s. dim.* tía; vieja; (E. U. del Sur) negra vieja.

aura [ǿrɑ], *s.* magnetismo animal; influencia psíquica; aura, céfiro; (med.) aura epiléptica o histérica.

aural [ǿral], *a.* auditivo, auricular, del oído.

aurantiaceous [ɔ̀rænti-éiʃʌs], *a.* (bot.) auranciáceo.

aurate [ǿrit], *s.* (quím.) aurato.

aurated [ǿreitid], *a.* con orejas. *V.* AUREATE.

aureate [ǿrit], *a.* áureo, dorado; espléndido.

aurelia [ɔrílja], *s.* (ent.) crisálida, ninfa.

aureola [ɔríolɑ], **aureole** [ǿriʊl], *s.* aureola, auréola, corona.

auric [ǿrik], *a.* de oro, del oro; (quím.) áurico.

auricle [ǿrikl], *s.* (anat.) aurícula o ala del corazón; aurícula o pabellón de la oreja.

auricula [ɔríkyʊ̀lɑ], *s.* (bot.) oreja de oso; (zool.) apéndice en forma de oreja.

auricular [ɔríkyʊ̀lɑ(r)], *a.* auricular; oíble; confidencial, secreto, dicho al oído.

auricularly [-li], *adv.* al oído, secretamente.

auriculate(d [ɔríkyʊ̀leit(id], *a.* orejudo; en forma de oreja.

auriferous [ɔríferʌs], *a.* (poét.) aurífero.

auriform [ǿriform], *a.* en forma de oreja.

Auriga [ɔráigɑ], *s.* (astr.) Auriga.

aurist [ǿrist], *s.* (med.) aurista, otólogo.

aurochs [ǿraks], *s.* (zool.) uro, bizonte europeo.

aurora [ɔrǿrɑ], *s.* aurora, alba, alborada.—**a. australis,** aurora austral.—**a. borealis,** aurora boreal.

auroral [ɔrǿral], *a.* matutino; rosáceo.

aurum [ǿrɑm], *s.* (quím.) oro.

auscultate [ǿskʌlteit], *va.* y *vn.* (med.) auscultar.

auscultation [-éiʃən], *s.* (med.) auscultación; atención.

auspicate [ǿspikeit], *va.* inaugurar o principiar con buenos auspicios.

auspice [ǿspis], *s.* auspicio, presagio; protección, favor, dirección, auspicio (gen. *pl.*).—**under the auspices of,** bajo los auspicios de, (Am.) auspiciado por.

auspicial [ɔspíʃal], *a.* perteneciente al auspicio.

auspicious [ɔspíʃʌs], *a.* feliz, favorable; benigno, propicio.

auspiciously [-li], *adv.* con buenos auspicios, auspiciosamente, felizmente.

auspiciousness [-nis], *s.* prosperidad; buenos auspicios.

austere [ɔstír], *a.* austero, severo, rígido; rudo, adusto; agrio, ácido, acerbo.—**austerely** [-li], *adv.* austeramente.—**austereness** [-nis], **austerity** [ɔstériti], *s.* austeridad, rigorismo, severidad.

Austin Friars [ǿstin fráiɑrz], *s. pl.* frailes Agustinos.

austral [ǿstral], *a.* austral, meridional.

Australian [ɔstréljan], *a.* y *s.* australiano.

Austrian [ǿstrian], *a.* y *s.* austríaco.

Austro-Hungarian [ǿstrouhʌŋgérian], *a.* y *s.* austrohúngaro.

autarchy, autarky [ǿtarki], *s.* autarquía, independencia económica (de un país).

authentic(al [əθéntįk(ąl], *a*. auténtico, legítimo, fehaciente, original.

authentically [-į], **authenticly** [-lį], *adv*. auténticamente.

authenticalness [-ąlnįs], **authenticity** [əθentí-sįtį], *s*. autenticidad.

authenticate [əθéntįkejt], *va*. autenticar, autorizar, refrendar.

authentication [-éįşǫn], *s*. (for.) autenticación, refrendación.

author [óθǫ(r)], *s*. autor; escritor.

authoress [-įs], *s*. autora, escritora.

authoritarian [əθariţériąn], *s*. y *a*. autoritario, autoritarista, defensor de la autoridad absoluta o excesiva.—**authoritarianism** [-įzm], *s*. autoritarismo.

authoritative [əθárįtejtįv], *a*. autorizado, que autoriza; autoritario; positivo, perentorio, terminante.—**authoritatively** [-lį], *adv*. autorizadamente.—**authoritativeness** [-nįs], *s*. calidad de autorizado o autoritario.

authority [əθárįtį], *s*. autoridad; autorización; dominio, jurisdicción, mando, poder, férula; perito, experto; facultad; representación; junta, comisión, cuerpo directivo, departamento.—*pl*. funcionarios, autoridad pública.—**I have it from the best a.**, lo sé de buena tinta; lo tengo de buena fuente o mano.—**printed by a.**, impreso con licencia.

authorization [əθǫrįzéįşǫn], *s*. autorización, sanción, legalización.

authorize [óθǫrajz], *va*. autorizar, facultar, apoderar, sancionar, acreditar, otorgar, legalizar.

authorship [óθǫršįp], *s*. estado, calidad o profesión de autor; invención; paternidad literaria.

auto [ótǫų]. **I.** *s*. (fam.) automóvil, auto. **II.** *vn*. (fam.) pasear o viajar en automóvil.

Autobahn [ótoban], *s*. (alem.) autoestrada, autopista.

autobiographic(al [otobajográefįk(ąl], *a*. autobiográfico.

autobiography [otobajágrąfį], *s*. autobiografía.

autoboat [ótoboųt], *s*. lancha o bote automóvil.

autobus [-bʌs], *s*. bus, autobús, autoómnibus.

autocade [-kejd], *s*. desfile de automóviles.

autocar [-kar], *s*. (coche) automóvil; autocar.

autochthon [otákθǫn], *s*. autóctono.

autochthonal, autochthonous [-ąl, -ʌs], *a*. autóctono.

autochthonism [-įzm], **autochthony** [-į], *s*. autoctonía.

autoclave [ótoklejv], *s*. autoclave, *f*., marmita hermética.

autocoherer [otokohírœ(r)], *s*. (rad.), autocohesor, autodetector.

autocracy [otákrąsį], *s*. autocracia.

autocrat [ótokræt], *s*. autócrata, *m.f*.

autocratic(al [otokrǽtįk(ąl], *a*. autocrático.

auto-da-fé [otoụdąféj], *s*. auto de fe.

autodidact [ótodįdækt], *s*. autodidacto.—**autodidactic** [-dæktįk], *a*. autodidacto; autodidáctico.

autodrome [ótodroųm], *s*. (dep.) autódromo.

autodyne [ótodajn], *a*. (rad.) autodino.

autogamous [otágąmʌs], *a*. (bot.) autógamo, autofecundante.

autogamy [otágąmį], *s*. (bot., zool.) autogamia, autofecundación.

autogenesis [otodżénesįs], *s*. (biol.) autogénesis.

autogenous [otádżenʌs], *a*. autógeno.—**a. soldering**, (elec.) soldadura eléctrica autógena.

autogiro, autogyro [otodżájroų], *s*. (aer.) autogiro (es marca de fábrica).

autograph [ótogræf]. **I.** *a*. y *s*. autógrafo. **II.** *va*. autografiar; escribir o inscribir una celebridad su autógrafo o firma (en un libro, etc.).

autographic(al [otográfįk(ąl], *a*. autógrafo; autográfico; (tlg.) autorregistrador; que recibe o transmite en facsímile.

autography [otágrąfį], *s*. autografía.

autoinfection [otoųįnfékşǫn], *s*. autoinfección.

autointoxication [-įntaksįkéįşǫn], *s*. autointoxicación, autoenvenenamiento del organismo.

autoist [ótojst], *s*. (fam.) automovilista.

automat [ótomæt], *s*. artificio o mecanismo automático; restaurante de servicio mecánico.

automatic(al [ǫtomǽtįk(ąl], *a*. automático.

automatism [otámąţįzm], *s*. (fisiol., filos. y psic.) automatismo.

automaton [otámąţan], *s*. autómata, *m*.

automobile [otomóųbil]. **I.** *s*. automóvil, coche.—**a. horn**, bocina, klaxon. **II.** *a*. = AUTO-MOTIVE.

automobiling [-įŋ], *s*. automovilismo.

automobilism [-įzm], *s*. automovilismo.

automobilist [-įst], *s*. automovilista.

automotive [otomóųtįv], *a*. automotor, automotriz, automóvil, automovilista.

autonomic [otonámįk], *a*. autonómico.

autonomist [otánomįst], *s*. autonomista.

autonomous [-mʌs], *a*. autónomo.

autonomy [-mį], *s*. autonomía.

autoplasty [ótoplæstį], *s*. (cir.) autoplastia.

autopsy [ótapsį], *s*. autopsia, necropsia.

autostrada [ótostrada], *s*. (ital.) autopista.

autosuggestion [-sʌgdżéschǫn], *s*. autosugestión.

autotherapy [-θérąpį], *s*. (med.) autoterapia.

autotomy [otátomį], *s*. (biol.) autotomía.

autotoxemia [ototaksímįą], *s*. autointoxicación.

autotruck [ótotrʌk], *s*. autocamión, *m*.

autotype [-tajp], *s*. facsímil(e), copia exacta.

autotypy [-į], *s*. autotipia.

autumn [ótʌm], *s*. otoño.

autumnal [otámnąl], *a*. otoñal, autumnal.

auxiliary [ogzílyąrį]. **I.** *a*. auxiliar; auxiliatorio, subsidiario. **II.** *s*. auxiliador, coadyuvante, sufragáneo.

avail [ąvéįl]. **I.** *va*. aprovechar, beneficiar, valer. **II.** *vn*. valer, servir, ser útil o ventajoso.—**to a. oneself of**, valerse de, aprovecharse de, servirse de.—**not to a. oneself of**, desperdiciar.—**it avails nothing**, de nada sirve. **III.** *s*. provecho, utilidad; eficacia.—*pl*. beneficios, producto (de una venta).—**to no a.**, en vano; sin resultado.

available [-ąbl], *a*. aprovechable, disponible, asequible, accesible, utilizable.

availableness [-nįs], **availability** [-bílįtį], *s*. disponibilidad, calidad de aprovechable; eficacia, valor.

availably [-ąblį], *adv*. eficazmente, provechosamente, útilmente.

avalanche [ǽvąlænch], *s*. lurte, alud, *m.;* (fig.) torrente, torbellino; (gal.) avalancha.

avarice [ǽvąrįs], *s*. avaricia, codicia, sordidez.

avaricious [ævąrįšʌs], *a*. avaro, avariento, codicioso, miserable.—**avariciously** [-lį], *adv*. avaramente, avarientamente.—**avariciousness** [-nįs], *s*. avaricia.

Avars [avárz], *s. pl*. (hist.) ávaros.

avast [ąvǽst], *interj*. (mar.) ¡forte! ¡basta!

avatar [ævątár], *s*. (mit.) avatar (encarnación de Vichnú); encarnación.

avaunt [ąvónt], *interj*. (ant.) ¡fuera! ¡atrás! ¡vete!

Ave Maria, Ave Mary [ávįmąríą o éįvį mérį], *s*. (igl.) avemaría.

avenaceous [ævęnéįšʌs], *a*. (bot.) avenáceo; de avena.

avenge [ąvéndż], *va*. y *vn*. vengar, vindicar.

avengement [-męnt], *s*. venganza.

avenger [-œ(r)], *s*. vengador.

avens [ǽvįnz], *s*. (bot.) gariofilea.

aventail [ǽvįntéįl], *s.* = VENTAIL.

aventurin(e [ąvénchųrįn], *s*. (min.) venturina.

avenue [ǽvęnjų], *s*. avenida, calzada; alameda, carrera; vía, entrada, pasadizo.—**a. of trade**, ruta comercial.

aver [ąvǿr], *va*. asegurar, afirmar; declarar.

average [ǽvęrįdż]. **I.** *s*. promedio, término medio; cosa o persona ordinaria o de término medio; (com.) avería; compensación por averías.—**a. bond**, fianza que se da al capitán de un barco por indemnización de averías.—**general**

a., (mar.) avería gruesa o común.—**on an a.,** como promedio, por término medio.—**petty a.,** avería ordinaria, gastos menores. **II.** *a.* medio, de término medio: común, ordinario, corriente, típico.—**a. speed,** velocidad media. **III.** *va.* calcular el término medio o hallar el promedio de; prorratear, promediar, tantear; ascender por término medio a (tanto).—**to a. 50 miles per hour,** sacar un promedio de 50 millas por hora. **IV.** *vn.* ser por término medio.

averment [ₐvᵊrmᵊnt], *s.* aseveración, declaración, afirmación; (for.) alegato, adveración.

Avernus [ₐvᵊrnʌs], *s.* averno; (poét.) Infierno.

Averr(h)oism [ₐvᵊróújzm], *s.* averroísmo.—**Averr(h)oist(ic** [-ístjk], *s.* y *a.* averroísta.

averse [ₐvᵊrs], *a.* adverso, contrario, enemigo.

aversely [-lj], *adv.* con repugnancia.

averseness [-njs], *s.* V. AVERSION.

aversion [ₐvᵊrʒₒn], *s.* aversión, aborrecimiento, repugnancia, antipatía, renuencia, mala gana, despego, desvío; inquina, tirria, odio.

avert [ₐvᵊrt], *va.* desviar, apartar, separar; prevenir, impedir, conjurar.

avian [éjvjₐn], *a.* perteneciente a las aves; avícola.

aviary [éjvjₑrj], *s.* pajarera, avería, averío.

aviate [éjvjeit], *vn.* volar en avión.

aviation [ejvjéjʃₒn], *s.* aviación.

aviator [éjvjeitₒ(r)], *s.* aviador.—**aviatress** [-trjs], **aviatrix** [-trjks], *s.* aviadora, aviatriz.

aviculture [éjvjkʌlchₑ(r)], *s.* avicultura.

aviculturist [-kʌlchₑrjst], *s.* avicultor, ra.

avid [ǽvjd], *a.* ávido, ansioso, codicioso.

avidity [ₐvídjtj], *s.* avidez, ansia, codicia.

avocado [ævokádoų], *s.* (bot.) aguacate, palta.

avocation [ævokéjʃₒn], *s.* distracción, diversión, pasatiempo; (úsase incorrectamente en lugar de **vocation** para denotar una profesión u ocupación seria); avocamiento o avocación.

avocet, avoset [ǽvoset], *s.* (orn.) avoceta.

avoid [ₐvójd], *va.* evitar, salvar, eludir, esquivar, evadir; guardarse, librarse o zafarse de; (for.) anular, invalidar, dejar sin efecto.

avoidable [-ₐbl], *a.* evitable, eludible; (for.) anulable, revocable, que puede ser cancelado.

avoidance [-ₐns], *s.* evitación, acción de evitar o de eludir; (for.) anulación, invalidación.

avoider [-œ(r)], *s.* el que evita o evade.

avoidless [-ljs], *a.* (poét.) inevitable, irremediable.

avoirdupois [ævₒdₑpój z], *s.* sistema de pesos vigente en Inglaterra y los E. U., cuya unidad es la libra de 16 onzas; (fam.) peso, gordura.

avouch [ₐváųch], *va.* afirmar, sostener; alegar, testimoniar, protestar; confesar, reconocer.

avow [ₐváų], *va.* reconocer, admitir, confesar.

avowable [-ₐbl], *a.* que se puede declarar.

avowal [-ₐl], *s.* confesión, admisión.

avowed [-d], *a.* reconocido, admitido.

avowedly [-jdlj], *adv.* sin rebozo, reconocida o confesadamente.

avulsion [ₐvʌlsₒn], *s.* arrancamiento o separación violenta; (cir. y for.) avulsión.

avuncular [ₐvʌŋkyųlₐ(r)], *a.* de o como un tío.

await [ₐwéjt], *va.* y *vn.* aguardar, esperar, estar aguardando.—**awaiting,** en espera de.

awake [ₐwéjk], **awaken** [-ₑn]. **I.** *va.* (*pret.* AWOKE o pp. AWAKED) despertar (al que está dormido); mover, excitar. **II.** *vn.* despertar(se), dejar de dormir.

awake, *a.* despierto, desvelado.—**to be a.,** velar.

awakener [-nₒœ(r)], *s.* despertador.

awakening [-jŋ], *s.* despertamiento.

award [ₐwórd], *va.* y *vn.* otorgar, conferir, conceder, (Am.) discernir; premiar; (for.) adjudicar.

award, *s.* sentencia, laudo, decisión, adjudicación, concesión; premio.

awarder [-œ(r)], *s.* juez árbitro.

aware [ₐwér], *a.* enterado, sabedor.

awareness [-njs], *s.* conocimiento; (filos.) mera conciencia de un hecho, sin atención.

awash [ₐwáʃ], *a.* y *adv.* (mar.) a flor de agua.

away [ₐwéj]. **I.** *adv.* lejos; a lo lejos; ausente, fuera; de distancia, vg. *two miles away,* a dos millas de distancia; alejándose, en dirección opuesta, vg. *away from the sun,* alejándose del sol, en dirección opuesta a la del sol; continuamente, con empeño, vg. *he is working away,* él está trabajando con ahinco; (fam.) sin empacho, lo que, o cuanto, se quiera (a veces enfático y no se traduce), vg. *talk away,* diga lo que quiera, eche usted lo que quiera, diga usted. Se usa después de muchos verbos para indicar alejamiento o acción lenta continua, vg. *to go away,* alejarse, irse; *to take away,* arrebatar, quitar; *to wither away,* irse marchitando. Frases de esta clase se dan bajo los verbos respectivos. A veces el verbo se suprime por elipsis, vg. *let us* (go) *away,* vámonos; *whither* (are *you going*) *away?* ¿adónde va Vd.? **II.** *interj.* ¡fuera de aquí! ¡márchese Vd.! ¡vámonos!—**a. with you!** ¡márchese Vd.! ¡lárguese Vd.!

awe [ɔ]. **I.** *s.* temor reverente; pavor.—**a.-inspiring,** imponente.—**a.-struck,** despavorido, aterrado, espantado.—**to stand in a. of,** temer; reverenciar sumisamente. **II.** *va.* aterrar, infundir miedo o respeto, aterrorizar.

aweary [ₐwírj], *a.* (poét.) cansado, fatigado.

aweather [ₐwéðœ(r)], *adv.* (mar.) a barlovento.

aweigh [ₐwéj], *adv.* (mar.) ú. del ancla cuando suelta el fondo y está pendiente.

awesome [ósʌm], *a.* terrible, aterrador, pavoroso; que infunde temor reverencial.

awful [ófuₗ], *a.* tremendo; terrible; majestuosamente abrumador; (fam.) muy malo, enorme.

awfully [-lj], *adv.* terriblemente, horrorosamente; (fam.) muy, excesivamente.

awfulness [-njs], *s.* veneración, respeto o temor reverencial; (fam.) enormidad.

awhile [ₐhwájl], *adv.* un rato, algún tiempo.—**not yet a.,** por ahora no, todavía no.

awhirl [ₐhwœrl], *adv.* en rotación; en giro, en torbellino.

awkward [ókwₐrd], *a.* desmañado, desgarbado, torpe, chambón, chabacano; embarazoso, difícil, delicado, peliagudo.

awkwardly [-lj], *adv.* torpemente, desmañadamente; embarazosamente, en una posición difícil, delicada.

awkwardness [-njs], *s.* torpeza, desmaña.

awl [ɔl], *s.* lezna, (a)lesna; subilla, punzón; (mec.) lengüeta.

awn [ɔn], *s.* (bot.) arista.

awning [ónjŋ], *s.* toldo, tendal, entalamadura, marquesina; toldo voladizo (sobre puertas y ventanas); (Am.) carpa; (mar.) toldo, toldilla, cenefa, tienda, carroza.—**to cover with an a.,** entoldar, entalamar.

awoke [ₐwóųk], *pret.* de TO AWAKE.

awry [ₐráj], *adv.* y *a.* oblicuo, sesgado, torcido, oblicuamente, de través; fuera de razón, erradamente, descaminadamente.

ax, axe [æks], *s.* (*pl.* **axes** [ǽksjz]) hacha, segur, *f.*—**to have an a. to grind,** tener algún fin interesado, ir taimadamente tras algo.

axes [æksjz], *s. pl.* de AXIS.

axhammer [ǽkshæmœ(r)], *s.* (alb.) piqueta o martillo de dos bocas o filos.—**axhammered** [-d], *a.* (piedra) trabajada con tal herramienta.

axial [ǽksjₐl], *a.* axil.—**a.-flow turbine,** turbina paralela o axial.—**a. skeleton,** esqueleto de la cabeza y el tronco, sin las extremidades.

axil [ǽksjl], *s.* (bot.) axila.

axile [ǽksjl], *a.* (bot.) axilar.

axilla [æksílₐ], *s.* (anat., zool., bot.) axila; sobaco.

axillar(y [ǽksjlₑr(j)], *a.* (anat., zool., bot.) axilar; sobacal.

axinite [ǽksjnajt], *s.* (min.) axinita.

axiom [ǽksjₒm], *s.* axioma, *m.*, postulado, sentencia.

axiomatic(al [-ǽtjk(ₐl)], *a.* axiomático.

axiometer [æksjámetœ(r)], *s.* (mar.) axiómetro.

axis [ǽksjs], *s.* (mat., bot., etc.) eje; (anat.) axis.

segunda vértebra cervical; (zool.) venado o ciervo de manchas blancas de la India: (A.) Eje, alianza militar entre Alemania, Italia y el Japón.—**a.-cylinder**, (anat.) eje de una fibra nerviosa.—**axes of coordinates**, (mat.) ejes de coordenadas.

axle [ǽksl], s. eje (de un vehículo); eje, árbol, peón (de una rueda o máquina).—**a. bar**, eje de hierro de una rueda.—**a. box**, (mec.) caja de eje, buje.—**a. shaft**, (aut.) puente o eje trasero.

axletree [-tri], s. eje (de ruedas de carruaje).

axman [ǽksmạn], s. hachero; leñador.

axoid [ǽksọid], **axoidean** [æksóidiạn], a. (anat.) axoideo.

axolotl [ǽksolatl], s. (zool.) (Am.) ajolote.

axon(e [ǽksan], s. (anat.) axón.

axonometry [æksonámetrị], s. (mat.) axonometría.

ay [ei], interj. (ant.) ¡ay!—**ay me!** ¡ay de mí!

ay, aye [ei], adv. (poét.) siempre, por siempre.—**for aye**, por siempre jamás.

aye, ay [ai]. **I.** adv. sí. **II.** s. voto afirmativo.

aye-aye [áiai], s. (zool.) aye-aye.

azalea [azéiliạ̈], s. (bot.) azalea.

azarole [ǽzạroụl], s. (bot.) acerola.

azimuth [ǽzịmʌθ], s. (astr. y top.) acimut, azimut.—**a. compass**, brújula de azimut.—**a. dial**, gnomon.

azimuthal [-mʌ́θạl], a. acimutal, azimutal.

azoic [azóụik], a. (geol.) azoico; sin vida; (quím.) azoico.

azonic [eizánịk], a. que no es local.

azote [ǽzoụt], s. (quím.) ázoe, nitrógeno.

azoth [ǽzaθ], s. (alquimia) azogue, mercurio.

azotic [ạzátịk], a. (quím.) azoico, azoado, nítrico.

azotize [ǽzotaịz], va. (quím.) azoar, nitrogenar.

Aztec [ǽztek], a. y s. azteca, mf.

azure [ǽẓụr]. **I.** a. y s. azulado, claro, azul celeste, cerúleo; (blas.) azur, blao. **II.** va. azular.

azurine [ǽẓụrịn]. **I.** a. azulado. **II.** s. (quím.) azurina.

azurite [ǽẓụraịt], s. (min.) azurita, malaquita azul.

azygous [ǽzịgʌs], a. y s. (anat.) (vena) ácigos.

azym [ǽzịm], **azyme** [ǽzaịm], s. pan ázimo o ácimo, pan sin levadura.

azymic [æzịmịk], a. azímico.

azymous [ǽzịmʌs], a. ázimo, sin levadura.

B

b [bi], s. b; (mús., B) si.

baa [ba]. **I.** s. be (balido). **II.** vn. balar.

Baalist, Baalite [béjạlịst, -ait], a. y s. baalita, mf.

babbitt [bǽbịt]. **I.** s. metal antifricción para cojinetes (ll. t. **B. metal**). **II.** va. revestir de metal antifricción, forrar con metal blanco.

babble [bǽbl], va. y vn. balbucear; charlar, parlar, bachillear, garlar; murmurar (un arroyo).

babble, s. charla, parla, balbuceo, bachillería, charlatanería; susurro, murmullo.

babbler [bǽblœ(r)], s. charlador, garlador, charlatán, hablador; parlero, bachiller, trapalón.

babbling [bǽblịŋ]. **I.** a. murmurante, balbuciente. **II.** s. cháchara, garrulería, balbucencia.

babe [beib], s. criaturita, nene, bebé, rorro.

Babel, Babeldom [béibẹl, -dọm], s. Babel; **b.**, confusión, desorden.

babirous(s)a, babirus(s)a [bæbịrúsạ̈], s. (zool.) babirusa.

Babism [bábịzm], s. babismo, doctrina persa.

baboon [bæbún], s. (zool.) mandril, papión, m.

baboosh, babouche [bæbúš], s. babucha, pantufla.

baby [béịbị]. **I.** s. criatura, crío, nene, nena, pequeñuelo, rorro, bebé, (Am.) guagua, mf. **II.** a. de niño, semejante a un niño; de, para o como nene; pequeño; de tierna edad; infantil.—**b. act**, acción infantil; ley (f.) de exculpa-

ción de menores.—**b. basket**, cesto de ajuar para nene.—**b. beef**, ternerillo para el matadero; su carne.—**b. blue**, azul claro.—**b. bond**, bono de bajo valor nominal (gen. 50 o 100 dólares).—**b. buggy, b. carriage**, cochecillo de nene.—**b. farm**, casa en que se crían por paga niños ajenos.—**b. grand piano**, piano de media cola.—**b. ribbon**, bocadillo, cintilla muy angosta.—**b. talk**, habla de nene o de chiquillo, media lengua, tono infantil.—**b. tooth**, diente de leche o mamón. **III.** va. tratar como niño; mimar.

babyhood [-hụd], s. niñez, infancia.

babyish [-ịṣ̌], a. niñero; pueril, infantil.

babyishness [-ịšnịs], s. puerilidad, niñada.

Babylonian [bæbịlóụnịạn], a. babilónico; fastuoso.

baccalaureate [bækạlórịịt], s. bachillerato.

baccara(t [bækạrá], s. bacará, m., juego de naipes.

baccate [bǽkeịt], s. (bot.) abayado, parecido a una baya.

bacchanal [bǽkạnæl], **bacchanalian** [-éịlịạn]. **I.** s. bacanal, f. **II.** a. bacanal, báquico; ebrio.

Bacchanalia [-éịlịạ̈], **Bacchanals** [bǽkạnælz], s. pl. bacanales, f.

bacchant, bacchante [bǽkạnt, bækǽntị], s. bacante, ménade; persona disoluta o borracha.

Bacchic(al [bǽkịk(ạl], a. báquico.

bacciferous [bæksífẹrʌs], a. que produce bayas.

baccivorous [bæksívọrạs], a. que se alimenta de bayas.

bachelor [bǽčẹlọ(r)], s. soltero, (fam.) celibato, mancebo; bachiller.—**b.'s-button**, (bot.) aciano, azulejo.—**bachelors' apartments, rooms**, etc., apartamientos, cuartos, etc., para solteros.—**to receive the b.'s degree**, bachillerarse.

bachelordom [-dọm], s. el mundo de los solteros; soltería.

bachelorhood [-hụd], s. celibato, soltería; bachillerato.

bachelorship [-šịp], s. celibato, soltería; bachillerato.

bacillary [bǽsịlẹrị], a. bacilar.

bacillus [bæsíLʌs], s. (pl. BACILLI) bacilo, bacteria.

back [bæk], s. espalda; lomo, espinazo (de un animal); respaldo, (r)espaldar (de un asiento, etc.); dorso, envés, revés (de la mano, letra de cambio, etc.); reverso, lado de atrás; parte posterior o de atrás, trasera; lomo (de una montaña, de un cuchillo, de un libro); (teat.) foro; (arq.) trasdós (de un arco); (dep.) zaguero, defensa, m. (fútbol, pelota).—**to b.**, espalda con espalda.—**at one's b.**, detrás de uno (sea persiguiéndolo, sea apoyándolo).—**behind one's b.**, por detrás, a espaldas de uno, sin conocimiento de uno (con la implicación de perfidia o cobardía).—**in the b. of one's mind**, en lo recóndito del pensamiento.—**on one's b.**, a cuestas, boca arriba, de espaldas.—**to be, o lie, on one's b.**, estar en cama; estar postrado, ser impotente.—**to break the b. of**, deslomar, agobiar.—**to carry on the b.**, llevar o traer a lomo o a cuestas.—**to cast behind the b.**, olvidar y perdonar, echar pelillos a la mar.—**to get, o put, one's b. up**, (fam.), obstinarse.—**to see the b. of**, deshacerse o librarse de.—**to turn one's b. (on)**, volver la(s) espalda(s) (a); irse; huir; abandonar, desdeñar o negarse (a uno).—**to turn one's b. to**, volverse de espaldas a.—**with one's b. to the wall**, acosado, a raya, en situación desesperada.

back, a. trasero, posterior, de atrás; dorsal; del interior; atrasado; anterior, pasado (apl. al tiempo); apartado, lejano.—**b. door**, puerta de atrás, puerta falsa o de servicio; (fig.) surtida; modo indirecto e indigno.—**b. comb**, peineta.—**b. court**, trascorral.—**b. draft**, explosión de gases de combustión; corriente de aire invertida.—**b. excentric**, (m. v.) excéntrica de inversión o de cambio de marcha.—**b. electromotive force,** fuerza contraelectromotriz.—**b. filling,** (const.) relleno de respaldo.—**b. number,** número atrasado (de un periódico); persona desprestigiada o rezagada.—**b. page,** página izquierda.—**b. pay,** sueldo retrasado.—**b. pitch,** distancia entre dos hileras paralelas de remaches.—**b. pressure,** (m. v.) contrapresión.—**b. seat,** asiento de atrás; posición inferior o de poca monta.—**b. sight,** (top.) visual inversa, visual de comprobación u orientación dirigida hacia atrás.—**b. stairs,** escalera de atrás; escalera secreta; medios indirectos y solapados.—**b. step,** (mil.) marcha atrás, paso a retaguardia.—**b. stream,** contracorriente; remolino.—**b. street,** calle apartada o no central.—**b. stroke,** revés; (en el nadar) de espaldas.—**b. talk,** respuesta insolente.—**b. tooth,** muela, diente molar.—**b. yard,** trascorral.

back. I. *adv.* atrás, detrás; a alguna distancia (de); otra vez, de nuevo; de vuelta, de regreso. Después de un verbo indica en general retrocesión, y a veces equivale al prefijo *re*, vg. *to come back*, regresar; *to give back*, devolver; *to beat back*, rechazar.—**b. and forth,** de arriba para abajo, de una parte a otra; de uno a otro.—**b. in 1800,** allá por el año de 1800.—**as far b. as 1800,** ya en 1800, desde 1800.—**in b. of,** detrás de, tras de. **II.** *interj.* ¡atrás!

back. I. *va.* mover, empujar o tirar hacia atrás; hacer retroceder, acular; reforzar; (a veces con **up**) sostener, apoyar, defender, respaldar, guardar las espaldas (a uno); favorecer, apostar a (en carreras, etc.); endosar, certificar al reverso; montar (un caballo).—**to b. the wrong horse,** apostar por el mal caballo; apoyar el partido o bando que pierde; escoger mal. **II.** *vn.* (a veces con **up**) recular, retroceder, ciar.—**to b. and fill,** (mar.) fachear y marcar en el viento; ir de un lado a otro; vacilar.—**to b. down, to b. out,** volverse atrás, abandonar una empresa o resolución.—**to b. water,** (mar.) impulsar un barco hacia atrás, recular, ciar; (fig.) retractarse, desdecirse, cantar la palinodia.

backache [bǽkejk], *s.* dolor de espalda.
backbite [bájt], *va.* y *vn.* (*pret.* BACKBIT; *pp.* BACKBITTEN) difamar, calumniar solapadamente, murmurar, maldecir, morder.—**backbiter,** *s.* murmurador, calumniador, detractor, maldecidor, malsín, tijera.—**backbiting,** *s.* murmuración, difamación, calumnia.—**backbitingly,** *adv.* calumniosamente.
backboard [bórd], *s.* respaldo, forro, espaldar.
backbone [boun], *s.* (anat.) espina, espinazo, columna vertebral, cerro, raquis; firmeza, nervio; fundamento; sostén.—**to the b.,** hasta la médula.
backbreaking [bréjkiŋ], *a.* agobiante, abrumador.
backdown [daun], *s.* (fam.) cesión; rendición; palinodia, retractación.
backed [t], *a.* apoyado, respaldado.
backer [œ(r)], *s.* sostenedor, defensor, auxiliador, partidario; (com.) refaccionista, aviador; (fam.) caballo blanco; (dep.) sostenedor, apostador.
backfield [fild], *s.* en el fútbol, terreno detrás de la línea; los defensas que ocupan tal posición.
backfire [fajr]. **I.** *s.* quema que se hace para detener otra; medida o acción defensiva; (m. comb. int.) encendido o explosión prematura en el cilindro o tubo de escape; explosión en la parte de atrás de un arma de fuego. **II.** *vn.* hacer una quema para detener otra; (m. comb. int.) tener explosiones prematuras; (fig.) ser contraproducente, salir el tiro por la culata, fracasar.

backgammon [gǽmon], *s.* juego de chaquete.—**b. board,** tablas reales.
background [graund], *s.* antecedentes, *m. pl.*; fundamento, raíz, base, *f.*; medio, circunstancias rodeantes; posición subordinada; olvido, oscuridad; (b. a.) fondo; último término, lontananza, lejos.
backhanded [hǽndjd], *a.* dado con el revés de la mano; inclinado a la izquierda; falto de sinceridad; irónico.—**b. blow o stroke,** revés.
backhouse [haus], *s.* trascuarto; dependencia que sirve de retrete; el común, la necesaria.
backing [iŋ], *s.* apoyo, sostén, garantía; refuerzo; (Am.) refacción, avío; retroceso; respaldo, forro, espaldar; (enc.) lomera.
backlash [lǽsh], *s.* (mec.) marcha muerta, juego entre dientes; retroceso con sacudimiento y vibración.
backlog [lag], *s.* tronco trasero en una hoguera; soporte; (com.) cúmulo de pedidos por llenar.
backmost [moust], *a. super.* de más atrás.
backpiece [pis], **backplate** [plejt], *s.* (arm.) espaldar, espaldarón.
backsaw [sɔ], *s.* sierra de trasdós.
backset [set], *s.* contratiempo, contrariedad, revés, infortunio, recaída; remolino.
backshop [sap], *s.* trastienda; rebotica.
backside [sajd], *s.* envés, revés, vuelta, espalda; trasero, culo, nalgas, *pl.*
backslide [slajd], *vn.* reincidir, volver a las andadas.
backslider [œ(r)], *s.* apóstata, *mf.*; reincidente.
backsliding [iŋ], *s.* apostasía; reincidencia.
backspacer [spéjsœ(r)], *s.* tecla de retroceso.
backstairs [stérz], *a.* (fig.) secreto, clandestino.
backstay [stej], *s.* soporte, refuerzo posterior; tirante; (mar.) burda, brandal, traversa.
backstitch [stjch]. **I.** *s.* pespunte, punto atrás. **II.** *va.* y *vn.* pespuntar.—**backstitching** [iŋ], *s.* pespunte, acción de pespuntar.
backstop [stap], *s.* (dep.) reja o valla para detener la pelota; zaguero (en la pelota); *catcher* (en el béisbol).
backswept [swept], *a.* (aer.) que tiene el borde delantero inclinado hacia el eje lateral del avión.
backsword [sord], *s.* sable, alfanje.
backtrack [træk], *vn.* desandar, volver atrás en el camino ya andado; retirarse.
backward [bǽkwərd], *a.* vuelto o dirigido hacia atrás; retrógrado, que retrocede; retraído, corto; lerdo, pesado, tardo, atrasado, tardío.—**b. motion,** retroceso, retrocesión.—**backward(s,** *adv.* de espaldas, (hacia) atrás; atrasadamente, (fam.) redro, a reculones.—**to go b. and forward,** ir y venir, adelantar y retroceder.—**to go o move b.,** cejar, retroceder.
backwardation [éjshon], *s.* (en la bolsa) aplazamiento de la entrega de acciones, con premio pagado por el vendedor por la demora; dicho premio.
backwardly [lij], *adv.* con repugnancia, de mala gana; torpemente.
backwardness [njs], *s.* torpeza, pesadez; negligencia; atraso, retraso.
backwash [bǽkwash], *s.* agua lanzada hacia atrás por remos, hélices, etc.
backwater [wotœ(r)], *s.* contracorriente, *f.*; remolino; agua de rechazo (de una turbina, etc.); remanso.
backwoods [wúdz], *s.* región apartada, gen. en lo más denso de un bosque; fragosidades, *f. pl.*
bacon [béjkon], *s.* tocino.—**to bring home the b.,** (fam.) tener éxito; ganar el premio gordo.—**to save one's b.,** (fam.) salvar el pellejo.—**to sell one's b.,** (fam.) venderse.
Baconian [bejkóunjan], *a.* y *s.* baconiano, baconista.
bacteria [bæktírja], *s. pl.* de BACTERIUM.
bacterial [l], *a.* bacteriano, bactérico.
bactericidal [isájdal], *a.* bactericida.
bactericide [bæktírjsajd], *s.* bactericida.

Para la pronunciación véase la clave al principio del libro.

bacterin [bǽktęrįn], s. vacuna bacteriana.
bacteriological [bæktįrįoládźįkąl], a. bacteriológico, microbiológico.
bacteriologist [-álodźįst], s. bacteriólogo.
bacteriology [-álodźį], s. bacteriología, microbiología.
bacteriolysis [-álįsįs], s. bacteriólisis.
bacterioscopy [-áskopį], s. bacterioscopia, estudio microscópico de las bacterias.
bacteriotherapy [-oθérąpį], s. bacterioterapia.
bacterium [bæktírįʌm], s. (pl. BACTERIA) bacteria, microbio.
Bactrian [bǽktrįąn], a. y s. bactriano.
baculiform [bækįúlįform], a. derecho, recto.
bad [bæd]. I. a. mal(o), perverso, depravado; infeliz, desgraciado; dañado, podrido; nocivo, dañoso; indispuesto, enfermo.—**b. blood**, animosidad, encono, mala sangre.—**b. child**, niño travieso, pilluelo.—**b. coin**, moneda falsa. —**b. debt**, deuda incobrable.—**b. form**, mala educación, mal gusto, falta de formalidad o de etiqueta, cosa que no se mira bien.—**b.-looking**, mal parecido, feo, fachoso.—**from b. to worse**, de mal en peor.—**very b.**, pésimo.— **with b. grace**, de mala gana. II. s. (con the) lo malo; la perdición; gente mala.—**to the b.** (con to be), (estar o quedar) peor; perder o salir perdiendo.
bade [bæd], pret. de TO BID.
badge [bædź], s. escarapela, insignia, condecoración, divisa, distintivo, símbolo, placa.
badge, va. condecorar, dar una insignia.
badgeless [-lįs], a. sin divisa.
badger [-œ(r)]. I. s. (zool.) tejón, tasugo. II. va. molestar, cansar, fatigar, fastidiar.
badigeon [bądídźọn], s. (alb.) gabarro.
badinage [bædįnáź], s. jocosidad, burla, chanza, chirigota; cháchara.
badly [bǽdlį], adv. mal, malamente.—**b. off**, mal en sus negocios; mal de fortuna; maltrecho.— **to need b.**, necesitar con urgencia.—**very b.**, pésimamente.
badminton [bǽdmįntọn], s. (juego de) raqueta y volante; cierta bebida o refresco.
badness [bǽdnįs], s. maldad; demasía.
baffle [bǽfl]. I. va. frustrar, impedir, desconcertar, desbaratar, contrariar. II. vn. luchar en vano. III. s. (mec.) cualquier artificio que sirve para desviar, guiar o regular el flujo de un gas o líquido; (m. v.) contrapuerta (del hogar); placa de desviación o de choque (llamada t. b. **plate**); reductor de velocidad o de tiro.—**b. tube**, conducto con placas de desviación para reducir la temperatura de los gases.—**b. wall**, superficie o tabique de choque o desviación.
baffler [bǽflœ(r)], s. impedimento, contrariedad; desconcertador, desbaratador; el que desbarata o frustra.
baffling [bǽflįŋ], a. desconcertador, desconcertante.
bag [bæg]. I. s. saco, costal, talega, fardel; bolsa, bocha (en la ropa); zurrón; cogida, redada (caza, pesca); presa, botín; saquito de mano; (zool.) bolsita o vejiguilla de algunos animales; ubre; bolsa (de un marsupial).—**b. net**, nasa. —**to be in the b.**, (fam.) ser cosa segura.—**to hold the b.**, (fam.) quedar manivacío; pagar los vidrios rotos.—**to pack up bag and baggage**, liar el hato, liar el petate, tomar el tole. II. va. ensacar, enzurronar, entalegar, imbursar; coger, capturar, cazar, cobrar. III. vn. hacer bolsa o pliegue (la ropa); abotagarse, hincharse.
bagasse [bągǽs], s. bagazo, gabazo (de azúcar); brisa, orujo (de uvas); (b)orujo (de oliva).
bagatelle [bægatél], s. bagatela, fruslería.
bagful [bǽgfuł], s. saco, zurronada, talega.
baggage [bǽgįdź], s. equipaje, maletas, pl., etc., (fam.) petate; (mil.) bagaje; (fam.) ramera, prostituta.—**b. car**, o **wagon**, furgón, vagón de equipajes.—**b. check**, marbete, placa,

contraseña de equipaje.—**b. master**, (f.c.) factor.—**b. room**, depósito de equipajes.
bagging [bǽgįŋ], s. arpillera, malacuenda.—**b. at the knees**, rodillera.
baggy [bǽgį], a. flojo; bombacho, holgado(ropa).
bagman [bǽgmąn], s. (Ingl.) agente viajero.
bagnio [bǽnyou], s. lupanar, burdel; cárcel, f.; casa de baños.
bagpipe [bǽgpaip], s. gaita, cornamusa.
bagpiper [-œ(r)], s. gaitero.
bah! [ba], interj. ¡bah!
bail [béjl]. I. s. (for.) caución, fianza; fiador; anillo, aro; soporte arqueado de un toldo; pared exterior (de un castillo); patio; tabique de tablas suspendidas; asa, cogedero (de cubo, caldero); división entre los compartimentos de un establo; achicador, cubo o vertedor para achicar (agua).—**b. bond**, (for.) caución, escritura de fianza.—**on b.**, (for.) bajo fianza. —**to go b. for**, salir fiador de. II. va. (for.) caucionar, dar fianza o salir fiador por otro; poner en libertad bajo fianza; entregar (mercancías) bajo contrato de depósito; afianzar, asegurar, zunchar con aros o fajas; desaguar, vaciar.—**to b. out**, achicar, baldear, sacar el agua de.—**to b. up**, zunchar; detener. III. vn. —**to b. out**, (aer.) descender o saltar en paracaídas.
bailable [-ąbl], a. caucionable.
bailee [béjlí], s. (for.) depositario.
bailer, **bailor** [béjlœ(r)], s. (for.) fiador; el que entrega mercancías a otro bajo contrato de depósito.
bailey [béjlį], s. pared exterior, o patio de un castillo feudal; tribunal de justicia; cárcel, f.
bailie, **baillie** [béjlį], s. alcalde, baile.
bailiff [béjlįf], s. alguacil, corchete; baile, ministril; mayordomo.
bailing [béjlįŋ], s. (mar.) achique, achicadura.
bailiwick [béjlįwįk], s. alguacilazgo, bailiazgo; bailía; mayordomía; (fig.) especialidad.
bailment [béjlmęnt], s. (for.) depósito, entrega en calidad de depósito; libertad bajo fianza.
bailsman [béjlzmąn], s. (for.) fiador.
bairn [bern], s. (Esco.) niño.
bait [bejt]. I. va. cebar, dar un pienso; poner cebo para atraer animales; azuzar; atormentar, molestar, acosar. II. vn. hacer parada o alto para tomar un refrigerio; (cetr.) aletear. III. s. cebo, carnada; anzuelo, añagaza, señuelo; refrigerio o refresco en una jornada; pienso.— **to take the b.**, tragar el anzuelo, caer en un lazo.
baize [bejz], s. bayeta.—**green b.**, tapete verde.
bake [bejk]. I. va. cocer o asar en horno; (Am.) hornear; desecar, endurecer, calcinar. II. vn. hornear (como oficio). III. s. cosa cocida en horno.
baked [-t], pp. y a. (coc.) al horno; asado o cocido en horno.—**b. eggs**, huevos al plato.—**b. on**, (ind.) aplicado en caliente.
bakelite [béjkęlajt], s. bakelita o baquelita [marca de fábrica].
baker [béjkœ(r)], s. hornero, panadero, tahonero. —**a b.'s dozen**, trece, docena de fraile.—**b.'s peel**, pala de horno.
bakery [-į], **bakehouse** [béjkhaųs], s. horno, panadería, tahona.
baking [béjkįŋ], s. hornada; cocimiento; cocción. —**b. pan**, tortera o tartera.—**b. powder**, levadura en polvo.—**b. soda**, bicarbonato de sosa.—**b. tin**, chapa de enhornar.
baksheesh, **bakshish** [bǽkšíš], s. propina.
balance [bǽląns]. I. s. (fís.) balanza; cotejo; equilibrio; balance; péndola, volante de reloj; (astr.) Libra; (com.) balance; saldo, resto, alcance.—**b. of power**, (pol.) equilibrio militar y económico.—**b. of trade**, balanza del comercio.—**b. sheet**, balance, avanzo.—**b. weight**, contrapeso.—**b. wheel**, balancín, rueda catalina; volante; péndola de reloj.—**to**

strike a b., hacer o pasar balance. **II.** *va.* equilibrar, poner en equilibrio; balancear, contrapesar; (com.) dar finiquito, saldar: nivelar (el presupuesto, etc.); pesar; considerar, examinar. **III.** *vn.* equilibrarse, estar en equilibrio, ser de igual peso, etc.; contrarrestarse; (com.) igualarse, saldarse; vacilar, dudar; balancearse, agitarse, mecerse.

balancer [-œ(r)], *s.* pesador; fiel de balanza; equilibrista.

balancing [-iŋ]. **I.** *s.* equilibrio; balance; balanceo, nivelación. **II.** *a.* compensador, equilibrador.—**b. flap,** (aer.) alerón. **b. pole,** balancín.

balas [bǽlas], *s.* balaj(e), rubí de color morado.

balata [bǽlatǝ], *s.* (bot.) balata; su jugo.

balbriggan [bælbrígǝn], *s.* cierto tejido de algodón (o lana) para ropa interior, medias, etc.

balcony [bǽlkoni], *s.* balcón; antepecho; galería; (teat.) galería, anfiteatro.

bald [bold], *a.* calvo, morondo; escueto, pelado, desnudo, pelón, raído; desabrido, grosero.—**b.-faced,** cariblanco, careto.—**b.-headed,** calvo. —**to become b.,** calvar, encalvecer.

baldachin [bǽldakin], *s.* (arq.) dosel, baldaquín; (igl.) palio, pabellón.

balderdash [bóldœrdæŝ], *s.* (fam.) disparate, jerigonza; mezcolanza, calabriada.

baldhead [bóldhed], *s.* persona calva.

baldly [-li], *adv.* chabacanamente, groseramente.

baldness [-nis], *s.* calvicie, alopecia, pelona.

baldpate [-peit], *s.* =BALDHEAD; (orn.) cerceta norteamericana.

baldric [bóldrik], *s.* tahalí; (astr.) zodíaco.

bale [béil]. **I.** *s.* fardo, frangote; tercio (de tabaco); bala, paca (de algodón); bala (de papel). —**b. fire,** lumbrada, luminaria; pira funeraria. **II.** *va.* embalar, empaquetar, enfard(el)ar. *V.* BAIL.

baleen [balín], *s.* (com.) ballena.

baleful [béilful], *a.* funesto, maligno, pernicioso.

balefully [-i], *adv.* funesta o perniciosamente.

baling [béiliŋ], *s.* embalaje, enfardeladura. *V.* BAILING.—**b. press,** prensa para balas.

balk, baulk [bok]. **I.** *va.* frustrar, desbaratar, impedir, poner obstáculo; amontonar formando lomo. **II.** *vn.* plantarse, (Am.) empacarse, rebelarse (un caballo); resistirse.

balk, *s.* obstáculo, impedimento, contrariedad, fracaso, yerro; lomo entre surcos; (carp.) viga. —**b.-line,** cabaña, casa (en el billar).

Balkan [bólkǝn], *a.* y *s.* balcánico, balkánico.

balky [bóki], *a.* rebelón; harón; (Am.) empacón.

ball [bol]. **I.** *s.* bola, pelota, globo; bala de cañón; juego de pelota, de béisbol, etc.; manera de arrojar la pelota; yema (del dedo); copa, trago de licor con hielo y agua (llamado también **high b.**); baile; (agr.) cepellón.—**b.-and-socket joint,** articulación esférica, rótula.— **b. bearing,** cojinete de bolas.—**b. blue,** añil. —**b. cartridge,** cartucho o cápsula con bala. —**b. cock,** llave o válvula de flotador.—**b. extractor,** (cir.) sacabala.—**b. flower,** (arq.) decoración en forma de bola con flores.—**b. governor,** regulador de bolas o de fuerza centrífuga.—**b. gown,** traje de baile.—**b. mold,** balero.—**b. of yarn,** ovillo (de hilo).— **b. valve,** válvula esférica; válvula de flotador. **II.** *va.* y *vn.* apelotonar(se), convertir o convertirse en bolas.—**to b. up,** (fam.) embrollar, confundir.

ballad [bǽlad], *s.* balada, copla, trova, cantinela; canción, chanzoneta; jácara, romance.—**b. monger,** coplista, vendedor de coplas o canciones, etc.—**b. singer,** jacarero, cantor de coplas, jácaras, etc.—**b. writer,** coplero, escritor de canciones, romances, etc.

ballast [bǽlast]. **I.** *s.* (mar.) lastre, zahorra; (f. c.) balasto.—**b. bed,** firme (de carretera). —**b. lighter,** lanchón de deslastrar.—**b. ports,** portas de lastrar.—**to go in b.,** ir en lastre.—

washed b., lastre lavado, o guijarro. **II.** *va.* (mar.) lastrar; (f. c.) balastar; (fig.) asegurar, sostener, reforzar.

ballasting [-iŋ], *s.* acto de lastrar o balastar; (f. c.) balasto; (mar.) lastre.

ballerina [bælerínǝ], *s.* bailarina.

ballet [bǽlei], *s.* baile, bailable, bailete, ballet; cuerpo de baile.—**b. dancer,** bailarín, bailarina.

ballista [balístǝ], *s.* ballesta; balista.

ballistic [balístik], *a.* balístico.

ballistics [-s], *s.* balística.

ballonet [bælonét], *s.* (aer.) globillo compensador, que va dentro de un dirigible para regular el ascenso, etc.

balloon [balún], **I.** *s.* globo aerostático, aeróstato; (quím.) redoma, balón.—**b. barrage,** (mil.) barrera de globos cautivos contra ataques aéreos.—**b. bed,** amarradero para dirigibles.— **b. jib,** (mar.) foque balón.—**b. tire,** neumático o llanta balón. **II.** *vn.* ascender o viajar en un globo aerostático; hincharse como globo.

balloonist [-ist], *s.* aeronauta, *mf.*

ballot [bǽlot]. **I.** *s.* balota; papeleta, cédula o boleta para votar; (Am.) bolita; voto; votación, (Am.) balotaje.—**b. box,** urna electoral, cántaro. **II.** *vn.* y *va.* balotar; insacular, sacar; votar.—**balloting** [-iŋ], *s.* votación, insaculación, (Am.) balotaje.

ballplayer [bólpleiœ(r)], *s.* basebolista; jugador de béisbol, etc.; pelotari (de pelota vascuence).

ballroom [-rum], *s.* sala o salón de baile.

ballyhoo [bǽlihu]. **I.** *s.* (fam.) alharaca; bombo. **II.** *va.* bombear, dar bombo, ensalzar exageradamente.

balm [bám], *s.* bálsamo, ungüento balsámico y fragante; balsamita mayor; (bot.) cidronela, melisa, toronjil.—**b. of Gilead,** opobálsamo, bálsamo de Judea, o de la Meca; bálsamo de Canarias; abeto balsámico.

balmoral [bælmárǝl], *s.* especie de faldas de lana rayada; borceguí; gorra escocesa.

balmy [-i], *a.* balsámico; aromático, fragante; calmante, reparador; (Am.) tonto, alocado.

balneary [bǽlniǝri], *a.* y *s.* balneario.

balneotherapy [bælnioθérǝpi], *s.* (med.) balneoterapia.

balsa [bólsǝ], *s.* balsa; (Am., bot.) balso.

balsam [bólsǝm]. **I.** *s.* bálsamo; ungüento.—**b. apple,** (bot.) balsamina, momórdiga.—**b. fir,** (bot.) abeto balsámico.—**b. of fir,** bálsamo del Canadá.—**b. of Mecca** = BALM OF GILEAD. —**b. of Peru,** bálsamo del Perú. **II.** *va.* untar con bálsamo, embalsamar.

balsamic [bolsémik], *a.* balsámico. *V.* BALMY.

balsamiferous [bólsǝmífǝrǝs], *a.* balsamífero.

balsamine [bólsǝmin], *s.* (bot.) balsamina.

Baltic [bóltik], *a.* báltico.

baluster [bǽlǝstœ(r)], *s.* (arq.) balaustre.

balustered [-d], *a.* balaustrado, barandado.

balustrade [-tréid], *s.* balaustrada, barandilla.

bamboo [bæmbú], *s.* (bot.) bambú, bambuc.

bamboozle [bæmbúzl], *va.* (fam.) capotear, engañar; burlar, embaucar.

bamboozler [-lœ(r)], *s.* (fam.) engañador, embaucador.

bambusaceous [bæmbjuséiŝʌs], *a.* bambusáceo, semejante al bambú, de la familia del bambú.

ban [bæn]. **I.** *s.* bando, edicto, proclama, pregón; excomunión; entredicho; tejido de abacá.— **bans of marriage,** amonestaciones, proclamas.—**to publish the bans,** amonestar, correr las amonestaciones. **II.** *va.* encartar, proscribir; prohibir; excomulgar, anatematizar.

banal [béinǝl], *a.* trivial, vulgar; feudal.

banality [bǝnǽliti], *s.* trivialidad, vulgaridad.— *pl.* lugares comunes.

banana [bǝnǽnǝ], *s.* (bot.) plátano, guineo; banana, banano; cambur.—**b. oil,** acetato de amilo.—**b. plantation,** platanar.—**b. tree,**

banano, bananero, plátano.—**red b.,** cambur morado.

banc [bæŋk], *s.* (for.) tribunal.—**court in b.,** tribunal en pleno.

band [bænd]. **I.** *s.* faja, fleje, venda, tira, lista, vencejo, cordón, correa, cinta, franja, precinta; abrazadera, zuncho; lazo, enlace, unión, conexión, coyunda; cuadrilla, gavilla, partida, bandería; (mús.) banda, charanga, música; murga; (arq.) filete, listón.—**b. brake,** freno de cinta.—**b. iron,** fleje.—**b. pulley,** polea para correa ancha, tambor de transmisión.—**b. saw,** sierra de cinta, sierra sin fin.—**b. wagon,** carro de banda de música; (fig.) partido o bando de la multitud (**to get on the b. wagon,** adherirse a la causa popular, seguir la corriente).—**b. wheel,** rueda de la correa o de transmisión. **II.** *va.* congregar, abanderizar; fajar, vendar, atar, precintar. **III.** *vn.* asociarse, ir en pandilla o en manada.

bandage [bǽndidʒ]. **I.** *s.* (cir.) vendaje, venda, faja, longuetas. **II.** *va.* (cir.) vendar.

bandanna [bændǽnə], *s.* pañuelo de hierbas.

bandbox [bǽndbaks], *s.* caja redonda u ovalada para sombreros, gorras, cuellos, etc.

bandeau [bændóu], *s.* cinta o faja para la cabeza.

banderole [bǽndҽroul], *s.* banderola, corneta.

bandit [bǽndit], *s.* bandido, bandolero, atracador.

banditry [-ri], *s.* bandolerismo, bandidaje.

bandlet [bǽndlit], *s.* (arq.) filete, listón.

bandmaster [bǽndmæstœ(r)], *s.* músico mayor.

bandog [bǽndog], *s.* mastín, perro de presa atado.

bandoleer, bandolier [bændolír], *s.* bandolera.

bandoline [bǽndolin], *s.* bandolina.

bandore [bǽndɔr], *s.* (mús.) bandurria.

bandsman [bǽndzman], *s.* músico de banda.

bandstand [bǽndstænd], *s.* quiosco de música.

bandy [bǽndi]. **I.** *va.* cambiar, trocar; pelotear; pasar de uno a otro. **I.** *s.* juego parecido al **hockey;** palo corvo para ese juego. **III.** *a.* arqueado, combado; estevado.—**b.-legged,** estevado, zámbigo o zambo, zanquituerto.

bane [béjn], *s.* tósigo, veneno; ruina, daño.

baneberry [-beri], *s.* (bot.) yezgo, actea.

baneful [-ful], *a.* pernicioso, dañino, mefítico, ponzoñoso, mortal, funesto.

banefulness [-fulnis], *s.* calidad de pernicioso o ponzoñoso.

banewort [-wœrt], *s.* (bot.) cualquiera planta venenosa (belladona, dulcamara, etc.).

bang [bæŋ]. **I.** *va.* arrojar, disparar, golpear con ruido; cascar, sacudir, zurrar; cortar el cabello en cerquillo; derrabar (un caballo, etc.). **II.** *vn.* hacer estrépito; saltar. **III.** *s.* puñada, porrazo; detonación; ruido de un golpe; (gen. *pl.*) fleco, flequillo o cerquillo de cabello sobre la frente; salto, brinco. **IV.** *adv.* con un golpe violento; con estrépito; de repente. **V.** *interj.* ¡pum!

bangle [bǽŋgl], *s.* ajorca, brazalete sin cierre.

bang-up [bǽŋʌp], *a.* (fam.) de primera; por todo lo alto.

banian [bǽnyan], *s.* (bot.) baniano, higuera de Bengala; baniano, comerciante de la India oriental; bata, ropón.

banish [bǽniʃ], *va.* desterrar, deportar, proscribir, confinar; relegar, ahuyentar.

banishment [-mҽnt], *s.* destierro, deportación, extrañación, expulsión.

banister [bǽnistҽ(r)], *s.* baranda, pasamano.

banjo [bǽndʒou], *s.* (E. U.) banjo, especie de guitarra con caja redonda a modo de pandero.

bank [bæŋk], *s.* orilla, ribera, margen, *mf.* (de un río, lago, arroyo, etc.); terreno, loma; bajo, bajío, banco (de arena, etc.); banda (de mesa de billar); banca (dinero del banquero en el juego); banco de remeros en una galera; serie, hilera; (mús.) teclado; (aer.) inclinación lateral de un aeroplano en una curva; (com.) banco, casa de banca, mesa de cambios; (elec.) batería (de lámparas).—**b. acceptance,** giro contra

un banco aceptado por éste.—**b. account,** cuenta de banco, o en un banco.—**b. bill,** billete de banco; obligación de banco (expedida o aceptada por un banco).—**b. book,** libreta de depósitos del depositante.—**b. discount,** descuento en el cual se deduce del valor nominal el interés de éste hasta la fecha de vencimiento.—**B. for, u of, International Settlements,** Banco de Arreglos Internacionales.—**b. guaranty,** seguro (de un depositante) contra quiebra (del banco).—**b. holiday,** día de fiesta para los bancos, en que éstos se cierran; período en que los bancos están cerrados.—**b. money,** valores de banco.—**b. note,** billete de banco.—**b. of circulation** = B. OF ISSUE.—**b. of deposit,** banco de depósito.—**b. of issue,** banco de emisión.—**b. paper,** papel moneda; obligaciones negociables en los bancos.—**b. rate,** tipo de descuento de un banco, o de los bancos.—**b. roll,** rollo de billetes de banco; (fig.) caudal, fortuna.

bank [bæŋk]. **I.** *va.* represar, estancar o resguardar con dique o reparo; amontonar, apilar; (agr.) acogombrar, aporcar (plantas); depositar en un banco.—**to b. (up) a fire,** cubrir un fuego (con cenizas). **II.** *vn.* ocuparse en negocios de banca, ser banquero; (aer.) inclinar al virar.—**to b. on,** (fam.) apostar a; tener absoluta confianza en. **III.** *va. y vn.* (aer.) ladear(se).

bankable [-abl], *a.* recibidero por un banco.

banker [-œ(r)], *s.* banquero; cambista.

banking [-iŋ]. **I.** *s.* banca, operaciones de banco.—**b. indicator,** (aer.) inclinómetro, indicador de inclinación lateral o de viraje.—**b. rudder,** (aer.) alerón. **II.** *a.* bancario.—**b. house,** casa de banca.

bankrupt [-rʌpt]. **I.** *s. y a.* quebrado, en quiebra, fallido, insolvente.—**fraudulent b.,** alzado.—**to go,** o **become b.,** hacer bancarrota, quebrar. **II.** *va.* hacer quebrar, arruinar.

bankruptcy [-si], *s.* (com.) bancarrota, quiebra.

banner [bǽnœ(r)]. **I.** *s.* bandera, insignia, estandarte, pendón, gonfalón. **II.** *a.* excelente, sobresaliente, principal, digno de llevar la bandera. **III.** *va.* proveer de bandera.

banneret [bǽnœret], *s. dim.* bandereta, pendoncito; caballero con bandera.

bannerol [bǽnœroul], *s.* banderola.

banns [bænz], *s. pl.* amonestaciones. *V.* BAN.

banquet [bǽŋkwit]. **I.** *s.* banquete, festín. **II.** *va. y vn.* banquetear.

banquette [bæŋkét], *s.* (fort.) banqueta, terraplén; (E. U. del Sur) acera; andén; cupé.

bantam [bǽntam]. **I.** *s.* gallinilla de Bantam; persona pequeña y pendenciera. **II.** *a.* diminutivo.—**bantamweight** [-weit], *s.* boxeador de peso gallo (que no pasa de 118 libras).

banter [bǽntœ(r)], *va. y vn.* zumbar(se), dar matraca, fisgar, chotear, torear, tomar el pelo a, embromar.

banter, *s.* zumba, burla, fisga, matraca, chunga.

banterer [-œ(r)], *s.* zumbón, burlón, fisgador.

bantling [bǽntliŋ], *s.* chicuelo, rapaz, mocoso.

banyan, *s. V.* BANIAN.

baobab [béjoubæb], *s.* (bot.) baobab.

baptism [bǽptizm], *s.* (igl.) bautismo; bautizo.

baptismal [bæptízmal], *a.* bautismal.—**b. name,** nombre de bautismo o de pila.

Baptist [bǽptist], *s.* bautista.—**Saint John the B.,** San Juan Bautista.

baptist(e)ry [-ri], *s.* (igl.) bautisterio.

baptistic [bæptístik], *a.* bautismal; perteneciente a los bautistas.

baptize [bæptájz], *va.* bautizar, (fam.) (a)cristianar.

baptizer [-œ(r)], *s.* bautizante, bautista.

bar [bar], *s.* barra; varilla; barr(ill)a, tabl(ill)a o pastilla (de chocolate, etc.); palanca; lista, faja; valla, barrera; bocado (del freno); barra, banco de arena, lodo, etc.; cantina; bar, mostrador de taberna; obstáculo, impedimento; **reja**; tranca, barrote; balaústre; tribunal (de justicia, de la opinión pública); abogacía, foro, curia, cuerpo de abogados licenciados; (for.) foro, estrados; recinto de los acusados; (mús.) barra, raya de compás; (arq.) listón de marco de ventana; (metal.) barra, lingote; (fís.) = ATMOSPHERE, unidad de presión.—**b. association**, colegio de abogados.—**b. bell**, palanqueta de gimnasio.—**b. iron**, hierro forjado en barras. —**b. loom**, telar de barras.—**b. magnet**, barra imanada.—**b. shot**, (arti.) bala enramada, palanqueta.—**b. sight**, mira de atrás (de un cañón).—**b. winding**, (elec.) arrollamiento de barras.—**b. silver**, plata en barras.—**at b.**, (for.) en pleno tribunal.—**in b. of**, para impedir; como razón suficiente para impedir.—**to be admitted**, o **called, to the b.**, recibirse de abogado.

bar, va. (a)trancar, barrear, impedir, estorbar, obstruir, obstar, prohibir; exceptuar, excluir. —**to b. out**, excluir, cerrarle la puerta a.

bar, prep. excepto, salvo.—**b. none**, sin excepción.

barb [barb]. I. s. púa; lengüeta (de saeta, anzuelo, etc.); caballo berberisco; (bot.) barba, arista; (vet.) tolano.—pl. cendal (de pluma). —**b. bolt**, perno dentado, garfio. II. va. armar con lengüetas; hacer incisivo o mordaz.

barbarian [barbérjan], a. y s. bárbaro, barbárico.

barbaric [barbérjk], a. de ruda magnificencia.

barbarism [bárbarizm], s. barbarie; barbarismo.

barbarity [barbérjtj], s. barbaridad, ferocidad.

barbarize [bárbarajz], va. y vn. barbarizar.

barbarous [bárbarʌs], a. bárbaro, inculto; barbárico; cruel, inhumano; de sonido áspero y bronco.—**barbarously** [-lj], adv. bárbaramente.

barbarousness [-njs], s. barbarie, barbarismo.

barbate [bárbejt], a. barbado; (bot.) barbado, aristado.

barbecue [bárbjkju]. I. va. asar un animal entero; (Am.) hacer barbacoa. II. s. animal asado entero; barbacoa; asado al asador.

barbed [barbd], a. barbado, armado con lengüetas o púas; bardado. V. BARD.—**b. wire**, alambre de púas (para cercas).

barbel [bárbel], s. barbilla de ciertos peces; (ict.) barbo, comiza; (vet.) tolano.

barber [bárbœ(r)]. I. s. barbero, peluquero; (fam.) rapador, rapista.—**b. fish** (ict.) barbero.—**b.'s itch**, herpes o tiña tonsorial.—**b. shop**, peluquería, barbería. II. va. afeitar y cortar el pelo.

barberry [bárberj], s. (bot.) bérbero, agracejo.

barbet [bárbet], s. (orn.) ave tropical; variedad del perro de lanas.

barbette [barbét], s. (fort.) barbeta.—**en b.**, a barbeta.

barbican [bárbjkan], s. (fort.) barbacana; tronera, aspillera.

barcarol(l)e [bárkaroʊl], s. (mús.) barcarola.

bard [bárd]. I. s. poeta, m., bardo, vate; barda, arnés, jaez, arreo; (coc.) albardilla; (ict.) mustela de río. II. va. poner barda a un caballo; enjaezar; (coc.) emborrazar, poner albardilla.

bardic, **bardish** [-jk, -jʃ], a. que pertenece a los bardos o poetas.

bare [bér]. I. a. desnudo; raso, pelado; raído, gastado, usado; liso, llano; sencillo, simple; desarmado; descarnado; descubierto; público; mero, puro, solo.—**b. of money**, sin un cuarto, sin blanca.—**to be b. of**, estar desprovisto de. —**to lay b.**, desnudar, descubrir. II. va. desnudar, descubrir, despojar.—**to b. one's head**, descubrirse.

bareback [-bæk], a. y adv. (montado) en pelo, en cerro, sin silla.—**barebacked** [-bækt], a. desensillado, sin silla, en cerro.

bareboned [-boʊnd], a. muy flaco, descarnado.

barefaced [-fejst], a. descarado, desfachatado, insolente, atrevido; raído.—**barefacedly** [-lj],

adv. descaradamente; a cara descubierta.—**barefacedness** [-njs], s. descaro, descoco, desfachatez.

barefoot, **barefooted** [-fut, -jd], a. descalzo.

bareheaded [-hedjd], a. descubierto, sin sombrero.

barelegged [-legjd], a. en pernetas, en piernas.

barely [-lj], adv. sola, mera, escasamente.

barenecked [-nekt], a. descotado, con escote.

bareness [-njs], s. desnudez, desabrigo; flaqueza; laceria, miseria.

bareribbed [-rjbd], a. muy flaco; esquelético.

bargain [bárgjn]. I. s. convenio, concierto, pacto; negocio, trato de compra o venta; ganga, barata, chiripa, precio muy ventajoso para el comprador; artículo a precio reducido.—**b. day**, día de gangas, día de precios rebajados.—**b. driver**, regateador.—**b. sale**, venta a precios rebajados, saldo, barato.—**at a b.**, baratísimo, con gran rebaja, de lance o de ocasión.— **to give into the b.**, dar de más o de ñapa, o por añadidura.—**to make a b.**, hacer un convenio o un trato.—**to strike a b.**, cerrar un trato, llegar a un convenio; hallar una ganga, comprar muy barato. II. va. y vn. concertar, contratar, negociar, tratar; regatear.—**to b. away**, permutar, vender; dar por una bicoca, sacrificar, vender regalado.

bargainee [-i], s. (for.) el que pacta para comprar; el contratante comprador.

bargainer [-œ(r)], s. el que hace un pacto de compra o venta.

bargaining [-jŋ], s. regateo; trato.

bargainor [-ǫ(r)], s. (for.) el que pacta para vender; el contratante vendedor.

barge [bárdʒ], s. (mar.) alijador, bombo, lanchón, barcaza, gabarra; chata.—**b. board**, (arq.) alero.—**b. canal**, canal interior para barcos de carga.—**bargeman** [-man], **barger** [-œ(r)], s. barquero, lanchero.—**bargemaster** [-mæstœ(r)], s. patrón de barca o lanchón.

baric [bérjk], a. barométrico; (quím.) de bario.

barilla [barílja], s. barrilla (planta o cenizas), sosa, mazacote, natrón.—**b. pits, b. plantation**, barrillar.

barite [bérajt], s. (min.) baritina. V. BARYTES.

baritone [bérjtoʊn], s. (mús.) barítono, bajete.

barium [bérjʌm], s. (quím.) bario.

bark [bark]. I. s. corteza, cáscara (de árbol); ladrido, ladra, latido (del perro, etc.); (mar.) barca, buque de tres palos; (fam.) tos, f.—**b. beetle**, escarabajo horadador que ataca el abeto.—**b. mill**, triturador de casca.—**his b. is worse than his bite**, perro ladrador, poco mordedor. II. va. descortezar, raspar, raer; cubrir con corteza; encostrar; curtir o teñir en una infusión de cortezas. III. vn. ladrar, latir; vociferar; (fam.) toser.—**to b. up the wrong tree**, (fam.) ir descaminado, tomar el rábano por las hojas.

barkeeper [bárkipœ(r)], s. tabernero, cantinero.

barkentine [bárkentin], s. (mar.) bergantín.

barker [bárkœ(r)], s. ladrador; descortezador; vociferador; (fam.) gritón, esp. el que vende o anuncia algo a gritos.

barking [bárkjŋ]. I. s. ladrido, ladra, latido. II. a. ladrador, ladrante.

barky [bárkj], a. cortezudo.

barley [bárlj], s. cebada, alcacer.—**b. dealer**, cebadero.—**b. field**, cebadal.—**b. sugar**, una especie de alfeñique.—**b. water**, hordiate.

barleycorn [-korn], s. grano de cebada; tercio de pulgada; ancho de un grano de cebada (como 4 mm.).—**B.**, o **John B.**, personificación del licor, Baco.

barm [barm], s. jiste; levadura; espuma.

barmaid [bármejd], cantinera, moza de taberna.

barmy [bármj], a. espumoso; activo; veleidoso.

barn [barn], s. granero, pajar, troje, f., henil, hórreo; establo (para ganado); cobertizo para coches de tranvía.—**b. owl**, autillo, especie de

lechuza.—**b. swallow,** (orn.) golondrina norteamericana.
barnacle [bárnak̯l], *s.* (zool.) broma, lapa, escaramujo, percebe; (orn.) barnacla; (herr.) acial.—
pl. (fam.) anteojos, antiparras.
barnstorm [bárnstɔrm], *vn.* andar representando
en poblaciones pequeñas.
barnstormer [-œ(r)], *s.* actorzuelo, actor de poca
monta; actor ambulante, cómico de la legua.
barnyard [bárnyard], *s.* patio de granja.—**b.
fowl,** aves (*f. pl.*) de corral.
barograph, barometrograph [bǽrɔgrǽf, bæro-
métrɔgrǽf], *s.* barógrafo, barometrógrafo.
barology [barálodʒi̯], *s.* barología.
barometer [barámɛtœ(r)], *s.* barómetro.
barometrical [bæ-rométrik̯ạl], *a.* barométrico.
barometry [barámɛtri̯], *s.* barometría.
baron [bǽrọn], *s.* barón.
baronage [-idʒ], **barony** [-i̯], *s.* baronía.
baroness [-i̯s], *s.* baronesa.
baronet [-ɛt], *s.* título hereditario de barón en
Inglaterra.—**baronetage** [-idʒ], **baronetcy,
baronetship** [-si̯, -ši̯p], *s.* dignidad o patente
de *baronet.*
baronial [baróuni̯ạl], *a.* pert. a barón o baronía.
baroque [baróuk̯], *a.* (b. a.) barroco.
baroscope [bǽroskoup̯], *s.* baroscopio.
barouche [barúš], *s.* birlocho, milord.
barracan [bǽrakæn], *s.* barragán.
barrack [bǽrak̯]. **I.** *s.* (gen. *pl.*) (mil.) cuartel;
caserna; barraca. **II.** *va. y vn.* acuartelar(se),
abarracar(se).
barracoon [bærakún], *s.* barracón.
barrage [baráʒ], *s.* (hidr.) presa de contención;
(mil.) cortina de fuego, fuego concentrado de
artillería, fuego de barrera.—**b. balloon,** globo
de cortina contra aeroplanos, del cual van sus-
pendidos alambres o redes.
barrator [bǽratọ(r)], *s.* picapleitos; trapacero;
camorrista; (for.) el culpable de baratería.
barratry [-tri̯], *s.* (for.) baratería.
barrel [bǽrɛl]. **I.** *s.* barril o barrica, candiota,
bocoy, tonel; tambor de reloj; tímpano del
oído; capacidad de un barril; cubeta, rodillo,
tambor de cabrestante o molinete; cañón de
escopeta; cañón de pluma; cuerpo de bomba.—
b. maker, barrilero.—**b. organ,** organillo.—
b. process, (min.) extracción del oro y la
plata por tratamiento en cilindros giratorios.—
b. roll, vuelta de un avión alrededor de su
eje longitudinal.—**b. vault,** (arq.) bóveda en
cañón. **II.** *va.* envasar, embarrilar, entonelar.
barren [bǽrẹn]. **I.** *a.* estéril, infructuoso, árido,
improductivo, infecundo. **II.** *s.* (gen. *pl.*)
tierras estér:les; eriales.—**barrenly** [-li̯], *adv.*
infructuosamente, estérilmente.—**barrenness**
[-nịs], *s.* esterilidad, infecundidad, aridez.
barrette [barét], *s.* broche para el cabello.
barretter [bǽrịtœ(r)], *s.* (elec.) detector de
oscilaciones eléctricas.
barricade [bǽrikéi̯d]. **I.** *s.* barrera, empalizada,
barricada, valla. **II.** *va.* obstruir; cerrar con
barricadas, barr(e)ar.
barrier [bǽriœ(r)], *s.* barrera, valla; cerca; (fort.)
espaldón; fortaleza; impedimento, obstáculo,
estacada, atasco; término, límite.
barring [bári̯ŋ], *prep.* salvo, excepto, quitando.
barrister [bǽrịstœ(r)], *s.* abogado.
barroom [bárrum], *s.* taberna, cantina, bar.
barrow [bǽroụ], *s.* angarillas, *f. pl.*; parihuela(s);
carretilla; madriguera (de animal); vestido de
niño; túmulo; escurridor; marrano o puerco
castrado.
barshot [báršat], *s.* (arti.) palanqueta.
bartender [bártendœ(r)], *s.* tabernero, cantinero.
barter [bártœ(r)]. **I.** *vn.* baratar, traficar, feriar,
trujamanear. **II.** *va.* trocar, cambiar, conmutar,
cambalachear, permutar. **III.** *s.* cambio, trueque, permuta, barata, cambalache.
barterer [-œ(r)], *s.* traficante, baratador, cambalachero.

bartizan [bártizan], *s.* garita (de un castillo).
barycentric [bærịséntrik̯], *a.* (fís.) baricéntrico.
baryta [bæráịtǎ], *s.* (quím.) barita.
barytes [bæráịtiz], *s.* (min.) baritina.
barytic [bærịtik̯], *a.* barítico.
barytone [bǽrịtoụn], *s.* (mús.) barítono, bajete.
basal [béịsạl], *a.* fundamental; básico.
basalt [bǽsɔlt], *s.* basalto.
basaltic [bæsɔ́ltik̯], *a.* basáltico.
bascule [bǽskịul], *s.* palanca basculante u
oscilante.—**b. bridge,** puente levadizo.
base [béịs]. **I.** *a.* que sirve de base; de referencia;
bajo, ruin, vil, villano, rastrero; humilde; bajo
de ley, de mala ley; (mús.) bajo, grave.—
b. bullion, plomo en bruto que contiene plata,
antimonio, etc.—**b. circle,** (mec.) círculo
primitivo (de una rueda dentada).—**b. course,**
(arq.) hilada inferior, primera hilada.—**b.
court,** patio; tribunal inferior.—**b. line,** (top.)
línea de base; línea del saque (tenis).—**b.
metal,** metal común (no precioso); (fig.) cosa
o persona de poco mérito. **II.** *s.* base, *f.,*
cimiento, fundamento; (arg. y mec.) basa,
base, fundación, lecho, pedestal, pie, *m.,*
zócalo; (mil., quím., mat.) base; (mús.) bajo,
grave; (béisbol) base, cada uno de los cuatro
puestos que forman cuadro. **III.** *va.* (a menudo
con **on**) basar, apoyar, fundar o fundamentar
(en).
baseball [-bɔ́l], *s.* béisbol o basebol; pelota de
baseball.—**b. player,** basebolista, jugador de
béisbol, etc.
baseboard [-bɔrd], *s.* (arq.) zócalo; plancha que
sirve de base; tabla o listón de resguardo en la
base de una pared; rodapié, *m.,* friso inferior.
baseborn [-bɔ́rn], *a.* bajo, plebeyo; bastardo.
baseburner [-bœrnœ(r)], *s.* horno de alimentación automática.
baseless [-lịs], *a.* desfondado; infundado, sin
fundamento o base.
basely [-li̯], *adv.* bajamente, vilmente.
basement [-mẹnt], *s.* (arq.) basamento; cuarto
bajo, sótano.
baseness [-nịs], *s.* bajeza, vileza, ruindad.
bash [bǽš]. **I.** *s.* golpe aplastante. **II.** *va.* golpear
fuertemente; despedazar, quebrar a golpes.
bashaw [bąšɔ́], *s.* bajá, *m.*
bashful [-fụl], *a.* vergonzoso, ruboroso, tímido,
corto, encogido; esquivo.—**bashfully** [-li̯], *adv.*
tímidamente, turbadamente, modestamente.—
bashfulness [-nịs], *s.* vergüenza, timidez,
cortedad, encogimiento; esquivez.
basic [béịsik̯], *a.* fundamental; (quím.) básico.
basidium [bąsíḍiam], *s.* (bot.) báside, célula
esporífera de algunos hongos.
basify [béịsifaị], *va.* (quím.) basificar.
basil [bǽzịl], *s.* (bot.) albahaca, alábega; (carp.)
filo achaflanado de escoplo o cepillo; badana.
basilar [bǽsịlä(r)], **basilary** [-ɛrị], *a.* basilar.
Basilian [bæsíli̯ạn], *a. y s.* (igl.) basilio.
basilic [bąsílik̯], *s.* (arq.) basílica; (anat.) vena
basílica.
basilic(al [-ạl], *a.* (anat.) basílica; (arq.) pert.
a una basílica; real, regio; (farm.) basilicón.
basilica [bąsílikạ], *s.* (arq.) basílica; túmulo
endoselado; (**B.**) basílicas (leyes).
basilicon [-ɔn], *s.* (farm.) ungüento basilicón.
basilisk [bǽsịlisk̯], *s.* (zool.) basilisco, régulo.
basin [béịsịn], *s.* (al)jofaina, bacía, palangana
(para lavar, etc.); cubeta; pila (para agua
bendita); pila(r), pilón, taza, tazón (de fuente,
etc.); estanque, represa, dársena; charca, laguna; (geog.) cuenca de un río, hoya, valle;
(anat.) cavidad de la pelvis; platillo de balanza.
basinet [bǽsịnet], *s.* (arm.) bacinete, capacete.
basis [béịsịs], *s.* base, *f.,* fundación; fundamento,
principio fundamental; elemento principal.
bask [bǽsk̯]. **I.** *va.* asolear, calentar al sol. **II.** *vn.*
tomar el sol.—**basking shark,** tiburón gigante
del Atlántico septentrional.
basket [bǽskịt]. **I.** *s.* cesta, cesto, canasta,

cuévano; cestada; guarnición reticulada o cazoleta de la espada (llamada también **b. hilt**); la espada que la tiene; (aer.) barquilla (de un dirigible o globo).—**b. carriage**, jardinera, carrito de junco.—**b. maker**, o **seller**, canastero, cestero.—**b. making**, cestería.—**b. work**, (labor de) cestería. **II**. *va*. encestar, encanastar.

basketball [-bɔl], *s*. baloncesto, basketbol, basquetbol.—**b. player**, basquetbolista.

basketful [-fŭl], *s*. cestada.

basketry [-rɪ], *s*. fabricación de cestas.

Basque [bæsk], *a*. y *s*. vasco, vascongado (apl. esp. a las personas); vascuence, éuscaro, éusquero (apl. esp. al idioma).

basque, *s*. especie de jubón o chaqueta de mujer.

bas-relief [barɪlíf], *s*. (b. a.) bajo relieve o bajorrelieve, entretalladura.

bass [bæs], *s*. (ict.) lobina; (bot.) tilo (= BASS-WOOD); líber (= BAST).

bass [bejs]. **I**. *a*. (mús.) bajo, grave.—**b. drum**, bombo.—**b. horn**, tuba.—**b. string**, bordón.—**b. viol**, violón; violoncelo. **II**. *s*. bajo (apl. a la voz, instrumento o músico.)

basset [bǽsɪt]. **I**. *s*. juego de naipes, algo parecido al faraón o las pintas; tipo de pachón, casta de perro de caza, de piernas cortas y orejas largas; (geol., min.) afloramiento.—**b. horn**, (mús.) clarinete de tenor. **II**. *vn*. (min., geol.) aflorar, campear.

bassinet [bæsɪnét], *s*. cuna; cesto de ajuar para nene; cochecillo de niño; (arm.) *V*. BASINET.

basso [bǽsoŭ], *s*. (mús.) bajo.—**b.-rilievo** [-rɪlívoŭ], *s*. (b. a.) bajo relieve.

bassoon [bæsún], *s*. (mús.) bajón, fagot, piporro.

basswood [bǽswŭd], *s*. (bot.) tilo americano.

bast [bæst], *s*. (bot.) líber; estera, cuerda, etc., hecha de líber.

bastard [bǽstǝːd]. **I**. *s*. bastardo, hijo natural. **II**. *a*. bastardo, borde, ilegítimo, noto; falso, espurio; degenerado; anormal; (impr.) bastardo.—**b. file**, lima bastarda.—**b. title**, (impr.) anteportada.

bastardize [-ajz], *va*. y *vn*. probar que alguno es bastardo; bastardear; abastardar.

bastardly [-lɪ], *adv*. como bastardo.

bastardy [-ɪ], *s*. bastardía.

baste [bejst], *va*. (cost.) hilvanar, bastear, embastar; (coc.) pringar, lard(e)ar, emborrazar; (fam.) dar de palos.

bastile, bastille [bæstíl], *s*. bastilla, castillo, fortaleza; prisión.

bastinado [bæstɪnéjdoŭ]. **I**. *s*. paliza, bastonazo. **II**. *va*. bastonear, dar una paliza.

basting [béjstɪŋ], *s*. (cost.) hilván, basta, embaste; (coc.) emborrazamiento, acto de pringar o lardear; (fam.) paliza.—**b. thread**, hilo de hilvanar.

bastion [bǽschǝn], *s*. (fort.) bastión, *m*., baluarte.

bat [bæt]. **I**. *s*. garrote, palo con que se juega baseball (ll. t. *bate* en algunas partes); paleta (para el juego de cri(c)quet); raqueta (para ciertos juegos); (zool.) murciélago; algodón o lana en hojas (= BATTING); tejoleta, pedazo de ladrillo; albarda; (fam.) parranda.—**to go on a b.**, (fam.) ir de parranda.—**to go to b. for**, (fam.) volver por, salir a la defensa de. **II**. *va*. y *vn*. dar, golpear, volear o batear con un *bat*; pestañear (los ojos).

Batavian [batéjvjan], *a*. y *s*. bátavo, de Batavia.

batch [bæch], *s*. cochura, hornada, tanda; número o cantidad de cosas que se reciben, se despachan o se confeccionan de una vez.

bate [bejt]. **I**. *va*. minorar, disminuir; rebajar el precio; (ten.) poner en remojo; separar y ablandar (yute).—**with bated breath**, pasmado, con aliento entrecortado. **II**. *vn*. minorarse, mermar; aletear (= TO BAIT).

batfowling [bǽtfaŭlɪŋ], *s*. caza nocturna de aves con lumbre.

bath [bæθ], *s*. baño; cuarto de baño; bañadera; (fot., quím.) baño, solución.—*pl*. balneario,

establecimiento de baños.—**b. keeper** o **attendant**, bañero.—**Knight of the B.** (K. B.), Caballero de la Orden del Baño.—**to take a b.**, bañarse.

bathe [bejð]. **I**. *va*. bañar, lavar. **II**. *vn*. bañarse.

bather [-œ(r)], *s*. bañista, bañador.

bathhouse [-haŭs], *s*. casa de baños; casilla o desvestidero en un balneario.

bathing [béjðɪŋ]. **I**. *s*. baño. **II**. *a*. de baño.—**b. place** o **resort**, bañadero, baño, balneario.—**b. robe** = BATHROBE.—**b. suit**, traje o malla de baño.—**b. trunks**, calzón de baño.

bathometer [bæθámetœ(r)], *s*. batómetro.

bathorse [bǽthɔrs], *s*. acémila.

bathos [béjθas], *s*. paso de lo sublime a lo ridículo.

bathrobe [bǽθroŭb], *s*. bata de baño, albornoz, *m*.

bathroom [-rum], *s*. (cuarto de) baño.

bathtub [-tʌb], *s*. bañadera, baño, bañera, tina.

bathymeter [bæθímetœ(r)], *s*. batómetro.

bathymetry [-trɪ], *s*. batometría, determinación de profundidades en el mar.

bating [béjtɪŋ], *prep*. excepto, exceptuando, deduciendo.

batiste [bætíst], *s*. (tej.) batista, holán, holanda.

baton [bætán]. **I**. *s*. bastón de mando; (mús.) batuta. **II**. *va*. bastonear.

Batrachia [bætréjkjǎ], *s*. *pl*. (zool.) batracios.

batrachian [-n], *a*. y *s*. batracio.

batsman [bǽtsman], *s*. el que volea la pelota con el *bat* en el béisbol o cri(c)quet.

battalion [bætǽlyǝn], *s*. (mil.) batallón.

batten [bǽtɛn]. **I**. *s*. lata, tabla de chilla, listón, alfa(r)jía, taujel, tablilla, tejamanil. **II**. *va*. cebar, engordar; (agr.) abonar la tierra; (carp.) listonar, construir con lata, tablillas, o tablas de chilla.—**to b. down the hatches**, (mar.) cerrar las escotillas y asegurarlas con listones de madera. **II**. *vn*. engordar, ponerse gordo; medrar a expensas de otro; saciar un deseo malsano.

batter [bǽtœ(r)]. **I**. *va*. apalear, cascar, golpear batir, cañonear; romper, desmenuzar; destruir, demoler, derribar, mellar, estropear, majar. **II**. *vn*. golpear, majar; inclinarse hacia arriba y atrás. **III**. *s*. (coc.) albard(ill)a; batido, pasta culinaria; golpeo, golpeadura; batidor de yeso; (tip.) estropeo de tipos o de una plancha; (ing. y arq.) talud, *m*., declive de un parapeto; (dep.) *v*. BATSMAN.

batterer [-œ(r)], *s*. apaleador.

battering piece [-ɪŋ pis] o **gun** [gʌn], *s*. (arti.) pieza de batir.—**b. ram**, ariete, brigola.—**b. train**, batería de sitio.

battery [bǽtœrɪ], *s*. (arti. y mec.) batería; (for.) agresión; (elec.) pila; batería, acumulador.

batting [bǽtɪŋ], *s*. el acto de apalear, golpear, etc.; guata, algodón o lana en hojas o en rama; (dep.) voleo.

battle [bǽtl]. **I**. *s*. batalla, combate; lucha, lidia.—**b. array**, orden de batalla.—**b. ax(e)**, hacha de armas.—**b. cruiser**, crucero acorazado o de combate.—**b. cry**, grito de guerra.—**b. fleet**, escuadra o flota de combate.—**b. front**, frente de combate.—**b. piece**, (b. a.) cuadro que representa una batalla.—**b. royal**, riña promiscua, pelotera.—**to do b.**, batallar, luchar.—**to offer b.**, presentar batalla. **II**. *vn*. batallar, luchar, combatir. **III**. *va*. luchar o batirse con; (fort.) almenar.

battled [-d], *a*. almenado.

battledore [-dor], *s*. raqueta.—**b and shuttlecock**, raqueta y volante (juego).

battlefield [-fild], **battleground** [-graŭnd], *s*. campo de batalla.

battlement [-mɛnt], *s*. muralla almenada, almenaje; pretil con cresteria.

battlemented [-id], *a*. almenado.

battleplane [-plejn], *s*. avión (*m*.) de combate.

battler [bǽtlœ(r)], **battling** [bǽtlɪŋ], *a*. y *s*. batallador.

battleship [-ʃɪp], *s*. acorazado.

battlewagon, (fam.) = BATTLESHIP.
battology [bætálodżị], *s.* batología.
battue [bætú], *s.* batida (de caza); matanza inicua.
batty [bǽtị], *a.* de o como el murciélago; (fam.) chiflado.
bauble, bawble [bóbl], *s.* bujería, chuchería, fruslería, futesa, friolera; varilla de bufón.
baulk, *vn.* = BALK.
bauxite [bóksajt], *s.* (min.) bauxita.
Bavarian [bạvérịan], *a.* y *s.* bávaro.
bawd [bód]. **I.** *s.* alcahuete, alcahueta, rufián, tercero. **II.** *vn.* alcahuetear.
bawdily [-ịlị], *adv.* obscenamente.
bawdiness [-ịnịs], *s.* alcahuetería; obscenidad.
bawdry [-rị], *s.* alcahuetería, rufianería.
bawdy [-ị], *a.* indecente, obsceno, impúdico.—**b. house**, lupanar, burdel, mancebía.
bawl [ból]. **I.** *va.* pregonar;—**to b. someone out**, (fam.) regañar; poner como chupa de dómine. **II.** *vn.* gritar, vocear, chillar, desgañitarse; (fam.) llorar a moco tendido. **III.** *s.* gritería, vocería.
bawler [-œ(r)], *s.* voceador, vocinglero, alborotador, gritador, chillón.
bay [bej]. **I.** *a.* bayo. **II.** *va.* ladrar a, acorralar. **III.** *vn.* ladrar, aullar. **IV.** *s.* bahía, ancón, cala, ensenada, rada; abra; entrada (de agua en tierra, de un valle en el flanco de una montaña, etc.); ladrido, aullido; caballo bayo; acorralamiento; pajar de almacenar heno; corona de laurel; (bot.) laurel; (*pl.*) corona de laurel, renombre; (arq.) intercolumnio, crujía, entrepaño; vano; recuadro; (hidr.) agua de una entrada o compartimiento a la cabeza de una esclusa, a la entrada de una turbina, etc.; (ing.) ojo de puente; (mar.) cierta parte del buque [que sirve de hospital.—**b. rum**, ron con aceite esencial de laurel o de malagueta.—**b. salt**, sal marina.—**B. State**, estado de Massachusetts (E. U.).—**b. tree**, laurel.—**b. window**, mirador, ventana saliente, balcón cerrado.—**b. work**, entramado.—**at b.**, acosado, acorralado; a raya.
bayadere [bejɐdịr], *s.* bayadera.
bayberry [béjberị], *s.* (bot.) fruto o baya del laurel; variedad de arrayán brabántico o de mírica cerífera.—**b. tallow**, cera del arrayán brabántico o de la mírica cerífera.
baying [béjiŋ], *s.* ladrido.
bayonet [béjọnịt]. **I.** *s.* bayoneta. **II.** *va.* cargar o herir con bayoneta.
bayou [báju], *s.* (E. U. del Sur) ensenada, brazo de río, etc., de aguas algo estancadas.
baywood [béjwụd], *s.* caoba tosca de Campeche y Honduras.
baza(a)r [bazár], *s.* bazar, feria; a veces, tómbola.
bazooka [bạzúkạ], *s.* (mil.) bazuco, cierto cañón antitanque portátil que dispara cohetes.
bdellium [délịʌm], *s.* bedelio, gomorresina.
be [bi], *vn.* (*ind.* AM, ART, IS; ARE; *pret.* WAS, WAST, WERT; WERE; *subj.* BE, WERE, WERT; *pp.* BEEN) ser; estar; haber; hacer; tener; existir; encontrarse, hallarse, verse, andar, resultar. Son éstos los verbos más empleados. Ejemplos generales del uso de *ser* y *estar*: *he is a doctor*, es médico; *he is old*, es viejo; *he is from Madrid*, es de Madrid; *it is I*, soy yo; *it is they*, son ellos; *it is 2 o'clock*, son las dos; *ice is cold*, el hielo es frío; *it is possible*, es posible; *the door was opened by*, la puerta fué abierta por; *so be it* (o *be it so*), sea, así sea; *he is tired*, él está cansado; *he is in Sevilla*, está en Sevilla; *he is about to do it*, está para hacerlo; *he is for doing it*, está por hacerlo; *he is dead*, está muerto; *the coffee is cold*, el café está frío; *it's all right*, está bien; *the door is open*, la puerta está abierta. Con el expletivo *there* equivale al impersonal *haber*, pero concuerda en número con el substantivo que le sigue, vg., *there is a man in the room*, hay un hombre en el cuarto; *there are two*

men, hay dos hombres. Con ciertas expresiones impersonales se emplea el verbo *hacer*, vg., *it is cold today*, hace frío hoy; *it is good weather*, hace buen tiempo; *it is sunny*, hace sol; *it is a long time*, hace mucho tiempo. Con algunos adjetivos, esp. cuando indican sensaciones, forma frases que se traducen por *tener* seguido del substantivo correspondiente, vg., *to be hungry and cold*, tener hambre y frío; *to be desirous of*, tener ganas de; *to be successful*, tener éxito; *to be unlucky*, tener mala suerte; *to be right*, tener razón; *to be in a hurry*, tener prisa; *to be 10 years old*, tener 10 años. Con algunos verbos neutros es equivalente al auxiliar *to have*, haber: *he was gone*, se había ido; *the time is come*, ha llegado el tiempo. Seguido de infinitivo equivale a veces a: 1) deber, tener que, vg., *I am to be there*, debo (o tengo que) estar allí. 2) *can*, *could*, vg., *how am I to know it?* ¿cómo puedo saberlo? *what were we to do?* ¿qué podíamos hacer? 3) *to be going to*, ir a, vg., *he was to speak that evening*, iba a hablar esa noche. Seguido de *being* y un participio forma frases de construcción pasiva, vg., *the house is being built*, la casa se está construyendo. Seguido de gerundio, forma frases equivalentes a estas últimas, vg., *the house is building*, la casa se está construyendo. También seguido de gerundio, indica a veces un acto que acaba de ejecutarse o se piensa ejecutar pronto, vg., *I am sending you the book under separate cover*, le envío el libro en otra cubierta; *we are dining at home tonight*, esta noche comemos (o comeremos) en casa. Seguido de *to be* y un participio en frases impersonales equivale a *ser* de seguido de infinitivo reflexivo, vg., *it is to be regretted*, es de sentirse; *it is to be noted*, es de notarse. En otros casos se emplea gran variedad de verbos para traducir el verbo *to be*. Ejemplos de éstos se dan a continuación: *how much is it (worth)?* ¿cuánto vale? *it's all over*, se acabó; *I am very sorry*, lo siento mucho; *we are agreed*, quedamos de acuerdo o conformes; *he is obliged to go*, se ve obligado a ir; *she is disposed to sell it*, se halla dispuesta a venderlo; *they are here*, se encuentran aquí; *English is spoken here*, aquí se habla inglés; *he is looking for it*, va (anda, sigue) buscándolo; *two were hurt and one killed*, resultaron dos heridos y un muerto; *have you been here long?* ¿lleva Ud. mucho tiempo aquí? *I'm not too well these days*, no ando muy bueno estos días; *they are no more*, ya no existen. Para las expresiones **to be in**, **off, out, up**, *V.* IN, OFF, etc.
beach [bich]. **I.** *s.* costa, ribera, playa, orilla.—**b. comber**, vago de las playas o puertos; buscador de pecios, etc.; (E. U.) ola encrestada.—**b. robe**, albornoz, *m.*—**b. wagon**, cierto tipo de automóvil. **II.** *va.* impeler o arrastrar a la playa. **III.** *vn.* varar, encallar o dar en la playa.
beached [-t], *a.* varado, encallado.
beachhead [-hed], *s.* (mil.) cabeza de playa; punto de avanzada establecido en una playa al efectuarse una invasión.
beachy [bíchị], *a.* playado.
beacon [bíkọn]. **I.** *s.* (mar.) baliza, boya; faro, fanal, almenara, ángaro, alcandora, atalaya; señal luminosa, luz; guía.—**b. fire**, fuego de señal o alarma. **II.** *va.* abalizar; señalar con almenara; iluminar, guiar.
beaconage [-ịdż], *s.* derechos de faros.
bead [bid]. **I.** *s.* cuenta, cañutillo, chaquira, agallón, rocalla, abalorio; burbuja; espuma; bolita, gota, glóbulo; saliente, pestaña, listoncillo o tira convexa; mira globular de un arma; (aut.) pestaña o reborde de un neumático; (arq.) moldura convexa; (quím.) botón, glóbulo de bórax, etc. empleado en el análisis al soplete para determinaciones por el color; (min.) glóbulo de metal precioso obtenido por

copelación.—*pl.*, rosario.—**b. tree**, (bot.) cinamomo.—**to draw a b. on**, apuntar a con un arma de fuego.—**to say**, *o* **tell, one's beads**, rezar el rosario. II. *va.* adornar con abalorios; redondear los bordes (de un tubo ensanchado, etc.); proveer de molduras convexas, pestañas, etc. (*v.* I.). III. *vn.* ser espumoso, formar espuma; burbujear.

beading [bídiŋ], *s.* abalorio; preparación para formar espuma en los licores; (arq.) listón, astrágalo, tondino; moldura convexa; pestaña, reborde.

beadle [bídl], *s.* pertiguero o macero, muñidor, bedel, alguacil, ministril.

beadleship [-ŝip], *s.* bedelía.

beadwork [bídwœrk], *s. V.* BEADING.

beady [bígl], *a.* parecido a abalorio; que tiene espuma o jiste.

beagle [bígl], *s.* especie de sabueso pequeño; (fig.) alguacil, corchete; (ict.) tiburón pequeño.

beak [bik], *s.* (zool.) pico, hocico, rostro; (fam.) rostro; cabo, promontorio (de tierra); pico (de jarro, retorta o vaso; (mar.) beque, espolón, rostro (de navío).—**b. iron**, (pico de) bigornia.

beaked [-t], *a.* picudo.

beaker [bíkœ(r)], *s.* vaso o copa de boca ancha; (quím.) vaso picudo para los análisis.

beam [bím]. I. *s.* viga, tablón, trabe, *f.*; (*pl.*) envigado; vigueta; rayo, destello (de luz); (mar.) bao; manga de un buque; (tej.) enjulio, vara o plegador (de telar); astil o cruz de balanza; brazo de una báscula o romana; palanca oscilante; lanza de coche; (rad.) rayo radiogoniométrico.—**b. balance**, balanza de cruz o brazos.—**b. compass**, compás de regla o de barra.—**b. engine**, máquina de balancín.—**b. sea**, mar de costado.—**b. tree**, (bot.) mostajo, mostellar.—**on the b.**, (mar.) por el través; (fam.) listo, al tanto o al corriente.—**to be on her b. ends**, (mar.) estar de costado, estar ladeado (apl. a los barcos). II. *vn.* destellar, fulgurar; estar rebosando de alegría. III. *va.* envigar; emitir, despedir (rayos de luz, etc.).—**to b. a broadcast**, (rad.) dirigir una radiodifusión hacia un punto determinado.

beaming [-iŋ], *a.* radiante; brillante; alegre.

beamy [-i], *a.* radiante; alegre, vivo; macizo, como viga; astado (venado); (mar.) ancho de manga.

bean [bin]. I. *s.* (bot.) haba, habichuela, alubia, judía, frijol, fréjol (*V.* KIDNEY B., STRING B.); grano, semilla, almendra (de café, cacao, etc.); (fam.) cabeza, testa.—**b. pole**, rodrigón.— **in the b.**, en grano. II. *va.* (fam.) dar en la cabeza con la pelota (béisbol).

bear [ber], *va.* (*pret.* BORE; *pp.* BORNE, O BORN) sostener, aguantar, sustentar; llevar, cargar; mostrar, dar muestras; soportar, sufrir, tolerar, conllevar, sobrellevar; sufragar (los gastos); asumir o tener una obligación, carga o responsabilidad; usar alguna insignia de autoridad o distinción; (com)portarse, conducirse (como *vr.*); profesar o tener (amor, odio); tener, guardar (relación, etc.); producir, rendir; parir, dar a luz (en este sentido, el *pp.* es **born**); dar (testimonio); ejercer por derecho o autoridad; ser susceptible de admitir; llevar, tener (una marca, inscripción, etc.); impeler, empujar; deprimir; (com.) hacer bajar el valor, jugar a la baja.—**to b. a hand**, ayudar, echar una mano.—**to b. arms**, servir de soldado.— **to b. away**, llevarse; ganarse.—**to b. company**, acompañar.—**to b. date**, estar fechado. —**to b. down**, reducir a un lugar inferior, hundir, deprimir; derribar, vencer, postrar.— **to b. in**, socavar, aflojar (el carbón de una mina).—**to b. in mind**, tener presente o en cuenta.—**to b. interest**, devengar interés.— **to b. off**, contener, separar; ganar, llevarse (un premio, etc.); (mar.) salvar, apartarse de,

para no rozar o chocar.—**to b. out**, sostener, apoyar; confirmar; hacer llevadero.—**to b. the bag**, tener la bolsa, dominar o manejar los fondos.—**to b. up**, sostener.—**to b. witness**, atestiguar, testimoniar.

bear, *vn.* padecer, sufrir; aguantar, soportar; fructificar, dar fruto; dirigirse o encaminarse; tener o llevar cierta dirección, señalar (vg. *the ship bears north*, el barco lleva dirección norte; *this line bears east*, esta línea tiene dirección, o rumbo, este); demorar.—**to b. away**, (mar.) desatracar, cambiar la dirección de un barco, sobre todo a sotavento.—**to b. back**, retroceder, retirarse.—**to b. down on**, *o* **upon**, acosar, atacar despiadadamente, caer sobre.—**to b. off**, (mar.) alejarse.—**to b. on**, referirse a, atañer.—**to b. up**, cobrar ánimo, resignarse; (mar.) = TO B. AWAY.—**to b. upon**, (mil.) estar dirigido a, dominar.—**to b. with**, tener paciencia con, ser indulgente con.

bear, *s.* (zool.) oso; (com.) bajista.—(**B.**, astr.) Osa.—**b. account**, (com.) cuenta de especulación a la baja.—**b.-baiting**, deporte de atormentar osos cautivos, gen. con perros.—**b. cub**, osezno.—**b. den**, osera.—**b. garden**, patio de osos; (fam.) Babel, campo de Agramante.— **b.'s-breech**, (bot.) branca ursina, acanto.— **b.'s-ear**, (bot.) oreja de oso, aurícula.—**b.'s-foot**, (bot.) eléboro negro.

bearable [bérabl], *a.* sufrible, soportable.

bearberry [bérberj], *s.* (bot.) gayuba, aguavilla, uvaduz.

bearbind [-bajnd], *s.* (bot.) correhuela.

beard [bírd]. I. *s.* barba o barbas; (bot.) raspa, arista; lengüeta de flecha; barbas de pluma. II. *va.* arrancar las barbas, mesar; retar.

bearded [-id], *a.* barbado; barbudo; (bot.) aristado; (bot.) caudato.

beardless [-lis], *a.* imberbe, barbilampiño, (cari)lampiño; (bot.) derraspado.—**b. wheat**, trigo chamorro.—**b. youth**, rapagón.

bearer [bérœ(r)], *s.* portador, dador; faquín; andero, camillero; árbol fructífero; (tec. y mec.) soporte, caballete; asiento; viga maestra de apoyo; (print.) calzo. *V.* PALLBEARER.—**b. stock**, acciones (*f. pl.*) al portador.

bearing [bériŋ]. I. *s.* aguante, paciencia, sufrimiento; porte, maneras, presencia, talante; relación, conexión; fuerza, sentido, valor de una expresión; producción, fructificación, cosecha; gestación, preñez; (mec.) punto de apoyo; cojinete; soporte; (rad.) marcación; (arq.) apoyo, sostén; (mar.) orientación, marcación, situación, arrumbamiento, demora; (top. y mar.) rumbo.—*pl.* orientación, rumbo; línea de flotación (de un barco).—**b. cloth**, capa de cristianar.—**b. metal**, metal para cojinetes; metal antifricción.—**to find one's bearings**, orientarse.—**to have no b. on**, no tener relación con, no concernir.—**to lose one's bearings**, desorientarse; confundirse, aturdirse.— **to take a b.**, (top.) determinar un rumbo (de una línea).—**to take bearings**, abalizarse, marcarse; orientarse. II. *a.* de apoyo, de contacto; productivo.—**b. rein**, gamarra.—**b. surface**, superficie de apoyo; superficie de contacto o de rozamiento. A veces equivale a la *term.* "-ífero," vg., *gold-bearing*, aurífero.

bearish [bériŝ], *a.* osuno; rudo, áspero.

bearskin [bérskin], *s.* piel (*f.*) de oso; birretina, morrión de granadero o húsar, etc.; cierto género lanudo para sobretodos.

bearwood [bérwud], *s.* (bot.) arbusto cuya corteza es la cáscara sagrada. *V.* BUCKTHORN.

beast [bíst], *s.* bestia, bruto, res, *f.*, cuadrúpedo; hombre brutal.—**b. of burden**, acémila, cabalgadura, bestia de carga.—**b. of prey**, animal de rapiña.

beastlike [-lajk], *a.* bestial, abrutado.

beastliness [-linjs], *s.* bestialidad, brutalidad.

beastly [-li]. I. *a.* bestial, brutal; (fam.) muy

beat [bít], *va.* (*pret.* BEAT; *pp.* BEATEN, BEAT) batir (un metal, huevos, la costa, las alas, etc.); revolver; sacudir; percutir; pegar, aporrear, batanear, moler a palos; golpear; vencer, derrotar, ganarle a; llegar o acabar primero que; correr, recorrer, andar por; indicar, marcar (tiempo, el compás, etc.); (fam.) sobrepasar, dejar atrás (en cuanto a calidad, etc.); confundir, estar más allá de los alcances o capacidad de; (vulg.) engañar; (caz.) ojear, montear, dar una batida; (mil.) tocar (tambor u otro instrumento); (agr.) trillar; (ind.) abatanar; espadillar, agranar, majar.—**to b. all hollow,** (fam.) dejar tamañito.—**to b. an alarm,** (mil.) tocar alarma.—**to b. a parley,** (mil.) pedir parlamento.—**to b. a retreat,** batirse en retirada, emprender la retirada.—**to b. black and blue,** acardenalar.—**to b. down,** abatir; regatear, lograr rebaja regateando.—**to b. off,** rechazar.—**to b. out of,** privar de.—**to b. the band,** (fam.) hasta más no poder, con sumo ahinco o empeño.—**to b. the Dutch,** (fam.) ser extraordinario o sorprendente.—**to b. the record,** sobrepujar el record, alzar el record.—**to b. time,** marcar el compás.—**to b. up,** sorprender (al enemigo); batir (huevos, etc.)

beat, *vn.* latir, palpitar, pulsar; batir (el sol, las olas, etc.); golpear repetidamente; ganar, vencer; dar un toque (de tambor, etc.); poderse batir o revolver; sonar; (mar.) tentar el vado; voltejear; (caz.) correr; mover las matas, ramas, etc., para levantar la caza.—**to b. about,** barloventear; andar buscando.—**to b. about the bush,** andarse por las ramas; divagar, andar con rodeos.—**to b. against,** chocar contra.—**to b. it,** (fam.) escurrirse; poner pies en polvorosa.

beat. I. *s.* golpe; pulsación, latido; sonido repetido; toque de tambor; (mil.) ronda; distrito vigilado por un sereno o policía; (fam.) noticia que publica un periódico antes que los demás. —**b. reception,** (radtlf.) recepción heterodina. **II.** *a.* (fam.) fatigado, rendido de cansancio.

beaten [-ɘn]. **I.** *pp.* de TO BEAT. **II.** *a.* trillado, asendereado; batido, vencido; (met.) batido.

beater [-œ(r)], *s.* martillo, maza, pisón, golpeador; batidor, batidera, agitador, sacudidor, molinillo; apaleador; (caz.) ojeador, batidor.

beatific(al [biɘtífik(ɘl], *a.* (teol.) beatífico.

beatifically [-i], *adv* beatíficamente.

beatification [biɘtifikéiṣɘn], *s.* beatificación.

beatify [biɐtifai], *va.* (teol.) beatificar.

beating [bítiŋ], *s.* paliza, zurra, somanta, tunda; latido, pulsación; golpeo, batidura; (caz.) ojeo.

beatitude [biɐtitiud], *s.* beatitud; beatificación. —**the Beatitudes,** las bienaventuranzas.

beau [bou], *s.* (*pl.* BEAUX *o* BEAUS) galán, petimetre, lindo, pisaverde, currutaco; cortejo; (fam.) cuyo.—**b. ideal,** bello ideal.—**b. monde,** gente de moda.

beauteous [biútiʌs], *a.* bello, hermoso.

beauteousness [-niṣ], *s.* belleza, encantos.

beautician [biutíṣɘn], *s.* embellecedor, persona que se ocupa en el trabajo de salones de belleza.

beautification [-fikéiṣɘn], *s.* embellecimiento.

beautifier [biútifaiœ(r)], *s.* hermoseador.

beautiful [biútiful], *a.* bello, hermoso, precioso, venusto, pulcro.—**the b.,** lo bello.

beautifully [-i], *adv.* bellamente.

beautifulness [-niṣ], *s.* belleza.

beautify [biútifai], **I.** *va.* hermosear, embellecer, acicalar, adornar. **II.** *vn.* hermosearse, pulirse, maquillarse.

beauty [biúti], *s.* belleza, beldad, hermosura, venustidad, preciosidad.—**b. contest,** concurso de pulcritud.—**b. parlor,** *o* **salon,** salón de belleza.—**b. sleep,** primer sueño, el de antes

de media noche.—**b. spot,** parche o lunar postizo.

beaver [bívœ(r)], *s.* (zool.) castor; piel (*f.*) de castor; (arm.) babera, baberol; (fam.) chistera, sombrero de copa; (tej.) cierto paño grueso de lana.

beaverboard [-bord], *s.* cartón de fibras para tabiques, paredes interiores, etc. [marca de fábrica].

beavered [-d], *a.* con babera; acastorado.

bebeerine [bibírin], *s.* (quím.) bebirina.

becalm [bikám], *va.* y *vn.* calmar, serenar, sosegar; encalmarse (tiempo o viento).—**becalmed,** *a.* y *pp.* quedado sin viento.

became [bikéim], *pret.* de TO BECOME.

because [bikóz], *conj.* y *adv.* porque, pues, que. —**b. of,** a causa de, por causa o motivo de.

beccafico [bekɐfikou], *s.* (orn.) papaũgo.

bechance [bicĵéns], *va.* y *vn.* acaecer, acontecer.

beck [bék]. **I.** *va.* y *vn.* = BECKON. **II.** *s.* señas, ademán; riachuelo; valle; (tint.) cubeta.—**at one's b. and call,** a disposición de uno, a la mano.

beckon [-ɘn]. **I.** *va.* llamar o mandar con (o por) señas. **II.** *vn.* hacer señas o ademanes. **III.** *s.* seña, ademán, indicación de cabeza o mano.

becloud [bikláud], *va.* obscurecer, anublar.

become [bikám]. **I.** *va.* (*pret.* BECAME; *pp.* BECOME) convenir a, sentar a; caer o ir bien a; ser propio de. **II.** *vn.* hacerse, ponerse, tornarse, volverse; convertirse en, llegar o pasar a ser; (fil.) devenir. Seguido de un adjetivo, se traduce a veces por un solo verbo que indica el cambio correspondiente: vg., *to b. acute,* agudizarse; *to become angry,* enojarse; *to b. excited,* agitarse; *to b. exhausted,* agotarse; *to b. grave,* agravarse; *to b. hard,* endurecerse; *to b. intimate,* intimarse; *to b. longer,* alargarse; *to b. impatient,* impacientarse; *to become old,* envejecer; *to b. poor,* empobrecer(se); *to b. shorter,* acortar(se); *to b. soft,* suavizarse; *to b. stout,* engordar; *to b. sour,* agriarse; *to b. thin,* adelgazar(se), enflaquecer(se); *to become useless,* inutilizarse; *to b. worse,* empeorar(se).—**to b. of,** ser de, hacerse: *what will become of me?* ¿qué será de mí? *what has become of John?* ¿qué se ha hecho (o qué hay de) Juan?

becoming [-iŋ]. **I.** *a.* correcto, decoroso, propio; decente, conveniente; que sienta bien, que va bien.—**to be b.,** caer, ir o sentar bien. **II.** *s.* transformación, paso de un estado a otro.

becomingly [-li], *adv.* decorosamente, correctamente; a propósito.

becomingness [-niṣ], *s.* decoro, corrección; propiedad, compostura.

bed [béd]. **I.** *s.* cama, lecho, yacija; (geol.) capa, estrato, yacimiento; madre, *f.,* álveo, cauce (de río); (mec.) asiento, banco, lecho, fondo; armadura, fundación, base, *f.,* cimiento; arriate, cama, macizo (de jardín); tablar de una huerta; tonga, tongada, camada; (min.) yacimiento, capa, venero, veta; (alb.) capa; (ing.) firme; (impr.) carro, tabla.—**b. joint,** (const.) junta horizontal; (geol.) grieta paralela al terreno. —**b. linen,** ropa de cama.—**b. of roses,** (fig.) canonjía, situación de holganza.—**to go to b.,** acostarse.—**to keep to one's b.,** guardar cama. **II.** *va.* acostar, poner en cama; cohabitar; dar cama a; sembrar en un macizo; meter; asentar, apoyar; (const.) labrar o preparar la superficie de. **III.** *vn.* acostarse; cohabitar; descansar, apoyarse.

bedabble [bidæbl], *va.* rociar, mojar, salpicar.

bedaub [bidób], *va.* salpicar, ensuciar, embarrar, embadurnar; vilipendiar.

bedazzle [bidæzl], *va.* deslumbrar.

bedbug [bédbʌg], *s.* (ent.) chinche, *f.*

bedchamber [bédcheimbœ(r)], *s.* dormitorio, alcoba; (Méx.) recámara.

bedclothes [bédklouðz], *s. pl.* ropa de cama (sábanas, mantas, etc.); (Am.) cobijas.

bedding [bédiŋ], s. colchones y ropa de cama; paja para el ganado; asiento, fundamento; (arq.) empotramiento; (geol.) estratificación.

bedeck [bidék], va. adornar, engalanar, acicalar.

bedevil [bidévil], va. endemoniar, endiablar, maleficiar; hechizar; enloquecer; atormentar.

bedew [bidjú], va. rociar, regar.

bedfellow [bédfelou], s. compañero o compañera de cama; asociado.

bedhangings [bédhæŋiŋz], s. pabellón, cortinas de cama.

bedhead [bédhed], s. cabecera de cama.

bedim [bidím], va. obscurecer, ofuscar.

bedizen [bidáizn], va. acicalar, ataviar vistosamente.

bedlam [bédlam], s. casa de orates; manicomio; bullicio, Babel; desbarajuste.

bedlamite [-ait], s. loco, orate.

Bedouin [béduin], s. beduíno; vago.

bedpan [bédpæn], s. silleta para enfermos, chata.

bedplate [bédpleit], s. (mec.) bancaza, cama, platina, plancha de asiento.

bedpost [bédpoust], s. poste de la cama.

bedquilt [bédkwilt], s. cubrecama, colcha.

bedraggle [bidrǽgl], va. ensuciar o manchar arrastrando por el suelo o el lodo, etc.

bedrid (den [bédrid(en], a. postrado en cama.

bedrench [bidrénch], va. calar, empapar.

bedrock [bédrak], s. (min.) lecho de roca; roca firme; (fig.) fundamento, base, f.; lo último.

bedroom [bédrum], s. alcoba, cuarto de dormir, dormitorio; (Méx.) recámara.

bedside [bédsaid], s. lado de cama; cabecera.

bedsore [bédsɔr], s. llaga causada por la prolongada permanencia en el lecho.—**to contract bedsores**, decentarse, encentarse.

bedspread [bédspred], s. sobrecama, cobertor, vánova.

bedspring [bédspriŋ], s. colchón de muelles o de tela metálica.

bedstead [bédsted], s. cuja, armadura de la cama.

bedtick(ing [bédtik(iŋ], s. cotí, cutí.

bedtime [bédtaim], s. hora de acostarse.

bee [bi], s. (ent.) abeja; (fam.) reunión, tertulia; manía, chifladura; (mar.) aleta del bauprés (ll. t. **b. block**).—**b. bread**, polen almacenado por las abejas.—**b. eater**, (orn.) abejaruco.—**b. fly**, (ent.) mosca abeja.—**b. glue**, cera aleda, tanque.—**b. line**, línea recta, derechura.—**to have a b. in one's bonnet**, o **head**, estar destornillado; estar haciendo castillos en el aire o lleno de esperanzas vanas.

beech [bich], s. (bot.) haya.—**b. forest**, hayal, hayedo.—**b. mast** = BEECHNUT.—**b. oil**, aceite de fabuco.

beechen [-en], a. de haya.

beechnut [-nʌt], s. fabuco, hayuco, nuez de haya.

beef [bif]. I. s. carne (f.) de vaca o de res; res, f. (buey, toro, vaca); (fam.) fuerza muscular; jactancia; queja.—**b. cattle**, ganado vacuno de ceba, o de engorde.—**b. extract**, extracto de carne (de buey).—**b. stew**, platillo.—**b. tea**, caldo, cocina.—**b.-witted**, lerdo, estúpido. II. vn. (fam.) jactarse; quejarse.

beefeater [bífitœ(r)], s. el que come carne de vaca; persona rolliza; (fam.) un inglés (apodo); (Ingl.) alabardero de palacio; guardia de la Torre de Londres.

beefsteak [bífsteik], s. bistec, biftec, (Am.) bife.

beehive [bíhaiv], s. colmena, corcho.

beekeeper [bíkipœ(r)], **beemaster** [bímæstœ(r)], s. colmenero, abejero, apicultor.—**b.-keeping** [-iŋ], s. cría de abejas, apicultura.

been [bin], pp. de TO BE.

beer [bir], s. cerveza, malta.—**b. garden** o **parlor**, cervecería (lugar donde se sirve cerveza).—**b. leaven**, cervesina.—**b. saloon**, taberna, cantina.

beestings [bístiŋz], s. calostro.

beeswax [bízwæks]. I. s. cera de abejas. II. va. encerar.

beeswing [bízwiŋ], s. flor (f.) o nata (de vino añejo).

beet [bit], s. (bot.) remolacha, betarraga; (Méx.) botabel, f.—**b. root**, o **beetroot**, (raíz de la) remolacha.—**b. sugar**, azúcar de remolacha.

beetle [bítl]. I. s. (ent.) escarabajo, coleóptero; pisón, pala, moza, maza, aplanadera; martinete; mallo; batán; estúpido, imbécil.—**b.-browed**, cejudo; adusto.—**b.-headed**, lerdo, pesado. II. vn. combar, sobresalir; (ind.) abatanar. III. va. golpear o majar con pisón, etc.; (ind.) (a)batanar; estampar (paño).

beetling [bítliŋ]. I. a. saliente, pendiente, colgante. II. s. (tej.) bataneo, estampación.—**b. machine**, (tej.) batán; máquina de estampar.

beetradish [bítrædiš], **beetrave** [bítreiv], s. V. BEET.

beeves [bivz], s. (pl. de BEEF) ganado; reses, f. pl.

befall [bifól], vn. (pret. BEFELL; pp. BEFALLEN) suceder, acontecer, sobrevenir.

befit [bifít], va. convenir, sentar o venir bien, cuadrar, ser propio o digno de.

befitting [-iŋ], a. conveniente, propio, digno.

befog [bifág], va. aneblar, envolver en niebla; confundir, obscurecer.—**to b. the issue**, salirse por la tangente.

befool [bifúl], va. engañar, embaucar; entontecer.

before [bifór]. I. adv. delante, al frente; antes, anteriormente, con prioridad; (mar.) de proa.—**b.-cited** o **-mentioned**, antemencionado, susodicho. II. prep. delante de, enfrente de, frente a; ante, en presencia de; antes de.—**b. the mast**, (mar.) a proa del palo.—**b. the wind**, viento en popa. III. conj. antes que, primero.

beforehand [-hænd]. I. adv. de antemano, a prevención, previamente, con antelación. II. a. acomodado, con recursos.

befoul [bifául], va. ensuciar, emporcar.

befriend [bifrénd], va. favorecer, patrocinar, amparar, proteger.

befuddle [bifʌdl], va. confundir, ofuscar.

beg [beg]. I. vn. mendigar, pordiosear, vivir de limosna.—**to b. off from**, rogar (uno) que se le exima de; excusarse de; evadir con súplicas. II. va. rogar, pedir, suplicar, implorar, mendigar.—**to b. the question**, cometer petición de principio.—**to b. (leave) to**, permitirse.

began [bigæn], pret. de TO BEGIN.

beget [bigét]. I. va. (pret. BEGOT—ant. BEGAT; pp. BEGOTTEN) engendrar, procrear; producir, causar, suscitar (odios, etc.). II. vn. padrear.

begetter [-œ(r)], s. engendrador, procreador.

beggar [bégə(r)]. I. s. mendigo, mendigante, pobre, pordiosero; gallofo.—**beggardom, beggarhood** [-dam, -hud], pobrismo o pobrería; (Méx.) chinaca. II. va. empobrecer, arruinar; apurar, agotar.—**to b. description**, no haber palabras para describir.

beggarliness [-linis], **beggary** [-i], s. mendicidad o mendiguez, pordiosería, pobreza absoluta.

beggarly [-li]. I. a. pobre, miserable. II. adv. pobremente.

begging [bégiŋ]. I. a. mendicante. II. s. mendicación, pordioseo.—**to go b.**, andar mendigando.

begilded [bigíldid], a. dorado.

begin [bigín], va. y vn. (pret. BEGAN o BEGUN; pp. BEGUN) comenzar, empezar, principiar o ponerse (a); iniciar, entablar (un negocio, etc.); (for.) incoar (un pleito); nacer; salir (en el juego).—**not to b. to**, no . . . ni con mucho (he cannot begin to do what we need, él no puede hacer lo que necesitamos, ni con mucho).—**to b. with**, en primer lugar, para empezar.

beginner [-œ(r)], s. iniciador, originador; principiante; novicio, neófito, novato; (com.) meritorio.

beginning [-iŋ], s. comienzo, iniciación, principio, origen; albor(es); génesis.—**from b. to end**, de pe a pa, de cabo a rabo.—**in the b.**, al principio.

begone! [bigón], *interj.* ¡fuera! ¡vete! ¡largo!

begonia [bigóuniả], *s.* (bot.) begonia.

Begoniaceæ [bigouniéị̈ṣ̈iị], *s. pl.* (bot.) begoniáceas.

begot [bigát], *pret.*; **begotten** [-ẹn], *pp.* de TO BEGET.

begrime [bigráịm], *va.* ensuciar, tiznar.

begrudge [bigrʌ́dž], *va.* envidiar el bien ajeno; regatear, repugnar, tasar.

beguile [bigáịl], *va.* engañar, seducir; defraudar; entretener, pasar el tiempo, divertir.

beguiled [-d], *a.* y *pp.* engañado, iluso.

beguilement [-mẹnt], *s.* engaño, seducción.

beguiler [-œ(r)], *s.* engañador, seductor.

begun [bigʌ́n], *pp.* y *pret.* de TO BEGIN.

behalf [bihǽf], *s.* (precedido de **in**, **on** *o* **upon**) por; a favor, en nombre, interés o defensa de, en pro de; de parte de.

behave [bihéịv], *va.* y *vn.* proceder, obrar, conducirse, (com)portarse (bien o mal), vadearse. —**b.!** ¡estése Vd. quieto! ¡pórtate bien!

behavior [-yọ(r)], *s.* proceder, porte, conducta, comportamiento; (mec.) funcionamiento.

behaviorism [-yọrịzm], *s.* (psic.) sistema que sostiene que la psicología debe fundarse exclusivamente en el análisis de los actos objetivamente observables.—**behaviorist** [-yọrịst], *s.* partidario de esta teoría.

behead [bihéd], *va.* decapitar, descabezar, degollar.

beheading [-iŋ], *s.* decapitación, degüello.

beheld [bihéld], *pret.* y *pp.* de TO BEHOLD.

behest [bihést], *s.* mandato, precepto, requerimiento.—**at the b. of**, a instancia de.

behind [biháịnd]. **I.** *adv.* atrás, detrás; en o a la zaga; hacia atrás; por detrás; en pos; con retraso. **II.** *prep.* tras, detrás de; después de.— **b. one's back**, en ausencia o a espaldas de uno.—**b. time**, tarde.—**b. the times**, atrasado (de noticias).—**b. the scenes**, entre bastidores.

behindhand [-hænd]. **I.** *adv.* con atraso, con retraso, atrasadamente. **II.** *a.* atrasado, retrasado.—**to be b.**, atrasarse, retrasarse.

behold [bihóụld], *va.* (*pret.* y *pp.* BEHELD) mirar, ver, contemplar, catar.—**b.!** *interj.* ¡mirad! ¡mire Vd.! ¡he aquí!

beholden [-ẹn], *a.* obligado por gratitud.

beholder [-œ(r)], *s.* espectador.

behoof [bihúf], *s.* provecho, utilidad, ventaja.

beho(o)ve [bihúv, bihóụv], *vn. impers.* tocar, corresponder, incumbir, importar, ser útil o necesario.

beige [beịž]. **I.** *a.* de color de lana, entre gris y pardo; de color rojo amarillento o de canela; (neol.) beige. **II.** *s.* cierto tejido de lana.

being [bíiŋ]. **I.** *ger.* de TO BE.—**for the time b.**, por el momento, por ahora; por entonces.—**it b. that**, siendo así que. **II.** *s.* ser, ente, criatura; existencia, vida.—**the Supreme B.**, Dios.

bejewel [bidžúẹl], *va.* enjoyar.

belabor [biléịbọ(r)], *va.* apalear, pegar, cascar; trabajar, elaborar.

belated [biléịtid], *a.* demorado, atrasado, tardío; cogido o sorprendido por la noche.

belay [biléị], *va.* (*pret.* y *pp.* BELAYED O BELAID) amarrar dando vueltas a una cabilla, etc.; bloquear, cercar.—**belaying pins**, (mar.) cabillas.

belch [bélch]. **I.** *va.* arrojar, echar de sí; vomitar. **II.** *vn.* regoldar, eructar; vomitar; salir con fuerza (una llama, etc.).

belch(ing [-iŋ], *s.* regüeldo, eructo, eructación.

beldam(e [béldam, -eịm], *s.* vieja bruja.

beleaguer [bilígœ(r)], *va.* sitiar, bloquear.

beleaguerer [-œ(r)], *s.*; **bcleaguering** [-iŋ], *a.* sitiador.

belemnite [bélẹmnaịt], *s.* (min.) belemnita.

belfry [bélfrị], *s.* campanario, torre, *f.*

Belgian [béldžẹn]. **I.** *a.* belga, bélgico. **II.** *s.* belga.

Belial [bílịal], *s.* Belial; Satanás; ángel caído.

belie [bilái], *va.* desmentir; dar un mentís a; calumniar; disfrazar; defraudar (una esperanza).

belief [bilíf], *s.* fe, *f.*, creencia, crédito; confianza; convencimiento; credo, religión; opinión, parecer.

believable [bilívạbl], *a.* creíble.

believe [bilív], *va.* y *vn.* creer; confiar en o fiarse de; opinar; tener por.—**to b. in**, creer en; ser partidario de; aprobar; tener fe en o a.

believer [-œ(r)], *s.* creyente, fiel.

believingly [-iŋlị], *adv.* con fe o creencia, confiadamente.

belittle [bilítl], *va.* deprimir, achicar, rebajar, dar escasa importancia a.

bell [bel], *s.* campana; campanilla; (elec.) timbre; esquila, cencerro (de ganado); cascabel; campanada; (mús.) pabellón (de instrumento de viento); címbalo; brama (ú. esp. del ciervo en celo).—**b. bird**, (orn.) campanero.—**b.-bottomed trousers**, especie de pantalón bombacho.—**b. boy**, botones, mozo de hotel encargado de llevar recados, etc.—**b. buoy**, (mar.) boya sonora o de campana.—**b. clapper**, badajo.—**b. cow, horse, mule**, julo, manso.—**b. crank**, cigüeña, torniquete; palanca angular.—**b. founder**, campanero.— **b. glass**, campana de cristal.—**b. hop = B. BOY.**—**b. metal**, bronce de campanas.—**b.-mouthed**, abocinado, acampanado.—**b.-ox**, cabestro.—**b. pull**, cuerda o tirador de campana.—**b. ringer**, campanero.—**b. ringing**, campaneo.—**b. rope = B. PULL.**—**b.-shaped**, acampanado, campanudo.—**b. stroke**, campanada.—**b. tower**, campanario.—**b. tree**, (mús.) chinescos.—**to bear away the b.**, ganar el premio, llevarse la palma.—**to bear the b.**, ser el primero, ir en la delantera.

bell. **I.** *va.* acampanar; encascabelar; poner campana a.—**to b. the cat**, poner el cascabel al gato. **II.** *vn.* (bot.) crecer en figura de campana; acampanarse; florecer; bramar (ciervo, etc.).

belladonna [beladánạ], *s.* (bot.) belladona.

belle [bel], *s.* beldad, mujer bella.

belleric [belérịk], *s.* (bot.) belérico, mirobálano.

belles-lettres [bellétr], *s.* bellas letras.

bellflower [bélflaụœ(r)], *s.* (bot.) ruiponce o rapónchigo; campánula; variedad de manzana.

bellhanger [bélhæŋœ(r)], *s.* campanillero.

bellhanging [-iŋ], *s.* instalación de campanas.

bellicose [bélikoụs], *a.* belicoso, bélico, guerrero.

bellied [bélịd], *a.* ventrudo, barrigón; panzudo; combado, convexo.

belligerence, -cy [bilídžẹrẹns, -ị], *s.* beligerancia.

belligerent [-ẹnt]. **I.** *s.* beligerante. **II.** *a.* beligerante, belicoso, guerrero.

bellman [bélmạn], *s.* campan(ill)ero, pregonero.

bellow [béloụ]. **I.** *vn.* bramar, berrear, mugir, rugir; vociferar, gritar. **II.** *s.* bufido, bramido, rugido.

bellower [-œ(r)], *s.* bramador; vociferador.

bellowing [-iŋ]. **I.** *s.* V. BELLOW. **II.** *a.* bramador, rugiente.

bellows [-z], *s.* (*sing.* y *pl.*) fuelle, barquín, pava. —**b. maker**, folle(te)ro, barquinero.—**b. pocket**, (sast.) bolsillo de fuelle.—**to blow with b.**, (a)follar.

bellwether [bélwɛðœ(r)], *s.* (carnero o morueco) manso.

belly [bélị]. **I.** *s.* (*pl.* BELLIES) vientre; barriga, tripa, panza; estómago; entrañas; combadura, barriga de una botella, etc.; pandeo; seno (de vela); frente, parte (*f.*) anterior; caja de eje; (min.) ensanche (de una veta).—**b. god**, glotón; epicúreo.—**b.-pinched**, hambriento.—**b.**

worm, lombriz intestinal. **II.** *vn.* pandear. **III.** *va.* combar, inflar, hinchar.

bellyache [-eĭk], *s.* dolor de vientre.

bellyband [-bænd], *s.* cincho, ventrera, tripero; cincha, barriguera (para caballo, etc.).

bellybound [-baʊnd], *a.* estreñido de vientre.

bellyful [-fʊl], *s.* panzada, hartazgo; suficiencia.

belong [bilóŋ], *vn.* pertenecer; tocar, atañer, convenir, concernir, incumbir; residir en, ser (natural) de.—**to b. in,** pertenecer a (una clase, etc.).

belonging [-iŋ]. **I.** *a.* perteneciente. **II.** *s.* pertenencia, propiedad.—*pl.* posesiones, anexos, anexidades; bártulos.

beloved [bilʌv(i)d]. **I.** *a.* caro, dilecto, querido, amado. **II.** *s.* persona amada.

below [bilóu]. **I.** *adv.* abajo, bajo, debajo, más abajo; en el infierno. **II.** *prep.* bajo, debajo de; después de.—**b.-cited** o **-stated,** más adelante, o más abajo mencionado.—**b.** par, a descuento, a menos de su valor nominal.—**b. zero,** bajo zero.

belt [bɛlt]. **I.** *s.* cinto o cinturón, faja, ceñidor, cincho, pretina; estrecho; tira; (mec.) correa de transmisión; (geog.) zona, faja; (mar.) faja de la coraza en la línea de flotación; (fam.) golpe.—**b. course,** (arq.) faja o banda horizontal.—**b. line,** o **b. railroad,** vía de circunvalación.—**b. saw,** sierra sin fin o de cinta.—**b. shaft,** árbol de transmisión. **II.** *va.* fajar; ceñir; cercar, rodear; poner correa a (una máquina); unir o conectar por correa; (fam.) golpear, herir.

belting [-iŋ], *s.* correaje, correas de transmisión.

beluga [bilúgặ], *s.* (ict.) ballena blanca; esturión blanco.

belvedere [belvǐdír], *s.* torre, *f.,* mirador.

bemire [bimáịr], *va.* enlodar, embarrar, entarquinar, encenagar, emporcar.

bemoan [bimóụn], *va.* lamentar, deplorar.

bemoaner [-œ(r)], *s.* lamentador, plañidor.

bemoaning [-iŋ], *s.* lamento, lamentación.

bench [bɛnch]. **I.** *s.* banco, banca; bancada, banqueta, escaño; banco de carpintero; serie de bancos para la exhibición de animales; ramo, división (de un cuerpo deliberante, etc.); (for.) tribunal.—**b. mark,** (top.) punto de referencia de cota conocida.—**b. plane,** (carp.) garlopa.—**b. root,** (agr.) raíces trabadas o deformadas.—**b. screw** o **vise,** tornillo de banco.—**b. show,** exposición de perros u otros animales.—**b. warrant,** auto de prisión.—**the King's,** o **Queen's, B.,** tribunal superior de justicia. **II.** *va.* exhibir (animales); asentar sobre un banco; proveer de bancos, etc.; poner en un tribunal; (dep.) sacar del juego (a un jugador). **III.** *vn.* ocupar un banco.

bencher [-œ(r)], *s.* (Ingl.) decano de los colegios de abogados; frecuentador de tabernas; barquero.

bend [bɛnd]. **I.** *va.* (*pret.* y *pp.* BENT) encorvar, curvar, cimbrar, doblar, plegar, torcer, combar, empandar, pandear, acodillar; dirigir o encaminar; inclinar (la cabeza); dedicar, aplicar; doblegar, sujetar, vencer; humillar, hacer bajar; (mar.) entalingar, amarrar, envergar (vela, cable, etc.).—**to b. the brow,** fruncir el entrecejo.—**to b. the oars,** hacer fuerza de remos. **II.** *vn.* encorvarse, doblarse, agarbarse, combarse, torcerse; doblegarse, someterse. **III.** *s.* comba(dura), corva, encorvadura, curvatura; vuelta, curva; recodo; codillo; (mar.) nudo, gaza; cinta; (blas.) barra diagonal.

bendable [-ặbl], *a.* flexible, plegable.

bender [-œ(r)], *s.* torcedor; doblador; flexor.

bending [-iŋ]. **I.** *s.* comba; codillo; doblamiento, encorvadura, (in)flexión, cimbra, cimbreo; declive; rodeo, vuelta. **II.** *a.* flexor, de flexión.—**b. hammer,** copador.—**b. machine,** máquina de curvar.—**b. moment,** (mec.) mo-

mento flexor.—**b. strength,** resistencia a la flexión.

bends [-z], *s.* (med.) *V.* CAISSON DISEASE.

beneath [biníθ], *adv.* y *prep.* bajo, abajo, debajo (de); en lo más hondo; indigno de.

benedick [bénịdịk], **benedict** [-t], *s.* (recién) casado.

Benedictine [-díktin], *s.* y *a.* benedictino, benito.

benediction [-díkṣọn], *s.* bendición; gracia.

benefaction [-fǽkṣọn], *s.* beneficio, favor, gracia, merced, beneficiación.

benefactor [bénịfæktọ(r)], *s.* benefactor, bienhechor, beneficiador; fundador; patrón.—**benefactress** [-trịs], *s.* bienhechora; fundadora, patrona.

benefice [bénịfịs], *s.* (igl.) beneficio, prebenda.

beneficed [-t], *a.* (igl.) beneficiado, prebendado.

beneficence [bịnéfịṣẹns], *s.* beneficencia; caridad.

beneficent [-ẹnt], *a.* benéfico; caritativo.

beneficently [-li], *adv.* benéficamente.

beneficial [benịfíṣặl], *a.* beneficioso, provechoso, útil, ventajoso.—**beneficially** [-i], *adv.* beneficiosamente, provechosamente.

beneficiary [benịfíṣặri]. **I.** *s.* beneficiario; (igl.) beneficiado; feudatorio. **II.** *a.* beneficial.

benefit [bénịfit]. **I.** *s.* beneficio, servicio; disfrute, logro, valimiento, utilidad, provecho, ventaja; pro, bien, privilegio; gracia; (teat.) función de beneficio.—**b. society,** sociedad benéfica o de beneficencia.—**for the b. of,** en pro de, a beneficio de.—**b. of clergy,** cierta inmunidad del clero.—**without b. of clergy,** (casamiento) sin sanción de la iglesia. **II.** *va.* beneficiar, aprovechar. **III.** *vn.* aprovecharse o utilizarse; prevalerse o disfrutar (de).

benevolence [bịnévọlẹns], *s.* benevolencia; bondad, caridad; gracia, merced.—**b. society** = BENEFIT SOCIETY.

benevolent [-ẹnt], *a.* benévolo, caritativo.

Bengal [bengśl], *s.* (tej.) especie de muselina (antes ll. bengala).—**B. light,** luz de Bengala.

Bengalese [bengặlíz], **Bengali** [bengólị], *s.* y *a.* bengalí.

bengaline [béngalin], *s.* (tej.) bengalina.

benighted [bináịtịd], *a.* anochecido, sorprendido por la noche; rodeado de tinieblas; ignorante.

benign [bináịn], *a.* benigno, afable, humano; saludable (clima, etc.); (med.) benigno, ligero.

benignant [bịnígnặnt], *a.* benéfico, propicio, saludable; benigno.

benignity [bịnígnịtị], *s.* benignidad, bondad, dulzura; salubridad.

benignly [bináịnlị], *adv.* benignamente.

benison [bénịṣọn], *s.* bendición.

benjamin [béndžặmịn], *s.* (bot.) benjuí; **(B.)** hijo menor y favorito.

benne [bénị], *s.* (bot.) alegría, ajonjolí, sésamo.

bent [bent]. **I.** *s.* encorvadura, curvatura, comba; afición, genio, inclinación, propensión, tendencia; grado máximo de tensión; (ing.) palizada o sostén de viaducto; (bot.) especie de hierba. **II.** *a.* curvo, encorvado, torcido, combo, gacho; inclinado, determinado, resuelto; (mar.) amarrado, entalingado.—**b. on,** o **upon,** resuelto a, empeñado en, propenso a. **III.** *pret.* y *pp.* de TO BEND.

benthos [bénθas], *s.* (biol.) fauna y flora del fondo del mar.

benumb [bịnʌm], *va.* entorpecer, pasmar, entumecer, envarar, aterir.

benumbedness [-dnịs], **benumbment** [-mẹnt], *s.* entumecimiento, pasmo.

benzaldehyde [benzǽldẹhaịd], *s.* (quím.) benzaldehido, aldehido benzoico.

benzamide [benzǽmịd], *s.* (quím.) benzamida.

benzene [bénzin], *s.* benceno, bencina (C_6H_6).—**b. nucleus, b. ring,** núcleo o anillo bencénico, en forma de hexágono.

benzil, benzyl [bénzịl], *s.* (quím.) bencilo.—**benzilic** [benzílịk], *a.* bencílico.

benzin(e [bénzin], *s.* bencina (gen. del petróleo).
benzoate [benzóujt], *s.* (quím.) benzoato.
benzoic [benzóujk], *a.* (quím.) benzoico.
benzoin [bénzojn], *s.* (quím.) benzoína; (bot.) benjuí. *V.* SPICEBUSH.
benzol(e [bénzoul], *s.* (quím.) benzol, benceno.
bequeath [bikwíð], *va.* (for.) dejar, legar, mandar, donar (en testamento); transmitir.
bequeather [-œ(r)], *s.* testador; el que lega o dona.
bequest [bikwést], *s.* (for.) manda, donación o legado.
berate [biréjt], *va.* zaherir, reñir, regañar, poner a uno como nuevo.
Berber [bœrbœ(r)], *s.* y *a.* bereber, berberisco, berberí.
berberidaceous [bœrbęridéjšas], *a.* (bot.) berberídeo.
berberin(e [bœrbęrin], *s.* (quím.) berberina.
bereave [birív], *va.* (*pret.* y *pp.* BEREFT) despojar, privar; desolar, acongojar, afligir (esp. por la muerte).
bereavement [-męnt], *s.* pérdida muy sensible, privación, despojo, desamparo; aflicción, desgracia, luto, duelo.
beret [beréj], *s.* boina; gorra vizcaína.
berg [bœrg], *s.* témpano de hielo.
bergamot [bœrgamat], *s.* (bot.) bergamota; el bergamoto y su fruto; rapé perfumado con bergamota; tapiz ordinario.—**b. mint,** (bot.) sándalo (especie de hierbabuena).
beriberi [bérjbéri], *s.* (med.) beriberi.
Berlin [bœrlín], *s.* berlina (coche y auto); estambre.—**B. blue,** azul de Prusia.—**B. wool,** estambre.
berm [bœrm], *s.* (fort.) lisera, berma.
Bernardine [bœrnardjn], *a.* y *s.* bernardo (monje o monja).
bernicle [bœrnjkl], *s.* *V.* BARNACLE.
berry [bérj], I. *s.* baya; grano (de café, etc.)—Avignon berries, granas de Aviñón.—**b. bush,** arbusto frutal.—**b.-like,** abayado. II. *vn.* producir bayas; coger fresas, moras, etc.
berserk [bœrsœrk], *a.* frenético, enloquecido.—to go b., enloquecerse con violencia.
berserker [-œ(r)], *s.* fiero guerrero escandinavo.
berth [bœrθ], I. *s.* (mar., f.c., aer.) cama, litera; camarote; (mar.) anclaje, amarradero, atracadero, dársena; (fam.) empleo, destino.—to give a wide b. to, apartarse de, ponerse a resguardo de. II. *va.* (mar.) atracar, llevar al puerto; dar anclaje a; dar camarote, pasaje o empleo a. III. *vn.* atracar, llegar a puerto; ocupar un camarote, etc.; proporcionar o dar litera, anclaje o empleo.
Bertha [bœrθə], *s.* (fam.) Berta gran granada Krupp; cañón Krupp de gran calibre.
bertha, *s.* cuello ancho o capita de mujer.
berthage [bœrθədž], *s.* anclaje.
berthing [bœrθiŋ], *s.* disposición de los camarotes y literas; (mar.) anclaje; obra muerta.
beryl [béril], *s.* (min.) berilo.
beryllium [beríljam], *s.* (quím.) berilio, glucinio.
beseech [bisích], *va.* (*pret.* y *pp.* BESOUGHT) suplicar, rogar, implorar, exhortar, conjurar.
beseecher [-œ(r)], *s.* rogador, suplicante.
beseeching [-iŋ], I. *s.* ruego, súplica, instancia. II. *a.* suplicante, de súplica.
beseem [bisím], I. *va.* cuadrar, parecer bien. II. *vn.* parecer; ser decente o decoroso.
beset [bisét], I. *va.* (*pret.* y *pp.* BESET) acosar, perseguir; bloquear, obstruir; rodear; engastar, adornar o aderezar (con piedras preciosas, etc.). II. *a.* acosado; obseso; adornado, engastado.—besetting sin, vicio habitual y dominante.
beside [bisájd], I. *adv.* cerca, al lado, a la mano. II. *prep.* al lado de; junto a; en comparación de.—b. himself, fuera de sí.—b. the mark o the point, impertinente, que no viene al caso.
besides [-z], I. *adv.* también, además, (de)más,

a más. II. *prep.* además de, a más de, amén de; sobre, por encima de; excepto, fuera de.
besiege [bisídž], *va.* (mil.) sitiar; (fig.) asediar, acosar.—besieger [-œ(r)], *s.* sitiador; asediador.
besmear [bismír], *va.* ensuciar, embadurnar.
besmirch [bismœrch], *va.* manchar, ensuciar.
besom [bízǫm], I. *s.* escoba; (bot.) retama. II. *va.* barrer.
besot [bisát], *va.* embeleñar; entontecer; embrutecer; infatuar.
besottedly [-idlj], *adv.* estúpida o fatuamente.
besottedness [-nis], *s.* entontecimiento, embrutecimiento, fatuidad.
besought [bisát], *pret.* y *pp.* de TO BESEECH.
bespangle [bispængl], *va.* adornar con lentejuelas o brichos.
bespatter [bispǽtœ(r)], *va.* salpicar, manchar; di(s)famar.
bespeak [bispík], *va.* (*pret.* BESPOKE; *pp.* BESPOKE o BESPOKEN) encomendar, encargar o apalabrar algo de antemano; indicar, demostrar; predecir, adivinar; (poét.) hablar a.
bespectacled [bispéktakld], *a.* que lleva gafas.
bespread [bispréd], *va.* (*pret.* y *pp.* BESPREAD) cubrir.
besprinkle [bispríŋkl], *va.* rociar, regar.
Bessemer steel [bésęmœ(r) stíl], *s.* acero fundido según el procedimiento Béssemer.
bessemerize [-ajz], *va.* (fund.) someter al procedimiento Béssemer.
best [best], I. *a.* y *adv. super.* de GOOD y WELL: mejor, del mejor modo, óptimo, óptimamente, superior(mente).—b. bower, (juego) = JOKER; (mar.) ancla de ayuste.—b. girl, (fam.) amiga preferida, novia.—b. man, padrino de boda.—b. seller, favorito, el que más se vende o de los que más se venden (apl. sobre todo a libros).—b. of all, lo mejor de todo, lo mejor es que.—as b. one can, como mejor pueda uno.—it is b., eso es lo mejor; lo mejor es.—the b. part of, lo mejor de; la mayor parte de, casi todo (*the best part of a month,* casi todo un mes).—you had b. do it, mejor sería que Vd. lo hiciera.—you know b., Vd. sabe mejor que nadie (lo que conviene hacer, etc.) II. *s.* el (lo) mejor, los mejores, etc.—at (the) b., a lo más, cuando más o mucho, a mejor andar, aun en el mejor caso o en las mejores circunstancias;—for the b., con las mejores intenciones; conducente o encaminado al bien o a buenas cosas (*everything is for the best,* todo sucede para los mejores fines, todo resulta bien a la larga).—to be at one's b., lucirse, estar uno en su máximo, obrar con su acostumbrada habilidad o maestría, hacer lo mejor.—to do one's b., hacer lo posible, esmerarse.—to get the b. of, llevar(se) la ventaja o la mejor parte a, vencer a.—to make the b. of, sacar el mejor partido de, aprovechar bien; salir lo mejor posible (de un mal paso o negocio).—to the b. of my knowledge, según mi leal saber y entender.—with the b., como el que más. III. *va.* aventajar, vencer, ganar a.
bestead [bistéd], *va.* y *vn.* (*pret.* BESTEADED; *pp.* BESTEADED o BESTED) beneficiar, aprovechar, servir.
bestead, *a.* (ú gen. con ill o sore) colocado, situado; acosado, cercado.
bestial [béschal], *a.* bestial, brutal; abrutado.—bestiality [-jáliti], *s.* bestialidad, brutalidad.—bestialize [-ajz], *va.* embrutecer.—bestially [-j], *adv.* bestialmente.
bestir [bistœr], *va.* mover, menear, incitar.—to b. one's self, menearse, afanarse.
bestow [bistóu], *va.* conceder, conferir, cola(ciona)r (un beneficio eclesiástico o grado de universidad); otorgar, agraciar; dar, donar, regalar; dedicar, emplear, gastar.—to b. in abundance, colmar (de).

bestowal [-ạl], *s.* dádiva, presente, gracia; colación (de grados, etc.).

bestower [-œ(r)], *s.* donador, regalador.

bestraddle [bịstrǽdl], *va. V.* BESTRIDE.

bestrew [bịstrú], *va.* (*pret.* BESTREWED; *pp.* BESTREWED, BESTREWN) rociar, esparcir, derramar.

bestride [bịstrájd], *va.* (*pret.* BESTRODE O BESTRID; *pp.* BESTRID(DEN) montar o colocarse a horcajadas en (o sobre); cruzar de un tranco.

bet [bet]. I. *s.* apuesta, postura, parada.—**it's a good b.**, es cosa segura. II. *vn.* apostar.—**to b. on**, apostar a. III. *va.* apostar, poner, ir (en el juego).—**how much do you b.?** ¿cuánto va? ¿cuánto apuesta Vd.?—**what do you bet that John won't come?** ¿a que no viene Juan?—**you b. (your life)**, (fam.) claro, ya lo creo.

beta [béịtạ], *s.* beta (letra griega).—**b. rays**, (fís.) rayos beta.

betaine [bịtéịịn], *s.* (quím.) betaína.

betake [bịtéịk], *vr.* (*pret.* BETOOK; *pp.* BETAKEN) recurrir, acudir; irse, trasladarse; aplicarse a, darse a, emprender.

bête noir [beịt nwár], *s.* (fr.) coco; cosa o persona detestada o temida.

betel [bítẹl], *s.* (bot.) betel.—**b. nut**, fruto de la areca o bonga.—**b. palm**, areca, (Fil.) bonga.

bethel [béθẹl], *s.* capilla para marineros; lugar santificado; (Ingl.) capilla de los disidentes.

bethink [bịθịŋk]. I. *va. y vr.* (*pret. y pp.* BETHOUGHT) recordar, acordarse de; recapacitar, hacer memoria; considerar. II. *vn.* pensar, reflexionar.

Bethle(he)mite [béθlị(he)maịt], *s.* betlemita. *V. t.* BEDLAMITE.

betide [bịtájd], *va. y vn.* suceder (a), acontecer (a); (*a veces erróneamente*) presagiar, indicar.

betimes [bịtáịmz], *adv.* con tiempo, en sazón; pronto, temprano.

betoken [bịtóụkẹn], *va.* significar, prometer, dar muestras de, presagiar.

betony [bétonị], *s.* (bot.) betónica.

betook [bịtúk], *pret.* de TO BETAKE.

betray [bịtréị], *va.* traicionar, vender; revelar, descubrir; engañar; seducir; mostrar, dejar ver.

betrayal [-ạl], *s.* traición, perfidia; engaño; seducción, abuso de confianza; prevaricación.

betrayer [-œ(r)], *s.* traidor; seductor; prevaricador.

betroth [bịtróθ], *va. y vr.* desposar(se), contraer esponsales; comprometerse, dar palabra de casamiento.—**betrothal** [-ạl], *s.* esponsales, desposorio, compromiso, noviazgo.—**betrothed** [-t], *pp. y s.* prometido, novio, futuro.

better [bétœ(r)]. I. *a. y adv. compar.* de GOOD y WELL: mejor, de mejor modo; más bueno o bien; superior(mente).—**b. and b.**, de mejor a mejor.—**b. half**, cara mitad (esposo o esposa), costilla, oíslo, media naranja (ú. gen. de la esposa).—**b. late than never**, más vale tarde que nunca.—**b. off**, en mejores circunstancias; más acomodado; mejor librado.—**it is b. that**, más vale que.—**no b. and no worse**, ni mejor ni peor.—**the b. part of**, la mayor parte de, casi todo.—**to be b.**, estar mejor (de salud).—**to be b. than**, ser mejor que; valer más que.—**to know b.**, estar mejor enterado; saber que no se deben hacer ciertas cosas.—**to think b. of**, tener mejor opinión de (uno); repensar (algo) y mudar de parecer, plan, etc.—**you (had) b. do it**, más vale hacerlo; sería mejor, o prudente, que Vd. lo hiciera. II. *s.* superioridad, ventaja; persona superior (a uno).—**for the b.**, hacia cosas o condiciones mejores.—**so much**, o **all the b.**, tanto mejor, mejor que mejor.—**to change for the b.**, mejorar(se).—**to get the b. of**, aventajar, ganarle a, vencer a.—**our betters**, nuestros superiores. III. *va.* mejorar; aventajar,

exceder.—**to b. oneself**, mejorar de situación, adelantar. IV. *vn.* mejorarse, progresar.

better *o* **bettor**, *s.* apostador, ponedor.

betterment [-mẹnt], *s.* mejora, mejoría; mejoramiento, adelantamiento, superación.

betting [bétịŋ], *s.* apuesta; (el) apostar.

betulaceous [betịuléịsạs], *a.* (bot.) betuláceo.

betulin [bétịulịn], *s.* (quím.) betulina.

between [bịtwín]. I. *adv.* en medio, de por medio, entremedias, entre los dos. II. *prep.* entre.—**b. decks**, (mar.) entrepuentes.—**b. now and then**, de aquí a entonces, de acá para allá.—**b. the devil and the deep (blue) sea**, entre la espada y la pared.—**b. you and me**, entre nos, entre usted y yo; en confianza; acá para los dos. A veces se agregan palabras expletivas, que no se traducen, vg., **b. you and me and the lamppost.**—**in b.**, en medio (de).

betwixt [bịtwíkst], *adv. y prep. V.* BETWEEN.—**b. and between**, a medias; así así; ni lo uno ni lo otro.

bevel [bévẹl]. I. *s.* bisel, chaflán; derrame, sesgo (de puerta o ventana); falsa escuadra; rueda dentada cónica.—**b. gear(ing**, engranaje cónico.—**b. protractor, b. square**, falsa escuadra, falsarregla, saltarregla.—**b. wheel**, rueda cónica de engranaje. II. *a.* sesgo, chaflanado, biselado. III. *va.* sesgar, (a)chaflanar, (a)biselar; inclinar; (arq.) falsear. IV. *vn.* inclinarse.

bevelling [bévelịŋ], *s.* chaflán, bisel; (arq.) falseo.

beverage [bévịrạdž], *s.* brebaje, bebida, po(ta)ción.

bevy [bévị], *s.* bandada; hato; grupo de mujeres.

bewail [bịwéịl], I. *va.* lamentar, deplorar, llorar. II. *vn.* plañir, querellarse.

bewailing [-ịŋ], *s.* lamentación, lloro.

beware [bịwér], *va. y vn.* (*defect.; sólo se usan el inf. y el impv.*) guardarse, cuidarse de, estar alerta contra; recelarse, precaverse; *impv.* ¡guarda! ¡cuidado (con)! ¡ojo alerta! ¡mucho ojo!

bewilder [bịwíldœ(r)], *va.* aturdir, aturrullar, desatinar, azorar, dejar perplejo.—**bewilderment** [-mẹnt], *s.* aturdimiento, azoramiento, perplejidad.

bewildering [-ịŋ], *a.* que pone a uno perplejo.

bewitch [bịwích], *va.* embrujar, aojar, maleficiar; encantar, hechizar, arrobar, fascinar, embelesar.—**bewitcher** [-œ(r)], *s.* encantador, brujo, hechicero.—**bewitchment** [-mẹnt], *s.* encantamiento, hechizo; aojo; embeleso, encanto.—**bewitching** [-ịŋ], *a.* encantador, hechicero.—**bewitchingly** [-lị], *adv.* hechiceramente, de un modo encantador.

bey [beị], *s.* bey.

beyond [bịjánd]. I. *adv.* más allá, más lejos; allende, allá lejos. II. *s.* lo que está más allá; vida futura. III. *prep.* más allá de, tras; después de; sobre; fuera de; superior a; no capaz o susceptible de.—**b. compare**, incomparable(mente).—**b. (a) doubt**, fuera de duda, sin lugar de duda.—**b. dispute**, incontestable.—**b. expression**, indecible(mente).—**b. measure**, sobremanera, desmesuradamente.—**b. my reach**, fuera de mi alcance.—**b. question**, indiscutible.—**b. the hour**, después de (o pasada) la hora.—**b. the seas**, ultramarino.—**(from) b. the grave**, de ultratumba.—**it is b. me**, no está en mi mano; es cosa que no entiendo, etc.

bezant [bézạnt], *s.* besante, moneda bizantina; (blas. y arq.) bezante, roel.

bezel [bézẹl]. I. *va.* sesgar, (a)biselar, (a)chaflanar. II. *s.* bisel; (joy.) engaste, chatón; faceta o bisel; sello de oro grabado.

bezique [bịzík], *s.* juego de naipes.

bezoar [bízoụr], *s.* bezar o bezoar; antídoto.

bezoardic [bezoárdịk], *a.* bezoárico.

bi- [baị]. *prefijo* que significa dos o doble; (quím.) bi-, di-.

biangular [-éŋɡiulǎ(r)], *a.* biangular.

biannual [-ǽnyuạl], *a.* semianual, semestral; (*t. a veces*, bienal, dosañal).

bias [báịạs]. **I.** *s.* sesgo, oblicuidad; parcialidad, preferencia, predisposición, prejuicio.—**to cut on the b.**, sesgar, cortar al sesgo, o al soslayo. **II.** *a.* sesg(ad)o, diagonal, terciado. **III.** *va.* (*pret.* y *pp.* BIAS(S)ED) influir, predisponer, torcer.

bib [bịb]. **I.** *s.* babador, babero, pechero; grifo, espita (*V.* BIBCOCK); (ict.) faneca. **II.** *va.* y *vn.* beber a menudo, beborrotear, empinar el codo.

bibasic [baịbéịsịk], *a.* (quím.) bibásico.

bibb [bịb], **bibcock** [-kak], *s.* grifo o espita de boca dirigida hacia abajo.

bibber [-œ(r)], *s.* bebedor.

Bible [báịbl], *s.* Biblia; historia sagrada.—**B.,** o **b., paper,** papel indio, especie de papel para libros ligero, delgado, opaco y durable.

Biblical [bịblịkạl], *a.* bíblico.

bibliographer [bịblịáɡrafœ(r)], *s.* bibliógrafo.

bibliographic(al [-oɡrǽfịk(ạl], *a.* bibliográfico.

bibliography [-áɡrafị], *s.* bibliografía.

bibliomania [-oméịnịạ], *s.* bibliomanía.

bibliomaniac [-jæk], *s.* bibliómano.

bibliophile [bịblịofaịl], *s.* bibliófilo.

bibliopole [-opoụl], **bibliopolist** [-ápoḷịst], *s.* librero (esp. de libros raros).

bibulous [bịbyũḷạs], *a.* bebedor, borrachín; relativo al beber; absorbente.

bicapsular [baịkǽpsịulǎ(r)], *a.* (bot.) bicapsular.

bicarbonate [baịkárbonịt], *s.* (quím.) bicarbonato.

bice [baịs], *s.* color azul o verde pálido.

bicentenary [baịséntẹnẹrị], **bicentennial** [-ténịạl]. **I.** *a.* que ocurre cada 200 años. **II.** *s.* segundo centenario.

bicephalous [baịséfạḷạs], *a.* bicéfalo, bicípite.

biceps [báịseps], *a.* y *s.* (anat.) bíceps, lagarto.

bichloride [baịklóraịd], *s.* (quím.) bicloruro.

bichromate [baịkróụmeịt], *s.* (quím.) bicromato.

bicipital [baịsịpịtạl], *a.* (anat.) bicípite.

bicker [bịkœ(r)]. **I.** *vn.* altercar, repiquetearse, argumentar trivialmente; murmurar (arroyo); charlar, gorjear (pájaros); brillar, flamear, chisporrotear (llama). **II.** *s.* altercado, quisquilla, discusión ociosa; corrida.

bickerer [-œ(r)], *s.* camorrista.—**bickering** [-ịŋ], *s.* riña o disputa ociosa, guerra de palabras.

bickern [bịkœrn], *s.* pico de bigornia o yunque.

bicolor, bicolored [baịkÁlọ(r), -d], *a.* bicolor, de dos colores.

biconcave [baịkánkeịv], *a.* bicóncavo.

biconvex [-veks], *a.* biconvexo.

bicornous [baịkórnạs], *a.* bicorne.

bicron [báịkran], *s.* (fís.) bicrón, milimicrón, millonésima de milímetro.

bicuspid [baịkÁspịd]. **I.** *a.* bicúspide. **II.** *s.* una de las dos muelas inmediatas al colmillo.

bicycle [báịsịkl]. **I.** *s.* bicicleta, biciclo, velocípedo. **II.** *vn.* andar o montar en bicicleta.

bicycling [-ịŋ], *s.* (bi)ciclismo.

bicyclist, [-lịst], **bicycler** [-œ(r)], *s.* biciclista.

bid [bịd]. **I.** *s.* postura, licitación, propuesta, oferta.—**higher b.,** alzamiento, mejora, puja. **II.** *va.* (*pret.* BADE o BID; *pp.* BIDDEN o BID) ofrecer, pujar, licitar; decir (en el juego); pedir, rogar; convidar; mandar, ordenar; proclamar; dar (la bienvenida, el saludo, etc.).—**to b. adieu,** farewell, good-bye, decir adiós a, despedirse de.—**to b. defiance,** desafiar.—**to b. up,** pujar u ofrecer más. **III.** *vn.* hacer una oferta.—**to b. fair,** prometer, dar indicios de o tener probabilidad de.

bidder [-œ(r)], *s.* postor, licitador, pujador.— **the highest b.,** el mejor postor, rematante.

bidding [-ịŋ], *s.* orden, *f.*, mandato; invitación; licitación, postura.

biddy [bịdị], *s.* (fam.) gallina; (fam.) criada (irlandesa).

bide [baịd]. **I.** *va.* (*pret.* BODE o BIDED; *pp.* BIDED) (ant.) encontrar; sufrir, aguantar. —**to b. one's time,** esperar o aguardar el momento oportuno. **II.** *vn.* (ant.) residir; quedarse.—**to b. by,** sostenerse en, cumplir con.

bident [báịdẹnt], *s.* bidente.

bidental [baịdéntạl], **bidentate** [-teịt], *a.* bidente, bidentado.

bidet [bịdét], *s.* caballito, jaca; bidé.

biding [báịdịŋ], *s.* espera; residencia, estancia.

biennial [baịénịạl]. **I.** *a.* bienal, dosañal; (bot.) bienal, bisanuo, bisanual. **II.** *s.* planta bienal; exámenes bienales.

bier [bir], *s.* andas funerales, féretro.—**b. bearer,** andero.

biestings, *V.* BEESTINGS.

bifer [báịfœ(r)], *s.* planta bífera.—**biferous** [-ʌs], *a.* que fructifica dos veces.

bifid [báịfịd], *a.* (bot.) bífido, bipartido.

bifilar [baịfáịlǎ(r)], *a.* bifilar.

biflorous [baịflórạs], *a.* (bot.) bifloro.

bifocal [baịfóụkạl]. **I.** *a.* bifocal. **II.** *s. pl.* anteojos de lentes bifocales.

biform(ed [báịform(d], *a.* biforme, de dos formas.

bifront [báịfrʌnt], *a.* bifronte, de dos frentes.

bifurcate [báịfœrkeịt], *vn.* bifurcarse.

bifurcate *a* [-ịd], *a.* bifurcado.

bifurcation [-éịʂọn], *s.* bifurcación.

big [bịg], *a.* grande, gordo, grueso, abultado, voluminoso; lleno; noble, magnánimo; hinchado, fatuo.—**b. brother,** hermano mayor o grande, considerado como protector, etc.—**b. bug,** (fam.) persona de influencia o importancia.—**b. business,** el alto comercio; negocio en grande escala; empresa o empresas comerciales dominadoras o acaparadoras.—**b. end,** (m. v.) cabeza (de la biela).—**b. finger,** dedo pulgar o gordo.—**b. game,** animales de caza mayor.—**b. gun,** **b. shot,** (fam.) persona de alto coturno; gran punto.—**b. prize,** el gordo (lotería).—**b.-sounding,** altisonante.— **b. stick,** garrote, machete; (fig.) poder de coacción.—**b. talk,** baladronadas, bravatas, roncas, *f. pl.*; lenguaje altisonante.—**b. toe,** dedo pulgar del pie.—**b. with,** (fig.) preñado o lleno de, que encierra mucho o muchos (resultados, etc.).—**b. with child, b. with young,** preñada.—**b. words,** disputa acalorada, palabras mayores; palabras campanudas.—**to speak,** o **talk b.,** (fam.) echarla de sabihondo o importante; echar roncas o bravatas, baladronear, fanfarronear. Con participios derivados de substantivos, indica gran tamaño del objeto denotado por el substantivo: *big-mouthed*, boquigrande; *big-bellied*, barrigón, ventrudo; *big-boned*, huesudo; *big-footed*, de pies grandes; *big-headed*, cabezón; engreído; *big-hearted*, valeroso; magnánimo.

bigamist [bịɡạmịst], *s.* bígamo.—**bigamous** [-mạs], *a.* bígamo.—**bigamy** [-mị], *s.* bigamia.

bigger [bịɡœ(r)], *a. compar.* de BIG: mayor, más grande.—**biggest** [bịɡịst], *a. superl.* de BIG: (el) mayor, (el) más grande.

biggin [bịɡịn], *s.* cafetera; gorra; capillo de niño.

biggish [bịɡịʂ], *a.* grandote.

bighorn [bịɡhọrn], *s.* (zool.) carnero de grandes cuernos de las Montañas Roqueñas (E. U.).

bight [baịt], *s.* (anat.) codillo; (mar.) presilla, seno de un cabo; (geog.) caleta, ensenada, (Cuba) caney.

bigly [bịglị], *adv.* pomposa o engreídamente.

bigness [bịgnịs], *s.* grandor; grandeza; tamaño (grande o pequeño); importancia.

bignonia [bịgnóụnịạ], *s.* (bot.) bignonia.

bignoniaceous [-éịʂạs], *a.* (bot.) bignoniáceo.

bigot [bịɡọt], *s.* fanático, persona intolerante.

bigoted [-ịd], *a.* fanático, intolerante.

bigotry [-rị], *s.* fanatismo, intolerancia.

bigwig [bígwig], s. (fam.) hombre de fuste.

bike [baik], s. (fam.) bicicleta.

bilabial [bailéibiạl], a. (fon.) bilabial (como la b y la p).

bilabiate [-iịt], a. (bot.) bilabiado.

bilander [bilandœ(r)], s. (mar.) balandra.

bilateral [bailǽtęrạl], a. bilateral.

bilberry [bílberi], s. (bot.) arándano.

bilbo [bílbou], s. (poét.) espada (de Bilbao, España.)

bilboes [-z], s. pl. (mar.) cepo con grillos.

bile [báil], s. bilis, hiel, f.; cólera, ira, mal genio. —**b. duct,** (anat.) conducto biliar.

bilestone [-stóun], s. = GALLSTONE.

bilge [bildż]. **I.** vn. (mar.) abrirse una vía de agua, hacer agua; combar; hacer barriga. **II.** va. (mar.) quebrar el pantoque (de un buque); hacer combar. **III.** s. (mar.) pantoque, sentina; (ton.) barriga de barril.—**b. keel,** quilla de pantoque.—**b. pump,** bomba de carena.—**b. water,** agua de pantoque.

biliary [bílieri], a. biliar, biliario.

bilingual [bailingwạl], a. bilingüe.

bilingualism [-izm], s. bilingüismo.

bilious [bíly^s], a. bilioso.

biliousness [-nịs], s. estado bilioso.

biliteral [bailítęrạl], a. bilítero, de dos letras.

bilk [bilk]. **I.** va. engañar, defraudar, estafar. **II.** s. trampista, estafador; estafa, trampa.

bill [bil]. **I.** s. proyecto de ley; ley, f.; certificado; escrito, documento; declaración, formulación; pedimento; lista, cédula; cartel, aviso; pico o rostro (de ave); uña (de ancla); (agr.) podón, podadera, hocino; pica (arma); alabarda (arma); billete de banco; (com.) cuenta, factura, nota, minuta; letra; giro; (Ingl.) pagaré; (for.) pedimento, reclamo; (teat.) cartel, programa, m.—**b. book,** (com.) libro de obligaciones (cuentas por pagar, por cobrar, etc.).— **b. broker,** corredor o agente de cambios, agiotista.—**b. form** = BILLHEAD.—**b. of attainder,** (for.) decreto de proscripción y confiscación.—**b. of credit,** carta de crédito; (E. U.) billete de banco emitido por un estado. —**b. of debt,** pagaré en pago de una deuda.— **b. of entry,** cuenta o lista de artículos recibidos en la aduana.—**b. of exchange,** letra de cambio, cambial, libranza.—**b. of fare,** lista de platos o comidas, minuta, menú.—**b. of particulars,** (for.) declaración o exposición detallada del demandante o demandado.—**bills payable,** efectos a pagar.—**bills receivable,** efectos a cobrar.—**b. rendered,** cuenta antes girada.—**b. of health,** patente o certificado de sanidad.—**b. of indictment,** (for.) acusación oficial escrita.—**b. of lading,** conocimiento de embarque.—**b. of material,** (const.) lista de material o de piezas.—**b. of rights,** declaración de derechos; ley fundamental.—**b. of sale,** escritura de venta. **II.** va. cargar en cuenta; enviar una cuenta a; anunciar por carteles; (com.) facturar, adeudar. **III.** vn. juntar el pico (las palomas, etc.); (fig.) acariciarse, besarse (a veces **b. and coo**).

billboard [-bord], s. cartelera; (mar.) apeadero de la uña del ancla.

billed [-d], a. picudo.

billet [-ịt]. **I.** s. billete, esquela; (mil.) boleta; (fam.) colocación, empleo; zoquete de leña; (arq.) tipo de moldura; (fund.) lingote, tocho, changote.—**b. doux,** carta amorosa. **II.** va. (mil.) alojar, aposentar.

billfold [-fould], s. cartera para billetes, (Am.) billetera.

billhead [-hɛd], s. modelo o encabezamiento de factura.

billhook [-huk], s. (agr.) hocino, (navaja) podadera.

billiard [bílyạrd]. **I.** s. (E. U. fam.) carambola. **II.** a.—**b. ball,** bola de billar.—**b. cue,** taco.

—**b. hall,** o **room,** (sala de) billar.—**b. player,** billardista.—**b. table,** (mesa de) billar.

billiards [-z], s. billar.

billingsgate [-iŋzgeit], s. lenguaje bajo y soez (como el que usan las pescaderas en el mercado **Billingsgate** de Londres).

billion [bílyọn], s. (arit.) billón, bicuento; millón de millones (en España e Inglaterra); mil millones (en Francia y los E. U.).

billionth [-θ], a. y s. billonésimo; (en Francia y los E. U.) milmillonésimo.

billow [bílou]. **I.** s. oleada, ola; onda; golpe de mar. **II.** vn. ondular o hincharse como una ola.

billowy [-i], a. ondulado, ondeante, undísono.

billposter [bílpoustœ(r)], **billsticker** [-stịkœ(r)], s. cartelero, fijador de carteles.

billy [bíli], s. porra, cachiporra (de policía, etc.) —**b. goat,** (fam.) cabra macho, cabrón.

bilobate [bailóubeit], a. bilobulado, de dos lóbulos.

bilocular [bailákyülǽ(r)], a. (bot.) bilocular.

bimanous [bímạnạs], a. (zool.) bímano.

bimembral [baimémbrạl], a. bimembre.

bimestrial [baiméstriạl], a. bimestre, bimestral.

bimetallic [baimetǽlịk], a. bimetálico; bimetalista.—**bimetallism** [baimétạlizm], s. bimetalismo.—**bimetallist** [-ịst], s. bimetalista.

bimonthly [baimʌ́nθli], a. y adv. bimestral(mente), cada dos meses; a veces, bimensual(mente), dos veces cada mes.

bimotored [baimóutœœrd], a. de dos motores.

bin [bin]. **I.** s. hucha, arcón, arca; depósito; barril, cajón; sección de una bodega. **II.** va. ahuchar, guardar en hucha o arcón, etc.

binary [báinạri], a. binario, doble.—**b. measure,** (mús.) compás binario.—**b. star,** estrella doble.

binate [báineịt]. **I.** a. (bot.) doble, apareado. **II.** vn. (igl.) binar.

binaural [binórạl], a. de dos orejas; para ambos oídos.—**b. stethoscope,** fonendoscopio.

bind [báind]. **I.** va. (pret. y pp. BOUND) atar, liar, precintar, apretar, amarrar; juntar, unir, enlazar, vincular; ligar; ceñir; envolver; obligar, precisar, comprometer; (cir.) vendar; (cost.) ribetear, guarnecer; (med.) constipar, estreñir; trabar, trincar; encuadernar, empastar; (agr.) agavillar (las mieses); escriturar o contratar (a alguno); (for.) compeler.—**to b. over,** obligar a comparecer ante el juez.—**to b. up in,** dedicarse con afán a (una cosa). **II.** vn. endurecerse; trabarse; pegarse; ser obligatorio; comprometerse. **III.** s. lazo, ligadura; (mús.) ligado.

binder [-œ(r)], s. encuadernador, (Am.) empastador; atadero; enlazador; capa interior, sobretripa (de cigarro); (agr.) atador, agavilladora; (carp.) traviesa, ligazón, f.; (cost.) ribeteador.

bindery [-œri], s. taller de encuadernación.

binding [-iŋ]. **I.** s. ligazón, f.; ligamiento; enlazamiento, atadura; venda, tira, faja, cinta, ligadura; encuadernación, empastadura; (cost.) ribete, guarnición; galón; (mar.) ligazón.— **full b.,** pasta entera.—**half b.,** media pasta. **II.** a. obligatorio; valedero, válido; constipante, que estriñe.—**b. beam,** (carp.) crucero.—**b. post,** **b. screw,** (elec.) tornillo de conexión o de contacto, borne.—**b. streaks,** (mar.) cuerdas o esloras.—**b. wire,** alambre para atar.

bindweed [-wid], s. (bot.) correhuela o corregüela, enredadera, altabaquillo.

binge [bindż], s. (fam.) parranda.

binnacle [bínakl], s. (mar.) bitácora.

binocle [bínokl], s. (ópt.) binóculo, gemelos.

binocular [bínákyülǽ(r)]. **I.** a. binocular. **II.** s. anteojo, microscopio, gemelos, lente, mf., etc., para ambos ojos.

binomial [bainóumiạl]. **I.** a. de dos nombres.— **b. theorem,** binomio de Newton. **II.** s. (álg.) binomio.

binoxide [baináksaid], s. (quím.) bióxido.

bioblast [bájoblæst], *s.* bioblasto.

biochemistry [-kémįstrį], *s.* bioquímica.—**biochemical** [-įkal], *a.* bioquímico.

biodynamics [-dajnæmįks], *s.* biodinámica.

biogenesis [-dżénesįs], *s.* (biol.) biogénesis.

biogeny [bajádżenį], *s.* biogenia.

biogenous [bajádżenʌs], *a.* (bot.) biógeno.

biographer [bajágrafœ(r)], *s.* biógrafo.

biographical [bajográfįkal], *a.* biográfico.—**b. sketch,** semblanza.

biography [bajágrafį], *s.* biografía.

biologic(al [bajoládżįk(al], *a.* biológico.

biology [bajálodżį], *s.* biología.

biologist [-dżįst], *s.* biólogo.

biomechanics [bajomękénįks], *s.* biomecánica.

biometry [bajámetrį], *s.* cálculo de la duración probable de la vida; estadística biológica.

bionomy [bajánomį], *s.* bionomía.

biophysics [bajofísįks], *s.* biofísica.

bioplasm [-plæzm], *s.* (biol.) bioplasma, protoplasma reproductivo.

biostatics [-stétįks], *s.* (biol.) estudio de la relación entre estructura y función, biostática.

biota [bajóŋtä], *s.* seres organizados, o flora y fauna (de una región, época, etc.).—**biotic** [bajátįk], *a.* (biol.) biótico, propio de la vida.

biotite [bájotajt], *s.* (min.) biotita.

bipartible [bajpártįbl], *a.* divisible en dos.

bipartisan, bipartizan [-tįząn], *a.* compuesto de o representante de dos partidos políticos.

bipartite [-tajt], *a.* bipartido, bífido.

biped [bájped], *s.* bípedo.

bipedal [-al], *a.* bípede, bípedo.

bipetalous [bajpétalʌs], *a.* (bot.) bipétalo.

bipinnate [bajpíneįt], *a.* (bot.) bipinado.

biplane [bájplejn]. I. *a.* biplano. II. *s.* (aer.) biplano.

bipolar [bajpóŋlä(r)], *a.* bipolar.

biquadratic [bajkwadrétįk]. I. *s.* (álg.) ecuación del cuarto grado. II. *a.* del cuarto grado.

birch [bœrch]. I. *s.* (bot.) abedul y su madera; vara de abedul (como férula).—**b. bark,** corteza de abedul. II. *va.* castigar, fustigar.

birchen [-ęn], *a.* de abedul.

bird [bœrd], *s.* ave, *f.,* pájaro; (fam.) tipo, persona rara o singular.—**b. bath,** alberquilla o pila de baño para pájaros.—**b. bolt,** saetilla roma de matar pájaros.—**b. cage,** jaula.—**b.-eyed,** de ojos de pájaro; penetrante, observador.—**b. fancier** o **seller,** pajarero.—**b. of freedom,** (E. U.) águila.—**b. of Jove,** águila.—**b. of Juno,** pavo real.—**b. of Minerva,** búho.—**b. of paradise,** ave del paraíso, manucodiata.—**b. of passage,** ave de paso.—**b. of prey,** ave de rapiña.—**b.'s-eye,** moteado; visto de arriba y rápidamente; general, o sin pormenores; (bot.) ojo de pájaro; especie de primavera o verónica.—**b.'s-eye view,** vista de pájaro.—**b.'s-foot,** (bot.) pie de pájaro.—**b.'s nest,** nido de pájaro.—**b. shot,** perdigón.—**b. spider,** (ent.) migala.—**a b. in the hand is worth two in the bush,** más vale pájaro en mano que buitre volando.—**birds of a feather flock together,** cada cual con los de su oficio; Dios los cría y ellos se juntan.

bird, *vn.* pajarear, andar a caza de pájaros.

birdcall [-kɔl], *s.* reclamo; (a)ñagaza.

birdcatcher [-kæchœ(r)], **birder** [-œ(r)], *s.* pajarero, parancero, chuchero.

birding [-įŋ], *s.* caza de pájaros.—**b. piece,** escopeta.

birdlime [-lajm], *s.* liga, liria, hisca, ajonje, almuérdago.

birdling [-lįŋ], **birdlet** [-lįt], *s.* pajarillo.

birdman [-mæn], *s.* pajarero; ornitólogo; aviador.

birdseed [-sid], *s.* alpiste; cualquier grano menudo de alimentar pájaros.

birdwoman [-wųmąn], *s.* vendedora de pájaros; aviatriz.

birectangular [bajrektǽŋgyųlä(r)], *a.* (mat.) birrectángulo.

birefringence [bajręfríndżęns], *s.* (ópt.) birrefringencia, doble refracción.—**birefringent** [-ęnt], *a.* birrefringente, de doble refracción.

bireme [bájrim], *s.* (mar.) birreme (galera).

biretta [bįrétä], *s.* (igl.) birreta, birrete, bonete.

birr [bœr]. I. *s.* zumbido. II. *vn.* zumbar.

birth [bœrθ], *s.* nacimiento, natío, natal; principio, origen, *f.;* parto, alumbramiento; camada, lechigada; linaje, alcurnia.—**b. certificate,** acta, fe, *f.,* o partida de nacimiento.—**b. control,** limitación del número de nacimientos, o de la fecundidad, prevención voluntaria de la preñez; esterilidad voluntaria.—**b. rate,** natalidad, proporción de nacimientos.—**by b.,** de nacimiento.—**to give b. to,** parir, dar a luz.

birthday [-dej], **birthnight** [-najt], *s.* cumpleaños, natal, natalicio.—**b. present,** cuelga.

birthmark [-mark], *s.* estigma, *m.,* marca de nacimiento.

birthplace [-plejs], *s.* suelo nativo, patria, cuna.

birthright [-rajt], *s.* derechos de nacimiento; naturalidad; primogenitura, mayorazgo.

birthwort [-wort], *s.* (bot.) guaco, aristoloquia.

bis [bįs], *adv.* e *interj.* bis; repítase; ¡otro!

Biscayan [bįskéjąn], *a.* y *s.* vizcaíno.

biscuit [bískįt], *s.* galleta; bizcocho, molleta, bollo; (cerá.) bizcocho; color moreno pálido.

bisect [bajsékt], *va.* bisecar, dividir en dos partes iguales.—**bisecting line,** (geom.) bisectriz.

bisection [-sǫn], *s.* bisección.

bisector [-tǫ(r)], *s.* (geom.) bisectriz.

bisexual [bajséksųal], *a.* y *s.* bisexual, hermafrodita.

bishop [bíšǫp]. I. *s.* (igl.) obispo, diocesano; alfil (en el ajedrez); bebida de vino caliente con especias.—**to become a b.,** obispar. II. *va.* hacer obispo.

bishopric [-rįk], *s.* obispado, episcopado, mitra.

bisk [bįsk], *s.* = BISQUE.

bismuth [bízmʌθ], *s.* bismuto.

bison [bájsǫn], *s.* (zool.) bisonte.

bisque [bįsk], *s.* sopa o caldo; guisado a modo de pepitoria; (cerá.) bizcocho; ventaja (en el tenis y otros juegos).

bissextile [bajsékstįl], *a.* y *s.* (año) bisiesto.

bister, bistre [bístœ(r)], *s.* bistre.

bistort [bístɔrt], *s.* (bot.) bistorta.

bistoury [bístorį], *s.* (cir.) bisturí.

bisulcate [bajsʌlkejt], *a.* bisulco; de pesuñas partidas.

bisulfate, bisulphate [-fejt], *s.* (quím.) bisulfato.

bisulfide, bisulphide [-fajd], *s.* (quím.) bisulfuro.

bisulfite, bisulphite [-fajt], *s.* (quím.) bisulfito.

bit [bįt]. I. *s.* (mec.) taladro, broca, lengüeta; hoja de corte; bocado o embocadura del freno; paletón de una llave; parte o porción pequeña; trozo, miaja, pizca, triza, jota, ápice; bocadito; poquito; momento; moneda pequeña, ardite.—**b. by b.,** a poquitos.—**not a b.,** nada, ni miaja, ni pizca.—**to do one's b.,** ayudar uno en lo que pueda; servir uno a su patria.—**to smash to bits,** hacer añicos.—**to take the b. between the teeth,** rebelarse; desbocarse.—**two bits,** (E. U., fam.) 25 centavos. II. *va.* enfrenar; refrenar. III. *pret.* y *pp.* de TO BITE.

bitbrace [-brejs], *s.* = BITSTOCK.

bitch [bįch], *s.* perra; (vulg.) ramera, zorra.

bite [bajt]. I. *va.* y *vn.* (pret. BIT; pp. BITTEN o BIT) morder, mordiscar, atarazar, dentellear; picar, mordicar (un insecto); picar (el mar); picar, re(s)quemar (la pimienta, etc.); (mec.) agarrar, sujetar; corroer (un ácido); murmurar o satirizar, hincar el diente; engañar, clavar, defraudar.—**to b. the dust,** morder el polvo, morir, caer vencido. II. *s.* mordedura, tarascada, dentellada; mordisco; bocad(ill)o, piscolabis, tentempié, *m.;* picada, picadura; resquemo; (mec.) asimiento, cogedura.

biter [-œ(r)], *s.* mordedor.

biting [-įŋ], *a.* penetrante; mordaz, mordedor.

mordiente, picante, cáustico.—**bitingly** [-lĭ]‧ *adv.* mordazmente, con mofa; satíricamente.—
bitingness [-nĭs], *s.* resquemo, causticidad, mordacidad.
bitstock [bítstak], *s.* manubrio de taladro, berbiquí.
bitt [bĭt]. **I.** *va.* (mar.) abitar, tomar la bitadura. **II.** *s.* (mar.) abitón, bita (*ú. gen. en plural*).
bitten [bítĕn], *pp.* de TO BITE.
bitter [bítœ(r)]. **I.** *a.* agrio, amarg(os)o, áspero; agudo, cruel, severo; mordaz, satírico; rudo; enconado, encarnizado; penoso, desagradable. —**b. apple,** (bot.) coloquíntida, tuera, alhandal.—**b. cold,** frío picante.—**b.-sweet,** agridulce.—**to the b. end,** sin tregua, hasta vencer o morir, sin piedad. **II.** *s.* amargor, amargo, amargura.—*pl.* **bitters,** bíter, amargos, licor de raíces amargas. **III.** *va.* y *vn.* agriar(se), amargar(se).
bitter-ender [-éndœ(r)], *s.* persona porfiada e intransigente.
bitterish [-ĭš], *a.* amargoso.
bitterly [-lĭ], *adv.* amarga, agriamente.
bittern [-n], *s.* (orn.) avetoro, alcaraván, bitor, árdea; agua madre de sal; composición amarga para adulterar la cerveza.
bitterness [-nĭs], *s.* amargo(r) o amargura; acritud; acíbar, hiel, *f.*; angustia, aflicción; odio, rencor o encono; severidad, dureza de genio; mordacidad.
bittersweet [-swit], *s.* (bot.) dulcamara.
bittervetch [-vech], *s.* (bot.) alcarceña.
bitterwood [-wụd], *s.* (bot.) tiquistiquis.
bitterwort [-wǫrt], *s.* (bot.) genciana.
bitumen [bĭtjúmĕn], *s.* betún.
bituminize [-ajz], *va.* embetunar, bituminizar.
bituminous [-ʌs], *a.* bituminoso, abetunado.— **b. coal,** carbón bituminoso, hulla grasa.
bivalence, bivalency [bívalĕns, -ĭ], *s.* (quím.) bivalencia.—**bivalent** [-ĕnt], *a.* bivalente.
bivalve [bájvælv], **bivalvular** [bajvélvjulạ(r)], *a.* bivalvo, bivalvular.—**bivalve,** *s.* molusco bivalvo.
bivouac [bívụæk]. **I.** *s.* (mil.) vivac o vivaque. **II.** *vn.* vivaquear.
biweekly [bajwíklĭ], *a.* quincenal, de cada dos semanas; (erróneamente) bisemanal.
bizarre [bĭzár], *a.* grotesco, caprichoso, fantástico.
blab [blǽb]. **I.** *va.* revelar, divulgar indiscretamente. **II.** *vn.* chismear, comadrear, parlar ociosamente.
blab, blabber [-œ(r)], *s.* chismoso, parlador, hablador, descosido.
blab, blabbing [-ĭŋ], *s.* habladuría.
black [blǽk]. **I.** *va.* dar o teñir de negro; dar betún y lustre a (los zapatos), embetunar, dar bola, embolar, tiznar.—**to b. out,** apagar las luces (en precaución contra bombardeo aéreo). **II.** *vn.* ennegrecerse, negrear, atezarse.—**to b. out,** apagarse las luces (de tablero de instrumentos, etc.); desmayarse, privarse.—**to b. up,** pintarse de negro.
black. I. *s.* negro, atramento (color); (blas.) sable; negro (hombre); luto; mancha.—**in b. and white,** por escrito.—**in the b.,** (com.) del lado del haber, sin deudas. **II.** *a.* negro, obscuro; puro (café); *a*)tezado, tiznado; horrible, atroz, funesto; triste; ominoso, tétrico; perverso.— **b. and blue,** acardenalado, amoratado, lívido. —**b. art,** nigromancia, magia negra.—**b.-bearded,** barbinegro.—**b. beetle,** cucaracha. —**b. belt,** (E. U.) región de los negros.—**b. bile,** atrabilis.—**b. bread,** pan de centeno.— **b.-damp,** gas (de anhídrico carbónico) de las minas de carbón.—**b. death,** (hist.) la peste europea del siglo XIV.—**b. diamond,** carbonado, diamante negro; *pl.* carbón mineral.— **b. eye,** ojo amoratado por un golpe.—**b.-eyed,** ojinegro.—**b.-eyed pea,** (bot.) garbanzo.—**b.-faced,** carinegro.—**b. flag,** bandera (de) pirata. —**b. friar,** (igl.) fraile dominicano.—**B. Fri-

day,** viernes santo; viernes aciago o fatal.— **b.-haired,** pelinegro.—**B. Hand,** sociedad anarquista y gen. terrorista.—**b.-hearted,** perverso, malvado.—**b. japan,** laca japonesa. —**b. lead,** grafito; lápiz, *m.*—**b. letter,** (impr.) letra gótica antigua.—**b. light,** rayos ultraviolados (del espectro).—**b. list,** lista negra (de personas sospechosas, enemigas, etc.); *va.* poner en tal lista; proscribir.—**b. magic,** teurgia. *V.* B. ART.—**b. Maria,** (fam.) vagón negro de prisión; (mil.) granada humeante.—**b. market,** bolsa negra, venta clandestina de artículos de contrabando o fuera de la ley; estraperlo.— **b. marketeer,** estraperlista.—**b. mass,** misa de difuntos.—**b. monk,** benedictino.—**b. pepper,** pimienta negra.—**b. pope,** "papa negro," general de los jesuítas.—**b. pudding,** morcilla. —**b. rust,** (agr.) carbón (honguillo y enfermedad que causa).—**b. sheep,** el hijo malo.— **B. Shirt,** camisanegra (fascista italiano).— **b. spruce,** abeto falso o negro.—**b. vomit,** vómito negro, fiebre amarilla.—**b. widow,** cierta araña muy venenosa.
blackamoor [-ạmur], *s.* negro, esp. el de África; persona de piel negra o morena.
blackball [-bǫl]. **I.** *s.* bola negra; bola de betún. **II.** *va.* dar bola negra; votar en contra de; dar bola o betún a (los zapatos).
blackberry [-berĭ], *s.* (bot.) (zarza)mora.
blackbird [-bœrd], *s.* (orn.) mirlo o merla.
blackboard [-bǫrd], *s.* pizarra, encerado.
blackcap [-kæp], *s.* el que lleva gorra negra; (orn.) paro, silvia; (bot.) frambueso negro y su fruta.
blackcock [-kak], *s.* gallo silvestre.
blackdamp [-dæmp], *s. V.* BLACK-DAMP y CHOKE-DAMP.
blacken [-ĕn]. **I.** *va.* dar de negro o teñir de negro; betunar; atezar; ennegrecer u obscurecer; difamar, denigrar. **II.** *vn.* ennegrecerse, obscurecerse.
blackener [-ĕnœ(r)], *s.* ennegrecedor; denigrador, difamador.
blackening [-ĭŋ], *s.* ennegrecimiento, atezamiento.
blackguard [blǽgạrd]. **I.** *s.* canalla, hombre vil y desvergonzado, pelagatos. **II.** *va.* denostar, abusar vilmente.
blackhead [blǽkhed], *s.* (med.) espinilla, comedón; enfermedad infecciosa de los pavos; (orn.) pato marino.
blacking [-ĭŋ], *s.* betún, bola de zapatos.
blackish [-ĭš], *a.* negruzco, bruno.
blackjack [-džæk]. **I.** *s.* (bot.) pequeño roble; (min.) blenda; pabellón pirata; cachiporra pequeña de mango flexible; escudilla de metal charolado. **II.** *va.* atracar con cachiporra.
blackleg [-leg], *s.* petardista; fullero, tramposo; (fam.) esquirol; (vet.) morriña negra.
blacklist [-lĭst], *va. V.* BLACK LIST.
blackly [-lĭ], *adv.* tétrica o lúgubremente; airada u hoscamente; atroz o perversamente.
blackmail [-mejl]. **I.** *s.* chantaje, exacción por medio de amenazas. **II.** *va.* arrancar dinero por chantaje, o sea, con amenaza de escándalo o de denuncia.
blackmailer [-œ(r)], *s.* chantajista.
blackness [-nĭs], *s.* negrura; obscuridad.
blackout [-ạụt], *s.* apagón, apagamiento total de luces (como defensa contra ataque aéreo); censura de noticias, movimientos de buques, etc., por razones de seguridad; (teat.) mutación al oscuro; desmayo o vértigo (de los aviadores, etc.).
blacksmith [-smĭθ], *s.* herrero, herrador, chispero, forjador.—**b.'s shop,** herrería.
blacksnake [-snejk], *s.* culebra negra; látigo, fuete de cuero retorcido o acordonado.
blackthorn [-θǫrn], *s.* (bot.) endrino.
bladder [blǽdœ(r)], *s.* (anat.) vejiga, vesícula;

bolsa; ampolla.—**b. senna,** (bot.) espantalobos.

bladderwort [-wœrt], *s.* (bot.) utricularia.

blade [bléjd], *s.* hoja (de espada, navaja, etc.); pala (de remo, etc.); ala o (p)aleta (de hélice, turbina o ventilador); (bot.) brizna, mata, paja; espada, espadachín; calavera, tronera.

bladebone [-boʊn], *s.* (anat.) omóplato, escápula.

bladed [-jd], *a.* que tiene hojas.

bladesmith [-smjθ], *s.* espadero.

blain [blejn], *s.* (med.) llaga, ampolla.

blamable [bléjmạbḷ], *a.* culpable, censurable.

blamableness [-njs], *s.* culpabilidad.

blamably [-blj], *adv.* culpablemente.

blame [bléjm]. I. *va.* (in)culpar, echar la culpa a, censurar, tachar. II. *s.* (in)culpación, reproche, reprobación, censura; culpa, falta, delito.

blameful [-fụl], *a.* censurable, culpable; censurador.—**blameless** [-ljs], *a.* inculpable, inculpado, intachable.—**blamelessly** [-lj], *adv.* inculpablemente.—**blamelessness** [-njs], *s.* inculpabilidad.—**blamer** [-œ(r)], *s.* censurador, tachador.

blameworthy [-wœrðj], *a.* culpable, censurable. —**blameworthiness** [-njs], *s.* culpabilidad, censurabilidad.

blanch [blǽnch]. I. *va.* blanquear; hacer palidecer; (coc.) pelar, mondar; escaldar; (fig.) paliar. II. *vn.* albear, blanquear, perder el color; palidecer.

blancher [-œ(r)], *s.* blanqueador.

blanching [-jŋ], *s.* blanquecimiento, blanqueo.— **b. liquor,** agua de blanquear.

blancmange [blạmánž], *s.* (Fr.) manjar blanco.

bland [blǽnd], *a.* blando, suave, dulce, fonje.

blandish [-jš], *va.* engatusar, acariciar, halagar o lisonjear.—**blandisher** [-œ(r)], *s.* zalamero, halagador, lisonjeador.—**blandishment** [-mẹnt], *s.* blandura, halago, requiebro, zalamería.

blandly [-lj], *adv.* blandamente, suavemente.

blandness [-njs], *s.* suavidad, blandura.

blank [blǽŋk]. I. *a.* en blanco, no escrito; vacío, sin adorno; sin interés; confuso, turbado; pálido, descolorido.—**b. cartridge,** cartucho sin bala. —**b. check,** cheque en blanco; carta blanca.— **b. endorsement,** endoso al portador.—**b. form,** blanco, esqueleto.—**b. page,** (impr.) guarda.—**b. signature,** firma en blanco.— **b. verse,** verso blanco, libre o suelto. II. *s.* blanco, espacio, laguna, hueco; (arq.) vano; suerte o cédula de la lotería que no gana nada; papel o forma en blanco; pedazo de tejo o metal de forma apropiada para trabajarlo, cospel (de moneda); centro de blanco (en el tiro). III. *va.* (gen. con **out**), obstruir; borrar; sacar o cortar a punzón o a troquel; (fam.) maldecir, renegar; (dep.) vencer al contrario, impidiendo que éste gane un solo tanto.

blanket [blǽŋkjt]. I. *s.* manta, frazada, cubierta de lana o algodón, cobertor; manto, velo que oculta o cubre; (Am.) cobija; mantilla, envoltura para las criaturas; (imp.) mantilla, bayeta; (ing.) capa bituminosa.—**to throw a wet b. on,** poner peros a; aguar la fiesta. II. *va.* cubrir con manta; mantear; (mar.) quitar el viento un buque a otro; (rad.) paralizar (un radiorreceptor) por medio de fuertes señales o interferencia. III. *a.* general; comprensivo; irrestricto, incondicional, absoluto.—**b. ballot,** papeleta que tiene los nombres de todos los candidatos.—**b. clause,** (for.) cláusula referente a una clase entera de objetos o condiciones, que no se especifican una por una.

blanketing [-jŋ], *s.* manteamiento.

blankly [blǽŋklj], *adv.* en blanco; confusa o estúpidamente; directamente, sin ambages.

blankness [-njs], *s.* blanco, hueco, laguna, espacio; turbación, confusión.

blare [blɛr]. I. *va.* y *vn.* hacer sonar a modo de trompeta. II. *s.* sonido como de trompeta; fragor.

blarney [blárnj]. I. *s.* adulación, lisonja, zalamería. II. *va.* y *vn.* lisonjear, engatusar, engaitar.

blasé [blazéj], *a.* hastiado, gastado.

blaspheme [blǽsfím], *va.* y *vn.* vilipendiar; blasfemar, decir blasfemias, renegar.

blasphemer [-œ(r)], *s.* blasfemo, blasfemador, renegador.—**blaspheming** [-jŋ]. I. *s.* blasfemia, acto de blasfemar. II. *a.* blasfemo.

blasphemous [blǽsfjmʌs], *a.* blasfemo, impío.— **blasphemously** [-lj], *adv.* blasfemamente.

blasphemy [blǽsfjmj], *s.* blasfemia, reniego.

blast [blǽst]. I. *s.* ráfaga, golpe de aire, bocanada, ventada, ventolera; resoplido; soplo (de un fuelle, soplete, etc.); (min.) carga de un taladro; voladura (de roca, etc.); explosión; sonido o toque repentino (de corneta, etc.); influjo maligno; (agr.) tizón, añublo; (fund.) carga, hornada; inyección de aire.—**b. draft,** tiro forzado o de ventilador.—**b. furnace,** horno de cuba, alto horno.—**b. hole,** (min., etc.) taladro (agujero), barreno, hornillo; (hidr.) agujero de entrada de una bomba.—**b. indicator, b. meter,** indicador de tiro.—**b. pipe,** tubo de escape.—**at full b.,** a todo tiro, a pleno tiro (apl. a hornos, hogares de caldera, etc.).—**in full b.,** en pleno ejercicio, en plena marcha. II. *va.* volar, reventar, hacer saltar, barrenar (roca o mina); secar, agostar; añublar, atizonar los granos; maldecir, infamar. III. *vn.* (agr.) añublarse, secarse, marchitarse, perderse.

blasted [-jd], *a.* añublado, marchito; maldito.

blastema [blǽstímạ], *s.* (biol.) blastema, *m.*

blaster [blǽstœ(r)], *s.* (min.) barrenero, pegador.

blasting [blǽstjŋ], *s.* (min. y mil.) voladura; (ing.) trabajo con barrenos; (agr.) marchitamiento, marchitez.—**b. cap,** cápsula de explosión, detonador.—**b. charge,** carga explosiva.—**b. fuse,** espoleta de barreno.—**air b.,** sopladura.

blastocyst [blǽstosjst], *s.* (embr.) blastocisto.

blastoderm [-dœrm], *s.* (embr.) blastodermo.

blastogenesis [-džénesjs], *s.* (biol.) blastogénesis.

blastomere [-mir], *s.* (embr.) blastómero.-

blastula [blǽschulạ], *s.* (embr.) blástula.

blat [blǽt], *va.* y *vn.* balar, mugir; (fam.) decir o hablar sin consideración.

blatant [bléjtạnt], *a.* bramante; vocinglero.

blather [blǽðœ(r)]. I. *va.* y *vn.* charlar, charlatanear. II. *s.* charla, charlatanería, tonterías.

blatherskite [-skajt], *s.* fanfarrón; fanfarronada.

blaze [bléjz]. I. *s.* llama, llamarada, fogarada, fogata, hoguera; incendio; luz brillante; ardor; estrella o mancha blanca en la frente del caballo o la vaca; señal hecha en los troncos de los árboles, para servir de guía en un bosque; arranque (de ira, etc.).—**blazes!** (fam.) ¡chispas! ¡maldito sea!—**in a b.,** en llamas, resplandeciente. II. *va.* templar (acero); encender, inflamar; publicar, proclamar; marcar los árboles para que sirvan de guía en un bosque. III. *vn.* encenderse en llama; arder con llama; inflamarse, llamear o flamear, resplandecer, lucir.—**to b. away,** or disparando.

blazer [-œ(r)], *s.* chaqueta ligera de franela o seda; brasero, braserillo.

blazing [-jŋ], *a.* flameante; en llamas.

blazon [bléjzọn]. I. *va.* blasonar; adornar, decorar, publicar, proclamar. II. *s.* blasón, heráldica; divulgación, publicación.

blazoner [-œ(r)], *s.* autor de heráldica; heraldo; blasonador.

blazonry [-rj], *s.* blasón, heráldica; boato.

bleach [blích]. I. *va.* blanquear al sol, emblanquecer, colar (ropa), curar (tela), aclarar (el pelo); descolorar. II. *vn.* ponerse blanco, descolorirse; palidecer. III. *s.* blanquimiento.

bleacher [-œ(r)], *s.* blanqueador.—*pl.* (E. U.) gradería, gradas o tendido de sol (para ver los deportes).

bleachery [-ẹrj], *s.* blanquería.

bleaching [-in̦], s. blanqueo, blanqueamiento.— **b. powder,** cloruro de cal.

bleak [blík]. I. a. desierto, desabrigado, yermo; frío, helado.—**b. region,** páramo, paramera, (Am.) puna. II. s. (ict.) albur, breca, dardo.

bleakness [-njs], s. desolación; intemperie, destemplanza; frío, frialdad.

blear [blír], **bleared** [-d], a. legañoso; nublado; bañado en lágrimas.—**b.-eye,** s. (med.) legaña, blefaritis.—**b.-eyed,** a. legañoso, pitarroso, cegajoso; torpe de entendimiento.

blear, va. hacer legañoso; ofuscar; nublar.

blear(i)ness [-(i)njs], s. legaña, turbación de la vista.

bleat [blít]. I. s. balido. II. vn. balar.—**bleating** [-in̦]. I. s. balido. II. a. balante, balador.

bleb [bleb], s. ampolla, vejiga, burbuja.

bleed [blíd]. I. va. (pret. y pp. BLED) sangrar (a una persona, una planta, etc.); arrancar dinero a; (fam.) pegar un sablazo.—**to b. white,** desangrar; agotar; arrancar hasta el último céntimo a. II. vn. sangrar, desangrarse, echar sangre; derramar su sangre; sufrir; exudar (apl. a las plantas).—**to b. at,** echar sangre por.—**to b. to death,** morir desangrado.

bleeder [-œ(r)], s. sangrador, sajador, flebótomo; persona que padece de hemofilia.

bleeding [-in̦], s. (cir.) sangría; sangradura; flujo de sangre.—**b. heart,** (bot.) dicentra.

blemish [blémij̦]. I. va. dañar, manchar, empañar; denigrar, infamar. II. s. tacha, defecto, desperfecto, lunar, borrón, maca; deshonra.

blemishless [-ljs], a. sin tacha, inmaculado.

blench [blench]. I. vn. cejar, recular, retroceder, acobardarse. II. va. y vn. = TO BLANCH.

blend [blénd]. I. va. (pp. BLENDED O BLENT) mezclar, combinar; (pint.) casar o matizar colores; templar. II. vn. mezclarse, fundirse. III. s. mezcla, mixtura; (pint.) degradación, matiz, m.

blende [blénd], s. (min.) blenda.

blender [-œ(r)], s. mezclador.

blennorrhagia [blenǫréidȝiạ̈], s. (med.) blenorragia.

blennorrhea [blenǫrîạ̈], s. (med.) blenorrea.

blenny [bléni], s. (ict.) blenia.

blent [blent], pret. y pp. de TO BLEND.

blepharitis [blefạrái̦tjs], s. (med.) blefaritis.

bless [blés], va. bendecir; hacer feliz; santiguar; sanctificar, consagrar; alabar, exaltar, glorificar.—**b. me!** interj. ¡válgame Dios!—**God bless him,** que Dios le bendiga, bendito sea.

blessed [-jd], a. bendito, santo, santísimo; glorioso, beato, bienaventurado; feliz; escogido; (irón.) condenado, maldito, ni un solo. . . .—**b. be!,** ¡bien haya . . . !

blessedly [-lj], adv. bienaventuradamente, dichosamente, felizmente.

blessedness [-njs], s. felicidad, santidad, beatitud, gloria, bienaventuranza.

blessing [-in̦], s. bendición; beneficio, bien; gracia, favor divino; santiguada; culto.

blesser [-œ(r)], s. bendecidor; bienhechor.

blest [-t], part. adj. = BLESSED.

blet [blet]. I. vn. pasarse, echarse a perder, podrirse (la fruta). II. s. podredumbre incipiente.

blew [blu], pret. de TO BLOW.

blight [blájt]. I. s. (agr.) añublo, tizón; alheña, roya; (ent.) pulgón; (fig.) contratiempo, mala suerte, plaga. II. va. atizonar, agostar, esterilizar, añublar; ajar, marchitar (esperanzas o expectativas). III. vn. atizonarse, añublarse, agostarse.

blimp [blimp], s. (aer.) pequeño dirigible fláccido.

blind [blájnd]. I. va. cegar, enceguecer, quitar la vista a; vendar; obcecar, ofuscar; deslumbrar, (mil.) blindar. II. a. ciego; obcecado, ignorante, insensato; confuso, difícil de entender, ilegible, ininteligible; tapado, sin salida; oculto, secreto; obscuro, tenebroso.—**b. alley,** callejón sin salida.—**b. asylum,** asilo de (o para) ciegos.

—**b. flying,** (aer.) vuelo a ciegas, o sin visibilidad.—**b. gut,** (anat.) intestino ciego.—**man's buff,** juego de la gallina ciega, (Méx.) moma.—**b. of one eye,** tuerto.—**b. side,** el lado débil o de menor peligro aparente.—**b. spot,** (anat.) punto ciego; (rad.) lugar donde la recepción es mala.—**b. window,** (arq.) ventana figurada. III. s. biombo, pantalla, venda, velo, cualquiera cosa que estorba la vista o quita la luz; celosía, persiana (de ventana); persona ciega; huta, paranza o tollo donde se esconde el cazador; evasiva, pretexto, engaño; disfraz, m., tapujo; anteojera (de caballo).—pl. (fort.) blindajes, blinda.

blindage [-jdȝ], s. (mil.) blindaje, blinda.

blinded [-jd], a. enceguecido, cegado.

blinder [-œ(r)], s. anteojera, (Am.) visera (de caballo)

blindfold [-foųld]. I. va. vendar de ojos; despistar, ofuscar. II. a. con los ojos vendados; ofuscado; a ciegas, sin saber. III. s. ardid, m., engaño, superchería.

blinding [-in̦]. I. a. que ciega; cegador; deslumbrador. II. s. acción de cegar; (ing.) guijo (para carreteras).

blindly [-lj], adv. ciegamente, a ciegas.

blindness [-njs], s. ceguedad o ceguera.

blindstitch [-stjch], va. (cost.) coser de modo que no se vean las puntadas.

blink [blin̦k]. I. vn. pestañear, parpadear; disimular; fulgurar, centellear. II. va. guiñar; mirar con los ojos entreabiertos; eludir, hacer la vista gorda; paliar, cohonestar. III. s. pestañeo, guiñada; destello, reflejo, ardentía.

blinker [-œ(r)], s. el que pestañea, guiña, etc.; lo que fulgura o centellea; aparato que transmite señales por lámparas eléctricas; anteojera (de caballo); (fig.) pantalla; coqueta.—pl. (fam.) gafas.

bliss [blís], s. gloria, bienaventuranza; felicidad, arrobamiento, deleite.

blissful [-fųl], a. bienaventurado, dichoso.—**blissfully** [-lj], adv. felizmente.—**blissfulness** [-njs], s. suprema felicidad.

blister [blístœ(r)], s. ampolla, vejiga, flictena (en la piel); ampolla, burbuja (en el metal, esmalte, etc.); (mar.) cámara de aire o de agua que protege de torpedos la quilla de un acorazado.—**b. beetle o fly,** (ent.) cantárida, carraleja, cubillo.—**b. copper,** cobre metálico de superficie negra ampollada, refinado por calcinación.—**b., o blistering, plaster,** vejigatorio, (parche de) cantárida(s).—**b. steel,** acero cementado. II. vn. ampollarse, avejigarse. III. va. ampollar, avejigar; aplicar vejigatorio o cantárida.

blistering [-in̦], a. vejigatorio; que levanta ampollas.

blistery [-i], a. vejigoso.

blithe(ful [blájð(fųl], a. alegre, contento, gozoso, jacarandoso.—**blithely** [-lj], adv. alegremente.

blitheness [-njs], s. **blithesomeness** [-sʌmnjs], s. alegría, júbilo, gozo, jovialidad, despejo.

blithesome [-sʌm], a. = BLITHE.

blitzkrieg [blítskrig], s. (mil.) guerra relámpago.

blizzard [blízạrd], s. ventisca; chubasco de nieve; descarga cerrada; golpe violento; desastre.

bloat [blóųt]. I. va. hinchar, henchir; ahumar, curar (arenques, etc.). II. vn. entumecerse, hincharse, abotagarse; engreírse. III. s. (med., vet.) timpanitis; (fam.) calavera, borrachín.

bloated [-jd], a. hinchado, abotagado, túmido.

bloatedness [-njs], s. turgencia, hinchazón, f., tumefacción.

bloater [-œ(r)], s. (ict.) arenque ahumado.

blob [bláb], s. gota, burbuja, pompa; ampolla.

blobber, blobber lip. V. BLUBBER, etc.

bloc [blak], s. grupo político, "bloc."—**en b.,** en conjunto, global; enterizo, de una pieza.—**in**

b., en una pieza, en monobloque (apl. a los cilindros de un motor, etc.)

block [blak], *s.* cualquier obstáculo, obstrucción o impedimento; bloque, trozo, canto; toza, zoquete (de madera); témpano (de hielo); bloque de cilindros de un motor (llám. t. **cylinder b.** y **motor b.**); manzana de casas, (Am.) cuadra; isla; horma de sombrero; estampa, dado; cepo (de yunque); tajo, tajón; garrucha; caja o cepo de polea; (mar.) cuadernal, motón; refuerzo (tira, tabla, etc.), cuña, calzo (de un cañón, etc.); soporte; armazón de soporte para trozas de madera; (carp.) cuña, zapata; lote o partida de varias cosas de una misma clase (acciones, etc.); tableta o bloc de papel; división, compartimiento; hilera, fila; boliche o bolín, en el juego de bochas; plataforma en que se vendían los esclavos en subasta; banco patibulario, patíbulo; (fam.) testa, cabeza; zopenco; (f. c.) tramo, sección o block en un sistema de señales; (imp.) montadura de una plancha electrotípica; plancha o estampa grabada para imprimir en tela o en papel.—**b. and tackle**, aparejo de poleas.—**b. anesthesia**, (med.) anestesia por bloqueo.—**b. letter** (impr.) tipo de madera.—**b. pavement** o **paving**, pavimento de bloques, entaragudo.— **b. pulley**, polea.—**b. signal**, (f. c.) señal que gobierna el movimiento de trenes en una sección o block.—**b. system**, (f. c.) sistema de señales por secciones o blocks.—**b. tin**, estaño puro o en lingotes.—**in (the) b.** = EN BLOC. —**on the b.**, puesto en pública subasta; de venta.

block, *va.* bloquear, obstruir, cerrar; (alb.) tapar, tapiar, condenar; (tip.) montar una plancha; cerrar una forma; (sombr.) conformar; (carp.) reforzar un ángulo; calzar una rueda; (dep.) parar la pelota.—**to b. in**, *o* **out**, delinear, esbozar.—**to b. up**, (en)tupir.—**to b. the way**, cerrar el paso.

blockade [-éjd]. I. *s.* bloqueo, asedio, cerco; bloque; obstrucción. II. *va.* bloquear, asediar, poner cerco a.

blockader [-œ(r)], *s.* bloqueador.

blockhead [-hed], *s.* tonto, estúpido, mentecato, zopenco, zoquete, camueso.

blockhouse [-haus], *s.* (fort.) blocao, fortín.

blockish [-iš], *a.* estúpido, tonto.

blockishness [-njs], *s.* estupidez, tontería.

blond, blonde [bland], *a.* y *s.* rubio, blondo, (Am.) catire.—**b. lace** o **blonde**, blonda, blondina.

blood [blʌd]. I. *s.* sangre, *f.*; (poét.) púrpura; linaje o parentesco; ira, cólera; vida, temperamento, pasión; hombre animoso; jugo, o zumo (de plantas), savia (de árboles).—**b. bank**, depósito de sangre para transfusiones.—**b. bath**, (fig.) carnicería, matanza.—**b. clot**, coágulo.—**b.-colored**, sanguíneo.—**b. count**, recuento sanguíneo o globular.—**b. cupping**, ventosa sajada.—**b.-curdling**, horripilante; que hiela la sangre.—**b. donor**, el que da su sangre para transfusión.—**b. feud**, venganza de sangre.—**b. heat**, calor de sangre.—**b. horse**, caballo de pura raza.—**b. money**, precio que se pagaba como indemnización por un asesinato; dinero que se recibe por ayudar a la muerte o ruina de otro.—**b. poisoning**, (med.) septicemia, toxemia.—**b. pudding**, morcilla.—**b. pressure**, presión o tensión sanguínea o arterial.—**b. red**, color de sangre. —**b. relative**, pariente consanguíneo.—**b. relationship**, consanguinidad.—**b. serum**, suero sanguíneo.—**b.-stained**, manchado de sangre.—**b. stream**, caudal sanguíneo.—**b. test**, análisis de sangre, prueba sanguínea.—**b. transfusion**, transfusión de sangre.—**b. vessel**, vaso sanguíneo.—**to get one's b. up**, encendérsele a uno la sangre. II. *va.* sangrar; hacer olfatear sangre a un perro de caza.

blooded [-jd], *a.* que tiene sangre o temperamento de tal o cual carácter; de pura casta, de buena raza.

bloodflower [-flauœ(r)], *s.* (bot.) flor de la sangre.

bloodguilt, bloodguiltiness [-gilt, -jnjs], *s.* culpable de homicidio; asesinato.

bloodhound [-haund], *s.* sabueso.

bloodily [-jlj], *adv.* sangrientamente, cruentamente, encarnizadamente.

bloodiness [-jnjs], *s.* ensangrentamiento, sanguinolencia; calidad de sangriento.

bloodless [-ljs], *a.* exangüe, desangrado, muerto; incruento.

bloodletter [-letœ(r)], *s.* sangrador, flebótomo.

bloodletting [-jn], *s.* sangría, flebotomía.

bloodroot [-rut], *s.* (bot.) sanguinaria.

bloodshed (**ding** [-šed(jn), *s.* efusión o derramamiento de sangre; matanza.

bloodshedder [-œ(r)], *s.* homicida, *mf.*, asesino.

bloodshot [-šat], *a.* ensangrentado, inyectado de sangre.

bloodstain [-stejn], *s.* mancha de sangre.

bloodstone [-stoun], *s.* (min.) hematites, *f.*, sanguinaria, albín, heliotropo.

bloodsucker [-sʌkœ(r)], *s.* sanguijuela; usurero.

bloodthirstiness [-θœrstjnjs], *s.* encarnizamiento, sed de sangre.

bloodthirsty [-θœrstj], *a.* sanguinario, carnicero.

bloody [blʌdj]. I. *a.* sangriento; sanguinario, encarnizado, cruento; ensangrentado; sanguinolento; mezclado con sangre.—**b. flux**, flujo de sangre, disentería.—**B. Mary**, (hist.) María la Sanguinaria (María I de Ingl.).—**b.-minded**, cruel, sanguinario. II. *va.* ensangrentar.

bloom [blúm]. I. *s.* (bot.) floración, florecimiento, florescencia; cualquiera flor; vello o pelusilla de algunas frutas y hojas; belleza, lozanía; pasa de calidad superior; (fund.) tocho, lingote, changote.—**b. of youth**, lozanía de la juventud, flor (*f.*) de la edad.—**in b.**, florido, en flor. II. *va.* hacer florecer; aviciar; abigarrar. III. *vn.* florecer, florar, desabotonar; ostentar lozanía, lozanear.—**to b. out**, eflorecerse.

bloomer [-œ(r)], *s.* traje de mujer de falda corta y calzones anchos.—*pl.* calzones cortos y holgados; pantalones de mujer.

bloomery [-œrj], *s.* (metal.) forja; horno de pudelar.

blooming [-jn], *a.* en flor; lozano, fresco; próspero.—**bloomingly** [-lj], *adv.* florida, prósperamente.

bloomy [-j], *a.* florido; cubierto de pelusilla.

blossom [blásǫm]. I. *s.* (bot.) flor, *f.*, capullo, botón; floración. II. *vn.* florecer, echar flor, florar, desabotonar, reventar.

blossomy [-j], *a.* lleno de flores, floreciente.

blot [blat]. I. *va.* emborronar, manchar de tinta; chafarrinar, ensuciar, empañar; denigrar; secar con papel secante; obscurecer.—**to b. out**, rayar lo escrito, tachar; borrar. II. *vn.* correrse la tinta; pasarse (el papel). III. *s.* borrón; mancha, mancilla; testación, testadura; en ciertos juegos, peón o jugada arriesgada; lado flaco.

blotch [blach]. I. *s.* mancha, borrón, pintarrajo; pústula, roncha. II. *va.* marcar o cubrir con manchas o ronchas.

blotter [blátœ(r)], *s.* (papel) secante, teleta; borrador (para apuntar transacciones, arrestos, etc.).

blotting paper [blátjn péjpœ(r)], *s.* (papel) secante.

blouse [blaus], *s.* blusa; (mil.) guerrera.

blow [blóu], *s.* golpe; revés o contratiempo; ventarrón, vendaval; (re)soplido; trompada; tromp(et)azo; (bot.) floración, florescencia; (met.) mineral fundido de una hornada; (ing.) rotura de una ataguía; salida de gas; (fam.) fanfarronada; fanfarrón; (fam.) holgorio, parranda. Esta voz se traduce a menudo por medio del sufijo *-azo: blow with the fist,* puñetazo; *blow with a club,* porrazo.—**b. lamp,** lámpara de soldar.—**b.-off,** expulsión del agua, vapor, etc., por presión; aparato que sirve para esta operación.—**b.-off valve,** válvula de descarga o de purga.—**b.-out** = BLOWOUT.—**at a (single) b.,** de un golpe, de una vez, repentinamente.—**to come to blows,** venir a las manos, pelear.

blow. I. *va.* (*pret.* BLEW; *pp.* BLOWN) soplar, afollar; inflar, henchir (con aire); tocar o hacer sonar (un instrumento de viento); (bot.) aviciar; soplar (vidrio); limpiar con un chorro de vapor, aire, etc.; quitar soplando o por presión de vapor, etc.; depositar huevos en (apl. a insectos); divulgar; (fam.) gastar con profusión; (fam.) convidar (a tomar algo).—**to b. away,** quitar soplando.—**to b. down,** derribar (apl. al viento).—**to b. in,** meter soplando; (metal.) poner a funcionar (fam.) despilfarrar (dinero). —**to b. off,** (m. v.) vaciar, descargar o purgar (una caldera); limpiar con un chorro de vapor, aire, etc.—**to b. off steam,** dejar salir vapor; (fam.) desfogarse, soltar la lengua.—**to b. one's brains out,** levantarse la tapa de los sesos, darse un tiro.—**to b. one's nose,** sonarse, mocarse.—**to b. one's own horn,** *o* **trumpet,** alabarse, celebrar uno sus propias acciones.— **to b. out,** hacer salir soplando; apagar soplando; apagar, o suspender el funcionamiento de (un horno); vaciar o expeler por un chorro de vapor, etc.; (elec.) quemar (un fusible).— **to b. up,** inflar (sentido recto y figurado); volar o hacer saltar (una roca, un fuerte); (fam.) regañar; (foto.) hacer una ampliación de. **II.** *vn.* soplar; sonar (una corneta, etc.); jadear, bufar; ventear, correr (el viento); hacer viento (*it blows,* hace viento); ser llevado o levantado por el viento (polvo, etc.); salir, escapar (un gas); quemarse (un fusible); desabotonarse (una flor); (fam.) fanfarronear, echar roncas; (fam.) irse, marcharse.—**to b. great guns,** soplar (el viento) violentamente. —**to b. hot and cold,** estar entre sí y no, vacilar.—**to b. off,** (m. v.) descargarse.—**to b. out,** apagarse por causa del viento; (aut.) estallar, reventar; (elec.) quemarse, fundirse (un fusible).—**to b. over,** disiparse, pasar.—**to b. shut,** cerrarse por el viento (*the door blew shut,* el viento cerró la puerta).—**to b. up,** estallar, reventarse, hacer explosión; (fig.) frustrarse; fracasar.—**to b. upon,** desacreditar; denunciar.

blower [-œ(r)], *s.* soplador, aventador, fuelle; soplete; ventilador; tapadera de chimenea.

blowfly [-flai], *s.* (ent.) moscarda.

blowgun [-gʌn], *s.* cerbatana, bodoquera.

blowhole [-houl], *s.* respiradero; (fund.) escarabajo, ampolla, burbuja.

blowing [-iŋ]. **I.** *s.* soplo, soplido; sopladura. **II.** *a.* soplador.—**b. weather,** tiempo tempestuoso. —**b. fan,** soplador rotatorio, soplillo, aventador.

blown [-n], *pp.* de TO BLOW; *a.* jadeante; rendido.

blowout [-aut], *s.* limpia (de una caldera, etc.) por un chorro de vapor; (elec.) fundición (de fusible); bobina apagachispas (ll. t. **b. coil**); (aut.) revent(az)ón (de llanta); (fam.) festín, francachela.

blowpipe [-paip], *s.* soplete.

blowtorch [-tɔrch], *s.* lámpara de soldar, soplete.

blowtube [-tjub], *s.* caña de vidriero, cañón de soplar; cerbatana.

blowup [-ʌp], *s.* explosión; (fam.) acceso de ira.

blowy [-i], *a.* ventoso.

blowzy [bláuzi], *a.* coloradote; desaliñado, sucio.

blubber [blʌbœ(r)], *s.* esperma o grasa de ballena; (bot.) ortiga marina.—**b.-lip,** bezo, jeta, morro; (Cuba) bembo.—**b.-lipped,** befudo, jetón, hocicudo.

blubber. I. *vn.* llorar hasta hincharse los carrillos;

berrear, gimotear ruidosamente. **II.** *s.* gimoteo.

bluchers [blúchœrz], *s.* borceguíes; botines o medias botas.

bludgeon [blʌdʒ̩n]. **I.** *s.* porra, garrote, clava, estaca. **II.** *va.* apalear o aporrear; intimidar.

blue [blú]. **I.** *s.* azul; mujer pedante, doctora.— **the b.,** el cielo; el mar.—**out of the b.,** inesperado; de fuente desconocida.—*pl.* **the blues,** esplín, morriña, murria, melancolía. **II.** *a.* azul, indio, cerúleo, zarco; triste, melancólico; severo, estricto, puritano; fiel, leal; genuino; lívido, amoratado; literata, bachillera, erudita, sabida (mujer).—**b. baby,** criatura que padece de cianosis congénita.—**b.-black,** azul muy obscuro.—**b. blood,** sangre (*f.*) azul.—**b.-blooded,** de sangre azul.—**B. Book,** (Ingl.) Libro Azul (de informes oficiales); (E. U.) registro de los empleados del gobierno.—**b. devils,** melancolía; hipocondría; delírium tremens.—**b.-eyed,** garzo, ojiazul, ojizarco.— **b. fox,** zorro azul, raposo ferrero.—**b. gum,** (bot.) eucalipto; (med. *pl.*) descoloración de las encías.—**b. laws,** leyes puritánicas severas, sobre todo las relativas a la observancia del domingo.—**b. lead,** (min.) galena.—**b. ointment,** ungüento mercurial.—**b. paper,** papel heliográfico.—**b.-pencil,** *va.* marcar o corregir con lápiz azul; (fam.) desaprobar, criticar.—**b. plate,** plato grande, gen. azul, dividido en compartimentos, en los cuales se sirven a un tiempo varios alimentos que forman una comida.—**b. ribbon,** primer premio; de la mayor excelencia.—**b.-ribbon jury,** jurado especial, compuesto de personas selectas.—**b. streak,** relámpago, rayo; cosa hecha con gran rapidez; como un relámpago, a la carrera (*to talk a b. streak,* hablar por los codos, soltar la tarabilla).—**b. vitriol,** vitriolo azul.

blue. I. *va.* azular; pavonar (hierro y acero); añilar, lavar en agua de añil o azulada. **II.** *vn.* ponerse azul.

bluebell [-bel], *s.* (bot.) campanilla; almizcleña.

blueberry [-beri], *s.* (bot.) variedad de arándano.

bluebird [-bœrd], *s.* (orn.) azulejo norteamericano.

bluebottle [-batl], *s.* (ent.) moscón; (bot.) azulejo, liebrecilla, aciano, aldiza.

bluefish [-fiʃ], *s.* (ict.) pez azulado y plateado de la costa norteamericana del Atlántico.

blueing, *s. V.* BLUING.

bluejacket [-dʒækɪt], *s.* marinero de buque de guerra.

bluejay [-dʒei], *s.* (E. U., orn.) pájaro azul con copete.

blueprint [-prɪnt], *s.* heliografía; dibujo de ejecución.

bluestocking [-stakɪŋ], *s.* mujer docta; bachillera, literata, (fam.) marisabidilla.

bluestone [-stoun], *s.* (quím.) sulfato de cobre, vitriolo azul; (min.) arenisca arcillosa azulosa.

bluet [blúɪt], *s.* (bot.) planta de flores azuladas.

bluff [blʌf]. **I.** *a.* francote; escarpado, enhiesto. **II.** *s.* escarpa (dura), risco, morro, farallón; fanfarronada; fanfarrón; (E. U.) lance del *poker*. **III.** *va.* rechazar o impedir algo, valiéndose de una baladronada; conseguir algo a fuerza de descaro. **IV.** *vn.* alardear, baladronar.

bluffer [-œ(r)], *s.* baladrón, fanfarrón.

bluffness [-nɪs], *s.* franqueza; aspereza, rudeza.

bluing [blúɪŋ], *s.* azul o añil para lavandera; (Am.) azulillo; azulete; (metal.) pavón, pavonado.

bluish [blúɪʃ], *a.* azulado, azulino.

bluishness [-nɪs], *s.* color azulado.

blunder [blʌndœ(r)]. **I.** *va.* y *vn.* desatinar, disparatar, trabucar; divulgar sin consideración; equivocarse, confundir las especies. **II.** *s.* disparate, equivocación, error craso, patochada, trabucación.

blunderbuss [-bʌs], *s.* trabuco, encaro.

blunderer [-œ(r)], **blunderhead** [-hɛd], s. desatinado, chapuceador, trabucador; trabuco.

blunderingly [-ịŋlị], adv. desatinadamente.

blunge [blʌndʒ], va. (cerá.) mezclar la pasta.

blunger [-œ(r)], s. (cerá.) paleta para mezclar la pasta o arcilla con agua.

blunt [blʌnt]. I. a. boto, embotado, romo, obtuso; brusco, descortés; lerdo.—**to grow b.**, entorpecerse; embotarse. II. va. embotar, enromar, desafilar, despuntar; calmar o mitigar.

bluntly [-lị], adv. sin filo; lisa y llanamente, claramente; bruscamente.

bluntness [-nịs], s. embotadura; grosería, brusquedad, aspereza.

blur [blœr]. I. s. trazo borroso o confuso; borrón, mancha. II. va. hacer borroso o indistinto; embotar, entorpecer; empañar, manchar. III. vn. ponerse borroso.

blurb [blœrb], s. (fam.) bombo; noticia encomiástica de un autor o producto; advertencia que va en el forro de un libro.

blurred [blœrd], a. borroso, confuso.

blurt [blœrt], va. decir o soltar abruptamente.—**to b. out**, hablar sin consideración.

blush [blʌʃ]. I. vn. ruborizarse, sonroj(e)arse, sonros(e)arse, abochornarse. II. va. enrojar, embermejar; sonroj(e)ar. III. s. rubor, bochorno, sonrojo, sonroseo; color rojo.—**at, o on, first b.**, a primera vista.—**to put to the b.**, sacar los colores a la cara.—**blushful** [-fụl], a. modesto, ruboroso; encarnado.—**blushing** [-ịŋ]. I. s. sonrojo, rubor, erubescencia. II. a. erubescente; sonrosado.—**blushingly** [-lị], adv. ruborosamente.—**blushless** [-lịs], a. desvergonzado, descarado.

bluster [blʌstœ(r)]. I. s. ruido, tumulto; jactancia, fanfarria. II. vn. soplar con furia; fanfarrear, bravear. III. va. proferir con ira.

blusterer [-œ(r)], s. fanfarrón.

blustering [-ịŋ]. I. s. = BLUSTER. II. a. fanfarrón; jactancioso, hinchado, truculento; tempestuoso, ruidoso; tumultuoso; ventoso.

blusterous [-ʌs], **blustery** [-ị], a. V. BLUSTERING.

boa [bóụə], s. boa (sierpe); boa, m., prenda de piel o pluma para adorno o abrigo del cuello.

boar [bor], s. verraco; (S. A.) pecarí, saíno.—**wild b.**, jabalí, jabalina.

board [bórd], s. tabla; tablero; tablilla; mesa; comida, comidas, alimentos; hospedaje, pensión, pupilaje; tribunal, consejo, junta; cartón; (mar.) bordo; borda(da).—pl. tablazón, f.; (teat.) escenario, las tablas.—**b. and lodging**, mesa y habitación, cuarto y comidas, pensión completa.—**b. foot** (pl. **b. feet**), unidad de medida para madera—como 2360 cm. cúb. o 144 pulgs. cúb.—**b. meeting**, sesión de la directiva.—**b. of admiralty**, almirantazgo.—**b. of aldermen**, consejo municipal.—**b. of directors**, junta directiva; dirección, directorio.—**b. of education**, junta de educación.—**b. of health**, junta de sanidad.—**b. of trade**, (E. U.) junta de comercio; (Ingl.) ministerio de comercio.—**b. of trustees**, junta directiva, junta de síndicos.—**b. wages**, alojamiento y comida en pago de servicios; dinero que se da a los criados para mantenerse; sueldo o salario que escasamente alcanza para vivir.—**b. walk**, entablado de paseo, sobre todo a la orilla del mar.—(**bound**) **in boards**, (enc.) encartonado.—**on b.**, a bordo.—**to go by the b.**, (mar.) caer un mástil roto por el costado del buque; (fig.) arruinarse por completo, frustrarse, fracasar.

board. I. va. (mar.) abordar; subir (a un tren, etc.); (carp.) entablar, entarimar, enmaderar; dar manutención por dinero, hospedar, tomar a pupilaje. II. vn. ir a bordo; estar a pupilaje, posar.

boardable [-ạbl], a. accesible, abordable.

boarder [-œ(r)], s. huésped, pupilo, pensionista; (mar.) abordador.

boarding [-ịŋ], s. tablazón, f.; entablado; tabique de tablas; pupilaje; (mar.) abordaje.—**b. house**, casa de huéspedes, pensión, pupilaje.—**b. pike**, (mar.) botavante, chuzo de abordar.—**b. pupil**, o **student**, estudiante interno, pensionista.—**b. school**, escuela de internos, internado.

boarhound [bórhaụnd], s. perro jabalinero.

boarish [bórịʃ], a. cochino, sucio; brutal, cruel.

boast [bóụst]. I. vn. alardear, blasonar, cacarear; jactarse, preciarse, ufanarse, vanagloriarse (de).—**it is nothing to b. of**, no es gran cosa.—**to b. of being**, echarla de, echárselas de. II. va. decantar, ponderar, exaltar; ostentar; (esc. y cant.) desbastar. III. s. jactancia, ostentación, baladronada, bravata; alarde, vanagloria, cacareo.

boaster [-œ(r)], s. fanfarrón, jaque, baladrón.

boastful [-fụl], a. jactancioso.

boasting [-ịŋ], **boastfulness** [-fụlnịs], s. V. BOAST.

boastingly [-ịŋlị], **boastfully** [-fụlị], adv. jactanciosamente, ostentosamente, ufanamente.

boat [bóụt]. I. s. (mar.) buque, barco, bajel, navío, nave, f.; bote, barca, lancha, batel, chalupa.—**b. hook**, bichero, botador.—**b. race**, regata.—**b. song**, barcarola.—**b. train**, tren que enlaza con un barco.—**in the same b.**, en iguales circunstancias o apuros. II. va. poner o llevar a bordo.—**to b. oars**, desarmar los remos. III. vn. navegar, remar, ir en bote, barquear.

boatable [-ạbl], a. navegable para botes; que se puede transportar en botes.

boatage [-ịdʒ], s. barcaje, lanchaje; cabida o capacidad total de los botes de un buque.

boatful [-fụl], s. barcada.

boathouse [-haụs], s. cobertizo para botes.

boating [-ịŋ], s. ir o pasear en bote; manejo de un bote; transporte en bote.

boatload [-loụd], s. barcada.

boatman [-mạn], s. barquero, botero, lanchero, batelero, chalupero.

boatswain [bóụsn, bóụsʌn], s. contramaestre.—**b.'s chair**, balso.—**b.'s mate**, segundo contramaestre.

bob [bab]. I. va. y vn. menear(se) o mover(se) con sacudidas, o de arriba abajo; subir y bajar; pescar con corcho y cebo; desmochar, descolar, cercenar; cortar corto (apl. esp. a la piel y al rabo); golpear con algún objeto redondeado o nudoso; tocar ligeramente; dar con el codo o la mano.—**to b. up**, presentarse inesperadamente, surgir. II. s. corcho (en la pesca con anzuelo); cebo (gen. un manojo de lombrices o trapos); perendengue, zarcillo; borla; plomo de plomada; lenteja o disco del péndulo; (maq.) balancín; saludo, cortesía; cierto toque de campanas; (fam.) chelín (en Inglaterra); cola cortada de un caballo; pelo cortado corto.

bobbin [bábịn], s. canilla, broca; devanadera, carrete(l), argadijo, huso; bolillo, palillo, majaderillo (para hacer encaje); (elec.) carrete, bobina.—**b. winder**, devanador.

bobbinet (o **bobbin net**) [babịnét], s. encaje de imitación; punto de bobiné o de algodón.

bobby [bábị], s. (Ingl., fam.) policía (agente).—**b. pin**, especie de horquilla para sujetar el pelo.—**b. sox**, calcetines muy cortos.—**b. soxer**, (fam.) polla, mocita.

bobcat [bábkæt], s. (E. U., zool.) lince o gato montés.

bobolink [bábolịŋk], s. = REEDBIRD.

bobsled [bábsled], **bobsleigh** [-sleị], s. rastra corta; trineo de dos rastras.

bobstay [-steị], s. (mar.) barbiquejo.

bobtail [-teịl]. I. va. cortar la cola a. II. a. rabón, rabicorto; incompleto. III. s. animal rabicorto; rabo mocho.

bobwhite [-hwáįt], *s*. (E. U., orn.) codorniz común.

bobwig [-wįg], *s*. peluquín.

Boche, boche [baš], *s. y a*. (despec.) alemán.

bock [bák], **bock beer** [-bír], *s*. cerveza extrafuerte.

bode [boųd]. **I**. *pret. y pp*. de TO BIDE. **II**. *va*. presagiar, pronosticar, presentir. **III**. *vn*. predecir; prometer.—**to b. ill** (o **well**), ser de mal (o buen) agüero.

bodice [bádįs], *s*. corpiño, jubón, cuerpo de vestido, almilla, monillo; (Am.) talle.

bodied [bádįd], *a*. corpóreo; que tiene cuerpo.

bodiless [bádįlįs], *a*. incorpóreo; sin cuerpo.

bodiliness [bádįlįnįs], *s*. corporalidad, corporeidad—**bodily** [bádįlį]. **I**. *a*. corpóreo, corporal, físico. **II**. *adv*. corporalmente; en persona; en conjunto, en peso.

boding [bóųdįŋ]. **I**. *a*. ominoso, presagioso. **II**. *s*. presagio, pronóstico, (mal) agüero.

bodkin [bádkįn], *s*. (cost.) punzón; pasacintas. pasador o aguja de jareta; alfiler, espadilla o rascamoño para el tocado o sombrero; lezna para la cestería; (impr.) punzón o punta.

body [bádį], *s*. cuerpo; tronco; torso (de estatua); cadáver; realidad; una persona, un individuo; cuerpo, gremio, corporación; colección, agregado; cuerpo, consistencia, densidad, espesor, fortaleza; caja o cama de un carruaje; cuerpo (de prenda de vestir); (aut.) carrocería (sólo se aplica a coches, no a camiones, de los cuales se dice *caja*); parte (*f.*) principal o central; (mar.) quilla; vista de la quilla; (aer.) armazón (*f.*) de un aeroplano; (impr.) cuerpo (del tipo). —**b. cloth,** manta para caballos.—**b. exercises,** ejercicios corporales.—**b. of a church,** nave (*f.*) de una iglesia.—**b. of water,** extensión de agua.—**b. plan,** (mar.) corte transversal de un buque.—**b. politic,** estado o nación; entidad política.—**b. snatcher,** ladrón de cadáveres.—**in a b.,** en masa.

body, *va*. dar cuerpo o forma a; representar; formar un cuerpo, gremio, etc., de.

bodyguard [-gard], *s*. guardia de corps; comitiva.

Bœotian [bįoųšąn], *a. y s*. beocio; (fig.) palurdo, estúpido.

Boer [bor], *a. y s*. bóer, del Transvaal.

bog [bag]. **I**. *s*. pantano, fangal, atolladero, ciénaga, lodazal.—**b. bean,** (bot.) trifolio fibrino. —**b. oak,** lignito de encina.—**b. ore,** (min.) limonita.—**b. trotter,** (fam.) campesino irlandés. **II**. *va. y vn*. (a veces con **down**), hundir(se); atollar(se); atascar(se).

bogey, bogy [bóųgį], *s*. espectro, espantajo, coco.

boggle [bágl]. **I**. *va*. hacer una patochada. **II**. *vn*. recular, retroceder; cejar, vacilar.

boggle, *s*. retroceso de un caballo asustado; objeción, dificultad; patochada.

boggy [bágį], *a*. pantanoso, palustre, cenagoso.

bogie [bóųgį], *s*. carretilla o un taller de aserrar madera; vagoneta de carga; (f. c.) *bog(g)ie, m., truck,* carro giratorio.

bogland [báglænd], *s*. tierra pantanosa.

bogus [bóųgąs], *a*. (fam. E. U.), falso, espurio.

bohea [boųhí], *s*. té de calidad inferior.

Bohemian [boųhímįąn], *a. y s*. bohemi(an)o.

boil [bóįl]. **I**. *va. y vn*. hervir; bullir; cocer, salcochar o sancochar, herventar; (farm.) elijar; (fig.) agitarse, hervirle a uno la sangre.—**to b. away,** consumir un líquido a fuerza de cocerlo. —**to b. down,** reducir por cocción; reducir(se) a su más simple forma o expresión.—**to b. over,** borbotar, hervir hasta rebosar.—**to b. clear,** (azú.) melar. **II**. *s*. hervor, ebullición; (med.) divieso, furúnculo; (Cuba) nacido; (Méx.) clacota.

boiled [-d], *a*. (coc.) cocido, salcochado.

boiler [-œ(r)], *s*. marmita, olla, caldero; paila; (m. v.) caldera; (azú.) tacho.—**b. compound,** (m. v.) antiincrustante, desincrustante.—**b. head,** fondo de caldera.—**b. iron, steel,** palastro de hierro, acero, para calderas.—**b. jacket,** camisa de caldera.—**b. maker,** cal-

derero.—**b. plant,** instalación de calderas.— **b. room,** cámara o sala de calderas.—**b. shell,** cuerpo de caldera.

boiling [-įŋ], *s*. hervor, ebullición, cocción, cochura; hervidero.—**b. flask,** (quím.) balón. —**b. kettle,** caldero, marmita, hervidor.—**b. point,** punto de ebullición.

boisterous [bóįstœrᴧs], *a*. turbulento, ruidoso, revuelto, estrepitoso, tumultuoso, borrascoso, bullicioso.—**boisterously** [-lį], *adv*. ruidosamente, tumultuosamente.—**boisterousness** [-nįs], *s*. turbulencia, tumulto, vocinglería, bulla.

bola(s [bóųlä(s)], *s*. (Am.) boleadoras, *f. pl.*, aíllo.

bold [bóųld], *a*. arrojado, denodado, valiente; atrevido, audaz, osado, temerario; impudente, fresco, descarado; (mar.) escarpado, acantilado. —**b.-faced,** descarado, desvergonzado, insolente.—**b.-faced type,** (impr.) letra negra, negrilla.

boldface [-feįs], *s*. descaro; persona desfachatada; (impr.) = BOLD-FACED TYPE.

boldly [-lį], *adv*. libremente; osadamente, audazmente; descaradamente.

boldness [-nįs], *s*. arrojo, intrepidez; atrevimiento, osadía, audacia, denuedo; descaro.

bole [boųl], *s*. tronco de un árbol; especie de arcilla (ll. t. **Armenian bole,** bol(o) arménico).

bolero [boléroų], *s*. bolero (baile y chaquetilla).

bolide [bóųlaįd], *s*. bólido, meteoro.

Bolivian [bolívįąn], *s. y a*. boliviano.

boll [boųl]. **I**. *s*. antigua medida; (bot.) cápsula (de algodón, etc.).—**b. weevil,** gorgojo del algodón.—**b. worm,** gusano del maíz (que ataca también el algodón). **II**. *vn*. formarse en cápsulas; producir cápsulas.

Bolognese [boųloníz], *a. y s*. boloñés; de Bolonia.

bolometer [boųlámetœ(r)], *s*. (elec.) bolómetro, detector bolométrico de ondas.—**bolometric** [boųlométrįk], *a*. bolométrico.

boloney [boųlónį], *s*. (fam.) tonterías, hojarasca.

Bolshevik [báĺševįk], *s. y a*. bolchevique.—**Bolshevism** [-vįzm], *s*. bolchevismo.—**Bolshevist** [-vįst], *a. y s*. bolchevista.—**bolshevize** [-vaįz], *va*. hacer bolchevique.

bolster [bóųlstœ(r)]. **I**. *s*. travesero, almohadón; cabecero, cabezal; larguero, soporte, refuerzo; (cir.) cabezal; (mar.) almohada de los palos; borrenes de la silla de montar; (f. c.) solera de carro; (constr.) travesaño; canecillo; caballete. **II**. *va*. sostener, reforzar, auxiliar, apoyar.

bolstering [-įŋ], *s*. apoyadero, apoyo.

bolt [bóųlt]. **I**. *s*. (cerr.) cerrojo, pasador, pestillo, falleba; (carp.) perno, tornillo, chaveta, clavija; (arti.) lingote, proyectil cilíndrico; dardo, flecha; centella, rayo; suceso repentino; salto rápido; fuga; pieza o rollo (de paño); (mar.) perno, cabilla; tamiz muy fino para harina; (pol. E. U.) disidencia.—*pl.* (mar.) pernería.— **b. and nut,** perno y tuerca.—**b. clasp,** hembra.—**b. staple,** cerradero, picolete.—**b. from the blue,** suceso inopinado. **II**. *adv*. recto como una flecha, rígidamente.—**b. upright,** enhiesto, empinado. **III**. *va*. acerrojar, cerrar con cerrojo, echar el cerrojo; empernar; encabillar; cerner (harina); examinar, escudriñar; (pol. E. U.) disidir de; engullir, tragar sin mascar; soltar; arrojar, echar. **IV**. *vn*. saltar de repente; lanzarse; desbocarse (caballo); resistirse; caer como rayo.—**to b. in,** entrar de repente.—**to b. out,** salir de golpe.

bolter [-œ(r)], *s*. cedazo, criba; cordel de pescar; caballo que se desboca; (pol. E. U.) disidente.

bolthead [-hed], *s*. cabeza de perno; (quím.) matraz, *m*.

bolting [-įŋ], *s*. cerramiento; cernido o cernidura. —**b. cloth,** tela de cedazo, tamiz, *m*.—**b. house,** cernedero.

boltrope [-roųp], *s*. (mar.) relinga.

bolus [bóųlᴧs], *s*. bolo, píldora gruesa; bola.

bomb [bam]. **I**. *s*. bomba; granada; (piro.) petardo; (fig.) rayo, suceso inesperado y perturbador.—**b. bay,** (aer., mil.) recipiente o compartimiento para bombas, de apertura automática.—**b. carrier,** portabombas, *m.*—**b. ketch,** (mar.) bombarda, lancha bombardera o cañonera.—**b. rack,** (aer.) portabombas, *m.*—**b. release,** (aer.) lanzabombas, *m.*—**b. shelter,** refugio contra bomba(rdeo)s.—**b. thrower,** (arti.) mortero; (aer.) lanzabombas, *m.* **II.** *va.* (arti.) bombear; bombardear, sobre todo desde un avión.

bombacaceous [bambakéiŝʌs], *a.* (bot.) bombáceo.

bombard [bambárd], *va.* (arti.) bombardear, bombear.

bombardier [bambardír], *s.* bombardero.—**b. beetle,** (ent.) escarabajo bombardero o escopetero.

bombardment [bambárdment], *s.* bombardeo.

bombardon [bámbardon], *s.* (mús.) bombardón.

bombast [bámbæst], *s.* ampulosidad.—**bombastic** [-bǽstik], *a.* ampuloso, altisonante, retumbante, campanudo, culterano, (Am.) bombástico.

bombax [bámbæks], *s.* (bot.) ceiba.

bombazine [bambazín], *s.* (tej.) bombasí; alepín.

bomber [bámœ(r)], *s.* avión (*m.*) de bombardeo; bombardero (avión o aviador).

bombing [bámiŋ], *s.* bombardeo.

bombproof [bámpruf], **I.** *a.* a prueba de granadas o de bombas. **II.** *s.* abrigo contra bombas.

bombshell [bámŝɛl], *s.* bomba, granada.

bombsight [bámsait], *s.* (aer.) mira o visor de bombardeo.

bombyx [bámbiks], *s.* (ent.) gusano de seda, bómbice.

bona fide [bóuna fáidi], *a.* y *adv.* de buena fe, sin engaño, honradamente.

bonanza [bonǽnza], *s.* bonanza; mina o veta rica en mineral; (com. y fig.) operación lucrativa.

Bonapartist [bóunapartist], *a.* y *s.* bonapartista.

bonbon [bánban], *s.* bombón, confite, dulce.

bonbonnière [-yér], *s.* bombonera.

bond [bánd]. **I.** *s.* lazo, vínculo; unión, ligazón, *f.*; ligam(i)ento, nexo, nudo; traba, trabadura; cualquier cosa que une o liga; (arq.) aparejo, trabazón, *f.*; (elec.) conexión eléctrica de dos rieles; (quím.) grado de afinidad, enlace; (com.) bono, obligación, vale; título de la deuda; fiador; fianza, dita, recaudo.—*pl.* cadenas, cautiverio; (const.) maderamen, enmaderado.—**b. issue,** emisión de bonos.—**in b.,** en depósito; afianzado. **II.** *a.,* siervo; esclavizado, cautivo. **III.** *va.* unir; ligar estrechamente; conectar eléctricamente; afianzar, dar fianza; obligar por fianza; hipotecar; poner mercancías en depósito afianzado. **IV.** *vn.* unirse, adherirse.

bondage [-idz], *s.* cautiverio, esclavitud, servidumbre; obligación.

bonded [-id], *a.* garantido por obligación escrita; hipotecado; asegurado; depositado bajo fianza para el pago de derechos arancelarios.—**b. goods,** mercancías en depósito.—**b. warehouse,** almacén de depósito.

bonded debt, deuda consolidada.

bonder [-œ(r)], *s.* depositante de mercancías; (alb.) perpiaño.

bondholder [-houldœ(r)], *s.* tenedor de bonos, obligacionista, rentista.

bondmaid [-meid], *s.* esclava, sierva.

bondman [-man], *s.* esclavo, siervo.

bondsman [-zman], *s.* fiador, dita, garante.

bondstone [-stoun], *s.* (arq.) perpiaño, tizón.

bondswoman [-zwuman], *s.* fiadora, dita.

bone [bóun], *s.* hueso; espina del pez; cuesco de fruta; barba de ballena.—*pl.* esqueleto; dados; especie de castañuelas.—**b. black,** carbón o negro animal.—**b. dust, b. meal,** huesos molidos, harina de huesos.—**b.-dry,** enteramente seco; (fam.) que no vende ni gota (de licor); absolutamente temperante.—**b. of contention,** manzana de la discordia, asunto de disputa o desavenencia.—**b. porcelain,** porcelana de fosfato de cal, hecha con polvo de huesos.—**a b. to pick,** una cuestión que averiguar o arreglar.—**to have a b. to pick with someone,** tener alguna queja de él o satisfacción que pedirle.—**to make no bones of,** no andarse con rodeos, no tener empacho en.

bone. I. *va.* deshuesar, desosar; emballenar, poner ballenas (a un corsé, etc.); abonar con polvo de huesos; nivelar; alinear. **II.** *vn.* (fam.) quemarse las cejas estudiando.

boneache [-eik], *s.* dolor de huesos.

boneblack [-blæk], *s.* = BONE BLACK. *V.* BONE.

boned [-d], *a.* osudo, huesudo; sin huesos.

bonehead [-hɛd], *s.,* **boneheaded** [-id], *a.* (fam.) mentecato, imbécil.

bonelace [-leis], *s.* encaje de bolillos.

boneless [-lis], *a.* mollar, sin huesos.

boner [-œ(r)], *s.* (fam.) patochada, disparate.

boneset [-sɛt], *s.* (bot.) eupatorio.

bonesetter [-œ(r)], *s.* algebrista, ensalmador.

bonfire [bánfair], *s.* hoguera, fogata, fogarada.

bonhomie [banomí], *s.* afabilidad.

Boniface [bánifeis], *s.* hostelero, mesonero.

boning [bóuniŋ], *s.* acción de deshuesar o de emballenar; abono de tierras; nivelación por medio de estacas.

bonito [boníto u], *s.* (ict.) bonito, biza, especie de atún.

bon mot [ban móu], *s.* (fr.) agudeza, dicho agudo.

bonnet [bánit]. **I.** *s.* gorra, gorro, toca, boneta, sombrero de mujer; solideo, bonete; (fort.) bonete; (mec.) sombrerete; (mar.) boneta; (aut.) cubierta del motor. **II.** *va.* cubrir; apabullar. **III.** *vr.* tocarse, cubrirse.

bonnet rouge [banɛ rúẑ], *s.* (fr.) gorro encarnado; ultrarradical.

bonny [báni], *a.* bonito, lindo, gentil; alegre.

bonnyclabber [-klæbœ(r)], *s.* cuajo, leche cuajada.

bon ton [ban tán], *s.* el gran mundo; buen tono.

bonus [bóunʌs], *s.* bonificación, adehala; prima; dividendo; sobresueldo, sobresalario; (Am.) ñapa, contra.

bony [bóuni], *a.* osudo, huesudo, óseo, ososo.

bonze [banz], *s.* bonzo (sacerdote budista).

boo [bu]. **I.** *s.* bucheo, grita, rechifla. **II.** *va.* y *vn.* buchear, sisear, dar grita, rechiflar, silbar. **III.** *interj.* ¡fuera! ¡mira! ¡qué va! ¡bu!

boob [búb], *s.* (fam.) bobo, zopenco, papanatas.

booby [-i], *s.* y *a.* zote, bobo, pajuncio, papamoscas, gaznápiro; (orn.) pájaro bobo.—**b. prize,** premio que se da al peor jugador, en ciertos juegos.—**b. trap,** engañabobos.

boodle [búdl], *s.* (fam. E. U.) ganancias ilícitas; soborno; moneda falsa; (Am.) chanchullo; hato, partida, cuadrilla. *V.* CABOODLE.

boodler [búdlœ(r)], *s.* (fam. E. U.) el que se deja sobornar o practica desfalcos, etc.

book [búk]. **I.** *s.* libro; obra, tomo; libreta; libreto (de ópera).—**b. end,** sujetalibros.—**b.-learned,** erudito, leído; de ciencia aprendida en libros.—**b. learning,** saber aprendido en libros, teoría.—**b. lover,** bibliófilo.—**B. of Common Prayer,** ritual de la secta anglicana o episcopal.—**b. of pilotage,** derrotero.—**b. of rates,** arancel de aduana.—**b. of reference,** libro de consulta.—**b. plate,** ex libris.—**b. review,** reseña.—**b. satchel,** cartapacio.—**b. stand** o **stall,** puesto de libros.—**b. trade,** comercio de libros.—**by the b.,** según las reglas; con exactitud.—**to bring to b.,** traer a capítulo. **II.** *va.* asentar o notar en un libro o registro; inscribir; retener o sacar (pasaje, etc.), tomar (localidades); contratar o apalabrar (a un artista, conferenciante, etc.).

bookbinder [-baindœ(r)], *s.* encuadernador.

bookbinding [-baindiŋ], *s.* encuadernación.

bookcase [-keis], *s.* armario o estante para libros, librería.

bookie [-i], s. (fam.) V. BOOKMAKER (dep.).

booking [-iŋ], s. registro, asiento; compra o venta de billetes.—**b. clerk**, vendedor de billetes de pasaje o teatro; taquillero.—**b. office**, despacho o expendeduría de billetes; taquilla.

bookish [-iš], a. estudioso; libresco; versado en libros; pedante, teórico.

bookishness [-niš], s. estudiosidad; afición a los libros; falta de sentido práctico.

bookkeeper [-kipœ(r)], s. tenedor de libros.

bookkeeping [-kipiŋ], s. teneduría de libros, contabilidad.—**b. machine**, máquina contable.

booklet [-lit], s. libretín, folleto, opúsculo.

bookmaker [-meikœ(r)], s. el que hace libros; (dep.) corredor de apuestas, o apostador de profesión, esp. en las carreras de caballos.

bookmaking [-meikiŋ], s. ocupación del *bookmaker*.

bookmark [-mark], s. señal o marcador de libro.

bookrack [-ræk], s. atril; sostén para libros.

bookseller [-selœ(r)], s. librero.

bookstore [-stor], s. librería, almacén de libros.

bookworm [-wœrm], s. polilla o gusano que roe los libros; bibliófilo, ratón de biblioteca.

boom [bum]. I. s. (mar.) botalón; botavara; pescante, aguilón (de grúa); cordón, cabeza (de puente); cadena para cerrar un puerto o río, o para detener trozas; estampido; torrente crecido y bramador; (fig.) auge, actividad o prosperidad repentina.—**b. iron**, (mar.) zuncho de botalón.—**b. sail**, (mar.) vela cangreja. II. vn. hacer estampido; moverse con violencia; ir a velas desplegadas; (fam. E. U.) estar en auge, medrar. III. va. favorecer, anunciar, fomentar, bombear, dar bombo.

boomerang [búmęræŋ], s. bumerang (arma); (fig.) plan, argumento, etc., que resulta contraproducente.

boon [bun]. I. s. dádiva, don; gracia, merced; dicha, bendición. II. a. genial, festivo, convival.

boor [búr], s. patán, palurdo, rústico, villano.

boorish [-iš], a. rústico, agreste, grosero, tosco, villanesco; (Am.) guajiro, jíbaro.—**boorishly** [-li], adv. rústicamente, toscamente.—**boorishness** [-niš], s. rusticidad, tosquedad, grosería, patanería.

boost [búst]. I. va. (fam. E. U.) empujar, levantar; alzar desde abajo; fomentar, promover, bombear; hacer subir. II. s. alza; ayuda, asistencia.

booster [-œ(r)], s. impulsador, fomentador; (elec.) elevador de potencial o de tensión.—**b. battery**, (rad.) batería de conservación del voltaje en el detector.

boot [bút]. I. va. y vn. aprovechar, valer, servir, importar; calzarse uno las botas; (fam.) dar patadas a. II. s. bota, botín, botina (de mujer); calzado; borceguí; ganancia, provecho; adehala, refacción, (Am.) ñapa.—**b. hook**, tirabotas.—**b. maker**, zapatero.—**b. tree**, horma de botas.—**boots and saddles**, (mil.) botasilla (toque de clarín).—**bet your boots**, (fam.) no cabe duda; es cosa segura.—**to be in another's boots**, estar en el pellejo de otro.—**to b.**, además; por añadidura, de ñapa.—**to put the b. on the wrong leg**, culpar al inocente.

bootblack [-blæk], s. limpiabotas, (Am.) lustrabotas, embolador.

booted [-id], a. calzado con botas; (fam.) embotado.

bootee [-í], s. bota corta de mujer; calzado plástico para niños.

booth [buθ], s. garita, casilla; puesto o mesilla de venta; (tlf.) cabina; reservado en ciertos restaurantes, etc.

boothose [búthouz], s. calcetones.

bootjack [bútdžæk], s. sacabotas, descalzador.

bootleg [bútlɛg]. I. va. y vn. (fam. E. U.) contra-

bandear, esp. en licores. II. a. de contrabando.—**bootlegger** [-œ(r)], s. contrabandista de licores.—**bootlegging** [-iŋ], s. contrabando de licores.

bootless [bútlis], a. descalzo; inútil, sin provecho.

boots [buts], s. limpiabotas de hotel.

bootstrap [bútstræp], s. tirilla.

booty [búti], s. botín, despojo, presa.

booze [búz]. I. vn. embriagarse, emborracharse. II. s. bebida alcohólica; (fam.) borrachera, pítima.

boozer [-œ(r)], s. (fam.) bebedor, borrachín.

boozy [-i], a. (fam.) borracho, achispado, calamocano.

bopeep [boupíp], s. escondite (juego de niños).

boracic [borǽsik], a. bórico.

boracite [bóręsait], s. (min.) boracita, borato de magnesio.

borage [bóridž], s. (bot.) borraja.

boraginaceous [borædžinéišʌs], a. (bot.) borragíneo.

borate [bóreit], s. (quím.) borato.—**borated** [-id], a. boratado.

borax [bóræks], s. (quím.) bórax, borraj, atíncar.

border [bórdœ(r)]. I. s. orilla, (re)borde, faja, margen, *mf.*; arriate de un jardín; frontera, límite, confín; comarca, raya; (cost.) orla, guarnición, banda, cenefa, cerco, ribete, franja, farfalá, *f.*, dobladillo, repulgo; (blas.) bor(da)-dura. II. vn. confinar, comarcar, lindar; rayar, aproximarse, acercarse.—**to b. on**, o **upon**, lindar con, tocar; rayar en. III. va. (cost.) orlar, repulgar, guarnecer, ribetear; tocar o lindar con.

borderer [-œ(r)], s. habitante de tierras limítrofes o comarcanas; (cost.) orlador, ribeteador.

bordering [-iŋ]. I. s. (cost.) oladura. II. a. fronterizo, contiguo, lindante, confín, rayano.

borderland [-lænd], s. frontera, límite, confín.

borderline [-lain]. I. s. límite. II. a. limítrofe; dudoso.

bore [bor]. I. va. taladrar; barrenar, trepar, horadar, perforar; hacer o abrir a taladro o barrena; (ing., min.) sondear; (fam.) aburrir, fastidiar, cargar, dar la lata a. II. vn. hacer agujeros; adelantarse, avanzar.—**to b. from within**, atacar desde adentro por traición. III. pret. de TO BEAR. IV. s. taladro, barreno, agujero que se hace taladrando o barrenando; (arti.) calibre, alma, ánima; (mec.) diámetro interior (de un cilindro); luz o diámetro (de un pozo); ola grande causada por la marea; (fam.) machaca, pelmazo, latoso, chinche, persona pesada.

boreal [bórięl], a. septentrional, boreal.

Boreas [bórięs], s. cierzo, bóreas.

borecole [bórkoul], s. (bot.) variedad de col.

bored [bord], pp. y a. taladrado; aburrido, fastidiado.

boredom [bórdom], s. fastidio, aburrimiento, hastío, tedio; gente pesada en general.

borer [bórœ(r)], s. horadador; barrena; taladro, perforadora, broca; (min.) sonda; cualquier animal que horada; (ent.) barrenillo, insecto xilófago (horadador); (fam.) pelmazo, latoso, chinche.

boresome [bórsʌm], a. aburrido, cansado, fastidioso.

boric [bórik], a. bórico.

boride [bóraid], s. (quím.) boruro.

boring [bóriŋ]. I. s. trepa, horadación; taladro, barrenado, perforación; sondeo.—*pl.* taladrados; partículas que se desprenden al taladrar o barrenar.—**b. machine**, taladradora, etc. II. a. de taladrar; xilófago, horadador (insecto); pesado, aburrido(r). V. BORESOME.—**b. bar**, barra o árbol portabarrenas.—**b. block**, bloque de barrenar; portabarrenas.—**b. frame**, bastidor de perforadora.—**b. rod**, tientaguja, barra de perforadora.

born [born], a. nacido, nato; de nacimiento, por

naturaleza, destinado.—**to be b.**, nacer.—**to be b. again**, renacer, volver a nacer.

born, borne [bɔrn], *pp.* de TO BEAR.

borneol [bɔ́rnioυl], *s.* (quím.) borneol, producto del alcanforero de Borneo.

boron [bɔ́ran], *s.* (quím.) boro.

borough [bároυ], *s.* villa; municipio incorporado; barrio; distrito administrativo de una ciudad. —**municipal b.**, (Ingl.) corporación municipal.—**parliamentary b.**, (Ingl.) pueblo con derecho de representación en el Parlamento.

borrow [bároυ], *va.* y *vn.* pedir o tomar prestado (algo a alguien); tomar a préstamo; (fam.) sablear, sangrar (dinero); apropiarse, hacerse suyo; copiar.

borrow (pit) [-pit], *s.* (ing.) zanja de préstamo, zanja de que se saca tierra para terraplenes.

borrower [-œ(r)], *s.* prestatario, comodatario; el que pide o toma prestado; (fam.) sablista.

borrowing [-iŋ], *s.* acto de pedir o conseguir prestado; (fam.) sablazo.—*pl.* cantidades adeudadas.

boscage [báskidź], *s.* boscaje, espesura.

bosh [báʃ], *s.* (fam.) palabrería, tontería; (metal.) etalaje de alto horno.

bosk(et [básk(it], *s.* matorral, bosquete.

bosky [-i], *a.* frondoso, nemoroso; (Am.) boscoso.

bo's'n, bosun [bóυsn], *s.* (mar.) *abrev. de* BOATSWAIN.

Bosnian [báznian], *s.* y *a.* bosnio.

bosom [búzɔm]. **I.** *s.* seno, pecho, corazón; (fam.) buche, pechera, pechugo; amor, inclinación, cariño; (cost.) pechera. **II.** *a.* íntimo, querido; secreto.—**b. friend**, amigo íntimo; (fam.) amigote, compinche. **III.** *va.* abrazar; guardar en el pecho; ocultar.

boss [báʃ]. **I.** *s.* clavo o tachón; giba, joroba, corcova, protuberancia; copa (de freno); lomo (de libro); (arq.) pinjante; realce (de una piedra); (fam. E. U.) amo, capataz, *m.*, patrón; jefe, cabecilla; (pol.) cacique, (Am.) gamonal. —**b.-like, b.-ridden**, caciquil. **II.** *va.* trabajar en relieve, abollonar, relevar (*v.* EMBOSS); (fam. E. U.) regentear, mandar; dominar.

bossage [-idź], *s.* (arq.) almohadilla.

bossed [-t], **bossy** [-i], *a.* tachonado; turgente, abultado, saliente.

bossism [-izm], *s.* caciquismo, caudillismo, caudillaje, (Am.) gamonalismo.

bossy [-i], *a.* (fam.) mandón, autoritario.

bot, bott [bat], *s.* rezno, larva de estro.

botanic(al [botɛ́nik(al], *a.* botánico.

botanically [-i], *adv.* botánicamente.

botanist [bátanist], *s.* botánico, botanista.

botanize [-aiz], *vn.* herborizar.

botany [-i], *s.* botánica, fitología.

botch [bách]. **I.** *s.* remiendo, chapucería, chafallo. **II.** *va.* remendar, chapucear, chafallar.

botcher [-œ(r)], *s.* remendón, chapucero, chambón, chafallón.—**botchery** [-i], *s.* corcusido, culcusido.

botfly [bátflai], *s.* (ent.) estro, moscardón.

both [boυθ]. **I.** *a.* y *pron.* ambos (a dos), entrambos, los dos, dos [*both his sons are here*, sus dos hijos están (ambos) aquí].—**b. of**, los dos, ellos dos, ambos, etc.; *both of them*, ellos dos, los dos, ambos; *both of us*, nosotros dos. **II.** *conj.* y *adv.* tanto como, así como, a un mismo tiempo; *both he and I*, tanto él como yo; *both cheap and durable*, tanto barato como durable, a un mismo tiempo barato y durable.

bother [báðœ(r)]. **I.** *va.* y *vn.* incomodar(se), molestar(se); (fam.) marear(se).—**to b. about, o with**, molestarse o preocuparse con; hacer caso de. **II.** *s.* molestia, incomodidad, (fam.) lata, pejiguera.

botheration [-éiʃɔn], *s.* molestia, fastidio, vejación, disgusto, lata.

bothersome [-sʌm], *a.* molesto, fastidioso.

botryoidal [batriɔ́idal], *a.* arracimado, botriforme.

bottle [bátl]. **I.** *s.* botella; frasco.—**b. gourd**, (bot.) güira, calabaza vinatera.—**b. green**, verde botella.—**b. imp**, (fís.) diablillo de Descartes. **II.** *va.* (a veces con **up**) embotellar (un líquido, un ejército, una armada); envasar; enfrascar.

bottleflower [-flauœ(r)], *s.* (bot.) = BLUE BOTTLE.

bottleful [-fʊl], *s.* (contenido de una) botella.

bottleholder [-hoυldœ(r)], *s.* portabotellas; (fam.) partidario; padrino (en duelo); asistente o segundo de un pugilista.

bottleneck [-nɛk], *s.* cuello de botella; estrechura; obstrucción, impedimento, dificultad.

bottlenose [-noυz], *s.* (ict.) especie de delfín, marsopa o cachalote; nariz hinchada por el beber excesivo.

bottler [bátlœ(r)], *s.* embotellador.

bottling [bátliŋ], *s.* envase, acción de embotellar. —**b. machine**, embotelladora.

bottom [bátɔm]. **I.** *s.* fondo; suelo; lecho (de un río, lago, etc.); parte (*f.*) inferior, lo más bajo, pie, *m.*; (fam.) trasero, nalgatorio, culo, posadera/s; zanja, cimiento, fundamento; (mar.) casco, barco, buque; base, *f.*, motivo; hez, poso, sedimento (de licores); asiento de una silla; pie, *m.* (de página); (f. c.) balasto; (gen. *pl.*) tierra(s) baja(s).—**at b.**, en el fondo, en realidad.—**b. ice** = ANCHOR ICE.—**b. side up**, (fam.) patas arriba; (mar.) quilla arriba.—**to be at the b. of**, ser causa de; tener la culpa de. —**to go to the b.**, profundizar; (mar.) irse a pique.—**to touch b.**, tocar fondo. **II.** *a.* hondo, bajo; inferior, de abajo; ínfimo; fundamental; (fam.) último. **III.** *va.* poner fondo o asiento a; cimentar, fundar, apoyar, basar; (tec.) acabar, repasar. **IV.** *vn.* apoyarse.

bottomless [-lis], *a.* sin fondo; insondable.

bottomry [-ri], *s.* (com.) préstamo o contrato a la gruesa, o sobre casco y quilla.

botulism [báchʊlizm], *s.* (med.) botulismo.

boudoir [budwár], *s.* gabinete de señora, tocador.

bouffe [buf], *a.* bufo, cómico.

bough [báυ], *s.* (bot.) rama, ramo, cepo, brazo (de árbol).—**boughpot** [-pat], *s.* florero; ramillete.

bought [bɔt], *pret.* y *pp.* de TO BUY.

boughten [-ɛn], *a.* (fam.) comprado (a diferencia de lo casero).

bougie [búdʒi], *s.* (cir.) candelilla, tienta, sonda.

bouillon [búlyan], *s.* caldo, consumado.

boulder [bóυldœ(r)], *s.* canto rodado, pedrejón.

boulevard [búlevard], *s.* bulevar.

bounce [báυns]. **I.** *vn.* rebotar; brincar, saltar; lanzarse; echar fieros o bravatas; fanfarronear. **II.** *va.* hacer saltar o botar; (fam. E. U.) despedir, echar con cajas destempladas, poner de patitas en la calle. **III.** *s.* salto, brinco; (re)bote, repullo, respingo; golpazo, porrazo; fanfarronada; bola, mentira, filfa; echada, despedida.

bouncer [-œ(r)], *s.* guapo, fanfarrón; bola, filfa; embustero; (fam. E. U.) guardián fornido que echa a los alborotadores de un café.

bouncing [-iŋ], *a.* fuerte, vigoroso, robusto; gordiflón (bebé); exagerado; fanfarrón.

bound [báυnd]. **I.** *s.* límite, término, lindero; bote, brinco, corcovo, salto, resalto, rebote. **II.** *va.* deslindar, parcelar, confinar, limitar, ceñir; hacer saltar, botar. **III.** *vn.* saltar, brincar; botar; corvetear.

bound. I. *pret.* y *pp.* de TO BIND. **II.** *a.* atado, amarrado, sujeto, ligado; confinado; moral o legalmente obligado; encuadernado (libro); destinado; sentenciado; decidido, resuelto (a); puesto en aprendizaje; (med.) estreñido, estíptico.—**b. for**, (mar.) con destino a, rumbo a.—**b. up in**, absorto, engolfado, enfrascado en; inseparable de; muy consagrado a.—**it is b. to happen**, sucederá fatalmente o seguramente. —**to be b. for**, (fam.) ir a, ir para.

boundary [-ari]. **I.** *s.* límite, linde, lindero, frontera, confín, meta; término, coto; muga, mojón.—**b. line**, ámbito.—**b. marker**, o

stone, cipo, hito, mojón. **II.** *a.* limítrofe, fronterizo, divisorio.
bounded [-ịd], *a.* limitado, circunscrito.
bounden [-ẹn], *a.* obligatorio, preciso.
bounder [-œ(r)], *s.* (fam.) persona mal vestida o sin modales; presuntuoso.
bounding [-iŋ], *a.* que mueve a saltos; exuberante; que deslinda, limita, etc.
boundless [-lịs], *a.* ilimitado, infinito.—**boundlessness** [-nịs], *s.* inmensidad, infinidad.
bounteous [báuntịas], *a.* liberal, generoso, dadivoso, largo.—**bounteously** [-lị], *adv.* liberalmente, generosamente.—**bounteousness** [-nịs], *s.* munificencia o liberalidad, generosidad, largueza.
bountiful [báuntịfụl], *a.* liberal, dadivoso, generoso, copioso.—**bountifully** [-lị], *adv.* liberalmente, generosamente.—**bountifulness** [-nịs], *s.* generosidad, liberalidad, largueza, copiosidad.
bounty [báuntị], *s.* generosidad, liberalidad, dadivosidad, munificencia; merced, gracia; concesión, subvención, prima.—**b. money**, (mil.) enganche.
bouquet [bukéị], *s.* ramo o ramillete de flores; aroma, *m.*, perfume o nariz (del vino).
Bourbon [búrbọn], *s.* Borbón; conservador, recalcitrante.—**B. whisky**, aguardiente de maíz o de centeno.—**Bourbonic** [-bánịk], *a.* borbónico.—**Bourbonism** [búrbọnịzm], *s.* borbonismo.
bourdon [búrdọn], *s.* bordón; roncón de gaita; registro de órgano.—**B. ga(u)ge**, manómetro de Bourdon.
bourgeois [bœrdźóịs], *s.* (impr.) tipo de nueve puntos.
bourgeois [bųrźwá], *a.* y *s.* burgués; ordinario; comerciante, industrial.
bourgeoisie [-zí], *s.* clase media, burguesía.
bourgeon [bœrdźọn], *V.* BURGEON.
bourn(e [bourn], *s.* límite, linde; meta; arroyo, riachuelo.
bourse [burs], *s.* (com.) bolsa, lonja.
bouse [búz], **bousy** [-ị], *V.* BOOZE, BOOZY.
bout [baut], *s.* vez, turno; ataque (de borrachera, de enfermedad); curva o vuelta; encuentro, combate; asalto de esgrima o boxeo.
Bovidæ [bóủvịdị], *s. pl.* (zool.) bóvidos.
bovine [bóủvaịn]. **I.** *a.* bovino, boyuno, vacuno; paciente, sufrido; lerdo, bruto. **II.** *s.* bovino, bóvido.
bow [bau]. **I.** *va.* saludar; hacer reverencia o cortesía; doblar, inclinar; agobiar, oprimir, agravar. **II.** *vn.* inclinarse; arquearse, agacharse; doblarse, torcerse; agobiarse; ceder, someterse. **III.** *s.* saludo, reverencia, cortesía, venia, zalema; (mar.) proa, amura.—**b. chaser**, cañón de caza o de tiro hacia adelante.—**b. oar**, remo o bogador más cercano a la proa.—**on the b.**, (mar.) por la amura.—**to make one's b.**, presentarse, entrar; ser presentado.
bow [bou]. **I.** *s.* arco (para disparar flechas); (mús.) arco de violín; moño; lazada; lazo (de corbata, de cinta, etc.); arzón o fuste de silla.—*pl.* gafas (de anteojos). **II.** *a.* arqueado, encorvado.—**b. compass(es)**, bigotera, compás de bomba (compás pequeño de resorte).—**b. hand**, la mano del arco; (mús.) la mano derecha; (ballestería) la mano izquierda (de donde **on the b. hand**, erradamente, por el mal camino).—**b.-legged**, (pati)estevado, perniabierto.—**b. net**, nasa; red de pescar langostas; red para coger pájaros.—**b. pen** = B. COMPASS.—**b. saw**, sierra de arco.—**b. tie**, corbata en forma de lazo.—**b. window**, ventana saliente o arqueada; mirador. **III.** *va.* y *vn.* arquear(se), encorvar(se); tocar (el violín, etc.) con el arco.
bowdlerize [báủdlœraịz], *va.* recortar, mutilar o expurgar (un escrito).
bowel [báụẹl]. **I.** *s.* intestino, tripa.—*pl.* entrañas; (fam.) bandullo, mondongo. **II.** *va.* destripar.

bower [báụœ(r)]. **I.** *s.* glorieta, emparrado, cenador, enramada; morada retirada; (mar.) ancla de proa o de leva (ll. t. **b. anchor**).—**b. bird**, tilonorinco (pájaro australiano). **II.** *va.* emparrar.
bower [bóủœ(r)], *s.* músico de arco; arquero, hacedor de arcos.
bowery [báụẹrị]. **I.** *s.* cortijo, granja.—**the B.**, calle de Nueva York frecuentada en otros días por el pueblo bajo. **II.** *a.* frondoso, sombreado.
bowie knife [bóị naịf], *s.* cuchillo de monte.
bowknot [bóụnat], *s.* nudo corredizo, lazada.
bowl [boụl]. **I.** *s.* escudilla, cuenco; hueco, concavidad; tazón de fuente; palangana, jofaina (para lavarse); bolo, rulo, bocha, boliche (juego); copa, vaso (de vino, etc.); bol, ponchera; tabaquera (de pipa); paleta (de cuchara).—*pl.* juego de bolos; rodillos de calandria. **II.** *va.* (a veces con **over**) tumbar con una bola; derribar, abatir; hacer rodar; tirar las bolas. **III.** *vn.* bolear, jugar a las bochas.—**to b. along**, rodar rápida y llanamente (un coche, etc.).
bowlder [bóụldœ(r)], *s.* = BOULDER.
bowleg [bóụlẹg], *s.* pierna corva o estevada.
bowler [bóụlœ(r)], *s.* jugador de bolos o bochas; (Ingl.) sombrero hongo; (Am.) bombín.
bowline [bóụlịn], *s.* (mar.) bolina, boliche.
bowling [bóụliŋ], *s.* juego de bolos; bola, boleo, chirinola.—**b.-alley**, **b.-green**, bolera, boleo, boliche, mallo.
bowman [bóụman], *s.* arquero, flechero, asaeteador.
bowshot [bóụʃat], *s.* tiro de flecha.
bowsprit [báụsprịt], *s.* (mar.) bauprés.
bowstring [bóụstriŋ]. **I.** *s.* cuerda de arco; dogal para ahorcar. **II.** *va.* estrangular con cuerda.
bowwow [báụwáụ], *s.* **I.** *s.* ladrido, guau; (fam.) perro. **II.** *vn.* ladrar.
bowyer [bóụyœ(r)], *s.* arquero.
box [báks], *s.* caja, cajón; estuche; cofre, arca; palco de teatro; apartado (de correos); bofetada, manotazo, puñada, revés; establo; casilla; compartimiento, sección, recinto; cavidad, corte (en un árbol); (mar.) bitácora; (carr.) pescante; (impr.) cajetín; (mec.) buje, caja, cojinete, manguito; (bot.) boj(e).—**b. calf**, cuero de becerro curtido con cromo.—**b. camera**, cámara rígida o de cajón.—**b. car**, (f. c.) furgón, vagón cubierto.—**b. coat**, sobretodo (apl. esp. al de viaje).—**b. coupling**, acoplamiento de manguito.—**b. girder**, viga de cajón o tubular.—**b. kite**, cometa celular.—**b. office**, (teat.) taquilla, casilla, contaduría, (Am.) boletería.—**b. office success**, éxito de taquilla.—**b. plaiting**, (cost.) plegado, pliegue de tabla.—**to be in a b.**, hallarse en un aprieto o brete.
box. I. *va.* encajonar, embalar; apuñear, abofetear, sobar.—**to b. the compass**, (mar.) cuartear la aguja. **II.** *vn.* boxear.
boxer [-œ(r)], *s.* boxeador, púgil; embalador; (perro) bóxer; (B.) bóxer, miembro de la sociedad patriótica china de los boxers.
boxhaul [-hol], *va.* (mar.) virar en redondo; abroquelar.
boxing [-iŋ], *s.* encajonamiento, empaque, embalaje; madera para encajonar; box(eo), pugilato, pugilismo; (carp.) marco de puerta o de ventana; (mar.) escarpe.
boxthorn [-θorn], *s.* (bot.) arto(s), cambronera, tamujo.
boxwood [-wụd], *s.* (bot.) boj(e); especie de cornejo u otros arbustos; madera de boj.
boy [bóị], *s.* muchacho, niño, chico, rapaz, *m.*; hijo varón; mozo; criado, lacayo; (mar.) grumete.—**b. scout**, niño explorador.
boycott [-kat]. **I.** *va.* excluir, boicotear, boycot(e)ar. **II.** *s.* exclusión, boicoteo o boicot.
boyhood [-hụd], *s.* muchachez, puericia.
boyish [-iʃ], *a.* amuchachado, mucheril, pueril.

boyishly [-lį], *adv.* como muchacho.
boyishness [-nįs], *s.* muchachada, niñada, niñería, puerilidad; talante de muchacho.
bra [bra], *s. V.* BRASSIÈRE.
braccate [brǽkeįt], *a.* (orn.) (pati)calzado.
brace [bréįs]. **I.** *va.* ligar, asegurar; reforzar; fortalecer, vigorizar; (carp.) ensamblar, (Am.) empatar; (arq.) (ar)riostrar, atirantar; (mar.) bracear; cercar, rodear; (impr.) abrazar con llave o corchete. **II.** *vn.* (con **up**) (fam.) animarse, rehacerse. **III.** *s.* abrazadera, laña, grapón, broche, manija, traba, braza; (carp.) berbiquí; tornapunta; (arq.) riostra, tirante, puntal, viento; anclaje, silla, mordaza; can, canecillo; (carr.) sopanda; un par (de pistolas, perdices, etc.); (cir.) braguero; (impr.) corchete, llave, {}; (mús.) ligadura.—**b. bit**, taladro o barrena de berbiquí.—**b. drill**, parahuso.—*pl.* tirantes o tiradores del pantalón; (mar.) brazas.
bracelet [-lįt], *s.* brazalete, ajorca, pulsera, manilla; (arm.) brazal.
bracer [-œ(r)], *s.* brazal; (med.) medicamento tónico y fortificante; (fam.) bebida fortificante, copa, trago; abrazadera, afianzador, laña; cinto, venda.
brachial [bréįkįąl], *a.* braquial.
brachiopod [-opad], *s. y a.* (zool.) braquiópodo.
brachiotomy [-átomį], *s.* (cir.) braquiotomía.
brachium [bréįkįʌm], *s.* (anat.) brazo superior.
brachycephalic [brǽkįsefǽlįk], **brachycephalous** [-séfąlʌs], *a.* (anat.) braquicéfalo.
brachygrafy [brǽkįgrąfį], *s.* braquigrafía.
brachypodous [brǽkípǫdʌs], *a.* (zool. y bot.) braquípodo.
bracing [bréįsįŋ]. **I.** *a.* fortificante, tónico. **II.** *s.* amarra, ligazón, *f.*, refuerzo, trabazón, *f.*, arriostramiento; (mar.) braceaje.—**b. rope**, viento.
bracken [brǽkęn], *s.* (bot.) helecho; helechal.
bracket [brǽkįt]. **I.** *s.* ménsula, soporte asegurado en la pared; brazo o sostén de lámpara, candelabro, mechero de gas, etc., asegurado en la pared; consola, repisa, rinconera; (arq.) modillón, ménsula; clase, *f.*, grupo; categoría.—*pl.* corchetes, paréntesis angulares []. **II.** *va.* poner entre paréntesis; unir, juntar; poner en una misma clase.
brackish [brǽkįš], *a.* salobre, salado.
brackishness [-nįs], *s.* sabor salobre, salobridad.
bract [brǽkt], *s.* (bot.) bráctea.
bractlet [-lįt], *s.* (bot.) bractéola.
brad [brǽd], *s.* clavo de ala de mosca; puntilla, agujuela, hita, espiga, saetín.
bradawl [-ɔl], *s.* lesna o punzón para agujeros de clavos, etc.
bradypepsia [brædįpépsįą], *s.* (med.) bradipepsia.
bradypod [brǽdįpad], *s.* (zool.) bradipo, perezoso.
brag [brǽg]. **I.** *s.* jactancia, fanfarronada; farolero, fanfarrón; juego de naipes. **II.** *va.* y *vn.* jactarse (de), fanfarronear, blasonar, baladronear, darla (de), hacer alarde (de), preciarse (de); (fam.) farolear.
braggadocio [brægądóųšĵoųl], *s.* fanfarria, ronca, bravata; fanfarrón, baladrón, farolón.
braggart [brǽgąrt], *a.* jactancioso, bravucón.
braggart, bragger [brǽgœ(r)], *s.* jaque, matasiete.
braggartism [-įzm], *s.* jactancia o fanfarronería, vana ostentación.
braggingly [brǽgįŋlį], *adv.* jactanciosamente.
Brahman, Brahmin [brámįn], *s.* bracmán, brahmán, brahmín.
Brahmanic(al, Brahminic(al [bramǽnįk(ąl, -ínįk(ąl], *a.* bracmánico, brahmánico, brahmínico.
Brahmanism [brámįnįzm], *s.* brahmanismo.
braid [bréįd]. **I.** *va.* trenzar, entrelazar; (cost.) acordonar, trencillar, bordar con cordoncillo o de realce; galonear. **II.** *s.* galón, alamar, trencilla; trenza, crizneja.

brail [bréįl]. **I.** *va.* (mar.) cargar las velas. **II.** *s.* (ú. gen. en *pl.*) candaliza, cargadera.
braille [bréįl], *s.* escritura en relieve para uso de los ciegos.
brain [bréįn]. **I.** *s.* (anat.) cerebro, seso; encéfalo, meollo, sesera.—*pl.* sesos; (fig.) inteligencia, juicio.—**b. power**, capacidad mental.—**b. storm**, acceso violento pero transitorio de locura; confusión.—**b. tumor**, (med.) tumor cerebral.—**b. work**, trabajo u ocupaciones intelectuales.—**b. fever**, (med.) fiebre (*f.*) cerebral, meningitis. **II.** *va.* hacer saltar los sesos a; romper la crisma a.
brainless [-lįs], *a.* sin sesos; tonto, insensato.
brainpan [-pæn], *s.* (anat.) cráneo, sesera.
brainsick [-sįk], *a.* chiflado.—**brainsickness** [-nįs], *s.* enajenación mental; chifladura.
brainy [-į], *a.* (fam.) sesudo, inteligente.
braise [bréįz], *va.* (coc.) perdigar la carne y ponerla a hervir a fuego lento en cazuela.
braize [bréįz], *s.* (ict.) pargo.
brake [bréįk]. **I.** *s.* (bot.) helecho (*v.* BRACKEN); agramadera, agramador (para lino, cáñamo); jaral, matorral, mato, soto; (f. c., aut., etc.) freno; plancha (de diligencia); (mar.) guimbalete de bomba; amasadera; (agr.) grada, rastra; palanca, espeque.—**b. band**, cinta de freno.—**b. beam**, barra del freno.—**b. block**, portazapata de freno; zapata, mordaza.—**b. drum**, tambor de freno.—**b. efficiency**, rendimiento al freno.—**b. horsepower**, potencia al freno.—**b. lever**, palanca de freno.—**b. lining**, forro de freno.—**b. pedal**, (aut.) pedal de freno.—**b. rod**, varilla de freno.—**b. shoe**, zapata de freno, calzo. **II.** *va.* (f. c., aut.) (en)frenar; espad(ill)ar, tascar (cáñamo, lino); amasar pan; (agr.) gradar, desterronar con la grada.
brakeman [-mąn], *s.* (f. c., etc.) guardafrenos.
braky [-į], *a.* espinoso, jaroso, matoso.
bramble [brǽmbl], *s.* (bot.) zarza, cambrón.—*pl.* jijallar, zarzal.—**b. berry**, (zarza)mora.
brambled [-d], *a.* breñoso, zarzoso.
brambling [-blįŋ], *s.* (orn.) pinzón.
brambly [-blį], *a.* zarzoso.
bran [brǽn], *s.* salvado, afrecho.—**b. bread**, acemita.
branch [brénch]. **I.** *s.* rama (de árbol o familia); ramo (de árbol, ciencia, arte o industria); dependencia, división o sección; sarmiento (de vid, etc.); ramal, brazo; afluente, tributario (de río); (com.) sucursal, *f.*; (f. c.) ramal, bifurcación; (mil.) arma (de las fuerzas armadas); (elec.) derivación.—*pl.* ramas, ramaje. **II.** *a.* dependiente, tributario, sucursal.—**b. post office**, estafeta. **III.** *vn.* ramificarse; echar pitones, astas o ramas; (f. c.) empalmar.—**to b. off**, bifurcarse, separarse, dividirse.—**to b. out**, divergir, ampliar, extenderse. **IV.** *va.* ramificar, dividir en ramas; (elec.) derivar; (cost.) bordar.
brancher [-œ(r)], *s.* (cetr.) halcón ramero.
branchia [brǽŋkįą], *s.* branquia (de pez, etc.).
branchial [-l], *a.* branquial.
branchiferous [-kífęrʌs], *a.* branquífero.
branchiness [brénchįnįs], *s.* frondosidad.
branching [-įŋ], *s.* bifurcación, ramificación.
branchless [-lįs], *a.* sin ramas, desramado.
branchlet [-lįt], *s. dim.* ramita.
branchy [-į], *a.* ramoso.
brand [brénd]. **I.** *s.* tizón o tea; (poét.) espada, rayo; sello o marca de fábrica; calidad; hierro de marcar reses y la marca; estigma, mancha, baldón.—**b. goose**, (zool.) oca silvestre.—**brand(ing) iron**, hierro de marcar, (Am.) calimba, carimbo.—**b.-new**, enteramente nuevo, nuevecito, flamante. **II.** *va.* herrar, marcar con hierro candente, grabar a fuego, (Am.) calimbar; tildar, tiznar (de malo, etc.); infamar, desdorar.
branding [-įŋ], *s.* herradero, (Am.) hierra.

brandish [brǽndiŝ]. **I.** *va.* blandir, blandear, cimbrar, florear. **II.** *s.* (esgr.) floreo, molinete.

brandling [brǽndliŋ], *s.* (ent.) gusano para cebo; (ict.) esguín.

brandy [brǽndi]. **I.** *s.* brandy, coñac, aguardiente. **II.** *va.* conservar, mezclar o saborear con aguardiente.

bran-new [brǽnnjú], *a.* nuevecito, enteramente nuevo.

branny [brǽni], *a.* parecido al salvado.

brant [brænt], *s.* (orn.) oca silvestre.

brash [bræŝ]. **I.** *a.* quebradizo (madera); (fam.) impetuoso; temerario; descarado, insolente. **II.** *s.* (med.) acedía; erupción; montón de escombros.

brasier [bréiẑœ(r)], *s. V.* BRAZIER.

brass [bræs]. **I.** *s.* latón; bronce, azófar; cualquier objeto de latón; (fam.) descaro, desfachatez; calderilla (dinero); (fam.) el alto mando, la oficialidad (ll. t. **b. hats**).—*pl.* (mec.) bronces, (anillos de) cojinetes; (mús.) cobres (instrumentos).—**b. band**, banda (militar), charanga, murga.—**b. shop, trade** o **works**, latonería.—**b.-visaged**, descarado, descocado.—**to get down to b. tacks**, entrar en materia, ir al grano. **II.** *va.* revestir de latón.—**to b. it**, (fam.) = TO BRAZEN IT OUT.

brassard [brésard], *s.* (arm.) brazal, brazalete; brazal, faja que ciñe la manga.

brassart [brǽsạrt], *s.* (arm.) = BRASSARD.

Brassicaceæ [bræsikéiŝii], *s. pl.* (bot.) crucíferas.

brassie [brǽsi], *s.* uno de los palos o mazos en el juego de golf (ll. t. **brassy**).

brassière [brạzír], *s.* sostén; corpiño, justillo o ajustador para sostener los pechos.

brassiness [brǽsinịs], *s.* calidad de bronceado; (fam.) desfachatez, descaro; bajeza.

brassware [-wɛr], *s.* objetos de latón, latonería.

brassy [-i], **brassish** [-iŝ], *a.* de latón; (fam.) descarado, descocado, desvergonzado.

brat [bræt], *s.* (despec.) rapaz, mocoso.

brattice [brǽtịs]. **I.** *s.* (min.) ademe. **II.** *va.* ademar.

bravado [brạvádou], *s.* bravata, baladronada.

brave [bréiv]. **I.** *a.* bravo, valiente, denodado, alentado, animoso, esforzado; bizarro, gallardo. **II.** *va.* desafiar, arrostrar, acarar. **III.** *s.* valiente; guerrero (apl. a los indios norteamericanos).

bravely [-li], *adv.* brava, esforzada, valerosa o valientemente; bizarra o gallardamente.

bravery [-ɛri], *s.* valentía, valor, ánimo, aliento; bizarría, proeza, heroísmo; esplendor, magnificencia.

bravo [brávou]. **I.** *s.* asesino pagado o asalariado. **II.** *interj.* ¡bravo!

brawl [brǿl]. **I.** *s.* alboroto, disputa, camorra, quimera, pendencia, trapisonda. **II.** *vn.* alborotar, armar camorra, trapisondear, vociferar, vocinglear. **III.** *va.* decir gritando.

brawler [-œ(r)], *s.* camorrista, pendenciero.

brawling [-iŋ]. **I.** *s.* alboroto, vocinglería. **II.** *a.* pendenciero, vocinglero.

brawn [brǿn], *s.* músculo, fuerza muscular; pulpa; carne dura; carne de verraco.

brawniness [-iņịs], *s.* fortaleza, musculatura.

brawny [-i], *a.* fuerte, musculoso, membrudo.

braxy [brǽksi]. **I.** *s.* fiebre (*f.*) carbuncular del ganado lanar; (*f.*) lanar atacada de este mal. **II.** *a.* atacado de dicha fiebre.

bray [bréi]. **I.** *va.* majar, triturar, moler, pulverizar; emitir ruidos discordes. **II.** *vn.* rebuznar, roznar. **III.** *s.* rebuzno, roznido; ruido bronco.

brayer [-œ(r)], *s.* rebuznador; (impr.) rodillo.

braying [-iŋ], *s.* rebuzno, roznido; ruido bronco.

braze [bréiz], *va.* soldar con soldadura fuerte o de latón; broncear; hacer duro o descocado.

brazen [-ẹn]. **I.** *a.* (como) de latón; broncíneo; bronco; descarado.—**b.-browed, b.-faced,** *a.* descocado.—**b. face**, *s.* cara de vaqueta, sinvergüenza. **II.** *va.* hacer desvergonzado.—**to b. it out,** o **through,** hacer frente a; sostener o llevar a cabo con desfachatez.

brazenness [-nịs], *s.* descaro, desvergüenza.

brazier [bréiẑœ(r)], *s.* latonero, calderero; brasero, copa, maridillo, rejuela.

braziery [-i], *s.* latonería.

brazil, brazilwood [brạẑíl, -wụd], *s.* palo brasil.—**Brazil nut** [-nʌt], *s.* nuez del Brasil.

braziletto [-étou], *s.* (bot.) brasilete, brasil.

Brazilian [brạẑílịạn], *a.* y *s.* brasileño.

brazilin [brǽẑilịn], *s.* (quím.) brasilina.

brazing [bréiẑiŋ], *s.* soldadura fuerte.—**b. metal,** latón de soldar, soldadura de latón.

breach [brich]. **I.** *s.* rotura, fractura; quebrantamiento; infracción, violación; brecha, abertura; disensión, escisión, rompimiento de las relaciones; (mar.) rompiente, oleaje; salto de ballena.—**b. of faith,** o **of trust,** abuso de confianza, prevaricación.—**b. of promise,** incumplimiento de la palabra de casamiento.—**b. of the peace,** perturbación del orden público.—**more honored in the b. than in the observance,** que descuella más por lo que se viola que por lo que se observa (precepto, principio, etc.). **II.** *va.* hacer brecha; batir en brecha; aportillar.

bread [bréd], *s.* pan.—**b. and butter,** pan con mantequilla; (fig.) sustento diario; (usado como adjetivo, mercenario; menesteroso; relativo a la subsistencia).—**b. basket,** panera; (fam.) panza.—**b. corn,** o **grain,** cualquier grano de que se hace pan.—**b. crumb,** miga de pan; pan desmigado o rallado.—**b. line,** fila de menesterosos que piden pan donde se distribuye gratis.—**to earn one's b.,** o **one's b. and butter,** ganarse el pan o la vida.—**to know on which side one's b. is buttered,** saber dónde aprieta el zapato. **II.** *va.* dar pan a; (coc.) empanar, envolver en masa de harina.—**breaded cutlet,** chuleta empanada.

breadboard [-bord], *s.* tabla para amasar o cortar pan.

breadfruit [-frut], *s.* (bot.) árbol del pan y su fruto.

breadstuff [-stʌf], *s.* cereales, granos, harinas, etc., que sirven para pan.—*pl.* panes.

breadth [brédθ], *s.* anchura, ancho; holgura; envergadura; latitud; liberalidad; (cost.) paño, ancho de una tela.—**b. of beam,** (mar.) manga.

breadthwise [-waiz], *adv.* a lo ancho.

breadwinner [brédwinœ(r)], *s.* el que se gana la vida (para sí o para su familia); productor.

break [bréik], *va.* (*pret.* BROKE o BRAKE (poét.); *pp.* BROKEN o BROKE) romper, quebrar, fracturar, partir; romper, suspender (relaciones, etc.); infringir, violar (la ley, etc.); abrir brecha en; domar, amansar; degradar (a un oficial, etc.); quebrar, arruinar; cortar, interrumpir; dividir; reducir a fragmentos o partes, quebrantar; cambiar (un billete, etc.); moderar, amortiguar; exceder, ir más allá de; dar o comunicar suave o cautelosamente (una mala noticia, etc.); picar (piedra); descifrar (una llave); descomponer; anular (un testamento).—**to b. a house,** entrarse a una casa con intentos criminales.—**to b. a lance with,** batirse con.—**to b. a straw,** reñir.—**to b. asunder,** separar, partir, dividir.—**to b. bread,** comulgar o dar de comulgar.—**to b. bread with,** sentarse a la mesa o a comer con; gozar de la hospitalidad de.—**to b. camp,** levantar el campo.—**to b. down,** destruir, demoler, aportillar; desmembrar; descomponer (cifras, etc.).—**to b. ground,** abrir o remover la tierra, roturar; empezar a cavar; principiar una empresa; (mar.) levar ancla.—**to b. in,** forzar, romper o abrir empujando hacia adentro; domar, amansar, desbravar (caballos, etc.); adiestrar.—**to b. in o to pieces,** despedazar, hacer añicos, cascar, desbaratar, destrozar, frangir.—**to b. jail,** escaparse de la cárcel.—**to b. of a habit,** desacostumbrar(se), deshabituar(se).—**to b. off**, cortar; desgajar (un ramo); desentablar (un pacto, etc.); dejar sin concluir.—**to b. one's neck**, desnucarse; (fam.) romperse el alma, desalarse, precipitarse.—**to b. open**, abrir a la fuerza, forzar, descerrajar.—**to b. out**, forzar, quitar; aflojar, abrir; (mar.) sacar (carga) de la bodega. —**to b. the back**, derrengar, quebrar la espalda; agobiar, postrar; pasar de lo peor o más difícil (de un apuro).—**to b. the bank**, hacer saltar la banca (en el juego).—**to b. the heart of**, acongojar, matar (fig.) de dolor.—**to b. the ice**, pasar de las primeras dificultades; cobrar confianza; comenzar.—**to b. the record**, exceder o sobrepujar el record, superar la marca. —**to b. the tape**, llegar el primero a la meta (en una carrera).—**to b. up**, dividir en partes, desmenuzar, fraccionar, fragmentar; roturar (la tierra); abrir (una mina, etc.); desbaratar, desguazar (un buque); forzar (una puerta, etc.); disolver (un parlamento, etc.); desconcertar, confundir; levantar (casa, el campo, etc.).—**to b. upon the wheel**, enrodar.

break, *vn.* romperse, quebrarse, partirse; reventar (una apostema, etc.); quebrar, hacer bancarrota; descomponerse; fracasar, frustrarse; romper (con una persona, la costumbre, etc.); separarse, desprenderse violentamente; salir, brotar; apuntar, rayar (el día); saltar (un pez); estallar, brotar, florecer; desfallecer, descaecer; fallar (la voz); ceder, dispersarse; partir antes de tiempo.—**to b. apart**, desunirse.—**to b. away**, desprenderse; zafarse; escaparse; desaparecer, disiparse.—**to b. cover(t)**, salir (la caza) de su escondite.—**to b. down**, desbaratarse; irse abajo; perder la salud, el valor o el ánimo; abatirse, desesperarse; (mec.) descomponerse, sufrir una avería.—**to b. even**, (fam.) salir sin ganar ni perder.—**to b. forth**, salir, brotar; exclamar; prorrumpir.—**to b. from**, desprenderse de, desasirse.—**to b. in**, entrarse (sobre todo forzando puertas, etc.).—**to b. in upon**, aparecerse a de sopetón, sorprender; irrumpir; meter baza (en una conversación).— **to b. into**, soltarse en (risa, llanto), pasar repentinamente a; forzar, violentar.—**to b. loose**, separarse, desprenderse; escaparse o fugarse.— **to b. off**, separarse, desprenderse; desistir; interrumpirse; romper (con alguien).—**to b. open**, cascarse.—**to b. out**, brotarse; estallar (una guerra); empezar (una epidemia); echar a hablar, soltarse; (med.) salpullir, salir granos en el cuerpo; (arq.) sobresalir.—**to b. through**, abrirse paso o camino por (entre); salvar.—**to b. up**, desmenuzarse, hacerse pedazos o fragmentos; dispersarse; disolverse; levantarse (una sesión).—**to b. wind**, ventosear, peer.

break, *s.* rotura, rompimiento, ruptura; abertura, grieta, raja; comienzo, principio; pausa, intervalo, interrupción, solución de continuidad; vacío, claro, hueco; pifia, disparate (**to make a b.**, cometer un disparate o pifia, obrar con desacierto); gallo, nota falsa (en el canto); (elec.) interruptor, abertura, distancia entre contactos; (com.) baja (en el mercado); (fam.) chiripa, casualidad o coyuntura feliz.—**an even b.**, oportunidad igual o justa; empate; (salir, estar, etc.) sin ganar ni perder.—**b. of day**, alba, amanecer.—**to give one a b.**, mostrarse compasivo o servicial al que se halla en un apuro.

breakable [-ạbl], *a.* quebradizo, frágil, frangible, rompible.

breakage [-idẑ], *s.* fractura, rotura, rompimiento; desbarate, destrozo, estropicio; indemnización por cosas quebradas (en el tránsito, etc.).

breakax(e [-æks], *s.* (bot.) quiebrahacha, *m.*, jabí.

breakbone fever [-boṇ fívœ(r)], *s.* (med.) dengue.

breakdown [-dauṇ], *s.* vuelco, caída, derrumbamiento; desbarajuste, trastorno, fracaso; inte-

rrupción, paralización (de servicio, etc.); (mec.) avería (de motor, etc.); (com.) descomposición (de cifras, etc.); (E. U.) zapateado de negros; debilidad, agotamiento, postración.

breaker [-œ(r)], *s.* roturador; infractor; quebrantador, rompedor; (máquina) quebrantadora; (elec.) disyuntor; (mar.) bota de agua.—*pl.* rompientes, cachones (olas).

breakfast [brékfạst], **I.** *vn.* desayunarse, almorzar. **II.** *s.* desayuno, almuerzo.

breaking [bréikiṇ], **I.** *s.* fractura, quebradura, quebrant(amient)o; desgaje; rompimiento, ruptura (a veces con **off**); interrupción; doma, amansamiento (de caballos); (agr.) tierra roturada.—**b. load**, (ing.) carga de fractura.— **b. up**, cierre, disolución, dispersión; (agr.) rotura(ción), (mar.) desguace. **II.** *a.* quebrantante, quebrantador, rompiente, saltadizo.

breakneck [-nek]. **I.** *s.* despeñadero, precipicio. **II.** *a.* precipitado, rápido.

breakwater [-wotœ(r)], *s.* quebrantaolas, rompeolas, malecón, escollera, espolón.

bream [brim], *s.* (ict.) brema, pez (*m.*) de agua dulce. *V.* SEA BREAM.

bream, *va.* (mar.) limpiar fondos.

breast [brést]. **I.** *s.* pecho, seno; teta; pechuga de ave; pecho, corazón, interior del hombre; (arm.) peto; (arti.) testera; (arq.) toro; (min.) frente o cara de veta o filón; (carr.) comba del cubo de una rueda.—**b. collar**, (tal.) collera.—**b.-deep**, de hondura que llega o da al pecho.—**b. drill**, (mec.) berbiquí.—**b.-fed**, amamantado, criado a los pechos.—**b. harness**, (tal.) arnés de pretal. —**b.-high**, a altura de pecho; alto hasta el pecho.—**b. pump**, mamadera.—**b. strap**, (tal.) pechera, petral, zambarco.—**b. stroke swimming**, natación de pecho.—**b. wheel**, (hidr.) rueda de costado.—**to make a clean b. of**, confesar, reconocer con franqueza. **II.** *va.* arrostrar resueltamente; amamantar, dar el pecho a.

breastband [-bænd], *s.* (tal.) petral o pretal.

breastbone [-boṇ], *s.* (anat.) esternón.

breastfast [-fæst], *s.* (mar.) amarra del través.

breasthooks [-hụks], *s. pl.* (mar.) buzardas.

breastpin [-piṇ], *s.* broche, prendedor.

breastplate [-pleịt], *s.* peto; pretal; pectoral.

breastplow [-plau], *s.* arado de pecho.

breastrail [-reịl], *s.* antepecho.

breastsummer [-sʌmœ(r)], *s.* (arq.) solera, cabio superior de puerta o ventana.

breastwork [-wœrk], *s.* (mil., gen. *pl.*) trinchera, parapeto; antepecho; (mar.) propao.

breath [breθ], *s.* aliento, respiración, resuello; hálito, soplo; pausa, respiro; instante, momento.—**b.-taking**, conmovedor, pasmoso, sorprendente.—**in a b.**, de un resuello.—**in the same b.**, al mismo tiempo, a renglón seguido. —**out of b.**, sin aliento, sofocado, jadeante.— **under one's b.**, en voz baja.

breathable [bríðạbl], *a.* respirable.

breathe [bríð]. **I.** *vn.* respirar, resollar, alentar; vivir; descansar, tomar aliento; soplar, avahar; aspirar, exhalar. **II.** *va.* inspirar, respirar; exhalar; dar aire o desahogo; sugerir, revelar.— **to b. one's last**, dar el último suspiro, boquear, morir, expirar.—**to b. upon**, (fig.) empañar.

breather [-œ(r)], *s.* respirador; viviente; inspirador; tregua, descanso; (fam.) ejercicio violento.

breathing [-iṇ], *s.* respiración, respiro, resuello, vaharada; aire suave; inspiración; aspiración; comunicación; (fon.) aspiración.—**b. hole**, respiradero.—**b. place**, pausa, cesura; lugar de descanso.—**b. spell**, tregua, descanso, respiro, reposo.

breathless [bréθlịs], *a.* falto de aliento, sin resuello; jadeante; intenso, expectante; muerto.

breathlessness [-nịs], *s.* desaliento; muerte, *f.*

breccia [bréchiạ], *s.* (min.) (mármol) brecha.

bred [bred], *pret.* y *pp.* de TO BREED.

breech [brích]. **I.** *s.* trasero, posaderas, nalgas; (arti.) recámara, culata, cierre.—**b. block,** (arti.) obturador.—**b. cloth, b. clout,** culero, taparrabo.—**b.-loading,** (arti.) de retrocarga. **II.** *va.* poner calzones; zurrar; poner recámara a un arma.

breeches [-iz], *s. pl.* calzones, bragas, pantalones. —**b. buoy,** salvavidas en forma de bragas, boya pantalón.—**to wear the b.,** llevar los calzones.

breeching [-iŋ], *s.* (tal.) retranca, cejadero del arnés; zurra; (mar.) bragueros (*m. pl.*) de cañón.

breechloader [-lóudœ(r)], *s.* arma de retrocarga.

breed [bríd]. (*pret. y pp.* BRED). **I.** *va.* criar, engendrar, multiplicar, procrear; empollar; parir; ocasionar, producir; educar.—**to b. in-and-in,** procrear sin mezclar razas. **II.** *vn.* multiplicarse; padrear; empollar (abejas); parir; sacar cría. **III.** *s.* casta, raza, progenie, prole, *f.*; generación; lechigada; ralea.

breeder [-œ(r)], *s.* criador (de ganado, etc.), ganadero; padre, (animal) reproductor o semental; paridera (u. a., apl. a la hembra).

breeding [-iŋ]. **I.** *s.* cría; crianza, educación; modales, *m. pl.,* urbanidad. **II.** *a.* de criar, que cría. —**b. cage,** jaula de criar.—**b. place,** criadero.

breeze [bríz], *s.* brisa, aura, airecillo, oreo, orilla; (fam.) agitación, excitación; vago rumor, murmuración; cisco de coque; (ent.) tábano.

breezeless [-lis], *a.* sin aire.

breezy [-i], *a.* airoso, ventilado; animado, garboso, vivo.—**it is b.,** hace brisa.

bregma [brégmä], *s.* (anat.) bregma, *m.*

brethren [bréðrin], *s. pl.* hermanos, cofrades (miembros de una fraternidad, iglesia, etc.).

Breton [brétɔn], *a. y s.* bretón.

breve [briv], *s.* (mús.) breve; (pros.) marca de sílaba breve; (for.) escrito.

brevet [brévét]. **I.** *s.* (mil.) graduación honoraria (sin el sueldo correspondiente), grado. **II.** *a.* (mil.) graduado; honorario, de grado. **III.** *va.* (mil.) graduar, conferir grado honorario a.

breviary [brívieri], *s.* (igl.) breviario.

brevier [brevír], *s.* (impr.) breviario, tipo de ocho puntos.

brevipennate [brevipéneit], *s. y a.* (orn.) brevipenne, corredor.

brevirostral, brevirostrate [-rásträl, -reit], *a.* (orn.) corto de pico.

brevity [bréviti], *s.* brevedad; concisión.

brew [brú]. **I.** *va.* hacer cerveza o té, etc.; fraguar, urdir, tramar. **II.** *vn.* elaborar cerveza; formarse, prepararse: *a storm is brewing,* se prepara, o amenaza, una tormenta. **III.** *s.* mezcla.

brewage [-idž], *s.* brebaje.

brewer [-œ(r)], *s.* cervecero.—**b.'s grains,** hez o heces.—**b.'s yeast,** jiste, levadura de cerveza.

brewery [-i], *s.* cervecería, fábrica de cerveza.

brewhouse [-haus], *s.* = BREWERY.

brewing [-iŋ], *s.* elaboración de cerveza; cantidad de cerveza que se hace de una vez; señales de borrasca.

brewis [brúis], *s.* sopa; caldo espeso.

briar [bráiä(r)], *s.* V. BRIER.

bribe [bráib]. **I.** *s.* cohecho, soborno.—**b. money** (fam.) unto amarillo.—**to take bribes,** dejarse sobornar. **II.** *va.* cohechar, sobornar; (fam.) untar las manos o el carro.

briber [-œ(r)], *s.* cohechador, sobornador.

bribery [-eri], *s.* cohecho, soborno.

bric-a-brac [bríkäbræk], *s.* objetos de arte, artículos curiosos y de gusto; baratijas, chucherías.

brick [brík]. **I.** *s.* ladrillo; aglomerado (de carbón); (fam.) buen chico, persona simpática.—**b. clay, b. earth,** arcilla o barro de ladrillos.—**b. hammer,** aciche.—**b. ice-cream,** queso helado.— **b. pavement,** enladrillado.—**b. tea,** té prensado. V. BRIQUET(TE. **II.** *va.* (en)ladrillar.

brickbat [-bæt], *s.* tejoleta, tejuela.

brickkiln [-kil], *s.* horno de cocer ladrillos.

bricklayer [-leiœ(r)], *s.* albañil, (en)ladrillador.

brickmaker [-meikœ(r)], *s.* ladrillero.

brickmaking [-iŋ], *s.* fabricación de ladrillos.

brickwork [-wœrk], *s.* enladrillado, enladrilladura, albañilería, mampostería, obra de fábrica.

bricky [-i], *a.* ladrilloso.

brickyard [-yard], *s.* ladrillar; adobería.

bridal [bráidäl]. **I.** *a.* nupcial.—**b. bed,** tálamo. —**b. song,** epitalamio.—**b. trip,** viaje de novios. **II.** *s.* boda, fiesta nupcial.

bride [bráid], *s.* novia, desposada.—**bridecake,** torta o pan de la boda.—**bridechamber,** tálamo.

bridegroom [-grum], *s.* novio, desposado.

bridesmaid [-zmeid], *s.* madrina de boda, (poét.) pronuba.

bridesman [-zmän], *s.* padrino de boda.

bridewell [-wel], *s.* casa de corrección, calabozo.

bridge [bridž]. **I.** *s.* (ing., mar., mús., dent., etc.) puente, *mf.;* caballete de la nariz; diablo o violín (del billar); bridge (juego de naipes); (m. v.) altar (del hogar); (fund.) tabique; (f. c.) puente o travesaño elevado de señales.—**b. of boats,** puente de barcas.—**B. of Sighs,** Puente de los Suspiros.—**b. toll,** peaje, pontazgo.—**b. truss,** (ing.) viga.—**in b.,** (elec.) en paralelo. **II.** *va.* (a menudo con *over*), tender un puente sobre; salvar (un obstáculo); llenar (un vacío, etc.); ayudar a salir del paso; (elec.) conectar en paralelo.

bridgehead [-hed], *s.* (mil.) cabeza o cabecera de puente (defensas a la entrada de un puente).

bridgeward [-word], *s.* custodio de puente; (cerr.) guarda principal de una llave.

bridgework [-wœrk], *s.* (ing.) construcción de puentes; puente dental.

bridging [-iŋ], *s.* (ing.) construcción de puentes; (arq.) puntales separadores.—**b. brace,** péndola.

bridle [bráidl]. **I.** *s.* brida o freno del caballo; freno, sujeción; (mar.) frenillo.—**b. curb,** barbada.—**b. hand,** mano izquierda.—**b. path,** camino de herradura.—**pl. bridles,** (mar.) poas. **II.** *va.* embridar, enfrenar; arrendar; reprimir, refrenar. **III.** *vn.* levantar la cabeza, erguirse; (mar.) afrenillar, acorullar (los remos).

bridler [bráidlœ(r)], *s.* enfrenador; refrenador.

bridoon [bridún], *s.* (tal.) bridón, filete.

brief [bríf]. **I.** *a.* breve, conciso, corto, lacónico, sucinto, sumario; fugaz, pasajero, rápido. **II.** *s.* epítome, resumen; (for.) escrito, relación, alegato, memorial, informe; (igl.) breve o buleto apostólico.—**b. case, b. bag,** cartera.—**in b.,** en resumen, concisamente.—**to hold no b. for,** no ser defensor de, no estar defendiendo. **III.** *va.* abreviar, epitomar; (mil.) dar instrucciones.

briefing [-iŋ], *s.* (mil.) órdenes (*f. pl.*) o instrucciones.

briefless [-lis], *a.* (abogado) de secano, sin clientes.

briefly [-li], *adv.* brevemente, sucintamente, someramente; en resumen.

briefness [-nis], *s.* brevedad, concisión, laconismo.

brier [bráiœ(r)], *s.* (bot.) escaramujo, agavanzo, rosal silvestre; zarza.

briery [-i], *a.* zarzoso, espinoso.

brig [brig], *s.* (mar.) bergantín; prisión militar.

brigade [brigéid], *s.* brigada.

brigadier [brigädír], *s.* (mil.) brigadier.—**b. general,** general de brigada.

brigand [brígänd], *s.* bandido, bandolero.

brigandage [-idž], *s.* salteamiento, bandolerismo, bandidaje.

brigandine [-in], *s.* cota de malla.

brigantine [brígäntin], *s.* (mar.) bergantín goleta.

bright [bráit], *a.* claro, lustroso, brillante, (re)luciente; subido (apl. a colores); preclaro, eximio; vivo, alegre; talentoso, inteligente, listo; halagüeño, feliz.—**b.-eyed,** ojialegre.

brighten [-ęn]. I. *va*. pulir o abrillantar; alegrar, consolar; ennoblecer o hacer ilustre; mejorar; avivar. II. *vn*. (a veces con **up**) aclarar, despejarse (el cielo); avivarse, animarse.

brightly [-lį], *adv*. brillante o lucidamente.

brightness [-nįs], *s*. lustre, esplendor, brillantez, luz, lucidez; resplandor, claridad; agudeza o viveza de ingenio.

Bright's disease [bráįts dįzíz], *s*. (med.) albuminuria, nefritis.

brill [brįl], *s*. (ict.) especie de rodaballo.

brilliance [brílyąns], **brilliancy** [-į]. *s*. brillantez, brillo, fulgor, resplandor; esplendor, lustre.

brilliant [brílyąnt]. I. *a*. brillante, refulgente; talentoso; excelente. II. *s*. (joy.) brillante; diamante; (impr.) tipo de 3½ puntos.

brilliantine [-in], *s*. brillantina.

brilliantly [-lį], *adv*. espléndidamente, brillantemente.

brilliantness [-nįs], *s*. brillantez, brillo.

brim [brįm]. I. *s*. borde, orilla, margen, *mf*., labio de un vaso; ala de sombrero. II. *va*. llenar hasta el borde. III. *vn*. rebosar; estar de bote en bote.

brimful [-fúl], *a*. lleno hasta el borde; colmo.

brimless [-lįs], *a*. sin labio, borde o ala.

brimmer [-œ(r)], *s*. copa o vaso lleno.

brimming [-įŋ], *a*. lleno hasta el borde.

brimstone [-stoųn], *s*. azufre; marimacho.

brinded [brįndįd], *a*. moteado, mosqueado.

brindle [brįndl], *s*. remiendo; animal mosqueado. —**brindled** [-d], *a*. mosqueado, abigarrado.

brine [bráįn]. I. *s*. salmuera, agua cargada de sal; el mar; (poét.) lágrimas, *f. pl*. II. *va*. salar, remojar en salmuera.

brinepit [-pįt], *s*. pozo de agua salada.

bring [brįŋ]. I. *va*. (*pret. y pp*. BROUGHT) traer; llevar; conducir; inducir, persuadir; aportar; causar, producir, rentar, valer, venderse a (buen precio, etc.).—**to b. about**, efectuar, poner por obra; lograr, realizar; dar lugar u origen a, causar.—**to b. around** = TO B. ROUND.—**to b. away**, llevar una cosa de donde estaba.—**to b. back**, traer de vuelta, devolver.—**to b. down**, matar (caza); hacer bajar; deprimir, humillar; continuar, prolongar.—**to b. down the house**, promover grandes aplausos.—**to b. forth**, producir; parir; dar a luz; poner de manifiesto.—**to b. forward**, empujar; (com.) llevar una suma a otra cuenta (**brought forward**, suma y sigue, suma anterior).—**to b. home**, demostrar indisputablemente; hacer sentir o ver claramente.—**to b. home the bacon**, (fam.) llevarse el premio.—**to b. in**, presentar (una cuenta, etc.); producir; recoger; entrar, meter; servir (una comida); introducir (una moda, etc.); dar (un fallo); presentar, entablar (juicio, queja, etc.).—**to b. into play**, poner en juego.—**to b. near**, acercar, llegar, arrimar.—**to b. off**, llevar a cabo, lograr el éxito de; llevarse; librar, rescatar; disuadir.— **to b. on**, acarrear; causar; comenzar; ocasionar; inducir.—**to b. oneself to**, resolverse a.—**to b. out**, presentar; sacar a luz; publicar; sacar; poner de manifiesto; hacer resaltar; (teatro) poner en escena; revelar, descubrir.— **to b. over**, persuadir, convertir; traer.—**to b. round**, ganar, convertir, persuadir; curar; sacar bien.—**to b. suit**, entablar o seguir pleito. —**to b. to**, sacar de un desmayo; reanimar; (mar.) ponerse a la capa o en facha.—**to b. to book**, obligar a dar cuenta.—**to b. to light**, descubrir, revelar; hacer ver.—**to b. to pass, realizar**, efectuar.—**to b. to ruin**, perder, arruinar.—**to b. to task**, reprender, regañar, censurar.—**to b. to terms**, hacer ceder o convenir; someter.—**to b. under**, sojuzgar, someter.—**to b. up**, (hacer) subir; criar, educar; traer a colación o discusión; hacer parada. —**to b. upon one's self**, acarrearse, buscarse; incurrir (en).—**to b. up the rear**, cubrir o ir a la retaguardia.

bringer [-œ(r)], *s*. portador.

bringing-up [-įŋ áp], *s*. crianza, educación.

brininess [bráįnįnįs], *s*. salobridad, sabor de sal.

brinish [bráįnįš], *a*. salado, salobre.

brink [brįŋk], *s*. orilla, margen, *mf*., borde, extremidad.—**on the b. of**, al borde de; a punto de.

briny [bráįnį], *a*. salado, salobre.—**the b. deep**, el mar.

brioche [brióųš], *s*. brioche, pasta de harina, huevos y mantequilla.

briquet(te [brįkét], *s*. aglomerado (de carbón).

brisk [brįsk]. I. *a*. vivo, activo, animado, avispado, enérgico; rápido; efervescente (licor); frescachón (viento). II. *va*. (con **up**), avivar, animar, acelerar; atizar. III. *vn*. (con **up**), animarse.

brisket [brįskįt], *s*. pecho de un animal o un pedazo cortado de él.

briskly [brįsklį], *adv*. vivamente, aprisa.

briskness [brįsknįs], *s*. viveza, actividad, vivacidad, despejo, gallardía.

bristle [brįsl]. I. *s*. cerda; seda o seta (de jabalí); (fam.) porcipelo.—*pl*. cerdamen (para brochas, etc.). II. *va*. erizar, poner tieso. III. *vn*. erizarse. —**to b. up**, montar en cólera, encresparse; hacer ademán de resolución.—**to b. with**, estar erizado o rodeado de (dificultades, etc.).

bristletail [-teįl], *s*. (ent.) lepisma.

bristly [brįslį], *a*. cerdoso, hirsuto, erizado.

Bristol board [brįstql bqrd], *s*. bristol, cartulina bristol.—**B. brick**, piedra silícea para limpiar cuchillos.—**B. paper** = B. BOARD.

britannia [brįtǽnįą], *s*. (metal.) metal inglés; aleación de estaño, cobre, antimonio, bismuto, etc.

Britannic [brįtǽnįk], *a*. británico.

British [brįtįš]. I. *a*. británico; inglés. II. *s. pl*. el pueblo inglés.

Briton [brįtǫn], *a. y s*. britano, inglés.

brittle [brįtl], *a*. quebradizo, quebrantable, friable, frágil, frangible, bronco, vidrioso.—**b. star**, *s*. (zool.) ofiuro.—**brittleness** [-nįs], *s*. fragilidad, friabilidad.

broach [brouč]. I. *s*. (carp.) broca, mecha; escariador; espetón, lezna, punzón; terraja de relojero; (joy.) prendedor, broche; (arq.) aguja, chapitel. II. *va*. mencionar por primera vez; introducir; hacer público; espetar, ensartar; espitar un tonel; decentar, encentar; escariar.

broad [brǫd], *a*. ancho, anchuroso, amplio, extenso, vasto; claro; general, comprensivo; liberal, tolerante; descomedido, rudo, tosco, indelicado; lleno, abierto (apl. a letras y sonidos); pronunciado, marcado (apl. a la pronunciación, tono, etc.); pleno (*in broad daylight*, en pleno día, a la luz del sol).—**b.-backed**, lomudo.—**b.-blown**, enteramente formado. —**b.-breasted**, ancho de pechos.—**b.-brimmed**, de borde ancho; de alas anchas.— **b.-chested**, ancho de pecho.—**B. Church**, iglesia o doctrina liberal o tolerante.—**b.-faced**, **b.-fronted**, cariancho; frontudo (de animales).—**b. gauge**, *s*. (f. c.) vía ancha; *a*. de vía ancha.—**b.-horned**, corniabierto.—**b. jump**, (dep.) salto largo o de longitud.— **b.-leafed**, **b.-leaved**, de hojas anchas.—**b.-minded**, tolerante, liberal, despreocupado, de manga ancha.—**b. seal**, sello real o nacional. —**b.-shouldered**, espaldudo, costilludo.—**as b. as (it is) long**, igual en todos los sentidos, lo mismo del un modo que del otro.

broadax(e [-æks], *s*. hacha de carpintero; doladera.

broadbrim [-brįm], *s*. sombrero de ala ancha; sombrero de cuáquero.—**broadbrimmer** [-brįmœ(r)], *s*. (fam.) cuáquero.

broadcast [-kæst]. I. *va. y vn*. (*pret. y pp*. BROADCASTED), esparcir, diseminar; propalar; (agr.) sembrar al voleo; (rad.) perifonear, (ir)radiar, (radio)difundir, emitir, transmitir. **II.** *s.* (agr.) siembra al voleo; (rad.) emisión, transmisión, (radio)difusión, perifonía. **III.** *adv.* esparcidamente; por todas partes. **IV.** *a.* esparcido, difundido; (rad.) radiado, radioemitido, etc.

broadcaster [-œ(r)], *s.* (rad.) radiodifusor.

broadcasting [-kæstiŋ]. **I.** *s.* (agr.) siembra al voleo; (rad.) perifonía, (radio)difusión, transmisión. **II.** *a.* (rad.) emisor, (radio)difusor.—**b. station,** difusora, emisora.

broadcloth [-kloθ], *s.* (tej.) cierto paño fino.

broaden [-ₑn], *va.* y *vn.* ensanchar(se), engrosar(se), ampliar(se), dilatar(se).

broadening [-iŋ], *s.* ensanchamiento, ensanche, ampliación.

broadish [-iš], *a.* algo ancho.

broadloom [-lum], *a.* (alfombra) tejida en telar ancho y en color sólido.

broadly [-li], *adv.* anchamente, ampliamente; de una manera general; groseramente.

broadness [-nįs], *s.* ancho o anchura; liberalidad, liberalismo; amplitud; grosería.

broadside [-said], *s.* (mar.) costado de un buque; (mar. y arti.) andanada, batería; (fam.) represión severa; (impr.) pliego suelto; hoja grande impresa en un solo lado (ll. t. **broadsheet**).

broadsword [-sord], *s.* espadón, montante, (fam.) chafarote.

broadtail [-teil], *s.* carnero de Bujaria; caracul (astracán de la mejor calidad).

broadwise [-waiz], *adv.* a, o por, lo ancho.

brocade [brokéid]. **I.** *s.* brocado. **II.** *va.* espolinar; decorar con brocado.

brocaded [-id], *a.* espolinado.

brocage [bróukidž], *s.* = BROKERAGE.

brocatel [brakatél], *s.* (tej.) brocatel.

broccoli [brákoli], *s.* (bot.) bróculi, brécol, brecolera.

brochure [brošúr], *s.* folleto; bosquejo.

brock [brák], *s.* (zool.) tejón.

brocket [-it], *s.* gamo de dos años.

brogan [bróugan], *s.* zapato basto.

brogue [broug], *s.* abarca; zapato grueso; acento o pronunciación dialectal (apl. esp. al acento irlandés).

broil [bróil]. **I.** *s.* riña, camorra, pendencia; alboroto, tumulto; carne, etc., asada al fuego o a la parrilla; calor intenso. **II.** *va.* asar sobre las ascuas o en parrillas; emparrillar, soasar, tostar, turrar. **III.** *vn.* asarse; padecer calor.

broiler [-œ(r)], *s.* parrilla(s); pollo asadero; camorrista; (fam.) día muy caluroso.

broiling [-iŋ], *a.* extremamente cálido; tórrido.

brokage [bróukidž], *s.* = BROKERAGE.

broke [bróuk]. **I.** *vn.* hacer de corredor. **II.** *pret.* de TO BREAK. **III.** *a.* (fam.), sin blanca, sin un real, pelado, tronado; (Am.) en la lata.

broken [-ₑn], *a.* y *pp.* de TO BREAK; quebrado, roto; imperfecto; suelto, separado; interrumpido; domado; mal pronunciado, chapurrado; barrancoso; irregular, áspero, disparejo; quebrado (apl. al terreno); desalentado; debilitado; agotado; arruinado. (*V.* BROKE).—**b. ashlar,** mampostería de piedras de distintos tamaños. —**b.-backed,** deslomado; (mar.) quebrantado. —**b.-down,** decrépito, estropeado, agotado; descorazonado, afligido; arruinado.—**b.-faced,** desbocado (herramienta).—**b.-hearted,** angustiado, traspasado de dolor.—**b. language,** lenguaje chapurrado, hablado con acento extranjero.—**b. line,** línea quebrada.—**b.-lipped,** desbocado (jarro).—**b. sleep,** sueño interrumpido o intranquilo.—**b.-up,** desguazado (buque).—**b. voice,** voz cascada.—**b. wind,** (vet.) huélfago.—**b.-winded,** falto de resuello; (vet.) atacado de huélfago.—**b.-winged,** aliquebrado.

brokenly [-li], *adv.* interrumpida o desbaratadamente, etc.; a ratos.—**brokenness** [-nįs], *s.* desigualdad.

broker [bróukœ(r)], *s.* (com.) corredor; cambista.

brokerage [-idž], *s.* (com.) corretaje, correduría.

broma [bróumą], *s.* harina de cacao; bebida que con ella se hace; (med.) alimento sólido.

bromal [bróumæl], *s.* (quím.) bromal.

bromate [bróumeit]. **I.** *va.* tratar con bromo. **II.** *s.* (quím.) bromato.

bromatology [broumątálodži], *s.* bromatología.

brome grass [bróum græs], *s.* (bot.) bromo.

bromeliaceous [broumiliéišias], *a.* (bot.) bromeliáceo.

bromic [bróumik], *a.* (quím.) brómico.

bromide [bróumaid], *s.* (quím.) bromuro; (fam.) Perogrullo, formalista; perogrullada.—**b. paper,** (fot.) papel de gelatinobromuro.

bromidic [bromídik], *a.* (fam.) trivial, cansado.

bromine [bróumin], *s.* (quím.) bromo.—**b. water,** agua bromurada.

brom(in)ism [bróum(in)izm], *s.* (med.) bromismo.

bromoform [bróumoform], *s.* (quím.) bromoformo.

bronchi [bránkai], *s. pl.* de BRONCHUS.

bronchia [bránkią], *s. pl.* (anat.) subdivisiones de los bronquios.

bronchial [-l], *a.* bronquial.—**b. pneumonia,** (med.) bronconeumonía, broncopulmonía (ll. t. **bronchopneumonia**).—**b. tubes,** bronquios.

bronchiole [-kioul], *s.* (anat.) bronquiolo.

bronchitis [-káitis], *s.* (med.) bronquitis.

bronchocele [-kosil], *s.* (med.) bocio, papera.

bronchoscope [-koskoup], *s.* broncoscopio.

bronchotomy [-kátomi], *s.* (cir.) traqueotomía, broncotomía.

bronchus [-kʌs], *s.* (anat.) bronquio.

bronco, broncho [bránkou], *s.* (E. U. del oeste) potro cerril o mesteño.—**b.-buster,** (fam.) domador de tales caballos; vaquero.

broncorrhea [-koríą], *s.* (med.) broncorrea.

bronze [bránz]. **I.** *s.* bronce; (b. a.) objeto de bronce; color de bronce.—**b.-colored,** bronceado. **II.** *va.* broncear; pavonar; tostar por el sol.

bronzing [-iŋ], *s.* bronceado.

brooch [brouch], *s.* (joy.) broche, prendedero, alfiler de pecho, pasador.

brood [brúd]. **I.** *va.* empollar, incubar; cobijar; acariciar; tolerar. **II.** *vn.* empollar, aclocar(se). —**to b. over,** cavilar o rumiar (con cuidado, melancolía, amargura, etc.). **III.** *s.* cría, pollada; empolladura (de abejas); nidada, camada, ventregada; progenie, raza, ralea. **IV.** *a.* clueca. —**b.-mare,** yegua madre o paridera.—**brooding hen,** clueca, llueca.

brooder [-œ(r)], *s.* clueca; incubadora; rumiador.

broodiness [-inįs], *s.* cloquera; melancolía.

broody [-i], *a.* clueca; rumión, rumiador.—**to become b.,** enclocar(se), encloquecer.

brook [brúk]. **I.** *s.* arroyo, riachuelo; (Am.) cañada, quebrada. **II.** *va.* sufrir, aguantar, tolerar.

brooklet [-lit], *s.* arroyuelo.

brooklime [-laim], *s.* (bot.) becabunga.

brooky [-i], *a.* lleno de arroyos.

broom [brúm]. **I.** *s.* (bot.) hiniesta, retama; escoba.—**b. brush** = BRUSH BROOM.—**b. corn,** (bot.) variedad de sorgo, millo de escoba, carquexia.—**b. maker,** escobero.—**b. rape,** (bot.) orobanca. **II.** *va.* barrer.

broomstick, broomstaff [-stik, -stæf], *s.* palo de escoba.

broomy [brúmi], *a.* retamero.

broth [broθ], *s.* caldo.

brothel [bróθel], *s.* burdel, lupanar, mancebía.

brother [brʌðœ(r)]. **I.** *s.* hermano; cofrade, colega, *m.*; fraile, fray.—**b.-in-law,** cuñado, hermano político.—**B. Jonathan,** (fam.) el hermano Jonatás (los E. U.). **II.** *va.* hermanar; llamar, tratar o recibir como a un hermano.

brotherhood [-hud], *s.* fraternidad; hermandad; hermanazgo; confraternidad, cofradía, congregación.—**brotherless** [-lįs], *a.* que no tiene

hermanos.—**brotherlike** [-lajk], *a.* fraternal.—
brotherliness [-linjs], *s.* fraternidad.—**brotherly** [-li]. **I.** *a.* fraternal, fraterno. **II.** *adv.*
fraternalmente.

brougham [brúąm], *s.* (carr. y aut.) berlina.

brought [brot], *pret.* y *pp.* de TO BRING.

brow [bráụ], *s.* ceja; (fig.) sienes, *f. pl.*, frente, *f.*,
rostro, semblante; cresta, cima, cumbre.—**b.
band**, (tal.) frontalera.

browbeat [-bit], *va.* imponerse a; intimidar, acobardar; mirar con ceño torvo.

browbeating [-bitiŋ].**I.** *s.* ceño, capote; intimidación. **II.** *a.* ceñudo, ceñoso.

brown [bráụn]. **I.** *a.* pardo, castaño, moreno.—
b. bear, oso pardo.—**b. Betty**, pudín de manzana y pan.—**b. bread**, pan bazo o moreno.—
b. coal, lignito.—**b. coat**, (alb.) segunda capa
de enlucido.—**b.-eyed**, ojimoreno.—**b. holland**, holanda cruda.—**b. ochre**, ocre carmelita.—**b. paper**, papel de estraza.—**b. race**,
raza malaya.—**b. shirt**, camisaparda, nazi.—**b.
study**, ensimismamiento, meditación profunda.
—**b. sugar**, azúcar moreno, negro o terciado.
—**to do (up) b.**, (fam.) engañar como a un
chino; poner los puntos sobre las íes. **II.** *s.* color
pardo, moreno o castaño. **III.** *va.* poner moreno
o tostado; broncear; quemar (el sol); (coc.)
perdigar.

brownie [-i], *s.* duende moreno y benéfico.

brownish [-iš], *a.* que tira a moreno.

brownness [-njs], *s.* color moreno.

brownout [-aụt], *s.* apagamiento parcial de luces
como medida de conservación de electricidad.

brownstone [-stoụn], *s.* piedra arenisca de color
pardo rojizo.

brownwort [-wœrt], *s.* (bot.) escrofularia.

browse [bráụz]. **I.** *va.* y *vn.* ramonear, rozar,
tascar, herbajar; (a veces con **around, about**
u **on**) curiosear (en una biblioteca, librería o
tienda); hojear (un libro). **II.** *s.* pimpollos,
renuevos o ramones que roza el ganado.

browsing [-iŋ], *s.* ramoneo, ramón.

brucite [brúsajt], *s.* (min.) brucita.

bruin [brúin], *s.* oso.

bruise [brúz]. **I.** *va.* magullar, golpear, contundir,
machacar, machucar, abollar, majar; pulverizar. **II.** *s.* magulladura, contusión; maca (del
fruto); abolladura.

bruiser [-œ(r)], *s.* púgil; machacador, majador.

bruising [-iŋ], *s.* pugilato; magullamiento, machucamiento; (ten.) majadura del cuero; acto
de agramar; prensado de uvas.

bruit [brut]. **I.** *s.* (ant.) ruido, rumor, noticia,
fama; [brwi] (med.) sonido que se oye por la
auscultación. **II.** *va.* esparcir, divulgar, publicar.

Brumaire [brųmér], *s.* brumario (mes).

brumal [brúmąl], *a.* brumal, invernal, invernizo.

brume [brúm], *s.* bruma, neblina.

brumous [-ʌs], *a.* brumoso.

brunet(te [brunét], *a.* y *s.* moreno, trigueño.

brunt [brʌnt], *s.* embate más fuerte; lo más reñido o duro (de un ataque, choque, etc.).

brush [brʌš]. **I.** *s.* cepillo, escobilla, bruza;
(pint.) brocha, pincel; cola (de zorro, etc.);
(elec.) escobilla; escaramuza, pelea, haz (*m.*)
de leña menuda; matorral, monte, breñal.—
b. broom, escobilla, cepillo. **II.** *va.* (a)cepillar;
limpiar con cepillo; quitar frotando (con un
trapo, la mano, etc.); frotar, rozar, restregar;
bruzar, (impr.) brozar; rasar; pintar con brocha.
III. *vn.* moverse apresuradamente.—**to b.
aside**, echar a un lado.—**to b. away**, restregar
duro.—**to b. up**, retocar, refrescar, repasar.

brusher [-œ(r)], *s.* acepillador; (impr.) brozador.

brushwood [-wụd], *s.* matorral, breñal, zarzal;
broza, ramojo, ramalla.

brushy [-i], *a.* matoso, cubierto de matojos.

brusk *o* **brusque** [brʌsk]. **I.** *a.* brusco, rudo.
II. *va.* tratar con rudeza.

brusqueness [-njs], *s.* brusquedad.

Brussels [brʌsęlz], *s.* Bruselas.—**B. carpet**, alfombra de Bruselas.—**B. lace**, encaje de
Bruselas.—**B. sprouts**, (bot.) bretones.

brutal [brútąl], *a.* brutal, bestial, cruel, salvaje.

brutality [brutǽlįtį], *s.* brutalidad; barbaridad.

brutalize [brútąlajz]. **I.** *va.* embrutecer; tratar
con crueldad. **II.** *vn.* embrutecerse.

brutally [brútąlį], *adv.* brutalmente.

brute [brút]. **I.** *s.* bruto, bestia. **II.** *a.* brutal;
bruto.—**b. force**, fuerza bruta.

brutify [-įfaị], *va.* y *vn.* embrutecer(se), (fam.)
arrocinar(se).

brutish [-iš], *a.* brutal, bestial; abrutado; irracional; sensual, salaz.—**brutishly** [-lį], *adv.*
brutalmente.—**brutishness** [-njs], *s.* brutalidad.—**brutism** [-izm], *s.* bruteza, brutalidad.

bryonin [brájonįn], *s.* (quím.) brionina.

bryony [brájonį], *s.* (bot.) brionia, nueza.

bryozoan [brajozóµan], *a.* y *s.* (zool.) briozoario.

bub, bubby [bʌb, -į], *s.* (fam.) hermanito; chicuelo.

bubal, bubalis, [bjúbąl, -įs], *s.* (zool.) búbalo.

bubble [bʌbl]. **I.** *s.* burbuja, ampolla; borbollón;
bagatela; engañifa; pompa.—**b. tube**, tubo de
nivel de burbuja; el nivel mismo. **II.** *vn.* burbujear, hacer ampollas; bullir, hervir; murmurar
el río; brotar, surgir (el agua); trinar los pájaros.
—**to b. over**, (fig.) rebosar, estar en efervescencia.—**to b. up**, ampollarse. **III.** *va.* hacer
bullir, etc.

bubbler [bʌblœ(r)], *s.* surtidor de beber agua.

bubbling [bʌbliŋ]. **I.** *s.* burbujeo. **II.** *a.* burbujeante.

bubbly [bʌblį], *a.* burbujeante, espumoso.

bubo [bjúboụ], *s.* (med.) incordio, bubón, caballo.

bubonic [bjubánįk], *a.* bubónico.

buccal [bʌkąl], *a.* bucal.

buccaneer [bakanír], *s.* bucanero, filibustero.

Buccinum [bʌksįnʌm], *s.* (zool.) buccino.

bucentaur [bjuséntor], *s.* bucentauro.

Bucephalus [bjuséfąlʌs], *s.* bucéfalo; (fam.) caballo malo.

buck [bʌk]. **I.** *s.* (zool.) gamo; buco o macho (de)
cabrío, cabrón; macho de algunos otros animales (ciervo, antílope, liebre, *f.*, conejo, etc.);
(E. U.) indio o negro varón y adulto; petimetre;
banquillo de aserrar leña; lejía; colada; corcovo, salto de carnero del potro cerril; potro
(de gimnasio); caja de carruaje; (fam.) dólar.—
b. private, soldado raso. **II.** *va.* colar, enjebar,
enlejiar; empuchar; (mil.) castigar atando los
codos, muñecas y rodillas; topetar, acornear;
tirar el caballo al jinete por las orejas; romper
mineral con martillo. **III.** *vn.* corcovear, saltar
violentamente; (fam.) resistir tenazmente.—**to
b. up**, (fam.) animarse, rehacerse; acicalarse.

buckaroo [bʌkarú], *s.* vaquero; amansador.

buckbasket [bʌkbæskįt], *s.* cesto de la colada.

buckbean [bʌkbin], *s.* (bot.) trébol de pantano.

buckboard [bʌkbord], *s.* (E. U.) carretón o carruaje sin muelles o ballestas.

bucket [bʌkįt], *s.* cubo, cubeta, balde, pozal; contenido de un balde; (hidr.) cangilón; arcaduz,
m.; paleta o álabe (de turbina u otra rueda);
émbolo de (con) válvula de una bomba elevadora; (ing.) cucharón, cubo (de draga, excavadora, etc.); cuja (de lanza).—**b. chain**, (ing.)
cadena o transportador de cangilones.—**b.
excavator**, excavadora de cucharón.—**b. shop**,
(E. U.) oficina o agencia donde se hacen apuestas relativas a los valores de la lonja, en forma
de transacciones ficticias (la ley la prohibe
como casa de juego).—**b. wheel**, rueda de
cangilones, noria.

bucket, *va.* y *vn.* sacar o llevar (agua, etc.) en
cubos; (fam.) cabalgar duro, precipitarse; dirigir un *bucket shop*; estafar.

bucketful [-fụl], *s.* contenido de un balde; cantidad que cabe un cubo.

buckeye [bʌkaị], *s.* (bot.) castaño de Indias.

buckhorn [bʌkhorn], *s.* cuerno de gamo.—**b.**

plantain, (bot.) estrellamar (ll. t. **buck's thorn**).

buckle [bʌkl]. **I.** s. hebilla; arricés; comba, pandeo. **II.** va. (en)hebillar, abrochar con hebilla; embrazar. **III.** vn. doblarse, encorvarse; combarse, pandearse; prepararse.—**to b.** (**down**) **to,** dedicarse con empeño a.—**to b. with,** empeñarse, encontrarse con.

buckler [bʌklœ(r)], s. escudo, broquel, adarga, rodela.—**b. maker** o **wearer,** broquelero.

buckling [-iŋ], s. comba, pandeo.

buckram [bʌkram], s. (tej.) bucarán, bocací, zangala; tiesura, arrogancia, excesiva formalidad.

bucksaw [bʌksɔ], s. sierra bracera o de bastidor.

buckshot [bʌkʃat], s. posta, perdigón grande.

buckskin [bʌkskin], s. piel (f.) de ante.—pl. calzones de ante o de badana.

buckthorn [bʌkθɔrn], s. (bot.) ladierno, tamujo, cambrón, espino.

bucktooth [bʌktuθ], s. diente saliente.

buckwheat [bʌkhwit], s. (bot.) alforfón, trigo sarraceno.—**b. coal,** antracita menuda.

bucolic]bjukálik]. **I.** a. bucólico, pastoril. **II.** s. bucólica.

bud [bʌd]. **I.** s. pimpollo, brote, cogollo, botón, gema o yema de las plantas; capullo de una flor; niña que entra en la sociedad. **II.** vn. brotar, germinar, crecer, florecer, abotonar, pimpollecer. **III.** va. (agr.) injertar o ingerir de escudete.

Buddha [búdǝ], s. Buda.—**Buddhic** [búdik], **Buddhistic** [budʃstik], a. búdico.—**Buddhism** [búdizm], s. budismo.—**Buddhist** [-ist], s. y a. budista.

budding [bʌdiŋ]. **I.** a. en capullo. **II.** s. brotadura; injerto de escudete; (bot.) gemación.

buddle [bʌdl]. **I.** s. (min.) lavadero, artesa. **II.** va. lavar el mineral.

buddy [bʌdi], s. (fam.) camarada, m., compañero; soldado; niño, muchachito.

budge [bʌdʒ]. **I.** va. mover. **II.** vn. moverse, menearse; hacer lugar. **III.** a. guarnecido con piel de cordero. **IV.** s. piel (f.) de cordero, baldés.

budget [bʌdʒit]. **I.** s. presupuesto; colección de noticias, etc.; morral, saco. **II.** va. presuponer, presupuestar.

budgetary [-eri], a. presupuestario, presupuestal.

buff [bʌf]. **I.** s. piel (f.) de ante, búfalo, etc.; pulidor rotatorio, rueda pulidora; color de ante; (med.) linfa cuajada.—**b. coat,** coleto; (fig.) soldado.—**in b.,** en cueros. **II.** a. de ante; anteado. **III.** va. pulimentar, pulir o bruñir; (ten.) raer el cuero; parar un golpe; amortiguar un choque.

buffalo [bʌfalou]. **I.** s. (zool.) búfalo; bisonte norteamericano.—**b. moth,** (ent.) antreno, polilla de las alfombras.—**b. robe,** piel (f.) de búfalo o bisonte con pelo. **II.** va. (fam.) confundir; intimidar; capotear.

buffer [bʌfœ(r)], s. pulidor; rueda de pulir; amortiguador de choques, parachoques; (f. c.) tope.—**b. block,** (f. c.) tope.—**b. state,** estado o país que sirve de valla entre dos naciones rivales.

buffet [buféi], s. aparador, copero; repostería, alacena; caja de órgano.—**b. car,** (f. c.) vagón donde se sirven refrigerios.—**b. lunch,** o **supper,** comida de fiambres, etc., en que cada cual se sirve.

buffet [bʌfit]. **I.** s. bofetada; (fam.) sopapo; embate. **II.** va. abofetear; dar golpes; luchar contra. **III.** vn. combatir a puñadas.

buffeter [-œ(r)], s. púgil, abofeteador.

buffeting [-iŋ], s. mano (f.) de bofetadas; zurra.

buffing [bʌfiŋ]. **I.** s. (ten.) raspado del cuero; separación de dicho raspado; pulimentación.—**b. block,** (f. c.) = BUFFER BLOCK.—**b. spring,** resorte amortiguador. **II.** a. de pulir; pulidor.

buffoon [bʌfún], s. bufón, juglar, histrión, m., truhán.—**to act** o **play the b.,** chocarrear,

truhanear, bufonearse.—**buffoonery** [-eri], s. bufonada, chocarrería, juglaría, truhanería.—

buffoonlike, buffoonish, [-laik], [-iʃ], a. bufo, bufonesco, truhanesco, chocarrero, burlesco.

buffy [bʌfi], a. anteado.—**b. coat,** (med.). V. BUFF.

bug [bʌg], s. cualquier insecto; bicho, sabandija (cucaracha, chinche, etc.); (fam.) microbio.—**to be a b. for,** (fam.) ser entusiasta de.—**to be bugs about,** (fam.) enloquecer o apasionarse por.—**b. house,** (vulg.) manicomio.

bugaboo, bugbear [-ǝbu, -ber], s. espantajo, coco, bu.

buggery [bʌgeri], s. vicio contra natura; sodomía; bestialidad.

buggy [bʌgi]. **I.** s. coche ligero, calesa; carro; (f. c.) vagón de cola. **II.** a. lleno de chinches u otros insectos; (vulg.) bobo, destornillado.

bugle [bjúgl], **bugle horn** [-hɔrn], s. cuerno de caza, bocina; (mil.) corneta, trompeta, clarín.—**b. call,** toque o llamada de corneta; clarinada.

bugle. **I.** s. cañutillo; abalorio; (bot.) consuelda menor. **II.** a. de abalorio.

bugler [bjúglœ(r)], s. trompetero, clarín, corneta, m.

bugloss [bjúglas], s. (bot.) buglosa, lengua de buey.

buhl [búl], **buhlwork** [-wœrk], s. taracea.—**b.-saw,** segueta.

buhrstone [bœrstoun], s. V. BURRSTONE.

build [bild]. **I.** va. y vn. (pret. y pp. BUILT) edificar, fabricar, construir, erigir, labrar, obrar; formar; cimentar; fundar.—**to b. on** o **upon,** edificar o levantar sobre; contar con, confiar en.—**to b. up,** reconstruir, vigorizar; formar de piezas; (mec.) armar; hacer la propaganda, o crear la atmósfera por. **II.** s. estructura; forma, figura, hechura o fachada (de una persona).—**b.-up,** noticias halagadoras de alguien o de algo.

builder [-œ(r)], s. arquitecto, maestro de obras, constructor.

building [-iŋ]. **I.** s. casa, fábrica, edificio, local; obra, construcción, edificación. **II.** a. constructor; de construcción; para construcciones; de o relativo a casas o edificios.—**b. site,** terreno para construir.—**b. tile,** bloque hueco de hormigón o de arcilla.—**b. trade,** ramo de la construcción.

built [bilt], pret. y pp. de to BUILD.—**b.-in,** como parte de la estructura, hecho en la estructura misma.—**b.-up,** compuesto de varias partes, piezas o capas; armado.

bulb [bʌlb], s. (bot.) bulbo o cebolla; (anat.) bulbo; (fís.) cubeta, bola, ampolleta (de termómetro o barómetro); lámpara termiónica; (elec.) ampolla, bomb(ill)a, foco, lámpara (de luz eléctrica); pera de goma (de jeringa o pipeta); pelota de goma (de vaporizador, etc.); ensanche, protuberancia.—**b. angle,** (constr.) escuadra con un ala ensanchada.—**b. syringe,** jeringa de pera.

bulbar [-ǝ(r)], a. bulbar; pert. a un bulbo.

bulbose [-ous], **bulbous** [-ʌs], **bulby** [-i], a. bulboso; que produce o nace de bulbos.

Bulgar [bʌlgar], s. y a. búlgaro.

Bulgarian [bʌlgérian], s. y a. búlgaro.

bulge [bʌldʒ]. **I.** s. pandeo, comba, saliente, teso; (mar.) V. BILGE.—**to get the b. on one,** (fam.) aventajar a uno. **II.** va. y vn. combar(se), pandear(se).

bulginess [-inis], s. pandeo, combadura.

bulgy [-i], a. combo, pandeado; saliente.

bulimia [bjulímia], s. (med.) bulimia, hambre canina.

bulimic [bjulímik], a. bulímico; voraz.

bulk [bʌlk]. **I.** s. volumen, tamaño, bulto, masa, mole, f., tomo; balumba; corpulencia; parte principal, tronco; la mayor parte, el grueso; la mayoría; (mar.) capacidad o carga de un buque; (mar.) bodega; barriga o comba en un edificio; tabanco.—**in b.,** a granel, suelto; en grueso, en globo. **II.** va. amontonar; estimar la capacidad o carga. **III.** *vn.* hincharse; aumentar de bulto; cobrar o ser de peso o importancia.

bulkhead [-hɛd], *s.* (mar.) mamparo; muro de contención ribereño; entrada exterior, gen. inclinada, que da acceso a una bodega, sótano, etc.

bulkiness [-inɪs], *s.* volumen o bulto, masa, magnitud.

bulky [-ɪ], *a.* voluminoso, abultado; corpulento, macizo, pesado, difícil de manejar.

bull [bʊl]. **I.** *s.* (zool.) toro; macho (de elefante, ballena, etc.); (T., astr.) Tauro; diploma, *m.*; bula pontificia; (fam.) disparate, pata de gallo; palabras pomposas y vanas; detective; (com.) alcista.—**b. account**, (com.) cuenta de especulación al alza.—**b. baiting**, combate de toros y perros.—**b. calf**, ternero.—**b. chain**, cadena para arrastrar trozas con perros.—**b.-faced**, cariancho.—**b. moose**, macho de anta; (fam. pol., E. U., **B. M.**) progresista (partido fundado por Teodoro Roosevelt).—**b. ring**, plaza de toros, redondel.—**b.'s eye**, claraboya, tragaluz; linterna sorda; centro de blanco; tiro que da en el blanco; (astr.) Aldebarán; (mar.) guardacabo, motón ciego. **II.** *va.* (com.) jugar al alza; hacer subir el valor.

bulla [bʊlə], *s.* bula (medalla; sello de documento pontificio); (med.) flictena, ampolla.

bullary [bʊlarɪ], *s.* (igl.) bulario.

bulldog [bʊldɔg], *s.* perro dogo o de presa, buldog; revólver de calibre grande.

bulldoze [bʊldoʊz], *va.* (E. U.) intimidar.

bulldozer [-œ(r)], *s.* rasadora.

bullet [bʊlɪt], *s.* bala (de fusil o pistola); plomada de pescador.—**b. mold**, turquesa.—**b. screw**, sacabalas.—**b.-proof**, a prueba de bala.

bulletin [bʊlɪtɪn], *s.* boletín; comunicado.—**b. board**, tablilla en que se fijan listas, noticias, etc.

bullfight [bʊlfaɪt], *s.* corrida de toros, lidia.—**bullfighter** [-œ(r)], *s.* torero, toreador, diestro.—**b.'s garb**, traje de luces.—**bullfighting** [-ɪŋ], *s.* tauromaquia, toreo, toros.

bullfinch [bʊlfɪnʃ], *s.* (orn.) pinzón real.

bullfrog [bʊlfrag], *s.* rana toro, mugidora o bramadora.

bullhead [bʊlhɛd], *s.* (ict.) siluro, bagre; (orn.) chorlito; (fam.) zote, torpe.

bullheaded [-ɪd], *a.* de cabeza grande o ancha (como el toro); obstinado, terco.

bullion [bʊljən], *s.* (com.) metálico; oro o plata en barras.—**b. fringe**, galón o franja de oro.

bullish [bʊlɪʃ], *a.* disparatado; (com.) en alza.

bullock [bʊlɔk], *s.* (zool.) buey, toro castrado.—**b.'s heart**, (bot.) guanábana.

bullpen [bʊlpen], *s.* toril; (fam.) prevención de policía.

bully [bʊlɪ]. **I.** *s.* espadachín, fanfarrón, jaque, matón, rufián, matasiete.—**b.** (beef), carne (f.) de vaca en lata o en adobo. **II.** *a.* (fam.) magnífico, excelente. **III.** *va.* intimidar, amedrentar. **IV.** *vn.* bravear, gallear, fanfarronear.

bullyrag [-ræg], *va.* molestar, atormentar; dar una broma a.

bulrush [bʊlrʌʃ], *s.* (bot.) junco, enea; (bib.) papiro.

bulwark [bʊlwərk]. **I.** *s.* (fort.) baluarte, bastión, *m.*; malecón; (fig.) propugnáculo; (mar.) amurada. **II.** *va.* abaluartar, poner baluartes.

bum [bʌm]. **I.** *va.* (fam.) sablear, obtener (algo) de gorra o de sablazos. **II.** *vn.* (fam.) holgazanear, parrandear; vivir a expensas de otro. **III.** *s.* (fam.) holgazán, vago; borrachín; sablacista, gorrón; borrachera. **IV.** *a.* (fam.) de calidad muy inferior.

bumbailiff [bʌmbéiljif], *s.* corchete, alguacil.

bumblebee [bʌmblbi], *s.* (ent.) abejorro, abejarrón.

bumboat [bʌmboʊt], *s.* (mar.) bote vivandero.

bumkin [bʌmkin], *s.* (mar.). *V.* **BUMPKIN.**—**b. shrouds**, obenques de los pescantes de amura.

bummer [bʌmœ(r)], *s.* (fam.) holgazán.

bump [bʌmp]. **I.** *s.* tope(tazo), porrazo, choque, encontrón, sacudida, trompazo, coscorrón; chichón; protuberancia. **II.** *va. y vn.* chocar contra; entrechocarse; topar o topetar(se) con.—**to b. off**, (fam.) matar, despachar; morirse.

bumper [-œ(r)]. **I.** *s.* copa o vaso lleno; lo que da golpes; (f. c. y mar.) tope; (aut.) parachoques, paragolpes. **II.** *a.* (fam.) lleno; excelente, muy grande o abundante.

bumpkin [-kin], *s.* patán, rústico; (mar.) pescante de la amura del trinquete.

bumptious [-ʃʌs], *a.* engreído, envanecido, presuntuoso.—**bumptiousness** [-nɪs], *s.* presunción, engreimiento.

bumpy [-ɪ], *a.* desigual, que tiene baches (camino).

bun, bunn [bʌn], *s.* bollo, buñuelo; (rabo de) conejo o ardilla; moño o castaña (de pelo).

bunch [bʌnʃ]. **I.** *s.* haz, *m.*, manojo, atado; ristra (de cebollas, etc.); mazo, montón; racimo; macolla; bulto o tumor; (fam.) manada (de gente). **II.** *va.* agrupar, juntar, amontonar. **III.** *vn.* arracimarse, amacollarse.

bunchiness [-inɪs], *s.* calidad de ser racimoso o nudoso.

bunchy [-ɪ], *a.* racimoso o arracimado, amacollado.

bunco [bʌŋkoʊ] = **BUNKO.**

buncombe, bunkum [bʌŋkʌm], *s.* palabrería.

bundle [bʌndl]. **I.** *s.* atado, lío, mazo, haz, *m.*, manojo, paquete, envoltorio, fardo, bulto. **II.** *va.* liar, atar, enfardelar, empaquetar, envolver; (con off), despedir con cajas destempladas o con prisa; (con up), arropar bien. **III.** *vn.* (gen. con off), liar y marcharse; liarlas; escabullirse, largarse.

bung [bʌŋ]. **I.** *s.* tapón, tarugo, bitoque. **II.** *va.* atarugar.

bungalow [bʌŋgaloʊ], *s.* en la India, choza con galerías; (E. U.) casa de un piso.

bunghole [bʌŋhoʊl], *s.* boca de tonel, canillero.

bungle [bʌŋgl]. **I.** *va.* chapucear, chafallar, estropear. **II.** *vn.* hacer chapucerías. **III.** *s.* chapucería, chabacanería.—**bungler** [bʌŋglœ(r)], *s.* chapucero, chambón.—**bungling** [bʌŋglɪŋ], *a.* chapucero, chambón.—**bunglingly** [-lɪ], *adv.* chapuceramente, chabacanamente.

bunion [bʌnjən], *s.* adrián, juanete (del pie).

bunk [bʌŋk]. **I.** *s.* tarima, litera; (fam.) baladronada, faramalla, palabrería vana; hojarasca. **II.** *vn.* dormir en litera; acostarse. **III.** *va.* (fam.) embaucar; estafar.

bunker [-œ(r)]. **I.** *s.* arcón; carbonera; (mar.) pañol del carbón; (fort.) fortín; (golf) hoya de arena. **II.** *vn.* (mar.) rellenar las carboneras.

bunko [-oʊ]. **I.** *va.* (fam.) estafar. **II.** *s.* estafa.

bunny [bʌnɪ], *s.* (fam.) gazapo, conejito; ardilla.

Bunsen burner [bʌnsœ bœrnœ(r)], *s.* lámpara o mechero (de) Bunsen.

bunt [bʌnt]. **I.** *va.* topetar; empellar; (baseball) golpear ligeramente la pelota para que ruede muy poco. **II.** *vn.* (mar.) hincharse. **III.** *s.* hinchazón, *f.*; barriga o seno de una vela o una red; (agr.) añublo, tizón; empellón, topetazo; (baseball) golpecito muy suave.

bunting [-ɪŋ], *s.* lanilla, estameña, colgaduras, banderas; (orn.) calandria.—**b. iron**, caña para soplar vidrio.

buntline [-laɪn], *s.* (mar.) briol.

buoy [bɔɪ o bʊɪ]. **I.** *s.* (mar.) boya, baliza.—**b. rope**, orinque. **II.** *va.* aboyar, abalizar; mantener a flote.—**to b. up**, apoyar o sostener. **III.** *vn.* boyar, flotar.

buoyage [-idʒ], *s.* sistema (*m.*) de boyas; abalizamiento.

buoyancy [-ansɪ], *s.* flotabilidad; flotación; alegría, animación; (aer.) fuerza ascensional; (fís.) presión o empuje hacia arriba.

Para la pronunciación véase la clave al principio del libro.

buoyant [-ąnt], *a.* boyante; campante, alegre, animado, vivaz.

bur, burr [bœr]. **I.** *s.* (bot.) escobilla, carda, cabeza erizada de la cardencha; capullo de la castaña, etc.; (tej.) nudillo; vilano o milano del cardo; mota; (mec.) disco; arandela. **II.** *va.* (tej.) desmotar; (dent.) raspar con el buril.

burbot [bœrbǫt], *s.* (ict.) mustela.

burden [bœrden]. **I.** *s.* carga, peso, gravamen; cuidados y aflicciones del ánimo; (mar.) porte, capacidad, tonelaje; (poét.) estribillo, bordón, retornelo. **II.** *va.* cargar, agobiar, gravar.

burdensome [-sʌm], *a.* gravoso, pesado, oneroso, molesto.—**burdensomeness** [-nįs], *s.* molestia, pesadez.

burdock [bœrdak], *s.* (bot.) bardana, lampazo.

bureau [bįúrou], *s.* cómoda, tocador; buró, escritorio, bufete; oficina, agencia, negociado, despacho; ramo, división, departamento.

bureaucracy [bįųrákrąsi], *s.* burocracia.

bureaucrat [bįúrekræt], *s.* burócrata, *m.*

bureaucratic [-krǽtįk], *a.* burocrático.

burette [bįųrét], *s.* (quím.) bureta, probeta.

burg [bœrg], *s.* villa, aldea, ciudad.

burgeon [bœrdʒǫn]. **I.** *vn.* y *va.* brotar, retoñar, germinar. **II.** *s.* retoño, yema.

burgess [bœrdʒįs], *s.* burgués, ciudadano libre; (pol.) diputado por un *borough*.

burgessship [-šįp], *s.* oficio y calidad de diputado de *borough*.

burgh [bœrg], *s.* = BOROUGH.

burgher [-œ(r)], *s.* ciudadano, vecino de un *burgh*.—**burghership** [-šįp], *s.* ciudadanía.

burglar [bœrgląr], *s.* ladrón.—**b. alarm**, alarma contra ladrones.—**b.-proof**, a prueba de ladrones.

burglarious [bœrglérįʌs], *a.* referente a un escalo.

burglary [bœrgląri], *s.* robo con escalo; hurto.

burgomaster [bœrgomæstœ(r)], *s.* burgomaestre.

burgonet [bœrgonet], *s.* (arm.) borgoñeta.

burgrave [bœrgrejv], *s.* burgrave.

burgraviate [-gréjvįąt], *s.* burgraviato.

Burgundian [bœrgándįąn], *s.* y *a.* borgoñón.

Burgundy [bœrgʌndį], *s.* Borgoña.—**B. helmet**, celada borgoñona.—**B. wine**, vino de Borgoña.

burial [bérįąl], *s.* entierro, inhumación.—**b. ground, b. place**, cementerio, camposanto.

burier [bérįœ(r)], *s.* enterrador, sepulturero.

burin [bįúrįn], *s.* (b. a.) buril, cincel.

burl [bœrl]. **I.** *va.* (tej.) desmotar, despinzar, desborrar. **II.** *s.* (tej.) borra, nudillo, mota; (carp.) nudo; chapa de madera nudosa.

burlap [bœrlæp], *s.* (h)arpillera, cañamazo, rázago.

burler [bœrlœ(r)], *s.* desmotador.

burlesque [bœrlésk]. **I.** *a.* burlesco, paródico.—**b. show**, (teat.) espectáculo de variedades (o *varietés*) de carácter burlesco. **II.** *s.* parodia. **III.** *va.* chufar, parodiar.

burletta [bœrlétą], *s.* zarzuelita.

burling iron [bœrlįŋ ái̯œrn], *s.* (tej.) despinzadera, (des)pinzas, desmotadera.

burly [bœrlį], *a.* corpulento, fornido; nudoso.

Burman [bœrmąn], *a.* y *s.* birmano.

Burmese [bœrmís], *a.* y *s.* birmanés.

burn [bœrn]. **I.** *va.* (pret. y pp. BURNED o BURNT) quemar, abrasar; incendiar; cocer (ladrillos, etc.), calcinar; (cir.) cauterizar.—**to b. away**, quemar o disipar lentamente con el calor o el fuego.—**to b. daylight**, perder tiempo.—**to b. on**, (tec.) soldar.—**to b. one's boats**, quemar las naves.—**to b. out**, quemar, destruir quemando; hacer salir con fuego.—**to b. the midnight oil**, quemarse las cejas.—**to b. to a crisp**, carbonizar.—**to b. to ashes**, reducir a cenizas. **II.** *vn.* quemarse; arder; consumirse; encenderse; abrasarse; (elec.) formar arco en las escobillas.—**to b. out**, quemarse; apagarse; pasarse (el fuego); (elec.) fundirse (un fusible, etc.).—**to b. up**, quemarse o consumirse por completo.—**to b. with**, arder de, abrasarse de

(celos, ira, etc.). **III.** *s.* quemadura; marca de hierro candente.

burnable [-ąbl], *a.* combustible.

burner [-œ(r)], *s.* quemador, abrasador; quemador de lámpara, mechero (de gas, etc.).

burnet [bœrnįt], *s.* (bot.) pimpinela.

burning [bœrnįŋ]. **I.** *s.* ardor; quemadura; quemazón, *f.,* abrasamiento; quema, incendio; (cer.) cocción. **II.** *a.* abrasador, ardiente; quemante, vehemente.—**b. glass**, espejo o vidrio ustorio.

burnish [bœrnįš]. **I.** *va.* bruñir, pulir, acicalar, pulimentar, (fot.) satinar. **II.** *vn.* tomar lustre. **III.** *s.* bruñido, satinado.—**burnisher** [-œ(r)], *s.* bruñidor, pulidor; acicalador; (fot.) satinador.

burnoose, burnous [bœrnús], *s.* albornoz, *m.*

burnsides [bœrnsai̯dz], *s. pl.* patillas.

burnt [bœrnt], (*pret. y pp.* de TO BURN) quemado; abrasado; cocido; calcinado.—**b. offering**, o **sacrifice**, holocausto.

burr [bœr]. **I.** *s.* (V. BUR) rebaba del metal; zumbido; (dent.) buril; (carp.) roldana de perno, virola; canal auricular; sonido fuerte de la **r**; protuberancia; nudo (de un árbol); raíz de las astas de un ciervo. **II.** *va.* y *vn.* pronunciar la erre con sonido gutural; zumbar.

burro [bœrou], *s.* burro.

burrow [bœrou]. **I.** *s.* madriguera, conejera; cueva, vivar. **II.** *va.* hacer cueva(s) en; hacer (ex)cavando. **III.** *vn.* amadrigarse; encuevarse; minar, horadar.

burrstone [bœrstoun], *s.* piedra de molino.

bursa [bœrsą], *s.* (anat.) bolsa o saco.

bursar [bœrsą(r)], *s.* tesorero (esp. de una universidad u orden religiosa; (Esco.) becario.

bursary [-į], *s.* tesorería; (Esco.) beca. *V.* BURSAR.

burse [bœrs], *s.* bolsa; (igl.) bolsa del corporal.

burst [bœrst]. **I.** *va.* (*pret. y pp.* BURST) romper; reventar.—**to b. open**, forzar, romper (una puerta, etc.). **II.** *vn.* reventar(se); estallar; volarse; hacer explosión.—**to b. into**, deshacerse en (lágrimas), desatarse en (improperios, amenazas, etc.).—**to b. out**, reventarse, estallar; desatarse, prorrumpir, soltar.—**to b. through**, irrumpir. **III.** *s.* reventón, estallido, explosión; supremo esfuerzo; (mil.) sucesión de tiros de una arma automática.

burthen [bœrðen], *s.* y *v.* = BURDEN.

burton [bœrtǫn], *s.* (mar.) polispasto.

bury [bérį], *va.* enterrar, inhumar, sepultar; soterrar, esconder, ocultar.—**to be buried in thought**, estar absorto en la meditación.—**to b. the hatchet**, hacer la paz.

burying [-įŋ], *s.* entierro; exequias.—**b. ground, b. place**, cementerio, camposanto.

bus [bʌs], *s.* (aut.) ómnibus, bus, autobús, (Am.) camión, *m.,* (Cuba) guagua.—**b. bar**, (elec.) barra colectora.—**b. boy**, ayudante de restaurante.—**b. line**, ruta, línea o compañía de autobuses.

bush [bųš]. **I.** *s.* arbusto, mata; matorral; terreno cubierto de malezas; (Cuba) manigua; ramo colgado a las puertas de las tabernas; hopo de zorra; (mec.) *V.* BUSHING.—**b. bean**, frijol enano. **II.** *vn.* crecer espeso o contiguo. **III.** *va.* forrar con metal; poner grano a un cañón, buje a una rueda, tejuelo a un eje, etc.; apoyar, sostener con matas; (agr.) gradar o igualar el terreno arrastrando matas; labrar (piedra) a escuadra con martillo.

bushel [bųšel], *s.* medida de áridos (Ingl., 36.35 litros; E. U., 35 litros).

bushhammer [bųšhæmœ(r)], *s.* pica, escoda.

bushing [bųšįŋ], *s.* (mec.) forro de metal; manguito; casquillo de cojinete; boquilla, guía, dado, tejo, tejuelo; (arti.) grano de un cañón.

bushman [bųšman], *s.* campesino; habitante del bosque; (B.) salvaje nómada sudafricano.

bushmaster [bųšmæstœ(r)], *s.* (zool.) serpiente muy grande y venenosa de la América tropical.

bushwhacker [bʊ́shwækœ(r)], *s.* montonero; guerrillero; cuchillo para cortar malezas, etc.

bushy [bʊ́shi], *a.* matoso; copudo; peludo.

busily [bízili], *adv.* solícitamente, diligentemente; atareadamente.

business [bíznjs], *s.* oficio; asunto, cuestión; tarea, trabajo; (com.) negocio(s), comercio.—**b. man**, comerciante, negociante, hombre de negocios.—**b. suit**, terno, traje ordinario o de calle.—**b. transaction**, contratación, negociación.—**b. is b.**, la cuenta es cuenta.—**to be one's b.**, importarle o atañerle a uno.—**to make it one's b.**, proponerse.—**to mean b.**, hablar en serio; formalizarse.—**to send about one's b.**, enviar a paseo.

businesslike [-laik], *a.* formal, directo; práctico, sistemático, bien ordenado o administrado.

busk [bʌsk], *s.* ballena o acero de corsé.

buskin [bʌ́skin], *s.* borceguí; coturno; (teat.) tragedia.

buskined [-d], *a.* de alto coturno; trágico.

busman [bʌ́smən], *s.* conductor de autobús.

buss [bʌs], I. *va.* y *vn.* (fam.) besar. II. *s.* beso sonado.

bust [bʌst], *s.* (b. a.) busto; retrato o fotografía de busto; pecho de mujer; (fam.) fracaso; borrachera.

bust, (fam. y vulgar). I. *va.* reventar; degradar (a un oficial); domar (un potro). II. *vn.* reventarse; quebrarse; arruinarse, quedar sin un real; salir mal.

bustard [bʌ́stärd], *s.* (orn.) avutarda.

buster [bʌ́stœ(r)], *s.* (vulg. o fam.) cosa notable, maravilla. *V.* BRONCO y TRUST.

bustle [bʌ́sl], I. *vn.* bullir, menearse, no parar. II. *s.* bullicio, animación, bulla, ruido; (cost.) caderillas, tontillo, polisón.

bustler [bʌ́slœ(r)], *s.* bullebulle, *mf.*

busy [bízi], I. *a.* ocupado; activo, laborioso; bullicioso; entremetido. II. *va.* ocupar, emplear. III. *vr.* ocuparse.—**busybody** [-badi], *s.* entremetido, refitolero, chismoso.—**busybrain** [-brein], *s.* proyectista.—**busyness** [-njs], *s.* ocupación.

but [bʌt], I. *conj.*, *prep.* y *adv.* pero, mas; sin embargo; excepto, menos; solamente, no más que; sino; que no (*there was nobody* but *was tired*, no había nadie que no estuviese cansado); sin que, sin (*he never speaks* but *he yells*, nunca habla sin gritar, o sin que grite).—**b. for**, a no ser por.—**b. that**, que no; sino que; si no fuera porque.—**cannot b.**, no puedo (puede, etc.) menos de, o dejar de (*I could not* but *laugh*, no pude menos de reír; *it cannot* but *be true*, no puede dejar de ser cierto).—**none b.**, solamente. II. *s.* pero, objeción.

butadiene [bjutadáijin], *s.* (quím.) butadieno.

butane [bjútein], *s.* (quím.) butano.

butcher [bʊ́chœ(r)], I. *s.* carnicero, cortador, jifero; hombre sanguinario; (fam.) chapucero.—**b. bird**, (orn.) alcaudón, desol·ador.—**b.'s block**, tajo.—**b.'s broom**, (bot.) brusco.—**b.'s knife**, jifero.—**b.'s shop**, carnicería. II. *va.* matar reses; dar muerte cruel; hacer una carnicería en; (fam.) chapucear.—**butchering** [-iŋ], *s.* carnicería, matanza.—**butcherly** [-li], *a.* perteneciente al carnicero; cruel, inhumano, sangriento.—**butchery** [-i], *s.* carnicería, matanza; oficio de carnicero; matadero.

butler [bʌ́tlœ(r)], *s.* despensero, mayordomo; repostero; cillerero (de un monasterio).—**b.'s pantry**, despensa, repostería.—**butlerage** [-idž], *s.* departamento del despensero; (Ingl.) antiguo derecho sobre vinos.—**butlership** [-šip], *s.* oficio de despensero.—**butlery** [-i], *s.* despensa.

butt [bʌt], I. *s.* cabo, extremo; (carp.) cabeza o tope de tablón; empalme plano; (arm.) culata, coz; mocho de un taco de billar; mango de látigo, etc.; blanco, hito; límite, fin, término; bota, pipa, tonel; topetada, topetazo, mochada;

estocada; punta o colilla (de cigarro).—**b. and b.**, a(l) tope.—**b. cut**, primera troza arriba de la cepa.—**b. end**, cabo, mango, mocho, tope, extremo mayor; cabeza (de biela).—**b. hinge**, bisagra.—**b. joint**, junta a tope o de yuxtaposición.—**b. maker**, pipero, tonelero.—**b. of ridicule**, hazmerreír.—**b. weld**, soldadura a tope. II. *va.* top(et)ar; (mar.) topar; acornear, mochar; apoyar; (mec.) juntar a tope. III. *vn.* top(et)ar, embestir, acornear; sobresalir.—**to b. against**, confinar o empalmar con; estrellarse contra.—**to b. in**, (fam.) entremeterse, meter baza, meter su cuchara(da).

butte [bjut], *s.* monte aislado.

butter [bʌ́tœ(r)], I. *s.* mantequilla, manteca de vaca; (quím.) manteca; topador, acorneador, el que da topetazos.—**b. bowl** o **dish**, mantequ(ill)era.—**b. knife** o **spreader**, cuchillo mantequillero.—**b. mold** o **print**, molde para mantequilla. II. *va.* untar con manteca; (fam.) adular.

buttercup [-kʌp], *s.* (bot.) ranúnculo, botón de oro.

butterfat [-fæt], *s.* grasa de mantequilla.

butterfly [-flai], *s.* (ent.) mariposa.—**b.-like**, (bot.) amariposado.—**b. screw**, tornillo con aletas.—**b. valve**, válvula de mariposa o de estrangulación.

butterine [-in], *s.* (oleo)margarina.

butteris [-js], *s.* (herr.) pujavante.

buttermilk [-milk], *s.* suero de manteca.

butternut [-nʌt], *s.* (bot.) nogal blanco americano; nuez oleosa del mismo.

butterscotch [-skach], *s.* dulce de azúcar con mantequilla; bombón escocés.

buttery [-i]. I. *s.* despensa; bodega, botillería. II. *a.* mantecoso; (fam.) adulador, zalamero.

buttock [bʌ́tɔk], *s.* nalga, trasero; anca; *pl.* posaderas, (fam.) asentaderas; (mar.) llenos de popa.

button [bʌ́tɔn], I. *s.* botón; tirador de puerta; (elec.) botón de timbre; botón o zapatilla de florete; cascabel de crótalo; (arti.) cascabel; (agr.) botón o capullo.—*pl.* **buttons**, paje, lacayo, (fam.) botones.—**b. maker** o **seller**, botonero. II. *va.* abotonar. III. *vn.* abotonarse.—**buttonhole** [-houl], I. *s.* ojal, presilla. II. *va.* (cost.) hacer o abrir ojales; abrochar, atacar; importunar, fastidiar; (esgr.) dar botonazos.

buttonhook [-huk], *s.* abotonador, abrochador.

buttonwood [-wud], *s.* (bot.) plátano de Occidente; plátano falso, sicómoro.

buttress [bʌ́trjs], I. *s.* sostén, apoyo, refuerzo; (arq.) contrafuerte, estantal, machón, botarel, estribo; (geog.) contrafuerte, estribo. II. *va.* afianzar, apoyar, estantalar, sostener.

butyl [bjútil], *s.* (quím.) butilo.—**b. alcohol**, alcohol butílico (ll. t. **butylic alcohol**).

butylene [-in], *s.* (quím.) butileno.

butyraceous [bjutiréišjʌs], o **butyrous** [bjútirʌs], *a.* manteeoso, butiráceo.

butyric [bjutírik], *a.* butírico.

butyrin(e [bjútirin], *s.* (quím.) butirina.

butyrometer [bjutirámetœ(r)], *s.* butirómetro, medidor de la grasa de la leche.

butyryl [bjútiril], *s.* (quím.) butirilo.

buxom [bʌ́ksɔm], *a.* frescachona, rolliza, mocetona; alegre, jovial, retozona.

buy [bái], I. *va.* (*pret.* y *pp.* BOUGHT) comprar, mercar; sobornar.—**to b. a pig in a poke**, cerrar un trato a ciegas.—**to b. in**, comprar (en una subasta) por cuenta del dueño; comprar acciones (en una compañía, etc.).—**to b. off**, librarse de, con dinero, comprar (a una persona). —**to b. on credit** o **trust**, comprar al fiado.— **to b. out**, comprar la parte de (un socio).—**to b. up**, acaparar. II. *vn.* hacer compras, comprar. III. *s.* compra; (fam.) compra ventajosa, ganga.

buyable [-abl], *a.* comprable.

buyer [-œ(r)], *s.* comprador, marchante.

buying [-iŋ], *s.* compra.

buzz [bʌz]. **I.** *s.* zumbido; susurro, murmurio.—
b. bomb, bomba planeadora o voladora. *V.*
ROBOT BOMB.—**b. saw,** sierra circular. **II.** *vn.*
zumbar, zurri(a)r; cuchichear, susurrar.

buzzard [bʌ́zərd], *s.* (orn.) especie de halcón o
milano; gallinazo.

buzzer [bʌ́zœ(r)], *s.* zumbador; murmurador;
(elec.) zumbador.

buzzing [-ɪŋ]. **I.** *a.* zumbador. **II.** *s.* zumbido,
zurrido.

by [baɪ]. **I.** *prep.* por (cuando denota el agente, el
instrumento, la causa, el modo y el medio por
el cual se ejecuta alguna cosa); a, en; para;
por, junto a, cerca de, al lado de (cuando denota
proximidad); a, de, con, en; según, de acuerdo
con. Antes de gerundio indica manera, y no se
traduce (*by studying, you will learn,* estudiando,
Vd. aprenderá). **II.** *adv.* cerca, al lado; aparte,
a un lado.—**b. and b.,** pronto, luego.—**b. and
large,** en todo respecto, de una manera general.
—**b. day, b. night,** de día, de noche.—**b.
God!,** ¡por Dios!—**b. heaven!,** ¡vive Dios!—**b.
itself,** de por sí.—**b. means of,** mediante.—
b. much, con mucho.—**b. one's self,** solo, sin
ayuda.—**b. the dozen,** por docenas.—**b. the
light of,** a la luz de.—**b. the way,** en el camino; entre paréntesis; de paso.—**b. then,** para
entonces.—**b. this time,** ahora, a la hora de
ésta, ya.—**b. way of,** por vía de.

by, bye [baɪ]. **I.** *a.* apartado, secundario; incidental; secreto. **II.** *s.* asunto secundario; (dep.)
meta; jugador no pareado (en un torneo, etc.).
—**by the bye,** de paso, entre paréntesis. **III.**
interj. by(e)-by(e)!, (fam.) ¡adiós!

by-bidder [báɪbɪdœ(r)], *s.* postor simulado (en
una subasta).

by-blow [báɪbloʊ], *s.* golpe de lado o accidental;
hijo ilegítimo.

by-channel [báɪchænel], *s.* contracanal.

by-election [baɪɪlékʃon], *s.* elecciones especiales,
sobre todo para llenar puestos vacantes.

bygone [báɪgon], *a.* pasado.—**let bygones be
bygones,** olvidemos lo pasado; peli:los a la mar.

by-lane [báɪleɪn], *s.* vereda, camino retirado.

by-law [báɪˈlɔ], *s.* estatutos o reglamentos.

by-name [báɪneɪm], *s.* sobrenombre; apodo.

by-pass [báɪpæs]. **I.** *s.* camino de paso o al largo
de una carretera, etc.; desvío; (mec. y elec.)
derivación.—**b.-pass valve,** (m. v.) válvula
auxiliar o de derivación; (hidr.) válvula de
sobrecarga o adicional. **II.** *va.* desviar; evitar;
pasar por alto o alrededor de (un obstáculo,
etc.).

by-path [báɪpæθ], *s.* senda, vereda.

by-play [báɪpleɪ], *s.* (teat.) escena muda, juego
escénico; pasatiempo; diversión.

by-product [báɪpradʌkt], *s.* producto accesorio,
residuo, derivado.

by-road [báɪroʊd], *s.* atajo, andurrial.

Byronic [baɪrɑ́nɪk], *a.* byroniano; romántico,
apasionado, cínico, libre.

bystander [báɪstændœ(r)], *s.* mirón.—*pl.* circunstantes.

by-street [báɪstrit], *s.* callejuela, calle desviada.

by-view [báɪvju], *s.* fin particular, propio interés.

byway [báɪweɪ], *s.* camino desviado.

byword [báɪwœrd], *s.* objeto de burla u oprobio;
apodo; mote; máxima, refrán; perogrullada.

Byzantian, Byzantine [bɪzǽnʃɪən, bɪzǽntɪn], *a.*
y *s.* bizantino.—**B. Greek,** romeo.

Byzantinism [-ɪzm], *s.* bizantinismo.

C

c [si], *s.* c; (mús., C) do.

cab [kæb], *s.* cab, cabriolé; coche de punto, simón;
taxi; (f. c.) puesto del maquinista; casilla del
conductor de un autocamión.—**c. stand,** punto
de coches.

cabal [kəbǽl]. **I.** *s.* cábala, intriga, maquinación.
II. *vn.* intrigar, maquinar, tramar.

cabala [kǽbələ], *s.* cábala (entre los judíos).

cabalism [-ɪzm], *s.* cabalismo.—**cabalist** [-ɪst], *s.*
cabalista.—**cabalistic**(al [-ɪstɪk(əl], *a.* cabalístico.—**cabalistically** [-ɪ], *adv.* cabalísticamente.

caballer [kəbǽlœ(r)], *s.* cabalista, maquinador.

cabaret [kæbəréɪ], *s.* cabaret, café cantante, café
concierto.

cabaret [kǽbəret], *s.* taberna; juego de té o de
café.

cabas [kəbá], *s.* cabás; bolsa de labor.

cabbage [kǽbɪdʒ]. **I.** *s.* (bot.) berza, col, repollo;
sisa.—**c. beetle, c. bug, c. worm,** etc., nombres de varios insectos y orugas que atacan la
col.—**c. butterfly,** piéride (*f.*) de las coles;
mariposa blanca.—**c.-headed,** repolludo. **II.**
va. sisar (los sastres); hurtar. **III.** *vn.* (agr.)
repollar.

cabby [kǽbɪ], *s.* (fam.) cochero de punto.

cabin [kǽbɪn]. **I.** *s.* barraca, cabaña, choza, tugurio; (mar.) cabina, cámara, camarote.—**c.
boy,** (mar.) paje de escoba; camarero.—**c.
class,** (mar.) de una sola clase.—**c. cruiser,**
crucero de placer. **II.** *vn.* vivir en cabaña o
choza. **III.** *va.* encerrar en cabaña o choza.

cabinet [kǽbɪnɪt]. **I.** *s.* (pol.) gabinete, ministerio; sala donde se exhiben objetos artísticos;
escaparate, vitrina, estuche; armario; estante;
caja o mueble (de radio, etc.); (impr.) chibalete.
—**c. council,** consejo de ministros o de gabinete.—**c. wood,** madera de ebanistería. **II.** *a.*
ministerial; (b. a.) digno de figurar en una sala;
secreto, reservado.

cabinetmaker [-méɪkœ(r)], *s.* ebanista.—**cabi-
netmaking** [-ɪŋ], *s.* ebanistería.—**cabinetwork** [-wœrk], *s.* ebanistería, marquetería.

cable [kéɪbl]. **I.** *s.* cable, *m.*; (mar.) cable, maroma,
amarra; telégrafo submarino; cablegrama, *m.*—
c. address,dirección cablegráfica.—**c. bitt,**bitadura.—**c. car,** vagón movido por tracción de
cable.—**c. grip,** grapa, fiador de cable.—**c.
railroad,** ferrocarril de tracción o de cable;
ferrocarril funicular.—**c.'s length,** cable, me-
dida longitudinal ($\frac{1}{10}$ de milla náutica). **II.** *va.*
y *vn.* cable(grafi)ar, telegrafiar por cable; proveer de o atar con cables.

cablegram [-græm], *s.* cablegrama, *m.*, cable.

cablet [kéɪblet], *s.* (mar.) estacha.

cableway [-weɪ], *s.* alambrecarril, cable aéreo de
transporte.

cabman [kǽbmən], *s.* cochero de punto, simón.

cabochon [kǽbəʃan], *s.* (joy.) cabujón.

caboodle [kəbúdl], *s.* (fam.) hato, cuadrilla, conjunto de gente o cosas.

caboose [kəbús], *s.* (mar.) fogón o cocina; (f. c.)
vagón de cola en un tren de carga.

cabotage [kǽbotaʒ], *s.* (mar.) cabotaje.

cabriolet [kæbrɪoléɪ], *s.* cabriolé.

cacao [kəkéɪoʊ], *s.* (bot.) cacao (árbol y semillas).
—**c. butter,** manteca de cacao.—**c. plantation,** cacahual.

cachalot [kǽʃalat], *s.* (ict.) cachalote.

cache [kæʃ]. **I.** *va.* depositar en un escondrijo.
II. *s.* escondite, escondrijo; víveres, *m. pl.*,
tesoro, etc., escondidos en tal sitio.

cachectic(al [kəkéktɪk(əl], *a.* caquéctico.

cachet [kæʃéɪ], *s.* sello (de carta, etc.); distintivo.

cachexia [kəkéksɪə], *s.* (med.) caquexia.

cachinnation [kækɪnéɪʃɒn], *s.* carcajada.

cacique [kəsík], *s.* cacique; (orn.) oropéndola.

caciquism [-ɪzm], *s.* caciquismo.

cackle [kǽkl]. **I.** *vn.* cacarear; reírse; chacharear.
II. *s.* cacareo; charla, cháchara.

cackler [kǽklœ(r)], *s.* cacareador; chacharero,
parlanchín.

cackling [-ɪŋ], *s.* cacareo; cháchara.

cacochymia [kækokímɪə], *s.* (med.) cacoquimia.

cacodemon [kækodímɒn], *s.* diablo, espíritu
malo.

cacodyl [kǽkodɪl], *s.* (quím.) cacodilo.

cacodylate [-eɪt], *s.* (quím.) cacodilato.

cacodylic [kækodílɪk], *a.* (quím.) cacodílico.

cacography [kækágrafi], *s.* cacografía.

cacomistle [kǽkomįsl], *s.* (zool.) basáride, *f.*, (Mex.) cacomixtle.

cacophonous [kækáfonʌs], *a.* cacofónico.

cacophony [kækáfoni], *s.* cacofonía.

cactaceous [kæktéişʌs], *a.* cácteo.

cactus [kǽktʌs], *s.* (bot.) cacto.

cad [kæd], *s.* persona de modales groseros.

cadastral [kadǽstral], *a.* catastral.

cadastre, cadaster [kadǽstœ(r)], *s.* catastro.

cadaver [kadǽvœ(r)], *s.* cadáver.

cadaverous [-ʌs], *a.* cadavérico.

caddie, caddy [kǽdį]. **I.** *s.* muchacho que en el juego de golf lleva los palos.—**c. bag** = GOLF BAG. **II.** *vn.* servir de *caddie*.

caddish [kǽdįş], *a.* grosero, mal educado.

caddy [kǽdį], *s.* bote, lata, cajita para té.

cade [kejd]. **I.** *a.* manso, domesticado; mimado. **II.** *s.* cordero manso; (bot.) variedad de enebro.

cadence, cadency [kéjdens, -į], *s.* cadencia, ritmo, modulación.—**cadent, cadential** [-ent, kadénşal], *a.* cadente, cadencioso.

cadenza [kadénzä], *s.* (mús.) cadencia.

cadet [kadét], *s.* (mil.) cadete; segundón, hijo o hermano menor; (fam.) alcahuete.

cadge [kædž], *va.* y *vn.* (fam.) pedir; vivir de gorra.

cadi [kádį], *s.* cadí.

cadmia [kǽdmįä], *s.* cadmía.

cadmium [kǽdmįʌm], *s.* (quím.) cadmio.

cadre [kǽdr(į)], *s.* núcleo; armazón, *f.*, plan; (mil.) cuadro, conjunto de jefes.

caduceus [kadúsįʌs], *s.* caduceo.

caducous [kadúkʌs], *a.* caduco; perecedero; transitorio; (bot.) caduco.

caducity [kadúsįtį], *s.* caducidad; caduquez; senectud; (for.) caducidad.

cæcal [síkal], *a.* cecal.

cæcum [síkʌm], *s.* (anat.) (intestino) ciego.

Cæsarean [sįzérįan], *a.* cesáreo.—**C. operation, C. section,** (cir.) operación cesárea; histerotomía.

Cæsarism [sízarįzm], *s.* cesarismo.

cæsura [sįzúrä], *s.* (poét.) cesura.

cæsium [sízįʌm], *s.* (quím.) cesio.

café [kæféj], *s.* café, cantina, restaurante.—**c. au lait,** café con leche.—**c. chantant,** café cantante.—**c. noir,** café puro, negro o tinto.

caffein [kǽfin], *s.* cafeína.

cafeteria [kæfetírįä], *s.* cafetería, restaurant donde los parroquianos se sirven a sí mismos.

caftan [kǽftan], *s.* vestimenta turca.

cage [kéjdž]. **I.** *s.* jaula, gayola; (fam.) trena, prisión; camarín de ascensor; fogaril. **II.** *va.* enjaular.

cageling [-lįŋ], *s.* pájaro enjaulado.

cahoot [kahút], *s.* (fam.) compañía; colusión.—**to be in** o **to go cahoots,** formar compañía, asociarse, confabularse.

caïque [kaík], *s.* (mar.) caique.

cairn [kɛrn], *s.* montón de piedras para señal.

caisson [kéjson], *s.* arcón; (mil.) furgón; cajón de municiones; (ing.) cajón neumático y sumergible dentro del cual se hacen cimientos bajo el agua; (mar.) camello; compuerta de dique; (arq.) artesón.—**c. disease,** (med.) parálisis que afecta a veces a los que trabajan en cámaras de sumersión.

caitiff [kéjtįf], *a.* y *s.* vil, miserable, belitre.

cajole [kadžóųl], *va.* lisonjear, adular; halagar, engatusar, lagotear, gitanear.

cajoler [-œ(r)], *s.* adulador, zalamero.

cajolery [-į], *s.* adulación, lisonja; requiebro, zalamería, carantoñas, engatusamiento.

cajuput [kǽdžųpʊt], *s.* (bot.) cayeputi.

cake [kéjk]. **I.** *vn.* conglutinarse, aterronarse (apl. al carbón), formar costra. **II.** *s.* tort(it)a, bizcocho, bollo, pastel, hojaldre, *mf.*, pastelillo; tabl(et)a (de chocolate, etc.); pastilla o pan de jabón, de cera, etc.; terrón.

cakewalk [-wok], *s.* cierto baile; orig., marcha o danza de negros, en que se premiaba con un pastel a la pareja que mejor se contoneaba.

calaba [kǽlabä], *s.* (bot.) calaba, *m.*, calambuco.

calabash [-bæş], *s.* (bot.) calabacera (planta cuyo fruto es la calabaza); calabaza (planta y fruto); (Am.) calabaza, güiro (árbol y fruto).—**c. bottle,** calabacino, güiro.—**bottle c.,** calabaza vinatera.

calaboose [kǽlabus], *s.* (fam.) calabozo, cárcel, *f.*

Calabrian [kaléjbrįan], *a.* y *s.* calabrés.

caladium [kaléjdįʌm], *s.* (bot.) caladio.

calamanco [kǽlamǽŋkoų], *s.* (tej.) calamaco.

calamar, calamary [kǽlamar, -mɛrį], *s.* (zool.) calamar, chipirón. *V.* SQUID.

calamine [kǽlamajn], *s.* (min.) calamina.

calamint [kǽlamįnt], *s.* (bot.) calamento.

calamitous [kalǽmįtʌs], *a.* calamitoso.

calamity [kalǽmįtį], *s.* calamidad.

calamus [kǽlamʌs], *s.* (bot.) cálamo aromático.

calash [kalǽş], *s.* calesa, carretela; capota de carruaje; capota de señora.

calcaneum [kælkéjnįʌm], *s.* (anat.) calcáneo; calcañar.

calcar [kǽlkar], *s.* (zool., bot.) espolón; (vid.) carquesa; (met.) horno de reverbero.

calcareous [kælkérįʌs], *a.* calcáreo, calizo, calero.

calceate, calced [kǽlsįejt, kælst], *a.* (igl.) calzado.

calcic [kǽlsįk], *a.* cálcico.

calciferous [kælsífɛrʌs], *a.* que contiene cal.

calcification [-fįkéjşon], *s.* calcificación; petrificación.

calcify [kǽlsįfaj], *va.* y *vn.* calcificar; hacer(se) pétreo, depositando cal, *f.*

calcimine [kǽlsįmajn]. **I.** *s.* lechada.—**coat of c.,** tendido. **II.** *va.* (alb.) dar lechada, tender.

calcinable [kælsájnabl], *a.* calcinable.

calcinate [kǽlsįnejt], *va.* = CALCINE.

calcination [-éjşon], *s.* calcinación.

calcinatory [kælsínätorį], *s.* calcinatorio.

calcine [kǽlsajn], *va.* y *vn.* calcinar(se).

calcite [kǽlsajt], *s.* (min.) calcita.

calcium [kǽlsįʌm], *s.* (quím.) calcio.—**c. carbide,** carburo de calcio.—**c. light,** luz de calcio.

calcspar [kǽlkspar], *s.* (min.) calcita, espato calizo.

calculable [kǽlkjulabl], *a.* calculable.

calculate [-lejt]. **I.** *va.* calcular, computar, tantear; preparar, disponer, proyectar; (fam.) suponer, creer. **II.** *vn.* calcular.

calculated [-įd], *pp.* de TO CALCULATE; proyectado, ideado.—**to be c. to,** tener la probabilidad de, conducir a, ser a propósito para.

calculating [-įŋ], *ger.* y *a.* de calcular; que calcula; interesado, artero.—**c. machine,** aritmómetro, máquina de calcular, calculadora.

calculation [-léjşon], *s.* cálculo, cómputo.

calculative [-lätįv], *a.* pert. al cálculo.

calculator [-lejto(r)], *s.* calculista; calculador, (máquina) calculadora; libro de cálculos hechos.

calculi [-laj], *s. pl.* de CALCULUS.

calculist [-lįst], *s.* (mat.) el que es versado en el cálculo; matemático.

calculous [-lʌs], *a.* (med.) calculoso.

calculus [-lʌs], *s.* (mat. y med.) cálculo.

Calderonian [kældɛróųnįan], *a.* calderoniano.

caldron [kóldron], *s.* caldera o caldero, paila.

Caledonian [kæledóųnįan], *a.* y *s.* caledonio, escocés.

calefacient [kælįféişent], *a.* calentador.

calefaction [-fékşon], *s.* calefacción.

calefactory [-féktorį]. **I.** *a.* calentador. **II.** *s.* (igl.) calefactorio.

calembour [kǽlembúr], *s.* equívoco, retruécano.

calendar [kǽlįndä(r)]. **I.** *s.* calendario; almanaque; lunario; lista o tabla de pleitos; orden (*f.*) del día.—**c. year,** año civil, año corriente o natural (el que principia el 1° de enero). **II.** *va.* poner en el calendario o en una lista.

calender [kǽlįndœ(r)]. **I.** *s.* calandria, satinador. **II.** *va.* aprensar, calandrar, cilindrar, satinar.—

calenderer [-œ(r)], *s.* aprensador, el que calandra.

calends [kǽlịndz], *s. pl.* calendas.—**on the Greek c.**, en las calendas griegas, nunca.

calendula [kạléndʒụlạ̈], *s.* (bot.) caléndula, maravilla.

calf [kǽf], *s.* (*pl.* CALVES [kævz]), (zool.) becerro, ternero; cervatillo, ballenato, etc.; piel (*f.*) de becerro; (anat.) pantorrilla; (fam.) bobo, mentecato.—**c.-bound**, encuadernado en piel.—**c. love**, (fam.) amor pueril.—**c.'s foot jelly**, gelatina de manos de ternera.

calfskin [-skịn], *s.* (ten.) becerrillo, piel (*f.*) de becerro, curtida.

caliber, calibre [kǽlịbœ(r)], *s.* (arti.) calibre; diámetro interior (de cañón, bala, etc.); calibre, aptitud, capacidad.—**ball c.**, vitola.—**calibrate** [-breịt], *va.* calibrar; graduar; regular; rectificar (graduaciones, dimensiones, etc.).—**calibration** [-bréịṣọn], *s.* calibración; rectificación, corrección.

calico [kǽlịkọụ], *s.* (tej.) calicó, indiana, zaraza; percal, estampado, cotonada, angaripola.

calif, califate, *s.* = CALIPH, CALIPHATE.

Californian [kælịfórnịạn]. I. *s.* y *a.* californiano, californio. II. *a.* califórnico.

caliga [kǽligạ̈], *s.* cáliga.

caliginous [kạlídʒịnʌs], *a.* caliginoso.

calipash [kǽlịpæš], *s.* substancia verdusca gelatinosa de la tortuga próxima a la concha superior.

calipee [kǽlịpị], *s.* substancia amarillenta de la tortuga próxima a la concha inferior.

caliper [kǽlịpœ(r)], *s.* (gen. *pl.*) calibrador, calibre.—**inside c.**, compás de calibres.—**outside c.**, compás de gruesos.

caliph [kéịlịf], *s.* califa, *m.*

caliphate [-eịt], *s.* califato.

calisaya [kælịséịyạ̈], *s.* (bot.) calisaya.

calisthenic [kælịsθénịk], *a.* calisténico.

calisthenics [-s], *s.* calistenia; gimnasia.

calix [kéịlịks], *s.* (igl.) = CHALICE; (bot., anat.) = CALYX.

calk, caulk [kɔk], *va.* calafatear, acollar (buques, etc.); rellenar, tapar; (mec.) apretar a martillo; hacer ramplón en la herradura; (vet.) herir con el ramplón.

calk [kælk], *va.* marcar con tiza; calcar.

calk, calkin [kók, -ịn], *s.* ramplón de herradura.

ca(u)lker [-œ(r)], *s.* calafate, calafateador.—**c.'s boy**, calafatín.

ca(u)lking [-ịŋ]. I. *s.* calafateadura, calafateo. II. *a.* de calafatear.—**c. auger**, aviador.—**c. chisel, o iron**, calador, escoplo de calafatear.—**c. hammer**, martillo de biselar.

call [kɔl]. I. *va.* llamar (*he called me*, me llamó; *he called me his friend*, me llamó su amigo; *they called him John*, lo llamaron Juan; *this is called cement*, esto se llama cemento); decir, denominar, nombrar, apellidar, titular; calificar (de), tratar (de); citar; convocar; invocar; telefonear; llamar, atraer; pronunciar, enunciar, o decir en alta voz; suponer aproximadamente, dar como valor aproximado; exigir el pago de, cobrar; pasar (lista); recibir, admitir (de abogado, etc.).

call. II. *vn.* llamar, dar voces, gritar; ir, venir (a ver a alguien), estar (en alguna parte a ver a alguien); personarse, presentarse.—**to c. a bluff**, cogerle la palabra a un baladrón.—**to c. a bond**, avisar que un bono se pagará.—**to c. a halt**, detenerse, parar; (con **on**) detener, poner fin a.—**to c. after**, llamar a.—**to c. again**, llamar de nuevo; volver.—**to c. at**, ir a; parar en; (mar.) hacer escala, tocar (en un puerto).—**to c. attention to**, llamar la atención sobre.—**to c. away**, llamar (a alguien de alguna parte); *I was called away to Boston*, me llamaron de Boston.—**to c. back**, mandar volver; revocar, retirar.—**to c. down**, hacer bajar; (fam.-regañar, reñir.—**to c. for**, requerir,

pedir; exigir, necesitar; ir o venir por.—**to c. forth**, hacer salir, sacar, poner de manifiesto; provocar, originar.—**to c. in**, hacer entrar, pedir (a uno) que entre; recoger; llamar (un médico, etc.); (com.) retirar; exigir la presentación (de bonos, etc.).—**to c. in doubt**, *o* **in question**, poner en duda.—**to c. into (being, existence**, etc.) dar el ser, producir, crear; poner en.—**to c. it a day**, (fam.) parar (en el trabajo).—**to c. it quits**, (fam.) parar (en el trabajo); dejar la reyerta, dejar de reñir o de altercar.—**to c. names**, insultar con epítetos ofensivos.—**to c. off** = TO C. AWAY; distraer; suspender; aplazar; desistir de.—**to c. on, o upon**, visitar a; pedir a, exhortar, exigir; pedir la cooperación de; invocar, apelar a; en la voz pasiva, **to be called on o upon**, tener la obligación de.—**to c. one's own**, disponer de, tener.—**to c. out**, gritar, vocear; hacer salir; llamar de afuera; poner de manifiesto; desafiar.—**to c. the roll**, pasar lista.—**to c. together**, convocar.—**to c. to account**, llamar a cuentas; censurar, impugnar, regañar.—**to c. to meeting**, citar a junta.—**to c. to memory**, *o* **to mind**, recordar.—**to c. to order**, llamar al orden; abrir la sesión, dar principio a las deliberaciones.—**to c. to the bar**, recibir de abogado; en la voz pasiva **to be called to the bar**, ser admitido como abogado, recibirse de abogado.—**to c. to the colors**, llamar al servicio militar.—**to c. to witness**, tomar por testigo.—**to c. up**, hacer subir; recordar, evocar; citar, llamar a comparecencia; poner (un proyecto) en discusión; exigir la consideración o discusión de (un proyecto, etc.); llamar por teléfono.

call, *s.* llamada; llamamiento; citación; convocatoria; reclamo de un ave; vocación; seña, señal, *f.*, aviso; silbo, señuelo, balitadera; visita; (mil.) toque, llamada; acción de pasar lista; exigencia; (com.) demanda, pedido; contrato, obligación; mandato de presentación de bonos, etc., para redimirlos; conversación o llamada telefónica.—**c. bell**, timbre de llamada.—**c. bird**, pájaro de reclamo.—**c. boy**, (teat.) traspunte; (fam.) botones.—**c. button**, botón de llamada.—**c. down**, (fam.) regaño.—**c. loan**, préstamo pagadero a solicitud.—**c. money**, dinero listo para prestar cuando se pida, o a la orden.—**c. note**, reclamo (de ave).—**at c.**, *o* **on c.**, a requerimiento, a solicitud, al pedir (apl. a obligaciones de pago).—**to make o pay a c.**, hacer una visita; (mar.) hacer escala.—**to sound a c.**, hacer llamamiento.—**within c.**, al alcance de la voz.

calla (lily) [kǽlạ̈], *s.* (bot.) cala, lirio de agua.

callable [kȯlạbl], *a.* que puede ser llamado, etc.; (com.) pagadero o amortizable a solicitud.

caller [kȯlœ(r)], *s.* llamador; visita, visitante.

calligraph [kǽlịgræf], *s.* ejemplar o muestra de caligrafía.—**calligrapher** [kạlígrạfœ(r)], *s.* calígrafo.—**calligraphic** [-grǽfịk], *a.* caligráfico.—**calligraphy** [kạlígrạfị], *s.* caligrafía.

calling [kȯlịŋ], *s.* profesión, vocación, oficio, empleo; llamamiento; acción de llamar, visitar, etc. *V.* CALL.—**c. card**, tarjeta de visita.

calliope [kælǽịopị], *s.* (mús.) especie de órgano con una serie de silbatos de vapor.

calliper, *s.* = CALIPER.

callisthenic(s, *a.* y *s.* = CALISTHENIC(S.

callosity [kælásịtị], **callousness** [kǽlʌsnịs], *s.* callo, callosidad, dureza; insensibilidad.

callous [kǽlʌs], *a.* calloso, córneo, encallecido.—**callously** [-lị], *adv.* insensiblemente, duramente.

callow [kǽlọụ], *a.* implume; joven, inexperto.

callus [kǽlʌs], *s.* callo, dureza; (cir.) callo.

calm [kám]. I. *s.* calma, serenidad, sosiego, tranquilidad; sangre fría. II. *a.* calmado, calmoso, compuesto, quieto, tranquilo, sereno, bonancible. III. *va.* tranquilizar, aquietar; apaciguar, calmar; aplacar, sosegar. IV. *vn.* (gen. con

down), calmarse, componerse, serenarse; abonanzarse.—**calmer** [-œ(r)], *s.* apaciguador, pacificador.—**calmly** [-lị], *adv.* sosegadamente. —**calmness** [-nịs], *s.* = CALM.

calmative [-ǎtịv], *a.* y *s.* calmante, sedante.— **calmy** [-ị], *a.* (poét.) tranquilo, apacible.

calomel [kǎlomɛl], *s.* calomel, calomelanos, *m. pl.*

calorescence [kælọrésçns], *s.* conversión de rayos caloríficos en rayos luminosos.

caloric [kạlórịk]. **I.** *a.* referente al calor. **II.** *s.* calórico; calor.

caloricity [kælọrísịtị], *s.* (fisiol.) caloricidad.

calorie [kǎelọrị], *s.* (fís.) caloría.

calorific [kælọrífịk], *a.* calorífico.

calorification [-kéịšọn], *s.* calorificación.

calorifics [-s], *s.* termología, ciencia del calor.

calorimeter [-ímɛtɔ(r)], *s.* calorímetro.

calorimetric [-ímɛtrịk], *a.* calorimétrico.

calorimetry [-ímɛtrị], *s.* calorimetría.

calorize [kǎelọraịz], *va.* alear superficialmente con aluminio por tratamiento térmico.

calory [kǎelọrị], *s.* = CALORIE.

calotte [kạlát], *s.* solideo; (arq.) sombrerete; cascarón o casquete.

caltha [kǎelθǎ], *s.* (bot.) calta.

caltrop [kǎeltrọp], *s.* (mil.) abrojo; (bot.) tríbulo, abrojo.

calumet [kǎelyụmɛt], *s.* calumet, pipa ceremonial de los indios de Norte América.

calumniate [kạlÁmnịeịt], *va.* y *vn.* calumniar.

calumniation [-éịšọn], *s.* calumnia.

calumniator [-eịtọ(r)], *s.* calumniador.

calumniatory [-ạtorị], **calumnious** [-ʌs], *a.* calumnioso, injurioso, difamatorio.—**calumniously** [-lị], *adv.* injuriosamente, calumniosamente.—**calumniousness** [-nịs], *s.* calumnia, maledicencia, infamación.

calumny [kǎelʌmnị], *s.* calumnia, difamación.

Calvary [kǎelvạrị], *s.* Calvario.

calve [kæv], *vn.* parir la vaca.

Calvinism [kǎelvịnịzm], *s.* calvinismo.

Calvinist [-ịst], *a.* y *s.* calvinista.—**Calvinize** [-aịz], *va.* enseñar la doctrina de Calvino.

calvities [kælvíšịịz], *s.* (med.) calvicie.

calx [kælks], *s.* (*pl.* CALXES o CALCES) (min.) cenizas o residuos; cal, *f.,* yeso.

calycle [kǎelịkl], *s.* (bot.) calículo.

calyx [kéịlịks], *s.* (bot.) cáliz, *m.;* (anat.) pelvis del riñón.

calycular [kạlíkyụlǎ(r)], *a.* (bot.) calicular.

cam [kæm], *s.* (mec.) leva, levador, cama.—**c. gear**, (aut.) engranaje del eje de levas; (mec.) distribución por levas.—**c. shaft**, (aut.) eje de levas.—**c. wheel**, rueda de (con) levas.

camaraderie [kạmǎrádɛrị], *s.* camaradería, compañerismo.

camber [kǎembœ(r)]. **I.** *s.* comba, combadura, convexidad, curvatura, peralte, alabeo. **II.** *vn.* y *va.* combar(se), arquear(se).

cambist [kǎembịst], *s.* (com.) cambista.

Cambrian [kǎembrịạn], *s.* y *a.* (geol.) cámbrico, cambriano; pert. a, o habitante del país de Gales.

cambric [kéịmbrịk], *s.* batista, holanda, cambray.

came [keịm], *pret.* de TO COME.

camel [kǎemɛl], *s.* (zool.) camello; (mar.) cajón sumergible para alzar un buque hundido; camello.

camellia [kạmílịǎ], *s.* (bot.) camelia.

camelopard [kạmílopard], *s.* (zool.) camello pardal, camelopardal, jirafa; (**C.,** astr.) Camaleopardo.

cameo [kǎemịọụ], *s.* camafeo.

camera [kǎemɛrǎ], *s.* cámara fotográfica; (arq.) sala abovedada; (anat.) cavidad; (for.) cámara particular para los jueces.—**c. lucida**, cámara lúcida.—**c. obscura**, cámara obscura.

cameral [kǎemɛrạl], *a.* relativo a una cámara, oficina o tesorería.

cameralistic [-ịstịk], *a.* perteneciente a la hacienda pública.

cameraman [kǎemɛrạmæn], *pl.* -**men**, *s.* fotógrafo (apl. esp. al de cinematógrafo y al de cámara portátil); operador cinematográfico.

camion [kǎemịọn], *s.* camión, *m.;* autocamión militar.

camisado [kæmịséịdoụ], *s.* (mil.) encamisada.

camise [kạmís], *s.* camisón o bata holgada.

camisole [kǎemịsoụl], *s.* cubrecorsé; camiseta; bata.

camlet [kǎemlịt], *s.* (tej.) c(h)amelote; barragán.

camomile [kǎemomaịl], *s.* (bot.) camomila, manzanilla.

camouflage [kǎemụflaž]. **I.** *s.* (mil.) camuflaje, disfraz (*m.*) de protección; simulación, fingimiento, engaño. **II.** *va.* (mil.) camuflar, disfrazar con camuflaje; encubrir bajo falsas apariencias.

camp [kæmp]. **I.** *s.* (mil.) campo, (a)campamento, real(es); vida o servicio militar, vida de cuartel; tienda(s) o cabaña(s) donde se vive transitoriamente en el campo; caserío, ranchería, alojamientos (como cerca de las minas); colonia (como las escolares de verano); campo, terreno (de actividad, de acción); cuerpo, agrupación, partido; división (de una confraternidad).—**chair**, silla ligera plegadiza de tijera.—**c. follower**, acompañante civil, persona que, sin ser militar, acompaña a un ejército (criado, vendedor, mujer de soldado, etc.).—**c. meeting**, reunión religiosa en el campo.—**c. stool**, catrecillo. **II.** *vn.* acampar; (gen. con out) vivir transitoriamente en tiendas. **III.** *va.* acampar, alojar.

campaign [kæmpéịn]. **I.** *s.* (mil.) campaña; (pol., etc.) campaña; propaganda. **II.** *vn.* hacer campaña o propaganda.—**campaigner** [-œ(r)], *s.* el que hace campaña; propagandista; veterano.

campanero [kæmpạnéịroụ], *s.* (orn.) campanero.

campaniform [kæmpǎenịform] = CAMPANULATE.

campanile [kæmpạnílị], *s.* campanario, campanil.

campanologist [kæmpạnálodžịst], *s.* campanólogo.

campanology [-džị], *s.* arte de fundir y de tañer las campanas; campanología.

campanula [kæmpǎenyụlǎ], *s.* (bot.) campánula.

campanulate [-leịt], *a.* (bot.) acampanado, campanudo.

campeachy, campeche [kæmpíchị], *s.* = LOGWOOD.

camper [kǎempœ(r)], **camper-out** [-áụt], *s.* persona que acampa o vive transitoriamente en tienda (toldo), choza rústica o campamento (gen. por placer).

campestral [kæmpéstrạl], *a.* campesino, campestre.

campfire [kǎempfaịr], *s.* hoguera o fogata que se enciende en el campo o en un campamento, sea por placer, sea para cocinar; reunión.—**C. girl**, niña de la organización Camp Fire Girls, que es semejante a la de las niñas exploradoras (*girl scouts*).

camphene [kǎemfin], *s.* (quím.) canfeno.

camphine [kǎemfin], *s.* aceite de trementina rectificado.

camphor [kǎemfọ(r)]. **I.** *s.* alcanfor.—**c. ball** = MOTH BALL.—**c. oil**, esencia de alcanfor.—**c. tree**, (bot.) alcanforero. **II.** *va.* alcanforar.

camphorate [-eịt]. **I.** *a.* alcanforado. **II.** *s.* canforato. **III.** *va.* alcanforar.

camphoric [kæmfárịk], *a.* (quím.) canfórico.

campus [kǎempạs], *s.* (E. U.) terreno de un colegio o universidad.

camshaft [kǎemšæft], *s.* = CAM SHAFT.

camwood [kǎemwụd], *s.* madera roja de Angola.

can [kæn]. **I.** *s.* lata, bote de lata.—**c. hooks**, (mar.) gafas.—**c. opener**, abrelatas. **II.** *vn. defectivo usado como verbo auxiliar sólo con las formas* CAN *y* COULD *en el pres. y pret. de indicativo o subjuntivo y en el condicional* poder: saber (*I can go*, puedo ir; *I can read*, sé leer; *I can but speak*, sólo puedo, o no puedo más que, hablar; *I cannot but do it*, no puedo menos de hacerlo;

could I but speak! ¡si pudiera hablar siquiera! *if
I could only write!* ¡quién supiera escribir! *I
could do it,* pod(r)ía o sab(r)ía hacerlo. III. *va.*
enlatar, envasar o conservar en latas; (fam.)
despedir (de un empleo). *V.* CANNED.

Canaanite [kéinanait], *s.* cananeo.

Canadian [kanéidian], *a.* y *s.* canadiense.

canaille [kanéil], *s.* canalla, gentuza.

canal [kanǽl]. I. *s.* canal; buzón, cacera, caz, *m.;*
(anat.) canal, conducto, meato; (arq.) estría,
media caña.—**c. rays,** (fís.) iones positivos o
un tubo de vacío con un cátodo perforado. II.
va. acanalar, canalizar.

canalage [-idż], *s.* construcción de canales; canalización; sistema (*m.*) de canales; derechos
de transporte por un canal.

canaliculate [kænalíkiuleit], *a.* acanalado, estriado.

canalization [kænalizéiśǫn], *s.* canalización.

canalize [kanǽlaiz], *va.* canalizar.

canard [kanárd], *s.* canard, embuste, filfa; (aer.)
aeroplano de mando delantero, de motor propulsor.

canary [kanéri], *s.* (orn.) canario; color de canario; vino de Canarias.—**c. seed,** alpiste,
triguera.

cancan [kǽnkæn], *s.* cancán (baile).

cancel [kǽnsel]. I. *va.* cancelar, revocar, rescindir; tachar, borrar; invalidar, anular; (mat.)
suprimir. II. *s.* (impr. y enc.) supresión; (mús.)
becuadro.

cancellate [-eit], *a.* reticular, celular, poroso.

cancellation [-éiśǫn], *s.* cancelación, rescisión;
retículo; (mat.) supresión de factores comunes.

cancer [kǽnsœ(r)], *s.* (med.) cáncer, cancro;
(astr., C.) Cáncer.

cancerate [-eit], *vn.* cancerarse.

canceration [-éiśǫn], *s.* principio o formación de
cáncer.—**cancerism** [-izm], *s.* (med.) cancerismo.—**cancerous** [-ʌs], *a.* canceroso.—**can-
cerousness** [-nis], *s.* cancerismo, calidad de
canceroso.

cancriform [kǽnkrifǫrm], *a.* cancriforme, cancroideo.

cancroid [kǽnkroid]. I. *s.* (med.) cancroide;
cancro. II. *a.* cancroideo.

candelabrum [kændeléibrʌm], *s.* candelabro.

candent [kǽndent], *a.* candente.

candescence [kændésens], *s.* candencia.

candid [kǽndid], *a.* cándido, candoroso, sincero.

candidacy [kǽndidasi], **candidature** [-dachur],
s. candidatura.

candidate [-deit], *s.* candidato, pretendiente.

candidly [kǽndidli], *adv.* cándidamente, candorosamente, ingenuamente.—**candidness** [-nis],
s. candidez, ingenuidad, sinceridad.

candied [kǽndid], *a.* confitado, almibarado, garapiñado, escarchado.

candle [kǽndl]. I. *s.* vela, bujía, candela; (fís.)
bujía, unidad lumínica.—**c. drippings,** moco.
—**c. end,** cabo de vela.—**c. extinguisher,**
matacandelas.—**c. foot,** (fís.) bujía-pie; *V.*
FOOT CANDLE.—**c. grease,** sebo.—**c. hour,**
bujía-hora.—**c. power,** intensidad de la luz, o
potencia lumínica, expresada en bujías.—**c.
snuff,** pabilo.—**c. snuffer,** despabilador.—**not
to hold a c. to someone,** (fam.) no llegar a la
suela del zapato de uno.—**the game is not
worth the c.,** no vale la pena.—**to hold a c.
to,** comparar una persona o cosa con otra. II.
va. probar (huevos, etc.) al trasluz.

candleberry [-beri], *s.* (bot.) mírica cerífera,
árbol de la cera (ll. t. **c. myrtle, c. tree**);
especie de aleutina (ll. t. **candlenut tree**).

candleholder [-hǫuldœ(r)], *s.* portavela, candelero.

candlelight [-lait], *s.* luz de vela; luz artificial;
oración, entrada de la noche.

candlelighter [-laitœ(r)], *s.* encendedor de velas;
(igl.) acólito.

Candlemas [-mas], *s.* Candelaria.

candlestick [-stik], *s.* candelero, palmatoria.

candlewick [-wik], *s.* pabilo.

candor [kǽndǫ(r)], *s.* candidez, candor, sinceridad.

candy [kǽndi]. I. *s.* bombón, dulce.—**c. pull,**
(fam.) tertulia en que se hace melcocha.—**c.
shop o store,** bombonería, confitería, dulcería.
II. *va.* almibarar, confitar, garapiñar. III. *vn.*
acaramelarse.

candytuft [-tʌft], *s.* (bot.) carraspique.

cane [kéin]. I. *s.* caña; bengala; bejuco; bastón,
báculo; caña de azúcar; pezón; tallo; (tej.)
urdimbre.—**c. chair,** silla de junco.—**c. juice,**
guarapo.—**c. knife,** machete.—**c. maker o
seller,** bastonero.—**c. mill,** trapiche, ingenio
de azúcar.—**c. press,** prensa de exprimir caña.
—**c. rack o stand,** bastonera.—**c. sugar,**
azúcar de caña. II. *va.* bastonear, apalear;
poner asiento o espaldar de mimbre, bejuco,
etc.

canebrake [-breik], *s.* cañaveral.

canella [kanélä], *s.* (bot.) canela (ll. t. **c. bark**).

canephoros [kanéfǫras], *s.* canéfora.

Canicula [kaníkiulä], *s.* (astr.) Canícula, Sirio.

canicular [-(r)], *a.* canicular.

Canidæ [kǽnidi], *s. pl.* (zool.) cánidos, *m. pl.*

canine [kéinain]. I. *a.* canino, perruno.—**c. appetite,** hambre canina.—**c. tooth,** colmillo,
(diente) canino. II. *s.* perro, can; colmillo
(diente).

Canis [kéinis], *s.* (zool.) género de los cánidos;
(astr.) el can.—**C. Major,** (astr.) Can Mayor.
—**C. Minor,** Can Menor.

canister [kǽnistœ(r)], *s.* bote, frasco o lata para
té, tabaco, etc.—**c. shot,** (bote de) metralla.

canities [kaníśjiz], *s.* canicie.

canker [kǽnkœ(r)]. I. *s.* (med.) llaga gangrenosa;
úlcera en la boca; (bot.) cancro, enfermedad
de los árboles frutales. II. *vn.* gangrenarse. III.
va. gangrenar, roer, corromper; contaminar.—
cankered [-d], *a.* ulcerado; maligno, corrompido.—**cankerous** [-ʌs], *a.* gangrenoso, corrosivo.

cankerworm [-wœrm], *s.* (ent.) especie de oruga.

canna [kǽnä], *s.* (bot.) planta de las canáceas.

cannabic [kǽnæbik], *a.* cañameño, canabíneo.

Cannabis [kǽnæbis], *s.* (bot.) cáñamo.—**c.
indica,** cáñamo de la India; haxix.

Cannaceæ [kanéisji], *s. pl.* (bot.) canáceas.

cannaceous [kanéisas], *a.* (bot.) canáceo.

canned [kænd], *pp.* y *a.* en conserva, en lata(s).—
c. goods, conservas alimenticias, alimentos
enlatados.—**c. music,** (fam.) música en discos.

cannel [kǽnel], **cannel coal** [-kǫul], *s.* carbón
mate, hulla de llama brillante, rica en substancias volátiles.

canner [kǽnœ(r)], *s.* el que enlata conservas.

cannery [-i], *s.* fábrica de conservas.

cannibal [kǽnibal], *s.* caníbal, antropófago.—
cannibalism [-izm], *s.* canibalismo.

cannikin [kǽnikin], *s.* lato o vaso de metal; balde
de madera.

cannily [kǽnili], *adv.* sagazmente. (*V.* CANNY.)

cannon [kǽnǫn]. I. *s.* oreja de campana; (arti.)
cañón; (mec.) manguito, cañón, guardaeje;
(billar) carambola.—**c. ball,** (arti.) bala de
cañón.—**c. bone,** (anat.) canilla, caña.—**c.
metal,** bronce de cañón.—**c. shot,** bala de
cañón; alcance de un cañón. II. *va.* y *vn.* cañonear.

cannonade [-éid]. I. *va.* cañonear. II. *s.* cañoneo.

cannoneer [-ír], *s.* artillero.

cannonry [-ri], *s.* cañonería; cañoneo.

cannot [kǽnat], *contr.* de CAN y NOT. *V.* CAN.

cannula [kǽniulä], *s.* (med.) cánula.

canny, cannie [kǽni], *a.* (Esco.) sagaz, prudente,
cuerdo; agradable; garboso; digno.

canoe [kanú]. I. *s.* canoa, piragua; (Méx.) chalupa. II. *va.* y *vn.* llevar o pasear en canoa.

canoeist [-ist], *s.* canoero, piragüero.

canon [kǽnǫn], *s.* canon; regla o precepto; (igl.)

canon o **cánones; canónigo**; (impr.) canon, tipo grande; (mús.) canon.—**c. law**, derecho canónigo.

canoness [-is], *s.* (igl.) canonesa.

canonic(**al** [kǎnǎnik(ąl], *a.* canónico.—**canonically** [-i], *adv.* canónicamente.

canonicals [-z], *s. pl.* hábitos eclesiásticos.

canonicate [-eit], *s.* canonjía.

canonist [kǽnǫnist], *s.* canonista.—**canonization** [-izéişǫn], *s.* canonización.—**canonize** [-ajz], *va.* canonizar.—**canonry** [-ri], **canonship** [-şip], *s.* canonjía, canonicato, prebenda.

canopied [kǽnopid], *a.* endoselado.

canopy [kǽnopi]. I. *s.* dosel, pabellón (de cama, etc.); baldaquín, palio; cielo; (arq.) cobertizo de puerta, etc.; (elec.) campana (de una guarnición, etc.).—**c. of heaven**, capa del cielo. II. *va.* endoselar.

canorous [kǎnóurʌs], *a.* canoro.

can't [kænt], (fam.) *contr.* de CANNOT.

cant [kænt]. I. *s.* canto, esquina, chaflán; desplomo, sesgo, inclinación, oblicuidad; tumbo, vaivén; tabla, toza, etc., descanteada; hipocresía, gazmoñería; jerga, jerigonza, germanía, caló; lenguaje afectado o hipócrita.—**c. hook**, garfio. *V.* PEAVEY. II. *va.* poner al sesgo o inclinar; oblicuar; ladear; arrojar, lanzar; voltear, invertir; chaflanar, descantear. III. *vn.* hablar con gazmoñería; hablar en jerga.

Cantabrian [kæntéjbriǎn], *a.* y *s.* cantábrico, cántabro.

cantaloupe [kǽntạloup], *s.* (bot.) variedad de melón.

cantalever, cantaliver, *s. V.* CANTILEVER.

cantankerous [kæntǽŋkẹrʌs], *a.* avinagrado, quisquilloso, quimerista, pendenciero.

cantata [kæntátạ], *s.* (mús.) cantata.

canted [kǽntid], *a.* oblicuo, inclinado; (arq.) chaflanado.

canteen [kæntín], *s.* cantina, taberna; cantimplora.

canter [kǽntœ(r)]. I. *s.* medio galope. II. *vn.* andar el caballo a paso largo y sentado.

canterbury [kǽntẹrbẹri], *s.* estante para música, libros, etc.—**c. bell**, (bot.) campánula.

cantharides [kænθǽridiz], *s. pl.* (farm.) cantáridas.

cantharis [kǽnθạris], *s.* (zool.) cantárida, insecto coleóptero que se emplea en la medicina como vejigatorio.

canthus [kǽnθʌs], *s.* (anat.) ángulo o rabo del ojo.

canticle [kǽntikl], *s.* cántico, canto.—*pl.* **Canticles**, el Cantar de los Cantares.

cantilever [kǽntilevœ(r)], *s.* (ing.) viga voladiza; (arq.) canecillo, modillón; voladizo; consola, soporte.—**c. bridge**, puente de contrapeso o de vigas voladizas.—**c. roof**, cubierta volada.

cantle, cantlet [kǽntl, -let], *s.* trozo, pedazo, fragmento, porción; arzón trasero de la silla.

canto [kǽntou], *s.* (mús. y poét.) canto.

canton [kǽntǫn], *s.* cantón, distrito; (blas.) cantón.—**C. crêpe**, burato.—**C. flannel**, moletón o muletón.

canton [kæntán], *va.* acantonar, acuartelar.—**cantonal** [kǽntǫnạl], *a.* cantonal.—**cantonalism** [-izm], *s.* (pol.) cantonalismo.—**cantonment** [kæntánmẹnt], *s.* (mil.) acuartelamiento, acantonamiento.

cantor [kǽntǫr], *s.* chantre.

Canuck [kạnʌ́k], *s.* y *a.* (fam.) (E. U.) canadiense; (Can.) canadiense de origen francés.

canvas [kǽnvạs], *s.* (tej.) lona; cañamazo; (pint.) lienzo, cuadro; (mar.) lona, vela, velamen.

canvasback [-bæk], *s.* (orn.) variedad de pato marino norteamericano.

canvass. I. *s.* correría en solicitud de votos, opiniones, pedidos, etc.; examen, inspección; investigación, escrutinio; encuesta. II. *va.* escudriñar, examinar; recorrer un distrito o comarca solicitando votos, pedidos, etc.

canvasser [-œ(r)], *s.* solicitador (de votos, pedidos, etc.); (E. U.) agente electoral.

cany [kéini], *a.* lleno de, o hecho de, cañas.

canyon, cañon [kǽnyǫn], *s.* garganta, congosto, desfiladero, (Am.) cañón.

canzonet [kænzǫnét], *s.* cancioncilla, copla.

caoutchouc [kạuchúk], *s.* caucho, goma elástica.

cap [kæp]. I. *s.* gorro, gorra, montera; casquete, birrete; tapa; bonete, capelo; cima, cumbre, *f.*; (arq.) capitel; (mec.) casquete, casquillo, cornilla, sombrerete, chapaleta; guardapolvo de reloj; cápsula (de botella); chapa (de brújula); (fot.) tapa (de lente); (mar.) tamburete (de palo; (aut.) tapa (de biela).—**c. and gown**, toga y bonete (traje académico).—**c. paper**, papel de estraza. El nombre se aplica además a ciertos tamaños de papel de escribir.—**c. screw**, tornillo grande sin tuerca; tornillo con ranura.—**c. of liberty**, gorro frigio.—**the c. fits**, viene de perilla.—**to make the c. fit**, darse por aludido.—**to set one's c. for**, proponerse conquistar a uno para novio.—**to put on one's thinking c.**, reflexionar con madurez. II. *va.* cubrir con gorra; poner tapa; coronar, poner cima o remate; saludar a uno; dar la última mano, acabar; sobrepujar.—**to c. the climax**, pasar del límite, para colmo (de ridiculez, sinrazón, etc.). III. *vn.* descubrirse para saludar.

capability [keipạbíliti], *s.* capacidad, idoneidad, aptitud, inteligencia.

capable [kéipạbl], *a.* capaz; apto, hábil, idóneo, competente; suficiente.—**capableness** [-nis], *s.* capacidad, idoneidad, competencia.

capacious [kạpéişʌs], *a.* capaz, espacioso.—**capaciously** [-li], *adv.* capazmente, holgadamente.—**capaciousness** [-nis], *s.* capacidad, cabida.

capacitance [kạpǽsitạns], *s.* (elec.) capacitancia.

capacitate [-teit], *va.* capacitar, habilitar, hacer capaz, autorizar.

capacitive [-itiv], *a.* (elec.) relativo a la capacidad.—**c. coupling**, (radtlg.) acoplamiento de (por) condensadores.

capacity [-iti], *s.* capacidad, cabida, espacio(sidad), porte; inteligencia, aptitud, disposición, suficiencia; alcance; facultad, poder; potencia(lidad), rendimiento; calidad, condición, carácter; empleo, destino; (mar.) tonelaje, buque.—**c. load**, carga máxima; capacidad de transporte.—**in the c. of**, en calidad de.

cap-a-pie [kæpạpí], *adv.* de pies a cabeza; (armado) de punta en blanco.

caparison [kạpǽrisǫn]. I. *s.* caparazón, paramento, gualdrapa, telliz, *m.* II. *va.* enjaezar, engualdrapar; (fam.) vestir soberbiamente.

cape [keip], *s.* (geog.) cabo, angla; capa corta, capotillo, esclavina, manteleta. *V.* CAPESKIN.

caper [kéipœ(r)]. I. *s.* cabriola, zapateta; travesura; (bot.) alcaparra, tápara.—**to cut a c.**, cabriolar; corcovear, trenzar. II. *vn.* cabriolar; triscar, chozpar; travesear.

caperbush [-buş], *s.* (bot.) alcaparro.

caperer [-œ(r)], *s.* bailarín, chozpón, saltarín.

capeskin [kéipskin], *s.* cierta piel de cabra, ovejas, etc., para guantes.

capias [kéipias], *s.* (for.) orden de arresto.

capillaceous [kæpiléişias], *a.* capilar.

capillarimeter [-ạrímetœ(r)], *s.* (fís.) capilarímetro.

capillarity [-ériti], *s.* capilaridad.

capillary [kǽpileri]. I. *a.* capilar. II. *s.* (anat.) (vaso) capilar.—**c. attraction**, capilaridad.

capilliform [kạpíliform], *a.* (bot.) capiliforme.

capital [kǽpitạl]. I. *a.* capital; principal; excelente, magnífico.—**c. letter**, (letra) mayúscula o versal.—**c. punishment**, pena capital o de muerte.—**c. ship**, acorazado mayor.—**c. sin**, pecado mortal.—**c. stock**, (com.) capital; capital nominal en acciones, o valor nominal total de las acciones (de una compañía). II. *s.* capital, *f.* (ciudad), cabecera (de un territorio o distrito); (arq.) capitel o chapitel; (com.) capital, *m.*, fondo, principal; caudal, recursos; (fort.) capital.—**to make c. (out) of,** aprovecharse de.

capitalism [-ĭzm], *s.* capitalismo.

capitalist [-ĭst], *s.* capitalista.—**capitalistic** [-ĭstĭk], *a.* capitalista (sistema, teoría, etc.).

capitalization [-ĭzéĭşǫn], *s.* capitalización; empleo de letras mayúsculas.

capitalize [-aĭz], *va.* capitalizar; principiar una palabra con mayúscula.

capitally [-ĭ], *adv.* excelente o capitalmente.

capitate [kǽpĭteĭt], *a.* (bot.) capitado.

capitation [-éĭşǫn], *s.* capitación.

capitol [kǽpĭtǫl], *s.* capitolio.

Capitoline [-aĭn], *a.* capitolino.

capitula [kapĭchulặ], *s. pl.* de CAPITULUM.

capitular [-(r)], *a.* y *s.* capitular.

capitularly [-lĭ], *adv.* capitularmente.

capitulary [-lerĭ]. I. *a.* capitular. II. *s.* capitular; ordenanza real (gen. *pl.*).

capitulate [kapĭchuleĭt], *vn.* (mil.) capitular.

capitulation [-éĭşǫn], *s.* capitulación.

capitulator [-eĭtǫ(r)], *s.* capitulante.

capitulum [-ʌm], *s.* (bot., anat.) cabezuela, capítulo; (igl.) capítula.

capon [kéĭpan], *s.* capón.

caponier(e [kæpǫnír], *s.* (fort.) caponera.

caponize [kéĭpǫnaĭz], *va.* capar (gallos).

capote [kapóut], *s.* capote; especie de bonete ajustado con cintas; (carr.) capota.

cappadine [kǽpadĭn], *s.* cadarzo.

Cappadocian [kæpadóuşĭan], *a.* y *s.* capadocio.

capparidaceous [kæparĭdéĭşʌs], *a.* (bot.) caparídeo.

Capparis [kǽparĭs], *s.* (bot.) alcaparro.

capper [kǽpœ(r)], *s.* gorrero; soldador de latas de conserva.

capping [kǽpĭŋ], *s.* (arq.) coronamiento.

capreolate [kǽprĭoleĭt], *a.* (bot.) que tiene zarcillos.

capriccio [kaprĭchĭou], *s.* (mús.) capricho.

caprice [kaprís], *s.* capricho, antojo, fantasía.

capricious [kaprĭsʌs], *a.* caprichoso, antojadizo.

capriciously [-lĭ], *adv.* caprichosamente.

capriciousness [-nĭs], *s.* calidad de caprichoso.

Capricorn [kǽprĭkǫrn], *s.* (astr.) Capricornio; (ent.) especie de escarabajo cerambícido.

caprificate [kǽprĭfĭkeĭt], *va.* (agr.) cabrahigar.

caprification [-éĭşǫn], *s.* (agr.) cabrahigadura, caprificación.

caprifig [kǽprĭfĭg], *s.* cabrahigo (árbol y fruto).

capriform [-fǫrm], *a.* capriforme.

Caprifoliaceæ [kæprĭfouliéĭşĭi], *s. pl.* (bot.) caprifoliáceas.—**caprifoliaceous** [-ŝĭʌs], *a.* caprifoliáceo.

caprine [kǽpraĭn], *a.* caprino; caprario.

capriole [kǽprĭoul], *a.* capriola; zapateta.

capsicum [kǽpsĭkʌm], *s.* (bot.) pimiento, ají.

capsize [kǽpsáĭz], *va.* y *vn.* volcar(se); trastornar, poner patas arriba; (mar.) zozobrar.

capstan [kǽpstan], *s.* cabrestante, argüe; (min.) malacate.—**c. barrel,** cuerpo de cabrestante. —**c. bars,** barras del cabrestante.—**to rig the c.,** guarnir el cabrestante.

capstone [kǽpstoun], *s.* (arq.) coronamiento.

capsular(y [kǽpsĭulặr(ĭ], *a.* capsular.

capsulate(d [-eĭt(ĭd], *a.* cerrado en forma de cápsula; encerrado en una cápsula.

capsule [kǽpsĭul], *s.* (bot.) cápsula, cajilla, celdilla, vaina; (anat. zool., quím., farm.) cápsula.

captain [kǽptĭn]. I. *s.* capitán. II. *va.* capitanear.—**captaincy** [-sĭ], **captainship** [-ŝĭp], *s.* capitanía.

caption [kǽpşǫn], *s.* encabezamiento; título; (cine) subtítulo; captura, prisión.

captious [kǽpŝʌs], *a.* quisquilloso, caviloso; capcioso.—**captiously** [-lĭ], *adv.* cavilosamente; capciosamente.—**captiousness** [-nĭs], *s.* cavilosidad; capciosidad.

captivate [kǽptĭveĭt], *va.* cautivar, captar, fascinar.

captivating [-ĭŋ], *a.* cautivador, cautivante, encantador, seductivo, atractivo.—**captivation** [-éĭşǫn], *s.* encanto, fascinación.

captive [kǽptĭv], *s.* y *a.* cautivo.—**c. balloon,** globo cautivo o de observación atado a tierra.

captivity [kǽptĭvĭtĭ], *s.* cautiverio o cautividad, prisión; obsesión, fascinación.

captor [kǽptǫ(r)], *s.* apresador, aprehensor.

capture [kǽpchǔ(r)]. I. *s.* captura, apresamiento, aprehensión, prisión; captación; (mil.) toma; presa, botín. II. *va.* capturar, apresar, prender; (mil.) tomar; (mar.) detener.

capturer [-œ(r)], *s.* *V.* CAPTOR. (Am.) captor.

capuche [kapúŝ], *s.* capucha, capucho.

capuchin [kǽpĭuchĭn], *s.* monje capuchino; capuchón o capotillo con capucha; (orn.) paloma copetuda; (zool.) mono capuchino, cébido o sapajú; **C.,** (monje) capuchino, (monja) capuchina.

capucin [kǽpĭusĭn], *s.* color anaranjado; (bot.) capuchina.

capybara [kæpĭbárặ], *s.* (zool.) capibara, ca(r)-pincho, capiguara.

car [kar], *s.* coche; automóvil; tranvía; carro, carreta; coche, vagón, furgón (de f. c.); barquilla (de globo); camarín o caja (de ascensor).

carabao [karặbáou], *s.* (zool.) carabao.

Carabidae [karébĭdĭ], *s. pl.* (ent.) carábidos.

carabineer [kærặbĭnír], *s.* (mil.) carabinero.

caracal [kǽrakæl], *s.* (zool.) caracal.

carack [kǽræk], *s.* (mar.) carraca.

caracara [karặkárặ], *s.* (orn.) caracará.

caracole [kǽrakoul]. I. *s.* escalera de caracol; (equit.) caracoleo. II. *vn.* caracolear.

caracul [kǽrakụl], *s.* caracul, astracán (piel).

carafe [karéf], *s.* garrafa.

caramel [kǽramel], *s.* caramelo; azúcar quemado; dulce de azúcar, leche, mantequilla, etc.

caramelization [-ĭzéĭşǫn], *s.* caramelización.

caramelize [-aĭz], *va.* caramelizar, acaramelar.

carapace [kǽrặpeĭs], *s.* carapacho, concha, coraza.

carat [kǽrặt], *s.* (joy.) quilate; silicua (peso).

caravan [kǽravẹn], *s.* caravana; cáfila.

caravaneer [-ír], *s.* caravanero.

caravansary [-vǽnsặrĭ], *s.* caravanera, caravasar, caravanseray; posada grande.

caravel [kǽravẹl], *s.* (mar.) carabela.

caraway (seed) [kǽrặweĭ sĭd], *s.* (bot.) alcaravea, carvi.

carbamid(e [karbémaĭd], *s.* (quím.) carbamida, urea.

carbarn [kárbarn], *s.* cochera de tranvías.

carbid(e [kárbaĭd], *s.* (quím.) carburo.

carbine [kárbaĭn], *s.* carabina.—**carbineer** [karbĭnír], *s.* (mil.) carabinero.

carbinol [kárbĭnoul], *s.* (quím.) carbinol.

carbo [kárbou], *s.* residuo carbonoso de destilación.

carbohydrate [-háĭdreĭt], *s.* (quím.) hidrato de carbono.

carbolic [karbálĭk], *a.* (quím.) carbólico, fénico. —**c. acid,** carbol, fenol, ácido fénico.

carbolize [kárbolaĭz], *va.* impregnar con fenol.

carbon [kárbǫn], *s.* copia en papel carbón; (quím.) carbono; (elec.) carbón (de batería, de filamento, de lámpara de arco.)—**c. black,** negro animal o de humo.—**c. copy,** copia en papel carbón.—**c. diamond,** carbonado.—**c. dioxide,** anhídrido carbónico.—**c. light,** (elec.) lámpara de arco.—**c. monoxide,** (mon)óxido de carbono.—**c. paper,** papel carbón, usado en máquinas de escribir y en fotografía.—**c. pencil,** carbón, carboncillo.—**c. steel,** acero ordinario (no de aleación; puede llamarse acero carbono).—**c. tube,** (quím.) vaso de vidrio empleado en la determinación del carbono del acero.

carbonaceous [-éĭŝʌs], *a.* carbonoso.

carbonado [-éĭdou], *s.* carbonado, diamante negro.

Carbonarism [-áriẓm], *s.* carbonarismo.

carbonate [-eit]. I. *s.* carbonato. II. *va.* carbonatar.

carbonic [karbánik], *a.* carbónico.—**c. acid,** ácido carbónico, (impropia pero muy comúnmente) anhídrido carbónico (ll. t. **c.-acid gas**).

carboniferous [karbɒnífɡrʌs], *a.* carbonífero; (geol.—**C.**) carbonífero.

carbonite [-ait], *s.* carbonita (explosiva).

carbonization [-izéiʃɒn], *s.* carbonización, carboneo.—**carbonize** [-aiz], *va.* carbonizar.

carbonyl [-il], *s.* (quím.) carbonilo.

carborundum [karbɒrándʌm], *s.* carborundo (carburo de silicio). (Es nombre de fábrica.)

carboy [kárboi], *s.* garrafón, damajuana.

carbuncle [kárbʌŋkl], *s.* (joy.) carbúnculo o carbunclo; (med.) carbunc(l)o, avispero.

carbuncular [karbʌŋkjulä(r)], *a.* carbuncal.

carburate, carburation, carburator = CARBURET, *va.,* CARBURETION, CARBURETOR.

carburet [kárbjuret]. I. *s.* carburo. II. *va.* carburar.

carburetant [-ant], *s.* (quím.) carburante.

carbureter, carburet(t)or [-œ(r)], *s.* (m. comb. int.) carburador.

carburetion [-réʃɒn], *s.* carburación.

carburize [kárbjuraiz], *va.* carburar.

carcass, carcase [kárkəs], *s.* res muerta; armazón, *f.,* corpanchón, caparazón (de ave); esqueleto; (mar.) casco o armazón; (arti.) carcasa; (aut.) armazón o esqueleto (de neumático).

carcel [kársel], *s.* (elec.) carcel, patrón Carcel de intensidad lumínica.—**c. lamp,** lámpara Carcel.

carcinoma [karsinóumä], *s.* (med.) carcinoma, *m.,* cáncer.

carcinomatous [-tʌs], *a.* canceroso.

card [kard]. I. *s.* tarjeta, papeleta; ficha; aviso, anuncio; programa, *m.;* naipe, carta; (fam.) chusco, persona rara; cartón, cartulina; cardencha, carda; almohaza; peine.—**c. catalogue,** fichero.—**c. game,** juego de naipes.—**c. index,** índice en tarjetas, fichero.—**c. party,** tertulia de baraja, partida de juego.—**c. sharp,** fullero, tahur.—**c. table,** tapete verde, mesa de juego.—**to be in u on the cards,** ser probable; figurar en el programa.—**to have a c. up one's sleeve,** tener algo (plan, etc.) en reserva.—**to lay o put one's cards on the table,** revelar uno francamente sus designios, recursos, etc.—**to play (at) cards,** jugar a los naipes.—**to speak by the c.,** hablar con conocimiento de causa. II. *va.* cardar, carduzar; almohazar.

cardamom [kárdamɒm], *s.* (bot.) cardamomo.

Cardan joint [kárden], *s.* junta universal, articulación o junta cardánica.—**C. shaft,** eje cardánico.—**C.'s suspension,** cardán.

cardboard [kárdbɒrd], *s.* cartón, cartulina.

cardcase [kárdkeis], *s.* tarjetero.

carder [kárdœ(r)], *s.* card(uz)ador.—**c. bee,** abejorro.

cardia [kárdiä], *s.* (anat.) cardias.

cardiac [kárdiæk]. I. *a.* cardíaco; rel. al cardias o al corazón. II. *s.* cordial; (fam.) persona afecta de enfermedad cardíaca.

cardialgia [kardiéldżiä], *s.* (med.) cardialgia, acedía.

cardigan [kárdigan], *s.* chaqueta o chaleco de punto.

cardinal [kárdinal]. I. *a.* cardinal, fundamental; rojo vivo; (igl.) cardenalicio.—**c. number, point, virtue, wind,** número, punto, virtud, viento cardinal. II. *s.* (igl.) cardenal; púrpura; capa de mujer del siglo XVIII.—**c. bird,** (orn.) cardenal.—**c.'s hat,** capelo.

cardinalate [-eit], **cardinalship** [-ʃip], *s.* cardenalato, capelo.

carding [kárdiŋ], *s.* cardadura; cardón.—**c. machine,** carda mecánica.

cardiograph [kárdiogræf], *s.* cardiógrafo.

cardiography [kardiágrafi], *s.* cardiografía.

cardiology [-álodżi], *s.* cardiología, ciencia del corazón.

cardiopathy [-ápaθi], *s.* cardiopatía.

cardioscope [kárdioskoup], *s.* cardioscopio.

carditis [kardáitis], *s.* (med.) carditis.

cardmaker [kárdmeikœ(r)], *s.* fabricante de naipes o de cardas, cardero.

cardoon [kardún], *s.* (bot.) cepacaballo, cardo.

care [ker]. I. *s.* cuidado, solicitud; atención, cautela, detenimiento, mira, pulso, vigilancia; ansiedad, inquietud, zozobra; cargo, custodia; cuenta.—**(in the) c. of,** al cuidado de.—**take c.!,** ¡cuidado!, ¡mira!, ¡ojo!.—**under his c.,** a su cargo.—**without c.,** sin cuidado(s).—**to take c.,** tener cuidado.—**to take c. of,** cuidar de, correr con, guardar, encargarse de, mirar por.—**to take c. not to,** guardarse de. II. *vn.* tener cuidado, ansiedad o interés por algo o alguien; querer, tener ganas de (hacer algo); importarle a uno; estimar, apreciar, hacer caso.—**to c. for,** cuidar de; desear, gustar; interesarse en; gustarle a uno (una cosa, una persona).

careen [karín]. I. *va.* (mar.) carenar. II. *vn.* echarse de costado, dar a la banda. III. *s.* carena(dura).—**careenage** [-idż], *s.* (mar.) carenero; gasto de carena.—**careening** [-iŋ], *s.* (mar.) carena(dura).—**c. gear,** aparejo de carenar.—**c. wharf,** carenero, despalmador.

career [karír]. I. *s.* carrera, curso, corrida; profesión.—**c. diplomat,** diplomático profesional. II. *vn.* correr a carrera tendida.

carefree [kérfri], *a.* sin cuidados, alegre.

careful [kérful], *a.* cuidadoso; curioso, esmerado; solícito; cauteloso, prudente.—**to be c.,** tener cuidado.—**carefully** [-i], *adv.* cuidadosamente, detenidamente, esmeradamente.—**carefulness** [-nis], *s.* cuidado, cautela, atención.

careless [kérlis], *a.* descuidado, negligente, indiferente, remiso; desatento, desaplicado, atolondrado; inconsiderado.—**to be c.,** descuidar.—**carelessly** [-li], *adv.* descuidadamente, negligentemente; sin esmero.—**carelessness** [-nis], *s.* descuido, negligencia, indiferencia; desaseo, desaliño.

caress [karés]. I. *va.* acariciar, halagar, mimar. II. *s.* caricia, halago, mimo, cariño.

caresser [-œ(r)], *s.* acariciador.

caressing [-iŋ], *a.* acariciador, mimador.

caressingly [-li], *adv.* cariñosamente, con mimo.

caret [kéret], *s.* (impr.) signo de intercalación (∧).

caretaker [kérteikœ(r)], *s.* curador, celador, guardián, vigilante, velador, casero.

careworn [kérwɒrn], *a.* cargado de cuidados; agobiado de inquietud; trasojado.

carfare [kárfer], *s.* dinero para el tranvía, autobús, etc.; pequeña cantidad de dinero.

cargo [kárgou], *s.* (com.) carga(zón), *f.,* cargamento; consignación.—**c. boat,** barco de carga.

Carib [kérib], **Caribbean** [kæribíän], *s.* y *a.* caribe.—**C. sea,** mar Caribe o de las Antillas.

caribou [kéribu], *s.* (zool.) caribú.

caricatural [kérikachurạl], *a.* caricatural, caricaturesco.—**caricature** [kérikachur]. I. *s.* caricatura. II. *va.* caricaturar, caricaturizar.—**caricaturist** [-ist], *s.* caricaturista.

caries [kériiz], **cariosity** [kęriásiti], *s.* (med.) caries, *f.;* cariadura (del hueso); neguijón (de los dientes).

carillon [kérilan], *s.* carillón, conjunto de campanas acordadas; toque o sonido de ellas.

carinate [kérineit], *a.* aquillado.

carious [kériʌs], *a.* (med.) cariado.—**to grow c.,** cariarse.—**cariousness** [-nis], *s.* (med.) caries, *f.*

carking [kárkiŋ], *a.* penoso, inquietante.

carl [karl], *s.* (ant.) patán, rústico; villano.

carline thistle [kárlin θisl], *s.* (bot.) carlina.

Carlism [kárlizm], *s.* carlismo.

Carlist [-ist], *a.* y *s.* carlista.

carload [kárloud], *s.* galerada; (f. c.) vagonada, furgón entero.

Carlovingian [karlovíndżian], *a.* y *s.* carlovingio.

carmagnole [karmanyóчl], *s.* carmañola.
carman [kármæn], *s.* empleado de tranvía; carretero, carromatero, carretonero.
Carmelite [kármεlait]. **I.** *s.* carmelita (monje o monja). **II.** *a.* carmelito, carmelitano.—**C. order,** Carmen.
carminative [karmínativ], *a. y s.* (med.) carminativo.
carmine [kármin], *s.* carmín, carmesí, albín.
carminic [karmínik], *a.* carmínico.
carminite [kárminait], *s.* (min.) carminita.
carnage [kárnidž], *s.* carnicería, matanza.
carnal [kárnal], *a.* carnal; lascivo, sensual.—**c. knowledge** o **union,** coito, cópula; comercio sexual.
carnality [karnǽliti], *s.* carnalidad, lujuria, concupiscencia, lascivia.
carnalize [kárnalaiz], *va.* excitar la sensualidad.
carnally [kárnali], *adv.* carnalmente.
carnation [karnéišon], *s.* (pint.) encarnación, encarnado; (bot.) clavel doble, clavellina.
carnelian [karnílyan], *s.* (min.) cornalina, carniola.
carneous [kárnias], *a.* carnoso; encarnado.
carnification [karnifikéišon], *s.* carnificación.
carnify [kárnifai], *va. y vn.* criar carne, carnificarse.
carnine [kárnain], *s.* (quím.) carnina.
carnival [kárnival], *s.* carnaval, carnestolendas, *f. pl.*; holgorio.
Carnivora [karnívorä], *s. pl.* (zool.) carnívoros.
carnivorous [-ʌs], *a.* carnívoro, carnicero.
carnose [kárnoчs], *a.* carnoso, carnudo.
carnosity [karnásiti], *s.* carnosidad.
carnotite [kárnotait], *s.* (min.) carnotita.
carob [kærob], *s.* (bot.) algarrobo.—**c. bean,** algarroba, garrofa.
caroche [karóчch], *s.* carroza.
carol [kærol]. **I.** *s.* villancico; canto alegre. **II.** *va.* cantar villancicos. **III.** *vn.* gorjear.
carol(l)er [-œ(r)], *s.* el que canta villancicos.
Carolingian [kærolíndžian], *a. y s.* carolingio.
Carolinian [kærolínian], *a. y s.* natural de la Carolina.
carom [kærom]. **I.** *s.* carambola. **II.** *vn.* carambolear, hacer carambola.
carotid(al [karátid(al], *a. y s.* (anat.) carótida.
carousal [karáчzal], *s.* festín, holgorio, parranda, francachela, (fam.) juerga, jarana.
carouse [karáчz]. **I.** *vn.* jaranear, andar de parranda; (fam.) correrla; embriagarse. **II.** *s.* parranda, francachela.
carousel, *s.* = CARROUSEL.
carouser [-œ(r)], *s.* bebedor, jaranero.
carp [karp]. **I.** *s.* (ict.) carpa. **II.** *vn.* censurar, criticar, vituperar.
carpal [kárpal]. **I.** *a.* (anat.) carpiano. **II.** *s.* hueso carpiano.
carpel [kárpεl], *s.* (bot.) carpelo.
carpellary [-εri], *a.* (bot.) carpelar.
carpenter [kárpεntœ(r)]. **I.** *s.* carpintero; (mar.) carpintero de ribera; (min.) ademador.—**c. bee,** abeja carpintera.—**c. bird,** (pájaro) carpintero.—**c.('s) scene,** (teat.) sala corta.—**c.'s shop,** carpintería.—**c.'s square,** cartabón. **II.** *vn.* carpintear.—**carpentry** [-tri], *s.* carpintería; obra de carpintero.
carper [kárpœ(r)], *s.* criticón; reparón, reparador.
carpet [kárpit]. **I.** *s.* alfombra, tapete.—**c. beetle,** (ent.) antreno.—**c. knight,** soldado de gabinete o de parada.—**c. maker,** alfombrero.—**c. sweeper,** barredera doméstica, abarredera de alfombras.—**to be on the c.,** estar sobre el tapete; (fam.) ser llamado a capítulo. **II.** *va.* alfombrar, entapizar.
carpetbag [-bæg]. **I.** *s.* saco de noche. **II.** *a.* (fam.) explotador; aventurero.
carpetbagger [-œ(r)], *s.* explotador; aventurero; (hist. E. U.) politicastro del norte que tras la

guerra de secesión iban al sur a intrigar y enriquecerse.
carpeting [-iŋ], *s.* tela o tejido para alfombras; alfombrado.
carpincho [karpínchoч], *s.* (zool.) capibara, carpincho.
carping [kárpiŋ], *a.* caviloso, criticón, reparón.
carpingly [-li], *adv.* cavilosamente, mordazmente.
carpology [karpálodži], *s.* (bot.) carpología.
carpophagous [karpáfagas], *a.* frugívoro.
carpophore [kárpofoчr], *s.* (bot.) carpóforo.
carpus [kárpʌs], *s.* (anat.) carpo, muñeca.
carrack [kærak], *s.* (mar.) carraca; galeón.
carrag(h)een [kæragin], *s.* musgo de Irlanda.
carriage [kæridž], *s.* carruaje, coche, carroza; vehículo; (Ingl. f. c.) vagón; cochecillo de niño; (arti.) cureña; (mec.) carro, carretilla, soporte; (com.) conducción, porte, acarreo, transporte; presencia, continente, (com)porte, aire de una persona; (aer.) barquilla; tren de aterrizaje.—**c. bolt,** perno de coche.—**c. door,** portezuela.—**c. and four,** carroza de cuatro caballos.—**c. free,** franco de porte.—**c. horse,** caballo de tiro.—**c. maker,** carrocero.—**c. paid,** porte pagado.—**c. pole,** pértigo.—**c. porch,** puerta cochera.—**c. shop,** carrocería.
carrier [kærioe(r)], *s.* (trans)portador; acarreador, trajinante, faquín; arriero, ordinario, carretero, cargador o conductor de carga o mercaderías; empresa de transporte (gen. se aplica a los ferrocarriles); mensajero, mandadero; (aer.) portaaviones, portavión, *m.;* (mec.) guiadera; portacaja; soporte; (med.) portador de gérmenes; agente transmisor o de propagación (de una enfermedad); (rad.) onda de transmisión.—**c. pigeon,** paloma mensajera o correo.
carrion [kærion]. **I.** *s.* carroña. **II.** *a.* que se alimenta de carroña; mortecino; podrido; asqueroso; vil.—**c. crow,** cuervo negro europeo.—**c. buzzard,** caracará, *m.;* aura, gallinazo.
carronade [kæronéid], *s.* (arti.) carronada.
carrot [kærot], *s.* (bot.) zanahoria, azenoria.
carroty [-i], *a.* amarillo rojizo; rufo, pelirrojo.
carrousel [kæruzél], *s.* tiovivo; justa, torneo.
carry [kæri], *va.* (*pret. y pp.* CARRIED) llevar, conducir, transportar, acarrear; cargar, ajobar; traer, llevar encima, tener consigo; contener; incluir, comprender; llevar aparejado; implicar, entrañar; dirigir, impulsar, mover, influir; aprobar (una moción); ganar (las elecciones); tomar, conquistar, conseguir, lograr; mantener; aguantar, sostener; portarse, comportarse; (com.) tener existencia o surtido de.—**to c. about,** llevar de un lado a otro, de acá para acullá.—**to c. all,** o **everything, before one,** vencer toda dificultad.—**to c. along,** llevarse consigo.—**to c. arms,** llevar armas; ser militar; cuadrarse.—**c. away,** llevar(se), quitar; arrebatar (de la vida); seducir, encantar, entusiasmar.—**to c. away the palm,** llevarse la palma, triunfar.—**to c. back,** (de)volver.—**to c. coals to Newcastle,** llevar hierro a Vizcaya, llevar leña al monte, perder el tiempo.—**to c. forward,** llevar, pasar ("suma y sigue," en las cuentas).—**to c. into effect,** realizar, ejecutar, llevar a cabo.—**to c. it,** ganar, quedar victorioso.—**to c. off,** alzar, llevar(se), entrar; ganar.—**to c. on,** continuar; ocuparse en, practicar, ejercer.—**to c. one's point,** ganar, triunfar; salirse uno con la suya.—**to c. out,** llevar a cabo, cumplir, desempeñar, verificar, realizar; llevarse, retirar, sacar; llevar hasta el fin.—**to c. over,** ganar (a una persona); traspasar; trasladar, pasar a otra cuenta o página; guardar, tener para más tarde; aplazar, dar plazo a.—**to c. the day,** salir adelante, ganar, triunfar.—**to c. the prize,** etc., ganar el premio, etc.—**to c. through,** llevar a cabo; tramitar; sostener, ayudar hasta el fin.—**to c. up,** llevar arriba; erigir.—**to c. up to,** ajustar

o amoldar a.—**to c. weight,** ser de peso o de influencia.

carry, *vn.* portear (como oficio); alcanzar, llegar, tener alcance (voz, tiro, etc.).—**to c. on,** continuar, funcionar, permanecer en el puesto o en la tarea; (fam.) travesear, comportarse escandalosamente.—**to c. over,** continuar, persistir, durar.—**to c. through,** conducir a algo, ser eficaz.

carry, *s.* transporte de una canoa en hombros; trecho no navegable de un río; alcance (de arma de fuego, pelota, etc.); (Esco.) celaje.

carryall [-ol], *s.* (carr.) faetón, góndola; maleta de gran cabida.

carry-over [-oцvœ(r)], *s.* sobrante; reserva; (contabilidad) suma que viene o pasa de la cuenta o página anterior; saldo anterior.

cart [kárt]. I. *s.* carro, carromato, carreta, carretón; tílburi; carretilla (de mano).—**c. horse,** caballo de tiro.—**c. load,** carretada.—**c. road,** camino carretero.—**c. rut,** carril, rodada.—**to put the c. before the horse,** trastrocar; empezar la casa por el tejado.—**to turn c. wheels,** voltear sobre manos y pies. II. *va.* carretear, acarrear. III. *vn.* usar carretas o carros.

cartage [-idž], *s.* carretaje, acarreamiento, acarreo, conducción, porteo, transporte.

carte [kart], *s.* tarjeta; papeleta; lista de platos; carta, mapa, *m.;* (esgr.) cuarta.—**a la c.,** a la carta.—**c. blanche,** carta blanca.—**c. de visite,** tarjeta de visita; (fot.) retrato de tarjeta.

cartel [kartél], *s.* cartel (para cambio de prisioneros; de desafío); (e. p.) sindicato o asociación comercial, trust; (pol.) convenio, acuerdo.—**cartelize** [kártęlaiz], *va.* y *vn.* incorporar(se) en un sindicato.

carter [kártœ(r)], *s.* carretero, carromatero.

Cartesian [kartížan], *s.* y *a.* cartesiano.—**C. devil, diver,** o **imp,** (fís.) diablillo cartesiano.

Cartesianism [-izm], *s.* cartesianismo.

cartful [kártfµl], *s.* carretada.

Carthaginian [karθadžíniąn], *a.* y *s.* cartaginés.

carthamus [kárθamʌs], *s.* (bot.) cártamo, alazor.

Carthusian [karθjúžan], *a.* y *s.* (igl.) cartujo, cartujano.—**C. order,** Cartuja.

cartilage [kártilidž], *s.* (anat.) cartílago, ternilla.

cartilaginous [-édžinʌs], *a.* cartilaginoso.

cartman [kártmæn], *s.* carretero.

cartogram [kártogræm], *s.* cuadro gráfico estadístico comparativo.

cartographer [kartágrafœ(r)], *s.* cartógrafo.—**cartography** [kartágrafi], *s.* cartografía.

cartographic(al [kartográfik(ąl], *a.* cartográfico.

cartomancy [kártomænsi], *s.* cartomancia.

carton [kárton], *s.* (caja de) cartón fino.

cartoon [kartún]. I. *s.* (pint.) cartón, boceto; caricatura. II. *va.* y *vn.* caricaturizar, hacer caricaturas; bosquejar.—**cartoonist** [-ist], *s.* caricaturista.

cartouch(e [kartúš], *s.* (arq.) cartela; (mil.) cartucho; cartuchera.

cartridge [kártridž], *s.* (armas) cápsula; cartucho.—**c. bag,** (arti.) saquete.—**c. belt,** canana, cartuchera.—**c. box,** cartuchera; caja de municiones.—**c. case,** cápsula de proyectil.—**c. fuse,** (elec.) tapón fusible.—**c. pouch,** cartuchera.—**c. shell,** = **c. case.**

cartulary [kárchµleri], *s.* cartulario.

cartway [kártwei], *s.* carril, camino carretero.

cartwright [kártrait], *s.* carretero.

caruncle [kérʌŋkl], *s.* carúncula, carnecilla.

caruncular [kærʌŋkiulǝ(r)], *a.* caruncular, parecido a una carúncula.—**carunculate** [-leit], *a.* carunculado, que tiene carúnculas.

carve [karv], *va.* y *vn.* esculpir; cincelar, tallar; labrar; entallar, grabar; cortar, trinchar carne.—**carved work,** entallado, obra de talla, escultura.

carvel [kárvęl], *s.* (mar.) carabela.—**c.-built,** (mar.) con juntas a tope.—**c. joint,** junta a tope.

carven [kárvęn], *a.* (poét.) esculpido, entallado, grabado.

carver [kárvœ(r)], *s.* escultor; grabador, entallador, tallista; trinchador; trinchante.

carving [kárviŋ], *s.* escultura, entalladura, talla; arte de trinchar.—**c. knife,** trinchante.—**c. table,** trinchero.

caryatid [kærję̃tid], *s.* (arq.) cariátide, *f.*

caryophyllaceous [kærjofiléiṣiąs], *a.* (bot.) cariofileo.

caryophyllin [-fílin], *s.* (quím.) cariofilina.

caryopsis [kærjápsis], *s.* (bot.) cariópside, *f.*

casal [kéisąl], *a.* (gram.) perteneciente a los casos.

cascabel [kǽskabel], *s.* (arti.) cascabel.

cascade [kæskéid]. I. *s.* cascada, catarata.—**in c.,** (elec.) en cascada. II. *vn.,* caer en forma de cascada.

cascara sagrada [kæskérǝ sągrádą], *s.* (farm.) cáscara sagrada.

cascarilla [kæskarílą], *s.* (bot.) cascarillo (arbusto); (farm.) cascarilla.

case [keis]. I. *s.* caso; ejemplo; asunto; acontecimiento, suceso; condición, estado, situación; argumento; (for.) causa, acción, pleito, proceso; (med.) caso; (gram.) caso; caja, estuche; vaina, funda, cubierta; caja de reloj, guardapolvo; (com.) cajón, caja de mercancías; (mec.) chaqueta, camisa, manguito, forro, cubierta; (carp.) cerco o marco (de ventana, puerta, etc.), bastidor; (impr.) caja; (fam.) persona rara o difícil.—**c. knife,** cuchillo de mesa; cuchillo provisto de vaina.—**c. law,** ley de precedentes, o fundada en decisiones y sentencias.—**c. of pistols** = BRACE OF PISTOLS.—**c. shot,** metralla.—**c. system,** sistema inductivo de enseñar el derecho basado en casos particulares más bien que en libros de texto.—**a c. in point,** ejemplo a la mano.—**in c.,** caso (de) que, por si (acaso).—**in any c.,** en todo caso, de todos modos, sea como fuere.—**in such a c.,** en tal caso.—**in the c. of,** en cuanto a, respecto a.—**such being the c.,** siendo así.—**the c. in point,** el caso en cuestión.—**to make out one's c.,** demostrar lo que uno se proponía. II. *va.* embalar, encajonar; enfundar; cubrir.

caseate [kéisieit]. I. *s.* (quím.) caseato. II. *vn.* caseificar(se).—**caseation** [-éiṣǫn], *s.* caseación, caseificación; (med.) degeneración en materia parecida al queso.

casefy [kéisifai], *va.* y *vn.* caseificar(se).

caseharden [kéishárdęn], *va.* (met.) templar superficialmente.—**casehardening** [-iŋ], *s.* temple superficial.

caseic [kéisiik o kasíik], *a.* (quím.) caseico.

casein [kéisiin], *s.* caseína.

casemate [kéismeit], *s.* (fort.) casamata.

casemated [-id], *a.* acasamatado.

casement [kéismęnt], *s.* puerta ventana; ventano; cubierta, caja.

caseous [kéisiʌs], *a.* caseoso, quesoso.

caserne [kązérn], *s.* (mil.) caserna, cuartel.

cash [kǽš]. I. *s.* dinero contante, numerario, efectivo; pago al contado; (com.) caja.—**c. account,** cuenta de caja.—**c. and carry,** pago al contado con transporte por el comprador.—**c. box,** caja.—**c. down,** dinero en mano; al contado, (fam.) a toca teja.—**c. keeper,** cajero.—**c. on hand,** (metálico) en caja.—**c. payment,** pago al contado.—**c. register,** caja registradora (de dinero).—**c. store,** tienda de ventas al contado.—**for c.,** al contado.—**in c.,** en efectivo.—**c. balance,** saldo (en) efectivo.—**c. on delivery** (C.O.D.), entrega contra reembolso, pago contra entrega. II. *adv.* al contado. III. *va.* cambiar, cobrar, hacer efectivo (un cheque, etc.).—**to c. in** (a veces con on), cambiar por dinero, hacer efectivo; sacar provecho (de).

cashbook [-bµk], *s.* libro de caja.

cashew, cashew nut [kǽʃǐu], s. (bot.) anacardo, (Am.) marañón, acajú, merey, pajuil.

cashier [kæʃír]. I. s. cajero, contador.—**c.'s check,** cheque de caja.—**c.'s office,** caja; contaduría. II. va. destituir; (mil.) desaforar, degradar.

cashmere [kǽʃmir], s. (tej.) casimir, cachemir(a).

cashoo [kaʃú], s. = CATECHU.

casing [kéiꞎiŋ], s. camisa, cubierta, funda, enfundadura, envoltura, forro; marco de ventana o puerta; (aut.) cubierta (de neumático); entubado de retención (en los pozos de petróleo, etc.).—pl. **casings,** tripas para embutidos.

casino [kaꞎínou], s. casino, círculo; quinta de recreo; casino (juego de naipes).

cask [kæsk]. I. s. pipa, barril, tonel, barrica, bocoy; cuba; casco; tina de tintoreras; contenido de una pipa, etc. II. va. entonelar, envasar, encubar.

casket [kǽskit], s. arquilla, cofrecito, escriño, estuche, joyelero; (E. U.) ataúd, m., féretro.

casque [kæsk], s. casco, almete, capacete.

cassation [kæséiꞎǫn], s. (for.) casación, anulación, revocación, abrogación.

cassava [kaꞎávǎ], s. (bot.) mandioca, (Am.) yuca; harina de la raíz de estas plantas.—**c. bread,** cazabe, casabe.

casserole [kǽꞎeroul], s. cacerola; (coc.) plato cocido en cacerola; (quím.) platillo con mango.

cassette [kæsét], s. cajita; (fot.) chasis o chasí.

cassia [kǽꞎǎ], s. (bot.) casia; cañafístula.

cassimere [kǽꞎimir], s. (tej.) casimir.

cassiterite [kæsítěrait], s. (min.) casiterita.

cassock [kǽꞎǫk], s. sotana, balandrán, casacón.

cassowary [kǽꞎoweri], s. (orn.) casuario.

cast [kæst], va. (pret. y pp. CAST) tirar, arrojar, botar, disparar, emitir, lanzar; soltar, despedir; echar, verter, derramar; tumbar, derribar; echar, bajar (el ancla); tirar (dados), echar (suertes); mudar (la piel); perder (pelo, dientes, etc.); desechar; volver, dirigir (la mirada o el pensamiento); colar, fundir, vaciar, moldear (metales); electrotipar, estereotipar; calcular; imputar, echar la culpa; (teat.) repartir (papeles de un drama); (for.) ganar un pleito; (agr.) aventar; dar (un voto); echar, depositar (una balota, etc.).—**to c. a glance** o **an eye over,** echar una ojeada a.—**to c. a shoe,** desherrarse, perder una herradura.—**to c. aside,** desechar. —**to c. away,** desechar, abandonar; echar a pique (un buque) (**to be c. away,** naufragar).—**to c. down,** abatir, derribar; descorazonar. —**to c. forth,** exhalar, despedir.—**to c. headlong,** precipitar.—**to c. in one's teeth,** echar en cara.—**to c. in the rôle of,** adjudicar el papel de.—**to c. lots,** echar suertes, sortear.— **to c. off,** abandonar, soltar; mudar (la pluma, etc.); descartar; desechar.—**to c. out,** echar fuera, arrojar.—**to c. up,** calcular, sumar (cuentas).

cast, vn. hacerse al molde; calcular, sumar; pronosticar, suponer; alabearse; pescar con caña, especialmente con cebo artificial.—**to c. about,** buscar medios, o trazas.—**to c. anchor,** anclar, dar fondo, fondear.—**to c. off,** (mar.) desamarrar, largar.

cast (pp. de TO CAST), a. vaciado, fundido.—**c. iron,** hierro colado, fundición.—**c.-iron,** a. de hierro colado; rígido; inflexible.—**c. net,** atarraya.—**c.-off,** a. descartado, (des)echado, de desecho (ropa, etc.). s. persona o cosa que no se necesita; (imp.) cálculo de espacio.— **c. steel,** acero colado, acero fundido.

cast, s. echada, lanzamiento, tiro, tirada; distancia, alcance; lo que se tira; fundición, pieza fundida o vaciada; plancha estereotipada; molde, forma; mascarilla; estampa, aspecto, formación; tinte, tono, matiz, m.; tendencia; (b. a.) impronta; (teat.) reparto de papeles; conjunto de actores en un drama o compañía.

elenco.—**c. maker,** moldeador.—**a c. of the eye,** defecto en la mirada, ligero estrabismo.

castanets [kæstanéts], s. pl. castañuelas, castañetas, palillos, (ant.) crótalos.

castaway [kǽstawei]. I. s. náufrago; réprobo, malhechor; proscrito. II. a. desechado, abandonado; perdido.

caste [kæst], s. casta; clase (f.) social.—**to lose c.,** desprestigiarse.

castellan [kǽstelan], s. castellán, castellano.

castellany [-ǐ], s. castellanía.

castellated [kǽstelějtid], a. encastillado.

caster [kǽstœ(r)], s. tirador, echador; adivino; calculador; fundidor, vaciador, moldeador.

caster, castor, s. rued(ecill)a o rodaja de mueble; ampolleta; pl. aceiteras, vinagreras, angarillas, convoy de mesa, taller.

castigate [kǽstigejt], va. castigar; corregir.

castigation [-éiꞎǫn], s. castigo, castigación.

castigator [-ǫ(r)], s. castigador.

castigatory [kǽstigatori], a. penal, correctivo.

Castile soap [kæstíl soup], s. jabón de Castilla.

Castilian [kæstíliǎn], s. y a. castellano.

casting [kǽstiŋ]. I. V. CAST (v. y s.). fundición, vaciado; pieza fundida o vaciada; sorteo (de suertes); (teat.) distribución (de papeles); arreglo; plan, modelo. II. a.—**c. line,** sedal, tanza.—**c. net,** atarraya, esparavel.—**c. vote,** voto decisivo o de calidad.

castle [kǽsl]. I. s. castillo; alcázar, palacio; torre (f.) o roque de ajedrez.—**c. builder,** proyectista imaginario, visionario.—**c. in the air** o **in Spain,** castillo en el aire. II. vn. enrocar (ajedrez).

castled [-d], a. fortificado, encastillado.

castlet [kǽslit], s. castillejo.

castor [kǽstǫ(r)], s. V. CASTER. (zool.) castor; pelo, paño o sombrero de castor; castóreo.— (C., astr.) Cástor.—**C. and Pollux,** (mit.) fuego de Santelmo; (astr.) Astillejos.—**c. bean** [bin], **c.-oil plant,** (bot.) ricino, higuera infernal; semilla de esta planta.—**c.-oil,** aceite de ricino, carapato.

castoreum [kæstóuriam], s. castóreo.

castorin [kǽstorin], s. (quím.) castorina.

castrametation [kæstramětéiꞎǫn], s. (mil.) castrametación.

castrate [kǽstrejt], va. castrar, capar.—**castration** [-éiꞎǫn], s. capadura, castración.—**castrator** [-ǫ(r)], s. castrador, capador.

castrensian [kæstrénꞎan], a. (mil.) castrense.

casual [kǽꞎual], a. casual, fortuito, ocasional; indiferente, de paso, como de paso (a veces con fingimiento), parentético; advenedizo, extraño; (víctima) de accidente.—**casually** [-ǐ], adv. casualmente.—**casualness** [-nǐs], s. contingencia.

casualism [-ǐzm], s. casualismo.

casualist [-ǐst], s. casualista.

casualty [-tǐ], s. accidente, desastre; siniestro; víctima (de un accidente, etc.); muerte violenta; (mil.) baja; casualidad, acaso, contingencia; (for.) caso fortuito.

casuist [kǽꞎuist], s. casuísta.

casuistic(al [-ístǐk(ǎl], a. casuístico.

casuistry [-tri], s. casuística, casuísmo.

cat [kæt]. I. s. (zool.) gato, (fam.) morrongo; mujer maliciosa y chismera, (fam.) perra, (mar.) gata.—**c.-o'-nine-tails,** disciplina o azote con nueve ramales.—**c.'s-eye,** (min.) cimófana, asteria, ojo de gato.—**c. nap,** sueño ligero y corto.—**c.'s paw,** (fam.) mano (f.) de gato; el inocente que sirve de instrumento a otro, para sacarle las castañas del fuego, etc.; (mar.) ventolina; cierto nudo.—**c. tackle,** (mar.) aparejo de gata.—**cats and dogs,** (fam., com.) acciones o títulos de poco o ningún valor.—**to rain c. and d.,** llover a cántaros.—**to bell the c.,** poner el cascabel al gato. —**to let the c. out of the bag,** revelar un secreto.—**to see which way the c. will jump,**

ver qué sesgo toma un asunto. **II.** *va.* azotar con *cat-o'-nine-tails;* (mar.) izar (el ancla) a la serviola con la gata.

catabolic [kætəbálik], *a.* catabólico.—**catabolism** [kætǽbolizm], *s.* (biol.) catabolismo o metabolismo destructivo del protoplasma.

catachresis [kætəkrísis], *s.* (ret.) catacresis.

catachrestic(al [-kréstik(əl], *a.* forzado, traído por los cabellos.

cataclysm [kǽtəklizm], *s.* cataclismo; diluvio, inundación; catástrofe, *f.*—**cataclysmal, cataclysmic** [kætəklízməl, -mik], *a.* referente al cataclismo; catastrófico.—**cataclysmist** [-mist], *s.* = CATASTROPHIST.

catacombs [kǽtəkoumz], *s. pl.* catacumbas.

catacoustics [kætəkústiks], *s.* (fís.) catacústica.

catadioptric(al [kætədaiáptrik(əl], *a.* (ópt.) catadióptrico.

catadioptrics [-triks], *s.* (ópt.) catadióptrica.

catafalque [kǽtəfælk], *s.* catafalco, túmulo.

Catalan [kǽtələn], *s.* y *a.* catalán.

Catalanism [-izm], *s.* catalanismo.

Catalanist [-ist], *a.* y *s.* catalanista.

catalectic [kætəléktik], *a.* (poét.) cataléctico.

catalepsy [kǽtələpsi], *s.* (med.) catalepsia.—**cataleptic** [-léptik], *a.* cataléptico.

catalog(ue [kǽtəlag]. **I.** *s.* catálogo, lista, nómina, nomenclatura, elenco. **II.** *va.* catalogar.

catalog(u)er [-œ(r)], **catalog(u)ist** [-ist], *s.* catalogador.

cataloguing [-iŋ], *s.* catalogación.

Catalonian [kætəlóunjən], *a.* y *s.* catalán.

catalpa [kətǽlpə], *s.* (bot.) catalpa.

catalysis [kətǽlisis], *s.* (quím.) catálisis.

catalyst [kǽtəlist], *s.* (quím.) catalizador.

catalytic [-lítik], **I.** *a.* (quím.) catalítico. **II.** *s.* (quím.) catalizador; (med.) restaurativo.—**catalyzer** [kǽtəlaizœ(r)], *s.* (quím.) catalizador.

catamaran [kætəmərǽn], *s.* (mar.) catimarón; balsa o jangada de tozas o de dos cascos unidos.

catamenia [kætəmínjə], *s. pl.* menstruación.

catamite [kǽtəmait], *s.* sodomita, *m.*

catamount [-maunt], *s.* (zool.) gato montés, lince, puma.

catamountain [-máuntin], *s.* (zool.) pantera, leopardo, gato montés.

cataphract [-frækt], *s.* armadura de escamas de metal.

cataplasm [-plæzm], *s.* cataplasma.

catapult [-pʌlt]. **I.** *s.* catapulta, trabuquete; tirador; (aer.) aparato para lanzar al aire un avión desde la cubierta de un portaaviones. **II.** *va.* arrojar con catapulta, o con violencia.

cataract [-rækt], *s.* catarata, cascada; (med.) catarata.

catarrh [kətár], *s.* (E. U.) catarro crónico; (Ing.) catarro o romadizo fuerte.

catarrhal [-al], *a.* catarral, catarroso.

catarrhine [kǽtərain], *a.* y *s.* (zool.) catirrino.

catastasis [kætǽstəsis], *s.* (ret. y drama) catástasis.

catastrophe [kətǽstrofi], *s.* catástrofe, *f.;* cataclismo.—**catastrophic** [kætəstráfik], *a.* catastrófico.—**catastrophism** [kætǽstrofizm], *s.* (geol.) teoría que atribuye a catástrofes repentinas los cambios geológicos.—**catastrophist** [-ist], *s.* partidario de esa teoría.

catbird [kǽtbœrd], *s.* (orn.) tordo mímo.

catboat [-bout], *s.* (mar.) laúd, *m.*

catcall [-kɔl], *s.* silba, grita, pito, (re)chifla. **II.** *vn.* silbar, rechiflar, sisear.

catch [kæch]. **I.** *va.* (pret.·y *pp.* CAUGHT) coger, agarrar, asir; atrapar; alcanzar; prender, capturar; pillar, pescar; sorprender, coger desprevenido; (mec.) enganchar, endentar, engarzar; comprender, discernir; contraer, ser atacado o contagiarse de (una enfermedad). —**to c. cold,** resfriarse, tomar frío, constiparse. —**to c. fire,** inflamarse, encenderse.—**to c. hold of,** agarrar(se a), asir(se de).—**to c. it,**

(fam.) ganarse una zurra, un regaño, etc.—**to c. one's eye,** llamar la atención; ver por casualidad.—**to c. sight of,** ver, alcanzar a ver.—**to c. the,** o **one's, breath,** suspender el resuello.—**to c. up,** alcanzar; acoger con entusiasmo. **II.** *vn.* enredarse, engancharse; (mec.) endentar, engranar; prender (fuego); agarrar; ser contagioso.—**to c. at,** tratar de coger o agarrarse de, echar mano de.—**to c. on,** (fam.) comprender, ver, caer en la cuenta.—**to c. up,** salir del atraso; ponerse al día.—**to c. up with,** alcanzar; marchar (con la época, etc.); comprender.

catch, *s.* acción de coger; lo que se coge (pescados, etc.); cogida, pesca, pez, *m.,* redada; toma-(dura); presa, botín; captura, prendimiento; enganche; trampa, engañifa; (dep.) acto de parar la pelota al vuelo; (cost.) gancho, corchete; (mec.) leva, tope, retén; pasador, botón, fiador, tarabilla, pestillo, cerradera, detenedor, trinquete; alzaprima; lengüeta (de trampa); triquiñuela, trampa; impedimento, obstrucción; atractivo; buen partido.

catch, *a.*—**c. basin,** cisterna de desagüe a la cloaca (gen. en las esquinas).—**c. bolt,** picaporte.—**c. crop,** (agr.) siembra intermedia entre dos cosechas o siembras, o entre las hileras de la siembra principal.—**c. drain,** colector, cuneta o tubo de desagüe.

catchall [-ɔl], *s.* armario, cesto u otro receptáculo para varios objetos o retazos.

catcher [-œ(r)], *s.* el que o lo que coge, etc.; cogedor, prendedor, etc.; (baseball) catcher, parador o receptor de la pelota, situado detrás del *batter.*

catching [-iŋ]. **I.** *s.* (mec.) engranaje. **II.** *a.* contagioso, pegadizo, infectivo; cautivante.

catchment [-mont], *s.* desagüe; acción de coger.

catchpenny [-peni]. **I.** *s.* baratija, engañifa, sacadinero(s). **II.** *a.* de pacotilla.

catchpole, catchpoll [-poul], *s.* alguacil, agarrador.

catchup [-ʌp], *s.* = CATSUP.

catchword [-wœrd], *s.* (impr.) reclamo; (teat.) pie, *m.*

catchy [-i], *a.* atractivo; engañoso; irregular, interrumpido.

catechesis [kætəkísis], *s.* catequesis.

catechetic(al [-kétik(əl], *a.* catequístico.

catechetics [-kétiks], *s.* catequismo.

catechism [kǽtəkizm], *s.* catecismo.

catechist [-kist], *s.* catequista, catequizante.—**catechistical** [-kístikəl], *a.* catequístico.—**catechize** [-kaiz], *va.* catequizar.—**catechizer** [-œ(r)], *s.* catequizante.—**catechizing** [-iŋ]. **I.** *s.* catequismo. **II.** *a.* catequizante.

catechu [kǽtəchu], *s.* cato, cachú, cachunde.

catechumen [kætəkjúmen], *s.* catecúmeno.

catechumenical [-ménikəl], *a.* catecuménico.

categorematic [kætəgərimǽtik], *a.* (lóg.) categoremático.

categoric(al [kætəgárik(əl], *a.* categórico, rotundo.—**categorically** [-i], *adv.* categóricamente.

category [kǽtəgori], *s.* categoría, clase, *f.*

catenarian [kætinéirjən], *a.* catenaria; catenular; eslabonado.

catenary [kǽtinəri], *s.* y *a.* (geom.) catenaria.

catenate [kǽtineit], *va.* encadenar, concatenar.

catenation [-éiʃon], *s.* encadenamiento, encadenadura, engarce.

catenulate [kæténjuleit], *a.* catenular.

cater [kéitœ(r)], *vn.* y *va.* abastecer, proveer, surtir (de víveres, etc.); (con **to**) complacer a uno en sus gustos, etc.

cater-cornered [-kɔrnœrd], *a.* y *adv.* (fam.) en ángulo.

cater-cousin [-kʌzin], *s.* primo hermano; pariente lejano; amigo íntimo.

caterer [-œ(r)], *s.* (pro)veedor, surtidor, abastecedor, despensero.—**cateress** [-is], s. proveedora, etc.

caterpillar [kǽtœrpilǝ(r)], s. (ent.) oruga, gusano.
—**c. tractor**, tractor (de) oruga (es nombre de fábrica).

caterwaul [kǽtœrwɔl], vn. maullar.

caterwauling [-iŋ], s. maullido (del gato en celo).

catfish [kǽtfiŝ], s. (ict.) siluro, barbo, (Am.) bagre.

catgut [kǽtgʌt], s. cuerda de tripa usada en suturas quirúrgicas (ll. **catgut**) y en instrumentos músicos de cuerda.

Catharine wheel [kǽθrin hwil], s. rueda catalina; (arq.) rosa, rosetón; (piro.) rueda de fuegos artificiales.

catharpin [kǽtharpin], s. (mar.) jareta.

catharsis [kaθársis], s. (med.) catarsis, purga.

cathartic [kaθártik]. I. a. catártico, purgante. II. s. purga, purgante.

cathead [kǽthed], s. (mar.) serviola.

cathedra [kaθídrǝ], s. cátedra; sillón episcopal.

cathedral [kaθídrǝl]. I. s. catedral, seo, f. II. a. catedral(icio), episcopal; dogmático.—**c. chimes**, tubos metálicos acordados que se tañen con un martillo e imitan las campanas.

catheretic [kæθǝrétik], a. caterético, cáustico.

Catherine wheel, s. = CATHARINE WHEEL.

catheter [kǽθǝtœ(r)], s. (cir.) catéter, candelilla, algalia, sonda, tienta.

catheterism [-izm], s. cateterismo.

catheterize [-aiz], va. cateterizar.

cathetometer [kæθǝtámœtœ(r)], s. catetómetro.

cathode [kǽθoud], s. (elec.) cátodo.—**c. ray**, rayo catódico.

cathodic [kæθádik], a. catódico.

cathole [kǽthoul], s. gatera; (mar.) gatera.

catholic [kǽθolik]. I. a. católico, universal; liberal. II. s. y a. (**C.**) católico romano.

Catholicism [kaθálisizm], s. catolicismo.

catholicity [kæθolísiti], s. catolicidad.

catholicize [kaθálisaiz]. I. va. catolizar, convertir al catolicismo. II. vn. hacerse católico.

catholicly [kaθálikli], adv. católicamente.

catholicon [kaθálikon], s. catolicón; panacea.

cation [kǽtaion], s. (fís.) catión, m.

catkin [kǽtkin], s. (bot.) amento, candelilla.

catlike [kǽtlaik], a. gatesco, gatuno; furtivo.

catling [kǽtliŋ], s. gatito; (cir.) legra, bisturí.

catmint [kǽtmint], **catnip** [-nip], s. (bot.) calamento, nébeda.

Catonian [keitóuniǝn], a. catoniano.

catoptrical [kætáptrikǝl], a. catóptrico.

catoptrics [-triks], s. (ópt.) catóptrica.

catsup [kǽtsʌp], s. salsa de setas o de tomate.

cattail [kǽtteil], s. (bot.) espadaña, enea; amento.

cattish [kǽtiŝ], a. gatuno, gatesco. V. CATTY.

cattle [kǽtl], s. ganado (gen. se aplica sólo al vacuno), res, f.—**c. barn**, establo.—**c. bell**, esquilón.—**c. dealer**, ganadero.—**c. pest** o **plague**, morriña; comalia; glosopeda.—**c. pump**, bomba automática para ganado.—**c. raising**, ganadería.—**c. ranch**, ganadería, hacienda de ganado.—**c. rancher**, ganadero.—**c. range**, o **run**, potrero o campo para el ganado.—**c. rustler**, o **thief**, abigeo, cuatrero, ladrón de ganado.—**c. rustling**, o **stealing**, abigeato, hurto de ganado.—**c. show**, exposición de ganado.—**c. tick**, garrapata.—**c. wire**, alambre de púas.

cattleman [-mæn], s. ganadero.

catty [kǽti], a. gatesco; maliciosa y chismera.

catty-cornered = CATER-CORNERED.

catwalk [kǽtwɔk], s. acera o andén angosto de un puente; corredor o pasillo por la quilla de un dirigible.

Caucasian [kokéiʒǝn], a. y s. caucáseo, caucásico.

caucus [kókʌs], s. junta de un grupo o partido político para designar candidatos, discutir medidas, etc.

caudad [kódæd], adv. (anat.) hacia la cola.

caudal [kódǝl], a. caudal (de la cola).

caudate [kódeit], a. caudato, raboso.

caudex [kódeks], s. (bot.) tallo; tronco.

caudicle [kódikl], s. (bot.) caudícula.

caudle [kódl], s. cordial, bebida caliente de vino, huevos, etc.

caught [kot], pret. y pp. de TO CATCH.

caul [kol], s. (anat.) omento, redaño; amnios, f.

cauldron, s. = CALDRON.

caulescent [kolésǝnt], a. (bot.) caulescente.

caulicle [kólikl], s. (bot.) rejo.

cauliculus [kolíkiulʌs], s. (arq.) caulículo.

cauliferous [kolífɛrʌs], a. (bot.) caulífero.

cauliflower [kóliflauœ(r)], s. coliflor, f.

cauliform [kóliform], a. (bot.) cauliforme.

caulk, caulker, etc. = CALK, CALKER, etc.

causal [kózǝl], a. causal.

causality [kozǽliti], **causation** [kozéiŝǝn], s. causalidad; causa, origen, principio.

causally [kózǝli], adv. de un modo causal.

causative [kózǝtiv], a. causante, causativo.

cause [koz]. I. s. causa; autor; motivo, origen, porqué, razón, f.; (for.) causa, litigio, proceso. II. va. causar; acarrear, dar lugar a, motivar, ocasionar; hacer (to cause to move, hacer mover); mover, inducir, compeler.

causeless [-lis], a. sin causa; infundado, sin razón.—**causelessly** [-li], adv. infundadamente.

causer [-œ(r)], s. causador, causante, autor.

causerie [kouzɛrí], s. conversación, charla; discusión o deliberación de confianza; artículo breve.

causeway [kózwei], **causey** [kózi], s. arrecife; arriate, calzada, terraplén; acera.

causidical [kozídikǝl], a. (for.) causídico.

caustic(al [kóstik(ǝl], a. y s. cáustico.

causticity [kostísiti], **causticness** [kóstiknis], s. causticidad, mordacidad.

cauter [kótœ(r)], s. (cir.) instrumento para cauterizar; cauterio.

cauterization [kotœrizéiŝǝn], s. cauterización, cauterio.

cauterize [kótœraiz], va. cauterizar.

cauterizing [-iŋ]. I. s. cauterización. II. a. cauterizante.

cautery [kótœri], s. cauterio.

caution [kóŝǝn]. I. s. cautela, precaución; cuidado, recato; amonestación, advertencia, aviso. II. va. caucionar, precaver, prevenir, amonestar.

cautionary [-ɛri], a. preventivo, admonitorio, avisador.

cautious [kóŝʌs], a. cauto, cauteloso, circunspecto, precavido, prudente.

cautiously [-li], adv. cautamente, prudentemente.—**cautiousness** [-nis], s. cautela, previsión, prudencia, precaución.

cavalcade [kævǝlkéid], s. cabalgata.

cavalier [kævǝlír]. I. s. caballero; jinete; galán, cortejo; escolta, pareja de baile. II. a. caballeresco; altivo, desdeñoso; alegre, desenvuelto.—**cavalierly** [-li], adv. caballerescamente; altiva o desdeñosamente.

cavalla, cavally [kǽvælǝ, -li], s. (ict.) caballa.

cavalry [kǽvǝlri], s. (mil.) caballería, caballos.

cavalryman [-mǝn], s. (mil.) jinete; soldado de caballería.

cavatina [kæætátinǝ], s. (mús.) cavatina.

cave [keiv]. I. s. cueva, caverna.—**c. in**, hundimiento, atierre.—**c. dweller, c. man**, cavernícola; troglodita. II. vn. (gen. con in) hundirse; (fam.) ceder, rendirse; sufrir colapso. III. va. excavar; hacer hundirse.

caveat [kéivjæt], s. (for.) intimación a un juez o funcionario para que suspenda un procedimiento; (E. U.) inscripción previa en la oficina de patentes de un invento no perfeccionado todavía; amonestación, advertencia.

cavern [kǽvœrn], s. caverna, antro, gruta.—**cavernous** [-ʌs], a. cavernoso.

cavesson [kǽvɛsɔn], s. cabezón.

cavetto [kavétou], s. (arq.) caveto.

caviar [kǽvjar], s. cavial, caviar.
cavicorn [kǽvikɔrn], a. y s. (zool.) cavicornio.
cavil [kǽvil]. I. s. cavilosidad, cavilación, vanas sutilezas. II. vn. cavilar, sutilizar, buscar quisquillas.
cavil(l)er [-œ(r)], s. hombre caviloso, reparón.—**cavil(l)ing** [-iŋ]. I. s. cavilación, cavilosidad. II. a. caviloso, reparón.—**cavil(l)ingly** [-li], adv. cavilosamente.
cavity [kǽviti], s. cavidad; hueco, oquedad; seno.
cavort [kavɔ́rt], vn. (fam. E. U.) corvetear, travesear.
cavy [kéivi], s. (zool.) (Am.) agutí, cobayo, conejillo de Indias, paca, tepeizcuinte; ca(r)-pincho, capiguara o capibara.
caw [kɔ]. I. vn. graznar. II. s. graznido.
cay [kei o ki], s. cayo, peñasco o isleta.
cayenne [keién], s. (bot.) pimentón.—**c. pepper**, pimentón (ll. t. **red pepper**).
cayman [kéiman], s. (zool.) caimán.
cazique [kazík], s. = CACIQUE.
cease [sís]. I. vn. cesar, desistir o dejar de, parar; fenecer. II. va. discontinuar, parar, suspender.
—**without c.**, sin cesar.
ceaseless [-lis], a. incesante.—**ceaselessly** [-li], adv. perpetuamente, incesantemente.
cebid [síbid], a. y s. (zool.) cébide.
cecum, s. = CÆCUM.
cedar [sída(r)], s. (bot.) cedro (árbol y madera); tuya.—**c. bird**, (orn.) pájaro del cedro.—**c. chest**, cajón de cedro a prueba de la polilla.—**c. cone**, cédride, f.—**c. of Lebanon**, cedro de Líbano.—**c. oil**, cedrelón, cedróleo.
cedarn [-n], a. (poét.) cedrino.
cede [sid], va. ceder, traspasar, transferir.
cedilla [sidílá], s. zedilla, cedilla.
cedrine [sídrin], a. (bot.) cedrino.
cedrium [sídriʌm], s. cedria.
cedrol [sídrol], s. (quím.) cedróleo.
ceil [síl], va. entablar; poner cielo raso.
ceiling [-iŋ], s. techo interior o cielo raso; forro; cima; límite superior, colmo; (mar.) entabladura interior; (aer.) techo; altura máxima que un avión puede alcanzar; límite de visibilidad.
—**c. price**, precio máximo.
celadon [sélàdan], s. verdeceledón.
celandine [sélàndain], s. (bot.) celidonia, glaucio, golondrinera.
celature [sélachur], s. arte de grabar o repujar los metales; repuijado.
celebrant [sélèbrant], s. celebrante.—**celebrate** [sélèbreit]. I. va. celebrar, solemnizar; festejar; alabar, encomiar. II. vn. celebrar; (fam.) ir de parranda, echar una cana al aire.—**celebrated** [-id], a. célebre, famoso.—**celebration** [-éiʃon], s. celebración.—**celebrator** [-ɔ(r)], s. celebrador, celebrante.
celebrity [selébriti], s. celebridad, fama, renombre; persona célebre.
celeriac [selériæk], s. (bot.) arracacha.
celerity [seleríti], s. celeridad, prontitud.
celery [séleri], s. (bot.) apio.
celestial [seléschal]. I. a. celeste; celestial, empíreo, divino.—**C. Empire**, China.—**c. sphere**, esfera celeste. II. s. morador del cielo; (C.) chino.
celestially [-i], adv. celestialmente.
celestite [sélestait], s. (min.) celestina.
celiac [síljæk], a. (anat.) celiaco. V. COELIAC.
celibacy [sélibạsi], s. celibato, soltería.—**celibate** [sélibit], a. y s. célibe, soltero.
cell [sel], s. celda (de convento); (pol.) célula (comunista, etc.); celda, calabozo; (biol.) célula, glóbulo; nicho, cavidad; alvéolo; (api.) celdilla, vasillo; castillo (de la reina); (elec.) par, elemento de una pila; (aer.) celda.
cellar [séla(r)], s. sótano, bodega, cueva, cillero.
cellarage [-idʒ], s. cueva, sótano, candiotera; almacenaje en una bodega a gastos de esto.
cellarer [-œ(r)], **cellarman** [-man], s. bodeguero; cillerero (de monasterio); repostero.

cellaret(te [selarét], s. armario para licores.
cellist [chélist], s. violoncelista.
cello [chélou], s. (mús.) violoncelo.
cellophane [sélofein], s. celofán o celofano (es nombre de fábrica), papel transparente impermeable de envolver.
cellular [séljulá(r)], a. celular, celuloso.
cellulate(d [séljuleit(id], a. celulado.
cellule [séljul], s. celulilla.
celluloid [séljuloid], s. celuloide (es nombre de fábrica); (fam.) película de cinema.
cellulose [séljulous]. I. a. celular, celuloso.—**c. acetate**, (quím.) acetocelulosa. II. s. celulosa.
Celt [selt], s. celta; hacha prehistórica de piedra.
Celtiberian [seltibérian], a. y s. celtíbero, celtibérico, celtiberio.
Celtic [séltik], a. céltico.
Celt(ic)ism [sélt(is)izm], s. celtismo.
Celt(ic)ist [sélt(is)ist], s. celtista.
cement [sément]. I. s. cemento; mortero, argamasa; cemento (del diente); aglutinante; vínculo; (fund.) cemento.—**c.-like**, cementoso.—**c. steel**, acero cementado.—**c. tile**, baldosín o loseta de cemento, mosaico. II. va. pegar, aglutinar, argamasar; estrechar, asegurar; (fund.) cementar. III. vn. pegarse, aglutinarse; unirse.
cementation [sementéiʃon], s. ligazón, f., aglutinación; (fund.) cementación.
cementite [siméntait], s. (metal.) carburo de hierro del acero antes de endurecerse.
cemetery [séməteri], s. cementerio, campo santo.
cenacle [sénakl], s. cenáculo.
cenobian [senóubian], a. cenobial.
cenobite [sénobait], s. cenobita, m.
cenobitic(al [senóubitik(al], a. cenobítico.
cenobitism [sénobaitizm], s. cenobitismo.
cenobium [senóubiʌm], **cenoby** [sénobi], s. cenobio, monasterio.
cenotaph [sénotæf], s. cenotafio.
Cenozoic [sinozóuik], s. y a. (geol.) cenozoico; terciario.
cense [sens], va. incensar, turibular.
censer [-œ(r)], s. (igl.) incensario, turíbulo, naveta.—**c. bearer**, turibulario, turiferario.
censor [-ǫ(r)]. I. s. censor; censurador, crítico; escrutinador. II. va. censurar, someter a la censura.
censorial [sensórial], a. censorio.
censorious [-ʌs], a. severo, rígido; crítico, hipercrítico.—**censoriously** [-li], adv. severamente, críticamente.—**censoriousness** [-nis], s. inclinación a censurar.
censorship [sénsorʃip], s. censura o censoría.
censual [sénsual], a. censual (pert. al censo).
censurable [sénʃúrabl], a. censurable.—**censurableness** [-nis], s. calidad de censurable.—**censurably** [-bli], adv. censurablemente.
censure [sénʃú(r)]. I. s. censura, reprimenda, reprobación, crítica, zaherimiento. II. va. censurar, reprender, criticar, reprobar, fiscalizar, tachar, zaherir.—**censurer** [-œ(r)], s. censurador, represor, criticador, zaheridor.—**censuring** [-iŋ], a. censurante, zaheridor.
census [sénsʌs]. I. s. censo, empadronamiento, registro.—**c. list**, padrón.—**c. taker**, empadronador.—**c. taking**, encabezamiento. II. va. empadronar, encabezar, hacer el censo.
cent [sént], s. centavo (moneda).
cental [-al], s. quintal. V. HUNDREDWEIGHT.
centare [sénter], s. = CENTIARE.
centaur [sénta(r)], s. centauro; (C.; astr.) centauro.
centaury [-i], s. (bot.) centaura.
centenarian [senténérian], s. y a. centenario, quintañón.
centenary [sénteneri], **centennial** [senténial]. I. a. centenario, secular. II. s. centenar(io).
center, centre [séntœ(r)]. I. s. centro; medio, mitad, corazón, eje, yema; (arq.) cimbra; (top.) eje vertical (de un teodolito, etc.); (mec.) punta (de torno); centro, portapuntas (de torno).—**c.**

of **curvature**, (mat.) centro de curvatura.—**c. of figure**, centro de figura, centro geométrico. —**c. of gravity**, centro de gravedad.—**c. of gyration**, (mec.) centro de giro.—**c. of inertia, c. of mass**, centro de masa, centro de gravedad. —**c. of lift**, (aer.) punto de sustentación.— **c. of motion**, centro de rotación, punto fijo. —**c. of population**, centro de población, centro de gravedad de una región cuya superficie se considera proporcional a la población. II. *a.* central; relativo al centro.—**c. bit**, barrena de guía.—**c. lathe**, torno de puntas.—**c. line**, eje (de una vía, una caldera, etc.); línea central.—**c. punch**, punzón de marcar o de perforar; granete.—**c. rail**, (f. c.) riel central (para corriente eléctrica, cremallera, etc.). III. *va.* centrar, centralizar; concentrar; determinar el centro de; (arq.) cimbrar. IV. *vn.* concentrarse; estar o colocarse en el centro.—**to c. round**, girar en torno de; versar sobre.

centerboard [-bɔrd], *s.* (mar.) orza de deriva o de quilla.

centering [-iŋ], *s.* enfocamiento; determinación del centro de un objeto; acción de centrar; (arq.) cimbra de arco; maderamen de cimbra.

centerpiece [-pis], *s.* paño (gen. encaje u otra labor) para el centro de la mesa; cualquier cosa que va en el centro; centro de mesa (vaso, florero, ramillete, etc.).

centesimal [sentésimal]. I. *a.* centesimal; centésimo, centeno, céntimo. II. *s.* centésimo.

centiare [séntjer], *s.* centiárea.

centigrade [-grejd], *a.* centígrado.—**c. scale**, escala centígrada.

centigram(me [-græm], *s.* centigramo.

centiliter, centilitre [-litœ(r)], *s.* centilitro.

centime [sántim], *s.* céntimo.

centimeter, centimetre [séntimitœ(r)], *s.* centímetro.—**c.-gram-second** (**C. G. S.**), (fís.) centímetro-gramo-segundo; cegesimal.

centipede [-pid], *s.* (zool.) centípedo, ciempiés.

centner [séntnœ(r)], *s.* quintal; dracma.

cento [séntou], *s.* centón.

centrad [séntræd], *adv.* (zool.) hacia el centro.

central [séntral]. I. *a.* central, céntrico.—**C. American**, centroamericano.—**c. heating**, calefacción central.—**c. station**, central (f.) de electricidad. II. *s.* central (f.) de teléfono; telefonista; (com.) caucho.—**centralism** [-izm], *s.* (pol.) centralismo.—**centralist** [-ist], *s.* centralista.—**centrality** [sentrǽliti], *s.* centralidad.—**centralization** [sentralizéišon], *s.* centralización.—**centralize** [-ajz], *va.* centralizar.—**centralizer** [-œ(r)], *s.* centralizador.—**centrally** [-i], *adv.* centralmente.

centre [séntœ(r)] = CENTER.

centric(al [séntrik(al], *a.* central, céntrico.

centrically [-li], *adv.* centralmente.

centrifugal [sentrífjugal]. I. *a.* centrífugo.—**c. force**, fuerza centrífuga.—**c. pump**, bomba centrífuga.—**c. sugar**, azúcar separada del líquido por acción centrífuga. II. *s.* máquina centrífuga, o su cilindro; (Am., azú.) centrífuga. —*pl.* azúcar centrífuga.

centrifugalize [-ajz], *va.* centrifugar.

centrifuge [séntrifjudž]. I. *a.* centrífugo. II. *s.* (máquina) centrífuga o separadora. III. *va.* centrifugar, someter a acción centrífuga.

centripetal [sentrípetal], *a.* centrípeto.

centrist [séntrist], *s.* (pol.) centrista, del centro.

centrobaric [sentrobǽrjk], *a.* (mec.) centrobárico.

centroid [séntrojd], *s.* centroide.—**centroidal** [séntrojdal], *a.* relativo al centroide.

centrosome [séntrosoṃ], *s.* (biol.) centrosoma, *m.*

centrosphere [séntrosfir], *s.* (geol.) la parte central o núcleo de la tierra; (biol.) esfera de atracción.

centumvir [sentámvir], *s.* centunviro.—**centumvirate** [-ejt], *s.* centunvirato.

centuple [séntjupl]. I. *a.* céntuplo, centuplicado. II. *va.* centuplicar.

centuplicate [sentjúplikejt]. I. *a.* y *s.* céntuplo, centuplicado. II. *va.* centuplicar.

centuplication [-kéjšon], *s.* centuplicación.

centurial [sentjúrial], *a.* secular.

centurion [sentjúrjon], *s.* centurión, *m.*

century [sénchuri], *s.* centuria; siglo.—**c.-old**, secular.—**c. plant**, (bot.) pita, maguey, agave, *f.* (ll. t. **c. aloe**).

cephalad [séfalæd], *adv.* (anat.) hacia la cabeza.

cephalalgia [sefalǽldžjǝ], *s.* (med.) cefalalgia.

cephalic [sefǽljk], *a.* (anat.) cefálico.

cephalitis [sefalájtis], *s.* (med.) cefalitis.

cephalopod [séfalopad], *a.* y *s.* (zool.) cefalópodo.

cephalothorax [-θóuræks], *s.* (zool.) cefalotórax.

cephalous [séfalʌs], *a.* (zool.) que tiene cabeza.

Cepheus [sífjʌs], *s.* (astr.) Cefeo.

ceraceous [siréišʌs], *a.* ceráceo.

cerambycid [serǽmbisid], *a.* y *s.* (ent.) cerambícido.

ceramic [sirǽmjk], *a.* cerámico.

ceramics [-s], *s.* cerámica; alfarería.

ceramist [sérǝmist], *s.* ceramista.

cerargyrite [serárdžirajt], *s.* (min.) plata córnea.

cerastes [serǽstiz], *s.* (zool.) cerasta, ceraste.

cerate [síreit], *s.* (farm.) cerato, ceroto.

cerated [-id], *a.* encerado.

Cerberean [sœrbíriǝn], *a.* parecido al (can)-cerbero o relativo a él.

cercopithecus [sœrkopiθíkʌs], *s.* (zool.) cercopiteco.

cere [sir], *va.* envolver (esp. un cadáver) en un lienzo impregnado con cera. *V.* CERECLOTH y CEREMENT.

cereal [síriǝl]. I. *a.* cereal. II. *s.* cereal, grano.

cerebellar [serebélǝ(r)], *a.* cerebeloso, perteneciente al cerebelo.

cerebellitis [-ájtis], *s.* (med.) cerebelitis.

cerebellum [serebélʌm], *s.* (anat.) cerebelo.

cerebral [sérebral], *a.* cerebral.

cerebrate [sérebrejt], *vn.* exhibir o experimentar actividad mental; pensar.

cerebration [-éjšon], *s.* cerebración, actividad funcional del cerebro; función cerebral.

cerebrin [sérebrin], *s.* (quím.) cerebrina.

cerebritis [serebrájtis], *s.* (med.) cerebritis.

cerebrospinal [serebrouspájnal], *a.* cerebroespinal.—**c. axis**, eje cerebroespinal.

cerebrum [sérebrʌm], *s.* (anat.) cerebro, encéfalo.

cerecloth [sírklǝθ], *s.* encerado, hule.

cerement [sírment], *s.* enceramiento; mortaja encerada.

ceremonial [seremóunjal], *a.* y *s.* ceremonial; rito externo o ritual.

ceremonious [-móunjʌs], *a.* ceremonial; ceremonioso.—**ceremoniousness** [-njs], *s.* ceremonia.—**ceremoniously** [-li], *adv.* ceremoniosamente.

ceremony [séremounj], *s.* ceremonia, ceremonial; cumplido, formalidad, etiqueta.

cereous [sírjʌs], *a.* cereo, de cera.

Cereus [sírjʌs], *s.* (bot.) género de cactos.

ceric [sírjk], *a.* (quím.) cérico.

ceriferous [sɛrífɛrʌs], *a.* cerífero.

cerin [sírjn], *s.* (quím.) cerina.

cerise [serís], *s.* y *a.* color de cereza.

cerite [sírajt], *s.* (min.) cerita.

cerium [sírjʌm], *s.* (quím.) cerio.

cernuous [sœrnjuʌs], *a.* (bot.) inclinado.

cero [sírou], *s.* (ict.) priste, pez sierra.

cerograph [sírogræf], *s.* grabado sobre cera.

cerography [sirágrafj], *s.* cerografía.

ceroplastics [siroplǽstjks], *s.* ceroplástica.

cerotic [sirátjk], *a.* (quím.) cerótico.

cerolein [sírolin], *s.* (quím.) ceroleína.

ceromancy [síromænsi], *s.* ceromancia, ceromancía.

cerotate [sírotejt], *s.* (quím.) cerotato.

certain [sœrtǝn], *a.* cierto, alguno, un tal; seguro; cierto, evidente, inevitable, indudable, positivo;

certero, puntual; fijo, determinado; vg. c. *friends of mine*, ciertos amigos míos, c. *ones say so*, ciertos (o algunos) lo dicen, *he owes me a c. sum*, me debe cierta suma (o un tanto), *a c. Mr. X*, un tal Sr. X; *I am c. of it*, estoy seguro de ello; *war is c.*, la guerra es cierta (inevitable, etc.), *it is c. that we exist*, es cierto (evidente) que existimos; *he is c. to do it*, no puede menos de hacerlo (o lo hará con toda seguridad); *with c. aim*, con puntería certera; *at a c. hour*, en hora determinada o fija.—**for c.,** de fijo, de seguro, con seguridad.—**certainly** [-lĭ], *adv.* (por) cierto, ciertamente, sin duda; seguramente, sin falta; con mucho gusto.—**certainty** [-tĭ], *s.* certeza, certidumbre; seguridad, cosa segura.—**to a c.,** indubitablemente.—**with c.,** a ciencia cierta.

certifiable [sœ̃rtĭfaĭạbl], *a.* certificable.

certificate [sœ̃rtĭfĭkĭt], **certification** [-éĭṣǫn], *s.* certificado, testimonio; atestiguación; (for.) adveración, auténtica, atestado, certificación, fe (*f.*), partida; acta notarial; (com.) bono, obligación.—**c. of baptism,** fe de bautismo.—**c. of death,** partida de defunción.—**c. of genuineness,** certificación de legitimidad (de firma); volante de autenticación.—**c. of marriage,** certificado de matrimonio, fe de casado.—**c. of residence,** carta de vecindad.

certificate [sœ̃rtĭfĭkeĭt], *va.* certificar. *V.* CERTIFY.

certificatory [-kątǫrĭ], *a.* certificatorio.

certifier [sœ̃rtĭfaĭœ(r)], *s.* certificador.

certify [sœ̃rtĭfaĭ], *va.* certificar, atestiguar, adverar, dar fe; afirmar, garantizar, responder de o por.

certiorari [sœ̃rṣĭǫréraĭ], *s.* (for.) auto de avocación.

certitude [sœ̃rtĭtĭud], *s.* certidumbre, certeza.

cerulean [sĕrúlĭạn], *a.* cerúleo.

cerumen [sĕrúmęn], *s.* cerumen, cerilla.

ceruse [sírus], *s.* cerusa, albayalde.

cerussite [-aĭt], *s.* (min.) cerusita, cerusa.

Cervantine [sœ̃rvéntĭn], *a.* cervantesco, cervantino.

Cervantist [-ĭst], *a. y s.* cervantista.

cervical [sœ̃rvĭkạl], *a.* (anat.) cervical, cérvico.

cervine [sœ̃rvĭn], *a.* cervino, cervuno, cérvido.

cervix [sœ̃rvĭks], *s.* (anat.) cerviz, nuca.

Cesarean, *a.* = CÆSAREAN.

cespitose [sĕspĭtoṳs], *a.* cespitoso, de cesped.

cess [ses]. **I.** *va.* amillarar. **II.** *s.* amillaramiento.

cessation [sɛséĭṣǫn], *s.* cese, cesación, paro, discontinuación.

cession [sɛ́ṣǫn], *s.* cesión, traspaso.

cessionary [-ęrĭ], *a. y s.* cesionario.

cesspipe [sɛ́spaĭp], *s.* tubo de desagüe.

cesspool [sɛ́spul], *s.* pozo negro de letrina.

cestode [sɛ́stoṳd], *a. y s.* (zool.) cestódo.

cestus [sɛ́stʌs], *s.* cesto de púgil; ceñidor, cinturón.

cesura, *s.* = CÆSURA.

cetacean [sĭtéĭṣạn], *a. y s.* (zool.) cetáceo.

cetaceous [sĭtéĭṣʌs], *a.* cetáceo.

cetyl [sĕtĭl], *s.* (quím.) cetilo.

chacma [chǽkmą], *s.* variedad de mandril o papión, *m.*

chaconne [ṣækán], *s.* chacona (baile y música).

chafe [chéĭf]. **I.** *va.* excoriar, rozar; calentar frotando; enfadar, irritar. **II.** *vn.* desgastarse, raerse; sahornarse; irritarse, acalorarse. **III.** *s.* sahorno, excoriación; acaloramiento, rabia.—**chafer** [-œ(r)], *s.* lo que roza o excoria; estufilla; (ent.) escarabajo.—**chafery** [-œrĭ], *s.* fragua o forja.

chaff [chǽf]. **I.** *s.* barcia, ahechaduras, granzas, paja, tamo; desperdicios, broza; cascabillo; burla, fisga.—**c. cutter,** (agr.) cortadora de forraje. **II.** *va.* y *vn.* fisgar, dar matraca.

chaffer [-œ(r)]. **I.** *vn.* regatear, baratear; andar en dimes y diretes. **II.** *s.* regateo.—**chafferer** [-œ(r)], *s.* regatero.

chaffinch [chǽfĭnch], *s.* (orn.) pinzón.

chafing [chéĭfĭŋ], *s.* sahorno, excoriación, rozadura; irritación, impaciencia.—**c. dish,** escalfeta, escalfador, chufeta.

chagrin [ṣạgrín]. **I.** *s.* mortificación, sofocón, disgusto, desazón, *f.* **II.** *va.* mortificar, enfadar.

chain [chéĭn]. **I.** *s.* cadena; grillo; lazo; serie o sucesión, encadenación; cordillera (de montañas); (tej.) urdi(e)mbre, *f.*; (top.) cadena (la cadena misma y su longitud tomada por unidad); cadena de Gunter (66 pies ing., o como 20.117 m.); *pl.* prisiones; esclavitud.—**c. drive,** (aut.) mando o transmisión por cadenas.—**c. gang,** cuadrilla de presidiarios encadenados entre sí.—**c. gear, c. gearing,** (mec.) transmisión por rueda y cadena.—**c. lightning,** relámpagos o relampagueo en zigzag.—**c. mail,** cota de malla.—**c. plate,** (mar.) vigota.—**c. pump,** noria.—**c. riveting,** remachado paralelo o de cadena.—**c. shot,** (mil.) bala encadenada o de cadena.—**c. stitch,** (cost.) punto de cadeneta.—**c. store,** tienda de un sistema de ellas pertenecientes a una misma empresa y todas de una misma clase.—**c. wheel,** rueda dentada para cadena. **II.** *va.* encadenar, aherrojar; esclavizar; enlazar, unir; (top.) medir con cadena.

chainless [-lĭs], *a.* desencadenado; sin cadenas.

chainman [-mąn], *s.* cadenero.

chainwork [-wœrk], *s.* cadeneta.

chair [chér], *s.* silla, asiento; silla de manos; cátedra (de profesor); sillón de la presidencia; por extensión, presidencia, presidente (de una junta, etc.); (f. c.) cojinete; base, *f.*, asiento.—**c. car,** (f. c.) coche salón.—**to take the c.,** presidir (una junta).

chairman [-mąn], *s.* presidente de una junta, persona que preside; silletero; sillero.—**chairmanship** [-ṣĭp], *s.* presidencia (de una junta directiva).—**chairwoman** [-wụmąn], *s.* presidenta.

chaise [ṣeĭz], *s.* silla volante, calesín, carrocín; silla de posta.—**c. longue,** especie de sofá, meridiana.

chalcedony [kælsĕdǫnĭ], *s.* (min.) calcedonia.

chalcocite [kælkosaĭt], *s.* (min.) calcosina o calcocita (mineral de sulfuro de cobre).

chalcograph [kælkogræf], *s.* grabado calcográfico.

chalcographer [kælkágrạfœ(r)], *s.* calcógrafo.

chalcography [-fĭ], *s.* calcografía.

chalcopyrite [kælkopáĭraĭt], *s.* (min.) calcopirita.

Chaldaic [kældéĭk], **Chaldean** [kældíạn], *a.* **Chaldee** [kældí], *a. y s.* caldeo, caldaico.

chalet [ṣæléĭ], *s.* chalet; casita de campo.

chalice [chǽlĭs], *s.* (igl.) cáliz, *m.*

chalk [chɔ̃k]. **I.** *s.* creta, greda; tiza, yeso.—**c. for cheese,** (fam.) gato por liebra.—**c. rock,** roca cretácea. **II.** *va.* enyesar, engredar; marcar o dibujar con tiza; poner tiza (al taco); apuntar, llevar cuenta. **III.** *vn.* ponerse gredoso.

chalkiness [-ĭnĭs], *s.* calidad de gredoso.

chalkstone [-stoṳn], *s.* tiza; (med.) concreción gotosa en las coyunturas.

chalky [-ĭ], *a.* cretáceo, gredoso, yesoso.

challenge [chǽlĭndž]. **I.** *va.* desafiar, retar; repugnar, poner en tela de juicio; merecer o exigir (atención, respeto, etc.); disputar, contradecir; (for.) recusar, tachar (testigos); (mil.) dar el quién vive, exigir el santo. **II.** *s.* desafío, reto; cartel de desafío; (for.) recusación, objeción; (mil.) quién vive; (dep.) concurso, oposición.—**beyond c.,** irrefutable.—**challengeable** [-ạbl], *a.* expuesto a desafío; recusable.—**challenger** [-œ(r)], *s.* desafiador, retador; demandante.

challis, challie [ṣǽlĭ], *s.* (tej.) chalí.

chalybeate [kạlĭbĭęt]. **I.** *a.* calibeado, ferruginoso. **II.** *s.* agua ferruginosa.

Chalybes [kǽlĭbĭz], *s. pl.* cálibes.

chalybite [kǽlĭbaĭt], *s.* (min.) siderita.

chamade [ṣạmád], *s.* (mil.) llamada.

chamber [chéĭmbœ(r)]. **I.** *s.* cámara; gabinete,

cuarto, alcoba, dormitorio; (for.) cámara, tribunal o sala de justicia; (arti.) cámara; (mec.) depósito, cilindro.—**c. concert**, concierto de salón.—**c. council**, junta secreta.—**c. counsel**, abogado consultor.—**c. music**, música de salón.—**c. of commerce**, cámara de comercio. —**C. of Deputies**, cámara de diputados.—**c. pot o vessel**, orinal, bacín, vaso de noche.—**c. practice**, práctica (de la abogacía) de oficina, profesión de abogado consultor. II. *va.* hacer la cámara de un cañón; proveer de cámara; ahuecar; ajustar a la cámara. III. *vn.* (arti.) ajustarse la carga en un cartucho.

chamberlain [-lịn], *s.* camarero; chambelán; camarlengo.—**chamberlainship** [-ŝịp], *s.* oficio o dignidad de camarero, chambelán, etc.

chambermaid [-mejd], *s.* camarera.

chameleon [kạmílịọn], *s.* (zool.) camaleón.

chambray [ŝæmbréj], *s.* (tej.) cierta tela de algodón.

chamfer [chæmfœ(r)]. I. *va.* (carp.) acanalar; (a)chaflanar, biselar, descantear. II. *s.* (carp.) canal, estría; bisel, chaflán.

chamfering [-iŋ], *s.* (arq.) derrame, derramo.

chamfrain [chæmfrejn], **chamfron** [chæmfrọn], *s.* (arm.) testera (del caballo). *V.* CHANFRIN.

chamois [ŝæmị], *s.* (zool.) ante, gamuza; piel (*f.*) de ante.—**c.-colored**, agamuzado.

chamomile, *s.* = CAMOMILE.

champ [chæmp]. I. *va.* morder, mascar, mordiscar. II. *vn.* bocezar (el caballo, etc.).—**to c. at restrictions**, (fig.) irritarse, impacientarse por trabas de una índole u otra. III. *s.* (fam.) campeón.

champagne [ŝæmpéjn], *s.* champaña, *m.*

champaign [ŝæmpéjn]. I. *s.* campiña. II. *a.* abierto o llano.

champak, champac [chæmpæk], *s.* (bot.) champaca.

champion [chæmpiọn]. I. *s.* campeón, paladín, adalid, *m.;* defensor, abogado; (dep.) campeón. II. *a.* supremo, sin par, de primera. III. *va.* defender, abogar por.—**championess** [-ɛs], *s.* campeona; defensora, abogadora.—**championship** [-ŝịp], *s.* campeonato.

chance [chæns]. I. *s.* azar, acaso, casualidad; fortuna, ventura; ocasión, oportunidad, coyuntura; riesgo, peligro; billete de lotería, rifa, etc.; probabilidad.—**by c.**, por casualidad, por ventura; de chiripa.—**c. medley**, (for.) accidente u homicidio en defensa propia, en una reyerta; (fig.) pura casualidad o confusión.—**there is no c.**, no hay esperanza.—**to take chances**, correr un albur, aventurarse; confiar en la suerte. II. *a.* casual, accidental, fortuito. III. *vn.* acaecer, suceder, acontecer.—**to c. to have**, tener por casualidad.—**to c. upon**, topar (con). IV. *va.* (fam.) probar, arriesgar.

chancel [chænsẹl], *s.* (igl.) presbiterio, antealtar.

chancellery [-ẹrị], *s.* cancillería.

chancellor [-ọ(r)], *s.* canciller o chanciller; magistrado (de ciertos tribunales); presidente o rector (de ciertas universidades).—**C. of the Exchequer**, (Ingl.) Ministro de Hacienda. —**chancellorship** [-ŝịp], *s.* cancillería, cancillerato.

chancery [chænsẹrị], *s.* chancillería; tribunal (de varias clases).—**in c.**, en litigio; en aprietos; debajo del brazo del contrario (dícese de la cabeza de un boxeador).

chancre [ŝæŋkœ(r)], *s.* (med.) chancro.—**chancrous** [-krʌs], *a.* chancroso.

chancroid [-krọjd], *s.* (med.) chancroide, chancro blando.

chancy [chænsị], *a.* (fam.) arriesgado, incierto; (Esco.) de buena suerte; que promete.

chandelier [ŝændẹlír], *s.* araña, lucerna, lustro; candelabro que se cuelga del techo.

chandler [chændlœ(r)], *s.* cerero ⌐ velero; tendero, vendedor; abastecedor de ₋uques, pro-

veedor de granos, etc.—**c.'s shop**, abacería, mercería, (Am.) pulpería.

chandlery [-ị], *s.* almacén, tienda, mercancías o comercio de un *chandler.*

chanfrin [chænfrịn], *s.* frente (*f.*) del caballo.

change [chéjndž]. I. *va.* cambiar, alterar, modificar, transformar, variar, convertir; reemplazar, substituir, trocar; cambiar (moneda).—**to c. color**, ruborizarse; demudarse, inmutarse, palidecer.—**to c. face**, o **front**, cambiar de opinión o de conducta, desdecirse, virar de bordo (fig.). —**to c. hands**, cambiar de dueño.—**to c. one's clothes**, mudarse.—**to c. one's mind**, mudar de opinión.—**to c. one's tune**, cambiar de tono o actitud.—**to c. trains**, cambiar de tren. II. *vn.* mudar, cambiar, alterarse; corregirse, transformarse, trocarse. III. *s.* cambio; alteración, cambiamiento, demudación, mutación, mudanza; substitución, reemplazo, permutación, trueque; muda (de ropa, voz, etc.); vuelta o sobrante de un pago; menudo, suelto o moneda suelta; novedad, variedad; vaivén, vicisitud; (com.) lonja o bolsa.—**c. of heart**, arrepentimiento.—**c. of life**, (med.) menopausia.—**c. of the moon**, interlunio, cuarto de luna.—**for a c.**, para variar, por cambiar, por variedad.— **on 'c.**, en la bolsa.

changeability [-abịlịtị], *s.* mutabilidad.

changeable [-ạbl], *a.* variable; inconstante, veleidoso, voluble; alterable, cambiable, mudable; (tej.) cambiante, tornasolado.—**changeableness** [-nịs], *s.* mutabilidad; volubilidad; inestabilidad.—**changeably** [-ạblị], *adv.* inconstantemente; variablemente.—**changeful** [-fụl], *a.* inconstante, variable, veleidoso; variado.— **changeless** [-lịs], *a.* inmutable.—**changeling** [-lịŋ], *s.* niño cambiado por otro.

changer [-œ(r)], *s.* cambiador; cambista.

channel [chænẹl]. I. *s.* canal; álveo, cauce, lecho, madre (*f.*) de un río; arroyada; (geog.) canalizo, estuario, estrecho; zanja, caño, cacera, saetín; conducto; (carp.) cacera, ranura; (arq.) estría; (tec.) hierro en U (ll. t. **c. iron**).—*pl.* (mar.) mesas de guarnición.—**c. of a block**, (mar.) cajera de motón.—**c. wale**, (mar.) cinta de la segunda cubierta. II. *va.* acanalar, estriar; surcar; encauzar, conducir.

channeling [-iŋ], *s.* canal o sistema (*m.*) de canales, etc.; encauzamiento; (arq.) estriadura.

channelization [-izéjŝọn], *s.* canalización, encauzamiento.

channelize [-ajz], *va.* canalizar, encauzar.

chant [chænt]. I. *va.* y *vn.* cantar; discantar. II. *s.* canto llano; salmo; sonsonete.

chantage [ŝántáž], *s.* chantaje, explotación con amenazas de difamación. *V.* BLACKMAIL.

chanter [chæntœ(r)], *s.* cantor, chantre, primicerio.

chantey [chæntị], *s.* (mar.) saloma.

chanticleer [chæntịklịr], *s.* gallo.

chantlate [chæntlịt], *s.* (arq.) alero.

chantress [chæntrịs], *s.* cantora, cantatriz.

chantry [chæntrị], *s.* capilla; dotación (de una capilla o altar) para celebrarse misas, gen. en sufragio del fundador; la capilla o los sacerdotes dotados así.

chaos [kéjọs], *s.* el caos; gran confusión o desorden.—**chaotic** [kejátịk], *a.* caótico.

chap [chæp]. I. *va.* hender, rajar, resquebrajar, agrietar. II. *vn.* rajarse, agrietarse, cuartearse; ponerse áspero el cutis por la frialdad.—**chapping of the hands**, hendir, grietas en las manos.—**to become chapped**, (a)grietarse. III. *s.* grieta, raja, rendija, hendidura; (fam.) mozo, chico; tipo.

chap, chop [chæp o chap], *s.* mandíbula; quijada (de animal); quijada o mordaza de un tornillo de banco.

chaparajos [chaparáhọus], **chaparejos** [-éjhọus], *s. pl.* (Am.) chaparreras, zamarros.

chapbook [chǽpbŭk], *s.* librito de romances, etc., antes vendido por los buhoneros. *V.* CHAPMAN.

chape [cheip], *s.* chapa; contera, regatón; patilla o charnela de hebilla.

chapel [chǽpęl], *s.* capilla; coro u orquesta de una capilla; (impr.) personal de una imprenta.—**c. of ease**, ayuda de parroquia.—**chapelmaster**, [-mǽstœ(r)], maestro de capilla. *V.* KAPELL-MEISTER.

chapelry [-ri], *s.* jurisdicción de una capilla.

chaperon [šǽpęroun]. **I.** *s.* acompañadora de señoritas; señora de compañía. **II.** *va.* acompañar y escudar a una o más señoritas en lugares públicos.

chapfallen, chopfallen [chǽpfolęn, chápfolęn], *a.* boquihundido; (fig.) cariacontecido, alicaído.

chaplain [chǽplin], *s.* capellán; capellán castrense.—**chaplaincy** [-si], **chaplainship** [-šip], *s.* capellanía.

chaplet [chǽplit], *s.* guirnalda, corona de flores; rosario; gargantilla, collar; (arq.) moldura de cuentas.

chapman [chǽpmąn], *s.* buhonero.

chappy [chǽpi], *a.* agrietado, rajado.

chaps [chæps], *s. pl.* = CHAPARAJOS.

chapter [chǽptœ(r)], *s.* capítulo; (igl.) capítulo, cabildo; sucursal (*f.*) de una confraternidad.—**c. and verse**, con sus pelos y señales.—**c. house**, sala capitular.—**to read one a c.**, leer a uno la cartilla.—**to the end of the c.**, hasta el fin.

char [char]. **I.** *va.* y *vn.* carbonear; carbonizar(se), chamuscar(se). **II.** *s.* carbón de leña.

char-à-banc, charabanc [šær a bæŋ(k)], *s.* (fr.) charabán.

character [kǽriktœ(r)]. **I.** *s.* carácter, índole (*f.*), genio; fama, reputación; referencia; testimonio de conducta; clave secreta; marca, distintivo; persona, sujeto; (lit.) personaje, parte, *f.*, papel; carácter de letra; (fam.) tipo raro u original.—**c. actor o part**, (teat.) característico. **II.** *va.* grabar, esculpir, imprimir; caracterizar.

characteristic\al [-štjk(ąl], *a.* característico, distintivo, propio.—**characteristic**, *s.* característica, distintivo, peculiaridad; (mat.) característica.—**characteristically** [-ali], *adv.* característicamente.—**characterization** [-izéišǫn], *s.* caracterización, descripción, representación.—**characterize** [-ąjz], *va.* caracterizar.—**characterless** [-lis], *a.* sin carácter.

charactery [kǽriktœri], *s.* simbolismo; uso de señales o símbolos para representar una idea.

charade [šąréjd], *s.* charada.

charbon [šárban], *s.* (vet.) fiebre esplénica, ántrax.

charcoal [chárkoul], *s.* carbón de leña, carbón vegetal o animal; carboncillo de dibujos; dibujo al carbón.—**c. burner**, carbonero (que hace carbón).—**c. burning**, quema de madera para hacer carbón.—**c. drawing**, dibujo al carbón.—**c. furnace, o oven**, horno de hacer carbón por destilación.—**c. iron**, hierro de carbón de leña (en que éste es el combustible).

chard [chard], *s.* (bot.) acelga; hoja de alcachofa.

chare [chɛr], *s.* tarea suelta o de ocasión, trabajo por ratos. *V.* CHARWOMAN.

charge [chárdž]. **I.** *va.* cargar (un horno, un acumulador, etc.); gravar, imponer a; instruir, dar órdenes o instrucciones; exhortar, pedir a, mandar; cobrar, pedir, llevar (precio); (com.) cargar, endeudar, poner en cuenta; atacar, embestir; preparar, apuntar (un arma); blasonar.—**to c. with**, confiar, encargar, recomendar; acusar o tildar de, imputar o hacer cargo a uno (de algo). **II.** *vn.* fijar, pedir (precio); cargarse; cargar (a la bayoneta, etc.); agacharse, tenderse (los perros).

charge [chárdž], *s.* carga, embestida, ataque; carga, tiro (de cañón); carga (de un horno, un acumulador, etc.); cargo, custodia; comisión, encargo, encomienda; persona o cosa de que

uno está encargado; obligación; (com.) precio, costa, (gen. *pl.*) honorarios, costos, gastos; partida o suma cargada en cuenta; impuesto, gravamen; instrucciones (a un jurado, etc.), admonición, orden, *f.*, mandato; cargo, acusación.—**c. account**, (com.) cuenta abierta.—**in c.**, encargado; interino.—**to lay the c. at one's door**, echarle a uno la culpa.—**to take c. of**, encargarse o hacerse cargo de.

chargeable [-ąbl], *a.* que puede cargarse o atribuirse; acusable, imputable; obligado, sujeto.

chargé d'affaires [šaržéjdæfér], *s.* encargado de negocios (de una legación).

charger [chárdžœ(r)], *s.* cargador; el o lo que carga, etc.; corcel, caballo de guerra.

charily [chǽrili], *adv.* cautelosamente. *V.* CHARY.

chariness [-nis], *s.* cautela; frugalidad.

chariot [chǽriǫt], *s.* carro (de dos ruedas); carroza.

charioteer [-ír], *s.* cochero; (poét.) automedonte, auriga, *m.*; (C., astr.) Auriga.

charism [kǽrizm], *s.* (teol.) carisma, *m.*

charitable [chǽritabl], *a.* caritativo, benéfico, limosnero.—**c. funds o establishments**, obras pías.—**charitableness** [-nis], *s.* caridad.—**charitably** [-bli], *adv.* caritativamente.

charity [chǽriti], *s.* caridad; limosna; benevolencia.—**c. box**, cepillo de los pobres.—**c. child o pupil**, doctrino, niño de la doctrina.

charivari [šariivarí o šarivári], *s.* cencerrada.

charlatan [šárlątan], *s.* charlatán, curandero.

charlatanic [-tǽnik], *a.* empírico.—**charlatanism** [-jzm], **charlatanry** [-ri], *s.* charlatanería, charlatanismo, embaimiento.

charlock [chárlǫk], *s.* (bot.) mostaza silvestre.

charlotte (russe) [šárlǫt (rús)], *s.* carlota (rusa); natilla o compota rodeada de bizcochuelo.

charm [chárm]. **I.** *s.* encanto, embeleso, hechizo; ensalmo, encantamiento; maleficio; talismán, amuleto; (joy.) dije. **II.** *va.* ensalmar, hechizar; aojar; cautivar, encantar, embelesar, prendar.

charmer [-œ(r)], *s.* encantador, hechicero, fascinador, seductor.

charming [-iŋ], *a.* encantador; fascinante, seductor.—**charmingly** [-li], *adv.* encantadoramente.

charnel [chárnęl]. **I.** *a.* sepulcral. **II.** *s.* (ll. t. **c. house**) carnero, osario.

charpie [šarpí], *s.* (cir.) hilas.

charring [chárịŋ], *s.* carboneo, carbonización.

charry [chárị], *a.* carbonoso.

chart [chart]. **I.** *va.* poner en una carta hidrográfica; trazar en un diagrama, etc. **II.** *s.* (mar.) carta de navegar o de marear; carta hidrográfica; mapa, *m.*, cuadro, plano.—**c. recorder**, registro gráfico.—**c. room**, (mar.) caseta de derrota.

chartaceous [kartéjšʌs], *a.* que tiene la textura de papel.

charter [chártœ(r)]. **I.** *s.* cédula, título, encartación, carta de privilegio; carta constitucional; (com.) fletamento.—**c. member**, miembro fundador u originario.—**c. party**, contrata de fletamento. **II.** *va.* estatuir; (com.) fletar un barco; alquilar un tren, etc.—**charterage** [-idž], *s.* fletamento.—**chartered** [-d], *a.* privilegiado; (mar.) fletado.—**charterer** [-œ(r)], *s.* fletador.

charterhouse [-haus], *s.* cartuja.

chartless [chártlis], *a.* sin rumbo, desorientado.

chartographer, etc. *V.* CARTOGRAPHER, etc.

chartreuse [šartrœz], *s.* licor preparado por los cartujos; color verdoso pálido; (C.) cartuja.

chartulary [kártjulări], *s.* cartulario.

charwoman [chárwumąn], *s.* fregatriz, mujer asalariada por hora o día para faenas domésticas.

chary [chǽri], *a.* cuidadoso, cauteloso, circunspecto; económico, frugal, parco.

chase [chéjs]. **I.** *va.* cazar; perseguir; (joy.) engastar, montar; cincelar, encajar; acanalar.—**to c. away, o off**, ahuyentar, espantar; disipar.

II. *s.* caza; persecución; montería, partida de caza; cinegética; cazadero; (impr.) rama; (mec.) ranura, muesca, encaje; (art.) caña de un cañón.

chaser [-œ(r)], *s.* cazador; perseguidor; (joy.) encajador, engastador, recercador; cincelador; persona o caballo que se dedica a carreras de obstáculos; (mar.) cazasubmarinos; cañón de caza (de proa) o guardatimón; (aer.) avión ligero de defensa y perseguida.

chasing [-iŋ], *s.* caza, seguimiento; (joy.) encajadura, engarce; cinceladura.—**c. tool**, encajador.

chasm [kæzm], *s.* abismo, precipicio, sima, grieta, hendidura, quiebra; vacío, laguna, blanco.

chasseur [šæsœr], *s.* cazador; (mil.) cazador.

chassis [šæsi], *s.* armazón, *f.*, bastidor, marco; (art.) riel de cureña; (aut.) chasis, *m.*; (fot.) chasis, portaplacas.

chaste [chéjst], *a.* casto; virtuoso, continente, púdico; puro; castizo, neto (estilo, etc.).—**c. tree**, (bot.) agnocasto, sauzgatillo.—**chastely** [-lị], *adv.* castamente, púdicamente; correctamente.

chasten [chéjsẹn], *va.* corregir, castigar; depurar, limpiar, purificar (estilo, etc.).

chastener [-œ(r)], *s.* castigador, corrector; depurador.—**chasteness** [chéjstnịs], *s.* pureza, castidad.—**chastening** [chéjsẹnịŋ], *s.* castigo, corrección; disciplina.

chastisable [chæstájzạbl], *a.* punible, castigable.

chastise [chæstájz], *va.* castigar, corregir.—**chastisement** [-mẹnt], *s.* castigo, corrección.—**chastiser** [-œ(r)], *s.* castigador.

chastity [chæstịtị], *s.* castidad, pureza, pudicicia.

chasuble [chæsjubl], *s.* (igl.) casulla.

chat [chæt]. **I.** *vn.* charlar, platicar. **II.** *s.* conversación, plática, charla; (orn.) pájaro.

chateau [šætóụ], *s.* = CASTLE.

chatelaine [šætẹlejn], *s.* castellana; (joy.) muelle de dijes.

chattels [chætẹlz], *s. pl.* bienes muebles, enseres.

chatter [chætœ(r)]. **I.** *vn.* castañetear o rechinar (los dientes); cotorrear, parlotear, charlar, (fam.) hablar por los codos; (mec.) vibrar. **II.** *s.* rechinido; garla, charla, cháchara; garrulería; vibración.—**chatterbox** [-baks], *s.* charlador, tarabilla, trápala, *mf.*—**chatterer** [-œ(r)], *s.* charlador, gárrulo, hablistán.—**chattering** [-iŋ]. **I.** *s.* chirrido; rechinamiento; garrulidad, cotorreo, picotería. **II.** *a.* locuaz, hablanchín.

chatty [chætị], *a.* hablantín, picotero, gárrulo.

chauffeur [šoụfœr], *s.* chófer o chofer, conductor de automóvil.

chauvinism [šóụvịnịzm], *s.* patriotería, chauvinismo.

chauvinist [-ịst], *a.* y *s.* patriotero, chauvinista.

chaw [cho]. **I.** *va.* (vulg.) mascar. *V.* CHEW. **II.** *s.* (vulg.) mascada, bocado.

cheap [chíp], *a.* barato; de pacotilla; común, vulgar.—**c. skate**, (fam.) tacaño.—**to feel c.**, avergonzarse, sentirse inferior.—**to hold c.**, tener en poco.

cheapen [-ẹn], *va.* y *vn.* abaratar(se), despreciar(se).

cheapening [-iŋ], *s.* abaratamiento (de precios).

cheaply [-lị], *adv.* barato, a bajo precio.

cheapness [-nịs], *s.* baratura, modicidad.

cheat [chít]. **I.** *va.* engañar, defraudar; timar, trampear; enfullar (en el juego); chasquear.—**to c. out of**, sacarle o quitarle (a uno) por engaño; privar de (gen. por engaño). **II.** *s.* trampa, fraude, engaño; trampista, timador. *V.* CHEATER.

cheater [-œ(r)], *s.* trampista, tramposo, fullero; estafador, embustero, engañador, defraudador.

cheatery [-œrị], *s.* fraude, trampa, fullería.

cheating [-iŋ], *s.* engaño, fraude, trampería.

check [chék]. **I.** *va.* contener, contrarrestar, detener, parar, poner coto o freno a, refrenar, reprimir; moderar, reportar; comprobar, confrontar, verificar y marcar; registrar, facturar (equipajes, etc.); dar a guardar (el sombrero,

etc.), recibiendo una contraseña de reclamo; rajar, agrietar; jaquear, dar jaque a (ajedrez).—**to c. off**, verificar y dar el visto bueno a. (*V.* t. C.-OFF).—**to c. up**, verificar, comprobar.—**to c. up on**, comprobar lo hecho por; seguir la pista a. **II.** *vn.* detenerse, pararse; corresponder, estar conforme; rajarse, agrietarse; dar jaque. **III.** *s.* lo que contiene o detiene; detención, contrarresto, refrenamiento, represión; rechazo; obstáculo, impedimento; contratiempo; verificación, comprobación, ensayo, prueba; (com)probador; contraseña, billete de reclamo (de equipajes, etc.); cuadro, jaquel (en tela, etc., de cuadros); jaque (ajedrez); ficha (en el juego); grieta, grietecilla filiforme (en acero, hormigón, etc.); (carp.) muesca, entalladura; cuenta (de restaurante); (mec.) tope; (com.) cheque; póliza, talón.—**c. boy (girl)**, mozo (moza) que recibe y guarda los sombreros, abrigos, etc. en restaurantes, etc. y da las contraseñas.—**c. list**, lista para la confrontación de nombres, etc.—**c. mark**, marca.—**c. nut**, contratuerca.—**c.-off**, recaudación de contribuciones de los obreros a los gremios, haciendo que los patrones las rebajen de los salarios.—**c. protector**, (com.) protectógrafo.—**c.-up**, examen, comprobación.—**c. valve**, válvula de retención.—**c. writer**, máquina de estampar cheques.—**in c.**, contenido, refrenado.

checkbook [-bụk], *s.* (libro) talonario, librete de cheques.

checker [chékœ(r)], *s.* refrenador; verificador, etc.

checker, chequer [chékœ(r)]. **I.** *va.* (a) taracear; formar escaques o cuadros; diversificar. **II.** *s.* cada pieza del juego de damas; escaque.—*pl.* juego de damas.

checkerberry [-berị], *s.* (bot.) gaulteria y su baya.

checkerboard [-bord], *s.* tablero de damas.

checkered [-d], *a.* escaqueado, jaquelado, ajedrezado; variado; de fortuna inconstante.

checking [chékịŋ], *s.* refrenamiento, etc.; comprobación, etc.; agrietamiento.—**c. account**, cuenta corriente (en un banco).

checkless [chéklịs], *a.* desenfrenado.

checkmate [-mejt]. **I.** *va.* dar (jaque) mate; desconcertar, derrotar. **II.** *s.* (jaque) mate.

checkrein [-rejn], *s.* (tal.) engallador; gamarra.

checkroom [-rum], *s.* guardarropa, *m.*; cuarto donde se deja algo a guardar, recibiendo una contraseña.

cheek [chík], *s.* carrillo, mejilla, cachete; (art.) gualdera de cureña; (mec.) quijada, montante, larguero; banzo, cárcel, *f.*; (fam.) tupé, descaro, desfachatez; jamba (de puerta o ventana), derrame; cachola (de mástil).—**c. by jowl**, (fam.) cara a cara; en estrecha intimidad.—**c. piece o strap**, (tal.) quijera.—**c. pouch**, (zool.) abazón.—**with (one's) tongue in (one's) c.**, fingidamente, irónicamente.

cheekbone [-boụn], *s.* pómulo, juanete.

cheeky [-ị], *a.* (fam.) descarado, desfachatado.

cheep [chip]. **I.** *vn.* piar, pipiar; chirriar. **II.** *s.* pío, piada; chirrido.

cheer [chír]. **I.** *s.* alegría, regocijo; banquete, festín.—*pl.* vivas, vítores, aplausos.—**to be of good c.**, estar alegre, o de buen ánimo. **II.** *va.* alentar, consolar, alegrar, regalar; vitorear, aplaudir. **III.** *vn.* alegrarse.—**to c. up**, animarse, avivarse, cobrar ánimo.—**c. up!** ¡ánimo, valor!

cheerer [-œ(r)], *s.* regocijador; vitoreador.

cheerful [-fụl], *a.* (fam.) alegre, animado, genial, gozoso, jovial.—**cheerfully** [-ị], *adv.* alegremente, con júbilo.—**cheerfulness** [-nịs], *s.* alegría, gozo, jovialidad.—**cheering** [-ị], *a.* alentador, confortativo.—**cheerless** [-lịs], *a.* triste, melancólico; inhospitalario.

cheery [-ị], *a.* = CHEERFUL.

cheese [chíz]. **I.** *s.* queso; (fam.) cosa o persona que vale.—**c. curds**, cuajadas.—**c. dish**, quesera.—**c. mite**, ácaro de queso.—**c. mold**, cincho, encella.—**c. parings**, cortezas de queso; (fig.) tacañería, mezquindad.—**c. rennet**, cuajaleche, *f.*—**c. vat**, quesera, formaje. **II.** *va.* (fam.)—**c. it**, calle, déjese de eso; márchese.

cheesecake [-keik], *s.* quesadilla.

cheesecloth [-klɒθ], *s.* estopilla de algodón.

cheesemonger [-mʌŋgœ(r)], *s.* quesero.

cheesy [-i], *a.* caseoso, quesero; (fam.) sin valor.

cheeta(h [chítạ], *s.* (zool.) especie de leopardo de Asia y África que se adiestra para la caza.

chef [šef], *s.* jefe; maestro de cocina; cocinero.

chef-d'œuvre [šedœvr], *s.* obra maestra.

chela [kílạ], *s.* (zool.) quelícero; pinza de langosta.

chela [chéjlạ], *s.* En India, semiesclavo, esclavo que se cría con una familia; discípulo; novicio.

chelonian [kẹlóunjạn] *a.* y *s.* (zool.) quelonio.

chemical [kémjkạl]. **I.** *a.* químico. **II.** *s.* producto químico; reactivo.—**chemically** [-i], *adv.* químicamente.

chemise [šẹmíz], *s.* camisa de mujer; (fort.) camisa.

chemisette [šemjzét], *s.* camiseta o camisolín de mujer.

chemism [kémjzm], *s.* afinidad o actividad química; fenómenos químicos.

chemist [kémjst], *s.* químico; farmacéutico.

chemistry [-ri], *s.* química.

chemotherapeutic [kemoθerạpjútjk], *a.* quimioterapéutico.

chemotherapy [-θérạpi], *s.* quimioterapia.

chenille [šẹníl], *s.* (tej.) felpilla.

chenopod [kínopad], *s.* (bot.) quenopodio.

chenopodiaceous [kinopodjéjậạs], *a.* (bot.) quenopodiáceo.

cheque [chɛk], *s.* (Ingl.) (com.) cheque o talón.

chequer, *va.* y *s.* = CHECKER.

cherish [chérjš], *va.* apreciar, estimar, fomentar; alimentar, abrigar, acariciar, regalar.

cheroot [šẹrút], *s.* (Filip.) trompetilla (cigarro).

cherry [chéri]. **I.** *s.* (bot.) cereza; cerezo (árbol y madera). **II.** *a.* hecho de cereza o de cerezo; de color de cereza.—**c. red**, rojo cereza.

chert [chœrt], *s.* (min.) variedad de calcedonia.

cherty [-i], *a.* que tiene cuarzo; pedernalino.

cherub [chérʌb], *s.* (*pl.* CHERUBIM) querubín, querub(e); (*pl.* CHERUBS) niño angelical, o sonrosado y mofletudo.

cherubic(al [cherúbjk(ạl], *a.* querúbico.

chervil [chœrvjl], *s.* (bot.) cerafolio, perifollo.

chess [chés], *s.* ajedrez, *m.*, escaques, *pl.*; (bot.) bromo.—**c. player**, ajedr(ec)ista.—**chessboard** [-bɔrd], tablero de ajedrez.—**chessman** [-mạn], trebejo, pieza de ajedrez.

chessel [chésẹl], *s.* encella.

chest [chest], *s.* arca, baúl, cofre, caja, cajón; (anat.) pecho, seno, tórax; tesoro; (mec.) receptáculo para gases o líquidos.—**c. cavity**, (anat.) cavidad torácica, caja del pecho.—**c. cold**, catarro bronquial.—**c. of drawers**, cómoda, buró.—**c. protector**, pechera, peto de lana para abrigo.

chestnut [chésnʌt]. **I.** *s.* (bot.) castaña; castaño (árbol y madera); color de castaña o marrón; (fam.) broma o frase gastada; (vet.) excrecencia córnea.—**to take, o pull, another's c.'s out of the fire**, sacarle a otro el ascua, dejar que otro saque el ascua por mano de uno. **II.** *a.* castaño; zaino.

chetah [chítạ], *s.* (zool.) = CHEETAH.

cheval [šẹvél], *s.* caballo, caballete; apoyo, sostén.—**c.-de-frise** = CHEVAUX-DE-FRISE.—**c. glass**, psique o psiquis, espejo móvil de cuerpo entero.

chevalier [šẹvạlír], *s.* caballero; galán.—**c. of industry**, caballero de industria, estafador.

chevaux-de-frise [šœvóudœfríz], *s. pl.* (mil.) caballo de Fris(i)a.

Cheviot [chévjot], *s.* (zool.) cordero de Escocia.

cheviot [šévjot], *s.* (tej.) cheviot.

chevron [šévrọn], *s.* (mil.) sardineta; (blas.) cheurón, cabrio; (arq.) cheurón; cabrio.

chevrotain [šévrotejn], *s.* (zool.) trágulo.

chevy [chévj], **chiv(v)y** [chjvj]. **I.** *va.* (Ingl.) acosar; cazar. **II.** *s.* caza; seguimiento; grito de caza.

chew [chú]. **I.** *va.* y *vn.* mas(ti)car; rumiar; (fig.) rumiar, meditar; (fam.) mascar tabaco o goma. —**to c. the cud**, rumiar; considerar despacio. —**to c. the rag**, (fam.) charlar, machacar o porfiar, dale que dale. **II.** *s.* mascadura; mascada (de tabaco).

chewer [-œ(r)], *s.* mascador; rumiante.

chewing [-ịŋ]. **I.** *s.* masticación, mascadura; rumia. **II.** *a.* mascador; de o para mascar.—**c. gum**, chicle, goma de mascar.

chewink [chjwíŋk], *s.* (orn.) variedad de pinzón.

chiaroscuro [kịạroskjúrou], *s.* claroscuro.

chiasm [kájæzm], **chiasma** [kạjézmạ], *s.* (anat., biol.) quiasma, *m.*, decusación.

chibouk [chjbúk], *s.* chibuquí, pipa turca.

chic [šịk o šjk]. **I.** *a.* gentil, elegante, mono. **II.** *s.* elegancia, buen tono, gentileza.

chicane [šjkéjn]. **I.** *s.* tramoya, trampa, argucia, sofistería. **II.** *va.* y *vn.* trampear, embrollar, cavilar, sutilizar, buscar escapatorias, (Am.) chicanear.

chicanery [-œri], *s.* trapacería, trampería, sofistería, sutileza, embrollo, trampa legal, cavilación, (Am.) chican(ead)a.

chick, chicken [chjk, -ẹn], *s.* polluelo o pollo, pollito; (fig.) jovencito, niño; (fam.) chica, polla.—**c. breast**, (med.) deformidad del pecho causada por la raquitis.—**c. coop**, pollera.—**c.-hearted**, cobarde, gallina, medroso.—**c. pox**, (med.) varicela, viruelas locas.

chickadee [-ạdi], *s.* (orn.) paro americano.

chickpea [-pi], *s.* (bot.) garbanzo.

chickweed [-wid], *s.* (bot.) pamplina.

chicle [chjkl], *s.* (bot.) chicle (ll. t. **c. gum**).

chicory [chjkori], *s.* (bot.) achicoria.

chide [chájd]. **I.** *va.* (*pret.* CHID o CHIDED; *pp.* CHID, CHIDDEN o CHIDED) increpar, reprender, regañar; ahuyentar. **II.** *vn.* regañar, refunfuñar.

chider [-œ(r)], *s.* represor, regañón, regañador.

chiding [-ịŋ]. **I.** *s.* increpación, regaño, reprimenda. **II.** *a.* increpador, increpante, regañón.

chidingly [-li], *adv.* en tono de represión.

chief [chíf]. **I.** *a.* principal, capital; primero, en jefe.—**c. clerk**, oficial mayor.—**c. judge**, o **c. justice**, presidente de sala; (E. U.) presidente de la corte suprema; (hist.) Justicia Mayor (de Aragón). **II.** *s.* jefe; adalid, *m.*, cabeza, cabecilla; caudillo; cacique; (com.) principal.— **c. of staff**, (mil.) jefe de estado mayor.—**c. pilot**, (aer.) piloto-jefe.—**in c.**, en jefe.

chiefless [-ljs], *a.* sin jefe.

chiefly [-li], *adv.* principalmente, mayormente.

chieftain [chíftjn], *s.* jefe, comandante; caudillo, capitán; cabeza.—**chieftaincy** [-si], **chieftainship** [-šjp], *s.* jefatura.

chiffer [šjfœ(r)], **chiffre** [šífr], *s.* (mús.) cifra.

chiffon [šjfán], *s.* (tej.) gasa, soplillo.

chiffonier [šjfonjr], *s.* mueble de cajonería, cómoda alta, a veces con espejo.

chigger, chigre [chjgœ(r)], *s.* = CHIGOE.

chignon [šínyan], *s.* moño, castaña, (Fil.) posó.

chigoe [chjgou], *s.* (ent.) nigua, pique.

chilblain [chjlblejn], *s.* (med.) sabañón.

child [chájld]. **I.** *s.* (*pl.* CHILDREN) niño o niña; hijo o hija; infante, párvulo, criatura, chiquillo. —**c.'s play**, niñería; de clavo pasado, muy fácil.—**with c.**, preñada, embarazada. **II.** *a.* del niño, de (los) niños.—**c. labor**, trabajo de menores.—**c. welfare**, bien del niño.

childbearing [-berjŋ], *s.* parto.

childbed [-bed], *s.* parto; sobreparto, puerperio. —**c. fever**, fiebre puerperal.

childbirth [-bœrθ], *s.* parto, alumbramiento.

Childermas Day [chjldœrmạs dej], **Childermastide** [-tajd], *s.* día (*m.*) de los inocentes.

childhood [cháildhụd], s. infancia, niñez.
childish [cháildiš], a. pueril, aniñado; frívolo, trivial.—c. action, chiquillada, muchachada, niñería.—childishly [-li], adv. puerilmente.—childishness [-niṣ], s. puerilidad, niñada.
childless [cháildliṣ], a. sin hijos.
childlike [-laịk], a. pueril, infantil.
children [chịldrẹn], s. pl. de CHILD.
Chilean [chílịan], a. y s. chileno.
chile, chili [chíli], s. (bot.) chile, ají.—c. sauce, ajiaco, ají, salsa de chile.
chiliad [kílịæd], s. mil; mil años.
chiliasm [kílịæzm], s. doctrina milenaria.
chiliast [kílịæst], s. milenario.
chill [chil]. I. a. frío, desapacible, desalentador. II. s. frío, (es)calofrío; tiritón; enfriamiento; estremecimiento.—chills and fever, fiebre (f.) intermitente. III. va. enfriar, resfriar, pasmar, helar; desanimar, desalentar; (fund.) templar superficialmente por enfriamiento rápido. IV. vn. calofriarse.
chilli [chíli], s. = CHILI.
chill(i)ness [chíl(i)niṣ], s. frialdad, calidad de frío.
chilly [chíli]. I. a. frío, calofriado; friolento. II. adv. fríamente.
chimb, chime [chaịm], s. (ton.) cabo o remate de barril o tina, más allá del jable o gárgol.
chime [chaịm]. I. s. juego de campanas; campaneo, repique, repiquete; armonía, ritmo; conformidad, analogía. II. va. tocar, tañer las campanas. III. vn. repicar, repiquetear (las campanas); sonar con armonía; convenir, concordar (frec. con with, o in with).
chimera, chimæra [kaịmírä], s. (mit.) quimera; monstruo imaginario; ilusión; (ict.) quimera, pez de los holocéfalos.
chimere [chịmír], s. sobrepelliz.
chimerical [kaịmérịkạl], a. quimérico, imaginario.—chimerically [-ị], adv. quiméricamente.
chimney [chímni], s. chimenea; bombillo o tubo de lámpara.—c. cap, o pot, o c. TOP.—c. corner, chimenea, hogar.—c. flue, cañón, humero de chimenea.—c. piece, campana o repisa de chimenea.—c. swallow, (orn.) golondrina. —c. sweep(er), limpiachimeneas, deshollinador.—c. swift, (orn.) especie de vencejo.—c. top, caperuza, remate o sombrerete de chimenea.
chimpanzee [chịmpænzí], s. (zool.) chimpancé.
chin [chịn]. I. s. barba, barbilla, mentón.—c. band, barbicacho.—c. cloth, babador.—c. music, (fam.) charla, cotorreo.—c. strap, carrillera, barboquejo.—to keep one's c. up, (fam.) no desanimarse. II. vn. (fam.) charlar, chismear.
china [chájnä], s. china, porcelana, loza.—C. clay, caolín.—c. closet, chinero.—C. ink, tinta china.—c. orange, naranja china; naranja dulce.—C. silk, china.—C. tree, chinaberry, aceqeraque, cinamomo.—c. wedding, vigésimo aniversario.
Chinaman [-mạn], s. chino.
chinaroot [-rut], s. (bot.) china.
chinaware [-wer], s. = CHINA.
chinch [chịnch], s. (ent.) chinche, f.—c. bug, (ent.) insecto hemíptero muy nocivo para el trigo, etc.
chinchilla [chịnchílä], s. (zool.) chinchilla y su piel; (tej.) cierto paño de lana a imitación de esta piel.
chine [chaịn]. I. s. espinazo; lomo; solomo; (top.) cumbre, cerro. II. va. deslomar.
Chinese [chaịníz]. I. a. chino, chinesco, sínico.—C. anise, badián.—C. lantern, farolillo de papel.—C. paper, papel de China o de arroz, m.—C. puzzle, problema arduo o enredado.—C. white, blanco u óxido de cinc. II. s. chino, lengua china.
chink [chịŋk], s. grieta, hendedura, resquebradura, rajadura; sonido metálico; tintín; (fam.)

dinero, blanca.—C. (desp.) chino. II. va. hender, rajar; llenar los resquicios en. III. va. y vn. (hacer) sonar, retiñir o tintinar (copas, monedas, etc.).
chinkapin, chinquapin [chịŋkạpịn], s. (bot.) castaño enano, y su fruto.
chinky [chíŋkị], a. hendido, rajado, resquebrajadizo.
chinned [chịnd], a. barbado.
chinse [chịnts], va. (mar.) calafatear, embromar costuras.
chintz [chịnts], s. (tej.) quimón, zaraza.
chip [chíp]. I. va. desmenuzar, picar; astillar, descantillar. II. vn. romperse, quebrarse, desconcharse.—to c. in, (fam.) poner la apuesta (en el juego); contribuir. III. s. brizna, astilla; pedacito; viruta; ficha, tanto (en el juego).—pl. chamada, doladura; támaras; patatas a la inglesa.—c. ax, o axe, azuela.—a c. of(f) the old block, de tal palo, tal astilla.—to carry a c. on one's shoulder, ser belicoso, contencioso o pendenciero.
chip, vn. y s. = CHIRP.—chipping sparrow, chippy, (orn.) variedad de gorrioncillo.
chipmunk [chípmʌŋk], s. (zool.) especie de ardilla.
chipper [chípœ(r)]. I. s. el o lo que desmenuza, etc. II. a. (E. U. fam.) vivo, alegre.
chipping [-iŋ], s. acción o efecto del verbo TO CHIP.
chirk [chœrk]. I. a. (fam.) alegre, jovial. II. va. y vn. (fam.) (con up) alegrar(se), avivar(se).
chirograph [kájrogræf], s. quirógrafo.
chirographer [kaịrágrạfœ(r)], s. escribano, escribiente.—chirography [-fị], s. quirografía; carácter de letra.
chiromancer [kájromænsœ(r)], s. quiromántico.
chiromancy [kájromænsị], s. quiromancía.
chiropodist [kaịrápodịst], s. pedicuro, callista.
chiropodous [-dʌs], a. (zool.) quirópodo.
chiropody [-dị], s. quiropodia.
chiropractic [kaịroprǽktịk], s. quiropráctica (método de tratamiento médico manipulando la columna vertebral); quiropráctico.—chiropractor [kájropræktǫ(r)], s. quiropráctico.
chiropter [kaịráptœ(r)], s. chiropterous [-ʌs], a. (zool.) quiróptero, alípedo (apl. a los murciélagos).
chirp [chœrp]. I. vn. chirriar, gorjear, pipiar, piar, chicharrear. II. s. chirrido; gorjeo; canto.
chirper [-œ(r)], s. chirriador, piador; pajarillo.
chirping [-iŋ]. I. s. chirrido, piada, parlería. II. a. que pía; parlero, gárrulo.
chirrup [chíŗʌp]. I. va. y vn. chirriar repetidas veces; gorjear, trinar. II. s. gorjeo, trino.
chisel [chízẹl]. I. s. escoplo, cincel, formón, buril. II. va. y vn. escoplear, cincelar, esculpir, burilar; (fam.) engañar, embaucar, obtener con fraude.—chisel(l)er [-œ(r)], s. el que escoplea, etc.; (fam.) engañador; oportunista.
chit [chịt]. I. s. (despec.) chiquilla, muchacha descarada; vale; apunte, billete; (bot.) tallo, botón. II. va. quitar los brotes o renuevos.
chitchat [chítchæt], s. cháchara, charla, palique.
chitin [kájtịn], s. (bioquím.) quitina.
chiton [kájtọn], s. túnica; (zool.) chitón.
chitterlings [chítœrlịŋz], s. pl. intestinos menudos del puerco, etc., cocidos o fritos.
chivalric [šívạlrịk], a. caballeresco.—chivalrous [-ŗʌs], a. caballeroso.—chivalry [-rị], s. caballería; caballerosidad, hidalguía.
chive [chaịv], s. (bot.) cebollino, cebollana.
chiv(v)y [chívị], va. y s. V. CHEVY.
chlamys [kléịmịs o klǽmịs], s. clámide, f.
chloral [klóṛạl], s. (quím.) (hidrato de) cloral.
chlorate [klóṛeịt], s. (quím.) clorato.
chloric [klórịk], a. clórico.
chlorid, chloride [klórịd, klóṛaịd], s. (quím.) cloruro.—c. of lime, cloruro de cal.
chloridize [klórịdaịz], chlorinate [-neịt], va. clorar, tratar con cloro; (metal.) clorurar.

chlorination [-néiṣọn], *s.* cloración; cloruración.—**chlorinator** [klórinẹitọ(r)], *s.* clorador, aparato de clorar.

chlorine [klórin], *s.* (quím.) cloro.

chlorite [klórait], *s.* (min.) clorita; (quím.) clorito.

chloroform [klóroform]. I. *s.* (quím.) cloroformo. II. *va.* cloroformizar.—**chloroformic** [-fórmik], *a.* cloroformico.—**chloroformization** [-iẓéiṣọn], *s.* cloroformización.

chlorometer [klórámetœ(r)], *s.* (quím.) clorómetro.—**chlorometry** [-tri], *s.* clorometría.

chlorophyl(l [klórofil], *s.* clorofila.

chlorophyllaceous [-éiṣị̀ʌs], *a.* clorofílico.

chlorosis [kloróuṣis], *s.* (med.) clorosis.

chlorotic [klorátik], *a.* clorótico.

chlorous [klórʌs], *a.* cloroso.

chock [chák]. I. *s.* calzo, cuña, tornapunta; (mar.) calzo; choque; cornamusa de guía. *V.* CHUCK. II. *va.* afianzar, soportar, calzar.

chock-full [-fúl], *a.* colmado, atestado, repleto, de bote en bote.

chocolate [cháklit], *s.* chocolate, (Am.) cacao.—**c.-colored**, achocolatado.—**c. cup**, pocillo, jícara.—**c. pot**, chocolatera.—**c. tree**, cacao (árbol).

choice [chóis]. I. *s.* elección, escogimiento, preferencia, selección; alternativa; opción; cosa elegida; lo selecto, lo más escogido; variedad, abundancia. II. *a.* escogido, selecto, exquisito, florido, granado.

choicely [-li], *adv.* escogidamente, primorosamente.—**choiceness** [-nis], *s.* delicadeza; discernimiento.

choir [kwair], *s.* (igl. y mús.) coro.—**c. boy**, infante o niño de coro.—**c. loft**, coro.—**c. master**, maestro de capilla.—**c. stalls**, sillería.

choke [chóuk]. I. *va.* y *vn.* ahogar, sofocar; asfixiar, estrangular; agarrotar; suprimir, oprimir, tupir; atragantarse, atorarse; (m. comb. int.) ahogar, obturar o cerrar (el carburador).—**to c. up**, cerrar, obstruir, obturar, tapar. II. *s.* estrangulación.—**c. coil**, (elec.) bobina de reactancia o de reducción.—**c.-full** = CHOCK-FULL.—**c. pear**, (bot.) ahogadera, pera áspera o ahogadiza.

chokedamp [-dœmp], *s.* (min.) gas asfixiante y no combustible (de anhídrido carbónico) de las minas de carbón, etc.

choker [-œ(r)], *s.* ahogador, agarrotador; (fam.) corbatín; cuello alto; corbata blanca; tapaboca, bufanda; gargantilla; (aut.) regulador de aire, obturador del carburador.

choking [-iŋ]. I. *a.* que ahoga, etc.; sofocante. II. *s.* ahogo; atragantamiento; estrangulación; obturación.—**c. coil**, (elec.) = CHOKE COIL.

choky [-i], *a.* sofocante.

cholagogue [káląɡaɡ], *a.* y *s.* (farm.) colagogo.

choler [kálœ(r)], *s.* cólera, ira.

cholera [kálęrą], *s.* (med.) cólera, *m.;* cólera-morbo; cólera asiático.—**c. morbus**, cólera-morbo.—**c. infantum**, cólera infantil, enteritis coleriforme de los niños.

choleraic [kalęréiik], *a.* colérico (referente al cólera).

choleric [kálęrik], *a.* colérico, irascible.

choleriform [kálęriform], *a.* coleriforme.

cholerine [kálęrin], *s.* (med.) colerín o colerina.

cholesterin [koléstęrin], **cholesterol** [-ol], *s.* (bioquím.) colesterina.

choline [kóulin], *s.* (bioquím.) colina.

chondroblast [kándroblæst], *s.* (anat.) condroblasto.

chondrology [kandráloḓi̧], *s.* condrología, condrografía.

choose [chúz]. I. *va.* (*pret.* CHOSE; *pp.* CHOSEN) escoger, elegir, preferir, seleccionar, triar, optar por; desear.—**cannot c. but**, no poder menos de. II. *vn.* preferir, querer.

chooser [-œ(r)], *s.* escogedor; elector.

choos(e)y [-i], *a.* (fam.) remilgado, melindroso.

choosing [-iŋ], *s.* escogimiento, (s)elección.

chop [cháp]. I. *va.* tajar, cortar, separar; picar carne; (carp.) desbastar; rajar, hender; hablar a borbotones.—**to c. off**, tronchar. II. *vn.* dar cuchilladas; interrumpir; virar (el viento).—**to c. about**, girar, virar.—**to c. in**, interrumpir.—**to c. logic**, discutir, disputar con argucias, sofistería o casuística. III. *s.* porción, parte, *f.;* tajada, posta de carne; chuleta o costilla; (mec.) quijada, mordaza (de tornillo, etc.).—*pl.* quijadas; boca, entrada (de cañón, canal, valle, etc.).

chopfallen, *a.* = CHAPFALLEN.

chophouse [-haus], *s.* bodegón, figón.

chopine [choupín], *s.* chapín.

chopped [chapt], *pp.* de TO CHOP.—**c. meat**, carne picada; picadillo.

chopper [chápœ(r)], *s.* tajador; cuchilla de carnicero.

chopping [chápiŋ]. I. *a.* variable (viento); picado (mar). II. *s.* tajadura, cortadura.—**c. block**, tajo de cocina, tajadero, picador.—**c. board**, tajadera.—**c. knife**, cuchilla, tajadera.—**c. bowl**, **c. tray**, artesilla de picar (carne, etc.).

choppy [chápi], *a.* rajado, hendido; picado, agitado (mar); variable (viento); (fig.) incoherente, abrupto.

chopsticks [chápstiks], *s. pl.* palillos chinos para comer.

choral [kóral], *a.* y *s.* (mús.) coral.

chord [kord]. I. *s.* cuerda, cordón; (mús.) cuerda; acorde; armonía; (geom.) cuerda; (aer.) cuerda del ala; (ing.) cordón, cabeza (de un puente de celosía); (fig.) fibra, cuerda sensible. II. *va.* (mús.) encordar. III. *va.* y *vn.* templar; armonizar.

chorda [kórḓą], *s.* (anat.) cuerda.—**c. dorsalis**, notocordio, cuerda dorsal o columna vertebral (embrionaria).

chordate [kórdeit], *a.* y *s.* (zool.) cordado.

chore [chor], *s.* tarea doméstica; quehacer, faena.

chorea [koríǎ], *s.* (med.) corea, baile de San Vito.

choree, choreus [korí, koríʌs], *s.* (pros.) coreo, troqueo, pie de verso (—◡).

choreography [koréġrǎfi], *s.* = CHOREOGRAPHY.

choreograph [kóriogrǽf], *s.* coreógrafo.

chore(o)graphic [kori(o)grǽfik], *a.* coreográfico.

choreography [koriǎgrǎfi], *s.* coreografía.

choriamb [kóriæmb], *s.* (pros.) coriambo.

choriambic [koriǽmbik]. I. *s.* (pros.) coriambo, pie de verso (—◡◡—). II. *a.* coriámbico.

chor(i)oid [kór(i)oid]. I. *a.* (anat.) coroideo.—**c. coat**, coroides, *f.*—**c. plexus**, plexo coroideo. II. *s.* coroides, *f.*

chorion [kórion], *s.* (anat.) corión, *m.*

chorist [kórist], **chorister** [kóristœ(r)], *s.* corista o clerizón.

chorographer [korágrǎfœ(r)], *s.* (geog.) corógrafo.

chorographical [korográfikąl], *a.* corográfico.

chorography [korágrǎfi], *s.* corografía.

chortle [chórtl], *vn.* y *s.* *V.* CHUCKLE.

chorus [kórʌs]. I. *va.* y *vn.* corear; componer o cantar música coreada; cantar o hablar a coro; hacer coro a. II. *s.* (mús. y teat.) coro; (poét.) estrambote, estribillo.—**c. girl**, (teat.) corista (cantante o bailadora).—**c. singer**, corista.—**in c.**, al unísono, todos juntos.

chose, chosen [chóuz, -ẹn], *pret.* y *pp.* de TO CHOOSE.—**chosen people**, pueblo escogido.

chose [ṣóuz], *s.* (for.) cualquier objeto de propiedad personal.

chough [chʌf], *s.* (orn.) chova.

chouse [cháus]. I. *va.* engañar, estafar. II. *s.* engaño, fraude, estafa; bribón, estafador.

chow [chau], *s.* perro de raza china; (fam.) comida.

chowchow [cháuchau], *s.* mezcla de encurtidos con mostaza. *V.* CHOW.

chowder [cháudœ(r)], *s.* sancocho de almejas, pescado o maíz, gen. con leche y patatas, etc.

chrestomathy [krεstámɑθi̯], s. crestomatía.

chrism [krízm], s. (igl.) crisma, mf.

chrismatory [krízmɑtori̯], s. (igl.) crismera.

chrisom [krízɔm], s. (igl.) ropaje de bautizar.

Christ [krai̯st], s. Cristo; el Mesías.—**the C. child**, el Niño Jesús.

christcross [krískrɔs], s. cristus (cruz puesta al principio del abecedario); señal (f.) de la cruz.

christen [krísęn], va. bautizar, cristianar.

Christendom [-dǫm], s. cristiandad, cristianismo.

christening [-i̯ŋ]. I. s. bautizo; bautismo, cristianismo. II. a. bautismal.

Christian [krísчhąn], a. y s. cristiano.—**C. name**, nombre de bautismo o de pila.

Christianism, Christianity [-i̯zm, krischчǽni̯ti̯], s. cristianismo, cristiandad.

Christianize [-ai̯z], va. cristianizar.

Christianlike [-lai̯k], a. cristiano.

Christianly [-li̯], adv. cristianamente.

Christless [krái̯stlεs], a. anticristiano, herético.

Christmas [krísmɑs], s. natividad de Jesús; (pascua de) Navidad.—**C. carol**, villancico, cántico de Navidad.—**C. Eve**, víspera de Navidad, nochebuena.—**C. gift o present**, aguinaldo.—**C. tree**, árbol de Navidad.

Christmastide [-tai̯d], s. pascuas, f. pl.

Christology [kristálodʒi̯], s. (teol.) cristología, parte de la teología que trata de la persona y atributos de Cristo; doctrina relativa a Cristo.

Christolatry [-álɑtri̯], s. cristolatría, adoración de Cristo.—**Christophany** [-áfɑni̯], s. cristofanía, aparición de Cristo.

chroma [króu̯mɑ], s. pureza o intensidad de color.

chromate [króu̯mei̯t], s. (quím.) cromato.

chromatic [krou̯mǽti̯k], a. cromático; (mús.) cromático.—**c. aberration**, (ópt.) cromatismo.

chromatics [-s], s. cromática, ciencia del colorido.

chromatin [króu̯mɑti̯n], s. (biol.) cromatina.

chromatism [-ti̯zm], s. (ópt.) cromatismo.

chromatology [-tálodʒi̯], s. cromatología.

chrome [króu̯m]. I. s. (quím.) cromo; (tint.) dicromato potásico.—**c. steel**, acero cromo (aleación de acero y cromo).—**c. yellow**, amarillo de cromo, cromato de plomo. II. va. (tint.) tratar con dicromato potásico.—**chromic** [-i̯k], a. crómico.

chromite [-ai̯t], s. (min., quím.) cromito.

chromium [-i̯ʌm], s. (quím.) cromo.—**c. steel**, = CHROME STEEL.—**to c. plate**, cromar.

chromo [króu̯mo], s. cromo, cromolitografía.

chromogenic [-dʒéni̯k], a. cromógeno.

chromolithograph [-li̯θogræf]. I. s. cromo, cromolitografía. II. va. cromolitografiar.—**chromolithographer** [-li̯θágrɑfœ(r)], s. cromolitógrafo.—**chromolithography** [-fi̯], s. cromolitografía.

chromoplasm [-plæzm], s. = CHROMATIN.

chromoscope [-skou̯p], s. cromoscopio.

chromosome [-sou̯m], s. (biol.) cromosoma, m.

chromosphere [-sfi̯r], s. (astr.) cromosfera.

chromotype [-tai̯p], s. cromotipia; cromolitografía.

chromotypography [-tai̯págrɑfi̯], s. cromotipografía.

chromous [króu̯mʌs], a. cromoso.

chronic [kráni̯k], a. crónico, inveterado.

chronicity [kroni̯síti̯], s. cronicidad.

chronicle [kráni̯kl]. I. s. crónica.—**Chronicles**, Paralipómenos. II. va. escribir, registrar o narrar en forma de crónica. III. vn. escribir crónicas.

chronicler [-klœ(r)], s. cronista, historiador.

chronogram [kránogræm], s. cronograma.

chronograph [-græf], s. cronógrafo.

chronographer [kranágrɑfœ(r)], s. cronologista.

chronography [-fi̯], s. cronografía.

chronologer [kronálodʒœ(r)], s. cronologista, cronólogo.—**chronologic(al** [kranoládʒi̯k(ɑl], a. cronológico.—**chronologically** [-i̯], adv. cronológicamente.—**chronology** [kronálodʒi̯],

s. cronología.—**chronologist** [-dʒi̯st], s. = CHRONOLOGER.

chronometer [kronámεtœ(r)], s. cronómetro.

chronometric(al [kranométri̯k(ɑl], a. cronométrico.

chronometry [kronámεtri̯], s. cronometría.

chronophotograph [kranofóu̯togræf], s. cada una de las fotografías que se sacan consecutivamente para el cinematógrafo.

chronoscope [kránoskou̯p], s. cronoscopio.

chrysalid [krísɑli̯d], **chrysalis** [-li̯s], s. (ent.) crisálida, palomilla.

chrysanthemum [krisǽnθęmʌm], s. (bot.) crisantemo, santimonia.

chrysoberyl [krísoberi̯l], s. (min.) crisoberilo.

chrysolite [-lai̯t], s. (min.) crisólito o crisolito; peridoto.

chrysoprase [-prei̯z], s. (min.) crisoprasa.

chub [chʌb], s. (ict.) leucisco.—**c.-faced**, cariancho.

chubby [-i̯], a. regordete, gordiflón, rechoncho.—**c.-cheeked**, mofletudo, molletudo.

chuck [chʌk]. I. vn. cloquear. II. va. sopapear, hacer la mamola; echar, tirar; sujetar o poner en el manguito portaherramienta. III. s. mamola, sopapo; echada; cloqueo; golpe seco; (mec.) manguito portaherramienta; cuña; calzo; mandril (de un torno); la carne (de res) entre el pescuezo y la espaldilla. V. WOODCHUCK.—**c.-full** = CHOCK-FULL.—**c. hole**, bache, hoyo en una rodada.

chuckle [chʌkl]. I. vn. reír entre dientes; cloquear. II. s. risa ahogada, risita.

chucklehead [-hed], s. (fam.) tonto, cabezota, mf.

chug [chʌg]. I. s. ruido sordo explosivo intermitente, resoplido de locomotora, etc.), traquéteo (ll. t. **chug-chug**). II. vn. traquear.

chum [chʌm]. I. vn. (fam.) ser camarada. II. s. (fam.) camarada, mf.; compinche; condiscípulo.

chummy [-i̯], a. (fam.) íntimo, sociable.

chump [chʌmp], s. zoquete, tronco, trozo de madera; lomo del carnero; (fam.) mastuerzo; cholla.

chunk [chʌŋk], s. pedazo corto y grueso, trozo, zoquete; animalote; (fam.) persona fornida.

chunky [-i̯], a. fornido, trabado, rechoncho.

church [chœrch]. I. s. iglesia (institución y edificio); templo; cualquier edificio consagrado al culto; culto público; el clero.—**c. book** o **register**, becerro, registro de parroquia.—**c. burial**, entierro según los ritos de la iglesia.—**c. calendar**, santoral.—**c. militant**, iglesia militante.—**C. of England**, iglesia anglicana.—**c. music**, música sagrada.—**c. school**, institución de enseñanza mantenida por una secta religiosa.—**c. triumphant**, iglesia triunfante.—**to go to c.**, asistir al servicio de iglesia (ir a misa, si es éste el servicio). II. va. llevar (una persona) a la iglesia a ciertos ritos practicados en su beneficio; ejecutar estos ritos.

churchgoer [-goу̯œ(r)], s. persona que asiste regularmente a la iglesia.

churching [-i̯ŋ], s. misa de parida.

churchlike [-lai̯k], a. como iglesia, propio de iglesia; eclesiástico.

churchman [-mąn], s. miembro de alguna iglesia; sacerdote, eclesiástico, clérigo.

churchwarden [-wǫrdęn], s. (igl.) capillero, obrero, fabriquero.

churchyard [-yard], s. cementerio (de parroquia).

churl [chœrl], s. patán, palurdo, paleto; avaro.

churlish [-i̯sh], a. grosero, patán, rudo, rústico; ruin, avaro.—**churlishly** [-li̯], adv. rudamente.—**churlishness** [-nąs], s. patanería, rusticidad, tosquedad; rudeza, grosería.

churn [chœrn]. I. s. mantequera. II. va. agitar, menear, revolver; mazar, batir manteca. III. vn. agitarse, revolverse.—**churning** [-i̯ŋ], s. batido; cantidad de manteca batida de una vez.—**churnstaff** [-stæf], s. batidera.

chute [shut], s. saetín; conducto, tubo; canal, f.;

sumidero, vertedero; rabión, *m.*, rápidos; tobogán; paracaídas.

chylaceous [kajléɟʃAs], *a.* quiloso.

chyle [kájl], *s.* (fisiol.) quilo.

chyliferous [-íɟɛɾas], *a.* quilífero.

chylifactive [-iɟǽktɟiv], *a.* quilifactivo, quilifaciente.

chylification [-iɟikéjʃɵn], *s.* quilificación.

chylify [káɟlifaj], *va.* y *vn.* quilificar(se).

chylous [káɟlAs], *a.* quiloso.

chyme [káɟm], *s.* (fisiol.) quimo.

chymiferous [-íɟɛɾas], *a.* quimífero.

chymification [-iɟikéjʃɵn], *s.* quimificación.

chymify [káɟmiɟaj], *va.* y *vn.* quimificar(se).

chymous [káɟmAs], *a.* quimoso.

cibol [síbɵl], *s.* (bot.) cebolleta; chalote.

ciborium [sibóuɾiAm], *s.* (arq.) dosel de altar, ciborio; (igl.) copón, sagrario.

cicada [sikéjdǎ], *s.* (ent.) cigarra o chicharra.

cicatrice [síkatɾis], *s.* (med.) cicatriz.

cicatricial [-tríʃal], *a.* cicatrizal.

cicatricle [síkatɾikl], **cicatricula** [-tríkjulǎ], *s.* (embr.) cicatrícula, galladura, meaja de huevo.

cicatrisive [-trájsiv], *a.* cicatrizativo.

cicatrix [síkatɾiks], *s.* cicatriz.

cicatrizant [-trájzant], *a.* y *s.* cicatrizante.

cicatrization [-trizéjʃɵn], *s.* cicatrización.

cicatrize [síkatrajz], *va.* y *vn.* cicatrizar(se).

cicely [sísɛlj], *s.* (bot.) perifollo.

cicerone [sisɛróuɲj], *s.* cicerone, guía, *mf.*

Ciceronian [sisɛróuɲjan], *a.* ciceroniano.

cicuta [sikjútǎ], *s.* (bot.) cicuta.

cider [sáɟdœ(r)], *s.* sidra.

ci-devant [sidɛván], *a.* (fr.) anterior, pasado.

cigar [sigár], *s.* cigarro, puro, tabaco, habano.—**c. case**, petaca, cigarrera.—**c. cutter**, cortacigarros, cortapuros.—**c. holder**, boquilla.—**c. lighter**, mechero automático; chofeta.—**c. maker**, cigarrero, tabaquero.—**c. store** *o* **shop**, tabaquería, cigarrería, estanco.

cigarette [sigarét], *s. dim.* cigarrillo, pitillo, pito. —**c. case**, pitillera, cigarrera.—**c. holder**, boquilla.—**c. paper**, papel de fumar.

cilia [síljǎ], *s. pl.* de CILIUM.

ciliary [síljɛɾj], *a.* ciliar.

ciliate [síljit], *a.* (bot., zool.) ciliado, pestañoso.

cilice [sílis], *s.* cilicio.

cilium [síljAm], *s.* (bot., zool.) pelito; pestaña.

Cimbri [símbraj], *s. pl.* cimbros.

Cimbrian [símbrjan], **Cimbric** [-ik]. I. *s.* cimbro, címbrico. II. *a.* cimbr(i)o, címbrico.

Cimmerian [simíɾjan], *a.* cimerio.—**C. darkness**, obscuridad espantosa.

cinch [sinch]. I. *va.* cinchar; (fam.) apretar, forzar. II. *s.* cincha, cincho; (fam.) ganga, breva, cosa fácil o segura.

cinching [-iɲ], *s.* cinchadura.

cinchona [sinkóuɲǎ], *s.* (bot.) quina, cincona.

cinchonin(e [sínkounin], *s.* (quím.) cinconina.

cinchonism [sínkonizm], *s.* (med.) quinismo.

cinchonize [sínkonajz], *va.* poner bajo la influencia de la quinina; tratar con quinina.

cincture [síŋkchŭ(r)]. I. *s.* cinto, ceñidor, cincho; cercado, cerca. II. *va.* ceñir, cercar, rodear.

cinder [síndœ(r)]. I. *s.* carbón; cernada; escoria; brasa; rescoldo.—**c.** cenizas, pavesas; escarbillos, carbón a medio quemar; escoria volcánica. —**c. track**, (dep.) pista para carreras a pie. II. *va.* reducir a cenizas, etc.

Cinderella [sindœrélǎ], *s.* la Cenicienta.

cinema [sínɛmǎ], *s.* cine.

cinematograph [sínɛmǽtogræf], *s.* cinematógrafo.—**cinematographer** [-matágrafœ(r)], *s.* cinematografista.—**cinematographic** [-mætográfik], *a.* cinematográfico.—**cinematography** [-matágrafj], *s.* cinematografía.—**cinem(at)ize** [sínɛm(at)ajz], *va.* filmar, adaptar para el cine.

cineraceous [sinɛréjʃAs], *a.* ceniciento.

cineraria [sinɛɾéɾjǎ], *s.* (bot.) cineraria.

cinerary [sínɛɾɛɾj], *a.* cinerario.

cineration [sinɛɾéjʃɵn], *s.* incineración.

cinereous [sinírjAs], *a.* ceniciento, cinéreo.

cineritious [sinɛɾíʃAs], *a.* cenizoso.

cingulum [síŋgiulAm], *s.* cíngulo; (anat.) cordón de fibras que une las circunvoluciones del cerebro.

cinnabar [sínabar], *s.* (min.) cinabrio.

cinnamate [sínameit], *s.* (quím.) cinamato.

cinnamic [sinǽmik], *a.* (quim.) cinámico; de canela.

cinnamon [sínamɵn], *s.* (bot.) canela; canelo (árbol).—**c. bear**, (zool.) variedad de oso norteamericano.—**c.-colored**, canelo, acanelado.—**c. stone** = ESSONITE.

cinquecento [chiŋkwɛchéntouʃ], *s.* siglo XVI del arte y la literatura italianos.

cinquefoil [síŋkfɔjl], *s.* (arq.) ventana de cinco puntas; (bot.) cincoenrama, quinquefolio.

cion [sáɟon], *s.* (anat.) úvula; (agr.) = SCION.

cipher [sáɟfœ(r)]. I. *s.* (arit.) cero; cifra arábiga; nulidad; cifra, clave, *f.*; monograma, *m.* II. *va.* calcular; cifrar con clave. III. *vn.* numerar.

cipolin [sípolin], *s.* cipolino (mármol).

Circassian [sœrkǽʃjan], *a.* y *s.* circasiano.

Circensian [sœrsénʃan], *a.* circense.

circinate [sœrsineit], *a.* (bot.) circinado.

circle [sœrkl]. I. *s.* (geom.) círculo; circunferencia, (fam.) redondel; esfera; anillo; disco; cerco, ruedo; ciclo; círculo (social), rueda, corro, agrupación, clase, *f.*; circunloquio, rodeo; (lóg.) círculo vicioso; (top., astr.) limbo, placa (de instrumento). II. *va.* circundar, ceñir, cercar, rodear.—**to c. the globe**, dar la vuelta al mundo. III. *vn.* dar vueltas, remolinear.

circled [-d], *a.* redondo; rodeado.

circlet [sœrklit], *s.* círculo, anillo; collar, brazalete; faja circular; cinta; corona.

circuit [sœrkit], *s.* circuito; vuelta, rodeo; gira; radio, ámbito; distrito, partido, jurisdicción (de juez, etc.); contorno; (elec.) circuito.—**c. breaker**, (elec.) contracircuitos, disyuntor, interruptor automático.—**c. court**, tribunal itinerario, corte (*f.*) de circuito.

circuitous [sœrkjútas], *a.* tortuoso.—**circuitously** [-lj], *adv.* tortuosamente.—**circuitousness** [-njs], *s.* tortuosidad, rodeo.

circulable [sœrkjulabl], *a.* que puede circular.

circular [sœrkjulǎ(r)]. I. *a.* circular; redondo; indirecto.—**c. letter**, circular, *f.*—**c. measure**, (geom.) medida (de un ángulo) en radianes.— **c. mil**, milipulgada circular.—**c. motion**, cerco, movimiento giratorio.—**c. plate**, disco.—**c. ring**, (geom.) corona circular.—**c. saw**, sierra circular o giratoria. II. *s.* circular, *f.*; carta, aviso o folleto circular.

circularity [-ǽritj], *s.* circularidad.

circularize [-ajz], *va.* hacer circular; enviar circulares a; anunciar por circulares.

circularly [-lj], *adv.* circularmente.

circulate [sœrkjuleit]. I. *va.* propalar, propagar, diseminar, divulgar; poner en circulación. II. *vn.* circular; propagarse.

circulating [-iɲ], *a.* circulante.—**c. decimal**, fracción decimal periódica.—**c. library**, librería circulante.—**c. medium**, moneda corriente.

circulation [-éjʃɵn], *s.* circulación; propaganda; moneda corriente.

circulatory [sœrkjulǎtɵrj], *a.* circulatorio, circulante, circular.

circumambiency [sœrkAmǽmbjɛnsj], *s.* medio ambiente.—**circumambient** [-bjɛnt], *a.* circumambiente.

circumambulate [-bjuleit], *vn.* andar al rededor.

circumcise [sœrkAmsajz], *va.* circuncidar, retajar.—**circumcised** [-d], *a.* circunciso.—**circumciser** [-œ(r)], *s.* circuncidante.—**circumcision** [-síʒɵn], *s.* circuncisión.

circumference [sœrkAmfɛɾɛns], *s.* circunferencia, periferia; perímetro; contorno; circuito, ruedo.

circumferential [-énʃal], *a.* circunferencial, referente a la circunferencia, periférico; con rodeo.

circumferentor [-entǫ(r)], s. (top.) brújula de agrimensor.

circumflex [sǽrkʌmfleks]. **I.** s. acento circunflejo; (impr.) capucha. **II.** a. (gram.) pronunciado con, o que lleva, acento circunflejo; (anat.) circunflejo, encorvado. **III.** va. marcar con acento circunflejo.

circumfluence [scœrkʌmflyens], s. derrame circular.—**circumfluent** [-ent], **circumfluous** [-ʌs], a. circunfluente.

circumfuse [scœrkʌmfjúz], va. verter o derramar al derredor.—**circumfusion** [-ʒǫn], s. esparcimiento en derredor.

circumjacent [-dʒéisent], a. circunyacente, circunstante, circunvecino.

circumlocution [-loukjúšǫn], s. circunlocución, circunloquio, rodeo, requilorios, ambages.

circumlocutory [-lákiutǫri], a. circunlocutorio, perifrástico.

circumnavigable [-nǽvigǎbl], a. circunnavegable.

circumnavigate [-nǽvigeit], va. circunnavegar. —**circumnavigation** [-éišǫn], s. circunnavegación.—**circumnavigator** [-ǫ(r)], s. circunnavegante; el que navega al rededor.

circumpolar [-póulǎ(r)], a. circumpolar.

circumrotation [-routéišǫn], s. rotación; circunvolución.—**circumrotatory** [-róutǎtǫri], a. giratorio, rotatorio.

circumscissile [-sísil], a. (bot.) dehiscente transversalmente.

circumscribable [-skrái̯bǎbl], a. circunscribible, circunscriptible.

circumscribe [-skrái̯b], va. circunscribir, circunferir, fijar, limitar.—**circumscribed** [-d], a. circunscri(p)to.—**circumscribing** [-iŋ], a. circunferente, circunscriptivo.

circumscription [-skrípšǫn], s. circunscripción; limitación, restricción; periferia.

circumscriptive [-skríptiv], a. circunscriptivo.

circumspect [scœrkʌmspekt], a. circunspecto, discreto.—**circumspection** [-spékšǫn], s. circunspección, prudencia, reserva, cautela; recato, decoro, compostura.—**circumspectly** [scœrkʌmspektli], adv. circunspectamente, con cautela.

circumstance [-stæns], s. circunstancia, incidente, acontecimiento; detalle, menudencia.— pl. medios, recursos.—**in easy circumstances**, acomodado.—**under no c.**, jamás; de ningún modo; sean lo que fueren las condiciones, etc.— **under the c.**, en las circunstancias presentes, siendo así las cosas.

circumstantial [-stǽnšǎl], a. circunstanciado, minucioso; indirecto, circunstancial.—**c. evidence**, prueba circunstancial o indiciaria, indicios vehementes. — **circumstantiality** [-ši̯ǽliti], s. minuciosidad.

circumstantially [-stǽnšǎli], adv. circunstanciadamente, minuciosamente.

circumstantiate [-stǽnši̯eit], va. relatar o apoyar circunstanciadamente, detallar.

circumvallate [-vǽleit], va. (fort.) circunvalar.— **circumvallation** [-éišǫn], s. circunvalación.

circumvent [-vént], va. cercar o estrechar con artificio engañoso; entrampar, enredar, embaucar; evadir, evitar; pasar alrededor de.— **circumvention** [-vénšǫn], s. trampa, enredo, estratagema.—**circumventive** [-véntiv], a. engañoso, delusorio.

circumvolution [-volúšǫn], s. circunvolución; vuelta, rodeo.

circumvolve [-válv], va. y vn. revolver, voltear, (hacer) girar, dar vueltas (a).

circus [scœrkʌs], s. circo; compañía (actores) y animales de circo; arena; hipódromo; plaza circular, redondel.—**c. track**, pista.

cirque [scœrk], s. círculo, anillo; circo; (geol.) anfiteatro natural (de erosión glaciaria).

cirrhose [síroυs], a. cirroso.

cirrhosis [siróυsis], s. (med.) cirrosis.

cirrhotic [sirátik], a. (med.) cirrótico.

cirriped [síriped], a. y s. (zool.) cirrípedo.

cirro-cumulus [síroki̯úmyǫlʌs], s. cielo aborregado.

cirrose, cirrous [síroυs, sírʌs], a. cirroso.

cirrus [sírʌs], s. (bot.) cirro, zarcillo; (zool.) cirro; (meteor.) cirros.

cisalpine [sisǽlpain], a. cisalpino.

cisandine [sisǽndin], a. cisandino.

cisatlantic [sisætlǽntik], a. cisatlántico.

cissoid [sísoid], s. (geom.) cisoide.

cist [sist], s. arquilla, estuche; sepulcro.

Cistercian [sistœ́ršǎn], a. y s. cisterciense.

cistern [sístœrn], s. cisterna, aljibe.

cistus [sístʌs], s. (bot.) cisto, cergazo.

citadel [sítǎdel], s. ciudadela, presidio.

citation [saitéišǫn], s. cita, mención; excerta; (for.) citación, comparendo, emplazamiento.

citatory [sáitǎtǫri], a. (for.) citatorio.

cite [sáit], va. citar, sacar, referirse a; (for.) citar.

citer [-œ(r)], s. citador.

cithara [síθǎrǎ], s. (mús.) lira griega; cítara.

cithern [síθœrn], s. (mús.) cítara.

citified [sítifaid], a. que tiene las costumbres o maneras de la ciudad; urbanizado.

citizen [sítizen], s. ciudadano; munícipe, vecino. —**citizenry** [-ri], s. la masa de ciudadanos.— **citizenship** [-šip], s. ciudadanía, avecindamiento; nacionalidad.—**c. papers**, carta de ciudadanía.

citrate [sítreit], s. (quím.) citrato.

citric [sítrik], a. (quím.) cítrico.

citrine [sítrin], a. cetrino.

citron [sítrǫn], s. (bot.) cidra; cidro.—**candied c.**, acitrón, cidra confitada; espejuelo.

citronella [-élǎ], **citronella grass** [-græs], s. (bot.) cidronela, toronjil.

citr(o)us [sítrʌs], a. (bot.) auranciáceo.—**citrus fruit**, cidra, limón, naranja, toronja, etc.

cittern [sítœrn], s. = CITHERN.

city [síti]. **I.** s. ciudad, población, urbe, f. **II.** a. municipal, ciudadano, de (la) ciudad; urbano. —**c. block**, isla.—**c. council**, ayuntamiento.— **c. district**, barrio.—**c. editor**, (E. U.) redactor encargado de las noticias locales; (Ingl.) redactor financiero.—**c. father**, miembro del ayuntamiento o cabildo; regidor.—**c. hall**, casa municipal o del ayuntamiento; casa consistorial. —**c. of the dead**, cementerio.—**c. planning**, urbanismo, urbanización.—**c. police**, guardia municipal.

civet [sívit], s. algalia, civeto (para los perfumes); (zool.) (ll. t. c. cat) algalia, m., gato de algalia, civeta.

civic [sívik], a. cívico; ciudadano, municipal.— **civicism** [sívisizm], s. civismo; principios de los derechos y deberes cívicos.—**civics** [síviks], s. cívica, ciencia del gobierno civil.

civies [síviz], s. pl. (fam.) traje de paisano. V. CIVVIES.

civil [sívil], a. civil, de lo civil, ciudadano; intestino, doméstico; civil, cortés, urbano.—**c. death**, (for.) muerte (f.) civil.—**c. engineer**, ingeniero civil, ingeniero de caminos y construcciones.—**c. engineering**, ingeniería civil. —**C. Guard** (en España), Guardia Civil, la Benemérita.—**c. law**, derecho civil.—**c. marriage**, matrimonio civil.—**c. power**, autoridad civil.—**c. procedure**, (for.) enjuiciamiento civil.—**c. service**, servicio civil oficial, ramo civil de la administración pública.—**c. war**, guerra civil.—**c. year**, año civil.

civilian [sivílyan]. **I.** s. paisano (no militar); civilista, jurisperito, jurisconsulto.—pl. los civiles, la población civil. **II.** a. civil.

civility [sivíliti], s. civilidad, cortesía, urbanidad.

civilization [-sivilizéišǫn], s. civilización.

civilize [sívilai̯z], va. civilizar.—**civilized** [-d], a. civilizado, culto.—**civilizer** [-œ(r)], s. civilizador.

civilly [sívili], adv. civilmente; cortésmente.

civism [sívizm], *s.* civismo, patriotismo.
civvies [sívi̱z], *s. pl.* de CIVVY; (fam.) traje de paisano (a distinción del militar).
civvy [sívi̱], *s.* paisano (no militar).
clabber [klǽbœ(r)]. I. *vn.* cuajarse. II. *s.* cuajo.
clack [klǽk]. I. *s.* ruido, golpeo; charla; triquitraque; tarabilla, cítola (de molino).—**c. valve**, válvula de charnela, chapaleta. II. *vn.* restallar; repiquetear, castañetear; charlar, picotear.
clad [klǽd], *a.* vestido, aderezado. *V.* CLOTHE.
claim [kléim]. I. *va.* demandar, pedir en juicio; reclamar, recabar, reivindicar; denunciar (una mina); alegar, sostener, pretender.—**to c. to be**, (fam.) echarla o echárselas de.—II. *s.* demanda, pedimento; reclamación, reclamo, petición; pretensión, título, derecho; (min.) pertenencia, denuncia.—**c. agent**, agente de reclamaciones.
claimable [-əbl], *a.* que se puede reclamar.
claimant [-ənt], **claimer** [-œ(r)], *s.* reclamante; demandante, pretensor, actor; (min.) denunciante.
clairvoyance [klɛrvóiəns], *s.* clarividencia.
clairvoyant [-ənt], *a.* clarividente.
clam [klǽm]. I. *s.* almeja, tel(l)ina, chirla.—**c. bed**, almejar. II. *vn.* pescar almejas.
clamant [kléimənt], *a.* clamante; urgente.
clambake [klǽmbeik], *s.* partida de campo en que se cuecen almejas sobre piedras muy calientes en un hoyo.
clamber [klǽmbœ(r)], *vn.* gatear, trepar, encaramarse.
clamminess [klǽminis], *s.* viscosidad.
clammy [klǽmi], *a.* viscoso, pegajoso.
clamor [klǽmo(r)]. I. *s.* clamor(eo), grita, gritería, vocería, vocinglería, algarabía; estruendo, fragor. II. *vn.* clam(ore)ar, gritar, vociferar.
clamorous [-ʌs], *a.* clamoroso, ruidoso, estruendoso, tumultuoso.—**clamorously** [-li], *adv.* clamorosamente; ruidosamente.
clamp [klǽmp]. I. *s.* montón (de mineral, de ladrillos, etc.); pisoteo, pisadas recias; (mec.) abrazadera; grapa, grampa; cárcel, *f.;* barrilete, prensa de sujeción; tornillo de banco; tornillo de sujeción, de fijación o de ajuste (ll. t. **c. screw**); sujetador, afianzador; brida; collar; pinzas, tenazas; mordaza. II. *va.* empalmar; lañar, asegurar, afianzar, abrazar; imponer con rigidez (una ley, restricción, etc.), sujetar. III. *vn.* pisar recio.—**to c. down** (on), (fam.) ponerse severo; apretar los tornillos (a).
clamshell [klǽmʃel], *s.* concha de almeja; (ing.) cucharón de quijadas (ll. t. **c. bucket**).
clan [klæn], *s.* tribu, *f.;* clan; fratría; casta; asociación, cuerpo o sociedad exclusivista.
clandestine [klændéstin], *a.* clandestino, furtivo, secreto, subrepticio, (fam.) de extranjis.—**clandestinely** [-li], *adv.* clandestinamente.—**clandestineness** [-nis], *s.* clandestinidad.
clang [klǽŋ]. I. *s.* sonido metálico o retintín (de trompetas, campanas, armas, etc.). II. *va.* y *vn.* (hacer) sonar, resonar o retumbar.
clangor [klǽŋgo(r)], *s.* estruendo, estrépito; (poét.) clangor. *V.* CLANG.—**clangorous** [-ʌs], *a.* estruendoso, estrepitoso.
clank [klǽŋk]. I. *s.* rechinamiento, ruido estridente o de choque de metales (cadenas, armas, etc.). II. *va.* y *vn.* (hacer) rechinar o resonar.
clannish [klǽniʃ], *a.* ref. o parecido al clan; gregario, unido; exclusivista.
clanship [klǽnʃip], *s.* unión bajo un jefe.
clansman [klǽnzmən], *s.* miembro de un clan.
clap [klǽp]. I. *va.* batir, golpear; cerrar de golpe; aplicar, pegar; aplaudir.—**to c. eyes on**, (fam.) echar la vista encima.—**to c. the hands**, batir palmas. II. *vn.* aplaudir, dar palmadas, palm(ot)ear; cerrarse ruidosamente; guachapear. III. *s.* ruido o golpe seco; trueno; palmada, palmoteo, aplauso; (med.) gonorrea.
clapboard [klǽbo̱rd], *s.* (tabla de) chilla.

clapper [klǽpœ(r)], *s.* palmoteador; badajo; tarabilla, cítola; tableta, tejoleta; aldaba; chapaleta.
clapping [klǽpiŋ], *s.* aleteo; palmoteo.
claptrap [klǽptræp], *s.* artificio para alcanzar populachería; faramalla, música celestial.
claque [klǽk], *s.* (teat.) claque, *f.,* alabarderos o aplaudidores de oficio; clac, sombrero de copa alta, que puede plegarse.
clarence [klǽrens], *s.* carruaje, clarens.
clarendon [klǽrendon], *s.* (impr.) letra negrilla.
claret [klǽrit], *s.* clarete, vino tinto.
clarification [klærifikéiʃon], *s.* clarificación.
clarify [klǽrifai], *va.* clarificar, defecar, purgar; aclarar; esclarecer.—**clarifying** [-iŋ], *a.* clarificativo; aclaratorio.
clarinet [klærinét], *s.* (mús.) clarinete.
clarinet(t)ist [-ist], *s.* clarinete.
clarion [klǽrion], *s.* (mús.) clarín.—**c. call**, clarinada. II. *a.* claro, sonoro, agudo o penetrante.
clarionet [klærionét], *s.* = CLARINET.
clarity [klǽriti], *s.* claridad.
clary [klǽri], *s.* (bot.) a(l)maro, salvia silvestre.
clash [klǽʃ]. I. *vn.* chocar, entrechocarse, encontrarse, batir; oponerse. II. *va.* batir, golpear. III. *s.* choque, fragor, encontrón, colisión; oposición, antagonismo, disputa, discordia.
clashingly [-iŋli], *adv.* en oposición, en conflicto; estrepitosamente, con fragor.
clasp [klǽsp]. I. *s.* broche, chapeta, corchete, presilla, gafete, traba, hebilla, abrazadera; cierre, cerradero; (mec.) grapa, cárcel, *f.* manija; abrazo.—**c. knife**, navaja, sobre todo la grande de una cuchilla. II. *va.* abrochar, encorchetar, enganchar; asegurar; abarcar, abrazar, embrazar, ceñir.
clasper [-œ(r)], *s.* el que o lo que abrocha o abraza, etc.; abarcador, abrazador, etc.
class [klæs]. I. *s.* clase, *f.;* condición, categoría, grado, rango; (mil.) promoción; orden, linaje, género; clase en las escuelas; (fam.) excelencia, elegancia.—**c. struggle, c. war**, lucha o guerra de clases (gen. se aplica a la entre el capital y el trabajo). II. *va.* clasificar, calificar, ordenar.
classic [klǽsik], *s.* autor clásico; obra clásica (apl. esp. a las griegas y latinas).
classic(al [-(ə)l], *a.* clásico.—**c. scholar**, humanista, erudito en las lenguas clásicas (latín y griego).—**c. style**, clasicismo.
classically [-əli], *adv.* clásicamente.—**classicism** [klǽsisizm], *s.* clasicismo.—**classicist** [-sist], *s.* clásico, clasicista.
classifiable [-fáiəbl], *a.* clasificable; calificable.
classification [fikéiʃon], *s.* clasificación.
classify [klǽsifai], *va.* clasificar, graduar, ordenar. —**classified advertisement section**, sección de anuncios (de un periódico).
classis [klǽsis], *s.* junta directiva en ciertas iglesias reformadas; (hist. romana) clase, *f.*
classmate [klǽsmeit], *s.* condiscípulo.
classroom [-rum], *s.* (sala de) clase, aula.
classy [klǽsi], *a.* (fam.) excelente; elegante.
clastic [klǽstik], *a.* clástico, quebradizo; compuesto de fragmentos.
clatter [klǽtœ(r)]. I. *vn.* resonar ruidosamente, matraquear, guachapear; chacolotear; gritar, charlar. II. *s.* ruido, estruendo; martilleo; gritería, charla ruidosa u ociosa; gresca, alboroto, bulla.
claudicant [klódikant], *a.* claudicante, cojo.—**claudicate** [-keit], *vn.* claudicar, cojear.—**claudication** [-kéiʃon], *s.* claudicación, cojera.
clause [kloz], *s.* cláusula; (gram.) cláusula, período, proposición de relativo, oración; (for.) artículo, condición, estipulación, inciso (de un documento).
claustral [klóstral], *a.* claustral.
claustrophobia [-rofóubiǝ], *s.* claustrofobia.
clavate(d [kléiveit(id], *a.* en forma de maza o clava; claveteado.
clavichord [klǽvikord], *s.* (mús.) clave, clavicordio.

clavicle [klǽvɪkl], *s.* (anat.) clavícula, islilla.
clavicular [klævɪ́kiʊlǎ(r)], *a.* clavicular.
clavier [klævír], *s.* (mús.) teclado; instrumento con teclado (clavicordio, piano, etc.).
claw [klɔ]. I. *s.* garra, garfa, presa, uña; pinza o tenaza (del cangrejo, etc.); (mec.) gancho, garfio, uña, diente, garabato; (bot.) pecíolo.—**c. bar**, sacaclavos de horquilla; espeque o pie (*m.*) de cabra con uña.—**c. coupling**, (aut.) acoplamiento de diente.—**c. hammer**, martillo de orejas; (fam.) casaca, frac.—**c. hand**, (med.) gafedad. II. *va.* arpar, gafar; desgarrar; arañar; rasgar, despedazar. III. *vn.* arañar.
clawed [-d], *a.* armado de garras o zarpas.
clay [kléi]. I. *s.* arcilla, argil(l)a, greda, barro, tiza; (fig.) el cuerpo humano.—**c.-cold**, frío helado; sin vida.—**c. marl**, marga.—**c. pigeon**, disco de arcilla, pichón de barro.—**c. pigeon shooting**, tiro de pichón.—**c. pit**, gredal, barrizal, barrera.—**c. stone**, piedra arcillosa. II. *va.* engredar; filtrar en barro (apl. al azúcar); (agr.) *V.* MARL.
clayey [-i], **clayish** [-iš], *a.* arcilloso, gredoso.
claymore [kléimor], *s.* espada escocesa.
clean [klín]. I. *a.* limpio; puro, inocente, honesto; aseado; desembarazado, despejado; neto, distinto, nítido; perfecto; completo; bien hecho; bien formado, simétrico; diestro; no endorsado (bono, etc.); con pocas correcciones o sin ellas (prueba de imprenta).—**c. acceptance**, (com.) aceptación absoluta o incondicional.—**c. bill**, o **c. bill of health**, patente limpia de sanidad. —**c. bill of lading**, conocimiento de embarque limpio o sin restricciones.—**c.-bred**, de pura raza.—**c.-cut**, bien definido, claro.—**c.-handed**, con las manos limpias, sin culpa.— **to make c.**, limpiar.—**to make a c. breast of it**, confesar de plano.—**to show a c. pair of heels**, tomar las de Villadiego. II. *adv.* limpiamente; enteramente.—**to come c.**, (fam.) confesar de plano. *va.* limpiar, asear, aderezar; purificar; abalear (el grano); depurar (oro, aire, etc.); mondar; escombrar; desengrasar, desenlodar, desempolvar; abrir, sacar el menudo a (un pollo, un pescado, etc.).—**to c. house**, (fig.) poner en orden; extirpar vicios, abusos, etc.—**to c. out**, vaciar; (fam.) sacarle hasta el último céntimo a.—**to c. up**, limpiar completamente, sanear; acabar, salir de (una tarea, etc.); recoger; desembarazar; (mec.) corregir, rectificar; (min.) recoger; (fam.) ganar, sacar de ganancia. IV. *vn.* (gen. con **up**) limpiar(se), asear(se).—**to c. up after one**, limpiar lo que uno ha ensuciado, o después que uno ha acabado (de hacer algo).
cleaner [-œ(r)], *s.* limpiador; mondador; sacamanchas; depurador (de aire, etc.).—**c's.** (shop), tintorería, tinte.
cleaning [-iŋ], *s.* aseo, limpia(miento), limpieza; monda(dura); desengrase; abaleo (del grano).
cleanlily [klénlili], *adv.* aseadamente.
cleanliness [-linis], *s.* limpieza, aseo, aliño; pulidez; compostura, decencia; tersura.
cleanly [-li]. I. *a.* limpio, aseado; puro, delicado. II. *adv.* [klínli] limpiamente, pulidamente, primorosamente, aseadamente.
cleanness [klínnis], *s.* limpieza, aseo; pureza.
cleansable [klénzǎbl], *a.* limpiable; purificable.
cleanse [klénz], *va.* limpiar, purificar; purgar, expurgar, absterger, depurar, mundificar.
cleanser [-œ(r)], *s.* evacuante, purgante; limpiador, purificador.
cleansing [-iŋ]. I. *s.* limpiamiento, detersión, purificación. II. *a.* detersorio, mundificativo.
clean-up [klínʌp], *s.* recogida; aseo o limpia general; recogida de metal o residuos útiles en molinos, etc.; (fam.) extirpación de enfermedades, vicios, etc.; (fam.) ganancia.
clear [klir]. I. *a.* claro; diáfano, lúcido, transparente; despejado, (d)escampado; raso, abierto, franco, libre; limpio, inocente; (com.)

neto, líquido; desempeñado, sin deudas; puro, sin mezcla; sin desperfectos; cierto, seguro; claro, distinto, constante, evidente, palmario, patente; sonoro; gráfico; completo, total.— **c.-cut**, bien cortado o definido, claro.—**c.-eyed**, penetrante, perspicaz.—**c.-headed**, inteligente, listo.—**c. of**, libre o separado de, a distancia de, sin tocar; salvando, evitando.— **c. profit**, beneficio neto.—**c.-sighted**, clarividente, perspicaz.—**c.-sightedness**, clarividencia.—**c. track**, vía libre.—**to be c.**, constar. II. *s.* claro, espacio entre objetos; tranzón; clara (del tiempo o cielo). III. *adv.* claramente; enteramente (gen. con *away, off, out*).
clear, *va.* desembarazar, despejar, quitar estorbos; limpiar, purificar, aclarar, disipar; justificar; absolver; desenredar, desembrollar (un negocio); satisfacer (una hipoteca); saltar o pasar por encima o un lado de, salvar, franquear; (agr.) tumbar, desmontar, desbrozar, rozar, mondar; (com.) despachar en la aduana; ganar, sacar, obtener una ganancia líquida.— **to c. away**, quitar (estorbos).—**to c. (a ship) for action**, ejecutar el zafarrancho de combate, despejar las cubiertas, alistar (un buque de guerra) para el combate.—**to c. (an equation) of fractions**, quitar los denominadores (de una ecuación).—**to c. out**, echar, sacar; vaciar; desocupar; despachar (un barco) en la aduana. —**to c. the decks** = TO C. FOR ACTION.—**to c. the table**, levantar la mesa.—**to c. up**, sacar estorbos de, desembarazar, escampar; apurar, dilucidar, explicar; arreglar (una deuda, etc.).
clear, *vn.* aclarar(se), serenar(se); clarear; desembarazarse, desenredarse; despacharse en la aduana; liquidar cuentas.—**to c. off**, o **up**, aclarar, abonanzar; despejarse o escampar (el cielo).—**to c. out**, despacharse y salir (un barco); irse, escabullirse, salirse.
clearage [klírɪdʒ], *s.* despejo; desmonte.
clearance [klírǎns], *s.* despejo; despacho de aduana; beneficio líquido; (mec., ing.) juego, espacio libre; (m. v.) espacio muerto (del cilindro); (hidr.) intersticio (de una turbina).— **c. papers**, certificación del pago de derechos de aduana.—**c. sale**, liquidación, (venta de) realización.
clearing [klírɪŋ], *s.* aclaramiento, despejo; calva; escampo; desmonte; (agr.) desbrozo, roza; claro, raso; espacio libre; justificación, vindicación; (com.) liquidación de balances.—**c. for action**, (mar.) zafarrancho.—**c. of fractions**, (álg.) supresión de denominadores.—**c. house**, banco de liquidación (entre bancos); bolsa de compensación.—**c. pan**, (azú.) paila de clarificar, clarificadora.
clearly [klírli], *adv.* claramente; evidentemente; libremente; llanamente; abiertamente.
clearness [klírnis], *s.* claridad; luz; perspicuidad.
clearstarch [klírstarch], *va.* y *vn.* almidonar.
clearstory [klírstorj], *s.* = CLERESTORY.
cleat [klit]. I. *s.* listón; abrazadera, manija, fiador, afianzador; mordaza; cepo; (mar.) cornamusa; tojino; castañuela; galápago; (elec.) puente, *mf.* II. *va.* abrazar, afianzar (a o con listón, etc.).
cleavage [klívɪdʒ], *s.* hendidura, resquebradura; (min.) crucero; (biol.) segmentación; (quím.) desdoblamiento, descomposición.
cleave [klív]. I. *va.* (pret. CLEFT, CLEAVED o CLOVE; *pp.* CLEFT, CLEAVED o CLOVEN) partir, tajar, rajar, hender; abrir en canal; penetrar, abrirse paso. II. *vn.* resquebrar, henderse, partirse. III. *vn.* (pret. y *pp.* CLEAVED) pegarse, unirse, ajustarse, adherirse.
cleaver [-œ(r)], *s.* hendedor, partidor; hacha, destral; cuchilla o cortante de carnicero.
cleavers [-œrz], *s.* (bot.) presera.
clef [klef], *s.* (mús.) clave, *f.*, llave, *f.*
cleft [kléft]. I. *pret.* y *pp.* de TO CLEAVE. II. *a.* agrietado, hendido, partido.—**c. grafting**, injerto de hendidura. III. *s.* grieta, fisura, aber-

tura, rajadura, rendija.—**c. palate**, fisura palatina, paladar hendido.

cleft-graft [-græft], *va.* injertar por hendidura.

clematis [klématis], *s.* (bot.) clemátide, *f.*

clemency [klémensi], *s.* clemencia, piedad, misericordia, indulgencia.

clement [klément], *a.* clemente, misericordioso, indulgente.—**clemently** [-li], *adv.* clementemente.

clench [klénch]. I. *va.* apretar o cerrar el puño o los dientes; asegurar; remachar. *V.* CLINCH. II. *s.* agarro.—**clencher** [-œ(r)], *s.* agarrador; remachador; (fig.) argumento sin réplica.

clepsydra [klépsidra], *s.* clépsidra.

cleptomania [kleptoméinia] = KLEPTOMANIA.

clerestory [klírstori], *s.* (arq.) piso más alto de una iglesia, etc., con una serie de pequeñas ventanas.

clergy [klérdži], *s.* clero, clerecía; clericatura.

clergyman [-man], *s.* clérigo; cura, *m.*, sacerdote, eclesiástico, ministro de Dios.

cleric [klérik]. I. *s.* clérigo. II. *a.* clerical.

clerical [-al]. I. *a.* clerical, eclesiástico; de dependientes (apl. al trabajo de oficinas).—**c. error**, error de copista o empleado. II. *s.* clérigo; (C., pol.) clerical.—*pl.* (fam.) traje de clérigo, ropa clerical.

clericalism [-izm], *s.* clericalismo.

clericalist [-ist], *s.* clerical, partidario del clericalismo.

clerk [klœrk], *s.* oficial de secretaría; amanuense, escribiente; dependiente, empleado de oficina; clérigo; escolar, estudiante; (for.) escribano, actuario.

clerkship [-šip], *s.* oficio u ocupación de dependiente, clérigo, o escribiente; escribanía; secretaría.

clever [klévœ(r)], *a.* diestro, hábil; avisado, listo, mañoso; inteligente.—**cleverly** [-li], *adv.* diestramente, hábilmente.—**cleverness** [-nis], *s.* talento; destreza, maña, habilidad, amaño.

clevis [klévis], *s.* abrazadera (del arado, etc.).

clew [klu]. I. *s.* ovillo; pista, indicio (gen. = CLUE); (mar.) puño (de vela).—**c. garnet**, palanquín, cargapuños.—**c. lines**, chafaldetes. II. *va.* (mar.) ovillar.

cliché [klišéi], *s.* frase gastada; (impr.) clisé.

click [klik]. I. *s.* golpe seco; (mec.) trinquete, seguro, gatillo, fiador, linguete; chasquido de lengua.—**c. beetle**, (ent.) escarabajo de resorte. II. *va.* y *vn.* (hacer) sonar con uno o más golpes secos; hacer tictac; piñonear (un arma de fuego); (fam.) venir pintiparado; dar golpe; tener buen éxito.

client [kláient], *s.* cliente; parroquiano.

cliental [-al], *a.* pert. al cliente o a la clientela.

clientele [-él], *s.* clientela.

clientship [-šip], *s.* clientela, patrocinio.

cliff [klif], *s.* risco, farallón, escarpa, escollera, acantilado, tajo.—**c. dweller**, hombre de las rocas, antiguo indio norteamericano que vivía en las rocas.

cliffy [-i], **clifty** [-ti], *a.* acantilado, escarpado, riscoso; escabroso.

climacteric [klaimækterik], *s.* período climatérico.

climacteric(al [-térik(al], *a.* climatérico.

climactic [klaimæktik], *a.* que tiene carácter de clímax.

climate [kláimit], *s.* clima, *m.*

climatic(al [klaimætik(al], *a.* climático.

climatologic(al [klaimatoládžik(al], *a.* climatológico.

climatology [-tálodži], *s.* climatología.

climax [kláimæks], *s.* clímax; punto culminante o crítico; colmo, culminación.

climb [klaim]. I. *va.* trepar, subir, escalar. II. *vn.* trepar, subir, gatear, encaramarse, elevarse.—**to c. down**, bajar; (fam.) desistir de una empresa o demanda, volverse atrás. III. *s.* trepa;

subida, ascenso.—**c. indicator**, (aer.) indicador de ascensión.—**climber** [-œ(r)], *s.* trepador, escalador; trepadera; (bot.) enredadera, trepadora; (orn.) trepador; arribista o arrivista, oportunista.—**climbing** [-iŋ]. I. *s.* trepa, subida, gateamiento.—**c. angle**, (aer.) ángulo de subida.—**c. irons**, trepadores, clavos para subir a los árboles, etc.—**c. rope**, cuerda de nudos. II. *a.* trepante, trepador; de subir; de ascensión.

clime [klaim], *s.* clima, *m.; (poét.) región.

clinch [klinch]. I. *va.* remachar, roblar, rebotar (clavos, etc.); agarrar; afirmar, fijar, afianzar; establecer, confirmar; (mar.) entalingar. II. *vn.* agarrarse; (fam.) abrazarse estrechamente; acapizarse. III. *s.* remache, robladura; (mar.) entalingadura; forcejeo, lucha cuerpo a cuerpo (esp. en el boxeo); (fam.) abrazo estrecho.

clincher [-œ(r)], *s.* rebotador, remachador; clavo remachado; clavo de remachar; (fam.) argumento decisivo.—**c. rim**, (aut.) aro con pestaña para neumático de talón.—**c. tire**, (aut.) neumático de talón.—**c. work**, obra con juntas de solapa; (mar.) tingladillo.

clinching [-iŋ], *s.* remachado o robladura; (mar.) solapadura.

cling [kliŋ], *vn.* (*pret.* y *pp.* CLUNG) asirse, adherirse, pegarse; persistir (memoria, olor, etc.); unirse.—**to c. to**, perseverar o persistir en; confiar en.

clinging [-iŋ], *a.* colgante, pendiente; adhesivo.

clingstone [-stoun], *s.* (bot.) violeto, peladillo, pavía (ll. t. **c. peach**).

clinic [klinik], *s.* (med.) clínica, consultorio, dispensario; (igl.) clínico.—**clinical** [-al], *a.* clínico.—**c. chart**, gráfica de un enfermo, en que se representan gráficamente la temperatura, pulso, etc.—**c. medicine**, clínica.—**c. thermometer**, termómetro clínico, o médico.—**c. ward**, clínica.

clinician [klinišan], *s.* clínico, médico que practica.

clink [kliŋk]. I. *va.* hacer sonar metales o chocar copas, etc. II. *vn.* retiñir, tintin(e)ar, resonar. III. *s.* tañido, (re)tintín, tintineo; (fam.) calabozo, cárcel, *f.*

clinker [-œ(r)]. I. *s.* lo que retiñe; escoria; pedazo de escoria o de lava porosa; ladrillo vítreo; ladrillo holandés; remachador; clavo de remachar. *V.* CLINCH.—**c.-built**, (mar.) de tingladillo.—**c. work**, = CLINCHER WORK. II. *vn.* formar escorias; obstruirse con escorias. III. *va.* causar la formación de escorias en.

clinkstone [-stoun], *s.* (petr.) perlita, fonolita.

clinometer [klainámetœ(r)], *s.* clinómetro.

clinometric [-ométrik], *a.* clinométrico.

clinometry [-ámetri], *s.* clinometría.

clip [klip]. I. *va.* esquilar, trasquilar; tijeretear; cortar a raíz; (a veces con **off**) cercenar, recortar; podar, mondar; pellizcar, escatimar, acortar; chapurrear; abrazar, ceñir, agarrar; (fam.) apuñear. II. *vn.* moverse o deslizarse con rapidez. III. *s.* tijeretada, tijeretazo, talla; recorte; trasquila, esquileo; cantonera; grapa, mordaza, pinza, sujetapapeles; sujetador; abrazadera; celeridad, rapidez; (fam.) puñada.

clipper [-œ(r)], *s.* cercenador, recortador; esquilador, trasquilador; maquinilla para cortar el pelo; cizalla; (mar., aer.) clíper.—*pl.* tijeras podadoras o de trasquilar, etc.

clipping [-iŋ], *s.* trasquila; recorte; cercenadura, retal; pellizcamiento; tijereteo.—**c. machine**, maquinilla de repelar.—*pl.* recortes; (agr.) desbroce; (met.) cizalla; (sast.) sisas.

clique [klik]. I. *s.* pandilla, camarilla, asociación exclusivista, compadraje. II. *vn.* (fam.) apandillarse.

clitoris [kláitoris], *s.* (anat.) clítoris, *m.*

cloaca [klouéika], *s.* cloaca; retrete; (zool.) cloaca.

cloak [klóuk]. I. *s.* capa, manto; velo; palio; excusa, disimulo.—**c.-and-sword play**, comedia de capa y espada.—**c. hanger**, cuelgacapas.—

c. rack, capero. II. *va.* encapotar; embozar; ocultar, encubrir, paliar.

cloakroom [-rum], *s.* guardarropa, ropería.

cloche [klouʂ], *s.* cobertura de forma acampanada; sombrero de mujer muy ajustado a la cabeza; (aer.) palanca de mando de campana.

clock [klák]. I. *s.* reloj (de mesa o pared); cuadrado (de las medias).—**c. dial** o **face,** esfera, muestra de reloj.—**c. weight,** pesa. II. *va.* medir o contar el tiempo de un acto.

clockmaker, clocksmith [-mejkœ(r), -smɪθ], *s.* relojero.

clockwise [-wajz], *a.* y *adv.* en el sentido de las agujas del reloj.

clockwork [-wœrk]. I. *s.* movimiento de reloj.—**like c.,** con gran regularidad y precisión. II. *a.* de movimiento regular.

clod [klád]. I. *s.* terrón, gleba; tierra, suelo, césped; masa, trozo; gaznápiro, zoquete.—**c. crusher,** desterronador, rodillo. II. *vn.* aterronarse; coagularse. III. *va.* tirar terrones.

cloddish [-iʂ], **cloddy** [-i], *a.* terroso; rústico.

clodhopper [-hapœ(r)], *s.* destripaterrones, patán; papanatas.—*pl.* zapatos para trabajos duros.

clodpate [-pejt], **clodpoll** [-poul], *s.* mentecato.

clog [klág]. I. *va.* cargar, embarazar, empachar; obstruir, entorpecer; apiñar, amontonar. II. *vn.* apiñarse, atestarse; agolparse, amontonarse; atorarse; obstruirse; atascarse. III. *s.* traba, obstáculo; carga, hipoteca; galocha, chapín, chanclo, zueco, zoclo.—**c. dance,** zapateado.—**c. dancer,** zapateador.

clogginess [-inɪs], *s.* embarazo, impedimento, obstáculo.

cloister [klójstœ(r)]. I. *s.* claustro; monasterio, convento. II. *va.* enclaustrar; proveer de claustros.—**cloistered** [-d], *a.* enclaustrado.—**cloisterer** [-œ(r)], *s.* monje, religioso.—**cloistral** [-trạl], *a.* claustral; retirado, solitario.—**cloistress** [-trɪs], *s.* monja.

clonic [klánɪk], *a.* (med.) clónico, convulsivo.

close [klouz]. I. *va.* cerrar; obstruir, tapar; concluir, terminar; clausurar; levantar (una sesión); fenecer; finiquitar (una cuenta).—**to c. out,** vender en liquidación; saldar por ventas (mercancías, géneros, etc.).—**to c. up,** cerrar, cerrar por completo. II. *vn.* cerrar(se); juntarse, unirse; terminar; fenecer; arreglarse (a veces con *on, upon* antes del sustantivo o frase que indica lo convenido).—**to c. in,** acercarse rodeando; cerrar (la noche).—**to c. in on,** o **to c. on,** o **upon,** rodear, estrechar.—**to c. with,** cerrar con (el adversario). III. *s.* fin, conclusión, terminación; caída (de la tarde); clausura; cierre, unión; lucha cuerpo a cuerpo; [klouʂ], cercado; atrio; recinto; coto; solar, parcela.

close [klous], *a.* cerrado; apretado; ajustado; justo, premioso; íntimo o estrecho (amistad, etc.); sofocante, pesado (tiempo); ahogado, mal ventilado; tupido, compacto, denso; incomunicado; inmediato, contiguo, cercano; unido; estrecho, angosto; breve, compendioso, sucinto; oculto, secreto; callado, reservado; limitado, restringido; avaro, tacaño; retirado, solitario; aplicado, atento, concienzudo; perfecto; notable, marcado; casi igual, casi empatado; parejo, igual; reñido (combate, elección, etc.); (com.) difícil de obtener (dinero).—**at c. range,** a quema ropa, a boca de jarro.—**c.-bodied,** ajustado; tupido.—**c. call,** (fam.) escape difícil o milagroso (**to have a c. call,** escapar en una tabla).—**c. combat,** combate cuerpo a cuerpo.—**c. corporation,** compañía o sociedad anónima cuyos dignatarios son por lo general dueños de las acciones.—**c.-coupled circuit,** (elec.) circuito compuesto de dos, uno abierto y otro cerrado.—**c. fertilization,** (bot.) autofecundación, fecundación por polen de la misma flor.—**c.-fisted,** tacaño, cicatero, apretado, miserable.—**c.-fitting,** ceñido al cuerpo, ajus-

tado, entallado.—**c. formation,** (mil.) columna cerrada.—**c.-grained,** compacto, denso, tupido.—**c.-hauled,** (mar.) de bolina, ciñendo el viento.—**c.-lipped, c.-mouthed,** callado, reservado, cauteloso en el hablar.—**c. order** = C. FORMATION.—**c.-packed,** apretado.—**c. quarters,** lugar estrecho; contacto íntimo en la lucha.—**c. season,** veda.—**c. shave,** afeitada lisa, a ras o a contrapelo; (fam.) = C. CALL.—**c. stool,** sillico, silla-retrete.—**c. study,** aplicación.—**c.-tongued** = C.-MOUTHED.—**c.-woven,** tupido, acipado.

close [klous], *adv.* cerca, de cerca; estrechamente, apretadamente.—**c. by,** muy cerca.—**c. to,** muy cerca de; junto a; arrimado o pegado a; a raíz de; en relaciones muy íntimas con.

closed [klouzd], *a.* cerrado; cerrada (vocal); concluso; vedado.—**c. car,** (aut.) coche cerrado.—**c. chapter,** asunto concluido.—**c.-coil,** (elec.) de arrollamiento cerrado.—**c. corporation,** = CLOSE CORPORATION.—**c. door,** (der. int.) puerta cerrada, restricción de derechos, etc. *V.* OPEN DOOR.—**c. issue,** asunto concluido.—**c. sea,** (der. int.) mar enteramente jurisdiccional.—**c. season,** veda.—**c. shop,** taller exclusivo, que no admite sino miembros de los gremios obreros; agremiación obligatoria.—**c. syllable,** (fon.) sílaba cerrada o trabada (que termina en consonante).

closely [klóuslɪ], *adv.* de cerca; estrechamente, contiguamente; fuertemente, sólidamente; atentamente; cuidadosamente.

closeness [-nɪs], *s.* contigüidad; estrechez; densidad; apretamiento; falta de ventilación; solidez, firmeza; reclusión, soledad; reserva; avaricia, tacañería; conexión, dependencia, unión; exactitud, fidelidad (de copia o traducción).

close-out [klóuz aut], *s.* (com.) liquidación.

closet [klázit]. I. *s.* gabinete; tocador; armario, alacena; común, excusado, retrete. II. *a.* secreto, confidencial; propio del gabinete; teórico, especulativo, contemplativo.—**c. drama,** comedia más para leída que para representada. III. *va.* encerrar o esconder en un retrete; encerrar a uno para conferenciar a puerta cerrada.

close-up [klóus ʌp], *s.* fotografía a quema ropa, de cerca; cosa vista o examinada de cerca.

closing [klóuzɪŋ]. I. *s.* cierre, acción de cerrar; final, conclusión; clausura; remate (de cuentas). II. *a.* de cierre; último, final; de clausura.—**c. price,** último curso (en la bolsa).

closure [klóuʐŭ(r)]. I. *s.* procedimiento parlamentario para poner término a un debate; clausura; encierro; cierre; fin, conclusión; (fon.) oclusión. II. *va.* y *vn.* poner fin a un debate, aplicando el *closure.*

clot [klat]. I. *s.* grumo, coágulo, cuajarón. II. *vn.* coagularse, cuajarse, aburujarse, engrumecerse.

cloth [kláθ], *s.* paño, tela, género tejido; mantel; vestido o ropa clerical; el clero; (mar.) paño de vela.—**c. binding,** encuadernación en tela.—**c. press,** prensa de paños.—**c. prover,** cuentahilos.—**c. yard,** yarda de 36 pulgadas, o tres pies.

clothbound [-baund], *a.* encuadernado en tela.

clothe [klouð], *va.* (pret. y *pp.* CLOTHED o CLAD) vestir; cubrir; arropar, apañar; trajear; revestir.—**to c. with authority,** investir de autoridad.

clothes [klóuz], *s. pl.* vestido, vestuario, indumentaria, vestimenta; ropaje; paños; ropa de toda especie; ropa de cama.—**c. beetle,** moza.—**c. cleaner,** quitamanchas, sacamanchas, *mf.*—**c. chest,** guardarropa, ropero, armario.—**c. closet,** cuarto guardarropa.—**c. dryer,** camilla; secadora (máquina).—**c. hamper,** canasta de la ropa.—**c. hanger,** colgador de ropa, percha.—**c. moth,** (ent.) polilla.—**c. pole,** apoyo de la tenedera.—**c. pounder,** moza.—**c. rack** o **tree,** percha, perchero.—**c. room,** ropería.—**c. wringer,** secadora, exprimidor.

clothesbars [-barz], s. secarropa de travesaños.

clothesbasket [-bæskịt], s. cesta de la ropa o colada.

clothesbrush [-brʌʃ], s. cepillo de ropa.

clotheshorse [-hɔrs], s. camilla, percha.

clothesline [-laịn], s. tendedera, cuerda.—**c. post**, poste, berlinga.

clothesman [-man], s. ropero, ropavejero.

clothespin [-pịn], s. pinzas de tendedera o para sujetar ropa.

clothespress [-pres], s. guardarropa, armario.

clothier [klóuδịœ(r)], s. pañero, ropero.—**c.'s store** o **trade**, ropería.

clothing [klóuδịŋ], s. vestidos, ropa; vestuario, indumentaria; ropaje.—**c. store**, pañería; ropería.

clotted, clotty [klátịd, klátị], a. grumoso, coagulado.

cloture [klóuchụr], s. V. CLOSURE (proced. parl.).

cloud [kláụd]. I. s. nube, f.; nublado, nubarrón; (joy.) mancha, nube; muchedumbre, multitud, enjambre.—**c.-capped**, altísimo, coronado de nubes.—**under a c.**, desacreditado, sospechoso.—**in the clouds**, quimérico, ilusorio; abstraído. II. va. anublar, aneblar, enturbiar, obscurecer, cegar; abigarrar, motear; empañar, manchar, difamar. III. vn. anublarse; obscurecerse.

cloudburst [-bœrst], s. turbión, m., chaparrón.

cloudily [-ịlị], adv. obscuramente; con mucha niebla.

cloudiness [-ịnịs], s. nebulosidad, obscuridad.

cloudless [-lịs], a. sin nubes, despejado, claro.

cloudy [-ị], a. nublado, nubloso, encapotado; nebuloso, vaporoso; turbio; obscuro, sombrío; lóbrego, tétrico; sospechoso; (pint.) nubarrado; (fot.) velado.

clout [klaụt]. I. s. (mec.) cibica, cibicón; (ballestería) blanco, o tiro que da en el blanco; (ant.) rodilla o trapo para limpiar; remiendo; pañal; culero, metedor; (fam.) golpe; bofetada; zoquete, gaznápiro.—**c. nails**, clavos de zapato. II. va. cubrir con paño, cuero, etc.; remendar o vendar (gen. toscamente) con trapo; tachonar con clavos; proteger con cibica; (fam.) golpear, abofetear.

clove, pret; **cloven**, pp. de TO CLEAVE.

clove [kloụv], s. clavo de especia; diente de ajo.—**c. pink** o **gillyflower**, (bot.) variedad de clavel.—**c. tree**, (bot.) clavero, giroflé o jiroflé.

cloven [klóụven], pp. y a. partido, hendido.—**c.-foot, c.-footed, c.-hoofed**, patihendido, bisulco; diabólico.—**to betray**, o **show, the c. foot**, (fam.) sacar la pata, enseñar la oreja.

clover [klóụvœ(r)], s. (bot.) trébol.—**to be**, o **live, in c.**, vivir en la abundancia.

clovered [-d], a. lleno de trébol.

clown [kláụn], s. patán, paleto; bufón, payaso, hazmerreír, truhán, (teat.) bobo, gracioso, bufo.

clownery [-œrị], s. rusticidad; payasada.

clownish [-ịʃ], a. rudo, grosero, tocho, zafio; tosco, basto; bufonesco, truhanesco.—**clownishly** [-lị], adv. toscamente, groseramente.—**clownishness** [-nịs], s. rusticidad, grosería; bufonada, bufonería, payasada.

cloy [klɔ́ị], va. empalagar; saciar, hartar, hastiar.

cloying [-ịŋ], **cloysome** [-sʌm], a. empalagoso.

club [klʌ́b]. I. s. clava, (cachi)porra, garrote, maza, tranca; club, círculo, tertulia; centro de reunión; palo o mazo (de golf); maza de gimnasia.—pl. bastos (de baraja).—**c. car**, (f. c.) coche club, arreglado como cuarto de club, con mesas de escribir, periódicos, etc.—**c. chair**, sillón de club, butaca.—**c. grass** o **rush**, (bot.) espadaña.—**c. law**, la ley del más fuerte; gobierno tiránico.—**c. moss**, (bot.) licopodio.—**c. steak**, pequeño biftec (del filete). II. vn. contribuir, o concurrir a gastos comunes; unirse o juntarse para un mismo fin. III. va. aporrear, golpear con garrote; escotar, pagar a prorrata la parte que a cada uno le toca.

clubbed [-d]. I. pp. de TO CLUB. II. a. en forma

de clava o maza; ahusado; de extremo ensanchado; (bot.) de raíces atacadas de hongos.

clubbist [-ịst], s. miembro de club o casino.

clubfoot [-fụt], s. pateta, m., pie zambo, torcido o de piña.—**clubfooted** [-ịd], a. patituerto.

clubhouse [-haụs], s. casino, club.

clubman, clubwoman, [-(wụ)man], s. clubista; miembro de un club o círculo, o adicto a la vida social.

cluck [klʌk]. I. va. y vn. cloquear; hacer clo clo la gallina clueca; imitar este sonido. II. s. cloqueo.

clue [klu], s. guía, norte; indicio, pista. V. CLEW.

clump [klʌmp]. I. s. grupo (de árboles o arbustos); zoquete, tarugo; aglutinación, masa; suela gruesa; pisada recia. II. va. y vn. aglutinar(se), arracimarse; andar torpemente con fuertes pisadas.

clumsily [klʌmzịlị], adv. zafiamente, groseramente; chapucera, chabacana o torpemente.

clumsiness [-ịnịs], s. zafiedad, desmaña.

clumsy [-ị], a. desmañado, chapucero, chabacano; incómodo, difícil de manejar.

clung [klʌŋ], pret. y pp. de TO CLING.

Cluniacensian [klunịạsénṣan], a. y s. cluniacense.

cluster [klʌ́stœ(r)]. I. s. racimo; piña; ramo, ramillete, macolla; grupo, agrupación; caterva, hato; enjambre (de abejas).—**c. pine** = SEASIDE PINE. II. vn. arracimarse, agruparse.—**clustered pier** o **column**, (arq.) pilar en haz, columnas agrupadas. III. va. apiñar, amontonar.

clustery [-ị], a. arracimado, botriforme; apiñado; agrupado.

clutch [klʌch]. I. va. agarrar; empuñar, apretar; embragar. II. vn. (con **at**) echar la garra a, tratar de empuñar. III. s. agarro, presa; uña, grapa, garra; nidada; (aut.) embrague.—**c. coupling**, (mec.) acoplamiento por garras; conexión de engranaje.—**to fall in the clutches of**, caer en las garras de.

clutter [klʌ́tœ(r)]. I. s. (fam.) baraúnda, batahola; desorden, confusión. V. CLATTER. II. vn. alborotar, hacer ruido o estrépito, menearse con bullicio, atropellarse. III. va. poner en desorden, trastornar.

clyster [klị́stœ(r)], s. clister o clistel, ayuda, enema, lavativa.

clyster(ize [-aịz], va. (med.) clisterizar.

coach [kóụch]. I. s. coche, carruaje; carroza; automóvil de dos puertas; (f. c.) vagón, coche ordinario de viajeros; preceptor; (dep.) entrenador.—**c.-and-four**, coche o carroza de cuatro caballos.—**c. box**, pescante.—**c. dog**, perro dalmático.—**c. horse**, caballo de coche.—**c. house**, cochera.—**c. step**, zancajera. II. va. llevar en coche; enseñar, preparar; aleccionar, amaestrar; (dep.) entrenar. III. vn. (fam.) pasear en coche; prepararse con un preceptor o (dep.) entrenarse; servir de preceptor o entrenador.

coacher [-œ(r)], s. preceptor; (dep.) entrenador; caballo de coche.

coachmaker [-meịkœ(r)], s. carrocero.

coachman [-man], s. cochero; (poét.) auriga, m.

coachmanship [-ʃịp], s. arte de cochear.

coachwhip [-hwịp], s. manopla (látigo).

coact [koụǽkt], va. y vn. promulgar (una ley) u obrar de concierto; cooperar.

coaction [koụǽkṣạn], s. coacción; compulsión, fuerza; acción concertada.

coactive [koụǽktịv], a. coactivo; cooperante.

coadjument [koụédȝụmẹnt], s. mutua y recíproca asistencia.—**coadjutant** [-tạnt], a. coadyuvante, auxiliar.—**coadjutor** [-tǫ(r)], s. coadjutor.—**coadjutrix** [-trịks], s. coadjutora.—**coadjuvancy** [-vạnsị], s. coadjutoría.—**coadjuvant** [-vạnt], a. coadyuvante, coadyutorio.

coadministrator [kóụædmịnịstreịtǫ(r)], s. coadministrador.

coadunate [koŭǽdžŭneįt], va. coadunar.

coadunation [-néįşŏn], s. coadunación.

coagent [koŭéįdžęnt], s. coagente, cooperador.

coagulability [koŭægįųlǎbílįtį], s. propiedad de coagularse; calidad de coagulable.

coagulable [koŭǽgįųĺǎbl], a. coagulable.

coagulant [-lǎnt], a. y s. coagulante.—**coagulate** [-leįt]. I. va. coagular, cuajar. II. vn. coagularse, cuajarse, espesarse.—**coagulation** [-léįşŏn], s. coagulación; cuajamiento; coágulo.—**coagulative** [-lǎtįv], a. coagulativo.—**coagulator** [-leįtǫ(r)], s. coagulante, coagulador.—**coagulin** [-lįn], s. (quím.) coagulina.—**coagulum** [-lʌm], s. coágulo, cuajarón.

coal [koŭl]. I. s. hulla, carbón, carbón de piedra o mineral, antracita; brasa.—**c. bin**, o **box**, arca o depósito de carbón, carbonera.—**c. black**, negro como tinta, absolutamente negro.—**c. breaker**, molino de carbón.—**c. brick**, aglomerado, carbón prensado.—**c. bunker**, (mar.) carbonera, pañol del carbón.—**c. dust**, polvo de hulla, cisco.—**c. field**, yacimiento de carbón.—**c. gas**, gas de hulla; gas del alumbrado.—**c. heaver**, cargador de carbón.—**c. man**, carbonero.—**c. measures**, (geol.) yacimientos de carbón; estratos carboníferos explotables.—**c. mine** o **pit**, carbonera, mina de carbón.—**c. miner**, carbonero.—**c. oil**, petróleo (esp. kerosina).—**c. pipe**, (min.) veta de carbón delgada e irregular.—**c. rake**, badila, hurgón.—**c. scuttle**, cubo de (para) carbón.—**c. ship**, barco carbonero.—**c. tar**, alquitrán de hulla, coaltar.—**c. tongs**, tenazas de chimenea. II. va. y vn. carbonear, carbonizar; proveer(se) de carbón.

coalesce [koŭǎlés], vn. unirse, juntarse, soldarse.

coalescence [-ęns], s. coalescencia, unión.

coalescent [-ęnt], a. coalescente.

coaling [kóŭlįŋ]. I. s. toma de carbón. II. a. de toma o aprovisionamiento de carbón.—**c. station**, puerto de toma de carbón.

coalition [koŭǎlíşŏn], s. coalición, liga.

coalitionist [-įst], s. coalicionista.

coaly [kóŭlį], a. carbonoso, hornaguero.

coaming [kóŭmįŋ], s. brazola, brocal.

coaptation [koŭǽptéįşŏn], s. (cir.) coaptación.

coarctate [koŭárkteįt], a. comprimido, contraído.

coarctation [-éįşŏn], s. (med.) contracción, estrechez.

coarse [kórs], a. basto, ordinario; tosco; vulgar, soez; grueso, burdo.—**c. count**, (tej.) número grueso o bajo (del hilo).—**c. file**, lima de desbastar.—**c.-grained**, de fibra o granulación gruesa.—**c. wool**, lana burda.

coarsely [-lį], adv. toscamente; groseramente.

coarseness [-nįs], s. calidad de basto o burdo; tosquedad, vulgaridad.

coassume [koŭǎsúm], va. asumir con otro.

coast [kóŭst]. I. s. costa; litoral.—**c. guard**, guarda de costas, servicio costanero; carabineros, m. pl.—**c. guard cutter**, guardacostas.—**c. trade**, cabotaje.—**the c. is clear**, ha pasado el peligro; no hay moros en la costa. II. va. (mar.) costear. III. vn. (mar.) navegar a lo largo de la costa; deslizarse cuesta abajo en un trineíllo raso u otro vehículo movido únicamente por la gravedad; seguir rodando libremente en bicicleta, automóvil, etc.

coastal [-ąl], a. cost(an)ero, costeño.

coaster [-œ(r)], s. piloto práctico; barco de cabotaje; habitante de la costa; deslizador.—**c. brake**, freno de bicicleta para marchar cuesta abajo (freno de retroceso con piñón libre).

coasting [-įŋ], s. (mar.) cabotaje; acto o diversión de deslizarse cuesta abajo.

coastline [-laįn], s. costa, litoral.

coastwise [-waįz], a. y adv. a lo largo de la costa; costanero.

coat [koŭt]. I. s. americana, chaqueta, saco (traje usual); frac, levita, casaca (traje ceremonial);

abrigo, paletó, capote; pelo, lana, pelaje; (mec.) cubierta o envoltura, funda, caperuza; túnica del ojo; revestimiento; (alb.) tendido; baño, capa o mano (de pintura, alquitrán, etc.).—**c. card**, figura (de la baraja).—**c. of arms**, (escudo de) armas.—**c. hanger**, percha, colgador.—**c. of mail**, arnés, cota (de malla).—**c. rack** o **stand**, perchero.—**c. room**, guardarropa; cuarto donde se dejan abrigo, sombrero, etc.—**c. tail**, faldón; pl. faldillas.—**to turn one's c.**, volver casaca, cambiar de partido. II. va. cubrir, vestir, revestir; bañar, dar una mano o capa de; azogar; (alb.) tender.

coatee [koŭtí], s. chaquet(ill)a, casaquilla.

coati [koátį], s. (zool.) coatí.

coating [kóŭtįŋ], s. revestimiento, capa, man'ǫ de pintura, etc.; (alb.) blanqueo, jalbegue; enlucido; (tej.) bayetón.

coauthor [koŭáθǫ(r)], s. coautor.

coax [kóŭks], va. y vn. instar; engatusar, enga(i)tar, lagotear.—**to like**, o **wait**, **to be coaxed**, hacerse de rogar.

coaxer [-œ(r)], s. engatusador, marrullero.

coaxial [koŭǽksįąl], a. coaxil, de un mismo eje.

coaxing [kóŭksįŋ], s. ruego; engatusamiento.

cob [kab], s. tusa o carozo de maíz; jaca, caballito; cisne macho; cierta gaviota negra; araña; peso duro o fuerte español; mezcla de arcilla y paja; azotazo.—**c. coal**, hulla en pedazos redondos.

cobalt [kóŭbǫlt], s. (quím.) cobalto.—**c. blue**, azul de cobalto.

cobaltic [kobáltįk], a. (quím.) cobáltico.—**cobaltine** [kóŭbǫltįn], **cobaltite** [kóŭbǫltaįt], s. (min.) cobaltina.—**cobaltous** [-tʌs], a. (quím.) cobaltoso.

cobble [kábl], va. remendar zapatos; chapucear; empedrar con guijarros.

cobble, cobblestone [-stoųn], s. guijarro.

cobbler [káblœ(r)], s. zapatero de viejo, remendón; chapucero.—**c. fish**, (ict.) zapatero.

cobelligerent [koŭbelídžęręnt], a. y s. cobeligerante.

cobnut [kábnʌt], s. (bot.) avellana grande.

cobra [kóŭbrǎ], **cobra de capello** [-dįkǎpélouų], s. (zool.) cobra, cobracapelo.

cobweb [kábwɛb], s. telaraña; añagaza.

cobwebbed, cobwebby [-d, -į], a. telarañoso.

cobwork [kábwœrk], s. estructura de trozas horizontales.

coca [kóŭkǎ], s. (bot.) coca, (Am.) cuca, hayo.

cocain, cocaine [koŭkéįn], s. (quím.) cocaína.

cocainize [-aįz], va. poner bajo la influencia anestésica de la cocaína.

coccid [káksįd], s. (ent.) insecto de los cóccidos.

cocciferous [kaksíferʌs], a. que produce bayas.

cocculus [kákįųlʌs], s. (bot.) coca de levante.

coccus [kákʌs], s. (bot.-biol.) coco (bacteria).

coccygeal [kaksídžįąl], a. (anat.) coccígeo, coxígeo; pert. al cóccix o coxis, m.

coccyx [káksįks], s. (anat.) cóccix, coxis, m.

cochin [kóŭchįn], s. y a. cochinchino (aplícase a las gallinas).

cochineal [kachįníl], s. cochinilla, grana, quermes (insecto y tinte o materia colorante).

cochlea [kákĺįǎ], s. (anat.) caracol (del oído).

cochlear [-(r)], a. coclear.

cochleat(ed) [kákĺeįt(įd)], a. acaracolado.

cock [kak]. I. s. (orn.) gallo; macho de cualquier ave (en palabras compuestas); caudillo, campeón; veleta, giraldilla; llave, f. grifo, espita (de agua, etc.); llave, percusor o martillo de armas de fuego; seguro (de armas de fuego); vuelta del ala del sombrero; montón de paja, heno, etc.; saeta, estilo o gnomon de reloj de sol.—**c. and bull story**, patraña, cuento exagerado o increíble.—**c.-brained**, temerario.—**c.-eyed**, bizco; (fam.) extravagante, loco, achispado.—**c. of the walk**, o **of the loft**, (fam.) gallito del lugar, quiquiriquí.—**c. robin**, (orn.) petirrojo (macho). II. va. montar o amartillar (un arma de fuego); levantar, erguir, enderezar; encandilar el sombrero; hacinar o amontonar heno. **III.** *vn.* entonarse, engreírse, gallear.

cockade [kakéid], *s.* escarapela, cucarda, pedrada.

cock-a-doodle-doo [kákạdudldú], *s.* quiquiriquí, canto del gallo.

cock-a-hoop [kakạhúp], *a.* alegre, triunfante, achispado, engreído.

cockatoo [kakạtú], *s.* (orn.) cacatúa.

cockatrice [kákạtris], *s.* (mit.) basilisco.

cockboat [kákboụt], *s.* (mar.) barquilla.

cockchafer [kákchẹifœ(r)], *s.* (ent.) abejorro (coleóptero), variedad de escarabajo.

cockcrow(ing [kákkroụ(iṇ], *s.* canto del gallo; la aurora.

cocked hat [kákt hǽt], *s.* sombrero de candil o de tres picos.—**to knock into a c. h.,** (fam.) destrozar, apabullar.

cocker [kákœ(r)]. **I.** *va.* acariciar, mimar. **II.** *s.* gallero; el que pelea gallos.—**c. spaniel,** perro cócker (apl. a una casta de perros de caza, de origen español).

cockerel [kákẹrẹl], *s.* pollo, gallo joven.

cocket [kákẹt], *s.* sello de la aduana.

cockfight(ing [kákfaịt(iṇ], *s.* riña de gallos.—**cockfighter** [-œ(r)], *s.* gallero.

cockhorse [kákhórs], *s.* caballito (juguete).

cockish [kákiš], *a.* (fam.) engreído, hinchado.

cockle [kákl]. **I.** *s.* coquina (molusco); cúpula de horno; barquichuelo; (bot.) vallico, zizaña, joyo; neguilla (del trigo). *V.* **corn c.**—**c. hat,** sombrero de peregrino (esp. el de Santiago de Compostela).—**the cockles of the heart,** (fig.) las entretelas del corazón. **II.** *va.* y *vn.* arrugar, hacer arrugas, plegarse; encresparse (olas).

cocklebur [-bœ(r)], *s.* (bot.) bardana o cadillo.

cockled [-d], *a.* granoso (apl. esp. al papel); arrugado, ondulado.

cockleshell [-šel], *s.* concha de coquina.

cockloft [kákloft], *s.* desván, zaquizamí.

cockmaster [kákmæstœ(r)], *s.* gallero.

cockmatch [kákmæch], *s.* riña de gallos.

cockney [kákni], *s.* londinense de clase popular y de dialecto o acento característico.

cockpit [kákpit], *s.* gallera; reñidero de gallos; (mar.) entarimado del sollado; parte baja de popa de la cubierta (de un yate); (aer.) cabina del piloto y copiloto; cámara, casilla.

cockroach [kákroụch], *s.* (ent.) cucaracha, curiana, corredera.

cockscomb [kákskoụm], *s.* cresta (de gallo); gorro de bufón; bufón; (bot.) cresta de gallo o gallocresta, amaranto, (Am.) moco de pavo. *V.* **coxcomb.**

cockspur [kákspœ(r)], *s.* espolón o navaja de gallo.

cocksure [kákšúr]. **I.** *a.* absolutamente seguro. **II.** *adv.* con entera seguridad.

cockswain [káksn], *s.* = **coxswain.**

cocktail [kákteịl], *s.* cocktail, coctel.

cocky [káki], *a.* confiado, engreído, hinchado.

coco(a, coco(a-palm [kóụkoụ], *s.* (bot.) coco, cocotero (árbol); coco (fruto).

cocoa, *s.* cacao molido o en polvo; bebida de cacao.—**c. bean,** grano de cacao, cacao en grano.—**c. butter,** manteca de cacao.

coco(a)nut [kóụkonᴧt], *s.* (bot.) coco (fruto).—**c. palm** o **tree,** coco(tero).—**c. plantation,** cocotal.

cocobolo [koụkobóụloụ], *s.* (bot.) cocobolo.

cocoon [kọkún], *s.* capullo del gusano de seda y de ciertos otros insectos u orugas.

cocoonery [-œri], *s.* criadero de gusanos de seda.

coctile [káktil], *a.* cocido en horno.

coction [kákšọn], *s.* cocción, cocimiento, cochura.

cod [kad], *s.* (ict.) abadejo, bacal(l)ao, curadillo; truchuela (bacalao curado).—**c.-liver oil,** aceite de hígado de bacalao.

coddle [kádl], *va.* criar con mimo o ternura excesiva; cocer a fuego lento (huevos, frutas, etc.).

code [koụd]. **I.** *s.* (for.) código, compilación; (tel.,

com., mil., etc.) código, cifra, clave, *f.* (*V.* **signal code).—c. letter,** carta en clave.—**c. of honor,** código del honor. **II.** *va.* cifrar, meter en forma de clave o cifra.

codefendant [koụdịféndạnt], *s.* (for.) coacusado, acusado con otro u otros.

codein(e [kóụdin], *s.* (quím.) codeína.

codex [kóụdẹks], *s.* códice.

codfish [kádfiš], *s.* (ict.). *V.* **cod.**

codger [kádżœ(r)], *s.* (despec.) chiflado; tipo.

codicil [kádisil], *s.* (for.) codicilo.

codification [kadịfịkéišọn], *s.* codificación (de las leyes).—**codifier** [kádịfaịœ(r)], *s.* codificador.—**codify** [kádịfaị], *va.* codificar, compilar (leyes).

codling [kádliṇ], *s.* (ict.) pijota; (bot.) manzana.

coed, co-ed [kóụéd], *s.* alumna de un plantel de coeducación.

coeducation [koụẹdżụkéišọn], *s.* coeducación; educación de ambos sexos en comunidad.

coeducational [-ạl], *a.* coeducativo, de coeducación.

coefficiency [koụịfíšẹnsị], *s.* coeficiencia.

coefficient [-ẹnt]. **I.** *a.* coeficiente; cooperador. **II.** *s.* (mat.) coeficiente.—**c. of discharge,** (hidr.) coeficiente de salida.—**c. of efficiency,** (mec.) rendimiento.—**c. of expansion,** coeficiente de dilatación.—**c. of friction,** (mec.) coeficiente de rozamiento.—**c. of (magnetic) leakage,** coeficiente de dispersión magnética.—**c. of safety,** coeficiente o factor de seguridad.—**c. of sensitiveness,** (elec.) coeficiente de sensibilidad.

coefficiently [-liị], *adv.* cooperativamente.

coelenterate [sịléntẹrẹit], *a.* y *s.* (zool.) celenterado.

coeliac [síliæk], *a.* (anat.) celíaco.—**c. artery,** (arteria) celíaca.—**c. flux** o **passion,** (med.) celíaca.

coenesthesis [sinesθísịs], *s.* (psic.) cinestesia.

coequal [koụíkwạl], *a.* mutuamente igual.

coequality [koụikwálịtị], *s.* igualdad.

coerce [koụœrs], *va.* forzar, obligar; coercer, constreñir; contener, refrenar; restringir.

coercible [-ịbl], *a.* coercible, coactible.

coercion [koụœršọn], *s.* coerción, coacción.

coercive [koụœrsịv], *a.* coercitivo; coactivo, obligatorio.

coessential [koụẹsénšạl], *a.* coesencial.

coessentiality [-šịélịtị], *s.* coesencia.

coetaneous [koụịtéịnịạs], *a.* coetáneo.

coeternal [koụitœrnạl], *a.* coeterno.

coeternity [-ịtị], *s.* coeternidad.

coeval [koụíval], *s.* y *a.* coevo, contemporáneo; *a.* coetvo.

coexecutor [koụịgzékịụtọ(r)], *s.* coalbacea, *m.*

coexist [koụịgzíst], *vn.* coexistir.—**coexistence** [-ẹns], *s.* coexistencia.—**coexistent** [-ẹnt], *a.* coexistente.

coextend [koụịksténd], *vn.* coextenderse.—**coextension** [-sténšọn], *s.* coextensión.—**coextensive** [-sténsịv], *a.* coextensivo.—**coextensively** [-liị], *adv.* coextensivamente.

coffee [kófị], *s.* café (grano, bebida y árbol).—**c. bean,** grano de café.—**c. berry,** fruto, cereza del cafeto.—**c. cake,** rosca que gen. se come con el café.—**c. grinder, c. mill,** molinillo de café.—**c. grounds,** posos, heces o asientos del café.—**c. grower, planter** o **worker,** cafet(al)ero, (Am.) cafetalista.—**c. industry,** industria cafet(al)era.—**c. plantation,** cafetal.—**c. roaster,** tambor, tostador.—**c. spoon,** cucharita de (o para) café.—**c. tree,** café, cafeto.

coffeehouse [-haụs], *s.* café (establecimiento).

coffeepot [-pat], *s.* cafetera.

coffer [kófœ(r)]. **I.** *s.* arca, cofre; (arq.) artesón hondo. *V.* **caisson.**—*pl.* tesoro, fondos. **II.** *va.* meter en arca; atesorar; (arq.) artesonar.—**coffered ceiling,** artesonado.

cofferdam [-dæm], *s.* (hidr.) ataguía.

coffin [kófịn]. **I.** *s.* ataúd, *m.,* féretro, caja (mortuoria); (vet.) uña del casco del caballo.—**c.**

bone, (vet.) bolillo. **II.** *va.* meter en ataúd; (fig.) encerrar, ocultar.

cog [kag]. **I.** *va.* puntear o poner dientes a una rueda; (carp.) ensamblar con espigas; (met.) desbastar con rodillo; engañar.—**to c. a die,** cargar un dado. **II.** *vn.* trampear, hacer fullerías. **III.** *s.* (mec.) diente, punto o álabe de rueda; cama, leva; (carp.) espiga; fraude, engaño; (mar.) botequín.—**c. railway,** ferrocarril de cremallera.

cogency [kóu̯dźęnsi], *s.* fuerza lógica o moral.

cogent [-ęnt], *a.* convincente, persuasivo.

cogged [kagd], *a.* dentado, engranado; fraudulento.—**c. dice,** brocha, dados cargados o falsos.

cogitable [kádźįtabl], *a.* cogitable.

cogitate [-teįt], *vn.* pensar, meditar, reflexionar.— **cogitation** [-téįšǫn], *s.* cogitación, reflexión, meditación, discurso.—**cogitative** [-teįtįv], *a.* cogitativo, reflexivo.

cognac [kóu̯ηjæk], *s.* coñac.

cognate [kágneįt], *a.* y *s.* cognado, consanguíneo; pariente, deudo; afín; semejante, análogo.

cognatic [kagnǽtįk], *a.* cognaticio.

cognation [-éįšǫn], *s.* cognación; origen común; afinidad, entronque.

cognition [-íšǫn], *s.* cognición, conocimiento.

cognitive [kágnįtįv], *a.* cognoscitivo.

cognizable [kágnįzabl], *a.* conocible; (for.) de la competencia de.—**cognizance** [-ans], *s.* conocimiento, comprensión; divisa, señal, *f.;* (for.) competencia, jurisdicción.—**cognizant** [-ant], *a.* sabedor, informado, impuesto (de).—**cognize** [kágnaįz], *va.* (re)conocer.

cognomen [kagnóu̯men], *s.* apellido, sobrenombre; apodo.—**cognominal** [kagnáminal], *a.* ref. al apellido, etc.—**cognominate** [-eįt], *va.* apellidar.—**cognomination** [-éįšǫn], *s.* sobrenombre, cognomento.

cognoscible [kagnásįbl], *a.* cognoscible, conocible.

cognoscitive [-tįv], *a.* cognoscitivo.

cognovit [kagnóu̯vįt], *s.* (for.) conocencia.

cograil [kágreįl], *s.* riel dentado, cremallera.

cogwheel [kághwil], *s.* rueda dentada.

cohabit [kou̯hǽbįt], *vn.* cohabitar.

cohabitant [-ant], *s.* convecino.

cohabitation [-éįšǫn], *s.* cohabitación, contubernio.

coheir [kou̯ér], *s.* coheredero.

coheiress [-įs], *s.* coheredera.

cohere [kohį́r], *vn.* adherirse, pegarse, unirse; enlazarse, adaptarse; conformar(se).

coherence, coherency [-ęns, -į], *s.* cohesión, coherencia, enlace; consecuencia; conformidad.

coherent [-ęnt], *a.* coherente; consecuente.

coherer [-œ(r)], *s.* (rad.) cohesor, radioconductor.

cohesion [kohíźǫn], *s.* cohesión, adhesión, unión.

cohesive [kohísįv], *a.* cohesivo, coherente, adherente.—**cohesively** [-lį], *adv.* coherentemente. —**cohesiveness** [-nįs], *s.* calidad y propiedad de cohesivo.

cohibit [kohíbit], *va.* cohibir; restringir.

cohibition [-bíšǫn], *s.* cohibición.

cohobate [kohóu̯beįt], *va.* (quím., farm.) cohobar.

cohort [kóu̯hǫrt], *s.* cohorte, *f.*

coif [kóįf], *s.* cofia, escofieta, toca, gorro, papalina.

coifed [-t], *a.* adornado con cofia.

coiffeur [kwafœ́r], *s.* peluquero, peinador.

coiffeuse [kwafœ́z], *s.* peluquera, peinadora.

coiffure [kwafyúr], *s.* tocado, peinado.

coign [kǫįn], *s.* esquina; saliente; cuña.—**c. of vantage,** posición ventajosa.

coil [kǫįl]. **I.** *s.* rollo; rosca, espiral; arrollamiento o muelle espiral; vuelta (de tal arrollamiento); serpentín; (mar.) aduja; (elec.) arrollamiento; bobina, carrete. **II.** *va.* enrollar, arrollar; (mar.) adujar (un cable). **III.** *vn.* enrollarse; enroscarse.

coin [kǫįn]. **I.** *s.* moneda acuñada, numerario; (fam.) blanca, dinero; (arq.) *V.* QUOIN.—**c. box,** (tel., etc.) caja recaudadora.—**c. holder**

o **purse,** monedero.—**in c.,** en efectivo.—**to pay one in his own c.,** pagar a uno en la misma moneda. **II.** *va.* acuñar; amonedar o moned(e)ar; inventar, forjar (palabras, mentiras).—**to c. money,** batir dinero; (fam.) enriquecerse rápidamente; (Ingl., fam.) falsificar dinero.

coinage [-įdź], *s.* acuñación; braceaje; monedaje; moneda; sistema monetario; invención.

coincide [kou̯įnsáįd], *vn.* coincidir, concurrir; convenir (con); estar de acuerdo.

coincidence [kou̯ínsįdęns], **-cy** [-į], *s.* coincidencia, concurrencia; casualidad; conformidad.

coincident [-dęnt], **coincidental** [-déntal], *a.* coincidente, concurrente; acorde.

coincidentally [-į], **coincidently** [-dęntlį], *adv.* coincidentalmente; al mismo tiempo.

coindicant [kou̯índįkant], *a.* concurrente, confirmante.

coindication [-kéįšǫn], *s.* indicio que coincide con otro.

coiner [kǫínœ(r)], *s.* acuñador; monedero falso; inventor, fabricador.

coinheritance [kou̯įnhérįtans], *s.* herencia en común.—**coinheritor** [-tǫ(r)], *s.* coheredero.

coinsurance [kou̯įnśúrans], *s.* seguro en que el asegurado figura como coasegurador.

coir [kǫįr], *s.* bonote, fibra extraída del coco.

coition [kǫíšǫn], *s.* coito, concúbito, cópula.

coitus [kóu̯įtas], *s.* = COITION.

coke [kǫu̯k]. **I.** *s.* cok, coque. **II.** *va.* y *vn.* convertir(se) en coque.

cola [kóu̯la], *s.* (bot., farm.) cola. *V.* KOLA.

colander [kÁlandœ(r)], *s.* colador, coladera, coladero; espumadera, escurridor.

colatitude [kou̯lǽtįtįud], *s.* (astr., naveg.) colatitud.

colchicum [kálchįkʌm], *s.* (bot.) cólquico.

colcothar [kálkoθậ(r)], *s.* (quím.) colcótar.

cold [kóu̯ld], *a.* frío; frígido, enfriado, helado; indiferente; esquivo; desalentador; desalentado; apartado, lejos (del objeto buscado); (quím.) en frío; débil (rastro o pista); (pint.) frío, que tira a azul; (fam.) asegurado; insensible; muerto.—**c. abscess,** absceso crónico.—**c.-blooded,** de sangre fría; en sangre fría; impasible, inhumano, cruel; friolento; espurio (de raza).—**c. chisel,** cortafrío.—**c. cream,** colcrén, crema (cosmético).—**c. cuts,** fiambres variados.—**c. dish o lunch,** fiambre.—**c.-drawn,** estirado en frío.—**c. feet,** (hort.) decaimiento debido a exceso de agua; (fam.) miedo, desánimo, cerote.—**c.-hearted,** insensible, impasible.—**c. meat,** carne fría, carne fiambre.—**c. press,** prensa de satinar en frío.— **c.-roll,** *va.* laminar en frío.—**c. saw,** sierra de cortar en frío.—**c.-short,** frágil, quebradizo.— **c. shoulder,** frialdad, indiferencia (vg., *to give one the cold shoulder,* tratar a uno con frialdad, despedirlo con cajas destempladas, o con desaire).—**c. steel,** armas blancas (espada, bayoneta, etc.).—**c. storage,** conservación en frigoríficos o instalaciones refrigerantes.—**c.-storage house o plant,** frigorífico, instalación refrigerante, enfriadero.—**c. wave,** ola de frío. —**in c. blood,** a sangre fría.—**to be c.,** tener frío; (con *it* por sujeto) hacer frío.—**to have, o know, c.,** (fam.) saber al dedillo.—**to leave one c.,** dejar frío o indiferente.—**to turn down c.,** (fam.) rechazar sin consideración.

cold, *s.* frío, frialdad; enfriamiento; esquivez; (med.) resfrío, resfriamiento, resfriado, catarro, constipado.—**c. in the head,** (med.) fluxión, romadizo, catarro.—**c. sore,** (med.) herpe labial, afección inflamatoria o fuego en los labios.—**to catch, o take, c.,** resfriarse, constiparse, acatarrarse.—**to leave out in the c.,** dejar colgado, dejar a la luna de Valencia.

coldly [-lį], *adv.* fríamente; indiferentemente.

coldness [-nįs], *s.* frialdad, frigidez, frío; tibieza, indiferencia, despego, esquivez.

cole [koʊl], *s.* (bot.) col, *f.*, berza, colza.

colegatee [koʊlegatíˈ], *s.* colegatario.

Coleoptera [koʊlɪáptœrä], *s. pl.* (ent.) coleópteros.—**coleopterous** [-ʌs], *a.* coleóptero.

coleorhiza [koʊlɪoráɪžä], *s.* (bot.) coleorriza.

coleseed [koʊlsid], *s.* semilla de col o colza.

coleslaw [koʊlslɔ], *s.* ensalada de col picada.

colessee [koʊlesí], *s.* coarrendatario; mediero.

colessor [koʊlésɒ(r)], *s.* coarrendador.

colewort [koʊlwœrt], *s.* (bot.) colza, berza.

colic [kálɪk], *s.* (med.) cólico, cólica; (vet.) torozón.—*a.* cólico (del colon); relativo al cólico.

colicky [-ɪ], *a.* que tiene o produce cólico; parecido al cólico.

coliseum [kalɪsíʌm], *s.* coliseo.

colitis [koláɪtɪs], *s.* colitis, inflamación del colon.

collaborate [koˈlæboreɪt], *va.* colaborar.—**collaboration** [-éɪšɒn], *s.* colaboración.—**collaborationist** [-ɪst], *s.* colaboracionista.—**collaborator** [-ɒ(r)], *s.* colaborador.

collagen [káladžen], *s.* (bioquím.) colágeno.

collapse [koˈlæps]. **I.** *s.* aplastamiento; derrumbamiento, desplome; hundimiento; fracaso, ruina; (med.) colapso, postración.—**c. ring**, (m. v.) anillo de refuerzo. **II.** *va.* hacer caer o arruinar; aplastar; juntar los lados opuestos de (un tubo, etc.); plegar, reducir a menor volumen doblando o desarmando (un bote portátil, etc.). **III.** *vn.* derrumbarse, desplomarse, caerse, hundirse, venirse abajo; arruinarse, fracasar; desfallecer, sufrir colapso; aplastarse; plegarse, doblarse.

collapsible [-ɪbl], *a.* que puede aplastarse, desarmarse, etc.; plegable (bote, etc.).—**c. hat, clac.** *V.* COLLAPSE, *va.*

collar [kálä(r)]. **I.** *s.* cuello (de camisa, levita, etc.); cuello postizo; cabezón; golilla; collar; collarín; collera, horcajo; (mec.) aro, anillo, cárcel, *f.*, zuncho, reborde, virola, manguito; (mar.) collar, encapilladura, gaza; (arq.) anillo, collarín.—**c. beam**, (arq.) entrecinta.—**c. button o stud**, botón del cuello.—**c. plate**, arandela.—**to slip the c.**, escaparse, desenredarse. **II.** *va.* poner cuello, collar, zuncho, etc.; arrollar y ceñir (carne, pescado); agarrar del cuello; (fam.) apercollar, acogotar.

collarband [-bænd], *s.* (cost.) tirilla de camisa.

collarbone [-boʊn], *s.* (anat.) calvícula, islilla.

collards [kálärdz], *s. pl.* (bot.) variedad de col rizada.

collaret(te [kalärét], *s.* collarín, collarejo.

collate [koˈléɪt], *va.* comparar, cotejar, compulsar, confrontar; (igl.) colacionar, colar.

collateral [koˈlétærəl]. **I.** *a.* colateral; subordinado, accesorio.—**c. security**, garantía subsidiaria. **II.** *s.* (com.) garantía, resguardo.—**collaterally** [-ɪ], *adv.* colateralmente, subsidiariamente.

collation [koˈléɪšɒn], *s.* cotejo, comparación; (igl.) colación; colación, merienda, refacción.

collator [koˈléɪtɒ(r)], *s.* el que coteja; (igl.) colador.

colleague [kálig]. **I.** *s.* colega, *mf.*, compañero. **II.** *vr.* coligarse; conspirar.

collect [koˈlékt]. **I.** *va.* (re)coger; acopiar, reunir, congregar, juntar; coleccionar; (re)copilar; cobrar, recaudar, percibir, colectar.—**to c. one's self**, volver en sí; reponerse. **II.** *vn.* congregarse, reunirse; acumularse. **III.** *a.* cobrable.—**c. on delivery** (C.O.D.), entrega contra reembolso; cóbrese al entregar. **IV.** [kálɛkt], *s.* (igl.) colecta.

collectable [koˈléktabl], *a.* cobrable, cobradero.

collected [-tɪd], *a.* reunido, juntado; sosegado, vuelto en sí.

collectedly [-ɪ], *adv.* juntamente; sosegadamente.

collectible [-tɪbl], *a.* cobrable, cobradero.

collection [-šɒn], *s.* colección, conjunto, acopi-(amient)o, agregación; cobro, cobranza, recaudación (impuestos, etc.); cuestación, colecta

(para obras pías, etc.); compilación, (re)copilación.

collective [koˈléktɪv]. **I.** *s.* (gram.) nombre o substantivo colectivo. **II.** *a.* colectivo; agregado, congregado.—**c. bargaining**, (e. p.) (con)trato colectivo (entre patronos y gremios, etc.).

collectively [-lɪ], *adv.* colectivamente, en masa.—**collectiveness** [-nɪs], *s.* colectividad.

collectivism [-ɪzm], *s.* colectivismo.—**collectivist** [-ɪst], *a.* y *s.* colectivista.

collectivity [-tɪvɪtɪ], *s.* colectividad.

collectivization [-zéɪšɒn], *s.* colectivización.

collectivize [koˈléktɪvaɪz], *va.* colectivizar.

collector [koˈléktɒ(r)], *s.* colector, coleccionador, coleccionista; cobrador, recaudador; compilador, recopilador; (elec.) colector.—**c. of customs o of a port**, administrador de aduanas.—**c. of taxes**, recaudador de contribuciones.—**c. of tithes**, diezmero.

collectorship [-šɪp], *s.* colecturía.

colleen [kálin o kalín], *s.* niña, muchacha.

collegatary [koˈlégaterɪ], *s.* (for.) colegatario.

college [kálɪdž]. **I.** *s.* colegio superior; colegio (de cardenales, etc.). **II.** *a.* de colegio; estudiantil.

collegial [koˈlídžɪal], *a.* colegial.

collegian [koˈlídž(ɪ)an], *s.* colegiate** [-dž(ɪ)ɪt], *s.* colegial, estudiante.—**collegiate**, *a.* colegiado.—**c. church**, colegiata.

collet [kálɪt], *s.* (mec.) collar, mandril, boquilla; (joy.) engaste.

collide [koˈláɪd], *vn.* chocar, topar; contradecir, estar en conflicto.

collie [kálɪ], *s.* perro de pastor.

collier [kálɪœ(r)], *s.* obrero de las minas de carbón; barco carbonero; mercader de carbón.

colliery [-ɪ], *s.* mina de carbón, (mina) hullera.

colligate [kálɪgeɪt], *va.* coligar, atar, juntar.

colligation [-éɪšɒn], *s.* coligación.

collimate [kálɪmeɪt], *va.* (ópt.) ajustar la visual de (un anteojo); alinear.—**collimation** [-éɪšɒn], *s.* colimación.—**collimator** [-ɒ(r)], *s.* (ópt.) colimador.

collinear [kalínɪä(r)], *a.* en línea recta; (mec.) que obran según una misma línea (apl. a fuerzas).

collineation [-éɪšɒn], *s.* alineación.

collision [koˈlížɒn], *s.* colisión, choque; impacción; encontrón, (fam.) trompada; oposición; antagonismo.

collocate [kálokeɪt], *va.* colocar.

collocation [-éɪšɒn], *s.* colocación.

collodion [koˈlóʊdɪɒn], *s.* (quím.) colodión, *m.*

colloid [kálɔɪd]. **I.** *a.* coloide, coloidal, coloideo; gelatinoso; no cristalizable; amorfo en parte. **II.** *s.* coloide, substancia gelatinosa.

colloidal [kálɔɪdal], *a.* (quím.) coloide, coloidal.—**c. fuel**, combustible eoloide (polvo de carbón suspendido en petróleo, alquitrán, etc.).

collop [kálɒp], *s.* bocado, tajada; pedacito.

colloquial [koˈlóʊkwɪal], *a.* familiar, dialogal.—**colloquialism** [-ɪzm], *s.* expresión familiar.—**colloquially** [-ɪ], *adv.* en lenguaje familiar, familiarmente.

colloquy [kálokwɪ], *s.* coloquio, conversación.

collotype [kálotaɪp], *s.* fotografía de colotipia.—**collotypy** [-ɪ], *s.* colotipia.

collude [koˈlúd], *vn.* coludirse, confabularse, obrar de connivencia.

collusion [koˈlúžɒn], *s.* colusión, confabulación, connivencia.—**collusive** [koˈlúsɪv], *a.* colusorio.—**collusively** [-lɪ], *adv.* colusoriamente.

collyrium [kalírɪʌm], *s.* (med.) colirio.

colocynth [kálosɪnθ], *s.* (bot.) coloquíntida.

cologne [koˈlóʊn], *s.* agua de Colonia (ll. t. **C. water**).

Colombian [kolámbɪan], *s.* y *a.* colombiano.

colon [kóʊlɒn], *s.* (gram.) dos puntos (:); (anat.) colon.

colonel [kœrnel], *s.* coronel.—**colonelcy** [-sɪ], **colonelship** [-šɪp], *s.* coronelía, (Am.) coronelato.

colonial [kolóu̯nni̯əl], a. colonial.—**c. period**, (Am.) coloniaje.

colonist [kálonist], s. colono.—**colonize** [-ai̯z]. I. va. colonizar, poblar. II. vn. establecerse en colonia.—**colonization** [-i̯zéi̯ʃən], s. colonización.—**colonizer** [-œ(r)], s. colonizador.

colonnade [kalǫnéi̯d], s. (arq.) peristilo, columnata.

colony [kálonı̯], s. colonia.

colophon [kálofan], s. (impr.) colofón.

colophony [kálofou̯nı̯], s. colofonía.

color [kʌ́lǫ(r)]. I. s. color, colores, pintura; matiz, m., tinta o tinte; (pint.) colorido; pretexto, tinte, viso, socolor; palo (en los naipes).—*pl.* bandera, estandarte; pabellón, insignia, enseña; servicio militar.—**c. bearer**, abanderado, portaestandarte.—**c.-blind**, daltoniano, acromatopo, acromatópsico.—**c.-blindness**, daltonismo, acromatopsia, incapacidad de distinguir los colores.—**c. chart**, cuadro de colores.—**c. filter**, (fot.) filtro cromofotográfico.—**c. guard**, guardia de la bandera.—**c. index**, índice colorimétrico.—**c. line**, línea de demarcación (esp. de distinción social y política) entre la raza blanca y las de color.—**c. photography**, cromofotografía, fotografía en colores.—**c. plate**, placa o grabado a color, o en colores.—**c. rinse**, teñido (para el pelo).—**c. screen**, (fot.) pantalla de color, pantalla de interceptación de colores.—**c. sergeant**, sargento abanderado.—**under c. of**, so color de, con pretexto de.—**with flying colors**, a banderas desplegadas; triunfantemente. II. va. colorar, dar color, colorir, teñir; iluminar; exagerar, embellecer, paliar, desfigurar. III. vn. colorearse; ruborizarse, encenderse, ponerse colorado.

colorable [kʌ́lǫrəbl], a. que puede ser colorado; especioso, plausible.—**colorably** [-əblı̯], adv. especiosamente.

coloration [-éi̯ʃən], s. coloración; colorido.

colorature [-əchu̯r], s. (mús.) floreos y cadencias en el canto; música de esta índole.—**c. soprano**, tiple o soprano (f.) especialista en tal música.

colored [-d], a. colorado; de color; negro (apl. a personas); especioso, engañoso; disfrazado, desfigurado, exagerado; adornado.

colorful [-fu̯l], a. lleno de colorido; vívido, dramático, pintoresco, variado.

colorific [-fi̯k], a. colorativo.

colorimeter [-ímetœ(r)], s. colorímetro.—**colorimetric** [-i̯métrı̯k], a. colorimétrico.—**colorimetry** [-ímetrı̯], s. colorimetría.

coloring [-ı̯ŋ]. I. s. colorante, color; coloración; estilo o aire particular; (pint.) colorido. II. a. colorante, colorativo.

colorist [-ı̯st], s. colorista.

colorless [-lı̯s], a. descolorido, incoloro.

colorman [-mən], s. el que hace y vende colores.

colossal [kolásəl], a. colosal, descomunal.

colosseum [kalǫsı̯ʌm], s. coliseo.

Colossian [kolásən], s. y a. colosense.

colossus [kolásʌs], s. coloso.

colostrum [kolástrʌm], s. calostro.

colporteur [kálpǫrtœ(r)], s. vendedor o repartidor de escritos religiosos.

colpotomy [kalpátomı̯], s. (cir.) colpotomía.

colt [kóu̯lt], s. (zool.) potro; mozuelo sin juicio; (mar.) azote con un nudo.

colter [-œ(r)], s. reja del arado.

coltish [-i̯ʃ], a. juguetón, retozón.

coltishly [-lı̯], adv. juguetonamente.

coltsfoot [-sfu̯t], s. (bot.) fárfara, tusílago.

Colubridae [kolúbrı̯di], s. pl. (zool.) colúbridos.

colubrine [kálı̯u̯brı̯n], a. culebrino; astuto.

columbarium [kalʌmbéi̯rı̯əm], s. columbario; (alb.) mechinal.

columbary [kálʌmbᴂrı̯], s. palomar.

Columbian [kolʌ́mbı̯ən], a. relativo a Cristóbal Colón; colombino.

columbine [kálʌmbaı̯n], a. columbino.

columbine, s. (bot.) aguileña o pajarilla.

columbium [kolʌ́mbı̯ʌm], s. (quím.) columbio.

columella [kalı̯u̯mélə], s. eje central, columnilla.

column [kálʌm], s. columna; pilar; (mil.) columna.

columnar [kolʌ́mnə(r)], a. columnario.

columned [kálʌmd], a. con columnas.

columniation [kolʌmni̯éi̯ʃən], s. columnata.

columnist [kálʌm(n)ı̯st], s. colaborador de un periódico encargado de una columna o sección permanente especial.

colure [kolı̯úr], s. (astr.) coluro.

colza [kóu̯lzə], s. (bot.) colza.

coma [kóu̯mə], s. (med.) coma, m.; (astr.) cabellera, cola; (bot.) manojito de hebras sedosas.

comate [kou̯méi̯t], s. camarada, mf., compañero.

comate [kóu̯mei̯t], a. cabelludo.

comatose [kóu̯mǝtou̯s], a. (med.) comatoso, letárgico.

comb [kóu̯m]. I. s. peine; peineta; almohaza; carda, rastrillo, carducha; cresta; (api.) panal; avispero.—**c.-brush**, limpiadera, bruza para limpiar peines.—**c. foundation**, (api.) panal artificial.—**c. maker**, peinero. II. va. peinar; cardar, carduzar; rastrillar; buscar por todas partes. III. vn. encresparse y romper las olas.

combat [kámbᴂt]. I. s. combate, lucha, batalla, pelea, pugna.—**c.-worthy**, apto para el combate. II. va. combatir, resistir, oponerse a, luchar contra. III. vn. combatir, contender, luchar, pelear.

combatable [-əbl], a. combatible.

combatant [kámbətənt], s. y a. luchador, combatiente; s. combatidor, campeón.

combative [kʌmbǝtı̯v], a. combativo, belicoso.

combativeness [-nı̯s], s. combatividad, acometividad, predisposición a la lucha.

comber [kóu̯mœ(r)], s. cardador; ola encrestada, cabrilla, rompiente.

combinable [kombái̯nəbl], a. combinable.

combination [kambı̯néi̯ʃən], s. combinación; unión, liga; mezcla; cábala; reunión.

combinative [kámbı̯nei̯tı̯v], a. combinatorio.

combinatorial [kǫmbai̯nətórı̯əl], a. (mat.) combinatorio.

combine [kámbai̯n], s. combinación; monopolio; (fam.) monipodio, pastel; (agr.) segadora con trituradora, máquina de segar provista de un mecanismo de trituración y limpia.

combine [kǫmbái̯n]. I. va. combinar; mezclar; reunir, aunar. II. vn. combinarse, unirse, aunarse, mancomunarse; maquinar, conspirar.

combined [-d], a. juntos, unidos; aunado, unido; compuesto; mixto.

combing [kóu̯mı̯ŋ], s. peinad(ur)a; cardadura.—*pl.* peinadura.

combustibility [kǫmbʌstı̯bílı̯tı̯], s. combustibilidad.—**combustible** [kǫmbʌ́stı̯bl], a. y s. combustible.—**combustion** [-chǫn], s. combustión; tumulto, alboroto.—**c. chamber**, (m. v.) cámara de combustión; (m. comb. int.) cámara de encendido o de explosión.

comby [kóu̯mı̯], a. (api.) en forma de panal.

come [kʌm], vn. (pret. CAME; pp. COME) venir, llegar, acercarse, acudir, avanzar; aparecer, salir; acontecer, suceder; entrar (en acción, etc.).—**c. what will**, venga lo que viniere.—**coming!** ¡voy!—**to c. about**, rodear; acaecer, efectuarse; (mar.) virar.—**to c. across**, atravesar; encontrarse, dar o topar con; (fam.) (a veces con **with**) pagar, entregar, desembolsar.—**to c. after**, seguir, venir detrás o después; venir por, en busca de.—**to c. again**, volver.—**to c. along**, venir; andar, caminar.—**c. along!** ¡ven! ¡anda! ¡vamos!—**to c. apart**, dividirse, partirse.—**to c. around** = TO C. ROUND.—**to c. asunder**, deshacerse, desunirse.—**to c. at**, alcanzar; conseguir; llegar a; atacar.—**to c. away**, retirarse, irse.—**to c. back**, retroceder volver; (fam.) rehabilitarse, recobrarse; reflorecer; dar una réplica mordaz.—**to c. back again,** volver, tornar a venir.—**to c. before,** venir antes, anteponerse.—**to c. between,** interponerse, inmiscuirse.—**to c. by,** pasar junto a; venir por; hacerse a, obtener.—**to c. down,** bajar, descender; desplomarse, demolerse; (fam.) perder fortuna, rango, etc.—**to c. down on,** *o* **upon,** caer sobre; (fam.) regañar. —**to c. downstairs,** bajar (de un piso a otro). —**to c. down with,** (fam.) enfermar de.—**to c. for,** venir a buscar; venir por.—**to c. forth,** salir; aparecer; adelantarse.—**to c. forward,** avanzar, medrar; adelantarse; ofrecerse.—**to c. from,** proceder, provenir o emanar de; ser o resultar de.—**to c. high or low,** venderse caro o barato.—**to c. home,** volver a casa; (fig.) tocar la cuerda sensible.—**to c. in,** entrar; llegar; desembocar; consentir, acceder; introducirse; empezar; encajar; parir la vaca; empezar a dar leche.—**c. in!** ¡pase Ud.! ¡adelante! —**to c. in for,** pretender, reclamar; corresponderle a uno; tener parte en, tocarle a uno.—**to c. in,** *o* **into, sight,** *o* **view,** aparecer, asomar, empezar a verse.—**to c. into,** entrar a; heredar, obtener.—**to c. into one's own,** recobrar uno o hacer reconocer sus derechos; ser reconocido, hacer valer sus méritos.—**to c. into the world,** venir al mundo, nacer.—**to c. into trouble,** meterse en trabajos; tener algún percance.—**to c. near,** acercarse; faltar poco para (*he came near killing himself*, faltó poco para que se matara; por poco se mata).—**to c. next,** venir después, ser el que sigue.—**to c. of,** proceder, venir de.—**to c. of age,** llegar a mayor edad.— **to c. off,** zafarse, soltarse, salir, separarse; salir (una mancha); salir (bien o airoso, etc.); verificarse, tener efecto.—**c. off!,** (fam.) ¡déjate de tonterías!.—**to c. on,** avanzar; marchar; medrar; (teat.) salir.—**c. on!,** ¡vamos! ¡ven! ¡venga! ¡ea!—**to c. one's way,** caerle a uno en suerte.—**to c. out,** salir; crecer; resultar, finalizar; trascender; ver la luz; hacerse público; manifestarse, declararse; debutar.—**to c. out at the small end of the horn,** salir perdiendo, llevarse lo peor.—**to c. out with,** publicar, revelar; decir, echar afuera.—**to c. over,** venir, cruzar; pasarle a uno.—**to c. over to,** pasarse a.—**to c. round,** acontecer o efectuarse; convenir, asentir; restablecerse; volver en sí; engatusar.—**to c. short of,** faltar (cambiando un poco el giro), no llegar a; estar lejos de; no tener más o suficiente.—**to c. through,** salir bien.—**to c. to,** recobrar los sentidos; ascender a; parar en.—**to c. to a head,** madurar, llegar a condición decisiva o definitiva, definirse; (med.) madurar.—**to c. to anchor,** anclar.— **to c. to an end,** acabarse; morir.—**to c. to an estate,** heredar.—**to c. to blows,** *o* **to close quarters,** venirse a las manos.—**to c. to grief,** fracasar; salir mal parado.—**to c. to grips with,** afrontar, atacar; habérselas con.—**to c. to hand,** llegar a manos (de uno), recibirse; venir a la mano.—**to c. to life,** nacer.—**to c. to life again,** renacer; revivir; resucitar.—**to c. to light,** descubrirse, darse a luz.—**to c. to mind,** venir a la memoria, ocurrirse.—**to c. to naught,** *o* **nothing,** *o* **to nought,** frustrarse, reducirse a nada; no quedar en nada.—**to c. to one's self,** volver en sí.—**to c. to pass,** suceder, acaecer, ocurrir.—**to c. to stay,** llegar para no volver más; ser permanente.—**to c. to together,** venir juntos; juntarse, reunirse.—**to c. to terms,** aceptar condiciones; convenirse; zanjar un negocio.—**to c. to the point,** llegar al punto; venir al caso; venir al grano.— **to c. to the rescue,** acudir (a uno).—**to c. true,** realizarse, resultar cierto.—**to c. under,** figurar entre.—**to c. undone,** deshacerse, desatarse.—**to c. up,** subir; aparecer; brotar; nacer; surgir; presentarse, ocurrir.—**to c. upon,** encontrarse con, dar con.—**to c. up-**

stairs, subir (de un piso a otro).—**to c. up to,** acercarse a; estar a la altura de; dar alcance; abordar (un buque).—**to c. up with,** alcanzar (a uno).—**to c. within,** estar abarcado o incluído en.

come-at-able [kʌmǽtəbl], *a.* (fam.) accesible; asequible, procurable.

comeback [kʌ́mbæk], *s.* (fam.) rehabilitación, vuelta al puesto u oficio (ú. gen. en dep.); respuesta aguda; motivo de queja.

comedian [kọmídịan], *s.* comediante, cómico, actor, recitante; autor cómico, comediógrafo. —**comedienne** [kọmídịen], *s.* comedianta, cómica, actriz.

comedietta [kọmidịétǎ], *s.* juguete cómico.

comedo [kámịdọu], *s.* (med.) comedón, espinilla.

comedown [kʌ́mdaụn], *s.* (fam.) revés de fortuna; humillación, chasco.

comedy [kámẹdị], *s.* comedia.

comelily [kʌ́mlịlị], *adv.* gentil o donosamente.

comeliness [kʌ́mlịnịs], *s.* gracia, donaire.

comely [kʌ́mlị], *a.* gentil, donoso, bien parecido.

come-off [kʌ́mɔf], *s.* salida, pretexto, escapatoria.

come-on [kʌ́mon], *s.* (fam.) añagaza, cebo; desafío; blanco, persona fácil de engañar.

comer [kʌ́mœ(r)], *s.* llegado; recién venido; (fam.) persona o cosa que promete.—**all comers,** (dep.) todos los aspirantes o contendientes.

comestible [kọméstịbl], *a.* y *s.* comestible.

comet [kámịt], *s.* (astr.) cometa, *m.*

cometary [kámịtặrị], *a.* (astr.) cometario.

comether [kọméðœ(r)], *s.* asunto, cuestión; relaciones de amistad; compañerismo.—**to put the c. on,** inducir a, ganarse a, engatusar a.

cometography [kamịtágrəfị], *s.* cometografía.

comfit [kʌ́mfịt], *s.* confite, dulce.

comfort [kʌ́mfọrt]. I. *va.* confortar, vivificar; animar, alentar, consolar; alegrar, solazar; (for.) ayudar, apoyar. II. *s.* confortación, consuelo, alivio; solaz, *m.,* satisfacción; bienestar, confort; comodidad, conveniencia, regalo; (for.) ayuda, colcha.—**c. station,** lavatorio con excusado.

comfortable [-əbl]. I. *a.* confortativo; confortable, cómodo; consolador; adecuado. II. *s.* cobertor, colcha.—**comfortableness** [-nịs], *s.* comodidad, bienestar.—**comfortably** [-blị], *adv.* cómodamente, confortablemente.

comforter [-œ(r)], *s.* confortador, consolador; (C.) el Espíritu Santo; (E. U.) cobertor, colcha; (Ingl.) bufanda, tapabocas; chupete.

comforting [-ịŋ], *a.* consolador, consolante, consolativo; confortador, confortante.

comfortless [-lịs], *a.* desconsolado, sin consuelo, inconsolable; sin confort, sin comodidades.

comfrey [kʌ́mfrị], *s.* (bot.) consuelda.

comic(al [kámịk(əl], *a.* cómico; burlesco, bufo, bufón; alegre, jocoso, gracioso.—**c. opera,** ópera bufa, ópera cómica.—**c. strip,** hilera (en un periódico) de cuadros episódicos humorísticos; ilustración humorística en escenas.

comic, *s.* actor cómico; bufo; comicidad, lo cómico (en la vida, arte, etc.); película chistosa. —*pl.* (fam.) tiras cómicas. *V.* COMIC STRIP.

comically [-ị], *adv.* burlescamente, cómicamente. —**comicalness** [-nịs], *s.* comicidad, gracia, chiste.

coming [kʌ́mịŋ]. I. *s.* venida, llegada; advenimiento.—**c. back,** vuelta, regreso.—**c. out,** (fam.) entrada en la sociedad; estreno, *debut.* II. *a.* próximo, que viene, venidero, entrante; (fam.) en camino de la fama o del poder.—**c. from,** procedente de.

comitia [kọmíṣịạ], *s. pl.* comicios.

comitial [kọmíṣạl], *a.* comicial.

comity [kámịtị], *s.* cortesía, urbanidad, bienquerencia; (for. inter.) cortesía, deferencia.

comma [kámǎ], *s.* (gram.) coma (,); (mús.) coma. —**c. bacillus,** (biol.) microbio del cólera.

command [kọmǽnd]. I. *va.* mandar, ordenar.

dictar, disponer, gobernar, imponer, regir; acaudillar, capitanear; (mil.) comandar; atraer; (fort.) dominar. **II.** *vn.* mandar, imperar, gobernar, reinar; imponerse. **III.** *s.* mando; mandamiento, mandato, orden, *f.*, ordenanza; autoridad, cargo, dirección, gobierno, imperio; comandancia, dominación; (mil.) comando; alcance, perspectiva; facilidad, recursos; disposición, órdenes.—**at one's c.,** a la disposición de uno; de que uno dispone.—**under the c. of,** al mando de.

commandant [kamandǽnt], *s.* comandante.

commandeer [kamǎnd(r], *va.* reclutar forzosamente; expropiar, sobre todo para usos militares.

commander [kǫmǽndœ(r)], *s.* comandante, capitán, caudillo, jefe; teniente de navío; comendador; maza para empedrar.—**c. in chief,** generalísimo, general en jefe, jefe supremo.

commandery [-i], *s.* comandancia; encomienda.

commanding [-iŋ], *a.* dominante, imperante, imperativo; imponente, convincente, atrayente; que manda.—**c. officer,** comandante en jefe.

commandingly [-li], *adv.* imperativamente.

commandment [-mǫnt], *s.* mandato, precepto. —**the Commandments,** los mandamientos.

commando [kǫmǽndou], *s.* cuerpo militar; comando(s), tropas especialmente adiestradas para realizar misiones difíciles y audaces, como incursiones repentinas, etc.; miembro de tales grupos (ll. t. **commandoman**); invasión.

commatic [kǫmǽtik], *a.* breve, sucinto.

commatism [kámatizm], *s.* concisión, brevedad.

commeasurable [komǽʒūrǎbl], *a.* conmensurable.

commemorable [kǫmémorǎbl], *a.* (con)memorable, memorando.—**commemorate** [-eit], *va.* conmemorar, rememorar, recordar.—**commemoration** [-éiʃǫn], *s.* conmemoración.—**commemorative** [-ǎtiv], *a.* conmemorativo. —**commemoratory** [-ǎtori], *a.* conmemoratorio.

commence [kǫméns]. **I.** *va.* comenzar, empezar, entablar, iniciar, (for.) incoar. **II.** *vn.* comenzar, empezar, principiar, ponerse (a hacer algo).

commencement [-mǫnt], *s.* principio, comienzo, inauguración; (escuelas, etc.) función de fin de año o de distribución de diplomas.

commend [kǫménd], *va.* encomendar, recomendar, encargar; alabar, ensalzar, loar.

commendable [-ǎbl], *a.* recomendable, loable, plausible; autorizado.

commendably [-ǎbli], *adv.* loablemente.

commendatary [-ǎteri], *s.* comendatario, beneficiado.

commendation [kamǫndéiʃǫn], *s.* recomendación, encomio, alabanza.

commendator [-éitǫ(r)], *s.* comendatario.

commendatory [kǫmǽndǎtori], *a.* (re)comendatorio; de comendatario; comendaticio.

commender [kǫmǽndœ(r)], *s.* alabador.

commensal [kamǽnsǎl], *s.* y *a.* comensal; (biol.) asociado.—**commensalism** [-izm], *s.* comensalía.

commensurability [kǫmǫnsȳrǎbíliti], **commensurableness** [kǫmǽnsȳrǎblnis], *s.* conmensurabilidad.—**commensurable** [-ǎbl], *a.* conmensurable, conmensurativo; proporcionado.

commensurate [kǫmǽnsȳreit, -it]. **I.** *va.* conmensurar. **II.** *a.* proporcionado.—**commensurately** [-li], *adv.* proporcionadamente.

commensuration [-éiʃǫn], *s.* conmensuración, proporción.

comment [kámǫnt]. **I.** *va.* comentar; glosar, explicar, anotar; discutir, juzgar, tratar de. **II.** *vn.* comentar.—**to c. on,** comentar, juzgar, expresar opinión acerca de. **III.** *s.* comentario, comento, glosa, explicación; observación.

commentary [kámǫnteri], *s.* comentario, glosa, anotación, interpretación.

commentator [-eitǫ(r)], **commenter** [-œ(r)], *s.* comentador, comentarista, glosador.

commerce [kámœrs], *s.* comercio, negocio, tráfico o tráfago; trato, correspondencia, conversación.—**c. destroyer** o **raider,** buque ligero y rápido para atacar o capturar buques mercantes.

commercial [kǫmǽršǎl]. **I.** *a.* comercial, mercantil; de negocios.—**c. affairs,** negocios.—**c. law,** derecho mercantil.—**c. traveler,** viajante de comercio. **II.** *s.* (rad.) programa, *m.*, anuncio o propaganda comercial.

commercialism [-izm], *s.* mercantilismo.—**commercialize** [-aiz], *va.* mercantilizar; hacer objeto de comercio; explotar un negocio, lanzar un producto al mercado.—**commercially** [-i], *adv.* comercialmente, mercantilmente.

commerge [kǫmœ́rdʒ], *vn.* mezclarse, unirse.

comminate [kámineit], *va.* conminar; anatematizar.—**commination** [-éiʃǫn], *s.* conminación, amenaza.

comminatory [kǫmínǎtori], *a.* conminatorio.

commingle [kǫmíŋgl]. **I.** *va.* mezclar. **II.** *vn.* mezclarse, compenetrarse, unirse; barajarse.

comminute [káminiut], *va.* moler, triturar.—**comminuted fracture,** fractura conminuta.

comminution [-iúʃǫn], *s.* trituración, división; atenuación; (cir.) fractura conminuta.

commiserable [kǫmízǫrǎbl], *a.* lastimoso.

commiserate [-eit], *va.* apiadarse, compadecerse (de uno).—**commiseration** [-éiʃǫn], *s.* conmiseración, piedad.

commissar [kamisár], *s.* comisario de gobierno, miembro del gabinete soviético.

commissariat [kamisériǎt], *s.* (mil.) comisaría, comisariato; Administración Militar; departamento de gobierno (en Rusia).

commissary [kámiseri], *s.* comisario, delegado; (mil.) comisario de guerra; proveeduría de ferrocarriles, colonias de mineros, etc.; *commissar* (en Rusia).—**c. general,** jefe superior de Administración Militar.—**commissaryship** [-ʃip], *s.* comisaría, comisariato.

commission [kǫmíʃǫn]. **I.** *s.* comisión; misión, encomienda, encargo; cometido; patente, *f.*, despacho, nombramiento; (com.) comisión; (for.) comisión, perpetración; (E. U.) junta de gobierno municipal.—**c. government** o **plan,** (E. U.) gobierno municipal dirigido por un administrador o gerente nombrado por una junta municipal o por el alcalde y un concejo. —**c. merchant,** (com.) comisionista.—**out of c.,** (fam.) inservible, inutilizado, arruinado.—**to put into c.,** poner (un buque) en servicio activo.—**to put out of c.,** jubilar, retirar del servicio; (fam.) arruinar; poner fuera de combate (en los dep.), acabar con, despachar. **II.** *va.* comisionar, encargar, autorizar, capacitar, facultar; diputar, nombrar; poner en servicio activo.—**commissioned officer,** (mil.) oficial (apl. al alférez y los oficiales y jefes de mayor grado, que son nombrados por nombramiento por escrito).

commissionnaire [-ér], *s.* mensajero; (Ingl.) soldado pensionado empleado como mensajero o en tareas sencillas.

commissional [-ǎl], *a.* comisionado.

commissioner [-œ(r)], *s.* comisario; comisionado, apoderado, factor; (E. U.) miembro de la junta municipal. (*V.* COMMISSION GOVERNMENT).—**c. of deeds,** notario federal autorizado.—**c. of patents,** comisionado de patentes.

commissure [kámiʃur], *s.* (anat.) comisura.

commit [kǫmít], *va.* cometer, perpetrar; confiar, depositar, entregar; encarcelar, encerrar; encargar, encomendar; trasladar, pasar, someter (a una comisión, etc.).—**to c. one's self,** soltar prenda, comprometerse, empeñarse; declararse.—**to c. to memory,** aprender de memoria.—**to c. to writing,** poner por escrito.

commitment [-mẹnt], **committal** [-ạl], *s.* perpetración, comisión; traslado a una comisión; (for.) auto de prisión; encierro, encarcelamiento; compromiso, promesa.

committee [kọmítị], *s.* comité, comisión, diputación, delegación; junta.—**c. of the whole**, comisión de la totalidad de los miembros de una asamblea reunidos en junta con carácter puramente deliberativo.—**C. of Ways and Means**, comisión de arbitrios.

committeeman [-mạn], *s.* miembro de una comisión.

commix [kọmíks], *va.* y *vn.* mezclar(se), unir(se).

commixture [-chū̆(r)], *s.* conmistión, mezcla.

commode [kọmóụd], *s.* cómoda; lavabo cubierto (con jofaina, bacín, etc.); sillico.

commodious [kọmóụdiạs], *a.* cómodo, conveniente, espacioso, holgado.—**commodiously** [-lị], *adv.* cómodamente, holgadamente.—**commodiousness** [-nịs], *s.* conveniencia, comodidad; holgura.

commodity [kọmádịtị], *s.* comodidad, conveniencia; artículo de comercio o de consumo (apl. gen. a los de primera necesidad), mercancía, mercadería, géneros.—**c. money**, (E. U.) propuesta moneda variable cuyo valor se fija en función del precio de los artículos de consumo de primera necesidad.

commodore [kámodor], *s.* (mar.) comodoro; jefe de escuadra.

common [kámọn]. **I.** *a.* común, corriente, familiar, frecuente, usual, ordinario; vulgar, trivial; público, general, comunal, concejil; bajo, inferior; adocenado; (gram.) común o apelativo.—**c. carrier**, cargador, port(e)ạdor, empresa de transporte público (no oficial).—**c. council**, ayuntamiento, concejo.—**c. councilman**, concejal.—**c. crier**, pregonero.—**c. denominator**, (arit.) común de denominadores.—**C. Era**, era vulgar o cristiana.—**c. fraction**, (arit.) quebrado.—**c. herd**, gentuza, común de las gentes.—**c. law**, derecho consuetudinario.—**c.-law marriage**, matrimonio consensual.—**c. noun**, (gram.) apelativo.—**c. pleas**, causas ajenas al dominio de la corona. *V.* COURT OF COMMON PLEAS.—**c. sense**, sentido común; (fam.) gramática parda.—**c. school**, escuela primaria elemental.—**c. soldier**, soldado raso.—**c. stock**, (com.) acciones ordinarias.—**in c.**, comunalmente; de mancomún. **II.** *s.* común, comunal; pastos comunes, (terrenos) baldíos.—**commonable** [-ạbl], *a.* común, comunal.—**commonage** [-ịdẓ], *s.* derecho de pastar en común; comunal o común.—**commonalty** [-ạltị], *s.* comunal, común, comunidad.

commoner [-œr], *s.* plebeyo, pechero, villano; comunero; el que tiene derecho de pastar en común; (Ingl.) miembro de la Cámara de los Comunes.

commonly [-lị], *adv.* comúnmente, usualmente; vulgarmente.

commonness [-nịs], *s.* comunidad; frecuencia; ordinariez, vulgaridad.

commonplace [-pleịs]. **I.** *a.* común, vulgar, trivial. **II.** *s.* apunte, nota; *pl.* lugares comunes.—**c. book**, minuta, libro de memoria.

commons [-z], *s. pl.* el vulgo o pueblo bajo; (Ingl.) la cámara baja; mesa redonda (esp. en una universidad); víveres, bucólica; baldíos, pastos comunes.—**the C.**, (Ingl.) la Cámara baja; (miembros de) la Cámara de los Comunes.

commonweal [-wil], *s.* el bien público.

commonwealth [-welθ], *s.* estado; nación; cosa pública; república.—**the C.**, (hist.) la república de Cromwell.

commorant [kámorạnt], *s.* y *a.* (for.) vecino.

commotion [kọmóụṣọn], *s.* conmoción, perturbación, tumulto, alteración, escándalo, revuelo.

communal [kámyụnạl], *a.* comunal, público.

communalism [-ịzm], *s.* teoría o sistema (*m.*)

de gobierno por *comunas* independientes dentro de una federación.

commune [kámyụn]. **I.** *s.* comunión, intimidad; (pol.) comuna (apl. esp. a la de París); la menor división política de ciertos países; distrito municipal, (gal. y Am.) comuna. **II.** [kọmịún], conversar, platicar; comunicarse, ponerse en contacto; (igl.) comulgar.

communicability [kọmjunịkạbílịtị], *s.* comunicabilidad.—**communicable** [kọmjúnịkạbl], *a.* comunicable; comunicativo.

communicant [-kạnt], *s.* comunicante; (igl.) comulgante.

communicate [-keịt]. **I.** *va.* comunicar, participar, dar parte de, hacer partícipe, notificar; transmitir, pegar (una enfermedad); (igl.) dar la comunión, comulgar. **II.** *vn.* comunicarse, tener correspondencia o ponerse al habla con; abrir, dar a; (igl.) comulgar.—**communication** [-kéịṣọn], *s.* comunicación; participación, transmisión; transfusión; comunicado, mensaje, parte; comercio, trato; acceso, paso.

communicative [-kặtịv], *a.* comunicativo; expansivo.—**communicativeness** [-nịs], *s.* comunicabilidad.—**communicatory** [-kặtorị], *a.* comunicatorio.

communion [kọmịúnyọn], *s.* comunión; contacto, intimidad; confraternidad; (igl.) comunión, eucaristía; congregación.—**c. altar**, comulgatorio, trato; acceso, paso.—**c. cup**, cáliz, *m.*

communiqué [kọmjunịkéị], *s.* comunicación, oficio.

communism [kámyụnịzm], *s.* (pol.) comunismo.

communist [-ịst], *a.* y *s.* comunista.—**communistic(al** [-ịstịk(ạl], *a.* pert. al comunismo; común; comunal.

community [kọmịúnịtị], *s.* comunidad, común, público; colectividad, cuerpo social; sociedad, generalidad; corporación, sociedad; comunidad, propiedad o goce común.—**c. center** o **house**, centro social, casa o sala de reuniones de una población, asociación, etc.—**c. chest**, fondo de contribuciones voluntarias para gastos municipales de caridad.—**c. of interest**, solidaridad.

communize [kámyụnạịz], *va.* comunizar, hacer común; hacer comunista.

commutability [kọmịutạbílịtị], *s.* conmutabilidad.

commutable [kọmịútạbl], *a.* conmutable.

commutate [kámyụteịt], *va.* (elec.) cambiar la dirección de una corriente.

commutation [-éịṣọn], *s.* conmutación; cambio, permuta, trueque; iguala; (elec.) conmutación o cambio de corriente; (for.) conmutación de pena, indulto parcial.—**c. ticket**, (f. c.) billete de abono.

commutative [kamịútặtịv], *a.* conmutativo.

commutator [kámyụteịto(r)], *s.* (elec.) conmutador; colector.—**c. bar**, o **segment**, segmento colector.

commute [kọmịút]. **I.** *va.* conmutar, cambiar, permutar, rescatar, substituir; igualar, ajustar; reducir (una pena); (elec.) cambiar. **II.** *vn.* conmutar, pagar por medio de conmutación; (f. c.) abonarse, viajar de un sitio a otro con billete de abono.

commuter [-œr], *s.* (f. c.) viajero abonado; (elec.) conmutador.

comose [kóụmoụs], *a.* (bot.) cabelludo.

compact [kámpækt]. **I.** *s.* pacto, avenencia, convenio, ajuste; neceser, cajita o estuche de afeites (polvo y colorete para la cara), polver(it)a de bolsillo; (cir.) compresa. **II.** [kọmpǽkt] compacto, firme, denso, apelmazado; cerrado, apretado; breve, compendioso; (con **of**) compuesto de. **III.** *va.* [kọmpǽkt] consolidar, apretar, comprimir; compaginar, componer.

compacted [kọmpǽktịd], *a.* consolidado, apretado, firme.

compactedly [-lị], *adv.* = COMPACTLY.

compactedness [-nịs], s. = COMPACTNESS.

compactible [-jbl], a. que se puede hacer compacto o reducido.

compactly [-lị], adv. sólidamente, densamente; reducidamente.

compactness [-nịs], s. compactibilidad, densidad, apelmazamiento, estrechez; tamaño reducido.

companion [kọmpǽnyọn], s. compañero; consorte, mf.; (con)socio; camarada, mf.; acompañante; caballero de una orden.—**c. hatch,** (mar.) cubierta de escotilla.—**c. ladder,** (mar.) escala de toldilla. V. COMPANIONWAY.

companionable [-ạbl], a. sociable.

companionably [-ạblị], adv. sociablemente.

companionate [-ịt], a. propio de, o compartido entre, compañeros.—**c. marriage,** matrimonio de compañerismo, en que los cónyuges no tienen hijos, impidiendo la concepción, pueden divorciarse por mutuo consentimiento, y no tienen obligaciones pecuniarias mutuas.

companionship [-ŝịp], s. compañerismo; camaradería; unión; compañía.

companionway [-weị], s. (mar.) escalera de la cámara.

company [kámpanị], s. compañía, acompañamiento; visitante, huésped, mf.; visita (personas); asociación, gremio; compañero, acompañante; (com.) compañía, empresa; (mil., teat.) compañía; (mar.) tripulación.—**c. union,** (E. U.) gremio interno, asociación de todos los obreros de una fábrica o compañía en forma de gremio particular, gen. controlado por los patronos para hacer oposición a los gremios o sindicatos generales.—**to bear** o **keep c.** **(with),** acompañar, asociarse (con); (fam.) cortejar, galantear.—**to part c.,** separarse; terminar una relación.

comparable [kámpạrạbl], a. comparable.

comparableness [-nịs], s. comparabilidad.

comparably [-blị], adv. comparablemente.

comparative [kọmpǽrạtịv], a. comparativo, relativo; comparado; (gram.) comparativo.—**c. literature,** literatura comparada.—**c. science,** ciencia de observación (esp. biol.).

comparatively [-lị], adv. comparativamente, relativamente.

comparator [kámpareịtọ(r)], s. comparador.

compare [kọmpḗr]. I. va. comparar; comprobar, compulsar, confrontar, cotejar, equiparar, graduar.—**to c. notes,** comparar datos e informes; atar cabos (dos o más personas). II. vn. poderse comparar; ser comparable; ser igual.—**not to be compared to,** o **with,** no poder compararse con, ir muy en zaga a.—**to c. favorably,** o **well, with,** no perder por comparación con, no ser inferior a.—**to c. with,** poderse comparar con, ser comparable con; ser o valer por comparación o comparado con (how does this house compare with mine? ¿qué tal es esta casa comparada con la mía?). III. s. comparación.—**beyond c.,** sin igual o rival; incomparablemente.

comparison [kọmpǽrịsọn], s. comparación, confrontación, cotejo, equiparación; (ret.) comparación, símil; metáfora.—**beyond c.,** sin comparación, incomparablemente; incomparable.—**in c. with** o **to,** comparado con.

compartment [kọmpártmẹnt], s. compartimiento, división, departamento; tablero; cajoncito, gaveta; (her.) cuartel.

compass [kámpạs]. I. va. conseguir, lograr; idear, maquinar; concebir, comprender; circundar, circuir, cercar; sitiar. II. s. círculo, circuito, ámbito; recinto; alcance; extensión; moderación, límites; (mús.) cuerda; extensión de la voz o de un instrumento; brújula; (gen. pl. compasses) compás.—**c. card,** rosa de los vientos.—**c. needle,** aguja de brújula; aguja imanada.—**c. saw,** serrucho de calar o de puñal, sierra de punta.—**c. surveying,** levan-

tamiento de planos con la brújula.—**c. timber,** madera curvada.

compassable [-ạbl], a. asequible.

compassion [kọmpǽŝọn], s. compasión, conmiseración, enternecimiento, lástima, piedad.

compassionable [-ạbl], a. lastimoso, digno de compasión.—**compassionate** [-ịt]. I. a. compasivo, compasible, misericordioso. II. [-eịt] va. compadecer.—**compassionately** [-ịtlị], adv. compasivamente.

compatibility [kọmpætịbílịtị], **compatibleness** [kọmpǽtịblnịs], s. compatibilidad.

compatible [kọmpǽtịbl], a. compatible.

compatibly [-blị], adv. compatiblemente.

compatriot [kọmpéịtrịọt], s. compatriota, mf., compatricio; a. y s. paisano, conterráneo.

compeer [kọmpír], s. igual; compañero.

compel [kọmpḗl], va. compeler, obligar, apremiar, constreñir, forzar, precisar; arrancar por la fuerza; dominar, someter.—**compellable** [-ạbl], a. que puede ser compelido.—**compellably** [-ạblị], adv. a viva fuerza.

compellation [kampẹléịŝọn], s. tratamiento; acción o modo de dirigir la palabra a una persona.

compeller [kọmpḗlœ(r)], s. compulsor, apremiador.

compelling [-ịŋ], a. apremiante, constrictivo, preciso, urgente.

compend [kámpẹnd], s. compendio.

compendious [kọmpḗndịʌs], a. compendioso, breve, sumario.—**compendiously** [-lị], adv. compendiosamente.—**compendiousness** [-nịs], s. brevedad.—**compendium** [kọmpḗndịʌm], s. compendio, epítome, resumen, sumario, extracto.

compensable [kọmpḗnsạbl], a. compensable.

compensate [kámpẹnseịt]. I. va. compensar, indemnizar; remunerar; (mec.) compensar. II. vn. compensar; (con for), igualar, equivaler.

compensating [-ịŋ], a. (fís., mec., etc.) compensador, compensativo, de compensación.

compensation [-séịŝọn]. I. s. compensación; remuneración; resarcimiento, indemnización, reparación, desagravio; (psic.) neutralización. II. a. (tec.) compensador, de compensación.

compensative [kọmpḗnsạtịv], a. = COMPENSATORY.

compensator [kámpẹnseịtọ(r)], s. compensador.

compensatory [kọmpḗnsạtọrị], a. compensatorio, compensativo, equivalente.

compete [kọmpít], vn. competir, concurrir, contender, rivalizar; (con for) disputarse.

competence, competency [kámpẹtẹns, -ị], s. suficiencia, competencia; subsistencia; (for.) competencia, capacidad.

competent [-ẹnt], a. competente, capaz, apto, adecuado, calificado; (for.) competente.

competently [-lị], adv. competentemente.

competition [-tíŝọn], s. competición, competencia, concurrencia; rivalidad; certamen, concurso, oposición.

competitive [kọmpḗtịtịv], a. que compite, competidor.—**c. examination,** examen de concurso u oposición.

competitor [kọmpḗtịtọ(r)], s. competidor, rival; antagonista, contrario, opositor.

compilation [kampịléịŝọn], s. compilación, recopilación, recolección.

compilatory [kọmpáịlạtọrị], a. perteneciente a una compilación o compilador.

compile [kọmpáịl], va. compilar, recopilar.

compiler [-œ(r)], s. compilador; recopilador.

complacence, complacency [kọmpléịsẹns, -ị], s. complacencia; satisfacción serena (de sí mismo).

complacent [-ẹnt], a. complaciente; satisfecho.—**complacently** [-lị], adv. complacientemente; con satisfacción.

complain [kọmpléịn], vn. quejarse, lamentarse; (for.) querellarse, demandar.

complainant [-ant], s. (for.) querellante, demandante, demandador.
complainer [-œ(r)], s. querellador, lamentador.
complaining [-iŋ], a. quejoso, lamentador.
complainingly [-li], adv. quejosamente.
complaint [kompléjnt], s. queja; lamento; querella, agravio; mal, enfermedad; (for.) demanda, queja.
complaisance [kompléjʒans], **complaisantness** [-antnis], s. afabilidad, cortesía, complacencia, contemplación; atención; cumplimiento. —**complaisant** [-ant], a. cortés, complaciente.— **complaisantly** [-li], adv. cortésmente.
complanate [kámplaneit], a. aplanado, llano.
complected [kompléktid], a. entretejido, enlazado; (fam.) = COMPLEXIONED.
complement [kámplement]. I. s. complemento; accesorio; cantidad o número completo; (biol., gram., geom.) complemento; (mar.) dotación. II. va. complementar, completar.
complemental [-méntal], a. completivo.
complementary [-méntari], a. complementario. —**c. angles, arcs, colors,** ángulos, arcos, colores complementarios.
complete [komplít]. I. a. completo; acabado, cabal, consumado, perfecto; entero, íntegro, lleno, plen(ari)o. II. va. completar, acabar, concluir, rematar, terminar; perfeccionar; complementar; cumplir (años).—**completely** [-li], adv. completamente, enteramente.—**completeness** [-nis], s. integridad, entereza, calidad de completo.
completion [komplíʃọn], s. acabamiento, cumplimiento, terminación, consumación, fin.
completive [komplítiv], a. completivo.
complex [kámpleks]. I. a. complejo, complexo; complicado, intrincado; múltiple, compuesto. —**c. fraction,** (arit.) fracción de términos fraccionarios.—**c. sentence,** (gram.) oración que contiene una o más proposiciones subordinadas. II. s. complexo, complejo; (psic.) complejo; grupo de ideas o tendencias reprimidas asociadas con un estado afectivo o emocional; (fam.) tema, m., obsesión.
complexion [komplékʃọn], s. tez; cutis (gen. m.), color; naturaleza; estado; carácter, calidad; (fisiol. ant.) complexión, constitución.
complexional [-al], a. complexional.
complexionally [-ali], adv. por complexión.
complexioned [-d], a. de tal o cual tez.
complexity [kompléksiti], **complexness** [-nis], s. complexidad, complejidad.
complexly [-li], adv. complexamente.
complexus [-as], s. complexo; complicación; (anat.) músculo complexo.
compliable [kompláiabl], a. = COMPLIANT.
compliance [-ans], s. docilidad, sumisión; complacencia; acatamiento; contemplación, condescendencia, anuencia, consentimiento.—**in c. with,** de acuerdo con, accediendo a; a tenor de.
compliant [-ant], a. dócil, obediente, sumiso; condescendiente, complaciente.—**compliantly** [-li], adv. rendidamente, complacientemente.
complicate [kámplikeit]. I. va. complicar, enredar. II. a. complicado; (hist. nat.) plegado.
complicated [-id], a. complicado, enredado, revesado; complejo.
complicatedly [-li], adv. complicadamente.
complicatedness [-nis], s. complejidad.
complication [-éiʃọn], s. complicación; (med.) enfermedad concurrente con otra afección.
complicative [kámplikạtiv], a. que produce complicaciones.
complicity [komplísiti], s. complicidad, calidad de cómplice; complejidad, complicación.
complier [kompláiœ(r)], s. consentidor, contemporizador.
compliment [kámpliment]. I. s. galantería, lisonja, requiebro, flor, f., (fam.) piropo, chicoleo; favor, fineza; cumplimiento; cumplido; obse-

quio, regalo.—pl. recados, memorias; saludo. II. va. lisonjear, requebrar, galantear, (fam.) piropear, echar flores a; cumplimentar, felicitar; obsequiar. III. vn. hacer cumplimientos.
complimentary [-méntari], a. lisonjero, galante; cumplido, cortés, obsequioso; de obsequio, de regalo (billete, etc.).—**complimenter** [kámplimentœ(r)], s. adulador; cumplimentero.
complin(**e** [kámplin], s. (igl.) completas.
complot [kámplat]. I. s. conspiración, conjura(-ción), cábala, trama, (fam.) complot. II. [komplát], va. tramar. III. vn. conspirar, conjurar.
Complutensian [kamplyténsian], a. y s. complutense.
compluvium [kamplúvjʌm], s. (arq.) compluvio.
comply [kompláj], vn. obedecer, cumplir con, acatar, condescender, consentir.—**to c. with,** obrar de acuerdo con, acceder a, satisfacer.
component [kompóunent], a. y s. componente.
comport [kompórt], vn. y va. convenir, concordar; portarse, comportarse.
comportment [-ment], s. comportamiento.
compose [kompóuz]. I. va. componer, formar, integrar; redactar, escribir; ajustar, arreglar, ordenar; apaciguar, conciliar, sosegar. II. va. y vn. (mús. e impr.) componer.
composed [-d], a. sosegado, tranquilo, sereno; compuesto (de).—**composedly** [-idli], adv. tranquilamente, sosegadamente, con calma, serenamente.—**composedness** [-idnis], s. compostura, tranquilidad, serenidad, calma, mesura.
composer [-œ(r)], s. autor, escritor; conciliador, mediador; (mús.) compositor.
composing [-iŋ], ger. de TO COMPOSE.—**c. frame** o **stand,** (impr.) chibalete.—**c. rule,** (impr.) regleta, filete.—**c. stick,** (impr.) componedor.
Compositæ [kampáziti], s. pl. (bot.) compuestas.
composite [kompázit]. I. a. compuesto, formado de partes; mixto; (arq.) compuesto; (bot.) compuesta.—**c. carriage,** (Ingl., f. c.) coche mixto.—**c. number,** (arit.) número no primo. —**c. photograph,** o **c. portrait,** retrato compuesto o de superposición. II. s. compuesto, cosa compuesta; mixtura; (bot.) (planta) compuesta.
composition [kampozíʃọn], s. (en casi todas las acepciones) composición; tema, m., ensayo (estudiantil); componenda, arreglo, ajuste.— **c. book,** cuaderno.
compositive [kompázitiv], a. compositivo.
compositor [kompázitọ(r)], s. (impr.) cajista.
compost [kámpoust]. I. s. mezcla; (agr.) mantillo, abono, estiércol. II. va. abonar la tierra.
composure [kompóuʒạ(r)], s. compostura, serenidad, calma, sangre fría.
compote [kámpout], s. compota, dulce.
compotier [kampatír], s. dulcera, compotera.
compound [kampáund]. I. va. componer, combinar, mezclar, confeccionar; transigir, componer. II. vn. avenirse, transigir, arreglarse.
compound [kámpaund]. I. s. compuesto; mezcla, mixtura; preparación; palabra compuesta; (quím.) cuerpo compuesto, combinación; recinto, empalizada. II. a. compuesto; mezclado. —**c. circuit,** (elec.) circuito compuesto de uno cerrado conectado con uno abierto.—**c. engine,** (m. v.) máquina compound.—**c. fracture,** (cir.) fractura complicada o abierta (en que el hueso rompe los tejidos).—**c. interest,** (com.) interés compuesto.—**c. number,** (arit.) número denominado o complejo.—**c. sentence,** (gram.) cláusula compuesta.—**c. steel,** acero de aleación.—**c. winding,** (elec.) arrollamiento compound.
compoundable [kampáundabl], a. componible.
compounder [-œ(r)], s. mezclador; (for.) componedor, árbitro, mediador.
comprehend [kamprihénd], va. comprender, concebir, alcanzar; contener, encerrar, abarcar.

comprehensible [-síbl], *a.* comprensible, inteligible.—comprehensibleness [-nis], *s.* comprensibilidad.—comprehensibly [-síbli], *adv.* comprensiblemente.

comprehension [-śǫn], *s.* comprensión, entendimiento, inteligencia.

comprehensive [-sív], *a.* compre(he)nsivo, amplio; perspicaz.—comprehensively [-li], *adv.* comprensivamente. — comprehensiveness [-nis], *s.* extensión, alcance; comprensión, entendimiento.

compress [kǫmprés], *va.* comprimir, apretar, estrechar, condensar; abreviar, reducir.—compressed-air brake, drill, etc., freno, taladro, etc., de aire comprimido.

compress [kámpres], *s.* (med.) compresa, cabezal; prensa de embalar algodón, etc.

compressibility [kǫmpresibíliti], compressibleness [-présiblnis], *s.* compresibilidad.

compressible [-présibl], *a.* compresible, comprimible, apretadizo.

compression [-préśǫn], *s.* compresión, apretadura; condensación.

compressive [-présiv], *a.* compresivo.

compressor [-présǫ(r)], *s.* compresor.

comprisal [kǫmpráizǫl], *s.* inclusión, comprensión.

comprise, comprize [-práiz], *va.* comprender, contener, incluir, abarcar, abrazar; constar de.

compromise [kámpromaiz]. I. *s.* arreglo, acomodo, transacción, avenencia, componenda; término medio; compromiso, obligación. II. *va.* arreglar, acomodar, componer, zanjar; comprometer, exponer. III. *vn.* transigir, avenirse.

compromiser [-œ(r)], *s.* el que arregla o compone, etc.; comprometedor; compromisario.

compromising [-iŋ], *a.* comprometedor; transigente.

comptometer [kamptámetœ(r)], *s.* contómetro; (máquina) calculadora. (Es nombre de fábrica.)

comptroller [kǫntróulœ(r)], *s.* contralor, interventor; sobrestante.—C. of the Currency, (E. U.) interventor de los bancos nacionales.—comptrollership [-śip], *s.* contraloría, intervención.

compulsative [kǫmpálsativ], compulsatory [-satǫri], *a.* compulsivo, coactivo.

compulsively [-li], *adv.* por fuerza.

compulsion [-śǫn], *s.* compulsión, apremio, coacción, precisión, constreñimiento.

compulsive [-siv], *a.* compulsivo.—compulsively [-li], *adv.* compulsivamente.—compulsiveness [-nis], *s.* calidad de compulsivo.

compulsory [-sǫri], *a.* obligatorio.—compulsorily [-li], *adv.* obligatoriamente.

compunction [kǫmpáŋkśǫn], *s.* compunción, contrición, remordimiento, escrúpulo.—to feel c., compungirse.—compunctious [-śas], *a.* compungido, contrito; compungivo.

compurgation [kampœrgéiśǫn], *s.* compurgación.—compurgator [kámpœrgătǫ(r)], *s.* compurgador.

computable [kǫmpiútạbl], *a.* calculable.

computation [kampiutéiśǫn], *s.* computación, cálculo.—compute [kǫmpiút], *va.* computar, calcular.—computer [-œ(r)], *s.* calculador, calculista.

comrade [kámræd], *s.* camarada, *mf.*, compañero.—comradeship [-śip], *s.* compañerismo, camaradería.

con [kan], *va.* estudiar, leer con atención; (mar.) gobernar (el buque).

con, *adv.* y *s.* contra. *V.* PRO.

con. I. *a.* (fam., abrev. de CONFIDENCE).—c. game, estafa, timo, embaucamiento.—c. man, estafador. II. *va.* (fam.) estafar.

conarium [kǫnéiriʌm], *s.* (anat.) glándula pineal.

conation [kǫnéiśǫn], *s.* (psic.) voluntad, esfuerzo; cualquier inquietud o impulso mental.

concatenate [kankǽtęneit], *l. va.* concadenar, concatenar, encadenar. II. *a.* eslabonado.

concatenation [-éiśǫn], *s.* concatenación, eslabonamiento, sucesión, serie.

concave [kánkejv]. I. *a.* cóncavo. II. *s.* cóncavo, concavidad; línea o superficie cóncava.—concaveness [-nis], *s.* calidad de cóncavo, concavidad.—concavity [kankǽviti], *s.* concavidad.—concavo-concave [kankéjvoukankéjv], *a.* cóncavo-cóncavo, bicóncavo.—concavo-convex [-kanvéks], cóncavo-convexo.

conceal [kǫnsíl], *va.* ocultar, esconder, encubrir, callar, tapar, disimular.—concealable [-ạbl], *a.* ocultable, escondible.—concealer [-œ(r)], *s.* ocultador, encubridor.—concealment [-męnt], *s.* ocultación, escondimiento; secreto, encubrimiento; reticencia; escondrijo, escondite.

concede [kǫnsíd]. I. *va.* conceder, admitir. II. *vn.* asentir, convenir.

conceit [kǫnsít]. I. *s.* presunción, engreimiento, fatuidad, ínfulas, *f. pl.*, vanagloria; noción, idea, fantasía; pensamiento; capricho, chifladura; concepción, comprensión. II. *va.* conceptuar, concebir, imaginar; engreírse; encapricharse.

conceited [-id], *a.* vanidoso, engreído, fatuo, presumido, presuntuoso, pagado.—conceitedly [-li], *adv.* engreídamente.—conceitedness [-nis], *s.* presunción, vanidad.

conceivable [kǫnsívạbl], *a.* concebible, conceptible, imaginable.—conceivableness [-nis], *s.* conceptibilidad; calidad de concebible.—conceivably [-bli], *adv.* de un modo conceptible.

conceive [kǫnsív]. I. *va.* concebir, comprender, idear, formar idea; coger (odio, etc.); expresar; engendrar, concebir. II. *vn.* concebir, imaginar, pensar; concebir, quedar preñada la hembra.

concenter [kǫnséntœ(r)]. I. *va.* concentrar, enfocar. II. *vn.* reconcentrarse.

concentrate [kánsęntreit]. I. *va.* (re)concentrar; enfocar. II. *vn.* reunirse; reconcentrarse. III. *a.* concentrado. IV. *s.* (quím.) substancia o producto concentrado; (met.) gandinga; resultado de la concentración de minerales.

concentrated [-id], *a.* concentrado.

concentration [-éiśǫn], *s.* (re)concentración; recogimiento, abstracción.—c. camp, campo de concentración.—concentrator [-ǫ(r)], *s.* concentrador.

concentre [kǫnséntœ(r)], *v.* = CONCENTER.

concentric(al [kǫnséntrik(ạl], *a.* concéntrico.

concentrically [-i], *adv.* concéntricamente.

concentricity [-trísiti], *s.* concentricidad.

concentus [kǫnséntʌs], *s.* concento, armonía, consonancia.

concept [kánsept], *s.* concepto, noción, idea.

conceptacle [kǫnséptạkl], *s.* (bot.) conceptáculo.

conception [kǫnsépśǫn], *s.* concepción, idea, concepto, sentimiento; conocimiento, comprensión; (biol.) concepción, preñez.

conceptism [kánsęptizm], *s.* (lit.) conceptismo.

conceptive [kǫnséptiv], *a.* conceptivo.

conceptual [kǫnsépchuạl], *a.* conceptual, relativo al concepto; de carácter de concepto.—conceptualism [-izm], *s.* (fil.) conceptualismo.—conceptualist [-ist], *a.* y *s.* conceptualista.

concern [kǫnsœrn]. I. *va.* concernir, importar, interesar, tocar, atañer o incumbir, rezar con, pertenecer; afectar; mover, excitar, preocupar, inquietar, desasosegar.—as concerns = CONCERNING. II. *s.* asunto, negocio, ocupación; interés, incumbencia; empresa, establecimiento, casa de comercio; importancia, consecuencia; inquietud, ansiedad.—of what c. is it to you? ¿qué le importa? ¿qué más le da a Vd.?

concerned [-d], *a.* interesado; comprometido; ansioso, intranquilo.—as far as I am c., en cuanto a mí.—concernedly [-idli], *adv.* ansiosamente, etc.—concerning [-iŋ], *prep.* por lo concerniente a, respecto a, por (o en) lo que respecta a, sobre, acerca de, tocante a.

concernment [-męnt], *s.* concernencia, interés; asunto; importancia; ansiedad, cuidado.

concert [kǫnsœrt], *va.* concertar, acordar, ajustar.

concert [kánsœrt], *s.* concierto, convenio, acuerdo; (mús.) concierto.

concertina [kansœrtínə], *s.* (mús.) concertina.

concertmaster, concertmeister [kánsœrtmœstœ(r), kántsœrtmájstœ(r)], *s.* (mús.) concertino.

concerto [kǫnchértou], *s.* (mús.) concie.to.

concession [kǫnséšǫn], *s.* concesión, privilegio.

concessionaire [-ér], *s.* concesionario.

concessionary [-eri]. I. *s.* concesionario. II. *a.* otorgado por concesión.

concessive [kǫnsésiv], *a.* concesivo, concedente.

concessively [-li], *adv.* concesivamente.

conch [káŋk o kanch], *s.* caracol marino; concha; caracola, (Ant.) fotuto; (arq.) concha.

concha [-ə], *s.* (anat.) cavidad del pabellón de la oreja.

conchiferous [kaŋkífęrʌs], *a.* conchífero.

conchiform [káŋkiform], *a.* conquiforme.

conchoid [káŋkoid], *s.* (geom.) concoide, *f.*

conchoidal [kaŋkóidəl], *a.* concoideo.

conchologist [kaŋkálodžist], *s.* conquiliólogo.

conchology [-dži], *s.* (zool.) conquiliología.

conchy [kánchi], *s.* (fam.) = CONSCIENTIOUS OBJECTOR.

concierge [kansjérž], *s.* conserje, portero.—**conciergerie** [-œri], *s.* portería, conserjería.

conciliar [kǫnsíliə(r)], *a.* conciliar.

conciliate [kǫnsíliejt], *va.* conciliar, propiciar; granjear, ganar, atraer.

conciliation [-éišǫn], *s.* conciliación.

conciliative [-eitiv], *a.* conciliativo.

conciliator [-eitǫ(r)], *s.* conciliador.

conciliatory [-ǫtǫri], *a.* conciliatorio.

concise [kǫnsájs], *a.* conciso, breve, sucinto.—**concisely** [-li], *adv.* concisamente.—**conciseness** [-nis], *s.* concisión, brevedad, laconismo.

concision [kǫnsížǫn], *s.* concisión; corte, cortadura; circuncisión.

conclave [kánklejv], *s.* conclave.

conclavist [-ist], *s.* conclavista.

conclude [kǫnklúd]. I. *va.* concluir, acabar, dar cima a; inferir, colegir, sacar en limpio; decidir; hacer (arreglo, etc.); excluir; restringir, coartar. II. *vn.* finalizar, fenecer; inferir.

concluding [-iŋ], *a.* concluyente; último.

conclusion [kǫnklúžǫn], *s.* conclusión; desenlace; determinación, decisión; deducción, inferencia.—**in c.,** en conclusión, por último.—**to a c.,** hasta el fin, hasta llegar a un resultado definitivo.

conclusive [kǫnklúsiv], *a.* concluyente; conclusivo, decisivo; terminante.—**conclusively** [-li], *adv.* concluyentemente.—**conclusiveness** [-nis], *s.* calidad de concluyente o terminante.

concoct [kankákt], *va.* mezclar, confeccionar, forjar, fraguar, maquinar, trazar, proyectar, urdir.

concocter [-tœ(r)], *s.* maquinador; trazador.

concoction [-šǫn], *s.* mezcla o mixtura; maquinación, trama; trazo.

concoctive [-tiv], *a.* relativo a una mezcla, o un trazo.

concomitance, concomitancy [kǫnkámitǫns, -i], *s.* concomitancia.—**concomitant** [-tǫnt]. I. *a.* concomitante. II. *s.* concomitante, acompañamiento.—**to be a c. of,** concomitar.—**concomitantly** [-li], *adv.* acompañadamente.

concord [kánkord], *s.* concordia; armonía, buena inteligencia; (mús. y gram.) concordancia.

concordance [kankórdǫns], *s.* concordancias (índice); concordancia, conformidad, armonía.

concordant [-dǫnt], *a.* concordante, concorde consonante, conforme.—**concordantly** [-li], *adv.* concordemente, de común acuerdo.

concordat [kankórdæt], *s.* concordato.

concourse [kánkors], *s.* concurso, concurrencia, gentío; confluencia; campo o lugar de reunión; gran salón (de estación, etc.).

concrescence [kǫnkrésǫns], *s.* concrescencia; coalescencia; crecimiento.

concrete [kǫnkrít]. I. *va.* concretar; concrecionar, espesar; (alb.) cubrir con hormigón. II. *vn.* cuajar, condensarse, coagularse.

concrete [kánkrit]. I. *a.* concreto; cuajado; de hormigón. II. *s.* masa de azúcar que se forma hirviendo guarapo; concreción; término o número concreto; (constr.) hormigón, (Am.) concreto.—**c. block,** bloque hueco de hormigón.—**c. mixer,** hormigonera.—**c. steel,** hormigón armado.

concretely [-li], *adv.* concretamente.

concreteness [-nis], *s.* calidad de concreto.

concretion [kǫnkríšǫn], *s.* concreción; concreto, cuajo; (med.) cálculo.

concretive [kǫnkrítiv], *a.* formando concreciones.

concubinage [kankiúbinidž], *s.* concubinato, amancebamiento, abarraganamiento, barraganería.—**to live in c.,** amancebarse, abarraganarse.

concubine [kánkiubajn], *s.* concubina, manceba, barragana, amiga, daifa, coima.

concupiscence [kankiúpisęns], *s.* concupiscencia.

concupiscent [-ęnt], *a.* concupiscente.

concur [kǫnkœr], *vn.* concurrir, encontrarse, confluir; convenir, conformarse, hallarse de acuerdo; unirse, juntarse, adunarse.

concurrence, concurrency [-ęns, -i], *s.* concurrencia; coincidencia, casualidad; acuerdo, cooperación, ayuda; punto de intersección.

concurrent [-ęnt]. I. *a.* concurrente; concomitante, coexistente. II. *s.* concurrente; rival, competidor.—**concurrently** [-li], *adv.* concurrentemente.

concuss [kǫnkʌs], *va.* sacudir, perturbar; coercer, coaccionar.—**concussion** [kǫnkʌ́šǫn], *s.* concusión, sacudida; golpe; (med.) desorden funcional debido a concusión o golpe; (arti.) rebufo.—**c. of the brain,** conmoción cerebral.—**concussional** [-al], *a.* (med.) causado por o relativo a concusión.—**concussive** [-kʌ́siv], *a.* concusionario; (med.) que causa concusión.

condemn [kǫndém], *va.* condenar, afear, censurar, desaprobar; prohibir oficialmente el uso de; (for.) condenar; confiscar, expropiar.

condemnable [-nabl], *a.* culpable, censurable, condenable.

condemnation [kandemnéišǫn], *s.* condenación; confiscación.

condemnatory [kǫndémnatǫri], *a.* condenatorio.

condemner [kǫndémœ(r)], *s.* condenador.

condensability [kǫndensabíliti], *s.* condensabilidad.

condensable [kǫndénsabl], *a.* condensable.

condensate [-sejt], *s.* objeto condensado.

condensation [kandenséišǫn], *s.* condensación.

condensative [kǫndénsativ], *a.* condensativo.

condense [kǫndéns]. I. *va.* condensar, comprimir; espesar; reducir, abreviar. II. *vn.* condensarse, comprimirse, espesarse.—**condensed milk,** leche condensada.

condenser [-œ(r)], *s.* (mec., elec. y ópt.) condensador; refrigerador.

condensing [-iŋ], *a.* condensante.—**c. coil,** serpentín refrigerante.—**c. engine,** máquina de condensación.

condescend [kandisénd], *vn.* condescender.

condescendence [-ęns], *s.* condescendencia.

condescending [-iŋ], *a.* condescendiente.

condescension [-sénšǫn], *s.* condescendencia, complacencia, dignación.

condign [kǫndájn], *a.* condigno, merecido.

condignity [kǫndígniti] (teol.), **condignness** [kǫndájnnis], *s.* merecimiento.—**condignly** [kǫndájnli], *adv.* merecidamente, condignamente.

condiment [kándimęnt], *s.* condimento, guiso.

condition [kǫndíšǫn]. I. *s.* condición; estado, disposición, calidad, situación, paraje, circunstancia; categoría, linaje; estipulación; requisito;

examen de habilitación por presentar (apl. gen. al nuevo examen cuando el alumno ha fracasado en el ordinario). II. *va.* estipular, convenir; determinar, modificar; depender, hacer depender (gen. con **on**, *vg. his position is conditioned on his competence*, su puesto depende de su competencia); reprobar (a un estudiante); (com.) probar (telas, etc. para determinar su humedad); (ind.) rehumedecer (telas, etc.) por tratamiento químico; (a)condicionar (el aire, etc.).

conditional [-ạl], *a.* condicional.—**c. mode**, (gram.) modo potencial.

conditionality [-ǽlịtị], *s.* limitación.

conditionally [-ạlị], *adv.* condicionalmente.

conditioned [-d], *a.* condicionado, condicional; acondicionado.

conditioning [-iŋ], *s.* (a)condicionamiento.

condole [kọndóul], *vn.* condolerse, dar el pésame.

condolement [-mẹnt], **condolence** [-ẹns], *s.* condolencia, pésame.

condom [kándọm], *s.* condón, preservativo.

condominium [kandomínịʌm], *s.* condominio.

condonation, condonement [kandoẹnéiṣọn, kọndóunmẹnt], *s.* condonación, perdón, indulto.

condone [kọndóun], *va.* condonar, perdonar.

condor [kándọ(r)], *s.* (orn.) cóndor.

condottiere [kandattyéireị], *s.* condotiero, condottiere, jefe de mercenarios; soldado mercenario.

conduce [kọndiús], *vn.* conducir, tender.

conducive [-ịv], *a.* conducente.—**conduciveness** [-nịs], *s.* conducencia, tendencia.

conduct [kándʌkt], *s.* conducta, comporte, proceder; dirección, manejo, gobierno, gestión; conducción; (mil.) escolta, conducta, convoy.

conduct [kọndʌ́kt]. I. *va.* conducir, guiar, dirigir, gestionar, manejar. II. *vr.* comportarse, proceder; llevar; mandar (un ejército). III. *vn.* (fís.) ser conductor; (mús.) llevar la batuta.

conductance [-ạns], *s.* conducción, transmisión; (elec.) potencia conductora.

conductibility [-ịbílịtị], *s.* conductibilidad.

conductible [-ịbl], *a.* conductible.

conduction [kọndʌ́kṣọn], *s.* transmisión, conducción, traída.

conductive [-tịv], *a.* conductivo; (elec.) que obra por conducción.

conductivity [kandʌktívịtị], *s.* conductividad; conductibilidad.

conductor [kọndʌ́ktọ(r)], *s.* conductor, guía, *m.;* director de orquesta; (f. c., etc.) recogedor de billetes, cobrador, revisor; (arq.) canalón; (cir.) (con)ductor, sonda acanalada; (elec.) conductor.

conductress [-trịs], *s.* conductora, directora.

conduit [kándịt], *s.* conducto; arcaduz, *m.,* caño, cacera, canal, *f.;* presera; cañería, encañado, tubería; (elec.) tubo, caja o túnel para conductores.

condyle [kándịl], *s.* (anat.) cóndilo.

condyloma [kandịlóumạ̈], *s.* (med.) condiloma, *m.*

cone [koụn]. I. *s.* (geom., geol.) cono; cucurucho; pan (de azúcar); (bot.) cono, piña.—**c.-bearing**, (bot.) confero.—**c. bearing**, (mec.) cojinete de cono.—**c. brake**, freno de cono.— **c. clutch**, embrague de cono.—**c. coupling**, acoplamiento de cono.—**c. gear**, engranaje cónico.—**c. pulley**, polea escalonada o múltiple.—**c.-shaped**, cónico, coniforme. II. *va.* dar forma cónica; ahusar; biselar; arrollar en carrete cónico. III. *vn.* (bot.) producir piñas.

conepate [kóunẹipáteị], *s.* (Am. C.) (zool.) mapurite.

coney, *s.* = CONY.

confab, *contr.* de CONFABULATION, CONFABULATE.

confabulate [kọnfǽbịuleịt], *vn.* confabular; platicar, departir, conferir.—**confabulation** [-éiṣọn], *s.* confabulación, plática, conferencia.

confarreation [kọnfærịéiṣọn], *s.* confarreación.

confect [kọnfékt], *va.* confitar, confeccionar.

confection [kọnfékṣọn]. I. *s.* confitura, dulce;

(farm.) confección. II. *va.* confeccionar, confitar.—**confectionary** [-ạrị]. I. *a.* confitado. II. *s.* confitería; dulces.—**confectioner** [-œ(r)], *s.* confitero, repostero, dulcero.—**confectionery** [-ẹrị], *s.* dulces, confites; confitería, repostería.—**c. shop**, *o* **store**, confitería, dulcería.

confederacy [kọnfédœrạṣị], *s.* confederación, alianza, coalición, liga; cábala.

confederate [-eịt]. I. *va. y vn.* confederar(se), coligar(se), unirse. II. [-ịt]. *a. y s.* confederado, aliado; compinche, socio.

confederation [-éịṣọn], *s.* confederación.

confederative [-eịtịv], *a.* confederativo.

confer [kọnfœ́r]. I. *vn.* conferenciar; conferir, tratar, consultar. II. *va.* (gen. con **on** *o* **upon**) conferir, dar, otorgar (a), investir (con *o* de); colar *o* colacionar (un beneficio eclesiástico *o* grado de universidad).—**to c. holy orders**, conferir órdenes sagradas, ordenar.

conferee [kanfœrí], *s.* el que participa en una conferencia; el investido de algo.

conference [kánfœrẹns], *s.* conferencia, consulta, deliberación, entrevista, junta; conversación; el acto de conferir (*vn. y va.*).—**c. table**, mesa verde.

conferment [kọnfœ́rmẹnt], *s.* el acto de conferir.

conferrable [-ạbl], *a.* que puede conferirse.

confess [kọnfés]. I. *va.* confesar, reconocer. II. *vn.* confesarse; hacer una confesión, (fam.) cantar.

confessant [-ạnt], *s.* confesante.

confessed [-t], *a.* confesado, declarado, reconocido.

confessedly [-ịdlị], *adv.* reconocidamente, admitidamente, según se admite.

confession [kọnféṣọn], *s.* confesión; credo; (igl.) confesión.—**confessional, confessionary** [-ạl, -ẹrị]. I. *s.* confes(i)onario. II. *a.* confesional, referente a la confesión.

confessor [kọnféṣọ(r)], *s.* confesor; penitente; confesante.

confetti [kọnfétị], *s. pl.* confet(t)i; confites.

confidant(e [kạnfịdǽnt], *s.* confidente, confidenta.

confide [kọnfáịd]. I. *vn.* confiar, fiarse. II. *va.* fiar, confiar, depositar.

confidence [kánfịdẹns], *s.* confianza, fe, *f.,* hoto; seguro, seguridad; presunción; confidencia, secreto.—**c. game, c. man**, *V.* CON GAME, etc. —**in c.**, en confianza.—**in strict c.**, con la mayor reserva.

confident [-ẹnt]. I. *a.* cierto, seguro, confiado; presumido.—**to be c.**, confiarse. II. *s.* confidente.

confidential [-énṣạl], *a.* reservado, secreto, confidencial; íntimo.—**confidentially** [-ị], *adv.* en confianza, confidencialmente, en secreto.

confidently [-lị], *adv.* confiadamente.

confider [kọnfáịdœ(r)], *s.* el que confía.

confiding [-iŋ], *a.* confiado; crédulo.

configurate [kọnfígịureịt], *va.* configurar.

configuration [-éịṣọn], *s.* configuración; (astr.) aspecto, plantilla.

confinable [kọnfáịnạbl], *a.* limitable.

confine [kánfaịn]. I. *s.* (gen. *pl.*) confín, límite, término. II. [kọnfáịn], *va.* confinar; encerrar, aprisionar; limitar, restringir.—**to be confined**, estar de parto. III. *vn.* confinar, comarcar, lindar.

confineless [-lịs], *a.* ilimitado.

confinement [-mẹnt], *s.* prisión, encierro, emparedamiento; confinamiento; destierro, cautiverio; restricción; parto; sobreparto.

confirm [kọnfœ́rm], *va.* confirmar, corroborar; verificar, establecer; sancionar, revalidar *o* ratificar; fortalecer; (igl.) confirmar.—**confirmable** [-ạbl], *a.* capaz de ser confirmado *o* ratificado.

confirmation [kanfœrméịṣọn], *s.* confirmación; ratificación, revalidación; (igl.) confirmación.

confirmative [kọnfœ́rmạtịv], *a.* confirmativo.

confirmatively [-lị], *adv.* confirmativamente.

confirmatory [-ątǫri], a. confirmativo, confirmatorio.

confirmed [-d], a. comprobado, corroborado; ratificado; establecido, demostrado; inveterado, consumado.

confirmedness [-idnis], s. certeza, firmeza.

confiscable [kǫnfískąbl], a. confiscable.

confiscate [kánfiskeit], va. confiscar, comisar.

confiscation [-éişǫn], s. confiscación.

confiscator [-ǫ(r)], s. confiscador.

confiscatory [kǫnfískątǫri], a. que confisca.

confiteor [kanfítiǫ(r)], s. (igl.) confíteor.

confiture [kánfichur], s. confitura, dulce.

conflagration [kanflągréişǫn], s. conflagración, incendio.

conflict [kánflikt], s. conflicto, oposición, pugna, contienda, antagonismo; lucha.

conflict [kǫnflíkt], vn. luchar; contender, chocar, pugnar, estar en pugna.—**conflicting** [-iŋ], a. antagónico, encontrado; contradictorio.

confluence [kánfluęns], s. confluencia; concurso, concurrencia.

confluent [-ęnt]. I. a. confluente. II. s. río confluente.

conflux [kánflʌks], s. = CONFLUENCE.

conform [kǫnfórm]. I. va. conformar, ajustar, concordar. II. vn. conformarse, ajustarse, amoldarse; allanarse, acatar, someterse.

conformability, **conformableness** [-ąbíliti, -ąblnis], s. conformidad.

conformable [-ąbl], a. conforme, acorde, consonante, conveniente, correspondiente, proporcionado; sumiso.—**conformably** [-ąbli], adv. conformemente.

conformation [kanforméişǫn], s. conformación, figura, arreglo.

conformator [kánformeitǫ(r)], s. conformador.

conformist [kǫnfórmist], s. conformista.

conformity [-iti], s. conformidad, avenencia, conveniencia, concordancia; sumisión, acatamiento.—**in c. with**, en consonancia con, con arreglo a.

confound [kǫnfáund], va. confundir, embrollar; turbar, aturrullar, azorar, desconcertar; mezclar, trabucar.—**c. it!**, ¡caramba! ¡maldito sea!

confounded [-id], a. (fam.) maldito, condenado, (irón.) dichoso.—**confoundedly** [-li], adv. detestable, execrable u odiosamente.

confraternity [kanfrątérniti], s. cofradía, confraternidad, hermandad.

confrere [kánfrer], s. compañero, colega, m., socio.

confront [kǫnfrʌnt], va. afrontar, arrostrar, hacer frente a; carear; confrontar, cotejar, comparar.

confrontation [kanfrʌntéişǫn], **confrontment**, [kǫnfrʌntmęnt], s. confrontación; careo.

Confucian [kǫnfiúşiąn], s. y a. confuciano; partidario de Confucio.—**Confucianism** [-izm], s. confucianismo, doctrina de Confucio.

confuse [kǫnfiúz], va. confundir; aturdir, desorientar, distraer, (per)turbar, trastornar; desbarajustar, desordenar; mezclar, trabucar; obscurecer.

confused [-d], a. confuso, azarado, corrido, distraído, (per)turbado; turbio, indistinto.

confusedly [-idli], adv. confusamente; atropelladamente.—**confusedness** [-nis], s. = CONFUSION.

confusion [kǫnfiúžǫn], s. confusión, desorden, baraúnda, desbarajuste, trastorno; desorientación, (per)turbación, aturdimiento, azoramiento; vergüenza.—**c. of tongues**, confusión de las lenguas; torre (f.) de Babel.

confutable [kǫnfiútąbl], a. refutable.

confutation [kanfiutéişǫn], s. confutación.

confute [kǫnfiút], va. confutar, refutar, impugnar.

confuter [-œr], s. confutador.

congé [kánžei], s. despedida, despido; cortesía.

congeal [kǫndžíl]. I. va. congelar, helar; cuajar, coagular. II. vn. congelarse, helarse, cuajarse.

congealable [-ąbl], a. congelable.

congealing [-iŋ], **congealment** [-męnt], s. congelación, congelamiento.

congelation [kandželéişǫn], s. congelación.

congelative [kándželeitiv], a. congelativo.

congener [kándžęnœ(r)], s. congénere.—**congeneric** [kandžęnérik], **congenerous** [kandžénęras], a. congénere, congenérico.

congenetic [kandžęnétik], a. de igual origen.

congenial [kǫndžíniąl], a. congenial, análogo; simpático.—**congeniality** [-iáliti], **congenialness** [-nis], s. congenialidad, simpatía.

congenital [kǫndžénitąl], a. congénito.

conger, **conger eel** [kángœ(r), -il], s. (ict.) congrio.

congeries [kǫndžíriiz], s. congerie, cúmulo.

congest [kǫndžést]. I. va. apiñar, aglomerar; (med.) congestionar. II. vn. congestionarse.—**congested** [-id], a. (med.) congestionado; hiperémico; apretado, apiñado, obstruído.—**congestion** [kǫndžéschǫn], s. (med.) congestión; apiñamiento.—**congestive** [kǫndžéstiv], a. (med.) congestivo.

conglobate [kǫnglóubeit]. I. a. conglobado. II. va. y vn. conglobar(se).

conglobation [kanglóubéişǫn], s. conglobación.

conglomerate [kǫnglámęreit]. I. va. y vn. conglomerar(se), aglomerar(se), redondear(se). II. [-it], a. conglomerado; congregado, redondeado. III. [-it], s. conglomeración; (geol.) conglomerado.

conglomeration [-éişǫn], s. conglomeración.

conglomeratic [-ǽtik], a. conglomerado.

conglutinate [kǫnglútineit]. I. va. y vn. conglutinar(se); pegar(se). II. a. conglutinado.

conglutination [-éişǫn], s. conglutinación.

conglutinative [kǫnglútinątiv], a. conglutinativo.

congo [káŋgou] **eel o snake**, (E. U.) (ict.) cierta anguila anfibia.—**c. monkey**, (Am.) (zool.) congo.—**C. red**, rojo de Congo (tinte y reactivo).

Congo(l)ese [kaŋgo(l)íz], a. y s. congo(leño), congolés.

congratulant [kǫngrǽchuląnt]. I. a. (con)gratulorio. II. s. congratulador.

congratulate [-leit], va. (con)gratular, felicitar, cumplimentar.—**to c. on**, felicitar por.

congratulation [-léişǫn], s. congratulación; felicitación, enhorabuena, parabién.—**congratulator** [-leitǫ(r)], s. congratulador.—**congratulatory** [-lątǫri], a. congratulatorio.

congregate [káŋgrigeit]. I. va. congregar, convocar, juntar, reunir. II. vn. congregarse, juntarse, afluir. III. a. agregado, reunido.

congregation [-éişǫn], s. concurso, auditorio; asamblea, reunión; agregado, colección; (igl.) congregación; grey, f., conjunto de los fieles o miembros de una iglesia; feligreses.

congregational [-ąl], a. perteneciente a una congregación; (C.) congregacionalista.—**Congregationalism** [-izm], s. congregacionalismo.—**Congregationalist** [-ist], a. y s. congregacionalista.

congress [káŋgris], s. congreso, convención, concilio, asamblea; junta, conferencia; (C.) congreso, asamblea nacional; (E. U.) el senado y la cámara de representantes.—**in c. assembled**, en sesión plenaria.

congressional [kǫngréşǫnąl], a. perteneciente o relativo al congreso.—**C. district**, (E. U.) distrito electoral que envía un diputado a la cámara de representantes.

congressman [káŋgrisman], s. miembro de un congreso cualquiera; diputado al congreso; congresista. (En los E. U. apl. esp. a los miembros de la cámara de representantes.)—**c. at large**, (E. U.) diputado que representa todo un estado, en vez de un distrito electoral.

congresswoman [-wuman], s. mujer congresista.

congruence [káŋgruęns], **congruency** [-i], s. congruencia, armonía, consonancia, conveniencia, conformidad; (álg.) congruencia; (geom.) coincidencia, superponibilidad, igualdad.— **congruent** [-ęnt], **congruous** [kángruʌs], *a.* congruente, congruo, apto, apropiado; (álg.) congruente; (geom.) superponible, igual.— **congruously** [-li], *adv.* congruentemente, apropiadamente, armónicamente.—**congruousness** [-nis], *s.* = CONGRUENCE.

congruism [kángruizm], *s.* (teol.) congruísmo.

congruist [-ist], *s.* (teol.) congruísta.

congruity [kǫngrúiti], *s.* = CONGRUENCE.

conic [kánik]. I. *a.* cónico, coniforme.—**c. section,** sección cónica. II. *s.* cónica, sección cónica.

conical [-ạl], *a.* cónico.—**conically** [-ali], *adv.* á manera de cono.—**conicalness** [-nis], *s.* conicidad.

conics [-s], *s.* teoría de las cónicas.

conidium [konídiʌm], *s.* (bot.) conidio.

conifer [kóunifœ(r)], *s.* (bot.) confero.

Coniferæ [konífœri], *s. pl.* coníferas.

coniferous [konífęrʌs], *a.* confero.

coniform [kóuniform], *a.* coniforme, cónico.

con(i)ine [kóun(i)in], *s.* (quím.) conicina, cicutina.

conirostral [konirástrạl], *a.* (orn.) conirrostro.

conium [konáiʌm], *s.* (bot.) cicuta.

conjecturable [kǫndžékchųrạbl], *a.* conjeturable, presumible.

conjectural [-chųrạl], *a.* conjetural.—**conjecturally** [-i], *adv.* conjeturalmente, presunt(iv)amente.

conjecture [-chŭ(r)]. I. *s.* conjetura, presunción, barrunto. II. *va.* conjeturar, presumir, barruntar.—**conjecturer** [-rœ(r)], *s.* conjeturador.

conjoin [kǫndžóin]. I. *va.* juntar, unir; asociar; conectar. II. *vn.* confederarse, unirse, ligarse.

conjoint [kǫndžóint], *a.* asociado, confederado.

conjointly [-li], *adv.* unidamente, de mancomún.

conjugable [kándžugạbl], *a.* (gram.) conjugable.

conjugal [kándžugạl], *a.* conyugal, connubial, matrimonial, maridable, marital.—**c. bond,** maridaje.—**conjugally** [-i], *adv.* conyugalmente.

conjugate [kándžugeit]. I. *va.* (gram.) conjugar. II. *vn.* (biol.) unirse en conjugación. III. *s.* palabra análoga. IV. *a.* apareado; (mat.) conjugado.

conjugation [-éišǫn], *s.* conjunción, unión; (gram.) conjugación; (biol.) unión o fusión.

conjunct [kǫndžʌnkt], *a.* conjunto, allegado, unido.

conjunction [kǫndžʌnkšǫn], *s.* conjunción, unión, liga; (gram. y astr.) conjunción.

conjunctiva [kǫndžʌnktáivạ], *s.* (anat.) conjuntiva.—**conjunctival** [-l], *a.* conjuntival.

conjunctive [-tiv]. I. *a.* conjunto; conjuntivo; (gram.) de carácter de conjunción; conjuntivo o subjuntivo (modo). II. *s.* (gram.) palabra conjuntiva; conjunción.—**conjunctively** [-li], *adv.* conjuntamente, de mancomún.

conjunctivitis [-tiváitis], *s.* (med.) conjuntivitis.

conjunctly [-li], *adv.* (con)juntamente.

conjuncture [-chŭ(r)], *s.* coyuntura, oportunidad; unión, conexión.

conjuration [kandžuréišǫn], *s.* conjuro; sortilegio, encantación; arte de prestidigitación.

conjure [kǫndžúr]. I. *va.* rogar o pedir con instancia, conjurar; [kándžu(r)] exorcizar. II. *vn.* [kándžu(r)] conjurar; escamotear, hacer juegos de manos.—**to c. away,** exorcizar.—**to c. up,** evocar; suscitar.

conjurer [-œ(r)], *s.* conjurador, brujo, nigromante, sortílego; prestidigitador, jugador de manos.

conn [kan], *va.* (mar.) gobernar el buque.

connate [kanéit], *a.* congénito; innato; cognado; (bot.) connato.

connation [kanéišǫn], *s.* calidad de connato; unión congénita.

connatural [kanéchųrạl], *a.* connatural.

connaturalness [-nis], *s.* connaturalidad.—**connaturally** [-i], *adv.* connaturalmente.

connect [kǫnékt]. I. *va.* juntar, unir; relacionar; poner en comunicación; coordinar; aparear, reunir; (mec.) conectar, ensamblar, acoplar; (elec.) conectar. II. *vn.* unirse, juntarse; relacionarse; comunicarse; entroncarse, enlazarse, encadenarse; (f. c., etc.) empalmar.

connected [-id], *a.* unido, conexo; relacionado; encadenado, hilado; asociado; emparentado; coherente.—**to be c. with** (a firm, etc.), estar asociado con o empleado por (una casa, etc.).—**connectedly** [-li], *adv.* coherentemente; con ilación.

connecting [-iŋ], *a.* que une, conecta, etc.; de unión, conexión, etc.; conect(ad)or, conectivo; comunicante, comunicado.—**c. link,** nexo, eslabón.—**c. rod,** (m. v.) biela.

connection [kǫnékšǫn], *s.* conexión; unión o enlace; encadenamiento, ilación, coherencia; relación; parentesco; asociación, filiación; entronque; pariente; coito; (mec.) acoplamiento, junta, unión; (elec.) conexión; (f. c.) empalme.—**in c. with,** con respecto a, hablando de, a propósito de.—**in this c.,** con respecto a esto.

connective [kǫnéktiv]. I. *a.* conectivo, conexivo, conjuntivo. II. *s.* (bot.) conectivo; (gram.) palabra conjuntiva (conjunción, preposición, relativo).—**c. tissue,** (anat.) tejido conjuntivo.

connectively [-li], *adv.* conjunta, unidamente.

connector [kǫnéktǫ(r)], *s.* conector, conectador.

conner [kánœ(r)], *s.* el que lee con cuidado (V. CON); (mar.) observador; oficial de derrota.

connexion [kǫnékšǫn], *s.* = CONNECTION.

conning tower [kániŋ táuœ(r)], *s.* timonera blindada de un buque de guerra.

conniption [kǫnípšǫn], *s.* (fam.) berrinche, pataleta, histerismo (ll. t. **c. fit**).

connivance [kǫnáivạns], *s.* connivencia, consentimiento.—**connive** [kǫnáiv], *vn.* tolerar, consentir, disimular, hacer la vista gorda; coludirse.—**conniver** [-œ(r)], *s.* cómplice, *mf.*; consentidor.

connoisseur [kanisœr], *s.* perito, conocedor.

connotation [kanotéišǫn], *s.* connotación.

connotative [kánotęitiv], *a.* (gram.) connotativo.

connote [kǫnóut], *va.* connotar.

connubial [kǫnúbiạl], *a.* conyugal, connubial.

conoid [kóunoid], *s.* (geom.) conoide, *f.*—**conoidal** [konóidạl], *a.* conoidal.

conquer [kánkœ(r)]. I. *va.* conquistar; vencer, superar. II. *vn.* triunfar.—**conquerable** [-ạbl], *a.* vencible, conquistable, domable.—**conquering** [-iŋ], *a.* victorioso; conquistador.

conqueror [-ǫ(r)], *s.* conquistador; vencedor.

conquest [kánkwest], *s.* conquista.—**the C.** (hist.) la conquista de Inglaterra por Guillermo el Conquistador.

consanguineous [kansæŋgwíniʌs], *a.* consanguíneo.

consanguinity [-niti], *s.* consanguinidad.

conscience [kánšęns], *s.* conciencia (moral).—**c. clause,** cláusula de conciencia, cláusula de una ley que exime de observarla a aquellos a quienes su conciencia (sobre todo en materias religiosas) no se lo permita.—**c.-stricken** o **smitten,** remordido por la conciencia.—**in (all) c.,** en conciencia; en verdad; ciertamente.—**with c.,** a conciencia.

conscienceless [-lis], *a.* desalmado, sin conciencia.

conscientious [kanšiénšʌs], *a.* concienzudo, escrupuloso; detenido.—**c. objector,** pacifista por conciencia; recalcitrante por conciencia (apl. esp. al que rehusa servir de soldado por dictarle su conciencia que la guerra es una acción inmoral).—**conscientiously** [-li], *adv.* concienzuda o escrupulosamente; a conciencia.—**conscientiousness** [-nis], *s.* rectitud, equidad; escrupulosidad.

conscionable [kánšǫnạbl], *a.* justo, razonable.

conscionably [-blị], *adv.* en conciencia, razonablemente.

conscious [kánsʌs], *a.* consciente.

consciously [-lị], *adv.* conscientemente, con conocimiento, a sabiendas.—**consciousness** [-nịs], *s.* conocimiento, sentido; (psic.) conciencia (de sí mismo), estado consciente.

conscript [kánskrịpt]. **I.** *a.* conscripto.—**c. fathers**, padres conscriptos (apl. esp. a la Roma antigua); senadores o legisladores. **II.** *s.* conscripto, recluta, *m.*, quinto.

conscript [kɒnskrípt], *va.* reclutar, alistar.

conscription [kɒnskrípʃɒn], *s.* conscripción, reclutamiento, quinta, alistamiento.

consecrate [kánsẹkreịt]. **I.** *va.* consagrar, santificar; ungir; dedicar, ofrecer; canonizar. **II.** *a.* (poét.) consagrado.—**consecration** [-éịʃɒn], *s.* consagración; dedicación; canonización.—**consecrator** [-ọ(r)], *s.* consagrante.

consecution [kansịkiúʃɒn], *s.* sucesión; ilación; (mús.) serie de intervalos similares.

consecutive [kɒnsékyutịv], *a.* consecutivo; sucesivo.—**consecutively** [-lị], *adv.* consecutivamente, de seguida.

consensual [kɒnsénsuạl], *a.* (for.) consensual, (fisiol.) excitado por medio de acción simpática o refleja.

consensus [kɒnsénsʌs], *s.* consenso; acuerdo general; (fisiol.) simpatía.—**c. of opinion**, opinión general.

consent [kɒnsént]. **I.** *s.* consentimiento, anuencia, permiso, beneplácito, aquiescencia, asenso.—**by common c.**, de común acuerdo.—**silence gives c.**, quien calla otorga. **II.** *vn.* consentir, condescender, acceder.

consenter [-œ(r)], *s.* consentidor.

consentient [kɒnsénʃịẹnt], *a.* anuente, consintiente; unánime.

consequence [kánsẹkwẹns], *s.* consecuencia, resulta(do), conclusión; importancia, entidad.—**as a c. of**, por resultas de.—**in c.**, por consiguiente; de resultas (de).

consequent [-kwent]. **I.** *a.* consecuente, consectario, consiguiente, lógico. **II.** *s.* (lóg.) consiguiente; (mat.) consecuente.

consequential [-kwénsạl], *a.* consecuente, consiguiente; fachendista, engreído; importante.—**consequentialness** [-nịs], *s.* calidad de consecuente; fachenda, engreimiento.

consequently [kánsẹkwentlị], *adv.* por lo tanto, por ende, por consiguiente, en consecuencia.

conservable [kɒnsœ́rvạbl], *a.* conservable.

conservancy [-ạnsị], *s.* conservación; junta para la conservación y fomento de viveros y pesquerías, etc.

conservant [-ạnt], *a.* conservador.

conservation [kansœrvéịʃɒn], *s.* conservación, preservación; manutención; conservación e inspección de bosques, ríos, etc.

conservatism [kɒnsœ́rvạtịzm], *s.* conservatismo, tendencia conservadora; (pol.) moderantismo.

conservative [-tịv]. **I.** *a.* y *s.* conservador, moderado; preservativo. **II.** *a.* conservativo.

conservatoire [-twár], *s.* conservatorio de música.

conservator [kánsœrveịtọ(r)], *s.* conservador; defensor, protector.

conservatory [kɒnsœ́rvạtọrị]. **I.** *a.* conservatorio. **II.** *s.* invernáculo, invernadero, jardín de invierno; conservatorio, academia.

conserve [kɒnsœ́rv], *va.* conservar, preservar; hacer conserva.

conserve [kánsœrv], *s.* conserva, dulce; (farm.) confección.

conserver [kɒnsœ́rvœ(r)], *s.* conservador, conservante; conservero.

consider [kɒnsídœ(r)]. **I.** *va.* considerar, pensar, pesar, reparar o parar mientes (en); tomar en cuenta; distinguir, tratar con respeto; creer, opinar, tener por, dar por. **II.** *vn.* pensar, reflexionar, deliberar.

considerable [-ạbl], *a.* considerable; notable;

cuantioso, no poco.—**considerableness** [-nịs], *s.* importancia, entidad, valor.—**considerably** [-blị], *adv.* considerablemente.

considerate [-ịt], *a.* considerado, (muy) mirado.

considerately [-lị], *adv.* consideradamente.

considerateness [-nịs], *s.* consideración; circunspección, moderación.

consideration [-éịʃɒn], *s.* consideración; miramiento; deliberación; entidad, importancia; retribución, retorno, remuneración.

considering [-ịŋ], *prep.* en atención a, considerando, visto que, en vista de.—**consideringly** [-lị], *adv.* seriamente, atinadamente.

consign [kɒnsáịn], *va.* confiar, traspasar; relegar; (com.) consignar.

consignatary [kɒnsígnạtẹrị], *s.* = CONSIGNEE.

consignation [kansịgnéịʃɒn], *s.* consignación.

consignee [kɒnsaịní], *s.* consignatario; depositario, destinatario, receptor.

consigner, *s.* = CONSIGNOR.

consignment [kɒnsáịnmẹnt], *s.* (com.) consignación, partida, envío.

consignor [kɒnsáịnọ(r)], *s.* consignador.

consist [kɒnsíst], *vn.* consistir; armonizar, ser compatible con.—**to consist in**, consistir en, depender de.—**to c. of**, constar o componerse de, ser integrado por.

consistence, consistency [-ẹns, -ẹnsị], *s.* consistencia; correspondencia, compatibilidad, conveniencia; permanencia, estabilidad.

consistent [-ẹnt], *a.* consecuente, conveniente, armonizable; coherente, consistente, denso, uniforme.—**c. with**, compatible con, conforme a; sin detrimento de.

consistently [-lị], *adv.* conformemente; consecuentemente; firmemente, sin cejar.

consistorial [kansịstóụrịạl], *a.* consistorial.

consistory [kɒnsístọrị], *s.* consistorio; asamblea, junta, congreso.

consociate [kɒnsóụʃịẹịt] **I.** *va.* y *vn.* asociar(se), congregar(se). **II.** *a.* y *s.* asociado.—**consociation** [-éịʃɒn], *s.* asociación, sociedad.

consolable [kɒnsóụlạbl], *a.* consolable.

consolation [kansoléịʃɒn], *s.* consolación, consuelo, alivio, confortación, solaz, *m.*

consolatory [kɒnsóụlạtọrị], *a.* consolatorio.

console [kɒnsóụl], *va.* consolar; confortar.

console [kánsoụl], *s.* consola, mesa sostenida por cartelas o arrimada a la pared (ll. t. **c. table**); (mús.) caja del órgano; (arq.) cartela, ancón, canecillo, ménsula.

consoler [kɒnsóụlœ(r)], *s.* consolador, confortador.

consolidant [kɒnsálịdạnt], *a.* consolidativo.

consolidate [kɒnsálịdeịt]. **I.** *va.* consolidar; solidar, unir. **II.** *vn.* consolidarse, endurecerse.—**consolidated annuities** = CONSOLS; consolidados.

consolidation [-éịʃɒn], *s.* consolidación, unión, conjunción.

consolidative [-ịv], *a.* consolidativo.

consoling [kɒnsóụlịŋ], *a.* consolador, consolante, consolativo, confortador.

consols [kánsoụlz], *s. pl.* (Ingl.) títulos de la deuda consolidada.

consommé [kansɒméị], *s.* consumado, caldo.

consonance [kánsonạns], **consonancy** [-ị], *s.* consonancia, conformidad, armonía.

consonant [-ạnt]. **I.** *a.* consonante, cónsono, conforme, armonioso. **II.** *s.* (gram.) consonante, *f.*

consonantal [kansonántạl], *a.* pert. a las consonantes.—**consonantly** [kánsonạntlị], *adv.* conformemente, consonantemente.—**consonantness** [-nịs], *s.* consonancia, conformidad.

consort [kánsort], *s.* consorte o cónyuge, *mf.*; compañero, socio; (mar.) buque que acompaña a otro.

consort [kɒnsórt]. **I.** *vn.* asociarse, acompañarse, ir (con); armonizar. **II.** *va.* casar, juntar, asociar.

consortism [kánsɔrtįzm], *s.* (biol.) simbiosis.
consortium [kɔnsórsįʌm], *s.* consorcio, unión o asociación (esp. la marital); consorcio comercial ο financiero (apl. esp. a la asociación de bancos).
conspectus [kɔnspéktʌs], *s.* ojeada, vista general; sumario, digesto.
conspicuous [kɔnspíkyuʌs], *a.* conspicuo, visible, llamativo; descollante, eminente, notable.—**conspicuously** [-lį], *adv.* visiblemente, claramente.—**conspicuousness** [-nįs], *s.* claridad, visibilidad; evidencia; fama, nombradía.
conspiracy [kɔnspírəsį], *s.* conspiración, complot, conjura(ción), cábala, trama; concurrencia.
conspirant [kɔnspáįrənt], *a.* conspirante.
conspirator [kɔnspírətɔ(r)], *s.* conspirador.
conspire [kɔnspáįr]. I. *vn.* conspirar, conjurar(se); ligarse; concurrir, juntarse. II. *va.* maquinar, tramar, urdir; preparar.
conspirer [-œ(r)], *s.* conspirado(r), conjurado(r).
conspiringly [-įŋlį], *adv.* conspirando criminalmente; en conspiración.
constable [kánstəbl], *s.* condestable; alguacil, ministril.—**constableship** [-ŝįp], *s.* condestablía.
constabulary [kɔnstǽbyulerį]. I. *a.* perteneciente a los alguaciles. II. *s.* cuadrilla de alguaciles; guardia civil.
constancy [kánstənsį], *s.* constancia; lealtad.
constant [kánstənt]. I. *a.* constante, continuo, firme, invariable, leal, perseverante, permanente. II. *s.* y *a.* (mat.) constante, *f.*
constantly [-lį], *adv.* constantemente, de continuo.
constellation [kanstəléįsɔn], *s.* (astr.) constelación, asterismo; (fig.) pléyade, *f.*
consternate [kánstœrneįt], *va.* consternar.—**to be consternated,** consternarse.
consternation [-éįsɔn], *s.* consternación, terror, horror, aturdimiento.
constipate [kánstįpeįt], *va.* estreñir, constipar.—**constipation** [-éįsɔn], *s.* (med.) estreñimiento de vientre, constipación.
constituency [kɔnstítʃuənsį], *s.* (pol.) distrito electoral; grupo de comitentes o electores.
constituent [-ənt]. I. *s.* elemento, ingrediente o componente; (pol.) elector, votante; (for.) poderdante, causante, comitente, delegante, diputador, mandante, principal. II. *a.* constitutivo; elemental, esencial; constituyente (asamblea, etc.); elector.
constitute [kánstįtįut], *va.* constituir, formar; nombrar, diputar; hacer, dar poder a; establecer, dar, ejecutar (una ley, etc.).
constitution [kanstįtįúsɔn], *s.* constitución; complexión, condición, físico, naturaleza, temperamento (de una persona); (for.) ley, *f.,* estatutos.
constitutional [-əl]. I. *a.* constitucional; constituyente; complexional; legal.—**c. law,** derecho constitucional o político; constitución, ley orgánica. II. *s.* (fam.) caminata, paseo higiénico.
constitutionalism [-įzm], *s.* (pol.) constitucionalismo.—**constitutionalist** [-įst], *s.* constitucional.—**constitutionality** [-ǽlįtį], *s.* constitucionalidad, conformidad con la constitución.—**constitutionally** [-į], *adv.* constitucionalmente, legalmente.
constitutive [kánstįtįutįv], *a.* constitutivo; esencial, elemental; legislativo.
constrain [kɔnstréįn], *va.* constreñir, compeler, obligar, forzar; restringir, impedir, detener; estrechar, comprimir, apretar.
constrainable [-əbl], *a.* constreñible.
constrainedly [-įdlį], *adv.* constreñidamente, coactivamente, por fuerza.
constrainer [-œ(r)], *s.* el o lo que obliga, etc.
constraint [-t], *s.* constreñimiento, coacción, compulsión, apremio; coartación, represión.
constrict [kɔnstríkt], *va.* apretar, estrechar, ligar.
constriction [kɔnstríksɔn], *s.* constricción, contracción, encogimiento.
constrictive [-tįv], *a.* constrictivo.

constrictor [-tɔ(r)], *s.* constrictor; (zool.) boa constrictor.
constringe [kɔnstríndž], *va.* constreñir, comprimir, estrechar, ligar.
constringent [-ənt], *a.* constrictivo, constringente.
construct [kɔnstrákt], *va.* construir; edificar, fabricar, obrar; proyectar, idear, inventar, componer; (gram., geom.) construir.
constructer, constructor [-œ(r)], *s.* constructor.
construction [kɔnstrákšɔn], *s.* construcción; edificación, estructura, obra, fabricación; interpretación, explicación; (gram.) construcción.
constructional [-əl], *a.* referente a la construcción o a la interpretación.
constructive [kɔnstráktįv], *a.* constructivo, constructor; implícito, tácito, sobrentendido.
constructively [-lį], *adv.* constructivamente; por deducción.—**constructiveness** [-nįs], *s.* facultad de construcción; ingeniosidad, aptitud mecánica.
construe [kɔnstrú], *va.* construir, interpretar, explicar; traducir (esp. oralmente).
consubstantial [kansʌbstǽnšəl], *a.* consubstancial, coesencial.—**consubstantialism** [-įzm], *s.* (teol.) doctrina de la consubstanciación.—**consubstantiality** [-ŝįǽlįtį], *s.* consubstancialidad.
consubstantiate [-ŝįeįt], *va.* unir en una misma substancia o naturaleza.
consubstantiation [-ŝįéįšɔn], *s.* (teol.) consubstanciación.
consuetude [kánswįtįud], *s.* costumbre, hábito.
consuetudinary [-tįúdįnerį], *a.* consuetudinario, habitual.
consul [kánsʌl], *s.* cónsul.—**c. general,** cónsul general.
consular [kánsįulą(r)], *a.* consular.—**c. agent,** agente consular.—**c. invoice,** factura consular.
consulate [kánsįulįt], *s.* consulado.—**c. general,** consulado general.
consulship [kánsʌlŝįp], *s.* consulado (dignidad o puesto).
consult [kɔnsált]. I. *va.* consultar; considerar, estudiar, examinar. II. *vn.* consultarse, asesorarse, aconsejarse (con); conferenciar.
consultant [-ənt], *s.* consultante, consultor.
consultation [kansʌltéįšɔn], *s.* consulta(ción), junta; deliberación, sesión; (med.) junta de médicos.
consultative [kɔnsáltətįv], **consultatory** [-ɔrį], *a.* consultivo.—**consulter** [-œ(r)], *s.* consultor, consultante.—**consulting** [-įŋ], *a.* consultor, consultante.—**c. office,** consultorio.—**c. physician,** médico de apelación.
consumable [kɔnsúməbl], *a.* consumible.
consume [kɔnsúm]. I. *va.* consumir, apurar, comer, devorar; deshacer, desgastar, (mal)gastar, disipar. II. *vn.* consumirse, deshacerse.—**consumed** [-d], *a.* (fig.) absorto (por), entregado por completo (a), muy metido (en), muerto (de).—**consumedly** [-įdlį], *adv.* excesivamente, extremamente.—**consumer** [-œ(r)], *s.* consumidor; disipador, destructor.—**consumers' goods,** (e. p.) bienes de consumo.—**consuming** [-įŋ], *a.* consumidor, consuntivo.
consummate [kánsʌmeįt]. I. *va.* consumar, acabar, completar. II. [kansámįt], *a.* consumado, cabal, completo.—**consummately** [-lį], *adv.* consumadamente.—**consummation** [kansʌméįšɔn], *s.* consumación, acabamiento.
consumptible [kɔnsámptįbl]. I. *s.* cosa deteriorable o que se gasta. II. *a.* deteriorable, que se gasta con el uso o el tiempo.
consumption [kɔnsámpšɔn], *s.* consunción, apuramiento, destrucción, desgaste, gast(amient)o expendio, extinción; (e. p.) consumo; (med.) consunción, tisis, tuberculosis, tabes, *f.*
consumptive [kɔnsámptįv]. I. *a.* consuntivo, destructivo; rel. a la tisis. II. *s.* y *a.* (med.) (h)ético, tísico.—**consumptively** [-lį], *adv.* con-

suntivamente.—**consumptiveness** [-nįs], s. consunción.

contabescence [kantabésęns], s. (med.) contabescencia, tabes, f., marasmo, atrofia.

contact [kántækt]. I. s. contacto; tocamiento.— pl. relaciones.—**c. breaker**, (elec.) interruptor automático (ll. t. **contactor**). II. va. y vn. tocar(se); poner(se) en contacto; (fam.) establecer relaciones comerciales o sociales con.

contagion [kǫntéįdʒǫn], s. contagio; infección, peste, f.; virus; contaminación.

contagious [kǫntéįdʒʌs], a. contagioso, infeccioso, pegadizo, pegajoso, pestilencial.

contagiousness [-nįs], s. contagiosidad.

contain [kǫntéįn], va. contener, caber, tener cabida para; abarcar, incluir, envolver; encerrar, refrenar, reprimir; (mat.) ser exactamente divisible.—**containable** [-abl], a. contenible.

container [-œ(r)], s. recipiente, vasija; envase.

contaminate [kǫntǽmįneįt], va. contaminar, corromper, apestar, infestar; contagiar o inficionar; depravar, manchar, pervertir.

contamination [-éįšǫn], s. contaminación.

conte [kǫnt], s. cuento; narración breve.

contemn [kǫntém], va. despreciar, menospreciar.—**contemner** [-(n)œ(r)], s. despreciador, menospreciador.

contemplate [kántempleįt]. I. va. contemplar, estudiar, meditar; proponerse, proyectar, tener la intención de. II. vn. meditar, reflexionar.

contemplation [-éįšǫn], s. contemplación, especulación, meditación; intención, proyecto; expectación.

contemplative [kǫntémplǝtįv], a. contemplativo.

contemplatively [-lį], adv. con atención y cuidado; contemplativamente.

contemplator [kántempleįtǫ(r)], s. contemplador.

contemporaneity [kǫntemporǝnéįįtį], **contemporaneousness** [-réįnʌsnįs], s. contemporaneidad, calidad de contemporáneo.—**contemporaneous** [-réįnʌs], a. contemporáneo.—**contemporaneously** [-lį], adv. contemporáneamente.—**contemporary** [kǫntémporerį]. I. a. y s. contemporáneo, coetáneo. II. s. colega (apl. a periódicos).

contempt [kǫntémpt], s. desprecio, menosprecio, desdén.—**c. of court**, (for.) contumacia; rebeldía.

contemptibility [-įbįlįtį], **contemptibleness** [-įblnįs], s. vileza, bajeza, ruindad.

contemptible [-įbl], a. despreciable, desdeñable.

contemptibly [-įblį], adv. vilmente.

contemptuous [kǫntémpchuʌs], a. desdeñoso, despectivo, despreciativo.—**contemptuously** [-lį], adv. desdeñosamente.—**contemptuousness** [-nįs], s. desdén, desprecio, altanería.

contend [kǫnténd]. I. va. sostener o afirmar. II. vn. contender, disputar; competir, lidiar, forcejear, bregar, altercar.—**contending parties**, partes contenciosas o litigantes.

contendent, contender [-ęnt, -œ(r)], s. contendedor, contendiente, competitor.

content [kántent], s. cantidad, proporción; (gen. pl.) contenido; cabida, capacidad; área; volumen.

content [kǫntént]. I. a. contento, satisfecho.—**c. o not c.**, (Ingl.) voto en pro o en contra. II. va. (com)placer, contentar, satisfacer. III. s. contento, contentamiento, satisfacción.

contented [-įd], a. contento, satisfecho, placentero, tranquilo; resignado.—**contentedly** [-lį], adv. tranquilamente, contentamente.—**contentedness** [-nįs], s. contento, satisfacción.

contention [kǫnténšǫn], s. contención, contienda, disputa; tema; pretensión; lo que se pretende o sostiene; argumento.

contentious [kǫnténšʌs], a. contencioso, litigioso, disputador, pugnaz.—**contentiously** [-lį], adv. contenciosamente.—**contentious-**

ness [-nįs], s. espíritu de contradicción, pugnacidad.

contentment [kǫnténtmęnt], s. contentamiento, contento, satisfacción.

conterminal [kantœrmįnǝl], **conterminous** [-nʌs], a. contérmino, vecino, limítrofe; coextensivo.

contest [kántest], s. contienda, debate, disputa; batalla, conflicto, pugna, lid, torneo; certamen, competencia, concurso, oposición; litigio, pleito.

contest [kǫntést]. I. va. disputar; discutir, debatir; impugnar; litigar, pleitear. II. vn. contender, combatir, lidiar; competir, emular o rivalizar (con uno).

contestable [-abl], a. contestable.

contestant [-ant], s. contendiente, disputador; opositor; litigante.

contestation [kantestéįšǫn], s. contestación.

context [kántekst], s. contexto.

contextual [kǫntékschuǝl], a. relativo al contexto.

contextural [-ūrǝl], a. perteneciente a la contextura.

contexture [-ū(r)], s. contextura; entretejido, enlazamiento.

contiguity [kantįgįúįtį], s. contigüidad, inmediación, adyacencia, vecindad; continuidad.

contiguous [kǫntįgįuʌs], a. contiguo, adyacente, afín, (co)lindante, inmediato, rayano, vecino.—**contiguously** [-lį], adv. contiguamente, junto, al lado.—**contiguousness** [-nįs], s. contigüidad.

continence [kántįnęns], **continency** [-į], s. continencia, castidad, moderación, templanza.

continent [-ęnt]. I. a. continente, moderado, casto. II. s. (geog.) continente.—**the C.**, la Europa continental (en que se excluyen las Islas Británicas).

continental [kantįnéntǝl], a. continental; de la Europa continental.

contingence [kǫntíndʒęns], s. contacto, tangencia. (Rara vez hoy = CONTINGENCY.)

contingency [-į], s. contingencia, eventualidad, evento, casualidad, caso fortuito.

contingent [-ęnt]. I. a. contingente, contingible, eventual, casual, fortuito.—**c. liabilities**, pasivo eventual; compromisos imprevistos.—**c. (up)on**, dependiente de. II. s. contingencia, casualidad; contingente, cuota.—**contingently** [-lį], adv. contingentemente.

continual [kǫntínyuǝl], a. continuo, incesante.—**continually** [-į], adv. continuamente.

continuance [-ans], s. continuación; persistencia; prolongación; (for.) aplazamiento.

continuation [-éįšǫn], s. continuación, prolongación.—**continuative** [-eįtįv], a. continuativo.—**continuator** [-eįtǫ(r)], **continuer** [-œ(r)], s. continuador.

continue [kǫntínyu]. I. va. continuar; mantener, perpetuar, prolongar, vincular; (for.) aplazar. II. vn. continuar; durar, mantenerse, permanecer, persistir, quedar; (pro)seguir.

continued [-d], a. continuo, continuado, prolongado, seguido.—**c. fraction**, (mat.) fracción continua.—**to be c.**, continuará.

continuedly [-lį], adv. continuadamente.

continuity [kantįnįúįtį], s. continuidad; continuación, perennidad; coherencia, enlace; serie o sucesión ininterrumpida; (cine y radio) V. SCENARIO y SCRIPT.

continuous [kǫntínyuʌs], a. continuo, ininterrumpido, sin solución de continuidad.—**continuously** [-lį], adv. continuamente.

continuum [kǫntínyuam], s. continuo, cosa continua (en el sentido matemático).

contort [kǫntórt], va. torcer, retorcer.

contortion [kǫntóršǫn], s. contorsión.

contortionist [-įst], s. contorsionista.

contour [kántur]. I. s. contorno, perfil, ámbito; (top.) curva de nivel. II. va. contorn(e)ar, perfilar.

contraband [kántrabænd]. I. s. contrabando.

II. *a.* prohibido, ilegal.—**contrabandism** [-ȷzm], *s.* contrabando, matute.—**contrabandist** [-ȷst], *s.* contrabandista, matutero.

contrabass [kántrȧbejs], *s.* (mús.) contrabajo.

contraception [kantrȧsépșȯn], *s.* contraconcepción, prevención de la concepción o la preñez.

contraceptive [-séptȷv]. **I.** *a.* de contraconcepción, antipreñante, que impide la preñez. **II.** *s.* agente antipreñante.

contract [kȯntrǽkt]. **I.** *va.* contraer, reducir, apretar; fruncir, arrugar; abreviar, compendiar; contraer (una enfermedad, una deuda, esponsales); contratar, pactar. **II.** *vn.* contraerse, encogerse, acortarse; comprometerse por contrato.

contract [kántrækt], *s.* contrato, convenio, pacto, ajuste; contrata, escritura; esponsales.—**c. of bargain and sale,** contrato de compraventa.

contracted [kȯntrǽktȷd], *a.* contraído, contracto, abreviado; fruncido; estrecho; escaso.—**contractedly** [-lȷ], *adv.* estrechamente; de manera mezquina.—**contractedness** [-nȷs], *s.* contracción; estrechez; mezquindad.

contractile [kȯntrǽktȷl], *a.* contráctil.

contractility [-tílȷtȷ], *s.* contractilidad.

contracting [-tȷŋ], *a.* contractivo; contrayente; contratante.—**the c. parties,** los contratantes; los contrayentes (ú. esp. del matrimonio).

contraction [-šȯn], *s.* contracción; abreviación, encogimiento, estrechamiento, reducción.

contractive [-tȷv], *a.* contractivo.

contractor [-tȯ(r)], *s.* contratista, contratante; asentista; empresario, concesionario.

contractual [-chuȧl], *a.* contractual, relativo a contratos; de o por contrato.

contracture [-chŭr], *s.* (med.) contractura.

contradance [kántrȧdæns], *s.* contradanza.

contradict [kantrȧdíkt], *va.* contradecir, desmentir, negar; impugnar, repugnar, oponerse, contrariar, llevarle la contraria a uno.

contradicter [-œ(r)], *s.* contradictor.

contradiction [-díkșȯn], *s.* contradicción; contrariedad, impugnación, oposición; repugnancia; (fam.) renuncio.

contradictious [-díkȧas], *a.* contradictor.

contradictorily [-díktȯrȷlȷ], *adv.* contradictoriamente.

contradictoriness [-díktȯrȷnȷs], *s.* espíritu de contradicción; calidad de contradictorio.

contradictory [-díktȯrȷ]. **I.** *a.* contradictorio; contrario, opuesto. **II.** *s.* (lóg.) contradictoria.

contradistinction [-dȷstíŋkšȯn], *s.* distinción por contraste o calidades opuestas.—**in c. to,** a distinción de, a diferencia de, en contraste con.

contradistinguish [-dȷstíŋgwȷš], *va.* distinguir por el contraste de calidades opuestas.

contraindicant [-índȷkȧnt], **contraindication** [-índȷkéȷșȯn], *s.* (med.) contraindicante, contraindicación.

contraindicate [-índȷkeȷt], *va.* (med.) contraindicar.

contralto [kȯntrǽltoŭ], *s.* y *a.* (mús.) contralto; de contralto.

contraplex [kántrȧpleks], *a.* (tlg.) de transmisión simultánea en direcciones opuestas.

contraposition [-poŭzíšȯn], *s.* contraposición; contraste; antítesis.

contraption [kȯntrǽpșȯn], *s.* (fam.) artefacto.

contrapuntal [kantrȧpŭ́ntȧl], *a.* (mús.) pert. al contrapunto; polifónico.—**contrapuntist** [-pŭ́ntȷst], *s.* (mús.) contrapuntista.

contrariety [kantrȧráȷetȷ], *s.* contrariedad; oposición.

contrarily [kántrȧrȷlȷ], *adv.* contrariamente, opuestamente.—**contrariness** [-nȷs], *s.* contrariedad, oposición; testarudez.—**contrariwise** [-waȷz], *adv.* al contrario, al revés, a tuertas, inversamente, viceversa; perversamente.

contrary [kántrȧrȷ]. **I.** *a.* contrario; adverso; contradictorio; divergente.—**c.-minded,** de diversa opinión.—**c. to,** en oposición a; en violación de; al contrario de, al revés de, contra.

II. *s.* contrario; contraria.—**on the c.,** al o por el contrario; antes bien.—**to the c.,** en contrario.

contrast [kántræst], *s.* contraste, contraposición.

contrast [kȯntrǽst], *va.* y *vn.* contrastar.

contrastable [-ȧbl], *a.* contrastable.

contrasting [-ȷŋ], *a.* contrastador; contrastante; de contraste.

contravallation [kantrȧvæléȷșȯn], *s.* (fort.) contravalación.

contravene [kantrȧvín], *va.* contravenir.

contravener [-œ(r)], *s.* contraventor, infractor.

contravention [-vénșȯn], *s.* contravención o infracción.

contrayerva [-yœ́rvȧ], *s.* (bot.) contrahierba.

contredance [-dáns], *s.* contradanza.

contribute [kȯntríbȷut]. **I.** *va.* contribuir, aportar, donar, ofrendar. **II.** *vn.* contribuir, cooperar, concurrir; colaborar.

contribution [kantrȷbȷúšȯn], *s.* contribución, cooperación, aportación, aporte; cuota, dádiva, donativo; colaboración; artículo, escrito (con que se colabora).

contributive [kȯntríbȷutȷv], **contributory** [-tȯrȷ], *a.* cooperante o contribuyente.

contributor [-tȯ(r)], *s.* contribuidor, contribuyente; colaborador.

contrite [kántraȷt], *a.* contrito, atrito, penitente.—**contritely** [-lȷ], *adv.* contritamente.—**contriteness, contrition** [-nȷs, kȯntríșȯn], *s.* contrición.

contrivance [kȯntráȷvȧns], *s.* idea, plan, invención; invención, aparato, artefacto, dispositivo; traza, ingenio, artificio; estratagema.

contrive [kȯntráȷv]. **I.** *va.* idear, inventar, ingeniar, arbitrar; tramar, urdir. **II.** *vn.* darse maña o trazas (de), buscar un medio, maquinar.

contriver [-œ(r)], *s.* arbitrista, autor, inventor.

control [kȯntróŭl]. **I.** *s.* mando, dirección, dominio, control; influencia predominante; regulación, inspección, intervención; restricción, freno; contrarregistro, regulador; (mec., aut.) mando, gobierno; aparato o mecanismo de mando, gobierno o regulación; *pl.* mandos; (fis.) factor, causa, agente; (espiritismo) comunicante, agente que informa al médium.—**c. board,** cuadro de control.—**c. car,** (aer.) barquilla de gobierno o de dirección (de un dirigible).—**c. experiment,** experimento de eliminación, en que se omiten ciertos elementos o circunstancias cuya influencia se trata de estudiar.—**c. column,** (aer.) = C. STICK.—**c. gear,** (aut.) mecanismo de mando.—**c. lever o stick,** (aer.) palanca de mando o de gobierno.—**c. station,** puesto de mando. **II.** *a.* regulador; de gobierno; de comprobación. **III.** *va.* dominar, dirigir, gobernar, regular, controlar; comprobar, verificar, intervenir; tener a raya; tener predominancia en; reprimir, restringir.—**to c. one's self,** contenerse, refrenarse.

controllable [-ȧbl], *a.* gobernable, dominable, manejable.

controller [-œ(r)], *s.* interventor, contralor; director, superintendente, inspector, registrador; regulador; (fís.) factor, causa, agente; (mar.) retén de cadena; (elec.) combinador (de coche eléctrico). *V.* COMPTROLLER.

controllership [-šȷp], *s.* contraloría, mayordomía, veeduría; oficio y oficina de *controller.*

controlling [-ȷŋ], *a.* que manda, que gobierna; decisivo, determinante; predominante.—**c. interest,** (com.) mayoría, interés predominante.

controlment [-mȩnt], *s.* restricción, sujeción; superintendencia, inspección; comprobación.

controversial [kantrovœ́rsȧl], *a.* polemístico, contencioso.—**controversialist** [-ȷst], *s.* polemista.

controversy [kántrovœrsȷ], *s.* controversia, disputa, debate, polémica.—**controvert** [kantrovœ́rt], *va.* y *vn.* controvertir, disputar.—**controverter** [-œ(r)], **controvertist** [-ȷst], *s.*

controversista, argumentador, polemista.—
controvertible [-ịbl], *a.* controvertible, disputable, discutible.
contumacious [kantịuméịʃʌs], *a.* contumaz, rebelde, tenaz.—**contumaciously** [-lị],*adv.* contumazmente.—**contumaciousness** [-nịs], **contumacy** [kántịumạsị], *s.* contumacia, terquedad.
contumelious [kantịumílịʌs], *a.* contumelioso,
injurioso, ofensivo.—**contumeliously** [-lị],
adv. contumeliosamente.—**contumeliousness**
[-nịs], **contumely** [kántịumịlị], *s.* contumelia,
ultraje, injuria.
contuse [kọntúz], *va.* contundir, magullar.
contusion [kọntúʒọn], *s.* contusión.
contusioned [-d], *a.* contuso.
contusive [kọntúsịv], *a.* contundente.
conundrum [kọnʌ́ndrʌm], *s.* acertijo, adivinanza.
convalesce [kanvạlés], *vn.* convalecer.
convalescence [-ẹns], *s.* convalecencia.
convalescent [-ẹnt], *a.* y *s.* convaleciente.
convection [kọnvékʃọn], *s.* conducción, transmisión; (fís.) convección, difusión del calor por
circulación.
convene [kọnvín]. I. *va.* convocar, citar; aplazar,
emplazar. II. *vn.* juntarse, reunirse.
convener [-œ(r)], *s.* convocador.
convenience, conveniency [kọnvínyẹns, -ị], *s.*
conveniencia, comodidad, confort; lugar, oportunidad, utilidad.—**at one's c.**, cuando le sea
cómodo a uno.—**at one's earliest c.**, a la
primera oportunidad que uno tenga, tan pronto
como le sea posible.—**to suit one's c.**, convenir
algo a uno; hacer uno lo que le guste.
convenient [-ẹnt], *a.* conveniente, cómodo, útil,
oportuno.—**c. (to)**, cerca (de), a la mano.—
conveniently [-lị], *adv.* cómodamente; convenientemente.
convent [kánvẹnt], *s.* convento, monasterio.
conventicle [kọnvéntịkl], *s.* conventículo, conciliábulo.
convention [kọnvénʃọn], *s.* convención, asamblea, congreso, junta; convenio, avenimiento,
pacto; costumbre, precedente; convencionalismo, formalismo.
conventional [-ạl], *a.* convencional; estipulado,
convenido, corriente, tradicional; formalista.
conventionalism [-ịzm], *s.* convencionalismo;
formalismo; respeto a las costumbres.
conventionality [-ǽlịtị], *s.* formalidad; regla impuesta por la costumbre.
conventionalize [-ạịz], *va.* hacer convencional;
(b. a.) estilizar, representar de modo convencional.
conventionally [-ị], *adv.* convencionalmente.
conventual [kọnvénchuạl], *a.* y *s.* conventual.
converge [kọnvœ́rdʒ], *vn.* convergir, converger.
convergence, convergency [-ẹns, -ị], *s.* convergencia.
convergent [-ẹnt], **converging** [-ịŋ], *a.* convergente.
conversable [kọnvœ́rsạbl], *a.* conversable; sociable.—**conversableness** [-nịs], *s.* sociabilidad.
—**conversably** [-blị], *adv.* sociablemente,
afablemente.
conversant [kánvœrsạnt], *a.* (gen. seguido de
with) versado, experimentado, experto (en),
ocupado (en), conocedor o entendido (de).
conversation [-éịʃọn], *s.* conversación, plática,
tertulia; conferencia; trato carnal.
conversational [-ạl], *a.* perteneciente a la conversación; de conversación.
conversationalist [-ịst], *s.* conversador; el que
conversa con gusto o facilidad notable.
converse [kọnvœ́rs], *vn.* conversar; platicar; hacer
tertulia; departir, tener trato.
converse [kánvœrs]. I. *s.* conversación, plática,
(fam.) conversa; familiaridad, trato; (mat.,
lóg.) recíproca. II. *a.* traspuesto, inverso.—
conversely [-lị], *adv.* a la inversa, recíprocamente.

conversible [kọnvœ́rsịbl], *a.* convertible.
conversion [kọnvœ́rʃọn], *s.* conversión, transformación; mudanza; (mil., relig.) conversión;
(for.) apropiación ilícita de los bienes de otro;
(com.) conversión, canje, mudanza.
conversive [kọnvœ́rsịv], *a.* conversivo.
convert [kánvœrt], *s.* neófito, converso, prosélito.
convert [kọnvœ́rt]. I. *va.* convertir; transmutar,
transformar, cambiar, reducir (a); (fund.) convertir, cementar; (com.) convertir o cambiar
(valores). II. *vn.* convertirse, mudar.
converter, convertor [-œ(r)], *s.* (lenguaje común,
fund., elec.) convertidor.
convertibility [-ịbịlịtị], *s.* convertibilidad.
convertible [-ịbl], *a.* convertible, conversible,
cambiable, reducible; (aut.) transformable (de
cerrado en abierto y recíprocamente).—**con-
vertibly** [-ịblị], *adv.* recíproca o mutuamente.
convex [kánvɛks]. I. *a.* convexo, abombado; combado. II. *s.* convexidad.—**convexo-concave,
convexocóncavo.—convexo-convex,**biconvexo.
convexed [kánvɛkst], *a.* convexo.
convexity [kọnvéksịtị], **convexness** [kánvɛksnịs],
s. convexidad, comba(dura).
convexly [kánvɛkslị], *adv.* convexamente.
convey [kọnvéị], *va.* conducir, acarrear, transportar, llevar; transmitir; enviar; ceder, transferir, traspasar; comunicar; causar, dar (a
entender).
conveyable [-ạbl], *a.* conductible.
conveyance [-ạns], *s.* conducción, transporte;
conducta; vehículo; entrega, cesión, traspaso,
traslación de dominio; escritura de traspaso.
conveyancer [-œ(r)], *s.* escribano que hace escrituras de traspaso.—**conveyancing** [-ịŋ], *s.*
oficio de preparar escrituras de traspaso.
conveyer, conveyor [-œ(r)], *s.* conductor, mensajero; portador; cedente; (mec.) transportador.
convict [kọnvíkt], *va.* (for.) condenar; convencer
de culpa o delito; probar la culpabilidad.
convict [kánvịkt], *s.* reo convicto; penado, presidiario.—**c. system**, sistema (*m.*) penal.
convictable, convictible [kọnvíktạbl], *a.* a quien
se le puede probar un crimen.
conviction [kọnvíkʃọn], *s.* convicción, convencimiento; persuasión; (for.) convicción, prueba
y fallo de culpabilidad; fallo condenatorio.
convince [kọnvíns], *va.* convencer, persuadir.
convincible [-ịbl], *a.* convencible, que puede con-
vencerse; convincente.
convincing [-ịŋ], *a.* convincente, persuasivo.
convincingly [-lị], *adv.* convincentemente.
convincingness [-nịs], *s.* calidad de convincente.
convivial [kọnvívịạl], *a.* convival.
conviviality [-ǽlịtị], *s.* jovialidad, buen humor.
convocation [kanvokéịʃọn], *s.* convocación; aplazamiento, llamamiento; asamblea.
convoke [kọnvóụk], *va.* convocar, citar, aplazar.
convolute(d [kánvoḷịut(ịd]. I. *a.* convolut(ad)o,
arrollado sobre sí mismo. II. *s.* enroscadura.
III. *va.* y *vn.* V. CONVOLVE.
convolution [-lịúʃọn], *s.* repliegue, pliegue; enroscadura; (anat.) circunvolución (cerebral).
convolve [kọnválv]. I. *va.* arrollar, enrollar, retorcer. II. *vn.* retorcerse, enroscarse.
convolvulaceous [-vịuléịʃạs], *a.* (bot.) convolvu-
láceo.
convolvulus [-vịuḷʌs], *s.* (bot.) convólvulo.
convoy [kọnvóị], *va.* convoyar, escoltar.
convoy [kánvoị], *s.* convoy, conducta, escolta;
(mar.) conserva.
convulse [kọnvʌ́ls], *va.* convulsionar, dar convul-
siones, crispar; agitar violentamente.—**convulsed** [-d], *a.* convulso.—**to be c. with laughter**, morirse o desternillarse de risa.—**to be c.
with pain, rage**, etc., crisparse de dolor, ira,
etc.
convulsion [kọnvʌ́lʃọn], *s.* convulsión, espasmo;
conmoción; (geol.) cataclismo.
convulsionary [-ɛrị], **convulsive** [kọnvʌ́lsịv], *a.*
convulsionario, convulsivo, espasmódico.

convulsively [-lị], *adv.* convulsivamente.
cony [kóuni], *s.* (zool.) gazapo, conejo; especie de damán; piel (*f.*) de conejo.
coo [kú]. **I.** *vn.* arrullar; decir ternezas. **II.** *s.* arrullo.
cooer [-œ(r)], *s.* paloma, tórtola; requebrador, cortejo.
cooing [-iŋ], *s.* arrullo; halago, requiebro.
cook [kúk], *va.* y *vn.* cocer, cocinar; guisar, aderezar, adobar; (fam.) echar a perder (un proyecto, etc.).—**to c. one's goose,** (fam.) arruinar o matar a uno.—**to c. up,** (fam.) tramar; falsear. —**what's cooking?,** (fam.) ¿qué se trama? ¿qué pasa?
cook, *s.* cocinero, cocinera.
cookbook [-bụk], *s.* libro de cocina.
cookery [-œrị], *s.* arte de cocina; cocina.
cooking [-iŋ]. **I.** *s.* arte culinario; cocina; cocción. **II.** *a.* de o para la cocina.—**c. pan,** cacerola, cazuela.—**c. range o stove,** cocina (económica); fogón.—**c. utensils,** batería o utensilios de cocina.
cookshop [-šap], *s.* casa de comidas, bodegón.
cookstove [-stouv], *s.* = COOKING RANGE.
cooky, cookie [kúkị], *s.* gallet(it)a, bizcochito, pasta o torta para el té, etc.; pequeño bollo dulce.
cool [kúl]. **I.** *a.* fresco; tibio, indiferente.—**c.-headed,** sereno. **II.** *s.* frescura o fresco(r). **III.** *va.* enfriar, refrescar, refrigerar, orear, entibiar, atemperar; calmar.—**to c. one's heels,** (fam.) hacer antesala, esperar largo tiempo. **IV.** *vn.* refrescar, enfriarse, templarse, apaciguarse.
coolant [-ạnt], *s.* agente de refrigeración.
cooler [-œ(r)], *s.* enfriadera, cantimplora, garapiñera; enfriadero, refrigerador; (med.) refrigerante; (fam.) calabozo.
coolie, cooly [kúlị], *s.* culí, peón chino o indio.
cooling [kúliŋ]. **I.** *a.* refrescante, refrigerativo, refrigerante, frigorífico; atemperante, oreante. **II.** *s.* enfriamiento, refrigeración.—**c. coil,** serpentín refrigerante.—**c. system,** sistema (*m.*) de refrigeración.
coolish [kúlịš], *a.* fresco, fresquito.
coolly [kúlị], *adv.* frescamente, fríamente, serenamente, a sangre fría.
coolness [kúlnịs], *s.* fresco; frialdad, despego, tibieza; frescura, calma, serenidad, sangre fría.
coon [kun], *s.* (zool.) mapache (*V.* RACCOON); (E. U. fam. y desp.) negro.—**c. dog,** sabueso de cazar mapaches.—**c. skin,** piel (*f.*) de mapache. —**c.'s age,** (fam.) mucho tiempo.—**old c.,** viejo marrullero.
coop [kup]. **I.** *s.* caponera, gallinero; (fam.) cárcel, *f.*—**to fly the c.,** (fam.) fugarse, evadirse. **II.** *va.* (gen. con **in** o **up**) enjaular; encarcelar.
co-op, co-öp [kóuap], *s.* abrev. de COOPERATIVE.
cooper [kúpœ(r)]. **I.** *va.* y *vn.* hacer barriles, cubas, toneles, etc. **II.** *s.* barrilero, cubero, tonelero.
cooperage [-idž], *s.* tonelería, cubería.
coöperant [koápœrạnt], *a.* y *s.* cooperante.
coöperate [koápœrejt], *vn.* cooperar, coadyuvar.
coöperation [-réišọn], *s.* cooperación.
coöperative [-rặtịv]. **I.** *a.* cooperativo; cooperante, coadyutorio, coadyuvante. **II.** *s.* cooperativa (empresa, compañía, asociación cooperativa).
coöperator [-rejtọ(r)], *s.* cooperador.
coopering, coopery [kúpœriŋ, kúpœrị], *s.* = COOPERAGE.
coördinate [koórdịnejt]. **I.** *va.* coordinar. **II.** [-inịt], *s.* igual, semejante; (mat.) coordenada. **III.** *a.* coordenado; (mat.) relativo a las coordenadas.—**c. axes,** (mat.) ejes de las coordenadas. —**c. geometry,** geometría analítica.
coördinately [-nịtlị], *adv.* coordinadamente.
coördinateness [-nịs], **coördination** [-néišọn], *s.* coordinación, coordinamiento.
coördinating [-nejtiŋ], *a.* coordinador.

coördinative [-nặtịv], *a.* coordinativo.
coördinator [-nejtọ(r)], *s.* coordinador.
coot [kut], *s.* (orn.) negreta; fúlica, foja, falaris; especie de pato marino; (fam.) zopenco.
cootie [kútị], *s.* (ent., fam.) piojo.
co-owner [kouóunœ(r)], *s.* condueño, copropietario.
cop [kap]. **I.** *s.* montón; rimero; husada, rollo ahusado; tubo de enrollar (seda, etc.); (E. U. fam.) polizonte. **II.** *va.* (fam.) hurtar, llevarse; coger.
copaiba [kopáịbạ], *s.* (farm.) copaiba (bálsamo). —**c. tree,** copayero, copaiba.
copal [kóupạl], *s.* copal (resina).
coparcen(ar)y [koupársẹn(ẹr)ị], *s.* (for.) participación en una herencia de bienes raíces.
coparcener [koupársẹnœ(r)], *s.* (for.) coheredero.
copartner [koupártnœ(r)], *s.* copartícipe; (con)-socio.
copartnership [-šịp], *s.* (co)participación; compañía, sociedad, asociación.
cope [koup]. **I.** *s.* arco, bóveda, cúpula; cielo; (alb., arq.) albardilla; (igl.) capa pluvial. **II.** *vn.* (con **with**) contender o competir con, habérselas con, hacer frente a. **III.** *va.* (alb.) poner albardilla o caballete; (igl.) poner la capa pluvial.
copeck [kóupek], *s.* copec (moneda rusa).
copepod [kóupẹpad], *a.* y *s.* (zool.) copépodo.
Copernican [kopérnikạn], *a.* copernicano.
copestone [kóupstoun], *s.* (alb.) piedra de albardilla o caballete; (fig.) remate, última mano.
copier [kápịœ(r)], *s.* copiante, copista; copiador, plagiario.
copilot [kóupaịlọt], *s.* (aer.) segundo piloto.
coping [kóupiŋ], *s.* (alb.) albardilla; brocal, pozal.
copious [kóupịʌs], *a.* copioso, abundante, caudaloso, cuantioso, fecundo, fértil, profuso.
copiously [-lị], *adv.* copiosamente.
copiousness [-nịs], *s.* copia, copiosidad, abundancia, fertilidad, profusión.
coplanar [koupléịnặ(r)], *a.* (mat.) en un mismo plano.
copped [kapt], *a.* (ant.) copado, copetudo.
copper [kápœ(r)]. **I.** *s.* cobre; vasija de cobre; caldera; hierro de soldar, soldador con puntas de cobre; lámina de cobre; grabado en cobre; penique; (E. U.) centavo; (E. U., fam.) polizonte.—**c.-bottomed,** de fondo de cobre.— **c.-colored,** cobrizo, acobrado, acijado.—**c. glance,** (min.) calcocita.—**c. money,** calderilla.—**c. pyrites,** pirita de cobre, calcopirita. —**c. sulphate,** sulfato de cobre, cobre quemado; vitriolo azul. **II.** *a.* de cobre; cobrizo (en color). **III.** *va.* revestir de cobre.
copperas [-ạs], *s.* caparrosa, aceche, acije.
copperhead [-hed], *s.* culebra norteamericana muy venenosa; (E. U. pol.) apodo que se daba durante la guerra civil al habitante de los Estados del norte que simpatizaba con los confederados del sur.
copperish [-ịš], **coppery** [-ị], *a.* cobrizo, cobreño, encobrado.
copperplate [-plejt]. **I.** *s.* lámina de cobre para grabar; grabado en cobre (ll. t. **c. engraving**). **II.** *va.* grabar en cobre.
coppersmith [-smiθ], *s.* artífice en cobre, calderero.
coppice [kápịs], **coppice woods** [-wụdz], *s.* soto, tallar, maleza, bosquecillo, mato.
copra [káprạ], *s.* (com.) almendra del coco puesta a secar, copra.
coprolite [káprolajt], **coprolith** [-liθ], *s.* (pal. y pat.) coprolito.
coprophagous [kapráfạgʌs], *a.* coprófago.
coproprietor [kouproprájetọ(r)], *s.* copropietario.
copse [kaps], *s.* matorral, mata. *V.* COPPICE.
Copt [kápt], *s.* copto.
Coptic [-ịk]. **I.** *a.* copto, cóptico. **II.** *s.* copto.
copula [kápyʊlặ], *s.* (gram., lóg.) cópula; (anat.) ligamento.

copulate [-leit]. I. va. unir, juntar. II. vn. juntarse, copularse.

copulation [-léişǫn], s. cópula o coito; unión, ayuntamiento.

copulative [-lǎtiv]. I. a. (gram.) copulativo, conjuntivo. II. s. (gram.) palabra copulativa.

copulatory [-lǎtǫri], a. copulativo.

copy [kápi]. I. s. copia, traslado, trasunto; imitación, remedo; ejemplar (de una obra), número (de un periódico); muestra o modelo, plana; (impr.) original, material, manuscrito.—c. book, (com.) copiador (de cartas, cuentas, etc.); cuaderno de escritura. II. va. y vn. copiar, trasladar, transcribir; imitar, remedar, contrahacer.

copygraph [-græf], s. hectógrafo.

copyhold [-hould], s. (for.) especie de enfiteusis.

copyholder [-œ(r)], s. lector de pruebas (que lee al corrector); (imp.) divisorio, sujetacuartillas.

copying [-iŋ]. I. a. de copiar; para copias.—c. ink, tinta de copiar.—c. machine, ciclóstilo, hectógrafo; pantógrafo.—c. press, prensa de copiar. II. s. transcripción; imitación.

copyist [-ist], s. = COPIER.

copyright [-rait]. I. s. (derechos de) propiedad literaria; privilegio. II. va. sacar la propiedad literaria.—c. (by), es propiedad (de).—copyrighted, derechos registrados.

coquet [koket], vn. coquetear, hacer cocos o coqueterías, flirtear; jugar o entretenerse (con).

coquetry [kóuketri], s. coqueteo, coquetería.

coquette [koket], s. coqueta, carantoñera.

coquettish [-iş], a. coquetón, coquet(on)a.

coracle [kárakl], s. barquilla de cuero u hule.

coracoid [kárakoid], a. y s. (anat.) coracoides.

coral [kárạl]. I. s. coral. II. a. coralino, de coral.—c.-bearing, coralífero.—c. reef, arrecife y banco de coral.—c. snake, (Am., zool.) coral; coralillo.

coralline [-in]. I. a. coralino, de coral. II. s. coralina.

coralloid [-oid], a. coralino.

corban [kórbæn], s. (igl.) ofrenda, exvoto.

corbel [kórbęl]. I. s. (arq.) modillón, can, voladizo, repisa, saliente, f., retallo; zapata de sustentación bajo una viga. II. va. apoyar por medio de zapatas; disponer en forma de saliente o retallo; proveer de zapatas o de salientes. III. vn. sobresalir.

corbie [kórbi], s. (orn.) cuervo.—c. steps, corbiesteps, (arq.) retallos o salientes escalonados.

cord [kórd]. I. s. cordel, cuerda, cordón; soga; torzal; cordoncillo; (tej.) pana; (anat.) cuerda, cordón, tendón; (elec.) flexible; cuerda (medida de leña).—c. tire, (aut.) neumático de cordones. II. va. encordelar; acordonar, encordonar.

cordage [-idż], s. cordaje, cord(el)ería; (mar.) jarcias; cantidad de leña medida en cuerdas.

cordate [-eit], a. cordiforme.

corded [-id], a. encordelado; acordonado, encordonado, barrado, hecho de cuerdas.

corder [-œ(r)], s. encordonador.

cordial [kórdżạl]. I. s. cordial, licor. II. a. sincero, cordial; confortativo, vigorizante.

cordiality [-éliti], **cordialness** [-alnis], s. cordialidad, sinceridad.—**cordially** [-ạli], adv. cordialmente, sinceramente.

cordite [kórdait], s. cordita (explosivo).

cordon [kórdǫn], s. cordón; cíngulo; (mil.) cordón; (arq.) cordón.—**to form o throw a c. (a)round**, acordonar.

cordovan [kórdǫvạn], s. cordobán (cuero); (C.) a. y s. cordobés.

corduroy [kórdụroi], s. (tej.) pana.—c. road, camino con piso de troncos, estriberón.

cordwood [kórdwụd], s. leña apilada o vendida en cuerdas (v. CORD), o de apilar en cuerdas.

core [kor]. I. s. centro, corazón, alma; parte (f.) central; esencia, substancia; fondo, núcleo; (bot.) corazón (de manzana, etc.); (med.) foco (de absceso); (ing.) cilindro de roca sacado con un taladro anular; pared (f.) central (de una presa, etc.); interior, núcleo de un terraplén; (fund.) macho o ánima (de molde); (elec.) núcleo (de bobina, etc.); alma (de cable); (vet.) enfermedad de las ovejas causada por gusanos en el hígado.—c. bit, c. drill, taladro o barrena tubular.—c. transformer, (elec.) transformador de núcleo. II. va. quitar el corazón o centro (a menudo con out); despepitar (fruta); (fund.) formar con un macho.

cored [-d], a. (vet.) que tiene gusanos en el hígado (apl. a las ovejas); de núcleo, con núcleo; despepitado.

coregency [kourídżęnsi], s. corregencia.

coregent [-dżęnt], a. y s. corregente.

coreligionary [kourilidżǫnạri], **coreligionist** [-ist], s. correligionario.

coreopsis [korjápsis], s. (bot.) coreopsis, m.

corer [kórœ(r)], s. despepitador(a).

corespondent [kourispándęnt], s. (for.) cómplice del demandado en una demanda de divorcio.

coriaceous [korjéişias], a. coriáceo, correoso.

coriander [korjændœ(r)], s. (bot.) coriandro, cilantro, culantro.

Corinthian [korinθiạn]. I. a. y s. corintio, coríntico. II. a. (arq.) corintio; libidinoso, licencioso.

cork [kórk]. I. s. (bot.) corcho, corcha; tapón.—c. cutter o seller, taponero.—c. factory, industry o shop, taponería.—c. jacket, (chaleco) salvavidas de corcho.—c. oak, c. tree, (bot.) alcornoque. II. va. tapar con corcho; proveer de tapón; tiznar con corcho quemado.

corkage [-idż], s. acción de tapar con corcho; derechos de descorche, estipendio que se exige por descorchar una botella (en realidad, recargo de precio por botella).

corker [-œ(r)], s. tapador; (fam.) argumento irrefutable; cosa o persona extraordinaria.—**corking** [-iŋ], a. (fam.) magnífico, de primera.

corkscrew [-skru]. I. s. tirabuzón, sacacorchos. II. a. en forma de tirabuzón, en espiral.

corkwood [-wụd], s. (bot.) balso.

corky [kórki], a. de corcho, suberoso.

corm [kórm], s. (bot.) bulbo, cebolla.

cormorant [kórmorạnt], s. (orn.) cormorán, cuervo marino, corvejón; glotón o avaro.

corn [kórn], s. grano, cereal; (E. U.) maíz, m.; mies (no segada); callo (dureza en los pies).—c. brandy, aguardiente de cereales; whisky.—c. bread, pan de maíz, borona.—c. chandler (Ingl.) o dealer, triguero, revendedor de granos.—c. cockle, (bot.) neguilla (del trigo).—c. crake, (orn.) ave zancuda que habita los maizales.—c. cure, callicida.—c. cutter, máquina de cortar maíz; pedicuro, callista.—c. field, maizal.—c. flag, (bot.) estoque; ácoro palustre, falso o bastardo.—c. flour, harina de maíz u otro grano.—c. husk, perfolla del maíz.—c. land, tierra de pan llevar.—c. law, ley de granos.—c. marigold, (bot.) santimonia.—c. meal, harina de maíz.—c. mill, molino harinero.—c. on the cob, (Am.) mazorca tierna de maíz, elote.—c. plaster, emplasto para los callos.—c. protector, anillo adhesivo para los callos.—c. remedy o salve, callicida.—c. sheller, desgranadora de maíz.—c. shuck = c. HUSK.—c. silk, cabellos o barbas del maíz.—c. worm, gusano del maíz.

corn, va. curar, salar, acecinar; granular.

cornaceous [-éişiạs], a. (bot.) cornáceo, córneo.

corncob [-kab], s. tusa de maíz, carozo, zuro.

corncrib [-krib], s. granero para maíz, hórreo.

cornea [kórniạ], s. (anat.) córnea.

corned [kórnd], a. acecinado.—c. beef, cecina.—c. pork, puerco salado.

cornel [kórnel], s. (bot.) cornejo, sanguiñuelo, sangüeño.

cornelian [kornílyạn], s. (min.) cornalina, cornelina (= CARNELIAN).—c. cherry, c. tree, (bot.) = CORNEL.

corneous [kórnįʌs], *a.* córneo; calloso.
corner [kórnœ(r)]. I. *s.* esquina; esconce; rincón; cantón; encuentro; recodo, escondrijo; aprieto o apuro; (com.) acaparamiento, monopolio.—**c. bracket, cabinet, cupboard,** etc., cantonera, rinconera, consola angular, armario rinconero.—**c. plate,** cantonera, esquinal.—**to cut corners,** atajar, echar por el atajo; economizar.—**to drive into a c.,** poner entre la espada y la pared. II. *va.* arrinconar; acochinar (en el juego de damas); acorralar, poner en aprieto; copar; (com.) monopolizar, acaparar.
cornered [-d], *a.* anguloso, angulado, esquinado; copado; acorralado, en aprieto.
cornerstone [-stoųn], *s.* piedra angular o fundamental; primera piedra; recantón; mocheta.
cornerwise [-waįz], *adv.* diagonalmente.
cornet [kornét], *s.* (mil.) corneta; portaestandarte; (mús.) cornetín; cucurucho, cartucho.
cornet(t)ist [-įst], *s.* cornetín (el que lo toca).
cornflower [kórnflaųœ(r)], *s.* (bot) aciano, azulejo, botoncillo, liebrecilla.
cornice [kórnįs], *s.* (arq.) cornisa; sobrepuerta.
cornicle [kórnįkl], *s.* cuernecillo.
corniculate [kornįkįulįt], *a.* (bot.) corniculado.
Cornish [kórnįš]. I. *a.* de Cornualles. II. *s.* dialecto de Cornualles.
cornstalk [kórnstok], *s.* tallo del maíz.
cornstarch [kórnstarch], *s.* maicena, almidón de maíz, esp. el purificado para la mesa.
cornucopia [kornyųkóupįą], *s.* cornucopia, cuerno de la abundancia; alcartaz, *m.,* cucurucho.
cornute(d [kornįút(įd], *a.* córneo; calloso; (fam.) cursi.
corny [kórnį], *a.* córneo; calloso; (fam.) cursi.
corolla [korólą], *s.* (bot.) corola.
corollary [kárǫlerį], *s.* corolario.
corona [koróųną], *s.* (arq.) corona, alero; (astr.) corona, halo; (anat.) coronilla; (bot.) corona; (elec.) descarga luminosa en un conductor.—**C. Australis,** (astr.) Corona austral.—**C. Borealis,** Corona boreal.
coronal [káronąl]. I. *s.* (anat.) coronal; corona, guirnalda. II. [koróųnąl], *a.* coronal.
coronary [káronerį], *a.* (anat., etc.) coronario.
coronation [koronéįšǫn], *s.* coronación.
coroner [káronœ(r)], *s.* médico forense.—**c.'s inquest,** pesquisa dirigida por el médico forense.
coronet [káronet], *s.* corona de un título nobiliario; guirnalda, cintillo; (vet.) corona del casco.
coronium [koróųnįʌm], *s.* (quím., astr.) coronio.
corporal [kórporąl]. I. *s.* (mil.) cabo; (igl.) corporal (paño). II. *a.* corporal, corpóreo.—**corporality** [-ǽlįtį], *s.* corporalidad, corporeidad.—**corporally** [-ąlį], *adv.* corporalmente.
corporate [kórporįt], *a.* social; corporativo; colectivo; incorporado.—**c. name,** nombre de una corporación, compañía, etc.—**corporately** [-lį], *adv.* corporal o corporativamente; en corporación.
corporation [korporéįšǫn], *s.* corporación; sociedad mercantil (apl. a las muy grandes); cabildo; cuerpo, sociedad, gremio.
corporative [kórporeįtįv], *a.* corporativo.
corporeal [korpóųrįąl], *a.* corpóreo, material, tangible.—**corporeally** [-į], *adv.* materialmente, corporalmente.
corporeity [korporíįtį], *s.* corporeidad, materialidad.
corposant [kórpozænt], *s.* (mar.) fuego de Santelmo, Cástor y Pólux, helena.
corps [koųr], *s.* cuerpo, corps.—**c. de ballet,** cuerpo de baile.
corpse [korps], *s.* cadáver, cuerpo, difunto.
corpulence, corpulency [kórpįulęns, -į], *s.* corpulencia.—**corpulent** [-ęnt], *a.* corpulento.
corpus [kórpʌs], *s.* cuerpo; (anat.) lóbulo, tubérculo; (for.) bienes tangibles, corporales.—

C. Christi, (igl.) Corpus.—**c. delicti,** (for.) cuerpo del delito.—**c. juris,** (for.) cuerpo legal.
corpuscle [kórpʌsl], *s.* (fisiol.) corpúsculo, célula sanguínea; (fís., quím.) átomo; electrón.
corpuscular [korpʌ́skįulą(r)], *a.* corpuscular.
corral [korél]. I. *va.* acorralar. II. *s.* corral.
correct [korékt]. I. *va.* corregir, enmendar, rectificar; reformar; reprender, castigar; reparar, subsanar, remediar. II. *a.* correcto; exacto, justo; visto bueno (abrev. V⁰ B⁰); bueno, bien hecho; propio; culto (estilo, etc.).
correctable [-ąbl], *a.* corregible.
correction [korékšǫn], *s.* corrección, enmienda, rectificación; castigo, reforma; censura, pena.
correctional [-ąl]. I. *a.* correccional, penal. II. *s.* casa de corrección, reformatorio.
corrective [koréktįv]. I. *a.* correctivo, correccional, reformatorio. II. *s.* correctivo, castigo.
correctly [koréktlį], *adv.* correctamente; bien, apropiadamente.—**correctness** [-nįs], *s.* corrección; exactitud; validez.
corrector [koréktǫ(r)], *s.* corrector, corregidor, reformador, revisor, enmendador.
correlate [káręleįt]. I. *va.* correlacionar, poner en correlación. II. *vn.* tener correlación.—**correlate, correlative** [korélątįv], *a. y s.* correlativo.—**correlation** [koręléįšǫn], *s.* correlación.
correlatively [korélątįvlį], *adv.* correlativamente.
correlativeness [-nįs], *s.* correlación.
correspond [koręspánd], *vn.* corresponder, convenir, adaptarse; mantener correspondencia, escribirse.—**correspondence, correspondency** [-ęns, -į], *s.* correspondencia; relación; reciprocidad; (com.) correspondencia.—**correspondent** [-ęnt]. I. *a.* correspondiente; conforme, conveniente. II. *s.* correspondiente, corresponsal.—**correspondently** [-lį], *adv.* correspondientemente.
corresponding [-įŋ], *a.* correspondiente; corresponsal; similar; conforme, congruente.—**c. secretary,** secretario correspondiente.
correspondingly [-lį], *adv.* correspondientemente.
corridor [kárįdǫ(r)], *s.* corredor, galería, pasillo, pasadizo; (fort.) galería; (geol.) paso, vía de salida; tira de tierra de una nación que atraviesa el territorio de otra.
corrie [kórį], *s.* (geol.) = CIRQUE.
corrigible [kárįdžįbl], *a.* corregible.
corrival [korájvąl], *a. y s.* émulo, rival.
corroborant [koráborąnt], *a. y s.* corroborante; tónico.
corroborate [-eįt], *va.* corroborar, confirmar.—**corroboration** [-éįšǫn], *s.* corroboración, confirmación, fe, *f.*—**corroborative** [-ątįv], *a.* corroborativo, corroborante, confirmativo.—**corroboratively** [-lį], *adv.* corroborativamente.
corroborator [-eįtǫ(r)], *s.* corroborante.
corroboratory [-ątǫrį], *a.* = CORROBORATIVE.
corrode [koróųd], *va. y vn.* corroer(se).
corrodibility [-įbílįtį], **corrosibility** [korǫusįbįlįtį], *s.* calidad de corrosible.
corrodible, corrosible [koróųdįbl, -sįbl], *a.* corrosible.
corrosion [koróųžǫn], *s.* corrosión.
corrosive [koróųsįv], *a.* corrosivo, corroyente, mordicante; mordaz.—**c. sublimate,** sublimado corrosivo, solimán.—**corrosively** [-lį], *adv.* corrosivamente.—**corrosiveness** [-nįs], *s.* corrosividad, calidad de corrosivo o mordicante.
corrugate [kárugeįt], *va.* arrugar, acanalar; rizar, encarrujar.—**corrugate(d** [-įd], *a.* corrugado, arrugado, ondulado (apl. al hierro en lámina, etc.); acanalado, encarrujado.—**c. sheet-iron,** chapa ondulada.—**corrugation** [-éįšǫn], *s.* corrugación, arruga(miento).—**corrugator** [-ǫ(r)], *s.* lo que arruga, etc.; (anat.) corrugador.
corrupt [korʌ́pt]. I. *a.* corrompido, corrupto; contaminado, infecto, podrido, putrefacto, pútrido; (fig.) desmoralizado, depravado, sobornado, viciado. II. *va.* corromper; contaminar, depravar, infectar, podrir o pudrir; malear,

adulterar; sobornar, seducir, pervertir, viciar.
III. *vn.* corromperse, podrirse o pudrirse.—
corrupter [-œ(r)], *s.* corruptor, corrompedor,
seductor, pervertidor, sobornador.—**corruptibility** [-ibílitĵ], *s.* corruptibilidad.—**corruptible** [-ibl], *a.* corruptible.—**corruptibleness**
[-nis], *s.* corruptibilidad.—**corruptibly** [-ibli],
adv. corruptiblemente.—**corrupting** [-iŋ], *a.* corruptor, corrompedor, corrumpente.—**corruption** [korápṣon], *s.* corrupción, corruptela, descomposición, podredura; contagio, inmoralidad;
cohecho, soborno; depravación, maldad; perversión; pus, materia.—**corruptive** [korAptiv],
a. corruptivo.—**corruptless** [-lis], *a.* incorruptible, íntegro, recto.—**corruptly** [-li], *adv.*
corruptamente, corrompidamente.—**corruptness** [-nis], *s.* corrupción, putrefacción, infección; vicio.—**corruptress** [-ris], *s.* corruptora,
corrompedora.
corsage [korsáĵ], *s.* corpiño, cuerpo; ramillete
para la cintura, etc.
corsair [kórser], *s.* corsario, pirata, *m.*
corselet [kórslit], *s.* (arm.) coselete, peto; (ent.)
coselete; [kórsélet], faja o corsé ligero.
corset [kórsit], *s.* corsé; cotilla.—**c. cover**, cubrecorsé, corpiño, canesú, corpecico, justillo.—
c. factory o **shop**, corsetería.—**c. maker** o
seller, corsetero, corsetera.
Corsican [kórsikạn], *a.* y *s.* corso (de Córcega).
cortege [kortéĵ], *s.* comitiva, séquito.
cortex [kórteks], *s.* (bot.) corteza; (anat.) capa
externa de un órgano.
cortical [kórtikạl], *a.* cortical.
corticate(d [-kejt(id], *a.* cortezudo.
corticose [-koụs], *a.* parecido a una corteza.
corundum [korÁndAm], *s.* (min.) corindón.
coruscate [kórAskejt], *vn.* coruscar, fulgurar
coruscation [-éiṣon], *s.* coruscación, fulgor
corvette [korvét], *s.* (mar.) corbeta.
corvetto [korvétoụ], *s.* (equit.) corveta.
corvine [kórvain], *a.* corvino.
corymb [kórimb], *s.* (bot.) corimbo.
coryphæus [koriʃĺAs], *s.* corifeo.
coryphée [koriféi], *s.* primera bailarina.
coryza [koráizạ], *s.* (med.) coriza.
cosecant [kosíkạnt], *s.* (geom.) cosecante.
cosey [kóụzi], *a.* y *s.* = COZY.
cosher [kóụšœ(r)]. I. *va.* acariciar, mimar. II. *vn.*
(fam.) charlar, comadrear, chismear.
cosignatory [koụsignạtori], **cosigner** [koụsái-
nœ(r)], *s.* y *a.* cosignatario, cofirmante.
cosine [kóụsajn], *s.* (geom.) coseno.
cosmetic [kazmétik], *a.* y *s.* cosmético; *s.* afeite.
cosmic(al [kázmik(ạl], *a.* cósmico, vasto; armonioso, metódico, ordenado.
cosmism [kázmizm], *s.* teoría de la evolución
cosmogónica.
cosmogonal, cosmogonic(al [kazmágonạl, kaz-
mogánk(ạl], *a.* cosmogónico.
cosmogony [kazmágonj], *s.* cosmogonía.
cosmographer [kazmágrạfœ(r)], *s.* cosmógrafo.
cosmographical [kazmográfikạl], *a.* cosmográfico.
cosmographically [-i], *adv.* cosmográficamente.
cosmography [kazmágrafi], *s.* cosmografía.
cosmological [kazmolódžikạl], *a.* cosmológico.
cosmologist [kazmálodžist], *s.* cosmólogo.
cosmology [-dži], *s.* cosmología.
cosmopolitan [kazmopálitạn], **cosmopolite**
[kazmápolajt], *a.* y *s.* cosmopolita, *mf.*
cosmopolitanism [-izm], *s.* cosmopolitismo.
cosmorama [kazmorámạ], *s.* cosmorama, *m.*
cosmos [kázmas], *s.* cosmos, universo.
Cossack [kássæk], *a.* y *s.* cosaco.
cosset [kásit]. I. *s.* cordero criado sin la madre.
II. *va.* acariciar, mimar.
cost [kóst]. I. *s.* costa, coste, costo; precio, importe; gasto.—*pl.* (for.) costas, gastos.—**c.,
insurance and freight** (*c. i. f.*), costo, seguro
y flete (c. s. f.).—**c. of living**, coste de la vida.
—**c. price**, precio de coste.—**at all costs**,

cueste lo que cueste, a toda costa, a todo trance.
—**at c.**, a coste y costas.—**to my c.**, a mis
expensas; por mi daño. II. *vn.* (pret. y pp. COST)
costar.—**c. what it may**, cueste lo que cueste.
—**to c. dear**, costar caro, costar un ojo de la
cara. III. *va.* calcular el coste de.—**costing**
[-iŋ], *s.* cálculo de costes o gastos.
costal [kástạl], *a.* (anat.) costal.
costard [kástạrd], *s.* (bot.) variedad de manzana
inglesa; (fam.) cabeza, cholla.
costate [kástejt], *a.* con costillas.
coster(monger [kástœr(mAŋgœ(r)], *s.* vendedor
ambulante de frutas, legumbres, pescado, etc.
costive [kástiv], *a.* estreñido, estíptico.
costiveness [-nis], *s.* constipación o estreñimiento
de vientre.
costless [kóstlis], *a.* de balde, gratis.
costliness [kóstlinis], *s.* calidad de costoso; suntuosidad.
costly [kóstli], *a.* costoso, caro; suntuoso.
costmary [kástmeri], *s.* (bot.) atanasia.
costume [kástium]. I. *s.* traje, ropa, vestido; disfraz, *m.;* traje de época.—*pl.* indumentaria,
(teat.) vestuario.—**c. ball**, baile de trajes.
II. *va.* proveer de traje, disfraz, etc.
costumer [-œ(r)], *s.* sastre de teatro; el que hace,
vende o alquila trajes para bailes, etc.
costus(root [kástAs(rut], *s.* (bot.) costo.
cosy [kóụzi], *a.* y *s.* = COZY.
cot [kat], *s.* cabaña, choza; catre, camilla; dedal.
cotangent [koụtándžent], *s.* (geom.) cotangente.
cote [koụt], *s.* corral, aprisco.
cotemporaneous, cotemporary, *V.* CONTEM-
PORANEOUS, etc.
cotenancy [koụténạnsi], *s.* coinquilinato.
cotenant [-ạnt], *s.* coinquilino.
coterie [kóụteri], *s.* camarilla, círculo, tertulia.
coterminous [koụtœrminAs], *a.* = CONTERMI-
NOUS.
cothurnus [koθœrnAs], *s.* coturno.
cotill(i)on [kotílyon], *s.* (danz.) cotillón.
cotquean [kátkwin], *s.* cominero, cazolero.
cotrustee [koụtrAstí], *s.* fideicomisario o curador
en unión de otro.
cotta [kátạ], *s.* (igl.) sobrepelliz.
cottage [kátidž], *s.* casita, cabaña, choza, casucha; casa de campo, quinta.—**c. cheese**,
requesón; queso de bola.
cottager [-œ(r)], **cotter** [kátœ(r)], *s.* el que vive
en una cabaña, casa de campo, etc.
cotter [kátœ(r)], *s.* (mec.) chaveta, llave, *f.*,
pasador.—**c. pin**, chaveta.
cotton [kátọn]. I. *s.* algodón (planta y fibra); tela
de algodón; hilo de algodón; lanilla o pelillo
vegetal algodonoso.—*pl.* géneros de algodón;
ropa de algodón. II. *a.* de(l), para o rel. al algodón; algodonero.—**c. bagging**, lienzo de algodón para sacos, y los sacos mismos.—**c.
batting**, algodón en hojas o en rama.—**c. belt**,
(E. U.) región algodonera.—**c. boll** = BOLL
WEEVIL.—**c. cake**, torta de harina de semillas
de algodón.—**c. dealer**, algodonero.—**c. factory**, algodonería.—**c. flannel**, (tej.) moletón,
franela de algodón.—**c. gin**, despepitadora o
(Am.) desmotadora de algodón.—**c. moth**,
mariposa del gusano del algodón.—**c. opener**,
abridora, máquina para abrir y limpiar el algodón al desbalarlo.—**c. plant**, algodonero.—
c. plantation, algodonal.—**c. powder**, pólvora que contiene algodón pólvora.—**c. press**,
prensa o instalación de embalar algodón.—**c.
print**, (tej.) cotón, estampado.—**c. thistle**,
(bot.) toba, acantio, cardo borriquero.—**c.
tree**, viburno; ceiba y otros árboles bombáceos
análogos; álamo.—**c. waste**, desperdicios de
hilaza de algodón.—**c. weevil** = BOLL WEEVIL.
—**c. wool**, algodón en rama; (Ingl.) algodón
hidrófilo o absorbente.—**c. worm**, gusano de
las hojas (no de la cápsula) del algodón.
cotton. II. *vn.* convenir, avenirse; (fam.) pren-

darse de, coger cariño a uno. II. *va.* envolver o rellenar con algodón; mimar.

cottonlike [-laik], **cottony** [-i], *a.* algodonoso.

cottonmouth [-mauθ], *s.* (zool.) mocasín (serpiente).

cottonseed [-sid], *s.* semilla del algodón.—**c. meal,** harina de orujo o borujo de algodón.—**c. oil,** aceite de semillas de algodón.

cottontail [-teil], *s.* (E. U., zool.) conejo común.

cottonwood [-wud], *s.* (bot.) álamo americano.

cotyledon [katjlídọn], *s.* (bot.) cotiledón.

cotyledonous [-as], *a.* cotiledóneo.

couch [káuch]. **I.** *va.* acostar; poner en capas o tongadas; depositar; indicar, expresar; enristrar, poner (la lanza) en ristre; (cir.) batir las cataratas o nubes de los ojos. **II.** *vn.* acostarse, recostarse, tenderse, echarse; agacharse; agobiarse, doblarse. **III.** *s.* canapé, cama, lecho, reclinatorio, sofá, yacija; cubil, guarida (de fieras); tonga, tongada, capa.—**c. fellow,** compañero de cama.—**c. grass,** (bot.) grama.

couchant [-ạnt], *a.* (blas.) acostado.

coucher [-œ(r)], *s.* cartulario.

cougar [kúgä(r)], *s.* (zool.) cuguar(do), puma, *m.*

cough [kɔf]. **I.** *s.* tos, *f.,* pechuguera.—**c. drop,** pastilla para la tos. **II.** *vn.* toser. **III.** *va.* (con **up**) esputar; arrojar del pecho tosiendo; (fam.) pagar, entregar.—**to c. down,** hacer callar (a un orador) a fuerza de toses.

coughing [-iŋ], *s.* (acceso de) tos, *f.,* tosidura.

could [kud], *pret.* de CAN.

coulee [kúli], *s.* quebrada, cañada; río de lava.

coulisse [kulís], *s.* ranura de corredera; (teat.) bastidor.

couloir [kulwár], *s.* garganta, barranca; pasadizo, corredor; draga de cangilones.

coulomb [kulám], *s.* (elec.) culombio.

coulter [kóultœ(r)], *s.* = COLTER.

coumaric [kumárik], *a.* (quím.) cumárico.—**coumarin** [kúmạrin], *s.* (quím.) cumarina.

coumarou [kúmạru], *s.* (bot.) cumarú (árbol y semillas).

council [káunsil], *s.* concilio; consejo; concejo; cabildo, ayuntamiento, junta.—**c. board** o **table,** sesión del consejo; mesa del consejo.— **c. of war,** consejo de guerra.

councilman [-mạn], *s.* concejal, regidor.

council(l)or [-ọ(r)], *s.* concejal; consejero.

counsel [káunsẹl]. **I.** *s.* consejo; deliberación, determinación; secreto, sigilo; trama, plan, designio; abogado consultor, asesor.—**c. for the defense,** defensor.—**c. for the prosecution,** acusador; fiscal.—**to keep one's c.,** ser reservado, no decir nada.—**to take c.,** deliberar, aconsejarse. **II.** *va.* aconsejar, dirigir, guiar, asesorar.

counsel(l)or [-ọ(r)], *s.* consultor, consejero, consiliario; confidente; abogado, causídico; asesor. —**c. at law,** abogado.

counsellorship [-ṣip], *s.* cargo o dignidad de consejero, etc.

count [káunt]. **I.** *va.* contar, numerar; considerar, reputar; imputar, atribuir; escrutar (votos).— **to c. noses,** contar cabezas (personas).—**to c. out,** no contar (votos, etc.); declarar vencido (a un pugilista que no se levanta tras contar diez segundos). **II.** *vn.* contar; valer.—**to c. on** o **upon,** contar con, confiar en. **III.** *s.* cuenta, cuento, cómputo, cálculo; partida, cláusula; valor, cuantía; atención, cuidado; conde (título); (for.) demanda, cargo, capítulo; (tej.) número o tamaño (del hilo).—**c. palatine,** conde palatino.

countable [-ạbl], *a.* contadero, contable.

countenance [káuntẹnạns]. **I.** *s.* semblante, cara, talante, aspecto; continente, talante; protección, apoyo.—**out of c.,** desconcertado, turbado, corrido.—**to give c.,** apoyar, favorecer, proteger, auxiliar. **II.** *va.* sostener, apoyar, fomentar, aprobar.

counter [káuntœ(r)]. **I.** *s.* calculista; contador;

mostrador, tablero (de tienda, etc.); ficha, tanto; (mar.) bovedilla; lo opuesto, lo contrario (zap.) contrafuerte, calcañar; pecho del caballo; (mús.) contrapunto; (esgr.) contra. **II.** *adv* contra, al contrario.—**c. electromotive force,** fuerza contraelectromotriz.—**to run c.,** oponerse a, violar. **III.** *a.* contrario, opuesto.— **IV.** *va.* combatir; contradecir. **V.** *vn.* contraatacar; oponerse.

counteract [-ǽkt], *va.* contrariar, impedir; neutralizar, contrarrestar.

counteraction [-ǽkṣọn], *s.* oposición; impedimento.

counteractive [-ǽktiv]. **I.** *a.* contrario, opuesto. **II.** *s.* opositor.

counterapproach [-ạprouch], *s.* (fort.) contraaproches o contraataques (*pl.*), contratrinchera.

counterattack [-ạtǽk]. **I.** *s.* contraataque, ataque de reacción. **II.** *va.* y *vn.* contraatacar, hacer un contraataque.

counterattraction [-ạtrǽkṣọn], *s.* atracción contraria.

counterbalance [-bǽlạns]. **I.** *va.* contrabalancear, contrapesar, equilibrar; compensar. **II.** [-bǽlạns], *s.* contrapeso, equilibrio, compensación.

counterbore [-bóᵤr]. **I.** *s.* ensanche de la boca (de un tubo, agujero, etc.); barreno de ensanchar. **II.** *va.* ensanchar la boca de.

counterbrace [-breiṣ]. **I.** *va.* (mar.) contrabracear. **II.** *s.* contrabraza, contraamantillo.

counterchange [-chéjndž], *va.* trocar, cambiar.

countercharge [-chardž]. **I.** *s.* recriminación; (mil.) contraataque. **II.** *va.* (for.) reconvenir; (mil.) contraatacar.

countercheck [-chék]. **I.** *va.* contrastar, contrarrestar. **II.** *s.* oposición, repulsa, rechazo.

counterclaim [-kleim], *s.* contrarreclamación.

counterclockwise [-klákwajz], *a.* y *adv.* contrario, o en sentido contrario, al de las agujas del reloj; a la izquierda.

countercurrent [-kœrẹnt], *s.* contracorriente, *f.*

counterdie [-dai], *s.* contramatriz, punzón.

counterespionage [-éspiọnidž], *s.* contraespionaje.

counterevidence [-évidẹns], *s.* contraprueba.

counterfeit [-fit]. **I.** *va.* falsear, falsificar, forjar, contrahacer, imitar fraudulentamente. **II.** *vn.* fingir, disimular. **III.** *s.* impostura, contrahechura, falsificación; copia, imitación; moneda falsa. **IV.** *a.* falsificado, espurio, contrahecho.

counterfeiter [-œ(r)], *s.* falsario, falsificador; falseador, imitador; monedero falso.

counterfort [-fort], *s.* contrafuerte, estribo.

counterguard [-gard], *s.* (fort.) contraguardia.

counterinformation [-informéiṣọn], *s.* contraaviso.

counterirritant [-iritạnt]. *s.* (med.) contrairritante, revulsivo.

counterlight [-lait], *s.* contraluz.

countermand [-mǽnd]. **I.** *va.* contramandar, desmandar; revocar, invalidar, cancelar. **II.** *s.* contramandato, contraorden, *f.*

countermarch [-march]. **I.** *s.* contramarcha. **II.** *vn.* contramarchar.

countermark [-mark]. **I.** *s.* contramarca, contraseña. **II.** *va.* contramarcar, resellar.

countermine [-main]. **I.** *s.* contramina. **II.** *va.* contraminar; contravenir.

countermotion [-mouṣọn], *s.* movimiento contrario; proposición contraria.

countermove [-múv]. **I.** *va.* y *vn.* mover(se) en dirección contraria; usar de represalias. **II.** *s.* movimiento en dirección contraria; represalia.

counteroffensive [-ọfénsiv], *s.* (mil.) contraofensiva.

counteropening [-oᵤpẹniŋ], *s.* (cir.) contraabertura.

counterpane [-pein], *s.* colcha de cama, cubrecama; cobertor.

counterpart [-part], *s.* contraparte, *f.;* duplicado; equivalencia; copia, imagen, *f.*

counterplea [-pli], s. (for.) reconvención.
counterplot [-plat]. I. s. contratreta. II. va. contraminar.
counterpoint [-pǫint], s. (mús.) contrapunto.
counterpoise [-pǫjz]. I. va. equilibrar, contrapesar, contrabalancear. II. s. contrapeso; compensación, equilibrio; pilón de una romana.
counterpoison [-pǫjzǫn], s. contraveneno; antídoto.
counterpressure [-presūr], s. contrapresión.
counterproject [-prájᴇkt], s. contraproyecto.
counterproof [-pruf], s. contraprueba.
counterproposition [-prapozíŝǫn], s. contraproposición.
counterpunch [-pʌnch], s. contrapunzón.
counterreformation [-rᴇformȩ́jŝǫn], s. contrarreforma.
counterrevolution [-rᴇvolj̇úŝǫn], s. contrarrevolución.
counterscarp [-skarp], s. (fort.) contraescarpa.
counterseal [-síl]. I. va. contrasellar. II. s. contrasello.
countersense [-sᴇns], s. contrasentido, sentido opuesto.
countershaft [-ŝæft], s. contraeje, eje intermedio; (aut.) eje secundario del cambio de marcha.
countersign [-sajn]. I. va. visar, refrendar. II. s. (mil.) santo y seña, contraseña.
countersignature [-sígnachur], s. refrendata.
countersink [-sịŋk]. I. va. abocardar, avellanar. II. s. avellanador, punzón, granete, fresa.
counterstain [-stejn], s. contracoloración.
counterstroke [-strǫuk], s. contragolpe, revés; (m. v.) golpe o carrera de retroceso.
countersunk [-sʌŋk], pp. de COUNTERSINK.—**c. rivet**, remache fresado o de cabeza embutida.
—**c. screw**, tornillo avellanado.
countertenor [-tᴇnǫr], s. (mús.) contralto.
countertide [-tajd], s. (mar.) contramarea.
countertrench [-trench], s. (mil.) contratrinchera.
countervail [-vȩ́jl]. I. va. contrapesar, compensar. II. s. V. COUNTERBALANCE.
counterweight [-wejt], s. contrapeso, pesa.
counterwork [-wǫ́rk], va. contrarrestar, contrariar; contraminar.
countess [káuntịs], s. condesa.
countinghouse [káuntịŋhaus], s. despacho, escritorio, oficina.
countless [káuntlịs], a. innumerable, sin cuento.
countrified [kʌ́ntrịfajd], a. rústico, campesino, campestre, agreste.
country [kʌ́ntrị]. I. s. país, nación; región, tierra; patria; campo, campiña. II. a. rústico, rural, campesino; rudo o agreste; campestre, de campo.—**c. club**, club campestre.—**c. dance**, baile campestre, charrada; (Am.) changüí, guateque.—**c. gentleman**, propietario rico que vive en sus tierras.—**c. house**, casa de campo, quinta, villa.—**c. road**, camino vecinal.—**c. rock**, (min.) roca madre.—**c. squire**, caballero de provincia.
countryfolk [-foŭk], s. campesinos, labradores, gente (f.) del campo.
countryman [-man], s. paisano, compatriota, conciudadano, conterráneo; campesino, labrador, labriego, paisano, aldeano, patán, paleto.
countryseat [-sit], s. casa de campo, quinta(na), villa.
countryside [-sajd], s. campo; distrito rural.
countrywoman [-wụman], s. paisana, compatriota; aldeana, campesina, labriega.
countship [káuntŝịp], s. condado.
county [káuntị], s. condado, distrito territorial, jurisdicción.—**c. clerk**, secretario del condado.—**c. palatine**, palatinado.—**c. seat**, capital de condado, cabecera o cabeza de distrito.
coup [ku], s. estratagema, golpe maestro.—**c. de grâce**, golpe de gracia.—**c. d'état**, golpe de Estado.—**c. de main**, ataque o movimiento repentino e imprevisto.—**c. d'oeil**, mirada.

coupé [kupéj], s. cupé, berlina.
couple [kʌpl]. I. s. par, pareja; yunta (de bueyes, etc.); (mec.) par (de fuerzas, motor).—**married c.**, matrimonio, marido y mujer. II. va. acoplar, (a)parear, conectar, embragar, empalmar, ensamblar, enganchar; unir, juntar, casar. III. vn. juntarse, unirse formando un par; tener cópula o coito.
coupler [kʌ́plœ(r)], s. aparato de conexión o de acoplamiento; manguito; enganche.
couplet [kʌ́plịt], s. par, pareja; copla; cuplé; pareado, dístico, dos versos pareados.
coupling [kʌ́plịŋ], s. acoplamiento; pareo; junta o unión; conjunción, cópula; enlazamiento, embrague, empalmadura, ensamblaje, enganche.
—**c. pin**, (f. c.) pasador del enganche.
coupon [kúpan], s. cupón, talón.—**c. ticket**, billete talonario.
courage [kᴇ́rịdž], s. coraje, valor, denuedo, ánimo.
courageous [kᴇréjdžʌs], a. animoso, valiente, valeroso.—**courageously** [-lị], adv. valerosamente.—**courageousness** [-nịs], s. valor, intrepidez, brío.
courbaril [kúrbarịl], s. (bot.) curbaril.
courier [kúrjœ(r)], s. correo, estafeta, expreso, ordinario.
course [kors]. I. s. marcha; recorrido; vía, ruta, rumbo, dirección; serie; asignatura, curso (de estudios); curso, marcha (de los sucesos); transcurso (de tiempo); camino, proceder, conducta; método, sistema, m.; plato (cada uno de los que forman una comida); (dep.) carrera, corrida; estadio; cancha de golf; carga, encuentro (en un torneo, etc.); (mar.) deriva, derrota, derrotero, rumbo; (top.) línea (determinada por rumbo y distancia); (arq., alb.) capa, mampuesta, hilada; (min., geol.) buzamiento, dirección de un afloramiento según la horizontal transversal del filón; (min.) galería; (mar.) papahigo.—pl. menstruación, regla.—**in due c.**, a su tiempo, oportunamente.—**in the c. of time**, andando el tiempo.—**matter of c.**, cosa común y corriente, cosa de cajón.—**of c.**, por supuesto, naturalmente, desde luego, claro, por de contado.—**the last c.**, los postres. II. va. correr por, o sobre; hacer correr; cazar, dar caza, perseguir. III. vn. dirigirse o encaminarse; correr; dedicarse a la caza con perros.
courser [kórsœ(r)], s. (poét.) corcel; cazador de liebres, etc.; (orn.) especie de avefría, ave zancuda y corredora.
coursing [kórsịŋ], s. caza de liebres; (min.) ventilación.
court [kort]. I. s. (for.) tribunal, juzgado, (Am.) corte, f.; audiencia; sala de justicia; juez; corte; palacio; comitiva, séquito, cortejo; patio, atrio; frontón; cancha, campo o pista (de tenis); mansión suntuosa; callejuela; plazoleta; cortejo, galanteo.—**c. card**, figura (en la baraja).—**c. day**, día (m.) de reunión del tribunal; (día de) besamanos.—**c. dress**, traje de corte.—**c. guide**, guía oficial, guía de forasteros.—**c. lands**, tierras señoriales.—**c.-martial**, s. consejo de guerra, tribunal militar; va. seguir o someter a consejo de guerra.—**c. of appeal(s)**, audiencia; tribunal de apelaciones.—**c. of first instance**, tribunal de primera instancia.—**c. of last appeal**, tribunal supremo.—**c. of record**, tribunal de registro o de actas perpetuas.—**c. officer**, alguacil, ministril.—**c. plaster**, esparadrapo, tafetán inglés.—**to pay c. to**, hacer la corte a; cortejar, galantear.—**to put out of c.**, demostrar la falsedad de, invalidar. II. va. enamorar, galantear; hacer la corte; solicitar, pretender, buscar; inducir, incitar.
courteous [kértjas], a. cortés, atento, comedido.
courteously [-lị], adv. cortésmente.
courteousness [-nịs], s. cortes(an)ía, comedimiento.
courtesan [kóurtȩzạn], s. dama cortesana; mujer pública, prostituta.

---

courtesy [kə́ertε̞si]. **I.** *s.* cortesía, atención, obsequio, urbanidad, finura; gracia, favor, merced; consentimiento, beneplácito; cortesía, reverencia. **II.** *vn.* hacer una cortesía o reverencia. *V.* CURTSY.

courtezan, *s.* = COURTESAN.

courthand [kɔ́rthænd], *s.* letra gótica o de curia.

courthouse [-hau̯s], *s.* audiencia; palacio de justicia, tribunal.

courtier [-jœ(r)], *s.* cortesano o palaciego; cortejante, galán, obsequiante.

courtlike [-lai̯k], *a.* cortesano.

courtliness [-linis], *s.* cortesanía, cortesía, urbanidad; elegancia.

courtly [-li]. **I.** *a.* cortesano, elegante, galante, cortés. **II.** *adv.* cortésmente.

courtroom [-rum], *s.* sala de tribunal.—*pl.* estrados.

courtship [-ʃip], *s.* corte, *f.,* cortejo; galanteo; noviazgo, enamoramiento.

courtyard [-yard], *s.* patio, atrio.

cousin [kázịn], *s.* primo o prima.—**c. german,** primo hermano o carnal.—**cousinhood** [-hud], **cousinship** [-ʃip], *s.* primazgo.

cove [kouv]. **I.** *s.* abra, ancón, caleta, ensenada; (arq.) bovedilla. **II.** *va.* abovedar, arquear.

covenant [kávənənt]. **I.** *s.* contrato, ajuste, convenio, pacto; escritura de contrato; (bib.) alianza; testamento.—**C. of the League of Nations,** pacto fundamental de la Sociedad de las Naciones.—**the New C.,** el Nuevo Testamento. **II.** *va.* prometer, empeñar. **III.** *vn.* convenir, pactar, estipular.

covenantee [-í], *s.* (for.) contratante, pactante.

covenanter [-œ(r)], *s.* contratante, pactante; (C.) firmante del pacto escocés de la reforma religiosa.

covenantor [-ǫ(r)], *s.* el que debe cumplir lo estipulado en un pacto.

cover [kávœ(r)]. **I.** *va.* cubrir; tapar, ocultar; cobijar, abrigar, proteger; recubrir, revestir; forrar (un libro, paraguas, etc.); abarcar, abrazar; describir o investigar (apl. al trabajo de repórters); resarcir, compensar, indemnizar; recorrer, andar (distancias, etc.); cubrir (el macho a la hembra); empollar (huevos); cubrirse, ponerse el sombrero; (gen. con **up**) paliar, disimular, encubrir (delitos, etc.); copar (en el juego); (com.) cubrir, remesar fondos; (arti.) apuntar a, dominar, cubrir. **II.** *s.* cubierta, tapa, tapadera, cobertera, envoltura; sobre, sobrecarta; capa, pretexto, velo; abrigo, techado, albergue; cubierto (tenedor, cuchillo y cuchara); funda; forro; tapete, cobertor; (caz.) huidero, guarida; (bot., zool.) opérculo.—**c. charge,** (precio de) cubierto (apl. a restaurantes, etc.).—**c. crop,** (agr.) siembra de abono o de protección.—**c. glass,** tapa de vidrio (de la platina de un microscopio).—**to take c.,** buscar abrigo.—**under c.,** bajo techado, al abrigo; oculto, cubierto; secretamente; bajo sobre o cubierta (apl. a cartas, etc.).

coverage [-idź], *s.* (com.) amplitud o extensión del seguro abarcado por una póliza; fondos de reserva para hacer frente a obligaciones; reportaje periodístico o por radio de un suceso de cierta importancia.

covered [-d], *a.* cubierto, tapado; cubierto, tocado, con el sombrero puesto; (com.) asegurado, respaldado.—**c. wagon,** carromato, carro con toldo; (Ingl., f. c.) vagón cerrado.—**c. way,** (fort.) camino cubierto, estrada encubierta.—**c. wire,** alambre aislado.

covering [-iŋ]. **I.** *s.* ropa, abrigo; funda, cubierta, cobija, cobertura, envoltura; tegumento; cubrimiento; arropamiento. **II.** *a.* cubriente, cobijador, ocultador.

coverlet, coverlid [-lit, -lid], *s.* cobertura, colcha, sobrecama, cubrecama, cobertor, vánova.

coversed sine [kóuvœrst sai̯n], *s.* (geom.) cosenoverso.

covert [kávœrt]. **I.** *s.* cubierto o cubierta; refugio, asilo; guarida, huidero. **II.** *a.* cubierto, tapado; secreto, escondido; (for.) que está bajo la autoridad o protección del marido (apl. a la mujer casada).—**c. cloth,** (tej.) cierta tela asargada.—**c. coat,** gabán ligero.—**c. way** = COVERED WAY.

covertly [-li], *adv.* secretamente, en secreto.

coverture [kávœrchụr], *s.* cubierto; escondrijo, escondite; ocultación; (for.) estado o condición de una mujer casada.

covet [kávịt]. **I.** *va.* codiciar, apetecer, ambicionar; anhelar o aspirar con ansia. **II.** *vn.* ser codicioso, suspirar por.

covetable [-əbl], *a.* codiciable.—**covetous** [-ʌs], *a.* codicioso, ambicioso, sórdido.—**covetously** [-li], *adv.* codiciosamente, avariciosamente.—**covetousness** [-nis], *s.* codicia, avaricia; ambición, avidez, sordidez.

covey [kávị], *s.* banda(da), nidada, pollada.

cow [kau̯]. **I.** *va.* acobardar, intimidar. **II.** *s.* vaca; hembra de otros cuadrúpedos grandes.—**c. bell,** cencerro, esquila.—**c. dung,** boñiga.—**c. hand** = COWBOY.—**c. house,** boyera; establo para ganado; lechería.

coward [káu̯ạrd], *a.* y *s.* cobarde.—**cowardice** [-ịs], **cowardliness** [-linịs], *s.* cobardía.—**cowardly** [-li]. **I.** *a.* cobarde. **II.** *adv.* cobardemente.

cowbane [káu̯bei̯n], *s.* (bot.) cicuta.

cowboy [-bɔi̯], *s.* vaquero, gaucho (jinete ganadero), (Am.) tropero, hatero.

cowcatcher [-kæchœ(r)], *s.* (f. c.) trompa, rastrillo, quitapiedras, barredor (de locomotora).

cower [káu̯œ(r)], *vn.* agacharse, alebrarse.

cowherd [káu̯hœrd], *s.* vaquero, boyero, pastor de ganado vacuno.

cowhide [-hai̯d]. **I.** *s.* cuero, vaqueta; penca, zurriaga, corbacho. **II.** *va.* azotar, zurriagar.—**cowhiding** [-iŋ], *s.* zurribanda, pencazo.

cowl [kau̯l], *s.* cogulla, capucha, capilla, capuz, *m.;* cubierta; sombrerete de chimenea; (aut.) bóveda del tablero; (aer.) cubierta o caja del motor.

cowled [-d], *a.* encapuchado, encapuzado.

cowlick [káu̯lịk], *s.* mechón de pelo, remolino.

cowlike [-lai̯k], *a.* avacado.

cowling [káu̯liŋ], *s.* (aer.) cubierta o tapa. *V.* COWL.

cowman [káu̯mạn], *s.* ganadero, hacendado.

coworker [kou̯wœ́rkœ(r)], *s.* coadjutor, colaborador.

cowpea [káu̯pi], *s.* (bot.) especie de garbanzo.

cowpox [-paks], *s.* (med.) vacuna.

cowpuncher [-pʌnchœ(r)], *s.* (E. U., fam.) = COWBOY.

cowrie o **cowry** [káu̯rị], *s.* (zool.) ciprea o porcelana (molusco).

cowshed [-ʃed], *s.* establo de vacas, boyera.

cowslip [-slịp], *s.* (bot.) vellorita, hierba centella; (Ingl.) primavera o prímula.

coxa [káksạ], *s.* (anat.) cadera; hueso innominado.—**coxal** [-l], *a.* coxal, de la cadera.—**coxalgia** [kaksáldźịạ], *s.* (med.) coxalgia.—**coxalgic** [-dźịk], *a.* coxálgico.

coxcomb [kákskou̯m], *s.* mequetrefe, petimetre, narciso, lindo, sietemesino; fantasmón, farolón, fachendista; (bot.) = COCKSCOMB.—**coxcombical** [kakskámịkạl], *a.* fachendoso, fatuo.—**coxcombry** [kákskou̯mrị], *s.* fachenda, fatuidad.

coxswain [káksn o kákswei̯n], *s.* (mar.) patrón, nostramo, batelero, timonel (II. t. fam. **cox**).

coy, coyish [kɔ́i, -iʃ], *a.* recatado, modesto; tímido, esquivo.

coyly [-li], *adv.* con esquivez.—**coyness** [-nịs], *s.* timidez, esquivez; recato, modestia.

coyote [kai̯óu̯tị], *s.* (zool.) coyote.

coypu [kɔ́i̯pu], *s.* (zool.) coipo, coipú.

coz [kaz], *s.* (fam.) primo, prima.

cozen [kázẹn], *va.* engañar.—**cozenage** [-idź], *s.*

engaño, trampa, superchería.—**cozener** [-œ(r)], *s.* engañador, embaucador.

ozily [kóuzįlį], *adv.* cómoda, agradablemente.

oziness [-nįs], *s.* comodidad, intimidad.

ozy, cozey [kóuzį]. **I.** *a.* cómodo, agradable, íntimo, abrigado. **II.** *s.* abrigo de la cafetera, tetera, etc.

rab [krǽb]. **I.** *a.* agrio, áspero. **II.** *s.* (zool.) cámbaro, cangrejo de mar, (Am.) jaiba; (mec.) molinete, malacate, torno, cabrestante; (C., astr.) Cáncer; gruñón, persona malhumorada. —**c. apple,** (bot.) manzana silvestre.—**c. louse,** (ent.) ladilla. **III.** *vn.* pescar cangrejos, etc.; (fam.) regañar, estar de mal humor.

rabbed [-įd], *a.* avinagrado, áspero, ceñudo, bronco, hosco; enmarañado, escabroso, desigual.

rabby [-į], *a.* malhumorado, de mal genio.

rack [krǽk]. **I.** *s.* hendedura, grieta, raja (dura), cuarteadura, rendija, resquebradura; (alb.) llaga; crujido, chasquido, estallido; traque, trique, tris, *m.;* mentecatez, chifladura; mudanza de la voz.—**c. of doom,** juicio final. **II.** *a.* (fam.) de calidad superior, de primer orden, granado. —**c.-brained,** *a.* alelado, chiflado, mentecato. —**c. shot,** tirador certero. **III.** *va.* hender, rajar, (res)quebrajar; partir, romper, destruir; hacer chasquear, restallar o crujir; trastornar, enloquecer; decir o contar con gracejo.—**to c. a bottle,** despachar una botella.—**to c. a joke,** decir un chiste.—**to c. jokes,** gastar bromas.— **to c. up,** (fam.) elogiar, bombear o dar bombo a; echar a pique (un avión), hacer pedazos (un auto). **IV.** *vn.* reventar, abrirse, (a)grietarse; cuartearse, partirse, rajarse, resquebra(ja)rse; crujir, estallar, traque(te)ar.—**to c. down on,** (fam.) tratar con dureza, apretar los tornillos a. —**to c. up,** (fam.) estrellarse (un auto o avión).

rackajack, crackerjack [-ǎdʒæk]. **I.** *s.* (fam.) persona o cosa de marca mayor. **II.** *a.* muy superior, de primera, de más de marca.

rackbrain [-brein], *s.* (fam.) loco; destornillado.

racked [-t], *a.* (a)grietado, cuarteado; (fam.) destornillado, chiflado; (voz) desapacible.

racker [-œ(r)], *s.* especie de galleta o bizcocho; triquitraque (*V.* FIRECRACKER).—**c. bonbon,** bombón sorpresa.

cracking [-įŋ], *s.* agrietamiento; cracking, destilación fraccionada o de separación empleada en la transformación de los aceites pesados del petróleo en esencias.

crackle [krǽkl]. **I.** *va.* hacer crujir. **II.** *vn.* crujir, crepitar, chasquear, chascar, chillar, restallar. **III.** *s.* crujido, crepitación; superficie finamente estriada o rayada.—**c. ware,** artículos (de porcelana, vidrio, etc.) de superficie estriada o rayada.

crackling [krǽkliŋ]. **I.** *s.* crepitación, crujido; estall(id)o; chicharrón. **II.** *a.* crepitante.

cracknel [krǽknęl], *s.* galleta o bizcocho seco, (prov.) coscarana.—*pl.* chicharrones.

crackpot [krǽkpat]. **I.** *s.* (fam.) loco inofensivo; pobre diablo. **II.** *a.* extravagante, excéntrico.

cracksman [krǽksmąn], *s.* (fam.) ladrón.

crackup [krǽkΛp], *va., vn.; y s. V.* CRASH.

cracky [krǽkį], *a.* rajado; susceptible de rajarse.

cradle [kréidl]. **I.** *s.* cuna, brizo; infancia, niñez; origen; (cir.) tablilla para fracturas; arco de protección para una herida; (agr.) armadura (de guadaña), guadaña agavillada (ll. t. **cradle scythe;** (min.) artesa oscilante; (mar.) cuna o basada; (const.) plataforma colgante; (arti.) armazón de retroceso de la cureña; (m. v.) caballete de soporte (de una caldera). **II.** *va.* cunear. **III.** *vn.* mecerse en la cuna; segar con guadaña agavillada.

cradlesong [-sŋ], *s.* arrullo.

craft [krǽft], *s.* arte (gen. *f.*); artificio, astucia, treta; maña; habilidad, pericia; arte u oficio; gremio; (mar.) embarcación, barco (ú. t. como *pl.*).—**c. guild, c. union,** gremio de artesanos de un mismo oficio.—**the c.,** la masonería.

craftily [-įlį], *adv.* astuta o mañosamente.

craftiness [-nįs], *s.* astucia, maña.

craftsman [-smąn], *s.* artífice, artesano.

craftsmanship [-šįp], *s.* habilidad en el oficio, artístico, mano (*f.*) de obra.

crafty [-į], *a.* astuto, taimado, ladino, artificioso.

crag [krǽg], *s.* despeñadero, risco.—**cragged** [-įd], *a.* escabroso, peñascoso.—**craggedness** [-nįs], *s.* escabrosidad o fragosidad; aspereza, desigualdad.

cragginess [-nįs], *s.* escabrosidad o fragosidad; aspereza, desigualdad.

craggy [-į], *a.* escabroso, escarpado, desigual.

crake [kreik], *s.* (orn.) ave zancuda; (Ingl.) cuervo.

cram [krǽm]. **I.** *va.* rellenar, henchir, atestar, atracar, apretar, embaular, embutir; hartar, cebar; (fam.) preparar (a un estudiante) o aprender (un asunto) a la carrera. **II.** *vn.* hartarse, darse un atracón; (fam.) leer o estudiar con empeño. **III.** *s.* atracón, atestamiento, apret(ad)ura; (fam.) persona que se aprende atropelladamente algo o se lo hace aprender a otra (ú. esp. de estudiantes y maestros); (fam.) mentira, embuste.

crambo [-bou], *s.* (desp.) consonante (en verso); juego de hallar consonantes.

crammer [-œ(r)], *s.* = CRAM (persona); (fam.) mentiroso; (fam.) mentira, engaño; (mec.) apretador, comprimidor.

cramming [-įŋ], *s.* atestamiento, atestadura, apretamiento, apret(ad)ura; atracón; engullimiento, hartazgo; (fam.) repaso.

cramp [krǽmp]. **I.** *s.* (med.) calambre, rampa, retortijón; entumecimiento; sujeción; estrechez, aprieto; (mec., carp.) cárcel, *f.,* grapa de tornillo; gra(m)pa, laña.—**c. iron,** laña, grapa, gatillo. **II.** *a.* contraído; apretado. **III.** *va.* entumecer; dar calambre; sujetar; lañar; engrapar, engatillar; apretar.

crampfish [-fįš], *s.* (ict.) torpedo, tremielga.

crampon, crampoon [krǽmpŋ, kræmpún], *s.* (bot.) raicilla trepadora de la hiedra; (gen. *pl.*) púa o espolón para trepar o andar sobre el hielo; tenazas de garfios.

cranberry [krǽnberį], *s.* (bot.) arándano agrio de los pantanos.

crane [krein]. **I.** *s.* (orn.) grulla; (mec.) grúa, cabria; sifón o cantimplora; cigüeña o aguilón de chimenea; brazo de soporte; (mar.) abanico, arbotante.—**c. fly,** (ent.) típula.—**c.'s-bill,** (bot.) geranio, pico de cigüeña (ll. t. **cranesbill**). **II.** *va.* levantar con la grúa; estirar, extender (el cuello). **III.** *vn.* estirarse, alargarse.

cranial [kréinįąl], *a.* craneal, craneano, craniano.

craniological [-olád́ʒįkąl], *a.* craneológico.

craniology [-álodʒį], *s.* craneología.

craniometer [-ámetœ(r)], *s.* craneómetro.

craniometry [-ámetrį], *s.* craneometría.

craniotomy [-átomį], *s.* craneotomía; perforación del cráneo del feto. *V.* TREPANATION.

cranium [kréinįam], *s.* cráneo, casco, sesera.

crank [krǽŋk]. **I.** *s.* (mec.) manubrio, manija; cigüeña, manivela; (fam.) maniático; chiflado, persona caprichosa o malhumorada; capricho, chifladura.—**c. arm,** (brazo de la) manivela.— **c. axle,** eje motor acodado; (aut.) cigüeñal.— **c. brace,** berbiquí.—**c. pin,** perno, botón de manivela.—**c. axle,** (mar.) mal lastrado, instable. *V.* CRANKY.—**c.-sided,** (mar.) celoso, que aguanta poca vela por falta de estabilidad. **III.** *va.* (aut.) voltear el cigüeñal para hacer arrancar el motor.

crankcase [-keis], *s.* (aut.) cárter de cigüeñal.

crankiness [-įnįs], *s.* mal humor; chifladura; desequilibrio; calidad de caprichoso o singular.

crankshaft [-šæft], *s.* (aut.) cigüeñal.—**c. gear,** (aut.) engranaje del cigüeñal.

cranky [-į], *a.* chiflado, lunático; torcido; destartalado, inseguro; caprichoso, testarudo.

crannied [krǽnįd], *a.* grietoso, hendido.

cranny [krǽnį], *s.* grieta, hendedura, raja.

crape [kreip]. **I.** *s.* (tej.) crespón. *V.* CREPE. **II.** *va.* poner crespón (como señal de luto).

crapefish [kréipfiŝ], s. bacalao seco.
craps [kræps], s. juego de azar, jugado con dados (ll. t. **crap game** y **crap shooting**).
crapulence [krǽpyulęns], s. crápula.
crapulent [-ęnt], **crapulous** [-ʌs], a. crapuloso.
crash [krǽŝ]. I. vn. romperse, caerse estrepitosamente, estrellarse; estallar; fracasar; (com.) quebrar; (aer.) aterrizar bruscamente. II. va. romper o despedazar estrepitosamente, estrellar; abrirse (paso); (aer.) echar a pique.—**to c. the gate,** (fam.) colarse.
crash, crashing [-iŋ], s. estallido, estampido, estrépito, fragor; fracaso; (com.) crac, quiebra o bancarrota; (tej.) cutí burdo, lienzo basto; (aer.) aterrizaje violento.—**c. dive,** sumersión rápida (de un submarino).—**c. helmet,** casco.
crass [kræs], a. grueso, gordo; basto, tosco; espeso; craso; torpe.
crassamentum [-ʌmɛ́ntʌm], s. coágulo de la sangre.
crassness [-niŝ], s. crasitud.
crassulaceous [-yuléjŝʌs], a. (bot.) crasuláceo.
crate [kréit]. I. s. embalaje de tablas; cuévano, canasta, banasta; (Am.) guácal. II. va. entablar, embalar con tablas.
crater [kréitœ(r)], s. cráter; hoyo de bomba o mina; (arqueol.) crátera.
craunch [krɔnch], va. = CRUNCH.
cravat [krʌvǽt], s. corbata, corbatín; chalina.
crave [kréiv]. I. va. pedir humilde pero vehementemente; anhelar, desear. II. vn. (con **for**) pedir o desear con vehemencia, suspirar por.
craven [kréivņn], s. y a. cobarde, pusilánime.
craving [kréiviŋ]. I. s. (con **for**), regosto, sed, anhelo, deseo vehemente (de). II. a. insaciable; pedigüeño.
craw [krɔ], s. buche.
crawfish [krɔ́fiŝ]. I. s. (zool.) cangrejo de río, ástaco, langostín, langostino. II. vn. (fam.) volverse atrás, faltar a lo prometido.
crawl [krɔl]. I. vn. arrastrarse; andar a gatas, gatear; serpear; hormiguear; humillarse, pedir o someterse abyectamente; marchar paso a paso, a paso de tortuga; (fam.) volverse atrás. II. s. arrastramiento; pozo, corral (de agua).
crawler [-œ(r)], s. reptil; persona rastrera; (bot.) planta rastrera.
crawly [-i], a. (fam.) pavoroso; de pavor; que causa hormigueo.
crayfish [kréjfiŝ], s. = CRAWFISH.
crayon [kréjɔn]. I. s. lápiz, m., crayón; gis, m., tiza; dibujo al crayón. II. va. lapizar.
craze [kréjz]. I. va. enloquecer; dementar, enajenar; cuartear, grietar. II. vn. perder la razón; cuartearse, grietarse. III. s. locura, manía, demencia; delirio, furor; antojo, capricho, moda; grieta, cuarteadura (en la cerámica).
crazed [-d], a. enloquecido, loco, demente; grietoso.
crazily [-ili], adv. loca o insensatamente.
craziness [-iniŝ], s. locura, insania, demencia; desequilibrio mental; inseguridad.
crazy [-i], a. loco; extravagante; desvencijado, roto, dilapidado; (fam.) exagerradamente deseoso o ansioso.—**c. quilt,** (cost.) centón.
creak [krík], vn. crujir, rechinar, chirriar.
creaking [-iŋ]. I. s. crujido, rechinamiento, chirrido, estridor. II. a. crujidero, chirriadero.
creaky [-i], a. crujidero, chirriador.
cream [krím]. I. s. crema, nata; lo mejor, la nata y flor.—**c. cheese,** queso de nata.—**c. of tartar,** crémor tártaro.—**c. puff,** bollo de crema.—**c. sauce,** salsa de crema o leche, harina y manteca, etc.—**c. separator,** desnatadora. II. vn. criar nata. III. va. desnatar.
creamer [-œ(r)], s. jarrito para crema; desnatadora.
creamery [-œri], s. lechería, mantequería.
creamy [-i], a. que parece o contiene nata.
crease [krís]. I. s. pliegue, repliegue, doblez, m., arruga, plegadura; raya (del pantalón, etc.). II.

va. plegar, doblar; acanalar, estriar; arrugar (enc.) filetear.
creaser [-œ(r)], s. (enc.) fileteador; (cost.) marcador.
create [kriéit], va. criar o crear, producir, causar, originar, ocasionar; engendrar, procrear; crear, establecer; constituir, elegir, nombrar.
creatine [kríatin], s. (bioquím.) creatina.
creation [kriéiŝǫn], s. creación; universo; producción; obra; fundación; nombramiento, elección.
creationism [-izm], s. doctrina de la creación divina tanto del mundo como de las especies, opuesta a la teoría de la evolución.—**creationist** [-jst], s. partidario de dicha doctrina.
creative [kriéitiv], a. creador, criador.
creativeness [-niŝ], s. facultad creadora, genio inventivo.
creator [kriéitǫ(r)], s. creador, criador.—**the C.,** el Criador, el Creador, Dios.
creature [kríchŭ(r)], s. criatura; ser viviente, animal; bicho; hechura, paniaguado.
crèche [kreiŝ o krɛŝ], s. = DAY NURSERY; inclusa, casa de expósitos; nacimiento, belén.
credence [krídęns], s. creencia, asenso, fe, f., crédito.
credential [krędénŝal]. I. a. credencial. II. s. título.—pl. (cartas) credenciales.
credibility [kredjbíljti], s. credibilidad, verosimilitud.
credible [krédjbl], a. creíble.—**credibleness** [-niŝ], s. credibilidad; veracidad.—**credibly** [-blj], adv. creíblemente.
credit [krédjt]. I. s. crédito, fe, f.; reputación; encomio; buen nombre; confianza; influencia o autoridad; (com.) crédito; haber; saldo a favor; plazo.—**c. balance,** saldo acreedor.—**c. man,** investigador de créditos, o de ventas al fiado, que averigua hasta dónde puede concederse crédito.—**c. union,** banco cooperativo (gen. de obreros).—**on c.,** al fiado, a plazo(s).—**to give c.,** dar crédito; abonar; reconocer el mérito; hacer justicia; reconocer o nombrar como autor (de una obra, cita, etc.); citar o nombrar (una obra de que se copia, etc.). II. va. creer; atribuir; reconocer; acreditar, (con)fiar, dar fama o fe, honrar; (com.) abonar, (a)datar, bonificar, imputar; dar al fiado.—**to c. one with,** atribuir a uno; reconocer a uno (como autor, inventor, etc.); (com.) abonarle a uno.
creditable [-ạbl], a. estimable, honroso, apreciable, loable.—**creditability** [-ạbíljti], s. crédito, reputación.—**creditably** [-ạblj], adv. honorablemente, honrosamente; hábilmente.
credited [-jd], a. acreditado, estimado, reputado; creído; (com.) acreditado, abonado en cuenta; pasado al haber.
creditor [-ǫ(r)], s. acreedor; (com.) haber.
credo [krídou], s. (igl.) credo.
credulity [kredjúljti], **credulousness** [krédjulʌsniŝ], s. credulidad.
credulous [-ʌs], a. crédulo.
creed [krid], s. credo, creencia, profesión de fe, doctrina, religión.
creek [krik], s. abra, cala, caleta, ensenada; estero; riachuelo, rivera.
creel [kril], s. nasa o cesta de pescador; jaula de mimbres.
creep [kríp]. I. vn. (pret. y pp. CREPT) arrastrarse, serpear; gatear; deslizarse, insinuarse; sentir hormigueo; moverse o acercarse lenta y cautelosa o furtivamente; pedir o someterse abyectamente; humillarse; trepar; correrse (una cosa sobre otra); (elec.) desviarse (una corriente).—**to c. on,** acercarse insensiblemente.—**to c. out,** escurrirse; resbalarse hacia afuera.—**to c. up,** encaramarse, treparse; subir gradualmente. II. s. arrastramiento.—pl. (fam.) pavor, sobrecogimiento, crispatura; hormigueo.
creepage [-idź], s. = CREEPING.
creeper [-œ(r)], s. el que o lo que se arrastra; rep-

til; (bot.) enredadera, trepadora; (orn.) trepador; garfio, garabato; ramplón o espolón de zapato (para andar sobre el hielo).—*pl. V.* ROMPERS.
creephole [-hoυl], *s.* huronera; escapatoria, evasiva, pretexto.
creeping [-iŋ]. I. *a.* que se arrastra; rastrero; lento; pavoroso, crispador; (bot.) rastrera.—**c. palsy,** o **paralysis,** atrofia muscular progresiva.—**c. sickness,** (med.) ergotismo. II. *s.* pavor, crispatura, horror; hormigueo; escurrimiento, deslizamiento; arrastramiento; abyección; corredura (de una cosa sobre otra); (elec.) desviación (de una corriente); (fís.) ascenso por atracción capilar; (f. c.) resbalamiento longitudinal (de los rieles); (mec.) resbalamiento (de una correa).
creepingly [-liĵ], *adv.* a paso de tortuga; abyectamente.
creepy [-i], *a.* = CRAWLY.
creese [kris], *s.* (Filip.) cris.
cremate [krímejt], *va.* cremar, incinerar.—**cremation** [krimáişợn], *s.* cremación, incineración.—**crematorium** [krimạtóuriʌm], **crematory** [krímạtori], *s.* crematorio; horno crematorio o de incineración.
Cremona [krimóuṇạ], *s.* violín de Cremona.
crenate [krínejt(ịd], *a.* (bot.) dentado.
crenel(l)ate [kréneleJt], *va.* almenar; aspillerar.
crenel(l)e [krénel *o* krịnél], *s.* (fort.) almena; aspillera.
creole [kríoμl], *s.* y *a.* criollo.
creosol [kríosol], *s.* (quím.) creosol.
creosote [kríosoμt]. I. *s.* creosota.—**c. oil,** creosota cruda, sin refinar. II. *va.* creosotar.
crepe, crêpe [krejp], *s.* (tej.) crespón. *V.* CRAPE.—**c. de Chine,** crespón de China o de seda.—**c. paper,** papel delgado semejante al crespón.
crepitate [krépịtejt], *vn.* crepitar, chasquear; chisporrotear.—**crepitation** [-éişợn], *s.* crepitación, chasquido; chisporroteo.
crept [krept], *pret.* y *pp.* de TO CREEP.
crepuscular [krepΛskjulạ(r], *a.* crepuscular.
crepuscule [krepΛskjul], *s.* crepúsculo.
crescendo [kreʃéndoμ], *a.* y *s.* (mús.) crescendo.
crescent [krésợnt]. I. *a.* creciente. II. *s.* lúnula; creciente, *f.* (de la luna); media luna; (astr.) cuarto de luna; (blas.) creciente.
cress [kres], *s.* (bot.) lepidio, mastuerzo, berro.
cresset [krésịt], *s.* fanal o farol, fogaril; hachón, antorcha, antorchero.
crest [krést]. I. *s.* cresta; copete, penacho; crestón; cimera; (blas.) timbre; cima, cumbre; cresta de una ola. II. *va.* coronar; (blas.) timbrar. III. *vn.* encrestarse; encresparse; encopetarse.
crested [-ịd], *a.* crestado, encopetado, penachudo, moñudo; (blas.) timbrado.—**c. heron,** airón.
crestfallen [-folẹn], *a.* cabizbajo, abatido.
cretaceous [krẹtéiʃiʌs], *a.* cretáceo, gredoso.
Cretan [krítạn], *a.* y *s.* cretense, crético.
cretin [krítịn], *s.* cretino.
cretinism [-izm], *s.* cretinismo.
cretonne [krítan], *s.* (tej.) cretona.
crevasse [krẹvás], *s.* hendedura profunda en un helero o glaciar; (E. U.) brecha en un malecón.
crevice [krévịs], *s.* hendedura, grieta, rendija.
crew [kru], *s.* (mar.) tripulación o dotación; equipaje, marinería; tripulantes; cuadrilla, banda, hato.—**c. member,** tripulante.
crew, *vn. pret.* de TO CROW.
crewel [krúẹl], *s.* ovillo de estambre.
crib [krịb]. I. *s.* pesebre; pesebrera; camita de niño; arcón, artesa; granero; (min.) brocal de entibación; (hidr.) cofre, cajón; (constr.) armazón o cajón de sustentación; balsa pequeña; estribo flotante; choza, casucha, chiribitil; (fam.) ratería; plagio. II. *va.* estribar; entibar; enjaular; (fam.) hurtar; plagiar.
cribbage [kríbịdž], *s.* juego de naipes.
cribble [kríbl], *s.* criba, harnero.

cribwork [kríbwœrk], *s.* cajón o armazón de apoyo, gen. lleno de piedra.
crick [krịk], *s.* (med.) tortícoli; calambre muscular.
cricket [kríkịt], *s.* (ent.) grillo; (dep.) cri(c)quet; (fam.) juego limpio; cáncana, banquillo, taburete.
cricketer [-œ(r], *s.* jugador de cri(c)quet.
cricoid [krájkoịd], *a.* y *s.* (anat.) cricoides.
cried [krajd], *pret.* y *pp.* de TO CRY.
crier [krájœ(r], *s.* pregonero; baladrero.
crime [krájm], *s.* crimen, delito; pecado.
criminal [krímịnạl], *a.* y *s.* criminal, criminoso, facineroso, reo.—**c. case,** proceso, causa criminal.—**c. conversation,** adulterio.—**c. law,** derecho penal.—**criminalist** [-ịst], *s.* criminalista.—**criminality** [-ǽlịtị], *s.* criminalidad.—**criminally** [-lị], *adv.* criminalmente.
criminate [krímịnejt], *va.* acriminar, acusar.
crimination [-éişợn], *s.* acriminación, acusación.
criminative [-ặtịv], *a.* acusatorio.—**criminator** [-ejtọ(r], *s.* acriminador, acusador.
criminologist [-álodžịst], *s.* criminólogo.
criminology [-álodžị], *s.* criminología.
crimp [krịmp]. I. *va.* rizar, encrespar, engrifar; alechugar; doblar hacia dentro (el borde de un tubo, etc.); dar forma doblando; hacer incisiones en; enganchar (soldados y marineros). II. *a.* rizado; quebradizo, desmenuzable. III. *s.* rizador; el que sirve de señuelo en garitos, etc. (para enganchar marineros, etc.).—**to put a c. in,** (fam.) estorbar, poner obstáculos a.
crimper [-œ(r], *s.* = CRIMPING MACHINE; máquina para cerrar cápsulas doblando los bordes hacia adentro; rizador.
crimping [-iŋ], *ger.* de TO CRIMP.—**c. iron,** tenacillas de rizar.—**c. machine,** máquina de combar u ondular.
crimple [krímpl], *va.* y *vn.* encrespar, arrugar, rizar.
crimpy [krímpị], *a.* encrespado.
crimson [krímzọn]. I. *a.* y *s.* carmesí. II. *va.* teñir de carmesí. III. *vn.* enrojecerse; sonrojarse.
cringe [krịndž]. I. *vn.* retroceder, encogerse o temblar (ante un peligro, dolor, etc.); rebajarse, adular. II. *s.* adulación, bajeza.
cringer [-œ(r], *s.* adulador servil.
cringing [-iŋ], *a.* bajo, rastrero.
cringle [kríŋgl], *s.* (mar.) garrucho.
crinite [krájnajt], *a.* crinado, peludo.
crinkle [kríŋkl]. I. *vn.* serpentear; crujir (como la seda), crepitar. II. *va.* arrugar, rizar, acanalar. III. *s.* recodo; sinuosidad, ondulación.
crinkly [-klị], *a.* arrugado; ondulado; crujiente.
crinoid [krájnoịd], *a.* y *s.* (zool.) crinoideo.
crinoline [krínolịn], *s.* (tej.) crinolina; ahuecador o miriñaque.
cripple [krípl]. I. *s.* zopo, cojo o manco, tullido, estropeado, inválido. II. *va.* lisiar, derrengar, mutilar, estropear, encojar; tullir, baldar; descabalar.
crippled [-d], *a.* lisiado, estropeado, derrengado, zopo, mútilo; tullido; (mar.) desmantelado.
crisis [krájsịs], *s.* crisis; (med.) acme; (teat.) nudo.
crisp [krịsp]. I. *a.* quebradizo, frágil; tostado, quemado; crespo, rizado; terso, vigoroso; refrescante. II. *va.* encrespar, engrifar, torcer, rizar; undular; hacer quebradizo o frágil.
crispation [-éişợn], *s.* crispatura.
crisping [-iŋ], *ger.* de TO CRISP.—**c. iron, c. pin,** *s.* encrespador, rizador.
crispness [-nịs], *s.* rizado, encrespadurə; fragilidad.
crispy [-ị], *a.* crespo, rizado; desmenuzable, frágil; fresco, vigorizante.
crisscross [krískros], I. *a.* cruzado o entrelazado. II. *s.* cruz o firma del que no sabe escribir; líneas cruzadas; juego del tres en raya. III. *adv.* en cruz. IV. *va.* y *vn.* formar o marcar con líneas cruzadas.

crissum [krísʌm], *s.* (orn.) región anal; plumas anales.

criterion [kraitíriọn], *s.* criterio.

critic [krítịk], *s.* crítico; censor; crítica.

critical [-ạl], *a.* crítico; criticón, criticador; exacto, escrupuloso; difícil, peligroso; decisivo; (med.) crítico.

critically [-i], *adv.* críticamente; exactamente, rigurosamente.

criticaster [krítịkæstœ(r)], *s.* criticastro.

criticism [krítịsizm], *s.* crítica; juicio crítico (de un libro, etc.); censura.

criticize, criticise [-saịz]. **I.** *vn.* criticar; critiquizar. **II.** *va.* censurar, fiscalizar; poner reparos a.—**criticizer** [-œ(r)], *s.* crítico, criticador.

critique [krịtík], *s.* crítica; revista, juicio crítico.

croak [króụk]. **I.** *vn.* graznar, crascitar; croar; gruñir; (fam.) morir. **II.** *s.* graznido; canto de ranas.

croaker [-œ(r)], *s.* graznador; gruñidor, refunfuñador; (ict.) especie de roncador.

Croat [króụæt], **Croatian** [kroụéíṣiạn], *a.* y *s.* croata, *mf.*

crocein [króụsiịn], *s.* (quím.) croceína.

croceus [króụṣʌs], *a.* crocino, azafranado.

crochet [króụṣéị]. **I.** *va.* y *vn.* hacer ganch(ill)o o crochet. **II.** *s.* labor (*f.*) de gancho o crochet.—**c. needle,** aguja de gancho, ganchillo.

crock [krak], *s.* cazuela, orza; tiesto, casco; olla de barro; hollín; (fam.) bestia o persona agotada.

crockery [krákœrị], *s.* loza, vidriado, cacharros.

crocodile [krákodaịl], *s.* (zool.) cocodrilo o crocodilo; caimán.—**c. tears,** (fig.) lágrimas de cocodrilo, dolor fingido.

crocus [króụkʌs], *s.* (bot.) azafrán, croco.

croft [kroft], *s.* (Ingl.) pegujal, llosa.

croissant [krwasán], *s.* (Am., coc.) media luna, cuernito.

cromlech [krámlɛk], *s.* (arqueol.) crónlech, monumento megalítico; dolmen.

crone [kroụn], *s.* vieja arrugada.

crony [króụnị]. **I.** *s.* compinche, camarada, *mf.* **II.** *vn.* ser camarada(s); amigarse íntimamente.

crook [krụk]. **I.** *s.* curva(tura); gancho, garfio; cayado; (fam.) fullero, petardista. **II.** *va.* y *vn.* encorvar(se), corcovarse; doblar(se), torcer(se).

crookback [-bæk], *s.*, **crookbacked** [-bækt], *a.* jorobado, gibado, corcovado.

crooked [-ịd], *a.* corvo, encorvado, curvo; torcido; oblicuo, ladeado; pícaro, avieso, deshonesto, pervertido.—**c. legs,** patituerto.

crookedly [-lị], *adv.* torcidamente, de través; de mala manera; pícaramente.—**crookedness** [-nịs], *s.* (en)corvadura, corcova; corcovo, claudicación, perversidad; vuelta, sinuosidad.

crooklegged [-lɛgịd], *a.* patituerto, pernituerto.

crookneck [-nɛk], *s.* (bot.) calabaza de cuello retorcido.

croon [krún], *va.* y *vn.* canturrear; cantar canciones sentimentales con emoción exagerada.—**crooner** [-œ(r)], *s.* canturreador; cantante popular.—**crooning** [-ịŋ], *s.* canturreo.

crop [kráp]. **I.** *s.* cosecha, recolección, agosto; siembra, lo que se siembra; crecimiento de cabellos o barba; cortadura; látigo mocho; buche de ave.—*pl.* mieses, *f. pl.*; producción.—**c.-eared,** desorejado. **II.** *va.* segar, cosechar, recoger los frutos; pacer; cultivar; (a veces con **off**) (re)cortar, repelar, motilar, desorejar, rapar, trasquilar, rabotear, desmochar. **III.** *vn.* dar frutos, producir mieses; pacer; (gen. con **forth, out, up**) descubrirse, dejarse ver.—**to c. out,** (min.) aflorar.

cropper [-œ(r)], *s.* cultivador (*V.* t. SHARE CROPPER), planta de cosecha; obrero recortador; máquina recortadora; (fam.) caída de cabeza; (orn.) *V.* POUTER.—**to come, fall, get, a c.,** (fam.) caer de cabeza; fracasar.

croquet [kroụkéị]. **I.** *s.* juego de croquet, argoll **II.** *va.* apartar de una bolada la bola del co trario.

croquette [kroụkét], *s.* (coc.) croqueta.

crosier [króụžœ(r)], *s.* báculo pastoral, cayado d obispo; (C., astr.) Cruz del Sur.

cross [krós]. **I.** *s.* cruz (sentidos recto y figurado guión; (fig.) aflicción, pena; (C., astr.) cru aspa; mercado (donde hay cruz); pieza en cru tubo de unión en cruz; cruce; querella, encue tro; cruzamiento (de razas); (top.) escuadra c agrimensor; (elec.) cruzamiento o contacto c dos conductores. **II.** *a.* relativo o perteneciente a la cruz; atravesado; transversal, travese travieso; cruzado; opuesto, contrario, adverso contradictorio; malhumorado, de mal genio serio, enojado, enfadado.—**c. action,** (for. reconvención.—**c. arm,** cruceta, brazo en cru (elec., teleg.) traviesa de poste.—**c.-armed** cruzado de brazos.—**c.-bearer,** crucifera (tec.) barra o riostra transversal.—**c.-bedded** (geol.) de láminas o capas cruzadas.—**c. birth** (for.) contraquerella.—**c. birth,** (med.) fet atravesado.—**c. bond,** (elec.) conexión entre riel y el alimentador.—**c. bun,** bollo de vierne santo (marcado con una cruz).—**c.-com pound,** (m. v.) compound cruzada, cross compound.—**c.-country,** a campo traviesa (dep.) carrera de obstáculos, a campo traviesa —**c.-examination,** interrogatorio (esp. re pregunta).—**c.-examine,** *va.* interrogar (esp repreguntar).—**c.-eyed,** bizco, bisojo, estrá bico.—**c.-fertilization,** (bot.) alogamia, fe cundación por polinización cruzada (de un planta por otra); (zool.) fecundación de lo huevos de un animal por otro.—**c. fire,** (mil. fuego cruzado; ataque por varios lados.—**c. girder,** viga transversal.—**c. grain,** repelo fibras oblicuas.—**c.-grained,** vet(e)ado; repe loso, de fibra transversal u oblicua; intratable terco.—**c. hair** = CROSS WIRE.—**c.-interro gate,** (for.) *va.* = CROSS-EXAMINE.—**c.-inter rogatory** = CROSS-EXAMINATION.—**c.-lots,** a campo traviesa; (fam.) derecho, del modo má corto.—**c. multiplication,** multiplicación e cruz.—**c.-pollinate,** fecundar por polinizació de una planta por otra.—**c.-pollination,** poli nización cruzada (de una planta por otra).—**c. purpose,** propósito o hecho contrario.—**(at c. purposes,** involuntariamente en pugna, por vías opuestas).—**c.-question** = CROSS-EX AMINATION.—**c. reference,** referencia de un parte de un libro a otra.—**c. section,** sección o corte transversal.—**c.-sectional,** transversal de la sección transversal.—**c.-section paper** papel cuadriculado.—**c.-staff,** (top.) escuadra de agrimensor.—**c. stitch,** punto cruzado o de cruz, punto de escapulario.—**c. street** travesía, calle traviesa.—**c. stud,** aspa.—**c timber,** (mar.) bao.—**c. wire,** (top., astr.) hilo pelo (del retículo de un anteojo).

cross. I. *va.* cruzar; atravesar, salvar, traspasar marcar con una cruz; cruzar o mestizar (la castas); (gen. con **off** o **out**) tildar, tachar borrar con una raya; poner el trazo transversal a (una letra, gen. la *t*); pasar o mover de u lado a otro de; oponerse a, contrariar; hacer frente a.—**to c. one's mind,** ocurrírsele a uno pasarle a uno por la imaginación.—**to c. one's self,** persignarse; santiguarse; hacerse cruces. —**to c. swords,** medir las armas, reñir, con tender. **II.** *vn.* cruzar(se); cortarse, intersecarse (líneas, etc.).—**to c. over,** pasar de un lado a otro, ir al otro lado, pasar por encima.

crossbar [-bar], *s.* travesaño; tranca, aldaba (impr.) crucero, medianil.—**c. shot,** (arti.) palanqueta, bala enramada.

crossbeak [-bik], *s.* = CROSSBILL.

crossbeam [-bim], *s.* viga transversal; travesaño aldabía, través; puente, *mf.*

crossbill [-bịl], *s.* (orn.) piquituerto.

---

crossbolt [-boult], *s.* macho doble de dos direcciones (apl. a cerraduras).

crossbones [-bounz], *s. pl.* canillas cruzadas (símbolo de la muerte).

crossbow [-bou], *s.* ballesta (arma).—**crossbowman** [-man], *s.* ballestero (soldado).

crossbred [-bred], *s.* y *a.* cruzado (de raza), mestizo, mixto.

crossbreed [-brid]. I. *s.* planta o animal cruzados o mixtos; híbrido; mezclado. II. *va.* cruzar (animales o plantas).

crosscurrent [-kœrent], *s.* contracorriente, corriente contraria; tendencias o ideas encontradas.

crosscut [-kʌt], *s.* corte transversal; corte en cruz; atajo; (min.) galería transversal.—**c. chisel**, cincel agudo de ranuras.—**c. file**, lima de picadura cruzada.—**c. saw**, sierra de trozar (al través de la fibra).

crosse [kros], *s.* vilorto.

crossed [-t], *a.* cruzado; de través; transversal.—**c. belt**, (mec.) correa cruzada.

crosshead [-hed], *s.* (mec.) cruceta (esp. la de la biela); (imp.) título de columna (de periódico).

crossing [-iŋ], *s.* cruce, intersección; paso, vado (de un río); travesía, acción de cruzar; travesío, lugar por donde se cruza; cruzamiento o mestizaje (de razas); (f. c.) paso; cruce o cruzamiento (de dos vías).—**c. one's self**, santiguada, santiguamiento.

crossly [-lj], *adv.* enojadamente, con enfado.—**crossness** [-njs], *s.* enfado; mal humor.

crosspatch [-pæch], *s.* (fam.) gruñón, de mal genio.

crosspiece [-pis], *s.* pieza transversal; cruceta; travesaño; (carp.) crucero; peinazo (de puerta); (mar.) cruz de las bitas.

crossroad [-roud], *s.* cruce o junta de dos caminos, travesía.—*pl.* encrucijada; punto crítico, tiempo llegado de decidir.

crosstail [-tejl], *s.* cruceta.

crosstie [-taj], *s.* (f. c.) traviesa, durmiente.

crosstree [-tri], *s.* (mar.) cruceta, bao de gavia.

crossway [-wej], *s.* travesía, encrucijada.

crossways [-wejz], **crosswise** [-wajz], *adv.* de través, al través; de parte a parte; en cruz.

crossword puzzle [-wœrd pázl], *s.* crucigrama, *m.*, rompecabezas, palabras cruzadas.

crosswort [-wœrt], *s.* (bot.) cruciata.

crotalum [krátalʌm], *s.* crótalo.

crotch [krach], *s.* bifurcación, cruce, cruz; (anat., sast.) bragadura, entrepierna(s); (mar.) pique.

crotchet [kráchjt], *s.* rareza, excentricidad, chifladura; (mús.) semínima, negra; ganchito; instrumento de obstetricia.

crotchety [-j], *a.* excéntrico, raro, chiflado.

croton [króutɔn], *s.* (bot.) crotón.—**C. bug**, (ent.) cucaracha.—**c. oil**, aceite de crotontiglio o de crotón.

crouch [krauch], *vn.* agacharse, agazaparse, acuclillarse; (re)bajarse.

croup [krup], *s.* rabadilla, obispillo (de ave); anca, grupa (de caballo); (med.) crup o garrotillo.

croupier [krúpjœ(r)], *s.* (gal.) crupié, gurupié (el que ayuda al banquero en una casa de juego).

croupous [krúpʌs], **croupy** [-j], *a.* crupal, como de crup.—**c. cough**, tos perruna o crupal.

crow [krou]. I. *s.* (orn.) cuervo; corneja; cacareo, canto del gallo. *V.* CROWBAR.—**c.-quill**, pluma de ave; pluma fina de canutillo para dibujar.—**c.'s foot**, pata de gallo (arrugas); marca en forma de pata de gallo, o de rayas convergentes; (mil.) abrojo; (aer.) bolina. *V.* CROWFOOT.—**c.'s nest**, (mar.) cofa para la vigía.—**as the c. flies**, a vuelo de pájaro, en línea recta.—**to eat c.**, (fam.) cantar la palinodia. II. *vn.* (*pret.* CROWED o CREW) cacarear, cantar el gallo; (*pret.* CROWED) gallear, alardear, cantar victoria; bravear.

crowbar [króubar], *s.* pie (*m.*) de cabra; barra o palanca de hierro; descalzador.

crowd [kraud]. I. *s.* gentío, multitud, muchedumbre, tropel, tropa, turba(multa); bulla, tumulto; agolpamiento, apiñamiento, apretura; caterva, populacho, vulgo; antiguo instrumento parecido al violín. II. *va.* amontonar, atestar, apretar, apiñar.—**to c. sail**, (mar.) hacer fuerza de vela. III. *vn.* apiñarse, agolparse, (ar)remolinarse.

crowded [-jd], *a.* apiñado, apretado, atestado, amontonado; lleno, tupido, de bote en bote.

crowder [-œ(r)], *s.* amontonador.

crowfoot [króufut], *s.* (bot.) ranúnculo, botón de oro, arañ(uel)a; (mar.) araña; (mil.) abrojo.

crown [kraun]. I. *s.* corona; diadema; guirnalda, láurea; premio, galardón; monarca, *m.*, soberano; soberanía; coronilla, mollera, testa (de la cabeza); copa, cima; complemento, colmo; (Ingl.) moneda de plata (cinco chelines); copa de sombrero; corona del diente; (arq.) corona, coronamiento; (bot.) unión de tallo y raíz; (blas.) coronel; (fort.) corona.—**c. glass**, crown glass, vidrio de ornamentación y de instrumentos ópticos.—**c. grafting**, injerto de coronilla.—**c. lands**, (Ingl.) patrimonio de la corona.—**c. law**, (Ingl.) derecho penal.—**c. prince**, príncipe heredero.—**c. princess**, princesa heredera, o consorte del príncipe heredero.—**c. saw**, sierra tubular giratoria.—**c. wheel**, rueda coronaria o de escape; rueda de dientes perpendiculares a su plano. II. *va.* coronar; recompensar, premiar; completar.—**crowned head**, testa coronada.

crowner [-œ(r)], *s.* coronador; remate.

crowning [-iŋ], *s.* remate; coronamiento; coronación.

crownland [-lænd], *s.* patrimonio o tierras de la corona.

crownless [-ljs], *a.* sin corona.

crownlet [-ljt], *s.* corona pequeña.

crownwork [-wœrk], *s.* (dent.) corona artificial, trabajo en coronas artificiales; (fort.) corona, obra de corona(s).

croze [króuz]. I. *s.* (ton.) gárgol, jable, ruña(dura); argallera, jabladera. II. *va.* ruñar.

crozer [-œ(r)], *s.* (ton.) el que o lo que ruña; argallera, jabladera, ruñadera.

crozier [króużœ(r)], *s.* = CROSIER.

crucial [krúśąl], *a.* crucial, decisivo, conclusivo; cruzado, atravesado.

cruciate [krúśjejt], *a.* cruciforme; (bot.) crucífero.

crucible [krúsjbl], *s.* crisol; prueba severa.—**c. steel**, acero de crisol.

crucifer [krúsjfœ(r)], *s.* (igl.) cruciferario, crucero; crucífero; (bot.) planta crucífera.

Cruciferæ [krusjfœri], *s. pl.* (bot.) crucíferas.

cruciferous [-ʌs], *a.* (igl., bot.) crucífero.

crucified [krúsjfajd], *pp.* y *a.* crucificado.

crucifier [-fajœ(r)], *s.* crucificador, crucifixor.

crucifix [-fjks], *s.* crucifijo, Cristo.—**crucifixion** [-fjkśɔn], *s.* crucifixión.—**cruciform** [-form], *a.* cruciforme.—**crucify** [-faj], *va.* crucificar; aspar; atormentar; mortificar (las pasiones, etc.).

crude [krúd]. I. *a.* crudo; imperfecto; no sazonado, no refinado; tosco, mal acabado; bruto; zafio.—**c. gypsum**, aljez. II. *s.* petróleo bruto.

crudely [-lj], *adv.* crudamente.—**crudeness** [-njs], **crudity** [-jtj], *s.* crudeza, dureza.

cruel [krúęl], *a.* cruel, cruento, duro, fiero, inhumano, sin entrañas.—**cruelly** [-j], *adv.* cruelmente.—**cruelty** [-tj], *s.* crueldad, dureza, inhumanidad.

cruet [krújt], *s.* ampoll(et)a, vinagrera.—**c. stand**, angarillas, vinagreras, convoy de mesa.

cruise [krúz]. I. *vn.* (mar.) cruzar; viajar por mar, tierra o aire; (fam.) andar de arriba para abajo, vagar. II. *s.* crucero; viaje por mar, tierra o aire; (mar. mil.) acción de cruzar.—**cruising speed**, velocidad de crucero.

cruiser [-œ(r)], *s.* navegante; (mar.) crucero.

cruller [krʌlœ(r)], *s.* buñuelo, churro, almojábana.

crumb [krʌm]. I. *s.* miga, migajón; pizca, miaja, brote. II. *va.* migar, desmig(aj)ar; desmenuzar; (coc.) *V.* BREAD.

crumbable [-əbl], *a.* desmenuzable.

crumble [-bl]. I. *va.* desmig(aj)ar, desmenuzar, destrizar. II. *vn.* desmigajarse; desmoronarse, derrumbarse, hundirse.

crumbly [-bli], *a.* desmenuzable; friable.

crumby [-i], *a.* blando, miguero.

crumpet [krʌmpit], *s.* bollo blando.

crumple [krʌmpl]. I. *va.* arrugar, apañuscar, ajar. II. *vn.* contraerse, encogerse, aovillarse.

crunch [krʌnch], *va.* ronchar, tascar, cascar.

cruor [krúor], *s.* crúor, coágulo sanguíneo.

crupper [krʌpœ(r)], *s.* (tal.) grupera, baticola, ataharre, sotacola; grupa (de caballo).

crural [krúrəl], *a.* (anat.) crural, femoral.

crus [krʌs], *s.* (anat.) caña de la pierna; pedúnculo.

crusade [kruséjd]. I. *s.* cruzada. II. *vn.* cruzarse; hacer una campaña (contra algún abuso, etc.).

crusader [-œ(r)], *s.* cruzado.

cruse [krus], *s.* ampolleta, cantarillo, frasco, redomita, botellita.

crush [krʌʃ]. I. *va.* romper por compresión; aplastar, machacar; quebrantar, triturar; moler, majar; abrumar; vencer; debelar, reprimir; anonadar. II. *vn.* aplastarse; romperse o deformarse por compresión; avanzar empujando o aplastando.—**crushed rock o stone**, grava, piedra machacada o picada. III. *s.* estrujamiento o deformación por compresión o choque; apiñamiento, aglomeración (de gente); (fam.) afición súbita y violenta; el objeto de tal apasionamiento.—**c. hat**, sombrero flexible (que puede doblarse), clac.

crushable [-əbl], *a.* quebrantable, triturable.

crusher [-œ(r)], *s.* triturador; trituradora, quebrantadora (máquina); molino; (fam.) polizonte; (fam.) argumento o acontecimiento decisivo o abrumador.

crushing [-iŋ]. I. *a.* triturador, quebrantante o quebrantador; moledor o de moler; de compresión; abrumador, aplastante. II. *s.* trituración; quebrant(amient)o; anonadación.—**c. strength**, resistencia a la compresión.

crust [krʌst]. I. *s.* costra, encostradura, postilla (de llaga, etc.); corteza, canto, mendrugo de pan; pasta de una torta o pastel; capa (de terreno); sarro (de una vasija); (ent., zool.) caparazón, carapacho, concha. II. *va.* encostrar, incrustar. III. *vn.* encostrarse.

crustacean [krʌstéiʃiən], *a.* y *s.* (zool.) crustáceo.

crustaceous [-éiʃəs], *a.* crustáceo; conchado.

crustate [krʌsteit], *a.* cubierto con corteza o costra.

crustation [-éiʃən], *s.* incrustación, formación de costras; cobertura.

crustily [krʌstili], *adv.* enojada o broncamente.

crustiness [-nis], *s.* dureza de la costra; mal genio, aspereza.

crusty [-i], *a.* costroso; sarroso; rudo, brusco.

crutch [krʌch]. I. *s.* muleta; arrimo; muletilla, horquilla.—**crutches**, (mar.) horquillas. *V.* CROTCH. II. *va.* ahorquillar.

crux [krʌks], *s.* enigma, *m.*, misterio; problema arduo o peliagudo; lo esencial, el punto de partida.

cry [krái]. I. *va.* y *vn.* (*pret.* y *pp.* CRIED) gritar, vocear; pregonar; exclamar; lamentarse; llorar; aullar, bramar.—**to c. down**, culpar; hacer callar a uno a fuerza de voces; menospreciar; reprimir.—**to c. for**, clamar; pedir llorando; llorar de.—**to c. off**, renunciar; deshacer un trato, etc.—**to c. one's eyes out**, llorar amargamente.—**to c. out**, exclamar, gritar, vocear.—**to c. up**, alabar, decantar. II. *s.* (*pl.* CRIES) alarido, bramido, grito; lamento, lloro; gritería,

clamor; pregón, promulgación; muta, cuadrilla de perros de caza.—**a far c.**, camino largo, gran distancia o diferencia.—**in full c.**, acosando de cerca.—**within c.**, al alcance de oído.

crybaby [-beibi], *s.* niño llorón y gimoteador.

crying [-iŋ]. I. *s.* grito; llanto, lloro, lamento pregoneo. II. *a.* llorón; enorme, atroz; urgente

cryolite [kráiolait], *s.* (min.) criolita.

cryometer [kraiámœtœ(r)], *s.* criómetro, medidor de bajas temperaturas.

cryoscopy [kraiáskopi], *s.* (fís.) crioscopia.

crypt [kript], *s.* gruta, cripta; (med.) cripta, folículo, cavidad glandular.

cryptanalysis [-ænǽlisis], *s.* criptoanalítica.

cryptic(al [-ik(əl], *a.* escondido, secreto.

cryptically [-i], *adv.* ocultamente.

cryptogam [-ogæm], *s.* (bot.) criptógama.

Cryptogamia [-ogǽmiä], *s. pl.* (bot.) acotiledóneas.

cryptogamous [-ágamʌs], *a.* (bot.) criptógamo

cryptogram [-ogræm], *s.* cifra, criptograma, *m.*

cryptography [-ágrafi], *s.* criptografía.

crystal [krístəl], *s.* (quím.) cristal; (min.) cristal de roca; cristal de reloj.—**c. ball**, bola de cristal del adivino.—**c. detector, c. tube**, (rad.) detector de cristales; galena.—**c. gazing**, adivinación por medio de la bola de cristal.—**c. glass**, cristal.—**c. wedding**, décimoquinto aniversario.

crystal, o crystalline [-iŋ], *a.* cristalino; claro, transparente.—**c. lens**, (anat.) cristalino (del ojo).

crystallizable [-aizəbl], *a.* cristalizable.

crystallization [-izéiʃən], *s.* cristalización.—**crystallize** [-aiz]. I. *va.* cristalizar. II. *vn.* cristalizarse.—**crystallography** [-ágrafi], *s.* cristalografía.—**crystalloid** [-oid], *a.* y *s.* cristaloide.

cub [kʌb], *s.* cachorro; osezno; ballenato; (fam.) mozalbete torpe o inexperto.—**c. reporter** aprendiz (*m.*) de repórter.

Cuban [kjúbən], *s.* y *a.* cubano.

cubature [kjúbachur], *s.* (geom.) cubicación.

cubbyhole [kʌbihoul], *s.* armario o sitio pequeño y encerrado.

cube [kjub]. I. *s.* (geom. y mat.) cubo; sólido en forma de dado o hexaedro regular.—**c. root** raíz cúbica. II. *va.* cubicar; elevar al cubo.

cubeb [kjúbeb], *s.* (bot.) cubeba; cigarrillo medicinal.

cubic [kjúbik], *a.* cúbico.—**c. content**, volumen capacidad cúbica.—**c. equation**, ecuación de tercer grado.—**c. measure**, medida de capacidad.

cubical [-əl], *a.* cúbico. *V.* CUBIC.

cubically [-i], *adv.* cúbicamente.

cubicalness [-nis], *s.* calidad de cúbico.

cubicle [-l], *s.* cubículo, alcoba; compartimiento

cubicular [kjubíkjulä(r)]. I. *a.* perteneciente a la alcoba; privado. II. *s.* (hist.) cubiculario.

cubiculum [-lʌm], *s.* cubículo; (arqueol.) cámara de entierro.

cubiform [kjúbiform], *a.* cúbico.

cubism [kjúbizm], *s.* (b. a.) cubismo.—**cubis** [kjúbist], *a.* y *s.* cubista.

cubit [kjúbit], *s.* codo, antigua medida.

cubital [-əl], *a.* cubital; codal.

cuboid [kjúboid]. I. *a.* cúbico; (anat.) cuboides II. *s.* (anat.) (hueso) cuboides; (geom.) paralelepípedo rectangular.

cuckold [kʌkold]. I. *s.* marido cornudo; cabrón cuclillo. II. *va.* encornudar.

cuckoo [kúku]. I. *s.* (orn.) cuclillo o cuco; cuco (canto); (fam.) tonto, papanatas.—**c. clock** reloj de cuclillo, etc. II. *a.* (fam.) loco, chiflado

cucullate(d [kjúkjuleit(id], *a.* en forma de capucha; con capucha, encapuchado.

cuculliform [kjukúliform], *a.* de forma de capucha. *V.* CUCULLATE(D.

cucumber [kjúkʌmbœ(r)], *s.* (bot.) cohombro, pepino.

cucurbit [kjukœ́rbjt], *s.* cucúrbita, retorta de alambique; (bot.) planta de las cucurbitáceas.

cucurbitaceous [-éjšjʌs], *a.* (bot.) cucurbitáceo.

cud [kʌd], *s.* alimento que mastican por segunda vez los rumiantes.—**c.-chewing,** rumiante, rumiador.—**chewing the c.,** rumia(dura).—**to chew the c.,** rumiar; (fig.) meditar despacio; charlar.

cudbear [kʌ́dbɐr], *s.* (bot.) orchilla; (tint.) orcina.

cuddle [kʌ́dl]. I. *va.* abrazar con ternura, acariciar, mimar. II. *vn.* estar abrazados; arrimarse; ponerse juntitos. III. *s.* abrazo.

cuddy [kʌ́dj], *s.* (mar.) tumbadillo; fogón; armario, aparador.

cudgel [kʌ́džɛl]. I. *s.* garrote, estaca, palo, porra; (Am.) tolete.—**c. play,** lid deportiva con garrotes.—**to take up the cudgels,** (fig.) entrar en una controversia, entrar en la lucha; (con *for*) salir a la defensa (de). II. *va.* apalear, tundir, aporrear.—**to c. one's brains,** devanarse los sesos.

cudgeller [-œ(r)], *s.* apaleador, aporreador.

cudweed [kʌ́dwid], *s.* (bot.) lanaria, perpetua.

cue [kju], *s.* cola, rabo; coleta, trenza de cabello (*v.* QUEUE); (teat.) pie, apunte; indirecta, sugestión; genio, humor; taco de billar.—**c. ball,** pinta.

cuff [kʌf]. I. *s.* trompada, bofetón, manotada; puño de camisa; bocamanga; vuelta de pantalón.—*pl.* esposas, manillas.—**c. buttons** o **links,** gemelos. II. *va.* abofetear, manotear; maniatar. III. *vn.* dar de puñadas, luchar, boxear.

cuirass [kwjrǽs], *s.* coraza.

cuirassier [kwjrasír], *s.* coracero.

cuish [kwjš], **cuisse** [kwjs], *s.* (arm.) escarcela, muslera, quijote.

cuisine [kwjzín], *s.* cocina, arte culinario.

cul-de-sac [kʌ́l dœ sǽk], *s.* callejón o conducto cerrado o tapado en un extremo.

culex [kjúlɛks], *s.* (ent.) mosquito.

culinary [kjúljnɐrj], *a.* culinario.

cull [kʌl]. I. *va.* escoger, elegir, entresacar. II. *s.* cosa o animal inferior o sin valor.

cullender [kʌ́lɛndœ(r)], *s.* = COLANDER.

culler [kʌ́lœ(r)], *s.* escogedor.

cullet [kʌ́ljt], *s.* (vid.) vidrio de desecho.

cullis [kʌ́ljs], *s.* canal de tejado.

culm [kʌlm], *s.* (bot.) caña, tallo; antracita inferior; polvo o desperdicios de carbón; cisco.

culminate [kʌ́lmjnejt], *vn.* culminar; lograr o alcanzar, terminar (en); (astr.) culminar.

culmination [-éjšon], *s.* culminación, auge.

culottes [kulǽts], *s. pl.* falda pantalón.

culpability [kʌlpabjljtj], *s.* culpabilidad.

culpable [kʌ́lpabl], *a.* culpable.—**culpableness** [-njs], *s.* culpa, culpabilidad.—**culpably** [-blj], *adv.* culpablemente.

culprit [kʌ́lprjt], *s.* reo, delincuente, criminal.

cult [kʌlt], *s.* culto; homenaje; devoción.

cultism [-jzm], *s.* devoción a un culto; (lit.) cult(eran)ismo, gongorismo.

cultch [kʌlch], *s.* basura; hueva de molusco.

cultivable [kʌ́ltjvabl], *a.* cultivable.

cultivate [kʌ́ltjvejt], *va.* cultivar, culturar, beneficiar, lab(o)rar; estudiar, ejercer, practicar; darse a; criar (gusanos de seda, etc.); (agr.) dar las labores a.—**cultivated** [-jd], *a.* cultivado, culto (ú. de plantas, tierras, etc.); labrado; culto, ilustrado, instruido.

cultivation [-éjšon], *s.* cultivación, cultivo; labranza; labor, *f.*, mejora, adelantamiento; cultura; (agr.) labores.

cultivator [-ǫ(r)], *s.* cultivador, labrador, agricultor; cultivadora; escarificador, extirpador; azadilla.

cultural [kʌ́lchūrɐl], *a.* cultural, perteneciente a la cultura o al cultivo.

culture [kʌ́lchū(r)]. I. *s.* cultura; cultivación; cultivo (de bacterias, etc.); civilización; ilustración. II. *va.* educar, enseñar, criar; refinar.

cultured [-d], *a.* culto, ilustrado.

culverin [kʌ́lvɐrjn], *s.* (arti.) culebrina, moyana.

culvert [kʌ́lvœrt], *s.* alcantarilla, atarjea.

cumber [kʌ́mbœ(r)], *va.* oprimir, obstruir, embrollar, estorbar; molestar, incomodar.

cumbersome [-sʌm], **cumbrous** [kʌ́mbrʌs], *a.* pesado, engorroso, enfadoso, incómodo, fastidioso, molesto, difícil de manejar.

cumbersomely [-lj], **cumbrously** [-lj], *adv.* pesadamente, incómodamente.

cumbersomeness [-njs], *s.* incomodidad.

cumbrance [kʌ́mbrʌns], *s.* carga, impedimento, molestia. *V.* ENCUMBRANCE.

cum(m)in [kʌ́mjn], *s.* (bot.) comino (planta y semilla).

cumulate [kjúmyʊlejt], *va.* y *vn.* acumular(se), amontonar(se), hacinar(se).

cumulation [-léjšon], *s.* acumulación, amontonamiento, hacinamiento.

cumulative [-lǽtjv], *a.* (a)cumulativo.

cumulo-cirrus [kjumyʊlosírʌs], *s.* (meteor.) cirro, nubes (*f. pl.*) que los marinos llaman *colas de gato.*—**cumulo-nimbus** [-njmbʌs], *s.* nimbo, nube de lluvia.—**cumulo-stratus** [-stréjtʌs], *s.* estrato, masa nebulosa horizontal.

cumulus [kjúmyʊlʌs], *s.* montón; (meteor.) cúmulo.

cuneal [kjúnjɑl], **cuneate(d** [kjúnjejt(jd], **cuneiform** [kjúnijform], *a.* cuneiforme.

cunner [kʌ́nœ(r)], *s.* (ict.) pez lábrido o labroideo.

cunning [kʌ́njŋ]. I. *a.* astuto, artero, marrullero; socarrón, ladino, solapado; artificioso; hábil, sutil; sagaz; (E. U.) gracioso, divertido, mono (apl. gen. a los niños). II. *s.* astucia, ardid, *m.*, disimulo, artificio; bellaquería, malicia, marrullería; sagacidad.

cunningly [-lj], *adv.* astuta, hábil, graciosamente.

cup [kʌp]. I. *s.* copa; taza, jícara, pocillo; cubeta; (igl.) cáliz, *m.*; (bot.) cúpula; (fig.) suerte, *f.*, fortuna; trago; (med.) copa que se da como premio; (med.) ventosa.—**c.-shaped,** acopado.—**in his cups,** ebrio, chispo. II. *va.* aplicar ventosas; ahuecar en forma de taza, acopar.

cupbearer [-bɛrœ(r)], *s.* copero o escanciador.

cupboard [kʌ́bord], *s.* aparador, alacena, armario.

cupcake [kʌ́pkejk], *s.* pequeño bollo en forma de taza.

cupel [kjúpɛl]. I. *s.* (metal.) copela. II. *va.* copelar.

cupellation [-éjšon], *s.* (metal.) copelación.

cupful [kʌ́pful], *s.* contenido de una taza.

cupid [kjúpjd], *s.* cupido.

cupidity [kjupídjtj], *s.* codicia, avaricia.

cupola [kjúpolɑ], *s.* (arq.) cúpula, domo, cimborrio, media naranja; (fund.) cubilote, horno de manga; (mar.) cúpula, torre blindada (de acorazado).

cupper [kʌ́pœ(r)], *s.* aplicador de ventosas.

cupping [kʌ́pjŋ], *s.* reducción a forma acopada; (med.) sajadura o escarificación para ventosa; aplicación de ventosa.—**c. glass,** ventosa.

cupreous [kjúprjʌs], *a.* cobrizo, cobreño; cúprico.

cupric [kjúprjk], *a.* (quím.) cúprico.

cupriferous [kjuprífɛrʌs], *a.* cuprífero.

cuprite [kjúprajt], *s.* (min.) cuprita, mineral de óxido de cobre.

cupromanganese, cupronickel [kjupromǽŋganis, -njkɛl], etc. cupromanganeso, cuproníquel, etc. (aleación de cobre y manganeso, cobre y níquel, etc.).

cuprous [kjúprʌs], *a.* (quím.) cuproso.

cupule [kjúpjul], *s.* hueco acopado; (bot.) cúpula.

cupuliferous [-jfɛrʌs], *a.* (bot.) cupulífero.

cur [kœr], *s.* perro de mala ralea, gozque; canalla.

curable [kjúrɑbl], *a.* curable, sanable.—**curableness** [-njs], *s.* curabilidad.

curaçao, curaçoa [kjurɑsóʊ], *s.* curasao, curazao.

curacy [kjúrɑsj], *s.* (igl.) curato, oficio de cura.

curare [kurárj], *s.* curare (planta y veneno).

curassow [kjúrɑsoʊ], *s.* (orn.) guaco.

curate [kiúrit], *s.* teniente de cura; cura, *m.*
curateship [-šip], *s.* = CURACY.
curative [kiúrativ], *a.* curativo, sanativo.
curator [kiuréito(r)], *s.* curador; guardián, conservador, celador, encargado.
curatrix [-triks], *s.* curadora.
curb [kœrb]. **I.** *s.* barbada; freno con barbada; (fig.) sujeción, restricción; brocal de pozo; bordillo, orilla, encintado, o flanco (de acera); bolsín, lugar de la calle donde se hacen transacciones de lonja (ll. t. **c. market**); (vet.) corvaza. **II.** *va.* refrenar, contener, reprimir, poner freno o coto a.
curbing [-iŋ], *s.* refrenamiento. *V.* CURBSTONE.
—curbstone [-stouŋ], *s.* piedra que forma el reborde o flanco de la acera; encintado; guardacantón; brocal de pozo.
curculio [kœrkiúliouŋ], *s.* (ent.) curculio, especie de escarabajo.
curcuma [kœrkiumǎ], *s.* (bot.) cúrcuma.
curd [kœrd]. **I.** *s.* cuajada; requesón; grumo. **II.** *va.* cuajar, coagular.
curdle [kœrdl]. **I.** *vn.* cuajarse, coagularse, engrumecerse, arrequesonarse; (fig.) helarse (la sangre). **II.** *va.* coagular, cuajar, espesar.
curd(l)y [kœrd(l)i], *a.* cuajado, coagulado.
curé [kiuréi], *s.* (igl.) cura, *m.*
cure [kiúr]. **I.** *s.* cura, curación; remedio; cura (de la madera, etc.); cura, cuidado (del hormigón, etc.); vulcanización (del caucho o goma). **—c.-all**, panacea, catolicón, sánalotodo. **II.** *va.* curar, sanar; curar (la madera, la carne, etc.); vulcanizar. **III.** *vn.* curar, sanar; curarse (la madera, etc.); vulcanizarse.
cureless [-ljs], *a.* incurable.
curer [-œ(r)], *s.* sanador, remediador; ahumador, salador; preparador de salazones y conservas.
curettage [kiurétidž], *s.* (cir.) curetaje.
curfew [kœrfju], *s.* toque de queda.
curia [kiúriǎ], *s.* curia.
curial [-l], *a.* y *s.* curial.
curie [kiúri], *s.* (fís.) curie, *m.*, unidad de masa de emanación de radio.
curio [kiúriouŋ], *s.* objeto curioso y raro.
curiosity [kiuriásiti], *s.* curiosidad; rareza.
curious [kiúriʌs], *a.* curioso; entremetido, preguntón; cuidadoso, exacto; raro, singular; (fam.) excéntrico.**—curiously** [-li], *adv.* curiosamente; singularmente.**—curiousness** [-njs], *s.* curiosidad; extrañeza.
curl [kœrl]. **I.** *s.* bucle, rizo, sortija, tirabuzón (del cabello); (Am.) crespo; tortuosidad, sinuosidad, ondulación; enfermedad de árboles y plantas; alabeo (de la madera).**—c. paper**, papelito para rizar el pelo. **II.** *va.* rizar, encrespar, ensortijar, achulegar, ondear.**—to c. the lip**, fruncir el labio. **III.** *vn.* rizarse, enroscarse, encarrujarse.
curled [-d], *a.* rizado, crespo, ensortijado, escarolado.**—c. up**, abarquillado.
curlew [kœrlju], *s.* (orn.) zarapito, chorlito.
curlicue [kœrlikiu], *s.* retortijón, enroscadura.
curliness [kœrlinjs], *s.* ensortijamiento.
curling [kœrliŋ], *s.* ensortijamiento; (dep.) juego parecido al chito, que se juega con piedras sobre el hielo.**—c. irons, o c. tongs**, encrespador, rizador, tenacillas.**—c. stone**, piedra con agarradera para el juego de *curling*.
curlingly [-li], *adv.* rizadamente.
curly [kœrli], *a.* rizado, crespo, rizo, rizoso.**—c.-hair(ed**, de pelo crespo.
curmudgeon [kœrmʌdžʌn], *s.* tacaño, cicatero; persona displicente e irascible.
currant [kœrǎnt], *s.* (bot.) grosella; uva o pasa de Corinto.**—c. bush**, grosellero.
currency [kœrensi], *s.* moneda corriente; dinero en circulación; uso corriente; valor corriente.
current [kœrent]. **I.** *a.* corriente, común; admitido, en boga; general, popular; circulante, corriente; presente, del día, de actualidad, actual, en curso.**—c. account**, cuenta corriente (en un banco).**—c. events**, sucesos de día, asuntos de la actualidad.**—c. exchange**, cambio corriente.**—c. money**, moneda legal.**—c. rate**, (com.) curso. **II.** *s.* corriente, *f.* (de agua, aire, etc.); rebalaje (de agua); (elec.) corriente; intensidad de la corriente; curso, marcha, progreso.**—c. meter**, (elec.) contador de intensidad; (hidr.) molinete hidrométrico, medidor de corriente; hidrómetro.**—c. wheel**, (hidr.) rueda de paletas planas movida por la corriente.
currently [-li], *adv.* corrientemente; generalmente; a la moda.**—currentness** [-njs], *s.* circulación; calidad de actual; aceptación general.
curricle [kœrikl], *s.* carrocín, carriola.
curricular [kʌríkyǔlǎ(r)], *a.* del plan de estudios o relativo a él.
curriculum [-lʌm], *s.* plan de estudios.
currier [kœrjœ(r)], *s.* (ten.) curtidor, zurrador, noquero; almohazador (de caballos).
curriery [-ri], *s.* tenería.
currish [kœriš], *a.* perruno; arisco; brutal.
curry [kœri]. **I.** *va.* (ten.) zurrar, adobar; (fam.) zurrar a uno la badana; almohazar (caballos) (coc.) condimentar con *curry*.**—to c. favor**, pedir o buscar favores adulando o abyectamente. **II.** *s.* (coc.) salsa usada en la India como condimento; plato sazonado con esta salsa.**—c. powder**, polvo de ciertas especias para preparar el *curry*.
currycomb [-kouŋ], *s.* almohaza, rascadera.
curse [kœrs]. **I.** *va.* maldecir, anatematizar, execrar, imprecar. **II.** *vn.* renegar, echar ternos, blasfemar. **III.** *s.* maldición; imprecación, anatema, *mf.*; terno, reniego, blasfemia; calamidad, azote.**—a c. on!**, ¡mal haya!
cursed [-id], *a.* maldito, abominable, execrable.**—cursedly** [-li], *adv.* miserablemente; abominablemente.**—cursedness** [-njs], *s.* malicia, perversidad; abominación, execración.
curser [-œ(r)], *s.* maldiciente.
cursing [-iŋ]. **I.** *s.* execración, maldición. **II.** *a.* maldiciente, blasfemador.
cursive [kœrsiv], *a.* y *s.* cursivo, corriente.**—c. hand**, letra cursiva.
cursorily [kœrsorili], *adv.* precipitadamente, de paso, de carrera.**—cursoriness** [-injs], *s.* precipitación, prisa; descuido.
cursory [-i], *a.* sumario, rápido, precipitado, de carrera, por encima.
curt [kœrt], *a.* corto, conciso; brusco, rudo, seco.
curtail [kœrtéil], *va.* cortar, abreviar, reducir, escatimar, cercenar, desmembrar; restringir.
curtailment [-ment], *s.* reducción, abreviación, rebajamiento.
curtain [kœrtin]. **I.** *s.* cortina, *pl.* cortinaje; velo (gal.) estor, transparente; (teat.) telón; (fort.) cortina.**—c. call**, llamada a la escena para recibir los aplausos.**—c. lecture**, regaño privado.**—c. of fire** = BARRAGE.**—c. raiser**, (teat.) pieza o representación preliminar.**—behind the c.**, entre bastidores; en secreto.**—to draw the c.**, correr un velo, ocultar. **II.** *va.* poner cortinas.**—to c. off**, separar por cortinas.
curtation [kœrtéišŏn], *s.* (astr.) curtación.
curtly [kœrtli], *adv.* brevemente; secamente, lacónica y bruscamente.
curtness [kœrtnjs], *s.* concisión, brevedad; brusquedad, rudeza, sequedad.
curtsy, curtsey [kœrtsi]. **I.** *s.* reverencia, cortesía. **II.** *vn.* hacer una cortesía o reverencia.
curule [kiúrul], *a.* curul.**—c. chair**, silla curul.
curvaceous [kœrvéišʌs], *a.* (fam.) de muchas curvas y redondeces (apl. a la mujer frescachona y rolliza).
curvate(d [kœrveit(id], *a.* corvo, encorvado.
curvation [kœrvéišŏn], *s.* curvidad, encorvadura, curvatura.
curvature [kœrvačhǔ(r)], *s.* curvatura, (en)corvadura, encorvamiento, corcova, comba; (arq.) cintra.

curve [kœrv]. **I.** *va.* combar, curvar, encorvar, torcer. **II.** *vn.* encorvarse, torcerse; voltear en curva. **III.** *a.* = CURVED. **IV.** *s.* curva; comba; combadura.

curved [-d], *a.* curvo, corvo, torcido, encorvado.

curvet [kœrvịt]. **I.** *s.* corveta, corcovo. **II.** *va.* y *vn.* corcovear, corvetear, cabriolar.

curvilinear [kœrvilíniặ(r)], *a.* curvilíneo.

curving [kœrviŋ]. **I.** *a.* curvo, onduloso. **II.** *s.* curvatura.

cushat [kʌ́ʃạt], *s.* (orn.) paloma torcaz.

cushion [kúʃọn]. **I.** *s.* cojín; almohadilla; bolo; b(ar)anda (de mesa de billar); (mec.) amortiguador; blandura o suavidad elástica. **II.** *va.* cubrir con cojines, poner cojines a; acojinar, amortiguar, suavizar; someter a acción amortiguadora.

cushy [kúʃị], *a.* (fam.) fácil, descansado, cómodo.

cusp [kʌsp], *s.* cúspide, *f.*; (astr.) cuerno de la luna.

cuspid [kʌ́spịd], *s.* colmillo, (diente) canino.

cuspidal [-ạl], *a.* puntiagudo.

cuspidate(d [kʌ́spịdeịt(ịd], *a.* cuspidado, cuspídeo.

cuspidor [kʌ́spịdọr], *s.* escupidera.

cuss [kʌs]. **I.** *s.* (fam.) terno, reniego; individuo o animal tunante o de poca monta. **II.** *va.* y *vn.* (fam.) maldecir.

cussedness [-idnịs], *s.* (fam.) malicia, tunantería.

custard [kʌ́stạrd], *s.* (coc.) flan, natillas.—**c. apple,** (bot.) guanábana, jachalí, anona.

custodial [kʌstóụdiạl], *a.* del custodio o de la custodia.

custodian [-diạn], *s.* custodio.

custody [kʌ́stọdị], *s.* custodia; guardia; cárcel, *f.*, prisión; cuidado; seguridad; recaudo.

custom [kʌ́stọm], *s.* costumbre, usanza, uso, hábito; clientela o parroquia de una tienda; venta, salida, despacho.—*pl.* (derechos de) aduana; derechos arancelarios o aduaneros.—**c.-built,** hecho a la orden.—**c.-free,** libre de derechos.—**c.-made,** hecho a la medida.—**c. tailor,** sastre ordinario (que hace ropa a la medida).—**c. work,** trabajo de cualquier clase hecho según pedido.—**to have the c. of,** soler, acostumbrar (hacer algo).—**customs union,** unión aduanera.

customable [-ạbl], *a.* adeudable; que debe pagar derechos de aduana.

customarily [-erịlị], *adv.* comúnmente, habitualmente, ordinariamente.

customariness [-erịnịs], *s.* frecuencia, hábito, costumbre.

customary [-erị], *a.* usual, habitual, acostumbrado; (for.) consuetudinario, a fuero.

customer [-œ(r)], *s.* parroquiano, cliente, marchante.

customhouse [-haụs], *s.* aduana.—**c. broker,** corredor de aduana.—**c. duty,** adeudo; *pl.* derechos arancelarios o de aduana.—**c. manifest,** manifiesto.—**c. officer,** o **inspector,** aduanero, vista, *m.*—**c. seal,** marchamo.

cut [kʌt], *va.* (*pret.* y *pp.* CUT) cortar; dividir, hender, partir, tajar; picar; rebanar; lastimar, herir; cincelar, grabar, labrar, tallar; desbastar; segar; recortar; negar el saludo a; extrañar; castrar (panales de miel, animales); levantar, alzar o cortar (los naipes); rebajar, reducir (los sueldos, gastos, etc.); faltar o no asistir a (la escuela, etc.); cortar (un traje); ejecutar, hacer (piruetas, etc.).—**to c. across,** cortar al través. —**to c. a figure,** descollar; hacer papel.—**to c. asunder,** separar cortando, despedazar.—**to c. away,** recortar, cercenar, quitar cortando. —**to c. capers,** cabriolar, hacer cabriolas.—**to c. down,** derribar cortando, tumbar; mermar, disminuir, rebajar, cercenar.—**to c. ice,** (fam.) valer, ser de importancia.—**to c. in,** (elec.) intercalar, conectar, introducir.—**to c. off,** quitar cortando; amputar; aislar, incomunicar; (tel.) cortar la comunicación; interrumpir,

suspender el abastecimiento (de vapor, agua, etc.); segar (fig.), destruir, arrebatar; interceptar; desheredar; terminar.—**to c. one's wisdom teeth,** (fam.) salirle a uno la muela del juicio, llegar a la edad de la prudencia, tener uso de razón.—**to c. open,** abrir cortando, dividir.—**to c. out,** quitar o sacar cortando; recortar; dar forma a (traje, bosque) cortando; preparar; labrar (el porvenir, etc.); (elec.) poner fuera de circuito, desconectar; (fam.) desbancar, suplantar (apl. gen. a asuntos de amores); excluir; suprimir; separar; (fam., con *it* por acusativo) no hablar más de eso, callarse, dejarse de eso.—**to c. short,** interrumpir; terminar repentina o prematuramente; abreviar; cortar a raíz; despedazar (fig., un libro, una reputación); (fam.) afligir, acongojar.

cut. **I.** *s.* corte; cortadura, (Am.) cortada; incisión; tajo, tajadura; ofensa, zaherimiento, cosa o palabra hiriente; desaire; falta, ausencia (de una clase, etc.); pedazo, cosa cortada; tajada, rebanada; atajo; figura, hechura; moda; forma; reducción, rebaja (de sueldos, gastos, etc.); (impr.) clisé; grabado, figura; (joy.) talla. **II.** *a.* cortado, tallado; labrado, tallado; capado, castrado; reducido, rebajado (apl. a precios); (fam.) achispado.—**c. and dried,** preparado, arreglado o convenido de antemano; de ordenanza.—**c. diamond,** diamante tallado.—**c. gear,** (mec.) dientes tallados a máquina.—**c. glass,** cristal tallado.—**c.-price, c.-rate,** a precio reducido.—**c. sugar,** azúcar en terrones. —**c. tobacco,** picadura de tabaco.

cutaneous [kịutéịnịʌs], *a.* cutáneo.

cutaway [kʌ́tạweị], **c. coat,** *s.* chaqué o chaquet, levita de faldones sesgados o abiertos.

cute [kịut], *a.* (fam.) cuco, mono, lindo; listo.

cuticle [kịútịkl], *s.* cutícula; película.

cuticular [kịutíkyǔlặ(r)], *a.* cuticular.

cutis [kịútịs], *s.* cutis, *mf.*; dermis, *mf.*

cutlass [kʌ́tlạs], *s.* alfanje, machete, chafarote.

cutler [kʌ́tlœ(r)], *s.* cuchillero.

cutlery [kʌ́tlœrị], *s.* cuchillería.

cutlet [kʌ́tlịt], *s.* (coc.) chuleta, costilla.

cutoff [kʌ́tạf], *s.* brazo de río que atraviesa una punta de tierra; laguna que queda cuando un río cambia su cauce; atajo; (m. v.) cortavapor; cierre a la admisión; punto de expansión; punto de cierre a la admisión; grado de admisión.— **c. valve,** válvula de expansión; válvula de cierre a la admisión.

cutout [kʌ́taụt], *s.* recortado; (elec.) cortacircuitos, fusible, disyuntor, interruptor, desconectador; (mec., aut.) escape libre.—*pl.* figuras recortables (para niños).—**c. muffler,** silenciador con válvula de escape libre en el tubo de escape.

cutpurse [kʌ́tpœrs], *s.* cortabolsas, carterista.

cutter [kʌ́tœ(r)], *s.* cortador; herramienta o máquina para cortar; cuchilla; fresa; hierro, hoja (parte cortante de una herramienta); grabador, tallador; pequeño trineo; (mar.) cúter; escampavía, guardacostas.—**c. bar,** portacuchilla, portahierro.

cutthroat [kʌ́tθrout], *s.* asesino.

cutting [kʌ́tiŋ]. **I.** *a.* cortante; de cortar; incisivo, hiriente, mordaz; penetrante; amargo, penoso. **II.** *s.* cortadura; corte; incisión; sección; recorte; viruta, retazo; alce (de naipes); (joy.) talla; (agr.) plantón, estaca de plantar.—**c. edge,** corte, filo, tajador.—**c. tool,** herramienta de filo.

cuttlebone [kʌ́tlboun], *s.* jibión, *m.*

cuttlefish [-fiʃ], *s.* (ict.) pulpo, jibia, sepia.

cutup [kʌ́tʌp], *s.* (fam.) = CIANITA.

cutwater [kʌ́twɔtœ(r)], *s.* (mar.) tajamar; nariz de puente.

cutwork [kʌ́twœrk], *s.* (cost.) calado.

cutworm [kʌ́twœrm], *s.* (ent.) agrotis, *m.,* larva destructora de las plantas tiernas.

cyanamide [saiánɛmaid], *s.* cianamido.

cyanate [sáianeit], *s.* (quím.) cianato.

cyanic [saiánik], *a.* (quím.) ciánico; (bot.) azul.

cyanid(e [sáianaid], *s.* (quím.) cianuro.

cyaniding [-iŋ], *s.* (metal.) cianuración.

cyanite [sáianait], *s.* (min.) cianita.

cyanogen [saiénodźin], *s.* cianógeno.

cyanosis [saianóusis], *s.* (med.) cianosis.

cyanotype [saiénotaip], *s.* fotografía de cianuro.

cyanuric [saianiúrik], *a.* cianúrico.

cycad [sáikæd], *s.* (bot.) cicadácea.—**Cycadaceæ** [-éiʃii], *s. pl.* (bot.) cicadáceas.

cyclamen [síklamin], *s.* (bot.) ciclamino, pamporcino, artanica o artanita.

cycle [sáikl]. **I.** *s.* ciclo; período; (elec.) período; bicicleta, triciclo, velocípedo. **II.** *vn.* mover o pasar por ciclos; andar en bicicleta, etc.

cyclecar [-kar], *s.* motocicleta o automóvil pequeño de tres o de cuatro ruedas.

cyclic(al [síklik(al], *a.* cíclico.

cycling [sáikliŋ], *s.* (dep.) ciclismo, velocipedismo.

cyclist [sáiklist], *s.* ciclista, velocipedista.

cycloid [sáikloid], *s.* (geom.) cicloide, *f.*

cycloid(al [saiklóid(al], *a.* cicloidal, cicloideo.

cyclometer [saiklámɛtœ(r)], *s.* ciclómetro u odómetro.

cyclometric [saiklométrik], *a.* ciclométrico.

cyclometry [saiklámetri], *s.* ciclometría.

cyclonal [saiklóunal], **cyclonic** [saiklánik], *a.* ciclonal.

cyclone [sáikloun], *s.* ciclón, prester, huracán.—**c. cellar,** sótano de refugio contra un ciclón.

cyclopedia [saiklopídiɛ], *s.* enciclopedia.

cyclopedic [-pídik], *a.* enciclopédico.

Cyclopean [-píɛn], **Cyclopic** [saiklápik], *a.* gigantesco; ciclópeo, pert. a los cíclopes.

Cyclops [sáiklaps], *s.* (mit.) Cíclope.

cyclorama [saiklórámɛ], *s.* ciclorama, *m.,* panorama, *m.*

Cyclostomata [-stóumɛtɛ], *s. pl.* (ict.) ciclóstomos.

cyclostyle [-stail], *s.* ciclostilo, ciclóstilo.

cyclotron [-tran], *s.* (fís.) ciclotrón.

cygnet [sígnit], *s.* (orn.) pollo del cisne.

cylinder [sílindœ(r)]. **I.** *s.* cilindro; rodillo, rollo; tambor.—**c. block,** bloque de cilindros.—**c. bore,** diámetro interior del cilindro.—**c. head,** fondo del cilindro; culata del cilindro (esp. en aut.).—**c. metal,** hierro de cilindros; ferromanganeso.—**c. oil,** aceite de cilindros, aceite lubricante espeso. **II.** *va.* cilindrar; proveer de cilindro(s).

cylindric(al [silíndrik(al], *a.* cilíndrico.

cylindricity [-drísiti], *s.* cilindricidad.

cylindroid [sílindroid]. **I.** *s.* (geom.) cilindroide. **II.** *a.* cilindroideo.

cyma [sáimɛ], **cymatium** [siméiʃiʌm], *s.* (arq.) cimacio, gola.—**c. reversa,** talón.

cymbal [símbal], *s.* (mús.) címbalo, platillo.

cymbalist [-ist], *s.* cimbalero, cimbalista.

cyme [saim], *s.* (bot.) cima.

cymophane [sáimofein], *s.* (min.) cimófana, crisoberilo.

cynegetic [sinɛdźétik], *a.* cinegético.

cynegetics [-s], *s.* cinegética.

cynic [sínik], *s.* cínico.—**cynic(al** [sínik(al], *a.* cínico, sarcástico, pesimista.—**cynically** [-i], *adv.* cínica o sarcásticamente.—**cynicism** [sínisizm], *s.* cinismo.

cynosure [sáinoʃur], *s.* miradero, blanco; lo que sirve de guía; (astr.) Cinosura, Osa Menor.

cyperaceous [saipɛréiʃiʌs], *a.* (bot.) ciperáceo.

cypher [sáifœ(r)], *s., va.* y *vn.* = CIPHER.

cypress [sáipres], *s.* (bot.) ciprés.—**c. nut,** piñuela.

Cyprian [síprian], *a.* y *s.* cipri(n)o, chipriota, *mf.*

Cyrenaic [sirɛnéik], *a.* y *s.* cirenaico, cireneo.

cyst [sist], *s.* (med., zool.) quiste; zurrón.

cystectomy [sistéktomi], *s.* (cir.) cistectomía.

cystic [sístik], **cystous** [sístʌs], *a.* cístico.

cystitis [sistáitis], *s.* (med.) cistitis.

cystocarp [sístokarp], *s.* (bot.) cistocarpo.—**cystocele** [-sil], *s.* (med.) cistocele, *f.,* hernia de la vejiga.—**cystoma** [sistóumɛ], *s.* (med.) cistoma, *m.*—**cystoscope** [sístoskoup], *s.* cistoscopio.

cystotomy [sistátomi], *s.* (cir.) cistotomía.

Cytherean [siθériɛn], *a.* citéreo.

cytisus [sítisʌs], *s.* (bot.) cítiso, borne, codeso.

cytoblast [sáitoblæst], *s.* (biol.) citoblasto, núcleo (de una célula).

cytology [saitálodźi], *s.* (biol.) citología.

cytoplasm [sáitoplæzm], *s.* (biol.) citoplasma, *m.*

czar [zar], *s.* zar.—**czarevitch** [zárévitch], *s.* zarevitz, hijo del zar.—**czarevna** [zarévnɛ], *s.* hija del zar.—**czarina** [zarínɛ], *s.* zarina.—**czarism** [zárizm], *s.* zarismo.

Czech [chék], *s.* y *a.* checo.—**Czechoslovak(ian** [-oslovák(iɛn], *s.* y *a.* checo(e)slovaco.

D

d [di], *s.* d; (mús., **D**) re.

D, *a.* en D, de forma de D.—**D valve,** válvula de corredera.

dab [dæb]. **I.** *va.* frotar suavemente con algo blando; picar, golpear. **II.** *s.* mamola, sopapo, golpecito; picada, picotazo; untadura; brochazo; punzón(azo); (fam.) perito; (ict.) barbada.

dabber [-œ(r)], *s.* (impr.) bala.

dabble [dæbl]. **I.** *va.* rociar, salpicar; mojar. **II.** *vn.* chapotear; meterse en algún asunto o negocio; especular, jugar a la bolsa.

dabbler [dæblœ(r)], *s.* aficionado; el que se dedica a algún negocio, arte, etc., de modo superficial o inexperto.

dabster [dǽbstœ(r)], *s.* = DABBLER; (fam.) perito.

dace [deis], *s.* (ict.) albur, dardo, breca.

dachshund [dákshunt], *s.* especie de pachón, perro de patas muy cortas y torcidas.

Dacian [déiʃian], *s.* y *a.* dacio.

dactyl [dǽktil], *s.* (pros.) dáctilo (—◡◡).

dactylic [dæktílik], *a.* dactílico.

dactylography [-lágrafi], *s.* dactiloscopia (sistema de identificación por las impresiones digitales); dactilología. *V.* DACTYLOLOGY.

dactylology [-lálodźi], *s.* dactilología.

dactyloscopy [-láskopi], *s.* dactiloscopia.

dad [dæd], **daddie, daddy** [dǽd, -i], *s.* (fam.) papá, papaíto, taita, (Am.) tata.—**daddy-longlegs** (zool.) falangio, segador, arácnido de cuerpo corto y largas patas; (ent.) típula.

dado [déidou], *s.* (arq.) dado, neto; friso, rodapié, arrimadillo.

daedal [dídal], *a.* primoroso, intrincado; artístico, ingenioso.

daemon [dímon], *s.* numen; demonio, familiar.

daffodil [dǽfodil], *s.* (bot.) narciso atrompetado.

daffy [dǽfi], *a.* (fam.) = DAFT.

daft [dæft], *a.* bobo; venático, chiflado; demente.

dagger [dǽgœ(r)], *s.* daga, puñal; (impr.) cruz, obelisco [†].—**to be at daggers drawn,** estar a matar(se), o de uñas.—**to look daggers at,** mirar con odio.

daggle [dǽgl]. **I.** *va.* embarrar, enfangar, ensuciar arrastrando. **II.** *vn.* embarrarse, enfangarse.

dago [déigou], *s.* (fam. y desp., E. U.) italiano; español; portugués.

daguerreotype [dægérotaip], *s.* daguerrotipo.

dahlia [dályä], *s.* (bot.) dalia; pigmento violado.

daily [déilị]. **I.** *a.* diario, cotidiano, diurno. **II.** *s.* diario (periódico). **III.** *adv.* diariamente.

dainties [déintịz], *s.* chochos, confites, golosinas.

daintily [déintịlị], *adv.* delicadamente; regaladamente.—**daintiness** [-nịs], *s.* pulidez, delicadeza.

dainty [déintị]. **I.** *a.* delicado, exquisito, refinado; regalado, gustoso, sabroso; melindroso; afectado. **II.** *s.* regalo, bocado exquisito, gollería, golosina.

dairy [déri], *s.* lechería; quesera o quesería; vaquería, (Arg.) tambo.—**dairymaid** [-meid], *s.* lechera, mantequera, vaquera.—**dairyman** [-man], *s.* lechero, mantequero, vaquero, (Arg.) tambero.

dais [déis], *s.* tablado, grada, estrado; dosel, pabellón, palio, baldaquín.

daisy [déizị], *s.* (bot.) margarita; (fam.) primor.

dale [deil], *s.* vallecico, valle.

dalles [dælz], *s. pl.* cañada; recial.

dalliance [dǽlịạns], *s.* tardanza, dilación; regodeo, retozo, jugueteo; coqueteo.

dally [dǽlị], *vn.* tardar, entretenerse; perder el tiempo, holgar, retozar.

Dalmatian [dælméiṣịạn], *a.* y *s.* dálmata, dalmático; perro dalmático.

dalmatic [dælmǽtịk], *s.* dalmática.

daltonism [dáltọnịzm], *s.* (med.) daltonismo, acromatopsia.

dam [dæm]. **I.** *s.* madre (en ganadería); yegua; (hidr.) (re)presa, embalse, pantano, dique; (fund.) dama. **II.** *va.* (hidr.) represar, estancar, embalsar; cerrar, tapar.

damage [dǽmịdž]. **I.** *s.* daño, perjuicio, deterioro, estropeo, damnificación; pérdida; (com.) avería, siniestro, quebranto.—*pl.* daños y perjuicios; indemnización. **II.** *va.* dañar, averiar, deteriorar, estropear, lesionar, perjudicar, empecer, damnificar. **III.** *vn.* dañarse, averiarse.

damageable [-ạbl], *a.* susceptible de daño o de indemnización.—**damaged** [-d], *pp.* y *a.* averiado, deteriorado, etc.

damaging [-ịŋ], *a.* perjudicante, perjudicial.

daman [démạn], *s.* (zool.) damán (especie de marmota de Asia y África).

Damascene [dæmạsín]. **I.** *va.* V. DAMASKEEN. **II.** *a.* damasceno, amaceno; damasquino.

damask [dǽmạsk]. **I.** *s.* (tej.) damasco. **II.** *a.* adamascado, damasquinado.—**d. rose,** rosa de damasco o encarnada.—**d. steel,** acero damasquino. **III.** *va.* hacer labor de ataujía; (tej.) adamascar; florear, matizar.

damaskeen [dæmạskín], *va.* hacer labor de ataujía.—**damaskeening** [-ịŋ], *s.* ataujía.

damassin [dǽmạsin], *s.* (tej.) damasina.

dame [deim], *s.* dama, señora; (fam.) tía.

damn [dæm]. **I.** *va.* condenar a pena eterna; maldecir; reprobar; vituperar.—**d. it!** (fam. o vulg.) ¡maldito sea! ¡cáspita! **II.** *vn.* echar ternos, renegar. **III.** *s.* maldición; (fam.) ardite, pito (**that is not worth a damn,** eso no vale un pito).

damnable [dǽmnạbl], *a.* condenable; detestable; infame.—**damnably** [-ạblị], *adv.* horriblemente, de un modo abominable.—**damnation** [-éiṣọn], *s.* condenación, maldición.—**damnatory** [-ạtọrị], *a.* condenatorio.

damned [dæmd]. **I.** *a.* condenado, réprobo; maldito; detestable, vil, del diablo.—**the people be d.,** llévese el diablo al pueblo, un pito me importa el pueblo, al diablo con el pueblo. **II.** *adv.* (fam.) sumamente; como un diablo.

damnify [dǽmnịfai], *va.* (for.) dañar, perjudicar, lastimar, injuriar.

damp [dæmp]. **I.** *a.* húmedo, mojado. **II.** *s.* humedad; exhalación deletérea; desaliento, abatimiento.

damp, dampen [-ẹn]. **I.** *va.* humedecer, mojar; enfriar, desanimar, desalentar; apagar; amortiguar; cubrir el fuego. **II.** *vn.* humedecerse.—**to d. off,** (agr.) podrirse por el pie, por los ataques de honguillos.

dampening [-ẹnịŋ]. **I.** *s.* humectación o humedecimiento. **II.** *a.* humectativo.

damper [-œ(r)], *s.* apagador; amortiguador; registro, regulador de tiro de chimenea; apagador del piano, sordina; desalentador.

damping [-ịŋ], *s.* (elec.) amortiguación, diminución de la amplitud de las ondas.

dampness [-nịs], *s.* humedad; relente.

damsel [dǽmzẹl], *s.* damisela, doncella.

damson [dǽmzọn], *s.* (ciruela) damascena, damasco.

dance [dæns]. **I.** *vn.* bailar, danzar, tripudiar; saltar, brincar. **II.** *va.* hacer bailar o saltar.—**to d. attendance,** servir humilde y constantemente. **III.** *s.* danza, baile, tripudio.—**d. hall,** salón de baile.

danceable [-ạbl], *a.* bailable.

dancer [-œ(r)], *s.* danzante, bailador; bailarina; bailarín, saltarín.—*pl.* parejas de baile.

dancing [-ịŋ]. **I.** *s.* baile. **II.** *a.* de baile; que baila; danzante.—**d. girl,** bayadera; bailarina.—**d. master,** maestro de baile.—**d. partner,** pareja (de baile).—**d. pumps,** escarpines.—**d. school,** escuela de baile.

dandelion [dǽndịlaiọn], *s.* (bot.) diente de león, o amargón.

dander [dǽndœ(r)], *s.* caspa; (fam.) ira, enojo.—**to get one's d. up,** (fam.) irritar a uno.

dandify [dǽndịfai], *va.* acicalar, repulir, vestir como un lechuguino o petimetre.

dandle [dǽndl], *va.* mecer; hacer saltar sobre las rodillas; mimar, acariciar.

dandler [dǽndlœ(r)], *s.* niñero.

dandruff [dǽndrʌf], *s.* caspa.

dandy [dǽndị]. **I.** *s.* petimetre, currutaco, lechuguino, gomoso, caballerete. **II.** *a.* (fam.) magnífico, rebueno, de (re)chupete.—**d. fever,** dengue.

dandyism [-ịzm], *s.* dandismo.

Dane [dein], *s.* danés, danamarqués.

danger [déindžœ(r)], *s.* peligro, riesgo.—**there is no d.,** no hay miedo, no hay cuidado.

dangerous [-rʌs], *a.* peligroso, arriesgado; grave, serio, de cuidado.—**dangerously** [-lị], *adv.* peligrosamente, gravemente, seriamente.—**dangerousness** [-nịs], *s.* peligro, gravedad.

dangle [dǽŋgl]. **I.** *va.* colgar, suspender, columpiar. **II.** *vn.* pender, columpiarse, bambolearse; andar al retortero; irse tras una dama.

Danish [déinịṣ]. **I.** *a.* danés, dánico, dinamarqués. **II.** *s.* danés, lengua dinarquesa.

dank(ish [dǽŋk(iṣ], *a.* húmedo, liento.

dank(ish)ness [-(iṣ)nịs], *s.* = DAMPNESS.

danseuse [dansœz], *s.* bailarina, saltatriz.

Dantean [dǽntịạn], **I.** *a.* dantesco. **II.** *s.* dantista.

Dantesque [dæntésk], *a.* dantesco.

Danubian [dænjúbịạn], *a.* danubiano.

Daphne [dǽfnị], *s.* (bot.) rododafne.

dapper [dǽpœ(r)], *a.* apuesto, gallardo, gentil; limpio, aseado; vivaracho.

dapple [dǽpl], *va.* salpicar, pintar con manchas redondas, motear.

dapple(d [-(d], *a.* rodado, habado, tordo, salpicado.—**d.-gray, d.-grey,** rucio moteado.

dare [dér]. **I.** *vn.* (*pret.* DURST o DARED; *pp.* DARED) osar, atreverse, arriesgarse.—**I dare say,** me figuro; no tengo duda. **II.** *va.* arrostrar, hacer frente a; desafiar, retar. **III.** *s.* reto, desafío.

daredevil [-devil], *a.* y *s.* atrevido, temerario, osado.

daring [dérịŋ]. **I.** *a.* osado, atrevido, temerario;

emprendedor; (fam.) de pelo en pecho. **II.** *s.* osadía, bravura, atrevimiento.—**daringly** [-li], *adv.* atrevidamente, osadamente.

dark [dárk]. **I.** *a.* obscuro; negro (sentido recto y fig.); negruzco; pardo, trigueño, moreno; enigmático; secreto; ciego, ignorante; triste; desconsolador; atroz, siniestro, funesto.—**D. Ages,** edad del obscurantismo, edad media.—**d. horse,** caballo que no promete pero que sale ganador; (pol. E. U.) competidor o candidato desconocido o inesperado, candidato de componenda.—**d. lantern,** linterna sorda.—**d. meat,** (coc.) carne del ave fuera de la pechuga.—**d. slide,** (foto.) portaplacas.—**to grow d.,** anochecer, o(b)scurecer.—**to keep it d.,** ocultar algo. **II.** *s.* obscuridad; tinieblas, *f. pl.;* noche, *f.;* anochecer; ignorancia; secreto; (pint.) sombra muy obscura.—**in the d.,** a o(b)scuras; a ciegas, a tientas.—**to be (left) in the d.,** ignorar, no comprender, quedarse en ayunas o a buenas noches.

darken [-en]. **I.** *va.* obscurecer, ennegrecer, ensombrecer, cegar, obcecar, ofuscar; confundir, embrollar; denigrar, manchar; (fig.) contristar, entristecer. **II.** *vn.* obscurecerse, anochecerse.

darkling [-lin]. **I.** *adv.* a obscuras. **II.** *a.* obscuro, obscurecido; que pasa o está a obscuras.

darkly [-li], *adv.* obscuramente; secreta u ocultamente; con misterio o amenaza.

darkness [-nis], *s.* obscuridad, sombra, tinieblas; opacidad; obcecación u ofuscación; ceguera; ignorancia; secreto.

darkroom [-rum], *s.* (foto.) cámara o(b)scura.

darksome [-sam], *a.* (poét.) obscuro, opaco, sombrío; malvado, perverso.

darky [dárki], *s.* (fam.) negro, (Cuba) moreno.

darling [dárlin]. **I.** *a.* querido, amado. **II.** *s.* el predilecto, el querido, el favorito; (fam.) pichón, pichona.—**my d.,** vida mía, amor mío.

darn [darn]. **I.** *va.* zurcir, remendar; (fam.) maldecir. En leng. fam. ú. eufemísticamente en vez de DAMN en imprecaciones, reniegos, etc. *V.* DAMN, DAMNED. **II.** *s.* (fam.) ardite, pito.—**I don't give a d.,** no me importa un bledo.

darned [-d]. **I.** *a.* (fam.) maldito; dichoso. **II.** *adv.* (fam.) sumamente.—**a d. sight (more),** (fam.) muchísimo (más).

darnel [dárnel], *s.* (bot.) cizaña, cominillo, rabillo, joyo.

darner [dárnœr)], *s.* zurcidor o zurcidora.

darning [dárnin]. **I.** *a.* de zurcir.—**d. needle,** aguja de zurcir, aguja capotera; (ent.) libélula. **II.** *s.* zurcidura, zurcido, remiendo, recosido.

dart [dárt]. **I.** *s.* dardo, saeta, flecha, venablo, virote; tragacete; banderilla (de torero); movimiento rápido; (cost.) sisa.—**d. thrower,** banderillero. **II.** *va.* lanzar, tirar; flechar. **III.** *vn.* lanzarse, arrojarse, precipitarse; volar como dardo o saeta.

darter [-œr)], *s.* flechador, flechero; (ict.) pez pequeño americano; (orn.) pájaro-culebra.

Darwinian [darwínian]. **I.** *a.* darwiniano o darviniano. **II.** *a.* y *s.* darwinista o darvinista.

Darwinism [dárwinizm], *s.* darwinismo.

dash [déš]. **I.** *va.* arrojar, tirar, lanzar; quebrar, estrellar, romper; magullar; reprimir, desanimar; frustrar; desvanecer (esperanzas) rociar, salpicar; mezclar; adulterar; sazonar.—**to d. off,** escribir de prisa.—**to d. out,** tachar.—**to d. to pieces,** hacer añicos. **II.** *vn.* chocar, estrellarse, romperse (olas, etc.); arrojarse, lanzarse; saltar; zabullirse.—**to d. out,** salir precipitadamente. **III.** *s.* arremetida, arranque, ataque; incursión; colisión, choque, embate; revés, contrariedad; guión, *m.*, raya o línea; tilde, *f.,* tildón; fachenda, gran papel, ostentación, rumbo; brío, energía, empuje; mezcla, condimento, sabor; poquito, pequeña cantidad; (dep.) carrera corta y rápida (*100 meter dash,* 100 metros planos); (aut.) tablero de instru-

mentos.—**at one d.,** de un golpe.—**to cut a d.,** hacer gran papel.

dashboard [-bord], *s.* guardafango o parafango; (aut.) tablero de instrumentos.

dashing [-in]. **I.** *a.* precipitado, arrojado; vistoso, aparatoso, ostentoso; brioso, vivo; animoso, arrollador. **II.** *s.* embate, reventazón, maretazo (de las olas).

dashpot [-pat], *s.* (mec.) amortiguador.

dastard [dástard], *s.* collón, cobarde.

dastardize [-aiz], *va.* acobardar, amedrentar.

dastardliness [-nis], *s.* cobardía, pusilanimidad.

dastardly [-li], *a.* cobarde, pusilánime, tímido.

dasyure [désiyur], *s.* dasiuro (marsupial arbóreo).

data [détə *o* déitə], *s.* (*pl.* de DATUM) datos, detalles; antecedentes.

dataria [datériə], *s.* (igl.) dataría (tribunal).—**datary** [déitari], *s.* datario (prelado).

date [déit]. **I.** *s.* data, fecha; plazo; cita, compromiso; período, duración; tiempo, época; (bot.) dátil.—**d. line,** línea de cambio de fecha; data (de carta, documento, etc.).—**d. palm,** (bot.) datilera, palmera.—**d. shell,** (zool.) dátil de mar.—**at an early d.,** en próxima fecha.—**(down) to d.,** hasta la fecha, hasta ahora.—**out of d.,** anticuado, desusado, atrasado, pasado de moda.—**up to d.,** hasta ahora; al día, a la última.—**to make a d.,** (fam.) citar a uno. **II.** *va.* datar, fechar, poner fecha a; contar, computar; (fam.) dar cita a uno. **III.** *vn.* (con from) datar de(e), remontarse a.

dated [-id], *a.* fechado; (fam.) citado.—**to be d.,** tener fecha de; estar pasado de moda. *V.* OUT OF DATE.

dateless [-lis], *a.* sin fecha.

dater [-œr)], *s.* fechador, estampilla de fechar.

dative [déitiv], *a.* y *s.* (gram.) dativo.

datum [déitəm], *s.* dato.—**d. plane,** (top.) plano de referencia, plano de cota cero, plano de nivel.

Datura [datiúrə], *s.* (bot.), datura, estramonio.

daub [dób]. **I.** *va.* embadurnar; untar, manchar, embarrar; pintorrear; dar lechada; cubrir, disfrazar. **II.** *s.* unto, embarradura; mezcla o argamasa barata; pintarrajo, mamarrachada.

dauber [-œr)], *s.* embadurnador, pintor de brocha gorda, pintorreador, mamarrachista; cepillo para dar betún al calzado, etc.

daubing [-in], *s.* mortero, estuco; afeite; mamarracho.

dauby [-i], *a.* viscoso, pegajoso; pintarrajado.

daughter [dótœr)], *s.* hija.—**d.-in-law,** nuera.

daughterly [-li], *a.* como (una) hija; filial.

daunt [dónt], *va.* acobardar, desanimar; espantar, intimidar, atemorizar.

dauntless [-lis], *a.* intrépido, impávido.

dauntlessness [-nis], *s.* intrepidez, valor.

dauphin [dófin], *s.* delfín.

dauphiness [-nis], *s.* delfina.

davenport [dévenport], *s.* canapé cama; escritorio pequeño adornado.

davit [dévit], *s.* (mar.) pescante de bote.

daw [dó], *s.* (orn.) corneja.

dawdle [dódl], *vn.* perder tiempo, haronear.

dawdler [dódlœr)], *s.* haragán, gandul.

dawn [dón]. **I.** *vn.* amanecer, alborear, clarear, rayar o romper el alba; apuntar, asomar, mostrarse.—**to d. on,** u **upon one,** caer uno en la cuenta, empezar uno a ver o comprender. **II.** *s.* alba, aurora, madrugada; principio, comienzo, albores, crepúsculo (matutino).—**at d.**—al amanecer, de madrugada.

dawning [-in], *s.* alborada.

day [déi], *s.* día, *m.;* luz del día; período, época; jornada, horas de trabajo; lid, lucha, combate; vida.—**d. after d.,** día tras día.—**d. after tomorrow,** pasado mañana.—**d. bed,** sofá cama.—**d. before yesterday,** anteayer.—**d. blindness,** (med.) hemeralopia; por confusión, nictalopia. *V.* NYCTALOPIA.—**d. by d.,** día por día.—**d. in, d. out,** día tras día, sin cesar.—

d. labor, trabajo a jornal.—**d. laborer,** jornalero, peón, bracero.—**d. letter,** telegrama largo que se envía con ciertas restricciones por precio menor que el corriente.—**d. nursery,** lugar donde se cuidan niños durante las horas de trabajo de los padres, casa o sala de cunas.—**d. of doom,** día del juicio.—**d. of reckoning,** día de ajustar cuentas; (fig.) día de la justicia.—**days of grace,** días de gracia.—**days of obligation,** fiestas de guardar.—**d. scholar,** alumno externo.—**d. school,** escuela de externos; escuela de semana (no dominical); escuela diurna (en que se enseña de día).—**d. star,** lucero del alba.—**d. telegram = D. LETTER.**—**d. wages,** jornal.—**a d. off,** un día de asueto o de descanso.—**by d.,** de día.—**every other d.,** un día sí y otro no, cada dos días.—**from d. to d.,** de día en día, de un día para otro.—**in our day(s),** en nuestro tiempo.—**in (the) days of old,** en la antigüedad.—**on the following d.,** al otro día.—**one of these days,** un día de éstos.—**some fine d.,** el día menos pensado; el mejor día.—**the d. before,** la víspera.—**this d. week,** hace ocho días; de hoy en ocho días.—**to call it a d.,** (fam.) cesar de trabajar.—**to gain the d.,** salir vencedor, triunfar.—**to this d.,** hasta el día de hoy.

daybook [-buk], s. diario (libro); libro de cuentas diarias.

daybreak [-breik], s. amanecer. V. DAWN.—**at d.,** al amanecer, al alba, al romper el día, a la primera luz.

daydream [-drim], s. ensueño, ilusión, quimera.

dayfly [-flai], s. (ent.) efímera, cachipolla.

daylight [-lait], s. luz del día, luz natural.—**d.-saving time,** tiempo (hora) de verano (en que los relojes se ponen con una hora de adelanto).—**in broad d.,** en pleno día.

daylong [-loŋ]. I. a. de todo el día. II. adv. el día entero; (fam.) todo el santo día.

dayspring [-spriŋ], s. aurora, amanecer, alba.

daytime [-taim], s. día.—**in the d.,** de día.

daze [deiz]. I. va. ofuscar, aturdir, privar, trastornar. II. s. deslumbramiento, ofuscamiento.

dazzle [dézl], va. deslumbrar, ofuscar, encandilar; (mil.) camuflar, disfrazar.—**dazzlement** [-ment], s. deslumbramiento; traslumbramiento.—**dazzling** [dézliŋ], a. deslumbrador.

deacon [díkon], s. diácono.—**deaconess** [-is], s. diaconisa.—**deaconry** [-ri], **deaconship** [-sip], s. diaconato, diaconado, diaconía.

dead [déd], a. muerto, difunto, fallecido, finado; inerte; inanimado; entumecido; inactivo; sin uso; marchito, seco (flores, hojas, etc.); completo; silencioso; certero, seguro, indudable; absoluto; monótono; profundo, hondo (silencio, calma); (for.) privado de derechos civiles; apagado (carbón, sonido, etc.); mortal; desechado, descartado, inútil; insensible; estéril; (elec.) inactivo, sin corriente (apl. a alambres desconectados y a accesorios, como ciertas lámparas, puramente ornamentales).—**d. beat,** (fam.) gorrero, petardista.—**d. block,** (f. c.) bloque amortiguador.—**d. calm,** calma profunda; (mar.) calma chicha.—**d. center,** (m. v.) punto muerto.—**d. certainty,** certeza completa.—**d. earth,** (elec.) tierra (conexión con tierra) perfecta.—**d. end,** extremo cerrado; callejón sin salida.—**d. ground,** (elec.) = D. EARTH.—**d. freight,** (mar.) falso flete.—**d. heat,** carrera que resulta en un empate.—**d. letter,** letra muerta (ley, etc.); carta devuelta o no reclamada.—**d.-letter office,** oficina de cartas no reclamadas, sección de rezagos.—**d. lift,** acto de alzar a pura fuerza de brazo; grande urgencia o emergencia.—**d. load,** (ing.) carga fija.—**d. man's handle,** (elec.) manubrio de interrupción automática (que corta la corriente cuando el conductor lo suelta).—**d. march,** marcha fúnebre.—**d. point = DEAD**

CENTER.—**d. reckoning,** (mar.) estima.—**d. rising,** (mar.) delgado, línea del arrufo.—**d. short circuit,** (elec.) cortocircuito sin resistencia.—**d. shot,** tirador certero.—**d. stick,** (aer.) hélice parada.—**d.-stick landing,** (aer.) aterrizaje con motor muerto.—**d. stop,** parada repentina o en seco.—**d. water,** agua tranquila; marea muerta; (mar.) reveses, estela.—**d. weight,** carga onerosa; peso muerto, peso propio de un vehículo (sin la carga).—**d. work,** trabajo preliminar.—**to be d.,** haber muerto; no existir ya; estar muerto.—**to be d. against,** estar completamente opuesto a.

dead. I. adv. entera o absolutamente; del todo; brusca o repentinamente; sumamente; (mar.) exactamente.—**d.-beat, d.-tired,** (fam.) agotado, muerto de cansancio.—**d.-broke,** (fam.) sin tener para un bocado.—**d.-drunk,** borracho de remate.—**d.-hearted,** empedernido.—**d. (-set) against,** completamente hostil u opuesto a. II. s. (con the) lo más silencioso, desolador, etc. (vg. the dead of night, el profundo silencio de la noche; in the dead of winter, en la yema o lo más inclemente del invierno).—**the d.,** los muertos.

deadbeat [-bit], a. (elec.) aperiódico (apl. a galvanómetros, descargas, etc.).

deadborn [-born], a. nacido muerto.

deaden [-en], va. amortiguar, amortecer; desvirtuar; retardar, parar; apagar, quitar brillo, sonido, etc.; hacer insípido (el vino, la cerveza).

deadeye [-ai], s. (mar.) vigota, liebre, f.

deadfall [-fol], s. cierta trampa que aplasta con su peso a la caza.

deadhead [-hed], s. (fam.) gorrero, parásito, sanguijuela; (mar.) boya en forma de bloque de madera; poste o bloque de amarra; (fund.) mazarota; depósito de mazarota.

deadlight [-lait], s. (mar.) postigo o porta de correr.

deadline [-lain], s. límite absoluto; línea vedada; fin del plazo, término.

deadliness [-linis], s. calidad de mortífero.

deadlock [-lak], s. detención, paro; estancación, desacuerdo insuperable o persistente que interrumpe una negociación, etc.

deadly [-li]. I. a. mortal, mortífero, letal; (med.) fulminante.—**d. nightshade,** (bot.) belladona.—**d. sin,** pecado mortal. II. adv. mortalmente; sin vigor; excesivamente.

deadness [-nis], s. inercia; pérdida de vida; amortiguamiento, entumecimiento.

deaf [déf], a. sordo.—**d. and dumb, d.-mute,** sordomudo.—**d.-mutism,** (med.) sordomudez.—**to make o become d.,** ensordecer.

deafen [-en], va. asordar, ensordecer.

deafening [-iŋ], a. ensordecedor.

deafness [-nis], s. sordera; ensordecimiento.

deal [díl], s. parte, f., porción, cantidad indefinida; turno o acción de tallar (en el juego); pacto o convenio secreto; (com.) trato, negociación.—pl. tablones de pino.—**a d., a good, o great d. (of),** mucho, bastante.—**a square d.,** (fam.) V. SQUARE.

deal. I. va. (pret. y pp. DEALT) distribuir, repartir; dar, tallar (naipes); dar, asestar (un golpe, etc.).—**to d. out,** dispensar. II. vn. traficar, tratar, gestionar, negociar; intervenir, mediar; ser mano (en el juego de baraja).—**to d. by,** portarse para con, tratar a.—**to d. in,** negociar o comerciar en.—**to d. with,** tratar con o a; tratar de; ocuparse en o de; entenderse con; habérselas con; entender en; versar sobre; abordar (un tema o problema).

dealer [-œ(r)], s. comerciante, negociante, mercante, traficante; expendedor; tallador (en el juego). V. JOBBER.

dealing [-iŋ], s. proceder, conducta, comportamiento; trato, comunicación; tráfico, comercio, negocio.—pl. negocios; relaciones; transacciones.

dean [dín], *s.* (igl.) deán; decano.
deanery [-œri], **deanship** [-ŝip], *s.* (igl.) deanato; decanato.
dear [dír]. I. *a.* querido, amado, caro; amable; caro, costoso (ú. t. como *adv.*). II. *s.* persona querida, bien amado, dueño.—**d. me!** ¡Dios mío! ¡válgame Dios!—**my d.**, querido mío; amigo mío. —**my d. sir(s)**, (com., etc.) muy señor(es) mío(s), o nuestro(s).
dearly [-li], *adv.* tiernamente, cariñosamente; costosamente.—**dearness** [-njs], *s.* cariño, amor, afecto; benevolencia; carestía.
dearth [dœrθ], *s.* carestía, escasez; hambre, *f.*
deary, dearie [díri], *s.* (fam.) queridito, corazón.
death [déθ], *s.* muerte, *f.;* (fig.) la descarnada, parca; defunción, fallecimiento; asesinato; mortalidad; mortandad, estrago; condenación, muerte eterna.—**d. benefit fund**, fondo de defunción.—**d. certificate**, partida de defunción, fe de óbito.—**d.-dealing**, mortífero.—**d. knell = D. TOLL.—d. mask**, mascarilla.—**d. penalty**, pena de muerte; pena capital o de la vida.—**d. rate**, mortalidad, proporción de defunciones.—**d. rattle**, estertor.—**d.'s-head**, calavera.—**d. to!**, ¡muera!—**d. toll**, doble, toque de difuntos.—**d. trap**, casa o lugar peligroso o inseguro, amenaza constante.—**d. warrant**, sentencia de muerte; fin de toda esperanza.—**d. wound**, herida mortal.—**to (the) d.**, hasta la muerte; muchísimo, sumamente.— **to be in the d. house**, estar (un reo) en (la) capilla.
deathbed [-bed], *s.* lecho mortuorio o de muerte.
deathful [-ful], *a.* mortal; mortífero.
deathfulness [-njs], *s.* calidad de mortal; apariencia de muerte.
deathless [-ljs], *a.* inmortal.—**deathlike** [-lajk], *a.* sepulcral; cadavérico; mortal.—**deathly** [-li]. I. *a.* como la muerte; letárgico; cadavérico; mortal; fatal. II. *adv.* mortalmente, gravemente.
deathwatch [-wach], *s.* vela(ción) de un moribundo o cadáver; guardia de un reo de muerte; (ent.) anobio.
debacle [dibákl], *s.* desbordamiento; derrumbamiento; alud, *m.;* desastre, caída, ruina.
debar [dibár], *va.* excluir, privar.
debark [dibárk], *va.* y *vn.* desembarcar(se).
debarkation [-éjŝon], *s.* desembarque.
debase [dibéjs], *va.* rebajar, abatir, deshonrar, envilecer, degradar, prostituir; adulterar o falsificar.—**debasement** [-ment], *s.* envilecimiento, degradación; adulteración, falsificación.—**debaser** [-œr)], *s.* el que degrada o envilece; falsificador.—**debasing** [-iŋ], *a.* degradante, envilecedor.
debatable [dibéjtabl], *a.* discutible, disputable.
debate [dibéjt]. I. *s.* discusión, debate, disputa, polémica. II. *va.* disputar, controvertir; considerar. III. *vn.* deliberar, discutir; pensar, reflexionar.
debater [-œr)], *s.* polemista, ergotista.
debauch [dibóch], *va.* corromper, relajar, pervertir; seducir, violar; sobornar, sonsacar.— **debauch(ery** [-œri], *s.* libertinaje, licencia, vicio; lujuria; crápula; seducción; corrupción. —**debauchedly** [-idli], *adv.* licenciosamente.— **debauchee** [debochí], *s.* calaverón, libertino. —**debaucher** [dibóchœr)], *s.* corruptor; seductor, burlador.
debenture [dibénchu(r)], *s.* (com.) obligación; bono, vale, acción; abonaré expedido por la aduana para el reintegro de derechos pagados; abonaré u orden de pago del gobierno.
debilitant [dibílitant], *a.* y *s.* (med.) debilitante, calmante.
debilitate [-tejt], *va.* debilitar, enervar, extenuar, aflojar.—**debilitation** [-téjŝon], *s.* debilitación, extenuación, enflaquecimiento.—**debility** [-ti], *s.* debilidad, extenuación, descaecimiento, languidez.

debit [débit]. I. *s.* (com.) débito, cargo, adeudo, egreso; data; debe (de una cuenta).—**d. balance**, saldo deudor. II. *va.* adeudar, cargar en cuenta.
debonair(e [debonér], *a.* afable, cortés, complaciente; alegre, vivo; garboso.
debonairly [-li], *adv.* cortésmente; complacientemente; alegremente.
debouch [dibúŝ], *vn.* desembocar, descargar, salir.
debouchment [-ment], *s.* desembocadura; boca de un desfiladero, etc.; salida.
debris, débris [dábrí], *s.* enrona, escombros, desecho, ripio, restos, ruinas; (geol.) despojos, deyecciones.
debt [dét], *s.* deuda, débito; obligación.—**to run into d.**, endeudarse, entramparse.
debtor [-o(r)], *s.* deudor; cargo, "Debe."
debunk [dibʌŋk], *va.* (fam.) bajar del pedestal, poner en su sitio verdadero; traer a la realidad.
debut, début [dábjú], *s.* debut; (teat.) estreno.— **to make one's d.**, debutar.
débutant, *m.* débutante, *f.* [déjbjutant], debutante, principiante, el o la que se estrena.
decade [dékejd], *s.* decenio, década.
decadence, decadency [dikéjdęns(i o dékądęns(i], *s.* decadencia, ocaso.
decadent [-ent], *a.* decadente, decaído.
decagon [dékagan], *s.* (geom.) decágono.
decagram(me [dékagræm], *s.* decagramo.
decahedron [dekahídron], *s.* decaedro.
décalage [dekaláž], *s.* (aer.) decalaje, ángulo entre las alas (de un aeroplano).
decalcomania [dikælkoųméjnią], *s.* calcomanía.
decaliter, decalitre [dékąlitœ(r)], *s.* decalitro.
decalogue [dékąlag], *s.* decálogo.
decameter, -metre [dékąmitœ(r)], *s.* decámetro.
decamp [dikǽmp], *vn.* decampar; huir, fugarse; tomar las de Villadiego.
decampment [-ment], *s.* acción de decampar.
decanal [dékąnąl], *a.* que pertenece al deanato o al decanato.
decant [dikǽnt], *va.* decantar, trasegar.
decantation [dikæntéjŝon], *s.* decantación; trasiego.
decanter [dikǽntœ(r)], *s.* garrafa, ampolla.
decapitate [dikǽpitejt], *va.* decapitar, degollar, descabezar.—**decapitation** [-éjŝon], *s.* de capitación, degüello, descabezamiento.
decapod [dékapad], *s.* y *a.* (zool.) decápodo.
decarbonate [dikárbonejt], *va.* descarbonatar, eliminar el anhídrido carbónico de.
decarbonize, decarburize [-bonajz, -bųrąjz], *va.* descarbonizar, descarburar.
decarbonization, decarburization [-éjŝon], *s.* descarburación.
decare [déker], *s.* decárea.
decastere [dékastir], *s.* decastéreo.
decasyllable [dékąsiląbl], *s.* decasílabo.
decay [dikéj]. I. *vn.* decaer, declinar, venir a menos, desmoronarse; deteriorarse; carcomerse, cariarse (dientes, huesos); pudrirse, dañarse, picarse; pasarse, marchitarse. II. *va.* arruinar, destruir, echar a perder, cariar. III. *s.* decaimiento, menoscabo, decadencia, mengua; corrupción, descomposición, podredumbre, putrefacción; caries, *f.* (de dientes, huesos); vejez, pobreza.
decayed [-d], *a.* decaído; cariado, pútrido.
decease [disís]. I. *s.* muerte, *f.*, fallecimiento, defunción, óbito. II. *vn.* morir, fallecer.
deceased [-t], *s.* y *a.* muerto, difunto, finado.
decedent [disídent], *s.* (for.) finado.
deceit [disít], *s.* engaño, dolo, fraude, embuste (ría), falacia, impostura, trampa, superchería.
deceitful [-ful], *a.* engañoso, falso; mentiroso, solapado; ilusorio, engañador.
deceitfully [-li], *adv.* engañosamente.
deceitfulness [-njs], *s.* falsía, falacia, fraudulencia, duplicidad; apariencia engañosa.
deceivable [disívąbl], *a.* engañadizo, cándido.

deceivableness [-nịs], s. facilidad de ser engañado, candidez.

deceive [dịsív], va. engañar, embaucar, embelecar, defraudar, burlar, seducir.

deceiver [-œ(r)], s. engañador, impostor, embelecador, tramoyista, burlador, seductor.

decelerate [disélereịt], va. y vn. retardar(se), disminuir la velocidad.

December [dịsémbœ(r)], s. diciembre; (fig.) vejez.

decemvir [dịsémvœ(r)], s. decenviro.—**decemviral** [-ạl], a. decenviral, pert. al decenvirato. —**decemvirate** [-eịt], s. decenvirato.

decency [dísẹnsị], **decentness** [dísẹntnịs], s. decencia, recato, decoro; pudor, honestidad.

decennary [disénạrị], a. y s. decenario.—**decennial** [-ịạl]. I. a. decenal, decenario. II. s. decenio, decen(ar)io.—**decennium** [-ịʌm], s. decenio, década.

decent [dísẹnt], a. decente, honesto, decoroso; razonable, módico.

decently [-lị], adv. decentemente.

decentralization [disentrạlịzéịṣọn], s. descentralización.—**decentralize** [diséntrạlạịz], va. descentralizar.—**decentralizing** [-ịŋ], a. descentralizador.

deception [dịsépṣọn], s. decepción, engaño, impostura, fraude, superchería, trapisonda.

deceptive [dịséptịv], a. falaz, engañoso, ilusorio.

deceptively [-lị], adv. falaz o engañosamente.

dechristianize [dikrístyạnaịz], va. descristianizar.

deciare [désịẹr], s. deciárea.

decidable [dịsáịdạbl], a. que se puede decidir.

decide [dịsáịd], va. y vn. decidir, determinar, concluir, venir en, resolver, juzgar, sentenciar.

decided [-ịd], a. decidido; determinado, resuelto; incontestable, indudable; categórico, inequívoco.—**decidedly** [-lị], adv. decididamente, categóricamente, indudablemente.

decidua [dịsídžuạ], s. (anat.) (membrana) caduca.

deciduous [-ʌs], a. deciduo, caduco, caedizo.

decigram(me [désịgræm], s. decigramo.

deciliter, decilitre [désịlitœ(r)], s. decilitro.

decimal [désịmạl], s. y a. decimal.—**decimally** [-ị], adv. decimalmente.

decimate [désịmeịt], va. diezmar.—**decimation** [-éịṣọn], s. gran mortandad; diezmo.—**decimator** [-ǫ(r)], s. gran destructor.

decimeter, decimetre [désịmitœ(r)], s. decímetro.

decipher [dịsáịfœ(r)], va. descifrar, interpretar; desenvolver, aclarar.—**decipherable** [-ạbl], a. descifrable.—**decipherer** [-œ(r)], s. descifrador.

decision [dịsížọn], s. decisión, resolución, determinación; firmeza, entereza; (for.) decreto, fallo, auto, sentencia, definición, providencia, laudo.

decisive [dịsáịsịv], a. decisivo; conclusivo, terminante, perentorio.—**decisively** [-lị], adv. decisivamente.—**decisiveness** [-nịs], s. autoridad decisiva; firmeza, entereza.

decistere [désịstịr], s. decistéreo.

deck [dék]. I. va. vestir, ataviar, engalanar. II. s. (arq.) cubierta; baraja, monte; (mar.) cubierta; puente, mf.; (f. c.) techo de un vagón.—**d. bridge**, (f. c.) puente de tablero superior.—**d. cabin**, camareta.—**d. chair**, silla de cubierta. —**d. compartment**, (aut.) compartimiento de equipajes.—**d. hand**, marinero de cubierta. —**on d.**, (mar.) sobre cubierta; (fam.) listo para la acción; disponible.

decker [-œ(r)], s. el o lo que adorna, atavía, etc. —**two-d., three-d.**, (mar.) navío de dos o tres puentes.

deckhouse [-haụs], s. (mar.) camareta alta.

deckle [dékl], s. (pap.) cubierta, bastidor rectangular.—**d. edge**, barba, borde sin cortar del papel hecho a mano.—**d.-edged paper**, papel de barbas.

declaim [dịkléịm]. I. va. recitar. II. vn. declamar, perorar, arengar.

declaimer [-œ(r)], s. declamador, perorador.

declamation [deklạméịṣọn], s. declamación, peroración, arenga.

declamatory [dịkléẹmạtọrị], a. declamatorio.

declarable [dịklérạbl], a. declarable.

declaration [deklạréịṣọn], s. declaración; aserción; explicación, exposición; manifiesto.

declarative [dịklérạtịv], a. declarativo, expositivo, testificativo.—**declaratorily** [-tọrịlị], adv. en forma de declaración.—**declaratory** [-tọrị], a. declaratorio; afirmativo, demostrativo.

declare [dịklér], va. y vn. declarar, afirmar, manifestar, proclamar; deponer, testificar.

declaredly [-dlị], adv. declaradamente, abiertamente, explícitamente.

declarer [-œ(r)], s. declarador; declarante, deponente.

declension [dịklénṣọn], s. (gram.) declinación, desinencia; decadencia, decremento, menoscabo; inclinación, declive.

declinable [dịkláịnạbl], a. declinable.

declination [deklịnéịṣọn], s. declinación; descenso, declive; inclinación; decadencia; decremento, deterioro; excusa; renuncia; desviación; descarrío; (astr., fís.) declinación.

declinatory [dịkláịnạtọrị], a. que envuelve excusa o renuncia.

declinature [-chur], s. negativa, renuncia; (for.) declinatoria, recusación.

decline [dịkláịn]. I. va. no aceptar; rehusar, rehuir, rechazar; (gram.) declinar. II. vn. rehusar, negarse; no aceptar; declinar, inclinarse hacia abajo, bajar; menguar, decaer, desmejorar, venir a menos; desviarse, apartarse. III. s. declinación, decadencia, menoscabo, descaecimiento; descenso, declive; caída (de la tarde, etc.); (med.) consunción; período en que una enfermedad va cediendo.

declinometer [deklịnámetœ(r)], s. declinómetro; declinatorio.

declivity [dịklívịtị], s. declive, declividad.

declivitous, declivous [-tʌs, dịkláịvʌs], a. inclinado, clivoso.

declutch [dịklʌch], vn. (mec.) desembragar.

decoct [dịkákt], va. hacer un cocimiento de; reducir por medio de la cocción; condensar.

decoction [dịkákṣọn], s. cocimiento; decocción; cocción o hervor.

decode [dịkǫud], va. descifrar.

decohere [dikohír], va. y vn. (elec.) volver el cohesor a su posición normal.—**decoherence** [-ẹns], **decohesion** [dikohížọn], s. descohesión. —**decoherer** [-œ(r)], s. descohesor, aparato para restablecer el cohesor a su posición normal.

decollate [dịkáleịt], va. degollar.—**decollation** [dikaléịṣọn], s. degollación, degüello.

décolletage [deịkaltáž], s. (cost.) escotadura, escote; traje escotado.

décolleté [deịkaltéị], a. (cost.) escotado.

decolor, decolorate [dikʌlọ(r), -eịt], **decolorize** [-aịz], va. de(s)colorar, descolorir; blanquear; clarificar (azúcar).

decolorant [-ạnt], a. y s. descolorante.

decoloration [-éịṣọn], s. descoloramiento, descolorimiento, decoloración.

decomposable [dikǫmpóụzạbl], a. corruptible; descomponible.

decompose [-póụz]. I. va. descomponer; pudrir. II. vn. pudrirse, corromperse.

decomposite [dikómpzịt]. I. a. compuesto de compuestos. II. s. palabra o cosa compuesta así.

decomposition [dikampozíṣọn], s. descomposición; corrupción, putrefacción.

decompound [dikǫmpáụnd]. I. va. componer de cosas ya compuestas; descomponer. II. a. (bot.) varias veces compuesto. III. s. = DECOMPOSITE. —**decompoundable** [-ạbl], a. capaz de componerse de compuestos; descomponible.

decompression [dikǫmpréṣọn], s. descompresión.

decontaminate [dikǫntémịneịt], va. desinfectar;

neutralizar (gases tóxicos, etc.).—**decontamination** [-éjṣǫn], s. desinfección; neutralización.—**d. squad**, equipo de desinfección.

decontrol [dikǫntróul]. **I**. s. terminación del control. **II**. va. terminar el control de.

decorate [dékoreit], va. decorar, adornar, embellecer, guarnecer; condecorar.

decoration [-éjṣǫn], s. decoración, ornamentación; adorno, ornamento; (cost.) guarnición; condecoración, insignia.—**D. Day**, (E. U.) el 30 de mayo, día señalado para decorar las tumbas de los soldados muertos en campaña.

decorative [dékorǫtiv], a. decorativo, ornamental.

decorator [dékoreitǫ(r)], s. decorador, adornista.

decorous [dékoras], a. decoroso, púdico; correcto.

decorously [-li]. adv. decorosamente, correctamente.—**decorousness** [-nis], s. decoro. V. DECORUM.

decorticate [dikórtikeit], va. descortezar, descascarar; pelar, mondar.—**decortication** [-éjṣǫn], s. descortezamiento, peladura.—**decorticator** [-ǫ(r)], s. descortezador, mondador, pelador.

decorum [dikóram], s. decoro, honor, honestidad, pudor; corrección, circunspección, conveniencia.

decoy [dikój]. **I**. va. atraer con señuelo o añagaza, reclamar (pájaros); (fam.) entruchar. **II**. s. añagaza, señuelo, reclamo; (fam.) entruchón; lazo, trampa; entruchada.—**d. duck**, o **pigeon**, cimbel.—**d. partridge**, perdigón.

decrease [dikrís]. **I**. vn. decrecer, menguar, mermar, minorarse, disminuir. **II**. va. disminuir, reducir, mermar. **III**. [díkris], s. decremento, di(s)minución; merma, mengua; menguante, f. (de la luna); descaecimiento, decadencia.

decreasing [-iŋ], a. decreciente, menguante.

decree [dikrí]. **I**. va. y vn. decretar, determinar, mandar, ordenar. **II**. s. decreto, edicto, mandato, ley, f.; auto, pragmática.

decrement [dékrǫmǫnt], s. decremento.

decrepit [dikrépit], a. decrépito, caduco.

decrepitate [-eit], va. y vn. (hacer) decrepitar.

decrepitation [-éjṣǫn], s. (quím.) decrepitación.

decrepitude [-tjud], s. decrepitud, senectud, caducidad.

decrescendo [deikreṣéndou], (mús.) = DIMINUENDO.

decrescent [dikrésǫnt], a. menguante.

decretal [dikrítal]. **I**. a. decretal. **II**. s. decretal, f., decretero (gen. pl.).

decretist [dikrítist], s. decretista, decretalista.

decretive [dikrítiv], a. decretal; decretorio.

decretorily [dekrǫtórili], adv. definitivamente.

decretory [dékrǫtǫri], a. decretorio, definitivo, decisivo, crítico.

decrial [dikrájal], s. vituperio; censura.

decrier [dikrájœ(r)], s. vituperador, censurador.

decry [dikráj], va. desacreditar, vituperar, afear, rebajar; condenar o desvalorizar oficialmente.

decubitus [dikjúbitas], **decumbence, decumbency** [dikámbǫns, -i], s. decúbito.

decumbent [-bǫnt], a. decumbente; recostado.

decumbiture [-bichǫ(r)], s. tiempo que el enfermo guarda cama.

decuple [dékjupl], **I**. a. y s. décuplo. **II**. va. decupl(ic)ar.

decurion [dikjúrjǫn], s. decurión, m.

decurionate [-it], s. decurionato.

decurrent [dikǿrǫnt], **decursive** [dikǿrsiv], a. (bot.) decurrente.

decury [dékyǫri], s. decuria.

decussate [dikáseit]. **I**. va. y vn. cruzar(se), entrelazar(se). **II**. a. entrecruzado; (bot.) decus(ad)o.—**decussation** [dikaséjṣǫn], s. cruzamiento; decusación.

dedicate [dédikeit], va. dedicar; aplicar, consagrar, destinar, enderezar, ofrecer.—**dedication** [-éjṣǫn], s. dedicación, consagración; dedi-

catoria.—**dedicative** [-tiv], a. dedicativo.—**dedicator** [-tǫ(r)], s. dedicante.—**dedicator:** [dédikatǫri], a. dedicatorio.

deduce [didjús], va. deducir, colegir, conclui: inferir; sacar; derivar.

deducible [-jbl], a. deducible.

deduct [didákt], va. deducir, restar, su(b)strae: rebajar, descontar.

deduction [didákṣǫn], s. deducción; su(b)strac ción; descuento, rebaja; conclusión, inferencia

deductive [didáktiv], a. deductivo.—**deduc tively** [-li], adv. deductivamente, por deducción

deed [did]. **I**. s. acto, hecho; realidad; hazaña proeza; (for.) escritura.—**d. of gift**, instru mento o escritura de donación.—**d. of release** acta de cesión.—**in d.**, de veras, en verdad; d hecho. **II**. va. (for.) hacer una escritura d cesión o traspaso.

deem [dim], va. y vn. juzgar, considerar, cree: estimar.

deep [díp]. **I**. a. profundo, hondo; sagaz, astut: subido, intenso (color); excesivo; concienzudo profundamente aplicado o consagrado; ronco (mús.) grave, profundo.—**d. blue**, turquí.— **d. in**, absorto en (la meditación, el estudio) cargado o lleno de (deudas); muy metido envuelto en (política, etc.).—**d. mourning** luto riguroso.—**d. red** = CRIMSON.—**d. sea** alta mar.—**d.-sea**, a. de las profundidades de mar; de aguas profundas de mar.—**d.-sea lead**, o **line**, sondaleza de mar para grande profundidades. **II**. adv. profundamente; (co into), hasta tarde (de la noche, etc.).—**d. drawing**, (mar.) de mucho calado.—**d.-laid** dispuesto con sagacidad o astucia.—**d.-seated** arraigado profundamente. **III**. s. profundi dad(es); piélago, mar, mf.; fondo del ma: abismo, sima.

deepen [-ǫn]. **I**. va. profundizar, ahondar; obs curecer; entristecer. **II**. vn. hacerse más hondo más profundo o más intenso.

deeply [-li], adv. profundamente, hondamente, fondo; sumamente, intensamente; obscura mente; sagazmente.

deepness [-nis], s. profundidad, hondura; in tensidad; malicia.

deer [dír], s. venado, ciervo.—**d. lick**, salegar.

deerhound [-haund], s. galgo de cazar venado:

deerskin [-skin], s. piel (f.) de venado, correal.

deerstalking [-stokiŋ], s. caza de venados a acecho.

deface [diféjs], va. mutilar, estropear, afear.

defacement [-mǫnt], s. deterioro, estrope: mutilación, afeamiento; deformación.

defacer [-œ(r)], s. el que deteriora, estropea afea.

de facto [d-féktou], (for.) de hecho.

defalcate [difálkeit], vn. desfalcar, malversar.

defalcation [-éjṣǫn], s. desfalco, malversación defraudación.—**defalcator** [dífælkeitǫ(r)], desfalcador.

defamation [defǫméjṣǫn], s. di(s)famación infamación, denigración, calumnia.

defamatory [difǽmatǫri], a. calumnioso, difams torio.

defame [diféjm], va. di(s)famar, infamar, amen guar, desacreditar, deshonrar, denigrar; calum niar.

defamer [-œ(r)], s. infamador, calumniador.

default [difólt]. **I**. s. omisión, descuido, negl gencia; incumplimiento (de una obligación pago, etc.); insolvencia; defecto, falta; (for rebeldía, contumacia.—**by d.**, (for.) en rebe día.—**in d. of**, por falta de; por faltar.—**in d whereof**, en cuyo defecto. **II**. va. y vn. faltar delinquir; dejar de cumplir; no pagar; (for condenar en rebeldía.

defaulter [-œ(r)], s. el delincuente; defraudado desfalcador; (for.) rebelde, contumaz.

defeasance [difízǫns], s. anulación, abrogació revocación, nulidad.

defeasible [difízibl], *a*. anulable, revocable.
defeat [difít]. **I.** *s*. derrota; frustración; (for.) anulación; rechazamiento. **II.** *va*. derrotar, vencer; frustrar; desechar; (for.) anular, abrogar.
defeatism [-izm], *s*. actitud o confesión de derrota o impotencia; derrotismo.—**defeatist** [-ist], *s*. y *a*. (el) que se declara vencido o impotente, o desea la derrota (de la patria, causa, etc.); derrotista.
defecate [défĕkejt]. **I.** *va*. defecar, clarificar, purgar, purificar, depurar. **II.** *vn*. purificarse, clarificarse; exonerar el vientre.
defecation [-éjŝǫn], *s*. defecación, purificación, clarificación; exoneración del vientre.
defecator [-ǫ(r)], *s*. (azú.) defecadora.
defect [difékt], *s*. defecto, falta, imperfección, tacha; pero; omisión.
defection [difékŝǫn], *s*. defección, apostasía; deserción, abandono.
defective [diféktiv]. **I.** *a*. defectivo, defectuoso; falto, corto; anormalmente escaso o falto de inteligencia; (gram.) defectivo. **II.** *s*. persona de baja mentalidad o físicamente defectuosa.—**defectively** [-li], *adv*. defectuosamente, deficientemente.—**defectiveness** [-nis], *s*. deficiencia, falta, imperfección.
defence, defenceless, etc. = DEFENSE, etc.
defend [difénd], *va*. defender, amparar, proteger, guardar; mantener, sostener.—**defendable** [-abl], *a*. defendible, defendedero.—**defendant** [-ant]. **I.** *a*. que defiende; que está a la defensiva; (for.) acusado. **II.** *s*. (for.) demandado, acusado, reo, procesado.—**defender** [-œ(r)], *s*. defensor, defendedor, campeón, protector, patrono.
defense [diféns], *s*. defensa, amparo, protección; vindicación o justificación; resistencia, resguardo o reparo; (for.) defensa.—*pl*. (fort.) defensas, obras de fortificación.—**d. attorney,** (for.) abogado defensor.—**defenseless** [-lis], *a*. indefenso o inerme.—**defenselessly** [-li], *adv*. indefensamente.—**defenselessness** [-nis], *s*. desvalimiento, desamparo, abandono.—**defensible** [-ibl], *a*. defendible, defendedero; sustentable.
defensive [-iv]. **I.** *a*. defensivo; vindicativo. **II.** *s*. defensiva.—**to be,** o **stand, on the d.,** estar, o ponerse, a la defensiva.—**defensively** [-li], *adv*. defensivamente.
defensory [-ǫri], *a*. defensivo, justificativo.
defer [difœr]. **I.** *va*. diferir, dilatar, aplazar, postergar, retrasar; remitir. **II.** *vn*. demorarse, aguardar; (con **to**) deferir, ceder, acatar, asentir, consentir.
deference [défĕrens], *s*. deferencia, acatamiento, condescendencia, obsequio, respeto.
deferent [-ent], **deferential** [-énŝal], *a*. deferente, respetuoso.
deferentially [-i], *adv*. deferentemente.
deferment [difœrment], *s*. aplazamiento, dilación, postergación.
deferred [difœrd], *a*. y *pp*. de TO DEFER.—**d. payment,** pago aplazado; pago a plazos.—**d. shares,** o **stock,** acciones postergadas.
deferrer [difœrœ(r)], *s*. tardador; hombre moroso.
defiance [difájans], *s*. desafío, reto; oposición obstinada.—**in d. of,** a despecho de.—**to bid d. to,** o **to set at d.,** desafiar; despreciar.
defiant [-ant], *a*. desafiador, retador.
deficiency [difíŝensi], *s*. defecto, imperfección; deficiencia, falta, carencia; déficit.
deficient [-ent], *a*. deficiente; defectuoso.
deficiently [-li], *adv*. deficientemente.
deficit [défisit], *s*. déficit; descubierto.
defier [difájœr(r)], *s*. desafiador, retador.
filade [defiléjd], *va*. (mil.) desenfilar, proteger contra fuego de enfilada.—**defilading** [-iŋ], *s*. desenfilada, desenfilamiento.
file [difájl o difaíl]. **I.** *vn*. (mil.) desfilar. **II.** *s*. desfiladero, hoz.
file [difáil], *va*. manchar, profanar, viciar; co-

rromper, violar, estuprar.—**defilement** [-ment], *s*. contaminación, violación, profanación.—**defiler** [-œ(r)], *s*. corruptor, violador, estuprador.
definable [difájnabl], *a*. definible.
define [difájn]. **I.** *va*. definir, describir, explicar; circunscribir; delimitar, determinar, fijar. **II.** *vn*. definir.—**definer** [-œ(r)], *s*. definidor.—**defining** [-iŋ], *a*. definidor.
definite [définit], *a*. definido, determinado, preciso.—**d. article,** (gram.) artículo definido o determinado.
definitely [-li], *adv*. definidamente, determinadamente, ciertamente.—**definiteness** [-nis], *s*. exactitud, precisión.
definition [definíŝǫn], *s*. definición; decisión o determinación; (ópt.) precisión.
definitive [difínitiv]. **I.** *a*. definitivo, decisivo, perentorio, terminante; en firme. **II.** *s*. lo que define.—**definitively** [-li], *adv*. definitivamente.—**definitiveness** [-nis], *s*. calidad de definitivo.
definitor [definájtǫ(r)], *s*. (igl.) definidor.
deflagrable [déflagrabl], *a*. combustible.
deflagrate [-grejt], *va*. y *vn*. (hacer) deflagrar.
deflagration [-gréjŝǫn], *s*. deflagración.
deflagrator [-grejtǫ(r)], *s*. deflagrador.
deflate [difléjt], *va*. desinflar, deshinchar; contraer, reducir (valores, etc.).—**deflation** [-éjŝǫn], *s*. desinflación, deshinchadura; contracción.
deflect [difiékt], *va*. y *vn*. desviar(se), apartar(se), ladear(se), torcer(se).
deflection, deflexion [difiékŝǫn], *s*. desviación, desvío, torcimiento; (ing.) flecha.—**d. angle,** ángulo de desviación.
deflective [difiéktiv], *a*. que desvía, desviador.
deflorate [difióreįt]. **I.** *a*. (bot.) que ha cesado de florecer. **II.** *va*. = DEFLOWER.
defloration [deflǫréjŝǫn], *s*. desfloración, desflorecimiento; selección; epítome.
deflower [difláuǫœ(r)], *va*. desflorar; ajar, quitar la flor o lustre; desvirgar, estuprar, violar.—**deflowerer** [-œ(r)], *s*. estuprador, violador.
defluxion [difiákŝǫn], *s*. destilación; reuma.
defoliate [difóuljeįt]. **I.** *a*. deshojado. **II.** *va*. y *vn*. deshojar(se).
defoliation [-éjŝǫn], *s*. (bot.) defoliación.
deforce [difórs], *va*. (for.) detentar, usurpar.—**deforcement** [-ment], *s*. usurpación, detentación.—**deforciant** [difórŝant], *s*. detentador.
deforest [difárist], *va*. talar bosques, desmontar. (Am.) desboscar.
deforestation [-éjŝǫn], *s*. desmonte, despoblación arbórea.
deform [difórm], *va*. de(s)formar, disformar, desfigurar, degradar, afear.
deformability [-abíliti], *s*. deformabilidad.
deformable [-abl], *a*. deformable.
deformation [difǫrméjŝǫn], *s*. deformación, alteración, desfiguración; (mec.) deformación.
deformed [difórmd], *a*. deformado, desfigurado; deforme, contrahecho, disforme.—**deformedly** [-idli], *adv*. feamente, deformemente.—**deformedness** [-idnis], *s*. deformación.
deforming [-iŋ], *a*. deformador, afeador.
deformity [-iti], *s*. deformidad, disformidad; deformación; fealdad; persona o cosa disforme.
defraud [difród], *va*. defraudar, estafar, engañar.
defrauder [-œ(r)], *s*. defraudador, estafador.
defraudment [-ment], *s*. defraudación.
defray [difréj], *va*. costear, sufragar, subvenir.—**defrayer** [-œ(r)], *s*. el que costea o sufraga.—**defrayment** [-ment], **defrayal** [-al], *s*. pago o subvención de gastos.
defrock [difrák], *va*. = UNFROCK.
defrost [difróst], *va*. descongelar, deshelar.
deft [déft], *a*. diestro, hábil; mañoso, apto.
deftness [-nis], *s*. destreza; habilidad; maña.
defunct [difáŋkt], *a*. y *s*. difunto.
defy [difáj], *va*. desafiar, retar, atreverse con; arrostrar; despreciar; contravenir.
degeneracy [didžénĕrasi], *s*. degeneración; de-

gradación, depravación.—**degenerate** [-eit].
I. *vn.* degenerar; (biol.) bastardear. II. [-it],
s. y *a.* degenerado.—**degenerately** [-li], *adv.*
degeneradamente; indignamente; vilmente.—
degenerateness [-nis], *s.* degeneración.
degeneration [-éişon], *s.* degeneración.
degenerative [-eitiv], *a.* degenerativo.
deglutinate [diglútineit], *va.* despegar; extraer
o separar el gluten (del trigo, etc.).
deglutition [diglutíşon], *s.* deglución.
degradation [degrądéişon], *s.* degradación; deposición; degeneración; diminución; descenso;
corrupción; (pint.) degradación.
degrade [digréid]. I. *va.* degradar, privar, deponer; minorar, rebajar, reducir; (pint.) degradar, atenuar; (biol.) reducir de clase superior a inferior. II. *vn.* degenerar; abellacarse,
envilecerse.
degrading [-iŋ], *a.* degradante.—**degradingly**
[-li], *adv.* degradantemente.
degree [digrí], *s.* grado (en todas sus acepciones);
título; cuantía.—**by degrees**, de grado en grado,
gradualmente, poco a poco.—**in the highest
d.**, en sumo grado.—**to a d.**, algo, bastante,
hasta cierto punto; sumamente.—**to take a
d.**, graduarse.
degression [digréşon], *s.* decrecimiento; descenso;
disminución progresiva (en los impuestos).
degressive [digrésiv], *a.* decreciente; que disminuye progresivamente, o por grados.
dehisce [dihís], *vn.* (bot.) abrirse.
dehiscence [-ens], *s.* hendedura, grieta; (bot.)
dehiscencia.—**dehiscent** [-ent], *a.* dehiscente.
dehorn [dihórn], *va.* descornar.
dehortation [dihortéişon], *s.* disuasión.
dehumanize [dihiúmąnaiz], *va.* deshuman(iz)ar,
embrutecer.
dehydrate [dihájdreit], *va.* deshidratar.
dehydration [-éişon], *s.* deshidratación.
dehydrator [dihájdreitǫ(r)], *s.* deshidratador.
dehydrogenize [dihájdrodżenajz], *va.* (quím.)
deshidrogenar, quitar el hidrógeno a.
deice [diáis], *va.* (aer.) descongelar.—**deicer**
[-œ(r)], *s.* descongelador, dispositivo antihielo.
deicide [díisaid], *s.* deicida, *m.*; deicidio.
deictic [dájktik], *a.* demostrativo; (lóg.) directo.
deific(al [diíffik(al], *a.* deífico, divino.
deification [-éişon], *s.* deificación, divinización;
apoteosis.
deifier [díifaiœ(r)], *s.* el que deifica; idólatra, *m.*
deiform [díiform], *a.* deiforme, divino.
deify [díifai], *va.* deificar, divinizar, endiosar.
deign [dein], *va.* y *vn.* dignarse, condescender.
deism [díizm], *s.* deísmo.—**deist** [díist], *s.*, **deis-
tic(al** [diístik(al], *a.* deísta.
deity [díiti], *s.* deidad, divinidad, numen.—**the
D.**, Dios.
deject [didżékt], *va.* abatir, afligir; desanimar,
desalentar, descorazonar.—**dejected** [-id], *a.*
acongojado, abatido, desalentado, desanimado.
dejecta [-ą], *s. pl.* excrementos.
dejectedly [-idli], *adv.* abatidamente, descorazonadamente, afligidamente.
dejection [didżékşon], *s.* melancolía, desaliento;
(med.) deyección, deposición, evacuación.
de jure [didżúri], (for.) legalmente, legítimamente; de derecho.
dekagram, dekaliter, etc. = DECAGRAM, etc.
delaine [diléin], *s.* (tej.) muselina de lana.
delate [diléit], *va.* delatar, denunciar; divulgar.
delation [diléişon], *s.* (for.) delación, acusación,
denunciación.
delay [diléi]. I. *va.* dilatar, diferir, demorar, retardar, postergar, atrasar, retrasar; entretener.
II. *vn.* tardar, demorarse. III. *s.* dilación, tardanza, demora, retraso, atraso, retardación.
dele [díli]. I. *va.* (impr.) suprimir. II. *s.* dele,
signo (δ).
delectable [diléktąbl], *a.* deleitable, delicioso.
delectableness [-nis], *s.* calidad de deleitoso.
delectably [-bli], *adv.* deleitosamente.

delectate [dilékteit], *va.* deleitar.
delectation [-éişon], *s.* deleitación, deleite.
delegacy [délęgąsi], *s.* delegación; carácter d
delegado; cuerpo de delegados.
delegant [délęgant], *s.* delegante.
delegate [délęgeit]. I. *vn.* delegar, diputar, com:
sionar. II. *a.* y *s.* delegado, diputado; comisari
—**delegation** [-éişon], *s.* delegación, diputació
representación; comisión.
delegatory [délęgątori], *a.* delegatorio.
delete [dilít], *va.* suprimir, borrar, tachar.
deleterious [delętíriąs], *a.* deletéreo, nocivo
perjudicial, pernicioso.
deletion [dilíşon], *s.* supresión, borradura.
delf(t [delf(t], *s.* loza fina.
deliberate [dilíbęreit]. I. *va.* y *vn.* deliberar, con
siderar, reflexionar; consultar, aconsejarse
vacilar. II. [dilíbęrit], *a.* pensado, reflexionad
premeditado; circunspecto, cauto.—**deliber
ately** [-li], *adv.* deliberadamente o con premedi
tación.—**deliberateness** [-nis], **deliberatio**
[-éişon], *s.* deliberación, reflexión; premedita
ción; intención.—**deliberative** [dilíbęrątiv], *d*
deliberativo.
delible [délibl], *a.* deleble.
delicacy [délikąsi], *s.* delicadeza, finura; suav
dad, sensibilidad; ternura; delicadez, fragilida
o friabilidad; nimiedad, escrupulosidad; mir;
miento o consideración; bocado exquisit
golosina, golería.
delicate [délikit], *a.* delicado; fino, suave, ligero
pulido, fino (como modales, etc.); tierno; escrt
puloso; mirado, considerado; de buen gusto
exquisito.
delicately [-li], *adv.* delicadamente, sutilment
delicateness [-nis], *s.* delicadez(a), molicie.
delicatessen [delikątésęn], *s.* manjares delicado
esp. fiambres; tienda donde se venden.
delicious [dilíşʌs], *a.* delicioso, sabroso, exqu
sito, rico.—**deliciously** [-li], *adv.* delicios;
mente; sabrosamente.—**deliciousness** [-nis], *:*
calidad de ser delicioso; delicia.
delight [dilájt]. I. *s.* delicia, deleite, delectació
encanto. II. *va.* deleitar, encantar, recrear. III
vn. deleitarse, recrearse, complacerse (en).
delighted [-id], *a.* encantado, contentísimo.—**t
be d.** to (seguido de infinitivo), tener much
gusto en; alegrarse muchísimo de, estar encar
tado de.
delightful [-ful], *a.* delicioso, deleitable, encar
tador.—**delightfully** [-i], *adv.* deliciosament
deleitosamente.—**delightfulness** [-nis], *s.* de
licia, deleite, encanto.—**delightsome** [-sʌm
a. = DELIGHTFUL.
delimit [dilímit], *va.* delimitar, fijar límites.—
delimitation [-éişon], *s.* delimitación.
delineament [dilíniąment], **delineation** [-éişon
s. delineación, delineamiento; boceto, diseñ
bosquejo, esquicio; descripción.
delineate [dilínieit], *va.* delinear, trazar, diseña
describir.
delineator [-ǫ(r)], *s.* delineador, delineant
diseñador, dibujante, descriptor.
delinquency [dilíŋkwęnsi], *s.* delincuencia.
delinquent [-ent]. I. *a.* delincuente; descuidad
negligente; culpable; adeudado y no pagad
moroso en el pago. II. *s.* delincuente.
deliquesce [delikwés], *vn.* liquidarse, derretirs
licuarse.—**deliquescence** [-ens], *s.* (quín
delicuescencia o licuación.—**deliquescer**
[-ent], *a.* delicuescente.
delirious [dilíriʌs], *a.* delirante, desvariado.
delirium [dilíriʌm], *s.* delirio, desvarío; devane
—**d. tremens**, (med.) delírium tremens.
deliver [dilívœ(r)], *va.* librar, libertar; entrega
rendir; comunicar, etc.; recitar, pronuncia
decir; dictar (una conferencia); descargar; da
asestar (un golpe, etc.); despachar (un pedid
transmitir (energía, etc.).—**to d. of a bab**
partear.—**to d. over**, entregar; traspasar.—
to d. the goods, (fam.) cumplir; hacer

prometido o esperado.—**to d. up**, entregar.—
to be delivered (of a child), alumbrar, parir;
dar a luz, dar nacimiento a.
deliverance [-ạns], *s.* rescate; liberación, salvación; dictamen, declaración formal.
deliverer [-œ(r)], *s.* entregador, librador; libertador, salvador; relator, comunicante.
delivery [-i], *s.* liberación, rescate; entrega; lo
entregado; capacidad; producción; salida (vg.
d. pipe, tubo de salida); traspaso, dación; rendición; alumbramiento, parto; modo de obrar,
expresarse o cantar; expedición, desembarazo;
(for.) entrega, cesión; (com.) remesa; distribución o reparto (del correo); (mec.) descarga,
impulsión, proyección.—**d. room**, sala de
alumbramiento (en un hospital).—**d. truck**,
camión (*m.*) o camioneta de reparto.
deliveryman [-mạn], *s.* recadero, entregador.
dell [del], *s.* vallejuelo, cañada.
delouse [diláus], *va.* despiojar, espulgar.
Delphian, Delphic [délfiạn, délfik], *a.* délfico.
delphinium [delfíniʌm], *s.* (bot.) = LARKSPUR.
delta [déltạ], *s.* delta (letra griega); (geog.) delta,
mf.—**d. connection**, (elec.) conexión en triángulo o en delta.
deltaic [deltéjik], **deltic** [déltik], *a.* deltaico.
deltoid(al [déltojd(ạl], **I.** *a.* deltoideo, deltoides,
triangular. **II.** *s.* (anat.) deltoides.
delude [diljúd], *va.* deludir, engañar, alucinar.
deluded [-id], *a.* y *pp.* iluso, engañado.
deluder [-œ(r)], *s.* delusor, engañador.
deluge [déljudž]. **I.** *s.* diluvio, inundación; golpe,
calamidad. **II.** *va.* inundar.
delusion [dilúžọn], *s.* error, embaimiento; ilusión; decepción, engaño.
delusive [dilúsiv], **delusory** [dilúsori], *a.* engañoso, delusivo, delusor(io), ilusivo, ilusorio.
delusively [-li], *adv.* delusoriamente.
de luxe [dilúks], *a.* de lujo, lujoso, ostentoso.
delve [delv], *va.* y *vn.* cavar; penetrar, ahondar;
sondear, inquirir.
demagnetization [dimægnetizéišọn], *s.* desi-
man(t)ación.—**demagnetize** [dimǽgnetajz],
va. desiman(t)ar.
demagogic(al [demagádžik(ạl], *a.* demagógico.
demagogism [démagagizm], **demagoguery**
[-gageri], **demagogy** [-gadži], *s.* demagogia.
demagog(ue [démagag], *s.* demagogo.
demain [diméjn], *s.* = DEMESNE.
demand [dimǽnd]. **I.** *va.* exigir, reclamar o pedir
perentoriamente; (for.) demandar, requerir,
recuestar; interrogar. **II.** *s.* demanda, exigencia; petición; (for., e. p.) demanda; pedido.—
on d., a la presentación, a solicitud.—**to be
in d.**, tener demanda, ser solicitado.—**deman-
dant** [-ạnt], *s.* (for.) demandante, demandador.
—**demander** [-œ(r)], *s.* exactor; demandador;
pedigüeño, pedigón.—**demanding** [-iŋ], *a.*
demandante, exigente.
demarcate [dimárkejt], **demark** [dimárk], *va.*
demarcar, deslindar; separar, distinguir.
demarcation, demarkation [-éišọn], *s.* demarcación, deslinde; limitación.
démarche [demárš], *s.* proceder, medida; diligencia; cambio de proceder o de política.
demean [dimín], *vr.* portarse, conducirse; *va.* y
vr. rebajar(se), degradar(se).
demeanor [-ọ(r)], *s.* conducta, comportamiento,
proceder; porte, aire, semblante.
dement [dimént], *va.* y *vn.* dementar(se), enlo-
quecer(se).
demented [-id], *a.* demente, falta de juicio.
dementia [diménšiạ], *s.* demencia, locura.—**d.
præcox**, demencia precoz.
demerit [dimérit], *s.* demérito, desmerecimiento.
demersed [dimœrst], *a.* (bot.) sumergido.
demesne [diméjn, dimín], *s.* heredad; tierra solariega; región; dominio, reino. *V.* DOMAIN.
demi [démi], *prefijo*, semi, medio.
demigod [-gad], *s.* semidiós, (poét.) semideo.
demigorge [-gordž], *s.* (fort.) semigola.

demijohn [-džan], *s.* castaña, damajuana.
demilitarization [dimilitạrizéišọn], *s.* desmilitarización.
demilitarize [dimilitạrajz], *va.* desmilitarizar.
demilune [démiljun], *s.* (astr. y fort.) media luna.
demimondaine [demimandéjn], *s.* mujer mundana, dama cortesana.—**demimonde** [démi-
mand], *s.* mujeres de la vida airada.
demise [dimájz]. **I.** *s.* muerte, *f.*, defunción,
fallecimiento; sucesión o transmisión de la
corona; (for.) traslación de dominio. **II.** *va.*
legar, dejar en testamento; transferir, ceder,
arrendar.
demisemiquaver [démisemikwejvœ(r)], *s.*
(mús.) fusa.
demission [dimíšọn], *s.* dimisión, abdicación.
demit [dimít], *va.* y *vn.* dimitir, renunciar, hacer
dejación de un empleo o comisión.
demitasse [démitæs], *s.* tacita de (o para) café.
demiurge [démiœrdž], *s.* (fil.) demiurgo.
demobilization [dimoубilizéišọn], *s.* desmovili-
zación.—**demobilize** [dimoubilajz], *va.* (mil.)
desmovilizar, poner (un ejército) en pie de paz.
democracy [dimákrạsi], *s.* democracia.—**democrat** [démokræt], *s.* demócrata, *mf.*—**demo-
cratic(al** [demokrǽtik(ạl], *a.* democrático,
demócrata.—**democratically** [-i], *adv.* democráticamente.—**democratization** [-izéišọn], *s.*
democratización.—**democratize** [dimákrạtajz],
va. y *vn.* democratizar(se).
demoded [dimóудid], *a.* anticuado, de moda
pasada.
demographic [dimogrǽfik], *a.* demográfico.
demographist [dimágrạfist], *s.* demógrafo.
demography [-fi], *s.* demografía.
demolish [dimáliš], *va.* demoler, arruinar, arrasar, derribar, derrocar, derruir.—**demolisher**
[-œ(r)], *s.* destructor, demoledor.—**demolish-
ing** [-iŋ], *a.* demoledor, destructor.—**demol-
ishment** [-mẹnt], **demolition** [demolíšọn], *s.*
demolición, destrucción, derribo, arrasamiento.
demon [dímọn], *s.* demonio, diablo, familiar.
demonetization [dimanetizéišọn], *s.* desmonetización.
demonetize [dimǽnetajz], *va.* desmonetizar;
suspender la circulación de (una moneda);
quitar el valor normal a.
demoniac(al [dimóунjæk, dimonájạkạl], *a.*
demoníaco, endemoniado.—**demoniac**, *s.*
energúmeno; demoníaco.
demonism [dímọnizm], *s.* creencia en demonios;
demonología; demonolatría.
demonolatry [-álạtri], *s.* demonolatría.
demonology [-álodži], *s.* demonología.
demonstrability [dimanstrạbíliti], *s.* demostrabilidad, calidad de demostrable.
demonstrable [dimánstrạbl], *a.* demostrable.
demonstrableness [-nịs], *s.* demostrabilidad.—
demonstrably [-bli], *adv.* demostrablemente.
demonstrate [démọnstrejt], *va.* (de)mostrar,
probar, hacer ver, poner de manifiesto.
demonstration [-éišọn], *s.* demostración; muestra, manifestación; exposición, presentación;
(mil.) demostración de fuerza; manifestación
pública.
demonstrative [dimánstrạtiv], *a.* demostrativo.
demonstratively [-li], *adv.* demostrativamente.
demonstrator [démọnstrejtọ(r)], *s.* el que de-
muestra; expositor (el que explica); maestro o
profesor de una ciencia objetiva, demostrador
(apl. esp. al de anatomía); manifestante.
demoralization [dimarạlizéišọn], *s.* desmoralización.
demoralize [dimárạlajz], *va.* desmoralizar, corromper; descorazonar; (fam.) desarreglar o
desbarajustar.—**demoralizing** [-iŋ], *a.* des-
moralizador.
Demosthenic [demosθénik], *a.* demostino.
demote [dimóut], *va.* rebajar en grado o en clase.
demotic [dimátik], *a.* demótico.

---

demotion [dimóuşọn], s. descenso de rango, categoría o empleo; (mil.) degradación.

demount [dimáunt], va. desmontar, desarmar (una máquina, un mueble, etc.).

demountable [-ạbl], a. desmontable, desarmable.

demulcent [dimÁlsẹnt], a. y s. (med.) emoliente, demulcente, dulcificante.

demur [dimœ́r]. **I.** vn. y va. objetar, poner dificultades; vacilar; aplazar o suspender (ante una duda, etc.); (for.) excepcionar, alegar excepción en el juicio. V. DEMURRER. **II.** s. duda; escrúpulo; vacilación; objeción.

demure [dimiúr], a. serio, formal, grave; recatado, modesto; gazmoño, pacato.—**demurely** [-li], adv. modestamente; con gazmoñería.—**demureness** [-nis], s. gravedad, recato; gazmoñería.

demurrage [dimœ́ridź], s. demora, detención; (com.) estadía.—**demurral** [-ạl], s. demora, detención; vacilación; objeción.—**demurrer** [-œ(r)], s. el que alega excepción o pone objeciones; (for.) excepción; admisión de los hechos aducidos por la parte contraria, pero negando que sean causa suficiente de litigio.

demy [dimái], s. papel (de) marquilla; becario de Oxford.

den [den], s. caverna, guarida, escondrijo; rincón, retrete; (fam.) cuchitril, pocilga, gazapera.

denarius [dinérias], s. denario.

denary [dénạri]. **I.** a. decimal, denario. **II.** s. decena.

denationalization [dinǽsọnạlizéişọn], s. desnaturalización, pérdida o cambio de nacionalidad.

denationalize [-lajz], va. desnacionalizar, desnaturalizar; cambiar la nacionalidad.

denaturalization [dinǽchụrạlizéişọn], s. desnaturalización.

denaturalize [-lajz], va. desnaturalizar; desfigurar.

denature [dinéichụ(r)], va. (quím.) desnaturalizar, alterar (el alcohol, etc., esp. haciendo que no se pueda comer o beber).

dendriform [déndriform], a. dendriforme.

dendrite [déndrajt], s. (min.) dendrita, planta fósil; arborescencia; (anat., fisiol.) prolongación arborizada de la célula nerviosa.

dendritic [dendrítik], a. dendrítico.

dendroid [déndrojd], a. dendroide(o), arborescente.

dendrolite [déndrolajt], s. dendrita, planta o rama fósil o petrificada.

dendrology [dendrálodźi], s. dendrografía.

dendrometer [dendrámtœ(r)], s. dendrómetro.

denegation [deneǵéişọn], s. denegación.

dengue [déngei], s. (med.) dengue.

deniable [dináiạbl], a. negable.

denial [dináiạl], s. negación, negativa, desmentida, contradicción; negativa, denegación.

denier [dináiœ(r)], s. negador, contradictor.

denier [denír], s. antiguo penique de plata; (tej.) unidad de peso del hilo de seda, rayón, etc.

denigrate [dénigrejt], va. ennegrecer; denigrar.

denigration [-éişọn], s. denigración.

denim [dénim], s. (tej.) cierta tela basta y resistente de algodón.

denitrification [dináitrifiķéişọn], s. desnitrificación, eliminación del nitrógeno.—**denitrify** [-faj], va. desnitrificar.

denization [denizéişọn], s. naturalización, ciudadanía.

denizen [dénizẹn]. **I.** s. ciudadano, habitante, residente; (Ingl.) extranjero naturalizado; planta, palabra, etc., naturalizadas. **II.** va. naturalizar.

denominable [dináminạbl], a. denominable.

denominate [dináminejt]. **I.** va. denominar, nombrar. **II.** a. denominado.

denomination [-éişọn], s. denominación, título, designación; secta; religión.—**denomina-**

tional [-ạl], a. sectario.—**denominationalism** [-izm], s. sectarismo.

denominative [-eitiv], a. denominativo.

denominator [-eitọ(r)], s. (arit.) denominador.

denotable [dinóutạbl], a. capaz de ser denotado o distinguido.

denotation [dinotéişọn], s. denotación.

denotative [dinóutạtiv], a. denotativo.

denote [dinóut], va. denotar, designar, marcar, señalar, simbolizar.

denouement [denúman], s. éxito; desenlace, desenredo, solución, catástrofe, f.

denounce [dináuns], va. denunciar, delatar, (fig.) soplar; denunciar (una mina); atacar, censurar; amenazar; significar la resolución de terminar (un pacto, tratado); promulgar.

denouncement [-ment], s. denuncia, denunciación, soplo; ataque, censura; declaración de la intención de terminar (un tratado, etc.); (min.) denuncio.

denouncer [-œ(r)], s. denunciador, delator.

de novo [di nóuvou], adv. (lat.) de nuevo; desde el principio.

dense [déns], a. denso, compacto, espeso, tupido; cerrado, estúpido.

densely [-li], adv. densamente.

denseness [-nis], **density** [-iti], s. densidad; espesura; estupidez.

densimeter [densímetœ(r)], s. (fís.) densímetro.

dent [dent]. **I.** s. abolladura; mella; hendidura; hoyo; (mec.) diente, indentación.—**d. corn**, (bot.) maíz dentado o hendido, maíz ordinario de forraje. **II.** va. y vn. abollar(se), mellar(se).

dental [déntạl]. **I.** a. dental, dentario.—**d. chair**, sillón de dentista.—**d. floss**, seda floja dental. —**d. plate**, dentadura postiza. **II.** s. (fon.) (letra) dental.

dentalization [-izéişọn], s. (fon.) dentalización.

dentate(d [déntejt(id], a. dentado; (blas.) danchado, dantellado o dentellado, endentado.

dented [déntid], a. abollado; mellado, dentellado.

denticle [déntikl], s. dientecillo; (arq.) dentículo.

denticulate(d [dentíkyulejt(id], a. (bot.) dentado, dentellado, denticular; (arq.) con dentículos, de dentículos.—**denticulation** [-éişọn], s. (arq.) formación de dentículos; obra de dentículos, que tiene dentículos; (anat., zool.) denticulación.

dentiform [déntiform], a. denticular.

dentifrice [-fris], a. y s. dentífrico.

dentil [déntil], s. (arq.) dentículo, dentellón.

dentilabial [dentiléibiạl], a. y s. (fon.) (letra) labiodental.—**dentilingual** [-língwạl], a. linguodental.

dentin(e [déntin], s. (anat.) dentina.

dentirostral [dentirástrạl], a. (zool.) dentirrostro.

dentist [déntist], s. dentista, odontólogo.

dentistry [-ri], s. cirugía dental, odontología.

dentition [dentíşọn], s. dentición; dentadura.

dentoid [déntojd], a. denticular; parecido a un diente.

denture [dénchụ(r)], s. dentadura (esp. la postiza).

denudate [diniúdejt]. **I.** va. = DENUDE. **II.** a. desnudo; despojado, deshojado.

denudation [-éişọn], s. denudación.

denude [diniúd], va. desnudar, despojar, desvestir; dejar desnudo.

denunciate [dinánşiejt], va. y vn. denunciar, amenazar.—**denunciation** [-éişọn], s. denunciación, acusación.—**denunciator** [-eitọ(r)], s. denunciador, denunciante.—**denunciatory** [-ạtọri], a. denunciatorio, conminatorio.

denutrition [dinutríşọn], s. (med.) desnutrición.

deny [dináj]. **I.** va. negar; rehusar o denegar; renunciar, desconocer; negarse a, no dejarse ver de.—**to d. one's self**, hacer abnegación de sí mismo; negarse. **II.** vn. negar.

deobstruent [diábstruẹnt], a. y s. (med.) desopilativo, desobstruyente; aperitivo.

deodar [díodar], *s.* (bot.) cedro deodara o de la India.

deodorant [dióudŏrant], *a.* y *s.*, **deodorizer** [-raizœ(r)], *s.* desodorante, desinfectante.—**deodorization** [-riẓéiẟŏn], *s.* desinfección, sahumerio.—**deodorize** [-ọraiẓ], *va.* desinfectar, sahumar.

deontology [diantálodẕi], *s.* deontología.

deoxid(iz)ation [diaksid(iz)éiẟŏn], **deoxygenation** [-dẕinéiẟŏn], *s.* desoxidación, desoxigenación.

deoxidize [diáksidaiz], **deoxidate** [-deit], **deoxygenate** [-dẕeneit], **deoxygenize** [-dẕenaiz], *va.* (quím.) desoxigenar, desoxidar.

depart [dipárt], *vn.* irse, marchar(se), partir, salir; apartarse, desviarse, salirse; morir.—**the departed**, los difuntos o muertos.

department [-ment], *s.* departamento; compartimiento; división, ramo; sección (en una tienda, etc.); oficina, despacho, negociado; ministerio; distrito, provincia.—**d. store**, bazar, tienda mixta, almacén de departamentos.—**D. of Justice**, Ministerio de (Gracia y) Justicia.—**D. of Labor**, M. del Trabajo.—**D. of Public Works**, etc., M. de Fomento.—**D. of State**, M. de Estado.—**D. of the Interior**, M. de la Gobernación o de lo Interior.

departmental [-méntal], *a.* departamental; del departamento, ramo, etc.; divido u organizado en departamentos; oficinesco, ministerial.

departure [dipárchu(r)], *s.* partida, salida, ida, marcha; desviación, divergencia; (mar. y top.) coordenada de longitud, distancia entre los dos meridianos que pasan por el extremo de una recta; (mar.) posición o coordenadas (longitud y latitud) de un barco a su salida.

depauperate [dipópœreit], *va.* empobrecer, depauperar.

depauperize [-aiz], *va.* sacar del pauperismo; limpiar de pobres o indigentes.

depend [dipénd], *vn.* pender, colgar.—**to d. (up)on**, depender de; atenerse a, confiar en, contar con, estar seguro de; tener por necesario; necesitar (de); ser mantenido por.

dependability [-abíliti], *s.* confiabilidad.

dependable [-abl], *a.* confiable, seguro.

dependance, dependancy, dependant. *V.* DEPENDENCE, DEPENDENCY, etc.

dependence [-ens], *s.* confianza, seguridad; dependencia; posesión, colonia; subordinación; sostén, apoyo; (for.) litispendencia.

dependency [-i], *s.* dependencia, pertenencia, sucursal; edificio anexo; posesión, colonia.—*pl.* anexidades.

dependent [-ent]. **I.** *a.* dependiente, subalterno; subordinado, sujeto; condicional, contingente; necesitado; pendiente, colgante. **II.** *s.* dependiente, subalterno; persona que hay que mantener; mantenido, manutenido.

dependently [-li], *adv.* dependientemente.

depending [-iṇ], *a.* pendiente; colgante, suspendido; dependiente.—**d. on**, según.

depict [dipíkt], **depicture** [dipíkchu(r)], *va.* pintar; representar; retratar; describir.

depilate [dépileit], *va.* depilar, quitar o hacer caer el vello o pelo.

depilation [-éiẟŏn], *s.* depilación.

depilatory [dipílatŏri]. **I.** *s.* depilatorio, atanquía. **II.** *a.* depilatorio.

deplete [diplít], *va.* agotar, disipar; vaciar; (med.) depauperar.—**depletion** [diplíẟŏn], *s.* vaciamiento; agotamiento; (med.) depauperación, depleción.

depletive, depletory [diplítiv, -ŏri], *a.* depletivo, depletorio; que vacía o agota.

deplorable [diplórabl], *a.* deplorable, lamentable; lastimoso.—**deplorableness** [-nis], *s.* estado deplorable.—**deplorably** [-bli], *adv.* deplorable o lastimosamente.

deplore [diplór], *va.* deplorar, lamentar, dolerse (de), sentir en el alma.

deploy [diplói], *va.* y *vn.* (mil.) desplegar(se).

deploy, deployment [-ment], *s.* (mil.) despliegue.

deplumate [diplúmeit], *a.* sin plumas, desplumado.

deplumation [-éiẟŏn], *s.* (zool.) muda, desplumadura.

deplume [diplúm], *va.* desplumar.

depolarization [dipóularizéiẟŏn], *s.* (fís.) despolarización.—**depolarize** [-aiz], *va.* despolarizar.—**depolarizer** [-aiẓœ(r)], *s.* despolarizador.

depone [dipóun], *va.* y *vn.* (for.) deponer. *V.* DEPOSE.

deponent [-ent], *a.* y *s.* (for.) deponente, declarante; (gram.) verbo deponente.

depopulate [dipápyuleit], *va.* y *vn.* despoblar(se).

depopulation [-léiẟŏn], *s.* despoblación; despueble, despueblo.—**depopulator** [-leitọ(r)], *s.* despoblador.

deport [dipórt]. **I.** *va.* deportar, desterrar, extrañar, relegar. **II.** *vr.* (com)portarse, conducirse.

deportation [-éiẟŏn], *s.* deportación, destierro, extrañamiento, relegación.

deportee [-í], *s.* deportado, desterrado.

deportment [-ment], *s.* proceder; conducta, comportamiento; porte.

deposable [dipóuzabl], *a.* capaz o digno de ser depuesto.—**deposal** [dipóuzal], *s.* = DEPOSITION.

depose [dipóuz]. **I.** *va.* deponer, destituir; destronar; degradar; (for.) deponer, declarar, atestiguar. **II.** *vn.* deponer, testificar.

deposit [dipázit]. **I.** *va.* depositar; consignar, confiar; (quím.) precipitar, asentar. **II.** *vn.* depositarse, sedimentarse. **III.** *s.* depósito; sedimento, poso, heces, *f. pl.*; (quím.) precipitado; (geol., min.) yacimiento, filón; (com. y for.) depósito; prenda, señal, *f.*, arras, *f. pl.*

depositary [-ạri], *s.* depositario, guardián; almacén, depósito.

deposition [depozíẟŏn], *s.* (for.) deposición o testimonio, declaración; deposición o destitución; depósito, acumulación; (b. a.) desprendimiento de la cruz; (igl.) deposición eclesiástica.

depositor [dipázitọ(r)], *s.* depositador o depositante; cuentacorrentista.

depository [-tŏri], *s.* depositaría, depósito, almacén; depositario, guardián.

depot [dípou], *s.* pósito, depósito, almacén; (f. c. E. U.) estación, paradero.

depravation [deprəvéiẟŏn], *s.* depravación, corrupción, perversión, estragamiento, vicio.

deprave [dipréiv], *va.* depravar, corromper, estragar, pervertir, viciar.—**depraved** [-d], *a.* depravado, perverso.—**depravedly** [-idli], *adv.* depravadamente.—**depravedness** [-idnis], *s.* depravación, estragamiento, corrupción.

depraver [-œ(r)], *s.* depravador.

depravity [diprévịti], *s.* depravación.

deprecate [déprẹkeit], *va.* deprecar; lamentar, desaprobar.

deprecation [-kéiẟŏn], *s.* deprecación; desaprobación.—**deprecative** [-keitiv], **deprecatory** [-katŏri], *a.* deprecativo; de desaprobación.—**deprecator** [-keitọ(r)], *s.* deprecador, deprecante; desaprobador.

depreciate [dipríẟieit]. **I.** *va.* depreciar, rebajar, abaratar; menospreciar, desapreciar. **II.** *vn.* bajar de precio, abaratarse; depreciarse.

depreciation [-éiẟŏn], *s.* depreciación; desaprecio, descrédito, desestimación; baja, reducción de precio.

depreciative, depreciatory [-ạtiv, -ạtŏri], *a.* despreciativo, despectivo.

depreciator [-eitọ(r)], *s.* despreciador.

depredate [déprideit], *va.* y *vn.* depredar, pillar, saquear.

depredation [-déiẟŏn], *s.* depredación, pillaje.

depredator [-tọ(r)], *s.* depredador.

depredatory [-tŏri], *a.* de depredación.

depress [diprés], *va.* deprimir, abatir; bajar, inclinar; abaratar, rebajar el precio de; desalentar o desanimar; humillar; (mat.) reducir el grado de.
depressant [-ant], *s.* y *a.* (med.) deprimente, debilitante; sedativo, calmante.
depressed [-t], *a.* deprimido; rebajado; desanimado, alicaído; (bot.) deprimido, hundido.
depression [dipréşon], *s.* depresión; abatimiento; hondonada, bajo; (com., mar., ast.) depresión. **—d. of the horizon, o of the visible horizon,** (mar.) depresión de horizonte.
depressive [-siv], *a.* depresivo; deprimente.
depressor [-ǫ(r)]. I. *a.* depresor.—**d. nerve,** nervio depresor o de Cyon. II. *s.* depresor; (anat.) músculo depresor; (cir.) depresor.
deprivable [dipráivabl], *a.* amovible, revocable.
deprivation [deprivéişon], *s.* privación, carencia, pérdida.
deprive [dipráiv], *va.* privar, despojar; excluir; impedir; destituir.
depth [depθ], *s.* profundidad; hondura; fondo; espesor, grueso (de una cosa); parte interior o recóndita; lo más profundo o intenso; viveza (del color); gravedad (del sonido); sagacidad, penetración; (mar.) puntal.—**d. bomb, o d. charge,** carga de profundidad, bomba o granada contra submarinos.—**d. of field, o focus,** (ópt., fot.) profundidad de foco.—**d. of the hold,** puntal de la bodega.—**beyond, o out of one's d.,** en agua más honda que uno, o que se lo traga; más allá de los alcances de uno.
depurant [dépjurant], **depurative** [-eitiv], *a.* y *s.* (med.) depurativo, depurador, que purifica.
depurate [-eit], *va.* (med.) depurar, purificar.
depuration [-éişon], *s.* depuración, purificación.
deputation [depjutéişon], *s.* diputación, delegación, comisión.
depute [dipjút], *va.* diputar, delegar, comisionar.
deputize [dépjutaiz]. I. *va.* = DEPUTE. II. *vn.* hacer de diputado o delegado.
deputy [dépjuti], *s.* diputado; delegado, comisionado, enviado, agente; (for.) (lugar)teniente, personero.—**d. governor,** teniente gobernador.
deracinate [dirásineit], *va.* desarraigar.
deraign [diréin], *va.* probar, vindicar; reclamar.
derail [diréil], *va.* y *vn.* (hacer) descarrilar.
derailment [-mənt], *s.* descarrilamiento.
derange [diréindž], *va.* desarreglar, desordenar; descomponer; trastornar.—**derangement** [-mənt], *s.* desarreglo, desorden; descompostura; desbarajuste; locura, enajenación mental, desvarío.
derby [(E. U.) dœrbi, (Ingl.) dárbi], *s.* sombrero hongo; (D.) carrera Derby, famosa carrera anual de caballos; (alb.) llana.
derelict [dérelikt]. I. *a.* negligente, remiso; derrelicto. II. *s.* delincuente; persona negligente, infiel, o abandonada; (for.) derrelicto, buque u objeto abandonado.
dereliction [derélikşon], *s.* negligencia culpable; desamparo, abandono; dejación.
deride [diráid], *va.* ridiculizar, escarnecer, burlarse o mofarse de.—**derider** [-œ(r)], *s.* burlón, zumbón; ridiculizador, mofador, escarnecedor.—**deriding** [-iŋ], *a.* mofador.—**deridingly** [-li], *adv.* irrisoriamente, con mofa.
derision [diríżon], *s.* irrisión, mofa, escarnio.
derisive [diráisiv], **derisory** [-sori], *a.* irrisorio, burlesco.
derisively [-li], *adv.* irrisoriamente.
derivable [diráivabl], *a.* derivable, deducible.
derivation [derivéişon], *s.* derivación; deducción; (gram.) derivación, etimología; (biol.) descendencia; (med.) derivación, revulsión.
derivative [dirívativ]. I. *a.* derivativo; derivado. II. *s.* derivativo; (gram., quím.) derivado; (mat.) derivada.
derive [diráiv]. I. *va.* deducir (una conclusión, una fórmula); establecer (una fórmula); (gram.) derivar; (quím.) derivar, obtener (un compuesto de otro); (elec.) derivar.—**to d. from,**

deber a; hacer provenir de; sacar (ganancia etc.) de. II. *vn.* provenir, emanar, descender
derived [-d], *a.* derivado; obtenido; originario resultante; (elec.) derivado.
derm [dœrm], **derma, dermis** [-ă, -is], *s.* dermis *fm.,* cutis, *mf.*
dermal, dermic [-al, -ik], *a.* dérmico, cutáneo.
dermatitis [-atáitis], *s.* (med.) dermitis, derma titis, inflamación de la piel.
dermatologist [-tálodžist], *s.* dermatólogo.
dermatology [-tálodži], *s.* dermatología.
derogate [dérogeit], *vn.* (con from) detraer, detractar.—**derogation** [derogéişon], *s.* detracción; derogación.—**derogative** [dirágativ] **derogatory** [-tori], *a.* derogatorio.
derrick [dérik], *s.* grúa, cabria, trucha, (mar.) abanico; percha de carga; torre o armazón de taladrar situada en la boca de un pozo arte siano, de petróleo, etc.).
dervish [dœrviš], *s.* derviche, santón.
descant [déskænt]. I. *s.* comentario, disertación (mús.) discante. II. [desként], *vn.* discurrir comentar; (mús.) discantar.
descend [disénd], *va.* y *vn.* descender, bajar (con from) descender, desviarse; (con to) re bajarse a, descender a; (con on o upon) invadir caer en o sobre; (astr.) declinar, ponerse.
descendant [-ant]. I. *s.* descendiente, vástago II. *a.* = DESCENDENT.
descendent [-ent], *a.* descend(i)ente; originario (de).—**descendible** [-ibl], **descendable,** *a.* que se puede descender o heredar; heredable; legable.
descending [-iŋ], *a.* descend(i)ente.
descent [disént], *s.* descenso, bajada; descendimiento, descensión; declive; alcurnia, origen descendencia, posteridad, sucesión; rebajamiento, humillación, degradación; (for.) herencia; (mil.) invasión, incursión.
describable [diskráibabl], *a.* descriptible.
describe [diskráib], *va.* describir, pintar, retratar
describer [-œ(r)], *s.* descriptor.
descrier [diskráiœ(r)], *s.* descubridor.
description [diskrípşon], *s.* descripción; trazado representación; clase, *f.,* género, naturaleza.
descriptive [-tiv], *a.* descriptivo.—**d. anatomy, geometry,** etc., anatomía, geometría, etc., descriptiva.
descry [diskrái], *va.* columbrar, avistar, divisar descubrir.
desecrate [désikreit], *va.* profanar, violar.
desecration [-éişon], *s.* profanación, desacato.
desensitize [disénsitaiz], *va.* desensibilizar.
desert [dézœrt]. I. *s.* desierto, yermo; páramo II. *a.* desierto, yermo, desolado; del desierto
desert [dizœrt]. I. *s.* merecimiento o mérito.—**to get one's d.,** llevar su merecido. II. *va.* desamparar, dejar solo, abandonar. III. *va.* y *vn.* (mil.) desertar, desbandarse.—**deserter** [-œ(r)], *s.* desertor.—**desertion** [dizœrşon], *s.* deserción defección, abandono.
deserve [dizœrv]. I. *va.* merecer. II. *vn.* tener merecimientos.—**deserved** [-d], *a.* merecido condigno.—**deservedly** [-idli], *adv.* merecidamente, condignamente.
deserver [-œ(r)], *s.* merecedor.
deserving [-iŋ]. I. *a.* meritorio; acreedor, merecedor o digno. II. *s.* mérito, merecimiento.—**deservingly** [-li], *adv.* dignamente, merecidamente.—**deservingness** [-nis], *s.* merecimiento
desiccant [désikant], *a.* y *s.* (med.) descante.
desiccate [-keit]. I. *va.* desecar, enjugar; secar pasar. II. *vn.* resecarse.
desiccation [-éişon], *s.* desecación; resecación.
desiccative [-keitiv], **desiccatory** [-katori], *a.* desecativo.
desiccator [désikeitǫ(r)], *s.* aparato para desecar (azú.) evaporadora.
desiderate [disídereit], *va.* desear, querer, apetecer, anhelar; faltar, necesitar.—**desiderative** [-iv]. I. *a.* desiderativo. II. *s.* objeto de deseo

(gram.) verbo desiderativo.—**desideratum** [-réjtʌm], *s.* desiderátum.

design [dizájn]. **I.** *va.* idear, inventar, concebir; proyectar, calcular (una máquina, un puente); destinar, dedicar; diseñar, delinear. **II.** *vn.* hacer proyectos, diseños, planos, planes. **III.** *s.* proyecto, cálculo (de máquinas, puentes, etc.); disposición, arreglo, hechura, construcción; plan; propósito, intención, motivo, fin, designio; plano; diseño, croquis, *m.*, trazo, delineación.— **by o through d.**, intencionalmente, adrede.— **to have designs on**, tener la mira en.

designable [-ʌbl], *a.* designable.

designate [dézignejt], *va.* apuntar, señalar; distinguir; designar, nombrar, destinar.

designation [-éjʂọn], *s.* designación, señalamiento, título, nombramiento.

designative [-ejtiv], *a.* designativo, especificativo.

designedly [dizájndli], *adv.* adrede, de propósito, de industria, de intento, intencionadamente.

designer [dizájnœ(r)], *s.* dibujante; diseñador; proyectista (de máquinas, obras, etc.); delineador, tracista; inventor; maquinador.

designing [-iŋ], *a.* insidioso, astuto, artero, intrigante.

designingly [-li], *adv.* insidiosamente.

desilverize [disílvœrajz], *va.* desplatar, extraer o separar la plata de.

desinence [désinɛns], *s.* (gram.) desinencia.

desirability [dizajrabíliti], **desirableness** [dizájrablnjs], *s.* calidad de deseable, apetecible o provechoso; conveniencia.

desirable [-ʌbl], *a.* deseable, de desearse, apetecible, conveniente.

desirably [-bli], *adv.* deseablemente.

desire [dizájr]. **I.** *s.* deseo, anhelo, apetencia, antojo, gana, voluntad. **II.** *va.* desear, anhelar, apetecer, querer. **III.** *vn.* sentir deseo.

desirous [-ʌs], *a.* deseoso, anheloso.—**desirously** [-li], *adv.* deseablemente, ansiosamente, con deseo.—**desirousness** [-njs], *s.* deseo vivo, anhelo.

desist [dizíst], *vn.* desistir, cesar; pararse.—**desistance** [-ʌns], *s.* desistencia, cesación.

desk [desk], *s.* escritorio, pupitre, bufete, buró; mesa, carpeta.—**d. clock**, reloj de sobremesa. —**d. pad**, carpeta.—**d. work**, trabajo de escritorio.

desman [désmʌn], *s.* (zool.) desmán.

desmography [desmágrafi], *s.* (anat.) desmografía.

desmoid [désmojd], *a.* (anat. y med.) ligamentoso; fibroso.

desolate [désolejt]. **I.** *va.* desolar o arrasar; despoblar, devastar, arruinar; desconsolar; abandonar. **II.** [désọlit], *a.* desolado; desierto, solitario; solo, abandonado, triste.—**desolately** [-li], *adv.* desoladoramente.—**desolateness** [-njs], *s.* desolación; desconsuelo; soledad.

desolater, desolator [désolejtœ(r)], *s.* desolador, asolador.—**desolation** [-éjʂọn], *s.* desolación, asolación; aflicción, desconsuelo, soledad.

despair [dispér]. **I.** *s.* desesperación. **II.** *vn.* desesperar, perder toda esperanza, desesperanzarse.

despairing [-iŋ], *a.* desesperante; desesperado; sin esperanza.—**despairingly** [-li], *adv.* desesperadamente.

despatch, despatcher = DISPATCH, etc.

desperado [despȩréjdou], *s.* malhechor, bandido temerario.

desperate [déspȩrit], *a.* desesperado; arrojado, arriesgado o temerario; irremediable, desesperanzado, perdido; furioso, violento, terrible; (for.) incobrable.—**desperately** [-li], *adv.* desesperadamente; perdidamente.—**desperateness** [-njs], *s.* temeridad, arrojo, furia, violencia.— **desperation** [-éjʂọn], *s.* desesperación, furor, encarnizamiento.

despicable [déspikʌbl], *a.* despreciable, vil.

despicableness [-njs], *s.* vileza, ruindad, bajeza.

despicably [-bli], *adv.* vilmente, bajamente.

despisable [dispájzʌbl], *a.* despreciable.

despise [dispájz], *va.* despreciar, menospreciar.

despisement [-mȩnt], **despisal** [-ʌl], *s.* desprecio. —**despiser** [-œ(r)], *s.* despreciador.

despite [dispájt]. **I.** *s.* despecho, malquerencia, aversión, inquina. **II.** *prep.* a despecho de, a pesar de, pese a, no obstante.

despiteful [-fʉl], *a.* malicioso, rencoroso, vengativo, maligno.—**despitefully** [-i], *adv.* malignamente, maliciosamente.—**despitefulness** [-njs], *s.* malignidad, rencor, odio, inquina.

despoil [dispójl], *va.* despojar, expoliar; robar.

despoiler [-œ(r)], *s.* pillador, saqueador, robador.

despoliation [dispouljéjʂọn], *s.* despojo.

despond [dispánd], *vn.* desalentarse, abatirse; perder la esperanza, desesperarse, abandonarse.

despondence, despondency [-ȩns(i], *s.* desaliento, descaecimiento, abatimiento, melancolía.

despondent [-ȩnt], **desponding** [-iŋ], *a.* desalentado, abatido, desesperanzado.

despondently, despondingly [-li, -iŋli], *adv.* desalentadamente.

despot [déspat], *s.* déspota, *m.*, tirano.—**despotic(al** [despátik(ʌl], *a.* despótico.—**despotically** [-i], *adv.* despóticamente.—**despoticalness** [-njs], *s.* despotismo.—**despotism** [déspọtizm], *s.* despotismo, tiranía; absolutismo; cesarismo; autocracia.—**despotize** [-ajz], *vn.* despotizar.

despumation [despjumȩ́jʂọn], *s.* despumación.

desquamate [déskwȩmejt], *vn.* (med.) exfoliarse. **II.** *prep.* a despecho

desquamation [-éjʂọn], *s.* (med.) descamación, exfoliación.

dessert [dizœ́rt], *s.* postre, sobrecomida.— **dessertspoon** [-spun], *s.* cuchara de postre, cuchara de tamaño intermedio entre la de sopa y la cafetera.

destination [destinéjʂọn], *s.* destinación, destino; paradero; meta.

destine [déstin], *va.* destinar; dedicar, consagrar; predestinar.

destiny [-i], *s.* destino, hado, sino, suerte, *f.*

destitute [déstitjut], *a.* destituído, indigente, necesitado, menesteroso; (con **of**) falto, desprovisto de.

destitution [-tjúʂọn], *s.* destitución, privación; miseria, indigencia, inopia.

destroy [distrój], *va.* destruir, destrozar, desbaratar, consumir, acabar con, dar al traste con; invalidar; exterminar, matar.

destroyer [-œ(r)], *s.* destruidor, destructor; (mar.) cazatorpedero, destróyer, destructor.

destructibility [distrʌktibíliti], *s.* destructibilidad.—**destructible** [-jbl], *a.* destructible.

destruction [distrʌ́kʂọn], *s.* destrucción, ruina, demolición, desolación, destrozo, exterminio.

destructionist [-ist], *s.* destructor; revolucionario, enemigo de las instituciones actuales.

destructive [distrʌ́ktiv], *a.* destructor, destructivo, destruyente; dañino; fatal, ruinoso; subversivo.—**d. distillation**, (quím.) destilación seca.

destructively [-li], *adv.* destructivamente.—**destructiveness** [-njs], *s.* espíritu de destrucción; destructividad.

desuetude [déswitjud], *s.* desuso.

desulfur(ize, desulphur(ize [disʌ́lfjʉr(ajz], *va.* (quím.) desulfurar, desazufrar.

desulphurization [-izéjʂọn], *s.* desulfuración.

desultorily [désʌltọrili], *adv.* sin plan ni ilación, inconexamente, inmetódicamente.—**desultoriness** [-njs], *s.* falta de plan; desconexión.

desultory [désʌltọri], *a.* inconexo; caprichoso, variable, casual, sin método; parentético.

detach [ditætch], *va.* separar, despegar o desprender; (mil.) destacar.

detachable [-ʌbl], *a.* separable, desmontable, de quita y pon, de quitapón.

detached [-t], *a.* suelto, distinto, separado.

detachment [-mȩnt], *s.* separación, despegadura; (mil.) destacamento.

---

detail [djtéjl]. **I.** *va.* detallar, particularizar, pormenorizar, razonar, circunstanciar; (mil.) destacar. **II.** *s.* detalle, pormenor; (mil.) destacamento; (b. a.) detalle.—**d. drawing**, dibujo especificado.—**in d.**, en detalle, por menudo, detallada o minuciosamente.

detain [djtéjn], *va.* detener, retardar, contener, atrasar; represar, retener.—**detainer** [-œ(r)], *s.* (for.) detentador, retenedor; detención.

detect [djtékt], *va.* descubrir, averiguar, echar de ver; hallar; (rad.) rectificar.

detecter [-œ(r)], *s.* = DETECTOR.

detection [djtékʃọn], *s.* averiguación, descubrimiento; detección; (rad.) rectificación.

detective [-tjv]. **I.** *a.* hábil para descubrir o averiguar.—**d. story**, novela policíaca.—**d. work**, detectivismo. **II.** *s.* detective, agente de policía particular o secreta.

detector[-tọ(r)],*s.*descubridor,averiguador; (m.v.) indicador de nivel; (mar.) detector de torpedos; (elec.) detector; (rad.) rectificador.

detent [djtént], *s.* (mec.) retén, trinquete; fiador, seguro; escape de un reloj.

detention [djténʃọn], *s.* detención, retención; arresto, encierro; (com. y mar.) estadía; (for.) detentación.

detentive [djténtjv], *a.* que retiene o asegura.

deter [djtœr], *va.* disuadir; acobardar; desanimar. —**to d. from**, disuadir de, impedir.

deterge [djtœrdʒ], *va.* deterger; (med.) absterger.

detergent [-ẹnt], *a.* y *s.* detergente, detersivo; detersorio; abstergente.

deteriorate [djtjrjoréjt], *va.* y *vn.* deteriorar(se), menoscabar(se), desmejorar(se), empeorar(se). —**deteriorating** [-jŋ], *a.* que deteriora, perjudicial.—**deterioration** [-réjʃọn], *s.* deterioro, deterioración, desperfecto, desmejora, empeoramiento, menoscabo.—**deteriorative** [-rejtjv], *a.* = DETERIORATING.

determent [djtœrmẹnt], *s.* disuasión.

determinable [djtœrmjnạbl], *a.* determinable; terminable.—**determinably** [-blj], *adv.* determinablemente.

determinant [-ạnt]. **I.** *a.* determinativo. **II.** *s.* causa determinante; (mat.) determinante.

determinate [-jt], *a.* determinado, definido; decidido, resuelto; concluyente; (bot.) de inflorescencia limitada.—**determinately** [-ljְ], *adv.* determinadamente.—**determinateness** [-njs], *s.* calidad de determinado.

determination [-éjʃọn], *s.* determinación, empeño; resolución, decisión; definición; (for.) decisión, fallo, sentencia; (lóg.) especificación; (med.) congestión.

determinative [djtœrmjnạtjv], *a.* determinativo, determinante.

determine [djtœrmjn]. **I.** *va.* determinar, decidir, resolver; (for.) definir, sentenciar, concluir, terminar; restringir. **II.** *vn.* (for.) terminar, acabar, concluir; resolverse, decidirse.

determined [-d], *a.* determinado, decidido, empeñado, resuelto.

determinism [-jzm], *s.* (fil.) determinismo, negación del libre albedrío.—**determinist** [-jst], *s.* y *a.* (fil.) determinista.

deterrent [djtérẹnt], *a.* y *s.* (lo) que disuade.

detersion [djtœrʃọn], *s.* (med.) detersión.

detersive [djtœrsjv], *a.* y *s.* detersivo, detersorio, detergente, abstergente.

detest [djtést], *va.* detestar, aborrecer, abominar, odiar.—**detestable** [-abl], *a.* detestable, aborrecible.—**detestableness** [-njs], *s.* calidad de detestable, odiosidad.—**detestably** [-ablj], *adv.* detestablemente.—**detestation** [-éjʃọn], *s.* detestación, execración.

dethrone [djθróųn], *va.* destronar, desentronizar.

dethronement [-mẹnt], *s.* destronamiento.

detinue [détjnju], *s.* (for.) detentación; auto contra el detentador de alguna cosa.

detonate [détonejt]. **I.** *vn.* detonar, estallar, hacer explosión. **II.** *va.* hacer estallar.

detonating [-jŋ], *a.* detonante.—**d. fuse**, mecha de explosión o detonante.—**d. gas**, gas o mezcla detonante (dos volúmenes de hidrógeno y uno de oxígeno).—**d. powder**, pólvora detonante.—**d. tube**, eudiómetro detonante.

detonation [-éjʃọn], *s.* detonación.

detonator [-ẹjtọ(r)], *s.* explosivo detonante o de explosión instantánea; detonador, explosor, mezcla o artefacto para producir explosión; (f. c.) señal detonante.

detorsion [djtórʃọn], *s.* acto de destorcer; destorcedura; (med.) destorsión.

detour [djtúr]. **I.** *s.* desviación, vuelta, rodeo. **II.** *va.* y *vn.* (hacer) desviar o rodear.

detract [djtrékt]. **I.** *va.* detraer, disminuir o quitar. **II.** *vn.* detraer, detractar, denigrar.—**to d. from**, disminuir, hacer desmerecer, calumniar, desvirtuar, quitar mérito a, afear.

detracter, detractor [-œ(r)], *s.* detractor, di(s)famador, infamador, calumniador, murmurador.

detraction [djtrékʃọn], *s.* detracción, denigración; calumnia, maledicencia, difamación.

detractive [djtréktjv], **detractory** [-orj], *a.* difamatorio, derogatorio, denigrante.—**detractively** [-jvlj], *adv.* difamatoriamente.

detrain [djtréjn], *va.* y *vn.* (hacer) salir del tren.

detriment [détrjmẹnt], *s.* detrimento; daño, perjuicio; desmedro.—**to the d. of**, con menoscabo de, en daño de.

detrimental [-mántạl], *a.* perjudicial, dañoso; nocivo; desventajoso.

detrital [djtrájtạl], *a.* detrítico.

detrition [djtríʃọn], *s.* desgaste.

detritus [djtrájtạs], *s.* (geol., med.) detrito, detritus; escombros, desperdicios.

detrude [djtrúd], *va.* empujar o lanzar hacia abajo o hacia afuera; mandar, derribar.

detruncate [djtrʌ́ŋkejt], *va.* destroncar, mochar, cercenar, recortar, podar; decapitar.

detruncation [-éjʃọn], *s.* destroncamiento, recorte, poda.

detrusion [djtrúʒọn], *s.* empuje hacia afuera o hacia abajo.

detune [djtjún], *va.* (rad.) desintonizar, destemplar, poner fuera de sintonización.

deuce [djús], *s.* dos (en naipes o dados); pata (en otros juegos); (fam.) demonio, diantre, demontre, pateta.

deuced [-jd], *a.* maldito, endemoniado; excesivo.

deuterogamist [djuterágạmjst], *s.* deuterógamo, el que contrae segundas nupcias.

deuterogamy [-ágạmj], *s.* deuterogamia, segundas nupcias.

Deuteronomy [-ánomj], *s.* Deuteronomio.

deuton [djútạn], *s.* (fís.) deutón.

deutoplasm [djútoplæzm], *s.* (embr.) deutoplasma, *m.*

deutoxide [djutáksajd], *s.* (quím.) deutóxido.

devaluate [divǽlyuejt], *va.* depreciar, desvalorizar, rebajar el valor.—**devaluation** [-éjʃọn], *s.* depreciación, desvalorización.—**devalue** [divǽlyu], *va.* depreciar.

devastate [dévạstejt], *va.* devastar, asolar.—**devastating** [-jŋ], *a.*, **devastator** [-ọ(r)], *s.* devastador, asolador.—**devastation** [-éjʃọn], *s.* devastación, desolación, asolación, ruina.

develop [divélọp]. **I.** *va.* desenvolver, desarrollar; desplegar; descubrir; fomentar; producir; perfeccionar, mejorar; ensanchar; urbanizar; establecer; realizar, efectuar; explotar (minas, etc.); (fot.) revelar.—**developing bath**, (fot.) baño revelador. **II.** *vn.* progresar; avanzar; formarse, crecer, desarrollarse, evolucionar.

developer [-œ(r)], *s.* (fot.) revelador, baño.

development [-mẹnt], *s.* desarrollo, evolución; fomento; producción; cambio; acontecimiento nuevo; explotación; mejora; ensanche; urbanización, caserío nuevo, colonia; (f. c.) desarrollo (vía curva en pendiente); (fot.) revelado, revelamiento.

developmental [-méntạl], *a.* relativo al desarrollo; evolucionista.

devest [djvést], *va.* y *vn.* (for.) enajenar(se).

deviate [dívjeịt], *va.* y *vn.* desviar(se), apartar(se), divergir, descarriar(se), extraviar(se).

deviation [-éịṣọn], *s.* desviación, divergencia; deriva; desvío, extravío, error; (astr.) receso.

device [djváịs], *s.* invento, invención; aparato, dispositivo, artefacto, artificio; plan, traza, proyecto; expediente, recurso; ardid; dibujo o patrón (de tela o bordado); lema, *m.,* divisa, mote, cifra, empresa.—*pl.* voluntad, deseo, inclinación.

devil [dévịl]. **I.** *s.* diablo; demonio; (fam.) pateta; aprendiz (*m.*) de imprenta; manjar muy sazonado con picante; (mec.) terraja para labrar tornillos de madera; máquina de moler o desgarrar; máquina de descargar granos. (Apl. a varias otras máquinas, cuya clase gen. se indica por un modificativo.)—**d. dog,** (fam.) soldado de marina norteamericana.—**d. worship,** adoración de espíritus malos; demonolatría.—**d.'s advocate,** (igl. y fig.) abogado del diablo.—**d.'s darning needle,** (ent.) caballito del diablo, libélula; (bot.) peine de Venus.—**a poor d.,** un pobre diablo.—**between the d. and the deep sea,** entre la espada y la pared.—**the d.!** (fam.) ¡caramba! ¡diablos!—**the D.,** Satanás.—**the d. take the hindmost,** quien se quede atrás, que pague el pato; quien se quede en zaga, con el diablo se las haya; el que venga atrás, que arree.—**the d. to pay,** la(s) de Dios en Cristo. **II.** *va.* condimentar con mucho picante; someter a la acción de una máquina *devil;* (fam.) atormentar.

devilfish [-fịṣ], *s.* (zool.) raya grande del golfo de México y otras mares calientes; pulpo.

deviling [-iŋ], **devilkin** [-kịn], *s.* diablillo.

devilish [-iṣ], *a.* diabólico; perverso; travieso; excesivo.—**devilishly** [-lị], *adv.* diabólicamente, endiabladamente.—**devilishness** [-nịs], *s.* diablura; perversidad.

devilment [-mẹnt], **devilry** [-rị], **deviltry** [-trị], *s.* diablura; travesura; conducta atolondrada; maldad; demonología.

devious [dívịas], *a.* desviado, descarriado, extraviado; tortuoso; errante.—**deviously** [-lị], *adv.* tortuosamente.—**deviousness** [-nịs], *s.* extravío, descarrío; desviación.

devisable [djváịzạbl], *a.* que se puede inventar; (for.) que se puede legar.

devisal [djváịzạl], *s.* invención; (for.) legado o manda.

devise [djváịz]. **I.** *va.* idear, inventar, proyectar; (for.) legar. **II.** *vn.* formar proyectos; maquinar. **III.** *s.* (for.) legado de bienes raíces.

devisee [-f], *s.* (for.) legatario.

deviser [-œ(r)], *s.* inventor, autor.

devisor [-ọ(r)], *s.* testador que lega bienes raíces.

devitalize [djváịtạlạịz], *va.* quitar vitalidad.

devitrification [djvítrịfịkéịṣọn], *s.* desvitrificación.—**devitrify** [-faị], *va.* desvitrificar, quitar al vidrio su transparencia.

devoid [djvóịd], *a.* libre, exento; desprovisto (de).

devoir [devwár], *s.* homenaje; deber.—*pl.* recados.

devolution [devoljúṣọn], **devolvement** [djválvmẹnt], *s.* entrega, traspaso; (for.) devolución; (biol.) degeneración.

devolve [djválv]. **I.** *va.* transmitir, traspasar, entregar. **II.** *vn.* (seguido de **to, on** o **upon**) recaer, pasar a, tocar, incumbir a.

Devonian [devóụnịạn], *a.* y *s.* devoniano, devónico.

devote [djvóụt]. **I.** *va.* dedicar; consagrar; condenar. **II.** *vr.* dedicarse, entregarse, consagrarse (a).

devoted [-ịd], *a.* devoto, ferviente; adicto, afecto; condenado.—**devotedly** [-lị], *adv.* devotamente.—**devotedness** [-nịs], *s.* devoción; dedicación; afecto.

devotee [dɛvotí], *s.* devoto; adicto, aficionado; beato; fanático.

devotion [djvóụṣọn], *s.* dedicación; devoción, piedad; celo; afecto; constancia.—*pl.* preces, rezo.—**devotional** [-ạl], *a.* devoto, piadoso, religioso.

devour [djváụr], *va.* devorar, tragar, engolfar, engullir; consumir, destruir.—**devourer** [-œ(r)], *s.* devorador, engullidor, tragón; destructor.—**devouring** [-lị], *a.* devorador.—**devouringly** [-lị], *adv.* devoradoramente.

devout [djváụt], *a.* devoto, pío, piadoso.

devoutly [-lị], *adv.* devotamente, piadosamente.

devoutness [-nịs], *s.* piedad, devoción.

dew [dju]. **I.** *s.* rocío, relente, sereno.—**d. point,** temperatura a que se forma el rocío. **II.** *va.* rociar; apaciguar, refrescar. **III.** *vn.* rociar.

Dewar vessel [djúạ(r) véṣẹl], *s.* (quím.) frasco de Dewar, frasco Dewar.

dewberry [djúberị], *s.* (bot.) zarzamora.

dewclaw [-klɔ], *s.* dedo rudimentario, uña, espolón o casco falso que tienen ciertos animales.

dewdrop [djúdrạp], *s.* gota de rocío; (poét.) aljófar.

dewlap [djúlæp], *s.* papada.

dewlapped [-t], *a.* papudo.

dewy [djúị], *a.* rociado; lleno de rocío; (poét.) aljofarado.

dexiocardia [dɛksjokárdịạ], *s.* (med.) dexiocardia, desviación del corazón hacia la derecha.

dexter [dékstœ(r)]. **I.** *a.* diestro o derecho; favorable, propicio. **II.** *adv.* a la derecha.

dexterity [dɛkstérịtị], **dexterousness** [dékstẹrạsnịs], *s.* destreza, habilidad, acierto, maña, tino, (Am.) atingencia.

dexterous [dékstẹrạs], *a.* diestro, hábil, experto; mañero.—**dexterously** [-lị], *adv.* diestramente.

dextrad [dékstræd],*"adv.* (anat.) a la derecha.

dextral [dékstrạl], *a.* derecho; diestro; propicio.

dextrin [dékstrịn], *s.* (quím.) dextrina.

dextrocardia [dɛkstrokárdịạ], *s.* = DEXIOCARDIA.

dextrose [dékstroụs], *s.* (quím.) dextrosa o glucosa.

dey [deị], *s.* bey o dey.

diabase [dáịabeịs], *s.* (geol.) diabasa.

diabetes [dajạbítịz], *s.* (med.) diabetes, *f.*

diabetic [dajạbétịk], *a.* y *s.* (med.) diabético.

diabolic(al [dajạbálịk(ạl], *a.* diabólico.

diabolically [-i], *adv.* diabólicamente.

diabolicalness [-nịs], *s.* calidad de diabólico.

diabolism [dajébolịzm], *s.* perversidad, iniquidad; acción diabólica; hechicería, brujería; demonolatría; posesión demoníaca.

diabolo [djébolou], *s.* diábolo (juego y juguete).

diacaustic [dajạkɔ́stịk], *a.* (fís.) diacáustico.

diachylon [dajékịlan], **diachylum** [-ʌm], *s.* (farm.) diaquilón.

diaconal [dajékonạl], *a.* diaconal.

diaconate [-neịt], *s.* diaconato.

diacoustics [dajạkústịks], *s.* (fís.) diacústica.

diacritic(al [dajạkrítịk(ạl]. **I.** *a.* (gram. y med.) diacrítico; diagnóstico. **II.** *s.* (gram.) signo diacrítico.

diactinic [dajæktínịk], *a.* (fot.) diactínico.

diadelphous [dajạdélfʌs], *a.* (bot.) diadelfo.

diadem [dáịạdɛm], *s.* diadema.

diæresis o **dieresis** [dajérịsịs], *s.* (gram.) diéresis; crema, puntos diacríticos.

diagnose [dajægnóụs], *va.* (med.) diagnosticar.

diagnosis [-ịs], *s.* (med.) diagnosis, diagnóstico.

diagnostic [dajægnástịk]. **I.** *s.* (med.) diagnóstico. **II.** *a.* diagnóstico, diacrítico.

diagnosticate [-eịt], *va.* = DIAGNOSE.

diagnostician [-tíṣọn], *s.* diagnosta, *mf.*—**diagnostics** [-íks], *s.* diagnosis, arte de diagnosticar.

diagonal [dajégonạl], *a.* y *s.* diagonal, *f.;* (mat.) diagonal.—**d. cloth,** diagonal (tela).

diagonally [-ị], *adv.* diagonalmente.

diagram [dáịạgræm], *s.* diagrama, *m.,* esquema, *m.,* gráfico.

diagrammatic [daiagræmǽtik], *a.* esquemático, gráfico.

diagraph [dáiagræf], *s.* diágrafo.

dial [dáial]. **I.** *s.* reloj de sol, cuadrante, gnomon; muestra, esfera de reloj; (rad., neol.) dial. conmutador; (tel.) disco de llamada; (min.) brújula.—**d. hum,** (tel.) señal (*f.*) de llamada. —**d. telephone,** teléfono automático. **II.** *va.* (rad.) sintonizar; (tel.) discar, marcar el disco de llamada.

dialect [dáialekt]. **I.** *s.* dialecto. **II.** *a.* dialectal.

dialectic(s [-léktik(s], *s.* dialéctica, lógica.

dialectic(al [-(al], *a.* dialéctico, lógico.

dialectician [-tíšon], *s.* dialéctico, lógico.

dialectology [-tálodži], *s.* (filol.) dialectología.

dialist [dáialist], *s.* constructor de relojes solares.

dial(l)ing [-liŋ], *s.* gnomónica, levantamiento del plano de una mina; (rad.) sintonización; (tel.) acción de discar o de marcar el número de llamada.

dialog, *s.* y *v.* = DIALOGUE.

dialogic(al [-ládžik(al], *a.* dialogal, dialogístico.

dialogism [daiélodžizm], *s.* dialogismo.

dialogist [-ist], *s.* dialoguista.

dialogically [daialádžikali], **dialogistically** [-lodžístikali], *adv.* en forma de diálogo.

dialogize [daiélodžaiz], *vn.* dialogar, dialogizar.

dialogue [dáialag]. **I.** *s.* diálogo, coloquio, interlocución. **II.** *va.* y *vn.* dialogar, dialogizar.

dialysis [daiélisis], *s.* solución de continuidad; (quím.) diálisis; (grám.) diéresis, crema; (ret.) asíndeton.

dialytic [daialítik], *a.* dialítico.

dialyze [dáialaiz], *va.* (quím.) dializar.

dialyzer [-œ(r)], *s.* dializador.

diamagnetic [daiamægnétik], *a.* diamagnético.— **diamagnetism** [-mǽgnetizm], *s.* diamagnetismo.

diamantine [dáiamæntin], *a.* diamantino.

diameter [daiémetœ(r)], *s.* diámetro, calibre.

diametral [daiémetral], **diametrical** [daiamétrikal], *a.* diametral.—**diametrically** [-i], *adv.* diametralmente.

diamide [daiémaid], *s.* (quím.) diamida.

diamine [dáiamin], *s.* (quím.) diamina.

diamond [dáiamond]. **I.** *s.* diamante; brillante; cortavidrios; oros (de baraja); (impr.) tipo de letra de 4 o 4½ puntos; (geom.) rombo.—**d. anniversary,** aniversario 60 o 75.—**d.-bearing,** diamantífero.—**d. chip,** chispa.—**d. cutter,** diamantista.—**d. drill,** taladro de punta de diamante.—**d. wedding,** aniversario 60 o 75. **II.** *a.* (a)diamantado; rombal. **III.** *va.* adiamantar, adornar con diamantes.

diandrous [daiéndrʌs], *a.* (bot.) diandro.

dianthus [daiénθʌs], *s.* (bot.) clavel de China.

diapason [daiapéizon], *s.* (mús.) diapasón.

diaper [dáiapœ(r)]. **I.** *s.* lienzo adamascado; servilleta; culero, pañal, braga; (b. a.) arabesco, adorno, labor, *f.* **II.** *va.* y *vn.* labrar, formar arabescos, adamascar; poner pañales (a una criatura).

diaphaneity [daiafaníti], *s.* diafanidad.

diaphanous [daiéfanʌs], *a.* diáfano o transparente; terso, claro.

diaphoresis [daiaforísis], *s.* (med.) diaforesis, sudor.—**diaphoretic(al** [-rétik(al], *a.* y *s.* diaforético, sudorífico.

diaphragm [dáiafræm], *s.* (anat., fot., mec., etc.) diafragma, *m.*—**d. pump,** bomba de membrana.

diaphragmatic [-frægmǽtik], *a.* diafragmático.

diaphysis [daiéfisis], *s.* (anat.) diáfisis.

diapophysis [daiapáfisis], *s.* (anat.) diapófisis.

diapositive [-pázitiv], *s.* (foto.) diapositiva.

diarchy [dáiarki], *s.* diarquía.

diarist [dáiarist], *s.* diarista.

diarrhea, diarrhœa [daiaríə], *s.* (med.) diarrea.

diarrheal [-l], **diarrheic** [-ik], *a.* diarreico, diárrico.

diarthrosis [daiarθróusis], *s.* (anat.) diartrosis.

diary [dáiari].°*s.* diario, jornal.

diaspore [dáiaspor], *s.* (min.) diásporo.

diastase [dáiasteis], *s.* (bioquím.) diastasa.

diastasis [daiéstasis], *s.* (cir.) diastasis.

diastole [daiéstoli], *s.* (fisiol., pros.) diástole, *f.*

diastolic [daiastálik], *a.* (fisiol.) diastólico.

diastrophism [daiéstrofizm], *s.* dislocación; (geol.) deformación o transformación de la corteza terrestre.

diastyle [dáiastail], *s.* (arq.) edificio diástilo.

diatessaron [daiatésaran], *s.* (mús.) diatesarón.

diathermanous [daiaθérmanʌs], *a.* diatérmano.

diathermia [-miə], **diathermy** [-mi], *s.* (med.) diatermia, termopenetración eléctrica.

diathermic [-mik], *a.* diatérmico.

diathesis [daiéθesis], *s.* (med.) diátesis.

diathetic [daiaθétik], *a.* (med.) diatésico.

diatom [dáiatoum], *s.* diatomea.

diatomaceous [daiatoméišʌs], *a.* pert. a, o que contiene, diatomeas o sus restos fósiles.

diatomic [daiatámik], *a.* (quím.) diatómico.

diatonic [daiatánik], *a.* (mús.) diatónico.

diatonically [-ali], *adv.* diatónicamente.

diatribe [dáiatraib], *s.* diatriba.

dibble [dibl]. **I.** *s.* (agr.) plantador, punzón de madera para plantar; almocafre. **II.** *va.* plantar con el punzón de madera; almocafrar.

dibstone [díbstoun], *s.* taba.

dice [dais]. **I.** *s.* (*pl.* de DIE) dados; terna (juego). —**d. box,** cubilete de dados. **II.** *vn.* jugar a los dados. **III.** *va.* cortar en forma de cubos menudos.

dicer [-œ(r)], *s.* jugador de dados.

dichotomize [daikátomaiz], *va.* separar, dividir.

dichotomous [-mʌs], *a.* dicotómico.

dichotomy [-mi], *s.* dicotomía.

dichroic [daikróuik], **dichroitic** [-króitik], *a.* (fís.) dieroico.

dichroism [dáikroizm], *s.* (fís.) dicroísmo.

dichromate [daikróumeit], *s.* (quím.) dicromato, bicromato.

dichromatism [-matizm], *s.* dicromatismo, incapacidad de percibir más de dos colores del espectro.

dichromic [-mik], *a.* dicromático, de dos colores; que sufre dicromatismo.

dick [dik], *s.* (fam.) detective; mozo, hombre.

dickens [díkenz], *s.* (fam.) el diablo, el demontre, mengue.—**the d.!,** *interj.* ¡caramba!, ¡diantre!

dicker [díkœ(r)]. **I.** *va.* regatear, (fam.) cambalachear. **II.** *s.* cambalache, chama; decena; partido.

dick(e)y [díki], *s.* camisola; pechera postiza; delantal; babero; asno; (carr.) zaga.—**d.-bird,** pajarito.

dick(e)y, *a.* (fam.) dudoso, arriesgado; inseguro; mal de salud.

diclinous [dáiklinʌs], *a.* (bot.) diclino.

dicotyledon [daikatilídon], *s.* (bot.) dicotiledón(eo).

dicotyledonous [-ʌs], *a.* dicotiledón(eo).

dicta [díktə], *s. pl.* de DICTUM.

dictaphone [díktafoun], *s.* dictáfono, fonógrafo de dictado (es nombre de fábrica).

dictate [díkteit]. **I.** *va.* y *vn.* dictar; mandar, imponer(se). **II.** *s.* dictamen; máxima, precepto, dictado (ú. gen. en el *pl.*).

dictation [-éišon], *s.* dictado; mando arbitrario. —**dictator** [díkteitœ(r)], *s.* dictador; el que dicta o prescribe.

dictatorial [diktatórial], *a.* dictatorial, dictatorio.

dictatorially [-i], *adv.* dictatorialmente.

dictatorship [díkteitœršip], *s.* dictadura.

dictatory [díktatori], *a.* dictatorio, dominante.

diction [díkšon], *s.* dicción, estilo; locución, lenguaje.

dictionary [-eri], *s.* diccionario, léxico.

dictum [díktʌm], *s.* sentencia, aforismo; (for.) fallo.

did [did], *pret.* de TO DO.

didactic(al [daidǽktik(al], *a.* didáctico.
didactically [-i], *adv.* didácticamente.
didactics [-s], *s.* didáctica.
didapper [dáidæpœ(r)], *s.* (orn.) somormugo.
diddle [dídl]. I. *va.* (fam.) engañar, entrampar. II. *vn.* perder tiempo; vacilar; menearse con sacudidas.
didst [didst], (ant. y poét.) 2a. *pers. pret.* de TO DO.
didymium [daidímiam], *s.* (quím.) didimio.
die [dái], *vn.* (*ger.* DYING) morir(se), expirar, fallecer; marchitarse, secarse; pasarse, desvirtuarse (un licor, un reactivo).—**to d. away, down, o out,** acabarse o desaparecer gradualmente; pasar.—**to d. hard,** luchar hasta la muerte.—**to d. the death,** sufrir la pena de muerte.—**to be dying,** estar agonizante.—**to be dying to,** (fig., fam.) estarse muriendo (de curiosidad, deseo, etc.) por, anhelar.
die. I. *s.* (*pl.* DICE) dado (para jugar); suerte, *f.*, azar.—**the d. is cast,** la suerte está echada. —(*pl.* DIES) cuño, matriz, troquel; molde, estampa; cojinete o caja de terraja; (arq.) cubo. II. *va.* cortar o estampar con troquel.
die-hard [-hard], *a.* y *s.* reaccionario, irreconciliable, intransigente; oposicionista reacio.
dielectric [daiɛléktrik], *a.* dieléctrico.
dieresis [daiérɛsis], *s.* = DIÆRESIS.
dies [dáiz], *s.* día, días.—**d. non,** (for.) día feriado.
Diesel engine o motor [dízɛl], *s.* motor Diésel.— **dieselize** [-aiz], *va.* proveer de motor(es) Diésel.
diesinker [dáisinkœ(r)], *s.* grabador en hueco.
diesis [dáiɛsis], *s.* (mús.) diesi, *f.*; (impr.) obelisco doble.
diestock [dáistak], *s.* (mec.) terraja.
diet [dáiɛt]. I. *s.* (med.) dieta, régimen alimenticio; dieta (asamblea).—**d. kitchen,** cocina de hospital, o institución de caridad donde se preparan alimentos especiales para los enfermos pobres. II. *va.* adietar, poner a dieta. III. *vn.* adietarse, estar a dieta.
dietary [dáiɛteri]. I. *a.* dietético; alimenticio. II. *s.* dieta medicinal.
dietetic(al [daiɛtétik(al], *a.* dietético.
dietetics [-s], *s.* (med.) dietética.
dietician, dietitian [daiɛtíʃan], *s.* dietista, dietético, especialista o versado en dietética.
dieting [dáiɛtin], *s.* dieta.
differ [dífœ(r)], *vn.* diferir; diferenciarse, distinguirse; disentir, discrepar.—**to d. from,** diferir de.—**to d. from, o with,** no estar de acuerdo con; contender, desavenirse.
difference [-ɛns]. I. *s.* diferencia; distinción (de personas, etc.); discrepancia; desacuerdo, disputa; (arit.) residuo.—**it makes no d.,** no importa. II. *va.* diferenciar, distinguir.
different [-ɛnt], *a.* diferente, distinto, vario.
differential [-ɛnʃal]. I. *s.* (mat., mec.) diferencial, *f.* II. *a.* (fís., mat., mec., etc.) diferencial; preferente.—**d. calculus,** (mat.) cálculo diferencial. —**d. duties,** (e. p.) derechos diferenciales de entrada, en que se tienen en cuenta no sólo la naturaleza de los artículos gravados, sino también su procedencia.—**d. gear,** (mec.) engranaje diferencial.—**d. rates,** (f. c.) flete preferente o rebajado (concedido a determinadas regiones); flete menor o rebajado (de dos o más vías competidoras).
differentially [-i], *adv.* diferencialmente.
differentiate [-énʃeit], *va.* y *vn.* diferenciar(se), distinguir(se); cambiar(se), modificar(se).
differentiation [-éiʃon], *s.* diferenciación.
differently [dífɛrɛntli], *adv.* diferentemente.
difficult [dífikʌlt], *a.* difícil; apurado, penoso.
difficulty [-i], *s.* dificultad; obstáculo, tropiezo; inconveniente, oposición, reparo; riña o pelea.— *pl.* aprieto, apuro, brete.
diffidence [dífidɛns], *s.* falta de confianza en sí mismo; timidez, modestia, encogimiento, cortedad, apocamiento, vergüenza.—**diffident** [-ɛnt], *a.* desconfiado de sí mismo; tímido o

modesto.—**diffidently** [-li], *adv.* tímidamente, modestamente.
diffract [dífrækt], *va.* (fís.) difractar.
diffraction [dífrǽkʃon], *s.* (fís.) difracción.
diffractive [-tiv], *a.* difrangente, difringente.
diffuse [dífjúz]. I. *va.* difundir, esparcir; desparramar, dispar; derramar o verter; repartir; divulgar, propagar. II. *vn.* difundirse; disiparse. III. [dífjús], *a.* difundido, esparcido; difuso, prolijo; (med.) no localizado.
diffused [dífjúzd], *a.* difundido o extendido; difuso.—**d. light,** luz difusa.—**diffusedly** [dífjúzidli], *adv.* difusamente.—**diffusedness** [-nis], *s.* dispersión, esparcimiento; prolijidad.
diffusely [dífjúsli], *adv.* difusamente, copiosamente; prolijamente.—**diffuseness** [-nis], *s.* prolijidad, difusión.
diffuser [dífjúzœ(r)], *s.* difundidor, esparcidor; difusor.
diffusible [dífjúzibl], *a.* difusible.
diffusion [dífjúʒon], *s.* difusión; dispersión, esparcimiento, propagación; prolijidad.
diffusive [dífjúsiv], *a.* difusivo.—**diffusively** [-li], *adv.* difusamente.—**diffusiveness** [-nis], *s.* dispersión; difusión.
dig [dig]. I. *va.* (*pret.* y *pp.* DUG O DIGGED) cavar, excavar; ahondar; escarbar; jadiar, mullir; minar; extraer.—**to d. out,** desentrañar.—**to d. up,** desenterrar (sentidos recto y fig.); (fam.) aflojar la mosca; reunir (dinero).—**to d. up the hatchet, o the tomahawk,** declarar o emprender la guerra. II. *vn.* cavar; (fam.) trabajar (esp. estudiar) con desafuero, como un peón, sudar la gota gorda; (mec.) entrar demasiado (apl. a herramientas cortantes).—**to d. in,** (mil., fam.) afosarse, enterrarse, abrirse trincheras. III. *s.* empuje; puñetazo; (fam.) observación sarcástica; estudiantón.
digastric [daigǽstrik], *a.* (anat.) digástrico.
digest [dáidʒɛst], *s.* compendio, resumen; recopilación, digesto (de leyes, etc.).
digest [daidʒést]. I. *va.* recopilar, abreviar y clasificar; codificar; asimilar; meditar, rumiar; sufrir, tolerar; (fisiol., quím. y fig.) digerir; cocer. II. *vn.* digerirse; asimilarse.
digestant [-ant], *s.* digestivo.
digester [-œ(r)], *s.* digestor (aparato).
digestibility [-ibíliti], *s.* digestibilidad.
digestible [-ibl], *a.* digerible, digestible.
digestion [daidʒéschon], *s.* digestión; asimilación; (quím.) digestión; absorción.
digestive [daidʒéstiv], *a.* y *s.* digestivo.
digger [dígœ(r)], *s.* cavador; azadón; excavadora.
digging [dígin], *s.* acción de cavar; cavadura.—*pl.* lo que se saca excavando; minas, lavaderos de oro, etc.; (fam.) domicilio, vivienda.
digit [dídʒit], *s.* dedo; (astr. y mat.) dígito.
digital [-al]. I. *a.* digital, dígito, dactilar. II. *s.* tecla (de piano); (fam.) dedo.
digitalin [-téilin], *s.* (quím., farm.) digitalina.
digitalis [-téilis], *s.* (bot.) dedalera, digital, *f.*
digitate(d [-teit(id], *a.* (bot., zool.) digitado.
digitation [-téiʃon], *s.* (biol.) digitación.
digitigrade [-tigreid], *a.* (zool.) digitígrado.
diglot [dáiglat], *a.* bilingüe.
diglyph [dáiglif], *s.* (arq.) diglifo.
dignified [dígnifaid], *a.* serio, grave; digno, decoroso; augusto, majestuoso, noble.
dignify [dígnifai], *va.* dignificar, honrar, exaltar.
dignitary [dígniteri], *s.* dignatario.
dignity [dígniti], *s.* dignidad; elevación, nobleza, majestuosidad; rango, puesto o cargo elevado.
digraph [dáigræf], *s.* (fon.) grupo indivisible de dos letras, y con un solo sonido (v.g. la **ch** española o la **th** inglesa).
digress [digrés], *vn.* divagar.—**digression** [digréʃon], *s.* digresión o divagación.—**digressional** [-al] o **digressive** [digrésiv], *a.* digresivo.— **digressively** [-li], *adv.* digresivamente.
dihedral [daihídral], *a.* (geom., aer.) diedro.—**d. angle,** diedro, ángulo diedro.

dike [daik]. **I.** s. dique, malecón, represa; zanja, acequia; (geol.) veta. **II.** va. represar; canalizar; avenar, desaguar con zanjas.

dilacerate [dilǽsęreit], va. dilacerar.—**dilaceration** [-éişǫn], s. dilaceración, desgarro.

dilapidate [dilǽpideit]. **I.** va. dilapidar. **II.** vn. arruinarse.—**dilapidated** [-id], a. dilapidado, arruinado.—**dilapidation** [-éişǫn], s. dilapidación, ruina, estado ruinoso.—**dilapidator** [-eitǫ(r)], s. dilapidador.

dilatability [dailéitȧbíliti], s. dilatabilidad.

dilatable [-ȧbl], a. dilatable.

dilatant [-ȧnt], a. y s. dilatador.

dilatation [dilȧtéişǫn], **dilation** [dailéişǫn], s. dilatación, ensanche, ensanchamiento.

dilate [dailéit]. **I.** va. dilatar, amplificar, explayar, ensanchar, espaciar. **II.** vn. dilatarse, espaciarse, extenderse.

dilated [-id], a. dilatado, extendido; hinchado, prolijo, difuso.

dilatedly [-li], adv. dilatadamente.

dilater [-œ(r)], s. dilatador.—**dilative** [-iv], a. dilatativo.—**dilator** [-ǫ(r)], s. (anat., cir.) dilatador.

dilatorily [dílȧtǫrili], adv. dilatoria, lenta o detenidamente.—**dilatoriness** [-nis], s. dilación; lentitud, tardanza.—**dilatory** [-ǫri], a. dilatorio; tardo, lento.

dilemma [dilémȧ], s. dilema, m.; disyuntiva.

dilemmatic [dilemǽtik], a. dilemático.

dilettante [diletȧnti], s. y a. dilettante, aficionado.

dilettant(e)ism [-t(i)izm], s. diletantismo.

diligence [dílidȝens], s. diligencia, asiduidad; diligencia, coche grande.

diligent [-ęnt], a. diligente, aplicado, asiduo, negocioso, solícito; incansable, activo.—**diligently** [-li], adv. diligentemente, solícitamente.

dill [dil], s. (bot.) eneldo.—**d. pickle**, pepino encurtido y sazonado con semillas del eneldo.

dillydally [dílidæli], vn. (fam.) perder el tiempo; holgazanear, perecear; vacilar.

diluent [dílyuęnt], a. y s. diluente.

dilute [diljút]. **I.** va. desleír, diluir; aguar; rarificar. **II.** vn. desleírse, diluirse. **III.** a. diluído.

dilution [diljúşǫn], s. desleidura, desleimiento, dilución; solución atenuada; (e. p.) reemplazo de obreros expertos por inexpertos.

diluvial, diluvian [dilúvial, -ȧn], a. diluvial, diluviano.—**diluvium** [-ʌm], s. (geol.) diluvial; depósito no estratificado; depósito arrastrado por fuertes corrientes o por glaciares.

dim [dim]. **I.** a. obscuro, poco claro; borroso, confuso, indistinto; empañado; deslustrado; lerdo; cegato, turbio de vista; (fot.) velado. **II.** va. obscurecer; ofuscar; empañar; deslustrar; amortiguar o reducir la intensidad (de una luz). **III.** vn. obscurecerse, etc.

dime [daim], s. (hist.) diezmo; decena; (E. U. y Canadá) moneda de diez centavos.—**d. novel**, novela barata y sensacional.

dimension [diménşǫn], s. dimensión, extensión, tamaño.—**dimensional** [-ȧl], a. dimensional.

dimethyl [daiméθil], s. (quím.) dimetilo.

dimidiate [dimídieit]. **I.** va. dimidiar, demediar, promediar. **II.** a. partido por la mitad.

dimidiation [-éişǫn], s. acto de partir en dos mitades.

diminish [dimíniş]. **I.** va. disminuir, amenguar, (a)minorar; acortar; reducir; rebajar, degradar. **II.** vn. disminuir(se), menguar, (a)minorarse, decrecer.

diminishing [-iŋ], a. decreciente; diminutivo.—**d. return.** V. LAW.—**diminishingly** [-li], adv. decrecientemente.

diminuendo [diminyuéndou]. **I.** a. y adv. (mús.) que va disminuyendo. **II.** s. decrescendo.

diminution [diminiúşǫn], s. di(s)minución, amenguamiento, atenuación, rebaja, reducción, desmedro.

diminutive [dimíniutiv]. **I.** a. diminuto; dimi-

nutivo; pequeño, mezquino. **II.** s. (gram.) diminutivo.

diminutively [-li], adv. diminutamente, diminutivamente.—**diminutiveness** [-nis], s. pequeñez.

dimissory [dímisǫri], a. dimisorio; que despide o traslada.—**d. letter**, dimisorias, f. pl.

dimity [dímiti], s. (tej.) cotonía.

dimly [dímli], adv. obscuramente.

dimmer [dímœ(r)], s. lo que obscurece, mitiga o reduce (gen. la luz); (elec.) bobina de reacción reguladora; (aut.) reductor de intensidad (de las luces).

dimness [dímnis], s. ofuscamiento; obscuridad u obscurecimiento; deslustre.

dimorph [dáimǫrf], s. (min.) una de las dos formas de una substancia dimorfa.

dimorphism [daimǫrfizm], s. dimorfismo.

dimorphous [-fʌs], a. dimorfo.

dim-out [dím aut], s. obscurecimiento parcial de luces; alumbrado reducido (como medida de seguridad).

dimple [dimpl]. **I.** s. hoyuelo. **II.** va. y vn. formar o formarse hoyuelos.—**dimpled** [-d], **dimply** [-pli], a. que tiene hoyuelos.

din [din]. **I.** s. ruido, estrépito, clamoreo, alboroto. **II.** va. ensordecer, asordar; clamorear, aturdir. **III.** vn. alborotar; (re)sonar con estrépito.

dine [dain]. **I.** vn. comer (la comida principal).—**to d. out**, comer fuera de casa. **II.** va. dar de comer; dar un convite a.

diner [-œ(r)], s. el que come; (f. c.) coche comedor, vagón restaurante; restaurante construído a imitación de éstos.—**d.-out**, (fam.) persona que come fuera de casa.

dinette [dainét], s. comedorcillo; (Ingl.) almuerzo.

ding [diŋ]. **I.** va. y vn. repicar, (re)sonar (las campanas); (fam.) instar, urgir, reiterar fastidiosamente. **II.** vn. tintinear, sonido de las campanas.—**d.-a-ling**, tintín.

dingdong [díŋdaŋ]. **I.** s. dindán, tintín (sonido de las campanas), repique(teo). **II.** a. repetido; (fam.) reñido, disputado con calor. **III.** va. y vn. repiquetear; repetir con insistencia; fastidiar, machacar.

dinghy, ding(e)y [díŋgi], s. lancha, bote, chinchorro; (f. c.) vagón del servicio.

dinginess [díndȝinis], s. obscuridad; deslustre.

dingle [díŋgl], s. cañada, vallejuelo umbroso.

dingo [díŋgou], s. dingo, perro salvaje australiano.

dingy [díndȝi], a. empañado, deslustrado, deslucido; manchado, sucio; obscuro.

dining [dáiniŋ], ger. de TO DINE.—**d. car**, (f. c.) coche comedor.—**d. room**, comedor.

dinner [dínœ(r)], s. comida (principal); cubierto.—**d. coat** o **jacket**, smoking.—**d. pail**, portaviandas, o fiambrera.—**d. set**, vajilla.—**d. time**, hora de la comida, hora de comer.

dinosaur [dáinosǫr], s. (pal.) dinosauro.

dinothere [dáinoθir], s. (pal.) dinoterio.

dint [dint]. **I.** s. abolladura, mella; fuerza, eficacia.—**by d. of**, a fuerza de, a puro, de puro. **II.** va. abollar; imprimir, estampar.

diocesan [daiásęsȧn], a. y s. diocesano.

diocese [dáiosis], s. diócesis, obispalía.

diœcious, diecious [daíşʌs], a. (bot.) dioico.

Dionæa [daioníȧ], s. (bot.) dionea, atrapamoscas.

Dionysiac [daionísiæk], **Dionysian** [-níşȧn], a. dionisíaco.

diopter [daiáptœ(r)], s. (ópt.) dioptra.

dioptric(al [-trik(ȧl], a. dióptrico.

dioptrics [-triks], s. (ópt.) dióptrica.

diorama [daiorámȧ], s. diorama, m.

dioramic [-ræmik], a. dioramico.

diorite [dáiorait], s. (min.) diorita.

diosmose [daiásmous], **diosmosis** [-móusis], s. (fís.) ósmosis.

dioxide [daiáksaid], s. (quím.) bióxido.

dip [dip]. **I.** va. meter, sumergir; bañar, humedecer, mojar, zambullir; saludar con (la ban-

dera); (mar.) achicar, vaciar. **II.** *vn.* sumergirse;
zambullirse; hundirse; penetrar; empeñarse o
meterse en algún negocio; hojear (en un libro,
etc.); inclinarse hacia abajo. **III.** *s.* inmersión,
zambullida; baño corto; vela de sebo chorreada;
depresión; baño o líquido en que algo está sumergido; inclinación; caída, declivio o declive,
pendiente, *f.;* (fam.) carterista, ratero o rata,
m.; sombrero.—**d. of the horizon,** (mar.) depresión de horizonte.—**d. of the needle,** inclinación de la brújula.

dipetalous [daipétạlʌs], *a.* (bot.) dipétalo.
diphase [dáifeiz], *a.* (elec.) bifásico.
diphtheria [difθíriạ], *s.* (med.) difteria.
diphtherial [-l], **diphther(it)ic** [difθérik, difθi-
rítik], *a.* diftérico.
diphthong [dífθɒŋ], *s.* (gram.) diptongo.
diphthongization [-izéişɒn], *s.* diptongación.
diphthongize [-ạiz], *va.* diptongar.
diploma [diplóumạ], *s.* diploma, *m.;* pergamino,
título.
diplomacy [-si], *s.* diplomacia; tacto, cautela.
diplomat [díplomæt], **diplomatist** [diplóumạ-
tist], *s.* diplomático.—**diplomatic(al** [diplo-
mǽtik(ạl], *a.* diplomático.—**d. body o corps,**
cuerpo diplomático.—**diplomatically** [-i], *adv.*
diplomáticamente.—**diplomatics** [-s], *s.* diplomática.
diplopia [diplóupiạ], *s.* (med.) diplopía.
dipper [dípœ(r)], *s.* cazo, cucharón, cacillo.—**Big
D.,** (astr.) Carro, Osa Mayor.—**Little D.,** Osa
Menor.
dipping [dípiŋ], *a.* que se inclina; inclinado; de
inclinación; de sumergir.—**d. compass,** brújula
de inclinación.—**d. needle,** aguja (magnética)
de inclinación.
dipsacaceous [dipsạkéişʌs], *a.* (bot.) dipsáceo.
dipsomania [dipsoméniạ], *s.* dipsomanía.—
dipsomaniac [-méinjæk], *s.* dipsómano.—**dip-
somaniacal** [-mạnáiạkạl], *a.* dipsomaníaco,
dipsómano.
dipter [díptœ(r)], *s.* (ent.) díptero.—**Diptera** [-ạ],
s. pl. dípteros.—**dipteran** [-æn], *s. y a.* díptero.
—**dipterocarpaceous** [-rokạrpéişʌs], *a.* (bot.)
dipterocárpeo.—**dipterology** [-rálodʒi], *s.* dip-
terología.—**dipterous** [-rʌs], *a.* (ent., bot.)
díptero.
diptych [díptik], *s.* (igl.) díptica, díptico.
dire [dair], *a.* horrendo u horrible; de mal agüero;
deplorable, lamentable.
direct [dirékt]. **I.** *a.* directo; derecho; claro, inequívoco; en línea recta (descendencia, sucesión,
etc.).—**d. action,** acción directa, métodos sindicalistas extremos (huelgas generales, sabotaje,
y aun la fuerza), a diferencia de métodos políticos.—**d. current,** (elec.) corriente continua.
—**d. drive,** (aut., mec.) toma directa, de mando
directo.—**d. examination,** primer interrogatorio (de un testigo).—**d. hit,** blanco directo.—
d. object, (gram.) acusativo, complemento
directo.—**d. primary,** (E. U.) comicios que
nombran candidatos directamente.—**d. tax,**
contribución directa. **II.** *va.* dirigir; encaminar,
encauzar, orientar; gobernar, regentar; enviar
(una persona a otra, a un lugar, etc.). **III.** *vn.*
dirigir; servir de guía. **IV.** *adv.* directamente.—
d.-acting, (mec.) de acción directa.—**d.-
connected, d.-coupled,** (mec.) acoplado directamente, de acoplamiento directo; (elec.) conectado directamente; de conexión directa.
directer [-œ(r)], *s.* = DIRECTOR.
direction [dirékşɒn], *s.* dirección; rumbo; sentido;
gobierno, administración; orden, *f.,* instrucción,
mandato; designio, mira, fin; tendencia; sobrescrito, señas, *f. pl.*—*pl.* instrucciones.—**d.
finder,** (rad.) radiogoniómetro.—**directional**
[-ạl], *a.* director, directriz.—**d. aerial,** (rad.)
antena directriz.—**d. loop,** (rad.) radiogoniómetro.
directive [diréktiv]. **I.** *a.* directivo, directorio.
II. *s.* instrucción, mandato.

directly [diréktli], *adv.* directamente; inmediatamente, en seguida, al instante; exactamente,
precisamente; sin ambages.—**d. after(ward),**
acto continuo.—**d. opposite,** frente por frente
(de).
directness [-nis], *s.* derechura, rectitud.
director [dirékto̯(r)]. **I.** *s.* director; regente; administrador; caudillo, guía; vocal de una junta
directiva; director de orquesta. **II.** *a.* (mat.)
director, directriz.—**directorate** [-rit], *s.* dirección o junta directiva, directorio.
directorial [direktóriạl], *a.* directorio, directivo;
directorial.—**directorship** [diréktɒrşip], *s.* di-
rectorado, rectorado.
directory [-ɒri], *s.* directorio; guía comercial;
(igl.) añalejo.
directress [-ris], *s.* directora.
directrix [-riks], *s.* (geom. y arti.) directriz.
direful [dáirful], *a.* horrible, calamitoso, terrible.
—**direfulness** [-nis], **direness** [dáirnis], *s.*
horror, espanto.
dirge [dœrdʒ], *s.* endecha; canto fúnebre.
dirigible [díridʒibl]. **I.** *a.* dirigible. **II.** *s.* (aer.)
dirigible, aeronave, *f.,* aeróstato, globo aeros-
tático.
diriment [díriment], *a.* (for.) dirimente.
dirk [dœrk], *s.* daga, puñal; cutó.
dirt [dœrt]. **I.** *s.* lodo, barro; polvo; partículas
extrañas; basura, porquería; mugre, *f.;* excremento; tierra, marga; vileza, bajeza; calumnia.
II. *a.* hecho de tierra.—**d.-cheap,** baratísimo.
—**d. farmer,** (fam.) agricultor que se ocupa él
mismo en el trabajo material de la labranza.
dirtily [-ili], *adv.* puercamente, suciamente, vilmente.—**dirtiness** [-inis], *s.* suciedad; desaseo;
porquería; bajeza, villanía.
dirty [-i]. **I.** *a.* sucio; manchado, enlodado; indecente; puerco, cochino, bajo.—**d. trick,**
(fam.) perrada. **II.** *va.* emporcar, ensuciar,
manchar.
disability [disạbíliti], *s.* impotencia; inhabilidad,
inhabilitación; incapacidad, invalidez.
disable [diséibl], *va.* imposibilitar; inhabilitar,
incapacitar; (for.) incapacitar legalmente.
disabled [-d], *a.* incapacitado; lisiado.
disablement [-ment], *s.* impedimento; inhabilitación, invalidez.
disabuse [disạbjúz], *va.* desengañar, desilusionar;
sacar de un error.
disaccustom [disạkʌ́stʌm], *va.* desacostumbrar.
disadjust [disạdʒʌ́st], *va.* desajustar, trastornar.
disadvantage [disạdvǽntidʒ]. **I.** *s.* desventaja,
menoscabo; detrimento, disconveniencia.—**at
a d.,** en situación o circunstancias desventa-
josas. **II.** *va.* perjudicar, menoscabar, dañar;
estorbar.
disadvantageous [disædvạntéidʒʌs], *a.* desventajoso.
disadvantageously [-li], *adv.* desventajosamente.
disaffect [disạfékt], *va.* descontentar; desaficionar; hacer desleal; indisponer (se con); malquistar.—**disaffected** [-id], *a.* desafecto.—**dis-
affectedly** [-li], *adv.* con desafecto.—**disaffection** [-fékşɒn], *s.* desafección, desafecto, desafición, desamor, descontento; deslealtad.
disaffirm [disạférm], *va.* contradecir, negar, impugnar; (for.) anular; renunciar, rechazar.
disaffirmance [-ạns], **disaffirmation** [disæ-
fœrméişɒn], *s.* confutación, impugnación; anulación; renuncia.
disafforest [disạfárist], *va.* desacotar; desboscar.
disagree [disạgrí], *vn.* desconvenir; disonar; disentir, discrepar, diferir, desavenirse; contender,
altercar, estar en pugna.—**to d. with,** no estar
de acuerdo con; no sentar bien a, no probar,
hacer daño a (apl. a comidas, etc.).
disagreeable [-ạbl], *a.* desagradable; repugnante;
descortés, desapacible, rudo.—**disagreeableness** [-nis], *s.* desagrado; desabrimiento; desapacibilidad, rudeza.—**disagreeably** [-ạbli], *adv.*
desagradablemente.

disagreement [-mẹnt], *s.* desconformidad, desacuerdo, desavenencia; discordia; disensión; discordancia, discrepancia, disonancia.

disallow [disạlẹ́u], *va.* y *vn.* denegar, desaprobar; rechazar.—**disallowable** [-ạbl], *a.* negable; inadmisible; censurable.—**disallowance** [-ạns], *s.* denegación, prohibición, vedamiento.

disappear [disạpír], *vn.* desaparecer(se).

disappearance [-ạns], *s.* desaparición.

disappearing [-iŋ], *a.* que desaparece.—**d. bed,** cama engoznada que se oculta de día.—**d. gun,** cañón de cureña movible verticalmente, la cual baja y oculta el cañón después de la descarga.

disappoint [disạpọ́int], *va.* chasquear, frustrar; faltar a una cita con o promesa a; defraudar una esperanza; decepcionar, desilusionar.—**to be disappointed,** llevarse chasco o camelo; verse contrariado; quedar plantado o colgado.—**disappointment** [-mẹnt], *s.* desengaño, desilusión, decepción, contratiempo; chasco, camelo.

disapprobation [disæprobéịṣọn], **disapproval** [disạprúvạl], *s.* desaprobación, censura.

disapprobatory [disǽprobạtọrị], *a.* desaprobador, que desaprueba.

disapprove [disạprúv], *va.* y *vn.* desaprobar.

disapprovingly [-iŋlị], *adv.* con desaprobación.

disarm [disárm], I. *va.* desarmar; desguarnecer; (fig.) apaciguar, sosegar. II. *vn.* deponer las armas; licenciar tropas; reducir o limitar las fuerzas armadas de una nación.

disarmament [-ạmẹnt], *s.* desarme, desarmadura.

disarming [-iŋ], I. *s.* desarme, desarmamiento. II. *a.* que priva de armas, defensa, etc.; que quita ira o sospecha; ingenuo.

disarrange [disạréịndž], *va.* desarreglar, descomponer, des(bar)ajustar, desordenar, trastornar.—**disarrangement** [-mẹnt], *s.* desarreglo, desorden.

disarray [disạréị], I. *s.* desarreglo, desorden, confusión; desaliño, desatavío, (de) trapillo. II. *va.* desordenar, derrotar; desarreglar; desaliñar; desnudar.

disarticulate [disartíkyụleịt], *va.* y *vn.* desarticular(se), descoyuntar(se), desencajar(se).

disarticulation [-éịṣọn], *s.* desarticulación.

disassemble [disạsémbl], *va.* desarmar, desmontar (un reloj, una máquina, etc.).

disassembly [-blị], *s.* desarme (de una máquina).

disassociate [disạsóụṣieịt], *va.* disociar; desasociar.—**disassociation** [-éịṣọn], *s.* disociación.

disaster [dizǽstœr], *s.* desastre; siniestro.

disastrous [-trạs], *a.* desastroso, funesto.—**disastrously** [-lị], *adv.* desastrosamente.

disavow [disạváu], *va.* repudiar, desconocer; desaprobar; desautorizar.

disavowal [-ạl], **disavowment** [-mẹnt], *s.* repudiación; desautorización.

disband [disbǽnd], I. *va.* (mil.) licenciar las tropas, desbandar; despedir, expulsar. II. *vn.* dispersarse, desbandarse.

disbandment [-mẹnt], *s.* licenciamiento, desbandada.

disbar [disbár], *va.* (for.) excluir del foro.

disbarment [-mẹnt], *s.* (for.) exclusión del foro.

disbelief [disbịlíf], *s.* incredulidad, escepticismo.—**disbelieve** [disbịlív], *va.* y *vn.* descreer.—**disbeliever** [-œr], *s.* descreído, incrédulo.

disburden [disbœ́rdẹn], I. *va.* descargar, aligerar. II. *vn.* quitarse un peso de encima.

disbursable [disbœ́rsạbl], *a.* desembolsable, pagable.—**disburse** [disbœ́rs], *va.* desembolsar, pagar, gastar.—**disbursement** [-mẹnt], *s.* desembolso; gasto.—*pl.* (com.) egresos.—**d. office,** pagaduría.

disburser [-œr], *s.* pagador.

disc [disk], *s.* = DISK. (anat.) disco.

discalceate [diskálṣeịt], **discalced** [diskǽlst], *a.* (relig.) descalzado.

discant, *s.* y *verbo* = DESCANT.

discard [diskárd]. I. *va.* descartar; despedir, deponer. II. [diskárd], *vn.* descartarse (en el juego). III. [dískard], *s.* descarte (en el juego).—**to put,** o **throw, into the d.,** (fam.) echar a un lado, descartar.

discern [dizœ́rn], *va.* y *vn.* discernir, percibir, columbrar, distinguir.

discerner [-œr], *s.* discernidor.

discernible [-ịbl], *a.* perceptible, discernible.—**discernibleness** [-nịs], *s.* visibilidad, perceptibilidad.—**discernibly** [-ịblị], *adv.* perceptiblemente, visiblemente.

discerning [-iŋ], *a.* discernidor, discerniente, juicioso, sagaz, perspicaz.—**discerningly** [-lị], *adv.* juiciosamente, sagazmente.

discernment [-mẹnt], *s.* discernimiento; criterio.

discharge [dischárdž]. I. *va.* (arti., com., elec., mar., etc.) descargar; disparar; pagar, saldar; desempeñar, ejecutar, cumplir; relevar, exonerar, eximir, dispensar; absolver, dar libertad; desembarazar de alguna dificultad; despedir, remover; lanzar, arrojar; vomitar; vaciar; emitir, dar salida a; (tint.) descolorar, desteñir; (mil.) licenciar, dar de baja. II. *vn.* descargarse, soltarse; salir, vaciarse; desaguar; (tint.) correrse la tinta. III. *s.* (arti., elec., mar.) descarga; disparo; (com.) descargo; finiquito, carta de pago, quitanza; desempeño; separación, remoción, despedida, despido, deposición; (mil.) licencia absoluta; absolución, exoneración; derrame, desagüe; (hidr.) salida; gasto (cantidad que sale por unidad de tiempo); (tint.) antimordente, descolorante.—**d. cock,** grifo de purga.—**d. outlet,** escape, salida.

discharger [-œr], *s.* descargador; disparador; (fís.) excitador (de una botella de Leyden).

discharging arch [-iŋ arch], *s.* (arq.) sobrearco.

disciple [disáịpl], *s.* discípulo; apóstol; secuaz. II. *va.* hacer discípulos, convertir.

discipleship [-šịp], *s.* discipulado.

disciplinable [dísịplịnạbl], *a.* disciplinable.

disciplinal [dísịplịnạl], **disciplinarian** [-érịạn], **disciplinary** [-erị], *a.* disciplinal o disciplinario.—**disciplinant** [-ạnt], *s.* (igl.) disciplinante, flagelante.—**disciplinarian,** *s.* ordenancista; el que gobierna o enseña con rigor y exactitud.

discipline [dísịplịn]. I. *s.* disciplina; instrucción, enseñanza; orden, regla, conducta; educación; castigo; curso, materia (de estudio). II. *va.* disciplinar, instruir; castigar; corregir, reformar.

disclaim [diskléịm], *va.* repudiar, desconocer, rechazar; (for.) renunciar.—**disclaimer** [-œr], *s.* negador; (for.) renuncia, abandono.

disclose [disklóụz], *va.* descubrir, destapar, desvelar; exponer, revelar, publicar.

disclosure [disklóụžụr], *s.* descubrimiento, revelación, declaración.

discobolus [diskábolʌs], *s.* discóbolo, atleta que arroja el disco.

discoid [dískoịd], **discoidal** [diskóịdạl], *a.* discoidal, discoide, discoideo, de forma de disco.

discolor [diskʌ́lọr], *va.* y *vn.* descolorar(se), descolorir(se), desteñir(se).—**discoloration** [-éịṣọn], *s.* descoloramiento, descolorimiento; mancha.—**discolored** [-d], *a.* descolorido, descolorado, desteñido, pocho.—**discolorer** [-œr], *s.,* **discoloring** [-iŋ], *a.* descolorante.

discomfit [diskʌ́mfịt], *va.* derrotar; desconcertar, frustrar.—**discomfiture** [-fịchụr], *s.* derrota, desconcierto, desbarato, confusión.

discomfort [diskʌ́mfọrt]. I. *s.* incomodidad; malestar, molestia. II. *va.* incomodar; molestar; apenar, afligir.

discomfortable [-ạbl], *a.* incómodo, molesto.

discommode [diskọmóụd], *va.* incomodar, molestar, hacer mala obra o mal tercio.

discommodity [-mádịtị], *s.* incomodidad; desventaja, inconveniencia, inconveniente.

discompose [diskọmpóụz], *va.* turbar, desconcertar; descomponer, desarreglar.

discomposure [-póų̃ʒų̃(r)], *s.* descompostura, agitación, desorden; inquietud, destemple.

disconcert [dįskǫnsǿert], *va.* desconcertar, (per)turbar, confundir; correr; descomponer; destemplar.

disconcerting [-ịŋ], *a.* desconcertador, desconcertante.

disconformity [-fórmįtį], *s.* desconformidad.

disconnect [dįskǫnékt], *va.* desunir o separar; desarticular; disociar; (mec.) desacoplar, desconectar, desembragar, desencajar; (elec.) desconectar, desenchufar.

disconnected [-įd]. **I.** *pp.* de DISCONNECT. **II.** *a.* inconexo, incoherente.

disconnection, disconnexion, [-nékʂǫn], *s.* desconectación; desunión, separación; desembrague, desacoplamiento, desencajamiento; inconexión; (elec.) desconexión.

disconsolate [dįskánsǫlįt], *a.* desconsolado, inconsolable, desolado.—**disconsolately** [-lį], *adv.* desconsoladamente.—**disconsolateness** [-nįs], *s.* tristeza, desconsuelo, desconsolación.

discontent [dįskǫntént]. **I.** *s.* descontento, disgusto, desagrado. **II.** *a.* descontento; quejoso, disgustado. **III.** *va.* descontentar, desagradar, disgustar.

discontented [-įd], *a.* descontent(adiz)o; disgustado, malcontento.—**discontentedly** [-lį], *adv.* de mala gana, a regañadientes.—**discontentedness** [-nįs], **discontentment** [-mɛnt], *s.* descontento, mal humor.—**discontenting** [-įŋ], *a.* descontentador; que desagrada o no satisface.

discontinuance [dįskǫntínyuąns], **discontinuation** [-éįʂǫn], *s.* des-(o dis)continuación, cesación, interrupción, intermisión; suspensión; desabono.—**discontinuance,** (for.) sobreseimiento.

discontinue [dįskǫntínyu], *va.* y *vn.* descontinuar o discontinuar, interrumpir, parar, cesar; suspender; desabonarse.

discontinuity [dįskǫntįnįúįtį], *s.* discontinuidad.

discontinuous [dįskǫntínyuʌs], *a.* descontinuo.

discord [dískǫrd], *s.* discordia; desacuerdo, desavenencia, cizaña; (mús.) discordancia, disonancia.—**to sow d.,** cizañar.

discord [dįskórd], *vn.* desconvenir; discordar.

discordance, discordancy [-ąns, -į], *s.* discordia; discordancia; desafinación; disensión.—**discordant** [-ąnt], *a.* discorde, desacorde, desconforme; desavenido; discordante, disonante, desentonado.—**discordantly** [-lį], *adv.* discordemente.

discount [dískąųnt]. **I.** *va.* (com.) descontar; rebajar, deducir; desestimar, dar poca importancia a, considerar exagerado; anticipar. **II.** *s.* descuento; rebaja, menoscuenta.—**d. rate,** tipo de descuento.—**at a d.,** al descuento; bajo la par; depreciado; mal acogido.

discountable [dįskáųntąbl], *a.* (com.) descontable.

discountenance [dįskáųntɛnąns], *va.* desconcertar, correr; desfavorecer, desaprobar.

discourage [dįskǿrįdʒ], *va.* desalentar, desanimar, descorazonar, desmayar; desaprobar, oponerse a.

discouraged [-d], *a.* desanimado, desmayado.

discouragement [-mɛnt], *s.* desaliento, desánimo, desmayo.

discouraging [-įŋ], *a.* desalentador.

discourse [dįskórs]. **I.** *s.* discurso; plática, conversación; disertación; (lóg.) raciocinación. **II.** *vn.* discurrir, discursar; disertar; conversar, razonar. **III.** *va.* hablar de; proferir, expresar.

discourteous [dįskǿrtįʌs], *a.* descortés, grosero.—**discourteously** [-lį], *adv.* descortésmente.—**discourteousness** [-nįs], **discourtesy** [dįskǿrtɛsį], *s.* descortesía, desatención, grosería.

discous [dískʌs], *a.* (bot.) = DISCOID.

discover [dįskʌvœ(r)], *va.* descubrir, averiguar.

discoverable [-ąbl], *a.* que se puede descubrir.

discoverer [-œ(r)], *s.* descubridor; explorador.

discovery [-į], *s.* descubrimiento, hallazgo.

discredit [dįskrédįt]. **I.** *s.* descrédito, desconfianza; deshonra, oprobio. **II.** *va.* descreer, dudar; desautorizar, desvirtuar; desacreditar, difamar.

discreditable [-ąbl], *a.* vergonzoso, ignominioso.

discreet [dįskrít], *a.* discreto, circunspecto, cuerdo, juicioso, prudente, sesudo.

discreetly [-lį], *adv.* discretamente, cuerdamente.

discreetness [-nįs], *s.* discreción, prudencia.

discrepance, discrepancy [dįskrépąns, -į], *s.* discrepancia, diferencia; variante.

discrepant [-ąnt], *a.* discrepante.

discrete [dįskrít], *a.* distinto, desunido, separado; opuesto, contrario; (mat. y med.) discreto.

discretion [dįskréʂǫn], *s.* discreción, prudencia, sindéresis; albedrío; juicio.—**age of d.,** edad de discreción; (for.) edad legal.—**at d.,** a discreción; a voluntad.

discretional [-ąl], **discretionary** [-ɛrį], *a.* discrecional.—**discretionally** [-ąlį], *adv.* discrecionalmente, a discreción.

discretive [dįskrítįv], *a.* disyuntivo; separado; diferencial; que distingue.

discretively [-lį], *adv.* disyuntivamente, separadamente, de por sí.

discriminable [dįskrímįnąbl], *a.* discernible, distinguible, (Am.) discriminable.

discriminate [dįskrímįnɛįt]. **I.** *va.* discernir, distinguir; diferenciar, (Am.) discriminar; entresacar. **II.** [dįskrímįnɛįt], *vn.* distinguir; hacer distinciones parciales o injustas.—**to d. against,** hacer distinción en perjuicio de, tratar desfavorablemente o sin equidad. **III.** [-nįt], *a.* definido, distinguible; discernidor, discerniente.

discriminately [-lį], *adv.* con discernimiento; con distinciones; con parcialidad.

discriminateness [-nįs], *s.* discernimiento; distinción; favoritismo.

discriminating [-nɛįtįŋ], *a.* discerniente; mirado, capaz de distinguir claramente; característico, diferencial; preferente, parcial.

discrimination [-néįʂǫn], *s.* discernimiento, sindéresis; distinción, diferencia, (Am.) discriminación; parcialidad, favoritismo.

discriminative [-nątįv], **discriminatory** [-nątorį], *a.* discerniente, discernidor, (Am.) discriminador; parcial, injusto.

discriminatively [-lį], *adv.* con discernimiento; con parcialidad.

discrown [dįskráųn], *va.* destronar, derrocar.

discursive [dįskǿrsįv], *a.* digresivo; discursivo; razonador, razonado.—**discursively** [-lį], *adv.* razonadamente, o con ilación.—**discursiveness** [-nįs], *s.* calidad de digresivo; ilación.

discus [dískʌs], *s.* disco.—**d. thrower,** discóbolo. *V.* DISK.

discuss [dįskás], *va.* discutir, debatir, argüir, ventilar; tratar; (fam.) probar; catar.

discussion [dįskáʂǫn], *s.* discusión, debate; exposición, presentación, ventilación.

discutient [dįskįúʂįɛnt], *s.* y *a.* (med.) discusivo, resolvente, resolutivo.

disdain [dįsdéįn]. **I.** *va.* desdeñar, despreciar. **II.** *vn.* desdeñarse, esquivarse. **III.** *s.* desdén, desprecio, esquivez.—**disdainful** [-fųl], *a.* desdeñoso; altivo, altanero.—**disdainfully** [-lį], *adv.* desdeñosamente, con desprecio.—**disdainfulness** [-nįs], *s.* desprecio altanero.

disease [dįzíz], *s.* enfermedad, mal, afección, morbo, dolencia.—**d. germ,** germen o microbio patógeno. **II.** *va.* enfermar, hacer daño.—**diseased** [-d], *a.* enfermo; morboso, mórbido.

diselectrify [dįsįléktrįfaį], *va.* deselectrizar.

disembark [dįsembárk], *va.* y *vn.* desembarcar(se).

disembarkation [-éįʂǫn], *s.* desembarque o desembarco.

disembarrass [-bǽrąs], *va.* desembarazar; desenredar; descombrar, despejar, zafar.

disembarrassment [-mẹnt]. s. desembarazo, desenredo, desencogimiento.

disembody [-bádi̯]. va. librar, separar del cuerpo o de la carne: (mil.) licenciar, dispersar.

disembogue [-bóu̯g]. va. y vn. desembocar; descargar, desaguar, vaciar, derramar(se).

disemboguement [-mẹnt], s. desemboque, desagüe, salida al mar.

disembosom [-bú̯zǫm]. I. va. separar o sacar del pecho; revelar, (fam.) desembuchar. II. vr. desahogarse.

disembowel [-báu̯ẹl], va. desentrañar, destripar, sacar las entrañas a.—**disembowelment** [-mẹnt], s. desentrañamiento, destripamiento.

disembroil [-brói̯l], va. desembrollar; restablecer el orden de o en.

disemploy [-plói̯], va. privar de empleo o de trabajo.

disenchant [-chǽnt], va. desencantar, deshechizar; desilusionar.

disenchantment [-mẹnt], s. desencant(amient)o, deshechizo; desilusión, desengaño.

disencumber [-kámbœ(r)], va. desembarazar, descombrar.—**disencumbered** [-d], a. escueto. —**disencumbrance** [-brǎns], s. desembarazo, descombro.

disendow [-dáu̯], va. retirar la subvención a.

disengage [-géi̯dʒ]. I. va. desunir; desasir; soltar, desembarazar; (mec.) desembragar; desenganchar; librar, eximir. II. vn. librarse, zafarse, soltarse, desligarse; (mil.) romper el contacto con el enemigo.

disengaged [-d], a. desembarazado, libre; suelto; vacante; desocupado; sin empleo; manumiso.

disengagement [-mẹnt], s. soltura; desempeño, desembarazo, desocupación, ocio; desembrague.

disentail [-téi̯l]. I. va. (for.) desvincular; desamortizar. II. s. desvinculación; desamortización.

disentangle [-tǽngl], va. desenredar, desenmarañar, desanudar, desembrollar.—**disentanglement** [-mẹnt], s. desenredo, desembarazo.

disenthral(l [-θról], va. libertar, emancipar, manumitir.—**disenthral(l)ment** [-mẹnt], s. emancipación, manumisión.

disentomb [-túm], va. desenterrar, exhumar.

disentombment [-mẹnt], s. = DISINTERMENT.

disentrance [-trǽns], va. deshechizar, desilusionar; hacer volver en sí.

disestablish [disestǽbliš], va. separar (la iglesia del Estado).—**disestablishment** [-mẹnt], s. privación del apoyo de un Estado; separación (de la iglesia y el Estado).

disesteem [disestím]. I. s. desestima(ción). II. va. desestimar; desaprobar.

disfavor [disféi̯vǫ(r)]. I. va. desairar; desfavorecer. II. s. disfavor, malquerencia; desgracia; desaprobación.

disfiguration [disfi̯gyụréi̯šǫn], **disfigurement** [-mẹnt], s. desfiguración, deformidad; daño, deterioro.

disfigure [disfi̯gyụ(r)], va. desfigurar, afear.

disforest [disfárist], va. desmontar, talar, (for.) desacotar. V. DEFOREST y DISAFFOREST.

disfranchise [disfrénchai̯z], va. privar de derechos civiles, franquicias u otros privilegios.— **disfranchisement** [-mẹnt], s. privación de los derechos civiles, etc.

disgorge [disgórdʒ], va. vomitar; arrojar; desembuchar; devolver lo robado.

disgorgement [-mẹnt], s. vómito; entrega, devolución.

disgrace [disgréi̯s]. I. s. ignominia, vergüenza; deshonra, estigma, m., oprobio, mengua.—**in d.**, con ignominia; desacreditado, deslucido. II. va. deshonrar, causar oprobio; despedir con ignominia.

disgraceful [-fụl], a. vergonzoso, oprobioso.

disgracefully [-i̯], adv. vergonzosamente, ignominiosamente.—**disgracefulness** [-ni̯s], s. ignominia, vergüenza.

disgregation [disgrẹgéi̯šǫn], s. disgregación.

disgruntle [disgrántl], va. poner de mal humor, descontentar, disgustar, enfadar.

disguise [disgái̯z]. I. va. disfrazar, enmascarar, embozar; desfigurar; encubrir, ocultar. II. s. disfraz. m., máscara; embozo, velo.

disgust [disgást]. I. s. repugnancia; asco, náusea; disgusto, fastidio, hastío. II. va. repugnar, inspirar repugnancia o aversión; fastidiar, hastiar.—**disgusted** [-id], a. disgustado, fastidiado, chocado.—**disgusting** [-iṇ], a. repugnante; odioso; asqueroso, nauseabundo.—**disgustingly** [-li̯], adv. repugnantemente, asquerosamente.

dish [diš]. I. s. plato, fuente, f.; manjar, plato; vasija de bordes bajos; (quím.) cápsula (de evaporar, etc.); concavidad; artesa, gamella (de lavar mineral); caja de medir mineral.—pl. loza, vajilla de mesa.—**d. drainer** o **rack**, escurreplatos.—**d. warmer**, calientaplatos. II. va. servir en platos; formar una concavidad en; (fam.) engañar, burlar; (mec.) avellanar.—to **d. out**, servir (manjares); acanalar, ahondar. III. vn. deprimirse, ahondarse.

dishabille [disabíl], s. desabillé, vestido llano y casero; paños menores.—**in d.**, (fam.) de trapillo.

dishabituate [dishabíchu̯ei̯t], va. deshabituar.

disharmony [dishármoni̯], s. falta de armonía; discordia; incongruencia.

dishcloth [díškloθ], **dishclout** [-klau̯t], s. albero, estropajo, paño para lavar los platos.

dishearten [dishártẹn], va. desanimar, desalentar, descorazonar.

dished [dišt], a. cóncavo; ahondado.

dishevel [dišévẹl], va. desgreñar, desmelenar.

dishevel(l)ed [-d], a. desgreñado, despeinado; desarreglado; despeluzado.

dishful [díšfụl], s. contenido de un plato lleno; fuente, f., fuentada.

dishonest [disánist], a. no honrado, ímprobo, malo, pícaro; fraudulento, falso.—**dishonestly** [-li̯], adv. fraudulentamente, de mala fe.—**dishonesty** [-i̯], s. improbidad, picardía; dolo, fraude.

dishonor [disánǫ(r)]. I. s. deshonor, deshonra, desdoro, ignominia, infamia, mancha; afrenta. II. va. deshonrar, infamar; afrentar; profanar; (com.) no aceptar o no pagar (un giro).

dishonorable [-ạbl], a. deshonroso, indecoroso, ignominioso, vil; deshonrado, infamado.

dishonorably [-ạbli̯], adv. ignominiosamente, deshonrosamente.

dishpan [díšpæn], s. paila de fregar platos.

dishrag [-ræg], s. = DISHCLOTH.

dishtowel [-tau̯ẹl], s. albero, rodilla, paño para secar los platos.

dishwasher [-wašœ(r)], s. fregador(a) de platos; máquina de lavar platos.

dishwater [-wotǫ(r)], s. agua de lavar platos.

disillusion [disili̯úžǫn], **disillusionize** [-ai̯z], va. desilusionar, desengañar; desencantar.—**disillusion(ment** [-mẹnt], s. desilusión, desengaño, decepción; desencanto.

disimpassioned [disimpǽšǫnd], a. desapasionado, sin pasión, sereno.

disimprison [disimprízǫn], va. desencarcelar.

disinclination [disinklinéi̯šǫn], s. desafecto o desamor; aversión, desinclinación, mala gana.

disincline [-klái̯n]. I. va. desinclinar, malquistar, indisponer. II. vn. estar desinclinado, no tener ganas de.

disincorporate [-kórpǫrei̯t], va. desincorporar.— **disincorporation** [-éi̯šǫn], s. desincorporación.

disinfect [-fékt], va. desinfectar, desinficionar.— **disinfectant** [-ạnt], a. y s. desinfectante.— **disinfection** [-fékšǫn], s. desinfección, desinficionamiento.—**disinfector** [-féktǫ(r)], s. agente o aparato desinfectante.

disingenuous [-dʒényu̯ʌs], a. doble, falso, disimulado.—**disingenuously** [-li̯], adv. doblemente, falsamente.—**disingenuousness** [-nịs], *s*. doblez, astucia, mala fe.

disinherit [-hérịt], *va*. desheredar, exheredar.

disinheritance [-ạns], *s*. desheredación, exheredación.

disintegrate [dịsíntẹgreịt], *va*. y *vn*. desintegrar(se), desagregar(se), disgregar(se); desmoronarse, deshacerse.

disintegration [-éịṣọn], *s*. desagregación, disgregación.

disinter [dịsịntœr], *va*. exhumar, desenterrar.

disinterest [dịsíntœrest], *s*. desinterés; indiferencia, apatía; desventaja.

disinterested [-ịd], *a*. desinteresado, desprendido, imparcial, sin interés personal; indiferente.

disinterestedly [-lị], *adv*. desinteresadamente.

disinterestedness [-nịs], *s*. desinterés.

disinterment [dịsịntœrmẹnt], *s*. exhumación, desenterramiento.

disjoin [dịsdżóịn], *va*. desunir, apartar, separar, despegar, disgregar.

disjoint [dịsdżóịnt]. **I**. *va*. descoyuntar, dislocar, desarticular; desgozar, desunir, desarreglar; trinchar (un ave). **II**. *vn*. descoyuntarse, etc.—**disjointed** [-ịd], *a*. dislocado, descoyuntado; desarticulado.—**disjointedness** [-nịs], *s*. descoyuntamiento.

disjunct [dịsdżʌ́nkt], *a*. descoyuntado, dislocado.

disjunction [dịsdżʌ́nkṣọn], *s*. disyunción, descoyuntamiento, dislocación, disgregación.

disjunctive [dịsdżʌ́nktịv], *a*. y *s*. disyuntivo.

disjunctively [-lị], *adv*. disyuntivamente.

disk [dịsk], *s*. disco; redondo, rodaja, tejo; lenteja (de péndola); (igl.) patena; (bot., zool.) disco.—**d. harrow**, (agr.) cultivadora o escarificador de discos.—**d. jockey**, (fam., rad.) narrador de un programa basado en discos.—**d. record**, (mús.) disco.—**d. saw**, sierra giratoria.—**d. wheel**, rueda de disco.

dislikable [dịsláịkạbl], *a*. antipático.

dislike [dịsláịk]. **I**. *s*. aversión, antipatía, tirria. **II**. *va*. tener aversión a, no gustar de, querer mal.

disliked [-t], *a*. malquisto, malmirado.

dislocate [dịslokéịt], *va*. dislocar, descoyuntar.

dislocation [-éịṣọn], *s*. dislocación, descoyuntamiento, luxación.

dislodge [dịsládż]. **I**. *va*. desalojar, echar fuera. **II**. *vn*. desalojar, mudarse.

disloyal [dịslóịạl], *a*. desleal, falso, infiel, pérfido, traidor.—**disloyally** [-ị], *adv*. deslealmente.—**disloyalty** [-tị], *s*. deslealtad.

dismal [dízmạl]. **I**. *a*. triste, funesto, lúgubre. **II**. *s*. pantano, ciénago (del sur de los E. U.).—*pl*. (fam.) esplín, morriña, zangarriana.—**dismally** [-ị], *adv*. funesta o tristemente.—**dismalness** [-nịs], *s*. tristeza, melancolía; lobreguez.

dismantle [dịsmántl], *va*. desguarnecer, desamueblar; desmantelar; (mar.) desaparejar; (mec.) desmontar.

dismast [dịsmást], *va*. (mar.) desarbolar.

dismay [dịsméị]. **I**. *s*. desaliento, desánimo, desmayo, congoja; espanto, consternación. **II**. *va*. desanimar, espantar, aterrar.

dismember [dịsmémbœr], *va*. desmembrar.

dismemberment [-mẹnt], *s*. desmembración.

dismiss [dịsmís], *va*. despedir, echar, destituir, remover; descartar, echar a un lado; disolver (una junta, jurado, etc.); (mil.) licenciar, dar de baja.

dismissable, dismissible [-ạbl, -ịbl], *a*. destituíble.

dismissal [-ạl], **dismission** [dịsmíṣọn], *s*. despedida, remoción, destitución, deposición; liberación; acción de desechar, despedir o disolver.

dismissory, dismissive [dịsmísorị, -sịv], *a*. que despide, destituye o licencia; dimisorio.

dismount [dịsmáụnt]. **I**. *va*. desmontar; (mec.) desarmar; (arti.) desplantar. **II**. *vn*. desmontar o descabalgar, apearse; bajar.

disobedience [dịsobídịẹns], *s*. desobediencia.

disobedient [-ẹnt], *a*. desobediente.

disobediently [-lị], *adv*. desobedientemente.

disobey [dịsobéị], *va*. y *vn*. desobedecer.

disoblige [dịsobláịdż], *va*. desobligar, desplacer, no complacer.—**disobliging** [-ịŋ], *a*. poco complaciente, poco servicial.—**disobligingly** [-lị], *adv*. desatentamente.

disorder [dịsórdœr)]. **I**. *s*. desorden, desarreglo, desbarajuste, barullo; irregularidad; alboroto o motín; enfermedad; enajenación mental.—**in d.**, en desorden; a la desbandada. **II**. *va*. desordenar, desarreglar, desbarajustar; inquietar; perturbar.

disorderliness [-linịs], *s*. desorden, confusión; perturbación, turbulencia.

disorderly [-lị]. **I**. *a*. desordenado, desarreglado; turbulento, alborotador; escandaloso; inmoral; perturbador.—**d. conduct**, conducta escandalosa o contra la moral pública; desvergüenza.—**d. house**, casa de vicio (esp. burdel). **II**. *adv*. desordenadamente; turbulentamente; escandalosamente.

disorganization [dịsorganịzéịṣọn], *s*. desorganización; desarreglo, desorden.

disorganize [dịsórganaịz], *va*. desorganizar.

disorganizer [-œr)], *s*. desorganizador.

disorientate [dịsórịentéịt], *va*. desorientar.

disorientation [-éịṣọn], *s*. desorientación.

disown [dịsóụn], *va*. repudiar, negar, desconocer; renunciar, renegar de.

disparage [dịspérịdż], *va*. rebajar, menospreciar, deprimir, desdorar, desacreditar.

disparagement [-mẹnt], *s*. rebajamiento, menosprecio, detracción.

disparaging [-ịŋ], *a*. menospreciativo, detractivo.—**disparagingly** [-lị], *adv*. desdeñosamente; con desdoro.

disparate [díspạreịt], *a*. desigual, discorde; desemejante, diferente.

disparity [dịspérịtị], *s*. disparidad, desemejanza, desigualdad, diferencia, desproporción.

dispart [dịspárt]. **I**. *va*. despartir, apartar, dividir, separar. **II**. *vn*. partirse, dividirse, rajarse. **III**. *s*. (arti.) punto de mira.

dispartment [-mẹnt], *s*. despartimiento, división.

dispassionate [dịspéṣọnịt], *a*. desapasionado, imparcial.—**dispassionately** [-lị], *adv*. imparcialmente, sin pasión, desapasionadamente.

dispatch [dịspéch]. **I**. *va*. despachar, expedir; enviar, remitir; despedir; aviar, apresurar; concluir, rematar; matar. **II**. *s*. despacho; expedición; prontitud; parte, mensaje, comunicación, telegrama, *m.*; despedida, destitución; ejecución, muerte, *f.*; medio rápido de transporte.—**d. boat**, (mar.) aviso.

dispatcher [-œr)], *s*. despachador; expedidor; (f. c.) director del movimiento de trenes.

dispauperize [dịspópœraịz], *va*. suprimir el pauperismo en.

dispel [dịspél], *va*. dispersar; disipar, desvanecer.

dispensable [dịspénsạbl], *a*. dispensable.

dispensableness [-nịs], *s*. calidad de prescindible.

dispensary [dịspénsạrị], *s*. dispensario, clínica.

dispensation [dịspenséịṣọn], *s*. distribución, reparto; administración, gobierno; dispensación, dispensa o exención; (teo.) designio divino; acto o plan providencial; ley divina.

dispensator [dịspenseịtọr)], *s*. dispensador.

dispensatory [dịspénsạtorị]. **I**. *s*. farmacopea; dispensario. **II**. *a*. dispensador.

dispense [dịspéns], *va*. distribuir, repartir; administrar (justicia); dispensar, excusar, eximir.—**to d. with**, hacer caso omiso de, renunciar a, pasar sin, prescindir de.

dispenser [-œr)], *s*. dispensador.

dispeople [dịspípl], *va*. despoblar, yermar.

dispersal [dịspœrsạl], *s*. dispersión.

disperse [dịspœrs]. **I**. *va*. dispersar; disipar, esparcir; propalar; (ópt.) separar (la luz) en sus colores componentes. **II**. *vn*. dispersarse; disiparse; desaparecer. **III**. *a*. disperso.—**dis-**

persed phase, (quím.) estado coloide (el de una substancia suspendida en un líquido).
dispersedly [-ídlị], adv. esparcidamente.
disperser [-œ(r)], s. dispersador.
dispersion [dịspœ́rṣọn], s. dispersión; esparcimiento; difusión.
dispersive [dịspœ́rsịv], a. dispersivo.—**d. power,** (ópt.) poder dispersivo.
dispersoid [dịspœ́rṣọịd], s. (quím.) substancia en suspensión, coloide. V. DISPERSED PHASE.
dispirit [dịspírịt], va. desalentar, descorazonar.
dispiritedness [-ídnịs], s. desaliento, desánimo.
dispiriting [-ịŋ], a. desalentador.
displace [dịspléịs], va. dislocar; remover; desalojar, quitar el puesto a; (mar. y fig.) desplazar; (quím., farm.) colar.—**displaced persons,** los que huyen de su casa o patria ante una invasión u otra catástrofe, o que son llevados por el enemigo para trabajos forzados.—**displacement** [-mẹnt], s. desalojamiento; remoción; cambio de situación; (mar.) desplazamiento, tonelaje; (med.) desplazamiento, ectopia; (quím.) coladura; (geol.) falla, quiebra.—**displacer** [-œ(r)], s. (quím.) colador.
displant [dịsplǽnt], va. desarraigar.
display [dịspléị]. I. va. desplegar, abrir, extender; exhibir, mostrar, lucir, exponer; poner de manifiesto; (impr.) componer con tipo grande o de adorno. II. s. despliegue; exhibición, ostentación, manifestación; pompa o fausto.—**d. type,** (impr.) tipo de adorno.—**d. window,** escaparate.—**on d.,** en exhibición.
displease [dịsplíz], va. y vn. desagradar, desplacer, descontentar, disgustar.—**displeasing** [-ịŋ], a. desagradable, antipático, displicente.
displeasure [dịsplɛ́ẓ̇ụ(r)], s. desagrado, disfavor.
displume [dịsplúm], va. desplumar; degradar.
disport [dịspórt]. I. vn. y vr. entretenerse, retozar, divertirse. II. s. diversión, pasatiempo.
disposable [dịspóụẓạbl], a. disponible.
disposal [dịspóụẓạl], s. disposición; colocación, arreglo; distribución, repartimiento; venta; donación; enajenación.—**at your d.,** a su disposición.
dispose [dịspóụz]. I. va. disponer, arreglar, adaptar; inclinar el ánimo; ordenar, mandar. II. vn. disponer.—**to d. of,** acabar con, poner fin a; deshacerse o desprenderse de, dar, vender, enajenar, traspasar; disponer de, tener a su disposición.
disposition [dịspozíṣọn], s. disposición; arreglo, orden(ación); genio, natural, índole, f., modo de ser; inclinación, ánimo, propensión; tendencia.
dispositive [dịspázịtịv], a. dispositivo.
dispossess [dịspọẓɛ́s], va. desposeer, desalojar, desaposentar; (for.) desahuciar, lanzar.—**to d. one's self of,** desprenderse de.
dispossession [-zɛ́ṣọn], s. desposeimiento; (for.) desahucio, lanzamiento.
dispossessor [-zɛ́sọ(r)], s. desposeedor; desahuciador; quien desposee o desahucia.
dispraise [dịspréịz]. I. va. menospreciar; criticar, censurar. II. s. menosprecio; censura o desaprobación.
disproof [dịsprúf], s. confutación, refutación.
disproportion [dịspropórṣọn]. I. s. desproporción, desigualdad. II. va. desproporcionar.
disproportionable [-ạbl], **disproportional** [-ạl], **disproportionate** [-ịt], a. desproporcionado.—**disproportionableness** [-ạblnịs], **disproportionality** [-ǽlịtị], **disproportionateness** [-ịtnịs], s. desproporción, desigualdad.—**disproportionably** [-ạblị], **disproportionally** [-ạlị], **disproportionately** [-ịtlị], adv. desproporcionadamente.
disprovable [dịsprúvạbl], a. refutable.
disproval [dịsprúvạl], s. confutación, refutación.
disprove [dịsprúv], va. confutar, refutar.
disputability [dịspịụtạbílịtị], **disputableness**

[dịspịụtạblnịs], s. calidad de disputable, discutible, controvertible, contestable, opinable.
disputable [-ạbl], a. disputable.—**disputant** [-ạnt], a. y s. disputador.—**disputation** [-éịṣọn], s. disputa.—**disputatious** [-éịṣʌs], **disputative** [dịspịụtạtịv], a. disputador, litigioso, polémico.
dispute [dịspịút]. I. va. refutar, impugnar; disputar, luchar por. II. vn. disputar, discutir, controvertir, pleitear. III. s. disputa, discusión, altercado, contienda, controversia, polémica, reyerta; (for.) litigio, pleito.
disputer [-œ(r)], s. disputador; controversista.
disqualification [dịskwálịfịkéịṣọn], s. descalificación, inhabilitación; impedimento.
disqualified [-fạịd], a. descalificado, inhabilitado; incompetente.
disqualify [-faị], va. descalificar, inhabilitar.
disquiet [dịskwáịẹt]. I. s. inquietud, intranquilidad, desasosiego. II. va. inquietar, intranquilizar, desasosegar, (per)turbar.
disquieting [-ịŋ], a. inquietante.
disquietness [-nịs], **disquietude** [-jụd], s. inquietud, desasosiego, intranquilidad.
disquisition [dịskwịzíṣọn], s. disertación, disquisición.
disregard [dịsrịgárd]. I. va. desatender, desconocer, hacer caso omiso de, no hacer caso de; descuidar; desairar, despreciar. II. s. desatención, descuido, omisión; desprecio, desaire.—**disregardful** [-fụl], a. desatento; negligente.—**disregardfully** [-ị], adv. desatentamente.
disrelish [dịsrɛ́lịṣ]. I. s. repugnancia, aversión, disgusto; desazón, f., desabrimiento. II. va. sentir repugnancia o aversión a; desazonar.
disrepair [dịsrịpɛ́r], s. desarreglo, descompostura.
disreputability [dịsrépyụtạbílịtị], s. mala reputación.
disreputable [-ạbl], a. deshonroso, desdoroso; desacreditado, despreciable, bajo, vergonzoso; (fig.) desgarbado, dilapidado.
disreputably [-ạblị], adv. deshonrosamente.
disrepute [dịsrịpịút], s. descrédito, mala fama, mal nombre, desprestigio.—**to bring into d.,** desprestigiar, desacreditar.
disrespect [dịsrịspɛ́kt]. I. s. desatención, desacato, falta de respeto. II. va. desacatar, desairar; faltar al respeto a.—**disrespectful** [-fụl], a. irrespetuoso, irreverente.—**disrespectfully** [-ị], adv. irrespetuosamente.
disrobe [dịsróụb]. I. va. desnudar, desvestir; (fig.) despojar. II. vn. desnudarse.
disroot [dịsrút], va. desarraigar; desalojar.
disrupt [dịsrápt], va. romper; rajar, reventar, hacer pedazos; desorganizar, desbaratar.
disruption [dịsrápṣọn], s. desgarro, rotura; reventazón, f.; separación; desorganización o rompimiento; (elec.) interrupción (de un arco).
disruptive [dịsráptịv], a. desgarrador, destrozador, destructor, quebrantador, rajante.—**d. discharge,** (elec.) descarga violenta que vence la resistencia del aislamiento.—**d. spark,** (elec.) chispa de descarga.—**d. strength,** (elec.) resistencia dieléctrica, resistencia a la perforación por chispas.
dissatisfaction [dịsætịsfǽkṣọn], s. descontento, disgusto.—**dissatisfactoriness** [-torịnịs], s. incapacidad de contentar.—**dissatisfactory** [-torị], a. poco o nada satisfactorio.
dissatisfy [dịsǽtịsfaị], va. descontentar o desagradar.
dissect [dịsɛ́kt], va. anatomizar, disecar, dividir o cortar en pedazos; (fig.) criticar, analizar.—**dissecting knife,** escalpelo.—**d. room,** sala de disección, anfiteatro anatómico.
dissection [dịsɛ́kṣọn], s. disección, disecación, anatomía; análisis, mf.; objeto disecado.
dissector [dịsɛ́ktọ(r)], s. disecador, disector.
disseizin [dịsíẓịn], s. (for.) usurpación de tierras o heredades, o del dominio de éstas.
disseize [dịsíz], va. (for.) usurpar el dominio.

disseizor [-ǫ(r)], *s.* (for.) usurpador.

dissemble [disémbl], *va.* y *vn.* disimular, fingir, disfrazar, embozar, desmentir, encubrir; hacer la vista gorda.—**dissembler** [-blœ(r)], *s.* hipócrita, *mf.*, fingidor, disimulador.—**dissemblingly** [-blįnlį], *adv.* fingidamente, disimuladamente.

disseminate [disémįneįt], *va.* diseminar, esparcir, propagar, sembrar; divulgar, propalar.—**dissemination** [-éįşǫn], *s.* diseminación.—**disseminator** [-eįtǫ(r)], *s.* diseminador; propalador.

dissension [disénşǫn], *s.* disensión, desunión, desacuerdo, discordia; oposición.

dissent [disént]. I. *vn.* disentir, diferir, disidir; rehusar adhesión. II. *s.* disensión, disentimiento, desavenencia; disidencia.

dissenter [-œ(r)], *s.* disidente.

dissentient [disénşįent]. I. *a.* desconforme u opuesto. II. *s.* disidente.

dissentious [disénşʌs], *a.* contencioso, pendenciero.—**dissentiously** [-lį], *adv.* contenciosamente.

dissertate [dísœrteįt], *vn.* disertar.

dissertation [-éįşǫn], *s.* disertación, tesis.

dissertator [-ǫ(r)], *s.* disertador.

disserve [disœ́rv], *va.* deservir.—**disservice** [-įs], *s.* deservicio.—**disserviceable** [-ȧbl], *a.* perjudicial, dañoso.

dissever [disévœ(r)], *va.* partir, dividir, separar, desmembrar.

disseverance [-ȧns], *s.* división, separación.

dissidence [dísįdęns], *s.* disidencia.

dissident [-ęnt], *a.* y *s.* disidente.

dissilience, dissiliency [disílįęns, -į], *s.* (bot.) dehiscencia.—**dissilient** [-ęnt], *a.* dehiscente.

dissimilar [disímįlȧ(r)], *a.* disímil, desemejante.

dissimilarity [-lǽrįtį], *s.* desemejanza, disimilitud, diferencia, desconformidad, desigualdad.

dissimilarly [-lį], *adv.* desemejantemente.

dissimilate [disímįleįt], *va.* y *vn.* (fon.) disimilar(se).

dissimilation [-éįşǫn], *s.* (fon.) disimilación; (biol.) catabolismo.

dissimilitude [disimílįtįud], *s.* = DISSIMILARITY.

dissimulate [disímyųleįt], *va.* y *vn.* = DISSEMBLE.

dissimulation [-éįşǫn], *s.* disimulo, disimulación, disfraz, *m.*, hipocresía; tolerancia afectada.

dissimulative [-tįv], *a.*, **dissimulator** [-tǫ(r)], *s.* disimulador.

dissipate [dísįpeįt]. I. *va.* y *vn.* disipar(se), dispersar(se); desintegrar(se), desvanecer(se), evaporar(se). II. *va.* desperdiciar, derrochar, malgastar. III. *vn.* ser pródigo o disoluto.

dissipated [-įd], *a.* disipado, disoluto, crapuloso, relajado.—**dissipation** [-éįşǫn], *s.* disipación; libertinaje.

dissociable [disóųşȧbl], *a.* incongruo; insociable; separable.

dissocial [disóųşȧl], *a.* insociable, huraño.

dissociate [disóųşįeįt], *va.* disociar, dividir, separar, desunir, disgregar.—**dissociation** [-éįşǫn], *s.* disociación, separación, desunión, disgregación.

dissociative [-ȧtįv], *a.* disociador.

dissolubility [disȧlyųbílįtį], *s.* disolubilidad.

dissoluble [-bl], *a.* disoluble.

dissolute [dísoljut], *a.* disoluto, distraído, libertino, licencioso.—**dissolutely** [-lį], *adv.* disolutamente.—**dissoluteness** [-nįs], *s.* disolución, disipación, relajación, enviciamiento.

dissolution [-ljúşǫn], *s.* disolución; muerte, *f.*

dissolvable [dizȧ́lvȧbl], *a.* disoluble.

dissolve [dizȧ́lv]. I. *va.* disolver; disipar; dispersar; deshacer, desunir; derretir, desleír; (for.) derogar, revocar, anular; (fot.) desvanecer gradualmente una fotografía cinematográfica e irla cambiando en otra. II. *vn.* disolverse; descomponerse; descaecer, languidecer; desvanecerse.

dissolvent [-ęnt], *a.* y *s.* disolvente.

dissolving [-įn], *ger.* de TO DISSOLVE.—**d. view,**

(fot.) fotografía cinematográfica que gradualmente se desvanece y se va cambiando en otra.

dissonance, dissonancy [dísonȧns, -į], *s.* disonancia, desentonación; desconcierto, discordia.

dissonant [-ȧnt], *a.* disonante, discordante; contrario, discorde, opuesto.

dissuade [diswéįd], *va.* disuadir, desaconsejar, desviar, apartar.—**dissuasion** [-żǫn], *s.* disuasión.—**dissuasive** [-sįv]. I. *a.* disuasivo. II. *s.* disuasión, consejo.

dissyllabic [disįlǽbįk], *a.* disílabo.

dissyllable [disílȧbl], *s.* (gram.) disílabo.

dissymmetric(al [disįmétrįk(ȧl], *a.* disimétrico, no simétrico.—**dissymmetry** [disímetrį], *s.* disimetría, falta de simetría.

distaff [dístæf], *s.* rueca.—**d. side,** línea femenina.

distal [dístȧl], *a.* (biol.) distante del centro.

distance [dístȧns]. I. *s.* distancia; alejamiento; lejanía, lontananza; tirada, trecho; intervalo; respeto, miramiento; esquivez, frialdad, altivez.—**at a d.,** lejos, remoto; a lo largo.—**in the d.,** en lontananza, a lo lejos.—**to keep one's d.,** mantenerse a distancia; no familiarizarse. II. *va.* alejar, apartar; espaciar; tomar la delantera, dejar atrás, (sobre)pasar; adelantarse (a).

distant [dístȧnt], *a.* distante, alejado, apartado, lejano, remoto; serio, esquivo, extraño.—**to be d. with one,** tratar a uno con frialdad.

distantly [-lį], *adv.* a distancia, de lejos; en lontananza.

distaste [distéįst], *s.* fastidio, aversión, disgusto.

distasteful [-fųl], *a.* desabrido, desagradable.

distastefulness [-nįs], *s.* aversión, desagrado.

distemper [distémpœ(r)]. I. *s.* destemplanza o destemple; mal, morbo; (vet.) moquillo; enfermedad infecciosa; (fig.) mal humor, destemplanza; perturbación política; (pint.) templa; pintura al temple. II. *va.* destemplar, desordenar, perturbar; enfermar.

distemperature [-ȧchų(r)], *s.* destemplanza, desarreglo; indisposición, dolencia; desorden.

distend [disténd], *va.* tender, ensanchar, dilatar, inflar, hinchar; (med.) distender.

distensibility [-sįbílįtį], *s.* dilatabilidad.

distensible [disténsįbl], *a.* dilatable, (med.) distensible.—**distension, distention** [-şǫn], *s.* dilatación, inflación, (med.) distensión.

distich [dístįk], *s.* (poét.) dístico.

distichous [-ʌs], *a.* (bot.) dístico.

distil(l [distíl]. I. *va.* destilar; alambicar, alquitarar. II. *vn.* destilar; exudar, gotear.—**distillable** [-ȧbl], *a.* destilable.—**distillate** [dístįleįt], *s.* líquido o producto de destilación.—**distillation** [-éįşǫn], *s.* destilación; alambicación.

distillatory [-ȧtorį], *a.* destilatorio.

distiller [-œ(r)], *s.* destilador, refinador; condensador de alambique.

distillery [-œrį], *s.* destilería, destilatorio, refinería.—**distilling** [-įn], *a.* destilador, destilatorio.—**d. vessel,** destiladera.

distinct [distínkt], *a.* distinto, claro, preciso; diferente, diverso.—**d. from,** distinto a.

distinction [distínkşǫn], *s.* distinción; discernimiento, juicio; distintivo; honor, alto rango.—**in d. from** o **to,** a distinción de.

distinctive [distínktįv], *a.* distintivo, característico, privativo, de distinción.

distinctively [-lį], **distinctly** [-lį], *adv.* distintamente, claramente.

distinctness [-nįs], *s.* distinción, claridad.

distinguish [distíngwiş], *va.* distinguir, diferenciar, discernir; clasificar, marcar; honrar; individuar, singularizar.—**distinguishable** [-ȧbl], *a.* distinguible, discernible, perceptible.

distinguished [-t], *a.* distinguido, notable, famoso, prestigioso; caracterizado; especial, marcado, señalado.—**as d. from,** a distinción de, a diferencia de.

distinguishing [-įn], *a.* distintivo, que distingue.

distomatous [daįstámȧtʌs], *a.* (zool.) dístomo.

distort [distórt], *va.* (re)torcer; deformar; falsear,

pervertir, tergiversar.—**distortion** [distórʃǫn], *s.* esguince, contorsión, torcimiento; deformación; perversión, tergiversación; (med.) detorsión.

distract [distrǽkt], *va.* distraer; perturbar, interrumpir; enloquecer, volver loco.—**distracted** [-id], *a.* aturrullado, aturdido; demente.—**distractedly** [-li], *adv.* locamente.—**distraction** [distrǽkʃǫn], *s.* distracción, confusión, perturbación; frenesí, locura; desorden, alboroto; diversión, pasatiempo.—**distractive** [-tiv], *a.* que distrae, perturba o enloquece.

distrain [distréin], *va.* y *vn.* (for.) embargar, secuestrar.

distrainer [-œ(r)], *s.* (for.) embargador.

distraint [-t], *s.* (for.) embargo, secuestro.

distraught [distrɔ́t], *a.* = DISTRACTED.

distress [distrés]. I. *s.* pena, dolor; angustia, zozobra; desgracia, miseria, apuro, escasez; peligro; (for.) embargo, secuestro.—**d. signals,** señales (*f.*) de socorro o de peligro.—**to put in in d.,** (mar.) entrar de arribada. II. *va.* angustiar, afligir; poner en aprieto; (for.) embargar, secuestrar.

distressful [-ful], *a.* = DISTRESSING.

distressfully [-i], *adv.* acongojadamente, desdichadamente.

distressing [-iŋ], *a.* penoso, congojoso, aflictivo.

distributary [distríbjuteri]. I. *a.* distributivo. II. *s.* brazo de río que no se reúne con éste.

distribute [distríbjut]. I. *va.* distribuir, (re)partir; clasificar, arreglar, disponer. II. *vn.* hacer distribución; (impr.) distribuir.—**distributer** [-œ(r)], *s.* distribuidor, repartidor, dispensador.

distribution [-bjúʃǫn], *s.* distribución, (re)partición, repartimiento; colocación, arreglo, disposición, clasificación; esparcimiento; (arq., impr.) distribución.

distributive [distríbjutiv], *a.* distributivo.

distributively [-li], *adv.* distributivamente.

district [dístrikt], *s.* distrito, comarca, partido o territorio; barriada, barrio (de ciudad); región, jurisdicción.—**d. attorney,** fiscal de un distrito judicial.

distrust [distrást]. I. *va.* desconfiar, recelar, sospechar. II. *s.* desconfianza, recelo, sospecha, suspicacia, cavilación; descrédito.

distrustful [-ful], *a.* desconfiado, receloso, caviloso; suspicaz, sospechoso; difidente o modesto. —**distrustfully** [-i], *adv.* desconfiadamente.—**distrustfulness** [-nis], *s.* desconfianza, sospecha.

disturb [distœ́rb], *va.* disturbar, alborotar, alterar, conmover, (per)turbar; distraer, interrumpir; inquietar, desasosegar; desordenar, revolver.—**disturbance** [-ạns], *s.* disturbio, conmoción, perturbación, confusión, desorden, alboroto, tumulto, revuelo; perplejidad, irresolución.—**d. of the peace,** alteración del orden.—**disturber** [-œ(r)], *s.* perturbador, inquietador, desbaratador.—**disturbing** [-iŋ], *a.* perturbador, inquietante.

disulfate, disulphate [disʌlfeit], *s.* (quím.) bisulfato.—**disulfid(e** [-fid, -faid], *s.* (quím.) bisulfuro.

disunion [disyúnyǫn], *s.* desunión; disociación, separación; discordia, desavenencia.

disunionist [-ist], *s.* (pol.) separatista.

disunite [disyunáit]. I. *va.* desunir; disociar, separar; dividir; desavenir. II. *vn.* desunirse, separarse; desavenirse.

disunity [disyúniti], *s.* desunión, separación.

disuse [disyús]. I. *s.* desuso, deshabituación. II. [disyúz], *va.* desusar, desacostumbrar; cesar de usar; desechar (ropa, etc.).

disutility [disyutíliti], *s.* (e. p.) incomodidad; inconveniencia, impedimento.

disutilize [disyútilaiz], *va.* inutilizar.

disyoke [disyóuk], *va.* desuncir.

ditch [ditʃ]. I. *s.* zanja, caz, *m.*, acequia, regadero; cuneta; trinchera; (fort.) foso, cárcava; (hidr.)

presa, badén.—**to the last d.,** hasta quemar el último cartucho, sin cejar. II. *va.* zanjar, acequiar, abarrancar; (fam.) abandonar, desembarazarse de, dar calabazas a.

ditcher [-œ(r)], *s.* cavador de zanjas; máquina de hacer zanjas.

ditheism [dáiθiizm], *s.* diteísmo, creencia en un dios bueno y uno malo.

dither [díðœ(r)]. I. *s.* temblor; (fam.) agitación. —**to be (all) in a d.,** (fam.) estar sumamente nervioso o agitado. II. *vn.* temblar, tiritar; vibrar; molestarse.

dithionic [daiθaiánik], *a.* (quím.) ditiónico, hiposulfúrico.

dithyramb [díθiræm(b)], *s.* ditirambo.

dithyrambic [diθiræmbik]. I. *s.* ditirambo. II. *a.* ditirámbico.

ditone [dáitoun], *s.* (mús.) dítono.

dittany [dítani], *s.* (bot.) díctamo.

ditto [dítou]. I. *s.* ídem; el o lo mismo; marca (") o abreviatura (*id.*) que se usa en lugar de *ídem;* (fam.) duplicado, copia fiel. II. *va.* duplicar, copiar. III. *adv.* como ya se dijo; asimismo.

ditty [díti], *s.* (mús.) cantinela.—**d. bag, d. box,** (mar.) saco, caja de costura.

diuresis [daiyurísis], *s.* (med.) diuresis.

diuretic [daiyurétik], *a.* y *s.* (med.) diurético.

diurnal [daiœ́rnạl]. I. *a.* diurno; de día. II. *s.* (igl.) diurno.

diurnally [-i], *adv.* diariamente.

diuturnal [daiyutœ́rnạl], *a.* diuturno.

diuturnity [-niti], *s.* diuturnidad.

diva [dívạ], *s.* diva, cantatriz afamada.

divagate [dáivageit], *vn.* vagar perdido; divagar. —**divagation** [-éiʃǫn], *s.* divagación.

divalent [daivéilẹnt], *a.* (quím.) bivalente.

divan [dáivæn *o* divǽn], *s.* diván; cámara; café, fumadero; otomana.

divaricate [daivérikeit]. I. *va.* y *vn.* bifurcar o bifurcarse. II. *a.* esparrancado.

divarication [-éiʃǫn], *s.* bifurcación.

dive [dáiv]. I. *vn.* za(m)bullirse, echarse o tirarse de cabeza; bucear; sumergirse, enfrascarse, profundizar; (aer.) picar, descender en fuerte declive con la cabeza hacia abajo. II. *s.* za(m)bullidura, buceo; enfrascamiento; (fam.) garito, leonera, lupanar; (aer.) picada, descenso rápido de cabeza.—**d. bomber,** (aer.) avión (*m.*) de bombardeo en picada.—**d. bombing,** (mil.) bombardeo en picada.

diver [-œ(r)], *s.* za(m)bullidor, buceador, buzo; (orn.) somorgujo.

diverge [divœ́rdʒ], *vn.* divergir, diferir, desviarse.

divergence, divergency [-ẹns, -i], *s.* divergencia. —**divergent** [-ẹnt], *a.* divergente.

divers [dáivœrz], *a.* varios, diversos.

diverse [divœ́rs], *a.* diverso; multiforme, variado. —**diversely** [-li], *adv.* diversamente, distintamente.

diversification [-ifikéiʃǫn], *s.* diversificación, variación.—**diversify** [-ifai], *va.* diversificar, variar, matizar.

diversiform [-iform], *a.* diversiforme.

diversion [divœ́rʃǫn], *s.* desviación; diversión, divertimiento, distracción, entretenimiento.

diversity [divœ́rsiti], *s.* diversidad, variedad; diferencia, desemejanza, distinción, divergencia.

divert [divœ́rt], *va.* desviar, apartar; divertir, distraer, recrear.—**diverting** [-iŋ], *a.* divertido, entretenido, recreativo.

divertisement [-izmẹnt], *s.* diversión, holgura; divertimiento; intermedio de baile.

divertissement [divertismán], *s.* (teat.) entretenimiento; pieza o representación ligera; (mús.) divertimiento, pieza ligera; baturrillo.

divertive [divœ́rtiv], *a.* diversivo; recreativo, divertido.

divest [divést], *va.* desnudar; despojar; desposeer.

divestiture [-itʃu(r)], *s.* despojo; (for.) desposeimiento.

dividable [diváidạbl], *a.* divisible.

divide [diváid]. I. *va.* dividir; (des)partir, desmembrar, desunir, separar; deslindar; graduar; repartir, compartir. II. *vn.* dividirse. III. *s.* (geog.) vertiente, *f.;* divisoria; cordillera o cresta divisorias de dos cuencas o valles.—**the Great D.**, (E. U.) los montes Rocosos.

divided [-id], *pp.* de TO DIVIDE.—**d. skirt,** falda pantalón.

dividedly [-li], *adv.* separadamente; por separado.

dividend [dívidend], *s.* (arit. y com.) dividendo.

divider [diváidœ(r)], *s.* (re)partidor, distribuidor, desmembrador; divisor.—*pl.* compás de división, compás de punta fija o seca.

dividing [-in], *a.* divisor(io).

divi-divi [dívi-dívi], *s.* (bot.) dividivi.

divination [divinéishon], *s.* (a)divinación.

divine [diváin]. I. *a.* divino. II. *s.* sacerdote, ministro del culto; teólogo. III. *va.* adivinar; vaticinar.

divinely [-li], *adv.* divinamente.—**divineness** [-nis], *s.* divinidad.

diviner [-œ(r)], *s.* adivino, agorero; adivinador, conjeturador.—**divineress** [-es], *s.* adivina, profetisa, sibila.

diving [dáivin], *s.* za(m)bullida, za(m)bullimiento; buceo; (aer.) picada (= DIVE).—**d. beetle,** escarabajo acuático.—**d. bell,** campana de buzo.—**d. board,** trampolín o plataforma de saltar al agua.—**d. suit** o **dress,** escafandra o vestidura de bucear.

divining [diváinin], *ger.* de TO DIVINE.—**d. rod,** vara de adivinar, vara mágica; (min.) vara buscadora, que sirve para determinar la presencia de agua o mineral subterráneos.

divinity [divíniti], *s.* divinidad; deidad, numen; teología; atributo divino.

divinize [dívinaiz], *va.* divinizar.—**divinization** [-nizéishon], *s.* divinización.

divisibility [divizibíliti], **divisibleness** [diví-ziblnis], *s.* divisibilidad.

divisible [-bl], *a.* divisible; (for.) dividuo.

division [divíshon], *s.* división; distribución, repart(imient)o; ramo, negociado, departamento; sección; parte, *f.,* grupo; desunión; desacuerdo, disensión; (pol.) votación por grupos; (arit., mil., mar.) división.—**d. of labor,** (e. p.) división del trabajo.

divisional, divisionary [-al, -eri], *a.* divisional, divisorio.

divisive [diváisiv], *a.* divisivo.

divisor [diváizo(r)], *s.* (arit.) divisor.

divorce [divórs]. I. *s.* divorcio. II. *va.* divorciar; divorciarse de.—**divorceable, divorcible** [-abl], *a.* que se puede divorciar.—**divorcee** [-í], *s.* esposa divorciada.—**divorcement** [-ment], *s.* divorcio.—**divorcer** [-œ(r)], *s.* divorciador.

divulgation [diválgéishon], *s.* divulgación.

divulge [diváldʒ], *va.* divulgar, revelar, propalar.—**divulger** [-œ(r)], *s.* propalador.

divulsion [diválshon], *s.* arrancamiento; (cir.) dilaceración, divulsión, desgarro.

Dixie [díksi], *s.* el sur de los Estados Unidos.

dixit [díksit], *s.* afirmación dogmática.

dizen [dízen], *va.* ataviar, adornar.

dizzily [dízili], *adv.* vertiginosamente.

dizziness [dízinis], *s.* vértigo, vahído o vaguido; desvanecimiento.

dizzy [dízi]. I. *a.* vertiginoso, vaguido, desvanecido. II. *va.* causar vértigos o vahídos: aturdir.

do [du], *va.* (*pret.* DID; *pp.* DONE), hacer (justicia, bien, mal, un favor, el honor, daño, etc.); ejecutar; causar (peligro, daño, etc.); cumplir con (un deber, etc.); rendir, tributar (homenaje, etc.); cocinar (*to be done,* estar cocinado, asado, etc.); componer, arreglar (la cama, un cuarto); aprender (una lección); hacer, ejecutar (un ejercicio, una suma); terminar; dejar de (*she has done weeping,* ella ha dejado de llorar); traducir; hacer de, desempeñar el papel de; agotar, abrumar; recorrer, andar (una distancia); (fam.) visitar, explorar,

ver (como turista, etc.); (fam.) engañar, estafar; (fam.) (seguido de una expresión de tiempo) cumplir una condena de (el tiempo mencionado), estar o pasar en la cárcel o el presidio (el tiempo mencionado), vg., *he did a year in the penitentiary,* estuvo un año en la penitenciaría.—**to d. away with,** quitar, suprimir.—**to d. down,** (fam.) ganar a; engañar, embaucar.—**to d. in,** (fam.) pegarle a; despachar, matar; embaucar.—**to d. one's best, one's level best,** o **one's utmost,** hacer uno cuanto pueda, hacer lo posible.—**to d. over,** volver a hacer, hacer de nuevo; repetir; cubrir, revestir.—**to d. reverence,** rendir homenaje; inclinarse.—**to d. sewing, washing,** etc., coser, lavar, etc.—**to d. to death,** matar, despachar.—**to d. up,** componer, arreglar, poner en orden; planchar; envolver; (fam.) fatigar, cansar.—**to d. (up) brown,** (fam.) hacer perfectamente; embaucar.—**to have nothing (something) to d.,** no tener nada (tener algo) que hacer.

do, *vn.* conducirse; hacerlo, pasarlo (bien o mal); hallarse, estar (bien, mal, etc.: *to be doing,* ir; vg. *the patient is doing well,* el enfermo va bien); moverse; hacer algo, no estar ocioso; obrar, actuar; ser suficiente; servir; (con *to*) que hacer (*what is to do?* ¿qué hay que hacer?).—**to do by,** tratar a, portarse con.—**to d. for,** servir o bastar para; (en la voz pasiva, **to be done for,** estar arruinado o echado a perder; estar muerto o desahuciado).—**to d. with,** tratar, entenderse, habérselas con.—**to d. without,** pasarse sin; prescindir de.—**to have done,** haber terminado; desistir; no seguir adelante.—**to have done with,** haber terminado con; no tener más que ver con.—**to have to d. with,** tener que ver con; tener que entenderse o habérselas con; tratar de (*arithmetic has to do with numbers,* la aritmética trata de los números).—**how do you do?** ¿cómo está Vd.? buenos días, etc.—**that will d.,** eso basta; eso sirve; (fam.) deja, déjate de eso; calla, no digas más.—**that will never d., that won't d.,** eso no se hace; eso no se hace así; así no se irá a ninguna parte.—**what are you going to d. about it?,** ¿qué piensa Vd. hacer? ¿qué puede Vd. hacer? ¿qué (se) le ha de hacer?

do, *aux.* Como auxiliar, *do* se emplea:—1°. Para indicar interrogación o negación: *do you see?* ¿ve usted? *I do not see,* no veo; *she did not come,* ella no vino. 2°. Como reproductor del verbo, para evitar su repetición: puede entonces traducirse repitiendo el verbo, o por los adverbios *sí, no,* o por el verbo *hacer: do you see him?* ¿lo ve usted?—*I do, I do not,* lo veo, no lo veo (o sí, no); *he was working busily, as he was in the habit of doing,* trabajaba activamente, como lo solía hacer. 3°. Antes de un verbo, para dar mayor fuerza a su significado: *he does write well,* él ciertamente escribe bien; *I do tell the truth,* yo sí digo la verdad; *do sing for us,* le ruego que nos cante; *do come tomorrow,* venga mañana sin falta. El traductor puede escoger la palabra o forma enfática que le parezca más apropiada. 4°. Expletivamente, después de adverbios y conjunciones, cuando el sujeto va después del verbo: *nor do I believe,* ni creo yo; *seldom did he complain,* él rara vez se quejaba.

do [dou], *s.* (mús.) do.

doable [dúabl], *a.* factible.

do-all [dúol], *s.* factótum.

doat, doating, doaty = DOTE, DOTING, etc.

dobbin [dábin], *s.* caballo dócil y fiel; caballo de labor; rocín.

docile [dásil], *a.* dócil, sumiso; fácil de manejar.—**docility** [dasíliti], *s.* docilidad.

docimastic [dasimǽstik], *a.* docimástico.

docimasy [dásimasi], *s.* docimasia, docimástica.

dock [dak]. I. *s.* (bot.) bardana, lampazo; muñón de la cola cercenada de un caballo; (tal.) codón; (mar.) dique, dársena; desembarcadero, muelle; (for.) barra; banquillo de los acusados. —d.-tailed, o docked, curto, rabón, rabicorto. II. *va.* cortar, cercenar; descolar, derrabar; reducir, rebajar (sueldo, etc.); (for.) rescindir; (mar.) poner en dique; (*va.* y *vn.*) entrar en muelle, atracar.

dockage [dákidž], *s.* entrada de un buque en dique; muellaje; reducción, rebaja; impurezas.

docker [dákœ(r)], dockman [dákmạn], *s.* estibador, trabajador de muelle.

docket [dákịt]. I. *s.* minuta, sumario, extracto; rótulo, marbete; (for.) lista, turno, orden del día. II. *va.* extractar, hacer el sumario o minuta; rotular; dar turno, poner en el orden del día.

dockyard [dákyard], *s.* (mar.) astillero, arsenal.

doctor [dáktọ(r)]. I. *s.* doctor; médico. II. *va.* (fam.) medicinar, recetar; alterar y adulterar; reparar, componer. III. *vn.* tomar medicinas; practicar la medicina.

doctoral [-ạl], *a.* doctoral.—doctorate [-ịt], *s.* doctorado.—doctoress [-ịs], *s.* doctora o médica.—doctorship [-ŝịp], *s.* doctorado.

doctrinaire [daktrịnér], doctrinarian [-ịạn], *a.* y *s.* doctrinario; visionario, teorista.

doctrinairism [-ịzm], *s.* doctrinarismo.

doctrinal [dáktrịnạl], *a.* doctrinal; didáctico o instructivo.

doctrinally [-ị], *adv.* doctrinal o magistralmente.

doctrine [dáktrịn], *s.* doctrina, dogma, *m.*; teoría.

document [dákyụmẹnt]. I. *s.* documento. II. *va.* documentar; probar con documentos.

documental [-méntạl], documentary [-méntạrị], *a.* documental.

documentation [-éịŝọn], *s.* documentación.

dodder [dádœ(r)], *s.* (bot.) cúscuta.

dodder [dádœ(r)], *vn.* temblar, vacilar.

doddered [-d], *a.* decrépito, quebrantado.

doddering [-ịŋ], *a.* temblón, senil; sandio.

dodecagon [dodékạgạn], *s.* dodecágono [dodịkégọnạl], *a.* (geom.) dodecágono.—dodecahedron [dodekạhídrọn], *s.* (geom.) dodecaedro. —dodecasyllable [-sịlạbl], *s.* (verso) dodecasílabo.

dodge [dádž]. I. *va.* escabullirse, regatear (el cuerpo); esquivar, soslayar (una dificultad); evadir; seguir con disimulo. II. *vn.* hacer quites; dar un quiebro o esquinazo; trampear, entrampar. III. *s.* regate; evasiva; esquinazo.

dodger [-œ(r)], *s.* trampista, sablacista; cartel o anuncio pequeño.

dodo [dóụdoụ], *s.* (orn.) cierta ave ya extinta; (fam.) vejestorio.

doe [doụ], *s.* (zool.) gama; hembra del gamo, de la liebre, del conejo, del canguro y del antílope. —d. rabbit, coneja.

doer [dúœ(r)], *s.* hacedor; actor, agente; persona activa.

does [dʌz], 3a. *pers. del pres. de indic. de* TO DO.

doeskin [dóụskịn], *s.* ante, piel (*f.*) de gama; tejido fino de lana.

doff [dɑf], *va.* quitar; quitarse (el sombrero, la ropa, etc.).

dog [dóg], *s.* (zool.) perro, can; macho de algunos cuadrúpedos (zorro, lobo, chacal, etc.); sujeto despreciable, calavera o ligero de cascos; (mec.) grapa, cárcel, *f.*, barrilete; fiador, garra, trinquete; diente, perno; morillo; (astr.) Can (Mayor o Menor).—*pl.* tenazas de tracción.— d. ape o baboon, (zool.) mandril.—d. biscuit, canil, moyana.—d.-cheap, muy barato, regalado.—d. days, canícula, días caniculares. —d. dung o excrement, canina.—d.-ear o DOG'S EAR.—d. fancier, perrero.—d. fennel, (bot.) = MAYWEED.—d. fox, zorro macho; zorro azul.—d. grass, grama y otras clases de yerba.—d. hook, gancho, gancho de arrastre. —d. iron, morillo; llave de destornillar; gafa; grapa.—d. kennel, perrera.—d. Latin, latinajo, latín macarrónico.—d.-rose, (bot.) escaramujo, zarzaperruna, zarzarrosa.—d.'s

age, (fam.) mucho tiempo.—d.'s ear, esquina doblada de una hoja de un libro.—d. sledge o sled, trineo tirado por perros.—d.'s life, (fam.) vida miserable.—d.'s meat, comida de perros; comida de desperdicios para perros.—D. Star, (astr.) Sirio; Proción, *m.*—d.'s tongue, (bot.) cinoglosa.—d.'s tooth, (bot.) diente de perro. —d.-tired, cansadísimo.—a dead d., (fam.) una persona caída (que ha perdido su importancia o influencia).—a d. in the manger, el perro del hortelano.—d. eat d., destrucción mutua.—every d. has his day, a cada cual le llega su turno o su San Martín.—to drive to the dogs, arruinar.—to go to the dogs, estar arruinado o perdido.—to throw to the dogs, tirar o descartar como inútil.—to put on (the) d., (fam.) darse ínfulas.

dog, *va.* seguir los pasos o pisadas de alguno a, espiar, perseguir; (mec.) asegurar o afianzar con grapa, barrilete, etc.

dogbane [-bẹịn], *s.* (bot.) matacán.

dogberry [-berị], *s.* (bot.) cornejo y su fruto.

dogbolt [-boụlt], *s.* (mec.) perno dobladizo para unir piezas en ángulo recto.

dogcart [-kart], *s.* carrito tirado por perro(s); dócar o dogcart, coche de dos ruedas con dos asientos situados espalda con espalda.

doge [doụdž], *s.* dux.

dogfight [dógfajt], *s.* riña de perros; refriega; (mil.) combate violento entre aviones de caza, etc.

dogfish [dógfịŝ], *s.* (ict.) lija, cazón, melgacho, tollo; tiburón pequeño.

dogged [dógịd], *a.* terco, tenaz.—doggedly [-lị], *adv.* tenazmente.—doggedness [-nịs], *s.* tenacidad, terquedad, pertinacia.

dogger [dógœ(r)], *s.* (mar.) dogre, urca.

doggerel [dógœrẹl], *s.* coplas de ciego, aleluyas.

doggery [dógœrị], *s.* los perros; farsante, trampista; conducta soez; (vulg.) garito, leonera.

doggish [dógịŝ], *a.* perruno; gruñón, regañón.

doggy [dógị], *s.* (fam.) perro; perrito.

doghouse [dóghaụs], *s.* perrera, caseta de perro. —in the d., (fam.) en disfavor.

dogma [dógmạ], *s.* dogma, *m.*

dogmatic(al [dogmétịk(ạl], *a.* dogmático.

dogmatically [-lị], *adv.* dogmáticamente.—dogmaticalness [-nịs], *s.* magisterio; calidad de dogmático.—dogmatics [-s], *s.* (teol.) estudio de los dogmas y doctrinas de una religión.— dogmatism [dógmạtịzm], *s.* dogmatismo.— dogmatist [-tịst], *s.* dogmatizador; dogmatista. —dogmatize [-tạịz], *va.* y *vn.* dogmatizar.— dogmatizer [-œ(r)], *s.* dogmatizador, dogmatizante.

dogskin [dógskịn], *s.* piel (*f.*) de perro.

dogsleep [-slip], *s.* sueño fingido; sueño intranquilo o interrumpido.

dogtooth [-tuθ], *s.* diente canino, colmillo.

dogtrick [-trịk], *s.* perrada, perrería.

dogtrot [-trat], *s.* trote suave.

dogvane [-vẹịn], *s.* (mar.) cataviento.

dogwatch [-wach], *s.* (mar.) guardia de cuartillo.

dogwood [-wụd], *s.* (bot.) cornejo, sanguiñuelo.

doily [dóịlị], *s.* paño pequeño de adorno o para poner platos; frutero, servilletita.

doing [dúịŋ]. I. *ger.* de TO DO.—nothing d., a menudo con there is, was, etc.) (fam.) no hay (había, etc.) nada; nada de eso.—something d., (fam.) algo pasa (pasaba, etc.).—to be up and d., moverse, darse prisa, rebullirse. II. *s.* acción, hecho.—*pl.* acciones, obras; (fam.) acontecimientos, cosas (que ocurren).—great d., (fam.) grande actividad; grandes (o muchas) cosas; tremolina.

doit [dọịt], *s.* blanquillo (moneda); pizca, ápice.

dolce [dóụlchị], *a.* (mús.) dolce, dulce.—d. far niente [-farnịéntị], dulce ociosidad.

doldrums [dáldramz], *s. pl.* (mar.) zona de calmas ecuatoriales; (fam.) murria.—to be in the d., tener murria.

dole [dóul]. **I.** *s.* distribución, repartimiento en raciones o pequeñas porciones; dádiva, don, limosna; (poét.) suerte, *f.*, hado; angustia, congoja. **II.** *va.* (gen. con *out*) repartir, distribuir, dar (gen. de limosna).

doleful [-ful], **dolesome** [-sʌm], *a.* dolorido, lúgubre, funesto, melancólico, triste.—**dolefully** [-li], **dolesomely** [-li], *adv.* tristemente.—**dolefulness** [-nis], **dolesomeness** [-nis], *s.* tristeza.

dolerite [dálgrait], *s.* (min.) dolerita.

dolichocephalic, dolichocephalous [dalikose-fǽlik, -sɛ́fʌlʌs], *a.* (anat.) dolicocéfalo, dolicocefálico.

doll [dal]. **I.** *s.* muñeca. **II.** *va.* y *vn.* (gen. con *up*), (fam.) engalanar(se), acicalar(se), emperejilar(se).

dollar [dálạ(r)], *s.* dólar; duro, peso.—**d. diplomacy**, diplomacia del dólar o mercantilista, cuyo único móvil son los intereses comerciales; imperialismo del dólar, que se aprovecha del poder o la superioridad financieros.—**d. mark**, el signo $.

dolly [dáli], *s.* (fam.) muñequita; (min.) revolvedor de mineral; (mec.) cazoleta de remachar; remachador; rodillo, plataforma de (con) rodillo; (constr.) bloque de protección para la cabeza de un pilote; (f. c.) locomotora de maniobras o de arrastrar mineral.—**d. tub**, tina de lavar mineral.

dolman [dálmạn], *s.* dormán, dolmán.

dolmen [dálmɛn], *s.* (arqueol.) dolmen.

dolomite [dálomait], *s.* (min.) dolomía.

dolomitic [dalomítik], *a.* dolomítico.

dolor [dóulọ(r)], *s.* (poét.) dolor, pena.

dolorous [-ʌs], *a.* lastimoso; triste.—**dolorously** [-li], *adv.* dolorosamente.

dolphin [dálfin], *s.* (zool.) delfín, golfín, puerco marino, tonina; (mar.) poste de amarra; boya de anclaje; ⟨astr.⟩ Delfín.—**d. striker**, (mar.) moco del bauprés.

dolt [dóult], *s.* bobalicón, mastuerzo, bodoque.

doltish [-iš], *a.* lerdo, estúpido, memo, tonto.

doltishness [-nis], *s.* estupidez, tontería.

domain [doméin], *s.* dominio; imperio, soberanía; propiedad, heredad, finca.

domanial [-iạl], *a.* perteneciente al dominio o a la finca.

dome [doum], *s.* (arq.) cúpula, cimbor(r)io, dom(b)o; (m. v., fund.) cúpula; (geol.) techo, bóveda (de una caverna, etc.); (aut.) techo; (poét.) edificio majestuoso.—**d. light**, (aut.) lámpara de techo.

domesday [dúmzdei], *s.* = DOOMSDAY.

domestic [doméstik]. **I.** *a.* doméstico, casero; nacional, del país, interior, interno; intestino.—**d. commerce**, comercio interior. **II.** *s.* doméstico, criado, fámulo, sirviente.—*pl.* artículos del país.

domestically [-ạli], *adv.* domésticamente.

domesticate [-eit], *va.* domesticar; amansar, domeñar, desembravecer; hacer adquirir costumbres domésticas.

domestication [-éišọn], *s.* domesticación.

domesticity [domestísiti], *s.* domesticidad.

domical [dóumikạl], *a.* en forma de cúpula o que la tiene.

domicile [dámisil]. **I.** *s.* domicilio, residencia. **II.** *va.* y *vn.* domiciliar(se), tener domicilio (en).

domiciliary [-sílieri], *a.* domiciliario.

domiciliate [-sílieit], *va.* y *vn.* domiciliar(se), avecindar(se), establecer(se); domesticar.

domiciliation [-éišọn], *s.* fijación de domicilio.

dominant [dáminạnt]. **I.** *a.* dominante. **II.** *s.* (mús.) dominante, *f.*

dominate [dáminẹit], *va.* y *vn.* dominar.

domination [-éišọn], *s.* dominación, dominio, imperio; tiranía; gobierno, autoridad.—*pl.* (rel.) dominaciones.

dominative [-tiv], *a.* dominativo, dominante; imperioso, altivo.

dominator [-tọ(r)], *s.* dominador.

domineer [dɑminír], *va.* y *vn.* dominar, tiranizar.—**domineering** [-iŋ], *a.* dominante, tiránico, mandón.

dominical [domínikạl], *a.* dominical.

Dominican [domínikạn], *a.* y *s.* dominicano (natural de la República Dominicana); (igl.) dominic(an)o (de la orden de Santo Domingo).

dominie [dámini], *s.* dómine; (fam.) clérigo.

dominion [domínyọn], *s.* dominio; territorio; distrito; (for.) posesión, propiedad, dominio.

dominium [domíniạm], *s.* (for.) dominio.

domino [dáminou], *s.* dominó (disfraz); persona que lo lleva; máscara; ficha del juego de dominó.—*pl.* **dominoes**, dómino o dominó (juego).

don [dan], *va.* vestirse, ponerse, calar.

don [dan], *s.* caballero, señor; don (título); personaje de alta categoría; (Ingl.) rector de universidad.

donate [dóuneit], *va.* donar, contribuir.

donation [-éišọn], *s.* donación, don(ativo), dádiva.

Donatism [dánạtizm], *s.* donatismo.

Donatist [-ist], *a.* y *s.* donatista.

donative [dánạtiv], *s.* donativo.

donator [dóuneitọ(r)], *s.* donador.

done [dʌn], *pp.* de TO DO y *a.* hecho, ejecutado; dado (decreto, etc.); fecho; convenido; acabado, concluído; bien cocido o asado; (fam.) fatigado, consumido.—**d. for**, (fam.) agotado, rendido; desahuciado; vencido, fuera de combate; muerto.—**d. up**, envuelto; (fam.) fatigado.

donee [douní], *s.* donatario.

donjon [dándžọn], *s.* = DUNGEON.

donkey [dáŋki], *s.* (zool.) asno, burro, borrico, jumento, pollino; persona tonta o terca.—**d. boiler**, (mar.) caldera auxiliar.—**d. engine**, máquina pequeña auxiliar; (m. v.) máquina de alimentación.

donor [dóunọ(r)], *s.* donador, donante.

donship [dánšip], *s.* nobleza, caballería.

don't [dount], *abrev.* de **do not**.

doodle [dúdl], *va.* y *vn.* (fam.) garrapatear.

doom [dum]. **I.** *va.* sentenciar a muerte; predestinar a la ruina o destrucción; condenar, destinar. **II.** *s.* sentencia, juicio, condena; predestinación; sino, hado; perdición, ruina.

doomsday [dúmzdei], *s.* día del juicio universal.—**D. Book**, (Ingl.) registro del gran catastro hecho por orden del rey Guillermo el Conquistador.

door [dór], *s.* puerta; portal, zaguán; entrada; acceso.—**d. catch**, golpete; cierre.—**d. check**, amortiguador de puerta (para cerrarla suavemente).—**d. closer**, cierrapuertas.—**d. latch**, pestillo.—**d. mat**, felp(ud)o, ruedo.—**d. panel**, tablero.—**out of doors**, afuera, al aire libre.—**to lay at one's d.**, echarle a uno la culpa de.—**to lie at one's d.**, tener uno la culpa de.—**within doors**, adentro (de la casa).—**without doors**, afuera (de la casa).

doorbell [-bɛl], *s.* timbre de llamada.

doorcase [-keis], *s.* marco de puerta, jambaje.

doorframe [-freim], *s.* marco de puerta.

doorjamb [-džæm], *s.* jamba, batiente, quicial.

doorkeeper [-kipœ(r)], *s.* portero; (igl.) ostiario.

doorknob [-nab], *s.* tirador, botón o perilla de puerta.

doorman [-mạn], *s.* portero.

doornail [-neil], *s.* clavo grande de clavar puertas.—**as dead as a d.**, (fam.) absolutamente muerto.

doorplate [-pleit], *s.* placa de puerta, con el nombre del dueño de la casa.

doorpost [-poust], *s.* jamba de puerta.

doorsill [-sil], *s.* umbral, solera de puerta.

doorstep [-step], *s.* escalón de la puerta delantera.

doorstop [-stap], *s.* tope de puerta.

doorway [-weị], *s.* entrada, puerta; vano de puerta; portal.

dooryard [-yard], *s.* patio de entrada, enfrente de la puerta principal.

dope [dóup]. **I.** *s.* pasta o preparación semiflúida; grasa lubricante; pasta de opio; material absorbente que se mezcla con los explosivos; (aer.) material para revestir la tela de aeroplanos y dirigibles; (fam.) narcótico, estimulante; informes, datos, *m. pl.;* tonto, lerdo.— **d. fiend,** (fam.) morfinómano, persona que tiene el vicio de los narcóticos o estimulantes. —**d. racket,** tráfico ilícito en narcóticos. **II.** *va.* (fam.) pronosticar; formar el plan de (gen. con *out*); (fam.) estimular o entorpecer con un estimulante o narcótico. **III.** *vn.* (fam.) tener el vicio de los narcóticos.

dop(e)y [-ị], *a.* (fam.) narcotizado; aletargado.

dor, dorbug [dór, -bʌg], *s.* escarabajo.

Dorian [dórịạn], **Doric** [dórịk], *a.* dórico, dorio.

dormancy [dórmạnsị], *s.* sueño, letargo; quietud; suspensión, estado latente.

dormant [dórmạnt], *a.* durmiente; latente; inactivo.—**d. partner** = SILENT PARTNER.

dormer [dórmœ(r)], *s.* (arq.) viga maestra; gablete.—**d. window,** buharda, lumbrera, ventana vertical de buhardilla de gablete.

dormitive [dórmịtịv], *a.* y *s.* dormitivo, soporífero.

dormitory [dórmịtorị], *s.* dormitorio.

dormouse [dórmaus], *s.* (zool.) lirón.

dorp [dorp], *s.* aldea, lugarcito.

dorr, dorrbeetle = DOR.

dorsad [dórsæd], *adv.* (anat.) hacia la espalda.

dorsal [dórsạl], *a.* dorsal, espinal.

dorsum [dórsam], *s.* (anat.) dorso, espalda, lomo.

dory [dórị], *s.* (ict.) gallo, ceo; (mar.) bote pescador de fondo plano y estrecho, costados altos y acampanados, proa aguda y popa en V.

dosage [dóusịdʒ], *s.* (med., farm.) dosificación, posología; toma de un medicamento en dosis regulares.

dose [dous]. **I.** *s.* (med.) dosis; (fig.) píldora, mal trago; ingrediente que se agrega al vino. **II.** *va.* administrar una dósis; dividir en porciones dosimétricas. **III.** *vn.* medicarse con frecuencia.

dosimetric [dosịmétrịk], *a.* dosimétrico.

dosimetry [dosịmetrị], *s.* (med.) dosimetría.

doss [das], *s.* (Ingl., fam.) dormidero, lugar donde dormir (gen. se entiende que es malo); cama; sueño.—**d. house,** posada de mala muerte.

dossal, dossel [dásạl], *s.* (igl.) dosel, colgadura.

dosser [dásœ(r)], *s.* cuévano, serón. *V.* DOSSAL.

dossier [dásịęr], *s.* (for.) pieza de autos, expediente, documentos, papeles; historial.

dossil [dásịl], *s.* (cir.) lechino; tarugo.

dost [dʌst], *2da. pers. pres. ind. de* TO DO.

dot [dat]. **I.** *s.* punto; (mús.) puntillo; dote, *mf.*— **d. and dash,** punto y raya.—**on the d.,** en punto, a la hora exacta.—**to a d.,** perfectamente, absolutamente. **II.** *va.* punt(e)ar; poner punto a (una letra).

dotage [dóutịdʒ], *s.* chochera, chochez, ñoñería, ñoñez; cariño excesivo; extravagancia.

dotal [dóutạl], *a.* dotal.

dotard [dóutạrd], *s.* viejo chocho, ñoño.

dotation [dotéịʃạn], *s.* dotación.

dote [dóut], *vn.* chochear, caducar; devanear.— **to d. upon,** amar con exceso, estar chiflado por.

doter [-œ(r)], *s.* = DOTARD.

doth [dʌθ], (ant.) *3a. pers. pres. ind. de* TO DO.

doting [dóutịŋ], *a.* locamente cariñoso o enamorado, caducante, bobo, chocho; podrido o pudriéndose de viejo (apl. a las plantas).— **dotingly** [-lị], *adv.* con cariño excesivo, ciegamente.

dotted [dátịd], *a.* punteado, de puntos; mosqueado.—**d. line,** línea de puntos, línea para la firma.

dotterel [dátẹrẹl], *s.* (orn.) variedad de chorlito o ave fría.

doty [dóutị], *a.* manchado, descolorido por putrefacción incipiente (apl. a la madera).

double [dʌbl], *a.* doble, doblado, dupl(icad)o, dúplice; dos veces; ambiguo; engañoso; (bot.) doble; (mús.) una octava más bajo.—**d.-acting,** (mec.) de doble efecto.—**d. barrel,** escopeta de dos cañones.—**d.-barreled,** de dos cañones.—**d. bass,** (mús.) contrabajo, violón. —**d.-beat valve,** válvula de campana.—**d. bed,** cama ancha, para dos personas.—**d. boiler,** baño de María.—**d.-bottom,** (mar.) de carena doble.—**d.-break switch,** interruptor doble (para ambos polos del generador).— **d.-breasted,** (sast.) cruzado, de dos hileras de botones (saco, americana, etc.).—**d. chin,** papada.—**d. consciousness,** (psic.) doble personalidad.—**d.-cross,** *s.* traición hecha a un cómplice: *va.* traicionar (a un cómplice).— **d.-current dynamo,** o **generator,** dínamo (*f.*) doble o de dos corrientes (continua y alterna). —**d. dagger,** (impr.) obelisco doble.—**d.-dealer,** hombre falso, traidor.—**d.-dealing,** doblez, segunda intención, falsía, perfidia.— **d.-decker,** de dos puentes o pisos (ú. de ciertos autobuses y tranvías (con imperial).—**d. eagle,** (E. U.) doble águila, moneda de oro de 20 dólares.—**d.-edged,** de dos filos.—**d.-ended,** de extremos iguales.—**d.-ender,** cosa que tiene extremos iguales; (f. c.) locomotora de dos direcciones; (mar.) barco de dos direcciones (de timón en ambos extremos).—**d. entry,** partida doble (en contabilidad).—**d.-faced,** de dos caras; acabado por ambos lados; doble, falso, hipócrita.—**d.-feature,** (cine) función de dos películas de largo metraje.—**d.-flow turbine,** turbina de dos corrientes contrarias.— **d.-header,** tren con dos locomotoras; dos partidos (de béisbol, etc.) jugados sucesivamente.—**d. house,** casa gemela, casa de familia separada de otra idéntica por una pared medianera.—**d.-jointed,** de articulaciones dobles.— **d.-lock,** echar dos vueltas a la llave, cerrar con dos machos; asegurar doblemente.—**d. meaning,** equívoco, ambigüedad, segunda intención, doble sentido.—**d.-minded,** vacilante, inconsecuente.—**d.-pole switch,** interruptor bipolar.—**d.-quick,** (mil.) paso ligero o rápido. —**d.-riveting,** remachado doble.—**d. star** = BINARY STAR.—**d. the amount,** el doble o duplo.—**d. thread,** filete doble (tornillos).— **d.-throw switch,** (elec.) interruptor, o conmutador, de dos direcciones.—**d. time,** (mil.) = D.-QUICK; (e.p.) pago doble (por el tiempo en exceso de las horas regulares del trabajo).— **d.-tongued,** falso, pérfido.—**d. track,** vía doble.—**d.-track,** de vía doble.—**d.-wound,** (elec.) de doble arrollamiento.

double, *adv.* doblemente; dos veces; dos juntos; en par. Empléase sobre todo en adjetivos compuestos, como los que se dan anteriormente, con el adjetivo.

double. I. *s.* doble, duplo; pliegue, plegadura, doblez, duplicado; (teat.) contrafigura; copia, retrato (persona muy parecida a otra); (fig.) aparecido, fantasma.—*pl.* (en el tenis) juego de dobles.—**men's, women's, mixed doubles,** dobles de caballeros, señoras, mixtos. **II.** *va.* doblar, duplicar; redoblar, repetir; pasar por, doblar, remontar.—**to d. up, u over,** doblar, plegar, replegar. **III.** *vn.* doblarse, duplicarse; volver atrás.—**to d. up,** doblarse; dormir dos en una misma cama o cuarto.

doubleness [-njs], *s.* doblez, dobladura.

doubler [dʌblœ(r)], *s.* doblador, plegador, plegadera; duplicador; (elec.) excitador.

doublet [dʌblịt], *s.* par, pareja; jubón, ropeta; (joy.) doblete.

doubling [dʌblịŋ], *s.* doblez, pliegue; vuelta para huir; rodeo, artificio; (cost.) forro; (mar.) embono.

doubloon [dʌblún], *s.* doblón español.

doubly [dÁblị], *adv.* doblemente, dobladamente, al o en doble; por duplicado; con dolo.

doubt [dáut]. **I.** *va.* y *vn.* dudar; desconfiar. **II.** *s.* duda, dubitación; incertidumbre, irresolución; (for.) dubio.—**if, o when, in d.,** en caso de duda.—**no d., without d.,** sin duda.—**there can be no d.,** no cabe duda.

doubtable [-ạbl], *a.* dudable.—**doubter** [-œ(r)], *s.* el que duda.

doubtful [-fụl], *a.* dudoso, dudable, dubitable, dubitativo; ambiguo; incierto.—**doubtfully** [-ịị], *adv.* dudosamente.—**doubtfulness** [-nịs], *s.* duda, difidencia; calidad de dudoso.

doubtingly [-ịnlị], *adv.* dudosamente.

doubtless [-lịs]. **I.** *a.* cierto; confiado. **II.** *adv.* indubitablemente, sin duda.—**doubtlessly** [-lị], *adv.* indubitablemente; presumible o probablemente.

douceur [dusœr], *s.* (fr.) dulzura; recompensa, gratificación; soborno.

douche [duš]. **I.** *s.* ducha, regadera. **II.** *va.* y *vn.* duchar(se).

dough [dóu], *s.* pasta, masa, amasijo; cochura; (fam.) pecunia.—**d.-faced,** de cara pastosa.

doughboy [-boị], *s.* (fam.) soldado norteamericano de infantería.

doughnut [-nʌt], *s.* buñuelo, rosca, especie de churro o rosquilla frita.

doughtily [dáutịlị], *adv.* con denuedo.

doughtiness [dáutịnịs], *s.* valentía, denuedo.

doughty [dáutị], *a.* bravo, valeroso, denodado.

doughy [dóuị], *a.* pastoso.

douma [dúma], *s.* = DUMA.

dour [dụr *o* daụr], *a.* terco; difícil, trabajoso; riguroso, fuerte; hosco.

dourine [durín], *s.* (vet.) durina, sífilis equina.

douse [daụs]. **I.** *va.* za(m)bullir, empapar, meter en el agua; (mar.) recoger; arriar (velas); (fam.) extinguir, apagar (luces); (fam.) quitar(se) (el sombrero, etc.). **II.** *vn.* caer al agua.

dove [dʌv], *s.* (orn.) paloma, tórtola; persona pura y amante; símbolo de la paz. (**D.,** igl.) Espíritu Santo.—**dovecot, dovecote** [-kat, -kout], *s.* palomar.—**dovelike** [-laịk], *a.* columbino.

dovetail [dʌvteịl]. **I.** *s.* (carp.) ensambladura a cola de milano; cola de milano, o de pato.—**d. hinges,** bisagras de cola de pato.—**d. plane,** guillame de ensamblar. **II.** *va.* machihembrar o ensamblar a cola de milano; ajustar, amoldar. **III.** *vn.* (a veces con *into*) unirse a cola de milano; ajustarse; corresponder, estar de acuerdo.

dovetailed [-d], *a.* machihembrado; denticulado.

dowable [dáuạbl], *a.* capaz de ser dotado.

dowager [dáuạdźœ(r)], *s.* viuda con viudedad (apl. esp. a reinas, etc., vg. **d. queen,** reina viuda); (fam.) matrona respetable.

dowdy [dáudị]. **I.** *a.* zafio, desaliñado, sucio. **II.** *s.* pazpuerca, estropajosa, maritornes.

dowel [dáuẹl]. **I.** *s.* (carp.) taco, tarugo, clavija, espiga; nudillo; torillo; barra de alineación que atraviesa una junta de dilatación (ll. t. **d. pin**). **II.** *va.* sujetar o alinear con tarugos, etc.; empernar, enclavijar.

dower [dáuœ(r)]. **I.** *s.* viudedad; bienes gananciales de una viuda; don, beneficio; prendas personales. **II.** *va.* señalar viudedad o legar bienes gananciales; (fig.) dotar, adornar, favorecer. —**dowerless** [-lịs], *a.* sin viudedad.

dowery [dáuẹrị], *s.* = DOWRY.

down [dáun]. **I.** *adv.* abajo; hacia abajo; (mar.) a o hacia sotavento (el timón). Después de un verbo indica a menudo diminución, reducción, etc., vg. *to boil down,* reducir o mermar hirviendo; (fig.) compendiar, reducir a su más simple expresión; *to cut down,* recortar, rebajar. En leng. familiar se usa (sobre todo con referencia a posición en el mapa) en el sentido de "allá," "por allá," "en," y a veces no se traduce; vg. *down South,* (allá) en el sur; *I went down to Texas,* fuí a Tejas.—**d. below,**

allá abajo; más abajo.—**d. from,** desde.—**d. grade** = DOWNGRADE.—**d. the river, the stream,** etc., río abajo, agua(s) abajo, etc.— **d. to,** hasta.—**d. to date,** hasta la fecha, hasta nuestros días.—**d. on one's knees,** de rodillas. **II.** *interj.* ¡abajo!, ¡a tierra!—**d. the helm!,** (mar.) ¡la caña a sotavento!—**d. with . . . !** ¡abajo! ¡muera! **III.** *prép.* en sentido descend(i)ente; por, al largo de, hacia, bajo. **IV.** *a.* pendiente; descendente; abatido, alicaído; de abajo; (dep.) atrasado, atrás.—**d. and out,** (fam.) fuera de combate (esp. en el boxeo); vencido irremisiblemente; arruinado.—**d. in the mouth,** cariacontecido.—**d. payment,** primer plazo, paga al contado.—**d. train,** tren descendente.—**to be d. on,** (fam.) tener inquina a. **V.** *s.* plumón, flojel; bozo, vello; lana fina o pelo suave, pelusa; (bot.) vilano o milano (de cardo, etc.); revés de fortuna, baja, caída; colina, duna; (football) colocación de la pelota en el suelo para una rebatiña.—**d. bed,** edredón, colchón de pluma. **VI.** *va.* derribar, echar por tierra; vencer; beber; (fam.) tragar, aceptar o creer sin examen.—**to d. tools,** declararse en huelga.

downcast [-kæst]. **I.** *a.* inclinado, descendente; bajo; cabizbajo, mustio, deprimido, abatido. **II.** *s.* derribo; ruina; (min.) pozo de ventilación.

downcomer [-kʌmœ(r)], *s.* (m. v.) tubo de descenso; (metal.) tubería de gases combustibles.

downed [-d], *a.* cubierto o henchido con plumón.

downfall [-fɔl], *s.* caída; ruina.

downgrade [-greịd]. **I.** *a.* y *adv.* pendiente abajo, cuesta abajo. **II.** *s.* cuesta abajo, bajada, descenso.

downhaul [-hɔl], *s.* (mar.) cargadera.

downhearted [-hartịd], *a.* abatido, desmayado, descorazonado.

downhill [-hịl]. **I.** *a.* pendiente, inclinado, en declive. **II.** *s.* declive, bajada. **III.** *adv.* cuesta abajo, ladera abajo.

downiness [dáunịnịs], *s.* vellosidad.

down-lead [dáunlịd], *s.* (rad.) = LEAD-IN.

downpour [-pɔr], *s.* aguacero, chaparrón.

downright [-raịt]. **I.** *a.* vertical; claro, categórico; absoluto, completo. **II.** *adv.* claramente; completamente.

downstairs [-stérz]. **I.** *adv.* abajo, en el piso de abajo. **II.** *s.* piso inferior, primer piso.

downstream [-strím], *adv.* agua(s) o río abajo.

downthrow [-θrou], *s.* derribo.

downtown [-táun]. **I.** *a.* y *adv.* de o en la parte baja de la ciudad; del centro. **II.** *s.* parte baja de la ciudad; distrito del comercio.

downtrod(den [-trad(ẹn], *a.* pisoteado, atropellado; oprimido, esclavizado.

downward [-wẹrd], *a.* inclinado, descendente.

downward(s [-z], *adv.* hacia abajo.

downy [dáunị], *a.* velloso, felpudo; blando, suave; dulce, tranquilo.

dowry [dáurị], *s.* dote, *mf.;* dotación; arras, *f. pl.*

dowse [daụs], *va.* = DOUSE.

doxology [daksálodźị], *s.* (igl.) gloria; Gloria Patri; Gloria in excelsis.

doxy [dáksị], *s.* opinión; doctrina, creencia; (fam.) amante, querida; ramera.

doze [douz]. **I.** *vn.* dormitar, adormitarse. **II.** *s.* sueño ligero; sopor, adormecimiento.

dozen [dázẹn], *s.* docena.

doziness [dóuzịnịs], *s.* somnolencia, modorra.

dozy [dóuzị], *a.* adormecido, soñoliento, amodorrado.

drab [dræb]. **I.** *a.* parduzco; monótono; seco, ordinario, sin atractivos. **II.** *s.* color entre gris y amarillento; pipa de saladar; mujer desaliñada; ramera.

drabble [drǽbl], *va.* arrastrar, embarrar.

drabbler [drǽblœ(r)], *s.* (mar.) vela barredera.

drachm [dræm], *s.* = DRAM y DRACHMA.

drachma [drǽkmạ], *s.* dracma; antigua medida griega de peso; en griego moderno, gramo.

Draconian [dreikóuniǎn], a. draconiano, cruel.
dracunculus [dreikúnkyулʌs], s. (bot.) dragontea; (zool.) dracúnculo, parásito nemátodo.
draff [dræf], s. desperdicios; heces.
draffy [-į], a. inútil, despreciable.
draft, draught [dræft]. I. s. corriente (f.) de aire; tiro (de chimenea, etc.); succión, aspiración; trago, bebida; (mar.) calado; tracción, tiro, tirón, estirón; estiramiento; (mil.) ateleje (esp. de la artillería); carga, carretada; redada; traza, trazado, delineación, dibujo, esquicio; plan, plano; anteproyecto; borrador, minuta, apuntación; esquema; proyecto, propuesta (de ley, reglamento, etc.); (com.) giro, libranza, letra de cambio; libramiento, póliza, orden (f.) de pago; (mil.) reclutamiento, quinta, conscripción, leva; destacamento.—pl. juego de damas.
—**d. ale**, cerveza del tonel.—**d. animal**, animal de tiro.—**d. board**, (mil.) junta de reclutamiento.—**d. dodger**, (mil.) el que rehuye el servicio militar obligatorio.—**d. furnace**, alto horno.—**d. gauge**, indicador de tiro.—**d. horse**, caballo de tiro.—**on draught**, por vaso, sacada del barril (cerveza). II. va. hacer un borrador, minuta, apuntación de; redactar, escribir; bosquejar, delinear; dibujar; (mil.) reclutar, quintar; destacar; (tej.) hacer pasar entre los lizos del telar.
draftboard, draughtboard [-bɔrd], s. tablero de damas.
draftee [dræftí], s. recluta, m., conscripto, quinto.
draftsman, draughtsman [dræftsmǎn], s. dibujante, dibujador, diseñador, delineante, delineador; peón o pieza en el juego de damas.
drafty, draughty [dræftį], a. que causa, o está expuesto a, una corriente de aire.
drag [dræg]. I. va. arrastrar, tirar; (mar.) rastrear; (agr.) rastrillar.—**to d. in**, traer por los cabellos.—**to d. on o out**, prolongar. II. vn. arrastrar por el suelo; (mar.) garr(e)ar; ir tirando, avanzar penosa o lentamente; atrasarse, ir en zaga; retrasarse; (fig.) decaer la acción o interés; pasar con penosa lentitud, ser interminable. III. s. (mar.) rastra; draga; jábega, brancada; (agr.) rastrillo; rastra; (carr.) galga; narria; carruaje alto de cuatro caballos; rastro, pista; caza con perros que siguen un rastro artificial; (fund.) marco o parte inferior de una caja de moldear; (min.) hierro de limpiar pozos; (fig.) rémora, traba; cosa que retarda el movimiento o acción; (aer.) resistencia al avance.
—**d. anchor**, (mar.) ancla flotante.—**d. chain**, (f. c.) cadena de acoplamiento.—**d. hook**, garfio, rebañadera.—**d. link**, (mec.) contramanivela; (f. c.) barra de enganche.—**d. sail o sheet**, (mar.) ancla flotante.—**d. seine** = DRAGNET.—**d. wire**, (aer.) tirante de tracción.
dragbar [-bar], s. (f. c.) barra de enganche.
dragbolt [-boult], s. (f. c.) pasador de enganche.
dragging [-iŋ], s. arrastre, rastra.
draggingly [-lį], adv. arrastrando, a la(s) rastra(s).
draggle [drægl], va. y vn. ensuciarse arrastrando.
draggletail [-teįl], s. mujer desaliñada o puerca.
dragline [dræglaįn], s. draga o cangilón de arrastre; (aer.) = GUIDE ROPE.
dragnet [drægnet], s. brancada, red barredera, boliche; (fig.) pesquisa, sistema o artificio para recoger datos, coger personas sospechosas, etc.
dragoman [drægomǎn], s. dragomán, trujamán.
dragon [drægon], s. dragón; (zool.) dragón; hombre o mujer feroz; (bot.) dragontea; (D., astr.) Dragón.—**d. balloon**, (aer.) globo cometa.—**d.'s blood**, (bot.) sangre de drago.—**d.'s mouth**, (bot.) dragón, becerra, boca de dragón.—**d. tree**, drago.
dragonfly [-flaį], s. (ent.) libélula, caballito del diablo.
dragoon [drægún]. I. s. (mil.) dragón. II. va. acosar, intimidar.
dragrope [drægroup], s. (aer.) sonda.
drain [dreįn]. I. va. desaguar, (de)secar, encañar,

avenar; escurrir, apurar, sacar (el agua, aceite, etc.); sanear; (min.) achicar; (mec.) purgar; agotar, (de)sangrar, empobrecer, disipar.—**to d. off**, sacar, vaciar. II. vn. desaguarse, vaciarse; (a veces con off) escurrirse, salir (el agua). III. s. desagüe; desaguadero, cacera, reguera; tubería o zanja de desagüe; escurridor; sumidero; desangre; agotamiento; (cir.) desagüe. IV. a. de desagüe, de drenaje o avenamiento.—**d. cock**, (m. v.) llave (f.) de purga.—**d. plug**, tapón de desagüe.
drainable [-abl], a. desaguable.
drainage [-idʒ], s. desagüe, avenamiento, drenaje; saneamiento; arroyada, cuenca de un río.
drainboard [-bɔrd], s. escurridero para fuentes y platos.
drainer [-œ(r)], s. coladero, colador.
drainpipe [-paįp], s. tubo o tubería de desagüe.
draintile [-taįl], s. atanor, tubo de desagüe o drenaje hecho de barro cocido u hormigón.
drake [dreįk], s. (orn.) pato o ánade macho.
dram [dræm], s. dracma (⅛ de onza) (v. DRACHMA); trago de aguardiente; porción pequeña.
drama [drámǎ], s. drama, m.
dramatic(al [drǎmǽtįk(ǎl], a. dramático.—**d. art**, dramática.—**d. quality**, dramatismo.
dramatically [-ǎlį], adv. dramáticamente.
dramatics [-s], s. dramática, dramaturgia.—pl. piezas representadas por aficionados.
dramatism [drǽmǎtįzm], s. dramatismo.
dramatis personæ [drǽmǎtįs pœrsóuni], s. pl. (teat.) personajes dramáticos.
dramatist [drémǎtįst], s. dramaturgo, comediógrafo.—**dramatize** [-taįz], va. dramatizar.—**dramatization** [-tįzéįʃon], s. dramatización.
dramaturge, dramaturgist [-tœrdʒ, -įst], s. dramaturgo.
dramaturgy [-į], s. dramática, dramaturgia.
dramshop [drémʃap], s. cantina.
drank [drænk], pret. de TO DRINK.
drape [dreįp], va. vestir; colgar, entapizar; formar ropaje o pliegues artísticos en un ropaje o colgadura.—**draper** [-œ(r)], s. pañero.—**drapery** [-į], s. ropaje, cortinas, colgaduras, tapicería; pañería; paños.
drastic [drǽstįk]. I. a. extremo, fuerte; (med.) drástico. II. s. (med.) drástico, purgante poderoso.
draught [dræft], s. y v. = DRAFT.
draughtsman [dréftsmǎn], s. peón del juego de damas. V. DRAFTSMAN.
Dravidian [drǎvídįǎn], s. y a. dravidiano, drávida.
draw [drɔ], v. (pret. DREW; pp. DRAWN) tirar, arrastrar; atraer; estirar; sacar (clavo, agua, pistola, consecuencia); inferir, deducir, colegir; desenvainar (espada o daga); hacer salir; chupar o mamar; aspirar, respirar, inspirar (apl. al aliento); cobrar (un sueldo); sacarse (un premio); sortear (lotería, jurado, etc.); procurarse, proporcionarse (medios o recursos); correr o descorrer (cortinas); dibujar; trazar, hacer (descripción, etc.); redactar, escribir o extender; alargar, estirar (metales, tejidos, etc.); (com.) devengar, redituar (intereses); retirar (fondos); girar, librar; tender (un arco); hacer un cocimiento; destripar (aves, etc.); (en el billar) picar bajo; (mar.) calar.—**to d. along**, arrastrar.—**to d. aside**, correr (un telón); llevar aparte.—**to d. asunder**, separar.—**to d. away**, quitar, llevarse; disuadir; distraer.—**to d. back**, reintegrarse de, recibir devuelto.—**to d. breath**, respirar, tomar aliento, resollar.—**to d. forth**, hacer salir, sacar.—**to d. in**, atraer; seducir, embaucar.—**to d. it fine**, (fam.) hilar muy delgadito.—**to d. it mild**, decir sin exagerar, moderarse.—**to d. lots**, echar suertes, sortear.—**to d. near**, acercar, arrimar.—**to d. off**, sacar, extraer; retirar; trasegar, vaciar, decantar (licores); distraer; disuadir.—**to d. on**, ocasionar.—**to d. out,**

sacar; alargar, extender; sondear; sonsacar.—
to d. over, persuadir, sonsacar.—**to d. the
curtain**, correr el telón; (fig.) correr el velo (ya
para tapar, ya para destapar).—**to d. the line**
(a menudo con *at*) hacer la cruz, no pasar o ir
más allá (de).—**to d. the long bow**, exagerar.
—**to d. to an issue**, acabar, concluir.—**to d.
up**, tirar hacia arriba, subir tirando; redactar;
extender (un giro o documento); (mil.) formar;
(for.) levantar (acta).

draw, *vn.* tirar arrastrando; atraer gente, concurrencia; tirar bien (el fuego, la chimenea);
encogerse, arrugarse; adelantarse, moverse;
dibujar; echar suertes; sacar la espada; ir al
robo (en los naipes); (mar.) calar; (com.) girar.
Con ciertos adverbios indica movimiento, vg.,
to draw nigh, o *near*, acercarse; *to draw away*,
alejarse.—**to d. against**, (com.) girar contra o
sobre (fondos).—**to d. aside**, hacerse a un
lado, retirarse.—**to d. back**, retroceder; cejar.
—**to d. off**, retirarse.—**to d. on**, acercarse;
(com.) girar contra (persona, casa).—**to d. to
a head**, (med.) madurar, empezar a supurar;
aproximarse o llegar a un estado, situación,
etc., definitivos, estar al culminar o (fig.) al
reventar.

draw, *s.* tirada, tiro, tracción, arrastre; función
muy favorecida, que atrae mucha gente; (en
el billar) retroceso; (en los naipes) robo; (en
damas y ajedrez) tablas; (en dep., votaciones)
empate; (en juegos de azar) suerte, *f.*, premio;
(tej.) pasada, carrera; parte levadiza o giratoria de ciertos puentes; (E. U.) barranco,
arroyo.—**d. poker**, juego de *poker*, con opción
de descartarse e ir al robo.—**d.-well**, pozo de
noria.

drawback [-bæk], *s.* (com.) rebaja, descuento;
reintegro de derechos de aduana; desventaja,
inconveniente.

drawbar [-bar], *s.* (f. c.) barra de tracción.

drawbench [-bench], *s.* (mec.) hilera (máquina
de estirar); banco de estirar.

drawbridge [-brídʒ], *s.* puente levadizo o giratorio.

drawee [droí], *s.* (com.) girado, librado.

drawer [dróœ(r)], *s.* gaveta, cajón; extractor;
(com.) librador, girador.—*pl.* calzoncillos;
pantalón.

drawgear [drógir], *s.* (f. c.) aparato de tracción
o de enganche.

drawing [dróiŋ]. I. *s.* dibujo; tiro, tirante; (met.,
tej.) estiramiento, estirado; sorteo (de lotería,
jurado, etc.); extracción, saca. II. *ger.* de TO
DRAW.—**d. account**, cuenta corriente.—**d.
awl**, lezna de ojo.—**d. bench** = DRAWBENCH.
—**d. block**, tambor de estirar.—**d. board**,
tablero de dibujar; (tej.) = DRAWING FRAME.—
d. compass, compás portalápiz.—**d. frame**,
(tej.) estirador; carda mecánica.—**d. knife** =
DRAWKNIFE.—**d. paper**, papel de dibujo.—**d.
pen**, tiralíneas.—**d. press**, prensa de cortar y
estampar metal en lámina.—**d. room**, sala (de
una casa), estrado; recibimiento (sala y acción
o función); (f. c.) compartimiento particular
de un coche dormitorio.—**d. table**, mesa de
dibujar.—**d. triangle**, escuadra.

drawknife [drónaif], *s.* cuchilla desbastadora de
dos mangos (ll. t. **drawshave**).

drawl [drol]. I. *va.* pronunciar despacio. II. *vn.*
arrastrar las palabras. III. *s.* enunciación penosa y lenta.

drawn [dron], *pp.* de TO DRAW y *a.* desenvainado;
destripado, desentrañado; movido, inducido;
(dib.) tirado, trazado; contraído, ojeroso (de
dolor, cansancio, etc.); empatado (deportes,
tablas, etc.); indeciso (el triunfo); abierto
(un puente); estirado; fundido, derretido.—**d.
butter**, mantequilla derretida.—**d.-out**, estirado; extendido, prolongado; fastidioso, latoso.
—**d. work**, (cost.) labor de calado.

drawplate [dróplejt], *s.* (mec.) hilera (placa

perforada de estirar); (f. c.) plancha de enganche (de la locomotora).

drawtube [drótjub], *s.* tubo telescópico de enchufe, esp. el portalentes del microscopio.

dray [dréj]. I. *s.* carro, carretón, camión pequeño,
rastra; narria. II. *va.* acarrear.

drayage [-idʒ], *s.* acarreo, carretaje, arrastre.

drayhorse [-hors], *s.* caballo de tiro.

drayman [-man], *s.* carromatero, carret(on)ero.

dread [dréd]. I. *s.* miedo, terror, pavor, espanto;
asombro. II. *a.* terrible, espantoso; venerable.
III. *va.* y *vn.* temer, tener miedo o temor (de).

dreadful [-ful], *a.* terrible, espantoso, medroso.

dreadfully [-li], *adv.* terrible u horrendamente.

dreadfulness [-nis], *s.* terribilidad, horridez.

dreadless [-lis], *a.* intrépido, sin temor.

dreadlessness [-nis], *s.* intrepidez, arrojo.

dreadnaught, dreadnought [drédnot], *s.* el que
nada teme; paño muy doble; capote de capucha; (mar.) dreadnaught, grande acorazado.

dream [drím]. I. *s.* sueño, ensueño.—**d. world** =
DREAMLAND. II. *va.* y *vn.* (*pret.* y *pp.* DREAMED
y DREAMT) soñar; ver en sueños; (a veces con
up) idear, imaginar, forjar, fantasear.—**to d.
of**, soñar con.

dreamer [-œ(r)], *s.* soñador; visionario, utopista.

dreamily, dreamingly [-ili, -iŋli], *adv.* como en
sueños.

dreamland [-lænd], *s.* región de los sueños.

dreamless [-lis], *a.* sin sueños.

dreamlike [-lajk], *a.* como soñado; vaporoso,
nebuloso, vago.

dreamt [dremt], *pret.* y *pp.* de TO DREAM.

dreamy [drími], *a.* desvariado; soñador, contemplativo; propio de un sueño.

drear [drir], *a.* (poét.) = DREARY.—**drearily** [-ili],
adv. funestamente, tristemente.—**dreariness**
[-inis], *s.* tristeza; lobreguez.

dreary [-i], *a.* triste, melancólico; monótono,
pesado.

dredge [drédʒ]. I. *va.* dragar; rastrear; (coc.)
polvorear. II. *s.* draga; pontón de dragar; rastra; brancada.

dredger [-œ(r)], *s.* el que draga o rastrea; pescador de ostras; draga; pontón de limpia; (coc.)
polvorera.

dredging [-iŋ], *pa.* y *s.* dragado.—**d. box**, (coc.)
polvorera.—**d. bucket, grab** o **scoop**, cucharón o cubo de draga.—**d. machine**, draga.
—**d. tube**, caño o tubo de una draga de succión.

dreggish [drégiš], **dreggy** [drégi], *a.* que abunda
en heces; borroso, turbio; feculento.

dregs [dregz], *s. pl.* hez, heces; poso, sedimento;
madre (del vino); feculencia; escoria, barreduras, desperdicio; chusma, gentuza, populacho.

dreibund [drájbunt], *s.* triple alianza.

drench [drénch]. I. *va.* empapar, ensopar, calar,
mojar; (vet.) purgar con violencia. II. *s.* tragantada; mojada; (vet.) bebida purgante;
inundación, diluvio; (ten.) solución para remojar pieles.

drenching [-iŋ]. I. *a.* mojador.—**a d. rain**, una
lluvia torrencial, chaparrón. II. *s.* mojad(ur)a,
empapamiento.

dress [dres]. I. *va.* (*pret.* y *pp.* DRESSED y DREST)
vestir; ataviar, adornar, engalanar; (mar.)
empavesar (un buque); curar (las heridas);
almohazar (las caballerías); preparar, arreglar;
cocinar, guisar; aderezar, aliñar (la ensalada);
poner (la mesa); amortajar (un cadáver);
peinar, arreglar (el pelo); podar; cultivar (un
jardín); (ten.) adobar y curtir (pieles); preparar, agramar, rastrillar (lino, cáñamo);
(carp.) desbastar o azolar (madera); (cant.)
labrar (piedra); (alban.) allanar, aplanar, revocar; (mil.) alinear.—**to d. down**, (fam.) poner
como nuevo, o como chupa de dómine. II. *vn.*
vestirse; componerse, ataviarse; (mil.) formar
en línea, alinearse.—**d. left, right!** (mil.) ¡a
la izquierda, a la derecha, alinearse!—**to d. up**,

(fam.) vestirse de etiqueta, prenderse de veinticinco alfileres, endomingarse. III. *s.* vestido, traje, hábito; ropa(je), indumentaria; vestuario.—**d. ball,** sarao, baile de etiqueta.—**d. circle,** (teat.) anfiteatro, galería o grada principal.—**d. coat,** frac, casaca.—**d. form,** (cost.) maniquí.—**d. goods,** géneros para vestidos.—**d. hanger,** percha.—**d. parade,** (mil.) parada.—**d. rehearsal,** (teat.) ensayo final o general.—**d. suit,** traje de etiqueta.—**d.-suitcase,** maleta plana.

dresser [drésœ(r)], *s.* el que suele acicalarse; ayuda de cámara, moza de cámara; tocador; mesa de cocina; aparador; cocinero; (ten.) zurrador, adobador de pieles.

dressing [drésiŋ], *s. y pa.* adorno, aderezamiento; desbaste (de la madera, piedra, etc.); peinadura (del pelo); (mar.) empavesado; (tej.) aderezo; (ten.) adobo; (coc.) condimento, aliño, salsa; relleno; (cir.) hilas, vendajes, etc.; (agr.) abono, estercoladura; poda; (fam.) (gen. con *down*) rapapolvo, regaño.—*pl.* (arq.) molduras, adornos.—**d. case,** neceser, tocador.—**d. chisel,** desbastador.—**d. gown, jacket,** o **sack,** peinador, bata.—**d. room,** trasalcoba, cuarto de vestir o de tocador; vestuario; (teat.) camarín.—**d. table,** mesa de tocador; (min.) mesa de limpiar y concentrar (mineral, etc.).

dressmaker [drésmejkœ(r)], *s.* modista; costurera.

dressmaking [-iŋ], *s.* arte de modista; oficio de costurera; corte y confección de vestidos.

dressy [drési], *a.* (fam.) acicalado, peripuesto; elegante, vistoso, que viste mucho.

drew [dru], *pret.* de TO DRAW.

dribble [dríbl]. I. *vn.* gotear; escurrir; bab(os)ear. V. DRIVEL. II. *va.* hacer gotear; (dep.) avanzar el fútbol o baloncesto a trechos. III. *s.* goteo; baba; llovizna. V. DRIBLET.

driblet [dríblịt], *s.* trozo, pedacito, pizca; pico (de dinero); gota.

dried [drajd]. I. *pret. y pp.* de TO DRY. II. *a.* seco; (de)secado; enjuto; paso (ú. de la fruta).—**d. beef,** tasajo, cecina, (Am.) charque o charqui.—**d. fig,** higo paso.—**d. peaches,** orejones.—**d. plums,** ciruelas pasas.

drier, driest, *a. y comp. y superl.* de DRY.

drift [dríft]. I. *s.* todo objeto llevado por una corriente (nubes, restos de un naufragio, etc.); montón formado por el viento, el mar o el deshielo (ventisquero, dunas, alud, témpano, etc.); rumbo, tendencia, objeto; impulso, impulsión móvil; (mec.) mandril de ensanchar (agujeros para remaches, etc.); escariador; (min.) galería horizontal; socavón; rumbo (de una galería); (geol.) terrenos de acarreo, esp. los arrastrados por ventisqueros; (ing.) túnel de comunicación (entre otros dos) o de exploración; (arq.) empuje horizontal de un arco; (aer.) deriva, abatimiento, movimiento o velocidad lateral; (mar.) deriva, abatimiento; dirección de la corriente; red flotante (ll. t. **d. net**).—**d. anchor,** ancla flotante.—**d. angle,** (aer.) ángulo de deriva.—**d. avalanche,** alud, *m.*—**d. bar,** (aer.) varilla de deriva.—**d. ice,** hielo flotante o a la deriva.—**d. meter** o **indicator,** (aer.) derivómetro, indicador de deriva.—**to get the d.,** comprender (el objeto o lo esencial de algo). II. *va.* impeler, llevar; apilar, amontonar; (min.) abrir un socavón o galería. III. *vn.* (aer., mar.) abatir, derivar, devalar o davalar; apilarse, amontonarse; flotar a la ventura o sin rumbo; ir arrastrado por la corriente; ventiscar (nieve).

driftage [-idž], *s.* (mar., aer.) deriva; (arti.) desviación; lo llevado por una corriente, etc.

driftbolt [-boųlt], *s.* perno largo; botapernos, clavo o perno para sacar pernos empujándolos.

drifting [-iŋ]. I. *a.* flotante, a flote; movedizo

(arena, etc.); (fig.) instable, errante, vagabundo. II. *s.* (aer., mar.) deriva, abatimiento.

driftway [-wej], *s.* (min.) galería horizontal (gen. galería de avance o exploración); socavón, rompimiento, contramina; (mar.) deriva.

driftwind [-wịnd], *s.* ventisca.

driftwood [-wụd], *s.* madera flotante o arrojada a la playa por el agua; cosa instable; basura.

drill [dríl]. I. *va.* (mec.) taladrar, perforar, horadar, fresar, barrenar; hacer a barrena; (agr.) sembrar, plantar en hileras o surcos; derramar gota a gota; disciplinar, ejercitar, instruir; (mil.) enseñar el ejercicio. II. *vn.* (mil.) hacer el ejercicio; plantar en surcos; gotear. III. *s.* (mec.) taladro, perforadora, fresa, broca, barrena; parahuso; (min.) sonda; (joy.) árbol; (agr.) sembradora mecánica; hilera de semillas sembradas con esa máquina; (zool.) dril, especie de mono; (mil.) ejercicio; disciplina, pericia; (tej.) dril, tela cruda.—**d. brace,** berbiquí.—**d. instructor** o **sergeant,** (mil.) sargento instructor.—**d. plow,** arado sembrador.—**d. press,** taladradora, perforadora.

driller [-œ(r)], *s.* taladrador, etc.

drilling [-iŋ], *s.* barrenado, perforación, trepa; material extraído por un taladro; instrucción; (mil.) ejercicio; (tej.) dril.—**d. machine,** taladradora.

drillmaster [-mæstœ(r)], *s.* el que enseña el ejercicio militar u otros ejercicios.

drillstock [-stak], *s.* portabarrena; mango de taladro.

drink [dríŋk]. I. *va. y vn.* (*pret.* DRANK, (ant.) DRUNK; *pp.* DRUNK, (ant.) DRUNKEN) beber; brindar por; (fam.) trincar, empinar el codo, echar un trago; chupar, absorber (agua, como la tierra).—**to d. away,** beberse (su sueldo, etc.), gastar en beber.—**to d. down,** tragar; beber; ahogar (el dolor, etc.) en vino.—**to d. in,** chupar; absorber.—**to d. off,** o **up,** beber de un trago o a grandes tragos.—**to d.** (to) **the health of,** beber a la salud de, brindar por. II. *s.* bebida; poción; trago, copa.—**d. money,** propina.

drinkable [-abl]. I. *a.* potable, bebedero, bebedizo, bebible. II. *s.* bebida.

drinker [-œ(r)], *s.* bebedor; borracho, borrachín.

drinking [-iŋ]. I. *s.* acción de beber (apl. esp. a las bebidas alcohólicas). II. *a.* de beber, para beber.—**d. cup, glass, taza,** vaso de beber agua.—**d. fountain,** surtidor; fuente pública (para beber agua).—**d. place, trough,** abrevadero.—**d. water,** agua potable.

drip [dríp]. I. *va. y vn.* (*pret. y pp.* DRIPPED o DRIPT) verter o caer gota a gota, gotear, chorrear, destilar, rezumar; escurrir. II. *s.* gotera; reguero; humedad condensada; chorrera; goteadero, escurridero; (arq.) alero, vierteaguas.—**d. band,** o **flap,** faldilla de escurrimiento (de un dirigible).

dripping [-iŋ], *s.* chorreo, chorreadura; gotera; rezumadero.—*pl.* (coc.) pringue.—**d. pan,** grasera, pringuera.—**d. place,** rezumadero.

dripstone [-stoųn], *s.* (arq.) alero, vierteaguas, escurridero (cuando es de piedra).

drive [drajv]. I. *va.* (*pret.* DROVE; *pp.* DRIVEN) empujar, impeler, impulsar; echar, arrojar; estimular; llevar, conducir, gestionar; compeler, forzar, inducir (a); esclavizar, errear; meter, clavar, hincar; guiar, conducir, manejar (caballos, coche, automóvil, etc.); abrir (un túnel, socavón); (mec.) actuar, mover.—**to d. a good bargain,** hacer un buen negocio.—**to d. a hard bargain,** regatear mucho.—**to d. a point home,** remachar el clavo.—**to d. away,** ahuyentar, desterrar.—**to d. back,** rechazar.—**to d. crazy,** sacar de sus casillas, o de tino.—**to d. in,** o **into,** meter a macha martillo.—**to d. mad,** volver loco.—**to d. off,** ahuyentar, apartar.—**to d. to cover,** poner fin o coto a.—**to d. to the dogs,** arruinar, desesperar.—**to d. to the wall,** acosar, poner entre la espada y la pared. **II.** *vn.* ser impelido o empujado; arrojarse o moverse violentamente; andar o ir de paseo (en coche, etc.), cochear; (saber) conducir o manejar (un automóvil, etc.).—**to d. at,** aspirar a, tender a, proponerse.—**to d. away,** trabajar asiduamente.—**to let d.** (at), asestar un golpe, etc., (a). **III.** *s.* jornada o paseo en coche; calzada para coches; urgencia, presión, exigencia; impulso, tendencia, anhelo; manada de reses; montón de leños o trozas de árboles (que flotan en un río); (com.) saldo, liquidación, venta a bajo precio; (mil.) rebato, embate, ataque violento y rápido; (fig.) campaña vigorosa para lograr algún fin; (aut.) conducción, gobierno; mecanismo de dirección o de transmisión; asiento del conductor; (mec.) accionamiento, mando; mecanismo de transmisión o de impulsión (ll. t. **d. gear,** o **driving gear**).—**d. lever,** palanca de impulsión.—**d. shaft,** árbol o eje de transmisión.

drive-in [-in], *s.* cine al aire libre, o puesto de refrescos, cuyos clientes no necesitan dejar sus automóviles.

drivel [drível]. **I.** *vn.* babear, babosear, desbabar; bobear, chochear. **II.** *s.* baba; ñoñería, cháchara.

drivel(l)er [-œ(r)], *s.* fatuo, simple; baboso.

driveling [-iṇ], *a.* baboso; ñoño, chocho.

driven [drívẹn], *pp.* de TO DRIVE.—**d. pulley,** polea impulsada.—**d. snow,** nieve apretada. —**d. well,** pozo perforado o de tubo.

driver [drájvœ(r)], *s.* el que conduce o gobierna un vehículo; cochero, carruajero; mayoral (de diligencia); carret(on)ero; (aut.) conductor, chofer o chófer, piloto, guía, *mf.;* (f. c.) maquinista; rueda motriz (de locomotora); (mec.) rueda (o cualquiera otra pieza) impulsora; polea impulsora; hincador, martinete; (mar.) maricangalla.—**d.'s seat,** pescante (de un coche de tiro); (aut.) asiento del conductor.

driveway [drájvwẹi], *s.* vía de acceso a una cochera o garaje; calzada para coches.

drivewell [-wel], *s.* = DRIVEN WELL.

driving [drájviṇ]. **I.** *s.* conducción, manejo de coches u otros vehículos; hincadura; acción de impulsar, actuar y demás acciones comprendidas en TO DRIVE. **II.** *a.* motor, motriz; impulsor; enérgico; batiente, impetuoso, violento (lluvia, tempestad, etc.); (mec.) de actuación, de dirección, de mando, etc. (*V.* TO DRIVE).—**d. axle,** eje de las motrices.—**d. belt,** correa de transmisión.—**d. gear, d. shaft,** *V.* DRIVE.—**d. license o permit,** (aut.) licencia de conductor. —**d. pulley,** polea impulsora.—**d. wheel,** rueda motriz; volante.—**to go (out) d.,** ir de paseo.

drizzle [drízl]. **I.** *va.* rociar, salpicar. **II.** *vn.* lloviznar, molliznar, (Am.) garuar.—**drizzling rain,** llovizna. **III.** *s.* llovizna, molli(z)na, cernidillo, (Am.) chipichipi, garúa.

drizzly [drízlj], *a.* lloviznoso.

drogue [droug], *s.* (aer., mar.) ancla flotante.

droll [dróul]. **I.** *a.* drolático, festivo, jocoso, chancero, chistoso; raro. **II.** *s.* chusco, bufón. **III.** *vn.* bromear, chancear, chocarrear.

drollery [-œrj], *s.* chuscada, chocarrería, bufonería.

dromedary [drámẹdẹrj], *s.* (zool.) dromedario.

drone [droun]. **I.** *s.* (ent.) zángano, abejón; zangandungo, haragán; roncón de gaita; zumbido. —**d. fly,** abejorro, moscardón. **II.** *vn.* zanganear, holgazanear; zumbar; producir un ruido zumbador, sordo o monótono.

drool [drul]. **I.** *vn.* babear. **II.** *s.* babeo. *V.* DRIVEL.

droop [drup]. **I.** *va.* inclinar, bajar. **II.** *vn.* inclinarse, caer; colgar, pender; descaecer, decaer; desanimarse; consumirse, marchitarse.— **drooping lashes,** pestañas caídas. **III.** *s.* inclinación, caimiento.

drop [dráp]. **I.** *s.* gota; pizca; (joy.) pendiente, *f.,* zarcillo; caída, caimiento; pendiente, declive; pastilla; (com.) baja, caída; (mec.) artefacto (plataforma, martillo, etc.) que cae o se abre hacia abajo; (elec.) indicador de disco levadizo (en el tablero de un ascensor, hotel, etc.).—*pl.* (med.) dosis en gotas.—**d. annunciator,** (elec.) indicador de disco.—**d. box,** buzón.—**d. by d.,** gota a gota.—**d.-center rim,** llanta de canal. —**d. cover,** tapa caediza.—**d. curtain,** (teat.) telón de boca.—**d.-forge,** *va.* forjar a martinete; forjar a troquel.—**d. forging,** forjadura o forjado a martinete.—**d. glass,** cuentagotas, bureta, pipeta.—**d. hammer,** martinete.—**d. of a sail,** (mar.) caída de una vela.—**d. press** = DROP HAMMER.—**d. scene,** (teat.) telón de foro.—**d. sulphur,** tin, azufre, estaño granulado vaciándolo fundido en agua fría.—**d. valve,** válvula de cierre por gravedad.—**to d. get,** o **have, the d. on,** (fam.) tener indefenso, o en posición desventajosa. **II.** *va.* (*pret.* y *pp.* DROPPED o DROPT) verter a gotas; soltar, dejar caer; abandonar, desprenderse de; renunciar a, desistir de; despedir, echar; (ant.) polvorear, rociar; escribir (una esquela); parir los animales; (fam.) tumbar, derribar de un tiro.— **dropped eggs,** huevos escalfados.—**to d. a courtesy,** hacer una cortesía.—**to d. a hint,** soltar una indirecta.—**to d. anchor,** anclar.— **to d. a subject,** poner fin a una cuestión, cambiar de asunto.—**to d. the curtain,** correr el telón, echar un velo. **III.** *vn.* gotear, chorrear; bajar, descender; caer; cejar, parar, detenerse.—**to d. in,** entrar al pasar.—**to d. off,** decaer; dispersarse; quedar dormido; morir de repente.—**to d. out,** desaparecer; separarse, retirarse; quedarse atrás.

droplet [-lịt], *s.* gotita.

droplight [-lait], *s.* (elec.) lámpara movible unida a un cordón de derivación; lámpara colgante; cordón para dichas lámparas.

dropper [-œ(r)], *s.* cuentagotas.

dropping [-iṇ], *s.* acción o resultado de caer, gotear, etc.; estilicidio.—**d. bottle,** o **tube,** (frasco) cuentagotas, bureta, (Am.) gotero.— *pl.* excrementos de animales.

dropsical [drápsịkạl], **dropsied** [drápsịd], *a.* (med.) hidrópico.

dropsy [drápsị], *s.* (med.) hidropesía.

dropwort [drápwœrt], *s.* (bot.) filipéndula.

droshky, drosky [dráskị, dráskị], *s.* carruaje ruso de cuatro ruedas; coche de plaza.

dross [drós], *s.* escoria; horrura, espuma; basura, borra; sedimento, hez.

drossiness [-iṇịs], *s.* calidad de impuro.

drossy [-ị], *a.* que tiene escoria, espuma o heces; impuro.

drought, drouth [draụt, draụθ], *s.* seca, sequía; aridez, sequedad; (raro) carestía, escasez; sed. —**droughty, drouthy** [-ị, -ị], *a.* seco; árido; (raro) sediento.

drove [dróuv], *s.* manada, recua, arria, piara, tropa, vacada; gentío, muchedumbre; cincel de pedrero.

drove [dróuv], *pret.* de TO DRIVE.

drover [-œ(r)], *s.* ganadero.

drown [draụn]. **I.** *va.* ahogar, anegar; sumergir; inundar. **II.** *vn.* anegarse; ahogarse.

drowning [-iṇ], *s.* ahogamiento, anegación.

drowse [draụz]. **I.** *va.* adormecer, modorrar. **II.** *vn.* amodorrarse, adormecerse. **III.** *s.* modorra.

drowsily [-ị1ị], *adv.* soñolientamente.

drowsiness [-iṇịs], *s.* somnolencia o soñolencia, modorra, letargo, pesadez.

drowsy [-ị], *a.* soñoliento, amodorrado; soporífero.

drub [dráb]. **I.** *va.* apalear, sacudir, pegar, tundir, zurrar. **II.** *s.* porrazo.—**drubbing** [-iṇ], *s.* paliza, zurra, tunda, azotaina; derrota decisiva.

drudge [dráдz]. **I.** *vn.* afanarse, fatigarse; insudar. **II.** *s.* ganapán; marmitón, galopín.

drudgery [-œri], *s.* faena o trabajo penoso, tráfago.

drudgingly [-iŋli], *adv.* laboriosa o penosamente.

drug [drʌg]. **I.** *s.* droga, medicamento; artículo
de poca venta o demanda; narcótico; estimulante.—**d. fiend**, morfinómano.—**d. habit**,
morfinomanía, vicio de los narcóticos.—**d.
store**, farmacia, botica, droguería. **II.** *va.*
mezclar con drogas; narcotizar; poner narcótico
en. **III.** *vn.* tomar drogas (esp. narcóticos).

drugget [drʌgit], *s.* (ant., tej.) droguete; cierta
alfombra de India.

druggist [drʌgist], *s.* droguero, droguista, (E. U.)
boticario, farmacéutico.

Druid [drúid], *s.* druida, *m.*—**Druidess** [-is], *s.*
druidesa, sacerdotisa entre los druidas; profetisa.—**druidic(al** [druídik(al], *a.* druídico.—
druidism [drúidizm], *s.* druidismo.

drum [drʌm]. **I.** *s.* tambor, redoblante, caja,
(fig.) parche; (mec.) tambor, cilindro, rodillo;
bobina (de cable); (com.) cuñete o barrilito;
(arq.) campana; vaso de capitol, cuerpo de
columna; (anat.) tímpano (del oído).—**d.
major**, (mús., mil.) jefe o director de una
banda en las paradas, etc.; (ant.) tambor
mayor. **II.** *va.* y *vn.* tocar el tambor; tamboril-
lear, repetir, machacar; teclear; (com.) solicitar
parroquianos o pedidos.—**to d. out**, (mil.)
expeler a tambor batiente.

drumbeat [-bit], *s.* toque de tambor.

drumfire [-fair], *s.* (mil.) fuego graneado.

drumhead [-hed], *s.* piel, *f.*, parche, cara o
cabeza del tambor; (anat.) tambor, tímpano
(del oído).—**d. courtmartial**, consejo de
guerra de campaña, en el campamento o en la
línea de batalla.

drummer [-œ(r)], *s.* tambor, redoblante; (com.)
viajante.

drumstick [-stik], *s.* palillo, baqueta o bolillo de
tambor; (fam.) pierna (de un ave cocida).

drunk [drʌŋk]. **I.** *pp.* de TO DRINK. **II.** *a.* borracho, ebrio, beodo. **III.** *s.* (fam.) borrachín,
cuba, pellejo; (fam.) borrachera, holgorio,
parranda.

drunkard [-ərd], *s.* borracho, borrachín.

drunken [-ən], *a.* ebrio, borracho.

drunkenly [-li], *adv.* ebriamente.—**drunkenness**
[-nis], *s.* embriaguez, beodez; crápula.

drupaceous [drupéiʃias], *a.* (bot.) drupáceo.

drupe [drup], *s.* (bot.) drupa.

dry [drai]. **I.** *a.* árido, seco, sediento; pobre, estéril, frío; jocoso, satírico; chocarrero; agudo,
incisivo; seco (hablando de vinos); (b. a.) duro,
crudo; (met.) impuro y basto; (fam. y pol.)
prohibicionista, partidario u observante de la
temperancia; (quím.) por vía seca.—**d. battery**, batería seca, pila seca.—**d. beef**, cecina,
charqui. *V.* DRIED BEEF.—**d. casting**, fundición en arena seca.—**d. cell**, (elec.) pila seca,
elemento seco.—**d. cleaner**, tintorero.—**d.
cleaner's**, tintorería.—**d. cleaning**, limpi(ez)a
en seco (*to dry-clean(se)*, limpiar en seco).—**d.
concentration**, (met.) separación por gravedad al aire.—**d. cup**, (med.) ventosa seca.—**d.
cupping**, aplicación de ventosas secas.—
d. distillation, (quím.) destilación seca.—**d.
dock**, dique de carena.—**d. farming**, cultivo
seco (sin riego).—**d. fruit**, frutas pasas.—**d.
goods**, (E. U.) mercancías generales, esp. telas,
ropa y menudencias; géneros; lencería, mercería; (Ingl.) víveres, comestibles, etc.—**d.
goods store**, lencería, mercería.—**d. ice**, hielo
seco, anhídrico carbónico solidificado (es
nombre de fábrica).—**d. kiln**, horno (para
secar madera aserrada).—**d. law**, ley prohibicionista (contra bebidas alcohólicas).—**d.
masonry**, construcción de fábrica a hueso.—
d. mass, (igl.) misa en seco.—**d. measure**,
medida o sistema de medidas para áridos.—**d.
nurse**, niñera (*to dry-nurse*, ser niñera de, o
cuidar de un niño sin darle de mamar).—**d.**

plate, (fot.) placa o plancha seca.—**d. rot**,
enfermedades de las patatas, etc., debidas a
honguillos; pudrimiento de la madera debido a
causas semejantes; (fig.) deterioro, desinte-
gración o corrupción interna y oculta.—**d.
season**, seca, sequía.—**d. shod**, a pie enjuto.
—**d. weight**, peso seco.—**as d. as dust**,
sumamente árido o pesado. **II.** *s.* (fam., pol.)
prohibicionista, nefalista. **III.** *va.* secar, desecar; pasar (fruta); enjutar, enjugar; desaguar;
dar sed; acecinar. **IV.** *vn.* secarse, enjugarse.—
to d. up, secarse (esp. completa o rápidamente).

dryad [dráiæd], *s.* (mit.) dríada, dríade, *f.*

dryer [dráiœ(r)], *s.* = DRIER.

drying [dráiiŋ]. **I.** *s.* secamiento, desecación;
pasera (de frutas). **II.** *a.* (de)secante, secador.
—**d. chamber**, estufa.—**d. kiln**, horno secador.—**d. room, shed, floor**, etc., secadero,
sequera, (de)secador; pasera (para frutas).

dryly [dráili], *adv.* secamente, fríamente.

dryness [dráinis], *s.* sequedad, aridez.

drysalter [dráisoltœ(r)], *s.* (Ingl.) traficante en
viandas saladas y secas; droguista.

dual [diúal], *a.* binario, doble; (gram.) dual.—**d.
control**, (aut., aer.) mando o control doble,
mandos gemelos.—**d. ignition**, (m. comb.
int.) encendido doble.—**d. personality**, personalidad doble o múltiple.—**d.-purpose**, que
sirve dos fines o funciones.

dualism [-izm], *s.* dualismo; dualidad.

dualist [-ist], *s.* dualista.

duality [diuéliti], *s.* dualidad.

dub [dʌb]. **I.** *va.* apellidar, dar apodo; armar
caballero; alisar; (carp.) aparar, azolar; (mar.)
aparar; (cine) doblar.—**to d. out**, (alb.) repellar, revocar. **II.** *vn.* redoblar. **III.** *s.* golpe,
empuje; toque de tambor; (fam.) chambón,
persona torpe.—**d.-a-d.**, rataplán.

dubbing [-iŋ], *pa.* y *s.* ceremonia de armar caballero; (ten.) adobo impermeable; (mar.) apa-
rado; (cine) doblaje.—**d. tool**, azuela.

dubiety [diubáieti], *s.* duda, incertidumbre.

dubious [diúbias], *a.* dudoso, dudable, dubitativo, indeciso, irresoluto; incierto; ambiguo.

dubiously [-li], *adv.* dudosamente.—**dubious-
ness** [-nis], *s.* duda, incertidumbre.

dubitable [diúbitabl], *a.* dubitable, dudable.

dubitably [-bli], *adv.* dudosamente.

dubitation [diubitéiʃøn], *s.* dubitación.

ducal [diúkal], *a.* ducal.

ducat [dʌkat], *s.* ducado (moneda).

duchess [dʌchis], *s.* duquesa.

duchy [dʌchi], *s.* ducado.

duck [dʌk]. **I.** *s.* (orn.) ánade, pato; acción de
agacharse; capuz o chapuz, *m.*; (tej.) dril, brin,
lona fina, loneta; (fam.) pichona, vida mía;
(mil., fam.) camión anfibio.—*pl.* (fam.) pantalones de dril.—**to make o to play at ducks
and drakes**, hacer saltar una piedra sobre el
agua; (fig.) derrochar. **II.** *va.* chapuzar, za(m)-
bullir; evitar (un golpe, deber, etc.). **III.** *vn.*
chapuzar(se), za(m)bullirse; agacharse.

duckbill [dʌkbil], *s.* (zool.) ornitorrinco, platipo.

ducking [dʌkiŋ], *s.* chapuz, *m.*, zambullida.—**d.
stool**, silla de chapuzar (antiguo castigo).

duckling [dʌkliŋ], *s.* anadino, anadeja, patito;
monina (voz cariñosa).

duckweed [dʌkwid], *s.* (bot.) lenteja de agua.

duct [dʌkt], *s.* conducto, canal, tubo.

ductile [-il], *a.* dúctil, flexible, blando, correoso,
dócil, tratable.—**ductility** [-iliti], *s.* ductilidad;
docilidad.

ductless [-lis], *a.*—**d. gland**, (anat.) glándula
endocrina (de secreción interna).

dud [dʌd]. **I.** *s.* (fam.) persona o cosa floja o
inútil; fiasco; (fam.) bomba o granada que no
estalla.—*pl.* (fam.) trapos, ping(aj)os, andrajos;
ropa vieja; bártulos. **II.** *a.* (fam.) sin fibra,
falto de energía.

dude [diud], *s.* petimetre, pisaverde, lechuguino.

Para la pronunciación véase la clave al principio del libro.

dudgeon [dʌ́dźǫn], *s.* inquina; enojo; (ant.) puño de daga.—**in high d.**, muy enojado.

dudish [djúdiš], *a.* lechuguino, afeetado.

due [dju]. **I.** *a.* debido, cumplido, vencido; pagadero; apto, propio, conveniente, oportuno; legítimo; esperado, que debe llegar.—**d. bill**, pagaré, abonaré.—**d. to**, ocasionado por, debido a, con motivo de.—**in d. time**, a su debido tiempo.—**to become o fall d.**, correr, cumplir, vencer. **II.** *adv.* exactamente.—**d. west**, (mar.) poniente derecho. **III.** *s.* deuda u obligación; derechos, tributo, impuesto.—*pl.* cuota.—**to get one's d.**, llevar su merecido (castigo).—**to give the devil his d.**, ser justo hasta con el diablo.

duel [djúel]. **I.** *s.* duelo, desafío; certamen. **II.** *vn.* batirse en duelo.—**duel(l)er** [-œ(r)], **duel(l)ist** [-ist], *s.* duelista.—**duel(l)ing** [-iŋ], *s.* desafíos, duelos.

duenna [djuénä], *s.* dueña.

duet [djuét], *s.* (mús.) dúo, dueto; pieza a cuatro manos.

duffel [dʌ́fel], *s.* (tej.) paño de lana basta; equipo, pertrechos.—**d. bag**, (mil.) talego para llevar efectos de uso personal.

duffer [dʌ́fœ(r)], *s.* (fam.) estúpido; inútil, chambón; vendedor ambulante de artículos de imitación o de relumbrón; estafador, farsante; cosa que no vale nada, basura.

dug [dʌg]. **I.** *pret.* y *pp.* de TO DIG. **II.** *s.* teta, ubre, *f.*

dugong [dúgǫŋ], *s.* (zool.) dugong(o), vaca marina.

dugout [dʌ́gaut], *s.* (mar.) piragua; cueva; (mil.) defensa subterránea, cueva de protección.

duke [djúk], *s.* duque.—**dukedom** [-dʌm], *s.* ducado.

dulcet [dʌ́lsit], *a.* dulce, suave, armonioso.

dulcification [dʌlsifikéišǫn], *s.* dulcificación.

dulcify [dʌ́lsifai], *va.* dulcificar, endulzar.

dulcimer [dʌ́lsimœ(r)], *s.* (mús.) dulcémele.

dulia [djuláiä], *s.* (igl.) dulía.

dull [dʌl]. **I.** *a.* embotado, obtuso, sin punta, sin filo, desafilado, romo (herramientas, etc.); apagado, sordo; lerdo, negado; insípido, soso, insulso; flojo, perezoso, pesado; lánguido; desvaído, mate, bajo (colores); insensible; triste, murrio; lento pero no intenso (dolor); deslustrado, empañado; opaco, obscuro, ofuscado, nebuloso; soñoliento, modorro; (com.) desanimado, paralizado, inactivo, muerto.—**d.-brained**, estúpido, tonto, lerdo.—**d.-browed**, cejijunto.—**d.-eyed**, ojiapagado.—**d. of hearing**, duro de oído, medio sordo.—**d. pain**, dolor sordo.—**d.-sighted**, cegato.—**d.-witted**, lerdo, estúpido. **II.** *va.* embotar, desafilar; enromar; entontecer; entorpecer, obstruir; contristar; amortiguar, aliviar, moderar, mitigar; ofuscar, deslumbrar; empañar, deslustrar; mermar, enfriar (el entusiasmo, etc.). **III.** *vn.* embotarse; ponerse romo, gastarse la punta o el filo; empañarse; apagarse, mitigarse.

dullard [-ärd]. **I.** *s.* bestia, estólido. **II.** *a.* estúpido.

dullhead [-hed], *s.* tonto, zopenco.

dully [-i], *adv.* lentamente; estúpidamente; sin brillo.

dul(l)ness [-nis], *s.* falta de punta o filo; estupidez; somnolencia, pereza, pesadez; prosaísmo; deslustre; (com.) depresión, desanimación.

dulse [dʌls], *s.* alga marina comestible.

duly [djúli], *adv.* debidamente, puntualmente, a su tiempo.

Duma [dúma], *s.* duma, parlamento ruso.

dumb [dʌm], *a.* mudo; callado; (fam.) estúpido.—**d. creature**, bestia, bruto.—**d. motions**, señas.—**d. show**, pantomima, signo, gesto.—**d.-waiter**, ascensor o estante giratorio para el servicio del comedor; montaplatos; especie de montacargas pequeño.—**to strike d.** = TO DUM(B)FOUND.—**dumbly** [-li], *adv.* mudamente.

—**dumbness** [-nis], *s.* mudez; silencio; estupidez.

dumbbell [-bel], *s.* pesa o palanqueta de gimnasia; (fam.) tonto, zopenco.

dumdum, dumdum bullet [dʌ́mdʌm búlit], *s.* (mil.) bala dumdum o bala de expansión.

dum(b)found [dʌmfáund], *va.* confundir, pasmar, dejar turulato o sin habla.

dummy [dʌ́mi]. **I.** *a.* fingido, falseado, imitado.—**d. car**, vagón que lleva su propio motor o locomotora. **II.** *s.* mudo; (fam.) estúpido, imbécil; testaferro; (teat.) personaje que no habla; ascensor doméstico; objeto simulado; maniquí para vestidos, cabeza para pelucas, etc.; figurón; (imp.) libro en blanco con o sin páginas de muestra que enseña la forma general de un libro; libro u hojas con galeras recortadas, ilustraciones, etc., pegadas por páginas; (f. c.) locomotora de máquina condensadora; (en ciertos juegos) naipes que están sobre la mesa; jugador inactivo o imaginario. DUMMY CAR: locomotora de máquina condensadora; (en ciertos juegos) naipes que están sobre la mesa; jugador inactivo o imaginario.

dump [dʌmp]. **I.** *va.* vaciar de golpe; descargar, verter; (com.) vender a precios inferiores a los corrientes. **II.** *s.* vaciadero; vaciamiento; (min.) terrero; (mil.) centro de allegamiento y distribución de pertrechos, depósito de municiones, etc.—*pl.* melancolía, morriña.—**d. body**, caja de volteo (de un camión).—**d., o dumping car, truck o wagon**, carro o vagón de volteo o de fondo caedizo, camión de volquete.—**to be in the dumps**, tener murria.

dumping [-iŋ], *s.* vaciamiento; (com.) inundación del mercado con artículos de precios rebajados, esp. para suprimir la competencia.

dumpish [dʌ́mpiš], *a.* estúpido, lerdo; murrio.—**dumpishness** [-nis], *s.* estupidez; murria.

dumpling [dʌ́mpliŋ], *s.* pudín de pasta rellena de fruta o carne.

dumpy [dʌ́mpi], *a.* regordete; melancólico; descontento, enfurruñado. *V.* DUMPISH.—**d. level**, (top.) nivel de Troughton (nivel de anteojo corto).

dun [dʌn]. **I.** *va.* importunar a un deudor; apremiar; salar y conservar pescado; obscurecer. **II.** *a.* bruno, pardo, castaño obscuro; sombrío. **III.** *s.* acreedor importuno; apremio; (arqueol.) loma fortificada.

dunce [dʌns], *s.* zote, zopenco, bolo, tonto.—**d. cap**, coroza (para los alumnos estúpidos o perezosos).

dunderhead, dunderpate [dʌ́ndœrhed, -peit], *s.* zamacuco, bodoque, badulaque. *V.* DUNCE.

dune [djun], *s.* duna, marisma, médano.

dunfish [dʌ́nfiš], *s.* bacalao seco.

dung [dʌŋ]. **I.** *s.* estiércol, fimo.—**d. heap, d. yard**, estercolero, muladar. **II.** *va.* y *vn.* estercolar.

dungaree [dʌŋgarí], *s.* (tej.) cierto paño basto de algodón.—*pl.* pantalones, zahones, mono, etc.

dungeon [dʌ́ndźǫn]. **I.** *s.* calabozo, mazmorra. **II.** *va.* encalabozar.

dungfork [dʌ́nfork], *s.* horca para estiércol.

dunghill [dʌ́nhil]. **I.** *s.* estercolero, muladar, basurero. **II.** *a.* bajo, vil.

dunk [dʌŋk], *va.* mojar, ensopar; tirar al agua.

dunnage [dʌ́nidź], *s.* equipaje; (mar.) abarrote.

dunnite [dʌ́nait], dunita, explosivo Dunn (explosivo compuesto en gran parte de ácido pícrico).

duo [djúou], *s.* (mús.) dúo.

duodecimal [-désimal], *a.* (arit.) duodecimal.

duodecimo [-désimou], *s.* libro en dozavo.

duodenum [-dínʌm], *s.* (anat.) duodeno.

duogravure [-greivur], *s.* fotograbado en un color con dos placas.

duologue [-lǫg], *s.* diálogo.

duotype [-taip], *s.* fotografía obtenida de dos fotograbados a media tinta.

dupe [djup]. **I.** *s.* incauto, primo, víctima de engaño o dolo. **II.** *va.* engañar, embaucar.

duple [djúpl], *a.* doble, duplo.

duplex [djúpleks], *a.* duplo; doble, dúplice; (tec.)

dúplex.—d. house, casa para dos familias.—
d. iron, fundición recalentada en horno eléctrico.—**d. telegraphy,** telegrafía dúplex.
duplicate [djúplikeit]. **I.** *va.* duplicar, copiar,
reproducir; repetir. **II.** [djúplikit], *s.* duplicado,
copia.—**in d.,** por duplicado. **III.** [djúplikit], *a.*
duplicado, doble, en pares.—**d. part,** pieza de
recambio o de repuesto.—**duplication** [-éişǫn],
s. duplicación; repetición, reduplicación; plegadura, pliegue, doblez, *m.*
duplicative [-eitiv], *a.* duplicativo.
duplicator [-eitǫ(r)], *s.* duplicador(a), copiador.
duplicity [djuplísiti], *s.* duplicidad, doblez, engaño, segunda intención.
durability [diurabíliti], *s.* estabilidad, permanencia; duración, durabilidad.
durable [djúrabl], *a.* durable, duradero.
durably [-bli], *adv.* duraderamente.
duralumin [djurǽlyǫmin] (nombre de fábrica),
s. duraluminio, cuproaluminio, aleación de
aluminio y cobre.
dura mater [djúrǻ méitœ(r)], *s.* (anat.) duramáter o duramadre, *f.*
duramen [djuréimɛn], *s.* (bot.) duramen.
durance [djúrans], *s.* cautividad, prisión; (tej.)
sempiterna (ll. t. **durant**).
duration [djuréişǫn], *s.* duración, dura.
duress [djúris, djurés], *s.* compulsión, coacción;
prisión, encierro.
during [djúriŋ], *prep.* durante, mientras.
durst [dœrst], *pret. irr.* de TO DARE.
dusk [dʌsk]. **I.** *a.* (poét.) obscuro. **II.** *s.* crepúsculo vespertino, oraciones, obscuridad.—**d.-
to-dawn,** (la) anochecer a (la) madrugada.—
at d., al anochecer.
duskily [-ili], *adv.* obscuramente.
duskiness [-nis], *s.* obscuridad.
dusky [-i], *a.* fusco, obscuro; moreno, pardo.
dust [dʌst]. **I.** *s.* polvo; polvareda; altercado;
cenizas, restos mortales; (fig.) abyección, humillación; basura, barreduras, tamo; escombros; oro en polvo; (fam.) dinero.—**d. band,**
guardapolvo (de reloj).—**d. bowl,** región en
que se producen a veces grandes vendavales de
polvo.—**d. brush,** plumero, cepillo de despolvar.—**d. cloak o coat,** guardapolvo.—**d.
cloud,** polvareda.—**d. devil,** remolino móvil
de arena.—**d. guard,** guardapolvo.—**d. storm,**
vendaval de polvo.—**to bite the d.,** morder el
polvo, morir o caer vencido.—**to kick up, o
raise, a d.,** armar un alboroto.—**to lick the
d.,** morder el polvo; humillarse con abyección.
—**to shake off the d.,** sacudir el polvo.—**to
throw d. in one's eyes,** embaucar. **II.** *va.*
despolvorear, despolvar, desempolv(or)ar, sacudir o quitar el polvo; espolvorizar, (es)polvo-
rear, aplicar polvos.—**to d. one's jacket,**
zurrar a uno.
dustbin [-bin], *s.* basurero, receptáculo para
polvo, barreduras, ceniza, etc.
dustcloth [-klɔθ], *s.* paño o trapo de despolvar.
duster [-œ(r)], *s.* el, la o lo que quita el polvo;
sacudidor; plumero; guardapolvo (prenda de
vestir); utensilio para espolvorear (insecticidas,
etc.).
dustiness [-nis], *s.* calidad de empolvado o
polvoroso.
dusting [-iŋ], *s.* desempolvoradura; polvoreamiento.—**d. powder,** polvo fino, talco; (med.)
epítema.
dustman [-man], *s.* basurero, barrendero.
dustpan [-pæn], *s.* pala de recoger la basura.
dusty [-i], *a.* empolvado, polvoroso, polvoriento.
Dutch [dʌch], *s.* y *a.* holandés; (fam.) alemán.—
D. bond, (alb.) aparejo longitudinal o de sogas
y tizones alternados.—**D. brass,** tombac (aleación de cobre y cinc).—**D. cheese,** queso de
Flandes o de bola; especie de requesón.—**D.
foil, gold, leaf o metal,** hoja de tombac.—**D.
tile,** azulejo.—**D. treat,** (fam.) convite a escote, convite en que cada cual paga por lo que

bebe o come.—**D. uncle,** mentor o crítico
severo.—**D. wife,** (Fil.) abrazador.—**in D.,**
(fam.) en disfavor.—**to beat the D.,** (fam.)
ser cosa sorprendente o inaudita.—**to go D.,**
(fam.) ir a medias. *V.* D. TREAT.
Dutchman [-man], *s.* holandés; (fam.) alemán.
duteous [djútiʌs], *a.* obediente, obsequioso,
respetuoso.
dutiable [djútiabl], *a.* imponible; sujeto a adeudo
o derechos de aduana.
dutiful [djútiful], *a.* deferente, respetuoso; concienzudo.—**dutifully** [-i], *adv.* obedientemente,
respetuosamente; concienzudamente.—**duti-
fulness** [-nis], *s.* obediencia; respeto; escrupulosidad.
duty [djúti], *s.* deber, obligación; cargo, incumbencia, quehacer(es); obediencia, sumisión,
acatamiento; (mil.) facción, servicio; carga,
impuesto, adeudo, derechos de aduana o de
puertas; (mec.) trabajo, servicio; (mec.) rendimiento; (ing.) cantidad de agua necesaria para
el riego de un área dada (gen. 1 acre).—**d.-
free,** (com.) franco, libre de derechos.—**in d.
bound,** moralmente obligado.—**off d.,** libre.
—**on d.,** de guardia o de servicio.—**to do d.
for,** servir de, hacer las veces de.
duumvir [djuʌmvœ(r)], *s.* duunvir(o).
duumvirate [-rit], *s.* duunvirato.
dwale [dweil], *s.* (bot.) belladona.
dwarf [dwɔrf]. **I.** *s.* enano, pigmeo. **II.** *a.* diminuto, enano, pigmeo. **III.** *va.* impedir el crecimiento de; empequeñecer, achicar. **IV.** *vn.*
empequeñecerse, achicarse.
dwarfish [-iş], *a.* enano, pequeño, diminuto.—
dwarfishly [-li], *adv.* como un enano.—**dwarf-
ishness** [-nis], *s.* pequeñez de estatura, (e)na-
nismo.
dwell [dwél], *vn.* (*pret. y pp.* DWELT O DWELLED)
habitar, morar, residir, vivir; (con **on o upon**)
espaciarse (en), tratar (de).
dweller [-œ(r)], *s.* morador, habitante.
dwelling [-iŋ]. **I.** *s.* morada, residencia; casa,
domicilio, vivienda. **II.** *a.* de habitación.
dwindle [dwíndl]. **I.** *vn.* menguar, disminuirse;
degenerar; decaer; consumirse. **II.** *va.* mermar.
dyad [dáiæd]. **I.** *a.* (quím.) bivalente. **II.** *s.*
(quím.) díada, átomo o cuerpo bivalente.
dye [dái]. **I.** *s.* (*pp. y pret.* DYED; *ger.* DYEING)
teñir, tinturar, (en)tintar, colorar. **II.** *s.* tinte;
tintura; color, matiz, *m.*—**to d. in** (the) **grain,**
o **in the wool,** teñir (la lana) en rama.—**dyed-
in-the-wool,** acérrimo, intransigente.
dyehouse [-haus], *s.* tintorería.
dyeing [-iŋ]. **I.** *s.* tintorería; tinte, teñidura,
tintura. **II.** *a.* colorante.
dyer [-œ(r)], *s.* tintorero.—**d.'s broom,** (bot.)
ginesta, retama de tintes o de tintoreros.—**d.'s
shop,** tintorería, tinte.—**d.'s weed,** (bot.)
gualda.
dyestuff [-stʌf], *s.* materia de tinte.
dyewood [-wud], *s.* madera de tinte.
dying [dáiiŋ]. **I.** *ger.* de TO DIE. **II.** *a.* moribundo,
agonizante; morte cino; mortal. **III.** *s.* muerte, *f.*
dyke [daik], *s.* = DIKE.
dynameter [dainǽmetœ(r)], *s.* (ópt.) dinámetro.
dynamic(al [dainémik(al], *a.* dinámico; eficaz.
dynamics [-s], *s.* dinámica; mecánica (estática y
dinámica).
dynamism [dáinamizm], *s.* (filos.) dinamismo.—
dynamist [-ist], *s.* dinamista.
dynamite [dáinamait]. **I.** *s.* dinamita. **II.** *va.*
volar con dinamita.—**dynamiter** [-œ(r)], *s.*
dinamitero.
dynamo [dáinamou], *s.* (elec.) dínamo, *f.*,
generador.
dynamoelectric(al [-ilɛktrik(al], *a.* dinamoeléctrico.
dynamogenesis [-dźénesis], *s.* (psic.) dinamo-
génesis, actividad muscular debida a estimulación de los sentidos.

dynamometer [dainəmámɛtœ(r)], s. dinamómetro.

dynamometric(al [-mométrik(əl], a. dinamométrico.

dynast [dáinæst], s. dinasta, m.

dynastic(al [dainæstik(əl], a. dinástico.

dynasty [dáinəsti], s. dinastía.

dyne [dain], s. (fís.) dina (unidad de fuerza).

dyscrasia [diskréiʒiə], s. (med.) discrasia.

dysenteric [disɛntérik], a. disentérico.

dysentery [dísɛnteri], s. (med.) disentería.

dyspepsia [dispépsiə], s. (med.) dispepsia.

dyspeptic [dispéptik], a. y s. dispéptico; mórbido, quejoso; indigesto.

dysphagia [disféidʒiə], s. (med.) disfagia.

dysphasia [disféiʒiə], s. (med.) disfasia.

dysphonia [disfóuniə], s. (med.) disfonía.

dyspnea, dyspnœa [dispniə], s. (med.) disnea.

dyspneal, dyspneic [-l, dispnfik], a. disneico.

dysuria [disyúriə], s. (med.) disuria.

E

e [i], s. e; (mús., E) mi.

each [ich]. I. a. cada, todo. II. pron. cada uno, cada cual, todos.—**e. for himself,** cada cual por su cuenta, o por su lado.—**e. other,** mutuamente, el uno al otro; unos a otros. III. adv. por persona, por cabeza, cada cual.

eager [ígœ(r)], a. ansioso, anhelante, deseoso; vehemente, impaciente.—**eagerly** [-li], adv. ansiosamente, con anhelo, afanadamente.—**eagerness** [-nis], s. ansia, avidez, anhelo, afán, ahinco; vehemencia.

eagle [ígl], s. (orn.) águila; (E. U.) águila, moneda de oro ($10); (E., astr.) Águila.—**e. boat,** especie de cazasubmarinos.—**e.-eyed,** de ojo avizor, vista de lince.—**e. owl,** (orn.) buharro, curuca, curuja.—**e. ray,** (ict.) águila, m.

eaglet [íglit], s. (orn.) aguilucho.

eaglestone [íglstoun], s. (min.) etites.

eaglewood [-wud], s. (bot.) palo (de) áloe, palo de águila, agáloco, calambac.

ear [r]. I. s. (anat.) oreja, pabellón; oído; asa, asidero (de jarro, etc.); (bot.) mazorca; espiga.—**e. muff,** orejera.—**e.-piercing,** penetrante (sonido).—**e. trumpet,** trompetilla, cuerno acústico, (Am.) bocina.—**by e.,** de oído; de oídas.—**by the ears,** en pugna abierta.—**to be all ears,** (fam.) abrir tanto oído; aguzar los oídos o las orejas.—**to have a good e.,** tener buen oído (para la música).—**to have one's e.,** tener influencia con uno, gozar de su confianza.—**to set by the ears,** enemistar, malquistar.—**up to the ears,** (fam.) en calzas prietas. II. vn. espigar, (Am.) muñequear (el maíz, etc.).

earache [íreik], s. (med.) otalgia, dolor de oído.

eardrop [írdrap], s. arete con adorno colgante.

eardrum [írdrʌm], s. (anat.) tímpano (del oído).

eared [ird], a. espigado; en mazorca.

earflap [írflæp], s. orejera (para proteger las orejas).

earing [íriŋ], s. (mar.) empuñidura.

earl [œrl], s. conde.—**e.-marshal,** rey de armas.

earlap [írlæp], s. = EARFLAP; (anat.) lóbulo o perilla de la oreja; pabellón.

earldom [érldʌm], s. condado.

earless [írlis], a. desorejado.

earlier [érli(œ(r)], a. y adv. comp. de EARLY: más temprano, antes; anterior, antiguo.—**earliest** [érliest], a. y adv. super. de EARLY: más temprano; más antiguo, más remoto; antiguo, primitivo.

earliness [érlinis], s. precocidad, anticipación; presteza, prontitud; calidad de temprano.

early [érli]. I. a. primitivo; tempran(er)o; avanzado, precoz, anticipado; matinal; cercano, próximo.—**e. bird,** (fig.) madrugador; el que llega temprano.—**e. fruit,** fruto temprano.—**e. riser,** madrugador.—**e. rising,** madrugada.—**the e. part of,** el principio de. II. adv. temprano, tempranamente, antes de la hora; al principio.—**as e. as possible,** lo más pronto posible.—**e. in,** a principios de, a primeras horas de.—**to be e.,** llegar temprano.

earmark [írmark]. I. s. marca en la oreja; señal inequívoca. II. va. señalar, marcar el ganado en la oreja para identificarlo; asignar o destinar fondos, etc., para un fin particular.

earn [œrn], va. ganar; merecer; captarse; devengar.

earnest [érnist]. I. a. serio, formal; extremo, fervoroso; activo, celoso, diligente; atento, cuidadoso; grave, importante. II. s. seriedad, buena fe; arras, f. pl., caparra, prenda, señal, f. (ll. t. e. money).—**e. money,** caparra.—**in (good) e.,** de buena fe, en conciencia; en serio, con formalidad, resuelto a perseverar.

earnestly [-li], adv. seriamente, de veras; encarecidamente.—**earnestness** [-nis], s. seriedad, formalidad, buena fe, ahinco, veras, f. pl.

earnings [érniŋz], s. pl. salario, estipendio, jornal, paga; (com.) ganancias, ingresos.

earphone [írfoun], s. (tlf., rad.) auricular; audífono. V. HEADPHONE.

earpick [írpik], s. mondaoídos, escarbaorejas.

earpiece [írpis], s. (tlf.) auricular, receptor.

earring [íriŋ], s. pendiente, arete, zarcillo.

earshot [írʃat], s. alcance del oído.

earsplitting [írsplitiŋ], a. penetrante, ensordecedor.

earth [érθ]. I. s. tierra (globo terráqueo); orbe; suelo; mundo, gente, f.; madriguera (de zorra, etc.); (elec.) tierra; (quím.) óxido metálico terroso.—**e.-eating,** geófago. II. va. cubrir con tierra; (elec., rad.) conectar con tierra. III. vn. retirarse debajo de tierra.

earthboard [-bord], s. orejera del arado.

earthborn [-born], a. terrígeno; bajo, innoble.

earthen [-ɛn], a. térreo, terreno, terrizo; de barro.

earthenware [-wɛr], s. loza de barro, cacharros.

earthiness [-inis], s. terrosidad.

earthliness [-linis], s. terrenidad, mundanalidad.

earthling [-liŋ], s. habitante de la tierra, ser mortal; persona mundana.

earthly [-li], a. terreno, terrero; terrenal, mundano.

earthnut [-nʌt], s. (bot.) castañuela; chufa; trufa; cacahuete, (Am.) maní.

earthquake [-kweik], s. temblor de tierra, terremoto, sacudimiento terrestre.

earthward [-wärd], a. y adv. hacia la tierra.

earthwork [-wœrk], s. (fort. e ing.) terraplén.

earthworm [-wœrm], s. lombriz de tierra.

earthy [-i], a. terroso, terrizo; mundano; grosero.

earwax [írwæks], s. cerumen, cera de oído.

earwig [írwig], s. (ent.) tijereta, cortapicos.

earwitness [írwitnis], s. testigo auricular.

ease [iz]. I. s. tranquilidad; ocio, reposo; comodidad, alivio, descanso; holgura; facilidad, desembarazo o desenvoltura, naturalidad.—**at e.,** con desahogo, descansadamente, a sus anchas.—**with e.,** con facilidad. II. va. aliviar, mitigar, suavizar, aligerar, descargar, desembarazar, facilitar.—**to e. away, u off,** aflojar gradualmente; (mar.) amollar, lascar, arriar (cable, cadena).—**to e. nature, u one's self,** hacer del cuerpo.—**to e. of,** (fam.) quitar por la fuerza; robar. III. vn. disminuir, apaciguarse.

easel [ízɛl], s. caballete de pintor; atril.

easement [ízmɛnt], s. alivio, apoyo, descarga; (for.) servidumbre.

easily [ízili], adv. fácilmente, aína; sobradamente.

easiness [ízinis], s. facilidad; suavidad; holgura, comodidad; tranquilidad, quietud; despejo, desembarazo, soltura.

east [ist]. I. s. este, levante, oriente, (mar.) leste.—**the E.,** el Oriente, el Levante; el este (de los E. U.).—**e. wind,** (l)este, levante, oriente. II. a. oriental, de oriente, levantino; del este. III. adv. hacia el este.

Easter [ístœ(r)], s. Pascua florida o de Resurrección.—**E. day,** día de Pascua.—**E. eve, E.**

Saturday, Sábado Santo o de Pasión.—E. **Sunday,** Domingo de Resurrección.

easterly [ístœrlį], *a.* y *adv.* oriental, del este, al este; hacia el este.—**e. wind,** aire de levante, solano.

eastern [ístœrn], *a.* oriental, (astr.) ortivo.

Easterner [ístœrnœ(r)], *s.* oriental; habitante del este (de los E. U.).

Eastertide [ístœrtaįd], *s.* aleluya, *m.*, tiempo de Pascua.

eastward [ístwärd]. **I.** *a.* de o en dirección oriental o este. **II.** *adv.* hacia el este.

easy [ízį]. **I.** *a.* fácil; cómodo, holgado; acomodado; complaciente, condescendiente; accesible o asequible; suelto, libre; tranquilo; aliviado; simple, natural; suave; manual, mañero; quedo; (com.) flojo; abundante; (fam.) blanco, confiado, fácil de engañar.—**e. chair,** butaca, sillón, poltrona.—**e. going,** de movimiento fácil o suave; lento, despacioso; calmado, sereno, filosófico.—**e. labor,** parto feliz.—**on e. street,** (fam.) en buenas circunstancias, acomodado. **II.** *adv.* e *interj.* despacio, qued(it)o.

eat [ít]. **I.** *va.* (*pret.* ATE, *pp.* EATEN) comer; corroer; consumir.—**to e. away, into,** o **through,** corroer, destruir.—**to e. breakfast, lunch, dinner, supper,** desayunarse, almorzar, comer, cenar.—**to e. crow,** (fam.) tragarse, tragar saliva.—**to e. humble pie,** humillarse y dar excusas.—**to e. one's heart,** sufrir uno la amargura en silencio.—**to e. one's words,** retractarse, cantar la palinodia.—**to e. up,** devorar, tragar, comer completamente. **II.** *vn.* comer; alimentarse, sustentarse; (fam.) ser comible; saber (a). **III.** *s. pl.* (fam.) refrescos, comestibles.

eatable [ítąbl]. **I.** *a.* comestible, comedero. **II.** *s. pl.* comestibles, víveres, vituallas.

eater [ítœ(r)], *s.* comedor.

eating [ítįŋ]. **I.** *s.* la acción de comer; cosa de comer; comidas. **II.** *a.* de comer; corrosivo; consumidor.—**e. house,** restaurante, bodegón, figón.

eaves [ívz], *s. pl.* socarrén, alero, tejaroz, *m.*

eavesdrop [-drap]. **I.** *s.* estilicidio. **II.** *vn.* escuchar a las puertas, fisgonear.—**eavesdropper** [-œ(r)], *s.* el que escucha escondido.

ebb [εb]. **I.** *vn.* menguar la marea, desplayar; decaer, disminuir. **II.** *s.* (mar.) menguante, reflujo; decadencia.—**e. of life,** vejez.—**e. tide,** (mar.) marea menguante.

ebenaceous [ebɛnéįšʌs], *a.* (bot.) ebenáceo.

ebon [ébɒn], *a.* de ébano, negro.—**ebonist** [-įst], *s.* ebanista.

ebonite [-aįt], *s.* ebonita, vulcanita.—**ebonize** [-aįz], *va.* ebanizar, dar la apariencia del ébano.

ebony [-į], *s.* (bot.) ébano.

ebullience, ebulliency [ibʌ́lyɛns, -į], *s.* ebullición; entusiasmo.

ebullient [-ɛnt], *a.* hirviente; entusiasta.

ebullition [ebʌĺįšɒn], *s.* ebullición; (fig.) viva emoción o agitación; entusiasmo.

eburnated [ébœrneįtįd], *a.* (med.) endurecido como hueso.

eburnean [ibœ́rnįɛn], **eburneous** [-įʌs], *a.* ebúrneo, marfileño.

écarté [eįkartéį], *s.* ecarté, juego de naipes.

eccentric [iksɛ́ntrįk], *s.* persona excéntrica o rara; (mec.) excéntrica.

eccentric(al [-ąl], *a.* (geom. y mec.) excéntrico; extravagante, excéntrico, estrambótico, estrafalario, raro.

eccentrically [-į], *adv.* excéntricamente.

eccentricity [iksɛntrísįtį], *s.* excentricidad.

ecchymosis [ɛkįmóųsįs], *s.* (med.) equimosis, *mf.*, moretón, aporisma, *m.*

ecclesia [iklízią], *s.* (hist.) asamblea popular; iglesia, cuerpo de los fieles.

Ecclesiastes [iklizįéstįz], *s.* (bib.) Eclesiastés.

ecclesiastic(al [-ǽstįk(ąl], *a.* eclesiástico.— **ecclesiastic,** *s.* eclesiástico, clérigo.—**ecclesi-**

astically [-į], *adv.* eclesiásticamente.—**ecclesiasticism** [-ǽstįsįzm], *s.* clericalismo, espíritu eclesiástico.

Ecclesiasticus [-ǽstįkʌs], *s.* (bib.) Eclesiástico.

ecclesiolatry [-álątrį], *s.* devoción excesiva a la Iglesia y a sus ritos.

ecclesiology [-álodʒį], *s.* ciencia del arte, arquitectura y decorado de iglesias.

echelon [éšęlan]. **I.** *s.* (mil.) escalón. **II.** *va.* (mil.) escalonar.

echidna [ikídną], *s.* (zool.) equidna, *m.* (mamífero).

echinate(d [ékįneįt(įd], *a.* erizado.

echinococcus [įkaįnokákʌs], *s.* equinococo.

echinoderm [ikáįnodœrm], *a.* y *s.* equinodermo.

echinoid [įkáįnoįd], *a.* y *s.* (zool.) equinoideo.

echinus [įkáįnʌs], *s.* (arq.) equino, gallón; (zool.) erizo, equino.

echo [ékoų]. **I.** *s.* eco, retumbo; (mús.) eco (de órgano).—**e. sounder,** (mar.) sonda acústica.—**to the e.,** estrepitosamente. **II.** *vn.* formar eco, repercutir, resonar, reverberar. **III.** *va.* repetir con aprobación; imitar servilmente; hacer eco a.

echoic [ekóųįk], *a.* (filol.) ecoico; onomatopéyico.—**echoism** [ékoųįzm], *s.* onomatopeya.

éclair [eįklér], *s.* bollo de crema o de natas.

éclaircissement [eįklɛrsismán], *s.* aclaración, explicación, ilustración.

éclat [eįklá], *s.* esplendor, magnificencia; aclamación, aplauso; renombre, celebridad.

eclectic [įklɛ́ktįk], *s.* y *a.* ecléctico.

eclecticism [-sįzm], *s.* eclecticismo.

eclipse [įklíps]. **I.** *s.* eclipse. **II.** *va.* eclipsar.

ecliptic [įklíptįk]. **I.** *s.* (astr.) eclíptica. **II.** *a.* eclíptico.

eclogue [éklag], *s.* égloga, écloga.

ecologic(al [ɛkoládʒįk(ąl], *a.* ecológico.

ecology [įkálodʒį], *s.* (biol.) ecología, mesología; relación entre un organismo y su medio.

economic(al [ikonámįk(ąl], *a.* económico; moderado, módico (ú. de precios, etc.); frugal, parco.

economically [-ąlį], *adv.* económicamente.

economics [-s], *s.* economía política.

economist [įkánomįst], *s.* economista.—**economize** [-maįz], *va.* y *vn.* economizar, ahorrar, endurar.—**economy** [-mį], *s.* economía; ahorro.

écraseur [eįkrazœ́r], *s.* (cir.) triturador.

ecru, écru [ékru, éįkru]. **I.** *a.* crudo, sin blanquear. **II.** *s.* color de lino o seda sin blanquear; géneros de lino crudo.

ecstasied [ékstąsįd], *a.* extático.

ecstasy [ékstąsį], *s.* éxtasi(s), *m.*, rapto, transporte, embeles(amient)o, arrebat(amient)o, arrobamiento.—**ecstatic(al** [ɛkstǽtįk(ąl], *a.* extático.

ectasis [éktąsįs], *s.* (pros.) éctasis; (med.) ectasia.

ecthyma [ɛkθáįmą], *s.* (med.) ectima, *m.*

ectoblast, ectoderm [éktoblæst, -dœrm], *s.* (biol.) ectoblasto, ectodermo.—**ectodermal** [-dœrmąl], **ectodermic** [-įk], *a.* ectodérmico.

ectogenous [ɛktádʒɛnʌs], *a.* (bact.) ectógeno.

ectoparasite [ɛktopɛ́rąsąįt], *s.* ectoparásito.

ectopia [ɛktóųpįą], *s.* (med.) ectopia.

ectoplasm [éktoplæzm], *s.* (zool., biol., bot.) ectoplasma, *m.*; (espiritismo) emanación o exhalación que, según algunos, se desprende del cuerpo del médium.

ectropion, ectropium [ɛktróųpįɒn, -pįʌm], *s.* (med.) ectropión, *m.*, inversión de los párpados.

Ecuadorian [ɛkwądórįąn], *a.* y *s.* ecuatoriano.

ecumenical [ɛkyuménįkąl], *a.* ecuménico.

eczema [ékzįmą], *s.* (med.) eczema.

eczematous [ɛkzémątąs], *a.* eczematoso.

edacious [įdéįšąs], *a.* voraz.—**edaciousness** [-nįs], **edacity** [įdǽsįtį], *s.* voracidad, glotonería.

eddy [édį]. **I.** *s.* remolino.—**e. current,** (elec.) corriente (*f.*) de Foucault, corriente parásita. **II.** *vn.* remolinar. **III.** *va.* remolinear.

edelweiss [éįdęlvaįs], *s.* (bot.) planta alpina.

edema [idímá], s. (med.) edema, m.

edematous [idémátas], a. (med.) edematoso.

Eden [ídęn], s. Edén.

Edentata [identéitá], s. (zool.) desdentados.

edentate [idénteit], a. desdentado.

edge [édž]. **I.** s. filo, corte; canto; borde, orilla, margen, mf., arcén; ribete; ventaja.—**e. tool,** herramienta o instrumento de filo.—**on e.,** de canto; impaciente, irritable; ansioso, perturbado.—**to have the e. on,** llevar ventaja a.—**to set the teeth on e.,** dar dentera. **II.** va. afilar, aguzar; (a menudo con *on*) aguijonear, incitar; (cost.) orlar, ribetear, guarnecer; abrirse (paso) marchando de lado. **III.** vn. avanzar de lado, escurrirse.

edged [-d], a. afilado, cortante.

edgeless [-lis], a. embotado, obtuso; sin filo.

edgeways, edgewise [-wejz, -wajz], adv. de filo o de canto, de lado o sesgo.

edging [-iņ], s. orla(dura), orilla, ribete, trepado, pestaña, guarnición.

edibility [edibíliti], **edibleness** [édiblnis], s. calidad de comestible.

edible [édibl], a. y s. comestible.

edict [ídjkt], s. edicto, decreto, mandato, orden(amiento); ordenación; ordenanza, bando; auto.

edification [edifikéišǫn], s. edificación.

edificatory [édifikatǫri], a. edificativo, edificante.

edifice [édifis], s. edificio.

edifier [édifaiœ(r)], s. edificante, edificador.

edify [édifaj], va. edificar; instruir.

edifying [-iņ], a. edificante, edificativo.—**edifyingly** [-li], adv. edificantemente, ejemplarmente.

edile [ídajl], s. V. AEDILE.

edit [édjt], va. redactar; dirigir (un periódico); corregir.

editing [-iņ], s. redacción; corrección.

edition [idíšǫn], s. edición; impresión; tirada.

editor [éditǫ(r)], s. redactor, compilador; director de un periódico o revista, etc.—**e. in chief,** jefe de redacción, redactor (en) jefe.

editorial [editórjal]. **I.** a. editorial.—**e. rooms** o **staff,** redacción.—**e. writer,** editorialista. **II.** s. editorial, artículo de fondo.

editorialize [-ajz]. **I.** va. escribir críticamente acerca de, en estilo de editorial. **II.** vn. (con *about* u *on*) escribir un editorial acerca de.

editorship [éditǫršip], s. cargo de redactor; dirección de un periódico.

educable [édžukabl], a. educable.

educate [édžukeit], va. educar, instruir, enseñar, doctrinar, dirigir, disciplinar, dar crianza a.

education [-éišǫn], s. educación, enseñanza, instrucción, crianza; ilustración, cultura.

educational [-al], a. docente; cultural; de enseñanza; educativo, (Am.) educacional.—**e. institution,** plantel.

educationalist [-alist], **educationist** [-ist], s. pedagogo, persona versada en asuntos de educación, educador, educacionista.

educative [édžukeitiv], a. educativo, educador.

educator [-keitǫ(r)], s. educador, pedagogo.

educe [idjús], va. educir; sacar, extraer.

eduction [idákšǫn], s. educción; (m. v.) = EXHAUST.

edulcorate [idálkoreit], va. (quím.) edulcorar, dulzurar, endulzar.—**edulcoration** [-éišǫn], s. edulcoración, dulcificación.—**edulcorative** [-iv], a. dulcificante.

eel [íl], s. (ict.) anguila, (Am.) anguilla.

eelpot [-pat], s. nasa para anguilas.

eelpout [-paut], s. (ict.) zoarces. V. BURBOT.

e'en [in], adv. contracción de EVEN.

e'er [er], adv. contracción de EVER.

eerie, eery [íri], a. pavoroso, misterioso; atemorizado.

efface [eféjs], va. borrar, raspar, destruir, tachar.

effaceable [-abl], a. deleble, que puede borrarse.—**effacement** [-męnt], s. tachón, raspadura.

effect [efékt]. **I.** s. efecto; impresión; eficacia,

eficiencia; tenor, significado, substancia; fuerza, vigor, operación; realización, cumplimiento.— pl. efectos, bienes, caudal.—**for e.,** para causar efecto.—**in e.,** en operación, vigente; en substancia, en realidad (nunca *en efecto,* en el razonamiento).—**into e.,** en vigor, en vigencia, en práctica, en operación.—**of no e.,** sin resultado, vano.—**to take e.,** salir bien, producir su efecto; ponerse en vigor.—**to the e. that,** de que, en el sentido de que. **II.** va. efectuar, realizar, ejecutar, llevar a cabo.

effecter [-œ(r)], s. causador, hacedor.

effective [-iv]. **I.** a. efectivo, eficaz; vigente, en vigor; de buen efecto, que causa buena impresión; real, verdadero; (mec.) útil, efectivo.—**e. weight,** peso útil.—**to make e.,** llevar a efecto; hacer cumplir. **II.** s. (com. y e. p.) metálico, numerario; (mil.) (gen. pl.) soldados o marineros disponibles para el servicio; ejército.—**effectively** [-li], adv. eficazmente.—

effectiveness [-nis], s. eficacia, eficiencia, efectividad.

effectless [-lis], a. ineficaz; sin resultado.

effectual [efékchual], a. eficaz.—**effectually** [-i], adv. eficazmente; efectivamente, de hecho.

effectuate [-chueit], va. efectuar, ejecutar.

effeminacy [eféminási], **effeminateness** [-itnis], s. afeminamiento, afeminación, molicie.

effeminate [eféminit], a. afeminado, adamado, amujerado, barbilindo.—**to make o become e.,** afeminar(se), adamarse.

effeminately [-li], adv. afeminadamente.

effendi [eféndi], s. efendi, título turco.

efferent [éfęrent], a. (fisiol.) eferente.

effervesce [efœrvés], vn. hervir, fermentar, estar en efervescencia.—**effervescence** [-ęns], s. efervescencia.—**effervescent** [-ęnt], a. efervescente.

effete [efít], a. usado, gastado, cascado; estéril, infructuoso.

efficacious [efikéiǎs], a. eficaz.—**efficaciously** [-li], adv. eficazmente.—**efficaciousness** [-nis], s.

efficacy [éfikasi], s. eficacia, eficiencia; fuerza, validez, virtud, virtualidad.

efficiency [efišęnsi], s. eficacia; eficiencia; fuerza, virtud; habilidad, competencia; economía; (mec.) rendimiento.

efficient [-ęnt], a. eficiente, eficaz, competente; (mec.) de gran rendimiento.

efficiently [-li], adv. eficientemente; eficazmente; con buen rendimiento.

effigy [éfidži], s. efigie, retrato, imagen, f.—**to burn** o **hang in e.,** quemar o ahorcar en efigie.

effloresce [eflorés], vn. florecer(se), echar flor; (quím.) eflorecerse.

efflorescence, efflorescency [-ęns, -i], s. eflorescencia; (med.) roncha; erupción; (bot.) florescencia.—**efflorescent** [-ęnt], a. (quím.) eflorescente; (bot.) en flor.

effluence [éfluęns], s. emanación, efluvio; efusión; emanación.—**effluent** [-ęnt]. **I.** a. efluente. **II.** s. líquido que sale.

effluvium [eflúvjam], s. efluvio, exhalación, emanación, tufo, vaho.

efflux [éflaks], s. efusión, emanación; flujo, derrame.—**effluxion** [efláksǫn], s. emanación, efluvio, exhalación, eflución.

effort [éfǫrt], s. esfuerzo, conato, empeño, gestión.

effortless [-lis], a. sin esfuerzo, fácil.

effrontery [efrántœri], s. desfachatez, impudencia, descaro, desvergüenza.

effulge [efáldž], va. y vn. lucir, brillar, resplandecer.

effulgence [-ęns], s. esplendor, fulgor, brillantez.—**effulgent** [-ęnt], a. resplandeciente, refulgente.

effuse [efjúz]. **I.** va. derramar, verter, esparcir, efundir. **II.** vn. emanar. **III.** a. (bot.) esparcido.

effusion [efjúžǫn], s. efusión, derrame; expansión; desahogo.

effusive [efjúsiv], a. expansivo, comunicativo, demostrativo.—**effusively** [-li], adv. demostrativamente, ardientemente.—**effusiveness** [-nįs], *s.* ardor o pasión.

eft [eft], *s.* (zool.) lagartija (acuática). *V.* NEWT.

egest [įdʒést], *va.* excretar, expeler.—**egesta** [-ǎ], *s. pl.* excremento.—**egestion** [įdʒéschǫn], *s.* defecación.

egg [ég]. I. *s.* huevo, postura, (Méx.) blanquillo. —**e. beater**, batidor de huevos.—**e. cell**, (biol.) célula reproductiva o embrionaria, huevo.—**e. coal**, antracita gruesa.—**e. cup**, huevera.—**e. dealer**, huevero.—**e. glass**, reloj de arena de 3 minutos para hervir huevos; huevera de vidrio.—**e.-laying**, *a.* ovíparo, ponedor, ponedero.—**e. laying**, *s.* postura.— **e.-shaped**, oviforme.—**e. stand**, huevera.— **e. store**, huevería.—**bad e.**, huevo podrido; (fam.) mala persona. II. *va.* (coc.) mezclar o cubrir con huevo; (E. U.) arrojar huevos a una persona; (seguido de **on**) hurgar, incitar, provocar. III. *vn.* coleccionar huevos de aves.

eggnog [-nag], *s.* ponche de huevo; yema mejida.

eggplant [-plænt], *s.* (bot.) berenjena.

eggshell [-šel], *s.* cáscara de huevo, cascarón.— **e. china**, loza muy fina.

egis, ægis [ídʒįs], *s.* égida, escudo.

eglantine [églạntạįn], *s.* (bot.) eglantina; escaramujo, agavanzo, galabardera, zarzarrosa.

ego [ígoų], *s.* (filos.) el yo.

egocentric [-séntrįk], *s.* y *a.* egocéntrico.

egoism [ígoųįzm], *s.* egoísmo.—**egoist** [-įst], *s.* egoísta.—**egoistic** [-įstįk], *a.* egoísta.—**egotism** [ígoųtįzm], *s.* egotismo, egolatría.—**egotist** [-įst], *s.*, **egotistic(al** [-įstįk(ǎl], *a.* egotista, ególatra.—**egotize** [-ạįz], *vn.* hablar o escribir mucho de sí mismo.

egregious [įgrídʒʌs], *a.* egregio; (desp.) extraordinario, insigne, estupendo, atroz, escandaloso.— **egregiously** [-lį], *adv.* egregiamente.

egress [ígres], **egression** [įgréšǫn], *s.* salida.

egret [ígret], *s.* moño, penacho, plumero; (orn.) airón.

Egyptian [įdʒípšạn], *a.* y *s.* egipci(an)o, egipcíaco, egiptano; gitano.

Egyptologist [įdʒįptálodʒįst], *s.* egiptólogo.

Egyptology [-dʒį], *s.* egiptología.

eh [eį], *interj.* ¿qué? ¿eh? ¿no?

eider, eider duck [áįdœ(r), -dʌk], *s.* (orn.) pato de flojel, eidero.—**e. down** [-daųn], edredón, plumazón, plumón; colcha de edredón.

eidograph [áįdogræf], *s.* = PANTOGRAPH.

eidolon [aįdóųlạn], *s.* representación, imagen, *f.*; fantasma, *m.*

eight [eįt], *a.* y *s.* ocho.—**e. hundred(th**, ochocientos.—**e.-sided**, octágono, ochavado.— **eighteen** [éįtín], *a.* y *s.* diez y ocho, dieciocho. —**eighteenth** [-θ], *a.* décimoctavo; dieciochavo; dieciocho (ordinal).

eightfold [éįtfoųld], *a.* óctuple, ocho veces tanto.

eighth [eįtθ], *a.* y *s.* octavo.

eightieth [éįtįeθ], *a.* octogésimo; ochenta (ordinal); ochentavo.

eighty [éįtį], *a.* y *s.* ochenta.

either [íðœ(r)]. I. *a.* y *pron.* uno u otro, cualquiera de los dos; uno y otro, ambos, entrambos. II. *conj.* o. III. *adv.* (después de *not, nor*) tampoco.

ejaculate [įdʒ&kyųleįt], *va.* exclamar, proferir; (fisiol.) eyacular.

ejaculation [-éįšǫn], *s.* jaculatoria (oración); exclamación; (fisiol.) eyaculación.

ejaculatory [-ạtorį], *a.* jaculatorio.

eject [įdʒékt], *va.* arrojar, lanzar, expeler, echar.

ejecta [-ǎ], *s. pl.* materias expelidas.

ejection [įdʒékšǫn], *s.* expulsión, evacuación.

ejectment [įdʒéktmạnt], *s.* (for.) desahucio; expulsión, exclusión.

ejector [įdʒéktǫ(r)], *s.* expulsador; (armas) eyector; (mec.) bomba de chorro (ll. t. **e. pump**).

eke [ík], *va.* (gen. con **out**) suplir lo que falta a; ganar (la vida) a duras penas.

elaborate [įlǽboreįt]. I. *va.* labrar, elaborar. II.

[įlǽborįt], *a.* elaborado, trabajado, detallado, primoroso; esmerado; estudiado.—**elaborately** [-lį], *adv.* primorosamente, con muchos detalles. —**elaborateness** [-nįs], *s.* esmero, perfección.— **elaboration** [-éįšǫn], *s.* elaboración; obra acabada.—**elaborative** [įlǽborạtįv], *a.* elaborativo. —**elaborator** [-eįtǫ(r)], *s.* elaborador; artífice.

eland [ílạnd], *s.* (zool.) grande antílope sudafricano.

elapse [įlǽps], *vn.* mediar, pasar, transcurrir.

elastic [įlǽstįk]. I. *a.* elástico.—**e. gum**, caucho. —**e. limit**, (tecn.) límite elástico; (com.) límite variable de emisión (de un banco).—**e. webbing**, elástico. II. *s.* cinta de goma, faja o tira de caucho.

elasticity [įlæstįsįtį], *s.* elasticidad.

elate [įléįt], *va.* exaltar, endiosar; alborozar; engreír, ensoberbecer.—**elated** [-įd], *a.* exaltado, triunfante, gozoso, alborozado.—**elatedly** [-lį], *adv.* exaltadamente, triunfantemente.

elaterin [elǽterįn], *s.* (quím.) elaterina.

elaterium [elạtíríạm], *s.* (bot.) elaterio; (farm.) purgante extraído del jugo de esta planta.

elation [įléįšǫn], *s.* júbilo, elación.

elbow [élboų]. I. *s.* codo; recodo, ángulo, codillo; brazo de sillón.—**e. grease**, (fam.) trabajo asiduo.—**e. pipe**, codo, tubo acodado.—**e. rest**, ménsula.—**at one's e.**, a la mano, muy cerca.—**out at e.**, andrajoso.—**up to the elbows**, hasta los codos. II. *va.* dar codazos; dar de(ll codo.—**to e. one's way**, abrirse paso codeando. III. *vn.* codear; formar recodos o ángulos.

elbowchair [-chœr], *s.* silla de brazos, poltrona.

elbowed [-d], *a.* acodado.

elbowroom [-rum], *s.* espacio suficiente; amplia oportunidad; libertad de acción.

elder [éldœ(r)]. I. *a. comp. irr.* de OLD: mayor, de más edad, más viejo; antiguo, anterior (ú. de tiempos, etc.).—**Pliny the E.**, Plinio el Viejo. II. *s.* anciano; señor mayor; jefe de tribu o familia; dignatario; funcionario eclesiástico, presbítero; (bot.) saúco, yezgo.—*pl.* ancianos, mayores, antepasados.

elderberry [-berį], *s.* (bot.) baya del saúco.

elderly [-lį], *a.* mayor, de edad madura o avanzada.—**an e. man**, un señor mayor.—**eldership** [-šįp], *s.* ancianidad; primogenitura presbiterado.

eldest [éldįst], *a. super.* de OLD: el mayor, primogénito.

Eleatic [eljǽtįk], *s.* y *a.* (fil.) eleático.

elecampane [elįkæmpéįn], *s.* (bot.) énula campana, olivarda.

elect [įlékt]. I. *va.* elegir, escoger, sacar (por votación). II. *a.* y *s.* (gen. *pl.*) electo o elegido; escogido, predestinado.—**bishop-e.**, obispo electo.

election [įlékšǫn], *s.* elección; (teol.) predestinación.

electioneer [-ŕ], *vn.* (pol.) solicitar votos; hacer campaña electoral.

elective [įléktįv], *a.* electivo; facultativo (curso, etc.).—**electively** [-lį], *adv.* electivamente.

elector [įléktǫ(r)], *s.* elector.

electoral [-ạl], *a.* electoral.—**e. college**, (E. U.) colegio electoral, asamblea de electores que elige al presidente.

electorate [-it], *s.* electorado; cuerpo o distrito electoral.

electric(al [įléktrįk(ạl], *a.* eléctrico; electricista; (fig.) vivo, fogoso, magnético; conmovedor, emocionante, excitante.—**e. balance**, puente de Wheatstone; electrómetro de balanza.—**e. bulb**, bombilla.—**e. cable**, cable conductor o e.—**e. candle**, bujía e., bujía de Jablochkoff. —**e. car**, tranvía e.—**e. chair**, silla e. o de electrocución.—**e. cooker**, cocina e.—**e. column**, pila voltaica.—**e. drill**, taladro o taladradora e.—**e. eel**, (ict.) gimnoto.—**e. engineer**, ingeniero electricista.—**e. engineering**, electrotecnia, ingeniería electricista.—e. eye, célula o tubo fotoeléctrico.—e. fan, ventilador e.—e. fish, pez e.—e. fixtures, instalación e. —e. furnace, horno e.—e. generator, generador e., dínamo, f.—e. heating, calefacción e. —e. heating pad, almohadilla e.—e. horn, bocina e.—e. light, luz e.—e. lighting, alumbrado e.—e. meter, contador de electricidad. —e. motor, electromotor, motor e.—e. plant, instalación e.—e. power, energía o fuerza e.— e. powerhouse, central, f.—e. ray, torpedo, tremielga.—e. refrigerator, nevera e., heladera automática.—e. rings, anillos de Nobili. —e. seal, piel de conejo a imitación de foca.— e. starter, (aut.) arranque e.—e. steel, acero hecho en el horno eléctrico.—e. switch, interruptor e.—e. tape, cinta aisladora o de aislamiento.—e. toaster, tostador e.—e. transcription, radiodifusión de un disco fonográfico especial; el disco mismo.—e. vane, o whirl, molinete e.—e. varnish, barniz aislador.—e. wave, onda e. o herziana.—e. welding, soldadura e.—e. wiring, instalación e.

electrically [-i], adv. por electricidad.—e.-controlled u operated, con o de mando eléctrico. —e.-heated, con calefacción eléctrica.

electrician [ilektríʃən], s. electricista.

electricity [-tríziti], s. electricidad.

electrification [ilɛ́ktrifikéiʃən], s. electrización; electrificación (aplicación de energía eléctrica a un f. c., etc.).

electrify [-fai], va. electrizar; electrificar (un ferrocarril, etc.); (fig.) avivar, inflamar el ánimo.

electrize [ilɛ́ktraiz], va. electrizar.—electrization [-trizéiʃən], s. electrización.—electrizer [ilɛ́ktraizœ(r)], s. electrizador.

electrobus [ilɛ́ktrobʌs], s. electrobús.

electrochemical [-kémikəl], a. electroquímico.

electrochemistry [-kémistri], s. electroquímica.

electrocute [ilɛ́ktrokjut], va. electrocutar.— electrocution [-kjúʃən], s. electrocución.

electrode [ilɛ́ktroud], s. electrodo.

electrodeposit [-dipázit], I. va. depositar electrolíticamente. II. s. deposición electrolítica. —electrodeposition [-depozíʃən], s. deposición electrolítica, galvanoplastia.

electrodynamic [-dainémik], a. electrodinámico.

electrodynamics, [-s], s. electrodinámica.

electrodynamometer [-dainamámetœ(r)], s. electrodinamómetro.

electrograph [-græf], s. electrógrafo, telégrafo registrador; gráfico de funcionamiento de un electromotor; cámara cinematográfica de luz de arco; radiografía.

electrokinetic [-kinétik], a. electrodinámico o electrocinético.—electrokinetics [-s], s. electrocinética, electrodinámica.

electrolier [-lír], s. candelabro o araña de lámparas eléctricas.

electrolysis [ilektrálisis], s. (quím.) electrólisis.

electrolyte [ilɛ́ktrolait], s. (quím.) electrólito.

electrolytic [-lítik], a. electrolítico.

electrolyzation [-izéiʃən], s. electrolización.

electrolyze [laiz], va. electrolizar.

electrolyzer [-œ(r)], s. electrolizador; (cir.) instrumento para el tratamiento electrolítico de la estrechez uretral.

electromagnet [-mægnit], s. (fís.) electroimán.

electromagnetic [-mægnétik], a. (elec.) electromagnético.

electromagnetism [-mægnetizm], s. electromagnetismo.

electrometallurgy [-métəlœrdʒi], s. electrometalurgia.

electrometer [ilektrámetœ(r)], s. electrómetro.

electrometric(al [-métrik(əl], a. electrométrico.

electrometry [ilektrámetri], s. electrometría.

electromotion [-móuʃən], s. circulación de una corriente eléctrica; movimiento producido por energía eléctrica.

electromotive [-móutiv], a. electromotor, electromotriz.—e. force, fuerza electromotriz.

electromotor [-móutor], s. motor eléctrico, electromotor.

electron [ilɛ́ktran], s. (fís. y quím.) electrón. V. ELECTRUM.—e. microscope, microscopio electrónico.—e. tube, (elec.) tubo de vacío; (rad.) tubo termiónico, válvula.—electronic [-tránik], a. electrónico.—electronics [-s], s. electrónica.

electronegative [ilektronégativ], a. electronegativo.

electropathy [ilektrápəθi], s. (med.) electroterapia.

electrophorus [-tráforʌs], s. (fís.) electróforo.

electrophysiology [ilektrofizjálodʒi], s. electrofisiología.

electroplate [-pleit], I. va. galvanizar. II. s. artículo galvanizado.—electroplating [-iŋ], s. galvanoplastia.

electropositive [-pázitiv], a. y s. electropositivo.

electropuncturation [-pʌŋktjuréiʃən], s. (cir.) electropuntura.

electroscope [-skoup], s. (fís.) electroscopio.

electrostatic [-stætik], a. electrostático.—electrostatics [-s], s. electrostática.

electrotechnics [-tékniks], s. electrotecnia.

electrotherapeutic(al [-θerəpjútik(əl], a. electroterápico.—electrotherapeutics [-s], electrotherapy [-θérəpi], s. electroterapia.

electrotonus [ilektrátonʌs], s. (fisiol.) cambio producido en un nervio por la corriente eléctrica.

electrotype [-taip], I. s. electrotipo; impresión de dicho grabado. II. va. electrotipar, reproducir por la electrotipia.—electrotyper [-taipœ(r)], s. el que hace electrotipos; baño para la electrotipia.—electrotypic [-típik], a. electrotípico.—electrotypy [-taipi], electrotyping [-taipiŋ], s. electrotipia, galvanoplastia.

electrum [ilɛ́ktrʌm], electron [ilɛ́ktran], s. plata alemana; oro argentífero; electro.

electuary [ilɛ́kchueri], s. (farm.) confección, electuario.

eleemosynary [elimásineri], a. caritativo; de caridad; que deriva o vive de limosna.

elegance, elegancy [éligəns, -i], s. elegancia.

elegant [-ənt], a. elegante.—elegantly [-li], adv. elegantemente, galanamente.

elegiac [elidʒáiæk], s. verso o poema elegíaco.

elegiac(al [-(əl], a. elegíaco.

elegize [élidʒaiz], va. y vn. hacer una elegía; lamentar, deplorar.

elegy [élidʒi], s. elegía, epicedio.

element [élimənt], s. elemento; componente, ingrediente; medio ambiente, centro, esfera de acción; celdilla o unidad morfológica; (elec.) elemento, par; (quím.) cuerpo simple.—pl. nociones, elementos, principios, rudimentos; intemperie; naturaleza, agentes naturales; los cuatro elementos (tierra, aire, fuego y agua); (igl.) el pan y el vino de la misa.—to be in one's e., estar en su centro o elemento.

elemental [eliméntəl], elementary [-təri], a. elemental, primordial, rudimentario.—elementary school, escuela primaria.

elemi [élimi], s. elemí.

elephant [élifənt], s. (zool.) elefante.

elephantiasis [elifæntáiəsis], s. (med.) elefancía, elefantíasis.

elephantine [elifæntin], a. elefantino.

Eleusinian [elyusíniən], a. eleusino.

elevate [éliveit], va. elevar; alzar, levantar, encumbrar, exaltar; animar, alegrar; inspirar.

elevated [-id], I. a. elevado, alzado, excelso, levantado, encumbrado, exaltado.—e. railroad, ferrocarril aéreo o elevado. II. s. (fam.) = E. RAILROAD.

elevation [elivéiʃən], s. elevación; exaltación, encumbramiento; altura; eminencia; alteza; (top.) cota; (dib.) alzado, proyección vertical;

(igl.) elevación (de la hostia; ll. t. **E. of the Host**).

elevator [élịveịtǫ(r)], s. ascensor; montacargas; elevador (esp. de granos); almacén o depósito de granos; noria; (aer.) timón de profundidad o elevador.—**e. operator**, ascensorista.—**e. shaft**, caja o pozo de ascensor.

eleven [ịléven], a. y s. once.

eleventh [-θ]. I. a. onceno, undécimo, once (ordinal).—**at the e. hour**, al último momento. II. s. y a. onzavo.

elf [élf], s. (pl. ELVES) elfo, duende, trasgo, hada, peri, f.; diablillo; enano.

elfin [-ịn]. I. a. de duendes. II. s. duendecillo; diablillo; niño travieso.

elfish [-ịš], a. aduendado, fantástico; travieso.

elfland [-lænd], s. tierra de las hadas, etc.

elflock [-lạk], s. greña de pelo.

elicit [ịlịsịt], va. (son)sacar, educir, atraer; producir, despertar.

elide [ịláịd], va. (gram.) elidir; (for.) anular.

eligibility [elịdžịbịlịtị], s. elegibilidad.

eligible [élịdžịbl], a. y s. elegible, preferible, deseable.—**eligibleness** [-nịs], s. elegibilidad.

eligibly [-blị], adv. de modo elegible.

eliminate [ịlímịneịt], va. eliminar, suprimir, quitar, prescindir de.—**elimination** [-éịšǫn], s. eliminación; supresión.—**eliminator**, (**-ing**) [-ǫ(r), -ịŋ], a. y s. eliminador.—**eliminatory** [-ạtǫrị], a. eliminatorio.

elision [ịlịžǫn], s. (gram.) elisión.

elite [eịlít], s. lo selecto, lo mejor, la flor y nata.

elixir [ịlịksœ(r)], s. elixir, elíxir; cordial, tónico.

Elizabethan [ịlịzabíθạn], a. isabelino (apl. esp. a la reina Isabel de Inglaterra o su tiempo).

elk [elk], s. (zool.) alce o anta; (N. A.) uapití.

ell [el], s. ana (medida de longitud); cualquier cosa en forma de L (ú. esp. de las alas de un edificio).

ellipse [elíps], s. (geom.) elipse, f.

ellipsis [elípsịs], s. (gram.) elipsis, eclipsis.

ellipsoid [elípsǫịd], s. (geom.) elipsoide.

ellipsoidal [elịpsóịdạl], a. elipsoidal.

elliptic(al [elịptịk(ạl], a. elíptico.

elliptically [-ị], adv. elípticamente.

elm [élm], s. (bot.) olmo.

elmy [-ị], a. ulmáceo.

elocution [elǫkịúšǫn], s. elocución; declamación.

elocutionary [-erị], a. declamatorio.

elocutionist [-ịst], s. declamador.

elongate [ịlóŋgeịt]. I. va. alargar; extender. II. vn. alargarse, prolongarse. III. a. = ELONGATED.

elongated [-ịd], a. alargado, extendido; apaisado.

elongation [-éịšǫn], s. alargamiento, prolongación; extensión; (astr.) elongación.

elope [ịlóụp], vn. fugarse con un amante; escapar, huir, evadirse.—**elopement** [-mẹnt], s. fuga.

eloquence [élǫkwẹns], s. elocuencia, oratoria, facundia, (fam.) labia.—**eloquent** [-ẹnt], a. elocuente.—**eloquently** [-lị], adv. elocuentemente.

else [éls]. I. a. otro; más.—**anything e.**, algo más; cualquiera otra cosa.—**nobody e., no one e.**, ningún otro.—**nothing e.**, nada más. —**what e.?**, ¿qué más?—**who e.?**, ¿quién más? II. adv. y conj. más, además; en vez de.—**or e.**, o bien, o en su lugar, de otro modo, en otro caso; si no.—**how e.?**, ¿de qué otro modo?

elsewhere [-hwer], adv. en, a o de otra parte.

elucidate [ịlịúsịdeịt], va. elucidar, dilucidar, aclarar, explanar, ilustrar.—**elucidation** [-déịšǫn]. s. elucidación, dilucidación, explanación, ilustración.—**elucidative, elucidatory** [-deịtịv, -dạtǫrị], a. dilucidador, explicativo.—**elucidator** [-deịtǫ(r)], s. dilucidador, expositor.

elude [ịlịúd], va. eludir, evadir, esquivar, evitar, sortear, su(b)straerse (a), dar esquinazo (a).

eludible [-ịbl], a. eludible, evitable.

elusion [ịlịúžǫn], s. evasión, escapatoria, fuga; esquinazo; fraude.

elusive [ịlịúsịv], **elusory** [ịlịúsǫrị], a. evasivo, esquivo, fugaz.

elution [ịlịúšǫn], **elutriation** [ịlịútrịéịšǫn], s. (quím.) levigación.—**elutriate** [-eịt], va. levigar.

elver [élvœ(r)], s. (ict.) angula, anguila joven.

elves [elvz], s. pl. de ELF.—**elvish**, a. = ELFISH.

Elysian [ịlịžịạn], a. ameno, delicioso.—**E. fields**, campos elíseos.

elytron, elytrum [élịtran, -trʌm], s. (ent.) élitro.

Elzevir [élzẹvịr], a. elzeviriano.

em [em], s. eme, f., nombre de la letra M; (impr.) eme, unidad de medida.

'em [em], pron. pl. (fam.) elisión de THEM.

emaciate [ịméịšịeịt]. I. va. extenuar, adelgazar. II. vn. enflaquecer(se).—**emaciate(d** [-(id], a. enflaquecido, flaco; (med.) extenuado.—**to be emaciated**, estar en los huesos.—**emaciation** [-éịšǫn], s. emaciación, enflaquecimiento, demacración, extenuación, acabamiento.

emanant [émạnạnt], a. emanante.—**emanate** [émạneịt], vn. emanar, derivar(se), proceder.— **emanation** [-éịšǫn], s. emanación, exhalación, efluvio, gas, tufo.—**emanative** [émạnạtịv], a. emanante.

emancipate [ịmǽnsịpeịt], va. emancipar; libertar, manumitir.—**emancipation** [-éịšǫn], s. emancipación; manumisión.—**emancipationist** [-ịst], a. y s. antiesclavista.—**emancipator** [-tǫ(r)], s. emancipador, libertador.

emarginate [ịmárdžịneịt]. I. va. quitar el margen, recortar. II. a. (bot.) recortado.

emasculate [ịmǽskyụleịt]. I. va. castrar, capar; afeminar, enervar; mutilar. II. a. afeminado; viciado; castrado.—**emasculation** [-léịšǫn], s. castradura, castración, afeminación; mutilación.

embalm [embám], va. embalsamar, conservar; (poét.) perfumar.—**embalmer** [-œ(r)], s. embalsamador.—**embalmment** [-ẹnt], s. embalsamamiento.

embank [embǽŋk], va. represar, terraplenar.

embankment [-mẹnt], s. malecón, riba, presa, dique; terraplén.

embargo [embárgǫu]. I. s. embargo, detención; prohibición. II. va. embargar, detener.

embark [embárk], va. y vn. (mar.) embarcar(se); aventurarse o lanzarse (a una política o empresa).

embarkation, embarcation [-éịšǫn], s. embarco; embarque.

embarrass [embǽrạs], va. turbar, aturdir, desconcertar; poner en aprieto; estorbar, embarazar.

embarrassment [-mẹnt], s. turbación, perturbación, perplejidad; compromiso; embarazo, estorbo; (com.) apuros, dificultades.

embassador [embǽsạdǫ(r)] = AMBASSADOR.

embassy [émbạsị], s. embajada.

embay [embéị], va. encerrar o abrigar (una armada) en una bahía; (fig.) rodear.

embattle [embǽtl], va. (mil.) formar en batalla; (fort.) almenar.—**embattled** [-d], a. en orden de batalla; ocupado por combatientes; (fort. y blas.) almenado.—**embattlement** [-mẹnt], s. almena; almenaje.

embed [embéd], va. encajar, encastrar, meter, enclavar, empotrar.—**embedment** [-mẹnt], s. empotramiento, encaje, enclavadura.

embellish [embélịš], va. hermosear, embellecer. —**embellishment** [-mẹnt], s. embellecimiento.

ember [émbœ(r)], s. ascua, pavesa, chispa.—pl. rescoldo.—**e. days**, (igl.) cuatro témporas.

embezzle [embézl], va. desfalcar.—**embezzlement** [-mẹnt], s. desfalco, peculado.—**embezzler** [-lœ(r)], s. desfalcador.

embitter [embịtœ(r)], va. amargar, agriar, acibarar.

emblaze [embléịz], va. adornar o embellecer suntuosamente; ensalzar; encender, inflamar.

emblazon [embléịzǫn], va. blasonar; esmaltar con colores brillantes; ensalzar, alabar.

emblazoner [-œ(r)], s. blasonador, decorador; heraldo.—emblazonment [-mᵊnt], s. blasonamiento.—emblazonry [-rᵢ], s. blasón.

emblem [émblᵊm], s. emblema, m., símbolo.

emblematic(al [emblᵊmétᵢk(ᵊl], a. emblemático.

emblematically [-ᵢ], adv. emblemáticamente.

emblematicize [-métᵢsaᵢz], va. dar carácter emblemático; alegorizar.

emblematize [emblémᵊtaᵢz], va. representar por medio de un emblema; simbolizar.

emblements [émblᵊmᵊnts], s. pl. (for.) cosecha; derecho de un arrendatario a su cosecha.

embodiment [embádᵢmᵊnt], s. incorporación; encarnación; personificación.

embody [embádᵢ]. I. va. dar cuerpo, informar; encarnar; incorporar; incluir, englobar, formular, sintetizar. II. vn. unirse, incorporarse.

embolden [embóᵤldᵊn], va. animar, envalentonar.

embolism [émbolᵢzm], s. (astr.) embolismo, intercalación; (med.) embolia.

embolismic [-ᵢzmᵢk], a. (astr.) embolismal.—e. year, año embolismal o de trece lunaciones.

embolus [émbolᴧs], s. (med.) émbolo, coágulo u obstrucción que causa embolia.

embonpoint [anbᴐnpwán], s. (fr.) redondez de cuerpo, gordura, corpulencia.

embosom [embúzᵊm], va. poner en el seno; envolver, encerrar, ocultar; querer, proteger.

emboss [embós], va. abollonar, repujar, relevar, realzar, estampar en relieve.

embossment [-mᵊnt], s. abolladura, realce, relieve, resalte.

embouchure [ambušúr], s. boca, desembocadura; (mús.) embocadura.

embowel [embáᵤᵊl], va. desentrañar, destripar.—embowelment [-mᵊnt], s. destripamiento.

embower [embáᵤœ(r)], va. emparrar, enramar.

embrace [embréᵢs]. I. va. abrazar; abarcar, rodear, ceñir, contener, comprender; admitir, recibir, adoptar, aceptar, aprovechar; (for.) cohechar, sobornar (un jurado, etc.). II. vn. abrazarse. III. s. abrazo.—embrace(ment [-mᵊnt], s. abrazo.—embracer [-œ(r)], s. abrazador; (for.) cohechador, sobornador.—embracery [-œrᵢ], s. (for.) cohecho, soborno.—embracing [-ᵢŋ]. I. s. abrazamiento; abarcamiento, abarcadura. II. a. comprehensivo.

embrasure [embréᶾᴜᵣ(r)], s. (fort.) tronera, aspillera, cañonera; (arq.) alféizar.

embrocate [émbrokeᵢt], va. (med.) embrocar, sobar con emolientes.—embrocation [-kéᵢšᴐn], s. embroca(ción).

embroider [embróᵢdœ(r)]. I. va. bordar, labrar, recamar; adornar retóricamente.—embroidered by hand, bordado a mano. II. vn. hacer bordadura o labor.

embroiderer, embroideress [-œ(r), -ᵢs], s. bordador, recamador; bordadora, labrandera.

embroidery [-ᵢ], s. bordado, bordadura, labor, f.; argentería (de plata u oro).—e. frame, bastidor.—e. yarn, hilo de bordar.—quill e., cañutería.

embroil [embróᵢl], va. embrollar, enredar, (fam.) liar; confundir; desentablar.

embroilment [-mᵊnt], s. alboroto, confusión; embrollo, intriga.

embrown [embráᵤn], va. y vn. hacer o volverse moreno u obscuro.

embryo [émbrᵢoᵤ]. I. s. embrión, m.; rudimento, germen, machuelo; principio. II. a. embrionario.

embryogeny [-ádᶾenᵢ], s. (biol.) embriogenia.

embryologist [-álodᶾᵢst], s. embriólogo.—embryology [-álodᶾᵢ], s. embriología.—embryonic [-ánᵢk], a. embrionario; rudimentario.

emeer [emír], s. V. EMIR.

emend [iménd], va. enmendar, corregir.

emendable [-abl], a. enmendable, corregible.

emendation [imendéᵢšᴐn], s. enmienda, enmen-

dación, corrección.—emendator [ímᴇndeᵢtᴐ(r)], s. corrector, enmendador.

emendatory [iméndᴅtorᵢ], a. enmendador.

emerald [émᵊrᴅld]. I. s. (min.) esmeralda; color de esmeralda; (Ingl.) tipo de 6½ puntos. II. a. de color de esmeralda.—e. green = Paris green.—E. Isle, Irlanda.

emerge [imœrdᶾ], vn. emerger, salir, brotar, surgir.

emergence [-ᵊns], s. emergencia, salida, surgimiento; aparición.

emergency [-ᵢ], s. emergencia, aprieto o necesidad urgente.—e. brake, freno de auxilio o de emergencia.—e. hospital, hospital de urgencia, casa de socorro.—e. landing, aterrizaje forzoso.—emergent [-ᵊnt], a. emergente; urgente; perentorio, repentino, subitáneo.

emeritus [imérᵢtᴧs], a. emérito, jubilado, retirado.

emersion [imœršᴐn], s. emersión; (astr.) emersión, reaparición.

emery [émᵊrᵢ]. I. va. esmerilar. II. s. esmeril.—e. cloth, tela de esmeril.—e. paper, papel (de) esmeril.—e. stone, muela de esmeril.—e. wheel, rueda de esmeril, disco de esmerilar.

emesis [émesᵢs], s. (med.) vómito.

emetic(al [imétᵢk(ᵊl], a. y s. emético, vomitivo.

emetin(e [émetᵢn], s. (quím.) emetina.

emeu [imju], s. (orn.) = EMU.

emigrant [émᵢgrᴅnt]. I. a. emigrante, (e)migratorio. II. s. emigrante, emigrado.—emigrate [-greᵢt], vn. emigrar, expatriarse.—emigration [-gréᵢšᴐn], s. emigración.

émigré [éᵢmigréᵢ], s. emigrado.

eminence [émᵢnᵊns], s. altura, cima, eminencia, encumbramiento, distinción; (E., igl.) eminencia (título).

eminent [-ᵊnt], a. eminente; prócer, relevante, supremo.—e. domain, (for.) dominio eminente.

eminently [-lᵢ], adv. eminentemente, en sumo grado.

emir [emír], s. emir o amir.

emissary [émᵢserᵢ]. I. s. emisario; agente secreto, espía, mf.; canal, desaguadero; orificio de salida; (anat.) conducto excretorio. II. a. perteneciente al emisario; enviado.

emission [imíšᴐn], s. emisión, salida; (com., med.) emisión; (mec.) escape.

emissive [imíšiv], a. emisivo.—e. power, (fís.) poder de irradiación.

emit [imít], va. emitir, arrojar, despedir, echar, exhalar; (com.) emitir.

emitter [-œ(r)], s. emisor.

emmenagogue [eménᴅgag], s. y a. (med.) emenagogo.

emmetropia [emetróᵤpiᴅ], s. emetropia, visión normal.—emmetropic [-trápᵢk], a. emétrope, normal (apl. al ojo).

emollescence [emolésᵊns], s. ablandamiento, reblandecimiento.

emollient [imályᵊnt], s. y a. emoliente.

emolument [imályᵤmᵊnt], s. emolumento, gaje; utilidad, provecho.

emotion [imóᵤšᴐn], s. emoción.—emotional [-ᴅl], a. emocional, emotivo, impresionable, sensible; sentimental.—emotionalism [-ᵢzm], s. sentimentalismo.—emotive [imóᵤtᵢv], a. emotivo; impresionable; emocionante.

empale [empéᵢl], va. = IMPALE.

empanel [empénᵊl], va. = IMPANEL.

empennage [anpenáᶾ], s. cola de un avión.

emperor [émpœrᴐ(r)], s. emperador.—e. moth, mariposa nocturna grande.

emperorship [-šᵢp], s. imperio, dignidad imperial.

empery [émpœrᵢ], s. (poét.) soberanía, dominio; imperio.

emphasis [émfᴅsᵢs], s. énfasis, m., relieve; intensidad; (fam.) recancanilla.—emphasize [-saᵢz], va. recalcar, acentuar, poner de relieve; hacer hincapié o insistir en; subrayar.

emphatic(al [ɛmfǽtɪk(ạl], a. enfático, categórico.

emphatically [-ị], adv. enfáticamente.

emphraxis [ɛmfrǽksịs], s. (med.) infarto, opilación.

emphysema [ɛmfịsímạ], s. (med.) enfisema, m., tumefacción.—emphysematous [-sémạtʌs], a. enfisematoso, hinchado.

emphyteusis [ɛmfịtjúsịs], s. (for.) enfiteusis.

emphyteuta [-tịútạ], s. (for.) enfiteuta, mf.

emphyteutic [-tịútịk], a. (for.) enfitéutico.

empire [ɛ́mpạịr], s. imperio.—e. cloth, tela barnizada aisladora.

empiric(al [ɛmpírịk(ạl]. I. a. empírico. II. s. empírico, medicastro, curandero.

empirically [-ị], adv. empíricamente.

empiricism [ɛmpírịsịzm], s. empirismo.

empiricist [-ịst], s. empírico; charlatán.

emplacement [ɛmpléịsmạnt], s. emplazamiento; (fort.) posición destinada a un cañón o batería.

emplastic [ɛmplǽstịk]. I. a. emplást(r)ico, glutinoso, pegajoso; estreñido. II. s. emplasto.

employ [ɛmplóị]. I. va. emplear; encargar; dar trabajo a; servirse o valerse de, usar; aplicar, dedicar, ocupar. II. s. empleo; servicio, encargo, ocupación, oficio.

employable [-ạbl], a. empleable.

employee, employé [-í], s. empleado, obrero; oficinista, dependiente.

employer [-œ(r)], s. el que emplea; amo, dueño; jefe, patrón, patrono, empresario.

employment [-mạnt], s. empleo, destino, puesto, plaza, colocación, uso, aplicación.

empoison [ɛmpóịzọn], va. corromper; inficionar.

emporium [ɛmpórịạm], s. emporio, plaza; bazar.

empower [ɛmpáụœ(r)], va. autorizar, facultar, comisionar, habilitar, dar poder, apoderar.

empress [ɛ́mprịs], s. emperatriz.

emptier [ɛ́mptịœ(r)], s. vaciador, vertedor.

emptiness [-nịs], s. vacío, vacuidad; futilidad.

empty [ɛ́mptị]. I. a. vacío; desocupado; vaco, vacante; vano, inútil; ignorante; hambriento; frívolo, superficial.—e.-handed, manivacío.—e.-headed, tonto. II. va. vaciar, evacuar, desocupar, descargar. III. vn. vaciarse; desaguar, desembocar.

emptying [-ịŋ], s. vaciamiento.—pl. (fam.) heces de la cerveza usadas como levadura (ll. t. emptings).

empurple [ɛmpœ́rpl], va. purpurar, teñir de púrpura.

empyema [ɛmpíímạ], s. (med.) empiema, m.

empyreal [ɛmpírịạl], a. empíreo.

empyrean [ɛmpịrịạn], s. y a. empíreo.

empyreuma [ɛmpịrúmạ], s. empireuma, m.

emu [ímịu], s. (orn.) ave (f.) grande de Australia parecida al avestruz o casuario.

emulate [ɛ́myụleịt], va. emular, competir o rivalizar con, imitar.

emulation [-éịšọn], s. emulación, rivalidad.

emulative [ɛ́myụlạtịv], a. emulador, émulo.

emulator [-leịtọ(r)], s. émulo, rival, competidor, emulador.

emulgent [ịmʎldʒạnt], a. (anat.) emulgente.

emulous [ɛ́myụlạs], a. émulo, rival.

emulously [-lị], adv. con emulación, a competencia.

emulsifier [ịmʎlsịfaịœ(r)], s. substancia emulsiva; emulsor, máquina para emulsionar.

emulsify [-sịfaị], va. emulsionar, convertir en emulsión, formar emulsión con o de.—emulsion [-šọn], s. emulsión.—emulsive [-sịv], a. emulsivo.

emunctory [ịmʎŋktọrị]. I. a. (anat.) excretorio. II. s. (anat.) emuntorio.

en [ɛn], s. ene, f., nombre de la letra N; (impr.) mitad de una eme.

enable [ɛnéịbl], va. habilitar, hacer capaz, capacitar, permitir, poner en situación de.

enact [ɛnǽkt], va. establecer, estatuir, promulgar, dar (una ley); decretar; (teat.) hacer el papel de; desempeñar la parte de.

enactable [-ạbl], a. que puede ser estatuído, efectuado o representado.

enactment [-mạnt], s. ley, f., estatuto; promulgación (de una ley).

enallage [ɛnǽlạdʒị], s. (gram.) enálage, f.

enamel [ɛnǽmẹl]. I. va. esmaltar; (a)charolar (cuero). II. s. esmalte; charol; esmalte (de los dientes).—e. work, esmalte.

enameler [-œ(r)], s. esmaltador.

enameling [-ịŋ], s. esmaltadura.

enamelware [-weịr], s. utensilios (m. pl.) de hierro esmaltado.

enamor [ɛnǽmọ(r)], va. enamorar.—enamored (of), enamorado o prendado (de).

enarthrosis [ɛnarθróụsịs], s. (anat.) enartrosis.

enate [ínẹit], s. pariente por descendencia materna común.—enation [inéịšọn], s. parentesco por madre.

encage [ɛnkéịdʒ], va. enjaular.

encamp [ɛnkǽmp], va. y vn. (mil.) acampar.

encamping [-ịŋ], s. castrametación.

encampment [-mạnt], s. (a)campamento, real; ranchería.

encase [ɛnkéịs], encasement = INCASE, etc.

encaustic [ɛnkɔ́stịk]. I. a. (pint.) encáustico. II. s. encausto, adustión, combustión.—e. painting, pintura al encausto.—e. tile, azulejo de colores.

encave [ɛnkéịv], va. encovar.

enceinte [ansǽnt]. I. a. (fr.) preñada, embarazada, encinta. II. s. (fort., arq.) recinto.

encephalic [ɛnsẹfǽlịk], a. (anat.) encefálico.

encephalitis [ɛnsẹfạláịtịs], s. (med.) encefalitis, inflamación del cerebro.—e. lethargica [-lịθárdʒịkạ], encefalitis letárgica o epidémica.

encephaloid [ɛnsẹfạlɔịd], a. encefaloideo.

encephalon [-lan], s. (anat.) encéfalo, cerebro.

enchain [ɛnchéịn], va. encadenar.

enchainment [-mạnt], s. encadenamiento.

enchant [ɛnchǽnt], va. encantar, hechizar; ensalmar; deleitar, fascinar, embelesar.—enchanter [-œ(r)], s. encantador, hechicero.—enchanting [-ịŋ], a. encantador.—enchantingly [-lị], adv. encantadoramente.—enchantment [-mạnt], s. encantamiento, hechicería, hechizo; ensalmo, fascinación, encanto, embeleso.—enchantress [-rịs], s. maga, bruja; encantadora, seductora, hechicera.

enchase [ɛnchéịs], va. engastar, embutir o incrustar, embeber.

enchorial [ɛnkóụrịạl], a. peculiar de un país, demótico; endémico; indígena, autóctono.

encircle [ɛnsœ́rkl], va. cercar, circuir, circundar, circunscribir, circunvalar, rodear.

encirclement [-mạnt], s. circunvalación; circunscripción; encerramiento, encierro, cerco, aislamiento.

enclave [ɛ́nkleịv]. I. s. región enclavada en territorio extranjero; barrio o distrito habitado por extranjeros o destinado a un objeto especial; (anat.) órgano enclavado en otro. II. s. [ɛnkléịv], va. establecer o encerrar dentro de territorio extranjero.

enclitic [ɛnklítịk], a. y s. (gram.) enclítico.

enclose [ɛnklóụz], va. cercar, circunvalar, circuir; rodear, circundar; encerrar; acompañar, incluir, remitir, adjuntar o enviar adjunta una cosa.

enclosure [ɛnklóụʒụ(r)], s. circamiento; cerca, vallado, tapia; cercado, corral; coto; recinto; (com.) adjunta, carta (etc.) inclusa, contenido.

encomiast [ɛnkóụmịæst], s. encomiasta, elogiador, panegirista.

encomiastic(al [ɛnkoụmịǽstịk(ạl], a. encomiástico.

encomium [ɛnkóụmịʌm], s. encomio, elogio.

encompass [ɛnkʌ́mpạs], va. cercar, circuir, circundar, rodear, encerrar; abarcar.—to e. the globe, dar la vuelta al mundo.

encore [áŋkọụr]. I. adv. otra vez, de nuevo.

II. *interj.* ¡otra! ¡que se repita! III. *s.* (teat.) repetición. IV. *va.* (teat.) pedir la repetición.

encounter [enkáuntœ(r)]. I. *s.* encuentro, choque; combate. II. *va. y vn.* encontrar; salir al encuentro de; dar, topar o tropezar con; batirse.

encourage [enkœridž], *va.* animar, alentar, confortar, fortalecer; estimular, incitar, fomentar; aprobar; dar pábulo, ánimos o alas a.

encouragement [-mênt], *s.* aliento, estímulo, incentivo, pábulo; fomento; tolerancia.

encouraging [-iŋ], *a.* animador, confortativo, alentador, halagüeño, favorable.—**encouragingly** [-lï], *adv.* alentadoramente.

encrinite [énkrinait], *s.* (zool.) crinoideo fósil.

encroach [enkróuch], *vn.* (con **on**) pasar los límites de, inmiscuirse en, intrusarse, usurpar.

encroachingly [-iŋlï], *adv.* por usurpación o intrusión.—**encroachment** [-mênt], *s.* usurpación, intrusión, abuso.

encrust [enkrást], *va.* = INCRUST.

encumber [enkámbœ(r)], *va.* embarazar, sobrecargar, gravar, estorbar, afectar, (fam.) entrampar.

encumbrance [-brans], *s.* embarazo, impedimento, estorbo; pensión, carga, gravamen.— **free from encumbrances,** libre de gravamen.

encyclical [ensíklikal], *s.* encíclica.

encyclopædia, encyclopedia [ensaiklopídiä], *s.* enciclopedia.

encyclopedic(al [-pídik(al], *a.* enciclopédico.

encyclopedism [-pídizm], *s.* enciclopedismo.

encyclopedist [-pídist], *s. y a.* enciclopedista.

encyst [ensíst], *va. y vn.* (cir., biol.) enquistar(se).

end [énd]. I. *s.* fin; extremidad; punta; cabo (del mundo); remate; conclusión, desenlace, efecto, final; fondo; finalidad, objeto, propósito; división, parte o ramo (de un negocio, empresa, etc.).—**e. for e.,** con los extremos invertidos.— **e. line,** línea de límite.—**e. on,** de punta; (mar.) de frente.—**e. paper,** (impr.) hoja en blanco.—**e. play,** (mec.) juego longitudinal.— **e. point,** (quím.) punto de evaporación completa.—**e. reaction,** (quím.) reacción al final del procedimiento.—**e. thrust,** empuje longitudinal.—**e. to e.,** cabeza con cabeza, punta con punta, por los extremos.—**at loose ends,** en desorden, desarreglado.—**at the e. of,** al cabo de.—**in the e.,** al fin, a la larga, al fin y al cabo.—**no e. of,** un sinfín de, muchísimo(s), la mar de.—**on e.,** de cabeza, de pie, derecho; de punta, erizado (el pelo).—**to make an e. of,** acabar con.—**to make both ends meet,** pasar con lo que se tiene.—**to no e.,** sin efecto, en vano.—**to put an e. to,** poner fin a.—**to the e. that,** a fin de que, para que, con objeto de. II. *va. y vn.* acabar, concluir, terminar, finalizar, cesar, fenecer, parar (en); morir(se).

end-all [-ol], *s.* conclusión definitiva, punto final.

endanger [endéindžœ(r)], *va.* poner en peligro, arriesgar, comprometer.

endear [endír], *va.* hacer(se) querer.

endearing [-iŋ], *a.* cariñoso.—**endearment** [-mênt], *s.* encariñamiento; caricia, fiesta.

endeavor [endévŏ(r)]. I. *s.* esfuerzo, conato, empeño. II. *va.* intentar, probar, pretender, tratar de. III. *vn.* esforzarse, hacer un esfuerzo (por).

endemic(al [endémik(al]. I. *a.* endémico. II. *s.* (med.) endemia.

ender [éndœ(r)], *s.* acabador.

endermic [endœrmik], *a.* endérmico.

ending [éndiŋ], *s.* fin, conclusión; cesación; terminación, suspensión; desenlace; (mús.) coda; (gram.) terminación, desinencia.

endive [éndaiv], *s.* (bot.) escarola, endibia.

endless [éndlis], *a.* sin fin; infinito; interminable, inacabable, continuo, perpetuo.—**e. chain, screw,** cable, cadena, tornillo sin fin.

endlessly [-lï], *adv.* infinitamente, sin fin, perpetuamente.—**endlessness** [-nis], *s.* perpetuidad; calidad de interminable.

endmost [éndmoust], *a.* extremo, último.

endoblast [éndoblæst], *s.* (biol.) endoblasto.

endocardiac, endocardial [-kárdiæk, -dial], *a.* endocardíaco.—**endocarditis** [-dáitis], *s.* (med.) endocarditis.—**endocardium** [-diʌm], *s.* (anat.) endocardio.—**endocarp** [-karp], *s.* (bot.) endocarpio.

endocrine [éndokrain], *s. y a.* endocrina (glándula).—**endocrinic** [-krínik], **endocrinous** [endákrinʌs], *a.* endocrino.—**endocrinology** [-álodžï], *s.* endocrinología.

endoderm [éndodœrm], *s.* endodermo, endoblasto.

endogamy [endágamï], *s.* endogamia, matrimonio dentro de la clase, casta, tribu, fratría, clan, etc.

endogen [éndodžin], *s.* (bot.) planta que se desarrolla por endogénesis.

endogenous [endádženʌs], *a.* (bot.) monocotiledóneo.

endogeny [-dženï], *s.* (biol.) endogénesis, reproducción por división interior.

endolymph [éndolimf], *s.* (anat.) endolinfa.

endometritis [-métráitis], *s.* (med.) endometritis, inflamación de la mucosa uterina.

endoparasite [-pérasait], *s.* endoparásito.

endoplasm [-plæzm], *s.* (biol.) endoplasma, *m.*

endorse, endorsee, etc. = INDORSE, etc.

endoscope [-oskoup], *s.* (med.) endoscopio.

endoskeleton [-skélœtɔn], *s.* (anat., zool.) neuroesqueleto.

endosmosis [endasmóusis], *s.* endósmosis.

endosmotic [-mátik], *a.* endosmótico.

endosperm [éndospœrm], *s.* (bot.) endospermo.

endothermic [-óœrmik], *a.* (quím.) endotérmico.

endow [endáu], *va.* dotar; fundar.

endower [-œ(r)], *s.* dotador.

endowment [-mênt], *s.* dotación; fundación.— *pl.* dotes, *f.,* prendas, gracias.—**e. insurance policy,** seguro, póliza dotal.

endue [endiú], *va.* (gen. con **with**) dotar, privilegiar; investir; poner(se), vestir(se); asumir.

endurable [endiúrabl], *a.* sufrible, soportable.

endurance [-ans], *s.* paciencia, sufrimiento; resistencia; duración, continuación.—**to be beyond o past e.,** ser insoportable o inaguantable.

endure [endiúr]. I. *va.* soportar, sufrir, resistir, sostener, (sobre)llevar, aguantar, tolerar. II. *vn.* durar, perdurar; sufrir, tener paciencia.

enduring [-iŋ], *a.* paciente, sufrido; durable, permanente; constante.

endways, endwise [éndweiz, -waiz], *adv.* de punta, de pie, derecho; longitudinalmente; cabeza con cabeza.

enema [énemä], *s.* (med.) enema, lavativa, ayuda.

enemy [énemi], *s.* enemigo; adversario; diablo.

energetic(al [enœrdžétik(al], *a.* enérgico, vigoroso.

energetically [-ï], *adv.* enérgicamente.

energetics [-s], *s.* (mec.) ciencia de la energía.

energize [énœrdžaiz]. I. *va.* excitar o dar energía; dar vigor o actividad. II. *vn.* obrar con energía.

energumen [enœrgiúmen], *s.* energúmeno, endemoniado.

energy [énœrdžï], *s.* energía, vigor, carácter, fibra; actividad; (mec.) energía, fuerza, potencia.

enervate [énœrveit]. 1. *va.* enervar o desnervar, debilitar, desmadejar; desvirtuar, embotar. II. [inœrveit], *a.* debilitado, enervado.

enervating [énœrveitiŋ], *a.* enervante, debilitante.

enervation [-éïšɔn], *s.* enervación; debilidad, desmadejamiento.

enfeeble [enfíbl], *va.* debilitar, enervar.

enfeeblement [-mênt], *s.* debilidad, desfallecimiento, endeblez, enervación, flojedad.

enfeoff [enféf], *va.* (for.) enfeudar.

enfeoffment [-mênt], *s.* (for.) enfeudación.

enfilade [enfiléid]. I. *s.* fuego o tiro de enfilada; ringlera, fila, hilera. II. *va.* (mil.) enfilar.

enfold [enfóuld], V. INFOLD.

enforce [enfórs], *va.* dar fuerza o vigor; poner en vigor; cumplimentar o hacer cumplir, observar o ejecutar (una ley); obtener o exigir por fuerza; hacer valer; hacer hincapié en.

enforcement [-ment], *s.* ejecución de una ley; observancia forzosa o coercitiva, coacción.

enfranchise [enfrénchajz], *va.* franquear, conceder franquicia o derechos civiles; libertar, manumitir, emancipar; adoptar, dar carta de naturaleza.—**enfranchisement** [-jzment], *s.* franquicia, ciudadanía; manumisión, emancipación.

engage [engéjdž]. **I.** *va.* ajustar, apalabrar, comprometer; contratar, escriturar; tomar en alquiler o a su servicio; ocupar, emplear; entretener, distraer; atraer, halagar, ganar; (mil.) librar o trabar (batalla o combate), entrar en lucha con, combatir; (arq.) empotrar, embeber; (mec.) engranar con, endentar con. **II.** *vn.* empeñarse, obligarse, dar palabra, comprometerse; ocuparse, estar atareado, entregarse a; pelear, venir a las manos.

engaged [-d], *a.* ocupado; comprometido, apalabrado; comprometido para casarse; (arq.) empotrado, embebido; (mec.) engranado, endentado (con).

engagement [-ment], *s.* ajuste, contrato; palabra de casamiento, esponsales, compromiso, noviazgo; cita, compromiso; obligación; (mec.) engranaje; (teat.) escritura, ajuste, contrato; (mil.) acción, batalla.—**e. ring**, anillo o sortija de esponsales.

engaging [-iŋ], *a.* atractivo, insinuante, agraciado, simpático.

engender [endžéndœ(r)]. **I.** *va.* engendrar, procrear. **II.** *vn.* engendrarse, producirse, causarse.

engine [éndžin], *s.* máquina, ingenio; locomotora; motor (esp. los de combustión interna); cualquier artefacto mecánico; instrumento, agente. —**e. builder**, fabricante de máquinas.—**e. driver**, (f. c.) maquinista.—**e. fitter**, montador.—**e. house**, casa de máquinas; estación de bomberos.—**e. lathe**, torno mecánico ordinario. —**e. room**, sala de máquinas; cuarto de la máquina.—**e.-room telegraph**, (mar.) campana o mecanismo de señales (entre el timonel o el puente y el maquinista).—**e. running**, manejo de máquinas.—**e.-sized**, aprestado a máquina (apl. al papel).—**e. trouble**, avería de motor.

engineer [-ír]. **I.** *s.* ingeniero; maquinista, mecánico.—**E. Corps**, (E. U.) Cuerpo de Ingenieros del ejército o de la armada.—**e.'s chain**, (top.) cadena de 100 pies, con eslabones de 1 pie.—**e.'s level**, nivel ordinario de topografía (a distinción de los de carpinteros, albañiles, etc.). **II.** *va.* gestionar, manejar, dirigir. **III.** *vn.* hacer de ingeniero o maquinista; darse maña.

engineering [-iŋ]. **I.** *s.* ingeniería; dirección, manejo. **II.** *a.* de o relativo a la ingeniería.

engineman [-man], *s.* maquinista.

enginery [-ri], *s.* artillería; maquinaria, ingenios de guerra; astucias, tretas.

engird [engérd], *va.* ceñir, cercar, rodear.

engirdle [-l], *va.* circundar, ceñir, rodear.

Englander [íŋglændœ(r)], *s.* natural de Inglaterra.

Englify [íŋglifaj], *va.* hacer inglés, inglesar.

English [íŋgliš]. **I.** *s.* y *a.* inglés; (en el billar) efecto.—**E. bond**, (alb.) aparejo inglés, o de hiladas alternadas de sogas y tizones.—**E. Channel**, Canal de la Mancha.—**E. type**, (impr.) atanasia. **II.** *va.* traducir al inglés.

Englishman [-man], *s.* inglés (hombre); (mar.) buque inglés.—**Englishwoman** [-wuman], *s.* inglesa.

engorge [engórdž], *va.* y *vn.* atracar, engullir.

engraft [engréft], *va.* (agr.) injertar; injerir o ingerir, inculcar.—**engraftment** [-ment], *s.* injerto.

engrail [engréjl]. **I.** *va.* dentar. **II.** *vn.* tener o formar borde dentellado o angrelado.

engrain [engréjn], *va.* pintar imitando la trepa de la madera. *V.* INGRAIN.

engrave [engréjv], *va.* grabar; cincelar, burilar, esculpir; tallar; (fig.) grabar (en la memoria, etc.).—**engraver** [-œ(r)], *s.* grabador.—**engraving** [-iŋ], *s.* grabado; lámina, estampa.

engross [engróus], *va.* poner en limpio, copiar o transcribir caligráficamente; absorber, embargar, preocupar; acaparar, monopolizar.— **engrosser** [-œ(r)], *s.* pendolista, calígrafo; monopolista, acaparador.—**engrossment** [-ment], *s.* monopolio; transcripción caligráfica; embebecimiento, embelesamiento, abstracción.

engulf [engálf], *va.* engolfar, sumergir, sumir.

enhance [enhéns], *va.* mejorar, acrecentar, encarecer, aumentar el valor de; realzar.

enhancement [-ment], *s.* acrecentamiento, encarecimiento, mejoría; realce.

enharmonic [enharmánik], *a.* (mús.) enarmónico.

enigma [inígmä], *s.* enigma, *m.*, (fam.) intríngulis, quisicosa.—**enigmatic(al** [enigmǽtjk(al], *a.* enigmático.—**enigmatically** [-i], *adv.* enigmáticamente.—**enigmatize** [inígmatajz], *vn.* usar de enigmas.

enjoin [endžójn], *va.* mandar, ordenar, prescribir; imponer.—**to e. from**, (for.) prohibir.

enjoy [endžój], *va.* gozar de, gozarse en; gustar de, gustarle a uno; disfrutar de, tener, poseer; saborear.—**to e. one's self**, gozar, divertirse.

enjoyable [-abl], *a.* deleitable, agradable.

enjoyment [-ment], *s.* goce, disfrute, placer; uso, usufructo.

enkindle [enkíndl], *va.* y *vn.* encender(se); arder.

enlace [enléjs], *va.* enlazar, entrelazar.

enlarge [enlárdž]. **I.** *va.* agrandar, aumentar, ensanchar; abultar, engrosar; ampliar o amplificar. **II.** *vn.* ensancharse o agrandarse; (gen. con on) explayarse (en), tratar detalladamente; exagerar.

enlargement [-ment], *s.* agrandamiento, ensanchamiento, ensanche, aumento, ampliación; liberación; dilatación, expansión; amplificación; (fot.) ampliación.

enlarger [-œ(r)], *s.* (fot.) ampliador(a), amplificador.

enlarging [-iŋ], *a.* ampli(fic)ador, ampliativo.

enlighten [enláiten], *va.* iluminar, instruir, informar, ilustrar, alumbrar, aclarar, esclarecer. —**enlightened** [-d], *a.* ilustrado, culto.—**enlightener** [-œ(r)], *s.* instructor, esclarecedor.— **enlightenment** [-ment], *s.* instrucción, ilustración, esclarecimiento; civilización, cultura.— **the E.**, el renacimiento del siglo XVIII.

enlist [enlíst]. **I.** *va.* alistar; (mar. y gal.) enrolar; (mil.) enganchar, reclutar; atraer, conseguir. **II.** *vn.* enrolarse; (mil.) sentar plaza; poner empeño en algo.—**enlistment** [-ment], *s.* alistamiento, enganche, enrolamiento.

enliven [enláiven], *va.* vivificar, animar, alentar; avivar, alegrar, regocijar.

enmesh [enméš], *va.* coger en la red; entrampar.

enmity [énmiti], *s.* enemistad, enemiga, desamor.

ennead [énjed], *s.* grupo de nueve; novena.

ennoble [enóubl], *va.* ennoblecer; esclarecer.

ennoblement [-ment], *s.* ennoblecimiento o esclarecimiento.

ennui [ánwi], *s.* aburrimiento, tedio, fastidio.

enologic(al [inoládžik(al], *a.* enológico.—**enologist** [ináladžist], *s.* enólogo.—**enology** [ináladži], *s.* enología.

enormity [inórmiti], **enormousness** [-mʌsnis], *s.* enormidad, demasía; atrocidad.—**enormous** [-mʌs], *a.* enorme, descomunal; perverso, atroz. —**enormously** [-li], *adv.* enormemente.

enostosis [enastóusis], *s.* (med.) enostosis.

enough [inʌ́f]. **I.** *a.* bastante, suficiente, asaz, harto.—**to be e.**, bastar. **II.** *s.* lo suficiente. **III.** *interj.* ¡basta! ¡no más! **IV.** *adv.* bastante,

harto, suficientemente.—**curiously e., strange
e.**, etc., cosa curiosa, extraña, etc. Estas expresiones pueden a veces traducirse cambiando
un poco el giro: lo curioso es que, es curioso que,
lo cual no deja de ser curioso, etc.

enounce [ináuns], va. declarar; anunciar.

enquire, enquirer, etc. = INQUIRE, etc.

enrage [enréidž], va. enfurecer, encolerizar.

enrapt [enrǽpt], a. arrebatado, extasiado.

enrapture [enrǽpchū(r)], va. arrebatar, enajenar,
embriagar, embelesar, arrobar, extasiar.

enrich [enrích], va. enriquecer; fecundar, fertilizar; adornar, embellecer.

enrichment [-mẹnt], s. enriquecimiento; abono,
beneficio; adorno, embellecimiento.

enrobe [enróųb], va. vestir, adornar.

enrol(l) [enróųl]. **I.** va. alistar, (gal.) enrolar;
empadronar, encartar, matricular; envolver, enrollar. **II.** vn. alistarse, enrolarse; inscribirse,
matricularse; (mil.) sentar plaza.—**enrol(l)er**
[-œ(r)], s. registrador, empadronador.—**enrol(l)ment** [-mẹnt], s. alistamiento, enrolamiento; empadronamiento, inscripción, matriculación; matrícula, padrón, registro.

enroot [enrút], va. arraigar, radicar.

en route [an rút], adv. en el camino; de tránsito.

ens [enz], s. (pl. **entia** [énšā]) ente, ser.

ensanguine [ensǽngwin], va. ensangrentar.

ensconce [enskáns], va. acomodar, situar; ocultar,
poner en seguro.

ensemble [ansámbl], s. conjunto; grupo; traje de
mujer compuesto de dos o más piezas.

ensheathe [enšíð], va. envainar.

enshrine [enšráįn], va. guardar como reliquia.

enshroud [enšráųd], va. amortajar; envolver,
ocultar, tapar.

ensiform [énsiform], a. (bot.) ensiforme.

ensign [énsaįn], s. bandera, pabellón, enseña;
insignia, divisa; [énsịn] (mil.) alférez, m.; subteniente.—**e. bearer,** abanderado.

ensigncy [-sị], s. alferazgo.

ensilage [énsịlidž]. **I.** s. (agr.) ensilaje. **II.** va.
ensilar.

enslave [ensléįv], va. esclavizar, avasallar.

enslavement [-mẹnt], s. esclavitud, cautiverio,
servidumbre; avasallamiento.

enslaver, (-ing) [-œ(r), -ịŋ], s. y a. avasallador.

ensnare [ensnér], va. entrampar, atrapar, enredar, insidiar; tender un lazo; engañar, embair.

ensoul [ensóųl], va. dar alma a; llevar al alma.

ensphere [ensfír], va. colocar en esfera; redondear.

ensue [ensiú], vn. seguir, suceder, sobrevenir.

ensure [enšúr], va. asegurar; garantizar.

entablature [entǽblachū(r)], s. (arq.) entablamento, cornisamento, solera.

entail [entéil]. **I.** s. (for.) vinculación, vínculo,
mayorazgo; herencia. **II.** va. vincular, asegurar,
perpetuar, transmitir, legar; acarrear, imponer,
ocasionar; envolver; (for.) vincular.

ental [éntạl], a. (anat. y zool.) de lo interior.

entangle [entǽŋgl], va. enredar, embrollar, enmarañar; intrincar; implicar.—**entanglement**
[-mẹnt], s. enredo, embrollo, complicación.

entasis [éntạsịs], s. (arq.) éntasis.

entelechy [entélẹki], s. (filos.) entelequia.

entente [antánt], s. pacto; alianza.—**e. cordiale,**
(fr.) pacto o convenio cordial o de amistad.

enter [éntœ(r)]. **I.** va. entrar a, por o en; penetrar;
meter, introducir; ingerir, insertar; asentar,
anotar, registrar; hacerse miembro de, ingresar
en; alistarse en, matricularse, afiliarse; (com.)
declarar, aduanar; (for.) incoar; registrar. **II.** vn.
entrar, introducirse, ingresar; (teat.) salir, entrar en escena.—**to e. into,** entrar en; formar
parte de; hacer, celebrar (un contrato, etc.).—
to e. on, o **upon,** comenzar, emprender.

enteralgia [enterǽldžiā], s. (med.) enteralgia.

enteric [entérịk], a. (anat.) entérico.—**e. fever,**
fiebre tifoidea.

entering [éntœriŋ], a. que entra; de entrada.—
e. chisel, gubia, cincel de mediacaña.—**e. edge,**

(aer.) borde de ataque (el anterior de un plano).
—**e. file,** lima plana de punta.—**e. tap,** macho
de aterrajado preliminar.—**e. wedge,** (fig.)
operación o medida que abre camino o prepara
el terreno; primer paso.

enteritis [enteráįtịs], s. (med.) enteritis.

enterocele [énterosil], s. (med.) enterocele.

enterocolitis [-koláįtịs], s. (med.) enterocolitis.

enteron [éntẹran], s. (anat.) canal intestinal.

enterotomy [entẹrátomị], s. (cir.) enterotomía.

enterprise [éntœrpraįz], s. empresa, demanda,
arresto; actividad, calidad de emprendedor.—
enterpriser [-œ(r)], s. emprendedor; progresista. V. ENTREPRENEUR.—**enterprising** [-ịŋ],
a. emprendedor, acometedor, esforzado.

entertain [entœrtéįn]. **I.** va. hospedar, festejar,
agasajar u obsequiar; entretener o divertir;
tomar en consideración; acariciar, abrigar.
II. vn. dar saraos, tertulias, comidas, etc.

entertainable [-ạbl], a. digno de tomarse en
consideración.

entertainer [-œ(r)], s. anfitrión, m.; festejador.

entertaining [-ịŋ], a. entretenido, chistoso,
gracioso, alegre, divertido, jovial.—**entertainingly** [-lị], adv. divertidamente, entretenidamente.

entertainment [-mẹnt], s. recibimiento, hospitalidad; convite, agasajo, festín, festejo, fiesta;
entretenimiento, diversión, pasatiempo, (Am.)
entretención; consideración.

enthetic [enθétịk], a. proveniente de agentes
externos; comunicado por inoculación (apl. a
enfermedades infecciosas).

enthral(l [enθról], va. dominar (el ánimo); esclavizar, sojuzgar.

enthrone [enθróųn], va. entron(iz)ar.

enthronement [-mẹnt], **enthronization** [-izéįšọn], s. entronización.

enthuse [enθiúz], va. y vn. (fam.) entusiasmar(se).

enthusiasm [-iæzm], s. entusiasmo.

enthusiast [-iæst], s. entusiasta, mf.; fanático.

enthusiastic(al [-iǽstịk(ạl], a. entusiástico, entusiasta; entusiasmado; caluroso.

enthymeme [énθịmim], s. (lóg.) entimema, m.

entice [entáįs], va. tentar, seducir, halagar, atraer,
sonsacar, (fam.) engatusar, entruchar.

enticement [-mẹnt], s. tentación, seducción,
sonsaca; reclamo, añagaza; atractivo.—**enticer**
[-œ(r)], s. seductor, tentador.—**enticing** [-ịŋ],
a. seductor.—**enticingly** [-lị], adv. seductoramente.

entire [entáįr], a. entero, cabal, completo, íntegro, intacto, todo, total; (vet.) entero, cojudo.
—**entirely** [-lị], adv. enteramente, íntegramente; del todo, de todo punto, por completo;
a fondo.—**entireness** [-nịs], s. entereza, calidad
de entero.—**entirety** [-tị], s. entereza, integridad, totalidad; cosa entera; todo.

entitle [entáįtl], va. titular; intitular; dar derecho; habilitar; autorizar.

entity [éntịtị], s. entidad; ente, ser.

entoblast [éntoblæst], **entoderm** [-dœrm], s.
endodermo.

entomb [entúm], va. enterrar, sepultar.

entombment [-mẹnt], s. entierro, sepultura.

entomogenous [entomádženʌs], a. (bot.) parásito de insectos (apl. a ciertos hongos).

entomologic(al [-moládžịk(ạl], a. entomológico.

entomologist [-málodžịst], s. entomólogo.

entomology [-džị], s. entomología.

entomophagous [-máfạgʌs], a. (zool.) entomófago, insectívoro.

entomophilous [-máfịlʌs], a. (bot.) entomófilo,
de polinización por insectos.—**entomophily**
[-fịlị], s. entomofilia, polinización por insectos.

entourage [anturáž], s. (fr.) compañía, cortejo,
séquito; medio ambiente.

entozoa [entozóųā], s. pl. entozoarios.—**entozoan** [-n], a. y s. entozoario.—**entozoic** [-ịk], a.
entozoico.

entr'acte [antrǽkt], s. (fr.) entreacto.

entrails [éntreɪlz], *s. pl.* entrañas, vísceras; tripas, intestinos.

entrain [entréɪn], *va. y vn.* despachar o ir por tren.

entrance [éntrəns], *s.* entrada; puerta, portal; zaguán; embocadura; ingreso; entrada en la aduana; (teat.) salida.—**e. examination**, examen de admisión, entrada o ingreso.—**e. fee**, cuota de entrada.—**e. forbidden**, o **no e.**, se prohíbe la entrada.

entrance [entréns], *va.* extasiar, fascinar, arrebatar, embelesar, hechizar.

entrancing [-ɪŋ], *a.* fascinador, hechicero.

entrant [éntrənt]. **I.** *a.* entrante. **II.** *s.* principiante, novicio; (dep.) competidor.

entrap [entrǽp], *va.* coger con trampa, entrampar.

entreat [entrít]. **I.** *va.* rogar, suplicar, implorar, impetrar, instar, solicitar, conjurar. **II.** *vn.* hacer una súplica, pedir un favor.

entreating [-ɪŋ], *a.* suplicante.—**entreatingly** [-lɪ], *adv.* suplicantemente.

entreaty [-ɪ], *s.* ruego, súplica, instancia, conjuro.

entree, entrée [ántreɪ], *s.* (fr.) entrada; privilegio de entrar; (coc.) principio o entrada.

entremets [ántrœmeɪ], *s.* (coc., teat.) entremés.

entrench [entrénch]. **I.** *va.* atrincherar. **II.** *vn.* atrincherarse; (con **on** o **upon**) invadir, infringir.

entrenchment [-mənt], *s.* atrincheramiento, trinchera; parapeto, reparo; infracción, invasión, transgresión.

entrepôt [ántrœpou], *s.* (fr.) factoraje; almacén.

entrepreneur [àntrœprœnœr], *s.* empresario (esp. de teatro), contratista.

entresol [éntrœsal], *s.* (arq.) entresuelo.

entropion [entrúpjan], *s.* (med.) entropión, *m.*, inversión de los párpados.

entropy [éntropi], *s.* (fís.) entropía.

entrust [entrᴧst], *va.* (con **to** o **with**) entregar, encargar (de), (con)fiar, depositar.

entry [éntri], *s.* entrada; acceso; vestíbulo, portal, pórtico, zaguán; ingreso; asiento, anotación o apuntamiento; (min.) bocamina; (mar.) registro, declaración de entrada; (com.) partida.

entwine [entwáɪn], *va.* entrelazar, entretejer.

entwist [entwɪst], *va.* torcer; ensortijar.

enucleate [injúkliejt]. **I.** *va.* descascarar; desenvolver; explicar; extraer el núcleo de; (cir.) extirpar, extraer sin cortar. **II.** *a.* sin núcleo.

enucleation [-éjʃən], *s.* (cir.) extracción de un tumor entero.

enumerate [injúmᴧreɪt], *va.* enumerar, contar.

enumeration [-éjʃən], *s.* enumeración, recuento, detalle; lista, catálogo; (ret.) recapitulación.

enumerative [-tiv], *a.* enumerativo.

enunciate [inᴧnʃjeɪt], *va.* pronunciar, articular (palabras); enunciar (teorías); proclamar.

enunciation [-éjʃən], *s.* pronunciación, articulación; enunciación; manifiesto.

enunciative [-ʃjeɪtiv], **enunciatory** [-ʃiatori], *a.* enunciativo, declarativo.

enure [enjúr], *va. y vn.* = INURE.

envelop [envélop], *va.* envolver; aforrar, cubrir.

envelope [énvéloup], *s.* envoltura; funda; cubierta; sobre (carta); (mat.) envolvente (curva); (bot.) túnica, envoltura.—**e. opener**, abrecartas.

envelopment [envélopmənt], *s.* envolvimiento; forro, funda, cubierta.

envenom [envénom], *va.* envenenar, emponzoñar, atosigar.

enviable [énvjabl], *a.* envidiable.

envious [énvjᴧs], *a.* envidioso.—**enviously** [-lɪ], *adv.* envidiosamente.—**enviousness** [-nɪs], *s.* envidia; calidad de envidioso.

environ [envaɪron], *va.* rodear, ceñir, envolver.

environment [-mənt], *s.* cercanía; ambiente o medio ambiente.

environs [-z], *s. pl.* alrededores, suburbios, contornos, cercanías, inmediaciones, afueras.

envisage [envɪzɪdʒ], *va.* hacer frente a; mirar; contemplar, representarse mentalmente.

envoy [énvoɪ], *s.* enviado, agente diplomático; mensajero; (poét.) tornada (ll. t. **envoi**).

envy [énvɪ]. **I.** *va.* envidiar; codiciar. **II.** *s.* envidia, emulación; (fam.) dentera; objeto de envidia.

enwrap [enrǽp], *va.* envolver; absorber, embargar.

enwreathe [enríð], *va.* enguirnaldar.

enzootic [enzoátɪk]. **I.** *a.* enzoótico, endémico (apl. a las enfermedades de los animales). **II.** *s.* (vet.) enzootia, enfermedad enzoótica o de carácter local (ll. t. **enzooty**).

enzym(e [énzaɪm, énzɪm], *s.* (bioquím.) enzima, fermento; (igl.) pan de levadura; pan eucarístico (en la iglesia oriental).

Eocene [íosin], *a. y s.* (geol.) eoceno.

Eolian [ióuljan], **Eolic** [iálɪk], *a. y s.* eolio, eólico.—**E. harp**, arpa eolia.

eolipile [iálpaɪl], *s.* (fís.) eolípila. *V.* AEOLIPILE.

eolith [íolιθ], *s.* (arqueol.) eolito.

eolithic [iolίθɪk], *a.* eolítico, relativo al principio de la edad de piedra.

eon, æon [íon], *s.* evo; eón.

eosin [íosɪn], *s.* (quím.) eosina.

eosinophil(e [iosínofɪl], *a. y s.* eosinófilo.

Eozoic [iozóujk], *s. y a.* (geol.) eozoico (apl. a los terrenos subyacentes al paleozoico).

epact [ípækt], *s.* (astr.) epacta.

epaulet [épolɛt], *s.* (mil.) charretera, capona.

ependyma [epéndjmᴧ], *s.* (anat.) epéndimo.

epenthesis [epénθesɪs], *s.* (gram.) epéntesis.

epenthetic [epenθétɪk], *a.* (gram.) epentético.

epergne [ipœrn], *s.* centro de mesa.

ephebe [efíb], *s.* (hist.) efebo, joven griego.

ephedrine [éfedrɪn], *s.* (quím.) efedrina.

ephemera [efémerᴧ], *s.* (med.) (fiebre) efémera o efímera; (fam.) causón; insecto efímero; cosa efímera.

ephemeral [-l]. **I.** *a.* efímero. **II.** *s.* cosa efímera.

ephemerid [efémerɪd], *s.* (ent.) efímera.

ephemeris [efémerɪs], *s.* (*pl.* EPHEMERIDES) efemérides, *f. pl.*, tablas astronómicas.

Ephesian [efíʒjan], *a. y s.* efesio, de Efeso.

ephete [éfit], *s.* (hist.) éfeta, *m.*, juez griego.

ephialtes [efiáltiz], *s.* efialtes, *f.*, pesadilla.

ephod [éfad], *s.* (igl.) efod, *m.*; superhumeral.

ephor [éfo(r)], *s.* éforo (magistrado griego); superintendente de obras públicas.

epiblast [épiblæst], *s.* (biol.) ectodermo.

epic(al [épik(al]. **I.** *a.* épico.—**e. poetry**, épica. **II.** *s.* poema épico, epopeya.

epicardium [epikárdjᴧm], *s.* (anat.) epicardio.

epicarp [épikarp], *s.* (bot.) epicarpio.

epicedium [episídjᴧm], *s.* epicedio, elegía.

epicene [épisin], *a.* (gram.) epiceno.

epicenter [épisɛntœ(r)], *s.* (geol.) epicentro.

epicure [épikjur], *s.* epicúreo; sibarita, *mf.*; gastrónomo.—**epicurean** [-ían], *a. y s.* epicúreo.

Epicureanism [-ízm], **epicurism** [épikjurizm], *s.* epicureísmo; gastronomía.

epicycle [épisaɪkl], *s.* epiciclo.

epicycloid [episáɪkloɪd], *s.* (geom.) epicicloide, *f.*

epidemic(al [epidémik(al]. **I.** *a.* epidémico, epidemial. **II.** *s.* epidemia, peste, *f.*, plaga.

epidermal [epidœrmal], *a.* epidérmico.

epidermic(al [-mjk(al], *a.* epidérmico.

epiderm(is [épidœrm, -dœrmɪs], *s.* (anat.) epidermis, cutícula; piel, *f.*; (bot.) epidermis.

epididymis [epidídjmɪs], *s.* (anat.) epidídimo.

epidote [épidout], *s.* (min.) epidota.

epigastric [epigǽstrɪk], *a.* (anat.) epigástrico.

epigastrium [epigǽstrjᴧm], *s.* (anat.) epigastrio.

epigenesis [epidʒénesis], *s.* (biol.) epigénesis.

epiglottis [epiglátɪs], *s.* (anat.) epiglotis, lengüeta.

epigram [épigræm], *s.* epigrama, *m.*—**epigrammatic(al** [epigramǽtik(al], *a.* epigramático.—**epigrammatically** [-lɪ], *adv.* epigramáticamente.—**epigrammatist** [epigrǽmatist], *s.* epigramatario, epigram(at)ista.

epigraph [épigræf], *s.* epígrafe, título; inscripción, epitafio.—**epigrapher, (-ist)** [epigrafoe(r), -ist], s. epigrafista.—**epigraphic** [epigréfik], a. epigráfico.—**epigraphy** [epígrafi], s. epigrafía.

epilepsy [épilepsi], s. (med.) epilepsia, alferecía, gota caduca o coral.—**epileptic(al** [epiléptik(al], a. y s. epiléptico.

epilogistic [epilodźístik], a. epilogal.

epilogize [epilodźaiz], va. y vn. epilogar; proveer (una obra) de un epílogo; (teat.) recitar un epílogo.

epilogue [épilag], s. epílogo.

epineurium [epinjúriʌm], s. (anat.) epineuro, envoltura de tejido conjuntivo que rodea un haz de nervios.

epinicion [epiníśion], s. epinicio, himno triunfal.

Epiphany [ipífani], s. (igl.) Epifanía, día de los Reyes.

epiphenomenon [epifinámenan], s. fenómeno secundario concomitante; (med.) epifenómeno.

epiphonema [epifonímǎ], s. (ret.) epifonema.

epiphysis [epífisis], s. (anat.) epífisis.—**e. cerebri**, glándula pineal.

epiphyte [épifait], s. (bot.) epífita, planta no parásita que vive en otra; hongo parásito de un animal.

epiphytic [-fítik], a. (bot.) epífito, epífito.

epiploon [ipíploon], s. (anat.) epíploon, epiplón.

episcopacy [ipískopasi], s. episcopado.

episcopal [-pal], a. episcopal; obispal.

Episcopalian [-péilian], a. y s. episcopal, perteneciente a la secta protestante episcopal.—**Episcopalianism** [-izm], s. episcopalismo, doctrina de la secta protestante episcopal.

episcopalism [-palizm], s. episcopalismo.

episcopally [-pali], adv. episcopalmente.

episcopate [-peit], s. obispado, episcopado.

episode [épisoud], s. episodio, lance, peripecia; digresión; (cine) V. SERIAL.

episod(i)al [-(i)al], **episodic(al** [episádik(al], a. episódico.—**episodically** [-i], adv. episódicamente.

epispastic [epispǽstik], a. y s. (med.) epispástico; vejigatorio, vesicante.

epistaxis [epistǽksis], s. (med.) epistaxis.

epistemology [epistimálodźi], s. epistemología, teoría del conocimiento.

epistle [ipísl], s. epístola, carta, misiva.

epistler [ipíslœ(r)], s. escritor de epístolas o cartas; (igl.) epistolero.

epistolary [ipístoleri], a. epistolar. II. s. (igl.) epistolario.

epistrophe [epístrofi], s. (ret.) epístrofe, f., conversión; (mús.) estribillo.

epistyle [épistail], s. (arq.) arquitrabe.

epitaph [épitæf], s. epitafio.

epitaphic [epitǽfik], a. relativo al epitafio.

epitasis [epítasis], s. (teat.) epítasis.

epithalamium [epiθaléimiam], s. epitalamio.

epithelial [epiθílial], a. epitelial.

epithelioma [epiθilióumǎ], s. (med.) epitelioma, m.

epithelium [epiθíliʌm], s. (anat.) epitelio.

epithem [épiθem], s. (med.) epítema.

epithet [épiθet], s. epíteto.

epitome [ipítomi], s. epítome, resumen, sumario, compendio.—**epitomize** [-maiz], va. epitomar, abreviar.—**epitomizer** [-œ(r)], **epitomist** [-mist], s. epitomador, abreviador, compendiador.

epitrochlea [epitráklǎ], s. (anat.) epitróclea, cóndilo interior del húmero.

epitrope [ipítropi], s. (ret.) epítrope, f.

epizoan [epizóuan], a. y s. epizoario.

epizootic [epizoátik], I. a. epizoótico. II. s. (vet.) epizootia (ll. t. epizooty).

epoch [épok], s. época, era, edad, período, siglo.—**e.-making**, que forma época, trascendental.

epochal [-al], a. que forma época, trascendental, memorable.

epode [époud], s. (poét.) epodo.

eponym [éponim], s. héroe, epónimo.

eponymous [epánimʌs], **eponymic** [eponímik], a. epónimo.

epopee [épopi], s. epopeya, poema épico.

Epsom salt(s [épsom solt(s], s. (quím.) sulfato de magnesia, sal de la Higuera, epsomita.

equability [ekwabíliti], **equableness** [ékwablnis], s. igualdad, uniformidad; ecuanimidad.—**equable** [ékwabl], a. igual, uniforme, ecuable, tranquilo.—**equably** [-bli], adv. igualmente.

equal [íkwal]. I. a. igual; parejo; adecuado, suficiente, adaptado.—**e. rights**, igualdad de derechos.—**to be e. to**, ponerse al nivel de, ser capaz de, sentirse con fuerzas para, servir para, poder hacer frente a, poder desempeñar o ejecutar. II. s. igual; cantidad igual. III. va. ser igual a; igualarse a, ponerse al nivel de; igualar, emparejar; compensar.—**not to be equalled**, sin igual. IV. vn. ser igual.

equalitarian [ikwalitérian], a. igualitario.

equality [ikwáliti], s. igualdad; uniformidad; paridad; lisura.

equalization [ikwalizéiśon], s. igualamiento, igualación, compensación.—**equalize** [íkwalaiz], va. igualar, hacer uniforme; compensar.

equalizer [-œ(r)], s. igualador, compensador; (elec.) conductor compensador o de compensación; dínamo compensadora.

equalizing [-iŋ], a. igualador; (tec.) compensador, de compensación.

equally [íkwali], adv. igualmente; por igual.

equalness [íkwalnis], s. uniformidad, igualdad.

equanimity [ikwanímiti], s. ecuanimidad.

equate [ikwéit], va. igualar, poner en ecuación.

equation [ikwéiśon], s. ecuación; igualdad; equilibrio.—**e. of time**, (astr.) ecuación de tiempo.

equator [ikwéito(r)], s. ecuador, línea.

equatorial [ikwatórial], a. y s. ecuatorial, f.

equerry [ékweri], s. caballerizo, palafrenero mayor.

equestrian [ikwéstrian]. I. a. ecuestre. II. s. jinete.

equestrianism [-izm], s. equitación.

equestrienne [ikwestrién], s. amazona.

equiangular [ikwiǽŋgjulǎ(r)], a. (geom.) equiángulo.

equidistance [ikwidístans], s. equidistancia.

equidistant [-ant], a. equidistante.

equidistantly [-li], adv. a una misma distancia.

equilateral [ikwilǽteral], a. y s. (geom.) equilátero.

equilibrant [ikwílibrant], s. (mec.) fuerza igual y contraria a la resultante de un sistema, fuerza equilibrante.

equilibrate [ikwilíbreit], I. va. equilibrar; compensar. II. vn. equilibrarse; estar en equilibrio.

equilibration [ikwilibréiśon], s. equilibración; equilibrio.

equilibrator [ikwiláibreito(r)], s. equilibrador; compensador.

equilibrist [ikwílibrist], s. equilibrista.

equilibrium [ikwilíbriʌm], s. equilibrio, balance.

equine [íkwain]. I. a. caballar, hípico, equino. II. s. caballo.

equinoctial [ikwináksǎl]. I. a. equinoccial.—**e. circle** o **line**, línea equinoccial, ecuador. II. s. línea equinoccial; tempestad equinoccial.

equinoctially [-i], adv. en dirección equinoccial.

equinox [íkwinaks], s. (astr.) equinoccio.

equip [ikwíp], va. equipar, pertrechar, aprestar, aparejar, proveer, dotar, habilitar, aviar.

equipage [ékwipidź], s. equipaje, equipo; tren; carruaje.

equipment [ikwípment], s. equipo, equipaje, habilitación; apresto, armamento; avíos; vestuario; adherentes, arreos; (mec.) equipo, tren, juego, conjunto de aparatos, accesorios, etc.

equipoise [íkwipoiz], s. equilibrio; contrapeso.

equipollence, equipollency [ikwipálens, -i], s. equipolencia o equivalencia.—**equipollent** [-ent], a. y s. equipolente.

---

equiponderance, equiponderancy [ikwipándœrąns, -i], s. equiponderancia.

equiponderant [-ąnt], a. equiponderante.

equiponderate [-eịt], vn. y va. equiponderar; hacer equiponderante; contrapesar.

equisetaceous [ekwisętéịsʌs], a. (bot.) equisetáceo.

equitable [ékwịtạbl], a. equitativo.—**equitableness** [-nịs], s. equidad, imparcialidad, justicia.—**equitably** [-blị], adv. equitativamente.

equitant [ékwịtạnt], a. (bot.) acaballado.

equitation [-éịsọn], s. equitación.

equity [ékwịtị], s. equidad, justicia; diferencia entre el valor de una propiedad y la cantidad por que está hipotecada.

equivalence, o **equivalency** [ikwívạlęns, -i], s. equivalencia.—**equivalent** [-ęnt], a. y s. equivalente.—**to be e.** (to), equivaler (a).—**equivalently** [-lị], adv. equivalentemente.

equivocal [ikwívọkạl]. I. a. equívoco, ambiguo. II. s. equívoco.—**equivocally** [-ị], adv. equívocamente, ambiguamente.—**equivocalness** [-nịs], s. ambigüedad.

equivocate [ikwívọkeịt], vn. usar palabras o frases equívocas o ambiguas.—**equivocation** [-éịsọn], s. equivocación, equívoco, anfibología.—**equivocator** [-tọ(r)], s. equivoquista, el que usa de equívocos.

era [írạ], s. era, época; (geol.) edad, época.

eradiate [iréịdịeịt], va. y vn. radiar, irradiar.

eradiation [-éịsọn], s. radiación.

eradicate [irédịkeịt], va. desarraigar, erradicar; destruir, extirpar.—**eradication** [-kéịsọn], s. erradicación, desarraigo, extirpación.—**eradicative** [-kạtịv], a. erradicativo.

erasable [iréịsạbl], a. borrable.

erase [iréịs], va. borrar, raspar, raer, tachar.

eraser [-œ(r)], s. raspador; goma de borrar.

erasion [iréịʒọn], s. (med.) extirpación o eliminación por raspadura.

Erasmian [irǽzmịạn], a. y s. erasmiano, erasmista.

erasure [iréịʒŋ(r)], s. raspadura, borradura.

ere [er]. I. prep. antes de. II. conj. antes que.

erect [irékt]. I. va. erigir, levantar, edificar, construir; enderezar; montar, instalar; erguir, enhestar o alzar; enaltecer. II. a. (e)recto, derecho, erguido, enhiesto; vertical; engallado, firme.

erectile [-ịl], a. eréctil.

erectility [-ịlịtị], s. erectilidad.

erecting [-ịŋ], a. edificante; (ópt.) de imagen recta (apl. a lentes, anteojos, telescopios).

erection [irékšọn], s. erección; montaje, instalación; elevación, erguimiento; estructura.

erective [-tịv], a. que tiende a erigir, etc.

erectness [-nịs], s. erección, erguimiento.

erector [-ọ(r)]. I. s. erector, edificador, montador. II. a. y s. (anat.) erector.

erelong [erlóŋ], adv. antes de mucho.

eremite [érịmạịt], s. ermitaño.

eremitic(al [erịmịtịk(ạl], a. eremítico.

erenow [ernáu], adv. antes de ahora.

erethism [éreθịzm], s. (med.) eretismo.

erg [œrg], s. (fís.) erg y ergio, unidad de energía.

ergosterin [œrgástęrịn], **ergosterol** [-ol], s. (quím.) ergosterina.

ergot [œrgọt], s. (bot.) cornezuelo de centeno.

ergotin(e [-ịn], s. (quím.) ergotina.

ergotinine [œrgátịnịn], s. (quím.) ergotinina.

ergotism [œrgọtịzm], s. (med. y fil.) ergotismo.

ergotize [-aịz], vn. (fil.) ergotizar.

ericaceous [erịkéịšʌs], a. (bot.) ericáceo.

eristic [erịstịk], a. erístico; pendenciero.

ermine [œrmịn], s. (zool.) armiño; piel (f.) de armiño; (fig.) toga, judicatura; pureza del cargo judicial.

ermined [-d], a. armiñado.

ern(e [œrn], s. (orn.) halieto.

erode [iróụd]. I. va. corroer, roer; comer. II. vn. (geol.) desgastarse.—**erodent** [-ęnt], a. (med.) corrosivo, cáustico.

erogenous [irádǽęnʌs], a. que despierta el deseo erótico.

erosion [iróụʒọn], s. corrosión; desgaste; (geol.) erosión.

erosive [iróụsịv], a. (med.) caterético; desgastador o corroedor.

erotic(al [erátịk(ạl], a. y s. erótico.—**eroticism** [erátịsịzm], **erotism** [érọtịzm], s. erotismo.—**erotomania** [eroụtoméịnịạ], s. erotomanía.

err [œr], vn. errar, equivocarse; descarriarse, pecar; errar, no dar en el blanco.

errancy [érạnsị], s. propensión a errar.

errand [érạnd], s. recado, mensaje, mandado, diligencia.—**e. boy,** mandadero, recadero.

errant [érạnt], a. errante, andante, errabundo, vagabundo, vagaroso; errático.—**errantry** [-rị], s. vida errante; caballería andante.

errata [iréịtạ], s. pl. de ERRATUM; fe de erratas.

erratic(al [irétịk(ạl]. I. a. errático, excéntrico; errante, vagabundo; (med.) errático. II. s. persona excéntrica; (geol.) canto rodado.—**erratically** [-ị], adv. de un modo errático; irregularmente.

erratum [iréịtạm], s. (pl. ERRATA) errata.

errhine [érạịn], a. y s. (med.) estornutatorio.

erring [œrịŋ], a. errado, errante, descarriado.

erroneous [eróụnịʌs], a. errado, erróneo, falso.—**erroneously** [-lị], adv. erróneamente.—**erroneousness** [-nịs], s. calidad de erróneo.

error [érọ(r)], s. error, equivocación, yerro; engaño; pecado.

ersatz [ersáts], a. y s. sintético, artificial; substitut(iv)o.

Erse [œrs], s. gaélico; lenguaje de los montañeses de Escocia.

erst [œrst], **erstwhile** [-hwaịl], adv. y a. (ant.) antiguamente, antes; en otro o de otro tiempo.

erubescence, erubescency [erụbésęns, -ị], s. erubescencia, rubor.

erubescent [-ęnt], a. erubescente, ruboroso.

eruct(ate [irákt(eịt], vn. y va. eructar, regoldar; arrojar, expeler, echar de sí.

eructation [-éịsọn], s. eructación, eructo, regüeldo.

erudite [érụdaịt], a. y s. erudito, letrado.

erudition [erụdịšọn], s. erudición; conocimientos.

eruginous [irúdǽịnʌs], a. ruginoso.

erupt [irápt], vn. salir con fuerza; hacer erupción.

eruption [irápšọn], s. erupción; irrupción.

eruptive [iráptịv], a. eruptivo.

eryngo [irịŋgoụ], s. (bot.) eringe, f., cabezuela, cardo corredor (ll. t. **eringo**).

erysipelas [erịsịpęlạs], s. (med.) erisipela.

erysipelatous [erịsịpélạtʌs], a. erisipelatoso.

erythema [erịθímạ], s. (med.) eritema, m.

erythr(a)ean [erịθríạn], a. de color rojo; (E.) a. y s. eritreo; rel. o pert. al Mar Rojo.

erythrin [erịθrịn], s. (quím.) eritrina.

escadrille [eskạdríl], s. escuadrilla aérea o naval.

escalade [eskạléịd]. I. s. (mil.) escalada. II. va. (mil.) escalar.

escalator [éskạleịtọ(r)], s. escalera mecánica, que funciona como una correa sin fin.

escal(l)op [eskálọp], va. y s. (coc.) = SCALLOP.

escapade [eskạpéịd], s. escapada, travesura; correría, aventura; fuga.

escape [eskéịp]. I. va. escaparse o librarse de; evadir, evitar, eludir, esquivar, salvar.—**to e. notice,** pasar inadvertido. II. vn. escapar(se), fugarse, huir(se), zafarse. III. s. escapada, huída, fuga, escapatoria, evasión, zafada; derrame; fuga o escape (de gas o líquido); escape (de reloj).—**e. hatch,** (mar.) escotilla de emergencia.—**e. outlet,** (m. v.) salida.—**to have a narrow e.,** escaparse en una tabla, salvarse por un pelo.

escapement [-męnt], s. escape de reloj, etc.

escarole [éskạroụl], s. (bot.) escarola.

escarp [eskárp]. I. va. (mil.) escarpar. II. s. escarpa.

escarpment [-męnt], s. escarpa, acantilado.

eschalot [ɛṣk̩lát], *s.* (bot.) escaloña.

eschar [éskar], *s.* (cir.) escara, costra.

escharotic [ɛskar̩átik̩]. **I.** *a.* escarótico. **II.** *s.* cáustico.

eschatology [ɛskatálodʒi̩], *s.* (teol.) escatología.

escheat [ɛschít]. **I.** *s.* (for.) reversión de bienes mostrencos o abintestatos al estado; confiscación de bienes. **II.** *va.* confiscar, apropriarse el estado de bienes mostrencos o abintestatos. **III.** *vn.* revertir al estado (bienes mostrencos o abintestatos).—**escheatable** [-ab̩l], *a.* confiscable; revertible al estado.

eschew [ɛschú], *va.* huir de, evitar, evadir.

escort [ɛskort], **I.** *s.* escolta, convoy; acompañante.—**e. ship**, barco escolta. **II.** [ɛskórt], *va.* escoltar, convoyar; acompañar, cortejar.

escritoire [ɛskr̩itwár], *s.* escritorio, escribanía, buró, arquimesa.

escrow [ɛskróu], *s.* (for.) plica.

esculent [éskiu̯lent], *a.* y *s.* comestible; comedero.

escutcheon [ɛskáchon], *s.* escudo de armas; guarnición.—**escutcheoned** [-d], *a.* blasonado.

Eskimo, Eskimau [éskimou̯], *s.* y *a.* esquimal.

esophagus [isáfag̩s], *s.* (anat., zool.) esófago, gola.

esoteric [esotérik̩], *a.* esotérico; oculto, reservado; confidencial.

espalier [ɛspǽlyœ(r)]. **I.** *s.* espaldar, espaldera, varaseto. **II.** *va.* hacer o formar espalderas.

esparto (**grass**) [ɛspártou̯], *s.* (bot.) esparto.

especial [ɛspéʃal], *a.* especial, particular; notable, sobresaliente.—**especially** [-i], *adv.* especialmente, señaladamente; sobre todo, máxime.

Esperantist [esperántist], *a.* y *s.* esperantista.

Esperanto [-tou̯], *s.* esperanto (lengua universal).

espial [ɛspái̯al], *s.* espionaje.

espionage [éspionidʒ], *s.* espionaje; acecho.

esplanade [esplanéid], *s.* ribera; (fort.) explanada, glacis.

espousal [ɛspáuz̩l], *s.* (a veces *pl.*) desposorio, esponsales, bodas; adhesión a una causa.

espouse [ɛspáuz], *va.* desposarse, casarse (con), contraer esponsales o matrimonio; defender, abogar por, abrazar (una causa).

esprit [esprí], *s.* (fr.) espíritu; chiste, agudeza.—**e. de corps**, compañerismo; espíritu de partido o de solidaridad.

espy [ɛspái̯]. **I.** *va.* divisar, alcanzar a ver, columbrar, descubrir. **II.** *vn.* mirar alrededor, observar.

esquire [ɛskwái̯r], *s.* título honorífico (se usa pospuesto al apellido y gen. se escribe Esq.); acompañante de una dama; (Ingl.) (ant.) hacendado; (hist.) escudero al servicio de un caballero.

essay [eséi̯], *va.* ensayar, probar, (in)tentar.

essay [ései̯], *s.* ensayo (literario); conato, esfuerzo, ensayo.—**e. writing**, ensayismo.—**essayist** [-ist], *s.* ensayista, escritor de ensayos.

essence [éṣens], *s.* esencia (de una cosa), ser, substancia; medula; (quím.) esencia; perfume.—**in e.**, en el fondo, esencialmente.

Essene [ɛsín], **Essenian** [-ian], *s.* y *a.* esenio.

essential [ɛsénʃal]. **I.** *a.* esencial, vital, indispensable, imprescindible, capital; constitutivo.—**e. oil**, aceite esencial. **II.** *s.* (gen. *pl.*) lo esencial, la substancia, los elementos, las necesidades.—**to stick to e.**, ir al grano.

essentiality [-ṣi̯éliti], *s.* calidad de esencial.—**essentially** [-i], *adv.* esencialmente.

essoin [esói̯n], *s.* (for.) excusa.

essonite [ésonai̯t], *s.* (min.) grosularia canela.

establish [ɛstábliʃ]. **I.** *va.* establecer, fundar, crear, constituir, erigir; sentar; consagrar; probar, demostrar; restablecer, solidar; ratificar, sancionar. **II.** *vr.* establecerse, instalarse, arraigarse, radicarse.

establishment [-ment], *s.* establecimiento (comercial, de educación, etc.); erección, fundación; institución; pensión o renta vitalicia.

estafet [ɛstafét], *s.* estafeta, correo.

estate [estéi̯t], *s.* bienes, propiedades, patrimonio, herencia; heredad, finca, fundo, hacienda; estado, clase o condición, posición.

esteem [estím]. **I.** *va.* estimar, apreciar, hacer caso de; reputar, juzgar; tener en o por, creer. **II.** *s.* estima(ción), aprecio; mérito; juicio, opinión.

ester [éstœ(r)], *s.* (quím.) éster.

esthesia [esθíʒi̯ạ], *s.* estesia, sensibilidad; capacidad de sentir.

esthete [ésθit], *s.* esteta, *mf.*, admirador del arte o de la estética.

esthetic [esθétik̩]. **I.** *a.* estético. **II.** *s.* esteta (persona), *mf.*; (fil.) estética.

esthetically [-ạli], *adv.* estéticamente.

esthetics [-s], *s.* (fil.) estética.

estimable [éstimab̩l], *a.* benemérito, estimable; calculable.

estimableness [-nis], *s.* estimabilidad.

estimate [éstimeit]. **I.** *va.* apreciar, (a)valuar o valorar, estimar, tantear, tasar; calcular (gen. aproximadamente); hacer un presupuesto. **II.** [éstimạt], *s.* avalúo, estimación, tanteo, tasa, cálculo; opinión; (com.) presupuesto.

estimation [estiméi̯ʃon], *s.* cálculo; presupuesto; estima, aprecio; opinión; suposición.

estimator [éstimeitọ(r)], *s.* estimador, calculador.

estival [éstival], *a.* estival, estivo, veraniego.—**estivate** [-veit], *vn.* veranear.—**estivation** [-véi̯ʃon], *s.* veraneo; veranada; (bot.) prefloración; (zool.) letargo o adormecimiento estival.

Est(h)onian [estóuni̯an], *a.* y *s.* estoni(an)o.

estop [estáp], *va.* (for.) impedir una afirmación contraria a otras anteriores.

estoppel [-el], *s.* (for.) acto o afirmación que no puede negarse posteriormente ante la ley; imposibilidad en que se coloca uno de negar lo que ha afirmado previamente.

estrange [stréi̯ndʒ], *va.* extrañar, apartar, alejar, malquistar o malmeter; enajenar.

estrangement [-ment], *s.* enajenamiento; extrañamiento, desvío, alejamiento.

estray [stréi̯], *s.* (for.) animal descarriado o mostrenco.

estuary [éschi̯ueri], *s.* estuario, estero, ría.

étagère [ei̯tæžér], *s.* (fr.) estante, juguetero.

et cetera, etc. [et séterạ], (lat.) etcétera, etc.

etch [ech], *va.* y *vn.* grabar, o hacer grabados, al agua fuerte.—**etcher** [-œ(r)], *s.* aguafuertista, acuafortista, grabador al agua fuerte.—**etching** [-iŋ], *s.* aguafuerte, *f.*, grabado al agua fuerte.

eternal [itérnal], *a.* eterno, eternal, inmortal, sempiterno.—**e. flower**, (bot.) perpetua.—**the E., Dios.**—**the E. City**, Roma.—**eternally** [-i], *adv.* eternamente.—**eternity** [-iti], *s.* eternidad.—**eternize** [-ai̯z], *va.* eternizar; perpetuar; inmortalizar.

etesian [itíʒan], *a.* y *s.* etesio, periódico (viento).

ethane [éθei̯n], *s.* (quím.) etano, dimetilo.

ether [íθœ(r)], *s.* éter.—**ethereal** [iθíri̯al], **ethereous** [iθíri̯as], *a.* etéreo.

etherealize [-ai̯z], *va.* hacer etéreo, espiritualizar; (quím.) convertir en éter.

etherealization [-izéi̯ʃon], *s.* efecto de hacer etéreo, etc.; conversión en éter.

etheriform [íθeriform], *a.* etéreo.

etherify [íθerifai̯], *va.* (quím.) eterificar.

etherism [íθœrizm], *s.* (med.) eterismo.

etherization [iθœrizéi̯ʃon], *s.* (med.) eterización.

etherize [íθœrai̯z], *va.* (med.) eterizar; (quím.) convertir en éter.

ethic [éθik]. **I.** *a.* = ETHICAL. **II.** *s.* = ETHICS.

ethical [éθikạl], *a.* ético, moral.—**ethically** [-i], *adv.* ética o moralmente.

ethicist [éθiṣist], *s.* ético moral.

ethicize [éθiṣai̯z]. **I.** *va.* dar carácter ético a. **II.** *vn.* tratar de la ética; discurrir sobre la moral.

ethics [éθiks], *s. pl.* ética, moral, *f.*

Ethiop [íθi̯ap], **Ethiopian** [iθi̯óupi̯an]. **I.** *s.* etíope, etiopio. **II.** *a.* etiópico.—**Ethiopic** [iθi̯ápik], *a.* y *s.* (lengua) etiópica.

ethmoid [éθmɔid], s. y a. (anat.) etmoides.
ethnarch [éθnark], s. etnarca, m.—ethnarchy [-i] s. etnarquía.
ethnic(al [éθnik(ąl], a. étnico; pagano, gentil.
ethnogeny [eθnádźeni], s. estudio del origen de las razas. V. ETHNOGRAPHY y ETHNOLOGY.
ethnographer [eθnágrąfœ(r)], s. etnógrafo.
ethnographic(al [eθnográefik(ąl], a. etnográfico.
ethnography [eθnágrąfi], s. etnografía.
ethnologic(al [eθnoládźik(ąl], a. etnológico.
ethnologist [eθnálodźist], s. etnólogo.
ethnology [-dźi], s. etnología.
ethological [eθoládźikąl], a. que trata del carácter.
ethology [iθálodźi], s. etología.
ethos [íθas], s. carácter, genio (de un pueblo, de una colectividad); rasgo distintivo.
ethyl [éθil], s. (quím.) etilo.—e. alcohol, alcohol etílico.—e. ether, éter.
ethylene [-in], s. (quím.) etileno.
ethylic [eθílik], a. etílico.
etiolate [itiolei̯t], va. y vn. blanquear(se).
etiolation [-éiśǫn], s. (bot.) palidez, descoloración.
etiology [itiálodźi], s. (med. y fil.) etiología.
etiquette [étįket], s. etiqueta.
Etruscan [itrắskąn], Etrurian [itrúrįąn], a. y s. etrusco.
étude [ei̯tiúd], s. (mús.) estudio.
etui, etwee [etwí], s. estuche, caja.
etymological [etįmoládźikąl], a. etimológico.
etymologically [-i], adv. etimológicamente.
etymologist [etįmálodźist], s. etimologista.
etymologize [-dźai̯z], va. etimologizar.
etymology [-dźi], s. etimología.
etymon [étįman], s. (gram.) raíz.
Euboean, Euboic [yubíąn, yubóųik], a. y s. eubeo, euboico.
eucaine [yukéin], s. eucaína, base de ciertos anestésicos locales.
eucalyptus [yukąlíptʌs], s. (bot.) eucalipto.
Eucharist [yúkąrįst], s. eucaristía.
Eucharistic(al [-ístik(ąl], a. eucarístico.
euchology [yukálodźi], s. (igl.) eucologio.
euchre [yúkœ(r)]. I. s. juego de naipes. II. va. en dicho juego, dar codillo; (fig.) ganar, vencer.
Euclidean, Euclidian [yuklídįąn], a. euclidiano, de Euclides.—E. geometry, geometría euclidiana.
eudemonic(al [yudįmánik(ąl], a. relativo a la felicidad; que tiene por fin la felicidad.
eudemonics [-s], s. tratado de la felicidad.—eudemonism [yudímǫnįzm], s. eudemonismo, doctrina según la cual la felicidad es el sumo bien.—eudemonist [-įst], s. eudemonista.
eudiometer [yudįámetœ(r)], s. (quím.) eudiómetro.
eugenic [yudźénik], a. eugenésico.—eugenics [-s], s. eugenesia (apl. esp. a la humana, que trata del perfeccionamiento de la raza).
eugenism [yúdźenįzm], s. condiciones eugenésicas; eugenesia.—eugenist [-įst], s. persona versada en eugenesia.
eugenol [yúdźenal], s. (quím.) eugenol.
eulogist [yúlodźįst], s. elogiador, panegirista.
eulogistic [-dźístik], a. laudatorio, encomiástico, (Am.) elogioso.—eulogize [-dźai̯z], va. elogiar, loar, encomiar, ensalzar, panegirizar, preconizar.—eulogy, eulogium [-dźi, yulóu̯dźįʌm], s. elogio, encomio, panegírico, apología.
eunuch [yúnʌk], s. eunuco, capón, espadón.
eupatorium [yupątóu̯rįʌm], s. (bot.) eupatorio.
eupatrid [yupétrįd; pl. EUPATRIDÆ], s. (hist.) eupátrida.
eupepsia [yupépsįȩ], s. (med.) eupepsia, digestión normal.—eupeptic [-tįk], a. eupéptico.
euphemism [yúfįmįzm], s. (ret.) eufemismo.
euphemist [-įst], s. el que emplea el eufemismo.—euphemistic(al [-ístik(ąl], a. eufemístico.—euphemize [-ai̯z], vn. hacer uso del eufemismo.
euphonic(al [yufánik(ąl], euphonious [yufóų-

niʌs], a. eufónico.—euphoniously [-li], adv. eufónicamente.—euphonize [yúfonai̯z], va. eufonizar.—euphony [yúfoni], s. eufonía.
euphorbia [yufórbįȩ], s. (bot.) euforbio.
euphorbiaceous [-éiśįʌs], a. euforbiáceo.
euphorbium [yufórbįʌm], s. (farm.) euforbio.
euphoria [yufórįȩ], euphory [yúfori], s. (psic.) euforia.
euphuism [yúfįuįzm], s. eufuismo, culteranismo, alambicamiento, gongorismo.—euphuist [-įst], s. eufuista, gongorista, culterano.—euphuistic [-ístįk], a. culterano, gongórico, alambicado.
Eurasian [yuréiźįąn], s. y a. eurasio, eurasiático; apl. a lo relativo a Eurasia (Europa y Asia) y también al mestizo de europeo y asiático.
eureka [yuríką], interj. ¡eureka! (¡lo he hallado!)
European [yuropíąn], s. y a. europeo.—E. concert, concierto europeo (relativo a la política europea en el Oriente).—E. plan, hospedaje sin alimentos, cuarto sin comida.—Europeanize [-ai̯z], va. europeizar.
eurythmic [yuríθmįk], a. eurítmico.
eurythmy [yuríθmį], s. (b. a.) euritmia.
Eustachian tube [yustéi̯kįąn tįub], s. (anat.) trompa de Eustaquio.
eustyle [yústai̯l], s. (arq.) éustilo.
eutectic [yu̯téktįk], a. (fís.) eutéctico, de máxima fusibilidad (apl. a aleaciones en que ciertas proporciones de los componentes dan el punto mínimo de fusión).
euthanasia [yu̯θąnéiźįȩ], s. eutanasia, muerte tranquila.
euthenics [yu̯θénįks], s. ciencia que trata de mejorar la raza humana mejorando las condiciones de la vida.
Eutychian [yutíkįąn], s. y a. eutiquiano.
euxenite [yúksęnai̯t], s. (min.) euxinita.
evacuant [įvékyuȩnt], a. y s. (med.) evacuante.
evacuate [-ei̯t]. I. va. evacuar, descoupar, vaciar; sacar. II. vn. vaciarse; desalojarse, retirarse.—evacuation [-éiśǫn], s. evacuación, desocupación.—evacuative [-ȩtįv], a. purgativo, evacuativo.—evacuator [-ei̯tǫ(r)], s. evacuador.—evacuee [įvækyuí], s. el que se aleja de su casa o país durante una evacuación.
evade [įvéid]. I. va. evadir, eludir o iludir, burlar, evitar, esquivar, rehuir. II. vn. usar de evasivas o efugios; deslizarse, escabullirse.
evaginate [įvédźįnei̯t], va. volver al revés, de adentro afuera.
evaluate [įvélyuȩit], va. avaluar, (e)valuar, valorar, tasar; (mat.) hallar el valor numérico de.—evaluation [-éiśǫn], s. avalúo, valoración; (mat.) determinación del valor numérico.
evanesce [įvanés], vn. desaparecer, disiparse, esfumarse; desvanecerse, evaporarse.—evanescence [-éns], s. disipación.—evanescent [-ént], a. evanescente, que se disipa o desvanece; (mat.) que se aproxima a cero; (biol.) instable.
evangel [įvéndźęl], s. buena nueva, evangelio; evangelista.
evangelic(al [-dźélįk(ąl], a. evangélico.
evangelically [-i], adv. evangélicamente.
evangelism [įvéndźęlįzm], s. evangelismo.
evangelist [-įst], s. evangelista; evangelizador.
evangelistary [-lístąrį], s. (igl.) evangeliario.
evangelization [-lizéiśǫn], s. evangelización.
evangelize [-lai̯z]. I. va. evangelizar. II. vn. predicar el evangelio.—evangelizer [-œ(r)], s. evangelizador.
evaporable [įvéporąbl], a. evaporable.
evaporate [-rei̯t], va. y vn. evaporar(se), (e)vaporizar(se); (de)secar(se); desvanecer(se).—evaporation [-réiśǫn], s. evaporación.—evaporative [-rȩtįv], a. evaporatorio.—evaporator [-rei̯tǫ(r)], s. evaporador; desecador; (azú.) desecadora, evaporadora.
evasion [įvéiźǫn], s. evasión, evasiva, efugio, escape, escapatoria.—evasive [įvéisįv], a. evasivo.—evasively [-li], adv. evasivamente.

eve [iv], *s.* (poét.) noche, *f.;* vigilia; víspera.—**on the e. of,** la víspera de, en vísperas de.

evection [ivékšǫn], *s.* (astr.) evección.

even [íven]. **I.** *a.* llano, plano, liso, nivelado; igual; uniforme; imparcial; apacible, inmutable; par (divisible por dos); recto, justo; constante, firme; redondo (número); situado al mismo nivel, parejo (con).—**of e. date,** de la misma fecha.—**to be e. with,** estar en paz con, estar mano a mano.—**to be e. with one,** cancelar la cuenta con uno; vengarse, pagar en la misma moneda.—**to make e.,** allanar, igualar, nivelar; compensar. **II.** *adv.* aun, hasta, también; incluso; siquiera; exactamente, precisamente, enteramente; de un modo igual y fácil.—**e. as,** así como.—**e. if,** aun cuando, aunque.—**e. now,** ahora mismo.—**e. so,** así; aun así, suponiendo que así sea.—**e. though** = EVEN IF.—**not e.,** ni siquiera, ni aun. **III.** *va.* (a veces con *up*) igualar, emparejar, allanar, enrasar, nivelar; unir; desquitar, liquidar cuentas.

evening [ívnin]. **I.** *s.* tarde, *f.;* noche, *f.* (primeras horas); vísperas. **II.** *a.* ocurriendo o visto de noche; vespertino.—**e. clothes,** o **dress,** traje de etiqueta, de ceremonia o de serio; frac; traje de noche o de cola (para señoras).—**e. party,** sarao, velada.—**e. star,** estrella vespertina, lucero de la tarde.

evenly [ívenli], *adv.* llanamente; igualmente; con suavidad; a nivel; imparcialmente.

evenness [-nis], *s.* igualdad, uniformidad; llanura, lisura; imparcialidad.

evensong [ívensǫn], *s.* vísperas, oraciones.

event [ivént], *s.* acontecimiento, acaecimiento, suceso; éxito, consecuencia, resultado.—**after the e.,** ya pasado, o ejecutado, el hecho.—**at all events, in any e.,** sea lo que fuere, en todo caso, de cualquier modo.—**in the e. of,** en caso de.

eventful [-fuḷ], *a.* lleno de acontecimientos; memorable.

eventide [íventaid], *s.* (poét.) caída de la tarde.

eventual [ivénchuǫḷ], *a.* consiguiente; eventual, contingente, fortuito.—**eventuality** [-éḷiti], *s.* eventualidad.—**eventually** [-i], *adv.* eventualmente, finalmente; con el tiempo.

eventuate [-eit], *vn.* acontecer, acaecer, suceder.

ever [évœ(r)], *adv.* siempre; alguna vez, en cualquier tiempo; en la (mi, su) vida; nunca (vg.: *the best book ever written,* el mejor libro que se haya escrito nunca). En oraciones interrogativas se emplea a veces como expletivo enfático para expresar sorpresa, dificultad, impaciencia, etc., y o no se traduce o se traduce introduciendo el verbo *poder* o el adverbio *nunca;* vg. *how did you ever do it?* ¿cómo lo hizo usted? o ¿cómo puede usted haberlo hecho?; *are you ever going to finish?* ¿no terminará usted nunca?.—**e. and anon,** de cuando en cuando, de vez en cuando.—**e. since,** desde que; desde entonces, después.—**e. so,** muy, -ísimo (*I am ever so happy,* soy muy feliz; *we saw ever so many things,* vimos muchísimas cosas; *I thank you ever so much,* muchísimas gracias, le agradezco mucho).—**as e.,** como siempre; (con *as*) tanto como, lo más, vg.: *run as fast as ever you can,* corra lo más aprisa que pueda).—**did you e.?** (fam.) ¿habráse visto? ¡qué cosa! ¡qué ocurrencia!—**for e. and a day,** interminablemente, eternamente.—**for e. and e.,** por siempre jamás, por los siglos de los siglos.—**hardly e.,** casi nunca.—**nor e.,** ni nunca.—**not e.,** nunca.—**scarcely e.,** casi nunca.

everglade [-gleid], *s.* terreno pantanoso cubierto de altas hierbas; paúl.

evergreen [-grin]. **I.** *a.* siempre verde, vivaz. **II.** *s.* (bot.) cualquier planta, arbusto o árbol que mantiene su verdor en todas las estaciones.

everlasting [-lǽstin]. **I.** *a.* eterno, sempiterno, perdurable, perpetua; fastidioso, pesado. **II.** *s.*

eternidad; (tej.) sempiterna; (bot.) siempreviva, perpetua.—**the E.,** Dios, el Ser eterno.

everlastingly [-li], *adv.* eternamente.

everliving [-lívin], *a.* inmortal, eterno, perdurable.

evermore [-mor], *adv.* eternamente; de todo tiempo.—**e.,** o **for e.,** para siempre jamás.

eversion [ivéršǫn], *s.* eversión; vuelta al revés.

evert [ivért], *va.* trastornar; voltear al revés.

every [évri], *a.* cada; todo, todos los.—**e. bit,** (fam.) enteramente.—**e. day, month,** etc., todos los días, meses, etc.—**e. now and then,** o **e. once in a while,** de cuando en cuando.—**e. one,** cada uno, cada cual; todos, todo el mundo.—**e. one of them,** todos, todos sin excepción.—**e. other,** cada dos, uno sí y otro no (*every other day,* un día sí y otro no).—**e. so often,** cada cierto tiempo, a intervalos fijos.—**e. which way,** (fam.) por todas partes, en toda dirección.—**e. whit,** enteramente.

everybody [-badi], *pron.* todos; todo el mundo; cada uno, cada cual.—**e. for himself,** cada cual por su cuenta; sálvese el que pueda.

everyday [-déi], *a.* de cada día, ordinario, diario, cuotidiano.

everyone [-wʌn], *pron.* todo el mundo; todos.

everything [-θiŋ], *pron.* y *s.* todo, cada cosa.

everywhere [-hwer], *adv.* en o por todas partes, por do(nde)quiera.

evict [ivíkt], *va.* desalojar, desaposentar, desahuciar; excluir, expulsar.

eviction [ivíkšǫn], *s.* desalojamiento; (for.) desahucio, evicción.

evidence [évidens]. **I.** *s.* evidencia; demostración; (for.) prueba; testimonio, deposición, declaración.—**to be in e.,** dejarse ver, mostrarse.—**to give e.,** dar testimonio, deponer, declarar. **II.** *va.* evidenciar, patentizar, probar.

evident [-ent], *a.* evidente, claro, manifiesto, palmario, palpable, patente.—**to be e.,** resaltar, saltar a la vista o a los ojos.

evidential [evidénšǫḷ], *a.* indicativo; de carácter de prueba, probatorio.

evidently [évidentli], *adv.* evidentemente.

evil [ívil]. **I.** *a.* malo; maligno, perverso; nocivo, perjudicial, pernicioso; aciago.—**e. deed,** malhecho.—**e. fame,** o **e. repute,** mala reputación.—**e. speaking,** maledicencia, murmuración.—**e. spirit,** demonio.—**the e. eye,** aojo, aojadura. **II.** *s.* mal; maldad, perversidad.—**sufficient unto the day is the e. thereof,** le basta al día su propio afán.—**the E. One,** el diablo, Satanás, el malo.—**the social e.,** la prostitución. **III.** *adv.* mal; malignamente.—**e.-eyed,** aojador.—**e.-favored,** repugnante, feo.—**e.-minded,** malicioso, mal intencionado.—**e.-starred,** desafortunado, de mala suerte.

evildoer [-duœ(r)], *s.* malhechor, persona perversa.

evilly [-i], *adv.* malamente; perversamente.

evilness [-nis], *s.* maldad.

evince [ivíns], *va.* hacer patente, probar terminantemente; revelar, indicar.—**evincible** [-ibl], *a.* demostrable.—**evincibly** [-ibli], *adv.* demostrablemente.—**evincive** [-iv], *a.* convincente.

eviscerate [ivíserejt], *va.* destripar, desentrañar.

evisceration [-éjšǫn], *s.* destripamiento.

evitable [évitabl], *a.* evitable.

evocation [evokéjšǫn], *s.* evocación o llamamiento; (for.) avocación.

evocative [ivákativ], *a.* evocador.

evoke [ivóuk], *va.* evocar, llamar.

evolution [evoliúšǫn], *s.* evolución, desarrollo; (mil.) evolución, maniobra; (mat.) extracción de raíces.—**evolutional** [-aḷ], **evolutionary** [-eri], *a.* evolucionista, evolucionario, evolutivo.—**evolutionism** [-izm], *s.* evolucionismo, teoría de la evolución.—**evolutionist** [-ist], *s.* y *a.* evolucionista.—**evolutive** [évoljutiv], *a.* evolutivo.

evolve [iválv]. **I.** *va.* desenvolver, desarrollar;

(biol.) producir por evolución; despedir (gases). **II.** vn. desarrollarse; evolucionar.

evolvent [-ęnt], s. y a. (geom.) evolvente.

evulsion [ivʌ́lşǫn], s. (cir.) evulsión, arranque.

ewe [yu], s. oveja.—**e. lamb**, cordera, borrega.

ewer [yúœ(r)], s. aguamanil, jarro, (Am.) múcura.

ex [ɛks]. **I.** a. ex, que fué. **II.** prep. (com. y fin.) sin incluir; sin participación en; libre de cargo o gravamen hasta salir de (un almacén, etc.). **III.** s. nombre de la letra X.

exacerbate [ɛgzǽscœrbejt], va. exacerbar; agravar.

exacerbation [-éįşǫn], s. exacerbación; agravación; exasperación, irritación.

exact [ɛgzǽkt]. **I.** a. exacto, cabal, correcto, fiel; justo, puntual; estrecho, estricto, riguroso. **II.** va. exigir, imponer.

exacter, exactor [-œ(r)], s. exactor, opresor.

exacting [-įŋ], a. exigente.

exaction [ɛgzǽkşǫn], s. exacción, extorsión.

exactitude [-títįud], s. exactitud, precisión, puntualidad, rectitud, fidelidad.—**exactly** [-lį], adv. exactamente.—**exactness** [-nįs], s. = EXACTITUDE.

exaggerate [ɛgzǽdžęrejt], va. y vn. exagerar, encarecer, engrandecer, ponderar.—**exaggeration** [-éįşǫn], s. exageración, encarecimiento, ponderación.—**exaggerative** [-įv], a. exagerativo.—**exaggeratively** [-lį], adv. exagerativamente.—**exaggerator** [-ǫ(r)], s. exagerador.

exalt [ɛgzólt], va. exaltar, elevar, enaltecer, empinar, ensalzar, promover, glorificar; alegrar o regocijar; reforzar, sublimar.

exaltation [-éįşǫn], s. exaltación, elevación; enaltecimiento; ensalzamiento; promoción; contento, regocijo.

exalted [-įd], a. exaltado, elevado, eminente.

exam [ɛgzǽm], s. (fam.) examen.

examinable [-įnȧbl], a. que se puede examinar; investigable, averiguable.

examination [-įnéįşǫn], s. examen; indagación, investigación; inspección, reconocimiento, registro; ensayo, prueba; (for.) interrogatorio.

examine [ɛgzǽmįn], va. examinar; indagar, inspeccionar; reconocer, registrar, revisar; explorar; preguntar, inquirir; ensayar, aquilatar, analizar; (for.) interrogar.—**examinee** [-í], s. examinando.—**examiner** [-œ(r)], s. examinador, indagador, inspector, escrutador.

example [ɛgzǽmpl]. **I.** s. ejemplo, ejemplar; paradigma, m.; muestra, dechado; escarmiento, lección.—**for e.**, por ejemplo, verbigracia.—**to set an e.**, dar ejemplo. **II.** va. ejemplarizar, dar ejemplo de.

exanimate [ɛgzǽnįmįt], a. exánime; sin ánimo.

exanimation [-éįşǫn], s. exanimación, muerte, f.; desmayo, síncope.

exanthem(a [ɛksǽnθɛm, -θímȧ], s. (med.) exantema, m., erupción, sarpullido.

exanthematous [-θémȧtʌs], a. exantemático.

exarch [ɛ́ksark], s. exarca, m.

exarchate [-ejt], s. exarcado.

exasperate [ɛgzǽspęrejt], va. exasperar, exacerbar, amostazar; irritar; agravar, amargar, agriar.—**exasperation** [-éįşǫn], s. exasperación, exacerbación, provocación, enojo; agravación, recargo.

excavate [ɛ́kskȧvejt], va. excavar, (so)cavar, zanjar; vaciar, ahondar.

excavation [-éįşǫn], s. excavación; desmonte, zanja; material extraído por excavación; (agr.) excava; (arq.) vaciado, excavación.

excavator [-ǫ(r)], s. excavador; (ing.) excavadora (máquina).

exceed [ɛksíd]. **I.** va. exceder; aventajar, sobrepujar, (sobre)pasar, superar; rebasar. **II.** vn. excederse, propasarse; preponderar.

exceeding [-įŋ], a. excesivo; extraordinario.

exceedingly [-lį], adv. excesivamente, por demás; sumamente, muy, -ísimo (he is exceedingly rich, él es sumamente rico, o riquísimo).

excel [ɛksél], va. y vn. aventajar, superar, vencer; ser superior a; campar, sobresalir.

excellence, excellency [ɛ́ksęlęns, -į], s. excelencia.—**His E.,** Su Excelencia.—**Your E.,** Vuestra Excelencia, vuec(el)encia; usía.

excellent [-ęnt], a. excelente, admirable, sobresaliente.—**excellently** [-lį], adv. excelentemente.

excelsior [ɛksélsįǫ(r)]. **I.** a. más alto; hacia arriba. **II.** s. madera en hebras para empaquetar.

excentric [ɛkséntrįk], a. = ECCENTRIC.

except [ɛksépt]. **I.** va. exceptuar, excluir, eximir, omitir. **II.** vn. (for.) excepcionar; recusar. **III.** prep. excepto, con excepción de, fuera de, menos, salvo; sino; fuera de que.—**excepting** [-įŋ], prep. a excepción de, salvo, exceptuando.—**exception** [ɛksépşǫn], s. excepción, salvedad; (for.) excepción, recusación; objeción.—**to take e.,** objetar, oponerse, desaprobar.

exceptionable [-ȧbl], a. recusable, tachable.

exceptional [-ȧl], a. excepcional.

exceptionally [-ȧl], adv. excepcionalmente.

exceptive [-tįv], a. que implica excepción; susceptible, quisquilloso.

exceptor [-tǫ(r)], s. el que pone excepciones.

excerpt [ɛksœ́rpt]. **I.** va. extractar. **II.** [ɛ́ksœrpt], s. extracto, excerta.

excerption [ɛksœ́rpşǫn], s. acto de extractar; extracto, excerta.

excerptive [-tįv], a., **excerptor** [-tǫ(r)], s. extractador.

excess [ɛksés]. **I.** s. exceso, demasía, nimiedad, sobra, superfluidad; excedente; inmoderación o destemplanza; desorden; transgresión; (com.) sobrante, superávit.—**to e.,** con, o en, demasía; en exceso; inmoderadamente. **II.** a. excesivo, sobrante; suplemental, de recargo.—**e. baggage o weight,** exceso de equipaje o de peso.—**e. fare,** suplemento (de trayecto o de cambio de clase).—**e. profits tax,** impuesto sobre ganancias excesivas, superiores al promedio durante cierto período de condiciones normales. **III.** va. (Ingl.) exigir como pago adicional a, hacer recargo a.

excessive [-įv], a. excesivo, demasiado, desmedido, inmoderado, nimio, sobrado.—**excessively** [-lį], adv. excesiva, demasiada o nimiamente; en demasía.

exchange [ɛkschéįndž]. **I.** va. cambiar; canjear, conmutar, trocar, permutar; hacerse, darse, etc. (vg. to exchange bows, hacerse cortesías).—**to e. cards,** desafiarse.—**to e. shots,** darse o tirarse pistoletazos o tiros.—**to e. signs,** hacerse señas.—**to e. words,** cambiar, cruzar, decirse algunas palabras. **II.** vn. hacer un cambio; recibirse en cambio. **III.** s. cambio, trueque, permuta, conmutación; canje (de periódicos, prisioneros, credenciales); periódico de canje; (com.) bolsa, lonja; cambio (de la moneda); centro; (oficina) central (f.) de teléfonos.—**e. on checks,** (com.) comisión de cobro de cheques foráneos.—**e. rate,** (com.) tipo de(l) cambio.—**in e. for,** a cambio de; a, o en, trueque de.

exchangeable [-ȧbl], a. cambiable.

exchanger [-œ(r)], s. cambista, cambiante.

exchequer [ɛkschékœ(r)], s. real hacienda, erario, tesorería; fondos; (E., Ingl.) tribunal de hacienda.—**e. bill,** (Ingl.) abonaré de la Tesorería.

excipient [ɛksípįęnt], s. (farm.) excipiente.

excisable [ɛksáįzȧbl], a. sujeto al derecho de sisa.

excise [ɛksáįz]. **I.** s. alcabala, sisa, impuesto sobre consumos o artículos de comercio interior; (Ingl.) oficina de recaudación de impuestos interiores. **II.** a. de o relativo a impuestos interiores. **III.** va. cortar; extirpar; borrar, expurgar; gravar, sisar, someter a impuesto.

exciseman [-man], s. oficial del resguardo.

excision [ɛksížǫn], s. (cir.) excisión; extirpación.

excitability [ɛksáįtȧbílįtį], s. excitabilidad.

excitable [-tȧbl], a. excitable.—**excitant** [-tȧnt], a. y s. excitante.

excitation [eksïtéïşǫn], s. excitación; instigación, incitamiento, suscitación.

excitative, excitatory [eksáïtǫtïv, -torï], a. excitativo, provocativo.

excite [eksáït], va. excitar; acalorar, provocar, suscitar, animar, estimular; (elec.) excitar.

excited [-ïd], a. excitado, agitado, acalorado.—**excitedly** [-lï], adv. agitadamente, acaloradamente.

excitement [-mǫnt], s. excitación; estimulación; agitación, conmoción; acaloramiento.

exciter [-œ(r)], s. incitador, agitador, instigador; (elec.) excitador, excitatriz, máquina excitadora.

exciting [-ïŋ], a. excitante, estimulante, incitante, provocativo; excitador; emocionante.—**excitingly** [-lï], adv. de un modo excitante o provocativo.

exclaim [ekskléïm], va. y vn. exclamar, clamar.

exclamation [eksklǫméïşǫn], s. exclamación; (gram.) interjección.—**e. point**, punto de admiración (!).

exclamative, exclamatory [eksklémǫtïv, -torï], a. exclamativo, exclamatorio; admirativo.

exclave [ekskléïv], s. parte de un país enclavada en otro, o situada dentro de otro.

exclude [eksklúd], va. excluir, desechar, rechazar; (biol.) expeler, arrojar.

exclusion [eksklúżǫn], s. exclusión; exclusiva; eliminación; recusación; expulsión.

exclusionist [-ïst], s. el que quiere excluir a otros.

exclusive [eksklúsïv], a. exclusivo, exclusivista; privativo; exceptuado; único; de moda.—**e. of**, exclusive, sin contar.—**exclusively** [-lï], adv. exclusivamente, exclusive.—**exclusiveness** [-nïs], s. exclusividad; exclusiva, repulsa; calidad de exclusivo.—**exclusivism** [-ïzm], s. exclusivismo.—**exclusivist** [-ïst], s. exclusivista.

excogitate [ekskádżïteït]. I. va. excogitar, inventar. II. vn. meditar.—**excogitation** [-éïşǫn], s. acción de excogitar.

excommunicable [ekskǫmïúnïkǫbl], a. digno de excomunión.—**excommunicate** [-keït]. I. va. excomulgar. II. a. y s. excomulgado.—**excommunication** [-kéïşǫn], s. excomunión.—**excommunicator** [-keïtǫ(r)], s. excomulgador.

excoriate [ekskórïeït], va. desollar, excoriar; sahornarse.—**excoriation** [-éïşǫn], s. desolladura, excoriación; sahorno.

excorticate [ekskórtïkeït], va. descortezar.

excortication [-éïşǫn], s. descortezadura.

excrement [ekskrïmǫnt], s. excremento, heces, f. pl.

excremental, excrementary [-méntǫl, -tǫrï], **excrementitial, excrementitious** [-tïşǫl, -tïşʌs], a. excrementicio, excrementoso.

excrescence, excrescency [ekskrésǫns, -ï], s. excrecencia, carnosidad, fungosidad.

excrescent [-ǫnt], a. superfluo, que forma excrecencia.

excreta [ekskrítǫ], s. pl. excreciones.

excretal [-l], a. de las excreciones.

excrete [ekskrít], va. excretar.—**excretion** [ekskríşǫn], s. excreción; excremento; (med.) emunción.—**excretive** [-tïv], **excretory** [ekskrïtorï], a. excretorio.—**e. organs**, emuntorios.

excruciate [ekskrúşïeït], va. atormentar.

excruciating [-ïŋ], a. agudísima (dolor), penosísimo; (fam. E. U.) extremado, afectado.—**excruciatingly** [-lï], adv. extremadamente, vivísimamente.—**excruciation** [-éïşǫn], s. tormento.

exculpable [ekskʌlpǫbl], a. disculpable.—**exculpate** [ekskʌlpeït], va. disculpar, justificar, sincerar.—**exculpation** [-péïşǫn], s. disculpa.—**exculpatory** [ekskʌlpǫtorï], a. disculpador, justificativo, sincerador.

excursion [ekskœrşǫn], s. excursión, romería, viajata; (mil.) correría; expedición; salida; digresión; (fís.) mitad del movimiento de osci-

lación; (mec.) recorrido, curso.—**e. train**, tren botijo o de recreo (con rebaja de precios).

excursionist [-ïst], s. excursionista, viajero.

excursive [ekskœrsïv], a. errante, vagante; (fig.) digresivo, errático.—**excursively** [-lï], adv. de un modo vago, digresivo.—**excursiveness** [-nïs], s. calidad de digresivo o errante.

excursus [ekskœrsʌs], s. apéndice explicativo; digresión.

excusable [ekskïúzǫbl], a. excusable, disculpable.

excusableness [-nïs], s. disculpabilidad.

excusably [-blï], adv. disculpablemente.

excusatory [-torï], a. apologético.

excuse [ekskïúz]. I. va. excusar, disculpar, dispensar; sincerar, justificar; eximir, exentar; paliar; despedir. II. [ekskïús], s. excusa, justificación; disculpa; pretexto.

execrable [éksïkrǫbl], a. execrable, execrando, vitando, aborrecible, abominable.

execrably [-blï], adv. execrablemente.

execrate [éksïkreït]. I. va. execrar, aborrecer, abominar; maldecir. II. vn. maldecir.—**execration** [-éïşǫn], s. execración, aborrecimiento; maldición.

executant [egzékyųtǫnt], s. (mús.) ejecutante.

execute [éksïkïut], va. ejecutar, llevar a cabo; cumplir; (mús. y teat.) ejecutar, desempeñar; (for.) legalizar, formalizar, otorgar un documento; ejecutar, ajusticiar (a un reo).

executed [-ïd], a. ejecutado; legalizado; fecho.

executer [-œ(r)], s. ejecutor; verdugo.

execution [eksïkïúşǫn], s. ejecución, cumplimiento; (for.) ejecución, mandamiento judicial; legalización, otorgamiento de un documento; ejecución (de la pena de muerte); (b. a.) ejecución, desempeño.

executioner [-œ(r)], s. verdugo; ejecutor.

executive [egzékyųtïv]. I. a. ejecutivo.—**e. board o committee**, junta directiva, (consejo de) dirección.—**E. Mansion**, Casa Blanca (del Presidente); casa oficial de un gobernador.—**e. power**, poder ejecutivo; gobierno.—**e. officer**, (mil.) oficial de mando. II. s. poder ejecutivo o la persona que lo representa (el Presidente, etc.); funcionario ejecutivo.

executor [-tǫ(r)], s. ejecutor; (for.) albacea, mf., testamentario.

executorship [-şïp], s. albaceazgo.—**executory** [-torï], a. ejecutorio, ejecutivo; administrativo.—**executrix** [-trïks], s. albacea (mujer), testamentaria.

exegesis [eksïdżísïs], s. exégesis.—**exegete** [éksïdżit], s. exegeta, m.—**exegetic(al** [-dżétïk(ǫl], a. exegético.—**exegetically** [-lï], adv. exegéticamente.

exegetics [-dżétïks], s. ciencia de la exégesis, o interpretación, sobre todo de la bíblica.

exemplar [egzémplǫ(r)], s. ejemplar, modelo o dechado.—**exemplarily** [-plerïlï], adv. ejemplarmente.—**exemplariness** [-nïs], s. ejemplaridad.—**exemplary** [-ï], a. ejemplar.

exemplification [egzémplïfïkéïşǫn], s. ejemplificación; (for.) copia certificada.—**exemplify** [-faï], va. ejemplificar, declarar, manifestar; trasladar, copiar.

exempt [egzémpt]. I. va. exentar, eximir, franquear. II. a. exento; libre, franco, inmune.

exemptible [-ïbl], a. exento, privilegiado, libre.

exemption [egzémpşǫn], s. exención, franquicia, dispensa, inmunidad, privilegio, relevación.

exequatur [eksïkwéïtœr], s. exequátur.

exequies [éksïkwïz], s. pl. exequias, funerales.

exercisable [éksœrsaïzǫbl], a. ejercitativo.

exercise [éksœrsaïz]. I. s. ejercicio; ejercicio corporal; gimnasia.—pl. exámenes; certamen literario; servicio religioso. II. va. ejercer; ejercitar, poner en ejercicio; formar, adiestrar, habituar; atarear; emplear; preocupar, causar ansiedad. III. vn. adiestrarse, ejercitarse; hacer ejercicio o gimnasia.

exercised [-d], a. agitado, intranquilo, inquieto.

exercitation [εgzœrsitéiʃǝn]. s. ejercicio, ejercitación, práctica; ensayo, discurso.

exergue [εgzœrg], s. exergo.

exert [εgzǽrt]. I. va. esforzar; ejercer. II. vr. empeñarse, esforzarse, hacer esfuerzo, apurarse.

exertion [εgzǽrʃǝn], s. esfuerzo, conato.—pl. gestiones, diligencias, pasos, medios.

exeunt [éksiʌnt], (lat.) (teat.) vanse.—**e. omnes,** vanse todos.

exfoliate [eksfóuljeit]. I. vn. (cir.) exfoliarse; escamarse. II. va. exfoliar, escamar.

exfoliation [-éiʃǝn], s. exfoliación.

exhalant [ekshéilǝnt], a. y s. exhalador.

exhalation [ekshǎléiʃǝn], s. exhalación, efluvio, emanación, vapor, vaho, tufo.

exhale [ekshéil]. I. va. exhalar, emitir, despedir, espirar. II. vn. vah(e)ar; disiparse, evaporarse, desvanecerse.

exhaust [εgzóst]. I. va. apurar, extraer, vaciar, agotar; acabar, gastar, consumir o disipar; empobrecer; (med.) depauperar, debilitar, enflaquecer, postrar. II. vn. (m. v.) escapar, descargarse (vapor). III. s. (m. v.) escape, educción; (fís. y mec.) vacío; succión, aspiración.—**e. chamber,** cámara de escape.—**e. curve,** o **line,** (m. v.) curva de escape.—**e. draft,** tiro de aspiración o por succión.—**e. fan,** ventilador aspirador.—**e. feed heater,** (m. v.) calentador de (con) vapor de escape.—**e. lap,** (m. v.) recubrimiento interior.—**e. lead,** (m. v.) avance al escape; (aut.) avance al encendido.—**e. pipe,** (m. comb. int.) tubo de escape.—**e. port,** lumbrera de escape o de educción.—**e. valve,** válvula de escape o de educción.

exhausted [-id], a. exhausto; agotado; postrado, rendido.

exhauster [-œ(r)], s. agotador; (mec.) aspirador, bomba.—**exhaustible** [-ibl], a. agotable.

exhaustion [εgzóschǝn], s. agotamiento; debilitación, postración, quebrantamiento; (mec.) aspiración, evacuación, vaciamiento.

exhaustive [εgzóstiv], a. agotador, apurador; exhaustivo; cabal, completo.—**exhaustively** [-li], adv. cabalmente, completamente, detenidamente, hasta agotar.—**exhaustiveness** [-nis], s. calidad de completo o cabal.—**exhaustless** [-lis], a. inagotable.

exhibit [εgzíbit]. I. va. exhibir; presentar, manifestar; mostrar; (for.) exhibir; (med.) administrar (un remedio). II. vn. dar una exhibición. III. s. cualquier objeto o instalación de objetos expuestos al público; manifestación; (for.) documento fehaciente presentado como prueba.

exhibiter, exhibitor [-œ(r)]. s. exhibidor, exponente, expositor; (for.) el que exhibe.

exhibition [eksjbíʃǝn], s. exhibición, exposición; manifestación, presentación u ostentación; (med.) administración de un remedio; (Ingl.) beca de merced, prebenda de estudiante.

exhibitioner [-œ(r)], s. estudiante pensionado.

exhibitionism [-izm], s. (psic. y pat.) exhibicionismo.—**exhibitionist** [-ist], s. exhibicionista.

exhibitive [εgzíbitiv], a. representativo.

exhibitory [-tori], a. que exhibe.

exhilarant [εgzílarǝnt]. I. a. regocijador; estimulante, vigorizante. II. s. lo que regocija.

exhilarate [-eit], va. alegrar, regocijar o alborozar; animar, estimular.

exhilarating [-iŋ], a. exhilarativo.

exhilaratingly [-li], adv. regocijadamente.

exhilaration [-éiʃǝn], s. regocijo, alborozo.

exhort [εgzórt], va. y vn. exhortar; dar admonestación o consejo.—**exhortation** [-éiʃǝn], s. exhortación.—**exhortative, exhortatory** [-ativ, -atori], a. exhortatorio.—**exhorter** [-œ(r)], s. exhortador.

exhumation [ekshiuméiʃǝn], s. exhumación.

exhume [ekshiúm], va. exhumar, desenterrar.

exhumer [-œ(r)], s. exhumador, desenterrador.

exigence, exigency [éksidʒɛns, -i], s. exigencia;

urgencia.—**exigent** [-ɛnt] a. exigente; urgente.—**exigible** [-ibl], a. exigible, exigidero.

exiguity [eksigiúiti], s. exigüidad.

exiguous [εgzígiuʌs], a. exiguo, pequeño.

exile [éksail]. I. s. destierro, expatriación; desterrado, expatriado. II. va. desterrar, expatriar.

exist [εgzíst], vn. existir, subsistir, vivir; encontrarse.—**existence** [-ɛns], s. existencia, ser, vida; entidad, ente.—**existent** [-ɛnt], a. existente.

existentialism [egzisténǎlizm], s. (fil.) existencialismo.

exit [éksit]. I. s. salida, salidero; partida, muerte, f.: (teat.) mutis, m., vase. II. vn. salir; morir.

exoderm [éksodœrm], s. ectodermo, exodermo.

exodus [éksodʌs], s. salida, emigración, éxodo; (E.) Éxodo, segundo libro del Pentateuco.

exogamy [ekságami], s. exogamia, matrimonio con miembros de tribus extrañas.

exogen [éksodʒin], s. (bot.) planta exógena.

exogenous [eksádʒinʌs], a. exógeno.

exonerate [εgzánereit], va. exonerar, descargar, disculpar; aliviar, relevar.—**exoneration** [-éiʃǝn], s. exoneración; exculpación, descargo.—**exonerative** [-tiv], a. exonerativo.

exophthalmos [eksafθálmas], s. (med.) exoftalmia.

exorable [éksorabl], a. exorable.

exorbitance, exorbitancy [εgzórbitǝns, -i], s. exorbitancia, exceso.—**exorbitant** [-ant], a. exorbitante, excesivo.—**exorbitantly** [-li], adv. exorbitantemente.

exorcise [éksorsaiz], va. exorcizar, conjurar.—**exorciser** [-œ(r)], **exorcist** [-ist], s. exorcista, conjurador.—**exorcism** [-izm], s. exorcismo, conjuro.

exordial [εgzórdiǝl], a. preliminar, previo.

exordium [-diʌm], s. exordio, preámbulo; (ret.) isagoge, f.

exoskeleton [eksoskélɛtǝn], s. (zool.) dérmatoesqueleto.

exosmose [éksasmous], **exosmosis** [-móusis], s. (fís., quím.) exósmosis o exosmosis.

exosmotic [-mátik], a. exosmótico.

exoteric(al [eksotérik(ǝl], a. exotérico, público.

exothermic [eksoθœrmik], a. (quím.) exotérmico.

exotic(al [εgzátik(ǝl], I. a. exótico; forastero, extraño. II. s. (bot.) planta exótica.

exoticism [εgzátisizm], **exotism** [égzotizm], s. exot(ic)ismo, exotiquez, exoticidad.

expand [ekspǽnd], va. y vn. extender(se), tender(se); dilatar(se); ensanchar(se); agrandar(se); abrir(se); (mat.) desarrollar; (mec.) abocardar.—**expanded metal,** metal desplegado.

expander [-œ(r)], s. (mec.) ensanchador; extensor.

expanding [-iŋ], a. de expansión, de dilatación; de ensanchar; regulable, ensanchable (apl. a varias herramientas de taladrar, ensanchar, etc., como barrenas, escariadores, etc., que pueden regularse para adaptarlas a agujeros de distintos diámetros).—**e. brake,** freno de cinta.—**e. pulley,** polea de diámetro regulable.—**e. tool,** ensanchador.

expanse [ekspǽns], s. extensión, espacio.

expansibility [-ibíliti], s. expansibilidad; dilatabilidad.

expansible [-ibl], a. expansible, dilatable.

expansion [ekspǽnʃǝn], s. expansión; ensanche; distención; aumento; prolongación; extensión (de terreno, etc.); (fís.) dilatación; (mat.) desarrollo.—**e. bolt,** perno de expansión o de ensanche.—**e. curve,** curva de expansión.—**e. engine,** máquina de expansión.—**e. joint,** junta de dilatación.—**e. valve,** válvula de expansión.

expansive [ekspǽnsiv], a. expansivo.—**expansively** [-li], adv. expansivamente.—**expansiveness** [-nis], s. expansibilidad, dilatabilidad.

expatiate [ekspéiʃieit], vn. espaciarse, extenderse, dilatarse; hablar o escribir mucho

expatiation [-éişǫn], *s.* digresión, difusión, prolijidad.

expatiatory [-ǎtǫrį], *a.* difuso, prolijo.

expatriate [ekspéįtrįeįt]. **I.** *va.* y *vr.* expatriar(se), desnaturalizar(se), desterrar(se). **II.** *s.* y *a.* expatriado, desnaturalizado, proscrito.

expatriation [-éişǫn], *s.* expatriación.

expect [ekspékt], *va.* esperar, aguardar; contar con; (fam.) suponer.—**expectance, expectancy** [-ǎns, -į], *s.* expectativa, esperanza.—**expectant** [-ǎnt]. **I.** *a.* expectante; preñada. **II.** *s.* el que espera.—**expectation** [-éişǫn], *s.* expectativa, esperanza; probabilidad.—**expectative** [-ǎtįv]. **I.** *a.* que hace esperar. **II.** *s.* expectativa.

expectorant [ekspéktǫrǎnt], *a.* y *s.* (med.) expectorante.—**expectorate** [-eįt], *va.* y *vn.* expectorar, esputar, (d)esgarrar, gargajear.—**expectoration** [-éişǫn], *s.* expectoración; esputo, gargajo.—**expectorative** [-eįtįv], *a.* y *s.* expectorante.

expedience, expediency [ekspídįens, -į], *s.* aptitud, propiedad; conveniencia, utilidad, comodidad; oportunidad.

expedient [-ęnt]. **I.** *a.* oportuno, conveniente; prudente, propio. **II.** *s.* expediente, medio, recurso.—**expediently** [-lį], *adv.* aptamente, convenientemente.

expediential [-énşǎl], *a.* de conveniencia, oportunista.

expedite [ekspįdaįt]. **I.** *va.* acelerar, apresurar, dar prisa; facilitar; despachar, expedir, cursar, dar curso a. **II.** *a.* expedito, suelto; listo, alerto; cómodo.

expediter [-œ(r)], *s.* despachador, expedidor.

expedition [ekspįdįşǫn], *s.* expedición; jornada de muchas personas; prisa, diligencia, despacho. —**expeditionary** [-erį], *a.* expedicionario.

expeditioner [-œ(r)], *s.* expedicionero.

expeditious [-díşǎs], *a.* pronto, suelto, expedito, expeditivo, sumarísimo.—**expeditiously** [-lį], *adv.* expeditamente, prontamente.

expel [ekspél], *va.* expeler, expulsar, echar; despedir.

expellable [-ǎbl], *a.* expulsable.—**expellant** [-ǎnt], *a.* expelente.—**expeller** [-œ(r)], *s.* expulsor.

expend [ekspénd], *va.* expender, gastar.

expenditure [-įchǔ(r)], *s.* gasto, desembolso, salida.

expense [ekspéns], *s.* gasto, coste, costa, costo; desembolso, egreso; detrimento, pérdida.—**at any e.,** a toda costa.—**at one's e.,** a costa o expensas de uno.

expensive [-įv], *a.* costoso; caro, dispendioso.— **expensively** [-lį], *adv.* costosamente.—**expensiveness** [-nįs], *s.* dispendio; calidad de costoso.

experience [ekspírįens]. **I.** *s.* experiencia, práctica; lance, caso, aventura, incidente; ejercicio espiritual; conocimiento experimental.—**e. is the mother of wisdom,** la experiencia es madre de la sabiduría. **II.** *va.* experimentar; conocer, sentir, sufrir.—**to e. religion,** convertirse, reformarse.

experienced [-t], *a.* experimentado, experto, perito; hábil; amaestrado o aleccionado, avezado, versado, veterano.

experiential [ekspįrįénşǎl], *a.* experimental, de observación.—**experientially** [-į], *adv.* experimentalmente, por observación.

experiment [ekspérįment]. **I.** *s.* experimento, experiencia, ensayo. **II.** [-ment], *vn.* experimentar, hacer una prueba, un experimento.

experimental [-méntǎl], *a.* experimental, de ensayo.

experimentalist [-įst], **experimenter** [-mentœ(r)], **experimentist** [-mentįst], *s.* experimentador.

experimentally [-méntǎlį], *adv.* experimentalmente.—**experimentation** [-mentéįşǫn], *s.* experimento, experimentación.

expert [ekspǿert]. **I.** *a.* experimentado, experto,

perito, diestro, hábil, práctico, advertido; pericial. **II.** [ekspǿert], *s.* experto, perito, juez, *m.*—**expertly** [ekspǿertlį], *adv.* expertamente, pericialmente.—**expertness** [-nįs], *s.* destreza, habilidad, pericia.

expiable [ékspįǎbl], *a.* que se puede expiar.

expiate [ékspįeįt], *va.* expiar, purgar, reparar, satisfacer.—**expiation** [-éįşǫn], *s.* expiación. —**expiator** [-eįtǫ(r)], *s.* el que expía, quien hace expiación.—**expiatory** [-ǎtǫrį], *a.* expiatorio.

expiration [ekspįréįşǫn], *s.* expiración; remate, terminación; (com.) vencimiento, cumplimiento; (fisiol.) espiración, muerte, *f.*

expiratory [ekspáįrǎtǫrį], *a.* rel. a la espiración.

expire [ekspáįr]. **I.** *va.* espirar, expeler (el aire respirado). **II.** *vn.* expirar, terminar, fallecer, morir; (com., for.) expirar, vencer, cumplir(se), caducar (un plazo); (fisiol.) espirar.

expiry [-į], *s.* terminación, expiración, caducidad (apl. esp. a contratos, pólizas, etc. que expiran después de cumplido su plazo).

explain [ekspléįn]. **I.** *va.* explicar, explanar, exponer, aclarar, dilucidar, ilustrar, interpretar. **II.** *vn.* dar una explicación.—**explainable** [-ǎbl], *a.* explicable.—**explanation** [eksplǎnéįşǫn], *s.* explicación, aclaración.—**explanatory, explanative** [eksplǎénǎtǫrį, -tįv], *a.* explicativo, aclarador.

expletive [ékspléįtįv]. **I.** *a.* expletivo. **II.** *s.* interjección, reniego; partícula expletiva, o ripio.

explicable [ékspľįkǎbl], *a.* explicable.

explicate [-keįt], *va.* explicar, interpretar, poner en claro.—**explication** [-kéįşǫn], *s.* explicación. —**explicative** [-kįtįv], **explicatory** [-kǎtǫrį], *a.* explicativo.—**explicator** [-keįtǫ(r)], *s.* expositor, ilustrador.

explicit [eksplísįt], *a.* explícito, claro, inequívoco. —**explicitly** [-lį], *adv.* explícitamente.—**explicitness** [-nįs], *s.* calidad de explícito, claridad.

explode [eksplóųd]. **I.** *va.* volar, fulminar, hacer estallar o saltar (una mina); refutar, desbaratar, confundir; expeler con violencia y estrépito. **II.** *vn.* volar, estallar, detonar, hacer explosión; reventar; desplomarse.

exploder [-œ(r)], *s.* explosor; causa de explosión.

exploit [ekspľǫįt]. **I.** *s.* hazaña, proeza. **II.** [ekspľǫįt], *va.* explotar, sacar partido o utilidad de (esp. de un modo abusivo o ilegítimo).—**exploitable** [-ǎbl], *a.* explotable.—**exploitation** [-éįşǫn], *s.* explotación, aprovechamiento.

exploiter [-œ(r)]. **I.** *s.* explotador. **II.** *va.* = EXPLOIT.

explorable [ekspľórǎbl], *a.* explorable.

exploration [ekspľoréįşǫn], *s.* exploración.

explorator [ékspľoreįtǫ(r)], *s.* explorador.

exploratory [ekspľórǎtǫrį], *a.* exploratorio.

explore [ekspľór]. **I.** *va.* explorar; averiguar; examinar, sondear; (Am., min.) catear. **II.** *vn.* dedicarse a exploraciones; hacer una investigación sistemática.

explorer [-œ(r)], *s.* explorador.

explosion [ekspľóųźǫn], *s.* explosión, voladura; detonación, reventón; (fon.) explosión.—**e. chamber,** (m. comb. int.) cámara de explosión.

explosive [ekspľóųsįv], *a.* y *s.* explosivo, fulminante; (letra) explosiva.—**e. ball, e. shell,** bala, granada explosiva.—**e. cotton,** algodón pólvora.

explosively [-lį], *adv.* con explosión.

explosiveness [-nįs], *s.* calidad de explosivo.

exponent [ekspóųnęnt], *s.* representante; expositor; (mat.) exponente.

exponential [eksponénşǎl], *a.* y *s.* (mat.) exponencial.

export [ekspórt]. **I.** *va.* (com.) exportar. **II.** [ékspǫrt], *s.* exportación.—**fcr e.,** exportable.— *pl.* artículos de exportación. **III.** *a.* pert. a la exportación.—**e. house,** casa exportadora.

exportable [ekspórtǎbl], *a.* exportable.

exportation [-éįşǫn], *s.* (com.) exportación.

exporter [-œ(r)], s. exportador.

exporting [-iŋ], a. exportador.

expose [ekspóuz], va. exponer, poner en peligro, arriesgar; poner de manifiesto, mostrar, descubrir; publicar, divulgar; revelar, desenmascarar; comprometer; abandonar (niños); (igl.) manifestar.

exposé [ekspozéi], s. revelación comprometedora o escandalosa.

exposed [ekspóuzd], a. expuesto, descubierto, no abrigado.

exposition [ekspozíšǫn], s. exposición, exhibición; análisis retórico; abandono (de niños).

expositive [ekspázitiv], a. expositivo.

expositor [-tǫ(r)], s. expositor; comentador.

expository [-tǫri], a. expositivo, explicativo.

expostulate [ekspáschulejt], vn. altercar, contender.—**to e. with**, reconvenir a, debatir con.

expostulation [-léišǫn], s. debate, reconvención, disuasión.—**expostulator** [-lejtǫ(r)], s. el que reconviene.—**expostulatory** [-lǫ̃tǫri], a. de reconvención.

exposure [ekspóužǫ(r)], s. exposición; acción de exponer o exponerse (al aire, agua); (estar expuesto a) la intemperie; orientación, situación; revelación, desenmascaramiento; (fot.) exposición.—**e. meter**, (fot.) exposímetro.

expound [ekspáund], va. exponer, explicar.

expounder [-œ(r)], s. expositor, intérprete.

express [eksprés]. I. va. expresar, manifestar; decir, proferir; representar; exprimir, prensar; extraer el jugo; enviar, expedir por expreso. II. vr. expresarse, producirse, explicarse. III. a. expreso; claro, explícito, especial; hecho de encargo; llevado por expreso; pronto, rápido, veloz; exacto, parecido, pintiparado. IV. adv. por expreso; expresa o especialmente. V. s. (tren, autobús o ascensor) expreso o exprés; expreso, servicio de porteo o de transportes de mercancías; mensajero.—**e. company**, compañía de porteo, de expreso.

expressage [-idž], s. porte por expreso; lo que se envía por expreso; servicio del expreso.

expressible [-ibl], a. decible; expresable; exprimible.—**expressibly** [-ibli], adv. de modo expresable o exprimible.

expression [expréšǫn], s. expresión; gesto, cara, semblante, talante; dicción, vocablo, término, palabra, voz, giro, locución; (b. a.) expresión; (farm.) expresión, zumo.

expressionism [-izm], s. postimpresionismo, nuevo impresionismo.

expressive [eksprésiv], a. expresivo.—**expressively** [-li], adv. expresivamente.—**expressiveness** [-nis], s. significación, expresión, energía.

expressly [eksprésli], adv. expresamente; explícitamente.

expressman [-man], s. empresario de expresos o servicio de porteo; repartidor de artículos enviados por dicho servicio; trajinante, ordinario.

expressness [-nis], s. exactitud, claridad.

expropriate [ekspróuprjeit], va. enajenar, expropiar.

expropriation [-éišǫn], s. enajenamiento, expropiación.

expugnable [ekspágnabl], a. (mil.) expugnable.

expulsion [ekspálšǫn], s. expulsión, echamiento.

expulsive [-siv], a. expulsivo.

expunge [ekspándž], va. borrar, cancelar, testar; expurgar, destruir.—**expunction** [ekspáŋkšǫn], s. borradura, canceladura.

expurgate [ékspœrgejt], va. expurgar, purificar.

expurgation [-éišǫn], s. expurgación, expurgo, purificación.

expurgator [-tǫ(r)], s. expurgador.

expurgatory [ekspœrgatǫri], a. expurgatorio.

exquisite [ékskwizit]. I. a. exquisito; almibarado, remilgado; intenso, excesivo, agudo.—**e. pain**, dolor agudísimo.—**e. pleasure**, vivo placer. II. s. elegante, petimetre.

exquisitely [-li], adv. exquisitamente, primorosamente.—**exquisiteness** [-nis], s. exquisitez, primor, delicadeza, excelencia, perfección.

exsanguine [eksæŋgwin], a. exangüe, anémico, desangrado.

exscind [eksínd], va. cortar, amputar; extirpar.

exsect [eksékt], va. (cir.) cortar, extirpar.

exsection [eksékšǫn], s. excisión, extirpación.

exserted [eksœrtid], a. (bot.) ex(s)erto.

exsiccant [eksíkant], a. y s. desecativo, desecante.

exsiccate [éksikejt], va. desecar, secar.

exsiccation [-éišǫn], s. desecación.

exsiccative [éksikǫtiv], a. desecativo, desecante.

extant [ékstant], a. estante, existente; viviente.

extemporaneous [ekstæmporéinjʌs], **extemporary** [ekstémporeri], a. repentino, improvisado, de improviso.

extemporaneously [-li], adv. repentinamente, de improviso.

extempore [ekstémpori]. I. a. sin estudio previo, improvisado. II. adv. de improviso, de repente, in promptu.

extemporize [ekstémporaiz], va. y vn. improvisar, repentizar.

extemporizer [-œ(r)], s. improvisador, repentista.

extend [eksténd]. I. va. extender, tender, alargar; ensanchar, amplificar; prolongar; proyectar; ampliar; ofrecer, conceder, dar o comunicar; explayar, dilatar; prorrogar, diferir. II. vn. extenderse; prolongarse, estirarse, dar de sí, prestar.—**to e. the arm, the hand,** alargar el brazo, tender la mano.—**to e. the time of payment,** dar prórroga, alargar el plazo.

extended [-id], a. extenso, prolongado, estirado, alargado; diferido; (impr.) tipo abierto.—**extendedly** [-li], adv. prolongadamente.—**extendible** [-id], a. extensible.—**extensibility** [eksténsibíliti], **extensibleness** [eksténsiblnis], s. extensibilidad.—**extensible** a. extensible.

extension [eksténšǫn], s. extensión; dilatación, expansión; aumento; prolongación; ensanche; adición, anexo; (com.) prórroga, respiro.—**e. arm,** brazo extensible.—**e. bar,** alargadera (de un compás).—**e. ladder,** escalera de alargar y acortar, o de largueros corredizos; escalera de tijera, o doble.—**e. table,** mesa de extensión, mesa con hojas de quitapón.—**e. tripod,** trípode con piernas de corredera, de alargar y acortar.—**e. line o wire,** (tel.) línea de extensión.—**e. tube,** tubo de prolongación.

extensity [-siti], s. extensión; (psic.) elemento de la sensación relativo al espacio; el espacio como parte de la sensación.

extensive [-siv], a. extens(iv)o, extendido, dilatado, amplio, anchuroso, vasto.—**extensively** [-li], adv. por extenso, extens(iv)a, extendidamente.—**extensiveness** [-nis], s. extensión; generalidad.

extensometer [ekstensámetœ(r)], s. extensómetro, medidor de dilatación o de deformaciones.

extensor [eksténsǫ(r)], s. (anat.) extensor.

extent [ekstént], s. extensión; alcance; grado, punto, límite; (for.) ejecución; entredicho, embargo.—**to a certain e.,** hasta cierto punto. —**to a great e.,** en sumo grado, grandemente. —**to the full e.,** en toda su extensión, completamente.

extenuate [ekstényuejt], va. minorar, mitigar, paliar, atenuar.—**extenuating** [-iŋ], a. atenuante, paliativo.—**extenuation** [-éišǫn], s. atenuación, paliación, mitigación.

exterior [ekstíriǫ(r)]. I. a. exterior, externo; visible, manifiesto.—**e. angle,** ángulo externo. II. s. lo exterior; aspecto, porte, exterioridad.

exteriority [-áriti], s. exterioridad.

exteriorization [-arizéišǫn], s. exteriorización.

exteriorize [ekstíriǫraiz], va. exteriorizar.

exteriorly [ekstíriǫrli], adv. exteriormente.

exterminate [ekstœrminejt], va. exterminar.

extermination [-éišǫn], s. exterminio, extirpación, destrucción total.

exterminator [-eįtǫ(r)], *s.* exterminador.
exterminatory [-ǎtǫrį], *a.* exterminador.
extern\e [ékstœern], *s.* alumno externo; médico o practicante de un hospital que no habita en el edificio.
external [ekstǿernąl]. **I.** *a.* externo, exterior; extranjero, exterior; objetivo.—**e. diameter**, diámetro exterior.—**e. ear**, (anat.) pabellón, oreja.—**e. trade**, comercio exterior o extranjero. **II.** *s.* lo exterior o externo; exterioridad.
externality [-nǽlįtį], *s.* exterioridad; percepción externa.
externalization [-nąlįzéįšǫn], *s.* exteriorización.
externalize [-nąlaįz], *va.* exteriorizar; (Am.) externar; dar cuerpo o forma.
externally [-nąlį], *adv.* exteriormente, externamente, de fuera.
exterritorial [eksterįtǿrįąl], *a.* extraterritorial.
extinct [ekstíŋkt], *a.* extinto; extinguido, apagado; abolido, suprimido.—**to become e.**, extinguirse; apagarse; caducar; morir, desaparecer.
extinction [ekstíŋkšǫn], *s.* extinción.
extinguish [ekstíŋgwįš], *va.* extinguir; apagar; sofocar; suprimir, destruir; obscurecer.
extinguishable [-ąbl], *a.* extinguible; apagable.
extinguisher [-œ(r)], *s.* extintor (de incendios); apagador; matacandelas, *f.*
extinguishment [-męnt], *s.* extinción; apagamiento; abolición, aniquilamiento; terminación; amortización (de una deuda, etc.).
extirpate [ékstœerpeįt], *va.* extirpar, arrancar, desarraigar; acabar con.
extirpation [-éįšǫn], *s.* extirpación, arrancamiento, (cir.) excisión, extirpación.—**extirpator** [-ǫ(r)], *s.* extirpador, arrancador.
extol [ekstóųl], *va.* ensalzar, enaltecer, exaltar, alabar, engrandecer, elogiar.
extort [ekstórt], *va.* extorsionar; sacar u obtener por fuerza; arrancar, arrebatar; sangrar, socaliñar, exigir dinero sin derecho.
extortion [ekstóršǫn], *s.* extorsión; exacción; concusión; gabela injusta.
extortionary [-erį], *a.* que implica extorsión, exacción o concusión.
extortionate [-įt], *a.* opresivo, injusto, gravoso.
extortioner [-œ(r)], **extortionist** [-įst], *s.* opresor, concusionario, socaliñero.
extra [éksträ]. **I.** *a.* extraordinario; suplementario, adicional, de más; de sobra, sobrante; de repuesto, recambio o reserva.—**e. charge**, recargo.—**e. edition**, extraordinario, edición extra.—**e. hand**, empleado supernumerario.—**e. pay, e. work**, paga, trabajo extraordinarios. **II.** *s.* exceso; recargo, sobreprecio; gasto extraordinario; suplemento o alcance de un diario; (fam.) extra, adehala, plus, (Am.) ñapa. **III.** *adv.* excepcionalmente, en exceso de lo corriente o estipulado, etc.
extract [ekstrékt], *va.* extraer, sacar (una muela, etc.); arrancar, educir, exprimir; extractar, compendiar, escoger (pasajes) y citar; (quím.) extraer; tratar para extraer por disolución; (mat.) extraer (una raíz).
extract [ékstrækt], *s.* extracto, excerta, resumen; cita; (quím.) extracto.
extractable, extractible [ekstréktąbl], *a.* extraíble, que se puede extraer.
extraction [-šǫn], *s.* extracción; saca; alcurnia, origen, descendencia; (quím.) extracción.
extractive [-tįv]. **I.** *a.* extractivo; extraente; que sirve para extraer o extractar. **II.** *s.* lo que puede extraerse o extractarse; (quím.) parte insoluble de un extracto.
extractor [-tǫ(r)], *s.* extractor, extractador, sacador; exprimidera; (cir.) fórceps; sacabalas; (arti.) sacatrapos; extractor de cartuchos.
extracurricular [ekstrąkʌríkyulą(r)], *a.* (actividad) que no forma parte de un plan de estudios.
extradite [ékstrądaįt], *va.* entregar, o reclamar, por extradición.

extradition [-díšǫn], *s.* extradición.
extrados [ekstréįdas], *s.* (arq.) extradós, trasdós.
extrajudicial [ekstrądžudíšąl], *a.* extrajudicial.
extrajudicially [-į], *adv.* extrajudicialmente.
extramundane [-mʌndeįn], *a.* extramundano.
extramural [-mįúrąl], *a.* situado extramuros.
extraneous [ekstréįnįʌs], *a.* extraño, externo, extranjero, extrínseco; ajeno; de afuera.
extraofficial [ekstrąofíšąl], *a.* extraoficial.
extraordinarily [ekstrórdįnerįlį], *adv.* extraordinariamente.—**extraordinariness** [-nerįnįs], *s.* singularidad, rareza.—**extraordinary** [-nerį], *a.* extraordinario, descomunal, particular, raro, singular; especial.
extraprofessional [-proféšąnąl], *a.* fuera de la profesión, ajeno a la profesión.
extraterritorial [-terįtórįąl], *a.* extraterritorial.
extraterritoriality [-ǽlįtį], *s.* extraterritorialidad.
extrauterine [-įútœerįn], *a.* extrauterino.
extravagance, extravagancy [ekstrǽvagąns, -į], *s.* lujo desmedido, profusión, derroche; extravagancia; disparate, locura, desbarro.—**extravagant** [-gąnt], *a.* extravagante, estrafalario; exorbitante; disparatado; pródigo, manirroto, gastador.—*s. pl.* (E., igl.) extravagantes, *f. pl.*—**extravagantly** [-lį], *adv.* extravagantemente; pródigamente, profusamente; estrafalariamente.—**extravagantness** [-nįs], *s.* extravagancia, desarreglo, exceso.
extravaganza [-gǽnzą], *s.* composición extravagante y fantástica.
extravasate [ekstrǽvąseįt], *va.* y *vn.* (med.) extravasarse, trasvenarse, extravenar(se) (sangre, etc.); (geol.) echar, emitir o salir (lava, etc.).
extravasation [-éįšǫn], *s.* (med.) extravasación.
extreme [ekstrím]. **I.** *a.* extremo, extremado, extremoso, último, postrero; riguroso, estricto, severo.—**e. unction**, (igl.) extremaunción. **II.** *s.* extremo, extremidad, ápice; fin, cabo.—**in the e.**, en o con extremo, en sumo grado.—**to go to extremes**, tomar medidas extremas; exagerar.
extremely [-lį], *adv.* extrem(ad)amente, sumamente, con o en extremo.
extremism [-įzm], *s.* extremismo, radicalismo.
extremist [-įst], *s.* y *a.* extremista, radical.
extremity [ekstrémįtį], *s.* extremidad; agudeza, rigor; necesidad, apuro.—*pl.* medidas extremas; (zool.) extremidades.
extricable [ékstrįkąbl], *a.* que se puede desenredar.
extricate [-eįt], *va.* desenredar, desembrollar; sacar (de una dificultad).
extrication [-éįšǫn], *s.* desembarazo, desenredo.
extrinsic\al [ekstrínsįk(ąl), *a.* extrínseco.
extrinsically [-į], *adv.* extrínsecamente.
extrorse [ekstrórs], *a.* (bot.) vuelto hacia afuera.
extroversion [ekstrovǿršǫn], *s.* (psic.) tendencia a ocuparse más en el mundo exterior que en el interior; (med.) extroversión.
extrovert [ékstrovœert]. **I.** *s.* (psic.) persona que se ocupa más en el mundo exterior que en el interior. **II.** [ekstrovǿert], *va.* volver hacia (a)fuera. **III.** *vn.* ocuparse en el mundo exterior.
extrude [ekstrúd]. **I.** *va.* forzar hacia fuera; echar, arrojar; (met.) estirar por presión. **II.** *vn.* salir fuera, sobresalir.—**extruded metal**, metal estirado por presión (forzado por orificios mediante presión hidráulica).
extrusion [ekstrúžǫn], *s.* expulsión; (met.) estiramiento por presión; (geol.) efusión de lava por grietas de rocas.
extrusive [ekstrúsįv], *a.* que tiende a sobresalir; que empuja hacia adelante.
exuberance, exuberancy [egzįúbœrąns, -į], *s.* exuberancia.—**exuberant** [-ąnt], *a.* exuberante, lujuriante, profuso.—**exuberantly** [-lį], *adv.* con suma abundancia.
exudate [éksjudeįt]. **I.** *va.* y *vn.* = EXUDE. **II.** *s.* exudado.

exudation [-éįŝǫn], *s.* exudación; exudado.
exude [eksįúd], *va.* y *vn.* exudar, sudar, transpirar; rezumarse, revenirse.
exult [egzʌlt], *vn.* exultar, regocijarse, alegrarse.—**exultance, exultancy** [-ạns, -į], *s.* = EXULTATION.—**exultant** [-ạnt], *a.* triunfante, regocijado, alborozado.—**exultation** [-éįŝǫn], *s.* exultación, regocijo, transporte; triunfo.—**exultingly** [-įŋlį], *adv.* con exultación.
exuviæ [eksįúvįį], *s. pl.* despojos de los animales.
exuviate [eksįúvįeįt], *va.* mudar, echar, soltar (las plumas, la piel, los cuernos, etc.).
exuviation [-éįŝǫn], *s.* la muda (de aves, crustáceos, etc.).
eyas [áįạs], *s.* halcón niego; pajarito en el nido.
eye [áį], *s.* ojo (de la cara, del queso, de aguja, de hacha, de armella, etc.); argolla; vista; aspecto, talante; juicio, discernimiento; concepto, opinión; orificio de observación (de un horno); vigilancia; quicio (de un gozne); (mec.) anillo, aro; (cost.) corcheta; (arq.) ojo de cúpula (abertura circular en la parte superior); (bot.) yema o botón.—**e.-minded,** (psic.) en que predominan las imágenes visuales como elementos de la memoria y otros fenómenos mentales.—**e. of a stay,** (mar.) ojo de un estay.—**e. of the anchor,** (mar.) ojo del ancla.—**e. opener,** todo lo que hace abrir los ojos, literal o figuradamente; cuento maravilloso, noticia increíble o inesperada; (fam.) copa de licor, trago.—**e. protectors,** anteojos de seguridad.—**e. shade,** visera, guardavista.—**e. socket,** (anat.) órbita o cuenca del ojo.—**e. splice,** (mar.) gaza.—**e. tube,** (ópt.) tubo del ocular.—**an e. for an e.,** ojo por ojo.—**before one's eyes,** a la vista, en presencia de uno.—**by e.,** a ojo.—**half an e.,** ojeada, vistazo.—**the e. of day, o of heaven, o of the morning,** el sol.—**to have a cast in the eye,** ser ligeramente bisojo, tener tendencia al estrabismo.—**to have in one's e.,** intentar, proponerse.—**to have one's e. on,** haberle echado el ojo a.—**to keep an e. on,** vigilar.—**to make eyes at,** mirar amorosamente o con codicia; comerse con los ojos.—**with an e. to,** con la intención de, pensando en, con vistas a.
eye, *va.* mirar de hito en hito, clavar la mirada a; hacer ojos o agujeros a.
eyeball [-bọl], *s.* (anat.) globo del ojo.
eyebar [-bar], *s.* barra de ojo (con un ojo en cada extremo).
eyebolt [-bọult], *s.* hembrilla, perno de ojo; (mar.) cáncamo.
eyebright [-braįt], *s.* (bot.) eufrasia.
eyebrow [-braụ], *s.* (anat.) ceja.
eyecup [-kʌp], *s.* ojera, copilla para los ojos.
eyeflap [-flæp], *s.* anteojera (de brida).
eyeglance [-glæns], *s.* ojeada, vistazo.
eyeglass [-glæs], *s.* (ópt.) ocular; anteojo.—*pl.* lentes, quevedos, anteojos, gafas.
eyehole [-họụl], *s.* (cost.) ojete; atisbadero.
eyelash [-læŝ], *s.* (anat.) pestaña.
eyeless [-lįs], *a.* ciego; sin ojos.
eyelet [-lįt], **I.** *s.* resquicio, abertura; (cost.) ojete; (mar.) ollao.—**e. punch,** sacabocados. **II.** *va.* (cost.) ojetear; abrir o poner ojetes en.
eyeleteer [-lįtír], *s.* ojeteador, punzón para abrir ojetes.
eyelid [-lįd], *s.* (anat.) párpado, pálpebra.
eyepiece [-pis], *s.* (ópt.) ocular.
eyeservant [-sœrvạnt], *s.* criado que sólo trabaja cuando lo vigilan.
eyeshot [-ŝat], *s.* alcance de la mirada.
eyesight [-saįt], *s.* vista; alcance de la vista.
eyesore [-sor], *s.* cosa que ofende la vista.
eyespot [-spat], *s.* ojo rudimentario; ojo embrionario.
eyestone [-stọụn], *s.* opérculo empleado para sacar del ojo objetos extraños menudos.
eyestrain [-streįn], *s.* vista fatigada.
eyestring [-strįŋ], *s.* (anat.) tendón del ojo.

eye-test chart [-tɛst chart], *s.* escala tipográfica oftalmométrica.
eyetooth [-tuθ], *s.* colmillo, (diente) canino.
eyewash [-waŝ], *s.* colirio, loción para los ojos; (fam.) patraña, embeleco.
eyewater [-wɑtœ(r)], *s.* colirio; lágrima; humor ácueo; (fam.) bebida espiritosa, ginebra.
eyewink [-wįŋk], *s.* guiñada; ojeada, vistazo.
eyewinker [-œ(r)], *s.* (anat.) pestaña.
eyewitness [-wítnįs], *s.* testigo ocular o presencial.
eyrie, eyry [érį], *s.* nido de ave de rapiña; cría de tales aves; sitio o castillo elevado. *V.* AERIE.

F

f [ɛf], *s.* f; (mús., F) fa.
fa [fa], *s.* (mús.) fa.
fabaceous [fạbéįŝįạs], *a.* (bot.) papilionáceo.
fable [féįbl], **I.** *s.* fábula, apólogo, conseja, cuento; leyenda, mito; falsedad, mentira. **II.** *va.* y *vn.* fingir, mentir, inventar o contar fábulas.
fabled [-d], *a.* legendario, mítico; ficticio, fabuloso.
fabric [fǽbrįk], *s.* tejido, tela, género, paño; fábrica, obra, edificio; manufactura; textura.—**f. gloves,** guantes de punto.
fabricant [-ạnt], *s.* fabricante.
fabricate [-keįt], *va.* fabricar; construir, hacer (apl. esp. a la fabricación en serie o en grande escala de piezas normalizadas intercambiables, y a la construcción de buques, edificios, máquinas, etc.—con dichas piezas); inventar (una mentira).
fabrication [-kéįŝǫn], *s.* fabricación; edificio; obra; mentira, fábula.
fabricator [-keįtǫ(r)], *s.* fabricador; embustero.
fabrikoid [-kọįd], *s.* fabricoide (nombre de fábrica), imitación de cuero hecha de tela revestida de una solución de piroxilina.
fabulist [fǽbyulįst], *s.* fabulista.—**fabulous** [-lạs], *a.* fabuloso, ficticio.—**fabulously** [-lį], *adv.* fabulosamente.—**fabulousness** [-nįs], *s.* fabulosidad.
façade [fạsád], *s.* (arq.) fachada, frontispicio o frontis, *m.*, frontera, portada, frente, haz.
face [féįs], *s.* cara, faz o haz; lado; superficie; facie (de un cristal); fachada, frontis, *m.*; frente (mil., constr.); aspecto, cariz, *m.*; apariencias; prestigio; muestra (de reloj); conocimiento inmediato, vista; descaro, desfachatez; mueca, gesto; (com.) valor neto; (impr.) ojo de la letra; (mec.) cabeza (de un diente de rueda); superficie de trabajo o de contacto (de la válvula de correderas); ancho (de una polea); cotillo o plano (de un martillo); (ing.) paramento (de un muro); fondo, frente, cara de trabajo (de galería, túnel, socavón, etc.).—**f. ache, f. ague,** neuralgia facial.—**f. angle,** (geom.) cara (de un ángulo poliedro).—**f. card,** figura (en la baraja).—**f. cloth,** paño de lavar la cara; sudario.—**f. cog,** diente lateral (de una rueda).—**f. down(ward),** boca abajo.—**f. guard,** careta, carilla, máscara.—**f. joint,** junta superficial o de paramento.—**f. lathe,** torno de plato.—**f. lifting,** (cir.) cirugía plástica de la cara, facioplastía.—**f. powder,** polvos de arroz, o de tocador.—**f.-saving,** que salva las apariencias.—**f. to f.,** cara a cara, faz a faz, frente a frente.—**f. value,** significado literal o al pie de la letra; (com.) valor nominal o facial.—**f. wheel,** coronaria, rueda de escape; rueda de amolar o pulir.—**in the f. of,** ante; luchando contra, a pesar de.—**on the f. of it,** según lo que se ve.—**to fly in the f. of,** ir contra viento y marea, nadar contra la corriente.—**to lose f.,** desprestigiarse.—**to one's f.,** en la cara de uno, en su presencia.
face. I. *va.* volver o mirar hacia; arrostrar, afrontar, enfrentar, encararse con, oponerse a, habérselas con; (for.) responder (a un cargo);

pulir, revestir, cubrir, forrar; (tec.) labrar, acabar, alisar.—**to f. it out,** hacer frente a todo, no cejar.—**to f. out,** persistir en o sostener descaradamente.—**to f. the music,** (fam.) hacer frente a las consecuencias.—**to f. with,** carear con. **II.** *vn.* volver la cara; dar, mirar (a, hacia).—**to f. about,** voltear la cara; cambiar de frente.

faceplate [-pleįt], *s.* placa de revestimiento o de protección; plato o disco (de torno).

facer [-œ(r)], *s.* el o lo que pule, labra, etc.; (fam.) puñetazo dado en la cara; percance o revés.

facet [fǽsįt]. **I.** *va.* (joy.) labrar facetas. **II.** *s.* faceta; (arq.) filete de las estrías de una columna; (ent.) faceta del ojo de un insecto.

faceted [-įd], *pp.* y *a.* labrado en facetas.

facetious [fasíṣas], *a.* salado, chistoso, gracioso.

facetiously [-lį], *adv.* chistosamente.

facetiousness [-nįs], *s.* sal, *f.,* chiste, gracia.

facial [féįṣạl]. **I.** *a.* facial.—**f. angle,** ángulo facial. **II.** *s.* (fam.) masaje facial.

facile [fǽsįl], *a.* fácil; obediente, dócil; vivo, listo; accesible, afable.

facilitate [fạsílįteįt], *va.* facilitar, allanar, expedir.—**facilitation** [-éįṣọn], *s.* facilitación.

facility [fạsílįtį], *s.* facilidad; destreza; docilidad; afabilidad.—*pl.* medios (de transporte, etc.).

facing [féįsįŋ]. **I.** *s.* paramento; revestimiento (const.) (gen. *pl.*) falso, bebederos, vueltas; cubierta; cara; encaramiento. **II.** *prep.* de cara (a), frente a; (mil.) de frente.

facsimile [fæksímįlį], *a.* y *s.* facsímil(e).

fact [fækt], *s.* hecho; realidad.—**f.-finding,** que determina los hechos.—**in (point of) f.,** en efecto, en realidad; de hecho.—**in the very f.,** en el mero hecho.—**the f. remains that,** ello es que, es un hecho que, a pesar de todo.

faction [fǽkṣọn], *s.* facción, bando, bandería, parcialidad; alboroto, tumulto.—**factional** [-ạl], *a.* faccionario.—**factionist** [-įst], *s.* faccioso.—**factious** [fǽkṣas], *a.* faccioso, sedicioso, revoltoso.—**factiously** [-lį], *adv.* sediciosamente.—**factiousness** [-nįs], *s.* espíritu de partido o facción.

factitious [fæktíṣas], *a.* facticio; artificial.

factitive [fǽktįtįv], *a.* (gram.) factitivo.

factor [fǽktọ(r)]. **I.** *s.* elemento, factor; agente comisionado; (mat.) factor; coeficiente.—**f. of safety,** coeficiente de seguridad. **II.** *va.* (mat.) descomponer en factores.

factorage [-įdž], *s.* (com.) comisión; factoraje.

factorial [fæktórįạl]. **I.** *s.* (mat.) factorial, *f.* **II.** *a.* pert. a un factor o a una fábrica.

factoring [fǽktọrįŋ], *s.* (mat.) descomposición en factores, factorización.

factorize [-aįz], *va.* (mat.) descomponer en factores; (for.) embargar en poder de un tercero; notificar, prevenir. *V.* **garnish.**—**factorization,** [-įzéįṣọn], *s.* descomposición en factores, factorización.

factorship [-šįp], *s.* agencia, factoría.

factory [fǽktọrį], *s.* fábrica, taller, manufactura; (gal.) usina; factoría.

factotum [fæktóųtʌm], *s.* factótum.

factual [fǽkchụạl], *a.* rel. a hechos; verdadero.

facula [fǽkyụlạ], *s.* (astr.) fácula.

facultative [fǽkʌlteįtįv], *a.* facultativo; (for.) potestativo.

faculty [fǽkʌltį], *s.* facultad, aptitud; claustro, facultad, cuerpo de doctores o maestros de una ciencia; cuerpo de profesores, profesorado; división o facultad (de leyes, medicina, etc.) en una universidad.

fad [fæd], *s.* novedad, moda; manía, chifladura.

faddish [-įš], *a.,* **faddist** [-įst], *s.* caprichoso; chiflado, aficionado a las novedades.

fade [féįd]. **I.** *va.* marchitar, poner pálido, descolorar; debilitar, desmejorar. **II.** *vn.* palidecer, descolorarse; decaer, marchitarse; (rad.) apagarse la intensidad.—**to f. in** (out), hacer aparecer (desaparecer) gradualmente (una

imagen cinematográfica).—**to f. away,** desvanecerse, desaparecer.—**f.-in,** (cine) aparición o aclaramiento gradual de la escena.—**f.-out,** desaparición u oscurecimiento gradual.

faded [-įd], *a.* descolorido, marchito.

fadeless [-lįs], *a.* que no palidece o se descolora.

fading [-įŋ], *s.* pérdida gradual de color, intensidad, etc.; (rad.) apagamiento o fluctuación en la intensidad de las señales.

fæcal, fæces, fæcula, *V.* **fecal, feces,** etc.

fäerie, faerie, faery [féįœrį], *s.* y *a.* (ant.) *V.* **fairy(land).**

fag [fæg]. **I.** *va.* fatigar, cansar; hacer trotar o trabajar a uno. **II.** *vn.* desfallecer de cansancio; trabajar como un galopín. **III.** *s.* faena penosa; esclavo, galopín, marmitón, ganapán; (Ingl.) estudiante que sirve a otro mayor; (fam.) cigarrillo.—**f. end,** cabo; cadillos, pestañas; sobra o desperdicio; (mar.) cordón.—**fagged out,** rendido, cansado.

fagot, faggot [fǽgọt]. **I.** *s.* haz, *m.,* manojo, gavilla de leña; (fort.) fajina; haz de barras de hierro o acero (120 libras de peso); (Ingl., desp.) vieja, bruja. **II.** *va.* liar, hacer líos o haces; recoger, recaudar.

Fahrenheit [fǽrenhaįt], *a.* Fahrenheit (grados, temperatura).—**F. scale,** escala de Fahrenheit.

faïence, faience [fayáns], *s.* loza fina.

fail [féįl]. **I.** *va.* abandonar, dejar; frustrar, chasquear; (fam.) reprobar, colgar (en los estudios); despedir por incompetente. **II.** *vn.* faltar, fallar, inutilizarse, romperse, ceder; frustrarse, malograrse; consumirse, acabarse, desvanecerse, decaer, menguar; (com.) quebrar, hacer bancarrota; salir mal, fracasar (en examen, etc.).—**(not) to f. to,** (no) dejar de. **III.** *s.* falta; defecto; fracaso.—**without f.,** sin falta.

failing [-įŋ]. **I.** *s.* falta, desliz, *m.;* defecto, flaqueza; decadencia, malogro. **II.** *a.* que mengua, decae (salud, etc.). **III.** *prep.* sin, faltando; en la ausencia de.

faille [faįl o feįl], *s.* (tej.) cierto tejido de seda o de rayón.

failure [-yụ(r)], *s.* fracaso, fiasco, malogro; suspenso (en un examen); falta, culpa, omisión, descuido, desliz, *m.;* (com.) quiebra, bancarrota; (mec.) avería, defecto (de motor, etc.).—**f. of issue,** (for.) el no dejar prole.—**f. to pay, etc.,** el no pagar, el dejar de pagar, la falta de pago, etc.

fain [féįn]. **I.** *a.* (ant., poét.) dispuesto, conforme, resignado; contento. **II.** *adv.* gustosamente, de buena gana.

faint [féįnt]. **I.** *vn.* desmayarse; desfallecer; desalentarse; descaecer, desvanecerse. **II.** *a.* lánguido, abatido, tímido; indistinto, tenue; débil, desfallecido.—**to be f. with,** morirse de, estar muerto de (hambre).—**f.-hearted,** medroso, pusilánime; apocado, desmazalado.—**f.-heartedly,** medrosamente.—**f.-heartedness,** miedo, pusilanimidad. **III.** *s.* faint(ing [-įŋ], (fig. y med.) deliquio, desmayo, desfallecimiento.—**f. fit,** o **spell,** (med.) síncope, desmayo, lipotimia.—**in a f.,** desmayado.

faintish [-įš], *a.* desfalleciente. *V.* **faint.**

faintly [-lį], *adv.* desmayadamente, débilmente; tenuemente, indistintamente.

faintness [-nįs], *s.* falta de claridad; languidez, desaliento; timidez.

faints [-s], *s. pl.* productos impuros y débiles del principio o del fin de la destilación.

fair [fer]. **I.** *a.* claro, despejado; limpio, terso; inmaculado; bonancible, favorable, próspero; rubio (es el sentido en que se toma gen. cuando se habla del aspecto de una persona); hermoso, perfecto, bello; recto, justo; imparcial; honrado, razonable, franco, cortés, liberal; corriente, regular, mediano, pasable, ordinario; bien formado; distinto; legible.—**f. and square,** honrado a carta cabal.—**f. complexion,** tez blanca (gen. se entiende además pelo rubio).—

f. name, nombre honrado, sin tacha.—**f. play,** proceder leal, juego limpio.—**f. sex,** bello sexo; las mujeres.—**f. to middling,** (fam.) bastante bueno.—**f. trade,** comercio internacional fundado en la reciprocidad; comercio legítimo.—**f.-weather,** buen tiempo, (mar.) bonanza.—**f.-weather friend,** amigo en la prosperidad.—**f. wind,** viento favorable.—**by f. means,** por medios rectos, honrados.—**to be in a f. way to succeed,** estar en buen camino de prosperar.—**to give a f. hearing,** oír, escuchar con imparcialidad.—**to give f. warning,** prevenir, advertir, avisar de antemano.—**to make a f. copy,** poner en limpio. II. *adv.* justamente, honradamente; claramente, perfectamente, exactamente; bondadosamente, bien.—**f.-complexioned,** de tez blanca.—**f.-haired,** de cabellos blondos o rubios; favorito.—**f.-minded,** imparcial, justo. III. *s.* mercado; feria; exposición regional; venta de caridad o en beneficio de una institución (ll. *bazar* en algunas partes); (poét.) mujer hermosa o amada.

fairground [férgraụnd], *s.* cercado al aire libre para feria, etc.

fairing [fériŋ], *s.* ferias, agasajos; (ing., aer.) miembro o estructura de líneas aerodinámicas, para reducir la resistencia al avance, etc.

fairish [férịṣ], *a.* así así, regular.

fairly [férlị], *adv.* imparcialmente; bastante, regularmente; justamente; honradamente; totalmente, cabalmente; claramente; favorablemente; primorosamente, bellamente.

fairness [férnịs], *s.* hermosura, belleza; honradez, candor; justicia, equidad, imparcialidad.

fairway [férweị], *s.* pasaje libre o despejado; cierta parte del campo de golf; (mar.) paso, canalizo.

fairy [férị]. I. *s.* hada, duende, trasgo. II. *a.* de duendes, de hadas.—**f. godmother,** hada madrina.—**f. tale,** cuento de hadas; burlería, patraña; mentira.

fairyland [-lænd], *s.* tierra de las hadas; región o sitio de belleza encantadora.

fairylike [-laịk], *a.* como hada.

faith [feịθ]. I. *s.* fe, *f.;* confianza; fe, religión, ley, *f.;* fidelidad, lealtad.—**f. cure,** curación por fe.—**in f.,** a la verdad.—**in good f.,** de buena fe.—**to break f. with,** faltar a la palabra dada a.—**upon my f.,** a fe mía. II. *interj.* en verdad.

faithful [-fụl]. I. *a.* fiel; leal; exacto, puntual; justo, recto; veraz. II. *s. pl.*—**the f.,** los fieles o creyentes; los partidarios leales.—**faithfully** [-ị], *adv.* fielmente, firmemente; puntualmente.—**faithfulness** [-nịs], *s.* fidelidad, honradez; exactitud.—**faithless** [-lịs], *a.* infiel, sin fe; pérfido, fementido.—**faithlessness** [-nịs], *s.* infidelidad, deslealtad, perfidia.

fake [feịk]. I. *s.* (mar.) aduja de cable; (fam.) falsificación, impostura; copia, imitación; filfa, patraña, farsa. *V.* FAKER. II. *va.* y *vn.* adujar, enroscar; (fam.) falsificar; chalanear; fingir, inventar; hurtar. III. *a.* falso, fraudulento.

faker [-œ(r)], *s.* (fam.) falsario, imitador; engañabobos; farsante; buhonero.

fakir [fạkír], *s.* faquir.

Falange [féịlændž], *s.* (pol.) Falange, *f.*

Falangist [fạléndžịst], *a.* y *s.* Falangista.

falcate(d [félkeịt(ịd], *a.* falcado, encorvado.

falcation [fælkéịṣọn], *s.* encorvadura.

falchion [fólchọn], *s.* cimitarra, falce.

falciform [félsịform], *a.* falciforme; falcado.

falcon [fólkọn], *s.* (orn.) halcón; (arti.) falcón.

falconer [-œ(r)], *s.* halconero, cetrero.

falconet [-et], *s.* (arti.) falconete.

falconry [-rị], *s.* halconería, cetrería.

falderal [féldẹræl], **falderol** [féldẹrạl], *s.* pamema, pampirolada; miriñaque, chuchería; estribillo sin sentido de canciones viejas.

faldstool [fóldstul], *s.* facistol, atril; faldistorio; silla de tijera.

fall [fọl], *vn.* (*pret.* FELL; *pp.* FALLEN) caer;

caerse; bajar, menguar, decrecer, disminuir; refluir (la marea); descaer; ceder, rendirse, entregarse; tocarle o corresponderle a uno; empezar, emprender, echar a.—**to f. aboard,** (mar.) abordar.—**to f. across,** encontrarse con por casualidad.—**to f. afoul of,** reñir con; habérselas con, enmarañarse con; (mar.) chocar con.—**to f. asleep,** dormirse.—**to f. astern,** (mar.) recular.—**to f. a prey to,** ser presa o víctima de.—**to f. away,** enflaquecer; marchitarse; apostatar, renegar.—**to f. back,** retroceder, recular, hacerse atrás, retirarse.—**to f. back on, o upon,** recurrir a, echar mano de; (mil.) replegarse hacia.—**to f. backward,** caer de espaldas.—**to f. behind,** rezagarse.—**to f. down,** prosternarse, postrarse; caerse; (fam.) (a veces con **on** o **in**) no tener el éxito deseado o esperado; fracasar.—**to f. due,** (com.) vencerse.—**to f. flat,** caer tendido, caer cuan largo es; no surtir efecto; tener mal éxito.—**to f. for,** (fam.) prendarse de; ser engañado por.—**to f. foul of** = TO FALL AFOUL OF.—**to f. from,** abandonar; faltar a; violar.—**to f. heir to,** heredar.—**to f. in,** caer dentro; desplomarse; ponerse en su lugar; (mil.) alinearse; expirar, terminar, caducar.—**to f. in for** = TO COME IN FOR.—**to f. in line,** formar cola; seguir la corriente; adherirse.—**to f. in love,** enamorarse.—**to f. in price,** abaratarse.—**to f. in with,** encontrarse con; convenir, estar de acuerdo con.—**to f. off,** caer, desprenderse; extrañarse, disgustarse; menguar, disminuir; decaer; (mar.) abatir.—**to f. on,** asaltar, echarse sobre; empezar, emprender; echar mano de, recurrir a; encontrar, descubrir.—**to f. on one's feet,** caer de pie; salir del trance.—**to f. out,** desavenirse, reñir, querellar; suceder; (mil.) salir de las filas.—**to f. over,** desertar; caer; tropezar; (fam.) adular servilmente.—**to f. overboard,** caerse al agua o al mar.—**to f. short,** faltar; ser deficiente; malograrse; errar (el tiro).—**to f. sick,** enfermar.—**to f. through,** abortar, fracasar, malograrse.—**to f. to,** caer en manos de; principiar a, echar a; empezar; tirarse sobre; cerrarse.—**to f. to one's lot, o share,** caber o caer en suerte a uno, tocarle a uno.—**to f. to the ground,** caerse; desplomarse; fracasar.—**to f. under,** caer debajo; incurrir en, estar sujeto a; ser del número de; estar comprendido en.—**to f. upon,** within,** estar dentro de, pertenecer a.

fall. I. *s.* caída, bajada, descenso; lapso, desliz, *m.;* (gen. *pl.*) salto de agua, cascada, catarata; otoño; decadencia, degradación; caída, desnivel; desembocadura de un río; (com.) baja o disminución de precio; pérdida en los fondos públicos; (mar.) tira de aparejo; (mús.) cadencia; bajada de tono, disminución del sonido.—**f.-trap,** (caza) trampa de golpe. II. *a.* otoñal.—**f. wheat,** trigo sembrado en el otoño.—**f. overcoat,** sobretodo de medio tiempo.

fallacious [fæléịṣas], *a.* falaz, sofístico, ilógico; engañoso, delusorio.—**fallaciously** [-lị], *adv.* falazmente; sofísticamente.—**fallaciousness** [-nịs], *s.* falacia, engaño; sofisma, *m.*

fallacy [félạsị], *s.* falacia; sofisma, *m.*

fallen [fólẹn]. I. *pp.* de TO FALL: caído. II. *a.* caído, postrado; arruinado; di(s)famado; deshonrado; muerto.

fallibility [fælịbílịtị], *s.* falibilidad.

fallible [félịbl], *a.* falible.

fallibly [-blị], *adv.* faliblemente.

falling [fóliŋ], *pa.* de TO FALL y *s.* caída; baja, disminución; cayente, que cae; (med.) prolapso.—**f. down,** desplome, derrumbamiento.—**f. off,** caída, decadencia, disminución.—**f. sickness, o evil,** epilepsia, mal caduco, gota coral.—**f. star,** exhalación, estrella fugaz.

Fallopian [fælóupịan] **tube,** *s.* (anat.) oviducto, trompa de Falopio.

fallow [fǽlou]. **I.** *a.* flavo, leonado; (agr.) barbechado; descuidado, abandonado.—**f. deer**, (zool.) corzo, paleto.—**f. finch**, (orn.) triguero. **II.** *s.* barbecho, añojal, tierra que descansa (ll. t. **f. ground, f. land**).—**to let lie f.**, dejar en barbecho. **III.** *va.* barbechar.

fallowing [-iŋ], *s.* barbechera.

false [fɔls]. **I.** *a.* falso, incierto, mentiroso; postizo, supuesto; de imitación; contrahecho, falseado; cuasi, (p)seudo; provisional, temporáneo; de refuerzo; de protección; (mús.) desafinado, falso, discordante.—**f. bottom**, fondo doble.—**f. claim**, pretensión infundada.—**f. colors**, bandera falsa.—**f. door**, puerta simulada.—**f. face**, máscara.—**f. floor**, subpiso.—**f.-heartedness**, perfidia.—**f. imprisonment**, prisión o detención ilegal.—**f. pretenses**, dolo, estafa.—**f. rib**, costilla falsa.—**f. step**, desliz, *m.*; error; imprudencia.—**f. teeth**, dentadura postiza.—**f. tooth**, diente postizo.—**f. window**, ventana simulada.—**to place in a f. light**, poner mal, desacreditar.—**to play f.**, engañar. **II.** *adv.* falsamente; pérfidamente.—**f.-faced**, hipócrita, falso.—**f.-hearted**, pérfido.

falsehood [-hud], *s.* falsedad.—**falsely** [-li], *adv.* falsamente.—**falseness** [-nis], *s.* perfidia, falsedad.

falsetto [fɔlsétou], *s.* (mús.) falsete.

falsework [fɔlswœrk], *s.* (constr.) andamiaje.

falsidical [fɔlsídikal], *a.* que da impresiones falsas; (psic.) ilusorio, enteramente imaginario.

falsifiable [fɔlsifaiabl], *a.* falsificable.

falsification [-fikéiʃon], *s.* falsificación; confutación.—**falsifier** [-faiœr(r)], **falsificator** [-fikeito(r)], *s.* falsificador; falsario.

falsify [fɔlsifai]. **I.** *va.* falsificar, adulterar; refutar, desmentir. **II.** *vn.* mentir.

falsity [fɔlsiti], *s.* falsedad, mentira.

falter [fɔltœ(r)]. **I.** *va.* balbucear. **II.** *vn.* vacilar; tartamudear. **III.** *s.* vacilación, temblor.

fame [feim]. **I.** *s.* fama. **II.** *va.* afamar; celebrar.

famed [-d], *a.* afamado, famoso, renombrado.

familiar [famílyą(r)]. **I.** *a.* familiar, íntimo; muy conocido; confianzudo.—**f. with**, acostumbrado a; versado o ducho en, conocedor de, al tanto de. **II.** *s.* amigo íntimo; demonio familiar; (igl.) familiar.

familiarity [famiļiǽriti], *s.* familiaridad, intimidad; confianza, llaneza; (con *with*) conocimiento (de).

familiarize [famílyąraiz], *va.* familiarizar, acostumbrar, avezar, habituar.

familiarly [-li], *adv.* familiarmente, amistosamente, íntimamente.

family [fǽmili]. **I.** *s.* familia; cuna, linaje, sangre, *f.*, raza; (biol.) familia. **II.** *a.* familiar, casero, de la familia.—**f. circle**, círculo familiar; (teat.) galería, gallinero, paraíso.—**f. man**, padre de familia.—**f. name**, apellido.—**f. skeleton**, secreto o motivo de vergüenza en una familia.—**f. tree**, árbol genealógico.—**in the f. way**, (fam.) encinta, embarazada.

famine [fǽmin], *s.* hambre, *f.*, carestía.

famish [fǽmiʃ], *va.* y *vn.* hambrear; matar o morirse de hambre.

famished [-t], *a.* famélico, hambriento.

famous [féiмʌs], *a.* famoso, afamado, célebre; (fam.) excelente.—**famously** [-li], *adv.* famosamente; (fam.) admirablemente, a las mil maravillas.

famulus [fǽmyuʌs], *s.* fámulo.

fan [fæn]. **I.** *s.* abanico; ventalle; (agr.) aventador, bieldo; (mec.) ventilador, volante de molino de viento; aficionado, entusiasta.—**f. belt**, (aut., etc.) correa del ventilador.—**f. blower**, ventilador.—**f. light**, o **window**, (arq.) abanico.—**f. palm**, (bot.) miraguano.—**f.-shaped**, en forma de abanico.—**f. sticks**, varillas de abanico.—**f. wheel**, ventilador. **II.** *va.* abanicar; ventilar; soplar; (agr.) aventar.

III. *vn.* (con **out**) desplegarse en forma de abanico.

fanatic [fanǽtik], *s.* fanático.—**fanatic(al** [-al], *a.* fanático.—**fanatically** [-i], *adv.* fanáticamente.—**fanaticism** [fanǽtisizm], *s.* fanatismo.

fancied [fǽnsid], *a.* imaginario.

fancier [fǽnsiœ(r)], *s.* criador y vendedor de aves y animales; aficionado; visionario.

fanciful [fǽnsiful], *a.* imaginativo, caprichoso; fantástico.—**fancifully** [-i], *adv.* caprichosamente.—**fancifulness** [-nis], *s.* calidad de imaginativo, caprichoso, fantástico o quimérico.

fancy [fǽnsi]. **I.** *s.* fantasía, imaginación, antojo, capricho; imagen, *f.*, idea; afición, afecto, gusto.—**f.-free**, libre del poder del amor.—**to take a f. to**, aficionarse a; antojarse de; coger cariño a. **II.** *a.* fantástico, imaginario; de fantasía; de ornato; bello, elegante; (com.) de capricho, de gusto, de lujo, costoso.—**f. ball**, baile de trajes.—**f. dress**, disfraz, *m.*, traje de capricho.—**f. goods**, objetos o artículos de fantasía.—**f. skating**, patinaje artístico.—**f. woods**, maderas preciosas. **III.** *va.* imaginar, suponer; gustar o encapricharse de, aficionarse a; antojarse, figurarse, fantasear; criar animales de tipo particular. **IV.** *vn.* tener un antojo o capricho; creer o imaginar algo sin pruebas.

fancywork [-wœrk],*s.* (cost.) labor, *f.*, confección.

fandango [fændǽŋgou], *s.* fandango (música y baile).

fane [fein], *s.* (ant. o poét.) templo, santuario.

fanfare [fǽnfer], *s.* son de trompetas; charanga; procesión o parada ruidosa; fanfarria.

fanfaron [fǽnfaran], *s.* fanfarrón; charanga.—**fanfaronade** [fænfaronéid], *s.* fanfarronada, fanfarronería.

fang [fæŋ], *s.* colmillo o diente (de un animal o serpiente); raíz de un diente.—**fanged** [-d], *a.* que tiene colmillos; colmilludo.

fangle [fǽŋgl], *s.* moda. V. NEWFANGLED.

fangless [fǽŋlis], *a.* sin colmillos.

fanion [fǽnyon], *s.* banderola.

fanlight [fǽnlait], *s.* V. FAN WINDOW.

fanlike [fǽnlaik], *a.* en forma de abanico.

fanner [fǽnœr], *s.* ventilador, aventador(a).

fantail [fǽnteil], *s.* (orn.) variedad de paloma de cola de abanico; pájaro matamoscas; (carp.) cola de milano.—**f. burner**, mechero de mariposa.

fantailed [-d], *a.* de cola en forma de abanico.

fan-tan [fæn tæn], *s.* cierto juego de naipes; juego chino.

fantasia [fæntéiʒiǎ], *s.* (mús.) fantasía.

fantasm, **fantasmagoria**, *s.* = PHANTASM, etc.

fantastic(al [fæntǽstik(al], *a.* fantástico, grotesco; caprichoso, caprichudo; ilusorio, imaginario.—**fantastically** [-i], *adv.* fantásticamente.—**fantasticalness** [-nis], *s.* calidad de fantástico, caprichoso, etc.

fantasy [fǽntasi], *s.* fantasía; ensueño, imagen, *f.*; capricho; dibujo fantástico (mús.) fantasía.

far [far]. **I.** *adv.* lejos; a lo lejos, en lontananza; en alto grado, muy, mucho.—**f. and away**, con o en mucho.—**f. and near, f. and wide**, por todas partes.—**f. away**, *adv.* muy lejos.—**f. be it from me**, lejos de mí, no permita Dios.—**f. better**, mucho mejor.—**f.-fetched**, forzado, traído por los cabellos.—**f.-flung**, vasto, extenso.—**f. from**, lejos de; ni con mucho.—**f. into**, hasta muy adentro de; hasta muy tarde de (la noche, etc.), hasta muy avanzado (el verano, etc.).—**f. off**, a gran distancia, en lontananza, a lo lejos.—**f.-reaching**, de mucho alcance, trascendente.—**as f. as, so f. as**, hasta; a la medida que, hasta donde, en cuanto a, según, que (*as far as I know*, según lo que sé, que yo sepa; *as far as I am concerned*, en cuanto a mí toca).—**by f.**, con mucho.—**from f.**, de(sde) lejos.—**in so f. as**, en cuanto a.—**so f., thus f.**, hasta ahora; hasta aquí; hasta ahí.—**so f. so good**, hasta ahora todo va

bien. II. *a.* lejano, distante, remoto; de grande alcance.—**F. East,** Extremo o Lejano Oriente. —**a f. cry,** una gran distancia (sentidos recto y figurado); gran diferencia (*it is a far cry*, hay gran distancia o diferencia).

farad [fǽræd], *s.* (elec.) faradio, farad, *m.*

faradic [fǽrædik], *a.* (elec.) farádico.

faradism [fǽrædizm], *s.* electricidad por inducción.

faradization [-izéișǫn], *s.* (med.) faradización, aplicación de una corriente farádica.

faradize [-aiz], *va.* (med.) faradizar.

faraway [fárǎwei], *a.* lejano, alejado; abstraído, distraído.

farce [fárs]. **I.** *va.* (coc., ant.) rellenar, embutir; (teat.) meter morcilla. **II.** *s.* (teat.) farsa, entremés, sainete; enredo, tramoya; (coc.) relleno de carne.

farcemeat [-mit], *s.* = FORCEMEAT.

farcical [-ikǎl], *a.* asainetado, burlesco, ridículo, bufo.—**farcically** [-i], *adv.* ridículamente.

farcing [-iŋ], *s.* (coc.) embutido, relleno.

farcy [fársi], *s.* (vet.) muermo.

fare [fér]. **I.** *vn.* pasarlo, irle o sucederle a uno (bien o mal); vivir (bien o mal); (gen. con **forth**) andar, ir, viajar. **II.** *s.* pasaje o tarifa (precio); pasajero; comida, vianda, mesa, plato.

farewell [-wél]. **I.** *interj.* ¡adiós! ¡vale! ¡vaya con Dios! **II.** *a.* de despedida.—**f. performance,** función de despedida. **III.** *s.* despedida, adiós. —**to bid f. to,** despedirse de.

farina [fǎríną], *s.* harina de cereales, patatas, nueces, etc.; fécula, almidón; (zool.) polvo harinoso.—**farinaceous** [fǽrinéiși̯ʌs], *a.* farináceo; harinoso.—**farinose** [fǽrinoṷs], *a.* farináceo; cubierto de polvo harinoso.

farm [fárm]. **I.** *s.* granja, labranza, hacienda, cortijo, finca, predio; terreno agrícola; (hist.) contribución; distrito de contribuciones.—**f. hand,** peón de granja, mozo de labranza, quintero, campesino, labrador.—**f. produce, o products,** productos agrícolas o de campo. **II.** *va.* cultivar, labrar la tierra; arrendar, tomar en arriendo.—**to f. out,** dar en arrendamiento.

farmer [-œr], *s.* labrador, labriego, granjero, campesino, colono, agricultor, hacendado.

farmerette [-ét], *s.* (fam.) agricultora, labradora.

farmhouse [-haṷs], *s.* alquería, quintería, granja.

farming [-iŋ]. **I.** *s.* cultivo, labranza; agricultura; recaudación o arrendamiento de contribuciones o rentas. **II.** *a.* agrícola; de labranza.

farmstead [-sted], *s.* alquería y sus dependencias; cortijo, cortijada, granja.

farmyard [-yard], *s.* corral de una granja.

farness [fárnis], *s.* distancia.

faro [féroṷ], *s.* faraón o golfo (juego de naipes).

farrago [fǎrágoṷ], *s.* fárrago, broza.

farrier [fǽriœr], *s.* herrador; mariscal, albéitar. —**f.'s parer,** pujavante.

farriery [-ri], *s.* herrería; albeitería, veterinaria.

farrow [féroṷ]. **I.** *s.* lechigada de puercos. **II.** *a.* horra; machorra. **III.** *va. y vn.* parir (apl. a la puerca).

farseeing [fársíiŋ], *a.* que ve a gran distancia; previsor, precavido.

farsighted [fársáitid], *a.* présbite; presciente, perspicaz.

farsightedness [-nis], *s.* presbicia; hipermetropía, vista cansada; perspicacia.

farther [fárðœr)]. **I.** *adv.* más lejos, a mayor distancia; más adelante; además de, demás de, ulteriormente.—**f. on,** más adelante. **II.** *a.* más lejano; ulterior, más alejado.

farthermost [-moṷst], *a.* más lejano o remoto.

farthest [fárðist]. **I.** *a.* (*super.* de FAR) más lejano o remoto; más largo o extendido. **II.** *adv.* más lejos, a la mayor distancia.

farthing [fárðiŋ], *s.* cuarto de penique; ardite, blanca.

farthingale [-geil], *s.* verdugado, guardainfante.

fasces [fǽsiz], *s. pl.* fasces, *f. pl.*

fascia [fǽși̯ą], *s.* (anat.) aponeurosis; (cir.) faja, venda; (arq.) faja, imposta; (astr.) faja alrededor de un planeta.

fascial [-l], *a.* (anat.) fascial, aponeurótico.

fasciate(d [fǽși̯eit(id], *a.* fajado, vendado.

fasciation [fǽși̯éișǫn], *s.* vendaje.

fascicle [fǽsikl], *s.* racimo, manojo; hacecillo; fascículo, entrega de una publicación; (anat.) fascículo; (bot.) glomérulo.

fascicular [fǽsikyulʌ(r)], *a.* fascicular, fasciculado.

fascinate [fǽsineit], *va.* fascinar, hechizar.— **fascination** [-éișǫn], *s.* fascinación, hechizo.— **fascinating** [-iŋ], *a.* fascinador, hechicero.

fascine [fæsín], *s.* (fort.) fajina; haz, *m.*

Fascism [fǽșizm], *s.* fascismo.—**Fascist** [-ist], *s.* y *a.* fascista.

fashion [fǽșǫn]. **I.** *s.* moda, estilo; elegancia, buen tono; forma, figura, hechura; modo, manera; gente (*f.*) de buen tono, alta sociedad. —**f. plate,** figurín, ilustración (grabado) de modas.—**f. shop,** tienda de modas.—**after a f.,** hasta cierto punto, en cierto modo; así así. —**in f.,** de moda.—**in the f. of,** a la moda de. —**out of f.,** fuera de moda, de moda vieja, pasado.—**to be in f.,** estar de moda, estilarse, usarse.—**to be the f.,** ser (de) moda. **II.** *va.* formar; adaptar; idear, inventar.

fashionable [-ąbl]. **I.** *a.* ajustado a la moda; de moda; elegante, de buen tono; que está en boga. **II.** *s.* lechuguino, currutaco.—**fashionableness** [-nis], *s.* gentileza, elegancia, buen tono.— **fashionably** [-ąbli], *adv.* a la moda.

fashionmonger [-mʌŋgœr)], *s.* petimetre.

fast [fæst]. **I.** *vn.* ayunar, hacer abstinencia. **II.** *s.* ayuno, abstinencia, vigilia; inedia; (mar.) lazo, amarra, cable.—**f. day,** día de ayuno, etc.— **to break one's f.,** romper el ayuno; desayunar. **III.** *a.* firme, seguro, fuerte; fijo, inmoble, estable; apretado; invariable; constante, fiel; indeleble, duradero, profundo (sueño); veloz, ligero, rápido; adelantado (reloj); gastador, pródigo; disoluto.—**f. and loose,** tira y afloja; inconstante.—**f. color,** color fijo o indeleble. —**f. friend,** amigo seguro.—**f. knot,** nudo apretado, firme.—**to be f.,** adelantar (un reloj) —**to make f.,** = TO FASTEN. **IV.** *adv.* fuertemente, firmemente; estrechamente, apretadamente; duraderamente; para siempre; profundamente; aprisa, rápidamente.—**f. by,** cerca de, junto a.

fasten [fæsn]. **I.** *va.* afirmar, asegurar, fijar, sujetar; ligar, pegar; echar el cerrojo, aldaba, etc., a; atar, amarrar; (mar.) trincar, abadernar; trabar, unir; abrochar.—**to f. a door,** cerrar una puerta.—**to f. in,** clavar, hincar.—**to f. one's eyes on,** fijar los ojos en.—**to f. on, o upon,** fijar en; imputar a.—**to f. with pegs, rivets, screws,** atarugar, remachar, atornillar. **II.** *vn.* fijarse, establecerse; agarrarse, asirse, pegarse.

fastener [-œr)], *s.* el que afirma o asegura; sujetador, asegurador, pasador, cerrojo, falleba, tarabilla; escarpador; fiador; afianzador.

fastening [-iŋ], *s.* artefacto de afianzar, unir o trabar; afianzador; traba; clavazón, *f.:* unión, ligazón, *f.*, atadura, cierre, cerradura, abrochamiento; (mar.) encapilladura, amarradura.

faster [fǽstœr)], *s.* ayunador.

fastidious [fæstídi̯ʌs], *a.* descontentadizo; despreciativo; melindroso, remilgado, mimoso, quisquilloso, dengoso.—**fastidiously** [-li], *adv.* melindrosamente.—**fastidiousness** [-nis], *s.* melindre(ría); dengue.

fastigiate [fæstídži̯eit], *a.* ahusado, de lados o flancos convergentes; (bot.) fastigiado.

fastigium [-dži̯ʌm], *s.* (arq., etc.) fastigio; frontón.

fasting [fǽstiŋ], *s.* ayuno, abstinencia.—**to be f.,** estar en ayunas.

fastness [fǽstnis], *s.* firmeza, fijeza, solidez;

fuerza; fortaleza, plaza fuerte; guájar, *mf.*, guájaras, *f. pl.*, fragosidad (de una sierra); celeridad, velocidad, rapidez; disipación, libertinaje.

fat [fæt]. **I.** *a.* gordo; corpulento, obeso; craso, grasiento, graso, mantecoso, pingüe; resinoso; tosco, lerdo, grosero; opulento, rico; ganancioso, provechoso, lucrativo; pura (cal); fértil (tierra); (impr.) ancho, abierto, claro. **II.** *s.* gordo, gordura; grasa, graso; manteca, sebo; lo más rico o provechoso de alguna cosa. **III.** *va.* y *vn.* engordar.

fatal [féjtəl], *a.* fatal; inevitable; mortal, mortífero, letal; funesto. *V.* FATEFUL.—**the f. sisters,** (mit.) las parcas.

fatalism [-jzm], *s.* (filos.) fatalismo.—**fatalist** [-jst], *s.* fatalista.—**fatalistic** [-ístjk], *a.* fatalista.

fatality [fejtǽljti], *s.* fatalidad, predestinación; desgracia, infortunio; muerte, *f.*

fatally [féjtəli], *adv.* fatalmente; mortalmente.

fatalness [-njs], *s.* fatalidad.

fate [féjt], *s.* hado, destino, sino; suerte, *f.*, fortuna, estrella; parca; muerte, *f.*, ruina.—**fated** [-jd], *a.* predestinado; fatal, aciago.

fateful [-ful], *a.* fatal, funesto; ominoso.

fathead(ed) [fǽthɛd(jd], *s.* y *a.* lerdo, estúpido.

father [fáðœ(r)]. **I.** *s.* padre; Dios padre; (igl.) padre (religioso, sacerdote, etc.); autor, creador o inventor de algo.—**f. confessor,** confesor, padre espiritual.—**f.-in-law,** suegro. **II.** *va.* engendrar, procrear, producir; apadrinar, prohijar, reconocer o adoptar como hijo; tratar como hijo.—**to f. on,** o **upon,** achacar, imputar, atribuir a.

fatherhood [-hud], *s.* paternidad.

fatherland [-lænd], *s.* (madre) patria, tierra natal.

fatherless [-ljs], *a.* huérfano de padre; sin padre conocido o responsable ante la ley.

fatherlike [-lajk]. **I.** *a.* como padre, con afecto paternal. **II.** *adv.* paternalmente.

fatherliness [-ljnjs], *s.* ternura o amor paternal.

fatherly [-li]. **I.** *a.* paternal, paterno. **II.** *adv.* paternalmente.

fathom [fǽðǫm]. **I.** *s.* (mar.) braza; toesa; alcance. **II.** *va.* sondar, sondear; profundizar, examinar a fondo, tantear; penetrar en, desentrañar, escudriñar.

fathomable [-əbl], *a.* sond(e)able, penetrable.

fathomless [-ljs], *a.* insondable; impenetrable.

fatidic(al) [fætjdjk(əl], *a.* fatídico.

fatigue [fətíg]. **I.** *s.* fatiga, cansancio; (mec.) pérdida de resistencia por esfuerzos continuos; (mil.) faena, fajina (ll. t. **f. duty**).—*pl.* (mil.) traje de faena. **II.** *va.* y *vn.* fatigar(se), cansar(se), rendir(se).

fatigued [-d], *a.* fatigado, cansado.

fatling [fǽtljŋ], *s.* cebón, ceboncillo; animal de ceba o de engorde.

fatly [fǽtli], *adv.* corpulentamente.

fatness [fǽtnjs], *s.* gordura, gordo, grasa, graso o graseza, pinguosidad; fertilidad, fecundidad.

fatten [fǽtn]. **I.** *va.* engordar, cebar; (agr.) abonar, fecundar, engrasar. **II.** *vn.* engordar, echar carnes, engrosarse; medrar, prosperar.

fattening [-jŋ]. **I.** *a.* engordador. **II.** *s.* ceba, engorde (del ganado).

fattiness [fǽtjnjs], *s.* gordura.

fattish [fǽtjš], *a.* gordi(n)flón, regordete; grasoso.

fatty [fǽti], *a.* craso, gras(ient)o; (fam.) gordi(n)flón; (quím.) graso; (med.) grasoso, adiposo.—**f. acid,** ácido graso.—**f. degeneration,** degeneración grasosa.—**f. tissue,** tejido adiposo.—**f. tumor,** lipoma, *m.*

fatuity [fətjújtj], *s.* fatuidad.

fatuous [fǽchuʌs], *a.* fatuo, insensato, necio, presumido; ilusorio, vacío.

fauces [fósjz], *s. pl.* (anat.) fauces, *f. pl.*

faucet [fósjt], *s.* espita, canilla, llave, *f.*, grifo.

faugh [fo], *interj.* ¡fo! ¡puf! ¡bah! ¡quita allá!

fault [fólt]. **I.** *s.* falta, culpa, yerro; defecto, tacha, pero, imperfección, falla, lunar; pérdida del rastro por los perros de caza; (geol.) falla; (elec.) fuga de corriente.—**at f.,** equivocado; culpable, responsable; extraviado; perplejo.—**in f.,** culpable, responsable.—**to a f.,** excesivamente, con exceso.—**to find f. with,** culpar; hallar defecto en. **II.** *va.* (geol.) producir falla en. **III.** *vn.* (geol.) quebrar, produciendo falla.

faultfinder [-fajndœ(r)], *s.* censurador, criticón; reparón; persona quejumbrosa.

faultfinding [-jŋ]. **I.** *s.* crítica por manía; manía de criticar. **II.** *a.* criticón, caviloso.

faultily [-jlj], *adv.* defectuosamente, erradamente.—**faultiness** [-jnjs], *s.* culpa; vicio, defecto.—**faultless** [-ljs], *a.* sin tacha, sin pero, impecable, perfecto.—**faultlessly** [-lj], *adv.* inculpadamente; perfectamente.—**faultlessness** [-njs], *s.* perfección; inculpabilidad.

faulty [-i], *a.* defectuoso, imperfecto; culpable.

faun [fon], *s.* (mit.) fauno.

fauna [fónǎ], *s.* (zool.) fauna.

fauteuil [foutœy], *s.* (fr.) sillón, poltrona; silla presidencial (de una academia, etc.); condición de académico (en Francia).

favonian [fejvóunjan], *a.* favorable, próspero.

favor [féjvǫ(r)]. **I.** *va.* hacer un favor; agraciar, favorecer, preferir, privilegiar; mirar con favor, apoyar, patrocinar, sufragar; facilitar, contribuir a, conducir a; usar con cuidado o precaución; (fam.) asemejarse, parecerse a. **II.** *s.* favor; fineza, cortesía; preferencia, favoritismo; protección, auspicio, apoyo; mitigación, lenidad o condescendencia; permiso o licencia; acomodación, facilitación; obsequio, agasajo; (com.) carta, grata, atenta.—**in f. of,** a favor de; (com.) pagadero a.—**to be in f. with,** disfrutar del favor o tener el apoyo de.—**to lose f.,** caer en desgracia.

favorable [-əbl], *a.* favorable, propicio.

favorableness [-njs], *s.* agrado, benignidad; calidad de favorable.—**favorably** [-əblj], *adv.* favorablemente, benignamente.

favored [-d], *a.* favorecido; valido; encarado.—**ill (well)-f.,** mal (bien) encarado o parecido.

favorite [-jt]. **I.** *a.* favorito, predilecto, preferido. **II.** *s.* favorito, privado, protegido, valido.

favoritism [-jzm], *s.* favoritismo; privanza.

favus [féjvǎs], *s.* (med.) favo, tiña.

fawn [fón]. **I.** *s.* (zool.) cervato, cervatillo; color del cervato. **II.** *vn.* parir la cierva; acariciar, halagar; popar, adular.

fawner [-œ(r)], *s.* adulador, adulón.

fawning [-jŋ], *s.* adulación, servilismo.

fawningly [-jŋlj], *adv.* servilmente.

fay [fej]. **I.** *s.* empalme, unión; (ant.) fe, *f.*; hada, duende. **II.** *va.* y *vn.* (mar.) unir, empalmar, juntar estrechamente (maderos); cuadrar, ajustar bien una pieza con otra.

faze [fejz], *va.* (fam.) perturbar, desconcertar.

fealty [fíalti], *s.* homenaje, fidelidad, lealtad.

fear [fjr]. **I.** *s.* temor, miedo, pavor, recelo; asombro.—**for f.,** por temor o miedo de.—**to be in f.,** tener miedo. **II.** *va.* y *vn.* temer, recelar.

fearful [-ful], *a.* medroso, miedoso; tímido, encogido; horrendo, espantoso, terrible; imponente, que inspira reverencia o temor respetuoso.—**fearfully** [-i], *adv.* temerosamente; terriblemente; (fam.) sumamente.—**fearfulness** [-njs], *s.* temor, miedo; calidad de espantoso, etc.

fearless [-ljs], *a.* intrépido; sin temor; desaprensivo.

fearlessly [-lj], *adv.* intrépidamente, sin miedo.

fearlessness [-njs], *s.* intrepidez, arrojo.

fearnaught, fearnought [-nɔt], *s.* = DREAD-NAUGHT.

fearsome [-sʌm], *a.* temible, espantoso; tímido, miedoso, asustado.

feasance [fízǎns], *s.* (for.) cumplimiento.

feasibility [fizjbíljtj], *s.* posibilidad.

feasible [fízjbl], *a.* factible, hacedero, practicable, agible, viable.—**feasibleness** [-njs], *s.* factibilidad, calidad de factible, etc.—**feasibly** [-blj], *adv.* de modo factible.

feast [físt]. I. *s.* fiesta; festejo, función; banquete; (fam.) comilona.—**f. day**, día (*m.*) de fiesta. II. *va.* festejar, banquetear, agasajar; regalar; recrear, deleitar. III. *vn.* comer opíparamente; gozarse, deleitarse.

feaster [-œ(r)], *s.* goloso; festejador.

feat [fit], *s.* hecho, acción; hazaña, proeza; valentía; juego de manos.—*pl.* suertes, *f. pl.*

feather [féðœ(r)]. I. *s.* pluma; plumaje; género, clase, *f.;* (mec.) cuña, rayo; nervio, refuerzo de eje; (carp.) lengüeta, barbilla.—**f. bed**, colchón de plumas, plumón.—**f. duster**, plumero. —**f. joint**, (carp.) encaje de barbilla y farda.— **f. key**, cuña de corredera.—**f. pillow**, edredón. —**a f. in one's cap**, un timbre para uno, un triunfo de uno.—**in high f.**, vivo, alegre.—**to cut a f.**, (mar.) cortar el agua, navegar con rapidez; estar hecho un brazo de mar.—**to show the white f.**, volver las espaldas, huir. II. *va.* emplumar, cubrir o adornar con plumas o algo parecido; volver la pala del remo al sacarla del agua, poniéndola casi horizontal; (carp.) machihembrar. III. *vn.* cubrirse de plumas; saltar o cristalizarse un líquido en forma de plumas.—**to f. one's nest**, hacer su agosto; sacar tajada, cuidar de sí.

featherbone [-boun], *s.* imitación de ballena para corsés, etc.

featherbrain [-brein], *s.* imbécil, tonto, casquivano.

feathered [-d], *a.* plumado; alado, (poét.) penígero; emplumado.—**f. game**, caza de pluma.— **f. tribe**, los pájaros.

featheredged [-edžd], *a.* en bisel, achaflanado.

feathering [-iŋ]. I. *s.* acto o efecto de emplumar(se); plumaje; (mús.) uso delicado del arco de violín. II. *pa.*—**f. float** o **paddle**, (hidr.) álabe o paleta movible.—**f. wheel** (o **screw**), rueda (o hélice, *f.*) de paletas movibles.

featherless [-ljs], *a.* desplumado; implume.

featherstitch [-stjch], *s.* (cost.) punto de espina o de París; punto ruso.

featherweight [-weit], *a.* y *s.* ligero de peso; de escasa importancia; (dep.) peso pluma.

feathery [-j], *a.* plumado, plúmeo, plumoso.

feature [fichü(r)]. I. *s.* rasgo, facción o carácter distintivo; lo más notable o conspicuo; (teat.) pieza o película principal.—*pl.* facciones, fisionomía, semblante, rostro; lineam(i)ento, aspecto. II. *va.* hacer conspicuo, dar importancia a; (fam.) asemejarse, parecerse a.

featured [-d], *a.* formado, cincelado; encarado; anunciado de modo conspicuo.

featureless [-ljs], *a.* sin rasgos o facciones características.

febricity [fjbrjsjtj], *s.* (med.) febricidad.

febrifacient [febrjféjšent], **febrific** [fjbrífjk], *a.* que produce fiebre.

febrifugal [fjbrífyugal], *a.* febrífugo.

febrifuge [fébrjfjudž], *a.* y *s.* (med.) febrífugo.

febrile [fíbrjl], *a.* (med.) febril.

February [fébruerj], *s.* febrero.

fecal [fíkal], *a.* fecal.

feces [físjz], *s. pl.* heces, *f. pl.*, excrementos; inmundicias; sedimento, poso.

fecula [fékyulä], *s.* almidón, fécula.

feculence [fékyulens], *s.* feculencia; poso; heces, *f. pl.*—**feculent** [-ent], *a.* feculento; inmundo.

fecund [fíkʌnd], *a.* fecundo, fértil.—**fecundate** [-eit], *va.* fecundar, fecundizar.—**fecundation** [-éišon], *s.* fecundación.—**fecundity** [fjkʌnditj], *s.* fecundidad; fertilidad, abundancia.

fed [fɛd], *pret.* y *pp.* de TO FEED.

federal [fédœral], *a.* federal.—**federalism** [-jzm], *s.* federalismo.—**federalist** [-jst], *a.* y *s.* federal(ista).—**federalization** [-jzéišon], *s.* federalización.—**federalize** [-ajz]. I. *va.* (con)-

federar, formar una federación de. II. *vn.* (con)federarse.

federate [fédœrjt]. I. *a.* (con)federado, aliado. II. [fédœrejt], *va.* = FEDERALIZE.—**federation** [-éišon], *s.* (con)federación, liga.—**federative** [-ejtjv], *a.* federativo.

fedora [fjdóurä], *s.* (sombrero de) fieltro.

fee [fí]. I. *s.* honorarios; gajes, emolumentos, estipendio; retribución, gratificación, propina; cuota de ingreso en un club, etc.; feudo; (for.) bienes, hacienda de patrimonio.— **f. farm**, dominio útil.—**f. simple**, dominio absoluto.—**f. tail**, herencia restringida a especificados herederos.—**in f.**, en propiedad. II. *va.* pagar, retribuir; dar propina; alquilar.

feeable [-abl], *a.* recompensable.

feeble [fíbl], *a.* débil; enfermizo, enclenque; flojo, endeble; tenue, delicado.—**f.-minded**, de inteligencia subnormal; irresoluto, vacilante. —**f.-mindedness**, inteligencia subnormal; irresolución.

feebleness [-njs], *s.* debilidad, endeblez, flaqueza, flojedad.—**feebly** [fíblj], *adv.* débilmente.

feed [fíd]. I. *va.* (*pret.* y *pp.* FED) alimentar, nutrir, dar de comer a; pensar, dar (un) pienso al ganado); mantener; (mec.) alimentar; avanzar. —**to be fed up on** o **with**, (fam.) estar harto o hastiado de. II. *vn.* comer; pacer, pastar (el ganado).—**to f. on**, o **upon**, alimentarse de. III. *s.* forraje, pienso; comida; alimentación; (mec.) avance.—**f. bag**, morral.—**f. cock** o **tap**, grifo de alimentación, llave (*f.*) de llenar. —**f. door**, (fund.) puerta de carga o de alimentación.—**f. pipe**, **pump**, **roll**, **valve**, etc., tubo, bomba, rodillo, válvula, etc., de alimentación.—**f. rack**, pesebre, comedero.—**f.-water heater**, (m. v.) recalentador de agua de alimentación.—**f. wire**, (elec.) alimentador.

feeder [-œ(r)], *s.* alimentador; cebador (de ganado); comedor (el que come); gorrista, parásito; afluente de un río; (f. c.) ramal tributario o alimentador; (elec., mec.) alimentador.

feedhead [-hed], *s.* (m. v.) depósito de alimentación; (fund.) canal de mazarota. V. SPRUE.

feeding [-iŋ]. I. *s.* alimentación; forraje, pasto; cebadura, alimento. II. *a.* alimenticio, de alimentación.—**f. bottle**, biberón, (Am.) mamadera.—**f. device**, (mec.) aparato de alimentación.—**f. dish**, o **trough**, comedero.

feedstuff [-stʌf], *s.* alimentos para ganado, forraje (en su sentido general).

feel [fíl]. I. *va.* (*pret.* y *pp.* FELT) sentir; experimentar, percibir; tocar, tentar, palpar, manosear (a veces con of); tomar (el pulso); examinar.—**to f. in one's bones**, tener uno fuerte presentimiento de, decírselo a uno el corazón.— **to f. one's oats**, estar vivaracho; engreírse.— **to f. one's way**, ir a tientas; proceder con tiento.—**to f. out**, sond(e)ar.—**to f. the effects of**, resentirse de. II. *vn.* sentirse, encontrarse, hallarse; ser (áspero, etc.) al tacto, estar, producir la sensación de (vg. *this feels rough*, esto está áspero, o es áspero al tacto; *the room feels warm*, el cuarto está caliente).— **to f. angry**, **happy**, etc., estar enfadado, contento, etc.—**to f. ashamed**, **joyous**, etc., avergonzarse, alegrarse, etc.—**to f. bad**, sentirse mal; estar triste, entristecerse; (con about), lamentar, sentir.—**to f. cold**, **hot**, **warm**, tener frío, mucho calor; (con *it* por sujeto) hacer frío, etc.—**to f. for**, condolerse de; buscar tentando.—**to f. hungry**, **thirsty**, tener hambre, *f.*, sed.—**to f. like** (**having** o **doing**), apetecer, sentir deseos de, tener gana(s) de, querer (a veces se cambia el giro: *I feel like walking*, doy ganas de andar; *I feel like a walk*, tengo gana de dar un paseo).—**how do you f.?**, ¿cómo está (o se siente) Vd.?—**how do you f. about it?**, ¿qué (tal) le parece a Vd.? ¿qué piensa u opina Vd. de ello? III. *s.* tacto, tocamiento; sensación, percepción.

feeler [-œ(r)], *s.* el que toca o palpa; probatura, tentativa, cebo; (ent., zool.) antena, tentáculo, palpo; (mec.) lámina calibradora.

feeling [-ịŋ]. I. *s.* tacto, tocamiento; palpamiento; sensación, percepción; sentimiento, sentido, sentir, sensibilidad, emoción; ternura, compasión; calor, pasión; opinión, presentimiento, sospecha.—**to hurt one's feelings**, herir el amor propio, tocar en lo vivo. II. *a.* sensible, tierno; conmovedor.

feelingly [-lị], *adv.* expresiva o vivamente; sensible o conmovidamente; tiernamente.

feet [fít], *s. pl.* de FOOT.

feetless [-lịs], *a.* sin pies.

feign [féịn], *va. y vn.* fingir, pretender, aparentar; (di)simular; inventar, idear o imaginar.

feignedly [-ịdlị], *adv.* fingidamente.

feignedness [-nịs], *s.* fingimiento, disimulo.

feigner [-œ(r)], *s.* fingidor.—**feigning** [-ịŋ], *s.* fingimiento.—**feigningly** [-lị], *adv.* fingidamente.

feint [féịnt]. I. *s.* ficción, disimulación, treta, artificio; (esgr.) finta; (mil.) ataque fingido o simulado. II. *vn.* hacer finta.

fel(d)spar [fél(d)spar], **feldspath** [-spæθ], *s.* (min.) feldespato.—**feldspathic** [-spǽθịk], *a.* feldespático.

felicitate [fịlísịtẹịt], *va.* felicitar, cumplimentar.

felicitation [-téịšọn], *s.* felicitación, enhorabuena.

felicitous [-tʌs], *a.* feliz, dichoso; bienaventurado; oportuno.—**felicitously** [-lị], *adv.* felizmente; con oportunidad.—**felicity** [-tị], *s.* felicidad, bienaventuranza, dicha; ocurrencia oportuna.

Felidæ [fílịdi], *s. pl.* (zool.) félidos, felinos.

feline [fílaịn], *a. y s.* gatuno, gatesco; felino.

fell [fel]. I. *s.* (cost.) sobrecostura; remate del tejido; pelo, vello; pellejo; cuero, piel, *f.;* páramo, erial; mineral fino. II. *a.* cruel, fiero, feroz; mortífero; destructor. III. *pret.* de TO FALL. IV. *va.* derribar, tumbar, cortar; acogotar (las reses); (cost.) sobrecargar, sobrecoser.—**to f. trees**, desmontar, talar.

fellah [félậ], *s.* en Oriente, patán, labriego.

feller [félœ(r)], *s.* el o lo que derriba, etc.; máquina taladora; pieza accesoria de una máquina de coser para hacer sobrecosturas.

felling [félịŋ], *s.* tala (de árboles), desmonte.

fellmonger [félmʌŋgœ(r)], *s.* mercader de pieles.

felloe [félou], *s.* pina (de rueda).

fellow [félou]. I. *a.* asociado; compañero de o en (cambiando un poco el giro; vg.: *fellow sufferer*, compañero en el sufrimiento); parejo, correspondiente.—**f. boarder**, compañero de pupilaje, comensal.—**f. citizen**, conciudadano.—**f. countryman**, compatriota, *m.*—**f. feeling**, simpatía, compasión, interés común.—**f. laborer**, colaborador.—**f. man, being, o creature**, prójimo, semejante.—**f. member**, compañero, colega, *mf.*—**f. partner**, consocio. —**f. scholar, f. student**, condiscípulo.—**f. traveler**, compañero de viaje; (pol.) correligionario, simpatizante.—Este adjetivo entra en la composición de otros vocablos y denota igualdad o compañerismo. II. *s.* compañero, camarada, *mf.;* igual; pareja; socio o individuo de un colegio, sociedad, etc.; (fam.) hombre, sujeto, tipo.—**a good f.**; (fam.) buen tipo, buen chico; desprendido.—**best f.**, (fam.) novio. III. *va.* aparear, hermanar, igualar a.

fellowship [-ŝịp]. I. *s.* confraternidad, compañerismo; coparticipación; asociación, mancomunidad; compañía, cuerpo, sociedad; colegiatura, plaza pensionada; beca.—**f. holder**, becario, beeado.—**good f.**, espíritu de paz o concordia. II. *va. y vn.* admitir, aceptar o unirse con otros en sociedad.

felly [félị], *s.* = FELLOE.

felly, *adv.* cruelmente, ferozmente.

felo-de-se [fílodịsí], *s.* (for.) suicida, *mf.*

felon [félọn]. I. *s.* reo, criminal, felón; (med.)

uñero, panadizo. II. *a.* malvado, criminal; traidor.

felonious [felóụnịʌs], *a.* felón, criminal; malvado, perverso.—**feloniously** [-lị], *adv.* criminalmente; malvadamente.

felony [félọnị], *s.* felonía, crimen, delito.

felsite [félsaịt], *s.* (petr.) petrosílice, *f.*

felt [félt]. I. *s.* fieltro. II. *pp. y pret.* de TO FEEL. III. *va.* hacer fieltro; cubrir con fieltro.

felting [-ịŋ], *s.* materiales para hacer fieltro; fieltro; (carp.) acción de rajar o aserrar al hilo.

felucca [felʌkậ], *s.* (mar.) falucho.

female [fímeịl]. I. *s.* hembra (mujer, animal o planta del sexo femenino). II. *a.* hembra; femenino; (bot.) pistilado, que tiene pistilos.—**f. dog, donkey**, etc., perra, burra, etc.—**f. fern**, helecho hembra.—**f. fish**, pez hembra.—**f. screw**, hembra de tornillo, tuerca.—**f. writer**, escritora.

feme [fem], *s.* (for.) mujer.—**f. covert**, mujer casada.—**f. sole**, soltera; mujer que vive sola.

feminality [feminǽlịtị], **femineity** [feminíịtị], *s.* femineidad; calidad de femenino.

feminine [fémịnịn]. I. *a.* femenino, femenil femíneo; mujeril; mujeriego; afeminado, (gram.) femenino. II. *s.* (gram.) (género) femenino.

femininity [feminínịtị], *s.* calidad o estado de femenino; el bello sexo.

feminism [fémịnịzm], *s.* caracteres femeninos; (pol.) feminismo; (med.) caracteres femeninos en el macho.—**feminist** [-ịst], *s. y a.* (pol.) feminista.

feminize [-aịz], *va. y vn.* afeminar(se).

femoral [fémoraḷ], *a.* (anat.) femoral.

femur [fímœ(r)], *s.* (anat.) fémur.

fen [fen], *s.* marjal, pantano, fangal.—**f. cress**, (bot.) berro pantanoso.—**f. duck**, ánade silvestre.—**f. fire**, fuego fatuo.

fence [féns]. I. *s.* cerca, cerco(ad)o, valla, vallado; estacada, palizada; seto; defensa, reparo; esgrima; comprador de efectos robados; (mec.) guarda, guía, resguardo.—**f. month o season**, tiempo de veda.—**f. rail o stake**, várgano.—**to be on the f.**, estar indeciso. II. *va.* (a menudo con *in*), cercar, vallar; defender, guardar, custodiar. III. *vn.* esgrimir, pelear; disputar, defenderse con respuestas evasivas; saltar cercas (un caballo).

fencer [-œ(r)], *s.* esgrimidor, esgrimista, floretista; cercador; caballo ágil para saltar cercas.

fencible [-ịbl], *a.* (Esco.) defendible.

fencing [-ịŋ], *s.* esgrima; esgrimidura; habilidad en el debate; materiales para cercas; vallador. —**f. bout**, asalto de armas.—**f. foil**, florete.— **f. master**, maestro de esgrima.—**f. school**, escuela de esgrima.

fend [fénd]. I. *va.* (con **off**) parar, apartar, rechazar. II. *vn.* esgrimir; resistir, resguardarse (de).—**to f. for one's self**, valerse, mirar por sí.

fender [-œ(r)], *s.* guardafuegos de chimenea francesa; (mar.) defensas, andullo, pallete; (aut., carr., etc.) alero, guardalodos, guardafango.—**f. bar**, o **f. rail**, batayola.—**f. beam**, espolón.—**f. pile**, pilote de protección.—**f. stone**, marmolillo.

fenestella [fenestélậ], *s.* ventanilla.

fenestra [fịnéstrậ], *s.* (anat.) ventana (del oído, etc.); orificio a modo de ventana; (ent.) mancha transparente de un órgano fenestrado.—**f. ovalis**, ventana oval.—**f. rotunda**, ventana redonda.—**fenestral** [-l], *a.* relativo a la estructura fenestrada; a modo de ventana.—**fenestrate** [fịnéstreịt], *a.* fenestrado.

fenestration [fenestréịŝọn], *s.* (arq.) ventanaje.

Fenian [fínịan], *s. y a.* feniano.—**Fenianism** [-ịzm], *s.* fenianismo.

fennec [fénịk], *s.* (zool.) feneco, zorro africano.

fennel [fénẹl], *s.* (bot.) hinojo.—**f. flower**, neguilla, ajenuz, *m.*—**f. giant**, cañaheja.

fenny [fénị], *a.* palustre, pantanoso.

fenugreek [fényuɡrik], s. (bot.) fenogreco, alholva.

feod, feodal, feodary [fiúd, -ᶏl, -ᶏri], etc. V. FEUD, etc.

feoff [fɛf o fif]. I. va. (for.) enfeudar. II. s. feudo.

feoffee [fɛfí], s. feudatario.

feoffor, feoffor [féfœ(r)], s. el que enfeuda.

feoffment [féfmᶒnt], s. (for.) feudo.

feral [fíᶏl], a. feral; salvaje; silvestre; fúnebre.

feria [fíriᶏ], s. feria; fiesta; (igl.) feria.—pl. **feriæ**, (hist.) días de fiestas.

ferial [fíriᶏl], a. (igl.) ferial.

ferine [fíraịn]. I. a. ferino, no domesticado; maligno. II. s. fiera.

ferineness [-nịs], **ferity** [fériti], s. fiereza, ferocidad.

ferment [fœrmᶒnt]. I. va. (hacer) fermentar; agitar; excitar, inflamar. II. vn. fermentar; rehervirse, revenirse; agitarse.

ferment [fœrmᶒnt], s. fermento; levadura; fermentación, agitación.

fermentability [-abíliti], s. fermentabilidad.—**fermentable** [-ᶏbl], a. fermentable.

fermentation [-éịʃᶒn], s. (quím.) fermentación; (fig.) efervescencia, agitación.

fermentative [-ᶏtịv], a. fermentativo, fermentante.—**fermentativeness** [-nịs], s. calidad de fermentativo.

fern [fœrn], s. (bot.) helecho, polipodio.

fernery [-œrị], s. lugar donde se crían helechos; helechal; puesto de helechos.

ferny [-i], a. abundante en helechos.

ferocious [fịróuʃᴧs], a. feroz, brutal, fiero, ferino.—**ferociously** [-lị], adv. ferozmente.—**ferociousness** [-nịs], **ferocity** [fịrásiti], s. ferocidad, ensañamiento, fiereza salvaje.

ferrate [férejt], s. (quím.) ferrato.

ferreous [fériᴧs], a. (quím.) ferrizo.

ferret [férit]. I. s. (zool.) hurón; (vid.) ferrete; (cost.) listón, bocadillo, hiladillo, ribete; filadiz, m. II. va. (con out) indagar, averiguar; huronear, cazar con hurones.

ferriage, ferryage [fériịdʒ], s. bareaje, lanchaje, peaje.

ferric [férịk], a. (quím.) férrico.

ferricyanic [feriṣajénịk], a. ferricianhídrico.

ferricyanide [-sájanajd], s. (quím.) ferricianuro.

ferriferous [ferífᶒrᴧs], a. ferrífero.

ferroalloy [feroalóị], s. aleación ferrosa.

ferrocalcite [-kᶏlsajt], s. (min.) ferrocalcita.

ferrochrome [férokroụm], **ferrochromium** [-króụmịᴧm], s. ferrocromo, aleación de hierro y cromo.

ferroconcrete [-kánkrit], s. hormigón armado.

ferrocyanide [-sájanajd], **ferroprussiate** [-prᴧsịejt], s. (quím.) ferrocianuro, ferroprusiato.

ferromagnetic [-mægnétịk], a. (fís.) ferromagnético.

ferromanganese [-mǽŋɡanịs], **ferrosilicon** [-sílịkᶒn], etc. s. ferromanganeso, ferrosilicio, etc., aleaciones de hierro y manganeso, silicio, etc.

ferrotype [-tajp], s. (fot.) ferrotipo.

ferrous [férᴧs], a. (quím.) ferroso.

ferruginous [ferúdʒịnᴧs], a. ferruginoso; mohoso, aherrumbrado.

ferrule [férụl], s. cuento, herrete, regatón, virola, casquillo; zuncho; marco de pizarra.

ferry [férị]. I. va. y vn. transportar de una a otra orilla; barquear; cruzar un río en embarcación; (aer.) transportar (tropas, etc.) por avión. II. s. medio de transporte a través de un río; paso, pasaje; embarcadero, balsadera; tra(n)sbordador; balsa.—**f. cable**, andarivel.

ferryboat [-boụt], s. barco o bote de paso (a través de un río).—**ferrying** [-iŋ], s. barqueo.—**ferryman** [-mᶏn], s. balsero, barquero; encargado de un paso (de río) o de un muelle de paso.

fertile [fœrtịl], a. fértil, fecundo, feraz.

fertilely [-i], adv. fértilmente, abundantemente.

fertileness [-nịs], **fertility** [fœrtílịti], s. fertilidad.

fertilization [-izéịʃᶒn], s. (biol.) fecundación;

(agr.) fertilización, abono.—**fertilize** [-ajz], va. fertilizar, fecundar; abonar.—**fertilizer** [-œ(r)], s. (agr.) abono; fructificador.

ferula [férụlᶏ], s. (bot.) férula, cañaheja; cetro.

ferule [férụl]. I. s. férula, palmeta, palmatoria. II. va. dar palmetazos.

fervency [fœrvᶒnsị], s. ardor, calor; celo, devoción.

fervent [-ᶒnt], a. ferviente, fervoroso; fogoso, vehemente; hirviente, ardiente.—**fervently** [-lị], adv. fervorosamente.—**ferventness** [-nịs], s. ardor, fervor.

fervid [fœrvịd], a. férvido, ardiente, fogoso.

fervidity, fervidness [fœrvídịti, fœrvídnịs], s. = FERVENCY.—**fervor** [fœrvᶒ(r)], s. fervor, devoción; ardor, calor, celo, vehemencia.

fescue [féskjụ], s. puntero.—**f. grass**, (bot.) cañuela.

festal [féstᶏl], a. festivo; de fiesta, de fiestas.

fester [féstœ(r)]. I. vn. enconarse, ulcerarse, supurar. II. va. enconar. III. s. llaga, úlcera.

festival [féstịvᶏl]. I. a. festivo. II. s. fiesta, festival, festividad.

festive [féstịv], a. festivo, alegre, regocijado.

festivity [festívịtị], s. regocijo, alegría, júbilo, alborozo; fiesta, festividad.

festoon [festún]. I. s. festón, guirnalda. II. va. festonear.—**festooned, o festoony**, afestonado.

fetal, fœtal [fítᶏl], a. (embr.) fetal.

fetation [fitéịʃᶒn], s. fetación, gestación.

fetch [féch]. I. va. ir a buscar, ir por; traer; coger; aportar, cobrar (la caza); conseguir; producir, venderse por; derivar, sacar, deducir; llegar a; (fam.) fascinar, cautivar.—**to f. and carry**, servir dócilmente; chismear.—**to f. a pump**, cebar una bomba.—**to f. a sigh**, exhalar un suspiro.—**to f. down**, bajar, abatir, humillar.—**to f. in**, entrar o meter dentro; cercar; incluir.—**to f. one's breath**, tomar aliento.—**to f. out**, sacar a luz, hacer resaltar.—**to f. round**, (fam.) traer a un arreglo, convencer; (hacer) volver en sí.—**to f. up**, educar, criar; parar, detener; recuperar. II. vn. moverse, menearse; (mar.) arribar, llegar.—**to f. away**, (mar.) soltarse, dar tumbos. III. s. acto de ir a buscar o de traer; tirada, alcance; estratagema, treta; aparecido, fantasma, m.

fetcher [-œ(r)], s. el que va por algo.

fetching [-ịŋ], a. (fam.) atractivo, encantador.

fete, fête [fejt]. I. va. festejar. II. s. fiesta.—**f. day**, día (m.) de fiesta; fiesta onomástica.

fetial [fíʃᶏl], a. fecial.

fetich [fítịʃ], s. = FETISH.

feticidal [fitịsáịdᶏl], a. feticida.

feticide [fítịsajd], s. (for.) feticidio; (med.) producción intencional del aborto.

fetid [fétịd], a. fétido, hediondo.

fetidity [fetídịti], **fetidness** [fétịdnịs], s. fetidez.

fetish [fítịʃ], s. fetiche.—**fetishism** [-ịzm], s. fetichismo.—**fetishist** [-ịst], s. fetichista.

fetlock [fétlᶏk], s. cerneja del caballo, espolón; trabón.—**f. joint**, menudillo.

fetor [fítᶒ(r)], s. hedor, fetor.

fetter [fétœ(r)]. I. va. engrillar, encadenar, trabar; impedir. II. s. traba, maniota, grillete, arropea, calceta; prisión.—**f. bone**, cuartilla.—pl. grillos, brete, cadenas; prisiones.

fetterless [-lịs], a. sin trabas; desenfrenado.

fetterlock [-lak], s. manea, maniota, trabón; cerneja.

fettle [fétl]. I. va. (fund.) poner brasca a. II. s. estado, condición.—**in fine f.**, en buena condición; de buen humor.

fettling [fétlịŋ], s. (fund.) brasca.

fetus, fœtus [fítᴧs], s. (embr.) feto.

feud [fiúd], s. contienda, enemistad entre familias, tribus, clases, etc.; (for.) feudo.

feudal [-ᶏl], a. feudal.—**feudalism** [-ᶏlizm], s. feudalismo.—**feudality** [fiudálịti], s. feudalidad.—**feudalize** [fiúdalajz], va. enfeudar.

feudary [fiúdᶏri]. I. a. feudal. II. s. vasallo; feudatario.—**feudatory** [fiúdątorị], _a._ y _s._ vasallaje, feudo, feudatario.

feudist [fiúdịst], _s._ (for.) feudista; (E. U.) el que lucha en contiendas o riñas. _V._ FEUD.

feuilleton [fœytón], _s._ folletín.

fever [fívœ(r)]. I. _s._ fiebre, _f._; calentura; ventolera, pasión.—**f. blister, f. sore,** escupidura, fuegos en los labios. II. _va._ causar fiebre.

feverish [-ịŝ], _a._ febril, febricitante, calenturiento; ardiente, ardoroso.

feverishly [-lị], _adv._ febrilmente.

feverishness [-nịs], _s._ estado febril, calentura.

few [fiú], _a._ y _pron._ o _s._ pocos; no muchos, contados.—**a f.,** (alg)unos, unos cuantos, unos pocos.—**in f.,** en una palabra.—**not a f.,** no pocos.—**quite a f.,** (fam.) bastantes, muchos. —**the f.,** la minoría, los menos.

fewer [-œ(r)], _a._ y _pron. comp._ de FEW: menos, no tantos.—**the f. the better,** cuantos menos mejor.—**fewest** [-ịst], _a._ y _pron. super._ de FEW: menos.

fez [fez], _s._ fez, _m._, gorro turco.

fiacre [fiákœ(r)], _s._ coche de plaza.

fiancé [fianséị], _s._ novio.—**fiancée,** _s._ novia.

fiasco [fiéskou], _s._ fiasco, fracaso; fracaso, botella.

fiat [fáịæt], _s._ fíat, orden, _f._, mandato.—**f. money,** billetes sin respaldo ni garantía emitidos por un gobierno.

fib [fịb]. I. _s._ embuste, filfa, bola, trufa. II. _vn._ decir mentirillas, embustear, trufar.

fibber [-œ(r)], _s._ mentiroso, trapacero, trufador.

fiber, fibre [fáịbœ(r)], _s._ fibra, hebra, hilaza, hilo, filamento.—**f. sandal,** alpargata.—**f. silk,** seda artificial hecha de celulosa.

fibriform [fáịbrịform], _a._ (de aspecto) fibroso.

fibril [fáịbrịl], _s._ fibrila, fibrilla, pelillo.

fibrillose [-ous], _a._ fibriloso.

fibrin [fáịbrịn], _s._ (bioquím.) fibrina.—**fibrinogen** [faịbrínodžen], _s._ (bioquím.) fibrinógeno.

fibrinous [fáịbrịnʌs], _a._ fibrinoso.

fibrocartilage [faịbrokártịlịdž], _s._ (anat.) fibrocartílago.

fibroid [fáịbroịd], _a._ fibroideo, fibroso.

fibroid, fibroma [faịbróụmä], _s._ (med.) fibroma, _m._, tumor fibroso.

fibrous [fáịbrʌs], **fibrose** [fáịbroụs], _a._ fibroso.

fibula [fịbyulä], _s._ (anat.) peroné; imperdible; (arqueol.) fíbula, hebilla, a manera de imperdible.

fibular [-(r)], _a._ peróneo.

fichu [fịŝu], _s._ pañoleta, fichú.

fickle [fịkl], _a._ voluble, inconstante, veleidoso.— **fickleness** [-nịs], _s._ inconstancia, veleidad.

ficoid (al [fáịkoịd, -kóịdạl], _s._ y _a._ (bot.) ficoideo.

fictile [fịktịl], _a._ plástico; figulino.

fiction [fịkŝọn], _s._ ficción, invención; literatura novelesca; novela, mentira, embuste, fábula; (for.) ficción de derecho.

fictional [-ạl], _a._ novelesco.

fictionist [-ịst], _s._ novelista.

fictitious [fịktíŝʌs], _a._ ficticio, contrahecho; fingido; fabuloso.—**fictitiously** [-lị], _adv._ ficticiamente.—**fictitiousness** [-nịs], _s._ calidad de ficticio.

fictive [fịktịv], _a._ fingido, ficticio, imaginario.

Ficus [fáịkʌs], _s._ (bot.) higuera.

fid [fịd], _s._ barra de sostén; tarugo, cuña.

fiddle [fịdl]. I. _s._ (fam.) violín; utensilio mecánico. —**f. block,** motón de poleas diferenciales.—**f. bow,** arco de violín.—**fit as a f.,** en buena condición física.—**to play first,** o **second, f.,** _V._ PLAY. II. _vn._ (fam.) tocar el violín; enredar, jugar nerviosamente con los dedos o manos, etc. III. _va._ (fam.) tocar en el violín; (con away) gastar ociosamente (el tiempo).

fiddlededee [-dịdí]. I. _interj._ ¡qué simpleza! II. _s._ disparate.

fiddle-faddle [-fædl]. I. _s._ (fam.) bagatelas, frioleras; desatino, dislate; chismoso; persona frívola. II. _vn._ disparatar; ajetrearse con fruslerías.

fiddler [fịdlœ(r)], _s._ violinista.

fiddlestick [fịdlstịk], _s._ arco de violín; bagatela. —**fiddlesticks!** _interj._ ¡disparate!

fiddlestring [-strịŋ], _s._ cuerda de violín.

fideicommissary [faịdịaịkámịserị], _s._ y _a._ (for.) fideicomisario.—**fideicommissum** [-kọmịsʌm], _s._ (for.) fideicomiso.

fidelity [fịdélịtị], _s._ fidelidad; veracidad.

fidget [fịdžịt]. I. _va._ molestar, inquietar. II. _vn._ ajetrearse, afanarse, cazcalear. III. _s._ (gen. _pl._) afán, agitación, inquietud, impaciencia.—**fidgety** [-ị], _a._ inquieto, agitado.

fiducial [fịdjúŝạl], _a._ fiduciario, de confianza; (mat.) fiducial.—**fiducially** [-ị], _adv._ confiadamente; confidentemente.

fiduciary [fịdjúŝịerị]. I. _a._ fiduciario; confidencial. II. _s._ (for.) fideicomisario, fiduciario.

fie! [faị], _interj._ ¡uf! ¡abrenuncio!

fief [fif], _s._ (for.) feudo.

field [fild]. I. _s._ campo, campiña; (agr.) campo, sembrado, terreno cultivado; (mil.) campo de batalla; batalla, campaña; (ópt.) campo de un anteojo; (elec.) inductor; (magn.) campo magnético; (dep.) campo del baseball fuera del cuadro; cancha, campo de juego; colectividad de competidores en carreras, etc.; todos los caballos que entran en una carrera aparte del favorito.—**f. artillery,** artillería rodada o de campaña.—**f. basil,** (bot.) clinopodio, albahaca silvestre.—**f. bean,** judía ordinaria blanca.—**f. day,** día de ejercicios atléticos o militares.—**f. glass,** gemelos de campaña, anteojo de larga vista.—**f. gun,** cañón de campaña.—**f. hospital,** hospital de sangre; ambulancia.—**f. kitchen,** cocina de campaña.—**f. lark,** (orn.) cugujada.—**f. magnet,** (elec.) inductor; (min.) imán para buscar hierro.—**f. marshal,** mariscal de campo.—**f. mouse,** (zool.) ratón campestre.—**f. officer,** coronel, teniente coronel o comandante.—**f. of fire,** (mil.) campo de tiro.—**f. of force,** campo de acción de una fuerza.—**fields of ice,** bancos de hielo.—**f. piece,** (arti.) pieza de campaña.—**f. sports,** diversiones de la caza y la carrera.—**f. trip,** excursión de estudios prácticos, fuera de la clase.—**f. of view,** campo visual.—**f. winding,** (elec.) arrollamiento del inductor.—**f. work,** (top.) trabajo de campo o en el terreno. —**to keep the f.,** mantenerse firme.—**to take the f.,** entrar en o salir a campaña. II. _va._ (dep.) parar y devolver la pelota; poner al aire libre. III. _vn._ (dep.) actuar como _fielder_; apostar al _field._ IV. _a._ campal; campestre, silvestre; (dep.) de, o pasando, en el campo; (mil.) pert. a la campaña o al servicio activo de combate.

fielder [-œ(r)], _s._ (dep.) jugador situado en el _field_ para interceptar la pelota; perro de caza.

fieldfare [fíldfer], _s._ (orn.) zorzal.

fieldwork [fíldwœrk], _s._ (fort.) obras de campo.

fiend [find], _s._ espíritu malo, el demonio; furia, arpía; (fam.) monomaníaco, esp. morfinómano. —**fiendish** [-ịŝ], **fiendlike** [-laịk], _a._ diabólico, perverso, malvado.—**fiendishness** [-nịs], _s._ maldad, perversidad.

fierce [fịrs], _a._ fiero, feroz; bárbaro, cruel; violento, furioso; vehemente, impetuoso.—**fiercely** [-lị], _adv._ furiosamente, ferozmente.—**fierceness** [-nịs], _s._ fiereza, ferocidad.

fieri facias [fáịeraị féịŝịas], _s._ (for.) auto ejecutorio.

fierily [fáịrịlị], _adv._ calurosa o ardientemente.

fieriness [-nịs], _s._ ardor, fogosidad, vehemencia.

fiery [fáịrị], _a._ ígneo; ardiente; encendido; vehemente, fogoso; feroz, furibundo.

fife [fáịf]. I. _s._ (mús. mil.) pífano, pito, flautín. II. _va._ y _vn._ tocar el pífano.

fifer [-œ(r)], _s._ (tocador de) pífano, pito.

fifteen [fịftín], _a._ y _s._ quince.

fifteenth [-θ], _a._ y _s._ décimoquinto; quince (ordinal); quinzavo.

fifth [fịfθ], _s._ y _a._ quinto; cinco (del mes); quinto de galón (licores).—**f. column,** quinta columna.—**f. columnist,** *a.* y *s.* quintacolumnista.—**f. wheel,** rodete; (fig.) supernumerario, persona o cosa superflua.

fiftieth [fíftieθ], *s.* y *a.* quincuagésimo; cincuenta; cincuentavo.

fifty [fífti], *a.* y *s.* cincuenta.—**f. f.,** (fam.) por igual, mitad y mitad.—**f.-f. solder,** soldadura de partes iguales de plomo y estaño.

fig [fig], *s.* (bot.) higuera; higo; (fam.) ardite, comino, bledo.—**figpecker,** *s.* (orn.) becafigo.

fight [fáit]. I. *va.* (*pret.* y *pp.* FOUGHT) pelear, combatir, reñir, luchar con; librar (una batalla); lidiar, sortear o correr (toros).—**to f. off,** rechazar.—**to f. out,** discutir, decidir por discusión; llevar la lucha hasta lo último, o hasta llegar a un resultado definitivo. II. *vn.* batallar, luchar, pelear, pugnar, reñir; torear, lidiar; hacer la guerra.—**to f. against odds,** luchar con desventaja.—**to f. shy of,** evadir. III. *s.* batalla, lucha, combate, lid, lidia; pugna, pelea, riña.—**to show f.,** mostrarse pugnaz, agresivo o dispuesto a defenderse.

fighter [-œ(r)], *s.* guerrero; peleador; batallador; lidiador, luchador, combatiente; duelista, espadachín.—**f. plane,** avión (*m.*) de combate o de caza.

fighting [-iŋ]. I. *a.* aguerrido, combatiente, batallador; agresivo; luchador; pugnante.—**f. cock,** gallo de pelea.—**f. pit o ring,** reñidero.—**f.-top,** (mar.) cofa militar. II. *s.* combate, querella, riña, el pelear.

figment [fígment], *s.* ficción, invención.

figuline [fígyulin], *s.* objeto figulino.

figural [fígyural], *a.* que tiene figuras.

figurant(e) [fígyurænt], *s.* (teat. y fig.) figurante, figuranta; (teat.) comparsa.

figurate [fígyureit], *a.* figurado; (mús.) floreado, embellecido.

figuration [-éiṣon], *s.* figuración; figura.

figurative [fígyurativ], *a.* figurado, metafórico; florido.—**figuratively** [-li], *adv.* figuradamente.—**figurativeness** [-nis], *s.* calidad de figurativo.

figure [fígyü(r)]. I. *s.* figura; forma, hechura; talle; representación, imagen, *f.*; tipo; maniquí; distinción, papel, viso; (arit.) cifra, guarismo, número; (danz.) mudanza; (com.) precio, valor; (gram.) figura gramatical; (astrol.) horóscopo.—**f. dance,** baile de figuras o de cuenta.—**f. (of) eight,** circuito en forma de ocho.—**f. of speech,** figura, metáfora, trope, etc.—**f. skating,** patinaje artístico.—**to cut a f.,** descollar, hacer figura o viso. II. *va.* figurar, delinear, formar; adornar con figuras; representar, simbolizar; calcular. —**to f. out,** hallar por cálculo, resolver.—**to f. up,** computar, calcular, sumar. III. *vn.* figurar; (fam.) figurarse, imaginarse; calcular, hacer cuentas; (mús.) florear.—**to f. on,** contar con; tomar en consideración.

figured [-d], *pp.* y *a.* adornado, floreado, labrado. —**f. velvet,** terciopelo estampado.—**f. silk,** seda floreada.

figurehead [-hed], *s.* caudillo nominal, figurón; figurante, figura decorativa; (mar.) mascarón o figurón de proa.

figurer [-œ(r)], *s.* calculista; modelador.

figurine [fígyurín], *s.* figurilla o imagen adornada con dorados o pintura.

figwort [fígwœrt], *s.* (bot.) escrofularia.

Fiji(an [fidži(an], *s.* habitante o lengua aborigen de las islas Fiji.—**Fijian,** *a.* de Fiji.

filament [fílament], *s.* filamento; hilacha.

filamentous, filamentose [filaméntʌs, -ous], *a.* filamentoso; hilachoso.

filar [fáilá(r)], *a.* perteneciente al hilo; filiforme; que contiene hilos.—**f. microscope,** microscopio de ocular reticulado.

filaria [filéiriá], *s.* (zool.) filaria.

filarial [-l], *a.* (zool. y med.) filárico.

filariasis [filaráiasis], *s.* filariasis.

filature [fílachü(r)], *s.* hilandería; fábrica de hilados.

filbert [fílbœrt], *s.* avellana.—**f. tree,** avellano.

filch [fílch], *va.* ratear, hurtar, sisar, soplar.—**filcher** [-œ(r)], *s.* ratero, garduño, ladroncillo. —**filchingly** [-iŋli], *adv.* rateramente.

file [fáil]. I. *s.* lima; escofina; archivo; ensartapapeles; guardapapeles; legajo o colección ordenada de periódicos o documentos; actas, *f. pl.*; protocolo (de notario, etc.); fila, hilera; catálogo, lista.—**f. cabinet o case,** archivador, casillero, fichero.—**f. card,** limpialimas; ficha (de fichero).—**f. clerk,** archivero.—**f. cutter,** picador de limas.—**f.-hard,** a prueba de lima. —**f.-soft,** que puede ser limado. II. *a.* de archivo, de o para archivar. III. *va.* limar; archivar; ensartar, enhilar; acumular; presentar, registrar, asentar, anotar; protocolar. IV. *vn.* (mil.) marchar en filas.—**to f. off,** (mil.) desfilar.—**to f. out,** salir en fila, desfilar.

filefish [fáilfiš], *s.* (ict.) lija.

filer [fáilœ(r)], *s.* limador; archivero.

filet [filéi o filéi] = FILLET.—**f. lace,** cierto tipo de encaje.

filial [fílyal], *a.* filial.

filially [-i], *adv.* filialmente.

filiation [filiéiṣon], *s.* filiación; adopción, prohijamiento; dependencia.

filibuster [fílibʌstœ(r)]. I. *vn.* ser filibustero; (E. U.) obstruir la aprobación de leyes, etc., en un cuerpo legislativo. II. *s.* filibustero, pirata, *m.*; obstruccionista; ejemplo de obstruccionismo.—**filibusterism** [-izm], *s.* filibusterismo; obstruccionismo.

filicide [fílisaid], *s.* filicidio; filicida, el o la que mata a su hijo.

filicinean [filisíniạn], *a.* (bot.) filicíneo.

filiform [fíliform], *a.* filiforme, nemátodo.

filigree [fíligri]. I. *s.* filigrana. II. *a.* afiligranado. III. *va.* adornar con, o trabajar en, filigrana.

filigreed [-d], *a.* afiligranado.

filing [fáiliŋ]. I. *s.* limado, acción de limar; acción de archivar; (gen. *pl.*) limaduras, limalla, raedura(s). II. *a.* de limar; de archivar.—**f. cabinet** = FILE CABINET.—**f. card,** ficha, tarjeta para archivo.

Filipino [filipínou], *s.* y *a.* filipino.

fill [fíl]. I. *va.* llenar; rellenar; henchir; satisfacer, contentar; desempeñar, ocupar (un puesto); preparar (una receta); empastar, rellenar, orificar (un diente); hinchar; macizar; terraplenar.—**to f. in,** terraplenar; rellenar; insertar.—**to f. out,** llenar, completar; llevar a cabo.—**to f. the bill,** (fam.) llenar los requisitos.—**to f. up,** colmar, repletar; llenar un blanco; tapar.—**to f. up the time,** emplear el tiempo. II. *vn.* (a menudo con *up*), llenarse; henchirse, ahuecarse; echar de beber, llenar el vaso; saciarse, hartarse. III. *s.* terraplén; hartura, hartazgo; abundancia.

filler [-œ(r)], *s.* lo que sirve para llenar o rellenar; henchidor, embudador, envasador; embudo.— *pl.* tripa (tabaco).—**f. rods,** varillas para soldadura.

fillet [fílet]. I. *s.* prendedero; venda, tira, faja, cinta; lista, listón; gusanillo de rosca; (coc.) filete, solomillo; (arq.) filete, tenia, listel; (enc.) nervio. II. *va.* vendar, fajar, atar o ceñir con venda, faja o cinta; (arq.) filetear.

filling [fíliŋ]. I. *s.* henchimiento; relleno; envase; empaquetadura; terraplén, rellenamiento (de tierra); tripa (tabaco); (dent.) orificación o empastadura; empaste.—**f. station,** (aut.) estación (de toma) de gasolina, aceite, etc. II. *a.* de llenar o rellenar; que llena.

fillip [fílip]. I. *va.* dar un capirotazo; tirar o impeler con un capirotazo; incitar, estimular. II. *s.* capirotazo, papirote; estímulo, aguijón.

fillister [fílistœ(r)], *s.* (carp.) guillame.

filly [fíli], *s.* potranca; (fam.) muchacha retozona.

film [fílm]. I. *s.* película, membrana, telilla; nube

(*f.*) en el ojo; (fot. y cine) película, film, cinta.—**f. pack**, (fot.) paquete de planchas fotográficas.—**f. play**, drama cinematográfico, película dramática.—**f. star**, (cine) estrella (actor o actriz). **II.** *va.* cubrir con película; fotografiar para el cine, cinematografiar, filmar, rodar (una película), poner en la pantalla o en el cine. **III.** *vn.* cubrirse de una película; (cine) hacer o dirigir películas.

filminess [-inis], *s.* apariencia de película.

filming [-iŋ], *s.* (cine) filmación.

filmize [-aɪz], *va.* fotografiar para el cine.

filmy [-i], *a.* membranoso, pelicular.

filose [fáiloʊs], *a.* filiforme.

filter [fɪltœ(r)]. **I.** *va.* filtrar, colar, destilar; depurar. **II.** *vn.* (in)filtrarse.—**to f. in** o **through**, infiltrarse; meterse, introducirse, colarse. **III.** *s.* filtro, destiladera, colador, filtrador; (elec., fot., ópt.) filtro.—**f. cloth**, tejido filtrante.—**f. paper**, papel de filtrar.

filterable, filtrable [fɪlt(œ)rəbl], *a.* filtrable.

filtering [fɪltœriŋ]. **I.** *s.* filtración. **II.** *a.* filtrante, filtrador.

filth [fɪlθ], *s.* suciedad, inmundicia, porquería, mugre, *f.*; corrupción, obscenidad.—**filthily** [-ili], *adv.* asquerosamente.—**filthiness** [-inis], *s.* inmundicia, suciedad.

filthy [-i], *a.* sucio, puerco, asqueroso, inmundo.

filtrate [fɪltreɪt]. **I.** *va.* y *vn.* filtrar(se). **II.** *s.* líquido filtrado.

filtration [-éiʃən], *s.* filtración, destilación.

fimbri(c)ate [fɪmbri(k)eɪt], *va.* franjear; ribetear.

fimbri(c)ate(d [-id], *a.* (bot., zool.) fimbriado, franjeado; recortado, laciniado.

fin [fɪn]. **I.** *s.* aleta; barba de ballena; (mec.) rebaba, apéndice en forma de aleta; peces.—**f.-footed**, palmeado. **II.** *va.* cortar las aletas (al pescado). **III.** *vn.* aletear, mover las aletas (los peces).

fin(e)able [fáinəbl], *a.* multable; refinable.

finagle [fínéigl], *va.* y *vn.* (fam.) embaucar; sacar (dinero, etc.) con engañifas.

final [fáinəl]. **I.** *a.* final, terminal; terminante, definitivo, concluyente, decisivo; mortal.—**f. cause**, (filos.) causa final. **II.** *s.* final; (a menudo *pl.*) el final o último (juego, examen, etc.), la prueba final.

finale [fináli], *s.* (teat.) final; (mús.) coda.

finalist [fáinəlist], *s.* finalista, el que toma parte en el juego decisivo de un torneo deportivo.

finality [fainéliti], *s.* finalidad; decisión, determinación.

finally [fáinəli], *adv.* finalmente, en fin, en conclusión, por último, al final, al cabo.

finance [finǽns]. **I.** *s.* ciencia o teoría de las operaciones y transacciones monetarias (hacienda, banca, etc.); (gen. *pl.*) asuntos monetarios o financieros; hacienda; fondos, recursos, finanzas. **II.** *va.* manejar (fondos); dirigir u ocuparse en operaciones financieras o monetarias para; financiar, pagar los gastos de, conseguir o suministrar fondos para. **III.** *vn.* ocuparse en operaciones financieras.

financial [finǽnʃəl], *a.* financiero, bancario, rentístico, monetario.

financially [-i], *adv.* financieramente, rentísticamente; en lo relativo a fondos.

financier [finǽnsir]. **I.** *s.* financiero, financista, rentista, hacendista. **II.** *va.* y *vn.* = FINANCE.

financing [finǽnsiŋ], *s.* financiación, financiamiento, (Am.) refacción.

finback [fínbæk], *s.* (zool.) yubarta.

finch [fɪnʃ], *s.* (orn.) pinzón, fringílido, fringilino.

find [fáind]. **I.** *va.* (*pret.* y *pp.* FOUND) encontrar, dar con, hallar; ver, descubrir; recobrar el uso de; averiguar, adquirir, saber; (for.) fallar, decidir; procurar, proveer; alimentar, mantener.—**to f. a way** (to), darse trazas (de).—**to f. fault with**, culpar; censurar; desaprobar, poner reparos a.—**to f. favor with** o **in the**

eyes of, caer en gracia a, granjearse la buena voluntad de.—**to f. one's self**, encontrarse (apl. a la salud); descubrir uno sus aptitudes.—**to f. out**, resolver; descubrir; atrapar, sorprender; adivinar; averiguar, saber, enterarse (de). **II.** *vn.* (for.) pronunciar sentencia o fallo. **III.** *s.* hallazgo, descubrimiento; encuentro.

finder [-œ(r)], *s.* el que encuentra; descubridor; (ópt.) anteojo buscador (de un telescopio); portaobjetos cuadriculado (de microscopio); (fot.) enfocador, (gal.) visor.

fin de siècle [fæn dœ syékl], *a.* (fr.) del fin del siglo XIX; moderno, al día; decadente.

finding [fáindiŋ], *s.* descubrimiento; hallazgo; (for.) fallo, sentencia, decisión, laudo; gasto, mantenimiento.—*pl.* herramientas y avíos de zapateros y talabarteros, etc.

fine [fáin]. **I.** *a.* fino; menudo; refinado, puro; excelente, admirable; bello, hermoso; selecto, escogido o primoroso; guapo, bien parecido o gallardo; claro, transparente; agradable.—**f. and dandy**, (fam.) muy bueno.—**f. arts**, bellas artes.—**f. cut**, picadura fina de tabaco, tabaco fino.—**f. gentleman**, (desp.) lechuguino.—**f. lady**, (desp.) mujer de ínfulas.—**f. writing**, estilo afectado o rebuscado. **II.** *s.* multa.—**in f.**, en resumen. **III.** *va.* afinar, refinar; multar.—**to be fined**, incurrir en multa. **IV.** *vn.* (con **down**) purificarse; adelgazarse; derretirse. **V.** *adv.* finamente; (fam.) de primera; muy bien (apl. a la salud); (billar) apenas tocando.—**f.-corded wool**, estambre.—**f.-drawn**, muy sutil o tenue.—**f.-grained**, de granulación fina; compacto, denso, tupido.—**f.-looking**, guapo, buen mozo, bien parecido.—**f.-tongued**, zalamero. **VI.** *interj.* ¡bien! ¡magnífico!

fine-draw [fáin dro], *va.* (*pret.* -DREW; *pp.* -DRAWN) (cost.) zurcir; (metal.) estirar en hilos finísimos; (fig.) hilar muy delgado en, sutilizar en.

finely [fáinli], *adv.* finamente; hermosamente, primorosamente; sutilmente.

fineness [fáinis], *s.* fineza, delicadeza; primor, excelencia; agudeza, sutileza; pureza, perfección; ley (*f.*) del metal; finura (de arena, cemento, etc.).

finer [fáinœ(r)]. **I.** *a.* *comp.* de FINE: más fino, mejor, más hermoso. **II.** *s.* refinador de metales.

finery [fáinœri], *s.* gala, adorno, atavío, aderezo.

finespun [fáinspan], *a.* sutil; alambicado.

finesse [fɪnés]. **I.** *vn.* valerse de subterfugios y artificios. **II.** *s.* artificio, treta; astucia, sutileza; tino, tacto, diplomacia.

finger [fíŋgœ(r)]. **I.** *s.* dedo; (mec.) dedo, brazo, uña, apéndice, saliente, etc. (pieza o parte que por su forma u oficio se asemeja a un dedo); ancho o largo del dedo (medida).—**f. bowl**, enjuague, enjuagatorio.—**f. board**, diapasón de violín o guitarra; teclado.—**f. mark**, impresión digital, marca que el dedo deja.—**f. post**, poste indicador.—**f. reading**, lectura de letras en relieve por el tacto.—**f. stall**, dedil.—**f. wave**, peinado al agua.—**to have a f. in the pie**, meter la cuchara; tener participación en un asunto.—**to have at one's fingers' ends**, o **f. tips**, tener en la punta de los dedos, saber al dedillo.—**to lay**, o **put, one's fingers on**, indicar exactamente. **II.** *va.* tocar, manosear; sisar, hurtar; (mús.) pulsar, tañer, teclear; hacer algo con los dedos.

fingerbreadth [-bredθ], *s.* anchura de un dedo.

fingering [-iŋ], *s.* manoseo; digitación; (mús.) dedeo; modo de tocar o pulsar un instrumento de música; (tej.) cierta lana gruesa para medias.

fingerless [-lis], *a.* sin dedos; adáctilo.

fingernail [-neil], *s.* uña del dedo.—**f. polish**, esmalte para las uñas.

fingerprint [-print]. **I.** *s.* impresión digital, huella dactilar o dactiloscópica. **II.** *va.* tomar las impresiones digitales de.

fingerprinting [-iŋ], s. dactiloscopia.

finial [fínjal], s. (arq.) pináculo; remate.

finical [fínikal], **finicky** [fíniki], a. melindroso, remilgado, dengoso, afectado, demasiado escrupuloso.—**finicality, finicalness** [-kǽliti, -njs], s. remilgo, melindre, afectación.—**finically** [-i], adv. melindrosamente.

finis [fínis], s. fin, conclusión.

finish [fíniš]. I. va. acabar, terminar, fenecer, rematar; pulir, perfeccionar, retocar; dar la última mano; (fam.) matar o hacer impotente, anonadar; vencer.—**to f. off**, completar, acabar (con); matar.—**to f. up**, dar la última mano a; retocar; terminar.—**to f. with**, terminar; reñir con. II. vn. acabar, finalizar, cesar; (raro) morir. III. s. fin, término, fenecimiento, remate; pulimento, última mano; acabado, capa superficial, revestimiento, enlucido o barnizado de acabado; (fam.) perdición, muerte, f.—**f. line**, (dep.) meta.—**to a, o the, f.**, hasta lo último, hasta el fin, hasta terminar.

finished [-t], a. acabado, perfeccionado, pulido.

finisher [-œ(r)], s. consumador; afinador, pulidor.

finishing [-iŋ]. I. s. acabamiento, consumación; colmo, perfección; última mano, repaso, afinación.—pl. accesorios de madera de un edificio. II. a. último; de remate, de acabado; de acabar.—**f. blow**, golpe mortal; golpe de gracia.—**f. coat**, última capa, capa de acabado; (pint.) última mano.—**f. school**, escuela de educación social para señoritas.—**to give the f. touch (to)**, dar el último toque, o la última mano o pincelada (a).

finite [fáinait]. I. a. finito, que tiene fin, término o límite.—**f. verb**, inflexión verbal que denota tiempo, número, persona, etc. (a distinción del infinitivo o los participios). II. s. cosa finita.—**the f.**, lo finito.—**finitely** [-li], adv. finita o limitadamente.—**finiteness** [-njs], s. calidad de finito, lo finito.

finless [fínljs], a. sin aletas, desaletado.

finlike [fínlaik], a. de forma de aleta.

Finn [fin], s. finlandés, finlandesa.

finned [find], a. aletado.

Finnic [fínik], a. y s. finés.

Finnish [fíniš], a. y s. finlandés.

finny [fíni], a. aletado, provisto de aletas; abundante en, o perteneciente a, peces.

fiord [fyord], s. fiord(o), ría orillada de altas rocas.

fir [fœr], s. (bot.) abeto; pino.—**f. tree**, abeto.

fire [fáir]. I. s. fuego; lumbre; conflagración, incendio, quema; combustión, ignición; chispa; ardor, pasión, viveza; desgracia, infortunio; rabia. II. a. de bomberos; de incendios; del servicio de incendios; refractario.—**f. alarm**, alarma o llamada de incendios.—**f. apparatus**, cualquier aparato para extinguir incendios.—**f. board**, mampara de chimenea.—**f. brick**, ladrillo refractario.—**f. bridge**, (m. v.) altar.—**f. brigade**, o **company**, cuerpo de bomberos.—**f. clay**, arcilla refractaria.—**f. department**, servicio de bomberos.—**f. door**, puerta de horno u hornillo; boca de hornalla; puerta contra incendios.—**f.-eater**, titiritero que finge tragarse brasas; jaque, matamoros, fierabrás; (fam.) bombero; (E. U.) partidario acérrimo de los estados del sur antes de la guerra civil.—**f. engine**, bomba de incendios.—**f. escape**, escal(er)a de incendios, aparato o escalera de salvamento.—**f. extinguisher**, extintor, matafuego, apagaincendios.—**f. insurance**, seguro contra incendios.—**f. opal**, ópalo de fuego.—**f. pan**, brasero, chofeta; fogón.—**f. plug**, boca de agua (para incendios).—**f. power**, (mil.) potencia de fuego.—**f.-resistive**, refractario. V. FIREPROOF.—**f. room**, cuarto de calderas.—**f. sale**, (com.) liquidación de mercaderías averiadas en un incendio.—**f. screen**, pantalla, mampara.—**f. ship**, brulote.—**f. shovel**, badil(a), pala de cocina.—**f. station** = FIRE-HOUSE.—**f. surface**, superficie de calefacción.

—**f. trap**, edificio sin medios adecuados de escape en caso de incendio.—**f. truck**, autobomba.—**f. wall**, cortafuego.—**f. water**, aguardiente.—**to be on f.**, estar ardiendo.—**to catch f.**, encenderse, inflamarse.—**to cease f.**, (mil.) cesar de disparar.—**to hang f.**, dar higa (la escopeta); (fig.) tardarse.—**to miss f.**, hacer fogonazo, dar higa; fallar el tiro; (fig.) fracasar.—**to open f.**, (mil.) hacer fuego, hacer una descarga.—**to set f. to, to set on f.**, pegar fuego a, incendiar.—**to take f.**, encenderse; acalorarse.—**under f.**, (mil., fig.) expuesto al fuego; atacado; censurado.

fire. I. va. incendiar, abrasar, quemar; encender; disparar, descargar, tirar (armas de fuego); animar, enardecer, excitar, incitar; (vet.) cauterizar, foguear; (fam.) despedir, echar (empleados).—**to f. off**, descargar, disparar, hacer fuego con; apagar (un horno).—**to f. up**, encender. II. vn. encenderse; inflamarse; disparar, hacer fuego; enardecerse, excitarse, enojarse.—**to f. up**, enfurecerse.

firearm [-arm], s. arma de fuego, boca de fuego.

fireback [-bæk], s. pared posterior de un horno u hogar.

fireball [-bol], s. bola de fuego (meteoro luminoso, rayo, etc.); (mil.) granada de mano.

fireboat [-bout], s. buque provisto de mangueras para incendios.

firebox [-baks], s. (m. v., hornos, etc.) caja de fuegos, hogar; caja para dar la alarma de incendios.

firebrand [-brænd], s. tea, tizón; incendiario.

firebug [-bʌg], s. (fam.) incendiario.

firecracker [-krækœ(r)], s. triquitraque, carretilla, trabuca, buscapiés, petardo.

firedamp [-dæmp], s. (min.) (fuego) grisú, mofeta inflamable.

firedog [-dog], s. morillo de hogar.

firefly [-flai], s. (ent.) luciérnaga, cocuyo.

fireguard [-gard], s. pantalla (de chimenea).

firehouse [-haus], s. estación de incendios o de bomberos.

fireless [-ljs], a. sin fuego; apagado.—**f. cooker**, cocina o cocinilla sin fuego, en que el calor se obtiene de receptáculos aisladores.

firelock [-lak], s. fusil de piedra o de chispa.

fireman [-man], s. bombero; fogonero.

fireplace [-pleis], s. hogar, chimenea (francesa).

fireproof [-pruf]. I. a. incombustible, calorífugo, a prueba de fuego, refractario.—**f. curtain**, telón de incendios. II. va. hacer incombustible.—**fireproofing** [-iŋ], s. acción de hacer incombustible; materiales refractarios.

fireside [-said]. I. s. hogar, fogón; sitio cerca de la chimenea; vida doméstica. II. a. casero, íntimo.

firetrap [-træp], s. edificio sin medios adecuados de escape en caso de incendio.

firewarden [-wordǝn], s. oficial o guardia encargado de prevenir o combatir incendios.

firewater [-wotœ(r)], s. aguardiente.

firewood [-wud], s. leña.

fireworks [-wœrks], s. pl. fuegos artificiales.

firing [fáiriŋ]. I. s. encendimiento; descarga, tiroteo; combustible, leña; cocción; acción de encender, disparar, etc. (v. FIRE, va.); cuidado del fuego de una caldera, etc. II. a. de disparar, encender, etc.—**f. iron**, cauterizador.—**f. kiln**, horno.—**f. line**, (mil.) línea principal de batalla.—**f. pin**, aguja de percusión.—**f. squad**, (mil.) pelotón de fusilamiento; piquete de salvas.

firkin [fœrkin], s. cuñete, barrilito.

firm [fœrm]. I. a. firme, fuerte; fijo, estable; consistente, sólido; constante, persistente; tenaz, inflexible.—**in f.**, (com.) en firme. II. s. (com.) casa, empresa (de comercio); firma, razón (f.) social (ll. t. **f. name**). III. adv. fijamente, firmemente. IV. va. y vn. fijar(se), afirmar(se); ponerse firme, adquirir solidez.

firmament [fœrmamǝnt], s. firmamento, cielo.

firmamental [-méntạl], *a*. del firmamento.

firman [fœ́rmạn], *s*. firmán.

firmer chisel [fœ́rmœ(r) chízẹl], *s*. formón ancho y corto.

firmly [fœ́rmlị], *adv*. firmemente, fijamente.

firmness [-nịs], *s*. firmeza; consistencia, dureza, estabilidad, fijeza, solidez; constancia, determinación, entereza, fortaleza, resolución, tesón.

first [fœ́rst]. **I.** *a*. primero; primario; primitivo, prístino, original, delantero, tempranо; excelente, principal, sobresaliente. **II.** *s*. el primero; el principio. **III.** *adv*. primero; en primer lugar; al principio; antes, anteriormente; por (o la) primera vez.—**f. aid**, primeros auxilios; primera ayuda o cura.—**f.-aid kit**, botiquín de urgencia o de primer auxilio; paquete de curación.—**f.-begotten, f.-born**, *a*. y *s*. primogénito.—**f.-class**, *a*. de primera clase o calidad; *adv*. (f. c., mar.) en primera.—**f. cousin**, primo hermano.—**f. day**, domingo.—**f. edition**, edición príncipe o primera.—**f. floor**, piso principal; piso bajo, (Am.) los bajos.—**f. fruits**, primicia.—**f.-hand**, directo; de fuentes originales; (com.) de primera mano.—**f. lady**, (E. U.) esposa del presidente o de un gobernador.—**f. lieutenant**, (mil.) teniente.—**f. mate u officer**, (primer) piloto.—**f. move o play**, salida (en ciertos juegos).—**f. name**, nombre de pila.—**f. of all**, en primer lugar, ante todo.—**f. or last**, tarde o temprano, un día u otro.—**f.-rate**, excelente, de primera clase; (fam.) muy bien.—**f. water**, la mejor calidad o clase (ú. esp. de brillantes y perlas).—**at f.**, al principio, al pronto.—**at f. blush o glance**, a primera vista, sin madura consideración.—**at f. hand**, de primera mano, directamente.—**from the (very) f.**, desde el principio; de buenas a primeras, a las primeras de cambio. —**in f. gear o speed**, (aut.) en primera

firstling [-lịŋ], *a*. y *s*. primogénito; primerizo.

firstly [-lị], *adv*. primeramente, en primer lugar.

firth [fœ́rθ], *s*. estero o brazo de mar.

fisc [fịsk], *s*. fisco, erario, hacienda pública.

fiscal [-ạl]. **I.** *s*. fiscal; ministro o secretario de hacienda. **II.** *a*. fiscal, perteneciente al fisco; rentístico.—**f. year**, año económico o fiscal.

fish [fịsh]. **I.** *s*. pez, *m*.; pescado; (mar.) jimelga, gemelo; (mec.) refuerzo; (f. c.) plancha de empalme, eclisa.—**f. bait**, cebo para pescar.—**f. ball o cake**, albóndiga de pescado y patata. —**f. car**, vivero; (f. c.) furgón para llevar pescado.—**f. culture**, piscicultura.—**f. davit**, (mar.) pescante.—**f. day**, día de pescado, día de vigilia.—**f. globe**, pecera.—**f. glue**, cola de pescado, colapez.—**f. hatchery**, piscifactoría, criadero, vivero.—**f. hawk**, (orn.) = OSPREY. —**f. joint**, (f. c.) junta de eclisa.—**f. market**, pescadería.—**f. oil**, aceite o grasa de pescado.—**f. pole**, caña de pescar.—**f. scale**, escama.—**f. spear** = FISHGIG.—**f. story**, cuento increíble, andaluzada.—**f. torpedo**, torpedo submarino pisciforme.—**f. trap**, garlito, nasa.—**f. wire**, (elec.) alambre para tirar conductores por tubos.—**neither f., flesh nor fowl**, ni carne ni pescado.—**to have (an)other f.** to fry, tener otras cosas en que pensar. **II.** *va*. pescar; buscar, coger; sacar (a menudo con *out*); intentar, alcanzar, obtener; reforzar, engimelgar; empalmar (rieles, etc.); (elec.) tirar (un conductor) por un tubo. **III.** *vn*. pescar.

fishbone [-boụn], *s*. espina de pescado.

fisher [-œ(r)], *s*. pescador; (zool.) marta de América.

fisherman [-mạn], *s*. pescador; barca pescadora.

fishery [-ị], *s*. pesca, pesquería; pesquera.

fishgig [-ḡịg], *s*. (mar.) fisga, arpón.

fishhook [-hụk], *s*. anzuelo, hamo, garfio.

fishing [-ịŋ]. **I.** *s*. pesca, pesquería. **II.** *a*. de pescar; pesquero (barco, industria).—**f. bait**, cebo, carnada.—**f. barge**, gánguil.—**f.-boat**, barca pescadora.—**f. eagle**, (orn.) = OSPREY.—

fly, mosca artificial.—**f. grounds**, pesquera.—**f. line**, cuerda, cordel o sedal de pescar.—**f. reel**, carretel.—**f. rod**, caña o vara de pescar. —**f. smack**, (Am.) balandro o queche.—**f. tackle**, avíos de pescar, aparejo de pesca.—**f. wire** = FISH WIRE.—**f. in troubled waters**, a río revuelto, ganancia de pescadores.

fishiness [-inịs], *s*. forma, olor o sabor de pescado.

fishlike [-laịk], *a*. semejante a los peces; a modo de pez.

fishline [-laịn], *s*. = FISHING LINE.

fishmonger [-mʌ̣ŋgœ(r)], *s*. pescadero.

fishplate [-pleịt], *s*. (f. c.) eclisa, placa de unión.

fishpond [-pand], *s*. nansa, vivero, corral.

fishskin [-skịn], *s*. piel (*f*.) de pescado, piel de lija.

fishwife [-waịf], **fishwoman** [-wụmạn], *s*. pescadora; mujer de lenguaje y modales soeces.

fishworm [-wœrm], *s*. lombriz que sirve de cebo para pescar.

fishy [-ị], *a*. pisciforme; que huele o sabe a pescado; abundante en peces; (fam.) inverosímil, inventado; sospechoso; mate, sin lustre.

fissate [fịseịt], *a*. hendido, grietado.

fissile [fịsịl], *a*. fisil, hendible, rajadizo.

fission [fịșọn], *s*. agrietamiento, fisura; (biol.) fisiparidad, reproducción por división; (fís. y quím.) fisión.

fissiparism [fịșíparịzm], **fissiparity** [-pérịṭị], *s*. (biol.) fisiparidad, reproducción por división.—

fissiparous [fịșíparạs], *a*. fisíparo.

fissipedal [fịșípedạl], *a*. (zool.) fisípedo, bisulco.

fissirostral [fịșirástrạl], *a*. (orn.) fisirrostro.

fissure [fịșǘ(r)]. **I.** *s*. grieta, hendedura, rajadura, fisura, quebradura; (anat.) cisura. **II.** *va*. hender. **III.** *vn*. agrietarse, cuartearse.

fist [fịst]. **I.** *s*. puño; (impr.) llamada, manecilla, ☞ **II.** *va*. (fam.) apuñear, dar puñetazos a.

fistic [-jk], *a*. relativo al puño o al pugilismo.

fisticuff [-ịkʌf]. **I.** *s*. puñada, puñetazo, (fam.) trompada.—*pl*. riña a puñetazos; boxeo. **II.** *va*. (fam.) apuñear. **III.** *vn*. venir a las manos.

fistula [fịschụlạ], *s*. (cir.) fístula.

fistular [-lạ(r)], *a*. fistular.

fistulate [-leịt], *a*. fistuloso, tubular.

fistulous [-lạs], *a*. fistuloso.

fit [fịt]. **I.** *s*. (med.) acceso, paroxismo; ataque (de una enfermedad, esp. de carácter histérico o epiléptico); pasión o capricho; arranque, arrebato; corte, talle o entalladura de un traje; ajuste, encaje; conveniencia, conformidad, adaptación; preparación; punto de saponificación.—**by fits (and starts)**, a tontas y a locas, espasmódicamente. **II.** *a*. apto, idóneo, a propósito, adecuado, conveniente, aprestado; hábil, capaz; compatible, apropiado, digno; decente; listo, preparado; en buena salud, bien.—**f. as a fiddle**, (fam.) en buena condición o disposición. —**f. to be tied**, (fam.) loco de atar; muy irritado, nervioso o impaciente.—**to see f.**, juzgar conveniente. **III.** *va*. ajustar, encajar, acomodar, conformar; igualar, adaptar, adecuar; surtir, proveer, equipar, aprestar; disponer, preparar; (cost.) entallar un vestido; calzar, vestir.—**to f. out**, equipar, habilitar; armar; tripular.—**to f. up**, ajustar, acomodar, componer; adornar, ataviar, alhajar; amueblar. **IV.** *vn*. convenir, venir bien, cuadrar; corresponder; compadecerse o compaginarse con; ajustarse, entallarse, venir, sentar o caer bien o mal.—**to f. into**, encajar en; concordar con.

fitch [fịch], **fitchet** [-ịt], **fitchew** [-u], *s*. (zool.) veso, turón.

fitful [fịtful], *a*. espasmódico; caprichoso; incierto, vacilante.—**fitfully** [-ị], *adv*. por intervalos; caprichosamente.

fitly [fịtlị], *adv*. aptamente, adecuadamente, propiamente, acertadamente.

fitness [fịtnịs], *s*. aptitud, idoneidad, adecuación, disposición, propiedad; conveniencia, correspondencia; oportunidad; adaptabilidad.

fitter [fịtœ(r)], *s*. ajustador; (mec.) armador, cerrajero, montador; proveedor; (cost.) entallador, cortador.

fitting [fítiŋ]. **I.** *a.* propio, digno, adecuado, conveniente. **II.** *s.* ajuste, encaje; tubo o pieza de unión o de conexión (en las tuberías); (cost.) entalladura, corte; prueba.—*pl.* guarniciones; accesorios; adjuntos o añadiduras; herrajes o avíos; herramientas.

fittingly [-liǰ], *adv.* propiamente, aptamente.

five [fáiv], *s.* y *a.* cinco.—**f.-finger, f.-leaf,** (bot.) cincoenrama.—**f. hundred,** quinientos; cierto juego de naipes.—**f.-spot,** cinco (en los naipes); (fam.) billete de cinco dólares o libras (ll. t. **fiver**).

fivefold [-fould], *a.* quíntuplo.

fives [fáivz], *s.* un juego de pelota; (vet.) adivas.

fix [fíks]. **I.** *va.* fijar; inmovilizar; asegurar, asentar; señalar (una fecha); arreglar, poner en orden; reparar, componer; calar (la bayoneta); estampar (en la mente, etc.); (quím. y foto.) fijar; (fam.) sobornar, cohechar; (fam.) castigar a uno, ajustarle las cuentas.—**to f. up,** componer, arreglar; equipar. **II.** *vn.* fijar el domicilio, establecerse; congelarse, cristalizarse, solidificarse.—**to f. on,** o **upon,** decidir, escoger, elegir. **III.** *s.* (fam.) apuro, aprieto; (fund.) brasca.

fixable [-ạbl], *a.* fijable.

fixation [fikséiʃọn], *s.* fijación; fijeza, firmeza, estabilidad; (quím.) fijación.

fixative [fíksạtiv]. **I.** *a.* que fija. **II.** *s.* (tint.) mord(i)ente; (fot., pint.) fijador, fijativo.

fixed [fíkst], *pp.* y *a.* fijo, arraigado, estable, permanente; determinado; (com.) a plazo fijo; perentorio.—**f. charges,** gastos fijos.—**f. idea,** idea persistente, obsesión.—**with f. bayonets,** con la bayoneta calada.

fixedly [fíksịdli], *adv.* fijamente; firmemente; ciertamente.—**fixedness** [-nịs], **fixity** [fíksịti], *s.* fijeza, firmeza; coherencia; fijación.

fixer [fíksœ(r)], *s.* (fot., etc.) fijador, fijativo.

fixing [fíksiŋ], *s.* acción de TO FIX en cualquier sentido; fijación.—*pl.* (fam.) jaeces, enseres, útiles, accesorios.—**f. bath** o **liquid,** (fot., pint.) = FIXER.

fixture [fíkschǔ(r)], *s.* cosa fija o enclavada en un sitio; sostén, brazo (de lámpara eléctrica o gas); adorno, trasto o mueble fijo en el suelo, la pared o el techo; empleado inamovible.—*pl.* habilitación de una tienda; instalación; muebles y enseres; guarniciones de alumbrado eléctrico y de gas (brazos, sostenes, accesorios, etc.).

fizgig [fízgig], *s.* arpón, dardo, fisga; buscapiés o carretilla; moza callejera.

fizz [fíz]. **I.** *vn.* sisear. **II.** *s.* siseo; efervescencia; gaseosa; champaña.

fizzle [fízl]. **I.** *vn.* sisear; (fam.) (a veces con **out**) hacer fiasco, quedar mal. **II.** *s.* siseo; agitación; (fam.) fiasco, fracaso.

fizzy [fízi], *a.* que sisea; efervescente.

fjord [fyord] = FIORD.

flabbergast [flǽbœrgæst], *va.* (fam.) dejar de una pieza, o hecho una pieza; aturrullar; pasmar.

flabby [flǽbi], *a.* flojo, lacio, fofo, blando. V. FLACCID.

flabellate [flạbéleit], **flabelliform** [-iform], *a.* flabeliforme.

flabellum [-ʌm], *s.* (igl.) flabelo.

flaccid [flǽksịd], *a.* flojo, endeble, débil, flaco, laso; (med.) fláccido.—**flaccidity** [-sídịti], *s.* flojedad, flaqueza, debilidad; (med.) flaccidez.

flag [flæg]. **I.** *va.* hacer señales con banderola; izar bandera; cazar con banderín; enlosar o adoquinar con lanchas, losas o lajas; hacer (a un tren) señal de parada. **II.** *vn.* flaquear, amilanarse; decaer, debilitarse; colgar, pender; vacilar. **III.** *s.* bandera; estandarte, pabellón; banderola; laja, lancha, baldosa, losa; cola de venado; (pl.) (orn.) plumas largas de las piernas; plumas secundarias del ala; (bot.) gladiolo, espadaña; ácoro, cálamo; (geol.) = FLAGSTONE, roca o piedra laminada; (mar.) = FLAGSHIP.—**F. Day,**

(E. U.) día de la bandera (14 de junio, aniversario de la adopción de la bandera norteamericana por los patriotas en 1777).—**f. officer,** (mar.) jefe de una escuadra (generalmente un almirante, vicealmirante o contraalmirante).—**f. of truce,** (mil.) parlamentario, bandera de parlamento.

flagellant [flǽdǎelạnt]. **I.** *a.* y *s.* flagelante. **II.** *s. pl.* (igl.) flagelantes, disciplinantes.—**flagellate** [-eit]. **I.** *va.* y *vr.* flagelar(se). **II.** *a.* (biol.) flagelado.—**flagellation** [-éiʃọn], *s.* flagelación.—**flagellator** [-eito(r)], *s.* flagelador.

flagelliform [flạdǎéliform], *a.* flageliforme.

flagellum [flạdǎélam], *s.* flagelo, azote; (biol.) flagelo; (bot.) renuevo, sarmiento.

flageolet [flædǎolét], *s.* (mús.) caramillo, chirimía, dulzaina.

flagging [flǽgiŋ]. **I.** *s.* enlosado; lajas para adoquinar. **II.** *a.* lánguido, flojo.

flaggy [flǽgi], *a.* parecido a la laja; que contiene espadañas o ácoros; lánguido, flojo.

flagitious [flạdǎíʃʌs], *a.* malvado, infame, atroz.

flagitiousness [-nịs], *s.* maldad, infamia, atrocidad.

flagman [flǽgmạn], *s.* el encargado de la bandera; (f. c.) guardavía, *m.*, vigilante.

flagon [flǽgọn], *s.* frasco, pomo.

flagpole [flǽgpoul], *s.* asta de bandera; (top.) banderola, jalón.

flagrancy [fléigrạnsị], *s.* notoriedad, escándalo, impudencia.—**flagrant** [-ạnt], *a.* notorio, escandaloso, público; flagrante.

flagrante delicto [flagrǽntị dịlíktou], *adv.* en flagrante, en fragante.

flagrantly [fléigrạntlị], *adv.* notoriamente.

flagship [flǽgʃip], *s.* (mar.) capitana, buque en que va el jefe de una escuadra; almiranta.

flagstaff [-stæf], *s.* asta de bandera.

flagstone [-stoun], *s.* losa grande de embaldosar; (geol.) laja, lancha.

flail [fleil]. **I.** *s.* (agr.) mayal, desgranador; (mil.) mangual. **II.** *va.* desgranar con mayal; azotar, batir.

flair [fler]. **I.** *s.* olfato; sagacidad; aptitud, inclinación, propensión. **II.** *va.* olfatear.

flak [flæk], *s.* (mil.) barrera antiaérea.

flake [fléik]. **I.** *s.* pedacito, escama, casquito; copo de nieve; hojuela, laminilla; (bot.) clavel rayado.—**f. of fire,** centella, chispa.—**f. of ice,** carámbano.—**f. white,** (pint.) albayalde. **II.** *va.* y *vn.* formar hojuelas o escamas; descascararse o desconcharse.

flaky [-i], *a.* lleno de cascajo o casquitos; escamoso; formando trepa.

flam [flæm]. **I.** *s.* (fam.) mentira, embuste, bola. **II.** *va.* y *vn.* (fam.) mentir, engañar, embaucar, engatusar.

flambeau [flǽmbou], *s.* antorcha, hachón; candelabro; caldero para hervir azúcar.

flamboyant [flæmbóiạnt], *a.* flamígero, flamante; extravagante, llamativo; (arq.) flamígero, flameante; de bordes ondulados.

flame [fléim]. **I.** *s.* llama(rada), flama; fuego; ardor, pasión; (fam.) persona amada.—**f.-colored,** de color de llama.—**f. thrower,** (mil.) lanzallamas. **II.** *va.* quemar, chamuscar; encender, tratar con la llama. **III.** *vn.* arder, flamear, llamear, encenderse; brillar, fulgurar; inflamarse.

flameless [-lịs], *a.* sin llama.

flamen [fléimen], *s.* flamen.

flaming [fléimiŋ], *a.* flamante, llameante; encendido, inflamado; excitante; apasionado.

flamingo [flạmíŋgou], *s.* (orn.) flamenco.

flamy [fléimi], *a.* inflamado, llameante.

flan [flæn *o* flan], *s.* cospel, tejo; (coc.) flan.

flange [flǽndǎ]. **I.** *s.* (mec.) pestaña, reborde; brida, orej(et)a, ala (de vigo, riel, etc.); herramienta para formar pestañas.—**f. coupling,** acoplamiento con anillos de rebordes.—**f. joint,** junta de pestañas remachadas o empernadas.—

f. nut, tuerca de reborde o de basa.—**f. pipe,** tubo con pestaña.—**f. rail,** riel en T.—**f. wheel,** rueda de pestaña. **II.** *va.* hacer pestaña o reborde a. **III.** *vn.* ensancharse en forma de pestaña.

flanged [-d], *a.* de reborde, que tiene reborde(s).

flanging [-iŋ], *s.* (arq.) derrame, vuelta, alféizar.

flank [flǽŋk]. **I.** *s.* ijar, ijada; flanco, costado; (mil., fort.) flanco, costado.—**f. attack,** flanqueo. **II.** *a.* lateral, de lado, de costado o por el flanco. **III.** *va.* orillar, estar a cada lado de; (mil.) flanquear. **IV.** *vn.* (con **on**) lindar con.—

flanker [-œ(r)], *s.* (fort.) flanco; flanqueador.—

flanking [-iŋ]. **I.** *a.* flanqueador, flanqueante. **II.** *s.* (mil.) flanqueo.

flannel [flǽnel], *s.* (tej.) franela, bayeta, muletón.

flannelet(te [-ét], *s.* (tej.) especie de franela o muletón.

flap [flǽp]. **I.** *s.* (sast.) cartera, golpe o portezuela; falda, faldilla, faldeta, faldón; ala de sombrero; hoja plegadiza de mesa; faldón de silla; oreja de zapato; mosqueador; revés, cachete; (aut.) faja de protección (de la cámara de aire); (cir.) colgajo.—**f. door,** trampa.—**f.-eared,** de orejas grandes y gachas.—**f.-mouthed,** morrudo, bezudo, hocicudo.—**f. valve,** chapaleta. **II.** *va.* batir, sacudir, golpear, pegar; agitar, columpiar; mosquear.—**to f. the wings,** aletear. **III.** *vn.* batir; gualdrapear (las velas), dar gualdrapazos o socolladas; colgar.

flapdoodle [-dudl], *s.* (fam.) tontería, disparate.

flapjack [-dʒæk], *s.* torta de sartén. *V.* PANCAKE.

flapper [-œ(r)], *s.* batidor; el que o lo que bate, golpea o sacude; recordatorio; patito, anadino, polluelo; (fam.) chica, poll(it)a; chica despreocupada; (fam.) mano, *f.*

flapping [-iŋ], *s.* batimiento, aleteo, aletazo; (mar.) gualdrapazo, socollada.

flare [flér]. **I.** *va.* encender; chamuscar; ensanchar, acampanar, abocinar. **II.** *vn.* lucir, brillar o destellar; fulgurar; deslumbrar; acampanarse; ensancharse hacia la boca; sobresalir.—**to f. up,** encenderse; encolerizarse. **III.** *s.* llama, llamarada, fulgor, brillo, destello; luz de Bengala, cohete de señales; brillantez, relumbrón; inclinación; derramo, ensanchamiento, ensanche.—**f.-up,** llamarada; arrebato de cólera; jarana.

flaring [-iŋ], *a.* rutilante, resplandeciente, fulgurante; chillón; acampanado, abocinado; que proyecta o sobresale.

flash [flǽʃ]. **I.** *s.* relámpago; llamarada, destello, fulguración, relumbrón, resplandor; viso; fucilazo; fogonazo; instante, tris, *m.*; (period.) breve despacho telegráfico; (cine) incidencia, incidente, proyección momentánea explicativa; estanque, esclusa, represa; golpe de agua.—**f. bulb, f. lamp,** (foto.) bombilla de magnesio.—**f. burner,** mechero de gas con encendedor eléctrico.—**f. flood,** avenida o inundación repentina y violenta.—**f. in the pan,** fogonazo; esfuerzo espasmódico que no logra nada.—**f. of light,** ráfaga.—**f. of lightning,** relámpago.—**f. of the eye,** ojeada, vistazo.—**f. of wit,** agudeza, rasgo de ingenio.—**f. point,** punto o temperatura de inflamación.—**f. test,** prueba del punto de inflamación; (por extensión) punto de inflamación.—**f. wheel,** rueda de canjilones para elevar agua. **II.** *a.* ladronesco, germanesco; falso; charro, chillón; (fam.) experto, listo. **III.** *va.* encender; quemar (pólvora); enviar o despedir con celeridad; sacar a relucir; hacer brillar; (elec.) tratar (un filamento de carbón) por la corriente eléctrica en una mezcla de hidrocarburos. **IV.** *vn.* relampaguear; brillar, fulgurar, destellar; pasar o cruzar como un relámpago.—**to f. in the pan,** dar higa (un fusil).

flashback [-bæk], *s.* (cine) = THROWBACK.

flashboard [-bord], *s.* tabla de contención puesta sobre una presa, etc., para ahondar el agua.

flasher [-œ(r)], *s.* (elec.) destellador (especie de

interruptor empleado en las lámparas de anuncios eléctricos).—**f. sign,** anuncio intermitente.

flashily [-ili], *adv.* con ostentación, con colores chillones.

flashing [-iŋ]. **I.** *a.* centellador, centellante; relampagueante. **II.** *s.* centelleo, coruscación, fulguración; relampagueo (*v.* FLASH); soplado del vidrio; (elec.) operación de reforzar los filamentos de lámparas incandescentes; (hidr.) golpe de agua; (arq.) vierteaguas, despidiente de agua, tabla o plancha de escurrimiento o de desviación (del agua).—**f. light, point** = FLASHLIGHT, FLASH POINT.

flashlight [-lajt], *s.* linterna eléctrica de bolsillo o portátil; reflector de luz intermitente o titilante (de un faro); luz giratoria de intensidad variable (para faros); (fot.) luz instantánea (de magnesio, etc.).—**f. photography,** fotografía instantánea de relámpago.

flashover [-ouvœ(r)], *s.* (elec.) formación de arco; descarga.

flashy [-i], *a.* charro, de oropel, de relumbrón.

flask [flæsk], *s.* frasco, redoma, botella, pomo; (fund.) caja de moldear.

flat [flǽt]. **I.** *s.* llanura; banco, bajío, escollo; cosa plana, v. gr.: palma de la mano, plano de una hoja cortante, barca chata, pala de remo, carro de plataforma, alma de botón; apartamiento, piso; (mús.) bemol; (fam.) mentecato; (agr.) semillero de cajón. **II.** *a.* plano, llano, liso; raso, chato, aplastado; tendido, extendido; arrasado; categórico; fijo; neto; insulso, insípido; (mús.) bemol(ado), desafinado (bajo); menor o disminuído.—**f.-bed press,** prensa de platina.—**f.-bottomed,** de fondo plano.—**f.-footed,** de pies planos, llanos o achatados; (fam.) inflexible, resuelto, determinado.—**f. nose,** nariz chata.—**f.-nosed,** chato, nacho, romo.—**f. rate,** tipo o tarifa fijos; precio alzado; tanto por unidad.—**f. roof,** azotea.—**f. tire,** (aut.) neumático desinflado, llanta reventada. **III.** *adv.* completamente; abiertamente, decididamente; (com.) sin interés. **IV.** *va.* (mús.) bemol(iz)ar, bajar de tono; allanar, aplastar, achatar. **V.** *vn.* (mús.) desafinar por lo bajo; aplastarse; atontarse.

flatboat [-bout], *s.* barco o bote de fondo plano.

flatcar [-kar], *s.* (f. c.) (vagón de) plataforma, *truck.*

flatiron [-ajœrn], *s.* plancha (de planchar).

flatland [-lænd], *s.* llano, llanura, llana(da).

flatly [-li], *adv.* horizontalmente, llanamente; de plano; categórica, rotunda o terminantemente; sin animación ni interés.—**flatness** [-njs], *s.* llanura, lisura, chatedad; desabrimiento, insipidez, insulsez.

flatten [-n]. **I.** *va.* allanar, aplastar, achatar, aplanar; tender; abatir; desabrir, desazonar; deprimir; (aer.) enderezar (un avión), poner horizontal. **II.** *vn.* aplanarse, igualarse; perder el sabor; evaporarse; (aer.) enderezarse, tomar la posición horizontal.

flatter [-œ(r)]. **I.** *a. comp.* de FLAT; más llano, insípido, etc. **II.** *s.* allanador; hilera de estirar alambre.

flatter. I. *va.* adular, lisonjear; hacerse una ilusión; favorecer. **II.** *vn.* adular, lisonjear.—**flatterer** [-œ(r)], *s.* adulador; lisonjero, zalamero.—**flattering** [-iŋ], *a.* lisonjero, halagüeño.—**flatteringly** [-li], *adv.* lisonjeramente, halagüeñamente.—**flattery** [-i], *s.* adulación, lisonja, halago.

flattish [flǽtiʃ], *a.* achatado.

flattop [-tap], *s.* (fam.) portaaviones.

flatulence, flatulency [flǽchulens, -i], *s.* flatulencia, ventosidad; hinchazón, presunción.

flatulent [-ent], *a.* flatulento, ventoso; hinchado, vano.

flatus [fléjtas], *s.* flato, ventosidad; hinchazón; ráfaga, soplo.

flatware [flǽtwer], *s.* vajilla de plata y porcelana.

flatwise [flǽtwajz], *adv.* de llano.

flaunt [flȯnt]. **I.** *va.* y *vn.* ostentar, lucir; desplegar, ondear. **II.** *s.* ostentación, alarde.

flautist [flȯ́tjst], *s.* (mús.) flautista.

flavescent [flejvésent], *a.* amarillento.

flavor [fléjvọr)]. **I.** *s.* sabor, gusto, gustillo; (coc.) sazón, sainete. **II.** *va.* saborear, sazonar, condimentar; (fig.) dar cualidad distintiva a una cosa.—**flavoring** [-jŋ], *s.* sainete, condimento. —**flavorless** [-ljs], *a.* sin sabor, insípido, soso.— **flavorous** [-ʌs], *a.* sabroso.

flaw [flȯ́]. **I.** *s.* defecto, imperfección, falta, mancha; grieta, pelo, paño, paja; (geol.) falla, mancha; (metal.) escarabajo, esponjadura, galleo; (mar.) ráfaga, racha. **II.** *va.* afear, estropear; agrietar. **III.** *vn.* agrietarse; ponerse defectuoso.

flawless [-ljs], *a.* entero, sin tacha.

flawy [-j], *a.* agrietado; defectuoso, lleno de faltas o tachas; (mar.) propenso a rachas.

flax [flǽks], *s.* (bot.) lino.—**f. brake**, agramadera. —**f. comb**, rastrillo.—**f. dresser**, rastrillador. —**f. dressing**, rastrilleo del lino.—**to brake f.**, agramar lino.—**to dress f.**, rastrillar lino.

flaxen [-ęn], **flaxy** [-j], *a.* de lino.—**f.-haired**, blondo, de pelo muy rubio.

flaxseed [-sid], *s.* (bot.) linaza, semilla de lino.— **f. oil**, aceite de linaza.

flay [fléj], *va.* desollar, despellejar; excoriar, escorchar.—**flayer** [-œr)], *s.* desollador.—**flaying** [-jŋ], *s.* desolladura, desuello; despellejadura; excoriación.

flea [flí], *s.* (ent.) pulga.—**a f. in one's ear**, amonestación desagradable; pulla; desaire.

fleabane [-bejn], *s.* (bot.) coniza, pulguera.

fleabite [-bajt], *s.* picadura de pulga.

flea-bitten [-bjtęn], *a.* picado de pulgas; salpicado (apl. al color de ciertos caballos).

fleam [flim], *s.* (vet.) fleme, lanceta.

fleawort [flíwœrt], *s.* (bot.) pulguera.

fleck [flék]. **I.** *va.* abigarrar, varetear. **II.** *s.* punto o lista de color, mancha, lunar; copo, vedija.

fleckless [-ljs], *a.* sin mancha.

flection [flékṣọn], *s.* flexión; corvadura; (gram.) (in)flexión.

flectional [-ạl], *a.* (gram.) flexional.

fled [fled], *pret.* y *pp.* de TO FLEE.

fledge [flédž]. **I.** *va.* criar las aves hasta que pueden volar; emplumar (saetas, dardos). **II.** *vn.* emplumecer, pelechar.—**fledged** [-d], *a.* plumado, plumoso; con bozo; alado; maduro, sazonado.

fledg(e)ling [-jŋ], *s.* y *a.* volantón; joven, novel, inexperto.

flee [flí]. **I.** *va.* (*pret.* y *pp.* FLED) huir de, escapar de, evitar. **II.** *vn.* huir; fugarse; desaparecer.

fleece [flís]. **I.** *s.* vellón, lana.—**f. wool**, vellón. **II.** *va.* esquilar, tonsurar; cubrir con lana o nieve; escamotear.

fleecy [-j], *a.* lanudo.—**f. clouds**, nubes aborregadas.

fleer [fljr]. **I.** *va.* mofar, burlar. **II.** *vn.* mofarse, burlarse. **III.** *s.* burla, mueca; risa falsa; el que huye.

fleet [flít]. **I.** *s.* (mar.) armada, escuadra; flota, flotilla; escuadra (de aviones), flota aérea; conjunto de coches, camiones, etc., que pertenecen a una misma empresa. **II.** *a.* veloz, rápido.— **f.-footed**, alípede; ligero.—**f.-winged**, alígero. **III.** *vn.* y *va.* volar; (hacer) pasar rápidamente; (mar.) despasar, cambiar.

fleeting [-jŋ], *a.* fugaz, efímero, huidizo, pasajero.

fleetingly [-lj], **fleetly** [-lj], *adv.* velozmente, fugazmente.

fleetness [-njs], *s.* ligereza, rapidez; agilidad.

Fleming [flémjŋ], *s.* flamenco.

Flemish [flémjṣ], *a.* y *s.* flamenco.—**F. bond** = DUTCH BOND.

flesh [fléṣ]. **I.** *s.* carne, *f.*; género humano; pulpa (de las frutas).—**f. and blood**, carne y hueso; sangre, *f.*, parentela, progenie.—**f. brush**, cepillo para frotar la piel.—**f. color**, color de carne, encarnado.—**f. fly**, (ent.) moscarda.—**f. of fowl** o **game birds**, carne de pluma.—**f. of hares**, etc., carne de pelo.—**f. wound**, herida superficial.—**in the f.**, vivo, carnal; en persona. —**to put on f.**, engordar, (fam.) echar carnes. **II.** *va.* hartar; incitar; meter en la carne (la espada, etc.); avezar, habituar; cebar; (ten.) descarnar, pelambrar.

fleshiness [-injs], *s.* carnosidad; corpulencia.

fleshings [-iŋz], *s. pl.* (teat.) calzas de punto de color de carne; (ten.) descarnaduras, piltrafas.

fleshless [-ljs], *a.* descarnado.

fleshliness [-ljnjs], *s.* carnalidad.

fleshly [-lj], *a.* carnal; corpóreo; sensual.

fleshpot [-pat], *s.* olla.—*pl.* vida regalada.

fleshy [-j], *a.* gordo, corpulento; corporal; carnal; carnudo, carnoso, pulposo; suculento.

fletcher [fléčœr)], *s.* flechero.

fleur-de-lis [flœrdœlí(s)],s.(blas.,bot.) flor de lis,*f.*

fleuron [flœrón], *s.* (arq.) florón.

flew [flu]. **I.** *pret.* de TO FLY. **II.** *s.* = FLUE.

flewed [flud], *a.* boquihendido.

flews [fluz], *s. pl.* belfos.

flex [fléks]. **I.** *va.* doblar, encorvar. **II.** *vn.* doblarse, encorvarse. **III.** *s.* doblez, encorvadura.

flexibility [-jbjljtj], **flexibleness** [fléksjblnjs], *s.* flexibilidad; docilidad.

flexi(b)le [fléksj(b)l], *a.* flexible; dócil; adaptable, doblegable; cimbreño, plástico.

flexion [flékṣọn], *s.* flexión.

flexor [fléksọr)], *s.* (anat.) músculo flexor.

flexuose [fléksḳọus], **flexuous** [-ṣuʌs], *a.* tortuoso; vario, inconstante; (bot.) flexuoso.

flexure [-ṣu̯r)], *s.* flexión; corvadura.

flick [flík]. **I.** *va.* dar ligeramente con un látigo, etc.; quitar con un golpecito, sacudir (la ceniza de un cigarro, etc.). **II.** *vn.* revolotear; moverse a tirones. **III.** *s.* golpecito, latigazo suave, (fam.) pasagonzalo.

flicker [-œr)]. **I.** *vn.* flamear; fluctuar, vacilar, aletear, revolotear. **II.** *s.* llama vacilante; pestañeo (de los párpados); (orn.) picamaderos. —*pl.* (fam.) cine.

flier [flájœr)], *s.* volador; ave voladora; aviador; aeroplano; fugitivo; (mec.) volante; (impr.) sacapliegos; hoja o papel volante; escalón, peldaño; (fam.) cosa veloz, v. gr.: buque rápido, caballo de carrera, tren expreso, etc.; (fam.) aventura, tentativa; operación arriesgada, esp. de bolsa.

flight [flájt], *s.* vuelo, volada; espacio recorrido por un proyectil, pájaro, aeroplano, etc.; carrera, raid, *m.*, viaje aéreo; escuadrilla aérea (ll. t. **f. squadron**); bandada de pájaros; ímpetu, arranque; tramo de escalera; huída, fuga; (for.) evasión, escape.—**f. deck**, (aer.) cubierta de despegue y aterrizaje (de un portaaviones).—**f. feather**, remera.—**f. leader**, (mil., aer.) jefe de patrulla o vuelo.—**f. path**, (aer.) trayectoria del centro de gravedad de un avión, línea de vuelo.—**f. strip**, (aer.) pista auxiliar de aterrizaje y despegue, al borde de una carretera.—**to put to f.**, ahuyentar.—**to take to f.**, huir, fugarse.

flightiness [-jnjs], *s.* veleidad, capricho.

flightless [-ljs], *a.* que no puede volar.

flighty [-j], *a.* volátil; voltario; travieso.

flimflam [fljmflæm]. **I.** *s.* (fam.) soflama; fraude, embaucamiento. **II.** *va.* soflamar; embaucar.

flimsily [fljmzjlj], *adv.* sin consistencia, endeblemente.—**flimsiness** [-njs], *s.* endeblez, falta de solidez o consistencia.

flimsy [fljmzj]. **I.** *a.* débil, endeble; baladí, frívolo. **II.** *s.* cierto papel delgado que usan los repórteres; noticia periodística escrita en este papel.

flinch [fljnch]. **I.** *vn.* vacilar; acobardarse; echar el cuerpo atrás; retroceder ante lo peligroso, difícil o desagradable. **II.** *s.* vacilación, titubeo; cierto juego de naipes.

flinder [flíndœ(r)], *s.* astilla, fragmento, tira.
fling [fliŋ]. I. *va.* (*pret.* y *pp.* FLUNG) arrojar, tirar, despedir; derribar, echar al suelo; sobrepujar, vencer.—**to f. about**, desparramar, esparcir.— **to f. away**, arrojar, desechar.—**to f. in one's face**, echar en cara; lanzar al rostro.—**to f. off**, engañar en la caza.—**to f. open**, abrir de repente.—**to f. out**, arrojar con fuerza; hablar violentamente, echar chispas.—**to f. up**, abandonar, dejar. II. *vn.* lanzar un arma arrojadiza; escarnecer, mofarse, murmurar; alborotarse, cocear, brincar, saltar, lanzarse. III. *s.* tiro; echada, echamiento; indirecta, sarcasmo, pulla; brinco, salto; coz; honda; desenfrenada libertad de acción; bravata, atrevimiento; baile escocés muy vivo.—**to have**, o **take, a f. at**, probar, aventurar (algo); echar una pulla a.—**to have one's f.**, calaverear, correrla.
flint [flint], *s.* pedernal; piedra de chispa; cualquiera cosa sumamente dura.—**f. glass**, cristal. —**f.-hearted**, empedernido.—**f. stone**, pedernal.
flintiness [-inis], *s.* excesiva dureza.
flintlock [-lak], *s.* llave (*f.*) o fusil de chispa.
flinty [-i], *a.* apedernalado o pedernalino; empedernido, inexorable.
flip [flip]. I. *va.* lanzar, soltar, tirar con un movimiento del pulgar y otro dedo; chasquear; dar un golpe rápido; quitar de golpe. *V.* FLICK. II. *vn.* dar un capirotazo; moverse a sacudidas. —**to f. up**, jugar a cara o cruz. III. *s.* pasangonzalo, capirotazo; bebida de vino, cerveza o ron con huevos, azúcar, etc.; (fam.) salto mortal. IV. *a.* (fam.) = FLIPPANT.
flippancy [flípansi], *s.* petulancia, impertinencia, ligereza irrespetuosa o impropia.—**flippant** [-ant], *a.* petulante, impertinente.—**flippantly** [-li], *adv.* petulante o impertinentemente.
flipper [flípœ(r)], *s.* aleta o pata de tortuga, ballena o de foca; (fam.) la mano.
flirt [flœrt]. I. *vn.* coquetear, galantear, flirtear; corretear, travesear; soñar con, o dejarse tentar por (una idea, etc.). II. *va.* tirar, sacudir o menear con ligereza. III. *s.* coqueta, coquetón; golpe o meneo rápido.
flirtation [-éiʃɔn], **flirting** [-iŋ], *s.* coquetería, coqueteo, galanteo, flirt(eo).—**flirtatious** [-éiʃʌs], *a.* coqueta, coquetón.
flit [flit]. I. *vn.* volar, revolotear; deslizarse, pasar rápidamente. II. *s.* movimiento o meneo rápido; aleteo.
flitch [flitʃ], *s.* hoja o témpano de tocino; a veces, lonja o cecina de carne de res o pescado; (carp.) costero.—**f. beam**, viga armada.
flitter [flítœ(r)], *s.* revoloteador; (fam.) harapo, andrajo; lentejuela, adorno de oropel.
flittermouse [-maus], *s.* (zool.) murciélago.
flitting [flítiŋ]. I. *s.* fuga, vuelo rápido. II. *a.* fugaz.
flivver [flívœ(r)], *s.* (fam.) automóvil o avión barato; (Am.) fotingo; (fam.) fiasco, fracaso, pifia.
flix [fliks], *s.* borra, tamo, pelusa.
float [flóut]. I. *va.* flotar, mantener o llevar a flote; (com.) emitir, poner en circulación; (alb.) enlucir con llana o talocha; regar; (dep.) cazar en bote. II. *vn.* flotar, sobrenadar; boyar; fluctuar; cernerse; nadar; hacer la plancha (en la natación). III. *s.* flotador; cualquier cosa que flota; balsa, boya, armadía, maderada; (mar.) jangada; salvavidas; corcho de una caña de pescar; palo (de remo); (alb.) regla o tabla aplanadora; aplanadera, llana de enlucir; (aer.) flotador (de hidroavión, *m.*); bote de cazar patos; carromato; carroza para espectáculos públicos. IV. *a.* de flotador (apl. a varios artificios mecánicos, como válvulas, indicadores de nivel, etc.).
floatable [-abl], *a.* flotable.
floatage [-idʒ], *s.* = FLOTAGE.
floatboard [-bɔrd], *s.* álabe, paleta de rueda.
floater [-œ(r)], *s.* flotador; (fam.) el que cambia a

menudo su domicilio, empleo o partido político; (fam.) el que vota fraudulentamente.
floating [-iŋ]. I. *s.* flote, flotación; plancha (natación); (alb.) revestimiento. II. *a.* flotante, boyante; a flote, suelto, no anclado; fluctuante, movible, variable; (com.) flotante, en circulación.—**f. battery**, (elec.) pila compensadora; (mil.) batería flotante.—**f. crane**, grúa flotante. —**f. debt**, deuda flotante.—**f. dock**, dique flotante.—**f. island**, isla flotante o artificial; (coc.) especie de flan en que flotan las claras de huevos batidas.—**f. kidney**, (anat.) riñón flotante.—**f. policy**, (com.) póliza flotante.—**f. population**, población flotante, de tránsito.—**f. rib**, (anat.) costilla flotante.—**f. taper**, mariposa (candelilla flotante en un vaso de aceite para conservar luz de noche).
floccose [flákous], *a.* (bot.) velludo.
flocculence [flákyulens], *s.* vellosidad.
flocculent [-ant], *a.* velludo, lanudo; parecido al flojel.
flock [flak]. I. *s.* hato, manada, rebaño (de ovejas); grey, *f.* (gen. de ganado menor; fig., de los fieles); bandada (de pájaros); congregación; multitud; borra, tamo, flojel, pelusilla; copo o vedija de lana.—**f. bed**, colchón de borra.—**f. paper**, papel aterciopelado.—**f. wool**, borra de lana. II. *vn.* afluir, congregarse, juntarse, reunirse, atroparse.
floe [flou], *s.* masa de hielo flotante.
flog [flág], *va.* azotar, vapular, tundir, flagelar.
flogging [-iŋ], *s.* azotaina o azotamiento, vapuleo, tunda, zurra, flagelación.
flood [flʌd]. I. *s.* diluvio; avenida, creciente, *f.*; inundación; plétora, abundancia; (min.) aguada; (med.) chorro, menstruo excesivo.— **f. control**, (ing.) control de los ríos con un sistema de presas y diques, etc.—**f. light**, reflector o lámpara proyectante de rayos concentrados, para iluminar objetos especiales.— **f. lighting**, sistema (*m.*) de alumbrado uniforme sin sombras; iluminación intensiva.—**f.-lit**, iluminado mediante reflectores.—**f. tide**, pleamar, *f.* II. *a.* inundar; anegar, apantanar, enaguazar; (com.) abarrotar (los mercados).
floodgate [-geit], *s.* compuerta de esclusa, paradera.
flooding [-iŋ]. I. *s.* inundación; (med.) hemorragia uterina; (com.) abarrotamiento. II. *a.* inundante.
floodmark [-mark], *s.* nivel de la marea alta.
floor [flɔr]. I. *s.* suelo, piso, entarimado, pavimento; piso de una casa (primero, segundo); (agr.) era; (mar.) fondo, plan; en una asamblea, lugar destinado a los diputados, y, por extensión, el uso de la palabra (*to have the floor*, tener la palabra).—**f. lamp**, lámpara de pie.—**f. leader**, (E. U., pol.) jefe de un partido político en el Congreso.—**f. mop**, escoba de bayeta.— **f. show**, atracciones (de cabaret, etc.).—**f. tile**, baldosín o loseta para pisos, mosaico.—**to ask for** (o **have**) **the f.**, pedir (o tener) la palabra. II. *va.* solar, tillar, entarimar; echar al suelo; (fig.) abrumar; vencer, derrotar; dejar confundido o turulato; poner en el suelo.
floorcloth [-klɔθ], *s.* hule para cubrir el suelo.
flooring [-iŋ], *s.* suelo, piso; pavimento, embaldosado, entablado; material para pisos.
floorwalker [-wɔkœ(r)], *s.* superintendente de una división de un bazar o gran tienda.
flop [flɔp]. I. *va.* batir, sacudir. II. *vn.* aletear; caer flojamente; colgar; caerse, venirse abajo; (fam.) pasarse de un partido a otro; fracasar, malograrse. III. *s.* (fam.) fracaso, fiasco.
flophouse [-haus], *s.* (fam.) posada de mala muerte, sobre todo para vagos.
flora [flɔrā], *s.* (bot.) flora.
floral [-l], *a.* floral.—**F. Games**, juegos florales.
Florentine [flɔrentin], *a.* y *s.* florentino, florentín.
florescence [flɔrésens], *s.* (bot.) florescencia, floración.—**florescent** [-ent], *a.* floreciente.

floret [flóret], *s*. (bot.) flósculo, florecilla.
floriculture [flórikalchu(r)], *s*. floricultura.
floriculturist [-kálchūrist], *s*. floricultor.
florid [flórid], *a*. florido; encarnado, rojo; vivo, figurado (estilo); (b. a.) florido.
floridity [floríditi], **floridness** [flóridnis], *s*. floridez.
floridly [-li], *adv*. floridamente.
floriferous [floríferas], *a*. florífero, florígero.
florin [flórin], *s*. florín (moneda).
florist [flórist], *s*. florista, florero, florera.—**f.'s shop** = FLOWER SHOP.
floscule [fláskjul], *s*. (bot.) flósculo.
floss [flós], *s*. seda floja; adúcar; atanquía, cadarzo; penacho del maíz; (fund.) escorias que sobrenadan.—**f. silk**, seda floja, borra de seda, filadiz, *m*.
flossy [-i], *a*. len; ligero, suave; (fam.) elegante.
flotage [flóutidž], *s*. objetos que flotan; pecio; flotación, flotadura, flotamiento.
flotation [flotéişon], *s*. flotación, flotadura, flotamiento; teoría de los cuerpos flotantes.
flotilla [flotíla], *s*. flotilla.
flotsam [flátsam], *s*. pecios; objetos flotantes.
flounce [flauns]. I. *va*. (cost.) guarnecer con volantes o vuelos. II. *vn*. pernear; brincar de impaciencia. III. *s*. (cost.) volante, fleco, farfalá, cairel.
flounder [fláundœ(r)]. I. *s*. (ict.) lenguado, rodaballo; tumbo, tropiezo. II. *vn*. forcejar torpe o atropelladamente; tropezar y caer.
flour [flaur]. I. *s*. harina; polvo; salitre fino.—**f. bin, f. dealer**, harinero.—**f. bolt o sieve**, tamiz, *m*., cedazo.—**f. mill**, molino harinero. II. *va*. pulverizar; rociar con harina. III. *vn*. dividirse en granos, pulverizarse.
flourish [flœriş]. I. *va*. florear, blandir, menear; embellecer. II. *vn*. florecer; medrar, prosperar; rasguear; jactarse; blandear; (mús.) florear. III. *s*. rasgo, plumada; rúbrica; floreo, adorno; (esgr.) molinete; (mús.) floreo, preludio.
flourishing [-iŋ], *a*. floreciente; próspero.
flourishingly [-li], *adv*. floridamente; prósperamente.
floury [fláuri], *a*. harinoso, farináceo.
flout [flaut]. I. *va*. y *vn*. tratar con desprecio; insultar; burlar(se) o mofar(se) (de), befar. II. *s*. mofa, befa, burla, escarnio.
flow [flóu]. I. *vn*. fluir, manar; correr; dimanar; seguirse; crecer (la mar), dilatarse; desdecirse, pasar.—**to f. from**, o **out**, brotar, salir, nacer, manar de.—**to f. into**, afluir, desembocar, desaguar a. II. *va*. inundar; derramar; hacer fluir. III. *s*. corriente, *f*., torrente; flujo; salida; flujo de la marea; afluencia; desagüe; abundancia, copia; (med.) menstruo; (hidr.) gasto, cantidad que sale o pasa por unidad de tiempo.
flowage [-idž], *s*. flujo, corriente, *f*.; derramamiento; líquido que sale o se derrama; (mec.) deformación por deslizamiento interno de las moléculas.
flower [fláuœ(r)]. I. *s*. (bot.) flor, *f*.; planta en flor; flor y nata; figura retórica; adorno, belleza.—*pl*. (quím.) flor; regla, menstruación.—**f. bed**, cuadro, macizo, era de jardín.—**f. bud**, capullo, botón de flor.—**f. de luce**, flor de lis, iris.—**f. garden**, jardín, vergel.—**f. girl**, florera, ramilletera.—**f. leaf**, pétalo.—**f. piece**, ramillete; (pint.) florero.—**f. shop**, tienda de flores; (Am.) florería.—**f. stalk**, pedúnculo, pezón.—**f. stand**, jardinera (mueble); puesto de (vender) flores.—**f. vase**, florero, jarrón, ramilletero.—**flowers of sulphur**, flor de azufre.—**flowers of zinc**, cinc sublimado. II. *va*. florear, espolinar. III. *vn*. florecer, florar, dar flor.
flowered [-d], *a*. floreado, espolinado.—**f. silk**, seda agrisetada.
floweret [-et], *s*. florecilla, florecita.
floweriness [-inis], *s*. abundancia de flores; floreo de palabras; estilo florido.

flowering [-iŋ]. I. *a*. (bot.) fanerógamo; floreciente, florido, en flor. II. *s*. floración, florescencia.
flowerless [-lis], *a*. (bot.) criptógamo; sin flores.
flowerpot [-pat], *s*. tiesto, maceta de flores.
flowery [-i], *a*. florido; ornado.
flowing [flóuiŋ]. I. *a*. corriente, flu(y)ente, manantial, manantío, ondeante, fluctuoso; suelto; colgante; flúido. II. *s*. derrame, salida; corriente *f*., flujo; fluidez.—**flowingly** [-li], *adv*. copiosamente.—**flowingness** [-nis], *s*. calidad de flúido; fluidez; dicción flúida.
flown [floun]. I. *pp*. de TO FLY. II. *a*. vidriado.
flu [flu], *s*. (fam., med.) influenza, gripe, *f*., trancazo.
flubdub(bery [flábdʌb(eri]. I. *s*. (fam.) tontería, dislate. II. *a*. tonto, inane.
fluctuant [flákchuant], *a*. fluctuante, fluctuoso.
fluctuate [-eit], *vn*. fluctuar; oscilar, ondear.
fluctuation [-éişon], *s*. fluctuación, oscilación.
flue [flu], *s*. humero, cañón de chimenea; tubo de caldera; pelusa, borra, tamo; (mec.) conducto, canal; (mús.) cañón de órgano.—**f. boiler**, caldera de tubos de humos o de conductos interiores.
fluency [flúensi], *s*. fluidez; afluencia, facundia, labia.
fluent [-ent], *a*. facundo, afluente; suelto, fácil, corriente; copioso; flúido, fluente.—**fluently** [-li], *adv*. con facundia o labia; corrientemente; de corrida.
fluff [flʌf]. I. *s*. pelusa, lanilla, pelillo, vello, borra, mota, tamo, plumón. II. *va*. mullir borra, plumón, etc.; ahuecar.—**fluffiness** [-inis], *s*. calidad de mullido o sedoso.—**fluffy** [-i], *a*. cubierto de plumón o vello; blando, mullido, esponjoso, ahuecado, suelto.—**f. hair**, cabello o pelo hueco.
fluid [flúid]. I. *s*. flúido; líquido; gas. II. *a*. flúido; líquido; gaseoso.—**f. dram**, o **drachm**, dracma flúida, la octava parte de una onza flúida.—**f. ounce**, medida de capacidad para líquidos (29.6 mililitros o centímetros cúbicos).
fluidify [flúidifai], *va*. fluidificar, licuar.
fluidity [flúiditi], **fluidness** [flúidnis], *s*. fluidez; liquidez; calidad de flúido, etc.
fluke [fluk], *s*. uña u oreja del ancla; uña del arpón; aleta de la cola de la ballena; (fam.) chiripa (en el billar), casualidad favorable; (ent.) tremátodo, lombriz del ganado lanar; (ict.) platija, lenguado.
flume [flum], *s*. saetín, caz, *m*., canal, acequia, presa, tragante; cañada con torrente, zubia; canal de descargar (carbón, etc.).
flummery [flámœri], *s*. (coc.) gachas de avena; especie de manjar blanco; (fam.) música celestial, pelitrique.
flung [flʌŋ], *pret*. y *pp*. de TO FLING.
flunk [flʌŋk]. I. *s*. (fam.) fracaso. II. *va*. (fam.) colgar, reprobar, suspender, dar calabazas (a un estudiante); despedir por incompetencia. III. *vn*. (fam.) fracasar, salir mal, recibir calabazas (en un examen, etc.); volverse atrás, desistir; ser despedido (de un colegio) por incompetencia.
flunk(e)y [flʌŋki], *s*. lacayo; adulón, lavacaras.
flunkyism [-izm], *s*. servilismo.
fluor [flúo(r)], *s*. (quím.) flúor.—**f. spar**, (min.) espato flúor, fluorina, fluorita.
fluorescence [fluorésens], *s*. (fís.) fluorescencia.
fluorescent [-ent], *a*. fluorescente.
fluoric [fluárik], *a*. (quím.) fluórico.
fluorid(e [flúorajd], *s*. (quím.) fluoruro.
fluorin(e [-in], *s*. (quím.) flúor.
fluorite [-ait], *s*. (min.) fluorita.
fluormeter [-mitœ(r)], *s*. (quím.) fluorómetro.
fluoroscope [-oskoup], *s*. fluoroscopio.
fluoroscopy [-áskopi], *s*. (med.) fluoroscopía.
flurry [flœri]. I. *s*. agitación, conmoción; ráfaga, racha. II. *va*. confundir, aturdir.
flush [flʌş]. I. *va*. abochornar, sonrojar; engreír,

alentar; igualar, nivelar o emparejar; inundar; limpiar con un chorro de agua; levantar, volar (aves de caza). II. *vn.* salirse, derramarse, llenarse de agua; (caza) echar a volar; sonrojarse, ponerse colorado. III. *a.* igual, parejo, ras, nivelado; copioso, abundante; rico, adinerado; robusto, lleno de vida.—**f. bolt,** perno de cabeza embutida.—**f. box,** (elec.) caja de inspección e introducción de conductores subterráneos, de tapa pareja con el pavimento.—**f. joint,** junta machihembrada ras en ras.—**f. rivet,** remache de cabeza embutida.—**f. switch,** (elec.) interruptor embutido de tapa al ras con la pared.—**f. tank,** depósito de agua para limpia (de inodoros, etc.).—**f. with,** a flor de, ras en ras o parejo con. IV. *s.* rubor, sonrojo, color (en las mejillas); animación, agitación, emoción; vuelo súbito de un pájaro o una bandada; floración; flujo rápido o copioso; copia, abundancia; flux (de naipes).

fluster [flΛstœ(r)]. I. *va.* y *vn.* confundir(se), aturdir(se). *V.* FUDDLE. II. *s.* confusión, aturdimiento.

flustered [-d], *a.* confuso, aturdido, agitado.

flute [flút]. I. *s.* (mús.) flauta, caramillo, tibia; zampoña; (arq.) estría; rizado, pliegue.—**f. stop,** flautado. II. *va.* estriar, acanalar, encañutar; (cost.) alechugar, rizar, plegar, (Méx.) encarrujar. III. *vn.* tocar la flauta.

fluted [-id], *a.* acanalado, ondulado.

flutelike [-laik], *a.* flaut(e)ado.

fluting [-iŋ], *s.* (arq.) estría, estriadura, acanaladura; (cost.) rizado, alechugado, encarrujado.—**f. iron,** hierro de rizar.—**f. plane,** cepillo bocel.

flutist [-ist], *s.* flautista.

flutter [flΛtœ(r)]. I. *va.* agitar, menear, sacudir; aturdir. II. *vn.* agitarse, menearse, alterarse; aletear, revolotear; flamear, undular (velas, banderas, etc.). III. *s.* alboroto, confusión; agitación; vibración; flameo, undulación.

fluvial [flúvial], **fluviatile** [-atil], **fluviatic** [-ætik], *a.* fluvial, fluviátil.

fluviograph [-ograf], *s.* fluviógrafo, fluviómetro.

flux [flΛks]. I. *s.* flujo; derretimiento, fusión; (med.) flujo, diarrea; (quím. y met.) fundente. II. *va.* fundir, derretir; fluidificar; mezclar con un fundente; (med.) purgar. III. *vn.* fluir; fluidificarse; fundirse.

fluxion [flΛksǫn], *s.* flujo; fusión; (med.) fluxión, congestión; (mat.) fluxión, derivada; diferencial.—**fluxional** [-al], *a.* variable, inconstante.

fly [flái]. I. *va.* (*pret.* FLEW; *pp.* FLOWN) hacer volar; elevar (una cometa, etc.); enarbolar; evitar, evadir, huir de; (impr.) sacar pliegos; (aer.) dirigir (un avión); cruzar o atravesar en avión. II. *vn.* volar; lanzarse, precipitarse; correr, pasar rápidamente; saltar, reventar, estallar; huir, escaparse; desaparecer, desvanecerse.—**to f. about,** (mar.) cambiar el viento con frecuencia.—**to f. around,** ir de un lado a otro.—**to f. at,** arrojarse o lanzarse sobre.—**to f. away,** irse volando; escaparse.—**to f. down,** bajar volando.—**to f.-fish,** pescar con moscas artificiales.—**to f. from,** huir de.—**to f. in the face of,** ir contra, hacer frente a.—**to f. into a passion o rage,** montar en cólera; irse del seguro.—**to f. off,** desprenderse súbitamente; separarse, sublevarse.—**to f. off at a tangent,** tomar repentinamente una resolución extraña, o salir con alguna extravagancia.—**to f. off the handle,** (fam.) perder la chaveta, irse del seguro.—**to f. on,** lanzarse sobre, arremeter a.—**to f. open,** abrirse repentinamente.—**to f. out,** dispararse, salir a espetaperros. *V.* TO FLY OFF THE HANDLE.—**to f. to arms,** correr a las armas.—**to f. to pieces,** romperse en añicos.

fly, *s.* (ent.) mosca; (dep.) mosca artificial (cebo para pescar); cabriolé, calesín, volanta; uno de varios objetos de movimiento rápido, v. gr.: 1) (impr.) sacapliegos; 2) brazo de romana; 3) rueda volante; 4) escape de reloj; 5) brazo de

veleta; 6) vuelo de una bandera; 7) lanzadera, etc.; (sast.) bragueta; vuelo de un proyectil, pelota, etc.; tapa del teclado de un piano; (teat.) bambalina.—**f.-bitten,** manchado por las moscas.—**f. blister,** cantárida (parche).—**f.-bynight,** persona o empresa poco segura; trampista, tramoyista.—**f.-fishing,** pesca con moscas artificiales.—**f. net,** mosquitero.—**f. paper,** papel para coger o matar moscas.—**f. press,** prensa de tornillo.—**f.-press worker,** (impr.) sacapliegos.—**f. sheet,** (impr.) hoja o papel volante.—**f. swatter,** matamoscas.—**on the f.,** al vuelo.

flyaway [-aweí], *a.* tremolante, ondeante, flameante; instable, inquieto; inconstante.

flyblow [-blou]. I. *s.* cresa, huevo de mosca. II. *va.* corromper la carne llenándola de cresas.

flyblown [-n], *a.* inficionado, contaminado.

flyboat [-bout], *s.* (mar.) filibote, especie de buque rápido; buque holandés de fondo plano.

flycatcher [-kæchœ(r)], *s.* (orn.) doral, muscaria, papamoscas.

flyer, *s.* = FLIER.

flyflap [-flæp], **flytrap** [-træp], *s.* mosqueador, espantamoscas, mosquero.

flying [-iŋ]. I. *a.* volante; volador; de volar; volátil; rápido, veloz; flotante, undulante; desplegado.—**f. boat,** hidroavión, *m.,* hidro(aero)-plano.—**f. bomb,** (mil.) bomba voladora. *V.* ROBOT BOMB.—**f. bridge,** puente volante.—**f. buttress,** (arq.) botarel, arbotante, contrafuerte volante.—**f. colors,** banderas desplegadas (*to come off with f. colors,* salir airoso de, tener éxito completo en).—**f. column,** (mil.) columna volante.—**f. field,** aeropuerto, campo de aviación.—**f. fish,** (ict.) volador, pez volante.—**F. Fortress,** (mil.) fortaleza aérea o volante.—**f. fox,** (zool.) murciélago frugívoro.—**f. jib,** (mar.) petifoque, cuarto foque.—**f. machine,** aparato volador o volante (de cualquier tipo).—**f. squadron,** escuadra ligera.—**f. squirrel,** (zool.) ardilla voladora.—**f. wing,** (aer.) ala volante.—**to shoot f.,** tirar al vuelo. II. *s.* vuelo.

flyleaf [-lif], *s.* (impr.) guarda de un libro.

flyspeck [-spek], *s.* mancha de mosca.

flyweight [-weit], *s.* (dep.) peso mosca.

flywheel [-hwil], *s.* (mec.) volante.

foal [foul]. I. *s.* potro; potrillo; buche. II. *va.* y *vn.* parir (una yegua o burra).

foam [fóum]. I. *s.* espuma.—**f. rubber,** caucho espumoso. II. *va.* hacer espuma. III. *vn.* espumar, echar espuma(rajos).

foamy [-i], *a.* espumajoso, espumoso.

fob [fab]. I. *s.* faltriquera del reloj.—**f. chain,** leopoldina, leontina. II. *va.* engañar, defraudar, pegársela a uno; (con **off**) entretener con engañifas.

focal [fóukal], *a.* focal; céntrico.—**f. distance, o length,** (ópt.) distancia focal.—**f. infection,** (med., dent.) infección focal.

focalize [-aiz], *va.* enfocar; concentrar; (med.) localizar, limitar a una área circunscrita.—**focalization** [-izéišǫn], *s.* enfoque; (med.) localización.

focus [fóukΛs]. I. *s.* foco; distancia focal.—**in f.,** enfocado.—**out of f.,** desenfocado. II. *va.* y *vn.* enfocar(se); concentrar(se).—**focusing** [-iŋ], *s.* enfoque.—**f. glass o lens,** (fot.) enfocador.

fodder [fádœ(r)]. I. *s.* forraje, pastura, pienso, herrén.—**f. plants,** plantas forrajeras. II. *va.* dar forraje a.

foe [fóu], **foeman** [-man], *s.* enemigo, adversario, antagonista.—**foelike** [-laik], *a.* hostil.

fœtus [fítas], *s.* feto.

fog [fág]. I. *s.* niebla, neblina, bruma; confusión, perplejidad; (fot.) velo.—**f. bank,** brumazón, masa densa de niebla.—**f. bell, signal, whistle,** campana, señal, *f.,* sirena de nieblas o de alarma. II. *va.* obscurecer; (fot.) velar. III. *vn.* ponerse brumoso; (fot.) velarse.

fog, *s.* segunda cosecha de hierba.
fogbound [-bɑund], *a.* rodeado o cubierto de niebla; parado (un buque o el tráfico) por la niebla.
foggily [-ili], *adv.* brumosamente.
fogginess [-inis], *s.* calidad de nebuloso, neblinoso o brumoso; nebulosidad.
foggy [-i], *a.* brumoso, brumal, neblinoso o nebuloso; obscuro; (bot.) mohoso; (foto.) velado.—**it is f.,** hace (o hay) niebla.
foghorn [-hɔrn], *s.* bocina, sirena de niebla.
fogy, fogey [fóugi], *s.* vejestorio; persona de ideas y costumbres atrasadas o anticuadas.
fogyism [-izm], *s.* cosas de viejos.
foible [tɔibl], *s.* lado flaco, flaqueza; parte media de la hoja de una espada.
foil [fɔil]. **I.** *va.* frustrar, contrarrestar, chasquear. **II.** *s.* hoja delgada de metal; oropel; chapa; pan u hoja de oro o plata; azogado de un espejo; (arq.) hoja, lóbulo; (esgr.) florete (caza) huella, pista, rastro; contraste.—**f.-wrapped,** envuelto en papel de estaño.
foiling [-iŋ], *s.* (caza) freza, rastro.
foist [fɔist], *va.* meter clandestinamente; (con *on*) encajar, imponer (a); meterle (a), engañar con.
fold [fɔuld]. **I.** *s.* doblez, *m.,* dobladura, (re)pliegue, arruga, recogido; abrazo; envoltorio; redil, corral, aprisco; hato, rebaño; (fig.) congregación de fieles. Usado como sufijo denota veces (*twofold,* dos veces, doble). **II.** *va.* doblar, plegar; abrazar, enlazar; cerrar, incluir, envolver, encerrar; arredilar, meter en redil.—**to f. the arms,** cruzar los brazos. **III.** *vn.* doblarse, plegarse, cerrarse.
folder [-œ(r)], *s.* plegador, doblador; (enc.) plegadera; hoja, circular, etc., plegadizas.
folderol [fóldɛral], *s.* = FOLDEROL.
folding [fóuldiŋ]. **I.** *a.* plegadizo, (re)plegable; doblador, plegador.—**f. bed,** cama plegadiza, catre de tijera, catricofre.—**f. camera,** cámara plegadiza.—**f. chair,** silla plegadiza; catrecillo.—**f. door,** puerta de dos hojas o plegadiza; puerta corrediza.—**f. knife,** navaja; cuchillo de caza.—**f. machine,** máquina de plegar, plegadora mecánica.—**f. rule,** metro plegable.—**f. screen,** biombo.—**f. seat,** asiento levadizo o plegable; (carr.) bigotera. **II.** *s.* plegado, plegadura, doblamiento; (re)pliegue.
foliaceous [fouljéiʃiʌs], *a.* (bot.) foliáceo; laminado.
foliage [fóuljidƷ], *s.* follaje, frondosidad, frondas; (b. a.) verdura.
foliate [-eit]. **I.** *va.* foliar; (arq.) adornar con hojas, lóbulos, etc.; (metal.) batir hoja; azogar un espejo. **II.** *vn.* echar flores; dividirse en capas laminadas; exfoliarse. **III.** *a.* frondoso; batido, laminado.
foliated [-id], *a.* (metal.) batido, laminado; (arq.) lobulado; azogado; chapeado; (bot.) foliado.
foliation [-éiʃən], *s.* foliación (de un libro, manuscrito, etc.); (metal.) batimiento; exfoliación; azogamiento; (bot.) foliación.
foliature [-əchur], *s.* foliatura.
folio [fóuliou]. **I.** *s.* infolio; folio, página; (for.) unidad para medir la extensión de un documento (Ingl. 90 palabras; E. U. 100 palabras); cartera para grabados, etc.—**in f.,** en folio. **II.** *a.* de a folio. **III.** *va.* foliar.
foliose [fóuljous], *a.* frondoso.
folk [fóuk]. **I.** *s.* gente, *f.;* nación, raza, pueblo.— *pl.* (fam.) parientes, parentela. **II.** *a.* de o pert. al pueblo; que tiene fuentes populares.—**f. dance,** baile popular.—**f. music,** música tradicional.—**folks say,** se dice, dicen, la gente dice.—**f. song,** cantar de gesta; canto popular, copla, jácara, romance.—**f. speech,** lenguaje vulgar.—**f. tale,** cuento tradicional, conseja.
folklore [-lor], *s.* folklore, tradiciones y leyendas populares; estudio de ellas.
folkloric [-lɔrik], *a.* folklórico. (*V.* FOLKLORE.)
folklorist [-lɔrist], *s.* folklorista. (*V.* FOLKLORE.)

folkway [-wei], *s.* cultura o costumbre que tienen en común los miembros de un mismo grupo social.
follicle [fálikl], *s.* (anat.) folículo; (bot.) folículo, hollejo; (ent.) capullo.
follicular [falíkyūlǟ(r)], *a.* folicular.
follow [fálou]. **I.** *va.* seguir, ir detrás de; venir después de; perseguir; ejecutar, poner por obra; observar, poner atención; resultar de, desprenderse, seguirse (*it follows,* síguese).—**to f. one's nose,** ir o seguir derecho.—**to f. out,** poner por obra, llevar hasta el fin.—**to f. suit,** jugar el mismo palo (en los naipes); seguir el ejemplo o la corriente; hacer lo mismo.—**to f. up,** perseguir con ahinco; llevar hasta el fin; continuar; reforzar. **II.** *vn.* seguir, ir detrás; seguirse.—**f. in one's tracks,** seguir a uno, seguir en las pisadas de uno.—**to f. on,** continuar, perseverar; seguir en la misma dirección (que otro).—**as follows,** como sigue(n).
follower [-œ(r)], *s.* seguidor; acompañante; secuaz, *m.,* sectario, partidario, parcial, adherente, adicto; ayudante; criado; (mec.) pieza impulsada; pola impulsada; bloque de protección de un pilote que se hinca.—*pl.* comitiva, séquito.
following [-iŋ]. **I.** *a.* siguiente; próximo; subsiguiente; consiguiente. **II.** *s.* adhesión; séquito, comitiva, cortejo; oficio, carrera, profesión.
follow-up [-ʌp]. **I.** *a.* de refresco, de empuje, uno más (dícese especialmente de una nueva carta o diligencia para promover un negocio). **II.** *s.* continuación de un esfuerzo inicial.
folly [fáli], *s.* tontería, locura, desatino, insensatez.
foment [fomént], *va.* fomentar, provocar, instigar; (med.) fomentar, dar baños calientes.
fomentation [-éiʃən], *s.* (med.) fomentación, fomento; provocación, instigación.
fond [fánd], *a.* aficionado, enamorado; tierno, cariñoso; querido, acariciado.—**to be f. of,** ser amigo de o aficionado a, ser afecto a, estar encariñado con.
fondant [-ant], *s.* pasta de azúcar que sirve de base a varios confites.
fondle [-l], *va.* mimar, acariciar, hacer fiestas a.
fondler [-œ(r)], *s.* acariciador.
fondling [-liŋ], *s.* acción de acariciar, etc.; favorito, querido, ser mimado.
fondly [-li], *adv.* aficionadamente, tiernamente, afectuosamente, cariñosamente.
fondness [-nis], *s.* afecto, afectuosidad, cariño, querencia, ternura; afición, apego, inclinación.
font [fant], *s.* pila de bautismo o de agua bendita; fuente, *f.;* (impr.) fundición, torta.
fontanel(le [fantənél], *s.* (anat.) fontanela.
food [fūd], *s.* alimento, comida, manjar, vianda, nutrimento; pasto de los animales; pábulo, materia.—**f. card,** cartilla de racionamiento.—**f. chopper,** máquina de picar carne, etc.—**f. for thought,** materia en que pensar, cosa que da que pensar.—**f. supply** o **supplies,** alimentación, comestibles, víveres.—**f. value,** valor nutritivo.
foodstuff [-stʌf], *s.* producto o substancia alimenticia.—*pl.* **foodstuffs,** víveres, comestibles.
fool [fūl]. **I.** *s.* tonto, necio, idiota, *mf.;* inocente, primo; bufón, truhán, payaso, (teat.) gracioso, bobo.—**f.'s cap,** gorro de bufón.—**f.'s errand,** empresa descabellada.—**f.'s gold,** pirita (de hierro o de cobre).—**f.'s paradise,** felicidad ilusoria.—**f. trap,** engañabobos. **II.** *va.* chasquear; embromar; engañar, embaucar.—**to f. away,** malbaratar, gastar a tontas y a locas. **III.** *vn.* tontear, divertirse, chancear.
foolery [-œri], *s.* tontería, bobería.
foolhardiness [-hardinis], *s.* temeridad.
foolhardy [-hardi], *a.* temerario.
fooling [-iŋ], *s.* broma, chacota; engaño.—**no f., without f.,** (fam.) sin broma, hablando en serio.
foolish [-iʃ], *a.* tonto; disparatado; bobo.—

foolishly [-liǰ], *adv.* tontamente.—**foolishness** [-niǰs], *s.* simpleza, tontería, disparate, bobería.

foolproof [-pruf], *a.* que los curiosos o chambones no pueden dañar o desarreglar; seguro.

foolscap [fúlzkæp], *s.* papel grande de escribir (35 × 43 centímetros), papel de oficio.

foot [fút], *s.* pie, *m.* (de animal, mesa, etc.); pata; peal (de media); base, *f.;* pie, medida lineal; (mil.) infantería; (pros.) pie.—**f.-and-mouth disease**, (vet.) fiebre aftosa, glosopeda, erupción vesicular que afecta sobre todo la boca y las pesuñas del ganado.—**f. bath**, pediluvio, baño de pies.—**f. brake**, freno accionado con el pie.—**f. by f.**, paso a paso; palmo a palmo, tenazmente.—**f.-candle**, bujía-pie, intensidad de la luz de una bujía normal a distancia de un pie.—**f. guard**, guardacascos, especie de bota para los caballos; cualquier cosa que protege los pies.—**F. Guards**, (Ing.) infantería de la guardia real.—**f.-loose**, sin trabas u obligaciones, libre, andariego.—**f. post**, cartero destre; el correo que lleva.—**f.-pound**, (mec.) pie-libra o libra-pie, *m.;* unidad de energía o trabajo—el ejecutado por una fuerza de 1 libra en una distancia de 1 pie (0.14 kgm.).—**f.-pound-second**, pie-libra-segundo (apl. al sistema de unidades en que las fundamentales son el pie, la libra y el segundo).—**f. race**, corrida o carrera pedestre.—**f. racing**, pedestrismo.—**f. rot**, (vet.) necrosis de las patas del carnero.—**f. rule**, pie, codo, regla de 1 pie dividida en pulgadas y fracciones (corresponde, en cuanto al uso, al doble decímetro).—**f. second**, pie por segundo.—**f. soldier**, infante, peón, soldado de infantería.—**f. stove**, estufilla para los pies, rejuela.—**f.-ton**, (mec.) pie-tonelada.—**f. tub**, baño de pies.—**f. warmer**, calientapiés.—**by f.**, a pie.—**on f.**, de pie; a pie; levantado, activo; progresando.—**to put one's best f. forward**, (fam.) esmerarse, poner sus cinco sentidos; poner todas sus fuerzas; andar con actividad, con la mayor diligencia posible.—**to put one's f. down**, (fam.) tomar una resolución decidida; poner su óbice.—**to put one's f. in it**, meter la pata, hacer una plancha.—**to set on f.**, iniciar, emprender, poner alguna cosa en movimiento, darle el primer impulso.—**to trample, o tread, under f.**, pisotear.—**under f.**, debajo de los pies; el suelo; con el pie sobre el pescuezo.—**with one f. in the grave**, moribundo, con un pie en el hoyo.

foot. I. *va.* recorrer, andar; hollar, pisotear; sumar y poner la suma al pie; poner pies a alguna cosa; (fam.) pagar (una cuenta); costear, sufragar. II. *vn.* (con **it**) andar, caminar, patear; (fam.) (con **up**) sumar guarismos.

footage [-idǰ], *s.* número de pies, longitud en pies; (min.) paga por pie (u otra unidad lineal) de trabajo; (cine) longitud en pies.

football [-bɔl], *s.* (dep.) fútbol o football, balompié, *m.*, balón.—**f. field**, campo de fútbol.—**f. player**, futbolista.

footboard [-bɔrd], *s.* pie (barandilla del pie) de cama; marchapié, *m.;* estribo; trasera (de coche); tabla del pescante para los pies del cochero; pedal.

footboy [-bɔi], *s.* lacayo, paje, volante, zagal.

footbreadth [-brɛdθ], *s.* ancho de un pie.

footbridge [-bridǰ], *s.* puente (*mf.*) para peatones.

footcloth [-klɔθ], *s.* alfombrilla; gualdrapa.

footed [-id], *a.* que tiene pies o patas; sumado.

footfall [-fɔl], *s.* paso, pisada (con respecto al ruido).

footgear [-giɾ], *s.* calzado.

foothill [-hil], *s.* colina al pie de una montaña.

foothold [-hɔuld], *s.* espacio en que cabe el pie; pie firme; posición establecida; chanclo de goma sin tacón.

footing [-iŋ], *s.* pie, *m.*, base, *f.*, fundamento; (arq.) zarpa; piso, paso; baile, danza; estado, condición; estribo; zócalo saliente; (arit.) suma

de una columna.—**on a war f.**, en pie de guerra.—**to be on equal f.**, estar en iguales condiciones o en pie de igualdad.—**to get a f.**, establecerse.

footless [-lis], *a.* sin pies; sin fundamento; (fam.) estúpido, chambón.

footlights [-laits], *s. pl.* (teat.) candilejas, luces del proscenio; (fig.) las tablas, el teatro.

footling [-liŋ], *a.* y *adv.* (obst.) con los pies hacia afuera; (fam.) tonto; fútil, trivial.

footman [-mạn], *s.* lacayo, criado de librea.

footmark [-mark], *s.* huella.

footnote [-nout], *s.* nota al pie de una página.

footpace [-peis], *s.* descanso de escaleras; paso lento.

footpad [-pæd], *s.* salteador de caminos.

footpath [-pæθ], *s.* senda para gente de a pie.

footprint [-print], *s.* huella, pisada, rastro.

footrail [-reil], *s.* rodapié, *m.*

footrest [-rɛst], *s.* rodapié, *m.;* escabel.

footrope [-roup], *s.* (mar.) marchapié, *m.;* relinga del pujamen.

foots [-s], *s. pl.* sedimentos, heces, *f. pl.*, poso.

footscraper [-skreipœr(r)], *s.* limpiabarros.

footsore [-sɔr], *a.* que tiene los pies doloridos o lastimados, despeado.

footstalk [-stɔk], *s.* (bot.) pedúnculo, pezón.

footstall [-stɔl], *s.* estribo para mujer; (arq.) plinto.

footstep [-stɛp], *s.* huella, pisada, paso.

footstool [-stul], *s.* escabel, escañuelo, banqueta.

footwalk [-wɔk], **footway** [-wei], *s.* senda, sendero, camino de peatones; acera.

footwear [-wɛr], *s.* calzado.

footwork [-wœrk], *s.* (dep.) juego o manejo de los pies en el boxeo, tenis, baile, etc.

footworn [-wɔrn], *a.* cansado de caminar, despeado; usado; asendereado, trillado.

foozle [fúzl]. I. *va.* y *vn.* chafallar, chapucear o hacer chapucerías, pifiar. II. *s.* chafallo, pifia; (fam.) chafallón.

fop [fɔp], *s.* petimetre, pisaverde, lechuguino.

foppery [-œriǰ], *s.* afectación en el vestir; perifollos.

foppish [-iʃ], *a.* vanidoso o fatuo; alechuguinado.—**foppishly** [-liǰ], *adv.* afectadamente; con perifollos.—**foppishness** [-niǰs], *s.* = FOPPERY.

for [fɔr]. I. *prep.* por; para; durante, por espacio de; de (*to cry for joy*, llorar de gozo); con, a pesar de, no obstante (*for all that*, con todo eso; *for all his arguments*, *I won't go*, a pesar de todos sus argumentos, no iré). Como regla general, empléase *por* cuando significa a causa de, en consideración a, con respecto o relación a, en cuanto a, en lugar o en nombre o representación de, en lugar o substitución de, a cambio de; empléase *para* cuando denota destinación, aplicación, dedicación, fin, intento, provecho, beneficio; vg.: *I speak for him*, hablo por él; *this is for him*, esto es para él. A veces conviene traducirlo por el dativo: *this is easy for me*, esto me es fácil; *do this for me*, hágame esto. Seguido de un substantivo o pronombre y un infinitivo, se traduce a veces por el dativo (*it is for you to decide*, a usted le toca decidir) o bien cambiando el giro y poniendo el verbo en subjuntivo: *the plan is for John to go*, el plan es que Juan vaya. II. *conj.* porque, puesto que, pues; (mat., lóg.) en efecto.

forage [fárjdǰ]. I. *va.* y *vn.* forrajear, proveer(se) de forraje; apacentar(se); (mil.) recorrer una comarca en busca de forraje y víveres; pillar, saquear. II. *s.* forraje.—**f. cap**, (mil.) kepi o quepí, gorra de visera.—**f. plant**, planta forrajera.

forager [-œ(r)], *s.* forrajeador.

foraging [-iŋ], *s.* forraje.

foramen [fɔréiṃɛn], *s.* foramen, apertura, agujero (ú. esp. en anat. y bot.).

foraminifer [fɔrạ̃míṇifœ(r)], *s.*, **foraminífera!**

[foraeminíferal], **foraminiferous** [-ʌs], *a.* (zool.) foraminífero.

forasmuch as [forazmʌch æz], *conj.* puesto que, por cuanto, ya que.

foray [fórei]. I. *s.* correría, irrupción; saqueo, pillaje. II. *va.* saquear, pillar, despojar.

forbad(e [forbǽd], *pret.* de TO FORBID.

forbear [fórbɛr], *s.* antepasado, antecesor.

forbear [forbér], *va.* y *vn.* (*pret.* FORBORE; *pp.* FORBORNE) abstenerse, contenerse, dejar de, reprimirse; mostrar paciencia o indulgencia.

forbearance [-ans], *s.* paciencia, clemencia, indulgencia o lenidad; abstención.—**forbearing** [-iŋ], *a.* paciente, indulgente.

forbid [forbíd], *va.* (*pret.* FORBAD(E; *pp.* FORBIDDEN) prohibir; impedir, estorbar; excluir de.

forbidden [-ən], *a.* prohibido, vedado, ilícito.—**f. fruit**, placer ilícito.

forbidding [-iŋ], *a.* prohibitivo; repulsivo, aborrecible, repugnante.

forbore [forbór], *pret.* de TO FORBEAR.

forborne [-n], *pp.* de TO FORBEAR.

force [fórs]. I. *s.* fuerza; vigor, reciura, robustez, brío; energía, animación; virtud, poder, potencia, eficacia; móvil, motivo; coacción, violencia; valor, validez, vigencia (de una ley); peso, importancia; (mil.) fuerzas, tropa.—**f. majeure**, fuerza mayor; (for.) caso fortuito.—**f. pump**, bomba impelente.—**by f. of**, a fuerza de.—**in f.**, vigente, en vigor.—**to be in f.**, regir. II. *va.* forzar; obligar, precisar, compeler, constreñir; violentar; violar; (mec.) impulsar; (coc.) rellenar, embutir, mechar; (agr.) forzar, hacer madurar temprano.—**to f. along**, hacer avanzar o adelantar.—**to f. away**, obligar a alejarse.—**to f. back**, rechazar, hacer retroceder.—**to f. down**, obligar a bajar.—**to f. from**, obligar a salir, echar de.—**to f. in**, o **through**, clavar, meter o entrar por fuerza.—**to f. on**, o **upon**, imponer a.—**to f. one's hand**, obligar a uno a hacer algo o a declarar su intención, contra su voluntad.—**to f. out**, arrancar, sacar u obtener por fuerza.—**to f. the issue**, hacer que el asunto se discuta o decida pronto; hacer que se vaya al grano sin demora.—**to f. up**, hacer subir por fuerza.

forced [-t], *a.* forzado, fingido; forzado, forzoso, obligatorio.—**f. feeding**, alimentación forzada.—**f. flowers**, flores (*f.*) de estufa.—**f. labor**, trabajos forzados o forzosos.—**f. landing**, (aer.) aterrizaje forzoso.—**by f. marches**, (mil.) a marchas forzadas.

forceful [-ful], *a.* enérgico; potente; violento.

forceless [-lis], *a.* endeble, débil.

forcemeat [fórsmit], *s.* (coc.) relleno, picadillo, salpicón; embutido, almóndiga.

forceps [fórseps], *s.* (cir.) fórceps, pinzas; (dent.) gatillo, tenazas.

forcer [fórsœr], *s.* forzador; (mec.) émbolo.

forcible [fórsibl], *a.* fuerte, potente; eficaz; violento; enérgico; de peso.—**forcibleness** [-nis], *s.* fuerza; violencia.—**forcibly** [-bli], *adv.* fuertemente; enérgicamente; forzosamente; violentamente.

forcing [fórsiŋ]. I. *a.* impelente; madurador; clarificador de vino. II. *s.* forzamiento; compulsión.—**f. bed**, almájara.—**f. house**, invernadero.

ford [fórd]. I. *s.* vado. II. *va.* vadear, esguazar.

fordable [-abl], *a.* vadeable, esguazable.

fore [for]. I. *a.* anterior, delantero; (mar.) proel, de proa.—**f. hatching**, escotilla de proa.—**f. part**, delantera.—**f.-topgallant**, juanete de proa.—**f.-topsail**, velacho. II. *adv.* (mar.) de proa.—**f. and aft**, de popa a proa. III. *s.* delantera, frente, *f.*; (mar.) trinquete.—**to the f.**, en primer plano, conspicuo, a la vista; a (la) mano, dispuesto; con vida. IV. *interj.* ¡ojo! (aviso en el juego de golf).

forearm [fórarm], *s.* (anat.) antebrazo.

forearm [forárm], *va.* armar de antemano.

forebear [fórbɛr], *s.* antepasado, ascendiente.—*pl.* mayores.

forebode [forbóud], *vn.* y *va.* pronosticar, presagiar, agorar, ominar; presentir, antever.—**foreboding** [-iŋ]. I. *s.* presentimiento, presagio; corazonada. II. *a.* presagioso, pronosticador, agorero, ominoso.

forebrain [fórbrein], *s.* (anat.) prosencéfalo, cerebro anterior.

forecast [fórkæst], *va.* y *vn.* (*pret.* y *pp.* FORECAST(ED) proyectar, trazar; prever, predecir, pronosticar.

forecast, *s.* pronóstico, prognosis, predicción; previsión; proyecto, traza, plan.

forecastle [fórkæsl o fóuksąl], *s.* (mar.) castillo de proa.

forecited [fórsaitid], *a.* precitado.

foreclose [forklóuz], *va.* impedir, excluir; (for.) entablar, sustanciar y decidir un juicio hipotecario.—**foreclosure** [forklóuzŭ(r)], *s.* (for.) juicio hipotecario.

foredeck [fórdek], *s.* (mar.) cubierta de proa.

foredoom [fórdum], *s.* predestinación, sino.

foredoom [fordúm], *va.* predestinar, predeterminar.

forefather [fórfaðœ(r)], *s.* ascendiente, antepasado.

forefinger [fórfiŋgœ(r)], *s.* dedo índice.

forefoot [fórfut], *s.* mano (*f.*) o pata delantera; (mar.) gorja, tajamar.

forefront [fórfrʌnt], *s.* frente, puesto delantero, primera fila.—**in the f.**, de, o en, primer plano.

foregather, *vn.* = FORGATHER.

forego [forgóu], *va.* y *vn.* (*pret.* FOREWENT; *pp.* FOREGONE) preceder; ir delante; privarse de, renunciar a; ceder, abandonar. *V.* FORGO.

foregoing [-iŋ], *a.* precedente, anterior.

foregone [forgán], *a.* predeterminado, decidido de antemano; inevitable, seguro.

foreground [fórgraund], *s.* (pint.) primer término o plano; frente.

forehand [fórhænd]. I. *s.* la parte anterior de la mano; cuarto delantero del caballo; posición superior o ventajosa. II. *a.* delantero; hecho o dado de antemano o anticipadamente; dado con la parte anterior de la mano.—**f. stroke**, (tenis) golpe dado con la raqueta extendida a la derecha del jugador (a no ser éste zurdo).

forehanded [fórhændjd], *a.* temprano; hecho en tiempo oportuno; previsor, prudente, ahorrador; acomodado, con recursos.

forehead [fórjd], *s.* la frente; parte delantera.

foreign [fárin], *a.* extranjero; exterior; extraño, advenedizo; ajeno, remoto.—**f. affairs**, negocios extranjeros.—**f.-built, f.-born**, etc., construido, nacido, etc., en el extranjero.—**f. commerce**, comercio exterior.—**f. exchange**, cambio extranjero.—**F. Office**, (Ingl.) Ministerio de Negocios Extranjeros.—**F. Service**, (E. U.) servicio diplomático y consular.—**f. to the case**, ajeno al caso.—**f. trade** = FOREIGN COMMERCE.

foreigner [-œr], *s.* extranjero, extraño, forastero.

foreignism [-izm], *s.* extranjerismo.

foreignness [-nis], *s.* calidad de extraño, extranjero, ajeno, etc.; inconexión.

forejudge [fordʒʌdʒ], *va.* prejuzgar.

forejudgment [-mǫnt], *s.* prejuicio.

foreknow [fornóu], *va.* prever, tener presciencia de.

foreknowable [-abl], *a.* que se puede prever.

foreknowledge [fornálidʒ], *s.* presciencia.

foreland [fórland], *s.* cabo, promontorio.

foreleg [fórleg], *s.* pierna o pata delantera, brazo.

forelock [fórlak], *s.* guedeja, vedeja; copete (de caballo); (mec.) chaveta.—**to take time by the f.**, asir la ocasión por el copete.

foreman [fórmąn], *s.* capataz, *m.*, aperador; encargado, mayoral, sobrestante; (impr.) regente; (for.) presidente del jurado.

foremast [fórmæst], *s.* (mar.) palo de trinquete.

forementioned [fórménṣǫnd], *a.* susodicho, precitado, antedicho.

foremost [fórmoụst], *a.* delantero; primero.

forename [fórneịm], *s.* primer nombre, nombre de pila.

forenamed [-d], *a.* susodicho, precitado, antedicho.

forenoon [fórnụn], *s.* la mañana.

forensic [forénṣịk], *a.* forense; causídico.—**f. medicine**, (for.) medicina legal.

foreordain [forordéịn], *va.* preordinar, predestinar.—**foreordination** [-dịnéịṣǫn], *s.* predeterminación; predestinación.

forepart [fórpart], *s.* delantera, parte primera.

forepeak [fórpik], *s.* (mar.) racel o delgado de proa.

forequarter [fórkwortœ(r)], *s.* cuarto delantero.

forerun [forrĂn], *va.* (*pret.* FORERAN; *pp.* FORERUN) preceder; adelantarse; anunciar.

forerunner [-œ(r)], *s.* precursor; presagio, pronóstico; (a)nuncio; (mil.) explorador.

foresaid [fórsed], *a.* antedicho, susodicho.

foresail [fórseịl], *s.* trinquete.

foresee [forsí]. **I.** *va.* (*pret.* FORESAW; *pp.* FORESEEN) prever, antever, prevenir, barruntar. **II.** *vn.* tener presciencia o previsión.

foreseer [-œ(r)], *s.* previsor.

foreshadow [forṣǽdoụ], *va.* prefigurar, anunciar.

foreshorten [forṣórtẹn], *va.* (pint.) escorzar.

foreshortening [-iŋ], *s.* (pint.) escorzo.

foreshow [forṣóụ], *va.* exhibir de antemano; prefigurar; presagiar, dar muestras de.

foresight [fórsaịt], *s.* previsión, prevención, perspicacia; presciencia; (top.) visual hacia adelante; visual de cota del ojo, para determinar la altura del ojo en la nivelación.

foresighted [fórsáịtịd], *a.* precavido; próvido.

foreskin [fórskịn], *s.* (anat.) prepucio.

forest [fárịst]. **I.** *s.* monte, bosque, selva, floresta. —**f. ranger**, guardabosque. **II.** *va.* arbolar.

forestaff [fórstæf], *s.* (mar.) ballestilla, radiómetro.

forestage [fórsteịdž], *s.* (teat.) proscenio, parte (f.) anterior del escenario (gen. enfrente del telón).

forestal [fárịstạl], *a.* forestal.

forestall [forstól], *va.* antuviar, anticipar; impedir, prevenir; (com.) acaparar, monopolizar, acaparar.—**forestaller** [-œ(r)], *s.* monopolista, acopiador.—**forestalling** [-iŋ], *s.* acción de antuviar, etc.; (com.) monopolio, acopio; estanco.

forestation [farịstéịṣǫn], *s.* silvicultura práctica; plantación o extensión de montes.

forestay [fórsteị], *s.* (mar.) estay del trinquete.

forestaysail [fórstéịseịl], *s.* (mar.) trinquetilla.

forester [fárịstœ(r)], *s.* silvicultor, ingeniero forestal o de montes; guardamonte, guarda (m.) forestal; habitante del bosque (hombre o animal).—**forestry** [-trị], *s.* silvicultura; ingeniería forestal o de montes.

foretackle [fórtækl], *s.* aparejo del trinquete.

foretaste [fórteịst]. **I.** *va.* gustar o conocer de antemano. **II.** [fórteịst], *s.* goce anticipado.

foretell [fortél], *va.* y *vn.* (*pret.* y *pp.* FORETOLD) predecir, pronosticar, profetizar, presagiar, vaticinar, adivinar.—**foreteller** [-œ(r)], *s.* profeta, *m.*—**foretelling** [-iŋ], *s.* profecía, pronóstico.

forethought [fórθot], *s.* presciencia, providencia, previsión, prevención; premeditación.

foretoken [fórtoụkẹn]. **I.** *s.* pronóstico, presagio, señal premonitoria. **II.** [fórtóụkẹn], *va.* prefigurar, presagiar, anunciar.

foretop [fórtap], *s.* copete (del caballo, etc.); (mar.) cofa de trinquete.

forever [forévœ(r)], **forevermore** [-mór], *adv.* siempre; para o por siempre; a perpetuidad.— **forever and a day**, o **forever and ever**, eternamente, por siempre jamás.

forewarn [forwórn], *va.* prevenir, advertir,

avisar.—**forewarning** [-iŋ], *s.* advertencia, aviso.

forewent [forwént], *pret.* de TO FOREGO.

forewoman [fórwụmạn], *s.* primera oficiala de un taller de mujeres.

foreword [fórwœrd], *s.* advertencia, preámbulo, prefacio, prólogo.

foreyard [fóryard], *s.* (mar.) verga del trinquete.

forfeit [fórfịt]. **I.** *s.* prenda; multa; confiscación, decomiso; pérdida legal de cosa o derecho por incumplimiento de obligaciones.—*pl.* juego de prendas. **II.** *a.* confiscado, perdido por incumplimiento. **III.** *va.* perder el derecho a, por incumplimiento o violación.—**forfeitable** [-ạbl], *a.* alienable, invalidable, revocable; perdible; confiscable.—**forfeiture** [fórfịchụ(r)], *s.* decomiso, multa, confiscación; pérdida legal.

forgather [forgǽðœ(r)], *vn.* reunirse, juntarse.

forgave [forgéịv], *pret.* de TO FORGIVE.

forge [fórdž]. **I.** *s.* fragua; forja, hornaza; herrería. **II.** *va.* forjar, fraguar; contrahacer, falsificar, falsear; inventar; tramar. **III.** *vn.* (gen. con **ahead**) avanzar despacio pero constantemente; (vet.) tropezarse (las bestias).

forger [-œ(r)], *s.* forjador, fraguador; falsificador.

forgery [-œrị], *s.* falsificación.

forget [forgét], *va.* y *vn.* (*pret.* FORGOT; *pp.* FORGOTTEN) olvidar(se de).—**f. it**, no piense más en eso; no se preocupe, descuide Vd.—**to f. all about it**, olvidarse de ello completamente.—**to f. one's self**, excederse, propasarse, desmedirse; ser distraído; olvidarse de sí mismo por los demás, ser abnegado.

forgetful [-fụl], *a.* olvidadizo.—**forgetfulness** [-nịs], *s.* olvido, descuido; calidad de olvidadizo.

forget-me-not [-mịnat], *s.* (bot.) miosota, nomeolvides, raspilla.

forgettable [-ạbl], *a.* olvidable.

forging [fórdžịŋ], *s.* forja(dura), pieza forjada; (vet.) tropezón o tropezadura.

forgivable [forgívạbl], *a.* perdonable.

forgive [forgív], *va.* (*pret.* FORGAVE; *pp.* FORGIVEN) perdonar, dispensar, condonar, remitir.

forgiveness [-nịs], *s.* perdón; remisión; clemencia, misericordia.

forgiver [-œ(r)], *s.* perdonador.—**forgiving** [-iŋ], *a.* perdonador, clemente, magnánimo.

forgo [forgóụ], *va.* (*pret.* FORWENT; *pp.* FORGONE) privarse de, renunciar a; abandonar.

forgot [forgát], *pret.*, **forgotten** [-ẹn], *pp.* de TO FORGET.

fork [fórk]. **I.** *s.* tenedor; (agr.) horca, horcón, horqueta, horquilla; horcadura (de árbol); bifurcación; confluencia de un río. **II.** *va.* hacinar o cargar con horca; ahorquillar.—**to f. out, u over**, (fam.) entregar, pagar. **III.** *vn.* ahorquillarse, bifurcarse.

forked [-t], *a.* horcado, ahorquillado, bifurcado, hendido; (bot.) bífido.—**f. stick** o **prop**, horcón, horquilla.

forkhead [-hed], *s.* lengüeta de saeta o flecha.

forlorn [forlórn], *a.* abandonado, olvidado, desamparado; infeliz, desdichado.—**f. hope**, (mil.) destacamento encargado de un servicio peligroso; empresa desesperada.

form [fórm]. **I.** *s.* forma; figura; hechura; hoja, modelo que ha de llenarse, (Am.) esqueleto; condición; estado; práctica, ritual, formalidad, ceremonia; estilo; horma, matriz, patrón; porte, conducta, modales; aparición, sombra; banco, asiento largo; (gram.) forma, inflexión; (impr.) forma; (constr.) molde; (fort.) cestón.— **f. letter**, (com.) carta general, que no requiere más cambio que el del nombre y dirección.—**in due f.**, en debida forma, en regla.—**for f's sake**, por pura fórmula.—**of f.**, de pura forma o de apariencia. **II.** *va.* formar, construir, labrar, modelar; idear, concebir; ordenar, componer, arreglar; hacer, constituir, integrar. **III.** *vn.* formarse.

formal [-ạl], *a.* formal, relativo a la forma; de

pura forma; exterior, superficial; metódico, regular; ceremonioso, cumplimentero, etiquetero; esencial, constitutivo.—**f. attire**, o **dress**, traje o vestido de etiqueta.—**f. call**, visita de cumplido o de cumplimiento.

formaldehyde [fɔrmǽldihaid], s. (quím.) formaldehido, aldehido fórmico.

formalin [fɔ́rmalin], s. (quím.) formalina, disolución de aldehido fórmico.

formalism [fɔ́rmalizm], s. formalismo.

formalist [-ist], s. formalista.

formality [fɔrmǽliti], s. formalidad, ceremonia, etiqueta, cumplido, cumplimiento.

formalize [fɔ́rmalaiz], I. va. formalizar. II. vn. ser formal o ceremonioso; afectar formalidad.

formally [fɔ́rmali], adv. formalmente; expresa o regularmente; con toda solemnidad.

format [fɔ́rmæt], s. formato, forma (detalles tipográficos, tamaño, etc., de un libro).

formate [fɔ́rmeit], s. (quím.) formiato.

formation [fɔrméiʂɔn], s. formación; desarrollo; disposición, arreglo; (geol.) formación.

formative [fɔ́rmativ], a. formativo.

formene [fɔ́rmin], s. (quím.) formeno, metano.

former [fɔ́rmœ(r)], I. a. primero; (con *the*) aquél, aquélla, aquéllos, etc.; pasado, anterior, antiguo, ex, que fué (*former teacher*, ex maestro, maestro que fué). II. s. formador, plasmador; molde, matriz.

formerly [-li], adv. antiguamente, en tiempos pasados, antes, un tiempo eso.

formic [fɔ́rmik], a. hormigoso; fórmico (ácido).

formicant [-kant], a. (med.) formicante.

formicary [-ikeri], s. hormiguero.

formicate [-keit], vn. hormiguear.—**formication** [-kéiʂɔn], s. hormigueo; (med.) formicación.

formidable [fɔ́rmidabl], a. formidable.

formidably [-bli], adv. formidablemente.

formless [fɔ́rmlis], a. informe, sin forma.

formula [fɔ́rmyula], s. fórmula, receta.

formulæ [-li], pl. de FORMULA.

formulary [-leri], I. a. formulario; formal; sujeto a fórmula. II. s. formulario.

formulate [-leit], va. formular.—**formulation** [-léiʂɔn], s. formulación.—**formulator** [-leitɔ(r)], s. formulador.

formulism [-lizm], s. formulismo.—**formulist** [-list], s., **formulistic** [-listik], a. formulista.

formulize [-laiz], va. formalizar; formular.

formyl [fɔ́rmil], s. (quím.) formilo.

fornicate [fɔ́rnikeit], vn. fornicar.—**fornicate(d** [-id], a. (arq.) fornicado, abovedado.—**fornication** [-kéiʂɔn], s. fornicio, fornicación; (arq.) bóveda.—**fornicator** [fɔ́rnikeitɔ(r)], s. fornicador.—**fornicatress** [-tris], s. fornicadora, concubina; manceba.

fornix [fɔ́rniks], s. (anat.) fórnix, f., trígono cerebral; (bot.) fórnix.

forsake [forséik], va. (pret. FORSOOK; pp. FORSAKEN) dejar, abandonar, desamparar, desertar; separarse de; renegar de; desechar, rechazar; dar de mano a.—**forsaken** [-ɛn], a. abandonado, desertado, desamparado.

forsooth [forsúθ], adv. ciertamente, en verdad.

forswear [forswér], I. va. (pret. FORSWORE; pp. FORSWORN) abjurar; renunciar o negar solemnemente.—**to f. one's self**, perjurarse. II. vn. perjurar(se).

fort [fɔrt], s. fuerte, castillo, fortaleza.

fortalice [fɔ́rtalis], s. fortín.

forte [fɔrt], s. fuerte (afición o mérito); (fig.) caballo de batalla.

forte [fɔ́rtei], a., adv. y s. (mús.) forte, fuerte.

forth [fórθ], adv. delante; adelante; fuera, afuera; a la vista, públicamente; hasta lo último.—**and so f.**, y así de lo demás; etcétera.

forthcoming [-kʌ́miŋ], I. a. futuro, próximo, venidero, que viene. II. s. aparición; acercamiento, proximidad.

forthright [-rait], I. a. directo, derecho; franco.

II. adv. directamente; francamente; en seguida, inmediatamente.

forthwith [-wíð], adv. inmediatamente.

fortieth [fɔ́rtieθ], s. y a. cuadragésimo; cuarentavo; cuarenta (ordinal).

fortifiable [fɔ́rtifaiabl], a. fortificable.

fortification [-fikéiʂɔn], s. fortificación; fortalecimiento; fortaleza, plaza fuerte.

fortifier [-faiœ(r)], s. fortificador; fortalecedor.

fortify [-fai]. I. va. fortificar; fortalecer; reforzar; corroborar. II. vn. construir defensas.

fortissimo [fortísimou], a. y adv. (mús.) fortísimo.

fortitude [fɔ́rtitiud], s. fortaleza; fuerza, ánimo.

fortnight [fɔ́rtnait], s. quincena, dos semanas.—**fortnightly** [-li]. I. a. quincenal, bisemanal. II. adv. quincenalmente. III. s. revista bisemanal.

fortress [fɔ́rtris], s. fuerte, fortaleza; plaza fuerte.

fortuitous [fortiúitas], a. fortuito, accidental, casual, eventual.—**fortuitously** [-li], adv. fortuitamente.—**fortuitousness** [-nis], s. calidad de fortuito.

fortuity [fortiúiti], s. caso fortuito; accidente.

fortunate [fɔ́rchunit], a. afortunado, dichoso, feliz, venturoso, bienhadado, fausto.

fortunately [-li], adv. afortunadamente.

fortune [fɔ́rchun]. I. s. fortuna; dicha, suerte, f., (buena)ventura; destino, sino; caudal, dinero, bienes.—**f. book**, libro de la buena ventura.—**f. hunter**, el que anda en busca de esposa rica.—**f. teller**, sortílego, adivino.—**f. telling**, buenaventura, sortiaria, sortilegio.—**to cost a f.**, costar un dineral, o un ojo de la cara. II. va. dotar con una fortuna.

fortuneless [-lis], a. sin fortuna, sin bienes.

forty [fɔ́rti], a. y s. cuarenta.—**f. winks**, siesta corta.

forum [fɔ́rʌm], s. plaza; foro; tribunal; reunión de debate, en que se discute un asunto.

forward [fɔ́rwærd]. I. a. adelante, en adelante, hacia adelante, más allá. II. a. delantero; (mar.) proel; precoz; adelantado; anterior; pronto, activo; desenvuelto, descocado; apresurado, vivo, listo; audaz, emprendedor; radical, exagerado.—**f. delivery**, (com.) entrega en fecha futura. III. s. (dep.) delantero. IV. va. reenviar; transmitir, remitir; apresurar, activar; fomentar.—**forwarder**, o **forwarding merchant**, comisionista expedidor.

forwardly [-li], adv. descocada o descaradamente.—**forwardness** [-nis], s. adelantamiento, progreso; prontitud, apresuramiento; precocidad; descaro, descoco, desenvoltura; audacia.

forwards [-z], adv. = FORWARD.

for(e)went [forwént], pret. de TO FOR(E)GO.

foss, fosse [fas], s. (fort.) foso.

fossa [fása], s. (anat.) fosa.

fossil [fásil], a. y s. fósil.—**fossiliferous** [-ífɛrʌs], a. fosilífero.—**fossilist** [-ist], s. paleontólogo.—**fossilization** [-izéiʂɔn], s. fosilización.—**fossilize** [-aiz]. I. va. fosilizar; petrificar; hacer anticuado. II. vn. fosilizarse, petrificarse.—**fossilology** [-álodʒi], s. paleontología.

fossorial [fasórial], a. cavador.—**f. wasp**, avispa cavadora.

foster [fástœ(r)]. I. va. criar, nutrir; dar alas, alentar, fomentar. II. a. Como adjetivo, se aplica comúnmente a nombres que por sí solos denotan parentesco, para expresar condición análoga debida a crianza o, general pero no necesariamente, adopción.—**f. brother, child, sister**, hermano, hijo, hermana de leche, adoptivos, o criados como hijos, etc.—**f. mother, father**, madre, padre adoptivos, o que han criado a los *foster children* correspondientes.—**f. earth**, (agr.) suelo o tierra de almáciga.—**f. home**, casa de crianza, donde se crían niños ajenos.—**f. nurse**, nodriza.

fosterage [-idʒ], s. crianza de niños ajenos; condición de ser hijo adoptivo; fomento.

fostering [-iŋ]. I. *a.* fomentador. II. *s.* fomento.

fosterling [-liŋ], *s.* = FOSTER CHILD.

Foucault current [fúkou̯ kǽrǫnt], *s.* corriente de Foucault, corriente parásita.

fought [fɔt], *pret.* y *pp.* de TO FIGHT.

foul [fau̯l]. I. *a.* sucio, puerco, impuro, inmundo; fétido, pestilente; viciado (aire); detestable, vil; injusto, sin derecho; enredado, atascado, obstruído; contrario, desagradable; obsceno; (impr.) lleno de errores y correcciones.—**f. bill of health**, (mar.) patente sucia.—**f. breath**, ocena, aliento fétido.—**f. dealing**, dolo, mala fe.—**f. language**, palabras injuriosas; lenguaje obsceno o soez.—**f.-mouthed**, mal hablado.— **f. play**, juego sucio o desleal; violencia, muerte violenta.—**f.-smelling**, hediondo, maloliente. —**f. weather**, mal tiempo.—**to fall f. of**, enredarse con; atacar; (mar.) abordar, chocar con. II. *s.* acción de ensuciar, de ludir o enredarse una cosa en otra; violación de las reglas establecidas. III. *va.* ensuciar, emporcar; (mar.) abordar, chocar, trabarse; (dep.) violar las reglas establecidas. IV. *vn.* ensuciarse; (mar.) chocar.

foulard [fu̯lárd], *s.* (tej.) fular.

foully [fáu̯li], *adv.* suciamente.—**foulness** [-nis], *s.* asquerosidad, porquería, pestilencia; vileza.

found [fáu̯nd], *pret.* y *pp.* de TO FIND.

found [fáu̯nd], *va.* cimentar, fundamentar; edificar; instituir, fundar, establecer; apoyar o vincular en; asentar, fijar; (fund.) fundir, derretir.

foundation [-éi̯šǫn], *s.* fundación, establecimiento; fundamento, base, *f.*, apoyo, entibo, polo; dotación; (mec.) asiento, lecho, pie, *m.*; (ing.) firme; cimentación o cimiento, embasamiento, fundamento; (cost.) forro, refuerzo.— **f. school**, escuela dotada.—**f. stone**, primera piedra.

founder [-œ(r)]. I. *s.* fundador; (fund.) fundidor; (vet.) despeadura. II. *va.* (mar.) hacer zozobrar; (vet.) despear los pies del caballo. III. *vn.* (mar.) irse a pique o a fondo, zozobrar; fracasar; desplomarse.

foundering [-iŋ], *s.* (mar.) zozobra.

founding [-iŋ], *s.* fundición.

foundling [-liŋ], *s.* niño expósito.—**f. hospital**, inclusa, casa de expósitos.

foundress [-ris], *s.* fundadora.

foundry [-ri], *s.* fundición (fábrica).—**f. iron**, fundición bruta de moldeo, o para piezas fundidas.

fount [fau̯nt], **fountain** [fáu̯ntin], *s.* fuente, *f.*; manantial, (poét.) fontana; pila.—**f. pen**, pluma estilográfica, pluma fuente.—**f. syringe**, (med.) jeringa o inyector de gravedad.

fountainhead [-hed], *s.* fuentes, *f. pl.*, cabeceras (de un río); fuente; origen.

four [fór], *a.* y *s.* cuatro.—**f.-cornered**, cuadrangular.—**f. flush**, (poker) lance con un flux de cuatro naipes.—**f.-flush**, (fam.) baladronear; exagerar uno su destreza, riqueza, etc.—**f.-flusher**, (fam.) baladrón, fanfarrón. —**f.-footed**, cuadrúpedo.—**f.-handed**, cuadrúmano; para o de cuatro jugadores; (mús.) de o a cuatro manos.—**f. hundred**, cuatrocientos; (fam.) la alta sociedad, la nata social. —**f.-in-hand**, carruaje tirado por cuatro caballos; corbata larga de nudo corredizo.— **f.-motored**, (aer.) cuatrimotores, de cuatro motores.—**f.-oared**, de cuatro remos.—**f. o'clock**, (bot.) dondiego de noche, arrebolera. —**f. of a kind**, cuatro de igual o de cuatro direcciones.—**f.-wheel**, de cuatro ruedas.—**f.-wheeler**, carruaje de cuatro ruedas.—**on all fours**, en las cuatro patas, a gatas; parejo, equivalente; sin discordancia; en completa armonía.—**to go on all fours**, gatear, andar a gatas.

fourfold [-fou̯ld], *a.* cuádruplo.—**fourpence** [-pens], *s.* (Ingl.) cuatro peniques.—**fourscore** [-skɔr], *a.* cuatro veintenas de; octogenario.—

foursome [-sam], *s.* grupo o juego de cuatro personas.—**foursquare** [-skwer]. I. *a.* cuadrangular; firme; franco; inequívoco. II. *adv.* sin ambages.

fourteen [fórtín], *a.* y *s.* catorce.

fourteenth [-θ]. I. *a.* catorceno, décimocuarto, catorce (ordinal). II. *s.* y *a.* catorzavo.

fourth [fórθ], I. *s.* y *a.* cuarto, cuarta parte; cuatro (del mes).—**f. arm**, (mil.) fuerzas aéreas.—**f. estate**, la prensa.—**the F.**, (E. U.) el 4 de julio.

fourthly [-li], *adv.* en cuarto lugar.

fowl [fáu̯l]. I. *s.* (orn.) gallo, gallina; pollo; aves (*f. pl.*) en general.—*pl.* volatería, aves de corral. II. *vn.* cazar (aves), ir de caza (de aves).

fowler [-œ(r)], *s.* cazador (de aves).

fowling [-iŋ], *s.* volatería, cetrería; caza (de aves). —**f. net**, red de cazar pájaros.—**f. piece**, escopeta; (pint.) bodegón de volatería.

fox [fáks]. I. *s.* (zool.) zorra, raposa; (fig.) zorro, bellaco, taimado.—**f. brush**, rabo de zorra.— **f. chase o hunt**, caza de zorras.—**f. den, hole o kennel**, zorrera, raposera. V. FOXHOLE, —**f. terrier**, fox térrier (perro).—**f. trot** (equit.) trote corto; *fox o foxtrot* (baile). II. *vn.* cazar zorras; raposear, usar de ardides o trampas; disimular; agriarse acedarse (la cerveza, etc.); ponerse rojizo, descolorarse (el papel). III. *va.* acedar; descolorar; emborrachar; (fam.) embaucar.

foxed [-t], *pp.* y *a.* descolorido (papel, libros, etc.).

foxfire [-fai̯r], *s.* luz fosforescente de la madera podrida.

foxglove [-glʌv], *s.* (bot.) dedalera, digital.

foxhole [-hou̯l], *s.* (mil.) trinchera individual.

foxhound [-hau̯nd], *s.* perro jateo, zorrero o raposero.

foxiness [-inis], *s.* zorrería, raposería; astucia; acedía, agrura; descolorimiento.

foxlike [-lai̯k], *a.* astuto, taimado bellaco.

foxtail [-tei̯l], *s.* (bot.) carricera.

foxwood [-wu̯d], *s.* madera podrida fosforescente.

foxy [-i], *a.* raposuno, zorruno; taimado, astuto; rojizo; agriado, tomado; descolorido, manchado.

foyer [fói̯œ(r)], *s.* recibimiento; salón de entrada (de hotel o casa); (teat.) (gal.) foyer, salón de descanso; (fund.) cubilote.

fracas [fréi̯kas], *s.* zacapela, riña.

fraction [frǽkšǫn]. I. *s.* (arit.) fracción, quebrado; fragmento, porción, trozo. II. *va.* fraccionar.

fractional [-al], *a.* fraccionario; fraccionado.— **f. distillation**, destilación fraccionada.—**f. numeral**, número quebrado o fraccionario.

fractionate [-ei̯t], *va.* fraccionar, fragmentar; (quím.) separar por destilación fraccionada.

fractious [frǽkšas], *a.* reacio; díscolo; rebelón.

fracture [frǽkchū(r)]. I. *s.* rotura, fractura, ruptura, rompimiento, quiebra, quebramiento; (cir.) fractura, rotura. II. *va.* y *vn.* fracturar(se), quebrar(se).

fraenum [frínʌm], *s.* frenillo (de la lengua).

fragile [frǽdžil], *a.* frágil, deleznable, friable, quebradizo.—**fragility** [frʌdžíliti], **fragileness** [frǽdžilnis], *s.* fragilidad.

fragment [frǽgmǫnt], *s.* fragmento; trozo.

fragmentary [-eri], *a.* fragmentario.

fragmentation [-éi̯šǫn], *s.* fragmentación.—**f. bomb**, (mil.) bomba de fragmentación.

fragrance, fragrancy [fréi̯grans, -i], *s.* fragancia, buen olor, perfume, aroma, *m.*—**fragrant** [-ant], *a.* fragante, oloroso, aromático.—**fragrantly** [-li], *adv.* con fragancia.

frail [fréi̯l]. I. *a.* frágil, quebradizo, deleznable; débil, delicado, endeble. II. *s.* canasta, junco, espuerta, sera.—**frailness** [-nis], **frailty** [-ti], *s.* fragilidad o friabilidad; flaqueza, debilidad.

frambesia [fræmbíźiə̯], *s.* (med.) frambesia. *V.* YAWS.

frame [fréim]. **I.** *va.* fabricar, formar, construir; armar; componer, ajustar; arreglar, dirigir; forjar, idear; enmarcar, encuadrar; (carp.) entramar; (gen. con **up**) fabricar, inventar (algo contra alguno); arreglar clandestinamente de antemano (el resultado de un juego, etc.); acusar o hacer condenar con pruebas inventadas a propósito, formar un complot contra.— **framed structure**, construcción reticulada o de celosía. **II.** *s.* marco; armazón; estructura; figura; arreglo, construcción; armadura, esqueleto, entramado, bastidor; banco de tornero; molde para barras de jabón; (tej.) telar; (impr.) chibalete; (cost.) bastidor para bordar; (mar.) cuadernas, ligazones, costillaje; (fig.) talante, disposición; cuadro, cerco (de puerta o ventana); cuadro (de bicicleta, etc.); forma, sistema, *m.* (de gobierno, etc.); tenor, alcance (de una ley, constitución, etc.); fotografía de una imagen transmitida por televisión; película de cine. *V.* FRAME-UP.—**f. house**, casa hecha de madera.—**f. of mind**, estado de ánimo.— **f. of reference**, (fís.) sistema de coordenadas. —**f. saw**, sierra bracera, sierra montada o de bastidor. **III.** *a.* reticulado, de celosía (dícese de las construcciones); de tablas, de madera; de entramado (casa).

framer [-œ(r)], *s.* constructor, armador; fabricante de marcos.

frame-up [-ʌp], *s.* (fam.) conspiración; fraude.

framework [-wœrk], *s.* armadura, armazón, esqueleto, entramado; sistema, *m.*, forma (de gobierno, etc.); tenor, alcance (de una ley, etc.).

framing [-iŋ], *s.* armadura, armazón.

franc [fræŋk], *s.* franco, moneda francesa, etc.

franchise [frǽnchaiz], *s.* derecho político; franquicia, privilegio; concesión; exención; encartación.

Franciscan [frænsískən], *s.* y *a.* franciscano.

francolin [frǽŋkolin], *s.* (orn.) francolín.

Francophile [frǽŋkofail], *a.* y *s.* francófilo.

Francophobia [-fóu̯biə̯], *s.* galofobia.

frangible [frǽndźibl], *a.* frangible; perecedero.

frangipani [frændźipáni], *s.* (Am., bot.) franchipanero; (Am.) franchipán (pomada aromática).

frank [fræŋk]. **I.** *a.* franco, sincero; francote, campechano. **II.** *s.* franquicia postal o de correos; carta franca. **III.** *va.* enviar (carta) exenta de franqueo.

Frank, *s.* franco, galo.

Frankenstein [frǽŋkenstai̯n], *s.* persona cuyas obras le causan su propia ruina.

frankfurter [frǽŋkfœrtœ(r)], *s.* salchicha de Fráncfort, especie de salchicha de carne de vaca y de puerco muy condimentada.

frankincense [frǽŋkinsens], *s.* incienso.

Frankish [frǽŋkiš]. **I.** *a.* franco (de los francos). **II.** *s.* la lengua de los francos.

franklin [frǽŋklin], *s.* (Ingl.) = FREEHOLDER.

frankly [frǽŋkli], *adv.* francamente.

frankness [-nis], *s.* franqueza, sinceridad, abertura, candor, ingenuidad.

frantic [frǽntik], *a.* frenético, furioso, rabioso.

frantically [-əli], *adv.* frenéticamente.

frap [fræp], *va.* (mar.) atortorar.

frappé [fræpéj]. **I.** *a.* refrescado con hielo, rozado (vino, champaña, etc.). **II.** *s.* refresco de zumo de frutas con azúcar, al cual se da cierto grado de congelación pastosa.

frat [fræt], *s.* (fam.) = FRATERNITY.

fraternal [frətœ́rnəl], *a.* fraternal, fraterno.—**f. order**, sociedad organizada para beneficios mutuos; sociedad secreta.

fraternally [-i], *adv.* fraternalmente.

fraternity [-niti], *s.* (con)fraternidad; hermandad, hermanazgo; gremio; congregación.

fraternization [frætœrnizéjšən], *s.* fraternización.

fraternize [-najz], *vn.* y *va.* (con)fraternizar, confraternar, hermanar(se).

fratricidal [frǽtrisajdəl], *a.* fratricida.

fratricide [-sajd], *s.* fratricidio; fratricida, *mf.*

fraud [fród], *s.* fraude, dolo, engaño, superchería, trampa; (fam.) farsante, engañador, timador. —**fraudful** [-fu̯l], *a.* pérfido, engañador; fraudulento.—**fraudfully** [-i], *adv.* engañosamente.—**fraudless** [-lis], *a.* sin fraude.— **fraudulence, fraudulency** [fródźu̯lens, -i], *s.* fraude, engaño.—**fraudulent** [-ent], *a.* fraudulento.—**fraudulently** [-li], *adv.* fraudulentamente.

fraught [frot], *a.* cargado, lleno, preñado (de).

fraxinella [frǽksinélə̯], *s.* (bot.) fresnillo.

fray [frej]. **I.** *s.* riña, refriega; raedura, desgaste. **II.** *va.* ludir, raer, tazar. **III.** *vn.* deshilacharse.

frazzle [frǽzl]. **I.** *va.* y *vn.* deshilachar(se); cansar(se). **II.** *s.* cosa deshilachada; hilachas, añicos; condición de estar rendido de cansancio.

freak [frík]. **I.** *s.* capricho, antojo; rareza, monstruosidad, curiosidad, extravagancia.—**f. of nature**, aborto de la naturaleza. **II.** *a.* raro; anormal. **III.** *va.* varetear; abigarrar, gayar.

freakish [-iš], *a.* caprichoso, antojadizo; raro, extravagante.—**freakishly** [-li], *adv.* caprichosamente.—**freaki(sh)ness** [-i(š)nis], *s.* calidad de caprichoso, monstruoso o ridículo.

freckle [frékl]. **I.** *s.* peca.—**f.-faced**, pecoso. **II.** *va.* motear. **III.** *vn.* ponerse pecoso.

freckled [-d], **freckly** [frékli], *a.* pecoso; moteado.

freckledness [frékldnis], *s.* estado de pecoso.

free [frí]. **I.** *a.* libre; despejado, franco; desocupado, vacante; licencioso, atrevido; liberal, generoso, exento, privilegiado; inmune; permitido; voluntario, discrecional; gratuito, de balde; gallardo, vivo, activo; zafo, flojo, suelto, desatado; escotero.—**f. and easy**, despreocupado; cómodo, fácil; sin restricción.—**f. enterprise**, libre empresa.—**f.-for-all**, (fam.) pelotera, contienda general.—**f. from**, libre o exento de; ajeno de.—**f. goods**, mercancías exentas de derechos.—**f.-hand drawing**, dibujo a pulso.—**f.-handed**, libre de manos; exento de trabas; liberal, dadivoso.—**f.-hearted**, franco, abierto.—**f. lance**, lanza, soldado libre; hombre despreocupado e independiente; persona sin empleo regular, que sirve a cualquiera que solicita sus servicios (apl. esp. a escritores y artistas).—**f. list**, (com.) lista de artículos exentos de derechos; lista de personas exentas de pago.—**f. liver**, comilón.—**f. of charge**, gratis, de balde.—**f. on board** (**f. o. b.**), (com.) franco a bordo (**f. a b.**), libre de gastos a bordo (**l. a b.**).—**f. port**, puerto franco.—**f. pass**, pase, permiso.— **f. press**, libertad de imprenta.—**f. school**, escuela gratuita.—**f.-spoken**, sin reserva, franco.—**f. state**, (hist., E. U.) estado no esclavista, o sin esclavos.—**f. thought**, librepensamiento.—**f.-tongued**, lenguaraz, deslenguado.—**f. trade**, (com.) libre cambio, libertad de comercio.—**f. trader**, librecambista.—**f. verse**, verso libre o suelto.—**f. wheeling**, rueda libre.—**f. will**, (libre) albedrío.—**to make f. with**, tomar libertades con; no gastar cumplidos. **II.** *va.* libertar; librar, rescatar; manumitir; desvedar; exentar, eximir; desembarazar, zafar. **III.** *adv.* libremente; gratis.

freeboard [-bord], *s.* (mar.) obra muerta.

freebooter [-bútœ(r)], *s.* saqueador; filibustero, forbante.

freebooting [-butiŋ], *s.* saqueo, pillaje.

freeborn [-born], *a.* nacido libre; (for.) ingenuo.

freedman [frídmən], *s.* liberto.

freedom [frídəm], *s.* libertad; exención, inmunidad; licencia, franqueza o familiaridad atrevida; facilidad, soltura.—**f. of a city,** concesión de inmunidades y privilegios especiales en una ciudad.—**f. of speech,** libertad de palabra.— **f. of the press,** libertad de imprenta.—**f. of the will,** libre albedrío.—**f. of worship,** libertad de cultos.

freehold [fríhoṵld], s. (for.) feudo franco, dominio absoluto.—**freeholder** [-œ(r)], s. dueño, propietario absoluto de una finca.

freely [frḯlḭ], adv. libremente; sin reserva; espontánea, desembarazada o gratuitamente.

freeman [frímạn], s. hombre libre; ciudadano.

Freemason [frímḗisọn], s. (franc)masón.

Freemasonry [-rḭ], s. (franc)masonería.

freeness [frínḭs], s. libertad; franqueza, sinceridad; liberalidad.

freer [fríœ(r)]. I. s. libertador. II. a. comp. de FREE; más libre.

freestone [frístoṵn]. I. s. piedra franca. II. a. y s. abridero (durazno).

freethinker [fríθḭŋkœ(r)], s. librepensador.

freethinking [-ḭŋ], s. librepensamiento.

freewill [fríwḭl], a. voluntario, hecho espontáneamente; pert. a la doctrina del (libre) albedrío.

freewoman [fríwṵmạn], s. mujer libre, no esclava; ciudadana.

freeze [fríz]. I. va. (pret. FROZE; pp. FROZEN) congelar, helar; garapiñar (líquidos); (com., etc.) congelar, estancar, inutilizar (fondos, crédito, precios, etc.); (fam.) no hacer caso a, tratar con desprecio.—**to f. out,** excluir o hacer salir tratando con frialdad o desprecio. II. vn. helarse; helar, escarchar.—**to f. to death,** morir de frío. III. s. helada.

freezer [-œ(r)], s. refrigerador, congelador; heladora, garapiñera, sorbetera.

freezing [-ḭŋ]. I. a. congelante, frigorífico; glacial.—**f. point,** punto de congelación. II. s. helamiento, congelación.

freight [fréit]. I. va. fletar; cargar. II. s. carga, cargazón; flete.—**f. car,** vagón, carro o furgón de carga.—**f. elevator,** montacargas.—**f. free,** libre de flete.—**f. home,** o **return f.,** flete de vuelta.—**f. outwards,** flete de ida.—**f. platform,** muelle.—**f. rates,** tarifas de flete.—**f. train,** tren de mercancías o de carga.—**by f.,** como carga.

freightage [-ḭdʒ], s. carga, cargamento; flete; transporte.—**freighter** [-œ(r)], s. fletador; cargador; buque de carga.

French [frénch], a. y s. francés; idioma francés. —**F. bean,** (bot.) judía, alubia, habichuela, fréjol.—pl. judías en lata tratadas químicamente.—**F. bread,** pan francés.—**F. doors** o **windows,** puertas vidrieras dobles.—**F. dressing,** salsa francesa para ensaladas.—**F. fried potatoes,** o **F. fries,** papas o patatas fritas en trozos.—**F. horn,** bocina, trompa.—**F. leave,** despedida a la francesa, a la chita callando.—**F.-like,** afrancesado, a la francesa.— **F. roof,** mansarda.

Frenchify [-ifai], va. afrancesar; agabachar.

Frenchman [-mạn], s. francés.

Frenchwoman [-wṵmạn], s. francesa.

Frenchy [-ḭ], s. y a. (desp.) franchute, gabacho.

frenetic [frḭnétḭk], **frenzied** [frénzid], a. frenético.

frenum [frínʌm], s. (anat.) frenillo.

frenzy [frénzḭ]. I. s. frenesí, locura, delirio, devaneo. II. va. volver loco; afectar con frenesí.

frequency [fríkwẹnsḭ], s. frecuencia; (elec.) frecuencia, número de períodos o ciclos por segundo.—**f. meter,** (elec.) frecuencímetro, medidor de frecuencia.—**f. modulation,** (rad.) frecuencia modulada, modulación de frecuencia.

frequent [-ẹnt], a. frecuente; usado, familiar, regular; habitual; persistente.

frequent [frḭkwént], va. frecuentar; concurrir a.

frequentation [-éishọn], s. frecuentación.

frequentative [-ạtḭv], a. y s. (gram.) frecuentativo.

frequenter [-œ(r)], s. frecuentador.

frequently [fríkwẹntlḭ], adv. frecuentemente.

fresco [fréskoṵ]. I. s. (b. a.) pintura al fresco. II. va. pintar al fresco.

fresh [frésh]. I. a. fresco, nuevo; reciente; recién llegado; refrigerante; puro (aire, agua); fresco (viento); recién parida (vaca); tierno (pan); lozano (flor, planta, etc.); sano, robusto; inexperto, novicio; (fam.) descocado, descarado; oficioso, entremetido.—**f. from,** acabado de llegar, sacar, etc., de.—**f. hand,** novicio.—**f. water,** agua dulce.—**f.-water,** de agua dulce; (fig.) inexperto; de poca monta. II. adv. = FRESHLY. III. s. avenida, riada, inundación; manantial; mezcla de agua dulce y salada en los ríos.

freshen [-ẹn]. I. va. refrescar, refrigerar. II. vn. refrescarse, avivarse.

freshet [-ḭt], s. avenida, crecida, creciente, f.

freshly [-lḭ], adv. frescamente; recientemente.

freshman [-mạn], s. estudiante de primer año.

freshness [-nḭs], s. frescura, frescor; lozanía, verdor; (fam.) descaro.

fret [frét]. I. va. gastar estregando, rabosear; raer, corroer; enojar, irritar; recamar, bordar en realce; adornar con calados. II. vn. gastarse, incomodarse, impacientarse, inquietarse; lamentarse.—**fretted,** calado. III. s. roce, rozamiento; raspadura, raedura; desgaste; irritación, enojo; hervor; (b. a.) relieve, realce, cinceladura; greca; calado; traste de guitarra. —**f. saw,** sierra de calados o de marquetería, segueta.

fretful [-fṵl], a. displicente, irritable, mohíno; inquieto; incómodo, molesto.—**fretfully** [-ḭ], adv. con mal humor; de mala gana.—**fretfulness** [-nḭs], s. mal humor; inquietud, desasosiego.

fretty [-ḭ], a. inquieto; irritable, malhumorado; (fam.) inflamado, apostemado.

fretwork [-wœrk], s. (b. a.) greca, adorno; calado.

Freudian [fróidiạn], a. y s. (psic.) freudiano.— **Freudianism** [-izm], s. freudismo, teoría de Freud.

friability [fraiạbílḭtḭ], s. friabilidad.

friable [fráiạbl], a. friable, desmenuzable.

friar [fráiạ(r)], s. fraile; (F.) Fray.—**friary** [-rḭ]. I. s. convento de frailes. II. a. frailero, frailesco.

fribble [fríbl]. I. vn. bobear. II. va. malgastar. III. a. vano, frívolo. IV. s. persona frívola; fruslería.

fricassee [frḭkạsí]. I. s. (coc.) fricasé. II. va. hacer fricasé.

fricative [fríkạtḭv], a. (gram.) fricativo.

friction [fríkshọn], s. fricción; frotación, frotamiento; roce; rozamiento, roce; ludimiento; disensión, desavenencia, falta de armonía. Se usa mucho adjetivadamente en mecánica, y casi siempre se traduce "de fricción", vg.: **f. clutch, cone, gearing,** embrague, cono, engranaje de fricción.—**f. band,** cinta de fricción (de un freno).—**f. block,** zapata (de un freno). —**f. factor,** coeficiente de rozamiento.—**f. matches,** fósforos de fricción.—**f. plate** o **point,** rozadero.—**f. tape,** (elec.) cinta aisladora adherente.

frictional [-ạl], a. de o producido por rozamiento, fricción o frotamiento.—**f. resistance,** resistencia de rozamiento.

Friday [fráidḭ], s. viernes.

fried [fraid], a. frito; freído (pp. de TO FRY).

friend [frénd], s. amigo, amiga; compañero, compadre; partidario, allegado; (F.) cuáquero. —**to become friends,** o **make friends with,** compadrar, trabar amistad (con); hacer las amistades (después de reñir).—**to have a friend at court,** tener al alcalde el padre, tener buenas aldabas.

friendless [-lịs], *a.* desamparado, desvalido, sin amigos.—**friendliness** [-lịnịs], *s.* amistad, amigabilidad.

friendly [-lị]. I. *a.* amigable, amigo, amistoso; servicial, favorable, benévolo, propicio. II. *adv.* amigablemente, amistosamente.

friendship [-ŝịp], *s.* amistad.

frieze [friz], *s.* (tej.) frisa; (arq.) friso, arrocabe.

frigate [frígịt], *s.* (mar.) fragata.—**f. bird**, (orn.) fragata, rabihorcado.

fright [frájt]. I. *s.* susto, espanto, terror, pavor; (fam.) espantajo, estantigua. II. *va.* = FRIGHTEN.

frighten [-ẹn], *va.* espantar, asustar, amedrentar, aterrorizar, amilanar, asombrar, dar miedo a.—**to f. away**, ahuyentar, espantar.

frightful [-fụl], *a.* espantoso, horroroso, terrible, tremebundo; feísimo.—**frightfully** [-ị], *adv.* espantosamente, terriblemente.—**frightfulness** [-nịs], *s.* horror, espanto; terror.

frigid [frídžịd], *a.* frío, frígido, gélido; indiferente.

frigidity [fridžídịtị], *s.* frialdad, frigidez, frío; indiferencia, falta de ardor; impotencia.

frigidly [frídžịdlị], *adv.* fríamente.

frigorific [frigorífịk], *a.* frigorífico.

frill [fril]. I. *s.* (cost.) lechuga, escarola; faralá, chorrera.—*pl.* (fam.) ringorrangos, arrequives. II. *va.* (cost.) alechugar, escarolar. III. *vn.* escarolarse.

fringe [frịndž]. I. *s.* (cost.) fleco, cairel, pestaña; orla, borde, margen, *mf.* II. *va.* guarnecer con fleco, cairelar; orlar.—**fringeless** [-lịs], *a.* sin fleco.—**fringy** [-ị], *a.* floqueado.

Fringillidae [frịndžílịdi], *s. pl.* (orn.) fringílidos. —**fringilline** [-aịn], *a.* fringilino, fringílido.

frippery [frípœrị]. I. *s.* prendería; trapería; baratillo; fruslería. II. *a.* despreciable, frívolo.

Frisian [frížạn], *a. y s.* frisón.

frisk [frịsk]. I. *vn.* saltar, brincar, cabriolar, triscar; retozar, travesear. II. *va.* (fam.) registrarle los bolsillos y la ropa a uno, en busca de armas ocultas, etc., o para robarle. III. *s.* retozo; brinco, salto.

frisker [-œ(r)], *s.* retozón, juguetón, zarandillo. —**frisket** [-ịt], *s.* (impr.) frasqueta; calzo, alza (ll. t. **f. sheet**).—**friskiness** [-inịs], *s.* calidad de retozón.—**frisky** [-ị], *a.* retozón, vivaracho, (en)revesado.

frit [frịt], I. *s.* (vid.) frita. II. *va.* fritar; derretir.

fritter [frítœ(r)]. I. *s.* (coc.) buñuelo, churro, fritillas, *f. pl.*, fritura, frisuelo, fruta de sartén; quesadilla; fragmento, trozo, triza. II. *va.* desmenuzar; desperdiciar.—**to f. away**, desperdiciar o malgastar a poquitos.

frivolity [frịvólịtị], *s.* frivolidad, liviandad.

frivolous [frívọlạs], *a.* frívolo, fruslero, liviano, vano, baladí.—**frivolously** [-lị], *adv.* frívolamente.—**frivolousness** [-nịs], *s.* frivolidad.

frizz, frizzle [friz, frízl]. I. *va.* frisar; rizar, encrespar. II. *s.* rizo, bucle.

frizzler [frịzlœ(r)], *s.* rizador, frisador.

frizz(l)y **frizz(l)(i)j**], *a.* rizado, frisado.

fro [frọu], *adv.* atrás, hacia atrás.—**to and f.**, de una parte a otra, de acá y allá.

frock [frak], *s.* (cost.) túnico, vestido de mujer o de niño; blusa.—**f. coat**, levita.

frog [frág], *s.* (zool.) rana; ranilla, horquilla (del casco del caballo); (f. c.) crucero, corazón, rana (de un desvío); (elec.) rana, desvío; (cost.) alamar, recamo.—**f. eye**, parches blancos hongosos del tabaco.—**f. in the throat**, carraspera.

frogfish [-fịŝ], *s.* (ict.) rana pescadora o marina, pejesapo.

froggy [-ị], *a.* lleno de ranas.

frogtongue [-tʌŋ], *s.* (med., vet.) ránula, sapillo.

frolic [frálịk]. I. *s.* juego, retozo, travesura. II. *a.* alegre, juguetón, travieso. III. *vn.* juguetear, retozar, triscar, jaranear.—**frolicsome** [-sʌm], *a.* juguetón, travieso, retozón.

from [fram], *prep.* de; desde; de parte de; a fuerza de; por, a causa de; según; con.—**f. behind**, desde atrás, por detrás.—**f. memory**, de memoria.—**f. now on**, de ahora en adelante, en lo sucesivo.—**f. nature**, del natural.—**f. off**, desde lejos, fuera de.—**f. on high**, desde lo alto.—**f. out**, de, desde, del fondo de.—**f. pity**, por piedad.

frond [fránd], *s.* (bot.) fronda, fronde; hoja.—**frondage** [-ịdž], *s.* frondosidad, follaje, frondas, *f. pl.*

frondescence [-ésẹns], *s.* (bot.) foliación; frondosidad.—**frondiferous** [-ífẹrạs], *a.* (bot.) frondífero, frondoso.—**frondose** [-ọus], *a.* (bot.) frondoso.

front [frʌnt]. I. *s.* frente, *f.*, faz, cara; audacia, descaro; (mil.) frente, *m.*; (arq.) frontispicio, fachada, portada, lienzo; (igl.) frontal; (teat.) sala, auditorio; (cost.) pechera, delantera, camisolín; (carr.) testera; (zap.) caña de una bota.—**f. axle**, (carr., aut.) eje delantero.—**f. door**, puerta principal o de entrada.—**f. drive**, (aut.) tracción delantera.—**f. rank**, primera fila.—**f. row**, delantera, primera fila.—**f. seat**, asiento delantero.—**from the f.**, de frente.—**in f.**, delante, (en)frente, frontero.—**in f. of**, (por) delante o enfrente de. II. *a.* anterior, delantero, frontero; frontal.—**f. room**, cuarto que da a la calle.—**f. view**, vista de frente. III. *va.* hacer frente a, mirar, dar o caer a; poner frente o fachada a; arrostrar. IV. *vn.* estar al frente de.

frontage [-ịdž], *s.* extensión lineal de frente.

frontal [-ạl]. I. *a.* frontero, anterior; (anat.) frental o frontal. II. *s.* (anat.) (hueso) frontal o coronal; frentero; (igl.) frontal; (arq.) frontón.

frontier [frʌntr]. I. *s.* frontera; raya, límite, término; confines de la parte civilizada o explorada de un país, fronteras de las tierras vírgenes. II. *a.* fronterizo; limítrofe; de exploración o colonización; de explorador o colonizador (con referencia a regiones incultas o inexploradas).—**f. town**, población fronteriza.—**frontiersman** [-zmạn], *s.* habitante de la frontera; colonizador; explorador.

frontispiece [frántịspịs], *s.* (arq., impr.) fachada, portada, frontis(picio) (de un libro o edificio).

frontlet [frántlịt], *s.* venda para la frente; frentero o frontero (para niños); (tal.) frontalera.

frost [fróst]. I. *s.* escarcha, rosada; helada, hielo. —**f. line**, profundidad a que llegan las heladas. II. *va.* escarchar; congelar; dañar (el frío); deslustrar (vidrio); (coc.) garapiñar (pasteles). III. *vn.* escarchar, helar, congelarse.

frostbite [-bajt]. I. *s.* congelación; lesión cutánea producida por el frío. II. *va.* congelar; dañar por el frío.

frostbitten [-bịtẹn], *a.* helado, congelado, quemado o marchitado por el hielo o la escarcha.

frosted [-ịd], *pa. y a.* escarchado; deslustrado; mate; (coc.) garapiñado.

frostiness [-inịs], *s.* escarcha.

frosting [-iŋ], *s.* en pastelería, capa de clara de huevo batida con azúcar; imitación de escarcha en los metales, vidrios, etc.

frostwork [-wœrk], *s.* garapiña; ramajes de la escarcha.

frosty [-ị], *a.* que tiene o parece escarcha; frío, indiferente; cano, canoso.

froth [fróθ]. I. *s.* espuma; bambolla, frivolidad. II. *vn.* espumar, hacer espuma; echar espuma.—**to f. at the mouth**, echar espuma por la boca.—**frothily** [-ịlị], *adv.* con espuma; frívolamente.—**frothiness** [-inịs], *s.* espumosidad; frivolidad.—**frothy** [-ị], *a.* espumoso; frívolo, vano.

frouzy [fráuzị], *a.* = FROWZY.

froufrou [frúfru], *s.* frufrú.

froward [fróuŵạrd], *a.* indócil, díscolo; insolente. —**frowardly** [-lị], *adv.* díscolamente; protervamente.—**frowardness** [-nịs], *s.* indocilidad; insolencia.

frown [fráun]. **I.** *va.* (gen. con **down, on** o **upon**) mirar con ceño o de mal ojo; desaprobar. **II.** *vn.* arrugar la frente, fruncir el ceño o entrecejo; enfurruñarse. **III.** *s.* ceño, entrecejo; esguince; desagrado, enojo.—**frowns of fortune,** reveses de fortuna.

frowning [-iŋ]. *a.* fosco, torvo, ceñudo.

frowningly [-lị], *adv.* con ceño, de mal ojo.

frowzy, frowsy [fráuzị], *a.* desaliñado, desaseado, sucio; mal peinado; maloliente.

froze [fróuz], *pret.* de TO FREEZE.

frozen [-ẹn], *pp.* de TO FREEZE.

fructiferous [frʌktíferʌs], *a.* fructífero.

fructification [frʌktịfịkéịʃọn], *s.* (bot.) fructificación; fruto.—**fructify** [-faị]. **I.** *va.* fertilizar, fecundar. **II.** *vn.* fructificar.

fructose [frʌktoụs], *s.* (quím.) fructosa, levulosa extraída de frutas o miel.

frugal [frúgạl], *a.* frugal.—**frugality** [frụgǽlịtị], *s.* frugalidad.—**frugally** [frúgạlị], *adv.* frugalmente.

frugivorous [frudʒívọrʌs], *a.* frugívoro.

fruit [frút]. **I.** *s.* fruto; fruta; frutas.—**f. basket,** frutero, cesta para frutas.—**f. bat,** (zool.) murciélago frugívoro.—**f.-bearing,** frutal, fructífero.—**f. cake,** torta o pastel de frutas. —**f. dealer,** frutero.—**f. dish,** plato frutero.— **f. dryer,** secador de frutas.—**f.-eating,** frugívoro.—**f. jar,** vaso o tarro para frutas.—**f. juice,** jugo o zumo de frutas.—**f. parer,** perero.—**f. piece,** (pint.) frutaje, frutero.— **f. press,** aparato para prensar frutas.—**f. stand,** puesto de frutas.—**f. store,** frutería. —**f. sugar** = FRUCTOSE.—**f. tree,** (árbol) frutal. **II.** *va.* y *vn.* (hacer) frutar, producir frutas; dar fruto.

fruitage [-ịdʒ], *s.* fruta; fruto.

fruiter [-œ(r)], *s.* (mar.) buque frutero.

fruiterer [-œ(r)], *s.* frutero.

fruitful [-fụl], *a.* feraz, fértil, fructífero; productivo; prolífico, fecundo; fructuoso, provechoso.

fruitfully [-lị], *adv.* fructíferamente; fructuosamente; fértilmente, prolíficamente.—**fruitfulness** [-nịs], *s.* fertilidad; fecundidad.

fruition [frụíʃọn], *s.* fruición; goce, gusto, complacencia.

fruitless [frútlịs], *a.* estéril, infructuoso, vano.

fruitlessly [-lị], *adv.* infructuosamente.

fruitlessness [-nịs], *s.* esterilidad; infructuosidad.

fruity [frútị], *a.* de olor o sabor de fruta.

frumentaceous [frumæntéịʃʌs], *a.* frumenticio.

frumenty [frúmẹntị], *s.* manjar hecho de trigo cocido con leche.

frump [frʌmp], *s.* mujer desaliñada o desaseada, vestida a la antigua y a veces regañona o chismosa.—**frumpish, frumpy** [-ịʃ, -ị], *a.* desaseado; pasado de moda (traje); a veces, malhumorado, de mal genio.

frush [frʌʃ], *s.* (vet.) arestín.

frustrate [frʌstreịt]. **I.** *va.* frustrar, burlar, desbaratar, privar; anular. **II.** *a.* (ant.) frustrado, burlado; nulo.—**frustration** [-éịʃọn], *s.* frustración, contratiempo, chasco; privación.— **frustrative** [-ịv], *a.* frustratorio.

frustum [frʌstʌm], *s.* (geom.) cono o pirámide truncados, tronco de cono o de pirámide.

frutescence [frụtésẹns], *s.* (bot.) calidad de fruticoso o leñoso.

frutescent [-ẹnt], *a.* (bot.) fruticoso.

fruticose [frútịkoụs], *a.* (bot.) fruticoso.

fry [fráị]. **I.** *s.* (*pl.* FRIES) (coc.) fritada, frito, fritura; (fam.) brete, sofocón.—*sing.* y *pl.* cría, boliche, morralla, pececillos recién nacidos; lechigada; enjambre, muchedumbre, *f.*—**small f.,** (fam.) chiquillería; gentecilla. **II.** *va.* freír. **III.** *vn.* freírse; achicharrarse.—**frying pan,** sartén, *f.*—**to fall out of the f. pan into the fire,** huir del fuego y dar en las brasas.

fucaceous [fjukéịʃʌs], *a.* (bot.) fucáceo.

fuchsia [fjúʃjạ], *s.* (bot.) fucsia.

fuchsin(e [fúksịn], *s.* (quím.) fucsina.

fucoid [fjúkoịd]. **I.** *a.* fucoideo. **II.** *s.* (bot.) alga parecida al fuco.—*pl.* fucoideas, fucáceas.

fucus [fjúkʌs], *s.* (bot.) fuco, ova.

fuddle [fʌdl]. **I.** *va.* emborrachar; confundir. **II.** *vn.* emborracharse.

fudge [fʌdʒ]. **I.** *s.* embuste, cuento; dulce de chocolate. **II.** *interj.* ¡quita allá!

Fuegian [fjuídʒịạn], *s.* y *a.* fueguino, de la Tierra del Fuego.

fuel [fjúẹl]. **I.** *s.* combustible; pábulo, aliciente. —**f. oil,** petróleo o aceite combustible, aceite de quemar. **II.** *va.* y *vn.* abastecer(se) o aprovisionar(se) de combustible.

fugacious [fjụgéịʃʌs], *a.* fugaz, fugitivo; efímero, transitorio.—**fugaciously** [-lị], *adv.* fugazmente.—**fugaciousness** [-nịs], **fugacity** [fjụgǽsịtị], *s.* fugacidad; calidad de fugitivo.

fugitive [fjúdʒịtịv]. **I.** *a.* fugitivo, huidizo, prófugo; fugaz, efímero, in(e)stable, pasajero, perecedero. **II.** *s.* fugitivo, tránsfuga.—**fugitiveness** [-nịs], *s.* fugacidad; calidad de fugitivo.

fugleman [fjúglmạn], *s.* (mil.) jefe de fila.

fugue [fjug], *s.* (mús.) fuga.

fulcrum [fʌlkrạm], *s.* (mec.) fulcro, punto de apoyo; guindaleta; (bot.) apéndice.

fulfil(l [fulfíl], *va.* colmar, llenar; cumplir; verificar, realizar.

fulfil(l)ment [-mẹnt], *s.* cumplimiento, desempeño, ejecución, realización, colmo.

fulgent [fʌldʒẹnt], *a.* fulgente, resplandeciente.

fulgurate [fʌlgjureịt], *vn.* fulgurar.—**fulgurating** [-iŋ], *a.* fulgurante; (med.) lancinante.— **fulguration** [-éịʃọn], *s.* fulguración; (med.) tratamiento o extirpación por medio de chispas eléctricas.

fulgurite [fʌlgjureịt], *s.* (geol.) fulgurita.

fuliginous [fjụlídʒịnʌs], *a.* fuliginoso, tiznado.— **fuliginously** [-lị], *adv.* de un modo fuliginoso.

full [ful]. **I.** *va.* dar amplitud; hacer espeso o grueso; (tej.) (a)batanar, enfurtir. **II.** *vn.* llenarse, espesarse; llegar la luna a su plenilunio. **III.** *a.* lleno; completo, cabal, repleto, cuajado, atestado; pleno; cumplido; amplio, ancho; rotundo; preñado; puro, sin mezcla; harto, ahíto; copioso, abundante; detallado, extenso; plenario; (fam.) borracho; maduro, perfecto; fuerte; suficiente; (mar.) desplegada, llena (vela).—**f. age,** mayoridad.—**f.-aged,** mayor de edad.—**f. binding,** (enc.) pasta entera.— **f. blast,** pleno tiro.—**f. blood,** sangre pura, raza pura; parentesco por ambos padres.—**f.- bloom,** abierta (una flor); maduro, cabal; desarrollado.—**f. brother, sister,** hermano (-na) de padre y madre.—**f. cock,** montado, amartillado.—**f. dress,** uniforme de gala; traje de etiqueta.—**f.-dress,** de etiqueta; (mil.) de parada, de gala.—**f. gallop,** galope tendido.—**f. house,** concurrencia plena, todos los puestos ocupados.—**f.-iength,** de tamaño natural, de cuerpo entero.—**f. load,** (mec.) plena carga; (aer.) peso total.—**f. moon,** plenilunio, luna llena.—**f. name,** nombre y apellido.—**f. of play,** muy juguetón o retozón. —**f. powers,** facultades amplias, plenos poderes.—**f. sail,** vela llena.—**f.-scale,** de, o en, tamaño natural; (fig.) en grande escala; de gran envergadura.—**f. scope,** carta blanca, rienda suelta.—**f. sea,** mar bravío.—**f.-size(d),** de tamaño natural.—**f. speed,** plena, o toda, velocidad.—**f. speed ahead!,** (mar.) ¡avante a toda máquina!—**f. stock,** (com.) acciones de valor nominal de 100 dólares.—**f. stop,** punto final.—**f.-tide** = HIGH TIDE.—**f. time,** tiempo o período completo, jornada completa, horas normales del trabajo.—**f. uniform,** uniforme de gala.—**f. weight,** peso cabal. **IV.**

s. lleno, complemento; colmo; saciedad; total, totalidad; plenilunio.—**in f.**, completamente, detalladamente; completo; total; por completo.—**to the f.**, enteramente, por completo; hasta no más. V. *adv.* enteramente, del todo, de lleno; totalmente, en pleno; derechamente.—**f.-blooded**, pletórico; sanguíneo; rubicundo; de sangre o raza pura; de raza (caballo).—**f.-blown**, abierta (una flor) del todo.—**f.-bound**, encuadernado en piel.—**f.-faced**, carilleno, carigordo; (impr.) letra negra.—**f.-fashioned**, ajustado en todas sus partes (apl. esp. a medias, etc.).—**f.-fledged**, completo, acabado.—**f.-grown**, maduro, crecido, completamente desarrollado.—**f.-manned**, con la dotación completa.—**f.-rigged**, (mar.) completamente equipado (de palos, velas, etc.).—**f. well**, muy bien, perfectamente.—**(at) f. blast**, a plena capacidad; sin coto, hasta más no poder.—**(at) f. speed**, a toda velocidad; a rienda suelta.—**in f. swing**, en plena operación.—**(under) f. sail**, a toda vela; con energía, resueltamente.

fuller [fúlœ(r)], *s.* batanero.—**f.'s earth**, (tej.) tierra de batán, galactita, arcilla grasa.—**f.'s thistle o teasel**, cardo de bataneros, palmar.

fullery [fúlœri], *s.* batán.

fulling [fúliŋ], *s.* abatanado, enfurtido.—**f. mill**, batán.

ful(l)ness [fúlnis], *s.* plenitud, copia, llenura, abundancia; hartura, saciedad; complemento.

fully [fúli], *adv.* entera o completamente; de lleno.

fulminant [fÁlminant], *a.* fulminante.

fulminate [-eit]. I. *va. y vn.* volar, hacer explosión, estallar; tronar, detonar; fulminar; condenar, censurar, o amenazar con vehemencia. II. *s.* (quím.) fulminato.

fulminating [-iŋ], *a.* fulminante.—**f. cap**, cápsula fulminante.—**f. compound**, **f. powder**, pólvora fulminante.—**f. mercury**, fulminato de mercurio.

fulmination [-éiṣon], *s.* fulminación; detonación.

fulminatory [-atori], *a.* fulminante, fulminoso, fulmíneo.

fulmine [fÁlmin]. I. *va.* fulminar. II. *vn.* tronar.

fulminic [fÁlmínik], *a.* (quím.) fulmínico.

fulsome [fúlsam], *a.* bajo, grosero, repugnante; de mal gusto, ofensivo (apl. esp. a los elogios excesivos o insinceros).—**fulsomely** [-li], *adv.* baja o groseramente; asquerosamente.—**fulsomeness** [-nis], *s.* asquerosidad; carácter repugnante u ofensivo.

fulvous [fÁlvas], *a.* leonado, amarillo rojizo.

fumaric [fiumárik], *a.* (quím.) fumárico.

fumarole [fiúmaroul], *s.* fumarola, grieta que arroja vapores volcánicos.

fumble [fÁmbl], *va. y vn.* chapucear; hacer las cosas sin habilidad o destreza; buscar a tientas (en el bolsillo, etc.); parar una pelota desmañadamente; tartamudear.—**to f. along**, andar a tientas.

fumbler [-blœ(r)], *s.* chapucero, desmañado.—**fumblingly** [-bliŋli], *adv.* chapuceramente.

fume [fium]. I. *s.* vapor, gas, humo; emanación; vaho, tufo; cólera, acaloramiento.—*pl.* (quím.) vapores. II. *va.* ahumar; sahumar; fumigar; avahar, exhalar. III. *vn.* humear; exhalar vapores; avahar; encolerizarse, enojarse.

fumigate [fiúmigeit], *va.* fumigar, ahumar; perfumar.—**fumigation** [-éiṣon], *s.* sahumerio, sahumo; (med.) fumigación.—**fumigator** [-eito(r)], *s.* fumigador.—**fumigatory** [-atori], *s. y a.* fumigatorio.

fuming [fiúmiŋ]. I. *s.* sahumerio; enojo. II. *a.* fumante, humeante.

fumitory [fiúmitori], *s.* (bot.) fumaria, palomina.

fumy [fiúmi], *a.* humoso, fumoso.

fun [fan]. I. *s.* broma, chacota, chanza, chiste, chuscada, burla; diversión, holgorio.—**for f.**,

o **in f.**, en broma.—**to be f.**, (fam.) ser divertido.—**to have f.**, (fam.) divertirse, pasar un buen rato.—**to make f. of**, burlarse de. II. *vn.* (fam.) chancear.

funambulatory [fiunǽmbiulatori], *a.* funambulesco; propio de volatines.—**funambulist** [-list], *s.* funámbulo, volatín o volatinero.

function [fÁŋkṣon]. I. *s.* (ing. ord., mat., fisiol., etc.) función. II. *vn.* funcionar.—**functional** [-al], *a.* funcional.—**functionary** [-eri], *s.* funcionario.—**functioning** [-iŋ], *s.* función, funcionamiento, marcha.

fund [fand]. I. *s.* fondo (dinero); caja (de caridad, etc.); acopio; reserva.—*pl.* fondos, dinero. II. *va.* consolidar (una deuda).

fundable [-abl], *a.* consolidable.

fundament [fÁndament], *s.* fundamento, principio, cimiento; (anat.) ano, (fam.) nalgas, trasero.

fundamental [fandaméntal]. I. *a.* fundamental; cardinal, esencial.—**f. colors**, colores elementales. II. *s.* fundamento.

fundamentalism [-izm], *s.* ortodoxia, fundamentalismo, adhesión a la interpretación literal de la Biblia (entre los protestantes).—**fundamentalist** [-ist], *s.* ortodoxo, fundamentalista, literalista.

fundamentally [-i], *adv.* fundamentalmente.

funded [fándid], *a.* consolidado; acumulado e invertido.—**f. debt**, deuda consolidada.

fundholder [fándhouldœ(r)], *s.* rentista.

fundus [fándas], *s.* fundamento, cimiento; (anat.) fondo; (for.) fundo.

funeral [fiúneral]. I. *a.* funeral, funerario, fúnebre.—**f. director**, empresario funerario, director de pompas fúnebres.—**f. home o parlor(s)**, funeraria, mortuoria.—**f. pile**, pira, hoguera.—**f. procession**, cortejo fúnebre. II. *s.* funeral, funerales, exequias; entierro; duelo.

funerary [fiúnereri], *a.* fúnebre; funéreo.

funereal [fiunírial], *a.* fúnebre; funéreo.

fungi [fándžai], *pl.* de FUNGUS.

fungicide [fÁndžisaid], *s.* fungicida, m., substancia para destruir hongos.—**fungiform** [-form], *a.* fungiforme, de forma de hongo.

fungoid [fáŋgoid], *a.* fungoso.

fungosity [faŋgásiti], *s.* fungosidad.

fungous [fáŋgas], *a.* fungoso; hongoso.

fungus [fÁŋgas]. I. *s.* (bot.) hongo; honguillo; moho; (med.) hongo, fungosidad. II. *a.* = FUNGOUS.

funicle [fiúnikl], *s.* cuerdecilla, funículo.

funicular [fiuníkiulā(r)], *a.* funicular.—**f. railway**, (f. c.) ferrocarril funicular.

funiculus [-las], *s.* (bot.) funículo; (anat.) funículo, cordón espermático; cordón umbilical.

funnel [fánel]. I. *s.* embudo, envasador; túnel, cañón, humero; chimenea de un vapor, etc.; (fund.) boca de carga.—**f.-shaped**, de forma de embudo, abocinado. II. *va. y vn.* encauzar(se), concentrar(se).

funnies [fániz], *s. pl.* láminas chistosas, tiras cómicas, caricaturas (de un periódico).

funny [fáni], *a.* cómico, divertido, gracioso, chistoso, ocurrente, chusco; (fam.) extraño, curioso.—**f. bone**, (fam.) cóndilo interno del húmero junto al cual pasa el nervio ulnar en el codo.—**f. business**, (fam.) treta; picardía, fraude.

fur [fœr]. I. *s.* piel, *f.* (para abrigo o adornos); borra, sarro, roya; (carp.) costilla; (med.) saburra. II. *va.* cubrir, forrar o adornar con pieles; depositar sarro; (alb.) separar de la pared con tiras los listones de enlucir; (mar.) forrar un buque; quitar incrustaciones a las calderas. III. *vn.* formarse incrustaciones.

furbelow [fœrbelou]. I. *s.* (cost.) farfalá, volante, (Cuba) vuelo. II. *va.* adornar con volantes.

furbish [fœrbiṣ], *va.* acicalar, pulir, limpiar.

furcate [fœrkeit], *a.* ahorquillado.

furcation [-éiṣon], *s.* bifurcación.

furfur [fǽrfœ(r)], s. (med.) fúrfura, caspa.

furfuraceous [-éįŝįʌs], a. furfuráceo, parecido al salvado o la caspa.

furious [fiúrįʌs], a. furioso, enfurecido, furibundo, rabioso.—**furiously** [-lį], adv. furiosamente.

furl [fœrl], va. plegar, recoger; (mar.) aferrar, empañicar.—f. **lines**, aferravelas.

furlong [fǽrlɔŋ], s. estadio (⅛ milla).

furlough [fǽrlou], I. s. (mil.) licencia. II. va. licenciar.

furnace [fǽrnįs], s. horno; hornillo; hogar (de caldera); calorífero (para calentar las habitaciones).—f. **bridge**, (m. v.) altar.—f. **charger**, cebadera.

furnaceman [-mạn], s. hornero (encargado de un horno).

furnish [fǽrnįŝ], va. surtir, suplir, suministrar, proporcionar; aparejar, equipar; amueblar.

furnished [-t], a. amueblado.

furnisher [-œ(r)], s. amueblador, decorador; proveedor.

furnishing [-įŋ], s. habilitación, equipo, suministro.—pl. equipos, accesorios, útiles, fornituras, avíos, adminículos, mobiliario.—f. **goods**, (com.) artículos para caballero.

furniture [fǽrnįchųr], s. mobiliario, mueblaje; muebles; ajuar; equipo; adornos, accesorios, avíos; (mil.) fornitura(s); (mar.) aparejo.—f. **factory** o **store**, mueblería.—f. **maker** o **seller**, mueblista.—f. **van**, carro de mudanzas.

furor(e [fiúror], s. furor, furia, rabia; frenesí; entusiasmo.

furred [fœrd], a. forrado o cubierto de piel; cubierto con sarro o (med.) con saburra (la lengua).—f. **game**, caza de pelo.

furrier [fǽrįœ(r)], s. peletero, manguitero.

furriery [-rį], s. peletería, manguitería.

furring [fǽrįŋ], s. forro o guarnición de pieles; incrustaciones de una caldera, y operación de limpiarla; sarro; (alb.) tiras o tablas que van bajo los listones de enlucido.

furrow [fǽrou], I. s. (agr.) surco; zanja; (fig.) arruga; (carp.) encaje, gárgol, muesca; (arq.) estría, mediacaña. II. va. surcar; estriar; arar.

furry [fǽrį], a. adornado con pieles; sarroso.

further [fǽrðœ(r)], I. a. (comp. de FAR) más; más distante; más amplio; adicional. II. adv. más lejos, más allá; nuevamente, con nuevos informes o detalles; además; aun; además de eso. III. va. adelantar, promover, fomentar, apoyar.

furtherance [-ạns], s. adelantamiento, promoción, ayuda, apoyo, fomento.

furtherer [-œ(r)], s. promotor, patrón, protector.

furthermore [-mór], adv. además; otrosí.

furthermost [-moụst], a. super. más lejano, más remoto.

furthest [fǽrðįst], a. y adv. super. más lejos, más remoto; extremo.

furtive [fǽrtįv], a. furtivo, latebroso, sigiloso.—**furtively** [-lį], adv. furtivamente.

furuncle [fiúrʌŋkl], s. (med.) furúnculo, divieso, nacido.

furuncular [fiųrʌ́ŋkyūlạ(r)], a. furunculoso.

fury [fiúrį], s. furia; frenesí, entusiasmo.

furze [fœrz], s. (bot.) tojo, hiniesta, árgoma, aliaga, aulaga, retama negra.

furzy [-į], a. retamoso; pert. al tojo, etc.

fuscous [fʌ́skʌs], a. fusco.

fuse [fiuz], I. va. y vn. fundir(se), derretir(se). II. s. espoleta, pebete, cebo, mecha, pajuela; (elec.) fusible, cortacircuitos.—f. **block**, o **board**, (elec.) tabla o bloque de fusibles.—f. **link**, (elec.) fusible.—f. **plug**, tapón fusible.—f. **wire**, alambre para fusibles.

fusee [fiųzí], s. fósforo de yesca o cartón; (arti.) espoleta, pipa; caracol o husillo de reloj; (f. c.) llama de señales.

fuselage [fiúzęlįdž], s. (aer.) fuselaje, huso.

fusel oil [fiúzęl ɔ́jl], s. (quím.) líquido que contiene principalmente alcohol amílico.

fusibility [fiuzįbílįtį], s. fusibilidad.

fusible [fiúzįbl], a. fusible, fundible.

fusiform [fiúsįform], a. fusiforme.

fusil [fiúzįl], s. fusil de chispa.

fusileer, fusilier [fiuzįlí̱r], s. (mil.) fusilero.

fusillade [fiuzįléįd], I. s. (mil.) descarga cerrada. II. va. fusilar; atacar con una descarga cerrada (de tiros, preguntas, etc.).

fusing [fiúzįŋ], a. fundente.—f. **point**, punto de fusión.

fusion [fiúžọn], s. fusión; fundición; unión.

fusionist [-įst], s. y a. (pol.) unionista, fusionista.

fuss [fʌs]. I. s. bulla, bullicio, alboroto; alharaca; ajetreo, agitación o actividad inútil.—f. **budget**, (fam.) persona exigente o fastidiosa.—**without f. or feathers**, (fam.) a la llana; sin alboroto, etc. II. va. (fam.) encocorar. III. vn. ajetrearse, agitarse, inquietarse por pequeñeces.

fussy [-į], a. inquieto, remilgado, exigente.

fust [fʌst], s. (arq.) fuste de la columna.

fustian [fʌ́schạn]. I. s. (tej.) fustán, pana; cultedad, culteranismo. II. a. hecho de fustán; culterano, altisonante, retumbante.

fustic [fʌ́stįk], s. (bot.) fustete.

fustigate [fʌ́stįgeįt], va. fustigar.

fustigation [-éįŝọn], s. fustigación, castigo o pena de azotes, palos o latigazos.

fustiness [fʌ́stįnįs], s. enmohecimiento; rancidez.

fusty [fʌ́stį], a. mohoso, rancio; fuera de moda; exageradamente atrasado en ideas, etc.

futile [fiútįl], a. vano, inútil; fútil, frívolo.

futility [fiųtílįtį], s. inutilidad, ineficacia; futilidad.

futtock [fʌ́tọk], s. (mar.) genol, estamenara, singlón, barraganete; arraigada.—f. **shrouds**, pernadas de las arraigadas.

future [fiúchụ(r)]. I. a. futuro, venidero, venturo; (gram.) futuro. II. s. el o lo futuro, porvenir; (com.) artículo de entrega futura.—**in f.**, en lo sucesivo o futuro; de aquí en adelante.—**in the near f.**, en fecha próxima.

futurism [-įzm], s. (b. a.) futurismo.—**futurist** [-įst], s. (b. a.) futurista; (teol.) el que cree que las profecías de la Biblia se cumplirán en lo futuro.—**futuristic** [-įstįk], a. futurista.

futurity [fiųtįúrįtį], s. lo futuro, porvenir.

fuze, fuzee [fiuz, fiuzí], s. = FUSE, FUSEE.

fuzz [fʌz]. I. vn. soltar pelusa o borra. II. s. pelusa, borra, tamo, vello.

fuzzball [-bɔl], s. (bot.) bejín.

fuzziness [-įnįs], s. vellosidad.

fuzzy [-į], a. velloso, cubierto de pelusa.

fyke [faįk], s. nasa para pescar.

fylfot [fílfat], s. svástica.

G

g [dži], s. g; (mús., G) sol.—**G clef**, clave (f.) de sol.—**G-man**, (E. U.) agente indagador, o detective, del Departamento de Justicia.—**G string**, primera cuerda del contrabajo, tercera del violoncelo, viola y guitarra, y cuarta del violín; pampanilla.

gab [gæb]. I. vn. parlotear, charlar, paliquear. II. s. (fam.) locuacidad, charla; (mec.) gancho.

gabardine [gǽbạrdín], **gaberdine** [gǽbœrdín], s. gabardina (tejido y sobretodo).

gabble [gǽbl]. I. va. y vn. charlar, cotorrear; graznar (los gansos). II. s. algarabía; cotorreo, charla; graznido.

gabbler [gǽblœ(r)], s. charlador, picotero.

gabion [géįbįọn], s. (fort.) gavión, m., cestón.

gable [géįbl], s. (arq.) gablete, aguilón, faldón, remate triangular de edificio o pared; pared lateral.—g. **end**, alero, socarrén, pared lateral de gablete o de remate triangular.—g. **roof**, tejado de caballete o de dos aguas.—g. **wall**, pared de caballete o de remate triangular, hastial.

gablet [géjblịt], *s.* (arq.) frontón, tímpano.

gaby [géjbị], *s.* (fam.) simplón, mentecato.

gad [gǽd]. **I.** *vn.* andorrear, callejear. **II.** *va.* (min.) romper (roca) con cuña o taladro. **III.** *s.* (min.) cuña, punzón, aguja, taladro, barra aguzada; lingote; aguijón, chuzo. **IV.** *interj.* (fam. o vulg.) ¡por Dios!

gadabout [-ạbaụt]. **I.** *a.* callejero, cantonero. **II.** *s.* placero, persona callejera; (fam.) pindonga.

gadder [-œ(r)], *s.* callejero, andorrero.

gadding [-iŋ], *s.* vagancia, briba.

gadfly [gǽdflaj], *s.* (ent.) tábano, moscardón.

gadget [gǽdʒịt], *s.* (fam.) dispositivo, artefacto, artificio, cosa (que no se nombra).

gadolinium [gædolíŋjʌm], *s.* (quím.) gadolinio.

Gael [géjl], *s.*, **Gaelic** [-ịk], *s.* y *a.* gaélico.

gaff [gǽf]. **I.** *s.* arpón o garfio; (dep.) espolón de acero (para gallos de pelea); (mar.) botavara. —**g. sail,** escandalosa, vela cangreja.—**to stand the g.,** (fam.) aguantar o resistir bien (penas, castigo, trabajo duro, chanzas, etc.). **II.** *va.* enganchar con garfio.

gaffer [gǽfœ(r)], *s.* viejo, vejete.

gag [gǽg]. **I.** *va.* amordazar; hacer callar; provocar bascas o náuseas; (teat.) meter morcilla. **II.** *vn.* nausear, arquear. **III.** *s.* mordaza; (vet.) acial; asco; lo que produce bascas; (teat.) morcilla; (fam.) chuscada; payasada; timo.— **g. law** o **ruling,** (fam.) ley (*f.*) de la mordaza; reglamento coartador o amordazante. *V.* CLOSURE.

gage [gejdʒ]. **I.** *s.* prenda, caución; guante, gaje, reto; (bot.) variedad de ciruela. **II.** *va.* (ant.) empeñar, dar en prenda; apostar.

gage, *s.* y *va.*, **gager,** *s.* = GAUGE, GAUGER.

gagger [gǽgœ(r)], *s.* el que amordaza.

gaiety [géjẹtị], *s.* jovialidad, alegría, alborozo; broma, algazara; viveza, ufanía.

gaily [géjlị], *adv.* alegremente, jovialmente.

gain [géjn]. **I.** *s.* ganancia, beneficio, provecho; lucro, usura; logro; (carp.) gárgol, ranura. **II.** *va.* ganar, reportar, lograr; granjear; vencer, conquistar; conciliar; propiciar; (carp.) hacer gárgoles.—**to g. ground,** ganar terreno.—**to g. the wind,** (mar.) ganar el barlovento.—**to g. weight,** echar carnes. **III.** *vn.* adelantar (un reloj); (con **in**) ganar, aumentar, crecer; (con **on** o **upon**) avanzar, adelantarse (a), aproximarse, acercarse.

gainable [-ạbl], *a.* ganable, asequible.

gainer [-œ(r)], *s.* ganador, el que sale ganando.

gainful [-fụl], *a.* lucrativo, ventajoso.—**gainfully** [-ị], *adv.* ventajosamente.—**gainfulness** [-nịs], *s.* provecho, ganancia.

gainless [-lịs], *a.* desventajoso; infructuoso.

gainlessness [-nịs], *s.* infructuosidad.

gainsay [géjnséj], *va.* (pret. y pp. GAINSAID) contradecir, negar; disputar; oponerse a; prohibir. —**gainsayer** [-œ(r)], *s.* contradictor.—**gainsaying** [-iŋ], *s.* contradicción, negación; oposición.

gait [gejt], *s.* marcha, paso, andadura; porte.— **at a good g.,** a buen paso.

gaiter [géjtœ(r)], *s.* borceguí, polaina, botín, botina.

gala [géjlạ], *a.* y *s.* (de) gala, (de) fiesta.

galactic [galǽktịk], *a.* (ga)láctico, ref. a la leche; (astr.) galáctico.

galactometer [gælæktámetœ(r)], *s.* (ga)lactómetro.

galantine [gǽlạntin], *s.* (coc.) galantina.

Galatian [galéjṣạn], *s.* y *a.* gálata, *mf.*

Galaxy [gǽlạksị], *s.* (astr.) Galaxia, Vía Láctea; (g.) grupo notable, constelación (fig.).

galbanum [gǽlbạnʌm], *s.* gálbano.

gale [géjl], *s.* viento fuerte, ventarrón; (fig.) algazara.

galea [géjljạ], *s.* yelmo, gálea, casco.

galena [galínạ], *s.* (min.) galena.

Galenic(al [galénịk(ạl], *a.* (med.) galénico.

Galenism [géjlẹnizm], *s.* (med.) galenismo.

Galenist [-ịst], *s.* galenista.

Galician [galíṣạn], *s.* y *a.* gallego.

Galilean [gælịlíạn], *s.* y *a.* galileo.

galilee [gǽl.lị], *s.* (arq.) galilea.

galimatias [gæliméjṣạs], *s.* galimatías (fam.).

galiot [gǽljọt], *s.* (mar.) galeota.

galipot [gǽlịpat], *s.* galipodio.

gall [gɔl]. **I.** *s.* hiel, *f.*, bilis; amargura, aspereza; odio, rencor; (fam.) descaro; (vet.) rozadura o matadura.—**g., g. apple,** (bot.) agalla.—**g. bladder,** (anat.) vesícula biliar, vejiga de la bilis.—**g. wasp** = GALLFLY. **II.** *va.* y *vn.* ludir, raspar; irritar, hostigar.

gallant [gǽlạnt]. **I.** *a.* galante, cortés; galanteador, cortejador; gallardo, bizarro, airoso. **II.** *s.* galán; cortejo; chichisbeo. **III.** [gạlǽnt], *va.* galantear, cortejar, requebrar.

gallant [gǽlạnt], *a.* valeroso, valiente.

gallantly [-lị], *adv.* valerosamente; galantemente.

gallantry [-rị], *s.* valentía, gallardía, valor; galantería, galanteo.

gallate [gǽlejt], *s.* (quím.) galato; agallato.

galleass [gǽljæs], *s.* (mar.) galeaza.

galleon [gǽljọn], *s.* (mar.) galeón.

gallery [gǽlẹrị], *s.* galería; tribuna; balcón corrido; pasadizo; crujía, corredor (apl. esp. al exterior); (b. a.) colección, galería; (teat.) paraíso, cazuela, gallinero; público que ocupa el paraíso o las tribunas; (fort.) galería; (min.) socavón, galería; (mar.) galería, crujía.

galley [gǽlị], *s.* (mar.) galera; fogón, cocina; (Ingl.) falúa; (impr.) galera.—**g. proof,** (impr.) galerada.—**g. slave,** galeote.

gallfly [gɔ́lflaj], *s.* insecto que produce las agallas.

gallic [gǽlịk], *a.* (quím.) agállico; (quím.) de o pert. al galio.—**g. acid,** ácido agállico.

Gallic(an [gǽlịk(ạn], *a.* galicano, galo.

Gallicism [gǽlịsịzm], *s.* galicismo.

Gallicize [gǽlịsajz], *va.* y *vn.* afrancesar(se).

galligaskins [gælịgǽskịnz], *s. pl.* botarga, calzacalzón.

gallinaceous [gælịnéjṣạs], *a.* (orn.) gallináceo.

galling [gɔ́lịŋ], *a.* irritante.

gallinule [gǽlịnjul], *s.* (orn.) polla de agua.

galliot [gǽljọt], *s.* = GALIOT.

gallipot [gǽlịpat], *s.* orza, bote, pote.

gallium [gǽljʌm], *s.* (quím.) galio.

gallivant [gælịvǽnt], *vn.* (fam.) callejear, pindonguear.

gallnut [gɔ́lnʌt], *s.* (bot.) agalla, bugalla.

Gallomania [gæloméjnjạ], *s.* galomanía.

gallon [gǽlọn], *s.* galón (Ingl. 4,546 litros; E. U. 3,785 litros); medida inglesa para áridos (⅛ bushel).

galloon [galún], *s.* (tej.) galón, trencilla.

gallop [gǽlọp]. **I.** *s.* galope. **II.** *vn.* galopar; ir aprisa. **III.** *va.* hacer galopar.

gallopade [gælopéjd], *s.* caracoleo; (danz.) galop.

Gallophile [gǽlofajl], *a.* y *s.* galófilo, francófilo.

Gallophobe [-foụb], *a.* y *s.* galófobo, francófobo.

Galloway [-wej], *s.* jaca escocesa.

gallows [gǽlouz], *s.* horca; armazón, montante.— **g. bird,** (fam.) malhechor digno de la horca.

gallstone [gɔ́lstoụn], *s.* (med.) cálculo biliario.

gally [gɔ́lị], *a.* amargo, como la hiel.

galop [gǽlọp], *s.* (danz. y mús.) galop.

galore [galɔ́r], *adv.* muchísimos; en abundancia.

galosh(e [galǽṣ], *s.* galocha, choclo, chanclo, zueco, zapatón.

Galtonian [gɔltóụnjạn], *a.* galtoniano.

galvanic [gælvǽnịk], *a.* galvánico.

galvanism [gǽlvạnịzm], *s.* (fís.) galvanismo.

galvanization [-ịzéjṣọn], *s.* galvanización.

galvanize [-ajz], *va.* galvanizar.—**galvanized iron,** hierro galvanizado.

galvanocautery [-okɔ́tœrị], *s.* (med.) galvanocauterio.

galvanometer [-námetœ(r)], *s.* galvanómetro.

galvanometric [-ométrịk], *a.* galvanométrico.

galvanometry [-ámetri̯], *s.* galvanometría.
galvanoplastic [-oplǽsti̯k], *a.* galvanoplástico.
galvanoplasty [-oplǽsti̯], *s.* galvanoplastia.
galvanoscope [-oskoṷp], *s.* galvanoscopio.
gam [gæm]. **I.** *s.* cardumen o banco (apl. sobre todo a las ballenas); (fam.) visita; (fam.) pierna. **II.** *vn.* reunirse en cardumen; visitarse.
gambado [gæmbéi̯doṷ], *s.* polaina.—*pl.* guardaestribos de cuero.
gambier [gǽmbi̯r], *s.* (bot.) gambir de la India, cato (arbusto) amarillo; (farm.) gambir.
gambit [gǽmbi̯t], *s.* (ajedrez) gambito.
gamble [gǽmbl]. **I.** *va.* jugar, aventurar o perder una cosa en el juego. **II.** *vn.* jugar por dinero. **III.** *s.* (fam.) jugada.
gambler [gǽmbloe(r)], *s.* jugador, tahur, garitero.
gambling [-i̯ŋ], *s.* juego (por dinero); tahurería. —**g. den, g. hell** (fam.), **g. house,** garito, casa de juego, matute, tahurería.—**g. table,** mesa de juego.
gamboge [gæmbóṷdʒ], *s.* gomaguta o gutagamba.
gambol [gǽmbol]. **I.** *vn.* brincar, saltar, chozpar, caracolear; juguetear, travesear. **II.** *s.* cabriola, brinco, zapateta, travesura.
gambrel [gǽmbrel], *s.* (zool.) corvejón, tarso, jarrete (esp. del caballo); garabato, gancho.— **g. roof,** (arq.) techo a la holandesa.
game [géi̯m]. **I.** *s.* juego; pasatiempo; partido o partida de juego; chanza, burla, mofa; caza (animales, antes o después de cazados).—**g. bag,** zurrón, morral.—**g. beater,** (caz.) ojeador.—**the g. is up,** se ha levantado la caza; (fam.) el proyecto se ha frustrado.—**g. of chance,** juego de azar.—**g. preserve,** coto, vedado (de caza).—**g. warden,** guardabosque, guarda de coto.—**to make g. of,** burlarse de, mofarse de. **II.** *va.* y *vn.* jugar; jugar fuerte. **III.** *a.* relativo a la caza o al juego; dispuesto a pelear; valeroso.—**g. bird,** ave (*f.*) de caza; gallo de pelea.—**g. fish,** pez (*m.*) difícil de pescar y que es por eso el favorito de los pescadores deportivos.—**to die g.,** morir peleando.
gamecock [-kak], *s.* gallo de pelea.
gamekeeper [-kipoe(r)], *s.* guardamonte, guardabosque.
gameness [-ni̯s], *s.* valor, resolución.
gamesome [-sʌm], *a.* juguetón, retozón.
gamesomeness [-ni̯s], *s.* festividad, alegría, jugueteo.
gamester [-stoe(r)], *s.* tahur; garitero.
gamete [gǽmit], *s.* (biol.) célula generadora.
gametogenesis [gæmetodʒénesi̯s], *s.* (biol.) gametogénesis.
gamin [gǽmi̯n], *s.* pilluelo, golfo.
gaming [géi̯mi̯ŋ], *s.* = GAMBLING.
gamma [gǽmá], *s.* gamma (letra griega).—**g. rays,** (fís.) rayos gama o gamma.
gammer [gǽmoe(r)], *s.* vieja; tía, abuelita.
gammon [gǽmon]. **I.** *s.* jamón; lance del juego de chaquete; (fam.) añagaza, trola, chasco. **II.** *va.* engañar, chasquear; ganar doble partida de chaquete; curar jamón; (mar.) trincar.— **gammoning** [-i̯ŋ], *s.* (mar.) trinca del bauprés.— **gammoning hole,** groera de trinca.
gamogenesis [gæmodʒénesi̯s], *s.* gamogénesis, generación o reproducción sexual.
gamopetalous [-pétaʌs], *a.* (bot.) gamopétalo.
gamosepalous [-sépaʌs], *a.* (bot.) gamosépalo.
gamut [gǽmʌt], *s.* (mús.) gama, escala.
gamy [géi̯mi̯], *a.* (coc.) manido, salvajino; (fam.) peleón, bravo, indómito.—**to be(come) g.,** husmear, oliscar (la carne).
gander [gǽndoe(r)], *s.* (orn.) ánsar, ganso.
gang [gæŋ]. **I.** *s.* cuadrilla, pandilla, partida, banda; revezo; juego (de herramientas, etc.); grupo; (min.) ganga.—**g. boss,** capataz (de obreros).—**g. plough,** o **plow,** arado de reja múltiple.—**g. saw,** sierra múltiple. **II.** *va.* y *vn.* abanderizar(se), formar cuadrilla; (con **up on**)

(fam.) atacar u obrar de concierto contra (alguien).
gangboard [-bord], *s.* (mar.) plancha, andamio. *V.* GANGPLANK.
gangling [gǽŋgli̯ŋ], *a.* delgaducho, larguirucho.
ganglion [gǽŋgli̯on], *s.* (anat.) ganglio.
ganglionic [-áni̯k], *a.* ganglionar.
gangplank [gǽŋplæŋk], *s.* pasamano, plancha.
gangrene [gǽŋgrin]. **I.** *va.* (med.) gangrenar. **II.** *vn.* gangrenarse. **III.** *s.* gangrena.
gangrenous [gǽŋgrinʌs], *a.* gangrenoso.
gangster [gǽŋstoe(r)], *s.* miembro de una cuadrilla de rufianes.
gangsterism [-i̯zm], *s.* bandolerismo organizado, pandillaje.
gangue [gæŋ], *s.* (min.) ganga.
gangway [gǽŋwei̯], *s.* (mar.) pasamano, portalón, tilla.
gannet [gǽni̯t], *s.* (orn.) especie de pájaro bobo, ave marina grande.
ganoid [gǽnoi̯d], *a.* (ict.) ganoideo.
gantlet [gǽntli̯t], *s.* (mil.) baquetas, *f. pl.*
gantry [gǽntri̯], *s.* caballete para barril, poíno; (f. c.) puente transversal de señales.—**g. crane,** puente grúa, grúa de puente.
gaol, gaoler [dʒéi̯l, -œ(r)] = JAIL, JAILER.
gap [gæp]. **I.** *s.* portillo, abertura, raja, resquicio, brecha; vacío, claro, laguna; quebrada; barranca, hondonada; (aer.) entreplano, distancia mínima entre los planos de un biplano. **II.** *va.* hacer una muesca o brecha en.
gape [géi̯p]. **I.** *vn.* bostezar; boquear; estar con la boca abierta; abrirse o estar abierta una cosa.—**to g. at,** embobarse, papar moscas. **II.** *s.* bostezo; boqueada; brecha, abertura, hendedura; (zool.) anchura de la boca abierta.
gaper [-œ(r)], *s.* bostezador; bobalicón, papamoscas.
gaping [-i̯ŋ], *a.* bostezante, boquiabierto.
gar [gar], *s.* (ict.) uno de varios peces ganoideos (lucio, sollo, aguja, etc.).
garage [gará̱ʒ], *s.* garaje, cochera para automóviles; taller mecánico o de reparaciones.
garb [garb]. **I.** *s.* vestido, vestidura, vestiduras, traje; forma literaria; apariencia exterior, aspecto. **II.** *va.* vestir, ataviar.
garbage [gárbi̯dʒ], *s.* basura, desperdicios, *m. pl.*; inmundicia.
garbel [gárbel], *s.* (mar.) aparadura.
garble [gárbl]. **I.** *va.* pervertir, mutilar (un texto, etc.); garbillar; entresacar, escoger. **II.** *s. pl.* (com.) desecho de especias y drogas.
garbler [gárbloe(r)], *s.* garbillador; pervertidor.
garboard (plank) [gárbord], *s.* (mar.) aparadura.
garden [gárdn]. **I.** *s.* huerta, huerto; jardín.—**g. balsam,** balsamina de jardín, nicaraguas.—**g. bed,** o **plot,** plantío; era, cuadro.—**g. mold,** tierra vegetal.—**g. of Eden,** paraíso terrenal. —**g. path** o **walk,** andador.—**g. stuff,** hortalizas, legumbres, verduras, *pl.*—**g. tools,** herramientas jardineras. **II.** *va.* y *vn.* cultivar jardines o huertos. **III.** *a.* común, ordinario; pert. a, o producido en, un jardín.
gardener [-œ(r)], *s.* jardinero; hortelano.
gardenia [gardíni̯á], *s.* (bot.) gardenia.
gardening [gárdni̯ŋ], *s.* jardinería; horticultura.
garfish [gárfi̯ʃ], *s.* (ict.) = GAR.
garget [gárget], *s.* (vet.) enfermedad del ganado, que consiste sobre todo en hinchazón de la garganta; inflamación de la ubre.
gargle [gárgl]. **I.** *va.* y *vn.* gargarizar, hacer gárgaras o gargarismos. **II.** *s.* gárgara, gargarismo; enjuague, colutorio.
gargoyle [gárgoi̯l], *s.* (arq.) gárgola, canalón.
garish [géri̯ʃ], *a.* deslumbrante; charro, llamativo, ostentoso, de mal gusto. *V.* GAUDY.
garishly [-li̯], *adv.* deslumbradora o llamativamente.—**garishness** [-ni̯s], *s.* relumbrón, oropel.
garland [gárlænd]. **I.** *s.* guirnalda, corona; lauro;

crestomatía; (arq.) festón; (mar.) roñada. **II.** *va.* enguirnaldar.

garlic [gárljk], *s.* (bot.) ajo.—**g. mustard**, aliaria.

garlicky [-j], *a.* que huele o sabe a ajo.

garment [gárment], *s.* prenda de vestir; vestido, vestidura.—*pl.* ropa, ropaje, vestimenta.

garner [gárnœ(r)]. **I.** *va.* acopiar; entrojar, almacenar el grano. **II.** *s.* granero, hórreo, acopio.

garnet [gárnjt], *s.* (min.) granate, almandina; color rojo; (mar.) aparejo de carga.

garnish [gárnjš]. **I.** *va.* (coc.) aderezar; guarnecer, ornar, ataviar; (for.) prevenir, notificar; aprestar. **II.** *s.* (coc.) aderezo; guarnición, adorno.—**garnishee** [-í]. **I.** *va.* (for.) embargar (sueldo, fondos, etc.) por entredicho. **II.** *s.* (for.) el que recibe un mandato de entredicho. —**garnisher** [-œ(r)], *s.* (coc.) aderezador; guarnecedor; (for.) el que obtiene un mandamiento de entredicho.—**garnishment** [-ment], *s.* ornamento, adorno; (for.) entredicho.

garniture [gárnjchur], *s.* guarnición, adorno, gayadura.

garret [gærjt], *s.* guardilla, buhard(ill)a, desván.

garrison [gérjson]. **I.** *s.* (mil.) guarnición, presidio. **II.** *va.* (mil.) guarnecer; guarnicionar, presidiar.

garrote [garóut]. **I.** *va.* agarrotar, dar garrote a; estrangular para robar. **II.** *s.* garrote.

garrulity [garúljtj], *s.* garrulidad, locuacidad.

garrulous [gérulʌs], *a.* gárrulo, lenguaz, locuaz.

garter [gártœ(r)]. **I.** *s.* liga, cenojil, ataderas, jarretera.—**G. King-at-arms**, rey de armas. —**g. snake**, nombre de una culebrilla no venenosa.—**the G.**, orden de la Jarretera, y su insignia. **II.** *va.* atar con liga o cenojil; investir con la orden de la Jarretera.

garth [garθ], *s.* patio (de un claustro).

gas [gæs], *s.* gas; (fam., esp. en aut.) gasolina; (fam.) cháchara, charladuría.—**g. bracket**, brazo de mechero de gas.—**g. buoy**, (mar.) boya de gas.—**g. burner**, boquilla, mechero de gas.—**g. carbon**, carbón de las retortas (en las fábricas de gas).—**g. concrete**, hormigón poroso.—**g. engine**, motor de gas, motor de combustión interna.—**g. fitter**, gasista, instalador de gas.—**g. fittings**, tubos y accesorios de distribución interior de gas.—**g. fixtures**, mecheros y accesorios de gas.—**g. helmet** = **g. mask.**—**g. holder**, gasómetro.—**g. jet**, mechero de gas o su llama.—**g. lighter**, encendedor de gas.—**g. machine**, máquina generadora de gas.—**g. main**, cañería maestra o alimentadora de gas.—**g. mantle**, mechero Auer.—**g. mask**, (mil.) careta antigás, careta de protección contra el gas.—**g. meter**, contador de gas.—**g. oil**, aceite para gas de alumbrado, obtenido del petróleo.—**g. pipe**, tubo o tubería de gas.—**g. producer**, gasógeno.— **g. range**, fogón o cocina de gas.—**g. station**, puesto, depósito o surtidor de gasolina (para automovilistas).—**g. tank**, gasómetro.—**g.- tight**, hermético.—**g. tube** = GASEOUS TUBE. —**g. works**, fábrica de gas.

gas. **I.** *va.* (tej.) exponer a una llama de gas o a calor fuerte para aflojar las fibras; chamuscar; (quím.) saturar de gas; (mil.) asfixiar, envenenar o atacar con gas. **II.** *vn.* desprender gas.

Gascon [gáskon], *a.* y *s.* gascón, gascones.

gasconade [-éjd]. **I.** *s.* gasconada, fanfarronada. **II.** *vn.* jactarse, fanfarronear.

gaseous [gésjʌs], *a.* gaseoso, gasiforme; aeriforme.—**g. tube**, (rad.) tubo o lámpara con exceso de gas, que estorba su funcionamiento.

gash [gæš]. **I.** *va.* dar una cuchillada, hacer un chirlo. **II.** *s.* cuchillada; incisión grande.

gasification [gæsjfjkéjšon], *s.* gasificación.

gasiform [gésjform], *a.* gasiforme.

gasify [-faj], *va.* gasificar; aerificar.

gasket [gæskjt], *s.* (mec.) relleno, empaquetadura.—*pl.* (mar.) tomadores, cajetas.

gaslight [gæslajt], *s.* luz de gas; mechero de gas.

gaslighting [-jŋ], *s.* alumbrado de gas.

gasman [gæsmæn], *s.* fabricante de gas; GAS FITTER.

gasogen(e [gæsodžin], *s.* = GAZOGENE.

gasoline [gæsolin], *s.* gasolina, gasoleno.

gasometer [gæsámœtœ(r)], *s.* gasómetro.

gasometry [-trj], *s.* gasometría.

gasp [gæsp]. **I.** *va.* y *vn.* emitir sonidos entrecortados; boquear, jadear. **II.** *s.* boqueada, jadeo.

gassing [gæsjŋ], *s.* tratamiento con gas; (mil.) ataque o asfixia con gas.

gassy [gæsi], *a.* gaseoso.

gast(e)ropod [gæst(e)ropad], *a.* y *s.* gasterópodo.

gastralgia [gæstréldžiʌ], *s.* (med.) gastralgia.

gastric [gæstrjk], *a.* gástrico.—**g. fever**, (med.) fiebre biliosa remitente; dispepsia aguda.—**g. juice**, jugo gástrico.

gastrin [gæstrjn], *s.* (bioquím.) gastrina, hormona que causa la secreción del jugo gástrico.

gastritis [gæstrájtjs], *s.* (med.) gastritis.

gastroenteritis [gæstroentgrájtjs]; *s.* (med.) gastroenteritis.

gastronomer, **gastronomist** [gæstránomœ(r), -mjst], *s.* gastrónomo.—**gastronomic(al** [gæstronámjk(ʌl], *a.* gastronómico.—**gastronomy** [gæstránomj], *s.* gastronomía.

gastroptosis [gæstraptóysjs], *s.* (med.) prolapso del estómago.

gastroscope [gæstroskoup], *s.* (med.) gastroscopio.

gastrotomy [gæstrátomj], *s.* (cir.) gastrotomía.

gastrula [gæstrulʌ], *s.* (embr.) gástrula.

gat [gæt], *s.* (fam.) revólver, pistola.

gate [géjt], *s.* puerta; entrada; portal; portón; (f. c.) barrera; rastrillo, poterna; compuertas de esclusa; vía, camino; garganta, paso; (fund.) vaciadero con un molde, conducto de colada.— **g. money** o **receipts**, (dep., etc.) entradas, ingresos de entrada.—**g. valve**, válvula de tipo de compuerta.

gatekeeper [-kipœ(r)], *s.* portero; (f. c.) guardabarrera.

gateway [-wej], *s.* entrada, puerta, paso (con portillo).

gather [gǽðœ(r)]. **I.** *va.* reunir, coger, recoger, ganar; acopiar, acumular; recaudar, recolectar; juntar, congregar; (cost.) fruncir; colegir, inferir, deducir.—**to g. breath**, tomar aliento. —**to g. dust**, cubrirse de polvo.—**to g. grapes**, vendimiar.—**to g. strength**, recuperarse, tomar fuerzas. **II.** *vn.* unirse, reunirse, juntarse, congregarse; amontonarse, acumularse; aumentarse; concentrarse, condensarse, contraerse; (med.) formarse pus. **III.** *s.* (cost.) frunce, pliegue, plegado.

gatherable [-abl], *a.* deducible; que puede juntarse o cosecharse.

gatherer [-œ(r)], *s.* colector, segador, vendimiador; recaudador, recolector; (cost.) fruncidor.

gathering [-jŋ], *s.* asamblea; reunión; agrupación; (re)colección, acopi(amient)o, amontonamiento, hacinamiento, acumulación; fruncimiento, contracción; cuesta, demanda, colecta; (med.) absceso; (cost.) fruncido.

Gatling gun [gǽtljŋ gʌn], *s.* (arti.) ametralladora Gatling.

gauche [góuš], *a.* zurdo, torpe.

gaucherie [-rj], *s.* torpeza.

gaud [gód], *s.* objeto charro, charrada, charrería.

gaudily [-jlj], *adv.* ostentosamente, fastosamente, charramente.

gaudiness [-jnjs], *s.* oropel, fausto, pompa; calidad de charro o fastuoso.

gaudy [-j], *a.* brillante, vistoso, lucido; llamativo, charro, chillón.

gauge [géjdž]. **I.** *s.* regla de medir; medida, norma, escantillón; calibrador, graduador; indicador; (mar.) calado; (m. v.) manómetro; (f. c.) ancho de la vía, entrevía, (Am.) trocha. —**g. cock**, (m. v.) grifo o llave de nivel.—**g. glass**, (m. v.) tubo indicador de nivel.—**g.

rod, calibre cilíndrico de diámetros.—**g. pressure,** (m. v.) presión manométrica. **II.** *va.* aforar, medir; graduar, calibrar, escantillar; estimar, apreciar, avaluar; (mar.) arquear.

gauger [-œ(r)], *s.* aforador, graduador, mojonero; (mar.) arqueador.

gauging [-iŋ], *s.* aforo, aforamiento; medición; (mar.) arqueaje.

Gaul [gól], *s.* Galia antigua, Francia; galo.

Gaulic [-ik], **Gaulish** [-iš], *a.* galicano, galo.

gaultheria [golθírjä], *s.* (bot.) gaulteria.

gaunt [gont], *a.* flaco, delgado, desvaído.

gauntlet [góntlịt], *s.* manopla; guantelete. **V.** GANTLET.

gauntry [góntri], *s.* = GANTRY.

gauze [góz], *s.* gasa, cendal.

gauziness [-inịs], *s.* diafanidad.

gauzy [-i], *a.* diáfano como gasa.

gavage [gæváž], *s.* alimentación forzada.

gave [geiv], *pret.* de TO GIVE.

gavel [gævẹl], *s.* mazo; mallo, mallete; (agr.) haz, *m.;* gavilla, mostela.

gavial [géjvịäl], *s.* gavial, cocodrilo del Ganges.

gavot(te [gavát], *s.* (danz. y mús.) gavota.

gawk [gók]. **I.** *s.* páparo, bobo, payo. **II.** *vn.* (fam.) papar moscas; bobear, cometer torpezas.

gawky [-i]. **I.** *s.* zote, papanatas. **II.** *a.* bobo, tonto, rudo, torpe, desgarbado.

gay [géi], *a.* alegre, festivo, gayo, ledo, ufano, llamativo; ligero de cascos, calavera.

gayety, gayly [-ẹti, -lị] = GAIETY, GAILY.

gaze [géiz]. **I.** *vn.* mirar con fijeza, clavar la mirada, contemplar. **II.** *s.* contemplación, mirada fija o penetrante.

gazehound [-haụnd], *s.* perro que sigue la presa con la vista.

gazelle [gazél], *s.* gacela, gacel.

gazer [géjzœ(r)], *s.* mirón.

gazette [gazét]. **I.** *s.* gaceta; nombramiento o anuncio oficial. **II.** *va.* publicar o anunciar en la gaceta; nombrar oficialmente.

gazetteer [gazet(r], *s.* gacetero; nomenclador o diccionario geográfico.

gazogene [gæzodžin], *s.* gasógeno, horno para la producción de gases combustibles.

gear [gír]. **I.** *s.* (mec.) engranaje, encaje; mecanismo de transmisión, de distribución o de gobierno; juego; rueda dentada; (mar.) aparejo, maniobra; en general, equipo, vestidos, adornos o atavíos, herramientas, aperos, utensilios caseros, arneses o aparejos de tiro.—*pl.* (mar.) drizas.—**g. box, g. case,** caja de engranajes; (aut.) caja de velocidades.—**g. changing** o **shifting,** cambio de velocidad o de marcha.—**g. cutter,** fresa para dientes de ruedas.—**g.-cutting machine,** máquina de fresar o cortar dientes.—**g. ratio,** relación de multiplicación.—**g.-shift lever,** (aut.) palanca de cambio de marcha.—**g. wheel,** rueda dentada.—**in g.,** en juego, engranado, encajado.—**out of g.,** fuera de juego, desencajado, desengranado.—**to put in g.,** relacionar, conexionar; engranar.—**to throw into g.,** poner en juego; engranar, embragar.—**to throw out of g.,** desengranar, desembragar; desencajar; desmontar. **II.** *va.* aparejar, enjaezar; equipar, preparar; montar, armar; (mec.) engranar, encajar, endentar, embragar. **III.** *vn.* venir o estar en juego; engranar; estar engranado.

gearing [-iŋ], *s.* (mec.) mecanismo o tren de engranaje; engranaje; (mar.) drizas y aparejos.

gecko [gékoụ], *s.* (zool.) salamanquesa.

gee [dži]. **I.** *va.* arrear hacia la derecha. **II.** *vn.* torcer hacia la derecha. **III.** *interj.* ¡arre!; (fam.) ¡cáspita! ¡caramba!

geese [gis], *s. pl.* de GOOSE.

Gehenna [gihénä], *s.* (bib.) gehena, *m.,* infierno.

geisha [géišä], *s.* bailarina y cantante del Japón.

gel [džel], *s.* (biol., quím.) substancia gelatinosa.

gelatin(e [džélạtin], *s.* gelatina, jaletina.

gelatinate, gelatinize [dželétineit, -naiz], *va.*

y *vn.* convertir o convertirse en substancia gelatinosa.

gelatinous [-nʌs], *a.* gelatinoso.

geld [géld], *va.* (*pret.* y *pp.* GELDED O GELT) (vet.) castrar, capar; (api.) castrar las colmenas.—**gelder** [-œ(r)], *s.* castrador, capador.—**gelding** [-iŋ], *s.* castración, capadura; animal capado.

gelid [džélịd], *a.* gélido.—**gelidity** [dželídịtị], **gelidness** [dželịdnịs], *s.* frío extremo.

gem [džem]. **I.** *s.* gema; joya, alhaja; preciosidad. **II.** *va.* adornar con piedras preciosas.

gemel [džémẹl], *a.* gemelo, mellizo.

gemellus [dželélʌs], *s.* (anat.) músculo gemelo.

geminate [džémịneit]. **I.** *va.* geminar. **II.** *a.* (bot.) geminado.

gemination [-éišọn], *s.* geminación.

Gemini [džémịnai], *s.* (astr.) Géminis, *m.*

gemma [džémä], *s.* (bot.) botón, yema.

gemmate [džémeit], *a.* que tiene yemas o botones.—**gemmation** [-éišọn], *s.* (zool., bot.) gemación.

gemmule [džémyul], *s.* (bot.) boncillo.

gemot [gẹmóụt], *s.* (ant.) asamblea.

gendarme [žándarm], *s.* gendarme, polizonte armado.—**gendarmerie** [-(œ)rí], *s.* gendarmería.

gender [džéndœ(r)], *s.* (gram.) género; (fam.) sexo.

gene [džin], *s.* (biol.) elemento determinante de la herencia, substancia, agente o factor generador determinante de los caracteres heredados.

genealogical [džżeniạládžịkạl], *a.* genealógico.—**g. tree,** árbol genealógico.

genealogist [dženiálodžịst], *s.* genealogista.

genealogy [-dži], *s.* genealogía.

genera [džénẹrä], *pl.* de GENUS.

generable [džénẹrạbl], *a.* generable.

general [džénẹrạl]. **I.** *a.* general, común, frecuente, usual.—**g. delivery,** lista de correos.—**g. officer,** (mil.) jefe de grado superior al de coronel.—**g. practitioner,** médico general.—**g. run,** generalidad.—**g. staff,** (mil.) estado mayor general. **II.** *s.* (mil.) general; generala (toque).—**in g.,** en general, por regla general.

generalissimo [-ísịmoụ], *s.* (mil.) generalísimo.

generality [-rélịtị], *s.* generalidad.

generalization [-izéišọn], *s.* generalización.

generalize [-aịz], *va.* generalizar; universalizar.

generally [-i], *adv.* generalmente, por lo común.

generalship [-šịp], *s.* generalato; táctica; habilidad en el manejo.

generate [džénẹreit], *va.* engendrar; producir, causar; (mec.) producir; (mat.) engendrar.

generation [-éišọn], *s.* generación; procreación, reproducción; (mat. y fís.) generación, producción.

generative [-eịtịv], *a.* generativo, genitivo; prolífico, fecundo.

generator [-eịto(r)], *s.* padre, procreador, engendrador; (elec.) generador, dínamo, *f.;* (mec.) generador; (mat.) generatriz.

generatrix [-éịtrịks], *s.* madre, procreadora; (mat.) generatriz; (elec.) generador, dínamo, *f.*

generic(al [džịnérịk(ạl], *a.* genérico.

generically [-i], *adv.* genéricamente.

generosity [dženẹrásịtị], *s.* generosidad, largueza.

generous [džénẹrạs], *a.* generoso; noble, magnánimo; amplio, holgado; estimulante.—**generously** [-lị], *adv.* liberalmente, generosamente.—**generousness** [-nịs], *s.* generosidad, liberalidad.

genesial [džịnísịạl], *a.* genésico.

genesis [džénẹsịs], *s.* génesis, origen, formación; (G.) Génesis, *m.,* primer libro del Pentateuco.

genet [džénịt], *s.* haca o jaca española; burra.

genet [džénịt], *s.* (zool.) jineta, gineta, y su piel.

genetic [džịnétịk], *a.* genesíaco; genético.

geneticist [džịnétịsịst], *s.* geneticista.

genetics [džịnétịks], *s.* (biol.) genética.

Genevan [dženívạn], *a.* y *s.* ginebrino, ginebrés; calvinista.

genial [dʒíːnjəl], a. genial, cordial, afable, alegre; confortante; nupcial; (anat., zool.) geniano.—**geniality** [dʒiːniæliti],̩ s. afabilidad.—**genially** [dʒíːniəli],̩ adv. genialmente, cordialmente.

geniculate(d [dʒiníkyuleit(id)], a. (biol.) geniculado, articulado, doblado.—**geniculation** [-éiʃən]. s. (biol.) geniculación, articulación, nudosidad.

genie [dʒíːni], s. (mit.) genio, demonio.

genii [dʒíːniai], s. pl. de GENIUS.

genista [dʒiníʃtə], s. (bot.) genista, retama.

genital [dʒénitəl]. I. a. genital. II. s. pl. órganos genitales, partes pudendas.

genitive [dʒénitiv], a. y s. (gram.) genitivo.

genius [dʒíːnjʌs], s. genio (fuerza intelectual extraordinaria); genio (sujeto dotado de esa fuerza; en esta acepción el plural es GENIUSES); prototipo; genio, numen; (b. a.) ángel, cupidillo.

Genoese [dʒenoíːz], a. y s. genovés.

genre [ʒáːnr], s. género, especie; (lit.) género; estilo o escrito costumbrista; (b. a.) de género (genre painting, cuadro de género).

gens [dʒenz], s. tribu, f., clan.

genteel [dʒentíːl], a. urbano, cortés, gentil; gallardo, airoso; elegante.—**genteelly** [-i], adv. cortésmente, gentilmente.—**genteelness** [-nis], s. gentileza, gracia, garbo.

gentian [dʒénʃən], s. (bot.) genciana.

gentile, Gentile [dʒéntail]. I. s. gentil; pagano. II. a. gentil, gentílico; (gram.) gentilicio.

gentilism [-izm], s. gentilismo, gentilidad.

gentilitious [dʒentilíʃʌs], a. gentilicio.

gentility [dʒentílity],̩ s. nobleza; gentileza; donosura, gracia, garbo, donaire.

gentle [dʒéntl], a. suave, apacible; dócil, manso; dulce, benévolo, benigno; bien nacido; cortés, comedido.—**the g. sex,** el bello sexo.

gentlefolk [-fouk], s. gente bien nacida.

gentleman [-mən], s. gentilhombre, caballero; hombre decente.—**g. in waiting,** gentilhombre de servicio.—**gentlemanlike** [-laik], a. acaballerado, caballeroso.

gentlemanliness [-linis], s. caballerosidad, hidalguía.

gentlemanly [-li], a. caballeroso, civil, urbano; hidalgo.

gentlemen [-men], s. pl. de GENTLEMAN; señores; (en cartas) muy señores míos (nuestros).—**g.'s agreement,** pacto de caballeros o de naciones, sin valor oficial pero que obliga moralmente.

gentleness [-nis], s. dulzura; docilidad, mansedumbre; urbanidad, delicadeza, nobleza.

gentlewoman [-wumən], s. señora, dama; dama de honor.

gently [-li], adv. dulcemente, suavemente; silenciosamente; mansamente; poco a poco, despacio, con tiento.

gentry [dʒéntri], s. clase media o acomodada; gente bien nacida y de buena crianza.

genuflect [dʒényuflekt], vn. doblar la rodilla.

genuflection [-flékʃən], s. genuflexión.

genuine [dʒényuin], a. genuino, verdadero, auténtico, legítimo; sincero.—**genuinely** [-li], adv. genuinamente; sinceramente.—**genuineness** [-nis], s. pureza, autenticidad, legitimidad.

genus [dʒíːnʌs], s. (biol.) género.

geocentric [dʒioséntrik], a. geocéntrico.

geochemical [-kémikəl], a. geoquímico, relativo a agentes geológicos y químicos.

geochemistry [-kémistri], s. geoquímica, geología química.

geode [dʒíoud], s. (geol.) geoda.

geodesist [dʒiádesist], s. geodesta, mf.

geodesy [-si], s. (mat.) geodesia.

geodetic(al [dʒiodétik(əl], a. geodésico.

geodynamics [-dainæmiks], s. geodinámica.

geogenic [-dʒénik], a. geogénico, geogónico.

geogeny [dʒiádʒeni], s. (geol.) geogenia.

geognosy [dʒiágnosi], s. (geol.) geognosia.

geographer [dʒiágrəfoe(r)], s. geógrafo.

geographic(al [dʒiográfik(əl], a. geográfico.—**g. mile** = NAUTICAL MILE.

geographically [-i], adv. geográficamente.

geography [dʒiágrəfi], s. geografía.

geoid [dʒíoid], s. geoide, la tierra considerada como sólido geométrico.

geologic(al [dʒiolódʒik(əl], a. geológico.

geologist [dʒiálodʒist], s. geólogo.

geologize [-dʒaiz]. I. vn. estudiar la geología. II. va. examinar geológicamente.

geology [-dʒi], s. geología.

geomancy [dʒíomænsi], s. geomancía.

geometer [dʒiámetoe(r)], s. geómetra.

geometric(al [dʒiométrik(əl], a. geométrico.

geometrically [-i], adv. geométricamente.

geometrician [dʒiametríʃən], s. geómetra, mf.

geometrid [dʒiómetrid], s. (ent.) geometrino.

geometry [dʒiámetri], s. geometría.

geomorphy [dʒíomorfi], s. geomorfía.

geophagous [dʒiáfagʌs], a. geófago.

geophysics [dʒiofíziks], s. geofísica, estudio de los caracteres y cambios físicos de la tierra—incluye la geografía física y la geodinámica.

geopolitics [-pálitiks], s. geopolítica.

geoponic(al [-pánik(əl], a. geopónico.

geoponics [-s], s. geoponía, agricultura.

georama [-rámə], s. georama, m., globo geográfico.

georgette [dʒordʒét], s. (tej.) crespón de seda de tejido fino (ll. t. **g. crepe**).

Georgian [dʒórdʒian], a. y s. georgiano.

georgic [dʒórdʒik]. I. a. geórgico. II. s. geórgica.

geoscopy [dʒiáskopi], s. geoscopia.

geosyncline [dʒiosínklain], s. (geol.) geosinclinal, pliegue cóncavo.

geotectonic [-tektánik], a. (geol.) geotectónico.

geothermic [-θέrmik], a. geotérmico.

geotropism [dʒiátropizm], s. (bot.) geotropismo, tendencia hacia el centro de la tierra.

geraniaceous [dʒereiniéiʃʌs], a. (bot.) geraniáceo.

geranium [dʒeréinjʌm], s. (bot.) geranio.

gerfalcon [dʒéérfolkən], s. (orn.) gerifalte.

germ [dʒéérm], s. germen; (biol.) embrión, m.; (bot.) yema, botón, simiente, embrión, ovario; principio, origen, rudimento; (med.) microbio.—**g. cell,** (biol.) célula embrionaria.—**g. plasm,** (biol.) germen plasma; parte (f.) del protoplasma que se transmite de generación a generación y es la causa de la herencia.

german [dʒéérmən], a. de unos mismos padres o abuelos.

German, s. y a. alemán; germánico, tudesco.—**G. measles,** (med.) rubéola.—**G. silver,** plata alemana, metal blanco.—**G. text,** (impr.) tipo alemán.—**G. tinder,** yesca.—**the g.,** el cotillón (baile).

germander [dʒéérmændoe(r)], s. (bot.) pinillo, maro, teucrio, zamarilla.

germane [dʒéérméin], a. pariente; afín; pertinente, relacionado, aplicable.

Germanic [dʒéérménik], a. germánico, alemanisco.

Germanism [dʒéérmənizm], s. germanismo.

germanium [dʒéérméinjʌm], s. (quím.) germanio.

Germanophile [dʒéérménofail], s. y a. germanófilo, partidario de los alemanes.

germicidal [dʒéérmisaidəl], a. germicida.

germicide [-said], s. germicida, m.

germiculture [-kʌlchū(r)], s. (biol.) germicultura, cultivo de bacterias.

germinal [dʒéérminəl], **germinative** [-eitiv], a. germinal, germinativo.—**germinate** [-eit], vn. germinar.—**germination** [-éiʃən], s. germinación.

gerrymander [gerimǽndoe(r)]. I. va. dividir (un estado, etc.) injusta o arbitrariamente en distritos electorales; tergiversar. II. [gérimændoe(r)], s. división arbitraria injusta en distritos electorales; tergiversación, argucia.

gerund [dʒérʌnd], s. (gram.) gerundio.
gerundive [dʒerʌndiv], s. (gram.) gerundio adjetivado.
gest [dʒest], s. (ant.) gesta, romance.
gestation [dʒestéjʃən], s. gestación, preñez, embarazo.
gestatory [dʒéstatori], a. gestatorio.
gesticulate [dʒestíkyuleit], vn. gesticular, accionar.—**gesticulation** [-éjʃən], s. gesticulación.—**gesticulator** [-eito(r)], s. gestero.—**gesticulatory** [-atori], a. gesticular.
gesture [dʒéschü(r)]. I. s. gesto, acción, ademán, signo. II. vn. accionar; gesticular o hacer gestos.
get [get], va. (pret. GOT; pp. GOT o GOTTEN) conseguir, obtener, adquirir; ganar; llevar (premio, ventaja, etc.); reportar, recibir; aprender de memoria; engendrar, procrear; mandar, disponer, hacer que; persuadir, inducir, incitar; procurar, lograr; traer, ir por; poner(se); entender.—**to g. across**, (fam.) hacer comprender; lograr.—**to g. a footing**, establecerse.—**to g. back**, recobrar.—**to g. by heart**, aprender de memoria.—**to g. down**, descolgar, bajar; tragar.—**to g. hold of**, apoderarse de, posesionarse de; coger; aprender.—**to g. in**, allegar, proveerse de; lograr dar, meter, etc. (un golpe, una observación, etc.).—**to g. it**, (fam.) recibir castigo o un regaño; (fam.) comprender.—**to g. off**, enviar; disponer de; librar, sacar (de un aprieto, etc.).—**to g. on**, ponerse (ropa).—**to g. one's goat**, (fam.) serle a uno inaguantable, fastidiarlo.—**to g. one's hand in**, aprender por experiencia o con la práctica.—**to g. on the brain**, tener (algo) metido en la cabeza.—**to g. out**, publicar, editar, sacar.—**to g. the better, o the best, of**, llevar ventaja a; engañar a; ganar a.—**to g. the sack**, (fam.) recibir calabazas.—**to g. the start of**, o **the jump on**, coger la delantera a.—**to g. the upper hand**, imponerse.—**to g. the worse, o the worst**, llevar la peor parte, quedar mal parado; perder.—**to g. up**, arreglar, preparar; idear, inventar; vestir, engalanar.—**to g. up steam**, levantar vapor.—**to g. wind of**, recibir aviso de, tener noticia de, descubrir.—**to have got**, (fam.) tener, poseer.—**g. you gone!** ¡váyase Vd.! ¡largo de aquí!
get, vn. ganar dinero; llegar; ponerse o volverse; hacerse, ser; hallarse, estar; introducirse, meterse.—**to g. about**, divulgarse, hacerse público; levantarse y moverse (un convaleciente).—**to g. abroad**, divulgarse.—**to g. ahead**, adelantarse, ganar la delantera.—**to g. ahead of**, adelantarse a; ganar a.—**to g. along**, adelantar; hallarse; ir pasando.—**to g. along well (badly) with**, llevarse bien (mal) con.—**to g. among**, hacerse uno de.—**to g. around** = TO GET ABOUT, TO GET ROUND.—**to g. at**, ir a; llegar a; atacar; averiguar, descubrir.—**to g. away**, irse; partir; huir, escaparse.—**to g. away with**, llevarse; vencer, ganarle a.—**to g. away with it**, salirse con la suya, llevar algo a cabo pasando por encima de todos o de todo.—**to g. back**, volver, regresar.—**to g. behind**, penetrar, enterarse de los secretos de; quedarse atrás.—**to g. better**, mejorar.—**to g. busy**, moverse, menearse, poner manos a la obra.—**to g. clear**, salir bien, quedar absuelto; vindicarse; zafarse, librarse.—**to g. down**, bajar, descender.—**to g. even with**, hacérselas pagar a; vengarse de.—**to g. forward**, adelantar, medrar.—**to g. home**, llegar a casa o a la meta.—**to g. in**, (lograr) entrar; llegar.—**to g. in the habit of**, acostumbrarse a, contraer el hábito de.—**to g. into**, entrar, penetrar; montarse en (cólera, etc.); meterse en.—**to g. in with**, relacionarse con.—**to g. left**, (fam.) quedarse colgado, o a la luna de Valencia.—**to g. loose**, o **free**, zafarse; quedar libre.—**to g. married**, casarse.

—**to g. near**, acercarse.—**to g. off**, salir de un asunto; escapar, huir; irse; salir; bajar(se), apearse.—**to g. on**, adelantar, medrar; ponerse encima de; subir; montar; entrar en un coche; armonizar.—**to g. on one's legs**, levantarse; mejorar de fortuna.—**to g. on one's nerves**, (fam.) irritar, cansar o fastidiar a uno.—**to g. on with**, llevarse bien con uno.—**to g. out**, salir, salirse; divulgarse.—**to g. out of**, evadir; evitar; escaparse de.—**to g. out of order**, descomponerse, desajustarse.—**to g. out of the way**, apartarse o hacerse a un lado.—**to g. over**, pasar por encima de; vencer (obstáculos); recuperarse de; olvidar.—**to g. ready**, aparejarse, disponerse (a).—**to g. rid of**, zafarse o librarse de, acabar con, quitar de encima.—**to g. round**, evadir, evitar; refutar.—**to g. square** = TO GET EVEN.—**to g. there**, (fam.) llegar al fin que se desea, salirse con la suya.—**to g. through**, pasar, penetrar; terminar.—**to g. through with**, acabar con.—**to g. to be**, llegar a ser, hacerse, ponerse (antes de a.).—**to g. together**, juntarse, reunirse, acercarse; cooperar, obrar de común acuerdo.—**to g. up**, levantarse; subir, ascender.—**to g. under the wire**, (fig.) llegar a tiempo.—**to g. under way**, partir, salir; (mar.) zapar, hacerse a la vela.—**to g. well**, curar, sanar, ponerse bueno.—**to have got to**, haber de, tener que.—**to tell one where to g. off**, decir a uno cuántas son cinco, ponerlo en su puesto, cantárselas claras.—**g. out!**, ¡fuera! ¡largo de aquí!—**g. up!**, ¡arre! (a las bestias).
get, s. engendro; engendramiento; raza; cría.
get-at-able [getétabl], a. accesible, tratable; obtenible, asequible.
getaway [gétawei], s. ida, partida; escape; comienzo (de una carrera); arranque (de un auto).
gettable [gétabl], a. obtenible, asequible.
getter [gétœ(r)], s. persona que consigue o logra.
getting [gétiŋ], s. ganancia; adquisición; procreación.
get-together [gétugeðœ(r)], s. tertulia, reunión social informal.
get-up [gétʌp], s. arreglo, disposición; atavío; traje.
gewgaw [gjúgɔ]. I. s. miriñaque, chuchería, friolera, adorno cursi. II. a. cursi, chillón.
geyser [gájzœ(r)], s. géiser, surtidor o fuente (f.) termal intermitente.
ghastliness [gǽstlinis], s. palidez cadavérica.
ghastly [gǽstli]. I. a. lívido; horrible. II. adv. horriblemente; lívidamente.
ghee [gi], s. aceite de manteca clarificada.
gherkin [gǿrkin], s. pepinillo, cohombrillo.
ghetto [gétou], s. ghetto, barrio de los judíos.
Ghibelline [gíbelin], a. y s. gibelino.
ghost [góust], s. aparecido, espectro, sombra, fantasma, m.; ánima en pena; alma, espíritu; imagen, traza leve; (foto. y ópt.) imagen falsa o secundaria; mancha.—**g. story**, cuento de fantasmas.—**g. writer**, escritor de artículos, discursos, etc., que salen bajo el nombre de otra persona.—**not a g. of a doubt**, ni sombra de duda.—**to give up the g.**, dar, o exhalar, el espíritu, morir(se).
ghostliness [-linis], s. calidad de espectral.
ghostly [-li], a. espectral, fantástico, de duendes o aparecidos.
ghoul [gúl], s. vampiro.—**ghoulish** [-iʃ], a. vampírico; horrible, brutal, asqueroso.
giant [dʒáiant]. I. a. gigante, gigantesco. II. s. gigante.—**g. fennel**, (bot.) cañaheja.—**g. powder**, variedad de dinamita.
giantess [-is], s. giganta.
giaour [dʒáur], s. infiel (en el sentido musulmán).
gib [gib]. I. s. (mec.) chaveta, cuña, contraclavija; aguilón, brazo de grúa.—**cotter (o key) and g.**, clavija y contraclavija. II. va. acuñar, asegurar con chaveta.

gibber [džíbœ(r)], *vn.* (fam.) farfullar. *V.* JABBER.

gibberish [-iš]. I. *s.* (fam.) farfulla, galimatías, jerigonza, jerga. II. *a.* falto de sentido, tonto, deshilvanado.

gibbet [džíbit]. I. *s.* horca, picota, patíbulo. II. *va.* ahorcar.

gibbon [gíbɒn], *s.* (zool.) gibón.

gibbosity [gibásiti], *s.* giba, corcova.

gibbous [gíbʌs], *a.* convexo; giboso, jorobado.

gibbousness [-nis], *s.* convexidad; corvadura.

gibe [džáib]. I. *va.* escarnecer, ridiculizar, mofarse de. II. *vn.* burlarse. III. *s.* escarnio, mofa.

gibingly [-iŋli], *adv.* con burla, burlonamente.

giblets [džíblits], *s. pl.* menudillos de ave.

gid [gid], *s.* (vet.) modorra, vértigo de los animales domésticos.

giddily [gídili], *adv.* vertiginosamente; atolondradamente.

giddiness [gídinis], *s.* vértigo, vahido, desvanecimiento; aturdimiento, atolondramiento, veleidad; devaneo, desvarío.

giddy [gídi], *a.* vertiginoso; voltario, voluble, inconstante; aturdido, atolondrado.—**g. girl**, muchacha casquivana.—**g.-brained, headed o pated**, ligero de cascos, frívolo.—**g.-head, o pate**, persona frívola, con los cascos a la jineta.

gift [gift]. I. *s.* donación; dádiva, regalo, obsequio; don, dote, *f.*, prenda.—**g. of tongues**, don de las lenguas. II. *va.* dotar; agraciar.

gifted [-id], *a.* talentoso, genial; agraciado.

gig [gig], *s.* birlocho, calesín, quitrín; máquina para tundir paño; (mar.) bote, lancha, falúa.

gigantean [džaigæntiạn], **gigantic** [džaigǽntik], *a.* gigánteo, gigantesco.

giggle [gígl]. I. *vn.* reírse tratando de suprimir u ocultar la risa; reírse sin motivo; reírse por nada. II. *s.* risa falsa, risita.

giggler [gíglœ(r)], *s.* persona de risa falsa o de risita.

gild [gild], *s.* = GUILD.

gild [gild], *va.* (*pret.* y *pp.* GILDED o GILT) dorar; iluminar; dar brillo o lustre.

gilder [-œ(r)], *s.* dorador; charolista.

gilding [-iŋ], *s.* doradura; dorado; latón de dorar (con como 95% de cobre) (ll. t. **g. metal**).

gill [džil], *s.* medida de líquidos (⅛ litro).

gill [gil], *s.* (ict.) agalla, branquia; barba (del gallo, etc.); (fam.) papada; (tej.) peine; (mec.) estría de chapa ondulada.

gillyflower, gilliflower [džíliflauœ(r)], *s.* (bot.) alelí.

gilt [gilt]. I. *pret.* y *pp.* de GILD. II. *a.* dorado, áureo.—**g.-edged**, de corte dorado; (fam.) de la mejor calidad.—**g. edges, o leaves**, cortes dorados. III. *s.* dorado; oro en hojuelas; oropel; falso brillo.

gilthead [-hed], *s.* (ict.) dorada; salema.

gimbals [džímbạlz], *s. pl.* (mar.) balancines de la brújula.

gimcrack [džímkræk]. I. *a.* cursi, de baratillo. II. *s.* chuchería, cosa cursi. *V.* GEWGAW.

gimlet [gímlit], *s.* barrena pequeña, taladro.

gimp [gimp], *s.* (tej.) bocadillo, alamar; (fam.) vigor, energía.—**g. nail**, tachuela para tapicería.

gin [džin]. I. *s.* almarrá, alijadora, despepitadora o (Am.) desmotadora de algodón; cabria, malacate, molinete, husillo; bomba movida por un molino de viento; martinete; trampa, armadijo; ginebra (licor de enebro).—**g. fizz**, bebida de ginebra y gaseosa. II. *va.* coger con trampa, despepitar, alijar o (Am.) desmotar (el algodón).

ginger [džíndžœ(r)], *s.* (bot.) jengibre.—**g. ale, beer, o pop**, cerveza de jengibre.

gingerbread [-bred], *s.* pan de jengibre.—**g. work**, adorno cursi, ostentoso, o falto de solidez.

gingerly [-li]. I. *a.* cauteloso, escrupuloso. II. *adv.* cautelosa o cuidadosamente.

gingersnap [-snæp], *s.* galletita de jengibre.

gingery [-i], *a.* parecido al jengibre; picante.

gingham [gíŋạm], *s.* guinga (tela).

gingili [džíndžili], *s.* (bot.) sésamo.

gingival [džindžáivạl], *a.* (anat. y fon.) gingival, perteneciente a las encías.

ginglymus [džíŋglimạs], *s.* (anat.) ginglimo.

ginseng [džínseŋ], *s.* (bot.) ginseng, ginsén.

gip [džip], *va.* destripar los pescados.

gipsy [džípsi], *s.* = GYPSY.

giraffe [džiræf], *s.* (zool.) jirafa; (**C.,** astr.) constelación Camelopardalis.

girandole [džírandoul], *s.* araña, candelabro; (piro.) girándula; (joy.) pendiente.

girasol [džírasạl], *s.* (min.) ópalo de fuego; (bot.) especie de girasol.

gird [gœrd]. I. *va.* (*pret.* y *pp.* GIRDED o GIRT) ceñir; cercar, rodear. II. *vn.* mofarse, burlarse.

girder [-œ(r)], *s.* (constr.) viga, carrera.—**g. bridge**, puente de vigas.—**g. rail**, riel de doble T para tranvías.

girdle [-l]. I. *s.* cinto, cinturón, ceñidor, cíngulo, pretina, faja, cincho; cintura; faja, corsé ligero; circunferencia, cerco, círculo, zona; zodíaco. II. *va.* ceñir, cercar, rodear, circundar, fajar.

girl [gœrl], *s.* muchacha, niña; (fam.) sirvienta, criada.—**g. scout**, niña exploradora.

girlhood [-hụd], *s.* doncellez; calidad o estado de muchacha; vida o edad de muchacha; la juventud femenina.

girlie [-i], *s.* (fam.) muchachita; chica.

girlish [-iš], *a.* de carácter de muchacha; característico de las muchachas; juvenil, propio de niña o joven.

girlishly [-li], *adv.* como una muchacha.

Girondist [džírándist], *s.* y *a.* girondino.

girt [gœrt]. I. *pret.* y *pp.* de TO GIRD. II. *a.* (mar.) amarrado. III. *s.* (constr.) viga, traviesa de piso. IV. *va.* = TO GIRD y TO GIRTH.

girth [gœrθ]. I. *s.* cincha; faja, cinto; periferia. II. *va.* cinchar, ceñir.

girthing [-iŋ], *s.* cinchadura.

gist [džist], *s.* substancia, quid, *m.*, busilis, *m.*

give [gív]. I. *va.* (*pret.* GAVE; *pp.* GIVEN) dar, donar; conceder, otorgar; sacrificar; pagar; producir o causar; dedicar, consagrar.—**to g. advice**, dar consejo; asesorar.—**to g. a good account of one's self**, salir bien, hacerlo bien. —**to g. a lift to one**, ayudar a uno a levantarse o a levantar algo; llevarle (en coche, etc.). *V.* LIFT, *s.*—**to g. a piece of one's mind to**, decir las verdades del barquero, decir cuántas son cinco.—**to g. a thought to**, pensar en, acordarse de (gen. en oración negativa).—**to g. away**, dar, regalar; deshacerse de; vender regalado (casi de balde); contar, divulgar (un secreto); descubrir, traicionar.—**to g. back**, restituir, devolver,—**to g. birth to**, dar a luz, parir; producir.—**to g. chase**, perseguir.—**to g. ear to**, prestar oídos a; escuchar.—**to g. effect to**, poner en ejecución.—**to g. fire**, mandar hacer fuego; disparar.—**to g. forth**, publicar, divulgar.—**to g. ground**, retirarse; ceder.—**to g. it to one**, (fam.) dar de palos a uno, echarle un sermón o (Am.) una raspa; poner a uno como nuevo; regañar a uno.—**to g. leave**, permitir; dar licencia.—**to g. line o rope**, dar rienda.—**to g. mouth to**, proferir, expresar.—**to g. notice**, advertir, hacer saber, informar.—**to g. off**, arrojar, echar, despedir; emitir.—**to g. one the cold shoulder**, recibir a uno fríamente.—**to g. one's self away**, (fam.) enseñar la oreja.—**to g. one's self up**, entregarse, rendirse; abandonarse, desesperarse.—**to g. out**, publicar, divulgar; proclamar; declarar, decir; repartir, distribuir.—**to g. over**, entregar; abandonar; desistir de; desahuciar.—**to g. pause**, dar en qué pensar; hacer pensar; ser peliagudo.—**to g. place**, ceder su puesto; ir seguido (de); dejar el puesto (a).—**to g. points**, dar ventaja, dar tantos (en

el juego); dar consejo, hacer indicaciones útiles.
—**to g. rein,** dar rienda (suelta); dar licencia, dar salida.—**to g. rise to,** dar lugar a, causar, ocasionar.—**to g. room,** hacer lugar; retirarse, apartarse.—**to g. the lie,** desmentir.—**to g. the rod,** azotar, castigar.—**to g. the sack** (fam.) dar calabazas.—**to g. the slip,** dar esquinazo; echar.—**to g. tongue,** empezar a ladrar.—**to g. up,** renunciar a; entregar; resignar; abandonar; dar por perdido; desahuciar.—**to g. up the ghost,** morir; desistir, darse por vencido.—**to g. vent to,** dar salida a; desatarse en.—**to g. voice to,** decir, expresar.—**to g. warning,** prevenir, advertir.—**to g. way,** ceder; cejar; retroceder; ceder su puesto; aflojarse; hundirse; bajar en, caer en (seguido de un número) (apl. a precios). **II.** *vn.* dar libremente, ser dadivoso; dar de sí, aflojarse; ablandarse; ceder; cejar, recular; desteñirse; aguarse; deteriorar.—**to g. back,** retirarse; cejar.—**to g. in,** ceder; acceder; asentir. —**to g. out,** faltar; consumirse, acabarse, agotarse; apagarse; perder las fuerzas; pararse (una máquina, un órgano).—**to g. over,** cesar, suspender; ceder.—**to g. up,** desistir, cejar; darse por vencido; perder la esperanza.

give, *s.* acción de dar de sí o de ceder físicamente (como una cuerda); elasticidad.

give-and-take [-əntéjk]. **I.** *s.* concesiones mutuas, componenda; réplicas y contrarréplicas. **II.** *a.* de componenda, de concesiones mutuas; de réplicas y contrarréplicas compensadas, de dares y tomares.

giveaway [-əwej], *s.* (fam.) revelación indiscreta; acción de dejar ver (algo que se trata de ocultar), o mostrar el juego; ganapierde (en el juego de damas).

given [-ən], *a.* y *pp.* de TO **GIVE;** dado; citado; especificado; (mat.) conocido.—**g. name,** nombre bautismal.—**g. that,** suponiendo que, sabiendo que.—**g. to,** adicto o aficionado a.

giver [-œ(r)], *s.* donador, dador, donante.

gizzard [gízərd], *s.* molleja (de ave); primer estómago (de un insecto).

glabrous [glébrəs], *a.* (zool., bot.) liso, calvo, llano; sin pelo ni pelusa.

glacé [glæséj], *a.* helado; garapiñado; liso y lustroso; glaseado.

glacial [gléjṣəl], *a.* glacial; (geol.) glaciario.—**g. acetic acid,** ácido acético puro o glacial.

glaciate [gléjṣjejt]. **I.** *va.* (geol.) cubrir con hielo glacial; producir sobre una superficie un efecto parecido al hielo. **II.** *vn.* helarse.

glaciation [-éjṣən], *s.* helamiento, congelación. —**glacier** [-œ(r)], *s.* helero, glaciar, ventisquero.—**glaciology** [-álodʒi], *s.* glaciarismo.

glacis [gléjsjs], *s.* (fort.) glacis (*m.*) o explanada.

glad [glæd], *a.* alegre, contento, gozoso; agradable; agradecido.—**to be g.,** celebrar, alegrarse, tener gusto (*I am glad to see you,* me alegro de ver a Vd.; *I shall be glad to go,* tendré gusto en ir).

gladden [-n], *va.* alegrar, regocijar, recrear.

gladdon [glædən], *s.* (bot.) lirio hediondo, jíribe; espadaña.

glade [glejd], *s.* claro, raso; ciénaga.

gladiator [glédjejtə(r)], *s.* gladiador, gladiator.

gladiatorial [glædjətórjəl], *a.* gladiatorio.

gladiolus [glædjóulʌs], *s.* (bot.) estoque; (anat.) mesosternón.

gladly [glédli], *adv.* alegremente; de buena gana, de buen grado, gustosamente.

gladness [-nis], *s.* alegría, placer, gozo.

gladsome [-sʌm], *a.* alegre, contento.—**gladsomely** [-li], *adv.* alegremente.—**gladsomeness** [-nis], *s.* alegría, regocijo.

glair [glér]. **I.** *s.* (coc., anc.) clara de huevo; cualquier substancia viscosa. **II.** *va.* untar con clara de huevo.

glairy [-i], *a.* viscoso, pegajoso.

glaive [glejv], *s.* (ant.) espada, espadón; alabarda.

glamo(u)r [glémo(r)]. **I.** *s.* encanto, hechizo; encantamiento, embeleso; brujería. **II.** *va.* hechizar, encantar.

glamorous [-ʌs], *a.* encantador, hechicero.

glance [gláns]. **I.** *s.* mirada, ojeada, vistazo; vislumbre; fulgor; desviación (por choque); (min.) mineral lustroso.—**g. coal,** antracita.— **at the first g.,** al primer aspecto, a primera vista. **II.** *va.* mirar de o al soslayo, o de refilón. **III.** *vn.* dar un vistazo o una ojeada; tocar o herir oblicuamente; brillar, centellear.—**to g. at,** hojear; referirse a, aludir a.—**to g. off,** desviarse (al chocar).—**to g. over,** echar un vistazo a; hojear (un libro).

glancing [-iŋ], *a.* oblicuo, de refilón (golpe).

gland [glænd], *s.* (anat. y bot.) glándula; bellota; (mec.) cuello, collarín, gola; casquillo del prensaestopas.

glanderous [glændərʌs], *a.* (vet.) muermoso.

glanders [glændœrz], *s.* (vet.) muermo.

glandiferous [glændíferʌs], *a.* (bot.) glandífero.

glandiform [glændjform], *a.* (bot.) glandiforme, abellotado.

glandular [glændʒulə(r)], **glandulous** [-lʌs], *a.* glanduloso, glandular, adenoso.

glandule [glændʒul], *s.* glandulilla.

glans [glænz], *s.* (*pl.* GLANDES) (bot.) bellota; (anat.) glande, bálano; clítoris, *m.*

glare [glér]. **I.** *vn.* relumbrar, brillar; tener colores chillones; (con at) mirar fija y penetrantemente, (fig.) echando fuego por los ojos. **II.** *s.* resplandor, viso; resol; deslumbramiento; mirada feroz y penetrante; superficie lisa y vidriosa. **III.** *a.* liso, lustroso y resbaladizo.

glaring [-iŋ], *a.* deslumbrador; evidente, notorio; de mirada penetrante.—**glaringly** [-li], *adv.* notoriamente, evidentemente; fijamente, penetrantemente.

glass [glás]. **I.** *s.* vidrio; vaso; copa; vidrio o cristal de ventana; espejo; lente, catalejo; ampolleta; anteojo; reloj de arena; contenido de un vaso o copa (*a glass of water,* un vaso de agua; *a glass of brandy,* una copa de brandy). —*pl.* **glasses,** anteojos, gafas; quevedos, lentes.—**g. blower,** soplador de vidrio, vidriero. —**g. blowing,** fabricación de objetos de vidrio. —**g. cutter,** diamante de vidriero.—**g. factory o shop,** vidriería, cristalería.—**g. furnace,** carquesa; horno de vidrio.—**g. roof,** montera.—**g. snake,** (zool.) lución, *m.*—**g. sponge,** esponja silícea.—**g. wool,** tela de vidrio. **II.** *a.* de vidrio.—**g. bead,** abalorio, cuenta de vidrio.—**g. case,** escaparate.—**g. window,** vidriera. **III.** *va.* glasear, satinar; cubrir con, encerrar en vidrio; reflejar.

glassful [-ful], *s.* vaso (contenido de un vaso).

glasshouse [-haus], *s.* vidriería; fábrica de vidrio o cristal; invernadero; galería fotográfica.

glassiness [-inis], *s.* vidriosidad.

glasslike [-lajk], *a.* transparente como vidrio; vidrioso, hialoideo.

glassmaker [-mejkœ(r)], **glassman** [-man], *s.* vidriero.

glassware [-wer], *s.* cristalería, vajilla de cristal.

glasswork [-wœrk], *s.* fabricación de vidrio; artículos de vidrio.—**glassworks** [-wœrks], *s.* fábrica de vidrio o cristales; vidriería, cristalería.

glasswort [-wœrt], *s.* (bot.) sosa, barrilla, almarjo, matojo, sapina.

glassy [-i], *a.* vítreo, cristalino, vidrioso, hialino.

Glauber's salt(s) [glóubœrz solt(s], *s. pl.* (farm.) sal (*f.*) de Gláuber, sulfato sódico cristalino.

glaucoma [glokóumə], *s.* (med.) glaucoma, *m.*

glaucous [glókəs], *a.* glauco, verde claro; (bot.) cubierto de una pelusilla blanca azulosa.

glaze [gléjz]. **I.** *va.* poner vidrios a una ventana; vidriar; barnizar; satinar, glasear; apomazar (cera); esmaltar. **II.** *s.* superficie lisa y lustrosa; barniz, *m.*, lustre; esmalte; capa de hielo.

glazed [-d], *a.* vidriado; satinado; glaseado.—**g.**

earthenware, vidriado.—**g. paper,** papel satinado.—**g. tile,** azulejo.

glazer [-œ(r)], *s.* el o lo que satina, pule, esmerila, etc.

glazier [gléiȝœ(r)], *s.* vidriero.—**g.'s shop,** vidriería.

glazing [gléiȝiŋ], *s.* vidriado, mogate; barnizado; satinado; superficie lustrosa; barniz, *m.,* lustre; vidriería, cristalería.

gleam [glím]. I. *s.* destello, fulgor, viso, centelleo. II. *vn.* centellear, fulgurar.

gleamy [-i], *a.* centelleante, fulgurante.

glean [glín], *va.* espigar, respigar; recoger, juntar; rebuscar.—**gleaner** [-œ(r)], *s.* espigadera; respigador, rebuscador, recogedor.—**gleaning** [-iŋ], *s.* espigueo, moraga, arrebañadura, rebusco.

glebe [glib], *s.* (poét.) gleba, césped, terrón; (Ingl.) tierras beneficiales.

glede [glid], *s.* (orn.) milano.

glee [gli], *s.* alegría, gozo, júbilo; (mús.) canción para voces solas.—**g. club,** coro.

gleeful [-ful], **gleesome** [-sʌm], *a.* alegre, gozoso, contento.

gleet [glít], *s.* (med.) gonorrea crónica, gota militar; blenorrea.

gleety [-i], *a.* blenorrágico.

glen [glen], *s.* hocino, hoyada, vallecico.

glengarry [glengéri], *s.* gorra escocesa.

glenoid [glínoid], *a.* que tiene una pequeña cavidad; (anat.) glenoideo.

gliadin [gláiadin], *s.* (bioquím.) gluten.

glib [glib], *a.* voluble, suelto de lengua.—**glibly** [-li], *adv.* volublemente.—**glibness** [-nis], *s.* volubilidad, facundia.

glide [gláid]. I. *vn.* resbalar, deslizarse, escurrirse; (aer.) planear. II. *s.* deslizamiento, escurrimiento; (aer.) planeo.

glider [-œ(r)], *s.* el o lo que se desliza; (aer.) planeador, deslizador, aeroplano de gravedad (sin motor).

gliding [-iŋ]. I. *s.* deslizamiento; (aer.) planeo. II. *a.* deslizador, deslizante, que se desliza; (aer.) de planear, planeador.—**g. angle,** (aer.) ángulo de deslizamiento, ángulo de planeo.—**g. boat,** (mar.) hidroplano que se desliza por la superficie del agua.—**g. machine,** (aer.) = GLIDER.

glimmer [glímœ(r)]. I. *vn.* rielar, centellear, brillar con luz vacilante. II. *s.* luz trémula; vislumbre, visión momentánea.—**glimmering** [-iŋ]. I. *a.* vacilante, luciente. II. *s.* vislumbre, viso.

glimpse [glímps]. I. *s.* ojeada, vistazo; vislumbre, resplandor fugaz; reflejo. II. *va.* vislumbrar, entrever; ver con una ojeada. III. *vn.* ojear, dar un vistazo; lucir a intervalos.

glint [glint]. I. *va.* reflejar. II. *vn.* lucir, brillar, destellar; saltar de rechazo. III. *s.* destello, viso, relumbre.

glioma [glaióumă], *s.* (med.) glioma, especie de tumor de ciertas partes del sistema nervioso.

glisten [glisn]. I. *vn.* brillar, resplandecer, rielar. II. *s.* brillo, centelleo, destello.

glister [glístœ(r)]. I. *vn.* (ant.) brillar, lucir. II. *s.* (ant.) brillo, destello.

glitter [glítœ(r)]. I. *vn.* resplandecer, centellear, relucir, relumbrar, rutilar, brillar. II. *s.* brillo, resplandor, oropel, centelleo.—**glittering** [-iŋ]. I. *s.* = GLITTER. II. *a.* reluciente, resplandeciente, coruscante.—**glitteringly** [-li], *adv.* lustrosamente, con lustre o brillo.

gloam [glóum], *vn.* obscurecerse, anochecer.—**gloaming** [-iŋ], *s.* crepúsculo vespertino, el anochecer, la oración.

gloat [glóut], *vn.* (con **on, over**) deleitarse, gozarse (en); regocijarse en el mal ajeno.

global [glóubal], *a.* global; esférico.

globate(d [glóubeit(id], *a.* esférico, globular.

globe [glóub], *s.* esfera, globo; pecera globular; globo o bomba de una lámpara.—**g. sight,**

(arm.) mira esférica.—**g. valve,** válvula esférica.

globefish [-fiš], *s.* (ict.) orbe.

globetrotter [-tratœ(r)], *s.* trotamundos.

globin [glóubin], *s.* (quím.) globina.

globose [glóubous], *a.* globoso, redondo.

globosity [globásiti], *s.* esfericidad, redondez.

globular [glábyulǎ(r)], *a.* globular, esférico.

globule [glábyul], *s.* glóbulo, globulillo.

globulin [-lin], *s.* (quím.) globulina.

globulose, globulous [-lous, -las], *a.* globuloso.

glomerate [glámęrit], *a.* aglomerado, conglomerado.

glomeration [-éišon], *s.* conglobación.

glomerule [glámęrul], *s.* (anat., bot.) glomérulo.

glonoin [glánoin], *s.* nitroglicerina o glonoína.

gloom [glúm]. I. *s.* obscuridad, lobreguez, tenebrosidad, tinieblas, *f. pl.;* melancolía, tristeza. II. *va.* y *vn.* encapotar(se), obscurecer(se); entristecer(se).

gloomily [-ili], *adv.* obscuramente; tétricamente, lúgubremente, tenebrosamente.

gloominess [-inis], *s.* obscuridad, tenebrosidad, lobreguez; melancolía, tristeza; adustez.

gloomy [-i] *a.* tenebroso, sombrío, lóbrego; nublado; triste, melancólico.

gloria [glóriǎ], *s.* tela de lana y seda usada para reemplazar la seda pura; (igl.) gloria; (b. a.) aureola.

glorification [-fikéišon], *s.* glorificación, apoteosis; (fam.) celebración, jolgorio.

glorify [-fai], *va.* glorificar, exaltar, alabar.

gloriole [glórioul], *s.* aureola.

glorious [glóriʌs], *a.* glorioso; (fam.) excelente, magnífico.—**gloriously** [-li], *adv.* gloriosamente.—**gloriousness** [-nis], *s.* gloria, calidad de glorioso.

glory [glóri]. I. *s.* gloria.—**to be in one's g.,** estar uno en sus glorias. II. *vn.* gloriarse, jactarse; deleitarse.

gloss [glos]. I. *s.* lustre, brillo; pulimento; barniz, *m.;* apariencia falaz, oropel; glosa, comentario; disculpa, paliativo. II. *va.* pulir, pulimentar, satinar, glasear; disculpar, paliar. III. *va.* y *vn.* glosar, comentar, postillar, escoliar.

glossa [-ǎ], *s.* (anat., zool.) lengua.—**glossal** [-al], *a.* pert. a la lengua, lingual.

glossarial [glaséjriǎl], *a.* referente a una glosa.

glossarist [glásǎrist], *s.* glosador.

glossary [glásǎri], *s.* glosario, nomenclador.

glossiness [glósiŋis], *s.* pulimento, lustre.

glossitis [glasáitis], *s.* (med.) glositis, inflamación de la lengua.

glossographer [glaságrafœ(r)], *s.* glosador, comentador.

glossography [-fi], *s.* arte de glosar o de hacer glosarios; (anat.) descripción de la lengua.

glossology [glasólodȝi], *s.* clasificación de las lenguas; filología comparada.

glossy [glósi], *a.* lustroso, glaseado, satinado; especioso, plausible.

glottal [glátal], **glottic** [glátik], *a.* glótico.

glottis [glátis], *s.* (anat.) glotis.

glove [glʌv]. I. *s.* guante.—**g. factory o shop,** guantería.—**g. fight,** boxeo con guantes.—**g. hook,** o **buttoner,** abotonador de guantes.—**g. maker,** guantero.—**g. money,** (Ingl.) gratificación a los criados; gajes.—**g. stretcher,** abridor de guantes.—**to be hand and g.,** ser inseparables, ser uña y carne.—**to handle with (kid) gloves,** tratar con muchos miramientos.—**to handle without gloves,** tratar sin contemplaciones. II. *va.* enguantar.

glover [-œ(r)], *s.* guantero.

glow [glóu]. I. *vn.* dar luz o calor sin llama; brillar o lucir suavemente; fosforecer; ponerse incandescente; enardecerse, agitarse. II. *s.* brillo sin llama; incandescencia; calor intenso; vehemencia.—**g. lamp,** lámpara incandescente.

glower [gláuœ(r)]. I. *vn.* mirar con ira o ceño. II. *s.* mirada ceñuda o amenazadora.

glowing [glóuįŋ], *a.* resplandeciente; incandescente, encendido; ardiente.—**glowingly** [-lį], *adv.* de un modo resplandeciente o vehemente.

glowworm [glóuwœrm], *s.* (ent.) luciérnaga, cocuyo.

gloxinia [glaksíniǎ], *s.* (bot.) (Am.) gloxínea.

gloze [glóuz]. I. *va.* paliar, colorear, excusar. II. *vn.* glosar, comentar; brillar, relucir.

glozing [-įŋ], *s.* paliativo; adulación.

glucina [glusáįnǎ], *s.* (quím.) glucina.

glucinum [-ʌm], *s.* (quím.) glucinio.

glucose [glúkōųs], *s.* (quím.) glucosa.

glucoside [glúkosạįd], *s.* (quím.) glucósido.

glucosuria [glukosįúriǎ], *s.* (med.) glucosuria.

glue [glú]. I. *s.* cola, ajícola; gluten. II. *va.* encolar; pegar con cola; engomar, aglutinar.

gluepot [-pat], *s.* cazo (de cola).

gluey [-į], **gluish** [-įš], *a.* viscoso, pegajoso, glutinoso.—**glueyness** [-įnįs], *s.* viscosidad, glutinosidad.—**gluing** [-įŋ], *s.* encoladura, encolamiento, pegadura.

glum [glʌm], *a.* malhumorado, displicente.

glumaceous [gluméįšįʌs], *a.* (bot.) glumáceo.

glume [glum], *s.* (bot.) gluma, cascabillo.

glumpy [glʌmpį], *a.* (fam.) malhumorado, de mal humor, murrio.

glut [glʌt]. I. *va.* hartar, saciar; colmar; atascar, atarugar.—**to g. the market**, (com.) inundar el mercado. II. *vn.* devorar, engullir. III. *s.* hartura, hartazgo; plétora; cuña de madera; (alb.) ripio de ladrillo.

gluteal [glutíạl], *a.* (anat.) glúteo, nalgar.

gluten [glúten], *s.* gluten.

gluteus [glutíʌs], *s.* (anat.) músculo glúteo.

glutinosity [glutįnásįtį], **glutinousness** [glútįnʌsnįs], *s.* glutinosidad, viscosidad.

glutinous [glútįnʌs], *a.* glutinoso.

glutted [glátįd], *a.* harto, ahíto.

glutton [glátǫn], *s.* glotón, trag(ant)ón, comilón; (zool.) glotón.

gluttonous [-ʌs], *a.* glotón; goloso.

gluttonously [-lį], *adv.* voraz o glotonamente.

gluttony [-į], *s.* glotonería, gula.

glycerate [glísereįt], *s.* (quím.) glicerato.

glyceric [glįsérįk], *a.* de glicerina.

glyceride [glísеraįd], *s.* (quím.) glicérido.

glycerin(e [-įn], *s.* glicerina.

glycerite [-aįt], *s.* (farm.) glicerito.

glycerol [-al], *s.* (quím.) glicerol.

glycogen [gláįkodzįn], *s.* (bioquím.) glicógeno.

glycol [-kal], *s.* (quím.) glicol.

glycolate [-koleįt], *s.* (quím.) glicolato.

glycolic [-kálįk], *a.* (quím.) glicólico.

glycosuria [-kosįúriǎ], *s.* (med.) glicosuria.

glyph [glįf], *s.* (arq.) glifo; estría.

glyptic [glíptįk], *s.* (gen. *pl.*) glíptica.

glyptodont [glíptodant], *s.* (pal.) gliptodonte.

glyptography [glįptágrafį], *s.* gliptografía.

gnarl [nárl]. I. *vn.* refunfuñar, gruñir. II. *va.* retorcer. III. *s.* nudo (en el árbol o la madera).

gnarled [-d], **gnarly** [-į], *a.* nudoso, retorcido.

gnash [næš], *va.* rechinar o crujir los dientes.

gnashing [-įŋ], *s.* rechinamiento o crujido de los dientes.

gnat [næt], *s.* (ent.) (Am.) jején; (Ingl.) mosquito.

gnaw [nó], *va.* roer; morder, mordicar; carcomer; corroer.—**gnawer** [-œ(r)], *s.* roedor.

gneiss [náįs], *s.* (geol.) gneis, *m.*—**gneissic** [-įk], *a.* (geol.) gnéisico.

gnetaceous [nįtéįšʌs], *a.* (bot.) gnetáceo.

gnome [nóųm], *s.* máxima, aforismo; gnomo, trasgo, enano; (orn.) especie de buho.

gnomic(al [-įk(ạl], *a.* sentencioso, gnómico.

gnomon [nóųman], *s.* gnomon; saeta.

gnomonic(al [nománįk(ạl], *a.* gnomónico.

gnomonics [-s], *s.* gnomónica.

Gnostic [nástįk], *s.* y *a.* gnóstico.

Gnosticism [nástįsįzm], *s.* gnosticismo.

gnu [nu], *s.* (zool.) gnú, especie de antílope o buey salvaje del África del Sur.

go [goų], *va.* (*pret.* WENT; *pp.* GONE) interesar; contribuir con, tener participación en; responder por; en el juego, ir, apostar, envidar.—to g. **bail**, salir fiador.—**to g. better**, apostar más.—**to g. halves**, ir a medias.—**to g. it**, (fam.) embestir, ir adelante; sufrir, soportar.—**to g. it alone**, obrar solo, sin ayuda.—**to g. one better**, aventajar, ir más allá.—**to g. one's way**, proseguir uno su camino.—**to g. shares**, o **snacks**, entrar o ir a la parte, ir a medias o a partes iguales.—**to g. the limit**, (fam.) ir hasta lo último o hasta el non plus ultra.—**to g. the rounds**, ir de ronda.—**to g. the way of all flesh**, o **of all the earth**, devolver el polvo al polvo, morir.—**to g. the whole hog**, (fam.) jugar el todo por el todo.

go, *vn.* ir, irse; andar; marchar; (mec.) funcionar, andar; acudir, recurrir; sentar, venir, ir, o caer bien; resultar (bien, mal), tener (buen, mal) éxito; ponerse (loco, etc.); cuajar, surtir efecto; ser ley, no cambiarse, ser terminante; guiarse; rezar, decir; irse, desaparecer; consumirse, acabarse; contribuir, concurrir, tender; morirse, estarse muriendo; venderse, tener venta; valer, ser válido, aceptarse.—**to g. about**, hacer, emprender; manejarse; dar rodeos; atender a; (mar.) virar de bordo.—**to g. about one's business**, meterse uno en lo que le importa.—**to g. abroad**, ir a otro país; divulgarse.—**to g. across**, cruzar.—**to g. after**, seguir a, ir tras de; ir por; caerle a, atacar.—**to g. against**, oponerse a, chocar con, ir en contra de.—**to g. ahead**, adelantar, seguir, proseguir.—**to g. all out**, (fam.) hacer un esfuerzo supremo; ir hasta el tope, o hasta lo último; poner toda la carne en el asador; jugar el todo por el todo.—**to g. along**, seguir, proseguir; irse, marcharse (gen. *impv.*).—**to g. along with**, acompañar a.—**to g. around**, alcanzar para todos; TO GO ROUND.—**to g. aside**, retirarse, separarse.—**to g. astray**, extraviarse; desmandarse; caer en la tentación, cometer un desliz.—**to g. at**, atacar, acometer; emprender; empezar, atacar (un problema, etc.); ejecutar, hacer.—**to g. away**, desaparecer; irse, marcharse.—**to g. back**, retirarse, retroceder; regresar; ceder, desistir, volverse atrás.—**to g. back of**, mirar más allá de; poner en tela de juicio.—**to g. back on one**, (fam.) faltar a lo pactado, traicionar.—**to g. back to**, remontarse hasta, datar de.—**to g. backward**, retroceder.—**to g. begging**, no tener demanda; no gustar.—**to g. behind**, ir atrás o atrás de; investigar las causas de o lo que está más allá de.—**to g. between**, interponerse entre, terciar; mediar entre.—**to g. by**, pasarse por alto; pasar por el lado de; pasar cerca, pasar (por aquí, por mi casa, etc.); ajustarse o atenerse a; regirse por.—**to g. by the board**, abandonarse; fracasar.—**to g. crazy**, o **daffy**, (fam.) volverse loco, enloquecerse, chiflarse.—**to g. deep (into)**, ahondar (en).—**to g. down**, bajar; descender; ponerse (el sol); hundirse; caer, caerse; (com.) quebrar, fracasar; (fam.) poderse tragar o creer, tragarse (cambiando el giro: *that does not go down with me*, eso no me lo trago yo); pasar por cierto; pasar (a la historia, etc.).—**to g. down on one's knees**, arrodillarse; implorar, rogar.—**to g. downstairs**, bajar (de un piso a otro).—**to g. far**, servir de mucho; alcanzar para mucho.—**to g. far towards**, ayudar o contribuir mucho a.—**to g. for**, favorecer; (fam.) embestir, atacar, acometer (real o figuradamente).—**to g. for a walk**, ir a pasear, dar un paseo.—**to g. forth**, salir; publicarse.—**to g. forward**, adelantar, adelantarse.—**to g. hard with one**, irle mal a uno; costarle a uno caro; ser para uno de graves consecuencias.—**to g. in**, entrar; encajar.—**to g. in and out**, entrar y salir; vivir; pasarlo.—**to g. in for**, (fam.) apoyar, favorecer, adherirse a; consagrarse a, tomar parte en, dedicar algún tiempo a; buscar, solicitar.—**to g. into**, participar en; investigar, discutir o ventilar; caber en; entrar en; ir o irse al.—**to g. into business**, emprender negocios.—**to g. into effect**, entrar en vigor.—**to g. into liquidation**, (com.) liquidarse, suspender negocios.—**to g. mad**, enloquecerse, perder el juicio.—**g. near**, acercarse.—**to g. off**, abandonar; dispararse, hacer explosión; morirse; irse, largarse, despedirse; tener efecto, salir o quedar (bien o mal).—**to g. on**, continuar, proseguir; ir adelante; progresar; entrar (un guante, etc.).—**to g. on strike**, declararse en huelga.—**to g. on the air**, hablar o dedicarse a hablar por radio; transmitirse por radio.—**to g. on the road**, viajar como agente o en el ejercicio de una profesión (esp. la del teatro).—**to g. on the stage**, hacerse actor.—**to g. out**, salir; apagarse, extinguirse.—**to g. out of fashion**, pasar de moda.—**to g. out of the way**, apartarse; descarriarse; molestarse.—**to g. over**, examinar, estudiar, repasar; recorrer; aplazar; pasarse (al otro lado, partido, etc.); pasar por encima de.—**to g. past**, pasar, pasar de largo.—**to g. round**, andar al rededor de; dar vueltas.—**to g. through**, realizarse, llevarse a cabo; registrar, examinar detenidamente; pasar, sufrir; atravesar; penetrar; pasar por; derrochar, malbaratar.—**to g. to**, o **toward**, dirigirse, acercarse o acudir a.—**to g. to bed**, acostarse, ir a acostarse.—**to g. together**, andar o ir juntos; armonizar entre sí, avenirse.—**to g. to law**, recurrir a los tribunales.—**to g. to one's head**, envanecer o engreír (a uno); subirse a la cabeza (dicho del vino).—**to g. to pieces**, desvencijarse, desbarajustarse (apl. esp. a la salud); confundirse, afligirse, echarse a morir.—**to g. to pot**, arruinarse.—**to g. to rack and ruin**, arruinarse.—**to g. to sea**, hacerse marino; viajar por mar.—**to g. to sleep**, dormirse.—**to g. to smash**, arruinarse, frustrarse, quebrar.—**to g. to the bottom**, irse a pique; profundizar.—**to g. to the country** = TO APPEAL TO THE COUNTRY.—**to g. to the wall**, quedarse atrás, darse por vencido; fracasar.—**to g. to war**, ir a la guerra; hacer guerra; (con **with**) hacer la guerra (a).—**to g. under**, quebrar, quedar arruinado, vencido o destruído; hundirse.—**to g. up**, subir; (fam.) quebrar, arruinarse.—**to g. up in smoke**, (fam.) esfumarse, malograrse.—**to g. upon an assumption**, proceder u obrar según una suposición.—**to g. upstairs**, subir (de un piso a otro).—**to g. up the spout**, (fam.) fracasar; evaporarse (fig.).—**to g. West**, (fam.) irse al otro mundo, morir.—**to g. with**, acompañar; seguir; armonizar con; (fam.) galantear.—**to g. without**, pasarse de o sin.—**to g. without saying**, sobreentenderse.—**to g. wrong**, salir mal, fracasar; perderse, irse a la mala vida; ir por mal camino.

go, s. (fam.) moda, usanza; energía, empuje; giro, marcha, curso; predicamento; pacto, convenio; buen éxito; oportunidad, turno.—**it is all the g.**, es la gran moda, hace furor.—**is it a g.?** ¿está resuelto? ¿estamos convenidos?—**it is no g.**, es inútil, esto no marcha.—**on the g.**, en actividad, moviéndose.

goad [góud]. I. s. aguijón, puya; focino para elefantes.—**g. spur**, acicate.—**g. stick**, garrocha, rejo. II. va. aguijonear, agarrochar; estimular, incitar.

goader [-œ(r)], s. agarrochador, garrocheador.

go-ahead [góu ahéd], a. (fam.) emprendedor, activo, enérgico.—**to get** (o **give**) **the g. signal**, recibir (o dar) la señal de permiso o de

consentimiento (para seguir adelante), o el visto bueno.

goal [góul], s. meta, fin, objeto, objetivo, propósito, finalidad; (fútbol) gol, tanto; portería, puerta.—**g. line**, raya de la meta.—**g. post**, poste de la meta.

goalkeeper [-kipœ(r)], s. (fútbol) portero, guardameta, m. (ll. t. goalie).

go-as-you-please [gou æz yu pliz], a. y adv. (fam.) al paso que uno quiera; libre, sin restricción.

goat [góut], s. (zool.) cabra; chivo; (fam.) víctima que carga con la culpa ajena.—**g. buck**, cabrón, macho cabrío.—**g. milker**, (orn.) chotacabras, f.—**g.'s hair**, pelote.—**g.'s rue**, (bot.) galega.—**g.'s-(t)horn**, (bot.) tragacanto, algalega.

goatbeard [-bird], s. (bot.) barba cabruna.

goatee [-í], s. pera, perilla.

goatherd [-hœrd], s. cabrero, cabrerizo.

goatish [-iš], **goatlike** [-laik], a. cabrerizo, cabrío, cabruno, chotuno, hircino; lascivo.

goatskin [-skin], s. piel (f.) de cabra.

goatsucker [-sakœ(r)], s. = GOAT MILKER.

gob [gab], s. pedazo; (min.) escombro; (fam.) marinero de guerra.

gobbet [gábit], s. pedazo, masa, bulto.

gobble [gábl]. I. va. engullir, tragar. II. vn. hacer ruido en la garganta como los pavos. III. s. voz del pavo.

gobbler [gáblœ(r)], s. glotón, tragón, tragador; pavo.

go-between [góubitwin], s. mediador; alcahuete.

goblet [gáblit], s. copa de mesa, vaso de pie.

goblin [gáblin], s. trasgo, duende.

goby [góubi], s. (ict.) gobio.

go-by [góubai], s. (fam.) desaire; esquinazo.

gocart [góukart], s. carretilla, andaderas.

god, God [gád], s. dios, Dios.—**G. be with you**, vaya Vd. con Dios.—**G.-fearing**, temeroso de Dios.—**G. forbid**, no lo quiera Dios.—**G.-forsaken**, dejado de la mano de Dios, desamparado.—**G.'s acre**, cementerio, camposanto.—**G.'s Day**, domingo; fiesta del Corpus.—**G.'s house**, iglesia, templo.—**G. willing**, Dios mediante, si Dios quiere.—**act of G.**, fuerza mayor.—**for G.'s sake**, por Dios, por el amor de Dios.

godchild [-chaild], s. ahijado, ahijada.

goddaughter [-dotœ(r)], s. ahijada.

goddess [-is], s. diosa.

goddesslike [-laik], a. de diosa; como de diosa.

godfather [-faðœ(r)], s. padrino.

Godhead [-hed], s. Deidad, Divinidad.

godless [-lis], a. sin Dios, ateo, infiel, impío.—**godlessness** [-nis], s. impiedad, ateísmo.

godlike [-laik], a. deiforme, de dios, como dios.

godlily [-lili], adv. piadosamente.

godliness [-linis], s. piedad, santidad.

godly [-li], a. divino; devoto, piadoso, religioso.

godmother [-maðœ(r)], s. madrina.

godown [godáun], s. almacén chino o indio.

godparents [gádpærents], s. pl. padrinos.

godsend [-send], s. divina merced; fortuna, buena suerte.

godship [-šip], s. divinidad.

godson [-san], s. ahijado.

Godspeed [-spíd], s. bienandanza.—**G.! o G. speed!** ¡buena suerte! ¡buen viaje!

Godward [-wird], adv. hacia Dios.

godwit [gádwit], s. (orn.) limosa.

goer [góuœ(r)], s. andador, paseante.

goffer [gáfœ(r)]. I. va. rizar, encrespar; estampar cuero. II. s. rizado.

go-getter [góugétœ(r)], s. (fam.) buscavida, sujeto emprendedor.

goggle [gágl]. I. va. y vn. torcer o abrir extremadamente los ojos. II. s. torcimiento de los ojos, mirada afectada.—pl. **goggles**, gafas; anteojos de camino; anteojeras.—**g.-eyed**, de ojos saltones.—**g.-eyes**, ojos saltones.

going [góuiŋ]. **I.** *a.* y *ger.* de TO GO; activo, que funciona.—**a g. concern**, una empresa que funciona o marcha. **II.** *s.* paso, andar, andadura; marcha, ida, partida; estado del camino.—**g. out**, salida.—**g. over**, recorrido.—**g. up**, subida.—*pl.* **goings**, idas y venidas.—**goings on**, (fam.) ocurrencias, sucesos; conducta.

goiter, goitre [góitœ(r)], *s.* (med.) bocio, papera.—**goitered** [-d], **goitrous** [góitrʌs], *a.* que tiene papera.

gola [góulȧ], *s.* (arq.) gola, cimacio.

gold [góuld], *s.* oro; color de oro.—**g.-bearing**, aurífero.—**g. brick**, añagaza, embuste.—**g. dust**, oro en polvo; (bot.) aliso; ombligo de Venus.—**g. embroidery**, argentería.—**g. fever**, fiebre (*f.*) de oro.—**g.-filled**, revestido de oro.—**g. filling**, (dent.) orificación, obturación de oro.—**g. foil**, oro batido o en hojas.—**g. lace**, galón o encaje de oro; entorchado.—**g. leaf**, pan de oro.—**g. mine**, arrugia.—**g. plate**, vajilla de oro.—**g.-plated**, dorado.—**g. point**, estado del cambio exterior en que los pagos pueden hacerse en oro no acuñado (oro en barras) sin perder.—**g. size**, cera de dorar.—**g. standard**, (com., e. p.) patrón de oro.—**g. stick**, (Ingl.) oficial de la corte; vara dorada que éste lleva.—**g. thread**, gusanillo de oro.—**g. work**, orfebrería.

goldbeater [-bitœ(r)], *s.* batihoja, *m.*, batidor de oro.

golden [-n], *a.* áureo, de oro, dorado; brillante; excelente, precioso; feliz; rubio, amarillento.—**g. age**, siglo de oro, siglo dorado.—**g. calf**, becerro de oro; riquezas, oro (fig.).—**G. Fleece**, (mit.) vellocino de oro.—**g. mean**, justo medio; moderación, prudencia.—**g. number**, (astr.) número áureo.—**g. oriole**, (orn.) oriol, oropéndola.—**g. rule**, regla áurea.—**g. thistle**, (bot.) cardillo.—**g. wedding**, bodas de oro.

goldfinch [-finch], *s.* (orn.) cardelina; pintacilgo.

goldfish [-fiʃ], *s.* (ict.) carpa pequeña de color rojo dorado; pececillo(s) de colores.

goldsmith [-smiθ], *s.* orífice, orfebre.

goldstone [-stoun], *s.* venturina.

golf [gálf]. **I.** *s.* golf, juego escocés.—**g. bag**, carcaj (para los palos).—**g. club**, palo, mazo o bastón para jugar al golf; grupo de personas que lo juegan.—**g. course**, o **links**, cancha de golf. **II.** *vn.* jugar golf.

golfer [-œ(r)], *s.* golfista, jugador(a) de golf.

Golgotha [gálgoθȧ], *s.* Calvario.

goliard [góuljard], *s.* bufón ambulante.

golosh [goláʃ], *s.* = GALOSH.

gomphosis [gamfóusis], *s.* (anat.) gonfosis.

gonad [gánæd], *s.* (anat.) gónado.

gondola [gándolȧ], *s.* góndola; (aer.) barquilla o cabina.—**g. car**, (f. c.) vagón largo de plataforma.

gondolier [gandolír], *s.* gondolero.

gone [gɔn], *pp.* de TO GO; ido; perdido, arruinado; pasado; apagado. Ú. a veces con *to be* en vez de *to have* para formar tiempos compuestos, *vg.*, *he was gone*, él se había ido.—**g. on**, (fam.) locamente enamorado de.—**to be g.**, haberse ido; faltar, haber desaparecido; haberse acabado.—**to be a goner**, (fam.) ser hombre perdido.

gonfalon [gánfalȧn], *s.* confalón, gonfalón, pendón.—**gonfalonier** [-ír], *s.* confalonier(o), gonfalonier(o).

gong [gaŋ], *s.* batintín, gongo, gong(om); tantan, tamtám.

Gongorism [gáŋgorizm], *s.* gongorismo, cult(eran)ismo.

goniometer [gouniámetœ(r)], *s.* goniómetro.

goniometric(al [-ométrik(ȧl], *a.* goniométrico.

goniometry [-ámetri], *s.* goniometría.

gonococcus [ganokákʌs], *s.* (bact.) gonococo.

gonophore [gánofour], *s.* (anat. bot.) gonóforo; prolongación del eje de la flor.

gonorrhea [ganoríȧ], *s.* (med.) gonorrea.

gonorrheal [-l], *a.* gonorreico.

goober [gúbœ(r)], *s.* (bot.) cacahuete.

good [gud]. **I.** *a.* bueno; apto, conveniente, ventajoso, útil; genuino, legítimo; de buena índole, dócil u obediente; hábil, capaz o competente; amplio, grande o considerable; digno.—**g. afternoon**, buenas tardes.—**g. and collectable**, (com.) valedero y cobrable.—**g. breeding**, (buena) educación, buenos modales.—**g. book**, o **G. Book**, Sagrada Escritura, Biblia.—**g. cheer**, buen ánimo, confianza (*to be of g.* cheer, tener buen ánimo, tener aliento); fiesta, festividad, festín; buenas viandas, buena mesa.—**g. day**, buenos días.—**g. enough**, suficientemente bueno, pasadero, suficiente.—**g. even, g. evening**, buenas noches (saludo).—**g. fellow**, campechano.—**g.-fellowship**, compañerismo, camaradería.—**g. for nothing**, inútil, sin valor; haragán, pelafustán.—**g. fortune**, dicha, suerte, *f.*—**G. Friday**, Viernes Santo.—**g. graces**, favor, amistad, consideración.—**g.-humored**, jocoso, vivo, jovial.—**g.-humoredly**, jocosamente, alegremente.—**g.-looking**, guapo, buen mozo, bien parecido.—**g. luck**, suerte, *f.*; Vd. lo pase bien; vaya Vd. con Dios.—**g. morning, g. morrow**, buenos días.—**g. nature**, bondad, buen corazón.—**g.-natured**, bonachón, afable, paciente.—**g.-naturedly**, tolerantemente, afablemente.—**G. Neighbor Policy**, la política del Buen Vecino.—**g. news!** ¡albricias!—**g. night**, buenas noches (despedida).—**g. offices**, buenos oficios.—**g. pay**, buena paga; buen pagador.—**G. Shepherd**, Buen Pastor (Jesucristo).—**g. speed**, buena suerte.—**g.-tempered**, de buen genio o carácter.—**g. time**, rato, día, etc., agradable o divertido; diversión, holgorio.—**g. times**, prosperidad, buen corazón.—**g. will**, buena voluntad; benevolencia; (com.) popularidad, reputación, buen nombre o crédito, bienquerencia; activo invisible, mayor valía o plusvalía.—**a g. deal**, mucho, bastante.—**a. g. turn**, un favor, una gracia.—**a g. way**, un buen trecho, larga distancia.—**a g. while**, un buen rato.—**as g. as** (seguido de participio), casi (*this is as good as done*, esto está casi terminado, o puede darse por terminado).—**in g. part**, en buena parte.—(to be) **in g. repute**, (tener) buena reputación.—**in g. time**, a tiempo, a propósito; con oportunidad.—**to be g. for**, servir para. **II.** *s.* bien; provecho, ventaja.—*pl.* V. GOODS.—**for g.**, permanentemente, para siempre; para no volver.—**for g., for g. and all**, terminantemente, una vez por todas.—**much g. may it do you**, que le aproveche.—(to be) **to the g.**, (tener) ganado, de sobra, en favor o al haber (de uno). **III.** *adv.* bien, rectamente.—**g. and** (antes de *a.* o *adv.*), bien, muy. **IV.** *interj.* ¡bueno! ¡magnífico! ¡muy bien!

good-by, good-bye [gud bái], *s.* e *interj.* adiós; hasta la vista, hasta luego; vaya Vd. con Dios.

goodish [gúdiʃ], *a.* algo bueno, regular; amplio.

goodliness [gúdlinis], *s.* belleza, hermosura, gracia, elegancia.

goodly [gúdli], *a.* hermoso, guapo, bien parecido; excelente; atractivo, agradable o vistoso; abultado; considerable; algo numeroso.—**a g. prospect**, hermosa perspectiva; buenas esperanzas.

goodman [gúdman], *s.* (ant.) señor; amo de casa.

goodness [gúdnis]. **I.** *s.* bondad, benevolencia; favor, fineza. **II.** *interj.* ¡Ave María! ¡Dios mío!

goods [gudz], *s. pl.* géneros, mercancías, existencias, efectos.—**g. shed**, almacén, cobertizo.—**g. train**, (Ingl.) tren de mercancías o de carga.—**g. truck, wagon**, o **van**, (f. c.) furgón.

goodwife [gúdwáif], *s.* (ant.) ama o señora de casa.

goody [gúdi], *a.* y *s.* bonachón, pazguato, Juan Lanas, mojigato.—**g.-g.**, santurrón, beato;

(como *interj.*) ¡magnífico!—*s. pl.* **goodies,** dulces.

gooey [gúi], *a.* (fam.) viscoso.

goof(er [gúf(œr], *s.* (fam.) bobo, simplón.

goofy [gúfi], *a.* (fam.) tonto, ridículo.

goon [gun], *s.* (fam.) terrorista al servicio de ciertos elementos en disputas obreras, etc.; ganso, pazguato.

goosander [gusǽndœ(r)], *s.* (orn.) mergánsar, patín.

goose [gus], *s.* (*pl.* GEESE [gis]) (orn.) ganso, ánsar, oca; plancha de sastre; bobo, necio; juego de la oca.—**g. barnacle,** (zool.) percebe, escaramujo.—**g. egg,** cero (en los juegos).—**g. flesh,** carne de gallina (aplicado a la piel humana).—**g. quill,** pluma de ave, pluma de ganso.—**g. skin** = GOOSE FLESH.—**g. step,** ejercicio en que uno descansa alternativamente sobre un pie y levanta el otro, como marcando el paso; (mil.) paso en que se mantienen las piernas tesas.

gooseberry [gúzberi], *s.* (bot.) uva espina o crespa; variedad de grosella blanca.

goosefoot [gúsfut], *s.* (bot.) chual, pata de ganso.

gooseherd [gúshœrd], *s.* ansarero.

gooseneck [gúsnɛk], *s.* (mar.) gancho de botalones; arbotante, cuello de cisne; pescante de bote; (tecn.) barra, tubo, etc., curvos; conexión en S o de doble codo con articulación universal.

goosewings [gúswiŋz], *s.* (mar.) calzones.

goosy [gúsi], *a.* tonto, estúpido; atacado de carne de gallina (apl. a personas).

gopher [góufœ(r)], *s.* (zool.) variedad de topo, de ardilla, de tortuga y de culebra.

gopherwood [góufœ(r)wud], *s.* (bot.) árbol de madera amarilla, fustete.

Gordian knot [górdiạn nat], *s.* nudo gordiano.

gore [gor]. I. *s.* sangre, *f.*, cuajarón; crúor; (cost.) cuchillo, nesga, sesga, fonas; pedazo de terreno triangular; (mar.) tabla triangular, cuchillo. II. *va.* herir con los cuernos; acornear; (cost.) poner nesga o cuchillo.

gorge [gordʒ]. I. *s.* (anat., zool.) gorja, gola, garganta, gaznate; (geog.) abra, desfiladero, barranco, cañada, quebrada; cuello de un vestido; trago, bocado; asco. II. *va.* engullir, tragar, atiborrar; hartar, saciar. III. *vn.* hartarse, saciarse.

gorgeous [górdʒʌs], *a.* vistoso, magnífico, suntuoso.—**gorgeously** [-li], *adv.* magníficamente, suntuosamente.—**gorgeousness** [-nis], *s.* esplendor, magnificencia, suntuosidad.

gorget [górdʒit], *s.* (arm.) gola, gorguera, gorjal; (cost.) gorguera; (orn.) collar de ciertas aves; (mil.) golilla; (cir.) cuchilla para fístulas.

Gorgon [górgọn], *s.* (mit.) Gorgona; (**g.,** fam.) esperpento; mujer muy fea.

Gorgonia [gorgóuniạ], *s.* (zool.) gorgonia.

Gorgonian [-n], *a.* (mit.) gorgóneo; (**g.,** zool.) pert. a los gorgónidos.

Gorgonzola [gorgonzóulạ], *s.* queso de Gorgonzola.

gorilla [gorílạ], *s.* (zool.) gorila, *m.*

gormand [górmạnd], *s.* glotón, goloso.—**gormandize** [-aiz], *vn.* glotonear.—**gormandizer** [-œr], *s.* glotonazo, tragamallas.

gorse [gors], *s.* (bot.) argomón, aulaga.

gory [góri], *a.* ensangrentado; sangriento.

goshawk [gáshɔk], *s.* (orn.) azor.

gosling [gázliŋ], *s.* (orn.) ansarino, gansarón.—**g. green,** color verdoso amarillento.

gospel [gáspel], *s.* evangelio; cosa cierta e indudable.—**g. truth,** verdad palmaria.

gospel(l)er [-œ(r)], *s.* (igl.) evangelista, evangelistero; (raro) misionero.

gossamer [gásạmœ(r)], *s.* hilo finísimo; telaraña; (tej.) gloria, gasa sutilísima; tela delgada impermeable.

gossamer(y [-i], *a.* sutil, delgado.

gossip [gásip]. I. *s.* chismografía, chisme(ría), chismorreo, murmuración, hablilla; chismoso, murmurador; padrino, madrina. II. *vn.* charlar; murmurar, chismear.

gossiping [-iŋ], **gossipy** [-i], *a.* chismero, chismoso, murmurador.

got [gat], *pret.* y *pp.* de TO GET.

Goth [gáθ], *s.* godo.—**Gothic** [-ik]. I. *a.* gótico. II. *s.* lengua goda.—**Gothicism** [-isizm], *s.* idioma godo; estilo gótico; barbarie.

gotten [gátn], *pp.* de TO GET.

gouache [gwaš], *s.* (pintura de) aguazo; aguada.

gouge [gaudʒ]. I. *s.* (carp.) gubia, mediacaña; ranura, canal (*f.*) o estría. II. *va.* escoplear con una gubia; arrancar, sacar, vaciar; sacar ventaja, engañar.

goulash [gúlaš], *s.* guiso húngaro, compuesto de ternera, patatas y harina con fuertes condimentos.

gourd [gord], *s.* (bot.) calabaza, calabacera; güiro, calabacino.

gourmand [gúrmạnd], *s.* glotón, goloso.

gourmet [gúrmei], *s.* (fr.) gastrónomo.

goût [gu], *s.* (fr.) gusto; inclinación.

gout [gáut], *s.* (med.) gota, artritis.—**g. of,** o **in, the feet,** podagra.

goutiness [-inis], *s.* (med.) afección gotosa.

gouty [-i], *a.* gotoso.

govern [gʌvœrn], *va.* y *vn.* gobernar; guiar, regir, dirigir, mandar; manejar; domar, embridar, enfrenar; (gram.) regir.

governable [-ạbl], *a.* dócil; manejable.

governance [-ạns], *s.* gobierno, ejercicio del poder, autoridad.

governess [-is]. I. *s.* aya, institutriz. II. *va.* y *vn.* instruir o enseñar como institutriz.

governing [-iŋ], *a.* gobernante, gobernador, gubernativo, regidor, regulador.

government [-mẹnt], *s.* gobierno, gobernación; dominio, autoridad; administración, dirección, manejo; conducta, porte; (gram.) régimen.—**g. bonds,** (com.) títulos de la deuda, bonos del gobierno o del Estado.—**for your g.,** (com.) para su gobierno.

governmental [gʌvœrnmén̄tạl], *a.* gubernamental, gubernativo.

governor [gʌvœrnọ(r)], *s.* gobernador; alcaide (de castillo); administrador; tutor, ayo; (mec.) regulador.

governorship [-šip], *s.* dignidad de gobernador; período que dura la gobernación; territorio sujeto a un gobernador.

gown [gáun]. I. *s.* traje de mujer; bata; túnica; toga, vestidura talar. II. *va.* y *vn.* poner o ponerse toga o vestido de mujer.

gowned [-d], *a.* vestido; togado.

gownsman [-zmạn], *s.* togado; paisano, civil.

grab [græb]. I. *va.* asir, agarrar; arrebatar; posesionarse. II. *s.* agarro, toma, asimiento; presa; arrebatiña; copo; (fam.) robo, sisa; (mec.) gancho, garfio.—**g. bucket,** (ing.) = CLAMSHELL BUCKET.

grabble [græbl], *vn.* ir a tientas; postrarse.

grace [greis]. I. *s.* gracia, garbo, donaire; favor, merced, indulgencia; concesión o privilegio; gana, disposición, talante; (teol.) gracia; (Ingl.) título de honor que se daba al soberano y se da a los duques y arzobispos, y equivale a Alteza; bendición (de la mesa), jaculatoria que se dice antes o después de comer.—**g. note,** (mús.) nota de adorno.—**g. stroke,** golpe de gracia.—**days of g.,** (com.) días de gracia.—**to say g.,** dar gracias o bendecir la mesa.—**with a bad (good) g.,** de mala (buena) gana.—*pl.* **good graces,** favor, amistad, bienquerencia.—**the Graces,** las tres Gracias. II. *va.* adornar; agraciar, favorecer.

graceful [-fụl], *a.* gracioso, agraciado, airoso, elegante, donairoso; fácil, natural; decoroso.—**gracefully** [-i], *adv.* graciosamente, donosamente, airosamente.—**gracefulness** [-nis], *s.* gracia, donosura, garbo, donaire, elegancia.

graceless [-lis], *a.* sin gracia, desagraciado,

desgarbado; réprobo, malvado; dejado de la mano de Dios.—**gracelessly** [-li], *adv.* desairadamente; depravadamente.—**gracelessness** [-njs], *s.* falta de gracia, garbo, etc.; depravación.

gracile [grǽsjl], *a.* grácil.

gracious [gréjšʌs], *a.* benigno, bondadoso; afable, cortés; gracioso, grato, agradable.—**g. me!** o **good(ness) g!** ¡válgame Dios! ¡caramba!

graciously [-li], *adv.* benignamente, cortésmente, gratamente.—**graciousness** [-njs], *s.* gracia, afabilidad, bondad, benignidad.

grackle [grǽkl], *s.* (orn.) especie de grajo.

gradate [gréjdejt]. **I.** *va.* graduar, (pint.) degradar. **II.** *vn.* graduarse, mezclarse.

gradation [-éjšǫn], *s.* graduación; paso gradual; grado; serie; (mús.) gradación; escalonamiento; (pint.) degradación (de tamaño, de color o de luz).

gradatory [grǽdǝtǫrj]. **I.** *a.* graduado o gradual; dispuesto para andar. **II.** *s.* (arq.) gradas, *f. pl.*

grade [gréjd]. **I.** *s.* grado, graduación; clase, *f.*; calidad; nota o calificación (en los estudios); animal de raza mixta; pendiente, *f.*; (f. c.) declive, rasante, *f.*; superficie del firme, del terreno, etc.—**g. crossing**, (f. c.) paso a nivel. —**g. of repose**, pendiente máxima de equilibrio, más allá de la cual un vehículo rueda por la sola acción de la gravedad.—**g. school**, escuela primaria.—**at g.**, a nivel.—**down g.**, pendiente descendente; cuesta abajo.—**highest g.**, de primera (clase o calidad).—**to make the g.**, lograr su propósito, vencer las dificultades. —**up g.**, pendiente ascendente; cuesta arriba. **II.** *va.* clasificar u ordenar según tamaño, calidad, etc.; graduar; (ing.) nivelar, explanar.—**to g. up**, cruzar castas de animales.

grader [-œ(r)], *s.* el o lo que clasifica, gradúa, etc.; alumno de cierta clase (en la escuela); (ing.) nivelador; grada; (agr.) separadora de granos.

gradient [gréjdjęnt]. **I.** *a.* ambulante, moviente; pendiente. **II.** *s.* (ing.) pendiente, *f.,* inclinación; (f. c.) declive; rampa, desnivel; (meteor.) grado del aumento o diminución (de temperatura, presión, etc.; diagrama (*m.*) que lo representa.—**g. post**, (f. c.) poste indicador del declive.

gradienter [-œ(r)], *s.* (top.) nivel de círculo vertical para establecer pendientes; tornillo tangencial micrométrico del tránsito (teodolito norteamericano) empleado para determinar ángulos de inclinación por sus tangentes y para calcular distancias horizontales.

gradin [gréjdjn], *s.* grada, escalón.—*pl.* gradería.

gradine [gradjn], *s.* gradina de escultor.

grading [gréjdjŋ], *s.* clasificación, gradación, arreglo según tamaño, etc.; (ing.) nivelación.

gradual [grǽdžuǝl]. **I.** *a.* gradual; graduado. **II.** *s.* (igl.) gradual.—**gradually** [-i], *adv.* gradualmente.—**gradualness** [-njs], *s.* calidad de gradual.

graduate [grǽdžuejt]. **I.** *va.* graduar (conferir un grado); graduar (dividir y señalar por grados); modificar, aumentar o disminuir gradualmente. **II.** *vn.* graduarse, recibirse; cambiar gradualmente. **III.** [grǽdžujt], *a.* graduado, recibido (de doctor, etc.).—**g. school**, escuela graduada. **IV.** *s.* el que se ha recibido en alguna facultad; (quím.) graduador; probeta, vasija o frasco graduados.

graduation [-éjšǫn], *s.* graduación.

graduator [grǽdžuejtǫ(r)], *s.* graduador.

graffito [grafítou], *s.* (arqueol.) inscripción tosca hallada en antiguos sepulcros y ruinas; (b. a.) obra esgrafiada. *V.* SGRAFFITO.

graft [grǽft]. **I.** *s.* (hort.) injerto; parte (*f.*) donde el injerto se aplica al patrón; mezcla; (cir.) transferencia de tejidos o piel de una parte del cuerpo (de un mismo o de otro individuo) a otra parte; el tejido así transferido; (fam.) dinero mal habido, esp. aprovechándose de

puestos públicos; concusión; peculado; latrocinio; soborno político. **II.** *va.* (hort.) injertar; ingerir; mezclar; (cir.) injertar, implantar un pedazo de piel u otro tejido de una parte del cuerpo a otra.—**to g. by approach**, injertar por aproximación. **III.** *vn.* injertar; transferir; (fam.) traficar con los puestos públicos, recibiendo sobornos; cometer concusión o peculado.

grafter [-œ(r)], *s.* injertador; (fam.) el que trafica con los puestos públicos; concusionario.

grafting [-jŋ], *s.* enjertación, ingeridura, injerto. —**g. knife**, abridor, ingeridor, navaja o cuchillo de injertar.—**g. twig**, estaca.

graham bread [gréjǝm bred], *s.* acemita, pan de acemite o de harina de trigo entero.

grail [gréjl], *s.* cáliz, *m.*—**the Holy G.**, el grial.

grain [gréjn]. **I.** *s.* grano (en todas sus acepciones); grano, peso equivalente a 0.06 gramos; finura (de una muela o piedra de esmerilar); fibra, veta, o trepa de la madera; el mármol, etc.; granilla del paño; flor (*f.*) del cuero; genio, disposición, índole, *f.*; (tint.) grana, cochinilla, color rojo.—*pl.* cereales, granos en general.— **g. alcohol**, alcohol etílico o de granos.—**g. cleaner**, aventador.—**g. elevator**, elevador de granos; depósito de granos con elevador.—**g. fork**, bieldo.—**g. moth**, polilla de granos.— **grains of paradise**, grana o granos del Paraíso; (card)amomo; malagueta.—**g. screen**, (fot.) pantalla reticular.—**g. weevil**, gorgojo de los granos.—**across the g.**, transversalmente a la fibra (de la madera).—**against the g.**, contra la dirección de la fibra, a contrapelo; con repugnancia, contra la inclinación o el carácter de uno.—**in g.**, de color rojo o vivo; arraigado; innato.—**with a g. of salt**, con reservas, recortándole o quitándole los adornos de la exageración; menos la tara (fig.). **II.** *va.* granular; granear; granelar; vetear, imitar la trepa de la madera, etc.

grained [-d], *a.* granular; áspero; teñido en rama.

grainer [-œ(r)], *s.* brocha o instrumento de granear; evaporadora de sal; solución de remojar.

grainy [-i], *a.* graneado; granoso.

gram [græm], *s.* (bot.) garbanzo de la India.

gram(me [græm], *s.* gramo.

grama grass [grámǝ grǽs], *s.* (bot.) grama.

gramercy [gramérsi], *interj.* (ant.) ¡muchas mercedes! ¡gracias!; ¡cielos!

graminaceous [græmjnéjšʌs], **gramineous** [graminjʌs], *a.* (bot.) gramíneo.

graminivorous [græmjnívǫrǝs], *a.* graminívoro.

grammar [grǽmǝ(r)], *s.* gramática; elementos de una ciencia.—**g. school**, (Ingl.) escuela de humanidades; (E. U.) escuela pública de enseñanza elemental.

grammarian [gramérjǝn], *s.* gramático.

grammatic(al [gramǽtjk(ǝl], *a.* gramatical.

grammatically [-i], *adv.* gramaticalmente.

grammaticalness [-njs], *s.* corrección gramatical.

gramophone [grǽmofoun], *s.* gramófono.

grampus [grǽmpʌs], *s.* (zool.) orco, orca.

granadilla [grænǝdíljǝ], *s.* (bot.) granadilla (flor y fruto).—**g. tree** o **wood**, granadillo.

granary [grǽnǝri], *s.* granero; hórreo, troj.

grand [grænd]. **I.** *a.* grande, grandioso; magnífico, majestuoso; ilustre, augusto.—**g. climacteric**, año 63 de la vida.—**g. duke**, gran duque. —**g. juror**, miembro de un *grand jury.*—**g. jury**, gran jurado de acusación.—**g. larceny**, robo que pasa de cierto valor.—**g. master**, gran maestre.—**G. Mogul**, gran mogol.—**g. opera**, (mús.) ópera.—**g. piano**, piano de cola. —**g. prize**, premio grande; premio gordo (en la lotería). **II.** *s.* piano de cola; (fam.) mil dólares.

grandam(e [grǽndæm, -ejm], *s.* abuela; anciana.

grandaunt [-ænt], *s.* tía abuela (hermana del abuelo o de la abuela).

grandchild [-chajld], *s.* nieto, nieta.

granddaughter [-dǝtœ(r)], *s.* nieta.

grandee [grændí], s. noble, grande.

grandeur [grǽndžǔ(r)], s. grandeza, grandiosidad, magnificencia, fausto.

grandfather [-fáðœ(r)], s. abuelo.—**g.**('s) **clock**, reloj de caja o de péndola.

grandiloquence [-ílokwęns], s. grandilocuencia.
—**grandiloquent** [-ęnt], **grandiloquous** [-ʌs], a. grandílocuo.

grandiose [-íoụs], a. grandioso; hinchado, bombástico.

grandly [-líi], adv. grandiosamente.

grandma [-ma], s. (fam.) abuelita.

grandmother [-mʌðœ(r)], s. abuela.

grandnephew [-néfịụ], s. sobrino (nieto de un hermano o de una hermana).

grandness [-nịs], s. grandiosidad.

grandniece [-nís], s. sobrina (nieta de un hermano o de una hermana).

grandpa [-pa], s. (fam.) abuelito.

grandparent [-pęręnt], s. abuelo, abuela.

grandsire [-saịr], s. abuelo, antepasado.

grandson [-sʌn], s. nieto.

grandstand [-stænd], s. andanada, tribuna, tendido, gradería de asientos principales para espectadores.

granduncle [-ʌŋkl], s. tío abuelo (hermano del abuelo o de la abuela).

grange [gréịndž], s. granja, cortijo, alquería, hacienda; (E. U.) logia de la sociedad *Patrons of Husbandry*, para el fomento de la agricultura.

granger [-œ(r)], s. granjero, labriego; (G., E. U.) miembro de una GRANGE.

granite [grǽnịt], s. granito.—**g. ware**, utensilios de hierro con esmalte de color de granito; obra de alfarería semejante al granito.

granitic(al [grænịtịk(ǫl], a. granítico.

granivorous [grænívorǎs], a. (zool.) granívoro.

granny [grǽnị], s. (fam.) abuelita; comadre, f.

granolite [grǽnolaịt], s. roca ígnea granosa.

grant [grǽnt]. I. va. conceder; acordar, permitir, otorgar, dispensar; ceder, transferir, transmitir el título de una propiedad, etc.; asentir, convenir en, dar de barato.—**to take for granted**, presuponer, dar por supuesto. II. s. concesión, dádiva, donación; otorgamiento, permiso, privilegio, subvención, franquicia, asenso, asentimiento; (for.) carta forera o de gracia; documento que confiere un privilegio o concesión.

grantable [-ǎbl], a. que se puede otorgar o conceder; concesible, dable, permisible.

grantee [-í], s. (for.) (con)cesionario, adjudicatario, donatario.

granting [-iŋ]. I. a. otorgante, cedente. II. s. otorgamiento, (con)cesión.—**g. that**, dado que, supuesto que.

grantor [-ǫ(r)], s. (for.) cesionista, otorgante, otorgador, donador, cedente.

granular [grǽnyụlǎ(r)], a. granoso, granular, granuloso.

granulate [-leịt]. I. va. granular; granear; granar (pólvora); (fund.) granallar. II. vn. granularse; (med.) encarnar.—**granulated** [-ịd], pp. y a. graneado, granulado; en grano; moteado.—**g. steel**, acero hecho con hierro granulado.

granulation [-léịšǫn], s. granulación; granazón; superficie granulada; (med.) granulación, encarnación; formación de tubérculos.

granule [grényul], s. gránulo, granito.

granulize [grényulaịz], va. granular; convertir en píldoras.

granulous [-lʌs], a. granuloso.

grape [gréịp], s. uva; vid.—**g. arbor**, parral.—**g. hyacinth**, (bot.) almizcleña.—**g. juice**, mosto, zumo de la uva.—**g. seed** o **stone**, granuja, simiente (f.) de uva.—**g. sugar**, glucosa, dextrosa.

grapefruit [-frut], s. (bot.) toronja.

grapery [-œrị], s. invernadero o criadero de uvas.

grapeshot [-šat], s. (art.) metralla.

grapevine [-vaịn], s. vid, parra; (fig.) noticia o chisme que circula por vías secretas.

graph [græf]. I. s. gráfica, representación gráfica; diagrama, m.; curva.—**g. paper**, papel cuadriculado. II. va. construir la gráfica de, representar gráficamente.

graphalloy [grǽfǎloị], s. aleación de grafito impregnado de metal.

graphic(al [grǽfịk(ǫl], a. gráfico.—**g. accent**, acento ortográfico.—**g. statics**, grafostática.

graphically [-ị], adv. gráficamente.

graphite [grǽfaịt], s. (min.) grafito, plombagina, lápiz (m.) (de) plomo.

graphitic [grǽfịtịk], a. grafítico.

graphology [grǽfálodžị], s. grafología.

graphomania [grǽfoméịnịǎ], s. grafomanía.

graphometer [grǽfámɛtœ(r)], s. grafómetro.

graphophone [grǽfofoụn], s. grafófono, especie de fonógrafo (es nombre de fábrica).

grapnel [grǽpnęl], s. (mar.) anclote, rezón; arpeo, cloque, rastra, rebañadera, garabato.

grapple [grǽpl]. I. va. agarrar, agarrafar, asir; amarrar. II. vn. agarrarse, engarrafarse; (mar.) atracarse, aferrarse, abordarse. III. s. lucha, riña, pelea; arpeo, garabato, gafa, cloque, rastra.

grappling [grǽplịŋ], s. (mar.) rezón; aferramiento.—**g. iron**, rezón, cloque, arpeo.

grapy [gréịpị], a. lleno o hecho de uvas.

grasp [grǽsp]. I. va. empuñar, asir, agarrar; apresar, coger, apoderarse de, usurpar, tomar; ver, entender. II. vn. agarrarse fuertemente. III. s. asimiento, agarro; presa; usurpación; puño, puñado; garras, f. pl.; comprensión.

grasper [-œ(r)], s. agarrador.

grasping [-iŋ], a. codicioso.

grass [grǽs]. I. s. hierba, herbaje; pasto; césped, m.—**g. green**, verde como la hierba.—**g. grown**, cubierto de hierba.—**g. mower**, dallador.—**g. widow**, mujer separada de su marido.—**g. widower**, marido separado de su mujer.—**to let the g. grow under one's feet**, perder el tiempo, haraganear. II. va. cubrir de hierba; blanquear lino; apacentar. III. vn. pacer; herbecer, cubrirse de hierba.

grasshopper [-hapœ(r)], s. (ent.) saltamontes, saltón, langosta; palanca de cada tecla del piano.

grassiness [-ịnịs], s. abundancia de hierba.

grassland [-lænd], s. prado, pradería.

grassless [-lịs], a. sin hierba.

grassplat [-plæt], **grassplot** [-plat], s. prado, terreno cubierto de césped.

grassy [-ị], a. herboroso; herbáceo.

grate [gréịt]. I. s. reja; verja, enrejado; (m. v.) parrilla de hogar.—**g. bar**, barra de parrilla. II. va. (coc.) rallar; raspar; frotar, hacer rechinar; enrejar; emparrillar. III. vn. rozar, ludir; raer; rechinar, chirriar; (gen. con **on** o **upon**) molestar, irritar.

grateful [gréịtfụl], a. agradecido, reconocido; grato, gustoso.—**to be g. to**, o **for**, agradecer.—**gratefully** [-ị], adv. agradecidamente, gratamente.—**gratefulness** [-nịs], s. gratitud; agrado.

grater [gréịtœ(r)], s. rallo, ralladora, raspador.

graticulate [gratịkyụleịt], va. cuadricular.

graticule [grǽtịkịul], s. ocular cuadriculado.

gratification [grætịfịkéịšǫn], s. satisfacción, complacencia; gratificación, recompensa.

gratify [grǽtịfaị], va. satisfacer, complacer, dar gusto; (ant.) gratificar, recompensar.

grating [gréịtịŋ]. I. a. rechinante, chirriante, discordante, mal sonante; irritante, ofensivo, áspero. II. s. reja, rejilla, verja, enrejado; emparrillado; escurridero; chirrido, rechinamiento; (ópt.) retícula de microscopio, etc.—pl. (mar.) ajedrez, m., enjaretado; (coc.) ralladura(s).

gratis [grǽtịs]. I. adv. gratis, de balde, de gracia. II. a. gratuito.

gratitude [grǽtịtjud], s. gratitud, reconocimiento.

gratuitous [grǽtịụịtʌs], a. gratuito; injustificado.

gratuitously [-lị], adv. gratuitamente.

gratuity [gratjúiti], *s.* gratificación; propina.

gratulate [grǽchuleit], *va.* (ant.) gratular(se); felicitar.—**gratulation** [-éişǫn], *s.* gratulación. —**gratulatory** [-ǫtǫri], *a.* gratulatorio.

gravamen [gravéimen], *s.* agravio; (for.) la parte más grave de una acusación.

grave [greiv], (*pret.* GRAVED; *pp.* GRAVED o GRAVEN) grabar; esculpir, cincelar; (mar.) despalmar.

grave [gréiv]. I. *s.* sepultura, sepulcro, tumba; (gram.) acento grave. II. *a.* grave, serio; solemne; (mús.) grave, bajo, profundo; (gram.) grave.

graveclothes [-klouŏz], *s. pl.* mortaja.—**gravedigger** [-djgœ(r)], *s.* sepulturero, enterrador.

gravel [grǽvel]. I. *s.* cascajo, grava, guijo; (med.) litiasis, mal de piedra, cálculos, *m. pl.*—**g. pit**, cascajar.—**g. walk**, o **path**, camino de grava, sendero de chinas o piedrecillas, paseo enarenado. II. *va.* (en)arenar; confundir, embarazar; (fam.) irritar.

gravelly [-i], *a.* cascajoso, guijoso.

gravely [gréivli], *adv.* seriamente, gravemente.

graven [gréivn], *pp.* de TO GRAVE.—**g. image**, estatua; ídolo.

graveness [gréivnis], *s.* gravedad, seriedad.

graver [gréivœ(r)], *s.* (b. a.) buril, chaple; punzón; gradino; cincel; grabador, cincelador.

graves [greivz], *s. pl.* residuo o sedimento del sebo o de pellas de manteca derretidos; chicharrones.

gravestone [gréivstoun], *s.* lápida sepulcral.

graveyard [gréivyard], *s.* cementerio.

gravid [grǽvid], *a.* grávida, preñada.—**gravidity** [grǽvíditi], *s.* gravidez, embarazo, preñez.

gravimeter [grǽvímetœ(r)], *s.* gravímetro.

gravimetric [grǽvimétrik], *a.* gravimétrico, relativo a la determinación por medio del peso.

gravimetry [grǽvímetri], *s.* gravimetría, determinación de pesos o densidades.

gravitate [grǽviteit], *vn.* gravitar, gravear; tender.

gravitation [-éişǫn], *s.* gravitación.

gravitational [-ǫl], *a.* de gravitación, referente a la gravitación.

gravity [grǽviti], *s.* (fís.) gravedad, pesantez; seriedad, gravedad; majestad; importancia.

gravy [gréivi], *s.* (coc.) salsa, jugo de la carne; caldo.—**g. boat**, o **dish**, salsera.

gravure [grǽvyúr, gréivyur], *s.* fotograbado.

gray [gréi]. I. *va.* y *vn.* poner(se) gris o cano; encanecer. II. *a.* gris, pardo; tordo, rucio; cano, encanecido.—**g.-bearded**, barbicano.— **g.-eyed**, ojizarco.—**G. Friar**, (igl.) fraile franciscano.—**g.-haired**, **g.-headed**, canoso, encanecido; envejecido.—**g. horse**, caballo tordo.— **g. matter**, (anat.) substancia gris; (fam.) inteligencia, sesos, *m. pl.* III. *s.* color gris; animal gris.

graybeard [-bird], *s.* barbicano; hombre entrado en años.

grayfish [-fiş], *s.* (ict.) lija, cazón.

grayhound [-haund], *s.* = GREYHOUND.

grayish [-iş], *a.* pardusco, gríseo, grisáceo, agrisado; entrecano; tordillo.

graylag [-læg], *s.* (orn.) ganso gris silvestre.

grayling [-lin], *s.* (ict.) tímalo.

graze [greiz]. I. *vn.* pacer, pastar; tascar; rozar, rasar. II. *va.* pastorear, apacentar, herbajar; dar pienso o forraje; pasar rozando, raspar, rasar. III. *s.* roce, raspadura; pasto, apacentamiento.

grazier [gréiʒœ(r)], *s.* ganadero.

grazing [gréiziņ], *s.* dehesa, pasto; apacentamiento.

grease [grís]. I. *s.* grasa, unto, sebo, manteca; pringue, *mf.*; (vet.) aguajas, *f. pl.*—**g. box**, o **cup**, (máq.) vaso de engrase, caja de grasa.— **g. spot** o **stain**, (mancha de) pringue, lámpara. II. *va.* engrasar, untar; lubricar; (fam.) untar las manos, sobornar con dinero.

greaser [-œ(r)], *s.* engrasador; lubricador; lubri-

cante; (E. U. despec.) apodo que se da a los hispanoamericanos.

greasily [-ili], *adv.* crasamente.

greasiness [-inis], *s.* calidad de grasiento; mugre, *f.*

greasing [-in], *s.* engrase, engrasamiento.

greasy [-i], *a.* grasiento, pringoso, mantecoso.

great [gréit], *a.* grande; magno; admirable, excelente; experto; favorito; (fam.) famoso, espléndido. Indica la tercera, cuarta o quinta generación, vg.: *great-grandson*, bisnieto; *great-grandfather*, bisabuelo; *great-great-grandfather*, rebisabuelo o tatarabuelo; *great-great-grandson*, rebisnieto o tataranieto.—**G. Bear**, (astr.) Osa Mayor, Septentrión, *m.*, Carro (Mayor).—**g.-bellied**, barrigudo; preñada.—**g. cattle**, ganado mayor.—**g. circle**, (geom. y astr.) círculo máximo.—**G. Dane**, mastín danés.—**g. grandsire**, bisabuelo.—**g. gross**, doce gruesas.—**g.-hearted**, generoso, noble; animado, de alma grande.—**G. Lakes**, los Grandes Lagos— Superior, Míchigan, Hurón, Erié y Ontario.— **G. Mogul**, gran mogol.—**g. nettle**, (bot.) ortiga mayor.—**g. primer**, texto (tipo de 18 puntos).—**g. pyramid**, pirámide (*f.*) de Cheops o Gran Pirámide.—**g. seal**, gran sello.—**G. Scott!** ¡válgame Dios! ¡qué cosa! ¡Jesús!—**G. Wall**, Gran Muralla (de China).—**G. War**, gran guerra (la de 1914).—**G. White Father**, Gran Padre Blanco, título que los indios dan al presidente de los E. U.—**G. White Way**, Broadway, calle principal de Nueva York.—a **g. deal**, mucho, gran cantidad.—a **g. many**, muchos.—a **g. way off**, muy lejos.—a **g. while**, largo rato.—the **g.**, los grandes.

greatcoat [-kout], *s.* levitón, casacón; gabán.

greaten [-n]. I. *va.* agrandar, engrandecer. II. *vn.* crecer, aumentarse.

greater [-œ(r)], *a. comp.* de GREAT: mayor, más grande.—**G. Britain**, el imperio colonial de la Gran Bretaña.

greatest [-ist], *a. super.* de GREAT: más grande; máximo; sumo.—**g. common divisor**, (arit.) máximo común divisor.

greatly [-li], *adv.* muy, mucho; grandemente, profundamente, magnánimamente; en gran parte.

greatness [-nis], *s.* grandeza; grandiosidad; magnitud, extensión; fausto.

greaves [grivz], *s. pl.* (arm.) grebas, canilleras, espinilleras; (coc.) chicharrones. *V.* GRAVES.

grebe [grib], *s.* (orn.) colimbo.

Grecian [gríşan], *s.* y *a.* griego, greco; helenista.

Grecianize [-aiz], **Grecize** [grísaiz], *va.* y *vn.* grecizar, greguizar.

Grecism [grísizm], *s.* grecismo, helenismo.

Greco-Latin [gríkoulǽtin], *a.* grecolatino.—**G.-Roman**, *a.* grecorromano.

greed [gríd], **greediness** [-inis], *s.* voracidad, gula; codicia, avidez, ansia, anhelo.

greedily [-ili], *adv.* vorazmente; ávida o codiciosamente; vehementemente.

greedy [-i], *a.* voraz, guloso; anhelante, ávido, codicioso.

Greek [grik]. I. *s.* griego, greco; helenista; (fam.) jerga, gringo, lenguaje o cosa ininteligible. II. *a.* griego, greco.—**G. calends**, calendas griegas.— **G. fire**, fuego griego.

green [grín]. I. *a.* verde (de color y de sazón); inexperto o novato; crudo; nuevo o fresco, reciente, acabado de hacer; pálido, descolorido; floreciente, lozano.—**g. barley**, (bot.) alcacer. —**g. cloth**, tapete verde, mesa de juego; (Ingl.) mayordomía de palacio.—**g.-colored**, verde, verdoso; pálido, enfermizo.—**g. corn**, maíz tierno; (Méx.) elote; (Ingl.) trigo nuevo.—**g.-eyed**, ojiverde; celoso.—**g.-eyed monster**, celotipia.—**g. goods**, verduras; (fam., E. U.) billetes de banco falsificados.—**g. hand**, novicio, tirón.—**g. laver**, alga marina comestible. —**g. lead ore**, (min.) piromorfita, fosfato de plomo.—**g. light**, luz verde; autorización para seguir adelante.—**g. sand** (no *greensand*), arena verde o húmeda; (fund.) arena de moldear, rica en sílice y mezclada con carbón pulverizado.— **g. vitriol**, (quím.) caparrosa o vitriolo verde. —**g. ware**, loza cruda. **II.** *s.* color verde; verdor, verdura; prado o pradera; césped, *m.*—*pl.* (coc.) verduras, hortalizas. **III.** *va.* pintar o teñir de verde. **IV.** *vn.* verdear.

greenback [-bæk], *s.* (E. U.) papel moneda, billete del gobierno o de un banco nacional.— **G. party**, (E. U.) partido político que sostenía que la moneda debía limitarse a billetes emitidos por el gobierno.

greenfinch [-finch], *s.* (orn.) verdecillo, verderón.

greengage [-geidʒ], *s.* (bot.) ciruela verdal.

greengrocer [-grousœ(r)], *s.* verdulero.—**greengrocery** [-i], *s.* (Ingl.) verdulería, tienda de legumbres y frutas.

greenheart [-hart], *s.* (bot.) bebeerú, especie de laurel de Guayana.

greenhorn [-horn], *s.* (fam.) tirón, novicio, aprendiz, *m.*; chambón; paleto, palurdo.

greenhouse [-haus], *s.* invernáculo, invernadero.

greening [-iŋ], *s.* acto de verdear; (bot.) variedad de manzana verdosa.

greenish [-iš], *a.* verdoso, verdusco.

greenly [-li], *adv.* nuevamente, recientemente; sin madurez.

greenness [-nis], *s.* verdura, verdor; vigor, frescura; falta de experiencia; novedad.

greenroom [-rum], *s.* (teat.) sala de espera de los actores.

greensand [-sænd], *s.* (geol.) arenisca verde.

greensick [-sik], *a.* clorótico.—**greensickness** [-nis], *s.* (med.) clorosis.

greenstone [-stoun], *s.* roca verde eruptiva (diorita, dolerita, etc.); jade, piedra nefrítica.

greensward [-sword], *s.* césped, *m.*

greenwood [-wud], *s.* selva frondosa.

greet [grit]. **I.** *va.* saludar, dar la bienvenida. **II.** *vn.* encontrarse y saludarse.

greeting [-iŋ], *s.* salutación, saludo; ¡salud!

gregarious [grigériʌs], *a.* gregario.—**gregariously** [-li], *adv.* gregariamente.—**gregariousness** [-nis], *s.* calidad de gregario.

Gregorian [grigórjan], *a.* gregoriano.

greisen [gráizn], *s.* (geol.) gres.

gremial [grímiʌl], *s.* (igl.) gremial.

grenade [grenéjd], *s.* (mil.) granada, bomba.

grenadier [grenadír], *s.* (mil.) granadero.

grenadine [grenadín], *s.* (tej.) granadina.

grew [gru], *pret.* de TO GROW.

grey [gréj], *a.* gris. *V.* GRAY.

greyhound [-haund], *s.* galgo; lebrel; vapor de alta mar muy veloz.

grid [grid], *s.* red; parrilla; reja, rejilla; (elec.) rejilla (de una pila); (rad.) parrilla, malla, ánodo auxiliar reticulado de la lámpara termiónica; (f. c.) GRIDIRON.—**g. accumulator**, (elec.) acumulador de rejilla.—**g. circuit**, g. **current**, etc., (rad.) circuito, corriente, *f.*, etc., de la parrilla.—**g. leak**, (rad.) resistencia de protección del circuito de la parrilla.—**g. potentiometer**, (rad.) potenciómetro regulador del voltaje de la parrilla.—**g. resistance**, (elec.) reóstato o resistencia de rejillas.

griddle [grídl], *s.* (coc.) tortera; tapadera de fogón.

griddlecake [-kejk], *s.* (coc.) tortita de harina que se asa en la tortera o sobre una plancha caliente; (Am.) arepa, tortilla. *V.* PANCAKE.

gridiron [grídaiœrn], *s.* parrillas; red (de vigas, tubos, etc.); (mar.) andamiada, basada de esqueleto; (f. c.) red de rieles; (teat.) telar; (dep.) campo demarcado para el juego de football.

grief [grif], *s.* pesar, aflicción, dolor, pesadumbre, sentimiento.—**g.-stricken**, des(cons)olado, apesadumbrado.—**to come to g.**, pasarlo mal; fracasar.

griefless [-lis], *a.* exento de pena.

grievance [grívʌns], *s.* injusticia, perjuicio; motivo de queja, agravio, ofensa.—**g. committee**, (e. p.) comité de reivindicaciones.

grieve [gríf]. **I.** *va.* afligir, lastimar; apesadumbrar. **II.** *vn.* apesadumbrarse, dolerse, penar.

grievingly [-iŋli], *adv.* apesaradamente.

grievous [grívʌs], *a.* penoso, doloroso, lastimoso; oneroso; fiero, atroz, cruel.—**grievously** [-li], *adv.* penosamente, lastimosamente, afligidamente.—**grievousness** [-nis], *s.* calidad de penoso, etc.

griffin [grifin], **griffon** [grifon], *s.* (mit. griega) grifo; (orn.) buitre; (fig.) guardián, vigilante.

grig [grig], *s.* (ent.) grillo; (ict.) anguila pequeña; persona alegre y vivaracha.

grill [gril]. **I.** *va.* grill, asar en parrillas; atormentar con fuego o calor; interrogar severamente y sin tregua. **II.** *s.* parrilla; manjar asado en parrillas. *V.* GRILLROOM.

grillade [-éjd], *s.* manjar asado en parrillas; carbonada.

grillage [grílidʒ], *s.* emparrillado; enrejado.

grille [gril], *s.* verja, reja.—**g. work**, enrejado.

grillroom [grílrum], *s.* *grillroom*; restaurante que se especializa en manjares asados en parrillas.

grim [grim], *a.* torvo, ceñudo; feo, horrendo; inflexible; formidable.—**g.-faced**, o **g.-visaged**, malcarado.

grimace [griméjs]. **I.** *s.* mueca, gesto, mohín, visaje. **II.** *vn.* gestear, gesticular, hacer muecas.

grimalkin [grimélkin], *s.* gatazo, gata vieja; mujer vieja.

grime [grajm]. **I.** *s.* tizne, mugre, *f.*, porquería. **II.** *va.* ensuciar, tiznar.

grimly [grímli], *adv.* torva o inflexiblemente, etc.

grimness [grímnis], *s.* calidad de torvo, feo, etc.; grima, horror, espanto.

grimy [grájmi], *a.* tiznado, sucio, manchado.

grin [grin]. **I.** *vn.* hacer muecas mostrando los dientes; sonreír satisfecha, aprobativa o sarcásticamente. **II.** *s.* mueca (de ira, dolor, etc.); sonrisa expresiva de satisfacción, aprobación, burla o sarcasmo (según el caso).

grind [grajnd]. **I.** *va.* (*pret.* y *pp.* GROUND) moler, quebrantar, triturar; pulverizar; picar (carne); hacer crujir o rechinar (los dientes); amolar, afilar; vaciar; frotar, rallar, estregar, refregar; pulir, esmerilar, bruñir; mascar; dar vueltas a un manubrio; gravar, acosar, molestar, agobiar, oprimir; (fam.) dar matraca. **II.** *vn.* hacer molienda; rozar, frotar, ludir; pulirse o deslustrarse con el roce; (fam.) empollar, estudiar excesivamente. **III.** *s.* molienda; (fam.) ajobo, trabajo pesado; (fam.) estudiantón, empollón.

grinder [-œ(r)], *s.* molinero, molendero; moledor; esmerilador; muela, piedra de molino o de amolar; molino, molinillo; amolador; muela, diente molar.

grinding [-iŋ]. **I.** *s.* pulverización, moledura, molienda, molimiento; amoladura; esmerilado, bruñido, pulimento. **II.** *pa.* de GRIND; moliente; de pulir, de esmerilar; de amolar; de moler.—**g. balls**, bolillas moledoras o pulverizadoras.— **g. lathe**, torno de pulir.—**g. machine**, esmeriladora.—**g. mill**, trapiche.—**g. plate**, disco para pulir vidrio.—**g. roll**, maza de trapiche.—**g. stand**, torno esmerilador.—**g. wheel**, muela; rueda de amolar o de esmerilar.

grindstone [-stoun], *s.* amoladera, muela, volandera; molejón; afiladera; esmeriladora.

gringo [gríngou], *s.* (desp.) *gringo*, yanqui, inglés.

grip [grip]. **I.** *s.* apretón de mano; empuñamiento, agarro; presa; modo de darse la mano; saco de mano; asidero, puño, mango; garras (fig.); (f. c.) mordaza de arrastre del cable de tracción; capacidad de agarrar y retener, o de comprender; (med.) GRIPPE.—**g. car**, coche o vagón de arrastre por cable (de un funicular).—**to be at grips**, estar en un cuerpo a cuerpo. **II.** *va.* agarrar, empuñar, asir, cerrar. **III.** *vn.* agarrarse con fuerza.

gripe [graip]. **I.** *va.* agarrar, empuñar; pellizcar; (mec.) morder; dar cólico; afligir, acongojar. **II.** *vn.* agarrar fuertemente; padecer cólico; (fam.) quejarse, refunfuñar de vicio. **III.** *s.* agarro, asimiento; sujeción; garra; (mec.) uña, grapa, abrazadera, freno de malacate; puño, mango, manija, agarradera; opresión; aprieto, apuro; (fam.) queja.—*pl.* dolor, cólico, retortijón, (vet.) torozón; (mar.) obenques o bozas de lancha; trincas.

gripman [grípman], *s.* (f. c.) el encargado de la mordaza de arrastre.

grippe [grip], *s.* (med.) gripe, *f.*, influenza.

gripper [grípœ(r)], *s.* el o lo que agarra, etc.; (impr. y mec.) uña.

gripping [grípiŋ]. **I.** *s.* acción de agarrar, asir, etc. **II.** *a.* muy emocionante (libro, drama, etc.).

grippy [grípi], *a.* (med., fam.) gripal, semejante a o con caracteres de gripe; tenaz, testarudo; avaro.

gripsack [grípsæk], *s.* (fam.) saco de noche, maletica.

grisette [grizét], *s.* griseta (tela); griseta, obrera o modistilla alegre (apl. esp. a la de París).

grisly [grízli], *a.* espantoso, terrible.

grison [gráison], *s.* (zool.) grisón, pequeño mamífero carnívoro.

grist [grist], *s.* molienda; provisión, abasto, suministro.

gristle [grísl], *s.* cartílago, ternilla.

gristly [grísli], *a.* cartilaginoso.

gristmill [grístmil], *s.* molino harinero.

grit [grít]. **I.** *s.* arena, cascajo; (geol.) arenisca silícea, asperón (ll. t. **gritrock** y **gritstone**); firmeza; entereza; valor, ánimo.—*pl.* sémola, farro. **II.** *va.* y *vn.* (fam.) rechinar o crujir (los dientes, etc.). *V.* GRATE y GRIND.

grittiness [-inis], *s.* contextura arenosa; fortitud, entereza.

gritty [-i], *a.* arenoso, arenisco; valeroso, esforzado.

grizzle [grízl], *s.* color gris; mezclilla.

grizzled [-d], *a.* tordillo, entrecano. *V.* GRIZZLY.

grizzly [grízli]. **I.** *a.* gríseo, pardusco.—**g. bear**, oso pardo. **II.** *s.* (min.) criba grande.

groan [groun]. **I.** *vn.* gemir; lanzar quejidos. **II.** *s.* gemido, quejido.

groat [grout], *s.* (Ingl.) moneda (cuatro peniques); bicoca, ardite.—*pl.* sémola, avena mondada.

grocer [gróusœ(r)], *s.* especiero, abacero.—**g.'s shop**, abacería, especiería, lonja o tienda de comestibles, ultramarinos o coloniales.

grocery (store) [-ri stor], *s.* abacería, especiería, (Am.) abarrote.—*pl.* **groceries**, especierías, comestibles, víveres; (Am.) abarrotes.

grog [grág], *s.* brebaje o bebida alcohólica, grog.

groggy [-i], *a.* medio borracho, calamocano; (dep.) vacilante; turulato.

grogram [grágram], *s.* (tej.) cordellate, gorgorán.

grogshop [grágšap], **groggery** [grágœri], *s.* taberna.

groin [groin]. **I.** *s.* (anat.) ingle, *f.*; (arq.) arista de encuentro, esquina viva; (ing.) espolón, dique, malecón. **II.** *va.* (arq.) formar aristas.

groined [-d], *a.* de arista (apl. a arcos, etc.).

grommet [grámit], *s.* anillo para cordones de talegas, velas, zapatos, etc.

groom [grúm]. **I.** *s.* mozo de mulas o de cuadra; establero; palafrenero; lacayo; novio.—**g. in waiting**, camarero de semana.—**g. of the bed chamber**, ayuda de cámara del rey.—**g. of the chamber**, caballerizo de cámara. **II.** *va.* cuidar, almohazar los caballos; (fam.) peinar y vestir, acicalar; (pol., etc.) preparar (para un cargo o puesto).

groomsman [-zman], *s.* padrino de boda.

groove [gruv]. **I.** *s.* muesca, encaje, rebajo, encastre, gárgol, acanaladura, canal, *f.*, caja, ranura, estría; surco; (arm.) rayadura; rutina.— **g. and tongue**, *s.* (carp.) ranura y lengüeta, unión machihembrada; *va.* machihembrar.—**g.**

grafting, injerto de canutillo. **II.** *va.* acanalar; (ton.) ruñar.

grooved [-d], *a.* acanalado.

grope [group], *va.* y *vn.* tentar, andar a tientas; buscar tentando.

gros, grosgrain [gróu(grein], *s.* (tej.) gro. *V.* GROGRAM.

grosbeak [gróusbik], *s.* (orn.) cardenal.

gross [gróus]. **I.** *a.* craso; grueso; espeso, denso; indecoroso, obsceno; tosco, grosero, descortés; lerdo, estúpido; (com.) bruto.—**g. amount**, importe bruto o total.—**g. ignorance**, ignorancia crasa.—**g. profit**, ganancia bruta, beneficio bruto.—**g. ton** = LONG TON.—**g. weight**, peso bruto. **II.** *s.* (*pl.* GROSS) gruesa (doce docenas); grueso, la mayor parte; la totalidad, el conjunto.—**by the g.**, por mayor; por gruesas.—**in g., in the g.**, en grueso, por junto, en conjunto.

grossly [-li], *adv.* en bruto; crasamente, toscamente, groseramente.

grossness [-nis], *s.* grosería, incivilidad, ordinariez; densidad; grosura.

grossularite [grásyülärait], *s.* (min.) grosularia.

grot [grat], *s.* (poét.) gruta. *V.* GROTTO.

grotesque [grotésk]. **I.** *a.* grotesco; (b. a.) grutesco. **II.** *s.* (b. a.) grutesco.

grotesquely [-li], *adv.* grotescamente.

grotesqueness [-nis], *s.* calidad de grotesco.

grotto [grátou], *s.* gruta, antro, covacha.

grouch [gráuch]. **I.** *s.* (fam.) gruñón, descontento.—**to have a g.**, estar de mal humor. **II.** *vn.* gruñir, refunfuñar, estar de mal humor. —**groucher** [-œ(r)], *s.* (fam.) gruñón, persona de mal humor.—**grouchy** [-i], *a.* (fam.) malhumorado.

ground [gráund]. **I.** *s.* tierra, terreno, suelo, territorio; base, *f.*, fundamento; razón, *f.*, motivo, causa; (pint.) fondo o campo; baño, capa; (elec.) (toma de) tierra; (rad.) tierra, objeto (tubería, calorífero, etc.) a que se ata el alambre de conexión con tierra; (mil.) campo de batalla; (*pl.*) poso, sedimento, heces, *f. pl.*; jardín, parque, terrenos; cancha (de juego).—**on, o upon, the g.**, en tierra, en el suelo.—**to be on one's own g.**, estar uno en su elemento.—**to break g.**, desmontar; roturar; empezar un trabajo.—**to come, o fall, to the g.**, caer al suelo; fracasar.—**to gain g.**, ganar terreno; hacer progresos.—**to give, o to lose, g.**, perder terreno, retroceder, atrasar.—**to stand, o to hold, one's g.**, mantenerse firme.—**to take the g.**, (mar.) encallar. **II.** *a.* situado en el suelo o al nivel del suelo; fundamental; de tierra; de base, primero (capa, etc.); (elec.) de conexión con tierra.—**g. clamp**, (elec.) tira de conexión con tierra.—**g. detector**, (elec.) detector de tierras.—**g. floor**, piso bajo, planta baja; (fam.) el sitio o puesto más ventajoso.—**g. hog**, marmota.—**g.-hog day**, (E. U.) día de la marmota (2 de feb.) en que, según la tradición, este animal descubre si el invierno será corto o largo.—**g. ice** = ANCHOR ICE.—**g. ivy**, (bot.) hiedra terrestre.—**g. lead** = **g. WIRE**.—**g. line**, (geom.) línea de (la) tierra.—**g. pine**, (bot.) pinillo.—**g. plate**, (elec.) placa de (conexión con) tierra; (f. c.) plancha de asiento; (arq.) carrera inferior.—**g. plot**, solar, lote; (arq.) plano.—**g. rent**, censo.—**g. speed**, (aer.) velocidad horizontal de un avión con respecto a la tierra.—**g. water**, agua subterránea; agua de pozo.—**g. wire**, (elec.) alambre de tierra. **III.** *va.* fundar, apoyar, establecer; (con **upon**) vincular en; enseñar los elementos de alguna ciencia; poner en tierra; (elec.) conectar con tierra. **IV.** *vn.* (mar.) encallar, embarrancar, varar, enarenar.

ground, *pp.* de TO GRIND.—**g. glass**, vidrio esmerilado o deslustrado.—**g. meat**, carne picada.

groundage [-idź], *s.* (mar.) derechos de puerto o de anclaje.

grounding [-iŋ], *s.* (mar.) encalladura.

groundless [-lįs], *a.* infundado.—**groundlessly** [-lį], *adv.* infundadamente, sin razón.—**groundlessness** [-nįs], *s.* falta de razón o fundamento.

groundling [-liŋ], *s.* animal o planta terrestre; (ict.) loche, loja; villano.

groundnut [-nʌt], *s.* (bot.) cacahuete, maní.

groundsel [-sęl], *s.* (bot.) zuzón, hierba cana.

groundsill [-sįl], *s.* (arq.) carrera inferior; solera, umbral.

groundwork [-wœrk], *s.* plan, plano, pie, *m.*, base, *f.*, fundamento, cimiento; principio, razón (*f.*) fundamental; firme (de carretera).

group [grúp]. I. *s.* grupo, agrupación, conjunto. II. *va.* y *vn.* agrupar(se), reunir(se).

grouper [-œ(r)], *s.* (ict.) mero; escorpina.

grouse [graus], *s.* (orn.) guaco; chachalaca; chocha; lagópodo.

grouse. I. *vn.* (fam.) quejarse. II. *s.* queja.

grout [graut]. I. *s.* (alb.) lechada; enlucido.—*pl.* sémola, farro; heces, *f. pl.*, sedimento. II. *va.* rellenar con lechada.

grove [grouv], *s.* arboleda, alameda, enramada, mata, soto, bosquecillo, boscaje.

grovel [grávęl], *vn.* serpear, arrastrarse; envilecerse, rebajarse.—**grovel(l)er** [-œ(r)], *s.* hombre servil y rastrero.—**grovel(l)ing** [-iŋ], *a.* servil, rastrero.—**grovel(l)ingly** [-lį], *adv.* servilmente, rastreramente.

grow [grou]. I. *va.* (*pret.* GREW; *pp.* GROWN) cultivar; criar; producir. II. *vn.* crecer; darse (frutas, plantas, etc.); (seguido de *adj.* o *adv.*) hacerse, volverse, ponerse (vg.: *to grow old*, ponerse viejo, envejecer; *to grow angry*, ponerse colérico, encolerizarse; *to grow crazy*, volverse loco, enloquecerse; *to grow late*, hacerse tarde; *to grow better*, ponerse mejor, mejorar); proceder, provenir, resultar; (con **to**) fijarse, arraigarse (en); llegar a (odiar, amar, etc.).—**to g. dark**, anochecer, obscurecer.—**to g. less**, disminuir.—**to g. long(er)**, alargarse.—**to g. loose**, aflojarse.—**to g. on**, o **upon**, desarrollarse en, ir dominando a, ir apoderándose de; ganar o aventajar a; hacerse cada vez más querido, admirable, etc., a.—**to g. out of**, resultar o provenir de, ser causado por, originarse en; brotar de; salir o pasar de con la edad (*he will grow out of this whim*, este capricho le pasará con la edad, o cuando crezca).—**to g. out of fashion**, o use, pasar de moda, caer en desuso.—**to g. sad**, entristecerse.—**to g. short(er)**, acortarse.—**to g. up**, crecer, desarrollarse, salir de la niñez; desarrollarse y establecerse (una costumbre, etc.).

grower [-œ(r)], *s.* cultivador, agricultor.

growing [-iŋ]. I. *s.* cultivo; cría; crecimiento, desarrollo. II. *a.* creciente; que crece, que aumenta.—**g. pains**, dolores asociados con el desarrollo físico de la niñez o adolescencia.

growl [graul]. I. *vn.* gruñir; rezongar, refunfuñar. II. *va.* decir gruñendo. III. *s.* gruñido; rezongo, refunfuño.

growler [-œ(r)], *s.* perro gruñidor; regañón, refunfuñador; (fam.) jarro para cerveza.

grown [groun], *a.* y *pp.* crecido, espigado, desarrollado; cubierto o lleno de hierbas, maleza, etc.—**g.-up**, crecido, adulto.

grownup [-ʌp], *s.* persona mayor.—*pl.* los grandes.

growth [grou¿], *s.* crecimiento, desarrollo; aumento; producto, producción; acrecencia.

grub [grʌb]. I. *va.* y *vn.* (agr.) rozar, descuajar, desyerbar, desmalezar; quitar insectos nocivos, descocar; (fam.) alimentar(se), manducar; cavar; emplearse en oficios bajos. II. *s.* (ent.) gorgojo; larva; (fam.) alimento, manducatoria; (E. U.) raíz arrancada.—**g. ax**, legón, picaza.—**grubbing hoe**, escarda, azada.

grubber [-œ(r)], *s.* desyerbador; arrancador de raíces.

grubby [-į], *a.* gusarapiento, gusaniento, cocoso, gorgojoso.

grudge [grʌdź]. I. *va.* envidiar, codiciar; escatimar, dar de mala gana. II. *s.* rencor, inquina, tema, tirria; renuencia, mal grado.

grudging [-iŋ], *s.* envidia, mala voluntad; refunfuño; repugnancia, aversión.—**grudgingly** [-lį], *adv.* de mala gana.

gruel [grúęl]. I. *s.* (coc.) atole, avenate. II. *va.* incapacitar, agotar; estropear, desbaratar.

gruel(l)ing [-iŋ], *a.* agotador, en que uno tiene que poner todas sus fuerzas; abrumador.

gruesome [grúsʌm], *a.* horrible, horripilante.

gruff [grʌf], *a.* ceñudo, áspero; (b)ronco (voz).—**gruffly** [-lį], *adv.* ásperamente.—**gruffness** [-nįs], *s.* aspereza, ceño, mal humor.

grum [grʌm], *a.* áspero, severo; gutural.

grumble [-bl]. I. *vn.* refunfuñar, gruñir, rezongar, quejarse. II. *s.* regaño, quejumbre, refunfuñadura.

grumbler [-blœ(r)], *s.* refunfuñador, gruñidor, rezongador, malcontento.

grumbling [-bliŋ]. I. *s.* queja, descontento, rezongo, refunfuñadura. II. *a.* quejumbroso.—**grumblingly** [-lį], *adv.* refunfuñando.

grume [grúm], *s.* grumo, cuajarón.

grumous [-ʌs], *a.* grumoso; (bot.) amacollado.

grumpy [grámpį], *a.* gruñón, quejoso, áspero.

grunt [grʌnt], *vn.* gruñir; arruar; refunfuñar.

grunt, *s.* gruñido; (ict.) nombre de un pez americano.

grunter [-œ(r)], *s.* gruñidor; cerdo.

gruntingly [-iŋlį], *adv.* gruñendo; regañando, refunfuñando.

gruntling [-liŋ], *s.* lechón, cochinillo.

Gruyère [grįyér], *s.* (queso) gruyere.

guacharo [gwácharou], *s.* (orn.) guácharo.

guaco [gwákou], *s.* (bot.) guaco.

guaiac(um [gwáįæk, -akam], *s.* (bot.) guayaco o guayacán; resina de este árbol.

guaiacol [gwáįakol], *s.* (quím.) guayacol.

guan [gwan], *s.* (zool.) pava.

guanaco [gwanákou], *s.* (zool.) guanaco.

guanin(e [gwánįn], *s.* guanina.

guano [gwánou], *s.* guano.

guarantee [gæręntí]. I. *va.* garantir, garantizar, respaldar; (for.) afianzar, responder de o por, salir fiador de; dar fianza o caución. II. *s.* garantía, fianza; (for.) persona de quien otra sale fiadora; úsase también en el sentido de GUARANTOR.

guarantor [gæręnto(r)], *s.* garante, fiador.

guaranty [gæręntį]. I. *s.* (for.) garantía, caución, fianza. II. *va.* garantizar.

guard [gárd]. I. *va.* y *vn.* guardar, custodiar, vigilar; atalayar; estar prevenido; guardarse.—**to g. against**, guardarse de. II. *s.* guarda, *mf.*; guardia; guardián, custodio; resguardo, protección, custodia, defensa; vigilancia; atalaya, *m.*, centinela, *mf.*; vigilante; precaución, cautela; estado de defensa; guarnición de un vestido o una espada; (f. c.) conductor de tren.—**g. mounting**, relevo de guardia o de centinela.—**on g.**, alerta; (esgr.) en guardia.—**to be off one's g.**, estar desprevenido.—**to be on one's g.**, estar alerta. III. *a.* de guardia, de protección.—**g. rail**, (f. c.) contracarril; barandilla.—**g. ship**, navío de guardia, o ronda de estación.

guarded [-įd], *a.* protegido, defendido; cauto, cauteloso, precavido.

guardedly [-lį], *adv.* cautelosamente.

guardedness [-nįs], *s.* cautela, precaución.

guardhouse [-haus], *s.* cuartel de la guardia; prisión militar.

guardian [gárdįan]. I. *s.* guardián, guarda, *mf.*, custodio; (for.) tutor o curador. II. *a.* que guarda, tutelar, etc.—**g. angel**, ángel de la guarda, ángel custodio.

guardianship [-šįp], *s.* tutela, patronato; (for.)

tutoría, curaduría; (igl.) guardianía; protección, amparo, guarda, custodia.

guardroom [gárdrum], s. cuarto de guardia; calabozo.

guardsman [gárdzmạn], s. soldado de guardia; centinela.

guava [gwávạ], s. (bot.) guayabo; guayaba.

guayule [gwayúlạ], s. (bot.) guayule.

gubernatorial [gịubœrnạtóriạl], a. gubernativo; del gobernador.

gudgeon [gʌdʒọn], s. (ict.) gobio; bobo, mentecato; chiripa, ganga; (mec.) muñón, gorrón, cuello de eje; (mar.) hembra (del timón).

Guelf, Guelph [gwelf], a. y s. güelfo.

guerdon [gœrdọn], s. (poét.) galardón, premio.

guerrilla [gɛrílạ]. I. s. (mil.) guerrillero. II. a. de guerrillas, de guerrilleros.

guess [gɛs]. I. va. y vn. conjeturar, suponer, barruntar; adivinar, acertar; (fam.) pensar, creer. —**to g. right**, acertar. II. s. conjetura, suposición; adivinación.

guesser [-œ(r)], s. conjeturador; adivinador.

guesswork [-wœrk], s. conjetura, ojo de buen cubero.

guest [gɛst], s. huésped, m., convidado, invitado; forastero, visita; pensionista o inquilino; animal parásito o intruso.—**g. chamber, g. room**, cuarto de reserva, cuarto para convidados.—**g. of honor**, huésped de honor, el agasajado, el festejado.—**g. rope**, (mar.) guía de falsa amarra (t. t. **guess-rope**).

guffaw [gʌfó]. I. s. carcajada, risotada. II. vn. reír a carcajadas.

guidance [gáidạns], s. guía, gobierno, dirección, conducta.

guide [gáid]. I. va. guiar, dirigir, encaminar, conducir, orientar; adiestrar; arreglar, gobernar. II. s. guía, mf., mentor; (mec.) corredera; (impr.) mordante.—**g. lines**, pauta, fals(ill)a (para escribir).—**g. rope**, cuerda lateral de guía; (aer.) cuerda de arrastre colgada de la barquilla para mantener un dirigible a una misma altura.

guideboard [-bɔrd], s. = GUIDEPOST.

guidebook [-bụk], s. guía del viajero.

guideless [-lịs], a. sin guía, sin gobierno.

guidon [gáidọn], s. (mil.) guión, m.; portaguión, m.

guidepost [gáidpoụst], s. hito, poste indicador.

guild [gịld], s. gremio, cuerpo, comunidad, hermandad, corporación.

guilder [gịldœ(r)], s. florín holandés. V. GULDEN.

guildhall [gịldhɔl], s. casa consistorial, casa de ayuntamiento.

guile [gáil], s. dolo o engaño; estratagema.—**guileful** [-fụl], a. aleve, engañoso.—**guilefully** [-i], adv. insidiosamente, engañosamente.—**guileless** [-lịs], a. sencillo, cándido.—**guilelessness** [-nịs], s. franqueza, sinceridad, candidez.

guillotine [gịlotin]. I. s. guillotina. II. va. guillotinar.

guilt [gịlt], s. delito, culpa(bilidad), delincuencia; pecado.

guiltily [-ili], adv. criminalmente, culpablemente.

guiltiness [-inịs], s. maldad; culpabilidad.

guiltless [-lịs], a. inculpable, inocente, libre de culpa; puro, sin tacha; virgen; ignorante, nesciente.—**guiltlessly** [-li], adv. inocentemente.—**guiltlessness** [-nịs], s. inocencia, inculpabilidad.

guilty [-i], a. reo, delincuente, convicto; culpable. —**to have a g. conscience**, remorderle a uno la conciencia, tener o sentir remordimiento (de conciencia).

guimpe [gæmp], s. (cost.) canesú.

guinea [gịni], s. guinea (unidad monetaria inglesa, 21 chelines).—**g. fowl, g. hen**, gallina de Guinea o pintada.—**g. grains**, malagueta.—**g. pepper**, (bot.) pimiento de Guinea.—**g. pig**, conejillo de Indias, cobayo, curí.—**g. worm**, filaria.

guise [gáiz], s. modo, manera; apariencia; máscara, capa, pretexto.—**under the g. of**, so color, bajo capa de.—**in this g.**, de este modo.

guiser [-œ(r)], s. disfrazado.

guitar [gitár], s. (mús.) guitarra, vihuela.—**g. player**, guitarrista, vihuelista.

gula [gịúlạ], s. (zool.) la parte superior de la garganta.—**gular** [-(r)], a. relativo o perteneciente a la garganta.

gulch [gʌlch], s. quebrada, cañada.

gulden [gụldẹn], s. gulden (moneda); florín (austríaco, alemán, etc.).

gules [gịulz], s. (her.) gules, m. pl.

gulf [gʌlf], s. golfo; seno; sima, abismo, vorágine, f.—**G. stream**, corriente (f.) del Golfo de Méjico.—**the G.**, (E. U.) el golfo de México.

gulfweed [-wid], s. (bot.) sargazo, alga marina.

gull [gʌl]. I. va. engañar, timar, estafar. II. s. (orn.) gaviota; bobo, bodoque, primo.

gullet [gʌlịt], s. (anat., zool.) fauces, f. pl., gaznate, gola; esófago; zanja, trinchera profunda.

gullibility [gʌlibịlịti], s. credulidad.

gullible [gʌlịbl], a. bobo, crédulo, simple.—**to be g.**, pecar de candoroso, tragar el anzuelo.

gully [gʌli]. I. va. formar canal. II. s. cárcava; arroyo; barranca, hondonada; zanja honda.

gulp [gʌlp]. I. va. (a veces con **down**) engullir, tragar; sofocar (un sollozo). II. vn. entrecortar el resuello. III. s. trago, sorbo, gorgorotada.

gum [gam]. I. s. goma; (anat.) encía (de la boca). —**g. arabic**, guacia, acacina, goma arábiga.— **g. dragon** o **tragacanth**, goma adragante, tragacanto.—**g. elastic**, goma elástica, caucho. —**g. lac**, goma laca.—**g. resin**, gomorresina.— **g. tree**, árbol que da goma.—**g. water**, aguagoma. II. va. engomar; pegar con goma; (tej.) aderezar.

gumbo [gʌmboụ], s. (bot.) quimbombó, quingombó; (coc.) sopa de pollo y quingombó; (agr.) suelo pegajoso; dialecto criollo de Luisiana, etc.

gumboil [gʌmbọil], s. (med.) flemón, párulis, m.

gumdrop [gʌmdrap], s. pastilla de goma.

gummiferous [gʌmífẹrạs], a. gumífero.

gumminess [gʌmịnịs], s. gomosidad.

gummy [gʌmi], **gummous** [gʌmʌs], a. gomoso; engomado.

gumption [gʌmpʃọn], s. (fam.) iniciativa; perspicacia; (pint.) arte de preparar colores.

gumshoe [gʌmʃú]. I. s. (fam.) zapato o chanclo de goma; polizonte, detective. II. a. (fam.) oculto, subrepticio; hecho con mucho tiento o muy cautelosamente. III. vn. (fam.) andar u obrar furtivamente.

gumwood [gʌmwụd], s. madera del árbol de goma.

gun [gʌn]. I. s. arma de fuego; cañón; fusil; escopeta de caza; (E. U., fam.) pistola o revólver; disparo de arma de fuego; cañonazo.—**g. barrel**, cañón de fusil o de escopeta.—**g. carriage**, cureña.—**g. deck**, (mar.) cubierta principal, batería.—**g. metal**, bronce de cañón; imitación de bronce (aleación parda).—**g. port**, porta, cañonera. II. va. hacer fuego a; cañonear, atacar con cañones; proveer de cañones. III. vn. cazar con escopeta o rifle.

gunboat [-boụt], s. (mar.) cañonero.

guncotton [-katn], s. algodón pólvora.

gunfire [-fạir], s. fuego de artillería; fuego (de armas de fuego en general).

gunflint [-flịnt], s. piedra de chispa, pedernal.

gunlock [-lak], s. llave (f.) de fusil.

gunman [-mạn], s. pistolero, bandido de calle o de ciudad, apache.

gunnel [gʌnẹl], s. (mar.) = GUNWALE.

gunner [gʌnœ(r)], s. (mar.) condestable, cabo de cañón; (mil.) artillero; escopetero.

gunnery [-i], s. artillería.

gunning [gʌnịŋ], s. (dep.) caza.

gunny [gʌni], s. yute; tejido basto para sacos; saco de (h)arpillera (lt. t. g. **bag** o **sack**).

gunpowder [gʌnpaụdœ(r)], s. pólvora.

gunpower, gun power [gánpaụœ(r)], *s.* (mar.) peso total de los proyectiles lanzados en una andanada por los cañones mayores de un barco de guerra.

gunshot [gánšat], *s.* tiro de fusil, alcance; escopetazo.

gunsmith [gánsmiθ], *s.* armero; escopetero.

gunstock [gánstak], *s.* caja de fusil o de escopeta.

Gunter's chain [gántœrz chejn], *s.* (top.) cadena de Gunter (2,0117 Dm.).

gunwale [gánl], *s.* (mar.) regala, borda.

gurgitation [gœrdžitéjšọn], *s.* ebullición violenta; vorágine, *f.*, remolino.

gurgle [gœrgl]. **I.** *vn.* gorgotear. **II.** *s.* gorgoteo, murmullo.

gurnard [gœrnärd], **gurnet** [gœrnịt], *s.* (ict.) trilla, alcotana.—**flying g.**, golondrina.

gush [gáš]. **I.** *va.* derramar, verter. **II.** *vn.* brotar, fluir, manar a borbotones, borbotar, borbollar, chorrear; (fam.) ser extremoso. **III.** *s.* chorro, borbotón; (fam.) efusión, extremo.

gusher [-œ(r)], *s.* pozo de chorro de petróleo.

gushing [-iŋ], *a.* borbotante; (fam.) extremoso.

gusset [gásịt], *s.* (cost.) escudete, contrete, cuchillo; codo de hierro, hierro angular de refuerzo.

gust [gást], *s.* ráfaga, racha, ventolera, bocanada, ventada; (mar.) fugada, sobreviento; acceso, arrebato; (ant.) gusto, sentido del paladar.

gustation [gastéjšọn], *s.* gustadura.

gustatory, gustative [gástạtọrị, gástạtịv], *a.* gustatorio, gustativo, del sentido del gusto.

gusto [gástou], *s.* gusto, placer.

gusty [gástị], *a.* borrascoso, chubascoso.

gut [gát]. **I.** *s.* (anat., zool.) intestino, tripa; cuerda de tripa; (mar.) estrecho.—*pl.* (fam.) entrañas; (fam.) valor, ánimo; resistencia. **II.** *va.* desventrar, destripar; desentrañar.

gutta [gátạ], *s.* (farm. y arq.) gota.

gutta-percha [-pœrchạ], *s.* gutapercha.

guttated [gátejtịd], *a.* goteado.

gutter [gátœ(r)]. **I.** *s.* canal, canalón, gotera; badén, cuneta; arroyo de la calle; arbollón, albañal, zanja, acequia; cámara; estría, canal de ebanistería. **II.** *va.* acanalar, estriar; poner canalones; construir albañales, etc. **III.** *vn.* acanalarse.

guttersnipe [-snajp], *s.* (fam.) golfillo, pilluelo.

guttural [gátụraḷ], *a.* gutural; (fon.) velar.—**gutturalness** [-njs], *s.* calidad de gutural.—**gutturally** [-ị], *adv.* guturalmente.

guy [gaj]. **I.** *s.* (ing., etc.) tirante, viento, guía; (mar.) retenida, patarráez, *m.*; (fam.) tipo, sujeto, tío; adefesio, ente ridículo, mamarracho. **II.** *va.* (mar.) sujetar con vientos o retenidas; (fam.) hacer burla o mofa.

guzzle [gázl]. **I.** *va. y vn.* beber mucho; tragar, engullir. **II.** *vn.* emborracharse.

guzzler [gázlœ(r)], *s.* bebedor, borrachín.

gym [džịm], *s.* gimnasio.

gymnasium [džịmnéjzịạm], *s.* gimnasio; (G.) escuela secundaria superior.

gymnast [džịmnast], *s.* gimnasta, *mf.*

gymnastic(al [džịmnǽstịk(ạḷ], *a.* gimnástico.

gymnastics [-s], *s. pl.* gimnasia, gimnástica.

gymnosophist [džịmnásofịst], *s.* gimnosofista.

gymnosperm [džịmnospœrm], *s.* (bot.) planta gimnosperma.

gymnospermous [-spœrmạs], *a.* (bot.) gimnospermo.

gynarchy [džájnärkị], **gyn(a)ecocracy** [-nịkákrạsị], *s.* ginecocracia.

gyneceum [-nísịạm], *s.* (bot.) gineceo.

gynecologist [-nịkálodžịst], *s.* ginecólogo.

gynecology [-džị], *s.* (med.) ginecología.

gyniatrics [-nịǽtrịks], *s.* ginecología aplicada.

gyp [džịp]. **I.** *s.* (fam.) timo; timador, trampeador. **II.** *va. y vn.* timar, trampear, embaucar.

gypseous [džịpsịạs], *a.* yesoso.—**gypsum** [džịpsạm], *s.* yeso, aljez, *m.*—**g. pit**, yesal.

gypsy [džịpsị]. **I.** *s.* gitano, cíngano; (fam.) tu-

nanta, pícara; (G.) el idioma de los gitanos; germanía, jerga. **II.** *a.* gitan(esc)o; picarón.

gypsydom [-dạm], (fam.), **gypsyhood** [-hụd], *s.* gitanismo, gitanería.

gypsyism [-ịzm], *s.* gitanismo.

gypsylike [-lajk], *a.* gitan(esc)o, agitanado.

gyral [džájrạḷ], *a.* giratorio; (anat.) referente a las circunvoluciones del cerebro.

gyrate [džájrejt], *vn.* girar, rodar.

gyration [-éjšọn], *s.* giro, vuelta, pirueta.

gyratory [džájrạtọrị], *a.* giratorio, rotativo.

gyre [džájr], *s.* giro, girada, vuelta.

gyrfalcon [džœrfolkọn], *s.* = GERFALCON.

gyrocompass [džájrokạmpạs], *s.* (mar.) compás giroscópico o brújula giroscópica.

gyroscope [-skoụp], *s.* giroscopio.

gyroscopic [-skápịk], *a.* giroscópico.

gyrostat [-stæt], *s.* giróstato.

gyrostatic [-stǽtịk], *a.* girostático, giroscópico.—**g. compass** = GYROCOMPASS.—**gyrostatics** [-s], *s.* (fís.) girostática.

gyve [džájv], *va.* engrillar, encadenar; apiolar.

gyves [-z], *s. pl.* grillos.

H

h [ejch]. **I.** *s.* h. **II.** (H) *a.* en H, en forma de H (apl. a vigas, postes, inducidos, etc.).

ha [ha], *interj.* ¡ah! ¡ja, ja!

habeas corpus [héjbịạs kórpạs], *s.* (for.) habeas corpus; auto de comparencia.

haberdasher [hǽbœrdæšœ(r)], *s.* camisero, mercero, tendero.—**haberdashery** [-ị], *s.* camisería, mercería.

habergeon [hǽbœrdžọn], *s.* cota de malla.

habiliment [hạbílịmẹnt], *s.* prenda de vestir.—*pl.* vestuario, ropa.

habilitate [hạbílịtejt]. **I.** *va.* pertrechar, habilitar, aviar. **II.** *vn.* hacerse idóneo.

habilitation [-éjšọn], *s.* habilitación; aptitud.

habit [hǽbịt]. **I.** *s.* hábito, costumbre; estado o condición habitual; carácter, manera de vivir (gen. *pl.*); vicio; vestido, hábito; (equit.) traje de amazona.—**h.-forming**, enviciador; que forma o crea hábito.—**by o from (force of) h.**, de vicio.—**to be in the h. of**, soler, acostumbrar.—**to fall**, o **get, in the h.**, dar en la flor. **II.** *va.* ataviar; vestir.

habitable [-ạbḷ], *a.* habitable.

habitableness [-njs], *s.* habitabilidad.

habitant [-ạnt], *s.* habitante, morador.

habitat [-æt], *s.* región donde crece y vive un animal o planta; habitación, morada.

habitation [-éjšọn], *s.* habitación, domicilio, morada.

habitual [hạbíchụạḷ], *a.* habitual, acostumbrado.

habitually [-ị], *adv.* habitualmente; de vicio.

habituate [-ejt], *va. y vn.* habituar(se).

habitude [hǽbịtjụd], *s.* hábito, costumbre.

habitué [hạbíchụéj], *s.* concurrente, parroquiano.

hachure [hæšúr], *s.* (dib.) líneas de sombra; líneas de declive (en dibujo topográfico). **II.** *va.* sombrear con líneas.

hack [hæk]. **I.** *s.* caballo de alquiler, rocín, cuartago; alquilón; (E. U.) simón o coche de alquiler; peón, trabajador; hacha, azuela, cuchilla; muesca, corte, tajo, cuchillada; puntapié en la canilla; tos seca; escritorcillo, autor mercenario.—**h. saw**, sierra para cortar metal.—**h. stand**, punto. **II.** *va.* tajar, cortar, picar; acuchillar, machetear; picar piedra; hacer muescas, mellar; alquilar (coche o caballo). **III.** *vn.* cortar; toser con tos seca; alquilarse, venderse. **IV.** *a.* = HACKNEY(ED).

hackamore [hǽkạmọr], *s.* especie de cabestro o ronzal para domar potros.

hackle [hǽkl]. **I.** *va.* rastrillar; mutilar; romper en pedazos. **II.** *s.* rastrillo; fibra no hilada; pluma(s) del cuello de ciertas aves; mosca para pescar.—**hackler** [hǽklœ(r)], *s.* rastrillador.

hackman [hǽkmạn], *s.* simón, cochero de alquiler o de punto.

hackmatack [hǽkmạtæk], *s.* (bot.) alerce.

hackney [hǽknị]. **I.** *s.* caballo de alquiler, rocín, cuartago; alquilón. **II.** *a.* alquilado; común.—**h. coach**, coche de alquiler, simón.—**h. coachman**, cochero de alquiler.—**h. writer**, escritor mercenario. **III.** *va.* repetir, gastar, vulgarizar; llevar en coche de alquiler.—**hackneyed**, *a.* trillado, resobado, manoseado, gastado, trivial, vulgar.

had [hæd], *pret.* de TO HAVE.

haddock [hǽdọk], *s.* (ict.) pez (*m.*) comestible semejante al bacalao o a la merluza.

hade [hejd], *s.* (geol.) buzamiento.

Hades [héjdiz], *s.* el otro mundo; los infiernos.

hæma-, hæmo-. (En composición, estas partículas se reemplazan generalmente por HEMA-, HEMO-.)

hafnium [hǽfnịʌm], *s.* (quím.) hafnio.

haft [hæft], *s.* mango, asa, puño, guarnición.

hag [hæg], *s.* bruja, hechicera.

haggard [hǽgạrd]. **I.** *a.* trasnochado, macilento, ojeroso, flaco, desfigurado; (cetr.) zahareño, montaraz, intratable. **II.** *s.* (orn.) falcón zahareño.

haggish [hǽgịš], *a.* feo como bruja.

haggle [hǽgl]. **I.** *va.* tajar, destrozar, machetear. **II.** *vn.* regatear; cavilar.

haggler [hǽglœ(r)], *s.* tajador; regatero.

hagiarchy [héjdžịarkị], **hagiocracy** [-ákrạsị], *s.* gobierno de (por) sacerdotes.

hagiographer [-ágrạfœ(r)], *s.* hagiógrafo.—**hagiography** [-ị], *s.* hagiografía.—**hagiolatry** [-álạtrị], *s.* culto de los santos.—**hagiology** [-álodžị], *s.* hagiología.

hah [ha], *interj.* = HA.

ha-ha [háha]. **I.** *s.* foso con escarpa, empalizada en zanja, cerca hundida. **II.** *interj.* ¡ja, ja, ja!

haik [hajk], *s.* jaique árabe.

hail [hejl]. **I.** *s.* granizo; saludo; grito, llamada.—**h. fellow**, compañero, camarada, *mf.*; sociable.—**H. Mary**, Ave María.—**within h.**, al habla, al alcance de la voz. **II.** *interj.* ¡salve! ¡saludl! **III.** *va.* saludar; aclamar; llamar.—**to h. a ship**, (mar.) ponerse al habla con un buque. **IV.** *vn.* granizar; vocear.—**to h. from**, venir o proceder de, ser oriundo de.

hailstone [-stoụn], *s.* piedra de granizo.

hailstorm [-stɔrm], *s.* granizada, pedrisquero.

hair [hér], *s.* pelo; vello; cabello, cabellera; cerda; hebra, fibra, pelillo, filamento; pelusa.—**h.-check**, grietecilla (**to h.-check**, agrietarse finamente, con grietecillas filiformes).—**h.-checking**, agrietamiento filiforme.—**h. dye**, tinte para el pelo.—**h. follicle**, folículo piloso.—**h. net**, albanega, redecilla, cofia.—**h. pencil**, pincel.—**h.-raising**, espeluznante, horripilante.—**h. remover**, depilatorio.—**h. ribbon**, cinta para el cabello.—**h. shirt**, cilicio.—**h. stroke**, rasgo muy fino.—**h. switch**, añadido.—**h. tonic**, vigorizador de cabello.—**h. trigger**, pelo (de armas de fuego).—**against the h.**, a contrapelo.—**to a h.**, exactamente, perfectamente.

hairbreadth [-bredθ], *s.* ancho de un pelo; casi nada.—**to have a h. escape**, escapar por un pelo.

hairbrush [-brʌš], *s.* cepillo para la cabeza.

haircloth [-klɔθ], *s.* tela de crin.

haircut [-kʌt], *s.* corte de pelo; rapadura.

hairdo [-du], *s.* peinado.

hairdresser [-drɛsœ(r)], *s.* peluquero, peinador o peinadora.—**h.'s shop**, peluquería.

hairdressing [-drɛsịŋ], *s.* peinado.

haired [-d], *a.* peludo, cabelludo.—**short-h.**, pelicorto.

hairiness [-inịs], *s.* pelaje.

hairless [-lịs], *a.* pelado, pelón, calvo; sin pelo.

hairpin [-pịn], *s.* horquilla, (Am.) gancho.

hairsieve [-sịv], *s.* tamiz (*m.*) de cerda.

hairsplitter [-splịtœ(r)], *s.* persona quisquillosa o pelillosa.—**hairsplitting** [-tịŋ]. **I.** *a.* quisquilloso. **II.** *s.* quisquilla; hilar muy delgado.

hairspring [-sprịŋ], *s.* pelo o muelle (de reloj).

hairy [-ị], *a.* peludo, velludo, velloso, cabelludo, peloso, piloso.

Haitian [héjtịạn], *a.* y *s.* haitiano.

hake [hejk], *s.* (ict.) merluza, pescada, pijota.

halation [hejléjšọn], *s.* (fot.) halo o aureola.

halberd [hǽlbœrd], *s.* alabarda.

halberdier [-ịr], *s.* alabardero.

halcyon [hǽlsịọn]. **I.** *a.* quieto, apacible, tranquilo.—**h. days**, días tranquilos. **II.** *s.* (orn.) alción, *m.*, martín pescador.

hale [hejl]. **I.** *a.* sano, robusto, fuerte. **II.** *va.* tirar de, arrastrar, halar.

half [hæf o haf]. **I.** *s.* (*pl.* HALVES) medio; mitad.—**h. and h.**, mitad y mitad; de medio a medio; en partes iguales; mezcla de dos cervezas o de otras cosas. *V.* HALVES. **II.** *a.* y *adv.* medio; casi; (en composición) semi.—**h.-baked**, a medio cocer, asar, etc.; incompleto; inmaturo.—**h. binding**, (enc.) media pasta, a la holandesa.—**h. blood**, mestizo; (for.) medio hermano, media hermana.—**h. boot**, borceguí, botín, zapata.—**h.-bred**, *a.* mestizo; incivil, inculto.—**h.-breed**, *a.* y *s.* mestizo, (Am.) cholo.—**h. brother**, hermanastro.—**h.-caste**, mestizo.—**h. close**, *va.* entornar.—**h.-closed**, *a.* entornado.—**h.-cock**, (arm.) montar en seguro.—**h.-cocked**, medio amartillado, montado en seguro.—**h.-hearted**, frío, indiferente; mezquino.—**h.-heartedly**, fríamente, sin entusiasmo.—**h.-heartedness**, frialdad, tibieza.—**h. holiday**, media fiesta.—**h. hose**, calcetines.—**h.-length**, (retrato) de medio cuerpo.—**h.-mast**, *s.* media asta (apl. a la bandera); *va.* poner a media asta.—**h. measure**, medida a medias; (fig. y fam.) paños calientes.—**h. moon**, semilunio; (fort.) media luna.—**h. mourning**, medio luto.—**h. note**, (mús.) mínima, blanca.—**h. open**, *va.* entreabrir.—**h. open(ed**, *a.* entreabierto).—**h.-past one, two**, etc., la una, las dos, etc., y media.—**h. pay**, media paga.—**h. price**, a mitad de precio.—**h. round**, semicircular.—**h.-round file**, lima de media caña.—**h.-seas over**, (fam.) achispado, medio borracho.—**h. sister**, hermanastra.—**h. sole**, media suela.—**h.-sole**, *va.* echar o poner media suela a.—**h.-staff** = H. MAST.—**h.-timer**, obrero que trabaja sólo la mitad del tiempo ordinario.—**h. tone**, fotograbado a media tinta; (mús.) semitono.—**h.-tone plate**, clisé fotograbado a media tinta.—**h.-witted**, bobo, alocado; imbécil.—**h. year**, semestre.—**h.-yearly**, semestral; semestralmente.

halfback [hǽfbæk], *s.* medio (en el fútbol).

halfpenny [héjpenị], *s.* (Ingl.) medio penique.

halfway [hǽfwéj], *a.* y *adv.* equidistante, a medio camino, hasta la mitad; parcial(mente).—**to go h., to meet one h.**, hacer concesiones en cambio de otras, estar dispuesto a hacer una componenda.

halibut [hǽlịbʌt], *s.* (ict.) hipogloso (pez grande, sin espinas, de carne muy estimada).

halitosis [hǽlịtóusịs], *s.* halitosis, ocena, mal aliento, aliento de mal olor.

halitus [hǽlịtʌs], *s.* hálito.

hall [hɔl], *s.* vestíbulo, zaguán, recibimiento; (ante)sala, antecámara; pasillo, pasadizo, corredor; salón, edificio (apl. a los destinados a reuniones, funciones, estudios, etc.); colegio; casa señorial.—**h. clock**, reloj de caja.

halleluiah, hallelujah [hǽlịlúýạ], *s.* aleluya.

halliard [hǽlyạrd], *s.* = HALYARD.

hallmark [hólmark], *s.* (marca de) contraste; marca de pureza o de buena calidad.

hallo, halloa [hạlóụ], *interj.* con que se llama o saluda: ¡hola! ¡oiga! ¡eh!

halloo [hạlú]. **I.** *s.* grita, vocería. **II.** *interj.* ¡sus!

¡busca! (voz de los cazadores). **III.** *va.* y *vn.* gritar, vocear, azuzar o llamar a gritos.

hallooing [-iŋ], *s.* grita, vocería.

hallow [hǽlou], *va.* consagrar, santificar; reverenciar.

Hallowe'en [-ín], *s.* víspera de Todos los Santos. —**Hallowmass** [-mɑs], *s.* (ant.) fiesta de Todos los Santos.

hallucinate [hæljúsineit], *va.* alucinar.

hallucination [-éiʃ ǝn], *s.* alucinación.

hallway [hólwei], *s.* pasadizo, pasillo; zaguán.

halo [héilou], *s.* halo, nimbo, aureola, corona.

halogen [hǽlodʒin], *s.* (quím.) halógeno.

halography [hælágrǝfi], *s.* (quím.) halografía.

haloid [hǽlɔid]. **I.** *a.* haloideo. **II.** *s.* sal haloidea.

halophilous [hælǽfilʌs], *a.* (bot.) halófilo.

halt [hɔlt]. **I.** *vn.* cojear, claudicar, renquear, vacilar; tartamudear; estar imperfecto; parar, hacer alto. **II.** *va.* parar, detener. **III.** *s.* cojera; detención; parada, alto. **IV.** *a.* cojo; lisiado.

halter [hóltœ(r)]. **I.** *s.* cabestro, ronzal, jáquima; cuerda de ahorcar, dogal; especie de corpiño: solera (de malla de baño). **II.** *va.* cabestrar; echar el ronzal; poner el dogal.

halting [hóltiŋ], *a.* claudicante, cojo; imperfecto; vacilante. —**haltingly** [-li], *adv.* a coxcojilla; vacilantemente.

halve [hæv], *va.* dividir en dos partes iguales; ser o formar la mitad de; (carp.) machihembrar.

halves [hævz], *s. pl.* de HALF. —**by h.,** a medias; por mitades. —**to go h.,** ir a medias.

halyard [hǽlyǝrd], *s.* (mar.) driza.

ham [hæm], *s.* jamón, pernil, nalgada; (anat.) corva. —*pl.* (fam.) nalgas. —*pl.* **h.** actor, comiquito.

hamadryad [hæmǝdráiæd], *s.* (mit.) hamadríada.

hamal [hǝmál], *s.* cargador; criado.

hamburg(**er** [hǽmbœrg(œr], *s.* carne picada de res, que se fríe o se asa en parrillas (ll. t. Hamburg steak).

hame [heim], *s.* (tal.) horcate.

Hamite [hǽmait], *s.* camita, descendiente de Cam; caucasiano antiguo del nordeste de África.

Hamitic [hæmítik], *a.* camítico.

hamlet [hǽmlit], *s.* aldea, villorrio, caserío.

hammer [hǽmœ(r)]. **I.** *s.* martillo; mazo (de madera); llave, *f.*, rastrillo o percutor de arma de fuego; macillo del piano; martinete; pilón o maza de martinete. —**h. and tongs,** (fam.) con violencia, bruscamente; en discordia, como perros y gatos. —**h.-hard,** endurecido o forjado en frío a martillo. —**h.-harden,** *va.* martillar en frío. —**h.-refined,** afinado a martillo. —**to come,** o **go, under the h.,** venderse en pública subasta. **II.** *va.* martillar; batir, golpear, cutir, machacar; clavar; forjar; repujar (metales). —**to h. one's brains,** devanarse los sesos. **III.** *vn.* martillar, dar golpes; repiquetear; (con away) trabajar asiduamente.

hammercloth [-klɔθ], *s.* paño del pescante de un coche.

hammerer [-œr)], *s.* martillador.

hammerhead [-hed], *s.* (ict.) cornudilla, pez martillo.

hammering [-iŋ], *s.* martilleo; ruido de martillazos; repujado. —**by h.,** a martillo.

hammock [hǽmɔk], *s.* hamaca; (mar.) coy.

hamper [hǽmpœ(r)]. **I.** *s.* canasta, cesto, cuévano; (mar.) aparejo; traba, impedimento. **II.** *va.* embarazar, estorbar; encestar, encanastar.

hamstring [hǽmstriŋ]. **I.** *s.* (anat.) tendón de la corva. **II.** *va.* desjarretar; incapacitar; mancar. —**hamstrung** [-strʌŋ], *pret.* y *pp.* de TO HAMSTRING.

hanaper [hǽnǝpœ(r)], *s.* canasto para documentos.

hand [hænd]. **I.** *s.* mano, *f.*; racimo (de plátanos); maña, destreza; ejecución, mano de obra; lado (derecho o izquierdo); operario, obrero; peón, jornalero, brazo, bracero; aguja, manecilla,

saeta (de reloj, etc.); carácter de letra: firma, rúbrica; palmo menor; dominación, poder, posesión; mano, en el juego; acción, trabajo, agencia. —**h. and glove,** uña y carne. —**h. and seal,** firma y sello. —**h. in h.,** parejas; junto; de concierto, de acuerdo. —**h. over head,** inconsideradamente. —**hands down,** sin dificultad, con los ojos cerrados (fig.). —**hands off,** no tocar; no meterse, abstenerse (cambiando un poco el giro). —**hands off policy,** política de no intervención. —**h. to h.,** cuerpo a cuerpo, brazo a brazo, a brazo partido. —**h.-to-mouth,** precario, incierto; impróvido. —**hands up!** ¡alce(n) las manos! (para seguridad de que quien recibe la orden no saca arma). —**all hands below!** ¡todo el mundo abajo! —**all hands on deck!** ¡todo el mundo arriba! —**at h.** o **near at h.,** a la mano, cerca, al canto. —**by h.,** a mano; con biberón. —**by the h.,** de la mano. —**from h. to h.,** de mano a mano. —**from h. to mouth,** de manos a boca. —**given under my h. and seal,** firmado y sellado de mi mano. —**in h.,** de contado, dinero en mano; entre manos. —**in one's h.,** en mano o manos de uno. —**off one's hands,** desechado; despachado. —**on all hands, on every h.,** por todas partes, por todos lados. —**on h.,** disponible; (com.) en existencia; en caja; pendiente, por hacer; por venir; presente, a la mano. —**on one's hands,** entre manos; a cargo de uno. —**on the one h.,** por una parte. —**on the other h.,** por otra parte; en cambio; al contrario. —**out of h.,** luego, inmediatamente; terminado; desbocado (fig.), incontenible. —**to be h. and glove,** o **h. in glove,** morder en un confite; ser íntimos o inseparables. —**to get the upper h.,** llevar la ventaja; tomar cuerpo, agravarse. —**to go h. in h.,** concertarse; ir de mano con. —**to h.,** a la mano; listo. —**to have a h. in,** tener mano o parte en. —**to have one's hands full,** estar ocupadísimo, tener muchísimo que hacer. —**to set the h. to,** meter mano en, emprender; firmar. —**under my h.,** firmado de mi puño y letra. **II.** *va.* dar, entregar, poner en manos de (alguien), pasar; conducir, guiar por la mano. —**to h. down,** transmitir; bajar, entregar o pasar de arriba abajo; (for.) publicar o dictar (un fallo). —**to h. in,** o **into,** dar la mano para entrar. —**to h. out,** entregar, dar. —**to h. over,** entregar, alargar. —**to h. round,** o **around,** hacer pasar, pasar de uno a otro. **III.** *a.* de mano; hecho a mano; para la mano; manual. —**h. basket,** cestilla, canastilla. —**h. bell,** campanilla. —**h.-embroidered,** bordado a mano. —**h. glass,** espejo de mano; lente de aumento; (gal.) lupa. —**h. grenade,** granada de mano. —**h. language,** lenguaje de los mudos. —**h. lead** = LEAD LINE. —**h. luggage,** equipaje o bultos (*m. pl.*) de mano. —**h. mill,** molinillo. —**h. organ,** organillo. —**h.-picked,** recogido o seleccionado a mano; selecto, escogido. —**h. sails,** (mar.) velas manuales. —**h. screw,** (carp.) tornillo de mano o de orejas; prensa de tornillos; cárcel, *f.*; (mec.) gato; cric. —**h. vise,** entenallas, *f. pl.*

handbag [-bæg], *s.* maleta, maletín, saco de noche; bols(it)a de mano, ridículo (de señora).

handball [-bɔl], *s.* pelota; juego de pelota.

handbarrow [-bærou], *s.* angarillas, *f. pl.*, parihuela.

handbill [-bil], *s.* hoja suelta o volante.

handbook [-buk], *s.* manual; prontuario; guía.

handbreadth [-bredθ], *s.* palmo menor.

handcart [-kart], *s.* carro o carretilla de mano.

handcuff [-kʌf]. **I.** *s.* manilla. —*pl.* esposas. **II.** *va.* maniatar.

handed [-id], *a.* que tiene manos; de mano.

handful [-ful], *s.* puñado, manojo; manípulo.

handicap [hǽndikæp]. **I.** *va.* (dep.) igualar a los competidores imponiendo ciertos impedimentos a los que llevan ventajas o dando a los otros ventajas especiales; de aquí, poner trabas u obstáculos, estorbar. **II.** *s.* (dep.) iguala que se hace imponiendo restricciones a los competidores que tienen **ventaja**; carrera con caballos de peso igualado; obstáculo, impedimento o desventaja; ventaja, (Am.) gabela.—**handicapped** [-t], *a.* impedido; que sufre de alguna inhabilidad (esp. física o mental).

handicraft [-kræft], *s.* mano, *f.*, mano de obra; oficio, arte mecánica.—**handicraftsman** [-smən], *s.* artesano, artífice.

handily [-li], *adv.* diestramente.

handiness [-nis], *s.* habilidad, destreza, maña; comodidad, conveniencia.

handiwork [-wœrk], *s.* artefacto, maniobra.

handkerchief [hǽŋkœrchif], *s.* pañuelo, moquero.

handle [hǽndl]. **I.** *va.* tocar, manosear; manipular, manejar; hacer tratable; tratar; dirigir; comerciar en; poner mango a. **II.** *vn.* usar las manos o trabajar con ellas; ser manejado. **III.** *s.* mango, puño, asa, manigueta, manubrio, tirador, agarrador, manija; astil (de hacha, etc.); (Am.) cacha (de arma blanca); (fam.) título.—**h. bar(s)**, guía(s) (de bicicleta).

handless [hǽndlis], *a.* manco.

handling [hǽndliŋ], *s.* manejo; manoseo, tocamiento; maniobra; manipulación; toque.

handmade [hǽndméid], *a.* hecho a mano.

handmaid [hǽndmeid], **handmaiden** [-ɡn], *s.* criada de mano, asistenta.

hand-me-down [-mi dəun], *a.* y *s.* (fam.) (traje, etc.) ya hecho, barato, o de segunda mano.

handout [-əut], *s.* (fam.) limosna de ropa o alimento dada a un pordiosero o vago.

handrail [-reil], *s.* pasamano, baranda(l).

handsaw [-so], *s.* serrucho, sierra de mano.

handsel, hansel [-sel, hǽnsel]. **I.** *s.* estrena, aguinaldo; estreno; prenda, señal, *f.*, arras, *f. pl.* **II.** *va.* dar estrenas o dádivas; estrenar.

handset [-set], *s.* teléfono que reúne el transmisor y el receptor en una sola pieza.

handshake [-šeik], *s.* apretón de manos.

handsome [hǽnsʌm], *a.* hermoso; excelente; amplio, liberal, generoso; elegante, fino.

handsomely [-li], *adv.* hermosamente; generosamente.—**handsomeness** [-nis], *s.* hermosura; generosidad.

handspike [hǽndspaik], *s.* palanca; espeque.

handspring [-spriŋ], *s.* voltereta sobre las manos.

handwork [-wœrk], *s.* obra hecha a mano.

handwriting [-raitiŋ], *s.* carácter de letra; letra, puño; escritura.

handy [-i], *a.* manual, manuable, fácil de manejar; próximo, a la mano; cómodo, útil; diestro, hábil, mañoso.—**h.-man**, hombre o mozo para tareas menudas varias.—**to come in h.**, caer bien, venir al pelo.

hang [hæŋ]. **I.** *va.* (*pret.* y *pp.* HUNG o HANGED) colgar, suspender; fijar (en la pared, etc.); empapelar (pared); poner colgaduras en; endoselar; ahorcar (en este último sentido es de preferirse el participio pasado HANGED).—**to h. fire**, fallar el tiro, hacer higa; estar una cosa en suspenso; vacilar.—**to h. out**, enarbolar; colgar.—**to h. up**, levantar, suspender en el aire; colgar; arrinconar, dejar pendiente, suspender; (fam.) empeñar.—**to h. with tapestry**, entapizar.—**h. it all!**, (fam.) ¡maldito sea! **II.** *vn.* colgar, pender, caer; fluctuar, vacilar, estar en duda; ser ahorcado; estar inminente, amenazar; (con **on** o **upon**) pegarse, agregarse a uno, ir al retortero; colgarse o abrazarse al cuello de uno; depender, estar pendiente de; (E. U.) no avenirse, no convenir.—**to h. around**, rondar, haraganear.—**to h. back**, rezagarse; plantarse, resistirse; vacilar.—**to h. down**, colgar, estar pendiente.—**to h. loose**, colgar flojamente.— **to h. in the balance**, estar pendiente de un hilo.—**to h. off**, no decidirse, hacerse el remolón.—**to h. on**, colgarse de, apoyarse en; quedarse, permanecer; insistir; persistir.—**to h. on the sleeve of**, estar sujeto a la voluntad de.—

to h. out, estar enarbolado o colgado; sobresalir; ser inflexible, no ceder; (fam.) pasar la noche, dormir, alojarse, frecuentar o haraganear en ciertos sitios.—**to h. over**, colgar arriba de; destacarse sobre; (fig.) cernerse sobre; amenazar.—**to h. together**, permanecer unidos; tener cohesión.—**to h. up**, (fam.) terminar una conversación telefónica colgando el auricular. **III.** *s.* caída (de un vestido); modo como cuelga una cosa; inclinación, declive; (fam.) maña, destreza; quid, *m.*, busilis, *m.*—**not to care, o give, a h.**, no importarle a uno un bledo.

hangar [hǽŋ(r)], *s.* cobertizo; (aer.) hangar.

hangbird [hǽŋbœrd], *s.* pájaro que fabrica nido colgante (ll. t. **hangnest**).

hangdog [hǽŋdog], *a.* y *s.* camastrón; (sujeto) ruin, vil, servil o solapado; avergonzado.

hanger [hǽŋœ(r)], *s.* soporte colgante; colgadero; barra, plancha, hierro, etc., de suspensión; artefacto de suspensión; (impr.) espito; alfanje.

hanger-on [-án], *s.* dependiente; mogollón, gorrista; familiar; paseante en corte.

hanging [hǽŋiŋ]. **I.** *s.* ahorcadura, muerte (*f.*) en la horca.—*pl.* colgaduras, tapices, cortinaje, etc. **II.** *a.* colgante, pendiente, suspendido; patibulario.—**h. sleeves**, (sast.) mangas perdidas.

hangman [hǽŋmən], *s.* verdugo.

hangnail [hǽŋneil], *s.* padrastro, respigón.

hangover [hǽŋouvœ(r)], *s.* sobra, algo que queda; (fam.) irritación o malestar que sigue a una borrachera, (Am.) goma.

hank [hæŋk]. **I.** *s.* madeja; cadejo; aduja, rollo de cuerda. **II.** *vn.* hacer madejas; adujar.

hanker [hǽŋkœ(r)], *vn.* (gen. con **for** o **after**) ansiar, apetecer.

hankering [-iŋ], *s.* anhelo, deseo, apetencia.

hanky [hǽŋki], *s.* (fam.) pañuelo.

Hansard [hǽnsərd], *s.* actas (*f. pl.*) del parlamento inglés; anseático, miembro del ansa.

hanse [hæns], *s.* (h)ansa; unión mercantil.

Hanseatic [hænsiǽtik], *a.* (h)anseático.—**H. League**, (h)ansa (ll. t. **Hanse**).

hansel [hǽnsel], *s.* y *va.* = HANDSEL.

hansom (**cab** [hǽnsǫm [kæb], *s.* cabriolé con el pescante en la zaga.

hap [hæp]. **I.** *s.* (ant.) lance, acaso; azar, suerte, *f.*, casualidad. **II.** *vn.* (ant.) acontecer.

haphazard [hǽphæzàrd]. **I.** *s.* suerte, *f.*, casualidad. **II.** *a.* casual, fortuito. **III.** *adv.* al acaso, a la ventura, al azar, casualmente.

hapless [hǽplis], *a.* desventurado, miserable.

haplology [hæplálodži], *s.* (filol.) haplología.

haply [hǽpli], *adv.* (ant.) quizá; casualmente.

happen [hǽpn], *vn.* acontecer, suceder, pasar, acaecer, sobrevenir; parar en; hallarse por casualidad en.—**to h. in**, entrar o llegar casualmente.—**to h. on**, encontrarse o tropezar con. —**no matter what happens**, suceda lo que suceda.

happening [-iŋ], *s.* suceso, acontecimiento.

happily [hǽpili], *adv.* feliz o dichosamente; afortunadamente.

happiness [-nis], *s.* felicidad, dicha, alegría.

happy [hǽpi], *a.* feliz, dichoso, alegre, contento; fausto; afortunado.—**to be h. to**, alegrarse de, celebrar, tener gusto en; tener la fortuna de.— **h. hunting grounds**, la tierra feliz de la caza, paraíso de los indios norteamericanos.—**h. medium**, justo medio.

happy-go-lucky [-goulʌki]. **I.** *a.* y *s.* descuidado, confiado en la buena ventura. **II.** *adv.* a la buena ventura; de cualquier modo.

hara-kiri [hárəkíri], *s.* harakiri, suicidio japonés que consiste en abrirse las entrañas.

harangue [hærǽŋ]. **I.** *s.* arenga, perorata. **II.** *va.* arengar a. **III.** *vn.* pronunciar un discurso.

harass [hǽrəs], *va.* acosar, fatigar, atormentar, atosigar, vejar; desolar; (mil.) hostigar, hostilizar, perseguir.—**harassment** [-mənt], *s.* hostigamiento; persecución; vejamen.

harbinger [hárbịndẕœ(r)]. **I.** *s.* precursor; presagio. **II.** *va.* presagiar, anunciar.

harbor [hárbọ(r)]. **I.** *s.* puerto; seguro; asilo, abrigo, albergue.—**h. dues,** derechos de puerto.—**h. master,** capitán de puerto.—**h. pilot,** práctico. **II.** *va.* abrigar, amparar; acoger, hospedar; guardar, conservar; profesar, acariciar. **III.** *vn.* ampararse, refugiarse.

harborage [-idẕ]. *s.* puerto; refugio, amparo, asilo.

harborer [-œ(r)], *s.* amparador, albergador, acogedor; encubridor.

harborless [-lịs], *a.* sin puerto; desamparado.

hard [hárd]. **I.** *a.* duro, endurecido; inflexible, tieso; difícil, arduo; empedernido; fuerte, recio, riguroso, severo; injusto, opresivo; ofensivo; áspero, tosco; vigoroso, sufrido; mezquino, miserable; cruda (agua); penoso; fuerte, fermentado (cidra, etc.); (fam.) malvado, perverso.—**h. and fast,** sin excepción; rígido; de calicanto, o a macha martillo.—**h. cash,** (com.) numerario efectivo, metálico.—**h. coal,** antracita.—**h. drink,** bebida fuertemente alcohólica; licor.—**h. drinking,** mucho beber.—**h.-heartedness,** insensibilidad, dureza, empedernimiento.—**h. labor,** trabajo forzado.—**h. lines, h. luck,** mala suerte.—**h. liquor,** licor (a diferencia de la cerveza y el vino).—**h. money = h. cash.**—**h. of hearing,** tardo o duro de oído, teniente.—**h. knot,** nudo apretado.—**h. rubber,** ebonita, vulcanita.—**h. sauce,** salsa espesa de azúcar y mantequilla.—**h. sausage,** salchichón.—**h. soap,** jabón duro.—**h. solder(ing),** soldadura fuerte o dura, o de alto punto de fusión.—**h. steel,** acero rico en carbono.—**h. to deal with,** intratable.—**h. usage,** mal trato, uso rudo.—**h. water,** agua cruda o gorda.—**h. words,** palabras injuriosas.—**h. work,** trabajo difícil; trabajo fuerte.—**h. worker,** trabajador muy asiduo.—**to be h. up,** (fam.) hallarse en apuros, estar a la cuarta pregunta. **II.** *adv.* diligentemente, con ahinco, con inquietud, con impaciencia, vejación o pesar; dificílmente; reciamente, con fuerza, con dureza, fuerte(mente), duro, duramente; (mar.) todo, enteramente.—**h. aport,** (mar.) a babor todo.—**h.-bitten,** (fam.) endurecido, aguerrido; tenaz, terco.—**h.-boiled,** bien cocido, duro (huevo); (fam.) rudo; terco, porfiado, (Am.) empecinado, petrificado.—**h. by,** inmediato, muy cerca.—**h.-drawn,** estirado en frío (alambre).—**h.-earned,** ganado con dificultad.—**h.-favored, o featured,** de aspecto áspero, cariaguño.—**h.-fisted,** de puños rudos; avaro, agarrado.—**h.-fought,** reñido.—**h.-handed,** de manos encallecidas o ásperas; cruel; despótico.—**h.-headed,** terco; perspicaz.—**h.-hearted,** empedernido.—**h.-heartedly,** empedernidamente.—**h. on the heels of,** a raíz de, inmediatamente después de.—**h. pressed, h. pushed,** escaso o falto de recursos, apurado.—**h.-set,** resuelto; inflexible, obstinado.—**h.-shell(ed,** con caparazón; porfiado, inflexible.—**h.-worked,** trillado, rancio (fig.).—**h.-working,** asiduo, que trabaja con tesón.—**to be h. put to it,** verse en calzas prietas.—**to drink h.,** beber con exceso.—**to rain h.,** llover a cántaros.—**to snow h.,** nevar copiosamente.—**to work h.,** aporrearse, trabajar con ahinco.

harden [-n]. **I.** *va.* endurecer, endurar; (med.) indurar; solidar; curtir, encallecer; robustecer; templar; hacer insensible o indiferente. **II.** *vn.* endurecerse, empedernirse.

hardening [-ịŋ], *s.* endurecimiento.—**h. of the arteries,** (med.) arteriosclerosis.

hardihood [-ịhụd], *s.* atrevimiento, temeridad.

hardiness [-inịs], *s.* ánimo, valor, intrepidez; robustez, vigor.

hardly [-lị], *adv.* mal, dificilmente, apenas, escasamente; no del todo; duramente, severamente.

hardness [-nịs], *s.* dureza, endurecimiento; firmeza, solidez; escasez, penuria; crueldad, rigor;

desabrimiento; obduración; crudeza (del agua); (b. a.) dureza, tosquedad.

hardpan [hárdpæn]. *s.* capa dura o roqueña debajo de terreno blando; base sólida; fondo.

hardship [-ṣịp]. *s.* penalidad, trabajo; privaciones, *f. pl.*; opresión, gravamen, injusticia.

hardtack [-tæk], *s.* bizcocho, galleta.

hardware [-wɛr], *s.* quincalla, ferretería, quincallería, herraje, conjunto de accesorios metálicos.—**h. store,** quincallería.

hardwareman [-mạn], *s.* quincallero, ferretero.

hardwood [-wụd], *s.* madera dura.

hardy [hárdị], *a.* fuerte, robusto, endurecido; bravo, intrépido; (bot.) resistente.

hare [hér], *s.* (zool.) liebre, *f.;* (astr.) constelación Lepus.—**h. and hounds,** juego en que se imita la caza de liebres.—**h.'s-ear,** (bot.) perfoliada.—**h.-hearted,** alebrado, medroso.—**h.-hunting,** lebrero.

harebell [-bel], *s.* (bot.) campanilla.

harebrained [-breịnd], *a.* cabeza de chorlito, ligero de cascos, tolondro.

harefoot [-fụt], *s.* pie (*m.*) de liebre; corredor ágil.

harefooted [-fụtịd], *a.* ligero, ágil.

harehound [-haụnd], *s.* lebrel, galgo lebrero.

harelip [-lịp], *s.* labio leporino.—**harelipped** [-lịpt], *a.* labihendido, de labio leporino.

harem [hérem], *s.* harén, serrallo.

haricot [hǽrịkoụ], *s.* guisado con habichuelas y otras legumbres; (bot.) frijol, habichuela.

hark [hárk], *vn.* escuchar, atender.—**to h. back,** volver al asunto o al punto de partida.

harken, hearken [-n]. **I.** *vn.* (poét.) escuchar, atender. **II.** *va.* (ant.) oír con atención.

harl [harl], *s.* hebras (*f. pl.*) de lino; filamento.

harlequin [hárlẹkwịn]. **I.** *s.* arlequín, bufón. **II.** *a.* multicolor; fantástico. **III.** *vn.* bufonearse.—**harlequinade** [-éịd], *s.* arlequinada, pantomima.

harlot [hárlọt]. **I.** *s.* ramera. **II.** *a.* meretricio.

harlotry [-rị], *s.* prostitución.

harm [hárm]. **I.** *s.* daño, perjuicio, mal. **II.** *va.* dañar, perjudicar; ofender, herir.

harmful [-fụl], *a.* dañoso, dañino, nocivo, perjudicial.—**harmfully** [-i], *adv.* dañosamente, perniciosamente.—**harmfulness** [-nịs], *s.* calidad de nocivo.

harmless [-lịs], *a.* innocuo; inofensivo, inocente; ileso, libre de daño; sano y salvo.—**harmlessly** [-lị], *adv.* inocentemente; sin daño.—**harmlessness** [-nịs], *s.* inocencia; innocuidad.

harmonic [harmánịk], *s.* (mús.) armónico, tono secundario.—*pl.* armonía.

harmonica [-ạ], *s.* (mús.) armónica.

harmonic(al [-(ạl], *a.* armónico.

harmonically [-i], *adv.* armónicamente.

harmonicon [-ọn], *s.* (mús.) armónica, organillo, orquest(r)ión.

harmonious [harmóụnịʌs], *a.* armónico; armonioso; simétrico, proporcionado.—**harmoniously** [-lị], *adv.* armoniosamente, armónicamente.—**harmoniousness** [-nịs], *s.* armonía.

harmonist [hármonịst], *s.* armonista.

harmonium [harmóụnịạm], *s.* (mús.) armonio.

harmonize, harmonise [hármonaịz]. **I.** *va.* armonizar, concertar, poner de acuerdo. **II.** *vn.* armonizarse, congeniar; armonizar, convenir, corresponder.—**harmonizer** [-œ(r)], *s.* conciliador; (mús.) armonista.

harmony [hármonị], *s.* armonía, acuerdo.

harness [hárnịs]. **I.** *s.* jaez (*m.*) o jaeces, arreos, guarniciones (*f. pl.*) de caballerías; (arm.) arnés; (mec.) aparejo; equipo; (fig.) servicio activo.—**h. maker,** guarnicionero, talabartero.—**h. room,** guarnicionería. **II.** *va.* poner las guarniciones a (una caballería); enjaezar; armar con arnés.

harp [hárp]. **I.** *s.* (mús.) arpa; (astr.) Lira. **II.** *vn.* tocar o tañer el arpa.—**to h. on, o upon,** repetir, machacar, porfiar.—**to h. on, o upon, one**

string, o the same string, estar siempre con la misma cantinela.

harper [-œ(r)], *s.* arpista.

harping [-iŋ], *s.* tañido del arpa; repetición enfadosa.—*pl.* (mar.) cucharros; jarretas.

harpist [-ist], *s.* = HARPER.

harpoon [harpún]. **I.** *s.* arpón, fisga.—**h. gun,** cañón para disparar el arpón.—**h. line o rope,** estacha. **II.** *va.* arponear.—**harpooner** [-œ(r)], *s.* arponero, fisgador.

harpsichord [hárpsikord], *s.* (mús.) clavicordio.

harpy [hárpi], *s.* arpía; (orn.) arpella.

harquebus [hárkwebʌs], *s.* arcabuz, *m.*

harquebusier [-ír], *s.* arcabucero.

harridan [hǽridan], *s.* vieja regañona, bruja.

harrier [hǽriœ(r)], *s.* lebrel pequeño; pillador, asolador; molestador; ave (*f.*) de rapiña.

harrow [hǽrou]. **I.** *s.* (agr.) grada, rastro, trilla; rodillo para desterronar; escarificador. **II.** *va.* (agr.) gradar; perturbar, atormentar.—**harrowing** [-iŋ]. **I.** *s.* (agr.) gradeo. **II.** *a.* horripilante, agudo, desgarrador.

harry [hǽri], *va.* pillar, asolar, saquear; acosar, molestar.

harsh [hárʃ], *a.* áspero, agrio, bronco, duro, riguroso, desagradable; tosco.—**harshly** [-li], *adv.* ásperamente, severamente, duramente, agriamente.—**harshness** [-nis], *s.* aspereza, rudeza, acerbidad; bronquedad; rigor, severidad.

hart [hárt], *s.* (zool.) venado, ciervo de cinco años.

hartshorn [-ʃorn], *s.* amoníaco; cuerno de ciervo; (bot.) variedad de llantén.

harum-scarum [hǽramskéram]. **I.** *a.* atolondrado, desbaratado. **II.** *s.* trueno, tronera, *mf.* **III.** *adv.* al tuntún, a troche y moche.

haruspex, haruspice [hærÁspeks, -pis], *s.* arúspice.

harvest [hárvist]. **I.** *s.* cosecha; siega, agosto; esquilmo, fruto, producto, recolección.—**h. bug,** (ent.) mita, arador.—**h. fly,** cigarra, chicharra.—**h. home,** (Ingl.) fiesta o coro de segadores.—**h. moon,** luna de la cosecha.—**h. mouse,** ratón del campo.—**h. time,** mies, *f.* **II.** *va.* recoger la cosecha, segar, esquilmar; cosechar; (fig.) recoger el fruto.

harvester [-œ(r)], *s.* agostero, cosechero, segador; cosechadora, segadora, máquina de segar.

harvestman [-man], *s.* cosechero, etc.; (ent.) falangia; típula.

has [hæz], 3*a. pers. pres. ind.* de TO HAVE.

hash [hæʃ]. **I.** *va.* picar, desmenuzar, hacer picadillo. **II.** *s.* picadillo, jigote.

hasheesh, hashish [hǽʃiʃ], *s.* haxix, hachich.

haslet [hǽslet], *s.* (coc.) asadura de puerco.

hasp [hæsp]. **I.** *s.* aldaba de candado; broche. **II.** *va.* abrochar; cerrar con aldaba.

hassock [hǽsok], *s.* banqueta, escabel; cojín; ruedo de estera.

hast [hæst], 2*a. pers. pres. ind.* de TO HAVE.

hastate [hǽstejt], *a.* (bot.) alabardado.

haste [hejst], *s.* prisa.—**in h.,** de prisa.

haste, hasten [héjsn]. **I.** *va.* acelerar, apresurar, activar; precipitar. **II.** *vn.* darse prisa, apresurarse, apretar el paso.

hastily [héjstili], *adv.* acelerada, apresurada o precipitadamente; a la carrera, a la ligera.

hastiness [-nis], *s.* prisa, prontitud; impaciencia.

hasty [héjsti], *a.* pronto; apresurado; precipitado, arrojado; temprano.—**h. pudding,** (coc.) papilla, gachas (*f. pl.*) de harina de maíz.

hat [hæt], *s.* sombrero; capelo, dignidad de cardenal.—**h. factory, o shop,** sombrerería.—**h. guard,** barboquejo.—**h. maker, o seller,** sombrerero.—**h. money,** (mar.) capa y sombrero, quintalada.—**hats off!** ¡descubrámonos! ¡descubrirse!—**to pass the h.** (around), pasar el cepillo, hacer una colecta.

hatable [héjtabl], *a.* odioso.

hatband [hǽtbænd], *s.* cinta del sombrero.

hatbox [-baks], **hatcase** [-kejs], *s.* sombrerera.

hatch [hæch]. **I.** *va.* criar pollos, empo ar, incubar

o encobar; fraguar, tramar, maquinar; sombrear con líneas. **II.** *vn.* empollarse, salir del cascarón; madurarse. **III.** *s.* cría, nidada, pollada; salida del cascarón; compuerta; portezuela; trampa; (mar.) escotilla, cuartel; (hidr.) paradera, compuerta.

hatchel [hǽchel]. **I.** *s.* rastrillo. **II.** *va.* rastrillar; (fig.) contrariar, impacientar.—**hatcheler** [-œ(r)]. *s.* rastrillador.—**hatcheling** [-iŋ], *s.* rastrillaje.

hatcher [hǽchœ(r)], *s.* empollador; incubadora.

hatchery [-i], *s.* incubadero; piscifactoría, vivero, criadero (esp. de peces).

hatchet [hǽchit], *s.* destral, machado, hacha pequeña.—**h. face,** cara delgada, cara de cuchillo. —**h.-faced,** de facciones enjutas.

hatching [hǽchiŋ], *s.* pollazón, incubación; (b. a.) sombreado, sombra hecha con líneas.

hatchway [hǽchwej], *s.* (mar.) escotilla.

hate [hejt]. **I.** *va.* odiar, aborrecer. **II.** *s.* odio, aborrecimiento.

hateful [-ful], *a.* aborrecible, odioso; maligno, rencoroso, malévolo.—**hatefully** [-i], *adv.* odiosamente.—**hatefulness** [-nis], *s.* odiosidad.

hater [-œ(r)], *s.* aborrecedor; enemigo.

hath [hæθ], (ant.) 3*a. pers. pres. ind.* de TO HAVE.

hatpin [hǽtpin], *s.* pasador o aguja de sombrero; rascamoño.

hatrack [hǽtræk], *s.* percha, cuelgasombreros.

hatred [héjtrid], *s.* odio, aborrecimiento, enemiga.

hatted [hǽtid], *a.* que lleva sombrero.

hatter [hǽtœ(r)], *s.* sombrerero.—**h.'s jack,** carda.

hauberk [hóbœrk], *s.* (arm.) plaquín, camisote.

haughtily [hótili], *adv.* arrogantemente.

haughtiness [-nis], *s.* arrogancia, soberbia, altanería, altivez; ínfulas, *f. pl.*; humos, *m. pl.*

haughty [hóti], *a.* arrogante; vano, entonado.

haul [hól]. **I.** *va.* tirar de, arrastrar; transportar; (mar.) halar, ronzar, aballestar, cazar.—**to h. aft the sheets,** (mar.) cazar las escotas.—**to h. down the colors,** arriar la bandera.—**to h. over the coals,** (fam.) culpar; regañar, echar una raspa a.—**to h. the wind,** (mar.) ceñir el viento. **II.** *s.* tirón o estirón, hala; arrastre, transporte; redada; (fam.) botín, presa, ganancia.

haulage [-idʒ], *s.* arrastre, acarreo, transporte; carretaje; coste o gastos de acarreo; (f. c.) precio que se paga por el uso de una vía férrea (gen. por los trenes de otra).

hauling [-iŋ], *s.* estirón, hala; acarreo, transporte, arrastre.—**h. line,** guía, cable portador.

haulm [hom], *s.* paja, rastrojo.

haunch [honch], *s.* (anat., zool.) anca, grupa, culata; pernil; (arq.) riñón de una bóveda.

haunt [hónt]. **I.** *va.* frecuentar; rondar; perseguir una idea a uno; obsesionar, obseder, causar obsesión; aparecerse en, andar por (apl. a los muertos que se suponen espantar como fantasmas). **II.** *s.* guarida, querencia; lugar que uno frecuenta.

haunted [-id], *a.* visitado por aparecidos; (sitio) donde se aparecen fantasmas o los muertos espantan.

haustellum [hostélʌm], *s.* trompa de las mariposas, moscas, etc.

hautboy [hóuboj], *s.* (mús.) oboe.

hauteur [hoytǽr], *s.* arrogancia, altivez.

have [hæv]. **I.** *aux.* (*pret. y pp.* HAD) haber. El pretérito **had** se usa a veces en vez de *if* (*had I been there,* si yo hubiera estado allí; *had it rained,* si hubiera llovido).—**had as soon, had as lief,** expresa buena voluntad, pero sin preferencia (*I had as lief go,* iré de buena gana, no tengo inconveniente en ir).—**had better,** (le, me, etc.) sería mejor o convendría (*you had better wait,* le sería mejor aguardar, mejor es que aguarde; *we had better ask,* mejor es que preguntemos).—**had rather,** más bien, (yo, etc.) preferiría (*I had rather go,* yo preferiría ir;

I had rather be free than famous, yo preferiría ser libre a ser famoso, más quisiera ser libre que famoso). **II.** *va.* tener, poseer; contar con; tomar (una bebida, etc.); recibir (carta, noticia etc.); tolerar, permitir; decir, asegurar; (fam.) vencer, ganar; engañar; saber, poseer (un idioma). Seguido de infinitivo indica, ya deseo, ya mandato (*I would have you come*, deseo que Vd. venga; *I will have my servant take the letter*, haré que mi criado lleve la carta). Antes de participio, equivale a "hacer" seguido de infinitivo (*I had the letter copied*, hice copiar la carta), o al tiempo del verbo correspondiente con dativo (*he had a leg broken*, le quebraron una pierna).—**to h. a care**, tener cuidado.—**to h. a grudge against**, tener tema o inquina a.—**to h. a mind to**, querer, tener ganas de.—**to h. a narrow escape**, escaparse en una tabla, salvarse por un pelo.—**to h. and to hold**, (for.) tener y poseer (en propiedad o en dominio).—**to h. an eye to**, vigilar, observar.—**to h. at**, dar (golpes, etc.) a, atacar.—**to h. at heart**, desear con vehemencia.—**to h. breakfast, lunch**, etc., desayunarse, almorzar, etc.—**to h. done (with)**, haber terminado; no tener más que ver con.—**to h. got to**, (fam.) tener que.—**to h. in hand**, estar ocupado en, tener entre manos.—**to h. it**, ganar; tener o ganar la ventaja; acertar, atinar, dar en el busilis, tener la solución de un problema; recibir golpes, castigo, etc. (Se emplea algún otro giro; vg. *he had it hard*, le dieron recio, le pegaron bien).—**to h. it in for**, tenérsela jurada a.—**to h. it out**, terminar el negocio, ponerle punto final, poner fin al asunto (por discusión, riña, etc.); decir verdades, cantar claro.—**to h. nothing on one**, no llevar ninguna ventaja a uno; no tener o saber nada contra uno.—**to h. on**, tener puesto (traje, etc.).—**to h. one's eye on**, vigilar, no perder de vista; haberle echado el ojo a.—**to h. one's self to blame**, tener la culpa.—**to h. one's way**, hacer uno lo que quiera; salirse con la suya.—**to h. recourse**, recurrir.—**to h. something on one**, llevar ventaja a uno; tener o saber algo contra uno.—**to h. to**, tener que deber.—**to h. to do with**, tener que ver con; tratar de, versar sobre.—**as fate, o fortune, would h. it**, quiso la suerte que, según quiso la suerte.—**rumor has it so**, así se dice; aseguran que es verdad.—**will h.**, deseo, desea, etc. (*I will have it so*, así lo quiero; *what will you have?* ¿qué desea Vd.?; *I will not have it*, no lo permito, o tolero). **III.** *s.* (fam.) el que tiene, el privilegiado (gen. en la frase **the haves and the have-nots**, los que tienen y los desposeídos).

havelock [hǽvlak], *s.* (mil.) cogotera.

haven [héjvn], *s.* puerto, fondeadero, abra; abrigo, asilo.

haversack [hǽvœrsæk], *s.* (mil.) mochila, barjuleta.

havoc [hǽvǫk]. **I.** *s.* estrago.—**to cry h.**, dar la orden de degüello y saqueo.—**to play h.**, hacer estragos. **II.** *va. y vn.* asolar, talar, hacer estragos.

haw [hɔ]. **I.** *s.* (bot.) acerola; baya o simiente (*f.*) del espino blanco; balbucencia. **II.** *va. y vn.* volver o hacer volver a la izquierda.—**to h. and gee**, ir de un lado a otro. **III.** *vn.* tartamudear.

Hawaiian [hawájyan], *a. y s.* hawaiano, hauaiano.

haw-haw [hɔ́hɔ́]. **I.** *s.* carcajada. **II.** *vn.* reír a carcajadas.

hawk [hɔ́k]. **I.** *s.* (orn.) halcón; gavilán; (alb.) tabla portamezcla.—**h.-eyed**, lince, de ojo avizor.—**h. moth**, (ent.) esfinge, *f.*—**h.-nosed**, aguileño, de nariz aguileña.—**h. owl**, (orn.) úlula, autillo.—**h. trainer**, halconero. **II.** *va. y vn.* cazar con halcón; pregonar mercancías;

gargajear, arrancar flema.—**hawking** [-iŋ], *s.* cetrería, halconería.

hawker [-œ(r)], *s.* buhonero; pregonero; halconero.

hawkweed [-wid], *s.* (bot.) pelosilla.

hawse [hɔ́z], *s.* (mar.) proa del buque; distancia, largo o cumplido de un cable.—**h. hole**, escobén.—**h. pipes**, bocinas o canales de los escobenes.—**h. plugs**, tacos de los escobenes.

hawser [-œ(r)], *s.* (mar.) cable, estacha.

hawthorn [hɔ́θɔrn], *s.* (bot.) espino, blanca espina, acerolo, oxiacanta.

hay [héj]. **I.** *s.* heno; paja de heno u otras hierbas para forraje, bálago.—**h. fever**, (med.) fiebre (*f.*) del heno, catarro anual de la nariz y los ojos.—**h.-spreader, h.-tedder**, esparcidora de heno.—**to make h. while the sun shines**, golpear el hierro cuando está en ascua, aprovechar la oportunidad, hacer su agosto. **II.** *va.* henear, ejecutar la operación del henaje.

haycock [-kak], *s.* almiar, niara.

hayfield [-fild], *s.* henar.

hayfork [-fɔrk], *s.* horca, bieldo, tridente.

haying [-iŋ], *s.* henaje.

hayloft [-lɔft], *s.* henal o henil, pajar.

haymow [-mau], *s.* henal. *V. t.* HAYSTACK.

hayrake [-rejk], *s.* rastrillo para heno.

hayrick [-rjk], *s.* = HAYSTACK.

hayseed [-sid], *s.* simiente (*f.*) de heno o de hierbas; (fam.) patán, rústico, paleto.

haystack [-stæk], *s.* niara, almiar; hacina de heno.

haywire [-wajr], *a.* (fam.) desarreglado; loco.

Haytian [héjtjan], *a. y s.* haitiano.

hazard [hǽzǝrd]. **I.** *s.* azar, albur, suerte, *f.*; peligro, riesgo; juego de azar a los dados; obstáculo (en el golf, etc.); acción de entronerar (en el billar). **II.** *va.* arriesgar, aventurar, exponer. **III.** *vn.* arriesgarse, aventurarse.

hazardous [-ʌs], *a.* arriesgado, peligroso.—**hazardously** [-lj], *adv.* peligrosamente, arriesgadamente.—**hazardousness** [-njs], *s.* riesgo, peligro; lo arriesgado.

haze [hejz]. **I.** *s.* niebla, bruma, calina; ofuscamiento mental. **II.** *vn.* abrumarse la atmósfera. **III.** *va.* dar culebra (en los colegios); (mar.) fatigar con trabajos pesados.

hazel [héjzl]. **I.** *s.* (bot.) avellano.—**h. grouse**, (orn.) ortega. **II.** *a.* castaño.

hazelnut [-nʌt], *s.* avellana.

haziness [héjzinjs], *s.* fosca, calígine, *f.,* calina.

hazing [héjzjŋ], *s.* culebra, culebrazo, novatada (en los colegios); acción o efecto de obligar a trabajar demasiado o en tareas desagradables; tunda, zurra.

hazy [héjzj], *a.* anieblado, brumoso; confuso, vago.

he [hi], *pron. pers.* él. Se emplea también para denotar el macho, vg.: *he-goat*, macho cabrío; *he-bear*, oso (macho).—**he-man**, (fam.) todo un hombre, hombre cabal.—**h. who, h. that**, el que, aquel que, quien.

head [héd], *s.* cabeza, testa; cima; parte (*f.*) superior o principal; título, encabezamiento; división sección (de un escrito, etc.); cabecera (de cama, mesa, río); fondo (de barril); tapa (de cilindro); (aut., etc.) culata (de cilindro) jefe, caudillo; director; res, *f.*, cabeza de ganado (en este sentido en el *pl.* es como el *sing.*); avance, progreso; crisis; astas (*f. pl.*) de ciervo o venado; punta (de flecha, etc.); puño (de bastón); (mar.) proa; fuente, *f.,* hacimiento; (hidr.) carga hidrostática o de presión, diferencia de nivel.—**h. fast**, (mar.) cabo de retenida de proa.—**h. of a sail**, gratil.—**h. of cabbage**, etc., repollo de col, etc.—**h. of hair**, cabellos *m. pl.,* cabellera.—**h. on**, de frente, cabeza con cabeza.—**h. or tail**, o **heads or tails**, cara y cruz, cara o sello.—**h. over heels**, precipitadamente, temerariamente.—**a h.**, por barba por persona.—**at the h. (of)**, al frente (de).—

from h. to foot, o to heels, de pies a cabeza.
—neither h. nor tail, ni pies ni cabeza.—off
one's h., (fam.) destornillado, loco.—on this
h., sobre este punto, asunto o particular.—
out of one's h., con el conocimiento perdido,
delirante.—over h. and ears, hasta las orejas.
—over one's h., por encima de uno, sin hacer
caso de uno; fuera del alcance de uno.—to
bring to a h., (med.) madurar; ultimar, traer
a un estado o situación decisivos.—to come
to a h., llegar a un estado definitivo, culminar;
(med.) madurar.

head, a. principal; de o para la cabeza; de frente;
(mar.) de proa; (hidr.) relativo a la carga hidrostática.—**h. cold**, (med.) romadizo, coriza.—
h. cook, primer cocinero.—**h. lamp** = HEAD-
LIGHT.—**h. money**, h. tax, capitación.—**h.
pin**, diez de bolos.—**h. post**, pilar o poste de
cabecera.—**h. resistance**, (aer.) resistencia
de proa o al avance.—**h. sea**, (mar.) mar o
marejada de proa.—**h. tone**, h. voice, voz de
cabeza.—**h. wind**, viento de frente, o en contra.

head. I. va. encabezar; mandar, dirigir, presidir;
interceptar, detener (gen. con off); descabezar,
degollar; formar o poner cabeza, puño, cabo
en o a; poner título; podar; (con in), recortar o
mochar (árboles). II. vn. dirigirse; (med.)
supurar; repollar, acogollarse (el col, etc.);
nacer en, salir o provenir de.—**to h. for**,
dirigirse o encaminarse a, hacer rumbo a.

headache [-ejk], s. (med.) dolor de cabeza,
jaqueca, cefalalgia.

headband [-bænd], s. cabezada de libro; venda,
cinta o faja para la cabeza.

headblock [-blak], s. bloque de levante bajo el
extremo de un madero, etc.; (f. c.) traviesa de
apoyo de las agujas de un cambiavía.

headboard [-bɔrd], s. cabecera de cama.

headcheese [-chiz], s. queso de cerdo.

headdress [-drɛs], s. cofia, tocado, redecilla o
escofieta.

headed [-jd], a. que tiene cabeza; titulado.—**h.
for**, en dirección a, con rumbo a.

header [-œ(r)], s. (ton.) el que pone fondos a las
cubas; caída o salto de cabeza, zambullida;
golpe en la cabeza; descabezador de las mieses;
cabecilla; (arq.) tizón, piedra o ladrillo a tizón;
(m. v.) colector, cámara de circulación.

headfirst [-fœrst], **headforemost** [-fɔrmoust],
adv. de cabeza.

headgear [-gjr], s. tocado o cofia de mujer; cabezada; (mar.) aparejo de las velas de proa.

head-hunter [-hʌntœ(r)], s. cazador de cabezas.

headiness [-injs], s. terquedad, obstinación; encabezamiento del vino.

heading [-iŋ], s. título, encabezamiento; membrete; (ton.) témpano, tapa; (min.) galería,
socavón; frente; (arq.) paramento o frente de
un tizón.—**h. bond**, (arq.) aparejo de tizones.
—**h. joint**, (carp.) junta de dos maderas con
las fibras en ángulo recto.

headland [-lænd], s. (geog.) promontorio, punta.

headledge [-ledź], s. (mar.) contrabrazola.

headless [-ljs], a. descabezado, degollado; acéfalo.

headlight [-lajt], s. linterna delantera; (aut.)
faro; (f. c.) farol, fanal; (mar.) farol de tope.

headline [-lajn], s. título, encabezamiento; titular, f.; epígrafe.

headlong [-lɔŋ]. I. a. temerario, arrojado; precipitado; precipitoso. II. adv. de cabeza; precipitadamente, de sopetón; sin pensarlo; de
hoz y de coz.

headman [-man], s. jefe, cabecilla.

headmaster [-mæstœ(r)], s. director de escuela.

headmistress [-mjstrjs], s. directora.

headmost [-moust], a. delantero, de la cabeza.

headphone [-foun], s. (tlf.) boquilla auricular o receptor que se asegura en la cabeza con
una cinta elástica.

headpiece [-pis], s. morrión, m., bacinete, casco;
(impr.) viñeta, cabecera; (fam.) cholla, mollera.

headquarters [-kwɔrtœrz], s. (mil.) cuartel
general; comisariato o jefatura (de policía,
etc.); oficina principal; centro de dirección o
de operaciones.

headrace [-rejs], s. saetín (de molino).

headrail [-rejl], s. (mar.) percha.

headrest [-rɛst], s. apoyo para la cabeza.

headrope [-roup], s. (mar.) relinga de gratil.

headsail [-sejl], s. (mar.) vela delantera.

headset [-sɛt], s. juego de headphones.

headshake [-śejk], s. cabezada.

headship [-śip], s. jefatura; supremacía.

headsman [-zman], s. verdugo; degollador.

headspring [-sprjŋ], s. fuente, f., origen.

headstall [-stɔl], s. cabezada del freno, testera,
jáquima, potrera.

headstock [-stak], s. portaherramienta (de un
torno, de cepilladora); (tej.) bastidor de la
carretilla de la despepitadora de algodón.

headstone [-stoun], s. lápida mortuoria; (arq.)
piedra angular; clave, f.

headstrong [-strɔŋ], a. terco, testarudo, obstinado, cabezudo, voluntarioso.—**headstrong-
ness** [-njs], s. terquedad, obstinación, testarudez.

headwaters [-wɔtœrz], s. pl. cabecera, fuentes,
f. pl.

headway [-wej], s. (mar.) salida, marcha de un
buque; avance, ímpetu; progreso; (f. c.) intervalo o distancia entre dos trenes; (ing.) elevación, espacio libre (debajo de un puente, etc.).
—**to make h.**, adelantar, progresar.

headwork [-wœrk], s. trabajo mental; obra intelectual; (arq.) cabeza de adorno en una clave.

heady [-j], a. temerario, arrojado; fuerte, encabezado (vino); violento, impetuoso; (fam.)
sesudo.

heal [hîl]. I. va. curar; remediar; reconciliar,
componer. II. vn. sanar; recobrar la salud.—
to h. up, cicatrizarse.

healable [-abl], a. curable, sanable.

heald [hild], s. (tej.) lizo.

healer [hîlœ(r)], s. sanador; curador.

healing [hîljŋ]. I. a. sanativo, curativo, cicatrizal.
II. s. cura, curación, cicatrización.

health [hélθ], s. salud; sanidad.—**h. department**, sanidad.—**h. officer**, sanitario, oficial
de sanidad o de cuarentena.—**h.-giving**,
salubre, saludable.—**h. resort**, lugar de curas,
colonia de enfermos.—**to be in good** (poor)
h., estar bien (mal) de salud.—**your h.!** ¡a su
salud!

healthful [-ful], a. sano, saludable, salubre.

healthfully [-j], adv. saludablemente.

healthfulness [-njs], s. salubridad, calidad de
saludable, higiénico, etc.

healthily [-jlj], adv. saludablemente.

healthiness [-injs], s. sanidad, estado sano, goce
de buena salud.

healthy [-j], a. sano; fuerte, de buena salud;
saludable.

heap [hîp]. I. s. montón, rimero, acervo; (fam.,
a veces pl.) gran cantidad, mucho(s); multitud,
gentío.—**in heaps**, a montones. II. va. amontonar, apilar, acumular; colmar, llenar completamente.

heaping [-jŋ]. I. a. llenado con exceso o hasta
que se desborde. II. s. amontonamiento.

hear [hjr]. I. va. (pret. y pp. HEARD) oír; oír decir;
escuchar; saber, tener noticia de; dar audiencia;
otorgar, conceder.—**to h. confession**, confesar.—**to h. it said**, oír decir.—**to h. mass**,
oír misa. II. vn. oír.—**to h. from**, saber de
(directamente, como por carta).—**to h. of**,
saber de (de oídas); tener noticia de.—**will
not**, o **won't**, **h. of it**, no quiere (quiero, etc.)
ni siquiera hablar de ello.

hearer [hjrœ(r)], s. oyente, oidor, escuchador.

hearing [hjrjŋ], s. oído; audiencia; (for.) vista
(de un pleito o causa); examen de testigos
acción de oír, audición; alcance del oído.—**in**

one's h., que uno oye u oyó.—**within h.**, al alcance del oído.

hearken [hárkn], *vn.* y *va.* = HARKEN.

hearsay [hírsei], I. *s.* rumor, voz común, fama.
—**by h.**, de oídas. II. *a.* de oídas.

hearse [hérs]. I. *s.* carro o coche fúnebre. II. *va.* colocar en un ataúd; enterrar, sepultar.

hearsecloth [-kloθ], *s.* palio, paño mortuorio.

hearselike [-laik], *a.* lúgubre, fúnebre.

heart [hárt], *s.* corazón; ánimo; (fig.) entraña(s).
—*pl.* copas (de baraja). (En lo que sigue se usa *c.* en vez de *corazón*).—**h. alive!** ¡Ave María! ¡caramba!—**h. and soul**, en cuerpo y alma.—**h. block**, (med.) bradicardia, retardación rítmica de los latidos del c.—**h. disease**, enfermedad del c.—**h. failure**, (med.) insuficiencia cardíaca; parálisis repentina del corazón.—**h.-rending**, agudo, desgarrador, que parte el c.—**h.-shaped**, cordiforme, cardiáceo, acorazonado, en forma de c.—**h.-to-h.**, sincero, franco.—**h. trouble**, enfermedad del c.—**h. whole**, desamorado; valiente, intrépido; sincero.—**h.-wounded**, herido en el alma.—**h.-worn**, agobiado.—**after one's own h.**, de todo el gusto de uno, que armoniza en todo con las ideas de uno.—**at h.**, en el fondo, esencialmente; en verdad.—**by h.**, de memoria.—**from one's h.**, de todo c., con sinceridad.—**out of h.**, descorazonado; en mal estado.—**to have one's h. in one's mouth**, o boots, tener el alma en un hilo, estar muerto de miedo.—**to one's h.'s content**, a sus anchas, sin restricción.—**with all one's h.**, con todo el c., de todo c.

heartache [-eik], *s.* angustia, congoja, pesar.

heartbeat [-bit], *s.* latido del corazón; profunda emoción.

heartbreak [-breik], *s.* angustia, pesar, dolor.

heartbreaking [-iŋ], *a.* congojoso, doloroso, desgarrador.

heartbroken [-broukn], *a.* acongojado, transido de dolor, muerto (fig.) de pesar.—**heartbrokenly** [-li], *adv.* con el corazón partido, dolorosísimamente.

heartburn [-bœrn], *s.* (med.) acedía, cardialgia.
—**heartburning** [-iŋ]. I. *s.* acedía; rencilla, animosidad. II. *a.* intenso, profundo, sentido.

hearted [-id], *a.* que tiene corazón.

hearten [-n], *va.* animar, alentar; confortar.

heartfelt [-felt], *a.* cordial, sincero; sentido.

heartgrief [-grif], *s.* congoja, angustia.

hearth [harθ], *s.* hogar, fogón, chimenea; hogar doméstico.—**h. money**, fogaje, tributo antiguo.

heartily [hártili], *adv.* cordialmente, de corazón.

heartiness [-injs], *s.* cordialidad, sinceridad.

heartless [-lis], *a.* sin corazón; empedernido, cruel; tímido, pusilánime.—**heartlessly** [-li], *adv.* cruelmente, sin piedad; pusilánimemente, tímidamente.—**heartlessness** [-nis], *s.* falta de corazón; falta de ánimo; empedernimiento.

heartsease [-siz], *s.* tranquilidad; (bot.) trinitaria, pensamiento.

heartsick [-sik], *a.* dolorido; desconsolado.

heartsore [-sor], *a.* afligido, acongojado.

heartstricken [-strikn], *a.* afligido, angustiado.

heartstrings [-striŋz], *s. pl.* fibras del corazón; (fig.) entretelas.

heartstruck [-strʌk], *a.* afligido, acongojado.

heartthrob [-θrab], *s.* emoción apasionada o sentimental; salto.

heartwood [-wụd], *s.* madera de corazón, duramen.

hearty [-i], *a.* cordial, sentido, sincero; sano, robusto, vigoroso; voraz; gustoso, grato.

heat [hít]. I. *s.* calor; acaloramiento, ardor, vehemencia; celo o brama (de los animales); (fund.) carga de un horno, hornada; colada; (dep.) carrera o corrida preliminar o eliminatoria.—**h. engine**, máquina térmica.—**h. exchanger**, recipiente de intercambio térmico.

compensador de temperatura.—**h. lightning**, fucilazos, relámpagos sin trueno.—**h. stroke**, insolación.—**h. unit**, unidad térmica.—**h. wave**, ola de calor.—**in h.**, en celo, salida (perra, gata, etc.).—**to be in h.**, estar en celo, (fig.) estar caliente o cachondo (un animal). II. *va.* calentar, caldear; acalorar; excitar. III. *vn.* calentarse; acalorarse.

heater [-œ(r)], *s.* calentador; calorífero; aparato de calefacción; estufa.

heath [hiθ], *s.* (bot.) brezo; brezal, matorral.—**h. cock**, (orn.) gallo silvestre, urogallo.

heathen [híðen], *s.* gentil, pagano.—**heathenish** [-iš], *a.* gentílico; pagano; bárbaro.—**heathenism** [-izm], *s.* gentilismo, paganismo.—**heathenize** [-aiz], *va.* y *vn.* hacer(se) pagano; gentilizar.

heather [héðœ(r)], *s.* (bot.) brezo, erica, urce.

heathery [-i], **heathy** [híθi], *a.* cubierto de brezos, matoso.

heating [hítiŋ]. I. *s.* calefacción; calentamiento, caldeo, calda. II. *a.* caluroso; calefaciente; de calefacción (superficie, área, etc.).—**h. pad**, almohadilla eléctrica.—**h. power**, potencia calorífica.

heatless [hítlis], *a.* frío, sin calor.

heave [hiv]. I. *va.* (*pret.* y *pp.* HEAVED o HOVE) alzar, levantar, elevar; (mar.) izar; virar; lanzar, echar fuera, arrojar; exhalar, prorrumpir.
—**to h. overboard**, echar al agua.—**to h. the lead**, escandallar.—**to h. a sigh**, exhalar un suspiro. II. *vn.* levantarse y bajarse alternativamente, v. gr., el pecho, el mar; suspirar hondo; palpitar; jadear, trabajar penosamente; tener náuseas; (mar.) virar.—**to h. in sight**, (mar.) aparecer, asomar.—**to h. to**, (mar.) ponerse al pairo o en facha. III. *s.* elevación; alzadura, levantamiento; henchidura de una ola; náusea, arcada; (geol.) falla.

heaven [hévn], *s.* cielo; gloria, paraíso.—*pl.* firmamento, las alturas.—**h.-born**, celeste, divino, angelical.—**h.-kissing**, que llega hasta el cielo.—**heavens!** ¡cáspita! ¡cielos! —**for h.'s sake!** ¡por Dios!

heavenliness [-linis], *s.* calidad de celestial.

heavenly [-li]. I. *a.* celeste; celestial. II. *adv.* celestialmente.

heavenward [-wạrd], *adv.* hacia el cielo.

heaver [hívœ(r)], *s.* (mar.) alzaprima; cargador.

heaves [hivz], *s. pl.* (vet.) huélfago o huérfano.

heavily [hévili], *adv.* pesadamente, lentamente; tristemente; excesivamente, sumamente.

heaviness [-nis], *s.* pesantez, peso; tardanza, torpeza; languidez, modorra; abatimiento o tristeza; opresión, carga.

heaving [hívin], *s.* acción del verbo TO HEAVE; palpitación; oleada.—**h. line**, estacha, cala-brote.

heavy [hévi]. I. *a.* pesado; grueso; fuerte; duro, riguroso, opresivo; molesto; denso, espeso; oneroso, gravoso; cargado, recargado; difícil; pesaroso, triste; considerable, importante; tardo, lento, estúpido; indigesto.—**h. artillery**, artillería gruesa.—**h. duty**, servicio o trabajo fuerte (de una máquina).—**h. earth**, (min.) barita.—**h. rain**, o **shower**, lluvia fuerte, turbión, *m.*, chaparrón, aguacero.—**h. sea**, oleada, ola fuerte.—**h. seas**, mar bravo o borrascoso.—**h. spar**, baritina, espato espeso.—**h. water**, agua que contiene deutóxido; agua superhidrogenada (H_2O_2). II. *adv.* = HEAVILY.—**h.-armed**, armado de armas o armadura pesadas.—**h.-handed**, torpe; opresivo.—**h.-hearted**, triste, abatido.—**h.-laden**, recargado; agobiado, oprimido.

heavyweight [-weit]. I. *a.* de peso pesado o máximo. II. *s.* boxeador de primer peso o de peso mayor.

hebdomad [hébdomæd], *s.* hebdómada.

hebdomadal [hebdámạdạl], **hebdomadary** [-deri], *a.* hebdomadario, semanal.

hebephrenia [hibęfrínią], *s.* (pat.) hebefrenia.
hebetation [hebitéişǫn], **hebetude** [hébitiud], *s.* estupidez, entorpecimiento.
Hebraic [hįbréįįk], *a.* hebreo, hebraico.
Hebraism [híbrįįzm], *s.* hebraísmo.
Hebraist [híbrįįst], *s.* hebraísta.
Hebraize [híbrįajz]. **I.** *va.* hebraizar, hacer hebreo. **II.** *vn.* volverse hebreo.
Hebrew [híbru], *s.* y *a.* hebreo; israelita; judío.
hecatomb [hékątum], *s.* hecatombe, *f.*
heckle [hékl], *va.* interrumpir con preguntas irrisorias y sátiras. *V.* HACKLE y HATCHEL.
hectare [hékter], *s.* hectárea.
hectic(al [héktįk(ąl], *a.* (med.) hético; agitado, turbulento.—**hectic,** *s.* (med.) tisis; fiebre hética; tísico.
hecto [hékto], *prefijo* que significa ciento.—
  hectogram(me [-græm], *s.* hectogramo.—
  hectoliter, hectolitre [-lítœ(r)], *s.* hectolitro.
  —**hectometer, hectometre** [-mitœ(r)], *s.* hectómetro.—**hectograph** [-græf], hectógrafo.
  —**hectowatt** [-wat], *s.* hectovatio.
hector [héktǫ(r)]. **I.** *s.* matasiete, matón, fanfarrón. **II.** *vn.* baladronear, bravear. **III.** *va.* amenazar, intimidar con bravatas.
heddle [hédl], *s.* malla, lizos de un telar.
hedge [hédʒ]. **I.** *s.* seto vivo, cerca, vallado de zarzas.—**h. garlic,** (bot.) aliaria.—**h. hyssop,** (bot.) graciola.—**h. marriage,** casamiento clandestino.—**h. mustard,** (bot.) jaramago, balsamita, sisimbrio.—**h. parson,** clérigo inculto. **II.** *va.* cercar con seto, vallar; defender, circundar; rodear. **III.** *vn.* ponerse al abrigo; cubrirse; compensar o igualar una apuesta o jugada de bolsa con otra en sentido contrario.
hedgeborn [-bǫrn], *a.* de baja ralea.
hedgehog [-hag], **hedgepig** [-pįg], *s.* (zool.) erizo.
hedgehop [-hap], *vn.* (aer., fam.) volar a ras de los árboles o setos.
hedger [-œ(r)], *s.* el que hace setos; el que compensa o iguala sus apuestas.
hedgerow [-rou], *s.* seto vivo.
hedging bill [hédʒįŋ bįl], *s.* podadera de setos.
hedonics [hįdánįks], *s.* ciencia del placer; parte (*f.*) de la ética que estudia el placer en su aspecto moral.
hedonism [hídonįzm], *s.* hedonismo.—**hedonist(ic** [-įst, -ístįk], *s.* y *a.* hedonista.
heed [híd]. **I.** *va.* atender, escuchar; observar, reparar (en), tener en cuenta. **II.** *vn.* prestar atención, hacer caso. **III.** *s.* cuidado, atención.
heedful [-fųl], *a.* atento, cuidadoso.—**heedfully** [-į], *adv.* atentamente, cuidadosamente.—
heedfulness [-nįs], *s.* cautela, atención, cuidado.
heedless [-lįs], *a.* desatento, descuidado; atolondrado, incauto.—**heedlessly** [-lį], *adv.* incautamente, descuidadamente.—**heedlessness** [-nįs], *s.* descuido, negligencia, imprudencia.
heel [híl]. **I.** *s.* (anat.) talón o calcañar; (zap.) tacón; talón de una media; pie, *m.*, parte (*f.*) inferior; (mar.) coz o pie de palo; (agr.) estaca, pie; (f. c.) talón (de una aguja).—**h. blank,** o **lift,** (zap.) tapa.—**heels over head,** patas arriba; precipitadamente, a tontas.—**down at the heels,** desvalido, en aprietos; desaliñado.—
to be at the heels of, perseguir estrechamente; seguir servilmente. **II.** *va.* poner talón a (zapatos o medias); asir, agarrar por los talones; poner espolones al gallo; (fam.) proveer de dinero.—**to be well heeled,** (fam.) estar bien provisto de dinero.—**to h. in,** (agr.) cubrir provisionalmente con tierra las raíces. **III.** *vn.* (mar.) inclinarse, tumbarse o escorar.—**to h. over,** zozobrar.
heeler [-œ(r)], *s.* gallo que clava bien los espolones; (fam.) paniaguado de un cacique político; (zap.) taconero; andarín.
heelpiece [-pis], *s.* talón.
heft [héft]. **I.** *s.* (fam.) peso, pesadez; (fam.) la mayor parte. **II.** *va.* (fam.) so(m)pesar.

hefty [-į], *a.* (fam.) un poco pesado; vigoroso; riguroso.
Hegelian [hejgéįlįąn], *a.* y *s.* hegeliano.
Hegelianism [-įzm], *s.* hegelianismo.
hegemony [hédʒįmoni], *s.* hegemonía.
hegira [hédʒįrą], *s.* héjira, (h)égira.
heifer [héfœ(r)], *s.* (zool.) vaquilla, novilla.
heigh-ho [háį hóų], *interj.* ¡ay! ¡oh!
height [háįt], *s.* altura, alto, altitud, elevación; estatura, talla; alzada (de caballo); (geog.) cerro, colina, eminencia; sublimidad; apogeo (de fama, etc.); colmo.—**h. gauge,** calibre de alturas.—**at the h. of** (spring, etc.), en plena (primavera, etc.).—**the h. of folly,** el colmo de la locura.
heighten [-n], *va.* realzar, levantar, elevar; mejorar; adelantar, ascender; sublimar, exaltar; avivar.
heinous [héįnąs], *a.* atroz, nefando, horrible.—
heinously [-lį], *adv.* atrozmente, horriblemente.—**heinousness** [-nįs], *s.* atrocidad, perversidad.
heir [ér], *s.* heredero.—**h. apparent,** heredero forzoso.—**h. at law,** heredero legal.—**h. presumptive,** presunto heredero.
heirdom [-dǫm], **heirship** [-šįp], *s.* herencia, derecho de heredar.—**heiress** [-įs], *s.* heredera.
—**heirless** [-lįs], *a.* sin heredero.—**heirloom** [-lum], *s.* bienes muebles heredados; herencia.
held [held], *pret.* y *pp.* de TO HOLD.
heliac(al [hílįæk, hįláįąkąl], *a.* (astr.) helíaco.
helianthemum [hilįænθǫmʌm], *s.* (bot.) heliantemo.
helianthus [-θʌs], *s.* (bot.) helianto, girasol.
helical [hélįkąl], *a.* espiral, helicoidal.
helicoid [hélįkojd]. **I.** *a.* helicoidal. **II.** *s.* (geom.) helicoide.
Helicon [hélįkan], *s.* (mit.) Helicón; (h., mús.) helicón.
helicopter [hélįkaptœ(r)], *s.* (aer.) helicóptero.
heliocentric(al [hįlįoséntrįk(ąl], *a.* heliocéntrico.
heliochromy [-kroųmį], *s.* heliocromía, fotocromía.
heliograph [-græf]. **I.** *s.* heliógrafo; helióstato. **II.** *va.* hacer señales con el heliógrafo o el helióstato.
heliographic [-gráfįk], *a.* heliográfico.
heliography [hilįágrafį], *s.* transmisión de señales por medio del heliógrafo; descripción de la superficie del sol.
heliogravure [hilįogravįúr], *s.* heliograbado.
heliolatry [hilįálatrį], *s.* culto del sol.
heliometer [hilįámetœ(r)], *s.* heliómetro.
helioscope [hílįoskoųp], *s.* helioscopio.
heliostat [-stæt], *s.* helióstato.
heliotherapy [-θérąpį], *s.* (med.) helioterapia.
heliotrope [-troųp], *s.* (bot.) heliotropo; olor o color de esta flor; (fís.) helióstato, heliógrafo; (min.) heliotropo, ágata verdosa.
heliotropism [hilįátropįzm], *s.* (bot.) heliotropismo.
heliotype [hílįotajp]. **I.** *s.* heliograbado. **II.** *va.* reproducir por medio de la heliotipia.
heliotypy [-į], *s.* heleotipia; procedimiento del heliograbado.
helium [hílįʌm], *s.* (quím.) helio.
helix [hílįks], *s.* hélice, *f.*, espira; (arq.) voluta; (anat.) hélice o hélix, reborde del pabellón de la oreja; (zool.) hélix, caracol de tierra.
hell [hél], *s.* infierno; tártaro, averno; garito; desván; cajón de sastre; (impr.) caja de letras inservibles.—**h.-doomed,** réprobo.—**h.-fire,** fuego o tormento del infierno.—**h. gate,** puerta del infierno.
hellbender [-bendœ(r)], *s.* (zool.) salamandra acuática.
hellborn [-bǫrn], *a.* infernal.
hellbox [-baks], *s.* (impr.) caja de tipo roto.
hellbroth [-broθ], *s.* caldo mágico maligno.
hellcat [-kæt], *s.* bruja; arpía, vieja viciosa; persona atolondrada o temeraria.

hellebore [hélibor], s. (bot.) eléboro, veratro.

Hellenic [helénik], a. heleno, helénico, greciano.

Hellenism [hélinizm], s. helenismo, grecismo.—**Hellenist** [-ist], s. helenista.—**Hellenistic** [-ístik], a. helénico.—**Hellenistically** [-ali], adv. a la manera de los griegos.—**Hellenize** [-aiz], va. y vn. helenizar, grecizar.

hellgrammite [hélgramait], s. (ent.) larva que se emplea como carnada en la pesca.

hellhound [hélhaund], s. (mit.) Cancerbero; demonio; perseguidor cruel.

hellish [héliš], a. infernal.—**hellishly** '-li], adv. infernal o diabólicamente.—**hellishnes** [-nis], s. malicia infernal, diablura.

hello [helóu], interj. V. HALLO y HOLLO.—**h. there!** ¡hola! ¡oiga!—**h.-girl,** (fam.) (chica) telefonista.

hellward [hélwärd], adv. hacia el infierno.

helm [helm], s. (mar.) timón, gobernalle, caña; (ant.) yelmo, capacete.—**h. port,** limera del timón.

helmet [hélmit], s. yelmo, celada, casco.—**h. flower,** (bot.) acónito, matalobos.

helmeted [-id], a. que lleva yelmo.

helminth [hélminθ], s. (zool.) lombriz, helminto.

helminthic [helmínθik], a. helminto; vermífugo.

helminthology [-θálodži], s. helmintología.

helmless [hélmlis], a. sin timón.

helmsman [hélmzman], s. timonero, timonel.

helot [hélot], s. ilota, mf.—**helotism** [-izm], s. ilotismo.—**helotry** [-ri], s. la clase ilota; servidumbre, esclavitud.

help [help]. I. va. ayudar, asistir, auxiliar, socorrer; aliviar; remediar, reparar; evitar; dejar de hacer.—**to h. down,** ayudar a alguno a bajar.—**to h. forward,** adelantar, activar, promover.—**to h. on,** ayudar.—**to h. one's self to,** servirse (carne, sopa, etc.).—**to h. one to,** servir a uno (carne, sopa, etc.); proporcionar.—**to h. out,** ayudar; ayudar a salir; sacar de algún peligro o mal paso.—**to h. over,** ayudar a salir de (una dificultad, etc.).—**to h. up,** ayudar (a una persona) a levantarse.—**cannot h.** (seguido de gerundio), no puedo (puede, etc.) dejar de, menos de (seguido de infinitivo) (I cannot help believing it, no puedo menos de creerlo; he could not help doing it, él no pudo dejar de hacerlo).—**I cannot h. it,** no puedo remediarlo.—**so h. me God,** así Dios me salve. II. vn. ayudar; contribuir; servir (en la mesa).—**to h. out,** ayudar. III. s. ayuda, auxilio, socorro; remedio; servidumbre, criados, sirvientes; empleados, dependientes; trabajadores.—**h.!** ¡socorro!—**by the h. of,** con ayuda de.—**there is no h. for it,** eso no tiene remedio.

helper [-œ(r)], s. auxiliador, ayudador; asistente, ayudante.

helpful [-ful], a. útil, servicial; provechoso; saludable.—**helpfulness** [-nis], s. calidad de provechoso, servicial, etc.; utilidad.

helping [-iŋ]. I. a. ayudador, auxiliante, auxiliadro)r. II. s. acción de ayudar, etc.; porción (de comida) que se sirve a uno o que uno se sirve de una vez. Conviene cambiar el giro: I have had two helpings of rice, me he servido (Vd. me ha servido, etc.) arroz dos veces.

helpless [-lis], a. desvalido; imposibilitado, impotente; inútil; irremediable.—**helplessly** [-li], adv. irremediablemente; desamparadamente.

helplessness [-nis], s. desamparo; impotencia.

helpmate [-meit], s. compañero; asistente, ayudante, auxiliador.

helter-skelter [héltœr skéltœr(r)], adv. a trochemoche, sin orden ni concierto, a la desbandada.

helve [helv]. I. s. astil de hacha o de destral; mango. II. va. poner mango o cabo a.

Helvetian [helvíšian], **Helvetic** [helvétik], a. y s. helvético, helvecio, suizo.

hem [hem]. I. s. (cost.) borde, dobladillo, bastilla, repulgo. II. interj. ¡ejem! V. AHEM. III. va.

(cost.) dobladillar, bastillar, repulgar; (gen. con **in**) rodear, encerrar. IV. vn. tartamudear; fingir tos, toser de fingido.

hemal [hímal], a. perteneciente a la sangre; relativo al lado del cuerpo que contiene el corazón.

hematemesis [hematémesis], s. (med.) hematemesis, vómito de sangre.

hematic [hímætik], a. hemático, de la sangre, que afecta la sangre.—**hematid** [hímætid], s. (anat.) hematíe, m., hematía, mf.

hematin [hémætin], s. (quím.) hematina.

hematite [-tait], s. (min.) hematites, f.

hematoblast [-toblæst], s. hematoblasto.

hematocele [-tosil], s. hematocele, tumor sanguíneo.

hematogenesis [-togénesis], s. hematogénesis, formación de sangre.

hematoid [-toid], a. hematoideo, de sangre o semejante a la sangre.

hematology [-tálodži], s. (med.) hematología.

hematoma [-tóuma], s. hematoma, m., tumor sanguíneo.

hematose [-tous], a. lleno o recargado de sangre; sanguíneo.

hematosis [-tóusis], s. (fisiol.) hematosis.

hematoxylin [-táksilin], s. hematoxilina, principio colorante del palo de Campeche.

hematuria [-tiúria], s. (med.) hematuria, orina con sangre.

hemi [hémi], prefijo que equivale a medio o semi.

hemialgia [-ældžia], s. hemialgia, dolor en un solo lado, esp. de la cabeza (ll. entonces t. **hemicrania**).

hemic [hímik o hémik], a. hémico, de la sangre, relativo a la sangre.

hemichordate [hemikórdeit], s. y a. (zool.) hemicordio.

hemicrania [-kréinia], s. (med.) hemicránea.

hemicycle [-saikl], s. hemiciclo.

hemihedral [-hídral], a. (min.) hemiédrico.—**hemihedrism** [-hídrizm], s. (min.) hemiedría.—**hemihedron** [-hídron], s. cristal hemiedro.

hemiplegia [-plídžia], **hemiplegy** [-plídži], s. (med.) hemiplejía.—**hemiplegic** [-k], a. hemipléjico.

hemipter [himíptœ(r)], s., **hemipteral** [-al], a., **hemipteran** [-an], s. y a., **hemipterous** [-ʌs], a. (zool.) hemíptero.

hemisphere [hémisfir], s. hemisferio.

hemispheric(al [-sférik(al], a. hemisférico.

hemispheroidal [-sfiróidal], a. hemisferoidal.

hemistich [-stik], s. (poét.) hemistiquio.

hemitropism [-tropizm], **hemitropy** [hemítropi], s. (min.) hemitropía.

hemlock [hémlak], s. (bot.) abeto, pícea; (bot.) cicuta.—**h. spruce,** (bot.) abeto del Canadá.

hemoglobin [himoglóubin], s. hemoglobina.

hemopathy [himápaθi], s. (med.) hemopatía.

hemophilia [himofília], s. (med.) hemofilia.

hemoptysis [himáptisis], s. (med.) hemóptisis, hemorragia pulmonar.

hemorrhage [hémoridž], s. (med.) hemorragia, flujo de sangre.—**hemorrhagic** [-rædžik], a. hemorrágico.

hemorrhoids [-roidz], s. pl. (med.) hemorroides, f. pl., almorranas.

hemorrhoidal [-róidal], a. hemorroidal.

hemostatic [-stætik], a. (med.) hemostático.

hemp [hémp], s. (bot.) cáñamo.—**h. beater,** espadador o espadillador.—**h. brake,** espadilla.—**h. breaker,** agramador.—**h. close, o h. field,** cañamar.—**h. comb,** rastrillo.—**h. comber,** rastrillador.—**h. cord,** bramante.—**h. dresser,** batidor.—**h. sandal,** alpargata, alpargate.

hempen [-n], a. cañameño.

hempseed [-sid], s. cañamón; (fam.) villano, malhechor.

hemstitch [hémstich]. I. va. (cost.) hacer una vainica en. II. s. (cost.) vainica.

hempy [hémpi], a. cañameño.

---

hen [hen], *s.* (orn.) gallina; hembra de cualquier ave. Se usa adjetivadamente en el sentido de hembra (*hen canary*, canario hembra).—**h. dung**, gallinaza.—**h. party**, (fam.) reunión (o tertulia) de señoras.

henbane [hénbejn], *s.* (bot.) beleño.

hence [héns], *adv.* de aquí; de aquí a (*two months hence*, de aquí a dos meses); desde aquí; fuera de aquí; de ahí que, por tanto, por esto, en consecuencia; de esto.

henceforth [-forθ], *adv.* (de aquí) en adelante, en lo futuro, en lo sucesivo.

henceforward [-fórwǎrd], *adv.* (de aquí) en adelante; de hoy más; en lo venidero.

henchman [hénchmǎn], *s.* hechura, paniaguado, secuaz (*m.*) servil.

hencoop [hénkup], *s.* gallinero.

hendecasyllable [hendekásjlǎbl], *s.*, **hendecasyllabic** [-sjlǽbjk], *a.* (poét.) endecasílabo.

henequen [hénekjn], *s.* (bot.) henequén.

henhouse [hénhaus], *s.* = HENCOOP.

henna [hénǎ], *s.* (bot.) alhefia, alcana.

hennery [hénceri], *s.* gallinero.

henotheism [hénoθijzm], *s.* henoteísmo, creencia en el poder alternativo de varios dioses, o en el poder de dioses regionales.

henpeck [hénpek], *va.* dominar e importunar la mujer al marido.—**henpecked** [-t], *a.* gurrumino.—**h. husband**, marido cuya mujer lleva los calzones, gurrumino.

henroost [hénrust], *s.* = HENCOOP.

hep [hep], *s.* (bot.) fruto del agavanzo. *V.* HIP. —**h. bramble**, o **brier**, escaramujo, agavanzo.

hep, *a.* (fam.) (gen. con to) conocedor de, al tanto de.

hepatic [hipǽtjk], *a.* y *s.* (bot. y med.) hepático.

hepatica [hipǽtjkǎ], *s.* (bot.) hepática.

hepatite [hépatajt], *s.* (min.) hepatita.

hepatitis [-tájtjs], *s.* (med.) hepatitis, inflamación del hígado.

hepatization [-tjzéjšǒn], *s.* (med.) hepatización.

hepatology [-tálodži], *s.* (med.) hepatología.

hepcat [hépkæt], *s.* (fam.) perito o aficionado del *jazz*.

heptachord [héptǎkord], *s.* (mús.) heptacordo.

heptad [héptæd], *s.* setena.

heptagon [héptǎgǎn], *s.* y *a.* (geom.) heptágono.

heptameter [heptǽmetœ(r)], *s.* **heptametrical** [heptǎmétrjkǎl], *a.* (poét.) heptámetro.

heptane [héptejn], *s.* (quím.) heptano.

heptarch [héptark], *s.* heptarca, *m.*

heptarchy [-j], *s.* heptarquía.

Heptateuch [héptǎtjuk], *s.* Heptateuco.

her [hœr], *pron.* (caso objetivo o acusativo de SHE) la, le, ella, a ella: *I saw her*, la vi; *I told her*, le dije; *this is for her*, esto es para ella; (caso posesivo o genitivo de SHE, y adjetivo posesivo) su, de ella: *her book, her house*, su libro, su casa (de ella).

herald [hérǎld]. **I.** *s.* heraldo, rey de armas; nuncio, precursor; publicador. **II.** *va.* anunciar, pregonar, proclamar.

heraldic [hérǎldjk], *a.* herádico, genealógico.

heraldry [hérǎldrj], *s.* heráldica, blasón.

heraldship [-šjp], *s.* oficio de heraldo.

herb [(h)œrb], *s.* hierba, yerba.

herbaceous [hœrbéjšjʌs], *a.* herbáceo.

herbage [(h)œrbjdž], *s.* hierba, herbaje; pasto.

herbal [(h)œrbǎl], *a.* herbario.—**herbalism** [-jzm], *s.* conocimiento de las hierbas.—**herbalist** [-jst], *s.* herbolario, herborizador, botánico herbario.

herbarium [hœrbérjʌm], *s.* herbario (seco).

herbary [hœrbǎrj], *s.* jardín de hierbas.

herbiferous [hœrbífgerʌs], *a.* herbífero.

herbivore [hœrbjvor], *s.* (zool.) herbívoro.

herbivorous [hœrbívǒrʌs], *a.* herbívoro.

herbless [(h)œrbljs], *a.* sin hierbas, yermo.

herborist [hœrborjst], *s.* = HERBALIST.

herborization [-rjzéjšǒn], *s.* herborización.

herborize [-rajz], *vn.* herborizar.

herborizer [-œ(r)], *s.* herborizador.

herbose [hœrbóųs], **herbous** [(h)œrbʌs] o **herby** [(h)œrbj], *a.* herboso, herbáceo.

herbwoman [(h)œrbwųmǎn], *s.* herbolaria.

herculean [hœrkjúljǎn], *a.* hercúleo.

herd [hœrd]. **I.** *s.* hato, grey, *f.*, manada, rebaño; vacada; piara (de cerdos); multitud, chusma; manadero, vaquerizo. **II.** *vn.* ir en manadas o hatos; asociarse. **III.** *va.* reunir el ganado en hatos o rebaños.

herdsman [-zmǎn], *s.* pastor, vaquero, vaquerizo, resero, manadero.

here [hjr], *adv.* aquí; acá; por aquí; ahora, en este momento, en este punto; ¡presente!—**h. and there**, acá y allá.—**h. goes!** ¡ahí va!—**h. I am**, aquí estoy, o heme aquí.—**h. is**, he aquí; aquí tiene Vd.—**h. is to you**, a la salud de Vd. —**that is neither h. nor there**, eso no viene al caso.

hereabouts [-ǎbáųts], *adv.* por aquí, en estas cercanías, por aquí cerca.

hereafter [hjrǽftœ(r)]. **I.** *adv.* (de aquí) en adelante, en lo sucesivo, en lo futuro. **II.** *s.* estado futuro; el más allá.

hereat [hjrǽt], *adv.* a esto, en esto, por eso.

hereby [hjrbáj], *adv.* por éstas, por la presente, por este medio, por este acto.

hereditable [hjrédjtǎbl], *a.* que puede ser heredado.—**hereditament** [herjdjtǎment], *s.* (for.) todo lo que puede heredarse.—**hereditarily** [hjrédjterjlj], *adv.* por herencia, hereditariamente.—**hereditary** [-terj], *a.* hereditario.

heredity [hjrédjtj], *s.* (biol.) herencia.

herefrom [hjrfrám], *adv.* de aquí, desde aquí; a causa de esto.

herein [hjrín], **hereinto** [hjríntu], *adv.* aquí dentro; incluso.

hereinafter [hjrjnǽftœ(r)], *adv.* después, más abajo, más adelante.

hereinbefore [hjrjnbjfór], *adv.* arriba, anteriormente, antes.

hereof [hjráv], *adv.* de esto, de eso, acerca de esto, de aquí.

hereon [hjrán], *adv.* sobre esto, sobre este punto.

heresiarch [hjrísjark], *s.* heresiarca, *m.*

heresy [héresj], *s.* herejía.

heretic [hértjk], *s.* hereje.—**heretical** [hjrétjk-ǎl], *a.* herético.—**heretically** [-j], *adv.* heréticamente.

hereto [hjrtú], *adv.* a esto, a este fin.

heretofore [hjrtufór]. **I.** *adv.* en otro tiempo, antes, en tiempos pasados; hasta aquí, hasta ahora. **II.** *s.* el tiempo pasado, antaño.

hereunder [hjrándœ(r)], *adv.* bajo esto, en virtud de esto.

hereunto [hjrántu], *adv.* a esto, a eso.

hereupon [hjrapán], *adv.* a esto; sobre esto.

herewith [hjrwíð], *adv.* con esto, junto con esto, incluso, adjunto.

heritable [hérjtǎbl], *a.* que se puede heredar.

heritage [hérjtjdž], *s.* herencia.

herma [hœrmǎ], *s.* (antig. gr.) herma, *m.* (ll. t. **hermes**).

hermaphrodite [hœrmǽfrodajt]. **I.** *a.* (zool. y bot.) hermafrodito. **II.** *s.* hermafrodito o hermafrodita, andrógino; (mar.) bergantín goleta.

hermaphroditic(al [-djtjk(ǎl], *a.* hermafrodita.

hermaphroditism, hermaphrodism [-dajtjzm, -djzm], *s.* hermafroditismo.

hermeneutic(al [hœrmjnjútjk(ǎl], *a.* hermenéutico.

hermeneutics [-s], *s.* hermenéutica.

hermetic(al [hœrmétjk(ǎl], *a.* hermético.—**the h. art**, alquimia.

hermetically [-j], *adv.* herméticamente.

hermit [hœrmjt], *s.* ermitaño, eremita, *m.*, anacoreta, *m.*—**h. crab**, (zool.) ermitaño, paguro.

hermitage [-jdž], *s.* ermita.

hermitess [-js], *s.* ermitaña.

hermitical [hœrmítjkǎl], *a.* eremítico.

hernia [hǽrniḁ], *s.* (med.) hernia.
hernial [-l], *a.* herniario.
hero [híroṵ], *s.* héroe; protagonista.—**h. worship**, culto extremado de los héroes.
Herodian [herádiḁn], *a. y s.* herodiano.
heroic(al [hiróṵik(ḁl], *a.* heroico, épico; grande, sublime; valeroso, magnánimo.—**heroically** [-i], *adv.* heroicamente.—**heroicalness** [-nis], *s.* heroicidad.
heroics [-s], *s. pl.* rimbombancia, ampulosidad.
heroin [héroin], *s.* (quím.) heroína, uno de los derivados acetílicos de la morfina.
heroine [héroin], *s.* heroína, protagonista.
heroism [héroizm], *s.* heroísmo, heroicidad; proeza.
heron [hérọn], *s.* (orn) garza; garzota.—**h.'s-bill**, (bot.) pico de garza.
heronry [-ri], *s.* lugar en que se crían las garzas o garzotas.
herpes [hǽrpiz], *s.* (med.) herpe, *mf.*
herpetic [hœrpétik], *a.* herpético.
herpetism [hǽrpetizm], *s.* (med.) herpetismo.
herpetography [hœrpetágrafi], *s.* (zool.) herpetografía; (med., zool.) herpetología.
herpetology [-táloǫj̇i], *s.* (zool.) herpetología, estudio de los reptiles.
herring [hériŋ], *s.* (ict.) arenque.
herringbone [-boṵn], *s.* espinapez, *m.;* punto espigado.
hers [hœrz], *pron. pos.* suyo, suya, de ella; el suyo, la suya, los suyos, las suyas (de ella).
herself [hœrsélf], *pron.* ella misma, ella, sí, sí misma. *V.* HIMSELF.
Hertzian [hértsiḁn], *a.* (fís.) herciano, hertziano.
hesitancy [hézitansi], *s.* hesitación, duda, irresolución, vacilación.—**hesitant** [-ḁnt], *a.* vacilante, indeciso.—**hesitate** [-eit], *vn.* vacilar, titubear; balbucear, tartamudear.—**hesitation** [-éiṣọn], *s.* irresolución, titubeo, vacilación; balbucencia.
Hesper [héspœ(r)], *s.* Héspero, estrella vespertina.
Hesperian [hespíriḁn], **I.** *a.* hespérido; occidental. **II.** *s.* habitante de un país occidental.
Hessian [héṣḁn], *s. y a.* de Hesse; (fam.) mercenario, venal; (*s.*) arpillera.—**H. crucible**, crisol de arcilla refractaria.—**H. fly**, (ent.) nombre de una mosca muy nociva al trigo.
hetæra [hetírḁ], **hetaira** [hetáirḁ], *s.* hetera, especie de cortesana griega.
heter(o [hétẹr(o], *prefijo* que significa otro, diferente.
heteroclite [-klait], *a.* heteróclito, irregular.
heterodox [-daks], *a. y s.* heterodoxo.
heterodoxy [-daksi], *s.* heterodoxia.
heterodyne [-dain], **I.** *s.* (rad.) heterodina, (generador) heterodino. **II.** *a.* heterodino.
heterogamous [heterágamʌs], *a.* (bot.) heterógamo.—**heterogamy** [-mi], *s.* heterogamia.
heterogeneity [heterodżiníiti], **heterogeneousness** [-dżíniʌsnis], *s.* heterogeneidad.
heterogeneous [-dżíniʌs], *a.* heterogéneo.
heterogenesis [-dżénesis], *s.* (biol.) heterogénesis, generación espontánea; heterogenia, producción de una especie por otra.
heteromorphic, heteromorphous [-mórfik, -fʌs], *a.* heteromorfo.
heteronomous [heteránomʌs], *a.* heterónomo.
heteronym [héterọnim], *s.* palabra que tiene la misma ortografía que otra, pero sonido y sentido diferentes, v. gr.: *lead* [lid], guiar, y *lead* [led], plomo.
heteroplasty [-plæsti], *s.* (cir.) heteroplastia.
Heteroptera [heteráptœrḁ], *s. pl.* (zool.) heterópteros.
hetman [hétmḁn], *s.* atamán, jefe cosaco.
heuristic [hjuríṣtik], *a.* heurístico, que ayuda al descubrimiento o interpretación de hechos y verdades.
hew [hjú], **I.** *va.* (pret. HEWED) *pp.* HEWN y HEWED) tajar, cortar, picar; hachear, desbas-

tar; azolar; trabajar una cosa.—**to h. a stone,** picar o labrar (una piedra).—**to h. in pieces,** destrozar, destroncar.—**to h. out,** hachear, cortar; modelar en bruto; abrir paso. **II.** *vn.* golpear.—**to h. right and left,** acuchillar a diestra y siniestra.
hewer [-œ(r)], *s.* cantero; picapedrero; desbastador.—**hewing** [-iŋ], *s.* tajadura; desbastadura, desbaste.
hex [heks]. **I.** *va.* (fam.) aojar, embrujar, hacer mal de ojo, echar el mal ojo a. **II.** *s.* (fam.) brujo, bruja; aojo.
hex(a [héks(ḁ], *prefijo* que significa seis.
hexachord [-kord], *s.* (mús.) hexacordo.
hexagon [-gan], *s.* (geom.) hexágono, exágono.
hexagonal [-ǽgonḁl], *a.* (h)exagonal, (h)exágono.
hexahedron [-hídrọn], *s.* (geom.) hexaedro.
hexameter [-ǽmetœ(r)], *s.* (poét.) hexámetro.
hexametric(al [-métrik(ḁl], *a.* hexamétrico.
hexangular [-ǽngiulḁ(r)], *a.* hexángulo.
hexapod [-pad], *a. y s.*, **hexapodous** [heksǽpodʌs], *a.* (zool.) hexápodo.
hexastyle [-stail], *s.* (arq.) hexástilo.
Hexateuc [-tiuk], *s.* Hexateuco, los seis primeros libros del Antiguo Testamento.
hexavalent [-véilẹnt], *a.* (quím.) hexavalente.
hey [hei], *interj.* ¡he! ¡eh! ¡oiga! ¡digo!
heyday [héidei]. **I.** *s.* colmo, apogeo de vitalidad y vigor. **II.** *interj.* ¡hola!
hiatus [haiéitʌs], *s.* laguna, vacío, solución de continuidad; (gram. y poét.) hiato.
hibernal [haibœrnḁl], *a.* hibernal, hiemal, invernizo, invernal.
hibernate [háibœrneit], *vn.* invernar; estar retirado e inactivo, vegetar.
hibernation [-éiṣọn], *s.* hibernación, invernada.
Hibernian [haibœrniḁn], *a. y s.* irlandés, hibernés.
Hibernianism, Hibernicism [-izm, -niṣizm], *s.* idiotismo irlandés.
hibiscus [haibískʌs], *s.* (bot.) hibisco.
hiccough, hiccup, hickup [híkʌp]. **I.** *s.* hipo. **II.** *vn.* hipar, tener hipo.
hick [hik], *a. y s.* (fam.) rústico, patán.
hickey [híki], *s.* encorvador tubular en T.
hickory [híkọri], *s.* (bot.) nogal americano.—**h. nut,** nuez del nogal americano.
hid [hid], *pret. y pp.* de TO HIDE.
hidden [-n], *a. y pp.* de TO HIDE; oculto, recóndito, escondido, secreto, latente.
hiddenly [-li], *adv.* escondidamente.
hide [háid], *s.* cuero, piel, *f.,* pellejo.—*pl.* corambre, *f.*
hide. I. *va.* (pret. HID; pp. HIDDEN o HID) esconder, ocultar, encubrir; (fam.) dar latigazos a (Am.) fuetazos. **II.** *vn.* esconderse, ocultarse, (con out) estarse escondido. **III.** *s.* escondite.
hide-and-seek [-ænd sík], *s.* juego del escondite.
hideaway [-ḁwei], *s.* escondite, escondrijo; fugitivo.
hidebound [-baund], *a.* obstinado, fanático, de ánimo estrecho; (vet.) de piel endurecida.
hideous [hídiʌs], *a.* horrible, espantoso, feo, deforme.—**hideously** [-li], *adv.* horriblemente.—**hideousness** [-nis], *s.* horribilidad; fealdad, deformidad.
hideout [háidaut], *s.* escondite.
hiding [háidiŋ], *s.* ocultación, encubrimiento; retiro, retrete; (fam.) zurra, paliza.—**h. place,** escondite.
hidrosis [hidróusis], *s.* sudor; sudor excesivo o anormal; cualquier enfermedad cutánea acompañada de sudor excesivo.
hie [hai]. **I.** *vn.* darse prisa, apresurarse. **II.** *va.* activar, apresurar; correr, pasar con rapidez.—**h. thee home,** apresúrate a volver a casa.
hierarch [háiẹrark], *s.* jerarca, *m.,* pontífice.—**hierarch(ic)al** [-árk(ik)ḁl], *a.* jerárquico.—**hierarchism** [-izm], **hierarchy** [-i], *s.* jerarquía.
hieratic(al [haiẹrǽtik(ḁl], *a.* hierático, sacerdo-

tal; consagrado.—**h.** **writing,** escritura hierática.

hierocracy [haierákrasi̯], *s.* supremacía eclesiástica, gobierno eclesiástico; jerarquía.

hieroglyph(ic [haierogliˈfik], *s.* jeroglífico.

hieroglyphic(al [-ąl], *a.* jeroglífico.

hieroglyphically [-i̯], *adv.* jeroglíficamente, simbólicamente.

hierology [haierálodʒi̯], *s.* hierología.

hieromancy [háieromænsi̯], *s.* hieroscopia.

Hieronymite [haierániˌmai̯t], *a.* y *s.* (igl.) jerónimo.

hierophant [háierofænt], *s.* hierofante.

hifalutin [haifalútin], *a.* = HIGHFALUTIN.

higgle [hígl], *vn.* regatear, altercar; andar en dimes y diretes; vender como buhonero.

higgledy-piggledy [-dipíglidi̯]. **I.** *adv.* (fam.) confusamente. **II.** *a.* revuelto. **III.** *s.* revoltillo.

higgler [híglœ(r)], *s.* zarracatín, regatón; buhonero.

high [hai̯], *a.* alto; de alto (con *to be,* que entonces es tener: *this is two inches high,* esto tiene dos pulgadas de alto); elevado; encumbrado o eminente, superior; sumo (sacerdote); supremo (tribunal, etc.); elevado, digno; caro (precio); (coc.) picante, muy sazonado; rico (en carbono, cemento, etc.); vivo, intenso; arrogante, estirado; fuerte, violento (viento); fuerte, oliscada (la carne); poderoso; (fam.) achispado.—**h.** **altar,** altar mayor.—**h. and dry,** en seco; en la playa; solo, sin recursos.—**h. and mighty,** (fam.) arrogante, hinchado.—**h. blood pressure,** (med.) hipertensión arterial.—**h. chair,** silla de altas patas.—**H. Church,** iglesia ortodoxa o ritualista (en la secta episcopal).—**h. comedy,** (teat.) alta comedia.—**h. command,** alto mando, comando supremo, suprema comandancia.—**h. day,** día de fiesta.—**h. explosive,** explosivo instantáneo de gran potencia.—**h. gear,** (aut.) posición de toma directa (**in h. gear,** en directa).—**h. hat,** sombrero de copa, (fam.) chistera.—**h. horse,** (fam.) actitud arrogante, presunción.—**h. jinks,** (fam.) bulla, retozo, francachela; hilaridad.—**h. jump,** salto de altura.—**h. life,** vida aristocrática, sociedad elegante, gran mundo.—**h. light,** (b. a.) toque de luz; cosa, acontecimiento o rasgo descollante.—**h. living,** abuso de ˙los placeres de la mesa, epicurismo.—**H. Mass,** misa cantada o mayor.—**h. noon,** pleno mediodía.—**h.-octane gas,** gasolina superoctana, o de elevado indicio de octano.—**h. pressure,** alta presión.—**h. priest,** sumo sacerdote.—**h. rank,** categoría, alto rango.—**h. relief,** (b. a.) alto relieve.—**h. road,** camino real; vía pública; carretera.—**h. school,** escuela secundaria.—**h. sea,** mar gruesa.—**h. seas,** alta mar, piélago.—**h.-speed steel,** acero rápido o de corte rápido.—**h. spirits,** alegría, buen humor (**in h. spirits,** alegre).—**h. steel,** acero rico en carbono.—**h. tide,** pleamar.—**h. time,** tiempo de no esperar más, tiempo de decidirse a hacer algo; (fam.) gran holgorio o parranda (**it is h. time to,** ya es hora de).—**h. treason,** alta traición, delito de lesa majestad.—**h. voltage,** (elec.) tensión alta.—**h. water,** marea alta; agua alta.—**h. words,** palabras ofensivas o ásperas.—**in h. terms,** en términos lisonjeros.—**the Most H.,** el Altísimo.

high, *adv.* altamente; muy, sumamente; a grande altura; arrogantemente; a precio elevado; lujosamente.—**h. and low,** de arriba abajo; por doquiera.—**h.-blooded,** de sangre azul, de noble alcurnia.—**h.-class,** de categoría o calidad superior; por todo lo alto.—**h.-colored,** subido de color.—**h.-explosive,** de alta potencia explosiva.—**h.-flown,** de alto vuelo; presuntuoso, altivo, orgulloso; hinchado.—**h.-frequency,** de alta frecuencia.—**h.-grade,** fino, de alta calidad.—**h.-grown,** muy crecido

o muy alto.—**h.-handed,** despótico, arbitrario.—**h.-heaped,** colmado.—**h.-hearted,** animoso, denodado.—**h.-heeled,** (zap.) de tacón alto.—**h.-keyed,** impresionable, sensitivo; (mús.) agudo.—**h.-minded,** magnánimo, noble; altivo.—**h.-necked,** (cost.) de escote subido.—**h.-pitched** = H.-KEYED.—**h.-powered,** de alta potencia.—**h.-pressure,** de alta presión.—**h.-priced,** caro.—**h.-proof,** de alta concentración, de mucho alcohol; muy rectificado.—**h.-seasoned,** picante.—**h.-sounding,** altisonante o retumbante.—**h.-spirited,** gallardo, bizarro.—**h.-stepping,** pisador (caballo); (fam.) de buen tono; de vida alegre.—**h.-strung,** muy nervioso, excitable o sensible.—**h.-tension,** de alta tensión.—**h.-test,** que bulle a baja temperatura y tiene propiedades antidetonantes (ú. de gasolina, etc.).—**h.-toned,** honorable, caballeroso; (mús.) agudo; (fam.) aristocrático, del buen tono.—**h.-wrought,** primorosamente labrado; muy agitado.—**on h.,** en las alturas, en el cielo.

high, *s.* alza, subida; punto o lugar alto; valor o precio máximo; naipe más alto; (fam.) escuela secundaria; (aut.) velocidad máxima.

highball [hái̯bol], *s.* whiskey con soda y hielo.

highborn [-born], *a.* noble, de alta alcurnia, linajudo.

highbred [-bred], *a.* de raza, de alcurnia pura; culto, bien educado.

highbrow [-brau̯], *s.* erudito engreído y arrogante; petulante.—**highbrowed** [-d], *a.* hinchado, arrogante.

higher [hái̯œ(r)], *a. comp.* de HIGH: más alto; superior (álgebra, matemáticas, etc.).—**h. bid.** V. BID.—**h. brackets,** clases (*f.*) o categorías superiores; gente (*f.*) de alta categoría.—**h. classes,** clases altas.—**h. criticism,** crítica textual (fundada en el texto) de la Biblia u otras obras.—**h. education,** enseñanza superior.—**h.-up,** (fam.) *a.* superior, de mayor jerarquía; *s.* funcionario de mayor jerarquía.

highest [hái̯ist], *a. superl.* de HIGH: más alto; sumo, supremo; mayor; máximo; de primer orden.—**h. common divisor,** o **factor,** (mat.) máximo común divisor.

highfalutin [haifalútin], *a.* (fam.) hinchado, pomposo, retumbante.

highflier [-flai̯œ(r)], *s.* pájaro de alto vuelo; extremista; despilfarrador.

highjack, hijack [-dʒæk], *va.* (fam.) saltear; atracar a mano armada un cargamento de mercancías, etc.—**highjacker,** **hijacker** [-œ(r)], *s.* (fam.) atracador, salteador (aplícase sobre todo al que roba a contrabandistas); ladrón de licores.

highland [-land], *s.* región montañosa.—*pl.* tierras altas; montañas.—**highlander** [-œ(r)], *s.* montañés, serrano, (Am.) arribeño; (H.) montañés de Escocia.—**highlandish** [-iš], *a.* montañés.

highlight [-lai̯t], *va.* poner de resalto o de relieve; subrayar; dar importancia o énfasis a.

highly [-li̯], *adv.* altamente; levantadamente, elevadamente; sumamente; arrogantemente, ambiciosamente; encarecidamente.

highness [-nis], *s.* altura, elevación; celsitud; Alteza (título).

hight [hai̯t], *a.* (ant.) llamado, nombrado.

highty-tighty [hái̯ti̯ tái̯ti̯] = HOITY-TOITY.

highway [hái̯wéi̯]. **I.** *s.* camino real; vía pública; carretera, calzada. **II.** *a.* caminero, carretero.—**h. robber** = HIGHWAYMAN.—**h. robbery,** salteo.—**highwayman** [-man], *s.* bandido, bandolero, atracador, salteador de caminos.

hike [hái̯k]. **I.** *s.* (fam.) caminata. **II.** *vn.* (fam.) dar una caminata; andar, caminar. **III.** *va.* (fam.) aumentar.

hiker [-œ(r)], *s.* caminador; andariego; el aficionado a las caminatas.

hilarious [hilérias], *a.* alegre, bullicioso.

hilarity [hilériti], s. hilaridad, júbilo, alborozo, regocijo bullicioso.

hill [hil]. I. s. collado, colina, cerro, cuesta, otero, altozano.—**h. of beans**, montoncillo de judías (sembradas). II. va. (agr.) aporcar, acogombrar. III. vn. amontonarse.

hillbilly [-bili], s. (E. U., fam.) patán serrano del Sur.

hilling [-iŋ], s. (agr.) amontonamiento, aporcadura.

hilliness [-inis], s. montuosidad.

hillman [-man], s. serrano, (Am.) arribeño.

hillock [-ɔk], s. altillo, loma, montecillo, otero.

hillside [-sajd], s. ladera, flanco de una colina.

hilltop [-tap], s. cima, cumbre de una colina.

hilly [-i], a. montañoso, montuoso.

hilt [hilt], s. (arm.) puño, empuñadura.—**up to the h.**, por completo; a fondo; (fam.) hasta las cachas.

hilted [-id], a. que tiene puño o guarnición.

hilum [hájlʌm], s. (bot.) ombligo de una semilla; núcleo de un grano de almidón; ojo de un fréjol; hilo; (anat. zool.) hilo.

him [him], pron. (caso oblicuo de HE) le, lo, a él.

himself [himsélf], pron. pers. (reflexivo en los casos oblicuos) él, él mismo, se, sí, sí mismo.—**by h.**, solo, por sí, por su cuenta.—**he h.**, él mismo; en persona.—**he said to h.**, se dijo a sí mismo.

hind [hájnd]. I. a. trasero, zaguero, posterior.—**h.-bow**, borrén trasero de la silla de montar.—**h.-foremost**, lo de atrás delante.—**h. leg**, pierna trasera.—**h. wheels**, juego trasero del coche. II. s. labrador; (zool.) cierva.

hindbrain [-brejn], s. (anat.) cerebelo; parte (f.) posterior del encéfalo.

hinder [híndœ(r)], I. va. impedir, estorbar, embarazar, obstruir, obstaculizar. II. vn. poner obstáculos, poner trabas; oponerse.

hinder [hájndœ(r)], a. posterior, trasero.

hinderer [híndœrœ(r)], s. obstructor, estorbador.

hindermost, hindmost [hájnd(œr)moṵst], a. postrero, último.

Hindi [híndi], s. indi, el idioma moderno del Indostán.

Hindoo, Hindu [híndu], s. y a. indostánico, indostanés, indostano.

hindquarter [hájndkwɔrtœ(r)], s. cuarto trasero (de res).

hindrance [híndrans], s. impedimento, obstáculo, estorbo.

hindsight [hájndsajt], s. alza o mira trasera (de arma de fuego); percepción tardía de lo que se debió hacer o decir, ya pasada la ocasión.

Hinduism [hínduizm], s. indoísmo.

Hindustani [hindustǽni], s. indostani, lengua principal de la India.

hinge [hindʒ]. I. s. gozne, gonce, pernio, bisagra; punto capital o principal.—**h. joint**, (anat.) gínglimo angular; (mec.) articulación de bisagra.—**h. post**, quicial(era). II. va. engoznar; enquiciar. III. vn. girar sobre un gozne; (con **on**) depender (de).

hinny [híni]. I. vn. (raro) relinchar. II. s. (zool.) mulo nacido de caballo y burra.

hint [hint]. I. va. insinuar, indicar, intimar, sugerir. II. vn. echar una pulla o indirecta.—**to h. at**, aludir a. III. s. indirecta, sugestión, pulla, insinuación.

hinterland [híntœrlænd], s. región interior (de un país, etc.).

hip [hip]. I. s. (anat.) cadera; (bot.) fruto del escaramujo; (arq.) caballete.—**h. bath**, baño de asiento, semicupio.—**h. bone**, cía, hueso de la cadera.—**h. joint**, (anat.) articulación ilíacofemoral; (ing.) nudo o articulación del extremo del cordón o cabeza superior de un puente y la pieza que apoya en el estribo.—**h. roof**, (arq.) techo a cuatro vertientes. II. va. descaderar; echar sobre la cadera; (arq.) construir un techo con cubierta a cuatro aguas.

hipped [-t], a. renco; (fam.) obsesionado; (fam. = HIPPISH.

hippish [-iš], a. (fam.) melancólico, abatido.

hippocampus [hipokémpʌs], s. (mit.) hipocampo; (ict.) hipocampo, caballo de mar (anat.) hipocampo (del cerebro).

hippocentaur [-séntœr], s. (mit.) hipocentauro

hippocras [hípokræs], s. (med.) hipocrás.

Hippocratic [-krǽtik], a. hipocrático.

hippodrome [-droṵm], s. hipódromo, circo.

hippogriff [-grif], s. (mit.) hipogrifo.

hippophagy [hipáfadʒi], s. hipofagia, costumbre de comer carne de caballo.

hippopotamus [hipopátamʌs], s. hipopótamo

hipshot [hípšat], a. renco.

hircine [hœrsin], a. cabrío, cabruno, cabrerizo hircino; lascivo, lujurioso.

hire [hájr]. I. va. alquilar, dar o tomar en arriendo arrendar; ajornalar, asalariar, contratar; sobor nar.—**to h. out**, alquilar(se). II. s. alquiler arriendo; salario, jornal; soborno.

hireling [-liŋ]. I. s. alquilón; persona asalariada II. a. mercenario, venal.

hirer [-œ(r)], s. alquilador, arrendador.

hirsute [hœrsiut], a. hirsuto, peludo, piloso.

hirsuteness [-nis], s. calidad de hirsuto, cerdoso etc.; vellosidad.

hirundine [hiróndin], a. de golondrina, seme jante a la golondrina.

his [hiz], a. y pron. pos. su, sus (de él); suyo, suya etc.; el suyo, la suya, los suyos, las suyas (de él)

Hispanic [hispǽnik], a. hispánico, hispano.—**Hispanicism** [-isizm], s. hispanismo, españolismo.

Hispaniolize [-jolajz], va. españolizar, hispanizar

Hispanophile [-ofajl], a. y s. hispanófilo.

hispid [híspid], a. (bot. zool.) híspido, cerdoso

hiss [his]. I. va. y vn. silbar, (re)chiflar; sisear. II s. silbido, silba; siseo.

hisser [-œ(r)], s. silbador.

hissing [-iŋ]. I. s. silbido, silba, (re)chifla; siseo II. a. silbador, silboso.

hissingly [-iŋli], adv. a silbidos.

hist [hist], interj. ¡chito! ¡chitón!

histogenesis [histodʒénesis], **histogeny** [histá dʒeni], s. histogenia, formación de los tejido vivos.

histologic(al [histoládʒik(al], a. histológico.

histologist [histálodʒist], s. histólogo.

histology [-dʒi], s. (biol.) histología.

histolysis [histálisis], s. (biol.) histólisis, disgre gación de los tejidos; (ent.) disolución de lo órganos larvales en la crisálida.

historian [histórian], s. historiador.

historic(al [histárik(al], a. histórico, historial.—**h. present**, (gram.) el presente usado metafóri camente en vez del pretérito, etc.

historically [-i], adv. históricamente.

historiographer [historiágrafœ(r)], s. historió grafo.

historiography [-fi], s. historiografía.

history [hístori], s. historia.—**h. piece**, (pint. cuadro o tapiz histórico.—**to have a h.**, se persona de historia (de malos antecedentes).

histrionic(al [histriánik(al], a. histriónico.—**his trionically** [-i], adv. cómicamente, teatral mente.—**histrionism** [hístrianizm], s. his trionismo.

hit [hit]. I. va. (pret. y pp. HIT) dar, pegar, gol pear; atinar, acertar; encontrar, dar con o en denunciar.—**to h. it off**, avenirse, simpatizar hacer buenas migas.—**to h. off**, improvisar describir o expresar bien o lucidamente; imitar remedar.—**to h. the mark**, dar en el blanco —**to h. the nail on the head**, dar en el hit o en el clavo.—**to h. the spot**, (fam.) satis facer por completo.—**to h. the target**, hace blanco.—**to h. the trail**, (fam.) ponerse e ruta. II. vn. rozar, chocar; acaecer o acontece felizmente, salir bien; encontrar por casualidad acertar.—**h. or miss**, al azar, a la ventura atolondradamente.—**to h. against**, dar contra alguna cosa, chocar.—**to h. on**, o **upon**, dar con, hallar; ocurrírsele a uno; acordarse de. **III.** *s.* golpe, choque, coscorrón; rasgo de ingenio.—**a lucky h.**, golpe de fortuna, ocurrencia feliz.—**to be**, o **make a h.**, (fam.) ser un exitazo, dar golpe.

hitch [híʧ]. **I.** *va.* atar, ligar; enganchar; (mar.) amarrar; mover a tirones. **II.** *vn.* moverse a saltos; rozarse los pies (los caballos); enredarse; (fam.) congeniar, llevarse bien con otro. **III.** *s.* alto, parada; tropiezo, dificultad, impedimento; tirón; (mar.) vuelta de cabo.

hither [híðœ(r)]. **I.** *adv.* acá, hacia acá.—**h. and thither**, **h.** and **yon**, acá y allá, de acá para allá. **II.** *a.* citerior.—**on the h. side of**, aquende, de este lado de.

hithermost [-moʊst], *a.* más cercano o próximo.

hitherto [-tú], *adv.* hasta ahora, hasta aquí.

hitter [hítœ(r)], *s.* golpeador.

Hittite [hítaɪt], *a.* y *s.* heteo, hitita, *mf.*

hive [haɪv]. **I.** *s.* colmena; enjambre de abejas; emporio.—*pl.* (med.) urticaria. **II.** *va.* (api.) enjambrar, encorchar; atesorar, acumular. **III.** *vn.* vivir juntos como en colmena.

ho [hoʊ], *interj.* ¡eh! ¡basta! ¡alto! *V.* WHOA.

ho, hoa, *interj.* ¡ha! ¡ah! ¡oh! ¡ja! ¡ja! *V.* HALLO.

hoar [hor], *a.* blanco, cano; nevado. *V.* HOARY.

hoard [hórd]. **I.** *va.* y *vn.* atesorar, acumular y guardar. **II.** *s.* provisión; montón; acumulamiento, repuesto; tesoro escondido.

hoarder [-œ(r)], *s.* atesorador.

hoarding [-ɪŋ], *s.* atesoramiento; cerca o valla provisional; tablilla o tablón de avisos.

hoarfrost [hórfrɒst], *s.* escarcha en agujas, helada blanca.

hoarhound [hórhaʊnd], *s.* (bot.) marrubio.

hoariness [hórɪnɪs], *s.* blancura; canicie.

hoarse [hórs], *a.* ronco, rauco.—**hoarsely** [-lɪ], *adv.* roncamente.—**hoarseness** [-nɪs], *s.* ronquera, carraspera.

hoary [hórɪ], *a.* blanco, blanquecino; cano, canoso; escarchado; venerable.

hoax [hoʊks]. **I.** *s.* engaño, burla, bola, petardo, mentira, (fam.) filfa. **II.** *va.* engañar, burlar.

hob [hab], *s.* repisa interior del hogar; cubo de rueda; (mec.) mandril para hacer roscas de tornillo; punzón de embutir; juego del chito; tángano o tango.—**to play h. with**, trastornar.

hobble [hábl]. **I.** *va.* poner trabas, maniotar. **II.** *vn.* cojear. **III.** *s.* cojera; traba, maniota; (fam.) dificultad, atolladero.—**h. skirt**, enagua apretada, ceñida o estrecha por abajo.

hobbledehoy [-dɪhóɪ], *s.* adolescente.

hobby [hábɪ], *s.* (fam.) tema, manía, chifladura; caballico (juguete); jaca; (orn.) sacre, halcón.

hobbyhorse [-hors], *s.* tema, manía; caballico (juguete); velocípedo.

hobgoblin [hábgablɪn], *s.* duende, trasgo.

hobnail [hábneɪl]. **I.** *s.* clavo de cabeza grande, para botas gruesas; patán, rústico. **II.** *va.* clavetear (suelas) con dichos clavos.

hobnob [hábnáb]. **I.** *vn.* beber juntos; tener intimidad, rozarse. **II.** *s.* charla amistosa. **III.** *adv.* a la diabla, a la ventura, al azar.

hobo [hóʊboʊ], *s.* (E. U.) vagabundo.

hock [hak]. **I.** *s.* vino del Rin; (zool.) tarso, corvejón, jarrete (del caballo, etc.); (anat.) corva.—**in h.**, (fam.) empeñado. **II.** *va.* desjarretar; (fam.) empeñar, dar en prenda.

hockey [hákɪ], *s.* (dep.) hockey.—**ice h.**, hockey sobre hielo.

hocus [hóʊkʌs], *va.* engañar, chasquear; atontar con drogas.—**h.-pocus**, treta, birlibirloque, pasapasa.

hod [hád], *s.* (alb.) esparavel; cubo (para carbón).—**h. carrier** = HODMAN.

hodgepodge [háʤpaʤ], *s.* almodrote, bodrio; baturrillo; (fam.) mezcolanza.

hodman [hádmən], *s.* peón de albañil, manobre.

hodometer [hoʊdámetœ(r)], *s.* (h)odómetro.

hoe [hóʊ]. **I.** *s.* azada, azadón, escardillo, legón. **II.** *va.* azadonar, sachar.—**hoeing** [-ɪŋ], *s.* sachadura.

hog [hág]. **I.** *s.* (zool.) cochino, puerco, cerdo, marrano; (fam.) persona sucia, tragona o egoísta; (mar.) escobón; (aer.) arqueo, comba vuelta hacia abajo.—**h. fennel**, (bot.) servato, ervato.—**the whole h.**, (fam.) llegar hasta el último límite. **II.** *va.* (mar.) afretar, limpiar fondos; partir una embarcación por el medio; rapar el pelo; (agr.) echar cerdos a o en. **III.** *vn.* arquearse, combarse.

hoggish [-ɪʃ], *a.* porcuno, porcino; egoísta; guloso, comilón.—**hoggishly** [-lɪ], *adv.* puercamente, cochinamente; vorazmente.—**hoggishness** [-nɪs], *s.* porquería, cochinada; glotonería; egoísmo.

hogherd [-hœrd], *s.* porquero, porquerizo.

hogpen [-pen], **hogsty** [-staɪ], *s.* pocilga.

hogshead [hágzhed], *s.* pipa, bocoy, tonel.

hoiden [hóɪdn]. **I.** *a.* atrevida, desenvuelta. **II.** *s.* muchacha traviesa, tunantuela. **III.** *vn.* retozar de un modo indecoroso.

hoi polloi [hóɪ pɔlóɪ], *s.* la chusma, las masas.

hoist [hóɪst]. **I.** *va.* alzar, elevar; izar, enarbolar. **II.** *s.* cabria, pescante, grúa, malacate, montacargas, elevador, ascensor; levantamiento, ascensión, enarboladura; medida vertical de una vela o una bandera.—**h. bridge**, puente levadizo.

hoister [-œ(r)], *s.* elevador, levantador; grúa; ascensor.

hoity-toity [hóɪtɪ tóɪtɪ]. **I.** *a.* atolondrado; fachendero, engreído. **II.** *interj.* ¡ola! ¡tate!

hokey pokey [hóʊkɪ póʊkɪ], *s.* helado de inferior calidad vendido en las calles; HOCUS-POCUS.

hokum [hóʊkʌm], *s.* (fam.) farsa, payasada; faramalla, farándula.

hold [hóʊld]. **I.** *va.* (*pret.* y *pp.* HELD; *pp.* (ant.) HOLDEN) tener; asir, coger, agarrar; retener, reservar; detener, contener; sostener, apoyar; tener de reserva; restringir, estrechar, limitar; encerrar; hacer, tener cabida o capacidad para; mantener; sostener, opinar; juzgar, reputar, entender; poseer, ocupar, disfrutar, gozar; celebrar (sesión, reunión); continuar, seguir; conservar; guardar, observar; obligar; hacer (responsable, etc.).—**to h. a bet**, o **a wager**, apostar.—**to h. a candle to**, (fam.) poder compararse con.—**to h. at bay**, (man)tener a raya.—**to h. back**, retener; contener.—**to h. down**, oprimir, tener sujeto; conservar, no perder.—**to h. forth**, expresar, publicar; mostrar.—**to h. hands**, cogerse de la mano; estar mano en mano.—**to h. in**, sujetar, refrenar, contener.—**to h. in affection, respect, etc.**, tener cariño, respeto, etc., a.—**to h. in play**, tener ocupado.—**to h. off**, apartar, alejar.—**to h. one's breath**, contener el aliento.—**to h. one's hand**, detenerse; abstenerse.—**to h. one's own**, o **one's ground**, mantenerse firme, defenderse bien; no salir perdiendo; resistir, aguantar (una enfermedad, etc.).—**to h. one's peace**, o **one's tongue**, callar, no decir nada.—**to h. out**, ofrecer, proponer; extender.—**to h. over**, tener suspendido o en suspenso; diferir, aplazar; (mús.) prolongar (una nota).—**to h. sway**, gobernar, mandar.—**to h. the bag**, o **the sack**, quedarse con las manos vacías; quedarse colgado.—**to h. up**, levantar, alzar; apoyar, sostener; asaltar para robar, saltear, atracar.—**to h. up one's hands**, alzar las manos en señal de sumisión; rendirse, darse por vencido.—**to h. up to**, exponer al (desprecio, etc.); poner en (ridículo).—**to h. water**, ser estanco (un cubo, etc.); (fig.) ser lógico o válido (un argumento); (mar.) ciar. **II.** *vn.* valer, ser válido, estar en vigor; mantenerse firme, sostenerse, aguantar; seguir, proseguir; estar en posesión; refrenarse, abstenerse; aplicarse, ser aplicable.—**to h. back,** detenerse, contenerse; abstenerse; cejar.—**to h. fast,** agarrarse bien.—**to h. fast to,** afirmarse en; agarrarse bien de.—**to h. forth,** arengar, exponer (uno) sus ideas.—**to h. good,** subsistir; aplicarse.—**to h. in,** contenerse, refrenarse.— **to h. off,** mantenerse a distancia.—**to h. on,** seguir, proseguir, persistir; detenerse; aguardar.—**to h. on to,** asirse de, agarrarse a.—**to h. out,** mantenerse firme, no cejar; durar; resistir, aguantar.—**to h. over,** continuar desempeñando un cargo después del término legal.—**to h. to,** pegarse, adherirse a.—**to h. together,** mantenerse o estar juntos o reunidos.—**to h. up,** cesar, parar.—**to h. with,** convenir con. III. *s.* presa, asimiento, agarro; asa, mango; influencia, dominio; freno; refugio; amparo; (ant.) fortificación; posesión, custodia; celda (en una prisión); (mar.) bodega, cala; (mús.) calderón, fermata.

hold! hold on! *interj.* ¡tente! ¡para! ¡quieto! (mar.) ¡top!

holdback [-bæk], *s.* restricción, freno; (carr.) cejadero.

holder [-œ(r)], *s.* tenedor, posesor; mantenedor; agarrador, agarradero, asidero, mango, asa; porta—(vg. *lamp holder,* portalámpara; *tool holder,* portaherramienta); sostén; (for.) tenedor; propietario; arrendatario; inquilino; (mar.) marinero de la bodega.—**h. of a bill,** tenedor o portador de una letra.—**h. of a share,** accionista.

holdfast [-fæst], *s.* (mec.) barrilete, grapón, grapa, laña; prensa, mordaza; sostén.

holding [-iŋ], *s.* tenencia, pertenencia, posesión; arrendamiento, inquilinato; celebración (de una sesión o reunión).—*pl.* valores habidos.— **h. company,** compañía tenedora (de acciones de otra).

holdup [-ʌp], *s.* (fam.) salteamiento, asalto de ladrones, atraco.—**h. man,** salteador, atracador.

hole [houl]. I. *s.* agujero, orificio; cavidad, hueco, hoyo; seno; perforación; pozo, charco (de un río, arroyo, etc.); cueva, madriguera, guarida (de animales); (fam.) atolladero, aprieto, brete.—**a h. to crawl out of,** escapatoria, excusa, refugio. II. *va.* agujerear, taladrar, perforar, horadar; meter una bola de billar en la tronera. III. *vn.* encuevarse; hacer un agujero u hoyo.

holiday [hálidei]. I. *s.* día festivo, fiesta, festividad; día feriado; aniversario.—**holidays,** vacaciones, asueto. II. *a.* alegre, festivo.

holily [hóulili], *adv.* piadosamente, santamente.

holiness [hóulinis], *s.* santidad, beatitud.—**His H.,** Su Santidad.

holing [hóuliŋ], *s.* perforación; taladro para alojar un clavo, perno, cabilla, etc.

holland [háland], *s.* (tej.) holanda.—**H. gin,** o **Hollands,** ginebra.—**Hollander,** *s.* holandés.

hollo, holl(o)a [hqlóu]. I. *interj.* ¡eh! ¡hola! II. *s.* grito, grita.

hollow [hálou], *a.* hueco, vacío; hundido; falso, insincero.—**h.-chested,** de pecho hundido.— **h.-hearted,** solapado.—**h. newel,** ojo de escalera.—**h. punch,** sacabocados.—**h. ware,** ollas, pucheros, marmitas. II. *s.* cavidad; depresión, concavidad; canal, *f.,* ranura; hueco; hoyo; valle; cañada. III. *va.* excavar; ahondar; ahuecar; acopar.

hollowness [-nis], *s.* cavidad, hueco, vacío; doblez, falsía.

holly [háli], *s.* (bot.) acebo; agrifolio.

hollyhock [-hak], *s.* (bot.) malva loca, real o rósea.

holm [houm]. *s.* isleta de río, mejana; vega ribereña; rambla.—**h. oak,** (bot.) encina.

holmium [hóulmiam], *s.* (quím.) holmio.

holocaust [hálokost], *s.* holocausto.

holocephalan [-séfalan], *a.* y *s.* (zool.) holocéfalo.

holograph [-græf], *s.* (for.) hológrafo.

holographic [-gréfik], *a.* hológrafo.

holohedron [-hídron], *s.* (crist.) holoedro.— **holohedral** [-hídral], *a.* holoédrico.

holophote [-fout], *s.* reflector o faro de rayos concentrados.

holophrasis [holáfrasis], *s.* holofrasia, polisintetismo.—**holophrastic** [halofrástik], *a.* holofrástico, polisintético.

holothurian [-θjúrian], *s.* (zool.) holoturia, cohombro de mar.

Holotricha [holátrika], *s. pl.* (zool.) holotricos, holotríquidos.

holster [hóulstœ(r)], *s.* pistolera, funda (de pistola).—**h. cap,** tapafunda.

holy [hóuli], *a.* santo, pío; puro, inmaculado; sacro, sagrado; consagrado, santificado; bendito.—**H. Communion,** sagrada comunión. —**h. cross,** santa cruz.—**h. cup,** cáliz, *m.*— **h. day,** fiesta de guardar, disanto.—**H. Father,** Santo Padre (el papa).—**H. Ghost,** Espíritu Santo.—**H. Grail,** grial.—**H. Innocents' Day,** día (*m.*) de los inocentes.—**h. lamb,** agnusdéi.—**H. Land,** Tierra Santa.—**H. Office,** Santo Oficio.—**h. of holies,** santo de los santos, sanctasanctórum.—**h. oil,** crisma, *mf.,* óleo santo.—**H. One,** Dios; Jesucristo.— **h. order,** o **orders,** orden sacerdotal.—**H. Roman Empire,** Sacro Imperio Romano.— **h. rood,** crucifijo; santa cruz.—**H. Sacrament,** el Santísimo.—**H. Saturday,** sábado santo.—**H. See,** Santa Sede.—**H. Spirit =** HOLY GHOST.—**H. Thursday,** jueves santo.— **h. water,** agua bendita.—**h.-water basin,** (igl.) pila.—**h.-water sprinkler,** hisopo.—**H. Week,** semana santa.—**H. Writ,** la Sagrada Escritura.

holystone [hóulistoun]. I. *s.* (mar.) piedra de cubierta. II. *va.* (mar.) dar piedra y arena.

homage [hámidʒ], *s.* homenaje, reverencia, culto.—**to do,** o **pay, h.,** acatar, rendir homenaje; rendir parias.

homager [-œ(r)], *s.* el que rinde homenaje.

home [houm]. I. *s.* hogar, casa; morada; patria, suelo patrio; domicilio, residencia; asilo, hospedería, albergue, refugio; (dep.) meta; límite o término.—**at h.,** en casa; en el país de uno; con toda comodidad; en su elemento; dispuesto a recibir visitas; recepción.—**at-h. day,** día (*m.*) de recibo.—**to hit,** o **strike, h.,** dar en el blanco; herir en lo vivo, llegar al alma. II. *a.* doméstico, de casa, casero; nativo, natal, indígena; regional; interior; nacional, del país; certero, eficaz, que da en el blanco, que llega a la meta.—**h. base,** (dep.) puesto del *batsman* en baseball.—**h.-born,** doméstico; nacido en casa.—**h.-bound,** en dirección a casa, hacia el hogar; imposibilitado de salir de casa.—**h.-bred,** nativo, natural; doméstico; casero, de casa; sencillo, inculto.—**h.-brew,** cerveza, etc., hecha en casa.—**H. Department,** H. **Office,** (Ingl.) Ministerio del Interior o de la Gobernación.—**h. economics,** ciencias domésticas.—**h. office,** oficina matriz.—**h. port,** (mar.) puerto nacional o de origen.—**h. rule,** (pol.) autonomía.—**h. ruler,** autonomista.—**h. run,** (dep.) en baseball, carrera del *batsman* alrededor del cuadro; carrera de regreso al punto de partida.—**H. Secretary,** (Ingl.) Secretario de lo Interior.—**h. stretch,** (dep.) último trecho de una carrera.—**h. town,** ciudad natal. III. *adv.* a casa; en casa; al país o en la tierra de uno; en el punto o lugar en que debe estar una cosa.

homeland [-lænd], *s.* patria, tierra natal; (Ingl.) Inglaterra (a distinción de las colonias).

homeless [-lis], *a.* destituído; sin casa ni hogar; mostrenco.

homelike [-laik], *a.* como de casa, semejante al hogar doméstico; sosegado y cómodo.

homelily [-lįlį], *adv.* llanamente, simplemente; como de casa; groseramente.

homeliness [-lįnįs], *s.* simpleza, sencillez; fealdad, mal aspecto.

homely [-lį], *a.* casero, doméstico; sencillo, liso, llano; feo; rústico, inculto, vulgar.

homemade [-mẹjd], *a.* casero, hecho en casa; fabricado en el país.

homeopathic, homœopathic [homjopǽθįk], *a.* (med.) homeópata, homeopático.—**homeopathically** [-ạlį], *adv.* homeopáticamente.—**homeopath(ist** [hóųmjopǽθ, -ápạθįst], *s.* homeópata, *mf.*—**homeopathy** [-ápạθį], *s.* homeopatía.

Homeric [homérįk], *a.* homérico.

homesick [hóųmsįk], *a.* nostálgico.—**to be h. for,** añorar, sentir nostalgia de.

homesickness [-nįs], *s.* nostalgia, añoranza.

homespun [-spʌn], **I.** *a.* casero, hecho en casa; basto, tocho. **II.** *s.* tela tejida en casa.

homestead [-stẹd], *s.* casa de habitación y sus terrenos; heredad; hogar.

homeward [-wạrd], *adv.* hacia casa, hacia su país; de vuelta.—**h.-bound,** de regreso.

homework [-wœrk], *s.* trabajo, tarea, estudio, etc., hechos en casa.

homicidal [hámįsajdạl], *a.* homicida, asesino.

homicide [hámįsạjd], *s.* homicidio; homicida, *mf.*

homiletic(al [hamįlétįk(ạl], *a.* referente a la oratoria sagrada.

homiletics [-s], *s.* oratoria sagrada.

homilist [hámįlįst], *s.* predicador de homilías.

homily [hámįlį], *s.* homilía; sermón.

homing [hóųmįŋ], *a.* mensajera (paloma).

hominy [hámįnį], *s.* maíz machacado.

homochromous [homokróųmʌs], *a.* (bot.) de un mismo color.

homodyne [hóųmodajn], *a.* (rad.) homodino.

homogen [-džįn], *s.* (biol.) estructura o parte homogénea.

homogeneity [-džènįįtį], *s.* homogeneidad.

homogeneous [-džínįʌs], *a.* homogéneo.—**homogeneously** [-lį], *adv.* homogéneamente.—**homogeneousness** [-nįs], *s.* homogeneidad.

homogenize [homádžẹnajz], *va.* hacer homogéneo, homogenizar.

homogenous [-nʌs], *a.* (biol.) de un mismo origen; de una misma estructura.

homograph [hámográef], *s.* vocablo homógrafo.

homographic [-gráefįk], *a.* homógrafo.

homologate [homálogẹjt], *va.* (for.) homologar.

homologation [-éjṣọn], *s.* (for.) homologación.

homologous [homálogʌs], *a.* homólogo.

homolog(ue [hámolag], *s.* cosa homóloga.

homonym [hámonįm], *s.* vocablo homónimo.

homonymous [hománįmʌs], *a.* homónimo; equívoco, ambiguo.

homonymy [-mį], *s.* homonimia; equivocación, ambigüedad.

homophone [hámofoųn], *s.* palabra o letra homófona.

homophonous [homáfonʌs], *a.* homófono.

homophony [-nį], *s.* homofonía; identidad de sonido de dos palabras de distinta significación.

Homoptera [homáptẹrạ], *s. pl.* (zool.) homópteros.—**homopterous** [-rʌs], *a.* homóptero.

homosexual [homosékṣụạl], *a.* homosexual, por el propio sexo, por individuos del mismo sexo (pasión).—**homosexual(ist** [-(įst], *s.* homosexual; sodomita, *mf.;* maricón.—**homosexuality** [-éljtį], *s.* homosexualidad, inversión sexual.

homosporous [homásporʌs], *a.* (bot.) homósporo.

homunculus [homʌ́ŋkjụlʌs], *s.* homúnculo.

Honduran [handúrạn], *a. y s.* hondureño.

hone [hoųn], **I.** *s.* piedra de afilar. **II.** *va.* afilar, asentar, pulir, esmerilar (navajas, etc.).

honest [ánįst], *a.* honrado, probo, recto; sincero; equitativo; honesta (mujer).

honestly [-lį], *adv.* honradamente; de veras; francamente; honestamente.

honesty [-į], *s.* honradez, probidad; franqueza; honestidad.

honey [hánį]. **I.** *s.* miel (*f.*) de abejas. Empléase a veces como voz de cariño, en el sentido de *vida mía, mi querido,* etc.—**h. ant,** (ent.) hormiga melífera.—**h. cell,** alvéolo.—**h.-colored,** melado, gilvo.—**h. creeper,** (orn.) pipí.—**h. flower,** (bot.) ceriflor.—**h. harvest,** recolección de la miel.—**h. jar,** parral.—**h.-like,** meloso.—**h.-mouthed,** adulador, melifluo.—**h.-pot,** colmena de abejas silvestres.—**h. stalk,** (bot.) trébol.—**h.-tongue,** lengua melosa. **II.** *va.* enmelar, cubrir con miel. **III.** *vn.* hablar con cariño.

honeybee [-bi], *s.* (ent.) abeja neutra u obrera.

honeycomb [-koųm], *s.* bresca, panal de miel; (fund.) escarabajo, rebollidura, magaña.

honeycombed [-d], *a.* apanalado, alveolar; poroso; (mar.) abromado; horadado por gusanos.

honeydew [-dju], *s.* ligamaza; secreción dulce de algunos insectos y plantas; (bot.) variedad de melón muy dulce (ll. t. **h. melon**).

honeyed [-d], *a.* dulce, meloso, melifluo.—**honeyedness** [-dnįs], *s.* dulzura, halago.

honeyless [-lįs], *a.* sin miel.

honeymoon [-mun], *s.* luna de miel.

honeysuckle [-sʌkl], *s.* (bot.) madreselva.

honeysweet [-swit], *a.* melar.

honeywort [-wœrt], *s.* (bot.) ceriflor, *f.*

honk [haŋk]. **I.** *s.* pitazo, sonido de la bocina de un automóvil; graznido. **II.** *va. y vn.* tocar o sonar la bocina; graznar.

honor [ánọ(r)]. **I.** *s.* honor, honra; honradez, rectitud; cargo, dignidad; lauro.—*pl.* distinción (en los estudios, etc.); en algunos juegos de naipes (whist, bridge, etc.), los cuatro o cinco naipes más altos; tantos adicionales, semejantes a los que se acusan en el tute.—**h. bright,** (fam.) de veras, a fe de caballero.—**in h. of,** en homenaje a, en obsequio de.—**on, o upon, my h.,** por mi fe, por mi palabra de honor.—**your H.,** usía, vuestra señoría (apl. a jueces, alcaldes, etc.). **II.** *va.* honrar; laurear, condecorar; respetar; (com.) honrar, aceptar, pagar, dar acogida a (una letra).

honorable [-ạbl], *a.* honorable; pundonoroso; honrado; honorífico, honroso.—**H.,** honorable (tratamiento).

honorableness [-nįs], *s.* honradez; honorabilidad; hombría de bien.—**honorably** [-blį], *adv.* honorablemente; honrosamente.

honorarium [anọrérịʌm], *s.* honorarios, *m. pl.*

honorary [ánọrẹrị], *a.* honorario, honorífico; honroso.—**h. president,** presidente de honor.

hooch [huch], *s.* (fam.) bebida fuertemente alcohólica; licor de contrabando.

hood [hụd]. **I.** *s.* capucha, capucho, capilla, capirote, caperuza; capirote (de halcón, etc.); muceta; (mar.) caperuza de palo; carroza de la escalera; fuelle de carruaje; (aut.) capota; cubierta del motor; campana del hogar; sombrerete de chimenea, etc.), cubierta, tapa. **II.** *va.* cubrir con caperuza, capucha o capirote; tapar, ocultar.

hooded [-id], *a.* provisto de, o en forma de, capucha, etc.—**h. cobra,** (zool.) haje, naja, cobracapelo.

hoodlum [húdlʌm], *s.* (fam.) pillo, tunante, rufián.

hoodman-blind [húdmạn blájnd], *s.* (ant.) juego de la gallina ciega. *V.* BLINDMAN'S BUFF.

hoodoo [húdu]. **I.** *va.* (fam.) aojar; traer mala suerte.—**hoodooed,** aojado. **II.** *s.* mal de ojo; aojador. *V.* VOODOO.

hoodwink [húdwįŋk], *va.* vendar los ojos; encubrir, tapar; engañar, mistificar, embaucar.

hoof [húf]. **I.** *s.* casco, uña, vaso (del caballo,

etc.); pezuña o pesuña (de los animales de pata hendida); animal ungulado.—**on the h.,** en pie (ganado), vivo.—**h.-and-mouth disease** = FOOT-AND-MOUTH DISEASE. II. vn. (fam.) (a veces con **it**) andar o ir a pie; bailar.

hoofbound [-baund], a. corto de cascos.

hoofed [-t], a. ungulado.

hook [húk]. I. s. gancho, garabato, garfio; anzuelo; grapón; garra; corchete, prendedero; atractivo, aliciente; (mús.) rabo de una corchea.—**h.-nosed**, de nariz aguileña.—**hooks and eyes**, (cost.) corchetes y corchetas, broches, gafetes.—**by h. or by crook**, a tuertas o a derechas, de un modo u otro.—**off the hooks**, (fam.) agitado, distraído.—**on one's own h.**, (fam.) por cuenta propia, sin depender de otro. II. va. enganchar, engafar, garfear; atraer, engatusar; encornar, dar una cornada, coger; pescar; encorvar; (fam.) birlar, hurtar.—**to h. up**, (mec., elec., etc.) conectar; (fam.) enganchar (las caballerías).

hookbill [-bil], s. pico encorvado.

hooked [-t], a. enganchado; encorvado, ganchudo, ganchoso; falcado.—**h. rug,** tapete tejido a mano.

hookedness [-idnis], s. encorvadura.

hooking [-iŋ], s. enganche, enganchamiento.

hookup [-ʌp], s. (rad.) circuito; conexión o combinación de difusoras; transmisión por varias emisoras conectadas en circuito.

hookworm [-wœrm], s. (zool.) anquilóstomo, lombriz intestinal.—**h. disease**, (med.) anquilostomiasis.

hooky [-i], a. ganchudo.—**to play h.,** hacer novillos o rabona, fumar la clase.

hooligan [húligan]. I. s. rufián, truhán. II. a. de rufianes, truhanesco.—**hooliganism** [-izm], s. truhanería, rufianismo.

hoop [hup]. I. s. aro; fleje, zuncho; (mec.) collar, collarín; anilla, argolla, vilorta; virola; (carr.) hierro de llantas; (joy.) sortija, ajorca; miriñaque; grito.—**h.-la!** ¡arriba! ¡upa!—**h. skirt**, miriñaque, verdugado, tontillo, guardainfante. II. va. poner aro a; (en)zunchar; cercar, ceñir. III. vn. gritar; ojear. V. WHOOP.

hooper [húpœ(r)], s. tonelero.

hoopoe, hoopoo [húpu], s. (orn.) abubilla.

hooray [huréi], interj. ¡hurra! ¡viva!

hoos(e)gow [húsgau], s. (fam.) cárcel, f., prisión.

hoot [hút]. I. vn. gritar, ulular, huchear; dar grita; (Ingl.) sonar la bocina o el pito. II. va. atacar o recibir con gritos de irrisión. III. s. grito, grita, ruido, clamor; sofión, m.—**h. owl,** buho que ulula.—**not to care**, o **give, a h.**, (fam.) no importarle a uno un bledo.

hooting [-iŋ], s. grito, grita.

hooves [húvz], s. pl. de HOOF.

hop [háp]. I. va. saltar, brincar; (fam.) alzar el vuelo en (un avión), poner en marcha; recoger lúpulo; mezclar el lúpulo en la cerveza. II. vn. saltar en un pie, andar a saltitos; cojear; (con **off**) hacerse al aire, alzarse o partir (en aeroplano). III. s. salto, brinco; (fam.) baile, sarao; (bot.) lúpulo; (aer.) trayecto de vuelo; (fam.) vuelo.—**hops**, (com.) lúpulo.

hopbine [-bain], s. vástago de lúpulo.

hope [húp]. I. s. esperanza, hoto, confianza; expectativa.—**h. box**, o **chest**, colección o acumulación de prendas de vestir, etc., que una joven hace en la esperanza de usarlas cuando se case.—**in hopes**, en o con la esperanza.—**to give h.,** esperanzar, dar o infundir esperanza(s). II. va. y vn. esperar, tener esperanza.—**to h. against h.,** esperar lo imposible.

hopeful [-ful]. I. a. esperanzado, confiado, lleno de esperanzas; que da esperanza o promete. II. s. (fam.) vástago, joven que promete.—**hopefully** [-i], adv. con esperanza.—**hopefulness** [-nis], s. esperanza; aspecto prometedor.

hopeless [-lis], a. desahuciado; desesperante, desespera(nza)do; incurable, desesperado; irreme-

diable, irreparable; con que o con quien no se puede hacer nada, que no tiene entrada.—**hopelessly** [-li], adv. sin esperanza, desesperadamente.—**hopelessness** [-nis], s. falta de esperanza o de remedio.

hopingly [-piŋli], adv. con esperanza.

hoplite [háplait], s. hoplita, m.

hopper [hápœ(r)], s. persona que salta a la pata coja; insecto saltador; (mol.) tolva, cibera.

hopple [hápl]. I. va. trabar o manear un caballo etc. II. s. traba, manea, maniota.

hopscotch [hápskách], s. coxcojilla, infernáculo o reina mora, a la pata coja.

horal [hóural], **horary** [-ari], a. horario; por horas.

Horatian [horéišian], a. horaciano.

horde [hórd]. I. s. horda; enjambre; hato o manada; aduar. II. vn. formar hordas.

horehound [hórhaund], s. (bot.) marrubio.

horizon [horáizon], s. horizonte.

horizontal [harizántal], a. y s. horizontal, f.—**h. bar**, barra fija (para la gimnasia).

horizontality [-éliti], s. horizontalidad.

horizontally [-i], adv. horizontalmente.

hormone [hórmoun], s. (bioquím.) hormón, hormona.—**hormonal** [hormóunal], a. hormonal.

hormonic [hormánik], a. hormónico.

horn [hórn]. I. s. cuerno, asta; cuerna, cacho; (zool.) tentáculo; palpo o antena; (música) trompa; corneta de monte, cuerno de caza; (fonóg., aut., etc.) bocina; callosidad o dureza en la piel; cuerno de la luna; vaso u objeto de cuerno; miembro (de un dilema); (aer.) palanca de gobierno.—pl. cornamenta, cornadura de un animal.—**h. fly**, mosca que se posa en enjambres sobre los cuernos del ganado vacuno.—**h. of plenty**, cuerno de la abundancia.—**h.-shaped**, corniforme, cornial.—**at the small end of the h.**, llevándose lo peor, perdiendo. II. va. poner cuernos; proveer de cuernos; dar una cornada; dar una cencerrada.

hornbeam [-bim], s. (bot.) carpe.

hornbill [-bil], s. (orn.) cálao.

hornblende [-blend], s. (min.) hornablenda.

hornblower [-blouœ(r)], s. trompetero, bocinero.

hornbook [-buk], s. cartilla.

horned [-d], a. cornudo, cornígero; encornado; enastado; de cuerno.—**h. cattle**, ganado vacuno.—**h. owl**, (orn.) especie de buho de los E. U.—**h. pout**, (ict.) siluro (ll. t. **hornpout**).—**h. toad**, (zool.) especie de iguana.

hornet [hórnit], s. (ent.) crabrón, avispa, avispón, moscardón.

hornish [hórniš], a. duro; córneo.

hornpipe [hórnpaip], s. (Ingl.) baile predilecto de los marineros, que ejecuta una sola persona; (mús.) especie de gaita o chirimía.

hornsilver [-sílvœ(r)], s. (min.) plata córnea.

hornswoggle [-swagl], va. engatusar, embaucar.

hornwork [-wœrk], s. (fort.) hornabeque u obra a cuerno.

horny [-i], a. hecho de cuerno; córneo; calloso.

horography [horágrafi], s. horografía, gnomónica.

horologe [hároloudž], s. reloj.—**horologer** [hárolodžœ(r)], **horologist** [-džist], s. relojero; el que profesa la horología o se dedica a ella.—**horologic(al** [-ládžik(al], a. referente a la gnomónica.—**horology** [horálodži], s. horología.

horometry [horámetri], s. horometría.

horoscope [hároskoup], s. horóscopo.

horrendous [haréndas], a. horrendo, espantoso.

horrent [hárent], a. erguido; horrendo.

horrible [háribl], a. horrible, horroroso, terrible.—**horribleness** [-nis], s. horribilidad.—**horribly** [-bli], adv. horriblemente.

horrid [hárid], a. horrible o hórrido; ofensivo, dañoso.—**horridly** [-li], adv. horriblemente.—**horridness** [-nis], s. horridez, horror.

horrific [harífik], a. horrífico.

horrify [hárifai], va. horrorizar, horripilar.

horrifying [-iŋ], a. horripilante.

horripilate [harípileit], va. y vn. horripilar(se).—
horripilation [-éiṣǫn], s. (med.) horripilación.
horrisonant [haríṣonạnt], a. horrísono.
horror [hárǫ(r)], s. horror.—**h.-stricken**, horrorizado.—**the horrors**, (fam.) melancolía, morriña; espasmo de horror.
hors d'oeuvres [ordǽvr], s. pl. (fr.) entremeses.
horse [hǫrs]. I. s. caballo; (mil.) caballería, caballos; potro (para la gimnasia); (carp.) caballete, borriquete, banco, bastidor, burro, borrico; tendedor, mesa de papel, etc.; (ten.) garatura o tabla de descarnar; (mar.) marchapié, guardamancebo, guindaste; manía, tema, chifladura, muletilla.—**h. aloes**, (bot.) acíbar caballuno.—**h. ant**, (ent.) hormiga roja.—**h. armor**, barda.—**h. artillery**, artillería montada o volante.—**h. bean**, (bot.) haba panosa o caballuna.—**h. block**, apeadero; montador, montadero.—**h. boat**, tafurea.—**h. bot**, (ent.) moscardón, estro.—**h. boy**, mozo de cuadra.—**h. breaker**, picador, amansador o domador de caballos.—**h. breeding**, cría caballar.—**h. brush**, bruza.—**h. car**, tranvía de fuerza de sangre; carro de transportar caballos.—**h. chestnut**, (bot.) castaño de Indias, y la castaña que produce.—**h. cloth**, manta de caballo.—**h. collar**, collera.—**h. dealer**, chalán.—**h. doctor**, albéitar; veterinario.—**h. drench**, toma de medicina para caballo.—**h. dung**, cagajón, estiércol de caballos.—**h.-faced**, de cara acaballada.—**H. Guards**, guardias montadas; (Ingl.) cuartel general del ejército.—**h. keeper**, establero, mozo de cuadra.—**h. litter**, litera montada o tirada por caballos.—**h. mackerel**, (ict.) caballa, sarda, chicharro.—**h. marine**, persona fuera de su elemento.—**h. mill**, tahona, molino de sangre.—**h. pistol**, pistola de arzón.—**h. power** = HORSEPOWER; fuerza de sangre.—**h. race**, carrera de caballos.—**h. racing**, carreras de caballos.—**h. sense**, (fam.) gramática parda, sentido común práctico.—**h. show**, concurso hípico.—**h. thief**, cuatrero.—**h. trader**, chalán, tratante de caballos.—**h. trappings**, arneses, gualdrapa.—**a h. of another color**, harina de otro costal, otra cosa, otro cantar.—**to get on, o mount, the high h.**, asumir una actitud arrogante.—**to h!** (mil.) ¡a caballo! II. va. montar a caballo; poner o llevar a caballo; (mil.) remontar, proveer de caballos; cubrir el caballo a la yegua; (mar.) calafatear; (fam.) forzar al trabajo. III. vn. cabalgar, andar a caballo; estar (la yegua) salida.
horseback [-bæk], s. lomo de caballo o asiento del jinete.—**to ride h.**, montar a caballo.
horsefair [-fer], s. feria de caballos.
horseflesh [-fleṣ], s. carne (f.) de caballo; conjunto de caballos; variedad de caoba de las Bahamas.
horsefly [-flai], s. (ent.) tábano, moscardón; rezno.
horsehair [-her], s. pelo de caballo (esp. de la crin y la cola); tela de crin.
horsehide [-haid], s. piel (f.) de caballo.
horsejockey [-dźaki], s. (dep.) jockey, yoquey.
horselaugh [-læf], **horselaughter** [-læftœ(r)], s. risotada, carcajada.
horseleech [-lich], s. (zool.) sanguijuela grande; gorrón; (ant.) albéitar, veterinario.
horseload [-loud], s. carga de caballo.
horseman [-mạn], s. jinete, caballero, caballista; (mil.) soldado de caballería.—**horsemanship** [-ṣip], s. manejo, equitación.
horsemint [-mint], s. (bot.) mastranzo.
horseplay [-plei], s. payasada.
horsepond [-pand], s. abrevadero, estanque donde beben los caballos.
horsepower [-pauœ(r)], s. (mec.) caballo de vapor o de fuerza.
horseradish [-rædiṣ], s. (bot.) rábano picante o rústico.
horseshoe [-ṣu], s. herradura; lo que tiene forma

de herradura.—**h. crab**, (zool.) límulo.—
horseshoer [-œ(r)], s. herrador.
horsetail [-teil], s. cola de caballo; (bot.) belcho.
horsewhip [-hwip]. I. s. látigo, (Am.) fuete. II. va. azotar, zurriagar, cruzar con látigo, dar fuetazos a.
horsewoman [-wụmạn], s. amazona.
horsiness [-inis], s. afición a los caballos.
horsing [-iŋ], s. asiento del amolador de cuchillos; vapuleo, azotes, m. pl.
horsy [-i], a. caballar, caballuno, chalán; hípico; aficionado a, o pert. a, los caballos.
hortation [hortéiṣǫn], s. exhortación.
hortative [hórtạtiv], **hortatory** [-tori], a. exhortatorio.
hortensial [horténṣạl], a. hortense, hortelano.
horticultural [hortikálchụrạl], a. hortícola.
horticulture [hórtikʌlchụ(r)], s. horticultura.
horticulturist [-kʌlchụrist], s. horticultor.
hortus siccus [hórtạs síkạs], s. herbario.
hosanna [hozǽnā], s. (igl.) hosanna, m.
hose [hóuz], s. calceta; medias o calzas, f. pl.; manguera, manga de bomba o de riego; tubo flexible de goma.—**h. reel**, carretel de manguera.
hoseman [-mạn], s. manguero.
hosier [hóuźœ(r)], s. mediero, calcetero.
hosiery [hóuźœri], s. calcetería.—**h. yarn**, hilo de punto o de calcetería.
hospice [háspiṣ], s. hospicio, hospedería.
hospitable [háspitạbl], a. hospitalario.—**hospitableness** [-niṣ], s. hospitalidad.—**hospitably** [-bli], adv. hospitalariamente.
hospital [háspitạl], s. hospital; clínica.—**h. ship**, buque hospital.—**h. wagon**, carro de ambulancia.—**h. ward**, sala o crujía de hospital.
hospitality [-tǽliti], s. hospitalidad.
hospitalization [-tạlizéiṣǫn], s. hospitalización; tratamiento de hospital.
hospitalize [háspitạlaiz], va. hospitalizar, enviar al hospital.
hospital(l)er [háspitạlœ(r)], s. hospitalario; hospiciano; hospitalero.
hospitium [haspíṣiʌm], s. hospicio.
host [houst], s. hospedero, mesonero, posadero, huésped, m.; anfitrión, m.; hueste, f.; multitud; (H., igl.) hostia.
hostage [hástidź], s. rehén, prenda, gaje.
hostel [hástel], s. posada, hostería; hotel; casa de huéspedes para estudiantes.
hostelry [-ri], s. fonda, mesón, hostal, parador.
hostess [hóustiṣ], s. posadera, mesonera, patrona, huéspeda, ama; anfitriona; maestra de ceremonias (en un cabaret, etc.); (aer.) mujer que atiende a los pasajeros.
hostile [hástil], a. hostil, enemigo, adverso.
hostilely [-li], adv. hostilmente.
hostility [hastíliti], s. hostilidad, enemiga.—pl. (actos de) guerra.
hostler [háslœ(r)], s. establero, palafrenero.
hot [hát], a. cálido, caliente; caluroso; ardiente, fogoso; picante, acre; violento, furioso; (fam.) intolerable; en caliente; (fam.) cercano (de algo que se busca).—**h. and heavy**, (fam.) furioso. —**h. baths**, caldas, termas.—**h. blast**, tiro de aire caliente.—**h.-blooded**, apasionado, de sangre ardiente.—**h. bulb**, (máq. comb. int.), tubo incandescente.—**h. chisel**, cincel para metal caliente.—**h. dog**, (fam.) = FRANKFURTER.—**h.-headed**, fogoso, exaltado.—**h.-livered**, irascible.—**h. mustard**, mostaza muy picante.—**h. pepper**, pimiento picante o de cornetilla.—**h. plate**, calorífero portátil de gas. —**h. pot**, **h. tube** = H. BULB.—**h.-press**, s. prensa de satinar papel en caliente; prensa térmica para la extracción del aceite; va. satinar (papel) en caliente.—**h. pursuit**, perseguimiento enérgico; (der. int.) perseguimiento extraterritorial de violadores del territorio nacional.—**h. riveting**, remachado en caliente.—**h.-roll**, laminar en caliente.—**h. saw**, sierra de

cortar metal en caliente.—**h. springs**, fuentes (f. pl.) de aguas termales.—**h.-water bottle**, calientapiés, o botella de caucho para agua caliente.—**h. wave**, ola de calor.—**h.-wire ammeter**, (elec.) amperímetro térmico.—**to be burning h.**, estar que quema; hacer mucho calor.—**to be in h. water**, (fam.) estar en ascuas o en calzas prietas.—**to get**, o **grow, h.**, calentarse; encenderse; hacer calor.

hotbed [-bɛd], s. (hort.) almajara, estercolero; (fig.) foco, plantel.

hotbox [-baks], s. (f. c., etc.) cojinete calentado excesivamente por fricción.

hotchpotch [háchpach], s. mezcolanza; sancocho. V. HODGEPODGE.

hotel [hotél], s. hotel; palacio; posada, fonda.—**h. keeper** o **manager**, hotelero, fondista.

hotfoot [hátfʊt], adv. (fam.) pronta o rápidamente.

hothead [-hɛd], s. persona fogosa, arrebatada, turbulenta o de mal genio; agitador, alborotador, bochinchero.

hothouse [-haʊs], s. invernadero, invernáculo, estufa.

hotly [-lɪ], adv. calurosamente; vehementemente; lascivamente.

hotness [-nɪs], s. calidad de caliente; calor.

hotspur [-spœ(r)], s. y a. temerario, impulsivo, atolondrado.

Hottentot [hátntat], s. y a. hotentote.

hound [haʊnd], I. s. sabueso, podenco; collón, hombre vil; (mar.) cacholas.—**h.'s-tongue**, (bot.) cinoglosa, viniebla.—**h.-tree**, (bot.) cornejo. II. va. cazar con perros; soltar los perros; seguir la pista; perseguir; azuzar.

hour [áʊr], s. hora.—pl. horas (rezos).—**h. angle**, (astr.) ángulo horario.—**h. circle**, (astr.) círculo horario.—**h. hand**, horario (del reloj).

hourglass [-glæs], s. ampolleta o reloj de arena.

houri [húrɪ], s. hurí, f.

hourly [áʊrlɪ], I. adv. a cada hora; por horas, frecuentemente. II. a. por horas, frecuente.

house [haʊs], I. s. casa; hogar, residencia, domicilio, vivienda; familia, linaje; casilla del tablero de ajedrez; (com.) casa de comercio, razón (f.) social, establecimiento mercantil; cámara de un cuerpo legislativo; (teat.) sala, público; (mec.) caja, cubierta.—**h. coat**, bata.—**h. duty**, (Ingl.) impuesto sobre las casas.—**h. fly**, mosca ordinaria.—**h. of cards**, castillo de naipes.—**H. of Commons**, Cámara de los Comunes.—**h. of correction**, reformatorio.—**h. of ill fame**, o **repute**, burdel.—**H. of Lords**, o of **Peers**, Cámara de los Lores o de los Pares.—**h. of prayer** = H. OF WORSHIP.—**H. of Representatives**, Cámara de Representantes.—**h. of worship**, iglesia, templo.—**h. painter**, pintor de brocha gorda.—**h. party**, convite de varios días; los convidados.—**h. physician**, médico residente o de asiento (en un hospital, casa, etc.).—**h. rent**, alquiler de casa.—**h. surgeon**, cirujano residente.—**h. tax** = H. DUTY. II. [haʊz], va. albergar, alojar; (agr.) entrojar; poner a cubierto; almacenar; (mar.) afianzar o cubrir cuando hay borrasca; (carp.) encajar. III. vn. residir, tener alojamiento.

houseboat [-boʊt], s. barco vivienda.

housebreaker [háʊsbrejkœ(r)], s. ladrón que escala una casa.—**housebreaking** [-ɪŋ], s. escalo.

household [-hoʊld], s. casa, familia.—**h. bread**, pan casero o bazo.—**h. duties**, quehaceres domésticos.—**h. furniture**, ajuar o menaje de casa.—**h. gods**, lares.—**h. goods**, mobiliario, enseres, bártulos.

householder [-œ(r)], s. amo de casa.

housekeep [-kip], vn. manejar casa, tener hogar propio; cocinar.

housekeeper [-œ(r)], s. ama de gobierno o ama de llaves; casera; mujer de casa.

housekeeping [-ɪŋ]. I. s. manejo de casa (se

subentiende que comprende la cocina).—**to begin h.**, poner casa.—**to break up h.**, levantar casa. II. a. doméstico, casero, de casa; provisto de facilidades para cocinar.

houseleek [-lik], s. (bot.) siempreviva o hierba puntera.

houseless [-lɪs], a. sin casa ni hogar.

housemaid [-mejd], s. criada.

houseroom [-rum], s. cabida de una casa.

housetop [-tap], s. tejado, techo, azotea.

housewarming [-wormɪŋ], s. tertulia con que se celebra el estreno de una casa.

housewife [-wajf], s. ama de casa; madre de familia; ama de gobierno o de llaves; agujetero; estuche o neceser de costura.

housewifely [-lɪ]. I. adv. con economía doméstica. II. a. económica y cuidadosa.

housewifery [-rɪ], s. gobierno de una casa; economía doméstica.

housework [-wœrk], s. tareas domésticas.

housing [háʊzɪŋ], s. alojamiento; abrigo, albergue; almacenaje; (mec.) muesca, rebajo, encaje; chumacera; caja; (aut.) caja, cárter; (arq.) nicho; (mar.) piola; mantilla, gualdrapa (de caballo).—**h. shortage**, falta o escasez de viviendas.

hove [hoʊv], pret. y pp. de TO HEAVE.

hovel [hʌvɛl]. I. s. cobertizo; choza, cabaña, bohío. II. va. abrigar en cabaña.

hover [hʌvœ(r)]. I. va. cubrir con las alas. II. vn. revolotear; cernerse (las aves, y fig.) rondar; estar suspenso; dudar.—**hovering** [-ɪŋ], s. revoloteo.

how [haʊ]. I. adv. cómo; cuán, cuánto; a cómo.—**h. about it?** ¿qué le parece? ¿y si lo hiciéramos?—**h. do you do?** ¿cómo le va a Vd.? ¿cómo está Vd.? para servir a Vd.—**h. do you sell them?** ¿a cómo los vende Vd.?—**h. early?** ¿cuándo, a más tardar?—**h. far?** ¿a qué distancia? ¿hasta dónde?—**h. late?** ¿a qué hora? ¿hasta qué hora? ¿cuándo?—**h. long?** ¿cuánto tiempo?—**h. many?** ¿cuántos?—**h. much?** ¿cuánto?—**h. now?** ¿y bien? ¿pues qué? ¿qué significa eso?—**h. often?** ¿cuántas veces?—**h. often!** ¡cuán a menudo! ¡con qué frecuencia!—**h. pretty!** ¡qué bonito!—**h. so,** (ant.) = HOWSOEVER.—**h. so?** ¿cómo así?—**h. soon?** ¿cuándo?—**h. well!** ¡qué bien! II. s. cómo, modo, manera.

howbeit [haʊbíjt], adv. sea como fuere, así como así; no obstante.

howdah [háʊdȡ], s. castillo que se pone sobre un elefante o camello.

howel [háʊɛl], s. (ton.) doladera.

however [haʊévœ(r)]. I. adv. como quiera que, de cualquier modo; por muy.—**h. much**, por mucho que. II. conj. no obstante, sin embargo.

howitzer [háʊɪtsœ(r)], s. (arti.) obús, bombero.

howl [háʊl]. I. vn. aullar, dar alaridos; ulular; rugir, bramar. II. va. gritar; (con down o out) condenar o echar a gritos. III. s. aullido, ululato; alarido; gemido; rugido; bramido.

howler [-œ(r)], s. aullador; gemidor; gritador; (fam.) adefesio ridículo; (zool.) mono chillón, araguato o aullador, (Am.) congo.

howlet [háʊlɪt], s. (orn., ant.) lechuza.

howling [háʊlɪŋ], s. aullido; grito; lamento.

howsoever [háʊsoévœ(r)], adv. = HOWEVER.

hoyden [hójdɛn], s., a., y vn. = HOIDEN.

hub [hʌb], s. (carr.) cubo de la rueda; por extensión, centro, eje; chito; calzo; manguito de doble bocina para juntas o empalmes; punzón para hacer troqueles.—**h.-and-spigot joint**, junta de enchufe de campana.—**the H.**, (E. U., fam.) la ciudad de Boston.

hubbub [hábab], s. grita, alboroto, bulla.

huckaback [hákabæk], s. (tej.) alemanisco; cierto género de lino o algodón (ú. esp. para toallas).

huckleberry [háklberɪ], s. (bot.) variedad de arándano, planta vacciniea.

hucklebone [-boṇ], s. (anat.) cía; taba.—pl. taba (juego de niños).

huckster [hʌ́kstœ(r)]. I. s. regatón, vendedor ambulante al pormenor, esp. de productos agrícolas; sujeto ruin. II. va. y vn. regatonear, andar menudeando.

hucksterage [-idǯ], s. regatonería.

huddle [hʌ́dl]. I. va. amontonar desordenadamente; atrabancar. II. vn. acurrucarse; apiñarse, amontonarse, agruparse. III. s. tropel, confusión, baraúnda; reunión, sobre todo de jugadores de futbol para recibir órdenes; (fam.) junta o reunión secreta.

hue [hju], s. matiz, m., tinta, tinte; grita, clamor.—**h. and cry**, alarma, somatén, alarida, vocería.—**many-hued**, matizado.

huff [hʌf]. I. s. enfado, enojo. II. va. hinchar, inflar; enfadar; maltratar, injuriar; soplar una dama en el juego. III. vn. ofenderse; hincharse; bufar. V. PUFF.

huffish [-iš], a. irascible; petulante.

huffishly [-li], adv. con petulancia; insolentemente; con enfado.—**huffishness** [-nis], s. petulancia, arrogancia, impertinencia.

huffy [-i], a. irascible, malhumorado.

hug [hʌg]. I. va. abrazar; abrazarse a; navegar muy cerca de (la costa).—**to h. one's self**, congratularse.—**to h. the wind**, (mar.) ceñir el viento. II. s. abrazo apretado.

huge [hjúdǯ], a. inmenso, enorme, vasto, colosal.—**hugely** [-li], adv. enormemente, inmensamente.—**hugeness** [-nis], s. enormidad, inmensidad.

hugger-mugger [hʌ́gœ(r) mʌ́gœ(r)]. I. s. confusión, desorden. II. a. secreto, reservado; dejado, descuidado. III. adv. secreta o confusamente.

Huguenot [hjúgənat], s. y a. hugonote.

hulk [hʌlk]. I. s. casco (de barco); carraca, barco viejo; armatoste; buque que sirve de cárcel; (fam.) sujeto gordiflón. II. vn. (gen. con up) convertirse en armatoste.

hulking [-iŋ], **hulky** [-i], a. tosco, grueso, pesado.

hull [hʌl]. I. s. cáscara, corteza; vaina de legumbre; casco (de un buque); flotador (de aeroplano); armazón, f. (de un dirigible rígido). II. va. pelar, mondar, descortezar, descascarar; dar un proyectil en el casco de un buque.

hullabaloo [hʌləbəlú], s: alboroto, batahola.

huller [hʌ́lœ(r)], s. descascarador.

hullo [hʌlóu], s. e interj. = HOLLO, HELLO.

hully [hʌ́li], a. cascarudo.

hum [hʌm]. I. va. canturrear, tararear. II. vn. zumbar; susurrar; hervir (fig.). III. s. zumbido, susurro; voz inarticulada (¡hum!); (fam.) engaño, filfa, burla, chasco. IV. interj. ¡ya! ¡hum!

human [hjúmən]. I. a. humano.—**h. race**, género humano. II. s. mortal, ser humano.

humane [hjuméjn], a. humano, benévolo, compasivo; humanitario.—**h. letters**, letras humanas.

humanely [-li], adv. humanitariamente.

humaneness [-nis], s. humanidad.

humanism [hjúmənizm], s. letras humanas; humanidad.

humanist [-ist], s. humanista.

humanitarian [hjumænitérjən]. I. a. humanitario. II. s. filántropo; el que cree que Jesucristo no fué más que un hombre; el que cree en la perfectibilidad de la naturaleza humana; el que basa la religión únicamente en la filantropía.

humanitarianism [-izm], s. humanitarismo.

humanity [hjumǽniti], s. humanidad; filantropía, benevolencia.—pl. **humanities**, humanidades.

humanize [hjúmənajz], va. y vn. human(iz)ar(se).

humankind [hjúmənkájnd], s. humanidad, género humano.

humanly [hjúmənli], adv. humanamente.

humble [hʌ́mbl]. I. a. humilde, modesto, sumiso.—**humble pie** [-páj], s. empanada de entrañas

de venado.—**to eat h. p.**, humillarse, pedir misericordia. II. va. humillar, postrar, someter. III. vn. bajar o doblar la cerviz.

humblebee [-bi], s. = BUMBLEBEE.

humbleness [-nis], s. humildad.

humbling [hʌ́mbliŋ], s. humillación, abatimiento, rendimiento.

humbly [hʌ́mbli], adv. humildemente.

humbug [hʌ́mbʌg]. I. s. farsa, patraña, fraude; farsante, embaucador. II. va. y vn. embaucar.

humdrum [hʌ́mdrʌm]. I. a. monótono, pesado, cansado. II. s. fastidio, aburrimiento; lata; charla o cantilena fastidiosa; posma, mf., zorrocloco, persona cargante.

humeral [hjúmeṛal], a. (anat.) humeral.

humerus [hjúmeṛas], s. (anat.) húmero.

humic [hjúmik], a. húmico, relativo al mantillo; (quím.) húmico.

humid [hjúmid], a. húmedo.—**h. process, way**, etc., (quím.) vía húmeda.

humidification [-ifikéjšǫn], s. humedecimiento.

humidifier [hjumídifajœ(r)], s. humedecedor.

humidify [-faj], va. humedecer.

humidity [-ti], **humidness** [hjúmidnis], s. humedad.

humidor [hjúmidor], s. bote o caja humectativos para tabaco, cigarros, etc.

humiliate [hjumíljejt], va. humillar, mortificar.

humiliation [-éjšǫn], s. humillación.

humility [hjumíliti], s. humildad, sumisión.

hummer [hʌ́mœ(r)], s. (orn.) colibrí.

humming [hʌ́miŋ]. I. s. zumbido, susurro, zurrido; canturreo, tarareo. II. a. zumbador; (fam.) muy activo, intenso, grande, etc.—**h. ale**, (fam.) cerveza fuerte y espumosa.—**h. bird**, (orn.) colibrí, pájaro mosca, tominejo.

hummock [hʌ́mǫk], s. montecillo, morón, colina, mogote.

humor [hjúmǫ(r)]. I. s. humor, carácter, índole, f.; humorada, fantasía, capricho; humorismo; sal, f., agudeza, chiste, jocosidad; (med.) humor; aguadija; erupción cutánea.—**to be in a bad h.**, o **out of h.**, estar de mal humor, o de malas pulgas. II. va. complacer, dar gusto; acceder; consentir en; mimar; adaptarse, acomodarse a; desempeñar bien.

humoral [-əl], a. (med.) humoral.

humoralism [-izm], s. (med.) humorismo.

humoresque [-ésk], s. capricho musical.

humorism [-izm], s. (med.) humorismo; ingenio, gracejo; gracia, chiste.

humorist [-ist], s. humorista; chocarrero.

humorous [-ʌs], a. humorístico, ocurrente, jocoso, chistoso; voluntarioso, caprichoso.—**humorously** [-li], adv. jocosamente; caprichosamente.—**humorousness** [-nis], s. jocosidad, gracejo, donaire; humorada.

humorsome [-sʌm], a. caprichoso.

humous [hjúmʌs], a. que contiene humus o mantillo.

hump [hʌmp]. I. s. giba, joroba, corcova; (f. c.) albardilla. II. vn. encorvarse, doblar la espalda.—**humped** [-t], a. jorobado, corcovado.

humpback [-bæk]. I. s. giba, joroba; jorobado.—**humpbacked** [-t], a. jorobado, giboso, corcovado.

humpy [-i], a. giboso.

humus [hjúmʌs], s. humus, mantillo.

Hun [hʌn], s. huno.

hunch [hʌnch]. I. va. empujar, dar empellones; doblar la espalda. II. vn. moverse o avanzar a tirones o a sacudidas; abalanzarse. III. s. giba, corcova; pedazo o trozo grueso; (fam.) corazonada, presentimiento.

hunchback(ed [-bæk(t] = HUMPBACK(ED.

hundred [hʌ́ndṛed]. I. a. (precedido de a o one) ciento, cien. II. s. ciento; (arit.) centena; centenar.—**by hundreds**, o **by centenares**.—**by the h.**, por ciento(s); por centenares.

hundredfold [-fould], s. céntuplo.

hundred-per-center [-pœrséntœ(r)], s. patriota

de ciento por ciento, sin mezcla de influencias ni predilecciones extranjeras.

hundredth [-θ], *a.* y *s.* centésimo, céntimo; ciento (ordinal).

hundredweight [-wejt], *s.* quintal; (E. U.' 100 libras (45.36 kg.); (Ingl.) 112 libras (50.8 kg.).

hung [hʌŋ], *pret.* y *pp.* de TO HANG.—**h. beef**, tasajo, cecina.—**h. jury**, (fam.) jurado en desacuerdo.

Hungarian [hʌŋgériạn], *a.* y *s.* húngaro.

hunger [hʌŋɡœ(r)]. I. *s.* hambre.—**h. strike**, huelga del hambre, huelga de inanición; recurso al suicidio por hambre (apl. a ciertos encarcelados). II. *va.* hambrear. III. *vn.* hambrear, tener hambre.—**to h. for**, tener sed de, anhelar.

hungrily [hʌŋgrịlị], *adv.* hambrientamente.

hungry [hʌŋgrị], *a.* hambriento; ganoso, deseoso; estéril, pobre.—**to be, o to feel h.**, tener hambre.

hunk [hʌŋk], *s.* (fam.) buen pedazo; rebanada gruesa.

Hunker [hʌŋkœ(r)], *s.* (hist. E. U.) conservador.

hunks [hʌŋks], *s.* avaro; persona malhumorada.

hunky [hʌŋkị], *a.* (fam.) muy bien hecho; en buen estado.—**h.-dory**, (fam.) a pedir de boca.

Hunnish [hʌnịṣ], *a.* huno.

hunt [hʌnt]. I. *va.* cazar; (per)seguir; recorrer buscando, registrar.—**to h. up**, buscar.—**to h. up and down**, buscar por todos lados. II. *vn.* cazar; hacer un registro minucioso; buscar.—**to h. after**, buscar, anhelar.—**to h. counter**, ir contra la pista. III. *s.* caza, cacería, montería; perseguimiento, acosamiento; asociación de cazadores.

hunter [-œ(r)], *s.* montero, cazador; podenco; caballo de caza.—**h.'s cap**, montera, gorra de caza.

hunting [-ịŋ], *s.* montería, caza, cacería.—**h. box**, pabellón de caza.—**h. case**, tapa de saboneta.—**h.-case watch**, saboneta.—**h. dog**, perro de caza, podenco.—**h. ground**, cazadero.—**h. horn**, corneta de monte, trompa de caza.—**h. horse**, caballo de caza.—**h. jacket**, cazadora.—**h. knife**, cuchillo de monte.—**h. lodge** = H. BOX.—**h. match, o party**, batida, partida de caza.—**h. season**, tiempo de caza.

huntress [-rịs], *s.* cazadora.

huntsman [-smạn], *s.* montero, cazador.

hurdle [hœrdl]. I. *s.* zarzo, valla, cañizo; encañado; adral; (dep.) valla portátil en carreras de caballos o personas; (mil.) fajina, cestón; (fig.) dificultad, obstáculo.—*pl.* salto de vallas, carrera de obstáculos (ll. t. **h. race**). II. *va.* hacer o colocar cañizos; vencer un obstáculo; (mil.) defender con fajinas. III. *vn.* saltar vallas.—**hurdler** [hœrdlœ(r)], *s.* (dep.) persona que toma parte en carreras de obstáculos.

hurdy-gurdy [hœrdịgœrdị], *s.* (mús.) organillo; especie de gaita, zanfonía.

hurl [hœrl]. I. *va.* tirar, lanzar, arrojar, echar; proferir (invectivas, etc.). II. *vr.* lanzarse, arrojarse, abalanzarse. III. *s.* tiro, lanzamiento.

hurling [-ịŋ], *s.* lanzamiento, tiro; antiguo juego parecido al football; en Irlanda, el juego llamado *hockey*.

hurly-burly [hœrlị bœrlị], *s.* batahola, baraúnda, alboroto.

hurra(h [hụrá]. I. *interj.* ¡viva! ¡hurra! II. *va.* y *vn.* aclamar, vitorear. III. *s.* viva, *m.*

hurricane [hœrịkejn], *s.* huracán, ciclón.—**h. deck**, (mar.) cubierta superior.

hurried [hœrịd], *a.* y *pp.* de TO HURRY; precipitado, apresurado, hecho de prisa.—**hurriedly** [-lị], *adv.* apresuradamente, precipitadamente.

hurry [hœrị]. I. *va.* y *vn.* apresurar(se); dar(se) prisa; afanar(se); (hacer) obrar a la carrera o con precipitación.—**to h. after**, correr detrás o en pos de.—**to h. away**, salir precipitadamente.—**to h. back**, volver de prisa; apresurarse a volver.—**to h. in**, (hacer) entrar de

prisa; entrar con precipitación en.—**to h. into**, arrastrar, impeler hacia.—**to h. off**, huir, sal[i] o hacer marchar de prisa.—**to h. on**, apresu[...] rar, precipitar; impulsar, empujar; apresurarse[...]—**to h. over**, (hacer) pasar rápidamente; des[...] pachar, expedir.—**to h. up**, apresurarse, dars[...] prisa. III. *s.* prisa, premura, precipitación.—**there's no h. about it**, no corre prisa.

hurry-skurry (o **scurry**) [-skœrị], *adv.* confusa[...] mente, en tropel.

hurt [hœrt]. I. *va.* (*pret.* y *pp.* HURT) dañar, hace[...] mal o daño, lastimar, lisiar, estropear, herir[...] injuriar, ofender; perjudicar, damnificar.—**to h. one's feelings**, apenar a uno; herirle a un[...] el amor propio, ofenderlo. II. *vn.* doler. III. *[s.]* lesión, herida, contusión, lastimadura; mal[...] daño, perjuicio, detrimento. IV. *a.* lastimad[...] herido, lisiado; perjudicado.

hurtful [-fụl], *a.* perjudicial, pernicioso, nociv[...] dañino.—**hurtfully** [-ị], *adv.* dañosamente, per[...] niciosamente, injuriosamente.—**hurtfulnes[s]** [-nịs], *s.* calidad dañosa o perjudicial; naturalez[...] dañina, peligrosa o perniciosa.

hurtle [hœrtl]. I. *vn.* lanzarse, arrojarse con vi[o]lencia. II. *va.* blandir; lanzar o arrojar.

hurtleberry [hœrtlberị], *s.* V. HUCKLEBERRY WHORTLEBERRY.

hurtless [hœrtlịs], *a.* inocente; ileso, intacto.

husband [hʌzbạnd]. I. *s.* marido, esposo. II. *v[a.]* ahorrar; manejar con economía; procurar ma[...] rido a; ser o pasar por marido de.

husbandman [-mạn], *s.* agricultor, granjero.

husbandry [-rị], *s.* labranza, agricultura; pro[...] ducción agrícola; frugalidad, parsimonia; eco[...] nomía doméstica.

hush [hʌṣ]. I. *va.* apaciguar, aquietar; hace[r] callar.—**to h. up**, tapar, ocultar, mantener se[...] creto. II. *vn.* estar quieto, callar, enmudece[r] estar callado. III. *s.* silencio, quietud.—**h. money**, dinero con que se compra el silencio d[e] alguien.—**h. boat, h. ship**, (fam.) barco a[r]mado disfrazado de barco mercante, esp. par[a] cazar submarinos.—**very h.-h.**, muy secret[o] IV. *interj.* ¡chist! ¡chito! ¡silencio!

husk [hʌsk]. I. *s.* cáscara, vaina, pellejo, hollej[o] bagazo; desperdicio. II. *va.* descascarar, des[...] vainar, pelar, mondar, despellejar, deshollejar[...]

husked [-t], *a.* que tiene cáscara, vaina o pellej[o] descascarado.—**husker** [-œ(r)], *s.* descascara[...] dor, desgranador; abridor de ostras.

huskily [hʌskịlị], *adv.* roncamente; secamente.

huskiness [hʌskịnịs], *s.* ronquera; calidad de ca[s]carudo o cortezudo.

husking [hʌskịŋ], *s.* acto de descascarar y de[s] granar maíz.—**h. bee**, reunión de vecinos par[a] desgranar maíz.

husky [hʌskị]. I. *a.* cascarudo, cortezudo; ronc[o] rauco. II. *a.* y *s.* (fam.) fuerte, fornido, tern[...]

hussar [hụzár], *s.* (mil.) húsar.

Hussite [hʌsajt], *s.* husita, *mf.*, discípulo de Hus[s]

hussy [hʌsị], *s.* buena pieza, tunanta, pícara.

husting [hʌstịŋ], *s.* asamblea, junta.—*pl.* (Ingl[.] tribuna pública para discursos electorales; con[...] sejo o tribunal de autoridades municipales.

hustle [hʌsl]. I. *va.* mezclar, confundir; empuja[r] atropellar, sacudir. II. *vn.* andar a empellone[s] (fam.) pernear, patear, moverse con actividad[...]

hustler [hʌslœ(r)], *s.* (fam.) trafagón, buscav[i]das, persona enérgica.

hut [hʌt]. I. *s.* choza, cabaña, barraca; huta, c[o]bertizo; (Am.) bohío.—**h. urn**, urna cineraria[...] II. *va.* y *vn.* alojar o vivir en una choza.

hutch [hʌch]. I. *s.* arca, cofre; artesa; cest[a] hucha; ratonera; conejera; amasadera; (mi[n.] cuba. II. *va.* guardar en cofre.

huzza [hʌzá], *vn.*, *s.* e *interj.* = HURRAH.

hyacinth [hájạsịnθ], *s.* (bot. y min.) jacinto.

hyacinthine [-sịnθịn], *a.* jacintino.

hyæna [hajínạ], *s.* = HYENA.

hyaline [hájạlịn], *a.* hialino, vítreo, vidrios[o] transparente.

hyalite [háiạlait], *s.* (min.) hialita.
hyalitis [haiạláitis], *s.* (med.) hialitis.
hyalograph [haiálogræf], *s.* hialógrafo.—**hyalography** [haiạlágrạfi], *s.* hialografía, hialotecnia.
hyaloid [háiạloid], *a.* hialoideo, hialino.—**h. membrane**, (anat.) hialoides, *f.*
hybrid [háibrid], *a.* y *s.* híbrido, mestizo.
hybridism [-izm], **hybridity** [haibríditi], *s.* hibridismo, hibridez, hibridación.
hybridization [-izéişọn], *s.* hibridación.
hybridize [-aiz], *va.* y *vn.* producir o generar híbridos; ser capaz de cruzamiento.
hybridizing [-iŋ], *s.* hibridación.
hybridous [-ʌs], *a.* híbrido.
hydatid [háidạtid], *s.* (med. y zool.) hidátide, *f.*
hydra [háidrạ], *s.* (zool.) hidra, polipo de agua dulce; (H., mit. y astr.) hidra.
hydracid [haidrésid], *s.* (quím.) hidrácido.
hydragogue [háidrạgag], *a.* y *s.* (med.) hidragogo.
hydrangea [haidréndʒiạ], *s.* (bot.) hortensia.
hydrant [háidrạnt], *s.* boca de riego; boca o toma de agua para incendios.
hydrargyric [haidrardʒírik], *a.* hidrargírico.
hydrargyrum [haidrárdʒirʌm], *s.* (quím.) hidrargiro, mercurio.
hydrate [háidreit]. **I.** *s.* (quím.) hidrato. **II.** *va.* hidratar.—**hydration** [haidréişọn], *s.* (quím.) hidratación.
hydraulic(al [haidrólik(ạl], *a.* hidráulico.—**h. brake**, freno hidráulico.—**h. cement**, cemento hidráulico.—**h. elevator**, ascensor hidráulico. —**h. forging**, forjadura hidráulica, forjadura en caliente por presión hidráulica.—**h. gauge**, manómetro hidráulico.—**h. gradient**, línea de alturas piezométricas.—**h. jack**, gato hidráulico.—**h. main**, receptáculo con agua para depurar el gas de alumbrado.—**h. mean depth**, o **mean radius** = H. RADIUS.—**h. mining**, minería hidráulica.—**h. power**, energía o fuerza hidráulica.—**h. press**, prensa hidráulica. —**h. radius**, radio hidráulico (medio), profundidad media (área dividida por el perímetro mojado).—**h. ram**, ariete hidráulico.—**h. valve**, válvula de máquina hidráulica; tapa acopada con los bordes sumergidos en agua.
hydraulic. I. *va.* excavar o demoler por chorros hidráulicos. **II.** *vn.* explotar minas por el método hidráulico.
hydraulician [-líşạn], *s.* hidráulico.
hydraulicking [haidrólikiŋ], *s.* (min.) minería hidráulica; explotación hidráulica.
hydraulics [-liks], *s. pl.* hidráulica.
hydrazine [háidrazin], *s.* (quím.) hidracina.
hydric [háidrik], *a.* (quím.) hídrico.
hydrid(e [háidraid], *s.* (quím.) hidruro.
hydriodic [haidriádik], *a.* (quím.) yodhídrico.
hydroaeroplane, hydroairplane [haidroéiẹroplein, -érplein], *s.* hidroaeroplano, hidroavión, *m.*
hydrobromic [-bróumik], *a.* (quím.) bromhídrico.
hydrobromide [-bróumaid], *s.* (quím.) bromhidrato.
hydrocarbon [-kárbọn], *s.* (quím.) hidrocarburo.
hydrocele [-sil], *s.* (med.) hidrocele, *mf.*
hydrocephalous [-séfalʌs], *a.* hidrocéfalo, hidrocefálico.—**hydrocephalus**, *s.* (med.) hidrocefalía.
hydrochlorate [-klóreit], *s.* (quím.) clorhidrato.
hydrochloric [-klórik], *a.* hidroclórico, clorhídrico.
hydrochlorid(e [-klóraid], *s.* clorhidrato.
hydrocyanic [-saiénik], *a.* cianhídrico o prúsico.
hydrodynamic(al [-dainémik(ạl], *a.* hidrodinámico.
hydrodynamics [-s], *s.* hidrodinámica.
hydroelectric [-iléktrik], *a.* hidroeléctrico.
hydrofluoric [-flụórik], *a.* (quím.) fluorhídrico.
hydrogen [-dʒin], *s.* (quím.) hidrógeno.
hydrogenate, hydrogenize [-dʒeneit, -dʒenaiz], *va.* (quím.) hidrogenar.
hydrogenous [haidrádʒenʌs], *a.* hidrogenado.

hydrographer [haidrágrạfœ(r)], *s.* hidrógrafo.
hydrographic(al [haidrográfik(ạl], *a.* hidrográfico.—**hydrography** [haidrágrạfi], *s.* hidrografía.
Hydroidea [haidróidiạ], *s. pl.* (zool.) hidroideos.
hydrokinetic [-kinétik], *a.* hidrocinético.—**hydrokinetics** [-s], *s.* hidrocinética.
hydrologic(al [-ládʒik(ạl], *a.* hidrológico.
hydrology [haidrálodʒi], *s.* hidrología.
hydrolysis [haidrálisis], *s.* hidrólisis.—**hydrolitic** [-lítik], *a.* hidrolítico.
hydromancy [háidromænsi], *s.* hidromancía.
hydromechanics [-mikéniks], *s.* hidromecánica.
hydromedusa [-midiúsạ], *s.* (zool.) hidromedusa.
hydromel [-mɛl], *s.* hidromel, aguamiel, *f.*
hydrometallurgy [-métạlœrdʒi], *s.* hidrometalurgia.
hydrometeor [-mítiọ(r)], *s.* hidrometeoro.
hydrometer [haidrámetœ(r)], *s.* areómetro.
hydrometric [haidrométrik], *a.* hidrométrico.—**h. pendulum**, péndulo hidrométrico.
hydrometry [haidrámetri], *s.* areometría, teoría y uso del areómetro.
hydropath [háidropæθ], **hydropathist** [haidrápạθist], *s.* hidrópata, *m.*
hydropathic [haidropéθik], *a.* hidropático.
hydropathy [haidrápạθi], *s.* (med.) hidropatía.
hydrophane [háidrofein], *s.* (min.) hidrófana.
hydrophobia [-fóubiạ], *s.* (med.) hidrofobia.
hydrophobic [-fóubik], *a.* hidrofóbico; hidrófobo.
hydrophone [-foun], *s.* (mar., hidr.) hidrófono, instrumento que sirve para escuchar sonidos transmitidos por el agua; (med.) estetoscopio de columna de agua.
hydroplane [-plein], *s.* hidroplano, hidroavión, *m.*
hydroponics [-pániks], *s.* (hort.) hidroponía.
hydroquinone [-kwínoun], *s.* (quím.) hidroquinona.
hydroscope [-skoup], *s.* instrumento para observar el fondo del mar.
hydrosphere [-sfir], *s.* hidrosfera.
hydrostat [-stæt], *s.* (m. v.) indicador eléctrico de nivel.
hydrostatic(al [-stétik(ạl], *a.* hidrostático.—**h. balance, joint, press, pressure**, balanza, conexión, prensa, presión hidrostática.—**hydrostatically** [-i], *adv.* hidrostáticamente.
hydrostatics [-s], *s.* hidrostática.
hydrosulphide [-sʌlfaid], *s.* (quím.) sulfhidrato, hidrosulfuro.
hydrosulphuric [-sʌlfiúrik], *a.* sulfhídrico.
hydrotherapeutic [-θerạpiútik], *a.* hidroterápico.
hydrotherapeutics, hydrotherapy [-s, -θérạpi], *s.* (med.) hidroterapia, hidropatía.
hydrothermal [-θórmạl], *a.* hidrotermal.
hydrothorax [-θóræks], *s.* (med.) hidrotórax.
hydrovane [-vein], *s.* timón horizontal para el movimiento vertical de un submarino.
hydrous [háidrʌs], *a.* acuoso, aguado; hidratado.
hydroxid(e [haidráksaid], *s.* (quím.) hidróxido.
hydroxyl [haidráksil], *s.* (quím.) oxhidrilo.
Hydrozoa [haidrozóụạ], *s. pl.* (zool.) hidrozoarios.
hyena [haiínạ], *s.* (zool.) hiena.
hyetal [háiịtạl], *a.* pluvial; lluvioso.
hygiene [háidʒin], **hygienics** [-éniks], *s.* higiene. *f.*—**hygienic** [-énik], *a.* higiénico.
hygienically [-ạli], *adv.* higiénicamente.
hygienist [háidʒienist], *s.* higienista.
hygrometer [haigrámetœ(r)], *s.* higrómetro.
hygrometric(al [haigrométrik(ạl], *a.* higrométrico.—**hygrometry** [haigrámetri], *s.* higrometría.
hygroscope [háigroskoup], *s.* higroscopio.
hygroscopic(al [-skápik(ạl], *a.* higroscópico.
hyli(ci)sm [háili(si)zm], *s.* materialismo.
hylotheism [háilọθiizm], *s.* panteísmo.
hylozoism [-zóụizm], *s.* hilozoísmo, doctrina según la cual la vida y la materia son inseparables.
hymen [háimẹn], *s.* himeneo; (anat.) himen.

hymeneal [-íal]. **I.** *s.* epitalamio. **II.** *a.* nupcial.
hymenium [haiméníʌm], *s.* (bot.) himenio.
Hymenoptera [-ápterą], *s. pl.* (ent.) himenópteros.—**hymenopteran** [-n], **hymenopterous** [-ʌs], *a.* himenóptero.
hymn [hím]. **I.** *s.* himno. **II.** *va.* alabar con himnos. **III.** *vn.* cantar himnos.
hymnal [-nal], *s.* himnario.—**hymnic** [-nik], *a.* perteneciente a los himnos.—**hymnology** [-nálodži], *s.* estudio, tratado o colección de himnos.
hyoid [háioid]. **I.** *s.* (anat.) hioides. **II.** *a.* hioides, hioideo.—**h. arch**, arco hioideo.
hyoscine [hájosin], *s.* (quím.) hioscina.
hyoscyamine [-sájamin], *s.* (quím.) hiosciamina.
hypallage [hipáladži], *s.* (gram. y ret.) hipálage, *f.*
hyperacidity [haipœrbœrǽsíditi], *s.* (med.) hiperacidez, exceso de ácido en el estómago.
hyper(a)emia [-ímią], *s.* (med.) hiperemia.
hyper(a)esthesia [-εsθížią], *s.* (med.) hiperestesia.
hyperbaton [haipœrbątan], *s.* (ret.) hipérbaton.
hyperbola [-bolą], *s.* (geom.) hipérbola.
hyperbole [-boli], *s.* (ret.) hipérbole, *f.*
hyperbolic(al [haipœrbálik(ąl], *a.* hiperbólico.
hyperbolically [-i], *adv.* hiperbólicamente.
hyperbolist [haipœrbolist], *s.* exagerador.
hyperborean [haipœrbórįan], *a.* y *s.* hiperbóreo.
hypercritic [haipœrkrítik], *s.*, **hypercritical** [-ąl], *a.* hipercrítico.—**hypercriticism** [-tisizm], *s.* hipercrítica.
hyperdulia [-djuláią], *s.* (igl.) hiperdulía.
Hypericaceæ [-ikéiṣii], *s. pl.* (bot.) hipericíneas.
hypericum [haipérikʌm], *s.* (bot.) hipérico.
hypermetrope [haipœrmétroup], *s.* hipermetrope, présbite o présbita.—**hypermetropia** [-mɛtróupią], *s.* (med.) hipermetropía, presbicia.
hyperope [-oup], **hyperopia** [-óupią] = HYPERMETROPE, HYPERMETROPIA.
hypertrophic [-tróufik], *a.* hipertrófico.
hypertrophy [haipœrtrofi]. **I.** *s.* (med.) hipertrofia; (fig.) aumento excesivo. **II.** *va.* y *vn.* hipertrofiar(se).
hyph(a)emia [haifímią], *s.* (med.) anemia; extravasación de la sangre, esp. en el ojo.
hyphen [háifęn]. **I.** *s.* guión, *m.* (-). **II.** *va.* = HYPHENATE.
hyphenate [-eit]. **I.** *va.* separar con guión. **II.** *s.* ciudadano norteamericano de origen extranjero. (El término, que es despectivo, alude al guión—*hyphen*—de la voz compuesta que indica las dos nacionalidades, como en *German-American*, ciudadano norteamericano de origen alemán.)
hyphenated [-id], *a.* (E. U.) de doble nacionalidad (apl. a extranjeros nacionalizados, esp. a los que prefieren su país natal al adoptivo).
hyphenation [-éiṣǫn], *s.* separación de sílabas con guiones.
hypnosis [hipnóuṣis], *s.* hipnosis.
hypnotic [hipnátik], *a.* hipnótico.
hypnotism [hípnotizm], *s.* hipnotismo.
hypnotize [hípnotaiz], *va.* hipnotizar.
hypnotizer [-œ(r)], *s.* hipnotizador.
hypo [háipou], *s.* (fot.) hiposulfito; (fam.) aguja o inyección hipodérmica.
hypoblast [háipoblæst], *s.* (biol.) hipoblasto, endodermo, endoblasto.
hypocaust [-kost], *s.* hipocausto.
hypochlorous [-klórąs], *a.* hipocloroso.—**hypochlorite** [-klórait], *s.* (quím.) hipoclorito.
hypochondria [-kándrią], **hypochondriasis** [-kandrájaṣis], *s.* hipocondría.
hypochondriac [-kándriæk], *s.* y *a.* hipocondríaco.
hypochondriacal [-kandrájakąl], *a.* hipocondríaco, hipocóndrico.
hypocondrium [-kándrįʌm], *s.* (anat.) hipocondrio.
hypocrisy [hipákriṣi], *s.* hipocresía, mojigatería.
hypocrite [hípokrit], *s.* hipócrita, *mf.*—**hypo-**

critical [-krítikąl], *a.* hipócrita, mojigato, gazmoño.—**hypocritically** [-i], *adv.* hipócritamente.
hypocycloid [haiposáikloid], *s.* (geom.) hipocicloide, *f.*
hypodermic [-dœrmik], *a.* hipodérmico.—**h. injection**, **syringe** (o simplemente **hypodermic**, *s.*) inyección, jeringa hipodérmicas.
hypogastric [-gǽstrik], *a.* hipogástrico.
hypogastrium [-gǽstrįʌm], *s.* (anat.) hipogastro.
hypogeal [-džíąl], *a.* subterráneo; (geol.) hipogénico, de formación subterránea, plutónico.
hypogene [-džin], *a.* (geol.) hipogénico, plutónico.
hypogeous [-džíąs], *a.* subterráneo; (bot.) de crecimiento subterráneo.
hypogeum [-džíʌm], *s.* (arq.) hipogeo.
hypoglossal [-glásąl]. **I.** *a.* (anat.) hipogloso. **II.** *s.* nervio hipogloso.
hypogynous [haipádžinąs], *a.* (bot.) hipógino.
hyponitrous [-nájtrąs], *a.* (quím.) hiponitroso.
hypophosphite [-fásfait], *s.* (quím.) hipofosfito.
hypophyge [haipáfjdži], *s.* (arq.) nacela.
hypophysis [haipáfiṣis], *s.* (anat.) hipófisis, glándula pituitaria (ll. t. **h. cerebri**); (bot.) hipófisis, célula proveniente del suspensor contiguo.
hypostasis [haipástaṣis], *s.* base, *f.*, fundamento; (teol.) hipóstasis; (med.) sedimento de la orina, etc.; hiperemia.
hypostatic(al [haipostǽtik(ąl], *a.* hipostático; constitutivo; personal.
hypostatically [-i], *adv.* hipostáticamente.
hypostatize [haipástataiz], *va.* objetivar, atribuir existencia real a.
hyposulphate [haiposálfeit], *s.* (quím.) hiposulfato.
hyposulphite [-sálfait], *s.* (quím.) hiposulfito.
hypotenuse [haipátinįus], *s.* (geom.) hipotenusa.
hypothec [haipáθik], *s.* (for.) hipoteca, prenda.
hypothecate [-eit], *va.* hipotecar, empeñar, pignorar.
hypothecation [-éiṣǫn], *s.* pignoración.
hypothecator [-tǫ(r)], *s.* el que pignora o da en hipoteca.
hypothenuse [haipáθinįus] = HYPOTENUSE.
hypothesis [haipáθesis], *s.* hipótesis, supuesto.
hypothetic(al [haipoθétik(ąl], *a.* hipotético.
hypothetically [-i], *adv.* hipotéticamente.
hypsometer [hipsámetœ(r)], *s.* hipsómetro.
hypsometric(al [hipsométrik(ąl], *a.* hipsométrico.
hypsometry [hipsámetri], *s.* hipsometría.
hyson [háisǫn], *s.* (com.) cha (*m.*) o te verde.
hyssop [híṣǫp], *s.* (bot.) hisopo.
hysterectomy [hịstɛréktomi], *s.* (cir.) histerectomía, extirpación del útero.
hysteresis [hịstɛríṣis], *s.* (fís.) histéresis.—**h. cycle**, ciclo o lazo de histéresis.—**h. loss**, pérdida por histéresis.—**h. loop** = H. CYCLE.
hysteria [hịstírią], *s.* (med.) histeria, histerismo; paroxismos histéricos; arrebatos nerviosos.
hysteric(al [hịstérik(ąl], *a.* histérico.
hysterics [-s], *s.* = HYSTERIA.
hysterotomy [hịstɛrátomi], *s.* (cir.) histerotomía; operación cesárea; incisión uterina.

I

i [ai], *s.* i.
I, *pron. pers.* (siempre con mayúscula) yo.
I, *s.* el ojo (en metafísica).
I, *a.* en I; de doble T.—**I bar**, barra de doble T.—**I beam**, **I girder**, viga de doble T.—**I iron** = I BAR.—**I rail**, riel de doble T.
iambic [aiǽmbik]. **I.** *a.* (poét.) yámbico. **II.** *s.* (pros.) yambo; verso yámbico.
iambus [aiǽmbąs], *s.* (pros.) yambo (ll. t. **iamb**).
Iberian [aibírįan], *a.* ibérico, ibero; *a.* y *s.* ibero.
ibex [áibeks], *s.* (zool.) íbice, cabra montés.
ibis [áibis], *s.* (orn.) ibis.
Icarian [aikérįan], *a.* icario; arriesgado.
ice [áis]. **I.** *s.* hielo; sorbete, granizada, garapiña,

(Am.) nieve, *f.*—**i. boat,** bote con patines que anda sobre el hielo, velero sobre hielo; barco rompehielos.—**i. box,** nevera, refrigerador.—**i. breaker,** buque o espolón rompehielos.—**i. chest** = I. BOX.—**i. cream,** helado, mantecado.—**i.-cream brick,** queso helado.—**i.-cream freezer,** heladora, sorbetera, garapiñera.—**i.-cream parlor,** heladería, tienda donde se sirve y se vende helado.—**i. drift, i. field, i. float, i. floe,** témpano, banco o masa de hielo flotante.—**i. hockey,** el juego del hockey sobre hielo.—**i. house,** nevera o nevería.—**i. pick,** punzón para romper hielo.—**i. plant,** (bot.) escarchada.—**i. skate,** patín de cuchilla, o para hielo.—**i. skating,** el patinar sobre hielo.—**i. water,** agua de nieve, agua enfriada con hielo.—**on thin i.,** en posición precaria.—**to cut no i.,** (fam.) no surtir efecto, no hacer mella. **II.** *va.* helar; congelar, refrigerar, enfriar con hielo; garapiñar; cubrir con alfeñique.

iceberg [-bœrg], *s. iceberg,* témpano grande de hielo flotante.

icebound [-baund], *a.* rodeado de hielo; pegado en el hielo o detenido por él.

iced [-t], *a.* escarchado, congelado; enfriado con hielo; cubierto con alfeñique.

Icelander [-lændœ(r)], *s.* islandés.

Icelandic [-lǽndịk], *a.* islandés.

Iceland moss [-lænd mɔs], *s.* (bot.) liquen o musgo de Islandia.—**I. spar** [-spar], *s.* (min.) espato de Islandia.

iceman [ᶐjsmæn], *s.* nevero, vendedor de hielo.

ichneumon [ịknjúmọn], *s.* (zool.) icneumón, mangosta (cuadrúpedo); icneumón (mosca) (ll. t. i. fly).

ichnographical [ịknogrǽfịkạl], *a.* icnográfico.

ichnography [ịknágrafị], *s.* (dib., arq.) icnografía.

ichor [ᶐjkọr], *s.* (med.) icor.

ichorous [ᶐjkọrʌs], *a.* icoroso.

ichthyocolla [ịkθjokólạ], *s.* colapez o cola de pescado.

ichthyoid [ᶆkθjọịd], *a.* y *s.* ictioideo.

ichthyol [ịkθjạl], **ichthyol oil,** *s.* (farm.) ictiol.

ichthyologic(al [ịkθjoládźịk(ạl], *a.* ictiológico.

ichthyology [ịkθjálodźịst], *s.* ictiología.

ichthyophagous [ịkθjáfagʌs], *a.* ictiófago.—**ichthyophagy** [-dźị], *s.* ictiofagía.

ichthyornis [ịkθjórnịs], *s.* (pal.) ictiornis, *m.*

ichthyosaur(us [ịkθjosór(ʌs], *s.* ictiosauro.

ichthyosis [ịkθjóʊsịs], *s.* (med.) ictiosis.

icicle [ᶐjsịkl], *s.* cerrión, *m.*, canelón, carámbano.

icily [ᶐjsịlị], *adv.* fríamente, frígidamente.

iciness [ᶐjsịnịs], *s.* frigidez; calidad de glacial.

icing [ᶐjsịṇ], *s.* capa de azúcar batida con clara de huevo (en tortas, etc.).

icon [ᶐjkạn], *s.* imagen, *f.,* representación; ilustración, grabado; icón, icono (imagen rusa).

iconoclasm [ᶐjkánoklæzm], *s.* iconoclas(t)ia.

iconoclast [-klæst], *s.* iconoclasta, *mf.*

iconoclastic [-klǽstịk], *a.* iconoclasta.

iconography [ᶐjkonágrafị], *s.* iconografía.

iconolater [-álatœ(r)], *s.* iconólatra, *mf.*

iconology [-álodźị], *s.* iconología.

icosahedron [ᶐjkosahídrọn], *s.* (geom.) icosaedro.

icteric(al [ịktérịk(ạl], *a.* y *s.* ictérico.

icterus [ᶆktẹrʌs], *s.* (med.) ictericia.

ictus [ᶆktʌs], *s.* (med.) acceso, paroxismo; pulsación, latido; (pros.) acento tónico.

icy [ᶐjsị], *a.* helado, frío, álgido.

idea [aịdíạ], *s.* idea; concepto; plan, propósito.—**ideal** [aịdíạl], *s.* y *a.* ideal; prototipo.—**idealism** [-ịzm], *s.* idealismo.—**idealist** [-ịst], *s.* idealista.—**idealistic** [-ịstịk], *a.* idealista.

ideality [aịdịǽlịtị], **idealness** [aịdịạlnịs], *s.* idealidad.

idealization [-ịzéịṣọn], *s.* idealización.

idealize [aịdíạlaịz], *va.* idealizar.

ideally [aịdíạlị], *adv.* idealmente.

ideate [aịdíịt]. **I.** *s.* objeto correspondiente a una idea. **II.** [aịdíeịt], *va.* concebir; pensar; recordar; idear. **III.** [aịdíeịt], *vn.* formar ideas, pensar.

ideation [aịdịéịṣọn], *s.* ideación.

identical [aịdéntịkạl], *a.* idéntico.—**i. with,** idéntico a.—**identically** [-ị], *adv.* idénticamente.—**identicalness** [-nịs], *s.* identidad.

identification [-fịkéịṣọn], *s.* identificación.—**i. papers,** cédula de identidad o de vecindad.

identifier [aịdéntịfaịœ(r)], *s.* identificador.

identify [-faị], *va.* identificar.

identity [-tị], *s.* identidad; (mat.) identidad, adecuación.

ideogram [ᶆdịogræm], *s.* = IDEOGRAPH.

ideograph [-græf], *s.* ideograma, *m.*

ideographic [ịdịográfịk], *a.* ideográfico.

ideography [ịdịágrafị], *s.* ideografía.

ideological [aịdịoládźịk(ạl], *a.* ideológico.

ideologist [aịdịálodźịst], *s.* ideólogo; idealista.

ideology [-dźị], *s.* ideología.

ides [aịdz], *s. pl.* idus o idos, *m. pl.*

idiocy [ᶆdịosị], *s.* idiotez, idiotismo, imbecilidad.

idiom [ᶆdịọm], *s.* modismo, idiotismo; habla, lenguaje, jerga; genio, índole (*f.*) de una lengua.

idiomatic(al [ịdịomǽtịk(ạl], *a.* idiomático.

idiopathic(al [ịdịopǽθịk(ạl], *a.* idiopático.

idiopathy [ịdịápaθị], *s.* idiopatía.

idiosyncrasy [ịdịosịŋkrạsị], *s.* idiosincrasia.

idiosyncratic [-krǽtịk], *a.* idiosincrásico.

idiot [ᶆdịọt], *s.* idiota, *mf.,* imbécil, necio.

idiotic [ịdịátịk], *a.* idiota, imbécil, tonto.

idiotism [ịdịótịzm], *s.* idiotismo, idiotez.

idle [aịdl]. **I.** *a.* ocioso, desocupado; sin colocación (dinero, etc.); perezoso, haragán; inútil, vano.—**i. current,** (elec.) corriente devaitada o anérgica.—**i. fellow,** haragán.—**i.-headed,** desrazonable.—**i.-pated,** majadero.—**i. pulley,** polea de guía; polea de tensión.—**i. wheel,** rueda intermedia o de transmisión. **II.** *vn.* holgazanear o haraganear; holgar, estar ocioso; (aut.) funcionar (el motor) en mínima, o a régimen mínimo, con el coche parado. **III.** *va.* (gen. con *away*) gastar ociosamente; dejar sin trabajo; poner en paro.

idleness [-nịs], *s.* ociosidad, ocio; pereza, holgazanería, haraganería, frivolidad; inutilidad.

idler [aịdlœ(r)], *s.* holgazán, azotacalles; (f. c.) furgón vacío; (mec.) = IDLE PULLEY, IDLE WHEEL.

idly [aịdlị], *adv.* ociosamente; desidiosamente; inútilmente, vanamente.

idol [aịdọl], *s.* ídolo.

idolater [aịdálatœ(r)], *s.* idólatra, *m.*—**idolatress** [-trịs], *s.* mujer idólatra.—**idolatrous** [-trʌs], *a.* idólatra, idolátrico.—**idolatrously** [-lị], *adv.* idolatradamente.—**idolatry** [-trị], *s.* idolatría.

idolize [aịdọlaịz], *va.* idolatrar.

idyl(l [ᶆdịl], *s.* idilio, égloga.

idyllic [aịdịlịk], *a.* idílico; pastoral, bucólico.

if [ịf]. **I.** *conj.* si; dado caso que, supuesto que; con tal que; aunque, aun cuando. Ú. elípticamente en vez de *if it is, if they are,* etc.; vg. *this, if true, is strange,* esto, si es cierto, es extraño. *If* introduce a veces una proposición de contraste numérico enfático, en el sentido de *cuando menos, ni uno menos;* vg. *she has fifty dollars, if she has one, o, if she has one cent,* ella tiene por lo menos cincuenta dólares, ella no tiene ni un centavo menos de, etc. **II.** *s.* hipótesis, suposición.

igloo [ịglu], *s.* iglú.

igneous [ịgnịʌs], *a.* ígneo, vulcanio.

ignis fatuus [ịgnịs fǽchụas], *s.* fuego fatuo.

ignitable, ignitible [ịgnáịtạbl], *a.* inflamable.

ignite [ịgnáịt]. **I.** *va.* encender, pegar fuego; (quím.) incinerar. **II.** *vn.* encenderse, inflamarse.—**igniter** [-œ(r)], *s.* deflagrador.

ignition [ịgnịṣọn], *s.* ignición, inflamación; (m. comb. int.) encendido.

ignivomous [ịgnívomʌs], *a.* (poét.) ignívomo.

ignobility [ịgnobịlịtị], *s.* villanía, bajeza.

ignoble [ịgnóʊbl], *a.* innoble, indigno; bajo, humilde.

ignobleness [-nįs], *s.* bajeza; calidad de plebeyo.

ignobly [-blį], *adv.* innoblemente.

ignominious [įgnomínįas], *a.* ignominioso.

ignominiously [-lį], *adv.* ignominiosamente.

ignominy [ígnomįnį], *s.* ignominia, infamia.

ignoramus [įgnoréįmas], *s.* ignorante, necio.

ignorance [ígnorąns], *s.* ignorancia; desconocimiento; rusticidad, falta de cultura.—**ignorant** [-ąnt], *a.* ignorante, indocto, ignaro, lego; zafio, inculto, rústico.—**i. of**, ajeno o desconocedor de.—**ignorantly** [-lį], *adv.* ignorantemente, neciamente, legamente.

ignore [ignór], *va.* desconocer, pasar por alto, no hacer caso de, desentenderse de; despreciar, desairar; ignorar; (for.) sobreseer; dar un fallo de "no ha lugar."

iguana [igwáną], *s.* (zool.) iguana.

iguanadon [įgwánodon], *s.* (pal.) iguanadonte.

ileac [ílįæk], *a.* ilíaco.

ileum [ílįʌm], *s.* (anat.) íleon (intestino).

ileus [ílįas], *s.* (med.) íleo, cólico miserere.

ilex [áįleks], *s.* (bot.) acebo; coscoja, encina.

iliac [ílįæk], *a.* (anat.) ilíaco.

Iliad [ílįąd], *s.* Ilíada.

ilium [ílįʌm], *s.* (anat.) íleon (hueso).

ilk [įlk]. I. *a.* (ant.) mismo. II. *s.* (fam.) raza, especie, clase, *f.*—**of that i.**, (fam.) del mismo nombre o especie.

ill [įl]. I. *a.* enfermo; malo; mal; nocivo, dañino.—**i. blood**, animosidad, inquina.—**i. breeding**, grosería, mala educación, malos modales.—**i. fame**, mala fama; reputación de inmoral (apl. esp. a la prostitución).—**i. nature**, mala disposición; malevolencia.—**i. repute** = I. FAME.—**i. temper**, mal genio.—**i. turn**, partida serrana, mala jugada.—**i. will**, mala voluntad, malquerencia, enemiga, ojeriza.—**in i. part**, en mala parte.—**to fall i.**, enfermar, caer enfermo. II. *s.* adversidad, calamidad; mal; malquerencia. III. *adv.* mal, malamente.—**i.-advised**, malaconsejado; mal pensado; desacertado.—**i.-affected**, descontento; malintencionado.—**i. at ease**, intranquilo, ansioso, inquieto; embarazado, confundido.—**i.-bred**, malcriado, descortés.—**i.-contrived**, mal pensado, mal dispuesto.—**i.-disposed** = I.-AFFECTED.—**i.-fated**, malogrado, malhadado, malaventurado.—**i.-favored**, feo, repulsivo.—**i.-founded**, mal fundado, infundado.—**i.-gotten**, mal habido.—**i.-grounded** = I.-FOUNDED.—**i.-humored**, malhumorado.—**i.-matched**, desigual. V. I.-SORTED.—**i.-minded**, maligno, malintencionado.—**i.-natured**, avieso.—**i.-omened**, de mal agüero o auspicio; malhadado.—**i.-pleased**, malcontento.—**i.-shaped**, malhecho.—**i.-sorted**, mal juntado; mal pareado, incompatible.—**i.-sounding**, malsonante.—**i.-spoken of**, de mala reputación.—**i.-starred**, malaventurado, desdichado.—**i.-tempered**, áspero, de mal genio, de malas pulgas, corajudo.—**i.-willed**, malévolo; de mal genio; renuente, maldispuesto.—**to make i.**, indisponer.—**to take (it) i.**, tomar a mal.

illation [įléįson], *s.* ilación, consecuencia, inferencia.

illative [ílątįv]. I. *a.* ilativo. II. *s.* conjunción ilativa.

illatively [-lį], *adv.* por ilación o inferencia.

illegal [ílígąl], *a.* ilegal, ilegítimo.

illegality [įlįgǽlįtį], **illegalness** [ílígąlnįs], *s.* ilegalidad; desaguisado.

illegally [-į], *adv.* ilegalmente.

illegibility [įledžįbílįtį], *s.* ilegibilidad.—**illegible** [įlédžįbl], *a.* ilegible.—**illegibly** [-blį], *adv.* ilegiblemente.

illegitimacy [įlįdžétįmąsį], *s.* ilegitimidad.

illegitimate [-mąt]. I. *a.* ilegítimo; espurio, falso; desautorizado. II. *va.* ilegitimar.—**illegitimately** [-lį], *adv.* ilegítimamente.—**illegitimation** [-méįson], *s.* ilegitimidad.

illiberal [įlíbęrąl], *a.* iliberal, mezquino; estrecho de miras.—**illiberality** [-ǽlįtį], *s.* tacañería ruindad; poquedad, apocamiento.—**illiberally** [-ąlį], *adv.* mezquinamente.

illicit [įlísįt], *a.* ilícito; ilegal.—**illicitly** [-lį], *adv.* ilícitamente.—**illicitness** [-nįs], *s.* ilicitud, calidad de ilícito; ilegalidad.

illimitable [įlímįtąbl], *a.* ilimitado; indefinido.

illimitably [-blį], *adv.* ilimitadamente.

illiquid [įlíkwįd], *a.* (com.) no realizable (fondos etc.); (for.) incierto, sin fundamento legal.

illiteracy [įlítęrąsį], **illiterateness** [-įtnįs], *s.* analfabetismo; ignorancia.—**illiterate** [-įt], *a.* y *s.* iliterato, analfabeto; ignorante.

illness [ílnįs], *s.* mal, enfermedad.

illogical [įládžįkąl], *a.* ilógico.—**illogically** [-lį], *adv.* ilógicamente.—**illogicality** [-ǽlįtį], **illogicalness** [-nįs], *s.* falta de lógica.

ill-treat [íltrít], *va.* maltratar, maltraer; acocear.—**ill-treated** [-įd], *a.* maltrecho.—**ill-treatment** [-męnt], *s.* maltrat(amient)o.

illume [įlįúm], *va.* (poét.) iluminar; dorar.

illuminant [įlįúmįnąnt]. I. *a.* iluminador, iluminante. II. *s.* substancia iluminativa.

illuminate [-eįt]. I. *va.* iluminar, alumbrar, aclarar, esclarecer; (b. a.) iluminar. II. *vn.* hacer luminarias.

illuminati [-éįtaį], *s. pl.* secta de los iluminados o alumbrados.

illuminating [-įŋ], *a.* iluminador, iluminativo.—**i. gas**, gas de alumbrado.

illumination [-éįson], *s.* iluminación, alumbrado; luminaria(s); brillo, esplendor; inspiración; (b. a.) iluminación en colores.

illuminative [-eįtįv], *a.* iluminativo.

illuminator [-eįto(r)], *s.* iluminador, reflector (lámpara, lente, etc.); (b. a.) iluminador.

illumine [įlįúmįn], *va.* iluminar.

Illuminism [-įzm], *s.* iluminismo.

illusion [įlįúžon], *s.* ilusión, ensueño; espejismo; engaño.—**to cause i.**, ilusionar.—**to have illusions**, ilusionarse.

illusive [įlįúsįv], *a.* ilusivo, ilusorio.—**illusively** [-lį], *adv.* ilusoriamente.—**illusiveness** [-nįs], *s.* ilusión, calidad de ilusorio; embaimiento.—**illusory** [įlįúsorį], *a.* ilusorio; engañoso.

illustrate [ílʌstreįt], *va.* ejemplificar; ilustrar, explicar, esclarecer con ejemplos; representar con grabados; ilustrar con grabados, etc.

illustration [-éįson], *s.* ejemplo, aclaración; (b. a.) grabado, ilustración, lámina.

illustrative [įlʌstrątįv], *a.* ilustrativo, ilustrador.

illustratively [-lį], *adv.* ilustrativamente.

illustrator [ílʌstreįto(r)], *s.* ilustrador.

illustrious [įlʌstríąs], *a.* ilustre, preclaro, insigne.—**illustriously** [-lį], *adv.* ilustremente.—**illustriousness** [-nįs], *s.* excelencia, grandeza.

image [ímįdž]. I. *s.* imagen, *f.,* efigie; simulacro; figura, retrato.—**i. worship**, culto de las imágenes. II. *va.* imaginar; formar imagen o idea clara de; representar en la mente; pintar (fig.) vívidamente; parecerse a.

imagery [-rį], *s.* imaginación, fantasía; conjunto de imágenes; exterioridad, apariencia; (b. a.) imaginería.

imaginable [įmǽdžįnąbl], *a.* imaginable.

imaginal [-nąl], *a.* relativo al insecto en su forma final o adulta. V. IMAGO.

imaginary [-nerį]. I. *a.* (leng. ord. y mat.) imaginario. II. *s.* (mat.) imaginaria, cantidad imaginaria.

imagination [-néįson], *s.* imaginación; imaginativa, inventiva.

imaginative [-neįtįv], *a.* imaginativo; imaginario.

imagine [įmǽdžįn]. I. *va.* imaginar; concebir; idear, inventar; figurarse, imaginarse. II. *vn.* imaginar, fantasear.

imagist [ímądžįst], *s.* poeta (*m.*) que escribe en verso absolutamente libre y con abundancia de imágenes o figuras.

imago [įméįgou], *s.* imagen, *f.;* (zool.) imago, forma adulta o final de un insecto.

imam [imám], *s.* imán (sacerdote, califa, etc. mahometanos).

imbecile [ímbisil], *a.* y *s.* imbécil.

imbecility [imbisíliti], *s.* imbecilidad.

imbed [imbéd], *va.* = EMBED.

imbibe [imbáib]. I. *va.* embeber, absorber; chupar; empapar(se), saturarse de; esponjarse; (fig.) empaparse de o en alguna idea. II. *vn.* (fam.) beber (vino); empinar el codo.

imbibition [imbibíson], *s.* imbibición.

imbricate(d [ímbrikeit(id], *a.* imbricado, encaballado, sobrepuesto.—**imbrication** [-éison], *s.* imbricación, superposición, traslapo.

imbroglio [imbróulyou], *s.* embrollo, enredo, lío.

imbrue [imbrú], *va.* mojar, teñir, manchar (de o con sangre).

imbrute [imbrút], *va.* y *vn.* embrutecer(se).

imbue [imbjú], *va.* calar, empapar, infiltrar; tinturar, teñir; imbuir, infundir.

imitability [imitabíliti], *s.* calidad de imitable.

imitable [ímitabl], *a.* imitable.

imitate [ímiteit], *va.* imitar, remedar, copiar, contrahacer.—**imitation** [-éison]. I. *s.* imitación. II. *a.* de imitación, imitado; falso (joya, etc.).—**imitative** [-iv], *a.* imitativo; imitatorio.—**imitator** [-o(r)], *s.* imitador.

immaculacy [imékyulasi], **immaculateness** [-litnis], *s.* pureza, inocencia.

immaculate [-lit], *a.* inmaculado, sin mancha.—I. **Conception**, (igl.) Inmaculada Concepción.

immaculately [-li], *adv.* inmaculadamente.

immanence, immanency [ímanens, -i], *s.* calidad de inmanente; inherencia.

immanent [-ent], *a.* inmanente, inherente.

immaterial [imatírial], *a.* inmaterial, incorpóreo; sin importancia, que no importa.—**to be i.**, no importar, no tener importancia, ser indiferente.

immaterialism [-izm], *s.* espiritualismo; idealismo.—**immaterialist** [-ist], *s.* espiritualista; idealista.

immateriality [-éliti], *s.* inmaterialidad, incorporeidad.—**immaterialized** [imatríalaizd], *a.* incorpóreo, espiritual.

immaterially [-i], *adv.* inmaterialmente.

immaterialness [-nis], *s.* inmaterialidad.

immature [imachúr], *a.* inmaturo, verde; prematuro; imperfecto.—**immaturely** [-li], *adv.* prematuramente; sin madurez.—**immatureness** [-nis], **immaturity** [-iti], *s.* calidad de inmaturo, falta de sazón.

immeasurability [imeźurabíliti], *s.* inconmensurabilidad.—**immeasurable** [iméźurabl], *a.* inmensurable, desmesurado.—**immeasurably** [-bli], *adv.* inmensamente, desmesuradamente.

immediacy [imídiasi], *s.* inmediación, proximidad, contigüidad.

immediate [imídiit], *a.* inmediato, cercano; perentorio, próximo, instantáneo, urgente; directo; intuitivo.—**i. truths**, verdades intuitivas.—**immediately** [-li], *adv.* inmediatamente, en seguida, en el acto, incontinenti; directamente, intuitivamente.—**i. after(ward)**, a continuación de, a raíz de; acto continuo, a renglón seguido.—**immediateness** [-nis], *s.* inmediación.

immedicable [imédikabl], *a.* incurable, irremediable.

immemorial [imimórial], *a.* inmemorial.

immemorially [-i], *adv.* inmemorablemente.

immense [iméns], *a.* inmenso, infinito, vasto.—**immensely** [-li], *adv.* inmensamente.—**immenseness** [-nis], **immensity** [-iti], *s.* inmensidad.

immensurability [imensurabíliti], *s.* inconmensurabilidad.

immensurable [iménsurabl], *a.* inmensurable.

immerge [iméerdź]. I. *va.* sumergir, zambullir. II. *vn.* hundirse, ocultarse, perderse de vista.

immerse [iméers], *va.* sumergir, zambullir, hundir; anegar, sumir; bautizar por la inmersión.

immersion [iméersón], *s.* inmersión, sumersión; bautismo por inmersión.

immesh [iméś], *va.* entrampar, enredar.

immethodical [imeθódikal], *a.* inmetódico.

immethodically [-i], *adv.* sin método.

immigrant [ímigrant], *s.* y *a.* inmigrante.

immigrate [ímigreit], *vn.* inmigrar.

immigration [-éison], *s.* inmigración.

immigratory [ímigratori], *a.* inmigratorio.

imminence [íminens], *s.* inminencia.

imminent [-ent], *a.* inminente.

immiscibility [imisibíliti], *s.* (quím. y fís.) inmiscibilidad.

immiscible [imísibl], *a.* inmiscible.

immission [imíson], *s.* inmisión, introducción, inyección.

immitigable [imítigabl], *a.* inmitigable.

immix [imíks], *va.* mezclar, juntar.

immobile [imóubil], *a.* inmóvil, inmovible.

immobility [-bíliti], *s.* inmovilidad.

immobilize [-aiz], *va.* inmovilizar; paralizar.

immoderate [imáderit], *a.* inmoderado, excesivo; desarreglado.—**immoderately** [-li], *adv.* inmoderadamente.—**immoderateness** [-nis], o **immoderation** [-éison], *s.* inmoderación, exceso, desarreglo.

immodest [imádist], *a.* inmodesto, impúdico, indecoroso, indecente; impudente, atrevido.—**immodestly** [-li], *adv.* inmodestamente.—**immodesty** [-i], *s.* inmodestia, impudicia, falta de pudor.

immolate [ímoleit], *va.* inmolar.—**immolation** [-éison], *s.* inmolación.—**immolator** [-o(r)], *s.* inmolador.

immoral [imáral], *a.* inmoral, licencioso, depravado, corrompido, vicioso.

immorality [imoréliti], *s.* inmoralidad.

immortal [imórtal], *a.* y *s.* inmortal.—**immortality** [-téliti], *s.* inmortalidad.—**immortalization** [-izéison], *s.* inmortalización, perpetuación.—**immortalize** [-aiz], *va.* inmortalizar.—**immortally** [-i], *adv.* inmortalmente.

immortelle [imortél], *s.* (bot.) siempreviva, perpetua.

immotile [imóutil], *a.* inmoto, fijo.

immovability [imuvabíliti], **immovableness** [imúvablnis], *s.* inmovilidad; inamovilidad; inmutabilidad; inalterabilidad; insensibilidad.

immovable [imúvabl]. I. *a.* inmóvil, inmovible, inamovible; inmutable, firme, inalterable; impasible, apático; (for.) inmueble. II. *s. pl.* inmuebles, bienes raíces.—**immovably** [-bli], *adv.* inmutablemente, inalterablemente.

immune [imjún], *a.* y *s.* inmune.

immunity [-iti], *s.* inmunidad; exención, franquicia, privilegio.

immunize [ímjunaiz], *va.* inmunizar.

immunization [-izéison], *s.* inmunización.—**immunology** [-álodźi], *s.* inmunología.

immure [imjúr], *va.* emparedar.

immutability [imjutabíliti], *s.* inmutabilidad, inalterabilidad; firmeza, constancia.—**immutable** [imjútabl], *a.* inmutable.—**immutably** [-bli], *adv.* inmutablemente.

imp [imp], *s.* diablillo, trasgo; picaruelo, tunantuelo.

impact [impékt], *va.* empaquetar.—**impacted**, *a.* impactado (diente, fragmento óseo, etc.).

impact [ímpækt], *s.* impacto, impacción, choque.—**i. excitation**, (rad.) excitación impulsiva.

impaction [impékson], *s.* impacción.

impair [impér], *va.* empeorar, dañar, perjudicar, menoscabar, deteriorar.—**impairment** [-ment], *s.* empeoramiento, deterioro, menoscabo.

impale [impéil], *va.* empalar; cercar, vallar.

impalement [-ment], *s.* empalamiento; empalizada.

impalpability [impælpabíliti], *s.* impalpabilidad.

impalpable [impælpabl], *a.* impalpable, intangible.

impanate [impéineit], a. (teol.) impanado, existente en el pan de la eucaristía.

impanation [-éişǫn], s. (teol.) impanación.

impanel [impǽnęl], va. (for.) formar la lista de los jurados; elegir (jurado).

imparity [impǽriti], s. desigualdad, desproporción; disparidad.

impart [impárt], va. impartir, comunicar, dar; conceder; compartir.

impartial [impárşǎl], a. imparcial.

impartiality [-şǐǎlǐtǐ], s. imparcialidad.

impartially [-i], adv. imparcialmente.

impartible [impártjbl], a. impartible, indivisible; comunicable; concedible, concesible.

impartment [impártmęnt], s. participación; comunicación.

impassability [impæsǎbǐlǐtǐ], **impassableness** [impǽsǎblnǐs], s. calidad de intransitable o de insuperable.—**impassable** [-ąbl], a. intransitable, impracticable; insuperable.

impasse [impǽs], s. atolladero, dificultad insuperable, desavenencia irreconciliable.

impassibility [impæsǐbǐlǐtǐ], **impassibleness** [impǽsǐblnǐs], s. impasibilidad.

impassible [-ibl], a. impasible.

impassion [impǽşǫn], va. apasionar; conmover o afectar fuertemente.

impassionable [-ąbl], a. conmovible.

impassioned [-d], a. apasionado, vehemente, extremoso.

impassive [impǽsiv], a. impasible.

impassiveness [-nǐs], s. impasibilidad.

impastation [impæstéişǫn], s. pasta, empaste.

impaste [impéist], va. hacer pasta; (pint.) empastar.

impatience [impéişęns], s. impaciencia.

impatient [-ęnt], a. impaciente; mal sufrido.

impatiently [-li], adv. impacientemente.

impeach [impích], va. acusar (a un funcionario ante un tribunal); poner en tela de juicio.—**impeachable** [-ąbl], a. delatable, censurable.—**impeacher** [-œ(r)], s. acusador, denunciador, delator.—**impeachment** [-męnt], s. acusación; imputación, delación, residencia.

impearl [impǽrl], va. aljofarar, emperlar.

impeccability [impękǎbǐlǐtǐ], s. impecabilidad.

impeccable [impékąbl], a. impecable.

impecuniosity [impǐkjunǐásǐtǐ], s. inopia.

impecunious [-kjúnǐʌs], a. pobre, indigente.

impedance [impídǎns], s. (elec.) impedancia.— **i. coil**, bobina de reacción.

impede [impíd], va. impedir, estorbar, dificultar.

impediment [impédjmęnt], s. impedimento; obstrucción, traba, cortapisa.

impedimenta [-méntǎ], s. pl. (mil.) impedimenta.

impeditive [impédǐtiv], a. impeditivo.

impel [impél], va. impeler, impulsar, empujar, mover; incitar.—**impellent** [-ęnt]. I. a. impelente; impulsor. II. s. empuje, motor, móvil. —**impeller** [-œ(r)], s. impulsor, motor.

impend [impénd], vn. pender; amenazar, amagar, ser inminente.—**impendence, impendency** [-ęns, -i], s. inminencia, amago, amenaza. —**impendent** [-ęnt], **impending** [-iŋ], a. inminente, amenazante; pendiente.

impenetrability [impęnętrǐbǐlǐtǐ], s. impenetrabilidad.—**impenetrable** [impénǐtrąbl], a. impenetrable.—**impenetrableness** [-nǐs], s. impenetrabilidad.—**impenetrably** [-bli], adv. impenetrablemente.

impenitence, impenitency [impénǐtęns, -i], s. impenitencia.—**impenitent** [-ęnt], a. y s. impenitente.—**impenitently** [-li], adv. sin contrición.

imperative [impérǎtiv]. I. a. imperativo, imperioso, imprescindible. II. s. mandato perentorio; (gram.) imperativo.

imperatively [-li], adv. imperativamente.

imperator [impęréitǫ(r)], s. (hist. rom.) emperador, *imperátor*.

imperceptibility [impœrsęptǐbǐlǐtǐ], **imperceptibleness** [-séptǐblnǐs], s. imperceptibilidad.

imperceptible [-ibl], a. imperceptible.—**imperceptibly** [-ibli], adv. imperceptiblemente.

imperceptive [-iv], a. incapaz de percibir.

imperfect [impœrfikt]. I. a. imperfecto, incompleto, defectuoso. II. s. (gram.) imperfecto.

imperfection [impœrfékşǫn], s. imperfección, desperfecto, defecto, mal, tacha, lunar.

imperfectly [impœrfiktli], adv. imperfectamente.

imperfectness [-nǐs], s. imperfección.

imperforate(d [impœrforeit(id], a. imperforado.

imperforation [impœrforéişǫn], s. imperforación.

imperial [impírǐǎl]. I. a. imperial. II. s. imperial; pera, perilla; (arq.) cúpula morisca; cosa superior en su clase.—**imperialism** [-izm], s. imperialismo.—**imperialist** [-ist], s. (pol.) imperial, imperialista.—**imperially** [-i], adv. imperialmente.

imperil [impéril], va. poner en peligro, arriesgar.

imperious [impírǐʌs], a. imperioso.—**imperiously** [-i], adv. imperiosamente.—**imperiousness** [-nǐs], s. autoridad, mando; arrogancia.

imperishable [impérǐşąbl], a. imperecedero.

imperium [impírǐʌm], s. (hist. rom.) imperio, mando absoluto; (for.) potestad, poder.

impermanence [impœrmąnęns], s. inestabilidad.

impermanent [-ęnt], a. que no es permanente.

impermeability [impœrmǐąbǐlǐtǐ], s. impermeabilidad.—**impermeable** [-ąbl], a. impermeable, impenetrable, a prueba de agua, etc.

impersonal [impœrsǫnąl], a. impersonal.

impersonally [-i], adv. impersonalmente.

impersonate [impœrsǫneit], va. personificar; (teat.) representar; imitar, remedar.

impersonation [-éişǫn], s. personificación; (teat.) representación, papel; imitación, remedo.

impersonator [-ǫ(r)], s. personificador; (teat.) intérprete, el que hace papel; imitador, remedador.

impertinence, impertinency [impœrtinęns, -i], s. impertinencia; insolencia.—**impertinent** [-ęnt], a. impertinente; oficioso; insolente, atrevido.—**impertinently** [-li], adv. impertinentemente; insolentemente.

imperturbability [impœrtœrbąbǐlǐtǐ], s. imperturbabilidad, serenidad.—**imperturbable** [-ąbl], a. imperturbable.—**imperturbably** [-bli], adv. imperturbablemente.—**imperturbation** [-béişǫn], s. calma, serenidad.—**imperturbed** [impœrtœrbd], a. sereno, sosegado.

impervious [impœrvǐʌs], a. impermeable.

imperviously [-li], adv. impenetrablemente.

imperviousness [-nǐs], s. impermeabilidad.

impetrate [impǐtreit], va. impetrar.—**impetration** [-éişǫn], s. impetración.—**impetrative** [-iv], a. impetrante.

impetuosity [impęchǔásǐtǐ], s. ímpetu, impetuosidad, violencia, vehemencia.

impetuous [impéchʉʌs], a. impetuoso, arrebatado.—**impetuously** [-li], adv. impetuosamente.—**impetuousness** [-nǐs], s. impetuosidad, arrojo.

impetus [impǐtʌs], s. ímpetu, impulso, impulsión.

imphee [imfi], s. caña de azúcar africana.

impiety [impáięti], s. impiedad, irreligiosidad.

impinge [impíndž], vn. (a veces con **on** o **upon**) tropezar, chocar (con o contra); violar, infringir.

impious [impiʌs], a. impío.—**impiously** [-li], adv. impíamente.—**impiousness** [-nǐs], s. impiedad.

impish [impiş], a. travieso, endiablado.

implacability [impleikąbǐlǐtǐ], **implacableness** [impléikąblnǐs], s. implacabilidad.

implacable [-ąbl], a. implacable; inexorable.—**implacably** [-bli], adv. implacablemente.

implacental [impląséntąl], a. y s. (zool.) implacentario, (mamífero) que no tiene placenta.

implant [implǽnt], va. (im)plantar, acodar, ingerir; inculcar.

implantation [-éįşǫn], *s.* injertación, (im)plantación; inculcación.

implausible [implóziþl], *a.* poco plausible.

implead [implíd], *va.* (for.) demandar, poner pleito.—**impleader** [-œ(r)], *s.* (for.) demandante, parte actora.

implement [implįmęnt]. **I.** *s.* herramienta, utensilio; elemento, instrumento (de guerra, etc.). —*pl.* utensilios, útiles, aperos, enseres, trebejos. **II.** *va.* poner en ejecución, completar, llevar a cabo; (for.) cumplir.

implicate [implįkęįt], *va.* implicar, envolver; enredar, embrollar.—**implication** [-éişǫn], *s.* deducción, inferencia; complicación; complicidad.

implicative [-įv], *a.* deductivo, que se infiere.—**implicatively** [-lį], *adv.* por deducción o inferencia.

implicit [implíşįt], *a.* implícito, sobrentendido; absoluto, sin reserva.—**i. faith,** fe ciega.

implicitly [-lį], *adv.* implícitamente, tácitamente; sin reserva.—**implicitness** [-nįs], *s.* calidad de implícito.

implied [impláįd], *a.* implícito, sobrentendido.—**to be i.,** sobrentenderse.

impliedly [impláįįdlį], *adv.* implícitamente.

imploration [imploréįşǫn], *s.* imploración.

implore [implór], *va.* implorar, suplicar, rogar.—**imploringly** [-įŋlį], *adv.* suplicantemente, con súplicas.

implosive [implóŭsįv]. **I.** *a.* (fon.) implosivo. **II.** *s.* implosiva.

impluvium [implúvįʌm], *s.* impluvio, estanque en el atrio de las casas romanas.

imply [impláį], *va.* querer decir; significar, denotar, argüir, entrañar, importar.

impolicy [impálįşį], *s.* impolítica, inoportunidad.

impolite [impoláįt], *a.* descortés, incivil, grosero.—**impoliteness** [-nįs], *s.* descortesía, desatención; falta de urbanidad.

impolitic [impálįtįk], *a.* imprudente, indiscreto; impolítico.

imponderability [impándœraþílįtį], *s.* imponderabilidad.—**imponderable** [-aþl]. **I.** *a.* imponderable, impesable. **II.** *s.* (gen. *pl.*) cosas, elementos, etc., imponderables.

imporosity [imporásįtį], *s.* falta de porosidad.

imporous [impórʌs], *a.* no poroso.

import [impórt]. **I.** *va.* (com.) importar; denotar, significar; importar, interesar. **II.** *vn.* convenir, importar, tener importancia.

import [ímport], *s.* sentido, significación; importancia, valor; (com.) importación.—*pl.* artículos importados.—**i. duty,** derechos de entrada o de importación.

importable [impórtaþl], *a.* (com.) importable.

importance [impórtans], *s.* importancia; consecuencia, alcance; consideración, fuste, tomo, peso, momento, cuantía; vanidad, presunción; fachenda.—**important** [-ant], *a.* importante; presuntuoso, fachendero.—**importantly** [-lį], *adv.* importantemente; engreídamente.

importation [-éįşǫn], *s.* (com.) importación, entrada; artículo importado.

importer [impórtœ(r)], *s.* importador.

importunate [impórchųnįt], *a.* importuno, pesado, insistente.—**importunately** [-lį], *adv.* importuna(da)mente. — **importunateness** [-nįs], *s.* importunidad.

importune [impǫrtjún], *va.* y *vn.* importunar, instar, porfiar, machacar.

importuner [-œ(r)], *s.* importunador.

importunity [-įtį], *s.* importunidad, porfía, (fam.) machaquería, importunación.

imposable [impóŭzaþl], *a.* imponible.

impose [impóŭz], *va.* imponer; hacer pasar como bueno; obligar a aceptar; (igl.) imponer las manos al obispo; (impr.) imponer.—**to i. on,** o **upon,** abusar de; engañar, embaucar.

imposer [-œ(r)], *s.* imponedor.

imposing [-įŋ], *a.* imponente; solemne, grandioso,

tremendo.—**i. stone,** o **table,** (impr.) piedra, o mesa, de imponer; platina.

imposition [impozíşǫn], *s.* imposición; impuesto, carga, tributo, gabela; abuso; impostura, engaño; (impr.) imposición.—**i. of hands,** (igl.) imposición de manos.

impossibility [impasįþílįtį], *s.* imposibilidad.

impossible [impásįþl], *a.* imposible; irrealizable, impracticable.—**it seems i.,** parece mentira.—**impossibly** [-blį], *adv.* imposiblemente.

impost [impoŭst], *s.* impuesto, tributo, gabela; (arq.) imposta.

impostor [impástǫ(r)], *s.* impostor, embaucador.

imposture [impáschȗ(r)], *s.* impostura.

impotence, impotency [ímpotęns, -į], *s.* impotencia; agenesia.—**impotent** [-ęnt], *a.* impotente.—**impotently** [-lį], *adv.* impotentemente.

impound [impáųnd], *va.* encerrar, acorralar; recoger (agua) en un depósito; represar, embalsar, rebalsar (aguas); aprisionar; (for.) depositar.—**impounding** [-įŋ], *s.* represa, embalse.

impoverish [impávœrįş], *va.* empobrecer, depauperar; menguar, deteriorar.—**impoverishment** [-męnt], *s.* empobrecimiento, depauperación.

impracticability [impráektįkáþílįtį], **impracticableness** [-aþlnįs], *s.* impracticabilidad.—**impracticable** [-aþl], *a.* impracticable; intransitable; intratable, irrazonable, terco.

imprecate [ímprįkęįt], *va.* imprecar, maldecir.

imprecation [-kéįşǫn], *s.* imprecación.

imprecatory [ímprįkątǫrį], *a.* imprecatorio.

impregnable [imprégnąþl], *a.* inexpugnable; impregnable.—**impregnably** [-blį], *adv.* inexpugnablemente.

impregnate [imprégnęįt]. **I.** *va.* empreñar, fecundizar; impregnar; imbuir. **II.** *a.* impregnado; preñada, embarazada.

impregnation [-éįşǫn], *s.* fecundación; impregnación; fertilización; infusión.

impresario [imprįsárjoų], *s.* (teat.) empresario.

imprescriptible [imprįskríptįþl], *a.* imprescriptible.

impress [imprés], *va.* imprimir, grabar, estampar; marcar; fijar; impresionar; inculcar; influir; (mil.) reclutar, enganchar; expropiar.

impress [ímpres], *s.* impresión, señal, *f.*, huella; empresa, divisa, lema, *m.*; (mil.) leva, enganche; expropiación.

impressibility [-íþílįtį], *s.* facilidad de impresionarse.—**impressible** [imprésįþl], *a.* impresionable; que se puede estampar.

impression [impréşǫn], *s.* impresión, estampa, sigilación; marca, señal, *f.*; huella; sello, estampado; impresión producida en el ánimo; idea o recuerdo vago; (impr.) impresión, edición.

impressionable [-aþl], *a.* impresionable, susceptible.

impressional [-al], *a.* referente a la impresión.

impression(al)ist [-(al)įst], *s.* (b. a.) impresionista.—**impressionism** [-izm], *s.* (b. a.) impresionismo.—**impressionistic** [-įstįk], *a.* (b. a.) impresionista.

impressive [imprésįv], *a.* impresionante, que causa impresión; solemne, grandioso, imponente.—**impressively** [-lį], *adv.* de modo poderoso o eficaz; imponentemente.—**impressiveness** [-nįs], *s.* calidad de causar impresión; grandiosidad.

impressment [imprésmęnt], *s.* expropiación; (mil.) leva, enganche; requisición, requisa.

imprest [ímprest], *s.* anticipo que hace el Erario.

imprimatur [imprįméįtœ(r)], *s.* imprimátur.

imprimis [impráįmįs], *adv.* en primer lugar.

imprint [imprínt], *va.* imprimir, estampar; fijar, grabar en el ánimo, etc.

imprint [ímprint], *s.* impresión, marca, señal, *f.*, huella; (impr.) pie (*m.*) de imprenta.

imprison [imprízɔn], va. encarcelar, poner preso, aprisionar, prender, arrestar.—**imprisonment** [-mɛnt], s. prisión, encarcelación, arresto, reclusión; carcelería.

improbability [imprábạbịlịtị], s. improbabilidad, inverosimilitud.—**improbable** [-bl], a. improbable, inverosímil, difícil.—**improbably** [-blị], adv. improbablemente.

improbity [impróụbịtị], s. improbidad.

impromptu [imprámptjụ]. I. a. impremeditado, improvisado. II. adv. de repente, en el acto. III. s. repente, ímpetu; improvisación.

improper [imprápœ(r)], a. impropio; indecoroso; incorrecto.—**i. fraction**, (mat.) quebrado impropio.—**improperly** [-lị], adv. impropiamente.

impropriate [impróụprịeịt]. I. va. apropiarse; expropiar o secularizar bienes eclesiásticos. II. a. secularizado.—**impropriation** [-éịṣɔn], s. secularización de bienes eclesiásticos.

impropriety [impropráịetị], s. impropiedad, incongruencia, indecoro.

improvability [imprúvạbịlịtị], **improvableness** [-blnịs], s. calidad de mejorable.—**improvable** [-bl], a. mejorable; laborable, cultivable.—**improvably** [-blị], adv. mejorablemente.

improve [imprúv]. I. va. mejorar; enmendar; perfeccionar, desarrollar, fomentar; utilizar; hacer más útil o valioso; (agr.) sanear, beneficiar, cultivar; (com.) subir, estar en alza.—**to i. the opportunity**, aprovecharse de la oportunidad, hacer su agosto. II. vn. mejorarse; mejorar; adelantar, progresar.—**to i. on**, o **upon**, mejorar, hacer mejor.

improvement [-mɛnt], s. mejora; mejoramiento; adelanto, progreso; alivio, mejoría; adición o cambio valioso; fomento; urbanización; (agr.) saneamiento, cultivo.—**i. on**, progreso sobre o con respecto a.

improver [-œ(r)], s. adelantador, mejorador, beneficiador; aprendiz(a), meritorio.

improvidence [imprávịdɛns], s. improvidencia, descuido, imprevisión, desprevención.—**improvident** [-ɛnt], a. impróvido.—**improvidently** [-lị], adv. impróvidamente.

improvisation [imprạvịzéịṣɔn], s. improvisación.—**improvise** [improváịz], va. improvisar.—**improviser** [-œ(r)], s. improvisador, repentista.

imprudence [imprúdɛns], s. imprudencia, indiscreción.—**imprudent** [-ɛnt], a. imprudente.—**imprudently** [-lị], adv. imprudentemente.

impudence [ímpịụdɛns], s. impudencia, descaro, desfachatez, atrevimiento; impudicia.—**impudent** [-ɛnt], a. impudente, descarado; impúdico.—**impudently** [-lị], adv. descaradamente, impudentemente; impúdicamente.

impudicity [impịụdịsịtị], s. impudi(ci)cia.

impugn [impjún], va. impugnar, refutar; (for.) redargüir.—**impugnable** [-abl], a. impugnable.—**impugnation** [impʌgnéịṣɔn], s. impugnación.—**impugner** [impjúnœ(r)], s. impugnador.—**impugnment** [-mɛnt], s. impugnación.

impulse [ímpʌls], s. impulso, ímpetu; estímulo, instigación, motivo; arranque, corazonada; pronto, repente.—**i. excitation**, (rad.) excitación impulsiva.

impulsion [impʌlṣɔn], s. impulsión, impulso.

impulsive [-sịv], a. impulsivo.—**impulsively** [-lị], adv. impulsivamente.

impunity [impịúnịtị], s. impunidad.

impure [impịúr], a. impuro; sórdido; impúdico, deshonesto; manchado por el pecado; incorrecto (lenguaje).—**impurely** [-lị], adv. impuramente.—**impureness** [-nịs], **impurity** [-ịtị], s. impureza; adulteración; torpeza, deshonestidad.

imputable [impịútạbl], a. imputable, achacable.

imputability [-bịlịtị], **imputableness** [-nịs], s. imputabilidad.

imputation [-éịṣɔn], s. imputación, acusación;

reconvención, censura.—**imputative** [impịútạtịv], a. imputativo, imputador.

impute [impịút], va. imputar, achacar, atribuir.

imputer [-œ(r)], s. imputador.

in [in]. I. prep. en, de, por, con, durante, mientras, dentro de, de aquí a (según que denote situación, división, estado, modo, disposición, duración, causa, objeto, fin, etc.), v. gr.: he is in Paris, está en París; the best hotel in Paris, el mejor hotel de París; in the morning, por la mañana; in writing, por escrito; in fun, in jest, en broma, por broma; in deference, por deferencia; in ink, con tinta; in anger, con ira; in his sleep, durante el sueño, cuando está dormido; he will come in a week, vendrá de aquí a una semana.—**i. as much as**, o **inasmuch as**, en cuanto, hasta donde; tanto como; como quiera que; puesto que, visto que, por cuanto, porque, a causa de que.—**i. so far as**, o **insofar as**, en cuanto (a), en lo que, hasta donde.—**i. that**, en que; por cuanto. II. adv. dentro, adentro; en casa, en su oficina, etc.; hacia adentro; en el poder; en su turno.—**i.-and-i.**, de una misma casta.—**i. here, there**, etc. aquí dentro, allí dentro, etc.—**i.-and-out**, que sale y entra alternativamente; a veces bueno y a veces malo; (mec.) de vaivén; (alb.) de sogas y tizones alternados verticalmente.—**to be i.**, haber entrado o llegado; estar (en casa, la oficina, etc.).—**to be i. for**, estar expuesto a, echarse a cuestas, estar metido en (trabajos, etc.).—**to be i. with**, gozar del favor de. III. s. rincón, recodo; miembro (de un partido) a quien se le ha dado empleo público; persona que está adentro; jugador del lado que lleva el bat.—**ins and outs**, interioridades, pormenores minuciosos. IV. a. de adentro; interior, interno; que está en el poder; que está en su turno.

inability [inạbịlịtị], s. inhabilidad, incapacidad, ineptitud; impotencia.

inaccessibility [inæksésịbịlịtị], s. inaccesibilidad.—**inaccessible** [-bl], a. inaccesible, inabordable.—**inaccessibly** [-blị], adv. inaccesiblemente.

inaccuracy [inækyụrạsị], s. inexactitud, incorrección, error.—**inaccurate** [-rịt], a. inexacto, erróneo.—**inaccurately** [-lị], adv. incorrectamente; inexactamente.

inaction [inækṣɔn], s. inacción.

inactive [inæktịv], a. inactivo, inerte.—**inactively** [-lị], adv. inactivamente.—**inactivity** [-tívịtị], s. inactividad, ociosidad.

inadequacy [inædịkwịsị], s. insuficiencia; falta de adecuación.—**inadequate** [-kwịt], a. inadecuado.—**inadequately** [-lị], adv. inadecuadamente.—**inadequateness** [-nịs], s. imperfección, falta de adecuación.

inadmissible [inædmísịbl], a. inadmisible.

inadvertence, inadvertency [inædvértɛns, -ị], s. inadvertencia.—**inadvertent** [-ɛnt], a. inadvertido, accidental; negligente, descuidado.—**inadvertently** [-lị], adv. inadvertidamente.

inadvisable [inædváịzạbl], a. inconveniente, poco aconsejable o prudente.

inalienable [inéịlịenạbl], a. inalienable, inajenable.—**inalienably** [-blị], adv. inalienablemente.

inalterability [inóltœrạbịlịtị], s. inalterabilidad.

inalterable [-bl], a. inalterable.

inamorata [inæmơrátạ], s. mujer amada; mujer enamorada.

inane [inéịn]. I. a. sandio, mentecato; inane, vacío, insubstancial. II. s. vacío; espacio infinito.

inanimate [inǽnịmịt], a. inanimado; exánime.

inanimateness [-nịs], **inanimation** [-éịṣɔn], s. inanimación, falta de animación, de vida.

inanition [inạníṣɔn], s. inanición; vaciedad.

inanity [inǽnịtị], s. inanidad, inania; inanición; insubstancialidad, sandez, mentecatada.

inappeasable [inapízabl], *a.* implacable.
inappetence, -cy [inápitens, -i], *s.* inapetencia.
inapplicability [inaplikabíliti], *s.* falta de aplicabilidad.
inapplicable [-bl], *a.* inaplicable.
inapposite [inapozit], *a.* inoportuno; inaplicable.
inappreciable [inaprísiabl], *a.* inapreciable, inestimable.
inapprehensible [inaprihénsibl], *a.* ininteligible, incomprensible.
inapproachable [inapróuchabl], *a.* inaccesible, inasequible.
inappropriate [inapróuprijt], *a.* inadecuado, impropio, inapropiado.—**inappropriately** [-li], *adv.* impropiamente, fuera del caso.—**inappropriateness** [-nis], *s.* impropiedad, incorrección.
inaptitude [ináptitjud], *s.* ineptitud.
inarable [inárabl], *a.* incultivable.
inarch [inárch], *va.* injertar por aproximación.
inarticulate [inartíkyulit], *a.* inarticulado.—**inarticulately** [-li], *adv.* de modo inarticulado.—**inarticulateness** [-nis], *s.* calidad de inarticulado.
inartificial [inartifísal], *a.* natural, simple, sencillo, sin artificio.
inasmuch as [inazmách az] = IN AS MUCH AS.
inattention [inaténson], *s.* desatención, distracción, inadvertencia.—**inattentive** [-tiv], *a.* desatento.—**inattentively** [-li], *adv.* descuidadamente, sin atención.
inaudibility [inódibíliti], **inaudibleness** [-blnis], *s.* calidad de inaudible.
inaudible [-bl], *a.* inaudible.
inaugural [inógjural], *a.* inaugural.
inaugurate [-eit], *va.* inaugurar; investir, instalar.—**inauguration** [-éison], *s.* inauguración, instalación, estreno; toma de posesión.
inauspicious [inospísas], *a.* impropicio, desfavorable, infeliz.—**inauspiciously** [-li], *adv.* desgraciadamente, bajo malos auspicios.—**inauspiciousness** [-nis], *s.* malos auspicios.
inbeing [ínbiin], *s.* inherencia, inseparabilidad.
inboard [ínbord], *a.* y *adv.* (mar.) interior, dentro del casco; (mec.) hacia dentro.
inborn [ínborn], *a.* innato, ingénito, connatural.
inbound [ínbaund], *a.* de entrada; de venida, que viene.
inbreathe [inbríð], *va.* inspirar; infundir.
inbred [ínbred], *a.* ínsito, innato; criado o nacido de padres de una misma raza o de razas muy semejantes.
inbreed [ínbríd], *va.* criar o producir sin mezcla de razas, o dentro de una misma raza.
Inca [ínka], **Incan** [-n]. I. *s.* inca, *m.*; orejón. II. *a.* incáico, incásico.—**Incaic** [inkéiik], *a.* = INCA(N).
incage [inkéidž], *va.* enjaular, encerrar.
incalculable [inkélkjulabl], *a.* incalculable.
incandesce [inkandés], *va.* y *vn.* encandecer(se), poner(se) incandescente.
incandescence, incandescency [-ens, -i], *s.* incandescencia.
incandescent [-ent], *a.* incandescente, candente.—**i. lamp,** lámpara incandescente.
incantation [inkantéison], *s.* encantación, conjuro, sortilegio.
incantatory [inkántatori], *a.* mágico.
incapability [inkéipabíliti], o **incapableness** [-blnis], *s.* incapacidad.
incapable [-bl], *a.* incapaz.
incapacitate [inkapásiteit], *va.* incapacitar, inhabilitar, imposibilitar.
incapacitation [-téison], *s.* inhabilitación.
incapacity [-ti], *s.* incapacidad.
incarcerate [inkársereit], *va.* encarcelar.
incarceration [-éison], *s.* encarcelación, encarcelamiento, prisión; (cir.) constricción o retención (de una hernia).
incardinate [inkárdineit], *va.* (igl.) incardinar; instalar, nombrar o ascender a cardenal.
incarnadine [inkárnadin]. I. *va.* encarnar, dar

color de carne. II. *s.* y *a.* (color) encarnadino, color de carne.
incarnant [inkárnant], *a.* y *s.* (cir.) encarnativo.
incarnate [inkárneit]. I. *va.* encarnar, tomar carne. II. [inkárnit], *a.* encarnado; personificado.
incarnation [-éison], *s.* encarnación; (cir.) encarnación, encarnamiento.
incase [inkéis], *va.* encajar, embutir, meter; encerrar, encajonar.
incasement [-ment], *s.* acción de encajar, meter o encerrar; introducción; cubierta, caja.
incautious [inkósas], *a.* incauto.—**incautiously** [-li], *adv.* incautamente.—**incautiousness** [-nis], *s.* falta de cautela, descuido.
incavation [inkavéison], *s.* ahuecamiento; depresión; hueco.
incendiarism [inséndiarizm], *s.* incendio malicioso; vicio de incendiar.
incendiary [inséndieri], *a.* y *s.* incendiario.
incense [ínsens], *s.* incienso.—**i. bearing,** turífero.
incense [inséns], *va.* exasperar, irritar, encolerizar; [ínsens] (igl.) incensar.
incensement [insénsment], *s.* ira, furia.
incensory [insénsori], *s.* incensario.
incentive [inséntiv]. I. *s.* incentivo, estímulo, aliciente. II. *a.* incitativo.
inception [insépson], *s.* principio, comienzo.
inceptive [-tiv], *a.* incipiente, incoativo.
inceptor [-to(r)], *s.* (Ingl.) examinando para recibir el grado de maestro o doctor en artes.
incertitude [insértitjud], *s.* incertidumbre.
incessant [insésant], *a.* incesante.
incessantly [-li], *adv.* incesantemente.
incest [ínsest], *s.* incesto.
incestuous [inséschuas], *a.* incestuoso.
incestuously [-li], *adv.* incestuosamente.
inch [inch]. I. *s.* pulgada (2.54 centímetros); pizca.—**i. by i.,** palmo a palmo, pulgada por pulgada.—**i. of water** = WATER INCH.—**i.-pound,** (mec.) pulgada-libra, unidad de momento y de energía cuando las de fuerza y longitud son la libra y la pulgada respectivamente.—**by inches,** paso a paso, con gran lentitud, (fam.) a poquitos.—**every i.,** cabal, en todo respecto (cambiando un poco el giro), *v. gr.: he is every inch a man,* es todo un hombre.—**within an i. of,** a dos dedos de, al (seguido de infinitivo). II. *a.* de una pulgada.—**i. board,** tablón de a pulgada. III. *va.* marcar por pulgadas. IV. *vn.* (con **along**) avanzar poquito a poquito.
inched [-t], *a.* dividido en pulgadas.
inchmeal [-mil], *adv.* (con **by**) poco a poco.
inchoate [inkóueit], *a.* principiado, incoado.
inchoately [-li], *adv.* en el primer grado.
inchoation [inkoéison], *s.* incoación, principio.
inchoative [inkóuativ], *a.* incipiente, incoativo.
inchworm [ínchwœrm], *s.* = MEASURING WORM.
incidence [ínsidens], *s.* incidencia; gabela, gravamen.—**i. wires,** (aer.) = STAGGER WIRES.
incident [-ent]. I. *a.* incidente; probable, acontecedero; casual, fortuito; concomitante. II. *s.* incidente; casualidad; acontecimiento, acaecimiento, peripecia, episodio, lance.
incidental [insidéntal]. I. *a.* incidental, incidente, contingente; concomitante.—**i. to,** que acompaña, anejo a, inherente a. II. *s. pl.* circunstancias imprevistas; imprevistos (gastos).
incidentally [-li], *adv.* incidentemente, incidentalmente; entre paréntesis.
incinerate [insínereit], *va.* incinerar.
incineration [-éison], *s.* incineración, cremación.
incinerator [-to(r)], *s.* incinerador.
incipience, incipiency [insípiens, -i], *s.* principio.
incipient [-ent], *a.* incipiente.—**incipiently** [-li], *adv.* en los comienzos.
incise [insáiz], *va.* tallar, grabar; cortar.

incised [-d], *a.* inciso, cortado; (bot., zool.) irregularmente denticular o serrado.

incision [insíẓon], *s.* incisión; cisura, cortadura; muesca; denticulación.

incisive [insáisiv], *a.* incisivo; mordaz; agudo.

incisor [insáizo(r)], *a.* y *s.* (diente) incisivo.

incisory [insáisori], *a.* (cir.) incisorio.

incitant [insáitant]. I. *a.* provocativo, incitante, incitativo. II. *s.* estímulo, incentivo.

incitation [insitéison], *s.* incitación, instigación.

incite [insáit], *va.* incitar, instigar.—**incitement** [-ment], *s.* incitación, instigación; estímulo, incentivo, aliciente.—**inciter** [-œ(r)], *s.* incitador, instigador.—**inciting** [-iŋ], *a.* estimulante o incitante.—**incitingly** [-li], *adv.* incitantemente.

incivility [insiviliti], *s.* incivilidad, descortesía.

inclemency [inklémensi], *s.* inclemencia, intemperie; crueldad, severidad.

inclement [-ent], *a.* inclemente, duro; riguroso, borrascoso.

inclinable [inkláinabl], *a.* favorable, inclinado a.

inclination [inklinéison], *s.* inclinación (de dos líneas, de un terreno); pendiente, *f.*, declive; inclinación, propensión; reverencia, venia; (fís.) inclinación (de la brújula).

inclinatory [inkláinatori], *a.* inclinado, ladeado.

incline [inkláin]. I. *va.* inclinar, ladear; doblar, doblegar. II. *vn.* inclinarse, ladearse, bajar, hacer pendiente; hacer reverencia o acatamiento; propender, tender a, tirar a (un color); sentir inclinación o predilección. III. [ínklain], *s.* declivio, declive, pendiente, *f.*; rampa.

inclined [inkláind], *a.* inclinado, oblicuo; propenso, proclive, afecto (a).—**i. plane**, plano inclinado.

inclinometer [inklinámetœ(r)], *s.* (aer.) inclinómetro.

inclose, inclosure = ENCLOSE, ENCLOSURE.

include [inklúd], *va.* incluir, encerrar; comprender, abarcar, abrazar, contener.

included [-id], *a.* incluído, comprendido; inclusive, incluso; (geom.) comprendido (ángulo).

including [-iŋ], *a.* inclus(iv)o, incluyente.

inclusion [inklúẓon], *s.* inclusión; contenido; (min.) partícula extraña, intrusión.

inclusive [inklúsiv], *a.* inclusivo.

inclusively [-li], *adv.* inclusivamente, inclusive.

incognito [inkágnitou], *adv.*, *a.* y *s.* incógnito; de incógnito.

incoherence, incoherency [inkohrens, -i], *s.* incoherencia, inconexión.—**incoherent** [-ent], *a.* incoherente, inconexo.—**incoherently** [-li], *adv.* incoherente o inconexamente, sin conexión.

incombustibility [inkombástibiliti], **incombustibleness** [-blnis], *s.* incombustibilidad.

incombustible [-bl], *a.* incombustible.

income [ínkʌm], *s.* renta, entrada, ingreso, rédito, censo; alimento asimilado.—**i. tax**, impuesto sobre rentas, impuesto de ingresos.—**i. tax return**, declaración del impuesto sobre la renta.

incomer [-œ(r)], *s.* recién llegado; intruso.

incoming [-iŋ]. I. *a.* entrante, que está por llegar. II. *s.* llegada, arribo, entrada.

incommensurability [inkoménsurabiliti], *s.* inconmensurabilidad. — **incommensurable** [-rabl], *a.* inconmensurable.

incommensurate [-rit], *a.* desproporcionado; inadecuado, insuficiente.—**incommensurately** [-li], *adv.* desproporcionadamente.

incommode [inkomóud], *va.* incomodar, desacomodar, molestar.

incommodious [-iʌs], *a.* incómodo, inconveniente, molesto.—**incommodiously** [-li], *adv.* incómodamente.—**incommodiousness** [-nis], **incommodity** [inkomáditi], *s.* incomodidad, inconveniencia, molestia.

incommunicability [inkomiúnikabiliti], **incommunicableness** [-blnis], *s.* incomunicabilidad.—**incommunicable** [-bl], *a.* incomunicable; indecible.—**incommunicably** [-bli], *adv.* incomunicadamente; sin comunicación.

incommunicado [-kádou], *s.* y *a.* incomunicado.

incommunicative [inkomiúnikeitiv], *a.* insociable, reservado.—**incommunicativeness** [-nis], *s.* insociabilidad, carácter intratable, reserva.

incommutability [inkomiútabiliti], *s.* inconmutabilidad.—**incommutable** [-bl], *a.* inconmutable.—**incommutably** [-bli], *adv.* inconmutablemente.

incomparable [inkámparabl], *a.* incomparable, sin igual.—**incomparableness** [-nis], *s.* excelencia incomparable.—**incomparably** [-bli], *adv.* incomparablemente.

incompatibility [inkompǽtibiliti], *s.* incompatibilidad.—**incompatible** [-bl], *a.* incompatible.—**incompatibly** [-bli], *adv.* incompatiblemente.

incompetence, -cy [inkámpitens, -i], *s.* incompetencia, incapacidad, inhabilidad, ineptitud, inepcia.—**incompetent** [-ent], *a.* incompetente, incapaz, inepto; (for.) inadmisible.—**incompetently** [-li], *adv.* incompetentemente.

incomplete [inkomplít], *a.* incompleto, imperfecto, descabal, parcial, trunco.—**incompletely** [-li], *adv.* incompletamente.—**incompleteness** [-nis], *s.* estado incompleto, calidad de incompleto.

incomplex [inkompléks], *a.* incomplejo.

incompliance [inkompláians], *s.* falta de condescendencia, indocilidad, desobediencia; inflexibilidad; terquedad.

incomprehensibility [inkamprihénsibiliti], **incomprehensibleness** [-blnis], *s.* incomprensibilidad.—**incomprehensible** [-bl], *a.* incomprensible.—**incomprehensibly** [-bli], *adv.* incomprensiblemente. — **incomprehension** [-hénson], *s.* incomprensión, falta de comprensión.

incomprehensive [-hénsiv], *a.* incomprensivo, limitado, de poco alcance.—**incomprehensiveness** [-nis], *s.* limitación, poco alcance.

incompressibility [inkomprésibiliti], *s.* incompresibilidad.—**incompressible** [-bl], *a.* incompresible, incomprimible.

inconceivable [inkonsívabl], *a.* inconcebible, inimaginable; increíble.—**inconceivability** [-biliti], **inconceivableness** [-blnis], *s.* inconcebibilidad.—**inconceivably** [-bli], *adv.* incomprensible o inconcebiblemente.

inconclusive [inkonklúsiv], *a.* inconcluyente, que no convence; inconcluso; indeciso.—**inconclusively** [-li], *adv.* de un modo que no convence; indecisamente; inconclusamente.—**inconclusiveness** [-nis], *s.* calidad de indeciso, inconcluso o inconcluyente.

incongruence, incongruity [inkáŋgruens, -grúiti], *s.* incongruencia, inconexión, discordancia, anomalía.—**incongruent** [-ent], **incongruous** [-ʌs], *a.* incongruente, incongruo, discordante, mal adaptado; inconsecuente; incoherente; (alg.) incongruente; (geom.) insuperponible.—**incongruently**, **incongruously** [-li], *adv.* discordantemente, inconexamente, contradictoriamente, inapropiadamente. —**incongruousness** [-nis], *s.* calidad de incongruente, discordante, inapropiado, anómalo, etc.

inconsequence [inkánsikwens], *s.* inconsecuencia.—**inconsequent** [-kwent], *a.* inconsecuente, ilógico.—**inconsequential** [-kwénšal], *a.* inconsecuente, inconexo; de poca importancia.

inconsiderable [inkonsídœrabl], *a.* insignificante, despreciable.—**inconsiderableness** [-nis], *s.* insignificancia.

inconsiderate [inkonsídœrit], *a.* irreflexivo; desconsiderado, malmirado; desatento.—**inconsiderately** [-li], *adv.* inconsideradamente; irreflexivamente.—**inconsiderateness** [-nis], **inconsideration** [-éišon], *s.* falta de consideración.

inconsistence, inconsistency [inkǫnsístǝns, -i], s. incompatibilidad, contradicción, inconsecuencia.—inconsistent [-ǝnt], a. incompatible, contradictorio, inconsecuente.—inconsistently [-li], adv. inconsecuentemente, contradictoriamente.

inconsolable [inkǫnsóulǝbl], a. inconsolable.

inconstancy [inkánstǝnsi], s. inconstancia.—inconstant [-ǝnt], a. inconstante, vario.—inconstantly [-li], adv. inconstantemente, volublemente.

inconsumable [inkǫnsiúmǝbl], a. inconsumible.

incontestable [inkǫntéstǝbl], a. incontestable, indisputable, inconcuso.

incontestably [-bli], adv. incontestablemente.

incontinence, incontinency [inkántinǝns, -i], s. incontinencia; lascivia; (med.) incontinencia.

incontinent [-ǝnt], a. incontinente, desenfrenado; incesante; (med.) incontinente; (raro) inmediato.—incontinently [-li], adv. incontinentemente; (ant.) inmediatamente, incontinenti.

incontrollable [inkǫntróulǝbl], a. ingobernable, irrefrenable.—incontrollably [-bli], adv. ingobernablemente, sin restricción.

incontrovertible [inkantrǫvǝ́rtibl], a. incontrovertible.—incontrovertibly [-bli], adv. indisputablemente.

inconvenience, inconveniency [inkǫnvíniǝns, -i]. I. s. inconveniencia, inconveniente; incomodidad, molestia. II. va. incomodar, estorbar, molestar.—inconvenient [-ǝnt], a. incómodo, molesto, inconveniente, inoportuno.—inconveniently [-li], adv. incómodo o molestamente.

inconvertible [inkǫnvǝ́rtibl], a. inconvertible.

inconvincible [inkǫnvínsibl], a. inconvencible, incontrastable.

incorporate [inkórpǫreit]. I. va. dar cuerpo o forma material; incorporar; formar corporación, gremio, etc.; comprender, encerrar. II. vn. incorporarse, unirse, asociarse. III. [-rit], a. incorporado; conmisto; incorporal, inmaterial; no constituído en corporación o asociación.

incorporation [-réiṣǫn], s. incorporación; organización, asociación.

incorporeal [inkǫrpóriǝl], a. incorporal, incorpóreo.—incorporeally [-i], adv. incorporalmente.

incorporeity [inkǫrpǫríiti], s. incorporeidad.

incorrect [inkǫrékt], a. incorrecto; falso, inexacto, erróneo; inmoral.—incorrectly [-li], adv. incorrectamente; inexactamente.—incorrectness [-nis], s. inexactitud; incorrección; impropiedad.

incorrigible [inkárid̦ẓibl], a. incorregible, empecatado.—incorrigibility [-bíliti], incorrigibleness [-nis], s. incorregibilidad.—incorrigibly [-bli], adv. incorregiblemente.

incorrupt [inkǫrápt], a. incorrupto; íntegro, probo.—incorruptibility [-ibíliti], s. incorruptibilidad.—incorruptible [-ibl], a. incorruptible, probo.—incorruption [-ṣǫn], s. incorruptness [-nis], s. incorrupción.

incrassate [inkráseit]. I. va. espesar, encrasar, incrasar. II. vn. espesarse. III. a. encrasado.

incrassation [-éiṣǫn], s. encrasación.

incrassative [-iv], a. incrasante.

increasable [inkrísǝbl], a. aumentable.

increase [inkrís], va. y vn. aumentar(se); multiplicar(se); acrecentar(se); incrementar; crecer, subir, arreciar (en intensidad, etc.).

increase [ínkris], s. aumento, incremento, crecimiento, acrecentamiento; ganancia, interés; multiplicación; progenie; productos agrícolas; (tecn.) adaptador, tubo cónico de unión.

increaser [inkrísœ(r)], s. lo que sirve para aumentar; (tecn.) refuerzo; adaptador, tubo cónico de unión.

increasing [-iŋ], a. creciente, acrecentador,

aumentativo.—increasingly [-li], adv. crecientemente; con creces; cada vez más.

increate [inkriéit], a. increado.

incredibility [inkrédibíliti], incredibleness [-blnis], s. incredibilidad.—incredible [-bl], a. increíble.—incredibly [-bli], adv. increíblemente.

incredulity [inkrid̦iúliti], incredulousness [inkréd̦iulʌsnis], s. incredulidad.

incredulous [inkréd̦iulʌs], a. incrédulo.

increment [ínkrimǝnt], s. incremento, aumento, adición, crecimiento.—incrementation [-éiṣǫn], s. incrementación.

incriminate [inkrímineit], va. (a)criminar o incriminar.—incrimination [-éiṣǫn], s. (a)criminación o incriminación.

incrust(ate [inkrást(eit], va. encostrar; incrustar.—incrustation [-éiṣǫn], s. encostradura, costra, incrustación, sarro.

incubate [ínkiubeit], va. y vn. empollar, incubar; pensar, madurar.—incubation [-éiṣǫn], s. incubación, empolladura; (med.) incubación.—incubator [-ǫ(r)], s. empollador; incubadora.

incubus [ínkiubʌs], s. íncubo; carga; (med.) pesadilla, íncubo.

inculcate [inkálkeit], va. inculcar.—inculcation [-éiṣǫn], s. inculcación.—inculcator [-ǫ(r)], s. inculcador.

inculpable [inkálpǝbl], a. inculpable.—inculpableness [-nis], s. inculpabilidad.—inculpably [-bli], adv. inculpablemente.—inculpate [inkálpeit], va. inculpar, imputar culpa a, incriminar.—inculpation [-éiṣǫn], s. inculpación.—inculpatory [inkálpǝtǫri], a. que inculpa.

incumbency [inkámbǝnsi], s. posesión o goce de un empleo; duración del mismo; incumbencia.

incumbent [-ǝnt]. I. a. obligatorio; colocado sobre, apoyado en, sostenido por.—to be i. (up)on one, incumbir a uno. II. s. (igl.) beneficiado; empleado con posesión de su cargo.

incumber, incumbrance, = ENCUMBER, ENCUMBRANCE.

incunabula [inkiunǽbiulǝ], s. pl. orígenes, cuna; incunables.—incunabular [-(r)], a. incunable.

incur [inkǝ́r], va. incurrir (en); atraerse.—to i. a debt, contraer una deuda.

incurability [inkiurǝbíliti], incurableness [-blnis], s. incurabilidad.—incurable [-bl]. I. a. incurable, insanable, irremediable. II. s. incurable.—incurably [-bli], adv. incurablemente.

incuriosity [inkiuriásiti], s. incuria, indiferencia.—incurious [inkiúriʌs], a. indiferente; incurioso, descuidado.—incuriously [-li], adv. sin curiosidad; descuidadamente.—incuriousness [-nis], s. falta de curiosidad o interés.

incursion [inkǝ́rṣǫn], s. incursión, correría.

incurvate [inkǝ́rveit], incurve [inkǝ́rv]. I. va. encorvar, doblar, torcer. II. a. encorvado, torcido.—incurvation [-éiṣǫn], s. encorvadura, curvatura; genuflexión.

incus [ínkʌs], s. (anat.) yunque (uno de los huesecillos del oído).

incuse [inkiúz]. I. a. incuso. II. s. medalla incusa, figura incusa. III. va. estampar golpeando.

indebted [indétid], a. adeudado, endeudado o en deuda; (fam.) entrampado; obligado, reconocido.—indebtedness [-nis], s. adeudo; deuda, pasivo; obligación.—indebtment [indétmǝnt], s. adeudo.

indecency [indíṣǝnsi], s. indecencia.—indecent [-ǝnt], a. indecente, indecoroso.—indecently [-li], adv. indecentemente, indecorosamente.

indecision [indiṣíẓǫn], s. indecisión, irresolución.—indecisive [indiṣáisiv], a. inciso, irresoluto.—indecisiveness [-nis], s. indecisión, irresolución.

indeclinable [indiklǽinǝbl], a. indeclinable.

indeclinably [-bli], adv. sin declinación.

indecorous [indékǫrʌs], a. indecoroso.—indec-

orously [-li], adv. indecorosamente.—**indecorousness** [-njs], **indecorum** [indikórʌm], s. indecoro, indecencia.

indeed [indíd], adv. verdaderamente, realmente, de veras, a la verdad, por cierto, sí tal, ya lo creo, claro está.—**i.?** ¿de veras? ¿es posible?—**no i.**, de ninguna manera; ¡quia!

indefatigability, indefatigableness [indifǽtigəbjliti, -blnjs], s. calidad de infatigable o incansable.—**indefatigable** [-bl], a. incansable.—**indefatigably** [-bli], adv. incansablemente.

indefeasibility [indifízibjliti], s. irrevocabilidad.—**indefeasible** [-bl], a. (for.) inabrogable, irrevocable.

indefectibility [indiféktibjliti], s. indefectibilidad.—**indefectible** [-bl], a. indefectible.—**indefectibly** [-bli], adv. indefectiblemente.

indefensible [indifénsibl], a. indefendible, insostenible.

indefensive [-siv], a. indefenso.

indefinable [indifáinabl], a. indefinible.

indefinite [indéfinit], a. indefinido, vago.—**i. article**, (gram.) artículo genérico, indefinido o indeterminado.—**indefinitely** [-li], adv. indefinidamente.—**indefiniteness** [-njs], s. calidad de indefinido.

indehiscence [indihísens], s. (bot.) indehiscencia.

indehiscent [-ent], a. (bot.) indehiscente.

indeliberate [indilíbərit], a. indeliberado, impremeditado.

indelibility [indélibiliti], s. calidad de indeleble.—**indelible** [-bl], a. indeleble.—**indelibly** [-bli], adv. indelebemente.

indelicacy [indélikəsi], s. indelicadeza, indecoro.

indelicate [-kit], a. indecoroso, inmodesto, falto de delicadeza.

indemnification [indémnifikéișon], s. indemnización.—**indemnify** [-fai], va. indemnizar.—**indemnity** [-ti], s. indemnización, resarcimiento; indemnidad.—**i. bond**, contrafianza.

indemonstrable [indimánstrəbl], a. indemostrable.

indent [indént]. I. va. dentar, endentar, mellar; (impr.) sangrar. II. vn. mellarse. III. s. mella, diente, muesca.

indentation [-éișon], s. indentación, mella, muesca, corte, hendedura, hueco, depresión.

indented [-id], a. dentado, enmuescado, serrado; (bot.) dentellado.

indention [indénșon], s. abolladura; mella; (impr.) sangría.

indenture [indéncḥu(r)]. I. s. (for.) escritura, instrumento, contrato, carta; partida, documento. II. va. escriturar, obligar por contrato.

independence, -cy [indipéndens, -i], s. independencia; posición holgada; bienandanza.—**I. Day**, (E. U.) fiesta de la independencia (4 de julio).

independent [-ent], a. independiente; libre; acomodado, capaz de mantenerse; altivo, altanero.—**independently** [-li], adv. independientemente; por separado; altivamente.—**i. seconds watch**, reloj de segundos muertos, reloj cronográfico.

indescribable [indiskráibabl], a. indescriptible.—**indescribably** [-bli], adv. indescriptiblemente.

indestructibility [indistráktibiliti], s. indestructibilidad.—**indestructible** [-bl], a. indestructible.

indeterminable [inditérminabl], a. indeterminable.—**indeterminate** [-nit], a. indeterminado.—**indeterminately** [-li], adv. indeterminadamente.—**indeterminateness** [-njs], s. indeterminación, duda.—**indetermination** [-éișon], s. indeterminación, duda.—**indetermined** [-d], a. indeterminado, irresoluto.

indeterminism [-izm], s. (fil.) indeterminismo.—**indeterminist(ic** [-ist, -ístik], s. y a. indeterminista.

index [índeks]. I. s. índice (indicio, tabla de materias, lista, indicador, manecilla, aguja);

elenco; dedo índice; (mat. y fís.) índice.—**i. card**, tarjeta o ficha para índices o archivos.—**i. correction**, corrección para eliminar el error instrumental.—**i. error**, error instrumental, error del cero (en el teodolito, etc.); error del índice (en el sextante).—I. **Expurgatorius**, Índice expurgatorio.—**i. finger**, dedo índice.—**i. gauge**, compás de graduación.—**i. hand**, indicador, aguja.—**i. number**, (com. e. p.) índice de precio, relación entre el precio de un artículo en un tiempo dado y un precio fijo tomado por unidad o patrón.—**i. plate**, círculo graduador. II. va. poner índice a; poner en un índice; indicar.

indexer [-œ(r)], s. el que hace índice o índices.

indexical [indéksikəl], a. en forma de índice; indicativo.

India [índiȃ], s. India.—I. **ink**, tinta china.—I. **paper**, papel de China.—I. **proof**, prueba en papel de China.—I. **rubber**, caucho, goma elástica.

Indiaman [-man], s. buque que hace el comercio con la India.

Indian [índian]. I. a. indio; indo, índico; indiano; (con referencia a la América) indígena.—**berries**, cocas de Levante.—I. **clubs**, mazas de gimnasia.—I. **corn**, (bot.) maíz, m., panizo, zara.—I.-**corn meal**, mañoco.—I. **cress**, (bot.) capuchina.—I. **fig.**, tuna, higo chumbo.—I. **file**, fila india; en hilera, en desfilada.—I.-**like**, aindiado.—I. **meal**, harina de maíz.—I. **millet**, (bot.) alcandía.—I. **pink**, (bot.) clavelón de Indias.—I. **red**, almagre.—I. **shot**, o **reed**, (bot.) cañácoro.—I. **summer**, (E. U.) veranillo de San Martín. II. s. indio, indo; piel roja, m. (indio norteamericano).

Indic [índik], a. índico; indio.

indicant [índikant], a. y s. indicante.

indicate [índikeit], va. indicar, señalar, designar, significar.—**indication** [-éișon], s. indicación, indicio, señal, f.

indicative [indíkativ], a. y s. indicativo.—**i. mode** (o **mood**), (gram.) modo indicativo.—**indicatively** [-li], adv. indicativamente.

indicator [índikeito(r)], s. indicador; índice, aguja; (m. v.) indicador; (quím.) indicador.—**i. card**, o **diagram**, (m. v.) diagrama (m.) o gráfica del indicador.—**i. telegraph**, telégrafo de agujas.—**i. weighing-machine**, balanza automática.

indicatory [índikatori], a. demostrativo, indicatorio.

indices [ídisiz], s. pl. de INDEX.

indicia [indíșiȃ], s. pl. indicios, señales, f. pl.

indicial [indíșal], a. indicativo, que indica; (anat.) índice, del índice.

indict [indáit], va. (for.) acusar ante el juez; procesar, encausar, enjuiciar.—**indictable** [-abl], a. encausable, procesable, denunciable.—**indictee** [-í], s. acusado, procesado.—**indicter** [-œ(r)], s. denunciante, fiscal, acusador.

indiction [indíkșon], s. indicción.

indictment [indáitment], s. (for.) sumaria o sumario; denuncia, acusación; proces(amient)o.

indifference [indíferens], s. indiferencia; apatía, despego, tibieza; mediocridad.

indifferent [-ent], a. indiferente; apático; neutral, imparcial; pasadero, mediano.

indifferentism [-izm], s. indiferencia habitual; (teol.) indiferentismo teológico, doctrina de que las diferencias de fe no son de importancia; (fil.) doctrina de que existir en el pensamiento y existir en la realidad son una misma cosa.

indifferently [-li], adv. indiferentemente; imparcialmente; pasaderamente, medianamente.

indigence, indigency [índidžens, -i], s. indigencia, penuria, inopia.

indigenous [indídženʌs], a. indígena, nativo, natural; innato.

indigent [índidžent], a. indigente, pobre, necesitado; falto.

Para la pronunciación véase la clave al principio del libro.

indigested [indįdžéstįd], *a.* no digerido; confuso, desordenado.

indigestible [-tįbl], *a.* indigesto, indigestible.

indigestion [-chọn], *s.* indigestión.

indignant [indígnạnt], *a.* indignado.—**indignantly** [-lį], *adv.* con indignación.

indignation [-éįshọn], *s.* indignación.

indignity [indígnįtį], *s.* indignidad, ultraje o afrenta, improperio; oprobio.

indigo [indįgou], *s.* añil, índigo.—**i. blue**, azul de añil.—**i. plant**, (bot.) añil, índigo, jiguilete.

indigotin [indígọtįn], *s.* (quím.) indigotina.

indirect [indįrékt], *a.* indirecto.—**indirection** [indįrékshọn], *s.* **indirectness** [-nįs], *s.* oblicuidad, rodeo, tortuosidad; conducta torcida; efugio; indirecta.—**indirectly** [-lį], *adv.* indirectamente.

indiscernible [indįzçérnįbl], *a.* indiscernible, imperceptible.

indiscreet [indįskrít], *a.* indiscreto.

indiscreetly [-lį], *adv.* indiscretamente.

indiscrete [indįskrít], *a.* que no está separado o desunido; compacto; homogéneo.

indiscretion [indįskréshọn], *s.* indiscreción.

indiscriminate [indįskrímįnįt], *a.* que no hace distinciones; promiscuo. — **indiscriminately** [-lį], *adv.* indistintamente, promiscuamente.—**indiscriminating** [-eįtįŋ], *a.* que no distingue.—**indiscrimination** [-éįshọn], *s.* falta de distinción.—**indiscriminative** [-įtįv], *a.* que no distingue.

indispensability, **indispensableness** [indįs-pénsạbįlįtį, -blnįs], *s.* calidad de indispensable, necesidad.—**indispensable** [-bl], *a.* indispensable, imprescindible; de rigor, forzoso, preciso.—**indispensably** [-blį], *adv.* indispensablemente.

indispose [indįspóųz], *va.* indisponer.—**indisposed** [-d], *a.* indispuesto; ligeramente enfermo.

indisposition [-íshọn], *s.* indisposición, malestar, destemplanza; falta de inclinación.

indisputable [indįspįutạbl], *a.* indisputable, irrefutable, incontestable.—**indisputableness** [-nįs], *s.* indisputabilidad.—**indisputably** [-blį], *adv.* indisputablemente.

indissolubility [indįsályọbílįtį], **indissolubleness** [-blnįs], *s.* indisolubilidad.—**indissoluble** [-bl], *a.* indisoluble, insoluble; estable.—**indissolubly** [-blį], *adv.* indisolublemente.

indistinct [indįstíŋkt], *a.* indistinto, confuso; obscuro, vago.—**indistinction** [indįstíŋkshọn], *s.* obscuridad, falta de claridad.—**indistinctly** [-lį], *adv.* indistintamente, confusamente, vagamente.—**indistinctness** [-nįs], *s.* falta de claridad, obscuridad.

indistinguishable [indįstíŋgwįshạbl], *a.* indistinguible.

indite [indáįt]. **I.** *va.* redactar, escribir. **II.** *vn.* poner por escrito.—**inditement** [-mẹnt], *s.* redacción.—**inditer** [-œ(r)], *s.* redactor, escritor.

indium [índįạm], *s.* (quím.) indio.

individual [indįvídžụạl]. **I.** *a.* solo, único, individual, particular, singular, individuo; para o de uno; personal; separado; para uno solo. **II.** *s.* individuo, particular, persona, sujeto.

individualism [-įzm], *s.* individualismo.—**individualist(ic** [-líst(įk], *s.* y *a.* individualista.

individuality [-ǽlįtį], *s.* individualidad, personalidad; individuación, particularidad; originalidad.

individualize [-aįz], *va.* individualizar, particularizar; individuar.

individually [-į], *adv.* individualmente, particularmente, personalmente.

individuate [indįvídžụeįt], *va.* individuar; individualizar.—**individuation** [-éįshọn], *s.* individuación; producción de individuos.

indivisibility [indįvízįbílįtį], *s.* indivisibilidad.—**indivisible** [-bl], *a.* indivisible.—**indivisibly** [-blį], *adv.* indivisiblemente, indivisamente.

Indo-Chinese [índou chaįníz], *a.* y *s.* indochino.

indocile [indásįl], *a.* indócil, cerril.

indocility [indosílįtį], *s.* indocilidad.

indoctrinate [indáktrįneįt], *va.* doctrinar, enseñar, disciplinar.—**indoctrination** [-éįshọn], *s.* instrucción, enseñanza.

Indo-European [índou yụropíạn], **Indo-Germanic** [-džœrmǽnįk], *a.* y *s.* indoeuropeo, indogermánico.

indolence [índolẹns], *s.* indolencia, desidia; (med.) ausencia de dolor.—**indolent** [-ẹnt], *a.* indolente, desidioso; (med.) sin dolor, insensible.—**indolently** [-lį], *adv.* indolentemente.

indomitable [indámįtạbl], *a.* indomable.

indoor [índọr], *a.* interno, interior, de casa; de puertas adentro; que se hace en la casa o bajo tech(ad)o.

indoors [índórz], *adv.* (a)dentro; en casa; bajo techo.

indorsable [indórsạbl], *a.* endo(r)sable; confirmable.

indorse [indórs], *va.* (com.) endosar; respaldar; garantizar, abonar; apoyar, sancionar.

indorsee [-í], *s.* (com.) endosado, endosatario.

indorsement [-mẹnt], *s.* (com.) endoso, endose; respaldo, rótulo; aval, garantía; sanción.

indorser, **indorsor** [-œ(r)], *s.* (com.) endosador, endosante.

indraft, **indraught** [índræft], *s.* absorción, succión, aspiración.

indrawn [índron], *a.* inspirado; introspectivo.

indubitable [indįúbįtạbl], *a.* indubitable.—**indubitableness** [-nįs], *s.* certeza.—**indubitably** [-blį], *adv.* indubitablemente.

induce [indįús], *va.* inducir, mover, incitar, persuadir; causar, producir; (lóg. y elec.) inducir.

inducement [-mẹnt], *s.* inducimiento, inducción; atractivo, móvil, aliciente; persuasión.

inducer [-œ(r)], *s.* el o lo que induce, persuade, etc.

inducible [-įbl], *a.* inducible; que se puede causar o producir.

induct [indʌkt], *va.* instalar; iniciar; (mil.) alistar para el servicio militar.

inductance [-ạns], *s.* (elec.) inductancia.—**i. coil**, bobina de inductancia o de reacción.

induction [indʌkshọn], *s.* introducción, preámbulo; instalación (en un puesto, dignidad, etc.); (elec. y lóg.) inducción.—**i. balance**, balanza de inducción.—**i. coil**, bobina de inducción.—**i. pipe**, **port**, **valve**, tubo, lumbrera, válvula de admisión.

inductive [indʌktįv], *a.* inductivo, ilativo; introductor; (elec.) inductivo, inductor, inductriz.—**inductively** [-lį], *adv.* inductivamente.

inductivity [-tívįtį], *s.* (elec.) inductividad.

inductor [indʌktọ(r)], *s.* (igl.) instalador; (elec.) inductor.

indue [indįú], *va.* vestir; investir; dotar. *V.* ENDUE.

indulge [indʌldž]. **I.** *va.* dar rienda suelta a; acceder a la voluntad o a los caprichos de (apl. esp. a la indulgencia excesiva de los padres); mimar, dar (a un niño) cuanto pide; gratificar, dejarse dominar por (el vicio, etc.); (igl.) conceder indulgencia a; (com.) dar plazo o prorrogar el plazo a. **II.** *vn.* (con **in**) entregarse a; gustar de.

indulgence, **indulgency** [-ẹns, -į], *s.* indulgencia, lenidad; gratificación; exceso; complacencia, favor; (com.) prórroga, extensión de plazo; (igl.) indulgencia.—**indulgent** [-ẹnt], *a.* indulgente.

indulgently [-lį], *adv.* indulgentemente.

indult [indʌlt], *s.* (igl.) indulto, dispensa.

indurate [índjureįt]. **I.** *va.* y *vn.* endurecer(se), empedernir(se). **II.** [índįurįt], *a.* duro, endurecido.

induration [-éįshọn], *s.* endurecimiento; dureza de corazón; (med.) induración, dureza.

industrial [indÁstriąl]. I. *a.* industrial. II. *s.* industrial; (com.) acción u obligación de una sociedad industrial anónima.—**industrialism** [-izm], *s.* industrialismo.—**industrialist** [-ist], *s.* industrial.—**industrialization** [-izéišǫn], *s.* industrialización.—**industrialize** [-aiz], *va.* industrializar.—**industrially** [-i], *adv.* industrialmente.

industrious [indÁstriʌs], *a.* industrioso, diligente, aplicado, hacendoso, laborioso.

industriously [-li], *adv.* industriosamente.

industry [índǫstri], *s.* industria; laboriosidad.

indwell [indwél], *va.* y *vn.* habitar, residir, morar. —**indweller** [indwelce(r)], *s.* habitante, morador.—**indwelling** [-iŋ], *a.* morador, residente.

inebriant [inǝ́briąnt]. I. *a.* embriagante, embriagador. II. *s.* lo que embriaga o inebria.

inebriate [inǝ́brieit]. I. *va.* inebriar, embriagar; infatuar, cegar. II. [inǝ́briit], *a.* ebrio, borracho. III. *s.* borracho, beodo.

inebriation [-éišǫn], **inebriety** [injbráieti], *s.* (in)ebriedad, embriaguez.

inedited [inédjtjd], *a.* inédito.

ineffable [inéfabl], *a.* inefable.—**ineffableness** [-nis], *s.* inefabilidad.—**ineffably** [-bli], *adv.* inefablemente.

ineffaceable [inefóisąbl], *a.* indeleble, imborrable.

ineffaceably [-bli], *adv.* indeleblemente.

ineffective [ineféktiv], *a.* ineficaz.

ineffectual [-chuąl], *a.* ineficaz; fútil.

ineffectually [-i], *adv.* ineficazmente.

ineffectualness [-nis], *s.* ineficacia.

inefficacious [inefikéišʌs], *a.* ineficaz.

inefficaciousness [-nis], *s.* ineficacia.

inefficacy [inéfikąsi], **inefficiency** [inefíšǫnsi], *s.* ineficacia; futilidad.

inefficient [inefíšǫnt], *a.* ineficaz.

inelastic [injlǽstik], *a.* inelástico.

inelasticity [-tísiti], *s.* falta de elasticidad.

inelegance, -cy [inéligąns, -i], *s.* inelegancia.— **inelegant** [-ąnt], *a.* inelegante, deslucido, falto de elegancia.—**inelegantly** [-li], *adv.* sin elegancia.

ineligibility [inélidžibíliti], *s.* inelegibilidad.

ineligible [-bl], *a.* inelegible.

ineloquent [inélokwęnt], *a.* infacundo.

ineluctable [injlÁktąbl], *a.* ineluctable, inevitable; irresistible.—**ineluctably** [-bli], *adv.* inevitablemente, ineluctablemente.

inept [inépt], *a.* inepto; absurdo.—**ineptitude** [-itjud], **ineptness** [-nis], *s.* ineptitud, inepcia, inhabilidad.—**ineptly** [-li], *adv.* ineptamente.

inequality [injkwáliti], *s.* desigualdad, disparidad; insuficiencia; aspereza, escabrosidad; injusticia.

inequitable [inékwitąbl], *a.* injusto.

inerrable [inérąbl], **inerrant** [-ąnt], *a.* inerrable, infalible.—**inerrancy** [-ąnsi], *s.* infalibilidad.

inert [inǝ́rt], *a.* inerte, inactivo.

inertia [inǝ́ršią], *s.* inercia, inactividad.

inertly [inǝ́rtli], *adv.* pesadamente, flojamente, indolentemente.—**inertness** [-nis], *s.* flojedad; falta de actividad.

inescapable [ineskéipąbl], *a.* ineludible.

inestimable [inéstimąbl], *a.* inestimable, inapreciable.—**inestimably** [-bli], *adv.* de modo inestimable.

inevitable [inévitąbl], *a.* inevitable, ineludible. —**inevitability** [-bíliti], **inevitableness** [-nis], *s.* inevitabilidad.—**inevitably** [-bli], *adv.* inevitablemente.

inexact [inegzǽkt], *a.* inexacto.—**inexactitude** [-itjud], **inexactness** [-nis], *s.* inexactitud.— **inexactly** [-li], *adv.* inexactamente.

inexcusable [inekskjúząbl], *a.* inexcusable, indisculpable, imperdonable.—**inexcusableness** [-nis], *s.* calidad de inexcusable.—**inexcusably** [-bli], *adv.* inexcusablemente.

inexhaustible [inegzóstibl], o **inexhaustive** [-tiv], *a.* inagotable.—**inexhaustibleness** [-nis], *s.* calidad de inagotable.

inexistence [inegzístęns], *s.* inexistencia.

inexistent [-ęnt], *a.* inexistente.

inexorable [inéksorąbl], *a.* inexorable.

inexorability [-bíliti], **inexorableness** [-nis], *s.* inexorabilidad, inflexibilidad.—**inexorably** [-bli], *adv.* inexorablemente.

inexpedience, inexpediency [inekspídięns, -i]. *s.* inoportunidad o inconveniencia.—**inexpedient** [-ęnt], *a.* inoportuno, inconveniente, impropio.

inexpensive [inekspénsiv], *a.* barato, poco costoso.

inexperience [inekspírięns], *s.* inexperiencia, impericia.—**inexperienced** [-t], **inexpert** [inekspǝ́rt], *a.* inexperto, novel, bisoño.

inexpertness [-nis], *s.* impericia.

inexpiable [inékspiąbl], *a.* inexpiable.

inexpiably [-bli], *adv.* de un modo inexpiable.

inexplicable [ineksplíkąbl], *a.* inexplicable.— **inexplicability, inexplicableness** [-bíliti, -nis], *s.* calidad de inexplicable.—**inexplicably** [-bli], *adv.* inexplicablemente.

inexpressible [ineksprésibl], *a.* indecible, inexpresable, inenarrable.—**inexpressibly** [-bli], *adv.* indeciblemente.

inexpressive [ineksprésiv], *a.* inexpresivo, falto de expresión; (raro) indecible.

inexpugnable [inekspÁgnąbl], *a.* inexpugnable.

inextensible [ineksténsibl], *a.* inextensible.

inextensive [-iv], *a.* inextenso.

inextinguishable [inekstíŋgwišąbl], *a.* inextinguible, inapagable.

inextirpable [inekstǝ́rpąbl], *a.* inextirpable.

inextricable [inékstrikąbl], *a.* inextricable, intrincado.—**inextricableness** [-nis], *s.* calidad de inextricable.—**inextricably** [-bli], *adv.* inextricablemente.

infallibility [infélibíliti], **infallibleness** [-blnis], *s.* infalibilidad.—**infallible** [-bl], *a.* infalible.— **infallibly** [-bli], *adv.* infaliblemente.

infamous [ínfąmʌs], *a.* infame; infamante, infamatorio.—**infamously** [-li], *adv.* infamemente.—**infamousness** [-nis], **infamy** [ínfąmi], *s.* infamia, ignominia, oprobio.

infancy [ínfąnsi], *s.* infancia, niñez; (for.) minoridad, minoría, menor edad.—**from i.**, desde pequeño.

infant [ínfąnt]. I. *s.* infante, niñito, criatura, nene; (for.) menor. II. *a.* infantil; menor de edad; de niños; naciente.

infanta [infǽntą], *s.* infanta.—**infante** [infǽnti], *s.* infante.

infanticidal [infǽntisaidąl], *a.* relativo al infanticidio; de infanticidio.—**infanticide** [-said], *s.* infanticidio; infanticida, *mf.*

infantile [ínfąntil], *a.* infantil.—**i. paralysis**, (med.) parálisis infantil o poliomielitis anterior aguda.—**i. scurvy**, escorbuto infantil o mal de Barlow.

infantilism [infǽntilizm], *s.* (med.) infantilismo.

infantry [ínfąntri], *s.* (mil.) infantería.

infarct [ínfárkt], *s.* (med.) infarto.

infarction [infárkšǫn], *s.* (med.) infartación.

infatuate [infǽchueit], *va.* infatuar, cegar, atontar.—**infatuate(d** [-id], *a.* infatuado, locamente enamorado.—**infatuation** [-éišǫn], *s.* infatuación; apasionamiento.

infeasibility [infízib́líti], **infeasibleness** [-blnis], *s.* impracticabilidad, infactibilidad.

infeasible [-bl], *a.* impracticable, infactible.

infect [infékt], *va.* infectar, inficionar, contagiar; (for.) exponer a pena o a proceso.

infection [infékšǫn], *s.* infección, contagio; lúe, *f.;* corrupción de costumbres; miasma, *m.;* (for.) tacha de ilegalidad.

infectious [infékšʌs], *a.* contagioso, pestilencial; (med.) infeccioso; (for.) antilegal, que viola la ley.—**infectiously** [-li], *adv.* infecciosamente. —**infectiousness** [-nis], *s.* carácter de infeccioso.—**infective** [inféktiv], *a.* infeccioso.

infecundity [ịnfịk*ŭ*ndịtị], *s.* infecundidad, esterilidad.

infelicitous [ịnfịlísịtʌs], *a.* infeliz, desgraciado; destinado, mal pensado.—**infelicity** [-tị], *s.* infelicidad, infortunio; falta de tino.

infer [ịnfǽr]. **I.** *va.* inferir, colegir, deducir, sacar, argüir. **II.** *vn.* sacar consecuencias o inferencias.—**inferable** [-ạbl], *a.* deducible.—**inference** [ínfẹrẹns], *s.* inferencia, deducción.—**inferential** [ịnfẹrénšạl], *a.* ilativo.—**inferentially** [-lị], *adv.* por inferencia.

inferior [ịnfírịọ(r)], *s.* y *a.* inferior; subordinado, subalterno.—**inferiority** [-árịtị], *s.* inferioridad.

infernal [ịnfǽrnạl], *a.* infernal.—**infernally** [-ị], *adv.* infernalmente.—**inferno** [ịnfǽrnou], *s.* infierno.

inferrible [ịnfǽrịbl], *a.* deducible, colegible.

infertile [ịnfǽrtịl], *a.* estéril, infecundo.

infertility [ịnfǽrtílịtị], *s.* esterilidad.

infest [ịnfést], *va.* infestar, plagar.

infestation [-éịšọn], *s.* infestación.

infestive [-ịv], *a.* triste, melancólico.

infeudation [ịnfịudéịšọn], *s.* (for.) enfeudación.

infidel [ínfịdel]. **I.** *s.* infiel; pagano, gentil; librepensador (en el sentido de descreído). **II.** *a.* infiel; librepensador; de infieles, de los infieles.

infidelity [ịnfịdélịtị], *s.* infidelidad, descreimiento; infidelidad conyugal.

infield [ịnfíld], *s.* los campos (de una granja) inmediatos a los edificios; (baseball) campo y jugadores situados dentro del cuadro o de la demarcación. *V.* OUTFIELD.

infighting [ínfaịtịŋ], *s.* boxeo cuerpo a cuerpo.

infiltrate [ịnfíltreịt], *va.* y *vn.* infiltrar(se); calar; penetrar, meter(se), introducir(se) en pequeño número por varias partes (dicho de los soldados en un ataque).

infiltration [-réịšọn], *s.* infiltración; (mil.) penetración de pequeñas fuerzas por varios puntos.

infinite [ínfịnịt]. **I.** *a.* infinito, ilimitado; innumerable; perfecto. **II.** *s.* infinito.—**infinitely** [-lị], *adv.* infinitamente.—**infiniteness** [-nịs], *s.* infinidad.

infinitesimal [ịnfịnịtésịmạl]. **I.** *a.* (mat.) infinitesimal.—**i. calculus**, (mat.) cálculo infinitesimal. **II.** *s.* cantidad infinitésima.

infinitive [ịnfínịtịv], *s.* y *a.* infinitivo.

infinitude [ịnfínịtịuˈ], *s.* infinidad.

infinity [ịnfínịtị], *s.* infinidad; infinito; sinfín.

infirm [ịnfǽrm], *a.* enfermizo, achacoso; instable, poco firme; (for.) anulable.—**infirmary** [-ạrị], *s.* hospital, enfermería, casa de salud.—**infirmity** [-ịtị], *s.* enfermedad, dolencia, achaque; flaqueza, fragilidad.—**infirmly** [-lị], *adv.* débilmente.

infix [ịnfịks], *va.* clavar, encajar; inculcar.

inflame [ịnfléịm]. **I.** *va.* inflamar, encender; enardecer, acalorar, azuzar; provocar, irritar. **II.** *vn.* arder, encenderse; (med.) inflamarse, hincharse.—**inflamer** [-œ(r)], *s.* inflamador.

inflammability, inflammableness [ịnflǽmạbịlịtị, -blnịs], *s.* inflamabilidad.

inflammable [-bl], *a.* inflamable.

inflammation [ịnflạméịšọn], *s.* inflamación.

inflammatory [ịnflǽmạtọrị], *a.* inflamatorio, inflamante; (med.) inflamatorio.

inflate [ịnfléịt], *va.* inflar, hinchar.—**inflated** [-ịd], *a.* hinchado, inflado; afectado, pomposo.—**inflating** [-ịŋ], *a.* inflativo; inflante.—**inflation** [ịnfléịšọn], *s.* inflación, hinchazón, *f.*; inflamiento; (e. p.) inflación monetaria, emisión excesiva de papel moneda; plétora.—**inflationist** [-ịst], *s.* inflacionista, partidario de la emisión de papel moneda.

inflect [ịnflékt], *va.* torcer, doblar; modular, acentuar; (gram.) declinar, conjugar.

inflection [ịnflékšọn], *s.* inflexión, dobladura; acento, modulación de la voz; (gram.) (in)flexión, conjugación, declinación, desinencia.—**inflectional** [-ạl], *a.* (gram.) flexional, que

tiene inflexiones.—**inflective** [-tịv], *a.* inflectivo, capaz de doblar o torcer; (gram.) = INFLECTIONAL.

inflexibility [ịnfléksịbịlịtị], **inflexibleness** [-blnịs], *s.* inflexibilidad.—**inflexible** [-bl], *a.* inflexible.—**inflexibly** [-blị], *adv.* inflexiblemente.

inflexion, s., inflexional, *a.* = INFLECTION(AL).

inflict [ịnflíkt], *va.* (gen. con **on**) infligir, imponer (a), descargar (contra).—**infliction** [-šọn], *s.* imposición, aplicación; pena, castigo.—**inflictive** [-tịv], *a.* inflictivo, que se impone o inflige.

inflorescence [ịnflorésẹns], *s.* (bot.) inflorescencia; florescencia.

inflow [ínflou], *s.* flujo, afluencia; entrada.

influence [ínflụẹns]. **I.** *s.* influencia, valimiento, influjo; ascendiente; (cam.) aldabas, *f. pl.* **II.** *va.* influir; inducir, persuadir; ejercer presión sobre.—**influential** [ịnflụénšạl], *a.* influ(y)ente, valido.—**influentially** [-ị], *adv.* influyentemente.

influenza [ịnflụénzạ], *s.* (med.) influenza, gripe, *f.*

influx [ínflʌks], *s.* (in)flujo; afluencia; instilación, intromisión; desembocadura, entrada.

infold [ịnfóuld], *va.* envolver; incluir; abrazar.

inform [ịnfórm]. **I.** *va.* informar, avisar, comunicar, enterar; poner al corriente, hacer saber; instruir, enseñar; informar o dar forma a, modelar; animar. **II.** *vn.* soplar; (con **on** o **against**) denunciar, delatar (a), sindicar.

informal [-ạl], *a.* informal, irregular; sin ceremonia, de confianza.

informality [-ǽlịtị], *s.* informalidad, irregularidad; acto sencillo, sin ceremonia.

informally [-ạlị], *adv.* informalmente; sin ceremonia.

informant [-ạnt], *s.* informante. *V.* INFORMER.

information [-éịšọn], *s.* informe, información, aviso; luz, razón, *f.*; saber, conocimiento(s); (for.) acusación, delación.—**i. bureau**, consultorio, oficina de información.

informative [-ạtịv], *a.* informativo.

informed [-d], *a.* informado; al corriente o al tanto (de).

informer [-œ(r)], *s.* delator, denunciante, denunciador; soplón; informante, informador, avisador, comunicante.

infraction [ịnfrǽkšọn], *s.* infracción, violación, contravención, quebrantamiento, transgresión; (cir.) infracción, fractura incompleta.—**infractor** [ịnfrǽktọ(r)], *s.* infractor, transgresor, contraventor.

inframaxillary [ịnfrạmǽksịlẹrị]. **I.** *a.* (anat.) inframaxilar. **II.** *s.* maxilar inferior.

infrangible [ịnfrǽndžịbl], *a.* infrangible, inquebrantable.—**infrangibleness** [-nịs], *s.* calidad de infrangible.

infraorbital [ịnfrạórbịtạl], *a.* (anat.) infraorbitario, situado debajo de la órbita del ojo.

infrared [ịnfrạréd], *a.* (fís.) infrarrojo o ultrarrojo.

infrequence, -cy [ịnfríkwẹns, -ị], *s.* rareza, raridad.—**infrequent** [-ẹnt], *a.* raro, infrecuente.—**infrequently** [-lị], *adv.* rara o infrecuentemente, rara vez, contadas veces.

infringe [ịnfríndž]. **I.** *va.* infringir, violar. **II.** *vn.* (con **on** o **upon**) violar.—**infringement** [-mẹnt], *s.* infracción, violación.—**infringer** [-œ(r)], *s.* violador, infractor.

infundibular, infundibuliform [ịnfʌndíbyụl*ǎ*(r), -lịform], *a.* infundibuliforme.

infundibulum [-lʌm], *s.* (anat.) infundíbulo.

infuriate [ịnfjúrịeịt], *va.* enfurecer, irritar.—**infuriated** [-ịd], *a.* enfurecido, furioso.

infuse [ịnfjúz], *va.* vaciar; (farm.) macerar; (con **into**) inculcar, infundir, imbuir; (con **with**) inspirar, dar, comunicar.

infusible [-ịbl], *a.* infusible, infundible.

infusibility [-ịbílịtị], **infusibleness** [-ịblnịs], *s.* infusibilidad.

infusion [infjúźǫn], s. infusión; instilación; (farm.) maceración.

infusive [infjúsjv], a. inspirador.

Infusoria [infjusóriạ], s. pl. (zool.) infusorios.—**infusorial** [-l], a. infusorio.—**i. earth,** tierra de infusorios.—**infusorian** [-n], s. y a. infusorio.

ingathering [ingǽðœriŋ], s. cosecha.

ingeminate [indźémineịt], va. reiterar, duplicar.—**ingemination** [-éịśǫn], s. repetición.

ingenerate [indźénǝreịt], a. innato, ingénito; increado.

ingenious [indźínịas], a. ingenioso; hábil; artificioso.—**ingeniously** [-l], adv. ingeniosamente.

ingeniousness [-njs], s. ingeniosidad, ingenio.

ingenuity [indźinịúịtị], s. ingeniosidad, inventiva.

ingenuous [indźényụas], a. ingenuo, sincero, cándido.—**ingenuously** [-l], adv. ingenuamente.

ingenuousness [-njs], s. ingenuidad, candidez.

ingest [indźést], va. (fisiol.) ingerir, introducir en el estómago.

ingesta [-ạ], s. pl. alimento tomado; (fig.) cosas ingeridas.

ingestion [indźéschǫn], s. ingestión, introducción de una cosa en el estómago.

ingle [íŋgl], s. llama; fuego; hogar.

inglorious [inglóriạs], a. afrentoso, ignominioso; obscuro.—**ingloriously** [-l], adv. ignominiosamente; obscuramente.—**ingloriousness** [-njs], s. ignominia; obscuridad.

ingoing [íŋgouịŋ]. I. a. entrante, que entra, pue llega. II. s. entrada, ingreso.

ingot [íŋgǫt], s. lingote; tejo de oro, galápago de cobre; barra de metal.

ingraft [ingrǽft], va. (agr.) injertar. V. ENGRAFT.

ingraftment [-mǝnt], s. injerto.

ingrain [ingreịn]. I. a. teñido en rama; inculcado. II. s. alfombra ordinaria.

ingrain [ingréịn], va. teñir en rama; teñir con grana o cochinilla; fijar o impregnar.

ingrate [ingreịt], a. ingrato.

ingratiate [ingréịśịeịt], va. recomendar; hacer aceptable.—**to i. one's self with,** insinuarse, hacerse a la buena voluntad de, conquistarse el favor de.—**ingratiating** [-ịŋ], a. insinuante.

ingratitude [ingrǽtịtjud], s. ingratitud, desagradecimiento, desconocimiento.

ingredient [ingrídịǝnt], s. ingrediente.

ingress [íŋgres], s. ingreso, entrada; acceso.

ingrowing [íŋgrouịŋ], a. que crece hacia dentro.—**i. nail,** uñero.

ingrown [íŋgroun], a. que va penetrando en la carne a medida que crece (v. INGROWING); congénito, natural.

ingrowth [íŋgrouθ], s. crecimiento hacia adentro; lo que crece hacia adentro.

inguinal [íŋgwịnạl], a. (anat.) inguinal, referente a la ingle.—**i. canal,** conducto inguinal.

ingulf [ingÁlf], va. sumir, sumergir, engolfar, tragar.

ingurgitation [ingœrdźịtéịśǫn], s. voracidad, glotonería, ingurgitación.

inhabit [inhǽbịt]. I. va. habitar, ocupar, poblar. II. vn. (ant.) habitar, vivir, residir.—**inhabitable** [-ạbl], a. habitable.—**inhabitance** [-ạns], s. habitación, morada, residencia.

inhabitant [-ạnt], s. habitante, poblador, residente, vecino.

inhabitation [-éịśǫn], s. habitación, acción de habitar.

inhabited [-ịd], a. poblado, habitado.

inhalation [inhạléịśǫn], s. inspiración; (med.) inhalación.

inhalator [inhạleịtǫ(r)], s. (med.) inhalador.

inhale [inhéịl], va. inspirar, inhalar, aspirar.

inhaler [-œ(r)], s. inhalador; aparato de inhalación.

inharmonic(al [inharmánịk(ạl], a. inarmónico.

inharmonious [-móụnịạs], a. discordante, disonante, dísono, inarmónico.—**to be i. (with),** disonar, desentonar (de).—**inharmoniously** [-l], adv. inarmónicamente, discordantemente.—**inharmoniousness** [-njs], s. desarmonía.

inhere [inhír], vn. ser inherente.—**inherence, inherency** [-ǝns, -ị], s. inherencia.—**inherent** [-ǝnt], a. inherente, inmanente; innato, esencial.—**inherently** [-lị], adv. inherentemente.

inherit [inhérịt]. I. va. heredar. II. vn. suceder como heredero.—**inheritable** [-ạbl], a. heredable.—**inheritably** [-ạblị], adv. por herencia.—**inheritance** [-ạns], s. herencia; patrimonio.—**inheritor** [-ǫ(r)], s. heredero.—**inheritress, -trix** [-rịs, -rịks], s. heredera.

inhesion [inhíźǫn], s. inherencia.

inhibit [inhíbịt], va. inhibir, prohibir, impedir.

inhibition [-íśǫn], s. inhibición, prohibición, impedimento.

inhibitory, inhibitive [-orị, -ịv], a. inhibitorio.

inhospitable [inháspịtạbl], a. inhospital(ario), inhospitable.—**inhospitableness** [-njs], s. **inhospitality** [inhaspịtǽlịtị], s. inhospitalidad.—**inhospitably** [-blị], adv. inhospitalariamente.

inhuman [inhjúman], a. inhumano, desalmado.—**inhumane** [inhjuméịn], a. inhumanitario.—**inhumanity** [inhjumǽnịtị], s. inhumanidad, crueldad.—**inhumanly** [-lị], adv. inhumanamente.

inhume [inhjúm], va. inhumar, enterrar, sepultar; (quím.) exponer a un calor constante enterrando el recipiente en tierra o estiércol caliente.

inhumation [-éịśǫn], s. inhumación.

inimical [inímịkạl], a. enemigo, hostil.—**inimically** [-ị], adv. enemigamente, hostilmente.

inimitability [inímịtạbílịtị], s. imposibilidad de ser imitado.—**inimitable** [-bl], a. inimitable.—**inimitableness** [-njs], s. calidad de inimitable.—**inimitably** [-blị], adv. inimitablemente.

inion [ínịǫn], s. (anat.) inio, inión, m.

iniquitous [iníkwịtạs], a. inicuo, perverso, malvado.—**iniquitously** [-lị], adv. inicuamente.—**iniquity** [iníkwịtị], s. iniquidad.

initial [iníśạl]. I. a. inicial, incipiente. II. s. (letra) inicial. III. va. poner las iniciales a o en; firmar con iniciales.

initially [-ị], adv. en primer lugar; en los comienzos; por modo inicial.

initiate [iníśịeịt]. I. va. iniciar, comenzar, entablar. II. a. y s. adepto, iniciado.

initiation [-éịśǫn], s. iniciación; comienzo.—**i. fee,** cuota de entrada o ingreso (en un club).

initiative [iníśịatịv]. I. a. iniciativo. II. s. iniciativa; originalidad; (der. y pol.) iniciativa, derecho (de una asamblea, etc.) de introducir propuestas, etc.; (gen. con the) iniciativa popular directa, derecho del pueblo de proponer directamente medidas legislativas, como en Suiza.

initiator [iníśịeịtǫ(r)], s. iniciador.

initiatory [iníśịatorị], a. iniciativo.

inject [indźékt], va. inyectar, jeringar; introducir.

injection [indźékśǫn], s. inyección; (med.) enema, jeringazo, clister, inyección, lavativa.

injector [indźéktǫ(r)], s. (mec. y med.) inyector.

injudicious [indźụdíśạs], a. indiscreto, poco juicioso, imprudente.—**injudiciously** [-lị], adv. indiscretamente, tontamente.—**injudiciousness** [-njs], s. indiscreción, imprudencia.

injunction [indźÁŋkśǫn], s. mandato, mandamiento; requerimiento; prohibición; (for.) entredicho, interdicto, embargo.

injure [índźur], va. injuriar, agraviar, ofender; perjudicar, dañar, damnificar, menoscabar; averiar, lesionar, lastimar.

injured [-d], a. herido, lesionado; ofendido.

injurer [-œ(r)], s. injuriador; perjudicador.

injurious [indźúrịạs], a. injurioso; dañoso, perjudicial, dañino, nocivo; lesivo.—**injuriously** [-lị], adv. dañosamente, perjudicialmente.—

injuriousness [-njs], s. calidad de perjudicial, etc.

injury [índʒuri], s. daño, avería, desperfecto; perjuicio, mal, detrimento, menoscabo; lesión.

injustice [indʒʌstis], s. injusticia.

ink [íŋk]. I. s. tinta; (zool.) tinta de calamar.—i., o **inking, ball,** bala de entintar.—**i. fountain,** (impr.) tintero de prensa.—i., o **inking, roller,** (impr.) rulo, rodillo. II. va. (a veces con **in**) entintar, dar tinta, pasar o linear en tinta.

inkhorn [-horn]. I. s. tintero de cuerno. II. a. pedantesco, pomposo.

inkle [íŋkl], s. cinta ancha de hilo.

inkling [íŋkliŋ], s. insinuación; sospecha; vislumbre, indicio, noción vaga.

inkmaker [íŋkmeikœ(r)], s. fabricante de tinta.

inkstand [-stænd], s. tintero; escribanía.

inkwell [-wel], s. tintero; frasco de tintero.

inky [-i], a. parecido a la tinta; manchado de tinta.

inlaid [inléid], pret. y pp. de TO INLAY.—**i. floor,** entarimado.—**i. work,** marquetería, encaje, embutido, taracea, incrustación, ataujía.

inland [ínlænd]. I. a. interior; del país, nacional, regional.—**i. commerce, duty, navigation,** etc., comercio, impuesto, navegación, etc. interior. II. s. el interior de un país. III. adv. tierra adentro.

inlander [-œ(r)], s. el que habita tierra adentro; (Am.) tierradentreño.

in-law [ínlə], s. (fam.) suegro, suegra; cuñado, cuñada.—pl. parientes políticos.

inlay [inléi], va. (pret. y pp. INLAID) embutir; (a)taracear, hacer ataujía o mosaico; incrustar.

inlay [ínlei], s. (a)taracea, embutido.

inlayer [ínleiœ(r)], s. incrustador, obrero que hace taracea.—**inlaying** [ínleiiŋ], s. incrustación; arte de ataracear, embutir o incrustar.

inlet [ínlet], s. entrada; abra, caleta, ensenada; estero, estuario; boca de entrada.

inly [ínli], adv. (poét.) interiormente; a fondo.

inmate [ínmeit], s. ocupante, residente (enfermo, si se trata de hospital; preso, recluso, encerrado, si de cárcel, etc.); inquilino, huésped, m.

inmesh [inméš], va. = ENMESH.

inmost [ínmoust], a. íntimo, recóndito, profundo.

inn [in], s. posada, fonda, mesón, hospedería.

innate [inéit], a. innato, ingénito, connatural.—**innately** [-li], adv. por modo ingénito.—**innateness** [-njs], s. calidad de innato.

innavigable [inévigabl], a. innavegable.

inner [ínœ(r)], a. interior.—**i. bark,** (bot.) líber. —**i.-spring mattress,** colchón de muelles.— **i. tube,** (aut.) cámara (de aire).

innermost [-moust], a. = INMOST.

innervate [ínœrveit], va. (fisiol.) inervar, proveer de nervios; causar inervación.—**innervation** [-éišơn], s. (fisiol.) inervación.—**innerve** [inœrv], va. inervar; estimular, vigorizar.

inning [íniŋ], s. en baseball y otros juegos, entrada, turno; por extensión, turno en el mando o gobierno; cosecha.—pl. tierras ganadas al mar.

innkeeper [ínkipœ(r)], s. posadero, mesonero, hospedero, hostelero.

innocence, innocency [ínosens, -i], s. inocencia.

innocent [-ent], s. y a. inocente.

innocently [-li], adv. inocentemente.

innocuous [inákiuʌs], a. innocuo, inofensivo.— **innocuously** [-li], adv. innocuamente, sin daño. —**innocuousness** [-njs], s. innocuidad.

innominate [inámineit], a. (anat.) innominado; anónimo.

innovate [ínoveit], va. innovar.—**innovation** [-éišơn], s. innovación; novedad.—**innovator** [-ơ(r)], s., **innovating** [-iŋ], a. innovador.

innoxious [inákšʌs], a. innocuo.

innuendo [inyuéndou], s. indirecta, insinuación.

innumerability [injúmerabíliti], s. innumerabilidad.—**innumerable** [-bl], a. innumerable.

innumerableness [-njs], s. innumerabilidad. —**innumerably** [-bli], adv. innumerablemente.—**innumerous** [-ʌs], a. innumerable, incontable.

inoculate [inákiuleit], va. y vn. (med.) inocular; fertilizar (el suelo) con bacterias; (fig.) imbuir, infundir; infectar, inficionar.

inoculation [-éišơn], s. (med.) inoculación; contaminación, infección; fertilización con bacterias.

inoculator [-ơ(r)], s. inoculador.

inodorous [inóudơras], a. inodoro.

inoffensive [inơfénsiv], a. inofensivo; inocente.— **inoffensively** [-li], adv. inofensivamente.— **inoffensiveness** [-njs], s. calidad de inofensivo.

inofficious [inơfíšʌs], a. (for.) inoficioso.

inoperable [inápœrabl], a. (cir.) inoperable.

inoperative [inápereitiv], a. ineficaz.

inopportune [inapơrtjún], a. inoportuno, a mal tiempo, intempestivo; inconveniente.—**inopportunely** [-li], adv. inoportunamente.—**inopportuneness** [-njs], s. inoportunidad.

inordinacy [inórdinisi], s. desarreglo, desorden; exceso.—**inordinate** [inórdinit], a. inordenado, desarreglado; excesivo.—**inordinately** [-li], adv. inordenadamente; desmedidamente.—**inordinateness** [-njs], s. desorden; exceso; demasía.

inorganic(al [inơrgénik(ạl], a. inorgánico.

inosculate [inákiuleit]. I. va. (anat., bot.) unir por anastomosis. II. vn. anastomosarse.— **inosculation** [-éišơn], s. inosculación, anastomosis.

inoxidize [ináksidaiz], va. hacer inoxidable.

inpatient [ínpeišẹnt], s. enfermo residente en un hospital.

inphase [ínfeiz], a. (elec.) de la misma fase.

input [ínput], s. dinero contribuido o gastado; (mec.) energía recibida por una máquina; (fisiol.) cantidad de sangre recibida por el cuerpo.

inquest [ínkwest], s. (for.) indagación, averiguación, examen, información o pesquisa judicial con ayuda de un jurado; jurado que hace dicha pesquisa; juicio de indemnización.

inquietude [inkwáiitjud], s. inquietud, desasosiego, descontento.

inquiline [ínkwilin], s. y a., **inquilinous** [-láinʌs], a. Dícese del animal que vive en el nido de otro.

inquirable [inkwáirabl], a. investigable.

inquire [inkwáir], va. y vn. inquirir, preguntar; averiguar.—**to i. about, after o for,** preguntar por.—**to i. into,** investigar, examinar, informarse.—**to i. of,** dirigirse a.

inquirer [-œ(r)], s. inquiridor, investigador, averiguador; preguntante, preguntador.

inquiry [-i], s. pregunta, interrogación; consulta; pesquisa, encuesta, indagación, averiguación; investigación, estudio.—**i. into,** investigación de, estudio de.

inquisition [inkwizíšơn], s. escudriñamiento, investigación, (I., igl.) inquisición, Santo Oficio.

inquisitional [-ạl], a. inquisitorial.

inquisitive [inkwízitiv], a. inquisitivo, preguntón; investigador.—**inquisitively** [-li], adv. inquisitivamente.—**inquisitiveness** [-njs], s. curiosidad, manía de preguntar.

inquisitor [-tơ(r)], s. inquisidor; juez investigador; inquiridor.

inquisitorial [-tórịal], a. inquisitorial.

in re [in rí], (lat.) concerniente o relativo a.

inroad [ínroud], s. incursión, irrupción; brecha.

inrush [ínrʌš], s. empuje, invasión.

insalivate [insǽliveit], va. insalivar.

insalivation [-éišơn], s. insalivación.

insalubrious [insạlúbriʌs], a. insalubre, malsano.

insalubrity [-briti], s. insalubridad.

insane [inséin], a. loco, insano, demente; de

locos o para locos.—**i. asylum**, casa de locos, manicomio.

insanity [insǽniti], s. locura, insania, demencia.

insatiable [insḗiʂiabl], a. insaciable, que no se sacia.—**insatiableness** [-nis], s. insaciabilidad. —**insatiably** [-bli], adv. insaciablemente.

insatiate [insḗiʂieit], a. insaciable.—**insatiately** [-li], adv. insaciablemente.

inscribable [inskráibabl], a. inscribible.

inscribe [inskráib], va. inscribir; grabar; dedicar; apuntar.

inscription [inskrípʂon], s. inscripción; rótulo, leyenda, letra, letrero; registro; dedicatoria.

inscriptive [-tiv], a. inscrito, inscripto.

inscrutability [inskrútabíliti], s. inescrutabilidad.

inscrutable [-bl], a. inescrutable.—**inscrutably** [-bli], adv. inescrutablemente.

insect [ínsekt], s. insecto, bicho.—**i. powder**, polvos insecticidas.

insectarium [-ériʌm], s. lugar donde se crían insectos.

insectean [insḗktian], **insectile** [-til], a. insectil.

insecticide [-tisaid], a. y s. insecticida, m.

insection [insḗkʂon], s. incisión.

Insectivora [insektívorạ], s. pl. insectívoros.

insectivorous [-ʌs], a. insectívoro.

insecure [insikiúr], a. inseguro.

insecurely [-li], adv. inseguramente.

insecurity [-iti], s. inseguridad, incertidumbre; peligro, riesgo.

insemination [inseminéiʂon], s. (in)seminación.

insensate [insénseit], a. insensato.

insensibility [insénsibíliti], s. insensibilidad.

insensible [-bl], a. insensible; imperceptible; impasible.—**insensibleness** [-nis], s. insensibilidad.—**insensibly** [-bli], adv. insensiblemente.

insentient [insénʂient], a. insensible; inanimado.

inseparability [inseparabíliti], **inseparableness** [-blnis], s. inseparabilidad.—**inseparable** [-bl], a. inseparable.—**inseparably** [-bli], adv. inseparablemente.

insert [insœrt], s. cosa insertada, intercalada, etc. (V. INSERT, va.); (enc.) hoja o lámina, etc., intercalada en un libro; (en el correo) circular o anuncio metido en un periódico o libro que se envía por correo; (cine) letrero explicativo proyectado sobre la pantalla.

insert [insœrt], va. insertar, ingerir; introducir, meter, encajar; intercalar.

insertion [insœrʂon], s. inserción, metimiento, introducción; (cost.) entredós; (bot.) inserción.

inserviceable [insœrvisabl], a. inservible.

inset [ínset], I. s. intercalación; flujo o marea montante; (enc.) = INSERT. II. va. = INSERT.

inshore [inʂór], I. a. cercano a la orilla. II. adv. hacia la orilla o cerca de ella.

inshrine [inʂráin], va. = ENSHRINE.

inside [insaid], I. a. interior, interno.—**i. play**, (dep.) juego con señales secretas convenidas de antemano.—**to have the i. track**, (dep.) seguir la pista interior en una carrera; tener ventaja sobre un competidor. II. s. el interior, la parte de dentro; contenido; forro; guarnición interior (de válvula, etc.).—pl. (fam.) entrañas; interioridades. III. adv. dentro, adentro, en el interior.—**i. out**, de dentro afuera; al revés. IV. prep. dentro de.

insider [-œ(r)], s. el que ocupa situación ventajosa, o posee informes secretos o de primera mano.

insidious [insídiʌs], a. insidioso, traidor, capcioso, solapado.—**insidiously** [-li], adv. insidiosamente.—**insidiousness** [-nis], s. calidad de insidioso.

insight [ínsait], s. discernimiento, perspicacia; penetración; comprensión; conocimiento, idea; percepción de la naturaleza interior de una cosa.

insightful [-ful], a. perspicaz, clarividente.

insignia [insígniạ], s. pl. insignias.

insignificance, **insignificancy** [insignífikans, -i], s. insignificancia.—**insignificant** [-ant], a. insignificante.—**insignificantly** [-li], adv. insignificantemente.

insincere [insinsír], a. insincero, hipócrita.—**insincerely** [-li], adv. sin sinceridad; (fam.) de dientes afuera.—**insincerity** [-sériti], s. insinceridad, falta de sinceridad, doblez, camandulería.

insinuate [insínyueit], I. va. insinuar, indicar, sugerir, dar a entender.—**i. one's self**, insinuarse, introducirse, congraciarse, intimar. II. vn. echar pullas o indirectas.

insinuating [-iŋ], a. insinuativo.

insinuation [-éiʂon], s. insinuación; sugestión, indirecta, pulla.

insinuative [-iv], a. insinuante, insinuativo.

insinuator [-o(r)], s. insinuante, insinuador.

insipid [insípid], a. insípido, soso, desab(o)rido. —**insipidity** [insipíditi], **insipidness** [insípidnis], s. insipidez, insulsez, sosería.—**insipidly** [-li], adv. insulsamente, insípidamente, sosamente.

insist [insíst], vn. insistir; persistir, porfiar; hacer hincapié (en).—**insistence, insistency** [-ens, -i], s. insistencia, porfía.—**insistent** [-ent], a. insistente, persistente; porfiado.

in situ [in sáitiu], (geol.) en el lugar de origen.

insnare [insnár], va. = ENSNARE.

insobriety [insobráieti], s. falta de sobriedad; embriaguez, borrachera.

insofar as, in so far as [insofáræz], en cuanto a, en cuanto, en lo que, hasta donde.

insolate [insoleit], va. insolar.

insolation [-éiʂon], s. acto de secar al sol, blanqueo; (med.) insolación.

insole [insoul], s. (zap.) plantilla, palmilla.

insolence [ínsolens], s. insolencia.—**insolent** [-ent], a. insolente, descarado, procaz.—**insolently** [-li], adv. insolentemente.

insolubility [insályubíliti], **insolubleness** [-blnis], s. insolubilidad.—**insoluble** [-bl], a. insoluble.

insolvable [insálvabl], a. inexplicable; insoluble; que no se puede saldar.

insolvency [insálvensi], s. insolvencia.

insolvent [-ent], a. insolvente.

insomnia [insámniạ], s. insomnio, desvelo anormal.—**insomniac** [-njæk], s. el que padece de insomnio.—**insomnious** [-niʌs], a. insomne, desvelado.

insomuch [insomʌ́ch], adv. (seguido de as o that) de manera que, de suerte que, en modo que, hasta el punto que.

inspect [inspékt], va. reconocer, registrar, revis(t)ar, inspeccionar.—**inspection** [inspékʂon], s. inspección; reconocimiento, registro.—**by i.**, a la simple vista.—**inspector** [inspékto(r)], s. inspector, registrador, superintendente, interventor, revisor.—**inspectorate** [-it], **inspectorship** [-ʂip], s. distrito, cargo o empleo de un inspector, (Am.) inspectoría.

insphere [insfír], va. = ENSPHERE.

inspiration [inspiréiʂon], s. inspiración; (poét.) estro, aflato, numen.

inspirational [-al], a. inspirativo; inspirado.

inspiratory [inspáiratori], a. inspiratorio.

inspire [inspáir], I. va. inspirar; animar, alentar, estimular; insinuar, sugerir; autorizar (por funcionarios públicos). II. vn. inspirar.—**inspirer** [-œ(r)], s. inspirador; insinuador.—**inspiring** [-iŋ], a. inspirador, animador, alentador; inspirativo, fortificante.

inspirit [inspírit], va. alentar, animar, vigorizar.

inspissate [inspíseit], va. espesar, condensar, incrasar.—**inspissation** [-éiʂon], s. condensación, acto de espesar.

instability [instabíliti], s. in(e)stabilidad.

instable [instéibl], a. in(e)stable, inconstante, insubsistente, mudable, variable.

install [instɔ́l]. *va.* instalar; montar; colocar.

installation [-éjʂǫn], *s.* instalación; montaje.

installer [-œ(r)], *s.* montador.

instal(l)ment [-mɛnt], *s.* instalación; entrega; plazo.—**i. plan**, pago por cuotas a plazos (por mensualidades, si los pagos son mensuales).—**on the i. plan**, con facilidades de pago; con pago por cuotas.

instance [ínstǫns]. **I.** *s.* ejemplo; caso; instancia, ruego, solicitación; (for.) instancia, expediente; ocasión, lugar.—**for i.**, por ejemplo, verbigracia.—**in the first i.**, desde el principio. **II.** *va.* poner por caso; ejemplificar; citar, mencionar.

instancy [-i], *s.* insistencia.

instant [ínstǫnt]. **I.** *a.* inminente, inmediato, perentorio; corriente, presente, actual. **II.** *s.* instante, momento, (fam.) santiamén.

instantaneous [-éjnjǫs], *a.* instantáneo.

instantaneously [-li], *adv.* instantáneamente.—**instantaneousness** [-njs], *s.* calidad de instantáneo.

instanter [instǽntœ(r)], **instantly** [ínstǫntli], *adv.* al instante, instantáneamente, incontinenti.

instate [instéjt], *va.* instalar, colocar.

instead [instéd], *adv.* en lugar, en vez, en cambio (de); en lugar de eso, ello, él, etc.

instep [ínstep], *s.* empeine o garganta del pie; parte (*f.*) anterior de la pata trasera.

instigate [ínstigejt], *va.* instigar, fomentar, incitar, provocar.—**instigation** [-éjʂǫn], *s.* instigación.—**instigator** [-ǫ(r)], *s.* instigador.

instil(l) [instíl], *va.* instilar; inspirar, inculcar, infundir.

instillation [-éjʂǫn], **instil(l)ment** [-mɛnt], *s.* instilación; insinuación.

instinct [ínstiŋkt], *a.* (con **with**) animado, impulsado, movido por.

instinct [ínstiŋkt], *s.* instinto.

instinctive [instíŋktiv], *a.* instintivo.—**instinctively** [-li], *adv.* instintivamente.

institute [ínstitjut]. **I.** *va.* instituir, fundar; iniciar; nombrar; (igl.) conferir un beneficio. **II.** *s.* instituto, establecimiento; regla, principio, máxima; reunión de maestros.—*pl.* (for.) instituta; instituciones.—**Institutes of Justinian**, Instituta de Justiniano.—**institutes of medicine**, instituciones de medicina.

institution [institjúʂǫn], *s.* institución; establecimiento; instituto; plantel (de educación, etc.); comienzo, acto incoativo; (for.) nombramiento de heredero; (igl.) institución canónica.—**institutional** [-ạl], o **institutionary** [-erị], *a.* institucional.—**institutive** [ínstitjutiv], *a.* instituente o instituyente; establecido, instituído.—**institutor** [-tǫ(r)], *s.* instituidor, institutor, fundador.—**institutress** [-trịs], *s.* fundadora.

instruct [instrʌ́kt], *va.* instruir, enseñar, educar, (a)doctrinar, disciplinar, aleccionar, amaestrar; dar instrucciones, dar órdenes, mandar.

instruction [instrʌ́kʂǫn], *s.* instrucción, docencia, educación, enseñanza; conocimiento, saber.—*pl.* instrucciones; órdenes, *f. pl.*; consigna.

instructive [-tịv], *a.* instructivo, aleccionador.—**instructively** [-li], *adv.* instructivamente.—**instructiveness** [-njs], *s.* calidad de instructivo.

instructor [-tǫ(r)], *s.* instructor, maestro, tutor.

instructress [-trịs], *s.* instructora, institutriz.

instrument [ínstrumɛnt]. **I.** *s.* instrumento; agente; (for.) instrumento, documento, escritura. **II.** [ínstrumɛnt], *va.* (mús.) instrumentar.

instrumental [instrumɛ́ntạl], *a.* instrumental; influyente, servicial, cooperador; conducente.—**to be i.**, contribuir a.—**instrumentalism** [-izm], *s.* (filos.) sistema (*m.*) que hace de la utilidad el criterio de la verdad; pragmatismo; humanismo.—**instrumentalist** [-jst], *s.* (mús.) instrumentista.—**instrumentality**

[-ǽliti], *s.* agencia, mediación, medio, arbitrio.—**instrumentally** [-i], *adv.* instrumentalmente.—**instrumentation** [-éjʂǫn], *s.* (mús.) instrumentación; ejecución instrumental; agencia.

insubordinate [insʌbɔ́rdinịt], *a.* insubordinado.

insubordination [-éjʂǫn], *s.* insubordinación.

insufferable [insʌ́fɛrạbl], *a.* insufrible.

insufferably [-bli], *adv.* insufriblemente.

insufficience, insufficiency [insʌfíʂɛns, -i], *s.* insuficiencia.—**insufficient** [-ɛnt], *a.* insuficiente; incapaz, inepto.—**insufficiently** [-li], *adv.* insuficientemente.

insufflate [insʌ́flejt], *va.* insuflar.—**insufflation** [-éjʂǫn], *s.* soplo, insuflación.—**insufflator** [insʌ́flejtǫ(r)], *s.* insuflador.

insular [ínsjulạ(r)], *a.* insular, isleño; estrecho de miras.—**i. sclerosis**, (med.) esclerosis cerebro-espinal.

insularity [ínsjulǽriti], *s.* calidad de insular o isleño; estrechez de miras.

insulate [ínsjulejt], *va.* aislar.—**insulating** [-iŋ], *a.* aislador, aislante.—**insulation** [-éjʂǫn], *s.* aislamiento.—**insulator** [-ǫ(r)], *s.* aislador.

insulin [ínsjulịn], *s.* (bioquím.) insulina, producto pancreático antidiabético.

insult [ínsʌlt], *s.* insulto, denuesto, improperio, ultraje, afrenta, agravio, injuria.

insult [insʌ́lt], *va.* insultar.—**insulter** [-œ(r)], *s.* insultador.—**insulting** [-iŋ], *a.* insultante.—**insultingly** [-li], *adv.* insultantemente.

insuperability, insuperableness [insjúpœrạbịliti, -blnịs], *s.* insuperabilidad.—**insuperable** [-bl], *a.* insuperable, incontrastable, invencible.—**insuperably** [-bli], *adv.* insuperablemente.

insupportable [insʌpɔ́rtạbl], *a.* insoportable, inaguantable o insufrible.—**insupportableness** [-njs], *s.* calidad de insoportable o inaguantable.—**insupportably** [-bli], *adv.* insoportablemente.

insuppressible [insʌprésịbl], *a.* que no se puede ocultar o suprimir.

insurable [insúrạbl], *a.* asegurable.

insurance [insúrǫns], *s.* garantía, seguridad; (com.) seguro, aseguramiento; sistema (*m.*) de seguros; prima o premio del seguro (ll. t. **i. premium**); cantidad total de seguro.—**i. agent**, agente de seguros.—**i. bonds**, bonos u otras propiedades en que las compañías de seguros pueden legalmente invertir sus fondos.—**i. broker**, corredor de seguros.—**i. company**, compañía de seguros.—**i. policy**, póliza de seguro.

insurant [insúrǫnt], *s.* asegurado.

insure [insúr]. **I.** *va.* (com.) asegurar; garantizar, afianzar; dar o tener seguridad de; lograr. **II** *vn.* asegurarse.

insurer [-œ(r)], *s.* asegurador.

insurgence, -cy [insœrdʓɛns, -i], *s.* insurrección, rebelión.

insurgent [-ɛnt], *a.* y *s.* insurgente, insurrecto.

insurmountable [insœrmáuntạbl], *a.* insuperable.—**insurmountably** [-bli], *adv.* insuperablemente.

insurrection [insœrékʂǫn], *s.* insurrección.—**insurrectional, insurrectionary** [-ạl, -erị], *a.* insurreccional, revolucionario, rebelde.—**insurrectionist** [-jst], *s.* insurrecto.

insusceptible [insʌséptịbl], *a.* no susceptible, insensible.

inswept [ínswept], *a.* (aut.) estrechado hacia adelante, más angosto adelante que atrás.

intact [intǽkt], *a.* intacto, íntegro, entero.—**intactness** [-njs], *s.* integridad.

intaglio [intǽljou], *s.* obra de talla o entalladura.

intake [ínteik], *s.* producto de una finca; (tej.) punto con que se empieza a estrechar; admisión; orificio de entrada, o de toma; aspiración; ingestión, absorción.

intangibility o **intangibleness** [intǽndʓịbỊliti, -blnịs], *s.* intangibilidad.

intangible [-bl], *a.* intangible; impalpable.

integer [íntȷdȝœ(r)], *s.* (número) entero.

integral [íntȷgrạl]. **I.** *a.* íntegro; integrante, inherente; (mat.) entero (número, función, etc.); integral (cálculo); (mec.) de una pieza. **II.** *s.* (mat.) integral, *f.*

integrality [ȷntȷgrǽlȷtȷ], *s.* integridad.

integrally [íntȷgrạlȷ], *adv.* integralmente.

integrand [íntȷgrænd], *s.* (mat.) función o diferencial (*f.*) por integrar.

integrant [íntȷgrạnt], *a.* integrante, constitutivo.

integrate [íntȷgreȷt]. **I.** *va.* integrar, formar un todo; (mat.) integrar. **II.** *vn.* integrarse, completarse.—**integrating** [-ȷŋ], *a.* integrante; de integración.—**integration** [-éȷȿọn], *s.* integración.—**integrator** [-ǫ(r)], *s.* integrador (instrumento).

integrity [íntégrȷtȷ], *s.* integridad, entereza.

integument [íntégyọmẹnt], *s.* integumento, túnica.—**integumental, integumentary** [-méntạl, -méntạrȷ], *a.* integumentario.

intellect [íntelɛkt], *s.* intelecto; intelectiva; inteligencia, entendimiento; persona o gente (*f.*) de talento.

intellection [ȷntelékȿọn], *s.* intelección.

intellective [-tȷv], *a.* intelectivo.

intellectual [ȷntelékƫuạl], *s. y a.* intelectual.—**intellectualism** [-ȷzm], *s.* intelectualismo.—**intellectualist(ic** [-ȷst, -ístȷk], *s. y a.* intelectualista.—**intellectuality** [-ǽlȷtȷ], *s.* intelectualidad.—**intellectually** [-ȷ], *adv.* intelectualmente.

intelligence [íntélȷdȝẹns], *s.* inteligencia; penetración, sagacidad; conocimiento; informe(s); noticia, aviso; correspondencia mutua, armonía, acuerdo; un ser inteligente; policía secreta.—**i. bureau** o **department,** oficina de información, indagación o espionaje.—**i. office** = **i. bureau;** (E. U. ant.) agencia de sirvientes.—**i. officer,** oficial o agente de la oficina de indagación.—**i. quotient,** cociente intelectual, edad intelectual.—**i. test,** examen de inteligencia.

intelligencer [-œ(r)], *s.* noticiero, mensajero; espía, *mf.*

intelligent [-ẹnt], *a.* inteligente; bien fundado, con conocimiento.—**intelligently** [-lȷ], *adv.* inteligentemente; con conocimiento del asunto.

intelligentsia [-éntsȷạ̈], *s. pl.* las clases cultas o ilustradas, la intelectualidad, los intelectuales.

intelligibility [-ȷbílȷtȷ], **intelligibleness** [-blnȷs], *s.* inteligibilidad; comprensibilidad, claridad.

intelligible [-bl], *a.* inteligible.—**intelligibly** [-blȷ], *adv.* inteligiblemente.

intemperance [íntémpœrạns], *s.* intemperancia; destemplanza; exceso en la bebida.—**intemperate** [íntémpœrȷt], *a.* destemplado; inmoderado, desmandado; intemperante; excesivo, desmedido.—**intemperately** [-lȷ], *adv.* destempladamente; inmoderadamente.—**intemperateness** [-nȷs], *s.* inmoderación, intemperancia; exceso, demasía.

intend [ínténd], *va.* intentar, tener intención de, pensar, proponerse; destinar; aplicar, determinar; querer decir; tener por objeto.

intendancy [ínténdạnsȷ], *s.* intendencia.

intendant [-ạnt], *s.* intendente, procurante.

intended [íntɛ́ndȷd]. **I.** *s.* (fam.) desposado, prometido, futuro. **II.** *a.* deseado, pensado, que se tiene en mira; encaminado a.—**intendedly** [-lȷ], *adv.* adrede, intencionalmente.

intendment [íntɛ́ndmẹnt], *s.* (for.) intento o espíritu de una ley.

intense [íntɛ́ns], *a.* intenso, fuerte, vivo, violento; extremado, sumo; esforzado; (fot.) duro (negativo).—**intensely** [-lȷ], *adv.* intensamente.—**intenseness** [-nȷs], *s.* calidad de intenso, intensidad.

intensification [-ȷfȷkéȷȿọn], *s.* intensificación, acrecentamiento, aumento; avivamiento.

intensifier [-ȷfaȷœ(r)], *s.* intensificador, acrecentador; (fot.) baño para reforzar un negativo.

intensify [-ȷfaȷ]. **I.** *va.* intensar, hacer más intenso, intensificar, acrecentar; avivar; (fot.) reforzar. **II.** *vn.* intens(ific)arse, volverse intenso.

intension [íntɛ́nȿọn], *s.* intensión; tensión; intensidad; (lóg.) contenido, comprensión.

intensity [íntɛ́nsȷtȷ], *s.* intensidad; (fot.) fuerza de un negativo.

intensive [íntɛ́nsȷv], *a.* intens(iv)o; entero, completo; (lóg.) relativo al contenido; (gram.) enfático.—**intensively** [-lȷ], *adv.* intensivamente.

intent [íntɛ́nt]. **I.** *a.* atento; asiduo, dedicado; (con **on**) decidido, resuelto a, empeñado en. **II.** *s.* intento, designio, intención, propósito.—**to all intents and purposes,** en realidad, en el fondo.

intention [íntɛ́nȿọn], *s.* intención; designio, fin, mira, propósito deliberado; (cir.) procedimiento de curación.—**by first, second i.,** (cir.) de o por primera, segunda intención.

intentional [-ạl], *a.* intencional.—**intentionally** [-ȷ], *adv.* intencionalmente, de intento, adrede.

intently [íntɛ́ntlȷ], *adv.* asiduamente; atentamente; resueltamente.—**intentness** [-nȷs], *s.* aplicación asidua, atención.

inter [íntœr], *va.* enterrar, sepultar, inhumar.

interact [íntœrǽkt]. **I.** *va.* obrar entre sí, o recíprocamente. **II.** [íntœrækt], *s.* (teat.) entreactọ intermedio.—**interaction** [-éȷkȿọn], *s.* interacción, acción recíproca.

interallied [-ælǽȷd], *a.* de los aliados.

interborough [-bʌ́roų], *a.* municipal, interseccional, que une las secciones o distritos (*boroughs*) de una gran ciudad.

interbreed [-bríd], *va. y vn.* = HYBRIDIZE.

intercalary [íntœrkạlerȷ], *a.* intercalar.—**intercalate** [-leȷt], *va.* intercalar.—**intercalation** [-léȷȿọn], *s.* intercalación.

intercede [íntœrsíd], *vn.* interceder.

interceder [-œ(r)], *s.* intercesor.

intercellular [-sélyǫlä(r)], *a.* intercelular.

intercept [-sépt]. **I.** *va.* interceptar; atajar, detener. **II.** *s.* (mat.) ordenada en el origen.—**interception** [-sépȿọn], *s.* interceptación; atajo.

intercession [-séȿọn], *s.* intercesión.—**intercessor** [-sésǫ(r)], *s.* intercesor.—**intercessory** [-rȷ], *a.* intercesor.

interchain [-chéȷn], *va.* encadenar, entrelazar.

interchange [-chéȷndȝ]. **I.** *va.* alternar; cambiar, trocar; permutar. **II.** *vn.* alternarse, trocarse. **III.** [íntœrcheȷndȝ], *s.* intercambio; comercio, tráfico.—**interchangeability** [-ạbílȷtȷ], **interchangeableness** [-chéȷndȝạ̈blnȷs], *s.* calidad de intercambiable.—**interchangeable** [-bl], *a.* intercambiable; de recambio; permutable; mutuo, recíproco.—**interchangeably** [-blȷ], *adv.* recíprocamente; intercambiablemente.

interchurch [-chœrch], *a.* relativo o común a varias iglesias o a las iglesias.

intercollegiate [-kǫlídȝȷȷt], *a.* intercolegiado, interescolar, de entre universidades o estudiantes.

intercolumnar [-kolʌmnä(r)], *a.* intercolumnar.

intercolumniation [-kolʌmnȷéȷȿọn], *s.* (arq.) intercolu(m)nio.

intercommunicate [-kọmúnȷkeȷt], *vn.* intercomunicarse, comunicarse con otro.—**intercommunication** [-éȷȿọn], *s.* comunicación mutua.

intercostal [-kástạl], *a.* intercostal.

intercourse [íntœrkors], *s.* comercio, tráfico; intercambio; comunicación; correspondencia, trato, roce; coito, cópula, trato sexual.

intercrop [-krap]. **I.** *va.* (agr.) hacer una siembra entre los surcos de otra; hacer siembra accesoria intermedia de cosecha rápida entre la cosecha de la siembra principal y el tiempo de sembrar para otra análoga. **II.** *s.* siembra de entre surcos; siembra accesoria de cosecha rápida.

intercross [-krós], *va.* entrecruzar; cruzar castas, hibridar.

intercrossing [-iŋ], *s.* cruzamiento.

intercurrent [-kœrɛnt], *a.* intercurrente.

intercutaneous [-kiutéiniəs], *a.* intercutáneo.

interdental [-déntəl], *a.* interdentario; (fon.) interdental.

interdependence [-dipéndɛns], *s.* dependencia mutua.—**interdependent** [-ɛnt], *a.* dependiente uno de otro.

interdict [-díkt], *va.* interdecir, entredecir; prohibir, vedar; poner entredicho.

interdict [íntœrdikt], **interdiction** [-díkʃɔn], *s.* veto, veda, prohibición; interdicto, entredicho.

interdictive [-díktiv], **interdictory** [-díktori], *a.* que interdice o veda.

interdigital [-dídʒitəl], *a.* interdigital.

interest [íntœrist]. I. *va.* interesar. II. *s.* interés; provecho; simpatía; (com.) interés, rédito; participación en una empresa; influencia, empeño, influjo.—**the interests**, las grandes empresas, los intereses creados del comercio y la industria, los capitalistas.—**to one's (own) i.**, en bien o provecho de uno, que le conviene.

interested [-id], *a.* interesado.

interesting [-iŋ], *a.* interesante, atractivo.—**in an i. condition**, en estado interesante, encinta.

interestingly [-li], *adv.* interesantemente, amenamente.

interfere [íntœrfír], *vn.* ingerirse, inmiscuirse, mezclarse, interponerse, meterse; intervenir; (con **with**) embarazar, impedir, estorbar; (fís.) interferir; (vet.) tropezarse, rozarse un pie con el otro los caballos.

interference [-ɛns], *s.* ingerencia, interposición, intromisión, intervención; obstáculo, impedimento; (fís., rad.) interferencia, interrupción.

interferential [-fiɾénʃəl], *a.* (fís.) interferente.

interfering [-fíɾiŋ], *s.* = INTERFERENCE; (vet.) alcance, tropezón, rozadura.

interferometer [-fiɾámetœr], *s.* instrumento para medir distancias, desplazamientos, etc., por medio de la interferencia; instrumento para el análisis espectral de gases incandescentes.

interfuse [-fiúz]. I. *va.* hacer fluir juntamente, fundir, mezclar. II. *vn.* fluir uno en otro; mezclarse.—**interfusion** [-fiúʒɔn], *s.* fusión íntima, mezcla, combinación.

interim [íntœrim], *a.* interino, intermedio, ínterin.—**i. certificate**, certificado provisional.—**in the i.**, en el ínterin, interinamente, entretanto.

interior [intírio(r)]. I. *a.* interior, interno. **I.** *s.* interior, parte (f.) de adentro.

interiorly [-li], *adv.* interiormente.

interjacent [íntœrdʒéisɛnt], *a.* interyacente, interpuesto.

interject [-dʒékt]. I. *va.* interponer, insertar. II. *vn.* interponerse, intervenir.

interjection [-dʒékʃɔn], *s.* (gram.) interjección; exclamación; intervención, interposición.

interjoin [-dʒóin], *va.* unir mutuamente.

interlace [-léis], *va.* entrelazar, entremezclar.

interlard [-lárd], *va.* (coc.) mechar; interpolar, insertar.

interleave [-lív], *va.* interfoliar, interpaginar, intercalar hojas en.

interline [-láin], *va.* interlinear; (cost.) entretelar.—**interlineal** [-líniəl], **interlinear** [-líniə(r)], *a.* interlineal.—**interlineation** [-éiʃɔn], *s.* interlineación.—**interlining** [-láiniŋ], *s.* interlineación; (cost.) entretela.

interlink [-líŋk], *va.* eslabonar.

interlock [-lák]. I. *va.* y *vn.* trabar, engranar, engargantar; unirse, entrelazarse; cerrar. II. [íntœrlak], *s.* traba; trabazón, f.; (cine) sincronización; (cine) sincronizador.

interlocking [-lákiŋ], *a.* que engranan, que se traban; de traba; de fijación mutua; de cierre.—**i. directorates**, juntas directivas entrelazadas de empresas comerciales, en que varios miembros lo son de juntas de empresas diferentes, las cuales pueden en realidad ser dominadas por unas mismas personas.

interlocution [-lokiúʃɔn], *s.* interlocución, diálogo, plática.

interlocutor [-lákiutɔ(r)], *s.* interlocutor.

interlocutory [-lákiutori], *a.* dialogístico; (for.) interlocutorio.

interlope [-lóup], *vn.* entremeterse sin derecho; traficar sin licencia.—**interloper** [íntœrloupœ(r)], *s.* entremetido, intruso; (com.) intérlope (ú. como *a.*).

interlude [-liud], *s.* blanco, intervalo; (teat.) intermedio, entremés, tonadilla; (mús.) interludio.

interlunar(y [-liúnər(i], *a.* interlunar.

intermarriage [-méridʒ], *s.* matrimonio de personas de distintas razas, o entre parientes.

intermarry [-méri], *vn.* casarse personas emparentadas o de distintas razas.

intermaxillary [-méksileri]. I. *a.* intermaxilar. II. *s.* hueso intermaxilar (ll. t. **i. bone**).

intermeddle [-médl], *vn.* injerirse, inmiscuirse, entremeterse.—**intermeddler** [-médlœ(r)], *s.* entremetido.—**intermeddling** [-iŋ], *s.* injerencia, entremetimiento.

intermediacy [-mídiəsi], *s.* calidad de intermedio; intervención, mediación.

intermedial, intermediate [-mídiəl, -mídiit], *a.* medianero, intermedio.—**intermediary** [-mídieri], *a.* y *s.* intermediario.—**intermediate** [-mídieit], *vn.* intervenir, (inter)mediar.—**intermediately** [-li], *adv.* por intervención.—**intermediation** [-éiʃɔn], *s.* intervención, mediación.

interment [íntœrmɛnt], *s.* entierro, sepultura.

intermezzo [íntœrmédzou], *s.* (mús.) intermedio.

interminable [íntœrmínabl], *a.* interminable.—**interminably** [-bli], *adv.* interminablemente.—**interminate** [íntœrminit], *a.* interminable.

intermingle [-míŋgl]. I. *va.* entremezclar, entreverar. II. *vn.* mezclarse.

intermission [-míʃɔn], *s.* intermisión, interrupción, tregua; (med.) intermitencia; (teat.) intermedio, entreacto.

intermissive [-mísiv], *a.* intermitente.

intermit [-mít]. I. *va.* intermitir, interrumpir, discontinuar. II. *vn.* interrumpirse, cesar.—**intermittent** [-ɛnt], *a.* intermitente.—**intermittingly** [-iŋli], *adv.* con intermisión, a intervalos.

intermix [-míks]. I. *va.* entremezclar, entreverar, entretejer, interpolar. II. *vn.* entremezclarse, compenetrarse.—**intermixture** [-chúr], *s.* entremezcladura; mezcla; compenetración.

intern [íntœrn]. I. *va.* encerrar, poner a buen recaudo; internar; meter en un campo de concentración. II. [íntœrn], *s.* interno, practicante de hospital (ll. t. **interne**).

internal [íntœrnəl], *a.* interno, interior; doméstico, intestino; íntimo.—**i.-combustion engine**, motor de combustión (interna).—**i. diameter**, diámetro interior.—**i. gear**, (mec.) engranaje de dientes interiores.—**i. revenue**, rentas interiores, rentas provenientes de impuestos sobre artículos y operaciones interiores.

internally [-i], *adv.* internamente; interiormente; adentro.

international [íntœrnéʃɔnəl]. I. *a.* internacional.—**i. law**, derecho de gentes, derecho internacional. II. *s.* (I.), Internacional (asociación).

internationalism [-izm], *s.* internacionalismo.—**internationality** [-éliti], *s.* internacionalidad.

internationalist [-ist], *s.* internacionalista.

internationalize [-aiz], *va.* internacionalizar.

internecine [íntœrnísin], *a.* mortífero, mutuamente destructor; sanguinario.

internee [íntœrní], *s.* (mil.) internado.

intern(e)ship [íntœrnʃip], *s.* internado.

internment [intɔ́ɹnmənt], s. encerramiento; internación; (mil.) internamiento.

internod(i)al [intɔɹnóud(i)əl], a. colocado entre dos nudos.—**internode** [íntɔɹnoud], s. (bot.) internodio, cañuto.

internuncio [-nʌ́nŝjou], s. internuncio.

interoceanic [-oŝiǽnịk], a. interoceánico.

interosseous [-ásɹʌs], a. (anat.) interóseo.

interpellant [-péḷənt], s. interpelante.—**interpellate** [-péḷeit], va. interpelar.

interpellation [-peḷéiŝon], s. interpelación.

interpenetrate [-pénịtreit], va. y vn. compenetrar(se).

interphone [-foun], s. teléfono de servicio interior.

interplane [-plein], a. situado entre dos planos.

interplanetary [-plǽneterị], a. interplanetario.

interplay [-plei], s. acción recíproca.

interplead [-plíd], vn. (for.) litigar entre sí varios demandantes, para determinar el mayor derecho a la demanda.—**interpleader** [- œ(r)], s. (for.) procedimiento para determinar cuál de varios demandantes tiene derecho a la demanda.

interpolate [intɔ́ɹpoleit], va. interpolar.—**interpolation** [-éiŝon], s. interpolación.—**interpolator** [-ọ(r)], s. interpolador.

interposal [intɔɹpóuzəl], s. interposición, mediación, intervención.—**interpose** [-póuz]. I. va. interponer; (cine) reemplazar gradualmente una figura por otra, o cambiar la una en la otra. II. vn. interponerse, intermediar, intervenir; interrumpir.—**interposer** [-œ(r)], s. mediador. —**interposition** [-poziŝon], s. interposición.

interpret [intɔ́ɹprịt], va. interpretar, descifrar, traducir; representar, ilustrar.

interpretable [-əbl], a. interpretable.

interpretation [-éiŝon], s. interpretación, traducción, explicación, exposición.

interpretative [-eịtịv], a. interpretativo.—**interpretatively** [-lị], adv. interpretativamente.

interpreter [-œ(r)], s. intérprete, traductor.

interregnum [intɔɹrégnʌm], s. interregno.

interrelated [-rịléịtịd], a. con relación recíproca.

interrogate [intérogeit]. I. va. interrogar, preguntar, examinar. II. vn. hacer preguntas.

interrogation [-éiŝon], s. interrogación, pregunta, pesquisa.—**i. point**, (impr.) interrogación, (punto) interrogante (?).

interrogative [intérágatịv]. I. a. interrogativo. II. s. palabra interrogativa.—**interrogatively** [-lị], adv. interrogativamente.

interrogator [intérogeitọ(r)], s. interrogante.

interrogatory [intérágatorị]. I. s. interrogatorio, examen. II. a. interrogativo.

interrupt [intɔrʌ́pt], va. interrumpir.—**interruptedly** [-ịdlị], adv. interrumpidamente, descontinuamente.—**interrupter** [-œ(r)], s. interruptor; (elec.) interruptor, disyuntor.— **interruption** [intɔrʌ́pŝon], s. interrupción.

interscapular [-skǽpyụlǽ(r)], a. interescapular.

interscholastic [-skolǽstịk], a. interescolar, de entre escuelas.

intersect [-sékt]. I. va. cortar. II. vn. (geom., etc.) cortarse, intersecarse.

intersection [-sékŝon], s. intersección; cruce (de calles, etc.), bocacalle.

interspace [-spéịs]. I. va. dejar espacio entre; llenar el espacio entre; espaciar. II. [íntɔɹspeịs], s. espacio intermedio; intersticio; intervalo.

intersperse [-spɔ́ɹs], va. esparcir, entremezclar; diseminar.—**interspersion** [-spɔ́ɹŝon], s. esparcimiento de una cosa entre otras.

interstate [íntɔɹsteịt], a. interestatal, entre estados, de entre estados (de un mismo país).

interstellar [-steḷǽ(r)], a. interestelar, intersideral.

interstice [intɔ́ɹstịs], s. intersticio.

interstitial [intɔɹstíŝəl], a. intersticial, que tiene intersticios.

intertexture [-tékschụ(r)], s. contexto, entretejedura, entretejimiento.

intertropical [-trápịkəl], a. intertropical.

intertwine, intertwist [-twáịn. -twíst], va. entretejer, entrelazar; (mar.) acolchar.

interurban [-ɔ́ɹbən], a. interurbano.

interval [íntɔɹvəl], s. intervalo; blanco, claro, hueco; (mús.) intervalo.—**at intervals**, a ratos; a trechos; aquí y allá.

intervene [intɔɹvín], vn. intervenir, mediar; atravesarse, interponerse; ocurrir, sobrevenir.—**intervening** [-ịŋ], a. intermedio, intercurrente, interjacente, interpuesto; interventor.

intervention [-vénŝon], s. intervención; mediación; interposición.

interventionism [-ịzm], s. intervencionismo.

interventionist [-ịst], s. partidario de la intervención; (med.) el que sostiene que una enfermedad debe atacarse en vez de dejarla seguir su curso natural; intervencionista, partidario del paternalismo o de la intervención del estado en disputas económicas.

intervertebral [-vɔ́ɹtębrəl], a. intervertebral.

interview [íntɔɹvịu]. I. s. entrevista, conferencia, abocamiento, interviú, f. II. va. entrevistar(se con), tener entrevista con, interviuvar.

interviewer [-œ(r)], s. entrevistador; reportero que se avista con personas para indagar opiniones, obtener información, etc.

intervocalic [-vokǽlịk], a. (fon.) intervocálico.

intervolve [-válv], va. envolver una cosa dentro de otra.

interweave [-wív], va. y vn. (pret. INTERWOVE o INTERWEAVED); pp. -WOVE(N) o -WEAVED) entretejer(se), entrelazar(se).—**interweaving** [-ịŋ], s. entretejimiento, entrelazamiento.—**interwoven** [-wóụvn], a. entrelazado, entretejido, vinculado.

interwreathe [-ríð], va. tejer en forma de guirnalda. V. INTERTWINE.

intestable [intéstəbl], a. legalmente ineapacitado para hacer testamento.

intestacy [intéstəsị], s. falta de testamento.

intestate [intésteịt], a. y s. intestado, abintestato.

intestinal [intéstịnəl], a. intestinal; interior, intestino.

intestine [intéstịn]. I. a. interior, intestino, doméstico; interno. II. s. (anat.) intestino, tripa.

inthrall, inthralment, etc. = ENTHRALL, etc.

intimacy [íntịmǽsị], s. intimidad, confianza.

intimate [íntịmịt]. I. a. íntimo; familiar; profundo (conocimiento).—**to become i.**, intimarse. II. s. amigo íntimo, confidente. III. [íntịmeịt], va. insinuar, indicar, intimar.—**intimately** [íntịmịtlị], adv. íntimamente.

intimation [intịméiŝon], s. insinuación, intimación, indirecta, pulla; indicio.

intimidate [intímịdeịt], va. intimidar, acoquinar.—**intimidation** [-éiŝon], s. intimidación.

intitle [intáịtl], va. = ENTITLE.

into [íntu], prep. en, dentro, adentro, hacia el interior (según que denote ingreso, penetración, inserción, inclusión, transformación o multiplicación).—**i. the bargain**, por añadidura.

intolerability [intálęrəbílịtị], **intolerableness** [-blnịs], s. intolerabilidad.—**intolerable** [-bl], a. intolerable, insufrible, inaguantable, insoportable.—**intolerably** [-blị], adv. intolerablemente.—**intolerance, intolerancy** [-əns, -ị], s. intolerancia.—**intolerant** [-ənt], a. y s. intolerante.—**intolerantly** [-lị], adv. con intolerancia.

intomb [intúm], va. enterrar, sepultar.

intonate [íntoneịt], va. entonar, solfear, cantar.—**intonation** [-éiŝon], s. entonación.

intone [intóụn], va. y vn. entonar; cantar o recitar en un solo tono; (igl.) salmear, salmodiar.

intortion [intɔ́ɹŝon], s. (bot.) intorsión.

intoxicant [intáksịkǽnt]. I. s. bebida alcohólica. II. a. = INTOXICATING.

intoxicate [-keịt], va. embriagar, emborrachar.—

intoxicated [-ịd], *a.* ebrio, embriagado, borracho, bebido.—**intoxicating** [-iŋ], *a.* embriagante, embriagador, emborrachador.—**intoxication** [-kéịşǫn], *s.* embriaguez, borrachez, beodez; (med.) intoxicación, envenenamiento.

intra-atomic [ịntrạ ætámịk], *a.* intraatómico, del interior del átomo.

intracardiac [-kárdịæk], *a.* (anat.) intracardíaco.

intracoastal [-kóȷstal], *a.* cercano a la costa.

intractability [ịntrǽktạbịlịtị], **intractableness** [-ạblnịs], *s.* intratabilidad, hurañería.—**intractable** [-bl], *a.* intratable.—**intractably** [-blị], *adv.* intratable o hurañamente.

intrados [ịntréịdas], *s.* (arq.) intradós.

intramolecular [ịntrạmǫlékȳụlǎ(r)], *a.* intramolecular.

intramural [-mịúrạl], *a.* situado intramuros; que se verifica dentro de un pueblo, o entre los estudiantes de un mismo colegio (deportes, etc.); (anat.) intramural.

intranquillity [ịntrænkwịlịtị], *s.* intranquilidad.

intransigence, -cy [ịntrǽnsịdźęns, -ị], *s.* intransigencia.—**intransigent** [-ęnt], *a.* y *s.*, **intransigentist** [-ịst], *s.* intransigente.

intransitive [ịntrǽnsịtịv], *a.* (gram.) intransitivo.

intransitively [-lị], *adv.* intransitivamente.

intransmutability [ịntrænsmịútạbịlịtị], *s.* intransmutabilidad.

intransmutable [-ạbl], *a.* intransmutable.

intravenous [ịntrạvínas], *a.* (anat.) intravenoso.

intrench, intrenchment = ENTRENCH, etc.

intrepid [ịntrépịd], *a.* intrépido, impávido.

intrepidity [ịntrepịdịtị], *s.* intrepidez.

intrepidly [ịntrépịdlị], *adv.* intrépidamente.

intricacy [ịntrịkạsị], **intricateness** [-kịtnịs], *s.* intrincación, intrincamiento, embrollo, enredo.

intricate [ịntrịkịt], *a.* intrincado, enredado.

intricately [-lị], *adv.* intrincadamente.

intrigue [ịntríg]. **I.** *s.* intriga, manejo, trama, cábala; arte, *mf.*, amaño; intriga amorosa, galanteo, lío; enredo de una comedia. **II.** *vn.* intrigar; tramar; tener intrigas amorosas. **III.** *va.* ganarse mañosamente, seducir; atraer, interesar; despertar la curiosidad de; poner perplejo.

intriguer [-œ(r)], *s.* intrigante, tracista, *mf.*

intriguing [-iŋ], *a.* intrigante; seductor.—**intriguingly** [-lị], *adv.* por medio de intrigas.

intrinsic(al [ịntrínsịk(ạl], *a.* intrínseco.

intrinsically [-ị], *adv.* intrínsecamente.

intrinsicalness [-nịs], *s.* calidad de intrínseco.

introduce [ịntrodịús], *va.* introducir, meter; implantar, injerir; presentar (una persona a otra); dar entrada; hacer adoptar, poner en uso.—**to i. a bill**, presentar un proyecto de ley.

introducer [-œ(r)], *s.* introductor; presentador.

introduction [-dǽkṣǫn], *s.* introducción; prefacio, proemio; implantación; presentación.

introductive [-tịv], *a.* introductivo.

introductory [-torị], *a.* de introducción, introductivo; preliminar.

introit [ịntróịt], *s.* (igl.) introito.

intromission [ịntromíşǫn], *s.* intromisión; introducción; admisión, iniciación.

intromit [-mịt]. **I.** *va.* introducir, insertar; enviar adjunto; dar entrada, admitir. **II.** *vn.* entremeterse, ingerirse.

introrse [ịntrórs], *a.* (bot.) introrso.

introspect [ịntrospékt]. **I.** *va.* mirar lo interior de alguna cosa. **II.** *vn.* hacer examen de introspección.—**introspection** [-spékṣǫn], *s.* introspección.—**introspective** [-spéktịv], *a.* introspectivo.

introversion [-vœ́rşǫn], *s.* vuelta hacia dentro; (psic.) introversión.

introvert [-vœrt]. **I.** *va.* volver hacia dentro. **II.** *vn.* (psic.) concentrarse en sí mismo, ocuparse más en el mundo interior que en el exterior. **III.** [ịntrovœrt], *s.* y *a.* (psic.) introverso, que tiene la tendencia a concentrarse en sí mismo.—**introverted** [-ịd], *a.* introverso.

intrude [ịntrúd]. **I.** *vn.* intrusarse, entremeterse, inmiscuirse. **II.** *va.* meter, forzar.

intruded [-ịd], *a.* (geol.) intrusivo.

intruder [-œ(r)], *s.* intruso, entremetido.

intrusion [ịntrúźǫn], *s.* intrusión, entremetimiento, impertinencia; (geol.) intrusión.

intrusional [-ạl], **intrusive** [ịntrúṣịv], *a.* intruso; (geol.) de intrusión, intrusivo.—**intrusively** [-lị], *adv.* intrusamente.—**intrusiveness** [-nịs]. *s.* tendencia a intrusarse.

intrust [ịntrást], *va.* = ENTRUST.

intubate [ịntịubeịt], *va.* (med.) intubar.—**intubation** [-éịṣǫn], *s.* intubación.

intuition [ịntịuíṣǫn], *s.* intuición.

intuitional [-ạl], *a.* intuitivo; de o por intuición. —**i. ethics**, doctrina de que los sentimientos e ideas morales son intuitivos.

intuitionalism [-ạlịzm], **intuitionism** [-ịzm], *s.* doctrina de que ciertas verdades fundamentales se adquieren por intuición; doctrina de que las ideas y sentimientos morales son intuitivos.

intuitive [ịntịúịtịv], *a.* intuitivo.

intuitively [-lị], *adv.* intuitivamente.

intumesce [ịntịuméṣ], *vn.* hincharse.—**intumescence, intumescency** [-ęns, -ị], *s.* intumescencia, hinchazón, *f.*—**intumescent** [-ęnt], *a.* intumescente; hinchado.

intussusception [ịntạssạsépṣǫn], *s.* (biol., med.) intususcepción.

intwine [ịntwaịn], *va.* y *vn.* = ENTWINE.

inula [ịnȳụlǎ], *s.* (bot.) énula campana, ínula.

inulin [ịnȳụlịn], *s.* (quím.) inulina.

inunction [ịnáŋkṣǫn], *s.* untura, frotación.

inundate [ịnándeịt], *va.* inundar, anegar.

inundation [-éịṣǫn], *s.* inundación.

inurbane [ịnœrbéịn], *a.* inurbano, descortés, incivil.—**inurbaneness, inurbanity** [-nịs, -bǽnịtị], *s.* inurbanidad.

inure [ịnȳúr]. **I.** *va.* avezar, acostumbrar, habituar. **II.** *vn.* tener efecto; quedar para, pasar (a). —**inured** [-d], *a.* avezado, hecho (a), endurecido, cursado.—**inurement** [-męnt], *s.* práctica, hábito, costumbre.

inurn [ịnœ́rn], *va.* poner en una urna cineraria.

inutility [ịnȳụtịlịtị], *s.* inutilidad.

invade [ịnvéịd], *va.* invadir.—**invader** [-œ(r)], *s.* invasor.

invaginate [ịnvǽdźịneịt]. **I.** *va.* envainar, enchufar; (cir.) invaginar. **II.** *a.* envainado, enchufado; invaginado.—**invagination** [-éịṣǫn], *s.* enchufamiento; intususcepción, invaginación.

invalid [ịnvǽlịd], *a.* inválido, nulo, írrito.

invalid [ịnvạlịd], *a.* y *s.* inválido, (persona) baldada, impedida o lisiada.—**i. chair**, sillón para inválidos.

invalid [ịnvạlịd], *va.* matricular en el registro de inválidos; lisiar, incapacitar.

invalidate [ịnvǽlịdeịt], *va.* invalidar, anular.

invalidation [-éịṣǫn], *s.* invalidación, irritación.

invalidism [ịnvǽlịdịzm], *s.* baldadura crónica.

invalidity [ịnvạlịdịtị], **invalidness** [ịnvǽlịdnịs]. *s.* (for.) nulidad; invalidez; falta de salud; inhabilitación, incapacidad.

invaluable [ịnvǽlyụạbl], *a.* inestimable, inapreciable.—**invaluably** [-blị], *adv.* inestimablemente.

invariability [ịnvérịạbịlịtị], **invariableness** [-blnịs], *s.* invariabilidad.—**invariable** [-bl], *a.* invariable.—**invariably** [-blị], *adv.* invariablemente.

invariant [ịnvérịạnt]. **I.** *a.* invariable, constante; (mat.) relativo a las invariantes. **II.** *s.* (mat.) invariante, *f.*

invasion [ịnvéịźǫn], *s.* invasión.

invasive [ịnvéịsịv], *a.* hostil; agresivo, invasor.

invective [ịnvéktịv]. **I.** *s.* invectiva, vituperio, filípica. **II.** *a.* ultrajante, injurioso.—**invectively** [-lị], *adv.* injuriosamente.

inveigh [ịnvéị], *vn.* prorrumpir en invectivas.

inveigher [-œ(r)], *s.* el que lanza una filípica.

inveigle [ịnvígl], *va.* seducir, engañar, engatusar.

—**inveiglement** [-mɛnt], s. engañifa, embaimiento.—**inveigler** [-glœ(r)], s. seductor.
inveil [invéil], va. cubrir con un velo.
invent [invɛ́nt], va. inventar; idear, discurrir.
inventible [-jbl], a. que puede ser inventado.
invention [invɛ́nʃǫn], s. invención, invento; inventiva, ingenio; mentira, falsedad, embuste.—I. **of the Cross,** (igl.) Invención de la Santa Cruz.
inventive [-jv], a. inventivo.
inventor [-ǫ(r)], s. inventor.
inventorial [inventóriạl], a. perteneciente al inventario.—**inventorially** [-i], adv. con inventario.
inventory [ínventǫri]. I. s. inventario. II. va. inventariar.
inverse [invœ́rs], a. inverso, invertido.—**i. ratio,** razón inversa.—**inversely** [-li], adv. inversamente.
inversion [invœ́rʃǫn], s. inversión, transmutación, trastrocamiento.
invert [invœ́rt]. I. va. invertir; volver al revés; trastrocar; transponer; (quím.) invertir. II. [ínvœrt], a. (quím.) invertido. III. s. (com.) invertosa, azúcar invertido; (psiq.) invertido, homosexual.
invertase [invœ́rteis], s. (quím.) invertasa, invertina.
invertebral, invertebrate [invœ́rtȩbrạl, -breit], a. y s. (zool.) invertebrado.
Invertebrata [-bréjtạ̈], s. pl. (zool.) invertebrados.
invertedly [invœ́rtidli], adv. invertidamente.
invest [invɛ́st], va. (com.) invertir, interesar, emplear o imponer dinero; (con **with** o **in)** vestir, cubrir, adornar, poner; investir, conferir, dar; (mil.) sitiar, cercar.
investigable [invɛ́stigạbl], a. averiguable, investigable, escudriñable.
investigate [invɛ́stigeit], va. investigar, indagar, averiguar; estudiar o analizar.—**investigating** [-iɳ], a. investigador, pesquisante.—**investigation** [-éjʃǫn], s. investigación, pesquisa, indagación, encuesta, averiguación; estudio, análisis, mf.—**investigative** [-jv], a. investigador.—**investigator** [-ǫ(r)], s. investigador; indagador, averiguador, pesquisidor.
investiture [invɛ́stịchur], s. investidura, instalación.
investment [invɛ́stmȩnt], s. (com.) inversión; (mil.) sitio, cerco; investidura, instalación; cubierta; envoltura.
investor [invɛ́stǫ(r)], s. (com.) inversionista, persona que invierte dinero; interesado.
inveteracy [invɛ́terạsi], **inveterateness** [-itnis], s. hábito o costumbre inveterada.—**inveterate** [-it], a. inveterado, arraigado, crónico, empedernido.—**inveterately** [-li], adv. inveteradamente.
invidious [invídiạs], a. denigrante, difamatorio; odioso.—**invidiously** [-li], adv. denigrantemente; odiosamente.—**invidiousness** [-nis], s. calidad de difamatorio.
invigorate [invígǫreit], va. vigorizar, fortificar.—**invigorating** [-iɳ], a. vigorizante, vigorizador, cordial, fortaleciente.—**invigoration** [-éjʃǫn], s. acto y efecto de vigorizar.
invincibility [invínsịbíliti], **invincibleness** [-blnis], s. calidad de invencible.—**invincible** [-bl], a. invencible.—**invincibly** [-bli], adv. invenciblemente.
inviolability [inviǫlạbílịti], **inviolableness** [-blnis], s. inviolabilidad.—**inviolable** [-bl], a. inviolable, inquebrantable.—**inviolably** [-bli], adv. inviolablemente.—**inviolate** [inviǫlit], a. inviolado, incorrupto, íntegro.
invisibility [invízịbílịti], **invisibleness** [-blnis], s. invisibilidad.—**invisible** [-bl], a. invisible.—I. **Empire** = KU KLUX KLAN.—**i. ink,** tinta simpática.—**invisibly** [-bli], adv. invisiblemente.
invitation [invịtéjʃǫn], s. invitación, convite.

invitatory [invájtạtǫri]. I. a. invitador, convidador. II. s. (igl.) invitatorio.
invite [invájt], va. convidar, invitar, brindar; atraer; provocar, incitar, tentar; instar.
inviter [-œ(r)], s. convidador, invitador.
inviting [-iɳ], a. atractivo, seductivo; incitante.—**invitingly** [-li], adv. de un modo atractivo.—**invitingness** [-nis], s. calidad de atractivo.
invocation [invǫkéjʃǫn], s. invocación; (for.) suplicatorio, exhorto, mandamiento.
invocatory [invákạtǫri], a. invocatorio.
invoice [ínvois]. I. s. (com.) factura.—**i. book,** libro de facturas.—**i. price,** precio de factura. II. va. facturar.
invoke [invóuk], va. invocar; (for.) expedir suplicatorio, exhorto o mandamiento.
involucel [invályusel], s. (bot.) involucela, involucro secundario.
involucral [invǫliúkrạl], a. involucral.—**involucrate** [-kreit], **involucred** [invǫliukœrd], a. involucrado.—**involucre** [-kœ(r)], **involucrum** [invǫliúkrʌm], s. (bot.) involucro; (anat.) envoltura.
involuntarily [inválʌnterịli], adv. involuntariamente.—**involuntariness** [-nis], s. involuntariedad.—**involuntary** [-eri], a. involuntario.
involute [ínvǫliut], a. intrincado; vuelto hacia dentro; enrollado en espiral.
involution [invǫliúʃǫn], s. envolvimiento; complicación, enredo; (mat.) elevación a potencias; teoría de las potencias; (mat. y med.) involución.
involve [inválv], va. envolver, enrollar; implicar, comprometer; entrañar, comprender; torcer, enredar, emmarañar, complicar; involucrar; (mat.) elevar a una potencia, hallar una potencia de.
involved [-d], a. complicado, difuso (apl. esp. al estilo); mezclado, comprometido (en un asunto).
involvedness [-jdnis], **involvement** [-mȩnt], s. envolvimiento; complicación, intrincación.
invulnerability [invʌlnȩrạbílịti], **invulnerableness** [-blnis], s. invulnerabilidad.—**invulnerable** [-bl], a. invulnerable.—**invulnerably** [-bli], adv. invulnerablemente.
inwall [inwɔ́l], va. rodear o proteger con muros.—**inwall** [ínwǫl], s. pared interior; revestimiento interior (de un horno, etc.).
inward [ínwạrd(z)], adv. hacia dentro, hacia lo interior; adentro.
inward. I. a. interior, interno. II. s. el interior. —pl. entrañas.—**inwardly** [-li], adv. interiormente, internamente.—**inwardness** [-nis], s. calidad, naturaleza o estado interior; lo interior; esencia; fondo.
inweave [inwív], va. entretejer, enlazar.
inwrap [inrǽp], va. envolver.
inwreathe [inríð], va. enguirnaldar.
inwrought [inrɔ́t], a. labrado, embutido, incrustado.
iodate [ájodeit]. I. s. (quím.) yodato. II. va. = IODIZE.
iodic [ajádịk], a. (quím.) yódico.
iodid(e [ájodaid], s. (quím.) yoduro.
iodin(e [ájodin], s. (quím.) yodo o iodo.
iodinate [ájodịneit], va. tratar o combinar con yodo.
iodism [ájodizm], s. (med.) yodismo.
iodization [ajodịzéjʃǫn], s. yoduración.
iodize [ájodaiz], va. (quím.) yodurar.
iodoform [ajódoform], s. (quím.) yodoformo.
iodometry [ajodámetri], s. (quím.) yodometría.
ion [ájǫn], s. (quím.) ion, m.
ionic [ajánịk], a. de o relativo a iones.
Ionic [ajánịk], **Ionian** [ajóunịạn], a. y s. jónico, jonio.
ionium [ajóunịʌm], s. (quím.) ionio, elemento radioactivo.
ionize [ájonaiz], va. ionizar, disociar en iones.—**ionization** [ajǫnịzéjʃǫn], s. ionización, disociación.

iota [aióutǝ], *s.* jota, ápice, tilde, punto.

I O U [ái óu yú] (abreviatura fonética de *I owe you*, yo le debo), *s.* pagaré, vale, abonaré.

ipecac [ípikæk], **ipecacuanha** [-yɹǽnǝ], *s.* (bot., farm.) ipecacuana.

Ipomœa [ipomíǝ], *s.* (bot.) convolvuláceas, *f. pl.*

I Q [ái kjú], abrev. de INTELLIGENCE QUOTIENT.

Iranian [airéinjǝn], *s. y a.* iranio; persa, *mf.*

irascibility [airǽsibíljti], **irascibleness** [-blnjs], *s.* irascibilidad.—**irascible** [-bl], *a.* irascible.

irate [áireit], *a.* encolerizado, airado.

ire [áir], *s.* ira, cólera.—**ireful** [-fyl], *a.* iracundo, colérico.—**irefully**]-i], *adv.* airadamente.

irenic(al [airénik(ǝl], *a.* pacífico, conciliador.

iridaceous [airidéisias], **irideous** [airídiAs], *a.* (bot.) iridáceo, irídeo.

iridectomy [airidéktomi], *s.* (cir.) iridectomía, escisión parcial del iris.

iridesce [iridés], *vn.* irisar.

iridescence [-ǝns], *s.* cambiante, tornasol.—**iridescent** [-ǝnt], *a.* iridiscente, tornasolado.

iridium [airídiAm], *s.* (quím.) iridio.

iris [áiris], *s.* (anat. y ópt.) iris, *m.;* arco iris; (bot.) (flor de) lis, *f.*, lirio, iris, *m.*—**i. root** = ORRIS-ROOT.

irisation [airiséisǝn], *s.* irisación.

Irish [áiriʃ], *a. y s.* irlandés, hibernés.—**I. moss**, musgo de Irlanda.—**I. potato**, patata blanca común.—**the I.**, los irlandeses.

Irishism [-izm], *s.* locución irlandesa; rasgo irlandés.

Irishman [-mǝn], *s.* irlandés.

Irishwoman [-wumǝn], *s.* irlandesa.

iritis [airáitjs], *s.* (med.) iritis.

irk [ǝrk], *va.* fastidiar, aburrir, cansar.

irksome [-sAm], *a.* tedioso, fastidioso, cansado.—**irksomely** [-li], *adv.* cansadamente, fastidiosamente.—**irksomeness** [-njs], *s.* calidad de tedioso.

iron [áiǝrn]. **I.** *s.* hierro, fierro (metal); hierro, hoja (parte cortante de una herramienta); hierro (pieza de construcción—escuadra, viga, etc.—de hierro o acero); plancha (de planchar); herramienta; utensilio; arma de hierro.—*pl.* hierros, grillos, cadenas.—**i. in the fire**, negocio, empresa, asunto a que atender.—**in irons**, aherrojado, en prisiones. **II.** *a.* férreo, de hierro; relativo al hierro.—**i. age**, edad de hierro.—**i. alum**, alumbre de pluma, alumbre ferropotásico.—**i.-bearing**, ferrífero.—**i. black**, polvo de antimonio.—**i.-bound**, unido o sujeto con hierro; escabroso; aherrojado; inflexible, rígido.—**i. dog** = FIREDOG.—**i. foundry**, fundición de hierro.—**i. horse**, (fig.) locomotora.—**i. law of wages**, la supuesta ley de que el salario tiende al mínimo necesario para la subsistencia.—**i. loss**, (elec.) pérdida en el hierro.—**i.-lung**, (med.) pulmón de acero, o mecánico; pulmotor.—**i. mill**, ferrería.—**i. ore**, mineral de hierro.—**i. rust**, herrumbre.—**i. sand**, arena ferruginosa; limaduras de hierro.—**i. scrap**, hierro forjado viejo; hierro colado de desecho.—**i. taste**, herrumbre. **III.** *va.* planchar; aherrojar, poner grilletes a.—**i. out**, planchar, emparejar, alisar; allanar.

ironclad [-klæd]. **I.** *a.* (mar. y elec.) acorazado; riguroso; leonino. **II.** *s.* (mar.) acorazado, blindado; horno para calcinar mineral de mercurio.

ironed [-d], *a.* (a)planchado; aherrojado; armado.

ironer [-œ(r], *s.* planchador(a).

ironic(al [airánik(ǝl], *a.* irónico.

ironically [-i], *adv.* irónicamente.

ironing [áiǝrnin]. **I.** *s.* planchado, acción de planchar; ropa por planchar. **II.** *a.* de planchar.—**i. board**, tabla o palo de planchar.

ironmaster [áiǝrnmæstœ(r], *s.* fabricante de hierro (apl. esp. a los grandes industriales).

ironmonger [-mAngœ(r], *s.* mercader o traficante en hierro; quincallero, ferretero.—**i.'s shop**, ferretería.

ironmongery [-i], *s.* ferretería, quincallería.

ironside [-said], *s.* hombre fuerte o terrible; héroe.—*pl.* (mar.) acorazado.—**Ironsides**, Oliverio Cromwell; caballería de Cromwell.

ironsmith [-smiθ], *s.* herrero.

ironstone [-stoun], *s.* mineral de hierro (gen. siderita o hematites).

ironware [-wer], *s.* artículos de ferretería.

ironwood [-wud], *s.* (bot.) palo hacha.

ironwork [-wœrk], *s.* herraje, obra de hierro.

ironworks [-s], *s.* fundición de hierro, ferrería.

ironwort [-wœrt], *s.* (bot.) siderita, sideritis.

irony [áironi]. **I.** *s.* ironía. **II.** [áiœrni], *a.* ferruginoso.

Iroquois [írokwɔi], *s. y a.* iroqués.

irradiance, irradiancy [iréidiǝns, -i], *s.* irradiación; lustre, esplendor.

irradiate [iréidieit]. **I.** *va.* irradiar, iluminar; inspirar; esparcir. **II.** *vn.* lucir, brillar. **III.** *a.* (poét.) resplandeciente.—**irradiation** [-éiʃǝn], *s.* irradiación; brillo, esplendor; iluminación.

irradiative [-iv], *a.* radiante, refulgente.

irrational [iréǝnǝl], *a.* irracional; absurdo, ilógico; (álg.) irracional.—**irrationality** [-ǽliti], *s.* irracionalidad.—**irrationally** [-ali], *adv.* irracionalmente.

irreclaimable [irikléimǝbl], *a.* incorregible; irredimible; inutilizable.—**irreclaimably** [-bli], *adv.* incorregiblemente; irremediablemente.

irreconcilable [irékǝnsáilǝbl]. **I.** *a.* irreconciliable, inconciliable; intransigente. **II.** *s.* (pol.) intransigente.—**irreconcilableness** [-njs], *s.* irreconciliabilidad.—**irreconcilably** [-bli], *adv.* irreconciliablemente.

irrecoverable [irikAvœrǝbl], *a.* irreparable o irrecuperable; incobrable.—**irrecoverableness** [-njs], *s.* calidad de irrecuperable.—**irrecoverably** [-bli], *adv.* irremediablemente, irreparablemente.

irrecusable [irikjúzǝbl], *a.* irrecusable.

irredeemable [iridímǝbl], *a.* irredimible; irremisible; inamortizable.—**irredeemably** [-bli], *adv.* de un modo irredimible; irremisiblemente.

irredenta [iridéntǝ]. **I.** *a.* irredento, irredimido. **II.** *s.* región irredimida.

Irridentist [-tjst], *a. y s.* (pol.) irredentista.

irreducible [iridiúsibl], *a.* irreducible; (mat.) irreductible.

irreflective [iriˈfléktiv], *a.* irreflexivo.

irrefragability [iréfragǝbíliti], *s.* irrefragabilidad.—**irrefragable** [-bl], *a.* irrefragable.—**irrefragably** [-bli], *adv.* irrefragablemente.

irrefrangible [irifrǽndʒibl], *a.* (ópt.) irrefrangible.—**irrefrangibility** [-bíliti], *s.* irrefrangibilidad.

irrefutable [iréfiutǝbl], *a.* irrefutable.

irrefutably [-bli], *adv.* irrefutablemente.

irregular [irégyǝlǝ(r], *a.* irregular; anormal.—**irregularity** [-ériti], *s.* irregularidad; demasía, exceso.—**irregularly** [-li], *adv.* irregularmente.

irrelative [irélǝtiv], *a.* inconexo, sin relación, regla, ni orden.

irrelatively [-li], *adv.* inconexamente.

irrelevancy [irélǝvǝnsi], *s.* inaplicabilidad; impertinencia, inconexión con algo alguno (a un asunto).—**irrelevant** [-ǝnt], *a.* que está fuera de lugar, ajeno, inaplicable, impertinente, que no viene al caso.—**irrelevantly** [-li], *adv.* inconexamente, impertinentemente, saliéndose del asunto.

irrelievable [irilívǝbl], *a.* irremediable, irreparable.

irreligion [irilídʒǝn], *s.* irreligión.—**irreligious** [-dʒǝs], *a.* irreligioso.—**irreligiously** [-li], *adv.* irreligiosamente.

irremediable [irimídiǝbl], *a.* irremediable.—**irremediableness** [-njs], *s.* calidad de irremediable.—**irremediably** [-bli], *adv.* irremediablemente.

irremissible [irimísibl], *a.* irremisible, imperdonable.—**irremissibleness** [-njs], *s.* irremisibilidad.—**irremissibly** [-bli], *adv.* irremisiblemente.

irremovable [ịrịmúvạbl], *a.* inamovible; inmutable.

irreparability [ịrépạrạbịlịtị], *s.* calidad de irreparable.—**irreparable** [-bl], *a.* irreparable.—**irreparably** [-blị], *adv.* irreparablemente.

irrepealable [ịrịpílạbl], *a.* inabrogable, irrevocable.

irreplaceable [ịrịpléịsạbl], *a.* irreemplazable, insu(b)stituíble.

irrepleviable [ịrịplévịạbl], *a.* (for.) irredimible.

irreprehensible [ịreprịhénsịbl], *a.* irreprensible.—**irreprehensibly** [-blị], *adv.* irreprensiblemente.

irrepressible [ịrịprésịbl], *a.* irreprimible, irrefrenable, indomable, incorregible.

irreproachable [ịrịpróychạbl], *a.* irreprochable, irreprensible, intachable.—**irreproachably** [-blị], *adv.* intachablemente.

irresistibility [ịrịzịstịbịlịtị], **irresistibleness** [-blnịs], *s.* irresistibilidad.—**irresistible** [-bl], *a.* irresistible, incontrastable.—**irresistibly** [-blị], *adv.* irresistiblemente.

irresoluble [ịrézoljubl], *a.* irresoluble.—**irresolubleness** [-nịs], *s.* calidad de irresoluble.

irresolute [ịrézoljut], *a.* irresoluto, vacilante, indeciso.—**irresolutely** [-lị], *adv.* irresolutamente.—**irresoluteness** [-nịs], *s.* irresolución, vacilación, indecisión.—**irresolution** [-ljúṣọn], *s.* irresolución, indecisión.

irresolvable [ịrịzálvạbl], *a.* irresoluble; que no puede descomponerse.

irrespective [ịrịspéktịv], *a.* (con of) con independencia de, sin consideración a, prescindiendo de.

irrespirable [ịrịspáịrạbl], *a.* irrespirable.

irresponsibility [ịrịspánsịbịlịtị], *s.* irresponsabilidad.—**irresponsible** [-bl], *a.* irresponsable.—**irresponsibly** [-blị], *adv.* irresponsablemente.

irretraceable [ịrịtréịsạbl], *a.* que no se puede desandar.

irretrievable [ịrịtrívạbl], *a.* irrecuperable, irreparable; incobrable.—**irretrievably** [-blị], *adv.* irreparablemente.

irreverence [ịrévẹrẹns], *s.* irreverencia.

irreverent [-ẹnt], *a.* irreverente.—**irreverently** [-lị], *adv.* irreverentemente.

irreversible [ịrịvérsịbl], *a.* no volvible o vertible; que no se puede volver al revés; irrevocable.

irreversibility [-bịlịtị], **irreversibleness** [-nịs], *s.* carácter o calidad de no ser volvible, etc.; irrevocabilidad.—**irreversibly** [-blị], *adv.* irrevocablemente.

irrevocability [ịrévokạbịlịtị], **irrevocableness** [-blnịs], *s.* irrevocabilidad.

irrevocable [-bl], *a.* irrevocable.

irrevocably [-blị], *adv.* irrevocablemente.

irrigable [ịrịgạbl], *a.* regadizo, regadío.

irrigate [ịrịgeịt], *va.* regar; bañar, mojar, humedecer; (med.) irrigar.—**irrigation** [-éịṣọn], *s.* riego, regadura; (med.) irrigación.—**irrigator** [-ọ(r), *s.* carro de riego; (med.) irrigador.

irritability [ịrịtạbịlịtị], *s.* irritabilidad.

irritable [-bl], *a.* irritable.—**irritableness** [-nịs], *s.* irritabilidad.

irritant [ịrịtạnt], *a.* y *s.* irritante, irritador.

irritate [ịrịteịt], *va.* irritar, exacerbar.—**irritation** [-éịṣọn], *s.* irritación, exacerbación.—**irritative** [-ịv], *a.* irritador, irritante.

irruption [ịrápṣọn], *s.* irrupción, invasión.

irruptive [-tịv], *a.* irruptor, invasor.

is [ịz], 3d. *pers. sing. pres. ind.* de TO BE.

isagogical [aịsagádẓịkạl], *a.* isagógico.

isagogics [-ịks], *s.* estudio crítico literario de la Biblia; introducción a la exégesis.

ischiatic [ịskịétịk], *a.* isquiático.

ischium [ịskịạm], *s.* (anat.) isquion, *m.*

Ishmaelite [ịṣmịelaịt], *s.* ismaelita, *mf.*

isinglass [áịzịnglæs], *s.* colapez, cola de pescado (ll. t. **i. glue**); (min.) mica.

Islam [ịslạm], **Islamism** [-ịzm], *s.* islam, islamismo.

Islamic [ịslǽmịk], *a.* islámico.—**Islamite** [íslamaịt], *s.*, **Islamitic** [ịslạmítịk], *a.* islamita, *mf.*

island [áịlạnd], *s.* isla, ínsula; zona (gen. plataforma o resalto) de seguridad o divisoria (en las calles y plazas).—**islander** [-œ(r)], *s.* isleño, insular.

isle [aịl], *s.* isla, ínsula.—**islet** [áịlịt], *s.* isleta, cayo.

ism [ịzm], *s.* doctrina, *ismo.*

isobar [áịsobar], *s.* línea isobárica.

isobaric [aịsobárịk], *a.* isobárico.

isocheimal [-káịmạl], *a.* isoquímeno.

isochromatic [-kromǽtịk], *a.* isocromático.

isochronal *o* **isochronous** [aịsákronạl, -ʌs], *a.* isócrono.—**isochronism** [-ịzm], *s.* isocronismo.—**isochronize** [-aịz], *va.* hacer isócrono, poner en sincronismo.

isoclinal [aịsokláịnạl], **isoclinic** [-klínịk], *a.* isoclinal, isoclino, de igual inclinación.—**i. line**, línea que une los puntos de igual inclinación de la brújula.

isocline [áịsoklaịn], *s.* (geol.) pliegue isoclinal.

isodynamic [-daịnǽmịk], *a.* isodinámico.

isogonal [aịságonạl], *a.* (geom.) isógono.

isogonic [aịsogánịk], *a.* isogónico.—**i. line**, línea isogónica.

isolate [áịsoleịt], *va.* aislar, separar, apartar; incomunicar.—**isolated** [-ịd], *a.* aislado, apartado; solitario, retirado; incomunicado.—**isolating** [-ịn], *a.* aislador.—**isolation** [-éịṣọn], *s.* aislamiento; incomunicación.—**isolationism** [-ịzm], *s.* aislacionismo, aislamientismo, prescindencia de otras naciones.—**isolationist** [-ịst], *s.* aislacionista, aislamientista, partidario del aislamiento.—**isolator** [áịsoleịtọ(r)], *s.* aislador.

isomeric [aịsomérịk], *a.* (quím.) isomérico.

isomerism [aịsámẹrịzm], *s.* (quím.) isomería.

isometric [aịsométrịk], **-cal** [-ạl], *a.* isométrico.

isometropia [aịsometrópịạ], *s.* isometropia, igualdad en la refracción de los dos ojos.

isomorphism [aịsomórfịzm], *s.* (min.) isomorfismo, isomorfía.—**isomorphous** [-fʌs], *a.* isomorfo.

isopod [áịsopạd], *s.* y *a.* (zool.) isópodo.

isosceles [aịsásẹliz], *a.* (geom.) isósceles.

isospore [áịsospoụr], *s.* (bọt.) isosporo.

isosporous [aịsásporạs], *a.* (bot.) isospóreo.

isotheral [aịsáθẹrạl], *a.* isótero.

isotherm [áịsoθœrm], *s.* línea isoterma.—**isothermal** [-θœrmạl], *a.* isotermo.

isotope [áịsotoụp], *s.* (quím.) isotopo.—**isotopic** [-tápịk], *a.* isotópico, isótopo.

isotropic [-trápịk], *a.* isótropo, isotrópico.

isotropy [aịsátropị], *s.* (fís.) isotropía.

Israelite [ịzrịelaịt], *s.* israelita, *mf.*

Israelitish, Israelitic [-ịṣ, ịzrịelítịk], *a.* israelita, israelítico.

issuable [ịṣuạbl], *a.* emisible.

issuance [ịṣuạns], *s.* emisión; promulgación; publicación; distribución.

issue [ịṣu]. **I.** *s.* (impr.) edición, tirada, impresión; número (de una revista, etc.); prole, *f.*, progenie, sucesión; (com.) emisión de valores; (for.) rentas, réditos, producto, beneficios; salida, egreso; (med.) flujo (de sangre, etc.); fuente, *f.*, principio, nacimiento; evento, consecuencia, resultado, éxito; decisión; tema (*m.*) de discusión, problema, *m.*; (med.) exutorio, fuente; (for.) punto en disputa.—**i. of blood**, pérdida de sangre.—**at i., o in i.**, en disputa. **II.** *va.* nacer, brotar, arrojar; dar; dictar, expedir, despachar; (com.) librar, emitir, poner en circulación; dar a luz, publicar. **III.** *vn.* salir, brotar, fluir, proceder, provenir; nacer; resultar; acabarse, terminarse, resolverse.

issueless [-lịs], *a.* sin sucesión.

isthmian [ịsmịạn], *a.* ístmico; *a.* y *s.* istmeño.

isthmus [ịsmạs], *s.* (geog., anat.) istmo.

istle [ịstlị], *s.* = IXTLE.

Istrian [ịstrịạn], *s.* y *a.* istrio.

it [ịt], *pron. neutro (pl.* THEY). Se aplica a cosas

inanimadas, a niños de teta y a los animales cuyo sexo no puede determinarse; por consiguiente corresponde en español a *él, ella, eso, ello, lo, la, le*, según los géneros y casos de las cosas a que se refiere; v. gr.: *have you the book?* —*I have it*, ¿tiene Vd. el libro?—Lo tengo. No se traduce cuando es sujeto gramatical de una oración que no tiene sujeto lógico (como las de verbos impersonales) o cuyo sujeto lógico (y gramatical en español) es un infinitivo o una frase: *it rains*, llueve; *it is late*, es tarde; *it is easy to promise*, es fácil prometer; *it is evident that he was there*, es evidente que él estaba allí. No se traduce cuando sigue a un *s.* y precede a un tiempo de *to be* seguido de infinitivo (*his duty it is to go*, su deber es ir). Tampoco se traduce cuando se refiere a la hora (*what time is it?* ¿qué hora es? *it is six o'clock*, son las seis); ni en las expresiones *who is it?* ¿quién es? *it is I*, soy yo; *it is they*, son ellos; *it was he who spoke*, fué él quien habló, y otras análogas.—**i. is . . . which**, o **that**, es lo que (*it is money that you need*, dinero es lo que Vd. necesita).—**is i.?** ¿sí? ¿de veras?—**is i. not** (so)? ¿no es verdad? ¿verdad? ¿no es así?—**is that i.?** ¿es eso?—**not to be in i. with**, (fam.) no poderse comparar con, ser muy inferior a.—**that is i.**, eso es.

Italian [itǽlyạn], *a.* y *s.* italiano.—**I. paste**, pasta de macarrones.—**Italianate** [-eįt]. I. *a.* italianizado. II. *va.* italianizar.—**Italianism** [-įzm], *s.* italianismo.—**Italianize** [-aįz], *va.* italianizar.

italic [itǽlịk], *a.* (impr.) bastardilla, itálica (letra): (I.) itálico, italiano.

italicize [itǽlịsaįz], *va.* poner en letra itálica o bastardilla; subrayar, dar énfasis.—**italics** [itǽlịks], *s. pl.* (impr.) letra itálica, bastardilla o cursiva.

Italiot, Italiote [itǽliat, itǽljout], *s.* italiota, *mf.*, antiguo habitante griego de Italia.

itch [ịch]. I. *s.* sarna, comezón, *f.*, picazón, *f.*; prurito.—**i. insect, i. mite**, (ent.) ácaro, arador. II. *vn.* picar; sentir picazón o comezón; antojarse, tener prurito por algo; desear vehementemente.

itching [-ịŋ], *s.* picazón, *f.*, comezón, *f.*, rascazón, *f.*; prurito, deseo vehemente.

itchy [-ị], *a.* sarnoso; picante, hormigoso.

item [áįtẹm]. I. *adv.* ítem; otrosí, aun más. II. *s.* partida; artículo; párrafo; detalle; renglón.

itemize [-aįz], *va.* detallar, especificar, particularizar, pormenorizar, circunstanciar.

iterable [ítẹrabl], *a.* iterable.

iterant [ítẹrạnt], *a.* iterativo.—**iterate** [ítẹreįt], *va.* repetir, (re)iterar; inculcar.—**iteration** [-éįṣọn], *s.* iteración, repetición.—**iterative** [-įv], *a.* iterativo; (gram.) frecuentativo.

itinerant [aįtínẹrạnt]. I. *s.* viandante. II. *a.* ambulante, errante.

itinerary [-rẹrị]. I. *s.* itinerario, ruta; relación de un viaje; guía de viajeros. II. *a.* itinerario, hecho en viaje.

itinerate [-reįt], *vn.* seguir una ruta o itinerario.

its [įts], *pron.* posesivo neutro (genitivo de *it*) su (de él, de ella, de ello), v. gr.: *a house with its furniture*, una casa con sus muebles.

itself [ịtsélf], *pron.* (se aplica solamente a las cosas) el mismo, la misma, lo mismo; v. gr.: *it moves of itself*, eso se mueve de sí, o por sí mismo; *she is virtue itself*, es la virtud misma.

ivied [áįvịd], *a.* cubierto de hiedra.

ivory [áįvọrị]. I. *s.* marfil.—*pl.* cosas hechas de marfil; bolas de billar; (fam.) los dientes. II. *a.* ebúrneo, de marfil.—**i. nut**, marfil vegetal, tagua.—**i. palm**, (bot.) tagua.

ivorylike [-laįk], *a.* ebúrneo, marfileño.

ivy [áįvị], *s.* (bot.) hiedra o yedra; cazuz, *m.*

ixtle [íkstlị], **ixtli**, *s.* istle, ixtle; fibra de Tampico o de istle.—**i. grass**, ixtle (la planta).

izzard [ịẓậrd], *s.* (ant.) la letra *z*.—**from A to i.**, de cabo a rabo, de pe a pa.

J

j [dẓeį], *s.* j.

jab [dẓǽb]. I. *va.* pinchar, punz.:r; (fam.) hurgonear. II. *s.* punzada, (fam.) hurgonazo, pinchazo.

jabber [dẓǽbœ(r)]. I. *va.* charlar; farfullar; chapurr(e)ar (un idioma); (fam.) disparatar. II. *s.* jerga, jerigonza, guirigay.

jabberer [-œ(r)], *s.* farfullador, parlanchín.

jabiru [dẓǽbịru], *s.* (orn.) jabirú, ave zancuda.

jaborandi [dẓǽboréndị], *s.* (bot.) jaborandi, pilocarpo.

jacamar [dẓǽkạmạr], *s.* (orn.) jacamar.

jacana [dẓǽkạna], *s.* (orn.) jacana, ave zancuda.

jacaranda [dẓǽkạréndậ], *s.* (bot.) jacaranda, abey.

jacent [dẓéįsẹnt], *pa.* yacente.

jacinth [dẓéįsịnθ], *s.* (min.) = ZIRCON.

jack [dẓǽk]. I. *s.* mozo; hombre; marinero; macho del burro y otros animales; (mec.) gato, cric; barrilete, cárcel, *f.*, prensa, burro, borriquete; sacabotas; martinete o macillo del piano; torno de asador; cota de malla; (dep.) boliche; sota (de la baraja); (mar.) bandera de proa; (tlf.) jack; (fam.) blanca, dinero; linterna manual de proyección (para cazar, etc.).—*pl.* juego de la taba.—**j. afloat**, (fam.) marinero.—**j. boots**, botas grandes y fuertes.—**j.-in-the-box**, caja de sorpresa, muñeco en una caja de resorte; (mec.) cric.—**j.-of-all-trades**, estuche; aprendiz (*m.*) de todo y oficial de nada.—**j.-o'-lantern**, fuego fatuo; linterna hecha de una calabaza, con cara grotesca.—**j. plane**, (carp.) garlopa, cepillo desbastador.—**j. rabbit**, (zool.) liebre americana.—**j. shaft**, eje intermedio.—**j.-tar**, (fam.) marinero.—**j. towel**, toalla de un rodillo giratorio. II. *va.* (gen. con **up**) soliviar con un cric; (fam.) subir (precios, sueldos); (fam.) sermonear.

jackal [-ạl], *s.* (zool.) chacal; adive o adiva.

jackanapes [-ạneįps], *s.* mequetrefe.

jackass [-æs], *s.* (zool.) garañón, **asno, borrico**, burro; (fig.) asno, tonto, necio.

jackdaw [-dɔ], *s.* (orn.) grajo, chova.

jacket [dẓǽkịt]. I. *s.* chaquet(ill)a, jubón, jaqueta; envoltura, cubierta; forro; pellejo; cáscara; forro o envoltura metálica (de acero, etc.) de una bala de plomo; (mec.) chaqueta, camisa. II. *va.* enchaquetar, proveer o cubrir de chaqueta, etc.

jackknife [dẓǽknaįf], *s.* navaja de bolsillo.

jackscrew [-skru], *s.* (mec.) gato, cric, lirón.

jacksnipe [-snaįp], *s.* (orn.) especie de becardón.

jackstaff [-stæf], *s.* (mar.) asta de bandera de proa o del bauprés.

jackstone [-stoụn], *s.* taba, pito, taquín.—*pl.* juego de la taba.

jackstraw [-strɔ], *s.* efigie de paja; espantapájaros.—*pl.* juego con pajitas.

Jacobin [dẓǽkobịn], *s.* (igl.) dominico; (pol.) jacobino; demagogo; (orn.) pichón capuchino.

Jacobinic(al [-bịnịk(ạl], *a.* jacobínico.

Jacobinism [-bịnịzm], *s.* jacobinismo.

Jacobite [-baįt], *a.* y *s.* jacobita, *mf.*

Jacob's-ladder [dẓǽkọbz lǽdœ(r)], *s.* (bot.) polemonio; (mar.) escala de jarcias.—**J.'s staff**, bordón de peregrino; bastón con estoque; báculo de Jacob; ballestilla; (top.) estaca con un regatón que se usa en vez de trípode.

jaconet [dẓǽkonẹt], *s.* (tej.) chaconada.

jac(ti)tation [dẓǽk(tị)téįṣọn], *s.* (med.) agitación, desasosiego; fanfarronería, jactancia.

jaculatory [dẓǽkịulạtọrị], *a.* disparado; jaculatorio.—**j. prayer**, fervorín, jaculatoria.

jade [dẓéįd]. I. *s.* rocín, jamelgo; mujercilla; picarona, mala pécora; (min.) jade; nefrita, piedra nefrítica, piedra de ijada, etc. II. *va.* cansar, acosar. III. *vn.* jadear, desalentarse.

jaded [-įd], *a.* rendido; saciado, ahito.

jadish [-ịṣ], *a.* viciosa (yegua); impúdica (mujer).

jag [dʒǽg]. **I.** *va.* dentar, mellar. **II.** *s.* diente, punta; perno de lengüeta; melladura, mella, muesca; (fam.) pítima, turca, chispa.

jagged [-jd], *a.* mellado, dent(ell)ado, serrado.— **j.-toothed,** helgado.—**jaggedness** [-nịs], *s.* melladura.—**jaggy** [dʒǽgị], *a.* = JAGGED.

jaguar [dʒǽgwar], *s.* (zool.) jaguar.

jail [dʒéjl]. **I.** *s.* cárcel, *f.*—**j. fever,** (med.) tifo.— **j. sentence,** condena. **II.** *va.* encarcelar, aprisionar.

jailbird [-bœrd], *s.* el que ha estado en presidio; presidiario, malhechor.

jailer [-œ(r)], *s.* carcelero.

jalap [dʒǽlạp], *s.* (bot., farm.) jalapa.

jalapin [-ịn], *s.* (quím.) jalapina.

jalop(p)y [dʒạlápị], *s.* (fam.) automóvil o avión viejo o en estado ruinoso; (Am.) fotingo.

jalousie [ʒálụzi], *s.* celosía.

jam [dʒæm]. **I.** *s.* compota, conserva; apretura, apiñadura, agolpamiento; atoramiento, atascamiento; atascadero (fig.), situación peliaguda. —**j. nut** = LOCK NUT. **II.** *va.* apiñar; acuñar, apretar, estrechar, apachurrar, estrujar; atorar, trabar; (rad.) enredar la transmisión de (una difusora), causar interferencia en, hacer ininteligible por ondas perturbadoras emitidas por otra difusora. **III.** *vn.* atorarse, trabarse, agolparse.

Jamaican [dʒạméjkạn], *a.* y *s.* jamaicano.

jamb(e [dʒæm], *s.* (arq.) jamba, quicial, montante, batiente (de puerta, etc.); (arm.) = JAMBEAU.

jambeau [dʒæmbóụ], *s.* (arm.) canillera, greba, espinillera, esquinela.

jamboree [dʒæmborí], *s.* lance del juego de *euchre*; reunión (inter)nacional de niños exploradores; (fam.) francachela.

jammed [dʒæmd], *a.* atorado, trabado; de bote en bote, repleto.

jangle [dʒǽŋgl]. **I.** *vn.* sonar en discordancia; reñir, altercar. **II.** *va.* hacer sonar de modo discordante. **III.** *s.* sonido discordante; disputa, querella, altercado; charla ociosa.

jangling [-glịŋ]. **I.** *a.* discordante. **II.** *s.* = JANGLE.

janitor [dʒǽnịtọ(r)], *s.* portero; conserje.

Janizary [dʒǽnịzerị], *s.* jenízaro.

Jansenism [dʒǽnsẹnịzm], *s.* jansenismo.

Jansenist [-ịst], *s.* y *a.* jansenista.

January [dʒǽnyụerị], *s.* enero.

Jap [dʒæp], *a.* y *s.* (fam.) japonés.

japan [dʒạpǽn]. **I.** *s.* charol; obra japonesa charolada. **II.** *va.* charolar; barnizar. **III.** *a.* (J.) japonés, japónico.—**J. earth,** tierra japónica, cato, catecú.

Japanese [dʒæpạnís], *a.* y *s.* japonés, japonense, japón, nipón.—**J. persimmon,** (bot.) níspero del Japón.

Japhetic [dʒéjfétịk], *a.* jafético.

japonica [dʒạpánịkạ], *s.* (bot.) camelia japonesa; membrillo japonés.

jar [dʒar]. **I.** *va.* sacudir, agitar, hacer vibrar o trepidar. **II.** *vn.* chirriar, hacer ruido desagradable; vibrar, trepidar; ludir, chocar; discordar. —**to j. on,** irritar, fastidiar. **III.** *s.* jarro o jarra; pote, tinaja, cántaro, tarro, botija; vibración, trepidación; sacudida; choque; pendencia, riña; chirrido, ruido desagradable.—**on the j.,** entreabierto.

jardinière [ʒardịnír], *s.* jardinera, florero.

jargon ╫dʒárgọn], *s.* jerga, jerigonza; caló.

jasmine [dʒǽsmịn], *s.* (bot.) jazmín.

jasper [dʒǽspœ(r)], *s.* (min.) jaspe.

jaundice [dʒóndịs]. **I.** *s.* (med.) ictericia, aliacán; celotipia, predisposición. **II.** *va.* causar ictericia; predisponer, torcer.

jaundiced [-t], *pp.* y *a.* ictérico, cetrino, aciguatado, aliacanado.

jaunt [dʒont]. **I.** *vn.* corretear, ir y venir. **II.** *s.* excursión, caminata, paseata.

jauntiness [dʒóntịnịs], *s.* viveza, gentileza, garbo, ligereza.

jaunty [dʒóntị], *a.* vistoso, airoso, garboso.

Javanese [dʒavạnís], *a.* y *s.* javanés, javo.

javelin [dʒǽvlịn], *s.* jabalina, venablo.

jaw [dʒó]. **I.** *s.* (anat.) maxilar, quijada, mandíbula; (mec.) boca, quijada, telera, mordaza; (fig., gen. *pl.*) abismo, fauces, *f. pl.*, garras; (fam.) charla, palabrería; vituperio. **II.** *a.* de (las) quijadas; de mordaza.—**j. clutch,** embrague de mordaza.—**j. crusher,** triturador de quijadas.—**j. teeth,** las muelas. **III.** *va.* y *vn.* (fam.) regañar, refunfuñar; charlar.

jawbone [-boụn], *s.* (anat.) maxilar, quijada, mandíbula (apl. esp. a la inferior).

jawbreaker [-brejkœ(r)], *s.* (fam.) terminacho impronunciable, trabalenguas; especie de dulce muy duro; (mec.) = JAW CRUSHER.

jay [dʒej], *s.* (fam.) rústico, chambón; simplón; (orn.) grajo; chova.

jaywalker [dʒéjwọkœ(r)], *s.* (fam.) persona que cruza la calle en puntos peligrosos.

jazz [dʒæz]. **I.** *s.* *jazz*, música popular sincopada; baile con música de *jazz*; estilo rimbombante y excéntrico. **II.** *va.* (a veces con **up**) convertir en *jazz*, o meter *jazz* en (una pieza), *jazzificar.* **III.** *vn.* bailar o tocar *jazz*; hacer algo desordenadamente.

jazzy [-ị], *a.* que tiene *jazz* o se parece al *jazz.*

jealous [dʒélʌs], *a.* celoso; envidioso.—**to be j.,** tener celos (de).—**to become j.,** encelarse.

jealously [-lị], *adv.* celosamente.

jealousy [-ị], **jealousness** [-nịs], *s.* celos, *m. pl.*, encelamiento, celotipia.

jean [dʒín], *s.* (tej.) cierta tela cruzada o asargada de algodón.—*pl.* ropa, esp. pantalones, hecha de esta tela.

jeep [dʒíp], *s.* (mil.) jip, yip (automóvil).

jeer [dʒír]. **I.** *va.* y *vn.* befar, mofar, escarnecer, burlarse. **II.** *s.* befa, mofa, burla, escarnio.—*pl.* **jeers,** (mar.) guindaste con sus drizas.

jeering [-ịŋ], *a.* mofador, escarnecedor.

Jehovah [dʒịhóụvạ], *s.* Jehová.

jehu [dʒíhịu], *s.* (fam.) cochero, auriga, *m.*

jejune [dʒịdʒún], *a.* falto; seco, estéril, árido; insípido.

jejuneness, jejunity [-nịs, -ịtị], *s.* carestía, esterilidad; aridez, sequedad; pobreza; tibieza.

jejunum [dʒịdʒúnạm], *s.* (anat.) yeyuno.

jellied [dʒélịd], *a.* gelatinoso.

jellify [dʒélịfaị], *va.* y *vn.* hacer(se) gelatinoso.

jelly [dʒélị]. **I.** *s.* jalea. **II.** *va.* y *vn.* convertir(se) en jalea.

jellyfish [-fịʃ], *s.* (zool.) medusa, aguamar.

jennet [dʒénet], *s.* jaca española; jumenta.

jenny [dʒénị], *s.* torno, máquina para hilar; hembra de ciertos animales; asna, burra, jumenta; (orn.) = WREN; (mec.) grúa locomóvil.

jeopard [dʒépạrd], **jeopardize** [-ajz], *va.* arriesgar, exponer, comprometer.—**jeopardy** [-ị], *s.* riesgo, peligro.

jerboa [dʒœrbóụạ], *s.* (zool.) jerbo, gerbo.

jeremiad [dʒerịmájæd], *s.* jeremiada.

jerk [dʒœrk]. **I.** *s.* tirón, sacudida, sacudimiento, vibración; salto, brinco, respingo; (mar.) socollada, gualdrapazo; (equit.) sobarbada. **II.** *va.* arrojar, dar un tirón, mover a tirones; sacudir, traquetear; atasajar carne, (Am.) charquear.— **jerked beef,** tasajo, cecina, (Am.) charque o charqui. **III.** *vn.* moverse a tirones.

jerkily [-ịlị], *adv.* a sacudidas.

jerkin [-ịn], *s.* justillo; chaquetón.

jerky [-ị], *a.* espasmódico.

jerry [dʒérị], *a.* de inferior calidad; mal hecho, hecho a la diabla.—**j.-build,** *va.* y *vn.* edificar a la diabla, mal o con malos materiales.—**j.-builder,** *s.* constructor de casas baratas de inferior calidad.

jersey [dʒœrzị], *s.* (tej.) estambre fino; camiseta, jubón o elástica de lana o de seda; (J., zool.) toro o vaca de la isla de Jersey (Ingl.).

jess [dʒes], *s.* (cetr.) pihuela.

jessamine [dʒésạmịn], *s.* (bot.) jazmín.

jest [džέst]. **I.** *vn.* bromear, jaranear, chancearse, (fam.) guasearse. **II.** *s.* chanza, broma.

jester [-œ(r)], *s.* bufón; burlón, fisgón, guasón.

jesting [-ɪŋ]. **I.** *s.* (el) chancearse, uso de chanzas. **II.** *a.* chancero, guasón; de chanza.

jestingly [-lɪ], *adv.* de burlas, por broma.

Jesuit [džέžuɪt], *s.* jesuíta, *m.; intrigante.—J.'s bark**, quina.—**Jesuitic(al** [-ítɪk(əl], *a.* jesuítico; ajesuitado.—**Jesuitically** [-lɪ], *adv.* jesuíticamente.—**Jesuitism** [džέžuɪtɪzm], *s.* jesuitismo.

jet [džɛt]. **I.** *s.* (min.) azabache; chorro; surtidor; caño de salida, boquilla; mechero (de gas).— **j.-black**, azabachado, negro como el azabache. **—j.-propulsion engine**, motor de propulsión "a chorro" de aire caliente. **II.** *va.* echar, arrojar, lanzar. **III.** *vn.* salir en chorro.

jetsam [džέtsam], **jetson** [-sǫn], *s.* (mar.) echazón, *f.;* (for.) pecio. *V.* JETTISON.

jettison [džέtɪsǫn]. **I.** *va.* (mar.) echar mercancías al mar. **II.** *s.* (mar.) echazón, *f.;* (for.) pecio.

jetton [džέtǫn], *s.* ficha.

jetty [džέtɪ]. **I.** *a.* de azabache; negro. **II.** *s.* malecón, rompeolas, dique, muelle, espolón.

Jew [džu], *s.* judío; israelita, *mf.*

jewel [džúęl]. **I.** *s.* joya, alhaja; gema, piedra preciosa; piedra (de reloj de bolsillo).—**j. box, case** o **casket**, joyero, joyelero, escriño. **II.** *va.* enjoy(el)ar, adornar con piedras preciosas.

jewel(l)er [-œ(r)], *s.* joyero, enjoyelador, diamantista, platero.—**jewelers' putty** = PUTTY POWDER.—**jeweler's shop**, joyería, platería.

jewel(le)ry [-rɪ], *s.* aderezo; joyas, *f. pl.*, pedrería; prendería; joyería.

Jewess [džúɪs], *s.* judía.

jewfish [džúfɪš], *s.* (ict.) guasa.

Jewish [džúɪš], *a.* judío, judaico; ajudiado.

Jewishly [-lɪ], *adv.* como judío, a la judía.

Jewry [džúrɪ], *s.* Judea; judería; ghetto.

jews'-harp [džúz harp], *s.* (mús.) birimbao.

Jezebel [džέžębel], *s.* mujer viciosa y cruel.

jib [džɪb], *s.* (mar.) foque.—**j. boom**, botalón de bauprés, tormentín.—**j. of a crane**, aguilón, pescante o pico de una grúa.

jibe [džaɪb]. **I.** *va.* y *vn.* = GIBE; (mar.) (hacer) moverse de un lado a otro una vela o su botavara, al efectuarse ciertas maniobras. **II.** *vn.* (fam.) concordar, estar conforme o de acuerdo.

jiffy [džífɪ], *s.* (fam.) instante, periquete.

jig [džɪg]. **I.** *s.* (mús. y danz.) jiga; chasco, bromazo, petardo; (min.) criba; anzuelo cargado de plomo; (mec.) conductor o guía para fabricar piezas idénticas.—**j. saw**, sierra de vaivén.— **the j. is up**, (fam.) se ha frustrado el proyecto; no hay más esperanza. **II.** *va.* (mús.) cantar o tocar una jiga; sacudir de abajo hacia arriba; separar minerales con criba; (mec.) formar o adaptar por medio de guías. **III.** *vn.* bailar una jiga; pescar con anzuelo emplomado.

jigger [džígœ(r)], *s.* bailador de jiga; cualquier utensilio que tiene movimiento de vaivén, v. gr., criba para minerales; rueda de alfarero; indicador eléctrico de precios; (mar.) aparejuelo, palanquín de socaire; (rad.) jigger, transformador Marconi; (ent.) nigua, pulga, garrapata u otra sabandija; (fam.) cosilla, chisme, chuchería; aparato, artefacto, herramienta.

jiggle [džígl], *va.* y *vn.* mover(se) ligeramente a tirones, de arriba abajo o de un lado a otro.

jigsaw puzzle [džígsɔ pʌzl], *s.* rompecabezas hecho de un cuadro pictórico en cartón o madera, cortado en pedazos irregulares con sierra de vaivén.

jill o **Jill** [džɪl], *s.* moza; querida; esposa.

jilt [džɪlt]. **I.** *s.* mujer que da calabazas a su pretendiente. **II.** *va.* despedir o dar calabazas; (fam.) plantar, dejar colgado. **III.** *vn.* coquetear.

jim-crow [džímkróu], *s.* encorvador de rieles.

jimmy [džími], *s.* ganzúa, pie (*m.*) de cabra (para forzar puertas, ventanas, etc.).—**j. bar** = CROWBAR.

jingle [džíŋgl]. **I.** *va.* y *vn.* retiñir, sonar o resonar; rimar. **II.** *s.* retintín, sonido metálico; cascabel; rima pueril, aleluya.—**jinglet** [-glɛt], *s.* escrupulillo de cascabel.

jingo [džíŋgou], *s.* jingoísta, partidario de una política exterior agresiva.—**by j.!** ¡caramba! ¡por Dios!

jingoism [-ɪzm], *s.* jingoísmo, política agresiva; odio de lo extranjero.

jingoist(ic [-ɪst (-ɪstɪk], *s.* y *a.* jingoísta.

jinni, jinnee [džɪní], *s.* (mit. mahom.) = GENIE.

jinny [džíni], *s.* (min.) máquina fija de arrastre; JINNY ROAD.—**j. road**, (min.) plano inclinado para arrastre por gravedad.

jinx [džɪŋks], *s.* y *va.* (fam.) = HOODOO.

jitney [džítni], *s.* (fam.) moneda de cinco centavos; (fam.) autobús.

jitter [džítœ(r)], *vn.* (fam.) estar nervioso, intranquilo, desasosegado.—**jitters** [-z], *s. pl.* (fam.) intranquilidad, desasosiego, inquietud; ataque de nervios, nerviosismos.—**jittery** [-i], *a.* (fam.) nervioso, inquieto.

job [džáb]. **I.** *s.* tarea; destajo; remiendo; agiotaje; (fam.) socaliña, engañifa; (fam.) empleo, ocupación, trabajo; tarea, empresa; suceso; circunstancia.—**j. lot**, mercancías varias vendidas en montón.—**j. printing**, impresión de remiendos. **—by the j.**, a destajo.—**on the j.**, en la tarea; en su puesto; (constr.) en el lugar de la obra. **II.** *va.* y *vn.* comprar al por mayor y revender al por menor; alquilar(se) al destajo; hacer destajo; especular con los fondos públicos.

jobber [-œ(r)], *s.* agiotador, agiotista; intrigante, destajero, destajista; remendero, remendón; (com.) negociante o traficante medianero, corredor.

jobbery [-œrɪ], *s.* engañifa; agiotaje.

jobbing [-ɪŋ], *s.* negocio de comprar por mayor y revender por menor; agio; cambalache.—**j. house**, (com.) casa medianera entre los fabricantes o importadores y los detallistas.

jobless [-lɪs], *a.* sin empleo, cesante.

Job's-tears [džóubztírz], *s. pl.* (bot.) lágrimas de David, o de Job.

jockey [džákɪ]. **I.** *s.* (dep.) jockey, yoquey; chalán; engañabobos, petardista. **II.** *va.* y *vn.* trampear, engañar; maniobrar hábilmente para sacar alguna ventaja.

jocose [džokóus], *a.* jocoso.—**jocosely** [-li], *adv.* jocosamente.—**jocoseness** [-nis], *s.* jocosity [džokásiti], *s.* jocosidad, alegría, chanza.

jocular [džákjulə(r)], *a.* jocoso, chancero; burlesco.—**jocularity** [-ériti], *s.* jocosidad.—**jocularly** [-li], *adv.* jocosamente.

jocund [džákənd], *a.* alegre, festivo, jovial.— **jocundity** [džokánditi], *s.* alegría, jovialidad.— **jocundly** [džákəndli], *adv.* alegremente.

jodhpurs [džádpœrz], *s. pl.* pantalón de montar.

jog [džág]. **I.** *va.* empujar; dar un golpecito para llamar la atención; excitar suavemente, estimular. **II.** *vn.* (con **on**, o **along**), moverse o ir despacio o a un trote corto. **III.** *s.* empujoncito, golpecito; estímulo; zangoloteo; trote lento; (mec.) muesca cuadrada.—**j. trot**, trote corto; pereza, lentitud; rutina.

joggle [džágl], *va.* y *vn.* empujar o moverse con sacudidas suaves.

John [džan], *s.* Juan. ú. para denotar un tipo nacional o genérico.—**j.-apple**, (bot.) especie de manzana tardía.—**J. Bull**, John Bull (Inglaterra; el pueblo inglés); (mec.) armazón (*f.*) de taladro.—**J. Chinaman**, cualquier chino; los chinos en general.—**J. Doe**, Fulano de Tal.— **J. Dory**, (ict.) dorado. *V.* DORY.—**J. Hancock**, la firma de una persona.

johnnycake [džánikejk], *s.* torta o pan de maíz.

join [džɔin]. **I.** *va.* juntar, unir, ensamblar, acoplar, empalmar; añadir; unir, casar; asociar; afiliarse, agregarse, incorporarse o unirse a, ingresar en, abrazar (un partido, etc.); empeñarse juntos, aunarse; chocar, embestir; lindar con.—to j. battle, librar batalla.—to j. company, incorporarse.—to j. issue, ponerse de acuerdo en algo como base de argumento; ponerse de punta; disputar.—to j. the colors, o (fam.) j. up, alistarse, enrolarse. II. vn. asociarse, unirse, juntarse, estar junto a; confluir.

joinder [-dœ(r)], s. = JOINING; (for.) junta, unión, asociación; aceptación por una de las partes de la alegación hecha por su contrario.

joiner [-œ(r)], s. ebanista, ensamblador, carpintero de blanco o de taller.

joinery [-i], s. ensambladura; ebanistería.

joining [-iŋ], s. unión, juntura, ensamblaje, trabamiento, cópula.—j. press, (carp.) cepo.

joint [dźóint]. I. s. juntura, junta, unión, empalme, ensambladura, acopladura; conexión, enganche; coyuntura, articulación; nudillo; gozne, bisagra; charnela; (alb.) degolladura: cuarto de un animal; encuentro de un ave; (bot.) nudo; (fam.) tugurio, garito.—out of j., desunido; descoyuntado, desbarajustado. II. a. unido, agrupado, colectivo; copartícipe; asociado; mixto; conjunto; de o por ambas cámaras (del congreso).—j. account, cuenta conjunta, mancomunada, o en participación.—j. (ad)venture, empresa o riesgo colectivos.—j. author, coautor.—j. bolt, perno para juntas en T.—j. commission, comisión mixta.—j. consent, común acuerdo.—j. file, lima de acanalar bisagras.—j. heir, coheredero.—j. meeting = J. SESSION.—j. owner, condómino, co(m)propietario.—j. pin, perno, clavija.—j. pipe, manguito, golilla.—j. possession, coposesión.—j. property, propiedad indivisa.—j. responsibility, responsabilidad solidaria.—j. session, sesión plena, sesión conjunta.—j. stock, capital social, fondos en común.—j.-stock company, compañía por acciones, sociedad anónima.—j. tenancy, tenencia en mancomún, con derecho absoluto del sobreviviente.—j. tenant, inquilino mancomunado, comunero. III. va. juntar, unir, agregar; formar nudos, articulaciones o coyunturas; descuartizar. IV. vn. unirse por medio de articulaciones.

jointed [-id], a. nudoso; articulado.

jointer [-œ(r)], s. (carp.) juntera.

jointly [-li], adv. (con)juntamente, colectivamente, de consuno, mancomunadamente.—j. and severally, (for.) todos y cada uno de por sí.—j. liable, (for.) solidario.

jointure [dźóinchū(r)], s. (for.) bienes parafernales.

joist [dźóist], s. (arq., carp.) viga, vigueta, cabio o cabrio, sopanda, carrera.

joke [dźóuk]. I. s. broma, burla, chanza, chiste, chuscada.—in j., en chanza, de broma. II. vn. bromear, chancear(se), (fam.) guasearse, gastar bromas.

joker [-œ(r)], s. burlón, bromista, chancero, guasón; naipe adicional en ciertos juegos; cláusula en un proyecto de ley que en efecto burla su intento; fallo o equivocación en un contrato que permite evadirlo.

jokingly [-iŋli], adv. de burlas, en chanza.

jollier [dźáliœ(r)], s. candonguero; lisonjeador.—jollification [-fikéišon], s. parranda, retozo, holgorio.—jolliness, jollity [-iŋis, -iti], s. jovialidad, broma, alegría, regocijo.

jolly [dźáli]. I. a. alegre, festivo, jovial; jaranero; divertido; (fam.) excelente, magnífico, de lo mejor.—j.-boat, (mar.) botequín, serení. II. adv. (fam.) muy, sumamente. III. va. y vn. (fam.) candonguear, engatusar con zalamerías; lisonjear, seguir el humor (a).

jolt [dźóult]. I. va. y vn. traque(te)ar, sacudir, dar sacudidas. II. s. sacudida, traque(te)o, salto.

jongleur [źáŋglœ(r)], s. trovador; bufón, juglar.

jonquil [dźáŋkwil], s. (bot.) junquillo.

josh [dźaš], va., vn. y s. (fam.) = BANTER.

joss [dźas], s. ídolo o dios chino.—j. house,

templo para ídolos chinos.—j. stick, pebete; pajuela perfumada que los chinos queman ante sus ídolos.

jostle [dźásl]. I. va. y vn. (r)empujar, empellar, codear. II. s. empellón, empujón.

jot [dźat]. I. s. jota, pizca, ápice, tilde, f. II. va. (con down) apuntar, tomar notas.

joule [dźaul o dźul], s. (fís.) julio.

jounce [dźauns]. I. va. y vn. sacudir, traquetear. II. s. sacudimiento, traqueteo.

journal [dźœrnal], s. diario, periódico diario; revista (publicación); acta; diario (apuntes personales); (com.) diario (libro); (mec.) gorrón, mangueta.—j. bearing, j. box, cojinete, chumacera, muñonera; (f. c.) caja de sebo.

journalism [-izm], s. periodismo, (Am.) diarismo; la prensa.—journalist [-ist], s. periodista.—journalistic [-ístik], a. periodístico.

journalize [-aiz]. I. va. (com.) pasar al diario. II. vn. apuntar en un diario.

journey [dźœrni]. I. s. jornada; viaje por tierra; camino, tránsito, pasaje. II. vn. viajar; recorrer un trayecto.—journeyer [-œ(r)], s. viajero.

journeyman [-man], s. oficial; mesero; jornalero.—j. tailor, oficial de sastre.—journeywork [-wœrk], s. jornal.

joust [dźʌst o dźaust]. I. s. justa, torneo. II. vn. justar, lidiar.—jousting field, liza.

jovial [dźóuvial], a. jovial.—joviality, jovialness [-ǽliti, -nis], s. jovialidad, regocijo, festividad.—jovially [-i], adv. jovialmente.

jowl [dźaul], s. carrillo; quijada; papada (del ganado); barba (de gallo); cabeza de pescado aderezada.

joy [dźói], s. alegría, júbilo, regocijo; felicidad.—j. ride, paseo subrepticio en automóvil, en que se violan las ordenanzas, esp. las que restringen la velocidad.—j. stick, (aer.) palanca de gobierno.

joyful [-ful], a. alegre, gozoso, regocijado; placentero, festivo.—joyfully [-i], adv. gozosamente.—joyfulness [-nis], s. gozo, júbilo.

joyless [-lis], a. triste, sin gozo.—joylessly [-li], adv. tristemente.—joylessness [-nis], s. tristeza, abatimiento.

joyous [-ʌs], a. alegre, gozoso.—joyously [-li], adv. gozosamente.—joyousness [-nis], s. gozo, dicha, alegría.

jubilant [dźúbilant], a. jubiloso, alborozado, regocijado, alegre.—jubilate [-eit], vn. alegrarse, regocijarse.—jubilation [-éišon], s. júbilo, regocijo.

jubilee [dźúbili], s. jubileo.

Judaic(al [dźudéijk(al], a. judaico.

Judaically [-i], adv. a manera de judío.

Judaism [dźúdjizm], s. judaísmo.—Judaize [dźúdjaiz], vn. judaizar.—Judaizer [-œ(r)], s. judaizante.

judge [dźʌdź], s. juez, m.; magistrado de un tribunal de justicia; magistrado de la corte suprema; perito.—J. Advocate, auditor de guerra.—to be no j. of, no ser juez en, no entender de, no conocer. II. va. juzgar; sentenciar, fallar. III. vn. juzgar.—judging by, o from, a juzgar por.

judg(e)ment [-mant], s. juicio, criterio, discernimiento; sentir, opinión, dictamen; (for.) fallo; sentencia; ejecutoria; juicio final.—j. day, día del juicio.—j. of God, juicio de Dios.—j. seat, tribunal.—to the best of one's j., según el leal saber y entender de uno.

judgeship [-šip], s. judicatura, magistratura.

judicable [dźúdikabl], a. que puede ser juzgado.—judicative [-tiv], a. judicativo.—judicatory [-tori]. I. s. tribunal de justicia; judicatura. II. a. judicial; jurídico.—judicature [-chur], s. judicatura, magistratura; juzgado.

judicial [dźudíšal], a. judicial.—j. astrology, judiciaria.—j. separation, separación legal o judicial (de marido y mujer)—exime a los cónyuges de sus deberes como tales, pero no disuelve el matrimonio.

judicially [-i], *adv.* judicialmente.

judiciary [dჳudíʃjeri]. **I.** *a.* judiciario; judicial. **II.** *s.* administración de justicia; judicatura; magistratura; poder judicial.

judicious [dჳudíʃʌs], *a.* juicioso, cuerdo, sensato, sesudo, atinado, circunspecto.—**judiciously** [-li], *adv.* juiciosamente, cuerdamente, atinadamente.—**judiciousness** [-nis], *s.* cordura, sensatez.

jug [dჳʌg]. **I.** *va.* introducir o cocer en una botija o cacharro; (fam.) encarcelar. **II.** *vn.* reclamarse (algunos pájaros); juntarse las perdices. **III.** *s.* botijuela, botijo; jarro, cacharro, cántaro, pote, porrón; reclamo del ruiseñor; (fam.) cárcel, *f.*

juggle [dჳʌgl]. **I.** *vn.* hacer juegos de manos, escamot(e)ar; engañar, hacer trampas. **II.** *s.* juego de manos, escamoteo; impostura, engaño.

juggler [dჳʌglœ(r)], *s.* prestidigitador, malabarista, escamoteador; impostor.

jugglery [-i], *s.* prestidigitación, juegos malabares, escamoteo; engaño, trampa.

Jugoslav [yúgosláv], *s.*, **Jugoslavian**, **Jugoslavic** [-ian, -ik], *a.* yugoeslavo.

jugular [dჳágyuljä(r)]. **I.** *a.* (anat.) yugular. **II.** *s.* vena yugular.

juice [dჳús], *s.* zumo; jugo, substancia; (fam.) electricidad.—**j. of the sugar cane,** zumo de caña, guarapo.

juiceless [-lis], *a.* seco, sin jugo.

juiciness [-inis], *s.* jugosidad, suculencia.

juicy [-i], *a.* jugoso, zumoso, suculento.

jujitsu [dჳudჳítsu], *s.* jiu-jitsu, método japonés de combatir brazo a brazo sin armas.

jujube [dჳúdჳub], *s.* azufaifa, yuyuba, jínjol, guinja.—**j. tree,** (bot.) guinjo, azufaifo.

juke box [dჳúk baks], *s.* (fam.) fonógrafo automático, provisto de una ranura por la cual se introduce una moneda, que lo hace funcionar.

julep [dჳúlip], *s.* (farm.) julepe; cierta bebida.

Julian [dჳúlyan], *a.* juliano.

julienne [dჳuljén], *s.* (coc.) sopa Juliana.

July [dჳuláj], *s.* julio.

jumble [dჳʌmbl]. **I.** *va.* mezclar, arrebujar, (fam.) emburujar; confundir. **II.** *vn.* mezclarse, revolverse, confundirse. **III.** *s.* mezcla, revoltillo, embrollo, mezcolanza; bollito delgado y dulce.

jumbo [dჳʌmbou]. **I.** *s.* (fam.) coloso, cosa o animal enorme. **II.** *a.* colosal, gigantesco.

jump [dჳʌmp]. **I.** *va.* saltar por encima de o al otro lado de; hacer saltar; saltarse, omitir; en el juego de damas, comer un peón.—**to j. one's bail,** fugarse uno estando bajo fianza.—**to j. the track,** (f. c.) descarrilar. **II.** *vn.* saltar, brincar; cabriolar; subir rápidamente (precios, etc.); (con **with**) convenir, concordar.—**j. at,** apresurarse a aprovechar.—**to j. on,** arremeter a; (fam.) poner como nuevo.—**to j. over,** saltar por encima de.—**to j. to a conclusion,** sacar precipitadamente una conclusión. **III.** *s.* salto, brinco, cabriola; repullo; (dep.) pista de saltos (esquí); (fam.) ventaja; (min.) falla de una vena.—**j. joint,** junta a tope; junta en ras.—**j. rope,** comba.—**j. spark,** (elec.) chispa en el entrehierro o en cualquier otro espacio de separación.—**on the j.,** de un salto, al vuelo.—**to get, o have, the j. on,** (fam.) tomar la delantera a, adelantársele a uno.

jumper [-œ(r)], *s.* saltador, brincador; blusa de obrero o de mujer; zamarra de pieles; narria, rastra; usurpador de una mina denunciada por otro; (mec.) barreta de mina, taladro de mano; (elec.) alambre de cierre.—*pl.* = ROMPERS.

jumping jack [-iŋ dჳæk], *s.* títere.

jumpy [-i], *a.* nervioso o excitable en exceso.

junction [dჳʌŋkʃən], *s.* conexión, junta, unión; trabadura, acopladura; bifurcación; (f. c.) entronque, empalme, confluencia de dos o más vías.—**j. box,** (elec.) caja de conexiones; caja de derivación.

juncture [dჳʌŋkchჳr], *s.* junta, juntura; coyuntura, articulación; ocasión, oportunidad; trance, momento o circunstancia críticos; exigencia.

June [dჳun], *s.* junio.—**J. bug,** (ent.) abejorro (coleóptero), variedad de escarabajo.

jungle [dჳʌŋgl], *s.* maraña, matorral, zarzal; (Am.) selva, bosque virgen, jungla.—**j. fever,** (med.) fiebre palúdica de la India.

jungly [dჳʌŋgli], *a.* enmarañado, lleno de matorrales.

junior [dჳúnyǫ(r)]. **I.** *s.* estudiante de penúltimo (gen. de tercer año); joven; (igl.) júnior. **II.** *a.* más joven; hijo (gen. en la forma abreviada jr. o Jr., v. gr. *Alexander Dumas, Jr.,* Alejandro Dumas, hijo); de penúltimo año (estudiante); menor; más nuevo o reciente; menos antiguo; posterior; segundo, subordinado, subalterno.—**j. college,** escuela semisuperior, en que se cursan sólo los dos primeros años de las escuelas superiores o universitarias; escuela de estudios universitarios de primero y segundo años.—**j. high school,** escuela secundaria inferior (escuela intermedia entre la elemental y la secundaria).—**j. partner,** socio menos antiguo, socio menor.

juniorate [-eit], *s.* (igl.) jovenado.

juniority [dჳunuyáriti], *s.* condición de *junior.*

juniper [dჳúnipœ(r)], *s.* (bot.) enebro; junípero.—**j. berry,** nebrina.—**j. oil,** miera.

junk [dჳʌŋk], *s.* (mar.) junco, champán; chicote; hierro viejo, chatarra; cecina; (fam.) cascajo, basura, hojarasca.—**j. dealer,** chapucero.

Junker [yúŋkœ(r)], *s.* joven noble alemán; aristócrata reaccionario alemán.

junket [dჳʌŋkit]. **I.** *va.* y *vn.* tener o dar un convite; festejar, obsequiar; andar de parranda. **II.** *s.* (coc.) manjar de leche, cuajo y azúcar.

junket(ing [-iŋ], *s.* festín, francachela; jira.

junkman [dჳʌŋkman], *s.* chapucero, traficante en hierro viejo, trapos, papeles, etc.

junta [dჳʌntä], *s.* junta, asamblea; tribunal.

junto [dჳʌntou], *s.* cábala, cabildeo.

jupon [dჳúpan], *s.* jubón.

jural [dჳúral], *a.* jurídico; rel. a la ley.

jurant [dჳúrant], *a.* juramentado.

Jurassic [dჳurǽsik], *a.* jurásico.

juratory [dჳúratori], *a.* juratorio.

jurel [hჳurél], *s.* (ict.) jurel, chicharro.

juridic(al [dჳurídik(al], *a.* jurídico, judicial.

juridically [-i], *adv.* jurídicamente.

jurisconsult [dჳurjskánsalt], *s.* jurisconsulto.

jurisdiction [-díkʃən], *s.* jurisdicción; potestad, poderío; fuero; competencia.—**jurisdictional** [-al], **jurisdictive** [-díktiv], *a.* jurisdiccional.

jurisprudence [-prúdǫns], *s.* jurisprudencia.—**jurisprudent** [-ǫnt], *a.* y *s.* jurisperito, jurisconsulto.

jurist [dჳúrist], *s.* jurista, jurisconsulto.

juristic [dჳurístik], *a.* jurídico.—**j. person,** persona jurídica, entidad jurídica.

juror [dჳúrǫ(r)], *s.* (for.) jurado (individuo).

jury [dჳúri], *s.* (for.) jurado (cuerpo e institución).—**j. box,** tribuna del jurado.

juryman [-man], *s.* jurado (persona).

jurymast [dჳúrimæst], *s.* (mar.) bandola.

just [dჳʌst]. **I.** *a.* justo, honrado, recto, justiciero; justificado; legal; legítimo, bien fundado; fiel, exacto, cabal. **II.** *adv.* justamente, exactamente; casi; sólo, no más que; apenas; simplemente; hace un momento.—**j. about,** poco más o menos; o poco menos (*this is just about right,* esto está bien, o poco menos).—**j. arrived,** recién llegado.—**j. as,** al momento que, al tiempo que; cuando; no bien; lo mismo que, semejante a.—**j. as you please,** como Vd. guste.—**j. beyond,** un poco más allá.—**j. by,** al lado, al canto, aquí cerca.—**j. now,** ahora mismo, en este mismo instante, poco hace.—**j. so,** ni más ni menos.—**to have but j. time,** tener el tiempo preciso.—**to have j.** (seguido de participio), acabar de (seguido de infinitivo): *I have just arrived*, acabo de llegar.

just [dʒʌst], *vn.* y *s.* = JOUST.

justice [dʒʌstis], *s.* justicia; razón, *f.*, derecho; (for.) juez, *m.*; magistrado:—**j. of the peace**, juez de paz, alcalde.

justiceship [-ʃip], *s.* justiciazgo, judicatura.

justiciable [dʒʌstiʃiabl], *a.* justiciable.

justiciary [-ʃiəri], *a.* judicial.

justifiable [dʒʌstifaiabl], *a.* justificable.—**justifiableness** [-nis], *s.* calidad de justificable.—**justifiably** [-bli], *adv.* justificadamente.—**justification** [-fikéiʃən], *s.* justificación; descargo, defensa; razón (*f.*) de ser.

justificative [dʒʌstifikeitiv], **justificatory** [-fikeitori], *a.* justificativo, defensivo.

justifier [-faiə(r)], *s.* justificador, justificante; calibrador; (impr.) justificador, ajustador.

justify [-fai], *va.* justificar, probar en justicia; sincerar, vindicar; absolver; (teol.) absolver, perdonar; (impr.) justificar, ajustar.

Justinian [dʒʌstinjən], *a.* justinianeo.—**J. Code**, Código Justinianeo.

justle [dʒʌsl], *s.* y *v.* = JOSTLE.

justly [dʒʌstli], *adv.* justamente, rectamente; a justo título; debidamente, dignamente; exactamente, precisamente.—**justness** [-nis], *s.* justicia; exactitud; propiedad; regularidad; primor.

jut [dʒʌt]. I. *vn.* (a veces con **out**) sobresalir, (re)salir, resaltar, proyectar, volar; combarse. II. *s.* salidizo, vuelo, retallo, resalto.—**j. window**, ventana saliente, mirador.

jute [dʒut], *s.* yute, cáñamo de las Indias.

juvenescence [dʒuvénésəns], *s.* rejuvenecimiento, renovación de la juventud.—**juvenescent** [-ənt], *a.* rejuveneciente, que se remoza.

juvenile [dʒúvənil], *a.* juvenil, joven.—**j. court**, tribunal juvenil o del niño; tribunal tutelar de menores.—*s.* mocito, joven; (teat.) galancete.

juvenility [-ʃliti], *s.* mocedad, juventud.

juxtapose [dʒʌkstəpóuz], *va.* yuxtaponer.

juxtaposition [-pouzíʃən], *s.* yuxtaposición, contigüidad.

K

k [kei], *s.* k.

Kabyle [kəbáil], *s.* cabila.

Kafir, Kaffir [kǽfœ(r)], *s.* cafre; infiel (entre los mahometanos).

kaiak [káiyæk], *s.* = KAYAK.

kail, kale [keil], *s.* (bot.) variedad de col rizada.

Kaiser [káizœ(r)], *s.* káiser, emperador alemán o austríaco.—**kaiserdom** [-dəm], *s.* puesto, oficio o dominio de un káiser; kaiserismo.

kaki [káki], *s.* (bot.) caqui, kaki, níspero del Japón.

kaleidoscope [kəláidoskoup], *s.* calidoscopio.

kaleidoscopic [-skápik], *a.* calidoscópico; variado, pintoresco.

kalends [kǽləndz], *s. pl.* = CALENDS.

kali [kǽli], *s.* (bot.) barrilla.

kalif, kalifate, = CALIF, CALIFATE.

kalium [kéiljəm], *s.* (quím.) potasio.

kalmia [kǽlmjə], *s.* (Am., bot.) kalmia.

Kalmuck [kǽlmʌk], *s.* y *a.* calmuco.

kalsomine [kǽlsomain], *v.* y *s.* = CALCIMINE.

Kamerad [kamœrát]. I. *s.* camarada (usado por los soldados alemanes en señal de rendición). II. *vn.* (k., fam.) rendirse, dar el *camarada*.

Kanaka [kǽnəkə], *s.* natural de las islas de Hawái.

kangaroo [kæŋgərú], *s.* (zool.) canguro.—**k. closure**, guillotina, limitación presidencial de la discusión de un proyecto a sus puntos principales.—**k. court**, tribunal irregular.

Kantian [kǽntjən], *a.* y *s.* kantiano, kantista.

Kantianism [-izm], *s.* kantismo.

kaolin [kéəlin], *s.* caolín.

Kapellmeister [kəpélmaistœ(r)], *s.* maestro de capilla; director de un coro, orquesta o banda.

kapok [kéipak], *s.* capoc, capoca o kapoc, especie de lana de ceiba.—**k. tree**, capoquero.

kappa [kǽpə], *s.* kappa (letra griega).

karakul [kǽrəkul], *s.* caracul, astracán (piel).

karat [kǽrət], *s.* (joy.) quilate.

karyokinesis [kærjokinísis], *s.* (biol.) cariocinesis, mitosis, multiplicación de las células por división indirecta.

kation [kǽtaiən], *s.* (fís.) catión, *m.*

katydid [kéitidid], *s.* (ent.) chicharra, cicada, insecto ortóptero.

kauri, kaury [káuri], *s.* (bot.) pino de la Nueva Zelandia, y su resina.

kayak [káiyæk], *s.* kayak, canoa de los esquimales.

kayo [kéióu], *s.* y *va.* (fam.) = KNOCKOUT.

kazoo [kəzú], *s.* chicharra (instrumento).

keck [kek], *vn.* arquear.

keckle [kékl], *va.* (mar.) aforrar un cable.

keddah [kédə], *s.* trampa de elefantes.

kedge [kedʒ], *s.* (mar.) anclote.

keel [kil]. I. *s.* (mar.) quilla. II. *va.* y *vn.* poner la quilla; (poét.) surcar el mar; dar carena.—**to k. over**, (fam.) volcarse; desplomarse; desmayarse.

keelage [-idʒ], *s.* (mar.) derechos de quilla.

keelhaul [-hɔl], *va.* (mar.) pasar por debajo de la quilla (castigo).

keelson [kélsən], *s.* (mar.) sobrequilla.

keen [kin], *a.* afilado; aguzado; agudo, penetrante, sutil, vivo; astuto, ladino; perspicaz; ansioso, vehemente; acre, mordaz, incisivo.

keenly [-li], *adv.* agudamente, profundamente; sutilmente; con viveza.

keenness [-nis], *s.* agudeza; sutileza, perspicacia, penetración; ansia, anhelo.

keep [kip], *va.* (*pret.* y *pp.* KEPT) conservar; quedarse con; guardar (una cosa, un secreto, un mandamiento, la cuaresma, cama, un rebaño); tener (criados, secretario, un perro); dirigir, manejar (hotel, tienda, etc.); alojar, dar hospedaje a por paga, tener (*he keeps boarders*, tiene huéspedes, da hospedaje, o tiene casa de huéspedes); llevar (cuentas, libros); cumplir (la palabra, una promesa); mantener; detener, demorar; contener; mantenerse en.—**to k. an eye on**, vigilar.—**to k. at bay**, tener a raya.—**to k. awake**, desvelar (ú. del café, etc.).—**to k. away**, tener o retener alejado; no dejar venir, entrar, etc.—**to k. back**, detener; ocultar; impedir; preservar, guardar o reservar; restringir.—**to k. bad**, o **late, hours**, acostarse tarde.—**to k. body and soul together**, vivir, ir viviendo, no pasar hambre.—**to k. cash**, ser cajero.—**to k. company**, acompañar; tener amores o casamiento arreglado.—**to k. company with**, pasar el tiempo en compañía de; (fam.) cortejar.—**to k. down**, sujetar; reprimir.—**to k. from**, mantener lejos de; impedir (cambiando el giro).—**to k. early**, o **good hours**, acostarse temprano.—**to k. house**, tener hogar propio; manejar casa.—**to k. in**, mantener dentro; no dejar salir.—**to k. in mind**, recordar; tener en cuenta.—**to k. informed (of)**, tener al corriente o al tanto (de).—**to k. off**, detener; tener a distancia; cerrar el paso a.—**to k. on**, mantener; continuar.—**to k. one's counsel**, callar, no decir nada.—**to k. one's countenance**, no alterarse, permanecer inmutable.—**to k. one's distance**, mantenerse dentro de propios límites, no tomarse libertades.—**to k. one's end up**, mantenerse en su puesto, no aflojar.—**to k. one's eyes open**, mantenerse alerta, no dormirse (fig.).—**to k. one's ground**, mantenerse en su puesto, defenderse bien.—**to k. one's hands off**, no tocar, no meterse en.—**to k. one's head**, no perder la cabeza, mantener su sangre fría.—**to k. one's temper**, contenerse; obrar con calma.—**to k. one's word**, cumplir su palabra, tener palabra. —**to k. open house**, mantener la puerta abierta (fig.), ofrecer hospitalidad o hacer invitaciones de continuo.—**to k. out**, no dejar entrar; excluir.—**to k. out of sight**, no dejar ver; quitar de delante.—**to k. pace with**, marchar con, ir al mismo paso que, correr parejas con.—**to k. step**, llevar o marcar el paso.—**to k. tally**, llevar la cuenta.—**to k. the ball rolling**, mantener el fuego ardiendo (fig.), mantener la animación, conversación, etc.—**to k. the bowels open**, mantener libre el vientre.—**to k. the land aboard**, (mar.) mantenerse inmediato a la costa.—**to k. the peace**, mantener la paz o el orden público.—**to k. the pot boiling**, ganarse la vida; mantener la actividad. —**to k. (the) score**, tantear, llevar la cuenta.— **to k. the wind**, navegar de bolina.—**to k. the wolf from the door**, guardarse del hambre o la pobreza.—**to k. time**, marcar la hora, andar (el reloj); llevar o marcar el compás.—**to k. track of**, seguir la pista a, no perder de vista. —**to k. under**, sujetar, oprimir.—**to k. up**, mantener, conservar.—**to k. up appearances**, salvar las apariencias.—**to k. up one's spirits**, mantener su valor, no desalentarse.

keep [kíp], *vn.* mantenerse, sostenerse; durar sin dañarse; acostumbrar, soler; continuar; perseverar; permanecer, quedarse.—**to k. along**, continuar, seguir, proseguir.—**to k. aloof**, permanecer apartado, no meterse, no tomar parte. —**to k. at it**, (fam.) perseverar, persistir.—**to k. at home**, quedarse en casa.—**to k. away**, mantenerse apartado, no acercarse.—**to k. from**, abstenerse de; no meterse en.—**to k. in**, permanecer dentro; estarse en casa.—**to k. off**, no entrar a; no tocar; no andar sobre o por; mantenerse fuera o lejos de.—**to k. on**, seguir, proseguir.—**to k. out of**, no meterse en, evitar. —**to k. out of sight**, mantenerse oculto, no mostrarse.—**to k. out of the way**, estarse o hacerse a un lado; esconderse, sacar el cuerpo.— **to k. to**, adherirse estrictamente a; seguir por. —**to k. up**, mantenerse firme; persistir; no cejar; estar de jarana.—**to k. up with** = TO K. PACE WITH.

keep, *s.* manutención, subsistencia; receptáculo, depósito; torreón, alcázar; castillo.—**for keeps**, para guardar, para quedarse con ello; permanentemente.

keeper [-œ(r)], *s.* guarda, *mf.*, guardián, custodio, defensor; alcaide, conserje; loquero; tenedor; carcelero; guardabosque; armadura (de un imán).—**k. of the great seal**, guardasellos del rey.—**k. of the keys**, llavero.—**k. of the records**, archivero.—**k.'s lodge**, casilla.

keepership [-šip], *s.* guardería, alcaidía.

keeping [-iŋ], *s.* cargo, custodia, mantenimiento; cuidado, preservación, defensa; guarda.—**in k. with**, en armonía con, de conformidad con, por el mismo estilo que, al mismo tenor que.

keepsake [-seik], *s.* regalo, recuerdo.

keeve [kiv], *s.* cuba en que fermenta la cerveza.

keg [keg], *s.* cuñete, barrilito, cubete, pipote.

keir [kir], *s.* cuba, tanque de blanquear.

kelp [kelp], *s.* algas marinas y sus cenizas, de las que se obtiene el yodo; sosa.

Kelt, Keltic [kélt, -ik], = CELT, etc.

kelter [kéltœ(r)], *s.* = KILTER.

Kelvin scale [kélvin skeil], *s.* (fís.) escala absoluta (de temperaturas).

ken [ken], **I.** *va.* (ant. y Esco.) saber, conocer; divisar. **II.** *s.* alcance de la vista; percepción mental.

kennel [kénel], **I.** *s.* perrera; jauría; canal, desagüe; zorrera; cuchitril. **II.** *va.* y *vn.* tener o estar en perrera.

kentledge [kéntledž], *s.* (mar.) enjunque.

kepi [képi], *s.* (mil.) quepis o kepis, *m.*

kept [kept], *pret.* y *pp.* de TO KEEP.—**k. mistress**, o **woman**, manceba, querida.

keramic [kirémik], *a.* = CERAMIC.

keratin [kérɑtin], *s.* (bioquím.) queratina.

keratitis [kerɑtáitis], *s.* (med.) queratitis.

keratosis [kerɑtóusis], *s.* (med.) queratosis.

kerbstone, *s.* (Ingl.) = CURBSTONE.

kerchief [kœrchif], *s.* pañuelo.

kerf [kœrf], *s.* corte que hace la sierra en la madera; cortadura que hace una máquina de tundir.

kermes [kœrmiz], *s.* (ent.) quermes, kermes, carmes, grana.—**k. oak**, (bot.) coscoja.—**k. berry**, grana, coscojo.

kermess [kœrmis], **kermis** [-is], *s.* quermese, *f.*, verbena, bazar, fiesta, romería.

kern [kœrn], *s.* (impr.) hombro de una letra; (ant.) patán; (hist.) soldado irlandés.

kernel [kœrnel]. **I.** *s.* almendra, pepita, meollo o semilla carnosa de cualquier fruto drupáceo; grano de maíz; (fig.) meollo, medula, núcleo. **II.** *vn.* formarse almendra; (agr.) granar.

kernel(l)ed [-d], *a.* que tiene almendra o pepita, etc.

kernelly [-i], *a.* almendrado; granado.

kerosene [kérosin], *s.* petróleo destilado, querosén, kerosena, (Am.) kerosén, kerosina, kerosene.

kersey [kœrzi], *s.* (tej.) buriel.

kerseymere [-mir], *s.* (tej.) casimir.

kestrel [késtrel], *s.* (orn.) cernícalo.

ketch [kech], *s.* (mar.) queche.

ketchup [kéchʌp], *s.* = CATSUP o CATCHUP.

ketone [kítoun], *s.* (quím.) quetona, acetona.

kettle [kétl], *s.* caldera, marmita, olla, perol, paila.—**(a fine) k. of fish**, lío, embrollo.

kettledrum [-drʌm], *s.* (mús.) timbal, atabal, tímpano; (fam.) tertulia de confianza por la tarde.

kettledrummer [-œ(r)], *s.* timbalero, atabalero.

kettleful [-ful], *s.* calderada.

kevel [kével], *s.* (mar.) manigueta.

key [ki]. **I.** *s.* llave, *f.*; clave, *f.*, buscapié, contracifra; fundamento; persona o cosa principal; tono (de la voz); estilo; tabla, cuadro; (mec.) llave, destornillador; chaveta; cuña; (arq.) clave, dovela; (enc.) clavija; (arti.) sotrozo; (elec.) llave, conmutador; tecla (del piano, de máquina de escribir o de las de componer y distribuir tipos); pistón o llave de los instrumentos de viento; (mús.) clave, llave, tono; (mar.) cayo, isleta; muelle.—**k. action**, teclado y mecanismo de un órgano o piano.—**k. bolt**, perno de chaveta.—**k. bugle**, corneta de llaves. —**k. rack**, llavero, taquilla.—**k. ring**, llavero. —**k. seat**, cajera de cuña.—**k. tone** = KEYNOTE.—**in k.**, templado, de acuerdo, en armonía.—**off (the) k.**, fuera del tono, destemplado. **II.** *a.* principal; que sirve de clave o de guía; fundamental; estratégico. **III.** *va.* enchavetar, calzar, acuñar; poner llaves; afinar, templar con llave.

keyboard [kíbord], *s.* teclado.

keyed [kíd], *a.* que tiene llaves o teclas; estirado; templado, afinado.—**k. up**, excitado, agitado.

keyhole [kíhoul], *s.* bocallave, *f.*, ojo de la cerradura.—**k. saw**, llave de punta o de calador.

keynote [kínout], *s.* (mús.) nota tónica; principio fundamental, piedra angular.—**k. address**, o **speech**, discurso de apertura (de una convención política, etc.), declaración de principios y programa.—**keynoter** [-œ(r)], *s.* orador que pronuncia el discurso de apertura, en que se enuncia el programa del partido, etc.

keystone [kístoun], *s.* (arq.) clave, llave (*f.*) de arco.

keyway [kíwei], *s.* = KEY SEAT.

khaki [káki], *s.* kaki, caqui (tela y color).

khan [kan], *s.* kan o khan (título); kan, posada o mesón en Turquía, etc.; caravanera.—**khanate** [-eit], *s.* kanato.

khedive [kedív], *s.* jedive (virrey).

kibe [káib], *s.* grieta en la piel; sabañón ulcerado.

kibed [-d], **kiby** [-i], *a.* lleno de sabañones.

kibitzer [kíbitzœ(r)], *s.* (fam.) mirón, espectador

molesto en los juegos de naipes; entremetido; (Arg.) pato.

kick [kík]. I. *va.* acocear, dar patadas a.—**to k. open**, abrir a patadas.—**to k. out**, echar a puntapiés o a patadas.—**to k. the bucket**, (fam.) irse al otro mundo, morirse, liarlas.—**to k. up a dust, o a row**, (fam.) armar un bochinche, ponerse por las nubes.—**to k. up one's heels**, (fam.) retozar, jaranear; morirse. II. *vn.* cocear, patear, dar o tirar coces; (fam.) respingar; oponerse; quejarse.—**to k. against the pricks**, cocear contra el aguijón.—**to k. over the traces**, rebelarse, abandonar o sacudir toda restricción. III. *s.* patada, coz; puntapié, *m.;* (fam.) respingo; oposición; (fam.) efecto estimulante del alcohol; placer (**to get a k. out of**, hallar placer en); estímulo, aliento, impulso; reculada, retroceso (de un arma de fuego); fondo entrante (de botella).—**k. plate**, placa de protección.

kickback [-bæk], *s.* (fam.) restitución gen. secreta de una parte del sueldo, honorarios, etc., que se deben al favor o protección de otra persona.

kicker [-œ(r)], *s.* coceador, pateador; (fam.) reparón, quejumbroso.

kicking [-iŋ], *s.* acoceamiento, pateadura; pataleo; (fam.) respingo, queja.—**k. coil** = CHOKING COIL.

kickshaw [-šɔ], *s.* bocado regalado, golosina; fruslería, bagatela; patarata.

kid [kid]. I. *s.* (zool.) cabrito, chiva, chivato; cabritilla (piel); carne (*f.*) de cabrito; (fam.) niño; muchachito; chico, chica; (mar.) gamella.—*pl.* guantes o zapatos de cabritilla.—**k. gloves, shoes, etc.**, guantes, zapatos, etc., de cabritilla.—**to handle with k. gloves**, (fam.) tratar con guantes blancos. II. *va. y vn.* parir (la cabra); (fam.) embromar, candonguear, tomar el pelo a; embaucar.

kidder [kídœ(r)], *s.* (fam.) chancero, bromista.

kiddishness [kídišnjs], *s.* (fam.) niñería, chiquillada, muchachada.

kidling [kídliŋ], *s.* (zool.) choto.

kidnap [kídnæp], *va.* secuestrar, raptar, (Am.) plagiar.—**kidnapper** [-œ(r)], *s.* ladrón de niños u otras personas, secuestrador, raptor.—**kidnapping** [-iŋ], *s.* secuestro, rapto, (Am.) plagio.

kidney [kídni], *s.* (anat.) riñón; índole, *f.*, clase, *f.*; temperamento.—**k. bean**, (bot.) judía, fríjol o fríjol ordinario, fréjol, alubia, habichuela.—**k. stone**, piedra nefrítica.—**k. vetch**, (bot.) vulneraria.

kidneyshaped [-šejpt], *a.* reniforme.

kidneywort [-wœrt], *s.* (bot.) ombligo de Venus.

kidskin [kídskin], *a. y s.* (de) cabritilla o baldés.

kier [kir], *s.* cuba o tanque de blanquear.

kilderkin [kíldœrkin], *s.* medio barril (medida).

kilerg [kílœrg], *s.* (fís.) kiloergio.

kill [kil]. I. *va.* matar; destruir; amortiguar; neutralizar; descartar; anular, cancelar, suprimir.—**to k. time**, (fam.) pasar el rato, hacer tiempo u hora.—**to k. two birds with one stone**, hacer de un camino dos mandados, matar dos pájaros de una pedrada o tiro. II. *s.* acción de matar; animal muerto (matado); arroyo, riachuelo.

killdee(r [kíldi(r), *s.* (orn.) frailecillo norteamericano, especie de ave fría o chorlito.

killed [kild], *pp. y a.* matado, muerto, occiso.—**k. in action**, (mil.) muerto en acción de guerra.

killer [kílœ(r)], *s.* matador; asesino, homicida, *mf.;* (fam.) matón.—**k. whale**, (zool.) orca.

killing [kíliŋ]. I. *a.* matador; destructivo; irresistible; (fam.) ridículo, risible. II. *s.* acto de matar, occisión, matanza.

kill-joy [kíl džoj], *s.* aguafiestas.

kiln [kíl(n)], *s.* horno, estufa; horno de cochura.

kilndry [-(n)draj], *va.* secar al horno.

kilo [kíloy], *s.* kilo(gramo); kilómetro; como prefijo = mil.

kiloampere [kíloæmpir], *s.* (elec.) kiloamperio.

kilocalorie [-kælori], *s.* (fís.) kilocaloría.

kilocycle [-sajkl], *s.* (elec.) kilociclo.

kilogram(me [-græm], *s.* kilo(gramo).

kilogrammeter [-græmítœ(r)], *s.* (mec. y fís.) kilográmetro.

kilojoule [-džul], *s.* (elec.) kilojulio.

kiloliter [-litœ(r)], *s.* kilolitro.

kilometer [-mitœ(r)], *s.* kilómetro.

kilometric [-métrik], *a.* kilométrico.

kilovolt [-voqlt], *s.* (elec.) kilovoltio.

kilovolt-ampere [-æmpir], *s.* (elec.) kilovoltamperio.

kilowatt [-wat], *s.* (elec.) kilovatio.

kilowatt-hour [-áur], *s.* (elec.) kilovatio-hora.

kilt [kilt]. I. *s.* tonelete; enagüillas, *f. pl.*, falda corta (como la de los escoceses serranos). II. *va.* sofaldar; (cost.) plegar, hacer pliegues anchos y planos.

kilter [kíltœ(r)], *s.* (fam.) buena condición, buen estado.—**out of k.**, desarreglado, descompuesto.

kimono [kimóqnoq], *s.* bata de quimón; quimono o kimono.

kin [kin]. I. *s.* parentesco, vínculo; parentela, familia, linaje.—**the next of k.**, los parientes (más) próximos. II. *a.* pariente, allegado.

kind [kajnd]. I. *a.* bueno, benévolo, bondadoso, amable; manso; afectuoso.—**k.-hearted**, bondadoso, de buen corazón.—**k.-heartedness**, benevolencia, bondad, buen corazón.—**k. regards**, cordial saludo, saludes, *f. pl.;* sentimientos de consideración. II. *s.* género, clase, *f.*, casta, índole, *f.*, suerte, *f.*, tenor, calidad.—**k. of**, (fam.) algo, un poco; en cierto modo.—**in k.**, del mismo modo, en la misma moneda (fig.); (e. p.) en especie (no en dinero).—**nothing of the k.**, nada de eso; no hay tal.—**of a k.**, de una misma clase.—**of the k.**, semejante, tal.

kindergarten [kíndœrgartin], *s.* kindergarten, escuela de párvulos, (Am.) jardín de infantes.

kindergart(e)ner [-gart(i)nœ(r)], *s.* maestro o niño de kindergarten.

kindle [kíndl]. I. *va.* encender; inflamar, enardecer. II. *vn.* prender, arder; inflamarse, avivarse.

kindler [kíndlœ(r)], *s.* encendedor (persona o cosa).

kindliness [kájndlinjs], *s.* benevolencia, bondad, benignidad; buena índole.

kindling [kíndliŋ], *s.* encendimiento; ignición; inflamación.—**k. wood**, leña menuda.

kindly [kájndli]. I. *adv.* amable o bondadosamente; cordialmente; favorablemente. Se emplea mucho en el sentido de *dígnese, sírvase, ojalá me haga el favor, etc.* II. *a.* bondadoso, benévolo; favorable, propicio; (min.) que promete; (hist.) lícito; legítimo.

kindness [kájndnjs], *s.* bondad, benevolencia, amabilidad, atención, favor, gracia.

kindred [kíndrjd]. I. *s.* parentesco, consanguinidad, cognación; parentela, casta, tribu, *f.* II. *a.* emparentado, deudo, consanguíneo, cognado; afín, hermano, parejo; conexo, congénere.

kinematic [kinjmætjk], *a.* cinemático.

kinematics [-s], *s.* (fís.) cinemática.

kinematograph [-mætogræf], *s.* cinematógrafo.

kinesiatrics [kinjsjætriks], **kinesitherapy** [-ϑérapi], *s.* (med.) cinesia o cinesia, cinesiterapia o kinesiterapia, tratamiento de las enfermedades por movimientos musculares.

kinesthesia [kinjsϑížjə], **kinesthesis** [-ϑísjs], *s.* cinestesia, sentido muscular, percepción de los movimientos musculares propios.

kinetic [kinétjk], *a.* cinético, dinámico.—**k. energy**, energía cinética.—**kinetics** [-s], *s.* cinética, dinámica.

kinetograph [kinétogræf], *s.* cinematógrafo; cinetógrafo (cinematógrafo parlante).

kinetoscope [-skoqp], *s.* cinetoscopio.

king [kiŋ], *s.* rey; en los naipes y el ajedrez, rey;

en el juego de damas, dama.—**k. at arms**, heraldo, rey de armas.—**k. crab**, (zool.) límulo. —**k. post**, (arq.) mangueta, nabo, montante, pendolón.—**k.-post bridge**, o **truss**, puente o armadura triangular de pendolón.—**k.'s English**, inglés (lenguaje) correcto.—**k.'s evil**, (med.) escrófula, lamparón.—**k.'s household**, casa real.—**k.'s yellow**, oropimento.—**the k.'s speech**, discurso de la Corona.

kingbird [-bœrd], *s.* (orn.) tirano.

kingbolt [-boʊlt], *s.* (carr.) pivote que une la caja al eje delantero; (constr.) perno real o pinzote; tirante.

kingcraft [-kræft], *s.* arte de reinar.

kingcup [-kʌp], *s.* (bot.) botón de oro.

kingdom [-dʌm], *s.* reino.

kingfisher [-fiʃœ(r)], *s.* (orn.) guardarrío, martín pescador, alción, *m.*

kinghood [-hʊd], *s.* dignidad real. *V.* KINGSHIP.

kinglet [-lit], *s.* reyezuelo; (orn.) abadejo, régulo.

kinglike [-laik], **kingly** [-li]. **I.** *a.* real, regio; majestuoso. **II.** *adv.* regiamente, majestuosamente.

kingpin [-pin], *s.* = KINGBOLT; pivote; el bolo delantero o central (en el juego de bolos); (fam.) gallo, persona más importante de una empresa.

kingship [-ʃip], *s.* majestad, dignidad real; monarquía; reino.

kink [kiŋk]. **I.** *s.* retorcimiento, ensortijamiento; (med.) torticolis, *m.;* (mar.) coca; (fam.) capricho, chifladura. **II.** *va.* y *vn.* formar cocas, ensortijarse, encarrujarse.

kinky [-i], *a.* ensortijado, encarrujado, grifo; (fam.) chiflado.

kino [kínoʊ], *s.* quino, zumo de ciertos árboles.

kinsfolk [kínzfoʊk], *s. pl.* parentela, parientes, *m. pl.*

kinship [kínʃip], *s.* parentesco.

kinsman [kínzmən], *s.* pariente, deudo.

kinswoman [-wʊmən], *s.* parienta.

kiosk [kiásk], *s.* kiosco o quiosco.

kip [kip], *s.* (ten.) piel (*f.*) de res pequeña.

kipper [kípœ(r)]. **I.** *s.* (ict.) salmón zancado; salmón o arenque ahumado. **II.** *va.* curar (pescado) al humo.

kirsch(**wasser** [kírʃ(vasœ(r)], *s.* kirsch.

kirk [kœrk], *s.* (Esco.) iglesia.

kismet [kízmet], *s.* hado, destino.

kiss [kis]. **I.** *va.* besar; en el billar, retrucar, tocarse suavemente dos bolas.—**to k. repeatedly**, (fam.) besuquear, besucar.—**to k. the dust**, morder el polvo.—**to k. the rod**, someterse a un castigo. **II.** *s.* beso, ósculo; en el billar, pelo, retruco; (coc.) merengue; dulce.

kisser [-œ(r)], *s.* besador, (fam.) besucador.

kit [kit], *s.* coldora, tineta; cubo; equipo, avíos, *m. pl.*, juego o caja de herramientas, medicinas, instrumentos, etc.; violín de tres cuerdas; tiple (guitarrita); gatito; (fam.) conjunto de cosas o personas; (fot.) marquito interior del chasís o portaplanchas.—**k.-cat**, (pint.) lienzo o retrato de medio cuerpo.

kitchen [kítʃen], *s.* cocina; fogón portátil.—**k. boy**, pinche, galopillo.—**k. garden**, huerta.—**k. maid**, fregona, fregatriz.—**k. police**, (mil.) trabajo de cocina; soldado que lo hace.—**k. range**, o **stove**, fogón, cocina económica.—**k. sink**, pila de cocina.—**k. stuff**, material o hierbas de cocina, legumbres; grasa, pringue, *mf.*—**k. utensils** = KITCHENWARE.

kitchener [-œ(r)], *s.* estufa de cocinar; cocinero.

kitchenette [-ét], *s.* cocina reducida o pequeña.

kitchenware [-wer], *s.* utensilios o trastos de cocina, batería de cocina.

kite [kait], *s.* cometa; (com.) papel negociable u obligación de valor dudoso; (orn.) milano; (mar.) sobrejuanete, foque volante.—**k. balloon**, **k. sausage**, globo cautivo, globo cometa.

kiteflying [-flaiiŋ], *s.* acción de remontar una cometa; (com.) negociación de pagarés sin valor; (pol.) sondeo de la opinión pública.

kith [kiθ], *s.* (ant.) conocidos, amistades, *pl.*—**k. and kin**, parientes y amigos.

kitten [kítn]. **I.** *s.* gatito. **II.** *vn.* parir la gata.—**kittenish** [-iʃ], *a.* juguetón, retozón.

kittiwake [kítiweik], *s.* (orn.) especie de gaviota.

kitty [kíti], *s.* gatito, minino; (en el juego, etc.) polla, puesta.

kiva [kívá], *s.* cámara de ceremonias de ciertos indios norteamericanos, con la entrada por arriba.

kiwi [kíwi], *s.* (orn.) kiwi, aptérix, pájaro áptero de Nueva Zelanda.

Klansman [klǽnzmən], *s.* miembro del KU KLUX KLAN.

kleptomania [klɛptoméiniá], *s.* cleptomanía.

kleptomaniac [-iæk], *a.* y *s.* cleptómano, cleptomaníaco.

knack [næk], *s.* tino, don, destreza, acierto, arte; treta; chuchería.

knaggy [nǽgi], *a.* nudoso; áspero.

knapping [nǽpiŋ], *s.* quebrantamiento o corte de piedras.—**k. hammer**, martillo de picapedrero.

knapsack [nǽpsæk], *s.* (mil.) mochila; barjuleta, alforja, fardel, morral.

knapweed [nǽpwid], *s.* (bot.) centaur(e)a negra.

knarled [narld], *a.* nudoso. *V.* KNURLED, GNARLED.

knave [néiv], *s.* bribón, pícaro, bellaco; sota de los naipes.—**knavery** [-œri], *s.* picardía, bellaquería, bribonada, tunantería.—**knavish** [-iʃ], *a.* bribón, pillo; travieso.—**knavishly** [-li], *adv.* bellacamente.

knead [níd], *va.* amasar, sobar, heñir.

kneader [-œ(r)], *s.* panadero, amasador.

kneading [-iŋ], *s.* amasadura, amasijo; soba.—**k. machine**, amasadera.—**k. table**, hintero.—**k. trough** [-trof], amasadera, artesa.

knee [ni], *s.* (anat.) rodilla, hinojo; codillo (de cuadrúpedos); (mec.) codo, codillo, ángulo, escuadra; (mar.) curva.—**k. bone**, (anat.) rótula.—**k. boss**, **guard**, **pad**, o **patch**, rodillera.—**k. breeches**, calzón corto.—**k.-crooking**, obsequioso.—**k.-deep**, metido hasta las rodillas.—**k.-high**, hasta la rodilla.—**k. jerk**, o **reflex**, reflejo rotuliano, patada o sacudida causada por golpe en el tendón de la rótula.—**k. joint**, articulación de la rodilla; junta de codillo.—**k.-jointed**, encorvado o angular.—**k. timber**, madera para curvas.—**k. tribute**, genuflexión.

kneecap [-kæp], *s.* rodillera; (anat.) rótula.

kneed [-d], *a.* articulado, acodillado.

kneel [níl], *vn.* (*pret.* y *pp.* KNELT o KNEELED) (a veces con **down**) arrodillarse, ponerse de rodillas o hinojos, doblar o hincar la rodilla, postrarse.

kneeler [-œ(r)], *s.* el que se arrodilla.

kneeling [-iŋ], *a.* arrodillado, de rodillas, de hinojos.

kneepan [nípæn], *s.* (anat.) rótula, choquezuela.

knell [nel]. **I.** *s.* doble, toque de difuntos; clamoreo; mal agüero. **II.** *va.* y *vn.* doblar, tocar a muerto.

knew [nju], *pret.* de TO KNOW.

Knickerbocker [níkœrbakœ(r)], *s.* descendiente de una de las primeras familias holandesas que se establecieron en Nueva York; neoyorquino.—(**k.**, *pl.*) calzón corto, bragas, pantalones (ll. t. **knickers**).

knickknack [níknæk], *s.* chuchería, baratija, bujería, juguete.

knife [naif]. **I.** *s.* cuchillo; navaja; (cir.) bisturí, escalpelo.—**k. edge**, filo, cuchillo; corte; (mec.) cuña o fiel de soporte.—**k. sharpener**, chaira, amolador, afilón.—**k. switch**, (elec.) interruptor de cuchillo. **II.** *va.* acuchillar; (fam.) frustrar o arruinar por intrigas.

knight [nait], *s.* caballero; campeón; caballo (del ajedrez).—**k. commander**, comendador.—**k. commandery**, encomienda.—**k.-errant**, caballero andante, aventurero.—**k.-errantry**, caballería andante.—**k. of St. Crispin**, zapatero.—K. of the Order of the Garter, caballero de la orden de la Jarretera.—k. of the shears, sastre.—K. Templar, Templario. II. *va.* armar caballero; condecorar; encomendar; (en Ingl.) hacer caballero, conferir el título de *Sir.*

knighthead [-hĕd], *s.* (mar.) guardaauprés.—**knightheads of the jeers,** (mar.) guindastes.

knighthood [-hųd], *s.* caballería; encomienda.

knightliness [-lįnįs], *s.* calidad de caballeresco.

knightly [-lį]. I. *a.* caballeresco. II. *adv.* caballerosamente, caballerescamente.

knit [nít], *va.* y *vn.* (*pret.* y *pp.* KNIT o KNITTED) hacer malla, hacer media o calceta, hacer punto de aguja; atar, enlazar, entretejer; contraer; unirse, trabarse.—k. **stockings,** medias de punto.—**knit**(ted) **goods,** o **fabrics,** géneros de punto o de tricot.—**to k.** the **brow,** fruncir las cejas, arrugar el entrecejo.

knitter [-œ(r)], *s.* calcetero, mediero.

knitting [-įŋ], *s.* unión o junta; acción de hacer calceta; trabajo de punto.—k. **machine,** máquina de hacer punto de media.—k. **mill,** fábrica de tejidos.—k. **needle,** aguja de medias o de hacer calceta, etc.—k. **work,** trabajo de punto, labor (*f.*) de calceta, tricot.

knives [najvz], *pl.* de KNIFE.

knob [náb], *s.* prominencia, bulto, protuberancia; nudo en la madera; borlita o borlilla; perilla, tirador (de puerta, ropero, etc.); botón; gorrón; montículo; (arq.) = KNOP; tojino.

knobbed [-d], **knobby** [-į], *a.* lleno de bultos o nudos; nudoso; montañoso.

knock [nák]. I. *va.* y *vn.* chocar, topar; tocar, llamar a una puerta; pegar, cutir; golpear, dar o pegar golpes, aporrear; (fam.) criticar, hablar mal de.—**to k. about,** (fam.) vagar, rodar.—**to k. down,** derribar, echar a tierra, tumbar; atropellar (con un coche, etc.); (mec., etc.) abatir, desarmar, desmontar.—**to k. down to the highest bidder,** (com.) rematar al mejor postor.—**to k. in,** (a)martillar; hacer entrar a golpes.—**to k. off,** hacer saltar una cosa a fuerza de golpes; (fam.) cesar, descontinuar, suspender; (fam.) hacer o ejecutar prontamente; rebajar, descontar.—**to k. on the head,** dar en la cabeza; frustrar.—**to k. out,** hacer salir a golpes; acogotar; destruir; dejar o poner fuera de combate (en el boxeo).—**to k. together,** construir toscamente o de prisa.—**to k. the bottom out of,** desfondar; (fam.) echar a perder, frustrar.—**to k. under,** someterse, rendirse. II. *s.* choque, golpe, porrazo, topetazo; aldabonazo, llamada, toque; (fam.) crítica dura.

knockdown [-daųn]. I. *a.* mínimo (apl. al precio mínimo a que se venderá una cosa en subasta); desarmable; abrumador. II. *s.* golpe que derriba o abruma; cosa desarmada.

knocker [-œ(r)], *s.* golpeador; llamador, aldaba, aldabón.

knocking [-įŋ], *s.* aldabazo, aldabonazo, llamada a la puerta.

knock-kneed [-nid], *a.* patituerto, (pati)zambo.

knockout [-aųt]. I. *a.* que pone fuera de combate; abrumador.—k. **drops,** (fam.) gotas narcóticas. II. *s.* golpe que pone fuera de combate; destapadero (lugar en una plancha donde puede botarse el metal a martillo para formar un agujero).

knoll [noųl]. I. *va.* y *vn.* (ant.) = KNELL. II. *s.* loma, otero; cumbre o cima de una loma; doble de las campanas.

knop [nap], *s.* = KNOB; (arq.) florón. *V.* FINIAL.

knosp [nasp], *s.* (bot.) capullo; (arq.) florón.

knot [nát]. I. *s.* nudo; lazo, vínculo; nudo de la madera o de plantas; enredo de un drama; dificultad; grupo, corrillo; quid, *m.,* (fam.) busilis, *m.;* moño o castaña; (mar.) milla náutica, nudo; (orn.) canuto.—k. **hole,** agujero que deja en la madera un nudo desprendido.—k.

wood, madera nudosa.—**knots of the log line,** nudos de la corredera. II. *va.* anudar; atar con nudos; enredar, juntar; fruncir (las cejas); hacer nudos en; intrincar; unir. III. *vn.* echar nudos las plantas; formar nudos; enredarse.

knotgrass [-græs], *s.* (bot.) centinodia, sanguinaria, sauquillo, grama.

knotless [-lįs], *a.* sin nudos.

knotted [-įd], *a.* nudoso, anudado.

knottiness [-inįs], *s.* abundancia de nudos; desigualdad; dificultad.

knotty [-į], *a.* nudoso; duro, áspero; intrincado, difícil.

knout [naųt], *s.* knut, azote, instrumento de suplicio usado antes en Rusia.

know [nóų]. I. *va.* (*pret.* KNEW; *pp.* KNOWN) conocer; saber; distinguir, discernir.—**to k. a thing or two,** saber algo, o una que otra cosa; tener buen juicio.—**to k. how to,** (antes de infinitivo) saber.—**to k. one's place,** conocer uno la posición que ocupa, saber con quién habla.—**to k. perfectly,** saber al dedillo.—**to k. the ropes,** conocer los detalles, estar al tanto, saber el juego (fig.).—**to k. what is what,** (fam.) saber cuántas son cinco, estar al corriente o al tanto.—**to k. where the shoe pinches,** saber uno dónde le aprieta el zapato, saber dónde está el busilis, o la dificultad. II. *vn.* saber.—**to k. best,** ser el mejor juez, saber lo que más conviene.—**to k. better,** saber que no es así; saber lo que debe hacerse, o cómo debe portarse (uno).—**to k. of,** saber de, tener noticia o conocimiento de; conocer de oídas.—**as far as I k.,** que yo sepa.—**to be in the k.,** estar informado; estar en el secreto.

knowable [-abl], *a.* conocible, cognoscible.

knower [-œ(r)], *s.* sabio, conocedor.

knowing [-įŋ], *a.* instruído, hábil, entendido; diestro; inteligente, sabio; sabedor, conocedor de; sabihondo; como de quien sabe (gen. desp.). II. *s.* conocimiento.

knowingly [-lį], *adv.* hábilmente; sabiamente; a sabiendas, con conocimiento de causa.

know-(**it-**)**all** [-it ɔl], *a.* y *s.* (fam.) sabihondo; sábelotodo; que presume de sabio sin serlo.

knowledge [nálįdž], *s.* conocimiento, saber, sapiencia; ciencia, erudición; inteligencia, destreza, pericia.—**to my k.,** que yo sepa.—**to the best of my k.,** según mi leal saber y entender.

know-nothing [nóų nʌθįŋ], *s.* ignorante; agnóstico; (**K.-N.**), (hist. E. U.) miembro de un partido secreto opuesto a la naturalización de extranjeros.

knuckle [nʌkl]. I. *s.* (anat.) nudillo, artejo, coyuntura, articulación de los dedos; jarrete de ternero o cerdo; (mec.) charnela; (mar.) codillo de una curva. II. *vn.* someterse, rendirse; abandonar la partida.—**to k. down,** o **to,** consagrarse o emprender con vehemencia.—**to k.** (**under**) **to,** doblegarse ante; ceder a.

knucklebone [-boųn], *s.* taba (de carnero).

knurl [nœr(l)], *s.* nudo, protuberancia.

knurled [nœrld], *a.* nudoso; estriado.

kob [kab], *s.* (zool.) antílope africano.

kobold [kóųbold], *s.* gnomo.

kohl [koųl], *s.* alcohol (afeite).

kohlrabi [kóųlræbį], *s.* (bot.) colirrábano.

kola (**nut** [kóųlạ (nʌt], *s.* (bot., quím., farm.) (nuez de) cola.

kope(**c**)**k** [kóųpɛk], *s.* copec (moneda rusa).

Koran [kórán], *s.* Corán, Alcorán.

Korean [korįan], *a.* y *s.* coreano.

kosher [kóųšœ(r)]. I. *a.* conforme al ritual judío. II. *s.* alimentos preparados de acuerdo con el ritual judío.

kotow [kotáų], **kowtow** [káųtaų]. I. *s.* postración china de homenaje, con la frente en el suelo. II. *vn.* arrodillarse y tocar el suelo con la frente (homenaje chino); doblar la rodilla (fig.), portarse servilmente.

koumis(s [kúmis], *s.* = KUMISS.

kraal [kral], *s.* población de hotentotes; corral, redil.

Krausism [kráusizm], *s.* (fil.) krausismo.

Krausist [-ist], *a.* y *s.* krausista.

kremlin [krémlin], *s.* kremlin, fortaleza de una ciudad rusa.

krypton [kríptan], *s.* (quím.) criptón.

Ku Klux Klan [kjú klʌks klǽn], *s.* (E. U.) sociedad secreta organizada en los estados del Sur después de la guerra civil para hostigar, amedrentar y alejar a los negros y a sus defensores, y revivida más tarde para hostilizar a los negros, judíos, católicos y extranjeros. Ll. t. **Ku-Klux** o **Kuklux**.

Kultur [kultúr], *s.* cultura, civilización.

kumiss, koomiss [kúmis], *s.* kumis, *m.*, leche fermentada de yegua, camella o vaca.

kümmel [kímel], *s.* cúmel (bebida).

Kurd [kúrd], *s.,* **Kurdish** [-iš], *a.* kurdo, curdo.

kymograph [káimogræf], *s.* instrumento para medir los movimientos de rotación de un aeroplano; (med.) cimógrafo o quimógrafo.

kyphosis [kaifóusis], *s.* (med.) cifosis.

Kyrie [kírji], *s.* (igl.) kirie, *m.*—**K. eleison,** kirieleisón.

L

l [el], *s.* l.

L [el]. **I.** *s.* ferrocarril elevado o aéreo; tubo en L o de ángulo recto. **II.** *a.* de o relativo a ferrocarril aéreo; en L, en forma de L.—**L.-head,** (m. comb. int.) culata en L, culata con válvulas de un mismo lado.—**L.-square,** escuadra de carpintero.

la [la]. **I.** *s.* (mús.) la. **II.** *interj.* exclamación de sorpresa.

labarum [lǽbarʌm], *s.* lábaro.

labdanum [lǽbdanʌm], *s.* ládano.

labefaction [læbifǽkšon], *s.* decadencia, decaimiento; enflaquecimiento; declinación.

label [léibel]. **I.** *s.* marbete, rótulo, etiqueta, letrero; marca. **II.** *va.* rotular o marcar; poner marbete o rótulo a; designar, clasificar.

labellum [lʌbélʌm], *s.* (bot.) labelo; (ent.) parte (*f.*) de la trompa de un insecto díptero.

labia [léibiǝ], *s. pl.* labios.

labial [léibiǝl]. **I.** *a.* labial; que tiene bordes. **II.** *s.* (fon.) letra labial.

labiate(d [léibieit(id]. **I.** *a.* labiado. **II.** *s.* (bot.) (planta) labiada.

labiodental [leibjodéntǝl]. **I.** *a.* labiodental. **II.** *s.* (fon.) articulación labiodental.

labionasal [-néizǝl]. **I.** *a.* labionasal. **II.** *s.* (fon.) sonido labionasal.

labium [léibjʌm], *s.* (*pl.* LABIA) labio.

labor [léibǝ(r)]. **I.** *s.* trabajo; las clases obreras, el obrerismo; mano (*f.*) de obra; labor, *f.*, tarea, faena; obra; quehacer, tráfago; aprieto, apuro; (dolores de) parto; (mar.) balanceo y cabeceo de un buque.—**L. Day,** (E. U.) Día del Trabajo. —**L. Party,** (Ingl.) laborismo, partido obrero. —**l.-saving,** que ahorra trabajo.—**l. union,** sindicato o gremio obrero. **II.** *vn.* trabajar; forcejar; estar de parto; (mar.) balancearse, cabecear, trabajar el buque contra mar y viento. **III.** *va.* elaborar, labrar, fabricar, pulir, perfeccionar; hacer trabajar, activar.

laboratory [lǽborǝtori], *s.* laboratorio, gabinete, oficina, taller.

labored [léibord], *a.* hecho con dificultad; forzado, antinatural.

laborer [léiborœ(r)], *s.* peón, jornalero, bracero; obrero, operario, trabajador.

laboring [léiboriŋ]. **I.** *s.* trabajo, esfuerzo. **II.** *a.* trabajador; de trabajo; obrero.—**l. beast,** bestia de carga.

laborious [lʌbórjʌs], *a.* laborioso, trabajoso, ímprobo, difícil, arduo; diligente, industrioso.—**laboriously** [-li], *adv.* laboriosamente.—**la-**

boriousness [-nis], *s.* laboriosidad, diligencia; dificultad.

Laborite [léiborait], *s.* (Ingl.) laborista, miembro o defensor del partido obrero o laborista.

laborsome [léiborsʌm], *a.* trabajoso, penoso, ímprobo, arduo.

labour [léibǝ(r)], *s.* y *v.* (Ingl.) = LABOR.

labradorite [lǽbradorait], *s.* (min.) labradorita.

labroid [lǽbroid], *a.* (ict.) labroideo, lábrido.

labrum [léibrʌm], *s.* (ent., zool.) labro.

laburnum [lʌbœrnʌm], *s.* (bot.) laburno, cítiso.

labyrinth [lǽbirinθ], *s.* laberinto, dédalo; (anat.) laberinto.

labyrinthic [-inθik], **labyrinthine** [-inθin], *a.* laberíntico, intrincado.

lac [læk], *s.* laca, goma laca.

lace [leis]. **I.** *s.* encaje; calados o galones (*pl.*); cuerda, cordón, cinta, agujeta; cordón del corsé o del zapato.—**l. bobbin,** bolillo, pasillo o majaderillo.—**l. edging,** o **trimming,** (cost.) puntilla, randa, adorno de encaje.—**l. frame,** telar para hacer encajes.—**l. pillow,** almohadilla para encajes.—**l.-winged,** (ent.) provisto de alas como de gasa o encaje. **II.** *va.* atar, ajustar, abrochar (corsé, zapatos, vestidos, etc.) con lazos o cordones; acordonar, enlazar; galonear, guarnecer con encajes, galones o cordones; entrelazar; rayar con líneas muy finas; (fam.) azotar.—**laced boot,** o **shoe,** borceguí. —**laced ruffles,** vueltas de encaje.

Lacedæmonian [læsedimóunjan], *s.* y *a.* lacedemonio, lacedemón.

laceman [léismǝn], *s.* el que hace o vende encajes, randas, etc.; cordonero, pasamanero.

lacerable [lǽserǝbl], *a.* lacerable.

lacerate [lǽsereit], *va.* lacerar, despedazar, desgarrar; lastimar.—**laceration** [-éišon], *s.* laceración, desgarradura, desgarro.

lacertian [lʌsœršjan], **lacertilian** [læsœrtiljan]. **I.** *a.* (zool.) lacertiano, lacertilio. **II.** *s.* lagarto.

lacewing [léiswiŋ], *s.* (ent.) crisopo.

lacewoman [-wumǝn], *s.* vendedora de encajes, randas, etc.; randera; pasamanera.

lacework [-wœrk], *s.* obra de encaje o parecida al encaje.

lachrymal [lǽkrimǝl]. **I.** *a.* lacrimal, lagrimal.— **l. caruncle,** (anat.) (carúncula) lagrimal. **II.** *s.* (anat.) lagrimal.—**lachrymation** [-méišon], *s.* lagrimeo, llanto, lloro.—**lachrymatory** [-mǝtori], *a.* y *s.* lacrimatorio.—**lachrymose** [-mous], *a.* lacrimoso, lagrimoso.

lacing [léisiŋ], *s.* acto de atar con cordones, en particular el uso de corsés; enlace, enlazadura, abrochamiento; cordón, cordoncillo; agujeta; galones (*pl.*) para uniformes, etc.; zurra, tunda.

lacinia [lʌsínjǝ], *s.* (bot.) lacinia.

laciniate(d [lʌsínjeit(id], *a.* laciniado.

lack [læk]. **I.** *va.* y *vn.* carecer, necesitar, faltar. **II.** *s.* falta, carencia, escasez, necesidad.

lackadaisical [lækǝdéizikǝl], *a.* lánguido; indiferente; soñador; sentimental.

lackaday [lǽkǝdei], *interj.* (ant.) ¡ay! ¡ay de mí! ¡mal día! ¡día aciago! ¡mal haya! *V.* ALACK.

lacker [lǽkœ(r)], *s.* y *va.* = LACQUER.

lackey [lǽki]. **I.** *s.* lacayo. **II.** *va.* y *vn.* servir como lacayo; ser criado.

lacking [lǽkiŋ], *a.* falto, faltante, carente, defectuoso.—**to be l.,** faltar, hacer falta; carecer de.

lackluster [lǽklʌstœ(r)], *a.* deslustrado.

Laconian [lʌkóunjan], *s.* y *a.* laconio.

laconic(al [lʌkánik(ǝl], *a.* lacónico.—**laconically** [-i], *adv.* lacónicamente.—**laconism** [lǽkonizm], *s.* laconismo.

lacquer [lǽkœ(r)]. **I.** *va.* barnizar; laquear, dar laca. **II.** *s.* laca, barniz, *m.*—**l.** o **l. work,** objetos (*pl.*) de laca.—**lacquered** [-d], *a.* laqueado, barnizado con laca.

lacquering [-iŋ], *s.* barnizado de laca.

lacrimal, lacrymal, etc. = LACHRYMAL, etc.

lacrosse [lʌkrós], *s.* (dep.) vilorta, cierto juego de

pelota común en el Canadá.—l. **stick**, vilorto.
lactary [lǽktəri]. I. a. lácteo. II. s. lechería.
lactase [lǽktejs], s. (quím.) lactasa.
lactate [lǽktejt]. I. s. (quím.) lactato. II. va. convertir en leche. III. vn. lactar, amamantar.
lactation [-éjʃən], s. lactancia, crianza; lactación.
lacteal [lǽktiəl], a. lácteo, quilífero.
lacteous [lǽktiʌs], a. lácteo, lactario.
lactescence [lǽktésəns], s. lactescencia.
lactescent [-ənt], a. lactescente, lácteo.
lactic [-ik], a. láctico.—l. **acid**, ácido láctico.
lactiferous [-fíɛrʌs], a. lactífero; (bot.) lechal.
lactifuge [-ifjudʒ], a. y s. lactífugo.
lactometer [-ámɛtœ(r)], s. lactómetro.
lactone [-oʊn], s. (quím.) lactona.
lactoscope [-oskoʊp], s. lactoscopio.
lactose [-oʊs], s. (quím.) lactosa, lactina, azúcar de leche.
lactucarium [-ʌkérjʌm], s. (farm.) lactucario.
lacuna [ləkjúnə], s. laguna, blanco, espacio; hoyo o hueco.
lacunar, lacunal [-(r), -l], **lacunose** [-oʊs], a. que tiene lagunas, claros u hoyos.
lacunar, s. (arq.) lagunar, lacunario, artesonado.
lacustral, lacustrine [ləkʌ́strəl, -trin], a. lacustre.
lacy [léjsi], a. de o parecido al encaje.
lad [lǽd], s. mozo, mozalbete, joven, chico.
ladanum [lǽdənʌm], s. ládano.
ladder [lǽdœ(r)], s. escalera o escala (de mano); carrera (en las medias).—l. **ropes**, (mar.) brandales.
lade [léjd]. I. s. canal de desagüe; embocadero, desembocadero. II. va. (pret. LADED; pp. LADED o LADEN) cargar; achicar; echar en.
laden [-n], a. cargado; abrumado, oprimido.
ladies' man [léjdiz mæn], **lady's man**, s. hombre galante o de salón, (fam.) Perico entre ellas.
lading [léjdiŋ], s. acción de cargar; carga, cargamento; achicamiento.
ladle [léjdl], s. cucharón, cuchara grande, cazo, paleta; (fund.) caldero, cazo o cuchara de colada; (hidr.) álabe, paleta; (arti.) cuchara. II. va. achicar; sacar o servir con cucharón.—
ladleful [-ful], s. cucharada.
lady [léjdi], s. señora, dama; (Ingl.) voz de tratamiento que se da a la esposa o hija de algún título del reino. ú. adjetivadamente para indicar sexo: a lady doctor, una doctora; a lady friend, una amiga.—**L. Day**, (igl.) (el día de la) Anunciación.—l. **fern**, (bot.) helecho hembra.—l. **finger**, (coc.) especie de torta o bizcocho largo y angosto; melindre; (Am.) plantilla.—l. **in attendance**, camarera mayor.—l. **in waiting**, azafata de una reina o princesa.—l.-**killer**, Don Juan, Tenorio; galanteador, coquetón.—l. **of the house**, ama o señora de la casa.—l.'s-**bower**, (bot.) la especie británica de la clemátide.—l.'s **maid**, doncella.—l.'s-**mantle**, (bot.) estrellada.—l.'s-**slipper**, (bot.) planta orquídea.—l.'s-**smock**, (bot.) cardamina.—l. **superior**, superiora.—l.'s **thumb**, (bot.) persicaria.—**Our L.**, Nuestra Señora.
ladybird [-bœrd], **ladybug** [-bʌg], **ladyfly** [-flaj], s. (ent.) mariquita.
ladylike [-lajk], a. delicado, tierno, elegante; afeminado, amujerado.
ladylove [-lʌv], s. amada, mujer querida.
ladyship [-ʃip], s. (Ingl.) señoría, usía, tratamiento que se da a las esposas e hijas de títulos del reino.
lag [lǽg]. I. s. retraso; (mec.) retardación de movimiento; listón de revestimiento o de forro de caldera.—l. **bolt**, l. **screw**, tornillo para madera con cabeza poligona y movido con llave inglesa. II. vn. retrasarse, rezagarse, quedarse atrás; remolonear, roncear.
lager [lágœ(r)], s. especie de cerveza.
laggard [lǽgərd]. I. a. tardo, perezoso, holgazán. II. s. rezagado, holgazán.—**lagger** [lǽgœ(r)], s. = LAGGARD.

lagging [lǽgiŋ], s. movimiento retardado; acción de rezagarse, etc.; envoltura; listones (pl.) de madera u otro material con que se forman revestimientos, forros, cubiertas, etc.
lagoon [lagún], s. laguna(jo), albufera, charca.
laic(al [léjik(əl], a. laico, lego, secular, seglar.—**laic**, s. lego, seglar.
laicism [léjisizm], s. laicismo, laicidad.
laid [léjd], pret. y pp. de TO LAY.
lain [lejn], pp. de TO LIE.
lair [ler], s. cubil, guarida, cueva de fieras.
laird [lerd], s. (Esco.) lord; hacendado.
laity [léjiti], s. laicidad, estado seglar; los legos.
lake [léjk], s. lago; (pint.) laca.—l. **dweller**, hombre lacustre.—l. **dwelling**, habitación lacustre.
lakelet [-lit], s. laguna, laguito.
lama [lámə], s. lama, m. (sacerdote budista).
La(ma)ism [lá(mə)jzm], s. lamaísmo.
Lamaist [-jst], a. y s. lamaí(s)ta.
Lamarckian [ləmárkiən], a. y s. lamarquiano, lamarquista.—**Lamarckism** [-kizm], s. (biol.) lamarquismo.
lamb [læm], s. cordero, borrego; (fig.) persona mansa o inocente.—l. **chop**, chuleta o costilla de carnero.—l. **fry**, turma, criadilla.—l.'s-**lettuce**, (bot.) colleja, valerianilla.—l.'s **quarters**, (bot.) chual.—**L. of God**, cordero de Dios, Cristo.—l.'s **wool**, añinos, pl.
lambaste [læmbéjst], va. (fam.) apalear, zurrar o reprender duramente.
lambda [lǽmdə], s. lambda (letra griega).
lambent [lǽmbənt], a. ligero, undulante; radiante; centelleante.
lambkin [lǽmkin], s. corderito, -illo, -ico.
lamblike [-lajk], a. manso; inocente; sumiso.
lambrequin [lǽmbrekin], s. guardamalleta, sobrepuerta; (blas.) lambrequín.
lambskin [lǽmskin], s. corderina, zamarro.
lame [lejm]. I. a. cojo, renco; lisiado, estropeado, derrengado; imperfecto.—l. **account**, relación imperfecta.—l. **duck**, (fam.) persona incapacitada; deudor insolvente; congresista o empleado público cesante, o que no ha sido reelegido.—l. **excuse**, disculpa frívola.—l. **expression**, expresión manca.—l. **verses**, versos cojos o defectuosos.—**to go l.**, cojear, andar cojeando, renquear. II. va. lisiar, estropear; encojar, derrengar.
lamella [lamélə], s. lamela, laminilla; hojuela.
lamellar [lǽmelə(r)], a. laminar.
lamellate(d [-ejt(id], a. laminado; hojaldrado.
lamellibranch [lǽmélibræŋk], s. y a. (zool.) lamelibranquio.
lamellicorn [-korn], s. y a. (ent.) lamelicornio.
lamelliform [-form], a. lameliforme.
lamellirostral [-rástrəl], a. (orn.) lamelirostro.
lamely [léjmli], adv. con cojera; defectuosamente; débilmente.
lameness [-nis], s. cojera, derrengadura; falta, defecto, imperfección.
lament [lǽmént]. I. va. y vn. lamentar(se); plañir, dolerse. II. s. lamento, queja.
lamentable [lǽméntəbl], a. lamentable, deplorable, desconsolador, lastimero, sensible.—**lamentably** [-bli], adv. lamentablemente.—**lamentation** [-éjʃən], s. lamentación, lamento.
lamented [lǽméntid], a. lamentado.—**lamenter** [-œ(r)], s. lamentador.—**lamenting** [-iŋ], s. lamentación.
lamina [lǽminə], s. lámina, hoja.—**laminable** [-bl], a. laminable.—**laminar** [-(r)], a. laminar.—**laminate(d** [-ejt(id], a. laminado.
laminitis [lǽminájtis], s. (vet.) despeadura.
Lammas [lǽmas], s. (igl.) festividad del día primero de agosto.
lammergeier [lǽmœrgajœ(r)], s. (orn.) quebrantahuesos, águila barbuda.
lamp [lǽmp], s. lámpara; velón, candil, quinqué; farol; linterna.—l. **burner**, mechero, piquera.—l. **chimney**, bombillo o tubo de lámpara.—

l. globe, globo, foco o bomba.—**l. holder,** portalámparas.—**l. post,** poste de farol de la calle.—**l. shade,** pantalla de lámpara.—**l. stand o table,** velador.—**l. wick,** torcida, mecha.

lampas [lǽmpəs], *s.* (vet.) inflamación en la parte superior de la boca de los caballos.

lampblack [lǽmpblæk], *s.* negro de humo.

lamplight [lǽmplajt], *s.* luz de una lámpara; luz artificial.—**lamplighter** [-œ(r)], *s.* farolero, lamparero; encendedor, cerillero.

lampoon [læmpún]. I. *s.* pasquín, libelo. II. *va.* satirizar, pasquinar.—**lampooner** [-œ(r)], *s.* pasquinero, escritor de pasquines.

lamprey [lǽmpri], *s.* (ict.) lamprea.

lanate(d [léjnejt(jd], *a.* lanoso; (bot.) lanudo.

lance [læns]. I. *s.* lanza; pica, asta; (cir.) lanceta; lancetazo, lanzada; (mil.) lanza, lancero.—**l. bucket,** cuja.—**l. rest,** o **socket,** ristre. II. *va.* lancear, dar una lanzada; penetrar, cortar; (cir.) abrir con lanceta.

lanceolate [-jolejt], *a.* (bot.) lance(ol)ado.

lancer [-œ(r)], *s.* alanceador; (mil.) lancero.—*pl.* (danz. y mús.) lanceros (ll. t. **lanciers**).

lancet [-jt], *s.* (cir.) lanceta; (arq.) arco puntiagudo; (ent.) trompetilla.

lancewood [-wŭd], *s.* palo de lanza; (bot.) yaya.

lancinate [lǽnsjnejt], *va.* lancinar.—**lancination** [-éjŝon], *s.* dolor lancinante.

land [lænd]. I. *s.* tierra; terreno; suelo, terruño; país, nación; región, territorio.—**l. agent,** corredor de fincas rurales.—**l.-based,** (aer., mil.) de tierra.—**l. breeze,** terral.—**l. forces,** (mil.) fuerzas terrestres.—**l. jobbing,** especulación en la compra y venta de bienes raíces.—**l. measure,** medidas agrarias.—**l. office,** oficina del catastro.—**l.-office business,** (fam.) grande actividad en los negocios, etc.—**l. of promise,** tierra prometida o de promisión.—**l. of the rising sun,** tierra del sol naciente (el Japón).—**l. plane,** (aer.) avión (*m.*) terrestre, o de tierra.—**l. poor,** poseedor de muchas tierras improductivas.—**l. surveying,** topografía; agrimensura.—**l. surveyor,** agrimensor.—**l. tax,** contribución territorial.—**l. wind,** terral.—**by l.,** por tierra. II. *va.* desembarcar; echar en tierra, (fam.) conseguir (un empleo, puesto, etc.); (fam.) plantificar (un golpe). III. *vn.* desembarcar; tomar tierra, aterrar; parar; ir a dar a (la cárcel, etc.); (aer.) aterrizar; amarar (un hidroavión).

landau [lǽndɔ], *s.* (carr.) landó.

landed [lǽndjd], *a.* hacendado.—**l. property,** predio; bienes raíces, *m. pl.*

landfall [lǽndfɔl], *s.* herencia de tierras; desprendimiento de tierras; (mar.) recalada; (aer.) aterrizaje.

landgrave [-grejv], *s.* landgrave.

landgraviate [-gréjvjejt], *s.* landgraviato.

landholder [-houldœ(r)], *s.* hacendado, terrateniente.

landing [-jŋ]. I. *s.* descanso, meseta, rellano (de escalera); desembarco, desembarque; desembarcadero o apeadero; paradero; (aer.) aterrizaje; amaraje (de un hidroavión). II. *a.* de desembarque; de aterrizaje.—**l. angle,** (aer.) ángulo de aterrizaje.—**l. craft,** barcaza militar de desembarque.—**l. field,** (aer.) campo de aterrizaje.—**l. forces,** (mil.) tropas de desembarco.—**l. gear,** (aer.) tren de aterrizaje.—**l. net,** salabardo, salabre.—**l. stage,** plataforma flotante de embarcar y desembarcar.—**l. wheels,** (aer.) ruedas de aterrizaje.

landlady [-lejdj], *s.* ama, casera, mesonera, posadera, patrona; arrendadora, propietaria.

landless [-ljs], *a.* sin bienes o sin tierras.

landlocked [-lakt], *a.* cercado de tierra; que viven en aguas cortadas de la mar (ú. de ciertos peces).

landlord [-lord], *s.* propietario o dueño de tierras o casas; arrendador; amo, huésped, posadero; casero, patrón.—**landlordism** [-jzm], *s.* autoridad del propietario; hacendados en general.

landlubber [-lʌbœ(r)], *s.* (desp.) marinero bisoño o de agua dulce.

land(s)man [-(z)mən], *s.* el que vive en tierra.

landmark [-mark], *s.* mojón, marca, coto, hito; señal, *f.;* (mar.) marca; punto o acontecimiento culminante; progreso o rasgo sobresaliente.

landowner [-ouṇœ(r)], *s.* hacendado, terrateniente, propietario.

landplane [-plejn], *s.* (aer.) aeroplano de tierra o terrestre (a distinción del hidroaeroplano).

landscape [-skejp]. I. *s.* paisaje, campiña, vista; (pint.) paisaje.—**l. architecture,** arte de modificar y hermosear un terreno, etc.—**l. painter,** paisajista (ll. t. **landscapist**). II. *va.* hermosear un terreno, parque o jardín, con árboles, arbustos, etc.

landslide, landslip [-slajd, -sljp], *s.* derrumbamiento, derrumbe, lurte.—**landslide victory,** victoria aplastante o arrolladora (esp. en elecciones).

Landsturm [lántŝtųrm], *s.* (mil.) leva, enganche general; últimas reservas.

landward [lǽndwərd], *adv.* hacia la tierra.

Landwehr [lántver], *s.* milicia disciplinada licenciada, que sirve de reserva en tiempo de guerra.

lane [lejn], *s.* senda, vereda; calle(juela), callejón; vía, ruta; zona (de tránsito).

langsyne [lǽŋsájn]. I. *adv.* mucho ha, tiempo ha. II. *s.* tiempo, tiempos (en la expresión escocesa *auld langsyne,* o *auld lang syne,* los felices tiempos de antaño).

language [lǽŋgwjdʒ], *s.* lengua(je), idioma, *m.*

langue d'oc [laŋ dák], *s.* lengua de oc, lemosín.

Languedocian [laŋgēdóuŝạn], *a.* y *s.* lemosín.

languet [lǽŋget], *s.* lengüeta, orejeta.

languid [lǽŋgwjd], *a.* lánguido.—**languidly** [-lj], *adv.* lánguidamente.—**languidness** [-njs], *s.* languidez.

languish [lǽŋgwjŝ], *vn.* languidecer, extenuarse, consumirse; agostarse, ponerse mustio; aflojar, encalmarse; mirar con ternura.

languishing [-jŋ]. I. *s.* languidez, flaqueza. II. *a.* lánguido, decaído.—**languishingly** [-lj], *adv.* lánguidamente.—**languishment** [-mẹnt], *s.* languidez, decaimiento, consumimiento.

languor [lǽŋgǫ(r)], *s.* desfallecimiento, languidez, debilidad, postración; indolencia.

languorous [-ʌs], *a.* lánguido, débil.

laniard [lǽnyärd], *s.* V. LANYARD.

laniary [léjnjerj]. I. *a.* propio para rasgar. II. *s.* colmillo, diente canino.

laniferous [lænífẹrʌs], **lanigerous** [-dʒẹrʌs], *a.* lanudo, lanoso, lanífero, lanuginoso.

lank [lǽŋk], *a.* flaco, seco, descarnado; delgado.—**l. hair,** cabellos largos y lacios.—**lankly** [-lj], *adv.* flacamente.—**lankness** [-njs], *s.* flacura; delgadez.—**lanky** [-j], *a.* larguiruƒho (fam.), langaruto, delgaducho.

lanner [lǽnœ(r)], *s.* (orn.) alcotán, borní.

lanolin(e [lǽnoljn], *s.* (farm.) lanolina.

lansquenet [lǽnskẹnet], *s.* sacanete, cascarela, parar (juegos de naipes); (ant.) lancero de a pie.

lantana [læntǽnə], *s.* (bot.) lantana.

lantern [lǽntœrn], *s.* linterna, farol; (mar.) faro, fanal; (arq.) linterna.—**l. maker,** linternero.—**l. jack,** fuego fatuo.—**l.-jawed,** carienjuto, carilargo, de quijadas largas y delgadas.—**l. pinion,** o **wheel,** (mec.) piñón de linterna.—**l. slide,** diapositiva.

lanthanum [lǽnθạnʌm], *s.* (quím.) lantano.

lanuginous [lạnjúdʒjnạs], *a.* lanuginoso.

lanyard [lǽnyärd], *s.* (mar.) acollador; cuerda, cabo; (artí.) cuerda y gancho de disparo.

Laodicean [lejạdjŝíạn], *a.* laodicense; tibio, indiferente.

lap [læp]. I. *s.* falda; regazo; seno, enfaldo; traslapo; (dep.) vuelta completa de la pista o redondel· (mec.) rueda de amolar, pulir o labrar joyas o metales; lamedura; susurro del agua; (m. v.) recubrimiento (de la válvula de corredera).—**l. dog**, perrillo faldero.—**l.-eared**, de orejas gachas o pendientes.—**l. hemmer**, rebatidor.—**l. joint**, junta de solapa, de traslapo o de recubrimiento.—**l. seam**, (cost.) costura rebatida.—**l. table** = LAPBOARD. **II.** *va.* traslapar; recubrir; envolver, cubrir, rodear; juntar a traslapo; pulir, labrar; lamer; tocar, besar (apl. al agua). **III.** *vn.* traslaparse; susurrar.

laparotomy [læpərátomĭ], *s.* (cir.) laparotomía.

lapboard [lǽpbərd], *s.* tabla faldera de sastre.

lapel [lȧpél], *s.* (sast.) solapa.

lapful [lǽpfŭl], *s.* halda(da), lo que puede caber en el regazo o enfaldo.

lapidary [lǽpĭderĭ]. **I.** *s.* lapidario; (ant.) tratado de las piedras preciosas y sus virtudes. **II.** *a.* lapidario; inscrito sobre piedra; lapídeo.

lapidate [lǽpĭdeịt], *va.* lapidar, apedrear.—**lapidation** [-éịṣǫn], *s.* lapidación, apedreamiento.—**lapideous** [lȧpĭdĭȧs], *a.* lapídeo, lapidoso.—**lapidescent** [-ésǫnt], *a.* que petrifica.—**lapidific** [-ĭfĭk], *a.* lapidífico.—**lapidification** [-ĭfĭkéịṣǫn], *s.* lapidificación.—**lapidify** [lȧpĭdĭfaị], *va.* y *vn.* lapidificar(se), petrificar(se).

lapin [lǽpĭn], *s.* (zool.) conejo y su piel.

lapis [léịpĭṣ], *s.* (lat.) piedra.—**l. infernalis**, piedra infernal, nitrato de plata.—**l. lazuli**, lapislázuli, lazulita.

Laplander [lǽplændœ(r)], **Lapp** [læp], *s.* lapón.

lappet [lǽpĭt], *s.* caída de toca o escofieta; doblez de una prenda de vestir; solapa; carúncula o barba de ciertas aves; (anat.) lóbulo.

lapsable [lǽpṣȧbl], *a.* (for.) prescriptible; susceptible de caer.

lapse [læps]. **I.** *s.* caída, lapso; intervalo de tiempo, curso, transcurso; desliz, *m.*, traspié, *m.*, equivocación, falta; (for.) prescripción, perención, caducidad de la instancia; translación de derecho o dominio.—**in the l. of time**, con el transcurso del tiempo, andando el tiempo. **II.** *vn.* pasar, transcurrir; decaer, deslizarse; caer en algún defecto, desliz o error; (for.) prescribir, caducar.

lapsed [-t], *a.* caído; deslizado; cumplido, caducado; omitido; (for.) prescrito.

lapstone [lǽpstoụn], *s.* piedra de batir el cuero.

lapwing [lǽpwĭŋ], *s.* (orn.) frailecico, ave fría.

lapwork [lǽpwœrk], *s.* obra entrelazada o entretejida; obra de tingladillo.

lar [lar], *s.* (*pl.* LARES) lar, dios doméstico.

larboard [lárbərd], *s.* (mar.) babor.—**l. watch**, guardia de babor.

larcener, larcenist [lársǫnœ(r), -ĭṣt], *s.* ladrón, ratero.—**larcenous** [-ȧs], *a.* ratero, hurtador, ladrón.

larceny [-ĭ], *s.* (for.) ratería, hurto.

larch [larch], *s.* (bot.) alerce, lárice.

lard [lárd]. **I.** *s.* manteca (de cerdo), lardo, (tocino) gordo.—**l. oil**, aceite de manteca de cerdo. **II.** *va.* (coc.) mechar; lardar o lardear; entreverar, guarnecer.

lardaceous [-éịṣȧs], *a.* lardáceo, lardoso, grasiento; (med.) craso, gordo.

larder [-œ(r)], *s.* despensa, reposte.

larderer [-œrœ(r)], *s.* despensero.

lardy [-ĭ], *a.* graso, lardoso, mantecoso.

large [lárdž]. **I.** *a.* grande; amplio, extenso, vasto; copioso, numeroso.—**l. bond**, bono mayor (de más de 1000 dólares).—**l.-handed**, de manos grandes; liberal, dadivoso.—**l.-headed**, cabezudo.—**l.-hearted**, magnánimo, desprendido o generoso.—**l. intestine**, (anat.) intestino grueso.—**l.-minded**, de ideas liberales.—**l. order**, (fam.) empresa o tarea peliaguda.—**l. scale**, en grande escala; de gran magnitud, envergadura o alcance.—**l.-size(d)**, grande, de tamaño grande.—**at l.**, en libertad, suelto; extensamente; sin limitación, libre; al acaso, (E. U.) que representa un todo (estado, región, etc.), a distinción del que representa una de las

divisiones (distrito electoral, etc.). **II.** *adv.* (mar.) con viento a la cuadra; (fam.) con jactancia.

largely [-lĭ], *adv.* grandemente; liberalmente; ampliamente; mayormente; en gran manera, considerablemente; muy.

largeness [-nĭs], *s.* grandor, extensión, amplitud, calidad de grande; liberalidad; grandeza de ánimo.

largess(e [lárdžĭs], *s.* don, dádiva, regalo; (ant.) largueza.

largo [lárgoụ], *a.* y *s.* (mús.) largo.

lariat [lǽrĭȧt], *s.* lazo, mangana; (Arg.) boleadoras, *f. pl.*

lark [lark], *s.* (orn.) alondra, calandria, terrera, zurriaga; (fam.) calaverada, francachela, parranda, holgorio.—**to be, o to go, on a l.**, andar de parranda, echar una cana al aire.

larkspur [lárkspœr], *s.* (bot.) espuela de caballero, consólida real.

larrup [lǽrȧp], *va.* (fam.) zurrar, tundir.

larva [lárvȧ], *s.* larva.—**larval** [-l], *a.* larval.

larvate(d [lárveịt(ịd], *a.* (med.) larvado.

laryngeal [lȧrĭndžĭȧl], *a.* laríngeo.

laryngitis [lǽrĭndžáịtĭṣ], *s.* (med.) laringitis.

laryngology [lǽrĭŋgálodžĭ], *s.* laringología.

laryngoscope [lȧrĭŋgoskoụp], *s.* laringoscopio.

laryngoscopy [lǽrĭŋgáskopĭ], *s.* laringoscopia.

laryngotomy [-gátomĭ], *s.* (cir.) laringotomía.

larynx [lǽrĭŋks], *s.* (anat.) laringe, *f.*

lascar [lǽskȧ(r)], *s.* láscar, lascar (marinero indio).

lascivious [lȧṣĭvĭȧs], *a.* lascivo.—**lasciviously** [-lĭ], *adv.* lascivamente.—**lasciviousness** [-nĭs], *s.* lascivia.

lash [lǽṣ]. **I.** *s.* látigo, flagelo, fusta, tralla (de látigo); azote, latigazo; chasquido; sarcasmo, invectiva; remate de las olas; pestaña (del ojo). **II.** *va.* dar latigazos; azotar, fustigar, flagelar; romper contra (como las olas); satirizar, censurar, reprochar; atar, ligar, (mar.) amarrar, trincar. **III.** *vn.* chasquear el látigo.—**to l. out**, desenfrenarse, desordenarse.

lashing [-ĭŋ], *s.* latigazo, azotamiento, castigo de azotes; represión dura; ligadura, atadura; (mar.) amarra(dura).

lass [lǽs], *s.* doncella, moza, muchacha, chica.

lassie [-ĭ], *s.* muchachita, mozuela.

lassitude [lǽṣĭtịud], *s.* lasitud, languidez.

lasso [lǽṣoụ]. **I.** *va.* (en)lazar, manganear. **II.** *s.* lazo, mangana, (Am.) guaso.

lassoer [-œ(r)], *s.* lazador.

last [lǽṣt]. **I.** *a.* último, postr(im)ero; extremo, final, supremo; pasado (*last week*, la semana pasada).—**l. but not least**, último en orden pero no en importancia.—**l. but one**, penúltimo.—**l. but two**, antepenúltimo.—**l. day**, día del juicio.—**l.-ditch** (defense, etc.) desesperado, a muerte.—**l. evening**, anoche, ayer por la noche.—**l. honors**, honores fúnebres.—**L. Judgment**, juicio final.—**l. night**, anoche.—**l. sleep**, la muerte.—**L. Supper**, última cena (de Jesucristo).—**l. word**, palabra o decisión final; (fam.) última moda; cosa inmejorable.—**that's the l. straw**, es el colmo; no faltaba más.—**to be on one's l. legs**, estar en las últimas, no poder más.—**to the l. ditch**, hasta la última trinchera o barricada; hasta quemar el último cartucho. **II.** *adv.* la última vez, finalmente, al fin.—**at l.**, por fin, al fin, al cabo, por último, a la postre.—**at long l.**, al fin, al fin (repetición enfática). **III.** *s.* fin, término; durabilidad; (lo, el) último; (zap.) horma.—**l. maker**, hormero.—**to see the l. of one**, no volver a ver a uno; librarse de uno.—**to the l.**, hasta el fin, hasta lo último. **IV.** *vn.* (per)durar, permanecer, subsistir. **V.** *va.* (zap.) ahormar.

lastage [-ĭdž], *s.* (mar.) espacio para la estiba.

laster [-œ(r)], *s.* (zap.) ahormador.

lasting [-ĭŋ]. **I.** *a.* duradero, durable, constante, perdurable. **II.** *s.* (tej.) sempiterna.—**lastingly**

[-li], *adv.* para siempre.—**lastingness** [-nis], *s.* duración, calidad de durable.

lastly [-li], *adv.* en conclusión, por fin, finalmente, por último.

latch [læch]. I. *s.* aldaba, aldabilla, cerrojo, picaporte. II. *va.* cerrar con aldaba.

latchkey [-ki], *s.* llavín; picaporte.

latchstring [-strin], *s.* cordón de aldaba.—**the l. is out,** venga Vd. cuando guste; será Vd. siempre bienvenido.

late [leit]. I. *a.* tardío; tardo, lento; último, postrero; difunto; reciente, moderno.—**l. arrival,** recién llegado.—**l. in years,** de edad avanzada o provecta. II. *adv.* tarde; poco ha, últimamente; antes.—**l. in the year,** al fin del año.—**of l.,** recientemente, últimamente.—**to be l.,** llegar tarde o con retraso, retrasarse, atrasar, estar atrasado; ser tarde.—**too l.,** (demasiado) tarde.

lateen [lætín], *a.*—**l. sail,** (mar.) vela latina o bastarda.—**l. yard,** entena.

lately [léitli], *adv.* poco ha, no ha mucho; recientemente, últimamente.

latency [léitensi], *s.* estado latente.

lateness [léitnes], *s.* calidad de tardo o de reciente; tardanza, retraso.

latent [léitent], *a.* latente, oculto, escondido.

later [léitœ(r)], *adv.* y *a.* (*comp.* de LATE) más tarde; luego, después; posterior, subsecuente.—**l. on,** más tarde, después.

lateral [lǽteral], *a.* lateral.—**laterally** [-i], *adv.* lateralmente.

Lateran [lǽteran]. I. *a.* lateranense. II. *s.* templo de San Juan de Letrán; palacio papal.

laterite [lǽterait], *s.* (geol.) laterita, arcilla roja ferruginosa.

latescent [leitésent], *a.* que se va obscureciendo u ocultando.

latest [léitist], *a.* y *adv.* (*superl.* de LATE) último; novísimo.—**at the l.,** a más tardar.

latex [léiteks], *s.* (bot.) látex, jugo lechoso y viscoso.

lath [læθ]. I. *s.* (carp., alb.) lata, listón.—**l. work,** enlatado, (en)listonado, listonería. II. *va.* enlatar, (en)listonar, hacer un enlatado a o en.

lathe [leið], *s.* (mec.) torno; (tej.) marco de telar.—**l. bed,** banco del torno.—**l. dog,** trinquete de mandril.—**l. drill,** torno de taladrar.

lather [lǽðœ(r)]. I. *va.* enjabonar para afeitar; (fam.) azotar. II. *s.* jabonadura, espuma de jabón. III. *vn.* espumar, hacer espuma.

lathing [lǽθin], *s.* (carp., alb.) = LATH WORK.

lathy [lǽθi], *a.* largo y delgado como un listón.

laticiferous [lætisíferas], *a.* (bot.) laticífero.

latifundium [lætifándiam], *s.* latifundio.

Latin [lǽtin]. I. *a.* y *s.* latino.—**L.-American,** *a.,* **L. American,** *s.,* latinoamericano. II. *s.* latín (lengua).—**Latinism** [-izm], *s.* latinismo.—**Latinist** [-ist], *s.* latinista, latino.—**Latinity** [latíniti], *s.* latinidad.—**Latinize** [lǽtinaiz]. I. *va.* latinizar. II. *vn.* latin(e)ar, emplear latinismos.

latirostral [lætiróstral], *a.* (orn.) latirrostro.

latish [léitiš], *a.* algo tarde, tardecito.

latitude [lǽtitiud], *s.* latitud, anchura; difusión; amplitud; libertad; (geog., astr.) latitud.

latitudinal [-tiúdinal], *a.* latitudinal.

latitudinarian [-érian], *a.* y *s.* latitudinario.—**latitudinarianism** [-izm], *s.* latitudinarismo.

latria [lætráiə], *s.* (igl.) culto de latría.

latrine [latrín], *s.* letrina.

latten [læten], *s.* latón en láminas; metal en lámina.—*pl.* láminas metálicas muy delgadas.

latter [lætœ(r)], *a.* posterior, más reciente, moderno.—**l.-day,** de nuestros días.—**L.-Day Saints,** mormones.—**the l.,** éste, esto.

latterly [-li], *adv.* recientemente; poco ha.

lattice [lætis]. I. *va.* enrejar, poner celosías; entrelazar, entretejer. II. *s.* celosía, enrejado de listoncillos, rejilla.—**l. bar,** listón de celosía, listón de sujeción (apl. esp. a los que, trabados,

unen dos piezas paralelas de una construcción). —**l. bridge,** puente de celosía.—**l. girder, l. truss,** viga de celosía.—**l. web,** alma de celosía.

latticework [-wœrk], *s.* enrejado(s); (mar.) enjaretado.

Latvian [lǽtvian], *s.* y *a.* latvio, de Latvia.

laud [lod]. I. *s.* (canto de) alabanza; loa.—*pl.* (igl.) laudes, *f. pl.* II. *va.* alabar, loar, elogiar.

laudability [lodabíliti], **laudableness** [lódablnes], *s.* calidad de laudable.—**laudable** [lódabl], *a.* laudable, loable.—**laudably** [-bli], *adv.* laudablemente.

laudanum [lódanʌm], *s.* láudano.

laudative, laudatory [lódativ, -ori], *a.* laudatorio, encomiástico, panegírico.

laugh [læf]. I. *vn.* reír, reírse.—**to l. at,** reírse, mofarse o burlarse de, ridiculizar.—**to l. at one to his face,** reírsele a uno en las barbas.—**to l. in one's sleeve,** reírse interiormente.—**to l. loudly, heartily u out,** reírse a carcajadas. II. *va.* decir o expresar riendo; causar o hacer (salir, callar, cesar) a risa o a carcajadas; ahogar en o con risa.—**to l. away, u off,** ahogar en risa; echar a risa o a risotadas.—**to l. down,** hacer callar a risotadas; matar o acabar con (una reforma, etc.) ridiculizando.—**to l. one out of countenance,** abochornar o confundir a uno a carcajadas.—**to l. to scorn,** ridiculizar, poner en ridículo. III. *s.* risa; risotada.

laughable [-abl], *a.* risible; divertido.

laugher [-œ(r)], *s.* reidor.

laughing [-in]. I. *s.* risa, reír. II. *a.* risueño, riente, reidor.—**l. eyes,** ojos alegres, reidores.—**l. gas,** gas hilarante, óxido nitroso.—**l. jackass,** (orn.) martín pescador australiano.—**it's no l. matter,** no es cosa de risa.

laughingly [-li], *adv.* riendo, con risa.

laughingstock [-stak], *s.* hazmerreír.

laughter [-tœ(r)], *s.* risa.

launch [lonch]. I. *va.* botar o echar al agua; dar principio a, acometer; lanzar, arrojar. II. *vn.* arrojarse, salir, lanzarse.—**to l. out for one's self,** emprender negocios por su cuenta. III. *s.* (mar.) botadura de un buque; lanzamiento; (mar.) lancha, chalupa.

launching [-in], *s.* lanzamiento; (mar.) botadura. —**l. ways,** (mar.) anguilas, parales.

launder [lóndœ(r)], *va.* lavar y planchar la ropa.

launderer [-œ(r)], *s.* lavandero.

laundress [lóndris], *s.* lavandera.

laundry [lóndri]. I. *s.* lavadero; lavandería, establecimiento de lavar ropa; tren de lavado; ropa lavada o para lavar. II. *va.* (fam.) = LAUNDER.

laundryman [-man], *s.* lavandero.

laundrywoman [-wuman], *s.* lavandera.

laureate [lóriit], *a.* y *s.* (poeta, etc.) laureado.

laureateship [-šip], *s.* dignidad de poeta laureado.

laureation [-éišon], *s.* acto de laurear, o de conferir algún grado académico.

laurel [lórel], *s.* (bot.) laurel, lauro; honor, distinción.—**l. crown,** o **wreath,** láurea, lauréola, laurel.—**l.-like,** láureo, lauráceo.

laurel(l)ed [-d], *a.* laureado.

Laurentian [lorénšian], *s.* y *a.* (geol.) laurentino.

lauric [lórik], *a.* (quím.) láurico.

laurustine [lórʌstin], **laurustinus** [-táinʌs], *s.* (bot.) durillo.

lava [lávə], *s.* lava.

lavabo [lavéibo], *s.* lavabo.

lavage [lǽvidž], **lavation** [lavéišon], *s.* lavadura, lavatorio, lavado.

lavalier(e [lævalír], *s.* (joy.) especie de medallón.

lavatory [lǽvatori], *s.* lavatorio, lavabo, lavamanos; lavadero; retrete.

lave [leiv], *va.* y *vn.* (poét.) lavar(se), bañar(se).

lavender [lévendœ(r)], *s.* (bot.) espliego, alhucema, lavándula; color de alhucema.—**l. cotton,** (bot.) santolina, guardarropa, *m.*—**l. water,** esencia de alhucema, (Am.) agua de lavanda.

laver [léĭvœ(r)], s. (ant. e igl.) aguamanil, jofaina, palangana; (bot.) ova, alga comestible.

lavish [lǽvĭš]. I. a. pródigo, gastador; profuso. II. va. disipar, malbaratar, prodigar.—**lavisher** [-œ(r)], s. pródigo, gastador.—**lavishly** [-lĭ], adv. pródigamente.—**lavishment, lavishness** [-mẹnt, -nĭs], s. prodigalidad, profusión.

law [lŏ], s. ley, f., estatuto; fuero; código de leyes; jurisprudencia, derecho, leyes (en general); tora o libro de la ley judía; (bib.) ley (de Moisés, del Antiguo Testamento).—**l.-abiding**, observante de la ley.—**l. day**, día en que están abiertos los tribunales.—**l. merchant**, ley mercantil; usos y costumbres, leyes y jurisprudencia mercantiles.—**l. of definite proportions**, ley de las proporciones definidas.—**l. of diminishing returns**, (e. p.) ley de utilidad o rendimiento decreciente; ley de que, pasado cierto límite, los productos de la tierra o de la industria dejan de aumentar proporcionalmente al aumento de capital y trabajo que se les consagre.—**l. of multiple proportions**, ley de las proporciones múltiples.—**l. of nations**, derecho internacional; derecho de gentes.—**l. of nature**, ley natural.—**l. school**, escuela de derecho.—**laws of motion**, leyes del movimiento.—**laws of war**, derecho de guerra.—**according to l.**, según derecho, conforme a la ley.—**to be a l. unto one's self**, no tener uno ni rey ni roque, ser uno su propio juez, hacer lo que le da la gana.

lawbreaker [-breĭkœ(r)], s. transgresor, infractor, violador de la ley.

lawful [-fụl], a. legal, lícito, legítimo, conforme a la ley; permitido, válido.—**l. goods**, géneros permitidos o lícitos.—**l. prize**, presa legítima.

lawfully [-ĭ], adv. legalmente, legítimamente, lícitamente.

lawfulness [-nĭs], s. legalidad, legitimidad.

lawgiver [-gĭvœ(r)], s. legislador.

lawless [-lĭs], a. ilegal; licencioso; forajido; desaforado, desmandado, de mal vivir.—**lawlessly** [-lĭ], adv. ilegalmente; licenciosamente.—**lawlessness** [-nĭs], s. desorden, licencia; desobediencia.

lawmaker [-meĭkœ(r)], s. legislador.—**lawmaking** [-ĭŋ]. I. s. legislación. II. a. legislativo.

lawn [lŏn]. I. s. prado, césped, m.; (tej.) linón, estopilla; episcopado anglicano.—**l. hose**, manguera de regar.—**l. mower**, cortadora de césped.—**l. sprinkler**, surtidor giratorio para regar el césped.—**l. tennis**, tenis (juego). II. a. de linón.

lawny [lŏnĭ], a. que tiene campos de césped; hecho o vestido de linón.

lawsuit [lŏsĭụt], s. pleito, litigio, juicio.

lawyer [lŏyœ(r)], s. abogado, jurisconsulto, legista, letrado.—**l.'s bill**, minuta.—**l.'s office**, bufete.

lax [læks], a. suelto, flojo, fláccido; laxo, relajado; vago, indeterminado; corriente de vientre.

laxation [lækséĭšọn], s. laxación.

laxative [lǽksạtĭv], a. y s. (med.) laxativo, laxante, purgante suave.

laxativeness [-nĭs], s. propiedad laxante.

laxity [lǽksĭtĭ], **laxness** [-nĭs], s. laxidad, laxitud; flaccidez, aflojamiento, flojedad; relajamiento; relajación, descuido, indiferencia.

laxly [-lĭ], adv. flojamente, sueltamente.

lay [leĭ], pret. de TO LIE.

lay [leĭ], va. (pret. y pp. LAID) poner, colocar; tender (tuberías, rieles, etc.), instalar; derribar; poner (un huevo, la mesa, etc.); matar; asentar (el polvo); enterrar; calmar, aquietar, sosegar, apaciguar; propagar (las plantas); imponer (cargas, tributos, etc.); (impr.) poner, calzar; proyectar, trazar, discurrir; imputar, atribuir; apostar; exhibir, presentar, exponer, hacer manifiesto.—**to l. a bill on the table**, encarpetar, dar carpetazo a un proyecto de ley.—**to l. against**, acusar de, achacar a.—**to l. apart**, reservar, poner aparte.—**to l. aside**, desechar,

echar o poner a un lado; arrinconar, abandonar; ahorrar.—**to l. a wager**, apostar.—**to l. away**, dejar, echar a un lado; guardar.—**to l. bare**, exponer, revelar, desnudar, poner al descubierto.—**to l. by**, poner a un lado, descartar; reservar, ahorrar.—**to l. claim to**, reclamar; pretender.—**to l. down**, abatir; abandonar; entregar, rendir, dimitir; sentar, formular; dictar, dar (la ley, etc.); proyectar; tragar; guardar, reservar; apostar.—**to l. eyes on**, ver.—**to l. hands on**, sentar la mano a, pegar a; tocar; coger, atrapar; (igl.) dar imposición de manos a, bendecir u ordenar por imposición de manos.—**to l. hold of**, asir, agarrar, coger; prender.—**to l. in**, proveerse de, comprar; (pint.) bosquejar.—**to l. level**, igualar, allanar; arrasar.—**to l. low**, derribar; matar.—**to l. off**, quitarse de encima; trazar, delinear; medir; despedir, suspender.—**to l. on**, descargar (golpes) sobre, pegar a; dar (pintura, etc.) a; distribuir (agua, gas); imponer a.—**to l. one's self out**, (fam.) esforzarse.—**to l. open**, descubrir, revelar, demostrar.—**to l. out**, gastar, emplear, desembolsar; exhibir, mostrar; trazar; proyectar; disponer, arreglar; amortajar.—**to l. over**, cubrir, sobreponer; aplazar.—**to l. siege to**, sitiar; importunar.—**to l. stress on**, insistir o hacer hincapié en.—**to l. the blame on**, echar la culpa a.—**to l. the foundation for**, echar los cimientos de.—**to l. to heart**, tomar a pechos.—**to l. to rest**, enterrar.—**to l. up**, guardar, atesorar, reservar; obligar a guardar cama; encerrar; guardar, poner a un lado; (mar.) desarmar.—**to l. wait**, formar emboscada; asechar.—**to l. waste**, asolar.

lay, vn. poner, aovar (las gallinas, etc.); apostar; (mar.) situarse, colocarse; (incorrecta pero muy frecuentemente) = TO LIE, acostarse, hallarse o estar acostado, etc.—**to l. about**, dar palos de ciego.—**to l. aft**, (mar.) ir a popa.—**to l. by** = TO L. TO.—**to l. for**, (fam.) asechar.—**to l. off**, parar (en el trabajo).—**to l. on**, virar hacia.—**to l. out**, procurar, esforzarse.—**to l. over**, demorarse, detenerse; sobrepasar.—**to l. to**, (mar.) estar parado o flotando en la dirección del viento, capear.

lay, a. laico, lego, secular, seglar; profano, incompetente.—**l. brother**, lego, converso, monigote.—**l. clerk**, capiscol, sochantre.—**l. days**, (mar.) estadía.—**l. figure**, maniquí, figurín.—**l. race**, (tej.) curso de la lanzadera.—**l. sister**, lega, (ant.) freila. II. s. caída, sesgo, dirección; contorno; (fam.) oficio, ocupación, negocio; cantidad determinada de hilo; (tej.) marco de telar; participación en una ganancia; trama (de un cable); canción, balada, lay.—**l. of the land**, (fig.) estado o disposición de las cosas.

layer [léĭœ(r)]. I. s. capa; estrato; (ten.) tina de remojar; (agr.) serpa, acodo; gallina ponedora. II. va. (agr.) acodar, amugronar.

layering [-ĭŋ], s. (agr.) acodadura.

layette [leĭyét], s. canastilla; ajuar para nene.

laying [léĭĭŋ]. I. s. colocación; postura (del huevo); (alb.) primera capa de un enlucido. II. a. situado; (mar.) anclado.—**l. hook**, manubrio del cordelero.—**l. on of hands**, imposición de manos.—**l. press**, (enc.) prensa de cepillo.—**l. top**, galapo.—**l. walk**, cordelería.

layman [léĭmạn], s. lego, seglar.

layoff [léĭɔf], s. cesantía o despido (de obreros).

layout [léĭạụt], s. plan, disposición, arreglo, trazado; equipo; (fam.) festín, banquete.

layover [léĭovœ(r)], s. parada temporal en un lugar.

lazar [léĭzạ(r)], s. (ant.) leproso, lazarino.

lazaret [læzạrét], **lazaretto** [-oṷ], **lazarhouse** [léĭzạrhaụs], s. lazareto, leprosería; (mar.) pañol.

laze [leĭz], vn. holgazanear, gandulear.

lazily [léĭzĭlĭ], adv. perezosamente.—**laziness** [-nĭs], s. pereza, holgazanería, desidia.

lazuli [lǽzyųlį], **lazulite** [-ąĭt], *s.* (min.) lazulita.
lazy [léįzį], *a.* perezoso, holgazán; pesado.
lea [lį], *s.* prado, pradera; llanura.
leach [lĭch]. I. *va.* filtrar; lixiviar; colar la ropa. II. *s.* cenizas (*f. pl.*) de lejía; lixiviación; colada. —l., l. **tub**, coladero, colador (de ropa, etc.).
leachy [-į], *a.* permeable, poroso.
lead [lĕd]. I. *s.* mina, núcleo o grafito del lápiz; (min.) plomo; (impr.) interlínea, regleta; (mar.) sonda, sondaleza, escandallo.—l.-**colored**, plomizo, aplomado.—l. **line**, sondaleza.—l. **pencil**, lápiz; lápiz portaminas.—l. **poisoning**, (med.) plumbismo, saturnismo.—l. **roofing**, plomería.—**to heave the l.**, (mar.) sond(e)ar, echar la sonda. II. *va.* (*pret. y pp.* LEADED) emplomar, forrar o guarnecer con plomo; (impr.) interlinear, regletear, espaciar verticalmente.
lead [lĭd]. I. *s.* primacía, primer lugar; dirección, mando; delantera; en el juego, mano, *f.*; salida (palo que juega el que es mano); (teat.) papel principal; protagonista; (mec.) avance (a la admisión, etc.); (elec.) alambre aislado de conexión.—l. **mare**, madrina.—**to take the l.**, adelantarse. II. *va.* (*pret. y pp.* LED) llevar de la mano, del cabestro, etc.; guiar, dirigir; mandar, acaudillar, encabezar; ir a la cabeza de: (mús.) llevar la batuta; enseñar, amaestrar, adiestrar; encauzar; derivar; llevar (buena, mala vida); atraer, inducir, mover; gastar o emplear el tiempo en alguna cosa.—**to l. along**, conducir, acompañar.—**to l. a new life**, enmendarse.—**to l. astray**, descarriar, seducir.—**to l. by the nose**, manejar a su gusto, llevar del cabestro, tener agarrado por las narices.—**to l. in**, o **into**, introducir en; llevar o conducir a.—**to l. off**, o **out**, desviar; principiar.—**to l. out of the way**, descarriar.—**to l. the way**, mostrar el camino, llevar la delantera, ir adelante. III. *vn.* mandar en jefe; guiar, enseñar el camino; sobresalir, ser el primero; ir adelante; conducir; dominar; ser mano en el juego de naipes.—**to l. off**, ir adelante; principiar.—**to l. on**, ir adelante, guiar, enseñar el camino.—**to l. (up) to**, conducir a, dar a.
leaded [lĕdįd], *pp. y a.* (impr.) interlineado; emplomado, plomado.
leaden [lĕdn], *a.* plomizo, plomoso, plúmbeo; aplomado; abatido, triste; pesado.—l.-**footed**, lento, tardo.—l.-**hearted**, insensible, empedernido.—l.-**pated**, l.-**skulled**, lerdo, estúpido.
leader [lĭdœ(r)], *s.* guía, *mf.*, conductor; guión, *m.*; jefe, caudillo, cabecilla, *m.*, líder; cosa principal o sobresaliente; lo mejor; (alb.) condutal, canalera, canalón, (tubo de) bajada; caballo delantero; (mús.) director de orquesta; primer violín, cornetín, etc.; (impr.) (*pl.*) puntos suspensivos; artículo de fondo; (mec.) rueda motriz; (min.) nervadura, vena, filón; (pesca) sedal corto de tripa unido al extremo del principal.
leaderless [-lįs], *a.* sin jefe o guía, etc.
leadership [-šĭp], *s.* dirección, primacía, hegemonía; jefatura, caudillaje, liderato.
lead-in [lĭd įn]. I. *a.* (elec.) de toma, de entrada (a un instrumento o aparato). II. *s.* conductor de entrada; (rad.) bajada, alambre de conexión de la antena con el receptor.
leading [lĭdįn]. I. *a.* director; principal, primero; capital; dominante, sobresaliente.—l. **article**, (period.) editorial, artículo de fondo.—l. **edge**, (aer.) borde de ataque.—l.-**in**, (elec.) de entrada.—l. **lady**, (teat.) dama, primera actriz.—l. **man**, jefe, cabecilla, *m.*; (teat.) galán, protagonista.—l. **question**, pregunta que sugiere o insinúa la respuesta.—l. **strings**, andadores.—l. **wheels**, ruedas delanteras de una locomotora. II. *s.* guía, conducción; dirección de orquesta.
leading [lĕdįn], *s.* emplomadura; (impr.) interlineación.
leadsman [lĕdzmąn], *s.* (mar.) sondeador.

leadwort [lĕdwœrt], *s.* (bot.) belesa, dentelaria, planta plumbagínea.
leady [lĕdį], *a.* aplomado, plomizo.
leaf [lĭf]. I. *s.* (*pl.* LEAVES) (bot.) hoja; fronda; pétalo; hoja, foja, folio (de libro); hoja o tabla (de mesa); hoja, ala, batiente (de puerta); hoja o plancha de metal.—l. **brass**, oropel.—l. **blade**, (bot.) lámina (parte ensanchada de la hoja).—l. **bud**, yema, botón de planta.—l. **gold**, oro en hojas.—l. **lard**, manteca en rama. —l. **of gold**, **silver**, hoja o pan de oro, plata.— l. **sheathe**, (bot.) vaina.—l. **tobacco**, tabaco en rama. II. *vn.* echar hojas; hacerse frondoso. III. *va.* hojear (un libro).
leafage [-įdž], *s.* follaje, frondaje, frondas, *pl.*
leafed [-t], *a.* hojudo, hojoso; frondoso.
leafiness [-inįs], *s.* follaje, frondaje.
leafless [-lįs], *a.* áfilo, sin hojas, deshojado.
leaflet [-lįt], *s.* (bot.) hojilla, hojuela; (impr.) folleto, hoja suelta.
leafstalk [-stǫk], *s.* (bot.) pecíolo, pezón.
leafy [-į], *a.* hojoso, frondoso; de forma de hoja.
league [lĭg]. I. *s.* liga, confederación, alianza; sociedad o asociación; pandilla; legua (unas 3 millas).—**L. of Nations**, Sociedad de las Naciones. II. *va. y vn.* aliar(se); confederar(se), asociar(se).
leagued [-d], *a.* confederado o aliado, (co)ligado; conjurado.
leaguer [-œ(r)], *s.* coligado, miembro de una liga.
leak [lĭk]. I. *s.* gotera en un techo; fuga o escape de gas, vapor, etc.; salida, fuga (lugar por donde algo se escapa); (mar.) vía de agua. II. *vn.* gotear; hacer agua; salirse, dejar escapar (el agua, vapor, etc.), tener fugas o salidas, escurrirse.—**to l. out**, (fig.) divulgarse, saberse, traslucirse.
leakage [-įdž], *s.* goteo, derrame, escape, fuga, salida; (magn.) dispersión; (elec.) fuga, escape; (com.) avería, pérdida, merma, derrame.
leaky [-į], *a.* llovedizo; resquebrajado; que se sale o deja fugar el contenido; permeable; (mar.) que hace agua; (fam.) locuaz, indiscreto.
lean [lĭn]. I. *vn.* (*pret. y pp.* LEANED O LEANT) apoyarse, recostarse, inclinarse; ladearse, encorvarse.—**to l. on**, o **upon**, apoyarse en; buscar o tener apoyo en.—**to l. over**, inclinarse. II. *va.* apoyar, reclinar; inclinar; encorvar. III. *a.* flaco; magro; enjuto, seco, delgado, momio, cenceño; pobre, improductivo; necesitado; de carestía, de hambre; deficiente, pobre (en el ingrediente principal); pobre en cemento (apl. al hormigón y al mortero).—l.-**witted**, tonto, necio. IV. *s.* carne mollar o magra; inclinación; propensión.
leaning [lĭnįn]. I. *a.* inclinado. II. *s.* ladeo; (a veces en plural) inclinación, propensión, tendencia; preferencia.
leanly [lĭnlį], *adv.* flaca o pobremente; sin gordura.
leanness [lĭnnįs], *s.* flacura; magrez; pobreza.
lean-to [lĭn tu], *s.* (arq.) colgadizo; tejado de una sola agua, o lo que lo tiene.
leap [lĭp]. I. *vn.* (*pret. y pp.* LEAPED O LEAPT) saltar, brincar, dar un salto o brinco; corvetear; brotar, salir con ímpetu; batir el corazón. II. *va.* (hacer) saltar; saltar, cubrir el macho a la hembra. III. *s.* salto, brinco; cabriola, zapateta. —l. **day**, día intercalar.—l. **year**, año bisiesto o intercalar.—**a l. in the dark**, un salto en el vacío.—**by leaps and bounds**, a saltos; a pasos agigantados.
leaper [-œ(r)], *s.* saltador, brincador.
leapfrog [-frag], *s.* salto, fil derecho, a la una la mula (juego de muchachos).
learn [lœrn], *va. y vn.* (*pret. y pp.* LEARNED O LEARNT) aprender; enterarse de, tener noticia de, saber; instruirse.
learnable [-ąbl], *a.* que puede aprenderse.
learned [-įd], *a.* docto, erudito, ilustrado, sabio. —**the l.**, los doctos, los sabios.
learnedly [-lį], *adv.* docta, erudita o sabiamente.

learner [-œ(r)], *s.* bisoño, principiante, tirón; aprendiz, *m.;* alumno, estudiante.

learning [-iŋ], *s.* saber, ciencia, erudición; ilustración, instrucción, sabiduría; aprendizaje.

leasable [lísąbl], *a.* arrendable, alquilable.

lease [lís]. **I.** *s.* (for.) arriendo, (escritura de) arrendamiento, censo; locación, inquilinato; (tej.) paso, cruce. **II.** *va.* arrendar, alquilar, dar o tomar en arriendo.—**l.-lend** = LEND-LEASE.

leasehold [-hoųld], *s.* censo, foro, inquilinato; (la tenencia de un) arrendamiento o arriendo.

leaseholder [-œ(r)], *s.* arrendatario.

leash [liš]. **I.** *s.* pihuela, traílla, correa; tres, par y medio; (tej.) lizo. **II.** *va.* atraillar.

least [líst]. **I.** *a.* (*super.* de LITTLE) mínimo; ínfimo; menos; el menor, el mínimo, el más pequeño.—**l. common multiple**, (mat.) mínimo común múltiplo, menor múltiplo común.—**l. squares**, (mat.) mínimos cuadrados.—**at (the) l.**, al menos, a lo menos, por lo menos, siquiera; cuando menos.—**not in the l.**, de ninguna manera, bajo ningún concepto.—**the l.**, el o lo menos. **II.** *adv.* menos.

leastways [-weįz], **leastwise** [-waįz], *adv.* al menos, por lo menos.

leather [léðœ(r)]. **I.** *s.* cuero, cordobán, piel, *f.,* curtido. **II.** *a.* de cuero.—**l. apron**, mandil.—**l. bag**, zurrón.—**l. beater**, batidor.—**l. belt**, correa.—**l. belting**, correaje.—**l. bottle**, zaque, bota.—**l. dresser**, curtidor, noquero.—**l. shield**, adarga.—**l. top**, (aut., carr.) capota.—**to dress l.**, zurrar, adobar o apellar pieles. **III.** *va.* forrar o guarnecer con cuero; hacer cuero; (fam.) dar una tunda.

leatherback [-bæk], *s.* (zool.) tortuga marina muy grande.

leatherette [-ét], *s.* cuero artificial.

leatherhead [-hed], *s.* (orn.) frailecico; (fam.) tonto, bodoque.

leathern [-n], *a.* de cuero; coriáceo.

leatherneck [-nɛk], *s.* (E. U. mil., fam.) = MARINE.

leatheroid [-ǫįd], *s.* imitación de cuero, de fibra vegetal.

leathery [-i], *a.* coriáceo, correoso.

leave [liv]. **I.** *s.* licencia, permiso, permisión, venia; despedida.—**l. of absence**, licencia, permiso.—**l.-taking**, despedida.—**by your l.**, con permiso de Vd.—**on l.**, (mil.) con licencia.—**to give l.**, permitir.—**to take l.**, despedirse. **II.** *va.* (*pret.* y *pp.* LEFT) dejar; abandonar; salir o partir de; separarse de; legar, mandar (en testamento).—**to l. alone**, dejar quieto o en paz; no meterse con, no mencallo.—**to l. behind**, dejar atrás; dejar en pos de sí.—**to l. in the dark**, dejar a oscuras.—**to l. in the lurch**, plantar, abandonar en un apuro.—**to l. no stone unturned**, no dejar piedra por mover. —**to l. off**, cesar, parar, suspender; dejar (un vicio, una costumbre).—**to l. out**, omitir, excluir.—**to l. out in the cold**, dejar colgado, olvidarse de.—**to l. undone**, no hacer, dejar de hacer; dejar sin terminar.—**to l. word**, dejar dicho. **III.** *vn.* irse, marcharse, salir, partir; (gen. con **off**) cesar, desistir; (*pret.* y *pp.* LEAVED) (a veces con **out**) echar hojas.

leaved [livd], *a.* hojoso; de hojas. *V.* TWO-LEAVED, THREE-LEAVED, etc.

leaven [lévn]. **I.** *s.* levadura, fermento. **II.** *va.* fermentar, leudar; imbuir, corromper, viciar.

leavening [-įŋ], *s.* fermento.

leaves [livz], *s. pl.* de LEAF.

leaving [lívįŋ], *s.* partida, marcha.—*pl.* sobras, desechos, desperdicios; residuo, sobra.

lecher [léchœ(r)], *s.* libertino.

lecherous [-ʌs], *a.* lujurioso, lascivo.—**lecherously** [-lį], *adv.* lujuriosamente.

lecherousness [-nįs], **lechery** [-į], *s.* lujuria, lascivia, salacidad.

lecithin [lésįθįn], *s.* (bioquím.) lecitina.

lectern [léktœrn], *s.* atril, facistol.

lection [léksǫn], *s.* (igl.) lección; letra de un texto.

lectionary [-erį], *s.* (igl.) leccionario.

lector [léktǫ(r)], *s.* (igl.) lector.

lectorate [-it], *s.* (igl.) lectorado.

lecture [lékchų(r)]. **I.** *s.* disertación, conferencia; lectura, instrucción, clase, *f.;* represión, (fam.) sermoneo, regaño.—**l. hall**, o **room**, aula, cátedra, salón de conferencias o de actos. **II.** *vn.* disertar, discursar; dar una conferencia; hablar ex cáthedra. **III.** *va.* reprender, (fam.) regañar, sermonear.

lecturer [-œ(r)], *s.* conferenciante, conferencista; catedrático; (igl.) lector.

lectureship [-šįp], *s.* (igl.) lectoría; cátedra.

led [lɛd], *pp.* y *pret.* de TO LEAD.

ledge [lɛdž], *s.* anaquel; borde, capa, tonga, tongada; retallo; arrecife; (mar.) lata de los baos.

ledger [lédžœ(r)], *s.* (com.) libro mayor; solera de emparrillado; traviesa de andamio. *V.* LEGER.

lee [li]. **I.** *s.* (mar.) sotavento; socaire. *V.* LEES. **II.** *a.* (mar.) sotaventado.—**l. shore**, (mar.) costa de sotavento.—**l. side**, banda de sotavento.—**l. tide**, marea de barlovento, marea de donde viene el viento.—**under the l.**, a sotavento.

leeboards [líbǫrdz], *s. pl.* (mar.) orzaderas.

leech [lich], *s.* (zool.) sanguijuela; gorrón; (med.) ventosa; (mar.) gratil; (ant.) médico.—**l. lines**, apagapenoles; (mar.) relinga de las caídas.—**l. rope**, relinga de las caídas.

leek [lik], *s.* (bot.) puerro, porro, ajete.

leer [lįr]. **I.** *s.* mirada de soslayo o de reojo. **II.** *vn.* mirar de soslayo, socarrona, maliciosa o lascivamente. **III.** *va.* atraer con tal mirada.

leery [lįrį], *a.* (fam.) astuto; sospechoso, receloso.

leeringly [lįrįnlį], *adv.* mirando de soslayo.

lees [liz], *s. pl.* heces, *f. pl.,* borra, sedimento, poso.

leeward [líwąrd o, entre marineros, lúąrd], *a.* (mar.) sotavento.—**l. tide**, marea en la dirección del viento.—**to fall to l.**, sotaventarse, abatir, decaer.—**to l.**, a sotavento.

leeway [líweį], *s.* (mar.) deriva, abatimiento, decadencia, desviación; riazgo, tiempo; libertad.

left [lɛft]. **I.** *pret.* y *pp.* de TO LEAVE.—**l. behind**, rezagado.—**l. off**, puesto a un lado o desechado. —**to be l.** (**over**), quedarse, sobrar. **II.** *a.* izquierdo, siniestro.—**l. bower**, triunfo que sigue al primero (*right bower*) en el *euchre*.—**l. drive**, (aut.) conducción a la izquierda.—**l. hand**, izquierdo (lado, etc.); con la mano izquierda; torcido hacia la izquierda (un cable, etc.); de movimiento hacia la izquierda.—**l. handed**, zurdo; torpe, desmañado; torcido, insincero, malicioso; de movimiento, funcionamiento, etc., hacia la izquierda.—**l.-handedness**, zurdería.—**l.-handed screw**, tornillo zurdo, tornillo a la izquierda.—**l.-hander**, zurdo (persona); zurdazo, golpe dado con la mano zurda.—**l. wing**, (pol.) bando izquierdista o radical, las izquierdas. **III.** *s.* mano izquierda o siniestra, lado izquierdo; (pol.) izquierda(s).—**at, on, o to the l.**, a la izquierda.

leftist [léftįst], *a.* y *s.* (pol.) izquierdista.

leftover [léftoųvœ(r)]. **I.** *s.* sobrante, sobra, rezago, resto. **II.** *a.* sobrante, sobrado.

leg [lɛg]. **I.** *s.* pierna; pata (de las aves y otros animales); remo (de caballo, etc.); pie (*m.*) o pata (de un mueble); pierna, pernil o pernera de pantalón; pierna (de compás, teodolito, etc.); caña de media o de bota; (mar.) bordada, pernada; (geom.) cateto; trayecto, jornada; (elec.) circuito derivado; alambre exterior de un circuito trifilar; (m. v.) placa de agua.—**l.-of-mutton sleeve**, (cost.) manga de jamón.—**not to have a l. to stand on**, no tener razón, defensa o argumento válidos.—**on, o upon, its legs**, en pie, firmemente establecido.—**on one's last legs**, acabándose; agonizante; sin recursos. —**to give l. bail**, (fam.) tomar las de Villadiego.—**to shake a l.**, (fam.) pernear, menearse. **II.** *vn.* (fam.) (gen. con **it**) andar; pernear.

legacy [légasi], s. legado, manda; herencia.—**l. duty**, derechos de herencia.

legal [lígal], a. legal, legítimo, lícito; jurídico.—**l. cap**, papel grande para documentos legales.—**l. capacity**, o **status**, (for.) personalidad.—**l. tender**, moneda de curso legal o forzoso.—**l. title**, título.

legalistic [-ístik], a. legalista.

legality [ligáliti], s. legalidad, legitimidad.

legalization [ligalizéişon], s. legalización; refrendación, refrendo.

legalize [-aiz], va. legalizar, autorizar, legitimar; refrendar; interpretar a la letra.

legally [-i], adv. legalmente; jurídicamente.

legate [légit], s. legado, enviado, embajador.

legatee [-í], s. (for.) legatario.

legateship [-šip], s. legacía.

legatine [légatin], a. hecho por un legado o que pertenece a él.

legation [ligéişon], s. legación, embajada, misión.

legato [ligátou], a. y s. (mús.) ligado.

legator [ligéito(r) o legátor], s. (for.) testador.

legend [lédžend], s. leyenda; letrero, inscripción, titulillo.—**legendary** [-eri], a. legendario.

leger [lédže(r)], a.—**l. lines**, (mús.) rayas adicionales al pentagrama.—**l. space**, espacio comprendido por esas rayas adicionales.

legerdemain [ledžœrdiméin], s. juego de manos, prestidigitación.

legged [légid], a. de piernas o pies. V. LONG-LEGGED, TWO-LEGGED, etc.

legging [légiŋ], s. polaina, sobrecalza, botín.

Leghorn [léghorn], s. sombrero de paja de Italia; casta de gallinas.

legibility [ledžibíliti], **legibleness** [-blnis], s. legibilidad.—**legible** [-bl], a. legible.—**legibly** [-bli], adv. legiblemente.

legion [lídžon], s. legión.—**legionary** [-eri], a. y s. legionario.

legionnaire [-ér], s. legionario.

legislate [lédžisleit], vn. legislar.—**legislation** [-éişon], s. legislación.—**legislative** [-iv], a. legislativo, legislador.—**legislator** [-ọ(r)], s. legislador.—**legislatorial** [-órial], a. de legislación o legislatura.—**legislatorship** [-oršip], s. oficio o dignidad de legislador.—**legislature** [lédžisleichür], s. legislatura, cuerpo legislativo, asamblea.

legist [lídžist], s. legista, jurisconsulto.

legitimacy [lidžítimasi], s. legitimidad.

legitimate [-mit]. I. a. legítimo; legal, lícito; auténtico, genuino.—**l. stage**, (teat.) las tablas (a distinción de la pantalla, el cine). II. [-meit], va. legitimar; legalizar.—**legitimately** [-mitli], adv. legítimamente.—**legitimateness** [-nis], s. legitimidad.—**legitimation** [-éişon], s. legitimación.—**legitime** [lédžitim], s. (for.) legítima.—**legitimist** [lidžítimist], s. (pol.) legitimista.—**legitimize** [-aiz], va. = LEGITIMATE.

legume [légium], **legumen** [legiúmen], s. (bot.) legumbre, leguminosa, vaina.

legumin [legiúmin], s. (bioquím.) legúmina.

leguminous [-ʌs], a. (bot.) leguminoso.

leisure [lížü(r)], s. ocio, ociosidad, holganza; comodidad.—**l. hours**, horas libres o desocupadas, ratos perdidos.—**at l.**, despacio, con sosiego, en un rato de ocio.—**to be at l.**, estar desocupado.

leisurely [-li]. I. a. pausado, deliberado. II. adv. despacio; cómoda o desocupadamente.

leitmotif [láitmotif], s. (mús.) motivo.

lemma [léma], s. (lóg. y mat.) lema, m.

lemna [lémna], s. (bot.) lenteja de agua.

lemnaceous [lemnéişʌs], a. (bot.) lemnáceo.

lemon [lémon]. I. s. (bot.) limón.—**l.-colored**, limonado, cetrino.—**l. drop**, pastilla de limón.—**l. squeezer**, exprimidera de limón.—**l. tree**, limonero, limón.—**l. verbena**, (bot.) luisa. II. a. de limón; hecho o sazonado con limón; cetrino.

lemonade [lemonéid], s. limonada.

lemur [límœ(r)], s. (zool.) lémur, maqui o maki.

lemures [lémyuriz], s. pl. (mit.) lémures.

Lemuria [limiúria], s. pl. (mit.) lemurias.

Lemuridæ [limiúridi], s. pl. (zool.) lemúridos.

lend [lénd], va. (pret. y pp. LENT) prestar, dar prestado.—**to l. a hand** (to), dar una mano, ayudar, arrimar el hombro.—**to l. aid**, dar ayuda, prestar auxilio.—**to l. an ear**, prestar atención, dar oídos.—**to l. countenance to**, apoyar.

lender [-œ(r)], s. prestador, prestamista; logrero, mutuante.

lending [-iŋ], s. empréstito, préstamo.

Lend-Lease Act [-lís ækt], (pol.) ley (f.) de préstamo y arriendo.

lene [líni]. I. a. (gram.) suave, no aspirado. II. s. consonante no aspirada.

length [léŋθ], s. longitud, largo(r); extremo, punto; extensión, distancia; espacio, duración de tiempo; alcance (de un tiro, etc.); (dep.) echada; (mar.) eslora (de un buque).—**at l.**, al fin, finalmente; extensamente, prolijamente.—**at full l.**, a lo largo, de todo el largo.

lengthen [-n]. I. va. alargar, estirar, extender; prolongar, dilatar. II. vn. alargarse, prolongarse.

lengthening [-iŋ]. I. s. alargamiento; prolongación. II. a. de alargar.—**l. bar, l. tube**, alargadera (de compás, retorta, etc.).

lengthways [-weiz], **lengthwise** [-waiz], adv. longitudinalmente; a lo largo, de largo a largo.

lengthy [-i], a. largo; prolijo, demasiado largo, larguísimo.

leniency [líniensi], s. suavidad, lenidad, indulgencia.—**lenient** [-ent], a. indulgente, lenitivo, clemente.

Leninism [léninizm], s. leninismo, sistema (m.) de Lenín.—**Leninite** [-ait], a. y s. leninista.

lenitive [lénitiv], s. y a. lenitivo.

lenity [léniti], s. lenidad, blandura.

lens [lenz], s. (ópt.) lente, mf., luna, lupa; objetivo; (anat.) cristalino.—pl. **lenses**, cristales de gafas o lentes.

lent [lent]. I. pret. y pp. de TO LEND; prestado. II. (L.), s. cuaresma, cuadragésima, cuarentena.

lentando [lentándou], a. y adv. (mús.) con lentitud creciente.

lenten [lénten], a. cuaresmal; escaso.

lenticular [lentíkyülá(r)], **lentiform** [léntiform], a. lenticular.

lentiginous [lentídžinʌs], a. (bot. y zool.) pecoso; casposo.

lentil [léntil], s. (bot.) lenteja.

lentiscus [lentískʌs], s. (bot.) lentisco.

lento [léntou], a. y adv. (mús.) lento, lentamente.

Leo [líou], s. (astr.) León.

leonine [líonain], a. leonino.

leopard [lépärd], s. (zool.) leopardo o pardal.—**l.'s-bane**, (bot.) dorónico.

lepadid [lépadid], s. (zool.) lápade, f., percebe.

leper [lépœ(r)], s. leproso, lazarino.

lepidolite [lépidolait], s. (min.) lepidolita.

Lepidoptera [lepidáptęra], s. (ent.) lepidópteros, diurnos.—**lepidopteran** [-n], s. y a. lepidóptero.—**lepidopterous** [-ʌs], a. lepidóptero.

lepidosiren [lepidosáiren], s. (zool.) lepidosirena.

leporine [lépǫrin], a. (zool.) lebruno, leporino.

leprology [leprálodži], s. leprología.

leprosarium [leprosęriʌm], s. leprosería, leprocomio, lazareto, hospital de leprosos.

leprose [léprous], a. (biol.) casposo, escamoso.

leprosy [léprosi], s. (med.) lepra.

leprous [léprʌs], a. leproso, lazarino.

leprousness [-nis], s. leprosidad.

Lepus [lípʌs], s. (astr.) Liebre, f.

Lesbian [lézbian], a. y s. lesbio, lesbiano.

Lesbianism [-izm], s. lesbianismo.

lese majesty [liz mædžisti], s. lesa majestad.

lesion [lížon], s. lesión.

less [les]. I. a. (comp. de LITTLE) menor, menos, inferior. II. adv. menos, en grado más pequeño; en grado más bajo.—**l. and l.**, de menos en menos, cada vez menos. **III.** *s.* el o lo menos: cantidad más pequeña o menor. **IV.** *prep.* menos; sin.

lessee [lɛsí], *s.* (for.) arrendatario, rentero, inquilino.

lessen [lésn]. **I.** *va.* (a)minorar, disminuir, mermar; menoscabar; rebajar, degradar. **II.** *vn.* mermar, disminuirse; degradarse, rebajarse.

lesser [lésœ(r)], *a.* (comp. de LITTLE) menor, más pequeño.—**l. prophets,** profetas (*m.*) menores.

lesson [lésọn], *s.* lección; instrucción, enseñanza; escarmiento; reprensión; (igl.) lección.

lessor [lésọ(r)], *s.* (for.) arrendante, arrendador, censualista, que da una cosa en arrendamiento.

lest [lɛst], *conj.* para que no, por miedo de, o de miedo que, no sea que.

let [lɛt]. **I.** *va.* (pret. y *pp.* LET) dejar, conceder, permitir; arrendar, alquilar, dar en arrendamiento. Como auxiliar, se usa para formar el subjuntivo e imperativo de algunos verbos anteponiéndolo al infinitivo: *let him go,* que se vaya; *let's eat,* vamos a comer; *let us fly,* huyamos; *let the children play,* que jueguen los niños; *let it be known,* sépase. Las circunstancias indican cuándo es auxiliar y cuándo no. Así, *let us see* puede significar "veamos," "vamos a ver" o "déjenos ver," según el caso. El infinitivo se usa a menudo elípticamente por sí solo en el sentido de "para arrendar," "se arrienda," "de alquiler," etc.—**to l. alone,** dejar en paz, no molestar; no tocar; no meterse con o en; sin hablar de; sin mencionar; mucho menos (*he cannot buy a horse, let alone an automobile,* no puede comprar un caballo, mucho menos un automóvil).—**to l. be,** no molestar; no meterse con.—**to l. blood,** sangrar.—**to l. bygones be bygones,** olvidar lo pasado.—**to l. down,** dejar caer; bajar; traicionar; abandonar; humillar.—**to l. fall a word,** soltar inadvertidamente una palabra.—**to l. fly,** (fam.) disparar.—**to l. go,** soltar.—**to l. good** (o **well**) **enough alone,** bueno está lo bueno, mejor es no menearlo (cambiando un poco el giro).—**to l. in,** dejar entrar, admitir, recibir; introducir; hacer entrar.—**to l. into,** dejar o hacer entrar en; dejar conocer; iniciar o admitir en.—**to l. it go at that,** conformarse con eso; no hacer o decir más, dejar pasar.—**to l. know,** hacer saber, avisar.—**to l. loose,** soltar, aflojar; desatar, desencadenar.—**to l. off,** disparar, descargar; (fam.) dejar salir o ir, dejar libre.—**to l. one's self go,** desatarse, dejar a la moderación.—**to l. out,** dejar salir; vaciar; poner en libertad, soltar; hacer salir; divulgar; arrendar, alquilar; largar (un rizo, etc.), aflojar.—**to l. the cat out of the bag,** revelar un secreto. **II.** *vn.* alquilarse o arrendarse.—**to let up,** (fam.) cesar; disminuir, moderarse. **III.** *s.* estorbo, impedimento.—**without l. or hindrance,** sin estorbo ni obstáculo.

letdown [létdaun], *s.* relajación, disminución, aflojamiento; (fam.) chasco; humillación.

lethal [líθal], *a.* letal.

lethargic(al [liθárdʒik(al], *a.* letárgico, aletargado, letargoso.—**lethargically** [-i], *adv.* letárgicamente.—**lethargize** [léθardʒaiz], *va.* aletargar.—**lethargy** [léθardʒi], *s.* (med.) letargo.—**to fall into a l.,** aletargarse.

Lethean [liθían], *a.* (poét.) leteo.

lethiferous [liθíferʌs], *a.* letífero, mortífero.

Lett [lét], *s.*, **Lettish** [-iʃ], *s.* y *a.* letón.

letter [létœ(r)]. **I.** *s.* letra; (impr.) carácter, tipo; carta, comunicación.—*pl.* (bellas) letras, literatura; erudición.—**l. book,** (com.) copiador de cartas.—**l. box,** buzón; apartado.—**l. carrier,** o **man,** cartero.—**l. case,** cartera, carpeta.—**l. drop,** buzón.—**l. file,** cartera, carpeta, guardacartas, archivo.—**l. of advice,** (com.) carta de aviso.—**l. of attorney,** poder, procuración.—**l. of credit,** carta de crédito.—**l. of introduction,** carta de presentación o de recomendación.—**l. of license,** moratoria, espera.—**l. of**

marque (and reprisal), carta de (contra)-marca, patente de corso.—**l. opener,** abrecartas, plegadera.—**l. paper,** papel de cartas.—**l. perfect,** exactísimo, muy perfecto; al dedillo; que sabe su papel, discurso, etc., de memoria.—**l. press,** prensa de copiar cartas.—**l. scale,** pesacartas.—**l. stamp,** matasellos, cancelador de sellos de correo; sello para fechar cartas en el correo.—**l. writer,** memorialista.—**letters dimissory,** dimisorias.—**letters of safe conduct,** (carta de) amparo, seguridad, guía, salvoconducto.—**letters patent,** título o patente de privilegio; ejecutoria (de nobleza).—**letters requisitorial,** exhorto.—**letters rogatory,** suplicatoria.—**to the l.,** al pie de la letra, a la letra. **II.** *va.* estampar con letras; rotular; poner letras, título o letreros a.

lettered [-d], *a.* letrado, instruido, erudito, literato, docto.

letterer [-œ(r)], *s.* el que pone letras y letreros (en un dibujo, etc.).

lettergram [-græm], *s.* telegrama largo, a manera de carta, que se envía con rebaja de precio pero sin garantía de entrega inmediata (puede llamarse carta telegráfica).

letterhead [-hed], *s.* membrete; hoja o pliego de papel con membrete.

lettering [-iŋ], *s.* letrero, inscripción, rótulo; estampilla; puesta de letras a un dibujo.

letterpress [-pres], *s.* impresión, impreso; texto (a distinción de grabados o figuras).—**l. printing,** impresión directa con tipo (a distinción de la hecha con planchas).

lettre de cachet [létr dœ kæʃéj], *s.* (fr.) carta real cerrada.

lettuce [létiʃ], *s.* (bot.) lechuga.

letup [létʌp], *s.* (fam.) diminución, calma; cesación, interrupción; descanso.

leucin(e [ljúsin], *s.* (bioquím.) leucina.

leucite [ljúsait], *s.* (min.) leucita.

leucocyte [ljúkosait], *s.* (anat.) leucocito.

leucocythemia [-θímiạ], *s.* (med.) leucocitemia.

leucoma [ljukóumạ], *s.* (med.) leucoma, *m.*, albugo.

leucorrhea [ljukoríạ], *s.* (med.) leucorrea.

leukemia [ljukímiạ], *s.* (med.) leucemia.

Levant [livǽnt]. **I.** *s.* levante, oriente. **II.** *a.* oriental.—**L. trade,** comercio de levante.

Levanter [-œ(r)], *s.* viento del levante.

Levantine [-in], *a.* y *s.* levantino, levantisco.

levator [livéitọ(r)], *s.* (anat.) músculo elevador; (cir.) levantador.

levee [lévi], *s.* corte, *f.,* besamanos, recepción; dique, malecón.

level [lévl]. **I.** *a.* plano, llano, igual, parejo; igual, uniforme; derecho, recto; honrado, probo; a nivel; horizontal.—**l. crossing,** (f. c.) paso a nivel.—**l.-headed,** juicioso, discreto.—**to do one's l. best,** (fam.) hacer uno lo sumo posible, o cuanto pueda. **II.** *s.* nivel (instrumento, altura); llanura; puntería; línea visual; (min.) galería horizontal, piso.—**on the l.,** abiertamente, sin dolo. **III.** *adv.* a nivel, ras; en derechura; con puntería; igualmente; lisa y llanamente. **IV.** *va.* igualar, allanar; nivelar; arrasar, derribar; apuntar, dirigir, asestar; proporcionar, adaptar, ajustar; igualar, emparejar; (alb.) enrasar. **V.** *vn.* apuntar (un arma); (top.) nivelar, hacer nivelaciones.—**to l. off,** (aer.) enderezarse para aterrizar.

level(l)er [-œ(r)], *s.* allanador, igualador, aplanador; nivelador; aplanadera.

level(l)ing [-iŋ]. **I.** *s.* igualación, allanamiento; nivelación; (alb.) enrasado. **II.** *a.* igualador; nivelador, de nivelar; de enrasar.—**l. course,** (alb.) enrase.—**l. line,** tendel.—**l. rod, staff,** o **pole,** (top.) jalón, mira de nivelar.

levelness [-njs], *s.* nivel, igualdad; horizontalidad.

lever [lévœ(r)], *s.* palanca; brazo; manecilla; escape de reloj.—**l. arm,** brazo de palanca.—**l. watch,** reloj de escape.

---

leverage [-idž], *s.* brazo de palanca; apalancamiento, acción de una palanca; sistema (*m.*) de palancas; influencia, poder, ventaja.

leveret [lévœret], *s.* (zool.) lebrato.

leviable [léviabl], *a.* exigible, tasable; imponible.

leviathan [liváia̱θa̱n], *s.* leviatán.

levigate [lévigeit], *va.* levigar; pulverizar.

levigation [-éiŝǫn], *s.* levigación; pulverización.

levirate [lévirit], *s.* levirato.

levitate [léviteit], *va.* y *vn.* alzar(se) o (hacer) subir contra la acción de la gravedad y sin medios físicos (apl. a los fenómenos espiritistas). —**levitation** [-éiŝǫn], *s.* suspensión o levantamiento de cuerpos pesados sin medios físicos.

Levite [líva̱it], *s.* levita, *m.*; (ant.) diácono.

Levitic [livítik-a̱l], *a.* levítico.

levity [léviti], *s.* levedad, ligereza; veleidad.

levulose [lévyûlǫus], *s.* (quím.) levulosa.

levy [lévi]. I. *va.* reclutar, enganchar; exigir contribuciones o tributos; (for.) embargar, ejecutar.—**to l. on**, gravar, imponer contribución sobre.—**to l. war**, guerrear, hacer la guerra. II. *s.* (mil.) leva, recluta, enganche; exacción de tributos; (for.) embargo, ejecución.

lewd [liúd], *a.* lujurioso, lascivo.—**lewdly** [-li], *adv.* lascivamente; impúdicamente.—**lewdness** [-nis], *s.* lascivia, lujuria, libídine, *mf.*; prostitución.

lewis(son [liújs(ǫn], *s.* clavija para alzar piedras; castañuela de cantera.

lewisite [liújsait], *s.* (mil.) cierto vesicante incoloro.

lexical [léksika̱l], *a.* lexicográfico.

lexicographer [-kágra̱fœ(r)], *s.* lexicógrafo.— **lexicographic** [-kográfik], *a.* lexicográfico.— **lexicography** [-kágra̱fi], *s.* lexicografía.—**lexicological** [-kolád̯žika̱l], *a.* lexicológico.—**lexicologist** [-kálod̯žist], *s.* lexicólogo.—**lexicology** [-kálod̯ži], *s.* lexicología.

lexicon [-kǫn], *s.* léxico, vocabulario, diccionario.

lex talionis [leks tælióu̯nis], *s.* ley (*f.*) o pena del talión.

Leyden jar [láid̯en d̯žar], *s.* (fís.) botella de Leiden.

liability [laia̱biliti], *s.* riesgo, exposición; obligación, responsabilidad; suma que una compañía de seguros está legalmente obligada a pagar.—*pl.* **liabilities**, (com.) pasivo, obligaciones a pagar.

liable [láia̱bl], *a.* sujeto, expuesto; obligado, responsable, deudor; propenso.

liaison [liéizǫn], *s.* concubinaje; enlace, vinculación, unión, coordinación; (fon.) unión de una consonante final a la vocal siguiente.—**l. officer**, (mil.) oficial de intercomunicación y coordinación.

liana, liane [liáng̯, liéng̯], *s.* (bot.) especie de bejuco, (gal.) liana, (Cuba) jagüey.

liar [láia̱r], *s.* embustero, mentiroso, falsario.

Lias [láia̱s], *s.* (geol.) lías.—**Liassic** [laiǽsik], *a.* y *s.* liásico.

libation [laibéiŝǫn], *s.* libación.

libel [láibel]. I. *s.* libelo; difamación. II. *va.* difamar, calumniar, injuriar; presentar una alegación contra una persona por conducta impropia, o contra un barco por deuda.—**libel(l)ant** [-a̱nt], *s.* (for.) el que presenta una demanda por libelo; actor o demandante ante el tribunal del Almirantazgo o ante un tribunal eclesiástico; libelista.—**libel(l)er** [-œ(r)], *s.* libelista, difamador.—**libel(l)ing** [-iŋ], *s.* difamación.— **libel(l)ous** [-ʌs], *a.* infamatorio, difamatorio, injuriante.

libellula [laibélyūla̱], *s.* (ent.) libélula.

liber [láibœ(r)], *s.* libro, registro; (bot.) líber.

liberal [líbera̱l], *a.* liberal, generoso, dadivoso, bizarro; abundante; (pol.) liberal; libre (traducción, etc.); noble, bien nacido.—**l. arts**, artes (*f.*) liberales.—**l.-minded**, tolerante.

liberalism [-izm], *s.* liberalismo.

liberality [-éliti], *s.* liberalidad.

liberalize [-a̱laiz], *va.* liberalizar.

liberally [-a̱li], *adv.* liberal o generosamente.

liberate [-eit], *va.* libertar, librar, redimir; manumitir; descargar.

liberation [-éiŝǫn], *s.* liberación, redención.

liberator [-eitǫ(r)], *s.* libertador.

libertarian [-térian]. I. *s.* el que defiende la libertad del individuo; el que cree en el libre albedrío. II. *a.* libertario; relativo a la doctrina que defiende el libre albedrío.

libertinage [líbœrtinid̯ž], *s.* libertinaje.

libertine [líbœrtin]. I. *a.* y *s.* libertino, disoluto. II. *s.* (for.) libertino, hijo de liberto.

libertinism [-izm], *s.* libertinaje; librepensamiento, abuso de la libertad del pensamiento.

liberty [líbœrti], *s.* libertad; exención, prerrogativa, inmunidad; osada familiaridad; liberación de presos o cautivos; licencia, permiso.—**L. Bell**, campana de la libertad (la que se repicó cuando los E. U. declararon su independencia). —**L. Bond**, bono de la libertad, nombre dado a los bonos emitidos por el gobierno de los E. U. durante la guerra mundial (1917 a 1919).—**L. Loan**, préstamo de la libertad, primera emisión de bonos de la libertad.—**to take the l. to**, permitirse.—**to take undue liberties**, propasarse.

libidinous [libídinʌs], *a.* libidinoso, lujurioso.— **libidinously** [-li], *adv.* libidinosamente.—**libidinousness** [-nis], *s.* lascivia, lujuria, libídine, *mf.*

Libra [láibra̱], *s.* (astr.) Libra.

librarian [laibrérian], *s.* bibliotecario.

librarianship [-šip], *s.* empleo de bibliotecario.

library [láibreri], *s.* biblioteca; librería; gabinete.

librate [láibreit], *vn.* balancear, oscilar.

libration [-éiŝǫn], *s.* balance; (astr.) libración.

libratory [láibra̱tǫri], *a.* de libración, oscilatorio; que balancea.

librettist [librétist], *s.* libretista.

libretto [librétou̯], *s.* (mús.) libro, libreto.

Libyan [líbia̱n]. I. *a.* líbico. II. *a.* y *s.* libio.

lice [lais], *s. pl.* de LOUSE, piojos.

licensable [láisensa̱bl], *a.* permisible.

license [láisens]. I. *s.* licencia, permiso; despacho, cédula, título; matrícula (para conducir un automóvil); licencia, libertinaje.—**l. plate**, (aut., etc.) placa. II. *va.* licenciar, dar licencia o permiso; autorizar, facultar; dar cédula, despacho o privilegio.

licensee [-í], *s.* persona que obtiene licencia o permiso; concesionario.

licenser [-œ(r)], *s.* el que da licencia.

licentiate [laisénšiit], *s.* licenciado.

licentious [laisénšʌs], *a.* licencioso, desenfrenado, distraído, disoluto.—**licentiously** [-li], *adv.* licenciosamente.—**licentiousness** [-nis], *s.* licencia, disolución, disipación, libertinaje.

lichen [láikęn], *s.* (bot.) liquen; (med.) salpullido causado por el calor; erupción papular.

licit [lísit], *a.* lícito.—**licitly** [-li], *adv.* lícitamente. —**licitness** [-nis], *s.* licitud, calidad de lícito.

lick [lik]. I. *va.* lamer, laminar; (fam.) cascar, dar una tunda o felpa; sobrepujar, vencer.—**to l. into shape**, (fam.) dar forma a.—**to l. the boots of**, (fam.) adular servilmente.—**to l. the dust**, morder el polvo. II. *vn.* flamear. III. *s.* lamedura, lengüetada; salegar, lamedero; (fam.) mojicón, bofetón.

licker [-œ(r)], *s.* lamedor, lamiente.

lickerish [líkœriš], *a.* apetitoso, aficionado a bocados regalados; goloso; salaz, libidinoso.

licking [líkiŋ], *s.* (fam.) tunda, paliza; derrota.

lickspittle [líkspitl], *s.* quitapelillos, parásito, hombre servil.

licorice [líkǫriš], *s.* (bot.) regaliz, *m.*, orozuz, *m.*, alcauyz, *m.*

lictor [líktǫ(r)], *s.* lictor.

lid [lid], *s.* tapa, tapadera; (anat.) párpado; (bot., zool.) opérculo; guardapolvo de reloj; (fam.) sombrero.

lie [lai]. I. *s.* mentira, embuste; desmentida,

mentís; postura, posición, yacimiento, caída; cubil; (f. c.) desviadero.—**to give the l. to,** dar un mentís a, desmentir. II. *vn.* (*pret.* y *pp.* LIED; *pa.* LYING) mentir.

lie, *vn.* (*pret.* LAY; *pp.* LAIN) echarse, tenderse; descansar recostado: apoyarse; acostarse, estar acostado o en cama; yacer, ubicar, estar situado; (ant.) pernoctar; consistir, depender; estar en, tocar o corresponder a; estar pendiente; (for.) ser sostenible o ejecutable.—**to l. about,** estar esparcido.—**to l. along,** dar a la banda.—**to l. at the heart,** ser objeto de afecto, ansiedad o deseo.—**to l. at the point of death,** estar expirando.—**to l. by,** estar cerca o a la mano; parar, descansar.—**to l. down,** echarse, acostarse; (fam.) ceder o someterse sin luchar; (fam.) ser negligente (en un deber o tarea).—**to l. in,** estar de parto.—**to l. in one,** depender de uno, estar de manos de uno.—**to l. in state,** estar en capilla o cámara ardiente, estar de cuerpo presente.—**to l. in wait,** espiar; asechar.—**to l. low,** estar postrado; permanecer oculto o en la oscuridad, ocultarse; no hacer ni decir nada, esperar; no dejarse ver las intenciones.—**to l. off,** descansar; contenerse al principio (de una carrera, etc.).—**to l. on,** o **upon,** ser obligatorio a, pesar sobre; depender de.—**to l. on one's head,** tener uno la culpa de.—**to l. on the oars,** cesar de remar; descansar del trabajo.—**to l. over,** aplazarse; (com.) caducar.—**to l. to,** (mar.) estar a la capa, ponerse en facha.—**to l. under,** estar bajo el peso de.—**to l. up,** descansar.—**to l. with,** vivir o dormir con; tocar o corresponder a.

lief [lif], *adv.* de buena gana, de buen grado.

liege [lídž]. I. *a.* ligio; feudatario. II. *s.* vasallo súbdito; señor feudal.—**liegeman** [-mạn], *s.* vasallo; secuaz leal.

lien [lin], *s.* (for.) embargo preventivo para el cobro de una deuda; obligación, gravamen.

lienteric [laiẹntẹríḳ], *a.* lientérico.

lientery [láiẹnterị], *s.* (med.) lientería, lientera.

lieu [lịu], *s.*—**in l. of,** en lugar de, en vez de.

lieutenancy, lieutenantship [liụtẹnạnsị, -ạntṣip], *s.* (lugar)tenencia; tenientazgo (**first l.**); alferazgo (**second l.**).

lieutenant [-ạnt], *s.* (primer) teniente (**first l.**); segundo teniente, subteniente, alférez (**second l.**), (lugar)teniente.—**l. colonel,** teniente coronel.—**l. general,** teniente general.—**l. governor,** (E. U.) vicegobernador, dignatario que reemplaza al gobernador cuando éste no puede funcionar; (Ingl.) lugarteniente del gobernador general de una colonia; gobernador de provincia.

life [láif]. I. *s.* vida; existencia, ser, vivir; conducta, modo de vivir; animación, ardor, vivacidad, viveza; duración; biografía.—**for l.,** de por vida, por toda la vida; vitalicio; para salvarse; hasta más no poder.—**for the l. of me,** por vida mía, a fe mía, en verdad.—**from l.,** del natural.—**to the l.,** al vivo, a lo vivo. II. *a.* de la vida; relativo a la vida; de toda la vida, vitalicio.—**l. annuity,** renta vitalicia.—**l. assurance** = L. INSURANCE.—**l. belt,** cinto de salvamento, cinturón salvavidas.—**l. boat** = LIFEBOAT.—**l. buoy,** boya oguindola salvavidas.—**l. expectancy,** promedio vital.—**l.-giving,** vivificante, vivificativo.—**l. guard,** (mil.) guardia de corps. *V.* LIFEGUARD y LIFESAVER.—**l. imprisonment,** cadena perpetua.—**l. insurance,** seguro de vida, o sobre la vida.—**l. line,** cuerda salvavidas; andarivel horizontal de verga; línea de la vida (en la quiromancia).—**l. net,** red de salvamento.—**l. policy,** póliza vitalicia o de seguro ordinario sobre la vida, pagadera sólo al fallecimiento del asegurado.—**l. preserver,** salvavidas.—**l. raft,** balsa salvavidas.—**l.-saving apparatus,** aparato salvavidas.—**l.-saving gun,** u **mortar,** cañón lanzacabos, u obús para lanzar proyectiles de salvamento.—**l.-saving station,** estación de

salvamento en la costa.—**l. sentence,** sentencia de prisión vitalicia.—**l.-size,** de tamaño natural.—**l. span,** duración máxima de la vida.

lifeblood [-blʌd], *s.* sangre (*f.*) vital; alma, nervio.

lifeboat [-bọut], *s.* bote o lancha salvavidas, de socorro, o de salvamento.

lifeguard [-gard], *s.* salvavidas (nadador experto empleado en las playas).

lifeless [-lịs], *a.* sin vida, muerto, exánime; inanimado; falto de vigor; agotado; falto de animación, sin vida, sin alma; inhabitado, sin ser viviente.—**lifelessly** [-lị], *adv.* sin vigor.

lifelessness [-nịs], *s.* falta de vida; falta de vigor o animación.

lifelike [-laịk], *a.* que parece vivo, natural.

lifelong [-lɔŋ], *a.* de toda la vida.

lifesaver [-sẹivœ(r)], *s.* miembro de una estación de salvamento. *V.* LIFEGUARD.

lifetime [-taịm]. I. *s.* curso de la vida; toda la vida.—**in our l.,** durante nuestra vida. II. *a.* vitalicio, de por vida, que dura toda la vida.

lifework [-wœrk], *s.* obra que abarca o requiere una vida entera; obra principal o total de la vida de uno.

lift [lịft]. I. *va.* alzar, levantar; quitar la presión; so(s)pesar; exaltar, ensalzar; enriscar; redimir (una hipoteca); (fam.) hurtar; plagiar.—**to l. a siege,** (mil.) levantar un sitio.—**to l. the hat,** quitarse el sombrero para saludar.—**to l. up,** alzar; solivicar.—**to l. (up) the hand,** prestar juramento levantando la mano; orar; hacer un esfuerzo.—**to l. up the voice,** levantar la voz; alzar el gallo. II. *vn.* hacer fuerza para levantar algo; disiparse (la niebla). III. *s.* esfuerzo para levantar; acción de alzar; lo que sirve para alzar (aparejo, gancho, etc.); elevación, altura a que algo se alza; soliviadura; alza, aumento; carrera (de un martinete, etc.); (aut.) manigueta de ventana; (Ingl.) ascensor; elevador, montacargas; (min.) diferencia de nivel; (min.) juego de bombas; (aer.) fuerza ascensional, componente vertical de la presión aerodinámica; sustentación.—**l. bridge,** puente levadizo.—**l. lock,** esclusa.—**l. pump,** bomba aspirante.—**l. valve,** válvula de movimiento vertical.—**l. wire,** (aer.) cable o cinta de sustentación.—**at one l.,** de un golpe.—**to give one a l.,** ayudar a uno; alentar o animar a uno; llevar a uno gratis en un vehículo.

lifter [-œ(r)], *s.* alzador, cualquier cosa que sirve para alzar; elevador; (fam.) ratero; (m. v.) brazo de la válvula de una máquina de balancín.

lifting [-ịŋ]. I. *s.* acción de alzar, etc.; levantamiento; soliviadura. II. *a.* de alzar o elevar.—**l. bridge,** puente levadizo.—**l. force,** o **power,** fuerza o poder ascensional o levantador(a).—**l. injector,** (m. v.) inyector aspirante.—**l. jack,** gato, cric.—**l. pump,** bomba aspirante.—**l. rod,** (m. v.) vástago vertical que en una máquina de balancín mueve el brazo de la válvula.

ligament [lígạmẹnt], *s.* (anat.) ligamento.

ligamental, ligamentous [ligạmɛ́ntạl, -tʌs], *a.* ligamentoso.

ligate [láigẹit], *va.* (cir.) ligar, atar con ligadura.

ligation [-éiṣ̣ọn], *s.* ligación; ligadura.

ligature [lígạchụr], *s.* (cir., mec. y mús.) ligadura; ligación; (impr.) letras ligadas, como æ, fi, fl, etc.

light [lait]. I. *s.* luz; claridad, resplandor; lumbre; farol, lámpara, candela, vela; luminar, notabilidad (dicho de los grandes hombres); claraboya, tragaluz; (vidrio de) ventana; fuego (de un cigarro, etc.); fósforo, cerilla; aspecto; situación, posición; punto de vista; día, *m.*, alba; (pint.) luz.—*pl.* *V.* LIGHTS.—**l. bulb,** (elec.) bombilla.—**l. buoy,** baliza o boya luminosa.—**l. dues,** **l. money,** derechos de faro.—**l. keeper,** torrero.—**l. port,** (mar.) portilla.—**l. pull,** tirador de lámpara, cadena o cuerda para encender y apagar una lámpara.—**l. quantum,** (fís.) = PHOTON.—**l. shaft,** lumbrera, toma de luz.—l. **vessel** = LIGHTSHIP.—l. **wave**, onda luminosa.—l. **year**, año-luz, unidad sideral de distancia, espacio que la luz recorre en un año. —**in the l. of**, a la luz de, según.—**in this l.**, desde este punto de vista.—**to give one a l.**, (fam.) dar lumbre a uno. II. *a.* ligero, leve, de poco peso; sutil; (mar.) boyante; llevadero; suelto, fácil; fútil, frívolo, superficial; ágil, desembarazado; inconstante, mudable; alegre, vivo; liviano, incontinente; claro (apl. esp. al color); de tez blanca; blondo, rubio.—l. **artillery**, (mil.) artillería ligera.—l. **complexion**, tez blonda.—l.-**headedness**, delirio; atolondramiento, aturdimiento.—l. **heavyweight**, (dep.) boxeador de peso medio (que no pasa de 175 libras).—l. **horse**, (mil.) caballería ligera.—l. **literature**, literatura amena, literatura ordinaria.—l. **opera**, (mús.) ópera ligera, opereta.—l. **sleep**, sueño ligero, (fam.) duermevela, *m.*—l. **soil**, (agr.) terreno árido.— **to make l. of**, hacer poco caso de, tomar en chanza. III. *va.* (*pret.* LIGHTED o LIT) encender; alumbrar, iluminar, lucir. IV. *vn.* encenderse, prender (el fuego o la luz); iluminarse; descender, posarse; apearse; (con **on** u **upon**), encontrarse con, hallar por casualidad, topar (con).— **to l. into**, (fam.) atacar o increpar duramente. —**to l. out**, (fam.) liarlas, poner pies en polvorosa, tomar las de Villadiego. V. *adv.* ligeramente; fácilmente.—l.-**fingered**, largo de uñas, ligero de dedos.—l.-**foot(ed**, l.-**heeled**, ligero de pies.—l.-**haired**, pelirrubio.—l.-**headed**, ligero de cascos, casquivano; delirante; atolondrado, aturdido.—l.-**hearted**, alegre, festivo. —l.-**legged**, ligero de piernas, activo.—l.-**minded**, voluble; atolondrado.—l.-**witted**, chalado, cascabelero.

lighten [láitn]. I. *va.* iluminar, alumbrar; aclarar; aligerar, quitar peso; (mar.) alijar, zafar; aliviar; alegrar, regocijar. II. *vn.* ponerse ligero disminuir de peso; relampaguear, centellear; aclarar.

lightening [-iŋ], *s.* alba, alborada; aligeramiento; alivio; (mar.) alijo.

lighter [láitœ(r)]. I. *a. comp.* de LIGHT; más ligero; más claro. II. *s.* (mar.) barcaza, chalana, gabarra, (lanchón) alijador; alumbrador, encendedor, mechero automático, (Am.) prendedor; mecha. III. *va.* y *vn.* transportar o llevar en chalana.

lighterage [-idž], *s.* (mar.) gastos de chalana, lanchaje, gabarraje; alijo.

lighterman [-man], *s.* (mar.) lanchonero, gabarrero.

lighthouse [láithaus], *s.* (mar.) faro, farola, fanal. —l. **keeper**, torrero.

lighting [-iŋ], *s.* alumbrado (eléctrico, de gas, etc.), luz (eléctrica, etc.); iluminación.—l. **effects**, (teat.) efectos de luz.—l. **technique**, técnica lumínica.

lightless [-lis], *a.* obscuro, sin luz.

lightly [-li], *adv.* ligeramente, levemente; prontamente, ágilmente; alegremente, de buena gana; sin seriedad, con liviandad, a la ligera; sin motivo; irrespetuosamente, con desprecio.

lightness [-nis], *s.* levedad, ligereza; agilidad, velocidad; inconstancia; frivolidad; liviandad.

lightning [-niŋ], *s.* relámpago; relampagueo; rayo.—l. **arrester, conductor, rod**, (elec.) pararrayos.—l. **beetle, l. bug**, (ent.) luciérnaga, cocuyo.—l. **proof**, a prueba de rayos.—l. **stone**, o **tube**, fulgurita.—l. **switch**, (rad.) interruptor de conexión de la antena con tierra.

lightroom [-rum], *s.* (mar.) pañol de los faroles; lampión (*m.*) de pañol de pólvora; linterna de un faro.

lights [-s], *s. pl.* pulmones, bofes, livianos.

lightship [-šip], *s.* buque faro o fanal.

lightsome [-sʌm], *a.* ligero, airoso; alegre, festivo; luminoso.—**lightsomeness** [-nis], *s.* claridad; alegría, jovialidad.

lightweight [-weit]. I. *a.* de poco peso; ligero (ú. de prendas de vestir); (dep.) de peso ligero (apl. a boxeadores); (fam.) de poca monta. II. *s.* boxeador de peso ligero (entre 127 y 135 libras).

lightwood [-wud], *s.* leña; (E. U. del Sur) pino resinoso. Apl. t. a otras maderas que contienen substancias volátiles inflamables.

lignaloes [lainélouz], *s.* (bot.) lináloe.

ligneous [lígniʌs], *a.* leñoso, lignario.

lignicole [lígnikol], *a.* (ent.) lignícola, que vive en la madera.—**ligniferous** [lignífɛrʌs], *a.* lignífero, leñífero.—**lignification** [-fikéišɔn], *s.* lignificación, conversión en madera.—**lignify** [lígnifai], *va.* y *vn.* lignificar(se), convertir(se) en madera.

lignin [lígnin], *s.* (bot., quím.) lignina.

lignite [lígnait], *s.* (min.) lignito.

lignum-vitæ [lígnʌm váiti], *s.* (bot.) guayaco, guayacán, palo santo.

ligroin(e [lígroin], *s.* ligroína, una de las fracciones del petróleo.

ligula [lígyulǎ], *s.* (bot.) lígula.

ligulate [lígyuleit], *a.* (bot.) ligulado.

ligule [lígyul], *s.* (bot.) lígula.

Ligurian [ligiúriʌn], *s.* y *a.* ligurio.

lik(e)able [láikǎbl], *a.* amable, simpático, agradable.

like [láik]. I. *a.* semejante, parecido, análogo, similar; igual; lo mismo que, equivalente; prometedor; (con **feel**) ganoso o deseoso (de), dispuesto (a) (*V.* FEEL LIKE).—l. **figures**, (geom.) figuras semejantes.—l. **for l.**, en la misma moneda.—l. **master, l. man**, tal para cual.—l.-**minded**, del mismo parecer.—**in l. manner**, análogamente, del mismo modo.—**to be as l. as two peas**, parecerse como dos gotas de agua.—**to be l.**, semejar(se). II. *s.* semejanza; semejante, igual; (con **the**) cosa o persona tal o semejante; gusto, simpatía (gen. en la frase **likes and dislikes**, simpatías y antipatías, gustos y aversiones).—**not to have one's l.**, no tener (uno) igual. III. *adv.* y *prep.* como, semejante a; a (la) manera de, a guisa de, en son de; al igual que, del mismo modo que, a semejanza de; (fam.) probablemente.—l. **a fury**, hecho una furia.—l. **anything**, o **everything**, muchísimo, hasta no más, hasta más no poder, como loco, etc.—l. **as**, (ant.) como, así como.—l. **mad**, como loco, furiosamente, vehementemente.—l. **this**, así, de este modo.—**that is (just) l. him**, eso es muy propio de él.— **what are they l.**? ¿cómo son ellos?

like. I. *va.* gustar de (*he likes the pleasures of the table*, él gusta de los placeres de la mesa); tener gusto en o afición a, hallar agrado en; aprobar; querer, amar, simpatizar con (una persona). Gen. se traduce por *gustar* (o *agradar, parecer bien*), pero con construcción distinta: el nombre o pronombre que en inglés es sujeto, en español es dativo, y el que en inglés es acusativo es en español sujeto: *I like this*, me gusta esto; *do you like music?* ¿le gusta a Vd. la música?; *he likes John and Mary*, le gustan Juan y María. En oraciones subjuntivas o condicionales, puede traducirse análogamente, o por "querer": *I should like to see him*, me gustaría (o quisiera) verlo; *what would you like to eat?* ¿qué quisiera Vd. (o le gustaría a Vd.) comer?—**to l. best, better**, gustar (a uno) más (*I like Japan better than China*, me gusta más el Japón que la China; *I like this best*, me gusta más esto, esto es lo que más me gusta). II. *vn.* (común en autores antiguos) gustar, agradar (*this likes me not*, esto no me gusta).—**as you l.**, como Vd. quiera, como Vd. guste, como le dé la gana.— **if you l.**, si le parece (bien).—**she had l. to die o have died**, (fam.) por poco se muere.

likelihood, likeliness [-lihud, -linis], *s.* probabilidad, verosimilitud; indicación.

likely [-li]. I. *a.* probable, verosímil, fácil; pro-

metedor; apto, idóneo, a propósito. **II.** *adv.*
probablemente.—**l. enough,** no sería extraño.

liken [-n], *va.* asemejar, comparar.

likeness [-nịs], *s.* semejanza, parecido; conformidad, igualdad; apariencia, aire; retrato.

likewise [-waịz], *adv.* también, asimismo, además, igualmente; ítem (más), otrosí.

liking [láịkịŋ], *s.* afición, gusto, agrado, inclinación; simpatía; preferencia.

lilac [láịlạk *o* láịlæk]. **I.** *s.* (bot.) lila, lilac, *f.*
II. *a.* de color de lila, de color morado claro.

liliaceous [lịlịéịṣịạs], *a.* (bot.) liliáceo.

lilied [lílịd], *a.* adornado con lirios.

Lilliputian [lịlịpịúṣạn], *a.* y *s.* liliputiense, enano.

lilt [lịlt]. **I.** *va.* y *vn.* cantar alegremente. **II.** *s.*
jácara; cadencia o movimientos ligeros y rítmicos.

lily [lílị], *s.* (bot.) lirio, azucena; (flor de) lis, *f.*—
l.-livered, cobarde, ruin.—**l. of the valley,**
lirio de los valles, muguete.

lilywort [-wœrt], *s.* (bot.) liliácea.

Lima [láịmạ], *s.*—**L. bean,** (bot.) especie de frísol, judía o haba.—**L. wood,** especie de brasilete.

limacine [límạsaịn], *a.* (zool.) pert. a las babosas.

Limax [láịmæks], *s.* (zool.) babosa, babaza.

limb [lịm]. **I.** *s.* miembro (del cuerpo); rama (de árbol); miembro, individuo; (top., astr., bot.) limbo; borde, orilla; (fam.) joven travieso.
II. *va.* desmembrar, despedazar.

limbed [-d], *a.* membrudo; ramoso.

limber [límbœ(r)]. **I.** *a.* flexible, cimbreño, blando.
II. *s.* (arti.) avantrén de cureña, armón. **III.** *vn.*
(con **up**) ponerse flexible.

limberness [-nịs], *s.* flexibilidad.

limbic [límbịk], *a.* límbico; marginal.

limbless [límlịs], *a.* desmembrado.

limbo [límbou], *s.* limbo; prisión.

limbus [límbạs], *s.* limbo; borde, orilla.

lime [láịm]. **I.** *s.* cal, *f.;* liga; (bot.) limón mejicano, limoncito (limón pequeño muy ácido);
lima (variedad dulce).—**l. burner,** calero.—**l.
nitrogen,** cianamida cálcica.—**l. pit,** calera,
cantera de cal; (ten.) pelambrera.—**l. tree,**
(bot.) lima, limero; tilia, tilo (= LINDEN).—**l.
twig,** vareta. **II.** *va.* encalar; untar o coger con
liga; (alb.) unir con argamasa, mortero o mezcla; (agr.) abonar con cal; (ten.) pelambrar.

limekiln [-kịl(n)], *s.* calera (horno de quemar caliza para extraer la cal).

limelight [-laịt], *s.* luz de calcio; posición conspicua, vista del público.

limen [láịmen], *s.* (psic.) umbral de la conciencia, punto en que un estimulante empieza a producir su efecto en la conciencia.

limerick [límẹrịk], *s.* lira o quintilla jocosa.

limestone [láịmstoụn], *s.* piedra caliza.

limewater [-wotœr)], *s.* agua de cal.

liminal [límịnạl], *a.* (psic.) relativo al umbral.

limit [límịt]. **I.** *s.* límite, término, fin; frontera,
confín, linde(ro); ámbito; aledaño, meta; limitación, restricción; colmo.—**to be the l.,** (fam.)
ser el colmo.—**to the l.,** hasta más no poder.
II. *va.* limitar, fijar; restringir, coartar.

limitable [-ạbl], *a.* limitable, restringible.

limitary [-ẹrị], *a.* limitáneo, fronterizo, limítrofe.

limitation [-éịṣọn], *s.* limitación; coartación, restricción.

limitative [-eịtịv], *a.* limitativo.

limited [-ịd], *a.* limitado, poco, escaso; reducido;
tasado; restricto; finito.—**l. company** (Ltd.),
l.-liability company, compañía de responsabilidad limitada al valor de las acciones de cada
socio.—**l. divorce,** divorcio restringido.—**l.
express,** o **train,** (f. c.) tren compuesto sólo de
coches de primera clase.—**l. partnership,**
sociedad en comandita.

limitedly [-lị], *adv.* limitadamente.

limiting [-ịŋ], *a.* que limita, etc.; restrictivo,
coartador; rayano, aledaño.—**l. adjective,**
(gram.) adjetivo determinativo.

limitless [-lịs], *a.* ilimitado.

limn [lịm], *va.* pintar, iluminar; dibujar; retratar.

limonene [límonin], *s.* (quím.) limoneno.

limonite [láịmonaịt], *s.* (min.) limonita.

limousine [lịmuzín], *s.* (aut.) limousine, *f.*

limp [lịmp]. **I.** *s.* cojera, claudicación. **II.** *a.* débil,
flojo; flexible (cuero, etc.); fláccido, lacio;
blando, débil de carácter. **III.** *vn.* cojear, claudicar, renquear; (mec.) cojear.—**limper** [-œ(r)], *s.*
cojo.

limpet [límpet], *s.* (zool.) lapa, lápade, *f.*

limpid [límpịd], *a.* limpio, cristalino, límpido.

limpidity [lịmpídịtị], **limpidness** [límpịdnịs], *s.*
limpidez, claridad; diafanidad, transparencia.

limping [límpịŋ], *a.* coj(uel)o, claudicante.

limpingly [-lị], *adv.* con cojera, cojeando.

limulus [límyulạs], *s.* (zool.) límulo.

limy [láịmị], *a.* calizo; viscoso, pegajoso.

linaceous [laịnéịṣịạs], *a.* (bot.) lináceo, líneo.

linage [láịnịdʒ], *s.* número de líneas.

linchpin [línchpịn], *s.* sotrozo, pezonera.

linden [líndẹn], *s.* (bot.) tilo, til(i)a, (Ch.) patagua.

line [laịn], *s.* (leng. ord., geom., f. c., mar., mil.,
elec.) línea; (geom.) línea recta (usada sola, la
palabra tiene casi siempre esta acepción); (ing.)
tubería, cañería; raya; veta; renglón; cuerda,
cordel, cabo; sedal (de pescar); frontera, límite;
línea, sucesión; (impr., etc.) línea, renglón;
(com.) renglón, ramo, clase, *f.;* surtido, artículos, *pl.;* (geog.) línea (equinoccial), ecuador;
curso, camino; (f. c., etc.) recorrido, trayecto;
método, plan; línea de conducta o de acción;
rumbo; hilera, fila; verso (una línea); especialidad, conocimientos, *pl.*—*pl.* contornos, apariencia; versos; (teat.) texto de un drama; parte
(*f.*) de un actor; curso, plan, método; (fam.)
certificado de matrimonio.—**l. drawing,** dibujo
de líneas, dibujo instrumental.—**l. engraving,**
(plancha para) grabado al buril.—**l. fishing,**
pesca con sedal y anzuelo.—**l. of apsides,**
(astr.) línea de los ápsides.—**l. of centers,**
(geom.) línea de los centros.—**l. of collimation,** (fís., astr., top.) línea de colimación o de
fe.—**l. of departure,** (arti.) dirección de salida
de un proyectil.—**l. of flotation,** (mar.) línea
de flotación.—**l. of force,** (fís., magn.) línea de
fuerza.—**l. of life,** línea de la vida (en la
quiromancia).—**l. of nodes,** (astr.) línea de los
nodos.—**l. of sight,** visual, *f.*—**l. shaft,** árbol
de transmisión.—**l. spacer,** interlineador (de
máquina de escribir).—**all along the l.,** en
toda la línea, en todos los ramos, abarcándolo
todo.—**along these lines,** en este sentido.—
in a l., en línea.—**in l.,** alineado; de acuerdo;
dispuesto.—**in l. with,** en línea recta con; en
armonía o de acuerdo con.—**in one's l.,** en la
especialidad o dentro de los conocimientos de
uno.—**on the lines of,** conforme a, a tenor de.
—**out of one's l.,** ajeno a la especialidad o
tarea de uno; (asunto) de que uno no entiende.

line. I. *va.* rayar, trazar líneas en; alinear; leer en
alta voz línea por línea; forrar, revestir; estar o
ir a lo largo o en los bordes o las orillas de.—**to
l. out,** marcar con rayas.—**to l. up,** alinear.
II. *vn.* alinearse; estar alineado; (gen. con **up**)
estar en fila, formar fila; formarse, ponerse en
formación.

lineage [línịdʒ], *s.* linaje, prosapia, alcurnia.

lineal [línịạl], *a.* lineal; descendiente, hereditario.

lineament [línịạmẹnt], *s.* lineamento, facción del
rostro.—*pl.* fisonomía.

linear [línịạ(r)], *a.* lineal; longitudinal; (zool. y
bot.) linear.—**l. equation,** ecuación de primer
grado.—**l. measure,** medida de longitud.

lineate(d [línịeịt(ịd], *a.* señalado con líneas.

lineation [-éịṣọn], *s.* delineación.

lined [laịnd], *a.* rayado; forrado.—**l. paper,** papel
rayado.

lineman [láịnmạn], *s.* (f. c., tlg., tlf.) recorredor
y reparador de la línea; (top.) cadenero.

linen [línen], *s.* (tej.) lienzo, lino; holanda; género de lino; ropa blanca.—**l. cambric,** (holán-) batista, cambray.—**l. damask,** damasco de hilo, alemanisco.—**l. draper,** lencero.—**l. goods,** géneros de lino, lencería.—**l. trade,** lencería.—**l. hosiery,** medias de hilo.—**l. prover,** cuentahilos.—**l. weaver,** tejedor de lienzos.

liner [láinœ(r)], *s.* vapor o avión (*m.*) de una línea establecida; delineador; rayador; forrador; forro; forro tubular de quitapón; placa de cuña; en baseball, pelota voleada horizontalmente.

linesman [láinzmạn], *s.* (f. c., tlg., tlf.) = LINE-MAN; juez (*m.*) de línea (en el fútbol, tenis, etc.). —**l.'s detector,** galvanoscopio probador.

line-up, lineup [láinʌp], *s.* formación, agrupación; fila; división definida en grupos o partidos.

ling [liŋ], *s.* (bot.) brezo; (ict.) curadillo.

linger [líŋgœ(r)]. **I.** *vn.* demorarse, dilatarse, ir despacio; subsistir, persistir. **II.** *va.* (con **out** o **away**) prolongar, dilatar, demorar.—**lingerer** [-œ(r)], *s.* el que se demora.

lingerie [lénžri], *s.* ropa blanca; ropa interior (esp. de mujer).

lingering [líŋgœriŋ]. **I.** *a.* lento, prolongado, moroso. **II.** *s.* tardanza, dilación.—**lingeringly** [-li], *adv.* lentamente, con dilación.

lingo [líŋgou], *s.* (fam.) jerga, algarabía.

lingua franca [-fræŋkạ], *s.* lengua franca.

lingual [líŋgwạl]. **I.** *a.* lingual. **II.** *s.* (fon.) letra lingual.

linguadental [liŋgwạdéntạl], *a. y s.* linguodental.

linguiform [líŋgwiform], *a.* lingüiforme, de forma de lengua.

linguist [líŋgwist], *s.* lingüista, poligloto, ladino.

linguistic [liŋgwístik], *a.* lingüístico.

linguistics [-s], *s.* lingüística.

liniment [línimẹnt], *s.* (farm.) linimento, untura.

lining [láiniŋ], *s.* forro; revestimiento; (sast.) tela para forros; camisa (de horno); (aut.) cinta (de freno); (mar.) embono; (min. y mar.) encofrado.

link [liŋk]. **I.** *s.* eslabón; vínculo; enlace, enganche; (top.) 0.01 de cadena de Gunter (201.2 mm.); (mec.) articulación, gozne; vástago de unión o transmisión; cada una de las partes de un sistema articulado; (m. v.) sector de la excéntrica; (fam.) salchichón; (ant.) hacha, antorcha.—*pl.* cancha de golf.—**l. block,** (m. v.) taco del sector de la excéntrica.—**l. fuse,** (elec.) fusible descubierto.—**l. motion,** (m. v.) distribución, sistema o mecanismo de distribución. **II.** *va. y vn.* enlazar(se), eslabonar(se), vincular(se), ligar(se), encadenar(se); unir(se).

linkage [-idž], *s.* eslabonamiento, encadenamiento; unión; (mec.) sistema articulado; (elec.) flujo magnético por espira de un arrollamiento.

linkboy [-boi], **linkman** [-mạn], *s.* paje de hacha.

linking [-iŋ], *s.* eslabonamiento; vinculación.

Linn(a)ean [liníạn], *a.* linneano, de Linneo.

linnet [línit], *s.* (orn.) jilguero, pardillo.

linoleum [linóuljạm], *s.* linóleo.

linotype [láinotaip], *s.* (impr.) linotipo (línea de tipos fundida en una sola pieza); linotipia, máquina de componer y fundir linotipos. (Es nombre de fábrica.)—**linotypist** [-ist], *s.* linotipista.

linseed [línsid], *s.* linaza, simiente (*f.*) de lino.—**l. meal,** harina de linaza.—**l. oil,** aceite de linaza.

linsey-woolsey [línzi wúlzi], *a. y s.* (tej.) (paño) de hilo o algodón y lana mezclados; basto.

linstock [línstak], *s.* botafuego.

lint [lint], *s.* hilacha; hilaza; plumón; (cir.) hilas; red.

lintel [líntẹl], *s.* (arq.) dintel, lintel; umbral; zapata.

linter [líntœ(r)], *s.* máquina desfibradora de algodón ya desmotado.—*pl.* fibra de residuo de algodón desmotado.

linty [línti], *a.* hilachoso.

lion [láiọn], *s.* (zool.) león; persona muy festejada;

(astr.) León.—**l. ant,** = ANT LION.—**l.-heart,** persona valerosa y noble.—**L.-Heart,** Corazón de León (Ricardo I de Inglaterra).—**l.-hearted,** valeroso y noble.—**l.'s share,** la parte del león, lo mejor.—**l.'s tooth,** (bot.) diente de león.

lioness [-is], *s.* (zool.) leona.

lionize [-aiz], *va.* poner en las nubes.

lionlike [-laik], *a.* de león, leonino.

lip [lip]. **I.** *s.* labio; por extensión, boca, habla; labio de una herida; borde; pico de jarro.—**l. devotion,** devoción de boca.—**l. good,** farisaico.—**l. reading,** interpretación del movimiento de los labios.—**l. salve,** ungüento para los labios.—**l. service,** alabanza, defensa o apoyo fingidos, de labios o dientes afuera; homenaje de boca, jarabe de pico.—**l. wisdom,** jarabe de pico, palabras vanas. **II.** *va.* tocar con los labios; besar; lamer (como las olas).

lipoma [lipóumạ], *s.* (med.) lipoma, *m.*

lipomatosis [-tóusis], *s.* degeneración crasa.

lipothymy [lipáθimi], *s.* lipotimia, síncope.

lipped [lipt], *a.* que tiene labios; (bot.) labiado; alabiado (ú. de monedas o medallas).

lipstick [lípstik], *s.* lapiz (*m.*) labial o de labios, barr(it)a de carmín (para pintarse los labios).

liquate [láikweit], *va.* (metal.) licuar, extraer por fusión.—**liquation** [-éišọn], *s.* (metal.) licuación.

liquefaction [likwifǽkšọn], *s.* licuación, licuefacción; liquidación, derretimiento.—**liquefiable** [-faiạbl], *a.* liquidable, licuable, licuefactible.— **liquefier** [-œ(r)], *s.*, **liquefying** [-iŋ], *a.* liquidador.—**liquefy** [-fai], *va. y vn.* liquidar(se), licuar(se), licuefacer(se); derretir(se), fundirse.

liquescence, liquescency [likwésęns, -i], *s.* licuescencia.—**liquescent** [-ęnt], *a.* licuescente.

liqueur [likœ́r], *s.* cordial, licor aromático.

liquid [líkwid], *s. y a.* líquido, flúido; (fon.) (consonante) líquida.—**l. air,** aire líquido o flúido.—**l. assets,** valores realizables.—**l. fire,** (mil.) fuego líquido, petróleo ardiendo.—**l. manure,** (agr.) agua de abono, estiércol líquido.—**l. measure,** medida para líquidos.—**l. securities** = L. ASSETS.

liquidambar [-æmbạr], *s.* liquidámbar.—**l. tree,** (bot.) ocozol, estoraque.

liquidate [-eit], *va.* liquidar, saldar cuentas; (fig.) liquidar, matar o destruir.—**liquidation** [-éišọn], *s.* (com.) liquidación.—**liquidator** [-eitọ(r)], *s.* (for.) liquidador.

liquidity [likwíditi], **liquidness** [líkwidnis], *s.* liquidez, fluidez.

liquor [líkọ(r)], *s.* licor, aguardiente; (farm.) solución, baño, licor.—**l. case,** licorera, cantina, frasquera.—**l. dealer, l. distiller,** licorista.—**l. shop,** licorería.

liquorice, *s.* = LICORICE.

lira [lírạ], *s.* lira (moneda).

lisle [lail], *s.* hilo o tejido de lino o algodón, usado esp. en calcetería y guantería.

lisp [lisp]. **I.** *va. y vn.* cecear; balbucir o balbucear. **II.** *s.* ceceo; balbuceo, balbucencia.

lisper [-œ(r)], *s.* ceceoso, el que cecea.

lisping [-iŋ]. **I.** *s.* ceceo. **II.** *a.* ceceoso; balbuciente.—**lispingly** [-li], *adv.* con ceceo.

lissom(e [lísạm], *a.* = LITHESOME.

list [list]. **I.** *s.* lista, elenco, catálogo, nómina; rol, matrícula; (tej.) orilla, borde del paño; lista, tira, cenefa; (arq.) filete, listel, orla, listón, barandal; (carp.) tabloncillo; (poét.) borde, límite; (mar.) recalcada, inclinación.—*pl.* liza, palestra.—**l. price,** precio de tarifa o corriente, precio de catálogo. **II.** *va.* registrar, poner en lista, matricular, inscribir; catalogar; (com.) cotizar, facturar; (mil.) alistar; cercar (liza) para torneos; guarnecer con listones o cenefas; (poét.) escuchar; (mar.) dar carena al buque. **III.** *vn.* (poét.) escuchar; (mar.) recalcar, acostar, inclinarse a la banda, escorar.

listed [-id], *a.* list(e)ado; (com.) cotizado.

listel [lístel], s. (arq.) listel, listón, filete.
listen [lísn], vn. (a veces con **to**) escuchar, oír; atender, prestar oídos a.—**to l. in**, (tlg., tlf.) escuchar a hurtadillas, intercalar o arreglar un instrumento receptor para enterarse subrepticiamente de comunicaciones enviadas a otras personas; (rad.) escuchar, ser radioyente.
listener [-œ(r)], s. escuchador, oyente.
listening [-iŋ], a. de escuchar, de escucha.—**l. cam, l. key, l. plug**, clavija de intercalación o de escucha, por medio de la cual el telefonista conecta su receptor con el circuito de un suscritor.—**l. post**, escucha.
lister [lístœ(r)], s. (agr.) arado sembrador.
Listerism [lístœrizm], s. listerismo (procedimiento antiséptico).
listing [lístiŋ], s. acción o efecto del verbo TO LIST; orilla de paño, tira, cenefa.
listless [lístlis], a. desatento; indiferente, descuidado.—**listlessly** [-li], adv. indiferentemente.—**listlessness** [-nis], s. descuido, indiferencia.
lit [lit], pret. y pp. de TO LIGHT; (fam.) achispado.
litany [lítani], s. (igl.) letanía.
liter [lítœ(r)], s. litro.
literacy [lítœrasi], s. capacidad de leer y escribir.
literal [lítœral], a. literal; a la letra, al pie de la letra; prosaico; positivista.—**literalism** [-izm], s. exactitud literal; (b. a.) realismo extremo.—**literalist** [-ist], a. y s. escrupulosamente exacto; positivista.—**literally** [-i], adv. literalmente.—**literalness** [-nis], s. exactitud literal; materialidad, positivismo.
literary [lítœreri], a. literario.—**l. property**, propiedad literaria.
literate [lítœrit], a. y s. literato, alfabetizado, alfabetista, que sabe leer y escribir.
literati [litœréitai], s. pl. literatos, doctos, eruditos.
literatim [-tim], adv. letra por letra, a la letra; literalmente.
literature [lítœrachur], s. literatura; obras literarias; trabajo literario; (com.) escritos de publicidad (circulares, catálogos, etc.).
lithagogue [líθagag], a. y s. (med.) litagogo.
litharge [líθardź], s. (quím.) litargirio.
lithate [líθeit], s. (med. y quím.) urato.
lithe [laið], a. flexible, delgado.
lithemia [liθímiä], s. (med.) litemia, exceso de uratos y ácido úrico en la sangre.
litheness [láiθnis], s. flexibilidad, flojedad.
lithesome [-sam], a. (poét.) flexible; ágil.
lithia [líθiä], s. (quím.) litina.
lithiasis [liθáiasis], s. (med.) litiasis, mal de piedra.
lithic [líθik], a. lítico.
lithium [líθiʌm], s. (quím.) litio.
lithograph [líθograef], I. va. litografiar. II. s. litografía (impresión).
lithographer [liθágrafœ(r)], s. litógrafo.
lithographic [liθográefik], a. litográfico.—**l. stone**, piedra litográfica.
lithography [liθágrafi], s. litografía (arte).
lithoid(al [líθoid, líθóidal], a. litoideo.
litholatry [liθálatri], s. culto de las piedras.
lithologic(al [liθoládźik(al], a. litológico.
lithologist [liθálodźist], s. litólogo.
lithology [-dźi], s. (geol.) litología; (med.) tratado sobre los cálculos.
lithontriptic [liθantríptik], a. y s. (med.) litotríptico, litagogo.
lithophyte [líθofait], s. (zool.) litófito.
lithoscope [-skoup], s. (cir.) litoscopio.
lithosperm [-spœrm], s. (bot.) litospermo.
lithosphere [-sfir], s. (geol.) litosfera.
lithotint [-tint], s. cromolitografía, litografía en colores.
lithotomist [liθátomist], s. (cir.) litotomista.
lithotomy [liθátomi], s. (cir.) litotomía, talla.
lithotrite [líθotrait], s. (cir.) litotritor.
lithotrity [liθátriti], s. (cir.) litotricia.
Lithuanian [liθyuéinian], s. y a. lituano.

litigant [lítigant], s. y a. litigante.—**litigate** [-eit], va. y vn. litigar, pleitear.—**litigation** [-éiśon], s. litigación, litigio, pleito.—**litigator** [-o(r)], s. litigante, pleiteador.
litigious [litídźʌs], a. litigioso.—**litigiously** [-li], adv. de un modo litigioso.—**litigiousness** [-nis], s. inclinación a pleitear.
litmus [lítmʌs], s. (quím.) tornasol en pasta.—**l. paper**, papel de tornasol.
litotes [lítotiz], s. (ret.) lítote, f.
litre [lítœ(r)], s. litro.
litter [lítœ(r)]. I. s. litera; camilla, parihuela, andas, pl.; cama de paja para las caballerías; parto; cría, camada, ventregada, lechigada; (fig.) objetos en desorden.—**l. bearer**, camillero, andero. II. va. parir; esparcir, poner en desorden; extender. III. vn. parir (los animales).
litterateur [litœratœr], s. literato.
little [lítl]. I. a. poco; pequeño; insignificante; apocado; despreciable, ruin, mezquino. Se traduce a menudo por una desinencia diminutiva: a little girl, una muchachita; a little watch, un relojito.—**L. Bear, L. Dipper**, (astr.) Osa Menor, Carro Menor, Cinosura.—**l. brain**, (anat.) cerebelo.—**L. Corporal**, Cabito (Napoleón).—**L. Entente**, Pequeña Alianza.—**l. finger, o toe**, dedo meñique.—**l. hours**, (igl.) horas menores.—**l. office**, (igl.) oficio parvo.—**l. one**, párvulo, niñito, muchachito.—**L. Red Ridinghood**, Caperucita Encarnada, o Roja.—**a l.** (seguido de sustantivo), un poco de.—**a l. (bit)**, un poco, un poquito, algún tanto, un tantico. II. adv. poco.—**l. do I care**, maldito lo que me importa. III. s. poco; una porción o parte pequeña.—**l. by l.**, o **by l. and l.**, poco a poco.
littleneck [-nek], s. (zool.) especie de almeja.
littleness [-nis], s. pequeñez, poquedad; ruindad, mezquindad, bajeza.
littoral [lítoral], s. y a. litoral.
liturgic(al [litœrdźik(al], a. (igl.) litúrgico.
liturgics [-s], s. ciencia de la liturgia.—**liturgist** [lítœrdźist], s. docto en la ciencia de la liturgia; liturgista, partidario de la liturgia.
liturgy [lítœrdźi], s. (igl.) liturgia.
livable [lívabl], a. habitable.
live [liv]. I. va. vivir, pasar, llevar (tal o cual vida).—**to l. down**, vivir hasta que se borre u olvide (una falta, un cargo, etc.) o hasta vindicarse de: ver desaparecer u olvidar con el tiempo.—**to l. out**, vivir hasta el fin de, sobrevivir a. II. vn. vivir, existir; habitar, morar, residir; mantenerse, subsistir; (mar.) salvarse.—**to l. downstairs (o upstairs)**, vivir en los bajos (altos).—**to l. fast**, vivir entregado a los placeres.—**to l. from hand to mouth**, vivir al día.—**to l. high**, darse buena vida; darse a los placeres de la mesa.—**to l. in**, vivir (uno) donde trabaja.—**to l. on**, vivir de.—**to l. out**, no vivir en la casa donde sirve (apl. a los criados).—**to l. together**, convivir.—**to l. up to**, vivir en conformidad con.—**to l. up to one's income**, gastarse toda la renta.—**to l. up to one's promise**, cumplir lo prometido.
live [laiv], a. vivo, viviente; de la vida, vital; encendido, en ascua; activo, listo; de interés actual; hirviendo de (fig.), repleto de; (impr.) útil, disponible; (arti.) cargado.—**l. axle**, eje motor.—**l. bait**, carnada viva (apl. esp. a pececillos que sirven de cebo en el anzuelo).—**l. box**, recipiente para el examen de animales microscópicos; cajón perforado para mantener vivos los pescados.—**l. coal**, ascua; brasa de carbón.—**l. load**, carga móvil, carga variable.—**l. oak**, (bot.) encina perenne (siempre verde) norteamericana.—**l. spindle**, huso o tambor (de torno).—**l. steam**, vapor vivo o de la caldera (no de escape).—**l. wire**, (elec.) alambre cargado o activo; (fam.) trafagón, persona lista o de grande actividad.
livelihood [láivlihud], s. vida, subsistencia.

liveliness [-nįs], *s.* vida, vivacidad, viveza, animación; agilidad, actividad.

livelong [lívloŋ], *a.* todo, entero.—**all the l. day**, todo el santo día.

lively [láįvlį]. **I.** *a.* vivo, vivaz, vivaracho; gallardo, airoso; rápido; animado, bullicioso. **II.** *adv.* enérgicamente; vivamente; aprisa.

liver [lívœ(r)], *s.* vividor; (anat., zool.) hígado; higadilla.—**l. complaint**, mal de hígado.—**l. extract**, (farm.) extracto hepático o de hígado.

livered [-d], *a.* de hígado. *V.* WHITE-LIVERED.

liveried [lívœrįd], *a.* que lleva librea.

liverwort [lívœrwœrt], *s.* (bot.) hepática.

liverwurst [-wœrst], *s.* salchicha de hígado.

livery [lívœrį], *s.* librea; uniforme; cochería de alquiler; (for.) entrega, acto de dar posesión de tierras; (ant.) ración.—**l. carriage**, o **l. coach**, carruaje de alquiler.—**l. horse**, caballo de alquiler.—**l. stable**, pensión de caballos; cochería de alquiler.

liveryman [-mąn], *s.* dueño de cochería de alquiler; criado de librea; (Ingl.) individuo de algún gremio.

lives [laįvz], *s. pl.* de LIFE, vidas.

livestock [láįvstak], *s.* ganado, ganadería.

livid [lívįd], *a.* lívido, cárdeno, amoratado.

lividity [livídįtį], **lividness** [lívįdnįs], *s.* lividez.

living [lívįŋ]. **I.** *s.* vida; (modo de) vivir; subsistencia, mantenimiento; vida, potencia vital; (Ingl., igl.) beneficio eclesiástico.—**l. in**, o **out**. *V.* TO LIVE IN, etc.—**the l.**, los vivientes, los vivos. **II.** *a.* y *ger.* vivo, viviente, con vida; animado; contemporáneo.—**l. language**, lengua viva.—**l. quarters**, vivienda.—**l. rock**, roca viva.—**l. room**, estancia, sala de confianza, cuarto general de habitación y recibo.—**l. wage**, (e. p.) salario vital, salario de subsistencia plena (inclusas las necesidades higiénicas, morales e intelectuales del obrero y su familia).

lixivial [lįksívįal], *a.* lixiviado.—**lixiviate** [-eįt], *va.* lixiviar; hacer lejía.—**lixiviation** [-éįşon], *s.* lixiviación.—**lixivium** [-Am], *s.* lixivio, lejía.

lizard [líząrd], *s.* (zool.) lagarto; lagartija; saurio.

llama [lámą], *s.* (zool.) llama.

lo [loų], *interj.* he aquí, cátate, ved aquí, mirad.

loach [loųch], *s.* (ict.) locha, lobo.

load [loųd]. **I.** *s.* carga; peso; (o)presión; (mec.) resistencia; (pint.) adición de color blanco, para obtener opacidad; (fam., gen. *pl.*) montón, montones, gran cantidad o número, muchísimo; (fam.) borrachera.—**l. line**, (mar.) línea de flotación; (mec.) línea o diagrama (*m.*) de cargas. **II.** *va.* y *vn.* cargar; recargar, agregar al premio de un seguro para cubrir ciertos gastos; (pint.) agregar color blanco para producir opacidad.

loader [-œ(r)], *s.* cargador, embarcador.

loading [-įŋ]. **I.** *a.* de cargar; que carga.—**l. coil**, (elec.) bobina que aumenta la inductancia de un circuito; (rad.) bobina de inducción para cambiar la longitud de la onda.—**l. platform**, **siding**, etc., plataforma, vía, etc., de carga. **II.** *s.* carga, cargo, acción de cargar; recargo aumentado al premio de una póliza para cubrir ciertos gastos; (rad.) cambio de la longitud de la onda de un instrumento; (aer.) = WING LOADING.

loadstar [loųdstar], *s.* = LODESTAR.

loadstone [-stoųn], *s.* piedra imán, calamita.

loaf [loųf]. **I.** *s.* (hogaza de) pan; torta; (fam.) = LOAFING.—**l. of sugar**, pan de azúcar.—**l. sugar**, azúcar de pilón. **II.** *vn.* haraganear, holgazanear.

loafer [-œ(r)], *s.* haragán, holgazán, vago, cantonero, arrimón, corrillero.—**loafing** [-įŋ], *s.* haraganería, holgazanería, ociosidad.

loam [loųm]. **I.** *s.* barro, marga; arcilla plástica; (fund.) tierra de moldeo.—**l. pit**, gredal. **II.** *va.* untar con marga; cubrir con arcilla o barro.—**loamy** [-į], *a.* margoso, gredoso, gredal.

loan [loųn]. **I.** *s.* préstamo; prestación, prestimonio; (com.) empréstito; (for.) mutuo, como-

dato.—**l. office**, casa de préstamos o empeños. —**l. shark**, (fam.) usurero. **II.** *va.* prestar.

loath [loųθ], *a.* poco dispuesto, renuente.

loathe [loųð]. **I.** *va.* detestar, abominar. **II.** *vn.* tener hastío, sentir fastidio, disgusto o aborrecimiento.—**loather** [-œ(r)], *s.* el que siente disgusto o aborrecimiento.—**loathful** [-fųl], *a.* lleno de tedio o aversión.—**loathing** [-įŋ], *s.* aversión, asco, hastío, repugnancia.—**loathingly** [-lį], *adv.* de mala gana, con repugnancia. —**loathsome** [-sʌm], *a.* aborrecible, repugnante, asqueroso.—**loathsomely** [-lį], *adv.* asquerosamente.—**loathsomeness** [-nįs], *s.* calidad de repugnante o asqueroso.

loaves [loųvz], *s. pl.* de LOAF.

lob [lab]. **I.** *s.* lombriz para cebo; en tenis, voleo alto y tendido de la pelota; en el *cricket*, voleo bajo. **II.** *va.* hacer un *lob* con la pelota.

lobar [loųbą(r)], *a.* lobular.

lobate(d [loųbeįt(įd], *a.* lobulado.

lobby [lábį]. **I.** *s.* paso, pasillo, corredor; salón de entrada (de un hotel); antecámara, vestíbulo; pórtico; (E. U., pol.) camarilla de cabilderos. **II.** *va.* y *vn.* (E. U., pol.) cabildear.

lobbying [-įŋ], *s.* (E. U., pol.) cabildeo.

lobbyist [-įst], *s.* (E. U., pol.) cabildero.

lobe [loųb], *s.* (anat., zool., bot.) lóbulo, lobo; lóbulo, perilla o pulpejo de la oreja; (aer.) saco de gas; compartimiento.

lobed [-d], *a.* lobado, lobulado.

lobelia [lobílją], *s.* (bot.) lobelia.

lobeliaceous [-lįéįšąs], *a.* lobeliáceo.

lobster [lábstœ(r)], *s.* (zool.) bogavante, cabrajo, langosta americana (con pinzas grandes).— **spiny l.**, langosta.

lobulate [lábyųleįt], *a.* lobulado.

lobule [lábjul], *s. dim.* lobulillo, lóbulo pequeño.

local [loųkąl]. **I.** *a.* local; vecinal; regional.—**l. attraction**, (top.) atracción anormal, perturbación (de la brújula) debida a la presencia de hierro en la vecindad; (fís., etc.) atracción de la plomada (por montañas, etc.).—**l. battery**, (tlg.) batería local, batería del receptor.—**l. call**, (tlf.) llamada urbana.—**l. color**, color local.—**l. government**, autonomía en asuntos puramente locales.—**l. horizon**, horizonte sensible.—**l. option**, (E. U.) derecho u obligación de una división territorial (distrito, ciudad, etc.) de establecer por sí y para sí ciertas ordenanzas (esp. las relativas a la venta de licores).—**l. remedy**, (med.) remedio tópico o externo.—**l. time**, hora local, tiempo local.—**l. train**, (f. c.) tren ómnibus, suburbano o de escala; tren que circula sólo en un tramo de un ferrocarril.—**l. value**, (arit.) valor relativo (de una cifra). **II.** *s.* (f. c.) = LOCAL TRAIN; sucursal (*f.*) de confraternidad, gremio obrero, etc.; (fam.) noticia de interés local.

locale [lokál], *s.* situación; localidad.

localism [loųkąlįzm], *s.* localismo; costumbre o locución local; provincialismo.

locality [lokélįtį], *s.* situación; localidad; lugar.

localization [loųkąlįzéįşon], *s.* localización.

localize [-aįz], *va.* localizar.

locally [-lį], *adv.* localmente.

locate [loųkeįt]. **I.** *va.* poner, colocar, situar, ubicar; (f. c.) trazar la vía de. **II.** *vn.* (fam.) establecerse, fijar su residencia.—**located** [-įd], *a.* sito, situado, ubicado.

location [lokéįşon], *s.* ubicación, colocación; sitio, localidad; situación, posición; (f. c.) trazado de la vía.

locative [lákątįv], *a.* y *s.* (gram.) locativo.

loch [lak], *s.* (Esco.) lago; ensenada.

lochia [loųkįą], *s. pl.* (med.) loquios.

lock [lak]. **I.** *s.* cerradura, cerraja; llave, *f.* (de las armas de fuego); chaveta; esclusa, compuerta; cámara de aire comprimido; abrazo estrecho y apretado; cerca, vallado; bucle, guedeja, mecha (de pelo); borla; vedija, vellón (de lana).—*pl.* cabellos.—**l. nut**, (mec.) contratuerca, tuerca de seguridad.—**l. step**, modo de andar un grupo a paso muy cerrado.—**l. stitch**, punto de cadeneta.—**l., stock and barrel**, (fam.) el todo; por completo.—**l. washer**, (mec.) arandela de seguridad.—**under l. and key**, bajo llave. II. *va.* cerrar con llave, acerrojar, candar; poner cerradura; hacer pasar por una esclusa; juntar, atar, entrelazar, trabar; (impr.) acuñar, cerrar la forma; abrazar; fijar, trincar; cerrar.—**to l. in**, encerrar, poner bajo llave; abrazar.—**to l. (one) out**, cerrar la puerta a uno; dejar en la calle; dejar sin trabajo. *V.* LOCKOUT.—**to l. up**, encerrar; encarcelar. III. *vn.* cerrarse con llave; unirse, enlazarse; trabarse; sujetarse.

lockage [lákįdz], *s.* materiales u obra de una esclusa; diferencia de nivel en un canal de esclusas; derechos o portazgo de esclusa.

locker [lákœ(r)], *s.* cajón, gaveta; alacena, ropero, armario; cerrador.—*pl.* (mar.) cajonada.

locket [lákįt], *s.* guardapelo, relicario, medallón.

locking [lákįŋ]. I. *s.* cierre; fijación; traba(dura). II. *a.* fijador, de fijación; de cierre; de traba.—**l. plate**, platillo fijador.—**l. wire**, (aer.) alambre fijador.

lockjaw [lákdžo], *s.* (med.) trismo, tétano(s).

locknut [láknʌt], *s.* = LOCK NUT.

lockout [lákaut], *s.* cierre (de fábrica); paro forzoso impuesto por los patronos; *lockout.*

lockram [lákram], *s.* (tej.) lienzo basto.

locksmith [láksmįθ], *s.* cerrajero.—**l.'s shop, o trade**, cerrajería.

lockup [lákʌp], *s.* calabozo; cárcel, *f.*; encarcelamiento.

locomobile [loukomóųbįl], *a.* y *s.* locomóvil, *f.*

locomotion [-móųşǫn], *s.* locomoción.

locomotive [-móųtįv]. I. *a.* locomotor, locomóvil. II. *s.* locomotora.—**l. boiler**, caldera de locomotora o de tipo locomotora.—**l. engine**, (máquina) locomotora.

locomotor [-móųtǫ(r)], *a.* locomotor, locomotriz.—**l. ataxia**, (med.) ataxia locomotriz.

locoweed [-wid], *s.* (bot.) una hierba venenosa.

locular [lákyŭlą(r)], *a.* locular, que tiene celdillas.

loculus [-lʌs], *s.* (biol.) lóculo, celdilla, cavidad.

locust [lóųkʌst], *s.* (ent.) langosta, langostón; saltamontes; (E. U.) cigarra.—**l., o l. tree**, (bot.) curbaril, robinia; algarrobo.—**l. bean**, algarroba.

locution [lokįúşǫn], *s.* locución; frase(ología).

locutory [lákyŭtǫrį], *s.* (igl.) locutorio.

lode [lóųd], *s.* (min.) filón, veta, vena, venero.

lodestar [-star], *s.* estrella de guía; estrella polar; Cinosura.

lodestone [-stoųn], *s.* piedra imán, calamita.

lodge [ládž]. I. *va.* alojar, hospedar, albergar; colocar; plantar, introducir, fijar; dar a guardar, poner a recaudo.—**to l. a complaint**, dar una queja. II. *vn.* vivir, morar, parar, hospedarse; tenderse, echarse. III. *s.* casa de guarda; pabellón; portería (de portero); casilla o casita accesoria; logia (de los francmasones, etc.).

lodg(e)ment [-mǫnt], *s.* colocación; hospedamiento; alojamiento; amontonamiento, acumulación; (mil.) posición establecida; atrincheramiento.

lodger [-œ(r)], *s.* huésped, *m.*, inquilino.

lodging [-įŋ], *s.* posada, hospedería; vivienda; albergue; hospedaje, (mil.) alojamiento; habitación, morada, residencia.—**l. house**, alberguería; casa de huéspedes o de pupilos.—**to take lodgings (in)**, alojarse, hospedarse (en).

loft [lɔft], *s.* piso, sobrado, desván; almacén.

loftily [-įlį], *adv.* elevadamente, levantadamente; hinchadamente.

loftiness [-įnįs], *s.* altura, elevación; excelsitud; altanería, orgullo; majestad.

lofty [-į], *a.* alto, altísimo, elevado, encumbrado; eminente, excelso; altivo, orgulloso.

log [lɔg]. I. *s.* leño, palo; tronco, t(r)oza, madero, rollo; (mar.) corredera; barquilla de la corredera (ll. t. **l. chip**).—**l. board**, (mar.) tableta de

bitácora.—**l. book**, cuaderno de bitácora; diario de navegación.—**l. cabin, l. hut**, cabaña rústica, (Am.) caney.—**l. driver, ganchero.—l. line**, (mar.) corredera.—**l. raft**, armadía.—**l. reel, carretel, devanadera. II. *va.* cortar (madera) en trozas y transportar; arrastrar (madera); (mar.) apuntar en el cuaderno de bitácora; indicar (cierta velocidad) en la corredera. III. *vn.* cortar, aserrar y transportar trozas; extraer madera.

loganberry [lóųgạnbęrį], *s.* (bot.) especie de zarzamora.

logarithm [lógạrįθm], *s.* (mat.) logaritmo.

logarithmic(al [-rįθmįk(ạl], *a.* logarítmico.

logbook, *s.* = LOG BOOK.

loge [louž], *s.* palco (de teatro).

logger [lógǫ(r)], *s.* talador, hachero, leñero; individuo o máquina que hacen el *logging.*

loggerhead [lógœrhęd], *s.* zote, necio; (zool.) tortuga marina (ll. t. **l. turtle**).—**at loggerheads**, en desacuerdo, en disputa; de uñas.

loggia [ládžą], *s.* (arq.) pórtico, galería abierta.

logging [lógįŋ], *s.* corte y transporte de trozas.

logia [lágįą], *s. pl.* de LOGION: máximas y palabras atribuidas a Jesucristo pero que no se hallan en los libros canónicos.

logic [ládžįk], *s.* lógica, dialéctica.—**logical** [-ạl], *a.* lógico, dialéctico; consecuente, natural.—**logically** [-į], *adv.* lógicamente.

logician [lodžíşạn], *s.* lógico, dialéctico.

logistics [lodžístįks], *s.* (mil.) logística, arte de transportes y abastecimientos.

logman [lógmạn], *s.* leñero, hachero. *V.* LOGGER.

logogram [lógogræm], *s.* abreviatura o signo que indica una palabra, como **lb., £, $**; logogrifo.

logography [logágrạfį], *s.* logografía.

logogriph [lógogrif], *s.* logogrifo, enigma, *m.*

logomachy [logámạkį], *s.* logomaquia; juego de formar anagramas.

Logos [lágạs], *s.* (teol.) Verbo; (fil.) el principio racional del universo.

logotype [lógotaįp], *s.* (impr.) logotipo.

logroll [lógroųl], *vn.* hacer rodar tozas; (pol., E. U.) entrar en o hacer por contubernio de ayuda recíproca (*V.* LOGROLLING).

logroller [-œ(r)], *s.* el que forma contubernio u obra por contubernio de ayuda recíproca.

logrolling [-įŋ], *s.* tarea de rodar tozas; contubernio de ayuda recíproca y trueque de votos, en que varios políticos convienen en apoyarse mutuamente, sobre todo en proyectos de ley propuestos en un cuerpo legislativo.

logwood [lógwụd], *s.* palo de Campeche o de tinte.

loin [loįn], *s.* (anat.) lomo.—**l. of beef**, etc., filete, salomillo, falda.—**to gird up one's loins**, apercibirse para la acción.

loincloth [-kloθ], *s.* pampanilla, taparrabo.

loiter [lóįtœ(r)]. I. *vn.* remolonear, ociar, holgazanear, haraganear, vagar. II. *va.* (con **away**) malgastar (tiempo).—**loiterer** [-œ(r)], *s.* vagabundo, haragán u holgazán.—**loitering** [-įŋ]. I. *a.* vago, haragán. II. *s.* vagancia.

loll [lal]. I. *vn.* apoyarse, recostarse, tenderse; pender, colgar, estar colgando (la lengua de un animal). II. *va.* dejar colgar (la lengua).

lollypop [lálįpạp], *s.* dulce en palito; variedad de caramelo, melcocha o arropía.

Lombard [lámbạrd], *s.* y *a.* lombardo.

Londoner [lándǫnœ(r)], *s.*, **Londonese** [-ís], *a.* londinense, londonense.

lone [loųn], *a.* solitario, solo; soltero.—**loneliness** [-lįnįs], *s.* soledad; tristeza del aislamiento.—**lonely** [-lį], *a.* solitario; solo, señero; triste.—**loneness** [-nįs], *s.* soledad; tristeza.

lonesome [-sʌm], *a.* solitario, desierto; triste.—**lonesomely** [-lį], *adv.* solitariamente; tristemente.—**lonesomeness** [-nįs], *s.* soledad; tristeza.

long [lɔŋ]. I. *a.* largo, luengo; de largo (a veces con *to be*, que entonces es tener: *this tape is 2* *inches long*, esta cinta tiene 2 pulgadas de largo); extenso, prolongado; tardío, dilatorio; excesivo, de más; remoto, distante; (com.) recargado, esperando alza de precios (apl. esp. al tenedor de valores de bolsa).—**l. clothes**, ropa talar; ropón de niño, pañales.—**l.-cut tobacco**, tabaco en hebras.—**l.-distance**, (tlf.) de larga distancia (apl. gen. a comunicaciones más allá de los límites dentro de los cuales se paga el abono ordinario); (dep.) de fondo (apl. a las carreras).—**l. division**, (arit.) división en que se escriben los productos parciales, división no abreviada.—**l. dozen**, docena del fraile; trece. —**l. hundred**, ciento veinte.—**l. measure**, medida de longitud.—**L. Parliament**, (hist.) Parlamento Largo.—**l. primer**, (impr.) entredós, letra de 10 puntos.—**l. staple**, fibra o hebra larga.—**l. stride**, zancada.—**l. suffering**, paciencia, resignación o fortitud en el sufrimiento.—**l. suit**, especialidad, fuerte (aquello en que uno sobresale).—**l. ton**, tonelada de 2240 libras (1.016,06 kg.).—**a l. time**, mucho tiempo, un largo rato.—**how l.**, de qué largo (medida). II. *adv.* a gran distancia; mucho, (durante) mucho tiempo.—**l. after**, mucho (tiempo) después.—**l. ago**, hace mucho, mucho (tiempo) ha.—**l.-bearded**, barbiluengo.—**l.-drawn**, lento, pesado, prolongado.—**l.-eared**, orejudo.—**l.-faced**, carilargo; (fam.) cariacontecido.—**l.-haired**, pelilargo.—**l.-headed**, dolicocéfalo; astuto, listo, sagaz.—**l.-legged**, zanquilargo.—**l. live!** ¡viva!—**l.-lived**, longevo, de larga vida.—**l.-necked**, cuellilargo.—**l.-range**, de largo alcance, de grandes alcances.—**l.-shanked** = L.-LEGGED.—**l.-sighted**, présbite; sagaz, previsor, precavido.—**l. since** = L. AGO. —**l.-standing**, de larga duración.—**l.-stapled**, de hebra larga.—**l.-suffering**, doliente, afligido; sufrido, paciente en el sufrimiento.—**l.-term**, (com.) a largo plazo.—**l.-tongued**, lenguaraz, chismoso.—**l.-winded**, largo, pesado, prolijo.—**all, o the whole, day, year**, etc., **l.**, todo el santo día, año, etc.—**as l. as**, mientras. —**before, o ere, l.**, en breve, antes de mucho. —**how l.**, cuánto tiempo.—**how l. is it since?** ¿cuánto (tiempo) hace que?—**not l. ago, o since**, no ha mucho.—**not l. before**, poco tiempo antes.—**so l. as**, mientras que, en tanto que. III. *s.* longitud, largo; (mús.) longa; (pros.) sílaba larga.—*pl.* (com.) los que guardan acciones en espera de alza.—**the l. and the short**, el meollo, la substancia. IV. *vn.* (con **for** o **to**) anhelar, suspirar (por), codiciar, apetecer, ansiar, desear con ansia; añorar.

longboat [lóŋboṵt], *s.* lancha, chalupa, falúa.
longbow [lóŋboṵ], *s.* arco para disparar flechas. —**to draw the l.**, exagerar, decir patrañas.
longe [lʌndž], *s.* (esgr.) estocada; pista; cuerda larga para adiestrar caballos.
longer [lóŋgœ(r)], **I.** *a. comp.* de LONG; más largo. II. *adv.* más tiempo, más rato.—**how much l.**, cuánto tiempo más.—**no l.**, ya no; no más.
longeron [lándžœran], *s.* (aer.) larguero.
longest [lóŋgịst], *a. y adv. super.* de LONG.—**at the l.**, a más tardar, cuando más.
longeval, longevous [lóndžíval, -as], *a.* longevo.
longevity [londžévịtị], *s.* longevidad.
longhand [lóŋhænd], *s.* escritura corrida, sin abreviaturas.
longhorn [-horn], *s.* animal cuernilargo (apl. esp. a ciertas razas de ganado vacuno).
longicorn [lándžịkorn], *a. y s.* (zool.) longicornio.
longimanous [landžímanʌs], *a.* (zool.) longimano.
longing [lóŋịŋ]. I. *s.* deseo vehemente, anhelo, ansia, ansiedad, pujo. II. *a.* anhelante, anheloso, ansioso, vehemente.
longingly [-lị], *adv.* vehementemente, anhelantemente.
longipennate [landžípéneịt], *s. y a.* (zool.) longi-

penne, de largas alas.—**longirostral [-rástral]**, *s. y a.* longirrostro, de largo pico.
longish [lóŋịš], *a.* algo largo, largucho.
longitude [lándžịtịud], *s.* (geog.) longitud.
longitudinal [-tịúdịnal]. I. *a.* longitudinal. II. *s.* (aer.) larguero.
longitudinally [-ị], *adv.* longitudinalmente, a lo largo.
Longobard [láŋgobard], *s.*, **Longobardian** [-bárdịan], *a.* longobardo. *V.* LOMBARD.
longshoreman [lóŋšorman], *s.* estibador, trabajador de muelle.
longspun [lóŋspʌn], *a.* = LONG-DRAWN. *V.* LONG.
longways [lóŋweịz], **longwise** [-waịz], *adv.* = LENGTHWISE.
loo [lu], *s.* cierto juego de naipes.
look [lúk]. I. *va.* mirar, pasar la vista a; causar (vergüenza, silencio, etc.) en, con la mirada; expresar, indicar con la mirada o el ademán.— **to l. a gift horse in the mouth**, mirarle el diente a caballo regalado.—**to l. daggers**, echar chispas; (con at) mirar con amenaza, o echando chispas.—**to l. in the face**, mirar cara a cara; mirar sin vergüenza.—**to l. one's age**, representar uno los años que tiene.—**to l. over**, examinar someramente, repasar, dar o echar un vistazo a, hojear (un libro, etc.).—**to l. up**, buscar, averiguar; (fam.) visitar (a uno). II. *vn.* mirar, ver; parecer, aparentar; poner cuida.lo; tener cuidado; lucir (bien o mal); tener o estar de buen o mal semblante o aspecto, tener cara de (sueño, cansado, etc.).—**to l. about**, mirar alrededor; observar.—**to l. about one**, estar alerta, tener vigilancia.—**to l. after**, cuidar, atender a, mirar (por), tener cuidado de; prestar atención; buscar, inquirir, investigar.—**to l. alike**, parecerse.—**to l. alive**, darse prisa.— **to l. at**, mirar, ver; tender la vista a; considerar; atender.—**to l. back**, reflexionar; mirar atrás.—**to l. down upon**, despreciar.—**to l. for**, esperar; buscar.—**to l. forward**, prever; mirar al o pensar en el porvenir.—**to l. forward to**, esperar.—**to l. into**, examinar, estudiar, averiguar.—**to l. like**, parecerse a; tener cara o traza de; dar o haber señales de (mejor es cambiar el giro: *it looks like rain*, parece que va a llover).—**to l. on**, considerar, estimar, juzgar; mirar, ver; ser espectador; dar o caer a.— **to l. out**, tener cuidado; (*l. out!* ¡cuidado! ¡guarda! ¡ojo!).—**to l. out for**, buscar; esperar; tener cuidado con.—**to l. out of**, asomarse a.— **to l. sharp**, tener ojo avizor.—**to l. through**, examinar, inspeccionar, hacer un registro de. —**to l. to**, cuidar de, velar por; atender a; hacer responsable; esperar de; acudir a.—**to l. up**, mirar hacia arriba; (fam.) mejorarse; alzarse (precios).—**to l. upon**, considerar, contemplar; estimar, dar o caer a.—**to l. up to**, respetar, estimar.—**as it looks to me**, a mi ver. III. *s.* mirada, ojeada, vistazo; (gen. *pl.*) aspecto, apariencia, semblante, cara, aire, ademán, traza, (fam.) pergeño.—**to have a l. at**, mirar, echar una ojeada a.
looker, looker-on [-œ(r), -œrán], *s.* mirador; mirón, espectador.
looking [-ịŋ]. I. *s.* miramiento; busca; examen, consideración. II. *a.* de para mirar.—**l. glass**, espejo.—**good (bad)-l.**, bien (mal) parecido, guapo, buen mozo (feo).
lookout [-aṵt], *s.* vigía, vigilancia; observación; mirador, garita, atalaya; avizorador, guardia, *mf.*, vigía, *mf.*, centinela, *mf.*—**that's his l.**, (fam.) eso le concierne a él; allá él, con su pan se lo coma.—**to be on the l.**, estar a la mira.
loom [lum]. I. *s.* telar; arte de tejer; (mar.) guión (*m.*) del remo; presencia, aparición.—**l. shuttle**, lanzadera mecánica. II. *va.* tejer. III. *vn.* asomar, aparecer en forma indistinta o exagerada; descollar, destacarse; (re)lucir.
looming [lúmịŋ], *s.* (ópt.) espejismo.
loon [lun], *s.* bobo, tonto; (orn.) somorgujo.

loony [lúni], *s.* y *a.* (fam.) bobo, loco rematado.

loop [lúp]. I. *s.* gaza, lazo, bucle; (cost., etc.) ojal, presilla, alamar; onda; punto; curva, vuelta; (mec.) abrazadera, anilla; (aer.) rizo; (f. c.) vuelta (de un desarrollo).—l. **aerial, o antenna**, (rad.) antena de cuadro.—l.-**the-l.**, (aer.) rizo; ferrocarril centrífugo con espiras verticales. II. *va.* asegurar con presilla; hacer gazas en; formar festones o curvas en.—**to l. in**, (elec.) intercalar (en un circuito).—**to l. the l.**, (aer.) hacer o rizar el rizo, dar una vuelta vertical. III. *vn.* andar haciendo curvas; formar gaza.

looper [-œ(r)], *s.* engazador; (ent.) = MEASURING WORM.

loophole [-hoųl], *s.* abertura, mirador; (fort.) aspillera, tronera; escapatoria, excusa.

loopholed [-d], *a.* que tiene troneras o aspilleras.

loose [lús]. I. *va.* desatar, desprender; desliar; aflojar; aliviar; soltar, libertar, librar; desenredar; desocupar.—**to l. one's hold**, soltar. II. *a.* suelto; desatado, desenredado; flojo, holgado; vago, indefinido; libre, relajado, disoluto; suelto, en libertad; descuidado, negligente, remiso.—l.-**bodied**, suelto, ancho, holgado (vestido).—l. **in the bowels**, suelto de vientre.— l.-**jointed**, desvencijado; suelto de coyunturas; de articulación o movimiento libre.—l.-**leaf**, de hojas sueltas o insertables (cuaderno, libro, etc.).—l. **morals**, moral relajada.—l. **pulley**, (mec.) polea loca.—l.-**reined**, a rienda suelta. —**at l. ends**, en desorden.—**to let, set, o turn l.**, soltar, libertar. *V.* TO BREAK, CUT, GET, HANG, WORK, etc. III. *s.* libertad; soltura. —**on the l.**, (fam.) libre; sin trabas; de holgorio, de parranda.

loosely [-li], *adv.* suelta o flojamente; sin cohesión; vaga o indefinidamente.

loosen [-ṇs], I. *va.* aflojar, soltar, desunir, desatar, desligar; solver; largar; laxar, relajar; ablandar; librar, libertar; soltar el vientre. II. *vn.* desunirse, aflojarse, desatarse, desasirse, separarse.

looseness [-ṇs], *s.* aflojamiento, flojedad, holgura; relajación, licencia; soltura; flujo de vientre; vaguedad.

loosening [-ṇiŋ]. I. *a.* laxante, relajante. II. *s.* aflojamiento, desatadura, desprendimiento, suelta; laxación, laxamiento, relajación.

loosestrife [-straif], *s.* (bot.) lisimaquia, salicaria.

loot [lút]. I. *va.* y *vn.* saquear; pillar; llevarse como botín. II. *s.* botín; saqueo, pillaje.— **looter** [-œ(r)], *s.* saqueador.—**looting** [-iŋ], *s.* saque(amient)o.

lop [lap]. I. *va.* (a veces con **off**) (des)mochar, (cha)podar; maestrear; cercenar, descabezar, descopar. II. *vn.* colgar, pender, caer flojamente. III. *s.* desmocha(dura); ramas podadas.—l.-**eared**, de orejas gachas o caídas.

lope [loųp]. I. *va.* y *vn.* (hacer) galopar o andar a paso largo y sentado. II. *s.* medio galope.

lophobranch [lóųfobræŋk], *a.* y *s.* (zool.) lofobranquio.

lopping [lápiŋ], *s.* poda, desmoche, chapado.—*pl.* desmocho.

lopsided [lapsáidid], *a.* más pesado de un lado que de otro; desequilibrado, desproporcionado.

loquacious [lokwéiʃʌs], *a.* locuaz, lenguaz.

loquaciousness [-ṇs], **loquacity** [lokwǽsiti], *s.* locuacidad, habladuría, charla, garrulidad.

lord [lórd]. I. *s.* señor; amo, dueño, patrón; castellano (de un castillo); marido; (Ingl.) lord (*pl.* lores).—**L.!**, o **good L.!** ¡Dios mío! ¡por Dios! —**L. Chamberlain**, camarero mayor.—**L. Chief Justice**, presidente del tribunal supremo de Inglaterra.—**L. High Chancellor**, ministro de justicia, o gran canciller.—**L. High Steward**, mayordomo mayor.—**L. Lieutenant**, virrey y gobernador de Irlanda.—**L. Mayor**, alcalde o corregidor de Londres.—**L. Privy Seal**, guardasellos.—**L.'s day**, domingo, día (*m.*) del Señor.—**L.'s Prayer**, padre nuestro.—

L.'s Supper, la última cena; Sacramento de la Eucaristía.—**L.'s table**, altar de la sagrada comunión; comunión, Eucaristía.—**Our L.**, Nuestro Señor.—**the L.**, el Señor.—**the L. of hosts**, Jehová.—**the Lords**, Cámara de los Lores. II. *va.* y *vn.* investir con la dignidad de lord; dar el título de lord; gobernar, mandar imperiosamente.—**to l. it over**, dominar, (en)señorear, mandar despótica o altaneramente, imponerse a.

lordliness [-liṇs], *s.* dignidad, señorío; altivez, orgullo.

lordling [-(l)iŋ], *s.* (desp.) hidalguillo, señorito, pequeño lord.

lordly [-li]. I. *a.* perteneciente a un lord; señoril; orgulloso, imperioso. II. *adv.* señorilmente; altiva o imperiosamente.

lordosis [lordóųsis], *s.* (med.) lordosis, encorvamiento de la columna vertebral de convexidad anterior.

lordship [lórdʃip], *s.* señorío, dominio, poder; señoría, excelencia.—**your l.**, usía; vuecencia.

lore [lor], *s.* erudición, saber, ciencia.

lorgnette [lornyét], *s.* impertinentes, *m. pl.;* gemelos de teatro con mango.

lorgnon [lornyón], *s.* = PINCE-NEZ.

lorica [loráikǝ], *s.* (arm.) loriga; (zool.) cubierta protectora.

loricate [lárikeit]. I. *va.* enchapar, planchear; esmaltar. II. *a.* lorigado; planchado, enchapado.

lorication [-éiʃǫn], *s.* enchapado; esmalte.

lorikeet [lárikit], *s.* (orn.) especie de perico.

loriot [lárjǝt], *s.* (orn.) oropéndola.

loris [lóųris], *s.* (zool.) especie de lemur.

lorn [lorn], *a.* sin parientes ni amigos. *V.* FORLORN.

lorry [lóri], *s.* (Ingl.) (auto)camión, *m.;* carro fuerte, carro de plataforma de cuatro ruedas.

lory [lóųri], *s.* (orn.) especie de loro o perico.

los(e)able [lúzǝbl], *a.* fácil de perder, perdidoso.

lose [lúz]. I. *va.* (*pret.* y *pp.* LOST) perder; malograr, malgastar (tiempo, etc.); entregar a la ignominia o a la ruina; quitar, hacer perder.— **to l. face**, desprestigiarse.—**to l. ground**, perder terreno.—**to l. heart**, desanimarse.— **to l. one's heart**, enamorarse.—**to l. one's mind**, enloquecerse.—**to l. one's temper**, perder los estribos, encolerizarse.—**to l. one's way**, perderse, andar perdido, desorientarse.— **to l. sight of**, perder de vista. II. *vr.* perderse, extraviarse. III. *vn.* perder, tener una pérdida; atrasar (un reloj).—**to l. out**, (fam.) llevarse chasco, ser derrotado.

loser [-œ(r)], *s.* perdedor, el que pierde algo o no logra lo que desea.—**losing** [-iŋ], *a.* perdidoso, perdedor, que pierde; vencido.

loss [los], *s.* pérdida; perdición; daño; privación; (com., etc.) siniestro.—l. **of face**, desprestigio. —**at a l.**, perdiendo, con pérdida; perplejo, indeciso, dudoso, en duda, sin saber qué hacer. —**at a l. to**, sin acertar a.—**it's your l.**, (fam.) Vd. se lo pierde.

lost [lost], *a.* y *pret.* y *pp.* de TO LOSE; perdido; extraviado, descarriado; desorientado; perplejo; malogrado; desperdiciado.—l. **cause**, causa desesperada; (hist. E. U.) la causa de los esclavistas.—l. **in thought**, absorto.—l. **motion**, (mec.) juego inútil, juego muerto, pérdida debida a conexiones flojas o inadecuadas.—l. **or not l.**, (com.) cláusula especial del seguro que cubre todos los riesgos.—l. **to**, insensible a; perdido para.—**not to be l. on, o upon**, no dejar de aprovechar a, no pasar inadvertido por.

lot [lat]. I. *s.* suerte, *f.*, hado, sino; lote, cuota, partija, partida, parte, *f.*, porción; solar de terreno; (fam., a veces *pl.*) gran cantidad; mucho(s); la mar de.—**a bad l.**, (fam.) mala persona; taifa.—**to cast, o throw in one's l. with**, compartir la suerte de. II. *va.* asignar, repartir (a veces por sorteo). III. *vn.* echar suertes.

lota(h [lóuṭä], s. escudilla de cobre.

loth [louθ], a. = LOATH.

Lothario [loθériou], s. libertino, seductor, Tenorio.

lotion [lóuṣon], s. (farm.) loción, agua.

lotos o **lotus** [lóuṭʌs], s. (bot.) loto, ninfea.—**l.-eater**, **l.-eating**, lotófago.—**l. tree**, loto, almez(o).

lottery [látœri], s. lotería, rifa.

lotto [látou], s. lotería, juego casero.

loud [láuḍ]. I. a. ruidoso, fuerte, recio; alta (la voz); (mús.) forte; turbulento, estrepitoso; (fam.) urgente; (fam.) charro, chillón, vulgar, llamativo, subido (colores, etc.).—**l. laugh**, risotada, carcajada.—**l.-voiced**, estentóreo. II. adv. ruidosamente, con ruido; en alta voz, a gritos.

loudly [-li], adv. ruidosamente, recio; en alta voz.

loudness [-nis], s. ruido, sonoridad; (fam.) vulgaridad, mal gusto.

loud-speaker [-spíkœ(r)], s. (radtlf.) altavoz, m., altoparlante; megáfono, amplificador de voz.

lough [lak], s. lago, laguna.

louis [lúi], s. luis de oro (moneda francesa).

lounge [láundž]. I. vn. haraganear, holgazanear, callejear; tenderse, repantigarse; ponerse uno a sus anchas. II. s. haraganería, holgazanería; sofá, m., canapé, yacija; salón de fumar.

lounger [-œ(r)], s. holgazán; azotacalles.

lour [láu(r)], vn. y s. = LOWER.

louse [láus], s. (ent.) piojo, (fam.) cáncano.

lousewort [-wœrt], s. (bot.) albarraz, m.; estafisagria; hierba piojera.

lousily [láuzili], adv. con piojería; (fam.) pésimamente.—**lousiness** [-inis], s. piojería.—**lousy** [-i], a. piojoso, piojento; (med.) pedicular; (fam.) astroso, miserable.

lout [láuṭ], s. patán, rústico, zafio.—**loutish** [-iš], a. rústico, tosco.—**loutishly** [-li], adv. groseramente.

louver [lúvœ(r)], s. (arq.) lumbrera, lucer(n)a, respiradero; especie de persiana, o serie de tablillas o listones dispuestos para que pase el aire y no la lluvia (ll. t. **l. boards**).

lov(e)ability [lʌvəbíliti], **lov(e)ableness** [-blnis], s. amabilidad, atractivo.—**lov(e)able** [-bl], a. amable; digno de ser amado.

lovage [lʌvidž], s. (bot.) ligústico.

love [lʌv]. I. va. amar, querer; (fam.) gustar mucho de, tener gran afición a. II. vn. amar, estar enamorado. III. s. amor, cariño, afecto, querer, devoción; pasión amatoria o sexual; el ser amado; (L.) Cupido, el amor dios; grande afición: (en tenis y otros juegos) falta, cero, nada.—**l. affair**, intriga amorosa, amorío.—**l. apple**, (bot.) tomate.—**l. bird**, (orn.) periquito.—**l. feast**, ágape.—**l.-in-a-mist**, (bot.) neguilla.—**l.-in-idleness**, (bot.) trinitaria o pensamiento silvestre.—**l. knot**, lazo de amor.—**l.-lies-bleeding**, (bot.) moco de pavo.—**l.-maker**, galanteador, enamorado.—**l.-making**, amorío, galanteo, amores, m. pl., corte, f.—**l. match**, matrimonio por amor.—**l. potion**, filtro de amor, bebedizo.—**l. set**, (tenis) partida ganada sin perder un solo juego.—**for l.**, por amor; con gusto; gratis, sin interés.—**for (the) l. of**, por amor de.—**for l. or money**, a cualquier precio; por buenas o por malas.—**in l. with**, enamorado de.—**not for l. or money**, por nada del mundo.—**to make l. to**, enamorar, cortejar, galantear, requerir de amores.

loveless [-lis], a. desamorado; desamorado.

loveliness [-inis], s. amabilidad, agrado, encanto; belleza.

lovelock [-lak], s. (ant.) rizo largo con lazo.

lovelorn [-lorn], a. abandonado de su amante; suspirando de amor.

lovely [-li], a. amable, cariñoso; hermoso, bello; (fam.) agradable, atractivo; ameno, deleitoso.

lover [-œ(r)], s. amante; galán; amigo, aficionado.

lovesick [-sik], a. enamorado, herido de amor.

lovesickness [-nis], s. mal de amores.

loving [lʌviŋ], a. amante, afectuoso, amoroso, cariñoso; aficionado; benigno, apacible.—**l. cup**, copa con varias asas, que pasa de mano en mano entre amigos; copa de premio (gen. l'. copa simplemente).—**l.-kindness**, benevolencia, favor o cariño afectuosos.

lovingly [-li], adv. afectuosamente, amorosamente.

lovingness [-nis], s. cariño, afecto.

low [lóu]. I. a. bajo, de poca altura o profundidad; bajo (tono, voz); hondo, profundo; económico, módico, barato; abatido, desanimado; gravemente enfermo; bajo, vil, rastrero, ruin; pobre, humilde; muerto; inferior; débil, debilitado.—**l. area**, área o región de baja presión barométrica.—**l. blood pressure**, hipotensión arterial.—**l. brass**, similor.—**l. (-carbon) steel**, acero pobre en carbono.—**L. Church**, iglesia o secta no ritualista.—**L. Churchman**, sectario opuesto al ritualismo.—**l. comedy**, farsa, sainete.—**l. count**, (tej.) número grueso o bajo (del hilo).—**L. Countries**, Países Bajos.—**l. down**, (fam.) bajo, vil.—**l. expressions**, expresiones vulgares.—**L. Latin**, bajo latín.—**l. latitude**, latitud cercana al ecuador.—**L. Mass**, (igl.) misa rezada.—**l. pressure**, baja presión.—**l.-pressure cylinder**, cilindro de baja presión.—**l. relief**, (b. a.) bajo relieve.—**l. spirits**, abatimiento.—**l. tide**, bajamar, f.—**l. trick**, perrada, mala pasada.—**l. water**, marea baja; nivel mínimo (de un río, lago, etc.).—**l.-water line** o **mark**, línea de nivel mínimo.—**in l. gear**, (aut.) en primera.—**in l. spirits**, abatido. II. adv. bajo, cerca del suelo; en la parte inferior; barato, a precio bajo; bajamente, vilmente; sumisamente; en voz baja; en tono profundo.—**l.-minded**, ruin.—**l.-necked**, escotado, de cuello bajo.—**l.-pitched**, de tono bajo; de poca inclinación o pendiente (tejado).—**l.-priced**, barato.—**l.-spirited**, abatido, acobardado.—**l.-waisted**, de talle bajo. III. vn. mugir, berrear. IV. s. mugido, mu, berrido; punto o lugar bajo; valor o precio mínimo; (aut.) primera velocidad; en los naipes, triunfo más bajo.—**l.-down**, (fam.) información confidencial o de primera mano; los hechos verdaderos.

lowborn [-born], a. de humilde cuna.

lowbred [-bred], a. malcriado; vulgar.

lowbrow [-brau]. I. s. (fam.) persona ajena a las cosas intelectuales. II. a. poco intelectual.

lower [lóuœ(r)]. I. va. agachar, humillar, abatir, deprimir; bajar, poner más bajo; rebajar, minorar, disminuir.—**to l. the flag**, abatir la bandera.—**to l. the sails**, (mar.) arriar las velas. II. vn. bajar, menguar, disminuirse. III. a. comp. de LOW; más bajo; bajero, inferior.—**l. berth**, cama o litera baja.—**l. case**, (impr.) caja baja, letras minúsculas.—**l. deck**, (mar.) cubierta inferior; (pl. Ingl.) tripulación.—**l. floor**, piso bajo.—**l. house**, cámara de representantes o diputados.—**l. mast**, (mar.) palo principal.—**l. world**, averno, los infiernos; la tierra.

lower [láuœ(r)]. I. vn. mirar sañudo, fruncir el ceño; encapotarse o encubrirse el cielo. II. s. ceño, sobreceño; aspecto amenazador.

lowerclassman [lóuœrklésmən], s. estudiante de primer o segundo año.

lowering [láuœriŋ], a. encapotado, nebuloso; amenazador.—**loweringly** [-li], adv. nubladamente; con ceño.

lowermost [lóuœrmoust], **lowest** [lóuist], a. super. de LOW: (el) más bajo, ínfimo.

lowing [lóuiŋ], s. mugido, mu, berrido, bramido.

lowland [lóuland], s. tierra baja.—**the Lowlands**, las tierras bajas de Escocia.

lowlander [-œ(r)], s. abajeño, llanero.

lowlily [lóulili], adv. humildemente; baja o vilmente.

lowliness [-nis], s. humildad; bajeza, vileza.

lowly [lóu̯li]. **I.** *a.* humilde; vil, bajo. **II.** *adv.* humildemente; vilmente.

lowness [lóu̯nis], *s.* bajura; bajeza o vileza, ruindad; villanía; humildad; sumisión; abatimiento, postración; baratura; gravedad o profundidad del tono; suavidad o debilidad del sonido.

loxodrome [láksodrou̯m], *s.* (mar.) loxodromia.

loxodromic [-drámik], *a.* loxodrómico.—**l. line,** línea loxodrómica.

loxodromics [-s], *s.* arte loxodrómico.

loyal [lói̯al], *a.* leal, fiel, constante.—**loyalist** [-ist], *s.* (pol.) realista; leal.—**loyally** [-i], *adv.* lealmente.—**loyalty** [-ti], *s.* lealtad, fidelidad, ley, *f.*

lozenge [lázendź], *s.* (geom.) rombo; (farm.) pastilla, rótula, tableta; (blas.) losanje, lisonja.

lozenged [-d], *a.* rombal.

lozengy [-i], *a.* (blas.) lisonjado.

lubber [lÁbœ(r)], *s.* gordiflón; bobalicón; patán; marinero de agua dulce.—**l.'s hole,** (mar.) boca del lobo.

lubberly [-li]. **I.** *a.* zafio, chabacano, poltrón. **II.** *adv.* toscamente, zafiamente.

lubricant [ljúbrikant], *s.* y *a.* lubri(fi)cante.

lubricate [ljúbrikeit], *va.* lubri(fi)car, engrasar.—**lubricating** [-iŋ], *a.* de lubricar, lubri(fi)cante. **lubricador.—lubrication** [-éiṣọn], *s.* lubri(fi)cación, engrasación, engrase.—**lubricative** [-ei̯tiv], *a.* lubricativo.—**lubricator** [-ọ(r)], *s.* lubricador, engrasador.

lubricity [ljubrísiti], *s.* lubricidad, lisura; veleidad, inconstancia; lujuria, lascivia.

lubricous [ljúbrikas], *a.* lúbrico; deslizadero; incierto; inconstante; lujurioso, lascivo.

lubritorium [ljubritóri̯am], **lubritory** [ljúbritori], *s.* cuarto o estación de lubricación de automóviles.

lucarne [ljukárn], *s.* ventanilla, buharda.

luce [ljus], *s.* (ict.) lucio.

lucent [ljúsent], *a.* luciente; luminoso; claro; transparente.

lucern(e [ljusǿrn], *s.* alfalfa.—**l. field,** alfalfal.

lucernal [ljusǿrnal], *a.* referente a lámparas.—**l. microscope,** microscopio proyector de lámpara.

lucid [ljúsid], *a.* luciente; diáfano; brillante; lúcido; cuerdo, de entendimiento claro.

lucidity [ljusíditi], **lucidness** [ljúsidnis], *s.* lucidez; claridad mental; transparencia; brillantez.

Lucifer [ljúsifœ(r)], *s.* lucero del alba; Lucifer, Luzbel.—**l.,** o **l. match,** fósforo de fricción.

Luciferian [-fíri̯an], *a.* luciferino, diabólico, endiablado.

luciferous [ljusíferas], *a.* lucífero.

lucifugous [-ugas], *a.* (biol.) lucífugo.

luck [lÁk], *s.* azar, acaso, casualidad; suerte, *f.;* (buena)ventura, dicha.—**for l.,** para que traiga suerte.—**to be in l.,** estar de buena suerte.—**to be out of l.,** estar de malas.

luckily [-ili], *adv.* por fortuna, afortunadamente, a o por dicha.

luckiness [-inis], *s.* buena suerte.

luckless [-lis], *a.* desafortunado, desgraciado.

lucky [-i], *a.* afortunado, dichoso, venturoso; propicio, favorable; que trae buena suerte.—**l. break,** (fam.) chiripa, feliz casualidad o coyuntura favorable.

lucrative [ljúkrativ], *a.* lucrativo, ganancioso.

lucratively [-li], *adv.* lucrativamente.

lucre [ljúkœ(r)], *s.* lucro, ganancia.

lucubrate [ljúkiubrei̯t], *va.* y *vn.* lucubrar.

lucubration [-éiṣọn], *s.* lucubración.

luculent [ljúkiulent], *a.* luciente, claro; evidente.

ludicrous [ljúdikras], *a.* ridículo, cómico, burlesco, risible.—**ludicrously** [-li], *adv.* ridículamente, cómicamente.—**ludicrousness** [-nis], *s.* ridiculez.

lues [ljúiz], *s.* (med.) lúe o lúes, *f.,* sífilis.

luetic [ljuétik], *a.* (med.) luético, sifilítico.

luff [lÁf]. **I.** *s.* (mar.) gratil; orza(da).—**l. tackle,** (mar.) aparejo de bolinear. **II.** *va.* (mar.) ceñir

el viento, orzar, bolinear.—**to l. alee,** o **round,** orzar a la banda.—**to l. up,** tomar por avante.

lug [lÁg]. **I.** *s.* (fam.) tirón, estirón; cosa tirada; cosa lenta y pesada; (fam.) porro, mostrenco; (mec., etc.) oreja; anillo, argolla; saliente; agarradera, asa; jamba de chimenea; correa de las varas de un carruaje. *V.* LUGSAIL, LUGWORM. **II.** *va.* tirar de (algo); (mar.) halar.—**to l. away,** u **off,** llevarse arrastrando.—**to l. in** o **into,** arrastrar hacia dentro; (fam.) introducir, traer a cuento, o por los pelos.

luggage [lÁgidź], *s.* equipaje; (fam.) trastos, petate.—**l. rack,** portaequipajes.—**l. van,** (Ingl.) furgón de equipajes.

lugger [lÁgœ(r)], *s.* (mar.) lugre.

lugsail [lÁgseil], *s.* (mar.) vela al tercio.

lugubrious [ljugiúbri̯as], *a.* lúgubre, lóbrego.

lugworm [lÁgwœrm], *s.* (zool.) lombriz de cebo.

lukewarm [ljúkwœrm], *a.* tibio, templado; indiferente, frío.—**lukewarmly** [-li], *adv.* tibiamente; indiferentemente.—**lukewarmness** [-nis], *s.* tibieza; indiferencia, frialdad.

lull [lÁl]. **I.** *va.* arrullar, adormecer; aquietar, calmar, moderar. **II.** *vn.* calmarse, sosegarse. **III.** *s.* momento de calma o de silencio.

lullaby [-abai], *s.* arrullo; canción de cuna, nana.

luller [-œ(r)], *s.* arrullador, niñero.

lumbago [lÁmbéi̯gou̯], *s.* (med.) lumbago.

lumbar [lÁmbá(r)], *a.* (anat.) lumbar, pert. a los lomos.—**l. puncture,** (cir.) punción lumbar.

lumber [lÁmbœ(r)]. **I.** *s.* madera aserrada; maderaje; armatoste; balumba; trastos o muebles viejos.—**l. dealer,** maderero, negociante en maderas.—**l. room,** camaranchón, cuarto de trastos. **II.** *va.* amontonar trastos viejos. **III.** *vn.* andar pesadamente: avanzar con ruido sordo.

lumberer [-œ(r)], *s.* = LUMBERMAN.

lumbering [-iŋ]. **I.** *s.* explotación de bosques maderables. **II.** *a.* que anda pesadamente; que hace o avanza con ruido sordo y continuo.

lumberjack [-dźæk], *s.* leñador, hachero.

lumberman [-man], *s.* leñador, hachero; negociante en madera, maderero.

lumberyard [-yard], *s.* maderería, depósito de maderas.

lumbricales [lÁmbríkéliz], *s. pl.* (anat.) músculos lumbricales.

lumen [ljúmin], *s.* (fís.) lumen, unidad de radiación de la luz; (fisiol.) cavidad o conducto de un órgano tubular, vaso sanguíneo, etc.

luminary [-eri], *s.* astro, luminar; lumbrera.

luminescence [-éṣeṇs], *s.* luminiscencia, emisión de luz sin incandescencia.—**luminescent** [-éṣent], *a.* luminiscente, luminoso sin incandescencia.

luminiferous [-ífẹras], *a.* luminífero.

luminist [-ist], *a.* y *s.* (pint.) luminista.

luminosity [-ásiti], *s.* luminosidad.

luminous [ljúminas], *a.* luminoso; lúcido.

luminously [-li], *adv.* luminosamente.

luminousness [-nis], *s.* luminosidad.

lummox [lÁmọks], *s.* (fam.) porro, sujeto torpe.

lump [lÁmp]. **I.** *s.* masa, bulto, burujón; protuberancia, hinchazón, *f.;* pitón; bollo; terrón; (fund.) lupia; (fam.) porro.—**l. coal,** carbón más grueso (el de mayores fragmentos que se produce).—**l. of sugar,** terrón de azúcar.—**l. sugar,** azúcar de terrón o en terrones.—**l. sum,** suma alzada, suma global o total.—**by the l.,** (com.) a bulto, en globo, a ojo, por grueso o por junto.—**in a l., in the l.,** todos juntos, sin distinción. **II.** *va.* amontonar, aborujar; comprar a bulto, en globo.—**to l. it,** (fam.) soportarlo, tragar saliva. **III.** *vn.* trabajar como estibador; aborujarse, apelotonarse, aterronarse.

lumper [-œ(r)], *s.* estibador, cargador de muelle.

lumpish [-iš], *a.* como masa o terrón, etc.; pesado, macizo; tosco; torpe, estúpido.—**lumpishly** [-li], *adv.* lerdamente, estúpidamente.—**lumpishness** [-nis], *s.* pesadez; estupidez; majadería.

lumpy [-ị], a. aterronado.

lunacy [ljúnạsị], s. locura, insania; frenesí.

lunar [ljúnạ̈(r)], a. lunar; lunario; lunado; lunático: (quím. y med.) relativo a la plata.—l. caustic, lunar cáustico, nitrato de plata.—l. year, año lunar (354⅓ días).

lunarian [ljunérịạn]. I. a. lunario. II. s. selenita, mf., supuesto habitante de la Luna.

lunary [ljúnạrị]. I. a. lunar. II. s. (bot.) hierba de la plata, lunaria anual.

lunate(d [ljúnejt(ịd], a. lunado.

lunatic [ljúnạtịk], s. y a. loco, lunático, orate, mf. —l. asylum, casa de locos, manicomio.

lunation [ljunéịṣọn], s. (astr.) lunación.

lunch [lʌnch], luncheon [-ọn]. I. s. almuerzo (comida del mediodía, gen. ligera); merienda, colación, refrigerio, (fam.) piscolabis, m., tentempie, m.—l. basket, fiambrera.—l. room, merendero. II. vn. almorzar; merendar.

lune [ljun], s. (geom.) lúnula.

lunette [ljunét], s. cualquier cosa de figura lunada; (forti.) luneta; (arq.) luneto, luneta.

lung [lʌŋ], s. pulmón.—l. trouble, (fam.) tisis.

lunge [lʌndʒ]. I. s. (esgr.) estocada; (fam.) embestida, arremetida. II. vn. (esgr.) irse a fondo, dar una estocada; abalanzarse, embestir.

lungmotor [lʌ́ŋmotọ(r)], s. = PULMOTOR.

lungwort [lʌ́ŋwœrt], s. (bot.) pulmonaria.

luniform [ljúnịform], a. lunado.

lunisolar [-sóulạ̈(r)], a. (astr.) lunisolar.

lunular, lunulate [ljúnyūlạ̈(r), -ejt], a. lunado.

lunule [ljúnjul], s. (anat.) lúnula, blanco de las uñas (ll. t. lunula).

luny [ljúnị], s. y a. loco; alocado.

Lupercalia [ljupœrkéjlịạ̈], s. pl. Lupercales, f. pl.

lupine [ljúpịn]. I. s. (bot.) a(l)tramuz, m., lupino. II. a. lupino, de lobo; voraz.

lupulin [ljúpịuljn], s. lupulino.

lupus [ljúpʌs], s. (med.) lupus; (L. astr.) el Lobo.

lurch [lœrch]. I. s. sacudida, vaivén; balance brusco; (mar.) bandazo, guiñada; en algunos juegos, partida doble; abandono.—to leave in the l., plantar, dejar en las astas del toro, o en la estacada. II. vn. andar tambaleando, haciendo eses, o con vaivén; (mar.) guiñar, cabecear, dar bandazos; ganar una partida doble.— lurcher [-œ(r)], s. = POACHER; acechador; rondador; ratero; perro de caza.

lure [ljur]. I. s. añagaza, señuelo, reclamo; armadijo; cebo; engaño; tentación. II. va. atraer, inducir, tentar.

lurid [ljúrịd], a. rojizo (cielo, etc.); cárdeno; fantástico, espeluznante.

lurk [lœrk], vn. espiar, acechar; esconderse.— lurking place, escondite, guarida; rincón; emboscada.

lurker [-œ(r)], s. acechador, espía, mf.

luscious [lʌ́ʌs], a. sabroso, delicioso, exquisito, rico; meloso; empalagoso.—lusciously [-lị], adv. sabrosa o melosamente.—lusciousness [-nịs], s. calidad de sabroso; melosidad; dulzura que empalaga.

lush [lʌʃ], a. suculento, jugoso; fresco y lozano; exuberante, lujuriante, profuso.

Lusitanian [ljusịtéjnịạn], a. y s. lusitano; portugués.

lust [lʌst]. I. s. anhelo vehemente, codicia; lujuria, concupiscencia, libídine, mf. II. vn. (a veces con for o after) codiciar, anhelar; lujuriar.

luster [lʌ́stœ(r)]. I. s. lustre, brillo; viso, aguas, f. pl.; realce, lucimiento, esplendor; araña de cristal; lustro. II. va. (a)lustrar.

lusterless [-lịs], a. sin brillo, mate, deslustrado.

lustful [lʌ́stful], a. lujurioso, sensual, lascivo, libidinoso.—lustfully [-ị], adv. lujuriosamente. —lustfulness [-nịs], s. lascivia, lujuria.

lustily [lʌ́stịlị], adv. fuertemente, vigorosamente.

lustiness [-nịs], s. lozanía, vigor, robustez.

lustral [lʌ́strạl], a. lustral, lústrico.

lustrate [lʌ́strejt], va. lustrar, purificar.

lustration [-éịṣọn], s. lustración.

lustre [lʌ́stœ(r)], s. = LUSTER.

lustrical [lʌ́strịkạl], a. (igl.) lustral.

lustrine [lʌ́strịn], lustring [lʌ́strịŋ], s. (tej.) lustrina.

lustrous [lʌ́strʌs], a. lustroso, brillante.

lustrum [lʌ́strʌm], s. lustro, quinquenio; lustración, purificación.

lusty [lʌ́stị], a. lozano, fuerte, robusto, vigoroso.

lute [ljut]. I. s. (mús.) laúd, m.; (quím.) luten, lodo para junturas; arandela de goma para cerrar tarros herméticamente; raspador de ladrillales. II. va. enlodar, tapar o embarrar con lodo o cemento; enrasar ladrillos. III. vn. tocar o tañer el laúd.

lutecium [ljutíṣịʌm], s. (quím.) lutecio.

lutein [ljútịịn], s. (bioquím.) luteína.

luteolin [ljútjolịn], s. (quím.) luteolina.

Lutheran [ljúθœrạn], s. y a. luterano.

Lutheranism [-ịzm], s. luteranismo.

luthern [ljúθœrn], s. (arq.) lumbrera, buharda.

lutist [ljútịst], s. tañedor de laúd.

lutose [ljútous], a. lodoso, cenagoso.

lux [lʌks], s. lux, unidad de intensidad luminosa, igual a una bujía-metro.

luxate [-ejt], va. dislocar, descoyuntar.

luxation [-éịṣọn], s. luxación, dislocación.

luxe [lʌks], s. lujo (esp. en la expresión de luxe, de lujo).

luxuriance, luxuriancy [lʌksúrịạns, -ị], s. exuberancia, lozanía; frondosidad; demasía.

luxuriant [-ạnt], a. exuberante, lozano, superabundante; superfluo; frondoso; lujuriante.

luxuriantly [-lị], adv. abundantemente; lozanamente.

luxuriate [-ejt], vn. ostentar lozanía; crecer o brotar con exuberancia; vivir con lujo; (fig.) gloriarse, complacerse.

luxurious [-ʌs], a. lujoso; sibarítico; exuberante; frondoso.—luxuriously [-lị], adv. con lozanía o exuberancia; frondosamente; lujosamente.— luxuriousness [-nịs], s. lujo, fausto.

luxury [lʌ́kṣụrị], s. lujo, fausto; gastos superfluos; manjar delicioso; cosa que deleita los sentidos. —l. tax, impuesto suntuario o sobre artículos de lujo.

lycanthrope [lájkænθroup], s. licántropo.

lycanthropy [lajkǽnθropị], s. (med.) licantropía.

lycée [liséị], s. (fr.) liceo, instituto de segunda enseñanza.

lyceum [lajsíʌm], s. liceo, ateneo; escuela secundaria; escuela de enseñanza por conferencias.

Lycian [lísịạn], s. y a. licio, de Licia.

lycopodium [lajkopóụdịʌm], s. (bot. y farm.) licopodio.

lyddite [lídajt], s. lidita (explosivo).

Lydian [lídịạn], a. y s. lidio, de la Lidia.

lye [laj], s. lejía; (Ingl., f. c.) desviadero.

lying [lájịŋ]. I. pa. de TO LIE, v. a. falso, mentiroso; echado, tendido, yacente; sito, situado.—l. down, acostado.—l.-to, (mar.) al pairo o en facha.—l.-in, parto.—l.-in hospital, hospital de parturientas, casa de maternidad.—l.-in woman, puérpera, mujer parida. II. s. mentira, embuste.

lyingly [-lị], adv. mentirosamente, falsamente.

lymph [lịmf], s. (anat., fisiol.) linfa, aguosidad.— l. duct, vaso linfático.

lymphadenoma [-ædịnóụmạ̈], s. linfadenoma, m.

lymphangitis [-ændʒájtịs], s. (med.) linfangitis.

lymphatic [lịmfǽtịk]. I. a. linfático; flemático. II. s. vaso linfático.

lymphatism [lịmfạtịzm], s. (med.) linfatismo.

lymphocyte [lịmfosajt], s. (anat.) linfocito.

lymphoid [lịmfɔjd], a. linfoideo.

lynch [lịnch], va. linchar.—l. law, (E. U.) ley (f.) de Lynch, suplicio impuesto por particulares sin procedimiento ni forma legal.

lynching [-ịŋ], s. linchamiento.

lynx [lịŋks], s. (zool.) lince.—l.-eyed, de ojos linces.

Lyonese [lajọníz], a. y s. lionés; de Lyón (Francia).

—**lyonnaise** [laiǫnéiz], *a.* a la lionesa (apl. a papas fritas con cebollas).

lyrate [láireit], *a.* de forma de lira.

lyre [lair], *s.* (mús.) lira; (**L.,** astr.) Lira.—**l. bird,** (orn.) pájaro lira.

lyric(**al** [lírik(ąl], *a.* lírico.—**l. poetry,** lírica.— **lyric,** *s.* poema lírico; (fam.) letra de una canción.—**lyricism** [lírisizm], *s.* lirismo.—**lyrist** [láirist], *s.* tocador de lira; [lírist], poeta lírico.

Lysimachia [laisiméikią], *s.* (bot.) lisimaquia.

lysin [láisin], *s.* (bioquím.) lisina.

lysis [láisis], *s.* (med.) lisis; (bioquím.) destrucción de células por una lisina.

lysol [láisal], *s.* lisol (nombre de fábrica), desinfectante extraído del alquitrán.

lyssa [lísą], *s.* rabia canina, hidrofobia.

lythraceous [liθréisiʌs], *a.* (bot.) litrarieo.

M

m [em], *s.* m.

ma [ma], *s. contr.* de MA(M)MA, mamá, *f.*

ma'am [mæm], *s. contr.* de MADAM, señora.

Mac, *prefijo,* que significa "hijo de" en nombres patronímicos escoceses o irlandeses (suele abreviarse así: **Mc, Mc,** o **M').**

macabre, macaber [mąkábr], *a.* macabro.

macadam [mąkǽdąm]. **I.** *s.* macádam, macadán. **II.** *a.* de macádam, macadamizado.—**macadamize** [-aiz], *va.* macadamizar.

macaque [mąkák], *s.* (zool.) macaco.

macaroni [mækąrǫúni], *s.* macarrones, *m. pl.;* mezcla estrambótica; pisaverde.—**m. wheat,** trigo para pastas.

macaronic [mækąrǫ́nik]. **I.** *s.* macarronea (composición burlesca). **II.** *a.* macarrónico; mezclado.

macaroon [mækąrún], *s.* almendrado, macarrón de almendras.

macassar [mąkǽsą(r)], *s.* aceite macasar.

macaw [mąkó], *s.* (orn.) guacamayo, macagua.

maccaboy [mǽkąbǫi], *s.* rapé macuba.

mace [meis], *s.* maza (insignia); (arm.) maza, clava, porra; forma de taco de billar; macis o macia (especia).—**macer,** o **mace bearer,** macero, ballestero.

Macedonian [mæsedǫ́unian], *a.* y *s.* macedón(io); *a.* macedónico.

macerate [mǽsereit], *va.* macerar.

maceration [-éiʃǫn], *s.* maceración.

Machiavel(l)ian [mækiavélian]. **I.** *s.* maquiavelista. **II.** *a.* maquiavélico.—**Machiavelism** [-izm], *s.* maquiavelismo.

machicolation [mąchikǫléiʃǫn], *s.* (fort.) matacán o ladronera.

machinate [mǽkineit], *va.* y *vn.* maquinar.— **machination** [-éiʃǫn], *s.* maquinación, intriga. —**machinator** [-tǫ(r)], *s.* maquinador.

machine [mąʃín]. **I.** *s.* máquina, aparato, ingenio; vehículo, coche, avión, *m.,* etc.; (pol.) camarilla. —**m. gun,** (mil.) ametralladora.—**m.-gun,** *va.* ametrallar, atacar con ametralladoras.—**m.-made,** hecho a máquina; mecánico.—**m. screw,** tornillo para metales.—**m. shop,** taller de maquinaria.—**m. tool,** máquina herramienta. **II.** *va.* fresar, trabajar a máquina.

machinery [-ǫri], *s.* maquinaria; mecánica; mecanismo, aparato; organización, sistema, *m.*

machinist [-ist], *s.* maquinista, mecánico; (teat.) tramoyista.

mackerel [mǽkǫrel], *s.* (ict.) escombro, caballa. —**m. sky,** cielo aborregado.

Mackinaw [mǽkinǫ], *s.* (mar.) especie de chalana, bote de fondo plano, proa aguda y popa cuadrada; manta gruesa de tela burda.—**M. coat,** especie de chamarra, saco corto de frente traslapado.

mackintosh [mǽkintaʃ], *s.* impermeable.

mackle [mǽkl]. **I.** *va.* y *vn.* (impr.) repintar, macular, remosquearse. **II.** *s.* maculatura.

macle [mǽkl], *s.* (min.) cristal gemelo; andalucita teselada; mancha oscura.

macramé [mǽkrąmei], *s. macramé,* trabajo de nudos.

macrobian [mąkrǫ́úbian], *a.* macrobio, longevo.

macrobiosis [mækrǫbaiǫ́úsis], *s.* longevidad.

macrobiotics [-baiátiks], *s.* macrobiótica.

macrocephalous [-séfąląs], *a.* macrocéfalo.

macrocosm [-kazm], *s.* macrocosmo.

macrocyte [-sait], *s.* (med.) macrocito.

macrograph [-græf], *s.* dibujo o fotografía de un objeto como aparece a la simple vista.—**macrography** [mąkrágrąfi], *s.* examen a la simple vista (a diferencia del microscópico).—**macrophysics** [-fíziks], *s.* macrofísica, estudio de los cuerpos que pueden observarse sin la ayuda del microscopio.

macroscopic [-skápik], *a.* macroscópico.

macruran [mąkrúrąn], *a.* y *s.* (zool.) macruro.

macula [mǽkyúlą], *s.* mácula, mancha, lunar.

maculate [-eit]. **I.** *va.* macular, manchar. **II.** *a.* manchado, maculado.—**maculation** [-éiʃǫn], *s.* mancha, mancilla, mácula, lunar.

mad [mæd], *a.* loco, demente, maniático, insano; furioso, rabioso; insensato, desesperado; (fam.) enojado, encolerizado; hidrófobo; bulliciosamente alegre.—**m. apple,** (bot.) berenjena; estramonio.—**m. as a hatter,** o **March hare,** loco de atar.—**m.-doctor,** alienista.—**like m.,** a la loquesca. *V.* LIKE.—**to go m.,** enloquecerse, volverse loco.

madam [mǽdąm], **madame** [mædǽm], *s.* madama, señora.

madapollam [mædąpáląm], *s.* (tej.) madapolán.

madbrain, madcap [mǽdbrein, -kæp], *a.* y *s.* fogoso; temerario; calavera, *m.,* tarambana, *mf.*

madden [mǽdn], *va.* y *vn.* enloquecer, enfurecer(se); exasperar.—**maddening** [-iŋ]. **I.** *a.* enloquecedor, que enfurece; exasperante, irritante. **II.** *s.* enloquecimiento, enfurecimiento.

madder [mǽdœr(r)], *s.* (bot.) rubia, granza.

made [meid], *pret.* y *pp.* TO MAKE; hecho, elaborado, fabricado, producido.—**m. mast,** (mar.) palo compuesto.—**m.-over,** rehecho; reformado.—**m.-to-measure, m.-to-order,** hecho a la medida o a la orden.—**m.-up,** artificial; ficticio; maquillado, pintado (el rostro); acabado; (con of) compuesto (de), integrado (por).

Madeira wine [mądírą], *s.* vino de Madera.

madhouse [mǽdhaus], *s.* manicomio.

madly [-li], *adv.* locamente; furiosamente.

madman [-mæn], *s.* loco, maniático, orate.

madness [-nis], *s.* locura, enloquecimiento, demencia, frenesí, insania; furor, furia, rabia.

madonna [mądáną], *s.* (ital.) señora, madama; imagen (*f.*) de la Virgen, madona.—**the M.,** la Madona, la Virgen María.—**M. lily,** (bot.) azucena.

madras [mǽdras o mądrǽs], *s.* (tej.) madrás, *f.*

madrepore [mǽdripǫr], *s.* (zool.) madrépora.

madreporic [-pórik], *a.* madrepórico.

madrigal [mǽdrigąl], *s.* (poét.) madrigal; (mús.) canción para varias voces.

Madrilenian [mædrilínian], *a.* y *s.* madrileño.

madroña [mądrǫ́únyą], *s.* (bot.) madroño.

madwort [mǽdwœrt], *s.* (bot.) aliso.

maelstrom [méilstrǫm], *s.* maelstrom; remolino.

mænad [mínæd], *s.* ménade, *f.,* bacante, *f.*

maestoso [maestǫ́úsǫu], *a.* (mús.) maestoso.

magazine [mægązín], *s.* almacén; (arti.) cámara o depósito para cartuchos en las armas de repetición; polvorín, pañol de pólvora o santabárbara; (impr.) revista.—**m. rifle,** rifle de repetición.

magazinist [-ist], *s.* el que redacta o escribe para las revistas.

magdalen [mǽgdalen], *s.* ramera arrepentida.

Magellanic [mædʒélænik], *a.* magallánico.

magenta [mądʒéntą], *s.* fucsina; color magenta.

maggot [mǽgǫt], *s.* (ent.) cresa; capricho, antojo. —**maggoty** [-i], *a.* gusaniento; caprichoso.

Magi [méidʒai], *s. pl.* magos, sabios.

Magian [méidźįąn], *s.* y *a.* mago.

magic [mǽdźįk]. I. *s.* magia, mágica; nigromancia; prestidigitación.—**m. square**, cuadrado mágico.—**m. wand**, varita o varilla mágica o de virtudes. II. *a.* mágico; encantador.—**m. lantern**, linterna mágica.

magical [-ąl], *a.* mágico; encantado.

magically [-į], *adv.* mágicamente, por arte de encantamiento.

magician [mądźíśąn], *s.* mago, mágico, nigromante; prestidigitador.

magisterial [mǽdźįst[rįął], *a.* magistral, magisterial; autoritario, absoluto.—**magisterially** [-į], *adv.* magistralmente.—**magisterialness** [-nįs], *s.* magisterio; autoridad magistral.

magistery [-tęrį], *s.* piedra filosofal; (quím.) magisterio, precipitado.

magistracy [-trǽsį], *s.* magistratura.

magistral [-trął]. I. *a.* magistral, magisterial; (farm.) magistral, preparado según prescripción. II. *s.* (farm.) magistral; (metal.) magistral, piritas de cobre pulverizadas.

magistrate [-treįt], *s.* magistrado; juez (*m.*) de paz.

magma [mǽgmą], *s.* magma, *m.;* (geol.) magma, materia fundida de que se forman las rocas ígneas; base vidriosa de una roca ígnea.

Magna Charta [mǽgną kártą], *s.* Carta Magna.

magnanimity [mǽgnąnįmįtį], *s.* magnanimidad.—**magnanimous** [mǽgnǽnįmᴀs], *a.* magnánimo.—**magnanimously** [-lį], *adv.* magnánimamente.

magnate [mǽgneįt], *s.* magnate.

magnesia [mǽgnísįą], *s.* (quím.) magnesia.

magnesian [-n], **magnesic** [mǽgnísįk], *a.* magnésico, magnesiano.

magnesite [mǽgnįsąįt], *s.* (min.) magnesita, espuma de mar.

magnesium [mǽgnísįᴀm], *s.* (quím.) magnesio.

magnet [mǽgnįt], *s.* imán, magneto; piedra imán.

magnetic(al [mǽgnétįk(ąl], *a.* magnético; atractivo.—**m. battery**, imán hojeado o compuesto.—**m. bearing**, rumbo magnético.—**m. creeping**, histéresis viscosa.—**m. explorer**, bobina de prueba.—**m. field**, campo magnético.—**m. flux**, flujo magnético.—**m. lag**, retardo de imanación.—**m. leakage**, dispersión magnética.—**m. needle**, brújula, calamita.—**m. pole**, polo magnético.—**m. pyrites**, pirita magnética.

magnetically [-į], *adv.* magnéticamente.

magnetism [mǽgnįtįzm], *s.* (fís.) magnetismo.

magnetite [-tąįt], *s.* (min.) magnetita.

magnetizable [-tąįząbl], *a.* magnetizable.

magnetization [-tįzéįśąn], *s.* magnetización, imanación.

magnetize [mǽgnįtąįz]. I. *va.* (fís.) magnetizar, imanar. II. *vn.* imanarse.

magnetizer [-œ(r)], *s.* magnetizador; imanador.

magneto [mǽgnítou], *s.* máquina magnetoeléctrica; (aut., etc.) magneto, *f.*

magnetodynamo [-dáįnąmou], *s.* magneto, *f.,* dínamo (*f.*) de imanes permanentes.

magnetoelectric [-įléktrįk], *a.* magnetoeléctrico.

magnetoelectricity [-įlektrįsįtį], *s.* magnetoelectricidad.

magnetogenerator [-dźénœreįtǫ(r)], *s.* = MAGNETODYNAMO.

magnetograph [-grǽf], *s.* (fís.) magnetógrafo, magnetómetro registrador.

magnetometer [mǽgnetámetœ(r)], *s.* (fís.) magnetómetro.

magnetomotive [mǽgnitoųmóųtįv], *a.* magnetomotriz (fuerza).

magneton [mǽgnetąn], *s.* (fís.) magnetón, elemento magnético semejante al electrón en electricidad.

magnetoscope [mǽgnįtoųskoųp], *s.* (fís.) magnetoscopio.

magnifiable [mǽgnįfaįąbl], *a.* magnificable, capaz de ser aumentado o enaltecido.

Magnificat [mǽgnįffįkat], *s.* (igl.) Magníficat.

magnification [-éįśǫn], *s.* (ópt.) amplificación, aumento; magnificación; enaltecimiento; alabanza, glorificación; exageración.

magnificence [mǽgnífįsęns], *s.* magnificencia.—**magnificent** [-ęnt], *a.* magnífico.—**magnificently** [-lį], *adv.* magníficamente, espléndidamente.

magnifier [mǽgnįfaįœ(r)], *s.* (ópt.) amplificador, vidrio de aumento; (ant.) exagerador; panegirista.

magnify [-faį], *va.* aumentar, amplificar; magnificar; (ant.) alabar; exagerar.

magnifying [-įŋ], *a.* amplificador, de aumento.—**m. glass**, vidrio de aumento, lente, *mf.,* lupa.

magniloquent [mǽgnílokwęnt], *a.* grandílocuo.

magnitude [mǽgnįtjud], *s.* magnitud.

magnolia [mǽgnóųlįą], *s.* (bot.) magnolia.

magnoliaceous [-éįśᴀs], *a.* (bot.) magnoliáceo.

magnum [mǽgnᴀm], *s.* botella de dos litros.

magpie [mǽgpaį], *s.* (orn.) urraca, picaza, pega, cotorra; (fig.) charlador, tarabilla.

maguey [mǽgweį o mągéį], *s.* (bot.) maguey, pita.

Magyar [mǽgya(r) o mádyar], *a.* y *s.* magiar.

maharaja [mąhąrádźą], *s.* maharajá, príncipe de la India.

mahatma [mąhǽtmą], *s.* título que se da en la India a los más elevados seguidores del budismo esotérico y la teosofía.

mahlstick [málstįk], *s.* (pint.) tiento.

mahogany [mąhágąnį], *s.* (bot.) caoba(na), caobo.

Mahometan [mąhámetąn], *a.* y *s.* = MOHAMMEDAN.

maid [meįd], *s.* doncella, soltera; (ant.) virgen, *f.;* doméstica, doncella, criada, sirvienta, (fam.) fámula; (ict.) lija.—**m. of all work**, criada para todo.—**m. of honor**, dama o doncella de honor.

maiden [méįdn]. I. *a.* virgíneo, virginal; soltera; prístino, primero, nuevo, inicial; intacto.—**m. name**, apellido de soltera.—**m. speech**, primer discurso de un orador. II. *s.* virgen, *f.,* doncella, joven soltera; zagala.

maidenhair [-her], *s.* (bot.) adianto, culantrillo.

maidenhead, maidenhood [-hęd, -hųd], *s.* doncellez, virginidad, flor, *f.*

maidenliness [-lįnįs], *s.* modestia, pudor.

maidenly, maidenlike [-lį, -laįk]. I. *a.* virginal, púdico, pudoroso. II. *adv.* modestamente.

maidhood [méįdhųd], *s.* virginidad.

maidservant [-sœrvąnt], *s.* criada, doméstica.

mail [méįl]. I. *s.* correo; correspondencia; mala, valija; (arm.) cota de malla.—**m. bag**, mala, valija; portacartas.—**m. carrier**, cartero.—**m. catcher**, (f. c.) garra para la correspondencia.—**m. chute**, buzón tubular.—**m. coach**, diligencia.—**m. order**, pedido de mercancías que se hace y se envía por correo.—**m.-order house**, casa de comercio o de ventas por correo.—**m. pouch**, **m. sack**, saco de lona para impresos, etc.—**m. steamer**, vapor correo.—**m. train**, tren correo. II. *va.* armar con cota de malla; echar al correo; enviar por correo.

mailable [-ąbl], *a.* que se puede enviar por el correo.

mailbox [-baks], *s.* buzón; apartado.

mailed [-d], *pp.* de TO MAIL, y *a.* cubierto con cota de malla.—**m. fist**, mano armada, espada desenvainada (fig.), fuerza bruta.—**mailing list**, *s.* lista de distribución (de personas a quienes se envía algo por correo).

mailman [-mæn], *s.* cartero.

mailplane [-pleįn], *s.* avión (*m.*) correo o postal.

maim [méįm]. I. *va.* mutilar, estropear, lisiar, mancar, tullir. II. *s.* mutilación. V. MAYHEM.

maimed [-d], *pp.* y *a.* mútilo, manco, zopo, mocho, contrecho.

maimedness [-(į)dnįs], *s.* mutilación, mancamiento, estropeamiento.

main [méįn]. I. *a.* principal, de mayor impor-

tancia.—m. **body**, grueso (de un ejército).—
m. **deck**, (mar.) cubierta principal.—m. **floor**,
primer piso.—m. **hatchway**, (mar.) escotilla
mayor.—m. **line**, (f. c.) línea troncal, (Am.)
tronco.—m. **office**, (com.) casa matriz.—m.
shaft, (min.) pozo maestro.—m. **street**, calle
(f.) mayor.—m. **tackle**, aparejo real.—m.-
topgallant, mastelero de juanete mayor.—m.-
topmast, mastelero mayor.—m. **topsail**, vela
de gavia.—m. **wale**, cinta principal o mayor.
—m. **wall**, pared maestra.—m. **yard**, verga
mayor.—by m. **force**, por la fuerza. II. s.
(poét.) océano, alta mar; (ant.) continente;
conducto, cañería maestra (de gas o agua);
fuerza, violencia; partida o riña de gallos; jugada de dados.—**for**, o **in**, **the m.**, mayor o
principalmente.

mainland [-lạnd], s. continente, tierra firme.

mainly [-lị], adv. principalmente.

mainmast [-mæst], s. (mar.) palo o árbol mayor.

mainsail [-seịl], s. (mar.) vela mayor.

mainsheet [-šịt], s. (mar.) escota mayor.

mainspring [-sprịŋ], s. móvil, motivo o causa
principales; (reloj.) muelle real.

mainstay [-steị], s. (mar.) estay mayor; soporte.

maintain [meịntéịn], va. tener, guardar, mantener; sostener, afirmar.

maintainable [-ạbl], a. defendible, sostenible.

maintainer [-œ(r)], s. mantenedor; defensor,
partidario, patrón.

maintenance [méịntẹnạns], s. mantenimiento,
apoyo, protección; manutención; sostén, sostenimiento; conservación (de una vía, máquina,
camino, etc.).

maintop [méịntạp], s. (mar.) cofa mayor o de
gavia.—m. **braces**, brazas de gavia.

maize [meịz], s. (bot.) maíz, m., zara.

majestic [mạdžéstịk], a. majestuoso.

majestically -[ạlị], adv. majestuosamente.

majesty [mædžịstị], s. majestad; majestuosidad.

majolica [mạdžálịkạ], s. (cerá.) mayólica.

major [méịdžọ(r)]. I. a. mayor, más grande (en
número, en cantidad, en extensión, en dignidad
o importancia); principal; (mús.) mayor, normal. II. s. (mil.) mayor, comandante; (for.)
mayor de edad.—m. **general**, general de división; (ant.) mariscal de campo.—m. **mode**, o
scale, (mús.) modo mayor. III. vn. (con in)
especializar en, estudiar como materia principal.
(Apl. a estudios de escuela y superiores.)

major-domo [-dóųmoų], s. mayordomo.

majority [mạdžárịtị], s. mayoría, el mayor número o la generalidad (de); pluralidad (de
votos); (for.) mayoría, mayor edad.

make [méịk], va. (pret. y pp. MADE) hacer; confeccionar, crear, elaborar, fabricar, producir;
efectuar, practicar; ser (buen material, empleado útil, mal maestro, etc.); formar, ser, ser
igual a (en arit.); compeler, forzar, obligar (a);
inducir, inclinar a; causar, ocasionar; poner
(triste, alegre); componer, trabajar; decir, pronunciar (un discurso, etc.); constituir, disponer,
aderezar; granjear, proporcionar; recoger, allegar; ganar; lograr; alcanzar, llegar a; atravesar,
pasar por, cruzar; (mar.) descubrir, avistar;
hacer (la cama, el tocado, etc.), arreglar; inferir,
deducir; adiestrar, enseñar; dar, prestar (excusas, juramento); andar, recorrer (leguas, distancia, etc.); dar (vueltas, revoluciones); cometer (error, equivocación). Seguido de acusativo modificado por un adjetivo indica acción
que causa la calidad o estado que el adjetivo
denota, y se traduce por "poner" o "hacer"
seguido del adjetivo, o por un solo verbo (to
make sad, poner triste, entristecer; to make
round, redondear, dar forma redonda; to make
public, hacer público, publicar).—**to m. a**
clean breast of, confesar, admitir francamente
un error.—**to m. a comeback**, (fam.) reponerse, rehabilitarse; replicar, redargüir.—**to m.**
a figure, hacer papel, hacer figura.—**to m. a**

fool of, engañar, embaucar; poner en ridículo.
—**to m. a fuss**, hacer alharaca, alharaquear.—
to m. again, rehacer, hacer de nuevo.—**to m.**
a great deal of = TO M. MUCH OF.—**to m. a**
hit, (fam.) causar buena impresión.—**to m. a**
litter, ensuciar, desordenar.—**to m. amends**,
indemnizar, resarcir, reparar, compensar.—**to**
m. a mistake, equivocarse.—**to m. a move**,
hacer una jugada; dar un paso, obrar; moverse.
—**to m. an appointment with**, citar.—**to m.**
and break, (elec.) abrir y cerrar un circuito.—
to m. angry, enojar.—**to m. a pass**, tirar una
estocada.—**to m. a point**, lograr (uno) su
objeto.—**to m. a point of**, dar importancia a;
esmerarse en; proponerse.—**to m. a practice**
of, acostumbrar, tener por costumbre.—**to m.**
a record, establecer un récord; tomar nota,
apuntar.—**to m. a (bad, good) show**, salir
(desairado, airoso), salir o hacerlo (mal, bien).
—**to m. a show of**, ostentar, hacer gala de;
poner en ridículo.—**to m. a stop**, detenerse;
hacer una pausa.—**to m. available to**, poner a
la disposición o al alcance de.—**to m. a wish**,
desear, pensar en algo que se desea.—**to m.**
both ends meet, pagar uno sus gastos, vivir
con lo que gana o tiene.—**to m. clear**, poner
claro; aclarar.—**to m. conspicuous**, destacar.
—**to m. difficult**, dificultar.—**to m. easy**, o
easier, facilitar.—**to m. effective**, hacer valer.
—**to m. evident**, evidenciar.—**to m. faces**,
hacer muecas, gestear.—**to m. fast**, amarrar,
afianzar, afirmar, asegurar.—**to m. friends**,
granjearse amigos; hacer amistad(es), amistarse.—**to m. fun of**, burlarse de.—**to m.**
good, mantener, defender; hacer bueno, probar; mejorar, cumplir; garantizar, responder de;
resarcir, indemnizar; lograr, llevar a cabo.—**to**
m. haste, darse prisa, apresurarse.—**to m.**
head, avanzar, progresar.—**to m. head**
against, hacer frente a, resistir a.—**to m.**
headway, adelantar.—**to m. hot**, calentar.—
to m. impossible, imposibilitar.—**to m. into**,
convertir en.—**to m. it a practice**, o **rule**,
tener o sentar por regla.—**to m. it hard**, o **hot**,
for one, causarle a uno trabajo, molestia o embarazo.—**to m. it one's business**, proponerse,
empeñarse, tomar como cosa suya.—**to m. it**
right, arreglar, pagar, compensar, indemnizar,
resarcir, etc. (según las circunstancias).—**to m.**
known, hacer saber; dar a conocer.—**to m.**
level, nivelar, allanar; (alb.) enrasar.—**to**
m. light of, burlarse de; no dar importancia a.
—**to m. little** (o **nothing**) **of**, hacer poco o
ningún caso de, despreciar.—**to m. love to**,
hacer el amor a, enamorar, cortejar.—**to m.**
money, ganar dinero.—**to m. much of**, dar
grande importancia a; estimar, apreciar; festejar; mimar, consentir.—**to m. neither head**
nor tail of, no comprender, no ver pies ni
cabeza a.—**to m. no bones of**, (fam.) no tener
escrúpulo, no pararse en pelillos acerca de.—
to m. no difference, no importar, ser indiferente, no importar.—**to m. nothing of**, no reparar en; no dar importancia a, no comprender.
—**to m. of**, sacar de, inferir, deducir, entender; aprovecharse de.—**to m. one**
of, ser o hacer uno de.—**to m. one's escape**,
escaparse, zafarse.—**to m. one's mark**, firmar
con una cruz; señalarse, distinguirse.—**to m.**
one's mouth water, hacerle o hacérsele a uno
la boca agua.—**to m. one's peace**, reconciliarse.—**to m. one's self known**, darse a
conocer.—**to m. one's self miserable**, entristecerse, afligirse.—**to m. one's self scarce**,
largarse, marcharse.—**to m. one's way**, avanzar; progresar; dirigirse; abrirse paso; salir bien.
—**to m. out**, comprender, descifrar, descubrir; divisar, columbrar; probar, justificar; suplir, abastecer, completar; componer, redactar;
escribir, hacer (recibo, etc.); llenar, formular,
extender (factura).—**to m. out of**, hacer o

formar de.—**to m. over**, rehacer, hacer de nuevo; ceder, traspasar; confiar.—**to m. progress**, progresar, hacer progresos.—**to m. ready**, preparar, alistar, aprestar; (impr.) imponer.—**to m. room**, abrir paso, hacer lugar.—**to m. room for**, dar paso a; dejar campo, lugar o puesto para; dar lugar o puesto a.—**to m. sail**, dar a la vela; largar (las) velas.—**to m. sense**, tener sentido (una frase); parecer acertado; (con *of*) comprender.—**to m. shift**, sacar partido; hacer lo posible; componérselas; (fam.) ir tirando.—**to m. short work of**, despachar pronto, disponer de (uno o algo) prontamente, sin rodeos.—**to m. sick**, enfermar; (fam.) fastidiar; inspirar desprecio; causar repugnancia. —**to m. slight of**, tener en poco, menospreciar. —**to m. speed**, darse prisa.—**to m. sport of**, burlarse de.—**to m. strong**, robustecer.—**to m. sure**, cerciorar, asegurar.—**to m. terms**, arreglarse.—**to m. the acquaintance of**, conocer a.—**to m. the best of**, sacar el mayor provecho de; hacer frente a, minorar en lo posible los efectos de.—**to m. (the) land**, descubrir la tierra, acercar la nave a la costa, tomar tierra.—**to m. the most of**, aprovecharlo todo; sacar el mejor partido de.—**to m. the worst of**, dar la peor apariencia a, menoscabar.—**to m. things hum**, (fam.) desplegar actividad.—**to m. time**, ir de prisa o velozmente.—**to m. tired**, cansar; fastidiar.—**to m. tracks**, alejarse de prisa.—**to m. uniform**, uniformar.— **to m. up**, reunir, formar; integrar (un comité, etc.); componer (un tren, etc.); completar; sumar; compensar, resarcir, indemnizar; recobrar (tiempo perdido, etc.); saldar, ajustar; conciliar, apaciguar; inventar (cuentos, etc.); (impr.) compaginar; enumerar, contar; afeitar, maquillar.—**to m. up one's mind**, resolverse, determinar.—**to m. use of**, servirse de, hacer uso de.—**to m. void**, anular, invalidar.—**to m. water**, hacer aguas, orinar; (mar.) hacer agua. —**to m. way**, abrir paso.—**to m. worse**, empeorar.

make, *vn.* (con **at, for**, o **toward**) dirigirse o encaminarse a, abalanzarse a; (con **for** o **to**) contribuir a, servir para, tender o propender a; crecer (la marea); formarse (el hielo).—**to m. after**, tratar de coger, seguir.—**to m. against**, estar en oposición a; ser contrario o nocivo a.— **to m. as if**, o **as though**, fingir(se), hacer como si.—**to m. away**, largarse, huirse.—**to m. away with**, derrochar; llevarse, hurtar; suprimir, matar.—**to m. away with one's self**, suicidarse; quitarse de en medio.—**to m. believe**, fingir.—**to m. bold**, atreverse (a); tomarse la libertad (de).—**to m. free with**, no gastar cumplidos con; servirse de sin pedir.— **to m. good**, salir bien o adelante, cumplir.— **to m. merry**, divertirse; regodearse.—**to m. off** = TO M. AWAY.—**to m. off with**, llevarse, quitar de delante, alzarse con; quitar.—**to m. out**, salir (bien o mal), tener (buen, mal) éxito. —**to m. sure**, asegurarse, cerciorarse.—**to m. up**, hacer las paces, echar pelillos a la mar; componerse con afeites, afeitarse, maquillarse. —**to m. up for**, compensar.—**to m. up to**, acercarse a; (fam.) obsequiar a; galantear.

make, *s.* hechura, forma, figura; estructura; fabricación, fábrica, producción, manufactura; producto; marca, nombre (de fábrica).—**m. and break**, (elec.), cortacircuitos, interruptor. —**on the m.**, (fam.) resuelto a sacar partido; en vías de ascender.

make-believe [-bilìv]. I. *a.* fingido, falso, de mentirillas. II. *s.* artificio, artimaña; pretexto; fingidor, hipócrita, *mf.*

makefast [-fæst], *s.* (mar.) amarradero.

maker [-œ(r)], *s.* hacedor; artífice; constructor; fabricante; autor; (for.) librador (de cheque, pagaré, etc.); otorgante (de escritura).—**the M.**, el Hacedor, Dios.

makeshift [-ṣìft]. I. *a.* temporal, interino, provisional. II. *s.* expediente, tapaagujeros.

make-up [-ʌp], *s.* conjunto; carácter, modo de ser; (impr.) imposición; (teat.) caracterización, modo de pintarse y arreglarse; mano (*f.*) de gato; afeite, pintura, maquillaje.

makeweight [-wejt], *s.* complemento de peso o contrapeso en una balanza; suplente.

making [-ìŋ], *s.* composición, estructura; hechura, confección, fabricación; preparación; formación; (a veces *pl.*) germen, elementos, ingredientes.—**m. iron**, hierro de calafate.—**in the m.**, haciéndose o formándose, en vía de construcción o de formación.—**the m. of**, la causa o el medio del buen éxito de; lo que hace (hizo, etc.) a (una persona).

Malabar [mǽlabar], *a.* malabar, malabárico.

Malaccan [mǝlǽkan], *a.* y *s.* = MALAY(AN.

malaceous [mǝléjʃas], *a.* (bot.) pomáceo.

malachite [mǽlakajt], *s.* (min.) malaquita.

malacology [-kǎlodʒị], *s.* (zool.) malacología.

malacopterygian [-kaptẹrídʒịan], *a.* y *s.* (zool.) malacopterigio.

malacostracan [-kástrakan], *s.* y *a.* (zool.) malacostráceo.

maladdress [mǽlǝdrés], *s.* descortesía, falta de tacto; desmaña, torpeza.

maladjusted [mǽlǝdʒʌstịd], *a.* de mal ajuste; inadapto; desadaptado.

maladjustment [-mẹnt], *s.* ajuste defectuoso; inadaptación; (biol.) desadaptación; desconformidad, discordancia.

maladministration [mǽlǝdmịnịstréjṣǝn], *s.* mala administración, desgobierno, mal manejo.

maladroit [mǽlǝdrójt], *a.* torpe, desmañado, falto de tino o de tacto.

malady [mǽlǎdị], *s.* mal, enfermedad, dolencia.

Malaga [mǽlǎgǎ], *s.* vino o uva de Málaga.

malaise [mǝléjẓ], *s.* indisposición, malestar.

malapert [mǽlapœrt], *a.* desvergonzado, descomedido, descarado.

malapropism [mǽlaprapịzm], *s.* despropósito; voz o expresión que resulta grotesca por su aplicación impropia.

malapropos [mǽlæpropóụ], *a.* impropio, fuera de propósito, despropositado.

malar [méjlạ(r)], *a.* (anat.) malar.—**m. bone**, hueso malar, pómulo.

malaria [mǝlérịǎ], *s.* (med.) paludismo, malaria; fiebre palúdica.—**malarial, malarious** [-l, -ʌs], *a.* palúdico, malárico.

malate [méjlejt], *s.* (quím.) malato.

Malay(an [mǝléj(ạn], *a.* y *s.* malayo, de Malaca.

malcontent [mǽlkǝntent], *a.* y *s.* malcontento.

male [mejl]. I. *a.* masculino; varón; macho; varonil; compuesto de varones; (bot.) estaminífero, que tiene estambres.—**m. issue**, hijos varones, sucesión masculina.—**m. screw**, tornillo. II. *s.* varón, hombre; animal macho.

malediction [mǽlịdịkṣǝn], *s.* maldición.

malefactor [mǽlịfæktǝ(r)], *s.* malhechor.

maleficence [mǝléfịṣens], *s.* maleficencia.

malefic(ent [mǝléfịk, -fịṣent], *a.* maléfico.

malevolence [mǝlévolẹns], *s.* malevolencia.— **malevolent** [-ẹnt], *a.* malévolo, maligno.— **malevolently** [-lị], *adv.* malignamente.

malfeasance [mǽlfìẓans], *s.* (for.) fechoría, desaguisado; acto ilegal o punible.

malformation [mǽlforméjṣǝn], *s.* formación defectuosa o anormal, deformidad.—**malformed** [mǽlfórmd], *a.* mal formado, contrahecho.

malic [méjlịk], *a.* (quím.) málico.

malice [mǽlịs], *s.* malicia, mala intención, malignidad.—**m. aforethought**, (for.) premeditación.

malicious [mǝlíṣʌs], *a.* malicioso, maligno, maléfico.—**maliciously** [-lị], *adv.* maliciosamente. —**maliciousness** [-nịs], *s.* mala intención, malicia.

malign [mǝláịn]. I. *a.* maligno; pernicioso, perjudicial. II. *va.* difamar; calumniar.

malignancy [mǝlígnǝnsi], *s.* malignidad, malicia, malevolencia; (med.) malignidad.

malignant [mǝlígnǝnt]. **I.** *a.* maligno, malévolo; perverso; nocivo; virulento.—**m. fever,** fiebre perniciosa.—**m. tumor,** tumor maligno. **II.** *s.* hombre malintencionado.

malignantly [-li], *adv.* malignamente.

maligner [mǝlájnœ(r)], *s.* detractor, difamador.

malignity [mǝlígniti], *s.* malignidad; virulencia.

malignly [mǝlájnli], *adv.* malignamente.

malinger [mǝlíngœœ(r)], *vn.* fingirse enfermo.

malingerer [-œœ(r)], *s.* remolón, (fam.) maula.

malison [mǽlizǝn], *s.* (poét.) maldición.

mall [mɔl], *s.* mazo, mallo; mallo (juego y terreno donde se jugaba); alameda, paseo; (hist.) tribunal de los francos. *V.* MAUL.

mallard [mǽlǝrd], *s.* (orn.) pato o ánade silvestre.

malleability, *o* **malleableness** [mǽliǝbiliti, -blnis], *s.* maleabilidad.

malleable [-bl], *a.* maleable; dúctil; dócil.—**m. cast iron,** fundición maleable, fundición dulce de moldeo.—**m. iron,** (E. U.) = M. CAST IRON; (Ingl.) hierro forjado.

malleate [mǽliejt], *va.* martillar.

mallein [mǽliin], *s.* (vet.) maleína.

malleolar [mæliólǝ(r)], *a.* (anat.) maleolar.

malleolus [-lʌs], *s.* (anat.) maléolo.

mallet [mǽlit], *s.* mazo, maceta, mallo, machote.

malleus [mǽliʌs], *s.* (anat.) martillo (del oído).

mallow [mǽlou], *s.* (bot.) malva.

malmsey [mámzi], *s.* malvasía (cierto vino).

malnutrition [mælnjutríʃǝn], *s.* desnutrición, nutrición defectuosa; alimentación deficiente.

malodorous [mælóudǝrǝs], *a.* hediondo, fétido, que huele mal; desagradable.

malpighiaceous [mælpigiéjʃiǝs], *a.* (bot.) malpigiáceo.

Malpighian [mælpígiǝn], *a.* (anat.) malpighiano, de Malpighi.

malposition [mælpozíʃǝn], *s.* (med.) posición anormal o defectuosa de un órgano, etc.

malpractice [mælprǽktis], *s.* (med. y cir.) malpraxis, tratamiento erróneo, perjudicial o ilegal; inmoralidad.

malt [mɔlt]. **I.** *s.* malta, *mf.*, cebada germinada; cerveza.—**m. extract,** extracto de malta.—**m. liquor,** cerveza.—**m. sugar,** (quím.) maltosa, azúcar de malta. **II.** *va.* hacer germinar la cebada; preparar el malta; tratar o mezclar con malta o extracto de malta.

Malta fever [mɔltǝ fívœœ(r)], *s.* (med.) fiebre (*f.*) de Malta o mediterránea.

maltase [mɔltejs], *s.* (bioquím.) maltasa.

Maltese [mɔltíz], *a.* y *s.* maltés; gato maltés.— M. cross, cruz de Malta.

maltha [mǽlθǝ], *s.* malta, betún fósil; variedad de ozocerita; brea mineral.

Malthusian [mælθjúʒiǝn], *s.* y *a.* maltusiano.— **Malthusianism** [-izm], *s.* maltusianismo.

maltman [mɔltmæn], **maltster** [mɔltstœ(r)], *s.* preparador de malta.

maltose [mɔltous], *s.* (quím.) maltosa.

maltreat [mæltrít], *va.* maltratar.

maltreatment [-mǝnt], *s.* maltrat(amient)o.

malvaceous [mælvéjʃiǝs], *a.* (bot.) malváceo.

malvasia [mælvǝsíǝ], *s.* (bot.) malvasía (uva).

malversation [mælvœœrséjʃǝn], *s.* malversación.

mamba [mǽmbǝ], *s.* (zool.) cobra surafricana muy venenosa.

Mameluke [mǽmǝljuk], *s.* mameluco.

mamey [mæméj *o* mamí], **mamey apple,** *s.* (bot.) mamey. *V.* MAMMEE y SAPODILLA.

mam(m)a [mámǝ *o* mǝmá], *s.* mamá, *f.*

mamma [mámǝ], *s.* (anat., zool.) mama, teta.

mammal [mǽmǝl], *s.* mamífero.

Mammalia [mæméjliǝ], *s. pl.* (zool.) mamíferos.

mammalian [-n], *a.* mamífero.

mammalogy [mæmálǝdʒi], *s.* (zool.) mamalogía.

mammary [mǽmǝri], *a.* mamario.

mammee [mæméj *o* mamí], *s.* (bot.) mamey.

mammiferous [mæmífœrǝs], *a.* mamífero.

mammiform [mǽmifɔrm], *a.* mamiforme; atetado.

mammilla [mæmílǝ], *s.* (anat.) pezón; mamila.

mammillary [mǽmilǝri], *a.* mamilar.

mammillate(d [-lejt(id], *a.* que tiene pezones; mamilado.

Mammon [mǽmǝn], *s.* espíritu de la codicia, becerro de oro; dios de las riquezas.

mammonist [-ist], *s.* avaro, codicioso.

mammoth [mǽmǝθ]. **I.** *a.* enorme, gigantesco. **II.** *s.* mamut, elefante fósil.

mammy [mǽmi], *s.* (fam.) madre, *f.*, mamá, *f.*; (E. U. del Sur) negra, ama, niñera o criada.

man [mæn], *s.* (*pl.* **men**) hombre; la humanidad o el género humano; varón; persona, sujeto; criado, servidor; peón (de ajedrez o de damas); soldado (vg.: *officers and men,* oficiales y soldados).—**m. about town,** el que frecuenta los clubs, teatros, etc.; paseante en corte.—**m. and wife,** marido y mujer.—**m.-at-arms,** soldado, hombre de armas (esp. el caballero armado).— **m.-eater,** antropófago; animal que ataca al hombre (apl. esp. a tiburones, tigres y leones).— **m. Friday,** criado fiel; secuaz (*m.*) servil.— **m.-hater,** misántropo; mujer que aborrece al sexo masculino.—**m.-hour,** unidad de trabajo hecho por un hombre en una hora.—**m.-killer,** homicida, *mf.*, asesino.—**m. midwife,** partero, comadrón.—**m. of all work,** hombre o criado para todo, (fam.) factótum.—**M. of Destiny,** Hombre del Destino (Napoleón).—**m. of God,** santo, profeta, *m.*; clérigo.—**m. of letters,** hombre de letras, literato.—**M. of Sorrows,** Jesucristo.—**m. of straw,** testaferro.—**m. of the world,** hombre de mundo.—**m.-of-war,** buque de guerra.—**m.-of-war bird,** (orn.) fragata, rabihorcado.—**m. power,** potencial humana; brazos, *m. pl.*; (mil.) fuerzas asequibles, gente (*f.*) de combate.—**m.'s estate,** edad viril.—as one m., todos a una, como un solo hombre, unánimemente.—the m. in the street, el común de las gentes.—the sick m. of Europe, el enfermo de Europa, Turquía, el sultán de la Puerta Otomana.—to a m., todos, sin excepción; hasta el último hombre.

man, *va.* (mar.) tripular, dotar, (a)marinar; armar; (mil.) guarnecer, poner guarnición a.—to m. the pumps, (mar.) armar las bombas.—to m. the yards, (mar.) disponer la gente sobre las vergas.

manacle [mǽnǝkl]. **I.** *s.* manilla.—*pl.* esposas. **II.** *va.* maniatar, poner esposas o manillas a.

manage [mǽnidʒ]. **I.** *va.* manipular, hacer andar o funcionar; manejar, dirigir, administrar, regentar, regir; gestionar, procurar; amansar, domar. **II.** *vn.* ingeniarse, arreglarse, componérselas; darse uno maña o trazas (de); llevar la batuta.

manageable [-ǝbl], *a.* manejable; dócil, tratable. —**manageableness** [-nis], *s.* calidad de manejable; docilidad; flexibilidad; mansedumbre.

management [-mǝnt], *s.* manejo, gobierno, dirección, administración; (com.) gerencia; gestión, negociación; proceder, conducta, régimen; uso, empleo; prudencia, destreza; dirección, cuerpo de directores; empresa (de teatro, etc.).

manager [-œœ(r)], *s.* administrador, director; empresario; superintendente; regente; (com.) gerente.

managerial [mænǝdʒíriǝl], *a.* directivo, administrativo.

managership [mǽnidʒœrʃip], *s.* gerencia.

managing [mǽnidʒiŋ], *a.* directivo, dirigente.— **m. expenses,** gastos de administración o dirección.—**m. partner,** (socio) gestor o gerente.

manatee [mǽnǝti], *s.* (zool.) manatí, vaca marina.

manchineel [mæntʃiníl], *s.* (bot.) manzanillo.

Manchurian [mæntʃúriǝn], *a.* y *s.* manchú; manchuriano.

mancipation [mænsipéjŝǫn], *s.* (for.) mancipación; emancipación de la patria potestad.

manciple [mǽnsipl], *s.* mayordomo de colegio.

mandamus [mændéjmʌs], *s.* (for.) mandamiento, carta orden, despacho.

mandarin [mǽndạriṇ], *s.* mandarín; (M.) lengua mandarina; (tint.) amarillo de mandarín; (bot.) (naranja) mandarina.

mandatary [mǽndạteri], *s.* (for.) mandatario.

mandate [mǽndejt]. I. *s.* mandato; mandado, encargo, comisión; legacía o mandato de la Sociedad de las Naciones. II. *va.* asignar por mandato.

mandator [mændéjtọ(r)], *s.* (for.) mandante.

mandatory [mǽndạtọri]. I. *a.* (for.) preceptivo, obligatorio. II. *s.* mandatario.

mandible [mǽndjbl], *s.* (anat. y zool.) mandíbula, quijada, maxilar inferior.

mandibular [mændíbyulạ̈(r)], *a.* mandibular.

mandibulate [-ejt], *a.* mandibulado.

Mandingo [mændíŋgou], *a.* y *s.* mandinga, *mf.*

mandolin [mǽndoliṇ], *s.* (mús.) mandolina, bandola, bandolín.

mandragora [mændrǽgọrạ̈], **mandrake** [mǽndrejk], *s.* (bot.) mandrágora.

mandrel [mǽndrẹl], *s.* (mec.) mandril, eje de torno.

mandrill [mǽndrjl], *s.* (zool.) mandril.

mane [mejn], *s.* crin o crines, *f. pl.*; melena.

maned [-d], *a.* crinado, crinito.

manège [mænéʒ], *s.* equitación, manejo; picadero.

manes [méjniz], *s. pl.* manes.

maneuver, manœuvre [mạnúvœ(r)]. I. *s.* (mar.) maniobra; (mar. y mil.) evolución; manejo, artificio. II. *va.* y *vn.* maniobrar; ejecutar maniobras o evoluciones; intrigar, tramar.

maneuverability [-abílịti], *s.* maniobrabilidad. —**maneuverable** [-ạbl], *a.* maniobrable.

manful [mǽnfụl], *a.* viril, varonil; valiente; resuelto.—**manfully** [-i], *adv.* viril, varonil o valientemente.—**manfulness** [-njs], *s.* virilidad; valentía; resolución.

manganate [mǽŋgạnejt], *s.* (quím.) manganato.

manganese [-nís], *s.* (quím.) manganeso.—**m. bronze**, bronce mangánico; (tint.) color pardo debido a sales de manganeso (ll. t. **m. brown**). —**m. steel**, acero mangánico, acero manganeso. —**m. spar**, rodonita, espato mangánico.—**m. sulphide**, sulfuro de manganeso, alabandina.

manganic [mæŋgǽnjk], *a.* mangánico.

manganite [mǽŋgạnajt], *s.* (min.) manganita; (quím.) manganito.

manganous [-nʌs], *a.* manganoso.

mange [mejndʒ], *s.* (vet.) roña, sarna, caracha.

mangel-wurzel [mǽŋgel wœ́rzẹl], *s.* (bot.) remolacha forrajera.

manger [méjndʒœ(r)], *s.* pesebre.

manginess [méjndʒinjs], *s.* sarnazo, roña.

mangle [mǽŋgl]. I. *va.* mutilar, destrozar, estropear, lacerar; echar a perder, chafallar; satinar, alisar, pasar las telas por la calandria. II. *s.* (mec.) calandria; lustrador; máquina de aplanchar, planchadora mecánica o automática.

mangler [mǽŋglœ(r)], *s.* destrozador, despedazador; lustrador.—**mangling** [-gliŋ], *s.* despedazamiento; acto de lustrar telas, planchar con planchadora mecánica, etc.

mango [mǽŋgou], *s.* (bot.) mango.

mangonel [mǽŋgonel], *s.* (mil.) catapulta.

mangosteen [mǽŋgostin], *s.* (bot.) mangostán.

mangrove [mǽŋgrouv], *s.* (bot.) mangle.

mangy [méjndʒi], *a.* sarnoso, roñoso.

manhandle [mǽnhændl], *va.* mover o manipular a brazo, sin fuerza mecánica; maltratar, tratar ruda o violentamente.

manhole [-hoụl], *s.* toma de aire (de una alcantarilla); boca o abertura de inspección de cloacas, alcantarillas, calderas, cañerías, cables telefónicos, etc.; registro, pozo de visita o de acceso; nicho (de refugio) en un túnel.

manhood [-hụd], *s.* naturaleza humana; los hombres; estado o condición de hombre; edad viril; virilidad; (for.) masculinidad; hombradía; valentía.

manhunt [-hʌnt], *s.* caza del hombre.

mania [méjnjạ̈], *s.* manía; locura, frenesí; tema.

maniac [méjnjæk], *a.* y *s.*, **maniacal** [mạnájạkạl], *a.* maniático, maníaco, loco, furioso.

Manichean [mænikíạn], *a.* y *s.*, **Manichee** [mǽnjki], *s.* maniqueo.

Manicheism [-jzm], *s.* maniqueísmo.

manichord [mǽnjkord], *s.* (mús.) manicordio.

manicure [mǽnjkjur]. I. *s.* manicura, cuidado de las manos y uñas. *V.* MANICURIST. II. *va.* cuidar y arreglar (manos y uñas). III. *vn.* hacer la manicura, ejercer el oficio de manicuro.— **manicurist** [-jst], *s.* manicuro, manicura, manicurista.

manifest [mǽnjfɛst]. I. *a.* manifiesto, claro, descubierto. II. *s.* (com.) manifiesto. III. *va.* manifestar; hacer patente; presentar el manifiesto de; poner o declarar en el manifiesto. IV. *vn.* hacer una manifestación o demostración pública; manifestarse (un espíritu).

manifestation [-éjŝọn], *s.* manifestación.

manifestly [-li], *adv.* manifiestamente.

manifestness [-njs], *s.* evidencia clara o patente; perspicuidad.

manifesto [mǽnjfɛstou], *s.* manifiesto, proclama.

manifold [mǽnjfoụld]. I. *a.* múltiple, multíplice, vario, numeroso; diverso. II. *va.* sacar varias copias al mismo tiempo. III. *s.* copia o duplicado; (mat.) agregado; (aut.) (tubo) múltiple. —**manifolder** [-œ(r)], *s.* copiador múltiple, policopia.

manifoldness [-njs], *s.* multiplicidad.

manikin [mǽnjkịn], *s.* pigmeo, enano; maniquí; muñeco. *V.* MANNEQUIN.

Manila [mạnílạ̈]. I. *s.* = M. HEMP, M. PAPER. II. *a.* manilense, manileño.—**M. cheroot**, trompetilla, cigarro filipino.—**M. hemp**, (bot.) abacá, cáñamo de Manila.—**M. paper**, papel de Manila.

manilla [mạnílạ̈], *s.* (joy.) manilla, ajorca; en algunos juegos de naipes, mala o malilla (ll. t. **manille**). *V.* MANILA HEMP, etc.

manioc [mǽnjak], *s.* (bot.) mandioca, (Am.) yuca.

maniple [mǽnjpl], *s.* (igl., mil.) manípulo.

manipular [mạnípyulạ̈(r)], *a.* manuable; perteneciente al manípulo.

manipulate [-lejt]. I. *va.* manipular; manejar. II. *vn.* trabajar con las manos.—**manipulation** [-léjŝọn], *s.* manipulación; manipuleo.— **manipulative, manipulatory** [-lejtiv, -lạtọri], *a.* manipulante.—**manipulator** [-lejtọ(r)], *s.* manipulador.

manito(u [mǽnjtoụ, -tu], *s.* espíritu; fetiche.

mankind [mænkájnd], *s.* la humanidad, el género humano; [mǽnkạjnd], los hombres, el sexo masculino.

manlike [mǽnlajk], *a.* varonil; hombruno.

manliness [mǽnljnjs], *s.* virilidad; hombradía; valor, valentía, ánimo.

manly [mǽnli], *a.* varonil, viril; animoso.

manna [mǽnạ̈], *s.* maná.—**m. sugar**, manita.

mannequin [mǽnekịn], *s.* mujer que se pone los trajes de venta para enseñarlos; maniquí.

manner [mǽnœ(r)], *s.* manera, modo; modo de ser; suerte, *f.*, jaez, *m.*, género, especie; traza, aire, ademán, porte.—*pl.* modales; costumbres; crianza, educación, urbanidad.—**after the m. of**, como, a la manera de, (cambiando un poco el giro) a la, a lo.—**after** (o **in**) **this m.**, así, de este modo.—**by all m. of means**, ciertamente; de todos modos; de cualquier modo.—**by no m. of means**, de ningún modo.—**in a m.**, en cierto modo, hasta cierto punto.—**in a m. of speaking**, como quien dice, por decirlo así.—**in such a m. as (to)**, de tal modo o suerte (que).—**in the m. of**, a fuer de, a guisa de, en son de.—**to**

the m. born, avezado (a ello) desde la cuna; de noble cuna, bien nacido.

mannered [-d], *a.* de modales, crianza, etc. (buenos, malos, etc.); amanerado; afectado.

mannerism [-izm], *s.* amaneramiento, manerismo; (teat.) latiguillo.—**mannerist** [-ist], *s.* manerista, artista amanerado.

mannerliness [-linis], *s.* urbanidad, cortes(an)ía.

mannerly [-li], I. *a.* cortés, urbano, atento, bien educado. II. *adv.* urbanamente.

mannish [mǽniʃ], *a.* ahombrado, hombruno, a lo hombre, machuno.—**m. woman,** varona, amazona, virago, *f.,* (fam.) marimacho.

mannite [mǽnait], **mannitol** [mǽnitol], *s.* (quím.) manita.

manœuvre, *s.* y *v.* = MANEUVER.

manometer [mǽnámetœ(r)], *s.* manómetro.

manometric(al [mænométrik(al], *a.* manométrico.

manor [mǽno(r)], *s.* feudo, señorío; finca solariega.—**m. house, m. seat,** solar, casa solariega.—**to the m. born** = TO THE MANNER BORN.

manorial [manóriəl], *a.* señorial, solariego.

mansard [mǽnsard], *s.* buhardilla, (galic.) mansarda.—**m. roof,** (arq.) techo Mansard, tejado abuhardillado o aguardillado.

manse [mæns], *s.* rectoría; (ant.) manso, masada.

manservant [mǽnsœrvant], *s.* criado.

mansion [mǽnʃon], *s.* hotel, casa grande y lujosa; solar, casa solariega; (raro) mansión, morada, residencia.

manslaughter [mǽnslɔtœ(r)], *s.* homicidio sin premeditación pero criminal.

manslayer [-sleiœ(r)], *s.* homicida, *mf.*

mantel(piece [mǽntel(pis], *s.* (arq.) repisa, mesilla o tablero de chimenea francesa; manto de la chimenea.

mantelet [mǽntelet], *s.* capotillo, manteleta; (mil.) mantelete, galápago.

mantelleta [mæntelétə], *s.* (igl.) mantelete.

mantelshelf [mǽntelʃelf], **manteltree** [-tri], *s.* = MANTELPIECE.

mantilla [mæntílə], *s.* mantilla, mantón.

mantis [mǽntis], *s.* (ent.) mantis religiosa, predicador, fraile rezador, (Arg.) mamboretá, *m.*

mantissa [mæntísə], *s.* (mat.) mantisa.

mantle [mǽntl], I. *s.* manto, manteo, capa; palio; (zool.) manto; (anat.) palio, corteza cerebral; caperuza de gasa incandescente, mechero Auer. II. *va.* y *vn.* cubrir, tapar; extender las alas; extenderse, desparramarse; ruborizarse, sonrojarse.

mantling [-liŋ], *s.* (blas.) mantelete, lambrequín.

mantua [mǽnchuə], *s.* manto. *V.* MANTLE.—**mantuamaker** [-meikœ(r)], *s.* mantero; modista.

Mantuan [mǽnchuən], *a.* y *s.* mantuano.

manual [mǽnyuəl], I. *a.* manual; manuable.—**m. alphabet,** alfabeto dactilológico (letras indicadas con los dedos).—**m. training,** enseñanza de trabajo manual; enseñanza de artes y oficios.—**m. work,** trabajo manual. II. *s.* manual; (mús.) teclado de órgano; (mil.) ejercicio de armas.

manubrium [manjúbriʌm], *s.* (anat., zool.) apófisis inferior del martillo; parte (*f.*) superior del esternón; manubrio (de las medusas); (bot.) manubrio.

manufactory [mænyufǽktori], *s.* fábrica, taller.

manufacture [-fǽkchu(r)]. I. *s.* fabricación, elaboración; manufactura, artefacto, obra hecha o fabricada. II. *va.* hacer, manufacturar, fabricar. III. *vn.* manufacturar, ser fabricante.

manufactured [-d], *a.* manufacturado, fabricado.

manufacturer [-œ(r)], *s.* fabricante, industrial.

manufacturing [-iŋ]. I. *a.* manufacturero, industrial, elaborador, fabril. II. *s.* fabricación, manufactura, elaboración.

manumission [mænyumíʃon], *s.* (for.) manumisión.

manumit [-mít], *va.* manumitir, emancipar.

manumitter [-œ(r)], *s.* manumisor.—**manumitted** [-id], *a.* manumiso.

manure [manjúr]. I. *va.* (agr.) abonar, estercolar. II. *s.* abono, estiércol, fimo.

manuscript [mǽnyuskript]. I. *a.* manuscrito, (por) escrito. II. *s.* manuscrito; (impr.) original.

Manx [mæŋks], *a.* y *s.* de la isla de Man: lenguaje y pueblo de dicha isla.—**M. cat,** (zool.) especie de gato doméstico de cola rudimentaria.

many [méni], *a.,* *pron.* y *s.* muchos, muchas. A menudo va seguido de nombre en singular con el artículo indeterminado, pero denota más de uno y se traduce en plural; v. gr.: *many a man,* muchos hombres. Forma con adjetivos en *-ed* derivados de sustantivos expresiones adjetivas, que se traducen por *de muchos* seguido del sustantivo correspondiente, o alguna otra expresión equivalente: *many-sided,* de muchos lados o aspectos, variado; *many-legged,* de muchos pies; *many-colored,* de muchos colores, multicolor, policromo.—**a great m.,** muchos, muchísimos.—**as m.,** igual número, otros tantos; más (*twice as many,* dos veces más).—**as m. as,** tantos como; cuantos; más que; hasta.—**how m.,** ¿cuántos?—**one, two,** etc., **too m.,** uno, dos, etc., de más o de sobra.—**so m.,** tantos.—**the m.,** la mayoría, la mayor parte de la gente; las masas, la muchedumbre.—**too m.,** demasiados.—**very m.,** muy muchos, muchísimos.

manyplies [-plaiz], *s.* (zool.) omaso, libro.

map [mæp]. I. *s.* mapa, *m.,* carta geográfica, plano topográfico.—**m. maker,** cartógrafo. II. *va.* trazar un mapa; (a veces con **out**) proyectar, hacer planes, formar (un plan).

maple [méipl], *s.* (bot.) arce, ácere, meple.—**m. sugar,** azúcar de arce.—**m. syrup,** jarabe de arce de azúcar.

mar [mar], *va.* echar a perder, estropear, dañar, malear, viciar, desfigurar; frustrar, aguar (gozo).

marabou(t [mǽrabu(t], *s.* (orn.) marabú; pluma de marabú.—**Marabout,** *s.* morabito, morabuto, anacoreta o santón mahometano.

maraschino [mǽraskínou], *s.* marrasquino.—**m. cherries,** cerezas confitadas en marrasquino.

marasmus [marǽzmʌs], *s.* (med.) marasmo, demacración.

marathon [mǽraθan], *s.* (dep.) maratón, *f.,* carrera pedestre de recorrido extenso (gen. de 42.186 metros, o de unas 26 millas).

maraud [marɔ́d]. I. *vn.* merodear, pecorear. II. *va.* saquear.—**marauder** [-œ(r)], *s.* merodeador.—**marauding** [-iŋ], *s.* merodeo, pillaje, pecorea.

maravedi [mǽravédi], *s.* maravedí (moneda).

marble [márbl]. I. *s.* mármol; bolita, canica o pita (de mármol, vidrio, etc., con que juegan los niños); (impr.) piedra de imponer.—*pl.* juego de bolitas, etc.—**m. cutter,** marmolista.—**m. work,** marmolería, obra de mármol.—**m. works,** marmolería (taller). II. *a.* marmóreo, de mármol.—**m.-hearted,** duro, empedernido. III. *va.* jaspear, crispir; empelechar.—**marbled leaves,** (enc.) cortes jaspeados.—**marbled paper,** papel jaspeado.

marbleize [-aiz], *va.* jaspear, crispir.

marbling [-bliŋ], *s.* marmoración, jaspeadura.

marbler [-blœ(r)], *s.* marmolista; jaspeador.

marbly [-bli], *a.* marmóreo, marmoleño.

marc [mark], *s.* orujo.

marcasite [márkəsait], *s.* (min.) marcasita.

marcel [marsél]. I. *va.* rizar el pelo a la Marcel. II. *s.* **m. (wave),** ondulado o rizado Marcel, peinado con ondulaciones.

marcescent [marsésənt], *a.* (bot.) marcescente.

march [márch]. I. *va.* poner en marcha, hacer marchar. II. *vn.* marchar, caminar; (con **upon** o **with**) lindar, estar contiguo o vecino.—**m. in,** entrar.—**to m. off,** irse, marcharse.—**to m. on,** marchar, caminar; seguir adelante.—**to m. out,** salir o hacer salir.—**to m. up,**

avanzar, adelantar. III. s. marcha; progreso, adelanto; (mil., mús.) marcha, pasodoble; frontera, lindero; (geog.) marca, provincia fronteriza; (M.) marzo.

marcher [-œ(r)], s. el que marcha a pie; rayano, habitante de una frontera o de una marca; (hist.) jefe de fuerzas que defendían una frontera.

marching [-iŋ]. I. s. marcha. II. pa. marchando, de o en marcha.—**m. order**, orden de marcha.

marchioness [máršǫnes], s. marquesa.

marchland [márčlænd], s. región fronteriza, frontera.

marchpane [márčpein], s. mazapán.

Marcionite [máršǫnait], s. marcionista.

marconigram [markóuŋigræm], s. marconigrama, m., radio(tele)grama, m.

Mardi gras [márdi grá], s. martes de carnaval.

mare [mer], s. yegua.—**m.'s-nest**, agua de cerrajas.—**m.'s-tail**, (bot.) cola de caballo.

marekanite [mærękǽnait], s. (min.) marecanita.

mareograph [mǽriǫgræf], s. mareógrafo.

margarate [márgǫreit], s. (quím.) margarato.

margaric [margǽrik], a. (quím.) margárico.

margarin [márgǫrin], s. (quím.) margarina.

margarin(e [márdžǫrin], s. margarina, mantequilla artificial, manteca falsificada.

margarite [márgǫrait], s. (min.) margarita.

margay [márgei], s. (zool.) margay, mamífero félido americano.

marge [mardž], s. (poét.) = MARGIN.

margent [márdžent]. I. a. marginal. II. s. apostilla, acotación.

margin [márdžin]. I. s. margen, mf., borde, orilla; reserva (para futuras contingencias); ganancia bruta; sobrante, excedente; (en el seguro) = LOADING. II. va. marginar, margenar, apostillar; poner borde o margen. III. vn. depositar fondos como margen para ciertas jugadas de bolsa.

marginal [-ạl], a. marginal.—**m. note**, margen, mf., apostilla, acotación.—**marginalia** [-éiliǫ], s. pl. notas o anotaciones marginales.—**marginally** [-ạli], adv. al margen.—**marginate(d** [-eit(id], a. marginado.

margrave [márgreiv], s. margrave.

margraviate [margréivieit], s. margraviato, dignidad y territorio de un margrave.

marguerite [margǫrít], s. (bot.) margarita.

Marian [mǽrian], a. (igl.) mariano; (Ingl.) adicto o referente a la reina Mary.

marigold [mǽrigould], s. (bot.) caléndula, clavelón, maravilla, flamenquilla.

marimba [mǫrímbǫ], s. (Am., mús.) marimba, especie de tímpano o xilófono.

marinade [mærinéid], s. escabeche.—**marinate** [mǽrineit], va. escabechar o marinar pescado o carne; (cocina) remojar en vino o vinagre con aceite, especias, etc.; sazonar de antemano (pollo, legumbres, etc.) con salsa francesa para ensaladas.

marine [mǫrín]. I. a. marino, marítimo, naval, náutico, de mar.—**m. belt**, (der. int.) aguas jurisdiccionales.—**m. boiler**, caldera marina. —**M. Corps**, (E. U.) Cuerpo de Infantería de Marina.—**m. engine**, máquina marina.—**m. insurance**, seguro marítimo.—**m. league**, legua marina (5.56 km.).—**m. stores** = NAVAL STORES. II. s. marino, soldado de marina; marina (mercante); (pint.) marina.

mariner [mǽrinǫ(r)], s. marinero, marino, nauta, m.—**m.'s compass**, brújula, compás de mar(ear).

Mariolatry [mæriálǫtri], s. (igl.) hiperdulía.

marionette [mærionét], s. marioneta, títere.

marital [mǽritạl], a. marital, matrimonial.

maritime [mǽritaim], a. marítimo, marino, naval.—**m. insurance**, seguro marítimo.—**m. law**, código marítimo.—**m. perils**, peligros y riesgos del mar.

marjoram [márdžǫrạm], s. (bot.) amáraco, me-

jorana o mayorana, sarilla, sampsuco. V. WILD M.

mark [márk]. I. s. marca; seña o señal, f.; rótulo; nota, importancia (a man of mark, un hombre de nota); calificación (de escuela, etc.); (hist.) límite, frontera; (dep.) línea de salida; fin, propósito; blanco o hito (a que se tira); marco (moneda); signatura, sigilación; señal o signo que sirve de firma (de quien no sabe escribir); depresión en el colmillo de una bestia, que indica edad.—**to be beside the m.**, no venir al caso.—**up to the m.**, (fam.) enteramente satisfactorio, perfectamente bueno o bien. II. va. marcar, señalar; indicar (emoción; precios); notar, acotar; advertir, observar; caracterizar; corregir o calificar (un examen).—**to m. down**, anotar, poner por escrito; marcar a un precio más bajo.—**to m. time**, (mil.) marcar el paso, llevar el compás (sin avanzar); (fig.) estar ocioso, hacer el tiempo.—**to m. out**, mostrar, señalar; elegir o escoger; cancelar, borrar. III. vn. advertir, notar, reparar.

markdown [-daun], s. reducción de precio.

marked [-t], a. marcado, notable.—**m. man**, hombre sospechoso o señalado como objeto de venganza.

markedly [-idli], adv. marcadamente.

marker [-œ(r)], s. marca, ficha; (de)marcador; tanteador, coime.

market [márkit]. I. s. mercado; plaza; feria; emporio; tienda (esp. carnicería o especiería).—**m. day**, día de mercado.—**m. garden**, huerta.—**m. place**, (plaza de) mercado; bazar.—**m. price**, precio corriente.—**m. rate**, tipo del mercado.—**m. stand**, banca de plaza; puesto en el mercado o la plaza.—**m. woman**, verdulera.—**in the m. for**, dispuesto a comprar.—**on the m.**, de o en venta. II. va. llevar al o vender en el mercado; vender; dar salida a; hallar mercado para. III. vn. comprar o vender en un mercado; hacer compras en un mercado o una tienda (apl. esp. a la compra de provisiones caseras).

marketable [-ǫbl], a. vendible, comerciable; corriente, de venta; venal.

marketer [-œ(r)], **marketman** [-mæn], s. placero.

marketing [-iŋ], s. despensa; gasto de plaza; compra o venta en el mercado.

marking [márkiŋ]. I. s. acción de marcar; marca; detalles y distribución de coloridos. II. a. de marcar; que marca.—**m. gauge**, gramil.—**m. ink**, tinta de marcar.—**m. iron**, hierro de marcar, cercador, ferrete.

marksman [márksman], s. tirador.

marksmanship [-šip], s. puntería; tino.

marl [márl]. I. s. marga, greda. II. va. (agr.) margar, abonar con marga; (mar.) trincafiar, empalomar.—**marlpit** [-pit], s. gredal, margal.

marlaceous [marléišǫs], a. margoso.

marlin [márlin], s. (ict.) especie de pez espada volante.

marline [márlin], s. (mar.) merlín.

marlin(e)spike [-spaik], s. (mar.) pasador.

marly [márli], a. margoso, gredoso.

marmalade [mármǫleid], s. mermelada.

marmatite [mármǫtait], s. (min.) marmatita.

marmoration [marmoréišǫn], s. marmoración.

marmoreal, o **marmorean** [marmóurial, -ạn], a. marmóreo, de mármol.

marmoset [mármozet], s. (zool.) titi.

marmot [mármǫt], s. (zool.) marmota.

Maronite [mǽronait], s. y a. maronita.

maroon [mǫrún]. I. va. abandonar a uno en una costa desierta. II. a. castaño. III. s. color castaño; (bot.) castaña; (negro) cimarrón; persona abandonada en una isla.—**marooner** [-œ(r)], s. pirata, m., filibustero. V. MAROON (persona).

marplot [márplat], s. aguafiestas.

marque [mark], s. corso. V. LETTER OF M.

marquee [markí], s. marquesina; gran tienda de campaña; toldo de ventana.

marquess [márkwịs], *s.* marqués.

marquetry [márkεtrị], *s.* marquetería, (a)taracea, embutido, mosaico de madera, etc.

marquis [márkwịs], *s.* marqués.—**marquisate** [-ịt], *s.* marquesado.—**marquise** [markíz], *s.* marquesa. V. MARQUEE.

marquisette [mark(w)ịzét], *s.* (tej.) cierto tejido fino.

marriage [mérịdƷ], *s.* matrimonio; casamiento, boda, himeneo, nupcias, *f. pl.*; maridaje; (fig.) enlace, íntima unión.—**m. articles,** contrato matrimonial o contratos esponsalicios.—**m. bell,** campana de bodas.—**m. licence,** licencia para casarse.—**m. portion,** dote, *f.,* arras, *f. pl.*—**m. rate,** nupcialidad.—**m. settlement,** capitulaciones, *f. pl.*—**m. song,** epitalamio.

marriageable [-abl], *a.* casadero, núbil.—**m. age,** nubilidad.

married [mérịd], *a.* casado; matrimonial, conyugal, connubial.—**m. couple,** cónyuges, *m. pl.,* marido y mujer, matrimonio.—**m. state,** estado o vida conyugal.—**to get m. (to),** casarse (con).

marron [mérọn], *s.* (piro.) petardo; color castaño, (gal.) marrón; (bot.) castaña.—**m. glacé,** castaña confitada, (gal.) marrón.

marrow [mérou], *s.* tuétano, medula o médula, meollo; substancia, esencia.—**marrowbone** [-boụn], *s.* caña o hueso medular.—*pl.* = CROSSBONES; (fam.) las rodillas o sus huesos.—**marrowfat** [-fæt], *s.* (bot.) especie de guisante.—**marrowish** [-ịš], *a.* meduloso.—**marrowless** [-lịs], *a.* falto de medula o tuétano.—**marrowy** [-ị], *a.* lleno de tuétano, meduloso; medular.

marry [mérị], **I.** *va.* casar, unir en matrimonio; casarse con; unir, juntar; (mar.) ayustar (cabos). **II.** *vn.* casarse. **III.** *interj.* (ant.) ¡canastos! ¡cáspita! ¡por mi fe! ¡justo!

Mars [marz], *s.* (mit. y astr.) Marte.

Marseillais(e [marseyé(z]. **I.** *a.* marsellés. **II.** *s.* la Marsellesa.

marsh [marš], *s.* marjal, pantano, fangal, ciénaga, marisma.—**m. fever,** (med.) malaria, paludismo.—**m. gas,** gas de los pantanos, metano.—**m. harrier,** (orn.) especie de busardo o circaeto.—**m. hen,** (orn.) polla de agua, rascón.—**m. mallow,** (bot.) malvavisco, altea.—**m. marigold,** (bot.) hierba centella, calta.

marshal [máršạl]. **I.** *s.* mariscal; bastonero o maestro de ceremonias; (mil.) mariscal; (E. U.) ministril; alguacil; jefe de policía en algunas ciudades. **II.** *va.* ordenar, poner en orden; formar (las tropas); reunir (argumentos); escoltar, guiar, dirigir, mandar. **III.** *vn.* juntarse, reunirse.

marshaller [-œ(r)], *s.* arreglador, ordenador.

marshalship [-šịp], *s.* mariscalía, mariscalato.

marshmallow [máršmælou], *s.* (bot.) malvavisco, altea; bombón o pastilla de altea (pastel de gelatina).

marshy [máršị], *a.* pantanoso, cenagoso.

marsupial [marsịúpịạl], *a.* y *s.* (zool.) marsupial.

marsupium [-pịʌm], *s.* bolsa de los didelfos.

mart [mart], *s.* mercado, emporio. V. MARQUE.

marteline [mártẹlịn], *s.* martellina.

marten [mártịn], *s.* (zool.) marta, fuina, garduña.—**m. fur,** piel (*f.*) de marta, vero.

martial [máršạl], *a.* marcial; guerrero, bélico, militar.—**m. law,** ley (*f.*) marcial, gobierno militar.

martialness [-nịs], *s.* marcialidad.

Martian [máršạn], *a.* de Marte, marciano.

martin [mártịn], **martlet** [mártlɛt], *s.* (orn.) avión, *m.,* arrejaco, vencejo.

martinet [martịnét], *s.* (mil.) ordenancista; [mártịnɛt], (mar.) apagapenol.

martingale [mártịngeịl], *s.* (tal.) (g)amarra; (mar.) moco del bauprés.

Martinmas [-mạs], *s.* (igl.) día (*m.*) de San Martín (11 de noviembre).

martyr [mártœ(r)]. **I.** *s.* mártir, *mf.* **II.** *va.* marti-

rizar; atormentar.—**martyrdom** [-dọm], *s.* martirio.—**martyred** [-d], *a.* mártir.—**martyrize** [-aịz], *va.* martirizar.—**martyrological** [-oládƷịkạl], *a.* perteneciente al martirologio.—**martyrologist** [-ólodƷịst], *s.* escritor de martirologios.—**martyrology** [-álodƷị], *s.* martirologio.

marvel [márvẹl]. **I.** *s.* maravilla, prodigio.—**m.-of-Peru,** (bot.) maravilla del Perú, arrebolera, dondiego de noche. **II.** *vn.* maravillarse, admirarse, pasmarse.—**to m. at,** admirarse de.

marvel(l)ous [-ʌs], *a.* maravilloso, prodigioso, portentoso; milagroso; increíble; (fam.) excelente.—**marvelously** [-lị], *adv.* maravillosamente.—**marvelousness** [-nịs], *s.* calidad de maravilloso; maravilla.

Marxian, Marxist [márksịạn, -ịst], *a.* y *s.* marxista.—**Marx(ian)ism** [-ịzm], *s.* marxismo.

marzipan [márzịpæn], *s.* mazapán.

mascara [mæskέrạ], *s.* tinte para las pestañas.

mascot [mέskạt], *s.* (fam.) mascota, el que o lo que trae buena suerte.

masculine [méskịulịn], *a.* masculino; varonil; macho, machuno.—**m. woman,** marimacho, mujer varonil, varona, amazona, virago, *f.*

masculinely [-lị], *adv.* varonilmente.

masculinity [-lịnịtị], *s.* masculinidad.

mash [mæš]. **I.** *s.* amasijo, masa; malta remojado, mosto; mezcla de granos molidos para la ganadería; baturrillo; (fam.) conquista amorosa.—**m. tub,** o **vat,** cuba de bracear o mezclar la cerveza, cuba del mosto. **II.** *va.* amasar, magullar, majar; elaborar cerveza, etc.; (fam.) hacer cocos, cocar, hacer una conquista amorosa.—**mashed potatoes,** puré de patatas o papas, patatas majadas.

masher [-œ(r)], *s.* majador, moledor, pistadero; (fam.) galanteador.

mashie, mashy [méšị], *s.* (dep.) cierto palo del golf.

mask [mæsk]. **I.** *s.* máscara, careta, carátula, antifaz, *m.*; disfraz, *m.*; mascarilla de una persona muerta; mascarada (*v.* MASQUERADE); máscara, *mf.* (persona disfrazada); (arq.) mascarón; (fig.) capa, color, pretexto, velo; (fort.) cubierta de ramaje, etc., para ocultar una batería; abrigo, parapeto provisional. V. MASQUE.—**masked ball,** baile de máscaras. **II.** *va.* enmascarar, disfrazar; encubrir, disimular. **III.** *vn.* encaratularse, andar enmascarado o disfrazado.

masker [-œ(r)], *s.* máscara, *mf.* (persona).

maskinonge [méskịnandƷ], *s.* (ict.) sollo.

masochism [mézọkịzm], *s.* masoquismo.

masochist [-kịst], *s.* masoquista.

mason [méịsọn], *s.* albañil; (M.) (franc)masón.—**m. bee,** (ent.) abeja albañila.—**m. bird,** (orn.) trepatroncos o herrerillo.—**m. wasp,** (ent.) avispa que construye celdas de barro.—**m.'s hammer,** piqueta.—**m.'s level,** nivel de albañil.—**m.'s measure,** o **rule,** regla, *s.* taujel.

masonic [meịsánịk], *a.* albañilesco, rel. o pert. a la albañilería o a los albañiles; masónico.

masonry [méịsọnrị], *s.* albañilería; mampostería (de piedra o de ladrillo); materiales de albañilería; (franc)masonería, masonismo.

Masora(h [masórạ], *s.* Masora.

Masorete [mésorit], *s.* masoreta, *m.*

Masoretic(al [mæsorétịk(ạl], *a.* masorético.

masque [mæsk], *s.* (hist.) cierta representación dramática (ll. t. **mask**); mascarada. V. MASQUERADE.

masquerade [mæskẹreịd]. **I.** *s.* mascarada, comparsa de máscaras, mojiganga; máscara, disfraz, *m.*—**m. ball** = MASKED BALL. **II.** *vn.* enmascararse, disfrazarse.

masquerader [-œ(r)], *s.* máscara, *mf.*

mass [mæs]. **I.** *s.* masa, montón, mole, *f.*; revoltijo, baturrillo; bulto, volumen; (mec.) masa; (igl., mús.) misa.—**m. book,** libro de misa; misal.—**m. formation,** (mil.) columna cerrada.—**m. for the dead,** misa de réquiem, de difuntos o de ánima.—**m. meeting**, reunión en masa, gran mitin, mitin popular.—**m. production**, producción en serie, fabricación en gran(de) escala.—**in m., in the m.**, en masa, en conjunto.—**the masses**, las masas, el pueblo, el vulgo. II. *va.* juntar, reunir en masa, amasar. III. *vn.* formarse, juntarse en masas.

massacre [mǽsəkœ(r)]. I. *s.* carnicería, matanza, destrozo. II. *va.* matar atrozmente, hacer una carnicería, destrozar.

massacrer [-krœ(r)], *s.* matador, asesino.

massage [məsáʒ]. I. *s.* masaje, soba, fricción. II. *va.* sobar, amasar, practicar el masaje.

massager [-œ(r)], **massagist** [-ʒist], *s.* masajista.

masseter [mæsítœ(r)], *s.* (anat.) masetero.

masseur [mæsœ́r], *s.* masajista (hombre).—**masseuse** [mæsœ́z], *s.* masajista (mujer).

massicot [mǽsikat], *s.* (quím.) masicote, almártaga.

massi(ve)ness [mǽsi(v)njs], *s.* peso, bulto, mole, *f.;* solidez.

massive [mǽsiv], **massy** [mǽsi], *a.* macizo, abultado, pesado, sólido.

mast [mæst]. I. *s.* (mar.) palo, mastelero, mástil, árbol; (bot.) bellota, fabuco, castaña.—*pl.* (mar.) arboladura.—**m. hole**, fogonadura.—**m. hoop**, garrucho. II. *va.* (mar.) arbolar un navío; colocar los palos.

mastaba(h [mǽstəbə], *s.* mastaba, *m.*, especie de capilla mortuoria de los antiguos egipcios.

masted [mǽstid], *a.* arbolado, provisto de palos.

master [mǽstœ(r)]. I. *s.* amo, dueño, señor; maestro, preceptor; ingenio; director, gobernador, jefe; señorito; patrono; (mar.) capitán, maestre, patrón, arráez, *m.;* perito, experto; oficial, maestro (de un oficio).—**m.-at-arms**, (mar.) sargento de marina.—**m. builder**, maestro de obras; contratista de construcciones; sobrestante de albañilería.—**m. mason**, (franc)masón de grado tres; maestro u oficial de albañilería.—**m. mechanic**, maestro mecánico.—**m. of**, profundo conocedor de; perito o docto en.—**M. of Arts**, maestro en artes.—**m. of ceremonies**, maestro de ceremonias.—**M. of Science**, maestro en ciencias.—**m. of the horse**, caballerizo mayor.—**M. of the Robes**, jefe de la guardarropa.—**m. workman**, maestro, sobrestante.—**the M.**, el Maestro (Jesucristo). II. *a.* maestro, magistral, superior, principal.—**m. clock**, reloj magistral.—**m. hand**, mano maestra, maestría.—**m. key**, llave maestra.—**m. stroke**, golpe maestro.—**m. touch**, golpe o destreza de maestro. III. *va.* vencer, domar; hacerse dueño de; dominar, conocer a fondo; ser maestro o perito en.

masterdom [-dəm], *s.* dominio, mando.

masterful [-fül], *a.* imperioso, dominante, arbitrario; perito, experto; sobresaliente, excelente.

masterless [-ljs], *a.* indómito, rebelde; mostrenco.

masterliness [-linjs], *s.* maestría, destreza.

masterly [-li]. I. *a.* magistral; maestro. II. *adv.* con maestría; maestro o magistralmente.

masterpiece [-pis], *s.* obra maestra o cumbre.

mastership [-ṣip], *s.* magisterio; maestría; superioridad, preeminencia.

masterwork [-wœrk], *s.* = MASTERPIECE.

masterwort [-wœrt], *s.* (bot.) imperatoria, astrancia.

mastery [-i], *s.* dominio, poder, gobierno; maestría, destreza, habilidad; superioridad, ventaja, victoria; conocimiento.

masthead [mǽsthed], *s.* (mar.) tope, espiga; vigía, *m.*, gaviero (persona).

mastic [mǽstik], *s.* (bot.) alfóncigo, almácigo, lentisco (árbol); almáciga, mástique, almástiga (resina); cemento bituminoso.

masticate [mǽstikeit], *va.* masticar, mascar, triturar.—**mastication** [-kéiʃən], *s.* masticación.—**masticator** [-keitə(r)], *s.* masticador.—**masticatory** [-kətəri], *a.* y *s.* masticatorio.

mastiff [mǽstif], *s.* (zool.) mastín, perro alano.

mastitis [mæstáitis], *s.* (med.) mastitis.

mastless [mǽstljs], *a.* que no produce bellotas, fabucos o castañas; (mar.) desarbolado.

mastman [mǽstmən], *s.* (mar.) gaviero.

mastodon [mǽstodən], *s.* mastodonte.

mastoid [mǽstoid], *a.* (anat.) mastoides, mastoideo, mastoidal.—**m. process**, (apófisis) mastoides.

mastoiditis [-áitis], *s.* (med.) mastoiditis.

masturbate [mǽstœrbeit], *vn.* masturbarse.

masturbation [-béiʃən], *s.* masturbación, onanismo.

masurium [məsúriʌm], *s.* (quím.) masurio.

mat [mæt]. I. *s.* estera, esterilla, felpudo; ruedo, redondel, baleo; rejilla, emparrillado; (mar.) pallete; orla, paspartú, borde de cartón alrededor de un grabado, etc.; mate del metal; herramienta para dar mate. II. *va.* enredar, desgreñar (pelo, lana, etc.); esterar; matar, producir (en los metales) una superficie mate. III. *vn.* enredarse, formarse greñas. IV. *a.* mate, sin lustre.

matador [mætədór], *s.* matador, diestro, primer espada, estoqueador; en juegos de naipes, matador.

match [mæch]. I. *s.* compañero, pareja; igual, semejante; competidor, contrincante; (dep.) partido; partida, juego, contienda, lucha, certamen; noviazgo, casamiento, alianza, boda; fósforo, cerilla, mecha, pajuela; (arti.) mecha, cuerda.—**m. board**, tabla de machihembrar, con ranura en un borde y lengüeta en el otro.—**m. box**, fosforera.—**m. cord**, mecha.—**m. mark**, (mec.) marca de apareamiento o de armar, que indica el orden o posición en que deben ponerse las piezas de un artefacto desarmado.—**m. point**, (dep.) tanto o punto decisivo.—**m. staff**, (arti.) botafuego.—**even m.**, partida igual; empate. II. *va.* hermanar, aparear, casar; igualar a, equiparar; ser igual a; competir con; hacer juego con.—**to m. horses**, emparejar caballos. III. *vn.* casarse; hermanarse, casar.

matchable [-əbl], *a.* que puede emparejarse con otro.

matching [-iŋ]. I. *a.* igual, parejo; que hace juego con. II. *s.* igualación, apareamiento, pareo, emparejamiento, hermanamiento.

matchless [-ljs], *a.* incomparable, sin igual, sin par, sin rival.—**matchlessly** [-li], *adv.* incomparablemente.—**matchlessness** [-njs], *s.* calidad de incomparable.

matchlock [-lak], *s.* llave (*f.*) de los mosquetes antiguos; mosquete.

matchmaker [-meikœ(r)], *s.* casamentero; fabricante de fósforos; (dep.) el que organiza luchas deportivas.—**matchmaking** [-iŋ], *s.* acción de andar arreglando bodas o haciendo casamientos; fabricación de fósforos.

matchmark [-mark]. I. *s.* = MATCH MARK. II. *va.* marcar, poner marcas de apareamiento en.

mate [meit]. I. *s.* consorte, *mf.*, cónyuge, *mf.*; camarada, *mf.*, compañero, compañera; macho o hembra entre los animales; mate (ajedrez); (mar.) piloto. II. *va.* casar, desposar; igualar; aparear; competir; en ajedrez, dar jaque mate. III. *vn.* casarse; aparearse (animales).

maté [mátei], *s.* (bot.) mate, te del Paraguay.—**m. drinker**, matero.—**m. gourd**, mate.

mateless [méitljs], *a.* solo, sin compañero, falto de consorte, desparejado.

materia medica [mətíriə médikə], *s.* (med.) materia médica.

material [mətíriəl]. I. *a.* material; físico, corpóreo; importante, substancial, esencial; serio, grave; tocante o pertinente al caso. II. *s.* material o ingrediente; materia o asunto; ropa, género, tela, tejido.

materialism [-izm], *s.* materialismo.

materialist [-ist], *s.* materialista.—**materialistic** [-ístik], *a.* materialista.

materiality [-élitì], s. materialidad, corporeidad; importancia.

materialization [-izéĵǫn], s. materialización; encarnación de un espíritu.

materialize [-aįz]. I. va. materializar; dar cuerpo, exteriorizar; hacer común o vulgar. II. vn. hacerse visible o corpóreo; verificarse, realizarse (planes, etc.); cuajar, encarnar; tomar forma; aparecer.

materially [-į], adv. materialmente, etc.

materialness [-nįs], s. = MATERIALITY.

matériel [mątįrįél], s. material(es), pertrechos, m. pl.

maternal [mątǫ́rnąl], a. maternal, materno.

maternally [-į], adv. maternalmente.

maternity [mątǫ́rnįtį], s. maternidad.—m. hospital, casa de maternidad, hospital de parturientes.

matgrass [mǽtgræs], s. = MATWEED.

mathematic(al [mæθįmǽtįk(ąl], a. matemático.

mathematically [-į], adv. matemáticamente.

mathematician [-mątįsąn], s. matemático.

mathematics [-mǽtįks], s. (pl.) matemática(s).

matico [mątíkoų], s. (bot.) matico, (Am.) mático.

matin [mǽtįn]. I. a. matutino. II. s. mañana.—pl. (igl.) maitines.

matinal [-ąl], a. matinal.

matinée [mætįnéį], s. (teat.) matiné, función de tarde; chambra; peinador.

mating [méįtįŋ], s. apareamiento; casamiento.—m. season, brama (de los animales).

matrass [mǽtrąs], s. (quím.) matraz.

matriarch [méįtrįark], s. matriarca, mujer que gobierna su familia y su tribu o clan.—**matriarchate** [-keįt], **matriarchy** [-kį], s. matriarcado, sistema en que la mujer da su nombre a sus hijos y la descendencia se determina por la línea materna; gobierno de las mujeres.

matrices [méįtrįsįz], s. pl. de MATRIX.

matricidal [meįtrįsáįdąl], a. referente al matricidio.

matricide [méįtrįsaįd], s. matricidio; matricida, mf.

matricula [mątríkyųlą], s. (hist.) matrícula.

matriculant [-ąnt], s. matriculado(r).

matriculate [-eįt]. I. va. y vn. matricular(se). II. s. y a. matriculado.—**matriculation** [-éįsǫn], s. matriculación.—**matriculator** [-ǫ(r)], s. matriculador.

matrimonial [mætrįmóųnįąl], a. matrimonial; conyugal, marital.—**matrimonially** [-į], adv. matrimonialmente.

matrimony [-monį], s. matrimonio, casamiento.

matrix [méįtrįks], s. (anat.) matriz, útero; matriz de la uña; (biol.) substancia intercelular; (impr. y fund.) matriz, molde; (min.) ganga, quijo; (dent.) molde.

matron [méįtrǫn], s. matrona; mujerona; ama de llaves; directora de instituto.

matronal [-ąl], a. matronal.

matronly [-lį], a. como de matrona; de alguna edad; materna(l); digna.

matronymic [mætronímįk], I. a. perteneciente al nombre de la madre o derivado de él. II. s. nombre así derivado.

matte [mæt], s. (fund.) mata; superficie mate.

matted [mǽtįd], a. enredado; enmarañado; enzarzado; esterado; de superficie mate, deslustrado.

matter [mǽtœ(r)]. I. s. materia; substancia; materia, asunto, cuestión; material; cosa, negocio; importancia, entidad; (med.) materia, pus; (impr.) tipo compuesto.—pl. la situación, las cosas; achaques (matters being so, así las cosas; in matters of chivalry, morality, etc., en achaques de caballería, moralidad, etc.).—m. of course, cosa natural o de cajón.—m. of fact, hecho positivo o cierto, realidad.—a m.-of-fact man, hombre positivista.—as a m. of fact, como cuestión de hecho; en realidad.—for that m., o for the m. of that, en cuanto a eso.—

in the m. of, en lo de, en cuanto a; en materia de.—(it is) no m., no importa.—no m. how (good, much, etc.) por (muy, mucho) que (no matter how far he goes, por lejos que él vaya; no matter how much you say, por mucho que Vd. diga).—small m., cosa de poca entidad.—to be something the m. with, tener algún defecto, achaque, etc.; pasarle algo a.—what is the m.? ¿qué pasa? ¿qué ocurre?—what is the m. with this (it, him, etc.)? ¿qué inconveniente tiene, qué defecto le encuentra a, por qué no, qué le parece (esto, él, etc.)?—what is the m. with you (him, her, etc.)? ¿qué (achaque) tiene Vd. (él, ella, etc.)? ¿qué le pasa a usted (él, ella, etc.)? II. vn. importar; convenir, hacer al caso; (med.) supurar, formar materia o pus.—what matters it?, o what does it m.? ¿qué importa?

matting [mǽtįŋ], s. estera; ester(ad)o; orla, paspartú, borde de cartón para un grabado, acuarela, etc.; superficie mate; (mar.) empalletado.

mattock [mǽtǫk], s. (agr.) zapapico, piqueta.

mattress [mǽtrįs], s. colchón; (hidr.) acolchado, defensa de ramas, varas y troncos trabados.

maturant [mǽchųrąnt], **maturative** [machúrątįv]. I. s. (cir.) madurativo. II. a. madurante.

maturate [mǽchųreįt]. I. va. (uso ord. y cir.) madurar. II. vn. madurar; supurar, formar pus.—**maturation** [-éįsǫn], s. maduración; supuración.

mature [mątįúr]. I. a. maduro, sazonado; juicioso; acabado, completo o perfecto; (com.) vencido, pagadero. II. va. madurar, sazonar. III. vn. madurar(se), sazonarse; (com.) vencer, cumplirse un plazo.—**maturely** [-lį], adv. duramente; sesudamente.—**matureness** [-nįs], s. madurez.

maturing [-įŋ], a. madurante, madurador.

maturity [-įtį], s. madurez; maduración; edad madura; perfección; (com.) vencimiento.

matutinal [mątįútįnąl], a. matutinal, matutino, matinal.

matweed [mǽtwid], s. (bot.) esparto, albardín.

matzoth [mátsoθ], s. pl. galletas de pan sin levadura.

maudlin [mǿdlįn]. I. a. sensiblero, sentimental en exceso; peneque, calamocano; (ant.) lloroso. II. s. (bot.) agérato, balsamita menor.

maul [mǫl]. I. va. apalear, aporrear; maltratar. II. s. mazo, machota, porra, mandarria.

maulstick [mǿlstįk], s. tiento (de pintor).

maunder [mǿndœ(r)], vn. divagar; obrar o hablar a tontas y a locas; mascullar; gruñir, refunfuñar.

Maundy [mǿndį], s. (igl.) mandato, lavatorio de pies.—M. Thursday, jueves santo.

Mauritanian [morįténįąn], a. y s. mauritano.

mausolean [mosolíąn], a. sepulcral.

mausoleum [-Am], s. mausoleo, mauseolo.

mauve [móųv], s. color de malva.

mauveine [-in], s. (quím.) malveína o mauveína, violeta de anilina.

maverick [mǽvœrįk], s. (E. U. del Oeste) res mostrenca, sin marca de hierro.

mavis [méįvįs], s. (orn.) malvís, m., zorzal.

maw [mǫ], s. gola, fauces, f. pl.; buche (esp. de las aves); estómago; cuajar.—m. o m. seed, semillas secas de amapola, para pájaros.

mawkish [mǿkįs], a. asqueroso, nauseabundo, repugnante; fastidiosamente sentimental; hostigoso.

mawkishness [-nįs], s. asquerosidad; sentimentalismo empalagoso.

maxilla [mæksílą], s. (anat., zool.) hueso maxilar.

maxillary [mǽksįlerį], s. y a. maxilar.—m. bone, maxilar.—m. sinus, antro o seno maxilar.

maxim [mǽksįm], s. máxima, adagio, aforismo, apotegma, m., sentencia; axioma, m.

maxima [mǽksįmą], s. pl. de MAXIMUM.

maximal [-į], a. máximo.

maximize [-aįz], va. y vn. llevar hasta el máximo; exagerar; interpretar liberalmente.

maximum [-ʌm], *s.* y *a.* máximo; *s.* máximum.

maxwell [mǽkswel], *s.* (elec.) máxwel, unidad de flujo magnético.

may [meɪ], *vn., irr.* y *def.* (*pret.* MIGHT) poder, tener facultad o permiso, ser posible, lícito o permitido (v. gr.: *I may go*, puede que yo vaya; *you may go*, puede Vd. marcharse; *may I come in?* ¿puedo entrar?; *it may be*, puede ser; *if I may say so*, si me es lícito decirlo). Usado elípticamente, y en ciertas cláusulas que denotan contingencia, se expresa poniendo el verbo en subjuntivo (v. gr.: *be the result what it may*, sea cual fuere el resultado; *suceda lo que suceda*; *come what may*, venga lo que venga; *I hope that you may come*, espero que Vd. venga; *though he may do it*, aunque lo haga; *in order that they may know it*, para que lo sepan). A veces denota deseo vivo, y se traduce por "ojalá," "Dios quiera," o se omite y el verbo se pone en subjuntivo, v. gr.: *may it be so*, ojalá que así sea; *may you live long and happy years*, viva Vd. largos y felices años.

May [meɪ]. **I.** *s.* mayo; (fig.) primavera de la vida. **—m., M. tree, Maybloom, maybush,** (bot.) = HAWTHORN.**—M. apple,** (bot.) mandrágora.**—M. basket,** mayo.**—M. beetle,** o **bug,** (ent.) = JUNE BUG.**—M. Day,** primero de mayo.**—M. drink** = M. WINE.**—M. fly,** (ent.) efímera, cachipolla.**—M. lady** = M. QUEEN.— **M. lily,** (bot.) lirio de los valles.**—M. queen,** maya, joven que preside la fiesta de mayo. **II.** *vn.* úsase sólo en la frase **to be,** o **go, a-maying,** coger flores la mañana del día primero de mayo.

Maya(n [máya(n], *a.* y *s.* maya, de los mayas.

maybe [méɪbɪ], (ant.) **mayhap** [-hæp], *adv.* acaso, quizá, tal vez.

Mayflower [méɪflaʊœ(r)], *s.* (bot.) (Ingl.) espino, acerolo; vellorita; calta; (E. U.) epigea; hepática; anemone, etc.

mayhem [méɪhem], *s.* (for.) mutilación criminal de una parte del cuerpo de otra persona.

maying [méɪɪŋ], *s.* festividad del primero de mayo.

mayonnaise [meɪonéɪz], *s.* (coc.) (salsa) mayonesa o mahonesa.

mayor [méɪo(r)], *s.* alcalde, corregidor.

mayoralty [-ltɪ], *s.* alcaldía, corregimiento.

Maypole [méɪpoʊl], *s.* mayo, poste o vara alta con adornos que se clava en el centro del lugar donde se celebran las fiestas del primero de mayo.

Maytide, Maytime [-taɪd, -taɪm], *s.* el mes de mayo.

mayweed [-wid], *s.* (bot.) manzanilla loca.

maz(z)ard [mǽzard], *s.* (bot.) guinda.**—m. tree,** guindo (especie de cerezo).

mazarine [mæzarín], *s.* color azul subido.

Mazdaism [mǽzdaɪzm], **Mazdeism** [-dɪɪzm], *s.* mazdeísmo, religión de los antiguos persas.

Mazda lamp [mǽzdā læmp], *s.* lámpara incandescente o de tungsteno (es nombre de fábrica).

maze [meɪz], *s.* laberinto; perplejidad, confusión. **—to be in a m.,** estar perplejo.

mazer [méɪzœ(r)], *s.* escudilla de madera.

mazurka [mazúrkā], *s.* mazurca (baile y música).

mazy [méɪzɪ], *a.* laberíntico; embrollado; perplejo.

me [mi], *pron. pers.* (caso oblicuo de I) me, mí; *do me the favor*, hágame Vd. el favor; *for me*, para mí; *with me*, conmigo.

mead [mid], *s.* aguamiel, *f.*, hidromel, aloja, meloja.

mead (poét.), **meadow** [médoʊ], *s.* pradera, pradería, vega, prado.**—m. crocus** = M. SAFFRON. **—m. lark,** (orn.) alondra de los prados.**—m. saffron,** (bot.) cólquico (otoñal), quitameriendas, *f.*

meadowsweet [-swit], **meadowwort** [-wœrt], *s.* (bot.) ulmaria, barba de cabra, reina de los prados.

meadowy [médoɪ], *a.* de pradera; como prado; lleno de prados.

meager, meagre [mígœ(r)], *a.* magro, flaco, enjuto; escaso, pobre; cuaresmal, de vigilia.— **meagerly, meagrely** [-lɪ], *adv.* pobremente, estérilmente.**—meagerness, meagreness** [-nɪs], *s.* flaqueza, flacura; escasez.

meal [mil], *s.* comida; (en general) sustento, vianda; harina.**—m. time,** hora de comer.

mealiness [-nɪs], *s.* calidad de harinoso, panoso o pastoso; melosidad.

mealman [-mæn], *s.* harinero.

mealy [-lɪ], *a.* harinoso, farináceo; panoso; pastoso; seco y desmenuzable; de pintas blancas.— **m.-mouthed,** pacato, tímido; meloso, falso.

mean [min]. **I.** *a.* humilde; mediano; inferior, pobre; bajo, vil; (fam.) malo, desconsiderado, indigno; desazonado, de mal humor; obscuro, despreciable; tacaño, mezquino, sórdido; insignificante; medio, intermedio; (mat.) medio.— **m.-born,** de humilde cuna; de baja estofa.— **m. pressure,** presión media.**—m. proportional,** (mat.) media proporcional.**—m.-spirited,** bajo, ruin.**—m. sun,** sol medio.**—m. time,** (astr.) tiempo medio.**—m. velocity,** velocidad media.**—m. wall,** pared medianera. **II.** *s.* medio (punto medio); medio (de una proporción); mediocridad, medianía;—*pl.* medio, recurso, modo, forma, instrumento, arbitrio, expediente; medios, posibles, caudal, fondos, recursos, riquezas.**—by all means,** sin duda, sin falta; por todos los medios posibles. **—by fair means,** por medios lícitos; a las buenas.**—by foul means,** por malos medios, por la fuerza.**—by means of,** por medio de, mediante.**—by no means, by no manner of means,** de ningún modo.**—by some means,** de alguna manera.**—by this means,** por este medio.**—to live on one's means,** vivir uno de sus rentas. **III.** *va.* (*pret.* y *pp.* MEANT) significar, querer decir, dar a entender; pensar, proponerse, pretender; destinar a; envolver, encerrar, traer o llevar consigo; decir de veras.— **to m. business,** estar resuelto; proponerse hacer lo que se dice; hablar en serio.**—I m. it,** hablo en serio o formalmente.**—I m. to go,** pienso ir.**—I didn't m. anything by it,** no lo dije por tanto.**—I didn't m. to do it,** lo hice sin pensar, o sin querer.**—what do you m.?** ¿qué quiere Vd. decir? ¿qué se propone Vd.?— **you don't m. it!** ¡calla! IV. *vn.* (con adverbio) tener intención o propósito, v. gr.: *he means well*, tiene buenas intenciones; *a well-meaning man*, un hombre de buena fe, bien intencionado.

meander [mɪǽndœ(r)]. **I.** *s.* meandro, laberinto, camino tortuoso.**—m. line,** (top.) línea quebrada auxiliar. **II.** *vn.* serp(ent)ear; caminar sin rumbo.

meandering [-ɪŋ], *a.* serpentino, tortuoso.

meaning [mínɪŋ]. **I.** *a.* significativo. **II.** *s.* intención, voluntad, designio; sentido, acepción, significación, significado.**—meaningful** [-ful], *a.* significante; intencionado.**—meaningless** [-lɪs], *a.* insensato; sin sentido, vacío.**—meaningly** [-lɪ], *adv.* significativamente; con intención.

meanly [mínlɪ], *adv.* bajamente, vilmente; con desprecio; pobremente, miserablemente; medianamente, mediocremente.

meanness [mínnɪs], *s.* bajeza; vileza; humildad; tacañería, miseria, mezquindad; mal genio.

meant [ment], *pret.* y *pp.* de TO MEAN.**—to be m. for,** o, ser para; servir para; haber nacido para; tener por objeto, aplicarse a; estar destinado o encaminado a.**—who is m.?** ¿de quién se trata?

meantime [míntaɪm], **meanwhile** [-hwaɪl]. **I.** *adv.* mientras tanto, entretanto, por de (o lo) pronto. **II.** *s.* ínterin.**—in the m.,** en tanto, mientras tanto, en el ínterin, hasta entonces.

measled [mízld], *a.* infestado de triquinas o helmintos (ú. esp. de la carne de cerdo).

measles [mízlz], *s. pl.* (med.) sarampión, *m.*;

alfombrilla; (vet.) enfermedad de los cerdos, etc., producida por las triquinas; (zool.) estas mismas triquinas; (bot.) cáncer de los árboles.

measly [mízli], *a.* infestada (carne) de triquinas; (fam.) despreciable, malísimo.

measurable [mézurabl], *a.* mensurable; (raro) moderado.—**measurableness** [-nis], *s.* mensurabilidad.—**measurably** [-bli], *adv.* mensurablemente; perceptiblemente, hasta cierto grado; (raro) con moderación.

measure [mézur(r)]. I. *s.* medida; unidad de medida; mensura; cantidad, dimensión, tamaño; graduación; disposición, provisión, expediente; recurso; compás, metro, cadencia; modo, grado; moderación; proyecto de ley; (mús.) compás.— *pl.* medios; (geol.) capas, yacimientos.—**beyond m.**, con exceso, sobremanera.—**for good m.**, para completar la cosa, de ñapa.—**in a great m.**, en gran manera; en gran parte.—**in some m.**, hasta cierto punto, en cierto modo. —**out of m.** = BEYOND M.—**to take measures**, tomar las medidas necesarias.—**to take one's m.**, o **the m. of**, (fig.) apreciar a uno en lo que vale; tomar las medidas a uno.—**to tread a m.**, bailar. II. *va.* medir, mensurar; señalar, distribuir; calibrar, graduar, tantear, estimar, juzgar, valuar; comparar, oponer; (mar.) arquear, cubicar (un navío).—**to m. one's length**, medir el suelo, caer tendido.—**to m. out**, asignar o dar según medida; medir (algo a alguien).—**to m. swords**, medir espadas. III. *vn.* medir, tener tal o cual dimensión.—**to m. up to**, elevarse a la altura de, ser igual a.

measured [-d], *pp.* y *a.* medido, moderado; uniforme; lento, rítmico; limitado, restringido.

measureless [-lis], *a.* inmensurable, ilimitado.

measurement [-ment], *s.* medición; dimensión; medida; (mar.) cubicación, arqueo.—**m. bill**, (mar.) certificación del porte de los buques.

measurer [-œ(r)], *s.* medidor, mensurador.

measuring [-in]. I. *s.* medición, medida. II. *a.* de medir.—**m. glass**, probeta o vaso graduados.—**m. tape**, cinta de medir.—**m. worm**, (ent.) geometrido, oruga geómetra.

meat [mit], *s.* carne, *f.;* vianda, sustento (en general); substancia, jugo; comida.—**m. ball**, albóndiga.—**m. chopper**, o **grinder**, aparato de picar carne.—**m. fly**, (ent.) moscarda.—**m. hook**, escarpia, garabato.—**m. market**, carnicería.—**m. packer**, empacador de carne.—**m. pie**, empanada, pastel de carne.—**m. pounder**, o **tenderizer**, mazo de la carne.—**m. safe**, fresquera.—**m. spit**, espiche, asador..

meatus [miétas], *s.* (anat.) meato.

meaty [míti], *a.* carnoso; jugoso, substancioso.

mechanic [mikánik]. I. *a.* mecánico, maquinal. II. *s.* mecánico, artesano, obrero, menestral.

mechanical [-al], *a.* mecánico, maquinal; automático; rutinario.—**m. drawing**, dibujo lineal. —**m. equivalent of heat**, equivalente mecánico del calor.—**m. pencil**, lápiz (*m.*) portaminas.—**m. man** = ROBOT.

mechanically [-i], *adv.* mecánicamente; maquinalmente.—**mechanicalness** [-nis], *s.* calidad de mecánico.

mechanician [mekanísan], *s.* mecánico, perito en la ciencia de la mecánica; maquinista.

mechanics [mikéniks], *s.* mecánica; maquinaria.

mechanism [mékanizm], *s.* mecanismo; maquinaria; dispositivo; técnica.

mechanist [-ist], *s.* mecanicista, el que sostiene que todos los fenómenos universales son puramente físicos o mecánicos.—**mechanistic** [-istik], *a.* mecanicista.—**m. system**, o **theory**, mecanicismo.

mechanization [-izésən], *s.* maquinismo; mecanización; (mil.) motorización.

mechanize [-aiz], *va.* construir mecánicamente; convertir en máquina; mecanizar; (mil.) motorizar.

Mechlin [méklin], *s.* encaje o puntas de Malinas.

mechoacan [michóuakan], *s.* (bot.) mechoacán.

meconic [mikánik], *a.* (quím.) mecónico.

meconium [mikóuniam], *s.* meconio, alhorre.

medal [médal], *s.* medalla, condecoración; insignia.

medallic [mid&lik], *a.* numismático, metálico.

medallion [midélyon], *s.* medallón; medalla.

medal(l)ist [médalist], *s.* numismático, coleccionista de medallas; grabador de medallas; el premiado con una medalla.

meddle [médl], *vn.* (gen. con **with** o **in**) (entre)meterse, ingerirse (en).

meddler [médlœ(r)], *s.* entremetido.

meddlesome [médlsʌm], *a.* entremetido, oficioso.—**meddlesomeness** [-nis], *s.* entremetimiento, oficiosidad.

meddling [médlin], *s.* entremetimiento, interposición impertinente y oficiosa.

Mede [mid], *s.* medo.

media [mídia]. I. *s.* (anat.) túnica media de un vaso. II. *s. pl.* de MEDIUM.

mediæval [midjíval], *a.* = MEDIEVAL.

medial [mídial], *a.* medio, del centro.

median [mídian]. I. *a.* del medio, que está situado en el centro. II. *s.* (geom.) mediana.

Median, *s.* y *a.* medo.

mediastinum [midiæstáinʌm], *s.* (anat.) mediastino.

mediate [mídieit]. I. *va.* y *vn.* mediar, intervenir, intermediar, interponerse. II. [mídiit], *a.* mediato, medio; interpuesto.

mediately [-li], *adv.* mediatamente.

mediation [-éisən], *s.* mediación, intercesión; interposición, intervención; tercería.

mediator [-eitɔ(r)], *s.* mediador, intercesor, medianero, abogado, avenidor, tercero, tratador.

mediatorial [-atɔrial], *a.* medianero.

mediatorship [-sip], *s.* oficio de mediador.

mediatress, mediatrix [mídieitris, -triks], *s.* medianera, abogada.

medic [médik], *s.* (bot.) alfalfa, mielga.

medicable [médikabl], *a.* medicable.

medical [médikal], *a.* médico, medicinal.—**m. attention**, asistencia facultativa.—**m. corps**, cuerpo de sanidad.—**m. examination**, reconocimiento médico.—**m. examiner**, médico forense.—**m. kit**, botiquín.—**m. man**, médico; médico general (que no es cirujano).—**m. jurisprudence**, medicina legal.—**m. school**, escuela de medicina.—**m. treatment**, medicación.—**medically** [-i], *adv.* en calidad de médico, facultativamente.

medicament [-ment], *s.* medicamento, remedio.

medicamental [-méntal], *a.* medicamentoso, curativo.

medicaster [médikæstœ(r)], *s.* medicastro, curandero.

medicate [médikeit], *va.* medicinar; hacer medicinal (alguna cosa).—**medication** [-éisən], *s.* medicación; medicamento.

medicative [-eitiv], *a.* medicinal.

medicinal [midísinal], *a.* medicinal, curativo.

medicinally [-i], *adv.* según la medicina.

medicine [médisin], *s.* medicina, medicamento, droga, remedio; medicina (arte o ciencia); (E. U.) entre los indios, ensalmo.—**m. ball**, pelota medicinal para gimnasia.—**m. cabinet**, **m. chest**, botiquín.—**m. dance**, baile ceremonial de indios.—**m. dropper**, cuentagotas.—**m. lodge**, casilla o tienda del exorcista.—**m. man**, exorcista, hechizador.—**to take one's m.**, tragar(se).

medicolegal [médikolígal], *a.* medicolegal.

medieval [midjíval], *a.* medi(o)eval.—**m. character**, o **quality**, medievalidad.—**medievalism** [-izm], *s.* medievismo.—**medievalist** [-ist], *s.* medievista.

mediocre [mídjokœ(r)], *a.* mediocre, mediano; vulgar, trivial, baladí.

mediocrity [midjákriti], *s.* mediocridad.

meditate [médịteịt]. **I.** *va.* meditar, idear, tramar. **II.** *vn.* meditar, reflexionar.

meditation [-éịšǫn], *s.* meditación, reflexión.

meditative [-tịv], *a.* meditativo, meditabundo, contemplativo, reflejo.—**meditatively** [-lị], *adv.* meditativamente.

Mediterranean [medịteréịnịan], *a.* mediterráneo. —**M. fever**, (med.) fiebre mediterránea, undulante o de Malta.

medium [mídịʌm]. **I.** *s.* (*pl.* MEDIUMS o MEDIA) medio; expediente; órgano, instrumento, intermediario; médium o medio (en el espiritismo); (fís.) medio ambiente; circunstancias rodeantes; (pint.) aceite.—**at a m.**, uno con otro, por término medio. **II.** *a.* mediano, intermedio; mediocre; (coc.) no muy cocido.—**m. fine**, entrefino.—**m.-sized**, de tamaño regular o mediano.

mediumistic [-ịstịk], *a.* de o relativo a médiums (en el espiritismo).

medlar [médlạ(r)], *s.* (bot.) níspero.

medley [médlị]. **I.** *s.* miscelánea, mezcla, mescolanza, ensalada, baturrillo, mixtifori; (mús.) miscelánea, pot-pourri. **II.** *a.* mezclado, confuso.

medulla [mịdʌ́lạ], *s.* (anat.) medula.—**m. oblongata**, medula oblonga(da).—**m. spinalis**, medula espinal.

medullary [médʌlerị], *a.* medular.

medusa [mịdịúsạ], *s.* (zool.) medusa, aguamala.

meed [mid], *s.* (poét.) premio, galardón.

meek [mík], *a.* manso, humilde, dócil.—**meekly** [-lị], *adv.* mansamente, humildemente.—**meekness** [-nịs], *s.* mansedumbre, humildad, docilidad.

meerschaum [míršǫm], *s.* (min.) magnesita, espuma de mar; pipa de espuma de mar.

meet [mit]. **I.** *va.* (*pret.* y *pp.* MET) encontrarse con; encontrar, topar o chocar con; convenir a, satisfacer, llenar (requisitos, etc.); pagar, saldar, honrar (un pagaré, etc.); sufragar, correr con, hacer frente a (los gastos, etc.); refutar, destruir con argumentos; combatir, batirse o pelear con; conocer o tratar personalmente (*I am glad to meet you*, me alegro de conocer a Vd.).—**to m. a charge**, refutar, responder a una acusación. —**to m. half way**, partir el camino con; partir la diferencia con; hacer algunas concesiones a. —**to m. the eye**, saltar a la vista.—**to go to m.**, ir o salir al encuentro de. **II.** *vn.* reunirse, juntarse; sesionar; verse; encontrarse; luchar, combatirse, batirse; entenderse, convenirse; confluir.—**to m. with**, juntarse con; encontrar; tener, sufrir (un accidente, una desgracia, etc.). —**to m. with one's match**, dar uno con la horma de su zapato.—**till we m. again**, hasta la vista, hasta más ver(nos). **III.** *a.* apto, idóneo, apropiado, conveniente.—**to be m.**, convenir. **IV.** *s.* encuentro; reunión deportiva; concurso, torneo; reunión de cazadores para una cacería, y lugar donde se reúnen.

meeting [mítịŋ], *s.* mitin; reunión, sesión; junta, asamblea, congreso; entrevista, conferencia; cabildo; (igl.) capítulo; confluencia de dos ríos; encuentro, duelo o desafío.—**m. of creditors**, concurso de acreedores.—**m. place**, lugar o sitio de reunión.—**to call a m.**, convocar o llamar a (una) junta.

meetinghouse [-haụs], *s.* capilla o templo protestante.

meetly [mítlị], *adv.* convenientemente.

meetness [mítnịs], *s.* aptitud, propiedad, conveniencia.

mega- [mégạ], prefijo o voz que indica grandeza, y que también se usa con los nombres de varias unidades mecánicas y eléctricas para indicar un millón; *vg. megadyne* [-daịn], megadina (un millón de dinas).

megacephalic [-sefálịk], **megacephalous** [-séfạlạs], *a.* = MEGALOCEPHALOUS.

megacycle [-saịkl], *s.* (fís.) megaciclo.

megafog [-fag], *s.* aparato megafónico de transmisión de señales a barcos en tiempo brumoso.

megalith [-lịθ], *s.* megalito.

megalithic [-líθịk], *a.* megalítico.

megalocephalous [-loséfạlạs], *a.* megalocéfalo.

megalomania [-méịnịạ], *s.* megalomanía.

megalomaniac [-méịnịæk], *s.* y *a.* megalómano.

megalosaur [-sǫr], *s.* (pal.) megalosauro.

megaphone [-foụn], *s.* megáfono, bocina, portavoz, *m.*

megapod [-pad], *a.* (zool.) megalópodo.

megapode [-poụd], *s.* (orn.) megápodo.

megascope [-skoụp], *s.* megascopio; cámara fotográfica ampliadora.

megatherium [-θịrịʌm], *s.* (pal.) megaterio.

megohm [mégoụm], *s.* (elec.) megohmio.

megrim [mígrịm], *s.* (med.) migraña, jaqueca, hemicránea; (ant.) capricho.—*pl.* melancolía, hipocondría.

mehari [mịhárị], *s.* (zool.) meharí, dromedario muy corredor del norte de África.

melancholia [melạŋkóụlịạ], *s.* (med.) lipemanía. —**melancholic** [-kálịk], *a.* melancólico, lipemaníaco.—**melancholically** [-ạlị], *adv.* de una manera melancólica.—**melancholy** [mélạŋkạlị]. **I.** *s.* lipemanía; melancolía, tristeza. **II.** *a.* melancólico.

Melanesian [melạníšịạn], *s.* y *a.* melanesio.

mélange [meịlánž], *s.* mezcla.

melanin [mélạnịn], *s.* (bioquím.) melanina.

melanite [-naịt], *s.* (min.) melanita, granate.

melanosis [-nóụsịs], *s.* (med.) melanosis.

melanuria [-nịúrịạ], *s.* melanuria o melanuresis, formación de pigmentos negros en la orina.

melaphyre [-faị(r)], *s.* (min.) meláfido.

melastomaceous [mịlæstoméịšạs], *a.* (bot.) melastomáceo.

mêlée [méịleị], *s.* rebujiña, pelotera.

meliaceous [milịéịšịạs], *a.* (bot.) meliáceo.

melic [mélịk], *a.* mélico, lírico.

melilot [mélịlat], *s.* (bot.) meliloto.

melinite [mélịnaịt], *s.* melinita (explosivo).

meliorate [mílyǫreịt]. **I.** *va.* mejorar; adelantar; bonificar. **II.** *vn.* mejorarse.—**melioration** [-éịšǫn], *s.* mejoramiento, mejora, adelanto.

melissa [melísạ], *s.* (bot.) melisa.

melliferous [melífẹrạs], *a.* melífero.

mellifluence [-flụens], *s.* melifluidad.—**mellifluent** [-ent], **mellifluous** [-ʌs], *a.* melifluo; dulce.

mellow [méloụ]. **I.** *a.* maduro, sazonado; meloso; tierno, blando, suave; pastoso, mantecoso; melodioso; blando, friable; mórbido; añejo, doncel (vino); calamocano. **II.** *va.* sazonar, madurar, ablandar, suavizar. **III.** *vn.* madurar(se).

mellowly [-lị], *adv.* suavemente, dulcemente.

mellowness [-nịs], *s.* madurez, sazón, *f.*; melosidad, suavidad; pastosidad, morbidez.

mellowy [-i], *a.* = MELLOW.

melodic [meládịk], *a.* melódico.

melodics [-s], *s.* (mús.) melopeya.

melodious [melóụdịạs], *a.* melodioso, canoro.— **melodiously** [-lị], *adv.* melodiosamente.— **melodiousness** [-nịs], *s.* melodía.

melodist [mélọdịst], *s.* melodista, compositor o cantor de melodías.—**melodize** [-daịz]. **I.** *va.* hacer melodioso. **II.** *vn.* hacer melodía.

melodrama [-dramạ], *s.* melodrama, *m.*—**melodramatic** [-drạmǽtịk], *a.* melodramático.— **melodramatically** [-ạlị], *adv.* melodramáticamente.—**melodramatist** [-drǽmạtịst], *s.* autor de melodramas.

melody [mélọdị], *s.* melodía; canción o aire melódico.

melon [mélǫn], *s.* (bot.) melón.—**m. dealer** o **grower**, melonero.—**m. patch**, melonar.

melopoeia [melọpíyạ], *s.* (mús.) melopeya.

melt [mélt]. **I.** *va.* derretir, fundir; liquidar; disolver; deshelar; ablandar, aplacar. **II.** *vn.* fundirse, derretirse; liquidarse; deshelarse; ablandarse; confundirse, mezclarse; consumirse, gastarse; (a veces con **away**) disiparse, desvanecerse.—**to m. into tears,** deshacerse en lágrimas. III. *s.* substancia derretida; fusión, derretimiento; (metal.) hornada.

melter [-œ(r)], *s.* fundidor; crisol.

melting [-iŋ]. **I.** *a.* fundente. **II.** *s.* derretimiento, fusión, fundición.—**m. pan,** cazo.—**m. point,** punto de fusión.—**m. pot,** crisol; amalgamación (de razas, etc.).

melton [mélton], *s.* (tej.) paño melton.

member [mémbœ(r)], *s.* miembro (del cuerpo, de una ecuación, etc.); parte (*f.*) de un todo; miembro, individuo, socio; pieza (de un puente, etc.).

membered [-d], *a.* provisto de o dividido en miembros; (blas.) membrado.

membership [-šip], *s.* calidad de miembro o socio; número de socios o miembros; personal.—**m. dues,** cuota.—**m. list,** nómina de socios.

membranaceous, *o* **membranous** [mémbranéišias, -nas], *a.* membranáceo, membranoso.— **membranous croup,** (med.) difteria.

membrane [mémbrein], *s.* membrana, capa de tejido delgado; panículo; trozo de pergamino.

membraniferous [membraníferas], *a.* que produce membranas.

memento [miméntou], *s.* recuerdo, recordatorio; (M., igl.) memento.

memo [mémou], *s. abrev.* de MEMORANDUM.

memoir [mémwar], *s.* memoria, informe, relación.—*pl.* memorias; (auto)biografía.

memorabilia [memorabília], *s. pl.* cosas dignas de recordación.

memorable [mémorabl], *a.* memorable.

memorably [-bli], *adv.* memorablemente.

memorandum [memoréndam], *s.* memorándum, memoria, nota, minuta, apuntación, volante.—**m. book,** memorándum, cartera de apuntes, libreta, carnet, mamotreto, prontuario.—**m. clause,** cláusula de exenciones (en una póliza), que exime de ciertas obligaciones al asegurador.—**m. pad,** tablilla o taco de apuntes.

memorial [mimórial]. **I.** *a.* conmemorativo; mnemotécnico.—**M. Day** = DECORATION DAY. **II.** *s.* monumento conmemorativo; trofeo; memorial, instancia, petición, recurso; (for.) nota, apuntamiento.

memorialist [-ist], *s.* memorialista; el que escribe memoriales o memorias; solicitante, suplicante.

memorialize [-aiz], *va.* presentar una petición o memorial a; conmemorar.

memoriter [mimóritœ(r)], *adv.* de memoria.

memorization [memorizéišon], *s.* aprendizaje de memoria.—**memorize** [mémoraiz], *va.* aprender de memoria.—**memorizer** [-œ(r)], *s.* el que aprende de memoria; el que tiene buena memoria.

memory [mémori], *s.* memoria, recuerdo; remembranza; retentiva.—**from m.,** de coro, de memoria.

men [men], *s. pl.* de MAN.

menace [ménis]. **I.** *va.* y *vn.* amenazar; bravear. **II.** *s.* amenaza, reto.

menad [mínæd], *s.* = MAENAD.

ménage [meináž], *s.* familia; manejo de casa, economía doméstica.

menagerie [menádžeri], *s.* colección de animales fieros o raros; casa de fieras. *V.* ZOO.

mend [ménd]. **I.** *va.* remendar; recoser, repasar, zurcir; arreglar, componer; mejorar; enmendar, reformar, remediar. **II.** *vn.* enmendarse, reformarse; mejorar; restablecerse. **III.** *s.* mejoría; reforma; remiendo.—**on the m.,** mejorándo(se).

mendable [-abl], *a.* reparable, componible, reformable, remediable.

mendacious [mendéišas], *a.* mendaz, mentiroso, embustero; falso.—**mendaciously** [-li], *adv.* mendazmente.—**mendaciousness** [-nis], **mendacity** [mendásiti], *s.* mendacidad; mentira.

Mendelism [méndelizm], *s.* mendelismo.

mender [méndœ(r)], *s.* componedor, reformador; reparador; remendón.

mendicancy [méndikansi], **mendicity** [mendísiti], *s.* mendicidad, mendiguez.

mendicant [méndikant], *a.* y *s.* mendicante, mendigante, mendigo.

mending [méndiŋ], *s.* compostura, composición, refección, adobe; recosido; ropa por zurcir, etc.

mendole [méndoul], *s.* (ict.) boga.

menhaden [menhéidn], *s.* (ict.) especie de sábalo.

menhir [ménhir], *s.* (arqueol.) menhir.

menial [mínial], *a.* y *s.* servil, bajo; doméstico, sirviente, criado, lacayo.

menially [-i], *adv.* servil o bajamente.

meningeal [miníndžial], *a.* meníngeo.

meninges [miníndžiz], *s. pl.* de MENINX; (anat.) meninges, *f. pl.*

meningitis [menindžáitis], *s.* (med.) meningitis.

meninx [míniŋks], *s.* (anat.) meninge, *f.*

meniscus [milゥískas], *s.* lúnula, media luna; (ópt., fís., anat.) menisco.

menispermaceous [menispœrméišias], *a.* (bot.) menispermáceo.

Mennonite [ménonait], *s.* y *a.* menonita, *mf.*

menology [minálodži], *s.* (igl.) menologio.

menopause [ménopaz], *s.* (fisiol.) menopausia.

menorrhagia [menoréidžiậ], *s.* (med.) menorragia.

menses [ménsiz], *s. pl.* menstruo, regla(s).

Menshevik [ménševik], *s.* menchevique, miembro (en Rusia) del partido radical moderado.— **Menshevism** [-vizm], *s.* menchevismo.

menstrual [ménstrual], *a.* menstrual, menstruo.

menstruate [-eit], *vn.* menstruar.

menstruation [-éišon], *s.* menstruación.

menstruous [-as], *a.* menstruo, menstruoso; (bot.) mensual.

menstruum [-am], *s.* (quím.) menstruo, disolvente.

mensurability [ménšurabíliti], *s.* mensurabilidad.—**mensurable** [-bl], *a.* mensurable.

mensural [ménšural], *a.* mensural.

mensuration [-éišon], *s.* medición, medida, mensura(ción); cálculo de magnitudes geométricas; aplicaciones geométricas.

mental [méntal], *a.* mental; intelectual; ref. a la mente o a la barba.—**m. blindness, m. deafness,** afección cerebral que impide la interpretación o identificación de las imágenes visuales o las impresiones auditivas.—**m. deficiency,** inteligencia subnormal.—**m. derangement,** desarreglo mental, alienación.—**m. healer,** curador mental, o por fe.—**m. healing,** arte de curar mediante procedimientos mentales.—**m. reservation,** reserva o restricción mental.— **m. test,** examen de inteligencia o capacidad mental.

mentality [mentáliti], *s.* mentalidad.

mentally [méntali], *adv.* mentalmente.

Mentha [ménậ], *s.* (bot.) menta, hierbabuena.

menthol [ménậl], *s.* (quím., farm.) mentol.

mentholated [-eitid], *a.* impregnado de mentol.

menthyl [ménậil], *s.* (quím.) mentilo.

mention [ménšon]. **I.** *s.* mención, recuerdo, alusión. **II.** *va.* mencionar, mentar, nombrar, aludir a.—**don't m. it,** no hay de qué, de nada.—**not to m.,** por no decir nada de; además.

mentionable [-abl], *a.* mencionable.

mentor [ménto(r)], *s.* mentor, ayo, guía, *mf.*

menu [ményu], *s.* lista de platos, menú; comida.

meow [miáu], *s.* y *vn.* = MEW.

Mephistophelian [mefistofílian], *a.* mefistofélico.

mephitic(al [mifítik(al], *a.* mefítico; viciado.

mephitis [mifáitis], *s.* vapor fétido; (min.) mofeta.—**mephitism** [méfitizm], *s.* mefitismo.

mercantile [mérkantil], *a.* mercantil, comercial.

mercantilism [-izm], *s.* mercantilismo.

mercenariness [mœrsęnęrinis], *s.* venalidad.

mercenary [-neri], **I.** *a.* mercenario; venal, interesado. **II.** *s.* mercenario.

mercer [mœrsœ(r)], *s.* (Ingl.) sedero, mercero.

mercerize [-aįz], va. mercerizar.

mercership [-šįp], **mercery** [-į], s. sedería, mercería.

merchandise [mɔ́ɹchəndaįz]. I. s. mercadería, mercancía(s), efectos, géneros. II. vn. traficar, comerciar, negociar.

merchant [mɔ́ɹchənt]. I. s. comerciante, mercader; tendero. II. a. mercante, mercantil.—**m. iron,** hierro o acero en barras de ciertos tamaños.—**m. marine, m. service,** marina mercante.—**m. tailor,** sastre comerciante (que vende géneros).—**m. vessel,** buque mercante.

merchantable [-əbl], a. comerciable; vendible; de recibo, corriente.

merchantlike [-laįk], a. propio de comerciantes.

merchantman [-mən], s. buque mercante.

merciful [mɔ́ɹsįfu̯l], a. misericordioso, compasivo.—**mercifully** [-lį], adv. misericordiosamente.—**mercifulness** [-nįs], s. misericordia, compasión.

merciless [mɔ́ɹsilįs], a. desapiadado, desalmado, inhumano, duro de corazón.—**mercilessly** [-lį], adv. sin piedad.—**mercilessness** [-nįs], s. falta de compasión, endurecimiento.

mercurial [mɔɹkįúɹįəl]. I. a. mercurial; vivo, activo, jovial; volátil; (M., mit., astr.) mercurial. II. s. (farm.) preparación mercurial.—**mercurialism** [-įzm], s. (med.) mercurialismo, estado causado por abuso del mercurio.—**mercurialize** [-aįz], va. (med.) someter a un tratamiento mercurial; (foto.) desarrollar con mercurio.

mercuric [mɔɹkįúɹįk], a. (quím.) mercúrico.

mercurize [mɔ́ɹkįuraįz], va. tratar o combinar con mercurio.

mercurous [mɔ́ɹkįúɹʌs], a. (quím.) mercurioso.

mercury [mɔ́ɹkįuɹį], s. (quím.) mercurio, azogue, hidrargir(i)o; (mit., astr.) Mercurio; (bot.) mercurial.—**m. chloride,** (quím.) sublimado corrosivo, solimán.—**M.'s wand,** caduceo.

mercy [mɔ́ɹsį], s. misericordia, clemencia, compasión; merced, gracia, perdón; arbitrio, discreción, poder.—**m. killing,** eutanasia.—**m. me!** ¡Ave María!—**m. seat,** propiciatorio.—**m. stroke,** golpe de gracia.—**at the m. of,** a la merced de, en el poder de.—**for m.'s sake!** ¡por piedad! ¡por Dios!—**to cry for m.,** cantar el kirieleisón.

mere [mįɹ]. I. a. mero, puro, simple, solo; sólo, no más que (lo mencionado). II. s. (poét. o ant.) laguna; el mar; (Ingl.) lindero, límite.—**merely** [-lį], adv. tan sólo, sola o meramente; simple o puramente.

meretricious [meɹįtɹíšʌs], a. meretricio; chillón.—**meretriciously** [-lį], adv. meretriciamente.—**meretriciousness** [-nįs], s. mal gusto; calidad de meretricio.

merganser [mɔɹgɛ́nsœ(r)], s. (orn.) mergo, mergánsar, gallipato, somorgujo.

merge [mɔ́ɹdž]. I. va. unir, fundir, combinar, fusionar. II. vn. unirse, fundirse, absorberse, mezclarse, fusionarse.

merger [-œ(r)], s. combinación, unión, consolidación, fusión, amalgamación comercial.

meridian [mįɹídįən]. I. s. (geog., astr., geom.) meridiano; (fig.) cenit, auge. II. a. meridiano; culminante, más alto.—**m. instrument,** meridiana, anteojo meridiano.—**m. line,** meridiana.—**m. sailing,** navegación según la meridiana, o siguiendo la meridiana.

meridional [-įoṇəl]. I. a. meridiano; meridional, pert. o rel. al Sur o Mediodía. II. s. meridional, habitante del Sur (esp. de Francia).—**meridionally** [-į], adv. en o según el meridiano.

meringue [meɹɛ́ŋ], s. (coc.) merengue.

merino [meɹínou̯]. I. a. merino; hecho de merino. II. s. (zool.) carnero merino; paño merino.

merit [mɛ́ɹįt]. I. s. mérito; merecimiento; premio.—**merits of a case,** (for.) méritos de un proceso.—**on its (his, etc.) own merits,** por sí mismo. II. va. merecer, ser digno de.

merited [-įd], a. merecido.

meritorious [meɹįtóɹįʌs], a. meritorio, benemérito.

meritoriously [-lį], adv. merecidamente.

meritoriousness [-nįs], s. merecimiento, mérito.

merle [mɔ́ɹl], s. (orn.) (poét.) merla, mirlo.

merlin [mɔ́ɹlįn], s. (orn.) esmerejón, azor.

merlon [mɔ́ɹlọn], s. (fort.) merlón, almena.

mermaid [mɔ́ɹmei̯d], s. sirena, pejemuller, f.

merman [-mæn], s. tritón.

Merovingian [meɹovíndžįən], a. y s. merovingio.

merrily [mɛ́ɹilį], adv. alegremente, con júbilo.

merriment [mɛ́ɹįmənt], s. alegría, júbilo, gozo, regocijo, alborozo; fiesta, diversión.

merry [mɛ́ɹį], a. alegre, festivo, divertido; feliz; gozoso, regocijado; risueño, placentero, agradable.—**m.-andrew,** bufón, truhán, chocarrero, mimo, payaso.—**m.-go-round,** tiovivo o tío vivo, caballitos; giro rápido, remolino.—**m. Christmas,** felices Pascuas.—**to make m.,** divertirse, regocijarse, ir de parranda.

merrymaker [-mei̯kœ(r)], s. fiestero, parrandista.—**merrymaking** [-įŋ]. I. s. fiesta, holgorio, regodeo, (fam.) gaudeamus. II. a. regocijado, parrandero.

merrythought [-θɔt], s. = WISHBONE.

mescal [meskǽl], s. (bot.) mezcal o mescal, variedad de pita; aguardiente obtenido de esta planta.

mesdames [mei̯dɛ́m], s. pl. de MADAM(E).

meseems [mįsímz], v. impers. (ant.) me parece, tengo para mí.

mesencephalon [mesɛnséfələn], s. (anat.) mesencéfalo, cerebro medio.

mesenchyma [mesɛ́ŋkįmə], s. (embr.) mesénquima.—**mesenchymatous** [-kímət̯ʌs], a. mesenquimatoso.

mesenteric [mesɛntéɹįk], a. mesentérico.

mesentery [-teɹį], s. (anat.) mesenterio, entresijo.

mesh [méš]. I. s. malla u ojo de una red; punto; obra de malla; redecilla; (mec.) engranaje.—pl. red, trampas, lazos.—**in m.,** (mec.) engranado. II. va. enredar, coger con red; (mec.) endentar. III. vn. enredarse; (mec.) endentar, engranar, engargantar.

meshy [-į], a. reticular, de malla.

mesial [mízįəl], a. mediano, del medio.—**m. plane,** plano mediano del cuerpo.

mesmeric [mezmɛ́ɹįk], a. mesmeriano, mesmerista.—**mesmerism** [mézmœɹįzm], s. mesmerismo.—**mesmerist** [-įst], s. mesmerista, magnetizador [-ai̯zœ(r)], s. mesmerista, magnetizador.—**mesmerize** [-ai̯z], va. magnetizar, hipnotizar.

mesne [min], s. intermed(iar)io.—**m. profits,** beneficios de una tierra durante ocupación ilícita.

mesoblast [mésoblæst], s. (embr.) mesoblasto.

mesocarp [-karp], s. (bot.) mesocarpio.

mesocephalic [-sefǽlįk], **mesocephalous** [-séfəlʌs], a. (anat.) mesocéfalo, mesocefálico.

mesoderm [-dœrm], s. (embr.) mesodermo.—**mesodermal** [-dœrməl], **mesodermic** [-dœrmįk], a. mesodérmico.

mesogastrium [-gǽstɹįʌm], s. (anat.) mesogastrio.—**mesogastric** [-gǽstɹįk], a. mesogástrico.

meson [mésən], s. = MESIAL PLANE.

mesoplast [-plæst], s. (biol.) núcleo celular.

Mesopotamian [-potéįmįən], a. y s. mesopotámico.

mesothoracic [-θoɹǽsįk], a. mesotorácico.—**mesothorax** [-θóɹæks], s. (zool.) mesotórax.

mesozoan [-zóu̯ən], a. y s. (zool.) mesozoario.

Mesozoic [-zóųįk], a. (geol.) mesozoico; secundario.

mesquite [meskít], s. (bot.) mezquite.

mess [mɛs]. I. s. plato (cantidad de vianda); ración, porción; rancho (comida o junta de personas que la toman a un tiempo); (fam.) comistrajo o matalotaje; (fam.) lío, confusión, revoltijo.—**m. hall,** comedor o sala de rancho para soldados, etc.; (mar.) rancho.—**m. kit,** utensi-

lios de cocina y valija en que se llevan. **II.** *va.*
dar de comer; dar rancho; (a veces con **up**)
desarreglar, desordenar, (fam.) embarrullar; ensuciar. **III.** *vn.* comer en rancho o hacer rancho;
arrancharse; hacer un revoltijo.—**to m. about**,
o **around**, ocuparse en fruslerías.

message [mésǐdž], *s.* mensaje; recado, parte,
mandado, aviso.

messenger [mésęndžœ(r)], *s.* mensajero, mandadero, propio, recadero; heraldo, nuncio; (mar.)
aparejo para levar el ancla.

Messiah [mesáįǎ], *s.* Mesías.—**Messianic** [mesj-
ǽnįk], *a.* mesiánico.—**Messianism** [mesáįan-
įzm], *s.* mesianismo.

messieurs [mésyœrz o mésœrz], *s. pl.* de **MON-
SIEUR**; ú. t. como *pl.* de **MISTER**, señores; se
escribe **Messrs.**, en abreviatura.

messmate [mésmejt], *s.* comensal.

messroom [-rum], *s.* = **MESS HALL**.

messuage [méswįdž], *s.* casa de vivienda y
anexas.

messy [mési], *a.* desordenado, desaliñado, sucio.

mestizo [mestízou], *a.* y *s.* mestizo; cambujo.

met [met], *pret.* y *pp.* de **TO MEET**.

metabolism [metǽbolįzm], *s.* (biol.) metabolismo; (ent.) metamorfosis.

metacarpal [metakárpal]. **I.** *a.* metacarpiano,
del metacarpo. **II.** *s.* cada hueso del metacarpo.

metacarpus [-kárpʌs], *s.* (anat.) metacarpo.

metacentre [-sentœ(r)], *s.* metacentro.

metachronism [metǽkronįzm], *s.* metacronismo.

metagenesis [metadžénesįs], *s.* metagénesis.

metageometry [-džiámetrį], *s.* geometría no
euclidiana.

metal [métal]. **I.** *s.* metal; liga, aleación; material
(piedra partida, escorias, etc.) para caminos
(*v.* **ROAD METAL**); (f. c.) balasto; vidrio en fusión; cualidad esencial (*v.* **METTLE**); (mar.) peso
de los proyectiles que un acorazado puede disparar a un tiempo.—**m. industry**, metalistería.
II. *va.* cubrir o proveer de metal; macadamizar
(un camino); (f. c.) balastar.

metalepsis [metalépsįs], *s.* (ret.) metalepsis.

metalled [métald], *a.* (f. c.) terraplenado, afirmado.

metallic [metǽlįk], *a.* metálico; libre, puro.

metalliferous [metalíferʌs], *a.* metalífero.

metallist [métalįst], *s.* metalario.

metallization [-ížēǐšǫn], *s.* metalización.

metallize [-ajz], *va.* metalizar.

metallography [metalágrafį], *s.* metalografía.

metalloid [métalojd]. **I.** *a.* metaloídico. **II.** *s.*
(quím.) metaloide.

metallotherapy [metæloθérapį], *s.* (med.) metaloterapia.

metallurgic(al [metalœrdžįk(al], *a.*, **metallurgist** [métalœrdžįst], *s.* metalúrgico.—**metallurgy** [-džį], *s.* metalurgia, metálica.

metalwork [métalwœrk], *s.* metalistería.—
metalworker [-œ(r)], *s.* metalista, metalario.

metamer [métamœ(r)], *s.* (quím.) cuerpo metámero.—**metamere** [-mir], *s.* (zool.) metámero,
somito.—**metameric** [-mérįk], *a.* metamérico;
(quím.) metámero, isómero.—**metamerism**
[metǽmœrįzm], *s.* (quím., zool.) metamería,
metamerismo; (zool.) estructura metamérica.—
metamerized [-ajzd], *a.* (zool.) metamerizado.

metamorphic [metamórfįk], *a.* metamórfico.—
metamorphism [-fįzm], *s.* (geol.) metamorfismo; metamorfosis.—**metamorphize**, **metamorphose** [-fajz, -fouz], *va.* metamorfosear.—
metamorphosis [-fosįs], *s.* metamorfosis;
mudanza de forma o estructura.

metaphor [métafǫ(r)], *s.* (ret.) metáfora.—
metaphoric(al [-fórįk(al], *a.* metafórico.—
metaphorically [-į], *adv.* metafóricamente.
—**metaphorist** [-forįst], *s.* metaforista.

metaphrase [métafrejz], *s.* metafrasis, traducción
literal.—**metaphrast** [-fræst], *s.* metafrasta,
mf.—**metaphrastic** [-fræstįk], *a.* metafrástico.

metaphysic(al [-fízįk(al], *a.* metafísico.

metaphysically [-į], *adv.* metafísicamente.

metaphysician [-fįzíšǫn], *s.* metafísico.

metaphysics [-fízįks], *s.* metafísica.

metaplasm [-plæzm], *s.* (gram.) metaplasmo;
(biol.) metaplasma, *m.*

metastasis [metéstasįs], *s.* metamorfosis; (med.)
metástasis; (biol.) metabolismo.

metatarsal [metatársal], *a.* metatarsiano.

metatarsus [-társʌs], *s.* (anat., zool.) metatarso.

metathesis [metéθesįs], *s.* (ret.) metátesis;
(quím.) substitución.

metathorax [metaθóræks], *s.* (zool.) metatórax.

Metazoa [-zóǎǎ], *s. pl.* (zool.) metazoarios.

mete [mit], *va.* (gen. con **out**) repartir, prorratear.

metempiric(al [metempírįk(al], *a.* (fil.) transcendental, que traspasa los límites de la experiencia.

metempsychosis [-psįkóųsįs], *s.* metempsicosis,
transmigración.

meteor [mítjǫ(r)], *s.* meteoro o metéoro; exhalación, estrella fugaz.

meteoric [mitjórįk], **meteoritic** [mitjǫrítįk], *a.*
meteórico; atmosférico, meteorológico.—**m.
iron**, o **stone**, aerolito.—**m. showers**, lluvia
de estrellas fugaces.

meteorism [mítjǫrįzm], *s.* (med.) meteorismo.

meteorite [mítjǫrajt], **meteorolite** [-olajt], **me-
teoroid** [-ojd], *s.* aerolito, meteorito, bólido.

meteorological [-oládžįkal], *a.* meteorológico.—
meteorologist [-álodžįst], *s.* meteorologista,
meteorólogo.—**meteorology** [-álodžį], *s.* meteorología.

meteorous [mítjǫrʌs], *a.* meteórico.

meter [mítœ(r)], *s.* (pros.) metro (medida del
verso); metro (medida de longitud); medidor,
mensurador; contador (de gas, agua, etc.).

meterage [-įdž], *s.* metraje.

methane [méθejn], *s.* (quím.) metano.

metheglin [miθéglįn], *s.* aguamiel, *f.*, hidromel.

methinks [miθíŋks], *v. impers.* (ant.) me parece.

method [méθǫd], *s.* método, medio, procedimiento, vía; orden, regularidad; ejecución,
técnica.

methodic(al [meθádįk(al], *a.* metódico, sistemático.—**methodically** [-į], *adv.* metódicamente.

methodics [meθádįks], *s.* metodología.

Methodism [méθǫdįzm], *s.* (igl.) metodismo.—
Methodist [-įst], *a.* y *s.* metodista.

methodize [-ajz], *va.* metodizar, ordenar.

methodology [meθǫdálodžį], *s.* metodología.

methought [miθót], *pret.* de **METHINKS**.

methyl [méθįl], *s.* (quím.) metilo.—**m. alcohol**,
alcohol metílico.—**m. orange**, anaranjado de
metilo.

methylamine [-amín], *s.* (quím.) metilamina.

methylate [-ejt]. **I.** *s.* (quím.) metilato. **II.** *va.*
mezclar con metilo o alcohol metílico.—**meth-
ylated spirit(s**, mezcla de alcohol etílico y
alcohol metílico, alcohol desnaturalizado.

methylene [-in], *s.* (quím.) metileno.

methylic [meθílįk], *a.* metílico.

meticulous [mitíkyulʌs], *a.* escrupuloso en demasía; (ant. o fig.) meticuloso.—**meticulously**
[-į], *adv.* escrupulosamente.—**m. clean**, de
limpieza exquisita.—**meticulousness** [-nįs], *s.*
escrupulosidad, delicadeza excesiva; (ant. o fig.)
meticulosidad.

métier [metyé], *s.* oficio, profesión.

metol [mítol], *s.* (quím., fot.) metol.

metonymical [metoním]kal], *a.* metonímico.—
metonymically [-į], *adv.* metonímicamente.—
metonymy [metánįmį], *s.* (ret.) metonimia.

metope [métopi], *s.* (arq.) métopa, plato.

metoposcopy [metopáskopį], *s.* metoposcopia.

metre [mítœ(r)], *s.* = **METER**.

metric(al [métrįk(al], *a.* métrico.—**m. system**,
sistema métrico.—**m. ton**, tonelada métrica de
1000 kg. (2204 libras).

metrically [-į], *adv.* métricamente.

metrician [metríšǎn], o **metrist** [mítrįst], *s.* versificador, metrista.

metrify [métrifai], *va.* metrificar, versificar.

metritis [mitráitis], *s.* (med.) metritis.

metrograph [métrogræf], *s.* (f. c.) metrógrafo.

metrological [-ládʒikal], *a.* metrológico.

metrology [metrálodʒi], *s.* metrología.

metronome [métronoum], *s.* (mús.) metrónomo.

metropolis [metrápolis], *s.* metrópoli, *f.; urbe, f.*

metropolitan [metropálitan]. I. *a.* metropolitano. II. *s.* (igl.) metropolitano; ciudadano de una metrópoli.

metrorrhagia [mitroréidʒiə], *s.* (med.) metrorragia.

mettle [métl], *s.* temple, brío, coraje, ardor, valor; vivacidad, fuego.—**on one's m.,** dispuesto a hacer lo mejor posible.—**to put on one's m.,** picar el amor propio de uno; estimularle; poner a prueba su valor, brío, etc.

mettled [-d], **mettlesome** [-sam], *a.* brioso, vivo, fogoso.—**mettlesomely** [-li], *adv.* briosamente, vivamente.—**mettlesomeness** [-nis], *s.* brío, fuego, vivacidad.

mew [mjú]. I. *s.* maullido, maúllo, miau (del gato); (orn.) gaviota, paviota; jaula, muda (esp. para aves de cetrería que mudan sus plumas); cercado o corral.—*pl.* establo, caballeriza. II. *va.* mudar; enjaular, encerrar. III. *vn.* maullar, miar, mayar (los gatos).

mewing [-iŋ]. I. *s.* maullido, maído; muda (ú. de las aves). II. *a.* maullador; que muda.

mewl [mjul]. I. *vn.* llorar como un niño; lloriquear. II. *s.* lloro de niño; lloriqueo.

Mexican [méksikan], *a.* y *s.* mejicano, mexicano.

mezereon [mizírion], *s.* (bot.) mecereo o mecereón, lauréola hembra.

mezzanine [mézanin], *s.* (arq.) entresuelo.

mezzo-rilievo [medzou rilyéivou], *s.* medio relieve.

mezzotint(o [mé(d)zotint, -tíntou], *s.* media tinta.

mi [mi], *s.* (mús.) mi.

miasm(a [máiæzm, maiæzmá], *s.* (*pl.* MIASMATA) miasma, *m.*, emanaciones mefíticas.

miasmal [-l], **miasmatic** [maiæzmætik], *a.* miasmático, infecto, palúdico.

mica [máika], *s.* (min.) mica.—**m. schist,** micacita, micasquisto.

micaceous [maikéiʃias], *a.* micáceo.

mice [mais], *s. pl.* de MOUSE.

Michaelmas [míkelmas], *s.* sanmiguelada.

microbe [máikroub], *s.* microbio.

microbial [maikróubial], **microbic** [-ik], *a.* micróbico, microbiano.

microbicide [-isaid], *s.* microbicida.

microbiological [-baioládʒikal], *a.* microbiológico.—**microbiologist** [-baiálodʒist], *s.* microbiólogo.—**microbiology** [-dʒi], *s.* microbiología.

microcephalic [-sefælik], **microcephalous** [-sefaᴧas], *a.* microcéfalo.—**microcephalism** [-sefalizm], *s.* (med.) microcefalia.

micrococcal [-kákal], *a.* micrococal.

micrococcus [-kákas], *s.* micrococo.

microcosm [-kazm], *s.* microcosmo.

microcosmic(al [-kázmik(al], *a.* microcósmico.

microcyte [-sait], *s.* (pat.) microcito.

microfarad [-færæd], *s.* (elec.) microfaradio.

microfilm [-film], *s.* microfilm.

microgram [-græm], *s.* microgramo.

micrograph [-græf], *s.* micrógrafo.

micrographer [maikrágrafœ(r)], *s.* micrógrafo.

micrographic [maikrográfik], *a.* micrográfico.

micrography [maikrágrafi], *s.* micrografía.

microhm [máikroum], *s.* (elec.) microhmio.

microlite [máikrolait], *s.* (geol.) microlito.

microlitic [-lítik], *a.* microlítico.

micrometer [maikrámetœ(r)], *s.* micrómetro.—**m. caliper, gauge,** o **gage,** compás micrométrico.—**m. screw,** tornillo micrométrico.

micrometric(al [maikrométrik(al], *a.* micrométrico.

micrometry [maikrámetri], *s.* micrometría.

micromillimiter [maikromílimitœ(r)], *s.* micra, micrón, micromilímetro.

micromotion [-mouʃon], *s.* movimiento de objetos diminutos amplificado con el microscopio.

micron [máikran], *s.* micra, micrón (millonésima de metro).

microörganism [maikroórganizm], *s.* microrganismo, microorganismo.

microphone [-foun], *s.* micrófono.

microphotograph [-fóutogræf], **microphotography** [-fotágrafi], *s.* microfotografía.

microphyte [-fait], *s.* (bot. y biol.) micrófito.

micropyle [-pail], *s.* (bot. y zool.) micrópilo.

micropyrometer [-pairámetœ(r)], *s.* (fís.) micropirómetro.

microscope [-skoup], *s.* microscopio.

microscopic(al [-skápik(al], *a.* microscópico.

microscopist [maikráskopist], *s.* microscopista.

microscopy [-kopi], *s.* microscopia.

microseism [máikrosaizm], *s.* microsismo.—**microseismometer**, **microseismograph** [-saizmámetœ(r), -sáizmogræf], *s.* microsismógrafo.

microsome [-soum], *s.* (biol.) microsoma, *m.*

microspore [-spɔr], *s.* (bot., zool.) microspora.

microtelephone [-télefoun], *s.* microteléfono.

microtome [-toum], *s.* micrótomo.

microvolt [-voult], *s.* (elec.) microvoltio.

microzyme [-zaim], *s.* microcima, microzima, *m.*

miction [míkʃon], **micturition** [miktjuríʃon], *s.* micturición, micción.

micturate [míktjureit], *vn.* orinar, mear.

mid [mid]. I. *a.* medio. úsase en composición.—**m.-age,** edad madura.—(**in**) **m. air,** (en) el aire.—**m.-course,** media carrera o medio camino.—**m.-Lent,** media cuaresma.—**m.-sea,** alta mar. II. *prep.* **m.** o **'m.** (poét.) entre, en medio de.

midbrain [-brein], *s.* (anat.) cerebro medio, mesencéfalo.

midday [-dei]. I. *s.* mediodía, *m.* (tiempo, hora). II. *a.* del mediodía, meridiano.

middle [mídl]. I. *a.* medio, intermedio, mediano; de en medio (the *middle drawer*, el cajón de en medio).—**M.-Age,** medieval.—**m.-aged,** de edad madura.—**M. Ages, Edad Media.—M. America,** Méjico y la América Central.—**m.-class,** de la clase media.—**m. class,** clase media, burguesía.—**m. distance,** (pint.) segundo término; (dep.) de medio fondo (carreras).—**m. ear,** (anat.) tímpano; oído medio.—**m. earth,** (poét.) tierra, el mundo.—**M. East,** los países del SO. del Asia (a veces también el Egipto).—**m. finger,** dedo del corazón.—**m. ground,** posición intermedia entre dos extremos; (pint.) segundo término.—**m. jib,** (mar.) segundo foque.—**M. Kingdom,** imperio chino.—**m. rail,** (f. c., elec.) riel central conductor.—**m.-shot wheel** = BREAST WHEEL.—**m.-sized,** de mediana estatura o tamaño.—**m. term,** (lóg.) término medio.—**m. wall,** tabique.—**M. West,** (E. U.) estados centrales del norte, el medio oeste. II. *s.* medio, centro, mitad, corazón; promedio; cintura.—*pl.* (agr.) lomos, caballones.—**m. of,** mediados de.—**m. of the road,** posición intermedia.—**m.-of-the-road,** que no está ni de un lado ni del otro; indeciso, vacilante.—**about,** o **towards the m. of,** a mediados de.

middleman [-mæn], *s.* intermediario; (com.) agente de negocios; corredor; revendedor.

middlemost [-moust], *a.* del medio; en el medio o más cercano al medio.

middleweight [-weit]. I. *a.* (dep.) de peso medio o mediano (hasta 160 libras). II. *s.* peso medio.

middling [mídliŋ]. I. *a.* mediano, regular, pasadero. II. *s. pl.* acemite.—**middlingly** [-li], *adv.* medianamente, regularmente, pasaderamente.

middy [mídi], *s. dim.* (fam.) guardia marina.—**m.,** o **m. blouse,** cierta blusa holgada para mujeres y niñas.

midge [mɪ̆dʒ], *s.* (ent.) especie de jején; enano.

midget [mɪ̆dʒɪ̆t], *s.* enanillo; chiquillo vivaracho.
—**m. submarine**, (mar.) submarino de tipo diminuto.

midheaven [mɪ̆dhɛ́vn], *s.* el medio del cielo; (astr.) el meridiano superior.

midiron [-aɪœrn], *s.* cierto mazo o palo del golf.

midland [-lənd]. I. *a.* mediterráneo, tierra adentro, interior. II. *s.* corazón de un país.

midmost [-mɒʊst], *a.* = MIDDLEMOST.

midnight [-naɪt]. I. *s.* medianoche, *f.* II. *a.* nocturno; negro.—**m. mass**, (igl.) misa del gallo.

midnoon [-nun], *s.* = MIDDAY.

midrib [-rɪb], *s.* (bot.) vena central.

midriff [-rɪf], *s.* (anat.) diafragma, *m.;* traje que deja descubierta una parte del diafragma.

midship [-ʃɪp]. I. *a.* (mar.) de, rel. a, o en medio del buque.—**m. beam**, bao maestro.—**m. frame**, cuaderna maestra. II. *s. pl.* baos maestros; el centro del buque.—**midships** [-s], *adv.* en o hacia el centro de la nave.

midshipman [-mən], *s.* (mar.) guardia marina, alférez alumno.

midst [mɪ̆dst]. I. *s.* medio, centro; (fig.) seno; presión, rigor.—**in our, their, your m.**, en medio de nosotros, ellos, ustedes.—**in the m. of**, en medio de, entre; rodeado de; en lo más (reñido, agitado, etc.) de. II. *adv.* (raro) en medio. III. *prep.* **m.**, o **'m.** (poét.) entre.

midstream [mɪ̆dstrím], *s.* el medio de una corriente.

midsummer [-sÁmœ(r)], *s.* solsticio estival; la mitad del verano; pleno verano.—**M. Day**, día (*m.*) de San Juan (24 de junio).

midway [-weɪ]. I. *s.* medio camino, mitad del camino; en una exposición o feria, avenida central dedicada a diversiones, curiosidades, etc. II. *a.* situado a mitad del camino. III. *adv.* en medio del camino; a medio camino.—**m. between**, equidistante de.

midweek [-wik]. I. *s.* medio o mediados de la semana.—**M.** (entre los cuáqueros) mitad de semana (miércoles). II. *a.* de la mitad de la semana.

Midwest [mɪ̆dwɛ́st], *s.* = MIDDLE WEST.

midwife [mɪ̆dwaɪf]. I. *s.* (*pl.* MIDWIVES) partera, comadre, *f.*, comadrona, matrona. II. *vn.* partear.—**midwifery** [-rɪ], *s.* obstetricia, partería.

midwinter [mɪ̆dwɪ́ntœ(r)], *s.* solsticio hiemal; mitad del invierno; pleno invierno.

mien [min], *s.* semblante, aire, talante, facha.

miff [mɪf]. I. *s.* (fam.) enojo, pique, riña por motivos frívolos. II. *va.* desagradar, enojar. III. *vn.* amoscarse.

might [maɪt], *pret. ind.* y *subj.* de MAY.—*s.* poder(ío).

might [maɪt], *s.* poder, fuerza.—**with m. and main**, con todas sus fuerzas, a más no poder.

mightily [-ɪlɪ], *adv.* poderosamente.

mightiness [-ɪnɪ̆s], *s.* poder(ío); potencia, fuerza; grandeza.

mighty [-ɪ]. I. *a.* potente, poderoso; fuerte, vigoroso; enorme; eficaz, importante. II. *adv.* (fam.) extremadamente, sumamente.

mignonette [mɪ̆nyɒnɛ́t], *s.* (bot.) reseda.

migraine [máɪgreɪn], *s.* (med.) migraña, hemicránea, jaqueca.

migrant [máɪgrənt]. I. *s.* el o lo que emigra; ave migratoria o de paso. II. *a.* = MIGRATORY o MIGRATING.

migrate [máɪgreɪt], *vn.* emigrar; trasplantarse.—**migrating** [-ɪŋ], *a.* migratorio, peregrino; de paso.

migration [-éɪʃɒn], *s.* (e)migración; trasplante.

migratory [máɪgrətɒrɪ], *a.* (e)migratorio; nómade.

mihrab [mírab], *s.* mihrab, hornacina de mezquita.

Mikado [mɪ̆kádoʊ], *s.* micado.

mike [maɪk], *s.* (fam.) = MICROPHONE.

mil [mɪl], *s.* milipulgada, milésima de pulgada.

milady [mɪ̆léɪdɪ], *s.* miladi, *f.*, dama noble inglesa.

Milanese [mɪ̆ləníz], *a.* y *s.* milanés, de Milán.

milch [mɪlch], *a.* lactífera, lechera, que da leche.—**m. cow**, vaca de leche.

mild [maɪld], *a.* suave, moderado, apacible, manso; benigno, blando, indulgente; leve, ligero.—**m. steel**, acero dúctil, acero pobre en carbono (menos de 0,25 por ciento).—**m. temperature**, blandura.

mildew [mɪ́ldjʊ]. I. *s.* añublo, moho, tizón, roya; mildeu o mildiú (de la vid). II. *va.* y *vn.* enmohecer(se), alheñar(se), añublar(se), atizonar(se).

mildly [máɪldlɪ], *adv.* suavemente, blandamente, con indulgencia.—**mildness** [-nɪ̆s], *s.* suavidad, lenidad; apacibilidad; mansedumbre, indulgencia.

mile [maɪl], *s.* milla (5,280 pies ingleses = 1,609 metros).—**m. post**, o **stone**, piedra miliaria, poste miliar, mojón, cipo, hito, pilar.

mileage [-ɪdʒ], *s.* longitud en millas; subsidio o derecho de tránsito por milla; (aut.) kilometraje, recorrido (apl. esp. a la duración de llantas medida por la distancia total que recorren).—**m. indicator**, (aut.) cuentakilómetros.—**m. ticket**, billete kilométrico.

Milesian [mɪ̆líʃɪ̆ən], *a.* y *s.* milesio, de Mileto; irlandés o hibernés.—**M. tale**, fábula milesia.

milfoil [mɪ̆lfɔɪl], *s.* (bot.) milenrama, aquilea.

miliaria [mɪ̆lɪérɪ̆ə], *s.* (med.) erupción miliar.

miliary [mɪ̆lɪerɪ], *a.* que se parece a una semilla de mijo; (med.) miliar.

milieu [milyœ́], *s.* medio ambiente.

militancy [mɪ̆lɪtənsɪ], *s.* militarismo; actitud belicosa o de combate.—**militant** [-ənt], *a.* militante, combatiente; belicoso, guerrero.

militarily [mɪ̆lɪterɪlɪ], *adv.* militarmente.

militarism [mɪ̆lɪtərɪzm], *s.* militarismo.

militarist [-ɪst], *s.*, **militaristic** [-ɪstɪk], *a.* militarista.

militarization [-ɪzéɪʃɒn], *s.* militarización.—**militarize** [-aɪz], *va.* militarizar.

military [mɪ̆lɪterɪ]. I. *a.* militar; guerrero, marcial; castrense; soldadesco, de tropa; de guerra.—**m. coup**, o **uprising**, golpe de cuartel.—**m. law**, código militar.—**m. man**, militar, soldado.—**m. police**, policía militar.—**m. stores**, municiones de guerra. II. *s.* ejército, milicia, soldadesca, tropa(s), los militares.

militate [mɪ̆lɪteɪt], *vn.* combatir, pelear; (con **against**) militar contra, oponerse a; (con **for**) militar en favor de.

militia [mɪ̆lɪ́ʃə], *s.* milicia, guardia nacional.—**militiaman** [-mən], *s.* miliciano.—*pl.* milicia.

milk [mɪlk]. I. *s.* leche, *f.;* (bot.) látex, jugo lechero.—**m.-and-water**, vacilante, débil de carácter.—**m. bag**, ubre, *f.*—**m. bar**, puesto donde se sirven leche y sus productos.—**m. can**, lechera, camella.—**m. crust**, (med.) lactumen.—**m. diet**, régimen lácteo.—**m. duct**, (anat., zool.) vaso lactífero; (bot.) vaso laticífero.—**m. fever**, (med.) fiebre láctea.—**m. food**, lacticinio.—**m. glass**, vidrio de criolita; ventosa de leche con que se extrae la leche de los pechos.—**m. leg**, (med.) edema doloroso puerperal.—**m.-livered**, timorato, miedoso.—**m. of almonds**, almendrada.—**m. of lime**, lechada de cal.—**m. of magnesia**, (farm.) leche de magnesia.—**m. pail**, colodra, ordeñadero.—**m. pan**, lechera.—**m. shake**, leche batida, batido de leche.—**m. sugar**, lactina, lactosa.—**m. tester**, lactómetro.—**m. thistle**, (bot.) titímalo, cardo lechero, lechetrezna.—**m. tooth**, diente de leche o mamón.—**m. vetch**, (bot.) astrágalo, tragacanto.—**m.-warm**, tibio.—**m.-white**, blanco como la leche.—**m.-white horse**, palomilla. II. *va.* ordeñar; (fam.) agotar, extraer de. III. *vn.* dar leche.

milker [-œ(r)], *s.* ordeñador; vaca (etc.) de leche. V. MILKING MACHINE.

milkiness [-ɪnɪ̆s], *s.* lactescencia.

milking [-iŋ], s. ordeño.—**m. machine**, máquina ordeñadora o de ordeñar.
milkmaid [-mejd], s. lechera.
milkman [-mæn], s. lechero.
milksop [-sap], s. marica, mantecón.
milkweed [-wid], s. (bot.) vencetósigo.
milkwort [-wœrt], s. (bot.) polígala.
milky [-i], a. lácteo, lactífero; lechoso, lacticíneo, lechar o lechal; blando, tierno, suave, tímido.— **M. Way**, (astr.) Vía Láctea, Galaxia.
mill [mȋl]. I. s. molino; taller, fábrica; (mec.) prensa; hilandería o tejeduría; fábrica de hilados o de tejidos; (fam.) pugilato; una milésima parte; (E. U.) milésimo de dólar.—**m. clack**, tarabilla, cítola.—**m. construction**, (arq.) construcción anticombustible, que en sí misma minora el peligro de incendio, sin ser de materiales incombustibles.—**m. dust**, harija. —**m. hand**, obrero.—**m. hopper**, tolva de molino.—**m. horse**, caballo de tahona.—**m. run** = MILLRACE; (min.) ensayo de molino.— **m. wheel**, rueda de molino.—**to go through the m.**, saber una cosa por experiencia. II. va. moler, desmenuzar; acordonar (moneda), estriar; fresar. III. vn. (a veces con **about** o **around**) (ar)remolinar(se), remolinear(se).
millboard [-bɔrd], s. cartón de encuadernar.
millcourse [-kɔrs], s. = MILLRACE.
milldam [-dæm], s. esclusa, represa; dique.
millenarian [milenérian], **millenary** [mȋleneri], a. y s. milenario.
millennial [milénial], a., **millennium** [-iʌm], s. milenario.
millepede [mȋlipid], s. (zool.) ciempiés.
millepore [-pɔr], s. (zool.) milépora.
miller [mȋlœr)], s. molinero, molendero, tahonero; (ent.) mariposa con manchas blancas.— **m.'s-thumb**, (ict.) especie de gobio o coto.
millesimal [milésimal], a. y s. milésimo.
millet [mȋlit], s. (bot.) mijo.
milliampere [mȋliæmpér], s. (elec.) miliamperio. —**milliam(pere)meter** [-(pir)mitœr)], s. (elec.) miliamperímetro.
milliard [mȋljard], s. mil millones.
milliare [mȋljer], s. miliárea.
milliary [mȋljeri], a. miliario, miliar.
millier [milyéi], s. tonelada métrica.
milligram(me [mȋligræm], s. miligramo.
milliliter, millilitre [-litœr)], s. mililitro.
millimeter, millimetre [-mitœr)], s. milímetro.
millimicron [-majkran], s. milimicrón.
milliner [mȋlinœr)], s. modista de sombreros.
millinery [mȋlineri], s. cintas, flores, etc., para sombreros de señora; ocupación o tienda de modista o sombrerera.—**m. department**, sección de sombreros (en una tienda).—**m. shop**, o **store**, sombrerería.
milling [mȋliŋ]. I. s. molienda, moledura; acordonamiento, acuñación; cordoncillo de la moneda; (metal.) fresado.—**m. about**, remolino. II. a. de moler, de fresar, etc. V. MILL, va.—**m. cutter**, o **tool**, fresa.—**m. machine**, fresadora.—**m. saw**, sierra circular de cortar metales.
million [mȋlyon], s. millón.
millionaire [-ér], s. y a. millonario, amillonado.
millioned [-d], a. amillonado.
millionth [-θ], s. y a. millonésimo.
millipede [mȋlipid], s. = MILLEPEDE.
millpond [mȋlpand], s. alberca, cubo.
millrace [-rejs], s. caz, m., saetín, canal de molino.
millstone [-stoun], s. muela, piedra molar o de molino.—**m. hammer**, o **pick**, martellina.
millwork [-wœrk], s. cualquier obra o producto de un molino, taller, etc.; maquinaria de molino.
millwright [-rajt], s. constructor de molinos; el instalador o encargado de la maquinaria en un molino, taller o fábrica.
milo [májlou], s. (bot.) especie de sorgo.

milord [milórd], s. milord.—pl. milores.
milreis [mȋlrejs], s. milréis, m. (moneda).
milt [mȋlt]. I. s. (anat.) bazo; lechecillas (f. pl.) de los peces. II. va. impregnar las huevas de los peces.
milter [-œr)], s. pez macho.—**m. and spawner**, pez macho y hembra.
Miltonian [miltóunian], **Miltonic** [miltánik], a. miltónico, miltoniano.
mime [majm], s. mimo; truhán, bufón, farsante; pantomima, farsa.
mimeograph [mȋmjográef]. I. s. mimeógrafo (es nombre de fábrica). II. va. reproducir con el mimeógrafo.
mimesis [mimísis], s. (ret.) mimesis; (biol.) mimetismo; (med.) simulación de una enfermedad por otra.
mimetic(al [mimétik(al], a. imitativo, mímico.
mimic [mȋmik]. I. va. remedar, imitar. II. s. mimo, pantomimo, remedador. III. a. mímico, imitativo, burlesco.—**mimically** [-ali], adv. burlescamente, mímicamente.—**mimicry** [-ri], s. mímica; bufonería; monería, remedo; (biol.) mimetismo.
mimodrama [mȋmodræma], s. mimodrama, m., zarzuela pantomímica con baile.
mimographer [mimágrafœr)], s. mimógrafo.
mimosa [mimóusa], s. (bot.) mimosa, sensitiva.
mimulus [mȋmjulʌs], s. (bot.) mímulo.
minacious [minéjsʌs], a. amenazador.
minaret [mȋnarét], s. (arq.) minarete, alminar.
minatory [mȋnatɔri], a. amenazador.
mince [mȋns]. I. va. desmenuzar, destrizar, capolar; picar (carne), hacer picadillo; medir (las palabras); paliar, atenuar.—**minced oath**, voto atenuado; eufemismo.—**without mincing words**, sin ambages. II. vn. ser afectado o melindroso en el modo de hablar, andar, etc. III. s. (raro) afectación.—**m. pie**, pastel relleno de picadillo de carne, fruta y especias.
mincemeat [-mit], s. carne picada con frutas, etc., para hacer pasteles.—**to make m. of**, destruir, aniquilar.
mincingly [-iŋli], adv. a pedacitos; a pasitos; con afectación.
mind [majnd]. I. s. mente, f., entendimiento, pensamiento, inteligencia; espíritu, ánimo; memoria, recuerdo; gusto, propensión, inclinación, afición, afecto; voluntad, gana; intención, resolución; opinión, criterio, juicio, parecer, dictamen.—**m. blindness** = MENTAL BLINDNESS.— **m. cure**, psicoterapia; sistema (m.) de curar que supone que toda enfermedad se debe a causas psicológicas.—**m. deafness** = MENTAL DEAFNESS.—**m. reader**, adivinador del pensamiento ajeno.—**m. reading**, adivinación del pensamiento ajeno.—**m.'s eye**, la imaginación. —**of one m.**, unánimes.—**out of m.**, olvidado. —**out of one's m.**, loco; fuera de juicio; desvariado.—**to call to m.**, recordar, traer a la memoria.—**to give someone a piece of one's m.**, decir a alguien cuántas son cinco, ponerlo como nuevo.—**to have a m. to**, tener gana de, querer; proponerse.—**to have in m.**, recordar; tener en consideración; pensar en.—**to have on one's m.**, tener mucho en las mientes, preocuparse con.—**to keep in m.**, tener presente o en cuenta.—**to my m.**, a mi ver, a mi juicio.—**to pass out of m.**, olvidarse.—**to set one's m. on**, aplicarse a; desear vivamente.—**with one m.**, unánimemente. II. va. notar, observar; atender a; cuidar; cuidarse de; (ant.) recordar; tener inconveniente en; oponerse a; hacer caso a o de; obedecer; (ant.) proponerse.—**to m. one's business**, meterse uno en lo que le importa.—**to m. one's P's and Q's**, poner los puntos sobre las íes, tener gran cuidado en lo que se hace o dice. III. vn. atender, obedecer, hacer caso; tener cuidado.—**never m.**, no importa; no se moleste, no se preocupe.
minded [-id], a. inclinado, dispuesto, propenso.

mindful [-fụl], *a.* atento, cuidadoso; memorioso.
mindfully [-i], *adv.* atentamente, cuidadosamente.—**mindfulness** [-nịs], *s.* calidad de cuidadoso o atento.
mindless [-lịs], *a.* sin mentalidad; descuidado, negligente; (raro) necio, insensato.
mine [majn]. **I.** *pron. pos.* mío, mía, míos, mías; el mío, etc.; lo mío: *this book is mine,* este libro es mío; *your book and mine,* su libro y el mío; *what's mine,* lo mío.—**of m.,** mío.—**it is m.** (seguido de infinitivo), a mí me toca o me cae en suerte; yo puedo a mi arbitrio. **II.** *a.* (ant.) mi, mío (ú. sólo ante vocal o *h,* o después del sustantivo: *mine eyes,* mis ojos; *lady mine,* señora mía).
mine [majn]. **I.** *s.* (min., fort., art.) mina; (mar.) mina submarina.—**m. detector,** detector de minas.—**m. field,** (mil., mar.) campo de minas explosivas.—**m. layer,** o **sower,** (barco) plantaminas, sembraminas o lanzaminas.—**m. sweeper,** dragaminas, barreminas.—**m. thrower,** obús, mortero de trinchera. **II.** *va.* minar; contraminar, zapar; destruir; extraer (mineral), explotar (una mina). **III.** *vn.* hacer una mina; explotar minas; dedicarse a la minería; hacer trabajos de zapa; dañar secretamente.
miner [-œ(r)], *s.* (min.) minero, barretero; (mil.) minador, zapador.—**m.'s inch** = WATER INCH.
mineral [mínẹrạl], *s.* y *a.* mineral.—**m. cotton,** = M. WOOL.—**m. oil,** petróleo.—**m. jelly,** vaselina, petroleína.—**m. kingdom,** reino mineral.—**m. pitch,** asfalto.—**m. right,** (for.) derecho al subsuelo.—**m. water,** agua mineral.—**m. wax,** ozocerita.—**m. wool,** lana de escoria.
mineralization [-izéjšọn], *s.* mineralización.
mineralize [-ajz], *va.* mineralizar.
mineralizer [-œ(r)], *s.* (quím.) mineralizador.
mineralogic(**al** [-ádžjk(ạl], *a.* mineralógico.—**mineralogist** [mínẹrálọdžist], *s.* mineralogista.
mineralogize [-džạjz], *vn.* recoger y estudiar minerales.
mineralogy [-dži], *s.* mineralogía.
mingle [míŋgl], **I.** *va.* mezclar, mixturar; confundir. **II.** *vn.* mezclarse, juntarse, incorporarse.—**m.-mangle,** mixtura, miscelánea, almodrote.
mingled [-d], *a.* mezclado, mixto; confuso.
miniate [míniẹjt]. **I.** *a.* rojo, miniado. **II.** *va.* miniar.
miniature [míniạchụr]. **I.** *a.* en miniatura. **II.** *s.* (b. a.) miniatura.—**m. painter,** miniaturista.—**to paint in m.,** miniar. **III.** *va.* representar en miniatura; reducir a escala pequeña.
minify [mínifaj], *va.* empequeñecer, achicar.
minikin [mínikịn]. **I.** *s.* cosa o persona menuda o chiquirritica. **II.** *a.* delicado; diminuto; afectado.
minim [mínịm]. **I.** *s.* (farm.) medida fluida (0.95 grano de agua; casi una gota); (mús.) mínima; (M., igl.) mínimo; pizca, jota, cosa o persona muy insignificante. **II.** *a.* mínimo, pequeñísimo.
minimal [-mạl], *a.* mínimo.
minimize [-majz], *va.* reducir al mínimo; achicar; menospreciar, tener en menos.
minimum [-mʌm], *s.* y *a.* mínimo; *s.* mínimum.
mining [májnịŋ]. **I.** *s.* minería, mineraje, laboreo o explotación de minas; (mil., mar.) acto de sembrar minas explosivas. **II.** *a.* minero, de mina.—**m. camp,** colonia de mineros.—**m. engineer,** ingeniero de minas.—**m. engineering,** ingeniería de minas.—**m. shares,** (Am.) barras.—**m. ship** = MINE LAYER.
minion [mínyọn]. **I.** *s.* privado, valido o paniaguado; esbirro; (impr.) miñona (tipo de 7 puntos); (min.) miñón, mena.—**m. of the law,** polizonte. **II.** *a.* delicado; elegante; bonito; querido.
minister [mínịstœ(r)]. **I.** *s.* ministro (en todas sus acepciones); (igl.) clérigo, pastor.—**M. of Foreign Affairs,** Ministro de Relaciones Exteriores.

—**M. of the Interior,** Ministro de la Gobernación o del Interior.—**M. of Public Works,** etc., Ministro de Fomento.—**M. of State,** Ministro de Estado.—**M. of the Treasury,** o **Exchequer,** Ministro de Hacienda. **II.** *va.* y *vn.* dar, administrar, suministrar; (ant.) surtir o proveer de. **III.** *vn.* atender, asistir, auxiliar; (igl.) oficiar, decir misa; tender, contribuir.
ministerial [mịnịstírịạl], *a.* ministerial; sacerdotal, parroquial.—**m. benches,** (Ingl.) bancos del gobierno (en la Cámara de los Comunes).
ministerially [-i], *adv.* ministerialmente.
ministerialism [-izm], *s.* ministerialismo.
ministrant [mínịstrạnt]. **I.** *a.* ministrante. **II.** *s.* ministrador; (igl.) oficiante.
ministration [-éjšọn], *s.* ministración; servicio; agencia; (igl.) ministerio, oficio eclesiástico.
ministry [mínịstri], *s.* ministerio, oficio, servicio; (pol.) ministerio, gabinete; (igl.) ministerio, clero; ayuda, intervención.—**M. of the Interior,** Ministerio de la Gobernación o del Interior.
minium [mínịʌm], *s.* (quím., min.) minio.
miniver [mínịvœ(r)], *s.* cierta piel, gen. blanca; (Ingl., zool.) armiño, con su piel blanca de invierno.
mink [miŋk], *s.* (zool.) visón, y su piel.
minnesinger [mínịsịŋœ(r)], *s.* trovador alemán medieval.
Minnie [mínị], *s.* (mil., fam.) = MINE THROWER.
minnow [mínou], *s.* (ict.) pez pequeño de agua dulce que se usa como cebo.
minor [májnọ(r)]. **I.** *a.* menor; secundario, inferior; leve (ofensa, etc.); (mús.) menor.—**m. key,** tono menor.—**m. mode,** modo menor.—**m. orders,** (igl.) (órdenes) menores, *f. pl.*—**M. Prophets,** profetas (*m.*) menores.—**m. term,** (lóg.) término menor (de un silogismo). **II.** *s.* menor (de edad); (lóg.) menor; (mús.) tono menor; asignatura(s) de importancia secundaria en un programa de estudios. **III.** *vn.* (con in) estudiar como materia secundaria. *V.* MAJOR.
Minorcan [mịnórkạn], *a.* y *s.* menorquín.
Minorite [májnọrajt], *s.* (igl.) menor, franciscano.
minority [majnárịti], *s.* minoridad, menoría o menor edad; minoría, los menos.—**m. report,** informe disidente.—**m. stockholders,** (com.) accionistas de la minoría.
Minotaur [mínọtor], *s.* (mit.) minotauro.
minster [mínstœ(r)], *s.* monasterio; basílica, catedral, *f.*
minstrel [mínstrẹl], *s.* trovador, cantor; (E. U.) cantor cómico que se tizna la cara e imita a los negros; (poét.) bardo.—**minstrelsy** [-sị], *s.* arte u ocupación del *minstrel;* gaya ciencia; canturía; compañía de *minstrels;* colección de cantos.
mint [mịnt]. **I.** *s.* casa de moneda, ceca; (fig.) mina, Potosí, dineral; (bot.) menta, hierbabuena; matapulgas.—**m. julep,** aguardiente de hierbabuena.—**m. master,** director de la casa de moneda. **II.** *va.* acuñar, amonedar; inventar, forjar, fraguar.
mintage [míntịdž], *s.* monedería, amonedación; braceaje; derechos de cuño, monedaje.
minter [míntœ(r)], *s.* acuñador; inventor.
minuend [mínyụend], *s.* (arit.) minuendo.
minuet [mínyụét], *s.* (danz. y mús.) minué, minuete.
minus [májnạs]. **I.** *prep.* menos (—); falto de; sin. **II.** *a.* (mat. y elec.) negativo; sin valor positivo; deficiente.—**m. lens,** (ópt.) lente divergente.—**m. sign,** (mat.) signo menos (—).—**to be, come out,** etc., **m. (something),** (fam.) haber perdido, salir perdiendo (algo). **III.** *s.* cantidad negativa; deficiencia; (mat.) signo menos (—).
minute [majnjút], *a.* menudo, pequeño, diminuto, minúsculo; nimio, minucioso, circunstanciado.
minute [mínịt]. **I.** *s.* minuto, momento, instante; (geom., etc.) minuto; (arq.) parte determinada del módulo; minuta, nota, apuntamiento.—*pl.*

minutas, actas; memoria auténtica.—**m. book,** minutario, libro de actas o de minutas.—**m. glass,** ampolleta de un minuto.—**m. gun,** cañón disparado de minuto en minuto.—**m. hand,** minutero.—**m. of arc,** (geom.) minuto de la circunferencia, arco de 1 minuto.—**m. steak,** filete al minuto.—**m. watch,** reloj de minutero.—**m. wheel,** rueda de los minutos.— **this (very) m.,** ahora mism(it)o. II. *va.* minutar, anotar, apuntar.

minutely [majnjútlj], *adv.* minuciosa, detallada o circunstanciadamente; ce por be, por menor, por menudo; [mínjtlj], por minutos, a intervalos de un minuto.

minuteman [mínjtmæn], *s.* (E. U., hist.) miliciano pronto para prestar servicio en el acto.

minuteness [majnjútnjs], *s.* minuciosidad; suma pequeñez.

minutia [mjnjúsjä], *s.* minucia, detalle menudo o minucioso.—*pl.* **minutiae** [-äji], minucias, menudencias, trivialidades.

minx [mjnks], *s.* moza descarada.

Miocene [májosin], *a.* (geol.) mioceno.

miracle [mírakl], *s.* milagro; maravilla; (teat.) auto dramático.—**m. monger,** milagrero.—**m. play,** auto, drama (*m.*) en que se representan episodios bíblicos o de personajes religiosos.— **m. worker,** taumaturgo.—**m. working,** taumaturgia.

miraculous [mjrǽkyulʌs], *a.* milagroso.

miraculously [-lj], *adv.* milagrosamente.

miraculousness [-njs], *s.* calidad de milagroso.

mirage [mjráž], *s.* espejismo, miraje.

mire [máj(r)]. I. *s.* cieno, lodo, fango, tarquín; lodazal, cenagal. II. *va.* encenagar, enlodar. III. *vn.* atorarse, atollarse, atascarse en el fango.

miriness [-jnjs], *s.* calidad de fangoso.

mirk [mǽrk], *s.,* **mirk(y** [-j], *a.* = MURK(Y).

mirror [mírọ(r)]. I. *s.* espejo, luna; ejemplar, modelo.—**m. frame,** marco; tremó.—**m. plate,** luna. II. *va.* reflejar, retratar.—**mirror-like** [-lajk], *a.* espejado.

mirth [mǽrθ], *s.* alegría, regocijo o júbilo.— **mirthful** [-fụl], *a.* alegre, regocijado, gozoso. —**mirthfully** [-jl], *adv.* alegremente, jovialmente.—**mirthless** [-ljs], *a.* triste, abatido.

miry [májrj], *a.* cenagoso, lodoso, fangoso.

misadventure [mjsạdvénchụ(r)], *s.* desgracia, contratiempo, percance, desventura, revés.

misadvised [mjsạdvájzd], *a.* malaconsejado.

misalliance [mjsạlájạns], *s.* matrimonio morganático, o con persona de clase inferior.

misanthrope [mísạnθroụp], **misanthropist** [mjsǽnθropjst], *s.* misántropo.—**misanthropic(al** [mjsạnθrápjk(ạl], *a.* misantrópico.—**misanthropy** [mjsǽnθropj], *s.* misantropía.

misapplication [mjsæpljkéjšọn], *s.* mala aplicación, mal uso.—**misapply** [mjsạpláj], *va.* hacer mal uso de; aplicar mal.

misapprehend [mjsæpṛjhénd], *va.* entender mal.

misapprehension [-hénšọn], *s.* error, concepto erróneo, falsa interpretación.

misappropriate [mjsạpróupṛjejt], *va.* malversar, distraer (fondos).—**misappropriation** [-éjšọn], *s.* malversación o distracción de fondos.

misbecome [mjsbjkʌ́m], *va.* no ser propio de, ser indigno de, no convenir a.

misbegot(ten [mjsbjgát(n], *a.* mal habido, ilegítimo; bastardo.

misbehave [mjsbjhéjv], *vn.* y *vr.* portarse mal.

misbehaved [-d], *a.* que se porta mal; reacio, travieso, malcriado.

misbehavior [-yọ(r)], *s.* desmán, mal comportamiento.

misbelief [mjsbjlíf], *s.* error; incredulidad; herejía, heterodoxia.—**misbelieve** [-lív], *vn.* estar en error; *va.* descreer.—**misbeliever** [-œ(r)], *s.* incrédulo; hereje.

miscalculate [mjskǽlkjulejt], *va.* calcular mal.

miscalculation [-éjšọn], *s.* error, mal cálculo; cuenta errada, yerro de cuenta.

miscall [mjskól], *va.* nombrar impropiamente.

miscarriage [mjskǽrjdž], *s.* aborto, malparto; fracaso, malogro; extravío, desmán.

miscarry [mjskǽrj], *vn.* frustrarse, malograrse, salir mal; abortar, malparir; extraviarse.

miscegenation [mjsjdženéjšọn], *s.* mezcla de razas.

miscellanea [mjsẹléjnjä], *s. pl.* miscelánea.

miscellaneous [-njʌs], *a.* misceláneo, mezclado; diverso.

miscellany [mjsẹlejnj], *s.* silva, miscelánea.

mischance [mjschǽns], *s.* desgracia, infortunio.

mischarge [mjschárdž], *va.* cargar indebidamente en cuenta.

mischief [míschjf], *s.* mal, daño; injuria, agravio; travesura, diablura, barrabasada; persona traviesa; (fam.) Barrabás.—**m.-maker,** dañador; chismoso, enredador.—**m.-making,** dañino, perjudicial.

mischievous [míschjvʌs], *a.* dañino, dañoso; malicioso o malévolo; chismoso o enredador; juguetón, travieso.—**-ly** [-lj], *adv.* perversamente; con o por travesura; dañoso o perjudicialmente. —**mischievousness** [-njs], *s.* malicia, perversidad; picardía, travesura.

miscibility [mjsjbjljtj], *s.* miscibilidad.

miscible [mjsjbl], *a.* miscible.

misclaim [mjskléjm], *s.* pretensión mal fundada.

misconceive [mjskọnsív], *va.* y *vn.* formar concepto erróneo, juzgar mal.

misconception [-sépšọn], *s.* concepto erróneo, equivocación, engaño; mala inteligencia; mala interpretación.

misconduct [mjskándʌkt], *s.* mala conducta o mal manejo, mal porte, extravío.

misconduct [mjskọndʌkt], *va.* y *vr.* conducir, administrar o manejar mal; portarse mal.

misconstruction [mjskọnstrákšọn], *s.* mala interpretación, error; mala construcción.

misconstrue [mjskọnstrú], *va.* interpretar erróneamente, entender mal; viciar el sentido.

miscount [mjskáụnt]. I. *va.* y *vn.* contar mal; equivocarse en la cuenta. II. *s.* yerro de cuenta, mal cálculo.

miscreant [mjskrjạnt], *s.* malandrín, malvado.

miscreated [mjskrjéjtjd], *a.* mal formado, deformado.

miscue [mjskjú]. I. *s.* (billar) pifia; (fam.) error, desacierto. II. *vn.* pifiar; (teat.) equivocarse de apunte.

misdate [mjsdéjt], *va.* fechar falsamente, o poner fecha equivocada.

misdeed [mjsdíd], *s.* fechoría, delito.

misdemean [mjsdjmín], *vn.* portarse mal.

misdemeanant [-ạnt], *s.* (for.) reo de delito menor.

misdemeanor [-ọ(r)], *s.* mala conducta; (for.) fechoría, delito de menor cuantía.

misdirect [mjsdjrékt], *va.* dirigir erradamente.— **misdirection** [-kšọn], *s.* mala dirección; informe falso.

misdo [mjsdú], *va.* y *vn.* (pret. MISDID; *pp.* MISDONE) errar, hacer mal o disparatadamente; faltar o delinquir.—**misdoer** [-œ(r)], *s.* malhechor, criminal.—**misdoing** [-jŋ], *s.* falta, mala acción; yerro.

mise en scène [miz an sén], *s.* (teat.) aparato escénico; puesta en escena.

misemploy [mjsẹmplój], *va.* abusar; emplear mal. —**misemployment** [-mẹnt], *s.* abuso.

miser [májzœ(r)], *s.* avaro, avariento, tacaño.

miserable [mízẹrạbl], *a.* miserable, desdichado, infeliz; pobre, menguado; sin valor; despreciable; lastimoso, lastimero.—**miserably** [-blj], *adv.* miserablemente.

Miserere [mjzẹríri], *s.* (igl.) miserere.

misericord [mjzẹríkórd], *s.* puñal con que se daba el golpe de gracia; relajación de una regla monástica; (arq., igl.) misericordia (de un asiento de coro) (ll. t. **miserere**).

miserliness [májzœrljnjs], *s.* avaricia, tacañería,

mezquindad, cicatería.—**miserly** [-li]. *a.* avariento, tacaño, mezquino.

misery [mízeri], *s.* miseria. desgracia; aflicción; calamidad; dolor continuo.

misfaith [misféiθ], *s.* falta de fe.

misfeasance [misfízans], *s.* (for.) acto legal hecho de una manera ilegal; infidencia.

misfire [misfáir]. I. *vn.* no dar fuego; no reventar. II. *s.* hecho de no reventar o dar fuego.

misfit [misfít]. I. *va.* y *vn.* ajustar o entallar mal, no sentar bien, no encajar. II. *s.* lo que no sienta, ajusta, entalla o encaja bien; mal ajuste; individuo que no se adapta bien al ambiente.

misfortune [misfórchun], *s.* desgracia, desdicha, contratiempo, percance, infortunio, revés.

misgive [misgív]. I. *va.* (*pret.* MISGAVE; *pp.* MISGIVEN) llenar de dudas o recelos; hacer temer o dudar. II. *vn.* ser receloso o tímido; faltar valor. —**misgiving** [-iŋ], *s.* recelo, duda, presentimiento, rescoldo; desconfianza, temor.

misgotten [misgátn], *a.* mal habido o adquirido.

misgovern [misgávœrn], *va.* desgobernar, gobernar o administrar mal.—**misgovernment** [-ment], *s.* desgobierno, mala administración.

misguidance [misgáidans], *s.* dirección errada; extravío, error.—**misguide** [misgáid], *va.* des(en)caminar, descarriar, extraviar; engañar, seducir.—**misguided** [-id], *a.* = MISLED.

mishap [mishǽp], *s.* desgracia, accidente, contratiempo.

mishear [mishír], *va.* y *vn.* (*pret.* y *pp.* MISHEARD) oír mal, trasoír, entreoír.

mishmash [míshmæsh], *s.* almodrote, mescolanza.

misinform [misinfórm], *va.* y *vn.* mal enterar o informar; dar informes erróneos.—**misinformation** [-éishon], *s.* información errónea.

misinterpret [misintérprit], *va.* y *vn.* interpretar mal, torcer, entender mal.—**misinterpretation** [-éishon], *s.* mala o falsa interpretación.

misjudge [misdʒádʒ], *va.* y *vn.* errar, juzgar mal.

misjudgment [-ment], *s.* juicio errado, equivocado o injusto.

mislay [misléi], *va.* (*pret.* y *pp.* MISLAID) colocar mal, extraviar, traspapelar, perder.

mislead [mislíd], *va.* (*pret.* y *pp.* MISLED) extraviar, descaminar, descarriar, despistar; conducir a conclusiones erróneas; alucinar, engañar, seducir, pervertir.

misleading [-iŋ], *a.* engañoso; de falsas apariencias.—**misled** [misléd], *a.* engañado, iluso, seducido.

mismanage [mismǽnidʒ], *va.* manejar o administrar mal.—**mismanagement** [-ment], *s.* mal manejo, mala administración, desgobierno, desconcierto.—**mismanager** [-œ(r)], *s.* mal administrador.

mismarriage [mismǽridʒ], *s.* mal matrimonio, matrimonio desacertado.

mismatch [mismǽch]. I. *va.* desigualar; malcasar; desproporcionar, deshermanar, desajustar. II. *s.* apareamiento o casamiento desigual o desproporcionado.

mismate [misméit], *va.* malcasar.

misname [misnéim], *va.* trasnombrar, equivocar el nombre.

misnomer [misnóumœ(r)], *s.* nombre inapropiado; (for.) nombre erróneo.

misogamist [miságamist], *s.* misógamo.

misogamy [-mi], *s.* misogamia.

misogynist [misádʒinist], *s.* misógino.

misogyny [-ni], *s.* misoginia.

misoneism [misonízm], *s.* misoneísmo.

misoneist(ic [-ist, -nístik], *s.* y *a.* misoneísta.

misplace [mispléis], *va.* colocar mal o fuera de su sitio; extraviar, traspapelar.

misprint [misprínt]. I. *va.* imprimir con erratas. II. *s.* (impr.) errata, error de imprenta.

misprision [mispríʒon], *s.* (for.) comisión u ocultación de un crimen o delito.

misprize [mispráiz], *va.* des(a)preciar.

mispronounce [mispronáuns], *va.* y *vn.* pronun-

ciar mal.—**mispronunciation** [-nʌnsiéishon], *s.* pronunciación incorrecta.

misproportion [mispropórshon], *va.* desproporcionar.

misquotation [miskwotéishon], *s.* cita falsa o equivocada.—**misquote** [miskwóut], *va.* citar falsa, equivocada o erróneamente.

misreport [misripórt]. I. *va.* dar una noticia falsa. II. *s.* informe falso o erróneo.

misrepresent [misreprizént], *va.* desfigurar, pervertir, tergiversar, disfrazar, falsificar.

misrepresentation [-éishon], *s.* falsedad, noticia o relación falsa, tergiversación.

misrule [misrúl]. I. *va.* y *vn.* gobernar mal; desgobernar. II. *s.* mal gobierno; desgobierno; confusión, desorden.

Miss [mis], *s.* (*pl.* MISSES) señorita (título que se da a una soltera: *Miss Brown*, la señorita Brown; *the Miss Browns* o *the Misses Brown*, las señoritas Brown); (m.), muchacha, jovencita.

miss. I. *va.* errar (el tiro, el golpe, etc.); no acertar con, no ver, no comprender; equivocar; perder (el tren, la función, un goce); echar de menos; pasar sin, abstenerse de, carecer de; pasar por alto, dejar de hacer.—**to m. fire**, fallar el tiro. —**to m. stays**, (mar.) faltar la virada, no virar. —**to m. the mark**, errar el blanco o el tiro.— **to m. the point**, no dar en el busilis, no comprender el verdadero sentido. II. *vn.* frustrarse, salir mal, malograrse; marrar, errar, faltar; fallar.—**to m. out**, (fam.) llevarse chasco; llegar tarde. III. *s.* malogro, fracaso, marra; pérdida, extravío; falta.

missal [mísal], *s.* (igl.) misal.

missend [misénd], *va.* (*pret.* y *pp.* MISSENT) enviar o dirigir mal.

misshape [misséip], *va.* deformar, desfigurar, afear.—**misshapen** [-n], *a.* disforme, deformado.

missile [mísil]. I. *a.* arrojadizo. II. *s.* proyectil; arma arrojadiza.

missing [mísiŋ], *a.* extraviado, perdido; desaparecido; ausente.—**m. link**, eslabón perdido o que falta.—**to be m.**, faltar, estar extraviado, etc.; haber desaparecido.

mission [míshon], *s.* misión (diplomática o religiosa, etc.); comisión; (mil.) salida de uno o más aviones para un ataque aéreo.—**m. school**, escuela de caridad, dirigida por misioneros, donde se da instrucción general y religiosa; escuela preparatoria para misioneros.

missionary [-eri]. I. *s.* misionario; (igl.) misionero. II. *a.* misional.—**m. station**, (igl.) misión.

missionize [-aiz], *vn.* misionar.

missis, missus [mísiz, mísaz], *s.* (fam. o dial.) esposa; señora o ama de casa.

missive [mísiv]. I. *a.* misivo, enviadizo. II. *s.* carta, misiva, comunicación escrita.

misspell [misspél], *va.* (*pret.* y *pp.* MISSPELLED o MISSPELT) deletrear mal, escribir con mala ortografía.—**misspelling** [-iŋ], *s.* deletreo erróneo, falta de ortografía.

misspend [misspénd], *va.* malgastar, malbaratar.

misstate [misstéit], *va.* relatar o exponer falsamente.—**misstatement** [-ment], *s.* relación equivocada o falsa, error, falencia, aserción errónea.

misstep [misstép]. I. *vn.* dar un paso en falso, tropezar. II. *s.* paso falso, desliz, *m.;* tropiezo.

missy [mísi], *s.* (fam.) señorita, niña.

mist [mist]. I. *s.* niebla, neblina, bruma, llovizna, calígine, *f.;* vapor, vaho. II. *va.* anieblar, anublar, empañar, obscurecer. III. *vn.* lloviznar.

mistakable [mistéikabl], *a.* confundible, equivocable, que puede ser equivocado.

mistake [mistéik]. I. *va.* (*pret.* MISTOOK; *pp.* MISTAKEN) equivocar, comprender mal; trabucar, tomar una cosa por otra. II. *vn.* errar, equivocarse, engañarse. III. *s.* equivocación, error, yerro, desacierto; errata.—**and no m.**, sin duda alguna, con toda seguridad.—**to make a m.**, equivocarse, desacertar.

mistaken [-n], *a.* erróneo, incorrecto; equivocado; errado, desacertado.

mistakenly [-lị], **mistakingly** [-iŋlị], *adv.* equivocadamente, erróneamente.

misteach [mịstích], *va.* (*pret.* y *pp.* MISTAUGHT) enseñar o instruir mal.

Mister [mịstœ(r)], *s.* señor (término de cortesía, cuya abreviatura es **Mr.**).

misterm [mịstœ́rm], *va.* trasnombrar, dar un nombre equivocado o impropio.

mistimed [mịstáịmd], *pp.* y *a.* inoportuno, extemporáneo, intempestivo, fuera de sazón.

mistiness [mịstịnịs], *s.* caligine, *f.*, nebulosidad, calidad de brumoso, etc.

mistletoe [mịsltoụ], *s.* (bot.) muérdago, liga.

mistook [mịstúk], *pret.* de TO MISTAKE.

mistral [mịstrạl], *s.* (viento) maestral o mi(n)stral.

mistranslate [mịstrænsl
éịt], *va.* traducir mal.

mistranslation [-éịṣǫn], *s.* traducción errónea.

mistreat [mịstrít], *va.* maltratar; abusar de.— **mistreatment** [-mẹnt], *s.* maltrat(amient)o.

mistress [mịstrịs], *s.* señora; dueña, ama; concubina, querida, cortejo, daifa; (Ingl.) maestra; (poét.) dama, mujer cortejada; (con *of*) conocedora (de) a fondo, perita (en); (M.), título que se da a las casadas y equivale en español a Señora (se escribe **Mrs.** y en este sentido se pronuncia *mịsịz*); aplicado a las solteras se escribe **Miss** (*v.* esta voz).—**M. of the Robes**, camarera mayor de una reina o princesa.—**M. of the Seas**, la Gran Bretaña.

mistrial [mịstráịạl], *s.* (for.) juicio nulo por causa de error o por desacuerdo del jurado.

mistrust [mịstrást]. **I.** *s.* desconfianza. **II.** *va.* desconfiar de, dudar de; sospechar, recelar.— **mistrustful** [-fụl], *a.* desconfiado; receloso.— **mistrustfully** [-ị], *adv.* desconfiadamente.— **mistrustfulness** [-nịs], *s.* desconfianza; recelo. —**mistrustingly** [-iŋlị], *adv.* con desconfianza.

misty [mịstị], *a.* brumoso, cali(gi)noso, nebuloso.

misunderstand [mịsʌndœrstǽnd], *va.* (*pret.* y *pp.* -STOOD) entender mal; tomar en sentido erróneo.

misunderstanding [-iŋ], *s.* concepto falso, equivocación, error, mala inteligencia; desavenencia, disensión.—**misunderstood** [-stúd], *a.* mal entendido o comprendido.

misusage [mịsyúsịdž], **misuse** [mịsyús], *s.* abuso; maltrato, estropeo.

misuse [mịsyúz], *va.* maltratar, tratar mal; estropear; abusar de.—**misused** [-d], *a.* maltrecho.

mite [maịt], *s.* pizca, triza, mota; blanca, ardite; óbolo; (ent.) ácaro, gorgojo, arador.

miter, mitre [máịtœ(r)]. **I.** *s.* (igl.) mitra; tiara (del Papa); dignidad de obispo; (mec.) inglete; (cost.) escudete, contrete.—**m. block, m. box**, caja de ingletes.—**m. gear**, (mec.) = BEVEL GEAR.—**m. joint**, junta a inglete. **II.** *va.* conferir una mitra a; adornar con mitra o algo parecido; (mec.) juntar con inglete; cortar ingletes.—**mitered, mitred** [-d], *a.* (igl.) mitrado.

mithridate [míθrịdeịt], *s.* (farm.) mitridato, antídoto.—**mithridatism** [-ịzm], *s.* mitridatismo.

mitigable [mịtịgạbl], *a.* mitigable.

mitigant [mịtịgạnt], *a.* mitigante, calmante.

mitigate [-geịt]. **I.** *va.* mitigar, calmar, suavizar, aplacar, atenuar. **II.** *vn.* mitigarse.—**mitigation** [-géịṣǫn], *s.* mitigación.—**mitigative, mitigatory** [-geịtịv, -gǽtǫrị], *a.* y *s.* mitigativo, lenitivo, calmante.—**mitigator** [-geịtǫ(r)], *s.* mitigador, lenitivo.

mitis [máịtịs], *s.* hierro forjado aluminico colado, fundición maleable Wittenstrom-Ostberg.—**m. casting**, pieza vaciada de hierro forjado aluminico; procedimiento de fabricación de estas piezas.—**m. metal** = MITIS.

mitosis [mịtóụsịs], *s.* (biol.) mitosis, cariocinesis.

mitral [máịtrạl], *a.* (anat.) mitral (válvula).

mitre [máịtœ(r)], *va.* y *s.* = MITER.

mitt [mịt], *s.* mitón, confortante, maniquete; guante especial para jugar al beisbol. *V.* MITTEN.

mitten [-n], *s.* guante con dedo para el pulgar, pero sin separaciones para los otros cuatro dedos; (fam.) calabazas, repulsa de un amante. —*pl.* (fam.) guantes para el boxeo; (fam.) las manos.—**to get (to give) the m.**, recibir (dar) calabazas.

mittimus [mịtịmʌs], *s.* (for.) auto o decreto de prisión.

mix [mịks]. **I.** *va.* mezclar, mixturar, inmiscuir; (fam.) embarullar, emburujar; aderezar (ensalada); amasar; hacer, confeccionar (hormigón, etc.); cruzar (animales); (con *up*) incorporar, asociar, unir, confundir; envolver. **II.** *vn.* mezclarse.—**to m. well**, hacer buenas migas. **III.** *s.* mezcla de ingredientes; proporciones de los ingredientes de una mezcla.—**m.-up**, (fam.) lío, confusión; agarrada, sarracina.

mixable [-ạbl], *a.* mezclable, miscible, que puede mezclarse.

mixed [-t], *a.* mezclado; mixto; misceláneo; (gen. con *up*) confundido; atolondrado; revuelto; envuelto (en).—**m. marriage**, matrimonio entre los de distintas razas o religiones.—**m. metal**, aleación.—**m. number**, número mixto.—**m. pickles**, encurtido mezclado (de varias legumbres).—**m. train**, tren mixto.

mixer [-œ(r)], *s.* mezclador, mixturero; (constr.) mezcladora, hormigonera.—**good m.**, (fam.) persona sociable y adaptable.

mixing [-iŋ]. **I.** *a.* mezclador. **II.** *s.* mezcla(dura), mezclamiento.

mixt (*pret.* y *pp. irr.* de TO MIX) = MIXED.

mixtilineal, mixtilinear [mịkstịlíniạl, -ạ̈(r)], *a.* (geom.) mixtilíneo.

mixture [mịkschụ(r)], *s.* mezcla(dura), mezclamiento; mixtura; mezcla, producto de ingredientes mezclados (hormigón, etc.); miscelánea, mescolanza, mixtifori. *V.* MIX.

mizen, mizzen [mịzn], *s.* (mar.) mesana.—**m. shrouds**, jarcia de mesana.—**m. topsail**, sobremesana.—**mizzenmast** [-mæst], *s.* palo de mesana.

mnemonic(al [nịmánịk(ạl], *a.* mnemotécnico.

mnemonics [-s], *s.* mnemónica.

moa [móụạ], *s.* (pal.) dinornis, *m.*, gran pájaro de Nueva Zelandia ya extinguido.

Moabite [móụạbaịt], *s.* y *a.* moabita, *mf.*

moan [móụn]. **I.** *s.* quejido, gemido, queja, lamento, plañido. **II.** *va.* lamentar, llorar, deplorar. **III.** *vn.* gemir, quejarse; lamentarse.

moanful [-fụl], *a.* lamentable, triste; quejumbroso.—**moanfully** [-ị], *adv.* lamentablemente; quejumbrosamente, con gemidos o quejidos.

moat [móụt]. **I.** *s.* (fort.) foso. **II.** *va.* rodear con fosos.

mob [máb]. **I.** *s.* chusma, populacho, gentuza; (fam.) turbamulta; multitud; cofia, toca o gorra de mujer (ll. t. **mobcap**).—**m. rule**, oclocracia. **II.** *va.* atropellar, hacer asonada a. **III.** *vn.* tumultuarse, formar un tropel, promover alborotos.

mobbish [-ịš], *a.* tumultuoso.

mobile [móụbịl], *a.* movedizo, movible, móvil; inconstante, variable.

mobility [mobílịtị], *s.* movilidad; volubilidad, instabilidad.

mobilization [-zéịṣǫn], *s.* movilización.

mobilize [móụbịlaịz], *va.* movilizar, poner en pie de guerra; poner en movimiento.

mobocracy [mabákrạsị], *s.* gobierno de (por) la muchedumbre; la muchedumbre gobernante.— **mobocrat** [mábokræt], *s.* partidario del gobierno de la muchedumbre; demagogo.

moccasin [mákạsịn], *s.* mocasín o mocasina; calzado de cuero sin curtir; (zool.) mocasín, serpiente venenosa.

mocha [móʊkǎ], s. moca o moka, m., café de Moca.

mock [mák]. I. va. mofar, escarnecer; remedar, imitar, copiar; engañar, burlar. II. vn. (con at) burlarse de, mofarse de, hacer mofa de. III. s. mofa, befa, escarnio, burla; mímica. IV. a. ficticio, falso, imitado; cómico, burlesco; irónico.—m.-**heroic**, (poét.) épico-burlesco.—m. **moon** = PARASELENE.—m. **orange**, (bot.) jeringuilla.—m. **privet**, (bot.) labiérnago.—m. **sun** = PARHELION.—m. **turtle soup**, sopa hecha con cabeza de ternera a imitación de tortuga.

mocker [-œ(r)], s. mofador, escarnecedor.

mockery [-i], s. mofa, burla, irrisión; remedo.

mocking [-iŋ], a. burlón, mofador.—m. **thrush**, (orn.) mirlo burlón.—**mockingbird** [-bœrd], s. (orn.) sinsonte; arrendajo.

mockingly [-ij], adv. burlonamente, con mofa.

mock-up [-ʌp], s. (mec., etc.) modelo en escala natural.

modal [móʊdǎl], a. modal.

modality [modǽliti], s. modalidad; carácter modal, diferencia accidental.

mode [moʊd], s. modo, manera, forma, vía; moda, uso, costumbre; (gram., filos., mús.) modo; (mús.) modalidad; (estadística) valor que ocurre con la mayor frecuencia.

model [mádel], I. s. modelo, ejemplar o patrón; (proto)tipo; muestra; horma; dechado, pauta, plantilla, figurín; mujer que sirve de figurín en tiendas de ropa; (b. a.) modelo vivo. II. a. modelo, ejemplar.—m. **house**, casa modelo.—m. **school**, escuela experimental o de práctica, anexa a una normal y que sirve tanto de modelo como de escuela de prueba en que los alumnos de la normal enseñan bajo la dirección de sus maestros. III. va. modelar; moldear; (b. a.) modelar; (fund.) hacer un molde de.

modeller [-œ(r)], s. modelador, trazador.

model(l)ing [-iŋ]. I. s. (b. a.) modelado. II. a. modelador.—m. **board**, terraja.

moderate [mádɛrit]. I. a. moderado, quieto, templado, tranquilo; regular, ordinario; razonable, sobrio; bonancible, suave; módico (en precio). II. s. (pol., etc.) moderado. III. [mádɛrejt], va. moderar, reprimir; templar, modificar; calmar; presidir. IV. vn. moderarse, calmarse, apaciguarse; presidir.

moderately [-ij], adv. moderadamente; razonablemente; módicamente; medianamente.

moderateness [-nis], s. moderación; modicidad.

moderation [-éjšǫn], s. moderación, medida; sobriedad, templanza, frugalidad, economía; presidencia, acto de presidir.—pl. (Ingl.) exámenes universitarios.—**in m.**, sin excesos, dentro de límites razonables.

moderatism [-izm], s. moderantismo.

moderator [mádɛrejtǫ(r)], s. moderador, moderante, concordador, árbitro; (mec.) regulador; presidente de una sesión, cuerpo legislativo o congregación presbiteriana; (Ingl.) examinador en las universidades.—m. **lamp**, lámpara de regulador.

moderatorship [-šip], s. oficio y dignidad de MODERATOR.

moderatrix [-triks], s. moderadora; presidenta.

modern [mádœrn]. I. a. moderno, reciente.—m. **improvements**, mejoras modernas.—m. **languages**, lenguas vivas. II. s. modernista.

modernism [-izm], s. modernismo; (M.), modernismo, en el sentido católico (sistema condenado por Pío X en 1907); (M.), modernismo, en el sentido protestante (sistema que niega la necesidad de los dogmas teológicos y la inspiración total de la Biblia).—**modernist**, M. [-ist], modernista, partidario del modernismo.—**modernistic** [-ístik], a. modernista; de vanguardia.—**modernity** [mádœrniti], s. modernidad; novedad.

modernization [-izéjšǫn], s. modernización.

modernize [-ajz], va. modernizar; resucitar.

modernness [-nis], s. calidad de moderno, modernidad; novedad.

modest [mádist], a. modesto, pudoroso, recatado, casto; humilde, sencillo, sin pretensiones.—**modestly** [-li], adv. modestamente.

modesty [-i], s. modestia, pudicicia, pudor, recato.—m. **piece**, bobillo (encaje).

modicum [mádikam], s. pitanza, bocado, porción pequeña; poco.

modifiable [mádifajǎbl], a. modificable.

modification [-fikéjšǫn], s. modificación.

modificative [-fikejtiv], a. modificativo.

modifier [-fajœ(r)], s. modificador; (gram.) modificante, palabra modificativa.

modify [-faj], va. modificar; cambiar; moderar.—**modifying** [-iŋ], a. modificante, modificativo.

modillion [modílyǫn], s. (arq.) modillón, can, cartela.

modish [móʊdiš], a. hecho o conforme a la moda.

modist [móʊdist], s. el o la que sigue la moda.

modiste [moʊdíst], s. modista.—m.'s **shop**, (Am.) modistería.—**modistry** [móʊdistri], s. modistería.

modular [mádžulǎ(r)], a. modular.

modulate [mádžulejt]. I. va. modular, entonar. II. va. y vn. (mús.) modular, cambiar de tono.—**modulating** [-iŋ], a. modulador.—**modulation** [-éjšǫn], s. (mús.) modulación; (arq.) módulo.—**modulator** [-ǫ(r)], s. modulador, gorjeador.

module [mádžul], s. (arq.) módulo.

moduli [-aj], s. pl. de MODULUS.

modulus [-ʌs], s. (mat., fís.) módulo; coeficiente.

modus [móʊdʌs], s. modo, manera.—m. **operandi**, modo de funcionar.—m. **vivendi**, convenio interino entre dos naciones, modus vivendi.

mofette [mofét], s. mofeta.

mogul [moɡʌl], s. mogol, personaje importante; naipe de la mejor calidad; locomotora de gran tamaño.—**the Great M.**, el Gran Mogol. V. MONGOL.

mohair [móʊhɛr], s. el pelo sedoso de la cabra de Angora; (tej.) tela hecha con dicho pelo, o imitación de esta tela.

Mohammedan [moʊhǽmɛdǎn], s. y a. mahometano, mahomético, muslime, agareno.

Mohammedanism [-izm], s. mahometismo.

Mohammedanize [-ajz], va. mahometizar.

Mohican, Mohegan [mohíkǎn, -ɡǎn], s. mohicano, miembro de cierta tribu india.

moiety [mójɛti], s. mitad.

moil [mojl]. I. vn. fatigarse, afanarse. II. s. faena, trabajo penoso; confusión, baraúnda; mancha.

moire, moiré [mwar, mwaréj], s. (tej.) muer, moaré, muaré.

moist [mojst], a. húmedo; lloroso; lluvioso.

moisten [mójsn], va. humedecer, humectar, mojar ligeramente.

moistener [-œ(r)], s. humedecedor, (re)mojador.—**moistening** [-iŋ], a. humectante, humectativo.

moistness [mójstnis], s. calidad de húmedo o mojado.—**moisture** [mójschǔ(r)], s. humedad.

molar, molary [móʊlǎ(r), -i], a. (anat., zool.) molar, referente a una muela; (med.) concerniente a una mola; (mec., fís.) relativo a la masa.—m. **(tooth)**, muela, diente molar.

molasses [molǽsiz], s. melaza, miel (f.) de purga.—m. **candy**, melcocha.

mold, molder, molding, etc. = MOULD, etc.

Moldavian [maldévjǎn], s. y a. moldavo.

mole [moʊl], s. lunar (en la piel); mancha; muelle, dique, malecón, espolón; (zool.) topo; (med.) mola.—m. **cricket**, (ent.) grillotalpa, cortón.—m.-**eyed**, (fam.) cegato.—m. **furs** = MOLESKIN.—m. **gray**, gris oscuro.—m. **rat**, (zool.) ratón topo.

molecast [-kæst], s. = MOLEHILL.

molecular [molékyulǎ(r)], a. molecular.

molecule [málikiul], s. (quím., fís.) molécula.
molehill [móulhil], molehole [-houl], s. to-p(in)era.
moleskin [-skin], s. piel (f.) de topo; (tej.) especie de fustán.—pl. pantalón u otras prendas de este paño.
molest [molést], va. molestar, vejar; faltar al respeto a (una mujer); meterse con, dañar.
molestation [-éjson], s. molestia, incomodidad, importunidad; vejación.
molester [-œ(r)], s. molestador, vejador.—molestful [-ful], a. molesto, vejatorio, enfadoso.
Molinism [móulinizm], s. (teol.) molinismo.
Molinist(ic [-ist, -istik], s. y a. molinista.
moll [mal], s. (fam.) compañera de un bandido, etc.; prostituta.
mollient [málient], a. molitivo. V. EMOLLIENT.
mollifiable [málifajabl], a. molificable.
mollification [-fikéjson], s. molificación, ablandamiento; mitigación.
mollifier [-fajœ(r)], s. ablandador, emoliente; mitigador, pacificador.
mollify [-faj], va. molificar, ablandar; apaciguar; aliviar; suavizar, mitigar.
Mollusca [maláskä], s. pl. (zool.) moluscos.
molluscan [-kan], a. y s. molusco.
molluscoid [-kojd], s. y a. (zool.) moluscoideo.
mollusk [málask], s. molusco, marisco, concha.
mollycoddle [málikadl]. I. s. (fam.) marica. II. va. y vn. consentir, mimar o tratar con mimo excesivo.
Moloch [móulak], s. Moloc, deidad de los fenicios, amonitas y moabitas; influencia perniciosa; (m., zool.) moloc, especie de saurio erizado.
molossus [molásas], s. (pros.) moloso.
molt, molting, v. y s. = MOULT, MOULTING.
molten [móulten], a. y pp. irr. de TO MELT; fundido, derretido (ú. de los metales).
moly [móuli], s. (bot.) planta fabulosa; ajo silvestre.
molybdate [molíbdejt], s. (quím.) molibdato.
molybdenite [-denajt], s. (min.) molibdenita.
molybdenum [-dēnam], s. (quím.) molibdeno.
molybdic [molíbdik], a. molíbdico.
moment [móument], s. momento, instante, rato; importancia, peso, entidad; (mec.) momento.—m. of a couple, (mec.) momento de un par.—m. of flexure, momento de flexión.—m. of inertia, momento de inercia.—m. of momentum, momento de la cantidad de movimiento.—m. of resistance, momento de resistencia, momento del par de las fuerzas elásticas.—for the m., de momento.
momentarily [-erili], adv. momentáneamente.—momentariness [-erinis], s. momentaneidad.—momentary [-eri], a. momentáneo.—momently [-li], adv. por momentos.
momentous [moméntas], a. importante, grave, trascendental.—momentously [-li], adv. con importancia, gravemente.—momentousness [-nis], s. importancia, gravedad.
momentum [moméntam], s. impulso, ímpetu; (mec.) cantidad de movimiento.
monachal [mánakal], a. monacal, monástico.
monachism [mánakizm], s. monaquismo.
monad [mánæd]. I. s. mónada (en todas sus acepciones). II. a. que se refiere a o consta de una mónada; (quím.) que tiene poder de combinación equivalente a uno, univalente.
monadelphous [manadélfas], a. (bot.) monadelfo.
monadism [mánædizm], monadology [manadálodži], s. (fil.) monadología.
monarch [mánärk], s. monarca, m.—monarch(ic)al [monár(ki)kal], a. monárquico.—monarchism [mánärkizm], s. monarquismo.—monarchist [-ist], s. y a. monárquico, monarquista.
monarchy [mánärki], s. monarquía.
monasterial [manastérial], a. monasterial, monástico.

monastery [mánasteri], s. monasterio, convento.
monastic(al [monástik(al], a. monástico.
monastically [-i], adv. monásticamente.
monasticism [-sizm], s. monacato, monaquismo.
monatomic [manatámik], a. (quím.) mon(o)atómico.
monazite [mánazajt], s. (min.) monacita.
Monday [mándi], s. lunes.
monetary [mánjteri], a. monetario, pecuniario.—m. standard, patrón o talón monetario.—m. unit, unidad monetaria.
monetization [-tizéjson], s. amonedación; monetización.
monetize [-tajz], va. monetizar; acuñar, amonedar.
money [máni], s. dinero; moneda; sistema monetario.—pl. moneys, pagos o recibos al contado; monies, dineros, efectivos y valores convertibles.—m. bill, ley (f.) de hacienda.—m. box, alcancía, hucha.—m. broker, corredor de cambios.—m. changer, dealer, o jobber, cambista.—m.-exchange house, casa de cambio.—m. in hand, dinero contante.—m. lender, prestamista, usurero.—money-maker, cosa con que se gana dinero; persona que gana y acumula dinero (gen. se usa en el sentido de persona metalizada o acaudalada).—m.-making, s. lucro, ganancia, prosperidad; a. ganancioso, lucrativo, provechoso.—m. market, mercado monetario.—m. of account, moneda imaginaria o no acuñada (p. ej. el mill, milésimo de dólar).—m. order, libranza o giro postal.—m. scales, pesillo para pesar el oro y la plata.—m.'s worth, valor cabal del dinero que se paga por algo.—to make m., hacer o ganar dinero, enriquecerse.
moneybag [-bæg], s. talega, bolsa, bolsón.—pl. (fam.) ricacho.
moneyed [-d], a. adinerado, dineroso, acaudalado, rico.—m. man, capitalista.
moneyer [-œ(r)], s. monedero, acuñador.
moneyless [-lis], a. falto de dinero, pobre.
monger [mángœ(r)], s. tratante, traficante.
Mongolian [mángal, mangóljan]. I. a. y s. mogol o mongol; idioma mogólico. II. a. mo(n)gólico.
mongoos(e [mángus], s. (zool.) mangosta.
mongrel [mángrel]. I. a. y s. mestizo, mixto. II. a. cruzado, atravesado, de raza indefinida.
'mongst [mángst], prep. (poét.) = AMONGST.
moni(c)ker [mánikœ(r)], s. (fam.) nombre; apodo.
monism [mánizm], s. (fil.) monismo; (biol.) unidad de origen.—monist [mánist], s., monistic [monístik], a. monista.
monition [moníson], s. amonestación, consejo; aviso legal u oficial; (igl.) monitorio.
monitor [mánitœ(r)]. I. s. amonestador, (ad)monitor; (mar.) monitor; (zool.) monitor, varano. II. va. amonestar; (rad., mil.) escuchar radiodifusiones (con fines de censura, análisis de su contenido militar o de propaganda, etc.). III. vn. hacer de amonestador, etc.; (rad.) probar un aparato transmisor escuchando en uno receptor.
monitory [mánitœri]. I. a. instructivo, monitorio. II. s. (igl.) monitorio.
monk [mánk], s. (igl.) monje, fraile.
monkery [mánkœri], s. vida monástica, frailía.
monkey [mánki]. I. s. (zool.) mono, mico, simio; (mec.) grapa, trinquete o fiador del martinete; martillo de martinete; (vid.) crisol para fundir el vidrio; (fam.) niño o sujeto travieso.—m. business, (fam.) tonterías; tretas.—m. flower, (bot.) mímulo.—m. fruit, (bot.) fruto del baobab.—m. jacket, chaqueta corta y muy ajustada de los marineros.—m. nut, (Ingl., bot.) cacahuete.—m. puzzle, (bot.) araucaria.—m. tricks, monerías.—m. wrench, llave inglesa.—to make a m. of, poner en ridículo.—to play the m., hacer monadas. II. va. y vn.

(fam.) remedar, imitar; hacer payasadas.—**to m. with,** meterse con; bregar con.

monkeyshine [-šajn], s. (fam.) monada, monería.

monkhood [mʌ́ŋkhụd], s. (igl.) monacato, monjía.

monkish [mʌ́ŋkjš], a. monástico, frailesco.

monkshood [mʌ́ŋkshụd], s. (bot.) napelo.

monobasic [manobéjsjk], a. (quím.) monobásico.

monocarpic [-kárpjk], a. (bot.) monocárpico.

monochlamydeous [-klạmídjʌs], a. (bot.) monoclamídeo.

monochord [mánokɔrd], s. (mús.) monocordio.

monochroic [-króụjk], **monochromatic** [-kromǽtjk], a. monocromático.

monochrome [mánokroụm], a. y s. monocromo.

monocle [mánokl], s. monóculo.

monoclinal [-klájnạl], s. y a. (geol.) monoclinal.

monoclinic [-klínjk], a. (crist.) monoclínico.

monocotyledon [-katjlídɔn], s. (bot.) monocotiledón(ea).

monocotyledonous [-ʌs], a. (bot.) monocotiledón(eo.

monocular [monákyụlạ(r)], **monoculous** [-lʌs], a. monóculo; de o para un ojo.

monocyle [mánosajkl], s. monociclo.—**monocyclic** [-sájkljk], a. monociclo; (elec.) monocíclico.

monodactylous [-dǽktjlʌs], a. (zool.) monodáctilo.

monodelphian [-délfjạn], s. y a. (zool.) monodelfo.

monody [mánodj], s. (mús.) monodía; elegía.

mon(o)ecious [moníšʌs], a. (bot.) monoico.

monogamist [monágạmjst], s. y a. monógamo.

monogamous [-mʌs], a. monógamo.

monogamy [-mj], s. monogamia.

monogenesis [manodžénesjs], s. (biol.) monogénesis, unidad de origen; doctrina de la descendencia de todos los seres vivos de una sola celdilla; reproducción asexual.

monogenism [monádženjzm], s. monogenismo, doctrina de la unidad de origen de toda la raza humana.

monogram [mánogræm], s. monograma, m., cifra.

monograph [-græf], s. monografía.

monographic [-grǽfjk], a. monográfico.

monohydrate [-hájdrejt], s. (quím.) monohidrato.—**monohydrated** [-jd], a. monohidratado.

monolater [monálạtœ(r)], s. el que adora sólo a uno de muchos dioses.—**monolatry** [-trj], s. adoración de sólo uno de varios dioses.

monolith [mánoljθ], s. monolito.—**monolithic** [-ljθjk], a. monolítico.

monologize [monálodžajz], vn. monologar, soliloquiar.

monologue [mánolag], s. monólogo, soliloquio.

monomachy [monámạkj], s. monomaquia.

monomania [manoméjnjạ], s. monomanía.

monomaniac [-méjnjæk], a. y s. monomaníaco.

monometallism [-métạljzm], s. monometalismo, teoría económica que defiende el uso de un solo metal como base monetaria.—**monometallist** [-jst], s. y a. monometalista.

monomial [monóụmjạl], s. (álg.) monomio.

monopetalous [manopétạlʌs], a. (bot.) monopétalo.

monophase [mánofejz], a. (elec.) monofásico.

monophobia [-fóụbjạ], s. (pat.) monofobia, terror de la soledad.

monophyletic [-fajlétjk], a. (biol.) monofilético, referente a un antepasado común y único.

monophyllous [-fílʌs], a. (bot.) monofilo.

Monophysite [monáfjsajt], s. (teol.) monofisita, mf.

monoplane [mánoplejn], s. (aer.) monoplano.

monoplegia [-plídžjạ], s. (med.) monoplejía.

monopolism [monápoljzm], s. monopolismo; sistema (m.), prácticas o existencia de los monopolios.

monopolist, monopolizer [-jst, -ajzœ(r)], s.

monopolista, monopolizador, acaparador.—**monopolistic** [-jstjk], a. monopolizador, acaparador.—**monopolization** [-jzéjšɔn], s. monopolización, acaparamiento.—**monopolize** [-ajz], va. monopolizar, acaparar, estancar.

monopoly [monápolj], s. monopolio, estanco.

monopteral [monáptẹrạl], a. (arq.) monóptero.

monorail [mánorejl], s. vía de un solo riel; grúa móvil de un solo riel o de monorrail. **II.** a. de un solo riel.

monorhymed [-rajmd], a. (pros.) monorrimo.

monosepalous [-sépạlʌs], a. (bot.) monosépalo.

monospermous [-spérmʌs], a. (bot.) monospermo.

monostrophe [-strof], s. (poét.) monóstrofe, f.

monosyllabic(al [-sjlǽbjk(ạl], a., monosilábico, monosílabo.—**monosyllable** [-sílạbl], s. monosílabo.

monotheism [-θjizm], s. monoteísmo.

monotheist [-θjjst], s. y a., **monotheistic** [-θjístjk], a. monoteísta.—**Monothelitism** [monáθelitjzm], s. (igl.) monotelismo.

monotone [-toụn], s. monotonía, uniformidad o igualdad de tono.

monotonic(al [-tánjk(ạl], **monotonous** [monátonʌs], a. monótono; machacón, unisonante.

monotony [monátonj], s. monotonía; unisonancia.

monotreme [mánotrim], s. (zool.) monotrema, m.

monotypal [-tajpạl], **monotypic** [-tjpjk], a. (biol.) monotipo, de una sola especie.

monotype [-tajp], s. (biol.) tipo único de su género o especie; (impr.) monotipia, máquina de componer que funde letras sueltas (es nombre de fábrica).

monotyper, monotypist [-œ(r), -jst], s. monotipista.

monovalent [-véjlẹnt], a. (quím.) monovalente, univalente.

monoxid(e [manáksajd], s. (quím.) monóxido.

Monseigneur [monsẹnyœ(r)], s. monseñor (título).

monsieur [mœsyœ], s. (fr.) señor.

Monsignor [mansjnyɔ(r)], s. (igl.) monseñor (título).

monsoon [mansún], s. monzón.

monster [mánstœ(r)]. **I.** s. monstruo. **II.** a. enorme, prodigioso, extraordinario.—**m. meeting,** junta magna.

monstrance [mánstrạns], s. (igl.) custodia, viril.

monstrosity [manstrásjtj], s. monstruo; monstruosidad.

monstrous [mánstrʌs], a. monstruoso.—**monstrously** [-lj], adv. monstruosamente.—**monstrousness** [-njs], s. monstruosidad.

montage [mantáž], s. (cine, etc.) montaje.

Montanist [mántạnjst], s. y a. (igl.) montanista.

monte [mántj], s. monte, juego de naipes.

month [mʌnθ], s. mes.—**m. of Sundays,** (fam.) largo tiempo.

monthly [-lj]. **I.** a. mensual; menstruo.—**m. allowance, payment, salary,** etc., mensualidad, mesada.—**m. rose,** (bot.) rosa de todo el año, rosa de China. **II.** s. publicación mensual.—pl. **monthlies,** (fisiol.) las reglas, menstruo. **III.** adv. mensualmente.

monticle [mántjkl], s. montículo, montecillo.

monument [mányụmẹnt], s. monumento; memoria, recuerdo; mojón, marca de límites, hito, (E. U.) parte (f.) del territorio del país reservada por el gobierno para usos nacionales.—**monumental** [-mǽntạl], a. monumental; conmemorativo; grandioso, descomunal.—**monumentally** [-j], adv. monumentalmente, a modo de monumento; (fam.) muy, en alto grado, descomunalmente.

moo [mu]. **I.** vn. mugir (la vaca). **II.** s. mu, mugido.

mood [múd], s. disposición de ánimo, talante, genio, humor; (lóg.) modo silogístico; (gram.)

modo.—**in a bad (good) m.**, de mal (buen) humor.

moodily [-ịliị], adv. caprichosamente; pensativamente.—**moodiness** [-inịs], s. capricho, extravagancia; mal humor; tristeza, cavilación, melancolía.

moody [-ị], a. fantástico, caprichoso; irritable, de mal humor; caviloso; triste, taciturno.

moon [mún], s. (astr.) luna; satélite; mes lunar.—**m.-blasted**, echado a perder por la influencia de la luna.—**m.-blind**, cegato, corto de vista.—**m. blindness**, ambliopía.—**m. daisy**, (bot.) margarita mayor.—**m. dial**, reloj lunar.—**m.-faced**, carilleno o carirredondo.—**m. fern**, (bot.) botriquio.—**m. knife**, (ten.) chifla.—**m.-mad**, **m.-struck**, lunático, loco.

moonbeam [-bim], s. rayo lunar.

mooncalf [-kæf], s. (ant.) monstruo; bobo, tonto.

mooned [-d], a. lunado.

moonfish [-fịʃ], s. (ict.) pez luna, m.

moonflower [-flaụœ(r)], s. (bot.) especie de ipomea.

moonless [-lịs], a. sin luna.

moonlight [-laịt]. I. s. luz de la luna. II. a. iluminado por la luna.

moonlit [-lịt], a. iluminado por la luna.

moonrise [-raịz], s. salida de la luna.

moonseed [-sid], s. (bot.) planta menispermácea.

moonset [-set], s. puesta de la luna.

moonshine [-ʃaịn], s. claridad de la luna; desatino, disparate; (fam.) música celestial; (E. U.) licor destilado ilegalmente.—**moonshiner** [-œ(r)], s. (E. U.) fabricante de licores ilícitos.

moonstone [-stoụn], s. (min.) adularia, ortosa.

moonwort [-wœrt], s. (bot.) lunaria; botriquio, especie de helecho.

moony [-ị], a. claro como la luna; lunático; bobo, simplón; soñador.

moor [múr]. I. s. (Ingl.) páramo, ciénaga; brezal, marjal; (M.) moro, sarraceno.—**m. buzzard**, (orn.) especie de busardo o circaeto.—**m. cock**, (orn.) macho del moorfowl.—**m. game** = MOORFOWL.—**m. hen**, (orn.) hembra del moorfowl; rascón, polla de agua. II. va. (mar.) amarrar, aferrar, atar con cables, afirmar con anclas. III. vn. (mar.) anclar, atracar; estar anclado.

moorage [-idʒ], s. (mar.) amarraje.

moorfowl [-faụl], s. (orn.) ave gallinácea parecida al tetrao, urogallo, ortega, chocha, etc.

mooring [-ịŋ]. I. s. (mar.) amarra, noray; cable o calabrote de amarrar. II. a. de amarre, de amarrar.—**m. berth**, amarradero.—**m. buoy**, boya de anclaje.—**m. guy**, (aer.) amarre de retenida (de un globo).—**m. harness**, (aer.) bandas para los cables o cuerdas de amarre (de un dirigible).—**m. mast o tower**, (aer.) torre (f.) o pilar de amarre para globos.—**m. rings**, (mar.) argollas de amarrar.

moorish [-ịʃ], a. pantanoso, cenagoso; árido; (M.), moro, morisco.

moorland [-lạnd], s. marjal; brezal; erial.

moory [-ị], a. pantanoso; moreno.

moose [mus], s. (zool.) anta, ante, alce.

moot [mut]. I. va. discutir, debatir. II. s. junta; discusión; lugar de reunión. III. a. discutible; discutido.—**m. court**, tribunal ad hoc, donde se ventilan pleitos supuestos para la enseñanza del derecho.

mop [máp]. I. s. aljofifa, estropajo; (mar.) lampazo; greña, mechón, cabellera revuelta y en desorden; mueca. II. va. aljofifar, fregar.—**to m. up**, vn. (mil.) acabar con el resto del enemigo.—**mopping-up**, (mil.) operación de limpiamiento.

mopboard [-bord], s. rodapié, friso.

mope [moụp]. I. va. abatir. II. vn. abatirse, desanimarse, estar tétrico, taciturno o apático. III. s. hombre abatido o desanimado.—pl. apatía, murria.—**m.-eyed**, cegato.

mopish [-ịʃ], a. abatido, melancólico, apático.—

mopishness [-nịs], s. abatimiento, apatía, desanimación.

moppet [mápịt], s. (ant.) nene, niña; (fam.) muñeca.

mopstick [mápstịk], s. mango de aljofifa.

moquette [mokét], s. moqueta.

moraine [moréịn], s. (geol.) morena.

morainic [-ik], a. (geol.) referente a una morena o formado por ella.

moral [márạl]. I. a. moral, ético; virtuoso; honrado, recto.—**m. faculty**, conciencia.—**m. philosophy**, ética.—**m. suasion**, persuasión, influencia moral.—**m. support**, apoyo moral. II. s. moralidad, moraleja.—pl. costumbres, conducta; ética, moral social.

morale [morél], s. moral, f., estado de ánimo, espíritu.

moralism [márạlịzm], s. enseñanza moral; acción o costumbre de moralizar; axioma moralizador; creencia en una moral sin carácter religioso.—**moralist** [-ịst], s. moralista, moralizador, ético; partidario del moralism.

morality [moréliị], s. ética, moral, f.; moralidad; moraleja; antiguo drama alegórico.

moralization [márạlịzéịʃọn], s. moralización.—**moralize** [-aịz], va. y vn. moralizar.—**moralizer** [-œ(r)], s. moralizador.

morally [márạlị], adv. moralmente.

morass [morǽs], s. cenagal, ciénaga, marisma.

moratorium [morạtóriạm], s. moratoria.

moratory [mórạtori], a. moratorio.

Moravian [moréịviạn], a. y s. moravo.

moray [móụreị], s. (ict.) morena.

morbid [mórbịd], a. mórbido, morboso, malsano.

morbidness [-nịs], **morbidity** [morbídịtị], s. morbidez, morbosidad, estado de enfermedad.

morbific(al [morbífịk(ạl], **morbose** [morbóụs], a. morbífico, mórbido, enfermizo.

morceau [morsóụ], s. (fr.) trozo, fragmento, pieza.

mordacious [mordéịʃʌs], a. mordaz.

mordacity [mordǽsịtị], s. mordacidad.

mordant [mórdạnt]. I. s. mordiente, mordente; (b. a.) agua fuerte. II. a. mordiente, ácido, corrosivo; acre, mordaz.

mordent [mórdạnt], s. (mús.) mordente.

more [mor]. I. a. (comp. de MUCH, MANY) más, adicional. II. adv. más, en mayor grado; además. III. s. mayor cantidad o número.—**more and m.**, de más en más, cada vez más.—**m. or less**, poco más o menos.—**no m.**, no más; ya no; se acabó.—**so much the m.**, tanto más, cuanto más.—**the m.**, tanto más.—**the m. . . ., the better**, cuanto más . . ., tanto mejor (the more you give, the better, cuanto (o mientras) más dé Vd., tanto mejor).—**the m. . . ., the less**, cuanto más . . ., tanto menos.—**the m. . . ., the m.**, cuanto más . . ., tanto más.—**to be no m.**, haber muerto; no existir ya.

moreen [morín], s. (tej.) filipichín; tabí.

morel [morél]. I. s. (bot.) colmenilla, cagarria. II. a. moreno, oscuro.

morel(le [morél], s. (bot.) hierba mora, solano.

moreover [moróụvœ(r)], adv. además, por otra parte.

mores [móriz], s. pl. costumbres (apl. esp. a las que envuelven sanción moral); leyes consuetudinarias.

Moresque [morésk]. I. a. morisco. II. s. (arq.) estilo morisco; (b. a.) arabesco.

morganatic [morgạnǽtịk], a. morganático.—**m. marriage**, matrimonio de la mano izquierda.

morgue [morg], s. necrocomio, depósito de cadáveres no identificados.

moribund [mórịbʌnd], a. moribundo.

morion [móụriọn], s. (arm.) morrión, m., casco.

Morisco [morískoụ]. I. a. morisco. II. s. morisco; arábigo; danza morisca; (arq.) arabesco.

Mormon [mórmọn]. I. s. mormón. II. a. mormónico.—**Mormonism** [-izm], s. mormonismo.

morning [mórnịŋ] (poét. **morn**). I. s. mañana

(primera parte del día). **II.** *a.* matutino, matinal, de mañana.—**m. coat**, chaquet o chaqué, levita.—**m. dress**, traje de mañana.—**m. glory**, (bot.) dondiego de día, dompedro, maravilla.—**m. gown**, bata.—**m. star**, (astr.) lucero del alba; (arm.) mangual.

Moro [mó⊍roʊ], *s.* y *a.* moro o mahometano filipino.

Moroccan [morákən], *s.* y *a.* marroquí(n), marrueco.

morocco [morákoʊ], *s.* marroquí, tafilete (cuero).

moron [móʊran], *s.* persona que padece deficiencia mental.

morose [moróʊs], *a.* áspero, malhumorado, arisco, hosco, adusto.—**morosely** [-li], *adv.* broncamente, ásperamente.—**moroseness** [-nis], *s.* mal humor, aspereza, acrimonia.

Morpheus [mórfiʌs], *s.* (mit.) Morfeo.

morphia [mórfiə], **morphin(e** [mórfin], *s.* morfina.—**m. addict**, morfinómano (ll. t. **morphinomaniac**).

morphinism [-izm], *s.* (med.) morfinismo.

morphological [morfoládžikəl], *a.* morfológico.

morphology [morfálodži], *s.* morfología.

morphosis [morfóʊsis], *s.* (biol.) morfosis.

morris *o* **morris dance** [máris dæns], *s.* (ant.) danza morisca; (Ingl.) mojiganga con cierto baile espectacular o fantástico.—**morris chair**, especie de poltrona o butaca.

morrow [mároʊ], *s.* mañana, *m.* (día que sigue al de hoy o a cualquier fecha o suceso de que se trata).—**good m.**, (ant.) buenos días.—**on the m.**, en el día de mañana; a raíz de, inmediatamente después (de).

morse [mors], *s.* (zool.) morsa. *V.* WALRUS.

Morse code [-koʊd], *s.* alfabeto telegráfico de Morse.

morsel [mórsel], *s.* bocado, manjar, presa.

mort [mort], *s.* toque de la trompa de caza al morir la res.

mortal [mórtəl]. **I.** *a.* mortal; letal, fatal; humano; (fam.) extremo, violento; prolijo, fastidioso.—**m. remains**, despojos mortales.—**m. sin**, pecado mortal. **II.** *s.* mortal, ser humano.

mortality [mortáliti], *s.* mortalidad; mortandad; humanidad.—**m. rate**, mortalidad.

mortally [mórtəli], *adv.* mortalmente, de muerte; (fam.) extremadamente, sumamente.

mortar [mórtə(r)], *s.* (farm.) mortero, almirez, *m.;* (arti.) mortero, obús (ll. t. **m. piece**); (alb.) mortero, argamasa, mezcla.—**m. bed**, (alb.) cuezo.—**m. board**, (alb.) esparavel (tabla con asa por debajo); gorro académico cuadrado.

mortgage [mórgidž]. **I.** *s.* (for.) hipoteca, gravamen.—**m. deed**, título de propiedad depositado en calidad de hipoteca.—**m. loan**, préstamo hipotecario. **II.** *va.* hipotecar, gravar (bienes raíces).

mortgageable [-əbl], *a.* hipotecable.

mortgagee [-i], *s.* acreedor hipotecario, persona a quien se le da una propiedad en hipoteca.

mortgager [-œ(r)], *s.* deudor hipotecario.

mortician [mortíšən], *s.* = UNDERTAKER.

mortiferous [mortíferas], *a.* mortífero.

mortification [mortifikéišən], *s.* mortificación, humillación, bochorno; (med.) mortificación, descomposición, gangrena; maceración.

mortify [mórtifai]. **I.** *va.* mortificar, humillar, abochornar; macerar o castigar (la carne); subyugar, domar (las pasiones); (med.) mortificar. **II.** *vn.* (med.) mortificarse, gangrenarse, corromperse.

mortifying [-iŋ], *a.* mortificador, humillante.

mortise [mórtis]. **I.** *s.* (carp.) mortaja, cotana, muesca, entalladura, gárgol; (mar.) alefriz, *m.* —**m. hole**, escopl(e)adura.—**m. lock**, cerradura embutida. **II.** *va.* escoplear, hacer muescas; engargolar, ensamblar.

mortmain [mórtmein], *s.* (for.) manos muertas; amortización.

mortuary [mórchueri]. **I.** *a.* mortuorio, funerario. **II.** *s.* depósito de cadáveres; osario. *V.* MORGUE.

mosaic [mozéijik], *a.* y *s.* mosaico, embutido, (de) encaje; (M.), *a.* mosaico, referente a Moisés.— **m. gold**, oro musivo.

Moslem [mázlem], *s.* y *a.* musulmán, muslime.

mosque [mask], *s.* mezquita.

mosquito [məskítoʊ], *s.* (ent.) mosquito, cénzalo, cínife, mosco, (Am.) zancudo.—**m. bar**, mosquitero.—**m. fleet**, escuadra de barcos relativamente menores.—**m. net** = M. BAR.—**m. netting**, gasa o redecilla para mosquiteros.

moss [mos]. **I.** *s.* (bot.) musgo, musco, moho; tremedal, ciénaga.—**m. agate**, (min.) ágata musgosa.—**m.-covered, m.-grown**, musgoso. —**m. rose**, rosa musgosa. **II.** *va.* cubrir de musgo.

mossiness [-inis], *s.* abundancia de musgo.

mosstrooper [-trupœ(r)], *s.* bandido, bandolero.

mossy [-i], *a.* musgoso.

most [moʊst]. **I.** *a.* (*superl.* de MUCH, MANY) más; lo más, los más, el mayor número (de); casi todo(s); la mayor parte de.—**for the m. part**, principalmente, generalmente; en su mayor parte. **II.** *adv.* más; sumamente, -ísimo (*most cruel*, muy cruel, cruelísimo); (fam.) casi.—**M. Reverend**, reverendísimo, ilustrísimo.—**the M. High**, el Ser Supremo, Dios. **III.** *s.* lo principal, la mayor parte, el mayor número, lo más, el mayor valor.—**at (the) m.**, a lo más, a lo sumo, cuando más.

mostly [-li], *adv.* en su mayor parte, casi todo(s), principalmente.

mote [moʊt], *s.* mota, átomo; punto; mecha; junta, asamblea.

mote [moʊt], *v.* (ant.) **so m. it be**, así sea, amén.

motet [motét], *s.* (mús.) motete.

moth [moθ], *s.* (ent.) alevilla; polilla; mariposa de varios gusanos.—**m. ball**, bola de naftalena o de alcanfor para la polilla.—**m.-eaten**, apolillado.

mother [mʌðœ(r)]. **I.** *s.* madre, *f.;* madre, tía, mujer vieja; madre del vino, zurrapa.—**M. Hubbard**, bata, ropón de mujer.—**m.-in-law**, suegra.—**m.-of-pearl**, nácar, madreperla.— **m.-of-thyme**, (bot.) serpol.—**M.'s Day**, día (*m.*) de la madre, o de las madres.—**m.'s mark**, estigma, *m.*, marca de nacimiento. **II.** *a.* madre; natural, nativo, natal, materno; vernáculo, nacional; metropolitano.—**m. church**, iglesia metropolitana.—**m. country**, madre patria; metrópoli, *f.*—**m. liquid, m. liquor**, (quím.) aguas madres.—**M. Superior**, superiora (de monjas, etc.).—**m. tongue**, lengua materna, madre o vernácula.—**m. water** = M. LIQUOR. —**m. wit**, chispa, ingenio. **III.** *va.* servir de madre a. **IV.** *vn.* criar madre, como el vino.

motherhood [-hud], *s.* maternidad.

motherless [-lis], *a.* huérfano de madre.

motherliness [-linis], *s.* maternidad, cariño o cuidado maternal.

motherly [-li]. **I.** *a.* maternal, materno. **II.** *adv.* maternalmente.

motherwort [-wœrt], *s.* (bot.) agripalma.

mothy [moθi], *a.* lleno de polilla, apolillado.

motif [motíf], *s.* motivo, asunto, tema, *m.*

motile [móʊtil], *a.* movible.

motility [motíliti], *s.* movilidad.

motion [móʊšən]. **I.** *s.* movimiento; meneo, aire, ademán; signo, señal, *f.*, seña; proposición o moción que se hace en una asamblea; (for.) pedimento.—**m. picture**, cine; fotografía cinematográfica; película.—**on the m. of**, a propuesta de.—**to set in m.**, poner en marcha. **II.** *vn.* hacer señas.

motionless [-lis], *a.* inmóvil, inmoble; yerto.

motivate [móʊtiveit], *va.* motivar, dar motivo para.

motive [móʊtiv]. **I.** *a.* motor, motriz.—**m. power**, fuerza motriz. **II.** *s.* motivo, móvil, razón, *f.*, porqué; pie, *m.*, tema, *m.*, idea, asunto; (mús.) tema, motivo.

motivity [motívitị], *s.* potencia motriz.

motley [mátlị]. I. *a.* abigarrado, gayado; mezclado, variado, diverso; vestido de colorines. II. *s.* traje abigarrado de payaso; botarga; payaso vestido de colorines; mezcla de colores.

motor [móụtọ(r)]. I. *s.* motor, el que o lo que mueve; (mec.) motor; (aut.) automóvil. II. *a.* motor, motriz; de motor, movido por motor (máquina).—**m.** boat, o launch, gasolinera, canoa o lancha automóvil.—**m.** bus, o coach, autobús, autocar.—**m.** car, auto(móvil).—**m.-driven**, movido por electromotor.—**m.** faculty, o function, (fisiol.) motricidad.—**m.** generator, (elec.) motogenerador.—**m.** nerve, (anat.) nervio motor.—**m.** oil, aceite lubricante de motores (gen. de gasolina).—**m.** ship, motonave, *f.*—**m.** spirit, esencia, combustible para motores de combustión interna (apl. gen. a la gasolina).—**m.** transport, transporte motorizado o por autocamiones.—**m.** truck, autocamión, *m.* III. *vn.* pasear, viajar o ir en automóvil.

motorcade [-kejd], *s.* procesión o desfile de automóviles.

motorcycle [-saịkl], *s.* motocicleta.

motorcyclist [-saịklịst], *s.* motociclista.

motordrome [-droụm], *s.* motódromo, autódromo, pista para carreras de automóviles.

motorist [-ịst], *s.* automovilista, motorista.

motorization [-ịzéịşọn], *s.* motorización.

motorize [-aịz], *va.* motorizar, proveer de autovehículos, o motovehículos; reemplazar por autovehículos, o vehículos automóviles.

motorman [-mạn], *s.* motorista, conductor (de tranvía o tren eléctrico).

mottle [mátl]. I. *va.* motear, abigarrar, jaspear. II. *s.* mancha, veta.—**mottled** [-d], *a.* moteado, jaspeado, vet(e)ado, pintado, pintojo.

motto [mátoụ], *s.* mote, lema, *m.*, divisa.

moufflon, mouflon [múflan], *s.* (zool.) musmón.

mo(u)ld [móụld]. I. *s.* tierra vegetal, humus, suelo, mantillo; molde, matriz, forma; plancha; modelo, patrón; (arq. y carp.) moldura; materia de que está hecha una cosa; (bot.) moho, verdín; mancha de orín.—**m.** shot, balines, *m. pl.*, posta. II. *va.* (a)moldar, moldear, vaciar, amasar, formar, plasmar; (arq. y carp.) moldurar, moldear; cubrir con mantillo; (mar.) galibar. III. *vn.* enmohecerse, florecerse.

mo(u)ldable [-ạbl], *a.* capaz de ser moldeado y amoldado.

mo(u)ldboard [-bọrd], *s.* orejera o vertedero del arado.

mo(u)lder [-œ(r)], *s.* moldeador, vaciador; amoldador, plasmador.

mo(u)lder [-œ(r)]. I. *vn.* convertirse en polvo, desmoronarse, consumirse. II. *va.* convertir en polvo, consumir, desgastar.

mo(u)ldering [-ịŋ], *s.* desmoronamiento.

mo(u)ldiness [-ịnịs], *s.* moho.

mo(u)lding [-ịŋ]. I. *s.* (arq. y carp.) moldura, bocel, ataire, lengüeta; amoldamiento; vaciado, vaciamiento. II. *a.* plasmante.—**m.** plane, bocelete, bocelón.

mo(u)ldy [-ị], *a.* mohoso, enmohecido, florecido.

moulin [mulén], *s.* pozo casi vertical que forma el agua en un ventisquero o glaciar.

moulinet [mulịnét], *s.* (esgr.) molinete; (mec.) tambor o rodillo de cabrestante.

mo(u)lt [móụlt], *vn.* mudar la pluma, desplumarse.—**mo(u)lting** [-ịŋ], *s.* muda (de pluma).

mound [maụnd]. I. *s.* montón de tierra; montículo, morón; baluarte, defensa, terraplén; túmulo.—**m.** builders, constructores de túmulos (apl. a los aborígenes de los E. U. que dejaron muchos túmulos sepulcrales y terraplenes de defensa). II. *va.* amontonar; atrincherar, fortalecer.

mount [máụnt]. I. *s.* monte, montaña; baluarte,

terraplén; montadura; caballería; montura; apeadero; (mil.) monta, toque de clarín. II. *va.* cabalgar, montar; armar; montar (una máquina, etc.); subir, alzar, elevar; enaltecer; subir a, trepar por; proveer de caballos; poner a caballo; (joy.) montar o engastar; (teat.) poner en escena; preparar una cosa para usarla o exhibirla; (fot.) pegar sobre cartulina; (mec.) montar, aparejar; (arti.) montar, armar; (mar.) montar, llevar (cañones).—**to m.** a cannon, (arti.) montar un cañón.—**to m.** guard, (mil.) montar la guardia. III. *vn.* subir, ascender, elevarse; montar a caballo; subir, montar, ascender (una cuenta, etc.).

mountable [-ạbl], *a.* que se puede montar o subir, etc.

mountain [máụntịn]. I. *s.* monte, montaña. II. *a.* montés, montañés; de montaña.—**m.** artillery, artillería de montaña.—**m.** ash, (bot.) especie de fresno o mostajo, serbal.—**m.** cat = m. lion o bobcat.—**m.** chain, sierra, cordillera, cadena de montañas.—**m.** climber, alpinista.—**m.** climbing, alpinismo.—**m.** dew, (fam.) whisky de contrabando.—**m.** goat, (zool.) cabra montés.—**m.** lion, (zool.) puma, *mf.*—**m.** railway, ferrocarril de cremallera.—**m.** sheep = bighorn.—**m.** side, valda o vertiente (*f.*) de una montaña.

mountaineer [-ịr], *s.* montañés, serrano.

mountainous [-as], *a.* montañoso, montuoso.

mountebank [máụntịbæŋk], *s.* charlatán, saltabanco(s), saltimbanco o juglar.

mounted [máụntịd], *a.* montado, (de) a caballo; armado; pegado. *V.* MOUNT.

mounter [-œ(r)], *s.* montador.

mounting [-ịŋ], *s.* monta; subida, ascensión; engaste, montadura; armadura; marco; montaje.—**m.** block, cabalgadero, montador o montadero.

mourn [móụrn]. I. *va.* lamentar, llorar, sentir. II. *vn.* lamentarse, dolerse; plañir; vestir o llevar luto.—**to m.** for, llevar luto por; lamentar, llorar.

mourner [-œ(r)], *s.* dolorido, doliente; persona que lleva el duelo en un funeral; lloraduelos, plañidera.

mournful [-fụl], *a.* triste, plañidero; apesadumbrado; funesto, deplorable; fúnebre, lúgubre, luctuoso.—**mournfully** [-ị], *adv.* tristemente.—**mournfulness** [-nịs], *s.* pesar, tristeza, melancolía, aflicción, desconsuelo, duelo, sentimiento.

mourning [-ịŋ]. I. *s.* luto; duelo; dolor, aflicción.—**in m.**, de luto. II. *a.* de luto, de duelo; fúnebre, luctuoso.—**m.** band, brazal de luto.—**m.** bride, m. widow, (bot.) escabiosa.—**m.** dove, (orn.) tórtola gemidora de los E. U.

mouse [máụs]. I. *s.* (*pl.* MICE) (zool.) ratón; (mar.) barrilete.—**m.-colored**, **m.-dun**, vellorio, pardusco, de color de rata.—**m.-ear**, (bot.) oreja de ratón, miosotis, vellosilla o pelosilla. II. *va.* y *vn.* cazar o coger ratones; cazar a hurtadillas, acechar; desgarrar, hacer trizas; (mar.) amarrar, hacer barriletes.—**to m.** a hook, amarrar un gancho.

mouser [-œ(r)], *s.* gato o perro ratonero.

mousehole [-hoụl], *s.* ratonera (agujero).

mousing [-ịŋ]. I. *a.* ratonero, taimado. II. *s.* caza de ratones; (mar.) acto de amarrar un gancho.—**m.** hook, gancho amarrado.

mousetail [-teịl], *s.* (bot.) miosuro, cola de ratón.

mousetrap [-træp], *s.* ratonera, trampa de ratones.

mousquetaire [muskœtér], *s.* (mil.) mosquetero; guante de mosquetero.

mousse [mus], *s.* (coc.) especie de crema.

mousseline [muslín], *s.* (tej.) muselina; vidrio de muselina. *V.* MUSLIN (GLASS).

moustache [mastéş] = MUSTACHE.

mousy [máụsị], *a.* ratonero, ratonesco.

mouth [máụθ]. I. *s.* boca; embocadura o desem-

bocadura de un río; labio, lengua, voz; mueca.
—m. **harp**, u **organ**, (mús.) armónica.—m.-
watering, que se le hace a uno agua la boca;
delicioso. II. [mauð], va. pronunciar, proferir,
vocear; mascar, comer; agarrar con la boca o
en la boca. III. vn. vociferar, hablar a gritos.
mouthed [-d], a. que tiene boca.
mouther [-œ(r)], s. orador afectado.
mouthful [máuθful], s. bocado; buchada; miaja,
migaja, pizca.
mouthless [-lis], a. desbocado, sin boca.
mouthpiece [-pis], s. (mús.) embocadura, boquilla, estrangul, bocal; embocadura (del freno);
(tel.) bocina; el que lleva la voz o habla por
otros, intérprete, vocero, portavoz, m.
mouthwash [-waš], s. (farm.) colutorio, enjuague.
mouthy [máuði], a. vociferador; bombástico.
mov(e)able [múvəbl]. I. a. móvil, movible;
movedizo, locomovible. II. s. pl. muebles, menaje, mobiliario, efectos.
movability [-bíliti], **movableness** [-blnis], s.
movilidad.
movably [-bli], adv. de un modo movible.
move [múv]. I. s. movimiento; paso; en varios
juegos, suerte, f., lance, jugada, turno.—**on
the m.**, en marcha, en movimiento; de viaje.
—**to get a m. on**, (fam.) rebullirse, darse
prisa.—**to make a m.**, dar un paso; hacer una
jugada. II. va. mover; remover; trasladar,
mudar; poner en otro sitio; menear, sacudir;
proponer, hacer una moción en una asamblea;
conmover, enternecer; inclinar, persuadir;
hacer mover el vientre; (mec.) accionar.—**to
m. to**, causar (cólera, compasión, lágrimas,
etc.) a. (A veces se traduce mejor por hacer o
poner, cambiando el giro; to move to anger,
poner colérico, hacer enojar; to move to tears,
hacer llorar.) III. vn. moverse; mudarse (de
casa); mudar de lugar o de postura; ir, andar,
caminar, ponerse en marcha; obrar, entrar en
acción; avanzar, progresar; exonerarse (el
vientre); jugar, hacer una jugada.—**to m.
away**, alejarse; irse; trasladarse; mudar de
casa.—**to m. forward**, adelantarse, avanzar.
—**to m. in**, entrar; entrar a habitar una casa.
—**to m. off**, quitarse o apartarse de.—**to m.
out**, desalojar.—**to m. round**, dar vueltas,
rodar.—**to m. to and fro**, zarand(e)arse, ir
de acá para allá.
movement [-mənt], s. movimiento; moción;
(mil.) maniobra, evolución; paso, acto, acción,
incidente; (mec.) movimiento; mecanismo;
juego; marcha (de reloj, etc.); (mús.) movimiento, compás o tiempo; (fisiol.) defecación,
cámara, evacuación, deposición; (com.) circulación; actividad.
mover [-œ(r)], s. motor, movedor, móvil; promotor, promovedor; autor de una moción; el
que se dedica a la traslación de muebles de un
sitio a otro.
movie [múvi], s. (fam.) función de cine; película.
—pl. (fam.) cine.—m. **camera**, cámara cinematográfica.—m. **film**, película, cinta.—m.
screen, pantalla de cine.
moving [múviŋ]. I. s. movimiento, moción;
actuación; mudanza, traslado, cambio de
domicilio. II. a. patético, conmovedor; motor;
que mueve o traslada; de mudanza (día, etc.).
—m. **picture**, película, cinematógrafo (en pl.,
cine).—m. **platform**, plataforma movible de
correa sin fin.—m. **sidewalk**, acera de correa
sin fin.—m. **staircase**, o **stairway** = ESCALA-
TOR.—m. **van**, camión (m.) de mudanza(s),
conductora de muebles.
movingly [-li], adv. patéticamente, conmovedoramente.
mow [mou]. I. va. (pp. MOWED y MOWN [moun])
segar, guadañar, dallar. II. vn. hacer muecas;
burlarse de. III. s. (ant.) mueca.

mow [mau]. I. s. granero, troj, f., hórreo, henil.
II. va. entrojar.
mower [móuə(r)], s. segador, dallador, guada-
ñero; guadañadora, segadora mecánica.
mowing [móuiŋ], s. siega; gesto, mueca.—m.
machine, guadañadora o segadora mecánica.
mown [moun], pp. irr. de MOW.
moxa [máksá], s. (cir.) moxa.
Mozarab(ic [mouzárəb(ik], s. y a. mozárabe.
mozetta [mozétá], s. (igl.) muceta.
mucedinous [miusédinas], a. mohoso.
much [mách]. I. a. mucho, abundante, copioso.
—m. **ado about nothing**, nada entre dos
platos; más es el ruido que las nueces. II. adv.
mucho, con mucho, en gran manera; casi;
(antes de pp.) muy (m.-loved, muy querido).—
m. **as**, por más que, a pesar de.—m. **of a
muchness**, (fam.) poco más o menos lo mismo,
casi igual.—m. **the same**, casi lo mismo; poco
más o menos lo mismo.—m. **too**, demasiado.
—**not so m. as**, no tanto como; ni siquiera.—
to be m. of a (seguido de sustantivo), ser muy,
ser todo un (he is much of a gentleman, es todo
un caballero; she is much of a woman, ella es
muy mujer).—**this m. more**, esto más, tanto
así más. III. s. mucho.
muchness [-nis], s. cantidad; magnitud.
mucid [miúsid], a. mohoso; mucoso, viscoso.
mucilage [miúsilidž], s. mucílago.
mucilaginous [-lǽdžinas], a. mucilaginoso.
mucilaginousness [-nis], s. calidad de mucilaginoso o viscoso.
mucin [miúsin], s. (bioquím.) mucina.
muck [mák]. I. s. abono, estiércol, fimo; porquería, basura.—m. **rake**, rastrillo para estiércol.—m. **rolls**, primeros rodillos de laminar. II. va. estercolar, abonar; ensuciar. III.
vn. (con about) (fam.) = POTTER.
mucker [-œ(r)], s. (fam.) sujeto vil o soez.
muckiness [-nis], s. suciedad, inmundicia.
muckrake [-reik], vn. (pol.) andar escarbando
para sacar trapos sucios al sol o a relucir.—
muckraker [-œ(r)], s. (pol.) escarbador de
vidas ajenas, averiguador y expositor de ruin-
dades.
mucksweat [-swet], s. sudor copioso.
mucky [-i], a. puerco, sucio, asqueroso.
mucoid [miúkoid], a. mucoideo, mucoso.
mucopurulent [miukopiúrulent], a. (pat.)
mucopurulento.
mucor [miúkə(r)], s. (med.) moco, mucosidad;
moho; (bot.) variedad de hongo.
mucosity [miukásiti], s. = MUCOUSNESS.
mucous [miúkas], a. mucoso, mocoso.—m.
membrane, (anat.) (membrana) mucosa (ll.
t. **mucosa**).
mucousness [-nis], s. mucosidad, viscosidad.
mucro [miúkrou], s. (bot., zool.) punta.—
mucronate(d [-neit(id], a. puntiagudo, mucronato.
mucus [miúkas], s. moco, mucosidad.
mud [mád]. I. s. fango, cieno, lodo, barro, limo,
légamo.—m. **bath**, baño de cieno.—m.
dauber, m. **wasp**, (ent.) especie de avispa.—
m. **hen**, (orn.) especie de polla de agua o de
pato marino.—m. **lighter**, gánguil, lancha
de draga.—m. **scow**, pontón, gánguil.—m.
scraper, limpiabarros.—m. **turtle**, (zool.)
tortuga de agua dulce.—m. **volcano**, cono
volcánico que arroja cieno. (Méx.) hornito.—
m. **wall**, tapia.—m.-**walled**, tapiado. II. va.
enlodar, embarrar; enturbiar, ensuciar.
muddily [-ili], adv. turbiamente.
muddiness [-inis], s. carácter de lodoso, etc.;
turbieza, suciedad; turbulencia.
muddle [mádl]. I. va. enturbiar; embriagar;
atontar; confundir, revolver. II. vn. estar confuso, inepto o atontado.—**to m. through**,
hacer algo malamente, salir del paso a duras
penas. III. s. chabacanería; embrollo, confusión.—m.-**headed**, estúpido, atontado.

muddy [mΛdi]. **I.** *a.* barroso, lodoso, fangoso; sucio, turbio; tonto, estúpido, confuso. **II.** *va.* enturbiar, ensuciar; entontecer, turbar.

Mudejar [muðéjhar], *s.* y *a.* mudéjar.

mudguard [mΛdgard], *s.* alero, guardabarros, guardafango.

mudhole [mΛdhoul], *s.* hoyo lodoso.

mudsill [mΛdsil], *s.* madero colocado en el suelo como cimiento; (E. U.) persona de baja condición social.

muezzin [mjuézin], *s.* (al)muecín, almuédano.

muff [mΛf]. **I.** *s.* manguito, estufilla; chabacanería, torpeza; en baseball, falta o falla; (fam.) torpe, zurdo. **II.** *va.* (fam.) hacer algo poco diestramente; desperdiciar (una ocasión); en baseball, dejar escapar la pelota.

muffin [mΛfin], *s.* (coc.) especie de panecillo; platito de barro.—**m. cap**, gorra redonda.

muffle [mΛfl]. **I.** *s.* horno de esmaltar, de arcilla o de copela; (zool.) hocico, morro; funda; tapujo.—**m. furnace**, mufla. **II.** *va.* embozar, arrebozar, tapar, encapotar; envolver, encubrir, apagar un sonido.—**to m. a drum**, enfundar o destemplar un tambor.

muffled [-d], *a.* apagado, sordo; embozado.—**m. drum**, tambor destemplado, tambor fúnebre. —**m. noise**, ruido sordo.—**m. oars**, remos silenciosos (cubiertos de trapos para ensordecer su ruido).

muffler [mΛflœ(r)], *s.* bufanda, tapaboca; (aut.) silenciador (mús.) sordina.

mufti [mΛfti], *s.* muftí, jurisconsulto musulmán; (mil.) traje de paisano.

mug [mΛg]. **I.** *s.* cubilete, pichel; (fam.) cara, boca; mueca. **II.** *va.* (fam.) fotografiar (esp. a los criminales); (fam.) atracar o asaltar con violencia.

mugginess [mΛginis], *s.* calor húmedo.

muggy [mΛgi], **muggish** [mΛgiš], *a.* húmedo, bochornoso, caluroso y sofocante (el tiempo).

mugwort [mΛgwœrt], *s.* (bot.) artemisa.

mugwump [mΛgwΛmp], *s.* (pol. E. U.) secuaz (*m.*) de un partido que se reserva el derecho de votar con entera independencia.

mulatto [mjulétou], *a.* y *s.* mulato.

mulberry [mΛlberi], *s.* (bot.) mora.—**m. tree**, morera o moral.

mulch [mΛlch]. **I.** *va.* cubrir (las plantas) con paja y estiércol, hojas, etc. **II.** *s.* estiércol y paja con que se protegen las plantas.

mulct [mΛlkt]. **I.** *s.* multa. **II.** *va.* multar.

mule [mjúl], *s.* (zool.) mulo, mula, macho, burdégano; planta o animal híbridos; especie de chinela, zapatilla o pantuflo sin talón; (fam.) sujeto terco o necio; (tej.) = M. JENNY.—**m. boy, m. driver** = MULETEER.—**m. chair**, jamugas, *f. pl.*—**m. jenny**, hiladora mecánica intermitente (en varias partes ll. selfactina).— **m. twist, m. yarn**, hilo de hiladora intermitente.

muleteer [mjuletír], *s.* mule(te)ro, arriero.

muliebrity [mjuliébriti], *s.* muliebridad; feminidad; calidad o estado de mujer.

mulier [mjúljer], *s.* (for.) mujer casada, esposa.

mulish [mjúliš], *a.* obstinado o terco como una mula; híbrido, mular; estéril.

mull [mΛl]. **I.** *s.* (tej.) muselina clara; (Esco.) cabo, promontorio. **II.** *va.* calentar vino con especias. **III.** *vn.* (gen. con **over**) rumiar, cavilar; afanarse mucho sin resultado.

mulla(h [mΛlá], *s.* título mahometano.

mulle(i)n [mΛljn], *s.* (bot.) verbasco, candelaria.

muller [mΛlœ(r)], *s.* moleta; pulverizador.

mullet [mΛlit], *s.* (ict.) múgil, mújol, cabezudo.

mulligatawny [mΛligatóni], *s.* sopa de arroz y carne sazonada con *curry*.

mullion [mΛljon]. **I.** *s.* (arq.) columna que divide el vano de una ventana; montante. **II.** *va.* dividir (una ventana) mediante una columna.

mulse [mΛls], *s.* clarea, vino mulso.

multicapsular [mΛltikǽpsjulá(r)], *a.* (bot.)

multicapsular, de muchas cápsulas o celdillas.

multicolored [mΛltikΛlord], *a.* multicolor, de varios colores, policromo.

multidentate [-dénteit], *a.* multidentado.

multiengined [-endžind], *a.* multimotor.

multifarious [-férjΛs], *a.* vario, multiplicado.— **multifariously** [-li], *adv.* diversamente.— **multifariousness** [-nis], *s.* diversidad; multiplicidad; variedad, desemejanza.

multifid(ous [-fid, -tífidΛs], *a.* multífido, dividido en muchas partes, lóbulos o porciones.

multiflorous [-flóras], *a.* multífloro.

multiform [-fǫrm], *a.* multiforme.

multigraph [-grǽf]. **I.** *s.* multígrafo (nombre de fábrica), aparato rotatorio que arregla tipo y lo imprime. **II.** *va.* multigrafiar, imprimir con multígrafo.

multilateral [-lǽterǫl], *a.* (geom.) multilátero; (pol.) = MULTIPARTITE.

multimillionaire [-miljǫnér], *s.* multimillonario.

multinominal [-náminǫl], *a.* que tiene muchos nombres; (mat.) multinomio.

multipara [mΛltípǫrǫ], *s.* (med.) mujer multípara.

multiparous [-Λs], *a.* multípara.

multipartite [mΛltipártait], *a.* que consta de muchas partes.

multiped [-pɛd], *a.* multípedo.

multiphase [-feiz], *a.* (elec.) polifásico.

multiplane [-plein], *s.* (aer.) poliplano.

multiple [mΛltipl]. **I.** *s.* múltiplo.—**in m.**, (elec.) en paralelo, en derivación. **II.** *a.* múltiple, multíplice; (mat.) múltiplo.—**m. circuit, connection, o series**, (elec.) circuito o conexión en serie múltiple o en paralelo.—**m.-way switch**, (elec.) interruptor de varias direcciones.

multiplex [mΛltipleks], *a.* multíplice; (tlg., rad.) múltiplex.

multipliable [-plaiǫbl], **multiplicable** [-plikǫbl], *a.* multiplicable.

multipliableness [-nis], *s.* calidad de multiplicable.

multiplicand [-plikǽnd], *s.* (mat.) multiplicando.

multiplicate [-plikeit], *a.* multiplicado; (bot.) replegado.

multiplication [-plikéišǫn], *s.* multiplicación.— **m. table**, tabla de multiplicar.

multiplicative [-plikeitiv], *a.* multiplicativo.

multiplicity [-plísiti], *s.* multiplicidad, sinnúmero.

multiplier [-plaiǫr)], *s.* multiplicador; (mat.) multiplicador; máquina de multiplicar.

multiply [-plai], *va.* y *vn.* multiplicar(se).

multiplying [-iŋ], *a.* multiplicador de multiplicación; reproductor; de propagación.—**m. glass**, espejo de varias facetas que multiplica el número de las imágenes.—**m. lens**, vidrio de aumento; (fot.) lente multiplicadora.

multipolar [-póulá(r)], *a.* multipolar.

multipresence [-prézǫns], *s.* ubicuidad.

multitube [-tjub], *a.* (rad.) de varias válvulas.

multitubular [-tjúbyúlá(r)], *a.* multitubular.— **m. boiler**, caldera de tubos de humos.

multitude [-tjud], *s.* multitud; vulgo.

multitudinous [-tjúdinΛs], *a.* numeroso.

multivalent [-véjlǫnt], *a.* (quím.) multivalente.

multure [mΛlchur], *s.* maquila; molienda.

mum [mΛm]. **I.** *interj.* ¡chito! ¡chitón! ¡silencio! **II.** *s.* cerveza fuerte y dulce; (fam.) mamá, *f.*; (bot., fam.) crisantemo. **III.** *a.* callado, silencioso—**mum's the word**, punto en boca.— **to keep m.**, callarse. **IV.** *vn.* enmascararse, disfrazarse; imponer silencio.

mumble [mΛmbl], *va.* y *vn.* barbotar, musitar, (fam.) bisbisar, hablar o decir entre dientes; murmurar, refunfuñar; (fam.) mascullar, mascar, mascujar.

mumbler [mΛmblœ(r)], *s.* el que barbota, etc.

mumbling [mámbliŋ], *s.* acción y efecto del verbo TO MUMBLE.

mumbo jumbo [mámbou dʒámbou], *s.* espantajo; coco; fetiche; sortilegio insensato; mojiganga.

mummer [mámœ(r)], *s.* máscara, *mf.*, momero: actor.

mummery [-i], **mumming** [mámiŋ], *s.* momería, mojiganga, disfraz, *m.*, mascarada.

mummification [mʌmifikéiʂon], *s.* momificación.

mummify [mámifai], *va.* y *vn.* momificar(se).

mummy [mámi]. **I.** *s.* momia. **II.** *va.* y *vn.* momificar(se).

mumpish [mámpiʂ], *a.* arisco, intratable, malhumorado.

mumps [mʌmps], *s.* (med.) papera, parótida.

munch [mʌnch], *va.* mascar enérgicamente.

mundane [mándein], *a.* mundano, terrenal.

mungo [máŋgou], *s.* (bot.) especie de garbanzo (ll. t. **mung(o) bean**); lana regenerada.

municipal [mjunísipal], *a.* municipal.—**m. building**, casa consistorial.—**m. council**, cabildo, concejo.—**m. government**, gobierno municipal; ayuntamiento, municipalidad.—**m. road**, camino vecinal.

municipality [-pæliti], *s.* municipio; municipalidad.

municipalization [-izéiʂon], *s.* municipalización.

municipalize [-ajz], *va.* municipalizar, transferir a la municipalidad.

municipium [mjunísipiʌm], *s.* (hist. rom.) municipio.

munificence [mjunífisęns], *s.* munificencia.—**munificent** [-ęnt], *a.* munífico, generoso, liberal.—**munificently** [-li], *adv.* munificamente.

muniment [mjúnimęnt], *s.* apoyo, defensa.—*pl.* (for.) título.

munition [mjuníʂon]. **I.** *s.* (gen. *pl.*) (mil.) municiones, pertrechos; equipo.—**m. bread**, pan de munición.—**m. ship**, navío almacén. **II.** *va.* municionar.

mural [mjúral]. **I.** *a.* mural; adosado a una pared; escarpado, vertical.—**m. circle**, (astr.) círculo mural.—**m. crown**, corona mural.—**m. painting**, cuadro mural.—**m. tablet**, tablilla fijada en una pared. **II.** *s.* (b. a.) = M. PAINTING.

murder [mœrdœ(r)]. **I.** *s.* asesinato.—**m. in the first degree**, homicidio premeditado.—**m. in the second degree**, homicidio impremeditado. **II.** *va.* asesinar; estropear. **III.** *vn.* cometer homicidio.

murderer [-œ(r)], *s.* asesino, homicida, *m.*, matador.—**murderess** [-is], *s.* asesina.—**murderous** [-ʌs], *a.* asesino; sanguinario, cruel; fatal.—**murderously** [-li], *adv.* sanguinariamente; asesinamente.—**murderousness** [-nis], *s.* instinto o instinto homicida.

murex [mjúreks], *s.* (zool.) múrice, conchil, púrpura.—**murexide** [mjuréksaid], *s.* (quím.) murexida.

muriate [mjúrieit], *s.* (quím.) muriato.

muriatic [-ǽtik], *a.* muriático, clorhídrico.

muricate(d [mjúrikeit(id], *a.* espinoso.

Muricidæ [mjurísidi], *s. pl.* (zool.) murícidos.

Muridæ [mjúridi], *s. pl.* (zool.) múridos.

murine [mjúrin], *s.* y *a.* (zool.) múrido.

murk(iness [mœrk(inis], *s.* obscuridad; lobreguez.

murk(y [-(i], *a.* obscuro, lóbrego; sombrío.

murmur [mœrmœ(r)]. **I.** *s.* murmullo, susurro; murmuración, queja. **II.** *vn.* murmurar, susurrar; refunfuñar; (con **at** o **against**) gruñir, quejarse de.—**murmurer** [-œ(r)], *s.* gruñidor, murmurador.—**murmuring** [-iŋ]. **I.** *s.* murmullo; murmureo; murmuración, queja. **II.** *a.* murmurante, susurrante.—**murmuringly** [-li], *adv.* con murmurio; quejumbrosamente.

murrain [mœrin], *s.* (vet.) morriña.

murre [mœr], *s.* (orn.) uria; especie de alca.

murrey [mœri], *a.* morado.

murr(h)ine [mœrin], *a.* múrrino.

musaceous [mjuzéiʂʌs], *a.* (bot.) musáceo.

muscadine [máskadin], *s.* (bot.) variedad de vid; mosqueruela, variedad de pera.

muscardine [máskardin], *s.* muscardina, enfermedad de los gusanos de seda.

muscat(el [máskæt, mʌskatél], *s.* (bot.) moscatel (uva y vino); especie de pasa.

muscid [másid], *a.* y *s.* (ent.) múscido.

muscle [másl], *s.* (anat.) músculo; fuerza muscular; (zool.) = MUSSEL.

muscoid [máskoid], **muscose** [máskous], *a.* musgoso.

muscosity [mʌskásiti], *s.* abundancia de musgo.

muscovado [mʌskovéidou], *s.* azúcar mascabado.

Muscovite [máskovait], *s.* y *a.* moscovita, *mf.*; *a.* moscovítico; (**m.**, min.) *s.* muscovita, mica potásica.

Muscovy duck [máskovi], *s.* (orn.) ánade o pato almizcleño.—**M. glass**, (min.) = MUSCOVITE.

muscular [máskjulǽ(r)], *a.* muscular; musculoso, vigoroso, fornido.

muscularity [-ǽriti], *s.* muscularidad, calidad de muscular o musculoso.

musculature [-achur], *s.* musculatura.

Muse [mjúz]. **I.** *s.* (mit.) musa; (**m.**) meditación o abstracción profunda; (poét.) estro, numen. **II.** (**m.**) *vn.* meditar, reflexionar, rumiar, estar absorto.—**to m. on, over,** o **upon**, meditar en.

museful [-ful], *a.* cogitabundo, pensativo.

musette [mjuzét], *s.* (mús.) especie de gaita o de chirimía.—**m.**, o **m. bag**, (mil.) mochila pequeña.

museum [mjuzíʌm], *s.* museo; gabinete.

mush [mʌʂ], *s.* (E. U.) especie de gachas o puches de harina de maíz; masa blanda y espesa; (fam.) sentimentalismo exagerado; (rad.) ruido como de chisporroteo debido a irregularidades del aparato transmisor.

mushroom [máʂrum]. **I.** *s.* (bot.) seta, hongo. **II.** *a.* hecho con hongos o setas; efímero, advenedizo; de desarrollo rápido. **III.** *vn.* recoger setas u hongos; tomar la forma de éstos; crecer o desarrollarse rápidamente.

mushy [máʂi], *a.* mollar, pulposo; (fam.) exageradamente sentimental.

music [mjúzik], *s.* música; composición musical; solfa; armonía, melodía.—**m. book**, libro de música.—**m. box**, o **musical box**, caja de música.—**m. cabinet**, musiquero.—**m. hall**, salón de conciertos; café concierto, café cantante.—**m. of the spheres**, armonía de las esferas celestes.—**m. paper**, papel de pauta. —**m. rack**, atril.—**m. school**, conservatorio de música.—**m. stand**, atril; tablado para una orquesta.

musical [-al], *a.* musical, músico; melodioso, canoro.—**m. comedy**, zarzuela.—**m. director**, director de música.

musicale [-ǽl], *s.* velada musical, concierto casero.

musically [-ali], *adv.* musicalmente, sonoramente.

musicalness [-alnis], *s.* armonía, melodía.

musician [mjuzíʂan], *s.* músico.

musing [mjúziŋ]. **I.** *a.* meditabundo, contemplativo, pensativo. **II.** *s.* cogitación, meditación.

musk [mʌsk]. **I.** *s.* almizcle; olor o perfume de almizcle; (zool.) almizclero.—**m. apple**, camuesa o manzana almizcleña.—**m. cat** = CIVET.—**m. cherry**, cereza almizcleña.—**m. deer**, almizclero.—**m. grape**, moscatel.—**m. melon**, melón.—**m. ox**, o **sheep**, carnero almizcleño.—**m. pear**, mosqueruela.—**m. rose**, mosqueta, rosa almizcleña.—**m. seed**, semilla del abelmosco. **II.** *va.* almizclar, perfumar con almizcle.

muskalonge [máskalandʒ], **muskellunge**

[-lʌndž], s. (ict.) especie de sollo muy grande.

musket [mʌ́skịt], s. mosquete, fusil; (orn.) gavilán macho.—**m. shot**, mosquetazo, fusilazo.

musketeer [-tị́r], s. mosquetero, fusilero.

musketry [-trị], s. mosquetería, fusilería.

muskiness [mʌ́skịnịs], s. olor de almizcle.

muskmelon [-mɛlọn], s. (bot.) melón.

muskrat [-ræt], s. (zool.) rata almizclera.

musky [-ị], a. almizclero (-cleño o -clado).

Muslem, Muslim, a. y s. = MOSLEM.

muslin [mʌ́zlịn]. I. s. (tej.) muselina; percal; (enc.) percalina. II. a. de muselina; de percal.—**m. glass**, vidrio de muselina.

musquash [mʌ́skwaš], s. (zool.) rata almizclera.

muss [mʌs]. I. s. (fam.) desorden, confusión; arrebatiña. II. va. (fam.) desordenar, desarreglar, descabellar, manosear, arrugar; ensuciar.

mussel [mʌ́sẹl], s. (zool.) mejillón, mítulo; almeja, tel(l)ina, chirla.

Mussulman [mʌ́salmạn], s. musulmán.

must [mʌst]. I. v. defect. cuyas formas equivalen a las de deber, tener que, haber de, deber de (I must write, debo escribir, tengo que escribir; it must be late, debe de ser tarde). También se traduce por las voces estar obligado, ser menester, necesario o preciso, convenir, etc. A veces se subentiende el infinitivo que le sigue [you must, Vd. debe (hacerlo, escribir, hablar, etc.); I must (go) to the city, debo partir para la ciudad].—**m. needs**, debe (debo, etc.) necesariamente o sin falta.—**it m. not be**, eso no puede ser, eso no debe permitirse. II. a. de carácter obligatorio, que obliga. III. s. necesidad, cosa obligatoria o indispensable.

must, s. mosto, zumo de la uva; moho.

mustache [mʌstǽš], **mustachio** [-joụ], s. bigote, mostacho; especie de mono; (gal.) soldado.—**mustached** [-d], a. mostachoso.

mustang [mʌ́stæŋ], s. potro mesteño o (semi)-salvaje, (Am.) mustango.

mustard [mʌ́stạrd], s. mostaza (planta, semilla y salsa); jenab(l)e.—**m. gas**, iperita o yperita, líquido para granadas de gas; gas mostaza, gas de iperita.—**m. paper, m. plaster**, sinapismo.—**m. pot**, mostacera.

Mustelidae [mʌstélịdị], s. pl. (zool.) mustélidas.

musteline, o **musteloid** [mʌ́stịlịn, -lọịd], a. (zool.) mustelino, que se parece a la comadreja.

muster [mʌ́stœ(r)]. I. va. reunir; (mil.) juntar para pasar revista, pasar lista, etc.—**to m. in**, o **into, service**, (mil.) alistar.—**to m. out (of service)** dar de baja.—**to m. up**, tomar (valor, fuerza, resignación, etc.). II. vn. (mil.) juntarse; pasar lista. III. s. (mil.) revista, muestra; rol, lista, reseña; alarde, muestra.—**m. book**, rol, lista.—**m. roll**, matrícula de revista; (mil.) muestra; (mar.) rol de la tripulación.—**to pass m.**, llenar los requisitos.

mustily [mʌ́stịlị], adv. con moho.

mustiness [mʌ́stịnịs], s. husmo; moho.

musty [mʌ́stị], a. mohoso; añejo; rancio; pasado; mustio, triste.

mutability [mjụtạbị́lịtị], s. mutabilidad.

mutable [mjụ́tạbl], a. mudable, inconstante, veleidoso.—**mutableness** [-nịs], s. mutabilidad, inconstancia.—**mutably** [-blị], adv. mudablemente.

mutant [mjụ́tạnt]. I. a. variable que sufre mutación. II. s. (biol.) mutante.

mutate [mjụ́tẹịt], va. y vn. transformar(se), alterar(se); (biol.) variar bruscamente.

mutation [-éịšọn], s. mudanza, alteración, cambio; (biol., etc.) mutación, variación brusca.

mute [mjụt]. I. a. mudo; callado, silencioso; (fon.) mudo. II. s. mudo; (fon.) letra muda; (mús.) sordina. III. va. (mús.) poner sordina a.

mutely [-lị], adv. mudamente.

muteness [-nịs], s. mudez, mutismo.

mutilate [mjụ́tịlẹịt], va. mutilar; truncar, tronchar, estropear.—**mutilated** [-ịd], a. mútilo, trunco, mocho.—**mutilation** [-éịšọn], s. mutilación.—**mutilator** [-ọ(r)], s. mutilador.

mutineer [mjụtịnị́r], s. amotinado(r), sedicioso.

mutinous [mjụ́tịnʌs], a. amotinado, sedicioso, turbulento, faccioso.—**mutinously** [-lị], adv. amotinadamente, sediciosamente.—**mutinousness** [-nịs], s. carácter sedicioso.

mutiny [mjụ́tịnị]. I. vn. amotinarse, rebelarse. II. s. motín, amotinamiento, insubordinación.

mutism [mjụ́tịzm], s. mutismo, mudez.

mutt [mʌt], s. (fam.) tonto, mentecato; perro atravesado o mestizo.

mutter [mʌ́tœ(r)]. I. va. y vn. murmurar, rezongar, refunfuñar, gruñir; bisbisar, hablar o decir entre dientes. II. s. refunfuñadura, gruñido.—**mutterer** [-œ(r)], s. rezongador, gruñón.—**muttering** [-ịŋ], s. rezongo; bisbiseo.

mutton [mʌ́tọn], s. carne (f.) de carnero.—**m. broth**, caldo de carnero.—**m. chop**, chuleta o costilla de carnero; pl. barba de chuleta.—**m. fish**, (ict.) barbero.—**m. fist** (fam.) manaza, mano grande y colorada; (impr.) manecilla.

muttony [-ị], a. de sabor de carnero.

mutual [mjụ́chụal], a. mutuo, mutual, recíproco.—**m. aid**, apoyo mutuo.—**m. company**, compañía mutual.—**m. help association**, mutualidad.—**m. insurance**, seguro mutuo.—**m. wall**, pared medianera.—**by m. consent**, de común acuerdo.

mutuality [-ǽlịtị], s. mutualidad; reciprocación, reciprocidad.

mutually [-ị], adv. mutuamente.

mutualness [-nịs], s. mutualidad.

mutuary [mjụ́chụẹrị], s. (for.) mutua(ta)rio.

mutule [mjụ́chul], s. (arq.) mútulo, modillón.

mutuum [mjụ́chụʌm], s. (for.) mutuo.

muzzle [mʌ́zl]. I. s. morro, hocico, jeta (de un animal); bozal, mordaza, frenillo; boca de arma de fuego.—**m.-loader**, arma que se carga por la boca.—**m. ring**, anillo de la boca de un cañón.—**m. velocity**, velocidad inicial o de salida. II. va. emboz(al)ar, abozalar, poner bozal; amordazar, imponer silencio. III. vn. hocicar.

muzzy [mʌ́zị], a. confuso; indistinto; peneque.

my [maị], a. pos. mi, mis.—**oh, my!** (fam.) ¡Ave María! ¡cáspita!

myasthenia [maịasθínịạ], s. miastenia, astenia muscular, debilidad muscular.

mycelium [maịsílịʌm], s. (bot.) micelión.

Mycenaean [maịsịníạn], a. micénico.

mycology [maịkálọdžị], s. (bot.) mic(et)ología.

mycosis [maịkóụsịs], s. (med.) micosis.

mydriasis [mịdráịạsịs], s. (med.) midríasis.

myelitis [maịẹláịtịs], s. (med.) mielitis.

mylodont [máịlọdạnt], s. (pal.) milodonte.

Mynheer [maịnhɛ́r], s. señor, título de cortesía en Holanda; (m.) holandés.

myocarditis [maịọkardáịtịs], s. (med.) miocarditis.

myocardium [-kárdịạm], s. (anat.) miocardio.

myograph [-græf], s. miógrafo.

myography [maịágrạfị], s. (anat.) miografía.

myology [maịálọdžị], s. (anat.) miología.

myoma [maịóụmạ], s. (med.) mioma, m.

myopathy [maịápạθị], s. (med.) miopatía.

myope, myops [máịọụp, -s], s. miope.

myopia [maịóụpịạ], **myopy** [máịọpị], s. miopía.

myopic [maịápịk], a. miope, corto de vista.

myoscope [máịọskọụp], s. = MYOGRAPH.

myosin [máịọsịn], s. (bioquím.) miosina.

myosis [maịóụsịs], s. (med.) miosis.

myosotis [maịọsóụtịs], s. (bot.) miosota o miosotis, raspilla, nomeolvides, f.

myotic [maịátịk], a. miótico.

myriad [mịrịạd]. I. s. miríada; diez mil; millares, un gran número. II. a. innumerable, numeroso.

myriagram [mịrịạgræm], s. miriagramo.

myrialiter [-litœ(r)], s. mirialitro.

myriameter [-mitœ(r)], *s.* miriámetro.

myriapod [-pad], *s.* y *a.* (zool.) miriápodo, miriópodo.

myrmidon [mœrmidon], *s.* esbirro, rufián.

myrobalan [majrábalan], *s.* (bot.) mirobálano(s).

myrrh [mœr], *s.* mirra, goma resinosa.

myrrhic [-ik], *a.* mirrado, mirrino.

myrtaceous [mœrtéjsjʌs], *a.* (bot.) mirtáceo.

myrtiform [mœrtiform], *a.* mirtino.

myrtle [mœrtl], *s.* (bot.) mirto, murto, arrayán. —**m. berry**, murtón, baya del mirto.—**m. wax**, cera del arrayán brabántico o de la mírica cerífera.

Myrtus [mœrtʌs], *s.* (bot.) murtilla.

myself [majsélf], *pron.* yo mismo; me, mí, mí mismo (*I said to myself*, me dije a mí mismo o para mí; *I myself did it*, yo mismo lo hice).

mystagogue [místagag], *s.* mistagogo.

mysterious [mistírjʌs], *a.* misterioso.—**mysteriously** [-li], *adv.* misteriosamente.—**mysteriousness** [-njs], *s.* misterio, calidad de misterioso.

mystery [místeri], *s.* misterio; arcano; (teat.) auto sacramental. *V.* MIRACLE PLAY.—**m. boat**, o **ship**, buque armado disfrazado de buque mercante indefenso.

mystic(al [místjk(al], *a.* y *s.* místico.—**mystically** [-i], *adv.* místicamente.—**mysticalness** [-njs], *s.* calidad de místico.

mysticism [-sizm], *s.* misticismo.

mystification [-fikéjʃən], *s.* ofuscación, confusión, perplejidad; mixtificación; superchería.—**mystify** [-faj], *va.* confundir, desconcertar, ofuscar; mixtificar.

myth [miθ], *s.* mito; fábula; ficción.

mythical [-ikal], *a.* mítico; fabuloso.

mythologic(al [miθoládʒik(al], *a.* mitológico.

mythologically [-i], *adv.* mitológicamente.

mythologist [miθálodʒist], *s.* mitólogo, mitologista.—**mythologize** [-dʒajz]. I. *va.* convertir en mito; interpretar mitológicamente. II. *vn.* explicar las fábulas mitológicas.

mythology [-dʒi], *s.* mitología.

mythopeic [miθopíjk], *a.* creador de mitos.

Myxomycetes [miksomajsítiz], *s. pl.* (bot.) mixomicetos.

N

n [ɛn], *s.* n.

nab [næb], *va.* (fam.) prender, atrapar, agarrar, echar mano a, echar el guante a.

nabob [néjbab], *s.* nabab(o); ricacho, fúcar.

nacelle [næsél], *s.* (aer.) barquilla.

nacre [néjkœ(r)], *s.* nácar, madreperla.

nacreous [néjkrjʌs], *a.* nacarado, nacarino.

nadir [néjdœ(r)], *s.* (astr.) nadir.

naevoid, *a.* **nævus**, *s.* = NEVUS.

nag [næg]. I. *s.* haca(nea), jaca o jaco, caballejo; (fam.) jamelgo, penco. II. *va.* y *vn.* (a veces con **at**) regañar, machacar, encocorar, sermonear.

naiad [néjvad], *s.* (mitol.) náyade, *f.*

naif [naíf], *a.* cándido, sencillo; (joy.) lustroso en bruto. *V.* NAIVE.

nail [néjl]. I. *s.* (anat.. zool.) uña; pezuña, garra; clavo; tachón, punta; roblón; medida de 2¼ pulgadas.—**n. bed**, (anat.) matriz de la uña.—**n. cleaner**, limpiauñas.—**n. extractor**, o **puller**, cazaclavos, pata de cabra, menestrete, arrancaclavos, desclavador.—**n. file**, lima para las uñas.—**n. hole**, clavera.—**n. plate**, metal en plancha para clavos.—**n. polish**, esmalte.—**n. scratch**, uñada, arañazo.—**n. set**, punzón, botador.—**on the n.**, luego, al instante, en el acto. II. *va.* clavar, enclavar, guarnecer o adornar con clavos; (fam.) = TO NAB.—**to n. a lie**, demostrar que una cosa es mentira.—**to n. down**, o **nail up**, sujetar con clavos; condenar (una ventana, etc.), clavándola.

nailbrush [-brʌʃ], *s.* cepillo para las uñas.

nailer [-œ(r)], *s.* fabricante de clavos.

nailery [-œri], *s.* fábrica de clavos.

nainsook [néjnsuk], *s.* (Am., tej.) nansú o nanzú.

naissant [néjsant], *a.* (blas.) naciente.

naive, naïve [naív], *a.* ingenuo, cándido.—**naively** [-li], *adv.* cándidamente, candorosamente.

naiveté [-téj], *s.* candidez, candor, ingenuidad.

naked [néjkid], *a.* desnudo; en carnes, en cueros, (fam.) en pelota; descamisado, indigente; descubierto, sin defensa; patente; simple.—**n. sword**, espada desnuda, desenvainada.—**the n. truth**, la verdad pura o desnuda.—**(with the) n. eye**, (a) simple vista.

nakedly [-li], *adv.* desnudamente; claramente.—**nakedness** [-njs], *s.* desnudez; partes pudendas.

nam(e)able [néjmabl], *a.* que puede recibir nombre, nombrable.

namby-pamby [næmbi pæmbi]. I. *a.* melindroso, afectado, insípido. II. *s.* pamplina, melindre; persona insípida o sentimental.

name [néjm]. I. *s.* nombre; apellido; (fam.) gracia; denominación; título; nombradía, fama, reputación, crédito; autoridad, poder, representación.—**n. day**, día (*m.*) del santo, días de uno, fiesta onomástica.—**n. plate**, rótulo, letrero, plancha con el nombre de uno. —**n. saint**, santo de uno.—**by u of the n. of**, llamado, nombrado.—**in n.**, de nombre.—**in the n. of**, en nombre de.—**to one's n.**, que pertenece a uno. II. *va.* nombrar, apellidar, llamar, poner nombre; mentar, mencionar; proferir; especificar, elegir, señalar, designar, fijar.

nameless [-ljs], *a.* sin nombre, innominado, anónimo; desconocido.

namely [-li], *adv.* señaladamente, especialmente; a saber, o sea, es decir.

namesake [-sejk], *s.* tocayo; homónimo.

nanism [néjnjzm], *s.* (e)nanismo, calidad de enano.

nankeen, nankin [nænkín], *s.* (tej.) mahón, nanquín.—*pl.* pantalón o traje de nanquín.

nanny [nænj], *s.* niñera.—**n. goat**, (zool.) cabra.

naos [néjas], *s.* templo; (arq.) nave, *f.*

nap [næp]. I. *s.* siesta, sueño ligero; vello de las plantas; (tej.) borra, lanilla, pelusa. II. *va.* (tej.) perchar, carmenar, sacar pelo. III. *vn.* dormitar, echar una siesta, descabezar el sueño; estar desprevenido, dormirse (fig.).—**to catch napping**, coger desapercibido.

Nap(a)ea [napíá], *s.* (mit. y bot.) napea.

nape [nejp], *s.* nuca, cogote, cerviz; testuz, *m.*

napery [néjpœri], *s.* ropa blanca; mantelería.

naphtha [næfθá], *s.* nafta.

naphthalene [-lin], *s.* (quím.) naftalina.

naphthol [næfθol], *s.* (quím.) naftol.

Nap(i)erian [nejpírjan], *a.* (mat.) neperiano, de Néper.

napiform [néjpiform], *a.* de forma de nabo.

napkin [næpkin], *s.* servilleta; sabanilla, to(b)alleta; pañal.—**n. ring**, servilletero.

napless [næpljs], *a.* sin vello o pelusa; raído.

napoleon [napóuljon], *s.* napoleón (moneda); juego de naipes; pastelito de hojaldre y crema.

Napoleonic [napouljánjk], *a.* napoleónico.

napped [næpt], *a.* peludo, velloso.

napper [næpœ(r)], *s.* el que duerme, sestea o tiene el sueño muy ligero; (tej.) perchador.

nappiness [næpjnjs], *s.* vellosidad.

nappy [næpj], *a.* = NAPPED; encabezado, fuerte (vino).

narcein(e [nársjin], *s.* (quím.) narceína.

narcissism [narsísjzm], **narcism** [nársjzm], *s.* narcisismo, admiración o enamoramiento de sí mismo.

narcissus [narsísʌs], *s.* (bot.) narciso.

narcosis [narkóusis], *s.* (med.) narcosis.

narcotic [narkátik], *s.* y *a.* narcótico.

narcotin(e [nárkotįn], *s.* (quím.) narcotina.—
narcotism [-įzm], *s.* narcotismo.—**narcotize**
[-aįz], *va.* narcotizar.—**narcotization** [narka-
tįzéįşǫn], *s.* narcotismo; narcotización.
nard [nárd], *s.* (bot.) nardo.
nardine [-įn], *a.* nardino.
nares [néįriz], *s. pl.* de NARIS, *s.* (anat.) orificio o
ventana de la nariz.
narg(h)ile [nárgįlį], *s.* narguile.
narrate [næréįt], *va.* y *vn.* narrar, relatar, relacionar, referir.—**narration** [næréįşǫn], *s.*
narración, relación.—**narrative** [nǽrątįv]. **I.**
a. narrativo. **II.** *s.* narración, narrativa, relato.
—**narratively** [-lį], *adv.* narrativamente.—
narrator [nǽréįto(r)], *s.* narrador, relatador.—
narratory [nǽrątǫrį], *a.* narratorio.
narrow [nǽrou]. **I.** *a.* angosto, estrecho; escaso,
limitado; apretado, encogido; tacaño, mez-
quino; de ideas poco liberales; próximo, cercano, aproximado; atento, escrupuloso.—**n.-
chested**, angosto de pecho(s).—**n. circumstances**, escasez pecuniaria, cortos posibles.
—**n. escape**, o (fam.) **squeak**, escapada en
una tabla.—**n.-gauge railway**, ferrocarril de
vía angosta.—**n.-hipped**, escurrido.—**n.-
minded**, apocado, mezquino; intolerante,
fanático, estrecho (de conciencia, etc.).—**n.-
mindedness**, estrechez de miras.—**n. pass**,
desfiladero, hoz.—**n. sea**, estrecho de mar.—
n.-spirited, *o* **n.-souled** = N.-MINDED.—**n.-
waisted**, ceñido. **II.** *s. pl.* bocal, pasaje angosto;
estrechura; desfiladero. **III.** *va.* estrechar,
angostar, contraer, encoger, disminuir; limitar.
IV. *vn.* estrecharse, encogerse, reducirse; reducir el número de puntos al hacer calceta;
(equit.) andar con las patas muy juntas.—**to
n. down to**, reducirse a.
narrowly [-lį], *adv.* estrechamente, angostamente, reducidamente; por poco, escasamente;
mezquinamente.
narrowness [-nįs], *s.* angostura, estrechura,
apretura; estrechez, pobreza.
narthex [nárθeks], *s.* (arq., igl.) pórtico.
narwhal [nárhwạl], *s.* (zool.) narval.
nary [nérį *o* néįrį], *a.* (dial.) ninguno, ni uno solo.
—**n. a thing**, maldita la cosa.—**n. a whit**, ni
pizca. *V.* NEVER A.
nasal [néįzạl]. **I.** *a.* (anat., fon.) nasal.—**n.
twang**, gangueo. **II.** *s.* (fon.) letra nasal;
(anat.) hueso de la nariz; (arm.) barra que
protege la nariz.
nasality [-ǽlįtį], *s.* sonido nasal; nasalidad.
nasalization [-įzéįşǫn], *s.* nasalización.
nasalize [-aįz], *va.* y *vn.* (fon.) nasalizar, ganguear, pronunciar con sonido nasal.
nasally [-į], *adv.* nasalmente, con gangueo.
nasard [nǽzạrd], *s.* (mús.) nasardo.
nascent [nǽsẹnt], *a.* naciente; creciente.
nastily [nǽstįlį], *adv.* puerca o asquerosamente.
nastiness [-nįs], *s.* suciedad, porquería.
nasturtium [nạstǽrşįʌm], *s.* (bot.) berro;
tropeolo, capuchina.
nasty [nǽstį], *a.* sucio, asqueroso; obsceno, indecente; impuro, sórdido; desagradable, ofensivo; avieso; intratable; detestable.
natal [néįtạl], *a.* nativo, natio; natal; (anat.)
nalgar, rel. a las nalgas. *V.* NATES.
natality [neįtǽlįtį], *s.* natalidad.
natant [néįtạnt], *a.* (bot.) nadante, flotante.
natation [neįtéįşǫn], *s.* natación.
natatorial [neįtạtǫ́rįạl], **natatory** [néįtạtǫrį], *a.*
natatorio; natátil.
natatorium [-tǫ́rįʌm], *s.* natatorio, piscina de
natación.
nates [néįtiz], *s. pl.* (anat.) nalgas, nalgatorio.
nation [néįşǫn], *s.* nación, país; pueblo, gente, *f.*
national [nǽşǫnạl]. **I.** *a.* nacional; gentilicio;
patriótico.—**n. anthem**, himno nacional.—
N. Army, (E. U.) ejército reclutado, parte del
ejército formada por reclutamiento.—**n. debt**,
deuda pública.—**N. Guard**, milicia nacional.

n. monument, (E. U.) terrenos nacionales
reservados, parte del territorio del país reservada por el gobierno para usos nacionales.—
n. park, (E. U.) vasta región de tierras nacionales, gen. con curiosidades naturales,
reservada por el gobierno para el público. **II.**
s. (con)ciudadano; súbdito.
nationalism [-įzm], *s.* nacionalismo; forma
reciente del socialismo; amor a la independencia nacional, patriotismo; idiotismo, costumbre, rasgo nacional peculiar o característico.—
nationalist [-įst], *s.* y *a.* nacionalista.
nationality [-ǽlįtį], *s.* nacionalidad; nación;
ciudadanía, patriotismo; naturaleza, naturalidad.—**by n.**, de nación.
nationalization [-įzéįşǫn], *s.* conversión en
nación, creación en nación; nacionalización,
puesta bajo la dirección o en poder de la
nación; (con)naturalización.
nationalize [-aįz], *va.* convertir en nación; nacionalizar, poner bajo la dirección o en poder
de la nación; naturalizar.
nationally [-į], *adv.* nacionalmente.
native [néįtįv]. **I.** *a.* nativo, natal, natural,
oriundo u originario; indígena, autóctono;
vernáculo; nacional, del país, patrio; (min.)
nativo, natío.—**n.-born**, natural, nativo.—**n.
country**, o **land**, patria, país natal, terruño,
origen.—**n. gold**, oro natío.—**n. place**, suelo
o tierra natal.—**n. silver**, plata nativa o virgen.
—**n. soil**, país natal. **II.** *s.* natural, *mf.*, indígena, *mf.*, vecino (de un lugar), nacional;
producto nacional.
natively [-lį], *adv.* naturalmente, originalmente,
originariamente.
nativeness [-nįs], *s.* calidad de nativo.
nativity [neįtįvįtį], *s.* nacimiento, natividad,
natalicio; (astr.) horóscopo; (N.) Navidad.
natrium [néįtrįʌm], *s.* (quím.) sodio.
natron [néįtrǫn], *s.* (min.) natrón.
nattily [nǽtįlį], *adv.* garbosamente.—**nattiness**
[-nįs], *s.* (fam.) garbo, gentileza.
natty [-į], *a.* elegante, garboso, galano, jarifo.
natural [nǽchụrạl]. **I.** *a.* natural, nativo; sencillo, inafectado; genuino, verdadero; normal,
ordinario; bastardo, natural; (mús.) natural.—
n. draft, *o* **draught**, tiro natural.—**n. features**, aspecto físico, geografía física.—**n. gas**,
gas natural.—**n. history**, historia natural.—
n. law, ley (*f.*) natural; derecho natural.—**n.
magic**, magia blanca.—**n. philosophy**,
física.—**n. resources**, riquezas naturales.—
n. science, ciencias naturales.—**n. selection**,
selección natural.—**n. theology**, teología
natural. **II.** *s.* idiota, *mf.*, simplón; persona
muy apta para hacer alguna cosa; (mús.) becuadro; tecla blanca; nota natural.
naturalism [-įzm], *s.* naturalismo.
naturalist [-įst], *s.* y *a.*, **naturalistic** [-įstįk], *a.*
naturalista.
naturalization [-įzéįşǫn], *s.* naturalización;
nacionalización; aclimatación.—**n. papers**,
carta de naturaleza.
naturalize [-aįz], *va.* naturalizar; nacionalizar;
habituar; aclimatar.
naturally [-į], *adv.* naturalmente; desde luego.
naturalness [-nįs], *s.* naturalidad; sencillez.
nature [néįchụ(r)], *s.* natura(leza); natural,
índole, *f.*, genio, carácter; especie, género,
clase, *f.*; naturalidad, espontaneidad.—**n.
study**, estudio objetivo de la naturaleza.—
from n., (b. a.) del natural.
naught [nǫt], *s.* nada; cero, la cifra 0.—**to come
to n.**, malograrse, frustrarse.—**to set at n.**,
hacer tabla rasa de.
naughtily [nǫ́tįlį], *adv.* pícara o traviesamente;
malvada o perversamente.
naughtiness [-nįs], *s.* maldad, perversidad;
picardía, travesura.
naughty [nǫ́tį], *a.* perverso; desobediente, dís-

colo; pícaro, travieso.—n. **boy,** picaruelo.—n. **trick,** picardihuela; pillada.

naumachy [nɔ́mǝki], s. naumaquia.

nausea [nɔ́si̯ǝ], s. náusea, basca, asco.

nauseant [-nt]. **I.** a. (med.) nauseante, nauseabundo. **II.** s. substancia que produce náuseas o bascas.

nauseate [nɔ́si̯ei̯t]. **I.** va. dar asco o disgusto, apestar. **II.** vn. nausear, asquear.

nauseating [-i̯n], **nauseous** [nɔ́si̯ʌs], a. nauseativo, nauseoso, nauseabundo, asqueroso, apestoso.—**nauseously** [-li̯], adv. nauseosa o asquerosamente.—**nauseousness** [-ni̯s], s. náusea, asquerosidad.

nautch [nɔch], s. baile de la India.—n. **girl,** bayadera, bailarina india.

nautical [nɔ́tikǝl], a. náutico, marino.—n. **cap,** gorra marina.—n. **mile,** milla marina o náutica, nudo (6080 pies).

nautics [nɔ́tiks], s. náutica.

nautilus [nɔ́ti̯lʌs], s. (zool.) nautilo, argonauta, m.

naval [néi̯vǝl], a. naval; de marina.—n. **auxiliary,** barco auxiliar.—n. **base, o station,** base (f.) naval; apostadero.—n. **law,** código naval.—n. **officer,** oficial de marina; (E. U.) capitán de puerto.—n. **stores,** artículos navales; productos resinosos.—n. **vessel,** barco de guerra.

navarch [néi̯vark], s. (hist. gr. y rom.) navarca, m.

Navarrese [næværíz], a. y s. navarro.

nave [nei̯v], s. (arq.) nave, f.; (carr.) cubo de rueda, maza.—n. **box,** buje, arandela, loriga.

navel [néi̯vl], s. (anat.) ombligo; centro, medio, parte (f.) interior.—n. **orange,** variedad de naranja sin semillas.—n. **string,** ombligo, cordón umbilical.—n.-**shaped,** umbilicado.

naveled [-d], a. umbilicado.

navelwort [-wœrt], s. (bot.) oreja de monje, ombligo de Venus.

navicert [névi̯sœrt], s. (Ingl.) certificado de navegación que permite pasar por el bloqueo británico.

navicular [nǝvíkyu̯lǝ(r)]. **I.** a. navicular; escafoides. **II.** s. (anat.) fosa o hueso navicular.

navigability [nævi̯gǝbíli̯ti̯], **navigableness** [-ǝblni̯s], s. calidad de navegable.

navigable [-ǝbl], a. navegable.

navigate [-ei̯t], va. y vn. navegar; marear.

navigating [-ei̯ti̯n], a. navegador, navegante.

navigation [-éi̯ʃǝn], s. navegación (de altura, costanera o aérea); náutica, mareaje; (raro) marina, naves, f. pl.

navigator [-ei̯tǝ(r)], s. navegador, navegante, mareante; piloto; tratado de náutica.

navvy [névi̯], s. (Ingl.) peón, bracero; máquina excavadora.

navy [néi̯vi̯], s. armada, marina de guerra, flota. —n. **bean,** (bot.) frijol blanco ordinario.—n. **blue,** azul oscuro.—N. **Department,** (E. U.) Ministerio de Marina.—N. **Office,** (Ingl.) Almirantazgo.—n. **yard,** arsenal, astillero.

nawab [nǝwɔ́b], s. nabab(o). V. NABOB.

nay [nei̯]. **I.** adv. no; de ningún modo; más aún, y aun. **II.** s. voto negativo; negación.

Nazarene [næzǝrín], a. y s. nazare(n)o.

Nazarite [næzǝrai̯t], s. nazare(n)o (sectario hebreo).

naze [nei̯z], s. cabo, promontorio.

Nazi [nátsi̯], s. y a. nazi, nazista.

Nazi(i)sm [nátsi̯(i)zm], s. nazismo.

Neanderthaloid [nejandœrtálɔi̯d], a. neandertaliano, del tipo del hombre de Neanderthal.

neap [nip], s. marea muerta (ll. t. n. tide).

Neapolitan [niǝpáli̯tǝn], a. y s. napolitano.

near [nír]. **I.** prep. cerca de, junto a, próximo a, cabe, por, hacia. **II.** adv. cerca; próximamente; (fam.) casi.—n. **at hand,** a (la) mano, cerca. **III.** a. cercano, próximo, inmediato, vecino; inminente; allegado; íntimo, estrecho; cica-

tero, tacaño; exacto; literal; imitado (near seal, imitación de piel de foca; near silk, seda imitada, imitación de seda); a punto de, por poco (cambiando el giro: we were in a near accident, por poco tenemos un accidente).—n. **beer,** (E. U.) cerveza no embriagante, de muy pequeña proporción de alcohol (puede llamarse cerveza aguada).—N. **East,** Levante.—n. **relation, o relative,** pariente cercano.—n. **wheel,** rueda izquierda. **IV.** va. y vn. acercar(se).

nearby, o near-by [-bai̯]. **I.** prep. cerca de. **II.** adv. cerca, a (la) mano. **III.** a. cercano, contiguo, próximo.

nearer [-œ(r)], a. (comp. de NEAR) más cercano; citerior.

nearest [-i̯st], a. (super. de NEAR) más cercano, próximo.

nearly [-li̯], adv. cerca, cerca de; estrechamente; mezquinamente; casi; íntimamente, de cerca; próximamente, aproximadamente.

nearness [-ni̯s], s. proximidad, cercanía; inminencia; parentesco cercano; amistad estrecha; mezquindad.

nearsighted [-sái̯ti̯d], a. miope, corto de vista.

nearsightedness [-ni̯s], s. miopía, vista corta.

neat [nit]. **I.** a. limpio, aseado, pulcro; bonito, pulido, lindo; neto, mondo, lirondo; puro, casto, natural; puro, sin mezcla; nítido, claro; gallardo; esmerado; perteneciente al ganado vacuno; (com.) neto. V. NET.—n. **cattle,** ganado vacuno.—n.-**handed,** diestro. **II.** s. ganado vacuno; vaca o buey. f.; n.'s-**foot oil,** aceite de pata de vaca.—n.'s **leather,** cuero de buey.—n.'s **tongue,** lengua de vaca.

'**neath** [niθ], forma apocopada de BENEATH.

neatherd [níthœrd], s. vaquero.

neatly [nítli̯], adv. pulidamente, nítidamente; primorosamente; limpiamente, aseadamente; elegantemente; diestramente, mañosamente.

neatness [nítni̯s], s. aseo, pulcritud, nitidez, limpieza; pulidez, elegancia, delicadeza.

neb [neb], s. pico, boca; punta, cabo. V. NIB.

nebula [nébyu̯lǝ], s. (astr.) nebulosa; (med.) opacidad ligera de la córnea, nube (f.) en los ojos; enturbiamiento de la orina; (farm.) preparado líquido para rociar.

nebular [-(r)], a. nebuloso.—n. **hypothesis,** (astr.) hipótesis nebular, hipótesis de Laplace.

nebulizer [-lai̯zœ(r)], s. rociador, pulverizador.

nebulosity [-lási̯ti̯], s. nebulosidad.

nebulous [-lʌs], a. nebuloso; nublo(so); vago.

necessarian [neseséri̯ǝn], s. y a. determinista.

necessarianism [-i̯zm], s. (filos.) determinismo.

necessarily [néseseri̯li̯], adv. necesariamente.

necessary [néseseri̯]. **I.** a. necesario, preciso, forzoso; inevitable.—**to be n.,** ser menester, hacer falta. **II.** s. lo necesario; requisito esencial.—pl. **necessaries,** cosas necesarias o imprescindibles.

necessitarian [nisesitéri̯ǝn], s. y a. (filos.) determinista.—**necessitarianism** [-i̯zm], s. determinismo.

necessitate [nisésitei̯t], va. necesitar, exigir.

necessitous [-tʌs], a. necesitado, indigente.

necessity [-ti̯], s. necesidad, precisión; indigencia. —pl. **necessities,** artículos de primera necesidad, requisitos indispensables.—**of n.,** forzosamente.

neck [nék]. **I.** s. (anat.) cuello, garganta, pescuezo; cuello, gollete (de una botella); mástil (de guitarra o violín); degüello; (arq.) collarino; (cost.) escote, escotadura, degolladura; (geog.) istmo, cabo, península; desfiladero.—n. **and crop,** todo junto y a un tiempo.—n. **and heels,** de pies a cabeza, del todo.—n. **and n.,** (dep.) parejos, con igual rapidez en una carrera. —n. **handkerchief** = NECKERCHIEF.—n. **line,** (cost.) escote.—n. **of land,** lengua de tierra.—n. **or nothing,** a toda costa.—n. **yoke,** yugo de colleras; (carr.) volea.—**in, u on**

the n. of, luego, inmediatamente después, a raíz de. **II.** *va.* degollar; agarrotar.

neckband [-bænd], *s.* (cost.) cabezón o tirilla de camisa.

neckcloth [-klɔθ], *s.* corbata, corbatín.

neckerchief [-œrchĭf], *s.* corbata, corbatín; especie de pañoleta; bobillo.

necklace [-lĭs], **necklet** [-lĭt], *s.* collar, gargantilla.

neckpiece [-pis], *s.* estola, boa o bufanda de piel; gorguera; gorjal.

necktie [-tai], *s.* corbata; (E. U. fam.) dogal.

neckwear [-wɛr], *s.* cuellos, corbatas, boas, *m. pl.*, etc.

necrologic(al [nɛkrolɑ́dʒĭk(ạl], *a.* necrológico.

necrologist [nɛkrɑ́lodʒĭst], *s.* registrador de defunciones.

necrology [nɛkrɑ́lodʒĭ], *s.* necrología.

necromancer [nɛ́kromænsœ(r)], *s.* nigromante, mago; (fam.) brujo.—**necromancy** [-sĭ], *s.* nigromancia, magia negra; brujería.—**necromantic** [-mǽntĭk], *a.* nigromántico.

necrophagous [nɛkrǽfagʌs], *a.* necrófago, que se alimenta de cadáveres.

necropolis [nɛkrɑ́polĭs], *s.* necrópolis.

necropsy [nɛ́krapsĭ], **necroscopy** [nɛkrɑ́skopĭ], *s.* (med.) necropsia, necroscopía, autopsia.

necrosis [nɛkrɑ́usĭs], *s.* (med.) necrosis, gangrena.

nectar [nɛ́ktạ(r)], *s.* (mit., fig. y bot.) néctar.—**nectarean** [nɛktɛ́rĭạn], **nectareous** [-ʌs], **nectarial** [-ạl], *a.* nectáreo.

nectarine [nɛ́ktạrĭn]. **I.** *a.* nectáreo, nectarino. **II.** *s.* (bot.) abridor, variedad de pérsico.

nectary [nɛ́ktạrĭ], *s.* (bot.) nectario; (ent.) tubo para miel.

née, o **nee** [nei], *a.* (fr.) nacida; se usa para designar el apellido paterno de una mujer casada: *Mrs. Kate Brown, née Smith,* la Señora Kate Smith de Brown.

need [nid]. **I.** *s.* necesidad; carencia, falta; pobreza, miseria; situación o momento de apuro.—**if n. be,** si hubiere necesidad, si fuere necesario.—**in case of n.,** en caso necesario.—**there is no n. to worry,** no hay para qué apurarse.—**to be in need,** tener necesidad; estar necesitado. **II.** *va.* necesitar, haber menester, requerir, exigir; faltar, hacer falta. Antes de infinitivo se emplea como una especie de auxiliar invariable, sobre todo en expresiones negativas, en el sentido de no haber que, no ser necesario, no deber: *he need not go,* no es necesario que él vaya; *it need not be done,* no hay que hacerlo, no es necesario que se haga. **III.** *vn.* ser necesario, precisarse; estar en la necesidad, carecer de lo necesario.

needer [-œ(r)], *s.* necesitado.

needful [-fŭl], *a.* necesario; necesitado.—**needfully** [-ĭ], *adv.* necesariamente.—**needfulness** [-nĭs], *s.* necesidad, calidad de necesario.

needily [-ĭlĭ], *adv.* pobremente.

neediness [-inĭs], *s.* necesidad, pobreza.

needle [nidl]. **I.** *s.* aguja (de coser, de media, de gancho, de fonógrafo, etc.); (mar.) aguja de marear, brújula; (arq.) aguja, chapitel; obelisco; roca o piedra acicular.—**n. bar,** portaaguja de una máquina de coser.—**n. file,** lima de aguja.—**n. gun,** fusil de aguja.—**n. holder,** portaagujas, palillo, acerico.—**n. lace,** encaje de, o a, mano.—**n. maker, seller, o user,** aguiero.—**n. of a balance,** lengüeta, fiel de la balanza.—**n. of a dial,** aguja o estilo de un reloj de sol.—**n. point** = N. LACE; cierto bordado de lona; punta de aguja del compás y otros instrumentos; (arq.) aguja, chapitel.—**n. prick,** aguijazo.—**n.-shaped,** acicular.—**n.-threader,** ensartador de agujas.—**n. valve,** (mec.) válvula de aguja o ahusada. **II.** *va.* coser, herir o punzar con aguja; aguijonear; vejar, atormentar. **III.** *vn.* trabajar con aguja; (quím., min.) cristalizarse en forma de agujas.

needlecase [-keis], *s.* agujetero, alfiletero.

needlefish [-fĭš], *s.* (ict.) aguja (paladar).

needleful [-fŭl], *s.* hebra de hilo.

needleman [-man], *s.* sastre.

needler [nidlœ(r)], *s.* agujero.

needless [nidlĭs], *a.* inútil, innecesario, superfluo, ocioso.—**n. to say,** inútil es decir(lo).

needlessly [-lĭ], *adv.* innecesariamente.

needlessness [-nĭs], *s.* superfluidad, inutilidad.

needlewoman [nidlwŭman], *s.* costurera.

needlework [-wœrk], *s.* costura; labor, *f.*, bordado de aguja.

needs [nidz], *adv.* necesariamente, de necesidad.

needy [nidĭ], *a.* necesitado, menesteroso.

ne'er [nɛr], *adv. contr.* de NEVER.—**n.-do-well.** **I.** *s.* haragán, (fam.) pelafustán. **II.** *a.* inútil, sin valor.

nefarious [nĭfɛ́rĭʌs], *a.* nefando, nefario.

nefariously [-lĭ], *adv.* nefariamente.

nefariousness [-nĭs], *s.* calidad de nefario.

negate [nĭgéit], *va.* negar; anular.

negation [nĭgéišọn], *s.* negación.

negative [nɛ́gạtĭv]. **I.** *a.* negativo (en toda acepción). **II.** *s.* negativa; denegación; veto, derecho de rehusar; (gram.) negación; (foto.) negativo o (prueba) negativa; (elec.) electricidad negativa. **III.** *va.* denegar, desaprobar, negar; oponerse a, votar en contra de; poner su veto a; contradecir.

negatively [-lĭ], *adv.* negativamente.

negativism [-ĭzm], *s.* negativismo.

neglect [nĭglékt]. **I.** *s.* descuido, negligencia; inobservancia; abandono, desdén, desprecio, indiferencia; desuso; preterición. **II.** *va.* descuidar, desatender; olvidar; dejar de; abandonar; desdeñar, despreciar; arrinconar; preterir.

neglecter [-œ(r)], *s.* descuidado, negligente; despreciador.

neglectful [-fŭl], *a.* negligente, descuidado.—**neglectfully** [-ĭ], *adv.* negligentemente, descuidadamente.—**neglectfulness** [-nĭs], *s.* negligencia, descuido, incuria, abandono.

negligee, négligé [nɛglĭʒéi], *s.* traje libre o inceremonioso; bata de casa.

negligence [nɛ́glĭdʒẹns], *s.* negligencia.

negligent [-ẹnt], *a.* negligente.

negligently [-lĭ], *adv.* negligentemente.

negligible [-ĭbl], *a.* despreciable, insignificante.

negotiability [nĭgóušĭạbĭlĭtĭ], *s.* negociabilidad.

negotiable [-ạbl], *a.* negociable.

negotiate [-eĭt]. **I.** *va.* (com.) negociar, cambiar; gestionar, agenciar; (dipl.) negociar; (fam.) ejecutar, vencer, disponer de, salvar, superar. **II.** *vn.* negociar.—**negotiating** [-ĭŋ], *a.* negociante, contratante.—**negotiation** [-éišọn], *s.* negociación; negocio, gestión, transacción.—**negotiator** [-eĭtọ(r)], *s.* negociador, gestor.

Negress [nígrĭs], *s.* negra.

Negrillo, Negrito [nĭgrílou, nĭgrítou], *s.* negrito africano o malayo de raza enana.

Negro [nígrou]. **I.** *s.* negro; (Cuba) bembo. **II.** *a.* negro, de raza negra; de negro; de los negros.

negroid [nígroĭd]. **I.** *a.* negroideo; parecido o rel. a los negros. **II.** *s.* persona de raza negroidea.

negrophile [nígrofaĭl], *s.* negrófilo, amigo o defensor de los negros.—**negrophobe** [-foŭb], *s.* y *a.* negrófobo, que teme u odia los negros.—**negrophobia** [-fóŭbị̆ạ], *s.* negrofobia, temor u odio de los negros.

negus [nígʌs], *s.* carraspada, sangría (bebida); (N.) negus, emperador de Abisinia.

neigh [nei]. **I.** *vn.* relinchar. **II.** *s.* relincho, hin.

neighbor [neibọ(r)]. **I.** *s.* vecino; prójimo. **II.** *va.* y *vn.* estar vecino o cercano a; ser vecino de; acercar; confinar. **III.** *a.* = NEIGHBORING.

neighborhood [-hụd]. **I.** *s.* vecindad; vecindario; barrio; cercanías, inmediaciones, alrededores.—**in the n. of,** (fam.) casi, como, aproximadamente. **II.** *a.* vecinal, del barrio.

neighboring [-ĭŋ], *a.* vecino, vecinal, próximo, rayano o cercano.

---

neighborliness [-linis]. *s.* cortesía de vecindad; buena vecindad; sociabilidad.

neighborly [-li]. *a.* sociable, amigable, como buen vecino.

neither [níðœ(r)]. **I.** *a.* ningún, ninguno de los dos. **II.** *conj.* ni; correlativo ordinario de NOR (v. gr.: *neither he nor she*, ni él ni ella); tampoco, ni siquiera (*neither will I do it*, yo tampoco lo haré). **III.** *pron.* ninguno, ni uno ni otro, ni el uno ni el otro.

Nemathelminthes [nɛmaθɛlmínθiz], *s. pl.* (zool.) nematelmintos.

nematode [nématoud], *s. y a.* (zool.) nemátodo.

Nemean [nimíən], *a.* nemeo.

Nemesis [némɛsis], *s.* (mit.) Némesis; (**n.**) justicia, venganza; agente de la justicia distributiva.

neo- [nio], *prefijo,* neo-, nuevo, reciente. Ú. en composición; v. gr.: *Neo-Catholic,* neocatólico.

neoclassic(al [-klǽsik(al], *a.* neoclásico.

neoclassicism [-sizm], *s.* neoclasicismo.

Neo-Latin [-lǽtin], *a.* neolatino.

neolith [nioliθ], *s.* herramienta u objeto neolíticos.

neolithic [niolíθik], *a.* neolítico.

neologic(al [niolódžik(al], *a.* neológico.

neologism [niálodžizm], *s.* neologismo.

neologist [-džist], *s.* neólogo.

neology [-dži], *s.* neología.

neomenia [niominíjá], *s.* (astr.) neomenia.

neon [nían], *s.* (quím.) neón, neo.—**n. lamp, light o tube,** lámpara o tubo neón.

neophyte [níofajt], *s.* neófito; novicio.

neoplasm [níoplæzm], *s.* (med.) neoplasma, *m.*

Neoplatonism [nioplɛ́jtonizm], *s.* neoplatonicismo.—**Neoplatonic** [-tánjk], *a.* neoplatónico.

neoteric [niotérjk], *a.* moderno, reciente.

Neozoic [niozóujk], *a.* (geol.) neozoico.

nepenthe(s [nipénθi(z], *s.* nepento, pócima que se suponía calmar las penas; (bot.) nepento.

nephew [néfju], *s.* sobrino.

nephology [nefálodži], *s.* tratado de las nubes.

nephoscope [néfoskoup], *s.* nefoscopio, que indica la dirección, elevación, etc., de las nubes.

nephralgia [nefréldžjá], *s.* (med.) nefralgia, neuralgia renal.

nephrectomy [nefréktomi], *s.* (cir.) nefrectomía, excisión del riñón.

nephrite [néfrajt], *s.* (min.) nefrita, piedra nefrítica o jade.

nephritic [nefrítik], *a. y s.* (med.) nefrítico.

nephritis [nefrájtis], *s.* (med.) nefritis.

nephrolith [néfroliθ], *s.* (med.) nefrolito.

nephroptosis [nefraptóusis], *s.* (med.) riñón flotante o móvil; nefróptosis.

nephrotomy [nefrátomi], *s.* (cir.) nefrotomía.

nepotism [népotizm], *s.* nepotismo, sobrinazgo.

Neptune [néptjun], *s.* (mit. y astr.) Neptuno; (fig.) océano, mar.

Neptunian [neptjúnjan], *a.* neptúneo; (geol.) neptúnico.—**N. theory,** (geol.) neptunismo.

Nereid [nírjid], *s.* (mit.) nereida.

nerita [nirájtá], *s.* (zool.) nerita.

Neronian [niróunjan], *a.* neroniano; sanguinario.

nerval [nérval], *a.* (anat.) nerval, nérveo.

nervate [nérvejt], *a.* (bot.) nervioso, nervado.

nervation [nœrvéjšƏn], **nervature** [nœrvachur], *s.* (bot.) nervadura; venación.

nerve [nœrv]. **I.** *s.* (anat. y bot.) nervio; vigor, fibra; valor, ánimo; (bot.) vena; (fam.) desfachatez, descaro, tupé.—*pl.* excitabilidad nerviosa.—**n. center,** (anat., fisiol.) centro nervioso. **II.** *va.* vigorizar, dar fuerza; animar, alentar.

nerved [-d], *a.* nervudo, nervoso; (bot.) nervioso.

nerveless [-lis], *a.* sin nervios; enervado; débil.

nerviduct [nérvidakt], *s.* (anat.) conducto óseo o cartilaginoso para dar paso a un nervio.

nervimotion [-móuʃƏn], *s.* (fisiol.) nervimoción.

nervine [nérvin], *a. y s.* (remedio) nervino.

nervosism [nérvosizm], *s.* (med.) nervosismo.

nervosity [nœrvásiti], *s.* nerv(i)osidad.

nervous [nérvʌs], *a.* nerv(i)oso; nervudo; excitado; vigoroso.—**n. breakdown, o prostration,** neurastenia.—**n. system,** sistema nervioso.

nervously [-li], *adv.* nerv(i)osamente.

nervousness [-nis]. *s.* nerv(i)osidad; vigor, fuerza; estado nervioso o irritable.

nervule [nérvjul], *s.* (anat.) nervezuelo, nérvulo.

nervure [nérvjur], *s.* (arq. y bot.) nervadura; (ent.) vena, nervadura.

nervy [nérvi], *a.* vigoroso; valeroso; que exige valor; (fam.) descarado; (Ingl.) excitable.

nescience [néšjens], *s.* nesciencia, ignorancia; agnosticismo.—**nescient** [-ent], *a.* nesciente.

ness [nɛs], *s.* promontorio, cabo.

nest [nɛst]. **I.** *s.* nido, nidal, ponedero (de gallinas); manida, madriguera; guarida; juego de objetos que encajan unos dentro de otros; (mec.) engranaje; (geol. y min.) bolsa.— **egg,** nidal, ponedero; (fig.) ahorros, *m. pl.*— **n. of drawers o boxes,** juego de gavetas o cajones. **II.** *va. y vn.* nidificar, anidar, hacer un nido; buscar nidos; alojar, anidarse, establecerse; colocar una serie de objetos uno dentro de otro.

nestful [-ful], *s.* nidada (de huevos, pollos, etc.).

nestle [nésl]. **I.** *va.* abrigar, poner en un nido; acariciar, mimar. **II.** *vn.* anidar(se); estar abrigado, como en un nido; apiñarse. *V.* SNUGGLE.

nestling [néstlin], *s.* (orn.) pollo, pichón, volantón.

Nestorian [nestórjan], *a. y s.* nestoriano.—**Nestorianism** [-izm], *s.* nestorianismo.

net [nɛt]. **I.** *s.* red; redecilla, albanega; malla; (fig.) trampa; (tej.) tul; (com.) líquido. *V.* NETWORK.—**n. fishing,** pesca con red.—**n. float,** boya. **II.** *va.* enredar, prender o coger con red; cubrir de red(es) u obra de malla; (com.) obtener, producir una ganancia líquida. **III.** *vn.* echar la red; hacer redes. **IV.** *a.* (com.) neto, líquido; (raro) limpio, puro; reticular, de punto de malla; cogido con red.—**n. amount,** importe neto.—**n. balance,** saldo líquido.—**n. earnings,** entrada o recaudación neta.—**n. embroidery,** bordado reticular.— **n. produce, o proceeds,** producto neto.—**n. profit,** ganancia o utilidad líquida, beneficio líquido.—**n. weight,** peso neto.

netful [nétful], *s.* redada.

nether [néðœ(r)], *a.* inferior, más bajo.—**n. lip,** labio inferior.—**n. millstone,** solera.—**n. world,** el otro mundo, la otra vida; infierno.

Netherlander [-lændœ(r)], *s.* holandés.

nethermost [-moust], *a.* lo inferior o más bajo.

netmaker [nétmejkœ(r)], *s.* redero, mallero.

netmaking [-in], *s.* confección de redes.

netted [nétid], *a.* cubierto o protegido por una red; reticular; enredado, cogido con red.

netting [nétin], *s.* red, randa, obra de malla; alambrado; operación de hacer redes o redecillas; pesca con redes; (mar.) jareta, ajedrez.— **n. needle,** aguja de tejer redes o mallas.

nettle [nétl]. **I.** *s.* (bot.) ortiga.—**n. rash,** urticaria.—**n. tree,** (bot.) almez(o), loto. **II.** *va.* picar con o como ortiga; irritar, provocar, espinar.

nettlesome [-sʌm], *a.* irritable; irritante.

nettling [nétlin], *s.* provocación, irritación.

network [nétwœrk], *s.* red, randa, malla; retículo; (anat.) plexo; (rad., f. c., etc.) cadena, red, sistema, *m.*

neume [njúm], **neuma** [-ǝ], *s.* (mús.) neuma, *m.*

neural [njúral], *a.* (anat., zool.) neural; nérveo o nervioso.—**n. arch,** arco neural.—**n. axis,** eje cerebroespinal.—**n. canal,** canal neural, canal medular.—**n. spine,** espina neural.

neuralgia [njuréldžjá], *s.* (med.) neuralgia.

neuralgic [-džik], *a.* neurálgico.

neurasthenia [njurəsθíniə], *s.* (med.) neurastenia.

neurasthenic [-θénịk], *a.* y *s.* neurasténico.

neuration [njuréiṣǫn], *s.* = NERVATION.

neuraxis [njuréksịs], *s.* (anat.) neuroeje, neuraxis, *m.*, eje cerobroespinal.

neuraxon [-sǫn], *s.* (anat.) neuraxón, axon.

neurectomy [njuréktomị], *s.* (cir.) neurectomía.

neurilemma [njurịlémə], *s.* (anat.) neurilema, *m.*

neuritis [njuráịtịs], *s.* (med.) neuritis.

neuroblast [njúroblæst], *s.* (embr.) neuroblasto.

neurography [njurágrafị], *s.* (anat.) neurografía.

neurologist [njurálodẓịst], *s.* (med.) neurólogo.

neurology [-dẓị], *s.* (anat.) neurología.

neuroma [njuróumə], *s.* (med.) neuroma, *m.*

neuron [njúran], *s.* (anat.) sistema (*m.*) cerebroespinal; neurona, célula con sus prolongaciones, etc.

neuropath [njúropæθ], *s.* (med.) neurópata, *mf.*

neuropathic(al [-pæθịk(al], *a.* neuropático; neurótico.—**neuropathology** [-pəθálodẓị], *s.* (med.) neuropatología.

neuropathy [njurápəθị], *s.* (med.) neuropatía.

Neuroptera [njuráptẹrə], *s. pl.* (ent.) neurópteros.—**neuropterous** [-ʌs], *a.* neuróptero.

neurosis [njuróusịs], *s.* (med.) neurosis.

neurotic [njurátịk], *a.* y *s.* (med.) neurótico.

neurotome [njúrotǫm], *s.* (cir.) neurótomo.

neurotomy [njurátomị], *s.* (cir.) neurotomía.

neuter [njútœ(r)]. **I.** *a.* neutro; neutral; (gram.) neutro; (bot. y zool.) sin sexo. **II.** *s.* género, verbo o palabra neutros; abeja neutra; animal neutro o castrado.

neutral [njútrəl]. **I.** *a.* neutral, neutro; indiferente, inactivo; mediano; (pint.) neutro, pardusco o azulado; (biol.) neutro, sin sexo; (quím.) neutro; (mec.) neutro (eje, plano, etc.). **II.** *s.* neutral.—**in n.** (aut.) en punto muerto.

neutrality [njutrélịtị], *s.* neutralidad, calidad de neutral; (quím.) calidad de neutro.

neutralization [-izéịṣǫn], *s.* neutralización.

neutralize [-aịz], *va.* neutralizar.

neutrally [-ị], *adv.* neutralmente.

neutron [njútran], *s.* (fís.) neutrón.

never [névœ(r)], *adv.* nunca, jamás; en la (o mi) vida; no, de ningún modo.—**n. again,** nunca más, otra vez no.—**n. a whit,** ni pizca.—**n. fear,** no hay cuidado, no hay miedo.—**n. mind,** no importa.—**n. so,** por muy, por mucho o por más que. Con *never* y un gerundio se forman compuestos que indican que la acción o condición denotadas por el verbo no se verifican o no se realizarán nunca, v. gr. *never-ceasing*, *never-ending*, que nunca termina, continuo, perpetuo, eterno; *never-erring*, que nunca falla, infalible; *never-fading*, que nunca se marchita, inmarcesible; *never-failing*, infalible, inagotable; *never-tiring*, incansable.

nevermore [-mór], *adv.* jamás, nunca más.

nevertheless [-ðélés], *adv.* no obstante, con todo, sin embargo, a pesar de eso.

nevoid [nívoịd], *a.* (med.) nevoideo.

nevus [nívʌs], *s.* (med.) nevo; marca de nacimiento.

new [njú]. **I.** *a.* nuevo; moderno; novicio; no habituado; fresco, reciente, recién hecho, recién cogido, etc.; otro, diferente, distinto.—**n. birth,** renacimiento; regeneración.—**N. Deal,** (pol., E. U.) *New Deal* (gen. se usa así la expresión, sin traducirla), política Roosevelt (del presidente F. D. Roosevelt).—**N. Dealer,** partidario del *New Deal*, roosveltista.—**n. departure,** nuevo sistema, nuevo método; nuevo derrotero; cambio, reforma.—**n.-delivered,** recién parida.—**N. Englander,** habitante de la Nueva Inglaterra.—**n.-fashioned,** de última moda.—**n.-fledged,** volantón, recién emplumado, novel.—**n.-formed,** reformado: formado de nuevo.—**N. Granadian,** neogranadino.—**n.-grown,** recién crecido; recién salido.—**n.-laid,** fresco (huevo); recién

puesto, colocado o tendido.—**n. learning,** nueva ciencia, renacimiento del saber; doctrinas de la reforma protestante; crítica bíblica moderna.—**N. Mexican,** neomejicano.—**n. moon,** luna nueva.—**n.-rich,** recién enriquecido.—**N. Style,** (cronología) estilo nuevo, estilo del calendario gregoriano.—**N. Testament,** Nuevo Testamento.—**N. World,** Nuevo Mundo.—**N. Year,** año nuevo.—**N. Year's (Day),** día de año nuevo.—**N. Year's gift,** aguinaldo.—**N. Yorker,** neoyorquino.—**N. Zealander,** neozelandés.—**what is n.?** ¿qué hay de nuevo? **II.** *adv.* nuevamente, de nuevo; (seguido de participio) recién.

newborn [-bɔrn], *a.* recién nacido.

newcomer [-kʌmœ(r)], *s.* recién llegado.

newel [njúęl], *s.* (arq.) nabo o bolo (de escalera); (carp.) poste con que termina la baranda de una escalera.

newest [njúịst], *a. superl.* de NEW; novísimo.

newfangled [njúfæ̃ngld], *a.* novelero; recién inventado, de última moda.

Newfoundland [njụfáụndlənd], *s.* perro de Terranova.

newish [njúịʃ], *a.* bastante nuevo.

newly [njúlị], *adv.* nuevamente, recientemente, recién.—**n. arrived,** recién llegado; advenedizo.

newlywed [-wed], *s.* recién casado, -da.

newness [njúnịs], *s.* novedad, calidad de nuevo; innovación; falta de práctica.

news [njúz], *s.* noticia, nueva; noticias (siempre en singular: *the news is this*, las noticias son éstas); cosa nueva, noticia fresca.—**n. agency,** agencia de prensa o de noticias.—**n. agent,** noticiero, agente de prensa.—**n. agent, dealer,** o **vender,** vendedor de periódicos.—**n. bureau,** sección de prensa.—**n. correspondent,** corresponsal (de noticias).—**n. writer,** gacetillero, noticiero.—**no n. is good n.,** la falta de noticias es buena noticia.—**what's the n.?** ¿qué hay de nuevo? ¿qué noticias hay?

newsboy [-boị], *s.* chiquillo vendedor de periódicos.

newscast [-kæst], *s.* (rad.) noticiario.

newscaster [-œ(r)], *s.* (rad.) noticiero que da y a veces comenta las noticias del día.

newsman [-mæn], *s.* = NEWSPAPER MAN.

newsmonger [-mʌ̃ngœ(r)], *s.* noticiero, novelero, gacetista, portanuevas, pilonero.

newspaper [-peịpœ(r)], *s.* periódico, diario; gaceta.—**n. clipping,** recorte de periódico.—**n. man,** periodista; reportero, repórter, noticiero.—**n. serial,** folletín.—**n. wrapper,** faja.

newsprint [-prịnt], *s.* papel para periódicos.

newsreel [-ril], *s.* (cine) noticiario, película que da las noticias del día.

newsroom [-rum], *s.* gabinete de lectura de periódicos; tienda de periódicos.

newsstand [-stænd], *s.* quiosco o kiosco, puesto o mostrador de periódicos, revistas, etc.

newsy [-ị], *a.* noticioso.

newt [njut], *s.* (zool.) tritón, especie de salamandra acuática.

Newtonian [njutóụnịən], *a.* y *s.* neutoniano.

next [nekst]. **I.** *a.* siguiente; entrante; próximo, contiguo, adyacente, inmediato, vecino; subsiguiente, futuro, venidero.—**n. day,** el o al día siguiente.—**n. door,** la puerta (o casa) siguiente.—**n. door to,** a la puerta (o casa) siguiente de; muy cerca de.—**n. month,** el mes entrante, próximo o que viene.—**n. of kin,** parientes más cercanos.—**n. time,** la próxima vez, otra vez.—**n. week,** la semana entrante.—**n. year,** el año entrante.—**the n. day before,** la víspera.—**the n. life,** la otra vida.—**to be n.,** seguir en turno, tocarle a uno. **II.** *adv.* luego, después, ahora, inmediatamente después, en seguida, a renglón seguido.—**n. best,** lo mejor después de eso, o a falta de eso. —**n. to,** junto a, al lado de; después de; casi.—

n. to impossible, punto menos que imposible.—**n. to nothing,** casi nada, poquísimo.—**what n.?** ¿y ahora (o luego) qué? III. *prep.* junto a, al lado de.

nexus [néksʌs], *s.* nexo, lazo, vínculo.

nib [nib]. I. *s.* asa de la guadaña; pico, punta, extremo; gavilán, punto o tajo de una pluma; pico de un ave; grano de cacao o de café. II. *va.* hacer punta a, aguzar; cortar la pluma.

nibble [níbl]. I. *va.* mordi(s)car, mordisquear, roer; pacer, tascar, rozar. II. *vn.* picar, morder (como el pez); (con at) criticar. III. *s.* roedura, ramoneo; mordisco, bocadito.

niblick [níblik], *s.* (dep.) uno de los palos del golf.

Nicaraguan [nikarágwan], *a.* y *s.* nicaragüense, nicaragüeño.

niccolite [níkolait], *s.* (min.) niquelina.

nice [náis], *a.* fino, sutil; delicado; diligente, solícito; circunspecto, cauto; exacto, concienzudo, escrupuloso; esmerado, pulcro, pulido, refinado; remilgado; tierno, frágil; agradable, lindo, bonito; simpático, gentil, amable.—**n. and,** (fam.) muy, bien.—**n. and warm,** calientito.—**n. distinction,** sutileza.—**n.-looking,** bien parecido.—**n. point,** punto delicado.

nicely [-li], *adv.* con finura; delicadamente; primorosamente; sutilmente; (fam.) muy bien.

Nicene [naisín], *a.* niceno.

niceness [náisnis], *s.* finura, gentileza, amabilidad; delicadeza; esmero, exactitud.

nicety [náiseti], *s.* finura, delicadeza, amabilidad; exactitud, esmero; refinamiento, atildadura; sutileza; remilgo.—**to a n.,** con la mayor precisión, en buen punto.

niche [nich], *s.* nicho, capilleta; hornacina.

nick [nik]. I. *s.* muesca, mella, corte, picadura, tarja; (impr.) cran del tipo; muesca en la cabeza de un tornillo; punto crítico, momento oportuno; jugada favorable.—(Old) N., el diablo, pateta.—**in the n. of time,** en el momento perentorio, a punto, a tiempo. II. *va.* mellar, cortar o hacer muescas, descantillar, tarjar; acertar, dar en el clavo; llegar a tiempo.

nickel [níkel]. I. *s.* (quím.) níquel; (E. U., fam.) moneda de níquel (5 centavos).—**n. bronze,** cuproníquel, aleación de cobre y níquel.—**n.-plate,** *va.* niquelar.—**n.-plated,** niquelado.—**n.-plating,** niquelado, niqueladura.—**n. silver,** metal blanco, plata alemana.—**n. steel,** acero níquel.

nicknack [níknæk], *s.* friolera, chuchería.

nickname [níknejm]. I. *s.* mote, apodo. II. *va.* motejar, apodar.

nicotia [nikóusiá], *s.* nicotina; (poét.) nicociana, tabaco.

nicotin(e [níkotin), *s.* (quím.) nicotina.

nicotinic [-tínjk], *a.* nicotínico (ácido).

nicotinism [níkotinizm], *s.* (med.) nicot(in)ismo.

nic(ti)tate [nik(ti)tejt], *vn.* pestañear, parpadear.—**nictitating membrane,** membrana nictitante.

nic(ti)tation [-éiṣon], *s.* nic(ti)tación, pestañeo.

nidificant [nídifikant], *a.* nidificante.

nidification [-éiṣon], *s.* nidificación.

nidify [nídifai], *vn.* nidificar, anidar.

nidus [náidʌs], *s.* nido; centro o foco de infección; (anat.) núcleo nervioso.

niece [nis], *s.* sobrina.

niello [niélou]. I. *s.* niel; nielado. II. *va.* nielar.

nifty [nífti], *a.* (fam.) elegante; excelente.

nig [nig], *va.* labrar (piedra) a pico.

nigella [naidżéliá], *s.* (bot.) neguilla.

niggard [nígard], *a.* y *s.* tacaño, mezquino.

niggard(li)ness [-(li)nis], *s.* tacañería, mezquindad, cicatería, miseria; escasez.

niggardly [-li]. I. *a.* tacaño, cicatero, mezquino, miserable; escaso. II. *adv.* tacaña o mezquinamente, con mezquindad o cicatería.

nigger [nígœ(r)], *s.* (desp.) negro, negra; uno de varios inventos mecánicos; (ent.) oruga negra.

—n. in the wood pile, (fam.) gato encerrado.—**n. heaven,** (fam.) paraíso, gallinero (en el teatro).

niggerism [-izm], *s.* carácter, sangre (*f.*), locución o idiotismo propio de los negros.

niggle [nígl]. I. *va.* burlarse de; engañar. II. *vn.* ocuparse en menudencias. III. *s.* letra menuda o metida.—**niggling** [nígliŋ]. I. *s.* (b. a.) minuciosidad. II. *a.* demasiado minucioso; remilgado.

nigh [nai]. I. *prep.* (ant.) cerca, no lejos de, cabe, junto a. II. *adv.* (ant.) cerca, inmediato; casi, cuasi. III. *a.* (ant.) cercano, próximo, vecino; de la izquierda (hablando de caballos o vehículos); allegado, íntimo.

night [náit]. I. *s.* noche, *f.*—**n. after n.,** noche tras noche.—**n. before last,** anteanoche.—**at n., by n.,** de noche, por la noche. II. *a.* nocturno; de noche; que funciona, se hace u ocurre de noche, o sirve para la noche.—**n. attack,** (mil.) trasnochada.—**n. bell,** campanilla para llamar por la noche.—**n. bird,** pájaro nocturno.—**n.-blind,** que no ve bien de noche. V. NYCTALOPIC.—**n. blindness,** defecto que consiste en la diminución de la visión durante la noche. V. NYCTALOPIA.—**n. blooming,** (bot.) noctífloro.—**n. brawler,** alborotador nocturno.—**n. chair,** sillico, silla-retrete.—**n. clothes,** camisa o traje de dormir.—**n. club,** café cantante, cabaret.—**n. commode,** o **stand,** mes(it)a de noche.—**n. dew,** sereno, relente.—**n. dial,** reloj lunar.—**n. glass,** catalejo nocturno.—**n. heron,** (orn.) garzota.—**n. key,** llavín, llave (*f.*) de noche.—**n. lamp,** o **light,** mariposa, lamparilla o luz de noche.—**n. latch,** o **lock,** cerradura de resorte.—**n. letter** = LETTERGRAM.—**n. life,** vida nocturna.—**n. owl,** (orn.) buho, mochuelo, lechuza; (fam.) trasnochador.—**n. piece,** (b. a.) cuadro o escena nocturna.—**n. rest,** reposo de la noche.—**n. robe** = NIGHTDRESS.—**n. school,** escuela nocturna o de noche.—**n. shift,** turno de noche.—**n. soil,** contenido de las letrinas, que sirve de abono.—**n. stool** = N. CHAIR.—**n. watch,** sereno, guardia o ronda de noche; trasnoch(e)o.—**to pass,** o **spend, the n.,** pernoctar; trasnochar.—**n. watchman,** sereno.

nightcap [-kæp], *s.* gorro de dormir; (fam.) trago que se toma antes de acostarse.

nightdress [-drɛs], *s.* camisón, camisa de dormir.

nightfall [-fol], *s.* anochecida, anochecer, caída de la tarde.—**at n.,** al anochecer.

nightgown [-gaun], *s.* = NIGHTDRESS.

nighthawk [-hok], *s.* (orn.) chotacabras, *f.*; pájaro insectívoro crepuscular de los E. U.; (fam.) trasnochador, nocherniego.

nightingale [-iŋgeil], *s.* (orn.) ruiseñor, filomela.

nightjar [-dżar], *s.* (orn.) chotacabras, *f.*

nightlong [-loŋ], *a.* y *adv.* de toda la noche, durante toda la noche.

nightly [-li]. I. *adv.* por las noches, todas las noches. II. *a.* nocturno, de noche.

nightmare [-mer], *s.* pesadilla.

nightshade [-ṣeid], *s.* (bot.) dulcamara, solano, hierba mora.—**deadly n.,** belladona, belladama.

nightshirt [-ṣœrt], *s.* camisa de dormir.

nighttime [-taim], *s.* noche, *f.*—**in the n.,** de noche.

nightwalker [-wokœ(r)], *s.* noctámbulo o (poét.) noctívago, sonámbulo; vago o mujer pública que calleja de noche; (ent.) lombriz nocturna de tierra, usada para cebo de pescar.

nightward [-ward], *a.* cercano o próximo a la noche.

nightwear [-wer], *s.* = NIGHT CLOTHES.

nigrescence [naigrésʌns], *s.* ennegrecimiento.

nigrescent [-ʌnt], *a.* nigrescente, negruzco.

nigrification [nigrifikéiṣon], *s.* ennegrecimiento.

nigrify [nígrifai], *va.* ennegrecer.

nihil [nájhi̠l], *s.* (lat.) nada.
nihilism [náj(h)i̠li̠zm], *s.* nihilismo.—**nihilist** [-i̠st], *s.*, **nihilistic** [-i̠sti̠k], *a.* nihilista.
nihility [najhíli̠ti̠], *s.* (estado de) la nada.
nilg(h)ai [ní̠lgaj], *s.* (zool.) especie de antílope.
nimble [ní̠mbl], *a.* vivo, listo, ágil, veloz, expedito.—**n.-fingered**, ligero de dedos.—**n.-footed**, ligero de pies, alípede.—**n.-pinioned**, de vuelo rápido.—**n.-witted**, vivo, despierto, inteligente.
nimbleness [-nj̠s], *s.* ligereza, agilidad, celeridad, presteza, expedición; destreza.
nimbly [ní̠mbli̠], *adv.* ligeramente, ágilmente.
nimbus [ní̠mbʌs], *s.* nimbo; aureola.
nincompoop [ní̠nko̠mpup], *s.* badulaque, simplón, tonto, pelele, majadero.
nine [nájn], *a.* y *s.* nueve.—**n. hundred**(th, novecientos—**the N.**, las nueve musas.
ninefold [-fo̠u̠ld], *a.* y *adv.* nueve veces.
ninepence [-pe̠n̠s], *s.* nueve peniques; real fuerte o media peseta.
ninepins [-pi̠n̠z], *s.* juego de bolos.
ninescore [-sko̠r], *a.* y *s.* nueve veces veinte.
nineteen [nájntí̠n], *a.* y *s.* diecinueve.
nineteenth [-θ], *a.* décimonono; diecinueveavo; diecinueve (del mes).
ninetieth [nájntje̠θ], *a.* nonagésimo, noventa; noventavo.
ninety [nájnti̠], *a.* y *s.* noventa.
ninny [ní̠ni̠], *s.* simple, mentecato, pelele, badulaque, papanatas, bobo.
ninth [nájnθ], *a.* nono, noveno; nueve (del mes).
ninthly [-li̠], *adv.* en no(ve)no lugar.
niobium [naj̠óu̠bi̠ʌm], *s.* (quím.) niobio, columbio.
nip [ni̠p]. I. *va.* pellizcar; asir, sujetar, agarrar; mordicar, (re)cortar, desmochar; helar, escarchar, marchitar.—**to n. in the bud**, cortar en flor.—**to n. off**, desmochar, despuntar. II. *va.* y *vn.* = TO TIPPLE. III. *s.* pellizco; pedacito; trago, traguito; uñada, dentellada; helada, escarcha; cogida; daño repentino de las plantas o sembrados.—**n. and tuck**, (E. U.) empate.
nipa [ní̠pä], *s.* (bot.) nipa.
nipper [ní̠pœ(r)], *s.* agarrador; pinza; boca de algunos crustáceos; pala, diente delantero del caballo.—*pl.* pinzas, tenazas, tenacillas.
nipping [ní̠pi̠n]. I. *s.* araño, rasguño, mordedura. II. *a.* mordaz, picante.
nippingly [-li̠], *adv.* mordazmente.
nipple [ní̠pl], *s.* pezón; tet(ill)a; pezón artificial; chimenea de arma de percusión; (mec.) tubo roscado de unión.—**n. shield**, pezonera.
nipplewort [-wœrt], *s.* (bot.) lámpsana.
Nipponese [ni̠paní̠z], *s.* y *a.* nipón, japonés.
Nipponism [ní̠pani̠zm], *s.* niponismo, japonismo.
Nirvana, o **nirvana** [ni̠rvá̠nä], *s.* nirvana, *m.*
nisus [nájsʌs], *s.* esfuerzo; contracción de los músculos en la evacuación del vientre o de la vejiga; apetito procreativo primaveral de las aves.
nit [ni̠t], *s.* liendre, *f.*; huevo de piojo.
niter, **nitre** [nájtœ(r)], *s.* (quím.) nitro, salitre o nitrato de potasio.—**n. bed**, nitral.
nitid [ní̠ti̠d], *a.* nítido, lustroso.
niton [nájtan], *s.* nitón, emanación del radio.
nitrate [nájtrejt], *s.* (quím.) nitrato, azoato.
nitric [nájtri̠k], *a.* (quím.) nítrico, azoico.—**n. acid**, ácido nítrico, agua fuerte.
nitrid(e [nájtri̠d], *s.* (quím.) nitruro.
nitrification [nájtri̠fi̠kéjʂo̠n], *s.* nitrificación.—**nitrify** [-faj], *va.* nitrificar, nitrogenar, azoar.—**nitrifier** [-œr)], *s.* nitrificador, substancia nitrogenada que sirve para nitrificar.
nitrile [nájtri̠l], *s.* (quím.) nitrilo.
nitrite [nájtrajt], *s.* (quím.) nitrito.
nitrobacteria [najtrobæktrí̠ri̠ä], *s. pl.* nitrobacterias (gen. se aplica a las nítricas).
nitrobenzine [-bénzi̠n], *s.* (quím.) nitrobencina.

nitrocellulose [-sélyu̠lou̠s], *s.* (quím.) nitrocelulosa.
nitrocotton [-kátn], *s.* algodón pólvora.
nitrogen [nájtrodʐi̠n], *s.* (quím.) nitrógeno, ázoe.—**n.-fixing**, nitrogenante, que fija o combina el nitrógeno atmosférico (apl. a bacterias).
nitrogenize [-ajz], *va.* nitrogenar, azoar.
nitrogenous [najtrádʐenʌs], *a.* nitrogenado, azoado.
nitroglycerin [najtroglíseri̠n], *s.* nitroglicerina.
nitrometer [najtrámetœ(r)], *s.* nitrómetro.
nitroprussiate [najtroprásje̠jt], *s.* (quím.) nitroprusiato.
nitrosyl [najtrósu̠si̠l], *s.* (quím.) nitrosilo.
nitrous [nájtrʌs], *a.* nitroso, salitroso.—**n. acid**, ácido nitroso.—**n. bacteria**, bacterias nitrosas.—**n. oxide**, óxido nitroso (ll. t. **laughing gas**).
nitty [ní̠ti̠], *a.* lendroso.
nitwit [ní̠twi̠t], *s.* (fam.) = NINNY.
nival [nájval], *a.* nevoso.
niveous [ní̠vi̠ʌs], *a.* níveo.
nix(ie [ní̠ks(i̠], *s.* genio de las aguas en la mitología alemana.—**nix. I.** *s.* (fam.) nitos, nada. **II.** *adv.* no, ni por pienso.
no [nou]. I. *adv.* no.—**n. more**, no más.—**n. more of that**, o of this, basta, bastante; no hablemos más de eso.—**n. sooner**, no bien.—**say n. more**, no diga más. **II.** *a.* ninguno, ningún. Gen. equivale a NOT y se traduce por no: *I have no time*, no tengo tiempo; *there is no bread*, no hay pan. A menudo se usa en expresiones elípticas en que es preciso suplir el verbo *ser, permitir, haber*, etc.: *no admittance*, no hay admisión, no se permite la entrada; *no public entrance*, ésta no es entrada pública; *no smoking*, no se permite fumar. Después de algunas preposiciones equivale a sin: *to no purpose*, sin objeto; *with no money*, sin dinero.—**n.-account**, (fam.) sin valor, despreciable.—**n. fooling**, (fam.) sin broma, de veras.—**n. man's land**, el campo que separa dos ejércitos enemigos.—**n. matter**, no importa; de ninguna importancia.—**n. matter how much**, por mucho que.—**n. . . ., n. . . ., sin . . .**, no hay [*no payment, no delivery*, sin pago no hay (o habrá) entrega].—**n. one**, nadie, ninguno.—**n. such thing**, no tal, no hay tal cosa.—**n. use** (con to be), inútil. **III.** *s.* (*pl.* NOES) no, voto negativo.—*pl.* nones.
Noachian [noéjki̠an], *a.* relativo a Noé.
Noah's ark [nóu̠ạz árk], *s.* (bib.) arca de Noé.
nob [nab], *s.* (fam.) la cabeza; noble, persona de viso.
nobby [nábi̠], *a.* (fam.) ostentoso, vistoso, jarifo.
nobiliary [nobíli̠eri̠], *a.* nobiliario.
nobility [nobíli̠ti̠], *s.* nobleza; hidalguía.
noble [nóu̠bl], *s.* y *a.* noble; hidalgo; (Ingl.) moneda antigua.—**n. extraction**, noble alcurnia, sangre (*f.*) azul.—**n. metals**, metales nobles (oro, plata o platino).—**n. opal**, ópalo noble.—**of n. descent**, linajudo, solariego.—**to make n.**, ennoblecer.
nobleman [-man], *s.* noble, hidalgo.
nobleness [-nj̠s], *s.* nobleza, caballerosidad.
noblesse [noblés], *s.* nobleza.
noblewoman [-wuman], *s.* mujer noble, hidalga.
nobly [nóu̠bli̠], *adv.* noblemente; espléndidamente.—**n.-born**, noble de nacimiento.
nobody [nóu̠bodi̠]. I. *pron.* nadie, ninguno.—**n. else**, nadie más, ningún otro. **II.** *s.* nulidad, persona insignificante o despreciable, (fam.) quídam.
noctambulism [naktæmbi̠u̠li̠zm], *s.* noctambulismo.
noctambulist [-i̠st], *s.* noctívago; somnámbulo.
noctiflorous [naktjflóras], *a.* (bot.) noctifloro, que florece de noche.
noctiluca [-ljúkä], *s.* (zool.) noctiluca.
nocturn [náktœrn], *s.* (igl.) nocturno (maitines).
nocturnal [naktœrnal], *a.* nocturno, nocturnal.

nocturne [náktœrn], *s.* (pint.) escena nocturna; (mús.) nocturno.

nocuous [nákyỵʌs], *a.* = NOXIOUS.

nod [nad]. I. *va.* (*pret.* y *pp.* NODDED) hacer una seña afirmativa o llamativa con la cabeza; inclinar la cima o parte superior (de una rama, etc.). II. *vn.* cabecear, doblar o inclinar la cabeza; descabezar el sueño, dormitar. III. *s.* cabeceo; cabezada; signo o seña con la cabeza; reverencia, inclinación de cabeza.—**to get the n.**, (fam.) recibir el visto bueno.

nodal [nóu̯dąl], *a.* nodal, rel. a un nodo; (anat.) nodátil, nudoso.

nodated [nóu̯dei̯ti̯d], *a.* nudoso.

nodding [nádi̯ŋ]. I. *a.* (bot.) inclinado, colgante. II. *s.* cabeceo; saludo con la cabeza.

noddle [nádl], *s.* (fam.) mollera, cabeza, chol(l)a.

noddy [nádi̯], *s.* papanatas; carruaje ligero de dos ruedas; (orn.) pájaro bobo. *V.* TERN.

node [nou̯d], *s.* bulto, protuberancia, chichón; nudo; (med.) nodo, nudo, tumor, dureza, nódulo; (astr.) nodo; (bot.) nudo; (geom.) nodo; (teat.) enredo, nudo, trama.

nodose [nóu̯dou̯s], *a.* nudoso.

nodosity [nodási̯ti̯], *s.* nudosidad.

nodular [nádʑỵlä(r)], **noduled** [nádʑuld], *a.* nodular, que tiene nódulos o nudillos.

nodule [nádʑul], *s.* nudillo, nódulo.

noetic [noéti̯k], *a.* mental, intelectual, noemático.

nog [nag], *s.* puntal; bloque de madera; (mar.) cabilla, clavija; cierta cerveza fuerte; (E. U.) = EGGNOG.

noggin [nági̯n], *s.* taza o pichel pequeños; cantidad pequeña de un licor. *V.* GILL.

nogging [nági̯ŋ], *s.* (alb.) encajadura de ladrillo.

nohow [nóu̯hau̯], *adv.* (fam.) de ninguna manera.

noise [nói̯z]. I. *s.* ruido; son(ido); bullicio, gritería. II. *va.* esparcir, divulgar; turbar con gritos o con estruendo. III. *vn.* hablar mucho o en voz alta; hacer ruido, meter bulla.

noiseful [-fu̯l], *a.* ruidoso.

noiseless [-li̯s], *a.* silencioso, sin ruido, quedo. **noiselessly** [-li̯], *adv.* sin ruido.—**noisily** [-i̯li̯], *adv.* ruidosa, bulliciosa o estrepitosamente.

noisiness [-i̯ni̯s], *s.* estrépito, ruido, barahunda.

noisome [nói̯sʌm], *a.* apestoso, fétido; nocivo, malsano.—**noisomely** [-li̯], *adv.* apestosamente; nocivamente.—**noisomeness** [-ni̯s], *s.* mal olor, fetidez, hedor, peste, *f.;* nocividad.

noisy [nói̯zi̯], *a.* ruidoso, turbulento, estrepitoso.

noli-me-tangere [nóu̯li̯ mi tǽndʑœri], *s.* (bot.) balsamina; (med.) noli me tángere.

nolition [nolíʃǫn], *s.* nolición.

nolle prosequi [náli̯ prási̯kwai̯], (for.) abandono de acción.—**nol-pros** [nal prás], *va.* (for.) abandonar una acción o un juicio.

nomad(ic [nóu̯mæd, noumǽdi̯k]. I. *a.* nómada o nómade, errante; trashumante (ganado). II. (**nomad**), *s.* nómada, *mf.,* nómade.

nomadism [nóu̯mædi̯zm], *s.* nomadismo; trashumación.

nomarch [námark], *s.* nomarca, *m.*

nomarchy [-i̯], *s.* nomarquía.

nom de plume [nám dœ plum], *s.* (fr.) seudónimo.

nome [nou̯m], *s.* provincia, nomo; nomarquía.

nomenclator [nóu̯mɘnklei̯tǫ(r)], *s.* nomenclador, nomenclátor.

nomenclature [-chụ(r)], *s.* nomenclatura.

nominal [námi̯nąl], *a.* nominal, aparente; titular; módico, insignificante.—**nominalism** [-i̯zm], *s.* nominalismo.—**nominalist** [-i̯st], *s.* nominal(ista).—**nominally** [-i̯], *adv.* nominalmente.

nominate [námi̯nei̯t], *va.* nombrar o nominar como candidato, designar; señalar.

nomination [-éi̯ʃǫn], *s.* nombramiento, nominación; propuesta.—**to put, o place, in n.,** proponer para candidato.

nominative [námi̯nąti̯v], *a.* y *s.* (gram.) nominativo.

nominator [-ei̯tǫ(r)], *s.* nominador.

nominee [nami̯ní], *s.* nómino, nombrado.

nomology [nomálodʑi̯], *s.* nomología, ciencia o formulación de las leyes de una ciencia.

non- [nan], partícula negativa que corresponde gen. a *in-, no* o a *falta de* en español.—**n. assumpsit,** (for.) alegación de que una persona no ha hecho una promesa.—**n.-Euclidean,** no euclidiano.

nonacceptance [nanæksép̣tąns], *s.* rechazo o falta de aceptación; recusación.

nonage [náni̯dʑ], *s.* minoridad.

nonagenarian [nanądʑenéri̯ąn], *a.* y *s.* nonagenario, noventón.

nonagesimal [-dʑési̯mąl], *a.* nonagésimo.

nonagon [nánągan], *s.* (geom.) nonágono, eneágono.

nonaggression [nanągréʃǫn], *s.* no agresión.

nonalcoholic [-ælkoháli̯k], *a.* no alcohólico.

nonappearance [-ąpíŗąns], *s.* ausencia; (for.) contumacia, rebeldía.

nonarrival [-ąrái̯vąl], *s.* falta de llegada.

nonassessable [-ąsésąbl], *a.* (com.) no susceptible de dividendos pasivos (ú. de acciones).

nonattendance [-ąténdąns], *s.* inasistencia, falta de asistencia, ausencia.

nonbreakable [-bréi̯kąbl], *a.* irrompible.

nonce [nans], *s.* tiempo, ocasión o propósito particular.—**n. word,** palabra ad hoc.—**for the n.,** por esta vez, por ahora, por el momento.

nonchalance [nánʃąląns], *s.* indiferencia.—**nonchalant** [-ąnt], *a.* indiferente, impasible.

noncombatant [nankámbątąnt], *s.* y *a.* no combatiente.

noncommissioned [-kǫmíʃǫnd], *a.,* **n. officer,** sargento o cabo; oficial subalterno nombrado por el jefe de un cuerpo (ll. t. **noncom** [fam.]).

noncomittal [-kǫmítąl], *a.* reservado, evasivo, que no se compromete expresando su opinión.

noncompliance [-kǫmplái̯ąns], *s.* incumplimiento, falta de cumplimiento, falta de obediencia.

non compos mentis [nan kámpos ménti̯s], *a.* (lat., for.) insano, falto de juicio.

nonconcurrence [-kankœŗens], *s.* falta de unión, combinación o cooperación; desacuerdo.

nonconducting [-kǫndʌ́kti̯ŋ], *a.,* **nonconductor** [-tǫ(r)], *s.* (fís., elec.) no conductor, mal conductor, aislador.

nonconformist [-kǫnfórmi̯st]. I. *a.* desconforme, disidente. II. *s.* disidente (de la iglesia anglicana).

nonconformity [-mi̯ti̯], *s.* desconformidad; disidencia (de la iglesia anglicana).

nonconsent [-kǫnsént], *s.* falta de consentimiento.

noncontagious [-kǫntéi̯dʑ̣ʌs], *a.* no contagioso.

noncoöperation [-koąpɘréi̯ʃǫn], *s.* falta de cooperación; (pol.) no cooperación con el gobierno, resistencia pasiva.

noncumulative [-kụ́myụląti̯v], *a.* (com.) no acumulable (apl. esp. a los intereses).

nondelivery [-di̯lívœri̯], *s.* falta de entrega.

nondescript [nándi̯skript]. I. *a.* inclasificable, de difícil clasificación o descripción. II. *s.* objeto o persona indescriptible, o que no pertenece a determinada clase o clasificación.

none [nʌn]. I. *pron.* nadie, ninguno; nada; nada de; no . . . nada, no . . . ninguno (*I have none,* yo no tengo ninguno, yo no tengo nada). —**n. of one's business,** cosa que a uno no le importa o atañe.—**n. of that,** nada de eso. II. *adv.* no, de ninguna manera, absolutamente no.—**n. the less,** no obstante, sin embargo; no menos.—**to be n. the better (worse),** (a menudo con **for,** con, a causa de, por) no hallarse mejor (peor), no salir o quedar mejor (peor) librado, no ganar (perder).

noneffective [nani̯fékti̯v], *a.* ineficaz; (mil.) no disponible, inhabilitado para el servicio activo. (En este último sentido, ú. t. como *s.*)

nonego [nanígou̯], *s.* (fil.) no yo, el mundo externo.

nonelectric [-ilḗktrik], a. (fís.) aneléctrico.
nonentity [-éntiti], s. la nada; persona o cosa de ningún valor, cero a la izquierda, nulidad.
nones [nounz], s. pl. nonas; (igl.) nona.
nonessential [nonʃénʃəl], s. y a. no esencial.
nonesuch [nʌnsʌch], a. y s. sin igual, sin par.
nonexistence [nanigzístəns], s. inexistencia.—**nonexistent** [-ənt], a. no existente, inexistente.
nonfeasance [-fízəns], s. (for.) incumplimiento, falta de cumplimiento.
nonfulfillment [-fulfílmənt], s. incumplimiento.
nonintervention [-intœrvénʃən], s. no intervención.
nonius [nóuniʌs], s. nonio. V. VERNIER.
nonjuror [nandʒúrɔ(r)], s. el que no presta juramento; (N., Ingl.) clérigo que no juró fidelidad al trono en 1688.
nonlegal [-lígəl], a. ilegal; no legal.
nonmetal [-métəl], s. (quím.) metaloide, elemento químico no metálico.
nonmoral [-márəl], a. no ético, fuera del dominio de la moral; amoral.
nonpareil [-pərél]. I. a. sin par, incomparable, sin rival. II. s. persona o cosa de incomparable mérito; (orn.) variedades de pinzón y de loro; (impr.) nomparell, f., tipo de seis puntos.
nonpartisan [-pártizạn], a. (pol.) independiente, no afiliado con ningún partido.
nonpayment [-péimənt], s. falta de pago.
nonperformance [-pœrfórmạns], s. falta de ejecución; incumplimiento.
nonplus [-plʌs]. I. s. perplejidad, incertidumbre; estupefacción. II. va. confundir, aplastar, dejar sin palabra.—**nonplus(s)ed** [-t], confundido, (fam.) turulato, estupefacto.
nonprofit [-práfit], a. que no proporciona ni busca provecho, utilidad o beneficio.
nonrecognition [-rekɔgníʃən], s. desconocimiento.
nonresidence [-rézidəns], s. ausencia, residencia en otra parte.
nonresident [-ənt], a. y s. ausente, no residente.
nonresistance [-rizístạns], s. obediencia pasiva, falta de resistencia.
nonrestraint [-ristréint], s. no compulsión, suavidad (apl. al tratamiento de locos).
nonrigid [-rídʒid], a. flexible; (aer.) fláccido (apl. a dirigibles).
nonrusting [-rástiŋ], a. inoxidable.
nonsectarian [-sektériạn], a. no sectario, que no pertenece a ninguna secta religiosa.
nonsense [nánsens], s. disparate, desatino; tontería, absurdo, necedad; (fam.) música celestial; bagatelas, fruslerías, jerigonza; interj. ¡bah!
nonsensical [-sénsikạl], a. disparatado, absurdo, desatinado.—**nonsensically** [-i], adv. disparatadamente, tontamente.—**nonsensicalness** [-nis], s. absurdidad; insensatez.
non sequitur [-sékwitœ(r)], (lóg.) falsa conclusión, conclusión que no se deduce de las premisas.
nonshatterable [-ʃǽtœrạbl], a. inastillable (vidrio).
nonskid(ding [nánskíd, -iŋ], a. antideslizante, antiresbaladizo.
nonslipping [-slípiŋ], a. no resbaladizo.
nonstop [nánstáp], a. y adv. directo, expreso; directamente; sin paradas o etapas; sin pararar(se).
nontransferable [-trænsfǽrạbl], a. intransferible.
nonsuit [-sjut]. I. s. (for.) abandono de acción; sobreseimiento; caducidad de la instancia. II. va. (for.) absolver de la instancia; sobreseer.
nontechnical [-téknikạl], a. no técnico.
nonunion [-yúnyɔn], a. no perteneciente a los gremios obreros, o que se opone a ellos; de fuera de los gremios.—**n. shop**, taller o fábrica que no emplea obreros agremiados, o en que los gremios prohiben que sus miembros trabajen. (Ú. gen. en el primer sentido.)

nonviable [-váiạbl], a. no viable, incapaz de vivir.
noodle [núdl], s. tallarín, pasta alimenticia, fideo; tonto, simplón, mentecato; (fam.) cabeza.
nook [nuk], s. rincón; escondrijo, traspuesta.
noon [nún]. I. s. mediodía, m.; las doce del día; (poét.) medianoche; (fig.) culminación, apogeo. II. a. = NOONDAY.
noonday [-dei]. I. s. mediodía, m. (mitad del día). II. a. meridional, de mediodía.
nooning [-iŋ], s. (siesta o comida del) mediodía.
noontide [-taid], **noontime** [-taim], s. = NOON.
noose [nus]. I. s. lazo corredizo, gaza; dogal.—**n. snare**, trampa. II. va. (en)lazar; coger con lazo corredizo o con trampa; ahorcar.
nopal [nóupạl], s. (bot.) nopal; higuera chumba.
nor [nɔr], conj. ni.—**nor I**, yo tampoco. V. NEITHER.
Nordic [nórdik], s. y a. nórdico; del noroeste de Europa (apl. esp. a pueblos y razas, más bien que a las lenguas).
noria [nóuriạ], s. noria, cenia.
norm [nɔrm], s. norma, pauta, modelo, tipo.
normal [nórmạl]. I. a. normal, regular, corriente; típico, ejemplar; perpendicular; (geom., quím.) normal.—**n. acid**, ácido normal (con las fracciones $\frac{1}{10}$, $\frac{2}{10}$, etc., decinormal, veintinormal, etc., o de un décimo, un veinteavo, etc., de la concentración normal).—**n. school**, (escuela) normal. II. s. estado normal; (geom.) normal, f.
normalcy [-si], **normality** [nɔrmǽliti], s. normalidad, estado de normal.
normalize [-aiz], va. normalizar, regularizar.
normally [-i], adv. normalmente.
Norman [nórmạn], a. y s. normando.
Norse [nɔrs], a. y s. escandinavo.
Norseman [-mạn], s. hombre del norte, normando, antiguo escandinavo.
north [nɔrθ]. I. s. norte, septentrión, m.; (poét.) cierzo.—**n.-northeast**, nornordeste.—**n.-northwest**, nornorueste.—**n. by east**, norte, cuarta nordeste.—**n. by west**, norte, cuarta noroeste.—**the N.**, (E. U.) los estados del Norte. II. a. septentrional, del norte.—**N. American**, norteamericano.—**N. Pole**, polo norte o ártico.—**N. Star**, estrella polar, la Polar.—**n. wind**, aquilón, norte, cierzo, septentrión, m., cierzo. III. adv. al norte, hacia el norte.
northeast [-íst], s. y a. nordeste.—**northeaster** [-œ(r)], s. tempestad nordestal.—**northeasterly** [-œrli], **northeastern** [-œrn], a. nordestal.
norther [nórðœ(r)], s. cierzo, nortada.
northerly [-li], **northern** [-n], a. septentrional, norteño, nórtico; nordista; del norte o hacia el norte.—**northern lights**, aurora boreal.
northern(er [nórðœrn(œ(r))], s. habitante del Norte.—**N.**, (E. U.) natural de los estados del Norte, nordista.—**northernmost** [-moust], a. superl. más septentrional, de más al norte.
northing [nórðiŋ], s. (mar.) derrota hacia el norte; diferencia de latitud norte.
northland [nórθlænd], s. tierra o región del norte; (N.) la península ocupada por Noruega y Suecia.
Northman [-mạn], s. = NORSEMAN.
northward(s [-wárd(z)], adv. hacia el norte.
northwest [-wést], s. y a. noroeste o norueste.—**n. by north**, noroeste, cuarta norte.—**n. by west**, noroeste, cuarta oeste.—**northwester** [-œ(r)], s. (viento) noroeste o maestral, cauro.—**northwesterly** [-œrli], a. hacia el noroeste o del noroeste.—**northwestern** [-œrn], a. del noroeste.
Norwegian [norwídʒiạn], s. y a. noruego.
nose [nóuz]. I. s. nariz; hocico de los animales; olfato; sagacidad; algo parecido a una nariz, v.gr.: proa de un buque; tobera o cañuto de fuelle; pico o boca (de cafetera, jarro, etc.); (aer.) extremo anterior o cabeza de un avión.—**n. bag**, morral, cebadera, caparazón.—**n. dive**,

(aer.) picada, descenso de cabeza o con gran inclinación.—**n. piece,** sobarba, muserola; portaobjetivo (de microscopio); extremo o boquilla de mang(uer)a.—**n ring,** nariguera, aro de nariz.—**n.-shaped,** narigudo.—**to look down one's n. at,** desdeñar, mirar con desprecio.— **to poke,** o **stick, one's n. into** = TO THRUST, etc. II. *va.* y *vn.* oler, olfatear, husmear, rastrear; entremeterse en asuntos ajenos; restregar la nariz contra; ganguear; encararse; oponerse, hacer frente; (con **out**) descubrir, averiguar; vencer por poco.—**to n. about,** husmear, curiosear.—**to n.-dive,** (aer.) picar, descender de cabeza.—**to n. in(to),** (mar.) avanzar, entrar al puerto, etc., con cuidado.

noseband [-bænd], *s.* muserola, sobarba.

nosebleed [-blid], *s.* (med.) epistaxis, hemorragia nasal; (bot.) milenrama.

nosegay [-geį], *s.* ramillete de flores.

noseless [-lįs], *a.* desnarigado; sin nariz.

nosepiece [-pis], *s.* = NOSE PIECE.

nos(e)y [-į], *a.* (fam.) curioso, entremetido, inquisitivo.

nosogeny [nosádžįnį], *s.* (med.) nosogenia.

nosography [noságrafį], *s.* (med.) nosografía.

nosological [nasoládžįkal], *a.* nosológico.

nosologist [nosálodžįst], *s.* (med.) nosólogo.

nosology [-džį], *s.* (med.) nosología.

nostalgia [nastáldžįą], *s.* nostalgia, añoranza.

nostalgic [-džįk], *a.* nostálgico.

nostoc [nástak], *s.* nostoc, género de algas.

nostology [nastálodžį], *s.* (med.) gerontología, ciencia de la senilidad.

nostril [nástrįl], *s.* ventana de la nariz; ollar.

nostrum [nástrʌm], *s.* remedio o medicina secreta o de patente; panacea, sánalotodo.

not [nat], *adv.* no; ni, ni siquiera (*not a word,* ni una palabra).—**n. a little,** no poco, bastante. —**n. any,** ninguno.—**n. at all,** nada; de ningún modo.—**n. but, in that,** no es (decir) que no (*not but that I shall go,* no es (decir) que no vaya).—**n. even,** ni siquiera.—**n. guilty,** no culpable; absuelto.—**n. one,** ni uno (solo).— **n. proved,** no proven, (for.) no convicto, absuelto.—**n. so much as,** ni siquiera.—**n. to,** sin, por no (*not to say bad,* por no decir malo; *not to mention more than two,* sin mencionar más que dos).—**is it n.?** ¿no es así? ¿no es eso? ¿verdad?—**I think n.,** no lo creo; creo que no.

notability [nóụtabílįtį], *s.* notabilidad.

notable [-bl]. I. *a.* notable, memorable, insigne, resaltante. II. *s.* notabilidad, celebridad (persona), personaje eminente.

notableness [-nįs], *s.* notabilidad.

notably [-blį], *adv.* notable o señaladamente.

notarial [notérįąl], *a.* notarial; notariado.

notarize [nóụtạraįz], *va.* (for.) autorizar ante notario.—**notary (public)** [nóụtạrį (pÁblįk], *s.* notario (público), escribano.

notation [notéįşǫn], *s.* notación; anotación; numeración escrita.

notch [nach]. I. *s.* muesca, corte, incisión, entalladura, escopleadura, espera, ranura, mortaja, hendidura; mella; (mar.) tojino; (geog.) desfiladero; (fam.) paso, grado. II. *va.* hacer muescas, entallar, escoplear; dentar, mellar.— **notched** [-t], *a.* (bot.) recortado.

note [nóụt]. I. *s.* nota; marca, señal, *f.;* (a)notación; apunte, memoria; comunicación, nota diplomática; billete, esquela, cartita; conocimiento, noticia, aviso; distinción, nota, importancia; (mús.) nota; tecla; tono; voz, acento; (com.) billete (de banco); letra; vale, pagaré, abonaré; (com.) agiotista.—*pl.* notas, solfa, pieza de música.—**n. broker,** (com.) agiotista.—**n. of hand** = PROMISSORY NOTE.—**n. of protest,** (acta o nota de) protesto.—**n. paper,** papel de cartas o esquelas.—**of n.** = NOTED. II. *va.* marcar, distinguir; reparar, observar, advertir; (a veces con **down**), apuntar, (a)notar, asentar, registrar.—**to n. an exception,** (for.) anotar en los

autos la excepción que pone una de las partes. —**to n. a protest,** protestar una letra o pagaré.

notebook [-bụk], *s.* libreta, memorándum, agenda, carnet, librito de memoria o de apuntes.

noted [-įd], *a.* notable, afamado, célebre, eminente, insigne, prestigioso, señalado.

notedly [-lįj], *adv.* notablemente.

noteless [-lįs], *a.* obscuro, desconocido.

noteworthy [-wœrðį], *a.* notable, digno de atención.

nothing [nÁθįŋ]. I. *s.* nada, ninguna cosa; la nada; nadería, friolera; nitos; cero.—**n. but,** sólo, no más que.—**n. doing.** V. DOING.—**n. else,** ninguna otra cosa; nada más.—**n. less than,** lo mismo que, no menos que.—**n. much,** no mucho, poca cosa.—**n. to boast,** o **speak, of,** poca cosa, no gran cosa.—**(there is) n. to,** o **in, it,** eso no vale nada, no asciende a nada.—**for n.,** gratis, de balde; inútilmente, sin provecho. —**that is to me,** eso nada me importa.— **there is n. else to do,** o **n. for it but,** no hay más remedio (que). II. *adv.* de ningún modo, en nada.—**n. daunted,** sin temor alguno, sin inmutarse.—**n. like,** ni con mucho, ni aproximadamente.

nothingness [-nįs], *s.* nada; la nada; nonada; insignificancia.

notice [nóụtįs]. I. *s.* nota, observación; atención; aviso, advertencia, reparo, anuncio, noticia, información, notificación; mención; artículo, suelto; ojo, llamada; consideración, cortesía.—**at the shortest n.,** al momento, tan pronto como sea posible.—**on short n.,** con poco plazo o tiempo, con poco tiempo de aviso.—**until further n.,** hasta más aviso. II. *va.* notar, advertir, reparar en, mirar, echar de ver, caer en la cuenta de; hacerse cargo de, atender a, cuidar de; mentar, hacer mención de; (fam.) tratar con atención.

noticeable [-ạbl], *a.* digno de atención, notable; perceptible, reparable.—**to be n.,** percibirse.

noticeably [-ạblį], *adv.* notablemente; perceptiblemente.

notification [nóụtįfįkéįşǫn], *s.* notificación; cita.

notify [-faį], *va.* notificar, avisar, advertir, participar, dar a conocer; prevenir; requerir, citar.

notion [nóụşǫn], *s.* noción; idea; parecer, opinión, entendimiento; preocupación; capricho, intención, inclinación.—*pl.* mercería, novedades, baratijas, fruslerías.—**notions counter,** sección de mercería (en una tienda).

notional [-ạl], *a.* nocional; imaginario, ideal; fantástico; caprichoso, chiflado, maniático.

notionally [-į], *adv.* idealmente.

notochord [nóụtokord], *s.* (anat., zool.) notocordio. V. CHORDA DORSALIS.

notoriety [nọụtoráịetį], *s.* notoriedad, publicidad (esp. de carácter escandaloso).

notorious [notórįas], *a.* notorio, público, conspicuo; escandaloso, sensacional; de mala fama.

notoriously [-lįj], *adv.* notoriamente.

notoriousness [-nįs], *s.* notoriedad, publicidad; mala reputación.

notus [nóụtʌs], *s.* noto, austro.

notwithstanding [natwįðstǽndįŋ]. I. *adv.* no obstante, sin embargo, empero. II. *prep.* a pesar de, a despecho de. III. *conj.* aun cuando, aunque, bien que; por más que.—**n. that,** aunque.

nougat [núgạt], *s.* nuégado, alajú.

nought [nọt], *s.* = NAUGHT.—**for n.** = FOR NOTHING.

noumenon [númenạn], *s.* (filos.) nóumeno.— **noumenal** [-ạl], *a.* relativo al nóumeno, de carácter de nóumeno.

noun [naụn], *s.* (gram.) nombre, su(b)stantivo.

nourish [nœrįš], *va.* nutrir, alimentar, dar alimento a; abrigar, alentar, fomentar.

nourishable [-ạbl], *a.* que se puede nutrir o fomentar.

nourisher [-œ(r)], *s.* nutridor, alimentador.

nourishing [-įŋ], *a.* nutritivo, alimenticio.

nourishment [-m̦ent], *s.* alimento; nutrición, alimentación; pasto, pábulo, fomento.

nova [nóuv̦ə], *s.* (astr.) nova, estrella transitoria.

Nova Scotian [-skóuʃ̦ən], *a.* y *s.* neoescocés.

Novatian [novéiʃ̦ən], *s.* y *a.* (igl.) novaciano.

novation [novéiʃ̦ən], *s.* (for.) novación.

novel [náv̦əl], **I.** *a.* novel, nuevo, original; reciente, moderno. **II.** *s.* novela; (for.) novela.—**n.-writing**, novelística.—**to write novels**, novelar.

novelette [-ét], *s.* novela corta.

novelist [-ist], *s.* novelista, novelador.

novelistic [-ístik], *a.* novelesco, roman(c)esco; novelístico.

novelize [-aiz], *va.* adaptar o escribir en forma de novela.

novelty [-ti], *s.* novedad; innovación.—*pl.* **novelties**, novedades, artículos de fantasía.

November [novémbœr)], *s.* noviembre.

novena [novín̦ə], *s.* (igl.) novena.

novenary [návin̦eri], **I.** *a.* que consta de nueve; de o rel. al número nueve. **II.** *s.* (igl.) novenario.

novennial [novén̦iəl], *a.* que ocurre cada noveno año o que dura nueve años.

novice [návis], *s.* novicio, novato, tirón, bisoño, principiante, aprendiz, *m.;* (igl.) novicio; neófito.

novitiate [noviʃ̦eit], *s.* (igl.) noviciado; novicio.

novocaine [nóuvokein], *s.* novocaína (nombre de fábrica de un anestésico local).

now [náu]. **I.** *adv.* ahora; ya, ora; hoy (día), actualmente, al presente; luego, al instante; después de esto; ahora bien, esto supuesto.—**n. and again, n. and then**, de vez en cuando, de cuando en cuando.—**n. . . ., n. . . ., ya . . .** ya, ora . . . ora, tan pronto . . . como, alternativamente (*now rich, now poor*, ya rico, ya pobre).—**n. or never**, ahora o nunca.—**n. then**, y bien, ahora bien, bien, pues bien.—**for n.**, por ahora, por el (o lo) pronto.—**from n. on**, de hoy, o de aquí en adelante.—**just n.**, ahora mismo, poco ha. *V.* JUST.—**until n.**, hasta ahora, hasta aquí. **II.** *conj.* (gen. con that) ya que, ahora que, puesto que. **III.** *interj.* ¡vamos! ¡vaya! **IV.** *s.* actualidad, momento presente.

nowadays [-ədeiz], *adv.* hoy (en) día.

noway(s [nóuwei(z], *adv.* de ningún modo.

nowhere [nóuhwer], *adv.* en ninguna parte.—**n. else**, en ninguna otra parte.—**n. near**, ni con mucho.

nowhither [nóuhwiðœr)], *adv.* hacia ninguna parte.

nowise [nóuwaiz], *adv.* de ningún modo, de ninguna manera, de modo alguno.

noxious [nákʃas], *a.* nocivo, malsano, mefítico, dañoso, pernicioso.—**noxiously** [-li], *adv.* perniciosamente.—**noxiousness** [-nis], *s.* nocividad.

nozzle [názl], *s.* lanza, boquilla (de mang(uer)a o pulverizador); boca, pitón; cañuto o tobera (de fuelle); pico o boca (de cafetera, etc.); (zool.) hocico, nariz; (fam.) nariz (de persona).

nuance [njúans], *s.* matiz, *m.*

nub [nʌb], *s.* protuberancia; nudo; (fam.) meollo.

nubbin [nʌbin], *s.* mazorca imperfecta de maíz; fruta imperfecta; pedacito saliente; tocón.

Nubian [njúbian], *s.* y *a.* nubio, nubiense.

nubile [njúbil], *a.* núbil, casadera, viripotente (ú. de la mujer).—**nubility** [njúbɪliti], *s.* nubilidad.

nubilous [njúbilʌs], *a.* (poét.) nub(i)loso; o(b)scuro.

nucha [njúkə], *s.* (anat.) nuca, cogote; testuz(o).

nuciferous [njusífɛras], *a.* que produce nueces.

nucleal [njúkliəl], **nuclear** [-ə(r)], *a.* nuclear(io). —**nuclear fission**, (fís.) fisión nuclear.

nucleate [njúkliejt], *va.* y *vn.* formar un núcleo.

nucleate(d [-ijd], *a.* (biol.) nucleado.

nuclein [njúkliin], *s.* (bioquím.) nucleína.

nucleolus [njuklíolas], *s.* (biol.) nucléolo.

nucleus [njúkliʌs], *s.* núcleo.

nude [njud], *a.* desnudo, nudo; escueto.—**the n.**, (b. a.) desnudo, figura humana desnuda.

nudge [nʌdʒ]. **I.** *va.* tocar ligera o disimuladamente con el codo. **II.** *s.* codazo ligero.

nudism [njúdizm], *s.* nudismo (culto o práctica). —**nudist** [njúdist], *s.* nudista; (b. a.) desnudista, partidario del desnudo.—**nudity** [njúditi], *s.* desnudez, calidad de desnudo.

nugatoriness [njúgatorinis], *s.* nulidad.

nugatory [-təri], *a.* ineficaz; nugatorio, frustráneo.

nugget [nʌgit], *s.* (min.) pepita, palacra(na).

nuggety [-i], *a.* en forma de pepitas.

nuisance [njúsans], *s.* incomodidad, molestia, estorbo; engorro, fastidio, lata; indecencia, porquería; (for.) perjuicio, daño, molestia o incomodidad que se causa al prójimo sin derecho para ello; (fam.) pelmazo, chinche (persona).

null [nʌl], *a.* nulo, inválido, írrito, sin fuerza legal.—**n. and void**, nulo y sin valor.

nullification [nʌlifikéiʃ̦ən], *s.* anulación, invalidación; (E. U. pol.) renuncia de un estado a obedecer las leyes federales.

nullify [nʌlifai], *va.* anular, invalidar, nulificar.

nullity [nʌliti], *s.* nulidad; (for.) acto o documento nulo y sin valor.

Numantine [njúmæntain], **Numantian** [njumǽnʃ̦ən], *a.* y *s.* numantino.

numb [nʌm]. **I.** *a.* aterido, entum(ec)ido, entorpecido; torpe. **II.** *va.* entumecer, entorpecer, adormecer.

number [nʌmbœr)]. **I.** *va.* numerar, contar; computar; incluir, contar, ascender a.—**numbering machine**, (impr.) máquina numeradora.—**n. stamp**, numerador. **II.** *s.* número; cifra, guarismo; cantidad, multitud, colección; (gram.) número; (impr.) número o ejemplar (de periódico); (poét., mús.) ritmo, cadencia.—*pl.* aritmética, ciencia de los números.—**Numbers**, Números, libro del Antiguo Testamento.—**numbers pool**, o **racket**, lotería ilegal en que se hacen apuestas sobre varias combinaciones numéricas.—**n. one**, (fam.) número uno, uno mismo, sí mismo.—**n. plate**, (aut.) placa con la matrícula, etc.—**a n. of**, varios.

numberer [-œr)], *s.* numerador, contador.

numberless [-lis], *a.* innumerable, sin número, sin cuenta, un sinnúmero de, un sinfín de.

numbfish [nʌmfiʃ̦], *s.* (ict.) torpedo.

numbness [-nis], *s.* entumecimiento, torpor, aterimiento, envaramiento, adormecimiento.

numen [njúmin], *s.* numen.

numerable [njúmerəbl], *a.* (e)numerable.

numeral [njúmerəl]. **I.** *a.* numeral, numérico, numerario. **II.** *s.* número, cifra, guarismo; nombre o adjetivo numeral.

numerary [njúmereri], *a.* numerario.

numerate [njúmereit], *va.* (e)numerar, contar.

numeration [-éiʃ̦ən], *s.* numeración hablada; enumeración.

numerator [-ọ(r)], *s.* contador; (mat.) numerador.

numeric(al [njumérik(əl], *a.* numérico.

numerically [-i], *adv.* numéricamente.

numerosity [njumerásiti], *s.* numerosidad.

numerous [njúmɛras], *a.* numeroso; muchos.—**numerously** [-li], *adv.* numerosamente, en gran número.—**numerousness** [-nis], *s.* numerosidad.

Numidian [njumídian]. **I.** *s.* y *a.* númida, *mf.* **II.** *a.* numídico.

numismatic(al [njumizmǽtik(əl], *a.* numismático.—**numismatics** [-s], **numismatology** [-tálodʒi], *s.* numismática.—**numismatist** [njumízmətist], *s.* numismático.

nummular [nʌmyūlə(r)], *a.* monetario; (med.) numular, numuláceo.

nummulite [-lait], *s.* (zool. y pal.) numulita.

numskull [nʌmskʌl], *s.* zote, bodoque.

nun [nʌn], *s.* (igl.) monja, religiosa; (orn.) una de

varias clases de aves—paro, pichón copetudo, paloma monjil o de toca, etc.—**n. buoy**, boya cónica.—**n.'s habit**, monjil.—**n.'s veiling**, (tej.) velo de monja.

nunciature [nʌ́nṣiạchụr], s. (igl.) nunciatura.

nuncio [nʌ́nṣiou], s. (igl.) nuncio.

nuncupative [nʌ́ŋkiupeịtịv], a. (for.) nuncupativo, verbal (testamento).

nunnery [nʌ́nœri], s. convento de monjas.

nunnish [nʌ́niṣ], **nunlike** [-laịk], a. monjil.

nuptial [nʌ́pṣạl], a. nupcial, esponsalicio.—**n. plumage**, plumaje de un ave durante la cría.—**n. song**, epitalamio.

nuptials [-z], s. pl. nupcias, boda.

nurse [nœrs]. **I.** s. ama de cría, nodriza; niñera; enfermera, enfermero; protector, padrino; fomentador.—**n. balloon**, globo nodriza, globo alimentador.—**n. child**, niño de teta.—**n. shark**, (ict.) especie de tiburón. **II.** va. criar, lactar, amamantar; alimentar, mantener; abrigar, acariciar; cuidar o asistir enfermos; fomentar, dar alas; cultivar (una planta). **III.** vn. cuidar de un enfermo; dar de mamar a un niño, criar; mamar, amamantarse; lactar.

nursemaid [-meịd], s. niñera.

nursery [nœ́rsœri], s. cuarto o aposento destinado a los niños; (agr.) plantel, plantío, plantario, almáciga, criadero, semillero; vivero, viveral; (fig.) plantel, semillero, seminario.—**n. school**, escuela de párvulos (gen. precede al kindergarten).—**n. tales**, cuentos de niños.

nurserymaid [-meịd], s. = NURSEMAID.

nurseryman [-mæn], s. (agr.) dueño o empleado de plantel o almáciga.

nursing [nœ́rsịŋ], s. crianza, lactancia.—**n. bottle**, biberón, (Am.) mamadera, tetero.—**n. home**, sanatorio particular.

nursling [nœ́rslịŋ], s. niño de teta; (fam.) crío.

nurture [nœ́rchụ(r)]. **I.** s. nutrimento; alimentación, nutrición; educación, crianza; fomento. **II.** va. nutrir, alimentar; criar; educar, enseñar fomentar, promover.

nut [nʌt], s. (bot.) nuez; avellana, almendra, nuez del Brasil, etc.; fruto parecido a la nuez; (mec.) tuerca, matriz, hembra de tornillo; (mús.) cejilla de violín o guitarra; talón del arco de violín (fam.) chiflado, loco; maniático; (fam.) cabeza.—**n. oil**, aceite de nueces.—**n. of an anchor**, (mar.) oreja de ancla.—**n. pine**, (bot.) pino piñonero.—**n. wrench**, (mec.) desvolvedor.—**a hard n. to crack**, problema (m.) difícil hueso duro de roer. **II.** vn. coger nueces.

nutant [niútạnt], a. (bot.) inclinado; (astr.) nutable.

nutation [niutéịṣọn], s. (astr., bot., med.) nutación; inclinación u oscilación habitual de la cabeza.

nutbrown [nʌ́tbraụn], a. avellanado.

nutcracker [-kræckœ(r)], s. cascanueces.

nutgall [-gol], s. (bot.) agalla.

nuthatch [-hæch], s. (orn.) pequeña ave trepadora, trepatroncos, (gal.) sítela.

nuthook [-hụk], s. horquilla para coger nueces.

nutmeat [-mit], s. carne (f.) o pierna de nuez.

nutmeg [-meg], s. (bot.) nuez moscada.—**n. tree**, mirística.

nutpecker [-pekœ(r)], s. = NUTHATCH.

nutpick [-pịk], s. instrumento para sacar la carne o pierna de nuez; (prov.) escoznete.

nutria [niútriạ], s. (zool.) el coipo y su piel. (La palabra española *nutria* designa más bien el *otter* y su piel).

nutrient [niútriẹnt]. **I.** a. nutricio, nutritivo. **II.** s. alimento nutritivo.—**nutriment** [-mẹnt] s. nutrimento, alimento.—**nutrimental** [-méntạl], a. nutrimental.

nutrition [niutríṣọn], s. nutrición, alimentación.

nutritious [niutríṣʌs], **nutritive** [niútrịtịv], a. nutricio, nutritivo, alimenticio, substancioso.

nutshell [nʌ́tṣel], s. cáscara de nuez o avellana.

—**in a n.**, en substancia, en pocas palabras, en su más simple expresión.

nuttiness [nʌ́tịnịs], s. sabor de nuez.

nutty [nʌ́tị], a. abundante en nueces; que sabe a nueces; (fam.) elegante, garboso; (con **on** u **over**) (fam.) entusiasta, loco (por); (fam.) chiflado, loco.

nux vomica [nʌks vámịkạ], s. (bot.) nuez vómica.

nuzzle [nʌ́zl], va. y vn. hozar, hocicar; frotar la nariz contra; mimar. V. SNUGGLE y CUDDLE.

nyctaginaceous [nịktạdźịnéịṣʌs], a. (bot.) nictagíneo.

nyctalopia [nịktạlóụpiạ], s. (med.) nictalopía (en la acepción de *night blindness*); por confusión, hemeralopía (en la acepción de *day blindness*). Es de notarse que las dos voces tienen en español una significación contraria a su acepción normal en inglés.

nyctalope [nịktạloụp], s., **nyctalopic** [-lápịk], a. nictálope; por confusión, hemerálope.

nyctalops [-laps], s. nictálope.

nylon [nájlạn], s. nilón (es nombre de fábrica).—pl. medias de nilón o de cristal.

nymph [nịmf], s. (mit.) ninfa; (poét.) mujer joven, zagala; (ent.) ninfa, palomilla, crisálida.

nympha [nịmfạ], s. (anat.) ninfa de la vulva; (zool.) ninfa, crisálida.

Nymphæa [nịmfíạ], s. (bot.) ninfea, nenúfar.

nymphæaceous [nịmfjéịạịạs], a. (bot.) ninfeáceo.

nymphal [nịmfạl], **nymphean** [nịmfíạn], a. perteneciente a las ninfas.

nymphomania [nịmfoméịnịạ], s. (med.) ninfomanía, furor uterino.

O

o [oụ], s. o.—**O**, cero; nulidad.

O! interj. ¡O! ¡oh!—**O that!**, ¡ojalá (que)!

oaf [oụf], s. zoquete, bobalicón; niño idiota o deforme.—**oafish** [-ịṣ], a. tonto, idiota.

oak [oụk], s. (bot.) roble, encina (árbol y madera).—**o. apple**, u **o. gall**, bugalla, agalla del roble.—**o. grove**, robledo, robledal, encinar.—**o. leather**, cuero curtido con cáscara de roble; (bot.) hongo duro y correoso que nace en los robles.—**o.-tanned**, curtido con corteza de roble.

oaken [-n], a. roblizo, de hojas o madera de roble; duro, fuerte.

oakum [óụkʌm], s. estopa, malacuenda.

oakwood [óụkị], a. duro, fuerte; que abunda en robles.

oar [ór]. **I.** s. remo; remero.—**o. blade**, pala de remo.—**o. stroke**, palada.—**to put in one's o.**, meter baza o su cucharada.—**to rest on one's** (o **the**) **oars**, V. TO LIE. **II.** va. y vn. bogar, remar.

oarage [-ịdź], s. conjunto de remos; palamenta.

oared [-d], a. provisto de remos; (zool.) que tiene pies parecidos a remos.

oarfish [-fịṣ], s. (ict.) regaleco.

oarlock [-lak], s. horquilla, chumacera. V. ROWLOCK.

oarsman [-zmạn], s. remero, remador.

oarsmanship [-ṣịp], s. arte de remar; destreza en remar.

oary [-i], a. formado como remo.

oasis [oéịsịs], s. oasis, m.

oast [oụst], s. horno para lúpulo, malta o tabaco.

oat(s [óụt(s], s. (bot.) avena; (poét.) avena, zampoña, dulzaina, poema pastoril.—**oats-peasbeans**, juego de niños que bailan y cantan en coro.—**off one's oats**, indispuesto, desganado.—**to feel one's oats**, (fam.) estar animoso o brioso; darse importancia.

oatcake [-keịk], s. torta de harina de avena.

oaten [-n], a. aveníceo, avenáceo, de avena.

oatfield [-fild], s. avenal.

oath [oụθ], s. juramento; reniego, terno, voto.—**o.-breaking**, violación de juramento, perjurio.—**on**, u **upon, o.**, bajo juramento.—**to**

take, o **make an,** o., jurar, prestar juramento.

oatmeal [óųtmil], s. harina de avena; gachas o puches de avena.—**o. gruel,** avenate, broma.

obbligato [abligátoų], s. (mús.) obligado.

obduracy [ábdįurặsį], s. obduración, obstinación, impenitencia, endurecimiento, dureza de corazón.

obdurate [ábdįurįt], a. obstinado, endurecido.— **obdurately** [-lį], adv. tercamente, obstinadamente.

obdurateness [-nįs] = OBDURACY.

obedience [obídįęns], s. obediencia, sumisión, acatamiento.—**obedient** [-ęnt], a. obediente, sumiso.—**obediently** [-li], adv. obedientemente.

obeisance [obéįsąns], s. cortesía, reverencia; homenaje, acatamiento, deferencia.

obelisk [ábelįsk], s. obelisco; aguja; (impr.) cruz, obelisco, obelo (†).

obelus [ábelʌs], s. obelo, obelisco, cruz o señal (como —, ÷ o †) puesto al margen.

obese [obís], a. obeso, gordo.—**obeseness** [-nįs], **obesity** [-įtį], s. obesidad, gordura, crasitud.

obey [obéį]. I. va. obedecer, cumplir; estar sujeto a, estar bajo el dominio de. II. vn. ser obediente.

obfuscate [abfʌskeįt], va. ofuscar, obcecar, cegar.

obfuscation [-éįṣǫn], s. ofuscación, ceguedad.

obi [óųbį], s. sortilegio practicado por los negros de las Antillas (ll. t. **obeah**); ancha faja japonesa.

obit [óųbįt], s. exequias, pl., funerales, pl.

obituary [obíchưerį]. I. a. obituario, necrológico. II. s. necrología, obituario; (igl.) obituario.— pl. (noticias) obituarias.

object [ábdʒekt], s. objeto, cosa, materia, sujeto; fin, objeto, propósito; blanco, punto; (gram.) complemento.—**o. ball,** mingo (en el billar).— **o. glass, o. lens,** (ópt.) objetivo.—**o. lesson,** lección práctica u objetiva.—**o. teaching,** enseñanza o método objetivo.

object [ǫbdʒékt]. I. va. objetar, oponer, aducir, poner reparos; tachar; imputar, hacer cargos. II. vn. oponerse, poner objeción, tener inconveniente.

objectify [ǫbdʒéktįfaį], **objectivate** [-įveįt], **objectivize** [-vaįz], va. objetivar; exteriorizar.— **objectification** [-fįkéįṣǫn], s. objetivación.

objection [ǫbdʒékṣǫn], s. objeción, reparo; réplica; tacha, defecto; inconveniente.

objectionable [-ạbl], a. objetable, reparable, inconveniente; defectuoso; reprensible.

objective [ǫbdʒéktįv]. I. a. objetivo.—**o. case,** (gram.) caso complementario.—**o. point,** punto objetivo, meta. II. s. (ópt., mil.) objetivo; (gram.) (caso) acusativo; punto objetivo, destinación; objetivo, objeto, propósito.

objectively [-lį], adv. objetivamente.

objectivism [-įzm], s. objetivismo.

objectivity [abdʒektįvįtį], s. objetividad.

objectless [ábdʒektlįs], a. sin objeto.

objector [ǫbdʒéktǫ(r)], s. impugnador, objetante.

objurgate [ábdʒœrgeįt], va. reprender, regañar, reconvenir o reprobar violentamente.

objurgation [-éįṣǫn], s. represión, reconvención, reprimenda.

objurgatory [ǫbdʒǽrgatǫrį], a. reprobatorio.

oblate [áblẹįt]. I. a. achatado por los polos; (igl.) consagrado al culto. II. s. (igl.) oblato, oblata.

oblation [abléįṣǫn], s. (igl.) oblación, ofrenda, sacrificio; eucaristía.

obligate [áblįgeįt], va. obligar, comprometer, empeñar; precisar, constreñir.

obligation [-éįṣǫn], s. obligación, compromiso, deber, incumbencia, promesa formal; agradecimiento.—pl. (com.) obligaciones y compromisos; pasivo.—**of o.,** obligatorio, de obligación, de precepto.—**to be under o. to one,** deber favores a uno.—**to put,** o **place, under o.,** hacer favores a; imponer obligación (legal o moral) a.

obligatoriness [ǫblígatǫrįnįs], s. obligatoriedad, calidad de obligatorio.

obligatory [-tǫrį], a. obligatorio, forzoso.

oblige [obláįdʒ], va. obligar, compeler, constreñir, apremiar; complacer, agradar, servir, hacer un favor. Ú. a menudo, esp. en la voz pasiva, para expresar agradecimiento, dar las gracias o pedir un favor; v. gr.: I am (much) obliged to you, muchas gracias, le agradezco mucho; you will greatly oblige me, me hará Vd. un gran favor, le agradeceré muchísimo, le quedaré muy reconocido.

obligee [ablįdʒí], s. (for.) obligado; el que es fiador de otro, o a quien se ha dado una fianza.

obliger [obláįdʒœ(r)], s. el que obliga.

obliging [-dʒįŋ], a. servicial, servidor, obsequioso, oficioso, condescendiente.—**obligingly** [-lį], adv. cortésmente, bondadosamente.—**obligingness** [-nįs], s. cortesía, condescendencia, bondad.

obligor [ablįgór], s. (for.) deudor, obligado.

oblique [ǫblík]. I. a. oblicuo, sesg(ad)o, diagonal, inclinado; indirecto, evasivo; solapado, doloso, siniestro; colateral (pariente); (gram., geom., mil., anat.) oblicuo.—**o. angle,** ángulo oblicuo. —**o.-angled,** oblicuángulo. II. vn. oblicuar, torcerse.—**obliquely** [-lį], adv. oblicuamente, al sesgo, al soslayo, de refilón; indirectamente, por rodeos.—**to place o.,** oblicuar, soslayar.— **obliqueness** [-nįs], **obliquity** [ǫblíkwįtį], s. oblicuidad, sesgo, sesgadura, desviación; (arq.) (es)viaje; aberración, extravío.

obliterate [ǫblítęreįt], va. borrar, testar, tachar; destruir, arrasar; (med.) obliterar.—**obliteration** [-éįṣǫn], s. cancelación, testación, extinción, destrucción; (med.) obliteración, extirpación.

oblivion [ǫblívįǫn], s. olvido.

oblivious [-ʌs], a. olvidadizo, desmemoriado; abstraído, absorto; que causa olvido.

oblong [áblǫŋ]. I. a. oblongo. II. s. cuadrilongo.

obloquy [áblokwį], s. deshonra, baldón; difamación, maledicencia, vilipendio público.

obnoxious [ǫbnáksʌs], a. ofensivo, odioso, detestable; sujeto, expuesto (a mal, daño, censura, etc.).—**obnoxiously** [-lį], adv. odiosamente.—**obnoxiousness** [-nįs], s. odiosidad.

oboe [óųbǫų], s. (mús.) oboe, obué.—**oboist** [óųbǫįst], s. oboe, oboísta (el que lo toca).

obol, obolus [ábǫl, -ʌs], s. óbolo (peso y moneda).

obole [ábǫl], s. (farm.) obolo (12 granos).

obovate [abóųveįt], a. (bot.) obovoide, trasovado.

obscene [ǫbsín], a. obsceno, indecente, impúdico, pornográfico; repugnante, asqueroso.—**obscenely** [-lį], adv. obscenamente.—**obsceneness** [-nįs], **obscenity** [ǫbsénįtį], s. obscenidad, indecencia, torpeza.

obscurant(ist [ǫbskįúrạnt(įst], a. y s. obscurantista.—**obscurantism** [-įzm], s. obscurantismo.

obscuration [abskįuréįṣǫn], s. obscurecimiento.

obscure [ǫbskįúr]. I. a. obscuro. II. va. obscurecer; ocultar, disfrazar, evadir, confundir (to obscure the issue, confundir o disfrazar el punto en debate).—**obscurely** [-lį], adv. obscuramente.

obscureness [-nįs], **obscurity** [-įtį], s. obscuridad; confusión, vaguedad; humildad.

obsecrate [ábsękreįt], va. obsecrar, suplicar, rogar, invocar.

obsecration [-éįṣǫn], s. obsecración, súplica; (igl.) cada ruego de la letanía.

obsequial [ǫbsíkwįạl], a. funeral, fúnebre.

obsequies [ábsįkwiz], s. pl. exequias, funeral(es), honras (funerales), ritos fúnebres.

obsequious [ǫbsíkwʌs], a. obsequioso, zalamero, servicial; servil, rendido.—**obsequiously** [-lį], adv. obsequiosa o servicialmente; servilmente. —**obsequiousness** [-nįs], s. obsequio; servilismo.

observable [ǫbzœ́rvǝbl], *a.* observable; perceptible; visible, conspicuo.—**observableness** [-nịs], *s.* calidad de observable o notable.— **observably** [-ǝblị], *adv.* notablemente, conspicuamente.

observance [-ǎns], *s.* observancia; acatamiento; rito o ceremonia; costumbre, uso.

observant [-ǎnt], *a.* observador, vigilante; observante, obediente.

observation [abzœrvéịšǫn], *s.* observación; reparo, advertencia; escrutinio, examen.—**o. balloon,** globo de observación.—**o. car,** (E. U., f. c.) coche trasero con mirador.—**to keep under o.,** vigilar.

observatory [ǫbzœ́rvǝtorị], *s.* observatorio; atalaya; mirador, miradero.

observe [ǫbzœ́rv], *va.* observar; advertir, notar, reparar, echar de ver, fijarse; atisbar, velar, vigilar; guardar (una fiesta); cumplir (un precepto).

observer [-œ(r)], *s.* observador; atisbador.

observing [-ịŋ], *a.* observador, atento, cuidadoso; observante.—**observingly** [-lị], *adv.* cuidadosamente, atentamente.

obsess [ǫbsés], *va.* obsesionar, obseder, causar obsesión.—**obsession** [ǫbséšǫn], *s.* obsesión.

obsidian [absídịan], *s.* (min.) obsidiana.

obsidional [absídịonạl], *a.* (mil.) obsidional.

obsolesce [absolés], *vn.* caer en desuso, desusarse. —**obsolescence** [-ǝns], *s.* estado o acto de caer en desuso.—**obsolescent** [-ǝnt], *a.* que va haciéndose anticuado.

obsolete [ábsolit], I. *a.* anticuado; (biol.) atrofiado, imperfecto. II. *s.* voz anticuada.

obsoleteness [-nịs], *s.* desuso; (biol.) desarrollo rudimentario e imperfecto.

obstacle [ábstǝkl], *s.* obstáculo; óbice, valla, traba, tropiezo, impedimento, dificultad, contrariedad.—**o. race,** carrera de obstáculos.

obstetric|al [ǫbstétrịk(ạl], *a.* obstétrico.

obstetrician [abstetríšǫn], *s.* especialista en obstetricia; partero, comadrón.

obstetrics [ǫbstétrịks], *s.* (med.) obstetricia.

obstinacy [ábstịnạsị], *s.* obstinación, porfía, terquedad, contumacia, tesonería, testarudez, tozudez.

obstinate [ábstịnịt], *a.* obstinado, terco, porfiado, tozudo, temático, temoso, contumaz, reacio.

obstinately [-lị], *adv.* obstinada o tercamente.

obstreperous [obstrépǝrʌs], *a.* estrepitoso, ruidoso, turbulento, alharaquiento.—**obstreperously** [-lị], *adv.* estrepitosamente, turbulentamente.—**obstreperousness** [-nịs], *s.* estrépito, bulla, baraúnda, alharaca.

obstruct [ǫbstrʌ́kt], *va.* obstruir, atorar, cerrar, impedir, dificultar, estorbar; atajar, detener.

obstructer, obstructor [-œ(r)], *s.* obstructor, el que estorba, impide o retarda.

obstruction [ǫbstrʌ́kšǫn], *s.* obstrucción, impedimento, estorbo, obstáculo, entorpecimiento. —**obstructionism** [-ịzm], *s.* (pol.) obstruccionismo.—**obstructionist** [-ịst], *s.* (pol.) obstruccionista.

obstructive [ǫbstrʌ́ktịv], I. *a.* obstructivo, obstructor; (med.) opilativo. II. *s.* impedimento. —**obstructiveness** [-nịs], *s.* calidad de obstructivo.

obstruent [ábstruǝnt], *a.* (med.) obstruyente, opilativo, astringente (agente o remedio).

obtain [ǫbtéịn], I. *va.* obtener, adquirir, conseguir, alcanzar, lograr. II. *vn.* prevalecer, privar, ser ley, moda o uso; presentarse.

obtainable [-ǝbl], *a.* obtenible, asequible.

obtainer [-œ(r)], *s.* obtentor, el que obtiene.

obtainment [-mǝnt], *s.* obtención, conseguimiento, consecución, logro.

obtrude [ǫbtrúd], I. *va.* imponer o introducir a la fuerza. II. *vn.* entrometerse, intrusarse.

obtruder [-œ(r)], *s.* entremetido, intruso.

obtruncate [abtrʌ́ŋkeịt], *va.* desmochar.

obtrusion [ǫbtrúžǫn], *s.* intrusión, entrometimiento.

obtrusive [ǫbtrúsịv], *a.* intruso, entrometido.

obtund [abtʌ́nd], *va.* embotar, amortiguar.

obturate [ábtjureịt], *va.* obturar, tapar.

obturation [-éịšǫn], *s.* obturación.

obturator [-ǫ(r)], *s.* obturador.

obtuse [ǫbtịús], *a.* obtuso (ángulo, etc.); romo, sin punta, embotado; lerdo, torpe; sordo, apagado (ruido).—**o.-angle(d)**, obtusángulo.

obtusely [-lị], *adv.* obtusamente; lerdamente.

obtuseness [-nịs], *s.* calidad de obtuso; embotadura, embotamiento; torpeza.

obverse [ábvœrs], I. *s.* anverso, frente. II. *a.* del anverso.

obversion [abvœ́ršǫn], *s.* vuelta que se da a un objeto para ponerlo de frente.

obvert [abvœ́rt], *va.* volver un objeto de frente a.

obviate [ábvịeịt], *va.* obviar, evitar, salvar.

obvious [ábvịʌs], *a.* obvio, evidente, claro, palpable.—**obviously** [-lị], *adv.* obvia o evidentemente.—**obviousness** [-nịs], *s.* claridad, evidencia.

oca [óụkǎ], *s.* (bot.) oca; caví.

ocarina [akǎrínǎ], *s.* (mús.) ocarina.

occasion [ǫkéịžǫn], I. *s.* ocasión, caso; acontecimiento; oportunidad, lugar, coyuntura; sazón, *f.,* tiempo oportuno; motivo, causa, razón, *f.;* necesidad.—**as o. requires,** en caso necesario, cuando llegue la ocasión.—**on o.,** en su oportunidad o a su debido tiempo; cuando se ofrece, ocasionalmente.—**on the o. of,** con motivo de. —**to give o.,** dar pie.—**to have o. to,** tener que, hacerle falta a uno, ofrecerse.—**to improve the o.,** aprovechar la ocasión. II. *va.* ocasionar, motivar, causar, acarrear.

occasional [-ạl], *a.* ocasional, casual, fortuito; alguno que otro; poco frecuente, que ocurre de cuando en cuando.—**o. verse,** poesía de circunstancia.—**occasionally** [-ị], *adv.* a veces, de vez en cuando, tal cual vez, a ratos.

occasioner [-œ(r)], *s.* ocasionador, causante, causador; causa, motivo.

occident [áksịdǝnt], *s.* occidente, ocaso, oeste.— **O.,** Europa y América, hemisferio occidental.

occidental [aksịdéntạl], *a.* occidental; occiduo.

occipital [aksịpịtạl], *a.* y *s.* (anat.) occipital; referente al occipucio.—**o. bone,** hueso occipital.

occiput [áksịpʌt], *s.* (anat.) occipucio, colodrillo.

occlude [aklúd], I. *va.* cerrar, tapar; (quím.) absorber; (med.) ocluir. II. *vn.* cerrar (los dientes).

occlusion [aklúžǫn], *s.* obstrucción; cerramiento; (med.) oclusión; (quím.) absorción de gases.

occlusive [aklúsịv], *a.* (fon., etc.) oclusivo.

occult [ǫkʌ́lt], *a.* oculto; visible sólo para los que tienen visión espiritual, según la teosofía.

occultation [akʌltéịšǫn], *s.* (astr.) ocultación; desaparición.

occultism [ǫkʌ́ltịzm], *s.* ocultismo.

occultist [-ịst], *s.* y *a.* ocultista.

occultness [-nịs], *s.* calidad de oculto.

occupancy [ákyǔpạnsị], *s.* ocupación, toma de posesión; tenencia.

occupant [-pạnt], *s.* ocupante; inquilino.

occupation [-péịšǫn], *s.* ocupación, toma de posesión; tenencia, inquilinato; ocupación, quehacer, trabajo; oficio, empleo, profesión.

occupational [-ạl], *a.* relativo a ocupaciones u oficio.—**o. disease,** enfermedad causada por el oficio u ocupación.

occupied [ákyǔpaịd], *a.* ocupado; atareado.

occupier [-paịœ(r)], *s.* ocupador. *V.* OCCUPANT.

occupy [-paị], *va.* ocupar, emplear (tiempo); estar instalado en, vivir en; apoderarse de; dar empleo, ocupación o trabajo a.—**to be occupied with,** ocuparse en.

occur [ǫkœ́r], *vn.* ocurrir, encontrarse, ofrecerse; suceder, acontecer, acaecer; aparecer; ocurrirse, venir a la imaginación o a la memoria.

occurrence [-ǝns], *s.* ocurrencia; suceso, caso, lance, incidente, acontecimiento, acaecimiento.

ocean [óu̱ʃạn], *s.* océano, mar, *mf.*, piélago; inmensidad.—**o.-going, o. liner**, tra(n)satlántico.

oceanic [ou̱ʃiénịk], *a.* oceánico; pelágico.

oceanographer [ou̱ʃạnágrạfœ(r)], *s.* oceanógrafo.—**oceanographic** [-ográfịk], *a.* oceanográfico.—**oceanography** [-ágrạfi], *s.* oceanografía.

ocellate(d [áseleit(ịd], *a.* ocelado; ojoso; manchado, rodado.

ocellus [oséḷʌs], *s.* (zool.) ocelo.

ocelot [óu̱selạt], *s.* (zool.) ocelote.

ocher, ochre [óu̱kœ(r)], *s.* ocre, sil, anorea, almagre.

ocherous, ochreous [-rʌs], *a.* ocroso.

ochlocracy [aklákrạsi], *s.* (pol.) oclocracia.

o'clock [ọklák], *loc. contr.* de OF THE CLOCK (según el reloj).—**what o. is it?** ¿qué hora es?—**it is eight o.**, son las ocho.

octagon [áktạgạn], *s.* (geom.) octágono.

octagonal [aktǽgonạl], *a.* octágono, octagonal.

octahedral [aktạhídrạl], *a.* octaédrico.

octahedron [-drọn], *s.* (geom.) octaedro.

octane [áktein], *s.* (quím.) octano.—**o. number, o rating**, número de octano.

octant [áktạnt], *s.* (astr., geom.) octante.

Octateuch [áktạtịuk], *s.* Octateuco.

octave [áktei̱v]. **I.** *s.* (mús. y poét.) octava; (igl.) ochava, octava de una fiesta.—**o. coupler**, (mús.) doblemano (*f.*) de órgano. **II.** *a.* octavo.

Octavian [aktéivịạn], *a.* octaviano.

octavo [aktéivou̱]. **I.** *a.* (impr.) en octavo. **II.** *s.* libro, folleto, etc., en 8vo.

octennial [aktⅇ́nịạl], *a.* que dura ocho años o que ocurre cada ocho años.

octet [aktét], *s.* (mús.) octeto.

octillion [aktíḷyọn], *s.* octillón; (E. U. y Fr.) unidad con 27 ceros; (Ingl.) unidad con 48 ceros.

October [aktóu̱bœ(r)], *s.* octubre.

octodecimo [aktodⅇ́sịmou̱], *a.* (impr.) en décimo-octavo; (escríbese por lo común 18mo y se llama **eighteenmo** [eitínmou̱]).

octogenarian [aktodẓenⅇ́rịạn], **octogenary** [aktádẓⅇnⅇri], *a.* y *s.* octogenario, ochentón.

octonary [áktonⅇri], *a.* ochavo.

octopetalous [aktopétạlʌs], *a.* (bot.) octopétalo.

octopod [áktopạd], *a.* y *s.* (zool.) octópodo.

octopus [áktopʌs], *s.* (zool.) pulpo, pólipo, jibia octópoda; (fig.) organización monopolizadora o absorbente.

octoroon [aktorún], *s.* mulato muy claro; (Cuba) ochavón.

octostyle [áktostai̱l], *s.* (arq.) octóstilo.

octosyllabic [aktosịlǽbịk]. **I.** *a.* octosílabo, octosilábico. **II.** *s.* octosílabo.

octroi [áktroi̱], *s.* fielato; derechos de puerta o de consumos.

octuple [áktu̱pl], *a.* óctuple, óctuplo.

ocular [ákyu̱lạ(r)]. **I.** *a.* ocular, visual. **II.** *s.* (ópt.) ocular.

ocularly [-li], *adv.* ocularmente; visiblemente.

oculist [ákyu̱lịst], *s.* oculista, oftalmólogo.

od [ad], *s.* fuerza misteriosa a que se atribuían los fenómenos del mesmerismo, llamada también **od(yl)ic force** y **astral fluid**.

odalisk, odalisque [óu̱dạlịsk], *s.* odalisca.

odd [ad]. **I.** *a.* impar; non, sobrante; y tantos, y pico (*forty odd*, cuarenta y tantos, cuarenta y pico); suelto (*an odd volume*, un tomo suelto; *an odd job*, una tarea suelta); casual, accidental; extraordinario, singular, raro, particular; excéntrico, extraño; ridículo, estrambótico.—**o. glove**, guante sin pareja.—**o. number**, non. **II.** *s. V.* ODDS.

oddity [ádịti], *s.* singularidad, particularidad, rareza; despropósito; ente singular.

oddly [ádli], *adv.* desigualmente; extrañamente; singularmente; estrambóticamente.

oddness [ádnịs], *s.* disparidad, desigualdad; singularidad, extravagancia, rareza.

odds [adz], *s. pl.* (y a veces *singular*) desigualdad, diferencia, disparidad, exceso; partido desigual,

apuesta desigual; ventaja, superioridad, exceso; riña, pendencia, disputa.—**o. and ends**, retazos, trozos, ñaque, zarandajas, sobras y picos, fragmentos sobrantes.—**by all o.**, con mucho, en todo; sin duda.—**it makes no o.**, es igual, da lo mismo.—**the o. are that**, las probabilidades son, o es lo más probable que.—**to be at o.**, estar de punta, de malas o encontrado(s).—**to give o.**, dar ventaja, puntos o (Am.) gabela (en un juego o apuesta).

ode [oud], *s.* (poét.) oda.

odeon [odían], **odeum** [odíam], *s.* odeón.

odious [óu̱djʌs], *a.* odioso, abominable, repugnante.—**odiously** [-li], *adv.* odiosamente, abominablemente.—**odiousness** [-nịs], *s.* odiosidad; odio.

odium [óu̱djʌm], *s.* odiosidad; odio; mala voluntad, malquerencia; oprobio.

odometer [odámⅇtœ(r)], *s.* (h)odómetro.

odometrical [adọmétrịkạl], *a.* hodométrico.

odontalgia [odantⅇ́ldẓịạ], *s.* (med.) odontalgia, dolor de muelas.

odontalgic [-ịk], *a.* odontálgico.

odontograph [odántograⅇf], *s.* (mec.) instrumento para trazar dientes de engranaje.

odontoid [odántoi̱d], *a.* odontoideo.

odontologist [odantálodẓịst], *s.* odontólogo, dentista.

odontology [-dẓi], *s.* (med.) odontología.

odontorrhagia [odantoréidẓịạ], *s.* (med.) odontorragia.

odontoscope [odántoskou̱p], *s.* odontoscopio.

odor [óu̱dọ(r)], *s.* olor; aroma, *m.*, perfume, fragancia; estimación; reputación.—**to be in bad (good) o.**, tener mala (buena) fama.

odoriferous [-ífⅇrʌs], *a.* odorífero.

odorless [-lịs], *a.* inodoro.

odorous [-ʌs], *a.* oloroso, odorante, fragante.

odorousness [-nịs], *s.* fragancia, aroma, *m.*

Odsbodikins [adzbádikịnz], *interj.* (ant.) ¡cuerpo de tal!

odyl(e [ádịl], *s. V.* OD.

Odyssey [ádịsi], *s.* Odisea u odisea, viaje largo.

œ, diptongo con que antes se escribían algunas voces de origen latino o griego que hoy se escriben con **e**, tales como **œconomics** y **œdema**.

œnological [inoládẓịkạl], *a.* enológico.

œnology [inálodẓi], *s.* enología.

œnometer [inámⅇtœ(r)], *s.* enómetro.

o'er [óu̱r], *contr.* poética de OVER.

œstrum [éstrʌm], *s.* brama, celo; estro.

œstrus [éstrʌs], *s.* (ent.) tábano.

of [av], *prep.* de. Este es el significado general de *of;* pero hay algunas expresiones, sobre todo con verbos, e idiotismos en que equivale a otra preposición o no se traduce (*to dream of*, soñar con; *to think of*, pensar en; *to rob a man of his money*, robar el dinero a un hombre; *to taste of*, saber a; *to smell of*, oler a; *sort of*, o *kind of*, (fam.) algo, un poco; *of course*, naturalmente; *of late*, últimamente). Tales formas se dan en los artículos sobre los verbos, sustantivos, etc., correspondientes. Cuando un gerundio sigue a un posesivo, el sustantivo que en español es el acusativo del verbo correspondiente va gen. precedido de *of;* la expresión resultante se traduce mediante el infinitivo o el subjuntivo del verbo español: *his writing of that letter*, el que él haya (hubiese) escrito esa carta; *our ordering of those articles*, el pedir (o haber pedido) nosotros esos artículos, o el que nosotros pidamos (hayamos pedido) esos artículos.—**o. an evening**, por la noche, algunas noches.—**o. myself, himself**, etc., por mí mismo, por sí mismo, etc.; solo, sin ayuda.—**o. the**, del, de la, de los, de las.—**it is five minutes of three**, faltan cinco minutos para las tres, son las tres menos cinco.—**it is very kind of you to do that**, es Vd. muy bondadoso en hacer eso.

off [ɔf]. **I.** *adv.* lejos, a distancia, fuera; enteramente, del todo; quitado, no puesto (*the lid is* *off*, la tapa está quitada; *my shoes are off*, estoy sin zapatos, me he quitado los zapatos); abandonado, frustrado (*the trip is off*, el viaje se ha abandonado, hemos desistido del viaje; *the wedding is off*, se ha deshecho la boda); de menos, de rebaja (*two per cent off*, rebaja o descuento de dos por ciento); a (con respecto a distancia: *two miles off*, a dos millas). Se une a muchos verbos para modificar su sentido, denotando ausencia, diminución, privación o distancia.—o. **and on**, de vez en cuando, algunas veces; a intervalos.—**how far o. is it?** ¿cuánto hay de aquí allá?—**to be o.**, irse, marcharse, partir, salir. II. *prep.* lejos de; fuera de; de; desde; frente a, a corta distancia de, cerca de (*off the coast*, cerca de la costa; *off New York*, frente a Nueva York).—**o. the track**, (fam.) despistado, por los cerros de Ubeda.—**from o.**, de.—**to be o.**, haber abandonado (*England is off the gold standard*, Inglaterra ha abandonado el patrón oro); (fam.) haber renunciado (al juego, tabaco, etc.).—**to be o. duty**, estar de asueto, no estar de servicio. III. *a.* derecho o de la derecha (hablando de una pareja de animales; o bien de las patas de los mismos, v. gr.: *the off ox*, el buey de la derecha; *off forefoot*, pata derecha delantera); de fiesta, de asueto (v. gr.: *an off day*, un día libre; *the off season*, la estación muerta); (fam.) equivocado, incorrecto (v. gr.: *off in his calculations*, errado en sus cálculos); (fam.) chiflado.—**o.-color**, desteñido, marchito; verde, obsceno; (joy.) de mal color.—**o. side**, lado derecho.—**o.-the-record**, extraoficial. IV. *interj.* ¡fuera! ¡vete! ¡vamos!—**o. with his head!** ¡que le corten la cabeza!—**o. with you!** ¡márchate! ¡fuera de aquí! ¡largo de ahí!

offal [5fәl], *s.* asadura, despojos de reses muertas; bazofia; desecho, desperdicio, relieves, *m. pl.*

offcast [5fkæst], I. *a.* desechado, descartado. II. *s.* cosa o persona descartada.

off-chance [5fchæns], *s.* posibilidad remota o escasa, improbabilidad.

offence, offenceless = OFFENSE, OFFENSELESS.

offend [ofénd], I. *va.* ofender, agraviar, ultrajar; irritar. II. *vn.* pecar, delinquir; desagradar, disgustar.—**to o. against**, faltar a.—**to feel offended**, o **take offense**, sentirse, agraviarse, picarse, ofenderse.

offender [-œ(r)], *s.* delincuente, transgresor, reo, pecador; ofensor, agraviador.

offense [oféns], *s.* ofensa; agravio, atentado, injuria, culpa, falta; cualquier delito o desaguisado.—**no o.**, sin ofender a Vd.; no lo dije por tanto.

offenseless [-lįs], *a.* inofensivo; innocuo.

offensive [-įv], I. *a.* ofensivo, desagradable; perjudicial; agresivo.—**o. odor**, olor desagradable.—**o. warfare**, guerra ofensiva. II. *s.* ofensiva, ataque.

offensively [-lį], *adv.* ofensivamente.

offensiveness [-nįs], *s.* calidad de ofensivo o desagradable.

offer [5fœ(r)], I. *va.* ofrecer, prometer, brindar, mandar; presentar (una moción, etc.), proponer; sacrificar, inmolar. II. *vn.* ofrecerse, ocurrir. III. *s.* oferta, ofrecimiento, promesa; envite; declaración de amor; esfuerzo, intento; (com.) oferta; proposición o propuesta.—**on o.**, a la venta, para vender.

offerer [-œ(r)], *s.* ofrecedor; oferente; licitador.

offering [-įŋ], *s.* ofrecimiento, oferta; sacrificio; ofrenda, oblación, tributo.

offertory [-torį], *s.* (igl.) ofertorio; ofrecimiento, ofrenda.

offhand [áfhænd], *a.* y *adv.* improvisado, de repente; sin preparación; sin pensarlo; sin cumplidos ni ceremonia.

office [áfįs], *s.* oficio; ministerio, empleo o cargo (sea público o privado); colocación, destino; oficina, despacho, bufete; escritorio; consultorio (de médico, etc.); agencia, negociado, departa-

mento; (igl.) oficios, función solemne, rezo.—*pl.* servicio, favor; buenos oficios; (Ingl.) cocina y cuartos del servicio.—**o. book**, (igl.) oficionario.—**o. boy**, chico de oficina, muchacho mandadero.—**o. building**, edificio de oficinas o de administración.—**o. clerk**, o **worker**, oficinista.—**o. copy**, (for.) copia certificada.—**o. hours**, horas hábiles, laborables o de oficina; (med.) horas de consulta o de clínica.—**o. hunter**, o **seeker**, pretendiente, buscaempleos.—**o. letter**, oficio.—**o. work**, trabajo de oficina; (ing.) trabajo de gabinete.—**to be in o.**, tener un empleo; estar en el poder.

officeholder [-houldœ(r)], *s.* empleado público, funcionario, burócrata, *mf.*

officer [áfįsœ(r)], I. *s.* oficial; funcionario; dignatario; empleado o dependiente de alguna categoría; guardia, *m.*, agente de policía; (mil.) oficial o jefe (desde alférez arriba).—**o. of the day**, (mil.) oficial de turno. II. *va.* mandar (como oficial o jefe); proveer de oficiales y jefes.—**officered** [-d], *a.* provisto de oficiales y jefes.

official [ofįšal], I. *a.* oficial; de oficio; autorizado; (farm.) oficinal.—**o. letters**, pliegos de oficio. II. *s.* oficial público; funcionario autorizado o ejecutivo; (Ingl.) provisor o juez eclesiástico.

officialdom [-dǫm], *s.* círculos oficiales; funcionarios públicos; oficialidad.

officialism [-įzm], *s.* estado, condición, costumbres oficiales; oficinismo; burocracia.

officiality [ofįšiálitį], *s.* (igl.) cargo de oficial o ministro de la curia; provisorato.

officially [ofįšalį], *adv.* oficialmente, de oficio.

officiant [ofįšįant], *s.* (igl.) oficiante.

officiate [ofįšįeįt], *vn.* (igl.) oficiar, celebrar (la misa); funcionar, ejercer o desempeñar un cargo.

officiating [-įŋ], *a.*, **officiator** [-ǫ(r)], *s.* oficiante.

officinal [ofįsįnal], I. *a.* (farm.) oficinal; (bot.) empleado en las artes o como medicamento. II. *s.* (farm.) medicamento oficinal.

officious [ofįšΛs], *a.* oficioso, entremetido, intruso; solícito.—**officiously** [-lį], *adv.* oficiosamente.—**officiousness** [-nįs], *s.* oficiosidad.

offing [5fįŋ], *s.* (mar.) franquía, mar afuera.—**in the o.**, visible pero algo lejos; en lontananza.

offish [5fįš], *a.* (fam.) esquivo, intratable, arisco.

offlet [5fįet], *s.* (hidr.) tubo o canal de desagüe.

offprint [5fprįnt], *s.* (impr.) tirada aparte de un artículo, etc.

offscouring [5fskaųrįŋ], **offscum** [5fskΛm], *s.* hez, desecho, basura, lavaduras, *f. pl.*

offset [5fset], *s.* balance, compensación, equivalencia, equivalente; (geog.) estribo, estribación; (top.) ordenada; (E. U.) terraplén; (hort.) pimpollo que sirve para la propagación (*V.* OFF-SHOOT); (mec.) cañería en S; (arq. e impr.) = SETOFF (*V.* también OFFSET, *a.*).

offset, *a.* fuera de su lugar; desalineado; (mec.) no paralelo; no convergente; (impr.) de calcado en lámina de caucho (procedimiento en que se imprime primero en una lámina de caucho, y luego con ésta en el papel. En algunas partes se usa el término inglés *offset*).

offset [ofsét], I. *va.* equiparar, compensar, contrapesar; neutralizar; medir la tierra por el procedimiento de ordenadas; terraplenar. II. [5fset], *vn.* (impr.) repetir; emplear el procedimiento *offset*.

offshoot [5fšut], *s.* renuevo, vástago; ramal.

offshore [5fšór], I. *adv.* de la costa, a corta distancia de la costa. II. *a.* terral (viento); costanero.

offspring [5fsprįŋ], *s.* hijo(s), vástago(s), casta, prole, *f.*, progenie o descendencia.

off-stage [5fstéįdž], *a.* (teat.) de escena dentro, de fuera del escenario.

often [5fn], **oftentimes** [-taįmz], (poét.) **oft-(times** [5ft(taįmz], *adv.* frecuentemente, a menudo, muchas veces.—**as o. as**, siempre que, tantas veces (o tan a menudo) como.—

how o.?, ¿cuántas veces? ¿con qué frecuencia?—**not o.**, rara vez.—**so o.**, tantas veces.—**too o.**, con demasiada frecuencia.

ogee [oud̄źí], *s.* (arq.) gola, cimacio; talón. *V.* CYMA.—**o. arch**, arco conopial o conopio.

ogival [oud̄źáiv̬l], *a.* ojival; aristado.

ogive [óud̄źa̬iv], *s.* (arq.) ojiva, arco apuntado; arista de arco carpanel.

ogle [óuḡl]. **I.** *va.* y *vn.* ojear, echar el ojo, comerse con los ojos a uno. **II.** *s.* ojeada, mirada expresiva de amor, coquetería o de atrevida familiaridad.

ogler [óuḡlœ(r)], *s.* el que echa el ojo, etc.

ogre [óuḡœ(r)], *s.* ogro, monstruo.

ogress [óuḡrịs], *s.* ogro hembra.

oh! [ou], *interj.* ¡oh!, ¡ay!

ohm [óum], *s.* (elec.) ohm(io).—**ohmic** [-ịk], *a.* óhmico.—**ohmmeter** [-mitœ(r)], *s.* ohmímetro, ohmiómetro.

oho [ohóu], *interj.* ¡ajá! ¡hola!

oidium [óidịaam], *s.* (bot.) oídio.

oil [ói̯l]. **I.** *s.* aceite; petróleo; óleo; esencia (de alcanfor, etc.).—**o. bag**, o **gland**, (bot., zool.) glándula oleífera.—**o.-bearing**, petrolífero; oleífero.—**o. beetle**, (ent.) carraleja.—**o. box**, lata de aceite; (f. c.) caja de aceite o sebo.—**o.-break switch**, (elec.) interruptor de aceite.—**o. burner**, quemador de petróleo.—**o.-burning**, de combustión de aceite o petróleo.—**o. cake**, bagazo, torta de borujo.—**o. car**, vagón tanque para petróleo.—**o. color**, color o pintura preparados con aceite. *V.* O. PAINTING.—**o. cruet**, aceitera, alcuza.—**o. cup**, (mec.) aceitera, copa de engrase, lubri(fi)cadora.—**o. engine**, motor de petróleo o de combustión.—**o. field**, yacimiento petrolífero.—**o. field worker**, obrero petrolero.—**o. gas**, gas de petróleo.—**o. groove**, (mec.) ranura de engrase.—**o. jar**, zafra.—**o. meal**, borujo molido, harina de borujo.—**o. mill**, molino de aceite, trujal, lagar, almazara.—**o. miller**, almazarero.—**o. of cedar**, cedreleón; (quím.) cedróleo.—**o. of vitriol**, aceite de vitriolo, ácido sulfúrico.—**o. of wintergreen**, aceite o esencia de gaulteria.—**o. paint** = o. COLOR.—**o. painting**, pintura o cuadro al óleo; arte de pintar al óleo.—**o. paint** = o. COLOR.—**o. pan**, recogedor de aceite.—**o. pipe**, tubo de engrase.—**o. pipe line**, oleoducto.—**o. press** = o. MILL.—**o. ring**, (mec.) anillo de lubricación.—**o. shop**, aceitería.—**o. stove**, estufa o cocina de petróleo.—**o. tank**, tanque, depósito de aceite (gen. de petróleo).—**o. tanker**, (mar.) petrolero.—**o. trough**, canal de aceite.—**o. well**, pozo de petróleo. **II.** *va.* (en)aceitar, engrasar, lubri(fi)car; (fig.) hacer liso, suave y agradable; ungir; untar (la mano), sobornar.

oilbird [-bœrd], *s.* (orn.) guácharo.

oilcan [-kæn], *s.* aceitera, lata de aceite, alcuza.

oilcloth [-kloθ], *s.* encerado, hule.

oiler [-œ(r)], *s.* aceitero; aceitador, engrasador, lubri(fi)cador; aceitera, alcuza; capa de hule; buque aceitero o petrolero.

oiliness [-inịs], *s.* ole(agin)osidad, untuosidad.

oiling [-iŋ], *s.* aceitado, engrase, lubricación.

oilman [-mæn], *s.* petrolero, aceitero, tratante en aceites; el que engrasa o lubri(fi)ca.

oilpaper [-peipœ(r)], *s.* papel encerado.

oilskin [-skịn], *s.* encerado, hule, tela impermeable.—*pl.* traje impermeable de este tejido.

oilstone [-stoun]. **I.** *s.* piedra afiladera o de amolar; asperón. **II.** *va.* afilar con asperón.

oily [ói̯li], *a.* aceitoso, oleoso, oleaginoso, oleario; pingüe, grasiento, craso; zalamero, hipócrita.—**o.-calm**, **o.-smooth**, tranquilo como una balsa de aceite.—**o. grain**, o **bean**, (bot.) ajonjolí, alegría. *V.* SESAME.

ointment [óintmẹnt], *s.* ungüento, untura.

O. K., **OK**, **okay** [óukéi]. **I.** *a.* y *adv.* (fam.) correcto; bueno, que sirve; que no está mal, pasadero; está bien, conforme. **II.** *s.* visto

bueno, V.° B.°; aprobación. **III.** *va.* dar o poner el visto bueno a, aprobar.

okapi [okápi], *s.* (zool.) okapí, rumiante del Congo semejante a la jirafa o cebra.

okra [óukrǎ], *s.* (bot.) quimbombó.

old [óuld], *a.* viejo, anciano, añoso, vetusto; antiguo; añejo, rancio (vino, etc.).—**o. age**, vejez, ancianidad, senectud, vetustez.—**o. bachelor**, solterón.—**o. boy**, (fam.) chico, mi viejo (expresión de amistad).—**O. Boy**, (fam.) el diablo.—**o.-clothes man**, ropavejero.—**o. country**, o. sod, terruño.—**o.-established**, establecido o reconocido desde hace largo tiempo.—**o.-fashioned**, chapado a la antigua; anticuado, fuera de moda.—**o.-fog(e)yish**, chapado a la antigua, engolillado.—**O. Glory**, (E. U.) la bandera de los E. U.—**O. Guard**, (E. U.) banda conservador del partido republicano.—**o. hand**, experto, (fam.) perro viejo.—**O. Harry**, (fam.) el diablo.—**o. lady**, anciana.—**o.-line**, conservador. *V.* O.-ESTABLISHED.—**o.-looking**, de aspecto viejo, que parece viejo.—**o. maid**, solter(on)a; la mona (juego de naipes).—**o.-maidish**, que parece u obra como solterona; melindroso, caprichoso.—**o. man**, viejo; (fam.) padre, esposo o jefe; (teat.) barba, *m.*—**O. Nick**, (fam.) el diablo.—**o. salt**, (fam.) lobo de mar.—**o.-school**, a la antigua.—**o. song**, bagatela.—**o. style**, estilo antiguo (de computar el tiempo); (impr.) tipo de forma antigua.—**O. Testament**, Antiguo Testamento.—**o.-time**, viejo, de tiempos pasados.—**o.-timer**, antiguo residente o concurrente.—**o. timber**, madera usada o de demolición.—**o. wheat**, trigo añejo.—**o. wife**, vieja (esp. la chismosa).—**o. wine**, vino añejo.—**o. wives' tale**, cuento de viejas.—**o. woman**, vieja; (teat.) característica.—**O. World**, Viejo Mundo.—**o.-world**, del Viejo Mundo.—**how o. is he, are you**, etc.? ¿cuántos años tiene él, Vd., etc.?—**of o.**, antiguo; antiguamente.—**to be . . . o.**, tener . . . de edad (*he is six years old*, él tiene seis años).—**to be o. enough**, tener bastante edad; no ser niño.—**to become**, o **grow, o.**, envejecer(se), encanecer; añejarse, gastarse.

olden [-n], *a.* (poét.) viejo, antiguo.—**o. days**, o **times**, tiempos pasados o antiguos.

oldish [-ị̄ʃ], *a.* avejentado, viejecillo.

oldness [-nịs], *s.* antigüedad; ancianidad, vejez; envejecimiento.

oleaceous [oliéiʃịas], *a.* (bot.) oleáceo.

oleaginous [oliédžịnas], *a.* ole(agin)oso, aceitoso.

oleaginousness [-nịs], *s.* ole(agin)osidad.

oleander [oliéndœ(r)], *s.* (bot.) adelfa, baladre.

oleaster [oliéstœ(r)], *s.* (bot.) oleastro, acebuche.

oleate [óuliẹit], *s.* (quím.) oleato.

olecranon [olékrạnan], *s.* (anat.) olécranon.

oleic [olíịk], *a.* (quím.) oleico.

olein [óuliịn], *s.* (quím.) oleína.

oleograph [óuliọgræf], *s.* oleografía.

oleomargarin(e [oliọmárdžạrịn], *s.* oleomargarina (manteca artificial).

oleometer [oliámetœ(r)], *s.* oleómetro.

oleoresin [oliọrézịn], *s.* oleorresina.

oleose, oleous [óulịous, -ʌs], *a.* oleoso.

olfaction [alféksọn], *s.* olfacción, acto de oler.

olfactory [alféktọri]. **I.** *a.* olfatorio, olfativo. **II.** *s.* olfato; órgano olfativo.

olibanum [olíbanʌm], *s.* incienso, olíbano.

oligarch [áligark], *s.* oligarca, *m.*

oligarchic(al [aligárkịk(ạl], *a.* oligárquico.

oligarchy [áligarki], *s.* oligarquía.

oligist [álidžịst], *s.* (min.) oligisto.

Oligocene [áligosin], *s.* y *a.* (geol.) oligoceno.

oligoclase [áligokleịs], *s.* (min.) oligoclasa.

olio [óuliọu], *s.* mezcla, miscelánea; (teat.) folla; (coc.) olla podrida, folla. *V.* OLLA.

olivaceous [alivéiʃịas], *a.* oliváceo.

olivary [álivẹri], *a.* oliviforme.—**o. body**, (anat.) oliva del bulbo o cuerpo olivar.

olive [áḷịv]. I. *s.* (bot.) olivo, oliv(er)a, aceituno (árbol); aceituna, oliva (fruto).—**o.-bearing,** olivífero.—**o. branch,** rama de olivo; (fig.) emblema (*m.*) de paz.—**o.-color(ed,** aceitunado.—**o. dealer,** aceitunero.—**o. drab,** color verdusco o verde amarillo oscuro; (mil.) uniforme de este color.—**o. grove,** olivar.—**o. oil,** aceite de oliva.—**o. press,** lagar, trapiche. —**o. presser,** lagarero.—**o. yard,** olivar. II. *a.* aceitunado.

olivine [áḷịvịn], *s.* (min.) olivino, peridoto.

olla [álạ], *s.* marmita, puchero, olla.—**o. podrida,** (coc.) olla podrida; (fig.) mistifori, mescolanza.

Olympiad [olímpịæd], *s.* olimpíada.

Olympian, Olympic u **Olympics** [-pịạn, -pịk], *a.* olímpico.—**O. games,** olimpíada, juegos olímpicos.

Olympus [-pʌs], *s.* Olimpo; cielo.

omasum [oméịsʌm], *s.* (zool.) omaso, libro, tercer estómago de los rumiantes.

ember, ombre [ámbœ(r)], *s.* tresillo o juego del hombre (naipes).

omega [omígạ], *s.* omega; (fig.) fin.

omelet(te [ámḷịt], *s.* tortilla de huevos.

omen [óụmịn]. I. *s.* agüero, augurio, anuncio, pronóstico, presagio. II. *va.* presagiar, augurar, ominar.

omened [-d], *a.* fatídico; augural, presagioso.

omental [oméntạl], *a.* (anat.) omental.

omentum [oméntʌm], *s.* (anat.) omento, redaño. —**the great o.,** epíploon, epiplón.

ominous [ámịnʌs], *a.* ominoso, siniestro, nefasto, de mal agüero; presagioso, pronosticador.— **ominously** [-lị], *adv.* ominosamente.—**ominousness** [-nịs], *s.* calidad de ominoso.

omissible [omísịbl], *a.* que se puede omitir o excluir.

omission [omíṣọn], *s.* omisión; supresión, exclusión; olvido, descuido.—**omissive** [omísịv], *a.* que omite o excluye; omis(iv)o, remiso.

omit [omít], *va.* omitir; prescindir de; suprimir, preterir, excluir; pasar por alto, olvidar.

omnibus [ámnịbạs]. I. *s.* (carr.) ómnibus, góndola; (teat.) palco grande al nivel del escenario. *V.* BUS y BUS BOY. II. *a.* que comprende varios asuntos (como proyecto de ley), o varias obras literarias reunidas en un mismo tomo.—**o. train,** (f. c.) tren de escala.

omnifarious [ámnịférịạs], *a.* omnímodo.

omnific [amnífịk], *a.* que todo lo crea.

omniform [ámnịform], *a.* omnímodo.

omnipotence, omnipotency [amnípọtẹns, -ị], *s.* omnipotencia; (O.), Dios.—**omnipotent** [-ẹnt], *a.* omnipotente.—**the O.,** Dios todopoderoso.

omnipresence [ámnịprézẹns], *s.* omnipresencia, ubicuidad.

omnipresent [-ẹnt], *a.* omnipresente, ubicuo.

omniscience, omnisciency [amníṣẹns, -ị], *s.* omnisciencia.

omniscient [-ẹnt], *a.* omniscio, omnisciente, omnisapiente.

omnium [ámnịʌm], *s.* (Ingl.) agregado de los diversos títulos de la deuda; total.—**o.-gatherum,** miscelánea, mare mágnum.

omnivorous [amnívọras], *a.* omnívoro; glotón.

omophagia [omoféjd̑ȥịạ], *s.* omofagia.

omoplate [óụmoplejt], *s.* (anat.) omoplato.

omphalic [amfálịk], *a.* (anat.) onfálico, umbilical.

on [an]. I. *prep.* sobre, encima de; en (*on the floor,* en el suelo; *on the train,* en el tren; *on the island,* en la isla; *on the wall,* en la pared; *on the committee,* en la comisión; *he is on his second year,* está en su segundo año; *on that occasion,* en esa ocasión; *on arriving,* en llegando); a, al (*on my arrival,* a mi llegada; *to bet on a horse,* apostar a un caballo; *on seeing,* al ver; *on seeing him,* al verlo; *on the right,* a la derecha); bajo, so, con, por (*on my responsibility,* bajo mi responsabilidad; *on pain of death,* bajo (so)

pena de muerte; *on his word,* por su palabra; *on my part,* por mi parte; *on your account,* por Vd.; *on all sides,* por todos lados; *on condition,* con la condición, con tal que; *on long terms,* con plazos largos); contra (*an attack on liberty,* un ataque contra la libertad; *draw on me,* gire contra mí). Gen. no se traduce cuando le sigue una expresión de tiempo: *on Monday,* (el) lunes; *on March third,* el tres de marzo; *on that day,* ese día.—**o. account,** a cuenta.—**o. an average,** por término medio.—**o. a sudden,** de golpe, de repente.—**o. credit,** al fiado.—**o. duty,** en servicio.—**o. fire,** ardiendo.—**o. foot,** a pie.—**o. guard,** en guardia; de guardia; alerta.—**o. hand,** a mano, disponible; (com.) en existencia.—**o. high,** en alto; en lo alto.— **o. horseback,** a caballo.—**o. purpose,** a propósito, adrede.—**o. record,** registrado; que consta; de que se tiene noticia.—**o. second thought,** después de reflexionar, reflexionando.—**o. the contrary,** por el contrario.—**o. the gad,** callejeando, correteando.—**o. the move,** moviéndose, andando.—**o. the road,** de viaje, viajando.—**o. the run,** corriendo; afanándose.—**o. time,** a la hora debida; puntualmente; (com.) a plazo, al fiado.—**o. to,** a, hacia.—**o. trust,** al fiado. II. *adv.* o *a.* puesto (*the lid is on,* la tapa está puesta; *with his hat on,* con el sombrero puesto); encendido (gas, etc.); en contacto (interruptor); en funcionamiento (radio, etc.); principiado, ocurriendo, verificándose (*the game is on,* el juego ha principiado, o se está jugando). Se usa con muchos verbos para indicar continuación o acción continua (*speak on,* continúe hablando), o posición o colocación sobre algo que se sobretiende (*the frying pan is on* [*the fire*], la sartén está sobre el fuego, o ya puesta). Se emplea pleonásticamente con ciertos comparativos, como "más" en español (*later on,* más tarde; *farther on,* más adelante). Indica la parte que va adelante en ciertos movimientos (*head on,* de cabeza).—**o. and off,** a intervalos, de vez en cuando.—**o. and on,** continuamente, sin cesar.—**and so o.,** y así sucesivamente, etcétera. III. *interj.* ¡adelante! ¡vamos!

onager [ánạdȥœ(r)], *s.* (zool. y mil.) onagro.

onagra [anégrạ], *s.* (bot.) onagra.

onanism [óụnạnịzm], *s.* onanismo; coito incompleto.

once [wʌns]. I. *adv.* y *s.* una vez; en otro tiempo, otras veces.—**o. a . . . always a . . .,** quien ha sido . . ., siempre lo será (*once a thief, always a thief,* quien ha sido ladrón, siempre lo será).—**o. and again,** varias veces.—**o. for all,** una vez por todas, por última vez, definitivamente.—**o. in a while,** de cuando en cuando.—**o. more,** otra vez.—**o.-over,** (fam.) ojeada, vistazo, examen rápido.—**o. too often,** una vez más de lo prudente; pasándose de los límites de la tolerancia.—**o. upon a time,** en otro tiempo; en tiempo de Maricastaña; érase que se era.—**at o.,** a un mismo tiempo, a la vez, de una vez, simultáneamente; en seguida, al instante, inmediatamente.—**for o.,** una vez siquiera; últimamente; al fin.— **this o.,** esta vez, siquiera esta vez. II. *a.* de otro tiempo, pasado, que fué. III. *conj.,* una vez que, tan pronto como.

oncology [aŋkálodȥị], *s.* (med.) oncología.

oncoming [ánkʌmiŋ]. I. *a.* próximo, venidero, cercano. II. *s.* proximidad, aproximación.

ondometer [andámẹtọ(r)], *s.* (elec.) ondómetro.

one [wʌn]. I. *a.* un, uno; solo, único; cierto, un tal; igual.—**o.-celled,** unicelular.—**o.-colored,** unicolor.—**o. day,** un día, cierto día; algún día, un día de éstos.—**o.-eyed,** tuerto, monóculo. —**o.-handed,** manco.—**o.-horse,** de (o tirado por) un caballo; (fam.) de poca importancia.— **o. hundred,** cien, ciento.—**o.-legged,** unípede, de un solo pie, o de una sola pata.—**o.-**

piece, de una (sola) pieza.—**o.-sided**, parcial, injusto, (for.) leonino; unilateral; de un solo lado; desigual.—**o.-story**, de un solo piso.— **o. thousand**, mil.—**o.-time**, antiguo, de otro tiempo, que fué.—**o.-track**, (f. c.) de una sola vía; estrecho; (fam.) que comprende o hace una sola cosa a la vez.—**o.-way**, de una sola dirección, de dirección única (calle); sencillo (billete).—**at o. and the same time**, a un mismo tiempo.—**at o. stroke**, de un golpe o tirón.—**it is all o. to me**, lo mismo me da; me es lo mismo.—**of o. height**, de un mismo alto. —**with o. accord**, de común acuerdo, unánimemente. **II**. *s.* y *pron.* uno; la una (hora). Ú. como reproductivo en casos en que en español se usa el artículo o el adjetivo sustantivado: *this one*, éste; *the white one*, el blanco; *the one that came*, el que vino; *the little one*, el chiquillo; *a better one*, uno mejor. Ú. indefinidamente en el sentido de "cosa," "chiste," "sujeto," "tipo," etc.: *this is a good one*, éste es un buen chiste (noticia, jugada, etc., según el caso); *he is a bad one*, es mal sujeto.—**o. and all**, todos, todos sin excepción.—**o. and the same**, idéntico.—**o. another** = EACH OTHER.—**o. by o.**, uno a uno, uno por uno.—**o. (for) each**, sendos (*tienen sendos libros*, they have a book each).—**o. or two**, unos pocos.—**o.'s**, de uno, su.—**o. to o.**, de punto por punto o parte por parte.—**all o.**, lo mismo.—**at o.**, a una; de común acuerdo.—**for o.**, por lo menos, uno de los que (*I for one don't believe it*, yo por lo menos no lo creo, yo soy uno de los que no lo creen).

oneiromancy [onái·roˈmænsj], *s.* oniromancía.

oneness [wǽnnjs], *s.* unidad; calidad de único.

onerous [ánerʌs], *a.* oneroso, gravoso, molesto, cargoso; (for.) gravable, sujeto a gravamen.

one's self, oneself [wʌnsɛlf], *pron.* se, sí, sí mismo, (a) uno mismo.—**with o.**, consigo.

one-step [wʌn step], *s. one-step*, cierto baile de salón en compás binario.

ongoing [ángou̯in], **I**. *a.* que marcha o va hacia adelante. **II**. *s.* movimiento hacia adelante.— *pl.* acontecimientos; negocios, asuntos.

onion [ʌnyɒn], *s.* (bot.) cebolla.—**o. bed**, cebollar.—**o. seed**, o **set**, cebollino.—**onionskin** [-skjn], *s.* binza, tela de cebolla; papel cebolla.

onlooker [ánlʌkœ(r)], *s.* espectador, observador.

only [óunlj], **I**. *a.* único, solo; singular, raro.—**o.-begotten**, unigénito.—**o. child**, hijo único. **II**. *adv.* (tan) sólo, solamente, únicamente; no más que (o de); no . . . sino.—**o. too** = ALL TOO (*v.* ALL).—**if o.**, ojalá, si (cambiando el giro: *if only he would come!* ¡ojalá que él venga! ¡si él viniera!)—**not o. . . . but also**, no sólo . . . sino también. **III**. *conj.* sólo que, pero.

onomancy [óunomænsj], *s.* onomancia.

onomastic [anoˈmæstjk], *a.* onomástico.

onomatopœia [anomatoˈpíə], *s.* (ret.) onomatopeya.—**onomatopœic**, **onomatopoetic** [-píjk, -poétjk], *a.* onomatopéyico.

onrush [ánrʌʃ], **onset** [ánsɛt], *s.* embestida, arremetida, carga, ataque; acceso; arranque.— **onset**, (med.) acceso, comienzo (de una enfermedad).

onshore [ánʃór], **I**. *adv.* de, a o hacia tierra. **II**. *a.* que está en tierra; que se mueve o se dirige hacia la orilla.

onslaught [ánslɔt], *s.* ataque furioso, embestida, arremetida, asalto.

onto [ántu], *prep.* encima de, sobre, en.

ontogeny [antádʒenj], *s.* ontogenia, ontogénesis.

ontologic(al [antoˈládʒjk(al], *a.* ontológico.

ontologism [antáloˈdʒjzm], *s.* (fil.) ontologismo.

ontologist [-dʒjst], *s.* ontólogo.

ontology [-dʒj], *s.* ontología.

onus [óunas], *s.* carga, responsabilidad.—**o. probandi**, (lat.) obligación de probar.

onward [ánwård], *a.* avanzado; progresivo. V. FORWARD.—**onward(s** [-(z], *adv.* adelante,

hacia adelante; progresivamente; en adelante.

Onychophora [anjkáforʌ], *s. pl.* (zool.) onicóforos.

onyx [ánjks], *s.* (min.) ónice, *mf.*, onique, *f.*, ónix, *mf.*; (med.) pus en la córnea del ojo.

oöcyte [óuosajt], *s.* (biol.) oocito.

oodles [údlz], *s. pl.* (fam.) gran abundancia, la mar (de).

oögonium [ouoɡóunjʌm], *s.* (bot.) oogonio.

oölite [óuolajt], *s.* (geol.) oolita.

oölitic [ouolítjk], *a.* oolítico.

oölogy [oálodʒj], *s.* (orn.) oología.

oolong [úloŋ], *s.* variedad de té negro.

oöphorectomy [ouoforéktomj], *s.* ovariotomía.

oöphoritis [ouoforájtjs], *s.* (med.) ooforitis, ovaritis.

oösperm [óuospœrm], *s.* (embr.) oospermo, huevo fecundado; (bot.) = OÖSPORE.

oösphere [óuosfjr], *s.* (bot.) oosfera, célula reproductiva antes de su fecundación.

oöspore [óuospor], *s.* (bot.) oosporo.

ooze [úz]. **I**. *va.* sudar; manar. **II**. *vn.* manar, fluir; escurrirse; exudar, rezumarse, trazumarse. **III**. *s.* cieno, fango, limo, lama; chorro suave.

oozy [-j], *a.* cenagoso, lamoso, legamoso; húmedo.

opacity [opásjtj], *s.* opacidad; obscuridad.

opal [óupʌl], *s.* (min.) ópalo.—**opalesce** [opalés], *vn.* irisar.—**opalescence** [-ɛns], *s.* opalescencia, calidad de opalino.—**opalescent** [-ɛnt], **opaline** [óupalin], *a.* opalescente, opalino, iridiscente.

opaque [opéjk], *a.* opaco; sin brillo, obscuro, mate.

opaqueness [-njs], *s.* opacidad.

ope [oup]. **I**. *va.* y *vn.* (poét.) abrir(se). **II**. *a.* abierto.

open [óupn]. **I**. *va.* abrir; desenvolver, destapar, desempaquetar; desplegar; establecer; inaugurar, iniciar, principiar; franquear, hender, cortar, rajar; romper; exponer, manifestar, descubrir, revelar; explicar; ensanchar, aumentar.—**to o. one's heart**, desabrocharse, franquearse; ser generoso.—**to o. the ball**, abrir el baile o romper a bailar; (fam.) dar comienzo. —**to o. the mouth**, hablar; revelar un secreto. —**to o. up**, explorar, descubrir, hacer accesible. **II**. *vn.* (a veces con **out**) abrirse, desplegarse, destaparse; descubrirse; dividirse, entreabrirse; aparecer, asomarse; desarrollarse, desenvolverse; empezar, comenzar; (teat.) debutar, estrenarse.—**to o. on**, o **upon**, caer, dar o mirar a.—**to o. with**, empezar con. **III**. *a.* abierto, libre, franco; público; descubierto; extendido, desplegado; desembarazado, (d)escampado (terreno); expuesto a un ataque; desnudo, visible; receptivo, dispuesto a, susceptible de; listo, aparejado; manifiesto, claro, patente, llano; sincero, franco; directo; suave; templado; (fon.) abierta (vocal); (com.) abierto, pendiente.—**o. air**, aire libre.—**o.-air**, al aire libre. *V*. OUTDOOR.—**o. circuit**, (elec.) circuito de corriente intermitente.—**o. coil**, (elec.) bobina abierta.—**o. car**, (aut.) coche abierto o descubierto.—**o. credit**, (com.) letra abierta.—**o. door**, (der. int.) puerta abierta, igualdad de derechos.—**o.-eyed**, alerta, vigilante, avizor; pasmado.—**o. face**, muestra (de reloj) sin tapa. —**o.-faced**, sin tapa; de cara franca.—**o.-handed**, generoso, dadivoso o liberal.— **o.-hearted**, ingenuo, sincero, abierto.— **o.-heartedness**, liberalidad, generosidad; franqueza.—**o. hearth**, (metal.) horno de reverbero.—**o.-hearth (steel, process**, etc.), (acero, procedimiento, etc.) Siemens-Martin. —**o. house**, casa abierta para todos. *V*. TO KEEP.—**o. letter**, carta abierta (de protesta o súplica).—**o. look**, mirada franca.—**o. market**, mercado (público).—**o. marks**, señales (*f. pl.*) evidentes.—**o.-minded**, razonable, liberal, imparcial, receptivo.—**o.-mouthed**, boquiabierto, con la boca abierta; bocudo; voraz, rapaz; clamoroso.—o. **notes**, (mús.) notas blancas (breves, semibreves y mínimas). —o. **pit**, (min.) tajo abierto.—o. **plumbing**, tuberías descubiertas.—o. **port**, puerto franco, puerto abierto al comercio extranjero.—o. **question**, cuestión discutible; asunto en duda. —o. **sea**, alta mar.—o. **season**, tiempo de caza o de pesca.—o. **secret**, secreto a voces o con chirimías; secreto conocido de todos, secreto de Anchuelo.—o. **sesame**, conjuro mágico para abrir puertas secretas; (fig.) palabra mágica, vara mágica.—o. **shame**, vergüenza pública.—o. **shop**, taller franco, en que se admiten obreros agremiados y no-agremiados.—o. **syllable**, (fon.) sílaba abierta o libre.—o. **winter**, invierno templado, sin heladas.—**in** o. **court**, en pleno tribunal.— **in the** o. **air**, al aire libre, al raso, a la intemperie.—**in the** o. **field**, a campo raso.—**it is** o. **to you to**, Vd. puede, Vd. tiene la libertad de.—**with** o. **arms**, con los brazos abiertos. **IV.** s. claro, raso, lugar abierto.—**in the open**, a campo raso; al descubierto, abiertamente.

opener [-œ(r)], s. abridor; (tej.) desmotadora.

opening [-iŋ]. **I.** s. abertura, brecha; boca, orificio; vano (de puerta o ventana); luz; abrimiento; claro, raso, campo abierto; abra, bahía; (min.) socavón, galería; principio, inauguración, apertura; oportunidad, coyuntura; empleo vacante. **II.** a. aperitivo.—o. **performance**, (teat.) estreno.—o. **play**, salida (naipes).—o. **price**, primer curso (en la Bolsa).

openly [-lĭ], adv. abiertamente, a las claras, al descubierto; públicamente.—**openness** [-nĭs], s. franqueza, sinceridad; publicidad.

openwork [-wœrk], s. enrejado; calado; (cost.) deshilado.

opera [ápęrą], s. (mús.) ópera.—o. **book**, libreto de una ópera.—o. **bouffe**, ópera bufa.—o. **cloak**, abrigo de señora para la salida del teatro.—o. **comique**, ópera cómica, zarzuela.— o. **glasses**, anteojo de teatro, gemelos de teatro.—o. **hat**, clac.—o. **house**, teatro de la ópera.—o. **singer**, operista, cantante de ópera.

operability [apęrąbĭlĭtĭ], s. (cir.) operabilidad, calidad de operable.—**operable** [-bl], a. operable.

operand [ápęrænd], s. (mat.) cantidad sometida a una operación.

operate [ápęrẹĭt]. **I.** va. hacer funcionar, mover, actuar; explotar; gobernar, dirigir, manejar; llevar a cabo, efectuar. **II.** vn. (con **in, on** o **upon**) obrar, operar; producir efecto; funcionar; (cir.) operar; (com.) operar, especular, jugar a la bolsa; (mil.) operar, maniobrar.— **operated by**, (mec.) accionado por.

operatic(al [apęrǽtĭk(ąl], a. de ópera.

operating [ápęrẹĭtĭŋ], a. operante, actuante, impulsante; operativo, operatorio, de operación; de funcionamiento, de explotación; de manejo, de servicio.—o. **expenses**, gastos de funcionamiento, de explotación o corrientes.— o. **room**, (cir.) sala de operaciones; (fot.) cuarto obscuro.—o. **table**, (cir.) mesa de operaciones.

operation [apęrẹĭşǫn], s. operación; explotación; marcha, funcionamiento; manejo, manipulación; acción, efecto; vigencia (de una ley); (cir.) operación.

operative [ápęrẹĭtĭv]. **I.** a. operativo, eficaz, activo; (cir.) operatorio. **II.** s. operario, obrero, artesano; detective. V. OPERATOR.

operator [ápęrẹĭtǫ(r)], s. operario, operante; maquinista; telegrafista; telefonista; ascensorista; escribiente con máquina; (cir.) operador, cirujano; (com.) agente, corredor de bolsa; (E. U.) explotador o empresario de minas.

opercular [opœrkĭulą(r)]. **I.** a. opercular, que tapa. **II.** s. opérculo (de los peces).

operculate(d [-eĭt(ĭd], a. operculado.

operculum [-ʌm], s. (bot., biol.) opérculo.

operetta [apęrétą], s. (mús.) opereta, zarzuela.

ophicleide [áfĭklaĭd], s. (mús.) oficleido, figle.

ophidian [offĭdĭąn], a. y s. (zool.) ofidio.

ophiolatry [afĭáląṭrĭ], s. ofiolatría, culto de las serpientes.

ophiology [afĭálodžĭ], s. ofiología, ciencia que trata de las serpientes.

ophite [áfaĭt], s. (petr.) ofita.

ophiuran [afĭyúrąn], s. (zool.) ofiuro.

ophiuroidean [afĭyuróĭdĭąn], a. y s. (zool.) ofiurídeo.

ophthalmia [afθǽlmĭą], s. (med.) oftalmía.— **ophthalmic** [afθǽlmĭk], a. oftálmico.—**ophthalmologic(al** [-moládžĭk(ąl], a. oftalmológico.—**ophthalmologist** [-málodžĭst], s. oftalmólogo.—**ophthalmology** [-džĭ], s. oftalmología.—**ophthalmometer** [-mámetœ(r)], s. (ópt.) oftalmómetro.—**ophthalmoscope** [afθélmoskoup], s. (ópt.) oftalmoscopio.—**ophthalmoscopy** [-máskopĭ], s. oftalmoscopia.

opiate [óupĭeĭt]. **I.** s. opiato, narcótico. **II.** a. opiado, narcótico, soporífico. **III.** va. (med.) administrar opio; (farm.) componer con opio.

opine [opáĭn], va. y vn. opinar, juzgar.

opinion [opĭnyǫn], s. opinión, concepto, parecer, sentir, ver; fama, reputación; dictamen.—**in my** o., a mi ver.—**to be of the** o., ser de opinión, opinar.—**to express an** o., dictaminar.

opinionated [-eĭtĭd], a. porfiado, obstinado, terco.

opinionate(d)ly [-eĭt(ĭd)lĭ], adv. porfiadamente, obstinadamente.

opinioned [-d], a. presumido; obstinado.

opium [óupĭąm], s. opio, meconio, anfión, m.— o. **eater**, el que toma opio por vicio.—o. **joint**, fumadero de opio.—o. **pipe**, pipa para fumar opio.

opobalsam [apobólsąm], s. opobálsamo.

opopanax [opápąnæks], s. (bot.) pánace, f.; (farm., etc.) opopánaco, opopánax (goma de la pánace).

opossum [opásʌm], s. (zool.) oposúm, zarigüeya.

oppilate [ápĭleĭt], va. obstruir.—**oppilation** [-éĭşǫn], s. opilación, obstrucción.

oppilative [ápĭleĭtĭv], a. (med.) opilativo.

opponency [opǫunęnsĭ], s. oposición.

opponent [-ęnt]. **I.** s. antagonista, contrincante, contrario; opositor; competidor. **II.** a. antagónico; opuesto, contrario; (anat.) oponente.

opportune [apǫrtĭún], a. oportuno, a propósito, conveniente.—**opportunely** [-lĭ], adv. oportunamente.—**opportuneness** [-nĭs], s. oportunidad.

opportunism [-ĭzm], s. (pol.) oportunismo.— **opportunist** [-ĭst], a. y s. oportunista.

opportunity [-ĭtĭ], s. oportunidad; lugar, ocasión.

opposable [opóuząbl], a. oponible.

oppose [opóuz]. **I.** va. oponer, resistir, combatir; oponerse a, hacer frente a, luchar contra, llevar la contraria; objetar, repugnar, impugnar, contrariar, contrarrestar. **II.** vn. oponerse, resistirse; argüir; obstar; estar frente a frente.

opposed [-d], a. opuesto, encontrado; contrario enemigo; en contra (de una proposición).

opposer [-œ(r)], s. opositor, opugnador, adversario, antagonista, rival.

opposite [ápozĭt]. **I.** a. opuesto, contrario, encontrado; fronter(iz)o, adverso, de cara, de enfrente, al otro lado.—o. **leaves**, hojas opuestas.—**the** o. **sex**, el otro sexo, el sexo opuesto. **II.** prep. del otro lado de; al frente de, enfrente de, frente a. **III.** s. (ant.) antagonista, adversario; contrario.—**the** o., lo opuesto, lo contrario.

oppositely [-lĭ], adv. enfrente, opuestamente.

oppositeness [-nĭs], s. contrariedad.

opposition [apozĭşǫn], s. oposición; contraste; contrariedad; aversión, repugnancia; óbice, impedimento; (astr.) oposición.—**opposi-**

tional [-al], *a.* de oposición; de la oposición.—
oppositionist [-ist], *a.* y *s.* (pol.) oposicionista, antiministerial.

oppress [oprés], *va.* oprimir, agobiar, gravar, supeditar, vejar; apretar, aprensar.

oppression [opréśon], *s.* opresión, supeditación, vejación; miseria, calamidad; presura, opresión de ánimo; fatiga; agobio, ahogo; pesadez.

oppressive [oprésiv], *a.* opresivo, opresor, tiránico; gravoso; agobiador, abrumador; sofocante.
—**oppressively** [-li], *adv.* opresivamente.—
oppressiveness [-nis], *s.* opresión.

oppressor [opréso(r)], *s.* opresor, tirano.

opprobrious [opróubrias], *a.* oprobioso, ignominioso, infamante.—**opprobriously** [-li], *adv.* oprobiosamente.—**opprobriousness** [-nis], *s.* oprobio.

opprobrium [opróubriam], *s.* oprobio, ignominia.

oppugn [opiún], *va.* opugnar, combatir.

oppugnancy [opágnansi], *s.* opugnación.

oppugner [opiúnœ(r)], *s.* opugnador.

opsonin [ápsonin], *s.* (bact.) opsonina.

opt [apt], *vn.* optar, escoger.

optative [áptativ], *a.* y *s.* (gram.) optativo.

optic(al [áptik(al], I. *a.* óptico, visorio, rel. a la vista o a la óptica.—**optic angle**, ángulo óptico.—**optic nerve**, nervio óptico.—**optical bench**, banco óptico.—**optical square**, escuadra de reflexión.—**optical telegraphy**, telegrafía óptica, sistema (*m.*) de señales ópticas.—**optic thalamus** (*pl.* **thalami**), tálamo óptico. II. *s.* (fam.) ojo.

optician [aptíśan], *s.* óptico.

optics [áptiks], *s.* óptica.

optimism [áptimizm], *s.* optimismo.—**optimist** [-ist], *s.*, **optimistic(al** [-istik(al], *a.* optimista.

optimum [áptimam], I. *a.* óptimo. II. *s.* óptimo; punto, grado, cantidad, etc., más propicios para un fin cualquiera.

option [ápšon], *s.* opción, elección, facultad de escoger; alternativa; (com.) opción, plazo para determinar.—**optional** [-al], *a.* opcional, optativo, facultativo, discrecional.—**optionally** [-i], *adv.* discrecionalmente, a voluntad.

optometer [aptámetœ(r)], *s.* (ópt.) optómetro.

optometrist [-trist], *s.* optómetra, *m.*, optometrista.—**optometry** [-tri], *s.* optometría.

optophone [áptofoun], *s.* optófono, instrumento por cuyo medio los ciegos reconocen la luz por el oído.

opulence, opulency [ápyulens, -i], *s.* opulencia, abundancia; lozanía; copia.—**opulent** [-lent], *a.* opulento.—**opulently** [-li], *adv.* opulentamente.

opuntia [opánśia], *s.* (bot.) tuna(l), nopal, chumbera.

opus [óupas], *s.* (*pl.* opera) obra o composición literaria o música.—**opuscle** [opásl], **opuscule** [opáskjul], *s.* opúsculo.

or [or]. I. *conj.* o, u; si no, de lo contrario. II. *s.* (blas.) oro (color amarillo).

orach [árak], *s.* (bot.) orzaga, armuelle, bledo.

oracle [árakl], *s.* oráculo.

oracular [orákyula(r)], *a.* oracular; fatídico; positivo, magistral, dogmático; obscuro, ambiguo.

oracularly [-li], *adv.* a modo de oráculo.

oral [óral]. I. *a.* oral; verbal, hablado, vocal; (anat., fon.) bucal; (for.) nuncupativo (testamento). II. *s.* examen oral.

orally [-i], *adv.* oral o verbalmente, de palabra.

orange [árandž]. I. *s.* (bot.) naranja; color de naranja.—**o. blossom**, azahar.—**o. color**, color de naranja.—**o.-colored**, (a)naranjado.—**o. dog**, oruga nociva a las naranjas.—**o. grove**, naranjal.—**o. grower**, o **seller**, naranjero.—**o. juice**, jugo de naranja.—**o. peel**, cáscara de naranja.—**o. pekoe**, cierto té negro de Ceilán o India.—**o. scale**, insecto cóccido que se cría en el naranjo.—**o. tree**, naranj(er)o.—**o. wife**, naranjera, vendedora de naranjas.

II. *a.* perteneciente a las naranjas; anaranjado.

orangeade [-éid], *s.* naranjada.

Orangeman [-man], *s.* orangista, protestante seguidor de Guillermo de Orange; miembro de la sociedad secreta irlandesa de los orangistas.

orangery [-ri], *s.* naranjal (invernáculo).

orang-(o)utan(g [orénqytæn, -tæŋ], *s.* (zool.) orangután.

oration [oréišon], *s.* oración, discurso solemne.

orator [árato(r)], *s.* orador; (for., Ingl.) suplicante.

Oratorian [aratórian], *s.* (igl.) oratoriano, sacerdote que pertenece a un oratorio.

oratorical [aratórikal], *a.* oratorio; retórico.—**oratorically** [-i], *adv.* oratoriamente.

oratorio [aratórjou], *s.* (mús.) oratorio.

oratory [áratori], *s.* oratoria, elocuencia; (igl.) oratorio, capilla; (O., igl.) oratorio, congregación.

orb [orb]. I. *s.* orbe, esfera, globo; astro; círculo, rueda; (poét.) ojo. II. *va.* (poét.) cercar, rodear, englobar; formar círculo.

orbed [-d], *a.* redondo, circular; esférico; redondeado; lleno; de ojos, que tiene ojos (ú. en composición).—**o. moon**, luna llena.

orbicular [orbíkyula(r)], *a.* orbicular, esférico.

orbicularly [-li], *adv.* orbicularmente.

orbicularness [-nis], *s.* esfericidad.

orbit [órbit], *s.* (astr. y anat.) órbita.

orbital [-al], *a.* (anat.) orbital, orbitario.

orca [órka], *s.* (zool.) orca, orco.

orcanet [órkanet], *s.* (bot.) orcaneta. *V.* ALKANET.

orcein [órsiin], *s.* (quím.) orceína.

orchard [órčard], *s.* huerto, vergel, pomar.—**orcharding** [-iŋ], *s.* horticultura, cultivo de huertos.—**orchardist** [-ist], *s.* horticultor, cultivador de huertos.

orchestra [órkistra], *s.* (mús.) orquesta; (teat.) platea, patio.—**o. circle**, (teat.) = PARTERRE.—**o. pit**, orquesta.—**o. seat**, luneta, butaca de platea.

orchestral [orkéstral], *a.* orquestal, instrumental, de orquesta.—**orchestrate** [órkistrejt], *va.* (mús.) orquestar, instrumentar.—**orchestration** [-éišon], *s.* (mús.) orquestación, instrumentación.

orchid [órkid], *s.* (bot.) orquídea.

orchidaceous [-éišias], *a.* orquídeo.

orchil [órkil], *s.* (bot.) orchilla, urchilla; orcina.

orch(i)otomy [ork(i)átomi], *s.* (cir.) orquiotomía, orcotomía.

orchis [órkis], *s.* (bot.) órquide; orquídea.

orchitis [orkáitis], *s.* (med.) orquitis.

orcin(e [órsin], **orcinol** [-oul], *s.* (quím.) orcina.

ordain [ordéin], *va.* ordenar, mandar; decretar, constituir, estatuir; (igl.) ordenar.

ordainer [-œ(r)], *s.* ordenador.

ordeal [órdjal], *s.* ordalía; juicio de Dios; prueba.

order [órdœ(r)]. I. *s.* orden, *m.*, arreglo, disposición; orden, *m.*, clase, *f.*, categoría, tipo; orden, *f.*, decreto, manda(mien)to, precepto; (arq., hist. nat.) orden, *m.*; (com.) pedido, encargo, comisión.—*pl.* órdenes sagradas, orden sacerdotal; sacramento.—**o. blank**, (com.) hoja de pedidos.—**o. book**, libro de pedidos.—**o. in council**, (Ingl.) orden (*f.*) real, con anuencia del consejo del rey.—**o. of battle**, (mil.) orden (*m.*) de batalla.—**o. of knighthood**, orden (*f.*) de caballería.—**o. of the day**, orden (*m.*) del día; (mil.) orden (*f.*) del día.—**O. of the Garter**, orden de la Jarretera.—**O. of the Golden Fleece**, orden del Toisón de Oro.—**a big, o large, o.**, (fig.) una tarea peliaguda.—**in (good) o.**, en regla, en orden, en buen estado.—**in o. to, in o. that**, para, a fin de, para que, porque, con (el) objeto de.—**on that o.**, de esa clase, de tal jaez.—**on the o. of**, de la clase de.—**till further orders**, hasta nueva orden.—**to give, o place, an o.**, hacer un pedido.—**to o.**, a propósito, especialmente; (com.) a la orden, por encargo especial, según se pida, a la medida (ropa que se manda hacer).—**to the o. of**, (com.) a la orden de. **II.** *va.* ordenar, mandar; ordenar, arreglar; mandar hacer; encargar, pedir (mercancías, un coche, una copa de vino, el almuerzo); (igl.) ordenar.—**o. arms!** (mil.) ¡descansen! (voz de mando); armas en descanso.—**to o. away**, despedir a uno, decirle que se vaya.—**to o. in**, mandar entrar; mandar traer.—**to o. out**, mandar salir; mandar llevar; echar.

orderer [-œ(r)], *s.* ordenador.

orderless [-ljs], *a.* desordenado, desarreglado.

orderliness [-linjs], *s.* orden, método.

orderly [-lj]. **I.** *a.* ordenado, metódico; bien arreglado; obediente, disciplinado; quieto o tranquilo.—**o. book**, (mil.) libro de ordenanzas.—**o. officer**, oficial del día. **II.** *s.* (mil.) ordenanza, *m.*, asistente; asistente en un hospital. **III.** *adv.* ordenadamente, metódicamente, en orden.

ordinal [órdjnal]. **I.** *a.* ordinal.—**o. numeral**, numeral ordinal. **II.** *s.* numeral ordinal; (igl.) ritual.

ordinance [órdjnans], *s.* ordenanza, ley, *f.*, auto, reglamento, estatuto; (igl.) rito, ceremonia del culto; (arq., pint., lit.) ordenanza, ordenación, disposición.

ordinand [órdjnænd], *s.* (igl.) ordenando, ordenante.

ordinarily [órdjnerilj], *adv.* ordinariamente.

ordinary [órdjnerj]. **I.** *a.* ordinario, común, corriente; tosco, burdo, plebeyo, vulgar; mediano, adocenado.—**o. shares**, (com.) acciones ordinarias. **II.** *s.* la masa, el vulgo; juez ordinario; (igl.) orden de la misa; comida o (ant.) fonda a precio fijo; mesa redonda.—**in o.**, en actual servicio, con ejercicio.—**out of the o.**, excepcional, inusitado.

ordinate [órdjnejt]. **I.** *a.* ordenado. **II.** *s.* (geom.) ordenada. **III.** *va.* ordenar; coordinar.

ordination [-éjșon], *s.* (igl.) ordenación, orden; ordenanza, arreglo, buen orden.

ordnance [órdnans], *s.* (mil.) artillería, cañones, *m. pl.*—**o. stores, o supplies**, pertrechos de guerra.

ordonnance [órdonans], *s.* (arq., pint.) ordenación, ordenanza; composición de lugar; ordenación, ordenanza, estatuto. *V.* ORDINANCE.

ordure [órdẕụ(r)], *s.* excremento, inmundicia.

ore [our], *s.* mineral, mena.—**o. crusher, o stamp**, bocarte, triturador. (Méx.) despuntador.

oread [óurjæd], *s.* (mit.) orea, oréade, *f.*, oreada, ninfa.

organ [órgan], *s.* (mús.) órgano; organillo, órgano de manubrio; (biol.) órgano; hablando de periódicos, órgano.—**o. blower**, entonador.—**o. builder**, organero.—**o. grinder**, organillero.—**o. pipe**, cañón de órgano.—**o. stop**, registro de órgano.

organdy [órgandj], *s.* (tej.) organdí.

organic(al [orgénjk(al], *a.* orgánico; organizado; sistematizado; constitutivo o fundamental; (quím.) orgánico, que contiene carbono.—**o. chemistry**, química orgánica.—**o. disease**, afección orgánica.—**o. law**, ley orgánica o fundamental.—**o. remains**, restos orgánicos, materias orgánicas.

organically [-lj], *adv.* orgánicamente.

organicism [orgénjsjzm], *s.* (med., filos.) organicismo.—**organicist(ic** [-jst, -jstjk], *a.* y *s.* organicista.

organism [órganjzm], *s.* organismo; (biol.) órgano, ser animal o vegetal.

organist [-jst], *s.* (mús.) organista.

organization [-jzéjșon], *s.* organización; estructura orgánica; constitución; organismo; sociedad, compañía; corporación; cuerpo, entidad.

organize [-ajz]. **I.** *va.* organizar, disponer, arreglar, constituir; abanderizar; (biol.) organizar. **II.** *vn.* organizarse, constituirse.

organizer [-œ(r)], *s.* **organizing** [-jŋ], *a.* organizador.

organogenesis [-odžénɛsjs], *s.* (biol.) organogenia.

organographic(al [-ogræfjk(al], *a.* organográfico.—**organography** [-ágrafj], *s.* (biol.) organografía.—**organology** [-álodžj], *s.* (biol.) organología.

organon, organum [-an, -ʌm], *s.* (filos.) sistema, *m.*, método (apl. esp. a la lógica de Aristóteles y a la inductiva de Bacon); medio (de conocer).

organotherapy [-oθérapj], *s.* (med.) organoterapia, opoterapia (ll. t. **opotherapy**).

organzine [órganzin], *s.* torzal; tela de torzal.

orgasm [órgæzm], *s.* excitación; (fisiol.) orgasmo.

orgeat [óržæt], *s.* horchata (bebida).—**o. maker, o seller**, horchatero.—**o. stand**, horchatería.

orgiastic [ordžjéstjk], *a.* orgiástico.

orgy [órdžj], *s.* orgía.—*pl.* **orgies**, orgías (esp. las bacanales de los antiguos).

oriel [óurjel], *s.* (arq.) mirador, camón (ventana).

orient [óurjent]. **I.** *a.* naciente; (poét.) ortivo, oriental; brillante, resplandeciente. **II.** *s.* oriente, naciente, este, levante; perla de gran brillo; brillo especial de las perlas.—**the O.**, el Oriente. **III.** *va.* orientar.

oriental [orjéntal], *a.* y *s.* oriental.—**orientalism** [-jzm], *s.* orientalismo.—**orientalist** [-jst], *s.* orientalista.—**orientalize** [-ajz], *va.* y *vn.* orientalizar(se).

orientate [óurjentejt]. **I.** *va.* orientar. **II.** *vn.* caer o mirar hacia el este.

orientation [-éjșon], *s.* orientación.

orifice [árifjs], *s.* orificio, abertura.

oriflamme [árjflæm], *s.* oriflama, estandarte.

origan [árjgan], **origanum** [aríganʌm], *s.* (bot.) orégano, mejorana silvestre.

Origenism [árjdžɛnjzm], *s.* (igl.) origenismo.

Origenist [-jst], *s.* y *a.* origenista.

origin [árjdžjn], *s.* origen, principio, génesis, procedencia, oriundez, ascendencia, cepa, tronco.

original [orídžjnal]. **I.** *a.* original, originario; prístino, primitivo, primero; radical; ocurrente.—**o. sin**, pecado original. **II.** *s.* original; prototipo; raíz; ejemplar; persona rara u original.

originality [orjdžjnéljtj], *s.* originalidad.

originally [orídžjnalj], *adv.* originalmente; en el principio.

originate [orídžjnejt]. **I.** *va.* originar, crear, inventar; producir, ocasionar, suscitar. **II.** *vn.* originarse, nacer, dimanar, emanar o provenir de.

origination [-éjșon], *s.* origen, principio; modo de propagar o de producir.

originator [-ọ(r)], *s.* originador, iniciador.

oriole [óurjoul], *s.* (orn.) oriol, oropéndola, lútea.

Orion [orájon], *s.* (astr.) Orión, *m.*

orison [árjzon], *s.* oración, plegaria, rezo.

orle [orl], *s.* (arq.) orla, filete, listón; (blas.) orla.

orlop [órlap], *s.* (mar.) sollado.

ormolu [órmolu], *s.* similor; bronce dorado; oro molido para dorar.

ornament [órnament]. **I.** *s.* ornamento, adorno, decoración, ornato; persona o cosa que honra o enaltece. **II.** [-ment], *va.* ornamentar, adornar, (ex)ornar.

ornamental [-méntal]. **I.** *a.* ornamental, decorativo, de adorno.—**o. painter**, adornista, decorador. **II.** *s.* cosa, planta, etc., de ornato o de adorno.

ornamentally [-j], *adv.* ornadamente.

ornamentation [-éjșon], *s.* ornamentación, decorado, exornación.

ornamented [órnamentjd], **ornate** [ornéjt], *a.* ornado, ornamentado, adornado.

ornateness [-njs], *s.* ornato, adorno, aparato.

ornery [órnœrj], *a.* (fam.) terco, intratable; vil; vulgar.

rnithologic(al [ɔrniθoládʒịk(ạl], a. ornitológico.
—**ornithologist** [-θálodʒịst], s. ornitólogo.—
ornithology [-dʒị], s. ornitología.

rnithomancy [ɔrniθomænsị], s. ornitomancía.

rnithopod [-θopad], s. y a. ornitópodo.

rnithopter [-θáptœ(r)], s. (aer.) ornitóptero.

rnithorhynchus [-θorịŋkʌs], s. ornitorrinco.

rogenesis [arodʒénesịs], **orogeny** [orádʒenị], s. (geol.) orogenia.

rogenic [arodʒénịk], a. orogénico.

rographic [arogrǽfịk], a. orográfico.

rography [orágrafị], s. orografía.

rology [orálodʒị], s. (geol.) = OROGRAPHY.

rometer [orámɛtœ(r)], s. barómetro de alturas.

ropharynx [orofǽrịŋks], s. (anat.) orofaringe, f.

rotund [óụrotʌnd]. I. a. rotundo, sonoro; retumbante. II. s. voz rotunda.

rphan [órfạn]. I. a. y s. huérfano.—o. asylum, hospicio, orfanato, asilo de huérfanos. II. va. dejar huérfano a.—**orphaned** [-d], a. huérfano.

rphanage [-idʒ], s. orfandad; orfanato(rio).

rphanhood [-hụd], s. orfandad.

Orphean [orfíạn], **Orphic** [órfịk], a. órfico.

rpiment [órpịmẹnt], s. (min.) oropimente.

rpin(e [órpịn], s. (bot.) telefio.

rrery [órẹrị], s. planetario.

rris [órịs], s. (bot.) lirio de Florencia; bocadillo y galón.—o. root, raíz de lirio o iris florentina.

rts [ɔrts], s. pl. sobras, desperdicios.

rthocephalic [ɔrθosefǽlịk], **orthocephalous** [-séfạlʌs], a. ortocéfalo.

rthochromatic [-kromǽtịk], a. (foto.) ortocromático.

rthoclase [órθokleịs], s. (min.) ortoclasa, ortosa.

rthodontia [-dánšịạ], s. (dent.) ortodontosia.

rthodox [órθodaks], a. ortodoxo; correcto, admitido, convencional.

rthodoxness [-nịs], s. calidad o condición de ortodoxo.

rthodoxy [-ị], s. ortodoxia.

rthodromic [-drámịk], a. ortodrómico.

rthodromics [-s], **orthodromy** [orθádromị], s. (mar.) ortodromia.

rthoepic(al [ɔrθoépịk(ạl], a. prosódico, ortológico.

rthoëpist [órθoepịst], s. ortólogo.

rthoëpy [órθoepị], s. ortología, prosodia.

rthogamy [orθágamị], s. (bot.) autogamia, autofecundación.

rthogonal [orθágonạl], a. ortogonal, ortogonio.

rthographer [orθágrafœ(r)], s. ortógrafo.—
orthographic(al [orθogrǽfịk(ạl], a. ortográfico.
—**orthographically** [-ị], adv. ortográficamente.
—**orthographist** [orθágrafịst], s. ortógrafo.—
orthography [-fị], s. ortografía.

rthop(a)edia [orθopídịạ], **orthop(a)edy** [órθopidị], s. (med.) ortopedia.

rthop(a)edic [-pídịk], a. ortopédico.

rthop(a)edist [-pídịst], s. ortopedista.

rthophony [orθáfonị], s. ortofonía, arte de pronunciar y articular bien; corrección de los vicios de la pronunciación.

rthophosphoric [orθofasfórịk], a. ortofosfórico.

rthopn(o)ea [orθapnḯạ], s. (med.) ortopnea.

rthopter [orθáptœ(r)], s.(aer.) = ORNITHOPTER; (ent.) ortóptero (ll. t. **orthopteron**).

Orthoptera [-ạ], s. pl. (ent.) ortópteros.—
orthopterous [-ʌs], a. ortóptero.

rthorhombic [orθorámbịk], a. ortorómbico.

rthoscopic [-skápịk], a. (ópt.) ortoscópico; de vista normal; para corregir defectos de la vista.

ortive [órtịv], a. (astr.) ortivo.

ortolan [órtolạn], s. (orn.) hortelano; verderol; emberizo.

oryx [óụrịks], s. (zool.) órix.

os [as], s. (L.) (anat., zool.) hueso; boca; abertura.

Osage [óụseịdʒ], s. osage, indio norteamericano. —**O. orange**, (bot.) árbol americano de las urticáceas, que se emplea para formar setos.

oscillate [ásịleịt]. I. va. balancear, hacer oscilar.

II. vn. oscilar, fluctuar; vibrar; vacilar; (elec.) producir corriente alterna.

oscillating [-ịŋ], a. oscilante.—o. engine, máquina de cilindros oscilantes.

oscillation [-éịšọn], s. oscilación, fluctuación; vibración; vacilación.

oscillator [-ǫ(r)], s. oscilador.

oscillatory [ásịlạtorị], a. oscilatorio, oscilante.

oscillograph [asịlográf], s. oscilógrafo.

osculate [áskịuleịt], va. y vn. besar; (geom.) tocar por osculación.

osculating [-ịŋ], a. (geom.) osculador, osculatriz.

osculation [-éịšọn], s. beso, ósculo; (geom.) osculación.

osculatory [áskịulạtorị], a. osculatorio.

osier [óụžœ(r)]. I. s. (bot.) mimbrera, sauce, sarga, salguera; mimbre. II. a. de mimbre, mimbreño.

osiery [-ị], s. mimbreral, mimbral.

osmazome [ásmạzoụm], s. osmazomo.

osmic [ásmịk], a. (quím.) ósmico.

osmium [ásmịụm], s. (quím.) osmio.

osmose [ásmoụs], **osmosis** [asmóụsịs], s. (quím., fís. y fisiol.) ósmosis.—**osmotic** [asmátịk], a. osmótico.

osprey [ásprị], s. (orn.) águila osífraga, halieto, quebrantahuesos, atahorma.

ossarium [osérịʌm], s. osario, osar.

ossein [ásịịn], s. (bioquím.) oseína.

osseous [ásịạs], a. huesoso, óseo, ososo.

ossicle [ásịkl], s. huesecillo.

ossiferous [asíférʌs], a. osífero.

ossific [asífịk], a. osífico.

ossification [-éịšọn], s. osificación.

ossified [ásịfaịd], a. osificado.

ossifrage [ásịfridʒ], s. (orn.) osífraga. V. OSPREY.

ossify [ásịfaị], va. y vn. osificar(se), convertir(se) en hueso o en substancia ósea.

ossuary [ásụerị], s. osario, osar.

osteal [ástịạl], a. osteico, óseo.

osteitis [astịáịtịs], s. (med.) ostetítis.

ostensible [asténsịbl], a. aparente; pretendido; (ant.) ostensible.

ostensibly [-blị], adv. pretendida o aparentemente.

ostensive [asténsịv], a. ostensivo. V. OSTENSIBLE.

ostentation [astentéịšọn], s. ostentación, boato, fausto, aparato, pompa, alarde.—**ostentatious** [-téịšʌs], a. ostentoso, ostentativo, fastuoso, faustoso.—**ostentatiously** [-lị], adv. ostentosa o pomposamente.—**ostentatiousness** [-nịs], s. calidad de ostentoso; fastuosidad, pomposidad.

osteoblast [ástịoblæst], s. (anat.) osteoblasto.

osteoclasis [astịáklạsịs], s. (cir.) osteoclasia; (anat.) resorción del tejido óseo.

osteogenesis [-dʒénesịs], **osteogeny** [-ádʒenị], s. (fisiol.) osteogenia, formación de los huesos.

osteography [-ágrafị], s. (anat.) osteografía.

osteologic(al [-olǽdʒịk(ạl], a. osteológico.

osteologist [-álodʒịst], s. osteólogo.

osteology [-álodʒị], s. (anat.) osteología.

osteoma [-óụmạ], s. (med.) osteoma, m.

osteomalacia [-omạléịšịạ], s. (med.) osteomalacia.

osteomyelitis [-omaịeláịtịs], s. (med.) osteomielitis.

osteopath [ástịopæθ], s. osteópata, mf.—**osteopathic** [-opǽθịk], a. osteopático.—**osteopathy** [-ápạθị], s. osteopatía.

osteotomy [astịátomị], s. (cir.) osteotomía.

ostiary [ástịerị], s. (igl.) ostiario.

ostiole [ástịoụl], s. (biol., bot.) ostíolo.

ostler [áslœ(r)], s. = HOSTLER.

ostosis [astóụsịs], s. (fisiol.) osificación.

ostracean [astréịsịạn]. I. a. ostráceo, conchudo. II. s. (zool.) ostráceo, ostra.

ostraceous [-sʌs], a. ostráceo, ostrero.

ostracism [ástrạsịzm], s. ostracismo.—**ostracize** [-saịz], va. desterrar, condenar al ostracismo.

ostrich [ástrịch], s. (orn.) avestruz, m., (Am.) ñandú, surí.

Ostrogoth(ic [ástrogaθ, -gáθįk], s. y a. ostrogodo.

otacoustic [otąkústįk]. **I.** a. otacústico. **II.** s. trompetilla.

otalgia [otáldžįą], s. (med.) otalgia.

other [Áðœ(r)]. **I.** a. y pron. otro, demás.—pl. (los o las) otros o demás.—**the o. day,** el otro día, hace poco. **II.** adv. (con **than**) otra cosa que (I cannot do other than praise him, no puedo hacer otra cosa que alabarlo, no puedo abstenerme de alabarlo). V. OTHERWISE.

otherness [-nįs], s. calidad de ser otro u otra cosa, existencia como cosa distinta de otras.

otherwise [-wajz]. **I.** adv. de otra manera, de otro modo; de lo contrario, si no; o bien.—**o. called,** o **known as,** alias, por otro nombre. **II.** a. otro, diferente.

otic [óųtįk], a. (anat.) ótico, auricular.

otiose [óųšįoųs], a. ocioso; holgazán; fútil; inútil.

otitis [otáįtįs], s. (med.) otitis.

otolith [óųtolįθ], s. (anat., zool.) otolito.

otologist [otálodžįst], s. otólogo, aurista.

otology [-džį], s. (med.) otología.

otorrhea, otorrhœa [otoríą], s. (med.) otorrea.

otoscope [óųtoskoųp], s. (med.) otoscopio.

otoscopy [otáskopį], s. (med.) otoscopia.

ottar [átą(r)], **otto** [átoų], s. aceite esencial.—**o. of roses,** aceite esencial de rosas. V. ATTAR.

otter [átœ(r)], s. (zool.) nutria, lutria; nutria de mar, lataz, mf.; su piel; (ent.) oruga de una mariposa nocturna; (mar.) artificio dragaminas. —**o.-colored,** alutrado.

Ottoman [átomąn]. **I.** a. y s. otomano, turco. **II.** s. (o.) otomana, diván, sofá, m.; escabel o escañuelo tapizado.

oubliette [ublįét], s. calabozo de prisión perpetua con entrada por arriba.

ouch [aųch]. **I.** s. (ant.) (joy.) montura, engaste; adorno de oro. **II.** interj. ¡huy! ¡ay, ay!

ought [ɔt], s. y adv. algo, alguna cosa; nada; cero. V. AUGHT y NAUGHT.—**for o. I know,** por lo que yo puedo comprender, en cuanto yo sé.

ought [ɔt]. **I.** aux. def. que se traduce por formas (gen. el presente de ind., el condicional y el pret. de subj.) de deber: you ought not to go, Vd. no debe (debiera, debería) ir; I ought to have gone, debí ir, he debido ir, debiera o debí(a) haber ido, hubiera debido ir. En la ética se usa como expresión de obligación moral, y a veces queda mejor traducido por "ser el deber," "tener obligación," cambiando un poco el giro. A veces se traduce por convenir, ser conveniente, menester o necesario, etc. **II.** s. deber, obligación.

ouija [wídžą], **ouija board** [-bɔrd], s. tabla de escritura espiritista (es nombre de fábrica).

ounce [aųns], s. onza (= 28.35 gramos, o $\frac{1}{16}$ de libra "avoirdupois"); (farm.) onza de farmacia (= 31.1 gramos, o $\frac{1}{12}$ de libra "troy": ll. t. **troy** o **apothecaries' o.**); pequeña porción, (fam.) pizca; (hist.) onza de oro española ($16); (zool.) onza; jaguar.

our, ours [aųr, -z], a. y pron. pos. nuestro, nuestra, nuestros, nuestras. Cuando no va seguido del substantivo, se emplea ours, v. gr.: your house is larger than ours, la casa de Vd. es mayor que la nuestra; this is ours, esto es nuestro; those cows are ours, aquellas vacas son nuestras.—**O. Father,** (teol.) Padre Eterno; padre nuestro o padrenuestro (oración).—**O. Lady,** Nuestra Señora (la Virgen).

ourang [urέŋ], s. = ORANG-OUTANG.

ourself [aųrsélf], pron. yo mismo, yo misma (en estilo oficial o regio).

ourselves [aųrsélvz], pron. recíproco o enfático, nosotros mismos, nosotras mismas. V. MYSELF.

ousel [úzęl] = OUZEL.

oust [aųst], va. desposeer, desahuciar, desalojar, desaposentar, echar fuera, despedir.

ouster [-œ(r)], s. (for.) desahucio, desposeimiento, despojo.

out [aųt]. **I.** adv. fuera, afuera; hacia fuera. Se emplea después de muchos verbos para indicar movimiento, dirección, etc., hacia fuera o situación fuera o afuera (to look out, mirar hacia fuera; to be out, estar afuera), o para cambiar parcial o totalmente el significado de ellos (to look out, tener cuidado; to be out, estar reñidos). Las frases en que sirve para este último objeto se dan con los verbos respectivos. **II.** prep. fuera de; más allá de; por (la puerta, ventana, etc.). V. FROM OUT. **III.** a. exterior, de afuera; ausente; fuera de moda; errado (en los cálculos, etc.); cesante; (declarado) en huelga; empleada (una criada, etc.).—**o. and away,** con mucho. —**o. and o.,** adv. a fondo; abiertamente; sin reserva.—**o.-and-o.,** a. cabal, completo; declarado, redomado, consumado.—**o. at interest,** puesto a interés.—**o. at the elbows,** agujereado, roto por los codos; andrajoso.—**o. at the heels,** con zapatos rotos.—**o. loud,** en voz alta. —**o. of,** fuera de; más allá de; sin (out of money, sin dinero, sin fondos); por (out of charity, por caridad; out of respect for you, por respeto a Vd.); seguido de un adjetivo, niega el estado o propiedad que éste denota (out of center, out of plumb, descentrado; out of vertical, no vertical, desviado de la vertical; out of true, no alineado o arreglado, desalineado, desarreglado).—**o. of breath,** sin aliento, jadeante.—**o. of character,** impropio, inconveniente.—**o. of commission,** fuera de servicio; desarreglado, que no funciona; fuera de combate.—**o. of danger,** fuera de peligro.—**o. of date,** pasado, anticuado.—**o. of doors** = OUTDOORS.—**o. of employment,** desacomodado; cesante.—**o. of fashion,** fuera de moda, pasado.—**o. of favor,** desvalido, desgraciado; desacreditado; menospreciado.—**o. of fuel, gas, etc.,** fuera de combustible.—**o. of hand,** luego, al punto; incontenible; desenfrenado.—**o. of his wits,** fuera de sí, insensato.—**o. of hope,** desesperanzado, sin esperanza.—**o. of humor,** de mal humor, enojado.—**o. of joint,** trastornado, desbarajustado.—**o. of measure,** desmesurado.—**o. of one's way,** apartado del camino de uno (gen. es mejor cambiar el giro: that store is out of my way, yo no paso por esa tienda); a un lado (poner, hacerse, etc., según el verbo).—**o. of order,** desordenado, descompuesto, desarreglado; fuera de orden.—**o. of patience,** sin paciencia, con la paciencia agotada (a veces es mejor cambiar el giro: I am out of patience, se me ha agotado la paciencia).—**o. of place,** fuera de lugar, impropio.—**o. of pocket,** perdidoso, perdiendo.—**o. of print,** agotada (una edición).—**o. of reach,** inaccesible, inasequible.—**o. of season,** que no se da o se produce (en una estación o tiempo dado).—**o. of sight,** fuera del alcance de la vista, invisible; (fam.) por las nubes (precios).—**o. of sorts,** indispuesto; descontento; (impr.) falta de un tipo o de una letra.—**o. of spirits,** triste, abatido, desalentado.—**o. of spite,** por despique.—**o. of stock,** (com.) sin existencia, agotada (la existencia de una mercancía).—**o. of style,** fuera de moda.—**o. of the way,** donde no estorbe; suprimido; hecho, despachado (a veces se cambia el giro: I am glad that work is out of the way, me alegro de haber salido de ese trabajo).—**o.-of-the-way,** a. lejano, apartado; inaccesible; extraordinario.—**o. of the woods,** libre de dudas, apuros o dificultades.—**o. of this world,** (fam.) el non plus ultra, de calidad superior, excelente.—**o. of time,** fuera de compás.—**o. of touch with,** apartado de, o alejado de; sin relaciones con; en desacuerdo con.—**o. of trim,** en mal estado; (mar.) mal estibado, equilibrado u orientado.—**o. of tune,** desentonado, desafinado; destemplado.—**o. of work,** sin trabajo.—**o. to o.,** de extremo a extremo, total.—**a way o.,** salida; escapatoria.

—**four o. of five,** de cada cinco, cuatro.—**the time is o.,** el tiempo (la hora) ha pasado; el plazo ha expirado.—**to be o.,** estar fuera o ausente; no estar en casa (o en el despacho, edificio, etc.); no estar de moda o en boga; quedar cesante; quedarse cortado; perder, haber perdido, salir perdiendo; estar apagado o extinguido; haberse agotado o acabado; haberse publicado, haber salido (un libro, un periódico); estar reñidos; (con **with**) estar reñido (con).—**to be o. of,** no tener más, habérsele acabado a uno (*we are out of coffee,* se nos ha acabado el café, no tenemos más café). IV. *interj.* ¡fuera!—**o. with it!** ¡fuera con ello! hable Vd. sin rodeos. —**o. upon thee!** (ant.) ¡vergüenza! V. *s.* exterior, parte (*f.*) de afuera; esquina, lugar exterior; exterioridad; cesante; dimisionario; (fam.) pero, defecto; (impr.) olvido, omisión; en baseball, el efecto de dejar fuera o echar a un jugador del lugar que ocupaba.—*pl.* (pol.) la oposición.—**at outs, u on the outs with,** reñido(s) con. VI. *va.* expulsar, desposeer, desalojar, echar fuera. VII. *vn.* salir; divulgarse, hacerse público.—**it will o.,** ello dirá; todo saldrá en la colada.—**to be o. to,** estar empeñado en o afanarse por (hacer o conseguir algo).

outbalance [aųtbǽlạns], *va.* sobrexceder, sobrepujar. V. OUTWEIGH.

outbid [aųtbíd], *va.* (*pret.* OUTBID; *pp.* OUTBID[DEN]) mejorar, pujar, ofrecer más dinero (en subasta, etc.).

outbidder [-œ(r)], *s.* pujador, ponedor, requintador.

outboard [áųtbords]. I. *a.* (mar.) fuera del buque. —**o. motor,** pequeño motor exterior, o fuera de bordo. II. *adv.* fuera del centro.

outbound [áųtbaųnd], *a.* de travesía; que sale, de salida. V. OUTWARD BOUND.

outbrag [aųtbrǽg], *va.* exceder o sobrepujar en fanfarronadas.

outbrave [aųtbréįv], *va.* sobrepujar en valentía, audacia o atavío; arrostrar los peligros.

outbreak [áųtbreįk]. I. *s.* erupción, brote, estallido; ataque violento; pasión; tumulto, disturbio; principio (de una guerra, epidemia, etc.). II. [aųtbréįk], *vn.* brotar; estallar; principiar.

outbred [áųtbred], *a.* criado o producido por mezcla de razas.—**outbreed** [aųtbríd], *va.* criar o producir por mezcla de razas.—**outbreeding** [-ịŋ], *s.* mezcla de razas.

outbuilding [áųtbįldịŋ], *s.* dependencia, accesoria, construcción exterior, anexo.

outburst [áųtbœrst], *s.* explosión, erupción, estallido; arranque.—**o. of laughter,** risotada, carcajada.

outcast [áųtkæst]. I. *a.* desechado, inútil; expulso, proscripto; perdido. II. *s.* paria, *mf.*

outclass [aųtklǽs], *va.* exceder, ser superior a.

outcome [áųtkʌm], *s.* éxito, resultado, suceso.

outcrop [aųtkráp], *vn.* (min.) asomar; aflorar.

outcrop [áųtkrap], *s.* (min.) afloramiento; crestón.

outcry [áųtkraį], *s.* clamor(eo); grita; alboroto; gritería, voc(ingl)ería; subasta.

outdare [aųtdér], *va.* atreverse más que; superar en osadía; desafiar.

outdate [aųtdéįt], *va.* anticuar.—**outdated** [-ịd], *a.* anticuado; fuera de moda.

outdistance [aųtdístạns], *va.* adelantarse a, pasar delante de, dejar atrás, distanciar, rezagar.

outdo [aųtdú], *va.* (*pret.* OUTDID; *pp.* OUTDONE) exceder, sobrepujar, descollar, eclipsar, veneer. —**to o. one's self,** superarse, excederse a sí mismo.

outdoor [áųtdor], *a.* externo, fuera de la casa, al aire libre.—**o. exercise,** ejercicio al aire libre.—**o. relief,** socorro a domicilio.—**o. sports,** juegos al aire libre o en campo abierto.

outdoors [áųtdórz]. I. *s.* el campo raso, el mundo de puertas afuera. II. *adv.* fuera de casa, al aire libre, al raso, a la intemperie.

outer [áųtœ(r)], *a.* exterior, externo.

outermost [-moųst], *a.* extremo; lo más exterior.

outface [aųtféįs], *va.* retar, desafiar; arrostrar; confundir, desconcertar. V. OUTSTARE.

outfall [áųtfol], *s.* salida, desembocadura.

outfield [áųtfild], *s.* campo abierto; campo contiguo; (dep.) campo y jugadores situados fuera del cuadro o de la demarcación.

outfielder [-œ(r)], *s.* en baseball y criquet, uno de los jugadores colocados fuera del cuadro.

outfit [áųtfịt]. I. *s.* equipo, apresto, tren; ropa, vestido, traje; habilitación; pertrechos, avíos, menesteres, *pl.*; (fam.) grupo, compañía; cuerpo o unidad militar. II. *va.* equipar, aviar, habilitar.

outfitter [-œ(r)], *s.* armador; abastecedor, proveedor, habilitador.

outflank [aųtflǽŋk], *va.* (mil.) flanquear; llevar la ventaja.

outflash [aųtflǽš], *va.* brillar más que, eclipsar.

outflow [áųtfloų], *s.* efusión, derrame, flujo; salida.

outgeneral [aųtdžénẹrạl], *va.* exceder en táctica militar o en habilidad.

outgo [aųtgóų]. I. *va.* exceder, aventajar, vencer. II. [áųtgoų], *s.* gasto, expendio. V. OUTLAY.

outgoer [-œ(r)], *s.* el que sale, parte o se va.

outgoing [-ịŋ]. I. *s.* ida, salida, partida. II. *a.* saliente, cesante; que sale, de salida.

outgrow [aųtgróų], *va.* (*pret.* OUTGREW; *pp.* OUTGROWN) crecer más que; pasar de la edad de, ser ya viejo para; botar o curarse de con la edad (*the boy has outgrown his clothes,* el muchacho ha crecido tanto que la ropa le está corta; *he will outgrow this ailment,* este achaque le pasará con la edad, o con el tiempo).

outgrowth [áųtgroųθ], *s.* excrecencia, nacencia; resultado, consecuencia.

outguard [áųtgard], *s.* (mil.) (guardia) avanzada.

outguess [aųtgés], *va.* = OUTWIT.

out-Herod [aųthérọd], *va.* sobrepasar o exceder en maldad, violencia o extravagancia.

outhouse [áųthaųs], *s.* dependencia, accesoria; retrete situado fuera de la casa.

outing [áųtịŋ], *s.* salida; paseo, caminata, jira, excursión, esparcimiento, explayamiento.

outland [áųtlạnd]. I. *s.* tierra vecina no cultivada u ocupada. II. *a.* = OUTLYING; (ant.) extranjero.

outlander [-œ(r)], *s.* extranjero; (fam.) = OUTSIDER.

outlandish [aųtlǽndịš], *a.* extraño, ridículo; de aspecto extranjero o exótico; remoto.

outlast [aųtlǽst], *va.* durar más que; sobrevivir a.

outlaw [áųtlo]. I. *s.* forajido, facineroso; proscrito. II. *a.* proscrito; fuera de la ley; rebelde. III. *va.* proscribir; declarar fuera de la ley.

outlawry [-rį], *s.* proscripción; encartamiento.

outlay [áųtleį]. I. *s.* desembolso, gasto, expendio, salida. II. [aųtléį], *va.* gastar; desplegar.

outlet [áųtlet], *s.* salida; orificio de salida; escape, desembocadero; desagüe; desaguadero; sangrador, tomadero; toma (de agua, corriente eléctrica, etc.); (min.) agolía.

outlie [aųtláį]. I. *va.* mentir más que; estar situado más allá de (un límite). II. *vn.* (ex)tenderse; dormir al raso, acampar en tiendas.

outline [áųtlaįn]. I. *s.* contorno, perfil; croquis, *m.*; esquicio, esbozo, bosquejo, plan general, reseña, trazo, traza(do). II. *va.* bosquejar, delinear, esbozar, esquiciar, reseñar, trazar.

outlive [aųtlív], *va.* sobrevivir a; durar más que.

outlook [áųtlụk], *s.* vista, perspectiva, aspecto; probabilidades, *f. pl.*; actitud; atalaya, vigía, garita; centinela, guardia. V. LOOKOUT.

outlying [áųtlaįịŋ], *a.* distante, remoto; lejos del centro; extrínseco; exterior, extranjero.

outmaneuver, outmanoeuvre [aųtmạnúvœ(r)], *va.* sobrepujar o aventajar en ejecutar maniobras o evoluciones.

outmarch [aųtmárch], *va.* dejar atrás a.

outmatch [aųtmǽch], *va.* exceder, prevalecer sobre.

outmeasure [aųtmɛ́ʒŋ(r)], *va.* exceder en medida.

outmoded [aųtmóụdįd], *a.* pasado de moda, de moda pasada, anticuado.

outmost [áųtmoųst], *a.* = OUTERMOST.

outnumber [aųtnʌ́mbœ(r)], *va.* exceder en número, ser más que.

outparish [áųtpærįʃ], *s.* parroquia rural.

outpatient [áųtpeįʃŋt], *s.* enfermo no hospitalizado, que recibe tratamiento en el hospital pero no reside en él.

outplay [aųtpléį], *va.* superar o vencer en un juego.

outpoint [aųtpóįnt], *va.* exceder en puntos al adversario; (mar.) ceñir el viento más que (otro buque).

outpost [áųtpoųst], *s.* (mil.) avanzada.

outpour [aųtpór]. I. *va.* y *vn.* chorrear, verter. II. [áųtpɔr], *s.* chorreo, chorro.

outpouring [-įŋ], *s.* chorro; efusión.

output [áųtpųt], *s.* producción total, rendimiento; capacidad, fuerza; (mec., elec.) potencia neta o útil; (fisiol.) lo que se expele por los pulmones, los riñones o la piel.

outrage [áųtreįdʒ]. I. *va.* ultrajar, injuriar; maltratar, violentar; violar, desflorar. II. *s.* ultraje, afrenta; desafuero, atropello; atrocidad; violación, rapto.

outrageous [aųtréįdʒʌs], *a.* ultrajoso, ultrajante, afrentoso, injurioso; atroz; desaforado.—**outrageously** [-lį], *adv.* ultrajantemente; atrozmente.—**outrageousness** [-nįs], *s.* calidad de ultrajante.

outrance [utráns], *s.* (fr.) el último extremo.

outrank [aųtrǽŋk], *va.* exceder en rango, grado, posición o importancia.

outré [utréį], *a.* (fr.) extremado, extravagante.

outreach [aųtrích], *va.* alcanzar, pasar, tomar la delantera a, exceder. *V.* OVERREACH.

outride [aųtráįd]. I. *va.* (*pret.* OUTRODE; *pp.* OUTRIDDEN) ganar la delantera a caballo; (mar.) resistir felizmente (a una tormenta). II. *vn.* cabalgar junto al estribo de un carruaje o delante de éste.

outrider [áųtraįdœ(r)], *s.* criado que cabalga al lado o delante de un carruaje; batidor; merodeador.

outrigger [áųtrįgœ(r)], *s.* saliente, vuelo; (mar.) horqueta, escora, tangón, cuerno; (Filip.) batanga; (mar.) pescante de banda para carenar; puntal de tope.—*pl.* (mar.) bordones, botantes.

outright [áųtraįt]. I. *a.* completo; directo; franco. II. [áųtráįt], *adv.* completamente; abiertamente; sin reserva; sin tardanza, al momento.

outrival [aųtráįvʌl], *va.* sobrepujar en excelencia, ganar, vencer.

outrun [aųtrʌ́n], *va.* (*pret.* OUTRAN; *pp.* OUTRUN) correr más que; pasar, ganar, exceder.

outsail [aųtséįl], *va.* (mar.) ser más velero que, dejar atrás, navegar mejor o más que.

outsell [aųtsél], *va.* vender más caro, más aprisa, o en mayor cantidad que.

outset [áųtset], *s.* principio; salida; estreno.

outshine [aųtʃáįn]. I. *va.* (*pret.* y *pp.* OUTSHONE) exceder en brillantez, dejar deslucido, eclipsar. II. *vn.* brillar, lucir, resplandecer.

outshoot [aųtʃút]. I. *va.* (*pret.* y *pp.* OUTSHOT) tirar mejor o más lejos que. II. *vn.* sobresalir. III. [áųtʃut], *s.* saliente, vuelo.

outside [áųtsáįd]. I. *a.* exterior, externo; superficial; extremo; ajeno, neutral.—**o. shutter,** contraventana. II. *s.* exterior, parte (*f.*) de fuera, superficie, sobrefaz; apariencia; extremo. —**at the o.,** (fam.) a lo sumo, a más tirar. III. *adv.* afuera, fuera; (teat.) al paño.—**o. of,** (fam.) con excepción de. IV. *prep.* fuera de, más allá de; (fam.) excepto.

outsider [-œ(r)], *s.* forastero, extraño; el que no pertenece a determinada sociedad, institución, etc.; entremetido, intruso.

outskirt [áųtskœrt], *s.* borde, linde.—*pl.* afueras, suburbios, cercanías, inmediaciones, arrabales.

outsmart [oųtsmárt], *va.* (fam.) vencer o ganar en destreza o maña.—**to o. one's self,** pasarse de listo.

outspeak [aųtspík]. I. *va.* hablar alto, hablar claro; hablar mejor o más tiempo que. II. *vn.* osar hablar.—**outspoken** [áųtspóųkn], *a.* abierto, franco(te); boquifresco.—**to be o.,** (fam.) no tener pelos en la lengua, no morderse los labios.

outspread [aųtspréd]. I. *va.* y *vn.* extender(se), difundir(se); desplegar(se). II. *a.* (ex)tendido, difuso; desplegado. III. *s.* extensión; despliegue, desplegadura; expansión.

outstanding [aųtstǽndįŋ], *a.* saledizo, saliente; destacado, descollante, relevante, sobresaliente, principal, prominente; que resiste; (com.) pendiente, no pagado.—**o. bills,** cuentas u obligaciones pendientes.—**o. claim,** (for.) activo.—**o. shares,** acciones en circulación o por redimir.

outstare [aųtstér], *va.* hacer bajar la vista mirando de hito en hito a uno.

outstart [áųtstart]. I. *s.* = OUTSET. II. [aųtstárt], *vn.* partir, ponerse en marcha. III. *va.* coger la delantera a.

outstay [aųtstéį], *va.* quedar(se) más tiempo que; durar o resistir más.

outstretch [aųtstréch], *va.* extender, alargar.

outstrip [aųtstríp], *va.* pasar, rezagar, distanciar, dejar atrás; aventajar, ganar.

outtalk [aųttók], *va.* hablar más o mejor que.

outturn [áųttœrn], *s.* producción; artículos producidos y entregados; resultado (en la venta y entrega de mercancías). *V.* OUTPUT.

outvalue [aųtvǽlyu], *va.* valer más que.

outvie [aųtváį], *va.* sobrepujar a.

outvote [aųtvóųt], *va.* ganar a, en el número de votos; dar más votos que.

outwalk [aųtwók], *va.* andar más que, dejar atrás.

outwall [áųtwol], *s.* pared exterior; antemural; exterior, parte externa.

outward [áųtwǝrd]. I. *a.* exterior, externo, visible; de hacia (a)fuera; aparente, superficial; extraño; extrínseco; (teol.) carnal, corpóreo.—**o. cargo,** o **freight,** cargamento o flete de ida. II. *adv.* fuera, afuera, exteriormente; superficialmente; (mar.) de ida; para el extranjero.—**o. bound,** con rumbo a un puerto extranjero; de ida, de salida; que sale.

outwardly [-lį], *adv.* exterior o aparentemente.

outwards [-z], *adv.* = OUTWARD.

outwatch [aųtwách], *va.* vigilar o velar más que.

outwear [aųtwér], *va.* (*pret.* OUTWORE; *pp.* OUTWORN) durar más que; gastar, consumir. *V.* OUTGROW.

outweigh [aųtwéį], *va.* preponderar; pesar más que; exceder en valor o importancia.

outwit [aųtwít], *va.* ser más listo que; llevar ventaja a; engañar a fuerza de tretas.

outwork [aųtwœrk], *va.* trabajar más que; acabar.

outwork [áųtwœrk], *s.* (fort.) obra exterior o accesoria.

outworn [aųtwórn], *a.* ajado, gastado, usado; anticuado; rendido de cansancio.

ouzel [úʒel], *s.* (orn.) mirlo, mirla o merla.

ova [óųvǝ], *s.* *pl.* de OVUM.

oval [óųvǝl]. I. *s.* óvalo. II. *a.* oval, ovalado.

ovally [-lį], *adv.* en figura de óvalo.

ovarian [ovérįǝn], *a.* ovárico.

ovariotomist [overįátomįst], *s.* ovariotomista.

ovariotomy [-mį], *s.* (cir.) ovariotomía.

ovaritis [ovaráitįs], *s.* (med.) ovaritis.

ovary [óųvǝrį], **ovarium** [ovérįʌm], *s.* (anat., bot.) ovario; (orn.) overa, huevera, madrecilla.

ovate [óųveįt]. I. *a.* (a)ovado. II. *va.* ovalar.

ovation [ovéįʃǫn], *s.* ovación.

ovational [-ǝl], *a.* ovante, triunfante.

oven [ʌvn], *s.* horno.—**o. wood,** hornija.

ovenbird [-bœrd], *s.* (orn.) (Am.) hornero.

ovenpeel [-pil], *s.* pala de horno.

over [óȝvœ(r)]. **I.** *prep.* sobre, encima, por encima de; allende, al otro lado de; a causa o por motivo de; a pesar de; más de; mientras, durante; por, en.—**o. all,** total, de extremo a extremo.—**o. a thousand,** más de mil.—**o. night,** durante la noche, hasta el otro día (cambiando el giro: *to stay over night,* pasar la noche).—**o. one's head,** sin contar con o hacer caso de uno.—**o. one's signature,** bajo su firma.—**o. the top,** (fam., mil.) al ataque, en el ataque, (ir, salir) a la carga (saliendo de las trincheras o defensas). **II.** *adv.* al otro lado; al lado, parte o partido contrario; enfrente; de arriba abajo; al revés; encima; más, de más, de sobra; otra vez, de nuevo; demasiado, excesivamente; acabado; terminado; a la vuelta, al dorso. Ú. mucho como prefijo equivalente a re-, sobre-, super-, trans-, ultra-, o para denotar superioridad o exceso, y a menudo puede traducirse por "demasiado" (*overkind,* demasiado bondadoso).—**o. again,** otra vez, segunda vez, de nuevo.—**o. against,** enfrente; en frente de; en contraste o comparación con.—**o. and above,** además de, en exceso de, por encima de; de sobra; (fam.) demasiado.—**o. and o.,** repetidas veces, una y otra vez.—**o. the leaf,** a la vuelta (de la página).—**o. there,** (fam.) en Europa, en el frente, en la línea de batalla.—**o. with,** (fam.) acabado.—**(all) the world o.,** en o por todo el mundo.—**to be (all) o.,** haber pasado; haberse acabado; terminar(se).—**to be o. and above,** sobrar. **III.** *a.* acabado, terminado; demasiado, excesivo; sobrante, en exceso de; superior; exterior.

overabound [-əbáȝnd], *vn.* sobre- o superabundar.—**overabundance** [-əbʌ́ndəns], *s.* sobre- o superabundancia, sobra, exceso, plétora.—**overabundant** [-ənt], *a.* sobre- o superabundante.

overact [-ǽkt], *va.* exagerar.

overage [-éȝdʒ], *a.* pasado de la edad requerida o debida; que tiene más edad que la normal o aceptable.

overall [-ɔ́l], *a.* que abarca o incluye todo; de un cabo a otro.—**o. length,** longitud total.

overalls [-ɔlz], *s. pl.* mono(s), traje de mecánico, etc.; zahones o zafones; sobrerropa; polainas impermeables.

overanxious [-ǽnkʃʌs], *a.* demasiado ansioso.—**overanxiously** [-li], *adv.* con excesiva ansiedad.

overarch [-árch], *va.* abovedar.

overarm [-arm], *a.* (baseball, etc.) tirada (la pelota) por lo alto.—**o. stroke swimming,** natación a la marinera.

overawe [-ɔ́], *va.* intimidar.

overbalance [-bǽləns]. **I.** *va.* y *vn.* preponderar; llevar ventaja; (hacer) perder el equilibrio. **II.** *s.* preponderancia.

overbear [-bér]. **I.** *va.* (*pret.* OVERBORE; *pp.* OVERBORNE) sojuzgar, reprimir; subyugar, oprimir, agobiar, vencer. **II.** *vn.* llevar demasiado fruto.—**overbearing** [-iŋ], *a.* ultrajoso, despótico; imperioso, altivo, dominante.

overbid [-bíd]. **I.** *va.* (*pret.* OVERBID; *pp.* OVERBID[DEN]) ofrecer más que, pujar. **II.** *vn.* ofrecer demasiado. **III.** [óȝvœrbíd], *s.* puja.

overbidding [-iŋ], *s.* puja.

overblow [-blóȝ]. **I.** *va.* (*pret.* OVERBLEW; *pp.* OVERBLOWN) dispersar; derribar o llevarse (el viento). **II.** *vn.* dispersarse; pasar; soplar con violencia (el viento).—**overblown** [-n], *a.* abierta (la flor) en exceso; cubierta (la carne) de eresas.

overboard [-bord], *adv.* (mar.) al mar, al agua.—**man o.!** ¡hombre al agua!

overboil [-bóȝl], *va.* hervir o cocer demasiado.

overbold [-bóȝld], *a.* temerario; descarado.

overbridge [-brídʒ], *s.* (f. c.) puente o paso superior.

overburden [-bœ́rdən]. **I.** *va.* sobrecargar; oprimir. **II.** [óȝvœrbœ́rdən], *s.* sobrecarga.

overcame [-kéȝm], *pret.* de TO OVERCOME.

overcapitalization [-kæpɩtəlɩzéȝʃən], *s.* exageración del capital, capitalización inflada.—**overcapitalize** [-kǽpɩtəlaɩz], *va.* exagerar el valor de, como capital; capitalizar en más de lo justo.

overcareful [-kérfʊl], *a.* demasiado cuidadoso.

overcast [-kǽst]. **I.** *va.* (*pret.* y *pp.* OVERCAST) anublar, obscurecer; entristecer; (cost.) sobrehilar; (cir.) cicatrizar; (enc.) hacer un doblez a (una hoja) para coserla. **II.** *vn.* anublarse. **III.** [óȝvœrkæst], *a.* (a)nublado, cerrado, cubierto, encapotado; sombrío.

overcasting [-iŋ], *s.* (cost.) sobrehilado, punto por encima.

overcautious [-kɔ́ʃʌs], *a.* demasiado prudente o precavido.

overcharge [-chárdʒ]. **I.** *va.* recargar el precio; cobrar más de lo justo; sobrecargar; oprimir; exagerar. **II.** [óȝvœrchardʒ], *s.* cargo excesivo; extorsión; cargo adicional; recargo de precio.

overcloud [-kláȝd]. **I.** *va.* cubrir de nubes, anublar; entristecer. **II.** *vn.* (a)nublarse, cerrarse.

overcoat [-kóȝt], *s.* sobretodo, gabán, abrigo, paletó.—**overcoating** [-iŋ], *s.* paño para gabanes.

overcome [-kʌ́m]. **I.** *va.* (*pret.* OVERCAME; *pp.* OVERCOME) vencer, rendir, sujetar, domar; sojuzgar, subyugar; superar, vencer, salvar (obstáculos). **II.** *vn.* sobreponerse; ganar, vencer; hacerse superior. **III.** *a.* agobiado; confundido.

overconfidence [-kánfɩdəns], *s.* presunción; demasiada confianza.—**overconfident** [-ənt], *a.* demasiado confiado.

overcrowd [-kráȝd], *va.* apiñar, atestar.—**overcrowded** [-ɩd], *a.* apiñado, atestado, repleto.

overdevelop [-dɩvélɔp], *va.* desarrollar excesivamente; (foto.) revelar demasiado.

overdo [-dú]. **I.** *vn.* (*pret.* OVERDID; *pp.* OVERDONE) hacer más de lo necesario; excederse, extralimitarse. **II.** *va.* agobiar, abrumar de trabajo; exagerar; (coc.) recocer, esturar, requemar; (poét.) eclipsar, sobrepujar.—**overdone** [-dʌ́n], *a.* (coc.) recocido, recocho, demasiado asado.

overdose [-dóȝs]. **I.** *va.* dar una dosis excesiva. **II.** [óȝvœrdoȝs], *s.* dosis excesiva.

overdraft [-dræft], *s.* (com.) giro o libranza en descubierto o en exceso de los fondos o el crédito disponibles.

overdraw [-drɔ́], *va.* (*pret.* OVERDREW; *pp.* OVERDRAWN) (com.) girar en descubierto, sobregirar, exceder, en un giro, del crédito disponible; estirar demasiado; exagerar en el dibujo, la descripción, etc.

overdress [-drés]. **I.** *va.* y *vn.* adornar o vestirse con exceso. **II.** [óȝvœrdres], *s.* prenda llevada sobre otra.

overdrink [-dríŋk], *vn.* (*pret.* OVERDRANK; *pp.* OVERDRUNK) beber con exceso, emborracharse.

overdrive [-dráɩv], *va.* (*pret.* OVERDROVE; *pp.* OVERDRIVEN) abrumar de trabajo; arrear y fatigar los animales; (mec.) hacer funcionar a más de la capacidad normal.

overdue [-djú], *a.* (com.) vencido y no pagado; retrasado.

overeat [-ít], *vn.* (*pret.* OVERATE; *pp.* OVEREATEN) comer con exceso, atracarse, tupirse, hartarse.

overestimate [-éstɩmeɩt]. **I.** *va.* presuponer, avaluar o estimar en valor excesivo; exagerar; tener en más de lo justo. **II.** [-éstɩmɩt], *s.* estimación, avalúo o presupuesto excesivos.

overexcite [-eksáɩt], *va.* sobre(e)xcitar.

overexcitement [-mənt], **overexcitation** [-eksaɩtéɩʃən], *s.* sobre(e)xcitación.

overexposure [-ekspóȝʒʊ(r)], *s.* (foto.) exceso de exposición.

overfatigue [-fatíg]. **I.** *va.* fatigar o cansar demasiado; rendir. **II.** *s.* fatiga excesiva.

overfeed [-fíd], *va.* alimentar con exceso, sobrealimentar, (med.) superalimentar.—**overfeeding** [-iŋ], *s.* sobre- o superalimentación.

overflow [-flóu]. I. *vn.* salir de madre; rebosar, desbordarse, derramarse. II. *va.* sobrellenar, inundar.

overflow [óuvœrflou], *s.* inundación, (a)venida, diluvio; rebosadura, rebosamiento, desbordamiento, derrame; exceso, superabundancia; desaguadero, escape, rebosadero, sumidero, aliviadero.—o. **pipe,** aliviadero de superficie.

overflowing [-flóuiŋ]. I. *a.* fuera de cauce (río); que rebosa, etc. II. *s.* superabundancia; rebosamiento; inundación, anegación, desbordamiento.—**to o.,** hasta derramarse; en exceso; en suma abundancia.

overflowingly [-li], *adv.* superabundantemente.

overgrow [-góu]. I. *va.* (*pret.* OVERGREW; *pp.* OVERGROWN) cubrir con plantas o hierba; crecer más que. *V.* OUTGROW. II. *vn.* crecer o desarrollarse con exceso. Se usa más como *pp.* (**overgrown**) : *garden overgrown with weeds,* jardín cubierto de herbaje.—**overgrown child,** niño grandullón o talludo.

overgrowth [óuvœrgrouθ], *s.* vegetación exuberante, (Cuba) manigua; crecimiento excesivo; exuberancia; (med.) hipertrofia.

overhand [-hænd], *a.* (dep.) voleada o tirada (la pelota) por lo alto; (cost.) sobrehilado; punto por encima, (galic.) surjete.

overhang [-hǽŋ]. I. *va.* (*pret.* y *pp.* OVERHUNG) sobresalir horizontalmente por encima de; colgar, suspender; mirar a, dar a, caer a; ser inminente, amenazar; poner demasiadas colgaduras en. II. *vn.* colgar o estar pendiente. III. [óuvœrhæŋ], *s.* (arq.) salidizo, alero; vuelo; (aer.) diferencia entre los largos de dos superficies de sustentación de un mismo lado del centro.

overhanging [-hǽŋiŋ], *a.* voladizo, saledizo, sobresaliente, pendiente; inminente.

overhasty [-héjsti], *a.* demasiado apresurado, precipitado.

overhaul [-hól], *va.* repasar, registrar, recorrer, trastejar; componer, remendar, reparar; desarmar y componer; alcanzar; (mar.) ir ganando un barco en la persecución de otro.—**to o. accounts,** revisar las cuentas.

overhaul [óuvœrhol], **overhauling** [-hóliŋ], *s.* recorrido, revisión, reparación, arreglo, compostura; alcance.

overhead [-héd]. I. *adv.* arriba, en lo alto; más arriba o hasta más arriba de la cabeza. II. [óuvœrhæd], *a.* de arriba; mediano, de término medio; aéreo (trole, etc.); (mec.) de techo.—o. **charges,** o **expenses,** gastos generales fijos (alquiler, alumbrado, calefacción, seguro, impuestos, etc.).—o. **crossing,** (ing.) paso superior.—o. **railway,** (Ingl.) ferrocarril aéreo o elevado. III. *s.* gastos generales (= OVERHEAD EXPENSES).

overhear [-hír], *va.* (*pret.* y *pp.* OVERHEARD) alcanzar a oír; oír por casualidad o espiando.

overheat [-hít], *va.* sobrecalentar; abochornar; acalorar, achicharrar; recalentar.—**to be overheated,** (vet.) encalmarse.—**overheating** [-iŋ], *s.* sobrecalentamiento; abochornamiento; acaloramiento excesivo, achicharramiento; recalentamiento; (vet.) encalmadura.

overhours [óuvœrau̯rz], *s. pl.* horas extraordinarias, fuera de reglamento.

overhung [óuvœrhʌŋ], *pp.* y *a.* colgado o suspendido por arriba.

overindulgence [-indʌldžəns], *s.* indulgencia o mimo excesivos; exceso o abuso (en el beber, etc.).

overissue [-íʃu]. I. *va.* (com.) emitir con exceso. II. [óuvœríʃu], *s.* emisión excesiva.

overjoy [-džói], *va.* alborozar, regocijar, arrebatar o enajenar de alegría.

overjoyed [-d], *a.* lleno de alegría, muy gozoso.

overkind [-káind], *a.* demasiado bondadoso.

overladen [-léjdn], *pp.* y *a.* sobrecargado. *V.* OVERLOAD.

overland [-lænd], *a.* y *adv.* por tierra.—o. **route,** ruta por la vía terrestre.

overlap [-lǽp]. I. *va.* sobreponer, solapar, traslapar. II. *vn.* sobreponerse, traslaparse. III. [óuvœrlæp], *s.* solapa(dura), solapo, traslapo.

overlapping [-iŋ]. I. *s.* = OVERLAP. II. *a.* a o de solapa, solapado, traslapado.

overlay [-léj]. I. *va.* (*pret.* y *pp.* OVERLAID) cubrir, sobreponer, extender sobre; dar una capa; dorar, platear; anublar, obscurecer; echar un puente sobre; (impr.) calzar.—**to o. with quicksilver,** azogar. II. [óuvœrlej], *s.* capa; (impr.) alza, calzo.

overlaying [-léjiŋ], *s.* (impr.) colocación de alzas o calzos; capa, dorado, plateado, azogamiento.

overleaf [-lif], *adv.* a la vuelta, al dorso.

overleap [-líp], *va.* saltar por encima de; omitir.

overlie [-láj], *va.* (*pret.* OVERLAY; *pp.* OVERLAIN) descansar, yacer o estar sobre; tenderse encima; sofocar echándose encima (v. gr., a un niño).

overlive [-lív]. I. *va.* sobrevivir a. II. *vn.* sobrevivir; vivir demasiado activa o lujosamente.

overload [-lóud]. I. *va.* sobrecargar, recargar. II. [óuvœrloud], *s.* sobrecarga, recargo, sobornal.

overlook [-lúk]. I. *va.* mirar desde lo alto; tener vista a, dar o caer a; dominar (con la vista); examinar, vigilar, cuidar de; pasar por alto, disimular, tolerar, perdonar; hacer la vista gorda; descuidar, no hacer caso de; no notar. II. [óuvœrluk], *s.* mirada desde lo alto; altura, punto de vista elevado, atalaya; inadvertencia; (bot.) planta trepadora leguminosa (*canavalia*).

overlooker [-lúkœ(r)], *s.* (Ingl.) = OVERSEER.

overlord [-lord]. I. *s.* señor. II. [óuvœrlórd], *va.* señorear.

overly [-li], *adv.* (fam.) muy, mucho, demasiado.

overlying [-lájiŋ], *pa.* de TO OVERLIE y *a.* puesto o situado encima de; superyacente.

overman [-man]. I. *s.* sobrestante; juez, *m.,* árbitro; superhombre. II. [-mæn], *va.* proveer de dotación excesiva.

overmaster [-mǽstœ(r)], *va.* señorear, dominar.

overmatch [-mǽch]. I. *va.* vencer, superar. II. [óuvœrmæch], *s.* el que puede más que otro; lucha de fuerzas desiguales.

overmeasure [-mę́ž(r)]. I. *s.* medida excesiva, colmo; sobrante, superávit. II. *va.* colmar; dar demasiada importancia a.

overmuch [óuvœrmʌ́ch], *a.* y *adv.* demasiado, más de lo suficiente; en demasía, con exceso.

overnice [óuvœrnájs], *a.* dengoso, remilgado, escrupuloso en exceso.—**overniceness** [-njs], *s.* dengue, remilgo, melindre, escrupulosidad.

overnight [-nájt]. I. *adv.* durante la noche; de noche, toda la noche; de la noche a la mañana. II. [óuvœrnajt], *a.* de una noche; de la noche anterior.—o. **bag,** o **case,** saco de noche.—o. **charge,** cargo por permanencia nocturna.—o. **guests,** huéspedes de una sola noche.—o. **train,** tren nocturno.

overpass [-pǽs]. I. *va.* atravesar, salvar, pasar al otro lado o por encima de; rebasar; transgredir; mirar con indiferencia, menospreciar; pasar por alto; omitir; sobrepujar, exceder; repasar, considerar. II. [óuvœrpæs], *s.* (f. c., ing.) paso de alto; puente o vía por encima de un ferrocarril, puente, etc.

overpay [-péj], *va.* pagar o retribuir con exceso.

overpayment [-ment], *s.* pago excesivo.

overpeopled [-pípld], *a.* poblado con exceso.

overplay [-pléj], *va.* hacer un papel con exageración; jugar mejor que, vencer; (golf) golpear la pelota más allá del *green.*

overplus [-plʌs], *s.* sobrante, superávit.

overpopulation [-papyuléjšǫn], *s.* exceso de población.

overpower [-páuœ(r)], *va.* subyugar, vencer, sobreponerse a; supeditar, oprimir, abrumar; dotar de poder o potencia excesivos.

overpowering [-iŋ], *a.* = OVERWHELMING.

overprize [-práįz], *va.* valuar o apreciar en más de lo justo.

overproduction [-prodákŝǫn], *s.* exceso de producción, sobre- o superproducción.

overproof [óųvœrprúf], *a.* de concentración alcohólica de más de 50 por ciento. *V.* PROOF SPIRIT.

overrate [-réįt], *va.* encarecer; exagerar el valor de.

overreach [-rích]. I. *va.* ser más listo o astuto que; engañar; extender, alargar o estirar demasiado; tirar alto; ir o pasar más allá de lo necesario; alcanzar, extenderse sobre.—**to o. one's self**, propasarse, excederse; aventurarse más allá de sus fuerzas; pretender demasiado; salir mal por exceso de astucia o de acción; pasarse de listo. II. *vn.* extenderse (sobre algo); (vet.) alcanzarse, rozarse la pata trasera con la delantera; (mar.) dar una bordada o virada más allá de lo necesario. III. *s.* (vet.) alcanzadura, rozadura.

override [-ráįd], *va.* (*pret.* OVERRODE; *pp.* OVERRIDDEN) pasar por encima, supeditar, vencer; poner a un lado, dar de mano a, rechazar arbitrariamente; anular, contrarrestar; reventar, fatigar un caballo.—**to o. one's commission**, extralimitarse, excederse.

overripe [-ráįp], *a.* demasiado maduro o pasado de maduro, (fam.) papandujo.

overrule [-rúl], *va.* (pre)dominar; ganar, vencer; gobernar, dirigir, regir; (for.) denegar, no admitir un alegato.

overrun [-rán]. I. *va.* (*pret.* OVERRAN; *pp.* OVERRUN) invadir, infestar; saquear, pillar, hacer correrías en; excederse; desbordarse; (impr.) retocar, recorrer. II. *vn.* rebosar; estar muy abundante.

overscore [-skór], *va.* rayar o señalar por encima con una raya alguna palabra o frase; borrar.

overscrupulous [-skrúpyųlʌs], *a.* demasiado escrupuloso.

oversea(s [óųvœrsí(z]. I. *adv.* allende los mares, ultramar. II. *a.* de ultramar, ultramarino; extranjero; (Ingl.) colonial.—**o. service**, (mil.) servicio en el extranjero o allende los mares.

oversee [-sí], *va.* (*pret.* OVERSAW; *pp.* OVERSEEN) inspeccionar, superentender, vigilar; descuidar, pasar por alto.

overseer [óųvœrsiœ(r)], *s.* sobrestante, capataz, *m.*; superintendente, veedor, inspector; mayoral.

oversell [-sél], *va.* vender demasiado, o más de lo que puede entregarse; vender a un precio más alto que otro.

overset [-sét]. I. *va.* (*pret. y pp.* OVERSET) volcar, voltear, derribar; trastornar, arruinar. *V.* UPSET. II. *vn.* volcarse, caerse; desarreglarse.

oversew [-soų], *va.* (cost.) sobrehilar.

overshade [-ŝéįd]. I. *va.* obscurecer, ensombrecer, sombrear. *V.* OVERSHADOW. II. *vn.* dar sombra.

overshadow [-ŝédoų], *va.* sombrear, asombrar; eclipsar, obscurecer; dominar; (fig.) proteger.

overshoe [-ŝu], *s.* chanclo; zapato de goma.

overshoot [-ŝút]. I. *va.* (*pret. y pp.* OVERSHOT) tirar por encima del blanco; ir más allá de, exceder; pasar rápidamente por encima.—**to o. one's self**, pasarse de listo. II. *vn.* pasar de raya.

overshot [-ŝat], *a. y pp.* excedido; exagerado.—**o. wheel**, (hidr.) rueda de alimentación o impulsión por arriba.

oversight [-sáįt], *s.* inadvertencia, descuido; vigilancia, cuidado.

oversize [óųvœrsáįz]. I. *a.* de mayor tamaño que el ordinario; extragrande. II. *s.* tamaño mayor que el regular; tamaño mayor.

overskirt [-skœrt], *s.* sobrefalda, faldellín.

oversleep [-slíp], *vn.* (*pret. y pp.* OVERSLEPT) dormir demasiado; no despertar a tiempo.

oversleeve [-slív], *s.* mangote, contramanga.

overspread [-spréd], *va.* (*pret. y pp.* OVERSPREAD) desparramar, esparcir, regar, tender.

overstate [-stéįt], *va.* exagerar.

overstatement [-mẹnt], *s.* exageración.

overstay [-stéį]. I. *vn. y va.* demorarse (en alguna parte); permanecer demasiado tiempo. II. *va.* (com., fam.) retener (valores de bolsa) demasiado tiempo, con pérdida consiguiente.

overstep [-stép], *va. y vn.* traspasar, transgredir, excederse, extralimitarse, propasarse.

overstock [-sták]. I. *va.* abarrotar. II. [óųvœrstak], *s.* surtido excesivo.

overstrain [-stréįn]. I. *va.* apretar o estirar demasiado. II. *vn.* esforzarse demasiado. III. [óųvœrstréįn], *s.* tensión o tirantez excesiva.

overstretch [-stréch], *va.* estirar demasiado.

overstrew [-strú], *va.* esparcir, desparramar.

overstrung [óųvœrstráŋ], *a.* demasiado tirante; muy sensible; hablando de pianos, que tiene dos juegos de cuerdas cruzadas oblicuamente.

overstuff [-stáf], *va.* atestar o llenar demasiado; rellenar (muebles).—**overstuffed** [-t], *a.* rellen(ad)o.

oversubscribe [-sʌbskráįb], *va.* su(b)scribir con creces, solicitar (bonos, etc.) en exceso de la emisión; contribuir más de lo pedido. Ú. gen. en la voz pasiva, y en la traducción se cambia el giro: *the loan has been oversubscribed*, la demanda de bonos del empréstito ha sido mayor que la oferta, las subscripciones al empréstito han excedido los bonos, ha habido subscripciones de sobra al empréstito, etc.

oversupply [-sʌplái]. I. *va.* abastecer, proveer o surtir en exceso. II. [óųvœrsʌplaį], *s.* surtido o provisión excesivos.

overt [óųvœrt], *a.* abierto, público, patente, evidente.—**o. act**, (for.) ofensa o transgresión premeditada; acto hostil.

overtake [-téįk], *va.* (*pret.* OVERTOOK; *pp.* OVERTAKEN) alcanzar, dar alcance a; atajar; (fam.) atrapar.—**overtaker** [-œ(r)], *s.* alcanzador.—**overtaking** [-įŋ], *s.* alcance.

overtax [-téks], *va.* oprimir con tributos; someter a esfuerzo excesivo o exigir esfuerzo excesivo de.

overthrow [-θróų]. I. *va.* (*pret.* OVERTHREW; *pp.* OVERTHROWN) echar abajo, abatir, demoler, derribar; derrocar, destronar; vencer. II. [óųvœrθroų], *s.* derribo, vuelco, derrocamiento; caída; derrota, ruina; subversión; destronamiento; (dep.) lanzamiento o voleo demasiado alto.

overtime [-taįm]. I. *s.* horas extraordinarias de trabajo; tiempo suplementario; pago por trabajo hecho fuera de las horas regulares. II. *adv.* fuera del tiempo estipulado. III. *a.* en exceso de las horas regulares de trabajo.

overtire [-táįr], *va.* fatigar demasiado, moler.

overtly [óųvœrtlį], *adv.* abierta, pública, patente o manifiestamente.

overtone [-toųn], *s.* (mús.) armónico.

overtop [-táp], *va.* dominar, descollar sobre, señorear, sobresalir entre; sobrepujar.

overtrain [-tréįn], *va. y vn.* entrenar(se) con exceso.

overture [óųvœrchųr], *s.* insinuación, proposición o propuesta formal; (mús.) obertura.

overturn [-tœrn]. I. *va.* volcar; echar abajo; trastornar, trabucar. II. *vn.* volcarse; (mar.) zozobrar. III. [óųvœrtœrn], *s.* vuelco, volteo; trastorno; (com.) = TURNOVER.

overturning [-tœrnįŋ], *s.* = OVERTURN.

overvalue [-vélyų], *va.* encarecer, ponderar; atribuir valor excesivo a.

overwatch [-wách], *va. y vn.* cansar a fuerza de vigilias; vigilar, celar.

overweening [-wínįŋ], *a.* presuntuoso, arrogante.—**overweeningly** [-lį], *adv.* arrogantemente.

overweigh [-wéį], *va.* pesar más que, preponderar; prevalecer contra; sobrecargar, oprimir.

overweight [-wejt]. I. *s.* exceso de peso; sobrepeso; preponderancia; superioridad. II. *a.* que pesa demasiado. III. [-wéjt], *va.* cargar excesivamente; preponderar; dar demasiada importancia a.

overwhelm [-hwélm], *va.* (a)brumar, agobiar; anonadar; sumergir, hundir.—**overwhelming** [-iŋ]. **I.** *a.* abrumador, opresivo; agobiante; irresistible, dominante, arrollador, (fam.) aplastante. **II.** *s.* (a)brumamiento; anonadación.—**overwhelmingly** [-li], *adv.* abrumadoramente; irresistiblemente.

overwork [-wǿrk]. **I.** *va.* (*pret.* y *pp.* OVERWORKED o -WROUGHT) hacer trabajar con exceso, esclavizar; elaborar la superficie de. **II.** *vn.* trabajar demasiado. **III.** [óʊvœrwǿrk], *s.* trabajo excesivo; trabajo hecho fuera de las horas reglamentarias.

overworn [-wórn], *a.* gastado por el trabajo; abrumado de fatiga.

overwrought [-rótl]. **I.** *pret.* y *pp.* de TO OVERWORK. **II.** *a.* sobre(e)xcitado; rendido o agobiado de trabajo; muy elaborado o labrado; recargado de adornos.

Ovidae [óʊvidi], *s. pl.* (zool.) óvidos.

Ovidian [ovídiạn], *a.* ovidiano, rel. a Ovidio.

oviduct [óʊvidʌkt], *s.* (anat.) oviducto.

oviferous [ovífɛrʌs], **ovigerous** [ovídžɛrʌs], *a.* (anat. y zool.) ovífero, ovígero.

oviform [óʊvifɔrm], *a.* oviforme.

ovine [óʊvaịn], *a.* (zool.) ovino, lanar, ovejuno.

oviparous [ovípạrʌs], *a.* (zool.) ovíparo.

oviposit [oʊvipázit], *vn.* (ent.) poner huevos.

oviposition, ovipositing [-pozíṣ̣ọn, -pázitiŋ], *s.* oviposición, (ent.) postura.

ovipositor [-tọ(r)], *s.* oviscapto, órgano que sirve a los insectos para depositar sus huevos.

ovoid(al [óʊvoịd, oʊvóịdạl], *a.* ovoide, aovado.

ovolo [óʊvoloʊ], *s.* (arq.) óvolo, equino, cuarto bocel.

ovoviviparous [oʊvovaịvípạrʌs], *a.* ovovivíparo.

ovulation [oʊvyuléịṣ̣ọn], *s.* ovulación.

ovule [óʊvjul], *s.* (biol.) óvulo.

ovum [óʊvʌm], *s.* (*pl.* OVA) (biol.) huevo; (arq.) óvolo.

owe [oʊ]. **I.** *va.* (*pret.* y *pp.* OWED) deber, adeudar; (con to) ser deudor a o de; estar obligado a.— **owing to,** debido a, con motivo de, por causa de.—**to be owing to,** ser debido, imputable o atribuíble a. **II.** *vn.* estar endeudado, deber.

owl [áʊl]. **I.** *s.* (orn.) lechuza, buho, mochuelo, oliva, autillo.—**o. train,** tren nocturno. **II.** *vn.* (Ingl.) matutear.—**owling** [-iŋ], *s.* (Ingl.) matute.

owlet [-ɛt], *s.* (orn.) hijuelo del buho.—**o. moth,** (ent.) mariposa nocturna.

owlish [-iš], **owl-like** [-laịk], *a.* semejante al buho.

owllight [-laịt], *s.* crepúsculo.

own [óʊn]. **I.** *a.* propio, particular, de mi (su, etc.) propiedad; peculiar, individual; mismo, verdadero, real: *he wrote it with his own hand,* lo escribió de su propio puño; *this is my own,* esto es mío propio; esto es lo mío; *Nero killed his own mother,* Nerón mató a su misma madre.— **o. cousin,** primo hermano, prima hermana.— **my** (**our,** etc.) **o.** (con respecto a la familia) los míos (nuestros, etc.).—**my o. self,** yo mismo. —**of one's o. motion,** espontáneamente, por propio impulso.—**on one's o.,** (fam.) por su propia cuenta o responsabilidad; con sus propios recursos. **II.** *va.* poseer, ser dueño de, tener; reconocer, confesar.—**owned by,** propiedad de. **III.** *vn.* (con to) admitir, confesar, reconocer.—**to o. up,** (fam.) confesar de plano.

owner [-œ(r)], *s.* dueño, señor, posesor, poseedor; amo, propietario.

ownerless [-lis], *a.* mostrenco.

ownership [-šip], *s.* propiedad, pertenencia.

ox [aks], *s.* (*pl.* OXEN) (zool.) buey.—**o. bot** = OXFLY.—**o. driver,** boyero.—**o.-eyed,** de ojos grandes.—**o. stall,** boyera, boyeriza, boíl.—**o. team,** yunta o yugada de bueyes.—**drove of oxen,** boyada.

oxacid [aksǽsid], *s.* (quím.) oxácido.

oxalate [áksạleịt], *s.* (quím.) oxalato.

oxalic [aksǽlik], *a.* oxálico.

Oxalidaceæ [-déịṣii], *s. pl.* (bot.) oxalídeas.

oxalis [áksạliṣ], *s.* (bot.) acedera.

oxaluria [aksạliúriä], *s.* (med.) oxaluria, exceso d oxalato cálcico en la orina.

oxblood [áksblʌd], *s.* color rojo obscuro.

oxbow [áksboʊ], *s.* collera de yugo.

oxcart [ákskart], *s.* carro tirado por bueyes.

oxen [áksn], *s. pl.* de OX.

oxeye [áksaị], *s.* (mar. y bot.) ojo de buey; (orn cierto pajarito, especie de gallineta.—**o. daisy** (bot.) manzanilla loca; ojo de buey.

oxfly [áksflaị], *s.* (ent.) estro.

Oxfordian [aksfórdiạn], *a.* y *s.* = OXONIAN.

oxgoad [áksgoʊd], *s.* aguijada, aguijón.

oxherd [ákshœrd], *s.* = O. DRIVER.

oxhouse [ákshaʊs], *s.* = O. STALL.

oxidable [áksidạbl], *a.* oxidable.

oxidant [áksidạnt], *s.* oxidante.

oxidase [áksideịs], *s.* (bioquím.) oxidasa.

oxidate [-deịt], *va.* = OXIDIZE.

oxidation [-déịṣ̣ọn], *s.* (quím.) oxidación.

oxide [áksaịd], *s.* (quím.) óxido.

oxidizable [áksidaịzạbl], *a.* oxidable.

oxidize [áksidaịz], *va.* (quím.) oxidar; oxigenar.— **oxidized silver,** plata oxidada.

oxidizer [-œ(r)], *s.* oxidante.

oxlip [ákslip], *s.* (bot.) prímula, primavera.

Oxonian [aksóʊniạn]. **I.** *a.* (Ingl.) oxfordiense perteneciente a Oxford o a su universidad. **II.** *s* oxfordiense, habitante de Oxford o estudiant de su universidad.

oxtail soup [áksteịl súp], *s.* sopa de rabo de buey

oxtongue [ákstʌŋ], *s.* (bot.) buglosa.

oxyacetylene [aksiæsétilin], *a.* oxiacetilénico.— **o. blowpipe,** o **torch,** soplete o pico de aceti leno.—**o. welding,** soldadura oxiacetilénica.

oxyacid [aksiǽsid], *s.* (quím.) oxácido.

oxychlorid(e [aksiklóraịd], *s.* (quím.) oxicloruro

oxygen [áksidžen], *s.* (quím.) oxígeno.—**o. aci** = OX(Y)ACID.—**o. tent,** (med.) tienda d oxígeno.

oxygenate [-eịt], *va.* oxigenar, oxidar.

oxygenation [-éịṣ̣ọn], *s.* (quím.) oxigenación, oxi dación.

oxygenic, oxygenous [aksidžénik, aksídženʌs] *a.* oxigenado, que contiene oxígeno.

oxygenizable [áksidženaịzạbl], *a.* oxigenable.— **oxygenize** [-aịz], *va.* = OXYGENATE.

oxyhemoglobin [aksihemoglóʊbịn], *s.* (quím. oxihemoglobina.

oxyhydrogen [aksihaịdrodžịn], *s.* (quím.) ga oxhídrico.—**o. blowpipe,** soplete oxhídrico.

oxymel [áksimel], *s.* (farm.) ojimiel.

oxysalt [áksiṣolt], *s.* (quím.) oxisal.

oxysulfid(e [aksiṣʌlfaịd], *s.* (quím.) oxisulfuro.

oxytocic [aksitóʊsịk], *s.* y *a.* (med.) oxitócico

oxytone [áksitoʊn]. **I.** *a.* (pros.) agudo. **II.** *s* palabra aguda.

oyer [óʊʝœr], *s.* (for.) audición, vista; audienci —**o. and terminer,** (Ingl.) audiencia; tribuna que se reúne dos veces al año en cada condado (E. U.) tribunal superior de jurisdicción crimi nal.

oyes, oyez [óʊʝes], *interj.* (for.) ¡oíd, oíd! (voz d los ujieres en los tribunales).

oyster [óịstœ(r)], *s.* (zool.) ostra, ostrón u ostiór *m.*—**o. bed,** ostral, criadero de ostras.—**o culture,** ostricultura.—**o. farm** = O. BED.— **o. farming** = O. CULTURE.—**o. fishery,** pes quería de ostras.—**o. fork,** desbullador.—**o grass,** (bot.) ova, ulva verde.—**o. house** *s.* ostrería.—**o. knife,** abreostras.—**o. plant** (bot.) salsifí.—**o. rake,** raño.—**o. shell** desbulla.—**o. tongs,** gafas para pescar ostras

oysterman [-mæn], *s.* ostrero.

ozæna, ozena [ozíṇä], *s.* (med.) ocena.

ozocerite [ozóʊkɛraịt], *s.* (min.) ozocerita.

ozonation [oʊzonéịṣ̣ọn], *s.* ozonización.

ozone [óʊzoʊn], *s.* (quím.) ozono.—**o. paper** papel para ozono, papel revestido de almidón yoduro potásico (ll. a menudo *ozonómetro*).

ozonic [ozániḳ], *a.* ozonizado; rel. al ozono.—**o. ether,** disolución de bióxido de hidrógeno en éter.

ozonization [oųzonįzéįṣǫn], *s.* ozonización.

ozonize [óųzonaįz], *va.* (quím.) ozonizar.—**ozonizer** [-œ(r)], *s.* ozonizador.—**ozonometer** [oųzonámetœ(r)]. *s.* ozonómetro, medidor de ozono.—**ozonous** [óųzonʌs], *a.* = OZONIC.

P

p [pi], *s.* p.

pa [pa], *s.* (fam.) papá.

pabulum [pǽbjulʌm], *s.* pábulo, alimento, pasto.

paca [pǽkä], *s.* (zool.) paca.

pace [péįs]. I. *s.* paso; marcha, modo de andar; (equit.) paso, portante, andadura; paso (medida de longitud); (arq.) estrado, tablado. II. *va.* recorrer o medir a pasos; marcar el paso; dirigir.—**to p. one's beat,** hacer la ronda. III. *vn.* pasear, andar, marchar; moverse con paso mesurado; (equit.) amblar.

pacemaker [-meįkœ(r)], *s.* el que marca el paso o da el ejemplo.

pacer [-œ(r)], *s.* caballo de paso de andadura; el que mide a pasos o marca el paso.

pacha [pǽṣá o pǽṣä], *s.* = PASHA.

pachyderm, *s.*, **pachyderm(at)ous** [pǽkįdœrm, pǽkįdœrm(at)ʌs], *a.* (zool.) paquidermo.

pacific [paṣífiḳ], *a.* pacífico.

pacificate [-eįt], *va.* pacificar.—**pacification** [pæṣįfiḳéįṣǫn], *s.* pacificación, apaciguamiento. —**pacificator** [paṣífiḳeįtǫ(r)], *s.*, **pacificatory** [-atǫrį], *a.* pacificador, apaciguador, sosegador. —**pacifier** [pǽṣįfaįœ(r)], *s.* = PACIFICATOR; chupador o (Am.) chupete (para niños).

pacifism [pǽṣįfįzm], *s.* pacifismo.—**pacifist** [-įst], *s.* y *a.* pacifista.—**pacifistic** [-ístįḳ], *a.* pacifista.

pacify [pǽṣįfaį], *va.* pacificar, apaciguar, calmar.

pacifying [-įŋ], *a.* pacificador, apaciguador, sosegador.

pacing [péįsįŋ], *s.* paso, andadura.

pack [pǽk]. I. *s.* lío, fardo; paquete; cajetilla o paquete de cigarrillos; baraja de naipes; muta, perrada, perrería o jauría (de perros); material de envolver o embalar; (med.) envoltura de sábanas o frazadas; hato o manada (de animales); cuadrilla, manga (de pícaros); grande extensión de témpanos flotantes.—**p. animal,** acémila, animal de carga.—**p. cloth,** (h)arpillera.—**p. load,** carga de una acémila.—**p. needle,** aguja de enjalmar, aguja de arria; almarada, saquera.—**p. train,** recua, reata. II. *va.* empacar, empaquetar; enfard(el)ar; embalar, envasar; encajonar, embaular; hacer (un baúl, maleta); llenar, atestar, apretar, colmar; (mec.) empaquetar una junta; despachar, enviar; cargar (una acémila); llevar sobre la espalda o lomo; hacer, formar, manipular o preparar fraudulentamente (naipes, un jurado, etc.); (med.) envolver en sábanas o frazadas.—**to p. off,** o **to send packing,** enviar, despedir, despachar; poner de patitas en la calle. III. *vn.* empaquetar; hacer el baúl, arreglar el equipaje; formar una masa compacta, consolidarse, conglomerarse; tomar soleta.—**to p. away,** u **off,** largarse, (fam.) tomar soleta.—**to p. up,** arreglar el equipaje.

package [-įdź]. I. *s.* fardo, bulto, lío; atado; paquete; cabo; (mar.) abarrote; embalaje, envase. II. *va.* empacar, empaquetar.—**packaging** [-įŋ], *s.* empaque, acto de empaquetar, embalar, etc.

packer [-œ(r)], *s.* embalador, empaquetador, empacador, enfardelador, envasador, (Méx.) arpillador.

packet [-įt]. I. *s.* paquete, fardo pequeño; paquete de cartas; mala, valija, correo.—**p., p. boat, p. ship, p. vessel,** paque(bote), correo marítimo. II. *va.* empaquetar, enfardelar.

packing [-įŋ]. I. *s.* embalaje; empaque(tamiento);

envase; enfardeladura; (mec.) empaquetadura, guarnición, estopada, relleno; (alb.) relleno, enripiado. II. *a.* de embalar; de enfardelar; de envolver; empacador.—**p. bag,** o **cloth,** halda.—**p. box, p. case,** caja de embalar; envase.—**p. effect,** (fís.) pérdida de masa debida a pérdida de energía.—**p. gland,** (mec.) prensaestopa, *m.*—**p. house,** o **plant,** empresa o planta empacadora; frigorífico; establecimiento donde se envasan conservas. —**p. leather,** cuero para empaquetadura.— **p. liquid,** líquido de obturación.—**p. needle** = PACK NEEDLE.—**p. paper,** papel de envolver.—**p. press,** prensa de embalar.—**p. ring,** (mec.) anillo de émbolo. *V.* PISTON RING.—**p. strip,** (mec.) cuña, tira de refuerzo.

packman [-mǫn], *s.* buhonero.

packsack [-sæk], *s.* especie de barjuleta.

packsaddle [-sædl], *s.* albarda, basto, enjalma, aparejo.—**p. maker,** albardero, enjalmero.

packthread [-θred], *s.* bramante, guita, hilo de acarreto.

pact [pækt], *s.* pacto, convenio, acuerdo, tratado.

pad [pæd]. I. *s.* cojinete o cojincillo, almohadilla: colchoncillo; postizo (de pelo); (sast.) relleno, almohadilla, bollo, hombrera; caderillas (*f. pl.*); tontillo (para ahuecar las faldas); (esgr.) peto, plastrón; (bot.) hoja grande de planta acuática; bloc (de papel); taco (de calendario); almohadilla (de entintar); paso o pisada amortiguados o sin ruido; pasta (de ciertos animales); rastro, huella. *V.* FOOTPAD.—**p. saddle,** albarda, lomillos, *m. pl.*—**p. saw,** serrucho de calar. II. *va.* forrar, rellenar, embrrar; aumentar (un escrito) con material superfluo; formar blocs de papel. III. *vn.* caminar (penosa o cansadamente); andar o trotar sin ruido; ser (o hacer de) salteador de caminos.— **padded** [-įd], *a.* acojinado, acolchado, rellen(ad)o, (galic.) capitoné.

padding [pædįŋ], *s.* (cost.) relleno, almohadilla (*V.* PAD); algodón guata; ripio (en un escrito).

paddle [pædl]. I. *va.* y *vn.* impeler, bogar o remar con canalete; chapotear, guachapear.—**to p. one's own canoe,** (fam.) bandearse por sí mismo, bastarse a sí mismo. II. *s.* canalete, zagual (de canoa), remo corto; (agr.) béstola, (ar)rejada o aguijada; (zool.) = FLIPPER.—**p. board, p. float,** paleta, álabe.—**p. box,** tambor (de rueda).—**p. wheel,** rueda de paletas.— **p.-wheel steamer,** vapor de ruedas.

paddler [pædlœ(r)], *s.* remero.

paddock [pædǫk], *s.* dehesa, parque.

paddy [pædį], *s.* arroz (*m.*) en cáscara, (Fil.) palay; (P., fam.) irlandés.—**p. field,** arrozal.

padlock [pædlǎk]. I. *s.* candado. II. *va.* echar el candado, cerrar con candado.

paduasoy [pædźuąsoį], *s.* (tej.) seda de Padua.

pæan [píąn], *s.* peán, himno.

pæon [píǫn], *s.* (pros. lat. y griega) peón.

pagan [péįgąn], *s.* pagano, gentil, infiel.—**pagan(ish)** [-(į)ṣ], *a.* pagano, gentílico, idólatra. —**paganism** [-įzm], *s.* paganismo, gentilismo o gentilidad.—**paganize** [-aįz], *va.* y *vn.* hacer(se) pagano, paganizar, gentilizar.

page [peįdź]. I. *s.* página, plana, llana o carilla (de libro); paje, escudero, criado.—**p. proof,** (impr.) pruebas de planas.—**full p.,** a toda plana. II. *va.* foliar, paginar; buscar llamando (en los hoteles).

pageant [pædźąnt], *s.* procesión cívica, manifestación imponente; pompa, celebridad; (teat.) espectáculo, aparato escénico.

pageantry [-rį], *s.* fasto, fausto, pompa; ostentación o aparato vanos.

pagedom [péįdźdǫm], **pagehood** [-hųd], *s.* escudería, escuderaje, oficio de paje.

paginate [pædźįneįt], *va.* paginar, foliar.

pagination [-éįṣǫn], *s.* paginación, foliación.

paging [péįdźįŋ], *s.* paginación.—**p. machine,** máquina de foliar.

pagoda [pəgóudǎ], *s.* pagoda.—**p. tree**, (bot.) sófora; (India) = BANYAN O BANIAN.

Pagurus [pəgiúrʌs], *s.* (zool.) paguro, cangrejo ermitaño.

Pahlavi [pálɑvi], *s.* y *a.* pelvi, antigua lengua persa.

paid [peid], *pret.* y *pp.* de TO PAY.—**p.-up share**, acción liberada.

paidology [paidálodži], *s.* (med.) paidología, estudio científico de los niños.

pail [péil], *s.* cubo, pozal, herrada, balde.

pailful [-ful], *s.* (lo que cabe en un) cubo, etc.

pain [péin]. **I.** *va.* doler (usado intransitivamente; *my stomach pains me*, me duele el estómago); causar dolor (*this pains me*, esto me causa dolor, o me duele); apenar, afligir. **II.** *vn.* doler. **III.** *s.* dolor; pena (castigo).—*pl.* V. PAINS.—**in p.**, con dolor.—**on p. of**, so pena de.—**to be in p.**, tener dolor, estar con dolor.

pained [-d], *a.* apenado, afligido.

painful [-ful], *a.* penoso, embarazoso; dolorido, afligido; doloroso, aflictivo; arduo, penoso, laborioso.—**to be p.**, doler.—**painfully** [-li], *adv.* dolorosamente; penosamente.—**painfulness** [-nis], *s.* calidad de penoso o doloroso.

painless [-lis], *a.* sin pena, sin dolor, indoloro.

painlessness [-nis], *s.* ausencia de dolor; (med.) anodinia.

pains [péinz], *s. pl.* trabajo, incomodidad, fatiga; esmero, cuidado; ansiedad, inquietud, solicitud; dolores de(l) parto; agujetas.—**to be at the p. of**, tomarse el trabajo de.—**to go to great p.** (to), afanarse o esforzarse (por), esmerarse (con o en).—**to have one's labor for one's p.**, trabajar de balde o en vano, no sacar nada.

painstaker [-teikœ(r)], *s.* trabajador asiduo o concienzudo, afanador.

painstaking [-iŋ]. **I.** *a.* cuidadoso, industrioso; afanoso, esmerado, concienzudo. **II.** *s.* esmero.

paint [péint]. **I.** *va.* pintar, colorar; untar, dar una capa o baño; retratar o copiar con colores; dedicarse a la pintura; afeitarse, pintarse el rostro, arrebolarse; describir.—**to p. the town red**, (fam.) ir de parranda, correrla.—**to p. with**, pintar con; dar una capa de; revestir de. **II.** *vn.* pintar, ser pintor; pintarse (el rostro). **III.** *s.* pintura; color; colorete, afeite, arrebol.—**p. box**, caja de colores o pinturas.—**p. tube**, tubo de color.

paintbrush [-brʌʃ], *s.* brocha, pincel.

painted [-id], *a.* pintado; de color.

painter [-œ(r)], *s.* pintor; (mar.) boza, amarra del bote o de la lancha.

painting [-iŋ], *s.* pintura (arte y oficio); coloración; cuadro o pintura.

paintress [-ris], *s.* pintora.

pair [per]. **I.** *s.* par; pareja, yunta; mancuerna; (pol.) en un cuerpo legislativo, dos miembros de opiniones contrarias, apareados para abstenerse de votar.—**p. of scales**, peso de cruz. —**a p. of scissors, of spectacles**, un par de tijeras, de anteojos. **II.** *va.* y *vn.* (a)parear(se); casar(se), hermanar(se), igualar(se).—**to p. off**, aparearse dos diputados de opiniones contrarias antes de la votación; retirarse de una reunión en parejas.—**to p. with**, hacer pareja con.

paisley [péizli], *s.* y *a.* (tejido, chal, etc.) de Paisley.

pajamas [pədžámǎz], *s. pl.* pijama o piyama, *m.*, traje de dormir; pijama, traje oriental.

pal [pæl], *s.* (fam.) compañero, amigote, compinche.

palace [pǽlis], *s.* palacio.

paladin [pǽlədin], *s.* paladín.

palæography, etc., *s.* = PALEOGRAPHY, etc.

palafitte [pǽləfit], *s.* (arqueol.) palafito.

palanquin [pælənkín], *s.* palanquín.

palatability [pælǎtǎbíliti], *s.* buen sabor.

palatable [pǽlǎtǎbl], *a.* sabroso, apetitoso, agradable, aceptable.

palatal [pǽlǎtǎl]. **l.** *a.* y *s.* (fon.) paladial. **II.** *a.* (fon.) palatal; (anat.) palatino, pert. al paladar.—**palatalize** [-aiz], *va.* (fon.) palatalizar.

palate [pǽlit], *s.* (anat.) paladar, bóveda palatina, techo de la boca, sentido del gusto; paladeo.

palatial [pǎléiʃǎl], *a.* palaciego, palatino; magnífico, suntuoso.

palatinate [pǎlǽtinit], *s.* palatinado.

palatine [pǽlǎtain], *a.* palatino; paladial.

palaver [pǎlǽvœ(r)]. **I.** *s.* palabrería, (fam.) labia; zalamería; embustes; conferencia, discusión. **II.** *va.* y *vn.* adular; engatusar; charlar.

pale [péil]. **I.** *a.* pálido; descolorido; claro; apagado, desmayado, mortecino, albarazado.—**p.-eyed**, de ojos sin brillo.—**p.-faced**, caripálido. —**p. green**, verde claro.—**p.-hearted**, pusilánime.—**p. wine**, vino clarete. **II.** *s.* estaca; palizada, estacada; valla, límite; espacio cerrado, literal o figuradamente; esfera, seno, gremio, sociedad; (blas.) palo.—**p. of the church**, gremio de la iglesia. **III.** *va.* empalizar, cercar, rodear; poner pálido, hacer palidecer; descolorar, descolorir. **IV.** *vn.* palidecer; perder el color.—**to p. into insignificance**, ser insignificante.

palea [péiliǎ], *s.* (bot.) glumilla.

paleface [péilfeis], *s.* caripálido (nombre que dan los indios a los blancos).

palely [péili], *adv.* pálidamente.

paleness [péilnis], *s.* palidez, descoloramiento.

paleobotany [peiliobátani], *s.* paleofitología, paleobotánica.

Paleocene [-osin], *a.* y *s.* (geol.) paleoceno; el terciario más antiguo.

paleograph [-ogræf], *s.* paleógrafo (persona); manuscrito antiguo.

paleographer [-ágrəfœ(r)], *s.* paleógrafo.

paleographic [-ográfik(ǎl], *a.* paleográfico.

paleography [-ágrǎfi], *s.* paleografía.

paleolith [-oliθ], *s.* paleolito, objeto pétreo de la edad de piedra.—**paleolithic** [-olíθik], *a.* paleolítico.

paleologist [-álodžist], *s.* paleólogo.

paleology [-álodži], *s.* paleología.

paleontographic(al [-antográfik(ǎl], *a.* paleontográfico.—**paleontography** [-antágrǎfi], *s.* paleontografía.

paleontologic(al [-antoládžik(ǎl], *a.* paleontológico.—**paleontologist** [-antálodžist], *s.* paleontólogo.—**paleontology** [-antálodži], *s.* paleontología.

Paleozoic [-ozóuik], *a.* (geol.) paleozoico.

paleozoology [-ozoálodži], *s.* paleozoología.

Palestinian [pælestíniǎn], *a.* y *s.* palestino.

palestra [pǎléstrǎ], *s.* palestra, gimnasio.

palette [pǽlit], *s.* (pint.) paleta, tabloza.—**p. knife**, espátula.

palfrey [pólfri], *s.* palafrén.

palfreyed [-d], *a.* montado en palafrén.

Pali [páli], *s.* pali (lengua).

palimpsest [pǽlimpsest], *s.* palimpsesto.

paling [péiliŋ], *s.* palenque, estacada, valla, cerca, (em)palizada.

palingenesis [pælindžénesis], *s.* palingenesia.

palinode [pǽlinoud], *s.* palinodia.

palisade [pæl<séid]. **I.** *s.* (em)palizada, estacada, frisa.—*pl.* farallón, risco. **II.** *va.* empalizar, estacar.

palisander [pælisændœ(r)], *s.* palisandro.

palish [péiliʃ], *a.* paliducho.

pall [pɔl]. **I.** *s.* paño mortuorio; (fig.) lo que ocasiona aflicción o tristeza; (igl.) hijuela, palia; palio. **II.** *va.* quitar el sabor; desalentar; saciar; hartar, empalagar. **III.** *vn.* hacerse insípido, perder el sabor.

palladium [pǎléidiʌm], *s.* paladión, *m.;* garantía, salvaguardia; (quím.) paladio.

pallbearer [pólbærœ(r)], s. andero, persona que va al lado del féretro.

pallet [pǽlit], s. jergón, camilla; (mec.) paleta de reloj, fiador de rueda, retén, linguete; eslabón de una cadena sin fin; torno de alfarero; (alb., pint.) paleta; (enc.) herramienta para dorar o inscribir los lomos de los libros; válvula de cañón de órgano.

pallette [pǽlit], s. (arm.) gocete.

palliate [pǽlieit], va. excusar, paliar; mitigar.

palliation [-éiṣǫn], s. paliación; mitigación.

palliative [-jv], a. y s. paliativo; a. paliatorio.

pallid [pǽlid], a. pálido, descolorido.

pallidity [pǽliditi], **pallidness** [pǽlidnis], s. palidez.

pallium [pǽliʌm], s. (igl.) palio; manto.

pall-mall [pélmél], s. (pala)mallo; galería o zona donde se juega.—**Pall Mall** s. nombre de una calle de Londres y del ministerio de guerra que estaba en ella.

pallor [pǽlǫ(r)], s. palidez.

palm [pam]. I. s. (bot.) palma, palmera, (Fil.) areca, burí o bulí; victoria; palma de la mano; ancho de la mano (medida); (mar.) rempujo; uña (del ancla).—p. **cabbage**, palmito.—p. **grove**, palmar.—p. **oil**, aceite de palma, aceite del Senegal.—P. **Sunday**, domingo de Ramos.—p. **wine**, vino de palmera. II. va. escamotar; (con **off**, **on** o **upon**) engañar, defraudar con; manejar, manosear, manipular; cubrir con palmas.

palmaceous [pælméiṣiʌs], a. (bot.) palmáceo.

palma Christi [pǽlmǎ krísti], s. (bot.) palmacristi, f., ricino.

palmar [pǽlmǎ(r)], a. (anat.) palmar.

palmary [pǽlmǎri], a. principal; digno del premio.

palmate(d [pǽlmeit(id], a. palm(e)ado.

palmer [pámœ(r)], s. palmero, peregrino, romero; fullero, tahur; palmeta.—p. **worm**, (ent.) cierta oruga velluda; gorgojo.

palmetto [pælmétou], s. (bot.) palmito, margallón; sombrero de palmito.—P. **State**, Carolina del Sur.

palmiferous [pælmíferʌs], a. (poét.) palmífero.

palmiped [pǽlmiped], a. y s. (zool.) palmípedo.

palmist(er [pámist(œr], s. quiromántico.

palmistry [-ri], s. quiromancia (o-cía).

palmitate [pǽlmiteit], s. (quím.) palmitato.

palmitic [pælmítik], a. (quím.) palmítico.

palmitin [pǽlmitin], s. (quím.) palmitina.

palmy [pámi], a. próspero, floreciente; triunfal; palmar.

palp [pælp], s. (zool.) palpo.

palpability [pælpǎbíliti], s. palpabilidad, evidencia, calidad de obvio, patente o palmar(io).

palpable [pǽlpǎbl], a. palpable, evidente.— **palpably** [-bli], adv. palpablemente, claramente.

palpate [pǽlpeit], va. palpar.—**palpation** [-éiṣǫn], s. palpamiento; (med.) palpación.

palpebra [pǽlpibrǎ], s. (anat.) pálpebra, párpado.

palpebral [-l], a. palpebral.

palpitate [pǽlpiteit], vn. palpitar, latir.—**palpitating** [-iŋ], a. palpitante, latiente.—**palpitation** [-éiṣǫn], s. palpitación; (med.) pulsación rápida del corazón.

palpus [pǽlpʌs], s. (zool.) palpo.

palsied [pólzid], a. perlático, paralítico, paraliticado; temblante.—**to become p.**, paraliticarse.

palsy [pólzi]. I. s. (med.) parálisis, perlesía; ineficacia; apatía. II. va. paralizar. III. vn. paraliticarse.

palter [póltœ(r)], vn. petardear, estafar, divertirse con alguno.—**palterer** [-œ(r)], s. petardista.

paltriness [póltrinis], s. vileza, mezquindad.

paltry [póltri], a. vil, miserable, mezquino.

paludal [palyúdǎl], **paludine** [pǽlyudin], a. palúdico, de los pantanos, palustre.—**paludism** [-dizm], s. (med.) paludismo, fiebre palúdica.—

paludous [-dʌs], a. palúdico; de los pantanos, que vive en los pantanos.

paly [péili], a. (poét.) pálido; (blas.) palado.

pampas [pǽmpʌz], s. pl. pampas.—p. **grass**, (bot.) cortadera argentina.

pampean [pæmpíǎn], a. y s. pampero, pampeano.

pamper [pǽmpœ(r)], va. mimar, consentir, tratar con mimo y regalo.

pamperer [-œ(r)], s. mimador.

pampero [pæmpéirou], s. pampero (viento, habitante).

pamphlet [pǽmflit], s. folleto; impreso.

pamphleteer [-r], s. folletista.

pan [pæn]. I. s. cacerola, cazuela, cuenco; barreño; perol; caldero; paila; cuenca; depresión; hondonada; (min.) gamella; cazoleta de un arma de fuego; (carp.) quicio. V. HARDPAN.— p. **pudding**, pudín cocido en el horno.—P.'s **pipes**, flauta del dios Pan. II. va. (min.) separar el oro en una gamella; cocer y servir en una cazuela; (fam.) alcanzar, sacar, lograr; (fam.) criticar o poner como nuevo. III. vn. (con **out**) dar oro la tierra o arena; (fam.) dar buen resultado o provecho.

panacea [pænǎsíǎ], s. panacea, sánalotodo o cúralotodo, remedio universal, catolicón.

panache [pǎnǽṣ], s. penacho, plumaje, plumero, airón; (fig.) = SWAGGER.

panada [pǎnádǎ], s. (coc.) panetela.

Panama hat [pǽnǎmá hǽt], s. (sombrero de) jipijapa, m.; panamá, m.—**Panamaian** [-máyǎn], **Panaman** [-mán], **Panamanian** [-mániǎn], s. y a. panameño.

Pan-American [pæn ǎmérikǎn], a. panamericano. —**Pan-Americanism** [-izm], s. panamericanismo.

Pan-Anglican [pæn ǽnglikǎn], a. pananglicano, relativo al conjunto de las divisiones de la iglesia anglicana.

panatela [pænǎtélǎ], s. panatela o panetela (cigarro).

pancake [pǽnkeik]. I. s. (coc.) fruta de sartén, hojuela, torta delgada de masa cocida rápidamente en la sartén, la callana o una plancha metálica, (Am.) panqué o panqueque, tortilla; (aer.) aterrizaje brusco casi vertical. II. a. plano. III. vn. (aer.) aumentar el ángulo de ataque al aterrizar.

pancratiast [pænkréiṣiæst], s. pancraciasta, m.

pancratic [pænkrétik], a. pert. al pancracio; atlético, gimnástico; (ópt.) ajustable.

pancratium [pænkréiṣiʌm], s. pancracio.

pancreas [pénkriǎs], s. (anat.) páncreas.

pancreatic [pænkriǽtik], a. pancreático.—p. **juice**, jugo pancreático.

pancreatin [pænkríǎtin], s. pancreatina.

panda [pǽndǎ], s. (zool.) panda, m. (ll. t. **lesser panda**).—**giant p.**, mamífero úrsido del Tibet.

pandanaceous [pændǎnéiṣiʌs], a. (bot.) pandáneo.

Pandean [pændíǎn], a. (mit.) del dios Pan.—P. **pipes**, = PAN'S PIPES.

pandect [pǽndekt], s. tratado, recopilación, digesto.—pl. **Pandects**, pandectas.

pandemia [pændímiǎ], s. (med.) pandemia.

pandemic [pændémik], a. pandémico, muy epidémico.

pandemonium [pændimóunjʌm], s. pandemónium, infierno; barahunda, batahola.

pander [pǽndœ(r)]. I. s. alcahuete, rufián, tercero. II. va. y vn. alcahuetear, rufianear.

panderage [-idʒ], **panderism** [-izm], s. alcahuetería, lenocinio.

panderess [-is], s. alcahueta.

pandiculation [pændikyǔléiṣǫn], s. pandiculación, desperezo.

pandore [pændór], s. (mús.) bandola, bandurria.

pandowdy [pændáudi], s. (coc.) cierto pastel o budín de manzanas.

pandy [pǽndi]. **I.** *s.* palmetazo. **II.** *va.* dar palmetazos (como castigo).

pane [pejn], *s.* hoja de vidrio o cristal de ventana o vidriera; entrepaño de puerta, etc.; cuadro, cuadrado, tablero; cara, lado, faz, faceta. *V.* PANEL y PEEN.—**paned** [-d], *a.* provisto de panes; hecho a cuadros.

panegyric [pænịdʒírịk], *s.*, **panegyric(al** [-(ạl], *a.* panegírico.—**panegyrist** [-ịst], *s.* panegirista.—**panegyrize** [pǽnịdʒịraịz], *va.* panegirizar.

panel [pǽnẹl]. **I.** *s.* (arq., etc.) panel; entrepaño, cuarterón, artesón, tablero, tabica; (elec.) panel, tablero; (pint.) tabla; (cost.) paño (en un vestido); cojincillo de silla de montar; cara de una piedra labrada; (ing.) recuadro, tramo (de puente); (aer.) pieza de tela de la envoltura (de un dirigible); (aer.) sección, cuadro (de un ala); (for.) jurado; lista oficial de personas que pueden servir como jurados.—**p. board,** tablero de cortacircuitos.—**p. discussion,** discusión de un tema o problema por oradores nombrados de antemano.—**p. doctor,** (Ingl.) médico de seguros.—**p. game,** modo de robar mediante postigos o puertas secretas en casas de mal vivir.—**p. house,** burdel donde se practica el robo antedicho.—**p. length,** (ing.) largo de los recuadros (de un puente). **II.** *va.* artesonar, formar tableros, cuarterones o artesones.

paneless [péjnlịs], *a.* sin cristales (ventana o vidriera).

panel(l)ing [pǽnẹlịŋ], *s.* artesonado.

panetel(l)a [pænẹtélạ], *s.* = PANATELA.

panful [pǽnful], *s.* contenido de una cazuela o cacerola; sartenada.

pang [pæŋ], *s.* angustia, congoja, dolor, tormento.—**pangs of childbirth,** dolores de parto.—**pangs of conscience,** remordimientos de conciencia.—**pangs of death,** ansias de la muerte, agonía.

pangenesis [pændʒénẹsịs], *s.* (biol.) pangenesia, pangénesis.—**pangenetic** [pændʒịnétịk], *a.* pangenésico, pangenético.

Pan-German [pændʒə́rmạn], *a.* pangermanista. —**Pan-Germanism** [-ịzm], *s.* pangermanismo.

pangolin [pæŋgóulịn], *s.* (zool.) pangolín.

panhandle [pénhændl]. **I.** *vn.* (fam.) mendigar en las calles. **II.** *s.* mango de cacerola, etc.; entrada angosta de un territorio en otro.— **panhandler** [-hændlœ(r)], *s.* (fam.) mendicante callejero, pordiosero.—**P. State,** (E. U.) Virginia Occidental.

Panhellenic [pænhẹlénịk], *a.* panhelénico, panhelenista.—**Panhellenism** [-hélẹnịzm], *s.* panhelenismo.—**Panhellenist** [-ịst], *s.* panhelenista.

panic [pǽnịk]. **I.** *a.* pánico. **II.** *s.* pánico; miedo o terror pánico; consternación; pánico o crisis comercial.—**p. grass,** (bot.) panizo, mijo, (a)daza.—**p.-stricken, p.-struck,** sobrecogido de terror, preso de pánico. **III.** *va.* consternar, sobrecoger de terror.

panicky [-ị], *a.* aterrorizado, consternado.

panicle [pǽnịkl], *s.* (bot.) panoja, panícula.

paniculate(d [pạnị́kyụleịt(ịd], *a.* (bot.) apanojado, paniculado.

Panicum [pǽnịkʌm], *s.* (bot.) panizo.

Pan-Islamism [pæníslạmịzm], *s.* panislamismo.

panjandrum [pændʒǽndram], *s.* persona hinchada; hombre mayúsculo (ú. jocosa o satíricamente); ceremonia ridículamente exagerada.

panniculus [pænị́kyụlạs], *s.* (anat.) panículo.

pan(n)ier [pǽnịœ(r)], *s.* cuévano, serón, cesto o cesta, canasta; (cost.) tontillo; armazón ligera; (ing.) cestón, gavión, *m.*—*pl.* angarillas.

pannikin [pǽnịkịn], *s.* cazo, cacillo.

panoply [pǽnoplị], *s.* panoplia.

panoptic(al [pænáptịk(ạl], *a.* panóptico.

panopticon [-an], *s.* panóptico.

panorama [pænorámạ], *s.* panorama, *m.*

panoramic [-ịk], *a.* panorámico.

Panslavic [pænslávịk], *a.* paneslavista.—**Pan slavism** [-ịzm], *s.* paneslavismo.

panspermatism [pænspə́rmạtịzm], *s.* (biol.) panspermia.

pansy [pǽnzị], *s.* (bot.) pensamiento, trinitaria

pant [pænt]. **I.** *vn.* (i)jadear, resollar, acezar anhelar; palpitar.—**to p. for o after,** suspirar por, desear con ansia. **II.** *s.* jadeo, resuello acezo; palpitación.—*pl.* (fam.) *V.* PANTS.

pantalet(te)s [pæntạléts], *s. pl.* pantalones largos de mujer, (Am.) pantaletas.—**pantaloon** [-lún], *s.* arlequín, bufón.—*pl.* pantalones

pantelegraph [-télịgræf], *s.* (elec.) pantelégrafo.

pantelephone [-télịfoun], *s.* panteléfono.

pantheism [pǽnθịịzm], *s.* panteísmo.—**pantheist** [-ịst], *s.* panteísta.—**pantheistic(al** [-ịstịk(ạl], *a.* panteísta, panteístico.

Pantheon, panteon [pǽnθịọn], *s.* panteón.

panther [pǽnθœ(r)], *s.* (zool.) pantera, leopardo (Am.) puma, *mf.*

panties [pǽntịz], *s. pl.* (fam.) pantalones (de mujer), (Am.) pantaletas.

pantile [pǽntaịl], *s.* teja cóncava o de canalón.

panting [pǽntịŋ]. **I.** *a.* jadeante, acezoso. **II.** *s.* jadeo, anhelación; (med.) disnea.—**pantingly** [-lị], *adv.* sin resuello, con anhelo.

pantler [pǽntlœ(r)], *s.* (ant.) panetero.

pantograph [pǽntogræf], *s.* pantógrafo; (f. c. eléct.) soporte articulado del vástago del trole.—**pantographic** [-gráfịk], *a.* pantográfico.

pantometer [pæntámetœ(r)], *s.* pantómetra, -tro.

pantomime [pǽntomaịm], *s.* mímica; (teat.) pantomima.—**pantomimic** [-mímịk], *a.* pantomímico.—**pantomimist** [-maịmịst], *s.* pantomimo.

pantoscopic [-skápịk], *a.* (ópt.) pantoscópico, bifocal.

pantry [pǽntrị], *s.* despensa, reposte(ría).

pants [pænts], *s. pl.* (fam.) pantalones; calzoncillos.—**p. (o pant) hanger,** percha.

pap [pæp], *s.* (ant.) pezón, teta; mogote; papilla, papas, *f. pl.*; gachas, puches; (ant.) carne, *f.* (de la fruta); (vet.) tolano.

papa [pápạ o papá], *s.* (fam.) papá o papa, *m.*

papacy [péjpạsị], *s.* papado, pontificado.

papain [pạpéịịn], *s.* (bioquím.) papaína.

papal [péjpạl], *a.* papal, pontifical.—**p. chamberlain,** camerlengo.—**papalism** [-ịzm], *s.* papismo.—**papalist** [-ịst], *a.* y *s.* papista.—**papally** [-ị], *adv.* papalmente.

papaveraceous [pạpœvẹréịʃạs], **papaverous** [pạpǽvẹrạs], *a.* (bot.) papaveráceo.

papaw [pạpɔ́], *s.* (bot.) lechosa, papaya; (E. U., bot.) asimina (ll. tb. **papaya** y **pawpaw**).—**p. tree,** lechoso, papayo.

paper [péjpœ(r)]. **I.** *s.* papel; memoria, artículo, disertación, ensayo; diario, periódico; (com.) valor, vale, letra o pagaré negociable; envoltorio; paquete, papel o papelito que contiene algo; (teat.) billete de favor, pase.—*pl.* papeles (valores, documentos, apuntes, etc.); credenciales; actas; carta de naturaleza.—**p. of needles,** cartón o paño de agujas.—**p. of tacks,** cajetilla de tachuelas.—**on p.,** escrito; por escrito; en lo escrito, en teoría. **II.** *a.* de papel; del o relativo al papel; para papel; para papeles; escrito.—**p. bag,** bolsa o saco de papel; papeleta.—**p. blockade,** (der. int.) bloqueo en el papel.—**p. book,** libro en blanco.—**p. -bound,** (enc.) en rústica.—**p. box,** caja de cartón.—**p. case,** papelera.—**p. clip,** sujetapapeles, sujetador, prendedero, clip.—**p. cone,** cucurucho.—**p. currency,** papel moneda.—**p. cutter,** cortapapel; (enc.) máquina de cortar papel.—**p. fastener,** cierre para muestras, etc.—**p. file,** papelera, guardapapeles.—**p. folder,** plegadera.—**p. hanger,** empapelador, papelista.—**p. hanging,** empapelado; oficio de empapelador; arte de empapelar.—**p.**

hangings, papel pintado o de empapelar.—**p. kite,** cometa de papel, (Am.) papalote.—**p. knife,** cortapapel; plegadera.—**p. maker,** o seller, papelero, papelista.—**p. (making) machine,** máquina papelera o para hacer papel continuo.—**p. mill,** fábrica de papel.—**p. money,** papel moneda.—**p. muslin,** lustrina.—**p. nautilus,** (zool.) argonauta.—**p. profits,** (com.) ganancias presuntas pero no realizadas aún.—**p. pulp,** pulpa para papel; pasta.—**p. punch,** perforador(a) de papel.—**p. ruler,** pauta; pautador (persona).—**p. stainer,** fabricante de papeles pintados.—**p. wasp,** (ent.) avispa.—**p. wedding,** primer aniversario de la boda.—**p. weight,** pisapapel. **III.** *va.* empapelar; cubrir con papel; pulir con papel de lija.

paperboard [-bǫrd], *s.* cartón.

paperer [-œ(r)], *s.* empapelador.

papering [-iŋ], *s.* empapelado.

papery [-i], *a.* parecido al papel.

papess [péipis], *s.* papisa.

papeterie [pǽpętri], *s.* cajita de papel y sobres.

papier-mâché [péipœr mǎséi], *s.* cartón piedra.

papilionaceous [papiljonéiśiʌs], *a.* (bot.) amariposado; papilionáceo.—**Papilionidæ** [-ánidi], *s. pl.* (ent.) papiliónidos, mariposas.

papilla [papílǎ], *s.* (zool., bot.) pezón, papila.

papillary [pǽpileri], **papillose** [-loųs], *a.* papilar.

papillitis [-láitis], *s.* (med.) (neuro)papilitis, neuritis óptica.

papilloma [-lóųmǎ], *s.* (med.) papiloma, *m.*

papist [péipist], *s.* (gen. desp.) papista.—**papistic(al** [peipístik(ạl], *a.* papista.—**papistry** [péipistri], *s.* (gen. desp.) papismo.

pap(p)oose [pæpús], *s.* niño de los indios norteamericanos.

pappose [pǽpoųs], **pappous** [pǽpʌs], *a.* velloso, velludo.

pappus [pǽpʌs], *s.* (bot.) vilano, papo.

pappy [pǽpi], *a.* como papilla; mollar, jugoso.

paprika [pǽprikǎ], *s.* pimentón.

Papuan [pǽpiuạn], *s. y a.* papú.

papula [pǽpyul(ǎ], **papule,** *s.* (med.) pápula.

papular [-ǎ(r)], **papulous** [-ʌs], *a.* papuloso, lleno de pápulas.

papyraceous [papiréiśiʌs], *a.* papiráceo; hecho de papiro. *V.* PAPERY.

papyrus [papáiras], *s.* (bot.) papiro; papel de papiro; documento escrito en papiro.

par [par], *s.* equivalencia, paridad, nivel; (com.) par, *f.*—**p. value,** valor a la par, valor nominal. —**above p.,** a premio, con prima.—**at p.,** a la par.—**below p.,** a descuento.—**to be on a p. with,** ser igual a, estar al par de, correr parejas con.

parablast [pǽrablæst], *s.* (embr.) parablasto.

parable [pǽrabl], *s.* parábola.

parabola [pǽrębolǎ], *s.* (geom.) parábola.

parabolic(al [pǽrębálik(ạl], *a.* parabólico.—**p. geometry,** geometría euclidiana.—**p. space,** espacio euclidiano.

parabolically [-i], *adv.* parabólicamente.

parabolist [pǽrębolist], *s.* parabolano.

paraboloid [-lǫid], *s.* (geom.) paraboloide.

paracentric(al [pǽraséntrik(ạl], *a.* paracéntrico.

parachronism [pǽréikronizm], *s.* paracronismo.

parachute [pǽrašut], *s.* paracaídas; (min.) cuba de seguridad.—**parachutist** [-ist], *s.* paracaidista.

Paraclete [pǽraklit], *s.* (igl.) Paráclito, Paracleto.

parade [paréid]. **I.** *s.* (mil.) parada, revista de tropas; desfile, procesión; cabalgata; paseo público; gala, ostentación, pompa, fachenda; (esgr.) parada, quite.—**p. ground,** plaza de armas.—**p. rest,** (mil.) descanso. **II.** *va. y vn.* (mil.) formar en parada; pasar revista; desfilar; pasear, cabalgar; hacer gala, alardear, ostentar.

paradigm [pǽradim], *s.* paradigma, *m.*, ejemplar.

paradigmatic [-digmǽtik], *a.* ejemplar.

paradise [pǽradais], *s.* paraíso; cielo; Edén; (teat.) paraíso.—**p. bird,** ave (*f.*) del Paraíso.

paradisiacal, paradisaic [-disáiakạl, -diséiik], *a.* paradisíaco, edénico.

paradox [pǽradaks], *s.* paradoja.—**paradoxical** [-dáksikạl], *a.* paradójico, paradojo.—**paradoxically** [-i], *adv.* paradójicamente.

paraffin(e [pǽrafin], *s.* parafina.

parage [pǽridž], *s.* (der. hist.) igualdad de sangre, de dignidad o terreno (entre coherederos).

paragenesis [pǽragdźénesis], *s.* (geol.) paragénesis.

paragoge [pǽragóydźi], *s.* (ret.) paragoge, *f.*

paragogic [pǽragádźik], *a.* paragógico.

paragon [pǽragan], *s.* modelo, ejemplar, dechado; (impr.) parangona (tipo grande de 20 puntos).

paragraph [pǽragræf]. **I.** *va.* dividir en párrafos. **II.** *s.* párrafo, parágrafo, aparte; suelto, gacetilla; (impr.) párrafo, calderón, el signo ¶.

paragrapher [-œ(r)], *s.* gacetillero.

paragraphic(al [-grǽfik(ạl], *a.* escrito en párrafos sueltos; gacetillesco.

paragraphically [-i], *adv.* por párrafos.

Paraguayan [pǽragwéiạn, -gwáiạn], *a. y s.* paraguay(an)o.

parakeet [pǽrakit], *s.* (orn.) perico, periquito.

paraldehyde [pǽréldihaid], *s.* (quím.) paraldehído.

paraleipsis [pǽraláipsis], *s.* (ret.) paralipse, *f.*

parallactic(al [-léktik(ạl], *a.* paraláctico.

parallax [pǽralæks], *s.* (astr.) paralaje, *f.*

parallel [pǽralel]. **I.** *a.* paralelo; igual; análogo, semejante.—**p. bars,** paralelas (gimnasia).—**p. motion,** mecanismo de movimiento paralelo.—**p. postulate,** postulado de las paralelas, o de Euclides.—**p. ruler,** regla para trazar rectas paralelas.—**p. sailing,** navegación paralela.—**p. series,** (elec.) = MULTIPLE SERIES. **II.** *s.* línea paralela; paralelo, cotejo; conformidad, semejanza; (geog.) paralelo (de latitud); igual, contraparte, *f.;* (fort.) paralela; (impr.) signo de esta forma ‖ .—**p. of latitude,** paralelo de latitud.—**in p.,** (elec.) en paralelo, en derivación. **III.** *va.* ser paralelo o igual a, correr parejas con; pararelar, poner en dirección paralela; parangonar, cotejar, poner en paralelo.

parallelepiped [-ępáipid], *s.* (geom.) paralelepípedo.

parallelism [-izm], *s.* paralelismo.

parallelly [-i], *adv.* paralelamente.

parallelogram [pǽralélogræm], *s.* (geom.) paralelogramo.

paralogism, paralogy [pǽrélodźizm, -dźi], *s.* (lógica) paralogismo.

paralogize [-dźaiz], *vn.* paralogizar.

paralysis [pǽrélisis], *s.* (med.) parálisis, perlesía; paralización, estancamiento.

paralytic(al [pǽralítik(ạl], *s. y a.* paralítico, perlático, tullido.

paralyzation [pǽrąlizéiśon], *s.* parálisis; paralización.

paralyze [pǽrąlaiz], *va.* paralizar.—**paralyzed** [-d], *a.* = PARALYTIC.—**paralyzing** [-iŋ], *a.* paralizador.

paramagnetic [pǽrąmægnétik], *a.* paramagnético.

paramecium [pǽramíśiʌm], *s.* (zool.) paramecio.

parameter [pǽrémetœ(r)], *s.* (geom.) parámetro.

paramo [párąmoų], *s.* páramo.

paramorphism [pǽramórfizm], *s.* (min.) paramorfismo, paramorfosis.

paramount [pǽramaunt]. **I.** *a.* superior, supremo, principalísimo. **II.** *s.* (lord) p., soberano.

paramour [pǽramur], *s.* amante, querido, (fam.) cortejo; querida, manceba.

paranoia [pǽrạnóiǎ], *s.* paranoia, esp. la persecutoria, o locura de persecución.—**paranoiac** [-nóiæk], **paranoic** [-nóiik]. **I.** *a.* paranoico, relativo a la paranoia. **II.** *s.* el que sufre de paranoia.

Pará nut [pará nʌt], *s.* = BRAZIL NUT.

paranymph [pǽrᵊnimf], *s.* paraninfo.

parapet [pǽrᵊpet], *s.* (arq.) baranda, antepecho, pretil, mampuesto; (fort.) parapeto, baluarte.

paraphernalia [pærᵊfœrnéiliᵊ], *s. pl.* atavíos, arreos; adornos, galas, insignias; (for.) bienes parafernales.

paraphrase [pǽrᵊfreiz]. **I.** *s.* paráfrasis. **II.** *va.* parafrasear.—**paraphraser** [-œ(r)], **paraphrast** [-fræst], *s.* parafraste, parafraseador.—**paraphrastic(al** [-frǽstik(ᵊl], *a.* parafrástico. —**paraphrastically** [-i], *adv.* parafrásticamente.

paraplegia [-plídʒiᵊ], *s.* (med.) paraplejía, -gia.

paraquet, *s.* = PAR(R)AKEET.

Pará rubber [pará rʌ́bœ(r)], *s.* = INDIA RUBBER.

parasang [pǽrᵊsæŋ], *s.* parasanga (5,250 metros).

parasceve [pǽrᵊsiv], *s.* (igl.) parasceve de los judíos; viernes santo.

paraselene [pærᵊselíni], *s.* (meteor.) paraselene, *f.*

parasite [pǽrᵊsait], *s.* parásito; (fam.) gorrista, gorrón, mogrollo.

parasitic(al [-sítik(ᵊl], *a.* parásito; gorrista; (med.) parasitario, parasítico.—**p. current,** (elec.) corriente de Foucault o parásita.

parasitically [-i], *adv.* a modo de parásito; a ufo.

parasiticide [-sítisaid], *a.* y *s.* parasiticida, *mf.*

parasitism [-saitizm], *s.* parasitismo.

parasitology [-saitalodʒi], *s.* (biol.) parasitología.

parasol [-sol], *s.* sombrilla, parasol, quitasol.

parasympathetic [-simpᵊθétik], *a.* (anat., fisiol.) parasimpático.

parathyroid [-θáiroid], *a.* y *s.* (anat.) paratiroides, *f.*

paratrooper [-trupœ(r)], *s.* (mil.) soldado del cuerpo de paracaidistas.—**paratroops** [-trups], *s. pl.* tropas de paracaídas.

paratyphoid [-táifoid], *s.* (med.) paratifoidea.

paravane [-vein], *s.* artificio para destruir minas submarinas o para atacar submarinos.

parboil [párboil], *va.* sancochar; medio cocer.

parbuckle [párbʌkl], *s.* cierto dispositivo que sirve para hacer subir o bajar barriles, etc., por un plano inclinado.

parcel [pársel]. **I.** *s.* paquete; lío, fardo, bulto; atado; porción, cantidad; partida.—*pl.* (for.) demarcación de linderos.—**p. of ground,** o **land,** parcela, tramo, lote de terreno, solar.— **p. post,** servicio de paquetes postales. **II.** *adv.* en parte, parcialmente.—**p.-gilt,** dorado en parte. **III.** *va.* (con out o into) partir, dividir, distribuir; liar, empaquetar; parcelar, dividir en parcelas.—**to p. the seams,** (mar.) aforrar las costuras.—**parcel(l)ing,** *s.* (mar.) precinta.

parcenary [pársᵊneri], *s.* (for.) herencia indivisa.

parcener [pársᵊnœ(r)], *s.* (for.) coheredero.

parch [párch]. **I.** *va.* (re)secar, agostar; tostar, quemar, abrasar; asol(an)ar. **II.** *vn.* tostarse, quemarse, abrasarse.—**to be parched with thirst,** morirse o estarse abrasando de sed.

parche(e)si [parchízi], *s.* parcheesi (juego).

parching [párchiŋ], *a.* abrasador, ardiente.

parchment [párchment], *s.* pergamino, vitela.

pard [pard], *s.* (ant., zool.) (leo)pardo; (fam.) asociado, compinche.

pardon [párdᵊn]. **I.** *va.* perdonar, absolver; indultar, amnistiar, remitir; disculpar, dispensar.—**p. me,** perdone Vd., Vd. dispense.—**to p. a criminal,** conceder gracia a un criminal. **II.** *s.* perdón, gracia, absolución, indulto, amnistía, remisión, venia.—**I beg your p.,** Vd. dispense, perdone Vd. (fórmula de cortesía).

pardonable [-ᵊbl], *a.* perdonable; venial.— **pardonableness** [-nis], *s.* disculpabilidad.— **pardonably** [-ᵊbli], *adv.* disculpablemente.

pardoner [-œ(r)], *s.* perdonador.

pardoning [-iŋ], *a.* indulgente, perdonante.

pare [per], *va.* (re)cortar; mondar (fruta); pelar

(patatas, etc.); chiflar (cuero, pieles, etc.); rallar, raspar; descantillar, desbastar.—**to p. a horse's hoof,** despalmar el casco de un caballo.—**to p. the nails,** cortar las uñas.

paregoric [pærᵊgórik]. **I.** *a.* paregórico, calmante. **II.** *s.* (farm.) elixir paregórico; anodino; tintura de opio alcanforada.

parenchyma [pᵊréŋkimᵊ], *s.* parénquima, *m.*

parenchymous [-mʌs], **parenchymatous** [pærᵊŋkímᵊtᵊs], *a.* (bot., zool.) parenquimatoso.

parent [pérᵊnt]. **I.** *s.* padre o madre; autor, causa, origen.—*pl.* padres. **II.** *a.* madre, matriz, materno, principal.—**p. complex,** (psic.) complejo Edipo.—**p. house,** casa principal.— **p. plant,** planta madre.—**p. speech,** lengua matriz o madre.

parentage [-idʒ], *s.* ascendencia, extracción, alcurnia, abolengo, nacimiento, origen. *V.* PARENTHOOD.

parental [pᵊréntᵊl], *a.* paternal o maternal.—**p. school,** reformatorio para jóvenes delincuentes.

parentheses [pᵊrénθesiz], *s. pl.* de PARENTHESIS.

parenthesis [-sis], *s.* paréntesis, *m.*

parenthetic(al [pærᵊnθétik(ᵊl], *a.* entre paréntesis.—**parenthetically** [-i], *adv.* entre paréntesis.

parenthood [pérᵊnthud], *s.* paternidad o maternidad, calidad de padre o madre.

parentless [pérᵊntlis], *a.* huérfano, sin padres.

parer [pérœ(r)], *s.* mondador, pelador.

paresis [pᵊrísis], *s.* (med.) paresia.

paresthesia [paresθíziᵊ], *s.* (med.) parestesia.

paresthetic [-θétik], *a.* parestésico.

paretic [pᵊrétik], *a.* (med.) parético.

par excellence [par éksᵊlᵊns], (fr.) por excelencia, sin rival.

parfait [parféi], *s.* (coc.) cierto postre congelado.

parget [párdʒet]. **I.** *va.* (alb.) enyesar, enlucir. **II.** *s.* yeso; mortero, argamasa; enlucido.

pargeting [-iŋ], *s.* (alb.) enyesado, enyesadura, enlucido; estuco; argamasa.

parhelion [parhíliᵊn], *s.* (meteor.) parhelia, -io.

pariah [páriᵊ o páráiᵊ], *s.* paria, *mf.*

Parian [périᵊn], *a.* y *s.* pario; de Paros.

parietal [pᵊráietᵊl]. **I.** *a.* paredaño; interno; (anat., bot., etc.) parietal. **II.** *s.* (anat.) parietal.

parietary [pǽrietᵊri], *s.* (bot.) parietaria.

pari-mutuel [pæri miúchᵊel], *s.* cierto sistema de apostar en las carreras de caballo; máquina para registrar las apuestas.

paring [périŋ], *s.* raspadura, peladura, mondadura, cáscara, recorte, desperdicio, desecho.— **p. knife,** cuchilleja; trinchete, chaira o corvillo (de zapatero); descarnador; chifla (para cueros); pujavante (de herrador).

Paris [pǽris], *n.* de París.—**P. green,** cardenillo arsenioso, aceto-arsenito de cobre, verde de París.—**P. white,** blanco de París.

parish [pǽriʃ]. **I.** *s.* parroquia, feligresía, curato; (E. U.) en Luisiana, jurisdicción o partido. **II.** *a.* parroquial, párroco.—**p. church,** parroquia, iglesia parroquial.—**p. clerk,** sacristán de parroquia.—**p. priest,** (cura) párroco.—**p. school,** escuela parroquial.

parishioner [pᵊríʃᵊnœ(r)], *s.* parroquiano, feligrés.

Parisian [pᵊríziᵊn], *a.* y *s.* parisiense.

parisyllabic [pærisilǽbik], *a.* (gram.) parisilábico.

parity [pǽriti], *s.* paridad, semejanza, igualdad; (com.) paridad, cambio a la par.

park [park]. **I.** *s.* parque; (mil.) parque de artillería, municiones, etc. **II.** *va.* cercar o cerrar un coto; estacionar (un coche) al borde de la acera o en un paradero; (fam.) depositar, guardar, dar a guardar por poco tiempo (algo que estorba). **III.** *vn.* (aut.) estacionarse.

parka [párkᵊ], *s.* cierta chaqueta de piel, o camisa larga de lana, con capucha.

parking [párkiŋ], s. estacionamiento (de un vehículo).—**p. place**, plaza de estacionamiento.—**no p.**, estacionamiento prohibido.

parkleaves [párklivz], s. (bot.) androsemo, castellar, todabuena o todasana.

parkway [párkwej], s. bulevar.

parlance [párlans], s. lenguaje, idioma, m.; dicción, modo de hablar; conversación. V. PARLEY.

parlay [párlej o párli], s. = PAROLI.

parley [párli]. I. vn. (mil.) parlamentar; discutir; conferenciar. II. s. (mil.) parlamento; conferencia, plática.

Parliament [párliment], s. (Ingl.) parlamento; (España) Cortes, f. pl.; cuerpo legislativo.—**member of P.**, parlamentario; diputado (a Cortes).

parliamentarian [-mentérian], s. parlamentario.

parliamentarily [-méntarili], adv. parlamentariamente.

parliamentarism [-tarizm], s. parlamentarismo.

parliamentary [-tari], a. parlamentario.—**p. law**, o **practice**, práctica parlamentaria.

parlor [párlo(r)], s. sala de recibo; salón; (Ingl.) sala de confianza; (igl.) parlatorio, locutorio.—**p. car**, (f. c.) coche salón.—**p. match**, mixto, fósforo.

parlormaid [-mejd], s. doncella.

parlous [párlas], a. (ant.) peligroso, temible; (fam.) muy astuto o perspicaz; horrible; sorprendente.—**parlously** [-li], adv. (fam.) sumamente.

Parmesan [parmizǽn], a. parmesano, de Parma.

Parnassian [parnǽsian]. I. a. del Parnaso; poético.—**P. school**, escuela parnasiana. II. s. poeta, m.; parnasiano.—**Parnassus** [parnǽsas], s. Parnaso.

parochial [paróukial], a. parroquial. V. PARISH.

parochially [-i], adv. por parroquias.

parodic(al [parádik(al], a. paródico.

parodist [párodist], s. parodista.

parody [párodi]. I. s. parodia. II. va. parodiar.

parol(e [paróul]. I. a. (for.) verbal, oral; escrito pero no sellado.—**p. contract**, contrato verbal o no perfeccionado.—**p. evidence**, prueba verbal.—**by p.**, de palabra. II. s. (for.) alegación o alegato.

parole [paróul]. I. s. palabra, promesa de honor de un prisionero; (mil.) santo y seña; (for.) caución juratoria. II. va. (mil. y penología) poner en libertad bajo palabra.

paroli [péroli], s. pároli (en el juego).

paronomasia [pæranoméiǯiǝ], s. (ret.) paronomasia.

paronomastic [-mǽstik], a. paronomástico.

paronychia [pæroníkiǝ], s. (cir.) panadizo.

paronym [péronim], s. voz parónima.—**paronymous, paronymic** [pæránimʌs, pæronímik], a. parónimo.—**paronymy** [pæránimi], s. paronimia.

paroquet [péroket], s. (orn.) periquito.

parotic [pærátik], a. (anat.) de la región auricular.

parotid [pærátid]. I. a. parotídeo, próximo a la oreja. II. s. (anat.) parótida (glándula).—**parotitis** [pæratáitis], **parotiditis** [pæratidáitis], s. (med.) parotiditis, parótida.

paroxysm [péroksizm], s. paroxismo, parasismo.

paroxysmal [-sízmal], a. paroxismal; (geol.) producido por una conmoción.

paroxytone [pæráksitoun], a. (gram.) paroxítono.

parquet [parkéj], s. (teat.) platea.—**p. circle**, (teat.) = PARTERRE.—**p. floor**, piso, entarimado o entablado de mosaico de madera.

parquetry [párketri], s. mosaico de madera.

parr [par], s. (ict.) esguín, murgón, salmoncillo.

parrakeet [pérakit], s. (orn.) perico, periquito.

parrel [pérel], s. manto de chimenea; (mar.) racamento.—**p. rope**, troceo.—**p. truck**, (mar.) troza.

parrhesia [paríǯiǝ], s. (ret.) parresia.

parricidal [pærisáidal], a. parricida.

parricide [périsaid], s. parricida, mf.; parricidio.

parrot [pérot]. I. s. (orn.) papagayo, loro, cotorra, (Am.) cata.—**p. disease**, o **fever**, psitacosis.—**p. fish** o **wrasse**, (ict.) escaro. II. va. y vn. repetir o hablar como loro; decir ociosidades.

parry [péri]. I. va. y vn. (esgr.) parar, rechazar, reparar, quitar. II. s. parada, quite, reparo.

parrying [-iŋ], s. parada, quite.

parse [pars], va. (gram.) analizar.

parsec [pársek], s. unidad astronómica igual a 206.265 veces la distancia del sol a la tierra.

Parsee, Parsi [pársi], s. parsi.

Parseeism, Parsiism [-izm]. s. parsismo, religión de Zoroastro.—**Parsic** [pársik], a. parsi.

parsimonious [pársimóuniǝs], a. parsimonioso, parco, frugal; mezquino cicatero, tacaño.—**parsimoniously** [-li], adv. parcamente; mezquinamente.—**parsimoniousness** [-nis], **parsimony** [-moni], s. parsimonia, parquedad; mezquindad.

parsing []pársiŋ], s. (gram.) análisis.

parsley [pársli], s. (bot.) perejil.

parsnip [pársnip], s. (bot.) chirivía, pastinaca.

parson [párson], s. clérigo; párroco, cura, m.

parsonage [-idǯ], s. rectoría, rectoral, f.

part [part]. I. s. parte, f.; porción, pedazo, trozo; miembro; pieza; región, lugar; (teat.) papel; interés, cuidado; obligación, deber; (mús.) parte; raya del cabello; (for.) parte; (mec.) pieza (de repuesto); (mat.) parte alícuota.—pl. partes, prendas personales, dotes, f. pl., c(u)alidades; distrito, paraje.—**p. and parcel**, parte integrante; uña y carne, carne y hueso.—**p. of speech**, parte de la oración.—**p. owner**, condueño.—**p. time**, tiempo o período incompleto (ú. esp. del empleo o trabajo). V. FULL TIME.—**p. way**, en parte, hasta cierto punto.—**by parts**, a o por partes.—**for my p.**, por mi parte, por lo que a mí toca, en cuanto a mí.—**for the most p.**, por la mayor parte, en su mayoría.—**in good** (**bad**) **p.**, sin ofenderse (ofendido), en buena (mala) parte.—**in p.**, en parte, parcialmente.—**it is the p. of wisdom**, la prudencia aconseja.—**on my p.**, de o por mi parte.—**to do one's p.**, cumplir uno con su obligación; hacer cuanto pueda, hacer de su parte.—**to meet p. way**, hacer algunas concesiones.—**to take p.** (**in**), tomar parte o participar (en). II. va. partir; repartir, distribuir; despartir, desunir, separar, dividir; romper, desprender; apartar.—**to p. company**, separarse.—**to p. the hair**, partir el pelo, hacerse la raya. III. vn. partirse; separarse; desprenderse, romperse, saltar, zafarse; despedirse; partir, irse; morir.—**to p. from**, despedirse de, decir adiós a.—**to p. with**, desprenderse o deshacerse de; enajenar.

partake [partéik], va. y vn. (pret. PARTOOK; pp. PARTAKEN) (a veces con **in** u **of**) participar (de), tener o tomar parte (en); tener algo de.

partaker [-œ(r)], s. participante, partícipe.

parted [pártid], a. partido, dividido, hendido; (ant.) ido, muerto.

parterre [partér], s. parterre, cuadro de jardín, macizo de flores; (teat.) parte (f.) de la platea detrás de las lunetas.

parthenogenesis, parthenogeny [parθenodǯénesis, -ǽdʒeni], s. (biol.) partenogénesis.—**parthenogenetic** [-nodʒenétik], a. partenogenésico, -genético.

Parthian [párθian], s. y a. parto.

partial [pársǝl], a. parcial, prevenido; parcial, no del todo o completo; muy o más aficionado (a), mejor dispuesto (hacia, para, con).—**p. differential**, (mat.) diferencial parcial.—**p. eclipse**, (astr.) eclipse parcial.—**p. fractions**, (mat.) fracciones parciales, fracciones en que puede descomponerse una fracción algebraica.—**p. payments**, pagos parciales.

partiality [parš(i)ǽliti], s. parcialidad; prejuicio, predilección, preferencia.

partially [páršali], adv. parcialmente, en parte; parcialmente, con parcialidad.

partible [pártibl], a. partible, divisible.

participant [partisipant], a. y s., **participator** [-peito(r)], s. participante, (co)partícipe.— **participate** [-peit], va. y vn. participar.— **participating** [-iŋ], a. = PARTICIPANT.—**p. stock**, acciones privilegiadas con participación en las ganancias, fuera del dividendo fijo que devengan.—**participation** [-péišon], s. participación; distribución, repartimiento.

participial [partisipiąl]. I. a. (gram.) participial. II. s. participio.

participially [-i], adv. participialmente.

participle [pártisipl], s. (gram.) participio.

particle [pártikl], s. partícula; pizca; (gram.) partícula; (mec.) punto material.

parti-colored [párti kalord], a. multicolor, abigarrado.

particular [partikyulą(r)]. I. a. particular, peculiar; en particular; individual, privado, privativo; singular, notable; distinguido, predilecto; preciso, exacto; delicado, escrupuloso; minucioso, detallado; exigente, quisquilloso.— **to be very p.**, ser exigente o descontentadizo; hilar delgado; hacer hincapié (en algo). II. s. particular(idad), detalle, pormenor; circunstancia; caso individual.—**in p.**, particularmente, en particular.—**to give, o go into particulars**, detallar circunstanciadamente.

particularism [-izm], s. individualismo, exclusivismo; (teol.) particularismo.

particularity [-lériti], s. particularidad, singularidad; minuciosidad; escrupulosidad; quisquillosidad.

particularize [-aiz], va. particularizar, singularizar, especificar, detallar.

particularly [-li], adv. particularmente, máxime.

parting [pártiŋ]. I. s. separación, división; marcha u partida; despedida; rompimiento, rotura; bifurcación (de una vía o camino); crencha, raya del pelo.—**to be at the p. of the roads**, u of the ways, haber llegado el tiempo de decidir definitivamente, o de que coja cada cual su camino. II. a. divisorio; de separación; de partida; de despedida; último, al partir.

partisan, partizan [pártizan]. I. a. partidario, parcial, adepto; (mil.) de guerrilla.—**p. vote**, votación de partido. II. s. partidario, secuaz, m., parcial, adepto; (mil.) guerrillero; (arm.) partesana; bastón de mando.

partisanship, partizanship [-šip], s. adhesión ciega a un partido, (Am.) partidarismo.

partition [partišon]. I. s. partición, repartimiento; división, separación; linde, demarcación; (alb.) tabique; (carp.) mampara; camón de vidrios; (for.) partija, (re)partición; (mús.) partitura.—**p. wall**, tabique; medianería, cerramiento. II. va. partir, dividir o separar; repartir, distribuir.—**to p. off**, tabicar, atajar.

partitive [pártitiv]. I. a. partitivo; (gram.) partitivo; distributivo. II. s. (gram.) palabra o caso partitivos.

partly [pártli], adv. en parte, en cierto modo.

partner [pártnœ(r)], s. socio; compañero; pareja (de baile, tennis, etc.); consorte, mf., cónyuge, mf.; interesado, partícipe; aparcero, parcionero.

partnership [-šip], s. (com.) compañía; sociedad, interés social; consorcio; aparcería; (arit.) regla de compañía.—**p. in commendam, p. en commandite**, sociedad comanditaria, o en comandita.

partook [partúk], pret. de TO PARTAKE.

partridge [pártridž], s. (orn.) perdiz.

parturient [partiúrient], a. parturienta, -te.

parturifacient [-iféišent], s. y a. (agente) parturifaciente, que induce o acelera el parto.

parturition [-išon], s. parto, parturición.

party [pártí]. I. s. partido (político, etc.); partida (de campo, teatro, etc.); tertulia, sarao, reunión, función o convite social; cuadrilla, bando o banda, facción, parcialidad; cuerpo; parte, f., partícipe; (mil.) partida, destacamento; (for.) parte, parte interesada; (fam.) persona, sujeto.—**p. in interest**, (for.) parte interesada; interesado.—**p. of the first (second) part**, (for.) primera (segunda) parte. Estas expresiones se usan en contratos, escrituras, etc., para distinguir las partes contratantes; pero al traducirlas debe cambiarse el giro, para que la frase se adapte a las formas castellanas; v. gr.: *a contract between N. N., party of the first part, and X. Y., party of the second part*, puede traducirse: "contrato entre N. N., por una parte, y X. Y., por otra parte"; o "contrato entre N. N., otorgante, y X. Y., concesionario," etc., según las circunstancias. Cuando en el cuerpo del documento se diga, *the said party of the first part*, etc., puede decirse: "el dicho N. N.," "dicho otorgante," "el mencionado otorgante," etc. II. a. de partido; (blas.) partido, dividido.—**p.-colored**, de varios colores.—**p. jury**, (Ingl.) jurado mixto (de ingleses y extranjeros).—**p. line, p. wire**, (elec.) línea de teléfonos agrupados en un mismo circuito y usados por dos o más abonados.—**p. line**, (pol.) posición oficial de un partido político, etc.; (for.) línea divisoria entre dos propiedades colindantes.—**p. man**, (pol.) hombre de partido, partidario.—**p. wall**, pared medianera.

parvenu [párvenįu], s. y a. advenedizo.

parvis [párvis], s. (arq.) atrio.

pas [pa], s. (fr.) paso; baile; precedencia.

paschal [péskal], a. (igl.) pascual.—**p. candle**, o **taper**, cirio pascual.—**p. lamb**, cordero pascual; (P. L.) Jesucristo; agnusdéi.

pasha [pašá o pášą], s. bajá.

pasquinade [pæskwinéid], **pasquin** [péskwin]. I. s. pasquín, pasquinada. II. va. pasquinar.

pass [pæs], va. (pp. PASSED O PAST) pasar; pasar de; pasar por; aprobar (un proyecto, a un alumno); dar, promulgar (una ley); pasar por alto; evacuar, orinar (sangre, etc.); ser aprobado en (un examen, una materia); llevar, conducir; transferir, trasladar; aventajar, exceder; dejar atrás; hacer pasar; consentir, tolerar; admitir, dar entrada.—**to p. a dividend**, no pagar dividendo.—**to p. a resolution**, tomar un acuerdo.—**to p. along**, pasar de uno a otro.—**to p. away**, gastar (el tiempo).—**to p. by**, dispensar, perdonar; omitir; pasar por alto.— **to p. each other, o one another**, cruzarse.—**to p. judgment** = TO P. SENTENCE.—**to p. muster**, pasar revista; valer algo; ser aceptado.—**to p. off**, dar o circular como legítimo lo que no lo es; encajar, colar (moneda falsa, etc.).—**to p. (something) on**, pasar (algo) de unos a otros; transmitir; pasar (algo) a otras personas.—**to p. one's self off as**, echarla o echárselas de.—**to p. one's word for another**, empeñar su palabra por otro.—**to p. over**, atravesar, cruzar, salvar, traspasar; omitir, pasar por alto; excusar.—**to p. sentence**, pronunciar sentencia, dar dictamen.—**to p. the buck**, (fam.) echarle la carga o el muerto a otro.—**to p. the hat**, (fam.) hacer la colecta, pasando el sombrero.—**to p. through**, pasar o hacer pasar por; penetrar.—**to p. up**, (fam.) rechazar, no aceptar (una oferta, etc.).

pass, vn. pasar; andar, correr, transcurrir (el tiempo, etc.); acontecer, ocurrir, suceder; transmitirse; ser aprobado (un proyecto, un alumno); ser admitido, aceptarse, correr; (fam.) colar; portearse (las aves); (esgr.) dar una estocada, hacer un pase; (naipes) pasar, abstenerse de hacer una jugada.—**to p. across**, cruzar.—**to p. along**, pasar de largo.—**to p. around**, circular.—**to p. away**, fallecer, morir; pasar, disiparse, desaparecer.—**to p. beyond**, pasar de; ir más allá de.—**to p. by**, pasar por el lado o cerca de, pasar de largo.—**to p. current**, ser corriente; aceptarse como bueno.—**to p. for**, pasar por, ser tenido o reputado por.—**to p. into**, pasar a; convertirse en.—**to p. off**, pasar, desaparecer (una enfermedad, tempestad, etc.); disiparse.—**to p. on**, seguir, continuar.—**to p. on, o upon**, formar juicio sobre, examinar y decidir sobre, dictaminar.—**to p. out**, salir; (fam.) desmayarse; morir.—**to p. over**, atravesar, cruzar.—**to p. through**, pasar por; atravesar; colarse.

pass, s. paso; (geog.) desfiladero, hoz, puerto; (mar.) rebasadero, pasaje; pase (billete, permiso: de manos, de esgrima); pase (en el juego); (mil.) licencia; salvoconducto; billete de favor o de cumplimiento; situación, estado (de los negocios, de las cosas); aprobación (en un examen).—**p. check**, billete de admisión.

passable [pǽsəbl], a. transitable; pasadero, regular.—**passably** [-bli], adv. pasaderamente.

passage [pǽsidž], s. pasaje; paso, pasada, tránsito; viaje, navegación, travesía; pasadizo, pasillo; callejón; pasaje (de un libro, etc.); trámite y aprobación de un proyecto de ley; (ant.) acontecimiento, episodio; encuentro personal, lance; pasa o migración de las aves; (anat.) meato, canal; (fisiol.) defecación, cámara, deposición.—**p. at arms**, paso de armas; riña.—**p. boat**, escorchapín.—**p. money**, pasaje.

passageway [-wej], s. pasadizo, pasaje.

passbook [pǽsbuk], s. libro de cuenta y razón; libreta de banco.

passé, passée [pæséj], a. pasado, pasada; anticuado, -da; marchito, -ta (fig.).

passementerie [pæsméntri], s. pasamanería.

passenger [pǽsəndžœr], s. pasajero, transeúnte, mf.; viajero, viandante, mf.—**p. car**, (aut., f. c.) coche de viajeros.—**p. miles**, (aer., f. c.) millas-pasajeros.—**p. office**, oficina de pasajes.—**p. pigeon**, (E. U., orn.) cierta paloma silvestre ya extinta.

passe partout [pæs partú], s. (fr.) paspartú; marco ligero de vidrio y cartón; llave maestra.

passer(-by) [pǽsœr)(-báj], s. transeúnte, mf., viandante, mf.

Passeres [pǽseriz], **Passeriformes** [pæserifórmiz], s. pl. (zool.) paserinos, pájaros (división de las aves).

passerine [pǽserin], a. y s. (orn.) paserino.

passibility [pæsibíliti], s. pasibilidad.

passible [pǽsibl], a. pasible.

passifloraceous [pæsiflœréišʌs], a. (bot.) pasifloreo, pasifloráceo.

passim [pǽsim], adv. (lat.) pássim, aquí y allá.

passing [pǽsiŋ]. I. a. que pasa; de paso, pasajero, transitorio, momentáneo; casual; corriente.—**p. grade**, calificación que permite ser aprobado (en un examen, etc.). II. adv. (ant.) eminentemente, sumamente. III. s. paso, pasada; transcurso o paso (del tiempo); tránsito; muerte, f.; aprobación (de una ley, de un estudiante, etc.); paso, ascenso de una clase a otra (en los estudios).—**p. bell**, toque de difuntos, posa, doble.—**in p.**, de paso, al paso; al pasar; entre paréntesis.

passion [pǽšọn], s. pasión; cólera, ira, saña; ardor; amor apasionado, o su objeto; manía; (P.) Pasión (de Cristo).—**p. flower**, (bot.) pasionaria, granadilla.—**P. play**, drama de la Pasión, drama religioso en que se representa la Pasión.—**p. vine** = **p. flower**.—**P. Week**, semana de Pasión, semana santa.

passional [-al], a. pasional, emotivo.

passionate [pǽšọnịt], a. apasionado; pasional; ardiente; impetuoso; colérico, arrebatado.—**passionately** [-li], adv. apasionadamente; ardientemente; coléricamente.—**passionateness** [-njs], s. apasionamiento, vehemencia, impetuosidad.

passionless [pǽšọnlịs], a. frío, sin pasiones.

passive [pǽsiv]. I. a. pasivo; inerte; (aer.) sin motor. II. s. (gram.) voz pasiva.—**passively** [-li], adv. pasivamente.—**passiveness** [-njs], **passivity** [pæsívịti], s. pasividad; inercia.

passkey [pǽski], s. llave maestra; llavín.

Passover [-ọuvœr)(r], s. (igl.) pascua de los hebreos.

passport [-pọrt], s. pasaporte; salvoconducto.

password [-wœrd], s. (mil.) palabra (de pase); santo y seña, contraseña.

past [pæst]. I. pp. y (raro) pret. de TO PASS. II. a. pasado, último; transcurrido; concluído; terminado; ex, que fué (presidente, director, etc.).—**p. master of**, experto o sobresaliente en.—**p. participle**, (gram.) participio pasivo.—**p. perfect**, pretérito perfecto.—**p. tense**, pretérito. III. s. (lo) pasado; antecedentes, m. pl., historia; (gram.) pretérito; pasado.—**in the p.**, antes, en tiempos pasados. IV. prep. más de, después de (tiempo); más allá de, fuera de (lugar); fuera de, sin.—**p. a doubt**, fuera de duda.—**p. bearing**, insoportable; infecundo.—**p. cure**, incurable.—**p. dispute**, incontestable, fuera de duda.—**p. hope**, sin esperanza.—**half (quarter, etc.) p. two**, las dos y media (cuarto, etc.).—**p. question**, fuera de duda, indudable.—**p. recovery**, desahuciado, sin remedio.—**p. remedy**, irremediable.

paste [pejst]. I. s. pasta; engrudo; (coc.) pasta; (joy.) imitación de piedras preciosas.—**p. brush**, empastador. II. va. engrudar, empastar, pegar, adosar.

pasteboard [-bọrd]. I. s. cartón. II. a. de cartón; acartonado.

pastel [pæstél]. I. s. (b. a.) pastel; pintura al pastel; clarioncillo (barra); (bot.) hierba pastel. V. WOAD. II. va. y vn. pintar al pastel.

pastel(l)ist [pæstelist], s. (b. a.) pastelista.

paster [pejstœr)(r], s. engrudador, persona que empasta; papel engomado por un lado.

pastern [pǽstœrn], s. cuartilla, trabadero o cerruma del caballo.—**p. bone**, (vet.) falange, f.—**p. joint**, articulación de las falanges.

pasteurization [pæstœrịzéjšọn], s. paste(u)rización.—**pasteurize** [-ajz], va. paste(u)rizar.—**pasteurizer** [-œr)(r], s. paste(u)rizador (aparato).

pastille [pǽstịl o pæstíl], s. pastilla, tableta; (b. a.) pastel.

pastime [pǽstajm], s. pasatiempo; distracción.

pastor [pǽstọr)(r], s. pastor espiritual, cura, m., párroco, clérigo; (orn.) estornino copetudo o rosado.

pastoral [-al]. I. a. (leng. ord. y poét.) pastoril, pastoral, pastoricio; (igl.) pastoral.—**p. life**, pastoría. II. s. (poét.) pastoral, f., bucólica; idilio, pastorela; (igl.) (carta) pastoral, f.—**pastorally** [-i], adv. pastoril o pastoralmente.

pastorate [-it], **pastorship** [-šip], s. curato; cura de almas.

pastourelle [pæsturél], s. (poét.) pastorela.

pastry [pejstri], s. (coc.) pastelería, pasteles, pl., pastas, pl.—**p. cook**, pastelero, repostero.—**p. shell**, pocito de hojaldre.—**p. shop**, pastelería, repostería.

pasturable [pǽschụrabl], a. pacedero.

pasturage [pǽschụridž], s. pastos, pl., pastura; pastoraje; apacentamiento, adehesamiento.

pasture [pǽschụr)(r]. I. s. apacentadero, dehesa, herbaje, pastura, pasto; apacentamiento, pacedura.—**p. ground**, dehesa, pradera, prado, pastizal, acampo. II. va. pastar, apacentar, pastorear, herbajar. III. vn. pastar, pacer.

pasturing [-iŋ], s. pastoreo; apacentamiento.

pasty [pejsti]. I. a. pastoso. II. s. pastel de carne.

pat [pæt]. I. a. exacto, oportuno, propio, pintiparado, a(l) pelo, bueno, cómodo; fijo, firme (V. TO STAND PAT).—**to have, o know p.**, (fam.) saber al dedillo. II. adv. justamente, convenientemente, a propósito. III. s. golpecito, palmadita; fiest(ecill)a, caricia, mamola; ruido ligero de pasos (*V.* PATTER); porción pequeña de mantequilla, etc., amoldada.—**p. on the back,** (fam.) felicitación, enhorabuena. **IV.** *va.* golpear ligeramente; allanar suavemente; dar palmaditas a, acariciar, pasar la mano sobre, hacer la mamola a.—**to p. one's self on the back,** esponjarse, hincharse. **V.** *vn.* golpear ligeramente.

Patagonian [pætɐɡóunįɐn], *s.* y *a.* patagón.

patch [pǽch]. **I.** *va.* remendar, apedazar, apañar; pegar; chapucear, chafallar; ponerse lunares postizos. **II.** *vn.* echar remiendos, hacer labor de retazos. **III.** *s.* remiendo; parche, apaño; material para remiendos; pieza embutida en taracea; lunar postizo; (farm.) parche, pegado; (med.) placa (en las mucosas); (agr.) mancha; sembrado (de trigo, etc.); (aer.) parche.—**p. of land,** o **ground,** pedazo de terreno.—**p. pocket,** (sast.) bolsillo sobrepuesto o de parche.—**tube p.,** (aut.) parche para cámara.

patcher [-œ(r)], *s.* remendón; chafallón.

patchouli [pǽchųlį], *s.* pachulí (planta y perfume).

patchwork [pǽchwœrk], *s.* obra o labor (*f.*) de retacitos; centón; remiendo, chapucería.

patchy [pǽchį], *a.* muy remendado; como de remiendos; deshilvanado.

pate [peįt], *s.* (fam.) cabeza; coronilla; seso(s).

pâté [patéį], *s.* (fr.) (coc.) pastelillo, empanada.

patella [pɐtélɐ], *s.* (anat.) rótula; (zool.) parte (*f.*) semejante a una copa; (arqueol.) cazoleta.

patellar [-(r)], *a.* (anat.) patelar, rotular.

paten [pǽtɐn], *s.* (igl.) patena.

patent [pǽtɐnt]. **I.** *a.* patente, manifiesto; público; patentado.—**p. insides** = PLATE MATTER. —**p. law,** ley (*f.*) de patentes; derecho patentario.—**p. leather,** charol.—**p. medicine,** remedio de patente.—**P. Office,** oficina de patentes. **II.** *s.* patente, *f.,* privilegio de invención; título, diploma, *m.,* despacho.—**p. applied for,** se ha solicitado patente. **III.** *va.* patentar.

patentable [-ɐbl], *a.* patentable.

patentee [-í], *s.* el que obtiene una patente.

patentor [-ǫ(r)], *s.* el que otorga una patente.

patera [pǽtɐrɐ], *s.* pátera.

paternal [pɐtœrnɐl], *a.* paternal, paterno.

paternalism [-įzm], *s.* gobierno paternal.

paternally [-į], *adv.* paternalmente.

paternity [pɐtœrnįtį], *s.* paternidad; linaje, alcurnia por parte de padre.

paternoster [péįtœrnástœ(r)], *s.* padrenuestro.

path [pæθ], *s.* senda, sendero; vereda; camino, vía; andador (en un jardín, etc.); línea; trayectoria.

pathetic(al [pɐθétįk(ɐl], *a.* patético o conmovedor.—**pathetically** [-į], *adv.* patéticamente.— **patheticalness** [-nįs], *s.* patetismo.

pathfinder [pǽθfaįndœ(r)], *s.* explorador; el que descubre, abre o traza nuevas rutas, etc.

pathless [pǽθlįs], *a.* sin camino, vereda o senda.

pathogene [pǽθodžin], *s.* microbio patógeno.

pathogenic [-dźénįk], *a.* patógeno.

pathogeny [pɐθádźenį], *s.* (med.) patogenia.

pathological [pæθɐládźįk(ɐl], *a.* patológico.

pathologist [pɐθálodźįst], *s.* patólogo.

pathology [-dźį], *s.* (med.) patología.

pathos [péįθas], *s.* rasgo conmovedor; lo que infunde tristeza, compasión, etc.; sentimiento.

pathway [pǽθweį], *s.* senda, vereda, andada.

patience [péįšęns], *s.* paciencia; sufrimiento.

patient [péįšęnt]. **I.** *a.* paciente, pacienzudo; asiduo, perseverante; sufrido. **II.** *s.* paciente, sujeto pasivo; (med.) paciente, enfermo, doliente.

patiently [-lį], *adv.* pacientemente.

patina [pǽtįnɐ], *s.* pátina.

patly [pǽtlį], *adv.* a propósito, convenientemente.

patness [pǽtnįs], *s.* oportunidad, conveniencia.

patois [pǽtwa], *s.* patuá, *m.,* jerga, dialecto.

patriarch [péįtrįark], *s.* patriarca, *m.*

patriarchal [-árkɐl], *a.* patriarcal.

patriarchate, patriarchship, patriarchy [-eįt, -šįp, -į], *s.* patriarcado.

patrician [pɐtríšɐn], *a.* y *s.* patricio.

patriciate [pɐtríšįeįt], *s.* patriciado.

patricide [pǽtrįsaįd], *s.* parricida, *mf.;* parricidio.

patrilineal [-línįɐl], *a.* de o por la línea paterna.

patrimonial [-móunįɐl], *a.* patrimonial.

patrimony [pǽtrįmonį], *s.* patrimonio.

patriot [péįtrįǫt], *s.* patriota, *mf.*

patrioteer [-ŗ]. **I.** *s.* (fam.) patriotero. **II.** *vn.* alardear de patriotismo, darse a la patriotería.

patriotic [peįtrįátįk], *a.* patriótico.—**patriotically** [-ɐlį], *adv.* patrióticamente.

patriotism [péįtrįǫtįzm], *s.* patriotismo, civismo.

patristic(al [pɐtrístįk(ɐl], *a.* patrístico.

patristic(s [-(s], *s.* (igl.) patrística, patrología.

patrol [pɐtróul]. **I.** *s.* patrulla; ronda.—**p. boat,** escampavía.—**p. plane,** avión patrullero, aparato de patrulla.—**p. wagon,** camión (*m.*) o diligencia de la policía. **II.** *va.* y *vn.* patrullar, rondar; hacer la ronda.

patrolman [-mɐn], *s.* patrullador, rondador; guardia (*m.*) municipal, agente o vigilante de policía.

patrology [pɐtrálodźį], *s.* (igl.) patrología.

patron [péįtrǫn], *s.* patrón, patrono, patrocinador, protector; padrino, apadrinador; cliente, parroquiano; (igl.) patrono.—**p. saint,** santo patrón; santo titular de una iglesia.

patronage [-įdź], *s.* patrocinio, amparo, auspicio, padrinazgo; mecenazgo; clientela, parroquia; (igl.) patronato, patronazgo.

patronal [-ɐl], *a.* patronal.

patroness [-įs], *s.* patrona, protectora; patrocinadora, madrina.

patronize [-aįz], *va.* patrocinar, proteger, apadrinar; auspiciar, apoyar, fomentar; condescender con altivez; tratar con arrogante condescendencia; ser concurrente a, o parroquiano de.

patronizer [-œ(r)], *s.* patrocinador.

patronizing [-įŋ], *a.* fatua o desdeñosamente condescendiente.—**patronizingly** [-lį], *adv.* con arrogante condescendencia, con aire de superioridad.

patronless [-lįs], *a.* desamparado.

patronymic [pætronímįk], *s.* y *a.* patronímico.

patten [pǽtɐn], *s.* zueco, chanclo, choclo, galocha; (arq.) cimiento, fundamento.

patter [pǽtœ(r)]. **I.** *vn.* hacer ruido acompasado; charlar, parlar.—**to p. with the feet,** patalear, patear. **II.** *s.* sucesión de golpecitos o palmaditas; pataleo; parlería, charla.

pattern [pǽtœrn]. **I.** *s.* modelo, pauta, norma; ejemplar; muestra; patrón, dechado; (mec.) molde, plantilla, escantillón. **II.** *va.* copiar, imitar; servir de ejemplo.

patty [pǽtį], *s.* (coc.) pastelillo, empanada, fajardo, torta.—**p. pan,** tartera.

patulous [pǽchųlɐs], *a.* abierto, extendido.

paucity [pósįtį], *s.* poquedad, escasez, corto número; exigüidad, insuficiencia.

pauldron [póldrǫn], *s.* (arm.) hombrera.

Pauline [pólaįn], *a.* referente a San Pablo.

paulownia [polóunįɐ], *s.* (bot.) paulonia.

paunch [pónch], *s.* panza, barriga, vientre; panza de los rumiantes; borde de una campana; (mar.) pallete, jimelga.

paunchy [-į], *a.* = POT-BELLIED.

pauper [pópœ(r)], *s.* pobre, *mf.,* indigente, *mf.* — **pauperism** [-įzm], *s.* pauperismo, indigencia. —**pauperization** [-įzéįšǫn], *s.* empobrecimiento.—**pauperize** [-aįz], *va.* depauperar, empobrecer.

pause [póz]. **I.** *s.* pausa; (pros.) hiato, cesura; irresolución, vacilación; (mús.) espera, fermata. **II.** *vn.* pausar, cesar, parar, detenerse; vacilar.

pausingly [-įŋlį], *adv.* por pausas; después de un intervalo.

pavan [pǽvan], s. (danz.) pavana.
pave [péiv], va. pavimentar, empedrar, enladrillar, adoquinar, enlosar, embaldosar.—**to p. the way**, facilitar, preparar el terreno, abrir el camino.—**paved road**, carretera pavimentada, camino asfaltado.
pavement [-ment], s. pavimento, empedrado, adoquinado, piso, suelo; pavimentación.
paver [-œ(r)], **pavier** [-yœ(r)], o **pavior**, s. empedrador, enlosador, solador.—**p.'s beetle**, pisón.
pavilion [pavílyon], s. pabellón, tienda de campaña; quiosco, glorieta, cenador de jardín; dosel; cobertizo; (anat.) pabellón de la oreja; (arq.) pabellón, ala.
paving [péiviŋ]. I. s. pavimento; pavimentación; material de pavimentar. II. a. de pavimentar, para pavimentos.—**p. hammer**, aciche.—**p. stone**, adoquín.—**p. tile**, baldosa, loseta.
pavis(e [pǽvis], s. pavés, escudo oblongo.
pavonine [pǽvonain], a. relativo al pavo real; iridescente.
paw [po]. I. s. garra, zarpa, pata; (fam.) mano(ta). II. va. y vn. patear, piafar; escarbar; (fam.) manosear.
pawl [pol], s. linguete, trinquete; fiador de rueda; paleta de reloj; diente de encaje, retén, seguro.
pawn [pon]. I. va. empeñar, pignorar, dar en prenda. II. s. prenda, empeño; peón de ajedrez. —**p. ticket**, papeleta de empeño.—**in p.**, en prenda.
pawnbroker [-broukœ(r)], s. prestamista sobre prendas, prendero, usurero; comodatario.
pawnee [poní], s. prestador, prestamista sobre prendas.—**P.**, tribu (f.) de indios norteamericanos.
pawner [pónœ(r)], s. empeñador, prendador.
pawnshop [pónšap], s. casa de empeños.
pax [pæks], s. (lat.) paz; (igl.) paz (patena y el acto de besarla en la misa).
pay [péi]. I. va. (pret. y pp. PAID) pagar; recompensar, remunerar, abonar, saldar (una cuenta); producir ganancia o provecho a; (mar.) embrear.—**to p. a call**, o **a visit**, hacer una visita. —**to p. a compliment**, hacer un cumplido, echar una flor; (fam.) chicolear, piropear.—**to p. attention**, prestar atención; fijarse o reparar (en), atender (a), hacer caso (de); galantear, cortejar.—**to p. back**, devolver, restituir, reembolsar; pagar en la misma moneda, vengarse de.—**to p. by instalments**, pagar a plazos.—**to p. cash**, pagar al contado.—**to p. court**, hacer la corte.—**to p. down**, pagar a buena cuenta o como primer plazo.—**to p. expenses**, cubrir los gastos.—**to p. for**, pagar, costear.—**to p. in full**, pagar por completo, pagar totalmente.—**to p. homage** (to), rendir homenaje o culto (a).—**to p. off** = TO P. OUT; pagar; pagar por completo; pagar a y despedir (el personal de un taller, buque, etc.); redimir (una hipoteca, etc.); vengarse de, ajustarle a uno las cuentas.—**to p. on account**, pagar a buena cuenta.—**to p. one's addresses to**, cortejar, pretender en matrimonio.—**to p. one's respects**, presentar u ofrecer sus respetos.—**to p. one's score**, pagar sus deudas, su escote.—**to p. (one) out**, vengarse de, desquitarse de.—**to p. out**, ir aflojando o dando (una cuerda), largar, arriar (un cabo).— **to p. reverence to**, rendir homenaje a; inclinarse ante.—**to p. the cost of**, costear.—**to p. up**, pagar por completo.—**to p. the fiddler**, o **the piper**, pagar el pato, pagar los vidrios rotos. II. vn. pagar; (a veces con **off**) compensar, ser provechoso o ganancioso, costearse; dar resultados, valer la pena.—**to p. by instalments**, pagar a plazos.—**to p. dear**, o **dearly**, costarle a uno caro.—**to p. in full**, pagar totalmente o del todo.—**to p. through the nose**, pagar excesivamente caro. III. s. paga, sueldo, salario, gaje(s), jornal; recompensa, galardón.

—**p. bill**, **voucher** o **warrant**, vale, boletín, póliza, libramiento.—**p. clerk**, pagador.—**p. dirt** (rock, etc.), (min.) tierra (roca, etc.) que da oro con ganancia.—**p. load**, carga de paga. —**p. list**, **p. roll**, nómina; lista de jornales.— **bad** (**good**) **p.**, mal (buen) pagador.
payable [-abl], a. pagadero, pagable; reembolsable.—**p. in advance**, pagadero por adelantado.
payday [-dei], s. día (m.) de pagos o de paga.
payee [peíí], s. tenedor, portador, persona a quien se paga o debe pagarse una letra, cheque, etc.
payer [péíœ(r)], s. pagador.
paying [péíiŋ], s. acto de pagar, etc.; (mar.) embreadura.—**p. teller**, pagador (de un banco).
paymaster [péimæstœ(r)], s. pagador, contador; (mil.) habilitado.—**p.'s office**, pagaduría.
payment [péiment], s. pago, paga; recompensa, premio.—**p. in advance**, anticipo, pago adelantado.—**p. in full**, pago total; saldo, finiquito.—**in part p.**, a buena cuenta.—**on the p. of**, mediante el pago de.—**to make p.**, efectuar un pago.—**to present for p.**, presentar al cobro.
paymistress [péimistris], s. pagadora.
pay-off [péí of], s. el acto o tiempo de pagar un sueldo, etc.; (fam.) resultado final; día (m.) de ajustar cuentas.
pea [pi], s. (bot.) guisante, chícharo, pésol.—**p. coal**, carbón muy menudo.—**p. green**, verde claro.—**p. gun** o **shooter**, bodoquera, cerbatana.—**p. jacket**, chaquetón de marinero.—**p. pod**, **p. shell**, vaina de guisante.—**p.-shaped**, pisiforme.—**p. weevil**, (ent.) gorgojo.
peace [pis]. I. s. paz; concordia; orden; descanso, reposo, tranquilidad; (fig.) oliva.—**p. at any price**, la paz a toda costa.—**p. be with you**, la paz sea con vosotros.—**p. establishment**, o **footing**, (mil.) pie (m.) de paz.—**p. offer**, oferta de paz.—**p. offering**, sacrificio propiciatorio.—**p. officer**, alguacil, guardia (m.) civil o municipal.—**p. overture**, sondeo de paz.— **p. pipe** = CALUMET.—**at p.**, en paz. II. interj. ¡paz! ¡silencio!
peaceable [písabl], a. tranquilo, pacífico, apacible. —**peaceableness** [-nis], s. tranquilidad, calidad de pacífico.—**peaceably** [-bli], adv. pacíficamente, tranquilamente.
peacebreaker [písbreikœ(r)], s. perturbador de la paz; alborotador.
peaceful [písful], a. tranquilo, apacible, pacífico. —**peacefully** [-i], adv. tranquilamente; pacíficamente.—**peacefulness** [-nis], s. quietud, calma.
peacemaker [písmeikœ(r)], s. pacificador; reconciliador.
peacetime [pístaim]. I. s. período o época de paz. II. a. relativo a, o propio de, paz; tal período.
peach [pích]. I. s. (bot.) durazno, melocotón, pérsico, abridero; color de durazno; (fam.) persona o cosa admirable.—**p. tree**, melocotonero; durazn(er)o, pérsico, abridor. II. vn. hacerse delator de un cómplice.
peachy [-i], a. semejante al durazno; (fam.) magnífico, excelente, muy agradable.
peacock [píkak]. I. s. (orn.) pavón o pavo real.— **p. fish**, (ict.) budión, m., doncella, pavo. II. vn. pavonear(se).
peafowl [pífaul], s. = PEACOCK o PEAHEN.
peahen [píhen], s. (orn.) pava real.
peak [pik]. I. s. cima, cumbre, pico, picacho; cúspide, f.; visera (de gorra); período álgido o culminante; máximo (ú. t. como a.); (mar.) penol, pico, espiga de vela; delgado o racel (de proa o de popa); uña del ancla.—**p. halyards**, (mar.) drizas de la pena.—**at p. level**, en auge de producción, en producción máxima, con el máximo de capacidad. II. vn. tener apariencia de enfermo. III. va. (mar.) amantillar el pico, levantar una verga contra el mástil.
peaked [pikt o píkid], a. puntiagudo, picoteado, picudo; (arq.) con caballete; [píkid], flacucho,

enfermizo.—**p. beard**, barba en punta.—**p. cap**, gorra de visera.

peal [pil]. I. *s.* repique de campanas; estruendo, estrépito.—**p. of laughter**, carcajada, risotada.—**p.-ringing**, repiqueteo. II. *va.* y *vn.* repicar, repiquetear; retronar.

pean [pían], *s.* = PÆAN.

peanut [pínʌt], *s.* (bot.) cacahué, cacahuete, maní.—**p. butter**, pasta de cacahuetes tostados.—**p. candy**, o **brittle**, crocante o guirlache de cacahuetes.—**p. gallery**, (fam., teat.) gallinero, paraíso.—**p. vender**, cacahuetero, manicero.

pear [per], *s.* (bot.) pera.—**p. orchard**, per(al)eda.—**p.-shaped**, piriforme.—**p. tree**, o **wood**, peral.

pearl [pɶrl]. I. *s.* perla, margarita, barrueco, aljófar; nácar, madreperla; (farm.) perla; (med.) catarata en el ojo; (impr.) perla, tipo de 5 puntos.—**p. barley**, cebada perlada.—**p. button**, botón de nácar.—**p.-colored**, perlino.—**p. fishery**, pesquería de perlas, (Am.) placer.—**p. oyster**, ostra que produce perlas.—**p. powder**, **p. white**, blanco de perla.—**p. seed**, aljófar, rostrillo. II. *va.* perlificar, aljofarar. *V.* PURL.

pearlash [-æš], *s.* carbonato potásico.

pearled [-d], *a.* perlado, aljofarado.

pearlstone [-stoun], *s.* (petr.) perlita, fonolita.

pearly [-i], *a.* perlino; aljofarado; nacarado.—**p. gates**, (fig.) cielo.—**p. nautilus**, (zool.) nautilo.

pearmain [pérmein], *s.* (bot.) pero.

peasant [pézant]. I. *s.* labriego, labrador, campesino, aldeano, villano. II. *a.* campesino, rústico.

peasantry [-ri], *s.* paisanaje, gente (*f.*) del campo, lugareños, (Am.) campesinaje, -ado.

peas(e)cod [pízkad], *s.* vaina de los guisantes.

peat [pít], *s.* turba.—**p. bog** o **bed**, turbal, turbera.—**p. (char)coal**, carbón de turba.—**p. moss**, musgo de pantano; turbera.

peaty [-i], *a.* turboso.

peav(e)y [pívi], *s.* garfio, palanca con gancho.

pebble [pébl]. I. *s.* guija(rro), china, piedrecica; cuero abollonado; pólvora gruesa; lente (*mf.*) de cristal de roca. II. *va.* granular, abollonar cuero; enchinar(rar); arrojar chinas o guijas a.

pebbly [pébli], *a.* guij(arr)oso, guijeño.

pecan [píkæn], *s.* (bot.) pacana (árbol y nuez).

peccability [pekəbíliti], *s.* fragilidad.

peccable [pékabl], *a.* pecable.

peccadillo [pekədílou], *s.* pecadillo.—**peccadillo(e)s** [-z], (fam.) peccata minuta.

peccancy [pékansi], *s.* calidad de pecaminoso; pecado, vicio, defecto.

peccant [pékant], *a.* pecador, pecante; corrompido; malsano, morboso.

peccary [pékari], *s.* (Am., zool.) pecarí, saíno.

peck [pék]. I. *s.* medida de áridos (¼ de *bushel*), celemín; montón, gran cantidad; pic(ot)azo, picotada. II. *va.* picotear; picar. III. *vn.* picotear; recoger (alimento) con el pico.—**to p. at**, regañar de continuo; (fam.) picar, mordiscar.

pecker [-ɶ(r)], *s.* picoteador; (zapa)pico; (orn.) pico verde, picamaderos.

pectate [pékteit], *s.* (quím.) pectato.

pecten [pékten], *s.* (anat., zool.) peine, o algo parecido; membrana del ojo de los pájaros y ciertos reptiles; hueso pubis; pecten, peine (*V.* SCALLOP).

pectic [péktik], *a.* (quím.) péctico (ácido).

pectin [péktin], *s.* (quím.) pectina.

pectinate(d [-eit(id], *a.* (anat., bot., etc.) pectiniforme, pectíneo, parecido a un peine.

pectineal [pektínial], *a.* (anat.) pectíneo, referente al músculo de este nombre; referente al hueso pubis.

pectineus [-ias], *s.* (anat.) pectíneo (músculo).

pectoral [péktoral]. I. *a.* pectoral.—**p. cross**, (igl.) pectoral.—**p. fin**, (ict.) aleta pectoral.

II. *s.* adorno para el pecho; (anat.) órgano o músculo pectoral; (farm.) pectoral; (arm.) peto.

pectose [péktous], *s.* (quím.) pectosa.

peculate [pékyuleit], *vn.* y *va.* desfalcar, malversar; hurtar, robar.—**peculation** [-éišon], *s.* (for.) peculado, malversación, desfalco.—**peculator** [-ǫ(r)], *s.* desfalcador, malversador.

peculiar [pikjúljǎ(r)]. I. *a.* (a veces con **to**) peculiar, privativo, particular, individual, propio (de); especial, singular, raro, extraordinario. II. *s.* propiedad particular; (Ingl., igl.) parroquia independiente.

peculiarity [pikjuliériti], *s.* peculiaridad, particularidad, singularidad; individualidad.

peculiarly [pikjúlyǎrli], *adv.* peculiarmente, particularmente.

peculium [pikjúljʌm], *s.* (for.) peculio, pegujal.

pecuniarily [pikjúnjerili], *adv.* pecuniariamente.

pecuniary [-ieri], *a.* pecuniario, monetario.

pecunious [-ias], *a.* rico, adinerado.

pedagogic(al [pedagádžik(al], *a.* pedagógico.

pedagogics [-džiks], *s.* pedagogía.

pedagogism [pédagagizm], *s.* sistema, *m.*, profesión, carácter o método de los pedagogos.

pedagogue [pédagag], *s.* pedagogo; maestro de escuela; pedante.

pedagogy [pédagoudži], *s.* pedagogía.

pedal [pédal]. I. *a.* del pie o del pedal.—**p. pipe**, cañón del órgano correspondiente a los pedales. II. *s.* pedal; (mús.) pedal; contra, *m.*, bajo de órgano.—**p. (point)**, (mús.) pedal. III. *vn.* pedalear.

pedant [pédant], *s.* pedante.—**pedantic(al** [pidántik(al], *a.* pedante(sco).—**pedantically** [-i], *adv.* pedantescamente.—**pedantism** [pédantizm], **pedantry** [-ri], *s.* pedantería, pedantismo.—**pedantize** [-aiz], *vn.* pedantear.

Pedata [pidéitǎ], *s.* *pl.* (zool.) pedatos.

pedate [pédeit], *a.* (zool.) que tiene pies; parecido a un pie; (bot.) palmeado.

peddle [pédl]. I. *va.* vender como buhonero; vender menudencias (esp. legumbres y frutas) de casa en casa. II. *vn.* ser buhonero.

peddler [pédlɶ(r)], *s.* buhonero, mercachifle, baratillero, (Am.) pacotillero, achín.—**peddlery** [-i], *s.* buhonería, (Am.) achinería.

peddling [pédliŋ], *a.* baladí, frívolo.

pederast [pédɶræst], *s.* pederasta, *m.*

pederasty [-i], *s.* pederastia.

pedestal [pédestal], *s.* (arq.) pedestal, basa, pilar, peana; (mec.) cojinete, soporte; caballete.

pedestrian [pidéstrian]. I. *s.* caminante, andante, pe(at)ón. II. *a.* pedestre; vulgar.

pediatric [pidiǽtrik], *a.* pediátrico.—**pediatrician** [pidiatríšan], **pediatrist** [pidiǽtrist], *s.* pediatra, *mf.*

pediatrics [-s], *s.* (med.) pediatría.

pedicel [pédisel], *s.* pedúnculo, pedículo, cabillo.

pedicellate [-eit], *a.* (bot., zool.) pedunculado.

pedicle [pédikl], *s.* (bot., zool.) pedículo, pedúnculo; (med.) pedículo.

pedicular, o **pediculous** [pidíkyuljǎ(r), -lʌs], *a.* piojoso; (med.) pedicular.

pedicure [pédikyur], *s.* quiropodia; pedicuro, callista.

pediform [pédiform], *a.* pediforme.

pedigree [pédigri], *s.* genealogía, linaje, estirpe, *f.*, árbol genealógico; ejecutoria.

pediluvium [pedilúvjʌm], *s.* (med.) pediluvio, baño de pies.

pediment [pédiment], *s.* (arq.) frontón, tímpano.

pedlar, **pedler** [pédlɶ(r)], *s.* = PEDDLER.

pedobaptism [pidobǽptizm], *s.* bautismo de los niños.

pedology [pidálodži], *s.* pedología, paidología, estudio de la niñez; pedología.

pedometer [pidámetɶ(r)], *s.* podómetro o pedómetro, (h)odómetro, cuentapasos; pedómetro (para medir los niños).

pedotrophy [pidátrafi], *s.* pedotrofia.

peduncle [pidʌŋkl], *s.* (anat., zool. y bot.) pedúnculo, pedículo.—**peduncular** [-kjulə̯(r)], *a.* peduncular.—**pedunculat(ed** [-kjuleı̯t(ı̯d], *a.* pedunculado.

peek [pik]. I. *vn.* atisbar. *V.* PEEP y PRY. II. *s.* atisbo, atisbadura.

peekaboo [píkabu]. I. *s.* escondite, juego de niños. II. *a.* (fam.) transparente (blusa, etc.).

peel [píl]. I. *va.* (a veces con **off**) descortezar, pelar, deshollejar, mondar. II. *vn.* desconcharse, descascararse, pelarse. III. *s.* corteza, cáscara; piel, *f.*, pellejo, hollejo; tel(ill)a de cebolla; pala de horno; (mar.) pala del remo; (impr.) espito, colgador.

peeler [-œ(r)], *s.* pelador, mondador, descortezador.

peeling [-ıŋ], *s.* peladura, mondadura, desconchadura, hollejo.

peen [pin], *s.* boca, corte o punta (del martillo).— **p. hammer**, martillo de punta, o de dos bocas.

peep [píp]. I. *vn.* atisbar, fisgar, mirar a hurtadillas; asomar, mostrarse; piar, pipiar.—**not to p.**, (fam.) no chistar. II. *s.* atisbo, atisbadura; mirada, ojeada; atisbadero; (arti.) mira; asomo; pío, piada de pájaros.—**p. show**, mundonuevo, tutilimundi.—**p. sight**, (arti.) mira o brújula de puntería.—**p. window**, postigo. *V.* PEEP-HOLE.—**at the p. of day**, al despuntar el día.

peeper [-œ(r)], *s.* atisbador, fisgón; (fam.) ojo; pollito que pía.

peephole [-houl], *s.* mirilla, atisbadero.

peeping [-ıŋ]. I. *a.* piador; piante. II. *s.* piada.

peer [pír]. I. *vn.* atisbar, fisgar, husmear; escudriñar; (poét.) asomar, salir, aparecer. II. *s.* par, igual; (Ingl.) par (título).

peerage [-ıdʒ], *s.* (Ingl.) dignidad de par; la grandeza, la nobleza.

peeress [-ıs], *s.* (Ingl.) mujer que tiene título de nobleza; paresa; mujer de un par.

peering [-ıŋ]. I. *a.* que atisba, etc. II. *s.* atisbadura.

peerless [-lıs], *a.* sin par, impar, incomparable.— **peerlessly** [-lı], *adv.* incomparablemente.— **peerlessness** [-nıs], *s.* calidad de incomparable.

peeve [pív]. I. *va.* y *vn.* (fam.) irritar(se), poner(se) de mal humor. II. *s.* (fam.) enojo, inquina, tema.

peevish [-ıš], *a.* malhumorado, displicente, rencilloso, enojadizo, de malas pulgas.—**peevishly** [-lı], *adv.* con displicencia y malhumor.— **peevishness** [-nıs], *s.* displicencia, mal humor.

peg [peg]. I. *s.* clavija, espiga, taco, sobina, espiga; tarugo; (zap.) estaquilla; espita (de cuba); colgadero; pernete, saetín; (mar.) cabilla; (mús.) clavija; (fig.) pretexto o excusa; (fam.) grado.—**p. ladder**, (min.) espárrago, escala de cotorra.—**p. leg**, pierna de palo; (fam.) el que la lleva.—**p. top**, peón, peonza.— **p.-top**, de forma de peón (pantalón o falda). —**to take down a p.**, humillar, bajarle a uno los humos. II. *va.* estaquillar, clavar; enclavijar (una guitarra, etc.); (mar.) encabillar; (a veces con **out**) estacar, jalon(e)ar; estabilizar, fijar o sostener el valor o precio de; (fam.) arrojar, asestar. III. *vn.* (gen. con **away**) afanarse; trabajar con ahinco.—**pegging awl**, estaquillador.

peganite [péganaı̯t], *s.* (min.) peganita.

Pegasean [pɛgasíən], *a.* pegaseo.

Pegasus [pégasʌs], *s.* (mit., astr.) Pegaso.

pegbox [pégbaks], *s.* clavijero (de guitarra, violín, etc.).

pegmatite [pégmataı̯t], *s.* (petr.) pegmatita.

peignoir [peı̯nwár], *s.* peinador, bata.

pejorative [pídʒoreı̯tıv]. I. *a.* peyorativo, despectivo, despreciativo. II. *s.* palabra despectiva.

pekan [pékan], *s.* (E. U., zool.) especie de marta.

pekin [pikín], *s.* pequín (tela de seda).

Pekingese [pikınʹíz]. I. *a.* de o rel. a Pekín o Peiping. II. *s.* natural o dialecto de Pekín; perro pequinés o pekinés.

pekoe [píkou], *s.* variedad de té negro.

---

pelage [pélıdʒ], *s.* pelaje.

Pelagianism [peléı̯dʒı̯anızm], *s.* pelagianismo.

pelagic [pelédʒık], **pelagian** [peléı̯dʒı̯an], *a.* pelágico, oceánico.—**Pelagian**, *a.* y *s.* pelagiano.

pelargonium [pelargóunı̯ʌm], *s.* (bot.) pelargonio.

Pelasgi [pılǽsdʒaı̯], *s. pl.* pelasgos.—**Pelasgian** [-dʒı̯an], *s.* y *a.*, **Pelasgic** [-dʒık], *a.* pelasgo; pelásgico (*a.*).

pelerine [pélerın], *s.* pelerina o esclavina.

pelf [pelf], *s.* dinero, riquezas mal adquiridas.

pelican [pélıkan], *s.* (orn.) pelícano, alcatraz, *m.* (quím.) alambique; (dent.) gatillo antiguo.

pelisse [pelís], *s.* pelliza; pellón o pellote.

pellagra [peléı̯gra], *s.* (med.) pelagra.

pellagrin [-grın], *s.*, **pellagrous** [-grʌs], *a.* (med.) pelagroso.

pellet [pélıt], *s.* pella, píldora, pelotilla, gránulo; bola, bolita; bodoque; perdigón.

pellicle [pélıkl], *s.* película, cutícula, panículo, túnica, hollejo; binza; lapa, tel(ill)a, nata.

pellicular [pelıkyūlə̯(r)], *a.* pelicular.

pellitory [pélıtorı̯], *s.* (bot.) parietaria, cañarroya. —**p. of Spain**, pelitre.

pell-mell [pélmél], *adv.* confusamente, atropelladamente, a trochemoche.

pellucid [pelı̯úsı̯d], *a.* pelúcido, transparente, diáfano; tra(n)slúcido; claro, cristalino.— **pellucidity** [-sídı̯tı̯], **pellucidness** [-nı̯s], *s.* diafanidad, transparencia; translucencia.

Peloponnesian [peloponíšı̯an], *s.* y *a.* peloponense; peloponesíaco (*a.*).

pelt [pelt]. I. *s.* pellejo, piel, *f.*, cuero, zalea; pelada; golpe, trastazo.—*pl.* corambre.—**at full p.** = AT FULL SPEED. II. *va.* apredrear, llover (piedras o algo análogo) sobre. III. *vn.* arrojar alguna cosa; caer con fuerza (la lluvia, etc.).

pelta [péltə̯], *s.* pelta, adarga ligera.

peltate(d [péltɛı̯t(ı̯d], *a.* escutiforme; (bot.) abroquelado, peciolado por el centro.

peltry [péltrı̯], *s.* peletería, pieles, pellejos, corambre; una sola piel.

pelvic [pélvık], *a.* (anat.) pelviano, pélvico.

pelvimeter [pelvímɛtœ(r)], *s.* pelvímetro.

pelvis [pélvıs], *s.* (anat.) pelvis.

pemmican [pémıkan], *s.* pemicán, especie de tasajo de los indios norteamericanos.

pemphigus [pémfıgas], *s.* (med.) pénfigo.

pen [pen]. I. *s.* pluma (para escribir), péndola, (poét.) péñola, cálamo; escritura, caligrafía; escritor; (orn.) péndola; (orn.) la hembra del cisne; corral, encerradero, pocilga, zahurda.—**p.-and-ink sketch**, boceto a pluma.—**p. name**, seudónimo.—**p. point**, pluma.—**p.-pusher**, escritor de (por) oficio.—**p. stroke**, plumada, plumazo. II. *va.* (pret. y *pp.* PENNED) escribir (con pluma); pergeñar, componer; (*pret.* y *pp.* PENNED o PENT) (a veces con **up**) encerrar, acorralar, enjaular.

penal [pínal], *a.* penal; sujeto a pena o castigo.— **p. code**, (for.) código penal.—**p. institution**, penal.—**p. servitude**, presidio, trabajos forzados.

penality [pinélıtı̯], *s.* penalidad.

penalize [pínalaı̯z], *va.* penar, penalizar, imponer pena a; castigar.

penalty [pénaltı̯], *s.* pena, castigo; (for.) penalidad, sanción; multa, pena pecuniaria; desventaja, inconveniente.—**on**, o **under p. of**, so pena de.

penance [pénans], *s.* penitencia.—**to do p.**, hacer penitencia o acto de contrición.

Penates [pinéı̯tiz], *s. pl.* (mit. rom.) penates.

pence [pens], *s. pl.* de PENNY.

penchant [pénchant o pansǽn], *s.* (fr.) propensión, inclinación, afición, tendencia.

pencil [pénsıl]. I. *s.* lápiz, *m.*; pincel fino; lápiz (labial, etc.); haz, *m.* (de luz, de rayos).—**p. box**, o **case**, estuche para lápices; lapicero.—**p. drawing**, o **sketch**, dibujo o boceto a lápiz.—

p. holder, lapicero, portalápiz, *m.*—**p. of rays,** (fís., geom.) haz de rayos.—**p. sharpener,** cortalápiz, afilalápices, sacapuntas.—**mechanical p.,** lapicero, lápiz mecánico, automático o de repetición. **II.** *va.* dibujar o escribir con lápiz; lapizar.

pend [pend], *vn.* estar pendiente de arreglo.

pendant [péndạnt]. **I.** *s.* cualquier cosa que cuelga o está pendiente de otra, v. gr.: (joy.) medallón, colgante, pinjante, pendiente, arete, zarcillo; apéndice; péndulo; (arq.) colgante; adorno que cuelga de un techo; (b. a.) uno de dos objetos que forman juego, (gal.) pandán; (elec.) araña (de luces); (mar.) amante; gallardete. **II.** *a.* = PENDENT.

pendency [péndẹnsị], *s.* calidad de pendiente o de colgante; suspensión.

pendent [péndẹnt]. **I.** *a.* pendiente, péndulo, colgante, suspendido; saledizo; (bot.) pendiente. **II.** *s.* = PENDANT.

pendentive [pendéntịv], *s.* (arq.) pechina.

pending [péndịŋ]. **I.** *a.* pendiente; colgante; indeciso. **II.** *prep.* durante, mientras; hasta.

pendragon [pendrǽgọn], *s.* jefe supremo.

pendular [péndẓ̱ụlạ̈(r)], *a.* pendular, con movimiento de péndulo.—**pendulosity** [-lásịtị], **pendulousness** [-lʌsnịs], *s.* calidad de colgante; suspensión.—**pendulous** [-lʌs], *a.* colgante, pendiente, péndulo.—**pendulum** [-lʌm], *s.* péndulo; péndola.

penetrability [pénạtrạbị̱lịtị], **penetrableness** [-blnịs], *s.* penetrabilidad.—**penetrable** [-bl], *a.* penetrable.

penetralia [penẹtréịlịạ], *s. pl.* penetrales.

penetrancy [pénẹtrạnsị], *s.* calidad de penetrante.—**penetrant** [-ạnt], *a.* penetrante.

penetrate [pénẹtreịt]. **I.** *va.* penetrar; taladrar, horadar; atravesar, calar; profundizar; conmover. **II.** *vn.* introducirse, penetrar, ahondar(se), adentrar(se), internar(se).—**penetrating** [-iŋ], *a.* penetrante; penetrador, agudo, perspicaz.—**penetration** [-éịsọn], *s.* penetración.—**penetrative** [-ịv], *a.* penetrativo.—**penetrativeness** [-nịs], *s.* aptitud de penetrar.

penguin [péngwịn], *s.* (orn.) pingüino, alca o pájaro bobo; (aer.) aeroplano de enseñanza, que no vuela; mujer (*f.*) del cuerpo de aviación de Inglaterra.

penholder [pénhoụldœ(r)], *s.* portaplumas, mango de pluma.

penicillate [penịsịleịt], *a.* (bot., zool.) penicilado, guarnecido de hebras finas.

penicillin [penịsịlịn], *s.* (bioquím.) penicilina.

peninsula [pịnịnsụlạ̈], *s.* península, penisla.

peninsular [-(r)], *a.* y *s.* peninsular.—**P. War,** guerras napoleónicas de España y Portugal.

penis [pínịs], *s.* (anat., zool.) pene, miembro viril.

penitence [pénịtẹns], *s.* penitencia; contrición.

penitent [-tẹnt]. **I.** *a.* penitente; contrito, compungido. **II.** *s.* penitente; arrepentido.

penitential [-ténsạl]. **I.** *a.* penitencial; de arrepentimiento. **II.** *s.* penitencial, libro de penitencias.

penitentiary [-ténsạrị]. **I.** *a.* penitenciario, de penitencia; de castigo, penal. **II.** *s.* penitenciaría, presidio; casa de corrección; (igl.) penitenciario (persona); penitenciaría (tribunal).

penitently [pénịtẹntlị], *adv.* con arrepentimiento, contrición o penitencia.—**penitentness** [-nịs], *s.* estado del penitente.

penknife [pénnaịf], *s.* cortaplumas, tajaplumas.

penman [pénmạn], *s.* pendolista o calígrafo; maestro de escritura; autor.

penmanship [-ŝịp], *s.* escritura, caligrafía; pluma, (carácter de) letra.

penna [pénạ̈], *s.* (orn.) pena.

pennant [pénạnt], *s.* (mar.) flámula, grímpola, gallardete, banderola, insignia; (mar.) amante, maroma corta; bandera (de escuela, etc.); (fig.) campeonato.—**broad p.,** (mar.) gallardetón, corneta.

pennate(d [pénẹịt(ịd], *a.* (bot., zool.) pinado, peniforme, de figura de pluma; alado, (poét.) penígero.

penner [pénœ(r)], *s.* autor, escritor; encerrador.

penniform [pénịfọrm], *a.* peniforme.

penniless [pénịlịs], *a.* sin dinero; sin un real; en la miseria; (fam.) tronado, pelado, en pelota.

pennon [pénọn], *s.* pendón, banderola, flámula; (blas.) pendón; (poét.) ala, *V.* PINION.

Pennsylvanian [pensịlvéịnịạn], *a.* y *s.* (E. U.) pensilvano.

penny [pénị], *s.* (*pl.* PENNIES, cuando denota número, y PENCE, cuando denota valor monetario) (Ingl.) penique; (E. U.) centavo; (España) cinco céntimos, (fam.) perra chica; dinero en general.—**p.-a-liner,** gacetillero.—**p. dreadful** = DIME NOVEL.—**p.-in-the-slot machine,** tragaperras.—**p. loaf,** rollo, bollo.—**p.-wise,** dícese del que por ahorrar poco se expone a perder mucho.—**p.-wise and pound-foolish,** que escatima en los gastos pequeños y derrocha sumas cuantiosas.

pennyroyal [-rójạl], *s.* (bot.) poleo.

pennyweight [-weịt], *s.* (joy.) escrúpulo o dinero (peso = 24 granos).

pennyworth [-wœrϑ], *s.* valor de un penique; cantidad pequeña.

penological [pinọládžịkạl], *a.* penológico.

penologist [pináludžịst], *s.* penalista, criminalista.

penology [-džị], *s.* penología.

pensile [pénsịl], *a.* pensil, colgante, suspenso.

pensileness [-nịs], *s.* calidad de colgante, etc.

pension [pénsọn]. **I.** *s.* pensión; cesantía, jubilación; (mil.) retiro; beca; juro.—**life p.,** pensión vitalicia. **II.** *va.* (a veces con off) (a)pensionar, jubilar.—**pensionary** [-erị]. **I.** *a.* pensionado. **II.** *s.* pensionado, pensionista; pensionario (magistrado).—**pensioner** [-œ(r)], *s.* pensionista, pensionado, jubilado; beca; jurista; (mil. y mar.) inválido.

pensive [pénsịv], *a.* pensativo, meditabundo.—**pensively** [-lị], *adv.* pensativamente.—**pensiveness** [-nịs], *s.* melancolía, tristeza; meditación profunda.

penstock [pénstak], *s.* compuerta de esclusa; paradera (del caz); portaplumas.

pent [pent], *a.*, *pret.* y *pp.* de TO PEN.—**p.-up,** acorralado, enjaulado, encerrado; detenido, reprimido.—**p. roof,** tejado de cola o de una sola vertiente.

pentachord [péntạkord]. **I.** *a.* de cinco cuerdas. **II.** *s.* (mús.) pentacordio, lira antigua.

pentacle [péntạkl], *s.* pentáculo, estrella de cinco (a veces seis) puntas.

pentad [péntæd], *s.* número cinco; grupo de cinco cosas; lustro; (quím.) átomo, radical o elemento que tiene fuerza de combinación de cinco.

pentadactyl [pentạdæktịl], *a.* (zool.) pentadáctilo, de cinco dedos.

pentadecagon [-dékạgạn], *s.* (geom.) pente- o pentadecágono, polígono de quince ángulos y lados.

pentagon [péntạgạn], *s.* (geom.) pentágono.

pentagonal [pentǽgọnạl], *a.* pentagonal, pentágono.

pentagram [péntạgræm], *s.* = PENTACLE.

pentahedron [-hídrọn], *s.* (geom.) pentaedro.

pentahedral, pentahedrous [-hídrạl, -hídrʌs], *a.* pentaédrico.

pentamerous [pentǽmẹrʌs], *a.* (bot., zool.) pentámero.

pentameter [-ɛtœ(r)], *s.* y *a.* (pros.) pentámetro.

pentane [pénteịn], *s.* (quím.) pentano.

pentapolis [pentǽpolịs], *s.* pentápolis.

pentarchy [péntarkị], *s.* pentarquía.

pentasyllabic [pentạsịlǽbịk], *a.* pentasílabo.

Pentateuch [péntạtịuk], *s.* Pentateuco.

pentathlon [pentǽϑlạn], *s.* pentatlo.

pentavalent [-véịlẹnt], *a.* (quím.) pentavalente.

Pentecost [péntịkọst], *s.* (pascua de) Pentecostés.

Pentecostal [-kóstạl], *a.* de Pentecostés.
penthouse [pénthaụs], *s.* techo inclinado; tejaroz, *m.*, tejadillo, colgadizo, cobertizo, sotechado, sobradillo; habitación construída en un techo.
pentosan [péntosæn], *s.* (quím.) pentosana.
pentose [péntoụs], *s.* (quím.) pentosa.
penult [pínʌlt], *s.* penúltima sílaba.
penultimate [pinʌltimịt], *a.* y *s.* penúltimo.
penumbra [pinʌmbrạ], *s.* (astr. y pint.) penumbra.
penurious [pinịúrịʌs], *a.* tacaño, miserable, cicatero; (raro) escaso.—**penuriously** [-lị], *adv.* escasamente; miserablemente.—**penuriousness** [-nịs], *s.* tacañería, ruindad, miseria; escasez, carestía.
penury [pényụrị], *s.* penuria, miseria, indigencia.
penwiper [pénwaịpœ(r], *s.* limpiaplumas.
penwoman [pénwụmạn], *s.* escritora. *V.* PENMAN.
peon [píọn], *s.* criado; peón.—**gang of peons**, peonaje, peonada.
peonage [-ịdż], *peonism* [-ịzm], *s.* condición o servicio de peón; sistema (*m.*) de emplear deudores (a veces presidiarios) como peones para que paguen con su trabajo lo que deben.
peony [píọnị], *s.* (bot.) peonia; saltaojos.
people [pípl]. **I.** *s.* pueblo, nación, población, grey, *f.*; los habitantes (de un país); gente, *f.*—**p. say**, dicen, se dice, dice la gente.—**many p.**, mucha gente, muchas personas.—**most p.**, la mayoría o el común de las gentes.—**one's p.**, la familia o parentela de uno.—**the p.**, el público, la gente; la colectividad.—**the common p.**, el pueblo, populacho o vulgo, la plebe o gente menuda. **II.** *va.* poblar, colonizar; habitar.
pep [pep]. **I.** *s.* (fam.) brío, espíritu; energía, fuerza, vigor. **II.** *va.* (con **up**) (fam.) animar, estimular, vigorizar.
peplum [péplʌm], *s.* peplo.
pepper [pépœ(r]. **I.** *s.* (bot.) pimienta, fruto del pimentero; pimiento, ají, chile.—**p.-and-salt cloth**, tejido mezclado de negro y blanco.—**p. pot**, pimentero; (coc.) ajiaco, sopa de carne y legumbres muy condimentada.—**p. mill**, pimentero de molinillo. **II.** *va.* sazonar con pimienta o ají; salpimentar; acribillar; sazonar (una conversación o escrito) con dichos picantes.
pepperbox [-baks], *s.* pimentero.
peppercorn [-korn], *s.* grano de pimienta; bagatela, chuchería.
peppergrass [-græs], o **pepperwort** [-wœrt], *s.* (bot.) lepidio, mastuerzo.
peppermint [-mịnt], *s.* (bot.) menta, hierbabuena.—**p. drop**, pastilla de menta.
peppery [-rị], *a.* picante; mordaz; de mal humor o genio.
peppy [pépị], *a.* (fam.) brioso, enérgico, vivo. *V.* PEP.
pepsin(e [pépsịn], *s.* (bioquím.) pepsina.
peptic [péptịk], *a.* péptico.
peptone [péptoụn], *s.* (bioquím.) peptona.
peptonic [peptánịk], *a.* peptónico.
peptonize [péptonaịz], *va.* peptonizar, -ificar.
per [pœr], *prep.* por.—**p. annum**, al año.—**p. capita**, por cabeza, por persona.—**p. cent**, por ciento.—**p. contra**, por el contrario; por otra parte.—**p. diem**, por día.—**p. se**, por sí mismo, en sí mismo.
peracid [pœrǽsịd], *s.* (quím.) perácido.
peradventure [pœrạdvénchụ(r]. **I.** *adv.* quizá, acaso, por ventura. **II.** *s.* posibilidad; duda.
perambulate [pœrǽmbjuleịt], *va.* y *vn.* recorrer, transitar, visitar; andar, deambular, pasearse.—**perambulation** [-éịṣọn], *s.* visita de inspección; paseo.—**perambulator** [-ọ(r], *s.* cochecillo de niño; (top.) podómetro.
perborate [pœrbóụreịt], *s.* (quím.) perborato.
percale [pœrkéịl], *s.* (tej.) percal.
percaline [pœrkạlín], *s.* percalina.
perceivable [pœrsívạbl], *a.* perceptible.

perceivably [-blị], *adv.* perceptiblemente.
perceive [pœrsív], *va.* percibir, columbrar; advertir, observar, percatar(se de); comprender.
perceiver [-œ(r], *s.*, **perceiving** [-ịŋ], *a.* perceptor.
percentage [pœrséntịdż], *s.* (com.) tanto por ciento, percentaje, porcentaje.
percept [pœrsept], *s.* (psic.) representación mental de lo percibido; el objeto percibido según lo da la percepción.
perceptibility [pœrséptibịlịtị], *s.* perceptibilidad.
perceptible [-tịbl], *a.* perceptible, sensible.
perceptibly [-tịblị], *adv.* perceptiblemente.
perception [-ṣọn], *s.* percepción; (for.) percibo.
perceptive [-tịv], *a.* perceptivo.
perceptivity [-tívịtị], *s.* perceptividad.
perch [pœrch], *s.* **I.** *s.* (ict.) perca, percha; medida de 16½ pies; alcándara, percha, varal, cetro (para las aves). **II.** *vn.* posarse, pararse, encaramarse; ponerse (las aves) en percha. **III.** *va.* emperchar.
perchance [pœrchǽns], *adv.* acaso, tal vez, quizá, por ventura.
Percheron [pœrchęran], *a.* y *s.* percherón (caballo).
perchlorate [pœrklóreịt], *s.* (quím.) perclorato.
perchloric [-rịk], *a.* perclórico (ácido).
perchlorid(e [-rịd o-raịd], *s.* (quím.) percloruro.
percipient [pœrsípịent], *a.* y *s.* percipiente.
percolate [pœrkoleịt]. **I.** *va.* y *vn.* (tras)colar, (in)filtrar, pasar, rezumarse. **II.** *s.* (farm.) percolado.
percolation [-éịṣọn], *s.* coladura, (in)filtración; (farm.) percolación.
percolator [-ọ(r], *s.* filtro, colador; cafetera filtradora o de filtro, percolador (de tamaño grande).
percuss [pœrkʌs], *va.* percutir, herir, golpear.
percussion [pœrkʌṣọn], *s.* percusión, choque; (med.) percusión.—**p. bullet**, bala explosiva.—**p. cap**, fulminante, pistón, cápsula, cebo percusor o fulminante.—**p. fuse**, pebete o fulminante de percusión o de choque.—**p. hammer**, percusor, percutor.—**p. instrument**, (mús.) instrumento de percusión (piano, tambor, etc.).
percussive [pœrkʌsịv], **percutient** [pœrkịúş̣ẹnt], *a.* percuciente.
percussor [pœrkʌsọ(r], *s.* percusor.
perdition [pœrdíṣọn], *s.* perdición; infierno.
perdu(e [pœrdịú], *a.* perdido de vista, escondido.
perdurable [pœrdịúrạbl], *a.* perdurable.
perdurably [-blị], *adv.* perdurablemente.
peregrinate [périgrịneịt], *vn.* peregrinar.—**peregrination** [-éịṣọn], *s.* peregrinación, -aje.
peregrin(e [périgrịn]. **I.** *a.* peregrino; extranjero; exótico, raro, extraño. **II.** *s.* (orn.) cierto halcón.
peregrinity [perịgrínịtị], *s.* peregrinidad.
peremptorily [pœrémptorịlị], *adv.* perentoriamente; absolutamente.
peremptoriness [-nịs], *s.* perentoriedad.
peremptory [-torị], *a.* perentorio; absoluto, rotundo, terminante, definitivo; dogmático, magistral.—**p. orders**, órdenes perentorias.—**p. sale**, venta forzosa.
perennial [pœrénịạl]. **I.** *a.* perenne, perennal; continuo, incesante, permanente, perpetuo; (biol.) que crece continuamente; (bot.) perenne, vivaz. **II.** *s.* (bot.) planta vivaz.
perennially [-ị], *adv.* perennemente.
perfect [pœrfịkt]. **I.** *a.* perfecto; completo, entero, cumplido, cabal, hecho y derecho; (bot.) completo; (gram.) perfecto; (fam.) muy grande, redomado. **II.** *s.* (gram.) tiempo perfecto.
perfect [pœrfékt o pœrfịkt], *va.* perfeccionar, mejorar.—**perfecting** [-ịŋ]. **I.** *s.* perfeccionamiento. **II.** *a.* perfeccionador.
perfecter [-œ(r], *s.* perfeccionador.
perfectibility [-tịbịlịtị], *s.* perfectibilidad.—**perfectible** [-tịbl], *a.* perfectible.
perfection [pœrfékṣọn], *s.* perfección.—**per-**

fectionism [-ízm], s. perfeccionismo.—**perfectionist(ic** [-ist, -ístik], s. y a. perfeccionista.

perfective [-tiv], a. perfectivo.—**perfectively** [-li], adv. con perfección.—**perfectly** [pǽrfiktli], adv. perfectamente, a la perfección; a fondo.

perfervid [pœrfǽrvid], a. muy férvido.

perfidious [pœrfídjʌs], a. pérfido, desleal, infiel, aleve, traidor.—**perfidiously** [-li], adv. pérfidamente.—**perfidiousness** [-njs], s. perfidy [pǽrfidi], s. perfidia, deslealtad, alevosía, traición.

perfoliate [pœrfóuljeit], a. (bot.) perfoliado.

perforate [pǽrforeit], va. perforar, agujerear, horadar, taladrar.—**perforating** [-iŋ], a. perforador, horadador.—**perforation** [-éiʃon], s. perforación, horadación.—**perforator** [-ọ(r)], s. perforador(a), horadador(a), taladrador(a).

perforce [pœrfórs], adv. por fuerza, forzosamente.

perform [pœrfórm]. I. va. ejecutar, hacer, realizar, poner por obra; desempeñar, llenar, cumplir; practicar, ejercer. II. vn. (teat.) representar, desempeñar un papel; tocar un instrumento músico; actuar, trabajar, funcionar.

performable [-ʌbl], a. ejecutable, realizable.

performance [-ʌns], s. ejecución, realización; desempeño, cumplimiento; actuación, funcionamiento, acción; capacidad; obra, acción, hecho, hazaña; (teat.) función, representación.—**first p.**, (teat.) estreno.

performer [-œ(r)], s. ejecutor, ejecutante; actor; músico; acróbata, mf.

perfume [pǽrfjum o pœrfjúm]. I. s. perfume, fragancia, aroma, m.; (quím.) esencia. II. [pœrfjúm], va. perfumar, sahumar, aromatizar.—**perfuming pan**, o **pot**, perfumador, cazoleja, sahumador.

perfumer [-œ(r)], s. perfumador, perfumero, perfumista.—**p.'s shop**, perfumería.

perfumery [-œri], s. perfumería; perfumes, pl.

perfumy [pǽrfjumi], a. perfumado; fragante.

perfunctorily [pœrfʌ́nktorili], adv. (raro) perfunctoriamente, por llenar las apariencias; de modo descuidado, negligente o rutinario.—**perfunctoriness** [-njs], s. descuido, superficialidad, indiferencia.—**perfunctory** [-tori]. I. a. (raro) perfunctorio; superficial, hecho sin cuidado, a la ligera; formulario. II. s. rutinero.

perfuse [pœrfjúz], va. cubrir; vaciar; regar, rociar; forzar (un líquido) por, hacer entrar en.

perfusion [pœrfjúʒon], s. acción de cubrir, vaciar o regar; perfusión; baño; aspersión; afusión; introducción de un líquido; líquido introducido; bautismo con agua rociada.

pergola [pǽrgolǎ], s. pérgola o pérgula, emparrado; cenador; balcón largo, galería exterior.

perhaps [pœrhǽps], adv. tal vez, quizá(s), acaso, por ventura.

peri [píri], s. (mit. pérsica) peri, f., hada.

periantí(ium [périænθ, -ǽnθjʌm], s. (bot.) periantio; perigonio.

pericardial, pericardiac [-kárdiạl, -djæk], a. pericardíaco, pericárdico.—**pericarditis** [-dájtis], s. (med.) pericarditis.—**pericardium** [-djʌm], s. (anat.) pericardio.

pericarp(ium [périkarp, perikárpjʌm], s. (bot.) pericarpio, folículo.—**pericarpial, pericarpic** [-piạl, -pjk], a. pericarpial, pericárpico.

perichondrium [-kándrjʌm], s. (anat.) pericondrio.

pericranium [-kréinjʌm], s. (anat.) pericráneo.

pericycle [périsaikl], s. (bot.) periciclo.

periderm [-dœrm], s. (bot., zool.) peridermo.

peridot [-dat], s. (min.) peridoto, crisólito, olivino.

peridotite [-dóutait], s. (min.) peridotita.

perigee [péridʒi], s. (astr.) perigeo.

perigon [-gan], s. (geom.) perígono, ángulo de 360°.

perigonium [-góunjʌm], s. (bot.) perigonio.

perigynium [-dʒínjʌm], s. (bot.) periginio.

perihelion [-híljon], s. (astr.) perihelio.

peril [péril]. I. s. peligro, riesgo, trance. II. va.

poner en peligro; arriesgar. III. vn. peligrar; correr peligro, estar en peligro o riesgo.

perilous [-ʌs], a. peligroso, arriesgado.

perilously [-li], adv. peligrosamente.

perilousness [-njs], s. calidad de peligroso; peligro.

perimeter [pœrímetœ(r)], s. perímetro.

perimetrical [perimétrikạl], a. perimétrico.

perineal [-níạl], a. (anat.) perineal.

perinephrium [-néfrjʌm], s. (anat.) perinefrio, tejido conjuntivo y adiposo que rodea el riñón.

perineum [-níʌm], s. (anat.) perineo.

period [píriọd], s. período; época, era, edad, tiempo; término, fin, conclusión; (gram.) período, cláusula; (impr.) punto (.); (med.) período; (mús.) período.—**the p.**, el día de hoy, la actualidad.—pl. (fisiol.) las reglas, menstruo.

periodic [pœraiádik], a. (quím.) peryódico.

periodic(al [piriádik(ạl], a. periódico.—**periodical**, s. periódico, publicación periódica.—**periodicalism** [-izm], s. periodismo.—**periodicalist** [-ist], s. periodista.

periodically [-i], adv. periódicamente.

periodicalness [-njs], s. periodicidad.

periodicity [piriọdísiti], s. periodicidad.

periodide [pœráiodaid], s. (quím.) peryoduro.

perioeci [períisai], s. pl. (geog.) periecos.

periosteal [periástiạl], a. perióstico.

periosteotome [-ástiotoụm], s. (cir.) periostiótomo, legra.—**periosteotomy** [-astiátomi], s. (cir.) periostiotomía, legración.

periosteum [-ástiʌm], s. (anat.) periostio.

periostitis [-astájtis], s. (med.) periostitis.

peripatetic [-patétik], a. y s. peripatético.—**P. philosophy**, o **Peripateticism**, peripat(e)tism)o.

peripatus [perípatʌs], s. (zool.) peripato, onicóforo.

peripetia [peripetáiǎ], s. peripecia.

peripheral, peripheric(al [periferạl, -férik(ạl], a. periférico, relativo a la periferia.

periphery [periferi], s. periferia, circunferencia; superficie exterior.

periphrase [périfreiz], va. y vn. perifrasear.

periphrase, periphrasis [périfrasis], s. perífrasis, circunlocución.

periphrastic(al [-frǽstik(ạl], a. perifrástico.

periphrastically [-i], adv. con perífrasis.

peripteral [periptẹrạl], a., peripteros [-tẹras], s. (arq.) periptero, (edificio) rodeado de columnas.

periptery [-tẹri], s. (aer.) región del aire alrededor de un avión agitada por remolinos.

periscii [perísiai], s. pl. (geog.) periscios.

periscope [périskoup], s. (ópt.) periscopio.

periscopic [-skápik], a. periscópico.

perish [péris], vn. perecer, morir, sucumbir, marchitarse, pasarse.—**p. the thought!** ¡Dios nos libre!

perishable [-ʌbl], a. perecedero, caduco; putrescible, expuesto a podrirse.—**p. goods**, mercancías de fácil descomposición (ll. t. **perishables**).

perishableness [-njs], s. fragilidad, caducidad, calidad de perecedero o putrescible.

perisperm [périspœrm], s. (bot.) perispermo.

perissodactyl(ous [perisodǽktil(ʌs], s. y a. (zool.) perisodáctilo.

peristalsis [periztǽlsis], s. (fisiol.) peristalsis, peristaltismo.—**peristaltic** [-tik], a. peristáltico.

peristole [perístoli], s. (fisiol.) perístole, f.

peristome [péristoum], s. (bot., zool.) perístoma, m.

peristyle [péristail], s. (arq.) peristilo.

perisystole [perisístoli], s. (fisiol.) perisístole, f.

peritoneal [peritoníạl], a. peritoneal.—**peritoneum** [-níʌm], s. (anat.) peritoneo.—**peritonitis** [-nájtis], s. (med.) peritonitis.

perityphlitis [peritifláitis], s. (med.) peritiflitis.

periwig [périwig], s. peluca, perico.

periwinkle [-wiŋkl], s. (zool.) litorina, margarita, caracolillo marino; (bot.) (vinca)pervinca.

perjure [pə́rdźur], va. y vr. perjurar(se).—**perjured** [-d], a. perjuro.—**perjurer** [-œ(r)], s. perjuro.—**perjury** [-i], s. perjurio.

perk [pœrk]. **I.** va. adornar, vestir; erguir, levantar la oreja o la cabeza, etc. **II.** vn. erguirse, pavonearse; (con **up**) animarse, avivarse.

perk(**y** [pœrk(i], a. gallardo, apuesto. V. PERT.

perlite [pə́rlait], s. (petrog.) perlita, fonolita.

permanence [pœrmánəns], **permanency** [-i], s. permanencia, estabilidad, durabilidad.

permanent [-ənt]. **I.** a. permane(cie)nte, duradero, persistente, fijo; indeleble.—**p. wave**, ondulación (u ondulado) permanente (del pelo). **II.** s. = P. WAVE.

permanently [-li], adv. permanentemente.

permanganate [pœrmǽŋgəneit], s. (quím.) permanganato.

permanganic [-gǽnik], a. permangánico.

permeability [pœrmiəbíliti], s. permeabilidad.

permeable [-bl], a. permeable.

permeameter [-émetə(r)], s. (fís.) permeámetro.

permeate [pœrmieit], va. penetrar, pasar a través de; estar difundido en, afectar, calar.

permeation [-éiʃən], s. penetración al través de los poros.

permeative [-iv], a. penetrativo, permeativo.

Permian [pœrmiən]. **I.** s. y a. (geol.) pérmico. **II.** a. permiano.

permissible [pœrmísibl], a. permisible, lícito.

permission [pœrmíʃən], s. permiso, licencia.

permissive [pœrmísiv], a. permisivo.—**permissively** [-li], adv. permisivamente.

permissory [pœrmísəri], a. por o con permiso; autorizado.

permit [pœrmít]. **I.** va. permitir, consentir, dejar, autorizar. **II.** [pœrmit], s. permiso, permisión, licencia, pase; (com.) cédula de aduana.—**permitter** [pœrmítœ(r)], s. permisor, permitidor.

permittance [pœrmítəns], s. (elec.) capacidad electro(e)stática.—**permittivity** [-tíviti], s. (elec.) inductividad específica.

permutable [pœrmiútəbl], a. permutable.

permutation [pœrmiutéiʃən], s. permuta, trueque; (mat.) permutación.

permutator [pœrmiutéitə(r)], s. (elec.) permutador, convertidor de núcleo magnético.

permute [pœrmiút], va. permutar, (tras)trocar.

permuter [-œ(r)], s. permutador.

pern [pœrn], s. (orn.) cierta ave de rapiña.

pernicious [pœrníʃʌs], a. pernicioso, dañoso, nocivo; fatal, mortal.—**p. anemia**, (med.) anemia perniciosa.—**perniciously** [-li], adv. perniciosamente.—**perniciousness** [-njs], s. perniciosidad.

pernickety [pœrníkęti], a. (fam.) quisquilloso, demasiado escrupuloso; difícil, delicado.

perone [péroni], s. (anat.) peroné.—**peroneal** [peróniəl], a. peróneo.—**peroneus** [perəníʌs], s. peróneo.

perorate [péroreit], vn. perorar.

peroration [-éiʃən], s. peroración.

peroxid(**e** [pœráksaid], s. (quím.) peróxido.—**p. of hydrogen**, agua oxigenada.—**p. blonde**, rubia oxigenada o de farmacia.

perpend (**stone**) [pœrpénd (stoun)], s. (alb.) perpiaño.

perpendicular [pœrpendíkyulə(r)]. **I.** a. perpendicular; vertical. **II.** s. perpendicular.—**perpendicularity** [-kériti], s. perpendicularidad.—**perpendicularly** [-li], adv. perpendicularmente; a plomo.

perpetrate [pə́rpetreit], va. perpetrar, cometer.—**perpetration** [-éiʃən], s. perpetración, comisión.—**perpetrator** [-ǫ(r)], s. perpetrador.

perpetual [pœrpéchuəl], a. perpetuo.—**p. calendar**, calendario perpetuo.—**p. motion**, movimiento perpetuo o continuo.

perpetually [-i], adv. perpetuamente.

perpetuate [-eit], va. perpetuar, eternizar; vincular.

perpetuation [-éiʃən], s. perpetuación.

perpetuity [pœrpętiúiti], s. perpetuidad.

perplex [pœrplέks], va. confundir, aturdir, aturrullar; intrincar, embrollar, enredar, enmarañar.

perplexed [-t], a. perplejo, confuso, suspenso; intrincado, enredado.—**perplexedly** [-idli], adv. perplejamente.—**perplexedness** [-njs], s. perplexity [-iti], s. perplejidad, confusión, duda.

perquisite [pœrkwizit], s. gajes, m. pl., percance(s), obvención, emolumento, plus, propina, adehala.

perron [pέron], s. (arq.) escalinata, gradas, f. pl.

perroquet [pέroket], s. (orn.) perico, periquito.

perry [péri], s. sidra de peras.

persecute [pə́rsękjut], va. perseguir; acosar, vejar; importunar.

persecution [-kiúʃən], s. persecución; vejación.

persecutive [-iv], a. perseguidor.

persecutor [-ǫ(r)], s. perseguidor; acosador.

Perseid [pə́rsjid], s. (astr.) perseida.

Perseus [pə́rsjus], s. (astr.) Perseo.

perseverance [pœrsęvírəns], s. perseverancia; persistencia, constancia; (teol.) perseverancia final (ll. t. **p. of the saints**, esp. entre los calvinistas, y **final p.**, entre éstos y los católicos).

persevere [-vír], vn. perseverar; persistir; obstinarse, cerrarse.—**persevering** [-iŋ], a. perseverante; persistente.—**perseveringly** [-li], adv. perseverantemente, persistentemente.

Persian [pə́rźən]. **I.** s. persa, mf., persiano; lengua persa; (tej.) persiana. **II.** a. persa, persiano, pérsico.—**P. blinds**, celosías, persianas.—**P. Gulf**, golfo Pérsico.—**P. lamb** = BROADTAIL.—**P. wheel**, noria.

Persic [pə́rsik], a. pérsico, persa, persiano.

persicary [pə́rsikęri], s. (bot.) persicaria, centinodia.

persienne [pœrsiέn], s. (tej.) persiana, tela oriental adornada.—*pl.* = PERSIAN BLINDS.

persiflage [pέrsiflaź], s. chulada, zumba, fisga, charla o burla baladí.

persimmon [pœrsímǫn], s. níspola (fruto del níspero); (bot.) níspero.

Persism [pə́rsizm], s. religión de los antiguos magos de Persia; modismo persa.

persist [pœrsíst], vn. insistir, porfiar, empeñarse; persistir, perseverar; perdurar.

persistence, persistency [-ęns, -i], s. insistencia, porfía; persistencia, perseverancia.

persistent, persisting [-ęnt, -iŋ], a. insistente; persistente, perseverante; permanente.

persistently [-li], adv. persistentemente; repetidamente.

person [pə́rsǫn], s. persona; (desp.) quídam, ente, tipo; (biol.) individuo.—**in p.**, en persona.—**in the p. of**, en lugar o representación de.

persona [pœrsóunə], s. persona; (biol.) individuo, organismo particular.—**p. ficta**, (for.) persona jurídica.—**p. grata**, persona grata.—**p. non grata**, persona no grata o no aceptada.

personable [pə́rsǫnəbl], a. guapo, bien parecido, bien apersonado.

personage [-idź], s. persona(je).

personal [pə́rsǫnəl]. **I.** a. personal; particular, privado; personalmente ofensivo o hiriente a la persona con quien se habla o discute; en persona (acción, comparecencia, etc.).—**p. effects**, bienes o efectos personales o de uso personal.—**p. equation**, ecuación personal.—**p. pronoun**, pronombre personal.—**p. property**, bienes muebles, (com.) acción nominativa. **II.** s. (period.) breve noticia de carácter personal.

personality [-éliti], s. personalidad, individualidad; alusión personal; personaje.

personalize [-aiz], va. personalizar; (ret.) personificar.

personally [-i̯], *adv.* personalmente.
personalty [-ti̯], *s.* (for.) bienes muebles.
personate [pœ́rsonei̯t]. I. *va.* hacerse pasar por; usurpar el nombre de; (teat.) desempeñar o hacer el papel de. II. *vn.* (teat.) representar. III. [-ni̯t], *a.* (bot.) personada.
personation [-éi̯ṣo̱n], *s.* personificación; (for.) usurpación del nombre de otro.
personator [-o̱(r)], *s.* el que se hace pasar por otro.
personification [pœrsáni̯fi̱kéi̯ṣo̱n], *s.* personificación; (ret.) prosopopeya.
personify [-fai̯], *va.* personificar.
personnel [pœrso̱nél], *s.* personal; dependencia, conjunto de empleados; tripulación; (Am., barb.) elenco (de una administración, compañía teatral, circo, etc.).
perspective [pœrspéktiv]. I. *s.* perspectiva; lejos. II. *a.* (pint.) en perspectiva; (geom.) proyecto. —**perspectively** [-li̯], *adv.* con arreglo a la perspectiva.
perspicacious [pœrspi̱kéi̯ṣʌs], *a.* perspicaz, sagaz.
perspicaciousness [-ni̯s], **perspicacity** [-kǽsi̯ti̱], *s.* perspicacia, perspicacidad, penetración.
perspicuity [-ki̱úi̯ti̱], *s.* perspicuidad, claridad, lucidez.
perspicuous [pœrspíkyu̯ʌs], *a.* perspicuo, claro, lúcido.—**perspicuously** [-li̯], *adv.* perspicuamente, claramente.—**perspicuousness** [-ni̯s], *s.* perspicuidad, claridad de estilo.
perspiration [pœrspi̱réi̯ṣo̱n], *s.* sudor, transpiración, perspiración.
perspirative, perspiratory [pœrspái̯rati̱v, -tori̱], *a.* sudorífico; perspiratorio.
perspire [pœrspái̯r], *va.* y *vn.* sudar, transpirar, perspirar, exhalar, excretar por la piel.
perspiring [-iŋ], *a.* sudoriento, sudor(or)oso.
persuadable [pœrswéi̯dab̦l], *a.* persuasible.
persuade [pœrswéi̯d], *va.* persuadir, inducir, reducir, imbuir, mover.—**persuader** [-œ(r)], *s.* persuadidor, persuasor, inducidor.—**persuasibility** [pœrswéi̯si̱bi̱li̱ti̱], *s.* calidad de persuasible.—**persuasible** [-b̦l], *a.* persuasible.—**persuasibleness** [-ni̯s], *s.* facilidad en dejarse persuadir.
persuasion [pœrswéi̯ʒo̱n], *s.* persuasión, inducción; creencia, opinión; credo, secta, denominación; persuasiva.
persuasive [-si̯v]. I. *a.* persuasivo. II. *s.* persuasiva.—**persuasively** [-li̯], *adv.* persuasivamente.—**persuasiveness** [-ni̯s], *s.* persuasiva.
persulphate, persulfate [pœrsʌ́lfei̯t], *s.* (quím.) persulfato.—**persulphide** [-fai̯d], *s.* (quím.) persulfuro.—**persulphuric** [-fi̱úri̱k], *a.* persulfúrico.
pert [pœrt], *a.* atrevido, descarado, petulante; (fam.) jovial, alegre.
pertain [pœrtéi̯n], *vn.* pertenecer, atañer, tocar, concernir, incumbir.—**pertaining to,** perteneciente, tocante, relativo o atinente a.
pertinacious [pœrti̱néi̯ṣʌs], *a.* pertinaz, porfiado, tenaz, terco.—**pertinaciously** [-li̯], *adv.* pertinazmente.—**pertinaciousness** [-ni̯s], **pertinacity** [-nǽsi̱ti̱], *s.* pertinacia.
pertinence, pertinency [pœ́rti̱nẹns, -i̯], *s.* pertinencia; oportunidad; correspondencia.
pertinent [-ẹnt], *a.* pertinente, a propósito, atinado.—**pertinently** [-li̯], *adv.* pertinentemente, oportunamente, atinadamente.
pertly [pœ́rtli̯], *adv.* descarada o petulantemente.—**pertness** [-ni̯s], *s.* descaro, desfachatez, petulancia; (fam.) viveza; desparpajo, dicacidad.
perturb [pœrtœ́rb], *va.* perturbar, agitar.
perturbable [-ab̦l], *a.* perturbable.
perturbation [-éi̯ṣo̱n], *s.* perturbación, agitación, inquietud; (astr.) perturbación, desviación.
perturbator [pœ́rto̱rbei̯to̱(r)], **perturber** [pœrtœ́rbœ(r)], *s.*, **perturbing** [-iŋ], *a.* perturbador.
pertussis [pœrtʌ́si̱s], *s.* (med.) tos ferina.
Perugian [pi̱rúdʒi̱an], *s.* y *a.* perusino; de Perusa.
peruke [pẹrúk], *s.* peluca, peluquín, perico.
perusal [pẹrúzal], *s.* lectura cuidadosa.

peruse [pẹrúz], *va.* leer con cuidado; examinar escudriñar, repasar, recorrer.
Peruvian [pẹrúvi̯an], *s.* y *a.* peruano, perulero.—**P. balsam,** bálsamo del Perú.—**P. bark,** quina(quina), cascarilla.
pervade [pœrvéi̯d], *va.* penetrar, ocupar, llenar.
pervasion [pœrvéi̯ʒo̱n], *s.* penetración.
pervasive [-si̯v], *a.* penetrante.
perverse [pœrvœ́rs], *a.* perverso; contrario, refractario, contumaz; molesto, petulante.
perversely [-li̯], *adv.* perversamente.
perverseness [-ni̯s], **perversity** [-i̱ti̱], *s.* perversidad, pravedad, protervia; terquedad, contumacia.
perversion [-ṣo̱n], *s.* perversión, corrupción.
perversive [-si̯v], *a.* perversivo.
pervert [pœrvœ́rt]. I. *va.* pervertir, corromper, viciar, infectar, inficionar; desnaturalizar; falsear. II. [pœ́rvœrt], *s.* perverso, depravado (moral o sexualmente); (rel.) renegado, apóstata, *mf.*
perverted [pœrvœ́rti̱d], *a.* pervertido, perverso, pravo, corrompido; desviado del camino recto.
perverter [pœrvœ́rtœ(r)], *s.* pervertidor.
pervertible [-i̱b̦l], *a.* pervertible.
pervious [pœ́rvi̯ʌs], *a.* pervio, permeable, penetrable.—**p. to light,** diáfano.
perviousness [-ni̯s], *s.* permeabilidad.
pesade [pẹsái̯d], *s.* (equit.) empinada, acto de encabritarse el caballo.
pesky [péski̱], *a.* (fam.) molesto, incómodo, cargante.
pessary [pésari̱], *s.* supositorio vaginal; (med.) pesario.
pessimism [pési̱mi̱zm], *s.* pesimismo.
pessimist [-i̱st], *s.*, **pessimistic** [-i̱sti̱k], *a.* pesimista.
pest [pest], *s.* persona o cosa molesta o nociva; molestia, (fam.) lata; (med.) peste, *f.*, pestilencia, plaga.—*pl.* insectos nocivos.
pester [péstœ(r)], *va.* molestar, vejar, cansar, incomodar, importunar; (fam.) amolar, cargar.
pesthouse [pésthau̯s], *s.* lazareto.
pestiferous [pẹstí̱fẹrʌs], *a.* pestífero.
pestilence [pésti̱lẹns], *s.* pestilencia.—**pestilent** [-ẹnt], **pestilential** [-lénṣal], *a.* pestilente, pestilencial; pernicioso, maligno; dañino, perjudicial.—**pestilently** [-li̯], *adv.* pestíferamente.
pestle [pésl]. I. *s.* mano (*f.*) de mortero o almirez; majadero, pistadero; martinete; triturador. II. *va.* majar, pistar, triturar, moler, machacar.
pet [pet]. I. *va.* mimar, acariciar. II. *vn.* acariciarse (los amantes); enojarse, atufarse. III. *a.* acariciado, mimado; favorito; domesticado.—**p. name,** diminutivo o epíteto cariñoso. IV. *s.* cualquier animal domesticado y mimado; favorito; niño mimado; enojo, enfado, berrinche.—**in a p.,** enojado, malhumorado.
petal [pétal], *s.* (bot.) pétalo, hoja.
petaled, petalous [-d, -ʌs], *a.* (bot.) provisto de pétalos.
petaliferous [-fẹrʌs], *a.* que tiene pétalos.
petalism [-i̱zm], *s.* (hist.) petalismo (destierro).
petaloid [-oi̯d], *a.* (bot.) petaloideo.
petard [pi̱tárd], *s.* (mil.) petardo; especie de triquitraque.—**hoist on (o with) one's own p.,** cogido en las propias redes.
petardeer [petárdi̱r], *s.* petardero.
petcock [pétkak], *s.* llave (*f.*) de escape; (m. v.) llave de purga, llave o grifo de desagüe.
petechiæ [pi̱tí̱ki̱i̯], *s. pl.* (med.) petequias.
petechial [pi̱téki̱al], *a.* (med.) petequial.
peter [pítœ(r)], *vn.* (con **out**) (fam.) disminuir poco a poco, acabarse; (min.) desaparecer una veta o filón.
Peter('s) pence [pítœr(z) pens], *s.* dinero de San Pedro.
petiolar [péti̱ola̱(r)], **petiolate** [-ei̯t], *a.* (bot.) peciolado.
petiole [péti̯ou̯l], *s.* (bot.) pecíolo.

petit [pẹtị], *a*. (for.) pequeño; menor.—**p. jury** = PETTY JURY.

petite [petít], *a*. (fr.) pequeña, chiquita.

petition [pẹtíʃọn]. **I.** *s*. memorial, instancia, solicitud, recurso, representación; pedimento, petición, demanda; súplica, ruego. **II.** *va*. suplicar, rogar; pedir, dirigir un memorial a.

petitionary [-ɛrị], *a*. demandante, suplicante, petitorio.

petitioner [-œ(r)], *s*. peticionario, suplicante, demandante.

petitory [pétịtorị], *a*. petitorio.

Petrarch(i)an [pịtrárk(i)ạn], *a*. petrarquesco.— **Petrarchist(ic** [pịtrarkịst, (-kịstịk], *a*. y *s*. petrarquista.

petrel [pétrẹl], *s*. (orn.) petrel.

petrescence [pịtrésẹns], *s*. petrificación.

petrescent [-ẹnt], *a*. que (se) petrifica; petrífico.

Petri dish [péjtri dịʃ], *s*. platillo de Petri para cultivos microbiológicos.

petrifaction, petrification [pétrịfǽkʃọn, -fịkéịʃọn], *s*. petrificación; fosilización; lapidificación; fósil.

petrifactive, petrifying [-fǽktịv, -faịịŋ], *a*. petrífico, petrificante.

petrify [-faị], *va*. y *vn*. petrificar(se), fosilizar(se), lapidificar(se).—**to be petrified with fear,** etc., quedarse paralizado o muerto de susto, etc.

petroglyph [pétroglịf], *s*. (arqueol.) petroglifo, escultura o inscripción en roca.

petrographic [-grǽfịk], *a*. petrográfico.

petrography [pịtrágrafị], *s*. petrografía.

petrol [pétral], *s*. (Ingl.) gasolina, (gal.) esencia.

petrolatum [petroléịtʌm], *s*. (farm.) petrolado o petrolato, ungüento de petróleo, vaselina.

petroleum [pịtróụlịʌm], *s*. petróleo, aceite mineral.—**p. ether,** nafta.—**p. jelly** = PETRO-LATUM.—**p. industry,** industria petrolera.

pétroleur [petrolǽr], *s*. petrolero (incendiario).

petrolic [pịtrálịk], *a*. petrolero.

petrology [pịtrálodžị], *s*. petrología, petrografía.

petrous [pétrʌs], *a*. petroso, pétreo.—**p. process,** (anat.) peñasco del temporal (ll. t. **petrosa**).

petticoat [pétịkout]. **I.** *s*. enaguas o (e)nagua(s); refajo, faldas, *f. pl.*; basquiña; (Am.) fustán; (fam.) mujer o muchacha; (elec.) campana (de aislador); aislador de campanas (ll. t. **p. insulator**); (locom.) tubo compensador de tiro (ll. t. **p. pipe**). **II.** *a*. de mujer, de mujeres; (elec.) de campana(s).

pettifog [pétịfag], *vn*. ser picapleitos, trapacear.

pettifogger [-œ(r)], *s*. leguleyo, picapleitos, (Am., fam.) tinterillo.—**pettifoggery** [-œrị], *s*. (fam.) triquiñuela de abogado, (Am.) tinterillada.

pettiness [pétịnịs], *s*. pequeñez, mezquindad.

petting [pétịŋ], *s*. acción de acariciar o mimar; mimo; caricias amorosas.

pettish [pétịʃ], *a*. enojadizo, quisquilloso; áspero, regañón. *V.* PETULANT.—**pettishly** [-lị], *adv*. ásperamente.—**pettishness** [-nịs], *s*. enojo; aspereza.

pettitoes [pétịtouz], *s. pl.* manos (*f. pl.*) o pies (*m. pl.*) de cerdo; a veces, dedos o pies humanos (esp. de niño).

petto [pétou], *s*. (ital.) pecho.—**in p.,** en lo interior del pecho, secreto, en sus adentros (de uno).

petty [pétị], *a*. insignificante, mezquino, despreciable; subordinado, inferior.—**p. cash,** (com.) caja chica; gastos menores de caja.—**p. jury,** jurado de juicio, compuesto de doce individuos, encargado de declarar y determinar el hecho.— **p. king,** reyezuelo.—**p. larceny,** o **theft,** hurto, ratería.—**p. officer,** suboficial, oficial subalterno de marina.—**p. prince,** principillo, principote.—**p. thief,** hurtador, ratero.—**p. treason,** traición menor.—**p. wares,** géneros menudos.

petulance, petulancy [péchụlạns, -ị], *s*. mal genio, impaciencia; (raro) petulancia.—**petu-**

lant [-ạnt], *a*. quisquilloso, enojadizo.—**petulantly** [-lị], *adv*. impacientemente, con aspereza.

petunia [pịtjúnịạ], *s*. (bot.) petunia.

pew [pịu], *s*. banco de iglesia.—**p. opener,** (igl.) ujier, acomodador.—**p. rent,** alquiler anual de un banco de iglesia.—*pl.* **pews,** la congregación.

pewee [píwị], *s*. (E. U.) (orn.) especie de tirano. *V.* PHŒBE.

pewholder [pịúhoụldœ(r)], *s*. arrendatario de un banco de iglesia.

pe(e)wit [píwịt], *s*. (orn.) = PEWEE; avefría, frailecillo; laro, pájaro reidor, especie de paviota.

pewter [pịútœ(r)], *s*. peltre; vajilla de peltre.

pewterer [-œ(r)], *s*. peltrero.

phænogam, etc. *V.* PHANEROGAM, etc.

phaeton [féị(ẹ)tọn], *s*. (carr.) faetón; (aut.) coche descubierto de turismo.

phagocyte [fǽgosaịt], *s*. (biol.) fagocito.

phalange [fǽlœndž], *s*. (anat.) = PHALANX; (pol.) falange ideada por Fourier. *V.* PHALANSTERY y FALANGE.

phalangeal [fạlǽndžịạl], *a*. (anat.) falangiano, falángico.

phalanger [-džœ(r)], *s*. (zool.) falangista (marsupial australiano).

phalanges [-džiz], *s. pl.* de PHALANX.

phalangian [-džạn], *a*. y *s*. (zool.) falángido; *s*. falangio (arácnido).

Phalangida [-džịdạ], *s. pl.* falángidos.

phalansterian [fælạnstǽrịạn], *s*. y *a*. falansteriano.

phalanstery [fǽlạnsterị], *s*. falansterio.

phalanx [féịlæŋks], *s*. (mil., anat., zool.) falange, *f*.

phallic [fǽlịk], *a*. fálico, relativo al falo o al falismo.

phall(ic)ism [fǽl(ịs)ịzm], *s*. falismo, culto del falo o principio generador de la naturaleza.

phallus [fǽlʌs], *s*. (anat., relig., bot.) falo.

phanerogam [fǽnẹrogæm], *s*. (bot.) fanerógamo.

Phanerogamia [-géịmịạ], *s. pl.* (bot.) fanerógamas, cotiledóneas.

phanerogamic, phanerogamous [-gǽmịk, -rǽgamạs], *a*. fanerógamo.

phantasm [fǽntæzm], *s.* phantasma [fæntǽzmạ], *s*. fantasma, *m*.—**phantasmal** [-tǽzmạl], *a*. = PHANTOM.

phantasmagoria [-górịạ], *s*. fantasmagoría.

phantasmagori(c)al [-górị(k)ạl], *a*. fantasmagórico; ilusorio.

phantasy [fǽntạsị], *s*. = FANTASY.

phantom [fǽntọm]. **I.** *s*. fantasma, *m*., espectro, sombra, visión; estantigua. **II.** *a*. fantástico, ilusorio, quimérico; semejante a un fantasma o espectro.

Pharaonic [ferịǽnịk], *a*. faraónico.

pharisaic(al [færịséịk(ạl], *a*. farisaico.—**pharisaically** [-ị], *adv*. farisaicamente.—**pharisaism** [fǽrịseịịzm], *s*. farisaísmo.

Pharisee [fǽrịsi], *s*. fariseo.

pharmaceutic(al [farmạsịútịk(ạl], *a*. farmacéutico.—**pharmaceutics** [-tịks], *s*. farmacia (ciencia).—**pharmaceutist** [-tịst], *s.* **pharmacist** [fármạsịst], *s*. farmacéutico, boticario.

pharmacognosy [-kágnosị], *s*. farmacognosia.

pharmacological [-kọládžịkạl], *a*. farmacológico. —**pharmacologist** [-kálodžịst], *s*. farmacólogo.—**pharmacology** [-džị], *s*. farmacología.

pharmacopœia [-kopíạ], *s*. farmacopea.

pharmacopolist [-kápolịst], *s*. boticario.

pharmacy [fármasị], *s*. farmacia; botica.

pharos [féịros], *s*. faro.

pharyngeal [farịndžịạl], *a*. (anat.) faríngeo.

pharyngitis [færịndžáịtịs], *s*. (med.) faringitis.

pharyngoscope [farịŋgoskoup], *s*. faringoscopio.

pharynx [fǽrịŋks], *s*. (anat.) faringe, *f*.

phase [feịz], *s*. fase, *f*., aspecto; (astr., fís., etc.) fase; (elec.) fase.—**p. angle,** ángulo de retraso, ángulo de diferencia de fases.—**p. displacement,** desplazamiento de fase.—**p. lag,** o **lagging,** retraso de fase.—**p. lead,** o **leading,** avance de fase.—**f. meter,** (elec.) fasímetro.— **to be in p.,** (elec.) tener una misma fase, estar en (concordancia de) fase.—**to be out of p.**, no tener una misma fase, discordar en fase.

phasis [féisis], s. (astr., etc.) fase, f.

pheasant [fézant], s. (orn.) faisán.

pheasantry [-ri], s. criadero de faisanes.

phenacetin [finésitin], s. (quím., farm.) fenacetina.

phenacite [fénasait], s. (min.) fenacita.

phenakistoscope [fenakístoskoup], s. fenaquistiscopio

phenazine [fénazin], s. (quím.) fenacina.

phenazone [fénazoun], s. (quím.) antipirina.

phenic [fínik], a. (quím.) fénico.

Phenician, Phenix, V. PHOENICIAN, PHOENIX.

phenol [fínol], s. (quím.) fenol, ácido fénico.

phenology [finálodži], s. (biol.) fenología, ciencia de los efectos del clima en el desarrollo de los seres organizados.

phenolphthalein [finolθélin], s. (quím., farm.) fenolftaleína.

phenomena [finámená], s. pl. de PHENOMENON. Ú. erróneamente en vez del sing.—**phenomenal** *[-nal], a. fenomenal.—**phenomenalism** [-izm], s. (filos.) fenomenalismo.—**phenomenalist** [-ist], s., **phenomenalistic** [-stik], a. fenomenalista.—**phenomenology** [-nálodži], s. (fil.) fenomenología.—**phenomenon** [-nan], s. fenómeno.

phenyl [fénil], s. (quím.) fenilo.

phenylacetic [-asítik], a. fenilacético, tolúico.

phenylamine [fenilamín], s. (quím.) fenilamina.

phenylene [fénilin], s. (quím.) fenileno.—**p. blue,** azul de fenileno.—**p. brown,** pardo de fenileno.

phenylic [fenílik], a. (quím.) fenílico, fénico.

phial [fáial], s. redoma, frasco. V. VIAL.

Philadelphian [filadélfian], a. filadelfo, de Filadelfia.

philander [filándœ(r)], vn. galantear.—**philander(er** [-œ(r)], s. amante; galán, coquetón; (zool.) filandro.

philanthropic(al [filanθrápik(al], a. filantrópico.—**philanthropist** [filénθropist], s. filántropo.—**philanthropy** [-θropi], s. filantropía.

philatelic(al [filatélik(al], a. filatélico.—**philatelist** [filátelist], s. filatelista.—**philately** [-li], s. filatelia.

philharmonic [filharmánik], a. filarmónico.

philippic [filípik], s. filípica; diatriba, invectiva.

Philippine [filipin], a. filipino.

Philistine [filístin], s. y a. filisteo; reaccionario, ultraconservador; prosaico, positivista; inculto, vulgar.

Philistinism [-izm], s. convencionalismo, formalismo; falta de cultura, positivismo vulgar, aspiraciones bajas.

philologic(al [filoládžik(al], a. filológico.

philologist [filálodžist], s. filólogo.

philology [-dži], s. filología, filológica.

philomel, philomela [fílomel, -mílá], s. (orn.) (poét.) filomela, ruiseñor.

philopena [filopíná], s. juego en que una persona paga una prenda a otra bajo ciertas condiciones; almendra doble que motiva este juego; regalo o prenda que paga el que pierde.

philosophaster [filasoféstœ(r)], s. filosofastro.

philosopher [filásofœ(r)], s. filósofo.—**p.'s stone,** piedra filosofal.

philosophic(al [filoséfik(al], a. filosófico.

philosophically [-i], adv. filosóficamente.

philosophism [filásofizm], s. filosofismo.—**philosophist** [-ist], s. (desp.) filosofastro.—**philosophize** [-faiz], vn. filosofar.—**philosophizer** [-œ(r)], s. filosofador.

philosophy [-fi], s. filosofía.

philter, philtre [fíltœ(r)]. I. s. filtro, hechizo, bebedizo. II. va. hechizar con filtro.

phimosis [faimóusis], s. (med.) fimosis.

phiz [fiz], s. (vulg.) fisonomía, facha, cara.

phlebitis [flibáitis], s. (med.) flebitis.

phlebology [flibálodži], s. (med.) flebología.

phlebosclerosis [flebosklíróusis], s. (med.) flebosclerosis, endurecimiento de las venas.

phlebotomist [flibátomist], s. flebotomiano, flebotomista, sangrador, (Am.) flebótomo.

phlebotomize [-maiz], va. sangrar.

phlebotomy [-mi], s. (med.) flebotomía.

phlegm [flem], s. (fisiol.) flema, gargajo; lentitud, cachaza, apatía; frialdad de ánimo.

phlegmasia [flegméižiá], s. flegmasía, flogosis.

phlegmatic(al [flegmétik(al], a. flemático; cachazudo.

phlegmon [flégman], s. (med.) flemón.

phlegmonous [-as], a. flemonoso.

phlogistic [flodžístik], a. (quím.) flogístico; (med.) inflamatorio.

phlogiston [flodžíston], s. (quím.) flogisto.

phlox [flaks], s. (bot.) flox.

phlyctena [fliktíná], s. (med.) flictena.

phobia [fóubiá], s. fobia; temor o aversión mórbidos.—**phobic** [-ik], a. fóbico, rel. a una fobia.

phoca [fóuká], s. (zool.) foca.

phocid [fóusid], a. y s. (zool.) fócido, focídeo.

phœbe (bird [fíbi (bœrd], s. (orn.) (Am.) febe, especie de papamoscas de los E. U.; aguador; (P., poét.) Febe, la Luna; (astr.) Febe o Febé (satélite de Saturno).

Phœbus [fíbas], s. (mit. y poét.) Febo, Apolo; el sol.—**Phœbean** [fíbian], a. febeo.

Phœnician [finíšan], a. y s., fenicio.

Phœnix, o phœnix [fíniks], s. (mit.) fénix; prodigio; (astr.) ave (f.) Fénix, constelación austral.—**P. column,** (arq.) columna redonda compuesta de hierros curvos en U unidos por sus pestañas.

phonate [fóuneit], va. y vn. articular, enunciar.

phonation [fonéišon], s. fonación.

phonautograph [fonótográf], s. fonautógrafo.

phone [foun], (contr. de TELEPHONE). I. s. (fam.) teléfono. II. va. y vn. telefonear.

phoneidoscope [fonáidoskoup], s. foneidoscopio.

phoneme [fóunim], s. (fon.) fonema, m.

phonendoscope [fonéndoskoup], s. (med.) fonendoscopio.

phonetic(al [fonétik(al], a. fonético.—**p. spelling,** escritura fonética.

phonetician [fonetíšan], s. fonetista, fonólogo.

phonetics [fonétiks], s. fonología, fonética.

phonetism [fóunetizm], s. fonetismo.

phoney [fóuni], a. = PHONY.

phonic [fánik], a. fónico.—**phonics** [-s], s. fónica.

phonism [fóunizm], s. (psic.) fonismo (sinestesia).

phonogenic [fonodžénik], a. fonogénico.

phonogram [fóunogræm], s. tipo que simboliza un sonido; fonograma, m.; reproducción fonográfica.

phonograph [fóunográf]. I. s. fonógrafo, gramófono. II. va. reproducir por medio del fonógrafo.—**p. record,** fonograma, m., disco (de fonógrafo).

phonographer [fonágrafœ(r)], **phonographist** [-fist], s. taquígrafo fonético; persona versada en el uso del fonógrafo.

phonographic(al [fonográfik(al], a. fonográfico.

phonography [fonágrafi], s. fonografía.

phonolite [fóunolait], s. (petr.) fonolita, perlita.

phonologic(al [fonoládžik(al], a. fonológico.

phonologist [fonálodžist], s. fonólogo.

phonology [-dži], s. fonología, fonética.

phonometer [fonámetœ(r)], s. fonómetro.

phonometric [fonométrik], a. fonométrico.

phonometry [fonámetri], s. (fís.) fonometría.

phonoscope [fóunoskoup], s. (fís.) fonoscopio.

phonotype [fóunotaip], s. (impr.) fonotipo; tipo empleado en la fonotipia.

phonotypic [-típik], a. fonotípico.

phonotypy [-taipi], s. (impr.) fonotipia, impresión con tipos que representan sonidos.

phony [fóuni], a. (fam.) falso, falsificado.

phosgene [fásdžin], s. (quím.) fosgeno (gas).

phosphate [fásfeit], *s.* (quím.) fosfato.—**f. rock,** roca fosfatada o rica en fosfato (gen. de calcio).

phosphated [-id], **phosphatic** [fasfǽtik], *a.* fosfático; fosfatado; fosforado.

phosphatize [fásfataiz], *va.* fosfatar, tratar con o reducir a fosfato.

phosphaturia [-tiúriä], *s.* (med.) fosfaturia, exceso de fosfatos en la orina.

phosphene [fásfin], *s.* (fisiol.) fosfeno, sensación de luz causada por presión en el ojo.

phosphid(e [fásfaid], *s.* (quím.) fosfuro.

phosphine [fásfin], *s.* (quím.) fosfina.

phosphite [fásfait], *s.* (quím.) fosfito.

Phosphor [fásfo(r)], *s.* Fósforo, lucero del alba, estrella matutina.—**p. bronze,** bronce fosforado.

phosphorate [fásforeit], *va.* (quím.) fosforar, combinar con fósforo.—**phosphorated oil,** (farm.) aceite fosforado.

phosphoresce [fasforés], *vn.* fosforescer.—**phosphorescence** [-éns], *s.* fosforescencia, ardentía.—**phosphorescent** [-ént], *a.* fosforescente.

phosphoric [fasfórik], *a.* fosfórico; fosforescente.

phosphorite [fásforait], *s.* (min.) fosforita.

phosphoroscope [fasfároskoup], *s.* fosforoscopio.

phosphorous [fásforas], *a.* fosforoso.

phosphorus [fásforas], *s.* (quím.) fósforo.

phosphuret [fásfjurit], *s.* (raro) = PHOSPHIDE.

phot [fat], *s.* unidad de luz, igual a 1 lumen por centímetro cuadrado.

photic [fóutik], *a.* fótico, relativo a la luz.

Photinia [fotiniä], *s.* (bot.) fotinia.

photo [fóutou], *s.* (fam.) foto, *f.,* fotografía.

photoactinic [-æktinik], *a.* fotoactínico.

photochemical [-kémikal], *a.* fotoquímico.

photochemistry [-kémistri], *s.* fotoquímica.

photochromy [-kromi], *s.* fotocromía.

photocollography [-kólagrafi], *s.* fotocolografía.

photodrama [-dramä], *s.* drama cinematográfico.—**photodramatist** [-drámatist], *s.* escritor de dramas cinematográficos.

photodynamic [-dainǽmik], *a.* fotodinámico.

photoelectric [-iléktrik], *a.* fotoeléctrico.—**p. cell,** célula fotoeléctrica.

photoelectron [-iléktran], *s.* (quím. fís.) fotoelectrón, electrón emitido por un metal iluminado.

photoengrave [-engréiv], *va.* y *vn.* fotograbar.

photoengraver [-œ(r)], *s.* fotograbador.

photoengraving [-iŋ], *s.* fotograbado.

photogen [-džen], *s.* (biol.) organismo fotógeno; aceite extraído de pizarras bituminosas, etc.

photogene [-džin], *s.* imagen (*f.*) persistente en la retina.

photogenic [-džénik], *a.* fotogénico.

photograph [-graf], *s.* I. *va.* fotografiar, retratar por la fotografía. II. *s.* fotografía (estampa), retrato.—**to sit for a p.,** retratarse.—**photographer** [fotágrafœ(r)], *s.* fotógrafo, retratista.

photographical [fotogréfikal], *a.* fotográfico.—**photographically** [-i], *adv.* fotográficamente.

photography [fotágrafi], *s.* fotografía (arte).

photogravure [-graviúr], *s.* fotograbado.

photokinetic [-kinétik], *a.* fotocinético.

photolithograph [-liθograf], *s.* I. *va.* fotolitografiar. II. *s.* fotolitografía (estampa).—**photolithographic** [-liθográfik], *a.* fotolitográfico.—**photolithography** [-liθágrafi], *s.* fotolitografía (arte).

photology [fotálodži], *s.* (fís.) fotología; óptica.

photolysis [fotálisis], *s.* fotólisis, descomposición química por la luz.

photomechanical [-mikǽnikal], *a.* (impr.) fotomecánico.

photometer [fotámetœ(r)], *s.* fotómetro.

photometric [fotométrik], *a.* fotométrico.

photometry [fotámetri], *s.* fotometría.

photomicrography [-maikrágrafi], *s.* fotomicrografía.

photomontage [-mantáž], *s.* (fot.) fotomontaje.

photon [fóutan], *s.* (fís.) fotón.

photophobia [fotofóubiä], *s.* (med.) fotofobia.

photophone [-foun], *s.* (fís.) fotófono.

photoplay [-plei], *s.* = PHOTODRAMA.—**photoplayer** [-œ(r)], *s.* actor de dramas cinematográficos, actor de cinematógrafo.—**photoplaywright** [-rait], *s.* = PHOTODRAMATIST.

photoprint [-print], *s.* impresión fototipográfica, fotocopia.

photoprocess [-prases], *s.* cualquier procedimiento foto(tipo)gráfico.

photorelief [-rilíf], *s.* impresión fotográfica de relieve; fotorrelieve (procedimiento).

photospectroscope [-spéktroskoup], *s.* fotospectroscopio.

photosphere [-sfir], *s.* (astr.) fotosfera.

photostat [-stæt], *s.* fotóstato (nombre de fábrica de una cámara de fotografía directa para reproducir documentos, grabados, etc., sin necesidad de negativo); fotocopia, fotoduplicación, reproducción fotostática.

photosynthesis [-sínθesis], *s.* (bot.) fotosíntesis.

phototelegraphy [-tilégrafi], *s.* fototelegrafía, telefotografía.

phototelephone [-téléfoun], *s.* = PHOTOPHONE.—**phototelephony** [-teléfani], *s.* fototelefonía, transmisión del sonido por medio de la luz.

phototherapeutics [-θerapiútiks], **phototherapy** [-θérapi], *s.* (med.) fototerapia.

phototype [-taip], *s.* clisé fototipográfico.

phototypography [-taipágrafi], *s.* fototipografía.

photozincography [-ziŋkágrafi], *s.* fotocincografía.

phragma [frǽgmä], *s.* (bot. y zool.) fragma.

phrase [fréiz], *s.* I. frase (en gram. se aplica esp. a la que no tiene verbo y a la compuesta de preposición y término); expresión o locución (a veces proverbial); fraseología; estilo, modo de hablar o de escribir; (mús.) frase musical. II. *va.* frasear; expresar, formular; (mús.) frasear, dividir en frases.

phraseogram [-iogrǽm], *s.* signo o combinación de signos taquigráficos que representa una frase.—**phraseograph** [-iográef], *s.* frase para la cual existe tal signo.

phraseology [-iálodži], *s.* fraseología; dicción, construcción, estilo.

phratry [fréitri], *s.* fratría (subdivisión tribal).

phrenetic [frinétik], *a.* frenético, delirante; fanático; (med.) atacado de fiebre cerebral.

phrenic [frénik], *a.* (anat., psic.) frénico, relativo al diafragma o a la mente (o inteligencia).

phrenitis [frináitis], *s.* (med.) fiebre (*f.*) cerebral; delirio, frenesí; inflamación del diafragma.

phrenologic(al [frenoládžik(al], *a.* frenológico.

phrenologist [frinálodžist], *s.* frenólogo.

phrenology [-dži], *s.* frenología.

phrenopathy [frinápaθi], *s.* (med.) frenopatía.

phrensied, phrensy = FRENZIED, FRENZY.

Phrygian [frídžian], *a.* y *s.* frigio.

phthalein [(f)θélin], *s.* (quím.) ftaleína.—**phthalic** [(f)θélik], *a.* (quím.) ftálico.—**phthalyl** [(f)θélil], *s.* (quím.) ftalilo.

phthisic(al [tízik(al], *a.* (med.) tísico; asmático.

phthisis [(f)θáisis], *s.* (med.) tisis.

phycology [faikálodži], *s.* (bot.) ficología, algología, ciencia de las plantas marítimas.

phylacter(y [filéktœr(i], *s.* filacteria.

phyllium [fíliam], *s.* insecto parecido a una hoja.

phyllode [fíloud], *s.* (bot.) filodio.

phyllomania [filoméiniä], *s.* (bot.) filomanía.

phyllome [fíloum], *s.* (bot.) hoja.

phyllophagous [filáfagas], *a.* (zool.) filófago.

phyllopod [fílopad], *a.* y *s.* (zool.) filópodo.

phyllotaxis [filotǽksis], *s.* (bot.) filotaxia.

phylloxera [filaksírä], *s.* filoxera.

phylogenesis [failodžénesis], **phylogeny** [failádženi], *s.* (biol.) filogenia.—**phylogenetic** [-dženétik], **phylogenic** [-džénik], *a.* filogenético, filogénico.

phylum [fáilAm], *s.* (biol.) filo, una de las divisiones primarias del reino animal o vegetal.

physic [fízik]. I. *va.* (med.) purgar; medicinar. II. *s.* purgante o purga; medicina; cualquier medicamento.

physical [fízikǎl], *a.* físico; corporal, corpóreo; material; natural.—**p. culture, education** o **training,** educación física.—**p. exercise(s),** ejercicio(s) corporal(es).—**p. geography,** geografía física.—**p. science,** ciencias físicas.—**p. therapy** = PHYSIOTHERAPY.—**p. training,** educación física.

physically [-i], *adv.* físicamente.

physician [fizísǎn], *s.* médico, doctor, facultativo.

physicism [fízisizm], *s.* fisicismo.

physicist [fízisist], *s.* físico.

physicky [fíziki], *a.* purgante.

physicochemical [fizikokémikǎl], *a.* fisicoquímico.

physics [fíziks], *s.* física.

physiocracy [fiziákrǎsi], *s.* fisiocracia.—**physiocrat** [fíziokræt], *s.* fisiócrata, *mf.*—**physiocratic** [-krétik], *a.* fisiocrático.

physiognomist [-ágnomist], *s.* fisonomista, fisónomo; fisiognomista (que se dedica a la fisiognomía).—**physiognomic(al** [-agnámik(ǎl], *a.* fisonómico; fisiognómico.

physiognomy [-ágnomi], *s.* fis(i)onomía (aspecto); fisiognomía (arte de juzgar del carácter, etc., de una persona por la observación de su apariencia exterior, esp. de las facciones).

physiographer [-ágrǎfœ(r], *s.* fisiógrafo.

physiographic(al [-ográfik(ǎl], *a.* fisiográfico.

physiography [-ágrǎfi], *s.* fisiografía.

physiologic(al [-oládžik(ǎl], *a.* fisiológico.

physiologically [-i], *adv.* fisiológicamente.

physiologist [-álodžist], *s.* fisiologista, fisiólogo.

physiology [-dži], *s.* fisiología.

physiotherapy [fizioθérǎpi], *s.* fisioterapia, tratamiento de las enfermedades por agentes físicos (calor, electricidad, luz, masaje, etc.).

physique [fizík], *s.* físico, figura, presencia.

phytivorous [fajtívorǎs], *a.* herbívoro, fitófago.

phytogenic [fajtodžénik], *a.* fitógeno, de origen vegetal.

phytogeography [-džiágrǎfi], *s.* (bot.) fitogeografía.

phytography [fajtágrǎfi], *s.* (bot.) fitografía.

phytoid [fájtojd], *a.* fitoideo.

Phytolaccaceæ [fajtolǎkéjsie], *s. pl.* (bot.) fitolacáceas.

phytology [fajtálodži], *s.* fitología, botánica.

phytonomy [fajtánomi], *s.* (bot.) fitonomía.

phytophagous [fajtáfagǎs], *a.* (zool.) fitófago.

phytosis [fajtóusis], *s.* (med.) fitosis.

phytotomy [fajtátomi], *s.* (bot.) fitotomía.

phytotoxin [fajtotáksin], *s.* fitotoxina, toxina obtenida de substancias vegetales.

pi, pie [paj]. I. *va.* (impr.) empastelar. II. *s.* (impr.) pastel; pi (letra griega); (mat.) pi, π (3,1416).

piacular [pajékyŭlǎ(r)], *a.* expiatorio; culpable, criminal.

piaffe [pjéf]. I. *vn.* (equit.) piafar. II. *s.* piafe (ll. t. **piaffer**).

pia mater [páiǎ méjtœ(r)], *s.* (anat.) piamadre o piamáter. *f.*—**pia-matral** [-méjtrǎl], *a.* piamátrico, pial.

pianism [pjénizm], *s.* (mús.) arreglo para piano; ejecución en el piano; técnica del piano.

pianissimo [pjanísimou], *adv.* y *a.* (mús.) muy suavemente, pianísimo.

pianist [pjénist], *s.* pianista.

piano [pjánou], *a.* y *adv.* (mús.) dulcemente, piano.

piano(forte [pjénou(fort], *s.* (mús.) pianoforte, piano.—**p. action,** mecanismo de piano.—**p. dealer,** o **maker,** pianista.—**p. player,** pianista; pianola, piano mecánico.—**p. stool,** taburete o banqueta de piano.—**p. tuner,** afinador.—**p. wire,** cuerda de piano.

pianola [pjanóulǎ], *s.* pianola, piano mecánico.

piarh(a)emia [piǎrímiǎ], *s.* (med.) piaremia, lipemia.

piaster, piastre [pjéstœ(r], *s.* piastra; peso.

piazza [pjézǎ], *s.* plaza; pórtico; portal, galería con arcadas; (E. U.) *V.* PORCH y VERANDA.

pibroch [píbrak], *s.* (Esco.) música marcial o fúnebre, tocada con la gaita.

pica [pájkǎ], *s.* (impr.) lectura, cícero (tipo de 12 puntos); (med.) pica, malacia.

picador [píkǎdor], *s.* picador (en la corrida de toros); (fig.) polemista listo o perspicaz.

Picard [píkard], *a.* y *s.* picardo, natural de Picardía; apl. t. a ciertos herejes del S. XV.

picaresque [pikǎrésk], *a.* picaresco.

picaroon [pikǎrún], *s.* picarón; ladrón; pirata, *m.*

picayune [pikǎyún]. I. *s.* (E. U.) medio real; cualquiera moneda, cosa o persona de poco valor. II. *a.* mezquino, insignificante, de poca monta.

piccalilli [píkǎlili], *s.* legumbres en escabeche.

piccolo [píkolou], *s.* (mús.) flautín.

piceous [písiǎs], *a.* píceo; inflamable; (zool.) de color de brea.

pick [pik]. I. *va.* picar, agujerear, romper con pico, picotear; hurtar, ratear; abrir (una cerradura) con ganzúa; escoger; coger, recoger; mondar o limpiar; descañonar (un ave).—**to p. a bone,** roer un hueso.—**to p. a bone with,** reñir o habérselas con.—**to p. a hole in one's coat,** denigrar a uno.—**to p. a quarrel (with),** meterse con, buscar camorra, armar pendencia.—**to p. off,** arrancar; ir escogiendo y matando uno a uno (en la guerra, etc.).—**to p. one's nose,** hurgarse las narices.—**to p. one's teeth,** mondarse o limpiarse los dientes.—**to p. out,** escoger, entresacar; señalar; tocar (una pieza) o cantar de oídas.—**to p. over,** examinar y escoger.—**to p. pockets,** ser carterista o ratero de faltriquera.—**to p. up,** alzar, recoger; aprender de oídas o con la práctica; coger; lograr obtener con trabajo; recobrar (las carnes, ánimo); entablar conversación con, sin presentación previa.—**to p. up speed,** acelerar la marcha, aumentar la velocidad.—**to have a bone to p. with one,** tener que ajustar cuentas (fig.) o habérselas con uno. II. *vn.* picar, comer bocaditos; hurtar.—**to p. and choose,** escoger esmeradamente.—**to p. at,** tirar de; criticar, regañar, sermonear.—**to p. on,** atormentar, molestar.—**to p. up,** restablecerse, recobrar la salud; cobrar carnes; (mec.) desarrollar velocidad. III. *s.* (zapa)pico (herramienta); ganzúa; escogido; derecho de elección; lo más escogido o granado, la flor (y nata); cosecha, cantidad de frutos, lúpulo, etc., que se recolecta de una vez o en una temporada; (tej.) golpe que empuja la lanzadera del telar; hilo de un tejido; (impr.) mancha en un pliego impreso.—**p. and p.,** alternación de hilos de diferentes colores.

pickaback, pickapack [píkǎbæk, píkǎpæk], *adv.* sobre los hombros, a cuestas.

pickaninny, pic(c)aninny [píkǎninj], *s.* negrito.

pickax(e [píkæks], *s.* zapapico, piqueta.

picked [pikt]. I. *pp.* y *a.* escogido, selecto. II. [píkjd], *a.* (ant.) espinoso, con púas; puntiagudo.

picker [píkœ(r], *s.* escogedor; escardador; (tej.) desmotadora, abridora. *V.* TO PICK y PICKING.—**p. of quarrels,** camorrista, pendenciero.

pickerel [píkerel], *s.* (ict.) pez algo parecido al lucio o sollo, pero de sólo dos pies de largo.

pickerelweed [-wid], *s.* (bot.) camalote, planta pontederiácea.

picket [píkit]. I. *s.* estaca puntiaguda, piquete; (mil.) piquete; (pol., e. p., etc.) piquete de vigilancia y propaganda, grupo de huelguistas o de cualquier bando, estacionado cerca de un establecimiento industrial, lugar de reunión de un cuerpo legislativo, etc., con el objeto de promover, de acción, de palabra o con la mera presencia, los intereses o propósitos de dicho bando.—**p. fence,** cerca de estacas puntiagudas.—**p. line**, (pol., e. p., etc.) línea de piquete. **II.** *va.* y *vn.* cercar con estacas o piquetes; (mil.) colocar de guardia; poner piquetes (cerca de); estacar (una bestia); (pol., e. p., etc.) desempeñar las funciones de un piquete o miembro de él; estacionar o poner piquetes de vigilancia y propaganda (en, cerca de, a, etc.).

picking [píkiŋ], *s.* acción y efecto de TO PICK en todas sus acepciones; v. gr.: recolección, cosecha; arrancamiento; picadura, roedura; limpia, monda; elección, escogido, (Am.) escogida; hurto, robo.—*pl.* desperdicios, residuos; hurtos, raterías; ganancias o beneficios de un oficio, etc.—**easy p.**, (fam.) tortas y pan pintado.

pickle [píkl]. **I.** *s.* salmuera, escabeche, adobo; encurtido, pepinillo; (fam.) lío, enredo, brete, apuro; (metal.) baño de ácido. **II.** *va.* escabechar, adobar, conservar, encurtir, salar, poner en salmuera o vinagre (a veces con especias); tratar con ácido por inmersión. **III.** *vn.* ratear, hurtar; comer poco.—**pickled** [-d]. **I.** *pp.* de TO PICKLE. **II.** *a.* (fam.) borracho.—**p. cucumbers**, pepinillos encurtidos.—**p. fish**, pescado en escabeche.—**p. herrings**, arenques salados.—**p. olives**, aceitunas en salmuera.—**p. oysters**, ostras encurtidas.—**p. salmon**, salmón escabechado.

pickler [píklœ(r)], *s.*, **pickling** [-liŋ], *a.* adobador.

picklock [píklak], *s.* ganzúa, llave falsa; ganzúa (fam.), ladrón; cierta lana escogida.

pickpocket [-pakit], **pickpurse** [-pœrs], *s.* cortabolsas, carterista, ratero de faltriquera, rata, *m.*

pickup [-Ap], *s.* (aut.) aceleración, pique; camión automóvil ligero para recoger y entregar mercancías; (radio) reproductor eléctrico de tono; fonocaptor; *pick-up* (aparato de fonógrafo); (fam.) mejora, recobro (en la salud, en los negocios, etc.); (fam.) bebida estimulante; (fam.) persona con quien se entablan relaciones o amistad casuales.

Pickwickian [pikwíkian], *a.* oculto, esotérico, no literal (apl. al sentido o acepción especial que se da a un vocablo empleado en cierta ocasión).

picnic [píknik]. **I.** *s.* partida de campo, jira campestre, romería, *picnic* o *pic-nic;* (fam.) tortas y pan pintado.—**p. grounds**, campo de excursión. **II.** *vn.* ir de romería.—**picnicker** [-œ(r)], *s.* participante en una jira campestre.

picoline [píkolin], *s.* (quím.) picolina.

picotee [píkotí], *s.* (bot.) clavel moteado.

picrate [píkreit], *s.* (quím.) picrato.

picric [píkrik], *a.* (quím.) pícrico (ácido).

picrite [píkrait], *s.* (petr.) picrita.

Pict(ish [píkt(iš], *s.* y *a.* picto.

pictograph [píktogræf], *s.* pictógrafo, representación pictográfica.—**pictography** [piktágrafi], *s.* pictografía, arte pictográfico.

pictorial [piktórial]. **I.** *a.* pictórico, gráfico. **II.** *s.* ilustración, publicación periódica que lleva muchas láminas y dibujos.

picturable [píkchūrabl], *a.* que puede dibujarse o pintarse.

picture [píkchū(r)]. **I.** *s.* pintura, cuadro; retrato, fotografía; (fig.) estampa, imagen, *f.;* ilustración, lámina, grabado; descripción; (cine) película, film.—*pl.* (fam.) cine.—**p. book**, libro con láminas o estampas.—**p. frame**, cuadro, marco. —**p. gallery**, pinacoteca, galería de pinturas.— **p. hat**, sombrero chambergo.—**p. house**, o (Ingl.) **palace**, teatro-cine, salón de cinematógrafo.— **p.-like**, semejante a una pintura.—**p. play**, drama o cuento cinematográfico.—**p. writing**, pictografía.—**to be in the p.**, figurar en el asunto.—**to be out of the p.**, no figurar ya en el asunto. **II.** *va.* pintar, dibujar; describir; imaginar.—**to p. to one's self**, imaginarse, representarse, concebir.

picturedrome [-droum], *s.* (Ingl.) teatro de cine.

picturesque [-ésk], *a.* pintoresco.

picturesqueness [-nis], *s.* carácter pintoresco.

picturize [-aiz], *va.* adaptar al cine.

piddle [pídl], *vn.* emplearse en bagatelas; picar o pellizcar la comida; (fam.) orinar.

piddler [pídlœ(r)], *s.* el que malgasta el tiempo en cosas baladíes; el que come sin ganas.

piddling [-liŋ], *a.* baladí, frívolo, trivial.

pidgin English [pídžin íŋgliš], *s.* inglés chapurrado usado en China.

pie [pai], *s.* (coc.) pastel; empanada; (orn.) marica, urraca; (impr.) *V.* PI.—**p. crust**, pasta.—**to have a finger in the p.**, meter cuchara, tener parte.

piebald [páibold]. **I.** *a.* pío; pintado, de varios colores; mezclado. **II.** *s.* caballo, mulo, etc., pío.

piece [pís]. **I.** *s.* pieza, pedazo, trozo, retazo, fragmento; sección, parte, *f.*, división; pieza (de paño, etc.); (arti.) pieza (cañón, fusil, escopeta); cualquier moneda; composición, obra, escrito; cualquier artefacto; (pint.) cuadro; (teat.) pieza; ficha (del dominó o de las damas).—**p. goods**, géneros que se venden por piezas.—**p. of advice**, consejo.—**p. of folly**, acto de locura. —**p. of furniture**, mueble.—**p. of ground**, solar, parcela.—**p. of news**, noticia, informe, especie.—**p. of wit**, chiste, agudeza.—**p. price**, precio por artículo o por obra hecha.—**p. wage**, paga por pieza o por obra.—**of a p. (with)**, de la misma clase (que), del mismo tenor (que).— **to come to pieces**, desarmarse, desbaratarse. **II.** *va.* apedazar, remendar; pegar, juntar, unir. —**to p. on**, juntar, pegar o poner a.—**to p. out**, completar a pedacitos; completar.—**to p. up**, apedazar, remendar; unir, juntar.

piecemeal [-mil], *adv.* y *a.* (hecho) gradualmente o poco a poco; por partes; a pedacitos, a remiendos; dividido; en pedazos; hecho trizas o añicos.

piecework [-wœrk], *s.* obra pagada por pieza, (trabajo a) destajo.

pied [paid], *a.* pío; de varios colores, pintado.

Piedmontese [pidmantíz], *s.* y *a.* piamontés.

pieplant [páiplænt], *s.* (bot.) ruipóntico.

pier [pir], *s.* (arq.) pila, machón, estribo; cepa; entrepaño de pared; (mar.) muelle, embarcadero, atracadero; espigón, escollera, espolón.— **p. glass**, espejo alto de pared, que por lo común va en un entrepaño.—**p. glass frame**, tremó o tremol.—**p. table**, consola.

pierage [píridž], *s.* muellaje, derechos de muelle.

pierce [pirs]. **I.** *va.* agujerear, taladrar, calar, pinchar; acribillar; atravesar, traspasar; abrir paso o camino.—**pierced with holes**, acribillado.— **pierced with sorrow**, traspasado de dolor. **II.** *vn.* penetrar, internarse, entrar a la fuerza.

piercing [-iŋ]. **I.** *a.* penetrante, agudo, cortante. **II.** *s.* penetración, horadación.—**piercingly** [-li], *adv.* penetrante o agudamente.

Pierian [paiírian], *a.* (poét.) pierio.

pietism [páietizm], *s.* piedad, devoción; mojigatería; (P.), pietismo.—**pietist** [-ist], *s.* devoto; beato, mísero; (P.), pietista.

piety [páieti], *s.* piedad, devoción, religiosidad; santidad.—**affected p.**, beatería, mojigatería.

piezoelectric [paiizoiléktrik], *a.* piezoeléctrico.

piezometer [paiezámetœ(r)], *s.* piezómetro; tubo indicador de presión.

piezometric(al [paiizométrik(al], *a.* piezométrico.

piffle [pífl], *s.* (fam.) palabrería, tontería(s).

pig [pig]. **I.** *s.* (zool.) lechón, cochinillo, porcino; cerdo, puerco, marrano; (fam.) persona soez; (fund.) lingote; molde de lingotes; metal bruto en lingotes (apl. esp. al hierro y al plomo).— **p.-headed**, terco, cabezudo.—**p. iron**, lead, hierro, plomo, en lingotes o para lingotes.—**a p. in a poke**, trato a ciegas, cosa que se quiere vender sin mostrarla. **II.** *vn.* parir la puerca; conducirse o vivir como cochinos.

pigeon [pídžon], *s.* (orn.) paloma, palomo; pichón; (fam.) primo, bobalicón.—**p.-breasted**, deformado de pecho por la raquitis.—**p. English**

= PIDGEON ENGLISH.—**p. fancy**, afición a la cría de palomas.—**p. hawk**, (orn.) azor, halcón palumbario.—**p.-hearted**, tímido; cobarde.— **p. house**, o **loft**, palomar.—**p.-livered**, manso. —**p.'s blood**, (joy.) rubí de color claro.—**p.- toed**, de pies de paloma, patituerto.

pigeonfoot [-fųt], *s.* (bot.) especie de geranio.

pigeonhole [-houḷ]. **I.** *s.* casilla.—*pl.* juego de boliche. **II.** *va.* proveer de casillas; encasillar, poner en una casilla; (fig.) archivar, relegar al olvido; dar carpetazo (a un proyecto de ley, etc.), (Am.) encarpetar.

pigeonry [-rį], *s.* palomar.

pigeonwing [-wįŋ], *s.* ala de paloma.

piggery [pígœrį], *s.* zahurda, chiquero.

piggie o **piggy** [pígi], **piglet** [píglit], *s. dim.* cochinillo.—**piggy bank**, (fam.) alcancía.

piggin [pígįn], *s.* cubeta, balde; cazo.

piggish [pígiṣ], *a.* cochino; voraz, guloso; codicioso; egoísta; puerco, sucio.—**piggishness** [-nįs], *s.* voracidad; porquería, suciedad.

pigment [pígmęnt], *s.* pigmento, color, pintura. —**pigmentary** [-erį], *a.* pigmentario.—**pigmentation** [-éiṣǫn], *s.* pigmentación; (med.) deposición excesiva de pigmento.

pigmy [pígmį], *s.* pigmeo.

pignoration [pignoréiṣǫn], *s.* pignoración.

pignoratitious [-ątíṣʌs], *a.* pignoraticio.

pignut [pígnʌt], *s.* (bot. E. U.) variedad de nogal de América y su nuez.

pigpen [-pen], *s.* zahurda, pocilga, chiquero.

pigskin [-skįn], *s.* piel (*f.*) de cerdo; (fam.) silla de montar; (fam.) fútbol.

pigstick [-stįk], *vn.* cazar jabalíes con venablo; matar cerdos.

pigsty [-stai], *s.* pocilga, gorrinera, cochitril.

pigtail [-teiḷ], *s.* cola de cerdo; coleta, trenza; chino; andullo de tabaco.

pigweed [-wid], *s.* (bot.) chual.

pike [paįk], *s.* (ict.) especie de lucio o sollo; pica, chuzo, guincho, garrocha; camino de barrera; carretera; peaje.

piked [páįkįd o paįkt], *a.* puntiagudo.

pikeman [páįkmąn], *s.* (mil.) piquero, chucero.

piker [páįkœ(r)], *s.* (fam.) el que se muestra tímido o tacaño en el juego, etc.

pikestaff [páįkstæf], *s.* asta de pica o chuzo, etc.; bordón, báculo herrado.

pilar [páįlą(r)], *a.* peludo, velloso.

pilaster [pįlǽstœ(r)], *s.* (arq.) pilastra, parástade.

pilchard [pįlchą̆rd], *s.* (ict.) sardina.

pile [paįl]. **I.** *s.* pila, montón, rimero, hacina; pira, hoguera; (ing.) estaca, pilote; edificio grande y macizo; pelo, pelaje; fibra, pelillo, pelusa; (arti.) montón de balas; (elec.) pila.—*pl.* (med.) hemorroides, *f. pl.*, almorranas.—**p. drawer**, aparato para arrancar pilotes.—**p. driver**, **p. engine**, martinete para clavar pilotes; martillo pilón.— **p. dwelling**, vivienda lacustre.—**p. hoop**, viorta, loriga o zuncho de pilote.—**p. shoe**, o **ferrule**, azuche.—**he has made his p.**, (fam.) tiene (bien) cubierto el riñón. **II.** *va.* hincar pilotes en; poner pelusa (a una tela); (a veces con **up**) amontonar, apilar; acumular. **III.** *vn.* (a veces con **up**) amontonarse; acumularse.

pileous [páįlįʌs], *a.* piloso, peludo, velloso.

pileus [páįlįʌs], *s.* (igl.) píleo; gorro o sombrero de fieltro sin ala; (bot.) sombrero de un hongo.

pilework [páįlwœrk], *s.* (ing.) pilotaje.

pilewort [páįlwœrt], *s.* (bot.) ficaria; celidonia menor (ll. t. **figwort**).

pilfer [pįlfœ(r)], *va.* y *vn.* ratear, hurtar, birlar, sisar.—**pilferer** [-œ(r)], *s.* ratero, birlador, buscón, sonsacador.—**pilfering** [-įŋ], *s.* ratería, sisa.

pilgrim [pįlgrįm]. **I.** *s.* peregrino, romero.—**p.'s staff**, bordón. **II.** *vn.* peregrinar, ir en romería.

pilgrimage [-įdž], *s.* peregrinación, romería.

piliferous, piligerous [pąilífęrʌs, pąilídžęrʌs], *a.* pilífero, peludo, velloso.

piliform [pįlifǫrm], *a.* piliforme.

---

piling [páįlįŋ], *s.* (ing.) pilotaje.

pill [pįl], *s.* píldora; desazón, *f.*, sinsabor, mal trago; (fam.) tragantona; (fam.) posma, persona fastidiosa.

pillage [pįlįdž]. **I.** *s.* pillaje, saqueo, merodeo, rapiña. **II.** *va.* pillar, saquear, entrar, meter o poner a saco. **III.** *vn.* merodear.

pillager [-œ(r)], *s.* pillador, saqueador, merodeador.

pillar [pįlą̆(r)], *s.* columna, pilar; poste; puntal; (biol.) columna; (fig.) soporte, sostén.—**Pillars of Hercules**, Columnas de Hércules.—**from p. to post**, de Ceca en Meca, de Herodes a Pilatos.

pillared [-d], *a.* sostenido por columnas.

pillbox [pįlbaks], *s.* caja para píldoras; (mil.) fortín armado de ametralladoras.

pillion [pįlyǫn], *s.* grupera; asiento trasero para pasajero o portaequipaje de motocicleta.

pilloried [pįlǫrįd], *a.* empicotado.

pillory [pįlǫrį]. **I.** *s.* pilorí, picota, cepo, argolla. **II.** *va.* empicotar; (fig.) exponer (a uno) a la mofa pública.

pillow [pįlou]. **I.** *s.* almohada, cabezal; almohadón, cojín; (mec.) cojinete, gorrón, dado, buje. —**p. block**, soporte; cojinete, tej(uel)o, chumacera.—**p. sham**, cubierta de adorno para almohada.—**p. slip** = PILLOWCASE. **II.** *va.* poner sobre una almohada, cojinete, etc.

pillowcase [-keis], *s.* funda de almohada.

pilocarpin(e [pąilokárpįn], *s.* (quím.) pilocarpina.

pilose [páįlous], *a.* piloso, velloso.

pilosity [pąilásįtį], *s.* vellosidad.

pilot [páįlǫt]. **I.** *va.* (mar.) pilot(e)ar, timonear; gobernar, dirigir, guiar; (aer.) pilot(e)ar, conducir, manejar. **II.** *s.* (mar.) timonel; piloto, práctico; consejero, guía, *mf.*; (aer.) piloto, aviador; (f. c.) trompa o quitapiedras (de la locomotora).—**p. balloon**, globo piloto, pequeño globo indicador de la dirección y velocidad del viento.—**p. bird**, (orn.) pájaro piloto. —**p. boat**, bote del práctico.—**p. bread**, **p. biscuit**, galleta.—**p. burner**, mechero encendedor, mechero pequeño que se mantiene encendido y sirve para encender otro mayor.—**p. chart**, carta de marear.—**p. engine**, locomotora piloto de descubierta, que va delante de un tren y lo guía.—**p. fish**, (ict.) piloto, romero. —**p. flag**, bandera en demanda de práctico.— **p. flame** = P. BURNER.—**p. house**, timonera. —**p. lamp**, (elec.) lámpara piloto.—**p. school**, escuela de pilotaje.—**p.'s mate**, piloto.—**p. valve**, (hidr.) válvula de mano auxiliar para hacer funcionar otra.—**p. wire**, (elec.) alambre piloto.—**coast p.**, piloto o práctico de costa. —**port** o **harbor p.**, práctico de puerto.—**sea p.**, piloto de altura.

pilotage [-įdž], *s.* pilotaje, practicaje.

pilotry [-rį], *s.* pilotaje (en toda acepción).

pilous [páįlʌs], *a.* piloso, peludo.

pimento [pįméntou], *s.* (bot.) pimienta de Jamaica. *V.* ALLSPICE y PIMIENTO.

pimiento [pįmyéntou], *s.* (bot.) pimiento.

pimp [pįmp]. **I.** *s.* alcahuete, rufián, tercero, (fam.) echacuervos. **II.** *vn.* alcahuetear, rufianear.

pimpernel [pímpœrnęl], *s.* (bot.) pamplina; anagálida; murajes, *m. pl.*

pimpinel [pímpįnél], *s.* (bot.) pimpinela.

pimping [pímpįŋ]. **I.** *a.* pequeño, fútil, mezquino, miserable. **II.** *s.* al●ahuetería.

pimple [pímpḷ], *s.* grano, barro, pupa, pústula.

pimply [pímplį], *a.* barroso, granujiento.

pin [pįn]. **I.** *s.* alfiler; prendedor, broche; (mec.) clavija, chaveta, perno, pasador, espiga; bolo; (mar.) cabilla; (mús.) clavija.—*pl.* (fam.) piernas.—**p. clover**, o **grass**, (bot.) alfilerillo.— **p.-connected**, con juntas de pasador; de ensamble articulado.—**p. connection**, junta de pasador o articulada.—**p. maker**, o **seller**, alfilerero.—**p. money**, (dinero para) alfileres. —**p. oak**, (bot.) pincarrasco.—**p. point**, punta de alfiler; minuciosidad.—**p.-point bombing,** (mil.) bombardeo aéreo de gran precisión.—**I don't care a p.,** no se me da un bledo, no me importa un pito.—**to be on pins and needles,** estar en ascuas, brasas, o espinas. II. *va.* prender con alfileres; fijar, clavar, enclavijar, sujetar.—**to p. down,** acosar; restringir.—**to p. in,** (alb.) llenar con ripio.—**to p. one's faith to,** u **on,** confiar absolutamente en.—**to p. up,** arremangar, recoger y asegurar con alfileres.

piña [pínyḁ], *s.* (bot.) piña, ananás.—**p. cloth,** piña.

pinaceous [painéiṣiʌs], *a.* (Am., bot.) pináceo.

pinafore [pínafor], *s.* delantal de niño.

pinang [pínæŋ], *s.* (Filip., bot.) areca.

pinaster [painǽstœ(r)], *s.* (bot.) pinastro, pino rodeno, aznacho.

pincase [pínkeis], *s.* alfiletero.

pince-nez [pæns nei], *s.* quevedos, lentes o anteojos de nariz (sujetados en la nariz).

pincers [pínsœrz], *s. sing.* y *pl.* pinzas, tenacillas; alicates, tenazas; (zool.) pinza(s), boca.—**p. movement,** (mil.) maniobra de pinzas.

pinch [pínch]. I. *va.* pellizcar; repizcar; apretar con pinzas o tenazas; oprimir, perseguir, estrechar; contraer, adelgazar; escatimar, limitar mucho los gastos; (fam.) prender, arrestar; hurtar, birlar.—**to p. one's self,** privarse de lo necesario.—**to p. out,** exprimir, hacer salir por presión. II. *vn.* pellizcar, apretar (*my shoes pinch,* me aprietan los zapatos).—**to p.-hit,** (baseball) batear por otro; (fig.) servir en lugar de otro en caso de necesidad. III. *s.* pellizco, repizco; pulgarada; (fam.) pizca; aprieto, apuro; dolor, tormento.—**p. bar,** palanca o barra con espolón.—**p. of snuff,** toma o polvo de rapé.—**in a p.,** en caso necesario, si es preciso.—**to be in a p.,** hallarse en un aprieto, en un apuro.

pinchbeck [-bek], *s.* similor, tumbaga; espurio.

pinchcock [-kak], *s.* abrazadera regulable de compresión, llave (*f.*) de pinzas.

pinchers [-œrz], *s. pl.* = PINCERS.

pinchfist(ed, pinchpenny [-fist(id, -peni], *s.* y *a.* avaro.

pincushion [pínkuṣǫn], *s.* acerico.

Pindaric [pindǽrik], *a.* (poét.) pindárico.

pindling [píndliŋ], *a.* (fam.) delicado, enfermizo.

pine [pain], *s.* (bot.) pino y su madera; piña, ananás.—**p. cone,** piña.—**p. grove,** pinar, pineda.—**p. kernel,** piñón.—**p. marten,** (zool.) marta cibelina o cebellina.—**p. needle,** pinocha.—**p. nut,** piña; piñón.—**p. resin,** zopisa, resina de pino.—**p. tree,** pino.—**P.-tree State,** (E. U.) Estado de Maine.

pine, *vn.* (con **away**) desfallecer, languidecer, consumirse; (con **for**) anhelar.

pineal [píniʌl], *a.* de figura de piña.—**p. body,** o **gland,** (anat. y zool.) glándula pineal.

pineapple [páinæpl], *s.* (bot.) piña, ananá(s), *m.*—**p. plantation,** (Am.) piñal.

pinene [páinin], *s.* (quím.) pineno, el elemento principal de la trementina, etc.

pinfeather [pínfeðœ(r)], *s.* cañón, flojel, pluma rudimentaria.

pinfold [pínfould], I. *s.* corral para animales mostrencos; redil. II. *va.* encerrar; encorralar.

ping [piŋ], *s.* silbido o zumbido de una bala.

ping-pong [-páŋ], *s.* ping-pong, juego de salón semejante al tenis que se juega sobre una mesa.

pinguid [píŋgwid], *a.* pingüe, craso, mantecoso.

pinhead [pínhɛd], *s.* cabeza de alfiler; objeto muy pequeño o insignificante; (fam.) bobalicón.

pinhole [pínhoul], *s.* agujero o pinchazo que hace el alfiler; agujero muy pequeño; (mec.) agujero para clavija, etc.; (fot.) punto transparente en una placa negativa.

piniform [páiniform], *a.* piniforme, en forma de cono.

pining [páiniŋ], *s.* languidez; anhelo.

pinion [pínyǫn], I. *s.* ala de ave; alón; piñón (pluma y último huesecillo del ala); (mec.)

piñón.—**p. drive,** (mec.) transmisión por engranajes. II. *va.* atar las alas; atar los brazos; maniatar.

pinioned [-d], *a.* alado; maniatado.

pinite [páinait], *s.* (min.) pinita; (quím.) pinita (ll. t. **pinitol**).

pink [piŋk]. I. *s.* (bot.) clavel; cualquier flor parecida al clavel; color de rosa; (pol., fam.) radical; (cost.) picadura; dechado, modelo; (Ingl.) casaquín encarnado de caza; (Ingl.) cazador de zorras; (mar.) pingüe (ll. t. **pinkie**).—**in the p. (of condition),** en el apogeo, en el mejor estado posible. II. *a.* (son)rosado, gilvo; (pol., fam.) radical, algo rojo.—**p.-sterned,** (mar.) de popa angosta.—**p. tea,** (fam.) té o recepción formal. III. *va.* herir con arma blanca, apuñalar; (cost.) picar, calar; ojetear.

pinkeye [píŋkai], *s.* (vet.) influenza o catarro epidémico de los caballos, acompañado de oftalmía; (med.) conjuntivitis purulenta contagiosa.

pinking [píŋkiŋ], *s.* (cost.) picadura, picado.—**p. iron,** picador, hierro de picar festones, etc.

pinkish [píŋkiṣ], *a.* que tira a rosado.

pinky [píŋki], *a.* rosado, gilvo.

pinna [pínḁ], *s.* (bot.) hojuela de hoja pinada; (anat.) oreja, pabellón; (zool.) ala, aleta.

pinnace [pínis], *s.* (mar.) pinaza.

pinnacle [pínakl], *s.* (arq.) pináculo, ápice, remate, fastigio; cima, cumbre.

pinnate(d [pínejt(id], *a.* (bot.) pinado.

pinnatifid [pinǽtifid], *a.* (bot.) pinatífido.

pinner [pínœ(r)], *s.* el que asegura con alfileres, pernos, clavijas, etc.; especie de toquilla.

pinnigrade [pínigreid], *a.* (zool.) que se mueve por medio de aletas o patas palmeadas.

pinniped [píniped], *s.* y *a.* (zool.) pin(n)ípedo.

pinnule [pínyul], *s.* (top., astr.) pínula; (zool.) aleta pequeña; (bot.) pínula, hojuela.

pinochle, pinocle [pínakl], *s.* cierto juego de naipes.

piñon [pínyon o pinyóụn], *s.* (bot.) pino piñonero, u otro pino que da piñones comestibles.

pinpoint [pínpoint], *s.* V. PIN POINT.

pinprick [pínprik], *s.* alfilerazo, pinchazo; molestia, irritación, antagonismo a poquitos.

pint [paint], *s.* (como medida para líquidos) pinta (⅛ galón), cuartillo; (para áridos) octava parte de un celemín.

pintail [píntejl], *s.* (orn.) ánade (*mf.*) de cola larga.

pintle [píntl], *s.* clavija, perno, pinzote; macho del timón.

pinto [píntoụ]. I. *a.* pintado, de varios colores. V. PIEBALD. II. *s.* animal pintado; (Am.) pinto (caballo; frijol).

pinwheel [pínhwil], *s.* (mec.) rueda de engranaje con clavijas en vez de dientes; girándula, rueda giratoria de fuegos artificiales; ventolera, molinete o rehilandero (juguete).

pinworm [pínwœrm], *s.* (zool.) oxiuro, gusano nemátodo o intestinal, ascáride, *f.*

piny [páini], *a.* pinoso.

pioneer [paiǫnir]. I. *s.* explorador, (neol.) pionero; iniciador, primer promotor; (mil.) gastador, zapador, palero. II. *va.* y *vn.* explorar; abrir un camino; guiar; introducir, promover.

pious [páiʌs], *a.* pío, piadoso, devoto.

piously [-li], *adv.* piadosamente.

pip [pip]. I. *s.* moquillo, pepita (de las aves); pepita, pipa o semilla de una manzana, naranja, etc.; punto de un naipe, dado o dominó. II. *va.* romper (un polluelo) el cascarón. III. *vn.* piar.

pipe [paip]. I. *s.* tubo, caño, conducto; tubería; cañería; pipa de fumar, (Am.) cachimbo; (mús.) caño (como de órgano, etc.); (mús.) caramillo, churumbela; (mar.) pito o silbato del contramaestre; silbo, silbido; pipa, casco, tonel.—*pl.* (mús.) gaita; tubería. V. P. LINE.—**p. bowl,** tabaquera.—**p. clip,** o **fastener,** escarpiador.—**p. cutter,** cortatubos.—**p. die** = P. STOCK.—**p. dream,** (fam.) sueño, ilusión.—**p. fitter,**

montador de tuberías.—**p. fitting,** instalación de tuberías; acoplamientos y accesorios de tuberías.—**p. layer,** tendedor o instalador de cañerías.—**p. laying,** instalación de cañerías. fontanería.—**p. line,** tubería, cañería; fontanería; oleoducto.—**p. of peace,** pipa de paz. *V.* CALUMET.—**p. organ,** órgano de cañones. —**pipes of Pan** = PAN'S PIPES.—**p. stock,** terraja.—**p. tree,** (bot.) lila; saúco; jeringuilla. —**p. wrench,** llave (*f.*) para tubos. **II.** *va.* tocar (flauta, caramillo o dulzaina, etc.); cantar con voz aguda; llamar con un pito o silbato· conducir por medio de cañerías o tubos; instalar cañerías en; (cost.) poner vivos. **III.** *vn.* tocar el caramillo o la gaita; pitar; gritar; (fund.) endurecerse en forma de tubo.—**to p. down,** (fam.) callarse.

pipefish [páipfiʃ], *s.* aguja, pez lofobranquio.

piper [páipœ(r)], *s.* flautista, gaitero.

piperaceous [pipœréiʃʌs], *a.* (bot.) piperáceo.

piperazin(e [pipérazin], *s.* (quím., farm.) piperacina.

piperin(e [pípœrin], *s.* (quím.) piperina.

piperonal [pipœronal], *s.* (quím.) heliotropina.

pipestem [páipstem], *s.* boquilla de pipa de fumar.

pipet(te [pipét], *s.* pipeta, probeta.

piping [páipiŋ]. **I.** *a.* muy caliente; que silba; agudo; pastoril.—**p. hot,** en (o muy) caliente; hirviendo. **II.** *s.* sonido de caramillo, etc.; (fam.) llanto, gemido; cañería, tubería; (cost.) vivo, cordoncillo; (fund.) burbujas e impurezas.

pipit [pípit], *s.* (orn.) especie de alondra.

pipkin [pípkin], *s.* pucherito, ollita.

pippin [pípin], *s.* (bot.) camuesa; fada.

pipy [páipi], *a.* que tiene tubos; tubular. *V.* PIPING.

piquancy [píkʌnsi], *s.* picante, sabor.

piquant [píkʌnt], *a.* picante; (ant.) áspero, mordaz.

piquantly [-li], *adv.* picantemente.

pique [pik]. **I.** *s.* pique, resentimiento, rencilla. **II.** *va.* picar, ofender, irritar; excitar (interés, curiosidad, etc.); (aer.) atacar picando, o de cabeza. **III.** *vn.* (aer.) picar, descender con grande inclinación hacia abajo. **IV.** *vr.* (gen. con **on** o **upon**) preciarse, jactarse; picarse, ofenderse.

piqué [pikéi], *s.* (tej.) piqué.

piquet [pikét], *s.* juego de los cientos.

piracy [páirʌsi], *s.* piratería; plagio.

pirate [páirit]. **I.** *s.* pirata, *m.*, corsario; plagiario. **II.** *va. y vn.* piratear; plagiar; pillar, robar.

piratical [pairétikʌl], *a.* pirático, raquero.

pirn [pœrn], *s.* (tej.) carrete; ovillo de hilo arrollado en la canilla.

pirogue [piróug̣], *s.* piragua (ll. t. **piragua**).

pirouette [piruét]. **I.** *s.* pirueta, girada, cabriola. **II.** *vn.* piruetear.

Pisan [pízan], *a. y s.* pisano; de Pisa.

piscary [pískʌri], *s.* (for.) privilegio de pesca en aguas ajenas; pesquera; pesquería.

piscatorial [piskʌtóriʌl], **piscatory** [pískʌtori], *a.* piscatorio.

pisces [písiz], *s. pl.* los peces; (astr. **P.**) Piscis, *m.*

pisciculture [písikʌlchu(r)], *s.* piscicultura.

pisciculturist [-kʌlchurist], *s.* piscicultor.

pisciform [-form], *a.* pisciforme, de forma de pez.

piscina [pisáinʌ], *s.* piscina, pecina; (igl.) piscina.

piscivorous [pisívorʌs], *a.* piscívoro.

pish [piʃ], *interj.* ¡bah! ¡quita allá!

pisiform [páisiform], *a.* pisiforme.—**p. bone,** (anat. y zool.) hueso pisiforme.

pismire [písmair], *s.* (ent.) hormiga.

pisolite [páisolait], *s.* (miner.) pisolita.

piss [pis]. **I.** *vn.* (vulg.) orinar. **II.** *s.* orina.

pistachio [pistáʃiou], *s.* (bot.) alfóncigo o pistachero (árbol).—**p. nut,** alfóncigo o pistacho.

pistil [pístil], *s.* (bot.) pistilo.

pistillary [-eri], *a.* perteneciente al pistilo.

pistillate [-eit], *a.* pistilado, con pistilos.

pistol [pístol]. **I.** *s.* pistola; revólver.—**p. case,**

pistolera.—**p. shooting,** tiro a pistola.—**p. shot,** pistoletazo, tiro de pistola. **II.** *va.* tirar con pistola.

pistole [pistóul], *s.* doblón de oro.

pistoleer [-[r], *s.* pistolero.

piston [pístọn], *s.* (mec.) émbolo, pistón; (mús.) llave (*f.*) o pistón.—**p. displacement,** capacidad embolar.—**p. pin,** (aut., etc.) eje del émbolo.—**p. ring,** anillo de empaquetadura del émbolo; aro de pistón.—**p. rod,** vástago del émbolo.—**p. (slide) valve,** distribuidor cilíndrico de émbolo.—**p. stroke,** embolada; golpe de émbolo.—**p. travel,** carrera del émbolo.

pit [pit]. **I.** *s.* hoyo; hoya, cárcava; foso; abismo; (pozo de) mina; hullera; cacaraña (originada por las viruelas, etc.); hueso de ciertas frutas; (teat.) platea, patio.—**p. coal,** carbón de piedra, hornaguera, hulla.—**p. game fowl,** gallo(s) de pelea.—**p. head,** pozo de mina.—**p. of the stomach,** boca del estómago.—**p. saw,** sierra cabrilla, sierra abrazadera.—**to be at the p.'s brink,** estar al borde del precipicio. **II.** *va.* marcar con hoyos; cacarañar; poner en un hoyo; incitar a pelear; deshuesar (una fruta).

pita [pítʌ], *s.* pita (planta y fibra).—**p. fiber, p. flax, p. hemp, p. thread,** pita (fibra). (*Pita* se aplica a veces a la cabuya y otras fibras análogas.)

pitapat [pítʌpæt]. **I.** *s.* taque taque, golpeteo, serie de golpecitos; palpitación. **II.** *vn.* andar a la carrerita, o con pasitos rápidos; golpetear; latir violentamente (el corazón). **III.** *adv.* a la carrerita, a pasitos cortos rápidos; golpeteando, taque taque.

pitch [pich]. **I.** *s.* grado de inclinación, pendiente, *f.*, declive; paso (de tornillo, de rueda dentada, de arrollamiento); (mús.) tono; diapasón; término, extremo, punto; en ciertos juegos, lanzamiento, echada, tiro; pez, betún, brea, alquitrán; resina.—**p.-black** = P.-DARK.—**p. chain,** cadena articulada que mueve una rueda dentada, cadena de engranaje.—**p. circle,** círculo o circunferencia primitivos (de una rueda dentada).—**p.-colored,** pizmiento, atezado.—**p.-dark,** obscuro como boca de lobo.—**p. line** = P. CIRCLE.—**p. of an arch,** relación entre la flecha y la luz o la semiluz de un arco (gen. se toma en este último sentido).—**p. of a roof,** inclinación o pendiente de un tejado.—**p. pine,** (bot.) pino tea.—**p. pipe,** diapasón de voz.—**p. tree,** (bot.) abeto píceo.—**highest p.,** (fig.) cima, pináculo; colmo.—**to the highest p.,** a lo sumo. **II.** *va.* tirar, arrojar; echar, botar; en el juego de baseball, lanzar o arrojar la pelota al *batsman*; clavar, plantar o fijar (estacas, etc.) en tierra; armar, asentar (tienda, etc.); colocar, formar, arreglar; embrear, empecinar, embetunar; (mús.) graduar el tono, dar el diapasón. —**to p. tents,** (mil.) armar las tiendas, acamparse. **III.** *vn.* arrojar por bajo mano; caerse hacia abajo; caer de cabeza; instalarse, fijarse, establecerse; hocicar, arfar, cabecear (el buque). —**to p. in,** (fam.) poner manos a la obra, emprender (algo) con ahinco.—**to p. into,** (fam.) arremeter a, embestir; desatarse contra, sermonear, zurrar.—**to p. (up)on,** escoger.

pitchblende [-blend], *s.* (miner.) pechblenda, pechurana, óxido natural de uranio.

pitched battle [picht bǽtl], *s.* batalla campal.

pitcher [pichœ(r)], *s.* jarro, cántaro; arrojador, botador; en baseball, el lanzador (el que tira la pelota al *batsman*); (bot.) ascidia.—**p. plant,** (bot.) sarracenia, planta provista de ascidias.

pitchfork [pichfork], *s.* (agr.) horca, horquilla; bielda, aviento, aventador; tridente.

pitchiness [pichinis], *s.* calidad de embreado o píceo; obscuridad; negrura, color de pez.

pitching [pichiŋ]. **I.** *a.* inclinado, en declive. **II.** *s.* acción del verbo TO PITCH; lanzamiento; embreadura, empecinamiento; revestimiento (de piedra, etc.); adoquinado; (mar.) arfada, cuneo, cabezada.

pitchstone [píchstoṇn], *s.* (petr.) vidrio volcánico.

pitchy [píchi], *a.* embreado; píceo, peceño, peciento; negro, obscuro.

piteous [pítiʌs], *a.* lastimero, lastimoso; (ant.) compasivo, tierno.—**piteously** [-li], *adv.* lastimosamente.—**piteousness** [-niṣ], *s.* calidad de lastimoso.

pitfall [pítfɔl], *s.* trampa, armadijo, hoya cubierta; añagaza; peligro latente.

pith [piθ]. I. *s.* meollo, medula o médula; (raro) medula espinal; tuétano; (fig.) meollo, corazón, fuerza, vigor; jugo; substancia, la parte esencial, el quid. II. *va.* quitar el meollo a (una planta); destruir los centros nerviosos de; atronar, descabellar, matar (ganado) cortando la medula espinal.

pithecanthrope, pithecanthropus [piθikǽnθroup, -θróupʌs], *s.* (pal.) pitecántropo.

pithily [píθili], *adv.* enérgica o sentenciosamente.

pithiness [píθiniṣ], *s.* energía, eficacia; calidad de meduloso, sentencioso, etc.

pithless [píθliṣ], *a.* falto de meollo; endeble.

pithy [píθi], *a.* enérgico, eficaz; meduloso, medulado, medular; expresivo, sentencioso.

pitiable [pítiạbl], **pitiful** [pítifụl], *a.* lastimoso, enternecedor, digno de compasión; compasivo (apl. sólo a **pitiful**); pobre, despreciable.—**p. object,** lástima.

pitifully [-li], *adv.* lastimosamente.

pitifulness [-niṣ], *s.* calidad de lastimoso, etc.

pitiless [pítiliṣ], *a.* desapiadado, empedernido, cruel, desalmado.—**pitilessly** [-li], *adv.* desapiadadamente, sin compasión.—**pitilessness** [-niṣ], *s.* crueldad, empedernimiento.

pitman [pítmạn], *s.* (*pl.* PITMEN) aserrador de foso; (min.) pocero; (mec.) (*pl.* PITMANS) biela.

pitpit [pítpit], *s.* (orn.) pitpit, pipí (ll. t. **guit-guit**).

pittance [pítạns], *s.* pitanza, ración, porción.

pitted [pítịd], *a.* picado, cacarañado, picoso (de viruelas); hoyoso; deshuesada (fruta).

pitter [pítœ(r)], *s.* deshuesadora (de cerezas, etc.).

pitter-patter [pítœ(r) pǽtœ(r)], *s.* serie rápida de golpecitos (como de la lluvia). *V.* PITAPAT.

pitting [pítiṇ], *s.* picadura(s) (de un metal), corrosión diseminada; deshuesamiento (de una fruta).

pituitary [pitiúitəri], *a.* pituitario.—**p. body, p. gland,** (anat. y zool.) glándula pituitaria.

pituitous [-tʌs], *a.* pituitoso.

pity [píti]. I. *s.* piedad, misericordia, lástima, compasión.—**for p.'s sake, from p.,** por piedad.—**it is a p.,** es lástima, es de sentirse.—**to have,** o **take, p. on,** tener piedad de, compadecer. II. *va.* compadecer, lastimar. III. *vn.* apiadarse, tener piedad o compadecerse de; enternecerse.

pityriasis [pitiráiạsiṣ], *s.* (med.) pitiriasis.

pivot [pívọt]. I. *s.* (mec.) espiga, espigón, gorrón, (gal.) pivote, muñón, pezón; eje o centro de rotación; punto o hecho fundamental, corazón (fig.), punto de partida.—**p. chair,** silla giratoria.—**p. collar** = P. HOLE.—**p. gun,** cañón giratorio, colisa.—**p. hole,** rangua, quicio, buje o cuenca de pivote o de eje.—**p. (man),** (mil.) guía, *m.,* centro de giro de una hilera. II. *va.* colocar sobre un eje, o por medio de un pivote; proveer de gorrón o espigón. III. *vn.* girar sobre un pivote.—**to p. on,** girar sobre; depender de, estribar en.

pivotal [-ạl], *a.* cardinal, fundamental, céntrico.

pix [piks], *s.* (igl.) píxide, *f.,* copón.

pixy, pixie [píksi], *s.* hada o duende travieso.

placability [plékạbílitị], **placableness** [-blniṣ], *s.* placabilidad; dulzura, clemencia.

placable [-bl], *a.* (a)placable.

placard [plǽkard]. I. *s.* cartel, letrero, anuncio, rótulo; (hist.) proclama, edicto. II. *va.* publicar por medio de carteles; fijar (cartel o aviso).

placate [pléikeit], *va.* aplacar, apaciguar, conciliar.

placation [pleikéiṣọn], *s.* aplacamiento.

place [pléis]. I. *s.* lugar, sitio, paraje, local, puesto; (mil.) plaza, fortaleza, puesto militar; calle corta; callejón; situación, posición; empleo, puesto, acomodo, colocación, destino; grado, rango, dignidad; espacio, cabida, asiento; cubierto (en la mesa); (mat.) decimal (*five-place table,* tabla de cinco decimales).—**p. card,** tarjeta (en la mesa).—**p. name,** nombre de lugar geográfico.—**p. of arms,** (fort.) plaza de formación del camino cubierto.—**in no p.,** en ninguna parte, en ningún sitio.—**in p.,** en su lugar; apropiado; in situ; en la obra (que se construye).—**in p. of,** en lugar de, en vez de.—**in that p.,** allí, allá.—**in the first p.,** en primer lugar.—**in the next p.,** luego, después.—**out of p.,** fuera de lugar o de propósito; impropio, indebido, intempestivo. II. *va.* colocar, poner, situar; instalar; dar colocación o empleo a; recordar pormenores o circunstancias acerca de; prestar a interés, invertir o poner (dinero) en un negocio; (com.) disponer de, vender, dar salida a.—**to p. across,** atravesar.—**to p. before,** anteponer.

placeman [-mạn], *s.* empleado público, funcionario, oficinista. (ú. gen. despectivamente).

placement [-mẹnt], *s.* acción del verbo TO PLACE; colocación; empleo.—**p. agency, p. office,** agencia de colocaciones o de empleos, donde se suministran sirvientes u otros empleados.

placenta [plạsẹ́ntạ], *s.* (anat. y zool.) placenta, pares o parias, *f. pl.;* (bot.) placenta.

placental [-l]. I. *a.* placentario, referente a la placenta; provisto de placenta. II. *s.* (zool.) placentario.

placentate [-teit], *a.* placentario, que tiene placenta.

placentation [plæsẹntéiṣọn], *s.* (bot.) placentación; (anat. y zool.) modo de formación e inserción de la placenta.

placer [plǽsœ(r)], *s.* (min.) placer, lavadero de oro, etc.—**p. mine,** placer de oro.—**p. mining,** minería de placer o de lavado.

placer [pléisœ(r)], *s.* colocador.

placet [pléiset], *s.* permiso.

placid [plǽsid], *a.* plácido, apacible, sereno.

placidity [plạsíditi], **placidness** [plǽsidniṣ], *s.* placidez, apacibilidad, serenidad.

placidly [-li], *adv.* plácida o apaciblemente.

placing [pléisiṇ], *s.* colocación; instalación.

placket [plǽkit], *s.* (cost.) abertura en la parte superior de una saya o enagua; bolsillo (de falda).

placoid [plǽkɔid], *a.* (zool.) placoideo.

plagal [pléigal], *a.* (mús.) plagal.

plagiarism [pléidʒ(i)ạrizm], *s.* plagio.—**plagiary, plagiarist** [-i, -ist], *s.* plagiario.—**plagiarize** [-aiz], *va.* y *vn.* plagiar.

plagioclase [pléidʒiokleis], *s.* (miner.) plagioclasa.

Plagiostomi [-ástomai], *s. pl.* (zool.) plagióstomos.

plague [pléig]. I. *s.* plaga, peste, *f.,* pestilencia; miseria, calamidad. II. *va.* vejar, importunar, fastidiar; apestar, infestar, plagar.

plaguily [-ili], *adv.* (fam.) molestamente.

plague(y) [-i], *a.* (fam.) enfadoso, molesto.

plaice [pleis], *s.* (ict.) platija, acedía.

plaid [plæd]. I. *s.* manta escocesa listada a cuadros; tartán o género listado a cuadros; muestra o diseño en forma de cuadros. II. *a.* a cuadros, cuadriculado.

plain [pléin]. I. *a.* llano, simple, sencillo; desnudo, escueto, sin adornos; franco; natural, ingenuo; corriente, ordinario o común; feo, de facciones ordinarias; puro, sin mezcla; rematado, acabado (loco, desatino, etc.); manifiesto, palpable, claro; humilde, de humilde cuna.—**p. as a pikestaff,** obvio, evidente.—**p. chant,** canto llano.—**p. clothes,** traje ordinario, o de paisano (a distinción de uniforme).—**p.-clothes man,**

detective, agente de policía secreta.—p. **dealer,** hombre sincero.—p. **dealing,** sinceridad, buena fe.—p.**-hearted,** bueno, sin doblez.—p.**-heartedness,** sinceridad.—p. **people,** gente sencilla, gente humilde; el común de las gentes. —p. **sailing,** camino fácil, cosa fácil, negocio liso y llano; coser y cantar.—p. **song** = P. CHANT.—p. **speaking,** franqueza.—p.**-spoken,** claro, franco(te).—p. **truth,** pura verdad.—p. **work,** costura sencilla, sin adorno. —in p. **English,** en romance, sin rodeos, en plata. II. *adv.* = PLAINLY. III. *s.* llano, llanura, planicie; vega; (Am.) pampa, sabana. IV. *va.* y *vn.* (ant.) lamentar(se).

plainly [-li], *adv.* llanamente; sencillamente; evidentemente; claramente, francamente.

plainness [-nis], *s.* simplicidad, llaneza, sencillez; franqueza; claridad; fealdad.

plainsman [pléinzmạn], *s.* llanero.

plaint [pléint], *s.* queja; (poét.) quejido, lamento; (for.) demanda.

plaintiff [-if], *s.* (for.) demandante, actor.

plaintive [-iv], *a.* dolorido, quejumbroso, élego.

plaintively [-li], *adv.* quejumbrosamente.— **plaintiveness** [-nis], *s.* calidad de quejumbroso.

plait [pléit]. I. *s.* (cost.) pliegue, doblez, *m.,* alforza, plegado; trenza.—p. **laces,** cordones, torzales. II. *va.* (cost.) plegar, alechugar, rizar, encañonar, encarrujar; tejer, trenzar.

plaiter [-œ(r)], *s.* plegador.

plaiting [-iŋ], *s.* plegadura, plegado; tejido; plegueria.—p. **machine,** plegador(a).

plan [plæn]. I. *s.* plan, designio, idea, proyecto, programa, *m.,* traza; plano, dibujo, diseño, bosquejo, esquema, *m.,* traz(ad)o; planta, proyección horizontal; (perspectiva) plano óptico, tabla. II. *va.* idear, proyectar, planear, discurrir, trazar, proponerse; hacer planes para; pensar, resolver. III. *vn.* hacer planes.

planchet [plénchịt], *s.* tejuelo, disco metálico.

planchette [plænšét], *s.* (top.) brújula de agrimensor; tabla de escritura mesmeriana o mesmerista.

plane [pléin]. I. *s.* superficie plana; nivel (de carácter, conducta, dignidad, etc.); (geom.) plano; (carp.) cepillo, garlopa; (bot.) plátano falso; (f. c., etc.) plano inclinado; (aer.) aeroplano; (aer.) plano, superficie de sustentación; (mec.) V. SURFACE PLATE.—p. **of projection,** plano de proyección.—p. **of sight,** plano visual, plano vertical de la línea visual. II. *a.* plano, llano; relativo al plano; (geom.) plano.—p. **angle,** ángulo plano.—p. **geometry,** geometría plana.—p. **sailing,** navegación sobre la carta de marear.—p. **surveying,** (top.) planimetría, topografía ordinaria, en que no se tiene en cuenta la curvatura de la tierra.—p. **table,** (top.) plancheta; (min.) plano inclinado.—p.**-tree,** plátano falso, sicómoro.—p. **trigonometry,** trigonometría rectilínea o plana. III. *va.* acepillar; desbastar; allanar, alisar; (impr.) tamborilear, igualar las letras del molde. IV. *vn.* alisar, acepillar; funcionar (una cepilladora, etc.); (aer.) planear; volar, viajar en avión.

planer [-œ(r)], *s.* acepillador(a), cepillo mecánico; (impr.) tamborilete, aplanador.

planet [plénịt], *s.* (astr.) planeta, *m.*—p. **gear,** (mec.) engranaje planetario.—p.**-stricken, p.-struck,** influído por los planetas; marchito; asombrado, atónito.—p. **wheel,** (mec.) rueda planetaria.

planetarium [plænetérịạm], *s.* (astr.) planetario.

planetary [plén̥eteri], *a.* (astr., mec.) planetario. —p. **gear,** engranaje planetario.

planetoid [plénetọid], *s.* planetoide, asteroide.

planifolious [plænịfóụlịạs], *a.* (bot.) planifoliado.

planimeter [plænịmetœ(r)], *s.* planímetro.

planimetry [-tri], *s.* planimetría, medida de las áreas planas.

planing [pléiniŋ], *s.* acepilladura, alisadura, desbastadura.—p. **bench,** banco de carpintero.—

p. **machine,** cepillo mecánico, (a)cepilladora.

planish [plénịš], *va.* alisar, pulir, aplanar; pulir perfectamente con rodillos.

planisher [-œ(r)], *s.* alisador, aplanador.

planisphere [plénịsfịr], *s.* planisferio.

plank [plæŋk]. I. *s.* tablón, tabla gruesa; tablaje, tablazón, *f.* (gen. en *pl.*); (pol.) cada uno de los principios que forman el programa de un partido.—p. **road,** camino de tablas. II. *va.* entablar, enmaderar; (min.) encofrar; (con **down**) (fam.) pagar; poner de golpe.

planking [-iŋ], *s.* tablaje, tablazón, *f.,* entabladura, forro; (min., etc.) encofrado.

plankton [plénˌktọn], *s.* (biol.) plancton o plankton, vegetación flotante marítima.

planned [plénd], *pp.* y *a.* ideado, planeado, proyectado, etc.—p. **economy,** (e. p.) economía dirigida.

planner [plénœ(r)], *s.* trazador, tracista, proyectista, planeador.

planning [-iŋ], *s.* planeamiento.

plano-concave [pleino kánkeịv], *a.* planocóncavo.—**plano-conical** [-kánịkạl], *a.* planocónico.—**plano-convex** [-kánvẹks], *a.* plano-convexo.

plant [plænt]. I. *s.* (bot.) planta, mata, vegetal; planta (industrial, etc.), fábrica; (mec.) instalación de maquinaria, etc.—p. **bed,** plantel de tabaco.—p. **house,** invernáculo, invernadero. —p. **louse,** (ent.) áfido, brugo, pulgón. II. *va.* plantar, sembrar; colocar, instalar; fijar, sentar, asegurar; plantar, dar o asestar (golpes); fundar, establecer; engendrar.

plantaginaceous [plæntạdžịnéịšʌs], *a.* (bot.) plantagináceo.

plantain [pléntịn], *s.* (bot.) plátano; llantén, plantaina.

plantar [pléntậ(r)], *a.* plantar.

plantation [plæntéịšọn], *s.* hacienda (esp. la en que se cultiva café, caña de azúcar, tabaco, etc.); (raro) plantación, siembra, plantío; criadero de árboles; (hist.) colonia.—p. **hoes,** azadones.

planter [pléntœ(r)], *s.* plantador, cultivador, sembrador; hacendado; colono.

plantigrade [pléntịgreịd], *a.* y *s.* (zool.) plantígrado.

planting [pléntiŋ], *s.* plantación, plantío.—p. **stick,** o **tool,** plantador.

plantlet, plantule [pléntlịt, -jul], *s.* (bot.) plantita, plantilla; plántula.

plaque [plæk], *s.* (b. a.) placa, plato decorativo; broche, medalla; (zool.) disco; (anat.) = PLATELET.

plash [plæš]. I. *s.* chapaleteo; charco, aguazal. II. *va.* y *vn.* chapalear, chapotear; enramar, entretejer (ramas); (pint.) manchar. V. SPLASH y PLEACH.

plashy [-i], *a.* pantanoso; mojado; manchado.

plasma, plasm [plézmạ, plézm], *s.* (biol.) plasma, *m.;* protoplasma, *m.;* (min.) prasma (m.) o plasma, *f.*—p. **cell,** célula plasmática.

plasmatic [plæzmétịk], **plasmic** [plézmịk], *a.* (biol.) plasmático, plásmico.

plasmodium [plæzmóụdiʌm], *s.* (biol.) plasmodio.

plasmosome [plézmosoụm], *s.* (biol.) plasmosoma, *m.*

plaster [plésstœ(r)]. I. *s.* yeso; (alb.) argamasa, mortero, mezcla; enlucido, estuco; (farm.) parche, emplasto.—p. **cast,** yeso, obra de escultura vaciada en yeso; (cir.) vendaje o apósito enyesado, tablilla de yeso; (dent.) modelo de yeso.—p. **of Paris,** yeso mate, sulfato de cal. II. *va.* (alb.) enyesar, enlucir, revocar, jaharrar; (fig.) embarrar, embadurnar; cubrir (paredes, etc., con carteles o anuncios); (med.) emplastar, poner emplastos.

plasterboard [-bọrd], *s.* plancha de yeso y fieltro que se emplea para tabiques.

plasterer [-œ(r)], *s.* revocador, yesero, enlucidor.

plastering [-iŋ], *s.* (alb.) enlucido, revoque, enyesado, jaharro; (med.) emplastadura.

plasterwork [-wœrk], *s.* enyesado, enlucido; yesería.

plastic [plǽstik]. **I.** *a.* plástico; formativo.—**p. art**, plástica.—**p. surgery**, cirugía plástica, anaplastia. **II.** *s.* materia plástica.

plasticity [plæstísiti], *s.* plasticidad.

plastid [plǽstid], *s.* (biol.) plastidio, plástido, elemento protoplasmático; célula.

plastron [plǽstrɔn], *s.* (arm.) peto; pechera, (gal.) plastrón; (zool.) peto, plastrón, concha inferior de las tortugas; (esgr.) perpunte.

plat [plæt]. **I.** *s.* solar, parcela; mapa (*m.*) o plano; trenza, cintilla. **II.** *va.* entretejer, trenzar; trazar el plano de; trasladar al papel. *V.* PLAIT y PLOT.

platanaceous [plætǝnéiʃʌs], *a.* (bot.) platáneo, platanáceo.

platan(e [plǽtǝn], *s.* = PLANE TREE.

platband [plǽtbænd], *s.* arriate de un jardín; (arq.) platabanda, faja de la cornisa.

plate [pléit]. **I.** *s.* plancha, chapa, lámina, placa; plat(ill)o (de mesa); contenido de un plato; plato (de comer); vajilla en general; plata; plaqué; (blas.) plata; platina (de una máquina neumática); (dep.) palio, copa de oro o plata dada como premio en regata o carrera; (impr.) estereotipo, clisé; electrotipo; ilustración, grabado; (dent.) dentadura postiza; (elec.) elemento de una pila; placa de acumulador; plancha de blindaje; (foto.) placa; (top.) placa, limbo (de un instrumento).—**p. armor**, blindaje.—**p. battery**, (rad.) batería de alta tensión, batería del ánodo o placa (de un tubo termiónico).—**p. circuit**, (rad.) circuito de la placa y el filamento.—**p. cultivation, p. culture**, platicultivo, cultivo de las bacterias en gelatina sobre láminas de vidrio.—**p. current**, (rad.) corriente (*f.*) de entre el filamento y la placa.—**p. girder**, viga de alma llena.—**p. glass**, vidrio cilindrado o en planchas; luna.—**p. holder**, (foto.) chasis, *m.*, portaplacas, bastidor.—**p. mark**, (marca de) contraste; línea del borde en relieve.—**p. matter**, planchas electrotípicas vendidas a varios periódicos para la publicación simultánea de un escrito.—**p. metal**, metal en planchas.—**p. paper**, papel de primera calidad para grabados.—**p. press**, prensa para grabados.—**p. printing**, impresión de grabados con planchas.—**p. rack**, escurreplatos; (foto.) bastidor para sostener las placas mientras se secan.—**p. rail**, riel plano; moldura plana o anaquel para platos ornamentales, etc.—**p. roller**, laminador.—**p. room**, repostería.—**p. shears**, cizalla.—**p. ship** = TREASURE SHIP.—**p. tracery**, (arq.) labor calada en una piedra.—**p. voltage**, (rad.) tensión de la batería de la placa.—**p. warmer**, calientaplatos.—**p. wheel**, rueda de disco lleno. **II.** *va.* planchear; revestir (un metal) con una capa de otro metal) por la galvanoplastia u otro procedimiento; vg.: argentear o platear (si el metal de revestimiento es plata); dorar (si dicho metal es oro); niquelar, platinar; batir hoja; unir con planchas de metal; (a veces con **out**) cultivar (bacterias) sobre una lámina; hacer una plancha electrotípica de (para imprimir).

plateau [plǽtou], *s.* mesa, meseta, rasa, altiplanicie, altiplano.

plated [pléitid], *a.* plateado, niquelado, etc., según el metal (vg.: *silver-plated*, plateado; *gold-plated*, dorado; etc.).—**p. ware**, plaqué.

plateful [pléitful], *s.* un plato lleno; ración.

platelet [pléitlit], *s.* (anat.) plaqueta.

platen [plǽtǝn], *s.* (impr. y mec.) platina; cuadro; cilindro o rodillo de caucho (de una máquina de escribir).

plater [pléitœ(r)], *s.* plateador (en gen., el que platea, dora, etc.); artífice que trabaja en metales en lámina; platero (que trabaja en plata, oro, joyas, etc.).

plateresque [plæterésk], *a.* (arq.) plateresco.

platform [plǽtform], *s.* plataforma, tablado, andamio; cadalso; tarima; (arti.) explanada; (fort.) terraplén; tribuna; (fig.) oratoria pública; (f. c.) andén; plataforma de un tranvía; (pol.) programa, *m.*, declaración formal de principios.—**p. car**, (f. c.) (vagón de) plataforma, batea, *truck.*—**p. scale**, báscula.

platinate [plǽtineit]. **I.** *s.* (quím.) platinato. **II.** *va.* platinar.

plating [pléitiŋ], *s.* arte o acción de revestir con una capa metálica (dorado, plateado, etc.); capa o revestimiento metálico; blindaje.

platinic [plætínik], *a.* (quím.) platínico.—**platiniferous** [plætiníferʌs], *a.* platinífero.—**platiniridium** [-airídiʌm], *s.* platiniridio, aleación de iridio y platino.—**platinize** [-aiz], *va.* platinar.—**platinoid** [-ɔid]. **I.** *a.* semejante al platino. **II.** *s.* platinoide.—**platinotype** [-otaip], *s.* (fot.) platinotipia; positiva platinotípica.—**platinous** [-ʌs], *a.* (quím.) platinoso.

platinum [plǽtinʌm], *s.* platino.—**p. black**, (quím.) polvo negro de platino.—**p. blond(e**, que tiene el pelo color platino.—**p. ore**, platina.—**p.-plated**, **p. plating**, platinado.—**p. point**, punta platinada.

platitude [plǽtitjud], *s.* perogrullada, trivialidad.

platitudinize [-tjúdinaiz], *vn.* decir perogrulladas o vejeces.—**platitudinous** [-nʌs], *a.* insípido, trivial, traqueado.

Platonic [platɔ́nik], *a.* platónico.—**P. year**, (astr.) año platónico.

Platonically [-ǝli], *adv.* platónicamente.

Platonism [pléitɔnizm], *s.* platonismo.

Platonist(ic [pléitɔnist, -ístik], *a.* y *s.* platónico.

platoon [platún], *s.* (mil.) pelotón.—**p. school**, escuela dividida en grupos (*platoons*) de alumnos, que se turnan en el uso de las aulas, talleres, etc.

platter [plǽtœ(r)], *s.* fuente, *f.*, platazo, platel.

platyhelminth [plætihélminθ], *s.* (zool.) platelminto.

platypus [plǽtipʌs], *s.* (zool.) platipo. *V.* DUCK-BILL.

platyrrhine [plǽtirain], *s.* y *a.* (zool.) platirrino.

plaudit [plɔ́dit], *s.* aplauso, aclamación.

plausibility [plɔzibíliti], **plausibleness** [plɔ́ziblnjs], *s.* admisibilidad o credibilidad aparente; verosimilitud. *V.* PLAUSIBLE.

plausible [-bl], *a.* que parece admisible, razonable, recomendable o digno de confianza, pero a veces no lo es; verosímil; (raro) de aceptación general; (ant.) plausible, digno de aplauso. *V.* SPECIOUS.

plausibly [-bli], *adv.* con carácter de admisible, etc.

plausive [plɔ́siv], *a.* plausivo, laudatorio.

Plautine [plɔ́tain], *a.* plautino, rel. a Plauto.

play [pléi]. **I.** *va.* jugar (algún juego); practicar (un deporte); mover (la pieza de algún juego); hacerle o jugarle a uno (una mala partida, etc.); (teat.) dar, representar, poner en escena; hacer o desempeñar (un papel); (mús.) ejecutar, tocar, tañer, sonar (pieza o instrumento); manejar, menear, manipular; valerse o hacer uso de; arrojar, echar, lanzar.—**to p. a card**, echar una carta (p. ej., el as de triunfo).—**to p. a part**, hacer o representar un papel.—**to p. a joke on**, hacer una burla a, dar una broma a.—**to p. a set, o game**, jugar un partido o una partida, echar una partida (de ajedrez, billar, etc.).—**to p. both ends against the middle**, poner uno de punta entre sí a sus rivales, meter discordia entre ellos.—**to p. cards**, jugar a los naipes.—**to p. down**, hacer poco caso de.—**to p. first fiddle**, llevar la batuta, ser el principal o la cabeza de una reunión, empresa, etc.—**to p. hide and seek**, jugar al escondite.—**to p. hooky**, (fam.) hacer novillos, bolas o rabona.—**to p. one a (bad, dirty, mean) trick**, engañar a uno, hacerle una mala jugada, pegarle un petardo.—**to p. second fiddle**, estar subordinado, hacer un papel secundario.—**to p. the devil**, o **the mischief, with**, perturbar, trastornar, desbaratar por completo, causar daño a.—**to p. the fool**, hacerse el tonto, hacer del bobo.—**to p. the game**, jugar limpio.—**to p. the knave**, engañar.—**to p. the lottery**, echar a la lotería.—**to p. the market**, (fam.) jugar a la bolsa.—**to p. the monkey**, hacer monadas.—**to p. (the) truant**, hacer novillos. —**to p. tricks**, hacer suertes; hacer travesuras. II. *vn.* jugar, juguetear; divertirse, entretenerse, recrearse; burlarse, chancearse, bromear; (mús.) tocar; (mec.) jugar, moverse, funcionar; portarse, conducirse; flotar, ondular, ondear; (teat.) representar.—**to p. at cards**, jugar a los naipes.—**to p. by** o **from ear**, tocar de oído.— **to p. fair**, jugar limpio.—**to p. false**, engañar. —**to p. fast and loose**, embaucar, no ser digno de confianza.—**to p. into the hands of one**, dar entrada a, ayudar; hacer a uno el caldo gordo.—**to p. off**, hacer alarde; pretender, ostentar.—**to p. on**, tocar (un instrumento).— **to p. to the gallery**, o **to the galleries**, obrar sin más motivo que el aplauso o la aprobación públicos.—**to p. up to**, (fam.) adular.—**to p. upon one**, burlarse de uno; explotar o abusar de su credulidad, amor, etc.—**to p. upon words**, hacer equívoco de vocablos. III. *s.* juego; jugada; recreo, diversión; (teat.) drama, *m.*, comedia, pieza; función, representación; (mec.) juego, espacio libre; funcionamiento, operación; rienda suelta, libertad de acción, vuelo; movimiento ligero y rápido; reflejo de colores o de luces; (teat.) ejecución, desempeño. —**p. actor**, actor, cómico.—**p. school**, escuela recreativa de chiquillos.—**p. upon words**, equívoco, retruécano; juego de palabras.—**at p.**, jugando.—**in p.**, en chanza, de burlas.

playable [-ȧbl], *a.* que puede ser jugado o tocado; (teat.) representable.

playbill [-bil], *s.* (teat.) cartel; programa, *m.*

playboy [-boi], *s.* (fam.) joven rico y algo disoluto; buscaplaceres; hombre de mundo.

playday [-dei], *s.* día (*m.*) de huelga o de asueto.

played [-d], *pp.* y *a.* jugado o tocado; ejecutado, representado.—**p. out**, agotado; acabado, concluido.

player [-œ(r)], *s.* jugador; actor, cómico, comediante, representante; (mús.) tocador, ejecutante, músico, instrumentista.—**p. piano**, pianola, piano mecánico o automático, autopiano.

playfellow [-felou], *s.* compañero de juego.

playful [-fμl], *a.* juguetón, retozón, travieso.

playgoer [-gouœ(r)], *s.* persona que frecuenta los teatros.

playground [-graund], *s.* patio o campo de recreo; campo de deportes o de juegos.

playhouse [-hauş], *s.* teatro; coliseo; casilla de recreo; casita en miniatura para niños.

playing card [-iŋ kard], *s.* naipe, carta.

playlet [-lit], *s.* drama corto.

playmate [-meit], *s.* = PLAYFELLOW.

plaything [-θiŋ], *s.* juguete; trebejo; niñería.

playtime [-taim], *s.* tiempo de recreo o para recreo; (teat.) hora de comenzar la función.

playwright [-rait], *s.* dramaturgo, autor dramático, comediógrafo.

plaza [pláźȧ], *s.* plaza.

plea [pli], *s.* argumento; ruego, súplica; disculpa; pretexto; (for.) alegato, defensa; respuesta o declaración (del acusado); acción, litigio, proceso.—**p. in abatement**, instancia de nulidad. —**p. of the crown**, (Ingl.) causa criminal.

pleach [plich], *va.* entretejer ramas.

plead [plíd], I. *va.* (for.) defender (un pleito, una causa); alegar; aducir como razón, motivo o excusa. II. *vn.* suplicar, implorar; abogar (por); declarar o responder el acusado si es culpable

o no.—**to p. guilty**, confesarse delincuente.— **to p. not guilty**, declararse inocente.

pleadable [-ȧbl], *a.* que se puede alegar en un pleito, o en defensa; alegable, abogable.

pleader [-œ(r)], *s.* abogado, defensor.

pleading [-iŋ]. I. *a.* suplicante, implorante. II. *s.* súplica, imploración; (for.) alegación, defensa; informe; abogacía.—*pl.* alegatos.

pleasant [plézȧnt], *a.* grato, agradable, gustoso, ameno, placentero; simpático, afable, tratable. —**p. journey** o **trip!** ¡feliz (o buen) viaje!—**p. weather**, buen tiempo.—**pleasantly** [-li], *adv.* agradablemente.—**pleasantness** [-nis], *s.* agradabilidad, agrado, amenidad; afabilidad.

pleasantry [-ri], *s.* chuscada, broma, humorada, agudeza, chanza.

please [plíz]. I. *va.* agradar, contentar; complacer, dar gusto, satisfacer, placer.—**to be easy (hard) to p.**, ser de buen (mal) contentar o contento.—**to be pleased to**, tener gusto en, o el gusto de; alegrarse de, complacerse en.—**to be pleased with**, estar satisfecho o contento de o con; gustarle a uno (cambiando el giro: *I am much pleased with this car*, me gusta mucho este coche).—**to p. one's self**, hacer uno su gusto sin miramientos por los demás. II. *vn.* agradar, satisfacer; querer, gustar. En el imperativo y con *if* se emplea por cortesía en el sentido de "hacer el favor," "tener la bondad," "servirse," etc.: *please speak slowly*, sírvase, o hágame el favor de, hablar despacio; *if you please*, o simplemente *please*, por favor, con permiso de Vd., si Vd. me hace el favor, si Vd. tiene la bondad.—**as one pleases**, como uno quiera o guste.

pleasing [-iŋ], *a.* complaciente; agradable, deleitable, grato, gustoso, ameno, placentero.—**to be p.**, gustar, dar gusto; caer bien.—**pleasingly** [-li], *adv.* agradablemente, donosamente.

pleasurable [plézůrȧbl], *a.* agradable, grato.— **pleasurably** [-bli], *adv.* agradable o gratamente.

pleasurableness [-nis], *s.* calidad de agradable.

pleasure [plézů(r)], *s.* placer, gusto, deleite; voluntad, arbitrio; complacencia.—**p. boat, trip**, etc., embarcación, viaje, etc., de recreo.—**p. lover**, o **seeker**, amante de los placeres; el que busca o anda tras los placeres.—**at one's (own) p.**, como uno quiera, como le plazca.—**at p.**, a voluntad.—**to take p. in**, complacerse o deleitarse en, tener gusto en.—**what is your p.?** ¿qué desea Vd.? ¿en qué puedo complacerle?— **with (great) p.**, con (mucho) gusto, con placer; que me place.

pleat [plít], I. *va.* (cost.) plegar, hacer pliegues, (gal.) plisar. II. *s.* pliegue.—**pleated** [-id], *a.* plegado.—**pleating** [-iŋ], *s.* (cost.) plegado, (gal.) plisado.

plebe [plib], *s.* (E. U. fam.) plebeyo, estudiante de primer año.

plebeian [plibían], *a.* y *s.* plebeyo; pechero.

plebeianism [-izm], *s.* plebeyismo; vulgaridad.

plebiscite [plébisait], *s.* (pol.) plebiscito.—**plebiscitary** [plíbişiteri], *a.* plebiscitario.

plebiscitum [plebisáitȧm], *s.* (hist.) plebiscito.

plebs [plebz], *s.* plebe, *f.*, populacho.

plectrum [pléktrȧm], *s.* (mús.) plectro, púa.

pledge [pledž]. I. *s.* prenda, señal, *f.*, arras, *f. pl.*, caución; empeño, fianza; rehén; compromiso; promesa, voto; brindis, *m.*—**to take the p.**, jurar abstenerse de bebidas alcohólicas, etc. II. *va.* prendar, pignorar, empeñar, dar en prenda; gravar, hipotecar; dar fianza; brindar por; prometer, comprometerse a, dar (la palabra).

pledgee [-í], *s.* (for.) depositario.

pledgeor [-ʒor], **pledgor** [-ʒor], *s.* (for.) prendador.

pledger [-œ(r)], *s.* el que empeña, promete, brinda, etc.; (for.) prendador.

pledget [plédžit], *s.* (cir.) tapón; (mar.) cordón de estopa para calafatear.

pledging [plédžiŋ], *s.* prendamiento, pignoración.

Pleiad [plíąd], s. (astr.) una de las Pléyades; (fig.) grupo de escritores o artistas destacados.

Pleiades [plíądiz], s. pl. (astr.) Pléyades, f. pl.

Pleistocene [plájstosin], a. y s. (geol.) pleistoceno.

plenarily [plínąrili], adv. plenariamente.

plenary [plínąri], a. plenario; entero, completo; absoluto; (for.) plenario.—**p. indulgence**, (igl.) indulgencia plenaria.—**p. powers**, plenos poderes.

plenipotential [plenipoténsąl], a. autorizado con poder pleno.

plenipotentiary [-śįęri], s. y a. plenipotenciario.

plenitude [plénįtjud], s. plenitud, abundancia.

plenteous [pléntįʌs], a. = PLENTIFUL.—**plenteously** [-lįi], adv. abundantemente.—**plenteousness** [-nįs], s. abundancia.

plentiful [pléntįful], a. copioso, abundante; fértil, feraz.—**plentifully** [-įi], adv. abundantemente, copiosamente.—**plentifulness** [-nįs], s. abundancia, copia; fertilidad.

plenty [pléntį]. I. s. copia, abundancia, profusión, afluencia. II. a. (fam.) copioso, abundante.

plenum [plínʌm], s. pleno, plenitud, plétora.

pleochroism [pliákrojzm], **pleochromatism** [pliokróumątizm], s. (crist.) pleocroísmo, propiedad de variar de color según la dirección de la luz.

pleonasm [plíonæzm], s. (gram. y ret.) pleonasmo. —**pleonastic** [plionéstįk], a. pleonástico.—**pleonastically** [-ąlį], adv. pleonásticamente.

pleroma [plįróumą], s. plenitud.

plesiosaur [plísįosor], s. (pal.) plesiosaur(i)o.

plessor [plésǫ(r)], **plexor** [pléksǫ(r)], s. (med.) plesor.

plethora [pléθorą], s. plétora, exceso, hartura.

plethoric [pleθórįk], a. pletórico, repleto.

plethysmograph [pleθízmogræf], s. (fisiol.) pletismógrafo.

pleura [plúrą], s. (anat., zool.) pleura.—**pleural** [-l], a. pleural; pleurítico.—**pleurisy** [plúrįsį], s. (med.) pleuritis, pleuresía.—**pleuritic(al** [plurítįk(ąl], a. pleurítico.

pleurocarpous [plurokárpʌs], a. (bot.) pleurocarpo, -pal.

pleurodont [plúrodant], a. y s. (zool.) pleurodonto.

pleurodynia [-dínįą], s. (med.) pleurodinia.

pleuron [plúran], s. (zool.) costado.

pleuronectid [pluronéktįd], s. (ict.) pleuronecto.

pleuropneumonia [-njumóunįą], s. (med. y vet.) pleuroneumonía.

pleurotomy [plurátomį], s. pleurotomía, incisión en la pleura.

plexiform [pléksįform], a. plexiforme, parecido a un plexo o red; reticular, complicado.

pleximeter [pleksímetǫ(r)], s. (med.) plexímetro o plesímetro.

plexus [pléksʌs], s. trabazón, f., entrelazamiento, red; (anat.) plexo.

pliability [plajabílįtį], s. flexibilidad, docilidad.

pliable [plájąbl], a. flexible; trefe; plegable, doblegable, dócil, manejable.—**pliableness** [-nįs], **pliancy** [plájąnsį], s. flexibilidad, docilidad, blandura.

pliant [plájąnt], a. flexible, doblegable, cimbreño; dócil, manejable, blando, tratable, manual.

plica [plájką], s. pliegue; (med.) plica.

plicate(d [plájkejt(įd], a. (bot. y zool.) plegado.

plication [plajkéjsǫn], s. plegadura, pliegue.

pliers [plájcerz], s. pl. alicates, tenacillas, tenazas.

plight [plajt]. I. va. empeñar o dar (palabra); prometer en matrimonio, contraer esponsales (gen. en la locución to plight one's troth). II. s. (raro) promesa, compromiso solemne; esponsales, promesa de matrimonio; situación, condición (gen. mala); apuro, aprieto.

plinth [plįnθ], s. (arq.) plinto, orlo; zócalo.

Pliocene [plájosin], a. y s. (geol.) plioceno.

plod [plád], vn. afanarse, ajetrearse, atrafagarse, trabajar con ahinco. V. TRUDGE y DRUDGE.

plodder [-œ(r)], s. trafagón; el que trabaja asidua y laboriosamente, o camina con dificultad.

plodding [-įn], s. tráfago, ajetreo, (Am.) atareo.

plop [plap]. I. va. y vn. (dejar) caer de golpe, con ruido apagado, un objeto al agua, etc. II. s. el ruido así producido. III. adv. de golpe; a plomo. IV. interj. ¡paf!

plosion, s., **plosive**, a. (fon.) = EXPLOSION, EXPLOSIVE.

plot [plát]. I. s. solar, parcela, porción de terreno; plano de un terreno; conspiración, complot, conjura(ción); (fam.) entruchada; argumento, enredo, trama (de drama o novela). II. va. tramar, urdir, fraguar; hacer el plano o dibujo de; transportar al papel. III. vn. conspirar, maquinar.

plotter [-œ(r)], s. conspirador, conjurado, tramador, maquinador.

plotting [-įn]. I. s. conspiración, maquinación; dibujo de planos; representación gráfica. II. a. que conspira; para planos o diagramas.—**p. paper**, papel cuadriculado.

plough [plau], etc. = PLOW, etc.

plover [plávœ(r) o plóyvœ(r)], s. (orn.) variedad de ave fría o avefría, frailecillo, chorlito.

plow [pláu]. I. s. arado; (P., astr.) Carro, Osa Mayor.—**p. alms**, contribución a la iglesia por cada arado.—**p. beam**, pértigo del arado.—**p. co(u)lter**, reja o cuchilla del arado.—**p. handle**, mancera, esteva.—**p. knife**, (enc.) lengüeta.—**P. Monday**, primer lunes después de la Epifanía.—**p. pin**, telera.—**p. plane**, (carp.) guillame, acanalador.—**p. press**, (enc.) ingenio.—**p. sole**, o **pan**, (agr.) capa compacta de tierra formada por el arado en el fondo del surco.—**p. staff**, arrejada. II. va. (agr.) arar, labrar, surcar; (mar. y fig.) surcar o cortar (las aguas).

plowable [-ąbl], a. arable, labrantío.

plowboy [-boj], s. yuguero, yuntero.

plower [-œ(r)], s. arador, surcador.

plowing [-įn], s. aradura, labranza; (fig.) reja.

plowland [-lænd], s. tierra labrantía o de pan llevar.

plowman [-mąn], s. arador, labrador; yuguero; patán, campesino.

plowshare [-šer], s. reja de arado.

plowtail [-tejl], s. mancera, mangorrillo.

plowwright [-rajt], s. fabricante de arados.

pluck [plák]. I. va. coger, arrancar; pelar; desplumar (aves); (mús.) puntear, pulsar o tocar (las cuerdas) con los dedos o el plectro; (fam.) robar, estafar, desplumar; (Ingl., fam.) dar calabazas en los exámenes.—**to p. up**, arrancar.—**to p. up courage**, (re)cobrar ánimo; hacer de tripas corazón, sacar fuerzas de flaqueza. II. vn. (con at) tirar de, dar un tirón. III. s. valor, ánimo, resolución; arranque, (es)tirón; asadura (hígado, corazón y bofes).

plucky [-į], a. animoso, denodado, resuelto.

plug [plág]. I. s. tapón, tarugo, taco; cuña; espita; (arti.) obturador; (dent.) obturador, empaste o empastadura; porción de tabaco comprimido; cala (de melón); cierre (de válvula); (elec.) enchufe, adaptador, tomacorriente; conectador; tapón (ll. t. **p. fuse**); (aut.) bujía; (fam.) rocín, penco; (fam.) sombrero de copa, chistera.—**p. board**, (elec.) conmutador de clavijas.—**p. clip**, contacto o terminal de tapón o botón eléctrico.—**p. fuse**, (elec.) fusible de tapón, tapón fusible.—**p. ga(u)ge**, calibre cilíndrico. —**p. jack**, (elec.) clavija-enchufe.—**p. key**, (elec.) clavija de conexión.—**p. tobacco**, tabaco curado y comprimido en forma de panes. II. va. atarugar, tapar, obturar; (dent.) orificar, empastar; (elec.) (con in) enchufar, conectar, insertar una clavija de conexión.—**to p. melons**, calar melones, etc.

plugger [-œ(r)], s. (dent.) obturador, orificador.

plum [plʌm], s. (bot.) ciruela; pruna; bruno (ll. t. **black p.**); pasas para guisar; (fig.) golosina, gollería; lo mejor; la nata; turrón, o puesto muy ventajoso; (bolsa) dividendo extraordinario; (fam. Ingl.) la cantidad de £100,000; riquezas, fortuna.—p. cake, bizcocho con pasas.—p. curculio, (ent.) curculio, gorgojo.—p. pie, pastel de ciruelas o de pasas. —p. pudding, budín o pudín inglés.—p. tree, ciruelo, cirolero; bruno.

plumage [plúmidž], s. plumaje, plum(aj)ería.

plumagery [-rį], s. plumajería.

plumb [plʌm]. I. a. perpendículo, a plomo; recto. —off p., out of p., no vertical, desviado de la vertical. II. s. plomada.—p. bob, plomo, plomada (pesa de ella).—p. level, nivel de albañil. —p. line, tranquil.—p. rule, (regla) plomada. III. adv. a plomo, verticalmente; (fam.) completa o rematadamente. IV. va. (mar. y fig.) sond(e)ar; (alb.) aplomar; (em)plomar, sellar con plomo; instalar cañerías.

plumbaginaceous [plʌmbædžinéišʌs], a. (bot.) plumbagináceo, plumbagíneo.

plumbago [plʌmbéigou], s. grafito, plombagina, lápiz, m. (de) plomo; (bot.) plumbagínea.

plumbean, o plumbeous [plʌmbian, -bias], a. plúmbeo, plomizo, plúmbico.

plumber [plʌmœ(r)], s. plomero, emplomador; fontanero; cañero, instalador de cañerías.

plumbic [plʌmbįk], a. plúmbico.

plumbiferous [plʌmbífęrʌs], a. plumbífero, que contiene plomo.

plumbing [plʌmįŋ], s. arte u oficio del plomero; plomería, instalación de cañerías; sistema (m.) de cañerías interiores; acción de sond(e)ar o aplomar.

plumbism [plʌmbįzm], s. (med.) plumbismo.

plumbless [plʌmlįs], a. insondable.

plumbum [plʌmbʌm], s. (quím.) plomo.

plumcot [plʌmkat], s. (bot.) injerto de ciruelo y albaricoque.

plume [plúm]. I. s. pluma; plumaje, penacho, plumero.—p. maker, plumista, plumario.—p. of feathers, plumero, penacho. II. va. adornar con plumas, emplumar, empenachar; desplumar, pelar; (raro) robar, desvalijar. III. vr. jactarse, vanagloriarse o preciarse. V. PREEN.

plumed [-d], a. emplumado, plúmeo, penachudo, empenachado.

plumeless [-lįs], a. implume.

plumery [-œrį], s. = PLUMAGE.

plumicorn [-įkorn], s. (zool.) copete, penacho.

plumigerous [-įdžęrʌs], a. (poét.) plumífero.

plumiped [plúmįped]. I. a. (orn.) plumípedo, calzado. II. s. ave calzada.

plumist [plúmįst], s. plumista, plumario, plumajero (ll. t. plumassier).

plummet [plʌmįt]. I. s. plomo, plomada, nivel; sonda, sondaleza. II. va. sond(e)ar. III. vn. caer a plomo o verticalmente.

plumose, plumous [plúmoųs, -mʌs], a. plúmeo.

plump [plʌmp]. I. a. rollizo, regordete; brusco, claro, francote; rotundo, categórico.—p.-faced, carilleno. II. adv. de golpe; a plomo; (todo) derecho, directamente. III. va. soltar, dejar caer, arrojar; engordar, hinchar. IV. vn. caer a plomo; hincharse, engordar, llenarse.

plumpness [-nįs], s. gordura, corpulencia.

plumpy [-į], a. rollizo, gordico, (fam.) gordiflón.

plumule [plúmįul], s. (bot.) plúmula; (orn.) plumón.

plumy [plúmį], a. plumado, plumoso, plúmeo.

plunder [plʌndœ(r)]. I. va. despojar, saquear, pillar, entrar, meter o poner a saco; expoliar. II. s. pillaje, saqueo, rapiña, robo; botín.

plunderer [-œ(r)], s. saqueador, pillador; ladrón.

plunge [plʌndž]. I. va. zambullir, sumergir, chapuzar; meter, hundir; arrojar, precipitar; sumir. II. vn. sumergirse, zambullirse; precipitarse, arrojarse; saltar, lanzarse; (mar.) hocicar. III. s. sumersión, zambullida; chapuz, m.; salto, arrojo, embestida; tanque para bañarse.—p. bath, baño de inmersión.

plunger [-œ(r)], s. buzo; (mec.) émbolo; chupón (ll. t. p. piston); cabeza del vástago (de ciertas válvulas); (hidr.) émbolo buzo; (fam.) jugador o bolsista desenfrenado.—p. pump, bomba de émbolo buzo.

plunk [plʌŋk]. I. va. (mús.) = TO PLUCK o TWANG; (fam.) golpear o arrojar fuerte o repentinamente. II. vn. (mús.) vibrar la cuerda punteada (de guitarra, etc.); (fam.) sonar como un golpe seco; caer a plomo o pesadamente. III. s. punteado de una cuerda; (fam.) golpe fuerte; ruido seco y repentino; dólar.

pluperfect [plupœrfįkt], a. y s. (gram.) pluscuamperfecto.

plural [plúrạl], a. y s. plural.—p. marriage, poligamia.—p. vote, derecho de dar más de un voto o de votar en varias partes.

pluralism [-įzm], s. pluralidad; ocupación o goce de más de un beneficio, puesto o destino a un mismo tiempo, (fam.) enchufe; (filos.) pluralismo, doctrina que sostiene que existe más de una substancia última (opuesto al monismo).—pluralist [-įst], s. el que ocupa más de un puesto a un mismo tiempo, (fam.) enchufista; (filos.) pluralista, partidario del pluralismo.

plurality [plurélįtį], s. pluralidad; mayoría relativa (de votos); multitud.

pluralize [plúrạlaįz], va. pluralizar.

plurally [plúrạlį], adv. en plural.

plus [plʌs]. I. prep. más (+); además de, con, con la añadidura de. II. a. (mat. y elec.) positivo; (fam.) y más, con algo de sobra; más otras cosas (gastos, ganancia, etc.).—p. fours, especie de calzones bombachos (para golf y otros deportes).—p. lens, (ópt.) lente convergente.—p. sign, (mat.) signo más (+).—to be, come out, etc., p. (something), (fam.) haber ganado, salir ganando (algo). III. s. signo más; cantidad positiva.

plush [plʌš]. I. s. (tej.) felpa; pana, tripe; (gal.) peluche. II. a. afelpado.

plushlike [-laįk], plushy [-į], a. felpudo, (a)felpado.

plutarchy [plútarkį], plutocracy [plutákrạsį], s. plutocracia.

plutocrat [plútokræt], s. plutócrata, m̥.

plutocratic [-krétįk], a. plutocrático.

Plutonian [plútóunįạn]. I. a. plutoniano; infernal; (geol.) plutónico. II. s. plutoniano; (geol.) plutonista.

Plutonic [plutánįk], a. (geol.) plutónico.—P. theory, plutonismo.

Plutonism [plútǫnįzm], s. (geol.) plutonismo.

Plutonist [-įst], s. (geol.) plutonista.

pluvial [plúvįạl], a. (mar.) pluvial; (geol.) pluviátil.

pluviogram [plúvįogræm], s. pluviograma, diagrama trazado por el pluviógrafo.

pluviograph [-ogræf], s. pluviógrafo, pluviómetro registrador.

pluviometer [-ámetœ(r)], s. pluviómetro.

pluviometric(al [-ométrįk(ạl], a. pluviométrico.

pluviometry [-ámetrį], s. pluviometría.

pluvious [plúvįʌs], a. pluvioso, lluvioso.

ply [plaį]. I. va. trabajar en con ahinco; ejercer, practicar; emplear, ocupar; manejar (la aguja, el remo); importunar, acosar (con preguntas, etc.); propinar, convidar a beber repetidas veces; atacar tenazmente; plegar. II. vn. ir y venir, hacer viajes regulares; estar constantemente ocupado o funcionando; solicitar o aguardar compradores; (mar.) barloventear; hacer la travesía. III. s. pliegue, doblez, m.; propensión, inclinación; capa (de tela, etc.).—two-ply, de dos capas, láminas, hilos, etc.

plywood [-wųd], s. madera terciada, compuesta de varias hojas o láminas superpuestas.

pneometer [niámetœ(r)], s. (fisiol.) neómetro.

pneuma [njúmạ], s. respiración, aliento; (filos.) pneuma, m.; alma, espíritu; (mús.) pneuma, m.

pneumatic(al [njumétįk(ạl], a. neumático.—p. tire, neumático, llanta neumática.

pneumatics [njumǽtiks], s. neumática.

pneumatology [njumətálodȝi], s. neumatología.

pneumatometer [-támetœ(r)], s. neumatómetro.

pneumatosis [-tóu̯sis], s. (med.) neumatosis.

pneumatotherapy [-toθérəpi], s. (med.) neumatoterapia.

pneumobacillus [njumobasíl̬ʌs], s. (bact.) neumobacilo, bacilo de Friedländer.

pneumococcus [-kákʌs], s. (bact.) neumococo.

pneumogastric [-gǽstrik]. I. a. neumogástrico. II. s. (anat.) nervio neumogástrico.

pneumograph[njúmogræf],s.(fisiol.)neumógrafo.

pneumonia [njumóu̯niə], s. (med.) (p)neumonía, pulmonía.

pneumonic [njumánik], a. (anat.) neumónico, pulmonar; (med.) neumónico, pulmoníaco.

pneumotherapy [njumoθérəpi], s. (med.) neumoterapia.

pneumothorax [-θóræks], s. (med.) neumotórax, acumulación de aire o gases en la cavidad pleural.

poa [póu̯ə], s. (bot.) poa, género de gramíneas.

poaceous [poéi̯ʃʌs], a. (bot.) gramíneo.

poach [póu̯ch]. I. va. (coc.) escalfar (huevos); robar caza de algún vedado; invadir. II. vn. cazar o pescar en vedado; atollarse o meterse en un fangal; encenagarse un terreno.

poacher [-œ(r)], s. cazador furtivo, el que roba caza o pesca en vedado.—poaching [-iŋ], s. hurto de caza en vedado.

pochard [póu̯chɑrd], s. (orn.) pato de mar.

pock [pak], s. (med.) pústula, postilla, viruela.— p.-marked, cacarañado, picado de viruelas.

pocket [pákit]. I. s. bolsillo, faltriquera; cavidad, receptáculo; (anat., med.) bolsa; (min.) bolsa; (min.) depósito de pepitas de oro; nasa para pescados; hoyo; hondonada, depresión; calle tapada o sin salida; tronera (de billar); (aer.) AIR POCKET.—p. battleship, acorazado de bolsillo.—p. clip, sujetador (de lápiz, etc.).— p. edition, edición de bolsillo.—p. flap, (sast.) golpe, cartera.—p. handkerchief, pañuelo de bolsillo.—p. lighter, encendedor de bolsillo.— p. money, alfileres, m. pl., dinero para gastos particulares.—p. picking, ratería de carterista, robo de faltriquera.—p. pistol, pistolete, cachorrillo.—p. veto, (E. U.) veto indirecto, o implícito, que consiste en no firmar el presidente una ley antes que el congreso se clausure, lo cual la invalida.—in p., con ganancia.—out of p., con pérdida. II. va. embolsar, meter en el bolsillo; tomar, apropiarse; entronerar, trucar (en el billar o trucos); tragarse (una injuria).

pocketbook [-buk], s. portamonedas, bolsa; cartera, (Am.) billetera; (fig.) dinero, recursos, m. pl.

pocketful [-ful], s. bolsillado, lo que cabe en un bolsillo.

pocketknife [-nai̯f], s. cortaplumas.

pockmark [pákmɑrk], s. cacaraña, hoyo que deja la viruela.—pocky [páki], a. (raro) cacarañado; sifilítico.

pod [pad]. I. s. (bot.) vaina (de legumbre), cápsula de una planta, silicua, hollejo; capullo (de gusano de seda); manada (de aves, focas, etc.); ranura o canal longitudinal (de ciertas brocas o barrenas); (fam.) panza.—p. auger, broca de media caña. II. vn. llenarse, hincharse; criar vainas.

podagra [podǽgrə], s. (med.) podagra, gota.

podagric(al [podǽgrik(əl], a. podágrico, gotoso.

podesta [podéstə], s. podestá, primer magistrado.

podgy [pádȝi], a. = PUDGY.

podiatrist [podái̯ətrist], s. podíatra, mf., podiatrista.—podiatry [-tri], s. (med.) podiatría.

podium [póu̯diəm], s. (arq.) podio; estrado (de director de orquesta); (anat. y zool.) pie, m.; (bot.) sostén, pecíolo.

podology [podálodȝi], s. (med.) podología.

podometer [podámetœ(r)], s. podómetro.

podophyllin [padofílin], s. (farm.) podofilina.

Podophyllum [-fíl̬ʌm], s. (bot.) género de los podófilos.

poem [póu̯im], s. poema, m.; poesía, composición poética.—pl. versos, rimas.

poesy [póu̯isi], s. (ant.) poesía; arte poética.

poet [póu̯it], s. poeta, m.—p. laureate, poeta laureado.

poetaster [-æstœ(r)], s. poetastro, coplero.

poetess [-is], s. poetisa.

poetic(al [poṷétik(əl], a. poético; poemático.—p. justice, justicia ideal, justa distribución del premio y del castigo.—p. licence, licencia poética.—p. vein, vena, numen poético.

poetically [-i], adv. poéticamente.

poetics [poṷétiks], s. (arte) poética.

poetize [póu̯itai̯z], vn. y va. poetizar; versificar.

poetry [póu̯itri], s. poética; poesía.

pogrom [póu̯grəm o pográm], s. (Rusia) pogrom, asonada de asesinato y despojo de los judíos.

poignancy [pói̯n(y)ənsi], s. acerbidad, picante; calidad de conmovedor o lastimero.—poignant [-ənt], a. acerbo, punzante, mordaz; conmovedor, que excita la compasión o lástima, etc.—poignantly [-li], adv. acremente; conmovedora o lastimeramente.

poilu [pwálu], s. poilu, soldado francés.

point [pói̯nt]. I. s. punto (en casi todas sus acepciones); punta, rasgo característico; fin, objeto, quid, m.; toque (that's just the point, ahí está el toque); herramienta puntiaguda (como un buril, punzón); (Ingl. f. c.) aguja (en plural, cambiavía); punta (de tierra), promontorio; peculiaridad, rasgo característico; grado (de una escala); sazón, f., ocasión, momento crítico; instante; agudeza, sal, f., chiste ingenioso; (mar.) rumbo, cuarta; (mús.) puntillo; en ciertos juegos, punto, tanto; (com.) entero, en la fluctuación de los valores; (gram.) cualquier signo de puntuación; (impr.) punto tipográfico (unidad de medida).—p. (lace), encaje hecho con aguja, encaje de punto, puntas, f. pl.—p. at issue, punto en cuestión.—p. by p., punto por punto.—p. of honor, pundonor, cuestión de honor.—p. of inflexion, (geom.) punto de inflexión.—p. of law, cuestión de derecho.—p. of order, cuestión de procedimiento, recurso al reglamento.—p. of support, punto de apoyo.—p. of view, punto de vista.—p. system, (impr.) sistema (m.) de medida (de tipos de imprenta) por puntos; sistema de Braille o de signos en relieve para la lectura de los ciegos.—at all points, por todos lados, enteramente.—at the p. of death, en artículo de la muerte, próximo a la muerte.—at the p. of the sword, a hierro y sangre, por la fuerza.—in p., al caso, a propósito; en cuestión, de que se trata.—in p. of, en cuanto a, tocante a.—in p. of law, como cuestión de derecho, desde el punto de vista del derecho.—on the p. of, a punto de.—to get the p., caer en la cuenta.—to get to the p., venir o ir al grano.—to give points, dar tantos (en el juego); dar información útil.—to see little p. in, no ver la utilidad de (algo).—to the p., al caso, a propósito: atinado, certero.—what's the p.?, ¿a qué viene eso? ¿de o para qué sirve? II. va. aguzar, afilar, sacar punta (a un lápiz, arma, etc.); (con at, to o toward) apuntar, señalar, indicar; encarar, dirigir, asestar; (gram.) puntuar; (alb.) unir con mortero, rellenar (juntas), llenar, fijar.—to p. out, apuntar, señalar, hacer notar u observar. III. vn. apuntar, señalar; hacer puntería; tender, propender o inclinarse a; dar, mirar a o hacia; parar y mostrar la caza (el perro); (med.) madurarse (un absceso).

point-blank [-blǽŋk]. I. a. horizontal; directo, claro, categórico. II. adv. a quema ropa, a boca de jarro, a tenazón; directamente, en línea recta; categóricamente, sin ambages. III. s. (raro) tiro a quema ropa, tiro asestado.

pointed [-id], a. puntiagudo, aguzado; en punta;

picante, satírico; directo, acentuado, enfático; (arq.) ojival, apuntado.—**pointedly** [-lị], *adv.* sutilmente; mordazmente; categóricamente.— **pointedness** [-nịs], *s.* agudeza, aspereza, acrimonia.

pointer [-œ(r)], *s.* afiladora; indicador, índice; manecilla, aguja o saeta (de reloj); fiel (de balanza); apuntador, puntero; punta, buril; (f. c.) palanca de aguja o cambiavía; perro de muestra o punta, ventor, pachón, braco; (fam.) indicación, observación o consejo útil.—*pl.* (P., astr.) las dos estrellas de la Osa Mayor que indican la polar.

pointillism [pwéntịlịzm], *s.* (pint.) puntillismo.

pointillist [-ịst], *s.* (pint.) puntillista.

pointing [pój̃ntịŋ], *s.* afiladura, aguzadura; señalamiento, indicación; puntería; punta (del perro de muestra); puntuación; (alb.) rejuntado, relleno de juntas; (med.) maduración de un absceso; (mar.) rabo de rata.—**p. trowel**, (alb.) espátula.

pointless [-lịs], *a.* obtuso, sin punta; insubstancial; insípido; inútil.

poise [pojz]. I. *s.* equilibrio, contrapeso; balanza; estabilidad; serenidad; reposo; porte, talante; duda, indecisión. II. *va.* equilibrar; estabilizar; suspender, mantener en equilibrio o suspendido (en alto o en el aire); (raro) pesar. III. *vn.* quedar en equilibrio; estar suspendido; cernerse (las aves).

poison [pójzọn]. I. *s.* veneno, tóxico, tósigo, ponzoña.—**p. ash, p. dogwood, p. elder, p. ivy, p. oak, p. sumac,** etc., variedades de zumaque, rus, toxicodendro o hiedra venenosos que causan erupción cutánea.—**p. gas,** gas tóxico.—**p. hemlock,** (bot.) cicuta.—**p. nut,** (bot.) nuez vómica.—**p.-pen letter,** (fam.) paulina, carta anónima ofensiva. II. *va.* envenenar, toxicar, (a)tosigar, emponzoñar; (fig.) corromper, inficionar.

poisoner [-œ(r)], *s.* envenenador.—**poisoning** [-ịŋ], *s.* envenenamiento, intoxicación, emponzoñamiento.—**poisonous** [-ʌs], *a.* venenoso, tóxico, emponzoñoso, deletéreo.—**poisonousness** [-nịs], *s.* venenosidad, toxicidad.

poitrel [pójtrel], *s.* (arm.) petral, antepecho.

poke [póụk]. I. *s.* empuje, empujón; hurgonada, hurgonazo; posma, *mf.*, hombre tardón o indolente; (ant.) barjuleta, bolsa; saquito; (ict.) vejiga de aire.—**p. bonnet,** papalina de mujer de ala abovedada. II. *va.* picar, aguijonear; atizar, hurg(one)ar; asomar, sacar (la cabeza, etc.).—**to p. fun at,** burlarse, mofarse de.— **to p. one's nose into,** meter las narices en; entremeterse, curiosear.—**to p. the fire,** hurgar la lumbre, atizar el fuego. III. *vn.* haronear; rezagarse; andar a tientas.

poker [-œ(r)], *s.* atizador o atizadero, hurgón(ero), espetón; (fam.) posma, *mf.*, perezoso; entremetido; persona tiesa; póker, juego de naipes. —**p.-faced,** (fam.) de rostro imperturbable o poco expresivo.—**p. picture,** pirograbado.—**p. work,** pirografía.

pokeweed [-wid], **pokeroot** [-rut], *s.* (bot.) hierba carmín, fitolaca (ll. su fruto **pokeberry**).

poking [-ịŋ]. I. *s.* hurgonada. II. *a.* = POK(E)Y.

pok(e)y [-ị], *a.* (fam.) flojo, pesado, lento; tedioso, sin interés; apretado, ahogado (cuarto); desaliñado (vestido).

Polack [póụlæk], *a. y s.* (fam. o desp.) (de origen) polaco.

polacre [polákœ(r)], *s.* (mar.) polacra.

Polander [póụlandœ(r)], *s.* polaco, polonés.

polar [póụlạ(r)], *a.* polar.—**p. bear,** (zool.) oso blanco.—**p. coördinates,** (mat.) coordenadas polares.—**p. curve,** curva dada en coordenadas polares.—**p. lights,** aurora boreal o austral.— **p. star,** (astr.) estrella polar (ll. gen. *la polar*).

polarimeter [-ịmɛtœ(r)], *s.* (ópt.) polarímetro.

Polaris [polérịs], *s.* (astr.) la (estrella) polar.

polariscope [polérịskoụp], *s.* (ópt.) polariscopio.

polarity [polérịtị], *s.* polaridad.

polarization [poulạrịzéịšọn], *s.* polarización.

polarize [póụlạraịz], *va.* polarizar.

polarizer [-œ(r)], *s.*, **polarizing** [-ịŋ], *a.* polarizador.

pole [póụl]. I. *s.* (geog. y elec.) polo; pértiga, vara larga, palo largo, asta, paral, estaca; balancín (de volatinero); poste (de telégrafos, etc.); medida de 16½ pies; (top.) jalón; (P.), polaco. —**p. bean,** (bot.) frijol de enrame, frijol trepador.—**p. of a coach,** lanza, pértigo o timón de coche.—**p. prop,** (carr.) tentemozo.—**p. vault,** (dep.) salto de altura (o a veces, de longitud) con garrocha. II. *va.* empujar, llevar, sostener o armar con palos; (metal.) revolver o agitar con varas. III. *vn.* impeler un barco con pértiga.

poleax(e [-æks], *s.* (mil.) antigua hacha de armas; (mar.) hach(uel)a de abordaje; cierta hacha de matadero.

polecat [-kæt], *s.* (zool.) veso; mofeta; turón.

polemarch [pálịmark], *s.* (hist. gr.) polemarca, *m.*

polemic(al [polémịk(ạl], *a.* polémico.

polemic [polémịk], *s.* polémica; polemista.

polemics [-s], *s.* polémica, dialéctica.

polemist [pálẹmịst], *s.* polemista.

polemoscope [polémoskoụp], *s.* (ópt.) polemoscopio.

polestar [póụlstar], *s.* (astr.) estrella polar.

police [polís]. I. *s.* policía.—**p. commissioner,** o **chief of p.,** jefe de policía.—**p. court,** tribunal de policía.—**p. dog,** perro de policía.—**p. force,** cuerpo de seguridad.—**p. headquarters,** comisariato o jefatura de policía; dirección de seguridad.—**p. inspector,** comisario de policía. —**p. officer** = POLICEMAN.—**p. station,** prevención; comisaría; cuartel de la policía. II. *s.* policíaco, (Am.) policial. III. *va.* apostar polizontes; poner o mantener servicio de policía en.

policeman [-mạn], *s.* policía, *m.*, agente de policía, guardia municipal o de seguridad, (fam.) polizonte.

policewoman [-wụmạn], *s.* policía (mujer).

policlinic [palịklínịk], *s.* (med.) dispensario anexo a un hospital; policlínica.

policy [pálịsị], *s.* prudencia, sagacidad; curso o plan de acción; política; regla, sistema, *m.*; costumbre; póliza de seguro; especie de lotería. —**p. holder,** asegurado, tenedor de póliza.—**p. player,** jugador de lotería, que apuesta sobre ciertas combinaciones numéricas.

poliomyelitis [palịomaịẹláịtịs], **polio** [póụlịoụ], *s.* (med.) poliomielitis, parálisis infantil.

Polish [póụlịš]. I. *a.* polaco, polonés. II. *s.* polaco (idioma).

polish [pálịš]. I. *va.* pulir, pulimentar, bruñir, limar, tersar; lustrar, dar lustre, embolar; educar; civilizar. II. *vn.* recibir lustre o pulimento. III. *s.* pulimento, bruñido, tersura, lustre; cultura, urbanidad; betún o bola para zapatos; embolada, acción de embolar (zapatos).

polished [-t], *pp. y a.* pulido, bruñido; terso; refinado, culto, urbano; cumplido, galante.

polishedness [-nịs], *s.* bruñidura, tersura; finura, cortes(an)ía, urbanidad.

polisher [-œ(r)], *s.* pulidor, pulidero, bruñidor.

polishing [-ịŋ]. I. *s.* bruñido, pulimento. II. *a.* pulidor, de pulir.—**p. bed,** bruñidor o pulidor mecánico; mesa de pulir.—**p. disk,** (dent.) disco pulidor.—**p. iron,** plancha o hierro de abrillantar.

polite [poláịt], *a.* cortés, urbano, bien educado, comedido, civil, atento, político.—**politely** [-lị], *adv.* cortésmente.—**politeness** [-nịs], *s.* cortesía, comedimiento, civilidad, urbanidad, buena crianza, educación.—**for p.' sake,** por cortesía; por política.

politic [pálịtịk], *a.* político, sagaz, astuto, hábil, ladino; apropiado, atinado.

political [polítịkạl], *a.* político.—(desp.) politiquero.—**p. economist,** crematólogo.—**p.**

economy, economía política, crematología o crematística.—**p. science,** ciencia política.
politically [-i], *adv.* políticamente.
politicaster [-kæstœ(r)], *s.* (desp.) politicastro.
politician [palitisən], *s.* político; estadista; (desp.) politicastro, politiquero.
politicize [politisajz], *vn.* politiquear (fam.).
politico [politikou]. **I.** *s.* (a veces desp.) = POLITICIAN. **II.** *a.* **p.-economical,** etc., políticoeconómico, etc.
politics [politiks], *s. sing.* o *pl.* política; asuntos, métodos o intereses políticos; (desp.) politiquería; rivalidades o maniobras de partido o facción.
polity [politi], *s.* constitución política, forma de gobierno; política.
polka [póu(l)kə]. **I.** *s.* (danz. y mús.) polca.—**p. dot,** (tej.) uno de una serie de lunares o puntos, de distribución uniforme en una tela; diseño formado por éstos. **II.** *vn.* polcar, bailar la polca.
poll [poul]. **I.** *s.* nómina, padrón, empadronamiento; matrícula; lista electoral; votación; escrutinio; encuesta (de la opinión pública); (anat.) cabeza, nuca; cotillo de destral o martillo.—*pl.* lugar donde se vota; urnas electorales; elecciones.—**p. evil,** (vet.) úlcera en la nuca (de un caballo).—**p. pick,** (min.) punterola.—**p. tax,** capitación. **II.** *va.* empadronar, matricular, registrar; dar o recibir (votos); someter a la votación de; determinar los votos de; escrutar; descabezar; podar, desmochar; descornar. *V.* POLLARD. **III.** *vn.* votar en las elecciones.
pollack [palək], *s.* (ict.) cierto pez semejante al bacalao o abadejo.
pollard [palərd]. **I.** *s.* árbol desmochado o descopado; res descornada; (ict.) leucisco; salvado. **II.** *va.* desmochar, podar.
pollen [palen], *s.* (bot.) polen.—**p. mass,** polinia.
pollex [paliks], *s.* (anat.) pólice, pulgar.
pollinate [palinejt], *va.* (bot.) polinizar, fecundar con polen; fecundar.—**pollination** [-éjʃən], *s.* polinación, polinización; fecundación.
polling [póuliŋ], *s.* votación; escrutinio.—**p. booth, p. place,** puesto o lugar de votación; (fig.) las urnas electorales.
pollinic [palinik], *a.* (bot.) polínico.
pollinium [paliniʌm], *s.* (bot.) polinia, masa coherente de granos de polen.
pollinosis [palinóusis], *s.* (med.) = HAY FEVER.
polliwig, polliwog o pollywog [paliwig, -wag], *s.* (zool.) renacuajo.
pollock [palək], *s.* = POLLACK.
pollute [poliút], *va.* manchar, ensuciar; contaminar o corromper; violar, deshonrar; profanar, mancillar.—**polluted** [-id], *a.* poluto, contaminado.—**pollutedness** [-idnis], *s.* calidad de poluto, etc.
polluter [poliútœ(r)], *s.* corruptor, contaminador; violador; profanador.
pollution [poliúʃən], *s.* contaminación, corrupción; violación; mancilla, mancha; contaminación, infección (del agua); (med.) polución.
Pollux [palʌks], *s.* (astr.) Pólux.
Polly, o polly [pali], *s.* (orn.) (fam.) cotorra, lorito o papagayo domesticado (ll. t. **poll parrot**).
Pollyanna [paliænə], *s.* nombre propio que se usa como personificación del optimismo excesivo.
polo [póulou], *s.* (dep.) polo (juego); polo (canto y baile popular de Andalucía).—**p. mallet,** taco o mazo.—**p. player, poloist** [-ist], polista.
polonaise [palonéjz], *s.* (sast.) polonesa; (mús.) polonesa, polaca.
polonium [polóuniʌm], *s.* (quím.) polonio.
poltroon(ish [paltrún(iʃ], *s.* y *a.* cobarde, pusilánime, menguado, mandria, (fam.) collón.
poltroonery [-œri], *s.* cobardía, pusilanimidad.
poly [pali], *s.* (bot.) zamarrilla; teucrio.
polyandry [paliændri], *s.* (sociol. y bot.) poliandria.—**polyandrous** [paliéndrʌs], *a.* poliándrico; (bot.) poliandro.
polyanthus [paliénθʌs], *s.* (bot.) primavera.

polyarchy [paliarki], *s.* (pol.) poliarquía.
polyatomic [-ətámik], *a.* (quím.) poliatómico.
polybasic [-béjsik], *a.* (quím.) polibásico.
polycarpous [-kárpʌs], *a.* (bot.) policárpico.
polychroism [palikrojzm], *s.* (min.) policroísmo.
polychromatic [-kromǽtik], *a.* policromático.
polychrome [-kroum], *s.* obra policroma.—**polychromic** [-króumik], *a.* policromo.
polyclinic [-klínik], *s.* policlínica; hospital; escuela de clínica.
polydactyl [-dǽktil], *a.* (zool.) polidáctilo.
polygala [poligalə], *s.* (bot.) polígala.
polygalaceous [-léjʃʌs], *a.* (bot.) poligaleo.
polygamist [poligamist], *s.*, **polygamous** [-mʌs], *a.* (sociol., bot. y zool.) polígamo.
polygamy [-mi], *s.* poligamia.
polygenesis [palidʒénisis], *s.* (biol.) poligénesis, doctrina de la pluralidad de orígenes.
polygenetic [-dʒenétik], *a.* relativo a la poligénesis.
polygenism [polidʒenizm], *s.* (biol.) poligenismo.
polygenist [-ist], *s.* poligenista.
polyglot [paliglat], *a.* y *s.* poligloto.—**p. Bible,** poliglota.
polygon [paligan], *s.* (geom.) polígono.
polygonal [poligonəl], *a.* poligonal, polígono.
Polygonum [-nʌm], *s.* género de las poligonáceas.—**polygonaceous** [-néjʃʌs], *a.* (bot.) poligonáceo.
polygraph [paligræf], *s.* policopia; polígrafo.
polygraphic(al [-grǽfik(əl], *a.* poligráfico.
polygraphy [poligrafi], *s.* poligrafía.
polygyny [polidʒini], *s.* poligamia por parte del hombre, posesión de varias esposas; (bot.) poliginia.
polyhedral, polyhedrous, polyhedric(al [palihidrəl, -drʌs, -drik(əl], *a.* poliédrico, poliedro.—**polyhedral angle,** ángulo poliedro.
polyhedron [-drọn], *s.* (geom.) poliedro.
polymer [palimœ(r)], *s.* (quím.) (cuerpo) polímero.—**polymeric** [palimérik], *a.* (quím.) polímero.—**polymerism** [polimerizm], *s.* polimerismo, polimería.—**polymerization** [palimerizéjʃən], *s.* polimerización.—**polymerize** [palimœrajz], *va.* y *vn.* polimerizar(se).
polymorph [palimorf], *s.* ser u organismo polimorfo.—**polymorphism** [-mórfizm], *s.* polimorfismo.—**polymorphous, polymorphic** [-mórfʌs, -fik], *a.* polimorfo.
Polynesian [paliníʒən], *s.* y *a.* polinesi(an)o.
polynomial [palinóumiəl]. **I.** *a.* de varios términos. **II.** *s.* (mat.) polinomio; vocablo científico compuesto de más de dos palabras.
polynuclear [-núkliə(r)], *a.* (med.) polinuclear.
polyorama [-orámə], *s.* poliorama, *m.*
polyp [palip], *s.* (zool.) pólipo, zoófito; (med.) pólipo; (ant.) pulpo. *V.* POLYPUS.
polypary [-ari], *s.* (zool.) polipero.
polypetalous [palipétalʌs], *a.* (bot.) polipétalo.
polyphase [-fejz], *a.* (elec.) polifásico.
polyphonic [-fánik], *a.* polifónico, polífono.—**polyphony** [polifoni], *s.* (mús.) polifonía.
polypodiaceous [-podiéjʃʌs], *a.* (bot.) polipodiáceo.
polypody [-poudi], *s.* (bot.) polipodio.
polypous [-pʌs], *a.* (zool.) poliposo.
polypus [-pʌs], *s.* (med.) pólipo; (zool.) pulpo; pólipo. *V.* POLYP.
polyscope [-skoup], *s.* (ópt. y med.) poliscopio.
polysepalous [-sépalʌs], *a.* polisépalo.
polysyllabic(al [-siləbik(əl], *a.* polisílabo.
polysyllable [-siləbl], *s.* polisílabo.
polysyndeton [-síndetan], *s.* (ret.) polisíndeton.
polytechnic [-téknik]. **I.** *a.* politécnico. **II.** *s.* escuela politécnica.
polytechnics [-s], *a.* politecnia.
polytheism [-θijzm], *s.* politeísmo.—**polytheist** [-θijst], *s.*, **polytheistic(al** [-θíístik(əl], *a.* politeísta.
polyuria [-yúriə], *s.* (med.) poliuria, secreción excesiva de orina.—**polyuric** [-rik], *a.* poliúrico.

polyvalent [-véi̯l̯e̯nt], a. (quím. y bact.) polivalente.

polyzoan [-zóu̯an], a. y s. (zool.) polizoo.

pomace [pʌ́mi̯s], s. bagazo de manzanas, uvas, etc., exprimidas; magma, m.

pomaceous [poméi̯s̄ʌs], a. (bot.) pomáceo.

pomade [poméi̯d], s. pomada.

pomander [póu̯mændœ(r)], s. bola de confecciones olorosas.—**p. box**, poma, pomo.

pomato [poméi̯tou̯], s. injerto de papa y tomate.

pomatum [poméi̯tʌm], s. pomada, manteca.

pome [poṳm], s. (bot.) pomo, fruta de pipa o pepita (manzana, pera, etc.).—**p.-bearing**, pomífero.

pomegranate [pʌ́mgræni̯t], s. (bot.) granada.— **p. flower**, granadino.—**p. tree**, granado.

pomelo [pʌ́melou̯], s. (bot.) toronja.

Pomeranian [pamœréi̯ni̯an], a. y s. pomerano; (zool.) pomeranio, perro de Pomerania.

pomiculture [póu̯mi̯kʌlchṳ(r)], s. pomicultura.

pomiferous [pomífeᵣʌs], a. (bot.) pomífero.

pommel [pʌ́mel̯]. I. s. pomo (de espada); perilla (de arzón); culata (de arma de fuego); (arq.) perilla, bolilla. II. va. cascar (fam.), aporrear.

pomological [poṳmolʌ́d̄ʒi̯kal̯], a. pomológico.

pomologist [pomʌ́lod̄ʒi̯st], s. pomólogo.

pomology [-d̄ʒi̯], s. pomología.

pomp [pamp], s. pompa, fa(u̯)sto, aparato, tren.

pompadour [pámpad̄or], s. copete (peinado).

pompano [pámpanou̯], s. (ict.) pámpano.

Pompeian [pampéi̯an], a. y s. pompeyano.

pompelmous [pámpelmu̯s], s. (bot.) toronja.

pompom, o pom-pom [pámpam] s. (arti.) cierto cañón antiaéreo automático.

pompon [pámpan], s. borl(it)a o madroño (adorno); (mil.) pompón (de chacó o morrión); (bot.) variedad pequeña de crisantema y de dalia.

pomposity [pampási̯ti̯], **pompousness** [pámpʌsni̯s], s. pomposidad, fa(u̯)sto, fastuosidad, ostentación; afectación; altisonancia (de estilo).

pompous [pámpʌs], a. pomposo, ostentoso.

pompously [-li̯], adv. pomposamente.

poncho [pánchou̯], s. poncho; capote de monte.

pond [pand], s. charca, laguna o lago pequeño, estanque.—**p. lily** = WATER LILY.

ponder [pándœ(r)]. I. va. pesar, estudiar, examinar, (fig.) rumiar. II. vn. (con **on** u **over**) considerar, deliberar, reflexionar (acerca de).

ponderable [-abl̯], a. ponderable.

ponderal [-al̯], a. ponderal, pert. a peso.

ponderosity [-ási̯ti̯], s. ponderosidad; pesadez, aridez.

ponderous [pándœᵣʌs], a. ponderoso, pesado; voluminoso; tedioso, cansado.—**ponderousness** [-ni̯s], s. ponderosidad; aridez, sequedad, pesadez (de estilo).—**ponderously** [-li̯], adv. pesadamente.

pondweed [pándwid], s. (bot.) potamogetón.

pone [poṳn], s. torta o panecillo de maíz.

pongee [pandʒí], s. cierta tela de seda o rayón.

poniard [pányard], I. s. puñal. II. va. apuñalar.

pontage [pánti̯dʒ], s. pontazgo, pontaje.

pontederiaceous [pantͤdiɾi̯éi̯s̄ʌs], a. (bot.) pontederiáceo.

Pontic [pánti̯k], a. póntico.

pontifex [pánti̯feks], s. pontífice, sumo sacerdote (apl. esp. al de los antiguos romanos).

pontiff [pánti̯f], s. pontífice; (arzo)bispo; el papa.

pontifical [pantífi̯kal̯], a. pontifical; pontificio, papal.—**p. mass**, misa pontifical.—**P. States**, (hist. y geog.) Estados pontificios.

pontifical, s. pontifical.—pl. pontificales.

pontificalia [-kéi̯li̯a], s. pl. (igl.) pontificales.

pontifically [pantífi̯kali̯], adv. pontificalmente.

pontificate [-kei̯t], s. pontificado.

pontil [pánti̯l], **ponty** [pánti̯], s. (vid.) pontil, puntel.

Pontine Marshes [pánti̯n mars̄i̯s], s. pl. (geog.) lagunas pontinas.

pontlevis [pantlévi̯s], s. puente levadizo.

ponton [pántan o pantún], s. (mil.) = PONTOON.

pontoon [pantún], s. (mil.) pontón; (mar.) pontón; chata, barcaza; (aer.) flotador (de un aeroplano).—**p. bridge**, puente de barcas o pontones.

pony [póu̯ni̯]. I. s. jaca, haca, caballito; (fam.) clave (f.) o traducción empleada a hurtadillas como ayuda de estudios; (fam.) copa o vaso pequeños, o el licor que se sirve en ellos. II. va. y vn. (fam.) traducir con clave o ayuda; (fam.) (con **up**) pagar. III. a. pequeño.—**p. engine**, locomotora de maniobras.—**p. express**, (E. U. del Oeste) antiguo sistema de llevar el correo, etc., por caballos ligeros.—**p. truck**, truck o bogie articulado.—**p. truss**, puente bajo sin refuerzos transversales superiores.

poodle [púdl̯], s. perro de lanas o de aguas.

pooh [pu], interj. ¡bah! ¡fu!

pooh-pooh [pú pú], va. y vn. desdeñar; hacer mofa (de).—**p.-p. theory**, la teoría de que el lenguaje tuvo su origen en interjecciones.

pool [pul]. I. va. formar una polla o puesta (en ciertos juegos); pagar a escote; mancomunar intereses. II. vn. formar un charco, resbalarse. III. s. charco, lagunajo; alberca, balsa; hoya, rebalsa; estanque; piscina (natatoria); (med.) rebalsa; el juego de trucos; en ciertos juegos, polla; en el billar, truco; piña, fusión de intereses o de empresas; combinación para especular en fondos o valores públicos.—**p. room**, sala de apuestas, donde se apuesta a carreras, etc., verificadas en otro lugar; sala de trucos (a veces de billar también).

poop [pup], s. (mar.) popa o toldilla; ventosidad.

poor [pur]. I. a. pobre, necesitado, indigente; deficiente, falto, escaso; en mal estado; de poco valor, de poco mérito; malo; de mala calidad, inferior; humilde; estéril (tierra); indispuesto, malo, enfermizo.—**p. box**, cepillo de pobres.— **p. devil**, pobre diablo.—**p. farm**, granja para alojar y mantener a los pobres.—**p. laws**, leyes (f.) de pobres o acerca de los pobres.—**p. rate**, contribución a la iglesia para limosnas; tasa o contribución para socorrer a los pobres. —**p.-spirited**, abatido, cobarde.—**p.-spiritedness**, poquedad, cobardía, pusilanimidad.— **p. thing**, pobrecito, pobrecillo.—**a p. horse**, un penco.—**a p. night**, una mala noche.—**a p. opinion of one**, mala opinión de uno. II. s. **the p.**, los pobres.

poorhouse [-hau̯s], s. hospicio, asilo, casa de caridad o de beneficencia.

poorly [-li̯]. I. adv. pobremente; malamente.—**p. off**, escaso de dinero. II. a. (fam.) indispuesto, enfermizo.

poorness [-ni̯s], s. pobreza, necesidad; deficiencia.

pop [páp]. I. s. chasquido, ruido seco, detonación; pistoletazo; taponazo; bebida gaseosa; (fam.) concierto popular. II. va. soltar, espetar, disparar; chasquear; hacer saltar un tapón.—**to p. the question**, (fam.) hacer una declaración de amor; pedir en matrimonio. III. vn. entrar o salir de sopetón; saltar un tapón; dar chasquidos o estallidos; detonar; reventar.—**to p. off**, (fam.) morir; dormirse.—**to p. up**, (fam.) aparecer de repente.

popcorn [-korn], s. maíz reventón de tostar o tostado; rosetas, flores o palomitas de maíz; (Am.) esquite.

pope o Pope [póu̯p], s. papa, m., sumo pontífice. —**p.'s head**, (Ingl.) escobillón para limpiar bóvedas.—**P.'s miter**, tiara.—**p.'s nose**, (fam.) obispillo o rabadilla de ave.

popedom [-dom], s. papado, papazgo.

popery [-œri̯], s. (desp.) papismo.

popgun [pápgan], s. cerbatana, tirabala, taco.

popinjay [pápindʒei̯], s. pisaverde, petimetre; (orn.) picamaderos verde; (ant.) loro, papagayo.

popish [póu̯pi̯s̄], a. (desp.) papal, papista.

poplar [páplə(r)], s. (bot.) álamo, chopo, pobo.

poplin [pápli̯n], s. (tej.) papelina; popelina.

popliteal [paplítiạl]. *a.* (anat.) poplíteo.

poppet [pápịt]. *s.* válvula de movimiento vertical (ll. t. **p. valve**); (mar.) columna de basada.

poppy [pápi], *s.* (bot.) adormidera, amapola.

poppycock [pápịkak]. *s.* (fam.) farsa, música celestial, farándula.

populace [pápyụlis], *s.* pueblo, plebe, *f.*; (desp.) populacho, chusma, vulg(ach)o, gentuza.

popular [pápyụlạ(r)], *a.* popular, democrático, comunero; populachero; preferido, estimado, de moda, en boga, favorecido.—**p. applause**, aura popular.—**p. front**, (pol.) frente (*f.*) popular.—**p.-priced**, de precio bajo o módico.—**to become p.**, generalizarse (ú. de deportes, etc.).

popularity [-lérịti]. *s.* popularidad, prestigio, boga, aura, aceptación o buena acogida general.

popularization [-lạrịzéịṣọn], *s.* popularización; divulgación, vulgarización.—**popularize** [pápyụlạraịz], *va.* popularizar, dar a conocer; divulgar, vulgarizar.—**popularizer** [-œ(r)], *s.*, **popularizing** [-ịŋ], *a.* popularizador; divulgador, vulgarizador.

popularly [-lị], *adv.* popularmente.

populate [pápyụleịt]. I. *va.* poblar. II. *vn.* (raro) multiplicarse, propagarse.—**populated** [-jd], *a.* poblado.—**populating** [-ịŋ]. I. *a.* poblador. II. *s.* población, población.

population [-léịṣọn], *s.* población; vecindario.

populator [pápyụleịtọ(r)], *s.* poblador.

Populism [pápyụlịzm], *s.* (pol. E. U.) populismo, partido semisocialista.—**Populist** [-ịst], *s.*, **Populistic** [-ịstịk], *a.* populista.

populous [pápyụlʌs], *a.* populoso, muy poblado.—**populously** [-lị], *adv.* con mucha gente.—**populousness** [-nịs], *s.* abundancia de población.

porbeagle [pórbigl], *s.* (ict.) especie de tiburón.

porcelain [pórsẹlịn], *s.* porcelana, china, loza fina.—**p. shell**, (zool.) porcelana, ciprea, concha de Venus (marisco).

porcelaneous [-léịnịʌs], *a.* de o como porcelana.

porcelanite [pórsẹlạnaịt], *s.* (petr.) porcelanita.

porch [porch], *s.* pórtico, vestíbulo, atrio, porche, entrada, (so)portal, propileo; corredor, galería (del frente o los lados de una casa).

porcine [pórsaịn], *a.* porcuno, porcino.

porcupine [pórkyụpaịn], *s.* (zool.) puerco espín(o).

pore [por]. I. *s.* poro. II. *vn.* (con **on, upon** u **over**) escudriñar, estudiar escrupulosamente.

porgy [pórdžị], *s.* (ict.) pargo.

poriness [pórịnịs], *s.* porosidad.

pork [pórk], *s.* carne (*f.*) de puerco; (pol., fam.) favores políticos otorgados por funcionarios públicos, honores mamados, canonjías.—**p. barrel**, (pol., fam.) partidas de favoritismo provincial, destinadas a determinadas localidades prescindiendo del bien general.—**p. chop**, chuleta o costilla de cerdo.—**p. sausage**, chorizo, embuchado, longaniza, salchicha.

porker [-œ(r)], *s.* (zool.) puerco, cerdo, cochino.

pornographer [pornágrạfœ(r)], *s.* pornógrafo.

pornographic [pornogræfịk], *a.* pornográfico.

pornography [pornágrạfi], *s.* pornografía.

porosity [pórạsịtị], **porousness** [pórʌsnịs], *s.* porosidad, esponjosidad.

porous [pórʌs], *a.* poroso, esponjoso, permeable.—**p. plaster**, (med.) emplasto o parche poroso.

porphyritic(al [porfịrítịk(ạl], *a.* porfídico.

porphyry [pórfịrị], *s.* (petr.) pórfido.

porpoise [pórpʌs], *s.* (zool.) puerco de mar, marsopa. *V.* DOLPHIN.

porridge [párịdž], *s.* gachas, puches, *mf. pl.*, potaje.

porringer [párịndžœ(r)], *s.* escudilla.

port [port]. I. *s.* puerto; (mar.) port(ill)a, portañola, tronera; portal, puerta; (m. v.) lumbrera; (mar.) babor; porte, talante; oporto (vino de Oporto).—**p. bar**, obstrucción (natural o artificial) a la entrada de un puerto.—**p. captain**, capitán de puerto.—**p. of call**, escala, puerto

de arribada.—**p. of destination**, puerto de destino.—**p. of entry**, puerto (marítimo o seco).—**p. side**, babor. II. *va.* y *vn.* (mar.) poner, o andar, a babor; (mil.) llevar un fusil terciado.

portable [pórtạbl], *a.* portátil (máquina de escribir, aparato de radio, etc.); (loco)móvil, rodado.

portableness [-nịs], *s.* propiedad de ser portátil.

portage [pórtịdž], *s.* porte(o), portaje, portazgo; transporte, acarreo.

portal [pórtạl], *s.* (arq.) portal, portada; vestíbulo.—**p. vein**, (anat.) vena porta.

portcrayon [pórtkréịọn], *s.* portalápiz (*m.*) de pintor.

portcullis [pórtkʌlịs], *s.* (fort.) rastrillo.

Porte (The) [port], *s.* la Puerta otomana.

porte-cochère [-koŝér], *s.* puerta cochera.

porte-monnaie [portmọnéị], *s.* portamonedas.

portend [porténd], *va.* pronosticar, presagiar.

portent [pórtent], *s.* presagio, augurio; prodigio, portento.

portentous [porténtʌs], *a.* ominoso, de mal agüero; prodigioso, portentoso.

porter [pórtœ(r)], *s.* port(e)ador; mozo de cordel o de cuerda, ganapán, faquín; mandadero; mozo de servicio (en trenes, hoteles, etc.); portero; cerveza oscura.—**p.'s lodge**, portería, garita.

porterage [-ịdž], *s.* oficio de faquín, portero, etc.; porte, portaje. *V.* PORTAGE.

porterhouse [-haụs], *s.* cervecería; bodegón.—**p. steak**, biftek de solomillo y filete.

portfire [pórtfaịœ(r)], *s.* (arti.) lanzafuego, botafuego.

portfolio [-fóụliọụ], *s.* cartera, carpeta, portapliegos; (fig.) ministerio.—**minister**, etc., **without p.**, ministro, etc., sin cartera, o sin departamento o ramo especial.

porthole [-houl], *s.* (mar.) port(ill)a, portañola, tronera.

portico [pórtịkọụ], *s.* (arq.) pórtico, porche, (so)portal, atrio.—**porticoed** [-d], *a.* provisto de pórtico(s).

portière [portịér], *s.* portier, cortina de puerta.

portion [pórṣọn]. I. *s.* porción, parte, *f.*; cuota; dote, *mf.* II. *va.* dividir, (re)partir; dotar.

portionless [-lịs], *a.* indotado.

Portland cement [pórtlạnd sịmént], *s.* cemento de pórtland.

portliness [pórtlịnịs], *s.* corpulencia; porte majestuoso.—**portly** [pórtlị], *a.* corpulento, grueso; majestuoso, serio, grave.

portmanteau [portmǽntọụ], *s.* portamanteo, manga, maleta ligera.—**p. word**, palabra que combina parcialmente otras dos (vg.: *brunch*, de *breakfast* y *lunch*).

Porto Rican [pórto ríkạn], *a.* y *s.* puertorriqueño, portorriqueño, borinqueño.

portrait [pórtrịt], *s.* retrato.—**p. painter**, retratista.—**to sit for a p.**, retratarse.

portraitist [-ịst], *s.* retratista.

portraiture [pórtrịchụ(r)], *s.* arte de hacer retratos; retrato; pintura, bosquejo.

portray [portréị], *va.* retratar, pintar.

portrayal [-ạl], *s.* representación gráfica, dibujo, pintura; descripción.

Portuguese [pórchụgịz], *a.* y *s.* portugués.

portulaca [porchụlǽkạ], *s.* (bot.) verdolaga.

pose [póụz]. I. *va.* (b. a.) colocar en cierta actitud o postura; proponer, afirmar; plantear (un problema); confundir con preguntas difíciles. II. *vn.* colocarse en cierta postura; tomar posturas afectadas; fachendear.—**to p. as**, pretender ser, hacerse pasar por, echárselas de, darlas de. III. *s.* postura, posición, actitud.

poser [-œ(r)], *s.* pregunta o problema (*m.*) difícil; (Ingl.) examinador; el que se coloca en cierta actitud; persona afectada o vanagloriosa (ll. t. **poseur**).

posit [pázịt], *va.* (lóg.) afirmar, proponer, sentar; disponer, colocar.

position [pozíʃǫn], *s.* posición, situación, ubicación: puesto, empleo, colocación, cargo, plaza; actitud; lo que uno sostiene.—**to be in** (a) **p. to,** estar en situación de, poder.

positive [pázjtiv]. I. *a.* positivo: real, verdadero; absoluto, inherente: explícito, categórico, imperativo. rotundo: expreso. escrito, convenido; (lóg.) afirmativo; (filos.) positivista: empírico, experimental; seguro, cierto, convencido; obstinado, terco, porfiado; (mat., elec., foto., gram.) positivo: (mec.) de acción directa, de transmisión rígida; de vaivén; de alimentación continua bajo presión (apl. a la lubricación).— **p. law,** derecho positivo. II. *s.* realidad, certeza; (foto.) positivo, prueba positiva; (gram.) grado positivo de comparación; (elec.) plancha, polo, etc., positivos.

positively [-li], *adv.* positiva o absolutamente; categórica o terminantemente; sin duda.

positiveness [-njs], *o* **positivity** [pazjtíviti], *s.* positivismo, positividad; seguridad, certeza, porfía.

positivism [pázjtivizm], *s.* positivismo; certidumbre; (filos.) positivismo.

positivist(ic [-jst, -jstjk], *s.* y *a.* (filos.) positivista.

positron [pázjtran], *s.* (fís.) posit(r)ón.

posology [posálodʒj], *s.* (med.) posología.

posse [pásj], *s.* posibilidad; pelotón; fuerza civil que el *sheriff* tiene autoridad de juntar para evitar desórdenes, tumultos, etc. (ll. t. **p. comitatus**).

possess [pozés], *va.* poseer; gozar, disponer (de); (como *vr.*), apoderarse, hacerse dueño (de); señorear, dominar; posesionar, poner (a uno) en posesión.

possessed [-t], *pp.* poseso, poseído.—**as one p.,** como energúmeno, o persona poseída del demonio.

possession [pozéʃǫn], *s.* posesión, dominio, (per)tenencia, goce; apoderamiento.—*pl.* patrimonio, propiedades, bienes.—**to put in p. of,** posesionar de.—**to take p. of,** hacerse dueño de. *V.* TO TAKE.

possessional [-ąl], *a.* posesional.

possessive [pozésjv]. I. *s.* y *a.* (gram., etc.) posesivo (pronombre). II. *a.* posesorio; posesional. —**p. case,** (gram.) genitivo.

possessor [pozésǫr], *s.* poseedor, posesor.

possessory [-j], *a.* posesorio.

posset [pásjt], *s.* bebida de leche cuajada y mezclada con cerveza o vino y especias.

possibility [pasjbíliti], *s.* posibilidad; contingencia; potencia(lidad); oportunidad.

possible [pásjbl], *a.* posible, potencial, dable, contingible.—**as far as,** o **as much as p.,** en lo posible.—**as soon as p.,** cuanto antes.—**to render p.,** posibilitar.

possibly [-blj], *adv.* posiblemente, quizá(s).

possum [pásʌm], *s.* (fam.) = OPOSSUM.—**to play p.,** (fam.) disimular; fingir (enfermedad, ignorancia, etc.).

post [póʊst]. I. *s.* poste, pilar, paral; (carp.) montante, pie derecho; (mil.) puesto, plaza, guarnición, avanzada; empleo, destino, cargo; correo, posta, estafeta, ordinario, propio.—**p. bag,** mala, valija.—**p. card,** (tarjeta) postal, *f.* —**p. chaise, p. coach,** silla o coche de posta.— **p.-free,** franco de porte.—**p. horse,** caballo de posta.—*pl.* posta.—**p. note,** pagaré de banco redimible en fecha dada; pagaré circulante emitido por un banco.—**p. office,** correo, casa de correos, administración de correos, estafeta. —**p.-office box,** apartado de correos, (Am.) casilla postal.—**p.-office order,** giro postal.— **p.-office savings bank,** caja postal de ahorros. —**p. road,** camino de posta o correo. II. *adv.* con rapidez; por la posta; de prisa. III. *va.* anunciar, pegar o fijar (carteles); cerrar o prohibir la entrada a (un terreno, etc.); estigmatizar, infamar públicamente; apostar, situar; echar al correo o a la estafeta; (com.) pasar los

asientos de un libro al libro mayor; (fam.) informar, tener al corriente, poner al tanto de. —**p. no bills,** se prohíbe fijar carteles. IV. *vn.* viajar en posta; (equit.) montar a la inglesa.

postage [-jdʒ], *s.* porte de correos, franqueo.—**p. free,** porte franco, franco de porte.—**p.** (pre-)**paid,** porte pagado.—**p. stamp,** sello de correo, (Am.) estampilla, timbre.

postal [-ąl], *a.* postal.—**p.** (**card**), postal, *f.*, o tarjeta postal.—**p. convention,** convenio postal.—**p.** (**money**) **order,** giro postal.—**p. tube,** cañuto para enviar papeles por correo.

post-bellum [póʊst bélʌm], *a.* de después de la guerra, posterior a la guerra.

postbox [póʊstbaks], *s.* buzón; apartado.

postboy [-bɔj], *s.* postillón. *V.* COURIER.

postcard [-kard]. *s.* = POST CARD.

postdate [-déjt]. I. *va.* posfechar. II. [póʊstdejt], *s.* posfecha.—**postdated** [-déjtjd], *a.* fechado posteriormente; con fecha adelantada.

postdiluvial, postdiluvian [-djlúvjal, -vjan], *a.* postdiluviano.

posted [póʊstjd], *a.* al corriente, al tanto (de), enterado; cerrado, vedado (terreno, etc.).

poster [póʊstœ(r)], *s.* cartel, cartelón, papelón, letrero, rótulo; fijador de carteles; correo; propio; caballo de posta.

poste restante [póʊst restánt], *s.* (fr.) posta restante, lista de correos.

posterior [pastírjo(r)], *a.* posterior.—*s.* *pl.* nalgas.

posteriority [pastjrjárjtj], *s.* posterioridad.

posterity [pastérjtj], *s.* posteridad.

postern [póʊstœrn], *s.* puerta trasera; (fort.) postigo, poterna.

postfix [póʊstfjks]. I. *va.* (gram.) añadir un sufijo. II. [póʊstfjks], *s.* sufijo, pos(t)fijo.

postgraduate [-grédʒujt]. I. *a.* post-graduado, de o para graduados (apl. a estudios superiores hechos después de recibir un grado). II. *s.* estudiante graduado que hace estudios superiores complementarios.

posthaste [póʊsthéjst]. I. *a.* urgente, apresurado. II. *s.* diligencia, presteza. III. *adv.* a toda prisa.

posthouse [-haʊs], *s.* posta, casa de postas.

posthumous [pástjumas *o* -chjumʌs], *a.* póstumo.

postil(late [pástjl(ejt], *va.* (a)postillar.

postil(l)ion [poʊstjlyǫn], *s.* postillón.

postimpressionism [poʊstjmprésǫnjzm], *s.* (b. a.) postimpresionismo.—**postimpressionist(ic** [-jst,-jstjk], *s.* y *a.* postimpresionista.

postliminium [-ljmjnjʌm], **postliminy** [-límjnj], *s.* (for.) postliminio.

postlude [-ljud], *s.* (mús.) postludio.

postman [-man], *s.* cartero; valijero.

postmark [-mark], *s.* sello o estampa de la oficina de correos; matasellos.

postmaster [-mæstœ(r)], *s.* administrador de correos.—**p. general,** director general de correos.

postmeridian [-mɛrídjan], *a.* postmeridiano, de la tarde.

post mortem [-mórtɛm], *adv.* (lat.) después de la muerte.—**p.-m. examination,** (med.) necropsia, autopsia.

postnatal [-néjtąl], *a.* postnatal, de después del nacimiento.

postnuptial [-nʌpʃąl], *a.* postnupcial o postconnubial, posterior al matrimonio.

postoperative [-ápratjv], *a.* (cir.) postoperatorio, de después de la operación.

postorbital [-órbjtąl], *a.* (anat.) postorbitario, postorbital (apl. esp. a la apófisis postorbital).

postpaid [póʊstpéjd], *a.* porte pagado, franco (de porte).

postpalatal [-pǽlatąl], *a.* y *s.* (fon.) pos(t)palatal.

postpone [-póʊn], *va.* diferir, aplazar; posponer; posponer.—**postponement** [-mɛnt], *s.* aplazamiento; postergación; posposición.

postposition [-pozíʃǫn], *s.* posposición.

postpositive [-pázjtjv], *a.* (gram.) pospositivo.

postprandial [-prǽndjąl], *a.* de sobremesa.

postscript [-skript], *s.* pos(t)data.

posttonic [-tánik] *a.* (filol.) postónico.

postulant [páschulant], *s.* postulante; (igl.) novicio -cia, postulante, -anta; postulador.

postulate [-eit], I. *va.* postular. II. *s.* (lóg. y geom.) postulado.—**postulation** [-éišon]. *s.* suposición, enunciado de una proposición que se da por sentada; (igl.) postulación.

posture [páschu(r)]. I. *s.* pos(i)tura, actitud; situación, estado, disposición. II. *va.* y *vn.* poner(se) en alguna postura. *V.* TO POSE.

postwar [póystwôr], *a.* de postguerra, de después de la guerra.—**p.** period, postguerra.

posy [póuzi], *s.* ramillete de flores; (ant.) mote o cifra en verso.

pot [pat]. I. *s.* marmita, olla; pote; piñata, cacharro, caldereta; jarro; tiesto (para flores); orinal, (Am.) tibor; cantidad contenida en una olla; (fund.) crisol (de horno); en el juego, (a)puesta, polla.—**p.-bellied**, panzudo, barrigón, tripudo, ventrudo.—**p. cheese**, requesón.—**p. companion**, compañero de taberna. —**p. lead**, grafito.—**p. metal**, aleación de cobre y plomo; vidrio que se colora cuando está fundido.—**p. roast**, (coc.) carne asada en marmita.—**p. shot**, tiro a mansalva, traidor, o que no pide destreza alguna.—**p.-valiancy, p.-valor**, *s.* valor postizo, debido al licor, valor de borracho.—**p.-valiant**, *a.* envalentonado por el licor.—**to go to p.**, (fam.) arruinarse, desbaratarse, irse a pique (fig.). II. *va.* (coc.) estofar, cocer en olla; plantar en tiestos; conservar en potes; (caz.) matar para llenar el morral (o la olla) más bien que por el deporte. III. *vn.* (fam.) tirar o disparar.

potable [póutabl]. I. *a.* potable, bebedizo.—**to make p.**, potabilizar. II. *s.* bebida.

potableness [-nis], *s.* potabilidad.

potash [pátæš], *s.* potasa (hidróxido de potasio, o potasa cáustica); carbonato de potasio.—**p. bulbs**, (quím.) tubo de bolas.

potassic [potéesik], *a.* (quím.) potásico.

potassium [potéesiAm], *s.* (quím.) potasio.—**p. bromide**, bromuro potásico.—**p. permanganate**, permanganato de potasio.

potation [potéišon], *s.* potación; bebida; trago.

potato [potéitou], *s.* (bot.) patata, papa, criadilla. —**p. beetle, p. bug**, (ent.) dorífora.—**p. blight**, enfermedad de las patatas.—**p. chips**, patatas fritas a la inglesa, frituras de papas, (Am.) papas doradas.—**p. flour**, (Am.) chuño. —**p. peeler**, o **slicer**, (máquina) mondadora o cortadora de patatas.—**p. rot** = P. BLIGHT.—**a small p.**, (fam.) cosa o persona de poca monta, nonada, nulidad.

potboiler [pátboilœ(r)], *s.* (fam.) obra artística o literaria hecha de prisa para ganarse la vida.

potboy [pátboi], *s.* (Ingl.) mozo de taberna.

poteen [potín], *s.* whisky irlandés de contrabando.

potency [póutensi], *s.* potencia, fuerza; actividad (de un veneno); poder, influjo, autoridad.

potent [póutent], *a.* potente, poderoso, eficaz.

potentate [póutenteit], *s.* potentado; potestad.

potential [poténšal]. I. *a.* potencial, posible; virtual; (fís.) potencial; (gram.) potencial; eficaz, poderoso.—**p. energy**, energía potencial. II. *s.* (gram.) modo potencial; (fís.) potencial; (elec.) potencial, tensión.

potentiality [-šiéliti], *s.* potencialidad, capacidad.—**potentially** [-šali], *adv.* potencialmente, en potencia, virtualmente.

potentilla [poutentíla], *s.* (bot.) potentila, planta rosácea; cincoenrama.

potentiometer [potenšiámetœ(r)], *s.* (elec.) potenciómetro.

potently [póutentli], *adv.* potentemente, poderosamente.

potentness [-nis], *s.* potencia, poder.

pothanger [páthæŋœ(r)], *s.* llares, *f. pl.*

pother [páðœ(r)]. I. *s.* baraúnda, alboroto; nube

(*f.*) asfixiante de polvo, humo o vapor. II. *va.* y *vn.* atormentar, aturdir; alborotar.

potherb [pát(h)œrb], *s.* hortaliza (v. gr. espinaca para la olla; tomillo para sazonar).

pothole [-houl], *s.* bache; hoya.

pothook [-huk], *s.* llares, *f. pl.*; garabato.

pothouse [-haus]. I. *s.* taberna, bodegón. II. *a.* de taberna; bajo, vulgar.

pothunter [-hantœ(r)], *s.* cazador que mira más a la ganancia que al deporte.

potion [póušon], *s.* poción, brebaje, pócima.

potlid [pátlid], *s.* cobertera o tapadera de olla.

potluck [-lak], *s.* comida ordinaria, sin preparación ni cumplidos.—**to take p.**, (fig.) hacer penitencia.

potpie [-pai], *s.* (coc.) pastel de carne.

potpourri [-púri o poupurí], *s.* baturrillo, miscelánea, revoltillo, (gal.) pot-pourri o popurrí.

potsherd [-šœrd], *s.* tiesto, casco.

pottage [pátidž], *s.* potaje, menestra, acemite.

potted [pátid], *pp.* de TO POT.—**p. meat**, conserva de carne condimentada o en gelatina.—**p. plants**, plantas en tiestos.

potter [pátœ(r)], *vn.* carecer de seriedad, ocuparse en fruslerías, ser frívolo; parlotear; haraganear, vagar.

potter [pátœ(r)], *s.* alfarero, ollero, alcarracero.— **p.'s clay**, arcilla, barro de alfareros.—**p.'s field**, cementerio de los pobres, hoyanca.—**p.'s ore**, alquifol.—**p.'s ware**, alfarería, cacharros, *m. pl.*—**p.'s wheel**, rueda de alfarero.

pottery [-i], *s.* alfarería; alfar (taller); ollería; cacharros, *m. pl.*

pottle [pátl], *s.* azumbre (antigua medida); pichel o cangilón que cabe dos litros; bebida alcohólica; cestilla para frutas.—**p.-bellied**, panzudo.

pouch [pauch]. I. *s.* saquito, bolsa; zurrón, morral (de caza, etc.); mala, valija (de correo); (anat., zool.) bolsa, saco, cavidad en forma de bolsa; abazón; (med.) bolsa; (bot.) silícula. II. *va.* embolsar; tragar, engullir. III. *vn.* formar bolsas.—**pouched** [-t], *a.* (zool.) que tiene bolsa (como el canguro, pelicán, etc.).

poudrette [pudrét], *s.* abono compuesto.

poulard [pulárd], *s.* polla capona.

poulp(e [pulp], *s.* (zool.) pulpo, pólipo.

poult [poult], *s.* pavipollo; polluelo.

poulterer [póultœrœ(r)], *s.* pollero, gallinero.

poultice [póultis]. I. *s.* (med.) cataplasma, emplasto, bizma. II. *va.* bizmar.

poultry [póultri], *s.* aves (*f. pl.*) de corral.—**p. dealer** o **raiser**, pollero, gallinero, recovero.— **p. manure**, gallinaza.—**p. market**, pollería, recova.—**p. yard**, corral, gallinero, pollero.

pounce [pauns]. I. *s.* zarpada; calada (del ave de rapiña); zarpa, garra; grasa, grasilla.—**p. bag**, cisquero o muñequilla de estarcir.—**p.**, o **pouncet, box**, cajita agujereada para polvos de sandáraca, o para perfumes. II. *va.* y *vn.* repujar (oro, plata, etc.); agujerear; (a veces con **on** o **upon**) saltar o abalanzarse sobre; calarse (el ave de rapiña); dar una zarpada; agarrar; entrar, saltar, etc., de repente; polvorear con grasilla; apomazar; alisar (un sombrero) frotándolo.

pound [páund]. I. *s.* libra (peso); libra esterlina; corral municipal o de concejo; depósito.—**p. avoirdupois**, libra de 16 onzas.—**p.-foolish**, gastador, derrochador. *V.* PENNY-WISE.—**p. net**, nasa de pescar.—**p. sterling**, libra esterlina (20 chelines).—**p. troy**, libra de 12 onzas. —**p. weight**, peso de una libra. II. *va.* golpear, batir; machacar, majar, moler, aporrear; encerrar; poner a buen recaudo. III. *vn.* golpear; latir con violencia (el corazón); andar pesadamente; avanzar continua o enérgicamente.

poundage [-idž], *s.* derecho de tanto por libra; costo de rescatar al ganado acorralado.

poundal [-al], *s.* (fís.) unidad de fuerza que, obrando durante un segundo sobre una masa de una libra, le da la velocidad de un pie por segundo.

poundcake [-kei̯k], *s.* (coc.) cierto bizcocho en que entra una libra de cada ingrediente principal (azúcar, mantequilla y harina).

pounder [-œ(r)], *s.* triturador(a); golpeador; majador, machaca(dera); mano (*f.*) de almirez o mortero; pala de lavar la ropa. Úsase en composición para denotar el número de libras: *thirty-six pounder,* cañón de a treinta y seis; *six-pounder,* pescado, bala, etc., de seis libras.

poundkeeper, poundmaster [-kipœ(r), -mæstœ(r)], *s.* guardián de un corral de concejo.

pour [pɔ́r]. I. *va.* derramar; verter, vaciar; trasegar; echar, escanciar (vino, etc.); emitir, arrojar; gastar pródigamente.—**to p. out of,** vaciar de. II. *vn.* fluir, correr, caer copiosa o rápidamente; llover a cántaros, diluviar; salir a borbotones.

pourer [-œ(r)], *s.* trasegador; vaciador; echador, escanciador.

pourparler [purparléi̯], *s.* (fr.) coloquio, conferencia (esp. diplomática) preliminar.

pout [páu̯t]. I. *s.* pucherito; berrinche; (ict.) especie de siluro o bagre; faneca. II. *vn.* hacer pucheritos, (fam.) pujar; estar con o de hocico; poner mal gesto, enfurruñarse; hinchar el pecho (apl. a las aves).

pouter [-œ(r)], *s.* el que hace pucheritos; (orn.) paloma buchona (ll. t. **p. pigeon,** o **pouting pigeon**).

poverty [pávœrti̯], *s.* pobreza, estrechez, necesidad, indigencia; falta, carencia.—**p.-stricken,** muy pobre.

powder [páu̯dœ(r)]. I. *s.* pólvora (explosiva o inflamable); (leng. ord., med., dent., etc.) polvo; polvos de tocador.—**p. box,** polvera, caja de los polvos (de tocador).—**p. chamber,** cámara de la pólvora en una mina o un arma de fuego.—**p. compact,** polvera de bolsillo.—**p. flask, p. horn,** frasco, cebador, chifle o cuerno para pólvora.—**p. magazine, p. room,** polvorín, pañol de pólvora, santabárbara.—**p. puff,** polvera o borla de polvos, (Am.) cisne, mota. II. *va.* pulverizar; empolvar; polvorear, espolvorear. III. *vn.* pulverizarse; ponerse polvos.

powdered [-d], *a.* pulverizado; en polvo.—**p. eggs, milk,** etc., huevos, leche, etc., en polvo.

powdermill [-mi̯l], *s.* fábrica de pólvora.

powdery [-i̯], *a.* polvoriento; empolvado; lleno de polvo; deleznable, quebradizo.

power [páu̯œ(r)], *s.* potencia, facultad, atribución, virtud; fuerza, pujanza; poder, poderío, potestad; mando, imperio, autoridad; ascendiente, influjo; potencia (nación); fuerza mecánica (a distinción de fuerza de sangre); (mat.) potencia; (mec.) potencia; fuerza motriz; energía; (ópt.) potencia (de una lente).—**p.-dive,** (aer.) *s.* ataque en picada; *vn.* picar o lanzarse (un avión) verticalmente a toda marcha sobre el blanco elegido.—**p. drill,** (mec.) taladradora de fuerza.—**p. factor,** (elec.) factor de potencia.—**p. house,** instalación o estación de energía o de fuerza motriz; central eléctrica o de electricidad.—**p. loading,** (aer.) carga normal por caballo de fuerza.—**p. of attorney,** (for.) poder, procura(ción).—**p. of the keys,** (igl.) llaves (*f. pl.*) de la Iglesia.—**p. plant** = P. HOUSE; (aut.) motor y sus accesorios.—**p. shovel,** (máquina) excavadora.—**p. tube,** (elec.) tubo generador, tubo de vacío generador de corriente alterna.—**p. transmission,** transmisión de energía.—**p. unit,** unidad motriz.—**in p.,** en el poder.—**the Great Powers,** las grandes potencias.—**the powers that be,** la(s) autoridad(es); los que mandan.—**to the best of one's p. (and ability),** con todo empeño, hasta donde uno pueda, hasta lo último de potencia, en lo sumo posible.—**under its own p.,** por sus propios medios.

powerboat [-bou̯t], *s.* canoa automóvil. V. MOTORBOAT.

powered [-d], *a.* (mec.) (con **by** o **with**) dotado de (motores); impulsado, propulsado, movido o accionado por.

powerful [-fu̯l], *a.* poderoso, potente, fuerte; influyente.—**powerfully** [-i̯], *adv.* poderosamente.—**powerfulness** [-ni̯s], *s.* poder(ío), potencia; fuerza.

powerhouse [-hau̯s], *s.* V. POWER HOUSE.

powerless [-li̯s], *a.* impotente; ineficaz.

powwow [páu̯wau̯]. I. *vn.* (entre los indios) conjurar las enfermedades con exorcismos; celebrar una junta; (fam. E. U.) deliberar con algarabía. II. *s.* curandero indio; exorcismo, baile, festín, holgorio; concilio; (fam.) cualquier mitín o junta.

pox [paks], *s.* (med.) cualquiera enfermedad que causa erupciones pustulosas (sífilis, viruelas, etc.).

pozz(u)olana [pats(w)ǫlánᵫ], *s.* (petr.) puzol(ana).

practicable [prǽkti̯kᵫbl], *a.* practicable, hacedero, factible, viable; accesible, transitable.

practicability [-bi̯li̯ti̯], **practicableness** [-blni̯s], *s.* calidad de practicable; factibilidad.—**practicably** [-bli̯], *adv.* posiblemente, práoticablemente.

practical [prǽkti̯kᵫl], *a.* práctico; de hecho, real; positivo, prosaico (a distinción de ideal, espiritual, teórico, etc.).—**p. joke,** burla, chanza, chasco.—**p. nurse,** enfermera práctica (no graduada).—**p. politics,** política de realidades; politiquería.

practicality [-kǽli̯ti̯], *s.* calidad de práctico; cosa práctica; espíritu práctico.

practically [-i̯], *adv.* prácticamente; en la práctica; por la práctica; virtualmente, en realidad; casi, poco menos que (a veces se cambia el giro: *he is practically dead,* está casi muerto, puede darse por muerto; *this is practically a refusal,* esto es realmente una negativa. Éste es el uso más general del adverbio, y debe cuidarse de no traducirlo por *prácticamente*).

practicalness [-ni̯s], *s.* calidad de práctico.

practice [prǽkti̯s]. I. *s.* práctica, uso, costumbre; ejercicio; experiencia; sistema, *m.,* regla, método; clientela.—**in p.,** en la práctica. II. *va.* y *vn.* practicar, ensayar(se), adiestrar(se), ejercitar(se); ejercer (una profesión); hacer ejercicios (en el piano, etc.); (raro) tramar; negociar secretamente.—**to p. at a target,** tirar al blanco.

practiced [-t], *a.* práctico, perito, experto, ejercitado; aprendido con la práctica o experiencia.

practicer [-œ(r)], *s.* practicante, practicador; el que ejerce una profesión; hombre artero.

practise [prǽkti̯s], *va.* y *vn.* = PRACTICE.

practitioner [prækti̯ʃǫnœ(r)], *s.* practicante; el que ejerce una profesión (médico, abogado, etc.).

praedial, *a.,* **praefect,** *s.* = PREDIAL, PREFECT.

prænomen [prinóum̵en], *s.* prenombre.

prætexta [pri̯tékstᵫ], *s.* (antiq. rom.) pretexta.

praetor [prítǫ(r)], *s.* (hist. rom.) pretor.—**praetorian** [pri̯tórᵫn]. I. *a.* pretoriano, pretorial, pretorio. II. *s.* pretoriano.—**praetorianism** [-i̯zm], *s.* pretorianismo.—**praetorium** [pri̯tóri̯ᵫm], *s.* pretorio.—**praetorship** [prítǫrʃi̯p], *s.* pretura, pretoría.

pragmatic [prægmǽti̯k], *s.* (for.) pragmática (ll. t. **p. sanction**); persona entremetida, porfiada o engreída.—**pragmatic(al** [-ᵫl], *a.* pragmático; práctico; entremetido, oficioso; activo, atareado; porfiado; engreído; dogmático.—**pragmatically** [-i̯], *adv.* pragmáticamente, etc.

pragmatism [prǽgmᵫti̯zm], *s.* (filos.) pragmatismo, doctrina que sostiene que el criterio de la verdad son los resultados prácticos.—**pragmatist(ic** [-ti̯st, -ti̯sti̯k], *s.* y *a.* pragmatista, partidario del pragmatismo o perteneciente a él.

Prairial [preri̯ál], *s.* pradial, noveno mes del calendario republicano francés.

prairie [préri̯], *s.* llanura, pradera, (Am.) pampa, sabana.—**p. chicken,** o **hen,** (orn.) especie de chocha.—**p. dog,** (zool.) especie de marmota de las llanuras norteamericanas.—**p. schooner,** V. SCHOONER.—**P. State,** (E. U.) el Estado de Illinois.—**p. wolf,** (zool.) coyote.

praise [préiz]. **I.** s. alabanza, elogio, loor, loa, encomio; fama, renombre. **II.** va. encomiar, alabar, loar, preconizar, ensalzar.

praiser [-œ(r)], s. loador, ensalzador, alabador.

praiseworthily [-wœrðili], adv. laudablemente.
—**praiseworthiness** [-nis], s. calidad de loable.
—**praiseworthy** [-i], a. digno de alabanza, laudable, loable, encomiable, plausible.

pralene [pralín], s. cierto dulce de azúcar con almendras, pacanas u otras nueces.

pram [præm], s. (fam.) = PERAMBULATOR.

prance [præns]. **I.** vn. cabriolar, trenzar, corvetear o gambetear (el caballo); cabalgar o andar garbosa u orgullosamente; bailar. **II.** s. cabriola, trenzado, corveta, gambeta.

prancer [-œ(r)], s. caballo pisador o que hace cabriolas, corvetas o gambetas.

prandial [prǽndiəl], a. pert. a una comida.

prank [præŋk]. **I.** va. hermosear, adornar. **II.** vn. emperejilarse, ataviarse con exceso. **III.** s. travesura, picardihuela; jugarreta.

prankish [-iš], a. travieso, retozón, revoltoso.

prankster [-stœ(r)], s. (fam.) persona traviesa, retozona, juguetona o chusca.

prase [preiz], s. (min.) prasio.

praseodymium [preiziodímiʌm], s. (quím.) praseodimio.

prate [préit]. **I.** vn. charlar, parl(ote)ar. **II.** s. charla.

prater [-œ(r)], s. hablador, charlatán, bachiller.

pratincole [prǽtiŋkoul], s. (orn.) pratíncola, m.

prating [préitiŋ], **prattling** [prǽtliŋ]. **I.** a. gárrulo, charlatán, (fam.) chacharero. **II.** s. = PRATE O PRATTLE.

pratique [prætík], s. (mar.) libre plática.

prattle [prǽtl]. **I.** vn. charlar, parlotear, (fam.) chacharear; balbucear; murmurar (un arroyo). **II.** s. parlería, parloteo, charla, garrulería, (fam.) cháchara.

prattler [prǽtlœ(r)], s. charlador, parlanchín.

prawn [pron], s. (zool.) camarón, quisquilla, esquila.

praxis [prǽksis], s. práctica, ejercicio; crestomatía.

pray [prei]. **I.** va. rogar, pedir, suplicar; implorar. **II.** vn. rezar, orar; (con for), hacer votos por. Se emplea como forma de cortesía en el sentido de "sírvase," "si me hace el favor," "sírvase decirme," "decidme," etc.

prayer [prér], s. oración, rezo, plegaria; súplica, ruego.—**p. beads,** rosario.—**p. book,** devocionario, oracional, horas, f. pl.—**p. desk,** reclinatorio.—**p. meeting,** reunión para ejercicios espirituales.

prayerful [-ful], a. piadoso, devoto.—**prayerfulness** [-nis], s. devoción; inclinación a rezar.—**prayerless** [-lis], a. sin rezo; que no reza.

praying [préiiŋ]. **I.** a. orante; que reza.—**p. mantis,** (ent.) = MANTIS. **II.** s. acción de rezar, etc.

preach [prích], va. y vn. predicar; sermon(e)ar.—**preacher** [-œ(r)], s. predicador.—**preaching** [-iŋ], s. predicación.—**p. friar,** (igl.) dominico.—**preachment** [-ment], s. prédica, plática o sermón; arenga.—**preachy** [-i], a. (fam.) sermoneador.

preadamite [priǽdamait], a. y s. preadamita, mf.—**preadamitic** [-mítik], a. preadamítico.

preamble [priǽmbl], s. preámbulo.

prearrange [priərréindž], va. arreglar de antemano, predisponer, prevenir.—**prearrangement** [-ment], s. arreglo o disposición previos.

prebend [prébend], s. (igl.) prebenda; prebendado.—**prebendal** [pribéndəl], a. perteneciente a la prebenda.—**prebendary** [prébenderi], s. prebendado.

Pre-Cambrian [pri kǽmbriən], s. y a. (geol.) precambriano, precámbrico.

precarious [prikériʌs], a. precario; peligroso, arriesgado.—**precariously** [-li], adv. precariamente.—**precariousness** [-nis], s. calidad de precario.

precast [prikǽst], a. prevaciado (apl. a construcciones y artefactos de hormigón, etc., hechos fuera de la obra y luego llevados a ella).

precaution [prikóšon], s. precaución.

precautionary [-eri], a. de precaución, preventivo, precautorio.

precede [prisíd]. **I.** va. anteceder, preceder; anteponer. **II.** vn. preceder; ir delante; tener la primacía; sobresalir.

precedence [-ens o présødens], **precedency** [-i], s. prioridad, anterioridad, antelación; precedencia, superioridad.

precedent [présødent]. **I.** s. precedente; antecedente; (for.) decisión judicial que forma jurisprudencia. **II.** [prisídent o présødent], a. precedente.

preceding [prisídiŋ], a. precedente, anterior.

precentor [prisénto(r)], s. (igl.) chantre, capiscol.

precept [prisept], s. precepto; ley, f. V. MAXIM.

preceptive [priséptiv], a. preceptivo.

preceptor [-tо(r)], s. preceptor.

preceptor(i)al [-tоrəl, -tóriəl], a. preceptoral.

preceptress [-tris], s. preceptora.

precession [prisésƏn], s. precedencia; (astr.) precesión (de los equinoccios).

precinct [prísiŋkt], s. recinto; distrito, barriada.

precious [préšəs]. **I.** a. precioso, preciado; de gran valor; caro, querido, amado.—**p. opal =** NOBLE OPAL.—**p. stones,** piedras preciosas. **II.** s. el bienamado o favorito. **III.** adv. (fam.) muy.

preciously [-li], adv. preciosamente.

preciousness [-nis], s. preciosidad.

precipice [présipis], s. precipicio, despeñadero.

precipitable [prisípitəbl], a. (quím.) que puede precipitarse.—**precipitance, precipitancy** [-itəns, -i], s. precipitación.

precipitant [-tənt]. **I.** a. precipitado, arrojado, arrebatado. **II.** s. (quím.) precipitante.

precipitantly [-li], adv. precipitadamente.

precipitate [-teit]. **I.** va. precipitar, despeñar, derrumbar, arrojar; acelerar, apresurar; (quím.) precipitar. **II.** vn. precipitarse; (quím.) precipitarse, depositarse. **III.** a. precipitado, atropellado. **IV.** s. (quím.) precipitado, depósito.

precipitately [-li], adv. precipitadamente.

precipitating [-iŋ], a. precipitante.

precipitation [-téišon], s. precipitación; derrumbamiento; rocío; cantidad de agua de lluvia; (quím.) precipitación.

precipitator [prisípiteito(r)], s. (quím.) precipitante.

precipitin [prisípitin], s. (bact.) precipitina.

precipitous [prisípitʌs], a. precipitoso, despeñadizo, escarpado; arrojado.

précis [preisí], s. (fr.) resumen, epítome.

precise [prisáis], a. preciso, exacto; justo, ni más ni menos; estricto, quisquilloso, escrupuloso; propio, mismísimo, idéntico.

precisely [-li], adv. precisamente, exactamente; justamente, cabalmente; formalmente.

preciseness [-nis], s. precisión, exactitud; escrupulosidad.

precisian [prisížan], s. rigorista; formulista.

precision [prisížƏn], s. precisión, exactitud, limitación exacta; escrupulosidad.

preclude [prikliúd], va. evitar, impedir; excluir.

precocious [prikóušʌs], a. precoz.—**precociousness** [-nis], **precocity** [prikósiti], s. precocidad.

precognition [prikagníšƏn], s. precognición.

pre-Columbian [prikolámbiƏn], a. precolombino.

preconceive [prikonsív], va. preconcebir; concebir, opinar o imaginar de antemano.

preconception [-sépšƏn], s. idea o proyecto preconcebidos; concepto anticipado; prejuicio.

preconcert [-sćrt], **I.** va. concertar de antemano. **II.** [prikánsœrt] s. acuerdo previo.

preconization [prikǫnizéiṣǫn], s. preconización.
preconize [príkǫnajz], va. (igl. y leng. ord.) preconizar; citar o elogiar públicamente.
preconsign [-sájn], va. consignar anteriormente.
precontract [-trǽkt]. I. va. contratar con anterioridad. II. [prikántrækt], s. contrato anticipado.
precool [prikúl], va. enfriar previamente; (com.) enfriar (frutas, etc.) antes de embarcar.
precordial [prikórdiǫl], a. (anat.) precordial.
precursive, precursory [prikœ́rsiv, -sorj], a. precursor.—**precursor** [-sǫ(r)], s. precursor.
predaceous [pridéiṣʌs], **predatory** [prédǫtorj], a. de rapiña, de presa, rapaz, voraz.
predate [pridéit], va. antedatar, poner fecha anterior a la verdadera; preceder (en tiempo).
predecease [pridiṣís]. I. va. y vn. premorir. II. s. (for.) premoriencia.—**predeceased** [-t], a. y s. premoriente; muerto antes que otro.
predecessor [prédiṣesǫ(r)], s. predecesor, antecesor; antepasado.
predesignate [pridézigneit], va. prefijar.
predestinarian [pridéstinǣrjǫn], a. y s. partidario de o relativo a la doctrina de la predestinación.—**predestinarianism** [-izm], s. fatalismo, doctrina de la predestinación.—**predestinate** [-eit]. I. va. predestinar. II. a. y s. predestinado.—**predestination** [-éiṣǫn], s. predestinación.—**predestinator** [-eitǫr)ǫ], s. predestinante.—**predestine** [pridéstin], va. predestinar.
predetermine [priditœ́rmin(e)it], a. predeterminado.—**predetermination** [-éiṣǫn], s. predeterminación.—**predetermine** [-min], va. predeterminar, prefijar.
predial [prídiǫl], a. predial.
predicable [prédikǫbl]. I. a. predicable. II. s. (lóg.) predicable; categorema.
predicament [pridíkǫment], s. dificultad, apuro, brete, compromiso; clase, f., categoría, situación, circunstancias; (lóg.) predicamento.
predicamental [-méntǫl], a. predicamental.
predicant [prédikǫnt], a. y s. predicante.
predicate [prédikeit]. I. va. proclamar; predicar; basar o fundar (una acción o declaración) en algo; afirmar un predicado. II. vn. afirmarse. III. [-kit], s. (gram. y lóg.) predicado, atributo.
predication [-kéiṣǫn], s. afirmación, aserción.
predict [pridíkt], va. predecir, pronosticar, profetizar, vaticinar.—**prediction** [-ṣǫn], s. predicción, pronóstico, profecía.
predictive [-tiv], a. que predice; profético.
predigest [prid(a)idʒést], va. digerir artificialmente.
predigestion [-dʒéschǫn], s. predigestión, digestión artificial o peptonización del alimento.
predilection [prediléksǫn], s. predilección.
predispose [pridispóuz], va. predisponer, prevenir.
predisposition [-pozíṣǫn], s. predisposición, propensión, inclinación, prevención.
predominance, -cy [pridáminǫns, -i], s. predominio, predominancia; ascendiente, influencia.
predominant [-ǫnt], a. predominante, prepotente.—**predominantly** [-li], adv. predominantemente.
predominate [-eit], vn. predominar, prevalecer, reinar.—**predomination** [-éiṣǫn], s. predominación; ascendiente.
preëminence [priémminǫns], s. preeminencia, supremacía.—**preëminent** [-ǫnt], a. preeminente, supremo; extraordinario, superlativo.—**preëminently** [-li], adv. preeminentemente; sumamente, extraordinariamente.
preëmpt [priémpt], va. asegurar el derecho de prioridad en la compra de terrenos públicos; adquirir o apropiarse de antemano (cualquier cosa).—**preëmptible** [-ibl], a. sujeto al derecho de prioridad.—**preëmption** [-ṣǫn], s. derecho de prioridad; adquisición o apropiación de una cosa, excluyendo a los otros.—**preëmptor** [-tǫ(r)], s. el que adquiere derecho de prioridad.

preen [prin], va. y vn. limpiar y componer sus plumas las aves; componerse; emperejilarse.
preëngage [priingéidʒ], va. apalabrar.
preëstablish [priistǽbliṣ], va. preestablecer.
preëxist [priigzíst], vn. preexistir.—**preëxistence** [-ǫns], s. preexistencia.—**preëxistent** [-ǫnt], a. preexistente.
prefabricate [prifǽbrikeit], va. fabricar de antemano (las piezas intercambiables de una casa, etc.).
preface [préfiṣ]. I. s. prefacio, prólogo, preámbulo, proemio. II. va. poner un prólogo a un libro; hacer un exordio a, decir por vía de introducción a, empezar (diciendo o escribiendo algo).
prefatory [préfǫtorj], a. preliminar; por vía de introducción.
prefect [prífekt], s. prefecto.
prefecture [prífekchǔ(r)], s. prefectura.
prefer [prifœ́r], va. (con **to**, **before** o **above**) preferir, anteponer (a); elevar, exaltar, adelantar, ascender; presentar, ofrecer; (for.) dar preferencia, v. gr. a un acreedor.—**to p. a charge**, (for.) presentar una denuncia.
preferable [préfrǫbl], a. preferible, preferente.—**preferably** [-bli], adv. preferible o preferentemente, de preferencia.
preference [préfrǫns], s. preferencia, predilección; prioridad, prelación; ventaja.—**p. shares**, o **stock**, (com.) acciones privilegiadas o preferidas.
preferent [-ǫnt], a. preferente.—**p. right**, prelación.
preferential [preferénṣǫl], a. preferente; privilegiado; parcial.—**p. ballot**, (E. U.) papeleta de *preferential voting*.—**p. voting**, votación en que el elector indica en su papeleta el candidato a quien realmente da su voto, y el que prefiere en caso de que aquél no obtenga la mayoría (puede llamarse votación de primera y segunda preferencia).
preferentially [-i], adv. preferentemente.
preferment [prifœ́rment], s. preferencia; promoción, elevación, ascenso, adelantamiento.
preferred [prifœ́rd], a. preferido, predilecto.—**p. shares**, o **stock**, (com.) acciones preferidas o preferentes.
prefiguration [prifigyǔréiṣǫn], **prefigurement** [-ment], s. prefiguración; prototipo.
prefigurative [-ǫtiv], a. que prefigura.
prefigure [prifigyǔ(r)], va. prefigurar, representar anticipadamente algo; representarse en la imaginación.
prefix [prifíks]. I. va. prefijar, anteponer. II. [prífiks], s. (gram.) prefijo, afijo.
prefloration [prifloréiṣǫn], s. (bot.) prefloración.
prefoliation [prifouliéiṣǫn], s. (bot.) prefoliación.
preformation [priforméiṣǫn], s. (leng. ord. y biol.) preformación, formación previa.
pregnable [prégnǫbl], a. expugnable, vulnerable.
pregnancy [prégnǫnsi], s. preñez, embarazo, gravidez; gestación; (fig.) fertilidad, fecundidad.
pregnant [prégnǫnt], a. preñada, embarazada, encinta, grávida (ú. t. en sentido figurado); fértil, copioso, fecundo.—**p. with**, repleto, lleno de.
pregnantly [-li], adv. abundante o plenamente.
preheat [prihít], va. calentar previamente.
prehensible [prihénsibl], a. capaz de ser aprehendido o asido.
prehensile [-sil], a. pre(he)nsil.
prehension [-ṣǫn], s. pre(he)nsión.
prehistoric(al [prihistárik(ǫl], a. prehistórico.
prehistory [prihístorj], s. prehistoria.
preignition [priigníṣǫn], s. (m. comb. int.) encendido anticipado.
prejudge [pridʒʌ́dʒ], va. prejuzgar.
prejudg(e)ment [-ment], s. prejuicio.
prejudice [prédʒudjs]. I. s. prevención, preju(d)icio, preocupación; parcialidad; perjuicio, detri-

mento. daño.—**in**, o **to**, **the p. of**, con perjuicio de.—**without p.**, (for.) sin detrimento de derechos, sin perjuicio o sin menoscabar. **II**. *va*. preocupar, prevenir, predisponer; perjudicar, dañar.

prejudicial [prĕdíṣǎl], *a*. perjudicial, dañable, lesivo.

prejudicially [-ĭ], *adv*. perjudicialmente.

prelacy [prélǎsi], *s*. (igl.) prelacía; episcopado.

prelate [prélĭt], *s*. prelado.—**prelateship** [-ṣip], *s*. prelacía, prelatura.—**prelatess** [-iṣ], *s*. prelada.

prelatic(al [prĭlǽtĭk(ǎl], *a*. prelaticio, de prelado.

prelature [prélǎchur], *s*. prelatura, prelacía.

prelection [prĭlékṣǒn], *s*. lección, conferencia.

prelector [-tǒ(r)], *s*. conferencista.

preliminarily [prĭlímineríli], *adv*. preliminarmente.

preliminary [-neri]. **I**. *a*. preliminar; preparatorio; proemial, introductorio. **II**. *s*. prèliminar.—*pl*. exámenes preliminares; (dep.) eliminatorias (pruebas).

prelude [préljud]. **I**. *s*. preludio, prelusión; presagio; (mús.) preludio. **II**. *va*. y *vn*. preludiar.

preludial [prĭljúdǐǎl], **prelusive** [prĭljúsiv], *a*. previo, introductorio, proemial.

premature [primǎchúr], *a*. prematuro, temprano.

prematurely [-li], *adv*. prematuramente.—**prematureness** [-niṣ], **prematurity** [-iti], *s*. madurez o sazón (*f*.) antes de tiempo.

premaxilla(ry [primǽksilǎ(ri], *s*. y *a*. (anat. y zool.) premaxilar, hueso intermaxilar; relativo a o delante de éste.

premedical [primédĭkǎl], *a*. preparatorio para el estudio de la medicina.

premeditate [primédĭteit], *va*. y *vn*. premeditar, pensar o deliberar de antemano.—**premeditatedly** [-idli], *adv*. premeditadamente.

premeditation [-éiṣǒn], *s*. premeditación.

premier [prímiœ(r)]. **I**. *s*. primer ministro, jefe de gobierno. **II**. *a*. primero, principal.

première [prĭmír o premiér], *s*. actriz protagonista; estreno (de un drama, etc.).

premiership [prímiœršip], *s*. dignidad u oficio de primer ministro.

premillennial [primĭlénǐǎl], *a*. anterior al milenario.—**premillennialism** [-izm], *s*. doctrina de que el milenario empezará con la segunda venida de Cristo.

premise [prémiṣ]. **I**. *va*. sentar o establecer como premisa. **II**. *s*. (lóg.) premisa.—*pl*. (for.) asertos, aserciones anteriores; parte (*f*.) de una escritura o título de dominio en que se expresan la fecha, los nombres de los individuos, la descripción de la propiedad, precio, etc.; predio rústico o urbano, casa, tierra, posesiones; local.—**in the(se) premises**, tocante al asunto de que se trata.—**of the p.**, de lo dicho.—**off the p.**, fuera del local o terreno.—**on the p.**, (presente) en el local, etc.

premium [prímiam], *s*. premio; remuneración; galardón; (com.) prima; premio; interés; agio.—**p. note**, pagaré otorgado en lugar del pago de primas de seguro.—**at a p.**, a premio; sobre la par; en gran demanda, muy solicitado.

premolar [primóulǎ(r], *a*. y *s*. premolar (diente).

premonition [primoníṣǒn], *s*. prevención, advertencia; presentimiento, corazonada.

premonitory [primáni̭tori], *a*. que advierte o anuncia; (med.) premonitorio.

Premonstratensian [primanstrǎténṣian], *s*. y *a*. (igl.) premo(n)stratense.

prenatal [prinéital], *a*. prenatal, antenatal, de antes del nacimiento.

prenotion [prinóuṣǒn], *s*. prenoción.

prentice [préntiṣ], *s*. (fam.) aprendiz, *mf*.

preoccupancy [priákyupǎnṣi], *s*. ocupación previa; preocupación.

preoccupant [-pǎnt], *s*. el que ocupa antes que otro.

preoccupation [-péiṣǒn], *s*. preocupación.

preoccupied [-paid], *a*. preocupado, absorto; ocupado anteriormente; puesto ya en uso.

preoccupy [-pai], *va*. preocupar; ocupar antes que otro.

preordain [priordéin], *va*. (teol.) preordinar; predestinar.

preordination [-dinéiṣǒn], *s*. (teol.) preordinación; predestinación.

prepaid [pripéid], *a*. porte pagado.

prepalatal [pripǽlǎtǎl], *a*. y *s*. (fon.) prepalatal, *f*.

preparation [prepǎréiṣǒn], *s*. preparación; preparativo; (farm.) preparado, confección.

preparative [pripǽrǎtiv]. **I**. *a*. preparativo, preparatorio. **II**. *s*. preparativo, apresto.

preparatively [-li], *adv*. anticipadamente.

preparator [pripǽrǎtǒ(r)], *s*. preparador de ejemplares de historia natural.

preparatorily [-torǐli], *adv*. preparatoriamente.

preparatory [-tori], *a*. preparatorio; previo, preliminar.—**p. school**, escuela de preparación para estudios universitarios.—**p. to**, como preparación, o preparándose, para; antes de.

prepare [pripér]. **I**. *va*. preparar, aprestar, apercibir; disponer, prevenir; aderezar, adobar, confeccionar, guisar. **II**. *vn*. prepararse, disponerse, hacer preparativos.

preparedly [-idli], *adv*. preventivamente.

preparedness [-niṣ], *s*. preparación, apercibimiento, prevención; preparación militar en tiempo de paz (ú. gen. en este sentido).

preparer [-œ(r)], *s*. preparador.

prepay [pripéi], *va*. (*pret*. y *pp*. PREPAID) pagar anticipadamente; antepagar; franquear (una carta).

prepayment [-mént], *s*. pago adelantado; franqueo.

prepense [pripéns], *a*. premeditado.—**with malice p.**, (for.) maliciosa y premeditadamente.

preponderance, -cy [pripándœrǎns, -i], **preponderation** [-éiṣǒn], *s*. preponderancia, predominio, prepotencia.—**preponderant** [-ǎnt], *a*. preponderante, predominante.—**preponderate** [-eit], *vn*. preponderar, pesar más; predominar, prevalecer.

preposition [prepozíṣǒn], *s*. (gram.) preposición.—**prepositional** [-ǎl], *a*. preposicional, prepositivo.

prepositive [pripázitiv]. **I**. *a*. (gram.) antepuesto, prefijo. **II**. *s*. partícula prepositiva.

prepossess [pripozés], *va*. predisponer, causar buena impresión; preocupar, tomar posesión antes que otro.—**prepossessing** [-iŋ], *a*. simpático, atractivo.

prepossession [pripozéṣǒn], *s*. impresión favorable; simpatía, predisposición favorable; preocupación, ocupación o posesión previa.

preposterous [pripástérǎs], *a*. absurdo, ridículo, descabellado.—**preposterously** [-li], *adv*. absurdamente.

prepotency [pripóutǒnsi], *s*. prepotencia, predominio.—**prepotent** [-ǒnt], *a*. prepotente.

prepuce [prípius], *s*. (anat.) prepucio, capullo.

Pre-Raphaelite [pri réfǎelait], *s*. y *a*. prerrafaelista.—**Pre-Raphaelitism** [-izm], *s*. prerrafaelismo.

prerequisite [prirékwizit]. **I**. *a*. previamente necesario. **II**. *s*. requisito previo.

prerogative [prirágativ]. **I**. *s*. prerrogativa, privilegio, distinción. **II**. *a*. privilegiado.

presage [présidż]. **I**. *s*. presagio. **II**. [priséidż], *va*. presagiar.—**presageful** [priséidżful], **presaging** [-iŋ], *a*. presagioso, présago.

presbyope [prézbioup], *s*. présbite, présbita, *mf*.—**presbyopia, presbyopy** [-óupiǎ, prézbioupi], *s*. (med.) presbiopia, presbicia.—**presbyopic** [-ápik], *a*. presbiópico, présbite.

presbyter [prézbitœ(r)], *s*. (igl.) presbítero, sacerdote.

presbyterial [-tíriǎl], *a*. presbiteral.

Presbyterian [-tíriąn], *a.* y *s.* presbiteriano.—
Presbyterianism [-izm], *s.* (igl.) presbiterianismo.

presbytery [prézbiteri], *s.* presbiterio; presbiterianismo; tribunal eclesiástico de los presbite-
rianos; (arq.) ábside, *mf.*, presbiterio.

preschool [prískúl], *a.* preescolar.

prescience [prísęns], *s.* presciencia.

prescient [prísęnt], *a.* presciente.

prescind [prisínd], *va.* y *vn.* (a veces con **from**)
prescindir (de); separar, abstraer.

prescribe [priskráib], *va.* y *vn.* prescribir, ordenar,
dictar; dar leyes o reglas; (med.) recetar, prescribir un remedio o tratamiento; (for.) prescri-
bir(se).

prescriptible [priskríptibl], *a.* prescriptible;
(for.) adquirible por prescripción.

prescription [-śǫn], *s.* prescripción, disposición,
precepto, regla; (med.) receta, récipe; (for.)
prescripción; perención, caducidad de la instancia.

prescriptive [-tiv], *a.* prescriptivo; sancionado,
autorizado por la costumbre; (for.) adquirido
por prescripción.

presence [prézęns], *s.* presencia; aspecto, porte;
asistencia; interesencia; aparición, aparecido.
—**p. chamber**, salón de audiencia.—**p. of
mind**, presencia de ánimo, serenidad.—**in the
p. of**, ante, a los ojos de.

present [prézęnt], **I.** *a.* presente; actual, corriente
(mes, semana, etc.); circunstante, interesente;
flagrante.—**p. company excepted**, mejorando
lo presente.—**p.-day**, actual, (del día) de hoy.
—**p. participle**, (gram.) participio activo o
(de) presente, gerundio.—**p. value, p. worth**,
valor actual (de un pagaré, etc.).—**at the p.
time**, hoy (por hoy), en la actualidad.—**to be
p. (at)**, asistir (a); presenciar; concurrir. **II.** *s.*
el presente, la actualidad; (gram.) tiempo
presente; regalo, presente, don, dádiva, obsequio.—*pl.* (for.) las escrituras presentes.—**at
p.**, al presente, actualmente, (por) ahora.—**for
the p.**, por ahora, por el (o lo) presente.—
know all men by these presents, conste por
la(s) presente(s).—**to all to whom these
presents shall come, greeting**, a cuantos las
presentes vieren, salud. **III.** [prizént], *va.* presentar, introducir, dar a conocer; dar, regalar,
obsequiar; manifestar, mostrar, exponer; representar, poner en escena (una ópera, etc.);
apuntar, asestar (arma); (for.) denunciar,
acusar.—**to p. a person to another**, presentar
a una persona a otra.—**to p. a person with a
thing**, regalar una cosa a alguien.—**to p.
arms**, (mil.) presentar las armas.—**to p. itself**,
ofrecerse, surgir.—**to p. one's self**, presentarse, personarse; comparecer.

presentable [-abl], *a.* presentable; decente.

presentability [-ǫbíliti], *s.* calidad de presentable.

presentation [prezęntéiśǫn], *s.* presentación;
introducción; entrega ceremoniosa de un obsequio; (teat.) exhibición, representación;
(med.) presentación del feto; (psic.) presentación.—**p. copy**, ejemplar de regalo con dedicatoria.—**on p.**, (com.) a presentación.—**the P.**,
(igl.) presentación.

presentative [prizéntativ], *a.* (filos.) concerniente a la presentación mental; (igl.) que tiene
derecho de presentación.

presentee [prezęntí], *s.* el quien se presenta u
obsequia algo; (igl.) presentado.

presenter [prizéntœ(r)], *s.* presentador, obsequiador.

presentiment [prizéntimęnt], *s.* presentimiento.

presently [prézęntli], *adv.* luego, ya, dentro de
poco, pronto.

presentment [prizéntmęnt], *s.* presentación,
introducción; representación; retrato; semejanza; conducta; (for.) denuncia, acusación.

preservable [prizǽrvǫbl], *a.* preservable, conservable.

preservation [prezœrvéiśǫn], *s.* preservación,
conservación, resguardo.

preservative [prizǽrvǫtiv], **I.** *a.* preservativo,
conservativo; (med.) profiláctico. **II.** *s.* preservativo; defensivo o defensa, salvaguardia.

preserve [prizǽrv], **I.** *va.* preservar, guardar;
resguardar, proteger; reservar, retener; conservar, mantener; (coc.) curar, sal(pres)ar; confitar, almibarar.—**preserved**, en conserva, en
almíbar.—**preserved meats**, viandas conser-
vadas. **II.** *vn.* hacer conservas de frutas. **III.** *s.*
(gen. *pl.*) conserva, dulce, compota, confitura;
(caz.) vedado, coto.—**p. jar**, o **dish**, dulcera,
compotera, orza, bote para conservas.

preserver [-œ(r)], *s.* preservador, conservador;
conservero; confitero.

preside [prizáid], *vn.* y *va.* (con **over** o **at**) presidir; gobernar; dirigir.

presidency [prézidęnsi], *s.* presidencia.

president [-dęnt], *s.* presidente; regente; rector
(de ciertas universidades).

presidential [-dénśǫl], *a.* presidencial.—**p. year**,
(E. U.) año de elecciones presidenciales.

presidentship [prézidęntśip], *s.* presidencia.

presider [prizáidœ(r)], *s.* presidente, el que
preside.—**presiding** [-iŋ]. **I.** *a.* presidente, que
preside.—**p. officer, judge**, etc., presidente.
II. *s.* presidencia, acción de presidir.

presidial [prisídiǫl], *a.* presidencial; de o pert. a
un presidio; (mil.) presidiado, guarnicionado.

presidium [prisídiʌm], *s.* (en Rusia) presidium,
comité administrativo de carácter gubernamental.

press [prés]. **I.** *va.* (a)prensar; apretar, comprimir;
estrujar, exprimir (jugo, etc.); pisar (la uva, el
acelerador, el pedal); oprimir (el botón); planchar (la ropa); lustrar, satinar; abrumar, afligir,
oprimir; compeler, obligar; apresurar, apremiar,
instar; acosar, perseguir; hostigar, fatigar;
recalcar, ajustar; (mil.) hacer levas, enganchar
soldados; abrazar, dar un apretón.—**pressed
for money**, apurado de dinero.—**to p. into
service**, enganchar (soldados); poner a trabajar.—**to p. the point**, apurar el punto, insistir
en el asunto. **II.** *vn.* pesar, ejercer presión;
urgir, apremiar; agolparse, apiñarse; ser importuno; influir en el ánimo.—**to p. forward,
to p. on**, avanzar, adelantarse; arremeter,
embestir. **III.** *s.* turba, muchedumbre; apiñamiento; empujón, apretón; prisa, presión,
urgencia; cúmulo de negocios; (mec.) prensa
(máquina); imprenta, estampa, prensa (periódica); escaparate, armario; (mil.) leva, enganche.—**p. agent**, agente de publicidad.—**p.
bed**, catricofre.—**p. box** o **gallery**, tribuna
de la prensa.—**p. clipping**, o **cutting**, recorte
de periódico.—**p. conference**, entrevista con
los periodistas.—**p. gang**, (mil.) patrulla de
reclutamiento.—**p. money**, (mil.) prima de
enganche.—**p. proof**, (impr.) prueba de prensa.
—**p. roll**, (pap.) cilindro.—**(to carry a) p. of
sail**, (mar.) (hacer) fuerza de vela.

pressboard [-bǫrd], *s.* especie de cartón.

presser [-œ(r)], *s.* prensador, satinador, lustrador; planchador; pisacostura o prensatelas de
una máquina de coser; prensa (para uva, etc.).

pressing [-iŋ]. **I.** *a.* urgente, apremiante, instante,
importante; importuno.—**p. boards**, cartones
de satinar; (enc.) tablillas.—**p. iron**, plancha.
II. *s.* prensado, prensadura; recalcadura;
(com)presión.—**p. out**, expresión, estrujadura
(del jugo, etc.).—**p. together**, apiñamiento
(de la gente).

pressingly [-li], *adv.* urgente o apremiantemente.

pressman [-man], *s.* prensador; (impr.) prensista,
tirador; (Ingl.) periodista.

pressmark [-mark]. **I.** *s.* marca de imprenta. **II.**
va. poner marca de imprenta a.

pressroom [-rum], *s.* taller de imprenta; sala o cuarto de las prensas.

pressure [préṣů(r)], *s.* presión; tensión; prensadura; urgencia, premura, prisa, apremio; ímpetu, impulso, apretón; carga, opresión; (elec.) fuerza electromotriz.—**p. circuit**, circuito derivado de un contador (que va al contador).—**p. coil**, bobina de tensión, bobina en derivación.—**p. cooker**, autoclave, *f.*; estufa o cocina de presión.—**p. gauge**, manómetro.—**p. group**, (pol. e. p., etc.) minoría que ejerce presión en los legisladores o la opinión pública para adelantar sus propios fines.—**p. nozzle**, (aer.) aparato para medir la presión del aire debida a la velocidad del avión.—**p. tube**, (quím.) probeta cerrada para reacciones a alta presión.—**p. wire**, alambre de derivación del voltímetro (que va al voltímetro).

presswork [préswœrk], *s.* (impr.) impresión, tiro, tirada; (ebanistería) encolado de chapas.

prester [préstœ(r)], *s.* (ant.) preste.—**P. John**, Preste Juan.

prestidigitation [prestididżitéiṣǫn], *s.* prestidigitación, juegos de manos.—**prestidigitator** [-didżiteitǫ(r)], *s.* prestidigitador, jugador de manos.

prestige [prestíż], *s.* prestigio, fama.

presto [préstoṷ]. **I.** *adv.* (mús.) presto; rápidamente. **II.** *interj.* ¡pronto!

presumable [prizįúmǎbl], *a.* presumible.

presumably [-blį], *adv.* presumiblemente.

presume [prizįúm]. **I.** *va.* presumir, suponer; atreverse a. **II.** *vn.* jactarse, presumir, preciarse en demasía; obrar presuntuosamente, propasarse; (con **on** o **upon**) abusar de.

presumed [-d], *a.* presunto, supuesto.

presumer [-œ(r)], *s.* el que presume, etc.; presumido; hombre arrogante o presuntuoso.

presumption [prizʌmpṣǫn], *s.* presunción, conjetura; suposición; (for.) presunción; presunción, engreimiento, soberbia, (fam.) penacho, copete.

presumptive [-tįv], *a.* presunto, presuntivo.

presumptively [-lį], *adv.* presuntivamente.

presumptuous [-chṷas], *a.* presuntuoso, presumido; insolente; atrevido.—**presumptuously** [-lį], *adv.* presuntuosamente.—**presumptuousness** [-nįs], *s.* presunción, presuntuosidad.

presuppose [prisʌpóṷz], *va.* presuponer.

presupposition [prisʌpoziṣǫn], *s.* presuposición, conjetura.

pretend [prįténd]. **I.** *va.* aparentar, fingir, (di)simular; alegar o afirmar falsamente. **II.** *vn.* fingir; hacer como si o como que; presumir, alardear.—**to p. to**, pretender, tener pretensiones a, reclamar, aspirar a.—**to p. to be**, echárselas de, darla(s) de, darse por, hacerse el o hacer (d)el.—**pretended** [-id], *a.* fingido, simulado, presunto, supuesto.—**pretender** [-œ(r)], *s.* pretendiente, pretensor; hipócrita, *mf.*; el que finge, etc.

pretense, pretence [prįténs o prítens], *s.* fingimiento; pretexto, excusa; máscara, capa, velo; pretensión (gen. mal fundada); ostentación; afectación, simulación.—**under false pretenses**, con falsas apariencias, con dolo.—**under p. of**, so pretexto de, so capa de, a título de.

pretension [prįténṣǫn], *s.* pretensión, demanda; pretexto; simulación, afectación; presunción.

pretentious [-šʌs], *a.* presuntuoso, presumido, de pretensiones.—**pretentiousness** [-nįs], *s.* presunción; ostentación; boato, lujo falso o de mal gusto.

preterit(e [prétęrit], *a.* y *s.* (gram.) pretérito.

preterition [pretęríṣǫn], *s.* preterición, pretermisión; (for. y ret.) preterición.

pretermission [pritœrmíṣǫn], *s.* pretermisión, omisión; (ret.) preterición.—**pretermit** [-mít], *va.* pretermitir, omitir, pasar por alto.

preternatural [-nǽchůrǎl], *a.* preternatural.—

preternaturally [-į], *adv.* preternaturalmente.—**preternaturalness** [-nįs], *s.* calidad de preternatural.

pretext [prítekst], *s.* pretexto, excusa, expediente, socolor, especie.—**under p. of** = UNDER PRETENSE OF.

pretor, pretorian, etc. = PRAETOR, etc.

prettify [prítįfai], *va.* alindar, hermosear, adornar.

prettily [-lį], *adv.* lindamente, bonitamente.

prettiness [-nįs], *s.* lindeza, galanura.

pretty [-į]. **I.** *a.* lindo, bonito, (fam.) mono; bastante, pasadero, regular; (iron.) bello, grande, bueno (*a pretty mess you made of the business*, bueno lo hizo Vd. del negocio).—**a p. penny**, (fam.) una buena suma, una buena talegada. **II.** *adv.* algo, algún tanto; un poco, bastante (*pretty good*, bastante bueno; *pretty tired*, un poco o algo, cansado).—**p. much**, bastante; casi.—**p. well**, medianamente, así así, tal cual.

pretzel [prétsęl], *s.* cierto bizcocho seco, salado por fuera, y usualmente en forma de nudo.

prevail [privéil], *vn.* reinar, regir, valer, prevalecer, preponderar; ser muy frecuente; estar en boga general; (con **over** o **against**) vencer a, triunfar de; sobresalir, predominar.—**to p. on**, **upon** o **with**, persuadir, inducir, convencer.

prevailing [-iŋ], *a.* prevaleciente, (pre)dominante, reinante; eficaz; muy esparcido, extendido, general o común.—**p. winds**, vientos dominantes.

prevalence, prevalency [prévǎlęns, -į], *s.* predominio, preponderancia; ocurrencia común, frecuencia; uso o aceptación general.

prevalent [-ęnt], *a.* reinante, muy general(izado), de frecuente ocurrencia; (raro) prevaleciente, predominante.

prevaricate [privǽrikeit], *vn.* engañar con embuste; mentir; (for.) prevaricar.—**prevarication** [-éiṣǫn], *s.* embuste, mentira; dolo; (for.) prevaricación.—**prevaricator** [-ǫ(r)], *s.* embustero, mentiroso; (for.) prevaricador.

prevenient [privínįęnt], *a.* preveniente; preventivo.

prevent [privént]. **I.** *va.* prevenir, precaver, evitar, impedir, desbaratar, excusar, remediar; (con **from**) impedir (a uno), estorbar, atajar. **II.** *vn.* empecer, obviar, obstar.—**preventable** [-ǎbl], **preventible** [-ibl], *a.* evitable.—**preventability** [-ǎbįlįtį], *s.* evitabilidad.—**preventative** [-ǎtįv], *a.* y *s.* = PREVENTIVE.—**preventer** [-œ(r)], *s.* estorbador; (mar.) soga, berlinga, cadena o perno auxiliar.—**p. brace**, (mar.) contrabraza.—**p. stay**, contraestay.

prevention [-ṣǫn], *s.* prevención, acción de evitar o impedir; obstáculo, estorbo.

preventive [-tįv]. **I.** *a.* impeditivo; (med., etc.) preservativo, profiláctico, preventivo. **II.** *s.* preservativo, profiláctico.—**preventively** [-lį], *adv.* preventivamente.

preventorium [-tórįʌm], *s.* (med.) preventorio, hospital profiláctico, donde se trata a personas desnutridas o que han estado expuestas al contagio.

preview o **prevue** [prívįu], *s.* vista o examen previo.

previous [prívįʌs], *a.* previo, anterior.—**p. question**, proposición de que se hace uso en las asambleas para poner fin a un debate.—**p. to**, antes de.

previously [-lį], *adv.* previamente, antes, con anterioridad, anteriormente, de antemano.

previousness [-nįs], *s.* prioridad, anterioridad.

prevision [privíżǫn], *s.* previsión.

prewar [príwór], *a.* de antes de, o anterior a, la guerra.

prey [prei]. **I.** *s.* presa; pillaje, rapiña, robo; víctima. **II.** *vn.* (con **on** o **upon**) devorar (la presa); rapiñar, pillar, robar; consumir, oprimir, agobiar.

priapism [práiapizm], *s.* (med.) priapismo.

price [práis], *s.* **I.** *s.* precio; costa, monta, importe,

valor.—p. **catalogue**, catálogo con precios.—
p. ceiling, máximo de precios.—p. **control**,
control de precios.—p. **current**, cotización,
lista o boletín de precios corrientes.—p.-**fixing**,
(Am.) valorización; fijación oficial o arbitraria
de precios.—p. **list**, lista de precios, tarifa.—
p. tag, o **ticket**, etiqueta o marbete.—at any
p., a toda costa, cueste lo que cueste; a todo
trance.—at the highest p., a las valías.—cost
p., precio de costo.—fixed, o set, p., precio fijo.
—lowest p., último precio.—selling p., precio
de venta (al menudeo).—to set a p. on one's
head, poner a precio la cabeza de uno, poner
talla a uno (apl. a criminales).—what's the p.
of this? ¿cuánto vale esto? II. va. valuar, (a)va-
lorar, (a)preciar, fijar o poner precio a; (fam.)
preguntar el precio de.

priceless [-lịs], a. inapreciable; sin precio.

prick [prík]. I. va. punzar, picar, pinchar; espinar;
aguij(one)ar (al ganado), espolear (al caballo),
agarrochar (al toro); marcar, indicar o calcar
con agujerillos (en una lista, un mapa, etc.);
causar una punzada (dolor punzante); (mar.)
compasar, trazar o puntear sobre la carta de
marear.—to p. off, o out, (agr.) transplantar
en el criadero.—to p. on, o forward, aguijonear, aguzar, incitar.—to p. up, enderezar,
erguir, aguzar, levantar (las orejas); (alb.) dar
la primera capa de enlucido a.—to p. up one's
ears, aguzar las orejas o los oídos, poner la
oreja, escuchar con ahinco. II. vn. causar o
sentir una punzada o dolor punzante; erguirse
o estar erguido; picarse (el vino); (ant.) correr
(a caballo). III. s. aguijón; acicate; garrocha;
puntura, picadura, punzad(ur)a, pinchazo,
garrochada o puyazo; agujerillo; (fig.) escozor,
resquemor, espina, remordimiento; pista, rastro (de liebre); blanco a que tiran los balles-
teros.

pricker [-œ(r)], s. punzón, aguijón, lesna; punzador; aguijoncador; picador, garrocheador;
(hist.) jinete. V. PRICKLE.

pricket [-it], s. candelero con punta en que se
inserta una bujía; (zool.) gamo de uno a dos
años.

pricking [-iŋ]. I. a. punzante, picante. II. s.
punzada, picad(ur)a, aguijadura.

prickle [príkl]. I. s. pincho, púa, espina. II. va.
y vn. producir o sentir picazón.

prickliness [-lịnịs], s. calidad de espinoso.

prickly [-lị], a. lleno de púas o puntas, espinoso.
—p. heat, erupción y picazón causada por el
calor.—p. pear, (bot.) nopal, tuna(l); higo
chumbo.—p. poppy, (bot.) argemone, f.,
chicalote.—p. thistle, acanto.

prickpunch [-pʌnch], s. punzón de acero.

pricktimber, prickwood [-tịmbœ(r), -wụd], s.
(bot.) bonetero.

pride [práịd]. I. s. orgullo; engreimiento, vanidad;
altivez(a), arrogancia, soberbia; dignidad,
amor propio, respeto de sí mismo; vigor, brío;
persona o cosa predilecta, la flor y nata, causa
de satisfacción; (ant.) majestuosidad, pompa,
aparato.—to take p. in, ufanarse o preciarse
de. II. vr. (gen. con on u upon), enorgullecerse
(de), jactarse (de).

prideful [-fụl], a. orgulloso, arrogante, vanidoso.

priedieu [prịdyœ́], s. (igl.) reclinatorio.

prier [práịœ(r)], s. escudriñador, atisbador, acechador, husmeador.

priest [prĭst], s. sacerdote; presbítero, cura, m.—
p.-ridden, dominado por sacerdotes o clérigos.

priestcraft [-kræft], s. (conocimiento del) arte y
prácticas sacerdotales; (desp.) intriga eclesiástica.

priestess [-ịs], s. sacerdotisa.

priesthood [-hụd], s. clero, sacerdocio.

priestliness [-lịnịs], s. comportamiento de un
sacerdote; carácter sacerdotal.

priestly [-lị], a. sacerdotal.

prig [prĭg], s. persona excesivamente escrupulosa,

formal, melindrosa o remilgada en su conducta,
habla, etc., y que parece pagada de su propia
rectitud, superioridad o erudición; pedante;
(ant.) = FOP.

priggish [-ịš], a. propio del prig; presumido,
afectado, gazmoño; pedantesco.

priggishness, priggism [-nịs, -ịzm], s. formalidad exagerada; melindre, remilgo; pedantería.

prim [prịm]. I. a. severamente modesto; etiquetero, relamido, estirado, (fam.) almidonado.
II. va. y vr. vestir(se) con recato; ponerse de
veinticinco alfileres. V. PRIMP. III. vn. y va.
fruncir los labios. IV. s. (bot.) = PRIVET.

primacy [práịmạsị], s. primacía; supremacía;
precedencia.

prima donna [primạ́ dánạ], s. primera cantatriz.

prima facie [práịmạ́ féịšiị], (lat.) a primera vista,
(de) prima facie.—p.-f. **evidence**, (for.) prueba
suficiente para justificar la presunción de un
hecho.

primage [práịmịdż], s. (mar.) capa, quintalada.

primal [práịmạl], a. prístino, primordial; principal.

primarily [-erịlị], adv. primariamente, en primer
lugar; originalmente; principalmente.

primariness [-erịnịs], s. primacía, prioridad,
supremacía.

primary [práịmerị]. I. a. primario, primero;
primitivo, prístino; radical, principal, fundamental; elemental, rudimental; (geol.) primario; (elec.) primario; inductivo.—p. **accent**,
(fon.) acento tónico.—p. **coil**, bobina primaria,
o del circuito primario.—p. **color**, (fís.) color
elemental, color espectral.—p. **education**,
primera enseñanza.—p. **feathers**, plumas
primarias.—p. **motion**, (astr.) movimiento
primario o aparente de la esfera celeste.—p.
necessities, artículos de primera necesidad.—
p. **planet**, planeta primario.—p. **point**, (com.)
centro de distribución de granos, etc.—p.
school, escuela primaria.—p. **union**, (cir.)
cura por primera intención. II. s. (lo) primero;
mitin de electores para elegir candidatos, delegados, etc.; comicios preliminares; (elec.) circuito primario; (astr.) planeta primario; (zool.)
pluma primaria de un ave; ala de un insecto.

primate [práịm(e)ịt], s. primate; (igl.) primado.
—pl. P. [práịmḗịtiz], (zool.) cuadrumanos, primates.

primateship [práịmịtšịp], s. (igl.) primacía.

primatial [praịméịšạl], a. primacial; primado.

prime [práịm]. I. s. la flor (de la vida, de la edad,
juventud); albor, principio; alba, aurora, amanecer; flor, nata, lo mejor, lo más escogido;
(igl.) (hora) prima; (arit.) número primo;
(esgr.) primera; (impr.) virgulilla, signo (′).
II. a. primero, principal; primoroso, de primera
clase o calidad, selecto; original, prístino;
(mat.) primo (número); (impr.) marcado con
el signo (′).—p. **conductor**, colector (de una
máquina eléctrica).—p. **cost**, costo de fábrica
o de producción.—p. **meridian**, primer meridiano, meridiano principal.—p. **minister**,
primer ministro.—p. **mover**, fuente (f.) natural de energía o fuerza motriz (agua, viento,
etc.); máquina generadora de energía (turbina,
máquina de vapor, etc.); móvil primero; alma,
palanca (de una empresa).—p. **vertical**, (astr.)
vertical primario. III. va. preparar, alistar;
informar; prevenir, dar instrucciones; cebar
(un arma de fuego, una bomba, etc.); (alb. y
pint.) imprimar; dar la primera capa; (impr.)
poner el signo (′). IV. vn. (m. v.) arrastrar
agua con el vapor; entrar una marea antes de
tiempo.—to be primed, (arti. y mec.) estar
cebado; estar listo o preparado.

primely [-lị], adv. (fam.) excelentemente.

primeness [-nịs], s. excelencia, primor, excelencia.

primer [prịmœ(r)], s. cartilla, libro primero de
lectura; devocionario; (impr.) V. LONG y
GREAT.

primer [práimœ(r)], *s.* (pint.) imprimador; (arti.) pistón, fulminante; cebador.

primeval [praimíval], *a.* primitivo, prístino.

primigenial [praimidžíniąl], *a.* primogénito; primigenio, primitivo.

priming [práimiŋ], *s.* preparación; (arti. y mec.) cebo; (m. v.) arrastre de agua con el vapor; (pint.) imprimación; primera capa.—**p. hole**, oído.—**p. horn**, cebador, chifle.—**p. tool**, imprimadera.—**p. tube**, estopín.

primipara [praimípąrą], *s.* primeriza, primípara.

primitial [praimíšąl], *a.* primicial.

primitive [prímitiv]. I. *a.* primitivo, primordial, original; (biol.) rudimentario; (gram.) primitivo. II. *s.* y *a.* (b. a.) primitivo (artista u obra).

primitively [-li], *adv.* primitivamente.

primitiveness [-nis], *s.* calidad de primitivo.

primitivism [-izm], *s.* primitivismo.

primitivist [-ist], *a.* y *s.* primitivista.

primitivity [-tíviti], *s.* = PRIMITIVENESS.

primness [prímnis], *s.* formalidad o gravedad afectada; escrupulosidad, remilgo. V. PRIM.

primogenitor [praimodžénitǫ(r)], *s.* progenitor.

primogeniture [-chų(r)], *s.* primogenitura; mayorazgo (ll. t. **right of p.**).

primonish [primániš], *va.* advertir, anunciar.

primordial [praimórdiąl]. I. *a.* primordial, primitivo. II. *s.* principio elemental.

primp [primp], *va.* y *vn.* (a veces con **up**) vestir(se) con afectación; acicalar(se); portarse afectadamente.

primrose [prímrouz]. I. *s.* (bot.) vellorita, primavera; color amarillo verdoso o rojizo claro. II. *a.* florido, gayo.—**p. path**, vida sensual.

primulaceous [primjuléišʌs], *a.* (bot.) primuláceo.

prince [prins], *s.* príncipe; monarca, *m.*, soberano. —**P. Albert (coat)**, levita.—**P. consort**, príncipe consorte.—**P. Rupert's drops**, lágrimas de Batavia.—**P. of Darkness**, Satanás. —**P. of Peace**, Jesucristo; Príncipe de la Paz (Manuel de Godoy).—**p. of the blood royal**, infante, príncipe de sangre real.—**P. of Wales**, Príncipe de Gales.

princedom [-dǫm], *s.* principado.

princelet [-lit], **princeling** [-liŋ], *s.* principillo.

princeliness [-linis], *s.* munificencia, nobleza, magnificencia.

princely [-li]. I. *a.* semejante a un príncipe, propio o digno de un príncipe, principesco, magnífico, regio. II. *adv.* principescamente.

princess [-is], *s.* princesa.—**p. royal**, hija mayor de un soberano.

principal [prínsipąl]. I. *a.* principal, esencial, capital; máximo; (arq.) maestro, toral. II. *s.* principal, jefe; director o rector (de escuela o colegio); (for.) causante, comitente, constituyente; (com.) capital o principal (puesto a interés); (arq.) jamba de fuerza.

principality [-pǽliti], *s.* principado, soberanía.

principally [-pli], *adv.* principalmente, mayormente, máxime.

principalness [-pąlnis], *s.* principalidad.

principle [prínsipl], *s.* principio, origen; fundamento, motivo, razón, *f.*; principio (regla, ley, teorema); (quím.) principio activo.—**in p.**, en principio.—**on general principles**, según, o de acuerdo con, principios generales; por sistema, según costumbre.

principle, *va.* imbuir, infundir principios o máximas a.—**(high-)principled** [-d], *a.* de principios, escrupuloso, probo.

prink [priŋk], *vn.* y *va.* ataviar(se), adornar(se); acicalar(se).

print [print]. I. *va.* estampar, imprimir; tirar, hacer una tirada; publicar, dar a la estampa; escribir a imitación de letras de molde; (foto.) imprimir, tirar una prueba; (fig.) imprimir o grabar en la memoria, etc.—**printed by**, impreso por; imprenta de.—**printed cotton**, (tej.) cotón, zaraza.—**print(ed) goods**, (tej.)

estampados.—**printed matter**, impresos. II. *vn.* ser impresor. III. *s.* impresión, estampa; tipo o letra de molde (v. gr. *small print*, tipo menudo); impreso, folleto, volante, periódico, alcance, etc.; papel de imprenta; impresión, marca, señal (*f.*) o huella; lámina, grabado; (tej.) estampado, indiana; molde; muestra, dibujo; (foto.) impresión, (prueba) positiva.— *pl.* prints, (tej.) estampados, cotonada, zarazas.—**p. butter**, mantequilla moldeada.—**p. maker**, o seller, estampero.—**p. shop**, estampería; imprenta (tipográfica).—**p. works**, (tej.) fábrica de estampados.—**in p.**, impreso; publicado; en letra de molde.—**out of p.**, (edición) agotada.

printable [-ąbl], *a.* imprimible.

printer [-œ(r)], *s.* impresor, tipógrafo.—**p.'s devil**, aprendiz (*m.*) de impresor.—**p.'s ink**, tinta de imprenta.—**p.'s mark**, pie (*m.*) de imprenta.—**p.'s proof**, prueba de imprenta.— **p.'s shooting stick**, (impr.) acuñador.

printery [-œri], *s.* imprenta; (tej.) taller de estampar géneros.

printing [-iŋ]. I. *s.* imprenta, tipografía; impresión; tiraje; estampa, impreso; (tej.) estampado. II. *a.* de imprenta, de imprimir.—**p. frame**, (foto.) marco de imprimir.—**p. ink**, tinta de imprenta.—**p. machine** = P. PRESS. —**p. office**, o **shop**, imprenta, tipografía.—**p. press**, prensa, máquina para imprimir o para estampar telas.—**p. types**, caracteres de imprenta, tipo.

prior [práiǫ(r)]. I. *a.* anterior, precedente, prior, previo.—**p. to**, antes de. II. *s.* (igl.) prior.

priorate [-it], *s.* (igl.) priorato, priorazgo.

prioress [-is], *s.* (igl.) priora.

priority [praiáriti], *s.* prioridad, precedencia, antelación, prelación.

priorship [práiǫršip], *s.* (igl.) priorazgo, priorato.

priory [práiǫri], *s.* (igl.) priorato, priorazgo.

prism [prizm], *s.* (geom.) y ópt.) prisma, *m.*

prismatic(al [prizmǽtik(ąl], *a.* prismático.

prismatically [-i], *adv.* prismáticamente; en forma de prisma.

prism(at)oid [prizm(ąt)oid], *s.* sólido prism(at)oideo.

prison [prízǫn], *s.* prisión, cárcel, *f.*, encierro.— **p. bird** = JAILBIRD.—**p. cell**, celda.—**p. fever**, (med.) tifo.—**p. guard**, guardia (*m.*) penal.—**p. house**, cárcel, prisión.—**p. ship**, pontón.—**p. term**, condena, período que por condena se pasa en una prisión.

prisoner [-œ(r)], *s.* preso, prisionero, recluso.— **p.'s base**, marro, (Am.) rescate, juego de muchachos.

pristine [prístin], *a.* prístino, primitivo.

prithee [príði], *v. contr.* de **I pray thee**, te ruego.

prittle-prattle [prítl prætl], *s.* (fam.) cháchara.

privacy [práivąsi], *s.* retiro, soledad, aislamiento; retraimiento; reserva, secreto; condición de estar solo y poder obrar privadamente.

private [práivit]. I. *a.* privado; particular (a distinción de público); personal; confidencial; secreto, oculto; solo, retirado; reservado, excusado; callado, reticente.—**p. affair**, o **business**, asunto privado.—**p. enterprise**, empresa particular.—**p. hearing**, audiencia secreta, a puertas cerradas.—**p. house**, casa particular.—**p. letter**, carta reservada.—**p. lodging**, habitación en una casa particular.— **p. mass**, misa privada o rezada (sin canto).— **p. office**, gabinete, despacho particular.—**p. person**, particular.—**p. school**, escuela particular.—**p. secretary**, secretario o secretaria particular.—**p. staircase**, escalera secreta o excusada.—**p. theatricals**, comedias caseras o de aficionados; teatro casero; función de aficionados.—**at one's p. expense**, a costa propia.—**to be p.**, estar solo(s); estar ocupado en asuntos privados. II. *s.* soldado raso.—*pl.*

partes pudendas.—**in p.**, particular o privadamente, en particular, en secreto, en reserva.
privateer [praįvətír]. I. *s.* corsario, armador. II. *vn.* corsear, armar en corso.—**privateering** [-įŋ], *s.* corso.—**privateersman** [-zmǫn], *s.* corsario.
privately [práįvįtlį], *adv.* privada o particularmente, secretamente, reservadamente.
privateness [-nįs], *s.* calidad de privado. V. PRIVACY.
privation [praįvéįşǫn], *s.* privación; carencia; estrechez, falta de bienestar.
privative [prívətįv]. I. *a.* privativo. II. *s.* negación; (gram.) prefijo o adjetivo privativo.—**privatively** [-lį], *adv.* privativamente.—**privativeness** [-nįs], *s.* calidad de privativo.
privet [prívįt], *s.* (bot.) alheña, ligustro.
privilege [prívįlįdž]. I. *s.* privilegio; gracia, prerrogativa; fuero; franquicia, patente, *f.*, inmunidad, exención, dispensa; indulto. II. *va.* privilegiar, exceptuar; (con **from**) exentar, eximir.
privileged [-d], *a.* privilegiado, inmune, franco, exento, libre.—**p. altar**, (igl.) altar privilegiado.—**p. debt**, (for.) deuda preferente.—**p. shares**, **p. stock**, (com.) acciones privilegiadas.—**p. witness**, (for.) testigo a quien las partes interesadas pueden impedir que declare.
privily [prívįlį], *adv.* privada o secretamente.
privity [prívįtį], *s.* informe reservado, secreto; (for.) relación mutua peculiar que existe entre individuos tocante a algún negocio.
privy [prívį]. I. *a.* (con **to**) confidente, cómplice (en); instruído, informado, enterado (en); (ant.) privado, secreto, excusado; particular, propio, personal.—**p. council**, consejo privado.—**p. purse**, (Ingl.) fondos para los gastos personales del rey; empleado que los maneja.—**p. seal**, sello privado (o pequeño). II. *s.* (for.) copartícipe; cómplice; retrete, necesaria, letrina, (lugar) excusado; (mar.) jardín.
prize [praįz]. I. *s.* premio, galardón; presa, botín; buque apresado; adquisición, ganancia, ventaja, buena suerte.—**p. court**, tribunal de presas.—**p. crew**, tripulación que lleva un buque apresado a su destino.—**p. fight**, pugilato, boxeo público entre profesionales.—**p. fighter**, boxeador, púgil, pugilista.—**p. fighting**, pugilismo.—**p. master**, capitán o cabo de presa.—**p. money**, parte (*f.*) de una presa.—**p. office**, negociado de las presas de guerra.—**p. ring**, liza o cuadrilátero de boxear; el boxeo como profesión.—**p. winner**, el premiado o vencedor en un concurso.—**p.-winning**, premiado. II. *va.* apreciar, estimar; valuar, tasar; alzaprimar.
prizer [-œ(r)], *s.* apreciador, valorador, tasador.
pro [proų]. I. *adv.* en favor; por. II. *s.* voto afirmativo; el que toma la afirmativa en un debate o votación.—**p. and con**, en pro (o en favor) y en contra.—**p. forma**, por fórmula; (com.) simulado.—**p. rata**, a prorrata.—**pros and cons**, el pro y el contra.—**p. tem**(**pore**, pro témpore, interino; interinamente.—**neither p. nor con**, ni en pro ni en contra.
pro, *a.* y *s.* (fam.) *contr.* de PROFESSIONAL.
probabilism [prábəbįlįzm], *s.* (fil.) probabilismo.
probabilist(**ic** [-bįlįst(įk], *s.* y *a.* probabilista.
probability [-bílįtį], *s.* probabilidad, verosimilitud.—**in all p.**, según toda probabilidad.
probable [-bl], *a.* probable, verosímil; fácil, regular.—**probably** [-blį], *adv.* probablemente.
probang [próųbæŋ], *s.* (cir.) sonda esofágica.
probate [próųbeįt]. I. *a.* (for.) testamentario.—**p. court**, tribunal de testamentarías. II. *s.* (for.) prueba plena y legal de la autenticidad de un testamento; competencia de un juez o tribunal en juicio testamentario. III. *va.* validar o legalizar (un testamento tras la muerte del testador).
probation [probéįşǫn], *s.* prueba, ensayo, tentativa; probación, noviciado; (en los tribunales juveniles) libertad condicional o vigilada.—**p. officer**, vigilante, agente de vigilancia (en algunas partes se llama *delegado de libertad vigilada*).—**probational** [-ǫl], **probationary** [-erį], *a.* probatorio.—**probationer** [-œ(r)], *s.* novicio; (for.) delincuente que goza de libertad condicional; aprendiz, *m.*, meritorio.
probationership [-şįp], *s.* noviciado.
probative [próųbətįv], *a.* probatorio.
probatory [-tǫrį], *a.* probatorio.
probe [proųb]. I. *s.* (cir.) sonda, tienta, cánula, exploratorio; prueba, ensayo; indagación.—**p. scissors**, tijeras de cirujano. II. *va.* (cir.) tentar, explorar, sond(e)ar; escudriñar, indagar.
probity [próųbįtį], *s.* probidad, hombría de bien.
problem [práblem], *s.* problema, *m.*; cuestión.
problematic(**al** [-mǽtįk(ǫl], *a.* problemático.
problematically [-į], *adv.* problemáticamente.
Proboscidea [proųbasídįə], *s. pl.* (zool.) proboscidios.—**proboscidean** [-n], *s.* y *a.* proboscidio.
proboscis [probásįs], *s.* proboscis, probóscide, *f.*, trompa (del elefante, etc.); (ent.) trompetilla; (fam.) nariz.
procaine [proųkéįn], *s.* procaína, novocaína.
procedural [prosídžųrǫl], *a.* de procedimiento, tocante al procedimiento.
procedure [prosídžų(r)], *s.* proceder, procedimiento, conducta; (for.) procedimiento(s) judicial(es), tramitación, vía judicial.
proceed [prosíd], *vn.* seguir (adelante), proseguir; marchar, adelantar, avanzar; proceder, obrar; (for.) empezar, instituir (una causa); (con **against**) proceder contra; tramitar; provenir, dimanar, proceder (de).—**to p. to blows**, llegar a las manos, acudir a los golpes.—**to p. to business**, ir a lo que importa; poner manos a la obra; entrar en materia.—**proceeding from**, procedente de; originario u oriundo de.
proceeding [-įŋ], *s.* procedimiento, conducta, proceder; transacción; (for.) trámite, procedimiento; proceso.—*pl.* actas, (for.) proceso, expediente, autos, actuaciones.
proceeds [próųsidz], *s. pl.* producto, réditos.
process [práses]. I. *s.* procedimiento, método, sistema, *m.*; proceso (conjunto o serie de fenómenos naturales); progreso, continuación, adelantamiento; curso, serie, sucesión; (for.) causa, proceso, expediente, autos; (anat. y zool.) apófisis, protuberancia, excrecencia; (bot.) apéndice.—**p. butter**, mantequilla de inferior calidad que se derrite con leche o crema para "renovarla."—**p. of law**, procedimiento legal.—**p. of time**, lapso o (trans)curso del tiempo.—**p. plate**, placa de fotografía lenta, empleada esp. para dispositivos.—**p. server**, portador de citaciones o notificaciones oficiales.—**in p. of time**, con el tiempo.—**in the p. (of)**, haciéndose, en vía de (fabricación, preparación, etc.). II. *va.* cocinar o esterilizar bajo presión; fotografiar; someter a algún procedimiento especial, tratar, industrializar, elaborar (dícese sobre todo de las materias primas que se elaboran o preparan para la industria o el mercado); (for.) procesar.
processal [prosésǫl], *a.* (for.) procesal.
processing [prásesįŋ], *s.* (ind.) elaboración (de materias primas, etc.); método particular de fabricar o preparar un producto.
procession [proséşǫn], *s.* procesión; cortejo; cabalgata; desfile de tropa; (teol.) procesión.
processional [-ǫl]. I. *a.* procesional. II. *s.* (igl.) himno; procesionario (libro).
processionary [-erį], *a.* procesional.—**p. moth**, (ent.) procesionaria.
proclaim [prokléįm], *va.* proclamar, anunciar, denunciar; promulgar; publicar, pregonar, vocear.
proclaimer [-œ(r)], *s.* proclamador.
proclamation [praklǝméįşǫn], *s.* proclamación; publicación; proclama, decreto, edicto, bando.

proclitic [proklítik], *a.* (gram.) proclítico.
proclivity [proklívįtį], *s.* propensión, proclividad.
proclivous [proklívᴧs], *a.* inclinado hacia adelante; proclive.
procœlia [prosílịạ], *s.* (anat.) procelio; (**P.**), *pl.* (zool.) procelios, suborden de cocodrilos.
proconsul [prokánsᴧl], *s.* procónsul.—**proconsular** [prokánsyᴜlạ(r)], *a.* proconsular.—**proconsulate, proconsulship** [-lịt, -sᴧlȿip], *s.* proconsulado.
procrastinate [prokrǽstįneįt], *va.* y *vn.* diferir, dilatar, trasmañanar, (fam.) perecear; ser moroso.—**procrastination** [-éįȿǫn], *s.* dilación, demora.—**procrastinator** [-eįtǫ(r)], *s.* hombre moroso.
procreant [próᴜkrịạnt], *a.* procreante.
procreate [próᴜkrįeįt], *va.* procrear, engendrar, criar.—**procreation** [-éįȿǫn], *s.* procreación.—**procreative** [-eįtįv], *a.* procreativo, procreador.—**procreativeness** [-nįs], *s.* facultad o potencia procreadora.—**procreator** [-eįtǫ(r)], *s.* procreador.
Procrustean [proᴜkrᴧstįạn], *a.* (mit.) de Procusto.
proctor [práktǫ(r)], *s.* (for.) procurador: apoderado, agente; censor de una universidad.
proctorage [-įdȝ], *s.* procuración.
proctorial [praktórịạl], *a.* referente al procurador o al censor académico.
proctorship [práktǫrȿip], *s.* procura(ción); procuraduría.
proctoscope [práktoskoᴜp], *s.* (med.) proctoscopio.
procumbent [prokᴧmbᴇnt], *a.* postrado, inclinado; (bot.) rastrero.
procurable [prokįúrạbl], *a.* procurable, asequible, proporcionable.
procuracy [prákyᴜrạsį], *s.* procuración; gestión, manejo de negocios.
procuration [-réįȿǫn], *s.* alcahuetería; (for.) procura(ción), poder.—**p. fee**, comisión sobre un préstamo.
procurator [-eįtǫ(r)], *s.* procurador, apoderado.
procuratorial [-rạtórịạl], *a.* hecho por procurador.
procure [prokįúr]. **I.** *va.* procurar, lograr, obtener, conseguir; causar, ocasionar. **II.** *va.* y *vn.* solicitar mozas para un lupanar, alcahuetear.
procurement [-mᴇnt], *s.* procuración, obtención, logro, consecución; solicitud, gestión.
procurer [-œ(r)], *s.* alcahuete, tercero, rufián.
procuress [-įs], *s.* alcahueta, tercera.
Procyon [próᴜsįạn], *s.* (astr.) Prución. *m.*
prod [prad]. **I.** *va.* punzar, picar, aguijonear. **II.** *s.* pincho, aguijada; picadura, pinchazo. *V.* GOAD.
prodigal [prádįgạl]. **I.** *a.* pródigo, derramado(r). **II.** *s.* pródigo, manirroto, derrochador.
prodigality [-gǽlįtį], *s.* prodigalidad; desperdicio.
prodigally [prádįglį], *adv.* pródigamente.
prodigious [prodídȝᴧs], *a.* prodigioso; ingente.
prodigiously [-lį], *adv.* prodigiosamente.
prodigiousness [-nįs], *s.* prodigiosidad.
prodigy [prádįdȝį], *s.* prodigio; portento, pasmo.
prodromal [prádromạl], **prodromic** [prodrámįk], *a.* (med.) prodrómico, premonitorio.
prodrome [próᴜdroᴜm], *s.* (med.) pródromo.
produce [prodjús]. **I.** *va.* producir; generar; causar, ocasionar; (com., etc.) rendir, rentar, redituar(r); mostrar, exhibir; introducir, presentar al público; (teat.) poner en escena; (geom.) prolongar. **II.** *vn.* producir; fructificar, dar frutos. **III.** [prádjus], *s.* producto, producción; fruto; productos agrícolas, provisiones.—**p. exchange**, lonja de víveres.
producer [prodjúsœ(r)], *s.* productor, producidor; gasógeno, generador de gas pobre.—**p. gas, gas pobre.—producers' goods**, (e. p.) elementos de producción (materias primas, maquinaria, etc.).
producible [-įbl], *a.* producible.

producibleness [-nįs], *s.* producibilidad.
producing [-įŋ], *a.* productor, producente, producidor.
product [prádᴧkt], *s.* producto; resultado, efecto, fruto; (com.) renta, rendimiento; (mat.) producto.
productile [prodᴧktįl], *a.* dúctil.
production [prodᴧkȿǫn], *s.* producción; producto; composición, obra del ingenio; (teat.) producción escénica, representación teatral.—**p. cost**, (com.) costo de fabricación.—**productive** [-tįv], *a.* productivo; generador; fértil, fecundo.—**productiveness** [-nįs], **productivity** [proᴜdᴧktívįtį], *s.* productividad; fertilidad, fecundidad.
proem [próᴜem], *s.* proemio, prefacio; exordio.
proemial [proᴜímįạl], *a.* proemial.
profanation [prafạnéįȿǫn], *s.* profanación.
profane [proféįn]. **I.** *a.* profano, secular; profano, blasfemo, irreverente; indecente; de reniegos. **II.** *va.* profan(iz)ar, violar; desacatar.
profanely [-lį], *adv.* profanamente.
profaner [-œ(r)], *s.* profanador, violador.
profaneness [-nįs], **profanity** [profǽnįtį], *s.* profanidad, blasfemia, impiedad; reniego, lenguaje profano; irreverencia, desacato.
profess [profés]. **I.** *va.* profesar, creer en; declarar, manifestar; fingir, aparentar; enseñar (como profesor); ejercer (una profesión); (igl.) profesar. **II.** *vn.* hacer profesión, declarar abierta o públicamente.
professed [-t], *a.* profeso, declarado, decidido; aparentado, (gal.) pretendido.
professedly [-įdlį], *adv.* declaradamente; aparentadamente, (gal.) pretendidamente.
profession [proféȿǫn], *s.* profesión, carrera, ocupación; profesión o protestación de la fe; declaración, manifestación; (igl.) profesión.—**the p.**, (fam., teat.) arte dramático; los cómicos en general.
professional [-ạl]. **I.** *a.* profesional, facultativo; de profesión (v. gr.: *professional gambler*, jugador de profesión). **II.** *s.* profesional; (dep.) deportista de profesión; (teat.) actor o actriz; perito en algún arte o profesión.
professionally [-į], *adv.* profesionalmente, en calidad de o como profesional.
professor [profésǫ(r)], *s.* profesor, catedrático.
professorate [-eįt], *s.* profesorado.
professorial [proᴜfesórịạl], *a.* profesoral, de profesor; pedagógico.—**professorship** [profésǫrȿip], *s.* profesorado, cátedra.
proffer [práfœ(r)]. **I.** *va.* proponer, ofrecer, brindar. **II.** *s.* oferta, propuesta, ofrecimiento.
proficiency [profíȿᴇnsį], *s.* aprovechamiento, adelant(amient)o; pericia, habilidad.
proficient [-ᴇnt], *s.* y *a.* experto, perito; aprovechado, proficiente, adelantado.
profile [próᴜfaįl]. **I.** *s.* contorno; recorte; perfil.—**p. paper**, papel cuadriculado.—**in p.**, de perfil. **II.** *va.* perfilar; recortar.
profit [práfįt]. **I.** *s.* provecho, pro, *mf.*, ventaja; fruto; beneficio; lucro, ganancia, utilidad.—**p. and loss**, (com.) lucros y daños, ganancias y pérdidas.—**p. sharing**, distribución de las ganancias con los empleados.—**p.-sharing system**, sistema cooperativo.—**clear p.**, beneficio neto. *V.* NET y GROSS. **II.** *va.* aprovechar a, servir. **III.** *vn.* sacar utilidad o provecho, ganar, lucrarse.—**to p. by**, sacar partido o provecho de, beneficiarse de.
profitable [-ạbl], *a.* provechoso, útil, beneficioso, ventajoso; productivo, lucrativo.—**profitableness** [-nįs], *s.* calidad de provechoso.—**profitably** [-ạblį], *adv.* provechosamente; lucrativamente.
profiteer [prafįtír]. **I.** *vn.* usurear, lograr, explotar con agio o buscando ganancias exorbitantes (apl. esp. a la usura que se aprovecha de una necesidad o calamidad nacional). **II.** *s.* usurero, logrero, explotador, acaparador, buitre (fig.),

vampiro (fig.).—**profiteering** [-ịŋ], *s.* usura, logrería, explotación.

profitless [práfịtlịs], *a.* infructuoso.

profitlessly [-lị], *adv.* infructuosamente.

profligacy [práflịgǎsị], *s.* libertinaje, desenfreno, disolución, crápula.

profligate [-gịt], *a.* y *s.* libertino, licencioso, relajado, perdido.—**profligately** [-lị], *adv.* disolutamente, licenciosamente.

profound [profáụnd], I. *a.* profundo; hondo; intenso; pesado (sueño). II. *s.* (poét.) sima, abismo; profundo, mar, *mf.*, océano.

profoundly [-lị], *adv.* profundamente.

profoundness [-nịs], *s.* profundidad.

profundity [profÁndịtị], *s.* profundidad, profundo; hondura.

profuse [profjús], *a.* profuso; pródigo.—**profusely** [-lị], *adv.* profusamente; pródigamente.

profuseness, profusion [-nịs, profjúžọn], *s.* profusión, abundancia; prodigalidad.

progenitor [prodžénịtọ(r)], *s.* progenitor.

progeny [prádženị], *s.* progenie, prole, *f.*, linaje.

prognathism [prágnạθịzm], *s.* prognatismo.

prognathous [-θʌs], *a.* (anat. y zool.) prognato.

prognosis [pragnóụsịs], *s.* (med.) pronóstico; prognosis, vaticinio, predicción; presciencia.

prognostic [pragnástịk]. I. *s.* pronóstico, presagio, señal, *f.*; predicción; (med.) síntoma (*m.*) determinante. II. *a.* pronosticador.

prognosticable [-ǎbl], *a.* pronosticable.

prognosticate [-ẹịt], *va.* pronosticar; presagiar; agorar, augurar.—**prognostication** [-kéịšọn], *s.* pronosticación; presagio, pronóstico, agüero.—**prognosticator** [-keịtọ(r)], *s.* pronosticador, vaticinador.

program(me [próụgræm]. I. *s.* programa, *m.*; agenda; plan, prospecto; (hist.) cartel.—**p. music,** música descriptiva. II. *va.* (Am.) programar.

progress [prágrẹs]. I. *s.* progreso; progresos, aprovechamiento, adelantamiento; desarrollo, mejoramiento; marcha, curso, carrera.—**to make 'p.,** hacer progresos, progresar. II. [progrés], *va.* adelantar, llevar adelante. III. *vn.* progresar; avanzar, marchar; adelantar, hacer progresos.

progression [progréšọn], *s.* progresión, adelantamiento, curso; (mat.) progresión.

progressional [-ạl], *a.* progresivo.

progressionist [-ịst], *s.* (pol.) progresista; (biol.) evolucionista; transformista.

progressive [progrésịv]. I. *a.* progresivo; progresista (t. *s.*). II. *a.* y *s.* (P., pol.) progresista.—**progressively** [-lị], *adv.* progresivamente.—**progressiveness** [-nịs], *s.* calidad de progresivo o progresista.—**Progressivism** [-ịzm], *s.* (pol.) progresismo, doctrinas del partido progresista.

prohibit [proụhíbịt], *va.* prohibir, vedar; impedir.

prohibition [proụ(h)ịbíšọn], *s.* prohibición, veda(miento); auto prohibitorio, entredicho o interdicto; veto; (E. U.) nefalismo obligatorio, prohibicionismo, prohibición legal de la manufactura y venta de bebidas alcohólicas.—**p. law,** ley antialcohólica.—**P. party,** (E. U.) partido prohibicionista, que aboga por la prohibición de bebidas alcohólicas.

prohibitionism [-ịzm], *s.* prohibicionismo.

prohibitionist [-ịst], *s.* y *a.* (E. U. pol.) prohibicionista, nefalista, afiliado al prohibicionismo.

prohibitive, prohibitory [proụhíbịtịv, -tọrị], *a.* prohibitivo, prohibitorio.

project [prodžékt]. I. *va.* proyectar; trazar, dibujar; idear; echar, arrojar, despedir. II. *vn.* resaltar, sobresalir, (re)salir, destacarse. III. [prádžekt], *s.* proyecto, plan; planta, plano, traza; empresa; (educ.) tema (*m.*) que se le asigna al alumno y que le exige iniciativa personal, la lectura de obras de consulta, etc.

projectile [prodžéktịl]. I. *s.* proyectil. II. *a.* proyectante; arrojadizo.

projecting [-tịŋ], *a.* proyectante (línea); saledizo, voladizo, saliente.

projection [-šọn], *s.* lanzamiento, echamiento; resalte; (arq.) vuelo, saliente, salidizo, retallo, proyectura; plan, proyecto; (geom.) proyección.—**p. machine,** proyector cinematográfico.

projector [-tọ(r)], *s.* proyectista; tracista; proyector (eléctrico, cinematográfico, etc.); aparato de proyección.

projecture [-chụ(r)], *s.* proyección; (arq.) proyectura, salidizo, vuelo.

prolapse [prolǽps]. I. *vn.* caer hacia adelante o afuera. II. *s.* (med.) prolapso, procidencia.

prolapsus [-ʌs], *s.* (med.) prolapso.

prolate [próụleịt], *a.* alargado hacia los polos.

proleg [próụleg], *s.* (ent.) pie abdominal o falso.

prolegomena [proụlegámena], *s. pl.* (*sing.* **prolegomenon**) prolegómenos.

prolepsis [prolépsịs], *s.* (ret.) prolepsis.

proleptic(al [proléptịk(ạl], *a.* proléptico, previo.

proletarian [proụletérịạn], *a.* y *s.* proletario.

proletariat [-ịat], *s.* proletariado; clase obrera.

prolicide [próụlịsaịd], *s.* infanticidio.

proliferate [prolífereịt], *va.* y *vn.* (biol., bot.) (re)producir(se); desarrollar(se) por la reproducción de células similares.

proliferating [-ịŋ], *a.* proliferante.

proliferation [-éịšọn], *s.* (biol., bot.) proliferación; multiplicación, reproducción.

proliferous [-ʌs], *a.* prolífero.

prolific(al [prolífịk(ạl], *a.* prolífico, fecundo, fértil.

prolifically [-ị], *adv.* prolíficamente.

prolification [-éịšọn], *s.* generación; fecundidad; (bot.) prolificación, proliferación.

prolificness [-nịs], *s.* fecundidad, fertilidad.

prolix [prolíks], *a.* prolijo, nimio, difuso.—**prolixity** [-ịtị], **prolixness** [-nịs], *s.* prolijidad, nimiedad.—**prolixly** [-lị], *adv.* prolijamente.

prolocutor [prolákjụtọ(r)], *s.* intercesor, portavoz, *m.*; presidente de una asamblea.

prolog(ue [próụlag]. I. *s.* prólogo, proemio, prefacio; (teat.) introito, loa. II. *va.* prolog(uiz)ar.—**prolog(u)ist** [-ịst], *s.* prologuista.—**prolog(u)ize** [-aịz], *va.* y *vn.* prolog(uiz)ar.

prolong [prolóŋ], *va.* prolongar, extender, dilatar.

prolongation [-géịšọn], *s.* prolongación.

prolonge [prolándž], *s.* (arti.) prolonga.

prolusion [prolịúžọn], *s.* prolusión, prelusión, preludio; ensayo preliminar.

promenade [pramenád]. I. *vn.* pasear(se). II. *s.* paseo (lugar y acto); caminata, vuelta.—**p. concert,** concierto durante el cual la gente pasea o baila.—**p. deck,** (mar.) cubierta superior o de paseo.—**p. roof,** azotea de baile y diversión.

promenader [-œ(r)], *s.* paseante.

Promethean [promíθịạn], *a.* de Prometeo.

prominence, prominency [prámịnẹns, -ị], *s.* eminencia, altura, relieve, distinción; prominencia, protuberancia, saledizo, resalto; (anat.) prominencia, apófisis, elevación.

prominent [-ẹnt], *a.* prominente, saliente, conspicuo, destacado, descollante, de viso; eminente, sobresaliente, distinguido.—**p. eyes,** ojos saltones.—**p. figures,** personalidades, figuras de relieve.

promiscuity [pramịskịúịtị], *s.* promiscuidad (apl. esp. a las relaciones sexuales).

promiscuous [promískyụʌs], *a.* promiscuo.—**p. intercourse,** relaciones sexuales promiscuas, libre amor.—**promiscuously** [-lị], *adv.* promiscuamente; sin distinción.—**promiscuousness** [-nịs], *s.* promiscuidad, confusión, mezcla.

promise [prámịs]. I. *s.* promesa, prometimiento, prometido, promisión; fe, *f.*, palabra dada; cosa prometida; expectativa, esperanza.—**p. of marriage,** palabra de matrimonio. II. *va.* y *vn.* prometer, ofrecer, mandar; dar o hacer concebir esperanzas.—**Promised Land**, Tierra Prometida o de Promisión.

promisee [-sí], *s.* (for.) persona que ha recibido una promesa.

promiser [-sœ(r)], **promisor** [-sɔr], *s.* prometedor.

promising [-siŋ], *a.* prometiente, prometedor, que promete, halagador, halagüeño.

promisorily [-sɔrili], *adv.* promisoriamente.

promissory [-sɔri], *a.* promisorio.—**p. note**, pagaré, vale, abonaré.

promontory [prámɔntɔri], *s.* (geog.) promontorio, punta, cabo; (anat.) promontorio, eminencia.

promorphology [proumɔrfálɔdži], *s.* (biol.) promorfología, morfología geométrica.

promote [promóут], *va.* promover, fomentar; provocar, suscitar; alentar, estimular; mejorar, adelantar, ascender; (com.) agenciar, gestionar; capitalizar y organizar (una empresa).

promoter [-œ(r)], *s.* promotor, promovedor; gestor, agente que se dedica a capitalizar y organizar empresas industriales; agente de negocios.

promotion [promóуšɔn], *s.* promoción, ascenso, adelant(amient)o; fomento.

promotive [promóутiv], *a.* promovedor, promotor.

prompt [prámpt]. I. *a.* pronto, listo, expedito; puntual.—**p. book**, (teat.) apunte, libro del apuntador o consueta.—**p. box**, (teat.) concha.—**p. cash**, pago al contado, inmediato.—**p. note**, (com.) nota de aviso, especie de memorándum o factura que se da a quien compra al fiado. II. *va.* impulsar, mover, incitar; indicar, sugerir, insinuar; soplar, decir en voz baja (en una clase); (teat.) apuntar.

prompter [-œ(r)], *s.* incitador, instigador; (teat.) apuntador, traspunte, consueta, *mf.*

promptitude, **promptness** [-itjud, -nis], *s.* prontitud, presteza; puntualidad.—**promptly** [-li], *adv.* prontamente, prestamente; puntualmente.—**p. at two o'clock**, a las dos en punto.

promulgate [promÁlgeit], *va.* promulgar, proclamar, publicar, pervulgar.

promulgation [-géišɔn], *s.* promulgación, proclama(ción), publicación.

promulgator [-geitɔ(r)], **promulger** [-džœ(r)], *s.* promulgador.

pronaos [pronéjas], *s.* (arq.) pronaos.

pronation [pronéišɔn], *s.* (fisiol.) pronación.

prone [próun], *a.* prono, postrado; inclinado, pendiente; prono, dispuesto, propenso.

proneness [-nis], *s.* postración; inclinación; propensión, tendencia.

prong [práŋ], *s.* púa, diente, punta (de tenedor, horquilla, etc.); pitón de asta; punta de colmillo.

prongbuck, **pronghorn** [-bʌk, -hɔrn], *s.* (zool.) antílope americano.

pronged [-d], *a.* dentado, provisto de púas.

pronominal [pronáminɐl], *a.* (gram.) pronominal.

pronoun [próunaun], *s.* (gram.) pronombre.

pronounce [pronáuns]. I. *va.* pronunciar; declarar; (for.) pronunciar, dar o dictar (sentencia). II. *vn.* pronunciar; hablar magistralmente.

pronounceable [-ɐbl], *a.* pronunciable.

pronounced [-t], *a.* pronunciado, marcado, fuerte, subido.—**pronouncement** [-mɐnt], *s.* proclama, manifiesto, declaración; anuncio formal; (for.) pronunciamiento.—**pronouncing** [-iŋ], *a.* de pronunciación, con la pronunciación.

pronucleus [proniúkliʌs], *s.* (embr.) pronúcleo.

pronunciamento [pronʌnsiɐméntou], *s.* proclama, manifiesto, declaración.

pronunciation [-éišɔn], *s.* pronunciación.

proof [prúf]. I. *s.* prueba, evidencia; probación; calificación; demostración; ensayo, experimento; impenetrabilidad; (impr.) prueba; graduación normal de licores alcohólicos; (foto. y b. a.) prueba; (mat.) prueba, comprobación. II. *a.* empleado en probar, cotejar o corregir; de comprobación; impenetrable; hecho a prueba de (agua, bomba, etc.); de prueba.—**p. plane**, (elec.) plano de prueba.—**p. sheet**, prueba (de imprenta); capilla.—**p. spirit**, licor de prueba (que contiene 50% de alcohol).—**to be p. against**, ser o estar a prueba de; (fig.) ser insensible a. III. *va.* probar; hacer (a) prueba de; impermeabilizar.

proofing [-iŋ], *s.* substancia o preparación impermeabilizadora o antipermeable.

proofless [-lis], *a.* falto de prueba, no probado; sin fundamento.

proofread [-rid], *va.* y *vn.* leer y corregir pruebas.—**proofreader** [-œ(r)], *s.* corrector de pruebas.—**proofreading** [-iŋ], *s.* corrección de pruebas.

prop [prap]. I. *va.* (a veces con **up**) sostener, apuntalar, afianzar; (min.) entibar; (mar.) escorar; (arq.) apear, acodalar; ahorquillar; (fig.) mantener, sustentar. II. *s.* apoyo, puntal, paral, apeo, codal; asnilla, madrina, sustentáculo; (min.) entibo, ademe; (mar.) escora; (agr.) rodrigón, tentemozo; (fig.) apoyo, amparo, báculo, sostén, soporte; (teat.) = PROPERTY.—*pl.* (fam.) piernas.

propædeutic(al [propidjútik(ɐl], *a.* propedéutico.—**propædeutics** [-tiks], *s.* propedéutica.

propagable [prápɐgɐbl], *a.* propagable.

propaganda [prapɐgǽndɐ], *s.* propaganda.

propagandism [-dizm], *s.* propagandismo, arte y práctica de la propaganda.

propagandist [-dist], *s.* y *a.* propagandista.

propagandize [-daiz], *va.* y *vn.* hacer propaganda (a o en).

propagate [prápɐgeit]. I. *va.* propagar, multiplicar, engendrar; diseminar; propalar. II. *vn.* propagarse, multiplicarse, reproducirse; cundir.

propagating [-iŋ], *a.* propagante.

propagation [-géišɔn], *s.* propagación, generación, reproducción; diseminación, difusión.

propagative, **propagatory** [-geitiv, -gɐtɔri], *a.* propagativo.

propagator [-geitɔ(r)], *s.* propagador.

propane [próupein], *s.* (quím.) propano.

proparoxytone [prouparáksitoun], *a.* (gram.) proparoxítono, esdrújulo.

propel [propél], *va.* propulsar, impeler, empujar.

propellent [-ɐnt]. I. *a.* motor, propulsor, impelente. II. *s.* agente impelente o impulsor.

propeller [-œ(r)], *s.* impulsor, propulsor; hélice, *f.* (de un buque, de un avión); (mar.) buque de hélice.—**p. shaft**, (aut.) eje de propulsión, eje cardán.

propelling [-iŋ], *a.* de impulsión, de propulsión.—**p. power**, fuerza propulsora.

propense [propéns], *a.* (ant.) propenso.

propension, **propensity** [propénšɔn, -siti], *s.* propensión, tendencia, proclividad, predisposición.

proper [prápœ(r)], *a.* propio, conveniente, debido, apropiado, adecuado; decoroso, decente, formal, correcto; justo, exacto; propiamente dicho; (her.) natural.—**p. fraction**, (mat.) quebrado propio.—**p. noun** o **name**, (gram.) nombre propio.—**properly** [-li], *adv.* propiamente, apropiadamente; en debida forma; correctamente, oportunamente, decorosamente.—**more p.**, mejor dicho.

properness [-nis], *s.* propiedad; decoro.

propertied [prápœrtid], *a.* propietario.

property [prápœrti], *s.* propiedad; hacienda, caudal, haberes, **m.** *pl.*, bienes (in)muebles; posesión, dominio, pertenencia; (teat.) (gen. *pl.* **properties**) aderezo, cualquier objeto necesario para la representación de una obra; (Am.) utilería.—**p. man**, (teat.) el encargado de los *properties*; (Am.) utilero.—**p. owner**, terrateniente, propietario (esp. de bienes raíces).

prophecy [práfɛsi], *s.* profecía, predicción.

prophesy [-sai], *va.* y *vn.* profetizar, predecir.

prophet [práfit], *s.* profeta, *m.*, vaticinador.

prophetess [-ɪs], *s.* profetisa, sibila.

prophetic(al [profétɪk(al], *a.* profético, profetal, sibilino.

prophetically [-i], *adv.* proféticamente.

propheticalness [-nɪs], *s.* calidad de profético.

prophylactic [proufjlǽktɪk], *a.* y *s.* profiláctico.

prophylaxis [-lǽksɪs], *s.* (med.) profilaxis.

prophyll [próufjl], *s.* (bot.) bractéola.

propinquity [propíŋkwiti], *s.* propincuidad, proximidad, cercanía; parentesco.

propionic [proupiánɪk], *a.* (quím.) propiónico.

propitiable [propíʃiabl], *a.* que se puede propiciar, propiciable, favorable.

propitiate [propíʃieit], *va.* propiciar, aplacar, conciliar.—**propitiation** [-éiʃǝn], *s.* propiciación.—**propitiator** [-eitǝ(r], *s.* propiciador.—**propitiatory** [-atǝri], *a.* y *s.* propiciatorio.

propitious [propíʃas], *a.* propicio, favorable; benigno; oportuno.—**propitiously** [-li], *adv.* propiciamente.—**propitiousness** [-nɪs], *s.* calidad de propicio.

propolis [prápolɪs], *s.* (api.) propóleos, cera aleda.

proponent [propóunɛnt], *s.* y *a.* proponente, proponedor.

proportion [propórʃǝn]. I. *s.* proporción; simetría; (h)armonía; (mat.) proporción.—*pl.* tamaño, dimensiones.—**in p.,** proporcionadamente; a prorrata.—**in p. as,** o **to, a** proporción que, a medida que o de.—**out of p.,** desproporcionado. II. *va.* proporcionar, armonizar.

proportionable [-abl], *a.* proporcionable, proporcionado.—**proportionableness** [-nɪs], *s.* calidad de proporcionado.—**proportionably** [-abli], *adv.* proporcionablemente, proporcionadamente.

proportional [-al]. I. *a.* proporcional.—**p. dividers,** compás de proporción.—**p. representation,** (pol.) representación proporcional. II. *s.* (mat.) número o cantidad proporcional.

proportionality [-ǽliti], *s.* proporcionalidad.

proportionally [-ali], *adv.* proporcionalmente.

proportionate [-it]. I. *a.* proporcionado, armónico. II. [-eit], *va.* proporcionar, ajustar.

proportioned [-d], *a.* proporcionado.

proportioning [-iŋ], *s.* proporción; dosificación.

proposal [propóuzal], *s.* propuesta, proposición; oferta; declaración (de amor, etc.).

propose [propóuz]. I. *va.* proponer; proponerse, pensar, tener intención de. II. *vn.* declararse (a una mujer).

proposer [-œ(r], *s.* proponente, proponedor.

proposition [prapozíʃǝn], *s.* proposición, propuesta; (lóg. y mat.) proposición; (ret.) exposición, propósito; (mús.) tema, *m.* En lenguaje familiar se emplea a veces con alguna vaguedad en el sentido de "cosa," "asunto," "problema," "sujeto," etc.: *the war was a serious proposition,* la guerra fué cosa seria; *the working of those mines was a complicated proposition,* la explotación de esas minas era un problema complicado; *that man seems to be a very tough proposition,* ese hombre parece ser tipo muy difícil.

propositional [-al], *a.* de carácter de proposición; relativo a la proposición.

propound [propáund], *va.* proponer; presentar.

propounder [-œ(r], *s.* proponente, proponedor.

propr(a)etor [prouprítǝ(r], *s.* (hist. rom.) propretor.

proprietary [propráieteri]. I. *a.* propietario; privilegiado, patentado (apl. esp. a remedios de patente). II. *s.* propietario, dueño; hacendados, propietarios; propiedad; remedio de patente.

proprietor [-tǝ(r], *s.* propietario, dueño, amo.

proprietorship [-ʃip], *s.* propiedad.

proprietress [-trɪs], *s.* propietaria, dueña, ama.

propriety [-ti], *s.* propiedad, corrección; decoro, decencia.—*pl.* **proprieties,** reglas, canones (del arte, sociales, etc.).

propulsion [propálʃǝn], *s.* propulsión; impulso, impulsión.

propulsive, propulsory [-sɪv, -sori], *a.* propulsor, impelente.

propyl [próupil], *s.* (quím.) propilo.

propylæum [prapjlíʌm], *s.* (arq.) propileo.

propylene [próupilin], *s.* (quím.) propileno.

prorate [prouréit], *va.* prorratear.

proration [prouréiʃǝn], *s.* prorrateo.

prorogation [prourogéiʃǝn], *s.* prórroga, prorrogación; (Ingl. pol.) suspensión de las sesiones del Parlamento.—**prorogue** [prouróug], *va.* (raro) diferir, aplazar; (raro) prorrogar; (Ingl. pol.) suspender las sesiones (del Parlamento).

prosaic [prozéiik], *a.* prosaico; insulso, trivial.

prosaically [-ali], *adv.* prosaicamente.

prosaism [próuziizm], *s.* prosaísmo.

proscenium [prosínjʌm], *s.* (teat.) proscenio.

proscribe [proskráib], *va.* proscribir; encartar; prohibir; condenar, reprobar.

proscriber [-œ(r], *s.* proscriptor.

proscription [proskrípʃǝn], *s.* proscripción; encartamiento; prohibición.

proscriptive [-tiv], *a.* que proscribe.

prose [prouz]. I. *s.* prosa; discurso pesado.—**p. writer,** prosista, prosador. II. *a.* de prosa, en prosa; insulso, pesado. III. *va.* y *vn.* escribir en prosa, o en estilo pesado; prosificar; prosaizar.

prosect [prosékt], *va.* preparar disecciones anatómicas.—**prosector** [-ǫ(r], *s.* prosector.

prosecute [prásikjut]. I. *va.* continuar, (pro)seguir, llevar adelante; (for.) acusar, encausar, enjuiciar, procesar. II. *vn.* querellarse ante el juez; seguir un pleito; fiscalizar.

prosecuting [-iŋ], *a.* (for.) acusante.—**p. attorney,** fiscal; abogado de la acusación.

prosecution [-kjúʃǝn], *s.* prosecución, (pro)seguimiento; (for.) procesamiento, institución de juicio, acusación; parte actora; fiscal.

prosecutor [prásikjutǫ(r], *s.* (for.) actor, acusador, demandante; acusador oficial, fiscal.

prosecutrix [-trɪks], *s.* acusadora, demandante.

proselyte [prásɛlait]. I. *s.* prosélito, converso. II. *va.* y *vn.* hacer prosélitos, convertir.

proselytism [-izm], *s.* proselitismo.

proselytize [-aiz], *va.* y *vn.* = PROSELYTE.

prosencephalon [prasɛnséfalan], *s.* prosencéfalo, parte anterior del cerebro (los hemisferios).

prosenchyma [praséŋkimä], *s.* (bot., biol.) prosénquima, *m.*

proser [próuzœ(r], *s.* prosista, prosador.

prosification [prouzifikéiʃǝn], *s.* prosificación.

prosifier [próuzifaiœ(r], *s.* prosificador.

prosify [-fai], *va.* prosificar; prosaizar.

prosily [-li], *adv.* prosaicamente.

prosiness [-nɪs], *s.* prosaísmo, calidad de prosaico; insulsez, aridez.

prosit [próusit], *interj.* (lat.) ¡buen provecho!

proslavery [prouslǽivœri]. I. *a.* esclavista. II. *s.* defensa de la esclavitud.

prosodist [prásodist], *s.* el versado en la prosodia o métrica.—**prosodic** [prasádik], *a.* prosódico, métrico.—**prosody** [prásodi], *s.* prosodia, métrica.

prosopopœia [prasopopíjä], *s.* (ret.) prosopopeya, personificación.

prospect [práspekt]. I. *va.* y *vn.* (min.) explorar, catear, buscar. II. *s.* perspectiva, vista, panorama, *m.;* probabilidad; expectativa, esperanza; situación, orientación; (min.) indicación o señal (*f.*) de veta o criadero; cata, producto de un mineral catado, muestra; (com.) comprador o parroquiano probable o de expectativa.

prospecter, prospector [-œ(r], *s.* (min.) explorador, buscador, (Am.) cateador.

prospecting [-iŋ], *s.* (min.) calicata, exploración en busca de minas, (Am.) cateo.

prospective [prospéktiv]. I. *a.* anticipado, venidero, en perspectiva; presunto, de expectativa.—**p. customer**, (com.) cliente presunto. *V.* PROSPECT. **II.** *s.* perspectiva, vista.

prospectus [prospέktʌs], *s.* prospecto.

prosper [práspœ(r)]. **I.** *va.* prosperar, hacer medrar. **II.** *vn.* prosperar, medrar, florecer.

prosperity [praspέriti], *s.* prosperidad.

prosperous [práspœrʌs], *a.* próspero, floreciente, venturoso; favorable o propicio.—**prosperously** [-li], *adv.* prósperamente.—**prosperousness** [-nis], *s.* prosperidad.

prostate (gland) [prásteit (glænd)], *s.* (anat.) próstata, glándula prostática.

prostatic [prostǽtik], *a.* prostático.

prosthesis [prásθesis], *s.* (gram., cir.) pró(s)tesis. —**prosthetic** [prasθέtik], *a.* (gram.) pro(s)tético.

prostitute [prástitiut]. **I.** *va.* y *vn.* prostituir(se); vender(se). **II.** *s.* prostituta, ramera, puta. **III.** *a.* prostituído, prostituto; venal, mercenario, degradado.

prostitution [-tjúṣon], *s.* prostitución.

prostrate [prástreit]. **I.** *a.* postrado, humillado, prosternado; (bot.) tendido. **II.** *va.* tender, postrar; demoler, derribar; arruinar; (med.) postrar, debilitar. **III.** *vn.* postrarse, prosternarse.

prostration [-éiṣon], *s.* postración, abatimiento, depresión; (med.) postración o adinamia.

prostyle [próuṣtail], *a.* y *s.* (arq.) próstilo.

prosy [próuzi], *a.* prosaico; insulso, árido.

protagonist [protǽgonist], *s.* protagonista.

protasis [prátasis], *s.* (gram. y drama) prótasis.

protean [próutian], *a.* proteico, proteiforme.

protect [protέkt], *va.* proteger, amparar, defender, (res)guardar; poner al abrigo o a cubierto (de).—**protected cruiser**, (mar.) crucero protegido, que tiene coraza acorazada a torres blindadas, pero poco o ningún blindaje en los costados.—**protected state**, (der. int.) protectorado (territorio).

protection [protέkṣon], *s.* protección, amparo; resguardo, defensa; salvoconducto, pasaporte, carta de seguridad; (e. p.) protección; proteccionismo.

protectionism [-izm], *s.* (e. p.) proteccionismo.

protectionist [-ist], *s.* y *a.* (e. p.) proteccionista.

protective [protέktiv]. **I.** *a.* protector; (e. p.) proteccionista. **II.** *s.* protección; lo que protege; (cir.) cubierta aséptica para una herida.

protector [-to(r)], *s.* protector, amparador.

protectorate [-it], *s.* protectorado.

protectorship [-ṣip], *s.* protectoría, protectorado.

protectress [-tris], *s.* protectora, (-triz).

protégé [próutãʒei], *s.* (fr.) protegido, paniaguado.

proteid(e [próutiid], *s.* (bioquím.) = PROTEIN.

proteiform [protíiform], *a.* proteiforme, proteico.

protein [próuti(i)n], *s.* (bioquím.) proteína.— **protein, proteinaceous** [-éiʌs], *a.* proteico.

Proterozoic [praterozóuik], *a.* (geol.) proterozoico.

protest [protέst]. **I.** *va.* protestar, declarar; (com.) protestar (una letra).—**to p. for non-acceptance**, protestar por falta de aceptación.—**to p. for non-payment**, protestar por falta de pago. **II.** *vn.* protestar. **III.** [próutest], *s.* protesta(ción); (com.) protesto.—**under p.**, bajo protesta.

Protestant [prátistant], *a.* y *s.* protestante.

Protestantism [-izm], *s.* protestantismo.

protestation [pratestéiṣon], *s.* protestación; protesta, declaración.

protester [protέstœ(r)], *s.* el que protesta.

protesting [-iŋ], *a.* protestante, protestativo.

protestingly [-li], *adv.* protestando, en tono de protesta.

prothallium [proθǽliʌm], *s.* (bot.) protalo.

prothesis [práθesis], *s.* (gram., cir.) = PROSTHESIS.

prothetic [proθέtik], *a.* = PROSTHETIC.

prothonotary [proθánoteri], *s.* (for., igl.) proto-

notario.—**p. warbler,** (E. U. orn.) pájaro cantor.

prothorax [proθóuræks], *s.* (ent.) protórax.

protoblast [próutoblæst], *s.* (biol.) protoblasto.

protochloride [-klóraid], *s.* (quím.) protocloruro.

protocol [próutokal]. **I.** *s.* protocolo, registro. **II.** *va.* protocol(iz)ar.

protohistory [-hístori], *s.* protohistoria.

protolithic [-líθik], *a.* del primer período de la edad de piedra.

protomartyr [-mártœ(r)], *s.* protomártir.

protometal [-metal], *s.* protometal.

proton [próutan], *s.* (fís. y chem.) protón.

protoplasm [próutoplæzm], *s.* (biol.) protoplasma, *m.*

protoplasmic, protoplasmal, protoplasmatic [-plǽzmik, -mal, -mǽtik], *a.* protoplásm(át)ico.

protoplast [-plæst], *s.* (biol.) protoblasto.

protosulphide [-sálfaid], *s.* (quím.) protosulfuro.

prototype [-taip], *s.* prototipo; arquetipo.

prototyp(ic)al [-táipal, -típikal], *a.* prototípico.

protoxid(e [protáksaid], *s.* (quím.) protóxido.

Protozoa [proutozóuã], *s. pl.* (zool.) protozo(ari)os.—**protozoan** [-n]. **I.** *a.* y *s.* protozoario. **II.** *s.* protozoo.

protract [protrǽkt], *va.* alargar, prolongar; (raro) demorar, dilatar; (top., etc.) trazar (un plano) por medio del transportador. *V.* PROTRUDE.

protracted [-id], *a.* largo, prolongado, lento.

protractile [-il], *a.* que se puede alargar hacia delante; (zool.) protráctil.

protraction [protrǽkṣon], *s.* prolongación, continuación; demora; (top., etc.) trazamiento (de un plano) con el transportador.

protractive [-tiv], *a.* que alarga, prolonga, etc.; dilatorio.

protractor [-to(r)], *s.* prolongador; (dib.) transportador (instrumento); (anat.) músculo extensor; (sast.) molde o regla.

protrude [protrúd]. **I.** *va.* empujar, sacar fuera. **II.** *vn.* salir fuera o sobresalir.—**protrusi(b)le** [-si(b)l], *a.* que puede sacarse o alargarse.— **protrusion** [-ʒon], *s.* acción de sacar o empujar hacia afuera; parte (*f.*) que sobresale; proyección; (med.) protrusión.—**protrusive** [-siv], *a.* que sobresale o tiende a sobresalir; que empuja hacia adelante.

protuberance, protuberancy [protiúberans, -i], *s.* protuberancia, prominencia, resalto.—**protuberant** [-ant], *a.* protuberante, prominente, saliente.—**protuberate** [-eit], *vn.* sobresalir, resaltar.

proud [práud], *a.* orgulloso; soberbio, arrogante, altivo, altanero, ufano; majestuoso; (poét.) brioso, pujante.—**p. flesh**, (cir.) tejido de granulación, bezo, carnosidad.—**to be p. (of)**, enorgullecerse, preciarse, ufanarse (de).—**proudly** [-li], *adv.* soberbiamente; orgullosamente.

provable [prúvabl], *a.* demostrable, comprobable.

prove [prúv]. **I.** *va.* (*pp.* PROVED o PROVEN) probar, demostrar; comprobar; acreditar, evidenciar, substanciar; poner a prueba, examinar, experimentar; (for.) abrir y hacer público (un testamento) (*V.* PROBATE); (impr.) sacar prueba de.—**proving ground**, campo de prueba. **II.** *vn.* resultar, venir a parar, salir (bien o mal); demostrar que es (capaz, etc.).

proven [-n], *pp.* y *a.* (com)probado; experimentado; (for.) probado, demostrado.—**not p.**, veredicto de no probado.

Provençal [prouvansál]. **I.** *a.* y *s.* provenzal. **II.** *s.* provenzal, lemosín (lengua de oc).

provender [próuvendœ(r)], *s.* forraje.

provenience [províniens], *s.* procedencia, origen.

proverb [práverb], *s.* proverbio; adagio, refrán. —**proverbial** [provérbial], *a.* proverbial; muy notorio.—**proverbialist** [-ist], *s.* refranista, (fam.) proverbista.—**proverbially** [-i], *adv.* proverbialmente.

provide [prováid]. **I.** *va.* proveer, proporcionar,

surtir, suplir, abastecer, suministrar; estipular.
II. *vn.* (con **for**) mantener, proveer lo necesario, sufragar gastos, abastecer de víveres; encargarse de; tener en cuenta; precaverse, tener cuidado, tomar precauciones, prepararse; disponer, dar disposiciones para, sobre, o con respecto a; providenciar, dar providencias para.—**to p. against**, precaver, prevenir algún riesgo.—**provided (that)**, con tal que, a condición que, siempre que.

providence [právidẹns], *s.* providencia; (raro) previsión; prudencia; frugalidad, economía; (**P.**) la Providencia, Dios.

provident [právidẹnt], *a.* próvido, providente; previsor; prudente; económico.

providential [-dénŝạl], *a.* providencial.

providentially [-i], *adv.* providencialmente.

providently [právidẹntli], *adv.* próvidamente.

provider [prováidœ(r)], *s.* proveedor, provisor, suministrador, abastecedor.

providing [-diṇ], *conj.* con tal que.

province [právins], *s.* provincia; obligación, incumbencia, competencia.—**that is not my p.**, eso no me toca, no es de mi incumbencia.

provincial [provínŝạl]. **I.** *a.* provincial; provinciano; rudo, campesino, grosero. **II.** *s.* provinciano; (igl.) provincial.—**provincialism** [-izm], *s.* provincialismo.—**provincialist** [-ist], *s.* provinciano.—**provinciality** [-ŝiéliti], *s.* carácter provinciano.

provincially [-ŝạli], *adv.* a modo provinciano.

provincialship [-ŝạlŝip], *s.* (igl.) provincialato.

provine [prováin], *va.* (agr.) amugronar.

provision [províẓọn]. **I.** *s.* provisión, aprovisionamiento, abastecimiento; medida, disposición, estipulación.—*pl.* provisiones, comestibles, víveres.—**till farther p. be made**, hasta más proveer.—**to make p. for** = TO PROVIDE FOR. **II.** *va.* proveer, abastecer, bastimentar.

provisional [-ạl], *a.* provisional, interino.—**provisionally** [-i], *adv.* provisionalmente, interinamente, por el (o lo) pronto.

proviso [prováiẓọu], *s.* estipulación, condición.

provisorily [-zoríli], *adv.* condicionalmente.

provisory [-i], *a.* provisional, (Am. o gal.) provisorio; condicional, que lleva estipulación.

provocation [pravokéiŝọn], *s:* provocación; excitación, estímulo.

provocative [provákạtiv]. **I.** *a.* provocativo, provocador. **II.** *s.* estimulante.—**provocativeness** [-nịs], *s.* calidad de provocativo.

provoke [provóuk]. **I.** *va.* provocar, irritar, encolerizar; excitar, incitar; causar, promover. **II.** *vn.* causar enojo, excitar cólera.—**provoker** [-œ(r)], *s.* provocador.—**provoking** [-iṇ], *a.* provocativo, provocante, irritante.—**provokingly** [-li], *adv.* provocativamente.

provost [právọst], *s.* preboste; (igl.) prepósito, pavorde; (Ingl.) director de colegio.—**p. marshal** [próuvọu márŝạl], (mil.) capitán preboste.

provostship [-ŝip], *s.* prebostazgo; prepositura.

prow [práu], *s.* (mar.) proa; tajamar.

prowess [-is], *s.* valentía; proeza, hazaña.

prowl [prául], *va.* y *vn.* rondar (para robar o vigilar); merodear; andar acechando; vagar.

prowler [-œ(r)], *s.* vago; rondador; merodeador.

proximal [práksimạl], *a.* (biol.) próximo.

proximate [práksimit], *a.* próximo, inmediato.

proximately [-li], *adv.* próxima o inmediatamente.

proximity [praksímiti], *s.* proximidad, cercanía, inmediación, propincuidad.

proximo [práksimou], *adv.* del o en el mes próximo.

proxy [práksi], *s.* apoderado, delegado, poderhabiente; procuración, poder.—**by p.**, por poder, mediante apoderado o substituto.

prude [prud], *s.* mojigata, remilgada, gazmoña.

prudence [prúdẹns], *s.* prudencia, cordura, juicio, discreción, circunspección, cautela.

prudent [-ẹnt], *a.* prudente, cuerdo, juicioso, discreto, circunspecto, caut(elos)o.

prudential [prudénŝạl], *a.* prudencial.

prudentially [-i], *adv.* prudencialmente.

prudently [prúdẹntli], *adv.* prudentemente.

prudery [prúdœri], *s.* melindre(ría), remilgo, gazmoñería, pudibundez, dengue.

prudish [prúdiŝ], *a.* gazmoño, remilgado, denguero.—**prudishness** [-nịs], *s.* = PRUDERY.

prune [prun]. **I.** *va.* y *vn.* (agri.) podar, cortar, (esca)mondar; expurgar. *V.* PREEN. **II.** *s.* (bot.) ciruela (pasa), pruna.—**p. tree**, variedad de ciruelo.

prunella, prunello [prunélạ, -ou], *s.* (tej.) sempiterna, rompecoches, (Am.) prunela.

pruner [prúnœ(r)], *s.* podador.

pruniferous [prunífẹrʌs], *a.* (bot.) que produce ciruelas.

pruning [prúniṇ], *s.* poda, (re)monda, escamonda.—**p. knife**, podadera, podón, márcola.—**p. shears**, podaderas, tijeras para podar.

prurience, pruriency [prúriẹns, -i], *s.* comezón, *f.*, prurito; sensualidad.—**prurient** [-ẹnt], *a.* salaz, lascivo; anheloso.

prurigo [pruráigou], *s.* (med.) comezón, *f.*, prurigo.

Prussian [prʌ́ŝạn], *a.* y *s.* prusiano.—**P. blue**, azul de Prusia; ferrocianuro férrico.

Prussianism [-izm], *s.* prusianismo, militarismo opresivo y ambicioso.

prussiate [prʌ́ŝieit], *s.* (quím.) prusiato.

prussic [prʌ́sik], *a.* (quím.) prúsico.

pry [prái]. **I.** *va.* y *vn.* espiar, acechar, atisbar, observar, registrar o escudriñar; (mec.) alzaprimar, apalancar.—**to p. apart**, separar.—**to p. off**, despegar.—**to p. into**, fisgar, fiscalizar, curiosear, entremeterse, (fam.) husmear.—**to p. out a secret**, arrancar un secreto. **II.** *s.* inspección, reconocimiento o registro escrupuloso; persona curiosa o entremetida; (mec.) palanca, barra, alzaprima.—**pryer** [-œ(r)], *s.* = PRIER.

prying [-iṇ]. **I.** *a.* curioso, entremetido, inquisitivo, husmeador. **II.** *s.* acción del verbo TO PRY; intromisión.

prytaneum [pritạníʌm], *s.* pritaneo (en Atenas).

psalm [sám], *s.* salmo; himno.

psalmbook [-buk], *s.* salterio. *V.* PSALTER.

psalmist [-ist], *s.* salmista.

psalmody [-odi *o* sálmodi], *s.* salmodia.

psalter [sóltœ(r)], *s.* salterio, salmodia.

psalterium [soltíriʌm], *s.* (zool.) libro, omaso, tercer estómago de los rumiantes.

psaltery [sóltœri], *s.* (mús.) salterio.

pseudo [sjúdou], *a.* (p)seudo, falso, pretendido. Se emplea en muchas palabras compuestas cuyo significado es obvio; v. gr.: *pseudo-apostle*, seudo apóstol, falso apóstol; *pseudo-emperor*, pretendido emperador; *pseudo-science*, falsa ciencia.

pseudomembrane [-mémbrein], *s.* (anat.) seudomembrana.

pseudomorph [-mɔrf], *s.* (min.) seudomorfo; forma irregular o falsa.—**pseudomorphous** [-mórfʌs], *a.* seudomorfo.

pseudonym [sjúdonim], *s.* seudónimo.

pseudonymous [sjudánimʌs], *a.* seudónimo.

pseudopod [sjúdopad], *s.*, **pseudopodal** [sjudópodạl], *a.* (biol.) seudópodo.

pshaw [ŝɔ], *interj.* ¡bah! ¡fuera! ¡quita allá!

Psittaci [(p)sítạsai], *s. pl.* (orn.) sitácidos.

psittacosis [(p)sitakóusis], *s.* (med.) (p)sitacosis.

psoas [(p)sóuæs], *s.* (anat.) psoas (músculo).

psoriasis [(p)soráiạsis], *s.* (med.) (p)soríasis.

psyche [(p)sáiki], *s.* psique o psiquis; mente, *f.*

psychiatric(al [saikiǽtrik(ạl], *a.* psiquiátrico.—**psychiatrist** [(p)saikáiạtrist], *s.* psiquiatra o psicópata, *mf.*—**psychiatry** [-tri], *s.* psiquiatría.

psychic(al [(p)sáikik(ạl], *a.* psíquico, anímico.

psychoanalysis [(p)saikoạnélisis], *s.* psicoanálisis.—**psychoanalyst** [-énạlist], *s.* psicoanalista; alienista.

Para la pronunciación véase la clave al principio del libro.

psychoanalyze [-ǽnǝlaiz], va. psicoanalizar, someter a psicoanálisis, examinar psicoanalíticamente.

psychogenesis [-dʒénɛsis], s. psicogénesis o psicogenia.—**psychogenic** [-dʒénik], a. psicogénico, psicógeno.

psychologic(al [(p)saikolǘdʒik(ǝl], a. psicológico.—**psychologist** [(p)saikǘlodʒist], s. psicólogo.—**psychology** [-dʒi], s. psicología.

psychometer [(p)saikǘmɛtœ(r)], s. psicómetro.—**psychometry** [-tri], s. psicometría.

psychopath [(p)sáikopæθ], s. psicópata, mf., el que sufre de enfermedad mental; psicópata, alienista.

psychopathology [(p)saikopǝθálodʒi], s. psicopatología, patología de la mente.

psychopathy [(p)saikápǝθi], s. psicopatía.

psychophysics [(p)saikofíziks], s. psicofísica.

psychophysiology [-fizjálodʒi], s. psicofisiología, fisiología psicológica.

psychosis [(p)saikóusis], s. psicosis.

psychotherapeutics [(p)saikoθerǝpiútiks], **psychotherapy** [-θérǝpi], s. psicoterapia.

psychotic [(p)saikátik]. I. s. y a. psicótico, psicopático, que sufre de enfermedad mental. II. a. psicótico, relativo a la psicosis.

psychrometer [(p)saikrámɛtœ(r)], s. psicrómetro.

ptarmigan [tármigǝn], s. (orn.) lagópodo.

pteropod [(p)téropǝd], s. y a. (zool.) pterópodo.

ptisan [tízǝn], s. (farm.) tisana.

Ptolemaic [talǝméijik], a. ptolemaico.

ptomain(e [tóumein], s. (bioquím.) (p)tomaína.

ptyalin [(p)táiǝlin], s. (bioquím.) (p)tialina.

ptyalism [-izm], s. (med.) (p)tialismo, salivación excesiva.

pub [pʌb], s. (Ingl., fam.) taberna.

puberty [piúbœrti], s. pubertad; pubescencia.

pubes [piúbiz], s. (anat.) pubes o pubis, m. (región).

pubescence [piubésɛns], s. pubescencia, pubertad; (bot.) pelusa, vello.—**pubescent** [-ɛnt], a. pubescente, púber(o); (bot.) pubescente, velloso.

pubic [piúbik], a. (anat.) pubiano, púbico.—**p. region**, pubis, m.

pubis [piúbis], s. (anat.) pubis, m. (hueso).

public [páblik]. I. a. público; común; notorio.—**p. conveyance**, vehículo (diligencia, ómnibus, etc.) del servicio público.—**p. employee**, burócrata, mf.—**p. health**, higiene pública.—**p. house**, posada, hostería, fonda; (Ingl.) cantina.—**p. lands**, tierras incultas nacionales, tierras baldías.—**p. law**, derecho público; derecho internacional.—**p. loan**, empréstito.—**p. notice**, cedulón, bando; manifiesto.—**p. officer**, funcionario público.—**p. prosecutor**, fiscal.—**p. rest room**, **p. toilet**, inodoro o retrete público; quiosco de necesidad.—**p.-spirited**, patriótico, de espíritu cívico o público.—**p. stores**, depósito aduanero.—**p. utility**, obra o empresa de servicio público.—**p. weal**, bien público.—**p. works**, obras públicas.—**the general p.**, el común de las gentes.—**to make p.**, publicar, sacar a plaza, poner de manifiesto. II. s. público.

publican [-ǝn], s. publicano; (Ingl.) mesonero, posadero, tabernero.

publication [pʌblikéiʃǝn], s. publicación; divulgación; promulgación; proclama(ción); revista, etc.

publicist [páblisist], s. publicista.

publicity [pʌblísiti], s. publicidad, notoriedad.—**p. bureau**, u **office**, agencia publicitaria.—**p. man**, o **agent**, agente de publicidad o propaganda.

publicize [páblisaiz], va. dar publicidad a, divulgar, publicar.

publicly [páblikli], adv. públicamente.

publish [pábliʃ], va. publicar, divulgar, propalar; promulgar; dar a conocer; dar a luz; editar.—to p. the banns, amonestar, correr las amonestaciones o proclamas.

publisher [-œ(r)], s. editor; publicador.

publishing [-iŋ], a. editorial, de publicaciones.—**p. house**, (casa) editorial, casa editora.

puccoon [pʌkún], s. (bot.) orcaneta, litospermo.

puck [pʌk], s. duende travieso; (dep.) disco de goma (en el hockey sobre hielo).

puckball [pákbɔl], s. (bot.) bejín.

pucker [pákœ(r)]. I. va. (cost.) fruncir, plegar, recoger, arrugar. II. s. (cost.) frunce o fruncido, fuelle, pliegue, arruga; (fam.) agitación.

puckish [pákiʃ], a. travieso.

pudding [púdiŋ], s. (coc.) budín, (neol.) pudín.—**p. dish** o **pan**, tortera, tartera.—**p. stone**, (geol.) pudinga.

puddle [pádl]. I. s. charco, poza; cimiento hidráulico. II. va. (fund.) pudelar; (hidr.) cimentar el fondo de un canal; enlodar, enfangar.

puddler [pádlœ(r)], s. (fund.) pudelador; horno de pudelar.

puddling [pádliŋ], s. (fund.) pudelación, pudelaje; cimiento hidráulico; (hidr.) cimentación.—**p. furnace**, horno de pudelar.

puddly [pádli], a. lodoso, cenagoso.

pudency [piúdensi], s. recato, pudor.

pudenda [piudéndǝ], s. pl. (anat.) órganos genitales.—**pudendal** [-dǝl], a. pudendo.—**pudendum** [-dʌm], s. vulva.

pudgy [pádʒi], a. (fam.) regordete, gordiflón.

pudicity [piudísiti], s. pudicicia, pudor.

pudu [piúdiu], s. (zool., Chile) pudú.

pueblo [pwébloų], s. pueblo, aldea; casa comunal o aldea de indios.—**P. Indians**, tribus indígenas agrícolas de México y el sur de los E. U.

puericulture [piúġrikǝlchŭ(r)], s. puericultura.

puerile [piúġril], a. pueril, infantil.

puerileness [-nis], **puerility** [-íliti], s. puerilidad; niñada, niñería.

puerilism [-izm], s. puerilismo, infantilismo.

puerperal [piuœrpérǝl], a. (med.) puerperal.—**p. fever**, fiebre (f.) puerperal.

puerperium [-píriʌm], **puerpery** [-pġri], s. (med.) puerperio, sobreparto.

Puerto Rican [pwértoų ríkǝn], a. y s. = PORTO RICAN.

puff [pʌf]. I. s. resoplido; soplo, bufido; bocanada, fum(ar)ada; (Am.) chupada, pitada (de cigarro, etc.); bombo o elogio exagerado; colcha o cobertor (de ejedrón, lana, etc.); (cost.) bollo, bullón; (coc.) especie de bollo o buñuelo. V. POWDER PUFF.—**p. adder**, víbora venenosa.—**p. box**, polvera.—**p. paste**, (coc.) hojaldre, mf.—**p. of wind**, racha, ráfaga, soplo; ventolera. II. va. (a veces con up) hinchar, inflar; engreír, envanecer; ensalzar, dar bombo; (cost.) abollonar; (Am.) chupar (pipa, etc.). III. vn. inflarse, hincharse; engreírse; bufar, dar bufidos; resoplar, resollar; jadear, hipar; echar bocanadas; fumar, (Am.) pitar.—**to p. away**, disipar a soplos.—**to p. up**, hincharse, henchirse, ahuecarse, esponjarse, engreírse.

puffball [páfbɔl], s. (bot.) bejín.

puffer [páfœ(r)], s. soplador; ponderador; (Am.) chupador; (for.) = BY-BIDDER.

puffily [páfili], adv. hinchadamente; jadeando.

puffin [páfin], s. (orn.) pufino.

puffiness [páfinis], s. hinchazón, f.; (med.) hinchazón, intumescencia, tumefacción.

puffy [páfi], a. hinchado, inflado, entumecido.—**p. style**, estilo campanudo.

pug [pʌg]. I. s. moño o castaña (del pelo); (alb.) torta.—**p. (dog)**, doguillo, perro pug.—**p. mill**, artesa de ladrillería; amasadera.—**p. nose**, nariz respingada.—**p.-nosed**, braco, nacho. II. va. (hidr.) cimentar; (alb.) embarrar, rellenar con torta o argamasa.

pugh [piu], interj. ¡puf! ¡uf! ¡fo!

pugilism [piúdʒilizm], s. pugilato, pugilismo, boxeo.—**pugilist** [-list], s. pugilista, púgil, boxeador.—**pugilistic** [-lístik], a. de pugilato.

pugnacious [pʌgnéiʃʌs], *a.* pugnaz, belicoso.
pugnacity [pʌgnǽsiti], *s.* pugnacidad.
puisne [pjúni], *a.* (for.) (juez) pedáneo.
puissance [pjúisʌns], *s.* (poét.) pujanza, poder.
puissant [-ʌnt], *a.* pujante, fuerte.
puke [pjuk]. I. *s.* vómito; (med.) vomitivo, emético. II. *va.* y *vn.* vomitar.
pulchritude [pʌlkritjud], *s.* pulcritud.
pule [pjul], *vn.* piar, pipiar; gemir, llorar.
pulex [pjúleks], *s.* (ent.) pulga.
pulicene [pjúlisin], **pulicose** [-kous], *a.* pulgoso.
puling [pjúliŋ]. I. *a.* piador, piante; llorón; enfermizo. II. *s.* piada, pío; lloriqueo, gimoteo.
pull [pul]. I. *va.* tirar de, tirar hacia sí, cobrar; halar, arrastrar; estirar, arrancar, sacar (dientes, etc.); pelar, desplumar (aves); (mar.) bogar o remar; (impr.) sacar (una prueba); (fam.) sorprender y copar un garito; prender (a uno); sacar (un arma).—**to p. a face,** hacer una mueca.—**to p. a long face,** poner la cara larga.—**to p. asunder,** o **away,** arrancar, separar o quitar con violencia.—**to p. back,** tirar hacia atrás; hacer recular o cejar.—**to p. down,** derribar, demoler; degradar, deponer; humillar, abatir.—**to p. in,** tirar hacia adentro; contener, refrenar.—**to p. in,** o **to, pieces,** hacer trizas, desgarrar, despedazar.—**to p. off,** arrancar; (fam.) efectuar, llevar a cabo.—**to p. one's leg,** (fam.) tomarle el pelo a uno.—**to p. one's self together,** recobrar la calma; arreglarse, componerse.—**to p. out,** sacar, arrancar.—**to p. the long bow,** exagerar, baladronear.—**to p. the trigger,** apretar el gatillo.—**to p. the wool over one's eyes,** engañar a uno como a un chino.—**to p. through,** sacar de dificultades o de un aprieto.—**to p. together,** llevarse bien; obrar armoniosamente.—**to p. up,** extirpar, desarraigar; contener, refrenar (un caballo); arrimar (una silla); subir (las persianas).—**p. up stakes,** (fam.) prepararse para partir, liar el petate, alzar tiendas (fig.). II. *vn.* tirar con esfuerzo; tironear, dar un tirón; ejercer tracción (un motor, etc.).—**to p. ahead,** marchar avante; (mar.) halar avante.—**to p. apart,** romperse por tracción.—**to p. for,** estar o abogar por (una persona).—**to p. in,** contenerse, refrenarse; llegar (un tren).—**to p. over to the left** (**right**), desviarse hacia la izquierda (derecha).—**to p. through,** salir de un trance o aprieto.—**to p. up,** detenerse, refrenarse, hacer alto. III. *s.* tirón, estirón; tirador (de puerta, etc.); tracción; (fam.) influjo, influencia; (impr.) impresión hecha con la prensa de mano; (dep.) ejercicio de remos, boga.—**p. box,** (elec.) caja de acceso a los conductores y tubos que los llevan.—**p. switch,** interruptor de tiro o de cadena.—**to have a p.,** (fam.) tener buenas aldabas o una buena cuña. IV. *interj.* ¡hala!
pullback [púlbæk], *s.* acción de tirar hacia atrás; rémora, estorbo.
puller [púlœ(r)], *s.* el o lo que tira, saca o arranca; extractor, arrancador, sacador.
pullet [púlit], *s.* polla, gallina a medio crecer.
pulley [púli], *s.* polea, trocla, garrucha; (mar.) motón, cuaderual; (anat.) tróclea.—**p. block,** aparejo de poleas); *pl.* (mar.) motonería.—**p. wheel,** roldana.—**set of pulleys,** poleame.
pullman [púlmʌn], *s.* (f. c.) coche salón; coche cama o dormitorio (ll. t. **P. car**).
pull-over [púl ouvœ(r)], *s.* elástica, jersey, *f.*
pullulate [pʌlyuleit], *vn.* pulular.
pulmometer [pʌlmámetœ(r)], *s.* (fisiol.) pulmómetro, espirómetro.
pulmonary [pʌlmoneri], *a.* pulmonar.
pulmonate [pʌlmoneit], *s.* y *a.* (zool.) pulmonado.
pulmonic [pʌlmánik]. I. *s.* (farm.) pectoral; (med.) pulmoníaco, el que tiene una afección pulmonar. II. *a.* pulmonar; pulmoníaco.
pulmotor [pʌlmoutɔ(r)], *s.* pulmotor (nombre de

fábrica), pulmón de acero, aparato de respiración artificial.
pulp [pʌlp]. I. *s.* pulpa; (bot.) pulpa; la carne o parte mollar de la fruta; (anat.) pulpa; pulpejo; (pap.) pulpa, pasta, lechada. II. *va.* reducir a pulpa; descerezar (café).
pulpiness [-inis], **pulpousness** [-ʌsnis], *s.* calidad de pulposo.
pulpit [púlpit], *s.* (igl.) púlpito; clero; ambón.— **the p.,** el clero; predicación.
pulpous [pʌlpʌs], **pulpy** [pʌlpi], *a.* pulposo, carnoso, mollar.
pulque [púlki], *s.* pulque.—**p. brandy,** mezcal.
pulpwood [pʌlpwud], *s.* (pap.) madera de pulpa.
pulsate [pʌlseit], *vn.* pulsar, latir rítmicamente.
pulsatile [pʌlsatil], *a.* pulsátil, pulsativo; latiente; (mús.) de percusión.
pulsating [pʌlseitiŋ], *a.* pulsativo.
pulsation [pʌlséiʃon], *s.* pulsación, latido.
pulsative [pʌlsativ], *a.* pulsativo.
pulsator [pʌlséitɔ(r)], *s.* lo que pulsa, late o golpea; (hidr.) pulsómetro.
pulsatory [pʌlsatori], *a.* pulsante, latiente.
pulse [pʌls]. I. *s.* pulso; pulsación, vibración; (bot.) legumbres colectivamente (garbanzos, habas, lentejas, etc.). II. *vn.* pulsar, latir, batir.
pulseless [-lis], *a.* sin pulso; falto de energía.
pulsimeter [pʌlsímetœ(r)], *s.* (med.) pulsímetro o pulsómetro, esfigmómetro.
pulsion [pʌlʃon], *s.* (pro)pulsión; impulso.
pulsometer [pʌlsámetœ(r)], *s.* (med.) pulsímetro, esfigmómetro; (hidr.) pulsómetro.
pultaceous [pʌltéiʃʌs], *a.* pultáceo; pulposo.
pulverizable [pʌlvɛraizabl], *a.* pulverizable, polvorizable.—**pulverization** [-éiʃon], *s.* pulverización, trituración.—**pulverize** [-aiz], *va.* pulverizar, reducir a polvo.—**pulverizer** [-œ(r)], *s.* pulverizador.
pulverulence [pʌlvérulens], *s.* pulverulencia, abundancia de polvo, polvareda.—**pulverulent** [-ɛnt], *a.* polvoriento, pulverulento.
puma [pjúmʌ], *s.* (zool.) puma, *mf.*
pumice [pʌmis], *va.* apomazar.—**p.** (**stone**), piedra pómez, pumita.
pumiceous [pjumíʃʌs], *a.* que contiene piedra pómez.
pummel [pʌmɛl], *va.* y *s.* = POMMEL.
pump [pʌmp]. I. *s.* (mec.) bomba, aguatocha, (mar.) pompa; (Am.) inflador (de neumático, etc.); (zap.) escarpín, zapatilla, servilla.—**p. barrel** = P. CYLINDER.—**p. brake,** o **handle,** guimbalete, manubrio de bomba; (art.) freno o amortiguador hidráulico.—**p. cylinder,** caja o cuerpo de bomba.—**p. dale,** (mar.) dala.—**p. plunger,** émbolo buzo de bomba.—**p. priming,** (pol., E. U.) "cebar la bomba," ayudar con fondos públicos para echar a andar las cosas (el comercio, la industria, etc.).—**p. rod,** o **spear,** vástago del émbolo de una bomba.— **p. water,** agua de pozo. II. *va.* y *vn.* dar a la bomba, (Am.) bombear; (fig.) sondear, tantear, sonsacar.—**to p. in,** inyectar (aire, etc.).—**to p. out,** achicar, sacar a bomba.—**to p. up,** inflar (un neumático, etc.).
pumper [-œ(r)], *s.* bombero; autobomba (del cuerpo de bomberos); sonsacador.
pumpernickel [pʌmpœrnikɛl], *s.* pan moreno.
pumping [pʌmpiŋ], *a.* de bombear.—**p. engine,** bomba de vapor.—**p. jack,** aparato de poleas de transmisión para actuar una bomba en un pozo profundo.
pumpkin [pʌmpkin o pʌŋkin], *s.* (bot.) calabaza (planta y fruto); calabacera (planta).—**p. pie,** (coc.) pastel de calabaza.
pun [pʌn]. I. *s.* equívoco, retruécano, juego de vocablos. II. *vn.* jugar del vocablo.
punch [pʌnch]. I. *va.* punz(on)ar, taladrar, horadar con punzón; sacar o cortar con punzón; aguijar o conducir (ganado); dar puñetazos, dar de puñadas, (fam.) apuñear.—**to p. a hole,** abrir un agujero. II. *s.* punzón, sacabocado(s),

máquina o instrumento de taladrar; ponche (bebida); puñada o puñetazo; (fam.) energía, actividad; vivacidad.—**punching bag,** pelota de boxeo; saco de arena.—**P. and Judy show,** títeres, *m. pl.*—**p. bowl,** bol, ponchera.—**p. die,** punzón de estampar.—**p. pliers,** sacabocado(s).—**p. press,** punzonadora.—**p. sinker,** tallador, abridor o grabador en hueco.

puncheon [pánchọn], *s.* pipa (medida de líquidos); punzón; contrapunzón, estampador; cuña; (carp.) pie derecho.

puncher [pánchœ(r)], *s.* punzón; (E. U.) vaquero, boyero.

punchinello [pạnchịnélọu], *s.* pulchinela, *m.*; títere.

punctate(d [páŋkteịt(ịd], *a.* punteado, mosqueado.

punctilio [pạŋktílịou], *s.* puntillo, punto.

punctilious [pạŋktílịạs], *a.* puntilloso, punt(u)oso, pundonoroso; etiquetero.—**punctiliousness** [-nịs], *s.* puntillo, pundonor.

punctual [páŋkchụạl], *a.* puntual; exacto.—**punctuality** [-élịtị], *s.* puntualidad; exactitud.—**punctually** [-ạlị], *adv.* puntualmente.

punctuate [-eịt], *va. y vn.* puntuar.

punctuation [-éịṣọn], *s.* (gram.) puntuación.

puncture [páŋkchụ(r)]. I. *va.* punzar; pinchar, perforar, agujerear, picar.—**punctured wound,** herida hecha con un instrumento puntiagudo. II. *s.* pinchadura, pinchazo, perforación; (med., etc.) puntura, punzad(ur)a, picad(ur)a; (cir.) punción; (zool.) hoyo.—**p.-proof,** a prueba de pinchazos (llanta, etc.).

pundit [pándịt], *s.* erudito; bracmán sabio.

pungency [pándžẹnsị], *s.* picante, punta, sabor, resquemo; acerbidad, acrimonia, mordacidad.

pungent [-ẹnt], *a.* picante; pungente, mordicante; acre, mordaz, acerbo; (zool.) punzante; (bot.) puntiagudo.

Punic [pịúnịk], *a.* púnico.

puniness [pịúnịnịs], *s.* encanijamiento.

punish [pánịš], *va.* castigar, penar, corregir.—**punishable** [-ạbl], *a.* penable, punible.—**punishability** [-ạbílịtị], **punishableness** [-ạblnịs], *s.* (for.) penalidad.—**punisher** [-œ(r)], *s.* castigador.—**punishment** [-mẹnt], *s.* castigo; pena, punición, justicia.

punitive, punitory [pịúnịtịv, -torị], *a.* penal, punitivo.

punk [páŋk]. I. *s.* yesca, hupe, *f.*, pebete. II. *a.* (fam.) muy malo, sin valor ni mérito.

punka(h [páŋkạ], *s.* abanico colgante.

punner, punster [pán(st)œ(r)], *s.* equivoquista.

punt [pánt]. I. *va.* impeler una batea apoyando una vara en el fondo del río; (dep.) dar un puntapié al balón en el aire. II. *vn.* cazar, pescar o ir en batea; despedir el balón con un puntapié; apuntar, en juegos de azar. III. *s.* (mar.) batea, barquichuelo de fondo plano; (dep.) puntapié dado al balón en el aire.

punter [-œ(r)], *s.* el que impele una batea; el que despide un balón a puntapiés; pelete (en juegos de azar).

punty [pántị], *s.* (vid.) pontil, puntel.

puny [pịúnị], *a.* encanijado; pequeño, diminuto; mezquino.—**p. child,** (fam.) redroj(uel)o, regojo.

pup [páp]. I. *vn.* parir la perra. II. *s.* cachorro, perrillo.—**p. tent,** (fam.) pequeña tienda de campaña.

pupa [pịúpạ], *s.* (ent.) ninfa, crisálida.

pupil [pịúpịl], *s.* (anat.) pupila, niña del ojo; (for.) pupilo; discípulo, alumno, escolar, educando.

pupilage [-ịdž], *s.* pupilaje.

pupil(l)ary, pupil(l)ar [-ẹrị, -ạ̈(r)], *a.* (anat. y for.) pupilar.—**p. margin,** borde de la pupila.

puppet [pápịt], *s.* títere, muñeco, monigote, maniquí, marioneta; persona servil, que sirve de instrumento a otra.—**p. valve** = POPPET VALVE.—**p. show,** función de títeres.

puppeteer [-ír], **puppetman** [-mæn], *s.* titiritero.

puppy [pápị], *s.* cachorro, perrillo; (despec.) fatuo, petimetre; monicaco, trompeta, *m.*—**p. love** = CALF LOVE.

puppyish [-ịš], *a.* parecido a un cachorro; fatuo.

puppyism [-ịzm], *s.* fatuidad.

purblind [pœrblaịnd], *a.* cegato.—**purblindness** [-nịs], *s.* ofuscamiento de la vista.

purchase [pœrchịs]. I. *va.* comprar, mercar; feriar; adquirir; (mec. y mar.) mover o sujetar con aparejo. II. *s.* compra, (fam.) merca; adquisición; (mec.) palanca, aparejo, maniobra.—**not to be worth a day's p.,** (fam.) estar en las últimas.

purchaseable [pœrchạ̈sạbl], *a.* comprable.

purchaser [-œ(r)], *s.*, **purchasing** [-ịŋ], *a.* comprador; adquiridor.—**purchasing power,** valor mercantil (de la moneda), poder adquisitivo; capacidad consumidora o de comprar.

pure [pịúr], *a.* puro (en todas sus acepciones); neto; castizo (idioma, etc.).—**p. mathematics,** matemáticas puras.—**pureblood** [-blʌd], **pureblooded** [-ịd], *a.* de sangre pura; castizo.

purebred [-bréd], **pure-breed** [-bríd], *s. y a.* (animal) de raza pura.

purée [pịuréị], *s.* (coc.) puré.

purely [pịúrlị], *adv.* puramente; meramente, simplemente; netamente.

pureness [-nịs], *s.* pureza.

purfle [pœrfl]. I. *s.* orla. II. *va.* orlar.

purgation [pœrgéịṣọn], *s.* purgación, purgamiento; purificación; (for.) purgación.

purgative [pœrgạtịv]. I. *a.* purgador, purgativo, purgante. II. *s.* (med.) purga, purgante.

purgatorial [-tórịạl], *a.* del purgatorio; purgativo, expiatorio.

purgatory [pœrgạtorị], *s.* purgatorio.

purge [pœrdž]. I. *va.* purgar, purificar, limpiar, clarificar, acrisolar; justificar; (med.) purgar. II. *vn.* purificarse. III. *s.* (med.) purga(nte), catártico; purgamiento, purgación.

purger [-œ(r)], *s.* purgador; purificador; (med.) purga(nte).

purging [-ịŋ]. I. *a.* purgativo, purgante. II. *s.* purgación; purificación, expiación; diarrea.

purifiable [pịurịfáịabl], *a.* purificable, depurable.—**purification** [-ịkéịṣọn], *s.* purificación, depuración; expiación; defecación.—**purificative, purificatory** [pịúrịfịkạ̈tịv, pịurịfịkạ̈torị], *a.* purificatorio, purificante.—**purificator** [pịúrịfịkeịtọ(r)], *s.* (igl.) purificador.—**purifier** [-fạịœ(r)], *s.* purificador.—**puriform** [-form], *a.* (med.) puriforme, que se parece al pus.

purify [-faị]. I. *va.* purificar; purgar, limpiar, defecar, refinar, clarificar; expiar; expurgar, depurar. II. *vn.* purificarse.—**purifying** [-ịŋ]. I. *s.* purificación. II. *a.* purificador; depurador.

purine [pịúrịn], *s.* (quím.) purina.

purism [pịúrịzm], *s.* purismo, casticismo.

purist [pịúrịst], *s.* purista, casticista.

Puritan [pịúrịtạn], *s. y a.* puritano.—**puritanic(al** [-ténịk(ạl], *a.* puritano; riguroso, severo, rígido.—**Puritanism** [-ịzm], *s.* puritanismo.

purity [pịúrịtị], *s.* pureza; casticidad (del idioma, etc.); limpieza (de sangre).

purl [pœrl]. I. *va.* (cost.) orlar, adornar con fleco; bordar con hilo de oro o plata. II. *vn.* murmurar o susurrar los arroyos; ondear, rizar; (ar)remolinar(se). III. *s.* murmullo, susurro; onda, rizo; (cost.) fleco de oro o plata, orla; pliegue de vestido; cierto encaje antiguo; cerveza aromatizada.

purlieus [pœrljuz], *s. pl.* cercanías, alrededores.

purlin(e [pœrlịn], *s.* (arq.) ejión, *m.*, jabalcón.

purling [pœrlịŋ]. I. *s.* murmullo, susurro, parlería (de un arroyo). II. *a.* murmurante, parlero.

purloin [pœrlóịn], *va.* hurtar, robar.

purloiner [-œ(r)], *s.* ladrón, ratero.

purparty [pœrpartị], *s.* (for.) parte, *f.*, división.

purple [pœrpl]. I. *a.* purpúreo, purpurino, morado; imperial, regio; brillante, vistoso; (ant.)

sangriento.—p. **heron**, (orn.) garza real. **II.** s. (zool.) púrpura, múrice (molusco); púrpura, (poét.) múrice (tinte y color); (hist. rom.) trábea; dignidad real o cardenalicia; (blas.) púrpura.—pl. (med.) = PURPURA. **III.** va. purpurar, teñir de púrpura.

purplish [pœrplíš], a. purpurino.

purport [pœrpórt]. **I.** s. significado, tenor, toque, substancia. **II.** [pœrpórt], va. y vn. significar, querer decir, implicar, dar a entender.

purpose [pœrpǫs]. **I.** s. propósito, fin(alidad), objeto, intención, mira, vista; resultado, utilidad; voluntad, resolución, determinación; uso, caso.—**p. clause, p. conjunction**, etc., (gram.) cláusula, conjunción, etc., final.—**for that p.**, a ese efecto.—**for what p.?** ¿con qué fin? ¿para qué?—**of p., on p.**, expresamente, de propósito, de intento, aposta.—**to come to the p.**, venir a cuento, o a(l) pelo.—**to no p.**, inútilmente, en vano, en balde.—**to the p.**, a o al propósito; al caso; al grano; de perilla.—**to very little p.**, casi para nada, con poco provecho. **II.** va. y vn. proponer(se), proyectar, intentar, designar o tener designio de.

purposeful [-fǔl], a. que tiene propósito o fin determinado.—**purposeless** [-lǐs], a. sin propósito ni fin determinado; vago.

purposely [-lǐ], adv. adrede, de intento, de industria, de propósito, expresamente.

purposive [-ǐv], a. dirigido o adaptado a un fin; intencional.—**purposively** [-lǐ], adv. con propósito, para un fin; intencionalmente.

purpura [pœrpiǔrǎ], s. (med.) púrpura; (**P.,** zool.) púrpura, múrice.

purpurate [-rejt], s. (quím.) purpurato.

purpuric [pœrpiúrǐk], a. (quím. y med.) purpúrico.

purpurin [pœrpiúrǐn], s. (quím.) purpurina.

purr [pœr]. **I.** s. ronroneo del gato; (aut.) zumbido del motor. **II.** vn. ronronear (el gato).

purse [pœrs]. **I.** s. bolsa, bolso o bolsillo; portamonedas; talega, bolsa de dinero; (fig.) peculio, riqueza; colecta, derrama.—**p. bearer**, tesorero.—**p. net**, o **seine**, manga de pescar.—**p.-proud**, envanecido por la opulencia.—**p.-shaped**, bursiforme.—**p. strings**, cerradero, cordones de la bolsa.—**to loosen the p. strings**, (fam.) aflojar o soltar la mosca. **II.** va. embolsar; fruncir, arrugar (la frente, los labios).

purseful [-fǔl], s. la cantidad que contiene una bolsa.

purser [-œ(r)], s. (mar.) contador, sobrecargo, comisario de a bordo.

pursiness [pœrsǐnǐs], s. disnea, asma, dificultad en la respiración; gordura; engreimiento.

purslane [pœrslejn], s. (bot.) verdolaga.

pursuable [pœrsiúabl], a. proseguible.

pursuance [-ǎns], s. prosecución, seguimiento, cumplimiento.

pursuant [-ǎnt]. **I.** a. consiguiente, conforme. **II.** adv. (con **to**) de acuerdo con, en cumplimiento de, según, con arreglo a.

pursue [pœrsiú], va. y vn. perseguir, dar caza, acosar; (pro)seguir, continuar; seguir (una carrera), dedicarse a, ejercer; (for.) demandar, poner pleito, procesar.

pursuer [-œ(r)], s. perseguidor.

pursuit [-t], s. (per)seguimiento, persecución, caza; práctica, ejercicio; prosecución; busca; ocupación; pretensión; conato, empeño.—**p. plane**, (aer., mil.) caza, m.—**in p. of**, en pos de.—pl. ocupaciones, estudios, investigaciones, actividades.—**p. of happiness**, busca de la felicidad o del bienestar.

pursuivant [pœrswǐvant], s. persevante.

pursy [pœrsǐ], a. asmático; obeso; engreído.

purulence, purulency [piǔrulęns, -ǐ], s. purulencia.—**purulent** [-ęnt], a. purulento.

purvey [pœrvéj], va. y vn. proveer, surtir, suministrar, abastecer.—**purveyance** [-ǎns], s. abastecimiento; abasto, suministro.—**purveyor**

[-ǫ(r)], s. proveedor, provisor, surtidor, abastecedor.

purview [pœrvjǔ], s. extensión, esfera, alcance; substancia de un estatuto; límite o alcance de una disposición legal.

pus [pʌs], s. (med.) pus, podre, f.

push [pǔš]. **I.** va. empujar, empellar, impeler; propugnar, promover, activar; oprimir, pulsar (el botón); apremiar, apretar, obligar, estrechar; importunar, molestar.—**to p. ahead**, o **through**, pujar.—**to p. away**, alejar, rechazar; apartar con la mano.—**to p. back**, rechazar, echar atrás.—**to p. down**, abatir, derribar.—**to p. in**, encajar, hacer entrar, introducir empujando.—**to p. off**, apartar con la mano; desalojar.—**to p. on**, incitar, aguijonear; apresurar.—**to p. one's self forward**, abrirse camino; entremeterse.—**to p. out**, empujar hacia fuera; echar, expulsar. **II.** vn. empujar; dar un empujón, dar empellones; apresurarse, darse prisa; acometer.—**to p. forward**, adelantarse dando empujones; avanzar, adelantar.—**to p. further**, seguir adelante.—**to p. in**, entremeterse.—**to p. off**, (mar.) desatracar.—**to p. on**, seguir adelante, avanzar. **III.** s. impulso; empuje, empujón, empellón; embestida, arremetida; apuro, aprieto; (fam.) energía, iniciativa; (mil.) ofensiva.—**p. button**, pulsador, botón de contacto, de presión o de llamada.—**p.-button switch**, (elec.) interruptor de botón.

pushball [-bǫl], s. (dep.) balón o pelota de viento, muy grande y pesado; juego en que se usa.

pushcart [-kart], s. carretilla de mano.

pusher [-œ(r)], s. empujador; (fam.) persona enérgica o agresiva; (f. c.) locomotora de empuje o trasera (ll. t. **p. locomotive**).—**p. airplane**, (aer.) avión propulsivo, el cual tiene la hélice detrás de las superficies de sustentación.—**p. grade**, (f. c.) pendiente (f.) que requiere locomotora de empuje.

pushing [-iŋ], a. impelente, empujador; activo, diligente, emprendedor; agresivo.—(**by**) **p.**, a empujones, a empellones.

pushpin [-pin], s. especie de chinche o alfiler de cabeza plana para clavar papeles, etc.; crucillo, juego de alfileres; niñería.

pusillanimity [piusilænímiti], s. pusilanimidad. —**pusillanimous** [-lénimʌs], a. pusilánime.

puss [pǔs], s. miz, m., minino, morro, micho, gata; liebre, f.; chica, mozuela; (vulg.) cara, boca.— **p. in the corner**, juego de las cuatro esquinas.

pussy [pǔsǐ], **pussycat** [-kæt], s. gatito, minino, etc.; (fam., bot.) amento de un sauce americano llamado pussy willow; cierto juego de niños.

pussyfoot [-fǔt]. **I.** vn. andar como el gato; (fam.) andarse con tiento, no declararse. **II.** a. (fam.) tímido, evasivo; prohibicionista.—**pussyfoot(er** [-œ(r)], s. (fam.) timorato, hombre de evasivas; (fam.) prohibicionista.

pussyfooting [-iŋ], s. subterfugio, evasiva; recurso a la evasión.

pustulant [pʌschǔlant], a. y s. (med.) pustulante.

pustular [pʌschǔlǎ(r)], a. (med.) pustuloso, postilloso, buboso.—**pustulate** [-lejt]. **I.** vn. formarse pústulas. **II.** a. pustuloso.

pustule [pʌschǔl], s. (med.) pústula, pupa, bubilla.—**pustulous** [-ʌs], a. puposo, pustuloso.

put [pǔt], va. (ger. PUTTING; pret. y pp. PUT) poner; situar, colocar; exponer, proponer, presentar para ser discutido; hacer, dirigir (una pregunta); expresar, declarar, interpretar; arrojar, lanzar (un peso, etc.); suponer.—**to p. about**, desconcertar; molestar.—**to p. across**, (fam.) realizar, llevar a cabo; hacer aceptar (algo).—**to p. after**, poner detrás de (sitio); posponer a (tiempo).—**to p. an end to**, poner fin a, terminar, acabar con.—**to p. a question**, hacer una pregunta o una interpelación.—**to p. aside**, deponer, descartar, desterrar; guardar, acumular.—**to p. a stop to,** poner coto o fin a; acabar con; impedir.—**to p. asunder,** separar, apartar; descasar.—**to p. away,** apartar, quitar; poner aparte; arrinconar, arrumbar; echar fuera, despedir; repudiar, rechazar; guardar, acumular; depositar.—**to p. back,** atrasar, retardar; devolver, reponer.—**to p. behind,** poner atrás; relegar a puesto o posición inferior. —**to p. by,** guardar; arrinconar; desviar, apartar.—**to p. down,** poner (en el suelo, etc.); sofocar, reprimir; deprimir, abatir, humillar, degradar; depositar; registrar, anotar, apuntar; rebajar, disminuir; hacer callar.—**to p. forth,** extender, alargar; publicar, dar a luz; producir, echar, brotar (retoños, etc.); presentar, proponer; ejercer; emplear.—**to p. forward,** adelantar; proponer, presentar (como candidato). —**to p. in,** poner en, echar en o a, meter; poner, insertar, ingerir, introducir, intercalar; presentar, hacer (reclamo, etc.); colocar (en un empleo, etc.); interponer (palabra, observación); (top., dib.) trazar (una curva, etc.); pasar o gastar (tiempo, haciendo algo).—**to p. in action,** actuar.—**to p. in a word for,** interceder por, hablar en favor de.—**to p. in an appearance,** aparecer, ir, llegar; (for.) comparecer.—**to p. in gear,** (aut.) hacer engranar. —**to p. in irons,** aherrojar.—**to p. in mind,** recordar.—**to p. in one's oar,** meter baza.—**to p. in order,** arreglar, ordenar.—**to p. in place,** colocar (en su sitio).—**to p. in, o into, practice,** poner en práctica, aplicar.—**to p. in print,** imprimir.—**to p. in the shade,** (fam.) eclipsar, dejar atrás o deslucido.—**to p. into,** meter dentro de, guardar en; expresar en.—**to p. into effect,** poner en práctica; poner en vigor.—**to p. into one's head,** meterle a uno en la cabeza.—**to p. in writing,** poner por escrito.—**to p. off,** diferir, dilatar, aplazar; desechar, apartar; evadir, entretener, salir de (con promesas); quitarse, desprenderse de (ropa, etc.).—**to p. on,** poner sobre; ponerse (ropa, etc.); calzar (zapatos, guantes, espuelas); echar o ganar (carnes); chantarse, vestir, armarse de; achacar, atribuir a; echar, poner, dar, aplicar (vapor, el freno, etc.); instigar a; engañar con; imponer, poner a; fingir, disimular; encender (las luces); (teat.) producir, representar, poner en escena.—**to p. on airs,** darse tono o ínfulas.—**to p. on one's thinking cap,** aguzar el seso, parar mientes.—**to p. on shore,** poner en tierra, desembarcar.—**to p. on the market,** lanzar al mercado.—**to p. on the spot,** poner en calzas prietas; matar.—**to p. one on, o to, one's mettle,** picar a uno el amor propio.—**to p. one's best foot forward,** (fam.) hacer uno lo sumo posible, poner sus cinco sentidos.—**to p. one's cards on the table,** jugar uno a cartas vistas, obrar franca y abiertamente.—**to p. one's foot down,** obstinarse; oponerse o negarse rotundamente; obrar resueltamente y sin cejar.—**to p. one's nose out of joint,** suplantar a uno; humillar, bajarle a uno los humos.—**to p. out,** brotar, echar (retoños); despedir, despachar, echar; apagar o matar (la luz, el fuego); publicar, dar a luz; cegar; borrar, tachar; cortar, confundir, desconcertar; dislocar, sacar de quicio; poner (dinero a interés), dar (a logro); extender, sacar, mostrar; enojar, irritar.—**to p. out of action,** poner fuera de combate.—**to p. out of all hope,** quitar la esperanza, desahuciar.—**to p. out of countenance, o face,** avergonzar; desconcertar.—**to p. out of doors,** poner en la calle.—**to p. out of joint,** dislocar.—**to p. out of one's head,** sacarse de la cabeza, dejarse de; hacer olvidar.—**to p. out of order,** descomponer, desordenar.—**to p. out of the way,** quitar de en medio, poner (algo) donde no estorbe; suprimir (matar).—**to p. over,** sobreponer; cubrir(se) con, echar(se) encima; dar a uno el

cargo de; diferir, dilatar; conducir al otro lado; (fam.) llevar a cabo, hacer pasar o triunfar.—**to p. (something) around,** cubrir o abrigar con (algo).—**to p. something (o one) over on someone,** (fam.) pegársela a uno; darle gato por liebre.—**to p. the hand to,** poner manos a, meter las manos en, emprender; meter la mano en, apropiarse.—**to p. through,** meter al través de; atravesar; hacer ejecutar; someter a; dar curso a, hacer atender; hacer aceptar, lograr, llevar a cabo.—**to p. to,** agregar, añadir; exponer o someter a; consignar a; echar, juntar (machos con hembras).—**to p. to bed,** acostar, poner en cama.—**to p. to death,** matar; ajusticiar, ejecutar.—**to p. to flight,** poner en fuga, ahuyentar.—**to p. together,** acumular, juntar; reunir; armar (una máquina); confeccionar; coordinar, arreglar.—**to p. to it,** causar dificultad a, poner en calzas prietas, poner a parir.—**to p. to rights,** poner en orden; componer; reconciliar.—**to p. to shame,** avergonzar.—**to p. to silence,** hacer callar.—**to p. to sleep,** adormecer, hacer dormir; poner fuera de combate (ú. esp. en el boxeo).—**to p. to the sword,** pasar a cuchillo.—**to p. to the test, to trial, u on trial,** poner a prueba.—**to p. to the vote,** someter a votación; proceder a votar acerca de.—**to p. to use,** usar, utilizar; sacar partido de.—**to p. two and two together,** atar cabos.—**to p. up,** poner en su lugar, guardar, conservar; preparar, confeccionar (vg. cónservas, remedios, etc.); construir, erigir; (mec.) montar (una máquina); proponer, presentar (como candidato); ofrecer, elevar; levantar (la mano); alojar, hospedar; envainar (la espada); oponer, ofrecer (resistencia); (fam.) poner dinero en una apuesta; (fam.) tramar, urdir.—**to p. up for sale,** poner en venta.—**to p. upon,** poner en, colocar encima de; atribuir o imputar a, acusar; embaucar; abusar de.—**to p. upon oath,** hacer prestar juramento.—**to p. up to,** incitar, instigar a; presentar o someter a; (fam.) dejar a uno (la decisión, elección, etc.); (fam.) enseñar, dar instrucciones a.—**to be hard p. to it,** estar en un brete, o muy apurado; hallarse en calzas prietas, serle a uno muy difícil.

put, *vn.* (mar.) dirigirse, seguir rumbo.—**to p. about,** (mar.) cambiar de rumbo, virar.—**to p. back,** retroceder; regresar; (mar.) volver a puerto.—**to p. forth,** partir; (mar.) zarpar.—**to p. in,** arribar, entrar; tocar en (un puerto); ponerse en salvo, esconderse.—**to p. in for,** pretender, solicitar; hacer oposición a algún destino.—**to p. into port,** (mar.) arribar, entrar de arribada.—**to p. off,** u **out,** partir, salir; (mar.) zarpar.—**to p. out,** salir, partir.—**to p. to sea,** salir a la mar, hacerse a la mar o a la vela.—**to p. up,** parar; hospedarse; detenerse (en combate), envainar la espada.—**to p. up with,** aguantar, tolerar, sufrir, resistir; conformarse con.

put, *s.* acción del verbo TO PUT en cualquiera de sus acepciones; golpe, tiro, lanzamiento; (E. U., com.) opción o privilegio que una persona adquiere pagando una prima a otra de venderle, dentro de un plazo determinado, un artículo por un precio estipulado; el mismo privilegio de compra se llama *call.*

put, *a.* fijo; en su sitio. *V.* TO STAY PUT.

putamen [pjutéjmɛn], *s.* (bot.) hueso, cuesco, núcleo; (anat.) capa externa del núcleo lenticular.

putative [pjútạtiv], *a.* putativo.

putlog [pútlag], *s.* (arq.) almojaya.—**p. hole,** mechinal.

putrefaction [pjútrɛfǽkṣɔn], *s.* putrefacción.

putrefactive [-tiv], *a.* putrefactivo.

putrefactiveness [-nịs], *s.* calidad de putrefactivo.

putrefiable [-faịạbl], *a.* que puede pudrirse.

putrefy [-faị]. *va.* y *vn.* pudrir(se).

putrescence [pjutrésęns], *s.* putrescencia, pudrición.—**putrescent** [-ęnt], *a.* putrescente.—**putrescible** [-ibl], *a.* putrescible.

putrid [pjútrid], *a.* podrido, pútrido, putrefacto.

putridity [pjutríditi], **putridness** [pjútridnęs], *s.* podredumbre, putridez; corrupción.

Putsch [puch], *s.* (alem.) alzamiento o rebelión con fines políticos.

putt [pʌt]. **I.** *s.* golpe suave que hace rodar la pelota hacia el hoyuelo (en el juego de golf). **II.** *va.* y *vn.* ejecutar este golpe.

puttee [páti *o* pʌtí], *s.* polaina.

putter [pátœ(r)]. **I.** *s.* uno de los palos del golf. **II.** *vn.* *V.* POTTER.

putting [pátiŋ], *s.* acción del verbo TO PUTT.—**p. green**, (golf) terreno nivelado y cubierto de hierba fina que rodea cada hoyuelo.

putting [pútiŋ], *s.* acción del verbo TO PUT.

putty [pʌti]. **I.** *s.* masilla de aceite; cemento (apl. esp. al de cal).—**p. coat**, revestimiento de cemento de cal dado a un enlucido.—**p. knife**, espátula (para masilla).—**p. powder**, cenizas de estaño. **II.** *va.* enmasillar, rellenar con masilla; revocar con cemento (gen. de cal).

put-up [pút ʌp], *a.* (fam.) tramado, urdido.—**p.-up job**, (fam.) trama, confabulación.

puzzle [pázl]. **I.** *s.* acertijo, adivinanza, rompecabezas; enigma, *m.*, misterio, (fam.) quisicosa; problema arduo. **II.** *va.* confundir, poner perplejo; enmarañar, enredar, embrollar.—**to p. out**, resolver, descifrar, desenredar. **III.** *vn.* estar perplejo.—**to p. over**, tratar de resolver, hincarle el diente a, devanarse los sesos sobre.

puzzlement [-męnt], *s.* perplejidad, maraña, enredo.

puzzler [pázlœ(r)], *s.* el o lo que confunde, etc.

puzzling [pázliŋ], *a.* confuso, nebuloso, enigmático, que pone a uno perplejo.

puzzolan(a [pútsolæn (-lænä], *s.* puzolana.

pycnometer [piknámetœ(r)], *s.* (fís.) picnómetro, frasco para pesos específicos.

pycnostyle [píknostail], *s.* (arq.) picnóstila, intercolumnio estrecho (de 1½ diámetros).

pyelitis [paięláitis], *s.* (med.) pielitis.

py(a)emia [paięmiä], *s.* (med.) piemia o piohemia, infección de la sangre por materias purulentas.

pygmean [pigmían], *a.*, **pygmy** [pígmi], *a.* y *s.* pigmeo, enano, liliputiense.

pyjamas [pidžámäz], *s. pl.* = PAJAMAS.

pylon [páilan], *s.* (arq. egipcia) pilón, portada con torres piramidales; (aer.) torre (*f.*) o poste de señal; soporte de la hélice de un dirigible.

pyloric [pailóris], *a.* (anat.) pilórico.—**p. valve**, esfínter pilórico.

pylorus [pailóras], *s.* (anat.) píloro.

pyogenesis [paiodžénęsis], **pyogenia** [-džíniä], *s.* (med.) piogénesis o piogenia, formación de pus.—**pyogenetic** [-dženétik], **pyogenic** [-dženik], *a.* piogénico, piógeno, que produce pus; relativo a la piogenia.

pyoh(a)emia [paiohímiä], *s.* (med.) = PY(A)EMIA.

pyorrhea [paiorríä], *s.* (med.) piorrea (apl. esp. a la alveolar).

pyramid [píramid]. **I.** *s.* pirámide, *f.;* (anat.) pirámide (de Malpighi, etc.). **II.** *va.* y *vn.* aumentar(se), acumular(se).—**pyramidal** [piråmidal], **pyramidical** [piramídikäl], *a.* piramidal.

pyramidally [piråmidali], *adv.* piramidalmente.

pyrargyrite [pairárdžirait], *s.* (min.) pirargirita, plata roja.

pyre [pair], *s.* pira, hoguera.

Pyrenean [pirenían], *a.* pirenaico, pirineo.

pyretic [pairétik]. **I.** *a.* (med.) pirético, febril. **II.** *a.* y *s.* febrífugo.

pyretology [pirętálodži], *s.* (med.) piretología.

pyrexia [pairéksiä], *s.* (med.) pirexia, fiebre, *f.*

pyridic [pairídik], *a.* (quím.) pirídico.—**pyridin(e** [píridin], *s.* (quím.) piridina.

pyriform [píriform], *a.* piriforme.

pyrite [páirait], **pyrites** [piráitiz *o* páiraits], *s.* (min.) pirita.—**iron pyrites**, marcasita.

pyritic, **pyritous** [pirítik, pírītas], *a.* piritoso.

pyro [páiro], *s.* (fam.) *contr.* de **pyrogallol.**

pyroacetic [-asítik], *a.* (quím.) piroacético.—**p. acid**, **o spirit**, ácido o espíritu piroacético.

pyroacid [-æsid], *s.* (quím.) ácido pirogenado.

pyrochemical [-kémikäl], *a.* relativo a los fenómenos químicos a altas temperaturas.

pyroclastic [-klæstik], *a.* (geol.) ígneo, volcánico.

pyrogallic [-gælik], *a.* pirogállico.—**p. acid**, **o pyrogallol** [-gæloul], ácido pirogállico, pirogallol.

pyrogenous [pairádženʌs], *a.* pirógeno, ígneo; febril.

pyrograph [páirogræf], *s.* pirografía, pirograbado (cosa pirograbada).—**pyrography** [pairágrafi], **pyrogravure** [pairográviur], *s.* pirografía, pirograbado (arte).

pyrolater [pairálatœ(r)], *s.* pirólatra, *mf.*

pyrolatry [-tri], *s.* pirolatría.

pyroligneous [pairolígniʌs], *a.* piroleñoso.

pyrolusite [-liúsait], *s.* (min.) pirolusita.

pyrolysis [pairálisis], *s.* pirólisis, descomposición química por el calor.

pyromagnetic [-mægnétik], *a.* piromagnético.

pyromancer [páiromænsœ(r)], *s.*, **pyromantic** [-mæntik], *a.* piromántico.—**pyromancy** [páiromænsi], *s.* piromancía.

pyromania [-méiniä], *s.* piromanía.

pyrometer [pairámetœ(r)], *s.* pirómetro.

pyromorphite [-mórfait], *s.* (min.) piromorfita.

pyrophone [-foun], *s.* (mús.) pirófono.

pyrophorus [pairáforas], *s.* (quím. y zool.) piróforo.—**pyrophosphoric** [-fasfórik], *a.* pirosfosfórico.

pyrophosphate [-fásfeit], *s.* (quím.) pirofosfato.

pyroscope [-skoup], *s.* (fís.) piroscopio.

pyrosis [pairóusis], *s.* (med.) pirosis.

pyrosphere [páirosfir], *s.* (geol.) pirosfera.

pyrostat [-stæt], *s.* (fís.) piróstato.

pyrotechnic(al [-téknik(äl], *a.*, **pyrotechnist** [-ist], *s.* pirotécnico.—**pyrotechny**, **pyrotechnics** [páirotekni, -téknics], *s.* pirotecnia.

pyroxene [páiraksin], *s.* (min.) piroxena, piroxeno.—**pyroxenic** [-énik], *a.* piroxénico.—**pyroxenite** [pairáksenait], *s.* (geol.) piroxenita.

pyroxylin [pairáksilin], *s.* piroxilina, algodón pólvora.

pyrrhic [pírik]. **I.** *a.* pírrico; *s.* pírrica (danza griega). **II.** *s.* (pros.) pirriquio. **III.** (P.) *a.* de Pirro.—**P. victory**, triunfo de Pirro, victoria demasiado costosa.

Pyrrhonean [piróuniän], **Pyrrhonist** [píronist], *a.* y *s.* pirrónico, pirroniano.

Pyrrhonism [píronizm], *s.* (fílos.) pirronismo.

pyruvic [pairúvik], *a.* (quím.) pirúvico.

Pythagorean [piθægoriän], *a.* y *s.* pitagórico.

Pythian [píθiän], *a.* pitio (pert. a Apolo o Delfos).

python [páiθan], *s.* (zool.) pitón, boa (serpiente); adivino, agorero.

pythoness [páiθonis], *s.* pitonisa (sacerdotisa).

pythonic [paiθánik], *a.* pitónico; profético; (zool.) rel. a los pitones.

pyuria [paiyúriä], *s.* (med.) piuria, pus en la orina.

pyx [piks], *s.* (igl.) copón, píxide, *f.*

pyxidium [piksídiʌm], *s.* (bot.) pixidio.

Q

q [kju], *s.* q.—**Q. boat**, **Q. ship** = MYSTERY BOAT.

qua [kwei *o* kwa], *adv.* como, en su calidad de.

quack [kwæk]. **I.** *vn.* graznar, parpar; charlatanear; echárselas de médico; curar empíricamente o con sortilegios. **II.** *s.* graznido del pato. **III.** *s.* y *a.* charlatán; saltabanco; curandero, matasanos; medicucho, medicastro.

quackery [-œri], *s.* charlatanismo, charlatanería; empirismo; fraude.

quad [kwad], *s.* (impr.) = QUADRAT; (fam.) = QUADRUPLET.

quadra [kwádrạ], *s.* (arq.) bastidor, marco; plinto.

Quadragesima [kwadrạdʒésimạ], *s.* (igl.) el primer domingo de la cuaresma; (ant.) cuadragésima, cuaresma.

quadragesimal [-l], *a.* cuadragesimal.

quadrangle [kwádræŋgl], *s.* cuadrángulo; (arq.) patio.—**quadrangular** [-ráŋgịulạ(r)], *a.* cuadrangular, cuadrángulo.

quadrant [kwádrạnt], *s.* (geom.) cuadrante, cuarta; (mec.) sector oscilante; (astr. y mar.) cuadrante de altura.—**q. electrometer**, electrómetro de cuadrante.

quadrantal [-réntạl], *a.* (mat.) cuadrantal.

quadrat [kwádrạt], *s.* (impr.) cuadrado, cuadratín.

quadrate [kwádreịt]. **I.** *a.* cuadrado. **II.** *s.* (anat.) hueso o musculo cuadrado; (astr.) cuadrado. **III.** *va.* y *vn.* cuadrar; conformar(se), adaptarse.

quadratic [kwadrétịk]. **I.** *a.* cuadrático, de segundo grado. **II.** *s.* ecuación de segundo grado.

quadratics [-s], *s.* parte (*f.*) del álgebra que trata de las (ecuaciones) cuadráticas.

quadrature [kwádrạchụr], *s.* (mat., elec. y astr.) cuadratura; (mec.) escuadreo.

quadrennial [kwadrénịạl], *a.* cuadrienal.

quadrennium [-ịʌm], *s.* cuadrienio, cuatrienio.

quadricentennial [kwadrịsenténịạl], *a.* y *s.* de o rel. al tiempo, espacio o aniversario de 400 años.

quadrifid [kwádrịfịd], *a.* (bot.) cuadrífido.

quadrifoliate(d [-fóụlịeịt(ịd], *a.* (bot.) cuadrifoliado.

quadriga [kwadráịgạ], *s.* cuadriga, cuadríyugo.

quadrilateral [kwadrịlétẹrạl], *a.* y *s.* (geom. y mil.) cuadrilátero.

quadrille [k(w)ạdríl], *s.* (danz. y mús.) contradanza, rigodón; cuatrillo, cascarela (juego de naipes); cuadrícula; cuadrilla de toreros.

quadrillion [kwạdrílyọn], *s.* cuatrillón (E. U. y Fr., unidad seguida de 15 ceros; Ingl., Alem. y Esp., unidad seguida de 24 ceros).

quadripartite [kwadrịpártaịt], *a.* cuadripartido.

quadrisyllable [-sịlạbl], *s.* cuadrisílabo.

quadrivalent [-véịlẹnt], *a.* (quím.) tetravalente.

quadrivium [kwadrívịʌm], *s.* cuadrivio.

quadroon [kwadrún], *s.* cuarterón.

Quadrumana [kwadrúmạnạ], *s. pl.* cuadrúmanos.

quadrumane [kwádrụmeịn], *s.* cuadrúmano.

quadrumanous [-rúmạnʌs], *a.* cuadrúmano.

quadruped [kwádrụped], *s.* y *a.* (zool.) cuadrúpedo.

quadrupedal [-rúpedạl], *a.* cuadrupedal.

quadruple [kwádrụpl]. **I.** *a.* cuádruple, cuádruplo. **II.** *s.* cuádruplo, cuatrotanto. **III.** *va.* y *vn.* cuadruplicar(se), cuatrodoblar(se).

quadruplet [kwádrụplịt], *s.* serie de cuatro cosas; cada uno de cuatro hijos nacidos de un parto; bicicleta de cuatro asientos.

quadruplex [-pleks]. **I.** *a.* cuádruple. **II.** *s.* (tlg.) (instrumento telegráfico) cuádruplex.

quadruplicate [kwadrúplịkeịt], *va.* cuadruplicar.

quadruplication [-éịsọn], *s.* cuadruplicación.

quadruply [kwádrụplị], *adv.* al cuádruplo.

quaestor [kwéstọ(r)], *s.* cuestor (romano).

quaestorship [-sịp], *s.* cuestura.

quaff [kwaf]. **I.** *va.* y *vn.* beber a grandes tragos, o repetidas veces. **II.** *s.* trago.

quagga [kwǽgạ], *s.* (zool.) cuaga, *m.*

quaggy [kwǽgị], *a.* pantanoso; blando.

quagmire [kwǽgmaịr], *s.* tremedal, tembladal, lodazal, cenagal, tollo, trampal; atolladero.

quahaug, quahog [kwóhag], *s.* almeja.

quail [kweịl]. **I.** *s.* (orn.) codorniz; perdiz.—**q. pipe**, reclamo de codornices. **II.** *vn.* acobardarse, descorazonarse; cejar.

quaint [kweịnt], *a.* de pristina belleza o amenidad; de curioso primor, de exquisito arcaísmo.—**quaintly** [-lị], *adv.* de modo amenamente arcáico, con la curiosa exquisitez de tiempos que fueron.—**quaintness** [-nịs], *s.* amenidad o belleza arcáica; rareza.

quake [kweịk]. **I.** *vn.* temblar; tiritar; estremecerse. **II.** *s.* temblor; estremecimiento.

Quaker [kwéịkœ(r)], *s.* y *a.* cuáquero o cuákero; temblador.—**Quakeress** [-ịs], *s.* cuáquera.—**Quakerism** [-ịzm], *s.* cuaquerismo.

quaking [kwéịkịŋ]. **I.** *s.* temblor. **II.** *a.* temblante, temblador.—**q. bog**, tremedal. *V.* QUAGMIRE.

quaky [kwéịkị], *a.* tembloroso, gelatinoso.

qualifiable [kwálịfaịạbl], *a.* calificable.

qualification [-fịkéịsọn], *s.* calificación, requisito; c(u)alidad, capacidad, idoneidad; habilitación; atenuación, mitigación; limitación; salvedad.—**without q.**, sin distingos o reparos.

qualificator [-fịkeịtọ(r)], *s.* (igl.) calificador.

qualified [-faịd], *a.* calificado, habilitado, idóneo, apto, competente; modificado; (for.) limitado, restringido.—**q. voter**, elector habilitado.

qualifier [-faịœ(r)], *s.* calificador, habilitador; (gram.) calificativo.

qualify [-faị]. **I.** *va.* capacitar, habilitar, hacer idóneo; calificar; modificar, limitar, restringir; templar, suavizar; diluir (un licor). **II.** *vn.* prepararse, habilitarse; llenar los requisitos; (E. U.) prestar juramento antes de entrar en funciones.

qualifying [-faịịŋ], *a.* preparativo; calificativo.

qualitative [-teịtịv], *a.* cualitativo.—**q. analysis**, análisis cualitativo.

quality [kwálịtị], *s.* c(u)alidad; clase, *f.*, casta, jaez, *m.*; propiedad, poder o virtud; categoría, distinción, alta posición social.

qualm [kwám], *s.* basca; escrúpulo o remordimiento de conciencia.—**qualmish** [-ịṣ], *a.* bascoso; escrupuloso.—**qualmishness** [-nịs], *s.* náusea.

quandary [kwándạrị], *s.* incertidumbre, duda, perplejidad; aprieto, apuro, brete.

quantitative [kwántịteịtịv], *a.* cuantitativo.—**q. analysis**, análisis cuantitativo.

quantity [kwántịtị], *s.* cantidad, cuantía, tanto; dosis; gran cantidad, gran número; (mús. y pros.) cantidad; (elec.) intensidad (de una corriente).—*pl* **quantities**, (fam.) gran cantidad, gran número.—**q. production**, fabricación o producción en serie, en masa o en grande.—**q. surveying**, medida y cálculo de materiales en las construcciones.—**q. theory**, (e. p.) teoría de que las variaciones en la cantidad de la moneda circulante son causa y no efecto de las variaciones en los precios.

quantum [kwántạm], *s.* (*pl.* QUANTA) tanto; cantidad; (fís., mec.) cuanto, quántum, unidad elemental de energía.

quarantine [kwárạntịn]. **I.** *s.* cuarentena; estación de cuarentena; aislamiento de dolientes de enfermedad contagiosa; prohibición de transportar animales o plantas enfermos que transmiten enfermedades. **II.** *va.* poner en cuarentena; aislar.

quarrel [kwárẹl]. **I.** *s.* reyerta, pendencia, riña, altercación, querella, camorra, disputa; diamante de vidrieros; flecha o instrumento cortante de cuatro aristas; vidrio, loseta o adoquín romboidal.—**to have no q. with**, no reñir con; no oponerse a; no censurar. **II.** *vn.* pelear, reñir; pendenciar, altercar, desamistarse, romper.

quarrel(l)er [-œ(r)], *s.*, **quarrel(l)ing** [-ịŋ], **quarrelsome** [-sʌm], *a.* altercador, quimerista, pendenciero.—**quarrelsomeness** [-nịs], *s.* pugnacidad.

quarrier [kwárịœ(r)], *s.* cantero, picapedrero.

quarry [kwárị]. **I.** *s.* cantera, pedrera; caza, presa; cuadrado, cuadro, rombo (de vidrio, teja, etc.). **II.** *va.* explotar (canteras).—**quarryman** [-mạn], *s.* cantero, picapedrero.

quart [kwort], *s.* cuarto de galón (como un litro); (mús.) cuarta; [kart] (esgr.) cuarta (ll. **t. quarte, carte**); en el juego de los cientos, cuarta.

quartan [kwórtạn]. **I.** *a.* cuartanal. **II.** *s.* (med.) cuartana (fiebre que recidiva cada cuatro días).

quartation [kwortéişǫn], *s.* (metal.) incuartación.
quarter [kwórtœ(r)]. **I.** *s.* cuarto, cuarta parte; arroba (cuarto de quintal); trimestre; cuarto de hora; cuarto de tonelada; (E. U.) moneda de 25 centavos (un cuarto de dólar); cuarto de luna; (mús.) semínima; (mar.) cuarta; origen, procedencia; región, comarca, distrito (v. gr.: *from all quarters*, de todas partes); barrio, barriada, vecindad; (carp.) cuarterón, entrepaño; (mar.) cuadra de popa; cuartel, merced o clemencia.—*pl.* domicilio, vivienda, morada; (mil.) cuartel; alojamiento.—**q.** cask, cuarterola.—**q. day**, día (*m.*) en que principia una estación del año; día en que se paga un trimestre.—**q.-deck**, (mar.) alcázar.—**q.-deck ladder**, escala del alcázar.—**q.-phase**, (elec.) bifásico.—**q. plate**, (foto.) placa de 3¼ por 4¼ pulgadas.—**q. point**, (mar.) cuarto viento o rumbo de la brújula.—**q. round**, (arq.) cuarto bocel, óvolo.—**q.-sawed**, aserrado en cuartones.—**q. section**, (E. U.) cuarto de una milla cuadrada (160 acres).—**q. sessions**, tribunal inferior que se reúne cada trimestre.—**q. tone**, (mús.) cuarto de tono.—**q. wind**, viento al anca o a la cuadra.—**to give no q.**, no dar cuartel.—**to take up quarters at**, alojarse en. **II.** *a.* cuarto. **III.** *va.* cuartear; descuartizar, hacer cuartos; dividir en cuatro partes iguales o en cuarteles; (mil.) acuartelar, acantonar; alojar, hospedar; (blas.) cuartelar.
quarterage [-idž], *s.* sueldo o salario trimestral; cuartel, alojamiento(s).
quartered [-d]. **I.** *pp.* de TO QUARTER. **II.** *a.* hecho de madera aserrada a lo largo en cuartos, para mostrar la veta; (blas.) acuartelado.—**q. oak**, roble aserrado de dicho modo.
quarterly [-lị]. **I.** *a.* trimestral.—**q. payment**, trimestre. **II.** *s.* publicación trimestral o cada tres meses. **III.** *adv.* trimestralmente; en cuartos, por cuartos.
quartermaster [-mæstœ(r)], *s.* (mil.) comisario ordenador.—**q.-general**, intendente de ejército.
quartern [kwórtœrn], *s.* (Ingl.) cuarta (parte); cuarto, cuarterón.—**q. loaf**, pan de cuatro libras.
quartet(te [kwortét], *s.* cuatro personas o cosas de una misma clase; (mús., poét.) cuarteto.
quartile [kwórtail], *s.* (astr.) cuadrado.
quarto [kwórtoụ]. **I.** *a.* (impr.) en cuarto. **II.** *s.* libro en cuarto.
quartz [kwórts], *s.* (min.) cuarzo, sílice, *f.*—**q. plate**, (elec.) placa eléctrica de cuarzo; condensador de cuarzo.—**quartziferous** [-ífɛɾʌs], *a.* cuarcífero.—**quartzite** [-ait], *s.* cuarcita.—**quartzose, quartzous, quartzy** [-oụs, -ʌs, -i], *a.* cuarzoso.
quash [kwaš], *va.* sofocar, reprimir; (for.) anular, invalidar, derogar.
quasi [kwéisai], *adv.* y *a.* cuasi, casi, como si fuera, al parecer; aparente, que parece.—**q. contract**, (for.) cuasicontrato.—**q. delict**, cuasidelito.
quassia [kwášịạ], *s.* (bot.) casia.
quassin [kwásịn], *s.* (quím., farm.) cuasina, elemento amargo de la casia.
quaternary [kwạtœrnạrị]. **I.** *a.* cuaternario; que consta de cuatro elementos. **II.** *a.* y *s.* grupo de cuatro; (Q., geol.) (período) cuaternario.
quaternion [-nịǫn], *s.* cuaternidad; fila o serie de cuatro; (mat.) cuaternio.
quaternity [-nịtị], *s.* cuaternidad.
quatrain [kwátrein], *s.* (poét.) cuarteto o cuartete (de versos endecasílabos); cuarteta o redondilla (de versos octosílabos).
quattrocento [kwatrochéntoụ], *s.* (b. a.) período cuatrocentista, Renacimiento (esp. italiano) del siglo XV.
quaver [kwéịvœ(r)]. **I.** *vn.* gargantear, gorjear, hacer quiebros, trinar; temblar, vibrar. **II.** *s.*

gorjeo, trino; trémolo, vibración; (mús.) corchea.
quavering [-iŋ]. **I.** *s.* gorgorito (fam.), trin(ad)o, gorjeo. **II.** *a.* trémulo, temblante.
quay [ki], *s.* muelle; (des)embarcadero.
quayage [kíidž], *s.* = WHARFAGE.
quean [kwin], *s.* mujercilla, piruja; moz(uel)a.
queasiness [kwízịnịs], *s.* propensión a la náusea.
queasy [kwízị], *a.* propenso a la náusea, bascoso; nauseabundo; delicado, fastidioso.
quebracho [keịbráchoụ], *s.* (bot.) quebracho.
Quechua(n [kéchwạ(n], *s.* y *a.* quichua, quechua.
queen [kwín], *s.* reina; en los naipes, figura de reina que equivale al caballo; la dama en el juego de damas y la reina en el ajedrez.—**Q. Anne's lace**, (bot.) dauco, zanahoria silvestre.—**q. (bee)**, abeja reina o maestra, enjambradera.—**q. cell**, maestral.—**q. consort**, esposa del rey.—**q. dowager**, reina viuda.—**q. mother**, reina madre.—**q. of the meadow**, (bot.) reina de los prados, espírea, ulmaria.—**q. olive**, aceituna de la reina.—**q. post**, (constr.) péndola.—**q.-post truss**, viga (de puente) o armadura (de techo) de dos péndolas.—**q. regent**, reina regente.—**q. regnant**, reina reinante.—**q.'s English**, inglés castizo o puro.—**Q.'s speech**, discurso de la Corona.—**q.'s ware**, vajilla de color de crema.
queenliness [-lịnịs], *s.* majestad de una reina.
queenly [-lị], *a.* como (de) reina; majestuoso, regio; propio de una reina.
queenship [-šịp], *s.* dignidad, dominio o poder de una reina.
queer [kwír]. **I.** *a.* extraño, raro; indispuesto, desfalleciente; (fam.) chiflado, excéntrico, estrafalario, estrambótico; (fam.) sospechoso, misterioso; (fam.) falso. **II.** *s.* (fam.) moneda falsa. **III.** *va.* (fam.) comprometer, poner a uno en mal lugar; echar a perder; (fam.) ridiculizar.
queerly [-lị], *adv.* extrañamente, estrafalariamente; sospechosamente.
queerness [-nịs], *s.* rareza, extrañeza, ridiculez.
quell [kwél], *va.* reprimir, sofocar, domar, sojuzgar; calmar, mitigar (un dolor).
queller [-œ(r)], *s.* opresor, domador, sojuzgador.
quench [kwénch], *va.* apagar, matar (luz, fuego); calmar, apagar (la sed); ahogar, sofocar; sosegar; extinguir; templar (hierro).
quenchable [-ạbl], *a.* apagable, extinguible.
quencher [-œ(r)], *s.* apagador.
quenching [-iŋ], *s.* apagamiento, extinción.
quenchless [-lịs], *a.* inapagable, inextinguible.
quercin [kwœrsịn], *s.* (quím.) quercina, amargo de roble.—**quercine**, *a.* relativo al roble o a la encina.
quercitrin [kwœrsịtrịn], *s.* (quím.) quercitrina.
quercitron [-trǫn], *s.* (bot.) roble negro americano y su cáscara; quercitrón.
Quercus [kwœrkʌs], *s.* (bot.) querco, género que comprende los robles y las encinas.
querist [kwírịst], *s.* inquiridor, preguntador.
querl, quirl [kwœrl]. **I.** *va.* torcer, enroscar. **II.** *s.* sinuosidad, enroscadura. *V.* TWIRL.
quern [kwœrn], *s.* molino de mano.
querulous [kwérulʌs], *a.* querelloso, quejicoso, (fam.) chinchoso.—**querulously** [-lị], *adv.* querellosamente, quejosamente.—**querulousness** [-nịs], *s.* disposición a querellarse o quejarse.
query [kwírị]. **I.** *s.* pregunta; duda; (impr.) signo interrogante (?). **II.** *va.* marcar con signo de interrogación; preguntar, indagar, pesquisar. **III.** *vn.* expresar una duda; preguntar.
quest [kwest], **I.** *s.* pesquisa, averiguación; busca. **II.** *vn.* y *va.* averiguar, investigar; buscar.
question [kwéschǫn]. **I.** *s.* pregunta, demanda; cuestión, asunto; problema, *m.*; debate, controversia; proposición que ha de discutirse en una asamblea; objeción, discusión.—**q.-begging**, de carácter de círculo vicioso.—**q. mark**, (signo de) interrogación, interrogante.—**a fair q.**, una pregunta legítima, justa o cuerda.—

beside the q., impertinente, ajeno al asunto. —**beyond**, o **without**, q., fuera de duda, indiscutible.—**in** q., de referencia, de que se trata; consabido, de marras.—**out of** q., sin duda, de veras.—**that is the** q., he ahí el problema, o la cuestión; ahí está el quid.—**there is no** q. **about it**, eso es indiscutible, está fuera de duda.—**to be out of the** q., ser indiscutible; no haber que pensar en.—**to put to the** q., interrogar; torturar; someter a votación.—**what is the** q.? ¿de qué se trata? II. *va.* preguntar, examinar, interrogar; dudar; poner en tela de juicio; desconfiar de; oponerse a, objetar; recusar. III. *vn.* inquirir, preguntar, escudriñar; dudar.

questionable [-abl], *a.* cuestionable, problemático, discutible, dudoso, sospechoso.

questionary [-eri]. I. *s.* cuestionario; catecismo; (igl.) bulero. II. *a.* interrogativo.

questioner [-œ(r)], *s.* preguntador, interrogador, inquiridor; preguntón.

questionless [-lis]. I. *a.* indubitable; que no pregunta. II. *adv.* indiscutiblemente, fuera de duda.

questionnaire [-ér], *s.* cuestionario, encuesta.

questor [kwéstọ(r)], *s.* cuestor. *V.* QUAESTOR.

que(t)zal [ke(t)sál], *s.* (orn.) quezal, quetzal(e).

queue [kju]. I. *s.* coleta, trenza (de pelo); fila, cola, hilera de personas, coches, etc. II. *vn.* (a veces con **up**) hacer cola, ponerse en fila.

quibble [kwíbl]. I. *vn.* sutilizar, buscar escapatorias; hacer uso de argucias o sofismas. II. *s.* evasiva, subterfugio, argucia, sutileza; equívoco.—*pl.* sofistería, retóricas.

quibbler [kwíblœ(r)], *s.* sofista; equivoquista.

Quichua(n [kíchwã(n], *s.* y *a.* quichua, quechua.

quick [kwik]. I. *a.* rápido, presto, veloz, acelerado, expedit(iv)o, listo, ágil; ardiente; penetrante, fino; irritable, petulante; disponible, efectivo; vivo.—**q. assets**, (com.) activo de rápida liquidación, lo que es de fácil conversión a efectivo.—**q.-fire**, **q.-firing**, (art.) de tiro rápido.—**q. freezing**, congelación rápida.— **q. grass** = COUCH GRASS.—**q. hedge**, seto vivo.—**q. march**, (mil.) paso doble.—**q. match**, estopín.—**q.-sightedness**, agudeza de vista, penetración.—**q. time**, (mil.) paso redoblado.—**q. on the draw**, **q. trigger**, impetuoso, impulsivo.—**q. with child**, embarazada, encinta.—**the q. and the dead**, los vivos y los muertos.—**to be q. about**, o **at**, hacer de prisa, despachar pronto. II. *s.* carne viva; lo más hondo o profundo (del alma, de la sensibilidad); lo más delicado.—**to cut (hurt, offend, etc.) to the q.**, herir en lo vivo, en el alma o profundamente. III. *adv.* con presteza, prontamente, velozmente.—**q.-sighted**, de vista aguda, penetrante.—**q.-tempered**, de genio vivo, de mal genio, irascible.—**q.-witted**, vivo de ingenio, listo, agudo, perspicaz.

quicken [-n]. I. *va.* vivificar, dar vida, resucitar; acelerar, urgir, avivar; excitar, aguzar, animar. II. *vn.* avivarse, vivificarse, revivir; moverse más aprisa; ser más sensitivo.

quickener [-œ(r)], *s.* vivificador, avivador.

quickening [-in], *s.* vivificación, avivamiento; primera señal de vida que da el feto.

quicklime [-laim], *s.* cal viva.

quickly [-li], *adv.* prontamente, pronto, aprisa.

quickness [-nis], *s.* presteza, vivacidad, prontitud, celeridad; sagacidad, viveza, penetración.

quicksand [-sænd], *s.* arena movediza.

quickset [-set], *s.* espino o abrojo con que se hace un seto.—**q. (hedge)**, seto vivo, (Am.) cerco.

quicksilver [-silvœ(r)]. I. *s.* azogue, mercurio. II. *va.* azogar.

quickstep [-step], *s.* (mús.) paso doble, pasacalle; (mil.) paso redoblado.

quid [kwid], *s.* mascada de tabaco; paja medio

mascada que cae de la boca de un caballo; rumiadura; substancia. *V.* QUIDDITY.

quiddity [kwídịti], *s.* esencia de una cosa; quid, *m.*, (fam.) busilis, *m.;* sutileza, equívoco.

quidnunc [kwídnʌŋk], *s.* curioso, insaciable; cuentista, chismero, portanuevas, (fám.) refitolero.

quiesce [kwaiés], *vn.* aquietarse, callarse; (gram.) hacerse muda una letra.—**quiescence, quiescency** [-ens, -i], *s.* quiescencia, quietud, reposo. —**quiescent** [-ent], *a.* quieto, inactivo; tranquilo; (gram.) mudo, que no se pronuncia; (ing.) estático, fijo.

quiet [kwáiet]. I. *a.* quieto, quedo; sereno, tranquilo, calmado; callado, silencioso; sencillo, modesto, sin ceremonia; ameno, apacible; (com.) inactivo (mercado, etc.).—**to be, o to keep, q.**, callarse; no hacer ruido. II. *s.* quietud; silencio; tranquilidad, calma.—**on the q.**, (fam.) a la sordina, a la chita callando, a cencerros tapados. III. *va.* acallar, (a)quietar, apaciguar; tranquilizar, calmar. IV. *vn.* (a veces con **down**) (a)quietarse, apaciguarse, calmarse.

quieting [-in], *a.* calmante.—**quietism** [-izm], *s.* quietismo.—**quietist** [-ist], *s.* y *a.* quietista.— **quietly** [-li], *adv.* tranquilamente; calladamente; sin ruido; sin alharaca.—**quietness, quietude** [-nis, -iud], *s.* quietud, sosiego, tranquilidad, paz.

quietus [kwaiítʌs], *s.* carta de pago, finiquito; descanso; muerte, *f.;* golpe decisivo.

quill [kwil]. I. *s.* pluma de ave; cañón de pluma; cañón o pluma para escribir; escritor; púa del puerco espín; canilla, broca, devanador, canutillo; estría, pliegue cilíndrico de un rizado.— **q. embroidery**, cañutería, bordado a canutillo. —**q. men**, gente de pluma.—**q. pen**, pluma de ave.—**the q.**, la pluma, la profesión literaria. II. *va.* desplumar; encanillar; (cost.) rizar, hacer un encarrujado.

quilling [-in], *s.* (cost.) rizado, encarrujado.

quilt [kwilt]. I. *s.* colcha, cobertor acolchado, edredón. II. *va.* (a)colchar, acojinar, estofar.

quilter [-œ(r)], *s.* acolchador; colchero.

quilting [-in], *s.* colchadura; material para colchas; hechura de colchas; (tej.) cotí, piqué.— **q. bee**, reunión de amigas para hacer colchas. —**q. cotton**, guata, algodón en rama u hojas para acolchar.

quina(quina [kínạ(kínạ], *s.* (bot.) quina(quina).

quinary [kwáinạri], *a.* y *s.* quinario.

quince [kwins], *s.* (bot.) membrillo.—**q. tree**, membrill(er)o.

quincentenary [kwinséntenẹri], *a.* y *s.* de o rel. al aniversario de 500 años.

quincuncial [kwiŋkʌnšạl], *a.* quincuncial, de figura de tresbolillo, al tresbolillo.

quincunx [kwíŋkʌŋks], *s.* quincunce, tresbolillo.

quinidin(e [kwínịdin], *s.* (quím.) quinidina o cincolina.

quinine [kwáinain], *s.* (qaím., farm.) quinina.

quinnat [kwínæt], *s.* (ict.) variedad de salmón del Pacífico.

quinol [kwínoụl], *s.* (quím.) hidroquinona.

quinone [kwinóụn], *s.* (quím.) quinona.

quinquagenarian [kwiŋkwạdżenérịạn], *a.* y *s.* quincuagenario.

Quinquagesima [-dżésịmạ], *s.* (igl.) quincuagésima.

quinquefoliate(d [kwiŋkwifóụlieịt(id], *a.* (bot.) quinquefoliado; quinquedigitado.

quinquennial [kwiŋkwénịạl]. I. *a.* quinquenal. II. *s.* quinquenio; quinto aniversario.

quinquennium [-iʌm], *s.* quinquenio.

quinquevalent [kwiŋkwẹvéịlent], *a.* (quím.) quinquivalente.

quinquina [kwiŋkwáinạ], *s.* (bot.) quina(quina).

quinsy [kwínzi], *s.* (med.) angina (tonsilar).

quint [kwint], *s.* registro de órgano; conjunto de cinco; (mús.) quinta; en algunos juegos de naipes, quinta; (fam.) = QUINTUPLET.

quintain [kwíntin], *s.* juego de lanza a caballo.

quintal [kwíntl̩], s. quintal, peso de 4 arrobas. V. HUNDREDWEIGHT.—**metric q.**, 100 kilos.

quintan [kwíntən]. **I.** a. de cada cinco días. **II.** s. (med.) fiebre (f.) intermitente que ocurre cada cinco días.

quintant [kwíntənt], s. (astr.) quintante.

quinte [kænt], s. (esgr.) quinta.

quintessence [kwíntésəns]. **I.** s. quinta esencia, quintaesencia. **II.** va. quintaesenciar.—**quintessential** [kwíntɛsɛ́nšl̩], a. quintaesenciado, depuradísimo.

quintet(te [kwíntɛ́t], s. cinco personas o cosas de una misma clase; (mús.) quinteto.

quintillion [kwíntílyən], s. quintillón (E. U. y Fr., sexta potencia de mil; Ingl., Alem. y Esp., quinta potencia de un millón).

quintuple [kwíntiupl̩]. **I.** a. y s. quíntuplo. **II.** va. y vn. quintuplicar(se).

quintuplet [-plit], s. quintupleta, bicicleta de asientos en tándem para cinco personas; uno de cinco hermanos mellizos.

quip [kwíp]. **I.** s. pulla, chufleta, escarnio, mofa, vaya. **II.** vn. echar pullas, mofarse.

quipster [-stœ(r)], s. pullista, mofador.

quipu [kípu o kwípu], s. (Perú) quipo.

quire [kwaɪr]. **I.** s. mano (f.) de papel (24 o 25 hojas); (enc.) cuadernos que forman un libro; libro. **II.** va. formar manos de papel.

quirk [kwœrk]. **I.** s. desviación, vuelta corta, recodo; arranque, capricho; plumada; pulla; evasiva, argucia, rodeo; (arq.) copada, caveto, avivador. **II.** va. acanalar, estriar.—**quirking plane**, cepillo de cavetos, avivador.

quirt [kwœrt]. **I.** s. látigo; (Méx.) cuarta. **II.** va. azotar con el látigo, (Am.) latiguear, cuartear.

quisling [kwízliŋ], s. quintacolumnista, traidor.

quit [kwit]. **I.** va. (pret. y pp. QUIT o QUITTED) dejar, parar, cesar o desistir de; dejarse de, soltar, dejar ir, abandonar; renunciar; evacuar, desocupar; irse, salir o marcharse de.—**q. your fooling, o nonsense,** déjate de tonterías.—**to q. scores,** ajustar cuentas.—**to q. work,** parar (en el trabajo). **II.** vn. desistir; parar; cejar; irse, quitarse; abandonar (una empresa, una causa, a sus amigos, etc.), zafarse.

quit, a. quito, libre, descargado, absuelto.—**to be quits,** estar en paz, no deberse nada, haberse vengado; empatar.—**to call it quits,** dar por terminado (un trabajo, etc.).—**to cry quits,** darse por buenos.

quitch (grass) [kwȳch (græs], s. (bot.) grama.

quitclaim [kwítkleɪm]. **I.** va. renunciar o ceder. **II.** s. (for.) renuncia; (com.) finiquito.

quite [kwaɪt], adv. completamente, enteramente, absolutamente, del todo; verdadera, efectiva o justamente; (fam.) bastante, asaz, harto, más bien.—**q. a bit,** considerable, bastante.—**q. the,** enteramente lo; justamente el (la).

quitrent [kwítrɛnt], s. (ant.) censo para librarse del servicio feudal; renta fija pagada sobre propiedad inmueble.

quittance [kwítəns], s. quitanza, finiquito, descargo, recibo; liberación; recompensa, remuneración.

quitter [kwítœ(r)], s. (metal.) escorias; el que se da por vencido o vuelve el rabo; desertor (de una causa, etc.).

quittor [-ǫ(r)], s. (vet.) inflamación de las patas de los caballos, sanos, etc.

quiver [kwívœ(r)]. **I.** s. carcaj, aljaba; temblor, tiritón. **II.** vn. temblar, estremecerse; palpitar.

quivered [-d], a. provisto de aljaba, carcaj o goldre; metido en aljaba.

quivering [-iŋ]. **I.** s. tremor, temblor. **II.** a. tremulante, trémulo, temblador; palpitante.

quixotic [kwiksátik], a. quijotesco.—**quixotically** [-əli], adv. quijotescamente.—**quixotism, quixotry** [kwíksǫtizm, -tri], s. quijotismo, quijotería.

quiz [kwīz]. **I.** s. examen o serie de preguntas; chanza, broma, guasa; zumbón, chancero,

guasón. II. va. examinar a un discípulo o clase; chulear, chancearse, tomar a guasa; mirar con aire burlón o zumbón.—**quizzing glass,** monóculo.

quizzical [kwízikl̩], a. burlón, zumbón, bromista; raro, extraño, estrambótico.

quodlibet [kwádlibɛt], s. cuodlibeto, sutileza; (mús.) fantasía, miscelánea.—**quodlibetic(al** [-bétik(əl], a. cuodlibético, cuodlibetal.

quoin [k(w)ɔin]. **I.** s. (arq.) adaraja, diente; mocheta, piedra angular; esquina, ángulo; clave (f.) de arco; (mec. e impr.) cuña. **II.** va. acuñar.

quoiner [-œ(r)], s. (impr.) acuñador.

quoit [kwɔit]. **I.** s. tejo, herrón; marrón.—pl. juego de tejos; marro. **II.** vn. jugar al tejo.

quondam [kwándam], a. antiguo, de otro tiempo, que fué.

quorum [kwórʌm], s. quórum.

quota [kwóutə], s. cuota o cota, cupo, escote; prorrata.—**q. of troops,** contingente de tropas.

quotable [kwóutəbl̩], a. citable; (com.) cotizable.

quotation [-éišǫn], s. citación; cita; texto citado; (com.) cotización.—**q. marks,** (impr.) comillas, el signo "".

quote [kwóut]. **I.** va. y vn. citar; repetir un texto; (com.) cotizar. **II.** s. (fam.) cita.—pl. (fam.) comillas.

quoter [-œ(r)], s. citador; (com.) cotizador.

quoth [kwouθ], pret. del verbo desusado TO QUETH.—**q. I,** dije yo.—**q. he,** dijo él.

quotha [kwóuθə], interj. (ant.) ¡de veras! ¡vaya!

quotidian [kwotídiən]. **I.** a. cotidiano, diario. **II.** s. (med.) calentura cotidiana.

quotient [kwóušɛnt], s. (mat.) c(u)ociente.

R

r [ar], s. r.—**the three R's,** (fam.) lectura, escritura y aritmética (reading, 'riting, 'rithmetic).

rabbet [ræbit]. **I.** va. (carp.) ensamblar a rebajo, encajar; hacer un rebajo. **II.** s. (carp.) rebajo, espera; encaje, ensambladura; batiente; (mar.) alefriz, m.—**r. plane,** guillame.

rabbi [ræbai], **rabbin** [ræbin], s. rabí, rabino.

rabbinic(al [ræbínik(əl], a. rabínico.

rabbinism [ræbinizm], s. rabinismo.—**rabbinist** [-ist], s. rabinista.

rabbit [ræbit], s. (zool.) conejo.—**r.-ear faucet,** grifo de aletas o de cierre automático.—**r. fever,** (med.) tularemia.—**r. fur,** conejuna.—**r. hole,** r. nest, conejera, madriguera.—**r. warren,** conejera, conejar.

rabble [ræbl̩]. **I.** s. canalla, chusma, populacho; (fund.) barra o agitador de pudelar, espetón. **II.** va. (fund.) pudelar, bracear, remover.

rabid [ræbid], a. (med.) rabioso; fanático, violento, feroz.

rabies [réibiz], s. (med.) rabia, hidrofobia.

raccoon, racoon [rækún], s. (zool.) mapache, oso lavador, perro mudo; (Hond.) racuna.—**r. skin,** mapache.

race [reis]. **I.** s. raza; estirpe, f.; casta; subespecie, variedad; calidad; nariz, sabor (del vino); carrera, corrida, regata, cualquier certamen de velocidad; curso, decurso de la vida; corriente (f.) de agua; canal estrecho, caz, m., saetín; (tej.) paso, carrera de la lanzadera.—**r. course,** hipódromo; velódromo; estadio; pista. —**r. glass,** binóculo para carreras.—**r. horse,** caballo de carrera.—**r. problem,** problema (m.) racial o de razas. V. RACISM.—**r. suicide,** suicidio de la raza, reducción voluntaria de la población; neomaltusianismo exagerado.—**r. track** = R. COURSE. **II.** va. (hacer) correr de prisa; competir con, en una carrera, echar carrera con. **III.** vn. correr de prisa; (mar.) regatear; (mec.) desbocarse; correr más de lo normal.

raceme [ræsím], s. (bot.) racimo.

racemiferous [ræsɛmífɛrʌs], a. racimífero.

racemose, racemous [ræsimoṇs, -mʌs], *a.* racimoso, racimado, racimal.

racer [réjsœ(r)], *s.* corredor; caballo de carrera.

raceway [réjsweị], *s.* caz, *m.*, saetín; (mec.) guía; (elec.) conducto o canal para conductores eléctricos.

rachialgia [rejkiǽldżịặ], *s.* (med.) raquialgia.

rachis [réịkịs], *s.* (bot.) raquis, *m.*, raspa; (zool.) cañón de pluma; (anat.) rachis, columna vertebral, espinazo.

rachitic [rækịtịk], *a.* (med.) raquítico; raquídeo.

rachitis [rækáịtịs], *s.* (med.) raquitis, raquitismo.

racial [réịṣạl], *a.* racial, étnico, de (la) raza o de (las) razas. *V.* RACIST.

racialism [-ịzm], *s.* distinción de razas; odios de raza.

racily [réịsịlị], *adv.* de una manera picante.

raciness [réịsịnịs], *s.* picante; nariz del vino.

racism [réịsịzm], *s.* racismo.—**racist** [-ịst], *a.* y *s.* racista.

rack [ræk]. I. *s.* bastidor, rambla; aparato para estirar; potro de tormento; dolor, pena, angustia; (mec.) cremallera o barra dentada; espetera, astillero, percha, cuelgacapas, soporte, sostén, colgador; armero (para armas de fuego); (coc.) morillos de asador; pesebre, comedero; (carr.) escaleta; celajes, *m. pl.;* (equit.) trote cochinero.—**r. and pinion,** engranaje de cremallera y piñón.—**r. and ruin,** (fam.) ruina completa, acabóse.—**r. bar,** cremallera.—**r. block,** (mar.) telera.—**r. rail,** riel de cremallera.—**r. railway,** ferrocarril de cremallera.—**racks of a cart,** adrales, laderas de carro.—**to be on the r.,** estar en el potro (fig.), estar en angustias. II. *va.* atormentar; despedazar, rasgar; extorsionar; estirar; mover con rueda y cremallera; agobiar, oprimir, vejar; hacer un enrejado para; (mar.) amarrar; trasegar, tra(n)svasar, zaquear (líquidos).—**to r. one's brains,** devanarse los sesos. III. *vn.* andar a trote cochinero.

racket [rækịt]. I. *s.* baraúnda, ruido, confusión; (fam.) francachela, parranda; raqueta, pala; zapato para andar sobre fango o nieve; (fam.) (contubernio o pandilla de) fraude sistematizado.—*pl.* juego parecido al tenis. II. *vn.* meter bulla.

racketeer [rækịtír]. I. *s.* contrabandista; socalifiero que se vale de la intimidación para sacar dinero a personas o a empresas comerciales, amenazándolas con la violencia o con la ruina de sus intereses. II. *vn.* ser *racketeer,* valerse de la intimidación para la exacción.—**racketeering** [-ịŋ], *s.* socaliña por intimidación.

rackety [rækịtị], *a.* (fam.) ruidoso.

racking [rækịŋ], *s.* tortura; trasiego (de licores).

rackrent [rækrent]. I. *s.* arriendo o arrendamiento exorbitante. II. *va.* rack-rent, exigir alquiler usurario.

rackwork [rækwœrk], *s.* mecanismo de engranaje de cremallera.

raconteur [rækantœr], *s.* cuentista, anecdotista.

racquet, *s.* = RACKET.

racy [réịsị], *a.* que tiene aroma (el vino); picante, chispeante (estilo o lenguaje); de raza; castizo.

radar [réjda(r)], *s.* radar.

radial [réịdịạl], *a.* radial; radiado.—**r. engine,** motor de cilindros radiales.

radian [réịdịạn], *s.* (geom.) radián, arco igual al radio.

radiance, radiancy [réịdịạns, -ị], *s.* brillo, resplandor, esplendor.

radiant [réịdịạnt]. I. *a.* radiante, radiosơ; resplandeciente, brillante; rebosante de alegría. II. *s.* (geom.) línea radial; foco irradiador; objeto radiante.

radiantly [-lị], *adv.* con brillo, con esplendor; con alegría.

Radiata [rejdịéịtặ], *s. pl.* (zool.) radiados.

radiate [réịdịeịt]. I. *va.* emitir, irradiar. II. *vn.* radiar, brillar.

radiate(d [-(ịd], *a.* radiado.

radiation [-éịṣọn], *s.* radiación, irradiación.

radiator [-ọ(r)], *s.* calorífero, aparato de calefacción; (aut., etc.) radiador.

radical [rædịkạl]. I. *a.* radical; (bot.) radical, raigal, radicoso; esencial, fundamental; completo, extremo.—**r. sign,** signo radical ($\sqrt{}$). II. *s.* radical; (gram.) radical, raíz de una palabra.

radicalism [-ịzm], *s.* radicalismo.

radicality [-kǽlịtị], **radicalness** [rǽdịkạlnịs], *s.* naturaleza radical o fundamental.

radically [rædịkạlị], *adv.* radicalmente.

radicant [rædịkạnt], *a.* (bot.) que echa raíces.

radicate [rædịkeịt]. I. *vn.* radicar(se), arraigar(se). II. *a.* arraigado.—**radication** [-kéịṣọn]. *s.* radicación, arraigue, arraigo.

radicle [rædịkl], *s.* (bot.) radícula, raiceja.

radii [réịdịaị], *s. pl.* de RADIUS: radios.

radio [réịdịoṇ]. I. *s.* radio, *f.* o *m.* (instrumento y transmisión); radiocomunicación (apl. esp. a la radiotelefonía).—**r. amateur, fan** o (fam.) **ham,** radioaficionado.—**r. announcer,** anunciador, locutor o prologuista.—**r. beacon,** radiofaro, fanal de radio.—**r. control,** gobierno o mando (de un mecanismo) por ondas hertzianas.—**r.-frequency,** frecuencia de las ondas de radiocomunicación.—**r. hookup,** circuito.—**r. link,** circuito radiotelefónico intercalado en otro circuito.—**r. listener,** radioyente, radioescucha, *mf.*—**r. receiver,** radiorreceptor.—**r. set,** radio (instrumento receptor o transmisor).—**r. station,** (estación) emisora o difusora.—**r. transmitter,** radiotransmisor.—**r. tube,** tubo termiónico, tubo o válvula de radio.—**by r.,** por radio, radiado. II. *va.* y *vn.* radiar, radiodifundir, comunicar o transmitir por radio.

radioactive [-ǽktịv], *a.* radi(o)activo.—**radioactivity** [-ǽktịvịtị], *s.* radi(o)actividad.

radioamplifier [-ǽmplịfajœ(r)], *s.* radioamplificador.

radiobroadcast [-brɔ́dkæst], *va.* radiar, radiodifundir, perifonear, difundir por radiotransmisión.—**radiobroadcaster** [-œ(r)], *s.* perifono, aparato de radiodifusión; radiodifusor, perifoneador, persona que habla en una difusora.—**radiobroadcasting** [-ịŋ]. I. *s.* perifonía, radiodifusión. II. *a.* perifónico, de radiodifusión, difusor.

radiocompass [-kʌmpạs], *s.* (rad.) radiogoniómetro, detector de dirección.

radioconductor [-kọndʌktọ(r)], *s.* (rad.) radioconductor.

radiodetector [-dịtéktọ(r)], *s.* (rad.) radiodetector, detector de ondas eléctricas.

radiogoniometer [-gounjámetœ(r)], *s.* (rad.) radiogoniómetro, detector de dirección.—**radiogoniometric(al** [-ométrịk(ạl], *a.* radiogoniométrico.—**radiogoniometry** [-ámetrị], *s.* (rad.) radiogoniometría.

radiogram [-græm], *s.* (rad.) radiograma, *m.,* radiotelegrama, *m.;* (fot.) radi(o)grafía.

radiograph [-græf]. I. *s.* radi(o)grafía, fotografía por medio de la radiactividad o con rayos X. II. *va.* (fot.) radi(o)grafiar, sacar una radiografía, hacer fotografías por medio de los rayos X; (rad.) radio(tele)grafiar.

radiographic(al [-grǽfịk(ạl], *a.* radi(o)gráfico.

radiography [rejdịágrạfị], *s.* radi(o)grafía, fotografía con substancias radiactivas o con rayos X.

Radiolaria [rejdịolérịặ], *s. pl.* (zool.) radiolarios. —**radiolarian** [-n], *s.* y ε. radiolario.

radiologist [rejdịálodʒịst], *s.* radiólogo.

radiology [-dʒị], *s.* radiología, ciencia de la radiactividad.

radiometer [rejdịámetœ(r)], *s.* radiómetro.

radiometry [-trị], *s.* radiometría.

radiophare [réịdịofer], *s.* radiofaro.

radiophone [-foṇn], *s.* (rad.) radiotéléfono;

aparato receptor o transmisor de la radiotelefonía; (fís.) radiófono.

radiophony [rɛ̞jdjáfonj], *s.* radiofonía.

radiophotography [rɛ̞jdjofotágrafj], *s.* radiofotografía, transmisión de fotografías por radio.

radioscope [-skoup], *s.* radioscopio.

radioscopy [rɛ̞jdjáskopj], *s.* radioscopia.

radiotelegram [rɛ̞jdjotél̞ḡræm], *s.* radio(tele)grama, *m.*

radiotelegraph [-téḡræf], *s.* radiotelégrafo, telégrafo sin hilos.—**radiotelegraphy** [-téḡrafj], *s.* radio(tele)grafía, telegrafía sin hilos.

radiotelephone [-téḷḟoun], *s.* radioteléfono.—**radiotelephony** [-téḷfonj], *s.* radiotelefonía.

radiotherapeutics [-θɛ̞rapjútj̞ks], **radiotherapy** [-θérapj], *s.* radioterapia, empleo terapéutico de los rayos X; raditerapia, empleo terapéutico de la radioactividad.

radiovision [-vj̞ȝon], *s.* radiovisión, transmisión de fotografías cinematográficas por radio.

radish [rǽdj̞ʃ], *s.* (bot.) rábano, rabanillo.

radium [rɛ̞jdjʌm], *s.* (quím.) radio.

radiumtherapy [-θérapj], *s.* (med.) radi(o)-terapia, radiumterapia.

radius [rɛ̞jdjʌs], *s.* radio; (geom. y anat.) radio.—**r. of curvature**, radio de curvatura.—**r. of gyration**, radio de giro.

radix [rɛ̞jdj̞ks], *s.* raíz; base, *f.* (de un sistema de numeración).

raffia [rǽfj̞ȝ], *s.* (bot.) rafia.

raffle [rǽfl]. I. *va.* (gen. con **off**) rifar, sortear. II. *s.* rifa, sorteo, lotería.

raft [ræft]. I. *s.* balsa, almadía o armadía; maderada, jangada, zatara.—**r. port**, (mar.) porta. II. *va.* convertir en balsa; transportar en balsa; pasar en balsa.

rafter [rǽftœ(r)], *s.* (arq.) cabrio, cabio, viga.

raftsman [rǽftsmȧn], *s.* almadiero, balsero; ganchero.

rag [ræg]. I. *s.* trapo, andrajo, harapo; (desp.) bandera, vela, periódico, capa; persona andrajosa; borde o canto mellado; risco; piedra granulosa; (fam.) broma, fisga. *V.* RAGTIME y RAGAMUFFIN.—~i. **baby** o **doll**, muñeca de trapo.—**r. bolt**, tornillo con garfios; perno para empotrar en piedra; (mar.) perno arponado.—**r. fair** o **market**, rastro, baratillo.—**r. money**, (fam.) papel moneda. II. *va.* rasgar; quebrantar, triturar; (fam.) regañar, sermonear; embromar, fisgar; poner en música sincopada, o musiquilla. III. *vn.* (fam.) tocar música sincopada o popular, tocar musiquilla; bailar.

ragamuffin [rǽgamʌfj̞n], *s.* galopín, golfo, pelafustán, pelagatos.

rage [rɛ̞jdȝ]. I. *s.* rabia, ira, furor, cólera; vehemencia, encarnizamiento; ardor, anhelo o entusiasmo; (fam.) boga, moda. II. *vn.* rabiar, bramar, encolerizarse, enfurecerse.

ragged [rǽgj̞d], *a* roto, rasgado, andrajoso, harapiento; mellado, desigual, escabroso o áspero.—**raggedly** [-lj], *adv.* andrajosamente; escabrosamente.—**raggedness** [-nj̞s], *s.* aspereza, escabrosidad; estado andrajoso.

raging [rɛ̞jdȝj̞ŋ], *a.* rabioso, furioso, bramador.

raglan [rǽglan], *s.* (sast.) raglán.

ragman [rǽgmæn], **ragpicker** [-pj̞kœ(r)], *s.* trapero.

ragout [rægú], *s.* (coc.) guisado.

ragstone [rǽgstoun], *s.* piedra de amolar.

ragtag [rǽgtæg], *s.* chusma, morralla.

ragtime [rǽgtajm], *s.* (mús.) tiempo sincopado; (fam.) música popular.

ragweed [rǽgwid], *s.* (bot.) ambrosía; (Ingl.) zuzón.

ragwort [rǽgwœrt], *s.* (bot.) zuzón.

raid [rɛ̞jd]. I. *va.* invadir; (fam.) entrar o apoderarse por fuerza legal.—**to r. the market**, (bolsa) tratar de trastornar los precios. II. *vn.* hacer una irrupción. III. *s.* (mil.) correría, irrupción, incursión; (fam.) invasión repentina, sorpresa.

raider [-œ(r)], *s.* el que hace correrías, etc.; (mar.) (buque) corsario.

rail [rɛ̞jl]. I. *s.* baranda, barandilla; (f. c.) riel, rail, carril; ferrocarril (medio de transporte); (mar.) batayola, cairel, galón, brazal; (orn.) rascón, ave zancuda.—**r. chair**, (f. c.) cojinete de riel.—**r. guard**, contracarril; (f. c.) rastrillo, limpiavía.—**r. train**, tren de laminadores de rieles.—**by r.**, por ferrocarril. II. *va.* (a veces con **in** u **off**) poner barandilla, barrera o verja a; transportar por ferrocarril. III. *vn.* (con **at** o **against**) denunciar, vilipendiar o quejarse de, abusiva o vehementemente.

railer [-œ(r)], *s.* murmurador, maldiciente.

railhead [-hed], *s.* término de la vía (los rieles) de un ferrocarril no terminado; (mil.) estación ferroviaria de víveres y municiones.

railing [-j̞ŋ], *s.* baranda, barandilla, pasamano; barra; cerca, verja, reja, enrejado; (f. c.) carriles, rieles; material para rieles.

raillery [rɛ̞jlœrj], *s.* chocarrería, fisga, zumba.

railroad [rɛ̞jlroud], *va.* proveer de ferrocarriles; transportar por ferrocarril; (fam.) apresurar, hacer algo rápidamente; hacer aprobar (una ley, etc.) con precipitación; (fam.) encarcelar falsamente.

railroad, railway [rɛ̞jlwej]. I. *s.* ferrocarril, vía férrea, camino de hierro. II. *a.* ferroviario, de ferrocarril, para ferrocarriles.—**r. car** o **carriage**, vagón o coche ferroviario.—**r. crossing**, paso a nivel.—**r. junction**, entronque.—**r. siding** o **switch**, apartadero, desviadero.—**railway spine**, (med.) desorden de la medula espinal debido a concusión.

raiment [rɛ̞jmȩnt], *s.* ropa, traje, indumento; prendas de vestir.

rain [rɛ̞jn]. I. *vn.* (*impers.*) llover.—**r. or shine**, que llueva o no; con buen o mal tiempo. II. *va.* derramar copiosamente.—**to r. cats and dogs**, o **pitchforks**, llover chuzos, llover a cántaros. III. *s.* lluvia.—**r.-and-wind storm**, turbonada.—**r. cape**, capa aguadera.—**r. ga(u)ge**, pluviómetro.—**r. water**, agua lluvia, agua llovediza.

rainbow [-bou], *s.* arco iris.—**r.-hued**, irisado, iridiscente.

raincoat [-kout], *s.* impermeable (sobretodo).

raindrop [-drap], *s.* gota de agua.

rainfall [-fol], *s.* aguacero; cantidad de lluvia que cae durante tiempo determinado.

raininess [-nj̞s], *s.* estado lluvioso.

rainproof [-pruf]. I. *a.* a prueba de la lluvia. II. *s.* capa o abrigo impermeable. III. *va.* hacer impermeable.

rainstorm [-storm], *s.* aguacero, temporal, chubasco, tempestad de agua.

rainy [-j], *a.* lluvioso, pluvioso.—**r. day**, (fig.) tiempo de escasez o necesidad.—**for a r. day**, por lo que pueda tronar.—**r. season**, época de las lluvias.

raise [rɛ̞jz]. I. *va.* levantar, alzar, poner en pie; elevar, erguir, empinar; construir, erigir; aumentar, subir; promover, ascender, encumbrar, ensalzar; animar, incitar; crear; causar, ocasionar; criar, cultivar; hacer concebir, inspirar, dar lugar a; hacer surgir, hacer brotar; vivificar, revivir; llamar, evocar; reclutar, alistar; allegar, reunir, recoger o juntar (dinero); poner fin a, abandonar; formar en relieve; ofrecer, presentar, suscitar; levantar (en la caza); fermentar (pan.).—**to r. a check**, raspar y aumentar la cantidad de un cheque, etc.—**to r. a dust**, (fam.) hacer grande alharaca.—**to r. an eyebrow**, (fam.) arquear las cejas.—**to r. an objection**, poner una objeción.—**to r. an outcry**, causar gritería, gritar.—**to r. a point**, presentar una cuestión, hacer una observación.—**to r. a racket, a row, a rumpus, Cain, the devil, the dickens, the mischief, the Old Boy**, etc., (fam.) armar un alboroto; causar gran conmoción, trastorno o desbarajuste: armar un lío.—**to r. a storm**, levantar cisco, promover desórdenes.—**to r. money on**, empeñar. obtener dinero prestado por.—**to r. steam**, levantar vapor, poner la caldera bajo presión.—**to r. the country**, sublevar, alborotar, revolucionar el país.—**to r. the dead**, despertar a los muertos.—**to r. the nap of the cloth**, perchar los paños, sacarles el pelo.—**to r. to a power**, (mat.) elevar a una potencia. **II.** *s.* levantamiento; alzamiento; aumento, subida; ascenso; tra·viesa (de una apuesta).

aised [-d], *a.* abollonado; en relieve; de resalto, de realce, que sobresale; (coc.) fermentado o leudo (pan).

aiser [-œ(r)], *s.* productor, cultivador; ganadero; educador; fundador.

aisin [réizin], *s.* pasa, uva seca.

aising [réiziŋ], *s.* acción de levantar, erigir, etc.; levantamiento; elevación; cría.

aison d'être [réizon détr], *s.* razón (*f.*) de ser.

aj [radž], *s.* (India) soberanía, señorío.

aja(h [rádžä], *s.* rajá, *m.* (príncipe o caudillo).

ake [reik]. **I.** *s.* (agr.) rastro, mielga, rastrillo; inclinación, desviación de la vertical; (aer.) inclinación del extremo de un plano de sustentación al plano de simetría; (geol., min.) lanzamiento o caída; calavera, *m.*, libertino, perdido. —**r. dredge**, draga barredera. **II.** *va.* (agr.) rastrillar; barrer, raspar, rascar, raer; atizar, hurgar (el fuego); (fig.) escudriñar; (mil.) enfilar, barrer.—**to r. out**, ahondar raspando. —**to r. over the coals,** (fam.) criticar severamente, despedazar, despellejar, poner como un trapo. **III.** *vn.* pasar el rastro o la mielga; rascar, ahorrar; pasar con rapidez o violencia; llevar una vida disoluta; (mar.) inclinarse.

ake-off [réik ɔf], *s.* (fam.) ganancia, tajada.

aker [réikœ(r)], *s.* raedera, raspadera; rastrilladora mecánica.

akish [réikiš], *a.* libertino, disoluto; airoso, garboso; (mar.) de mástiles muy inclinados; de aspecto velero y veloz.—**rakishness** [-nis], *s.* disolución, libertinaje; (mar.) caída, inclinación de los palos.

le [ral], *s.* (med.) estertor.

lly [réli]. **I.** *va.* (mil.) reunir y reanimar, rehacer; ridiculizar; dar matraca o zumba. **II.** *vn.* (mil.) reunirse, rehacerse; reanimarse; recobrar las fuerzas, revivir; chancearse, zumbarse. **III.** *s.* unión o reunión (de tropas dispersas o de gente); recuperación.

am [ræm]. **I.** *s.* (zool.) morueco, carnero padre; (mec.) martinete, pisón; ariete hidráulico; (mar.) espolón; buque con espolón; (mil.) ariete; (R., astr.) Aries. **II.** *va.* pisonear, apisonar, golpear con un pisón, espolón o ariete; meter por la fuerza, apretar; atacar (un arma de fuego); atestar, henchir; atracar.

amadan [rémadan], *s.* Ramadán.

mble [rémbl]. **I.** *vn.* vagar, callejear; divagar, ir por las ramas; dar vueltas, serpentear; discurrir. **II.** *s.* paseo; paseadero.—**rambler** [rémblœ(r)], *s.* vagabundo, callejero; paseador; divagador; (bot.) rosa trepadora.—**rambling** [-iŋ]. **I.** *s.* correteo, divagación. **II.** *a.* divagador, etc.

mbunctious [ræmbáŋkšʌs], *a.* (fam.) bullicioso, ruidoso; estrepitoso; ingobernable.

mekin [rémekin], *s.* (coc.) quesadilla; tazuela para quesadillas.

mie [rémi], *s.* (bot.) ramio; ramina.

mification [rémifikéišǝn], *s.* ramificación, ramal.—**ramify** [-fai], *va.* y *vn.* ramificar(se).

mmer [rémœ(r)], *s.* baqueta de fusil; atacador; pisón de empedrador; (mar.) espolón.

mmish [rémiš], *a.* arietino; rancio, que huele a carnero o chotuno; libidinoso, salaz.

mose [réimous], **ramous** [-mʌs], *a.* ramoso.

mp [ræmp]. **I.** *s.* rampa, declive. **II.** *vn.* saltar, brincar; agitarse, bramar; (bot.) trepar.

rampage [rémpeidž]. **I.** *s.* alboroto, agitación violenta, turbulencia. **II.** *vn.* bramar, enfurecerse, embestir a ciegas.

rampancy [rémpansi], *s.* exuberancia, superabundancia, extravagancia.

rampant [rémpant], *a.* exuberante; excesivo; desenfrenado; general y sin coto; ufano, lozano; (blas.) rampante.

rampart [rémpart]. **I.** *s.* (fort.) terraplén; muro, muralla; baluarte. **II.** *va.* murar, abaluartar.

rampion [rémpion], *s.* (bot.) rapónchigo.

ramrod [rémrad], *s.* baqueta, atacador, cargador.

ramshackle [rémšækl], *a.* desvencijado, destartalado, ruinoso.

ramulose, ramulous [rémiulous, -lʌs], *a.* (bot., zool.) ramoso.

ramus [réimʌs], *s.* (bot., anat.) ramal, ramificación.

ran [ræn], *pret.* de TO RUN.

ranch [rænch]. **I.** *s.* hacienda de ganado; granja; (Am.) estancia, rancho. **II.** *vn.* tener hacienda de ganado, ser hacendado.—**rancher** [-œ(r)], **ranchman** [-man], *s.* hacendado, ganadero; boyero; (Am.) estanciero, ranchero.

rancid [rénsid], *a.* rancio, rancioso.

rancidness, rancidity [-nis, rænsíditi], *s.* rancidez.

rancor [réŋkǫ(r)], *s.* rencor, enemiga, encono, inquina.

rancorous [-ʌs], *a.* rencoroso.

rancorously [-li], *adv.* rencorosamente.

rand [rænd], *s.* calzo del zapato.

random [réndǝm]. **I.** *s.* azar, casualidad.—**at r.**, a la ventura, al azar, a trochemoche. **II.** *a.* fortuito, impensado, casual; sin orden ni concierto.—**r. shot**, tiro sin puntería.

rang [ræŋ], *pret.* de TO RING.

range [réindž]. **I.** *va.* recorrer; batir (el monte); (mar.) costear; poner en posición; poner en fila; (a veces con *in*) alinear; arreglar, clasificar. **II.** *vn.* vagar; extenderse; estar en línea; ponerse al lado, adherirse; tener igual grado, estar a la misma altura; variar, fluctuar; (arti.) tener alcance (un proyectil).—**to r. by**, (mar.) pasar, dejar atrás. **III.** *s.* distancia que recorre alguna cosa; extensión, recorrido; trascurso, duración; límites, *m. pl.*; campo o esfera de actividad; excursión; vasta extensión de terrenos de pasto; alcance (de un arma o proyectil); fila, hilera, línea; clase, *f.*, orden; línea de un tiro de artillería; sitio para tirar al blanco; campo de tiro; dirección; cuerda (de la voz); cocina económica; (mar.) cornamusa.—**r. finder**, (arti.) telémetro.—**r. of mountains**, cadena de montañas, cordillera.—**r. pole**, (top.) jalón.—**r. stove**, cocina portátil.—**r. work**, (alb.) mampostería concertada, con hiladas de una misma altura.—**at close r.**, a quema ropa.—**to be within the r. of**, estar a tiro, al alcance de.

ranger [-œ(r)], *s.* guardabosque, guardamonte; batidor; recorredor, vigilante; perro ventor.

Ranidae [rénidi], *s. pl.* (zool.) ránidos.

rank [ræŋk]. **I.** *a.* lozano, exuberante, fértil; espeso, cerrado; rancio; fétido; grosero, indecente; acabado, rematado, insigne (cobarde, traidor, etc.); (mec.) profundo, hondo. **II.** *s.* línea, hilera; (mil.) grado, graduación, categoría; jerarquía, rango; posición (social, etc.); cuantía; calidad, distinción; (mil.) fila.—**the ranks, the r. and file**, la tropa, los soldados de fila; las masas; el cuerpo, los miembros ordinarios (de una asociación, etc.), a distinción de los dignatarios. **III.** *va.* clasificar, ordenar; colocar por grados; poner en fila; (mil.) tener un grado superior a. **IV.** *vn.* tener tal o cual grado o clasificación; ocupar (primer, segundo, etc.) lugar; figurar, contarse entre; (con **with**) estar al nivel (de); (con **high, low**), ocupar (alta, baja) posición.

ranker [-œ(r)], *s.* soldado; oficial que ha ascendido desde soldado raso.

rankish [-iŝ], *a.* algo rancio.

rankle [-l], *vn.* enconarse, inflamarse; causar encono, resentimiento o enojo.

rankly [-lį], *adv.* lozanamente; groseramente; ranciamente.—**rankness** [-nįs], *s.* exuberancia; fertilidad; rancidez, fetidez.

ransack [rǽnsæk], *va.* escudriñar, explorar, registrar a fondo; pillar, saquear.

ransom [rǽnsǫm]. I. *s.* rescate, redención. II. *va.* rescatar, redimir.—**ransomeless** [-lįs], *a.* sin rescate; irrescatable, irredimible.

rant [rǽnt]. I. *vn.* gritar, desvariar, delirar, (fam.) desparpajar. II. *s.* lenguaje campanudo, retumbante.—**ranter** [-œ(r)], *s.* vociferador, energúmeno.

ranula [rǽnyulǎ], *s.* (med., vet.) ránula, barbilla, sapillo.

ranunculaceous [rǎnᴧnḳiulḗiŝǎs], *a.* (bot.) ranunculáceo.—**ranunculus** [-lᴧs], *s.* (bot.) ranúnculo, botón de oro.

rap [ræp]. I. *va.* y *vn.* (*pret.* y *pp.* RAPPED) golpear, tocar, dar un golpe seco; proferir vivamente; (fam.) criticar, zaherir, echar púas.—**to r. at the door,** tocar o llamar a la puerta. II. *va.* (*pret.* y *pp.* RAPT) arrebatar; transportar con éxtasis (ú. esp. el *pp.*). III. *s.* golpe seco, taque; (fam.) crítica; medio penique falso; (fam.) fruslería, ardite (v. gr.: *I don't care a rap,* no me importa un bledo); madeja, cadejo de 120 yardas de hilo.—**r. on the nose,** papirote, pasagonzalo.—**r. on the knuckles,** golpecito sobre los artejos; reconvención.—**to take the r.,** (fam.) pagar el pato o los vidrios rotos.

rapacious [rǎpḗiŝᴧs], *a.* rapaz.—**rapaciously** [-lį], *adv.* con rapacidad.—**rapaciousness** [-nįs], **rapacity** [rǎpǽsįtį], *s.* rapacidad.

rape [réip]. I. *s.* violación, estupro; violencia, fuerza; rapto, robo; (bot.) nabo silvestre, colza; filtro para hacer vinagre; granuja.—*pl.* escobajo, raspajo.—**r. oil,** aceite de colza. II. *va.* violar, estuprar, desflorar.

rapeseed [-sid], *s.* (bot.) colza; nabina o simiente de colza o nabo silvestre.—**r. oil,** aceite de colza.

Raphaelesque [rǽfięlḗsk], *a.* rafaelesco.—**Raphaelism** [-izm], *s.* rafaelismo, estilo o escuela de Rafael.—**Raphaelite** [-ait], *s.* rafaelista.

raphe [réifi], *s.* (anat., bot.) rafe, torillo.

rapid [rǽpįd]. I. *a.* rápido, raudo, veloz.—**r.-fire gun,** o **r.-firer,** cañón de tiro rápido.—**r. transit,** tráfico o transporte rápido. II. *s. pl.* rabión, *m.,* recial, rápido.

rapidity [rǎpídįtį], **rapidness** [rǽpįdnįs], *s.* rapidez, velocidad.

rapidly [rǽpįdlį], *adv.* rápidamente, ligero.

rapier [réipįœ(r)], *s.* espadín; estoque.

rapine [rǽpįn], *s.* rapiña, robo.

rapist [réipįst], *s.* raptor, violador, estuprador.

rappee [rǽpí], *s.* rapé.

rapper [rǽpœ(r)], *s.* golpeador; medio espiritista; llamador, aldabón (de una puerta).

rapport [ræpórt], *s.* armonía, concordancia, simpatía.

rapprochement [raprόŝman], *s.* restablecimiento de las relaciones o la armonía (entre dos naciones); reconciliación; acercamiento.

rapscallion [ræpskǽlyǫn], *s.* bribón, pícaro.

rapt [ræpt], *pp.* y *a.* transportado, arrebatado o extasiado.—**r. in thought,** absorto.

raptorial [ræptóuriǎl], *a.* (orn.) de presa, de rapiña, rapaz.

Raptores [ræptóuriz], *s. pl.* aves (*f.*) rapaces.

rapture [rǽpchǔ(r)], *s.* rapto, enajenamiento, arrobamiento, embeleso, embriaguez, éxtasis, *m.*

rapturous [-ᴧs], *a.* arrobado, arrebatado, embelesado.—**rapturously** [-lį], *adv.* con éxtasis, con transportes, extáticamente.

rare [rer], *a.* raro; precioso; contado, extraordi-

nario, peregrino; (coc.) poco asado, a med asar; raro (de la atmósfera); esparcido.

rarebit [rérbįt], *s. V.* WELSH RABBIT.

raree-show [réri ŝǫu], *s.* tutilimundi, mundinov

rarefaction [réręfǽkŝǫn], *s.* rarefacción.

rarefiable [-fáiǎbl], *a.* capaz de rarefacción.

rarefy [-fai]. I. *va.* enrarecer, rarefacer, rarifica refinar, purificar. II. *vn.* rarificarse, etc.

rarely [rérlį], *adv.* raramente, rara vez, por rarez sólo de tarde en tarde; excelente o extrem mente.

rareness [-nįs], *s.* rareza, singularidad; escase excelencia.—**rareripe** [-raip]. I. *a.* precc temprano. II. *s.* legumbre o fruta precoz.

rarity [rérįtį], *s.* raridad, rareza; curiosidad, p ciosidad; tenuidad.

rascal [rǽskąl], *s.* pícaro, bribón, bellaco, pillo.

rascality [ræskǽlįtį], *s.* bellaquería, tunantuerí

rascallion [ræskǽlyǫn], *s.* villano, canalla, bel gante.

rascally [rǽskąlį], *a.* vil, bajo, ruin, truhanesco.

rase [reiz], *va.* = RAZE.

rash [ræŝ]. I. *a.* temerario, imprudente, arreb tado, precipitado. II. *s.* salpullido, erupción.

rasher [rǽŝœ(r)], *s.* lonja, magra, torrezno.

rashly [rǽŝlį], *adv.* temerariamente, imprudent mente.

rashness [-nįs], *s.* temeridad, imprudencia, pr cipitación.

Rasores [rǎsóuriz], *s. pl.* (orn.) gallináceas.

rasorial [rǎsóuriǎl], *a.* gallináceo.

rasp [ræsp]. I. *s.* escofina, raspa, raspador, lim tón, rallo, escarpelo; sonido estridente. II. *v* raspar, escofinar, rallar.

raspberry [rǽzberį], *s.* (bot.) frambuesa, zu güesa; (fam.) sonido de mofa.—**r. bus** frambueso.

rasper [rǽspœ(r)], *s.* raspador, rallo.

rasping [rǽspįŋ]. I. *a.* raedor, raspante; rone áspero; irritante. II. *s.* raspadura, raedura.

raspy [rǽspį], *a.* = RASPING.

rat [ræt]. I. *s.* (zool.) rata; (desp.) esquirol, que toma el lugar de un huelguista; (fam.) cobarde; desertor, renegado; (fam.) postiz para el pelo.—**r. catcher,** cazador de ratas. **r. dung,** cagarruta de ratas.—**r. poiso** arsénico, veneno para matar ratas.—**r.-ta file,** lima de cola de rata.—**r. trap,** ratonera. **to smell a r.,** recelar, haber gato encerrad II. *va.* y *vn.* (fam.) reemplazar obreros agremi dos por otros no agremiados; trabajar por jorn menor que el que fija un gremio; tomar el luga de un huelguista; cazar ratas; (pol. fam.) volv casaca.

ratable [réitǎbl], *a.* sujeto a contribución; ir ponible; valuable, que puede tasarse.

ratably [réitǎblį], *adv.* a prorrata.

ratafia [rǽtafíǎ], *s.* ratafía (licor).

ratan [rǽtǽn], *s.* = RATTAN.

ratany [rǽtanį], *s.* (bot.) ratania.

rataplan [rǽtąplǽn], *s.* rataplán, sonido d tambor. II. *vn.* tamborear, tabalear.

ratch [ræch], *s.* cremallera; rueda dentada c trinquete.

ratchet [rǽchįt], *s.* (mec.) trinquete, lingue retén.—**r. brace,** carraca, berbiquí de tr quete.—**r. drill,** taladro de trinquete.— **wheel,** rueda de trinquete.—**r. wrench,** lla (*f.*) de trinquete.

rate [réit]. I. *s.* tarifa, precio o valor fijo; coti ción; tasa; tipo (de interés, etc.); velocida proporción, tanto (por ciento, por unidad, etc contribución, impuesto; cuota; clase o clasific ción de un buque mercante o de guerra, o los miembros de la tripulación; error o var ción diaria de un reloj; modo, manera; (Ing contribución local. Se emplea a menudo, sob todo en plural, para denotar sumas de dine pagadas, exigidas, etc., regularmente, y pue traducirse por "precios," "salarios," "tarifa "honorarios," "sueldos," etc., según el caso.

r. of climb, (aer.) velocidad de ascenso.—**r. of exchange,** cambio (valor relativo de las unidades monetarias), tipo del cambio.—**r. of grade,** (f. c.) pendiente relativa, pendiente (subentendiéndose que se expresa en tanto por ciento, por kilómetro, etc.).—**r. of population,** aumento proporcional de la población (expresado gen. en tantos por 1000, por 100,000, etc.). —**at any r.,** de todos modos, sea como fuere, en todo caso.—**at no r.,** de ningún modo.—**at that r.,** en esa proporción; de ese modo; a ese paso.—**at the r. of,** a razón de. II. va. tasar, valuar; clasificar; imponer contribuciones, derecho, gravamen, etc.; determinar el error de (un reloj); considerar, justipreciar; calcular, estimar; fijar precio, tarifa, etc.; dar o determinar la capacidad normal de (una máquina). III. vn. ser considerado (como), tenido (por); estar clasificado (como). IV. va. y vn. regañar, reñir, sermonear.

rateable [-ᴀbl], a. = RATABLE.

ratel [réitᴇl], s. (zool.) ratel.

rather [ráᵭœ(r)]. I. adv. bastante, un poco, algo (she is rather pretty, ella es bastante bonita; I am rather tired, estoy un poco cansado); más bien, por mejor decir, mejor dicho (I am tired, or, rather, exhausted, estoy cansado, o mejor dicho, agotado); por el contrario, antes bien.— **r. than,** más bien que, primero que, en vez de, por no, antes que.—**the r., the r. as, the r. that,** tanto más cuanto que.—(I) had r., o **would r.,** prefiero, preferiría, más bien quisiera, de mejor gana (haría algo). II. interj. ¡ya lo creo!, ¡claro!, ¡mucho!

rathskeller [rátskɛlœ(r)], s. restaurante o cantina de sótano.

ratification [rᴂtᴉfᴉkéiʃᴏn], s. ratificación, aprobación, sanción.—**ratifier** [-faiœ(r)], s. ratificador.—**ratify** [-fai], va. ratificar, aprobar, confirmar, sancionar.—**ratifying** [-iŋ], a. ratificador, ratificatorio.

ratiné [rᴂtᴉnéi], s. (tej.) ratina.

rating [réitᴉŋ], s. justiprecio; apreciación; clasificación (de un buque, marinero, etc.); (mec.) capacidad o potencia normal o de régimen; fijación de impuestos; reprimenda, regaño, sermón.

ratio [réiʃiou], s. razón, f., relación, proporción; (mat.) razón.

ratiocinate [rᴂʃᴉásᴉneit]. I. vn. raciocinar, razonar. II. a. razonado.

ratiocination [-éiʃᴏn], s. raciocinio.

ration [rᴂʃᴏn o réiʃᴏn]. I. s. (mil.) ración.—**r. book** o **card,** cartilla o tarjeta de racionamiento. II. va. poner a ración; racionar; distribuir en raciones.

rational [rᴂʃᴏnᴀl], a. racional, cuerdo, juicioso; razonado; (mat.) racional.

rationale [rᴂʃᴏnᴂl], s. exposición razonada.

rationalism [rᴂʃᴏnᴀlizm], s. racionalismo.

rationalist [-ist], s. racionalista.

rationalistic(al [-istik(ᴀl], a. racionalista.

rationality [rᴂʃᴏnᴂliti], s. racionalidad.

rationalization [rᴂʃᴏnᴀlizéiʃᴏn], s. acción o efecto de explicar acciones, creencias, etc., de un modo racional(ista) o favorable; (mat.) supresión de radicales.—**rationalize** [-aiz]. I. va. hacer racional; interpretar o concebir racionalmente; buscar explicación racional o justificativa de; (mat.) hacer racional, quitar los radicales a. II. vn. profesar el racionalismo; emplear la razón y la lógica.

rationally [-i], adv. racionalmente.

rationing [rᴂʃᴏniŋ o réiʃᴏniŋ], s. racionamiento.

ratite [rᴂtait], s. y a. (orn.) corredora (ave).

Ratitæ [rᴂtáiti], s. pl. (orn.) corredoras.

ratlin(e [rᴂtlin], **ratling** [rᴂtliŋ], s. (mar.) rebenque, flechaste, frenillo.

ratoon [rᴂtún], s. retoño; soca de caña de azúcar.

ratsbane [rᴂtsbein], s. arsénico.

rattan [rᴂtᴂn], s. (bot.) roten, rota, bejuco; junquillo; bastón o varilla de roten.

ratter [rᴂtœ(r)], s. cazador de ratas; perro o gato ratonero; (fam.) desertor, renegado; esquirol.

rattle [rᴂtl]. I. va. hacer sonar como una carraca o matraca; batir o sacudir con ruido; (fam.) atolondrar, aturrullar; (con **off**) decir a la carrera; (mar.) proveer de, o atar con, rebenques. II. vn. matraquear, rechinar, guachapear; charlatanear, parlotear; moverse o funcionar con matraqueo.—**to r. away,** parlotear; rodar a distancia, haciendo ruido. III. s. cascabel (de crótalo); sonajero (juguete); matraca, carraca; parla, charla; bulla; estertor.—**r.-brained, r.-headed, r.-pated,** ligero de cascos, casquivano.—**r. snake,** (zool.) crótalo, culebra de cascabel.

rattlebox [-baks], s. cascabel (juguete); charlador.

rattled [-d], a. (fam.) aturdido, azarado, confundido.

rattlehead [-hed], **rattlepate** [-peit], **rattleskull** [-skᴧl], s. parlanchín; casquivano.

rattler [rᴂtlœ(r)], s. parlanchín, tarabilla; (zool.) crótalo; cosa que anda o funciona de prisa y con ruido.

rattlesnake [rᴂtlsneik], s. (zool.) culebra de cascabel, crótalo.

rattletrap [-trᴂp], s. coche u otro objeto destartalado; (fam.) parlanchín; la boca.—pl. chucherías.

rattling [rᴂtliŋ], a. ruidoso; vivo; (fam.) extremamente bueno, rápido, etc.

raucity [rósiti], s. ronquera; bronquedad.

raucous [rókᴀs], a. ronco, (poét.) rauco; bronco.

ravage [rᴂvidᴣ]. I. va. saquear, pillar; asolar, talar, destruir. II. s. ruina, estrago, destrucción; saqueo.

ravager [-œ(r)], s. saqueador; asolador.

rave [reiv]. I. vn. delirar, desvariar; devanear, disparatar; bramar, enfurecerse, salirse de sus casillas.—**to r. after,** querer a toda costa, despepitarse por.—**to r. over,** o **about,** entusiasmarse locamente por. II. s. (carr.) adral de un carro; (fam.) (objeto de un) amor o infatuación exagerada. V. BLURB.

ravehook [réivhuk], s. (mar.) descalcador.

ravel [rᴂvl]. I. va. deshilar, deshebrar, deshacer; (con **out**) desenredar, desenmarañar; enredar (acepción original). II. vn. (con **out**) deshilarse, destorcerse; deshacerse; (ant.) enredarse. III. s. V. RAVELING y RAVELMENT.

ravelin [rᴂvlin], s. (fort.) revellín.

ravel(l)ing [rᴂvliŋ], s. hilacha; deshiladura.

ravelment [rᴂvᴇlmᴇnt], s. maraña, enredo.

raven [réivn], I. s. (orn.) cuervo.—**r.'s-duck,** (tej.) loneta. II. a. negro y lustroso.

raven, ravin [rᴂvn o rᴂvin]. I. va. y vn. apresar, prender por fuerza; devorar. II. s. presa, botín, rapiña.

ravening [rᴂvᴇniŋ]. I. s. rapiña; rapacidad; voracidad. II. a. rapaz; voraz; (blas.) cebado.

ravenous [rᴂvᴇnᴀs], a. voraz, famélico; rapaz.— **ravenously** [-li], adv. vorazmente.—**ravenousness** [-nis], s. voracidad; rapacidad.

ravine [rᴀvín], s. barranca, cañada, hondonada, hoz.

raving [réiviŋ]. I. s. desvarío, delirio. II. a. delirante, desvariado.—**ravingly** [-li], adv. desvariadamente, locamente.

ravish [rᴂviʃ], va. arrebatar, atraer, encantar; violar, estuprar.—**ravisher** [-œ(r)], s. estuprador; arrebatador.—**ravishing** [-iŋ], a. arrebatador, embriagador.—**ravishingly** [-li], adv. arrobadoramente.—**ravishment** [-mᴇnt], s. rapto, transporte, arrobamiento; estupro, violación (de una mujer).

raw [ró]. I. a. crudo; pelado, despellejado; en carne viva; descarnado; desapacible, frío y húmedo; (com.) en bruto; fresco, nuevo; novato, bisoño (recluta, etc.); vulgar, tosco, brutal; (fam.) indecente; injusto.—**r. cotton,**

algodón en rama.—**r. flesh**, carne viva.—**r. gas**, gas sucio.—**r. hand**, novato, novicio.—**r. hemp**, cáñamo en bruto o sin peinar.—**r. material**, materia prima.—**r. silk**, seda en rama.—**r. spirits**, licores puros o sin mezcla. —**r. sugar**, azúcar bruto o mascabado.—**r. tallow**, sebo puro o en rama.—**r. weather**, tiempo crudo. **II.** s. carne viva o llagada; desolladura; (vet. y fig.) matadura; material en bruto; persona sin cultura.—**in the r.**, al desnudo; en su ser natural y crudo, etc.

rawboned [-bŏund], a. huesudo; flaco, desvaído.

rawhead [-hed], s. espectro, fantasma, espantajo.

rawhide [-haid]. **I.** a. de cuero sin curtir. **II.** s. cuero crudo; látigo hecho de este cuero.

rawish [-iṣ], a. algo crudo, un tanto crudo.

rawly [-li], adv. crudamente.

rawness [-nis], s. crudeza.

ray [rei]. **I.** s. rayo (de luz, calor, etc.); (geom.) radio; línea recta, hilera, raya; (bot.) lígula; (ict.) raya.—**r. filter**, pantalla fotocrómica.—**r. grass**, (bot.) vallico. **II.** va. y vn. emitir rayos; (ir)radiar; (fam.) radiografiar, fotografiar con los rayos X.

rayon [réiǫn], s. (tej.) rayón (fibra y tela).

raze [reiz], va. arrasar, demoler, derruir.

razee [raẓí]. **I.** va. rebajar un buque de guerra; reducir, cercenar. **II.** s. buque rebajado.

razor [réiẓǫ(r)], s. navaja de afeitar; colmillo del jabalí.—**r. blade**, hoja o cuchilla de navaja de seguridad.—**r. case**, navajero.—**r. clam, r. fish**, navaja (marisco).—**r. grinder**, vaciador de navajas de afeitar.—**r. shell** = R. CLAM.—**r. strap, r. strop**, asentador o suavizador.

razorback [-bæk], s. (zool.) yubarta; cerdo (semi)salvaje.

razorbill [-bil], s. (orn.) alca.

razz [ræz]. **I.** s. (fam.) crítica mordaz, desolladura, mofa, escarnio. **II.** va. (fam.) mofarse o burlarse de.

razzle-dazzle [ræzl dæzl]. **I.** va. (fam.) embriagar; deslumbrar; aturdir. **II.** s. (fam.) borrachera; aturdimiento; especie de tiovivo.

re [rei o ri]. **I.** s. (mús.) re. **II.** [ri], prep. (for., com.) acerca de, concerniente a.

reabsorb [riạbsŏrb], va. re(ab)sorber.

reabsorption [riạbsŏrpṣǫn], s. re(ab)sorción.

reaccess [riǽksịs], s. (med.) recidiva.

reach [rích]. **I.** va. alargar, llegar a o hasta; alcanzar, lograr, conseguir, obtener; penetrar.—**to r. out one's hand**, tender la mano.—**to r. the heart**, llegar al o tocar el corazón. **II.** vn. extenderse, llegar, alcanzar, penetrar; esforzarse; coger; (mar.) ceñir el viento, navegar de bolina.—**to r. after**, procurar obtener o coger, hacer esfuerzos por alcanzar o coger.—**to r. into**, penetrar en. **III.** s. alcance: extensión, distancia; poder, facultad; capacidad; (carr.) barra que une el juego posterior con la parte delantera; (mar.) bordada.—**beyond one's r., out of one's r.**, fuera del alcance de uno.—**within one's r.**, al alcance de uno; dentro del poder de uno.

reachable [-ạbl], a. asequible.

react [riǽkt], vn. reaccionar.

reactance [-ạns], s. (elec.) reactancia.—**r. coil**, bobina de reacción o de reactancia.

reaction [riǽkṣǫn], s. reacción.—**reactionary** [-ɛri]. **I.** a. reaccionario. **II.** s. (pol.) retrógrado. —**reactionist** [-ist], s. (pol.) reaccionario, retrógrado.

reactive [riǽktiv], a. reactivo.

reactivity [-tíviti], s. reactividad.

reactor [riǽktǫ(r)], s. el que reacciona; (quím.) reactivo; (elec.) = REACTANCE COIL.

read [rid]. **I.** va. (pret. y pp. READ [red]) leer; descifrar; marcar, indicar (the thermometer reads 20°, el termómetro marca 20°); (mús.) leer.—**to r. law**, estudiar derecho.—**to r. off hand**, leer de corrido.—**to r. one a lecture o lesson**, (fam.) sermonear, poner a uno como

nuevo.—**to r. one to sleep**, dormir o adormecer a uno leyéndole.—**to r. out**, expulsar (a un miembro de una asociación).—**to r. over**, leerlo todo, recorrer (un escrito).—**to r. proofs**, (impr.) corregir pruebas.—**to r. through**, leer de cabo a rabo.—**to r. through one**, calar a uno, conocer sus intenciones. **II.** vn. leer; (con **of o about**) saber, enterarse de (leyendo); leer, decir, rezar (the text reads thus, el texto reza, o dice, así); (mús.) saber leer e interpretar las notas; conferenciar en público; indicar; sonar (bien, mal) al leerlo; ser lectura (amena, difícil, etc.).—**to r. about**, leer acerca de; aprender leyendo.—**to r. between the lines**, leer entre líneas.—**to r. on**, proseguir o continuar leyendo.—**to r. to**, indicar hasta, tener apreciación de (apl. a instrumentos de medida).—**to r. to one's self**, leer para sí. **III.** [red], a. leído, instruido, ilustrado, erudito.

readable [rídạbl], a. leíble, legible; ameno, interesante, entretenido.

readability [ridạbílịti], o **readableness** [rídạblnịs], s. calidad de legible; interés, amenidad de estilo.

reader [rídǿe(r)], s. lector, leyente; declamador; libro de lectura (de texto); (impr.) corrector de pruebas; (igl.) lector.

readership [-ṣip], s. (igl.) lectoría.

readily [rédịli], adv. fácilmente; prontamente, luego; con placer, de buena gana.

readiness [rédịnịs], s. disposición, buena voluntad; prontitud; facilidad; aptitud, desembarazo.—**r. of wit**, viveza o vivacidad de ingenio.—**in r.**, listo, preparado.

reading [rídiŋ]. **I.** s. lectura; material de lectura; significado (de algo escrito); conferencia, disertación; lectura de un proyecto de ley; apertura de un testamento; estudio; lectura, indicación de un instrumento graduado; interpretación; leyenda, variante, f., glosa; solución de un enigma o acertijo; (teat.) desempeño o interpretación de un papel. **II.** a. de lectura.—**r. desk**, facistol, atril.—**r. glass**, vidrio de aumento; pl. carlita, lunetas para leer.—**r. matter**, material de lectura; sección de lectura (de un periódico).—**r. room**, sala de lectura.

readjust [riạdʤást], va. ajustar de nuevo; readaptar; (impr.) recorrer.—**readjustment** [-mǫnt], s. readaptación; (impr.) recorrido.

readmission [riạdmíṣǫn], s. readmisión.

readmit [riạdmít], va. admitir de nuevo.

ready [rédị]. **I.** a. listo, pronto, preparado, dispuesto, en condiciones de; inclinado, propenso; ágil, diligente, ligero; fácil; manuable, a la mano, al alcance; útil, disponible; (com.) contante, efectivo.—**r.-made**, ya hecho; confeccionado.—**r. money**, dinero contante: dinero al contado.—**r. payment**, paga inmediata.—**r. reckoner**, libro de cálculos hechos.—**r. reply o retort**, réplica pronta.—**r. wit**, genio agudo.—**r.-witted**, de ingenio vivo, pronto. **II.** va. preparar, apercibir, aparejar.

reaffirm [riạfǿerm], va. reafirmar, reiterar.—**reaffirmance** [-ạns], **reaffirmation** [riæfœrméiṣǫn], s. reafirmación, reiteración.

reagent [riéiʤǫnt], s. (quím.) reactivo.

real [ríạl]. **I.** a. real, verdadero, auténtico, genuino, legítimo, efectivo; inmueble; referente a bienes raíces (mat.) real.—**r. estate broker** = REALTOR.—**r. property**, o **r. estate**, bienes raíces o inmuebles; propiedad raíz, predio. **II.** s. real (moneda); (con the), (la) realidad, (lo) real. **III.** adv. (fam. e incorrecto) muy, bastante.

realgar [riǽlgǎ(r)], s. (min.) rejalgar, sandáraca

realism [ríạlizm], s. positivismo; espíritu práctico; verismo; (fil. y b. a.) realismo; reconocimiento o criterio de la realidad.

realist [-ịst], s. positivista, hombre práctico o de realidades; (fil. y b. a.) realista.

realistic [-ístik], *a.* práctico, de acuerdo con la realidad; natural, vivo; (fil. y b. a.) realista.

reality [riǽliti], *s.* realidad, verdad, veras, *f. pl.* —**in r.**, en realidad, de veras, efectivamente.

realizable [ríalaizabl], *a.* realizable, factible.

realization [rializéišon], *s.* realización, verificación; concepción, comprensión.

realize [ríalaiz], *va.* darse cuenta, hacerse cargo de; comprender; realizar, verificar, efectuar; dar vida; cumplir, llevar a cabo; ganar, reportar; (com.) realizar, convertir en dinero.

really [ríali], *adv.* realmente, verdaderamente.

realm [relm], *s.* reino, región, dominio; (zool.) extensión de una fauna.

realtor [ríalto(r)], *s.* corredor de bienes raíces (apl. esp. al que es miembro de la asociación de las Juntas de Bienes Raíces).

realty [ríalti], *s.* (for.) bienes raíces.

ream [rím]. I. *s.* resma (de papel). II. *va.* escariar, abocardar.

reamer [-œ(r)], *s.* escariador, ensanchador.

reanimate [riǽnimeit], *va.* reanimar, resucitar.

reannex [riǽnéks], *va.* volver a anex(ion)ar o unir.

reap [ríp]. I. *va.* segar; cosechar; obtener o sacar provecho de. II. *vn.* cosechar, hacer el agosto, hacer la cosecha; recibir (uno) la recompensa, o el fruto de su trabajo.

reaper [-œ(r)], *s.* segador; segadora mecánica.— **the Grim R.**, (fig.) la de la guadaña, la Muerte.

reaping [-iŋ], *s.* siega, cosecha.—**r. hook**, hoz, segadera.—**r. machine**, segadora.—**r. time**, siega.

reappear [riapír], *vn.* reaparecer.

reappearance [-ans], *s.* reaparición.

reappoint [riapóint], *va.* nombrar, designar o fijar de nuevo.

reapportion [riapóršon], *va.* proporcionar o repartir de nuevo.

reappraise [riapréiz], *va.* retasar.

reappraisement [-ment], *s.* retasa, revaluación.

rear [rír]. I. *a.* de atrás, trasero, posterior; último, de más atrás.—**r. admiral**, contra(a)lmirante. —**r. axle**, (carr., aut.) eje trasero, puente.—**r. axle shaft**, semieje trasero.—**r. guard**, (mil.) retaguardia.—**r. rank**, última fila.—**r. view**, vista posterior.—**r. wall**, pared trasera o posterior. II. *s.* fondo; espalda, parte (*f.*) de atrás o posterior; cola, trasera, zaga.—**r. drive**, (aut.) tracción posterior.—**r. sight**, alza (de armas de fuego).—**r. view mirror**, (aut.) espejo de retrovisión.—**to be in the r.**, estar detrás, o a la cola.—**to bring up the r.**, cerrar la marcha. III. *va.* levantar, alzar, erigir, construir; criar, educar. IV. *vn.* encabritarse, empinarse, arbolarse, irse a la empinada (el caballo); elevarse; exaltarse.

rearing [-iŋ], *s.* levantamiento; cría, crianza; encabritamiento, empinada.

rearm [riárm], *va.* (mil.) rearmar.—**rearmament** [-ament], *s.* rearme.

rearmost [rírmoust], *a.* último, de más atrás.

rearrange [riaréindž], *va.* volver a arreglar; cambiar el arreglo o el orden de; refundir.

rearward [rírwərd]. I. *a.* postrero, último. II. *adv.* hacia atrás. III. *s.* cola, retaguardia.

reascend [riasénd], *va. y vn.* subir de nuevo.

reason [rízon]. I. *s.* razón, *f.;* intelectiva; causa, motivo, porqué; moderación; argumento; sensatez; justicia; (lóg.) premisa.—**r. for existence, r. of being**, razón de ser.—**r. of state**, razón de estado.—**r. why**, el porqué.—**by r. of**, con motivo de, a causa de, en virtud de.— **in (all) r.**, con justicia, con razón.—**It stands to r.**, está puesto en razón.—**out of (all) r.**, fuera de razón, desrazonable.—**to bring to r.**, meter en razón. II. *va.* (a menudo con *out*) demostrar o concluir por el razonamiento; probar, argüir; persuadir; disuadir; deducir. III. *vn.* razonar, raciocinar; discurrir; argüir.

reasonable [-abl]. *a.* razonable, racional, justo; equitativo; módico; regular, mediano; prudencial.—**reasonableness** [-nis], *s.* racionalidad; razón, *f.;* moderación; justicia.—**reasonably** [-abli], *adv.* razonablemente; bastante.

reasoner [-œ(r)], *s.* razonador; argumentador.

reasoning [-iŋ], *s.* razonamiento, raciocinio.

reasonless [-lis], *a.* sin razón; desrazonable.

reassemble [riasémbl], *va.* juntar de nuevo.

reassert [riasœrt], *va.* reafirmar.

reassign [riasáin], *va.* asignar, destinar o repartir de nuevo.

reassume [riasiúm], *va.* reasumir.

reassumption [riasÁmpšon], *s.* reasunción.

reassurance [riašúrans], *s.* confianza establecida, tranquilidad; afirmación repetida, certeza restablecida; (com.) reaseguro.

reassure [riašúr], *va.* tranquilizar; (com.) reasegurar, volver a asegurar.

reassuring [-iŋ], *a.* tranquilizador.

reattachment [riatáchment], *s.* (for.) reembargo.

rebaptize [ribæptáiz], *va.* rebautizar.

rebate [ríbeit]. I. *va. y vn.* rebajar, descontar, hacer rebaja; reembolsar. *V.* RABBET. II. *s.* rebaja, descuento; di(s)minución, reducción; reembolso; (f. c.) detasa. *V.* RABBET.

rebec(k) [ríbek], *s.* (mús.) rabel.

rebel [rébel]. I. *a. y s.* rebelde; faccioso, insurrecto. II. [ribél], *vn.* rebelarse, sublevarse.

rebellion [ribélyon], *s.* rebelión, sublevación.

rebellious [-yas], *a.* rebelde, sublevado; insubordinado, refractario.—**rebelliously** [-li], *adv.* con rebeldía.—**rebelliousness** [-nis], *s.* rebeldía, insubordinación.

rebirth [ribœrθ], *s.* renacimiento.

reborn [ribórn], *a.* renacido.

reblossom [riblásom], *vn.* florecer de nuevo.

rebore [ribór], *va.* (mec.) rectificar (un cilindro).

rebound [ribáund]. I. *vn.* repercutir; (re)botar, resurtir, (re)saltar. II. *s.* repercusión; (re)bote, resurtida, resalto; rechazo.

rebounding [-iŋ], *s.* rebotadura, (re)bote.

rebroadcast [ribródkæst]. I. *va. y vn.* (rad.) redifundir; difundir de una difusora un programa o comunicaciones recibidas de otra. II. *s.* redifusión o retransmisión radiofónica.

rebuff [ribÁf]. I. *s.* desaire, repulsa, denegación; contariedad. II. *va.* rechazar, desairar.

rebuild [ribíld], *va.* (pret. y pp. REBUILT) reedificar, reconstruir.

rebuke [ribiúk]. I. *va.* increpar, reprochar, reprender, censurar, regañar. II. *s.* repulsa, reproche, increpación, represión, reprimenda.

rebus [ríbʌs], *s.* jeroglífico, logogrifo, acertijo; (fam.) quisicosa; (blas.) escudo alusivo al nombre de su dueño.

rebut [ribÁt]. I. *va.* (for.) refutar, contradecir. II. *vn.* replicar.

rebuttal [-al], *s.* refutación.

rebutter [-œ(r)], *s.* (for.) contrarréplica; el que la hace.

recalcitrant [rikǽlsitrant], *a.* recalcitrante.

recalcitrate [-treit], *vn.* recalcitrar.

recalescence [rikaléssns], *s.* recalescencia.

recall [rikól]. I. *va.* revocar, anular; llamar, hacer volver; recordar, rememorar, acordarse de; deponer, destituir de un cargo o empleo.—**to r. an ambassador**, retirar a un embajador. II. *s.* recordación; revocación; (mil.) toque o aviso de llamada; (pol. E. U.) derecho de deponer funcionarios o anular sus decisiones por votación popular.

recant [rikánt], *va. y vn.* retractar(se); desdecirse, desmentirse, cantar la palinodia.

recantation [-éišon], *s.* retractación.

recanter [-œ(r)], *s.* retrayente.

recap [rikǽp], *va.* recauchutar (neumáticos).

recapitulate [rikapíchuleit], *va.* recapitular.

recapitulation [-éišon], *s.* recapitulación.

recapitulatory [-atori], *a.* que recapitula.

recapping [rikǽpiŋ] *s.* (aut.) recauchutaje,

revestimiento o reconstrucción de neumáticos.

recapture [rikǽpchǔ(r)]. **I.** *va.* volver a tomar; represar. **II.** *s.* represa.

recast [rikǽst], *va.* (*pret.* y *pp.* RECAST) (fund.) volver a fundir; refundir, volver a escribir; volver a hacer; calcular de nuevo; (teat.) volver a repartir (papeles).

recede [risíd]. **I.** *vn.* cejar, retroceder; retirarse, alejarse; desistir, volverse atrás; desdecirse; inclinarse, desviarse. **II.** *va.* volver a ceder.

receipt [risít]. **I.** *s.* recibo, cobranza; descargo, recibí, carta de pago; receta, fórmula, récipe.—*pl.* ingresos, entradas.—**r. and outgo,** entrada y salida.—**r. book,** (farm.) recetario, registro de recetas; (com.) libro de recibos.—**r. in full (of all demands),** recibo por saldo de cuenta, quitanza, finiquito.—**on r. of,** al recibo de.—**to acknowledge r.,** (com.) acusar recibo. **II.** *va.* y *vn.* firmar o extender recibo; poner el recibí.

receipted [-id], *a.* que lleva el recibí.

receivable [risívǫbl], *a.* recibidero; admisible; (com.) por cobrar.

receive [risív], *va.* recibir; aceptar, admitir; cobrar, percibir; hospedar, acoger, agasajar; contener.—**received payment,** recibí.—**to r. the sacrament,** comulgar.

receiver [-œ(r)], *s.* recibidor, receptor; recipiente, campana (de máquina neumática, etc.); (elec.) receptor; (tlf.) auricular, receptor; (rad.) radiorreceptor; (for.) depositario, síndico, administrador judicial; liquidador; receptador (encubridor de artículos robados).—**r. general,** receptor o recaudador general.

receivership [-ŝip], *s.* (for.) receptoría; sindicatura; administración judicial.

receiving [-iŋ], *a.* recipiente, receptor; de recibir.—**r. set,** (rad.) radiorreceptor, aparato receptor.—**r. station,** (rad.) estación receptora.—**r. teller,** (com.) cobrador, recibidor.

recency [rísensi], **recentness** [rísentnis], *s.* novedad; fecha u origen reciente.

recension [risénŝǫn], *s.* revisión crítica; texto revisado.

recent [rísent], *a.* reciente.—**recently** [-li], *adv.* recientemente.—**r. born,** recién nacido.

receptacle [riséptakl], *s.* receptáculo, recipiente, vasija; (bot.) receptáculo, tálamo.

receptibility [riséptibíliti], *s.* capacidad para recibir, receptividad.

receptible [-bl], *a.* capaz de ser recibido.

reception [risépŝǫn], *s.* recepción, recibimiento, recibo; acogimiento, acogida; audiencia; recibimiento social, besamanos.—**r. day,** día (*m.*) de recibo.—**r. room,** recibimiento, gabinete.

receptionist [-ist], *s.* recibidor(a), recepcionista, persona que recibe las visitas en una oficina o casa de negocios.

receptive [riséptiv], *a.* receptivo.

receptivity [-tíviti], *s.* receptividad; sensibilidad.

recess [risés]. **I.** *s.* nicho, hueco; depresión, entrada; tregua, suspensión; vacación, recreación; recreo (escolar); retiro, lugar apartado, lugar o cosa recónditos. **II.** *vn.* suspender temporalmente (una sesión, el trabajo, etc.).

recession [riséŝǫn], *s.* receso, retirada, desistimiento; retracción; (for.) retrocesión; (com.) depresión temporal.

recessional [-al], *s.* himno que se canta después del servicio divino.

recessive [risésiv], *a.* de receso.

recherché [rœærŝéi], *a.* deseado, buscado; excelente; estudiado, refinado; forzado.

recidivist [risídivist], *s.* criminal reincidente.

recipe [résipi], *s.* récipe, receta de médico; fórmula; (coc.) receta.

recipient [risípient], *a.* y *s.* recibidor; recipiente.

reciprocal [risíprokal]. **I.** *a.* recíproco, mutuo; alterno, alternativo; permutable; (gram.) recíproco. **II.** *s.* (mat.) inverso (de un número—fracción cuyo numerador es 1 y cuyo denomi-

nador es el número).—**reciprocalness** [-nis], *s.* reciprocidad.—**reciprocally** [-i], *adv.* recíprocamente, mutuamente.

reciprocate [risíprokeit]. **I.** *va.* producir un movimiento de vaivén; permutar; corresponder. **II.** *vn.* alternar; ser recíproco; tener movimiento alternativo; estar a la recíproca.

reciprocating [-iŋ], *a.* de vaivén, alternativo; de movimiento alternativo.—**r. engine,** máquina oscilante o de cilindro, máquina de émbolo.

reciprocation [-éiŝǫn], *s.* reciprocación, reciprocidad; correspondencia (de amor, bondad, etc.); alternación.

reciprocity [resiprásiti], *s.* reciprocidad.

recision [risíʒǫn], *s.* rescisión; (cir.) resección.

recital [risáital], *s.* relación, narración; recitación; (mús.) recital.

recitation [resitéiŝǫn], *s.* recitación, declamación; clase, *f.*; acción de decir la lección en la clase.

recitative [résiteitiv, resitatív], *a.* y *s.* (mús.) recitativo, recitado.

recite [risáit], *va.* y *vn.* narrar, relatar, contar; recitar; declamar; citar; dar o decir la lección.

reciter [-œ(r)], *s.* recitador, declamador.

reckless [réklis], *a.* descuidado; temerario; atolondrado; derrochador.—**recklessly** [-li], *adv.* temerariamente; descuidadamente.—**recklessness** [-nis], *s.* temeridad; imprudencia; indiferencia.

reckon [rékǫn], *va.* y *vn.* contar, enumerar; calcular; estimar, considerar, suponer, creer; (con **on** o **upon**) contar con, fiar en.—**to r. with,** tener en cuenta; habérselas con.—**to r. without one's host,** hacer la cuenta sin la huéspeda.

reckoner [-œ(r)], *s.* contador, calculador.

reckoning [-iŋ], *s.* cuenta; tanteo, cómputo, cálculo; cuenta de gastos en una posada; ajuste de cuentas.—**(dead) r.,** (mar.) rumbo estimado, estima.—**r. book,** libro de cuenta y razón.—**day of r.,** día (*m.*) del juicio (final).—**everyone must pay his r.,** cada palo que aguante su vela.—**to be out in one's r.,** equivocarse en el cálculo.

reclaim [rikléim]. **I.** *va.* (for.) reclamar (derechos, etc.); (rei)vindicar; amansar, domesticar, domeñar; reducir; mejorar y utilizar (tierras), entarquinar (terrenos pantanosos), hacer labrantío o aprovechable; utilizar (material usado). **II.** *s.* = RECLAMATION.—**beyond r.,** perdido irreparablemente.

reclaimable [-abl], *a.* reclamable, mejorable, utilizable.

reclaimant [-ant], *s.* reclamante.

reclamation [reklaméiŝǫn], *s.* reclamación; (for.) reclamo; restauración; mejoramiento.

reclinate [réklineit], **reclined** [rikláind], *a.* reclinado, recostado.

reclination [reklinéiŝǫn], *s.* reclinación.

recline [rikláin]. **I.** *va.* reclinar, recostar. **II.** *vn.* recostarse.

recluse [riklíús]. **I.** *a.* recluso, solitario. **II.** *s.* solitario, eremita, *mf.*, emparedado; (fam.) cartujo.

recluseness [-nis], **reclusion** [riklúʒǫn], *s.* reclusión, retiro, aislamiento.

reclusive [riklíúsiv], *a.* recluso.

recognition [rekǫgníŝǫn], *s.* reconocimiento; admisión; confesión; agradecimiento; saludo.

recognizable [rékǫgnaizabl], *a.* que puede ser reconocido, recognoscible.

recognizance [rikágnizans], *s.* (for.) reconocimiento; obligación contraída.

recognize [rékǫgnaiz]. **I.** *va.* reconocer; admitir; confesar, conceder, comprender; (fil.) volver a conocer o percibir. **II.** [rikágnaiz], *vn.* (for.) subscribir una obligación auténtica; otorgar un reconocimiento.

recognizee [rikagnizí], *s.* (for.) aquel a cuyo favor se otorga un reconocimiento.

recognizor [rįkagnįzór], *s.* (for.) el que otorga un reconocimiento.

recoil [rįkóįl]. I. *s.* rechazo, reculada; (arti.) coz, retroceso, rebufo; repugnancia, temor.—**r. spring**, resorte para disminuir el rebufo. II. *vn.* recular; retirarse; cejar, retroceder; rebufar (un arma de fuego).

recoin [rįkóįn], *va.* resellar, acuñar de nuevo.

recoinage [-įdź], *s.* resello, nueva acuñación.

recollect [rɛkǫlɛ́kt], *va.* y *vn.* recordar, acordarse (de); [rįkǫlɛ́kt] recoger, reunir; juntarse de nuevo.

Recollect [rɛ́kǫlɛkt], *s.* y *a.* (igl.) recoleto.

recollection [rɛkǫlɛ́kšǫn], *s.* recuerdo, recordación, reminiscencia, memoria, acuerdo; (igl.) recolección.

recommence [rikǫmɛ́ns], *va.* y *vn.* empezar de nuevo.—**recommencement** [-mɛnt], *s.* acción de comenzar de nuevo.

recommend [rɛkǫmɛ́nd], *va.* recomendar; elogiar, encarecer; acreditar; aconsejar, sugerir.—**recommendable** [-ạbl], *a.* recomendable.—**recommendation** [-éįšǫn], *s.* recomendación; (fam.) carta de recomendación.—**recommendatory** [-ạtǫrį], *a.* recomendatorio.

recommender [-œ(r)], *s.* recomendante.

recommit [rikǫmį́t], *va.* cometer de nuevo; trasladar de nuevo (un proyecto, etc.) a una comisión; prender de nuevo (a alguno que estaba bajo fianza); enviar otra vez a la cárcel, al manicomio, etc.—**recommitment, recommittal** [-mɛnt, -ạl], *s.* nuevo traslado a una comisión; nuevo arresto, encarcelamiento, etc.

recompense [rɛ́kǫmpɛns]. I. *va.* recompensar; remunerar, retribuir, indemnizar, resarcir. II. *s.* recompensa, compensación, remuneración.

recompose [rikǫmpóųz], *va.* tranquilizar de nuevo; recomponer, rehacer.—**recomposition** [rikampozíšǫn], *s.* recomposición.

reconcilable [rɛ́kǫnsaįlạbl], *a.* reconciliable, componible; conciliable, compatible.—**reconcilableness** [-nįs], *s.* calidad de reconciliable o compatible.—**reconcilably** [-blį], *adv.* compatiblemente.

reconcile [rɛ́kǫnsaįl], *va.* (re)conciliar, componer; dirimir; compadecerse, avenir(se); ajustar, componer; resignarse; (igl.) reconciliar.—**reconcilement** [-mɛnt], *s.* reconciliación.—**reconciler** [-œ(r)], *s.* reconciliador; conciliador, pacificador.

reconciliation [-sįljéįšǫn], *s.* reconciliación; conciliación, ajuste; concordancia, conformidad.

reconciliatory [-sįljạtǫrį], *a.* reconciliador.

recondite [rɛ́kǫndaįt], *a.* recóndito; abstruso.

recondition [rikǫndíšǫn], *va.* (mec.) reacondicionar, rectificar, corregir.

reconduct [rikǫndɅ́kt], *va.* volver a conducir.

reconnaissance, reconnoissance [rįkánậsạns], *s.* (mil.) reconocimiento; (f. c., geol.) reconocimiento, exploración.

reconnoitre [rɛkǫnóįtœ(r)]. I. *va.* reconocer, explorar, inspeccionar. II. *vn.* practicar un reconocimiento; batir, descubrir el campo.

reconquer [rikánkœ(r)], *va.* reconquistar.

reconquest [rikánkwɛst], *s.* reconquista.

reconsider [rikǫnsídœ(r)], *va.* repensar; volver a considerar o discutir.—**reconsideration** [-éįšǫn], *s.* nueva discusión o consideración.

reconstitute [rikánstįtjut], *va.* reconstituir, reorganizar.—**reconstitution** [-tįúšǫn], *s.* reconstitución, reorganización.

reconstruct [rikǫnstrɅ́kt], *va.* reedificar, reconstruir; reconstituir.—**reconstructed ruby**, rubí artificial.—**reconstruction** [-kšǫn], *s.* reconstrucción; reconstitución.

reconvene [rikǫnvín], *va.* y *vn.* convocar, juntar(se) o reunir(se) de nuevo.

reconvey [rikǫnvéį], *va.* traspasar de nuevo; reponer, restituir.

record [rįkórd]. I. *va.* registrar, inscribir; protocolizar (documentos); archivar; apuntar; marcar, indicar; grabar, hacer un fonograma (impresión fonográfica) de.—**recorded music**, música en discos. II. [rɛ́kǫrd], *s.* registro; partida, inscripción, anotación; acta; documento; relación, crónica, historia; hoja de servicios, antecedentes de una persona; fonograma, *m.*, placa o disco fonográficos; (for.) memorial, informe, expediente; atestación, testimonio; memoria, recuerdo, recordación; (dep.) record.—*pl.* **records**, archivo; protocolo; actas, autos; fastos; memorias; datos.—**r.** lo que o lo que sobrepasa o sube el record.—**r.-breaking**, que pasa del record, que supera la marca.—**of r.**, (for.) que consta (en el expediente, la escritura, etc.).—**off the r.**, extraoficial.—**on r.**, registrado; de que hay o queda constancia; que la historia registra.—**to be of r.**, constar.

recorder [rįkórdœ(r)], *s.* registrador, archivero; (Ingl.) (for.) juez municipal superior que entiende en causas criminales; (mec.) indicador, contador; (mús.) flauta dulce; aparato inscriptor, trazador o grabador (de un fonógrafo, etc.).—**r. of deeds**, registrador de la propiedad.

recordership [-šįp], *s.* cargo de registrador o archivero.

recording [-įŋ], *a.* anotador, registrador; (fís., etc.) registrador (apl. a instrumentos).—**r. secretary**, secretario de actas, secretario escribiente.

recount [rįkáųnt]. I. *va.* referir, relatar; recitar; detallar; [rįkáųnt] recontar, hacer un recuento. II. [ríkaųnt], *s.* recuento.

recountal [rįkáųntạl], *s.* relato.

recoup [rįkúp]. I. *va.* (for.) retener para indemnizarse; reintegrarse, desquitarse de; reparar, indemnizar, resarcir; amortizar. II. *s.* desquite, reintegro, resarcimiento.—**recoupment** [-mɛnt], *s.* desquite; resarcimiento, reembolso.

recourse [rįkórs], *s.* recurso, remedio, auxilio, refugio; (for.) recurso.—**to have r. to**, recurrir a, apelar a, valerse de.—**without r.**, (com.) sin responsabilidad (de parte del endosante).

re-cover [rikávœ(r)], *va.* volver a cubrir o tapar.

recover [rįkɅ́vœ(r)]. I. *va.* recobrar, recuperar; amortizar; desempeñar; rescatar; reintegrarse o resarcirse; (for.) obtener fallo judicial contra alguien. II. *vn.* recobrar la salud; reponerse, restablecerse; (for.) ganar un pleito.

recoverable [-ạbl], *a.* recuperable, recobrable.

recovery [-į], *s.* recobro, recuperación; cobranza; rescate; restablecimiento; mejoría, convalecencia; (for.) fallo o decisión favorable; reivindicación.

recreancy [rɛ́krịạnsį], *s.* deslealtad; pusilanimidad.—**recreant** [-ạnt], *a.* y *s.* falso, desleal; cobarde.

recreate [rɛ́krįeįt], *va.* y *vn.* recrear(se), divertir(se), deleitar(se), refocilar(se); reanimar(se).

re-create [rikrįéįt], *va.* crear o criar de nuevo.

recreation [rɛkrįéįšǫn], *s.* recreación, recreo; pasatiempo, diversión; esparcimiento, holganza, huelga.—**recreation(al** [-ạl], *a.* recreativo.

re-creation [rikrįéįšǫn], *s.* nueva creación.

recreative [rɛ́krịeįtįv], *a.* recreativo, divertido.

recrement [rɛ́krįmɛnt], *s.* (med.) recremento; hez, escoria.

recremental [rɛkrįmɛ́ntạl], *a.* recrementicio.

recriminate [rįkrį́mįneįt], *va.* y *vn.* recriminar.

recrimination [-éįšǫn], *s.* recriminación.

recriminative, recriminatory [-ạtįv, -ạtǫrį], *a.*, **recriminator** [-eįtǫ(r)], *s.* recriminador.

recross [rikrós], *va.* volver a pasar o cruzar.

recrudesce [rikrįudɛ́s], *vn.* recrudecer(se), recidivar.—**recrudescence** [-ɛns], *s.* recrudecimiento, recrudescencia, recidiva.—**recrudescent** [-ɛnt], *a.* recrudescente.

recruit [rįkrįút]. I. *va.* y *vn.* (mil.) alistar, reclutar; restablecer, reparar; abastecer. II. *s.* (mil.) recluta, *m.*; novicio; renuevo, suministro.

recruiter [-œ(r)], *s.* reclutador.

recruiting [-iŋ], *s.* recluta, reclutamiento.

rectal [rḗktḁl], *a.* (anat.) rectal, del recto.

rectangle [rḗktæŋgl], *s.* rectángulo.—**rectangular** [rektǽngyṵlḁ(r)], *a.* rectangular.—**rectangularity** [-ǽriti], **rectangularness** [-nis], *s.* calidad de rectangular.

rectifiable [rḗktifaḭabl], *a.* rectificable.

rectification [-fikéi̯sǫn], *s.* rectificación, corrección, enmienda; enderezamiento; (quím.) rectificación, refinación; (geom.) rectificación.

rectifier [-faḭœ(r)], *s.* rectificador; refinador.

rectify [-faḭ], *va.* rectificar, corregir, enderezar, enmendar; (quím.) rectificar, refinar, depurar; (mat.) rectificar.

rectilineal, rectilinear [rektilíni̯al, -ḁ(r)], *a.* rectilíneo.

rectitude [rḗktitiud], *s.* rectitud; corrección.

rector [rḗktǫ(r)], *s.* (igl.) rector, cura párroco; prior, superior; rector de universidad.—**rectoral** [-ḁl], **rectorial** [rektóuri̯al], *a.* rectoral.—**rectorate, rectorship** [rḗktǫrit, -šip], *s.* rectorado, rectoría.—**rectory** [-i], *s.* rectoría.

rectrix [rḗktriks], *s.* (orn.) (pluma) timonera.

rectum [rḗktʌm], *s.* (anat.) recto.

recumbency [rikʌ́mbensi], *s.* reclinación.

recumbent [-ent], *a.* recostado, reclinado, echado.

recuperate [rikiúperei̯t], I. *va.* recuperar, recobrar. II. *vn.* recobrar la salud, reponerse.—**recuperation** [-éi̯sǫn], *s.* recuperación; recobro, rehacimiento.—**recuperative, recuperatory** [rikiúperḁtiv, -ḁtǫri], *a.* recuperativo.

recur [rikœ́r], *vn.* repetirse, volver a ocurrir, presentarse de nuevo; (med.) recidivar, recaer.

recurrence, recurrency [-ens, -i], *s.* repetición, reaparición; recurso; (med.) recidiva.—**recurrent** [-ent], *a.* periódico; recurrente.

recurve [rikœ́rv], *va.* y *vn.* encorvar, torcer o torcerse en sentido opuesto al ordinario; encorvarse hacia abajo.

recurvate, recurved, recurvous [-eit, -d, -ʌs], *a.* (bot.) encorvado anormalmente; (zool.) encorvado hacia arriba (el pico).

recusancy [rékiuzansi], *s.* recusación.

recusant [-ant], *s.* y *a.* recusante.

recusation [-éi̯sǫn], *s.* (for.) recusación.

red [red], I. *a.* encarnado, colorado, rojo, escarlata, sanguíneo, encendido; (pol. y e. p.) rojo (apl. esp. a los comunistas rusos y sus partidarios).—**r. ant,** hormiga colorada.—**R. Army,** el ejército rojo o soviético.—**r. ball,** mingo (en el billar).—**r. banana,** cambur morado.—**r.-bearded,** barbirrojo, barbibermejo.—**r.-bellied,** pechirrojo.—**r.-blooded,** animoso; viril.—**r. (blood) cell,** hematíe, *m.,* glóbulo rojo (de la sangre).—**r. brass,** latón cobrizo, latón rojo.—**r. cabbage,** lombarda.—**r. cedar,** cedro colorado; junípero; tuya de la costa del Pacífico.—**r. cent,** (E. U.) centavo.—**r. chalk,** creta roja.—**r. clover,** trébol morado.—**r. copper,** cuprita, óxido rojo de cobre.—**r. corpuscle,** corpúsculo o glóbulo rojo (de la sangre).—**r. coral,** coral rojo.—**R. Cross,** Cruz Roja; Cruz de San Jorge.—**r. deer,** ciervo común.—**r. flag,** bandera roja (apl. hoy gen. a la bandera socialista y de revolución social); señal (f.) de peligro; cosa que irrita o enfurece.—**r.-haired,** pelirrojo.—**r.-handed,** con las manos en la masa, o ensangrentadas; en flagrante.—**r.-hard,** duro en caliente, o cuando está caliente.—**r. hat,** (igl.) capelo o birreta de cardenal; cardenalato, dignidad de cardenal.—**r. heat,** calor rojo.—**r. herring,** arenque ahumado; artimaña para apartar la atención del asunto de que se trata (ú. esp. en la expresión **to draw a r. herring across the track,** distraer la atención, despistar).—**r.-hot,** candente, enrojecido al fuego; muy caliente; acérrimo, extremo; muy entusiasta o enardecido; fresco, reciente (informe, noticia, etc.).—**r. iron,** hematites, *f.*—**r. lead,** minio.

—**r.-lead pencil,** lápiz rojo.—**r.-letter,** marcado con letras rojas; dichoso, de buen agüero.—**r.-letter day,** día de fiesta, día de dos cruces; día feliz o de regocijo, día de piedra blanca.—**r. light,** luz roja empleada como señal de peligro, o, en los cruces de calles, para detener el tránsito.—**r.-light district,** barrio de los lupanares, o de mala vida.—**r. liquor,** acetato de alúmina.—**r. man,** indio norteamericano.—**r. mordant** = R. LIQUOR.—**r. mullet,** salmonete.—**r. ocher,** ocre rojo o quemado, almagre, almazarrón.—**r. pepper,** pimentón; pimiento, ají, chile.—**r. poppy,** amapola.—**R. Sea,** Mar Rojo.—**r.-short,** frágil o quebradizo en caliente.—**r. silver,** plata roja, pirargirita; proustita.—**r. sky,** arrebol.—**r. spider,** ácaro rojo, cresa roja.—**r. spruce,** pícea roja.—**r. tape,** balduque; expedienteo, rutina oficinesca, formalismo o formulismo.—**r. wine,** vino tinto.—**r.-winged,** alirrojo. II. *s.* color rojo; (pol. y e. p.) rojo, revolucionario.—**in the r.,** (fam.) en el debe; endeudado, perdidoso.—**out of the r.,** (fam.) en el haber.—**to see r.,** (fam.) enfurecerse. III. *va.* enrojar, pintar de rojo.

redact [ridǽkt], *va.* redactar.—**redaction** [-šǫn], *s.* redacción.—**redactor** [-tǫ(r)], *s.* redactor.

redan [ridǽn], *s.* (fort.) estrella.

redbait [rédbeit], *va.* perseguir a uno, tildándole de rojo o comunista, etc.

redbird [-bœrd], *s.* (orn.) cardenal.

redbreast [-brest], *s.* (orn.) petirrojo, pechirrojo.

redbud [-bʌd], *s.* (bot.) ciclamor.

redbug [-bʌg], *s.* (ent.) nigua.

redcap [-kæp], *s.* (orn.) cardelina; mozo de gorra roja que sirve al público en las estaciones de ferrocarril.

redcoat [-kout], *s.* (Ingl.) (fam.) soldado.

redden [rédn], I. *va.* rojear, teñir de rojo. II. *vn.* ponerse colorado; ruborizarse.

reddish [rédiš], *a.* rojizo, berme(jiz)o, buriel.

reddishness [-nis], *s.* bermejura. *V.* REDNESS.

reddle [rédl], *s.* almazarrón, almagre.

redeem [ridím], *va.* redimir; desempeñar; amortizar; rescatar; cumplir; resarcir; compensar.

redeemable [-abl], *a.* redimible, rescatable, amortizable.—**redeemableness** [-nis], *s.* calidad de redimible.

redeemer [-œ(r)], *s.* redentor o rescatador; (R.) Redentor, Salvador, Jesucristo.

redeeming [-iŋ], *a.* redentor; rescatador; atenuante.—**r. feature,** circunstancia atenuante; rasgo compensador o paliatorio.

redemption [ridémpšǫn], *s.* redención; rescate; desempeño; amortización de una deuda.

redemptional [-ḁl], *a.* redentor; que redime o se relaciona con la redención, rescate o amortización.

redemptioner [-œ(r)], *s.* emigrante que pagaba su pasaje a América con su servicio personal.

redemptive, redemptory [ridémptiv, -ǫri], *a.* = REDEMPTIONAL.

redevelop [ridivélǫp], *va.* volver a desarrollar; (fot.) volver a revelar después de tratamiento químico.

redhead [rédhed], *s.* persona de cabello rojo.—**redheaded** [-id], *a.* pelirrojo; irascible.

redhibition [redhibíšǫn], *s.* (for.) redhibición.

redhibitory [redhíbitǫri], *a.* redhibitorio.

redingote [rédiŋgout], *s.* redingote, levitón.

redintegrate [redintḗgreit], I. *va.* reintegrar, restablecer. II. *a.* reintegrado, restablecido; renovado.—**redintegration** [-éi̯sǫn], *s.* reintegración, reintegro; restauración, restablecimiento.

redirect [ridai̯rḗkt], I. *va.* dirigir de nuevo. II. *a.* (for.) dícese del segundo interrogatorio de un testigo por su abogado, después de las preguntas del contrario.

rediscount [ridískaunt], *s.* (com.) redescuento.

redivivus [redivái̯vʌs], *a.* redivivo.

redly [rédli], *adv.* rojizamente.

redness [rédnis], *s.* rojez, rojura, bermejura.
redolence, redolency [rédolens, -i], *s.* fragancia.
—**redolent** [-ent], *a.* fragante, oloroso.
redouble [ridʌbl]. **I.** *va.* redobl(eg)ar, reduplicar, aumentar; repetir. **II.** *vn.* redoblarse.
redoubt [ridáut], *s.* (fort.) reducto.
redoubtable [-abl], *a.* formidable, temible.
redound [ridáund], *vn.* (gen. con **to**) redundar (en), resultar (en), contribuir (a).
redowa [rédowä], *s.* (danz. y mús.) redova.
redraft [rídræft]. **I.** *s.* nuevo dibujo, copia o borrador; (com.) resaca. **II.** [rídræft], *va.* redactar, dibujar de nuevo. *V.* REDRAW.
redraw [ridró]. **I.** *va.* hacer un segundo dibujo o borrador. **II.** *vn.* (com.) resacar.
redress [ridrés]. **I.** *va.* enderezar; reparar, resarcir; remediar, compensar, desagraviar; hacer justicia; (aer.) enderezar. **II.** [rídres], *s.* reparación, satisfacción, desagravio; remedio; compensación.
re-dress [ridrés], *va.* y *vn.* vestir(se) de nuevo.
redresser [ridrésœ(r)], *s.* reparador, remediador.
redsear [rédsi(r)], *a.* (metal.) = RED-SHORT.
redshirt [-šœrt], *s.* (pol.) camisarroja; revolucionario (apl. esp. a los anarquistas y comunistas).
redskin [-skin], *s.* piel roja, *m.*, indio norteamericano.
redtop [-tap], *s.* (bot.) agróstide, *f.*
reduce [ridjús]. **I.** *va.* reducir; disminuir, aminorar, minorar, rebajar; abreviar, acortar, contraer; mermar; sujetar, someter, sojuzgar; (mil.) degradar; (mat., quím., cir. y b. a.) reducir. **II.** *vn.* reducirse, etc.; adelgazar.
reducer [-œ(r)], *s.* reductor; (mec.) manguito, unión o tubo de reducción.
reducible [-ibl], *a.* reducible.—**reducibleness** [-nis], *s.* calidad de reducible.
reducing [-iŋ], *a.* reductor, reductivo; de reducción (llama, agente, escala, etc.).
reduction [ridʌkšon], *s.* reducción; rebaja, di(s)minución; sujeción, toma, conquista; (mat., quím., cir. y b. a.) reducción.—**r. works**, fundición, horno de reducción.
reductive [-tiv], *a.* reductivo.
redundance, redundancy [ridʌndans, -i], *s.* redundancia; superfluidad; pleonasmo.—**redundant** [-ant], *a.* redundante; pleonástico.—**redundantly** [-li], *adv.* redundantemente, superfluamente.
reduplicate [ridjúplikeit]. **I.** *va.* reduplicar, repetir, multiplicar. **II.** *a.* reduplicado.—**reduplication** [-éišon], *s.* reduplicación, repetición.
redwing [rédwiŋ], *s.* (orn.) malvís, *m.*
redwood [-wud], *s.* (bot.) pino gigantesco de California.
reëcho [riékou], *vn.* responder, repercutir, resonar.
reed [ríd], *s.* (bot.) caña, cañuela, junquillo, (Am.) bejuco; (mús.) lengüeta; carrizal, dulzaina, churumbela, chirimía; por extensión, cualquier instrumento de boquilla; (min.) tubo para cebar un barreno; (arq.) baqueta, junquillo; (tej.) peine (cárcel); (poét.) flecha, saeta; barda; (zool.) abomaso.—**r. mace**, (bot.) anea, espadaña.—**r. organ**, armonio.
reedbird [-bœrd], *s.* (orn.) ave canora americana que se cría en los arrozales y praderas.
reedwork [-wœrk], *s.* lengüetería del órgano.
reedy [-i], *a.* semejante a, o abundante en, cañas, junquillos, etc.; de tono delgado y agudo.
reef [ríf]. **I.** *s.* arrecife, escollo, bajío; (min.) filón, vena metálica; (mar.) rizo.—**r. band**, faja de rizos.—**r. cringle**, anillo de vela.—**r. knot**, nudo de rizos.—**r. tackles**, (mar.) aparejuelos o palanquines de rizos.—**to run on a r.**, (mar.) tropezar en un escollo, (Am.) escollar.—**to take in a r.**, (mar.) tomar un rizo. **II.** *va.* (mar.) tomar rizos, arrizar, amainar o recoger (las velas).
reefer [-œ(r)], *s.* (mar.) rizador; (sast.) chaquetón;

(fam.) cigarrillo narcotizado con marijuana; (fam.) (f. c.) vagón o buque frigorífico.
reefy [-i], *a.* lleno de escollos.
reek [rík]. **I.** *va.* ahumar. **II.** *vn.* (gen. con **of** o **with**) humear, vah(e)ar; arrojar de sí un olor fuerte y desagradable. **III.** *s.* tufo; vaho, vapor; humo.
reeky [-i], *a.* tufoso, vaporoso, ahumado.
reel [ríl]. **I.** *s.* carrete, carretel, canilla, tambor; aspa(dera), aspador; devanadera; broca; película de cine; cierta danza muy viva, y su música. **II.** *va.* aspar, devanar. **III.** *vn.* hacer eses, tambalear, bambolear, rehilar, vacilar.
reëlect [riélékt], *va.* reelegir.
reëlection [riélékšon], *s.* reelección.
reëmbark [riimbárk], *va.* y *vn.* reembarcar.
reëmbarkation [-éišon], *s.* reembarco.
reënact [riinǽkt], *va.* promulgar de nuevo, revalidar (una ley); volver a realizar o representar algo.
reënactment [-ment], *s.* revalidación (de una ley); nueva realización o representación.
reënforce [riinfórs]. **I.** *va.* reforzar, fortalecer. **II.** *s.* refuerzo. *V.* REINFORCE.
reënforcement [-ment], *s.* refuerzo. *V.* REINFORCEMENT.
reëngage [riingéidž], *va.* reescriturar, contratar de nuevo.—**reëngagement** [-ment], *s.* (mil.) nuevo ataque; renovación de una contrata o escritura.
reënlist [riinlíst], *va.* y *vn.* (mil.) reenganchar(se), volver a alistar(se).—**reënlistment** [-ment], *s.* reenganche.
reënter [riéntœ(r)], *va.* reingresar; registrar o entrar de nuevo; (grabado) repasar con el buril.
reëntering [-iŋ], *a.* = REËNTRANT.
reëntrance, reëntry [-trans, -tri], *s.* segunda entrada; asiento repetido.—**reëntrant** [-trant], *a.* entrante (ángulo, etc.).
reëstablish [riistǽbliš], *va.* restablecer, instaurar. —**reëstablisher** [-œ(r)], *s.* restablecedor, restaurador.—**reëstablishment** [-ment], *s.* restablecimiento, restauración.
reeve [rív], *va.* (mar.) laborear, guarnir.
reëxamine [riigzǽmin], *va.* reexaminar, revisar, repasar.—**reëxamination** [-éišon], *s.* reexaminación, revisión, repaso, revista.
reëxport [riikspórt], *va.* reexportar.
reëxportation [-éišon], *s.* reexportación.
refection [rifékšon], *s.* refacción, colación.
refectory [riféktori], *s.* refectorio.
refer [rifœr]. **I.** *va.* referir, remitir, dirigir; trasladar, someter; asignar, atribuir. **II.** *vn.* referirse, remitirse, aludir; recurrir, acudir; indicar por medio de marcas; dar referencias.—**referred to**, mencionado; a que se hace referencia, a que uno se refiere.
referable [réferabl], *a.* referible, asignable.
referee [referí]. **I.** *s.* árbitro; (for.) arbitrador, (amigable) componedor, secuestro, ponente. **II.** *va.* y *vn.* arbitrar; servir de árbitro o juez.
reference [réferens]. **I.** *s.* referencia; recomendación, informe; remisión; alusión, mención; nota, marca o señal (f.) de referencia; persona a quien se puede acudir para referencia; fiador; (for.) arbitramento.—**r. mark**, (impr.) llamada (* † ‡ ‖ § ¶).—**r. table**, guión, *m.*—**in**, o **with**, **r. to**, respecto de, en cuanto a. **II.** *a.* de referencia; de consulta (libro, etc.).
referendum [referéndʌm], *s.* (dipl.) referéndum; (pol.) referéndum, plebiscito.
referent [réferent], *a.* referente.
referential [referénšal], *a.* referente.
referrible [rifœríbl], *a.* = REFERABLE.
refill [rifíl], *va.* rellenar, rehenchir, reenvasar.
refill [rifíl], *s.* repuesto, relleno.
refine [rifáin]. **I.** *va.* refinar, purificar, clarificar, depurar; afinar; acrisolar; pulir, perfeccionar. **II.** *vn.* sutilizar; purificarse, refinarse, pulirse.
refined [-d], *a.* refin(ad)o, afinado; fino, cortés.
refinement [-ment], *s.* refinamiento, cortesía,

cultura; refinación, refinadura, purificación; afinamiento, finura, filigrana; sutileza.

refiner [-œ(r)], *s.* refinador.

refinery [-œri], *s.* refinería.

refining [-iŋ], *s.* refinación, refinadura, depuración.

refit [rifít], *va.* reparar, componer, rehabilitar, recorrer, volver a equipar.

reflect [riflékt]. I. *va.* reflejar; reflexionar; indicar, manifestar (gen. en la voz pasiva **to be reflected**, manifestarse, verse, hacerse sentir); traer consigo, dar.—**to r. credit on one**, hacer honor a uno. II. *vn.* reflexionar, meditar, considerar; reflejar.—**to r. on**, o **upon**, desprestigiar, desdorar, perjudicar, herir; hacer desmerecer, desdecir de.

reflected [-id], *a.* reflejado, reflejo; (anat.) replegado.

reflecting [-iŋ], *a.* reflectante, reflector; reflexivo.

reflection [-šǫn], *s.* (fís., psic.) reflexión; reflejo; consideración, meditación, refleja; reproche, tacha, baldón; (anat.) repliegue; acción refleja. —**on** o **upon r.**, después de pensarlo; bien pensado.—**to cast r. on**, criticar, censurar. *V.* TO REFLECT ON.

reflective [-tiv], *a.* reflexivo; meditativo, meditabundo; reflector; reflejo.

reflectively [-li], *adv.* reflexivamente.

reflector [-tǫ(r)], *s.* (ópt.) reflector; reverbero; telescopio de reflexión.

reflex [rífleks]. I. *a.* reflejo.—**r. action**, acción refleja. II. *s.* acción refleja; reflejo, reverberación; (psic.) reflejo. III. [rifléks], *va.* replegar.

reflexion [riflékšǫn], *s.* = REFLECTION.

reflexive [rifléksiv], *a.* (gram.) reflexivo, reflejo; (fís.) reflector, de reflexión.

reflexively [-li], *adv.* reflexivamente.

reflorescence [riflorésǫns], *s.* acto de reflorecer.

reflourish [riflŏriš], *vn.* reflorecer.

reflow [riflóu], *vn.* refluir.

refluence, refluency [réfluęns, -i], *s.* reflujo.

refluent [-ęnt], *a.* refluente.

reflux [rífłaks], *s.* reflujo, menguante, *f.*

reforest [rifárist], *va.* restablecer bosques.—**reforestation** [-éišǫn], *s.* restablecimiento de bosques; repoblación forestal o arbórea.

re-form [rifárm], *va.* formar de nuevo, rehacer.

reform [rifárm]. I. *va.* y *vn.* reformar(se), corregir(se), convertir(se), enmendar(se), mejorar(se). II. *s.* reforma, enmienda, renovación, conversión.—**r. school**, reformatorio para jóvenes.

reformation [reforméišǫn], *s.* reforma(ción), corrección; (**R.** hist.) Reforma.

re-formation [riforméišǫn], *s.* nueva formación.

reformative [rifármativ], *a.* reformatorio.

reformatory [-ạtori]. I. *a.* reformatorio. II. *s.* reformatorio, casa de corrección.

reformer [-œ(r)], *s.* reformador, reformista.

reforming [-iŋ], *a.* reformatorio, reformador, reformista, renovador.

reformist [-ist]. I. *s.* reformista; religioso reformado. II. *a.* reformista, reformador.

refract [rifrékt], *va.* (fís., ópt.) refractar, refringir. —**refraction** [-šǫn], *s.* refracción.—**refractive** [-tiv], *a.* refringente, refractor.—**r. power**, poder de refracción.—**refractivity** [-tíviti], *s.* refractividad.

refractometer [-támetœ(r)], *s.* (fís.) refractómetro.

refractor [rifréktǫ(r)], *s.* telescopio de refracción.

refractorily [-ili], *adv.* tercamente, obstinadamente.—**refractoriness** [-inis], *s.* contumacia, terquedad, porfía.—**refractory** [-i], *a.* refractario, díscolo, contumaz, recalcitrante; (equit.) repropio; (quím.) refractario.

refrain [rifréin]. I. *vn.* refrenarse, abstenerse de, contenerse. II. *s.* (poét.) estribillo, bordón, contera; (fig.) cantilena o cantinela.

refrangibility [rifrǽndžibiliti], **refrangibleness** [-blnis], *s.* (fís.) refrangibilidad.—**refrangible** [-bl], *a.* refrangible.

refresh [rifréš]. I. *va.* refrescar, renovar, vivificar; templar el calor, enfriar; aliviar. II. *vr.* refrescarse, cobrar nuevas fuerzas.—**refresher** [-œ(r)], *s.* refresco; recordatorio, algo que ayuda a recordar.—**refreshing** [-iŋ], *a.* refrescante, refrescador, oreante; alentador, placentero.—**refreshment** [-męnt], *s.* refresco, refrigerio, refacción ligera, (fam.) tentempié, *m.*, piscolabis, *m.*—*pl.* refrescos.

refrigerant [rifrídžęrant], *a.* y *s.* refrigerante.

refrigerate [-eit], *va.* refrigerar, enfriar.

refrigerating [-eitiŋ], *a.* refrigerante, refrigerador, refrescador.—**r. chamber** o **vault**, cámara frigorífica.—**r. machine** refrigerador, instalación frigorífica.

refrigeration [-éišǫn], *s.* refrigeración, refrigerio, enfriamiento.

refrigerative [-ątiv], *a.* refrigerativo, refrigerante, frigorífico.

refrigerator [-eitǫ(r)], *s.* refrigerador, nevera; frigorífico; (quím.) refrigerante.—**r. car**, (f. c.) carro de refrigeración; furgón frigorífico.

refrigeratory [-ątori]. I. *s.* (quím.) refrigerante. II. *a.* refrigerativo, refrigerante.

refringence, refringency [rifríndžęns, -i], *s.* refringencia, refractividad, poder de refractar.

refringent [-ęnt], *a.* refringente.

refuel [rifiúęl], *va.* y *vn.* reabastecer(se) de combustible, gasolina, etc.

refuge [réfiudž], *s.* refugio, amparo, asilo, albergue; guarida; subterfugio, escapatoria.

refugee [refiudží], *s.* refugiado; asilado.

refulgence, refulgency [rifáldžęns, -i], *s.* refulgencia, fulgor, esplendor, brillantez.—**refulgent** [-ęnt], *a.* refulgente, resplandeciente.

refund [rifánd], *s.* reembolso, restitución.

refund [rifánd], *va.* restituir, reintegrar, reembolsar; amortizar; consolidar una deuda.

refundable [-ąbl], *a.* restituíble, reembolsable.

refurbish [rifœrbiš], *va.* restaurar, retocar.

refusable [rifiúząbl], *a.* recusable, denegable.

refusal [rifiúząl], *s.* negativa, denegación; nones, *m. pl.*; repulsa; desaire; opción, exclusiva.

refuse [rifiúz]. I. *va.* y *vn.* rehusar; rechazar; desechar; renunciar, recusar, denegar; negarse a; resistirse a; decir que nones. II. [rifiúz], *va.* (fund.) refundir. III. [réfius], *s.* desecho, basura, desperdicio; sobra, residuo.—**r. dump**, escombrera. IV. *a.* desechado, de desecho.

refutable [rifiútąbl], *a.* refutable, impugnable.

refutation [refiutéišǫn], **refutal** [rifiútąl], *s.* refutación, rebatimiento, respuesta, impugnación.

refutatory [refiútątori], *a.* refutatorio.

refute [rifiút], *va.* refutar, rebatir, repeler, impugnar, combatir, contradecir.

regain [rigéin], *va.* recobrar, recuperar.

regal [rígal]. I. *a.* real, regio. II. *s.* (mús.) organillo portátil.

regale [rigéil]. I. *va.* regalar, agasajar, festejar; recrear, deleitar. II. *vn.* regalarse, festejarse.—**regalement** [-męnt], *s.* regal(amiento), agasajo, festejo.

regalia [rigéiliạ], *s. pl.* regalía(s) (de la corona); insignias reales; insignias, distintivos; galas.—**in full r.**, (fig.) de punta en blanco.

regalism [rígalizm], *s.* regalismo.

regalist [-ist], *s.* y *a.* regalista.

regality [rigǽliti], *s.* realeza, soberanía.

regally [rígali], *adv.* regiamente; suntuosamente.

regard [rigárd]. I. *va.* observar, mirar; considerar, reputar, juzgar; respetar, venerar; tocar, respectar, atañer, concernir; referirse a, relacionarse con.—**as regards**, tocante a, en cuanto a, por (o en) lo que respecta a. II. *s.* miramiento, consideración, acatamiento; aprecio, estimación, respeto; referencia, relación; mirada.—*pl.* memorias, expresiones, afectos, recuerdos.—**in r. to** = WITH REGARD TO.—**in this r.**, a este respecto.—**to have r. to**, tener en cuenta.—**with (best, kind) regards**—fórmula que a veces se pone al fin de una carta y que puede traducirse por "con expresiones," "con amistoso saludo," "con sentimientos de consideración," "me es grato subscribirme," etc., según el grado de confianza, o no traducirse.—**without** (any) **r. to,** sin miramientos por, sin hacer caso de.— **with r. to,** (con) respecto a o de, en punto a, tocante a.—**with due r. for,** sin menoscabo de.

regardful [-fu̯l], a. atento; cuidadoso, mirado.— **regardfully** [-i̯], adv. atentamente.

regarding [-i̯ŋ], prep. relativo a, respecto de.

regardless [-li̯s]. I. a. descuidado, indiferente, desatento, negligente, omiso.—**r.** of, sin cuidado de, sin hacer caso de, haciendo caso omiso de; a pesar de. II. adv. con todo; prescindiendo de todo, a todo trance.

regardlessness [-ni̯s], s. descuido, negligencia; indiferencia.

regatta [rigǽtǎ], s. (dep.) regata.

regency [rídẓǝnsi̯], s. regencia.

regeneracy [ridẓénǝrǎsi̯], s. regeneración.

regenerate [-reit]. I. va. regenerar; reproducir; reengendrar. II. [-ri̯t], s. regenerado; reengendrado.

regenerateness [-ni̯s], **regeneration** [-éi̯sǫn], s. regeneración; renacimiento (espiritual).

regenerative [-ǎti̯v], a. regenerador, regenerativo.

regenerator [-eitǫ(r)], s. regenerador.

regent [rídẓǝnt]. I. a. regente, reinante. II. s. regente; gobernador, gobernante; regente de una universidad.

regentship [-ši̯p], s. regencia, cargo de regente.

regicidal [redẓi̯sái̯dǎl], a. regicida.

regicide [rédẓi̯sai̯d], s. regicidio; regicida, mf.

régime [reiẓím], s. régimen; administración; sistema (m.) social.

regimen [rédẓi̯men], s. (med.) régimen; gobierno metódico, sujeción, freno; (gram.) régimen.

regiment [rédẓi̯ment]. I. s. (mil.) regimiento. II. [rédẓi̯ment], va. (mil.) regimentar; reglamentar; dominar oficialmente.

regimental [-méntǎl], a. perteneciente a un regimiento.—pl. uniforme militar.

regimentation [-téi̯sǫn], s. (mil.) regimentación; reglamentación; dominio oficial.

region [rídẓǫn], s. región.—**regional** [-ǎl], a. regional.—**regionalism** [-i̯zm], s. regionalismo.

regionalist(**ic** [-i̯st, (-í̯sti̯k], s. y a. regionalista.

register [rédẓi̯stœ(r)]. I. s. registro, inscripción, matrícula; escalafón; lista, archivo, protocolo; libro de parroquia; registrador; indicador, contador; registro (de hornillo, de chimenea, etc.); reja regulable de calefacción; (impr. y enc.) registro; (mús.) registro (de la voz y del órgano); (mar.) matrícula; (com.) certificado de nacionalidad; cédula, albalá, mf., registro de aduana.—**r. book,** registro. II. va. registrar, inscribir, matricular, protocolar, encartar; (mar.) matricular, abanderar; indicar, marcar (según escala o graduación); manifestar, indicar.—**to r. a letter,** certificar una carta. III. vn. inscribirse; matricularse; (impr.) estar en registro.

registered [-d], a. registrado, inscrito, matriculado.—**r. bond,** (com.) título nominativo.—**r. holder,** (com.) tenedor inscrito.—**r. letter,** carta certificada, carta de valores declarados.

registrant [-trǎnt], s. el que se inscribe, etc.

registrar [-trar], s. registrador, archivero.

registration [-tréi̯sǫn], s. asiento, registro; inscripción, empadronamiento, encabezamiento.

registry [-tri̯], s. asiento, inscripción; matrícula; protocolo, registro; archivo; (aut., mar.) matrícula; patente de navegación.

regius [rídẓi̯ǎs] **professor,** s. real profesor (que ocupa una cátedra instituída por dádiva real).

reglet [réglet], s. (arq.) filete; (impr.) corondel, regleta.

regnant [régnǎnt], a. reinante; predominante.

regress [rigres]. I. s. regreso; (astr.) movimiento retrógrado, retrogradación. II. [rigrés], vn. regre-

sar; (astr.) retrogradar.—**regression** [rigrésǫn], s. regresión.—**regressive** [rigrési̯v], a. regresivo.

regret [rigrét]. I. s. pena, pesar, sentimiento; compunción, remordimiento.—pl. excusa cortés que se envía para rehusar una invitación. II. va. sentir, deplorar, lamentar.—**regretful** [-fu̯l], a. pesaroso.—**regretfully** [-i̯], adv. sentidamente.

regrettable [-ǎbl], a. lamentable, sensible.

regrettably [-ǎbli̯], adv. sensiblemente.

regular [régyu̯lǎ(r)]. I. a. regular, ordinario, normal, corriente; arreglado, ordenado, metódico; uniforme; formal, autorizado; (com.) mediano; (geom.) regular; (mil.) regular, de línea; (fam.) completo, cabal.—**r. army,** ejército permanente. II. s. (mil.) soldado de línea; obrero permanente; (igl.) regular.

regularity [-lǽri̯ti̯], s. regularidad; simetría, igualdad; método, orden.

regularization [-lǎri̯zéi̯sǫn], s. regularización.— **regularize** [-lǎrai̯z], va. regularizar.

regularly [-lǎrli̯], adv. regularmente o con regularidad; por lo regular, común o general.

regulate [-leit], va. regular(izar), (ar)reglar, reglamentar, ordenar, ajustar, controlar, disponer; moderar.

regulation [-léi̯sǫn]. I. s. regulación; reglamento, orden, f., regla; reglamentación.—pl. reglamento. II. a. reglamentario, de reglamento; corriente, ordinario, de ordenanza.

regulative [-lǎti̯v], a. regulativo, regulador.

regulator [-leitǫ(r)]. I. s. (tec.) regulador (de una máquina, turbina, etc.); registro (de reloj); cronómetro regulador. II. a. de regulación, regulador.—**r. valve,** (m. v.) válvula del regulador.—**regulatory** [-lǎtǫri̯], a. regulador; reglamentario, que reglamenta.

regulus [régyu̯lǎs], s. reyezuelo; (quím.) régulo; (min.) mata; (R., astr.) Régulo; (orn.) régulo, reyezuelo.

regurgitate [rigœ́rdẓi̯teit], va. y vn. (hacer) regurgitar o refluir.

regurgitation [-éi̯sǫn], s. regurgitación, reflujo.

rehabilitate [rihǎbíli̯teit], va. rehabilitar.

rehabilitation [-éi̯sǫn], s. rehabilitación; reeducación (de los heridos, etc.); (for.) reivindicación.

rehash [rihǽs]. I. va. recomponer, refundir. II. [ríhæs], s. refundición; fárrago.

rehearing [ríhri̯ŋ], s. (for.) revista.

rehearsal [ríhœrsǎl], s. (teat.) ensayo; recitación, relación.

rehearse [ríhœrs], va. y vn. (teat.) ensayar; repasar; repetir, recitar, referir.

reheat [ríhít], va. recalentar; recocer; calentar de nuevo.—**reheater** [-œ(r)], s. recalentador.— **reheating** [-i̯ŋ], s. recalentamiento; recocido.

reign [réin]. I. vn. reinar, imperar; prevalecer, predominar, estar en voga. II. s. reinado; soberanía, predominio.—**reigning** [-i̯ŋ], a. reinante, imperante.

reimburse [rii̯mbœ́rs], va. reembolsar, reintegrar, indemnizar.—**reimbursement** [-mǝnt], s. reembolso, reintegración, indemnización.

reimpression [rii̯mprésǫn], s. (impr.) reimpresión.

rein [rein]. I. s. rienda; brida; (fig.) dirección; sujeción, freno.—**to give free r. to,** dar rienda suelta a.—**to take the reins,** tomar las riendas. II. va. gobernar (un caballo); llevar las riendas de; refrenar, contener. III. vn. obedecer a las riendas.

reincarnation [rii̯nkarnéi̯sǫn], s. reencarnación.

reincorporate [rii̯nkórporeit], va. reincorporar.— **reincorporation** [-éi̯sǫn], s. reincorporación.

reindeer [réindi̯r], s. (zool.) reno, rangífero o rengífero, tarando.

reindorse [rii̯ndórs], va. (com.) contraendosar.

reinforce [rii̯nfórs], va. = REENFORCE; (ing.) armar, reforzar (hormigón).—**reinforced concrete,** hormigón o concreto armado.—**reinforcement** [-mǝnt], s. refuerzo; ayuda, socorro;

(ing.) armadura (del hormigón armado).—*pl.* (mil.) refuerzos.

reins [reįnz], *s. pl.* (ant.) (anat.) riñones, región renal; (fig.) entrañas; afectos, las pasiones.

reinsert [rijnsǿrt], *va.* insertar o ingerir de nuevo.

reinstall [rijnstǿl], *va.* reinstalar, rehabilitar, reponer, restablecer.—**reinstallment** [-mẹnt], *s.* reinstalación, rehabilitación, restablecimiento.

reinstate [rijnstéįt], *va.* reinstalar, rehabilitar, restablecer; en los seguros contra incendios, reparar o reponer lo dañado.

reinstatement [-mẹnt], *s.* reinstalación, rehabilitación, restablecimiento.

reinsurance [rijnšúŗąns], *s.* (com.) reaseguro.

reinsure [rijnšúŗ], *va.* reasegurar.

reintegrate [rijntẹgreįt], *va.* reintegrar.

reintegration [-éįšǫn], *s.* reintegración, reintegro.

reinvestment [rijnvéstmẹnt], *s.* reinversión.

reissue [rijšú]. **I.** *va.* volver a publicar o emitir. **II.** *vn.* volver a salir. **III.** *s.* reimpresión, nueva edición o emisión.

reiterate [rijtẹreįt], *va.* reiterar.—**reiteratedly** [-įdlį], *adv.* reiteradamente, repetidas veces.—**reiteration** [-éįšǫn], *s.* reiteración, repetición.

reject [rídžekt], *s.* persona o cosa no aceptada.

reject [rįdžékt], *va.* rechazar, recusar, rehusar, renunciar, rehuir, repeler; expeler, arrojar; (de)negar; desechar, despreciar; arrinconar, descartar; (mil.) excluir del servicio.

rejectable [-ạbl], *a.* recusable, inadmisible.

rejecter, rejector [-œ(r)], *s.* el que rechaza, recusa o desecha.

rejection [-šǫn], *s.* rechazamiento, desecho, exclusión, repudiación.

rejective [-tįv], *a.* que rechaza, rehusa o excluye.

rejoice [rįdžóįs]. **I.** *va.* regocijar, alegrar. **II.** *vn.* regocijarse, gozarse, alegrarse, jubilar.

rejoicing [-įŋ]. **I.** *s.* alegría, fiesta, regocijo, júbilo, festividad. **II.** *a.* gozoso, regocijado.

rejoin [rįdžóįn]. **I.** *va.* reunirse con, volver a la compañía de. **II.** *vn.* replicar; (for.) triplicar.

rejoinder [-dœ(r)], *s.* respuesta, réplica; (for.) tríplica, contrarréplica.

rejoint [rįdžóįnt], *va.* juntar de nuevo; (alb.) llenar las degolladuras con mortero.

rejuvenate [rįdžúvẹneįt], *va.* rejuvenecer, remozar.

rejuvenation [-éįšǫn], **rejuvenescence** [-ésẹns], *s.* rejuvenecimiento, remozamiento.

rekindle [rikíndl], *va.* volver a encender, reavivar, despertar.

relapse [rįlǽps]. **I.** *vn.* recaer; reincidir (en un error, etc.); (relig.) renegar; (med.) recidivar. **II.** *s.* recaída; reincidencia; (med.) recidiva, relapso, recaída.

relate [rįléįt]. **I.** *va.* relatar, referir, contar, narrar; relacionar; emparentar. **II.** *vn.* relacionarse con; concernir, tocar, referirse a.

related [-įd], *a.* relacionado, conexo; referido; afín o afine; emparentado, allegado.

relater [-œ(r)], *s.* relat(ad)or, narrador.

relating [-įŋ], *a.* (con to) referente o concerniente (a).

relation [rįléįšǫn], *s.* relación; referencia, alusión; relato, narración; parentesco; pariente.—*pl.* parentela, deudos, parientes; tratos, comunicaciones.—**in r. to**, con relación a, respecto a.

relational [-ạl], *a.* que guarda o expresa relación; relativo.

relationship [-šįp], *s.* relación; parentesco; entronque, enlace; allegamiento.

relative [rélạtįv]. **I.** *a.* (leng. ord. y gram.) relativo.—**r. wind,** (aer.) viento relativo. **II.** *s.* pariente, deudo, allegado; (gram.) relativo, pronombre relativo.—**relatively** [-lį], *adv.* relativamente.

relativism [-įzm], *s.* (fil. y fís.) relativismo, teoría de la relatividad en general, y de la relatividad del conocimiento en particular.—**relativist** [-įst], *s.* relativista.

relativity [relạtívįtį], *s.* relatividad.—**r. of**

knowledge, (fil.) relatividad del conocimiento.

relax [rįlǽks]. **I.** *va.* relajar, aflojar; mitigar; remitir; desatar; aliviar el estreñimiento; causar languidez; (fon.) relajar. **II.** *vn.* aflojar, ceder; esparcirse, descansar; mitigarse.

relaxation [rįlækséįšǫn], *s.* aflojamiento, flojedad; descanso, reposo; solaz, *m.*, recreo, distracción, esparcimiento; mitigación, lenidad; relajación, relajamiento de nervios, músculos, etc.

relay [ríleį]. **I.** *s.* relevo, remuda, parada, posta (de caballos, etc.); (m. v.) máquina auxiliar reguladora (ll. t. **r. cylinder**); (elec.) relevador, relais, relé.—**r. broadcast,** (rad.) difusión, por una difusora, de comunicaciones recibidas de otra; redifusión.—**r. race,** (dep.) carrera de relevos o de equipos. **II.** *va.* enviar por posta; retransmitir (un mensaje, etc.); [rįléį], volver a colocar.

release [rįlís]. **I.** *va.* soltar; poner en libertad; relevar, exonerar; renunciar a o abandonar; descargar (de una obligación); aliviar; poner en circulación, dar al público; (rilís], realquilar, volver a arrendar. **II.** *s.* liberación; exoneración; (com.) descargo; (for.) finiquito, quita; cesión (de un derecho); obra o pieza (de cine, fonógrafo, etc.) lista para darla al público; (m. v.) escape; (mec.) disparador, escape, trinquete.

releasee [rįlisí], *s.* (for.) persona a cuyo favor se otorga una escritura de cesión o finiquito.

releasor [rįlísǫ(r)], *s.* (for.) el que otorga una finiquito o acta de cesión.

relegate [rélẹgeįt], *va.* relegar; desterrar.

relegation [-éįšǫn], *s.* relegación; destierro.

relent [rįlént], *vn.* aplacarse, desenojarse; ceder, ablandarse, enternecerse.—**relentless** [-lįs], *a.* implacable, inexorable.—**relentlessness** [-nįs], *s.* calidad de implacable, inexorabilidad.—**relentlessly** [-lį], *adv.* implacablemente, sin piedad.

relevancy, relevance [rélẹvansį, -ạns], *s.* pertinencia.—**relevant** [-ạnt], *a.* pertinente, a propósito, apropiado; que hace o viene al caso.

reliability [rįláįạbĺįtį], **reliableness** [-blnįs], *s.* confiabilidad; calidad de seguro o digno de confianza; formalidad; precisión; veracidad.—**reliable** [-bl], *a.* seguro, digno de confianza, confiable, fidedigno, formal.—**reliance** [-ạns], *s.* confianza, seguridad.—**reliant** [-ạnt], *a.* confiado (en sí mismo).

relic [rélįk], *s.* reliquia, vestigio.

relict [rélįkt], *s.* viuda.—*pl.* restos mortales.

relief [rįlíf], *s.* ayuda, auxilio; alivio, consuelo; relevación, aligeramiento; socorro, limosna; solaz, *m.*, descanso; (mil.) relevo; (for.) desagravio, satisfacción, compensación, reparación; (b. a.) relieve, realce, resalte o resalto.—**r. agencies,** agencias de auxilio o de socorro.—**r. map,** mapa (*m.*) en relieve.—**r. train,** tren de socorro.—**r. valve,** (mec.) válvula de seguridad.—**on r.,** socorrido.—**to be on r.,** estar viviendo de socorro, recibir o percibir auxilio social.

relievable [rįlívạbl], *a.* consolable; aliviable.

relieve [rįlív], *va.* relevar, remediar, socorrer, aligerar, aliviar; descargar, exonerar; mitigar; suavizar; vivificar; realzar, poner en relieve, hacer resaltar; acopar; (mil.) relevar; (for.) reparar, desagraviar, hacer justicia.—**to r. nature,** hacer del cuerpo.

relieving arch [rįlívįŋ arch], *s.* (arq.) sobrearco, arco de descarga.—**r. tackle** [tǽkl], (mar.) pluma de chata de carena; aparejos de la caña del timón.

relievo [rįlívoų], *s.* (b. a.) relieve.—**r.-work,** obra de relieve, mazonería.

religion [rįlídžǫn], *s.* religión, fe, *f.*

religionism [-įzm], *s.* estricta, excesiva o falsa religiosidad; fariseísmo.

religionist [-įst], *s.* religionario.

religiosity [rįlįdžįásįtį], *s.* religiosidad.

religious [rįlídžʌs]. **I.** *a.* religioso, pío, devoto;

concienzudo, exacto, puntual. **II.** *s.* (igl.) religioso.—**religiously** [-li], *adv.* religiosamente.—**religiousness** [-nẹs], *s.* religiosidad, piedad.

relinquish [rịlínkwịš], *va.* abandonar, dejar, ceder; renunciar; despojarse de.—**relinquishment** [-mẹnt], *s.* abandono, dejación, renuncia.

reliquary [rélịkwẹrị], *s.* relicario.

relish [rélịš]. **I.** *s.* gusto, apetencia, sabor grato, dejo; sazón, *f.*, condimento; entremés; fruición, goce, saboreo, paladar; (carp.) hombro de espiga. **II.** *va.* saborear, paladear; gustar de; hacer algo con fruición; sazonar, condimentar. **III.** *vn.* saber bien, ser sabroso; gustar, agradar.

relishable [-abl], *a.* gustoso, sabroso.

reload [rilóụd], *va.* recargar; cargar de nuevo.

relucent [rịljúṣẹnt], *a.* reluciente.

reluctance, reluctancy [rịlʌ́ktạns, -ị], *s.* repugnancia, renuencia, desgana, disgusto.—**with r.**, de mala gana.—**reluctant** [-ạnt], *a.* renuente, maldispuesto, repugnante.—**reluctantly** [-lị], *adv.* de mala gana, a contrapelo, a regañadientes.

relume [rịljúm], *va.* volver a encender.

rely [rịláị], *vn.* (con **on** o **upon**) confiar o fiar en, contar con, fiarse de, atenerse a.

remain [rịméịn], *vn.* quedar, restar o faltar; sobrar; estarse, permanecer; persistir, continuar. —**to r. behind**, rezagarse, quedarse atrás.—**to r. silent**, callar(se), guardar silencio; no chistar.—**to r. undone**, quedar sin hacer.

remainder [-dœr)]. **I.** *s.* resto, restante, residuo, sobra(nte); rezago. **II.** *a.* restante, sobrante.

remaining [-ịŋ], *a.* restante, sobrante.

remains [-z], *s. pl.* restos, cadáver; sobras, despojos, vestigios, reliquias; remanente; obras póstumas; esqueletos humanos; ruinas.

remake [riméịk], *va.* rehacer.

reman [rimǽn], *va.* (mar., mil., etc.) volver a tripular, dotar, marinar, armar o guarnecer; poner un nuevo contingente en; alentar.

remand [rịmǽnd], *va.* enviar o mandar al punto de procedencia, devolver; (for.) reencarcelar; enviar a otro tribunal.

remand(ment [-mẹnt], *s.* (for.) reencarcelamiento; mandato judicial para el traslado a otro tribunal.

remark [rịmárk]. **I.** *s.* observación, advertencia, nota. **II.** *va.* hacer una observación, observar, advertir, notar, reparar, echar de ver.

remarkable [-abl], *a.* notable, interesante, extraordinario, admirable, marcado, señalado.—**remarkably** [-ablị], *adv.* notablemente.

remarker [-œr)], *s.* observador; anotador.

remarriage [rimǽrịdʒ], *s.* segundas nupcias.

remarry [rimǽrị], *va.* y *vn.* volver a casar o casarse; contraer segundas nupcias.

remediable [rịmídịabl], *a.* remediable, curable.

remedial [rịmídịal], *a.* reparador; terapéutico.

remedy [rémẹdị]. **I.** *s.* remedio, medicamento; cura; recurso.—**to be past r.**, no tener cura o remedio. **II.** *va.* curar, remediar, sanar; corregir.

remember [rịmémbœr)]. **I.** *va.* recordar, acordarse de, rememorar; tener presente o en cuenta; mentar, hacer presente, dar memorias (*remember me to her*, déle Vd. expresiones mías). **II.** *vn.* acordarse, hacer memoria.

remembrance [-brạns], *s.* memoria, retentiva; recordación; recuerdo; rememoración; conmemoración.—**remembrancer** [-œr)], *s.* recordador; recordatorio; (Ingl.) oficial de Hacienda o del Tribunal Supremo.

remind [rịmáịnd], *va.* recordar, hacer presente.—**reminder** [-œr)], *s.* recordativo, señal, *f.*, recordatorio; advertencia.—**remindful** [-fụl], *a.* recordativo, rememorativo; atento, cuidadoso.

reminisce [remịnís], *vn.* pensar en o hablar de cosas pasadas; recordar (uno) sus recuerdos.

reminiscence [-ẹns], *s.* reminiscencia, recuerdo. —*pl.* memorias.—**reminiscent** [-ẹnt], *a.* recordativo, rememorativo.

remise [rịmáịz]. **I.** *va.* (for.) restituir; ceder. **II.** *s.* restitución, cesión.

remiss [rịmís], *a.* remiso, descuidado, omiso; flojo.

remissibility [-ịbịlịtị], *s.* calidad de remisible o perdonable.—**remissible** [-ịbl], *a.* remisible.

remission [rịmíšọn], *s.* remisión, perdón; relevación, disminución; (com.) remesa; (med.) remisión.

remissive [rịmísịv], *a.* remisivo; que disminuye.

remissly [-lị], *adv.* remisamente.

remissness [-nẹs], *s.* flojedad, negligencia.

remissory [-orị], *a.* remisorio, remisivo.

remit [rịmít]. **I.** *va.* (com.) remesar; remitir, enviar; remitir, perdonar, condonar; exonerar, eximir; relajar, aflojar; (for.) referir, someter, trasladar. **II.** *vn.* (com.) hacer remesas; girar; disminuir; (med.) debilitarse, bajar, templarse (una fiebre, etc.).

remitment [-mẹnt], *s.* remisión, gracia, exoneración; remesa.—**remittal** [-al], *s.* cesión, renuncia, abandono; remesa.—**remittance** [-ạns], *s.* (com.) remesa, envío, giro, letra de cambio.—**remittence**, *s.* (med.) remitencia.—**remittent** [-ẹnt]. **I.** *a.* remitente. **II.** *s.* fiebre (*f.*) o calentura remitente.—**remitter** [-œr)], *s.* remitente; (for.) restitución.

remnant [rémnạnt], *s.* remanente, resto, residuo; dejo, vestigio; retal, retazo, maula.—**r. sale**, saldo.—**r. stand o store**, maulería.

remodel [rimádẹl], *va.* modelar de nuevo; rehacer, reconstruir; renovar, refaccionar.

remonetize [rimánẹtaịz], *va.* remonetizar.

remonstrance [rịmánstrạns], *s.* protesta; memorial, representación; reprensión, amonestación, reconvención; (igl.) *V.* MONSTRANCE.

remonstrant [-strạnt]. **I.** *a.* en son de protesta o de reconvención. **II.** *s.* peticionario, exponente.

remonstrate [-streịt], *vn.* protestar, objetar; (con *with*) reconvenir, (fam.) sermonear.

remora [rémọrạ], *s.* (ict.) remora.

remorse [rịmɔ́rs], *s.* remordimiento, compunción, cargo de conciencia.—**remorseful** [-fụl], *a.* lleno de remordimientos; arrepentido, compungido.—**remorseless** [-lịs], *a.* cruel, sin conciencia.—**remorselessly** [-lị], *adv.* sin remordimiento, sin piedad, des(a)piadadamente. —**remorselessness** [-nẹs], *s.* falta de piedad o remordimiento.

remote [rịmóụt], *a.* remoto, apartado, lejano, distante; leve, ligero; extraño, ajeno.—**(by) r. control**, (por) control remoto o a distancia.—**remotely** [-lị], *adv.* remotamente.

remoteness [-nẹs], *s.* calidad de remoto; lejanía.

remount [rimáụnt]. **I.** *va.* y *vn.* remontar; volver a subir; volver a engastar (piedras preciosas), pegar (fotografías), etc.; (mil.) remontar(se). **II.** *s.* (mil.) remonta.—**r. cavalry**, remonta.

removability [rịmúvạbịlịtị], *s.* removibilidad, amovilidad.—**removable** [-bl], *a.* removible; separable, de quita; transportable; amovible.

removal [rịmúvạl], *s.* acción de quitar, llevarse o levantar; remoción; removimiento; deposición; eliminación, extirpación; alejamiento, apartamiento; traslado, traslación, mudanza, cambio de domicilio; remudamiento; supresión.

remove [rịmúv]. **I.** *va.* remover, amover; quitar; suprimir, eliminar; alejar; mudar, cambiar, trasladar; alzar o levantar (la casa); destituir, deponer, derogar; apartar, desarrimar; sacar, extirpar, arrancar; desembarazarse de; poner fin a. **II.** *vn.* mudarse, trasladarse, alejarse; cambiar de sitio o domicilio. **III.** *s.* cambio de lugar, mudada; distancia, grado, paso, intervalo; grado de parentesco; plato o entrada que se quita en una comida.

removed [-d], *a.* apartado, alejado, distante; destituído; extraño.

remover [-œr)], *s.* quitador; apartador.

remunerable [rịmjúnẹrạbl], *a.* remunerable.

remunerate [-eịt], *va.* remunerar; premiar.—**remuneration** [-éịšọn], *s.* remuneración.—**remunerative** [-ạtịv], *a.* remuneratorio; lucrativo, remunerador.—**remunerator** [-eito̱(r)], *s.* remunerador.

Renaissance [renə̯sáns]. I. *s.* renacimiento. II. *a.* renacentista.

renal [rína̱l], *a.* renal; pert. a los riñones.

Renard [rénə̯rd], *s.* = REYNARD.

renascence [rinǽsns̱], *s.* renacimiento.

renascent [-ę̱nt], *a.* renaciente.

rencounter [renkáunto̱(r)]. I. *s.* encuentro casual; debate; combate, refriega, pendencia, riña. II. *va.* y *vn.* encontrar(se) por casualidad; acometer(se).

rend [rend]. I. *va.* (*pret.* y *pp.* RENT) rasgar, desgarrar; rajar, hender; lacerar, hacer pedazos; separar, desunir; arrancar. II. *vn.* rasgarse; rajarse; despedazarse.

render [réndœ(r)]. I. *va.* volver; poner; hacer; dar, suministrar, prestar, rendir; (mús., teat.) interpretar, ejecutar; traducir; devolver, restituir; derretir y clarificar; extraer por fusión; (com.) enviar, girar (una cuenta); (alb.) dar la primera capa de enlucido a.—**to r. assistance**, prestar auxilio, auxiliar.—**to r. into**, traducir o verter al.—**to r. justice**, hacer justicia. II. *s.* pago (esp. en forma de servicio); (alb.) capa de enlucido aplicada sin listonado.

rendezvous [rándə̯vu]. I. *va.* y *vn.* acudir, juntar(se), reunir(se). II. *s.* cita; reunión; lugar de la cita.

rendition [rendíʃǫn], *s.* versión o traducción; (mús., teat.) interpretación, ejecución; rendición, entrega; (com.) rendimiento, producción.

rendrock [réndrak], *s.* variedad de dinamita.

renegade [rénigeid], **renegado** [-géidǫu]. I. *s.* renegado, apóstata, *mf.*, elche; desertor. II. *a.* renegado, falso, traidor.

renege [riníg]. I. *va.* negar; renunciar; desertar. II. *vn.* renunciar (en el juego); faltar a la palabra dada. III. *s.* renuncio.

renew [rinjú]. I. *va.* renovar, reengendrar; restaurar, rehacer; reanudar; (com.) extender, prorrogar. II. *vn.* renovarse, recentarse, volver a empezar.

renewable [-ə̯bl], *a.* renovable.

renewal [-ə̯l], *s.* renovación, renuevo; reanudación; (com.) prórroga.

reniform [ríniform], *a.* reniforme.

renitency [rénitęnsi], *s.* renitencia.

renitent [-ę̱nt], *a.* renitente.

rennet [rénit], *s.* cuajo; (anat.) cuajar.

rennin [rénin], *s.* (bioquím.) fermento del cuajo; enzima del jugo gástrico que cuaja la leche.

renominate [rinámineit], *va.* nombrar de nuevo.

renomination [-éiʃǫn], *s.* (pol.) segundo nombramiento.

renounce [rináuns], *va.* renunciar; rechazar, repudiar, renegar, abnegar, abandonar, abjurar; abdicar; en los naipes, renunciar.

renouncement [-mę̱nt], *s.* renuncia(miento).

renovate [rénoveit], *va.* renovar, rehacer; limpiar; purificar.—**renovation** [-éiʃǫn], *s.* renovación, rehacimiento, compostura; renuevo; limpiadura.—**renovator** [-eito̱(r)], *s.* renovador.

renown [rináun], *s.* renombre, fama, nombradía.

renowned [-d], *a.* renombrado, famoso, célebre.

rent [rent]. I. *pret.* y *pp.* de TO REND. II. *s.* rasgón, rasgadura, desgarro; raja, grieta, cuarteadura; cisma, *m.*

rent [rént]. I. *s.* renta, rento, alquiler; censo; arrendamiento, arriendo; rédito.—**r. day**, día de pagar el arrendamiento.—**for r.**, para arrendar; se arrienda; de alquiler. II. *va.* alquilar, arrendar, dar o tomar en arrendamiento.

rentable [-ə̯bl], *a.* arrendable, alquilable.

rental [-ə̯l]. I. *s.* renta, rento; arrendamiento, alquiler; censo. II. *a.* censual; rentoso; rel. a rentas o alquileres.

renter [-œ(r)], *s.* rentero, inquilino, arrendatario; arrendador; arrendante.

renunciation [rinʌnsiéiʃǫn], *s.* renuncia, renunciación, renunciamiento.

reopen [rió̱upn], *va.* y *vn.* reabrir, volver a abrir(se); reanudar (una discusión, etc.).—**reopening** [-iŋ], *s.* reapertura.

reorganization [riórgąnizéiʃǫn], *s.* reorganización.—**reorganize** [-aiz], *va.* reorganizar.

reorganizer [-œ(r)], *s.* reorganizador.

rep [rep], *s.* (tej.) reps, cierta tela de cordoncillo.

repack [ripǽk], *va.* reempacar; reembalar.

repaid [ripéid], *pret.* y *pp.* de TO REPAY.

repaint [ripéint], *va.* repintar.

repair [ripér]. I. *va.* restaurar, reparar, aderezar, componer; remendar; (zap.) remontar; remediar, subsanar, enmendar; resarcir o indemnizar; restituir, restablecer; (mar.) carenar; embonar. II. *vn.* (con to) ir a, acudir a, dirigirse a. III. *s.* reparo, reparación, restauración; compostura, remiendo, recorrido; (mar.) carena; embonada; (zap.) remonta.—**r. ship**, buque taller.—**r. shop**, taller de reparaciones.—**out of r.**, descompuesto, en mal estado.

repairer [-œ(r)], **repairman** [-mæn], *s.* reparador, componedor, restaurador.

repairing [-iŋ], *s.* = REPAIR.

reparable [répą̯rąbl], **repairable** [ripérąbl], *a.* reparable.

reparation [repąréiʃǫn], *s.* reparación, satisfacción, resarcimiento; indemnización; saneamiento; restauración.

reparative [ripǽrątiv], *a.* reparativo, reparador, restaurativo.

repartee [repąrtí], *s.* respuesta o réplica aguda, vuelta, agudeza, discreteo.

repartition [ripąrtíʃǫn], *s.* repartimiento, repartición.

repass [ripǽs], *va.* repasar, volver a pasar.

repassage [-idž], *s.* repaso.

repast [ripǽst], *s.* comida, alimento, colación.

repatriate [ripéitrieit], *va.* repatriar.

repatriation [-éiʃǫn], *s.* repatriación.

repay [ripéi]. I. *va.* (*pret.* y *pp.* REPAID) pagar, devolver, reembolsar, retornar; recompensar; reintegrar; convenir o aprovechar a; pagar en la misma moneda. II. *vn.* pagar, hacer un pago.

repayable [-ə̯bl], *a.* pagable, reembolsable.

repayment [-mę̱nt], *s.* pago, retorno, devolución.

repeal [ripíl]. I. *va.* derogar, revocar, abrogar, abolir, anular, casar. II. *s.* revocación, derogación, abrogación.—**repealable** [-ə̯bl], *a.* revocable.—**repealer** [-œ(r)], *s.* revocador.—**repealing** [-iŋ], *a.* derogatorio.

repeat [ripít]. I. *va.* repetir; (re)iterar; reproducir; duplicar; volver a (hacer algo); repasar, ensayar. II. *s.* repetición; duplicado; (mús.) repetición, guión, *m.*

repeatedly [-idli], *adv.* repetidamente, repetidas veces, a menudo.

repeater [-œ(r)], *s.* repetidor; reloj de repetición; arma de repetición; (elec.) repetidor; (E. U. pol.) elector que vota varias veces en una misma elección.

repeating [-iŋ], *a.* repetidor; de repetición.—**r. circle**, (top., ast., etc.) círculo repetidor.—**r. coil**, (elec.) bobina acopladora de inducción.—**r. decimal**, (arit.) fracción decimal periódica.—**r. firearm**, arma de repetición.—**r. instrument**, instrumento repetidor.—**r. watch**, reloj de repetición.

repel [ripél]. I. *va.* repeler, rechazar, repulsar; resistir; alejar, ahuyentar; (med.) repercutir los humores. II. *vn.* ser repelente o repulsivo.

repellent [-ę̱nt], *a.* repelente, repulsivo; repercusivo; ahuyentador; impermeable. II. *s.* cosa repugnante o que causa aversión; tela impermeable; (med.) remedio repercusivo.

repent [rípęnt], *a.* (zool. y bot.) rastrero.

repent [ripę́nt], *va.* y *vn.* arrepentirse (de), dolerse (de); sentir.—**repentance** [-ąns], *s.* arrepentimiento, penitencia, compunción, contrición.—**repentant** [-ą̱nt], *a.* arrepentido, contrito.—**repenter, repenter** [-œ(r)], *s.* penitente, arrepentido.—**repentantly** [-ą̱ntli],

repentingly [-iŋli], *adv.* arrepentida o contritamente.

repeople [ripípl], *va.* repoblar.

repercussion [ripœrkáśǫn], *s.* repercusión, resonación, reverberación, rechazo; rimbombo, retumbo.

repercussive [-kásiv], *a.* repercusivo.

repertoire [répœrtwar], *s.* (mús. y teat.) repertorio.

repertory [-tǫri], *s.* depósito, colección; repertorio; inventario, lista, índice; almacén.

repetend [répitend], *s.* (mat.) período (de una fracción decimal periódica).

repetition [repitíśǫn], *s.* repetición, (re)iteración; repaso; redición.—**repetitious** [-ʌs], *a.* que abunda en repeticiones; redundante.

repine [ripáin], *vn.* afligirse, desconsolarse, apurarse, quejarse.—**repiner** [-œ(r)], *s.* el que se queja.—**repining** [-iŋ], *s.* pesar; queja, descontento.

replace [riplé̇s], *va.* reemplazar, substituir; suplir; reponer; renovar; poner nuevo (una parte o pieza de un mecanismo); devolver, reembolsar o restituir.—**replaceable** [-ǫbl], *a.* reemplazable, substituible; renovable.—**replacement** [-mǫnt], *s.* reemplazo, substitución; reemplazante; pieza de repuesto; restitución, reposición.

replait [riplé̇t], *va.* replegar.

replant [riplǽnt], *va.* replantar.

replenish [ripléniš], *va.* rellenar, rehenchir; llenar o surtir de nuevo.—**replenishment** [-mǫnt], *s.* relleno, rehenchimiento; acción y efecto de llenar o proveer.

replete [riplít], *a.* lleno, repleto; ahito.—**repletion** [riplíśǫn], **repleteness** [riplítnis], *s.* repleción, plenitud; ahito.

repleviable [riplévi̇ǫbl], *a.* (for.) reivindicable.

replevin [riplévin], *s.* (for.) reivindicación; auto de desembargo.

replevin, o **replevy** [riplévin, riplévi], *va.* (for.) desembargar; reivindicar.

replica [répliki̇ǫ], *s.* (b. a.) réplica, duplicado; copia, reproducción; (mús.) repetición.

replicate [réplikit], *a.* replegado.

replication [-kéiśǫn], *s.* réplica, replicato, respuesta; repetición; repliegue; (for.) réplica.

reply [riplái], I. *s.* respuesta, contestación; (for.) réplica, replicato. II. *vn.* y *va.* contestar, responder, reponer; (for.) replicar.

report [ripórt], I. *va.* informar acerca de, dar parte de, enterar de; comunicar; relatar, referir, contar; redactar un informe o dictamen; reseñar (un libro); propalar, divulgar; quejarse de, acusar, delatar, denunciar.—**to r. out**, devolver (un proyecto de ley, etc.) con informe o dictamen.—**to r. progress**, dar cuenta de la marcha de un asunto.—**it is reported**, corre la voz, se dice. II. *vn.* presentar informe o dictamen; servir como repórter o noticiero; comparecer, personarse. III. *s.* relato, parte, noticia, reporte, información; (mil. y period.) comunicado; reseña (de un libro); informe, dictamen, memoria; voz, rumor; reportaje (de periódico); fama, reputación; (for.) relación de pleitos o causas; estampido, estallido, trueno, estruendo.—**r. of a gun, musket, pistol**, cañonazo, escopetazo, pistoletazo.—**by r.**, según se dice.

reporter [-œ(r)], *s.* repórter, reportero; noticiero; (for.) relator.—**reporters' gallery**, tribuna de los periodistas.

reportorial [reportórial], *a.* reporteril.

repose [ripóuz], I. *va.* descansar, reclinar; poner (confianza o esperanza). II. *vn.* reposar, descansar; tener confianza en. III. *vr.* tenderse, reclinarse, recostarse. IV. *s.* reposo, descanso; tranquilidad, calma, quietud.

reposeful [-ful], *a.* reposado, descansado, calmoso, quieto, tranquilo.

reposit [ripázit], *va.* reponer; depositar.

reposition [ripozíśǫn], *s.* reposición, restablecimiento.

repositor [ripázitǫ(r)], *s.* reponedor.

repository [-tǫri], *s.* repositorio, depósito; almacén, tienda.

repossess [ripǫzés], *va.* recobrar, recuperar.

repossession [ripǫzéśǫn], *s.* recuperación.

repoussé [rœpuséi], *a.* y *s.* repujado.

reprehend [reprihénd], *va.* reprender, censurar, increpar, tachar, regañar.

reprehender [-œ(r)], *s.* reprendedor, reprensor.

reprehensible [-síbl], *a.* reprensible, censurable.—**reprehensibleness** [-nis], *s.* calidad de reprensible.—**reprehension** [-śǫn], *s.* reprensión, regaño, censura; (fam.) fraterna, repasata.—**reprehensive** [-siv], *a.* reprensor.

represent [reprizént], *va.* representar; figurar, pintar, simbolizar; significar, manifestar, exponer; [riprizént] presentar de nuevo.

representable [-ǫbl], *a.* representable.

representation [-éiśǫn], *s.* representación (en todas sus acepciones); [ri-] nueva presentación.

representative [-átiv], I. *a.* representativo, típico; representante. II. *s.* representante, gestor, apoderado, delegado, encargado; símbolo, tipo, ejemplar; (R.) diputado, representante (miembro de la Cámara de Representantes).

repress [riprés], *va.* reprimir, dominar, sofocar, moderar, represar; sojuzgar, sujetar; [riprés] volver a prensar, planchar, etc.

repression [ripréśǫn], *s.* represión.

repressive [riprésiv], *a.* represivo.

reprieve [riprív], I. *va.* (for.) suspender la ejecución de una sentencia; aliviar, librar temporalmente de peligro o dolor. II. *s.* suspensión temporal de una sentencia o de un dolor.

reprimand [réprimænd], I. *va.* reprender, regañar, reñir, reconvenir; (fam.) sermonear. II. *s.* reprimenda, reprensión, regaño, censura.

reprint [riprínt], I. *va.* reimprimir. II. [ríprint], *s.* reimpresión; tirada aparte (de un artículo).

reprisal [ripráizǫl], *s.* represalia.

reproach [ripróutš], I. *va.* reprochar, increpar, echar en cara, afear; vituperar, censurar. II. *s.* reproche, increpación; contumelia, vituperio; tacha, baldón, nota.—**above r.**, sin tacha.—**reproachable** [-ǫbl], *a.* censurable, reprensible.—**reproachableness** [-nis], *s.* reprensibilidad.—**reproachful** [-ful], *a.* increpante, reprensor, vituperioso; ceñudo.—**reproachfully** [-i], *adv.* vituperiosamente, contumeliosamente.—**reproachfulness** [-nis], *s.* calidad de vituperioso.

reproachless [-lis], *a.* intachable.

reprobate [réprobeit], I. *a.* y *s.* réprobo, malvado. II. *va.* reprobar, condenar; desaprobar.—**reprobation** [-éiśǫn], *s.* reprobación, desaprobación, condenación.—**reprobative** [-átiv], **reprobatory** [-átori], *a.* reprobador, reprobatorio.

reproduce [riprodiús], *va.* reproducir, reengendrar; duplicar, copiar.—**reproducer** [-œ(r)], *s.* reproductor; aparato reproductor (fonográfico, etc.).—**reproducible** [-ibl], *a.* reproductible.

reproduction [riprodákśǫn], *s.* reproducción; reminiscencia; (b. a.) copia, traslado, trasunto.—**reproductive, reproductory** [-tiv, -tori], *a.* reproductivo, reproductor.

reproof [riprúf], **reproval** [riprúvǫl], *s.* reprobación, reproche, reprensión.—**reprovable** [riprúvǫbl], *a.* reprochable, censurable, reprensible.

reprove [riprúv], *va.* reprobar, culpar, censurar; acusar, condenar.—**reprover** [-œ(r)], *s.* reprensor, reprobador, censor.

reptant [réptǫnt], *a.* (bot. y zool.) rastrero.

reptile [réptil], *s.* y *a.* (zool.) reptil; (fig.) bajo, vil, rastrero, traidor.—**Reptilia** [reptíliǫ], *s. pl.* reptiles.—**reptilian** [-n]. I. *s.* reptil. II. *a.* de reptil, de los reptiles.—**r. age**, (geol.) época mesozoica.

republic [ripáblik], *s.* república.—**republican** [-ǫn], *a.* y *s.* republicano; (orn.) republicano, que anida en manadas.—**republicanism** [-ızm], s. republicanismo.

republication [ripʌblįkéįşǫn], s. nueva publicación; reimpresión; (for.) renovación de un testamento.

republish [ripʌblį̧ş], va. publicar de nuevo; reimprimir; renovar.

repudiable [ripįúdįabl], a. repudiable.

repudiate [-eįt], va. repudiar, repeler; rechazar, renunciar; desconocer.—**repudiated** [-įd], pp. y a. marfuz.—**repudiation** [-éįşǫn], s. repudiación, repudio; rechazo, renuncia; desconocimiento.—**repudiator** [-ǫ(r)], s. repudiador; renunciante; desconocedor.

repugnance, repugnancy [rįpʌgnans, -į], s. repugnancia, repulsión; renitencia; mala gana, aversión.—**repugnant** [-ąnt], a. repugnante, repulsivo; antipático; opuesto, renitente; contrario, incompatible.—**repugnantly** [-lį], adv. con repugnancia, de mala gana.

repulse [rįpʌls]. I. s. repulsa, repulsión; denegación. II. va. repulsar, desechar, rechazar, repeler.

repulsion [-şǫn], s. (fís.) repulsión; rechazamiento; repugnancia, aversión.—**repulsive** [-sįv], a. repulsivo, repugnante, repelente.—**repulsiveness** [-nįs], s. carácter repugnante o repulsivo.

reputable [répyųt̹abl], a. honroso, honrado, respetable, estimable, intachable; lícito.—**reputably** [-blį], adv. honrosamente, honradamente.

reputation [repyųtéįşǫn], s. reputación; opinión, crédito, estimación, fama, prestigio, nombradía.

repute [rįpįút]. I. va. reputar, estimar, juzgar, tener por. II. s. fama, crédito, reputación, nota, estimación; opinión común.

reputed [-įd], a. considerado, tenido por; supuesto, putativo (padre, autor, etc.).—**to be r.,** pasar o quedar por; tener fama de.—**reputedly** [-lį], adv. según la opinión común; según se cree.

request [rįkwést]. I. s. súplica, ruego; petición, pedimento, instancia, solicitud; (com.) demanda.—**at the r. of,** o **by r.,** a petición, a solicitud de.—**in r.,** en boga, en demanda, pedido, buscado. II. va. rogar, pedir, suplicar, solicitar.

requiem (mass) [rīkwįem (mæs)], s. (igl. y mús.) misa de réquiem.

requirable [rįkwájrąbl], a. que se puede requerir o solicitar.

require [rįkwájr], va. requerir, demandar, pedir, obligar, exigir, necesitar.

requirement [-mẹnt], s. demanda, requerimiento, exigencia; requisito, necesidad; formalidad; estipulación.—**requirer** [-œ(r)], s. requeridor.

requisite [rékwįzįt]. I. a. necesario, forzoso, indispensable. II. s. requisito.—**requisitely** [-lį], adv. necesariamente.—**requisiteness** [-nįs], s. necesidad, precisión, calidad de indispensable.

requisition [rekwįzíşǫn]. I. s. pedimento, petición, demanda; (mil.) requisa, requisición; necesidad, requisito, menester; (com.) demanda, solicitud; (for.) requisitoria.—**in r.,** en demanda, pedido, buscado. II. va. (mil.) requisar.

requisitory [rįkwízįtorį], a. requisitorio.

requital [rįkwájtąl], s. retorno, paga, satisfacción; compensación; desquite; pena del talión.

requite [rįkwájt], va. pagar, (re)compensar, retornar, devolver; pagar en la misma moneda.

requiter [-œ(r)], s. el que (re)compensa o devuelve.

reredos [rírdas], s. (igl.) retablo.

reroute [rirút], va. dirigir por otra vía.

resale [ríseįl], s. reventa.

rescind [risínd], va. rescindir, anular, abrogar.

rescission [risíşǫn], s. rescisión, anulación, abrogación.

rescissory [risísorį], a. (for.) rescisorio.

rescript [rískript], s. rescripto, edicto, decreto.

rescue [réskįu]. I. va. rescatar, redimir; salvar;

librar, libertar. II. s. rescate, redención, salvación, libramiento, recobro; socorro.

rescuer [-œ(r)], s. salvador, rescatador, libertador.

research [rįsœrch]. I. s. investigación; averiguación, indagación, encuesta; rebusca(miento).—**r. station,** estación experimental. II. va. y vn. investigar.

researcher [-œ(r)], s. investigador.

researchful [-fųl], a. investigador, inquisitivo.

resection [rįsékşǫn], s. (cir.) resección.

reseda [rįsídą], s. (bot.) reseda, género de las resedas; gualda.—**resedaceous** [resįdéįşįʌs], a. resedáceo.

resemblance [rįzémblans], s. parecido, semejanza.—**resemble** [-bl], va. (a)semejarse a, parecerse a; salir (uno) a (su padre, etc.).

resent [rįzént], va. (re)sentirse de, ofenderse por, agraviarse o sentirse agraviado por.—**resentful** [-fųl], a. resentido, agraviado, ofendido.—**resentment** [-mẹnt], s. resentimiento, pique, enojo.

reservation [rezœrvéįşǫn], s. reservación; reserva, excepción, restricción (mental); (a veces pl.) pasaje, sitio, alojamiento, etc., reservados o retenidos de antemano por los viajeros; (E. U.) tierras nacionales reservadas por el gobierno (para indios, parques, escuelas, etc.).

reserve [rįzœrv]. I. va. reservar, guardar, retener, conservar; exceptuar, excluir. II. s. reserva, reservación; cautela, sigilo, reticencia, disimulación; (mil.) reserva, retén.—**r. bank,** banco de reserva.—**without r.,** sin reserva, sin excepción, enteramente.

reserved [-d], a. reservado; circunspecto, discreto; esquivo, callado, taciturno; disimulado; retenido, guardado.—**reservedly** [-įdlį], adv. reservadamente; con cautela.—**reservedness** [-nįs], s. reserva, cautela, sigilo.

reservist [-įst], s. (mil.) reservista; soldado o marinero de reserva.

reservoir [rézœrwwar], s. depósito; receptáculo; cubeta (de barómetro, etc.); (com.) surtido de reserva; (hidr.) depósito de abastecimiento; pantano, estanque, alberca; cisterna, charca, aljibe; cambija, arca de agua; presada (de molino); depósito de gas, petróleo, etc.).

reset [risét], va. (joy.) reengastar; montar de nuevo; (cir.) encasar, reducir (un hueso roto); (agr.) replantar. (Para otros muchos usos, v. TO SET.) II. s. (joy.) nuevo engaste o montadura. V. SET y SETTING.

reship [rįśįp], va. y vn. reembarcar.—**reshipment** [-mẹnt], s. reembarco, reembarque.

reside [rįzáįd], vn. residir, morar, vivir, habitar.

residence [rézįdẹns], s. residencia, morada, domicilio; casa; estancia, mansión; estada, quedada, permanencia; (igl.) presencia.—**r. hall,** dormitorio para estudiantes.—**in r.,** dícese del que reside en un sitio (casa, universidad, hospital, etc.) mientras cumple sus funciones allí.

residency [-į], s. V. RESIDENCE; en la India inglesa, habitación oficial del representante del gobernador general.

resident [-dẹnt]. I. a. residente; morador, habitador; permanente; inherente. II. s. habitante, vecino; (dipl.) ministro residente.

residential [-dénśal], a. perteneciente o relativo a la residencia; de habitación, de habitaciones, de viviendas.

residentiary [-dénśarį]. I. a. residencial. II. s. residente, habitante, vecino.

residual, residuary [rįzídžųąl, -erį], a. residual, restante.—**residual magnetism,** (elec.) magnetismo remanente.—**residuary legatee,** heredero universal.

residue [rézįdįu], s. residuo, resto, sobrante, remanente, superávit.

residuum [rįzídžųąm], s. residuo, resta; desperdicio, desecho.

re-sign [risáįn], va. firmar otra vez.

resign [rįzáįn]. I. va. resignar, dimitir, renunciar,

ceder, dejar, abandonar. **II.** *vr.* resignarse, rendirse, someterse, conformarse.

resignation [rezɪgnéɪʃən], *s.* dimisión, renuncia, dejación; resignación, conformidad.

resigned [rɪzáɪnd], *a.* resignado, conforme.

resignedly [-ɪdlɪ], *adv.* resignadamente.

resignee [rɪzaɪní], *s.* resignatario.

resigner [rɪzáɪnœ(r)], *s.* resignante.

resilience [rɪzílɪəns], **resiliency** [-ɪ], *s.* elasticidad, resorte, rebote; capacidad de recobrar la figura y el tamaño original después de deformación. —**resilient** [-ənt], *a.* elástico; (fig.) alegre, animado.

resin [rézɪn], *s.* resina, colofonia.

resinaceous [-éɪʃiʌs], *a.* resinoso.

resiniferous [-ɪfɛɾʌs], *a.* resinífero.

resinoid [-ɔɪd]. **I.** *a.* parecido a la resina. **II.** *s.* substancia resinosa; resina sintética; gomorresina. —**resinous** [rézɪnʌs], *a.* resinoso.— **resinousness** [-nɪs], *s.* calidad de resinoso.

resist [rɪzíst], *va.* y *vn.* resistir, rechazar, repeler; oponerse; impedir, detener, contrariar, negarse a; aguantar, soportar, hacer frente a.

resistance [-ʌns], *s.* (leng. ord. y tecn.) resistencia; defensa, oposición, fuerza contraria; aguante; repugnancia.—**r. box**, (elec.) caja de resistencias.—**r. coil**, bobina o carrete de resistencia.—**r. frame**, reóstato de cuadro, cuadro de resistencia.

resistant [-ənt], *a.* resistente.

resister [-œ(r)], *s.* resistidor, lo que o el que resiste.

resistibility [-ɪbílɪtɪ], *s.* resistibilidad.

resistible [-ɪbl], *a.* resistible.

resistivity [-ívɪtɪ], *s.* capacidad de resistencia; (elec.) resistividad, resistencia específica.

resistless [-lɪs], *a.* irresistible; indefenso.—**resistlessness** [-nɪs], *s.* calidad de irresistible.

resistor [-ǫ(r)], *s.* (elec.) resistencia.

resole [rɪsóʊl], *va.* (zap.) remontar, sobresolar; solet(e)ar (medias).—**resoling** [-ɪŋ], *s.* remonta; soleta.

resoluble [rézǫljubl], *a.* soluble; resoluble.

resolute [rézǫljut], *a.* resuelto, determinado, firme, denodado.—**resolutely** [-lɪ], *adv.* resueltamente.—**resoluteness** [-nɪs], *s.* resolución, determinación, denuedo, firmeza.

resolution [rezǫljúʃən], *s.* resolución, determinación, denuedo; propósito; resolución, acuerdo (de una junta o asamblea); (mat.) resolución (de un problema); disolución de un todo; análisis (químico, mecánico o mental); descomposición; (med.) resolución (de un tumor, etc.); (mec.) descomposición (de fuerzas, velocidades, etc.).

resolvable [rɪzálvəbl], *a.* resoluble.

resolve [rɪzálv]. **I.** *va.*, *vr.* y *vn.* resolver(se); acordar, tomar un acuerdo, determinar, decidir(se a); venir en (hacer algo); reducir, analizar; solucionar, explicar; descomponer (un cuerpo, una fuerza, etc.); disipar, desvanecer; (med.) resolver (tumores, etc.); (con *into*) transformarse en o reducirse a. **II.** *s.* resolución, determinación, propósito, acuerdo.

resolved [-d], *pp.* acordado, decidido; resuelto, decidido; fundido, liquidado; separado, dividido.—**it is r.**, resuélvese, queda acordado.

resolvedly [-ɪdlɪ], *adv.* resueltamente.

resolvent [-ənt], *a.* y *s.* resolvente; (med.) resolvente, resolutivo.

resonance [rézonʌns], *s.* resonancia.—**resonant** [-ənt], *a.* resonante, retumbante; sonoro.

resonate [-eɪt], *vn.* resonar.

resonator [-eɪtǫ(r)], *s.* resonador.

resorcin [rezórsɪn], *s.* (quím.) resorcina.

resorcinol [-oʊl], *s.* (quím.) resorcinol.

resorption [rɪsórpʃən], *s.* reabsorción, resorción.

resorptive [rɪsórptɪv], *a.* reabsorbedor.

resort [rɪzórt]. **I.** *vn.* (gen. con **to**) acudir, recurrir, frecuentar, concurrir; pasar a, recorrer a; hacer uso de, echar mano de. **II.** *s.* concurso,

concurrencia; punto de reunión; manida; recurso, medio, expediente, refugio; lugar de temporada, lugar frecuentado (gen. el objeto se indica por un substantivo modificativo: *summer resort*, lugar de veraneo; *health resort*, lugar de curación, colonia de enfermos).

re-sound [rɪsáʊnd], *va.* volver a sonar, sonar repetidas veces.

resound [rɪzáʊnd]. **I.** *va.* repetir, repercutir el sonido; cantar, celebrar. **II.** *vn.* resonar, retumbar; formar eco; tener resonancia; tener fama, ser celebrado.

resounding [-ɪŋ]. **I.** *a.* resonante; rimbombante. **II.** *s.* resonancia, resonación.

resource [rɪsórs], *s.* recurso, arbitrio, medio, expediente.—*pl.* fondos, recursos, posibles, medios pecuniarios; riquezas (inclusas las naturales).

resourceful [-fʊl], *a.* listo, ingenioso, mañoso.

resourceless [-lɪs], *a.* desprovisto de recursos o de medios.

respect [rɪspékt]. **I.** *va.* respetar, venerar, honrar, estimar; acatar, observar, guardar; respectar, tocar, corresponder, concernir, referir.—**as respects**, en cuanto a, en lo tocante a, por lo que respecta a. **II.** *s.* respecto, relación, motivo; respeto, estima(ción); reverencia, veneración, culto; acatamiento, consideración, miramiento, decoro; honra, homenaje.—*pl.* memorias, recuerdos, respetos, expresiones.—**r. of persons**, acepción de personas.—**in every r.**, por todos estilos.—**in other respects**, por lo demás, por otra parte.—**in r. that**, puesto que.—**in**, **o with, r. to**, con respecto a, tocante a.—**in some r.**, de algún modo, hasta cierto punto.— **in this r.**, a este respecto, en este sentido.— **out of r. for**, o to, en obsequio de, por consideración a.—**to have r. for**, tener respeto a. —**to have r. to**, referirse a.—**without r. to**, sin consideración de, sin distinción de, prescindiendo de.

respectability [-əbílɪtɪ], **respectableness** [-əblnɪs], *s.* respetabilidad, crédito.

respectable [-əbl], *a.* respetable, formal; estimable, apreciable, honroso; acreditado, autorizado; pasable, bastante bueno; considerable; mediano.—**respectably** [-əblɪ], *adv.* respetablemente; medianamente.

respecter [-œ(r)], *s.* respetador.—**r. of persons**, aceptor o aceptador de personas.

respectful [-fʊl], *a.* respetuoso, respetivo.

respectfully [-fʊlɪ], *adv.* respetuosamente.

respectfulness [-fʊlnɪs], *s.* respetuosidad, conducta respetuosa.

respecting [-ɪŋ], *prep.* con respecto a, en cuanto a, por lo que toca a, (en lo) tocante a.

respective [-ɪv], *a.* respectivo; particular, individual; sendos (*living in respective bunks*, acostados en sendas literas).

respectively [-ɪvlɪ], *adv.* respectivamente.

respirable [rɪspáɪrəbl], *a.* respirable.

respiration [rɪspɪréɪʃən], *s.* respiración, respiro.

respirator [réspɪreɪtǫ(r)], *s.* respirador.

respiratory [rɪspáɪrətǫrɪ], *a.* respiratorio.—**r. disease**, enfermedad de las vías respiratorias.

respire [rɪspáɪr], *va.* y *vn.* resollar, respirar; espirar, exhalar.

respite [réspɪt]. **I.** *s.* tregua, espera, pausa; plazo, prórroga, respiro. **II.** *va.* dar treguas, suspender o diferir, aplazar, prorrogar.

resplendence, **resplendency** [rɪspléndəns, -ɪ], *s.* resplandor, esplendor, fulgor, brillo.—**resplendent** [-ənt], *a.* resplandeciente, fulgurante.—**resplendently** [-lɪ], *adv.* esplendorosamente.

respond [rɪspánd]. **I.** *vn.* responder, contestar; reaccionar; corresponder; obedecer; acudir; venir bien, ajustarse. **II.** *s.* (igl.) = RESPONSORY.

respondent [-ənt]. **I.** *a.* respondedor, (cor)respondiente. **II.** *s.* (for.) demandado, apelado.

response [rispáns], *s.* respuesta, contestación.

responsibility [-jbjlítj], *s.* responsabilidad; obligación, deber; fideicomiso o depósito; solvencia.—**to assume r. for**, tomar por su cuenta.

responsible [-jbl], *a.* responsable; garante, fiable, solvente; autorizado; de responsabilidad.—**r. for**, responsable de; causa de; autor de; origen de.

responsibleness [-jblnjs], *s.* responsabilidad.

responsibly [-jblj], *adv.* con responsabilidad.

responsive [-jv], *a.* respondiente, respondedor; sensible, obediente; interesado; correspondiente, conforme.—**responsiveness** [-njs], *s.* correspondencia, simpatía, conformidad; sensibilidad; obediencia.

responsory [-orj], *s.* (igl.) responso(rio).

rest [rest]. I. *s.* descanso, reposo; holganza, huelga, inacción, tregua; paz, quietud, tranquilidad; sueño, paz (de los muertos); sustentáculo, apoyo, base, *f.*, soporte, arrimo, estribo; portaútil (de torno, etc.); cuja, ristre (de lanza); resto, residuo, sobra; excedente, sobrante, superávit; saldo semanal (del Banco de Inglaterra); posada, descansadero; parada, detención; (mús.) pausa; (poét.) cesura; (con *the*) los demás, los otros; lo demás; el resto.—**r. cure**, (med.) cura(ción) por el reposo y el sosiego.—**r. day**, día de descanso; domingo.—**r. room**, sala de descanso; retrete.—**a r.**, descanso.—**at r.**, en reposo; inactivo; tranquilo; en paz (apl. a los muertos); arreglado, terminado.—**without r.**, sin descanso, sin tregua. II. *vn.* descansar, reposar, holgar; echarse, dormir; yacer, reposar en el seno de la muerte; cesar, parar; estar en paz, vivir tranquilo; posar(se) o asentarse; descansar (sobre), apoyarse (en), cargar (sobre); confiar o fiar (en), contar (con); depender (de); quedar, permanecer; (for.) haber presentado una de las partes todas sus pruebas.—**to r. assured**, perder cuidado. III. *va. y vn.* descansar, proporcionar descanso, dejar descansar, poner, apoyar o asentar; (for.) terminar la presentación de pruebas.

restaurant [réstorant], *s.* restaurant(e), fonda.

restaurateur [restorátœr], *s.* dueño de un restaurante.

restful [réstful], *a.* reposado, quieto, tranquilo.

restfully [-j], *adv.* tranquilamente.

resting [réstjŋ]. I. *a.* quieto, inactivo. II. *s.* reposo, descanso.—**r. place**, descansadero; meseta de escalera; (fig.) la tumba.—**r. stage**, período de descanso.

restitution [restjtjúšon], *s.* restitución, restablecimiento; devolución, torna, reintegración; reparación, indemnización; recuperación, recobro; (fís.) elasticidad.

restitutive [réstjtjutjv], *a.* restitutorio, devolutivo.

restive [réstjv], *a.* obstinado, ingobernable; impaciente; inquieto; (equit.) repropio.

restiveness [-njs], *s.* impaciencia, inquietud.

restless [réstljs], *a.* inquieto, impaciente, intranquilo; bullicioso, revoltoso, levantisco; insomne, desvelado.—**restlessness** [-njs], *s.* inquietud, impaciencia, desasosiego; insomnio, desvelo.

restock [risták], *va.* volver a surtir; renovar.

restorable [ristórabl], *a.* restituíble.

restoration [restoréjšon], *s.* restauración, renovación, reparo; reintegración, instauración, rehabilitación, restablecimiento; (teol.) redención final; (R.), hist.) Restauración.

restorative [ristórɑtjv], *a. y s.* restaurativo.

restore [ristór], *va.* restaurar, rehacer, reparar, reconstruir o reedificar; reintegrar, restablecer, instaurar; restituir, devolver, reponer; [ristór] depositar o almacenar de nuevo.

restorer [-œ(r)], *s.* restaurador; restituidor.

restrain [ristréjn], *va.* refrenar, reprimir, contener, cohibir; represar; moderar, limitar,

coartar, restringir; (for.) prohibir o vedar a.—

restrainable [-abl], *a.* restringible.—**restrainedly** [-jdlj], *adv.* con restricción.—**restrainer** [-œ(r)], *s.* el o lo que refrena, etc.; (fot.) restringente.—**restraining** [-jŋ], *a.* restringente; coercitivo.

restraint [-t], *s.* sujeción, limitación, restricción, freno; coerción, prohibición.

restrict [ristríkt], *va.* restringir, limitar, confinar, coartar.—**restriction** [-šon], *s.* restricción, limitación, coartación.—**restrictive** [-tjv], *a.* restrictivo.—**restrictively** [-lj], *adv.* restrictivamente.

result [rizált]. I. *vn.* resultar; seguirse, inferirse; (con **in**) dar por resultado, venir a parar, acabar o terminar en, conducir a; causar. II. *s.* resultado, resulta; conclusión, deducción.—**as a r. of**, de resultas de, a consecuencia de.

resultant [-ant]. I. *a.* resultante. II. *s.* consecuencia, resultado; (mec.) resultante, *f.*

resulting [-jŋ], *a.* resultante; emergente; consecutivo a.—**r. use**, (for.) usufructo reversible.

resumable [rizjúmabl], *a.* que se puede reasumir o resumir; re(a)sumible.

resume [rizjúm]. I. *va.* reasumir; reanudar; recobrar, reocupar, recuperar; resumir, epitomar, recapitular, compendiar. II. *vn.* tomar el hilo; empezar de nuevo.

résumé [rezumméj], *s.* resumen, sumario, recapitulación.

resumption [rizámpšon], *s.* reasunción, reanudación, renovación; recobro.—**resumptive** [-tjv], *a.* que vuelve a tomar, asumir o resumir.

resupinate [risjúpjnejt], **resupine** [risjupájn], *a.* supino, boca arriba; (bot.) al revés, invertido.

resurface [risœrfjs], *va.* revestir, renovar la superficie de.

resurge [risœrdž], *vn.* resurgir, volver a alzarse o a subir.—**resurgence** [-ens], *s.* resurgimiento; reaparición; resurrección.—**resurgent** [-ent], *a.* resurgente, que surge de nuevo; resurrecto.

resurrect [rezœrékt], *va.* resucitar; desenterrar.

resurrection [rezœrékšon], *s.* resurrección; renovación, restablecimiento; (R.) Resurrección.

resurrectionist [-jst], *s.* el que resucita, vuelve al uso, o restablece (una doctrina, etc.); el que cree en la resurrección de la carne; el que desentierra y vende cadáveres.

resurvey [risœrvéj]. I. *va.* reexaminar, rever; (top.) volver a medir, deslindar o apear terrenos. II. [risœrvej], *s.* nuevo examen o estudio; (top.) nueva medición, nuevo deslinde.

resuscitate [risásjtejt], *va. y vn.* resucitar, reanimar, (hacer) revivir.—**resuscitation** [-téjšon], *s.* resucitación, resurrección; renacimiento, renovación.—**resuscitative** [-tɑtjv], *a.* resucitador, que reanima.—**r. faculty**, facultad reproductora de la mente.

ret [ret], *va.* enriar (cáñamo o lino).

retable [ritéjbl], *s.* (igl.) retablo.

retail [ritéjl]. I. *va.* vender al menudeo, o por menor, revender; detallar. II. *s.* menudeo, venta (al) por menor, reventa; detalle; (com.) detal(l).—**r. market**, (Am.) mercado minorista.

retailer [-œ(r)], *s.* comerciante al por menor, detallista, (Am.) minorista, lonjista, tendero, revendedor, mangón.

retain [ritéjn], *va.* retener, guardar, conservar, quedarse con; represar, detener, contener; contratar, ajornalar; ajustar (a un abogado).

retainable [-abl], *a.* que se puede retener.

retainer [-œ(r)], *s.* adherente, partidario; paniaguado; dependiente, criado, asistente; retenedor; iguala, anticipo que se da a un abogado al ajustar sus servicios.

retaining [-jŋ], *a.* que retiene o contiene; de retención, de contención.—**r. fee**, pago anticipado con que se ajusta a una persona.—**r. wall**, muro de sostenimiento o de contención.

retainment [-ment], *s.* retención; ajuste, empleo (de abogado).

retake [ritéik], *va.* (*pret.* RETOOK; *pp.* RETAKEN) volver a tomar; reasumir, recoger; represar; (fot. y cine) volver a fotografiar o filmar.

retaliate [ritǽlieit]. I. *va.* talionar. II. *vn.* desquitarse, vengarse; usar de represalias.

retaliation [-iéiṣǫn], *s.* talión, *m.*, revancha, desquite, despique; represalia; desagravio, satisfacción; pago, retorno.

retaliative [-iǎtiv], *a.* vengativo.

retaliatory [-iǎtǫri], *a.* que usa de represalias.

retard [ritárd]. I. *va.* retardar, atrasar, retrasar, demorar; aplazar, diferir, dilatar. II. *s.* retraso, atraso, dilación, demora.

retardation [-éiṣǫn], *s.* retardación, retardo, atraso, retraso.

retardative, *o* **retardatory** [-ǎtiv, -ǎtǫri], *a.* retardativo, retardatorio, retardador.

retarder [-œ(r)], *s.* retardador.

retch [réch], *vn.* arquear, basquear, nausear.—**retching** [-iṇ], *s.* arcada, basca(s), náuseas.

rete [ríti], *s.* (anat.) redecilla, plexo.

retention [riténṣǫn], *s.* retención, conservación; retentiva, memoria.—**retentive** [-tiv], *a.* retentivo.—**retentiveness** [-nis], *s.* retentiva.

retentivity [-tivjti], *s.* (magn.) retentividad.

reticence, reticency [rétisens, -i], *s.* reticencia, reserva; (ret.) reticencia.

reticent [rétisent], *a.* reticente, callado.

reticle [rétikl], *s.* (ópt.) retículo.

reticular [ritíkyūlǎ(r)], *a.* reticular.—**reticulate** [-leit], *va.* y *vn.* formar a modo de red.—**reticulate(d** [-(i)d], *a.* reticular.—**reticulation** [-léiṣǫn], *s.* disposición en forma de red.

reticule [rétikiul], *s.* ridículo, bolsa.

reticulum [ritíkyūlʌm], *s.* retículo (tejido); (anat.) retículo; redecilla, bonete de los rumiantes.

retiform [rétiform], *a.* reticular.

retina [rétinǎ], *s.* (anat.) retina.

retinitis [retinǎitis], *s.* (med.) retinitis, inflamación de la retina.

retinue [rétiniu], *s.* tren, comitiva, séquito, acompañamiento, corte, *f.*, mesnada.

retiral [ritáirǎl], *s.* retiro, retirada; (com.) recogida. *V.* RETIREMENT.

retire [ritáir]. I. *vn.* retirarse, irse a acostar; retirarse de la vida activa o de un empleo; jubilarse; retraerse, retroceder, recogerse, apartarse, separarse. II. *va.* (com.) recoger, retirar de la circulación; jubilar.

retired [-d], *a.* retirado; apartado, aislado; retraído; (com.) recogido; retirado, jubilado.—**r. life**, vida retirada o solitaria.—**r. officer**, oficial retirado.—**to put on the r. list**, dar el retiro, jubilar.

retiredly [-li], *adv.* retiradamente; privadamente.—**retiredness** [-nis], *s.* retiro, recogimiento, soledad.

retirement [-ment], *s.* retiro; retraimiento; recogida, recogimiento; lugar retirado; jubilación.

retiring [-iṇ], *a.* retraído, austero, recatado; modesto, discreto; referente a la jubilación.

retook [ritúk], *pret.* de TO RETAKE.

retorsion [ritórṣǫn], *s.* talión, *m.*, represalia.

retort [ritórt]. I. *va.* redargüir; devolver (un insulto); replicar, retorcer. II. *s.* redargución; réplica mordaz; (quím.) retorta; (metal.) cámara.

retorter [-œ(r)], *s.* el que replica o redarguye.

retortion [ritórṣǫn], *s.* retoreedura, retorcimiento; retorsión; represalia.

retouch [ritách]. I. *va.* retocar, modificar, limar, pulir; (fot.) retocar.—**retouching frame**, bastidor de retocar. II. *s.* retoque, última mano.

retoucher [-œ(r)], *s.* (fot.) retocador.

retouching [-iṇ], *s.* retocamiento.

retrace [ritréis], *va.* seguir (las huellas) retrocediendo; desandar, volver atrás; buscar el origen de; repasar un trazado; relatar, narrar.—**to r. one's steps**, volver sobre sus pasos.

retract [ritrǽkt]. I. *va.* retractar, retirar; retractarse de; retraer, encoger, esconder. II. *vn.* retractarse, desdecirse, cantar la palinodia; encogerse.—**retractable, retractible** [-abl], *a.* retractable; retráctil.—**retractile** [-il], *a.* retráctil.—**retraction** [-ṣǫn], **retractation** [-téiṣǫn], *s.* retracción; contracción; retractación.—**retractive** [-tiv], *a.* que tiende a retractar.—**retractor** [-tǫ(r)], *s.* el que o lo que retracta; (cir.) retractor; (anat.) músculo contractor.

retread [ritréd]. I. *va.* volver a pisar o andar; (aut.) renovar la superficie de rodadura (de un neumático). *V.* RECAP. II. [rítred], *s.* (aut.) *V.* RECAPPING.

retreat [ritrít]. I. *s.* retiro; soledad, retraimiento; refugio, asilo; (mil.) retirada; retreta; (igl.) retiro. II. *vn.* retirarse; retroceder, retraerse, refugiarse; cejar; (esgr.) dar un paso atrás; apartarse, inclinarse o prolongarse hacia atrás.

retrench [ritrénch]. I. *va.* cercenar, cortar, disminuir, abreviar; mondar o podar; (mil.) atrincherar. II. *vn.* reducirse, economizar o ahorrar.

retrenchment [-ment], *s.* cercenadura, cercenamiento; economía; rebaja, di(s)minución; (mil.) atrincheramiento, trinchera.

retribution [retribiúṣǫn], *s.* retribución, pago; justicia; justo castigo, pena incurrida.

retributive, retributory [ritríbyūtiv, -tǫri], *a.* retributivo, retribuyente.—**r. justice**, justicia distributiva.

retrievable [ritrívabl], *a.* recuperable; reparable.

retrievableness [-nis], **retrievability** [-bíliti], *s.* posibilidad de recuperación.

retrieval [ritrívǎl], *s.* cobranza, recobro, recuperación; reintegración; (caza) cobra.

retrieve [ritrív]. I. *va.* recuperar, recobrar; restaurar, reparar, remediar; cobrar (la caza). II. *vn.* cobrar la caza.

retriever [-œ(r)], *s.* perro cobrador o tomador; perdiguero.

retroact [rétroǽkt], *vn.* tener fuerza retroactiva.—**retroaction** [-ǽkṣǫn], *s.* (for.) retroactividad.—**retroactive** [-ǽktiv], *a.* retroactivo.

retrocede [-síd]. I. *va.* (for.) hacer retrocesión. II. *vn.* retroceder, recular.

retrocession [-séṣǫn], *s.* retrocesión, retroceso; contramarcha; (for.) retrocesión.

retrocognition [-kagníṣǫn], *s.* conocimiento supernormal (como el de los médiums) de lo pasado. (Puede llamarse *retrovidencia*.)

retroflex [-fleks], *a.* doblado hacia atrás.

retroflexion [-flékṣǫn], *s.* repliegue, flexión hacia atrás; (med.) retroflexión.

retrogradation [-grǎdéiṣǫn], *s.* retrogradación; retrogresión; degeneración.

retrograde [-greid]. I. *a.* retrógrado. II. *s.* = RETROGRESSION. III. *vn.* retrogradar, retroceder, desandar; degenerar; ciar.

retrogression [-gréṣǫn], *s.* retrogresión, retrogradación, retroceso, regresión.

retrogressive [-grésiv], *a.* retrógrado.

retrospect [-spekt], *s.* mirada retrospectiva.—**in r.**, mirando hacia atrás.

retrospection [-spékṣǫn], *s.* retrospección; ejercicio morboso de la memoria; consideración de cosas pasadas.

retrospective [-spéktiv], *a.* retrospectivo.

retrousse [rœtruséi], *a.* respingada, respingona.

retroversion [retrovérṣǫn], *s.* inclinación o miramiento hacia atrás; (med.) retroversión.

retrovert [rétrovœrt], *va.* desviar hacia atrás.

retry [ritrái], *va.* (for.) rever.

retting [rétiṇ]. I. *s.* enriado, enriamiento. II. *a.* de enriar; relativo al enriamiento.

return [ritœrn]. I. *va.* (de)volver; corresponder a, pagar, (re)tornar, dar en cambio, recompensar; dar (gracias, fallo, respuesta, etc.); rendir (informe); redituar, producir; (pol.) elegir, enviar (al congreso, etc.).—**to r. a call**, pagar una visita.—**to r. a kindness**, corresponder a un favor.—**to r. a verdict**, fallar; dar un veredicto. **II.** *vn.* volver, regresar, (re)tornar; reaparecer, presentarse de nuevo; responder; reponer, replicar; (for.) revertir.—**to r. home**, regresar a casa. **III.** [ritǿrn], *va.* y *vn.* doblar o volver de nuevo, dar otra vuelta o doblez. **IV.** *s.* vuelta, regreso, retorn(amient)o; torna, correspondencia (a un favor), pago, recompensa; respuesta; redargución; restitución, devolución; restablecimiento, reinstalación, instauración; reaparición; ganancia, utilidad, provecho, rédito; cambio, trueque, intercambio; estado, relación, informe o parte oficial; lista, nómina, padrón o censo; curva, vuelta; desviadero; (for.) reversión; diligencia; (arq.) ala; vuelta de moldura, marco, etc.; (pol.) elección.—*pl.* tablas estadísticas; resultado, cifras (de elecciones).—**r. address**, señas (*f. pl.*) del remitente.—**r. conductor**, (elec.) conductor de retorno.—**r. game, 'match**, etc.), juego (lucha, etc.) de desquite.—**r. request**, membrete en que se suplica la devolución de una carta al remitente, caso de no hallarse el destinatario.—**r. shock**, (elec.) choque de retroceso.—**r. stroke**, (mec.) golpe o carrera de retroceso.—**r. ticket**, billete de (ida y) vuelta.—**r. trip**, viaje de vuelta o de regreso.—**by r. mail, by r. of post**, a vuelta de correo.—**happy returns**, felices cumpleaños.—**in r.**, en cambio, en pago, en recompensa.

returnable [-əbl], *a.* restituíble, reintegrable, devolutivo; (for.) reversible; devolutivo, restitutorio.

returning [-iŋ], *s.* vuelta; restitución.—**on r.**, de vuelta.

retuse [ritjús], *a.* (bot.) achatado.

reunion [riyúnyǫn], *s.* reunión; reconciliación; tertulia; junta.

reunite [riyunájt]. **I.** *va.* reunir, juntar; volver a unir; reconciliar. **II.** *vn.* reunirse, reconciliarse.

revaluation [rivǽlyuéjṣǫn], *s.* revaluación.

revalue [rivǽlyu], *va.* revalorar.

revamp [rivǽmp], *va.* (zap.) poner capellada nueva a; remendar; (fig.) reorganizar, volver a construir, o adaptar a otro uso.

revanche [rəvánš], *s.* (fr.) venganza, revancha.

reveal [rivíl]. **I.** *va.* revelar; manifestar, descubrir, publicar, divulgar, dar a conocer. **II.** *s.* (arq.) costado de vano de puerta o ventana; (aut.) borde de ventana.

revealer [-œ(r)], *s.* revelador.

revealing [-iŋ], *a.* revelador, revelante.

reveille [révɛli], *s.* (mil.) diana; alborada.

revel [révɛl]. **I.** *vn.* jaranear, ir de parranda, gozarse (en). **II.** *s.* algazara, jarana, parranda.

revelation [-éjṣǫn], *s.* revelación; visión; (**R.**) Apocalipsis.

revel(l)er [-œ(r)], *s.* parrandista, borrasquero.

revelry [-ri], *s.* jarana, gresca, francachela, orgía, borrachera.

revenge [rivéndž]. **I.** *va.* vengar, vindicar; desquitarse, satisfacerse o vengarse de. **II.** *s.* venganza, desquite, vindicta, (gal.) revancha.—**revengeful** [-fụl], *a.* vengativo, vindicativo.—**revengefully** [-i], *adv.* vengativamente.—**revengefulness** [-nịs], *s.* calidad de vengativo; sed de venganza.

revenue [révenju], *s.* rentas públicas, ingresos del Erario; (com.) renta; rédito; entrada, ingreso, provento; recompensa, beneficio.—**r. cutter**, (mar.) escampavía, guardacostas.—**r. officer**, aduanero, empleado de aduana; resguardo; agente fiscal o del fisco.—**r. stamp**, sello fiscal, sello de impuesto.

reverberant [rivœ́rbẹrạnt], *a.* repercusivo; reverberante; retumbante, resonante.—**reverberate** [-ejt], *va.* y *vn.* retumbar, repercutir; reverberar, reflejar.—**reverberation** [-éjṣǫn], *s.* eco, repercusión; reverberación, reverbero;

reflexión.—**reverberator** [-ejtǫ(r)], *s.* reverberador, reverbero, reverberadero.

reverberatory [-ǻtori]. **I.** *a.* de reverbero, que reverbera o refleja. **II.** *s.* **r.** (**furnace**), horno de reverbero.

revere [rivír], *va.* reverenciar, venerar.

reverence [révrẹns]. **I.** *s.* reverencia, veneración; reverencia (inclinación del cuerpo); (**R.**, *igl.*) Reverencia (tratamiento).—**to pay r.**, rendir homenaje. **II.** *va.* reverenciar, venerar.

reverend [révrẹnd]. **I.** *a.* reverendo, venerable; (**R.**, *igl.*) Reverendo (tratamiento). **II.** *s.* (fam.) clérigo.

reverent [révrẹnt], *a.* reverente.—**reverently** [-li], *adv.* reverentemente.

reverential [revẹrénšạl], *a.* reverencial, respetuoso.—**reverentially** [-i], *adv.* con reverencia, respetuosamente.

reverie [révẹri], *s.* ensueño; embelesamiento, arrobamiento; (mús.) fantasía.

revers [rivír], *s.* (cost.) solapa, caída, vuelta (ll. t. **revere**).

reversal [rivœ́rsạl], *s.* reversión; inversión; (for.) revocación; (ópt.) cambio de una línea obscura en una brillante y viceversa.

reverse [rivœ́rs]. **I.** *va.* trastrocar, invertir; trastornar; (for.) revocar, anular; (mec.) invertir, dar contravapor. **II.** *vn.* invertirse; volver (a un estado anterior). **III.** *a.* reverso, inverso, invertido; opuesto, contrario; (mec.) de inversión, de marcha atrás, de contramarcha.—**r. curve**, (f. c.) curva en S.—**r. gear**, (mec.) mecanismo de marcha atrás.—**r. lever**, palanca de contramarcha.—**r. operation**, (mat.) operación inversa.—**r. running**, marcha hacia atrás.—**r. turn**, (aer.) maniobra de cambio de dirección. **IV.** *s.* lo contrario, lo opuesto; respaldo, dorso, reverso; reversión, inversión; contratiempo, revés, descalabro.

reversed [-t], *a.* = REVERSE; invertido, inverso.—**r. ogee**, (arq.) gola reversa.

reversely [-li], *adv.* al revés.

reversible [-ịbl]. **I.** *a.* volvible, versátil; (mec.) reversible; de vaivén; de dos caras; (for.) revocable. **II.** *s.* (tej.) género de dos caras.

reversibility [-ịbị́lịti], *s.* reversibilidad, invertibilidad, calidad de poder invertirse; (for.) revocabilidad, carácter de revocable o anulable.

reversing [-iŋ]. **I.** *a.* y *ger.* de TO REVERSE; de inversión, de cambio de marcha, etc.; (elec., mec.) inversor.—**r. mechanism**, inversor. *V.* REVERSE, *va.* y *a.* **II.** *s.* inversión; (mec.) cambio de marcha; (elec.) conmutación.

reversion [rivœ́rṣǫn], *s.* reversión; (biol.) atavismo; (for.) reversión; futura, derecho de sucesión.

reversionary [-ẹri], *a.* (biol.) atávico; (for.) reversible.

reversioner [-œ(r)], *s.* (for.) el que tiene derecho de reversión.

revert [rivœ́rt], *vn.* retroceder, volver, resurtir, recudir; (biol.) saltar atrás; (for.) revertir.

revertible [-ịbl], *a.* reversible.

revery [révẹri], *s.* = REVERIE.

revest [rivést], *va.* revestir; restablecer.

revet [rivét], *va.* (alb.) revestir.

revetment [-mẹnt], *s.* (alb., fort., ing.) revestimiento; muro de contención.

review [rivjú]. **I.** *va.* rever, remirar; repasar (estudios, etc.); revisar; censurar; reseñar, escribir una crítica o una síntesis de (un libro, etc.); criticar, analizar; (mil.) revistar, pasar revista a. **II.** *vn.* reseñar (libros), escribir (para) una revista. **III.** *s.* repaso; examen, análisis; reseña; revista, censura, juicio crítico; revista (publicación periódica); (mil.) revista, alarde, reseña, parada; (for.) revisión; (teat.) = REVUE.

reviewer [-œ(r)], *s.* crítico, revistero; revisor; examinador, inspector.

revile [rivájl], *va.* denigrar, vilipendiar, injuriar, denostar, oprobiar.—**revilement** [-mẹnt], *s.*

denuesto, vilipendio, injuria, oprobio.—**reviler** [-œ(r)], *s.* vilipendiador, denostador.—**revilingly** [-iŋli], *adv.* denigrantemente, injuriosamente.

revisal [riváizal], *s.* revista, revisión.

revise [riváiz]. I. *va.* revisar, rever, releer, repasar; corregir, enmendar.—**revised** [-d], revisado; corregido.—**Revised Version**, traducción corregida de la Biblia (hecha en los años 1870 a 1885; otra hecha en el año 1952). II. *s.* revista, revisión; (impr.) segunda prueba.

reviser, revisor [-œ(r)], *s.* revisor; (impr.) corrector de pruebas.

revision [rivíȝon], *s.* revisión, revista, repaso; enmienda; (impr.) corrección de pruebas.

revisionist [-ist], *s.* y *a.* revisionista.

revisit [rivízit], *va.* volver a visitar.

revisory [riváizori], *a.* revisor.

revitalize [riváitalaiz], *va.* (hacer) revivir, vivificar; dar un nuevo impulso a; (fig.) galvanizar.

revival [riváival], *s.* renacimiento, restauración, restablecimiento, renovación, reavivamiento; (teat.) reposición o reestreno de obras antiguas; despertamiento religioso.—**revivalist** [-ist], *s.* predicador que recorre un país para despertar la fe.

revive [riváiv]. I. *va.* hacer revivir, revivificar, (re)avivar, resucitar; restablecer, restaurar; despertar; hacer recordar, despertar la memoria; reponer (un drama). II. *vn.* revivir, resucitar; restablecerse, reanimarse; volver en sí, recobrar los sentidos; renacer.

reviver [-œ(r)], *s.* vivificador, resucitador.

revivification [rivivifikéiȝon], *s.* (re)vivificación.

revivify [-fai]. I. *va.* reavivar, revivificar, hacer revivir. II. *vn.* restablecerse, revivir.

revocable [révokabl], *a.* revocable.—**revocableness** [-nis], *s.* revocabilidad.

revocation [revokéiȝon], *s.* revocación; derogación.

revoke [rivóuk]. I. *va.* revocar, derogar, abrogar, anular. II. *vn.* en los juegos de naipes, renunciar o hacer un renuncio. III. *s.* renuncio.

revoker [-œ(r)], *s.* revocador; renunciante.

revolt [rivóult]. I. *vn.* rebelarse, sublevarse, amotinarse; sentir repugnancia o repulsión. II. *va.* rebelar, sublevar; causar asco o repugnancia; chocar, indignar. III. *s.* sublevación, rebelión, revuelta, alzamiento, amotinamiento. —**revolter** [-œ(r)], *s.* rebelde, sublevado, insurrecto.

revolting [-iŋ], *a.* odioso; repugnante, chocante, sublevante, asqueroso.

revolute [révoljut], *a.* (bot.) enrollado hacia atrás o abajo.

revolution [revoljúʃon], *s.* revolución, revuelta; (mec.) revolución, vuelta, volteo, giro; (astr.) revolución.—**revolutionary** [-eri], *a.* y *s.* revolucionario.—**revolutionist** [-ist], *s.* revolucionario.—**revolutionize** [-aiz], *va.* revolucionar, sublevar; trastornar, alterar radicalmente.

revolvable [riválvabl], *a.* giratorio.

revolve [riválv]. I. *vn.* girar, dar vueltas, rodar; moverse en ciclos, suceder periódicamente. II. *va.* voltear, hacer girar o rodar; revolver (en la cabeza), considerar bajo todos los aspectos.

revolver [-œ(r)], *s.* revólver (arma de fuego).

revolving [-iŋ], *a.* giratorio, rotativo, rotatorio, rotante.—**r. chair**, silla giratoria.—**r. fund**, (E. U.) fondos públicos especiales para préstamos.—**r. light**, luz giratoria.

revue [rivjú], *s.* (teat.) revista teatral; sainete de sucesos actuales o recientes.

revulsion [riválʃon], *s.* cambio repentino, reacción; removimiento, apartamiento, retroceso; reculada; (med.) revulsión, contrairritación.

revulsive [riválsiv], *a.* y *s.* (med.) revulsivo, revulsorio.

reward [riwórd]. I. *va.* premiar, galardonar, re-

compensar. II. *s.* premio, recompensa, galardón; hallazgo; merecido; pago, remuneración, gratificación.—**rewardable** [-abl], *a.* remunerable, digno de premio.—**rewarder** [-œ(r)], *s.* premiador, remunerador.

reweigh [riwéi], *va.* (com.) repesar.

Reynard [réinard], *s.* (zool.) zorro.

Rhaetian, Rhetian [ríʃan], *a.* y *s.* rético.

rhamnaceous [ræmnéiʃias], *a.* (bot.) rámneo.

rhapontic [ræpántik], *s.* (bot.) rapóntico.

rhapsodisc [ræpsodist], *s.* autor de rapsodias; rapsoda, *m.*—**rhapsodize** [-daiz], *va.* y *vn.* cantar o recitar rapsodias; escribir o hablar con entusiasmo extravagante.—**rhapsody** [-di], *s.* rapsodia.

rhatany [rǽtani], *s.* (bot.) ratania.

rhea [ríạ], *s.* (orn.) avestruz (*m.*) de la América del Sur, ñandú o nandú.

Rhenish [rénis]. I. *a.* renano. II. *s.* vino del Rin.

rhenium [ríniam], *s.* (quím.) renio.

rheometer [riámetœ(r)], *s.* reómetro.

rheophore [ríofor], *s.* (elec.) reóforo.

rheostat [ríostæt], *s.* (elec.) reóstato.

rheostatic [riostǽtik], *a.* reostático.

rhesus [rísas], *s.* (zool.) macaco de la India.

rhetoric [rétorik], *s.* retórica.—**rhetorical** [ritórikal], *a.* retórico.—**rhetorically** [-li], *adv.* retóricamente.—**rhetorician** [retoríʃan], *s.* retórico.

rheum [rum], *s.* (med.) reuma, *mf.*, fluxión, derrame catarral o mucoso.

rheumatic [rumǽtik], *a.* reumático.

rheumatism [rúmatizm], *s.* (med.) reumatismo.

rheumatoid [-tojd], *a.* reumatoideo.

rhinitis [raináitis], *s.* (med.) rinitis, coriza.

rhinoceros [raináseros], *s.* (zool.) rinoceronte.

rhinology [rainálodȝi], *s.* (med.) rinología.

rhinoplastic [rainoplǽstik], *a.* (cir.) rinoplástico. —**rhinoplasty** [ráinoplæsti], *s.* (cir.) rinoplastia.

rhinoscope [ráinoskoup], *s.* rinoscopio.

rhinoscopy [raináskopi], *s.* (med.) rinoscopia.

rhizocarpic [raizokárpik], **rhizocarpous** [-pas], *a.* (bot.) rizocárpeo.

rhizome, rhizoma [ráizoum, raizóumạ], *s.* (bot.) rizoma, *m.*

rhizopod [ráizopad], *s.* (zool.) rizópodo.

Rhodian [róudian], *s.* y *a.* rodio; caballero de la orden de Rodas, o San Juan de Jerusalén.

rhodic [róudik], *a.* (quím.) ródico.—**rhodium** [róudiạm], *s.* (quím.) rodio.

rhododendron [roudodéndron], *s.* (bot.) rododendro.

rhodonite [róudonait], *s.* (min.) espato mangánico.

rhomb(us [rámb(as], *s.* (geom.) rombo; (blas.) losange.

rhombic [rámbik], *a.* rombal.

rhombohedron [rambohídron], *s.* (geom.) romboedro.

rhomboid [rámbojd], *s.* (geom.) romboide.

rhomboidal [rambójdạl], *a.* romboidal.

rhubarb [rúbarb], *s.* (farm.) ruibarbo; (bot.) ruipóntico o rapóntico.

rhumb [ram], *s.* (mar.) rumbo.

rhyme [raim]. I. *s.* rima, consonancia, consonante; verso; poesía.—**without r. or reason**, sin ton ni son. II. *va.* rimar, versificar, metrificar, poner en verso; emplear como consonante. III. *vn.* rimar, consonar; corresponder, armonizarse.

rhymer [-œ(r)], **rhymster** [-stœ(r)], *s.* rimador, versificador; (desp.) coplero, poetastro.

rhythm [ríðm], *s.* ritmo, cadencia; armonía; (med.) periodicidad.—**rhythmic(al** [ríðmik(al], *a.* rítmico, cadencioso, cadente, armónico.—**rhythmically** [-li], *adv.* rítmicamente.

rialto [riǽltou], *s.* mercado, lonja.

rib [rib]. I. *s.* (anat.) costilla; (arq.) faja, listón, nervio, nervadura; cabrio, viga de tejado; arco; resalte, saliente; (mar.) cuaderna; varenga de hierro; varilla (de abanico o paraguas); tirante; (mec.) pestaña, reborde; (cost.) vivo; (bot.) costilla, nervadura de las hojas; (fam.) costilla, la mujer propia.—**r. grass**, (bot.) = RIBWORT. —**ribs of a ship**, (mar.) costillaje. II. va. marcar con rayas, listones o filetes; afianzar con rebordes o pestañas; proveer de nervios; (cost.) poner vivos; (fam.) embromar, burlarse de.

ribald [ríbₐld]. I. a. obsceno, lascivo, ribaldo. II. s. ribaldo, persona impúdica.

ribaldry [-ri], s. ribaldería, cinismo.

ribbon [ríbₒn]. I. s. cinta, listón, colonia; tira, banda, faja; galón.—pl. (fam.) riendas; perifollos.—**r. grass**, (bot.) alpiste. II. va. encintar. III. a. hecho de cinta; de forma de cinta.

ribwort [ríbwœrt], s. (bot.) llantén, zaragatona.

rice [ráis], s. (bot.) arroz, m.—**r. paper**, papel de paja de arroz; papel de China.—**r. planter** o **dealer**, arrocero.—**r. plantation**, arrocería. —**r. mill**, molino arrocero.

ricebird [-bœrd], s. (orn.) = REEDBIRD.

ricefield [-fild], s. arrozal.

rich [rích], a. rico; adinerado, acomodado, opulento; costoso, precioso; suntuoso, abundante, cuantioso; exquisito; gras(ient)o; vivo (color, etc.); muy sazonado, dulce, fuerte, etc.; fértil; (fam.) muy divertido; risible, ridículo.—**to become r.**, enriquecerse.

riches [-iz], s. pl. riqueza(s); bienes; opulencia.

richly [-li], adv. ricamente; copiosamente.

richness [-nis], s. riqueza, opulencia; suntuosidad; fertilidad; abundancia, copia.

ricinic [risínik], **ricinoleic** [risinóulijk], a. (quím.) ricinólico o ricinoleico (ácido).

ricinin(e [rísinin], s. (quím.) ricinina.

rick [rik]. I. s. (agr.) niara, fascal, hacina, fajina. II. va. hacer niaras o hacinas de.

rickets [ríkits], s. (med.) raquitis, raquitismo.

rickety [ríkiti], a. desvencijado, destartalado; (med.) raquítico.

ricochet [ríkošéi]. I. va. hacer fuego de rebote. II. vn. rebotar. III. s. (arti.) fuego de rebote.

rictus [ríktas], s. ensanche de la boca (en las aves).

rid [rid], va. (pret. y pp. RID o RIDDED) desembarazar, librar, quitar de encima, zafar.—**to r. one's self of**, **to get r. of**, salir, desembarazarse, zafarse, deshacerse de.—**to be r. of**, estar libre o exento de.

riddance [-ₐns], s. libramiento o preservación de un mal, peligro o pesadumbre; zafada.

ridden [rídn], pp. de TO RIDE.

riddle [rídl]. I. s. acertijo, enigma, m., adivinanza, rompecabezas; (fam.) busilis, m., quisicosa; misterio; criba o garbillo. II. va. resolver, adivinar; cribar, garbillar; acribillar. III. vn. hablar enigmáticamente.

riddler [rídlœ(r)], s. garbillador.

ride [ráid]. I. va. (pret. RODE; pp. RIDDEN) cabalgar, correr, dirigir o manejar (un caballo, etc.); ir montado en o sobre; hender o surcar (las olas).—**to r. down** u **over**, pasar por encima de, atropellar, pisotear, derribar y hollar (como en un ataque de caballería); tratar o mandar con arrogancia.—**to r. out**, hacer frente a, resistir bien (el viento).—**to r. shank's mare**, ir a pie.—**to r. the goat**, (fam.) ser iniciado (en sociedad secreta). II. vn. montar a caballo, cabalgar; pasear a caballo o en carruaje; ir en coche; flotar; (mec.) rodar, tener juego, funcionar.—**to r. at anchor**, (mar.) estar fondeado.—**to r. easy**, mantenerse bien al ancla; marchar suavemente.—**to r. horseback**, montar a caballo.—**to r. roughshod** (a menudo con over) obrar con indiferencia del prójimo, pisoteando los derechos ajenos. III. s. paseo a caballo o en coche; camino de herradura.—**to take for a r.**, (fam.) entre los gangsters, llevar a uno a paseo en coche, para matarle; engañar, tomar el pelo a uno.

rider [-œ(r)], s. caballero, cabalgador, jinete; amazona; persona que va en coche, bicicleta,

etc.; picador, (Am.) amansador; cosa que va montada sobre otra; pilón, pesa corrediza (de una balanza); hojuela pegada a un documento; aditamento, añadidura o adición a un proyecto de ley; (mar.) sobreplán, cochinata.

ridge [ridž]. I. va. (agr.) alomar, acaballonar; formar lomos o camellones; acanalar, arrugar, encaballar. II. vn. tener lomos o camellones. III. s. cerro, colina, cordillera, serranía; (mar.) escollo, arrecife; (cost.) arruga, costurón; (agr.) caballón, lomo, camellón; (arq.) caballete del tejado.—**r. cap**, cubierta de caballete. —**r. roof**, tejado a dos vertientes o a dos aguas. —**r. tile**, teja acanalada.

ridgeband [-bænd], s. (tal.) sufra.

ridgebeam [-bim], **ridgepiece** [-pis], **ridgepole** [-poul], s. (arq.) parhilera, cumbrera.

ridgerope [-roup], s. (mar.) cuerda de toldo.

ridgy [-i], a. acanalado; alomado; que se levanta con desigualdad, en forma de serranía.

ridicule [rídikjul]. I. s. ridículo, irrisión, mofa, rechifla. II. va. ridiculizar, poner en ridículo, escarnecer, mofarse de, rechiflar.

ridiculous [ridíkjūlᴀs], a. ridículo, risible, grotesco.—**ridiculously** [-li], adv. ridículamente. —**ridiculousness** [-nis], s. ridiculez, extravagancia.

riding [ráidiŋ]. I. s. paseo a caballo o en coche; cabalgata; camino de herradura; equitación, manejo; movimiento, marcha (de un vehículo). —**r. boots**, botas de montar.—**r. cloak**, r. **coat**, redingote.—**r. crop** = R. WHIP.—**r. habit**, (traje de) amazona, traje de montar.—**r. hood**, capirote, capotín, capuchón.—**r. horse**, caballo de silla, montura, caballería.— **r. party**, partida de cabalgata.—**r. school**, picadero, escuela de equitación.—**r. whip**, látigo de jinete. II. pa. cabalgante, caballero, montado (en caballo).

rifacimento [rifachiméntou], s. rehacimiento; adaptación.

rife [ráif], a. abundante, numeroso; corriente, reinante; (con with) lleno de.—**rifely** [-li], adv. abundantemente.—**rifeness** [-nis], s. abundancia.

Riff [rif], s., **Riffian** [rífiₐn], s. y a. rifeño.

riffle [rífl], s. rápido, rabión, m.; onda, rizo (del agua); cierto modo de barajar los naipes; (min.) ranura en el fondo de una gamella (para recoger el oro).

riffler [ríflœ(r)], s. escofina encorvada.

riffraff [rífræf], s. gentuza, canalla; desecho, desperdicio, ripio.

rifle [ráifl]. I. va. robar, pillar; arrebatar; (arti.) rayar (un arma). II. s. (arm.) rifle, fusil; espiral de rifle; (agr.) piedra de afilar guadañas.—**r. carbine**, carabina rayada.—**r. groove**, raya. —**r. pits**, pozos para rifleros.—**r. range**, campo de tiro; alcance de un tiro de fusil.—**r. shot**, fusilazo; tiro de fusil.

rifleman [-mₐn], s. riflero.

rifler [ráiflœ(r)], s. saqueador, salteador.

rift [rift]. I. s. hendedura, rendija, grieta, reventón; cuarteadura; vado; rompimiento, desacuerdo. II. va. hender, dividir, rajar, rasgar. III. vn. reventar, cuartearse, agrietarse, rajarse, abrirse.

rig [rig]. I. va. (a menudo con out u up) ataviar, adornar, vestir, acicalar; aparejar, equipar, armar; (mar.) enjarciar, guarnir; (aer.) armar, arreglar (un avión o un dirigible).—**to r. the market**, manipular la lonja, tramar para cambiar los precios. II. s. (mar.) aparejo; (fam.) traje; tren de carruaje o caballos; apresto, equipo; aparato de pesca.

rigadoon [rigadún], s. (danz. y mús.) rigodón.

rigger [rígœ(r)], s. (mar.) aparejador; (aer.) montador aeronáutico.

rigging [rígiŋ], s. (mar.) aparejo, cordaje, jarcia, enjarciadura; (mec.) aparejo (de poleas); equipo de arrastre (de trozas).

right [ráit]. **I.** *a.* recto, justo, equitativo; propio, conveniente; debido; correcto, exacto; fundado; verdadero, cierto, real, genuino; legal, legítimo; derecho, directo, en línea recta; ordenado, ajustado; derecho (lado, mano); sano; cuerdo; derecho (contrario de revés en las telas); que conviene, que se busca, que se quiere (a veces no se traduce, o se cambia el giro: *this is the right man*, éste es el hombre [que se busca]; éste es el hombre indicado, adecuado o que se necesita); (pol.) derechista, de las derechas.— **r. and left**, a diestra y siniestra.—**r. angle**, ángulo recto.—**r. ascension**, (astr.) ascensión recta.—**r. bower**, el mayor triunfo en el juego de *euchre*.—**r. cone, r. cylinder**, (geom.) cono, cilindro rectos.—**r. hand**, diestra.—**r.-hand**, de la mano derecha.—**r.-hand drive**, (aut.) conducción a la derecha.—**r.-hand man**, (fam.) hombre de confianza, brazo derecho.— **r. line**, línea recta.—**r. or wrong**, a tuertas o a derechas; con razón o sin ella; bueno o malo. —**r. side**, lado derecho; lado de afuera, cara; haz (de tela, etc.).—**r. triangle**, triángulo rectángulo.—**r. wing**, (pol.) bando derechista o moderado, las derechas.—**all r.**, bueno, enhorabuena, conforme.—**it is r.**, está bien; es justo.—**to be r.**, tener razón. **II.** *interj.* ¡bien! ¡bueno! **III.** *adv.* rectamente, justamente; exactamente, perfectamente, precisamente; bien; correctamente; debidamente; derechamente; en derechura; muy; inmediatamente, al instante, ahora mismo; mismo (vg. *right here*, aquí mismo).—**r. about**, vuelta a retaguardia; despedida.—**r. after**, a raíz de.—**r. afterward**, inmediatamente después.—**r. along**, sin interrupción, sin cesar; derecho, sin torcer. —**r.-angled**, rectangular, rectángulo.—**r.-angled triangle**, triángulo rectángulo.—**r. away**, ahora mismo, luego, ya, inmediatamente.—**r. down**, sin rodeos; sin demora.— **r.-handed**, (derecho (que usa la mano derecha); diestro, mañoso, hábil; de movimiento a la derecha, o de izquierda a derecha.—**r.-handed screw**, tornillo de rosca a la derecha.—**R.** Honorable, honorabilísimo, muy honorable. —**r.-minded**, recto, honrado.—**r. now, r. off**, al punto, inmediatamente.—**r. reverend**, reverendísimo. **IV.** *s.* derecho; justicia; rectitud; propiedad; dominio, título; poder, autoridad; privilegio, prerrogativa; opción; la diestra, la derecha (lo opuesto a la izquierda); (pol.) derecha(s), bando conservador o moderado.— **r. of assembly**, derecho de reunión.—**r. of search, r. of visit**, (mar.) derecho de visita. —**r. of way**, precedencia, prelación; (for.) servidumbre de paso; derecho a la vía; (f. c.) servidumbre de vía.—**by r., by rights**, de derecho, por derecho; propiamente, con razón. —**by r. of**, por razón de.—**in one's own r.**, por derecho propio de uno.—**of r.**, de derecho, según derecho.—**on the r.**, a la derecha.—**to be in the r.**, tener razón.—**to be within one's rights**, estar (uno) en su derecho.—**to have a r.**, tener derecho; (fam.) tener obligación.— **to put, o set, to rights**, arreglar, poner en orden.—**to the r.**, a la derecha. **V.** *va.* hacer justicia; enderezar, ajustar, corregir; (mar.) adrizar.—**to r. a wrong**, enderezar un entuerto, corregir un abuso.

rightabout [-əbaut], *s.* vuelta a la derecha, vuelta atrás, media vuelta.

righteous [ráichʌs], *a.* justo, recto, equitativo; virtuoso, honrado, probo.—**righteously** [-li], *adv.* virtuosamente, rectamente.—**righteousness** [-njs], *s.* rectitud, virtud, honradez, probidad.

righter [ráitœ(r)], *s.* enderezador de tuertos o agravios.

rightful [-ful], *a.* legítimo; recto.—**rightfully** [-i], *adv.* legítimamente, rectamente, justa-

mente.—**rightfulness** [-njs], *s.* virtud, justicia, rectitud.

rightist [-ist], *s.* y *a.* (pol.) derechista.

rightly [-li], *adv.* rectamente, justamente; con razón, con justicia; bien, como se debe; exactamente.

rightness [-njs], *s.* rectitud, justicia; derechura; propiedad.

rigid [rídžid], *a.* rígido, inflexible, tieso, yerto; austero, estricto, rigoroso.—**rigidity** [ridžíditi], **rigidness** [-njs], *s.* rigidez, inflexibilidad, tiesura; austeridad, rigor.—**rigidly** [-li], *adv.* rígidamente.

rigmarole [rígmǝroul], *s.* jerigonza, galimatías.

rigor [rígɘ(r)], *s.* rigor, inflexibilidad; inclemencia; severidad, austeridad; tesón, terquedad; rigor, exactitud; (med.) escalofrío.—**r. mortis**, rigor de la muerte, rigidez cadavérica.

rigorism [-izm], *s.* rigorismo.

rigorist [-ist], *s.* y *a.* rigorista.

rigorous [-ʌs], *a.* rigoroso o riguroso; recio (tiempo); estricto, severo.—**rigorously** [-li], *adv.* rigorosamente, severamente.—**rigorousness** [-njs], *s.* rigurosidad, severidad, rigor.

rile [rail], *va.* (fam.) sulfurar, encolerizar. *V.* ROIL.

rill [ril], *s.* riachuelo, arroyuelo, regajo.

rillet [-it], *s.* arroyuelo, regajo.

rim [rim]. **I.** *s.* canto, borde, margen, *mf.*, orilla; (carr.) llanta, aro; cerco, reborde, pestaña; ceja. **II.** *va.* proveer de canto, etc.; enllantar (una rueda).

rime, rimer, rimester = RHYME, etc.

rime [raim]. **I.** *s.* escarcha; grieta, hendedura, resquicio; peldaño de escala. **II.** *va.* y *vn.* cubrir(se) de escarcha. **III.** *va.* (carp.) avellanar, escariar. *V.* REAM.

rimer [-œ(r)], *s.* (carp.) avellanador.

rimose [ráimous], **rimous** [-mʌs], *a.* hendido, rajado, cuarteado.

rimple [rímpl]. **I.** *va.* arrugar. **II.** *s.* arruga. *V.* RIPPLE y RUMPLE.

rimy [ráimi], *a.* escarchado.

rind [raind]. **I.** *s.* corteza, pellejo, cuero, hollejo. **II.** *va.* descortezar, mondar, pelar, deshollejar.

rinderpest [ríndœrpest], *s.* (vet.) morriña.

ring [riŋ]. **I.** *s.* anillo, argolla, anilla; (joy.) sortija, anillo; circo, arena, liza; cerco; corro o corrillo de gente; camarilla, pandilla; ojera; campaneo, tañido o repique de campanas; juego de campanas; campanilleo, toque de campanilla; sonido metálico; rumor, clamor, estruendo; (mar.) arganeo, virola con chaveta.—**r. finger**, dedo anular.—**r. gauge**, calibre anular; (joy.) calibre para anillos.—**r.-shaped**, anular. **II.** *va.* (*pp.* y *pret.* RINGED) rodear, circundar, cercar; poner un anillo a, anillar, ensortijar; adornar con anillos; (hort.) quitar una tira circular de corteza. **III.** *vn.* moverse en círculo o en espiral; formar círculo. **IV.** *va.* (*pret.* RANG, RUNG; *pp.* RUNG) tocar, sonar, tañer, repicar (campanas); tocar (timbre o campanilla); anunciar, proclamar, celebrar (con repique de campanas); repetir, reiterar; llamar, convocar, por medio de una campana.—**to r. the bells in a peal**, tocar las campanas a vuelo.—**to r. up**, (fam.) llamar (a uno) por teléfono; (teat.) levantar (el telón). **V.** *vn.* sonar, tañer, campanillear; retumbar, resonar; zumbar (los oídos). —**to r. off**, terminar (una conversación telefónica); (fam.) cesar de hablar, etc.—**to r. true**, sonar bien (una moneda, etc.).

ringbolt [-boult], *s.* (mar.) cáncamo; armella.

ringbone [-boun], *s.* (vet.) sobrehueso de caballo.

ringdove [-dʌv], *s.* paloma torcaz, zurita o zorita.

ringed [-d], *a.* que lleva anillo (esp. de matrimonio); anular; (zool.) anillado.

ringent [ríndžent], *a.* (bot., zool.) bostezante.

ringer [ríŋœ(r)], *s.* campanero; (elec.) máquina de llamada.

ringing [ríŋiŋ]. **I.** *a.* resonante, sonoro, retumbante. **II.** *s.* campaneo, repique, retintín; toque; zumbido o silbido (de oídos).

ringleader [ríŋlidœ(r)], *s.* cabecilla, *m.*, abanderizador; promotor.

ringlet [ríŋlįt], *s.* anillejo, círculo; sortija, bucle, rizo; (Am.) crespo.

ringster [ríŋstœ(r)], *s.* (fam.) miembro de una pandilla o de una camarilla.

ringworm [ríŋwœrm], *s.* (med.) empeine, culebrilla, serpigo, tiña.

rink [riŋk], *s.* patinadero; sala o pista de patinar.

rinse [rįns], *va.* lavar, limpiar, deslavar, enjuagar, aclarar.

rinser [-œ(r)], *s.* lavandero.

rinsing [-iŋ], *s.* enjuague, enjuagadura, deslavadura.—*pl.* escurriduras.

riot [ráįǫt]. **I.** *s.* tumulto, sedición; alboroto, pelotera; motín, asonada, desorden, exceso; borrachera. **II.** *vn.* armar motines; alborotarse.

rioter [-œ(r)], *s.* alborotador; amotinador; bullanguero, jaranero, libertino.

riotous [-ʌs], *a.* sedicioso, faccioso; desenfrenado; desarreglado; bullicioso.—**riotously** [-lį], *adv.* disolutamente; bulliciosamente.—**riotousness** [-nįs], *s.* disolución; desenfreno, desorden.

rip [rip]. **I.** *va.* (con **up, open** u **off**) rasgar, rajar, romper; descoser, soltar; (con **out** o **away**) cortar, arrancar, destripar, destrozar; (carp.) aserrar con corte longitudinal.—**to r. off a plank**, (mar.) descoser un tablón.—**to r. out an oath**, jurar con violencia, jurar a la ligera, blasfemar. **II.** *vn.* rasgarse, rajarse, henderse, romperse. **III.** *s.* laceración, rasgadura, rasgón; (fam.) persona, caballo o cosa que no vale nada. —**r. cord**, (aer.) cuerda que sirve para abrir el paracaídas. V. RIPPING CORD.—**r. panel o strip,** V. RIPPING.

riparian [ripérįan], *a.* y *s.* ribereño.—**riparious** [-ʌs], *a.* (bot. y zool.) ribereña.

ripe [ráįp], *a.* maduro, sazonado; en sazón; hecho, acabado; pronto, preparado, a propósito; rosado, colorado; (agr.) espigado; (med.) maduro.

ripely [-lį], *adv.* maduramente; a propósito, en sazón.

ripen [-n], *va.* y *vn.* madurar, sazonar(se).

ripeness [-nįs], *s.* madurez, sazón, *f.*

ripening [-çnįŋ], *s.* maduración.

ripper [rípœ(r)], *s.* rasgador, desgarrador.

ripping [rípįŋ], *s.* rasgadura; deshiladura, descosedura.—**r. cord**, (aer.) cabo o cuerda de desgarre o de desinflación rápida (sirve para rasgar la faja de desgarre).—**r. iron**, (mar.) descalcador.—**r. panel o strip**, (aer.) faja de desgarre, parche de desinflación rápida.

ripple [rípl]. **I.** *va.* rizar, ondear; desgargolar el cáñamo. **II.** *vn.* agitarse, rizarse la superficie del agua; murmurar. **III.** *s.* escarceo, onda, rizo (del agua); murmullo; carda o peine para desgargolar.

riprap [rípræp]. **I.** *s.* (alb.) (cimiento de) piedras sueltas; ripio, rocalla, cascajo, broma. **II.** *va.* (alb.) construir de, o reforzar con, piedras sueltas, broma, etc.

ripsaw [rípsɔ], *s.* sierra para corte longitudinal de madera.

rise [ráįz]. **I.** *vn.* (*pret.* ROSE; *pp.* RISEN) ascender, subir, elevarse, remontarse; (mar.) altearse; levantarse, ponerse en pie; levantarse (de la cama); suspender una sesión; salir (el sol); nacer, salir o brotar (las plantas o los manantiales); levantarse, alzarse, amotinarse, sublevarse; surgir, aparecer, presentarse; sobrevenir, armarse, suscitarse (una disputa, etc.); medrar, mejorar de posición; hincharse, aumentar de volumen; encarecerse, subir (el precio); resucitar.—**to r. early**, madrugar.— **to r. late**, (fam.) pegársele a uno las sábanas. —**to r. to one's feet**, ponerse en pie, levantarse.—**to r. to the occasion**, estar a la altura de las circunstancias. **II.** *s.* ascensión, elevación;

levantamiento; crecimiento o desarrollo; cuesta, subida; nacimiento (de un manantial); altura, eminencia; inclinación, pendiente, *f.*; salida (de un astro); encarecimiento, subida, alza (de precios); crecida, creciente, *f.* (de un río, etc.); fuente, *f.*, principio, origen, manantial, causa; adelantamiento, medro; ascenso; elevación de la voz; (arq.) flecha de un arco; (carp.) altura de una contrahuella.—**r. and fall**, (mar.) pleamar y bajamar.—**r. of a hill**, pendiente (*f.*) de una colina.—**r. of ground**, elevación del terreno.—**r. of mercury, of temperature**, subida del mercurio, de la temperatura.—**to give r. to**, dar origen a, causar, motivar, ocasionar.

riser [ráįzœ(r)], *s.* el que se levanta; (carp.) contrahuella; soliviador; cosa que sirve para elevar; (arq.) tubería vertical; (elec.) conductor de un piso a otro; tubo ascendente; (fund.) = FEED-HEAD; respiradero.

risibility [rįzibílįti], *s.* risibilidad.

risible [rízįbl], *a.* risible.

rising [ráįzįŋ]. **I.** *a.* naciente; creciente; ascendiente; que se levanta; saliente; próspero.—**r. tide**, (in)flujo.—**r. vote**, votación en que los votantes se ponen de pie, un grupo tras el otro, para indicar su voto afirmativo o negativo. **II.** *s.* ascenso, subida; resurrección; renacimiento; levantada; solivio; levantamiento, insurrección; (astr.) orto, salida; acto de levantarse (una sesión, una persona); levadura, fermento; prominencia o protuberancia; (med.) lobanillo, lupia.

risk [rísk]. **I.** *s.* riesgo, peligro; contingencia; (en el juego, y fig.) albur.—**at all risks**, a todo trance.—**to run** o **take a r.**, correr peligro, arriesgarse.—**without r.**, a mansalva. **II.** *va.* arriesgar, aventurar, exponer.

risky [-į], *a.* peligroso, arriesgado, aventurado; imprudente, temerario.

risorial [raįsórįal], *a.* reidor; risible.

risqué [rįskéį], *a.* verde, colorado, libre.

rite [ráįt], *s.* rito, ceremonia.

ritornelle [ritornél], *s.* (mús.) retornelo.

ritual [ríchų̧al], *a.* y *s.* ritual, ceremonial.

ritualism [-įzm], *s.* ritualismo; ritualidad.— **ritualist** [-įst], *a.* y *s.* ritualista.—**ritualistic** [-įstįk], *a.* ritualista.—**ritually** [-į], *adv.* según el ritual, conforme a los ritos, de rúbrica.

rival [ráįval]. **I.** *s.* rival. **II.** *a.* émulo, competidor, opuesto. **III.** *va.* emular; competir con, rivalizar con. **IV.** *vn.* rivalizar.—**rivalry** [-rį], *s.* rivalidad, competencia, emulación.

rive [ráįv]. **I.** *va.* (*pret.* RIVED; *pp.* RIVED O RIVEN) rajar, hender. **II.** *vn.* henderse.

river [rívœ(r)]. **I.** *s.* río.—**r. basin**, cuenca de río. —**r. bed**, lecho, álveo, madre (*f.*) de un río.— **r. front**, tierra ribereña.—**r. horse**, hipopótamo.—**r. transportation**, transporte fluvial. —**down** (the) **r.**, río abajo.—**up** (the) **r.**, río arriba.

riverhead [-hed], *s.* fuente (*f.*) o nacimiento de río.

riverside [-saįd], *s.* orilla o margen (*mf.*) de un río; ribera.

rivet [rívįt]. **I.** *s.* remache, roblón.—**r. knob**, embutidera. **II.** *va.* remachar, robl(on)ar; (fig.) asegurar, afianzar.—**to r. the attention on**, fijar la atención en.

rivet(t)ing [-įŋ], *s.* remachado, remache, robl(on)adura.—**r. machine**, remachadora.

rivulet [rívyųlįt], *s.* riachuelo, arroyo, regajo.

roach [rǫuch], *s.* (ict.) escarcho; (ent.) cucaracha.

road [rǫud], *s.* camino, vía; carretera; ferrocarril. —*pl.* (mar.) rada; fondeadero.—**r. agent**, (fam.) salteador.—**r. mender**, peón caminero. —**r. metal**, material (grava, etc.) para caminos, macadán.—**r. roller**, rodillo (para caminos), rulo compresor, apisonadora.—**r. runner**, (orn.) cuclillo de tierra, (Am.) cachila, correcaminos.—**to be on the r.**, viajar de pueblo en pueblo en el ejercicio de una profesión (apl. esp. a los agentes viajeros y a las compañías cómicas).

roadbed [-bɛd], *s.* firme (de camino o carretera); (f. c.) explanación, balasto, asiento de los durmientes.

roadhouse [-haʊs], *s.* parador o posada en el campo, gen. con salón de baile, *bar* y atracciones.

roadside [-saɪd], *s.* orilla o borde del camino.— **r. inn**, venta, posada.

roadstead [-sted], *s.* (mar.) rada, fondeadero.

roadster [-stœ(r)], *s.* (aut.) coche abierto de turismo o de deporte; caballo o bicicleta para uso en las carreteras.

roadway [-weɪ], *s.* carretera, calzada (apl. esp. a la parte central o de tráfico).

roam [róʊm], *va.* y *vn.* vagar, andar errante.

roamer [-œ(r)], *s.* vago, vagabundo.

roan [róʊn], **I.** *a.* roano o ruano, rosillo, sabino. **II.** *s.* caballo ruano; color ruano; badana de color ruano.

roar [rór], **I.** *vn.* rugir, bramar. **II.** *s.* rugido, bramido; estruendo, estrépito.

roarer [-œ(r)], *s.* bramador.

roaring [-ɪŋ], **I.** *a.* rugiente, bramador; estrepitoso, ruidoso; (fam.) superlativo, inmenso. **II.** *s.* rugido, bramido; (vet.) ronquido.

roast [róʊst], **I.** *va.* (coc.) asar; tostar; calcinar; (fam.) hablar mal de; ridiculizar.—**to r. coffee**, tostar café. **II.** *a.* asado; tostado.—**r. beef**, carne de vaca asada, rosbif.—**r. meat**, asado; carne asada o buena para asar. **III.** *s.* asado.

roaster [-œ(r)], *s.* cocinero que asa; asador, tostador; pollo o lechón propio para asar.

roasting [-ɪŋ], **I.** *s.* acción de asar; tostadura; torrefacción; (metal.) calcinación; cocción; (fam.) desolladura, despellejadura.—**r. ear**, (coc.) mazorca de maíz. **II.** *a.* de asar; de calcinar; de cocción.

rob [rab], *va.* y *vn.* robar, pillar; saquear.—**to r. one of**, robar, hurtar o quitarle a uno (el dinero, etc.).

robalo [róʊbəloʊ], *s.* (ict.) róbalo.

robber [rábœ(r)], *s.* ladrón; salteador; caco.

robbery [-ɪ], *s.* robo, hurto, latrocinio.

robe [roʊb], **I.** *s.* manto; túnico o túnica; ropón, ropaje, toga, traje talar; bata; corte de vestido; manta de coche.—**r. of state**, traje de ceremonia.—**the (long) r.**, la curia. **II.** *va.* vestir de gala o de ceremonia; vestir, ataviar. **III.** *vn.* vestirse, ponerse traje; cubrirse.

robin [rábɪn], *s.* (orn.) pechicolorado, petirrojo.

roborant [rábɔrənt], *a.* (med.) roborante, roborativo.

robot [róʊbʌt], *s.* robot, hombre mecánico, autómata, *m.*; autómata (persona); (aer.) piloto mecánico.—**r. bomb**, (mil.) robot, bomba planeadora o voladora; avión (*m.*) cohete, sin piloto, cargado de explosivos.

robust [robʌ́st], *a.* robusto, vigoroso, fuerte.

robustness [-nɪs], *s.* robustez.

roc [rak], *s.* rocho, ruc (ave fabulosa).

rochet [ráchɪt], *s.* (igl.) roquete.

rock [rák], **I.** *s.* roca, peña, peñasco; arrecife, escollo, laja; (fig.) amparo, defensa, protección; (fam.) diamante; moneda.—**r. alum** (**roche alum**), alumbre de roca, jebe.—**r. bass**, (ict.) papagayo.—**r.-bound**, rodeado de peñascos. —**r. bottom**, s. el fondo, lo más profundo; *a.* mínimo, bajísimo.—**r. candy**, azúcar cande.— **r. crusher**, triturador, bocarte.—**r. crystal**, cristal de roca, cuarzo.—**r. dove**, paloma silvestre o de las rocas.—**r. drill**, perforadora de rocas.—**r. garden**, jardincito rocoso; jardín con adornos de piedras.—**r. oil**, petróleo.—**r. quartz**, cristal de roca.—**r.-ribbed**, fuerte, firme; intransigente.—**r. salt**, sal (*f.*) de piedra, o gema.—**r. water**, agua viva de roca.—**on the rocks**, (fam.) arruinado, tronado. **II.** *va.* mecer, cunear, balancear; arrullar; calmar, sosegar. **III.** *vn.* mecerse, bambolear, oscilar.

rocker [-œ(r)], *s.* cualquier cosa que mece o se

mece; cuna; columpio; cunera; mecedora (silla); soportes del asiento de una mecedora; (mec.) balancín; eje oscilante en sus cojinetes.—**r. arm**, brazo o palanca oscilante.—**r. cam**, leva oscilante.

rocket [rákɪt]. **I.** *s.* cohete, volador; (bot.) oruga, jaramago, roqueta.—**r. bomb**, (mil.) bomba cohete.—**r. plane**, (aer.) avión (*m.*) cohete. **II.** *vn.* volar o ascender verticalmente en el aire.

rockiness [rákɪnɪs], *s.* abundancia de rocas; naturaleza roqueña.

rocking [rákɪŋ]. **I.** *a.* mecedor; oscilante.—**r. chair**, mecedora, (Am.) columpio.—**r. horse**, caballo mecedor, caballico.—**r. shaft** = ROCKSHAFT.—**r. valve**, válvula oscilante. **II.** *s.* mecedura, balance, balanceo; tabaleo.

rockrose [rákroʊz], *s.* (bot.) estepa, cisto, cergazo.

rockshaft [ráksæft], *s.* eje que oscila en sus cojinetes.

rocky [rákɪ], *a.* peñascoso, roqueño, roquero, rocoso, pedregoso, pétreo, duro, endurecido.— **R. Mountains**, Montañas Rocosas o Roqueñas.

rococo [rokóʊkoʊ], *a.* y *s.* (estilo) rococó, barroco o churrigueresco.

rod [rad], *s.* vara, varilla; cetro; bastón de mando; vara de alcalde o de alguacil; disciplina(s); varilla de virtudes; caña de pescar; varilla o barra de cortina; vara de medir; medida de 16½ pies; jalón; (mec.) vástago, barra, varilla; azote; (fig.) disciplina, castigo; (bib.) vástago; alcurnia, linaje; raza, tribu, *f.*—**r. fishing**, pesca con caña.

rode [roʊd], *pret.* de TO RIDE.

rodent [róʊdɛnt], *a.* y *s.* (zool.) roedor.

rodeo [róʊdɪoʊ o roʊdéjoʊ], *s.* rodeo (de ganado); corral; función de vaqueros.

rodman [rádman], *s.* (top.) jalonero.

rodomontade [radomantéjd]. **I.** *s.* bravata, baladronada, fanfarronada. **II.** *vn.* baladronear, fanfarronear, bravear.

roe [róʊ], *s.* (zool.) corzo; hueva, freza, ovas de pescado.—**r. deer**, (zool.) corzo.

roebuck [-bʌk], *s.* (zool.) corzo.

Roentgen rays [réntgen réjz], *s. pl.* rayos X o de Roentgen.

rogation [rogéiʃon], *s.* (gen. *pl.*) (igl.) rogativa(s), rogación(es).

rogatory [róʊgətorɪ], *a.* rogatorio.

rogue [róʊg], *s.* bribón, pícaro, pillo, bellaco, golfo, maleante, villano; (fam.) tunantuelo, pilluelo, perillán; (for., Ingl.) pordiosero, vago; elefante feroz y peligroso.—**r.'s gallery**, galería de malhechores, retratos de malhechores que colecciona la policía para su identificación.

roguery [-œrɪ], *s.* picardía o bellaquería; tunantería; travesura, retozo.

roguish [-ɪʃ], *a.* picaresco, (fam.) belitre, tuno; travieso, juguetón.—**r. eyes**, ojos picarescos.— **roguishly** [-lɪ], *adv.* pícaramente, picarescamente.—**roguishness** [-nɪs], *s.* picardía, bellaquería.

roil [róɪl], *va.* enturbiar; vejar, irritar.

roily [-ɪ], *a.* turbio; agitado.

roister [róɪstœ(r)]. **I.** *vn.* bravear, fanfarronear. **II.** *s.* fanfarrón, baladrón.

rôle [roʊl], *s.* (teat.) papel, parte, *f.*, (Am.) rol.

roll [róʊl]. **I.** *va.* hacer rodar; volver, girar, voltear; arrollar o enrollar, abarquillar; (fund.) laminar; alisar, allanar, emparejar con rodillo; apisonar (el césped); liar (cigarrillos); envolver, fajar; redoblar (el tambor); vibrar la lengua (para pronunciar la **rr**) o la voz (para hacer un trino); mover (los ojos) hacia arriba, ponerlos en blanco.—**to r. up**, enrollar, arrollar; (fam.) acumular; revolver, revolverse. **II.** *vn.* rodar; agitarse (las olas); ondular, fluctuar, flotar; retumbar, retemblar; bambolearse, balancearse; arrollarse, abarquillarse, encarrujarse; dar un redoble de tambores.—**to r. about**, rodar, divagar, andar de acá para allá.—**to r. down,** bajar rodando.—**to r. in money,** nadar en la abundancia.—**to r. to a stop,** seguir rodando hasta pararse. **III.** *s.* rollo; rol, lista, nómina, matrícula, registro; (coc.) bollo, panecillo; (mec.) rodillo, cilindro de emparejar, allanar o laminar; laminador; maza de trapiche; redoble (de tambores); retumbo del trueno; balanceo, bamboleo; oleaje; (cir.) mecha; (arq.) voluta. —*pl.* archivos.—**r. call,** acto de pasar lista.— **r. film,** (fot.) película en rollo o sobre carrete. —**r. sulphur,** azufre en barretas.—**r.-top desk,** escritorio o pupitre de tapa rodadera o corrediza.

rolled [-d], *a.* enrollado, arrollado; alisado, allanado, emparejado; (fund.) laminado.—**r. oats,** avena aplastada que se usa como alimento.

roller [-œ(r)], *s.* rodillo, tambor, cilindro; arrollador, allanador, aplanadera; alisador; (impr.) rulo, rodillo; ola larga; (cir.) venda, faja; (mar.) polín, rollete, roldana.—**r. bearing,** cojinete de rodillos.—**r. bridge,** puente corredizo.—**r. coaster,** montaña rusa.—**r. mill,** molino de cilindros moledores (gen. para granos).—**r. skate,** patín de ruedas.—**r. towel,** toalla continua o sin fin.

rollick [rálik], *vn.* travesear, retozar, juguetear.

rollicking [-iŋ], *a.* jovial; juguetón, travieso, retozón.

rolling [róuliŋ]. **I.** *a.* rodador, rodante; rodadero; quebrado, undulado (terreno).—**r. kitchen,** (mil.) cocina de campaña. *V.* SOUP KITCHEN.— **r. mill,** (metal.) taller de laminar; laminador. —**r. pin,** rodillo de pastelero, rollo, fruslero, hataca.—**r. press,** laminador; calandria.—**r. stock,** (f. c.) material rodante.—**r. stone,** (geol.) galga, canto rodado (*a r. stone gathers no moss,* piedra movediza, nunca moho la cobija). **II.** *s.* rodadura; revuelco; balanceo, cuneo; enrollamiento; fajamiento; (aer.) escora lateral.

roly-poly [róuli pouli]. **I.** *a.* rechoncho, gordiflón. **II.** *s.* (coc.) pudín en forma de rollo; (fam.) persona gordiflona.

Romaic [rouméijk], *a.* romaico.

Roman [róumən]. **I.** *a.* romano; romanesco; católico romano.—**R. architecture,** arquitectura románica.—**R. candle,** candela romana. —**R. law,** derecho romano.—**R. letter,** (impr.) letra romana.—**R. nose,** nariz aguileña.—**R. numeral,** número romano.—**R. type,** (impr.) tipo romano.—**R. vitriol,** vitriolo azul, sulfato de cobre.

Romance, Romanic [roméns, roménik], *a.* romance; neolatino.

romance [roméns]. **I.** *s.* romance; novela, ficción, cuento, fábula; (mús.) romanza; aventura, drama, *m.*; episodio extraño y conmovedor; (fam.) amorío, idilio de amor.—**R. language,** lengua neolatina o románica. **II.** *vn.* mentir; fingir fábulas; hablar o pensar románticamente.—**romancer** [-œ(r)], **romancist** [-ist], *s.* romancero, novelista; romancista; embustero; visionario.

Romanesque [roumənésk], *a.* romanesco; (arq.) románico.

Romanism [róumənizm], *s.* catolicismo romano.

Romanist [-ist], *s.* y *a.* católico romano.

Romanization [-jzéjşơn], *s.* romanización.

Romanize [-ajz], *va.* y *vn.* romanizar; latinizar; latinear; convertir(se) al catolicismo; conformar(se) a la doctrina del catolicismo romano.

romantic(al [romántik(əl], *a.* romántico, novelesco, romancesco o romanesco; sentimental; fantástico.—**romantic(al)ly** [-i], *adv.* de un modo romántico.

romanticism [-tisizm], *s.* romanticismo.

romanticist [-ist], *s.* escritor romántico.

Romish [róumiş], *a.* romano.

Rom(m)any [rámani], *a.* y *s.* gitano.

romp [ramp]. **I.** *s.* muchacha retozona, saltabardales, *mf.*; retozo. **II.** *vn.* retozar, juguetear, travesear.

rompers [rámpœrz], *s. pl.* traje de juego para niñitos.

rompish [rámpiş], *a.* retozón.

rondeau, rondel [rándou, rándel], *s.* (poét.) rondel.

rondo [rándou], *s.* (mús.) rondó.

Röntgen rays = ROENTGEN RAYS.

rood [rud], *s.* cruz, crucifijo; cuarto de acre; pértica inglesa (entre 6 y 8 yardas).

roof [rúf]. **I.** *s.* tejado, tech(ad)o, techumbre, azotea; cubierta; (poét.) bóveda, cielo; tejadillo de un coche, imperial de una diligencia; casa, hogar, habitación.—**r. of the mouth,** cielo de la boca, bóveda palatina, paladar.—**r. garden,** jardín de la azotea; azotea de baile y diversión. —**r. paper,** papel cubretechos, papel para tejados.—**r. tile,** teja.—**r. tiler,** retejador.— **r. truss,** armadura de techo. **II.** *va.* techar; abrigar, alojar.

roofage [-idž], *s.* materiales para techos.

roofer [-œ(r)], *s.* techador, constructor de tejados.

roofing [-iŋ]. **I.** *s.* (arq.) techado, cubierta; material para techos; albergue. **II.** *a.* para techos o tejados, de techar.

roofless [-lis], *a.* destechado, sin techo; sin amparo, sin hogar.

rooftop [-tap], *s.* azotea; cumbrera; lo más alto de un techo.

rooftree [-tri], *s.* cumbrera.

rook [rúk]. **I.** *s.* (orn.) corneja, corvato; roque, torre (del ajedrez); fullero, trampista. **II.** *va.* enfullar, trampear.

rookery [-œrj], *s.* manada de cornejas; lugar donde procrean las aves marinas o las focas; casa destartalada y ruinosa; vecindario escuálido.

rookie, rooky [rúkj], *s.* (fam.) recluta, *m.*; novicio.

rooky, *a.* habitado por cornejas.

room [rúm]. **I.** *vn.* tener una habitación o aposento, alojarse. **II.** *s.* lugar; paraje, sitio, espacio, puesto; cuarto, aposento, sala, habitación, cámara, pieza; causa, motivo, razón, *f.*; tiempo, ocasión, oportunidad.—**there is no r. for doubt,** no cabe duda.

roomer [-œ(r)], *s.* huésped, *m.*, inquilino.

roomful [-ful], *s.* cuarto lleno.

roominess [-inis], *s.* espaciosidad, holgura, amplitud.

rooming house [-iŋ], *s.* casa de huéspedes.

roommate [-mejt], *s.* compañero de cuarto.

roomy [-j], *a.* espacioso, capaz, amplio, holgado.

roorback [rúrbæk], *s.* (pol. E. U.) noticia falsa, (fam.) filfa, tramoya.

roost [rúst]. **I.** *s.* percha de gallinero; lugar de descanso; sueño, descanso, reposo (de las aves domésticas). **II.** *vn.* dormir o descansar (las aves) en una percha.

rooster [-œ(r)], *s.* (orn.) gallo.

root [rút]. **I.** *s.* raíz (en todas sus acepciones); (mús.) base, *f.*—**r. and branch,** por completo. —**r. gall,** hinchazón (*f.*) de las raíces.—**r. hair,** (bot.) raicilla. **II.** *vn.* y *va.* echar o criar raíces, arraigar(se); hozar, hocicar (como los puercos). —**to r. for,** (fam.) aplaudir, alabar, vitorear; gritar por el éxito de.—**to r. up,** o **out,** arrancar de raíz, desarraigar; extirpar; desterrar.— **to take r.,** radicar, arraigar(se).

rootbeer [-bjr], *s.* bebida no alcohólica hecha de varias raíces.

rooted [-jd], *a.* radical; arraigado, con raíces.— **rootedly** [-lij], *adv.* radicalmente; fijamente.

rootlet [-ljt], *s. dim.* raicilla, radícula.

rootstock [-stak], *s.* (bot.) rizoma, *m.*; tallo subterráneo de una planta; (fig.) origen, *mf.*

rooty [-j], *a.* lleno de raíces; radicoso.

rope [róup]. **I.** *s.* soga, maroma; cuerda, cordel, cabo; driza, sirga; reata, cobra; sarta, ristra, trenza; hilera, fila.—**r. ladder,** escala de cuerdas.—**r. of onions,** ristra de cebollas.—**r. of**

pearls, sarta o hilo de perlas.—**r.'s end,** (mar.) chicote de cabo; látigo; latigazo; dogal.—**ropes of a ship,** (mar.) jarcia, cordaje.—**r. railway,** cable aéreo de transporte.—**r. sandal,** alpargata.—**r. shop o yard,** cordelería, soguería.—**r. yarn,** filástica.—**to be at the end of one's r.,** estar sin recursos; estar uno en las últimas. **—to know the ropes,** (fam.) estar al tanto de, estar bien familiarizado con algo. **II.** *va.* atar, amarrar con una cuerda; rodear con soga; (E. U.) coger con lazo.—**to r. in,** (fam.) atraer, embaucar, engañar.—**to r. off,** cercar con cuerdas.—**roper-in,** (fam.) gancho, donillero. **III.** *vn.* ahilarse, hacer hebras o madeja.

ropebands [-bændz], *s. pl.* (mar.) envergues.

ropedancer [-dænsœ(r)], *s.* volatín, bailarín de cuerda, funámbulo, maromero.—**r.'s pole,** balancín, balanza.

ropemaker [-meikœ(r)], *s.* cordelero, soguero.

ropery [-œri], *s.* cordelería.

ropewalk [-wɔk], *s.* cordelería, soguería.—**ropewalker** [-œ(r)], *s.* volatinero, maromero.

ropeway [-wei], *s.* cable aéreo; alambrecarril.

ropework [-wœrk], *s.* trabajo hecho de cuerdas.

ropiness [-inis], *s.* viscosidad; tenacidad.

ropish [-iŝ], **ropy** [-i], *a.* viscoso, pegajoso, glutinoso.

roquet [roukéi]. **I.** *va.* y *vn.* en el juego de *croquet*, dar o hacer chocar la bola del que juega contra otra. **II.** *s.* choque de dichas bolas.

rorqual [rórkwəl], *s.* (zool.) rorqual, yubarta.

rosaceous [rouzéiŝəs], *a.* (bot.) rosáceo.

rosanilin(e [rouzǽnilin], *s.* (quím.) rosanilina.

rosary [róuzəri], *s.* (igl.) rosario; guirnalda o corona de rosas; rosaleda, macizo o jardín de rosales; (fig.) crestomatía.

rose [rouz], *pret.* de TO RISE.

rose [róuz], *s.* (bot.) rosal; rosa; color de rosa; (arq.) rosetón; remate perforado de una regadera.—**r. apple,** pomarrosa.—**r. beetle, r. bug, r. chafer,** nombres de insectos que atacan al rosal.—**r. bush,** rosal.—**r.-colored,** color de rosa, rosado; róseo, halagüeño.—**r. garden,** rosaleda o rosalera.—**r. geranium,** geranio de rosa.—**r. of Jericho,** rosa de Jericó.—**r. mallow,** malva rósea, malvarrosa. *V.* HOLLYHOCK.—**r. of Sharon,** rosa de Siria.—**r. spray = ROSEHEAD.—r. water,** agua rosada, agua de rosas.—**r. window,** (arq.) rosetón (ventana).—**under the r.,** bajo cuerda, secretamente.

roseate [-iit], *a.* rosado; róseo.

rosebay [-bei], *s.* adelfa, baladre; rododendro.

rosebud [-bʌd], *s.* pimpollo, botón o capullo de rosa; niña adolescente.

rosebush [-buŝ], *s.* (bot.) rosal.

rosehead [-hed], *s.* boquilla de regadera.

rosemary [-mɛri], *s.* (bot.) romero, rosmarino.

roseola [rouzíolə], *s.* (med.) roséola.

roset [róuzet], *s.* rosicler.

rosette [rouzét], *s.* rosa, roseta; escarapela, moña; (arq.) rosetón, florón.

rosewood [róuzwud], *s.* palo de rosa; palisandro.

Rosicrucian [rouzikrúŝən], *s.* miembro de la secta secreta llamada Rosa Cruz.

rosied [róuzid], *a.* rosado, róseo.

rosin [rázin]. **I.** *s.* abetinote, resina. *V.* RESIN. **II.** *va.* dar con resina.

rosiny [-i], *a.* resinoso.

rossolis [rosólf], *s.* rosoli (licor) (ll. t. **rosolio**).

roster [rástœ(r)], *s.* (mil.) lista, rol; orden (f.) del día; registro, nómina, matrícula.

rostra [rástrə], *s. pl.* de ROSTRUM.

rostral [rástrəl], *a.* (zool.) rostral.

rostrate [rástreit], *a.* (zool., arq.) rostrado.

rostrum [rástrʌm], *s.* tribuna; (zool.) rostro, pico, hocico; (mar.) rostro, espolón.

rosy [róuzi], *a.* róseo, rosado, de color de rosa; sonrosado; sonrojado; (fig.) agradable, lisonjero; optimista.—**r. dream,** sueño dorado.—**r.-hued,** rosado.

rot [rat]. **I.** *vn.* pudrirse; echarse a perder; descom-

ponerse; corromperse; (vet.) padecer de morriña las ovejas. **II.** *va.* pudrir; enriar (cáñamo o lino). *V.* RET. **III.** *s.* putrefacción, podre(dumbre), descomposición; (vet.) morriña; (bot.) enfermedad de las plantas causada por los hongos; (fam.) tontada, sandez.

rota [róutə], *s.* rol, nómina, lista; orden (f.) del día, rutina; (R., igl.) Rota.

Rotarian [rotériən], *s.* y *a.* rotario.—**Rotarianism** [-izm], *s.* rotarismo.—**Rotary Club,** Club Rotario.

rotary [róutəri], *a.* giratorio, rotativo, rotatorio. **—r. engine,** máquina rotativa.—**r. press,** (impr.) prensa rotativa.—**r. pump,** bomba rotatoria.

rotate [róuteit]. **I.** *vn.* girar, dar vueltas; alternar(se). **II.** *va.* hacer girar, dar vuelta o vueltas a; alternar; (agr.) alternar, sembrar o cultivar en rotación. **III.** *a.* (bot.) de venas radiales (apl. a las hojas); en forma de rueda.

rotating [-iŋ], *a.* rotatorio, rotante.

rotation [routéiŝən], *s.* rotación, giro; turno; cambio, alternación, alternativa; (agr.) rotación.—**r. of crops,** rotación de cultivos.—**by r., in r.,** por turnos, alternadamente.—**in r.,** (agr.) en rotación.

rotative, rotatory [róutətiv, -təri], *a.* rotatorio, giratorio.

rotator [róuteitɔ(r)], *s.* lo que hace rodar o girar.

rote [rout], *s.* lo que se aprende de memoria.—**by r.,** de memoria o de coro; mecánicamente.

rotifer [róutifœ(r)], *s.*, **rotiferal, rotiferous** [routífɛrəl, -ʌs], *a.* (zool.) rotífero.

rotiform [róutiform], *a.* (bot. y zool.) rotiforme, de forma de rueda o estrella; radiado.

rotisserie [routísri], *s.* restaurante cuya especialidad son los asados; tienda donde se venden o se preparan asados.

rotogravure [routográvjúr], *s.* rotograbado, huecograbado.

rotor [róutɔ(r)], *s.* pieza giratoria; (hidr.) rotor, rueda móvil (de turbina); (elec.) rotor; pequeño motor para hacer girar discos, etc.—**r. ship,** barco de cilindros giratorios (*rotores*) movidos por el viento.

rotten [rátn], *a.* podrido, carroño, putrefacto; (fam.) malísimo, pésimo; dañado, en mal estado, descompuesto o podrido.—**rottenness** [-nis], *s.* podredumbre, putrefacción.

rottenstone [-stoun], *s.* trípoli o trípoli.

rotund [rotʌnd], *a.* rotundo, redondo; orbicular.

rotunda [-ə], *s.* rotonda o rotunda.

rotundity [-iti], *s.* rotundidad, redondez.

rouble [rúbl], *s.* = RUBLE.

roué [ruéi], *s.* libertino.

rouge [ruʒ]. **I.** *s.* color(ete), afeite, brasil; (joy.) colcótar. **II.** *a.* colorado, encarnado. **III.** *va.* y *vr.* arrebolar(se), pintar(se), dar(se) colorete.

rough [rʌf]. **I.** *a.* áspero; tosco; fragoso, escabroso; erizado; peludo, encrespado; duro, bronco, desapacible; bruto, tosco, cerril; rudo, inculto; grosero, brusco; tempestuoso, borrascoso, agitado; chapucero, mal acabado; aproximativo, general; preliminar, preparativo.—**r.-and-ready,** tosco o rudo pero eficaz, pronto pero tosco.—**r.-and-tumble,** desordenado, sin restricción ni regla; a topa tolondro; fuerte, resistente.—**r. coat,** primera capa (de enlucido, etc.).—**r. copy,** borrador, minuta.—**r.-cut, r.-dressed,** a medio pulir, a medio labrar.—**r. diamond,** diamante en bruto; persona ruda pero de buen fondo.—**r. draft,** boceto, bosquejo; borrador.—**r. going,** camino difícil o escabroso; cosa ardua.—**r. dressing o grinding,** desbaste.—**r. sea,** mar bravo o alborotado. **—r. sketch** = R. DRAFT.—**r. usage,** uso rudo, estropeo, maltrato.—**r. wind,** viento borrascoso.—**r. wine,** vino áspero.—**as, o at, a r. guess,** a ojo de buen cubero. **II.** *s.* estado tosco; matón, belitre, rufián.—**in the r.,** en bruto, sin pulimento. **III.** *va.* poner áspero, tosco, escabroso; labrar toscamente; (fam.) molestar, irritar.—**to r. a horse,** domar un caballo; herrarle de modo que no resbale en el hielo. *V.* ROUGH-SHOD.—**to r. it,** pasar trabajos, vivir sin comodidades.

roughage [- idʒ], *s.* alimento o forraje (salvado, paja, etc.) difíciles de digerir.

roughcast [-kæst]. **I.** *va.* bosquejar; picar, hacer áspero; dar una primera capa de mezcla gruesa. **II.** *s.* (alb.) mezcla o mortero gruesos; modelo tosco; obra sin acabar.

roughdry [-drái], *va.* secar (ropa) sin planchar.

roughen [-n], *va.* y *vn.* poner(se) áspero o tosco; picar, rascar.

roughhew [-hjú], *va.* desbastar.

roughhouse [-haus], *s.* (fam.) pelotera; algazara.

roughing-in [-iŋ in], *s.* primera capa de enlucido; aplicación de esta capa; colocación de las tuberías ocultas de un edificio.

roughly [-li], *adv.* ásperamente, rudamente; aproximadamente, de un modo general.

roughneck [-nek], *s.* (fam.) patán; rufián, truhán.

roughness [-nis], *s.* aspereza, rudeza, tosquedad, escabrosidad; severidad, dureza; ordinariez, bronquedad; chapucería; tempestad, tormenta.

roughride [-ráid], *va.* y *vn.* amansar; montar caballos indómitos; dominar, imponerse, dar la ley.

roughrider [-ráidœ(r)], *s.* picador o domador de caballos; jinete arrojado; *roughrider,* soldado voluntario norteamericano de caballería durante la guerra entre España y los E. U.

roughsetter [-sétœ(r)], *s.* (alb.) mampostero.

roughshod [-šád], *a.* herrado con púas o clavos que impiden resbalar en el hielo.—**to ride,** o **run, r. over,** andar u obrar sin hacer caso de dificultades; dominar, mandar a la baqueta; atropellar, tratar sin miramiento.

rouleau [rulóu], *s.* cartucho de dinero; rollo, cucurucho, alcartaz, *m.;* (fort.) fajina.

roulette [rulét], *s.* ruleta (juego); ruedecilla dentada de grabador, guarnicionero, etc.

Roumanian [ruméinian], *s.* y *a.* rumano.

round [ráund]. **I.** *a.* redondo, circular, cilíndrico, esférico, orbicular; rollizo; rotundo, lleno; sonoro; cabal; grande, cuantioso; liberal, amplio; franco, sincero, llano, ingenuo; vivo, veloz; justo, honrado.—**r. assertion,** afirmación clara y categórica.—**r. dance,** baile de parejas (vals, etc.); baile en círculo.—**r. hand,** letra redonda.—**r.-head screw,** tornillo de cabeza redonda.—**r. iron,** hierro redondo o en barras redondas.—**r. moulding,** bocel, torés.—**r. number,** número redondo; (*pl.* cifras globales).—**r. robin,** memorial firmado en rueda (con las firmas en rueda).—**r. shot,** bala rasa.—**r. sum,** cifra o suma redonda.—**r. table,** mesa redonda (sin ceremonia).—**R. Table,** (hist.) Tabla redonda; el rey Arturo y los caballeros de la Tabla redonda.—**r. timber,** madera en troncos.—**r. trip,** viaje redondo o de ida y vuelta.—**r.-trip ticket,** billete de ida y vuelta.—**to go r. and r.,** dar vuelta tras vuelta.—**to make r.,** redondear, dar figura redonda a. **II.** *s.* círculo, orbe, esfera; círculo de personas o cosas; redondez; vuelta, rodeo, giro, rotación, revolución; peldaño (de escala); listón o travesaño (de silla); rodaja de carne; (arq.) mediacaña; (mil.) ronda; andanada, salva, disparo, tiro, descarga; cartucho con bala; ruta, camino, circuito; rutina, serie; (dep.) tanda, suerte, *f.,* turno; asalto (boxeo); mano, *f.,* talla (naipes); (mús.) rondó; danza.—*pl. V.* ROUNDS. **III.** *adv.* alrededor, en derredor, por todos lados; a la redonda.—**r. about,** por el lado opuesto; por todos lados, a la redonda; en contorno.—**r.-faced,** carirredondo.—**r.-headed,** braquicéfalo; (bot.) repolludo.—**r.-headed bolt,** perno de cabeza de hongo.—**r.-shouldered,** cargado de espaldas.—**all-r.,** completo, que sirve para todo; cabal, experto en todos los detalles de su profesión u

oficio.—**all the year r.,** todo el año, el año entero. **IV.** *prep.* alrededor de; a la vuelta de. **V.** *va.* (a veces con *off*) (ar)redondear; moverse alrededor, cercar, ceñir, dar vuelta a; doblar (un cabo, una esquina); acabar, perfeccionar; (mar.) (con **in** o **down**) halar.—**to r. up,** recoger, juntar, reunir; aprehender, coger; recoger el ganado para reconocerlo, marcarlo, etc., (Am.) rodear (ganado). **VI.** *vn.* redondearse; desarrollarse, perfeccionarse; dar vueltas; rondar.—**to r. on,** volverse contra, cerrar, atacar.—**to r. out,** llenarse, redondearse.—**to r. to,** (mar.) orzar.—**to r. up,** colmar; (mar.) halar.

roundabout [-abaut]. **I.** *a.* indirecto, vago; desviado. **II.** *s.* chaqueta; tiovivo; rodeo.

roundel, o **roundelay** [-el, -elei], *s.* (mús.) melodía; rondó; baile en círculo.

rounder [-œ(r)], *s.* (fam.) libertino, calavera, *m.*

Roundhead [-hed], *s.* (Ingl.) (despec.) "cabeza redonda," apodo que se daba a los puritanos.

roundhouse [-haus], *s.* (mar.) chupeta, toldilla, tumbadillo; (f. c.) rotunda, casa de máquinas.

rounding [-iŋ], *s.* redondeamiento; curvatura; (mar.) forro o doblamiento de cable.

roundish [-iš], *a.* casi redondo, medio redondo.

roundly [-li], *adv.* redondamente; claramente, francamente; aproximadamente.

roundness [-nis], *s.* redondez.

rounds [-z], *s. pl.* recorrido, demarcación (de un sereno, policía, etc.); jiras, idas y venidas, salidas de costumbre (como las de un médico, un sacerdote).—**to do,** o **go, one's r.,** hacer uno su ronda o su jira.

roundsman [-zmạn], *s.* (E. U.) rondador de policía.

roundup [-ʌp], *s.* rodeo de ganado; recogida, junta; apresamiento, aprehensión.

roup [rup], *s.* (vet.) crup de las aves domésticas.

rouse [ráuz]. **I.** *va.* despertar, animar, excitar, suscitar, provocar; levantar (la caza); (mar.) halar o arronzar. **II.** *vn.* despertar(se), despabilarse, animarse, moverse.

rouser [-œ(r)], *s.* despertador, excitador; (fam.) cosa admirable o estupenda; bola, embuste.

rousing [-iŋ], *a.* vehemente, entusiasmador, entusiasta, ruidoso; activo, animado (el comercio); (fam.) estupendo; descarado.

roustabout [ráustạbaut], *s.* peón, gañán, mozo de tareas sueltas, obrero de muelle, etc.

rout [ráut]. **I.** *s.* rota, derrota, huída, destrozo; garulla, chusma; alboroto, tumulto, asonada. **II.** *va.* derrotar, desbaratar, destrozar; arrancar hozando.—**to r. out,** sacar a luz; forzar, echar, hacer salir.

route [rut o ráut]. **I.** *s.* ruta, vía, camino; (mar.) rumbo, derrota, derrotero; marcha, curso; itinerario, trazado, línea.—**en r. to,** en ruta a. **II.** *va.* dirigir o mandar por una ruta o vía específica.

routine [rutín], *a.* rutinario.

routine, *s.* rutina; costumbre, hábito.

rove [róuv]. **I.** *va.* (tej.) torcer el hilo antes de encanillarlo; ensartar, enhebrar. **II.** *vn.* corretear, vagar, vagabundear.—**to r. about the seas,** piratear. **III.** *s.* correría, paseo; (tej.) mechón, hebra, hilado; (mar.) arandela de remache.

rover [-œ(r)], *s.* errante, andorrero, vagabundo; persona inconstante; pirata, *m.;* flecha de arquero.

roving [-iŋ]. **I.** *s.* vagancia; (tej.) primera torsión. **II.** *a.* errante, vagabundo, andariego.

row [róu]. **I.** *s.* hilera, fila; paseo en lancha o bote; remadura. **II.** *vn.* (mar.) remar, bogar. **III.** *va.* conducir remando.

row [ráu]. **I.** *vn.* (fam.) pelearse, armar camorra o bochinche. **II.** *s.* camorra, bochinche, trifulca.

rowan [róuạn], *s.* (bot.) fresno.

rowboat [róubout], *s.* bote o lancha de remos.

rowdy [ráudi], *s.* y *a.* quimerista, alborotador,

(fam.) zaragatero, rufián.—**rowdyism** [-ĭzm], s. rufianismo, bellaquería, tunantería.

rowel [ráu̯ĕl]. I. s. rodaja de espuela; (vet.) sedal. II. va. espolear; (vet.) poner sedal.

rowen [ráu̯ĕn], s. segunda siega de heno.

rower [róu̯œ(r)], s. remero, bogador.

rowing [róu̯ĭŋ]. I. s. acción o deporte de remar. II. pa. remante.—**by r.**, a(l) remo, remando.

rowlock [róu̯lak], s. (mar.) chumacera, escalamera, encaje de remo.

royal [rói̯al]. I. a. real, regio, magnífico, magnánimo, excelente, superior.—**R. Highness**, Alteza.—**R. Household**, casa real.—**r. navy**, real armada.—**to have a r. time**, divertirse en grande, o a cuerpo de rey. II. s. tamaño de papel (19x24 pulgs. para escribir y de 20x25 para imprenta); (mar.) sobrejuanete; candil, o punta superior del asta del ciervo.

royalism [-ĭzm], s. realismo.—**royalist** [-ĭst], s. realista.

royally [-ĭ], adv. regiamente; a cuerpo de rey.

royalty [-tĭ], s. realeza, soberanía, majestad real; miembro(s) de la realeza; regalía; prerrogativas reales; participación, tanto por ciento de los ingresos;—pl. derechos de autor o de inventor.

rub [rʌb]. I. va. estregar, refregar, frotar, friccionar; tocar, ludir; raspar, raer; incomodar, fastidiar.—**to r. away**, quitar frotando.—**to r. down**, sobar, dar un masaje a (un atleta, etc.); limpiar, almohazar (un caballo, etc.); rebajar o alisar frotando.—**to r. in**, hacer penetrar por los poros frotando; (fam.) machacar.—**to r. off**, quitar; limpiar frotando.—**to r. out**, borrar.—**to r. the wrong way**, frotar a contrapelo; irritar, incomodar.—**to r. up**, aguijonear, excitar; retocar, repasar. pulir. II. vn. pasar raspando, rozar; ser desagradable o molesto; ir a contrapelo. III. s. frotación, ludimiento, roce, estregamiento; tropiezo, obstáculo o dificultad; sarcasmo, denuesto.

rubadub [rʌ́badʌb], s. tan(taran)tán, rataplán.

rubber [rʌ́bœ(r)]. I. a. de caucho o goma elástica; cauchero, gomero.—**r. band**, faja de goma o de caucho, elástico, goma.—**r. belt**, correa (de trasmisión) de caucho (más propiamente, de tela y caucho).—**r. belting**, correaje de caucho. —**r. boots**, botas de goma.—**r. bulb**, pera de goma.—**r. cement**, cemento o pasta de caucho y azufre.—**r. cloth**, tela engomada.—**r. dam**, (dent.) reparo de goma.—**r. eraser**, goma de borrar.—**r. heel**, tacón de goma.—**r. industry**, industria cauchera.—**r. plant** o **tree**, cauchera. —**r. plantation**, cauchal.—**r. stamp**, estampilla, fechador de goma; (fam.) el que imita o aprueba sin consideración las acciones de otros. —**to r.-stamp**, estampar con un sello de goma; (fam.) aprobar ciegamente.—**r. trader**, gomista, gomero. II. s. caucho, goma elástica, hule; fregador, frotador, masajista; goma de borrar; estropajo, aljofifa, estregadera; escofina; jugada final que decide un empate; partida de juego.—pl. chanclos, zapatos de goma.

rubberize [-ai̯z], va. engomar, cubrir o impregnar de caucho.

rubbery [-ĭ], a. semejante al caucho; de consistencia de caucho.

rubbing [rʌ́bĭŋ], s. fricción, frotación, frote, soba; roce; estregamiento.

rubbish [rʌ́bĭš], s. basura, desperdicio(s), desecho, escombro, cascajo, ripio; (fam.) tontería.

rubble [rʌ́bl], s. (alb.) mampuesto, piedra de cantera, piedra bruta o sin labrar; ripios, fragmentos de piedra y ladrillo para relleno; cascote, cascajo.—**r. masonry**, mampostería concertada (de piedras a medio labrar); mampostería de piedra bruta o de cantera (sin labrar).

rubblework [-wœrk], s. = RUBBLE MASONRY.

rubdown [rʌ́bdau̯n], s. fricción, masaje.

rube [rub], s. (fam.) aldeano, campesino, rústico.

rubefacient [rubĕ̯féi̯šĕnt], a. y s. (med.) rubefaciente.

rubefaction [-fǽkšǫn], s. (med.) rubefacción.

rubella [rubélȧ], s. (med.) rubéola.

rubescence [rubésĕns], s. rubescencia, rubicundez.

rubescent [-ĕnt], a. rubescente, sonrosado.

rubiaceous [rubĭéi̯šȧs], a. (bot.) rubiáceo.

rubicund [rúbĭkʌnd], a. rubicundo, rojizo.

rubicundity [-kʌ́ndĭtĭ], s. rubicundez.

rubidium [rubídi̯ʌm], s. (quím.) rubidio.

rubied [rúbĭd], a. adornado con rubíes; rubificado; (de) color de rubí.

rubiginous [rubĭdžĭnʌs], a. rubiginoso, herrumbroso.

ruble [rúbl], s. rublo, moneda rusa.

rubric [rúbrĭk]. I. a. rubro, rojo, rojizo. II. s. rúbrica; título, encabezamiento; división, sección; (igl.) rúbrica.—**rubrical** [-al], a. de rúbrica.—**rubricate** [-kei̯t]. I. a. iluminado, escrito o impreso de color rojo. II. va. marcar o iluminar con encarnado.

ruby [rúbĭ]. I. s. rubí; carmín, color encarnado vivo; (Ingl. impr.) V. AGATE. II. a. rúbeo, rojo. III. va. rubificar, enrojecer; arreglar.

ruche [ruš], s. (cost.) golilla, lechuguilla, (galic.) ruche, f.—**ruching** [-ĭŋ], s. (material para hacer) lechuguillas.

ruck [rʌk]. I. va. arrugar, ajar. II. s. arruga; muchedumbre; la masa de personas o cosas ordinarias.

rucksack [-sæk], s. mochila, morral.

ruction [rʌ́kšǫn], s. (fam.) alboroto; alharaca.

rudder [rʌ́dœ(r)], s. (mar.) timón, gobernalle; gobierno, dirección.

rudderhole [-hou̯l], s. (mar.) limera del timón.

rudderpost [-pou̯st], s. (mar.) codaste; madre (f.) del timón; (aer.) eje del timón. V. RUDDER-STOCK.

rudderstock [-stak], s. (mar.) cabeza del timón.

ruddiness [rʌ́di̯nĭs], s. rojez, rubicundez.

ruddy [rʌ́dĭ], a. rojo, rojizo; rubicundo.

rude [rúd], a. rudo, brusco, descortés; tosco, basto, chabacano, grosero; inculto; fuerte, vigoroso.—**rudely** [-lĭ], adv. rudamente, groseramente, toscamente, descortésmente.—**rudeness** [-nĭs], s. grosería; patanería, descortesía; rudeza, dureza, aspereza; rusticidad, tosquedad, crudeza.

rudiment [rúdĭmĕnt], s. rudimento; (biol.) embrión, m., germen.—**rudimental** [-méntal], a. = RUDIMENTARY.—**rudimentarily** [-méntarĭlĭ], adv. rudimentariamente.—**rudimentary** [-méntarĭ], a. rudimentario; germinal, embrionario.

rue [rú]. I. va. y vn. lamentar(se); arrepentirse (de); llorar, sentir, deplorar. II. s. amargura, decepción, chasco; arrepentimiento, pesar; acción de volverse atrás (en un negocio, etc.); (bot.) ruda.—**rueful** [-fl], a. lamentable, lastimoso; triste, apesarado; terrible.—**ruefully** [-lĭ], adv. tristemente.—**ruefulness** [-nĭs], s. tristeza, pena, pesar.

ruff [rʌf], s. (cost.) lechuguilla, gorguera, golilla, escarola; collarín de plumas o de pelo de algunos animales; gallineta de collar; pavo marino.

ruffed [-t], a. de collar, que tiene collar o collarín. —**r. grouse**, guaco norteamericano, especie de perdiz grande con collarín y moño.

ruffian [rʌ́fi̯an], a. y s. rufián, bergante, belitre.— **ruffianism** [-ĭzm], s. bellaquería.—**ruffianly**, **ruffianlike** [-lĭ, -lai̯k], a. forajido, arrufianado.

ruffle [rʌ́fl]. I. va. (cost.) fruncir un volante, rizar; ajar, arrugar, descomponer, desordenar; encrespar; desazonar, exhalar, irritar; vejar; redoblar (el tambor). II. vn. rizarse, arrugarse. III. s. (cost.) volante fruncido; desazón, f., enojo, enfado; escarceo del agua; redoble de tambor.

rufous [rúfʌs], a. rufo, bermejo, leonado.

rug [rʌg], s. alfombr(ill)a, ruedo, tapete; felpudo; manta de viaje.

rugate [rúgei̯t], a. = RUGOSE.

rugged [rʌ́gid], a. áspero, escarpado, escabroso, abrupto; tosco, basto; inculto; desapacible; bronco; descomedido, desvergonzado; arrugado, ceñudo, regañón; desgreñado; robusto, vigoroso; tempestuoso o borrascoso.—**ruggedly** [-li], adv. rudamente; ásperamente.—**ruggedness** [-nis], s. rudeza; aspereza, escabrosidad; robustez.

rugose, rugous [rúgoṣ, rúgʌs], a. rugoso, arrugado, rizado.

rugosity [rugásiti], s. rugosidad.

ruin [rúin]. I. s. ruina, caída; bancarrota; estrago, destrucción; tala, devastación; degradación, perdición.—pl. escombros, ruinas; vestigios. II. va. arruinar, devastar, destruir; dar al traste con, echar a perder; desbaratar; estropear; seducir, perder (a una mujer). III. vn. caer en ruinas, arruinarse; decaer.

ruination [ruinéiṣǫn], s. arruinamiento, ruina, perdición.

ruinous [rúinʌs], a. ruinoso, desmantelado; desastroso, fatal, funesto.—**ruinously** [-li], adv. perniciosa o ruinosamente.—**ruinousness** [-nis], s. arruinamiento; calidad de desastroso.

rulable [rúlạbl], a. gobernable, dirigible, dócil, manejable; permisible.

rule [rúl]. I. s. regla; gobierno, mando, poder, dominio, autoridad; soberanía; régimen, reinado; estatuto, precepto, canon; arreglo, regularidad, buen orden; (arq.) ságoma, escantillón; regla graduada, metro; regla de trazar líneas, pauta; (fig.) norma, guía, modelo; (for.) auto, fallo de un tribunal; (impr.) pleca, raya, filete; raya, línea trazada.—**r. book**, reglamento.—**r. of false position**, (mat.) regla de falsa posición.—**r. of the road**, reglamento del tráfico (apl. esp. al de automóviles).—**r. of three**, (mat.) regla de tres.—**rules and regulations**, reglamento.—**r. of thumb**, regla empírica; método empírico.—**as a r.**, por regla general, por lo general.—**to be the r.**, ser la regla; ser de reglamento. II. va. gobernar, mandar, regir; reprimir, contener; (for.) decidir, determinar, disponer; dirigir, guiar; arreglar, ordenar; rayar, reglar (papel).—**to r. out**, excluir; descartar; no admitir, desechar.—**to r. the roost** (o **roast**), (fam.) mandar, dominar, tener vara alta. III. vn. gobernar, mandar; establecer una regla, formular una decisión; prevalecer, estar en boga, privar; (com.) mantenerse a un tipo.—**to r. over**, mandar, gobernar, dominar.

ruled surface [-d sœ́rfis], s. (geom.) superficie reglada.

ruler [-œ(r)], s. soberano, príncipe; gobernador, gobernante; pauta, regla (para trazar líneas).

ruling [-iŋ]. I. s. (for.) decisión, fallo, disposición; rayadura; rayado. II. a. gobernante, imperante. —**r. grade**, (f. c.) pendiente determinante.—**r. machine**, máquina de rayar.—**r. pen**, tiralíneas.—**r. price**, (com.) precio predominante.

rum [rʌm]. I. s. ron; aguardiente de caña; cualquier bebida alcohólica. II. a. (fam.) extraño, singular.

Rumanian [ruméinian], s. y a. rumano.

rumble [rʌmbl]. I. vn. retumbar, rugir; avanzar con estruendo. II. va. hacer retumbar, etc. III. s. rumor, ruido sordo y prolongado; estruendo.—**r. (seat)**, (aut.) asiento trasero descubierto; pescante situado detrás de un coche.

rumbler [-blœ(r)], s. lo que hace un ruido sordo y continuo.—**rumbling** [-bliŋ]. I. s. ruido sordo y continuo, retumbo, rumor. II. a. rumoroso, retumbante y sordo.—**rumbly** [-bli], a. áspero, escabroso (ú. de un camino, etc.). V. RUMBLING.

rumen [rúmin], s. (zool.) rumen, panza.

ruminant [rúminạnt]. I. a. y s. (zool.) rumiante. II. a. (fig.) meditativo.

ruminate [rúminęit], va. y vn. rumiar; considerar, reflexionar.—**rumination** [-éiṣǫn], s. rumia, rumiadura; meditación.—**ruminative** [-ạtiv], a. reflexivo.

rummage [rʌ́midz]. I. va. y vn. revolver, explorar, escudriñar; (con **out** o **up**) hallar, desenterrar. II. vn. revolverlo todo en busca de algo. III. s. revuelta, trastorno, desorden.—**r. sale**, venta de cosas usadas o donadas con el fin de allegar fondos para obras caritativas; venta de rezagos o de artículos no reclamados.

rummy [rʌ́mi]. I. s. cierto juego de naipes; (fam.) borracho. II. a. pert. o semejante al ron; (fam.) extraño, raro.

rumor [rúmǫ(r)]. I. s. rumor, runrún. II. va. divulgar, propalar.—**it is rumored**, se dice, se rumorea, corre la voz o la especie.

rump [rʌmp], s. rabadilla u obispillo de ave; anca o grupa de caballo, etc.; nalgas; cadera de vaca; resto, retazo.

rumple [rʌmpl]. I. va. arrugar, ajar, chafar. II. s. arruga, doblez, m., ajamiento, estrujadura.

rumpus [rʌ́mpas], s. (fam.) batahola, zipizape.

rumrunner [rʌ́mrʌnœ(r)], s. importador de licor de contrabando; transportador de licor.

run [rʌn]. I. va. (pret. RAN; pp. RUN) correr, hacer correr (to run a horse, correr un caballo); mover, poner en movimiento; dejar correr o salir (agua de un grifo, etc.); meter, clavar, introducir; empujar, impeler, echar; cazar, perseguir; tirar, trazar (una línea, en el papel o el terreno); pasar (la vista); atravesar, cruzar; derramar, verter, manar; correr (un peligro); fundir, moldear; (cost.) bastear; tener o proponer como candidato; mandar, dominar; manejar, dirigir (una máquina, institución, empresa).—**to r. a blockade**, violar un bloqueo, burlar un bloqueo.—**to r. a level line**, (top.) hacer una nivelación, trazar una línea de cotas.—**to r. a race**, luchar a la carrera, a correr.—**to r. a risk**, correr riesgo o peligro.—**to r. a temperature**, tener fiebre.—**to r. down**, dar caza; (mar.) echar a pique; vilipendiar, difamar, hablar mal de; quebrantar, postrar; gastar (la salud, etc.).—**to r. in**, recorrer; encerrar; (fam.) prender; (impr.) = TO RUN ON.—**to r. into the ground**, meter en la tierra; extender hasta más abajo del suelo; (fam.) llevar al exceso.—**to r. off**, desviar; desecar, vaciar; repetir, decir de coro; imprimir. —**to r. on**, (impr.) poner de seguido, sin párrafo.—**to r. one's o, the, chances**, correr los riesgos.—**to r. out**, agotar; desperdiciar; (fam.) echar.—**to r. over**, atropellar, pasar encima de; hojear, repasar, revisar de prisa.—**to r. the danger**, correr el peligro.—**to r. the gantlet**, pasar por baquetas.—**to r. the hazard** = TO R. THE DANGER.—**to r. through**, ver, examinar, presentar, etc., a la ligera; atravesar, pasar de parte a parte; traspasar; hojear, leer por encima; gastar, derrochar, malbaratar.—**to r. up**, (cost.) remendar, repasar; incurrir, hacer subir (una cuenta); sumar, hacer una suma; montar o edificar de prisa; (mar.) izar (vela, bandera, etc.). II. vn. correr; pasar, deslizarse, volar; marchar, andar, funcionar, moverse (un buque, un reloj, una máquina); derretirse, fluir, gotear o chorrear; derramarse; correrse (un color, etc.); competir, lidiar (vg. to run a race, apostar a correr); ser candidato, presentarse (para presidente, etc.); (med.) supurar; (teat.) representarse consecutivamente; extenderse, ir, llegar (hasta), correr, transcurrir; inclinarse, tener predilección; continuar, durar; rezar, decir (the deed runs thus, la escritura reza así); ser, salir (mineral, carbón, tamaños, etc.); tener curso, circular; salirse, dejar fugar el agua, etc.; ir, andar, hallarse (en manadas, etc.).—**to r. about**, andar de lugar en lugar; andar de una parte a otra; corretear.—**to r. across**, atravesar corriendo; hallar; dar o tropezar con.—**to r. after**, ir tras de; seguir; perseguir; buscar, andar buscando.—**to r. against**, chocar, topar, dar contra; oponerse; ser contrario a.—**to r. aground**, (mar.) encallar.—**to r. ahead**, correr delante; llevar ventaja.—**to r. along**, correr a lo largo de; ir, correr.—**to r. amuck**, perder la chaveta, atacar a diestra y siniestra.—**to r. away**, huir; escaparse, zafarse; desbocarse.—**to r. away with**, arrebatar; fugarse con; (fam.) llevarse la palma en, monopolizar, ser el protagonista en.—**to r. back**, retroceder, volver atrás.—**to r. behind**, correr detrás; quedarse atrás; atrasarse; no hacer frente a sus gastos.—**to r. counter**, oponerse a; ir en contra de.—**to r. down**, acabarse la cuerda de (un reloj); dejar de funcionar por falta de vapor, agua, etc.; agotarse, debilitarse.—**to r. foul of**, (mar.) chocar, abordar.—**to r. (a)foul of the law**, meterse o habérselas con la policía.—**to r. in**, entrar; entrar al pasar; ir un momento.—**to r. in the blood, o in the family**, venir de casta, estar en la sangre.—**to r. into**, meterse de cabeza en; topar, chocar con(tra); pasar a, convertirse en; parar en; internarse en.—**to r. mad**, enloquecerse; ser atacado de hidrofobia.—**to r. off**, huir; derramarse, fugarse (un líquido); (com.) estar pagado (pagaré, etc.); agotarse; salirse de.—**to r. off the rails, u off the track**, descarrilarse.—**to r. off with**, huirse con.—**to r. on** = TO R. UPON; continuar.—**to r. out**, salir; salirse; esparcirse, escurrirse, derramarse; gastarse, acabarse; expirar, terminar.—**to r. out of**, no tener más, habérsele acabado a uno.—**to r. over**, rebosar, derramarse, salirse (un líquido); pasar al otro lado.—**to r. short**, hallarse falto o escaso, habérsele acabado a uno.—**to r. riot**, desenfrenarse, desmandarse, desaforarse; correr a rienda suelta.—**to r. through**, hallarse o ser manifiesto en todo un escrito, plan, etc.—**to r. to**, acudir a; correr a o hacia; tener inclinación o propender a.—**to r. to seed**, granar; agotarse.—**to r. true to type**, seguir o conservar el tipo, ser del tipo legítimo (apl. a plantas y animales); no desdecir de sus antecedentes o afiliados; obrar como era de esperarse o como de usanza.—**to r. up**, acudir; crecer, aumentar.—**to r. up against**, estrellarse contra.—**to r. up and down**, correr de una parte a otra; subir y bajar corriendo.—**to r. up into, o to**, subir o llegar hasta.—**to r. upon**, versar sobre, referirse a; correr por encima de.—**to r. wild**, volver al estado primitivo; desenfrenarse.—**to r. with**, estar saturado o empapado de; manar, abundar en.—**as they r.**, (com.) al barrer, sin escoger.—**to be running for**, ser, o estar de, candidato para. **III.** *a.* extraído; vaciado; derretido; (fam.) de contrabando.—**r. metal**, metal derretido. **IV.** *s.* corrida, carrera; curso, marcha; batida de caza; (mil.) marcha forzada; vuelta, viajecito, excursión, jornada; recorrido, trayecto; distancia; (mar.) singladura; (mec.) marcha, movimiento, funcionamiento; serie, continuación; duración, vida; hilo (del discurso); (teat.) serie de representaciones consecutivas de una pieza; lo que sale o se saca cada vez (hornada, vaciado, etc.); libre uso, discreción o libertad en el uso de algo; mando, dirección; carrera (en una media); carrera, *ron* (en el béisbol); asedio de un banco por los imponedores; terreno de pasto; migración; (ar)ribazón, *f.* (de peces); clase, *f.*, tipo; aspecto, carácter; producto al natural o como sale (de la mina, etc.); (min.) dirección; caída (de la caja de un elevador); galería inclinada, paso; distancia; (mús.) escala; (mar.) racel.—**r. of mine**, producto (mineral, carbón, etc.) tal como sale de la mina.—**in the long r.**, a la larga.—**the (common) run**, el común de las gentes; lo común, lo corriente.

runabout [ránəbạut], *s.* vagabundo; (carr.) birlocho; (aut.) coche pequeño de un solo asiento.

runagate [ránəgeit], *s.* (ant.) renegado, apóstata, *m.*; fugitivo; vagamundo.

runaway [ránəwei], **I.** *a.* y *s.* tránsfuga, *mf.*, fugitivo, desertor. **II.** *s.* fuga; rapto, secuestro; desbocamiento; caballo desbocado.—**r. infla-**

tion, (com.) inflación rápida.—**r. marriage, o r. match**, casamiento que sigue a un secuestro o fuga.—**r. race o victory**, victoria fácil y decisiva.

runcinate [ránsineit], *a.* (bot.) dentado hacia atrás.

rundle [rándl], *s.* peldaño de escal(er)a; rueda.

run-down [rándáun], *a.* agotado, debilitado; ruinoso, maltrecho; parado (un reloj, por habérsele acabado la cuerda).

rune [run], *s.* runa; misterio.

rung [rəŋ]. **I.** *pret.* y *pp.* de TO RING. **II.** *s.* peldaño de escala, travesaño de silla; listón, barrote.

runic [rúnik]. **I.** *a.* rúnico, runo. **II.** *s.* (impr.) tipo rúnico.

run-in [ránin], *s.* (fam.) reyerta, encuentro.

runlet, runnel [ránlit, ránəl], *s.* arroyuelo.

runner [ránœ(r)], *s.* corredor; peatón, andarín; pieza o parte giratoria o corrediza; correo, mensajero; (fam.) correve(i)dile, *mf.*; tránsfuga, *mf.*, o tránsfugo, fugitivo; contrabandista; maquinista o agente, factor; alguacil, corchete; corredera, volandera, muela (de molino); alfombra continua o pasacaminos; guía; anillo movible; pasador corredizo; hoja (de un patín); canal (para metal fundido); (bot.) sarmiento, tallo rastrero, serpa, jerpa; (hidr.) rueda móvil (de turbina); (aer.) patín o zapata de aterrizaje.—**r. of a tackle**, (mar.) amante de aparejo.

runner-up [-áp], *s.* jugador o equipo que queda en segundo lugar en un torneo.

running [rániŋ]. **I.** *s.* carrera, corrida, curso; matute, contrabando; funcionamiento o marcha (de una máquina); celo de ciertos animales; (med.) corrimiento; (mar.) laboreo.—**to be in the r.**, tener posibilidades de ganar. **II.** *a.* corredor; corriente; correntío, manantío (mapa); en marcha; que funciona (*this elevator not r.*, no funciona este ascensor); (med.) supurante; rápido, por encima; repetido.—**r. block**, polea movible.—**r. board**, estribo (de coche, locomotora).—**r. expenses**, gastos corrientes.—**r. fight**, combate en retirada.—**r. gate**, bebedero de orificio alimentador (de un molde).—**r. gear**, ejes y ruedas de un vehículo; tren de rodaje; mecanismo (a distinción de la armazón).—**r. hand**, letra corrida.—**r. knot**, nudo corredizo.—**r. lights**, luces de situación o de costado.—**r. title**, (impr.) título de página, titulillo.—**r. water**, agua corriente, agua viva.—**twice r.**, dos veces seguidas, consecutivas, o de corrido.

runoff [ránof]. **I.** *s.* agua de desagüe; (dep., equit.) carrera final y decisiva. **II.** *a.* final, decisivo; de desagüe.

runround [ránraund], *s.* (med., fam.) panadizo.

runt [rant], *s.* (fam.) redrojo; enano; (orn.) paloma.

runway [ránwei], *s.* lecho, madre, *f.*, cauce; senda; rampa; (aer.) pista (de aterrizaje); vía (gen. de rieles).

rupee [rupí], *s.* rupia (moneda).

Rupert's drops [rúpœrts draps], *s. pl.* lágrimas de Batavia.

rupestrian [rupéstriạn], *a.* rupestre.

rupture [rápchụ(r)]. **I.** *s.* rompimiento, rotura, fractura; reventazón, *f.*; ruptura, desavenencia; (med.) hernia, quebradura, (fam.) potra. **II.** *va.* romper, fracturar, quebrar; reventar. **III.** *vn.* abrirse, romperse, rajarse, reventar.

rural [rúrạl], *a.* rural, rústico, campesino, campestre.—**r. free delivery**, distribución gratuita del correo en regiones rurales.—**r. postman**, peatón, hijuelero.

rurally [-i], *adv.* ruralmente.

ruse [ruz], *s.* ardid, astucia, artimaña.

rush [rásh], *s.* ímpetu, embestida, acometida; prisa, precipitación; torrente, tropel, agolpamiento, asedio; tierra rica en oro; lucha, rebatiña; (bot.) junco, junquera, junquillo, enea; friolera, bagatela.—**r.-bottomed**, con asiento de enea.—**r. candle**, vela de junco y sebo.—**r. mat**, estera de junco.—**r. rope**, aderra.—**it is not worth a r.**, no vale un bledo o un ardite.—**there's no r. about it**, no corre prisa.—**with a r.**, de golpe; de repente. **II.** *vn.* lanzarse, abalanzarse, precipitarse; embestir, acometer; agolparse.—**to r. forward**, lanzarse.—**to r. in**, entrar precipitadamente o de rondón.—**to r. in upon**, sorprender.—**to r. out**, salir con precipitación.—**to r. through**, lanzarse por entre o a través de. **III.** *va.* empujar o arrojar con violencia; activar, despachar con prontitud, acelerar, precipitar; en el fútbol, llevar el balón a través del campo enemigo.—**to r. through**, ejecutar de prisa.

rusher [-œ(r)], *s.* embestidor; persona enérgica.

rushlight [-lait], *s.* vela de junco; luz débil.

rushy [-i], *a.* juncoso, juncino.

rusk [rʌsk], *s.* galleta, sequillo, rosca; bizcocho.

russet [rásit]. **I.** *a.* bermejo; burdo, tosco, grosero.—**r. leather**, cuero bermejo. **II.** *s.* color bermejo; paño burdo; cuero bermejo; (bot.) variedad de manzana.

russety [-i], *a.* bermejizo.

russia [rásḁ], *s.* piel (f.) de Rusia; vaqueta de Moscovia (ll. t. **R. leather**).

Russian [-n], *a.* y *s.* ruso.

rust [rʌst]. **I.** *s.* orín, herrumbre, moho; (bot.) añublo, tizón, roya; hongo que produce esa enfermedad. **II.** *va.* y *vn.* enmohecer(se), aherrumbrar(se); entorpecer(se), embotar(se).

rustic [rástik]. **I.** *a.* rústico, rural; agrario, agreste; aldeano, campestre, campesino; sencillo; inculto, palurdo.—**r. work**, cosas (muebles, adornos, etc.) hechas de madera al natural; mampostería acanalada o de juntas rebajadas. **II.** *s.* rústico, campesino, palurdo, villano.

rustically [-ali], *adv.* rústicamente.

rusticate [-eit]. **I.** *vn.* rusticar, veranear. **II.** *va.* enviar al campo; (Ingl.) expulsar de un colegio; (arq.) biselar las juntas.

rustication [-éişǫn], *s.* rusticación.

rusticity [rʌstísiti], *s.* rusticidad, rustiquez.

rustily [rástili], *adv.* con herrumbre, enmohecimiento o falta de uso.

rustiness [-nis], *s.* enmohecimiento, herrumbre; torpeza; falta de uso.

rustle [rásl]. **I.** *va.* y *vn.* susurrar, crujir (la seda), murmurar (las hojas); (fam.) = HUSTLE; (fam.) hurtar ganado. **II.** *s.* susurro, crujido, murmullo.

rustler [ráslœ(r)], *s.* (fam.) hombre activo o emprendedor; (fam.) abigeo, hurtador de ganado.

rustless [rástlis], *a.* sin herrumbre: inoxidable.

rustproof [rástpruf], *a.* inoxidable, a prueba de orín o herrumbre, etc.

rusty [rásti], *a.* mohoso, herrumbroso; rojizo o amarillento; entorpecido, torpe por falta de práctica; (bot.) añublado, atizonado.

rut [rʌt]. **I.** *va.* hacer rodadas o surcos. **II.** *vn.* bramar los venados, etc., estar en celo. **III.** *s.* rodada, surco, releje, bache, hoyo; rutina, costumbre, hábito arraigado; sendero trillado; brama, toriondez, celo (de los animales); mugido; bramido; ruido, batahola, alboroto.—**rutting time**, tiempo de brama, estación del celo, verriondez.

rutabaga [rutabéigḁ], *s.* (bot.) naba.

rutaceous [rutéişʌs], *a.* (bot.) rutáceo.

ruth [ruθ], *s.* (ant.) compasión; dolor, tristeza.

Ruthene [ruθín], *s.*, **Ruthenian** [-iạn], *s.* y *a.* ruteno.

ruthenium [-iʌm], *s.* (quím.) rutenio.

ruthless [rúθlis], *a.* cruel, despiadado, inhumano, insensible, empedernido.—**ruthlessly** [-li], *adv.* cruelmente, sin piedad.—**ruthlessness** [-nis], *s.* crueldad, empedernimiento.

rutile [rútil], *s.* (min.) rutilo o rútilo.

ruttish [rátiş], *a.* toriondo, salido, verriondo.

rutty [ráti], *a.* lleno de rodadas.

rye [rai], *s.* (bot.) centeno; whisky de centeno

(ll. t. **r. whisky**).—**r. field**, centenal.—**r. grass**, (bot.) ballico.—**r. straw**, paja centenaza.

ryot [ráiǫt], *s.* en la India, labrador, labriego.

S

s [es], *s.* **s.**—**'s**, de, el de (signo del posesivo: *this book is John's*, este libro es de Juan, o el de Juan).—**'s**, contr. de IS o HAS (*he's here*, está aquí; *he's lost it*, lo ha perdido).

S. I. *a.* en S, de forma de S.—**S bend**, codo, junta acodada.—**S brake**, freno de dos zapatas y palanca acodada.—**S-shaped**, sigmoideo. **II.** *s.* curva en S; junta en S o acodada; barra, tubo, etc., en S.

sabadilla [sæbạdílạ], *s.* (bot.) cebadilla.

Sabæan, Sabean [seibíạn], *a.* y *s.* sabeo.

Sabaoth [sébiạθ], *s. pl.* (bib.) ejércitos.

Sabbatarian [sæbạtériạn], *a.* y *s.* sabatario (apl. hoy a los que guardan santamente el domingo o el sábado, conforme a su religión).

Sabbath [sébạθ], *s.* día (*m.*) de descanso en cada semana (sábado entre los judíos, domingo entre los cristianos).

Sabbatic(al [sạbétik(ạl], *a.* sabático, sabatino.

saber [séibœ(r)]. **I.** *s.* sable. **II.** *va.* acuchillar, herir a sablazos.

Sabian [séibiạn], *a.* y *s.* sabeo.

Sabianism [-izm], *s.* sabeísmo.

sabine [séibain], *s.* (bot.) sabina.—**(S.)**, *s.* y *a.* sabino.

sable [séibl]. **I.** *s.* (zool.) cebellina, marta cebellina; su piel, *f.* **II.** *a.* (blas.) sable, negro.

sabot [sébou], *s.* zueco, almadreña.

sabotage [sébotaʒ]. **I.** *s.* sabotaje. **II.** *va.* y *vn.* cometer sabotaje (contra, en).

sabre [séibœ(r)], *s.* = SABER.

sabulous [sébiulʌs], *a.* sabuloso, arenoso.

sac [sæk], *s.* (bot., zool.) saco, bolsa, cavidad, receptáculo.

saccate [sékeit], *a.* (bot. y zool.) en forma de bolsa o saco; saculiforme; enquistado.

saccharate [sékạreit], *s.* (quím.) sacarato.

saccharic [sạkérik], *a.* (quím.) sacárico.

sacchariferous [sækạrífẹrʌs], *a.* sacarífero.

saccharification [sạkærifikéişǫn], *s.* (quím.) sacarificación.

saccharify [-fai], *va.* sacarificar.

saccharimeter, saccharometer [sækạríme-tœ(r), -ámetœ(r)], *s.* sacarímetro, sacarómetro.

saccharin [sékạrin], *s.* sacarina.—**saccharine, saccharous** [sékạrin, -ʌs], *a.* sacarino, azucarado.—**saccharoid** [-ɔid], *a.* sacaroideo.—**saccharose** [-ous], *s.* sacarosa.

saccharization [-izéişǫn], *s.* (quím.) sacarificación; fermentación.—**saccharize** [-aiz], *va.* sacarificar, convertir en azúcar; fermentar.

sacerdotal [sæscœrdóutạl], *a.* sacerdotal.

sacerdotalism [-izm], *s.* carácter y métodos sacerdotales; clericalismo.

sachem [séiçhem], *s.* cacique de ciertas tribus o confederaciones de indios norteamericanos.

sachet [sæşéi], *s.* perfumador, bolsita de polvo perfumado; (gal.) sachet.

sack [sæk]. **I.** *s.* saco, costal, talega; medida (variable); (mil.) saco, saqueo; botín; vino blanco generoso.—**s. coat**, saco, americana, chaqueta.—**s. race**, carrera de personas metidas en sacos.—**to get the s.**, (fam.) llevar calabazas; ser despedido (de un empleo).—**to hold the s.**, (fam.) quedar manivacío. **II.** *va.* ensacar, meter en un saco; empaquetar; envasar; saquear.

sackbut [-bʌt], *s.* (mús.) sacabuche.

sackcloth [-kloθ], *s.* (h)arpillera; cilicio.

sacker [-œ(r)], *s.* saqueador.

sackful [-ful], *s.* costal o saco lleno; lo que cabe en un saco.

sacque [sæk], *s.* saco, chaqueta.

sacral [séikrạl], *a.* (anat.) sacro.

sacrament [sǽkrəmənt], *s.* sacramento; eucaristía.—**sacramental** [-méntəl], *a.* sacramental. —**sacramentally** [-i], *adv.* sacramentalmente. —**sacramentarian** [-mentériən]. **I.** *a.* sacramental. **II.** *s.* sacramentario.—**sacramentary** [-méntəri]. **I.** *a.* sacramental. **II.** *s.* (igl.) sacramentario (libro).

sacrarium [səkréiriʌm], *s.* (igl.) sagrario; (arqueol.) capillita.

sacred [séikrid], *a.* (con)sagrado, sacro(santo), santo; inviolable.—**S. College**, (igl.) Colegio de cardenales.—**sacredly** [-li], *adv.* sagradamente, santamente.—**sacredness** [-nis], *s.* santidad, carácter de sagrado.

sacrifice [sǽkrifais]. **I.** *va.* y *vn.* sacrificar, inmolar; abandonar; (com.) malvender. **II.** *s.* sacrificio, inmolación.—**at a s.,** haciendo un sacrificio; perdiendo, con pérdida.

sacrificer [-œ(r)], *s.* sacrificador.—**sacrificial** [-fíʃal], *a.* sacrificador; de sacrificio, del sacrificio.

sacrilege [sǽkrilidʒ], *s.* sacrilegio.—**sacrilegious** [-lídʒʌs], *a.* sacrílego.—**sacrilegiously** [-li], *adv.* sacrílegamente.

sacrist [séikrist], **sacristan** [sǽkristən], *s.* (igl.) sacristán.

sacristy [-ti], *s.* (igl.) sacristía.

sacrosanct [sǽkrosæŋkt], *a.* sacrosanto.

sacrum [séikrʌm], *s.* (anat.) sacro.

sad [sæd], *a.* triste, melancólico, pesaroso; cariacontecido; conmovedor, lastimero, aciago, nefasto.

sadden [-n], *va.* y *vn.* entristecer(se); contristar(se); afligir, aquejar.

saddle [sædl]. **I.** *s.* silla de montar; enjalma; asiento, silla o sillín (de bicicleta); parte trasera de una res; (mec.) asiento, silla, soporte; cojinete, caballete de asiento (de una caldera); silla de los cilindros (de una locomotora); parte posterior del espinazo (de un ave); depresión, garganta, paso (de una montaña).—**s.-backed,** deprimido en la parte superior; ensillado; (caballo) de espalda baja y cuello largo; de espalda arqueada.—**s. cover,** acitara, telliz, *m.*—**s. gall,** matadura.—**s. horse,** caballo de silla, cabalgadura.—**s. maker** = SADDLER.—**s. of mutton,** lomo de carnero.—**s. pad,** baste, cojín.—**s. roof,** tejado de caballete o de dos aguas.—**to be in the s.,** (fig.) llevar las riendas, estar en el poder, tener la superioridad; estar listo. **II.** *va.* ensillar, enalbardar, aparejar; cargar, poner a cuestas.—**to s. with,** hacer cargar con; echar a cuestas a.

saddlebag [-bæg], *s.* alforja, jaque.

saddlebow [-bou], *s.* arzón, fuste delantero de la silla.

saddlecloth [-kloθ], *s.* sudadero, mantilla de silla.

saddler [sædlœ(r)], *s.* sillero, talabartero.

saddlery [-i], *s.* talabartería.

saddletree [sædltri], *s.* fuste de silla; tejuela, borrén.

Sadducean [sædyusən], *a.,* **Sadducee** [sædyusi], *s.* saduceo.—**Sadduceeism** [-izm], *s.* saduceísmo.

sadiron [sédaiœrn], *s.* plancha para la ropa.

sadism [séidjizm], *s.* sadismo, crueldad sexual.—**sadist** [séidist], *s.* sadista.—**sadistic(al** [seidístik(əl], *a.* sádico, sadista, sadístico.—**sadistically** [-li] *adv.* sadista o sadísticamente.

sadly [sǽdli], *adv.* tristemente.

sadness [sǽdnis], *s.* tristeza, melancolía.

safe [séif]. **I.** *a.* seguro; salvo, ileso, incólume; sin peligro, innocuo; intacto; leal, digno de confianza; cierto.—**s. and sound,** sano y salvo.—**s.-conduct,** salvoconducto, salvaguardia.—**s.-keeping,** guarda, depósito, custodia.—**s. load,** (ing.) carga de trabajo. **II.** *s.* caja de caudales, caja o cofre fuerte de hierro; despensa.

safeguard [-gard]. **I.** *s.* salvaguardia, *m.*; resguardo; carta de seguridad; defensor, escolta; defensa, abrigo. **II.** *va.* guardar, proteger, poner a salvo.

safely [-li]. *adv.* seguramente, sin peligro; a salvo, felizmente, sin novedad.

safeness [-nis], *s.* estado o condición de seguridad; ausencia o falta de peligro.

safety [-ti]. **I.** *s.* seguridad; protección; incolumidad; innocuidad; ausencia de todo mal, daño o perjuicio; salud (pública); fiador o seguro (de un arma de fuego). **II.** *a.* de seguridad.—**s. arch,** (arq.) arco de descarga.—**s. belt,** salvavidas; cinturón de seguridad.—**s. bolt,** cerrojo de seguridad, que no puede moverse desde el otro lado de la puerta; (arm.) fiador.—**s. deposit box o vault,** caja de seguridad (en un banco).—**s. device,** dispositivo de protección o de seguridad.—**s. factor,** coeficiente o factor de seguridad.—**s. fuse,** mecha de seguridad, mecha de quema lenta; (elec.) fusible.—**s. isle, o island,** isla o plataforma de seguridad (en el centro de una calle).—**s. lamp,** lámpara de seguridad.—**s. lock,** cerradura de seguridad; (arm.) seguro.—**s. match,** fósforo de seguridad (ll. en algunas partes fósforo sueco).—**s. pin,** imperdible.—**s. razor,** maquinilla de seguridad, navaja de afeitar de seguridad.—**s. stop,** mecanismo de detención o de parada.—**s. valve,** (mec.) válvula de seguridad.—**s. zone,** zona de seguridad o de peatones, demarcación (en una calle) para el uso exclusivo de peatones.

safflower [sǽflauœ(r)], *s.* (bot.) alazor, cártamo.

saffranin(e [sǽfranin], **saffron yellow,** *s.* (quím.) azafranina.

saffron [sǽfron]. **I.** *s.* (bot.) azafrán, croco. **II.** *a.* azafranado. **III.** *va.* azafranar.

sag [sæg]. **I.** *va.* combar, empandar. **II.** *vn.* combarse; estirarse y combarse en el centro; aflojarse, ceder, doblegarse; hundirse; desplomarse, desviarse de la vertical; rezagarse; vagar; (mar.) irse a la ronza, sotaventarse. **III.** *s.* comba; pandeo; flecha (de un cable, etc., combado).

saga [ságə], *s.* saga (leyenda).

sagacious [səgéiʃʌs], *a.* sagaz, perspicaz; ladino, vivo.—**sagaciously** [-li], *adv.* sagazmente, ladinamente.—**sagaciousness** [-nis], **sagacity** [səgǽsiti], *s.* sagacidad, perspicacia; astucia.

sagamore [sǽgəmor], *s.* cacique inferior. *V.* SACHEM.

sagapenum [sægǽpinəm], *s.* sagapeno.

sage [séidʒ]. **I.** *s.* (bot.) salvia; sabio, filósofo. **II.** *a.* sabio; grave; sagaz; cuerdo, prudente.—**sagely** [-li], *adv.* sabiamente; cuerdamente.—**sageness** [-nis], *s.* sabiduría.

sagebrush [-braʃ], *s.* (bot.) artemisia.

saggar, sagger [sǽgə(r)], *s.* receptáculo refractario de cocción.

sagittal [sædʒitəl], *a.* sagital.

sagittaria [sædʒitériə], *s.* (bot.) sagitaria, saetilla.

Sagittarius [-ʌs], *s.* (astr.) Sagitario.

sagittate [sǽdʒiteit], *a.* sagital.

sago [séigou], *s.* (bot.) sagú.

saguaro [səgwárou], *s.* (bot.) pitahaya.

sahib [sáib], *s.* señor (tratamiento persa e indio).

said [sed], *pret.* y *pp.* de TO SAY; el tal, el mencionado o citado; (for.) dicho, antedicho.—**s. and done,** dicho y hecho.

sail [séil]. **I.** *s.* (mar.) vela; buque, nave, *f.* (en esta acepción el plural es como el singular); excursión o paseo en barco; aspa, vela (de molino).—*pl.* velamen.—**s. loft,** tinglado o almacén de velas.—**s. yard,** verga.—**under full s.,** a toda vela, a todo trapo. **II.** *vn.* darse a la vela; zarpar; salir (un buque); navegar; dar un paseo o viajar por mar, río o lago; ir embarcado; flotar, mecerse en el aire; deslizarse.—**to s. against wind and tide,** ir contra viento y marea.—**to s. along the coast,** costear.—**to s. before the wind,** navegar viento en popa.—**to s. close with the wind,** ceñir el viento, bolinear.—**to s. into,** (fam.) embestir; criticar; sermonear.—**to s. under convoy,** navegar en conserva. **III.** *va.* gobernar (una embarcación); navegar por, surcar.

sailable [-ặbl], *a.* navegable.
sailboat [-boụt], *s.* barco de vela, balandro, velero.
sailcloth [-klɔθ], *s.* lona o paño para hacer velas.
sailer [-œ(r)], *s.* buque de vela.—**good s.**, velero.
sailfish [-fị̌s], *s.* (ict.) especie de pez espada volante.
sailing [-ịɳ]. **I.** *s.* salida, partida (de un buque); navegación, náutica; deporte de vela. **II.** *a.* de vela; de o relativo a la navegación.—**s. directions**, avisos o noticias marítimas.—**s. master**, piloto.—**s. orders**, orden (*f.*) de salida, últimas instrucciones que se dan al capitán de un buque.—**s. regatta**, regata de balandros, yates, etc.—**s. ship**, o **vessel**, buque de vela.
sailmaker [-meịkœ(r)], *s.* fabricante de velas, velero.
sailor [-ǫ(r)], *s.* marinero; marino.
sainfoin [séịnfoịn], *s.* (bot.) pipirigallo, esparceta.
saint [séịnt]. **I.** *s.* santo.—**s.'s day**, (día (*m.*) del santo. **II.** *a.* santo; como título (que generalmente se abrevia así: St.) San, Santo, Santa.—St. Andrew's cross, cruz de San Andrés.—St. Anthony's fire, (med.) fuego sacro, erisipela.—St. Bernard, perro de San Bernardo.—St. Elmo's fire, fuego de Santelmo; Cástor y Pólux.—St. George's Cross, cruz griega de la bandera inglesa.—St. John's bread, (bot.) algarroba.—St. John's wort, hierba de San Juan, hipérico, corazoncillo.—St. Valentine's Day, día de San Valentín (14 de febrero).—St. Vitus's dance, (med.) corea, baile de San Vito. **III.** *va.* (igl.) canonizar. **IV.** *vn.* (a veces con **it**) obrar como un santo.
sainted [-ịd], *a.* santo; bendito, canonizado; sagrado.—**sainthood** [-hu̯d], *s.* = SAINTSHIP.—**saintlike** [-laịk], *a.* de santo, como de santo.—**saintliness** [-lịnịs], *s.* santidad.—**saintly** [-lị], *a.* santo.—**saintship** [-sịp], *s.* santidad, carácter de santo.
Saint-Simonian [seịnt saịmóụnịạn], *s.* y *a.* sansimoniano.—**Saint-Simonianism** [-ịzm], *s.* sansimonismo.
saith [seθ], (ant.) 3*a. pers. pres. ind.* de TO SAY.
sake [seịk], *s.* causa, motivo, fin, objeto, razón, *f.*; amor, respeto, consideración. Ú. casi siempre en el caso posesivo precedido de *for*, y a veces no se traduce o se cambia el giro: *for your sake*, por Vd., por su bien, por consideración a Vd.; *for brevity's sake*, o *for the sake of brevity*, por brevedad, para mayor brevedad; *for policy's sake*, por política; *for the sake of peace*, por amor a la paz, por la paz, para conservar la paz; *for the sake of fostering education*, a fin de fomentar la educación.—**art for art's s.**, el arte por el arte.—**for conscience's s.**, por conciencia, para cumplir con la conciencia.—**for God's s.**, por Dios, por el amor de Dios.—**for mercy's s.**, por piedad, por misericordia.—**for the s. of**, en obsequio de.
saker [séịkœ(r)], *s.* (orn. y arti.) sacre.
sal [sæl], *s.* (quím. y farm.) sal, *f.*—**s. ammoniac**, sal amoníaco.—**s. soda**, sosa, carbonato de sodio.—**s. volatile**, carbonato amónico.
salaam, salam [sặlám]. **I.** *va.* y *vn.* hacer zalemas. **II.** *s.* zalema.
salability [séịlặbílịtị], **salableness** [-blnịs], *s.* facilidad de ser vendido; venta, salida.
salable [séịlặbl], *a.* vendible.
salacious [sặléịsʌs], *a.* salaz, lascivo, lujurioso.—**salaciously** [-lị], *adv.* salaz o lujuriosamente.—**salaciousness** [-nịs], **salacity** [sặlǽsịtị], *s.* salacidad, lascivia, lujuria.
salad [sǽlặd], *s.* ensalada.—**s. bowl, s. dish**, ensaladera.—**s. dressing**, salsa para ensalada; aderezo, aliño.—**s. oil**, aceite de comer, aceite de mesa.
salamander [sǽlặmǽndœ(r)], *s.* (zool.) salamandra; salamanquesa.—**s.'s hair**, o **wool**, (min.) asbesto, amianto.—**salamandrine** [sǽlặmǽndrịn], *a.* salamandrino, semejante a la salamandra; refractario.

salariat [sặléịrịạt], *s.* clases asalariadas no obreras (dependientes, profesionales, etc.).
salary [sǽlặrị], *s.* sueldo, salario, estipendio, paga.—**salaried** [-d], *a.* asalariado; con salario.
sale [seịl], *s.* venta; almoneda; liquidación, saldo; (com.) realización; venta a pública subasta; demanda, boga, mercado.—**s. by auction**, almoneda, subasta.—**s. on credit**, venta al fiado.—**s. on return**, (for.) retroventa.—**s. price**, precio de venta.—**s. representative**, agente de ventas.—**sales tax**, impuesto sobre ventas.—**for s.**, u **on s.**, de venta, en venta.
saleable, saleableness = SALABLE, -NESS.
saleratus [sælặréịtʌs], *s.* (quím., coc.) salerato, bicarbonato sódico o potásico.
Salesian [sặlíẓạn], *s.* y *a.* salesiano.
saleslady [séịlzleịdị], *s.* = SALESWOMAN.
salesman [-mạn], *s.* vendedor; dependiente de tienda, almacenista; viajante de comercio.
salesmanship [-mạnšịp], *s.* arte de vender.
salesroom [-rum], *s.* salón de ventas; lonja.
saleswoman [-wụmạn], *s.* vendedora; dependienta de tienda.
Salian [séịlịạn], *s.* y *a.*, **Salic** [sǽlịk], *a.* sálico.—**Salic law**, ley sálica.
salicaceous [sælịkéịšʌs], *a.* (bot.) salicíneo.
salicetum [sælịsítạm], *s.* salceda, saucedal.
salicin(e [sǽlịsịn], *s.* (quím.) salicina.
salicylate [sǽlịsịleịt], *s.* (quím.) salicilato.
salicylic [sælịsílịk], *a.* salicílico.
salience, saliency [séịlịẹns, -ị], *s.* calidad de sobresaliente; lo que sobresale; prominencia.
salient [-ẹnt]. **I.** *s.* saliente, *f.*, proyección, resalto; esquina, ángulo. **II.** *a.* saliente, saledizo, saltante; que sobresale; prominente, notorio.
saliferous [sặlífẹrʌs], *a.* (geol.) salífero.
salifiable [sélịfaịạbl], *a.* (quím.) salificable.
salify [sélịfaị], *va.* (quím.) salificar.
salina [sặláịnặ], *s.* salina (establecimiento); fuente (*f.*) de agua salina; salina marítima, charco artificial de agua de mar para obtener sal.
saline [séịlaịn], *a.* salino.—**salineness** [-nịs], **salinity** [sặlínịtị], *s.* salinidad.
salinometer [sælịnámetœ(r)], *s.* salinómetro.
salipyrin(e [sælịpáịrịn], *s.* (quím., med.) salipirina.
saliva [sặláịvặ], *s.* saliva; esputo.—**salivary** [sǽlịverị], *a.* y *s.* salival.—**s. gland**, glándula salival.—**salivant** [-ạnt], *s.* y *a.* (med.) sialogogo.—**salivate** [-eịt], *vn.* (med.) (de)salivar.—**salivation** [-éịšọn], *s.* (de)salivación; babeo.
salivous [sặláịvʌs], *a.* salivoso.
sallow [sǽloụ]. **I.** *a.* cetrino, pálido, lívido. **II.** *s.* (bot.) sarga, sauce.—**sallowness** [-nịs], *s.* palidez, amarillez, lividez.
sally [sǽlị]. **I.** *s.* (mil.) salida, surtida; paseo, excursión; ímpetu o arranque; humorada; salida de pie de banco; (arq.) saledizo, saliente, *f.*, vuelo.—**s. of wit**, agudeza, ocurrencia chistosa. **II.** *vn.* (a veces con *forth*) salir, hacer una salida; tener un arranque; avanzar con denuedo.
sallyport [-pɔrt], *s.* (fort.) surtida, poterna.
salmagundi [sælmặgándị], *s.* salpicón, picadillo; mescolanza.
salmon [sǽmọn], *s.* (ict.) salmón; color de salmón.—**s. trout**, trucha salmonada.
salmonet [-ẹt], *s.* salmón joven o aún pequeño.
salol [sǽloụl], *s.* (quím.) salol.
salon [sặlán], *s.* salón, sala; exposición anual de cuadros.
saloon [sặlún], *s.* salón, gran sala; cámara de un vapor; (E. U.) taberna, cantina; (Ingl.) (f. c.) coche salón.—**s. keeper**, tabernero, cantinero.
salpa [sǽlpặ], *s.* (zool.) salpa.
salse [sæls], *s.* volcán de cieno.
salsify [sǽlsịfị], *s.* (bot.) salsifí.
salt [sɔlt]. **I.** *s.* sal, *f.*; (quím.) sal; sabor, gusto; sal ática, agudeza, ingenio chispeante; (fam.) marinero; (fig.) reserva, duda. *V.* GRAIN.—*pl.* sales medicinales; en especial, sal de la Higuera, sulfato de magnesia.—**not worth one's s.**,

no valer uno el pan que come. **II.** *a.* salado; salobre; curado o conservado con sal.—**s. box,** salero de cocina.—**s.-bush,** (bot.) hierba de pasto.—**s. lick,** salegar, salero, lamedero.—**s. maker,** salinero.—**s. marsh,** saladar o marisma.—**s. meat,** carne salada, cecina.—**s. mine,** mina de sal; salina.—**s. pan,** caldera de saladar, salina.—**s. pit,** saladar, lagunajo; salina.—**s. pork,** tocino salado.—**s. rheum,** (med.) dermatosis reumática.—**s. shaker,** salero (de mesa).—**s. spring,** fuente (*f.*) de agua salada.—**s. tub,** saladero.—**s. water,** agua de mar, agua salada.—**s. well,** pozo de agua salada.—**s. works,** salina. **III.** *va.* salar, salpresar, marinar, arencar, curar con sal; (fig.) sazonar; purificar; poner mineral secretamente en una mina para darle valor.—**to s. away,** (fam.) reservar para uso futuro; ahorrar.

saltant [sǽltant], *a.* saltante.

saltation [sæltéiʃǫn], *s.* saltación, salto; palpitación; (biol.) variación brusca.

saltatorial [sæltǝtórial], **saltatory** [-tǫri], *a.* saltón.

saltcellar [sɔ́ltselǝ(r)], *s.* salero de mesa.

salted [sɔ́ltid], *a.* salado; (fam.) perito, experimentado.

salter [sɔ́ltœ(r)], *s.* salador; salinero, curador.

saltern [sɔ́ltœrn], *s.* salina (fábrica); saladar.

saltier [sǽltir], *s.* (blas.) sotuer.

saltigrade [sǽltigreid], *a.* saltígrado.

salting [sɔ́ltin], *s.* saladura.—**s. tub,** saladero.

saltish [-iʃ], *a.* salobre, un poco salado.

saltless [-lis], *a.* sin sal; soso, insulso, insípido.

saltness [-nis], *s.* sabor de sal; salsedumbre.

saltpan [-pæn], *s.* paila o receptáculo para evaporar agua salada; charco artificial de agua salada.—*pl.* salina (establecimiento).

saltpeter, saltpetre [-pítœ(r)], *s.* nitro, salitre.—**s. house** o **works,** nitrería; salitrería.—**s. maker** o **worker,** salitrero.

saltwort [-wœrt], *s.* (bot.) barrilla, sosa.

salty [sɔ́lti], *a.* salado; salobre.

salubrious [sǝljúbriǝs], *a.* salubre, salutífero, saludable, sano.—**salubriously** [-li], *adv.* salutíferamente.—**salubrity, salubriousness** [sǝljúbriti, -nis], *s.* salubridad.

salutariness [sǽlyutǝrinis], *s.* salubridad.

salutary [sǽlyutǝri], *a.* saludable; salubre, sano, salutífero.

salutation [-téiʃǫn], *s.* salutación, saludo; bienvenida, enhorabuena, parabién.

salutatory [sǝljútǝtǫri]. **I.** *a.* saludador. **II.** *s.* discurso de bienvenida.

salute [sǝljút]. **I.** *va.* y *vn.* saludar; (mil.) saludar; cuadrarse. **II.** *s.* salutación; saludo; (mil.) saludo, salva.

salvability [sælvǝbíliti], **salvableness** [-blnis], *s.* posibilidad de ser redimido o de salvarse.

salvable [-bl], *a.* que puede salvarse.

Salvador(e)an, Salvadorian [sælvǝdór(i)ǝn], *s.* y *a.* salvadoreño.

salvage [sǽlvidʒ]. **I.** *s.* salvamento.—**s. money,** derecho de salvamento. **II.** *va.* salvar; recobrar.

salvarsan [sǽlvǝrsæn], *s.* (farm.) salvarsán (es nombre de fábrica).

salvation [sælvéiʃǫn], *s.* salvación, salvam(i)ento; redención.—**S. Army,** Ejército de Salvación (organización religiosa).

Salvationist [-ist], *s.* miembro del Ejército de Salvación.

salve [sæv o sav]. **I.** *s.* emplasto, ungüento, pomada; socorro, remedio.—**S. Regina,** salve, *f.* (oración). **II.** *va.* curar (una herida) con ungüentos o emplastos; salvar; socorrer; remediar.

salver [sǽlvœ(r)], *s.* salva, salvilla, bandeja.

salvia [sǽlviǝ], *s.* (bot.) salvia.

salvo [sǽlvou], *s.* (mil.) salva de artillería; aplausos, aclamaciones populares; salvedad, reservación.

samara [sǽmǝrǝ], *s.* (bot.) sámara.

Samaritan [sǝmériṭǝn], *a.* y *s.* samaritano; persona benévola y caritativa.

samarium [sǝmériʌm], *s.* (quím.) samario.

sambo, zambo [sǽmbou, zǽmbou], *s.* zambo; persona de sangre india y negra o mulata; mestizo; (S., fam.) negro o mulato.

sambuca [sæmbiúkǝ], *s.* (mús.) sambuca.

same [séim], *a.* y *pron.* mismo; igual, idéntico.—**all the s.,** a pesar de eso, a pesar de todo.—**at the s. time,** a la vez, al mismo tiempo; no obstante.—**if it is the s. to you,** si le es a Vd. lo mismo, o igual; si Vd. no tiene inconveniente.—**it is all the s. to me,** para mí es todo uno; lo mismo me da.—**just the s.,** del mismo modo; a pesar de eso.—**much the s.,** casi lo mismo.—**much the s. as,** casi como.—**the s.,** lo mismo, el mismo, los mismos; otro tanto: todo uno.—**the s. as,** lo mismo que, (al) igual que; **el mismo, los mismos que.**—**the s.** old story, lo de siempre, el cuento eterno.

sameness [-nis], *s.* igualdad; identidad, parecido exacto; uniformidad monótona, monotonía.

samlet [sǽmlit], *s.* = SALMONET.

Samnite [sǽmnait], *s.* y *a.*, **Samnitic** [sæmnítik], *a.* samnita, *mf.*

Samoan [sǝmóuǝn], *s.* y *a.* samoano, de las islas de Samoa (Archipiélago de los Navegantes).

samovar [sǽmovar], *s.* samovar, urna rusa para agua caliente.

samp [sæmp], *s.* (E. U.) maíz triturado o molido bastamente; potaje del mismo.

sampan [sǽmpæn], *s.* (mar.) sampán, champán.

samphire [sǽmfair], *s.* (bot.) hinojo marino.

sample [sǽmpl]. **I.** *s.* muestra, prueba, espécimen; cata; patrón.—**s. book,** muestrario.—**s. room,** cuarto de muestras; (fam.) cantina, taberna, bar. **II.** *va.* sacar una muestra; probar, catar.

sampler [sǽmplœ(r)], *s.* probador, catador; (fam.) catacaldos; dechado, labor (*f.*) de las niñas.

sanative [sǽnǝtiv], *a.* curativo, sanativo.

sanatorium [-tóriʌm], *s.* sanatorio.

sanatory [-tǫri], *a.* sanador, sanitario.

sanbenito [sænbenítou], *s.* sambenito (capotillo de penitente).

sanctification [sǽnktifikéiʃǫn], *s.* santificación; consagración.—**sanctifier** [-faiœ(r)], *s.* santificador.—**sanctify** [-fai], *va.* santificar, consagrar.

sanctimonious [-móuniǝs], *a.* beato, mojigato, santurrón, santucho.—**sanctimoniously** [-li], *adv.* con mojigatería, santurronamente, taimadamente.—**sanctimoniousness** [-nis], **sanctimony** [sǽnktimouni], *s.* santurronería, beatería.

sanction [sǽnkʃǫn]. **I.** *s.* sanción; ratificación, confirmación; justificación: pena que la ley establece para el que la infringe. **II.** *va.* sancionar; autorizar, ratificar.

sanctity [sǽnktiti], *s.* santidad, santimonia.

sanctuary [sǽnkchuǝri], *s.* santuario; asilo, refugio sagrado.—**to take s.,** acogerse a sagrado.

sanctum [sǽnktʌm], *s.* paraje sagrado; retrete.—**s. sanctorum,** sanctasanctórum.

Sanctus [sǽnktʌs], *a.* (igl.) sanctus.—**S. bell,** campanilla que anuncia la elevación de la hostia.

sand [sænd]. **I.** *s.* arena; (fam.) fuerza de carácter; valor; (fam.) dinero contante.—*pl.* granos de arena; arenales; momentos de tiempo o de vida.—**s. ballast,** (mar.) sorra.—**s. bank,** banco o bajo de arena, placer, encalladero.—**s. bar,** barra, banco de arena.—**s. bath,** (quím.) baño de arena; (med.) arenación.—**s. blast,** soplador o aventador de arena para grabar el vidrio, mármol, etc.; chorro de arena; tempestad de arena.—**s. blasting,** limpiadura por chorro de arena.—**s. box,** salvadera, arenillero; (f. c.) arenero.—**s. dollar,** (zool.) especie de erizo pequeño de mar.—**s. dune,** algaida, médano.—**s. pit,** arenal, mina de arena, hoyo de donde se saca arena. **II.** *va.* (en)arenar; (gen. con **down**) alisar con papel de lija.

sandal [sǽndạl], *s.* sandalia, abarca: alpargata (de cáñamo) ; (Méx.) guarache o huarache, cacle.

sandalwood [-wụd], *s.* (bot.) sándalo.

sandarac(h [sǽndạræk], *s.* sandáraca.—**s. tree,** (bot.) tuya.

sandbag [sǽndbæg]. **I.** *s.* saco de arena. **II.** *va.* proveer de, atacar o golpear con sacos de arena.

sanded [sǽndịd], *a.* arenoso, arenisco, arenáceo.

sanders [sǽndœrz], *s.* (bot.) sándalo.

sandglass [sǽndglæs], *s.* reloj de arena, ampolleta.

sandiness [-ịnịs], *s.* naturaleza arenosa; rubio bermejizo.

sandpaper [-peịpœ(r)]. **I.** *s.* papel de lija. **II.** *va.* lijar.

sandpiper [-paịpœ(r)], *s.* (orn.) gallineta.

sandstone [-stoụn], *s.* piedra arenisca.

sandstorm [-storm], *s.* tempestad de arena.

sandwich [-wịch]. **I.** *va.* colocar entre dos capas: intercalar, insertar. **II.** *s.* (coc.)· emparedado, bocadillo, sandwich; combinación de cosas diferentes alternadas.—**s. man,** hombre que va por las calles con cartelones colgados por delante y por detrás.

sandy [-ị], *a.* arenoso, arenisco; rufo (color).

sane [seịn], *a.* cuerdo; sano.—**sanely** [-lị], *adv.* sanamente; cuerdamente.—**saneness** [-nịs], *s.* cordura.

sang [sæŋ], *pret.* de TO SING.

sangaree [sæŋgạrí], *s.* sangría (bebida).

sang-froid [san frwá], *s.* (fr.) sangre fría.

Sangreal [sǽŋgrịạl], *s.* grial.

sanguiferous [sæŋgwíf̱ęras], *a.* sanguífero.

sanguification [sæŋgwịfịkéịsọn], *s.* sanguificación.—**sanguify** [-faị], *va.* sanguificar.

sanguinariness [-nęrịnịs], *s.* calidad de sanguinario.—**sanguinary** [-nerị], *a.* sanguinario.

sanguine [sǽŋgwịn], *a.* confiado, lleno de esperanza; sanguíneo, sanguino(so); pletórico.—**sanguinely** [-lị], *adv.* ardientemente; confiadamente.—**sanguineness** [-nịs], *s.* plenitud de esperanza, confianza o entusiasmo; plétora.

sanguineous [sæŋgwínịʌs], *a.* sanguíneo, sanguinoso; sanguinolento.

sanguinolent [-olẹnt], *a.* sanguinolento.

Sanhedrin, Sanhedrim [sǽnhịdrịn, -drịm], *s.* sanedrín, sinedrio; cualquier asamblea.

sanicle [sǽnịkl], *s.* (bot.) sanícula.

sanies [séịnịiz], *s.* (med.) sanies, *f.*, icor.

sanious [séịnịʌs], *a.* (med.) sanioso, icoroso.

sanitarian [sænịtérịạn], *a.* y *s.* sanitario.

sanitarium [-térịʌm], *s.* sanatorio, enfermería.

sanitary [sǽnịterị], *a.* sanitario.—**s. corps,** cuerpo de sanidad.

sanitation [-téịsọn], *s.* saneamiento; aplicación práctica de la ciencia sanitaria.

sanity [sǽnịtị], *s.* cordura, juicio sano, sentido común, sensatez; sanidad.

sank [sæŋk], *pret.* de TO SINK.

Sanskrit, Sanscrit [sǽnskrịt], *s.* y *a.* sánscrito.

santalaceous [sæntạléịsʌs], *a.* (bot.) santaláceo.

santon [sǽntọn], *s.* santón; derviche oriental.

santonica [sæntǽnịkạ], *s.* (bot.) santónico.

santonin(e [sǽntọnịn], *s.* (quím., farm.) santonina.

sap [sæp]. **I.** *s.* savia; (fort.) zapa. **II.** *va.* zapar, minar. **III.** *vn.* hacer trabajos de zapa; obrar por bajo mano.

sapajou [sǽpạdžu], *s.* (zool.) sapajú, zambo.

sapanwood [sǽpạnwụd], *s.* (bot.) sapán, (Fil.) sibucao.

sapful [sǽpfụl], *a.* lleno de savia.

saphena [sạfínạ], *s.* (anat.) safena (vena).

saphenous [sạfínʌs], *a.* (anat.) safeno.

sapid [sǽpịd], *a.* sápido, sabroso.

sapidity, o sapidness [sæpídịtị, sǽpịdnịs], *s.* sapidez, sabor, gusto, sainete.

sapience [séịpịẹns], **sapiency** [-ị], *s.* sapiencia, sabiduría.—**sapient** [-ẹnt], *a.* sabio.

sapindaceous [sæpịndéịsʌs], *a.* (bot.) sapindáceo.

sapless [sǽplịs], *a.* seco, sin jugo.

sapling [sǽplịŋ], *s.* renuevo, vástago, serpollo; mozuelo, mozalbete.

sapodilla [sæpodị́lạ], *s.* (bot.) chicozapote, zapotillo.

saponaceous [sæponéịsʌs], *a.* jabonoso, saponáceo.

saponifiable [sạpánịfaịạbl], *a.* saponificable.

saponification [-fịkéịsọn], *s.* saponificación.

saponify [-faị], *va.* saponificar.

saponifier [-œ(r)], *s.* saponificador.

saponin [sǽponịn], *s.* (quím.) saponina.

saporific [sæporífịk], *a.* saporífero.

sapota [sạpóụtạ], *s.* (bot.) zapote, zapotero.

sapotaceous [sæpotéịsʌs], *a.* (bot.) sapotáceo.

sapper [sǽpœ(r)], *s.* (mil.) zapador, gastador.

Sapphic [sǽfịk]. **I.** *a.* sáfico. **II.** *s.* verso sáfico.

sapphire [sǽfaịr], *s.* (min.) zafiro, zafir; color de zafiro, cerúleo.

sapphirin(e [sǽfịrịn]. **I.** *a.* zafirino. **II.** *s.* (min.) zafirina.

Sapphism [sǽfịzm], *s.* safismo.

sappiness [sǽpịnịs], *s.* abundancia de savia, jugosidad; (fam.) sentimentalismo.

sappy [sǽpị], *a.* lleno de savia; jugoso; inmaturo; (fam.) ridículamente sentimental.

saprogenic [sæprodžénịk], **saprogenous** [sæprádžẹnạs], *a.* que produce putrefacción; que se origina de la materia orgánica en descomposición.

saprophyte [sǽprofaịt], *s.* (biol.) saprófito.

saprophytic [-fítịk], *a.* saprofítico.

sapsucker [sǽpsʌkœ(r)], *s.* (orn.) especie de pájaro carpintero que destruye la albura de los árboles.

sapwood [sǽpwụd], *s.* albura, alburno; (carp.) madera alburente, sámago.

saraband [sǽrạbænd], *s.* zarabanda.

Saracen [sǽrạsen], *s.* sarraceno.

Saracenic [særạsénịk], *a.* sarracénico.

sarbacane [sárbạkeịn], *s.* cerbatana.

sarcasm [sárkæzm], *s.* sarcasmo.—**sarcastic(al** [sarkǽstịk(ạl], *a.* sarcástico, mordaz.—**sarcastically** [-ị], *adv.* sarcásticamente.

sarcenet [sársnet], *s.* = SARSENET.

sarcocarp [sárkokarp], *s.* (bot.) sarcocarpio.

sarcocele [-sil], *s.* (med.) sarcocele.

sarcocol(la [-kúl(ạ], *s.* sarcocola.

sarcode [sárkoụd], *s.* sarcoda, protoplasma animal.

sarcologic(al [sarkolǽdžịk(ạl], *a.* sarcológico.

sarcology [sarkálodžị], *s.* (anat.) sarcología.

sarcoma [sarkóụmạ], *s.* (med.) sarcoma, *m.*

sarcomatous [sarkámạtạs], *a.* sarcomatoso.

sarcophagous [sarkáfạgạs], *a.* (zool.) carnívoro.

sarcophagus [sarkáfạgạs], *s.* sarcófago, lucillo; variedad de piedra caliza.

sarcotic [sarkátịk], *a.* y *s.* (med.) sarcótico.

sard [sard], *s.* (joy.) sardio.

sardine [sardín], *s.* (ict.) sardina; (joy.) sardio.

Sardinian [sardínịạn], *a.* y *s.* sardo.

sardonic [sardánịk], *a.* sardónico, burlón.

sardonyx [sárdonịks], *s.* (joy.) sardónice, *f.*

sargasso [sargǽsoụ], *s.* sargazo (alga).

Sarmatian [sarméịžịạn], *s.* y *a.* sármata, *mf.*

sarmentum [sarméntạm], *s.* (bot.) sarmiento.

sarmentose [-toụs], *a.* (bot.) sarmentoso.

sarracenia [særạsínịạ], *s.* (bot.) sarracenia.

sarsaparilla [sarsạpạrílạ], *s.* (bot.) zarzaparrilla.

sarsenet [sársnet], *s.* (tej.) tafetán de Florencia.

sartorial [sartórịạl], *a.* sartorio; de o relativo a sastres; de hechura de sastre.

sartorius [-rịʌs], *s.* (anat.) (músculo) sartorio.

sash [sæš], *s.* (mil.) faja, banda, trena; cíngulo, cinturón, ceñidor, cinto, cinta; (carp.) bastidor o marco de ventana.—**s. window,** ventana de guillotina.

sassafras [sǽsạfræs], *s.* (bot.) sasafrás.

Sassanid(e [sǽsạnịd], *a.* y *s.*, **Sassanian** [sæséịnịạn], *a.* sasánida, *mf.*

sat [sæt], *pret.* y *pp.* del verbo TO SIT.

Satan [séịtạn], *s.* Satanás, Satán, Luzbel, Luci-

fer.—**satanic(al** [seitǽnjk(ạl], _a._ satánico.—
satanically [-ị], _adv._ satánicamente.
satchel [sǽchẹl], _s._ maleta, maletín.
sate [seịt], _va._ hartar, saciar, repletar; hastiar.
sateen [sætín], _s._ (tej.) satén, rasete, (ant.) saetín.
sateless [séịtlịs], _a._ insaciable.
satellite [sǽtẹlaịt], _s._ satélite.
satiable [séịṣ̌iabl], _a._ saciable.
satiate [séịṣ̌ieịt], _va._ y _vn._ saciar(se); hartar(se),
ahitar(se), repletar(se).—**satiated** [-ịd], _a._
saciado; harto, ahito, repleto.—**satiation**
[-éịṣ̌ọn], _o_ **satiety** [sạtáịẹtị], _s._ saciedad; hartura, hartazgo.
satin [sǽtịn], _s._ (tej.) raso.—**satinet** [-ét], _s._
(tej.) satinete; rasete.—**satiny** [-ị], _a._ (tej.)
arrasado, asaetinado.
satire [sǽtaịr], _s._ sátira.—**satiric(al** [sạtírịk(ạl],
_a._ satírico.—**satirically** [-ị], _adv._ satíricamente.
—**satirist** [sǽtịrịst], _s._ escritor satírico.—
satirize [sǽtịraịz], _va._ satirizar.
satisfaction [sætịsfǽkṣ̌ọn], _s._ satisfacción, contento, complacencia, regocijo, ufanía; recompensa o reparación; desquite; desagravio;
finiquito, pago (de una deuda o cuenta).
satisfactorily [-trịlị], _adv._ satisfactoriamente.—
satisfactoriness [-trịnịs], _s._ calidad de satisfactorio.—**satisfactory** [-trị], _a._ satisfactorio,
satisfaciente; expiatorio; suficiente.
satisfied [-fạịd], _a._ satisfecho, contento; pagado.
satisfy [-faị], _I._ _va._ satisfacer, contentar; colmar,
saciar; convencer; recompensar, resarcir, pa-
gar. _II._ _vn._ satisfacer, causar satisfacción.
satisfying [-faịịŋ], _a._ satisfaciente.
satrap [séịtræp], _s._ sátrapa, _m._
satrapy [séịtrapị], _s._ satrapía.
saturable [sǽchụrạbl], _a._ saturable.
saturant [-rạnt], _I._ _a._ saturador. _II._ _s._ substancia
que neutraliza a otra.
saturate [-reịt], _I._ _va._ saturar; empapar, embeber,
impregnar; imbuir. _II._ _a._ saturado; intenso
(color).
saturated [-ịd], _a._ saturado; (ópt.) puro, sin
mezcla de blanco (apl. a colores).
saturation [-réịṣ̌ọn], _s._ saturación.
Saturday [sǽtœrdị], _s._ sábado.
Saturn [sǽtœrn], _s._ (astr.) Saturno.
Saturnalia [sætœrnéịlị̣ạ], _s._ _pl._ saturnales, _f._ _pl._
—**Saturnalian** [-n], _a._ saturnal, licencioso.
Saturnian [sætœrnị̣ạn], _a._ saturnal, saturnio;
feliz, dichoso.
saturnine [sǽtœrnaịn], _a._ saturnino; melancólico,
triste, silencioso; (ant., quím.) plomizo.—**s.
poisoning,** envenenamiento o intoxicación
por el plomo, saturnismo.
saturnism [sǽtœrnịzm], _s._ (med.) saturnismo,
envenenamiento con plomo.
satyr [séịtœ(r) _o_ sǽtœ(r)], _s._ (mit.) sátiro.
satyriasis [sætịráịạsịs], _s._ satiriasis.
satyric [sạtírịk], _a._ referente a los sátiros.
sauce [sós], _I._ _s._ (coc.) salsa, aderezo, aliño;
compota; (dial.) verduras, _f._ _pl._; (fam.) lenguaje descomedido. _II._ _va._ condimentar, sazonar; (fam.) ser respondón con, desvergonzarse
con o contra, decir insolencias a, deslenguarse
con.
sauceboat [-boụt], _s._ salsera.
saucebox [-baks], _s._ (fam.) muchacho descarado
y atrevido.
saucedish [-dịṣ̌], _s._ salsera; platillo dulcero.
saucepan [-pæn], _s._ cacerola, cazuela, perol.
saucer [sósœ(r)], _s._ platillo; salsereta.
saucily [sósịlị], _adv._ descarada o insolentemente.
sauciness [sósịnịs], _s._ insolencia, desmandamiento.
saucisse [sosís], _s._ (arti.) salchicha.
saucy [sósị], _a._ respondón, descarado, insolente.
sauerkraut [sáụrkraụt], _s._ (coc.) col fermentada.
saunter [sóntœ(r)], _vn._ vagar; andar despacio y
sin objeto; haraganear.
sauntering [-ịŋ], _s._ vagancia; paseo lento.
saurian [sóriạn], _s._ y _a._ (zool.) saurio.
sauropod [sóropad], _s._ y _a._ (pal.) saurópodo.

sausage [sósịdẓ̌], _s._ salchicha, embutido, chorizo,
longaniza, salchichón.—**s. balloon** = KITE
BALLOON.—**s. maker o seller,** salchichero,
choricero.—**s. shop,** salchichería, choricería.—
s. stuffer, jeringa choricera.
sauté [soụtéị], _va._ (coc.) saltear.
savage [sǽvịdẓ̌]. _I._ _a._ salvaje; silvestre; bárbaro,
inculto; brutal, feroz; enfurecido. _II._ _s._ salvaje.
—**savagely** [-lị], _adv._ bárbaramente, salvajemente, fieramente.—**savageness, savagery**
[-nịs, -rị], _s._ salvajismo; barbarie; ferocidad,
crueldad; los salvajes.
savanna(h [sạvǽnạ], _s._ sabana, pradera.
savant [sǽvạnt], _s._ sabio.
save [séịv]. _I._ _va._ salvar, librar; guardar, conservar, preservar, reservar; ahorrar, economizar;
evitar; aprovecharse de; proteger, eximir; dispensar (_save the word_, séame permitido el vocablo).—**God, o Heaven, s. the mark,** expresión
de desprecio o impaciencia; puede traducirse:
¡que mal haya! ¡maldita la cosa! ¡vaya! etc.,
según el caso.—**to s. appearances, to s.
(one's) face,** salvar las apariencias, cubrir el
expediente. _II._ _prep._ salvo, excepto. _III._ _conj._
sino, a menos que, a no ser que.
sav(e)able [-abl], _a._ conservable; que se puede
salvar o ahorrar.
save-all [-ol], _s._ baloncita, apuracabos; (mar.)
vela rastrera.
saver [-œ(r)], _s._ libertador; salvador; auxiliador;
economizador, ahorrador.
savin [sǽvịn], _s._ (bot.) sabina, junípero; cedro rojo.
saving [séịvịŋ]. _I._ _a._ ahorrativo, frugal, económico; salvador; calificativo.—**s. clause,** cláusula que contiene una salvedad o reserva. _II._ _s._
economía, ahorro; salvedad.—_pl._ ahorros,
economías; hucha.—**savings bank,** caja de
ahorros. _III._ _prep._ con excepción de, fuera de,
excepto, salvo.—**s. your reverence,** con perdón de Vd.
savingly [-lị], _adv._ económicamente, parcamente.
savingness [-nịs], _s._ ahorro, economía; frugalidad, parquedad.
savior [séịvyọ(r)], _s._ salvador.—**the Saviour,** el
Salvador, el Redentor (Jesucristo).
savor [séịvọ(r)]. _I._ _s._ sabor, sainete, dejo, gusto,
gustillo; olor, perfume. _II._ _va._ saborear, sazonar, dar sabor y gusto a. _III._ _vn._ (con of) saber
a, oler a, tener sabor, gusto u olor de; manifestar una calidad de.
savorily [-ilị], _adv._ con gusto, sabrosamente,
apetitosamente.
savoriness [-inịs], _s._ buen sabor; fragancia.
savory [-ị]. _I._ _a._ sabroso, apetitoso, gustoso, delicado; fragante. _II._ _s._ (bot.) ajedrea.
savoy [sạvóị], _s._ (bot.) variedad de col o berza
con hojas arrugadas.
Savoyard [-ạrd], _a._ y _s._ saboyano.
saw [so]. _I._ _s._ (carp.) sierra; dicho, decir, refrán,
proverbio, sentencia.—**s. cut,** corte de sierra;
muesca hecha con la sierra.—**s. swage, set,
o wrest,** triscador.—**s.-tooth(ed)** = SER-
RATE(D).—**s.-tooth roof,** (arq.) tejado en
diente de sierra. _II._ _va._ (_pp._ SAWED o SAWN)
serrar, aserrar. _III._ _vn._ ser serrado, (a)serrarse
(_this wood saws easily,_ esta madera es fácil de
aserrar); usar una sierra.
saw, _pret._ de TO SEE.
sawbuck [sóbʌk], _s._ (carp.) caballete o cabrilla
de aserrar, tijera; (E. U. fam.) billete de diez
dólares.
sawdust [sódʌst], _s._ (a)serrín, (a)serraduras.
sawer [sóœ(r)], _s._ aserrador. _V._ SAWYER.
sawfish [sófịṣ̌], _s._ (ict.) priste, pez sierra.
sawhorse [sóhọrs], _s._ (carp.) caballete o cabrilla
de aserrar, borriquete, burro.
sawmill [sómịl], _s._ aserradero; sierra de agua.
sawn [son], _pp._ _irr._ de TO SAW; aserrado.
sawpit [sópịt], _s._ aserradero.
sawwort [sówœrt], _s._ (bot.) serrátula.
sawyer [sóyœ(r)], _s._ aserrador; chiquichaque.

sax [sæks], s. martillo de pizarrero.

saxatile [sǽksətịl], a. (bot., zool.) saxátil.

saxhorn [sǽkshorn], s. (mús.) bombardino, bombardón.

saxicoline [sæksíkoḷịn], **saxicolous** [-ḷʌs], a. (bot., zool.) saxátil, que se cría en las rocas.

saxifragaceous [sæksịfragéiʃịʌs], d. (bot.) saxifragáceo.—**saxifrage** [sǽksịfrịdž], s. saxifraga.

Saxon [sǽeksọn]. I. a. sajón. II. s. sajón; lengua sajona; anglosajón.

saxophone [sǽeksofoụn], s. (mús.) saxófono.

say [séị]. I. va. (pret. y pp. SAID) decir; alegar, afirmar; hablar; recitar.—**to s. a lesson**, recitar una lección.—**to s. good-bye (to)**, despedirse (de).—**to s. in one's sleeve**, decir para su capote o para su sayo.—**to s. mass**, cantar misa.—**to s. nothing of**, sin mencionar.—**to s. one's prayers**, rezar, decir uno sus oraciones.—**to s. over again**, volver a decir, repetir.—**to s. the least**, por lo menos, si no algo peor.—**it is said, they s.**, se dice, dicen.—**so to s.**, por decirlo así.—**the book says so**, el libro lo reza.—**you don't s. (so)!**, ¡calle Vd.¡ ¡no es posible! II. vn. decir.—**s.!** I s.! ¡hola! ¡oiga! ¡digo!—**to s. on**, continuar hablando.—**to s. right**, decir bien, tener razón.—**to s. to**, decir a; opinar de.—**that is to s.**, es decir, esto es. III. s. uso de la palabra; decisión; expresión de opinión; discurso, afirmación; (fam.) turno de hablar.—**s.-so**, (fam.) opinión o juicio personal; declaración autorizada.

saying [-ịŋ], s. dicho, lo que se dice; aserto, relato; adagio, dicho, decir, refrán.—**as the s. is**, como dijo el otro, como dice el refrán.

'sblood, [zbḷʌd], interj. (ant.) ¡por Dios!

scab [skæb], s. (cir.) costra, escara; (vet.) roña, escabro; (fam.) hombre ruin o roñoso; (desp.) esquirol, obrero no agremiado que reemplaza a los agremiados en una huelga.

scabbard [skǽbạrd], s. vaina de espada, cuchillera, funda.

scabbed [skæbd], **scabby** [skǽbị], a. costroso, postilloso; sarnoso; tiñoso, roñoso; (fam.) vil, ruin.

scabbiness [-nịs], s. calidad de costroso, roñoso o tiñoso.

scabies [skéịbiz], s. (med.) sarna.

scabious [skéịbịʌs]. I. a. sarnoso. II. s. (bot.) escabiosa (ll. t. **scabiosa**).

scabrous [skéịbrʌs], a. escabroso, desigual, áspero.

scabrousness [-nịs], s. escabrosidad, aspereza.

scabwort [skǽbwœrt], s. (bot.) énula campana.

scad [skæd], s. (ict.) variedad de escombro; alosa; (fam., gen. pl.) la mar de, mucho (dinero, etc.).

scaffold [skǽfoụld]. I. s. andamio, tablado; cadalso, patíbulo. II. va. construir tablados o andamios para.

scaffolding [-ịŋ], s. castillejo, andamiada, andamiaje; andamio, armazón, bastidor de apoyo.

scaglia [skǽlyạ], s. piedra caliza italiana.

scagliola [skælyóuḷạ], s. (alb.) escayola, enlucido de imitación de piedra (mármol, granito, etc.).

scalar [skǽḷạ(r)]. I. a. (mat.) numérico, no vectorial. II. s. cantidad puramente numérica o no vectorial.

scal(l)awag [skǽḷạwæg], s. (fam.) tuno; bribón; res raquítica; (fam. E. U.) nombre despectivo aplicado a los republicanos del Sur después de la guerra de Secesión.

scald [skọld]. I. va. escaldar, quemar; (coc.) escalfar; lard(e)ar, pringar; limpiar con agua muy caliente. II. s. quemadura, escaldadura; escaldo, bardo escandinavo. III. a. tiñoso.—**s. head**, (med.) acores, usagre, tiña.

scale [skéịl]. I. s. escala; platillo de balanza; (gen. en pl.) balanza, báscula; (S., astr.) Libra; escama (de peces, reptiles); (med.) costra, costrita; (bot.) escama, hoja rudimentaria; incrustación (en las calderas); chispa; escama,

laminita, plancha, hojuela; escalón; escalada; (mat.) escala o pitipié; escala (de un mapa); escala, regla graduada; graduación, división; (mús.) escala, gama.—**s. insect**, (ent.) insecto cóccido, pulgón.—**on a large s.**, en grande escala, en grande.—**on a small s.**, en pequeña escala, en pequeño.—**to s.**, (dib.) según escala. II. va. escamar o des(es)camar; descortezar; pelar, descascarar, raspar; cubrir con escamas; incrustar o desincrustar; escalar; (a veces con off) medir según escala; dibujar según escala; (con down) reducir o rebajar según escala; pesar, romanar; tener (tanto) peso; graduar, igualar. III. vn. (a veces con off) descostrarse; desconcharse, pelarse, descascararse; exfoliarse; formarse incrustaciones o escamas; formar escalera; dar facilidad de subir; subir.

scalebeam [-bim], s. ástil o brazo de balanza.

scaled [-d], a. escamudo, escamoso; costroso.

scalene [skejlín]. I. a. (geom.) escaleno; (anat.) escaleno (músculo). II. s. triángulo escaleno.—**scalenus** [-ʌs], s. músculo escaleno.

scalepan [skéịlpæn], s. platillo de balanza.

scaler [skéịlœ(r)], s. escalador; rascador; escamador (de pescado); (dent.) instrumento para quitar el sarro.

scaliness [skéịlịnịs], s. escamosidad.

scaling [skéịlịŋ]. I. s. escamadura (del pescado); (mil.) escalamiento; (med.) descamación; exfoliación; medida o ajuste según escala. II. a. de escalar.—**s. ladders**, escalas de sitio o de bombero.

scall [skọl], s. (med.) tiña.—**scalled** [-d], a. tiñoso; costroso.

scallion [skǽlyọn], s. (bot.) chalote, ascalonia.

scallop [skǽlọp o skálọp]. I. s. (zool.) venera, pechina, pecten, peine (molusco); venera o concha (distintivo de los romeros); (cost.) festón, recorte, onda; platito en forma de concha para ostras. II. va. festonear, ondear; (coc.) asar ostras empanadas; cocer al horno (pescado, patatas, etc.) con migas de pan, salsa de crema, etc.

scalp [skælp]. I. s. (anat.) pericráneo; cuero cabelludo, piel (f.) que cubre el cráneo; (fig.) trofeo. II. va. escalpar, quitar el pericráneo con la cabellera (como hacían los indios); (fam.) comprar y revender (acciones, billetes de f. c., teatro, etc.) por una ganancia rápida, o a precios extraoficiales.

scalpel [skǽlpel], s. (cir.) escalpelo.

scalper [skǽlpœ(r)], s. (fam.) revendedor de acciones o billetes. V. SCALP, va.

scalping [skǽlpịŋ], s. acción de escalpar.—**s. iron**, (cir.) raspador.—**s. knife**, cuchillo que usaban los indios norteamericanos para desprender la piel del cráneo.

scaly [skéịlị], a. escamoso, conchado; herrumbroso; incrustada (caldera); (fam.) vil, ruin, deshonrado.

scammony [skǽmọnị], s. (bot.) escamonea.

scamp [skæmp]. I. s. bribón, pícaro. II. va. hacer (algo) o ejecutar (trabajo) descuidada o malamente, con intención de perjudicar al patrón; (fam.) chafalar, frangollar.

scamper [-œ(r)]. I. vn. escaparse, (d)escabullirse, huir. II. s. fuga, huída precipitada.

scamping [-ịŋ], s. mala ejecución del trabajo para perjudicar al patrón; producción de un obrero superior a la convenida con sus compañeros, para beneficiarse traicionándolos; sonsacamiento de los obreros de una compañía rival.

scan [skæn]. I. va. escudriñar, examinar, registrar; hojear, repasar; (poét.) escandir, medir (versos). II. vn. (poét.) ajustarse a las reglas de la métrica, tener la medida propia.

scandal [skǽndạl], s. escándalo; difamación, maledicencia; reproche, censura; oprobio, ignominia.—**s. bearer** = SCANDALMONGER.—**to raise a s.**, armar un alboroto.

scandalize [-aįz], *va.* escandalizar; difamar.
scandalmonger [-mʌŋgœ(r)], *s.* murmurador, propagador de escándalos.
scandalous [-ʌs], *a.* escandaloso; vergonzoso; calumnioso o difamatorio.—**scandalously** [-lį], *adv.* ignominiosamente; escandalosamente.—**scandalousness** [-nįs], *s.* carácter escandaloso.
scandent [skǽndent], *a.* (bot.) trepador.
scandic [skǽndįk], *a.* (quím.) escándico.
Scandinavian [skændįnéįvįan], *s.* y *a.* escandinavo.
scandium [skǽndįʌm], *s.* (quím.) escandio.
scansion [skǽnšơn], *s.* (poét.) escansión, acción de escandir; métrica.
scansorial [skænsórįal], *a.* (zool.; orn.) trepador.
scant [skǽnt], I. *va.* escatimar, limitar. II. *a.* escaso, escatimado, exiguo, limitado; insuficiente.—**s. of**, insuficientemente provisto de.—**a s.**, poco menos que.—**a s. two hours**, dos horas escasas.
scantily [-lį], *adv.* escasamente, parcamente, a duras penas.—**scantiness** [-nįs], *s.* escasez, insuficiencia, exigüidad.
scantling [-lįŋ], *s.* cuartón, madero, barrote; colección de cuartones; escantillón.
scanty [-į], *a.* escaso, escatimado, corto, insuficiente; económico, parco, estrecho.
scape [skéįp], *s.* (bot.) escapo, bohordo; (ent.) cuerno, antena; (orn.) cañón de pluma; (arq.) escapo, fuste de columna; vista escénica.
scapegoat [-goʊt], *s.* víctima propiciatoria; persona que paga por las culpas de otras; cabeza de turco.—**to be made the s.**, pagar el pato, o los vidrios rotos.
scapegrace [-greįs], *s.* persona incorregible; pícaro, travieso, bribón.
scaphoid [skǽfơįd]. I. *a.* navicular; escafoideo. II. *s.* (anat.) navicular o escafoides.
scapula [skǽpyūlä], *s.* (anat.) escápula, omoplato.
scapular [-lä(r)], **scapulary** [-lęrį]. I. *a.* escapular. II. *s.* (igl.) escapulario; (cir.) escapulario, vendaje para el hombro.
scar [skar]. I. *s.* cicatriz; chirlo, costurón; (Ingl.) peñasco, farallón.—**s. tissue**, tejido cicatrizal. II. *va.* marcar con una cicatriz.
scarab(**ee** [skǽrab(į], *s.* (ent.) escarabajo; (arqueol.) escarabajo sagrado de los egipcios.—**scarabæid** [skærabíįd], *s.* y *a.* escarabídeo.—**scarabæus** [-bíʌs], *s.* = SCARAB.
scaramouch [skǽramuš], *s.* pícaro, bribón; (S., teat.) fanfarrón cobarde; botarga, bufón.
scarce [skęrs], *a.* raro, escaso, contado.—**to make one's self s.**, (fam.) largarse, ausentarse.—**scarce**(**ly** [-lį], *adv.* escasamente, apenas, con dificultad, a duras penas, casi no, siquier(a); casi no, luego que.—**s. anything**, casi nada.—**s. ever**, casi nunca.—**scarceness**, **scarcity** [-nįs, -įtį], *s.* carestía, escasez; rareza.
scare [skęr]. I. *va.* asustar, espantar; amedrentar, intimidar.—**to s. away**, espantar, ahuyentar. II. *s.* susto, sobresalto, alarma, espanto.
scarecrow [-kroʊ], *s.* espantapájaros, espantajo; (fam.) esperpento, adefesio.
scarf [skárf]. I. *s.* banda, trena, faja; corbata, chalina; bufanda; (carp.) junta de solapa con bordes biselados o enmuescados; junta a diente de sierra (ll. t. **s. joint**). II. *va.* (carp.) ensamblar, empotrar, encabezar, empalmar, charpar; adornar con una banda.
scarfing [-įŋ], *s.* (carp.) acopladura, ensambladura, encabezadura, empalme.
scarfpin [-pįn], *s.* alfiler de corbata.
scarfskin [-skįn], *s.* (anat.) cutícula, epidermis.
scarification [skęrįfįkéįšơn], *s.* (cir.) escarificación, saja.—**scarificator** [-fįkeįtơ(r)], *s.* (cir.) escarificador.—**scarifier** [-faįœ(r)], *s.* sajador, escarificador; (agr.) escarificador.—**scarify** [-faį], *va.* (cir.) escarificar, sajar; (agr.) revolver la superficie del terreno; (fig.) criticar severamente.

scarious, **scariose** [skéįrįʌs, -oʊs], *a.* (bot.) escarioso; seco, delgado.
scarlatina [skarlǝtínä], *s.* (med.) escarlatina.
scarless [skárlįs], *a.* sin cicatrices; ileso.
scarlet [skárlįt]. I. *s.* escarlata, grana. II. *a.* de color escarlata.—**s. fever**, (med.) escarlatina, escarlata.—**s. oak**, (bot.) coscoja.
scarp [skarp]. I. *va.* escarpar, hacer escarpa, cortar en declive. II. *s.* (fort.) escarpa; declive, pendiente, *f.*, acantilado.
scarred, **scarry** [skard, skárį], *a.* que tiene cicatrices, cicatrizado.
scary [skęrį], *a.* (fam.) medroso, asustadizo.
scat [skæt]. I. *interj.* ¡zape! II. *va.* zapear, ahuyentar.
scathe [skéįð]. I. *va.* atacar con crítica mordaz. II. *s.* daño, perjuicio.
scatheless [-lįs], *a.* sano y salvo.
scathing [-įŋ], *a.* severísimo; que chamusca.
scatology [skǝtálodžį], *s.* escatología.
scatter [skǽtœ(r)]. I. *va.* esparcir, diseminar, regar, desparramar, desperdigar; disipar; dispersar.—**s.-brained**, atolondrado, casquivano, ligero de cascos. II. *vn.* dispersarse, esparcirse; disiparse.
scatterbrain [-breįn], *s.* (fam.) cabeza de chorlito.
scattered [-d], *a.* disperso, regado, esparcido, desparramado; apartado; irregular.
scattering [-įŋ], *s.* dispersión, esparcimiento; desparramamiento, desperdigamiento.
scatteringly [-įŋlį], *adv.* esparcidamente.
scaup [skɔp], *s.* (orn.) pato marino.
scavenge [skǽvįndž], *va.* recoger la basura; (m. comb. int.) dar salida a los gases (de los cilindros de un motor); (metal.) barrer, lavar.
scavenger [-œ(r)], *s.* basurero; animal que se alimenta de carroña (aura tiñosa, zopilote, etc.).—**s. beetle**, escarabajo clavicornio.
scenario [sįnérįoʊ], *s.* (teat.) argumento, libreto; película, drama, *m.*, guión (*m.*) o argumento para cinematógrafo.—**s. writer** o **scenarist**, peliculero, escritor de películas.
scend [send]. I. *vn.* (mar.) arfar, cabecear. II. *s.* arfada.
scene [sín], *s.* escena, vista, paisaje; (teat.) escena, cuadro (de un acto); escenario; decoración; teatro, lugar de un acontecimiento; arrebato, escándalo; lance.—**s. painter**, pintor escenógrafo.—**behind the scenes**, entre bastidores.
sceneful [-fʊl], *a.* abundante en escenas o en imágenes, *f. pl.*
scenery [-œrį], *s.* vista, paisaje; (teat.) decoraciones, decorado.
sceneshifter [-šįftœ(r)], *s.* (teat.) tramoyista.
scenic [sínįk]. I. *a.* escénico; teatral, dramático; pintoresco. II. *s.* paisaje cinematográfico.
scenographer [sįnágrafœ(r)], *s.* escenógrafo.
scenographical [sinográfįkạl], *a.* escenográfico.—**scenographically** [-į], *adv.* escenográficamente.
scenography [sįnágrafį], *s.* escenografía.
scent [sént]. I. *s.* olfato; olor, perfume, fragancia; mal olor; rastro, pista.—**to throw off the s.**, despistar. II. *va.* y *vn.* oler, olfatear, husmear, ventear; rastrear; perfumar; sospechar.
scentless [-lįs], *a.* sin olfato; inodoro, sin olor.
sceptic, **scepticism** = SKEPTIC, SKEPTICISM.
scepter, **sceptre** [séptœ(r)], *s.* cetro.
sceptered, **sceptred** [-d], *a.* que lleva o tiene cetro; real, regio, imperial.
schedule [skédžʊl]. I. *va.* incluir en una lista, catálogo, plan, programa (*m.*) o inventario; inventariar, catalogar; fijar el tiempo para. II. *s.* cédula; horario (de f. c., etc.); suplemento, aditamento; plan, programa; lista, catálogo, cuadro, descripción; (f. c.) cuadro de servicio de trenes.—**s. of charges**, tarifa.
schema [skímä], *s.* sumario, sinopsis, cuadro; diagrama, *m.*; esquema, *m.*
schematic [skimǽtįk], *a.* esquemático.
scheme [skím]. I. *s.* plan, proyecto, programa.

m., designio; planta, esquema, *m.*, modelo; diseño, bosquejo, traza, diagrama, *m.;* sistema, *m.*, arreglo, disposición; ardid, *m.*, treta, artificio. II. *va.* y *vn.* proyectar, trazar, discurrir, idear; urdir, tramar.

schemer [-œ(r)], *s.* proyectista; maquinador, intrigante, tracista, fraguador.

schism [sízm], *s.* cisma, *m.*; escisión.—**schismatic** [sizmǽtịk], *s.* cismático.—**schismatic(al** [-ạl], *a.* cismático.—**schismatically** [-lị], *adv.* cismáticamente, como cismático.—**schismatize** [sízmạtaịz], *vn.* dirigir, causar o fomentar un cisma.

schist [šịst], *s.* (geol.) esquisto.

schistic, schistose, schistous [-ịk, -ous, -ʌs], *a.* esquistoso.

schizocarp [skízokarp], *s.* (bot.) esquizocarpo.

schizophrenia [-frínịạ], *s.* esquizofrenia.

schizophrenic [-frénịk], *a.* y *s.* esquizofrénico.

schnap(p)s [šnæps], *s.* ginebra de Holanda.

scholar [skálạ(r)], *s.* escolar, alumno, estudiante, colegial; beca(rio); erudito, hombre de letras, docto, letrado, sabio, humanista.

scholarly [-lị]. I. *a.* erudito; ilustrado, docto. II. *adv.* eruditamente, doctamente.

scholarship [-šịp], *s.* saber, erudición; beca, plaza pensionada.—**s. holder**, beca(rio), becado.

scholastic [skolǽstịk]. I. *a.* escolástico, escolar; (filos.) escolástico; pedantesco. II. *s.* escolástico.—**scholastically** [-alị], *adv.* escolásticamente.—**scholasticism** [skolǽstịsịzm], *s.* escolasticismo.

scholia [skóulịạ], *s. pl.* de SCHOLIUM.

scholiast [-æst], *s.* escoliador, escoliasta.

scholium [-ʌm], *s.* escolio, glosa.

school [skúl]. I. *s.* escuela; colegio; alumnado; facultad de una universidad (la Facultad de Teología, Medicina, etc.); cardumen, banco de peces.—**s. of painting**, escuela de pintura.—**s. year**, año escolar.—**at, o in, s.**, en clase, en la escuela. II. *a.* escolar; de escuela; para escuela.—**s. board**, junta de educación.—**s. desk**, pupitre.—**s. teacher**, maestro o maestra de escuela.—**s. teaching**, enseñanza de escuela; profesión de maestro de escuela. III. *va.* instruir, enseñar, aleccionar, ad(i)estrar, amaestrar; disciplinar. IV. *vn.* ir o andar en manadas, como algunos peces; moverse en masa.

schoolbook [-bụk], *s.* texto de escuela.

schoolboy [-bɔị], *s.* muchacho de escuela, colegial.

schooled [-d], *a.* enseñado, amaestrado, aleccionado.

schoolfellow [-felou], *s.* condiscípulo.

schoolgirl [-gœrl], *s.* niña de escuela, colegiala.

schoolhouse [-haụs], *s.* escuela (edificio).

schooling [-ịŋ], *s.* instrucción elemental; educación, enseñanza; experiencia; precio de la escuela.

schoolman [-mạn], *s.* (filos.) escolástico.

schoolmaster [-mæstœ(r)], *s.* maestro de escuela.

schoolmate [-meịt], *s.* condiscípulo.

schoolmistress [-mịstrịs], *s.* maestra de escuela.

schoolroom [-rum], *s.* aula, sala de clase.

schooner [skúnœ(r)], *s.* (mar.) goleta; (E. U.) galera con toldo que usaban los emigrantes (ll. t. **prairie s.**); (fam.) vaso alto y grande para cerveza.

schorl [šɔrl], *s.* (min.) chorlo; turmalina.

schottische [šátịš], *s.* schotis o chotis, *m.*

sciagraphy [saịǽgrafị], *s.* esciagrafía.

sciatica [saịǽtịkạ], *s.* (med.) ciática.

sciatic(al [-ịk-ạl], *a.* (anat.) ciático, isquiático.—**s. nerve**, nervio ciático.

science [sáịens], *s.* ciencia; pericia, facultad.

scientific(al [saịentịfịk(ạl], *a.* científico.

scientifically [-lị], *adv.* científicamente.

scientist [sáịentịst], *s.* sabio, hombre de ciencia o científico.

scilicet [sịlịsɛt], *adv.* a saber.

scimitar, scimiter [sịmịtạ(r), -œ(r)], *s.* cimitarra.

scintilla [sịntílạ], *s.* centella, chispa.

scintillant [síntịlạnt], *a.* centelleante; titilante.—**scintillate** [-eịt]. I. *vn.* escintilar, chispear, centellear; titilar. II. *va.* destellar.—**scintillation** [-éịšọn], *s.* chispazo, centelleo, destello; titilación.

sciolism [sáịolịzm], *s.* conocimientos superficiales.

sciolist [-ịst], *s.* erudito a la violeta, semisabio.

scion [sáịọn], *s.* (agr.) púa, acodo, plantón, esqueje; vástago, renuevo, verdugo; hijo, hija o descendiente.

scirrhosity [s(k)ịrásịtị], *s.* calidad de escirroso.

scirrhous [s(k)ịrʌs], *a.* (med.) cirroso o escirroso, endurecido; canceroso.

scirrhus [s(k)ịrʌs], *s.* (med.) cirro o escirro.

scissel [sịsel], *s.* desperdicios o recortes de metal.

scission [sịžọn], *s.* escisión, corte, división, separación.

scissor [sịzọ(r)], *va.* cortar con tijeras, tijeretear.—**scissors** [-z], *s. pl.* tijeras.

scissure [sịšụr], *s.* cisura, hendedura; escisión, cisma, *m.;* ruptura.

sclera [sklírạ], *s.* (anat.) esclerótica.

scleroma [sklịróụmạ], *s.* (med.) escleroma, *m.*

sclerosis [-sịs], *s.* (med.) esclerosis.

sclerotic [sklịrátịk]. I. *a.* escleroso, indurado. II. *s.* (anat.) esclerótica, córnea opaca (ll. t. **sclerotica**).—**sclerotitis** [sklịrotáịtịs], *s.* esclerotitis, inflamación de la esclerótica.—**sclerotomy** [sklịrátomị], *s.* (cir.) esclerotomía.

scoff [skáf]. I. *vn.* (con at) mofarse o burlarse de; befar. II. *s.* mofa, escarnio, burla, befa; hazmerreír.

scoffer [-œ(r)], *s.* mofador, burlón, burlador.

scoffingly [-ịŋlị], *adv.* con mofa y escarnio.

scofflaw [-lɔ], *s.* burlador o violador de la ley.

scold [skóụld]. I. *va.* y *vn.* regañar, reñir, reprender, increpar; rezongar, refunfuñar. II. *s.* reñidor, regañón; mujer de lenguaje soez.

scolding [-ịŋ], *s.* regaño, reprensión.

scoliosis [skoụlịóụsịs], *s.* (med.) escoliosis, encorvadura lateral de la columna vertebral.

scollop [skálọp], *s.* y *v.* = SCALLOP.

Scolopendra [skạlopéndrạ], *s.* (ent.) género de las escolopendras o ciempiés.

scomber [skámbœ(r)], *s.* (ict.) escombro, caballa.

sconce [skans]. I. *s.* cobertizo, salidizo; (fort.) baluarte, fortín; (fam.) cabeza; seso, juicio, sentido; anaquel fijo; multa; cornucopia o candelabro de pared. II. *va.* abaluartar, fortificar con baluarte; multar.

sconcheon [skánchọn], *s.* (arq.) mocheta.

scoop [skúp]. I. *s.* pala de mano; cuchara o cucharón de draga; excavación, ahuecamiento; paletada, cucharada; cavidad, hueco; (mar.) vertedor, achicador; (fam.) hallazgo, ganancia; noticia que publica un periódico antes que los demás.—**air s.**, cuchara de aire (de un dirigible).—**s. net**, red barredera. II. *va.* sacar con pala o cuchara; achicar, vaciar; ahuecar, cavar, excavar.

scooper [-œ(r)], *s.* achicador, vaciador; cavador; cincel de grabador.

scoot [skút], *vn.* (fam.) largarse, tomar las de Villadiego; pasar, volar velozmente.

scooter [-œ(r)], *s.* monopatín, patinete (juguete de niños); velero de fondo plano que puede pasar velozmente sobre el hielo o el agua; (agr.) especie de arado empleado para hacer surcos.

scope [skoụp], *s.* alcance, extensión; campo, espacio o esfera de acción o aplicación; ámbito; (fig.) envergadura.

scorbutic(al [skɔrbịútịk(ạl], *a.* (med.) escorbútico.

scorbutus [skɔrbịútʌs], *s.* (med.) escorbuto.

scorch [skórch]. I. *va.* chamuscar, socarrar, aburrar, rescaldar, tostar; agostar, abrasar, quemar, picar (el sol); censurar, criticar cáusticamente. II. *vn.* quemarse, secarse; agostarse, abrasarse (apl. a las plantas); (fam.) ir en (en

coche o en bicicleta) con gran velocidad.—
scorched earth, tierra abrasada o chamuscada;
(mil.) política de arrasarlo todo en una región
antes de abandonarla al enemigo.

scorcher [-œ(r)], s. (fam.) día muy caluroso o
bochornoso; reproche o censura cáustica; automovilista o biciclista que va a toda velocidad.

scorching [-iŋ]. **I.** a. ardiente, abrasador, bochornoso. **II.** s. chamusquina; agostamiento.

score [skór]. **I.** s. muesca, canalita, entalladura;
señal, f., línea, raya; cuenta, tantos (en el
juego); (dep.) tanto, tanteo; resultado final;
deuda; inquina; controversia; cuenta y razón;
motivo, consideración; (mús.) partitura; veintena.—**s. board** o **keeper,** (dep.) tanteador.
—**on that s.,** a ese respecto, en cuanto a eso.
—**on the s. of,** con motivo de.—**on,** o **upon,
what s.,** con qué motivo, por qué razón.—**to
settle a s.,** ajustar cuentas; saldar una cuenta.
II. va. rayar, marcar con líneas, rayas o muescas; escoplear; azotar, censurar severamente;
(con **out**) borrar, tachar, testar; apuntar, sentar, poner en cuenta; tantear; ganar tantos en
un juego; alcanzar (un triunfo); (mús.) instrumentar.—**to s. a point,** (dep.) ganar un tanto;
obtener un triunfo. **III.** vn. marcar; llevar una
cuenta; marcar los tantos en un juego; llevar
ventaja en un juego; (fig.) recibir buena acogida, merecer aplausos; hacer muescas, rayas o
señales.

scorer [-œ(r)], s. marcador; tanteador; coime (en
el billar).

scoria [skóriä], s. escoria, horrura, cagafierro.—
pl. **scoriæ** [skórji], escorias volcánicas.

scoriaceous [-éiʃäs], a. escoriáceo.

scorification [-fjkéiʃǫn], s. escorificación.

scoriform [-fǫrm], a. escoriforme.

scorify [-fai], va. escorificar.

scorn [skórn]. **I.** va. y vn. despreciar, desdeñar;
escarnecer. **II.** s. desdén, desprecio, escarnio,
menosprecio.—**scorner** [-œ(r)], s. despreciador,
escarnecedor.—**scornful** [-fʊl], a. desdeñoso,
despreciativo.—**scornfully** [-i], adv. desdeñosamente, despreciablemente, despectivamente.
—**scornfulness** [-nis], s. desprecio, desdén.

Scorpio [skórpiou], s. (astr.) Escorpión, m.

scorpioid [-pioid], a. y s. (zool.) escorpiónido;
semejante al escorpión.

scorpion [-pion], s. (zool.) escorpión, m., alacrán;
látigo o azote; (S., astr.) Escorpión.—**s. fish,**
(ict.) escorpión.—**s. grass,** (bot.) miosotis o
nomeolvides.

Scorpionida [-piánidä], s. pl. (zool.) escorpioni-
deos.

scorpionwort [skórpiǫnwœrt], s. (bot.) escorpioide, f., alacranera.

scot [skat], s. escote; tasa, contribución; (S.)
escocés.—**s.-free,** libre de gravámenes; sano
y salvo.—**to go s. free,** salir enteramente libre,
sin pena alguna.

scotch [skach]. **I.** va. escoplear, hacer muescas o
cortes; herir ligeramente; picar piedra; calzar,
poner calza o galga; engalgar, apear (una
rueda); (fam.) frustrar. **II.** s. escopl(e)adura,
cortadura, corte, incisión; rasguño; trazo para
jugar al *hopscotch* o infernáculo; calzo o calza,
cuña, galga.

Scotch, Scottish [skach, skátiʃ]. **I.** a. escocés.—
S. fir, S. pine, pino albar.—**S. marriage,**
matrimonio por mero acuerdo, sin ceremonia
alguna.—**S. reel,** (danz. y mús.) especie de
contradanza, muy animada.—**S. snap,** (mús.)
ritmo peculiar de los cantos de Escocia.—**S.
thistle,** cardo, emblema (m.) nacional de Escocia. **II.** s. el pueblo escocés; la lengua escocesa.

Scotchman, Scotsman [skáchmǫn, skátsmǫn],
s. escocés.

scoter [skóutœ(r)], s. (orn.) foja, falaris.

scotia [skóuʃä], s. (arq.) escocia, nacela.

Scotism [skóutizm], s. escotismo.

Scotist [-ist], s. escotista.

Scotland Yard [skátlǫnd yárd], cuartel de policía
de Londres; la misma policía, esp. el cuerpo de
detectives.

scotoma [skotóumä], s. (med.) escotoma, m.

scotomy [skátomi], s. (med.) escotomía.

Scotticism [skátiʃizm], s. modismo, idiotismo o
provincialismo escocés.

scoundrel [skáundrǫl], s. pícaro, bribón, truhán.

scoundrelism [-izm], s. vida de bribón; bribones
colectivamente; truhanería, pillería.

scoundrelly [-i], adv. pícaramente.

scour [skáur]. **I.** va. y vn. fregar, estregar, limpiar;
blanquear; purgar; formar cauce; recorrer,
batir (el monte); ahuyentar, expeler; pulir,
alisar; quitar estregando; lavar con un chorro
o una corriente; limpiar (el trigo). **II.** s. reco-
rrida; barranco, zanja; limpiador (esp. de lana).
—pl. diarrea del ganado.

scourer [-œ(r)], s. limpiador, desengrasador,
sacamanchas; purgante eficaz; azotacalles.

scourge [skœrdʒ]. **I.** s. azote, flagelo, disciplinas,
f. pl.; castigo severo; plaga, calamidad.—**the
S. of God,** el azote de Dios (Atila). **II.** va.
azotar, flagelar; mortificar; acosar.

scouring [skáuriŋ], s. fregado, fregadura, estregadura; desengrase; purga.—pl. ripio.

scout [skáut]. **I.** s. (mil.) explorador, batidor;
(aer.) avión ligero de reconocimiento o caza;
niño de la asociación de Niños Exploradores.—
s. commissioner, director de un cuerpo de
niños exploradores.—**s. master,** jefe de tropa
de niños exploradores. **II.** va. y vn. (mil.) explorar; reconocer.—**to s. at,** burlarse de, escarnecer; rechazar con desdén.

scouting [-iŋ], a. y s. (de) reconocimiento, (de)
exploración.

scow [skau], s. chalana, lanchón.

scowl [skaul]. **I.** vn. mirar con ceño, fruncir el
ceño o el entrecejo, poner mal gesto, enfurruñarse; tener mal cariz. **II.** va. rechazar, repeler.
III. s. ceño, sobrecejo; mal cariz, m.

scrabble [skrǽbl]. **I.** va. y vn. escarabajear, garabatear, hacer garabatos; emborronar papel;
(ar)rebañar. V. SCRAMBLE y SCRIBBLE. **II.** s.
escarabajeo, garabat(e)o; (ar)rebatiña.

scrag [skrǽg], s. cualquier cosa flaca y basta o
áspera; el pescuezo.—**scragged, scraggly** [-id,
-li], a. áspero, escabroso; flaco, descarnado.—
scraggedness, scragginess [-idnis, -inis], s.
flaqueza, extenuación; aspereza, escabrosidad.
—**scraggy** [-i], a. áspero; desigual; flaco o descarnado.

scramble [skrǽmbl]. **I.** va. arrebatar, arrebañar,
recoger de prisa o confusamente; embrollar;
(coc.) hacer un revoltillo de (huevos).—**scrambled eggs,** revoltillo, huevos revueltos. **II.** vn.
trepar, subir gateando; (bot.) trepar; andar a
la rebatiña, bregar. **III.** s. trepa; contienda,
(ar)rebatiña.—**scrambler** [-blœ(r)], s. trepador;
el que anda a la rebatiña.

scrap [skrǽp]. **I.** s. migaja, mendrugo; pedacillo,
fragmento; material viejo o de desecho (apl.
esp. al hierro viejo); (fam.) riña, camorra.—pl.
cuero tostado (de tocino, etc.); basura, ripios,
desperdicios; sobras.—**s. heap** o **pile,** montón
de desechos, basura, hierro viejo; revoltillo.
—**s. iron** o **metal,** hierro viejo.—**s. of paper,**
(fig.) tratado o convenio sin valor.—**s. paper,**
papel de calidad inferior para apuntes, etc.;
papel de desecho. **II.** va. echar a la basura;
descartar; abolir, derogar; desguazar, desbaratar (un buque). **III.** vn. (fam.) reñir, armar
camorra.

scrapbook [-buk], s. álbum de recortes.

scrape [skréip]. **I.** va. y vn. raer, raspar, rascar,
rozar, arañar; (a veces con **up** o **together**)
(ar)rebañar, recoger; amontonar poco a poco;
rascar o tocar mal (un instrumento); restregar
los pies.—**to s. acquaintance,** trabar amistad; lograr amistarse.—**to s. along,** (fam.)

ganar la vida a duras penas.—**to s. down,** hacer callar (a un actor) con ruido de pies.—**to s. from, off,** o **out,** quitar raspando.—**to s. together,** arañar, juntar a poquitos (dinero, etc.). II. *s.* raspadura, raedura, rasguño, arañazo; ruido de raspar; restregadura de pies contra el suelo; enredo, lío, aprieto, apuro, embarazo.

scrapepenny [-peni], *s.* avaro, tacaño.

scraper [-œ(r)], *s.* rascador, raspador; estregadera, raedera; arañador, escarbador; (fam.) rascatripas, mal violinista; (mar.) rasqueta; (ten.) garatura, descarnador.

scraping [-iŋ], *s.* raedura, raimiento, raspadura; escarbo.—*pl.* ahorros; raspaduras, rebañaduras.

scrapple [skrǽpl], *s.* pasta frita de harina de maíz con carne picada de cerdo.

scrappy [skrǽpi], *a.* deshilvanado, incoherente, fragmentario; (fam.) reñidor, pendenciero.

scratch [skrǽch]. I. *va.* y *vn.* rascar, raspar, raer; arañar; rasguñar; rayar (el vidrio); escribir mal, garrapatear; escarbar; cancelar, borrar.—**to s. out one's eyes,** sacar a uno los ojos con las uñas. II. *s.* rasguño, arañazo; rascadura; marca o raya; tachón, borradura, tildón; (dep.) línea de partida en una carrera; en el billar, bambarria, chiripa.—*pl.* (vet.) galápago, espundia.—**s. awl,** punzón de marcar.—**s. coat,** capa de base de un enlucido.—**s. paper** o **pad,** papel o cuadernillo de apuntes.—**s. wig,** peluquín.—**from s.,** de nada; de los comienzos.—**up to s.,** en buenas o excelentes condiciones.

scratcher [-œ(r)], *s.* arañador; rascador; escarbador; (agr.) azadilla.

scratchwork [-wœrk], *s.* (b. a.) esgrafiado.

scrawl [skról]. I. *va.* garrapatear, garabatear. II. *s.* (gen. *pl.*) garabatos, garrapatos, escarabajos.

scrawler [-œ(r)], *s.* garabateador.

scrawniness [skrónin̩is], *s.* flacura, flaqueza.

scrawny [skróni], *a.* flaco y huesoso, flacucho.

screak [skrik]. I. *vn.* chirriar, rechinar; chillar. II. *s.* chirrido, rechinamiento.

scream [skrím]. I. *va.* y *vn.* chillar; gritar. II. *s.* grito, alarido, chillido; (fam.) cosa o persona divertidísima, que hace reventar de risa.

screamer [-œ(r)], *s.* chillón, chillador; (orn.) palamedea, especie de pájaro cornudo gritador; (fam.) cosa o persona divertidísima.

screaming [-iŋ]. I. *s.* gritería, grito(s), chillería, alarido(s); acción de gritar. II. *a.* gritador, que grita, chillador; (fam.) divertidísimo.

screech [skrích]. I. *vn.* chillar, ulular. II. *s.* chillido, ululato, estridor.—**s. owl,** (orn.) úlula, autillo, lechuza.

screechy [-i], *a.* chillante, chillón, agudo.

screed [skrid], *s.* escritura o discurso largos; diatriba, invectiva; arenga; (alb.) maestra.

screen [skrín]. I. *s.* cancel, biombo, mampara; pantalla; antipara, persiana; tabique, reja; albitana, cerca; reparo, abrigo, defensa; pantalla de chimenea; criba, cedazo, tamiz, *m.*; pantalla de cinematógrafo.—**s. plate,** (fot.) placa de filtros de colores.—**s. star,** (cine) estrella o astro de la pantalla.—**the s.,** el cine, el teatro de cinematógrafo, la pantalla, el celuloide. II. *va.* cribar, cerner, tamizar; ocultar, encubrir; escudar, proteger; (teat.) hacer una película de, poner en el cine.

screenings [-iŋz], *s. pl.* residuo, desperdicios de criba.

screw [skrú]. I. *s.* tornillo; rosca; hélice, *f.* (de buque o avión); (fam.) cicatero, tacaño. II. *a.* de tornillo, de rosca, roscado; para tornillos.—**s. bolt,** perno roscado.—**s. conveyor,** transportador de tornillo sin fin.—**s. driver,** destornillador.—**s. eye,** armella roscada.—**s. gear,** rueda dentada; engranaje de rueda dentada y tornillo sin fin.—**s. jack,** gato, cric.—**s. machine,** máquina de hacer tornillos; torno de roscar.—**s. nail,** tornillo para madera.—**s. pile,** pilote

con pie metálico de hélice.—**s. plate,** terraja.—**s. propeller,** hélice (de buque o avión).—**s. steamer,** vapor de hélice.—**s. stair,** escalera de caracol.—**s. stock,** terraja.—**s. tap,** macho de aterrajar.—**s. thread,** filete de tornillo o rosca (de tornillo).—**s. wheel,** rueda dentada.—**s. wrench,** llave (*f.*) de atornillar; llave inglesa.—**to have a s. loose,** (fam.) ser excéntrico o destornillado.—**to put the screws on,** apretar los tornillos; poner las peras a cuatro. III. *va.* atornillar; fijar con tornillos; torcer, retorcer; forzar, apretar, comprimir, oprimir, estrechar; apremiar; hacer visajes, gestos o contorsiones (con la cara, el cuerpo, etc.).—**to s. down,** atornillar, fijar con tornillo; (fam.) apretar los tornillos.—**to s. in,** hacer entrar una cosa en otra dándole vueltas como a un tornillo; insinuar.—**to s. off,** des(a)tornillar.—**to s. one's wits,** devanarse los sesos, descalabazarse.—**to s. out of someone,** sonsacar a uno; exigirle (dinero, etc.).—**to s. up,** excitar, aguijonear; torcer.—**to s. up one's courage,** hacer de tripas corazón. IV. *vn.* retorcerse o dar vueltas una cosa en forma de rosca o espiral; ejercer extorsión u opresión.

screwball [-bɔl], *s.* (fam.) loco, excéntrico.

scribble [skríbl]. I. *va.* y *vn.* escribir de prisa; borrajear, garrapatear, garabatear, escarabajear, emborronar. II. *s.* escrito mal pergeñado; garabat(e)o.

scribbler [skríblœ(r)], *s.* mal escritor.

scribe [skrajb]. I. *s.* escriba, *m.* (entre los hebreos); calígrafo; amanuense, escribiente, escribano; notario público; (fam.) autor, periodista. II. *va.* marcar, rayar, puntear; (carp.) juntar, ensamblar, ajustar.

scrim [skrim], *s.* cierto tejido de algodón o lino.

scrimmage [skrímidʒ], *s.* arrebatiña, reyerta.

scrimp [skrimp]. I. *va.* y *vn.* escatimar. II. *a.* escaso, reducido, corto. III. *s.* (fam.) avaro.

scrip [skrip], *s.* cédula; (com.) póliza, acción o certificado con carácter de vale o abonaré; vales o certificados fraccionarios de valores; esquela, apunte.—**s. holder,** tenedor de vales o certificados provisionales.

script [skript], *s.* letra cursiva; (impr.) plumilla inglesa; (for.) escritura; material escrito a máquina; sinopsis y argumento de un drama cinematográfico, guión (*m.*) de película; (teat.) manuscrito; (rad.) libreto.

scriptural [skríp̆chūṟạl], *a.* bíblico.

scripturally [-i], *adv.* conforme a la Biblia.— **Scripture** [skrípchū(r)], *s.* Escritura (la Biblia).

scrivener [skrívęncę(r)], *s.* plumista; notario; escribano, (fig.) tagarote; (ant.) corredor de cambios.

scrofula [skráfyųḷạ], *s.* (med.) escrófula.—**scrofulism** [-lizm], *s.* escrofulismo.—**scrofulous** [-ḷạs], *a.* escrofuloso.

Scrophularia [skrafjulérjạ], *s.* (bot.) (género de las) escrofularias.—**scrophulariaceous** [-jéj̇- śạs], *a.* (bot.) escrofulariáceo.

scrotal [skróųtạl], *a.* (anat.) escrotal.

scrotum [skróųtʌm], *s.* (anat.) escroto.

scrub [skráb]. I. *va.* fregar, estregar, estropajear; restregar; limpiar, depurar, lavar (un gas, etc.); limpiar fregando. II. *a.* achaparrado, desmirriado; inferior, mezquino.—**s. land,** chaparral, monte bajo.—**s. team,** (dep.) equipo compuesto de jugadores novicios o poco hábiles. **III.** *s.* estropajo, escoba vieja, aljofifa (de fregar); animal de raza mixta e inferior; persona mezquina; árbol achaparrado; monte bajo.

scrubber [-œ(r)], *s.* restregador; limpiasuelos; bruza; (quím. y metal.) limpiador, depurador.

scrubbing [-iŋ]. **I.** *s.* fregadura, fregado, estregadura; estropajeo (esp. del suelo). **II.** *a.* de estregar, de estropajear.—**s. brush,** bruza para el suelo, estregadera, cepillo limpiasuelos o de fregar.

scrubby [-i], *a.* estropajoso; despreciable; achaparrado.

scruff [skrʌf], *s.* nuca, pescuezo; (fund.) = DROSS.

scrumptious [skrʌmpŝʌs], *a.* (fam.) elegante; excelente, magnífico.

scrunch [skrʌnch]. **I.** *va.* y *vn.* = CRUNCH; (fam.) apretar, aplastar, arrugar. **II.** *s.* chasquido.

scruple [skrúpl]. **I.** *s.* escrúpulo; rescoldo; (farm.) escrúpulo (peso de 20 granos); cantidad ínfima. **II.** *vn.* escrupulizar, tener escrúpulos.

scrupulous [skrúpyŭlʌs], *a.* escrupuloso, concienzudo, exacto, puntilloso.—**scrupulously** [-li], *adv.* escrupulosamente.—**scrupulousness** [-nis], **scrupulosity** [-láṣiti], *s.* escrupulosidad.

scrutineer [skrutiŋír], *s.* escrutiñador.

scrutinize [skrútiŋaiẓ], *va.* escudriñar, escrutar.

scrutinizing [-iŋ], **scrutinous** [skrútiŋʌs], *a.* escudriñador, curioso.

scrutiny [skrútiŋi], *s.* escrutinio, escudriñamiento.

scud [skʌd]. **I.** *vn.* correr, volar o deslizarse rápidamente.—**to s. before the wind,** (mar.) correr viento en popa. **II.** *s.* carrera rápida; celajes, *m. pl.*

scuff [skʌf]. **I.** *va.* y *vn.* restregar; dañar(se) o poner(se) áspera una superficie con el uso o desgaste; arrastrar los pies; chancletear. **II.** *s.* desgaste (en una superficie); arrastramiento de los pies; chancleta.

scuffle [skʌfl]. **I.** *s.* rebatiña, forcejeo, refriega, pelea. **II.** *vn.* andar a la rebatiña, forcejear.

scull [skʌl]. **I.** *s.* (remo de) espadilla; botequín a dos remos. **II.** *vn.* bogar con espadilla; remar en botequín.

sculler [-œ(r)], *s.* bote de espadilla; remero de dicho bote o de un botequín a dos remos.

scullery [skʌlœri], *s.* espetera; fregadero.—**s. department** o **work,** sollastría.

scullion [skʌlyọn], *s.* marmitón, pinche, galopín de cocina, sollastre.—**s. wench,** fregona.

sculper [skʌlpœ(r)], *s.* buril, cincel (ll. t. **scauper**).

sculpin [skʌlpin], *s.* (ict.) coto espinoso.

sculptor [skʌlptọ(r)], *s.* escultor.—**sculptress** [-tris], *s.* escultora.—**sculptural** [skʌlpchŭral], *a.* escultural, escultórico.—**sculpture** [skʌlpchŭ(r)]. **I.** *s.* escultura; estatuaria, entalladura, grabadura, grabadura, *f.* **II.** *va.* esculpir, entallar, cincelar.—**sculpturesque** [-ésk], *a.* escultural, majestuoso.

scum [skʌm]. **I.** *s.* espuma, nata, hez, escoria.—**s. of metals,** escoria de metales.—**the s. of the people,** la hez del pueblo. **II.** *va.* y *vn.* espumar.

scumble [skʌmbl]. **I.** *va.* (pint.) dar glacis; (dib.) esfumar. *V.* STUMP. **II.** *s.* (pint.) glacis, *m.*, unión de colores; (dib.) esfumino.

scummy [skʌmi], *a.* espumoso, espumajoso.

scup [skʌp], *s.* (ict.) especie de pargo.

scupper [skʌpœ(r)], *s.* (mar.) imbornal o embornal.

scurf [skœrf], *s.* caspa; costra.—**scurfiness** [-nis], *s.* estado casposo o costroso.—**scurfy** [-i], *a.* casposo, costroso.

scurrility [skœríliti], *s.* grosería, insolencia, procacidad, desvergüenza.—**scurrilous** [skœriḷʌs], *a.* grosero, indecente, procaz; difamatorio.

scurrilously [-li], *adv.* injuriosa o groseramente.—**scurrilousness** [-nis], *s.* calidad de procaz o de insolente.

scurry [skœri]. **I.** *va.* poner en fuga, barrer. **II.** *vn.* echar a correr, escaparse, escabullirse. **III.** *s.* fuga precipitada; ventolera, remolino.

scurvied [skœrvid], *a.* escorbútico.

scurvily [skœrvili], *adv.* vilmente; groseramente; ignominiosamente.—**scurviness** [-nis], *s.* torpeza; vileza.

scurvy [skœrvi]. **I.** *s.* (med.) escorbuto. **II.** *a.* vil, ruin, despreciable.—**s. grass,** (bot.) coclearia.

scutate [skjútejt], *a.* (zool.) escutiforme; cubierto de placas en forma de escamas; (bot.) escuteliforme.

scutch [skʌch]. **I.** *va.* agramar, espadar, tascar, espadillar. **II.** *s.* estopa; agramaduras, *f. pl.*; agramadera; martillo de enladrillador.

scutcheon [skʌchọn], *s.* (blas.) escudo de armas; (zool.) escudete, escudo.

scutcher [skʌchœ(r)], *s.* agramadera; batidera; aventador.

scute [skjút], *s.* (anat., zool.) escud(ill)o, escudete.

scutellate(d [-ẹlejt(id], *a.* (zool.) escuteliforme; provisto de un escudete; cubierto de placas.

scutellum [skjutélʌm], *s.* (bot., zool.) escudete, escudillo.

scutiform [skjútifọrm], *a.* escutiforme.

scuttle [skʌtl]. **I.** *s.* escotillón; trampa; barreno, agujero; carrera corta; paso acelerado; cubo, balde.—**s. butt,** (mar.) pipa o tonel de agua de beber; (fam.) chismes, *m. pl.*; runrún. **II.** *va.* barrenar, dar barreno; echar a pique. **III.** *vn.* apretar a correr. *V.* SCURRY.

scythe [saiδ]. **I.** *s.* guadaña, dalle. **II.** *va.* guadañar.—**scythed** [-d], *a.* armado de guadaña, falcado.

Scythian [síθian]. **I.** *a.* y *s.* escita, *mf.* **II.** *a.* escítico.

'sdeath [zdeθ], *interj.* (ant.) ¡vive Dios!

sea [sí]. **I.** *s.* mar, *mf.*; océano, golfo, (poét.) ponto; agua(s); ola, oleada, oleaje, marejada; ola grande; la mar, abundancia excesiva o vasta extensión de una cosa. **II.** *a.* de mar, marino, marítimo; naval.—**s. anchor,** (mar., aer.) ancla flotante.—**s. anemone,** (zool.) anémone (*f.*) de mar.—**s. bank,** muralla de mar, rompeolas; orilla del mar.—**s. bass,** (ict.) especie de lobina o róbalo marino.—**s. bear,** (zool.) foca; oso polar.—**s.-beat(en,** azotado por las olas.—**s. biscuit,** galleta.—**s. blue,** azul marino, verdemar.—**s. boat,** buque marinero. —**s.-born,** nacido en la mar; marino.—**s.-borne,** transportado por mar.—**s. breach,** irrupción de mar que rompe un dique.—**s. bream,** (ict.) besugo, besuguete, chopa.—**s. breeze,** brisa de mar, virazón, *f.*—**s. brief,** (mar.) carta de mar o marítima.—**s. cabbage, s. colewort, s. kale,** (bot.) berza marina.—**s. calf,** (zool.) foca o becerro marino.—**s. captain,** capitán de buque de mar.—**s. card,** rosa náutica.—**s. chart,** carta de marear.—**s. coal,** carbón mineral.—**s. cob,** (orn.) gaviota.—**s. cock,** grifo de (comunicación con el) mar.—**s. compass,** brújula o aguja de marear.—**s. cow,** (zool.) vaca marina, dugongo, manatí; morsa. —**s. cucumber,** (zool.) holoturia, cohombro de mar.—**s. dog,** (zool.) foca común; (ict.) tiburón espinoso, perro de mar; (fam.) lobo de mar, marinero viejo; pirata, *m.*, filibustero.— **s. eagle,** (orn.) halieto.—**s. egg,** (zool.) erizo de mar.—**s. fan,** (zool.) gorgonia.—**s. fight,** combate naval.—**s. foam,** espuma de mar; magnesita.—**s. food,** pescado y mariscos comestibles.—**s. fowl,** ave marina.—**s.-gate,** oleada larga; punto de salida al mar; compuerta de marea.—**s. goose,** (orn.) pato marino, barnacla, *m.*; especie de fúlica o gallineta; (zool.) delfín.—**s. green,** verdemar, glauco.—**s. gull,** (orn.) gaviota.—**s. hare,** (zool.) liebre marina, huevo de pulpo.—**s. hedgehog,** (zool.) erizo de mar.—**s. hog,** (zool.) marposa.—**s. holly,** (bot.) cardo corredor, eringe, *f.*—**s. horse,** (ict.) caballo marino o hipocampo; (zool.) morsa; (erróneamente) hipopótamo; (mit.) hipocampo.—**s. legs**, (fam.) piernas de marino, pie marino.—**s. letter**, patente de mar.—**s. level**, nivel del mar.—**s. line**, horizonte; sondaleza.—**s. lion**, (zool.) foca, león marino.—**s. mew**, (orn.) gaviota.—**s. mile**, milla marina.—**s. moss**, ova, alga.—**s. nettle**, (zool.) acalefo, ortiga de mar.—**s. nymph**, (mit.) nereida.—**s. onion**, cebolla albarrana, escila marítima.—**s. ooze**, cieno de mar.—**s. otter**, (zool.) nutria de mar, lataz, *mf*.—**s. pass** = **s. LETTER**.—**s. pen**, pluma de mar (pólipo).—**s. pike**, (ict.) espetón; róbalo; merluza.—**s. pilot**, piloto de altura.—**s. power**, potencia naval.—**s. risk**, riesgo o peligro de mar.—**s. room**, espacio para maniobrar sin peligro, resguardo, franquía.—**s. rover** o **robber**, pirata, *m*.—**s. serpent**, sierpe marina (monstruo que algunos han creído ver); (S. S., astr.) Hidra.—**s. snake**, (zool.) hidra = **s. SERPENT**.—**s. salt**, sal marina.—**s. squirt**, (zool.) ascidia.—**s. star** = **STARFISH**.—**s. stores**, víveres para un viaje marítimo.—**s. swine**, (zool.) marsopa o puerco marino.—**s. term**, voz náutica.—**s. tortoise**, tortuga de mar.—**s.-tossed**, batido por el mar.—**s. trout**, (ict.) raño, baila.—**s. turtle** = **s. TORTOISE**.—**s. unicorn**, (zool.) narval.—**s. urchin**, (zool.) erizo de mar.—**s. valve** = **s. COCK**.—**s. wall**, malecón, muralla o dique de mar.—**s. water**, agua de mar, agua salada.—**s. wolf**, (zool.) lobo marino.—**at s.**, en el mar; perplejo, confuso, perdido.—**beyond sea(s)**, o **beyond the seas**, o **beyond the s.**, allende el mar; fuera de aguas jurisdiccionales; fuera de la jurisdicción (de un país, estado, etc.).

seaboard [-bord]. **I.** *a.* costanero, litoral. **II.** *s.* costa, playa; litoral.

seacoast [-ko̞ṣt], *s.* costa marítima, litoral.

seacraft [-kræft], *s.* barcos de mar; habilidad en la navegación.

seadrome [-dro̞m], *s.* (aer.) aeródromo flotante o marino; base (*f.*) de hidroaviones.

seafarer [-fe̞rœ(r)], *s.* marino, navegante.

seafaring [-fe̞ri̱ŋ]. **I.** *a.* marino, marinero, navegante, de mar. **II.** *s.* vida del marino o del mar.

seagirt [-gœrt], *a.* rodeado o cercado por el mar.

seagoing [-go̞u̱i̱ŋ], *a.* (marinero) de altura; navegante.

seal [si̱l]. **I.** *s.* sello; sigilo; signáculo; timbre; precinto; selladura, sigilación; firma; autenticación, fianza; sacramento; (hidr.) obturación; líquido obturador; substancia o artefacto de cierre; nema, cierre o sello de una carta; (zool.) foca.—**s. ring**, sortija con sello.—**under the hand and s. of**, firmado y sellado por. **II.** *va.* sellar, poner el sello, sigilar, precintar; estampar; concluir; poner fin; afirmar, confirmar; lacrar, cerrar una carta o un paquete (con lacre o goma); marchamar; (igl.) santiguar; bautizar; confirmar; guardar secreto; (mec.) tapar con chapaleta; obturar; tapar; (alb.) empotrar, encastrar.—**to s. up**, cerrar. **III.** *vn.* cazar focas.

sealed [-d], *a.* sellado o cerrado.—**s. orders**, instrucciones selladas.

sealer [-œ(r)], *s.* sellador; cazador de focas.

sealine [si̱li̱n], *s.* imitación de piel de foca hecha de pieles de conejo.

sealing [si̱li̱ŋ]. **I.** *s.* selladura; caza o pesquería de focas. **II.** *a.* de sellar; de tapar.—**s. liquid**, líquido obturador.—**s. wax**, lacre.

sealskin [si̱lski̱n], *s.* piel (*f.*) de foca.

seam [si̱m]. **I.** *s.* (cost.) costura; (fund.) rebaba; (cir.) sutura; (mec.) junta, costura (de un tubo, una caldera, etc.); grieta, hendedura; cicatriz, costurón; arruga; (geol. y min.) filón, vena, veta, criadero; capa delgada; yacimiento; (mar.) costura de los tablones. **II.** *va.* coser, juntar; señalar con cicatrices. **III.** *vn.* henderse, rajarse.

seamaid [si̱me̞i̱d], *s.* (poét.) nereida; sirena.

seaman [si̱man], *s.* marinero, marino, nauta, *m*.—**seamanlike** [-lai̱k], **seamanly** [-li̱], *a.* y *adv.* marino, marinesco; (como) de buen marino; a la marinera o marinesca.—**seamanship** [-ṣi̱p], *s.* náutica, marina, marinaje, marinería.

seamark [si̱mark], *s.* baliza, boya; señal, *f.*, faro.

seamless [si̱mlẹs], *a.* inconsútil, sin costura.—**s. tube**, tubo sin costura.

seamstress [si̱mstrẹs], *s.* costurera, labrandera; modistilla.

seamy [si̱mi̱], *a.* con costuras; (fig.) lo peor.—**the s. side**, el lado peor.

Seanad Eireann [sẹnad ẹran], *s.* (en Irlanda) cámara alta, senado.

séance [sẹjans], *s.* sesión (espec. de espiritistas).

seapiece [si̱pi̱s], *s.* (pint.) marina.

seaplane [si̱plẹi̱n], *s.* hidroavión, *m*.

seaport [si̱port], *s.* puerto de mar.

sear [si̱r]. **I.** *a.* seco, marchito, agostado. **II.** *s.* quemadura; (arm.) muelle real. **III.** *va.* agostar, secar, marchitar; tostar, chamuscar; cauterizar; endurecer, hacer insensible.

search [sœrch]. **I.** *va.* y *vn.* buscar, explorar, escudriñar; registrar (una casa); investigar, inquirir, indagar; (cir.) tentar.—**to s. after**, preguntar por; indagar, inquirir.—**to s. for**, buscar; solicitar, procurar.—**to s. into**, examinar, investigar.—**to s. out**, descubrir buscando. **II.** *s.* registro, visita, reconocimiento; pesquisa, indagación o investigación; búsqueda, busca, buscada.—**s. for arms**, cacheo.—**s. warrant**, (for.) auto que dispone que se haga un registro o reconocimiento.—**in s. of**, en busca de.

searchable [-a̱bl], *a.* que puede buscarse o registrarse; investigable.

searcher [-œ(r)], *s.* investigador, buscador, explorador, escudriñador, indagador, registrador; vista (*mf.*) de aduanas; inspector; (arti.) gato de registro; (cir.) explorador, tienta; (ópt.) buscador.

searching [-i̱ŋ], *a.* penetrante, escrutador; completo, cabal, minucioso, severo.

searchingly [-li̱], *adv.* minuciosamente; penetrantemente, de modo escrutinador.

searchlight [-lai̱t], *s.* (elec.) proyector, reflector, faro, foco eléctrico.

seascape [si̱skẹi̱p], *s.* (pint.) marina.

seashore [si̱ṣor], **seaside** [si̱sai̱d], *s.* playa, litoral, ribera, costa, orilla del mar.—**seaside pine**, (bot.) pino bravo o rodeno, pinastro.

seasick [si̱si̱k], *a.* mareado.—**to get s.**, marearse.

seasickness [-nẹs], *s.* mareo, mareamiento.

season [si̱zon]. **I.** *s.* estación (del año); sazón, *f.*, tiempo oportuno; temporada; época, momento, hora.—**s. cracks**, grietas longitudinales (de la madera, tubos metálicos, etc.).—**s. ticket**, billete de abono o de temporada.—**dull s.**, (com.) estación muerta.—**in due s.**, in s., en tiempo oportuno.—**in s.**, en sazón; a su tiempo.—**in s. and out of s.**, a todas horas, en tiempo y a destiempo.—**out of s.**, fuera de sazón; intempestivo, a destiempo.—**to be in s.**, ser de la estación o del tiempo debido. **II.** *va.* (coc.) sazonar, aliñar, aderezar, salar, condimentar; secar, curar (la madera); imbuir, persuadir, templar, moderar; aclimatar, habituar, acostumbrar. **III.** *vn.* secarse, endurecerse, curarse (madera); sazonarse, madurarse, habituarse.

seasonable [-a̱bl], *a.* oportuno; a propósito; de estación.—**seasonableness** [-nẹs], *s.* sazón, *f.*, oportunidad, tempestividad.—**seasonably** [-a̱bli̱], *adv.* en sazón, oportunamente, tempestivamente.

seasonal [-a̱l], *a.* estacional, de estación, de temporada.

seasoning [-i̱ŋ], *s.* (coc.) condimento, aliño, aderezo, sainete, sazón, *f.*; chiste, salsa o sal, *f.* (de un cuento, etc.); punto o madurez; aclimatación; desecación, cura (de la madera).

seat [sít]. **I.** *s.* asiento; silla, banco; escaño; (teat.) localidad; batalla (de la silla de montar); sillín (de bicicleta); (sast.) fondillos de los calzones; (anat.) nalga(s), asentaderas; sede, *f.* (de diócesis, etc.); sitio, paraje, lugar, situación; puesto; mansión, finca, quinta.—**s. back,** respaldo, espaldar.—**s. cover,** cubreasiento.—**s. of a valve,** asiento de una válvula.—**s. of war,** teatro de la guerra. **II.** *va.* sentar, asentar; colocar en asientos; tener asientos para; ajustar (una válvula) en su asiento; fijar, afianzar; establecer; arraigar; poner asiento a (una silla, etc.); echar fondillos a (un pantalón). **III.** *vn.* asentar, ajustar en su asiento (una válvula, etc.).

seating [-iŋ], *s.* acción de sentar(se), de poner asientos, etc.; material para entapizar muebles; (mec.) lecho, base, *f.*, asiento.—**s. capacity,** cabida (de personas sentadas), número de asientos.

seaward [síwȧrd]. **I.** *adv.* hacia el mar; mar adentro. **II.** *a.* dirigido hacia el mar.

seaware [síwer], *s.* algas arrojadas a la playa, que se usan para abono, etc.

seaway [síweį], *s.* ruta marítima; la alta mar; marcha de un buque por las olas; mar gruesa o alborotada.

seaweed [síwid], *s.* alga marina.

seaworthy [síwœrðį], *a.* marinero.—**seaworthiness** [-nįs], *s.* buen estado de una embarcación.

sebaceous [sįbéįšȧs], *a.* sebáceo.

sebacic [sįbǽsįk], *a.* sebácico.

sebiferous [sįbífɛrʌs], *a.* sebífero; cerífero.

seborrhea [sɛbȯríȧ], *s.* (med.) seborrea, secreción excesiva de substancias sebáceas en la piel.

secant [síkænt], *a.* y *s.* (geom.) secante.

secede [sįsíd], *vn.* separarse.

seceder [-œ(r), *s.* separatista.

secession [sįséšȯn], *s.* secesión.—**secessionism** [-įzm], *s.* (pol.) separatismo.—**secessionist** [-įst], *s.* (pol.) separatista, secesionista.

seclude [sįkljúd]. **I.** *va.* apartar, recluir o encerrar. **II.** *vr.* alejarse de otros.—**secluded** [-įd], *a.* alejado o apartado; retirado, solitario, recogido.

seclusion [sįkljúžȯn], *s.* reclusión, aislamiento, retraimiento, apartamiento, soledad; retiro.

seclusive [sįkljúsįv], *a.* retraído, amigo de la soledad.

second [sékȯnd]. **I.** *a.* segundo; secundario, subordinado; inferior; otro, igual, idéntico; de segundos; para segundos.—**S. Advent,** segundo advenimiento de Jesucristo.—**S. Adventist,** sectario que cree que el segundo advenimiento será en sus días, o antes de pasada la generación viviente.—**s. best,** el mejor después del primero; accésit; (ind. y com.) el número dos, segundo de primera (en calidad).—**s.-born,** segundogénito.—**s. cabin,** (mar.) segunda clase.—**s. cause,** causa secundaria.—**s. childhood,** senectud, chochez.—**s.-class,** de segunda clase; de grado inferior.—**s. fiddle,** segundo violín (ú. fig. en la expresión **to be, o to play, s. fiddle,** desempeñar un papel secundario, obedecer, etc.).—**s. floor o story,** (piso) principal; piso segundo.—**s. growth,** (agr.) bosque renacido.—**s. hand,** segundero (de reloj).—**s.-hand** = SECONDHAND.—**(at) s. hand,** indirectamente, por conducto ajeno; de oídas.—**s. lieutenant,** subteniente, alférez, *m.* —**s. mark,** signo de segundos (″).—**s. nature,** costumbre arraigada.—**s.-rate,** de segunda clase o categoría, de pacotilla.—**s. sheet,** (com.) segunda página de una carta, gen. escrita en papel sin membrete; cuartilla para copia de carbón.—**s. sight,** conocimiento de lo futuro; doble vista.—**s.-string** = s.-RATE. —**seconds pendulum,** péndulo de segundos (cuyas oscilaciones son de 1 segundo).—**every s. day,** cada dos días; un día sí y otro no.—**on s. thought,** después de repensarlo; después de

pensarlo bien.—**to be s. to none,** no ser inferior a nadie o a ningún otro, no ir en zaga a nada o nadie.—**to come off, o out, s.-best,** llevar lo peor, salir mal parado. **II.** *s.* segundo; momento, instante; brazo derecho; ayudante; defensor, sostenedor; padrino (en un desafío); segundo (de tiempo), (mús.) segunda; (geom.) segundo. **III.** *va.* apoyar, apadrinar, ayudar, favorecer; secundar o apoyar (una proposición); (a)segundar. **IV.** *adv.* en segundo lugar.

secondarily [-ɛrįlį], *adv.* secundariamente.

secondariness [-ɛrįnįs], *s.* calidad de secundario.

secondary [-ɛrį]. **I.** *a.* (leng. ord., elec., geol. y fís.) secundario, segundario; subordinado, subalterno; subsecuente; resultante; accesorio; (S., geol.) mesozoico.—**s. battery,** (elec.) acumulador; (mil.) batería secundaria de piezas de artillería.—**s. education,** segunda enseñanza.—**s. school,** escuela secundaria. **II.** *s.* lugarteniente, delegado, diputado, subalterno; (astr.) círculo secundario; planeta secundario; satélite; (orn.) pluma grande de la segunda articulación; (ent.) ala posterior; (elec.) secundario (circuito, bobina, etc.).

seconder [-œ(r)], *s.* el que apoya o secunda una proposición.

secondhand [-hǽnd], *a.* de segunda mano, o usado; indirecto, por conducto ajeno o de oídas.

secondly [-lį], *adv.* en segundo lugar.

secrecy [síkrɛsį], *s.* secreto; reserva; silencio, sigilo; clandestinidad; soledad, retiro.

secret [síkrįt]. **I.** *s.* secreto; callado, reservado; clandestino; escondido, oculto, recóndito.—**s. service,** policía secreta. **II.** *s.* secreto; sigilo; clave, *f.*—**in s.,** en secreto, en puridad.

secretarial [sɛkrɛtérįȧl], *a.* de secretario; de o para secretarios (escuela, etc.).

secretariat(e [sɛkrɛtérįȧt, -įįt], *s.* secretaría (oficina); secretariado; cuerpo de secretarios.

secretary [sékrɛtɛrį], *s.* secretario, secretaria; amanuense; secreter, buró, escritorio, pupitre, papelera.—**s. bird,** (orn.) serpentario.—**S. of Foreign Affairs,** Secretario o Ministro de Relaciones Exteriores.—**S. of State,** Secretario de Estado.—**S. of State for Air,** (Ingl.) Ministro de Aviación.—**S. of the Interior,** Secretario de lo Interior o de Gobernación.— **S. of the Navy,** Secretario de Marina.—**S. of the Treasury,** Secretario de Hacienda o del Tesoro.—**S. of War,** Secretario de Guerra.— **s.'s office,** secretaría.

secretaryship [-šįp], *s.* secretaría, secretariado.

secrete [sįkrít], *va.* esconder, ocultar, encubrir; recatar, callar; (fisiol.) secretar; segregar.

secretin [-įn], *s.* (bioquím.) secretina.

secretion [sįkríšȯn], *s.* (fisiol.) secreción; encubrimiento, ocultación, escondimiento.

secretive [sįkrítįv], *a.* callado, reservado; (fisiol.) secretorio.

secretiveness [-nįs], *s.* inclinación a ocultar o esconder.

secretly [sįkrítlį], *adv.* secretamente, a escondidas, de rebozo, en oculto, a puerta cerrada.

secretness [-nįs], *s.* secreto, sigilo.

secretory [sįkrítorį], *a.* secretorio.

sect [sɛkt], *s.* secta; partido, pandilla.

sectarian [sɛktérįȧn], *a.* y *s.* sectario, sectador.

sectarianism [-įzm], *s.* sectarismo.

sectary [séktȧrį], *s.* sectario; disidente.

sectile [séktįl], *a.* sectil.

section [sékšȯn]. **I.** *s.* sección, división; parte, *f.,* porción; lámina, tajada muy delgada; subdivisión, departamento, negociado; compartimiento; inciso, artículo (de una ley, etc.); tramo (de un terreno, etc.); (E. U.) división de terreno de 1 milla en cuadro (259 hectáreas o 640 acres); (dib.) corte, sección (gen. se entiende la transversal); (impr.) párrafo, signo §. —**s. cutter,** micrótomo. **II.** *va.* seccionar, dividir en secciones.

sectional [-al], *a.* regional, local; hecho de compartimientos.

sectionalism [-ĭzm], *s.* regionalismo; devoción exagerada a los intereses locales.

sector [sékto(r)], *s.* (geom. y mil.) sector; compás de proporción.

secular [sékyŭlạ(r)]. I. *a.* secular, seglar, laico o lego; profano, mundano; secular, centenario. II. *s.* seglar, lego.—**secularity** [-lĕrĭtĭ]. **secularness** [-nĭs], *s.* seglaridad, mundanalidad.—**secularly** [-lĭ], *adv.* seglarmente.—**secularization** [-ĭzéĭṣon], *s.* secularización, exclaustración.—**secularize** [-aĭz]. I. *va.* secularizar, exclaustrar. II. *vr.* aseglararse.

secularism [-ĭzm], *s.* secularismo, laicismo; exclusión de la religión en las escuelas y otras instituciones; librepensamiento (en el sentido de antagonismo a la religión).—**secularist** [-ĭst], *s.* secularista, partidario del secularismo.

secund [síkʌnd], *a.* (bot. y zool.) unilateral.

secundine [sékʌndĭn], *s.* (bot.) secundina; (zool.) (gen. *pl.*) secundinas, placenta.

secure [sĭkyúr]. I. *a.* seguro; tranquilo, confiado; descuidado; cierto, indudable; inexpugnable; firme, fuerte. II. *va.* asegurar, resguardar; salvar, proteger; asegurar, afianzar, fijar; garantizar; prender, coger; encerrar, aprisionar; procurarse, obtener, hacerse dueño de.

securely [-lĭ], *adv.* seguramente, firmemente, fuertemente; sin riesgo; tranquilamente.

secureness [-nĭs], *s.* seguridad, calidad de seguro; falta de cuidado.

security [-ĭtĭ], *s.* seguridad; seguro (social); afianzamiento, aseguramiento; firmeza; protección o defensa; tranquilidad, confianza; descuido; (for.) saneamiento; fianza, garantía, caución, prenda; fiador.—*pl.* (com.) valores, obligaciones, títulos.—**securities in hand**, valores en cartera.—**public securities**, efectos públicos.—**to give s.**, dar fianza; dar fiador.—**to stand s. for**, salir fiador de.

sedan [sĭdén], *s.* silla de manos, toldillo; litera (ll. t. s. **chair**); (aut.) sedán.

sedate [sĭdéĭt], *a.* sentado, sosegado, serio, formal.

sedately [-lĭ], *adv.* sosegadamente.

sedateness [-nĭs], *s.* compostura, formalidad.

sedative [sédạtĭv], *a.* y *s.* (med.) sedativo, sedante, dormitivo, calmante.—**s. salt**, (farm. ant.) ácido bórico.

sedentariness [sédẹnterĭnĭs], *s.* vida sedentaria; calidad de sedentario.—**sedentary** [-terĭ], *a.* sedentario; inactivo; (zool.) sedentario.

sedge [sédž], *s.* (bot.) juncia, junco, enea.—**s. warbler**, (orn.) curruca.

sedgy [-ĭ], *a.* abundante en juncias.

sediment [sédĭmẹnt], *s.* sedimento, poso, asiento, hez o heces, borra; (geol.) sedimento; tierras de aluvión; (quím.) depósito.—**sedimental** [-méntạl], **sedimentary** [-terĭ], *a.* sedimentario.—**sedimentation** [-téĭṣon], *s.* sedimentación.

sedition [sĭdĭṣon], *s.* sedición.—**seditious** [sĭdĭṣạs], *a.* sedicioso.—**seditiously** [-lĭ], *adv.* sediciosamente.—**seditiousness** [-nĭs], *s.* calidad de sedicioso.

seduce [sĭdĭús], *va.* seducir; corromper, pervertir, deshonrar.—**seducement** [-mẹnt], *s.* seducción.—**seducer** [-œ(r)], *s.* seductor, burlador.—**seducible, seduceable** [-ĭbl, -ạbl], *a.* seducible.

seduction [sĭdʌkṣon], *s.* seducción; deshonra.—**seductive** [-tĭv], *a.* seductivo, seductor; atractivo; persuasivo.—**seductress** [-trĭs], *s.* seductora.

sedulity [sĭdĭúlĭtĭ], *s.* diligencia, asiduidad o aplicación, ahinco.

sedulous [sédžŭlạs], *a.* asiduo, diligente, cuidadoso, hacendero, hacendoso.—**sedulously** [-lĭ], *adv.* diligentemente, asiduamente.—**sedulousness** [-nĭs], *s.* diligencia, asiduidad.

sedum [sídʌm], *s.* (bot.) género de las crasuláceas.

see [si], *va.* y *vn.* (*pret.* SAW; *pp.* SEEN) ver; discernir, columbrar, vislumbrar; mirar, observar; comprender, concebir, conocer.—*impv.* **see** (en citas) vide, véase.—**s.?** (fam.) ¿comprende? ¿sabe?—**to s. about**, pensar en; averiguar.—**to s. afar off**, ver de lejos, ver a lo lejos.—**to s. eye to eye**, estar enteramente de acuerdo.—**to s. fit**, creer conveniente.—**to s. (a person) home**, acompañar (a una persona) a su casa.—**to s. into**, penetrar, ver en lo interior de.—**to s. (a person) off**, ir a despedir (a una persona).—**to s. one another**, verse, visitarse.—**to s. one's way (clear) to**, saber uno cómo puede, o ver el modo de (hacer algo).—**to s. red**, echar chispas, montar en cólera.—**to s. service**, estar en servicio durante la guerra; pasar por trabajo o uso rudo o fuerte.—**to s. stars**, (fam.) ver las estrellas.—**to s. the back of**, deshacerse, salir de.—**to s. the light**, comprender, despertarse (fig.); nacer; darse a luz, publicarse.—**to s. the point**, comprender, ver el sentido o aplicación de lo dicho.—**to s. through (a proposition)**, comprender (una proposición).—**to s. through (a person)**, leer (fig.), verle el juego (fig.), adivinar la intención o el pensamiento (a una persona).—**to s. (a person) through**, ayudar (a una persona) a salir del paso, o hasta lo último.—**to s. (a thing) through**, llevar (una cosa) hasta el cabo; estar (en una cosa) hasta el fin o hasta lo último.—**to s. through a millstone**, tener mucha penetración.—**to s. to**, atender a, tener cuidado de; cuidarse de.—**to s. to it that**, atender a que, ver que, hacer que.—**I see**, ¡ya!, ya veo, comprendo.—**let me s., let us s.**, veamos, vamos a ver; déjeme pensar.

see, *s.* (igl.) silla, sede, *f.*

seed [síd]. I. *s.* semilla, simiente, *f.*; grano; semen, esperma; pepita, cuesco; progenie, prole, *f.*, generación; germen, origen, causa primitiva.—**s. bed**, sementera, semillero.—**s. bud**, botón, germen.—**s. corn**, trigo o maíz (*m.*) para sembrar.—**s. drill**, sembradera, máquina de sembrar.—**s. flat**, semillero de cajón.—**s. lac**, laca en grano.—**s. leaf**, (bot.) cotiledón.—**s. pearl**, aljófar, rostrillo.—**s. plant**, planta de semilla, que echa semillas.—**s. plot**, semillero.—**s. sowing**, siembra.—**s. vessel**, (bot.) pericarpio.—**to go, o run, to s.**, granar; agotarse, envejecerse. II. *va.* sementar, sembrar; despepitar; desgargolar (el lino). III. *vn.* hacer la siembra, granar.

seedcake [-kejk], *s.* torta de semillas aromáticas.

seeded [-ĭd], *a.* sembrado; despepitado.

seeder [-œ(r)], *s.* (agr.) sembrador; sembradora o sembradera, máquina de sembrar; despepitador(a).

seediness [-ĭnĭs], *s.* calidad de granado o semilloso; (fam.) desaliño, desaseo.

seedless [-lĭs], *a.* sin semillas; sin pepitas.

seedling [-lĭŋ], *s.* planta de semilla; planta de semillero; árbol de pie; planta recién nacida o joven; retoño, brote; grillo (tallo de semilla).

seedsman [-zmạn], *s.* sembrador; tratante en semillas o simientes.

seedtime [-tajm], *s.* sementera, siembra; tiempo de sembrar.

seedy [-ĭ], *a.* granado, semilloso, que tiene muchas semillas; (fam.) andrajoso, descamisado, zarrapastroso. *V.* SHABBY.

seeing [síĭŋ]. I. *s.* vista, visión, ver. II. *conj.*—**s. that**, visto que, siendo así que, puesto que, ya que. III. *a.* vidente, que ve.—**S. Eye dog**, perro amaestrado para conducir a un ciego.

seek [sík], *va.* y *vn.* (*pret.* y *pp.* SOUGHT) buscar; tratar de, esforzarse por; pedir, exigir, procurar, solicitar, pretender, aspirar a; investigar.—**to s. a person's life**, querer matar a una persona.—**to s. after**, buscar, tratar de obtener.—**to s. for**, buscar.

seeker [-œ(r)], *s.* buscador; investigador.—**s. after**, investigador de; buscador de.

seel [sil], *va.* (cetr.) tapar o coser los ojos, cegar.

seem [sím], *vn.* parecer; parecerle a uno.—**it seems**, parece, a lo que parece.—**it seems to me**, me parece.

seeming [-iŋ]. **I.** *s.* apariencia, parecer, exterior; apariencia falsa. **II.** *a.* aparente.—**seemingly** [-lị], *adv.* aparentemente.—**seemingness** [-nịs], *s.* apariencia; plausibilidad.

seemliness [-lịnịs], *s.* decoro, decencia; bien parecer; propiedad.

seemly [-lị]. **I.** *a.* decente, decoroso, correcto; conveniente. **II.** *adv.* decentemente; de manera conveniente.

seen [sin], *pp.* de TO SEE.

seep [síp], *vn.* filtrar, manar, brotar, salir; colarse, rezumarse, escurrirse.

seepage [-idź], *s.* coladura, escape, filtración; manadero (de petróleo, etc.).

seer [sịr], *s.* profeta, *m.*, vate; adivinador, vidente; [síœ(r)], veedor.

seersucker [sírsakœ(r)], *s.* (tej.) cierto tejido de lino o algodón.

seesaw [síso]. **I.** *s.* vaivén, balance, vibración; balancín de sube y baja, columpio de balancín o de tabla. **II.** *a.* de vaivén, de balance. **III.** *vn.* balancear, columpiarse; jugar en el columpio de tabla; vacilar, alternar.

seethe [síð]. **I.** *va.* remojar, empapar; hacer hervir; (farm.) elijar. **II.** *vn.* hervir, bullir; estar agitado. **III.** *s.* acción de hervir o bullir; estado de agitación.

seething [-iŋ]. **I.** *a.* hirviente o herviente, bullicioso. **II.** *s.* hervor, ebullición.

segment [ségmẹnt]. **I.** *s.* segmento; sección. **II.** *va.* y *vn.* segmentar(se).

segmental [segméntạl], **segmentary** [ségmẹnterị], *a.* segmentario.—**segmental arch**, (arq.) arco escarzano.

segmentation [-téịʃọn], *s.* acción de dividir(se) en segmentos o partes; (biol.) segmentación.

segregate [ségrẹgẹįt]. **I.** *va.* y *vn.* segregar(se), desagregar(se), separar(se). **II.** *a.* segregado, separado, apartado; selecto.—**segregation** [-géịʃọn], *s.* segregación, desagregación, separación.

Seidlitz powders [sédlịts páụdœrz], *s. pl.* (farm.) polvos de Seidlitz.

seignior [sínyọ(r)], *s.* señor.

seigniorage [-idź], *s.* señor(e)aje, monedaje; derecho de braceaje.

seigniory [-i], *s.* señoría, señorío.

seine [seịn]. **I.** *va.* y *vn.* pescar con jábega o red barredera. **II.** *s.* jábega, red, traína, tirona.

seism [sáịzm], *s.* sismo, terremoto, temblor de tierra.—**seismic(al** [sáịzmịk(ạl], *a.* sísmico.

seismogram [-mogræm], *s.* sismograma, *m.*, registro sismográfico.—**seismographer** [-mágrạfœ(r)], *s.* sismólogo.—**seismographic(al** [-mogræfịk(ạl], *a.* sismográfico.

seismograph, seismometer [-mogræf, -mámẹtœ(r)], *s.* sismógrafo, sismómetro.

seismologist [-málodźịst], *s.* sismólogo.

seismology [-dźị], *s.* sismología.

seizable [sízạbl], *a.* expuesto a ser asido o embargado; (for.) embargable.

seize [síz]. **I.** *va.* asir, agarrar, coger; apresar, capturar, prender; apoderarse de; aprovecharse de; comprender, darse cuenta de; (for.) secuestrar, embargar, (de)comisar, encautarse de (bienes, etc.); sobrecoger.—**to be seized**, o **seised, of**, (for.) obtener posesión de.—**to be seized with**, sobrecogerse de. **II.** *vn.* (gen. con *on* o *upon*) agarrar, coger; apoderarse de.

seizer [-œ(r)], *s.* agarrador; (for.) secuestrador.

seizin, seisin [sízịn], *s.* (for.) posesión (acto de poseer y cosa poseída); toma de posesión.

seizing [sízịŋ], *s.* toma de posesión; (mar.) trinca, traba; ligadura, aferramiento.

seizure [sízụ̆(r)], *s.* asimiento; aprehensión, prendimiento, prisión; captura, presa; (mil.) toma; (for.) embargo, secuestro, (de)comiso; (med.)

ataque, acceso, comienzo súbito de una enfermedad.

sej(e)ant [sídźạnt], *a.* (blas.) sentado.

selachian [sịléịkịạn], *a.* y *s.* (ict.) selacio.

seldom [séldọm], *adv.* raramente, rara vez, por rareza, pocas veces.

select [sẹlékt]. **I.** *va.* seleccionar, escoger, elegir, entresacar, optar (por). **II.** *a.* selecto, escogido, florido, granado.

selection [-ṣọn], *s.* selección o seleccionamiento, elección, escogimiento; trozo, pieza o escrito escogidos; (com.) surtido.

selective [-tịv], *a.* escogedor, que tiene la facultad o el poder de escoger; (biol.) selectivo.

selectman [-mạn], *s.* (E. U.) miembro del ayuntamiento, administrador municipal.

selectness [-nịs], *s.* calidad de selecto o escogido.

selector [-ọ(r)], *s.* escogedor; (elec.) selector.

selenic [sẹlénịk], *a.* (quím.) selénico.

selenid(e [sélẹnịd, -ạįd], *s.* (quím.) seleniuro.

selenite [sélẹnạịt], *s.* (min. y quím.) espejuelo, selenita; (S.) selenita, *mf.*, habitante de la luna.

selenium [selínị∧m], *s.* (quím.) selenio.

selenographic(al [selinográfịk(ạl], *a.* selenográfico.

selenography [selẹnágrạfị], *s.* selenografía.

self [sélf]. **I.** *a.* mismo; por sí mismo; idéntico, propio (desusado excepto en el compuesto **self-same**); (bot.) puro, no mezclado (colores). **II.** *s.* (*pl.* SELVES) uno mismo, sí mismo; (en composición) por sí mismo.—**the s.**, el yo, el propio yo. Se une a los pronombres personales, a algunos adjetivos posesivos y al pronombre *one* para formar pronombres reflexivos o para dar más fuerza a la expresión: *myself*, yo mismo, me; *himself*, *herself*, *itself*, se; *ourselves*, *yourselves*, *themselves*, nos, os, se; *one's self* o *oneself*, sí mismo, se. Véanse estos pronombres en sus respectivos lugares. Se separa a veces *self* del adjetivo posesivo, y entonces puede traducirse por el pronombre sencillo respectivo: *my wife and self*, mi esposa y yo; *my other self*, mi otro yo.—*my former self*, mi ser anterior; *your good self*, su buena persona. Antepuesto, *self* entra en muchas palabras con los significados de *por sí mismo*, *a sí mismo*, etc., y a menudo equivale al prefijo *auto*.—**s.-abased**, humillado por la conciencia de su propia falta o vergüenza. —**s.-abnegation**, abnegación.—**s. abuse**, censura de sí mismo; masturbación.—**s.-acting**, automático.—**s.-addressed envelope**, sobre con el nombre y dirección de uno.—**s.-affected**, amante de sí mismo.—**s.-assertive**, que se hace sentir; que hace sentir sus derechos o pretensiones.—**s.-assured**, = SELF-RELIANT. —**s.-binder**, (agr.) segadora agavilladora.— **s.-centered**, concentrado en sí mismo.—**s.-command**, dominio sobre sí mismo.—**s.-complacency**, complacencia en sí mismo. —**s.-complacent**, satisfecho de sí mismo, engreído.—**s.-conceit**, engreimiento, presunción, vanidad, arrogancia.—**s.-conceited**, presumido, arrogante, presuntuoso.—**s.-confidence**, confianza en sí mismo.—**s.-conscious**, consciente de sí mismo; concentrado en sí mismo, que obra con esfuerzo consciente y manifiesto por hacerlo bien; afectado, falto de naturalidad. —**s.-consistent**, consecuente consigo mismo. —**s.-contained**, completo, que contiene en sí todos sus elementos o accesorios; moderado, dueño de sí mismo; callado, reservado.—**s.-contradiction**, contradicción manifiesta.— **s.-contradictory**, antinómico.—**s.-control**, continencia; imperio sobre sí mismo.—**s.-convicted**, convicto por confesión propia; que se condena a sí mismo.—**s.-deception**, o delusion, engaño de sí mismo, vana ilusión.—**s.-defeating**, contraproducente.—**s.-defense**, defensa propia.—**s.-denial**, abnegación.—**s.-denying**, abnegado, desinteresado.—**s.-destruction**, suicidio.—**s.-determination**, libre determinación, autonomía, independencia.— **s.-devotion,** dedicación de una persona o sus deseos e intereses al servicio de una causa o de otra persona.—**s.-educated,** autodidacto.— **s.-esteem,** amor propio.—**s.-evident,** patente, evidente por sí mismo, que se cae de suyo.—**s.-examination,** examen de conciencia.—**s.-excitation,** (elec.) autoexcitación. —(to) **s.-excite,** (elec.) autoexcitar.—**s.-existent,** existente por sí mismo, eterno.—**s.-explaining,** que se explica por sí mismo.—**s.-expression,** modo de obrar según inclinación o carácter propios, expresión de la propia individualidad.—**s.-feeder,** de alimentación automática.—**s.-feeding,** de alimentación propia; (animal) criado o alimentado con alimentador automático.—**s.-governing,** autónomo.—**s.-government,** imperio sobre sí mismo; (pol.) autonomía.—**s.-help,** ayuda propia o de sí mismo.—**s.-heterodyne,** (rad.) autodino.— **s.-identity,** conciencia de la identidad del yo. —**s.-importance,** propia importancia; engreimiento.—**s.-induction,** (elec.) autoinducción. —**s.-indulgence,** complacencia excesiva para consigo mismo, falta de sobriedad, desenfreno. —**s.-indulgent,** sibarita, regalón; sensual.—**s.-instructor,** maestro de sí mismo, autodidacto. —**s.-interest,** propio interés.—**s.-liquidating,** de propia liquidación.—**s.-locking,** (de) cierre automático.—**s.-love,** egoísmo, amor propio, amor de sí mismo.—**s.-made,** que se ha levantado por sus propios esfuerzos.—**s.-moving,** automotor.—**s.-portrait,** autorretrato.—**s.-possession,** sangre fría, serenidad, aplomo.—**s.-preservation,** propia conservación.—**s.-propelled,** automóvil, locomóvil, de propulsión mecánica o automática.—**s.-regulating,** de regulación automática.—**s.-reliance,** confianza en sí mismo.—**s.-reliant,** confiado en sí mismo.—**s.-respect,** pundonor, dignidad, decoro, respeto de sí mismo, estimación propia.—**s.-respecting,** digno, pundonoroso.—**s.-restraint,** moderación, continencia. —**s.-righteous,** pagado de su propia rectitud; farisaico.—**s.-righteousness,** vanagloria de la rectitud o virtud propia; fariseísmo.—**s.-seeking,** s. egoísmo; a. egoísta, interesado.— **s.-sacrifice,** abnegación.—**s.-service,** a. sin empleados (apl. a ciertos restaurantes, tiendas, etc., donde uno se sirve a sí mismo).—**s.-starter,** (mec.) (de) arranque automático.— **s.-styled,** que se apellida o titula, que a sí mismo se llama.—**s.-sufficience, s.-sufficiency,** presunción, confianza desmedida en sí mismo; autarquía, autosuficiencia, capacidad de bastarse a sí mismo.—**s.-sufficient,** confiado en sí mismo; orgulloso, arrogante; autosuficiente, que se basta a sí mismo.—**s.-supporting, s.-sustaining,** que se sostiene o mantiene por sus propios esfuerzos o recursos. —**s.-taught,** autodidacto.—**s.-will,** obstinación, terquedad, porfía.—**s.-willed,** obstinado, tereo.—**s.-winding,** de cuerda automática (apl. a relojes).—**s.-worship,** egolatría, culto de sí mismo.—**s.-worshipper, s.-worshipping,** ególatra, mf.

selfheal [sélfhīl], s. (bot.) sanícula.

selfhood [sélfhụd], s. personalidad consciente; existencia independiente; egoísmo.

selfish [sélfịš], a. egoísta, interesado.—**selfishly** [-lị], adv. por egoísmo; interesada o egoísticamente.—**selfishness** [-nịs], s. egoísmo, egotismo, amor propio.

selfsame [sélfséịm], a. idéntico, mismísimo.

sell [sél]. I. va. (pret. y pp. SOLD) vender, despachar; (fam.) hacer aceptar o reconocer, convertir, convencer (ú. esp. en la voz pasiva **to be sold on,** estar convencido de, haberse convertido a).— to s., de venta, para la venta.—**to s. at auction,** almonedear, vender en pública subasta. —**to s. down the river,** (fam.) traicionar.—

to s. for a mere song, vender por una bicoca. —to s. (for) cash, o for ready money, vender al contado.—to s. on trust, fiar, vender al fiado.—to s. out, realizar, hacer venta de realización, liquidar lo que queda antes de cerrar una tienda; vender los bienes de un deudor para pagar; agotar (una edición, etc.); (fam.) venderse, hacer traición.—to s. short, (com.) vender acciones o efectos que uno no tiene y que espera comprar a bajo precio antes de hacer la entrega; (fig.) desestimar. II. vn. vender, traficar, hacer el comercio; venderse, tener buena venta (un artículo). III. s. (fam.) engaño, fraude.

seller [-œ(r)], s. vendedor.

selling [-iŋ]. I. s. venta, acción de vender. II. a. de venta; que vende.

sellout [sélaụt], s. (fam.) liquidación completa (de géneros); venta de todos los billetes disponibles.

Seltzer [séltsœ(r)], s. agua de Seltz, agua carbónica.

selvage [sélvịdẓ], s. (tej.) hirma, orillo de paño; borde, orilla, lista, orla; (min.) salbanda.

selves [sélvz], pl. de SELF.

semantics [sẹmǽntịks], s. semántica, estudio del desarrollo del significado de las palabras.

semaphore [sémạfọr], s. semáforo, telégrafo óptico; (f. c.) disco, telégrafo de señales.

semaphoric(al [-fórịk(ạl], a. semafórico.

semasiology [sẹmeịsiảlodẓị], s. semasiología.— **semasiologic(al** [-sịoládẓịk(ạl], a. semántico.

semblance [sémblạns], s. semejanza; exterior, aspecto, apariencia; además, velo; imagen.

semeiology [simaị̃álodẓị], **semeiotics** [-átịks], s. (med.) semeiología, semeiótica.

semen [símen], s. (fisiol.) semen, esperma; (bot.) simiente, f., semilla.

semester [sẹméstœ(r)], s. semestre.

semi- [sémị], prefijo, semi, medio.

semiannual [-ǽnyụạl], a. semestral, de cada seis meses.—**semiannually** [-ị], adv. semestralmente.

semiannular [-ǽnyụlạ(r)], a. semianular.

semiaxis [-ǽksịs], s. semieje.

semibreve [-brịv], s. (mús.) semibreve, f.—**s. rest,** aspiración de semibreve.

semicentennial [-sénténịạl], s. y a. cincuentenario.

semicircle [-sœrkl], s. semicírculo, hemiciclo.

semicircular [-sœrkịulạ(r)], a. semicircular.—**s. canals,** (anat.) canales semicirculares (del oído).

semicircumference [-sœrkΛmfẹrẹns], s. semicircunferencia.

semicolon [-koụlọn], s. punto y coma (;).

semidiameter [-daịémetœ(r)], s. semidiámetro.

semidiurnal [-daịœrnạl], a. semidiurno.

semidouble [-dΛbl]. I. a. (bot.) semidoble. II. s. (igl.) semidoble.

semifinal [-fáịnạl]. I. a. semifinal. II. s. pl. (dep.) partido, carrera, etc., antes de los finales.

semifloret [-flóret], s. (bot.) semiflósculo.

semifloscular, semifloscuolous [-fláskịulạ(r), -lΛs], a. (bot.) semifloscular.

semifluid [-flúịd], a. semifluído.

semiglobular [-glábyụlạr], a. semiesférico.

semilunar(y [-lịúnạr(ị], a. semilunar.

semilunation [-éịọn], s. semilunio.

semimanufactured [-mænyụfǽkchụrd], a. a medio acabar.

semimonthly [-mΛnθlị]. I. a. quincenal, bimensual. II. s. publicación quincenal. III. adv. quincenalmente, dos veces por mes.

seminal [sémịnạl], a. seminal, espermático; embrionario; elemental; (bot.) seminal, sementino.

seminar [sémịnạr], s. estudio superior que hace un grupo de estudiantes; dicho estudio, grupo, o la sala donde se reúne.

seminarist [-nẹrịst], s. seminarista.

seminary [-nẹrị]. I. s. seminario; colegio. V.

seminar. II. *a.* perteneciente a los seminarios.

semination [seminéişọn], *s.* sementera; diseminación, propagación; (biol.) seminación.

seminiferous [-níferʌs], *a.* seminífero.

seminific(al [-nífik(ạl], *a.* seminal, seminífero; sementino.

semiofficial [-ofṣ̌al], *a.* oficioso, semioficial.

semiology [simịólodẑị], **semiotics** [-átịks], *s.* (med.) semiología, semiótica.

semiordinate [semịórdịneịt], *s.* (geom.) semiordenada.

semiporcelain [-pórsẹlạn], *s.* porcelana falsa o imitada; loza de inferior calidad.

semiquadrate [-kwádreịt], **semiquartile** [-kwórtaịl], *s.* (astr.) semicuadrado.

semiquaver [-kweịvœ(r)], *s.* (mús.) semicorchea.

semiquintile [-kwíntaịl], *s.* (astr.) semiquintil.

semirigid [-rídẑịd]. I. *a.* (aer.) semirrígido. II. *s.* aeróstato semirrígido.

semisextile [-sékstaịl], *s.* (astr.) semisextil.

semispherical [-sférịkạl], *a.* semiesférico, hemisférico.

semisteel [-stil], *s.* acero pudelado.

Semite [sémaịt], *s.* semita, *mf.*

Semitic [sẹmítịk]. I. *a.* semítico, semita. II. *s.* semita; conjunto de las lenguas semíticas.— **Semitics** [-s], *s.* estudio de los semitas.

Semitism [sémịtịzm], *s.* semitismo.

semitone [sémịtoụn], *s.* (mús.) semitono.

semivocal [-vóụkạl], *a.* (fon.) semivocal.

semivowel [-vaụẹl], *s.* (fon.) letra semivocal.

semiweekly [-wíklị]. I. *a.* bisemanal. II. *s.* publicación bisemanal. III. *adv.* bisemanalmente.

semiyearly [-yírlị], *a.* semestral.

semolina [semolínɑ̈], *s.* sémola.

sempiternal [sempịtœ́rnạl], *a.* sempiterno.

sempstress [sémpstrịs], *s.* costurera.

senary [sénạrị], *a.* y *s.* senario.

senate [sénịt], *s.* senado; (S.) Cámara alta, junta directiva de algunas universidades; consejo, cuerpo legislativo; junta de personas venerables.— **s. house,** senado (sala).

senator [sénạtọ(r)], *s.* senador.

senatorial [senạtórịạl], *a.* senatoria, senatorial.

senatorship [sénạtọrşịp], *s.* senaduría.

senatus consultum [sịnéịtas kọnsΛltam], senadoconsulto.

send [sénd]. I. *va.* (*pret. y pp.* SENT) enviar, despachar, expedir, remesar, transmitir; echar, lanzar, arrojar, producir; difundir, extender, propagar; conceder, dar.— **to s. away,** despedir, poner en la calle.— **to s. back,** devolver; enviar de vuelta, enviar otra vez.— **to s. forth,** echar (retoños, etc.); emitir, despedir, exhalar (luz, vapores); enviar, despachar.— **to s. in,** hacer entrar; introducir.— **to s. in one's papers,** renunciar.— **to s. off,** despachar, expedir.— **to s. one about one's business,** enviar a paseo, echar o despachar a uno sin rodeos.— **to s. up,** enviar arriba; mandar subir; (mar.) izar; (fam.) enviar a la cárcel.— **to s. word,** mandar recado; avisar; enviar a decir. II. *vn.* enviar algún recado o recadero; (mar.) = SCEND.— **to s. for,** enviar a buscar, enviar por, hacer o mandar buscar.

sender [-œ(r)], *s.* remitente, expedidor; enviador; (elec.) transmisor.

send-off [-of], *s.* (fam.) despedida afectuosa.

sending [-ịŋ], *s.* remisión o remesa, envío; transmisión.

Senegalese [senịgalíz], *s.* y *a.* senegalés.

senescence [sẹnésẹns], *s.* senectud.

senescent [-ẹnt], *a.* que envejece.

seneschal [sénẹşạl], *s.* senescal.

senile [sínaịl], *a.* senil, caduco.

senility [sẹnílịtị], *s.* senilidad, senectud; ñoñez.

senior [sínyọ(r)]. I. *a.* mayor, de mayor edad; más antiguo; (E. U.) del último año en un colegio. II. *s.* señor mayor, anciano; decano; socio más antiguo o más caracterizado; (E. U.) escolar del último año en un colegio; (después de

un nombre, en la forma abreviada **Sr.**) padre.

seniority [sinyárịtị], *s.* antigüedad; ancianidad; decanato; prioridad.

senna [sénɑ̈], *s.* (bot.) sen o sena.

sensate [sénseịt], *a.* percibido por los sentidos.

sensation [senséịşọn], *s.* sensación, sentimiento; excitación.— **to be a s.,** dar golpe; ser un exitazo.— **sensational** [-ạl], *a.* relativo a la sensación; notable, sensacional; escandaloso.— **sensationalism** [-ịzm], *s.* (filos.) sensualismo.— **sensationalist** [-ịst], *s.* sensualista.— **sensationally** [-ị], *adv.* sensacionalmente.

sense [séns]. I. *s.* sentido; razón, *f.*, juicio; sensación; sentimiento; inteligencia, entendimiento; significado, interpretación; substancia; (geom. y mec.) sentido, dirección (el primer término es el más propio y preciso).— **s. impression,** sensación, impresión sensual.— **s. organ,** órgano de los sentidos.— **s. perception,** percepción sensual.— **in a s.,** hasta cierto punto.— **in no s.,** por ningún concepto.— **the senses,** los sentidos.— **to be out of one's senses,** haber perdido el juicio, no estar en sus cabales. II. *va.* percibir por los sentidos; (fam.) sentir, inferir intuitivamente; sospechar.

senseless [-lịs], *a.* insensible, privado, desmayado, sin conocimiento; sin sentido, absurdo; insensato, necio.— **senselessly** [-lị], *adv.* insensatamente.— **senselessness** [-nịs], *s.* tontería, insensatez.

sensibility [sénsịbịlịtị], *s.* sensibilidad; precisión (de instrumentos). V. SENSITIVENESS.

sensible [-bl], *a.* cuerdo, razonable; sensato; perceptible, sensible; sensitivo.— **s. note o tone,** (mús.) nota sensible o séptima.— **to be s. (of),** hacerse cargo de, estar persuadido de.— **sensibleness** [-nịs], *s.* sensibilidad; cordura, sensatez.— **sensibly** [-blị], *adv.* perceptiblemente, sensiblemente; cuerdamente.

sensitive [sénsịtịv], *a.* sensitivo; sensible, impresionable; susceptible; tierno, sentido; delicado; (fis., etc.) sensible (instrumento, etc.); (fot.) sensibilizado.— **s. plant,** (bot.) sensitiva, mimosa.— **sensitively** [-lị], *adv.* sensiblemente.

sensitiveness [-nịs], *s.* sensibilidad (de una persona, de un instrumento); susceptibilidad; finura, delicadeza; precisión.

sensitivity [sensịtívịtị], *s.* sensibilidad.

sensitization [-tịzéịşọn], *s.* (fot.) sensibilización.— **sensitize** [-taịz], *va.* sensibilizar.— **sensitized** [-d], *a.* sensibilizado.— **sensitizer** [-œ(r)] *s.* sensibilizador.

sensorial [sensórịạl], *a.* sensorio.

sensorium [-ịạm], *s.*, **sensory** [sénsọrị], *s.* y *a.* (anat.) sensorio.

sensual [sénşụạl], *a.* sensual, voluptuoso, lascivo, lujurioso; carnal.— **sensualism** [-ịzm], *s.* sensualismo; sensualidad.— **sensualist** [-ịst], *s.* sibarita, *mf.*; (filos.) sensualista.

sensuality [-éljtị], *s.* sensualidad, voluptuosidad, lascivia.

sensualize [-aịz], *va.* y *vn.* hacer sensual; volverse sensual.

sensually [-ị], *adv.* sensual o voluptuosamente.

sensuous [sénsụΛs], *a.* sensorio o sensitivo; tierno, sensible, apasionado.

sensuousness [-nịs], *s.* sensibilidad; sensualidad; afición a lo bello.

sent [sént], *pret. y pp.* de TO SEND.

sentence [séntẹns]. I. *s.* (gram.) oración, cláusula, período; dictamen, opinión, parecer; (for.) sentencia, fallo; condena (de presidio); máxima, sentencia o dicho; (mús.) frase, *f.* II. *va.* sentenciar, condenar.

sentential [senténşạl], *a.* (gram.) de la oración.

sententious [-ṣʌs], *a.* (gram.) de la oración, lacónico.— **sententiously** [-lị], *adv.* sentenciosamente.— **sententiousness** [-nịs], *s.* estilo sentencioso.

sentience [sénşịẹns], **sentiency** [-ị], *s.* conciencia, estado consciente; percepción; sensibilidad.—

sentient [-ent]. **I.** *a.* consciente. **II.** *s.* ser consciente; conciencia, sensibilidad mental.

sentiment [séntiment], *s.* sentimiento; afecto, simpatía; modo de sentir o de pensar, opinión, sentir, concepto; sentido, significado.

sentimental [-méntal], *a.* sentimental.—**sentimentalism, sentimentality** [-izm, -mentáliti], *s.* sentimentalismo.—**sentimentalist** [-méntalist], *s.* persona que se guía por sentimentalismo, sentimentalista.—**sentimentalize** [-méntalaiz], *va.* y *vn.* tratar u obrar sentimentalmente; atribuir sentimiento a.

sentimentally [-méntali], *adv.* sentimentalmente.

sentinel [séntinel], **sentry** [séntri], *s.* (mil.) centinela, *mf.*—**to stand sentry,** hacer o estar de centinela.—**sentry box,** garita de centinela.

sepal [sípal], *s.* (bot.) sépalo.

separability, separableness [séparabíliti, -blnis], *s.* calidad de separable; naturaleza separable.—**separable** [-bl], *a.* separable, partible, disgregable.—**separably** [-bli], *adv.* separablemente.

separate [sépareit]. **I.** *va.* separar, segregar, disgregar, disolver, partir, dividir; disociar, apartar, alejar, divorciar; desnatar (leche); descarriar (ganado). **II.** *vn.* separarse, desunirse. **III.** [séparit], *a.* separado, aparte, suelto; distinto, diferente; desunido, segregado.—**separately** [-li], *adv.* separadamente, por separado, uno a uno, aparte, de por sí.—**separateness** [-nis], *s.* estado de separación.—**separation** [-éisón], *s.* separación, segregación, disgregación; divorcio.—**separatist** [séparatist], *s.* (pol.) separatista; (igl.) cismático.—**separative** [-ativ], *a.* separativo, distintivo.

separator [sépareito(r)], *s.* separador; divisor, partidor; centrífuga (para desnatar leche).

separatory [-átori], *a.* separativo.—**s.** (o **separating**) **funnel,** (quím.) embudo de separación.

Sephardic [sifárdik], *a.* sefardí, sefardita.

Sephardim [-dim], *s. pl.* sefardíes, sefarditas, *mf.*

sepia [sípia]. **I.** *s.* (pint.) sepia; dibujo a la sepia; (ict.) sepia, jibia; jibión, *m.* **II.** *a.* de sepia.

sepoy [sípoi], *s.* cipayo, soldado indio.

sepsis [sépsis], *s.* (med.) sepsis, infección séptica causada por substancias pútridas.

sept [sept], *s.* clan, tribu, *f.*

septa [sépta], *s. pl.* de SEPTUM.

septal [séptal], *a.* (anat.) septal, rel. a un séptum.

septangle [séptangl], *s.* (geom.) heptágono.

septate [sépteit], *a.* tabicado, que tiene tabiques.

September [septémbœ(r)], *s.* septiembre.

septemia [septímiá], *s.* (med.) septicemia.

septenary [septénari]. **I.** *a.* septenario. **II.** *s.* septena; septenio.

septennial [septénial], *a.* sieteñal.

septet [septét], *s.* septena; (mús.) septeto.

septic [séptik], *a.* séptico.—**s. tank,** foso séptico.

septicemia [septisímiá], *s.* (med.) septicemia.—**septicemic** [-símik], *a.* septicémico.

septillion [septilyon], *s.* septillón; (E. U. y Fr.) unidad con 24 ceros; (Ingl.) unidad con 42 ceros.

septimole [séptimoul], *s.* (mús.) septillo.

septuagenarian [sepchuadżenérian], *a.* y *s.* septuagenario, setentón.

septuagenary [-édżenari], *a.* septuagenario.—**Septuagesima** [-adżésimá], *s.* septuagésima.—**septuagesimal** [-l], *a.* septuagésimo.

Septuagint [sépchuadżint], *s.* (bib.) versión griega de los Setenta.—**Septuagintal** [-dżíntal], *a.* relativo a, o según, la versión de los Setenta.

septum [séptam], *s.* (anat.) séptum, septo, tabique.

septuple [séptiupl]. **I.** *a.* séptuplo. **II.** *va.* y *vn.* septuplicar(se).

septuplet [-plet], *s.* (mús.) septillo.

sepulchral [sepálkral], *a.* sepulcral, fúnebre.

sepulcher, sepulchre [sépʌlkœ(r)]. **I.** *s.* sepulcro, sepultura. **II.** *va.* sepultar, enterrar.

sepulture [sépʌlchŭ(r)], *s.* inhumación, sepultura, entierro.

sequacious [sikwéiaas], *a.* secuaz; lógico.

sequel [síkwel], *s.* secuela, consecuencia, efecto; continuación.

sequela [sikwílá], *s.* adherente, secuaz, *mf.*; grupo de adherentes; consecuencia, inferencia; (med.) secuela.

sequence [síkwens], *s.* serie, orden de sucesión; arreglo; encadenamiento, ilación; efecto; en los naipes, runfla de un palo; (mús.) modulación; (igl.) secuencia.

sequent [síkwent], *a.* siguiente, subsiguiente.

sequester [sikwéstœ(r)]. **I.** *va.* separar, retirar, apartar; (for.) secuestrar. **II.** *vn.* (for.) renunciar una viuda a toda intervención en la liquidación de la herencia de su marido.

sequestrable [-trabl], *a.* secuestrable.

sequestrate [-treit], *va.* (for.) confiscar, comisar; secuestrar.

sequestration [-tréisón], *s.* (for.) embargo, secuestro, secuestración; reclusión, retiro.—**sequestrator** [síkwestreito(r)], *s.* secuestrador.

sequestrum [sikwéstrʌm], *s.* (cir.) secuestro.

sequin [síkwin], *s.* cequí (moneda); lentejuela, adorno reluciente para vestidos.

sequoia [sikwóiá], *s.* (bot.) abeto gigantesco de California.

seraglio [sirélyou], *s.* serrallo, harem o harén; palacio turco; mancebía, burdel.

seraph [séraf], *s.* (*pl.* -PHIM) serafín.—**seraphic** (**-al** [seréfik(al], *a.* seráfico.—**seraphically** [-i]. *adv.* seráficamente.

Serb [sœrb], **Serbian** [-ian], *s.* y *a.* servio.—**Serbo-Croatian** [-okroyéisán], *s.* y *a.* servocroata (idioma y raza).

sere [sir], *a.* seco, marchito, agostado. *V.* SEAR.

serenade [serenéid]. **I.** *s.* (mús.) serenata. **II.** *va.* dar serenata a.

serene [serín], *a.* sereno, despejado; sosegado, tranquilo.—**most s.,** serenísimo (título).—**serenely** [-li], *adv.* serenamente.—**sereneness** [-nis], *s.* serenidad de ánimo, tranquilidad, calma.

serenity [serényti], *s.* serenidad, bonanza; tranquilidad, calma, paz, quietud; presencia de ánimo; serenidad (título de algunos príncipes).

serf [sœrf], *s.* siervo.—**serfage** [-idż], **serfdom** [-dom], *s.* condición de siervo, servitud.

serge [sœrdż], *s.* (tej.) estameña, anascote.—**s. silk,** sarga, jerguilla.

sergean(t)cy [sárdżensi], *s.* = SERGEANTSHIP.

sergeant [sárdżent], *s.* (mil.) sargento; (ant.) alguacil, ministril; escudero; (Ingl.) abogado de primera clase (ll. t. **s. at law**).—**s. at arms,** (en un cuerpo legislativo) oficial de orden, que hace guardar el orden.

sergeantship [-śip], *s.* sargentía; grado de sargento.

serial [sírial]. **I.** *a.* de o en serie, de orden (número, marca, etc.); consecutivo; formando serie; que se publica por entregas; sucesivo. **II.** *s.* obra que se publica por entregas; (cine) drama cinematográfico de varias películas, película periódica o episódica.—**serially** [-i], *adv.* en serie; por serie; por entregas.

serialize [-aiz], *va.* publicar o arreglar en forma de serie.

seriatim [siriéitim], *adv.* en serie; uno tras otro.

sericate [sérikeit], *a.* sedoso; velludo.

sericeous [sirísas], *a.* sérico, sedoso, sedeño.

sericultural [serikálchŭral], *a.* sericícola.

sericulture [sérikʌlchŭ(r)], *s.* seri(ci)cultura.

series [síriz]. **I.** *s.* serie; sucesión, cadena; ciclo; (mat.) serie; progresión.—**in s.,** (elec.) en serie. **II.** *a.* en serie (arrollamiento, dínamo, etc.).—**s.-parallel,** (elec.) en serie-paralelo.—**s.-wound,** (elec.) arrollado en serie.

erin [sérịn], *s.* (orn.) verderón.

eringa [sérịŋgȧ], *s.* (bot.) siringa, variedad del árbol del caucho; jeringuilla. *V.* SYRINGA.

erio-comic(al [sịrịokámịk(ȧl], *a.* jocoserio.

erious [sírịⱥs], *a.* serio; formal, severo; grave, de peso, de consecuencia; verdadero, sincero. —**seriously** [-lị], *adv.* seriamente, en serio, de veras; formalmente; gravemente.—**seriousness** [-nịs], *s.* seriedad; formalidad, severidad; gravedad.

erjeant [sárdżęnt], *s.* = SERGEANT.

ermon [sœrmọn], *s.* sermón, prédica; sermoneo. —**S. on the Mount,** sermón del Monte.

ermonize [-aịz], *va.* y *vn.* predicar; sermonear.

ermonizer [-aịzœ(r)], *s.* sermoneador.

erology [sịrálodżị], *s.* (med.) serología, estudio de los sueros y sus efectos.

eron, seroon [sịróụn, sịrún], *s.* sera, serón.—**s. of cinnamon,** churla de canela.—**s. of cocoa,** sobornal de cacao.—**s. of indigo,** zurrón de añil.

serosity [sịrásịtị], *s.* (fisiol., med.) serosidad.

serotherapy [siroθérȧpị], *s.* (med.) s(u)eroterapia.

serotinous [sịrátịnⱥs], *a.* (bot.) serondo, serotino.

serous [sírⱥs], *a.* (fisiol.) seroso; icoroso.—**s. blood,** sanguaza.

serpent [sœrpęnt], *s.* serpiente (*f.*) o sierpe, *f.*; (piro.) buscapiés; (mús.) serpentón; persona traidora; Satanás; (S. astr.) Serpiente; (aer.) sonda corta, cable corto de arrastre. (*V.* TRAIL ROPE.)—**s. eater,** (orn.) serpentario.—**s. star,** (zool.) ofiuro.

serpentine [-tín *o* -táịn]. I. *a.* serpentino; caracoleado.—**s. marble,** serpentina (mármol).—**s. verse,** (poét.) verso que comienza y acaba con la misma palabra. II. *s.* (min.) serpentina. III. *vn.* serpentear.

serpiginous [sœrpídżịnⱥs], *a.* (med.) serpiginoso.

serpigo [sœrpáịgoụ], *s.* (med.) serpigo.

serrate(d [sérẹịt(ịd], *a.* dentellado; (anat., bot., etc.) serrado; (blas.) endentado.

serration [sɛréịṣọn], *s.* endentadura, recorte, recortadura.

serrature [sérȧchụr], *s.* (biol.) estructura serrada, endentadura.

serried [sérịd], *a.* apretado, apiñado, atestado.— **in s. ranks,** (mil.) en filas o hileras apretadas.

serriform [sérịform], *a.* serrado, dentado.

serum [sírⱥm], *s.* suero.—**s. sickness,** enfermedad causada por la inoculación de un suero.— **s. therapy,** (med.) sueroterapia, seroterapia.

servable [sœrvȧbl], *a.* servible.

servant [sœrvȧnt], *s.* criado, sirviente, fámulo, doméstico; servidor.—*pl.* servidumbre.—**s. girl, s. maid,** criada, sirvienta, doncella.—**s. man,** criado.

serve [sœrv]. I. *va.* servir a, estar al servicio de; servir en, estar encargado de; servir de o para, ser de alguna utilidad para; prestar culto a Dios; servir (la mesa); escanciar (vino, etc.); manejar, hacer maniobrar o funcionar (un cañón, etc.); agasajar, obsequiar, divertir; (for.) entregar (una citación o requerimiento); cumplir (una condena); (mar.) aforrar; recompensar; cubrir (el macho a la hembra).—**to s. an office,** desempeñar un cargo.—**to s. a warrant,** ejecutar un auto de prisión.—**to s. one a trick,** jugar a uno una mala partida.—**to s. one's time,** acabar el tiempo de servicio.—**to s. one's turn,** bastar, ser suficiente.—**to s. notice (on),** avisar o dar aviso, hacer saber, advertir, notificar.—**to s. time,** cumplir una condena en presidio.—**it serves you right,** (en tono de reproche) te está bien empleado; bien se lo merece Vd. II. *vn.* servir, ser criado; estar en sujeción; desempeñar los deberes de un empleo; servir a su país, en el ejército o en la marina; bastar, ser suficiente, útil o apto; (dep.) efectuar el saque, sacar o dar saque, servir la pelota; en ciertos juegos, servir con

naipe del mismo palo.—**to s. for,** servir de; hacer oficio de. III. *s.* saque (en el tenis o pelota).

server [-œ(r)], *s.* servidor; criado de mesa; mensajero, portador; (igl.) acólito; bandeja; pala (para pasteles, etc.); saque, *mf.* (en el tenis o pelota); macho de cría (gallo, toro, etc.).

Servian [sœrvịȧn], *s.* y *a.* servio. *V.* SERBIAN.

service [sœrvịs]. I. *s.* servicio; servidumbre; desempeño; oficio; auxilio, ayuda, favor; uso, utilidad, ventaja; vajilla, servicio de mesa, juego (de café, etc.); (igl.) servicio; (for.) obligación de un criado o arrendatario; entrega legal de una citación; (mar.) forro de cable o cabos; cubrición; precio que se paga por la cubrición de un macho de cría; (bot.) serbal. II. *a.* de servicio; ordinario (uniforme, etc.).— **s. book,** misal; libro litúrgico.—**s. ceiling,** (aer.) techo utilizable, altura límite para una velocidad dada.—**s. elevator,** montacargas.— **s. line,** línea del saque (tenis).—**s. man,** empleado o mecánico que hace reparaciones o mantiene el servicio; (mil.) = SERVICEMAN.— **s. pipe,** (hidr.) tubería de toma, tubería que va de la maestra a un edificio.—**s. record,** (mil.) hoja de servicios.—**s. station,** (aut.) estación de servicio, taller de reparaciones.— **s. tree,** (bot.) serbal.—**at your s.,** a su disposición, a sus órdenes, servidor de Vd.—**it is of no s.,** no vale nada, de nada sirve.—**out of s.,** sin acomodo, desacomodado; (mec.) que no funciona.—**to be of s.,** ser útil, servir.—**to hold a s.,** (igl.) celebrar un servicio.—**to see s.,** prestar servicios, servir. III. *va.* atender a; suministrar lo necesario a o para.

serviceable [-ȧbl], *a.* servicial, servible, útil; duradero.—**serviceableness** [-nịs], *s.* calidad de servicial o duradero.—**serviceably** [-ȧblị], *adv.* servicialmente, útilmente; duraderamente.

serviceman [-mæn], *s.* (mil.) individuo en el servicio militar o naval.

servient [sœrvịȧnt], *a.* (for.) subordinado.

servile [sœrvịl], *a.* servil, bajo, abyecto; excesivamente obediente o adulador; (gram.) que no pertenece a la raíz de la palabra, o que no se pronuncia.

servilely [-lị], *adv.* servilmente.

servileness [-nịs], **servility** [sœrvílịtị], *s.* servidumbre, esclavitud; bajeza, vileza.

serving [sœrvịŋ]. I. *a.* sirviente; ministrante.—**s. maid,** criada, sirvienta.—**s. mallet,** (mar.) maceta de forrar.—**s. man,** sirviente, criado. —**s. pantry,** antecomedor.—**s. stuff** o **ropes,** (mar.) forro de cabos.—**s. table,** trinchero. II. *s.* acción de servir, etc.; porción (de comida). *V.* HELPING.

servitor [sœrvịtọ(r)], *s.* servidor; ayudante; seguidor, secuaz, *m.*, partidario.

servitude [sœrvịtjụd], *s.* servidumbre; esclavitud; vasallaje; sujeción; trabajo forzado; (for.) servidumbre.

Servo-Croatian [sœrvo krouéịṣọn], *s.* y *a.* servocroata, *mf.*

servomotor [sœrvomóụtọ(r)], *s.* servomotor, motor auxiliar; motor de dirección (de un torpedo).

sesame [sésȧmị], *s.* (bot.) ajonjolí, sésamo, alegría. *V.* OPEN S.

sesamoid [sésȧmoịd], *s.* y *a.* (anat.) sesamoide(o).

sesquicentennial [séskwịsęnténịȧl]. I. *a.* de o pert. al cumplimiento de 150 años, o siglo y medio. II. *s.* aniversario o fiesta que conmemora tal ocasión.

sesquioxide [-áksaịd], *s.* (quím.) sesquióxido.

sesquipedal [-pẹdȧl], **sesquipedalian** [-pịdéịlịȧn], *a.* sesquipedal.

sessile [sésịl], *a.* (bot., zool.) sésil, sentado.

session [séṣọn], *s.* sesión; junta; tribunal inferior de la Iglesia presbiteriana; período escolar; (Ingl.) sala de justicia; término judicial.—**to hold a s.,** celebrar sesión, (Am.) sesionar.

sessional [-al], *a.* perteneciente a una sesión.

sesterce [séstœrs], *s.* sestercio (moneda romana).

sestertium [sestœ́rṣịʌm], *s.* mil sestercios.

sestet [sestét], *s.* las últimas seis líneas de un soneto; sextilla; (mús.) sexteto.

set [set], *va.* (*pret. y pp.* SET) poner; colocar, asentar; instalar, establecer; poner (una gallina) a empollar; meter, poner (fuego a una casa, etc.); fijar, inmovilizar, paralizar; embarazar, poner en aprietos; determinar, señalar; (con **on**) poner (la mente, la fe, el corazón, la esperanza) en algo, resuelta, firme o anhelosamente; montar, engastar (un diamante); adornar, aderezar (con piedras preciosas, etc.); arreglar; preparar (insectos, etc.); ajustar; alistar, arreglar, poner (una herramienta, un reloj, etc.); afilar, amolar (una navaja, etc.); (cir.) reducir, encasar, ensalmar (un hueso roto); (mec.) triscar (los dientes de una sierra); (impr.) componer (tipo); (constr.) depositar, colocar (piedras, etc.); (mar.) desplegar (velas); (mús.) dar (la nota o la clave); (mús.) poner música a; apostar; (con **at**) apreciar (en), valuar (en), estimar (en), dar por; (con **on**) poner (precio, límite) a; apuntar, señalar, parar (la caza); dar (ejemplo, regla); mostrar, enseñar, establecer; armar, poner (una trampa), tender (lazos); (top.) establecer o poner (un instrumento) en estación.—to s. **afire**, poner fuego a, incendiar.—to s. **afloat**, poner a flote; esparcir, hacer circular.—to s. **against**, indisponer, malquistar con; oponer u oponerse; contraponer a.—to s. **agoing**, hacer ir; poner en juego o movimiento; echar (algo) a andar; dar impulso a.—to s. **ajar**, entornar, entreabrir.—to s. **apart**, poner aparte.—to s. **a price on**, fijar precio a; poner a precio, ofrecer premio por.—to s. **aside**, dar de mano; poner a un lado o aparte; apartar; ahorrar; hacer caso omiso de; desechar, rechazar; abrogar, anular; destinar, reservar.—to s. **a task**, imponer una tarea.—to s. **at defiance**, retar, desafiar; desconocer, no hacer caso de.—to s. **at ease**, tranquilizar.—to s. **at liberty**, poner en libertad.—to s. **at naught**, despreciar, tener en nada.—to s. **at odds**, desunir, malquistar.—to s. **at rest**, poner en reposo; poner fin a.—to s. **at variance**, desunir, poner en contradicción o antagonismo.—to s. **back**, hacer retroceder; hacer perder lo ganado.—to s. **before**, presentar a, exponer ante; poner a la vista de.—to s. **by**, poner a un lado; guardar.—to s. **by the ears**, hacer reñir, malquistar.—to s. **down**, poner, colocar; poner por escrito; poner en tierra; apuntar, asentar; imponer, determinar; establecer, sentar, enunciar; censurar o humillar.—to s. **eyes on**, ver; mirar; clavar los ojos a.—to s. **fast**, sujetar, consolidar; adelantar (un reloj).—to s. **fire to**, poner o prender fuego a, incendiar; inflamar (las pasiones).—to s. **forth**, manifestar; exponer; promulgar; explicar; exhibir; ensalzar, alabar; publicar.—to s. **forward**, hacer adelantar o avanzar; promover, fomentar; empujar, impeler.—to s. **free**, poner en libertad.—to s. **great store by**, dar mucha importancia a.—to s. **in**, engastar.—to s. **in order**, arreglar, poner en orden.—to s. **light**, o **little, by**, menospreciar, dar poca importancia a.—to s. **milk**, poner leche a cuajar; cuajar leche.—to s. **off**, poner aparte, reservar, separar; comparar, contraponer; poner en relieve, hacer resaltar o destacarse; adornar, embellecer; disparar.—to s. **off against**, reemplazar por, dar como equivalente de.—to s. **on**, excitar, incitar, instigar contra; azuzar, echar (perros, etc.) a.—to s. **on end**, erizar, levantar el pelo.—to s. **one's cap at**, o **for**, (fam.) aspirar a, decidirse resueltamente a (casarse con cierto hombre, etc.).—to s. **one's course for**, hacer rumbo a.—to s. **one's face**, estar resuelto.—to s. **one's hand**, o **one's hand and seal to**, poner su

firma a, firmar; (fig.) aceptar, aprobar.—to **one's house in order**, poner su casa en orde[n] arreglar sus negocios; prepararse para la muert[e] —to s. **one's mind on**, aplicarse a.—to s. **one's teeth**, apretar los dientes.—to s. **one[']s] teeth on edge**, dar dentera.—to s. **on fire** pegar fuego a.—to s. **open**, abrir.—to s. **out** exponer, manifestar; equipar, armar; publicar promulgar; asignar, señalar; adornar, herme[ar] sear; (agr.) plantar, trasplantar.—to s. **over** traspasar, ceder; dar la dirección o el mando de —to s. **right**, colocar bien; enmendar, corregi[r] rectificar; desengañar.—to s. **sail**, hacerse a l[a] vela, zarpar.—to s. **store by**, dar valor o im[-] portancia a.—to s. **the pace**, dar el ejemplo.— to s. **the river**, the Thames, o **the world**, o[n] **fire**, hacer prodigios, ser el inventor de la pól[-] vora (gen. en la forma negativa, vg. *he wi[ll] never set the world on fire*, él no es una maravilla él no fué el inventor de la pólvora).—to s. **th[e] table**, poner la mesa.—to s. **the watch**, rend[ir] la guardia.—to s. **thinking**, hacer pensa[r] dar que pensar.—to s. **to music**, poner e[n] música.—to s. **to rights**, poner en orden.—t[o] s. **to work**, poner a trabajar; emplear, ocupa[r] —to s. **up**, ensalzar, exaltar, elevar; erigi[r] fundar, instituir, constituir; sentar, levanta[r] (tienda de campaña, etc.); enderezar, empinar[;] exponer y defender (una teoría, etc.); causa[r] producir, determinar; vender a subasta; (mec.[)] armar, montar; dar o pegar (un grito); estable[-] cer, abrir, poner (negocios, tienda, etc.); esta[-] blecer (a una persona); instalar; poner d[e] ejemplo o de modelo; (top.) poner en estació[n] (un instrumento); (impr.) poner en tipo; com[-] poner (tipo).—to s. **up the drinks**, (fam.[)] convidar (a beber).

set, *vn.* (astr.) ponerse (un astro); cuajarse, soli[-] dificarse; endurecerse; fraguar (el hormigó[n] etc.); fijarse; correr, moverse o fluir (una co[-] rriente); tender, inclinarse; aplicarse, dedicars[e] ponerse a; cambiar, alterarse, deformarse; em[-] pezar a crecer o desarrollarse; convertirse en fruto o semilla; (danz.) situarse enfrente de[l] compañero de baile; empollar (las aves); (fam.[)] sentar, ajustar, caer bien (una prenda de vestir[)] —to s. **about**, emprender, comenzar.—to s[.] **down**, (aer.) aterrizar.—to s. **forth**, avanza[r] ponerse en marcha.—to s. **in**, comenzar, apa[-] recer, sobrevenir; fluir (la marea); cerrar (l[a] noche).—to s. **off**, salir, partir.—to s. **on**, o[?] **upon**, salir, partir; empezar; acometer, atacar[.] —to s. **out**, salir, partir; emprender un viaje o u[n] negocio.—to s. **to**, aplicarse con vigor a[?] ponerse a (trabajar).—to s. **to work**, pone[r] manos a la obra; emprender el trabajo.—to s[.] **up**, establecerse; principiar, aparecer.—to s[.] **up for**, pasar plaza de, darla o echarla(s) de[,] pasar por.

set. **I.** *a.* resuelto, determinado; obstinado, terco[,] testarudo, inflexible, inadaptable; fijo, inva[-] riable; establecido, prescrito; regular, arreglado[,] ajustado; formal; meditado, estudiado; puesto[,] sentado, colocado; rígido, yerto, inmóvil; hecho[,] trabajado, construído, fabricado; (mec.) ar[-] mado; (joy.) montado, engastado.—s. **form**[,] formulario.—s. **price**, precio fijo.—s. **square**[,] (dib.) escuadra.—to **be** (all) s. to, estar listo o[?] preparado a.—to **be s. on**, estar resuelto a[.] **II.** *s.* juego, surtido, colección, serie, grupo[,] clase, *f.*; equipo; aparato (de radio); instru[-] mento, etc., con sus accesorios; recado; com[-] pañía, camarilla, cuadrilla, banda, hato, pan[-] dilla; círculo, centro, esfera, medio; (joy.[)] aderezo; (astr.) puesta; curso, movimiento[,] dirección, tendencia; encorvadura; porte; tris[-] camiento de los dientes de ciertas sierras; de[-] formación; (agr.) planta de trasplantar; bulbo[;] pie (*m.*) de árbol; fruto en estado rudimentari[o] (teat.) decoración; (sast.) *V.* FIT; (dep.) par[-] tida; (danz.) tanda; (tec.) endurecimiento (de la cola, etc.); fraguado (del cemento, etc.).—**s. of books**, colección de libros; juego de libros.—**s. of chairs**, *juego de sillas*.—**s. of china**, servicio de porcelana.—**s. of diamonds**, aderezo de diamantes; terno.—**s. of dishes**, vajilla.—**s. of drawing instruments**, estuche de compases.—**s. of horses**, tiro, tronco, pareja de caballos.—**s. of oars**, juego de remos.—**s. of stairs**, tramo de escalera.—**s. of surgical instruments**, instrumental.—**s. of teeth**, dentadura.

setaceous [sịtéịṣʌs], *a.* cerdoso, cerdudo.

setback [sétbæk], *s.* retroceso, revés, contrariedad; contracorriente, *f.*

setbolt [sétboụlt], *s.* (mar.) botador, perno de trabante.

setdown [sétdaụn], *s.* reprimenda; (fam.) peluca.

setiferous [sịtífɛɹʌs], *a.* cerdoso.

setiform [sịtịform], *a.* de forma de cerda.

setoff [sétɔf], *s.* compensación; contrapeso; adorno; relieve, realce; (arq.) saliente, *f.*, vuelo; (arq.) disminución progresiva; (for.) contrarreclamación; reconvención; (impr.) tiznadura.

seton [sịtọn], *s.* (cir. y vet.) sedal, fuente, *f.*

setose [sítoụṣ], *a.* cerdoso.

setout [sétaụt], *s.* salida; comienzo; (fam.) arreglos y equipo para un viaje; boato, aparato.

setscrew [sétskruː], *s.* (mec.) tornillo de sujeción o de presión.

settee [setí], *s.* banco; canapé.—**s. bed**, cama turca, cama sofá.

setter [sétœ(r)], *s.* (en composición) el que monta, pone, coloca o fija; perro de ajeo, perdiguero; espión, *m.*, espía, *mf.*; corchete, alguacil.

setting [sétịṇ], *s.* puesta de un astro, ocaso, postura; (constr.) fraguado (del hormigón, etc.); medio circundante, ambiente; (teat.) puesta en escena, decoraciones; (joy.) engaste, montadura; armadura, marco, guarnición; (fam.) nidada.—**s. of the wind, o current**, (mar.) dirección del viento o de la corriente.—**s. sun**, sol poniente.—**s. up**, establecimiento; (mec.) montaje.—**s.-up exercises**, calistenia, ejercicios físicos sin aparatos.

settle [sétl], **I.** *va.* colocar, asentar; fijar, asegurar; arreglar; establecer, estatuir; dar una profesión o estado a; casar; colonizar, poblar; clarificar, quitar la hez; sosegar, calmar, decidir, determinar; poner fin a, acabar; aclarar, resolver (dudas); solucionar (un problema); señalar, fijar; saldar, liquidar, finiquitar, ajustar, arreglar (cuentas); componer, redondear; dejar firme y transitable (un camino).—**to s. on, o upon**, dar en dote, señalar, asignar. **II.** *vn.* posarse, reposarse, asentarse; (quím.) depositarse, sedimentarse; hacer sedimento; arraigar, establecerse, radicarse, fijar su residencia; tomar estado; casarse; instalarse, poner casa; sosegarse, calmar; contraerse; decidirse, determinarse; liquidar con acreedores; saldar una cuenta.—**to s. differences**, avenirse, hacer las paces.—**to s. down**, asentarse; fijarse; posarse (un hidroavión o ave); cobrar juicio; ponerse a. **III.** *s.* banco, escaño.—**s. bed** = SETTEE BED.

settled [-d], *a.* fijo; establecido; arraigado, en orden; asentado; determinado, decidido; arreglado; saldado; poblado; seguro (tiempo).

settlement [-mẹnt], *s.* establecimiento, instalación; colonización; colonia; caserío, ranchería, poblado, pueblo; (for.) asiento, domicilio; (for.) dote (*mf.*) que se da en arras a una mujer; institución, centro de asistencia o servicio social; comunidad formada por un grupo religioso; (arq.) hundimiento, descenso, asiento de un edificio; acomodo, empleo, destino; ajuste, convenio, arreglo; (com.) saldo, liquidación, finiquito; pago.—**s. worker** = SOCIAL WORKER.

settler [sétlœ(r)], *s.* poblador, colono, colonizador; establecedor, fundador; árbitro, conciliador (de disputas).—**s. of averages**, medidor de averías.

settling [sétlịṇ], **I.** *s.* establecimiento, arraigo,

colonización; arreglo; conciliación; instalación; (arq.) sentamiento, hundimiento; ajustamiento.—*pl.* heces, *f. pl.*, zurrapas; sedimiento, poso. **II.** *a.* de asentar; de sedimentación; de clarificación.

set-to [séttú], *s.* lucha, combate; disputa.

setup [sétʌp], *s.* organización; arreglo, disposición; porte, presencia (de una persona); (metal.) máquina de comprimir para rebordear; (fam.) invitación (a beber); plan. (fam.) empresa o contienda fácil, o de éxito seguro.

setwall [sétwɔl], *s.* (bot.) valeriana.

seven [sévn], *s.* y *a.* siete.—**s. hundred(th)**, setecientos.—**s. o'clock**, las siete.—**the s. deadly sins**, los siete pecados capitales.—**the S. Hills**, las siete colinas (de Roma).—**the S. Seas**, todos los mares, el mundo entero.—**the S. Wise Men**, los siete sabios (de Grecia).—**the S. Wonders**, las siete maravillas.

sevenfold [-fóụld]. **I.** *a.* séptuplo. **II.** *adv.* siete veces.

sevenscore [-skɔr], *a.* y *s.* siete veintenas.

seventeen [sɛvntín], *a.* y *s.* diecisiete.

seventeenth [-θ]. **I.** *a.* décimoséptimo, diecisiete (ordinal). **II.** *s.* y *a.* diecisieteavo (fracción).

seventh [sévnθ]. **I.** *a.* séptimo.—**s. heaven**, (fig.) éxtasis, *m.* **II.** *s.* y *a.* (arit.) séptimo, la séptima parte; (mús.) séptima.—**seventhly** [-lị], *adv.* en séptimo lugar.

seventieth [sévntiịθ]. **I.** *a.* septuagésimo, setenta (ordinal). **II.** *s.* y *a.* setentavo (fracción).

seventy [sévntị], *a.* y *s.* setenta.

seventy-five [-fáịv], *s.* (arti.) cañón de 75 milímetros (ll. t. simplemente *setenta y cinco*).

sever [sévœ(r)]. **I.** *va.* separar, desunir, dividir, seccionar; cortar, romper. **II.** *vn.* separarse, desunirse; entreabrirse; partirse.

severable [-ʌbl], *a.* separable; excluíble.

several [sévœrʌl]. **I.** *a.* varios, diversos; distinto(s). respectivo(s). **II.** *s.* varios, cada uno en particular.—**severally** [-lị], *adv.* separada, distinta o individualmente; a parte, cada uno de por sí.—**joint(ly) and s.**, (for.) solidario; solidariamente, in sólidum.

severalty [-tị], *s.* (for.) posesión privativa de un terreno.

severance [sévœrʌns], *s.* separación, partición, división; (dipl.) ruptura o rompimiento (de relaciones).

severe [sẹvír], *a.* severo, riguroso; duro, cruel, acerbo, rígido, estricto, austero, escueto; grave, serio; recio, fuerte; bravo.—**severely** [-lị], *adv.* severamente, cruelmente, rigurosamente.

severeness [-nịs], **severity** [sẹvérịtị], *s.* severidad, rigor, crueldad; rigidez, rigorismo, exactitud, austeridad; seriedad, gravedad; inclemencia.

Sevillian [sẹvílyạn], *a.* y *s.* sevillano.

sew [soụ], *va.* y *vn.* (*pp.* SEWED O SEWN) coser.

sewage [sịúịdž]. **I.** *s.* aguas de albañal, aguas fecales; alcantarillado. *V.* SEWERAGE.—**s. disposal, s. purification**, depuración de aguas fecales. **II.** *va.* (agr.) abonar o regar con aguas fecales.

sewer [sóụœ(r)], *s.* (cost., enc.) cosedor.

sewer [sịúœ(r)]. **I.** *s.* albañal, cloaca, alcantarilla.—**s. gas**, emanaciones de las cloacas. **II.** *va.* alcantarillar; proveer de, o desaguar con, un sistema de cloacas.

sewerage [-ịdž], *s.* alcantarillado; sistema (*m.*) de cloacas.

sewing [sóụịṇ]. **I.** *s.* costura. **II.** *a.* de coser; para coser.—**s. basket**, cesta de costura.—**s. bee**, reunión de amigas para hacer costura.—**s. case**, neceser de costura.—**s. machine**, máquina de coser.—**s.-machine needle**, aguja de máquina de coser.—**s. press**, (enc.) telar.—**s. room, s. stand o table**, costurero.—**s. thread**, hilo de coser.

sex [sɛks], *s.* sexo.—**s. appeal**, atracción sexual.—**the fair s.**, el bello sexo.

sexagenarian [seksǎdženérịạn], *a.* y *s.* sexagenario, sesentón.

sexagenary [seksédženerị], *a.* y *s.* sexagenario.

Sexagesima [seksǎdžésịmǎ], *s.* (igl.) sexagésima.

sexagesimal [-l], *a.* sexagesimal.

sexangle [séksæŋgl], *s.* (geom.) hexágono.

sexed [sekst], *a.* sexuado.

sexennial [seksénịạl], *a.* que dura seis años, o acontece cada seis años.

sexless [sékslịs], *a.* neutro, sin sexo, asexual.

sext [sekst], *s.* (igl.) sexta (una de las horas menores); sexto (libro de decretos canónicos).

sextain [sékstejn], *s.* (poét.) sextilla.

sextant [sékstạnt], *s.* sextante (instrumento); (geom.) sextante.

sextet [sekstét], *s.* (mús.) sexteto.

sextile [sékstịl], *a.* y *s.* (astr.) (aspecto) sextil.

sextillion [sekstílyọn], *s.* sextillón; (E. U. y Fr.) unidad con 21 ceros; (Ingl.) unidad con 36 ceros.

sextodecimo [sekstodésịmọu], *a.* y *s.* dieciseisavo.

sexton [sékstọn], *s.* (igl.) sacristán; sepulturero.

sextuple [sekstjúpl], *a.* séxtuplo.

sexual [séksụạl], *a.* sexual.—*s.* **intercourse**, cópula, coito; comercio sexual.

sexuality [-ælịtị], *s.* sexualidad.

sexually [séksụạlị], *adv.* sexualmente.

sfumato [sfumáto], *a.* (pint.) esfumado.

sgraffito [zgrạffítou], *s.* (b. a.) obra esgrafiada.

shabbily [šébịlị], *adv.* zarrapastrosamente, andrajosamente; ruinmente, mezquinamente.

shabbiness [šébịnịs], *s.* desaseo, desaliño, estado zarrapastroso; ruindad, mezquindad.

shabby [šébị], *a.* usado, gastado, raído; desaseado, andrajoso, desharrapado, zarrapastroso; ruin, vil.—*s.* **genteel**, cursi.

shack [šæk], *s.* (fam.) choza, cabaña, casuca, casucha; casa destartalada.

shackle [šékl]. I. *va.* encadenar, aherrojar, atar; poner esposas o grilletes a; trabar; poner obstáculos, estorbar. II. *s.* grillete, grillo, esposa; maniota, arropea, trabón (para bestias); traba, impedimento; sujeción; (f. c.) cadena o perno de enganche.—*pl.* hierros, prisiones.—*s.* **bolt**, cáncamo de grillete; perno de horquilla; gancho o eslabón de candado.

shad [šæd], *s.* (ict.) alosa, sábalo, trisa.

shaddock [šédọk], *s.* (bot.) especie de cidro y su fruto algo parecido a la toronja.

shade [šéjd]. I. *s.* sombra; umbría; retiro; matiz, *m.*, tinte; ligera diferencia; un poco, cantidad pequeña; visillo, cortina, transparente (de ventana); pantalla de lámpara; visera; sombraje, umbráculo, toldo; (pint.) esbatimento; sombra, espectro, fantasma, *m.*; ficción, ilusión, imagen, *f.*—*pl.* (the shades) la obscuridad al anochecer; el báratro, el averno.—*s.* **tree**, árbol de sombra. II. *va.* sombrear, dar sombra; oscurecer; entoldar; resguardar de la luz; esconder, amparar; (b. a.) sombrear; matizar, casar bien los colores; rasguear (las letras).

shadeless [-lịs], *a.* privado de sombra.

shadily [-ịlị], *adv.* con sombra, en la sombra; (fam.) sospechosamente.

shadiness [-ịnịs], *s.* calidad de sombreado; (fam.) calidad de sospechoso o dudoso.

shading [-ịŋ], *s.* (b. a.) degradación, sombreado.

shadow [šédou]. I. *s.* sombra (proyectada por un objeto); obscuridad, sombrajo; imagen reflejada (en agua o espejo); sombra, aparecido; retiro reclusión; (pint.) sombra sombreado; vestigio pizca (*not a shadow of doubt*, ni sombra de duda) (fig.) refugio, amparo. II. *va.* anublar, obscurecer, dar sombra, sombrear; (con **forth** o **out**) indicar, representar vagamente; simbolizar; espiar, seguir a uno como su sombra; (b. a.) sombrear, matizar; esbatimentar. III. *vn.* anublarse, obscurecerse; cambiar gradualmente de color.

shadowbox [-baks], *vn.* **shadowboxing** [-ịŋ], *s.* (acción de) ejercitarse en el boxeo peleando con

un contrario imaginario; luchar contra enemigos imaginarios.

shadowgraph [-græf], *s.* silueta; (fís.) = RADIO GRAPH.

shadowy [-ị], *a.* sombroso, umbroso, umbrío obscuro, tenebroso; vago, indefinido; visionario indicador, simbólico.

shady [šéjdị], *a.* sombreado, sombrío, sombroso umbroso; (fam.) sospechoso; de dudosa mora lidad.—**on the s. side of**, pasado(s), más allá de (los cuarenta años, etc.).—**to keep s.**, (fam. guardar oculto.

shaft [šáft], *s.* flecha, dardo, saeta; (arq.) caña fuste de columna; columna, obelisco; chapite o aguja (de torre); (mec.) asta, eje, árbol; cual quier mango largo); barra, humero, cañón d chimenea; (carr.) limón o limonera, lanza, vara varas de las sillas de manos; cañón o tubo de pluma; caja, pozo (de ascensor); caña (de un hueso); (min.) pozo, tiro; (fund.) vientre (de ur alto horno); pozo de ventilación, respiraderc (en edificios de varios pisos).—*s.* **furnace** horno de alimentación superior o de carga po arriba.—*s.* **governor**, regulador axial (montado en el eje).—*s.* **horsepower**, potencia transmi tida por el árbol de transmisión, potencia al freno.—*s.* **pump**, bomba de pozo.

shafted [-ịd], *a.* provisto de eje(s), fuste(s), etc.

shafting [-ịŋ], *s.* (mec.) juego de ejes y correajes; sistema (*m.*) de ejes de transmisión; transmisión por eje o ejes.

shag [šæg]. I. *s.* mechón, pelo áspero y lanudo; tabaco desmenuzado; (tej.) felpa, tripe; velludo; (orn.) corvejón, cuervo marino. II. *va.* y *vn.* (pret. y *pp.* SHAGGED) hacer peludo, hacer escabroso, desigual.—*s.*-**haired**, hirsuto.

shagbark [šégbark], *s.* = HICKORY.

shagginess [šégịnịs], *s.* calidad de peludo o afelpado.

shaggy [šégị], *a.* peludo, velludo, hirsuto; afelpado, lanudo; de somonte, áspero.

shagreen [šạgrín], *s.* piel (*f.*) de zapa; lija; (ten.) chagrín; zapa, piel labrada de manera que forme grano como la de la lija.

shah [šạ], *s.* cha, *m.*, emperador de Persia.

shake [šéjk]. I. *va.* (pret. SHOOK; *pp.* SHAKEN) sacudir o menear, blandir, cimbr(e)ar; tra que(te)ar (un líquido); hacer temblar; lanzar, despedir con ímpetu; debilitar; hacer vacilar o flaquear, desalentar; despertar, excitar, agitar; (mús.) trinar (una nota); (fam.) desembarazarse o salir de, despedir.—**to s. a leg**, (fam.) bailar; menearse, darse prisa.—**to s. down**, hacer caer sacudiendo; (fam.) robar o sacar dinero a.—**to s. hands**, estrecharse la mano.—**to s. hands with**, dar o estrechar la mano a. El *impv.* shake hands with, se usa familiarmente para presentar una persona a otra, y puede traducirse por "tengo el gusto de presentar a."—**to s. off**, sacudir; arrojar con una sacudida; zafarse o salir de.—**to s. one's head**, cabecear, mover la cabeza.—**to s. the dust from one's feet**, sacudirse el polvo de los zapatos; marcharse para no volver.—**to s. to pieces**, sacudir hasta hacer pedazos.—**to s. up**, sacudir, remover; agitar; reorganizar; trastornar, cambiar bruscamente; (fam.) regañar, sermonear. II. *vn.* temblar; estremecerse; cimbr(e)arse; vacilar, titubear; (mús.) trinar; (Ingl.) rajarse, agrietarse (dicho de la madera); (fam.) dar(se) la mano.—**to s. with**, temblar o estremecerse de.—**to s. with cold**, tiritar.—**to s. with laughter**, desternillarse o reventar de risa.—**to s. in one's shoes**, o **boots**, temblar de miedo. III. *s.* sacudida; sacudimiento, traqueteo, meneo; vibración; temblor de tierra; temblor; apretón de manos; tabla de ripia; (fam.) periquete, instante; (ton.) duela; (mús.) trino; rajadura en una toza; bebida de leche batida con otros ingredientes.—**s.-down**, cama improvisada sobre sillas, o de paja; (fam.) robo; extorsión, socaliña mediante la intimidación.—**s.-up**, sacudida; reorganización o cambio de personal.—**no great shakes**, (fam.) no (es) gran cosa, no es cosa del otro jueves.—**the shakes**, (med.) (es)calofrío de la fiebre intermitente; (fam.) desasosiego; miedo.

shaken [-n], *pp.* de TO SHAKE; agitado; rajado o hendido (madero).

shaker [-œ(r)], *s.* temblador, temblón; sacudidor; espolvoreador; (S.) (E. U.) miembro de una secta religiosa.

Shakespearian [ʃeikspɾiən], *a.* perteneciente o relativo a Shakespeare.

shaking [ʃéikiŋ]. **I.** *s.* sacudimiento, sacudida; traqueteo; meneo, zaleo; concusión; temblor o estremecimiento. **II.** *a.* temblante, temblón, tembloroso, trepidante, vibrante.

shako [ʃékou], *s.* (mil.) chacó.

shaky [ʃéiki], *a.* trémulo; movedizo, vacilante, tambaleante, débil; agrietado, hendido; (com.) falto de crédito o solvencia.

shale [ʃeil], *s.* esquisto, pizarra.—**s. oil**, aceite de esquistos.

shall [ʃæl], *v. defec.* (sin infinitivo, pretérito, participio ni imperativo). Como *will*, sirve para formar el futuro de otros verbos, conjugándose los dos en esta forma: para indicar simplemente una acción futura o probable, *I shall, thou wilt, he will, we shall, you will, they will*; para denotar propósito o determinación, mandato, permiso o amenaza, *I will, thou shalt, he shall, we will, you shall, they shall*. Así, por ejemplo: *I shall die*, moriré (tiempo futuro); *I will die*, quiero morir; *he will die*, él morirá (tiempo futuro); *he shall die*, morirá, que muera (imperativo). V. WILL. Asimismo el tiempo futuro con *shall* se emplea a menudo, como el futuro en español, para indicar obligación o estipulación: *thou shalt not kill*, no matarás; *they shall not pass*, no pasarán; *the cement shall be Portland cement*, el cemento será cemento pórtland. También se usa como signo del subjuntivo: *when congress shall meet*, cuando el congreso se reúna.

shalloon [ʃalún], *s.* (tej.) chalón.

shallop [ʃélɔp], *s.* (mar.) chalupa.

shallot [ʃalát], *s.* (bot.) chalote, ascalonia.

shallow [ʃélou]. **I.** *a.* bajo, somero, vadoso, poco profundo; superficial.—**s.-draft**, (mar.) de poco calado.—**s.-brained**, **s.-pated**, ligero de cascos, bobo. **II.** *s.* (mar.) bajío.

shallowness [-njs], *s.* poca profundidad; superficialidad; frivolidad.

shaly [ʃéili], *a.* pizarreño, esquistoso.

sham [ʃæm]. **I.** *va.* y *vn.* simular, fingir.—**to s. Abra(ha)m**, fingirse enfermo. **II.** *s.* fingimiento, ficción, impostura, (fam.) bambolla, farsa. **III.** *a.* fingido, disimulado, supuesto; falso, postizo.—**s. fight**, (mil.) simulacro.—**s. quarrel**, contienda simulada.—**s. sale**, mohatra.

shaman [ʃámən], *s.* exorcista, hechicero.

shamble [ʃémbl]. **I.** *vn.* andar bamboleándose, vacilar. **II.** *s.* bamboleo, paso vacilante.

shambles [-z], *s. pl.* matadero, degolladero; carnicería; mercado de carne.

shame [ʃéim]. **I.** *s.* vergüenza; ignominia, deshonra; humillación, bochorno.—**it is a s.**, es una vergüenza; es una lástima.—**for s.! s. on you!**, ¡qué vergüenza!—**to put to s.**, avergonzar.—**what a s.!**, ¡qué lástima! **II.** *va.* avergonzar, abochornar; afrentar, deshonrar; (con **into** o **out of**) impeler a, por un sentimiento de vergüenza.

shamefaced [-feist], *a.* avergonzado, abochornado; tímido, vergonzoso; modesto, pudoroso.—**shamefacedly** [-li], *adv.* con rubor o modestia.—**shamefacedness** [-njs], *s.* timidez, vergüenza, rubor.

shameful [-ful], *a.* vergonzoso, escandaloso.

shamefully [-i], *adv.* vergonzosamente.—**shameless** [-ljs], *a.* desvergonzado, sin vergüenza,

descarado, impudente.—**shamelessly** [-li], *adv.* desvergonzadamente.—**shamelessness** [-njs], *s.* desvergüenza, impudencia.

shammer [ʃémœ(r)], *s.* impostor, fingidor.

shammy, shamois [ʃémi], *s.* (zool.) gamuza.—**s. leather** = CHAMOIS.

shampoo [ʃæmpú]. **I.** *va.* lavar la cabeza; dar champú; sobar. **II.** *s.* lavado de cabeza; champú; frotación, soba.

shamrock [ʃémrak], *s.* (bot.) trébol, trifolio; emblema (*m.*) de Irlanda.

shandygaff [ʃéndigæf], *s.* bebida de cerveza y otro líquido gaseoso.

shanghai [ʃéŋhai], *va.* (mar.) emborrachar o narcotizar y embarcar (a alguien contra su voluntad o su conocimiento); llevar a uno por engaño o coerción.

shank [ʃæŋk], *s.* caña o canilla de la pierna; zanca, pierna de las aves; (mec.) asta o astil, mango, vástago, caña, espiga; (impr.) cuerpo del tipo; (arq.) fuste, caña; (zap.) enfranque de la suela; rabo o cola de botón; (bot.) pecíolo.—**s. of an anchor**, (mar.) caña de ancla.

shanked [-t], *a.* que tiene caña, astil o mango.—**long-s.**, zancudo.

shan't, sha'n't [ʃænt]. (fam.) abreviación de SHALL NOT. V. SHALL.

shanty [ʃénti], *s.* casucha, choza, tabuquillo.

shapable, shapeable [ʃéipəbl], *a.* capaz de recibir una forma; bien formado.

shape [ʃéip]. **I.** *va.* formar; dar forma a; plasmar, labrar, ahormar, modelar; determinar; adaptar; dirigir; regular. **II.** *vn.* (a veces con **up**) empezar a tomar, formar o mostrar progreso; salir (bien o mal). **III.** *s.* forma, figura, aspecto; cuerpo, figura, hechura (de una persona); modelo; horma; molde; condición, estado; manera, modo.

shapeless [-ljs], *a.* informe; disforme.

shapelessness [-ljsnjs], *s.* deformidad, informidad.—**shapeliness** [-linjs], *s.* belleza de forma, proporción.

shapely [-li], *a.* bien formado, simétrico.

shaper [-œ(r)], *s.* conformador; máquina de tallar o estampar.

shard [ʃard], *s.* fragmento; casco; (zool.) elitro, escama, cáscara.

share [ʃér]. **I.** *va.* repartir; compartir, partir; hacer a escote; (con **in**) participar de, tener o tomar parte en. **II.** *vn.* participar o tener parte; terciar.—**to s. alike**, repartir igualmente, tener una parte igual. **III.** *s.* parte, *f.*, porción; cuota, cupo, escote; (com.) acción; interés, participación; (agr.) reja (del arado, etc.).—**s. and s. alike**, por igual, por partes iguales.—**s. crop** (**system**), (agr.) aparcería; cultivo de tierra ajena pagando al dueño con parte de lo producido.—**on shares**, a escote; con condición de tener una parte.—**to go shares**, ir a medias.

sharebone [-boun], *s.* (anat.) (hueso del) pubis.

sharecropper [-krapœ(r)], *s.* el que cultiva tierra ajena y paga alquiler con parte de los frutos.

sharecropping [-iŋ], *s.* (agr.) = SHARE CROP.

shareholder [-houldœ(r)], *s.* (com.) accionista.

sharer [-œ(r)], *s.* (co)partícipe, *mf.*, participante, *mf.*

shark [ʃark]. **I.** *s.* (ict.) tiburón, escualo; estafador, petardista; usurero; (fam.) perito, experto. **II.** *va.* y *vn.* estafar, petardear, hurtar; pescar tiburones.

sharker [-œ(r)], *s.* petardista, tahur, persona rapaz y astuta.

sharkskin [-skin], *s.* piel (*f.*) de lija; zapa; (tej.) cierto paño de algodón o rayón.

sharp [ʃarp]. **I.** *a.* agudo; puntiagudo, aguzado; cortante, afilado; perspicaz, sagaz; listo, vivo, astuto; fino de oído; penetrante; acre, agrio; incisivo, mordaz, sarcástico; severo, rígido; violento, animado, acalorado; vigilante, atento; distinto, claro, bien delineado o definido; (mús.) sostenido; agudo, punzante (dolor); anguloso (fragmento, arena); abrupto, fuerte, pronunciado (pendiente, *f.*, curva, etc.).—**s. features**, facciones enjutas.—**s. pain**, punzada; dolor agudo. **II.** *s.* (mús.) sostenido (♯); aguja de coser larga y delgada; estafador, fullero; (fam.) perito, experto. **III.** *adv.* = SHARPLY; (fam.) exactamente, en punto (apl. a la hora); (mús.) demasiado alto de tono.—**s.-edged**, afilado, aguzado.—**s.-eyed**, linceo, de vista penetrante. —**s.-nosed**, de nariz puntiaguda; de finísimo olfato.—**s.-pointed**, puntiagudo.—**s.-pointed pliers**, alicates de punta.—**s.-set**, ávido, ansioso.—**s.-sighted** = **s.-EYED**.—**s.-witted**, penetrante, perspicaz.—**look s.!**, ¡ojo! ¡aviva! ¡avizora! **IV.** *va.* (mús.) elevar medio tono; marcar un son sostenido. **V.** *vn.* (mús.) cantar o tocar más alto que el tono debido; engañar, trampear, petardear.

sharpen [-n]. **I.** *va.* afilar; aguzar, sacar punta a, amolar; adelgazar; (fig.) despertar, despabilar, aguzar (el apetito, el ingenio, etc.); hacer más severo, intenso, acre, fogoso o ansioso. **II.** *vn.* aguzarse; afilarse; agriarse, acedarse.

sharpener [-ǝnœ(r)], *s.* amolador, aguzador, afilador.

sharper [-œ(r)], *s.* tahur, fullero, petardista, estafador, caballero de industria.

sharply [-li], *adv.* (*v.* SHARP) con filo, corte o punta; prontamente; lacónicamente; brusca y mordazmente; severamente, rigorosamente; agudamente, vivamente; sutil o ingeniosamente.

sharpness [-nis], *s.* calidad de cortante, agudo, etc. (*v.* SHARP, *a.*); agudeza; sutileza, perspicacia, viveza; acrimonia, mordacidad; acritud, acidez; violencia, rigor; inclemencia.

sharpshooter [-šutœ(r)], *s.* tirador certero.

shastra [šǽstrǝ], *s.* colección de los libros sagrados y filosóficos de la India.

shatter [šǽtœ(r)]. **I.** *va.* destrozar, hacer pedazos, astillas o añicos; estrellar, romper, tro(n)zar; quebrantar (la salud); frustrar (esperanzas). **II.** *vn.* hacerse pedazos, quebrarse, romperse; estallar, dar un estallido. **III.** *s.* fragmento, pedazo.—**s.-proof glass**, cristal inastillable.— **to break into shatters**, hacer(se) pedazos o añicos.

shattery [-i], *a.* desmenuzable, quebradizo.

shave [šéjv]. **I.** *va.* (*pp.* SHAVED o SHAVEN) rasurar o afeitar; descañonar; (carp.) acepillar; desbastar; raspar; rebajar; rozar, pasar rozando; rebanar; (ten.) descarnar; (fam.) desollar a uno en un negocio, estafar; (fam.) comprar (obligaciones comerciales) con descuento exorbitante. —**clean-shaven**, barbirrapado. **II.** *vn.* rasurarse, afeitarse, hacerse la barba; llevarse la mejor parte en un trato. **III.** *s.* afeitado, (Am.) afeitada; afeitadura; (carp.) cuchilla desbastadora de dos mangos; viruta (de madera o metal); rebanada delgada; (fam.) descuento exorbitante; (fam.) acción de pasar raspando o casi tocando (literal y figuradamente); escape, zafada (gen. en la expresión **to have a close s.**, escapar por casualidad, salvarse en una tabla).

shaveling [-liŋ], *s.* mozalbete; (desp.) hombre rapado (presidiario); monje o fraile.

shaver [-œ(r)], *s.* barbero; afeitadora (máquina); (fam.) desollador (en los negocios), estafador; (fam.) jovencito, rapaz.

shaving [-iŋ]. **I.** *s.* afeitado, rasura(ción), (Am.) afeitada.—*pl.* raspaduras, acepilladuras, virutas, alisaduras. **II.** *a.* de afeitar, para afeitar.— **s. brush**, brocha de afeitar.—**s. cream**, crema de afeitar.—**s. dish**, bacía.

Shavian [šéjviǝn], *a.* perteneciente o relativo a George Bernard Shaw y sus obras.

shawl [šɔl], *s.* chal, mantón, pañolón.

shay [šej], *s.* (fam.) = CHAISE.

she [ši], *pron. fem.* ella; (delante de *who* o *that*) la, aquella (*she who speaks*, la que habla); hembra (en composición: **s.-ass**, borrica, burra.—*s.-*

cat, gata.—**s.-devil**, diabla.—**s.-goat**, cabra. —**s.-mule**, mula).

sheaf [šif]. **I.** *s.* (*pl.* SHEAVES) gavilla, haz, *m.*, garba, fajo, mostela; atado, paquete o lío; (mec.) roldana; manojo, colección. *V.* SHEAVE. —**s. of arrows**, haz de flechas. **II.** *va.* (agr.) agavillar, garb(e)ar.

shear [šir]. **I.** *va.* (*pp.* SHEARED o SHORN) tonsurar, rapar, esquilar, trasquilar; (tej.) tundir; cizallar, cortar (gen. con tijeras o cizallas); (mec.) someter a esfuerzo constante; (a veces con *off*) romper por fuerza cortante o por deslizamiento; estafar, petardear. **II.** *vn.* (mec.) romperse por deslizamiento o por esfuerzo cortante. **III.** *s.* tijeras, o una sola hoja de ellas; (mec.) esfuerzo cortante; fuerza cortante; deslizamiento, deformación debida al esfuerzo cortante. *V.* SHEARING y SHEARS.

shearer [-œ(r)], *s.* esquilador, trasquilador; tundidor (de tela).

shearing [-iŋ]. **I.** *s.* corte; tonsura, esquileo, trasquila(dura), trasquilón; (tej.) tundición, tundidura; cizallamiento; (mec.) deslizamiento; fractura por esfuerzo cortante. **II.** *a.* de deslizamiento; (mec.) cortante.—**s. machine**, esquiladora mecánica; máquina de cizallar; (tej.) tundidora.—**s. strength**, resistencia al deslizamiento.

shears [-z], *s. pl.* tijeras grandes; (mec.) cizallas; correderas de un torno; grúa de tijeras, machina, cabria (ll. t. **shear** o **sheer legs**).

sheatfish [šitfiš], *s.* (ict.) siluro.

sheath [šiθ], *s.* vaina; caja, manguito, funda, estuche, cubierta, envoltura.

sheathe [šíð], *va.* envainar; poner vaina, forro o cubierta; (mar.) aforrar, embonar.

sheathing [-iŋ], *s.* forro exterior, cubierta; (mar.) (a)forro, embono.—**s. nails**, clavos de entablar. —**s.**, o **s. boards**, tablas, enmaderado de un tejado o pared.

sheathless [-lis], *a.* sin vaina.

sheave [šiv]. **I.** *s.* (mec.) roldana; polea, garrucha, monopastos; rueda excéntrica o su disco. *V.* SHEAF. **II.** *va.* (agr.) garb(e)ar, agavillar.

shed [šéd]. **I.** *va.* (*pret.* y *pp.* SHED) arrojar, quitarse; desprenderse de, largar; mudar; verter, derramar; esparcir; dejar caer; exhalar. **II.** *vn.* mudar (los cuernos, la piel, las plumas). **III.** *s.* vertiente, *f.*; cobertizo, tinglado; tejadillo, colgadizo, salidizo; sombraje, cabaña o barraca; (aer.) hangar.

shedder [-œ(r)], *s.* derramador; animal que muda la piel, las plumas, etc.

shedding [-iŋ], *s.* derramamiento, vertimiento; muda (de plumas, etc.).

sheen [šín], *s.* resplandor, lustre, viso.

sheeny [-i], *a.* lustroso.

sheep [šíp], *s.* (*sing.* y *pl.*) oveja, carnero; ovejas; pécora; ganado lanar u ovejuno; (fig.) rebaño, grey, *f.*, congregación de fieles; papanatas, simplón; (enc.) badana.—**s. botfly**, mosca de carnero.—**s. dip**, decocción insecticida para el lavado de los carneros antes de la esquila.—**s. dog**, perro de pastor.—**s. dung**, sirle o sirria. —**s. ranch**, hacienda de ovejas.—**s. run**, dehesa de ovejas, carneril.—**s.'s eye**, mirada al soslayo; ojeada modesta y amorosa.—**s.'s leather**, badana.—**s. tick**, garrapata.

sheepcote [-kout], **sheepfold** [-fould], *s.* redil, corral, aprisco, majada, ovil.

sheephook [-huk], *s.* cayado, (prov.) gayata.

sheepish [-iš], *a.* avergonzado, corrido; tímido, pusilánime.—**sheepishly** [-li], *adv.* tímidamente.—**sheepishness** [-nis], *s.* timidez, cortedad, empacho.

sheepmaster [-mæstœ(r)], *s.* ganadero.

sheepshank [-šæŋk], *s.* pierna de carnero; (mar.) margarita, catabre.

sheepshead [-šɛd], *s.* (ict.) sargo.

sheepshearer [-šir œ(r)], *s.* esquilador.

sheepshearing [-iŋ], *s.* esquileo, trasquila.

sheepskin [-skįn], *s.* badana; (E. U. fam.) diploma, *m.*—**s. dressed with wool** o **undressed s.**, zalea, vellón, zamarra.

sheepwalk [-wɔk], *s.* dehesa de ovejas, carneril.

sheer [šįr]. **I.** *a.* puro, claro, consumado, cabal, completo; (tej.) ligero, fino, delgado; escarpado, enhiesto.—**s. hulk,** chata de arbolar.—**s. legs** = SHEERS.—**s. rail,** escaño. **II.** *adv.* de un golpe, de una vez. **III.** *s.* (mar.) arrufo, arrufadura, desviación, cambio de dirección. **IV.** *vn.* (mar.) alargarse, desviarse; torcer, doblar.

sheers [-z], *s.* cabria de arbolar, machina, grúa de tijeras.

sheet [šįt]. **I.** *s.* hoja, lámina, placa, chapa (de cualquier materia); sábana; pliego u hoja (de papel); diario; extensión de agua; (mar.) escota; (poét.) vela de navío).—**s. anchor,** (mar.) ancla mayor, ancla de la esperanza, (fig.) áncora de salvación.—**s. card,** cartulina en hojas.—**s. glass,** vidrio cilindrado o laminado.—**s. lightning,** fucilazo(s).—**s. metal (iron, steel,** etc.), metal (hierro, acero) laminado, en lámina o en planchas; palastro.—**s. music,** música (en hojas sueltas).—**s. of copy,** (impr.) cuartilla.— **s. pile,** tablestaca.—**s. piling,** tablestacas; empalizada, construcción de tablestacas. **II.** *va.* ensabanar, envolver en sábanas; amortajar; extender en láminas u hojas.

sheeting [-įŋ], *s.* lencería para sábanas; (metal.) laminado; (hidr. y min.) encofrado.

sheik [šik], *s.* jeque.

shekel [šékęl], *s.* siclo.—*pl.* (fam.) dinero.

sheldrake [šéldrejk], *s.* (orn.) cataraña; mergánsar, mergo.

shelf [šelf], *s.* (*pl.* SHELVES) anaquel, estante, repisa, tabla, entrepaño, poyata; bajío, banco de arena; vuelo; capa horizontal (de roca) saliente; (geol.) roca subyacente (de un depósito sedimentario).—**to put on the s.,** (fig.) archivar, arrinconar, olvidar.

shell [šel]. **I.** *s.* casco; cáscara (de nuez, de huevo, etc.); vaina, vainilla (de legumbres); (bot.) silicua; (zool.) concha, carapacho; marisco; cubierta, corteza; armazón, *f.*, armadura (de edificio, etc.); cualquier pieza hueca de paredes delgadas; esqueleto; cuerpo (de caldera); (fund.) camisa o revestimiento de horno; (arti.) bomba, granada, proyectil; cápsula para cartuchos; bote largo y angosto para regatas; (poét.) lira; (mar.) casco o caja de motón; pieza acopada o ahuecada. —**s. comb,** peineta.—**s.-lac,** laca en tablillas. —**s. shock,** neurosis de guerra, desorden especial nervioso o mental causado por heridas, concusión del aire, temor, excitación mental, etc., en los campos de batalla. **II.** *va.* descascarar, descortezar, desvainar, desgranar, deshollejar, mondar, pelar; encerrar en cáscara, vaina o cápsula; (arti.) bombardear, cañonear. **III.** *vn.* descascararse, desconcharse.—**to s. out,** (fam.) aflojar la mosca.

shellac [šelék]. **I.** *s.* laca, goma laca. **II.** *va.* revestir de laca, barnizar con laca.—**to take a shellacking,** (fam.) recibir una paliza, sufrir una derrota.

shellbark [šélbark], *s. V.* HICKORY.

sheller [šélœ(r)], *s.* desgranador; descascarador.

shellfire [šélfajr], *s.* (mil.) cañoneo con granadas; disparos de granadas.

shellfish [-fįš], *s.* mariscos, crustáceos, conchas.

shelling [-įŋ], *s.* descascaramiento; desgrane, desgranamiento; bombardeo.

shellproof [-pruf], *a.* a prueba de bomba.

shellwork [-wœrk], *s.* obra de concha.

shelly [šélį], *a.* conchado o conchudo; crustáceo.

shelter [šéltœ(r)]. **I.** *s.* resguardo, amparo, albergue, refugio, abrigo, asilo; guarida; protector, amparador. **II.** *va.* guarecer, abrigar, poner al abrigo o a cubierto, albergar, amparar, proteger, encubrir, ocultar, tapar.—**sheltered industries,** industrias no expuestas a la competencia extranjera. **III.** *vn.* refugiarse, guarecerse.

shelterer [-œ(r)], *s.* amparador, protector, el que guarece, cobija, acoge o recoge, etc.

shelterless [-lįs], *a.* desamparado, sin asilo; desabrigado.

shelve [šélv]. **I.** *va.* poner sobre un estante o anaquel; (fig.) poner a un lado, dar carpetazo, archivar, arrinconar, olvidar; proveer de estantes o anaqueles. **II.** *vn.* inclinarse, estar en declive.

shelves [-z], *pl.* de SHELF.

shelving [-įŋ]. **I.** *a.* inclinado. **II.** *s.* estantería, anaquelería; carpetazo; declive.

shelvy [-į], *a.* inclinado; que abunda en escollos, arrecifes o bancos de arena.

Sheol [šíoųl], *s.* báratro, infierno.

shepherd [šépœrd], *s.* pastor; zagal, ovejero; (fig.) párroco, cura, *m.*—**s. dog,** perro de pastor.— **s.'s crook,** cayado.—**s.'s hut,** tugurio.—**s.'s flute** o **pipe,** zampoña, caramillo.—**s.'s needle,** (bot.) aguja de pastor.—**s.'s pie,** especie de empanada.—**s.'s purse** o **pouch,** (bot.) bolsa de pastor.—**the (Good) S.,** Jesucristo.

shepherdess [-įs], *s.* pastora, zagala.

sherardize [šérądajz], *va.* galvanizar por el procedimiento Cowper-Coles (revestir de cinc por calentamiento con polvo de cinc en retortas cerradas; algunos usan *sherardizar*).

sherbet [šérbįt], *s.* sorbete.

sherd [šœrd], *s.* = SHARD.

shereef, sherif [šęríf], *s.* jerife.

sheriff [šérįf], *s.* administrador ejecutivo de un condado; alguacil mayor, (prov.) verguer(o).

sheriffalty, sheriffship, sheriffwick [-ạltį, -šįp, -wįk], *s. V.* SHRIEVALTY.

sheriffdom [-dǫm], *s.* jurisdicción del *sheriff.*

sherry [šérį], *s.* vino de Jerez.—**s. cobbler,** refresco hecho con vino de Jerez.

shew [šoų], *va.* (Ingl. o ant.) (*pret.* SHEWED; *pp.* SHEWN o SHEWED) = SHOW.

shewbread [šóųbred], *s.* pan(es) de proposición.

shibboleth [šįboliθ], *s.* palabra que sirve de santo y seña; lema, *m.;* rasgo distintivo.

shield [šíld]. **I.** *s.* escudo; broquel, tarja, rodela; égida, amparo; resguardo, reparo, defensa; protector, defensor; (blas.) escudo de armas.— **s.-bearer,** escudero. **II.** *va.* escudar, amparar, resguardar, defender, proteger.

shier, shyer [šáįœ(r)], *s.* caballo asustadizo.

shift [šįft]. **I.** *va.* cambiar; desviar; trasladar, transportar; mudar la ropa; (teat.) cambiar de decoración.—**to s. gears,** (aut.) cambiar de marcha.—**to s. into first,** (aut.) mover la palanca a primera velocidad.—**to s. into high,** (aut.) tomar la directa.—**to s. off,** diferir, aplazar; poner a un lado; librarse o salir de.—**to s. the helm,** cambiar el timón. **II.** *vn.* moverse, cambiar de puesto, mudarse; cambiar, variar, mudar; tergiversar, usar de frases equívocas.— **to s. about,** revolverse, girar.—**to s. for one's self,** ingeniarse, bandearse, valerse, darse maña, componérselas. **III.** *s.* cambio; mutación, desviación; su(b)stitución; trastrocamiento, trastrueque; recurso, expediente; ardid, *m.,* artificio; maña, subterfugio, fraude, evasión, excusa; camisa; turno o tanda de obreros; revezo.—**s. key,** tecla de mayúsculas (de una máquina de escribir).—**s. lock,** tecla de sujeción, sujetador. —**to make s.,** ingeniarse, arreglarse, hallar el medio de.—**to make s. without,** pasarse de.

shiftable [-ạbl], *a.* mudable; revecero.

shifter [-œ(r)], *s.* (mec.) desviador, disparador; (teat.) carpintero, tramoyista; zorrocloco.

shiftiness [-inįs], *s.* maña, astucia; calidad de mañoso, etc.; versatilidad.

shiftless [-lįs], *a.* inútil, incapaz; negligente, descuidado, perezoso; mal hecho, desaliñado.— **shiftlessly** [-lį], *adv.* negligentemente.—**shiftlessness** [-nįs], *s.* negligencia, pereza; inutilidad, incapacidad.

shifty [-į], *a.* mañoso, astuto, industrioso; versátil, mudable.

shillalah, shillelah [ʃiléjlä], s. palo, cachiporra.

shilling [ʃíliŋ], s. (Ingl.) chelín.

shilly-shally [ʃíli ʃǽlj]. I. vn. estar irresoluto, no saber qué hacer. II. s. vacilación, irresolución. III. a. irresoluto, indeciso, vacilante. IV. adv. irresolutamente.

shim [ʃim]. I. s. (mec.) cuña o chaveta delgada; plancha o tira de relleno. II. va. (a)cuñar; tapar, rellenar con una tira o tablilla.

shimmer [ʃímœ(r)]. I. vn. rielar. II. s. luz trémula; débil resplandor, vislumbre.

shimmy [ʃímj]. I. s. baile de movimientos temblorosos, baile nalgar; (fam.) camisa de mujer; (aut.) zigzagueo o bamboleo de las ruedas delanteras. II. vn. bailar el shimmy; (aut.) zigzaguear.

shin [ʃin]. I. s. espinilla, canilla.—**s. bone,** (anat.) tibia, canilla, caña. II. va. y vn. trepar.

shindig [ʃíndig], s. (fam.) festividad con baile.

shindy [ʃíndj], s. (fam.) zacapela. V. SHINDIG.

shine [ʃájn]. I. vn. (pret. y pp. SHONE) (re)lucir, brillar, fulgurar, alumbrar o relumbrar, resplandecer; sobresalir, distinguirse; hacer sol o buen tiempo; favorecer, ser propicio.—**to s. up to,** (fam.) engatusar, congraciarse con. II. va. reg. pulir, bruñir; dar lustre (a los zapatos), dar bola, embolar. III. s. resplandor, lustre, brillo; buen tiempo, claridad; embolada (del calzado), emboladura.—**to take a s. to,** (fam.) aficionarse de.

shiner [-œ(r)], s. el que o lo que brilla; (fam.) moneda de oro; (fam.) = BLACK EYE; (ict.) pez plateado.

shingle [ʃiŋgl]. I. va. cubrir con ripia; entejar con uralita o tejamaníes; cortar (el pelo) corto y en declive o en escalones; (metal.) cinglar, exprimir la escoria de. II. s. pelo corto en declive, o rebajado gradualmente; tabla de ripia o uralita. (Am.) tejamaní, tajamanil; (E. U.) muestra o letrero de oficina; china, cascajo.—**s. nail,** abismal.

shingles [-z], s. (med.) zoster, f., zona.

shining [ʃájniŋ]. I. a. brillante, radiante, resplandeciente, (re)luciente, lúcido. II. s. lucimiento, esplendor, lustre; resplandor, brillo.

shiny [ʃájnj], a. lustroso, brillante.

shinny [ʃínj]. I. vn. (gen. con up), trepar; jugar al shinny. II. s. juego de pelota o de hockey con palo encorvado.

Shinto [ʃíntou], **Shintoism** [-izm], s. sinto, sintoísmo.—**Shintoist** [-ist], a. y s. sintoísta.

ship [ʃip]. I. s. buque, barco, nave, f., bajel, navío; aeróstato, dirigible, nave aérea; aeroplano.—**s. biscuit, s. bread,** galleta, bizcocho.—**s. boy,** paje de escoba, grumete.—**s. breaker,** desguazador.—**s. carpenter,** carpintero de navío o de ribera.—**s. chandler,** proveedor de buques.—**s. chandlery,** almacén de efectos navales.—**s. fever,** tifo.—**s. money,** (Ingl.) impuesto de defensa naval, o para la armada.—**s. of the desert,** (fig.) camello.—**s. of the line,** navío de alto bordo o de línea.—**s. of war,** buque de guerra.—**s.-plane,** avión (m.) de cubierta, que puede despegar de o aterrizar en la cubierta de un buque o portaaviones.—**s. railway,** vía férrea para el transporte de embarcaciones.—**s.'s company,** tripulación.—**s.'s husband,** agente de un buque o empresa naviera.—**s.'s papers,** papeles o documentos legales de un buque.—**s. stores,** matalotaje.—**s.'s time,** hora local del buque.—**s. timber,** madera para construcciones navales. II. va. embarcar; (com.) enviar, despachar, remesar; (fam.) despedir, deshacerse de; (mar.) tripular, recibir a bordo la tripulación; embarcar (to ship a heavy sea, embarcar agua, encapillar un golpe de mar); armar, montar (mástiles, timón, remos).—**to s. oars,** armar los remos. III. vn. ir a bordo, embarcar; engancharse como marinero.

shipboard [-bərd], s. (mar.) bordo.—**on s.,** a bordo.

shipbuilder [-bildœ(r)], s. constructor de buques, arquitecto naval.

shipbuilding [-iŋ], s. construcción naval.

shipload [-loud], s. cargazón, f., cargamento que llena un buque; buque completamente cargado.

shipmaster [-mǽstœ(r)], s. (mar.) patrón, capitán de buque.

shipmate [-mejt], s. camarada (m.) de a bordo.

shipment [-ment], s. (com.) embarque; cargamento, partida; envío, despacho, consignación, remesa.

shipowner [-ounœ(r)], s. naviero, armador.

shipper [-œ(r)], s. (com.) embarcador, cargador, fletador; expedidor, remitente.

shipping [-iŋ]. I. s. buques; marina; tonelaje; (com.) embarque; envío, despacho. II. a. naval, marítimo, naviero, de marina mercante.—**s. agency,** agencia marítima.—**s. agent,** consignatario de buques.—**s. articles,** contrata de marinero.—**s. bill,** factura de embarque.—**s. charges,** gastos de embarque o de envío.—**s. clerk,** (com.) dependiente de muelle o de remesas.—**s. list** = **s. BILL.—s. master,** oficial que contrata marineros.—**s. receipt,** recibo de embarque.

shipshape [-ʃejp], a. en buen orden, bien arreglado.

shipway [-wej], s. (mar.) grada; canal para buques.

shipworm [-wœrm], s. (zool.) broma, tiñuela.

shipwreck [-rek]. I. s. naufragio; (com.) siniestro; desastre; desgracia, ruina. II. va. hacer naufragar o zozobrar, echar a pique.—**shipwrecked** [-rekt], a. naufragado.—**s. person,** náufrago.—**to be shipwrecked,** naufragar.

shipwright [-rajt], s. carpintero de ribera o de navío; constructor de buques.

shipyard [-yard], s. astillero, varadero, arsenal.

shire [ʃajr], s. (Ingl.) condado.

shirk [ʃœrk]. I. s. el que se evade de hacer algo. II. va. y vn. evadir(se de), eludir, evitar, esquivar, faltar a, desentenderse de, desatender.

shirker [-œ(r)], s. = SHIRK.

shirr [ʃœr]. I. va. (cost.) fruncir, gandujar; (coc.) escalfar huevos en crema de leche. II. s. (cost.) frunce, fruncimiento; hilo de goma tejido en una tela para hacerla elástica.

shirred [-d], a. (cost.) fruncido; (tej.) elástico.—**s. eggs,** huevos escalfados en crema.

shirt [ʃœrt], s. camisa de hombre; blusa o camisola de señora.—**s. bosom, s. front,** camisolín, pechera de camisa.—**s. store,** camisería.—**s. tail,** faldón.—**s. waist,** corpiño de mujer; cuerpo de camisa.—**in one's s. sleeves,** en mangas de camisa.

shirting [-iŋ], s. tela para camisas.

shirtless [-lis], a. descamisado; empobrecido.

shiver [ʃívœ(r)]. I. s. temblor, (es)calofrío, estremecimiento; brizna, astilla. II. vn. tiritar, temblar, calofriarse; cascarse, hacerse pedazos; estallar, estrellarse; (mar.) flamear (la vela). III. va. estrellar, romper, hacer astillas o añicos; vibrar, sacudir.—**shivering** [-iŋ], s. horripilación, calofrío, estremecimiento.—**shivery** [-i], a. trémulo, tembloroso; friolento, frío; friable, quebradizo.

shoal [ʃoul]. I. s. bajo, bajío, alfaque, banco de arena, cayo; multitud, muchedumbre o manada; banco de peces, cardume, cardumen. II. a. poco profundo, bajo. III. va. y vn. disminuir en profundidad; reunirse en gran número.

shoaliness [-injs], s. falta de profundidad; abundancia de bajos; calidad de somero.

shoaly [-i], a. lleno de bajos; vadoso; somero.

shoat, shote [ʃout], s. (zool.) cochinillo, gorrino.

shock [ʃák]. I. s. choque; sacudida, sacudimiento; concusión, golpe; susto, sobresalto, emoción; conmoción; ofensa; desazón, f.; (med.) choque, postración nerviosa; (elec.) choque; (agr.) fajina, hacina, fascal, tresnal; pelo tupido, greñas; perro de lanas. II. a. de choque; para choques; lanudo; desgreñado.—**s. absorber,**

(mec. y aut.) amortiguador.—s. **action**, (mil.) carga en columna cerrada.—s. **dog**, perro de lanas.—s. **troops**, tropas (escogidas) de asalto. III. *va.* y *vn.* sacudir, dar una sacudida; chocar, ofender, disgustar; conmover; escandalizar, horrorizar; (agr.) hacinar.

shocking [-iŋ], *a.* espantoso, horrible; chocante, ofensivo.

shockproof [-pruf], *a.* a prueba de choques.

shod [šad], *pret.* y *pp.* de TO SHOE.

shoddy [šádi]. I. *a.* de lana renovada o regenerada; falso, aparente. II. *s.* lana regenerada, y paño burdo de ésta; (fam.) ostentación vulgar, impostura.

shoe [šú]. I. *s.* zapato, botín, bota; calzado; herradura (de caballo); suela de trineo; zapata (de ancla, de freno mecánico, de contacto eléctrico, etc.); galga de carruaje; (aut.) llanta, cubierta (de neumático); (mar.) calzo, solera; (arq.) tornapunta; contera, regatón; canal para conducir trigo o mineral a la tolva, etc.—s. **black-ing**, bola, betún para zapatos.—s. **buckle**, hebilla de zapato.—s. **brush**, cepillo para sacar brillo (al calzado).—s. **of a wheel**, llanta.—s. **peg**, (zap.) puntilla, estaquilla.—s. **polish**, lustre, betún, bola.—s. **store**, zapatería.—s. **string**, s. **tie** = s. LACE.—s. **tree**, horma de zapatos; pernito.—**to be in his (their,** etc.**) shoes**, estar en su pellejo.—**to know where the s. pinches**, saber uno dónde le aprieta el zapato.—**to put on one's shoes**, calzarse. II. *va.* (*pret.* y *pp.* SHOD) herrar (un caballo); calzar (el ancla, a una persona); poner regatón a, proveer de regatón; enllantar o poner llantas a (una rueda).

shoeblack [-blæk], *s.* limpiabotas.

shoehorn [-hɔrn], *s.* calzador.

shoeing [-iŋ]. I. *s.* acto de herrar o de calzar. II. *a.* de herrar; de calzar.—s.-**horn**, calzador.

shoeless [-lis], *a.* descalzo, sin zapatos.

shoemaker [-meĭkœ(r)], *s.* zapatero.—s.'s **last**, horma.—s.'s **paring knife**, chaira o trinchete de zapatero.—s.'s **wax**, (zap.) cerapez, cerote.

shoemaking [-meĭkiŋ], *s.* fabricación de calzado, zapatería.

shoer [-œ(r)], *s.* herrador.

shogun [šóŭgʌn], *s.* general en jefe (del ejército japonés en tiempos pasados; taicún.—**shogunate** [-eĭt], *s.* taicunato, dignidad de taicún.

shole [šoŭl], *s.* solera, tornapunta.

shone [šoŭn], *pret.* y *pp.* de TO SHINE.

shoo [šu]. I. *va.* oxear (aves domésticas). II. *interj.* ¡ox(e)! ¡so! ¡fuera!

shook [šuk]. I. *pret.* de TO SHAKE. II. *s.* paquete de duelas, bocoyes o barriles abatidos; juego de tablas para hacer cajas.

shoot [šút]. I. *va.* (*pret.* y *pp.* SHOT) herir o matar con arma de fuego; fusilar, pasar por las armas; disparar, tirar; descargar; arrojar, lanzar, proyectar; emitir (un rayo); vaciar; empujar, hacer salir; traspasar, atravesar rápidamente; (min.) volar, hacer saltar, dar barreno; (carp.) ajustar (a una línea) cepillando; (cine) filmar (una escena o película).—**to s. a bolt**, echar, correr el pestillo.—**to s. down**, tumbar a balazos, derribar con armas de fuego.—**to s. off**, tirar, descargar (arma); llevarse.—**to s. the chute**, deslizarse en un tobogán de bote hacia el agua.—**to s. the rapids**, salvar el recial, bajar por los rápidos (de un río).—**to s. the works**, (fam.) jugar el todo por el todo, ir hasta el tope. —**to s. through**, atravesar, pasar de parte a parte.—**to s. up**, atacar a balazos (gen. en pandilla); entrar a (un pueblo) echando bala a diestra y siniestra. II. *vn.* tirar, disparar armas de fuego; pasar o correr rápidamente; salir, nacer, brotar, germinar; punzar (un dolor); sobresalir, destacarse.—**to s. at**, tirar a, hacer fuego o un tiro a.—**to s. forth**, lanzarse o abalanzarse.—**to s. out**, brotar, germinar.—**to**

s. over dogs, cazar con perros.—**to s. straight**, dar en el hito; (fam.) hablar y portarse honradamente.—**to s. up**, nacer, crecer; madurar. III. *s.* (agr. y bot.) vástago, pimpollo, retoño, renuevo, tallo, acodo, plantón, sarmiento (de vid); recial de un río; artesa inclinada; tiro, certamen de tiradores, tiro al blanco; (arq.) refuerzo de arco o bóveda; (zool.) = SHOAT.

shooter [-œ(r)], *s.* tirador.

shooting [-iŋ]. I. *s.* caza con escopeta; tiro, descarga; latido doloroso, punzada; (cine) filmación (de una escena). II. *a.* de tiro; de tirar.—s. **box** o **lodge**, pabellón de caza.—s. **gallery** o **grounds**, tiro (al blanco).—s. **match**, certamen de tiro al blanco.—s. **post** o **stand**, tiradero.—s. **star**, estrella fugaz.—s. **stick**, (impr.) desacuñador; (fam.) arma de fuego (esp. el revólver).—**by s.**, a tiros, a balazos.

shop [šáp]. I. *s.* tienda o almacén; taller; fábrica. II. *a.* de tienda; de taller; de o relativo a gremios obreros (*shop committee*, comisión del gremio, o de los gremios; *shop deputy* o *steward*, representante o delegado del gremio; *shop foreman*, jefe de talleres). III. *vn.* ir de tiendas o de compras, hacer compras; feriar.

shopboard [-bɔrd], *s.* tabla de sastre.

shopboy [-bɔi], *s.* mancebo, dependiente.

shopgirl [-gœrl], *s.* muchacha de tienda, dependienta.

shopkeeper [-kipœ(r)], *s.* tendero, mercader.

shoplifter [-liftœ(r)], *s.* ratero de tiendas, descuidero, mechero, mechera.

shoplifting [-liftiŋ], *s.* ratería en las tiendas.

shopman [-man], *s.* tendero; mercader; mancebo de tienda.

shopper [-œ(r)], *s.* comprador.

shopping [-iŋ], *s.* compras; acto de ir de tiendas.

shopwindow [-windoŭ], *s.* = SHOW WINDOW.

shopworn [-wɔrn], *a.* gastado, deteriorado con el trajín de la tienda; (fig.) traído y llevado.

shopwalker [-wɔkœ(r)], *s.* vigilante (para impedir raterías en tienda o almacén).

shopwoman [-wuman], *s.* tendera.

shore [šɔr]. I. *s.* costa, ribera, playa, orilla, litoral; (constr.) puntal; (mar.) escora; (min.) entibo, ademe.—**shore leave**, (mar.) licencia para ir a tierra.—**shore line**, contorno, borde de playa o ribera. II. *va.* apuntalar, acodalar; (min.) (a veces con **up**) ademar, entibar; (mar.) escorar; llevar a tierra, a la orilla.

shoreless [-lis], *a.* sin costa ni playa.

shoring [-iŋ], *s.* entibación, apuntalamiento.

shorn [šɔrn], *pp.* de TO SHEAR; mocho, chamorro.

short [šɔrt]. I. *a.* corto; bajo de estatura; diminuto, pequeño, reducido; falto, escaso; breve, conciso; brusco, seco; insuficiente, deficiente; próximo, cercano; menguado, corto de alcances; flaco (de memoria); (com.) falto de aquello que se vende y tiene que entregarse en cierto plazo; (pros.) breve; quebradizo.—s. **allowance**, media ración.—s.-**change**, engañar o defraudar al dar cambio; timar o estafar en pequeño.—s. **circuit**, (elec.) cortocircuito o corto circuito.—s.-**circuit**, *va.* y *vn.* poner(se) en cortocircuito. —s. **cut**, atajo; método o modo abreviado o corto; picadura de tabaco.—s. **division**, (arit.) división sencilla rápida, en que se escriben sólo las cifras del cociente y los residuos parciales, determinados mentalmente, o sólo aquéllas.—s. **money**, dinero prestado o para prestar a corto plazo (de pocos días).—s. **of**, lejos de; escaso de; inadecuado para; con excepción de, sin ir hasta; diferente de, sino, sólo (cambiando el giro: *nothing short of war*, sólo la guerra).—S. **Parliament**, (hist.) Parlamento Corto.—s. **rib**, (anat.) costilla falsa.—s. **sale**, venta de artículos que el vendedor no tiene aún.—s. **seller**, (com.) el que vende corto; el que vende acciones sin tenerlas.—s. **story**, cuento.—s. **subjects**, (cine) películas cortas.—s. **ton**, tonelada de 2000 libras (907 kg.).—s. **wave**, (rad.) onda corta.—**s.-weigh,** engañar en el peso.—**a s. time since,** poco ha que.—**a s. while,** un ratito.—**at s. notice** = ON S. NOTICE.—**in a s. time,** o **while,** en un rato; en poco tiempo; dentro de poco.—**in s. order,** prontamente.— **on s. notice,** prontamente, con poca demora, con poco tiempo de aviso.—**on s. term,** (com.) a corto plazo.—**to be s.,** estar escaso; para abreviar.—**to be s. of,** estar lejos de; no responder a; estar escaso de.—**to give s. shrift to, to make s. work of,** despachar sumariamente. —**to grow s.,** acortarse, menguar, disminuir. **II.** *s.* resumen, compendio; (pros.) sílaba o vocal breve; (com.) déficit; venta de aquello que no se posee y debe entregarse en cierto plazo; persona que contrae dicho compromiso; en el baseball, puesto que ocupa el *shortstop.*—*pl. V.* SHORTS. —**s. for,** forma abreviada de.—**for s.,** para abreviar, para mayor brevedad.—**in s.,** en suma, en resumen, en resumidas cuentas.—**the s. and the long of it,** el total, el todo, la substancia del asunto. **III.** *adv.* brevemente, breve.—**s.-bodied,** pequeño de estatura.—**s.-breathed,** asmático, corto de respiración, corto de resuello.—**s.-handed,** que carece de un número suficiente de operarios, marineros, etc. —**s.-lived,** de poca vida o duración; efímero.— **s.-nosed,** romo, chato, de nariz aplastada. —**s.-sighted** = SHORTSIGHTED.—**s.-stapled,** de hebra o fibra corta.—**s.-tailed,** rabicorto.— **s.-tempered,** irascible, irritable.—**s.-waisted,** corto de talle.—**s.-winded** = S.-BREATHED.— **s.-witted,** corto de alcances, limitado. **IV.** *va.* (elec.) poner en cortocircuito.

shortage [-idž], *s.* déficit; carestía, escasez, falta, merma.

shortbread [-bred], *s.* (coc.) tortita o galleta dulce hecha con manteca u otra grasa.

shortcake [-kejk], *s.* (coc.) torta de frutas.

shortcoming [-KAmiŋ], *s.* defecto; negligencia, descuido, omisión; falta, mengua.

shorten [-n]. **I.** *va.* acortar; encoger, abreviar, compendi(z)ar, resumir; reducir; impedir, limitar, restringir; (coc.) hacer tierna o deleznable (la pastelería) con mantequilla u otra grasa. **II.** *vn.* acortarse, abreviarse, disminuirse, encogerse.

shortening [-niŋ], *s.* acortamiento; disminución; abreviación; (coc.) manteca o mantequilla con que se hacen hojaldres, etc.

shorthand [-hænd]. **I.** *s.* taquigrafía, estenografía.—**to take s.,** **to write in s.,** taquigrafiar. **II.** *a.* taquigráfico.

shortly [-li], *adv.* presto, luego, al instante, dentro de poco; brevemente; en breve.—**s. after,** a poco de.—**s. afterward,** al poco rato.

shortness [-nis], *s.* cortedad; pequeñez; brevedad; deficiencia.—**for s.,** para mayor brevedad.

shortsighted [-sajtid], *a.* miope, cegato; falto de perspicacia.—**shortsightedness** [-nis], *s.* miopía, cortedad de la vista; falta de perspicacia.

shorts [-s], *s. pl.* calzones cortos flojos (traje de deporte, etc.); calzoncillos cortos; salvado; (cine) películas cortas.

shortstop [-stap], *s.* en el baseball, el jugador situado entre la segunda base y la tercera.

shot [šát]. **I.** *pret.* y *pp.* de TO SHOOT. **II.** *a.* (tej.) batido, tornasolado; relativo a o para perdigones.—**s. cartridge,** cartucho de perdigones. —**s. gage,** o **gauge,** vitola para calibrar proyectiles.—**s. locker,** (mar.) chillera; santabárbara, polvorín, pañol.—**s. plug,** tapabalazo.—**s. pouch,** perdigonera.—**s. samples,** (metal.) muestras en forma de perdigones o pulverizadas vaciando en agua el metal fundido.—**s. silk,** seda tornasolada.—**s. tower,** torre (f.) para hacer perdigones. **III.** *va.* cargar con perdigones. **IV.** *s.* perdigón; munición, perdigones; bala, proyectil; tiro, disparo; escopetazo; balazo; alcance (v. gr.: *within pistol shot,* a tiro de pistola); tirador; golpe, tirada, jugada (en el

billar); escote; (fam.) inyección, jeringa (de morfina, etc.); (fam.) trago o dedo (de licores) (fot.) vista; (min.) barreno.—**a good s.,** un tirador certero.—**a long s.,** apuesta arriesgada. —**bird s., fine s.,** munición (menuda), mostaza.—**like a s.,** como un rayo; disparado.— **not by a long s.,** (fam.) ni por asomo, ni por pienso.—**to have,** o **take, a shot at,** hacer un tiro a; echar una púa, burla o indirecta a.—**to put the s.,** (dep.) lanzar el peso.—**with shots,** a tiros.

shotgun [-gan], *s.* escopeta.

shot-put [-put], *s.* (dep.) lanzamiento del peso.

should [šud], *pret.* de SHALL. Úsase como auxiliar para formar los modos condicionales de otros verbos, con la misma distinción respecto de *would,* que tiene *shall* respecto de *will* en la formación del futuro de indicativo (*v.* SHALL); vg.: *I said that I should go,* dije que iría; *would you go if I should go?* ¿iría Vd. si yo fuese? Se usa muy frecuentemente como verbo defectivo con la significación de deber o haber de: *you should write to him at once,* debiera Vd. escribirle en seguida; *you should tell him,* Vd. debe (o debería) decirle; *the room should be kept open,* el cuarto debe mantenerse abierto. (No se cometa el error de creer que *should* equivale siempre a *debiera* o *debería,* pues a menudo equivale a *debe* o *deberá*).

shoulder [šóuldœ(r)]. **I.** *s.* (anat.) hombro; espalda; encuentro (de un ave); pernil, brazuelo o cuarto delantero (de un cuadrúpedo); (carp.) can, pie (*m.*) de amigo; espaldón de espiga; sostén, soporte, parte (*f.*) saliente.—**s. belt,** tahalí.—**s. blade,** o **bone,** (anat.) espaldilla, omoplato u omóplato, escápula, palet(ill)a.—**s. knot,** (mil.) charretera mocha, capona.—**s. pad,** (sast.) hombrera.—**s. strap,** correón (de los aguadores), etc.; (mil.) dragona; (sast.) hombrera, tirante.—**s. to s.,** hombro a hombro; unidamente.—**on one's shoulders,** a cuestas. —**to put one's s. to the wheel,** arrimar el hombro, echar una mano. **II.** *va.* echarse a la espalda, cargar a un hombro, llevar a hombros; (fig.) cargar con, asumir, tomar sobre sí.—**s. arms,** (mil.) armas al hombro. **III.** *vn.* hombrear.

shout [šáut]. **I.** *va.* y *vn.* vocear, gritar, baladrar, vociferar; vitorear, dar vivas.—**to s. one's self hoarse,** gritar hasta enronquecerse, desgañitarse. **II.** *s.* grito, baladro, alarido; aclamación. —**s. of applause,** viva, *m.*, ovación.

shouter [-œ(r)], *s.* gritador, baladrero, vociferador.

shouting [-iŋ]. **I.** *s.* vocerío, gritería; aclamación. **II.** *a.* que vocea, gritador, vociferador.

shove [šav]. **I.** *va.* y *vn.* empujar, empellar, impeler.—**to s. along,** empujar; hacer avanzar.— **to s. away,** rechazar, alejar.—**to s. back,** hacer retroceder.—**to s. forward** = TO S. ALONG.— **to s. from,** empujar, rechazar a empujones.— **to s. off,** echar afuera (una embarcación); alejarse de, dejar.—**to s. out,** empujar hacia afuera, hacer salir. **II.** *s.* empellón, empujón, empuje, impulso.

shovel [šável]. **I.** *s.* pala.—**s. hat,** sombrero de teja. **II.** *va.* traspalar.—**shovel(l)er** [-œ(r)], *s.* palero, paleador.—**shovelful** [-ful], *s.* palada.— **shovel(l)ing** [-iŋ], *s.* traspaleo.

shovelboard [-bord], *s.* tabla o mesa para jugar al tejo; juego de tejo (ll. t. SHUFFLEBOARD).

show [šóu]. **I.** *va.* (*pp.* SHOWN o SHOWED) mostrar, enseñar; hacer ver, señalar; exhibir, lucir, exponer, descubrir, manifestar, indicar; probar, demostrar; introducir, guiar, conducir; poner en escena, representar (un drama); poner, proyectar (una película); (com.) arrojar (un balance, o como resultado).—**to s. a clean pair of heels,** o **the heels,** escaparse.—**to s. cause,** (for.) rogar por la anulación de un decreto.—**to s. consideration,** o **regard, for,** guardar miramientos a.—**to s. displeasure,** poner mala cara.—**to s. fight,** ofrecer resistencia, mostrarse resuelto a pelear.—**to s. forth,** exponer, mostrar; publicar, manifestar.—**to s. in,** introducir, hacer entrar (a una persona).—**to s. one's cards,** o **hand,** mostrar el juego (fig.), dejarse ver sus intenciones.—**to s. one's face,** presentarse, aparecerse.—**to s. one's teeth,** enseñar los dientes.—**to s. off,** sacar a lucir.—**to s. spirit,** mostrar buen ánimo.—**to s. the door to,** echar, despedir.—**to s. to the door,** acompañar a la puerta.—**to s. up,** hacer subir (a una persona); denunciar, descubrir, arrancar la careta a. **II.** *vn.* parecer, tener apariencia o señales de; aparecer, mostrarse, asomar, dar señal.—**to s. off,** alardear, fachendear, pavonear.—**to s. through,** transparentarse; entreparecerse; entrelucir.—**to s. up,** presentarse, parecer, ir. **III.** *s.* exhibición, exposición; espectáculo público; (teat.) función; ostentación, boato, prosopopeya; señal, *f.,* indicación; apariencia, exterioridad; pretexto, máscara, velo; (fam. E. U.) oportunidad, suerte, *f.*—**s. bill,** cartel, cartelón, rótulo.—**s. card,** tarjetón, letrero.—**s. case,** vitrina, aparador, caja de muestras.—**s. window,** ventana o escaparate de tienda, vidriera.—**by s. of hands,** (votación) por manos levantadas.—**in open s.,** públicamente.

showbread [-brɛd], *s.* pan(es) de proposición.

showdown [-daun], *s.* declaración forzada (de recursos, intenciones, etc.); acción perentoria o definitiva.

shower [ʃáuœ(r)]. **I.** *s.* lluvia, chubasco, chaparrón; abundancia.—**s. bath,** (baño de) ducha. **II.** *va.* regar, mojar; derramar con abundancia. **III.** *vn.* llover, caer un chubasco; caer con profusión.

shower [ʃóuœ(r)], *s.* mostrador, el que muestra.

showerless [ʃáuœrlɪs], *a.* sin lluvia.

showery [ʃáuœrɪ], *a.* lluvioso, chubascoso.

showily [ʃóuɪlɪ], *adv.* ostentosamente, aparatosamente.—**showiness** [-nɪs], *s.* ostentación.

showing [ʃóuɪŋ], *s.* exhibición, exposición (de artículos de industrias y artes); proyección (de una película).—**to make a good s.,** lucirse.

showman [ʃóumạn], *s.* director de espectáculos; empresario de teatro, circo, museo, etc.

shown [ʃoun], *pp.* de TO SHOW.

showroom [ʃóurum], *s.* sala de exposición; cuarto de muestras (de mercancías).

showy [ʃóuɪ]. *a.* vistoso, aparatoso, ostentoso, suntuoso, rimbombante; chillón, charro.

shrank [ʃrænk], *pret.* de TO SHRINK.

shrapnel [ʃrápnɛl], *s.* (arti.) metralla; shrapnel, granada de metralla.

shred [ʃréd]. **I.** *va.* (*pret.* y *pp.* SHRED o SHREDDED) picar, desmenuzar, hacer tiras o trizas. **II.** *s.* triza, jirón, tira, retazo; fragmento, pizca.

shredded [-ɪd], *a.* trojezado, desmenuzado, hecho trizas.

shrew [ʃru], *s.* arpía, virago, mujer de mal genio; (zool.) musgaño, musaraña.

shrewd [ʃrúd], *a.* perspicaz, sagaz; astuto, sutil, (ant.) solapado; agudo, cortante.—**shrewdly** [-lɪ], *adv.* astutamente, sagazmente; solapadamente.—**shrewdness** [-nɪs], *s.* sagacidad, astucia, sutileza.

shrewish [ʃrúɪʃ], *a.* regañón(a), gruñidor(a).—**shrewishly** [-lɪ], *adv.* de muy mal humor, a regañadientes.—**shrewishness** [-nɪs], *s.* mal genio.

shrewmouse [ʃrúmaus], *s.* (zool.) musgaño, musaraña.

shriek [ʃrik]. **I.** *vn.* chillar, gritar. **II.** *s.* chillido, grito agudo.

shrievalty [ʃrívạltɪ], *s.* cargo o funciones de *sheriff.*

shrift [ʃrɪft], *s.* (igl.) (ant.) confesión; absolución.—**to make short s. of,** (fam.) despachar de prisa.

shrike [ʃraɪk], *s.* (orn.) pega reborda, alcaudón.

shrill [ʃrɪl]. **I.** *a.* chillón, estridente, agudo, penetrante.—**s.-tongued, s.-voiced,** de voz chillona. **II.** *va.* y *vn.* chillar.—**shrillness** [-nɪs], *s.* calidad de chillón.

shrimp [ʃrɪmp], *s.* (zool.) camarón, esquila; enano, hombre pequeño.—**shrimper** [-œ(r)], *s.* camaronero.

shrine [ʃraɪn], **I.** *s.* relicario, urna, altar, sepulcro de santo; sagrario, santuario, capilla, templete. **II.** *va.* = ENSHRINE.

shrink [ʃrɪŋk]. **I.** *vn.* (*pret.* SHRANK, SHRUNK; *pp.* SHRUNK, SHRUNKEN) encogerse, contraerse, acortarse; disminuir, mermar; (con **from**) evadir, apartarse o huir de; retroceder; temblar, estremecerse; retirarse; apocarse.—**to s. away,** desaparecer por grados; su(b)straerse, huir.—**to s. back,** retirarse, retroceder.—**to s. up,** estrecharse; encogerse, arrugarse; temblar, estremecerse. **II.** *va.* encoger, contraer, reducir.—**to s. on,** (mec.) montar en caliente (una llanta, una abrazadera, etc.).—**to s. up,** estrechar. **III.** *s.* encogimiento, acortamiento; contracción de nervios.

shrinkage [-ɪdʒ], *s.* encogimiento o contracción; reducción, di(s)minución; (com.) merma, pérdida.

shrinkingly [-ɪŋlɪ], *adv.* encogiéndose, acortándose; retrocediendo; encogida o tímidamente.

shrive [ʃraɪv], *va.* y *vn.* (*pret.* SHROVE o SHRIVED; *pp.* SHRIVEN o SHRIVED) (igl.) (ant.) confesar; oír en confesión; confesarse.

shrivel [ʃrívɛl]. **I.** *va.* arrugar, fruncir, doblar, encoger; estrechar; marchitar. **II.** *vn.* arrugarse, fruncirse, encogerse, deshincharse; marchitarse, avellanarse, acorcharse las frutas.

shriver [ʃráɪvœ(r)], *s.* confesor.

shroud [ʃraud]. **I.** *s.* mortaja, sudario; anillo de refuerzo (de una rueda dentada).—*pl.* (mar.) obenques, mostachos, jarcias. **II.** *va.* amortajar; (fig.) cubrir, ocultar.

shrove [ʃróuv], *pret.* de TO SHRIVE.—**Shrovetide** [-taɪd], carnaval, carnestolendas, *f. pl.*—**Shrove Tuesday,** martes de carnaval, martes de carnestolendas.

shrub [ʃrʌb], *s.* (bot.) arbusto.—**shrubbery** [-œrɪ], *s.* arbustos.—**shrubbiness** [-nɪs], *s.* abundancia de arbustos.—**shrubby** [-ɪ], *a.* cubierto de o abundante en arbustos; parecido a un arbusto; aparrado, fruticoso.

shrug [ʃrʌg]. **I.** *va.* encoger, contraer. **II.** *vn.* encogerse de hombros, o alzarse de hombros. **III.** *s.* encogimiento de hombros.

shrunk, shrunken, *pret.* y *pp.* de TO SHRINK.

shuck [ʃʌk]. **I.** *va.* descascarar, descortezar, pelar; desbullar, quitar la concha a una ostra. **II.** *s.* cáscara, vaina, hollejo; desbulla, concha de marisco.—**not worth shucks,** (fam.) no valer tres cominos.

shudder [ʃʌdœ(r)]. **I.** *vn.* estremecerse, temblar. **II.** *s.* temblor, estremecimiento.

shuffle [ʃʌfl]. **I.** *va.* y *vn.* barajar (naipes); mezclar, revolver; pasar, traspasar; restregar; esquivar, evadir; desordenar.—**to s. along,** arrastrar los pies, chancletear; ir tirando o pasando.—**to s. off,** soltar, echar a un lado, desprenderse o zafarse de.—**to s. up,** (fam.) frangollar, pergeñar, hacer una cosa de mala manera. **II.** *s.* barajadura; evasiva, embuste; salida; restregamiento de pies en el suelo, chancleteo.

shuffleboard [-bᴐrd], *s.* juego de tejo.

shuffler [ʃʌflœœ(r)], *s.* el que baraja, mezcla, arrastra los pies, etc.; embustero.

shuffling [ʃʌflɪŋ], *a.* lerdo, pesado; embustero; evasivo, (fam.) retrechero.

shun [ʃʌn], *va.* y *vn.* huir, rehuir, esquivar, evitar; retraerse, apartarse de.

shunt [ʃʌnt]. **I.** *va.* desviar; (f. c.) desviar, apartar; (elec.) shuntar, poner en derivación; evadir, eludir. **II.** *vn.* desviarse; mudar de curso o de opinión. **III.** *s.* desviación; (elec.) shunt, derivación.—**s. (-wound) dynamo,** dínamo (*f.*) con excitación en derivación. **IV.** *a.* (elec.) en derivación; de derivación.—**s.-wound**, de arrollamiento en derivación.

shunter [-œ(r)], *s.* (f. c.) guardaagujas.

shut [šát]. **I.** *va.* (*pret.* y *pp.* SHUT) cerrar; vedar; prohibir, impedir; negar la entrada; excluir; coger, agarrar (con algo que se cierra); plegar, doblar, cerrar (abanico, paraguas, etc.).—**to s. against**, cerrar a.—**to s. close**, cerrar bien.—**to s. from**, excluir.—**to s. in**, encerrar, confinar.—**to s. off**, impedir la entrada, interceptar; detener, cortar (el agua, etc.); interrumpir (a uno) en el teléfono, cortarle el circuito.—**to s. one's eyes to**, no hacer caso de; taparse los ojos (fig.).—**to s. out**, cerrar la puerta (a uno); excluir; ocultar, tapar.—**to s. out rain**, impedir que entre la lluvia.—**to s. up**, cerrar; hacer callar; acabar, terminar; tapar; encerrar; acorralar, recluir, aprisionar.—**to s. up shop**, cerrar la tienda; terminar el trabajo o cesar en él; desistir de una empresa.—**to half s.**, entornar. **II.** *vn.* cerrarse.—**to s. close**, cerrarse bien.—**to s. down**, cesar (en el trabajo), parar. —**to s. down on**, (fam.) hacer cesar, suprimir, reprimir.—**to s. up**, callarse; agotarse. **III.** *s.* cierre; término, fin; juntura; (fig.) horizonte. **IV.** *a.* cerrado, entornado; (pros.) sordo, poco sonoro; (gram.) sordo, cerrado.

shutdown [-daun], *s.* paro, cesación o suspensión de trabajo (en una fábrica, etc.).

shut-in [-in], *a.* y *s.* (persona) confinada en su casa o en un hospital por enfermedad, etc.

shutoff [-of], *s.* aparato para cerrar o cortar (el agua, gas, etc.).

shutout [-aut], *s.* (dep.) triunfo o partido en que el equipo contrario no registra tanto alguno. *V.* LOCKOUT.

shute [šut], *s.* trama de seda.

shutter [šátœ(r)], *s.* cerrador; persiana; hoja, contraventana; postigo; (foto.) obturador.

shuttle [šátl]. **I.** *s.* (tej.) lanzadera; (cost.) espolín, jugadera; lanzadera (de máquina de coser); tren de traspaso (entre dos vías férreas); tren que va y viene entre dos lugares cercanos (ll. t. **s. train**); compuerta corrediza. **II.** *va.* y *vn.* mover(se) alternativamente de un lado a otro o de una parte a otra; ir y venir.

shuttlecock [-kak], *s.* volante, rehilete.

shy [šái]. **I.** *a.* tímido; asustadizo; cauteloso, prudente; esquivo, arisco; vergonzoso, recatado; pudoroso, (fam.) ñoño; difícil, obscuro; poco prolífico o fértil; (fam.) falto, que falta (*I am shy a dollar*, me falta un dólar). **II.** *va.* (con **off** o **away**) hacer desviar, apartar; lanzar o arrojar. **III.** *vn.* respingar (un caballo); asustarse. **IV.** *s.* sobresalto; respingo; lanzamiento; (fam.) prueba, ensayo.

shyer [-œ(r)], *s.* caballo asustadizo.

shyly [-li], *adv.* cautelosamente; tímidamente.

shyness [-nis], *s.* timidez; recato; reserva; esquivez; vergüenza, (fam.) ñoñez.

shyster [šáistœ(r)], *s.* (fam. E. U.) picapleitos, trapisondista.

si [si], *s.* (mús.) si, séptima nota.

sialagogic [saialagádžik], *a.* **sialagogue** [saiélagag], *s.* sialagogo, que provoca la secreción de saliva.

Siamese [saiamíz], *a.* y *s.* siamés.

Siberian [saibíriąn], *a.* y *s.* siberiano.

sibilant [síbilant], *a.* sibilante.

sibilation [sibiléišœn], *s.* silbido.

sibyl [síbil], *s.* sibila, profetisa.—**sibylline** [-in], *a.* sibilino.

sic [sik], *adv. sic*, así dice.

sic, *va.* atacar, acometer (ú. esp. de los perros); azuzar, incitar a los perros para que acometan. *V.* SICK.

siccative [síkạtiv], *s.* y *a.* (pint.) secante, sicativo.

Sicilian [sisílyạn], *a.* y *s.* siciliano.

sick [sik]. **I.** *a.* enfermo; doliente, malo; nauseado; (con **of**) cansado, disgustado, fastidiado, harto; impuro, viciado; dañado, malo, imperfecto.—**s.**

at heart, afligido de corazón, angustiado.—**s bay**, (mar.) enfermería.—**s. bed**, lecho de enfermo.—**s. flag**, (mar.) bandera amarilla.—**s for**, deseoso de, suspirando por.—**s. headache** jaqueca con náuseas.—**s. leave**, licencia por enfermedad.—**s. rate**, proporción de enfermos.— **s. room**, cuarto del enfermo, enfermería —**s. to death**, enfermo de peligro, de muerte.— **the S. Man of Europe**, la Turquía (en tiempo de los sultanes), el imperio turco.—**to be s. a one's stomach**, tener náuseas. **II.** *va.* busca (ú. en imperativo para azuzar a un perro) excitar, incitar.

sicken [-n]. **I.** *va.* enfermar; dar asco; apestar debilitar, extenuar. **II.** *vn.* enfermarse; hartarse fastidiarse, cansarse; nausear, tener asco flaquear.

sickening [-nin], *a.* nauseabundo, repugnante asqueroso, apestoso.

sickish [-iš], *a.* enfermizo, delicado; nauseabundo excesivamente dulce o azucarado.

sickle [síkl], *s.* hoz, segadera, segur, falce, *f.*—**s. shaped**, falciforme.

sickliness [síklinis], *s.* calidad de enfermizo achaque, indisposición habitual; insalubridad.

sickly [síkli], *a.* enfermizo, achacoso; enclenque endeble; nauseabundo.

sickness [síknis], *s.* enfermedad, dolencia; náusea

side [sáid]. **I.** *s.* lado, costado; cara (de un sólido) flanco; costado, orilla, margen, *mf.*; falda, ladera; facción, partido, bando, parte, *f.*, causa lazo de parentesco; (mar.) costado, bordo banda.—**s. by s.**, lado a lado; hombro a hombro, juntos.—**by the s. of**, al lado de; cerca de. —**on all sides**, u on every s., por todos lados por todas partes.—**on that s.**, a, de, en o por ese lado.—**on the other s.**, del o al otro lado más allá; a la otra parte.—**on this s.**, a, de, en o por este lado; más acá. **II.** *a.* lateral; de lado oblicuo; secundario, incidental; auxiliar.—**s. arms**, armas de cinto, armas blancas.—**s. car**, sidecar, carro lateral (de una motocicleta).—**s. dish**, entremés.—**s. door**, puerta lateral.—**s. glance**, mirada de soslayo.—**s. graftage**, o **grafting**, (agr.) injerto de escudete.—**s. issue**, cuestión secundaria; incidente.—**s. light**, luz lateral; información o detalle incidental.—**s. line**, negocio o actividad incidentales; (dep.) línea que marca el límite del juego.—**s. pocket**, bolsillo lateral.—**s. road**, vereda, camino apartado.—**s. show**, función o exhibición secundaria.—**s. table**, trinchero, bufete, aparador.—**s. trip**, correría.—**s. wall**, pared lateral; pared, *f.*—**s.-wheel boat**, o **steamer**, **s.-wheeler**, vapor (buque) de ruedas laterales. —**s. whiskers**, patillas, (fam.) chuletas. **III.** *va.* y *vn.* (con **with**) tomar parte por, declararse por, unirse con, ser de la opinión de.

sideboard [-bord], *s.* aparador, bufete, copero.

sideburns [-bœrnz], *s. pl.* patillas.

sideface [-fejs], *s.* perfil.

sidehill [-hil], *s.* ladera, falda.

sideling [-lin]. **I.** *a.* oblicuo; inclinado. **II.** *adv.* de soslayo; oblicuamente, lateralmente.

sidelong [-lon]. **I.** *a.* lateral, de lado. **II.** *adv.* lateralmente, de lado.

sidereal [saidíriạl], *a.* sidéreo, sideral.

siderite [sídȩrait], *s.* (min.) siderosa o siderita.

siderography [sidȩrágrafi], *s.* grabado en acero blando.

siderostat [sídȩrostæt], *s.* (astr.) sideróstato.

siderurgical [sidȩrœrdžikạl], *a.* siderúrgico.

siderurgy [sidȩrœrdži], *s.* siderurgia.

sidesaddle [sáidsædl], *s.* silla de señora, silla de montar de lado, sillón; jamugas (*f. pl.*) para montar a mujeriegas.

sideslip [-slip]. **I.** *vn.* resbalar lateralmente. **II.** *s.* (aut.) resbalamiento o patinamiento lateral; (aer.) deslizamiento hacia adentro (en una curva).

side-step [-step]. **I.** *s.* paso lateral; paso a un

lado. **II.** *vn.* dar un paso lateral; hacerse a un lado. **III.** *va.* huir el cuerpo a; evitar, evadir.

sideswipe [-swaip], *va.* (fam.) chocar o rozar oblicuamente.

sidetrack [-træk]. **I.** *s.* (f. c.) apartadero, desviadero. **II.** *va.* (f. c.) meter en un apartadero; desviar; distraer (de un propósito); reducir a cosa secundaria, echar a un lado, arrinconar.

sidewalk [-wɔk], *s.* acera, orilla; andén; (Am.) vereda.

sideward(s [-wə̆rd(z], *adv.* de lado, de costado.

sideway(s [-wei(z], **sidewise** [-waiz], *a.* y *adv.* de lado, lateral(mente) de soslayo, oblicuamente, al través.

siding [sáidiŋ], *s.* (f. c.) apartadero, desviadero, vía muerta; (carp.) costaneras, entablado de los costados; adhesión a un partido.

sidle [sáidl], *vn.* andar o moverse de lado u oblicuamente; (con **up**) acercarse tímida o furtivamente.

siege [sidž], *s.* sitio, asedio, cerco; ataque (de una enfermedad).—**s. artillery,** (mil.) artillería de plaza o de sitio.

sienite [sáięnait], *s.* = SYENITE.

sienna [sienä], *s.* tierra de siena.

siesta [siéstä], *s.* siesta.

sieve [siv]. **I.** *s.* cedazo, tamiz, *m.*, criba, harnero, zaranda; canasto; persona gárrula o incapaz de guardar un secreto.—**s. cell,** (bot.) célula perforada.—**s. disk,** o **plate,** parte perforada de una célula.—**s. tissue,** tejido de células perforadas.—**s. tube, s. vessel** = S. CELL. **II.** *va.* = SIFT.

sift [sift]. **I.** *va.* cerner, cribar, a(h)echar, tamizar, zarand(e)ar; examinar, escudriñar; dividir, separar, entresacar.—**to s. out,** investigar. **II.** *vn.* caer o pasar al través de un tamiz o cedazo.

sifter [-œ(r)], *s.* cernedor, cribador; garbillador; escudriñador; tamiz, *m.*, harnero, cedazo, criba.

siftings [-iŋz], *s. pl.* granzas, cernidos o cerniduras, abaleaduras.

sigh [sái]. **I.** *vn.* suspirar; dar un quejido.—**to s. for,** anhelar, desear. **II.** *va.* (poét.) decir suspirando; lamentar. **III.** *s.* suspiro.

sighingly [-iŋli], *adv.* suspirando, entre suspiros.

sight [sáit]. **I.** *s.* vista; visión, perspectiva; ojo; escena, cuadro, espectáculo; aspecto, facha; concepto, parecer, modo de ver; puntería; mira, alza o punto (de armas de fuego); pínula (de una brújula de agrimensor, etc.); agujero o abertura para mirar.—**s. reader, s. reading,** lector, lectura a primera vista.—**s. unseen,** sin ser visto, sin verse.—**a s. of,** (fam.) gran cantidad o número de.—**after s.,** (com.) a . . . vista (*thirty days after sight,* a treinta días vista).—**at s.,** a la vista (giro, etc.); a primera vista; al ver, cuando se vea.—**by s.,** de vista.—**in s.,** visible; cercano.—**in s. of,** a vista de.—**out of s.,** fuera de vista, que no está a la vista.—**to be a s.,** (fam.) parecer o estar como un adefesio; ser extraordinario o extraño; tener aspecto maltrecho. **II.** *a.* visual; (com.) a la vista (*a sight draft,* una letra a la vista). **III.** *va.* ver, alcanzar con la vista, avistar, divisar; ver o descubrir con un instrumento; dirigir una visual; poner miras a un arma; apuntar; (com.) presentar (una letra) para su aceptación.—**to s. land,** (mar.) recalar. **IV.** *vn.* apuntar; dirigir una visual.

sighted [-id], *a.* (arm.) provisto de mira; con la mira arreglada para una distancia dada; que ve, que no es ciego; en composición, de vista (*sharp-s.,* de vista penetrante).—**s. for,** con la mira puesta para.

sightless [-lis], *a.* ciego; invisible.

sightliness [-linis], *s.* elegancia o hermosura; apariencia vistosa.

sightly [-li], *a.* vistoso, agradable a la vista.

sightseeing [-siiŋ]. *s.* acto de visitar objetos o puntos de interés.—**sightseer** [-siœ(r)], *s.* persona que visita puntos u objetos de interés.

sigmoid(al [sigmóid(ąl], *a.* (anat.) sigmoideo.

sigmoidoscope [-oskoup], *s.* sigmoidoscopio.

sign [sain]. **I.** *s.* signo; señal, *f.,* seña, signatura; muestra, letrero, rótulo, tablilla; firma, rúbrica; huella, vestigio, rastro, indicio, asomo.—**s. language,** dactilología, mímica.—**s. manual,** (Ingl.) firma del soberano; cualquier firma o rúbrica de propio puño.—**s. of the cross,** señal de la cruz.—**s. painter,** pintor de muestras o letreros.—**by signs,** por señas.—**the signs of the times,** las indicaciones de la actualidad, el rumbo de los acontecimientos, las orientaciones de la época.—**the signs of the zodiac,** los signos del zodíaco. **II.** *va.* firmar; rubricar, señalar, signar; subscribir (un tratado, etc.); (con **off** o **away**) firmar la cesión o traspaso de; poner una marca o firma. **III.** *vn.* firmar.—**to s. off,** (rad.) terminar, anunciar el fin de un programa o comunicación y cortar la transmisión.—**to s. on the dotted line,** firmar ciega y sumisamente.—**to s. up,** u **on,** contratarse, alistarse.

signal [sígnąl]. **I.** *a.* señalado, notable, insigne, memorable; de o para señales.—**s. box,** garita de señales.—**s. code,** código de señales.—**s. corps,** (mil. E. U.) cuerpo de señales y comunicaciones (inclusas las telegráficas, telefónicas, etc.).—**s. failure,** fracaso completo, (fam.) gran pifia.—**s. light,** fanal.—**s. service** = SIGNAL CORPS; sistema (*m.*) o servicio de señales.—**s. telegraph,** telégrafo óptico.—**s. tower,** garita alta de señales. **II.** *s.* seña, señal, *f.* **III.** *va.* y *vn.* hacer señas, señalar, indicar.

signalize [-aiz], *va.* señalar, distinguir; singularizar, hacer notable.

signally [-i], *adv.* insignemente, grandemente; señaladamente.

signalman [-mąn], *s.* guardavía, *m.*; señalador.

signalment [-mẹnt], *s.* marca, acción de poner marcas de identificación (apl. esp. a los criminales).

signatory [sígnątori], *a.* y *s.* firmante, signatario.

signature [sígnąchur], *s.* firma; rúbrica; (imp.) signatura; (mús.) signatura.

signboard [sáinbɔrd], *s.* muestra de establecimiento; tablero de anuncios.

signer [sáinœ(r)], *s.* firmante, signatario.

signet [sígnit], *s.* sello; signáculo; timbre, estampilla.—**s. ring,** sortija con sello.

significance, significancy [signífikąns, -i], *s.* significación; significado.—**significant** [-kąnt], *a.* significante, significativo.—**significantly** [-li], *adv.* significativamente; expresivamente.

signification [-kéišọn], *s.* significación o significado, sentido.

significative [signífikątiv], *a.* significativo; simbólico, emblemático.

signify [sígnifai]. **I.** *va.* significar, denotar, representar, simbolizar; expresar, manifestar, dar a entender. **II.** *vn.* significar; importar.

signpost [sáinpoust], *s.* poste o pilar de guía, que lleva letrero o señal, *f.;* hito.

silage [sáilidž], *s.* (agr.) ensilaje.

silence [sáiląns]. **I.** *s.* silencio; quietud; secreto; taciturnidad.—**s. gives consent,** quien calla otorga. **II.** *va.* imponer silencio, mandar o hacer callar; acorralar; sosegar, aquietar; (mil.) apagar el fuego de (la artillería enemiga).

silencer [-œ(r)], *s.* (tec.) silenciador, amortiguador de ruido.

silent [sáilẹnt], *a.* silencioso; callado, taciturno, sigiloso; quieto; sordo, mudo (sonido, letra, etc.); tácito.—**s. film** o **picture,** (cine) película muda.—**s. partner,** (com.) socio comanditario.—**s. partnership,** sociedad en comandita.—**to be,** o **keep, silent,** callar(se).

silentiary [sailénšiąri], *s.* silenciario.

silently [sáilẹntli], *adv.* silenciosamente, calladamente, callandico; tácitamente.

Silesian [sailíšąn], *s.* y *a.* silesio, silesiano.

silex [sáileks], *s.* (quím.) sílice, *f.*, pedernal; cierto vidrio resistente al fuego.

silhouette [silʉét] **I.** *va.* hacer aparecer en silueta. **II.** *s.* silueta.

silica [sílikä], *s.* (quím.) sílice, *f.*, pedernal.

silicate [sílikeit], *s.* (quím.) silicato.

siliceous [silíʃʌs], *a.* = SILICIOUS.

silicic [silísik], *a.* (quím.) silícico.

silicide [sílisaid], *s.* (quím.) siliciuro.

silicious [silíʃʌs], *a.* silíceo.—**s. earth**, tierra primitiva o sencilla de sílice o pedernal.

silicle [sílikl], *s.* (bot.) silícula.

silicon [sílikọn], *s.* (quím.) silicio.

siliqua [sílikwä], *s.* silicua (peso); (bot.) silicua.

silique [sílik], *s.* (bot.) silicua.

siliquous [sílikwʌs], **siliquose** [-kwọs], *a.* (bot.) silicuoso.

silk [sílk]. **I.** *s.* seda; tejido o hilo de seda.—*pl.* **silks**, sedería, géneros de seda. **II.** *a.* de seda; sedeño, sedoso, sedero, perteneciente o relativo a la seda.—**s. cotton**, lana vegetal.—**s.-cotton tree**, (bot.) árbol bombáceo (apl. más esp. a la ceiba).—**s. culture**, sericultura.—**s. dyer**, tintorero de sedas.—**s. goods**, géneros de seda, sedería.—**s. hat**, sombrero de copa, (fam.) chistera.—**s. mercer** = SILKMAN.—**s. plush**, felpa de seda.—**s.-producing**, (ent.) sericígeno, serígeno.—**s. serge**, sarga.—**s. skein**, capillejo.—**s. stocking**, media de seda.—**s.-stocking**, *a.* lujoso; aristocrático; *s.* aristócrata, *mf.*—**s. thrower**, devanador o torcedor de seda.—**s. throwing**, torcedura de la seda.—**s. throwster** = S. THROWER.—**s. twist**, torzal.—**s. weaver**, tejedor de seda.—**all s.**, de toda seda.

silkaline [-ạlin], *s.* tela de algodón mercerizada muy semejante a la seda.

silken [-n], *a.* de seda; sedoso, sedeño, sedero, sérico; lujoso.

silkiness [-iniṣ], *s.* calidad de sedoso, etc.; blandura, suavidad; molicie, afeminación.

silkman [-mạn], *s.* mercader de sedas, sedero.

silkweed [-wid], *s.* (bot.) asclepiada. *V.* MILKWEED.

silkworm [-wœrm], *s.* (ent.) gusano de seda.

silky [-i], *a.* asedado, sedoso, sedeño; de seda.

sill [sil], *s.* umbral de puerta; solera, mesilla, antepecho de ventana; (carp.) solera, viga de carrera.

sillabub [sílạbʌb], *s.* manjar de leche con vino o sidra.

sillily [sílili], *adv.* tontamente.

silliness [sílinis], *s.* simpleza, tontería, necedad, mentecatada.

silly [síli], *a.* necio, tonto, mentecato, bobo; simple, inocente, cándido; disparatado, ridículo.

silo [sáilou], *s.* (agr.) silo, silero.

silt [silt]. **I.** *s.* cieno, sedimento, aluvión, *m.* **II.** *va.* y *vn.* (a veces con *up*) obstruir(se) con sedimentos. **III.** *vn.* infiltrarse; manar.

silundum [silʌ́ndʌm], *s.* silundo, producto duro y refractario del horno eléctrico (carburo de silicio, a veces con oxígeno).

Silurian [silúriạn], *s.* y *a.* (geol.) siluriano, silúrico.

Siluric [silúrik], *a.* (geol.) silúrico.

silurid [silúrid], **silurus** [silúrʌs], *s.* (ict.) siluro.

silvan [sílvạn], *a.* = SYLVAN.

silver [sílvœ(r)]. **I.** *s.* plata; (com.) monedas de plata; vajilla de plata o plateada. **II.** *a.* de plata; argentado, argentino; plateado; blanco, cano.—**s. age**, edad de plata.—**s. bath**, (foto.) baño de plata.—**s.-bearing**, argentífero.—**s. beater**, batihoja, *m.*, batidor de plata.—**s. dollar**, peso fuerte o duro.—**s. embroidery**, argentería; escarchado.—**s. fir**, (bot.) abeto.—**s. fish**, (ent.) lepisma.—**s. foil**, hoja de plata.—**s. fox**, (zool.) zorro argentado y su piel.—**s. gray**, rucio (ú. del caballo).—**s. lace**, encaje o galón de plata.—**s. leaf**, hoja de plata.—**s. nitrate**, nitrato de plata; piedra infernal.—**s. paper**, papel plateado; (fot.) papel sensi-

bilizado con sales de plata; papel de seda para envolver artículos de plata.—**s. plate**, vajilla de plata o plateada.—**s.-plate**, *va.* platear.—**s.-plated**, plateado.—**s. print**, fotografía en papel de plata (sensibilizado con sales de plata).—**s. standard**, (e. p.) patrón o talón de plata.—**s. screen**, la pantalla cinematográfica.—**s. thistle**, (bot.) acanto.—**s.-tongued**, elocuente.—**s. voice**, voz argentina.—**s. wedding**, bodas de plata (vigésimoquinto aniversario).—**s. work**, orfebrería. **III.** *va.* platear, argentar; azogar (un espejo, etc.); blanquear.

silvering [-iŋ], *s.* capa o baño de plata; plateado o plateadura; azogamiento.

silversmith [-smiθ], *s.* platero, argentador, argentario, orfebre.—**s.'s roll**, cilindro de escarchar.—**s.'s shop**, platería.

silverware [-wer], *s.* plata labrada; vajilla de plata; artículos de plata.

silverweed [-wid], *s.* (bot.) argentina.

silvery [-i], *a.* plateado; argentino, argentado.

silvicultural [sílviḱʌlchurạl], *a.* de silvicultura, relativo a la silvicultura.—**silviculture** [-chur], *s.* silvicultura.—**silviculturist** [-ist], *s.* silvicultor.

simian [símiạn]. **I.** *s.* (zool.) simio. **II.** *a.* símico.

similar [símilä(r)], *a.* semejante, análogo, parecido, similar, símil; (geom.) semejante.

similarity [similáriti], *s.* semejanza, analogía.

similarly [símilạrli], *adv.* semejantemente, análogamente, asimismo, de igual manera.

simile [símili], *s.* (ret.) símil.

similitude [símílitjud], *s.* similitud, semejanza.

simioid, simious [símiɔid, símiʌs], *a.* símico.

simitar [símitä(r), *s.* cimitarra.

simmer [símœ(r)], *vn.* hervir a fuego lento.

simoniac [simóuniæk], *s.* y *a.*, **simoniacal** [saimonáiạkạl], *a.*, **simonist** [sáimonist], *s.* simoníaco, simoniático.—**simony** [sáimoni], *s.* simonía.

simon-pure [sáimọn pjúr], *a.* verdadero, puro, genuino.

simoom, simoon [simúm, simún], *s.* simún.

simp [simp], *s.* (fam.) simplón. *V.* SIMPLETON.

simper [símpœ(r)]. **I.** *vn.* sonreírse boba, afectada o fatuamente. **II.** *s.* sonrisa tonta.

simperingly [-iŋli], *adv.* sonriendo tontamente, con sonrisa necia o afectada.

simple [símpl]. **I.** *a.* simple; puro; sencillo; llano; mero; ingenuo, inocente, cándido; mentecato, necio; poco importante, insignificante, ordinario.—**s. contract**, (for.) contrato oral, o escrito pero no perfeccionado o sellado.—**s. engine**, (m. v.) máquina de simple expansión.—**s. equation**, (mat.) ecuación de primer grado.—**s.-hearted**, sencillo, ingenuo.—**s. interest**, (com.) interés simple.—**s. machines**, máquinas simples, mecanismos elementales—nombre que se da por costumbre a la palanca, el torno, el tornillo, la polea, la cuña y el plano inclinado.—**s.-minded**, cándido, confiado.—**s.-mindedness**, candor, sencillez.—**s. pendulum**, péndulo simple. **II.** *s.* simplón, bobo; (farm.) simple; (igl.) fiesta simple; persona de humilde alcurnia.—**the simples**, tontería, sandez.

simpleness [-niṣ], *s.* = SIMPLICITY.

simpleton [-tọn], *s.* simplón, gaznápiro, bobalicón, papanatas, zonzo.

simplicity [simplísiti], *s.* sencillez, llaneza, candor, inocencia; simplicidad; simpleza, bobería.

simplification [símplifiḱéiʃọn], *s.* simplificación.—**simplify** [-fai], *va.* simplificar.

simply [símpli], *adv.* sencillamente; simplemente; únicamente, solamente; tontamente.

simulacrum [simjulékrʌm], *s.* simulacro; farsa, apariencia.

simulant [símjulạnt]. **I.** *a.* que simula, imita o finge; de forma de. **II.** *s.* simulador.

mulate [-leit]. *va.* simular, fingir.—**simulated contract**, contrato simulado.

mulation [-léişǫn], *s.* simulación, fingimiento, imitación.

mulator [-leitǫ(r)], *s.* simulador.

multaneity, simultaneousness [sajmʌltʌníjti, -téjnjʌsnjs], *s.* simultaneidad.

multaneous [-téjnjʌs], *a.* simultáneo.—**simultaneously** [-lj], *adv.* simultáneamente.

n [sjn]. **I.** *s.* pecado, culpa; transgresión.—**s.-born**, nacido de pecado, adulterino.—**s. offering**, sacrificio o voto propiciatorio. **II.** *vn.* pecar.

inaic [sajnéjik], **Sinaitic** [sajnájtjk], *a.* sinaítico.

napism [sjnapizm], *s.* (med.) sinapismo.

nce [sjns]. **I.** *adv.* hace (*four days since*, hace cuatro días); desde entonces.—**s. when?, how long s.?**, ¿de(sde) cuándo acá?—**not long s.**, no hace mucho, hace poco. **II.** *prep.* desde, después de, a contar de. **III.** *conj.* desde que, después que; puesto que, como, comoquiera que, ya que, en vista de que.

ncere [sjnsír], *a.* sincero; genuino, verdadero; franco, cordial, abierto; serio.—**sincerely** [-lj], *adv.* sinceramente.—**sincereness** [-njs], **sincerity** [sjnsérjtj], *s.* sinceridad, integridad, cordialidad, franqueza, llaneza.

nciput [sjnsjpʌt], *s.* (anat.) sincipucio, coronilla.

ne [sajn], *s.* (mat.) seno.—**s. curve**, sinusoide, *f.*

ne [sájnj], *prep.* (lat.) sin.—**s. die**, indefinidamente, hasta nueva orden.—**s. qua non**, condición esencial.

necure [sájnjkjur], *s.* sinecura; prebenda, beneficio simple; (fam.) mina, pera, enchufe.

new [sjnyu]. **I.** *va.* fortalecer. **II.** *s.* (anat.) tendón; fibra, nervio, fortaleza, vigor.

newed [-d], **sinewy** [-j], *a.* nerv(i)oso, musculoso; fuerte, robusto, vigoroso.

nful [sjnfụl], *a.* pecaminoso; pecador.—**sinfully** [-j], *adv.* pecaminosa o pecadoramente, pecando.—**sinfulness** [-njs], *s.* perversidad, iniquidad, maldad, calidad de pecaminoso.

ng [sjŋ], *vn. y va.* (*pret.* SANG o SUNG; *pp.* SUNG) cantar; murmurar (el agua), gorjear (los pájaros), zumbar (los oídos).—**to s. a child to sleep**, arrullar a un niño.—**to s. out**, vocear, anunciar gritando.—**to s. out of tune, o false**, desafinar.—**to s. the same song**, cantar la misma cantinela, repetir la misma cosa.

inge [sjndž], *va.* chamuscar, socarrar, sollamar; quemar (las puntas del pelo).—**singeing** [-jŋ], *s.* socarra, chamusquina; quemado (del pelo).—**singer** [-œr], *s.* el o lo que chamusca o sollama.·

inger [sjŋœ(r)], *s.* cantor(a), cantante, *mf.*, cantatriz.

inghalese [sjŋgalíz], *s. y a.* cingalés.

inging [sjŋjŋ]. **I.** *s.* canto, música vocal; acción de cantar; zumbido (en los oídos). **II.** *a.* cantante, de canto; cantor; canoro.—**s. bird**, ave canora.—**s. book**, cuaderno de solfa, de canto.—**s. master**, maestro de canto.—**s. society**, orfeón, *m.*

ingle [sjŋgl]. **I.** *a.* único, solo; particular, singular, individual; aislado; simple, sencillo (no doble, etc.); célibe, soltero; puro, incorrupto; (mar.) single.—**s.-acting**, (mec.) de simple efecto.—**s. blessedness**, celibato, soltería, la (bendita) vida soltera.—**s. block**, (mec.) motón sencillo.—**s.-breasted**, (sast.) sencillo, de una sola hilera de botones (saco, americana, etc.).—**s. combat**, combate singular.—**s. entry**, (com.) partida simple.—**s.-entry**, por partida simple.—**s. file**, hilera; en hilera, uno tras otro; de reata (bestias); (mil.) por hileras, en desfilada.—**s.-handed**, solo, sin ayuda; manco.—**s.-hearted**, sencillo de corazón, ingenuo.—**s. life**, celibato.—**s. loader**, rifle de un solo cartucho.—**s.-minded**, concentrado en un solo objeto; ingenuo, sincero.—**s.-phase**, (elec.) monofásico.—**s.-phaser**, máquina monofásica.—**s.-pole**, unipolar.—**s.-screw**, (mar.)

de una hélice.—**s.-seater**, de un solo asiento.—**s. state** = s. LIFE.—**s. tax**, (e. p.) impuesto único.—**s.-throw**, de una dirección.—**s.-track**, de una sola vía.—**s.-valued**, (mat.) de un solo valor (función, variable).—**not a s.**, ni un, ni una. **II.** *va.* (gen. con **out**) singularizar; particularizar; separar, retirar; escoger; señalar con especialidad. **III.** *s.* billete de un dólar.—*pl.* juego sencillo, (juego de) individuales (en el tenis, etc.).

singleness [-njs], *s.* unidad; sencillez, llaneza; sinceridad, ingenuidad; soltería, celibato.

singlestick [-stjk], *s.* (esgr.) bastón.

singletree [-tri], *s.* (carr.) volea, balancín.

singly [sjŋglj], *adv.* individualmente, de uno en uno, uno a uno, separadamente.

singsong [sjŋsǫŋ], *s.* cadencia uniforme, sonsonete, tonillo.

singular [sjŋgjulạ(r)]. **I.** *a.* singular; aislado, aparte, peculiar; extraño, extraordinario, raro; sencillo, simple; único. **II.** *s.* (gram.) número singular.—**singularity** [-lérjtj], **singularness** [-njs], *s.* singularidad, rareza.—**singularize** [-ajz], *va.* singularizar, particularizar.—**singularly** [-lj], *adv.* singularmente, particularmente.

Sinic [sjnjk], *a.* sínico, chinesco, chino.

sinister [sjnjstœ(r)], *a.* siniestro.—**sinistrad** [-træd], *adv.* hacia el lado izquierdo del cuerpo.—**sinistral, sinistrorse** [-trạl, -trǫrs], *a.* siniestro, izquierdo.—**sinistrorsely** [-lj], *adv.* (bot.) sinistrórsum.—**sinistrous** [-trʌs], *a.* siniestro.—**sinistrously** [-lj], *adv.* siniestramente; hacia la izquierda.

sink [sjŋk]. **I.** *va.* (*pret.* SANK, SUNK; *pp.* SUNK, SUNKEN) hundir, sumergir; (mar.) echar a pique o a fondo; dar barreno (a un buque); sumir, ahondar; cavar, abrir (un pozo); clavar en tierra; deprimir, abatir, humillar; disminuir, bajar, rebajar; abatir, hacer bajar; derrochar, malbaratar; suprimir, ocultar, hacer desaparecer; arruinar; grabar en hueco. **II.** *vn.* hundirse, sumirse; (mar.) naufragar, zozobrar, anegarse, irse a pique; (arq.) (a)sentarse; introducirse, penetrar, caer; grabarse (en la memoria); descender, desaparecer; ponerse, tramontar (el sol); disminuir, menguar; debilitarse, sucumbir, perecer; dejarse caer, rendirse; abatirse, acoquinarse, amilanarse; decaer, empeorar.—**to s. down**, caer por grados; penetrar profundamente.—**to s. in**, (fam.) ser comprendido, calar.—**to s. into**, penetrar en, llegar a; caer en.—**to s. on one's knees**, caer de rodillas.—**to s. under**, atribularse en o con, anonadarse. **III.** *s.* sumidero, vertedero, derramadero; fregadero, pila de cocina; zahurda (fig.); cavidad; cauce, zanja.

sinkable [-ạbl], *a.* hundible, sumergible.

sinker [-œr(r)], *s.* el que o lo que hunde; grabador en hueco; plomada de pescar; (fam.) especie de buñuelo.

sinking [-jŋ]. **I.** *s.* hundimiento, sumergimiento; abertura (de un pozo, etc.); acción de hundir(se), echar a pique, etc. (*v.* SINK). **II.** *a.* que (se) hunde.—**s. fund**, fondo de amortización.

sinless [sjnljs], *a.* impecable; inmaculado.

sinlessness [-njs], *s.* impecabilidad.

sinner [sjnœ(r)], *s.* pecador, pecadora.

Sino-Japanese [sájno džæpạníz], *a.* sinojaponés.

Sinologist [sajnálodžjst], **Sinolog(ue** [sájnolag], *s.* sinólogo.—**Sinology** [sajnálodžj], *s.* sinología.

Sinophil(e [sájnofjl, -fajl], *s.* sinófilo, chinófilo, amigo o partidario de la China.

sinople [sjnopl], *s.* (min.; blas. ant.) sinople.

sinter [sjntœ(r)], *s.* (geol.) toba, incrustación.

sinuate [sjnyụejt]. *vn.* formar oblicuidades, sinuosidades o senos.—**sinuate(d** [-jd], *a.* tortuoso, sinuoso; (bot.) ondulado.—**sinuation** [-éjşǫn], *s.* tortuosidad, corvadura.

sinuosity [sjnyụásjtj], *s.* sinuosidad, tortuosidad.—**sinuous** [sjnyụʌs], *a.* sinuoso, tortuoso.

sinus [sáinʌs], *s.* curva, recodo; cavidad, abertura, hueco; (anat.) seno, cavidad hueca.

sinusoid [sáinʌsɔid], *s.* (mat.) sinusoide, *f.*

sinusoidal [-sóidɑl], *a.* sinusoidal.

sip [sip]. I. *va.* sorber, libar, chupar o churrupear. II. *s.* sorbo.

siphon [sáifon]. I. *s.* sifón, cantimplora. II. *va.* y *vn.* sacar líquidos con sifón. III. *a.* de sifón.—**s. bottle,** sifón (botella), botella de sifón.—**s. pipe, o trap,** desagüe de sifón o en U.

siphonage [-idʒ], *s.* desagüe o extracción por sifón; acción o funcionamiento del sifón.

siphonophore [saifánofor], *s.* (zool.) sifonóforo.

sipper [sípœ(r)], *s.* sorbedor.

sippet [sípit], *s.* sopita, sopilla, sopa; pizca.

sir [sœr]. I. *s.* señor, caballero; (Ingl.) sir, título que se antepone al nombre de pila de los barones y caballeros de las órdenes militares.

sirdar [sœrdár], *s.* sirdar, jefe; mozo de palanquín, cargador; criado.

sire [sair]. I. *s.* padre; progenitor; caballo padre; anciano; Señor, tratamiento del soberano. II. *va.* engendrar, producir (hablando esp. de caballos). III. *vn.* padrear.

siren [sáiren], *s.* (mit.) sirena; mujer peligrosa y hechicera; cantatriz de mérito; sirena eléctrica o de vapor, pito que se emplea en los buques, automóviles, fábricas, etc., para avisar.

siriasis [siráiasis], *s.* (med.) siríasis, insolación.

Sirius [sírias], *s.* (astr.) Sirio, Canícula.

sirloin [sœrloin], *s.* solomillo, lomo.

sirocco [sirákou], *s.* siroco, simún.

sirrah [sírɑ], *s.* (desp.) señoritingo, don Turuleque, u otra expresión despreciativa análoga.

sirup [sírʌp], *s.* jarabe, jarope, sirope.

sirupy [-i], *a.* semejante a jarabe, siruposo.

sisal [sísal], **s. hemp,** *s.* (bot.) henequén, cabuya.

siskin [sískin], *s.* (orn.) verderón.

sissy [sísi]. I. *s.* (fam.) hermanita; niñita. II. *s.* y *a.* (fam.) afeminado, adamado.

sister [sístœ(r)], *s.* hermana; (igl.) sor; monja.—**s.-in-law,** cuñada, hermana política.—**S. of Charity,** (igl.) hermana de la caridad.—**s. ships,** barcos gemelos.

sisterhood [-hud], *s.* hermandad; cofradía de mujeres o monjas; conjunto de hermanas.

sisterly [-li], *a.* con hermandad, como corresponde a hermanas, fraternal.

sistrum [sístrʌm], *s.* sistro, cascabel músico de los antiguos egipcios.

sit [sit]. I. *va.* (*pret.* y *pp.* SAT) sentar; dar asiento a; tener asientos o cabida para; cabalgar, sentarse en (un caballo, etc.).—**to s. out,** estarse (sentado) o aguantar (sentado) hasta el fin de; permanecer sentado durante; no tomar parte en. II. *vr.* sentarse. III. *vn.* sentarse; estar sentado; posarse, encobar, empollar (las aves); reunirse, celebrar junta o sesión; formar parte de un tribunal; sentar, venir (un vestido, etc.) bien o mal; montar, mantenerse a caballo; descansar, apoyarse.—**to s. at ease,** arrellanarse.—**to s. at meat, o at table,** sentarse a la mesa, o a comer.—**to s. by,** sentarse o estar sentado cerca de, junto a o al lado de.—**to s. down,** sentarse; detenerse, parar; residir.—**to s. down before (a city),** poner sitio a, sitiar (una ciudad).—**to s. down on, o upon,** sentarse en (fam.) reprimir; desairar, desechar.—**to s. for,** servir de modelo de.—**to s. for one's picture,** hacerse retratar.—**to s. in (on),** asistir como miembro de, ser miembro, o participar en las deliberaciones, de; reunirse en.—**to s. on, o upon,** (fam.) hacer callar a, aplastar (fig.), dejar feo a.—**to s. over (a cup of coffee, their cigars,** etc.), hablar de sobremesa (tomando una taza de café, fumando, etc.).—**to s. tight,** (fam.) esperar sin decir nada, esperar la jugada del contrario (fig.), tenerse firme.—**to s. up,** incorporarse; sentarse (el enfermo, sea en la cama, sea en una silla); velar, estarse levantado, no acostarse.—**to s.**

up and take notice, (fam.) abrir los oj (fig.), despertar (fig.), poner cuidado.—**s. stil** estése quieto, no se mueva; conserve Vd. asiento, no se levante Vd.

sit-down [-daun], *a.* que se hace (toma, etc sentado.—**s.-d. strike,** huelga de sentado huelga pasiva, sentada, o de brazos caídos, e que los huelguistas permanecen en el taller s trabajar.

site [sáit], *s.* asiento, solar; sitio, situación, loca

sith [siθ], (ant.) = SINCE.

sitter [sítœ(r)], *s.* el que se sienta o está sentad el que se hace retratar; el ave (*f.*) que empoll

sitting [sítiŋ]. I. *s.* acción o modo de sentars sentada delante de un retratista; sesión, junt legislatura; (a)sentada; empolladura; nidada cría. II. *a.* sentado.—**s. duck,** (fam.) blanc muy fácil para un ataque aéreo.—**s. roon** estancia, aposento.

situate [síchueit]. I. *va.* situar; fijar sitio o lug para. II. *a.* situado, sito, ubicado.

situation [-éiʃon], *s.* situación; ubicación, pos ción; (arq.) orientación, exposición; colocació plaza, empleo; incidente, peripecia.—**out of s.,** sin empleo, cesante.

situs [sáitʌs], *s.* situación, posición, colocación.

sitz bath [sits bæθ], *s.* baño de asiento o d caderas; semicupio; bidé.

six [siks], *a.* y *s.* seis.—**s. hundred(th,** sei cientos.—**s.-shooter,** (fam.) revólver de se tiros.—**s.-year period,** sexenio.—**at sixes an sevens,** a manga por hombro, en desorden; e desacuerdo.

sixfold [-fould], *a.* seis veces, seis veces más; d seis clases; séxtuplo.

sixpence [-pens], *s.* (Ingl.) moneda de plata (se peniques, o medio chelín).

sixpenny [-peni], *a.* que vale o se vende por se peniques; mezquino.

sixscore [-skór], *a.* y *s.* seis veintenas.

sixteen [-tín], *s.* y *a.* dieciséis.—**sixteent** [-tínθ]. I. *a.* décimosexto, dieciseiseno; diecisé (ordinal). II. *s.* y *a.* dieciseisavo.

sixth [siksθ]. I. *a.* sexto; seis (del mes). II. sexto; sexta parte; (mús.) sexta.—**sixthly** [-l adv.* en sexto lugar.

sixtieth [síkstjiθ]. I. *a.* sexagésimo, sesenta. II. *s.* y *a.* sesentavo.

sixty [síksti], *a.* y *s.* sesenta.

siz(e)able [sáizʌbl], *a.* de tamaño adecuad razonable o proporcionado; algo grande.

sizar [sáizₐ(r)], *s.* (Ingl.) estudiante con beca.

size [sáiz]. I. *s.* tamaño, medida, porte, capacida volumen, dimensiones; diámetro (de un tub alambre, etc.); cuerpo, talla, estatura; tipo d medida; número (de prendas de vestir); canti dad especificada; (pap. y tej.) apresto; cola sisa de doradores, cola de retazo; calibre diámetro interior.—**s. stick,** (zap.) cartabón.— **to s.,** del tamaño debido o exacto; segú medida. II. *va.* medir el tamaño de; calibra clasificar o separar según tamaño o estatura valuar, justipreciar; dar el tamaño debido reducir al tamaño debido; (pap. y tej.) apres tar; aderezar; (pint.) encolar; sisar; estofa aparejar.—**to s. down,** disminuir gradualment el tamaño de.—**to s. up,** tomar las medidas (fig.), justipreciar, juzgar.

sized [-d], *a.* dispuestos según tamaño o estatur (precedido de adjetivo) de tamaño (*good-sized* de buen tamaño; *large-sized,* de tamañ grande); calibrado; aprestado; encolado; sisad

sizer [-œ(r)], *s.* calibrador; pasabalas; encolador aprestador; sisador.

siziness [-inis], *s.* viscosidad.

sizing [-iŋ], *s.* encolado, aparejo, aderezo, estof calibradura; (pap. y tej.) apresto.

sizy [-i], *a.* viscoso, pegajoso.

sizz [siz], *vn.* silbar, chirlar, chirriar.

sizzle [sízl]. I. *va.* y *vn.* quemar(se) o chamus

car(se) produciendo chirrido o siseo. **II.** *s.* sonido como de siseo; calor excesivo.

skald [skɔld], *s.* escaldo, bardo escandinavo.

skate [skéịt]. **I.** *vn.* patinar. **II.** *s.* patín; (ict.) raya, *m.*—**skater** [-œ(r)], *s.* patinador.

skating [-iŋ]. **I.** *s.* patinaje, (el) patinar. **II.** *a.* de o para patinar.—**s. rink**, patinadero; pista o sala de patinar.

skedaddle [skịdǽdl], *vn.* (fam.) tomar las de Villadiego; largarse.

skee [ski], *s.* y *vn.* = SKI.

skeet [skit], *s.* (mar.) bañadera. *V.* TRAPSHOOTING.

skeg [skeg], *s.* (mar.) remate posterior de la quilla.

skein [skein], *s.* madeja, cadejo, capillejo.

skeletal [skélẹtạl], *a.* esquelético, de(l) esqueleto.

skeleton [skélẹtọn]. **I.** *a.* en esqueleto o armazón; encanutado.—**s. crew**, equipo mínimo.—**s. key**, llave maestra. **II.** *s.* esqueleto, osambre, osamenta; armazón o armadura; esbozo, esquema, *m.*

skeletonize [-aịz], *va.* sacar el esqueleto a o de, reducir (un cuerpo muerto) a su estructura ósea; reducir a las partes esenciales; disminuir, reducir; bosquejar.

skelp [skelp], *s.* tira o plancha metálica para tubos.

skeptic [sképtịk], *s.* y *a.* escéptico.—**skeptical** [-ạl], *a.* escéptico.—**skeptically** [-lị], *adv.* escépticamente.—**skepticism** [-tịsịzm], *s.* escepticismo.

sketch [skéch]. **I.** *s.* diseño, esbozo, bosquejo, dibujo, esquicio, trazado, boceto, croquis, *m.*; descripción a grandes rasgos; reseña; drama corto; (teat.) pieza corta o ligera; drama o cuadro dramático de radio. **II.** *va.* diseñar, dibujar, esbozar, trazar, esquiciar, delinear, bosquejar, hacer un croquis de; reseñar; describir a grandes rasgos.—**sketchily** [-ịlị], *adv.* de modo abocetado.—**sketchiness** [-nịs], *s.* modo abocetado de una obra artística.—**sketchy** [-i], *a.* bosquejado, esquiciado; incompleto, fragmentario.

skew [skjú]. **I.** *a.* oblicuo, sesg(ad)o. **II.** *s.* movimiento, curso o posición oblicuos; mirada de soslayo. **III.** *va.* sesgar, poner al sesgo. **IV.** *vn.* andar o moverse sesgadamente; mirar de soslayo.

skewback [-bæk], *s.* (arq.) sotabanco.

skewer [-œ(r)]. **I.** *s.* (coc.) brocheta o broqueta, palillo, pincho. **II.** *va.* espetar, embroquetar.

ski [ski]. **I.** *s.* ski, esquí, patín largo noruego de madera.—**s. jump**, pista de salto; el salto hecho con esquís. **II.** *vn.* esquiar, deslizarse o andar en esquís.

skiagraph [skáịạgræf], *s.* = RADIOGRAPH.

skiagraphy [skaịégrạfị], *s.* esciagrafía; esquiagrafía, fotografía por los rayos X.

skid [skịd]. **I.** *va.* sostener sobre polines o arrastrar o hacer deslizar sobre rodillos o trozas; (mar.) proveer de o proteger con varaderas o defensas. **II.** *vn.* deslizar; patinar (una rueda); (aut.) patinar o resbalar lateralmente. **III.** *s.* (mar.) defensa del costado, varadera; calzo; polín; rodillo; troza; tabla o madero inclinado de arrastre o deslizamiento; arrastradero; (aer.) patín.—**s. chains**, cadenas para impedir el deslizamiento o patinamiento.—**s. road**, arrastradero para trozas; camino con trozas transversales a intervalos.

skidding [-iŋ], *s.* deslizamiento, patinamiento, patinazo o patinaje.

skier [skíœ(r)], *s.* esquiador(a).

skiff [skịf], *s.* (mar.) esquife, botecillo, caique.

skiing [skíịŋ], *s.* acción de patinar con esquís; deporte de los esquís.

skil(l)ful [skịlfụl], *a.* diestro, hábil, experto, ducho. —**skil(l)fully** [-i], *adv.* diestramente.—**skil(l)-fulness** [-nịs], *s.* habilidad, destreza.

skill [skịl], *s.* habilidad, destreza, pericia, maña.

skilled [-d], *a.* práctico, instruído, experimentado, experto.—**skil(l)less** [-lịs], *a.* inexperto.

skillet [skịlịt], *s.* (coc.) cacerola o cazuela pequeña.

skim [skịm]. **I.** *va.* desnatar; (d)espumar; rasar, rastrear, tocar ligeramente; examinar superficialmente; hojear (un libro); echar una ojeada a.—**to s. the ocean**, (mar.) peinar las olas. **II.** *vn.* deslizarse o pasar rasando.—**to s. over**, resbalar, rozar; hojear; tocar ligeramente una cuestión. **III.** *s.* acción de desnatar; nata; escoria; desperdicios, inmundicias.—**s. milk**, leche desnatada.

skimmer [-œ(r)], *s.* (d)espumadera.

skimming [-iŋ], *s.* despumación.

skimp [skịmp]. **I.** *va.* escatimar; ejecutar con descuido. **II.** *vn.* ser tacaño; trabajar con descuido.

skin [skịn]. **I.** *s.* piel, *f.* (cutis, *mf.*, dermis, epidermis, tez), pellejo, tegumento; (ten.) piel, cuero; odre, pellejo o cuero para vino, etc.; piel, pellejo o corteza de algunas frutas; forros (de un buque); cáscara, costra; (fam.) avaro; petardista, estafador.—*pl.* pieles, corambre, *f.*—**s.-deep**, superficial.—**s. disease**, (med.) dermatosis.—**s. game**, (fam.) fullería.—**s. graft(ing)**, (cir.) injerto cutáneo.—**s. test**, (med.) prueba cutánea.—**s.-tight**, ajustado como un guante.—**by the s. of one's teeth**, por un tris, (salvarse) en una tabla, apenas, a duras penas. —**to be s. and bones**, estar en los huesos; no tener más que la piel y los huesos.—**to be, o to get, under one's s.**, irritar o fastidiar a uno.—**to save one's s.**, salvar el pellejo. **II.** *va.* desollar, despellejar; pelar, deshollejar; cubrir con piel; cubrir superficialmente; (fam.) agotar; (fam.) sacar dinero a, pelar; (fam.) aventajar, ganar. **III.** *vn.* cubrirse de pellejo o tegumento; cicatrizarse; mudar la piel; (fam.) ser embaucador o engañador; (fam.) (gen. con **out**) escabullirse.—**to s. over**, cicatrizarse; hacerse costras.

skinflint [skịnflịnt], *s.* avaro.

skink [skịŋk], *s.* (zool.) esquinco, sequinco o estinco.

skinless [skịnlịs], *a.* desprovisto de pellejo, despellejado; de piel muy delgada.

skinner [skịnœ(r)], *s.* desollador; (fam.) petardista, estafador; pellejero; peletero.

skinniness [skịnịnịs], *s.* flacura, extenuación.

skinny [skịnị], *a.* flaco; pellejudo.

skip [skịp]. **I.** *va.* saltar, omitir; saltar por encima de, pasar por alto; hacer saltar rozando, como una piedra sobre el agua. **II.** *vn.* saltar, brincar, cabriolar, triscar. **III.** *s.* cabriola, salto, brinco; omisión.

skipper [-œ(r)], *s.* saltador, brincador; (ict.) escombresoc(i)o; (ent.) gusanillo de queso; (apl. t. a varios otros insectos, mariposas, etc.); (mar.) patrón, mareante.—**s.'s daughters**, cabrillas de mar.

skipping [-iŋ], *s.* acción de saltar.—**s. rope**, comba, cuerda con que saltan los niños.

skippingly [-lị], *adv.* a saltos, a brincos.

skirmish [skœrmịʃ]. **I.** *s.* (mil.) escaramuza, refriega, zalagarda, guerrilla, tiroteo; choque, encuentro. **II.** *vn.* escaramuzar, escaramucear.

skirmisher [-œ(r)], *s.* escaramuzador.

skirret [skịrịt], *s.* (bot.) chirivía.

skirt [skœrt]. **I.** *s.* falda, faldellín, saya, refajo, enagua(s); (sast.) faldón; faldones de la silla de montar; orla, cenefa; orilla, margen, *mf.*, borde; (fam.) mujer, faldas (fig.).—**s. (board)** = BASEBOARD.—**s. dance**, (teat.) baile en que la bailarina hace graciosas posturas con su faldellín.—**skirts of a city**, contornos de una ciudad. **II.** *va.* poner enaguas a; proveer de borde, margen, etc.; seguir la orilla de; costear; (cost.) orillar; poner cenefa a. **III.** *vn.* (con *along, near*, etc.) moverse a lo largo de, ladear, (mar.) costear; escoger la lana separando la de inferior calidad.

skirting [-iŋ], *s.* enaguas (consideradas como

géneros); material para enaguas; rodapié, friso; *v.* BASEBOARD (ll. t. s. board).—*pl.* lana de inferior calidad.

skit [skįt], *s.* articulillo, suelto, pasquín; burla.

skitter [skįtœ(r)], *vn.* deslizarse saltando, ir saltando y rozando.

skittish [skįtįš], *a.* espantadizo; tímido; retozón; caprichudo, voluble.—**skittishly** [-lį], *adv.* caprichosamente.—**skittishness** [-nįs], *s.* calidad de espantadizo; desenvoltura; volubilidad, inconstancia.

skittles [skįtlz], *s. pl.* juego de bolos.

skive [skájv]. I. *va.* (ten.) raspar, adelgazar, chiflar, cortar en capas; (joy.) pulir. II. *s.* (joy.) disco para pulir el diamante.—**skiver** [-œ(r)], *s.* (ten.) el que raspa o adelgaza cueros; cuero hendido con cuchillo; (enc.) cuero para pastas; chifla, cuchillo de adelgazar.

skoal [skoŭl], *s.* e *interj.* brindis, *m.*; ¡salud!

skul(l)duggery [skʌldʌgœrį], *s.* (fam.) tretas, mañas.

skulk [skʌlk], *vn.* remolonear, (mar.) estar o ponerse al socaire; acechar; andar a sombra de tejado.

skunker [-œ(r)], *s.* socairero, remolón, el que rehuye el trabajo; acechador.

skull [skʌl], *s.* cráneo, casco, sesera; calavera.

skullcap [-kæp], *s.* casquete (gorro), (igl.) solideo; (anat.) sincipucio; (bot.) escutelaria.

skunk [skʌŋk]. I. *s.* (zool.) mofeta, (Am.) zorrino, zorrillo; (fam.) canalla, *m.*, persona ruin.—**s. cabbage**, (bot.) cierta hierba fétida. II. *va.* (fam.) ganar completamente a (en un juego) sin perder una jugada.

sky [skáj], *s.* cielo, firmamento, (poét.) éter.—**s.-blue**, **s.-colored**, azul celeste, cerúleo.—**s.-high**, por las nubes, tan alto como el cielo.—**s. pilot**, aviador; (fam.) clérigo.—**s. writing**, escritura aérea, formación de letreros o figuras con gases o vapores que se despiden de un avión. —**out of a clear s.**, de repente; inesperadamente.—**to praise to the skies**, poner en, o sobre, las nubes.

skyey [-į], *a.* (poét.) etéreo; del cielo; muy alto.

skylark [-lark]. I. *s.* (orn.) alondra, calandria. II. *vn.* (fam.) chacotear, jaranear.—**skylarking** [-įŋ], *s.* chacota, jarana.

skylight [-lajt], *s.* claraboya, tragaluz, lucera, lumbre(ra), buhardilla; luz cenital.

skyline [-lajn], *s.* horizonte; silueta; efecto de conjunto que dan edificios, árboles, etc., al destacarse contra el cielo.

skyman [-man], *s.* (fam.) aviador.

skyrocket [-rakįt], I. *s.* cohete, volador. II. *vn.* (fam.) subir rápidamente; ir a las nubes (precios); aumentar prodigiosamente (la producción, etc.).

skysail [-sejl], *s.* (mar.) monter(ill)a, (sobre)periquito.

skyscraper [-skrejpœ(r)], *s.* (mar.) = SKYSAIL; rascacielos, edificio sumamente alto.

skyward(s [-wǝrd(z], *adv.* hacia el cielo.

slab [slæb], *s.* costero; losa, plancha, tabla, laja, lancha o loncha, lastra.—**s. line**, (mar.) briol(ín).

slabber [slábœ(r)], *vn.* babear, salivar.—**slabberer** [-œ(r)], *s.* baboso.—**slabbering** [-įŋ], *s.* babeo.

slabby [slábį], *a.* espeso, viscoso; mojado.

slack [slæk]. I. *a.* flojo, laxo; débil, poco firme, aflojado; perezoso, negligente, remiso, tardo.—**s. ropes**, (mar.) cabos sueltos o en banda.—**s. water**, repunte de la marea; aguas represadas. —**s.-water navigation**, navegación por tramos. II. *s.* (mar.) seno de un cabo; flojedad; (com.) período de poca actividad, estación muerta o de calma; polvo de carbón, cisco, carbón menudo.—*pl.* pantalones flojos.

slack, slacken [slák, -n]. I. *va.* aflojar, relajar, desapretar; retardar; disminuir; descuidar; eludir.—**to slack lime**, apagar la cal. II. *vn.*

aflojarse, relajarse; (mar.) formar seno; disminuir; (a veces con *up*) mermar, menguar; retardarse; descuidarse, flojear; ceder, cejar.

slacker [-œ(r)], *s.* (fam.) el que elude su deber o el servicio militar en tiempo de guerra; tumbón; cobarde.

slackly [-lį], *adv.* flojamente.

slackness [-nįs], *s.* flojedad.

slag [slæg]. I. *s.* escoria (de metales o volcanes); chatarra, grasa, moco (de metales).—**s. heap**, escorial. II. *va.* escorificar.

slain [slejn], *pp.* de TO SLAY.

slake [slejk]. I. *va.* apagar (la cal, la sed); extinguir; remojar; desleír; calmar, moderar.—**slaked lime**, cal muerta o apagada. II. *vn.* apagarse (la cal).

slam [slæm]. I. *va.* cerrar de golpe; en los juegos de naipes, dar capote. II. *vn.* cerrarse de golpe y con estrépito. III. *s.* portazo; capote en el juego; (fam.) crítica severa.—**s.-bang**, (fam.) de golpe y porrazo.

slander [slándœ(r)]. I. *va.* calumniar, denigrar, difamar, infamar. II. *s.* calumnia, difamación. —**slanderer** [-œ(r)], *s.* calumniador.—**slandering** [-įŋ]. I. *s.* calumnia. II. *a.* calumnioso. —**slanderous** [-ʌs], *a.* infamatorio, calumnioso. —**slanderously** [-lį], *adv.* calumniosamente.

slang [slæŋ]. I. *s.* (gram.) vulgarismo; jerga, jerigonza, caló, germanía. II. *a.* vulgar, familiar; germanesco.

slangy [-į], *a.* vulgar en el lenguaje; que emplea vulgarismos, dicharachos, o habla en caló.

slant [slánt]. I. *va.* y *vn.* oblicuar, sesgar; inclinarse, sesgarse. II. *s.* oblicuidad, sesgo; inclinación; plano inclinado, declive; punto de vista, prejuicio; (fam.) mirada.

slant(ing [-(į)ŋ], *a.* de soslayo; sesgado, terciado, oblicuo; inclinado, en declive.

slantingly [-lį], **slantwise** [-wajz], *adv.* sesgadamente, oblicuamente, de o al través.

slap [slæp]. I. *va.* abofetear, acachetear, dar una palmada a (una persona) o en (la cara); poner o tirar violentamente. II. *s.* manotada, bofetada.—**a s. in the face**, bofetada; insulto. III. *adv.* de golpe y porrazo, de sopetón.

slapdash [-dæš], *a.* y *adv.* (fam.) chafallón, chapucero; de prisa, de una vez, de un golpe.

slapstick [-stįk], *s.* y *a.* (farsa) de carácter bufonesco, con muchos porrazos y otras acciones grotescas.

slash [slæš]. I. *va.* acuchillar, dar cuchilladas; cortar, hacer un corte largo en; azotar; rebajar, reducir radicalmente (sueldos, gastos, precios, etc.); criticar mordazmente. II. *vn.* tirar tajos y reveses. III. *s.* cuchillada; latigazo, azote; (sast.) corte, cortadura, cuchillo; entrada, abertura (en un bosque).—*pl.* ramas; matorral pantanoso.—**slashed** [-d], *a.* acuchillado; (bot.) laciniado.—**s. sleeves**, (sast.) mangas acuchilladas.—**slasher** [-œ(r)], *s.* acuchillador.

slat [slæt]. *s.* tablilla, loncha (de madera o metal).

slate [slejt]. I. *s.* pizarra, esquisto; pizarra para escribir; (E. U. pol.) lista de candidatos; candidatura; programa (*m.*) de partido.—**s.-colored**, apizarrado, pizarreño.—**s. pencil**, pizarrín.—**s. quarry**, pizarral, cantera de pizarra.—**s. roof**, empizarrado.—**to have a clean s.**, tener las manos limpias (fig.), no tener mácula.—**to wipe the s. clean**, empezar de nuevo, abrirse un nuevo derrotero. II. *va.* empizarrar; (ten.) quitar pelo a las pieles; (E. U. pol.) inscribir en una candidatura; redactar un programa de partido; inscribir u ofrecer para consideración; planear, proyectar, destinar.

slater [-œ(r)], *s.* pizarrero; raspador de pieles; crítico mordaz; (zool.) isópodo terrestre.

slating [-įŋ] *s.* empizarrado; pizarras; crítica pública y mordaz.

slattern [slétœrn]. I. *a.* puerco; desaliñado. II. *s.* mujer desaliñada.—**slatternliness** [-lįnįs], *s.* desatavío; desaliño.—**slatternly** [-li]. I. *adv.* desaliñadamente. II. *a.* puerco, desaliñado.

slaty [sléiti], *a.* pizarreño.

slaughter [slótœ(r)]. I. *s.* carnicería, matanza, (fam.) degollina. II. *va.* matar, sacrificar (las reses); hacer una carnicería; destrozar.— **slaughterer, slaughterman** [-œ(r), -man], *s.* jifero, matarife, matachín; matador; asesino; verdugo.—**slaughterous** [-ʌs], *a.* mortífero, destructivo.

slaughterhouse [-haus], *s.* matadero, rastro, degolladero, desolladero, (Am.) carnicería.

slaughtering [-iŋ], *s.* matanza, jifería (de reses).

Slav [slav], *a.* y *s.* eslavo.

slave [sléiv]. I. *s.* esclavo.—**s. ant,** (ent.) hormiga esclava.—**s. driver,** capataz (*m.*) de esclavos; persona opresiva o despótica.—**s.-making ant,** hormiga esclavizadora.—**s. trade,** trata de esclavos.—**s. trader,** negrero, traficante en esclavos. II. *vn.* trabajar como esclavo. III. *va.* esclavizar.

slaveborn [-born], *a.* nacido en la esclavitud.

slaveholder [-houldœ(r)], *s.* amo de esclavos.

slaver [-œ(r)], *s.* negrero, esclavista; (persona o buque) traficante de esclavos.

slaver [slǽvœ(r)]. I. *s.* baba. II. *vn.* bab(os)ear.

slaverer [-œ(r)], *s.* baboso; adulador, lavacaras.

slavering [-iŋ]. I. *a.* baboso. II. *s.* bab(os)eo.

slavery [sléivœri], *s.* esclavitud.

Slavic [slávik], *a. V.* SLAVONIC.

slavish [sléiviš], *a.* servil, abyecto; esclavizado.— **slavishly** [-li], *adv.* servilmente.—**slavishness** [-nis], *s.* servilismo.

Slavism [slávizm], *s.* eslavismo.

Slavonian [slavóunian], *a.* y *s.*, **Slavonic** [slavánik], *a.* esclavón, esclavonio; eslavo.

slaw [slɔ], *s.* (ensalada de) col picada.

slay [sléi], *va.* (*pret. y pp.* SLAIN) matar.

slayer [-œ(r)], *s.* matador; asesino.

sleave [slív]. I. *s.* seda en rama (ll. t. **s.,** o **sleaved, silk**). II. *va.* desenredar, desenmarañar.

sleaziness [slízinis], *s.* textura débil y ligera.

sleazy [slízi], *a.* baladí, delgado, ligero, tenue.

sled [sléd]. I. *va.* y *vn.* ir o llevar en trineo o narria. II. *s.* trineo, narria, rastra.

sledder [-œ(r)], *s.* el que va en un trineo o lo arrastra; animal de trineo, que arrastra trineos. —**sledding** [-iŋ], *s.* acción de ir en trineo o usarlo; marcha en trineo.—**rough s.,** marcha difícil.

sledge [sledž]. I. *va.* y *vn.* transportar o viajar en una narria. II. *s.* rastra, narria, trineo.—**s. hammer,** macho, mandarria, acotillo.

sleek [slík]. I. *a.* liso, bruñido, alisado; suave, blando, zalamero. II. *va.* alisar, pulir, suavizar.

sleekly [-li], *adv.* lisamente.

sleekness [-nis], *s.* lisura.

sleeky [-i], *a.* liso; taimado, mañoso.

sleep [slíp]. I. *va.* y *vn.* (*pret. y pp.* SLEPT) dormir (en toda acepción).—**to s. away,** disipar o malgastar el tiempo durmiendo.—**to s. like a log,** o top, dormir como un lirón.—**to s. off,** curar durmiendo (un dolor de cabeza, etc.); dormirla (la borrachera, etc.).—**to s. on,** seguir durmiendo.—**to s. on,** o **upon,** descuidarse o no hacer caso de; consultar con la almohada.— **to s. one's liquor away,** dormir la mona.— **to s. out,** dormir fuera de casa; saciarse de dormir.—**to s. over,** consultar con la almohada. —**to s. soundly,** dormir profundamente o a pierna suelta. II. *s.* sueño; dormida; descanso; reposo; muerte, *f.*

sleeper [-œ(r)], *s.* persona dormida o muerta; (f. c.) coche dormitorio, coche cama; (f. c.) traviesa, durmiente; viga; animal aletargado.

sleepily [-ili], *adv.* soñolientamente, con somnolencia, pesadez o torpeza.

sleepiness [-inis], *s.* somnolencia, sueño, modorra.

sleeping [-iŋ]. I. *s.* sueño. II. *a.* durmiente; dormido.—**s. bag,** especie de talego para envol-

verse por la noche cuando se duerme a la intemperie.—**s. car,** (f. c.) coche cama o coche dormitorio.—**s. draught,** bebida calmante, narcótico.—**s. partner** = SILENT PARTNER.—**s. potion** = DRAUGHT.—**s. sickness,** (med.) encefalitis letárgica, letargo epidémico.

sleepless [-lis], *a.* desvelado, insomne; de desvelo. —**sleeplessness** [-nis], *s.* insomnio.

sleepwalker [-wɔkœ(r)], *s.* so(m)námbulo.— **sleepwalking** [-wɔkiŋ], *s.* so(m)nambulismo.

sleepy [-i], *a.* soñoliento, amodorrado; soporífero, soporoso; letárgico.—**s.-head,** (fam.) dormilón.

sleet [slít]. I. *s.* cellisca, aguanieve, *f.*, agua nieve. II. *vn.* cellisquear, caer cellisca, etc.

sleetiness [-inis], *s.* estado del tiempo en que cellisquea.

sleety [-i], *a.* cubierto de cellisca.

sleeve [slív], *s.* (sast.) manga; (mec.) manguito; collar.—**s. band,** brazal; (sast.) vuelta de manga.—**s. coupling,** junta de manguito.—**s. garter,** sujetador de la manga de camisa.—**s. links, o buttons,** gemelos, (Am.) mancuernas. —**s. nut,** manguito de tuerca.—**to have up one's s.,** tener preparado en secreto.—**to laugh in,** o up, one's s., reírse con disimulo. —**to say in one's s.,** decir para su sayo o capote.

sleeveless [-lis], *a.* sin mangas.

sleigh [sléi]. I. *s.* trineo.—**s. bell,** cascabel.—**s. ride,** paseo en trineo. II. *vn.* pasearse en trineo.

sleighing [-iŋ], *s.* paseo en trineo; estado de los caminos que permite ir en trineo.

sleight [slait], *s.* habilidad, pericia, maña; ardid, artificio, estratagema.—**s. of hand,** juego de manos, prestidigitación.—**s. of hand artist** o **performer,** prestidigitador.

slender [sléndœ(r)], *a.* delgado; adelgazado, cenceño, esbelto; sutil, fino, ligero; flaco; delicado; escaso; pequeño, poco, corto, insuficiente; mediano.—**slenderly** [-li], *adv.* delgadamente, sutilmente, ligeramente.—**slenderness** [-nis], *s.* delgadez, sutileza; debilidad; escasez; pequeñez.

slept [slept], *pret. y pp.* de TO SLEEP.

sleuth [slúuθ]. I. *s.* detective; agente de policía secreta o investigador particular. *V.* SLEUTH-HOUND. II. *vn.* hacer de detective; seguir una pista o un rastro; (fam.) andar espiando o acechando.

sleuthhound [-haund], *s.* (perro) sabueso o ventor; (fam.) detective.

slew [slju]. I. *pret.* de TO SLAY. II. *va., vn.* y *s.* = SLUE. III. *s.* (fam.) un gran número de, la mar de.

sley [sléi], *s.* (tej.) peine, cárcel, *f.*

slice [sláis]. I. *va.* rebanar, cortar en tajadas; tajar, cortar. II. *s.* rebanada, tajada, lonja, raja; pala; espátula.—**s. bar,** hurgón, atizador.

slicer [-œ(r)], *s.* rebanador; (joy.) sierra circular.

slick [slik]. I. *va.* alisar, pulir. II. *vn.* (gen. con up) (fam.) componerse, acicalarse. III. *a.* liso, terso, lustroso; resbaladizo; meloso, untuoso, facundo; (fam.) diestro, mañoso; (fam.) de primera. IV. *s.* lugar lustroso o aceitoso (en el agua); formón ancho de alisar (ll. t. **s. chisel**).

slicker [slíkœ(r)], *s.* impermeable flojo; (fam.) embaucador, farsante.

slide [sláid]. I. *vn.* (*pret.* SLID; *pp.* SLID O SLIDDEN) resbalar, deslizarse, correrse, caer(se); patinar; escabullirse; salirse, escaparse; correr, pasar aprisa; pasar insensiblemente o gradualmente de un estado, tono, etc., a otro. II. *va.* hacer resbalar; meter o poner mañosa o suavemente (con let) dejar correr, no hacer caso de. III. *s.* tapa corrediza; (foto.) tapa del chasis o portaplacas; diapositiva; portaobjetos, platina de microscopio o linterna mágica; resbalón, resbaladura; resbaladero, deslizadero; (mec.) carro, guía de patín, cursor; plano inclinado; muesca, encaje (de un bastidor); (geol.) falla, dislocación; desmoronamiento, alud, *m.*; (mús.) ligado; bomba (de trombón, etc.). IV. *a.* corredizo; de corredera.—**s. bar,** guía, barra de guía; barra corrediza.—**s. bolt,** pestillo corredizo.—**s. box,** (elec.) caja de contacto en alambre de contacto corredizo.—**s. fastener** = ZIPPER.—**s. rail,** (f. c.) aguja de cambiavía. —**s. rest,** (mec.) soporte de corredera; carrillo portaherramientas (de torno).—**s. rod,** vástago de la válvula de corredera.—**s. rule,** regla de cálculo.—**s. shaft** = S. ROD.—**s. valve,** válvula de corredera.—**s.-valve rod** = S. ROD.—**s. wire,** (elec.) alambre de contacto corredizo; brazo (del puente de Wheatstone) de contacto corredizo.

slider [-œ(r)], *s.* resbalador; (mec.) cursor.
sliding [-iŋ]. **I.** *s.* desliz(amiento), resbalamiento. **II.** *a.* corredizo; resbaladizo, escurridizo; oscilante, variable, transitorio.—**s. door,** puerta corrediza o de corredera.—**s. friction,** rozamiento de resbalamiento.—**s. gear,** (aut.) cambio de velocidades con tren corredizo.—**s. knot,** nudo escurridizo.—**s. place,** sitio resbaladizo, resbaladero, deslizadero.—**s. scale,** escala móvil, en la cual los impuestos, jornales, etc., varían según los precios de los artículos de consumo, o, en el caso de los obreros, según los precios corrientes de lo que producen.

slight [sláit]. **I.** *a.* ligero, leve; pequeño, corto, fútil, débil, flojo, delgado. **II.** *s.* desaire, desatención, feo, desprecio. **III.** *va.* menospreciar, despreciar, desairar, dejar feo; desatender; descuidar.

slightingly [-iŋli], *adv.* con desprecio.
slightly [-li], *adv.* ligeramente; escasamente; descuidadamente.
slightness [-nis], *s.* pequeñez, insignificancia.
slim [slim], *a.* delgado; sutil, tenue; poco lógico, débil, baladí; delicado; insuficiente, escaso.
slime [sláim]. **I.** *s.* limo, lama, légamo, cieno, fango, babaza, tarquín, pecina; (raro) asfalto. **II.** *va.* y *vn.* enfangar, enlodar, ensuciar con limo, lama, légamo o babaza; deslamar.
sliminess [-inis], *s.* viscosidad; mucosidad, limosidad, limazo.
slimy [-i], *a.* viscoso, limoso, legamoso; mucoso.
sling [sliŋ]. **I.** *s.* honda; (cir.) cabestrillo; (mil.) charpa, portafusil; (E. U.) bebida alcohólica con azúcar y nuez moscada; (mar.) eslinga, balso.—**slings of the yard,** (mar.) cruz de la verga; estribos de las vergas. **II.** *va.* (*pret.* y *pp.* SLUNG) tirar con honda; tirar, arrojar; (mar.) embalsar, embragar, izar, eslingar; (cir.) poner en cabestrillo.
slinger [-œ(r)], *s.* hondero, pedrero.
slingshot [-šat], *s.* tirador.
slink [sliŋk]. **I.** *vn.* (*pret.* y *pp.* SLUNK) escabullirse, escaparse, escurrirse. **II.** *vn.* y *va.* (*pret.* y *pp.* SLINKED o SLUNK) (vet.) abortar, malparir. **III.** *s.* (vet.) abortón; sujeto ruin o apocado; cobarde. **IV.** *a.* (vet.) nacido antes de tiempo; inmaturo; flacucho; bajo, despreciable.
slip [slip]. **I.** *va.* (*pret.* y *pp.* SLIPPED) deslizar; llevar secretamente; soltarse, zafarse, desprenderse de, eludir, escapar de; soltar, desatar; (agr.) esquejar, cortar esquejes de; (mar.) largar o soltar (un cable o cabo); malparir (la bestia); escaparse a, pasar inadvertido por; irse de (la memoria, etc.); descuidar, dejar pasar; dislocar (un hueso).—**to s. a cog,** equivocarse.—**to s. in,** introducir o meter (esp. secretamente).—**to s. off,** quitarse de encima, soltar.—**to s. on,** ponerse (anillo, bata, etc.) de prisa.—**to s. one over on,** (fam.) engañar, pegársela (a uno).—**to s. one's arm around,** o **through,** pasar el brazo por (la cintura o el brazo de uno).—**to s. out,** sacar (esp. disimuladamente).—**to s. the cable,** (mar.) soltar el cable por ojo.—**to let s.,** revelar, dejar escapar sin querer (un secreto, etc.). **II.** *vn.* resbalar, deslizarse; tropezar, dar traspiés; escurrirse, salirse de su sitio; cometer un desliz; errar o equivocarse; huirse; largarse;

pasar sin ser visto; borrarse de la memoria, olvidársele a uno.—**to s. away,** escabullirse, huirse.—**to s. down,** dejarse caer; desguindarse, descolgarse (por una cuerda, etc.).—**to s. into,** introducirse, entrometerse; insinuarse. —**to s. out,** salir sin ser observado; escurrirse; dislocarse (un hueso); zafarse, soltarse; salirse.—**to s. through one's fingers,** perder uno, o írsele a uno, repentinamente, o en un abrir y cerrar de ojos.—**to s. up,** resbalar; (fam.) equivocarse; salir mal. **III.** *s.* resbalón; deslizamiento; tropiezo, traspié, *m.*; resbalamiento (de una rueda, de la hélice); patinamiento; velocidad retrógrada del agua tras un buque; (elec.) resbalamiento, *slip* (del inducido, etc.); desliz, *m.*, falta; platina (de microscopio, etc.); resbaladero; declive; falta, error; descuido, inadvertencia, lapso; (agr.) esqueje, estaca, plantón; escapada, huída; tira o pedazo; lengua de tierra; callejón; embarcadero; (geol.) falla, dislocación; (impr.) prueba, galerada; funda de almohada; bata o prenda de vestir holgada; combinación; mantilla de los niños; traílla de un perro; requesón de leche; boleta, papeleta, cédula; vástago, descendiente; mozuelo o mozuela, mozalbete.—**s. cover,** funda (de muebles, etc.).—**s. of the pen,** error de pluma. —**s. of the tongue,** lapsus linguæ.—**s. ring,** (elec.) anillo colector.—**s. stream,** (aer.) corriente retrógrada del aire.—**s. switch,** (f. c.) cruzamiento de (con) agujas; cruzamiento y cambiavías combinados.—**there's many a s. 'twixt the cup and the lip,** de la mano a la boca se pierde la sopa.—**to give one the slip,** zafarse o salir de uno, sacarle el cuerpo, darle esquinazo.
slipboard [-bord], *s.* corredera, tabla corrediza.
slipknot [-nat], *s.* lazo o nudo corredizo.
slip-on [-an], *s.* prenda de vestir fácil de ponerse o quitarse, o que se pone por la cabeza (blusa, jersey o *swéter,* etc.). (En el segundo caso ll. t. **pullover**).
slippage [-idž], *s.* resbalamiento; pérdida de velocidad o rendimiento debida al resbalamiento.
slipper [slípœ(r)], *s.* chinela, babucha, chancleta, pantufla; escarpín, zapatilla.
slippered [-d], *a.* con zapatillas o chinelas, etc.
slipperiness [slípœriŋis], *s.* calidad de resbaladizo; lubricidad; volubilidad.
slippery [slípœri], *a.* resbaladizo, resbaloso, deslizadizo; evasivo, astuto, zorro; voluble, voltario.—**s. elm,** (bot.) variedad de olmo y su corteza medicinal.
slipshod [slípšad], *a.* en chancletas; desaseado, desaliñado; descuidado; tosco, hecho a la diabla.
slipslop [-slap], *s.* (fam.) aguachirle, *f.*; dislate.
slip-up [-ʌp], *s.* (fam.) error, descuido.
slit [slit], **I.** *va.* (*pret.* y *pp.* SLIT) rajar, hender, tajar; cortar en tiras; rasgar (un vestido). **II.** *s.* raja; cortadura larga; hendedura, tajo; ranura, resquicio, quebradura, abertura.—**s. trench,** (mil.) zanja o trinchera estrecha. *V.* FOXHOLE.
slither [slíðœ(r)], *vn.* resbalarse, deslizarse, escurrirse por el suelo.
slitting [slítiŋ], *a.* de rajar, etc.—**s. file,** lima achaflanada.—**s. machine,** máquina de cortar metal, papel, etc., en tiras.—**s. saw,** sierra circular fina de cortar metales.
sliver [slívœ(r)]. **I.** *va.* y *vn.* cortar en tiras; desgajar(se), romper(se). **II.** *s.* brizna, astilla; lonja de pescado; torzal, mecha de fibras textiles; borde sin pulir de un tablón.
slob [slab], *s.* (fam.) sujeto desaliñado, estúpido o desmañado.
slobber [slábœ(r)]. **I.** *va.* babosear. **II.** *vn.* bab(os)ear. **III.** *s.* baba, bab(os)eo.
sloe [slou], *s.* (bot.) endrino; endrina.—**s.-eyed,** ojinegro, de ojos del color de endrino.
slog [slag]. **I.** *va.* pegar duro; aporrear. **II.** *vn.*

(gen. con **along** o **away**) andar pesadamente (como por el fango); afanarse, atrafagar.

slogan [slóuɡǎn], *s.* consigna; lema, *m.;* grito de combate.

sloop [slup], *s.* (mar.) balandra, chalupa.—**s. of war,** corbeta.

slop [slap]. **I.** *va.* verter, derramar; mojar, ensuciar, enlodar. **II.** *vn.* verterse, derramarse; chapotear, chapalear (por el fango, agua nieve, etc.). **III.** *s.* líquido derramado en el suelo; mojadura.—*pl.* agua sucia; aguachirle, *f.,* lavazas, zupia; (desp.) atole, gachas; té o café flojo; ropa mal hecha y barata; traje flojo; (mar.) ropa y otros efectos que se venden a los marineros.—**s. basin, s. bowl, s. bucket,** cubo o tina para agua sucia.—**s. jar,** tinaja de lavabo para aguas sucias.—**s. pail** = s. BUCKET.

slope [slóup]. **I.** *s.* (geol. y min.) buzamiento, inclinación; (f. c.) talud, *m.;* derrame, declive, bajada; cuesta, recuesto, costanera, loma, falda, ladera; (arq.) agua, vertiente, *f.* (de tejado); (fort.) rampa; escarpa. **II.** *va.* sesgar, cortar o partir en sesgo; formar en declive; escarpar; (cost.) escotar. **III.** *vn.* inclinarse, declinar, estar en declive; ir oblicuamente.—**sloping** [-iŋ], *a.* inclinado, (poét.) clivoso; deprimida (frente).—**slopingly** [-li], *adv.* sesgadamente, al sesgo; en declive.

sloppiness [slápinis], *s.* calidad de mojado y sucio; estado cenagoso; (fam.) desaliño.

sloppy [slápi], *a.* mojado y sucio; lodoso, cenagoso; (fam.) chapucero; (fam.) desaliñado.

slopshop [slápšap], *s.* bazar de ropa barata.

slopwork [slápwœrk], *s.* (fabricación de) ropa hecha y barata; chapucería.

slosh [slaš]. **I.** *va.* y *vn. V.* SPLASH. **II.** *s. V.* SLUSH; (fam.) bebida o comida floja e insípida.

slot [slat]. **I.** *s.* (mec.) muesca, ranura, canal, *f.,* abertura, hendedura; pista, rastro; tira de madera, tablilla.—**s. machine,** máquina de servicio automático, provista de una ranura por la cual se introduce una moneda, que la hace funcionar. **II.** *va.* ajustar en una ranura; acanalar, hacer una ranura en.

sloth [slóθ], *s.* pereza, haraganería, flojedad, acedia; (zool.) perezoso, perico ligero, calípedes.—**slothful** [-fṵl], *a.* perezoso.—**slothfully** [-li], *adv.* perezosamente, flojamente, haraganamente.—**slothfulness** [-nis], *s.* pereza.

slouch [slauč]. **I.** *s.* postura floja y descuidada; sujeto desmañado y desaliñado, o poco emprendedor y falto de energía. **II.** *vn.* y *va.* tenerse en postura dejada al andar o al estar de pie o sentado; poner gacho.—**s. hat,** sombrero gacho.

slough [slau], *s.* lodazal, cenagal o fangal; estado de desánimo, impotencia o degradación abismales; [slju] (E. U.) charca; pantano.

slough [slaf]. **I.** *va.* y *vn.* echar de sí una costra, tejido muerto, o la piel. **II.** *s.* piel o camisa que muda la serpiente; (med.) escara, tejido muerto.

sloughy [sláui], *a.* fangoso, pantanoso.

sloughy [sláfi], *a.* (med.) que tiene escara.

Slovak [slóuvæk], *s.*, **Slovakian** [slouvékian], *s.* y *a.* eslovaco.

sloven [slʌvn], *s.* persona desaseada.—**slovenliness** [-linis], *s.* desaliño, desaseo; suciedad, porquería; descuido, dejadez.—**slovenly** [-li]. **I.** *a.* desaliñado, puerco o sucio; dejado, descuidado. **II.** *adv.* desaliñadamente, suciamente.

Slovene [slóuvin], *s.* y *a.* esloveno.

slow [slóu]. **I.** *va.* y *vn.* (con **up** o **down**) retardar, aflojar (el paso), ir más despacio. **II.** *a.* lento, despacioso; pausado; tardo, tardío; atrasado (el reloj); calmoso, cachazudo; lerdo, estúpido.—**s. coach** o **slowpoke,** (fam.) indolente, perezoso.—**s. fire,** fuego lento.—**s. match,** mecha de quema lenta.—**s. motion,** velocidad reducida. **III.** *adv.* despacio, lentamente.—**s. paced,** pesado en el andar.—**s.-witted,** torpe, estúpido.—**to go s.,** atrasar, estar atrasado (el reloj).

slowly [-li], *adv.* despacio, lentamente, pausadamente.

slowness [-nis], *s.* lentitud, morosidad, retraso, tardanza, dilación; cachaza; pesadez, torpeza.

slub [slʌb]. **I.** *va.* torcer la lana. **II.** *s.* mechón.

slubber [-œ(r)], *s.* (tej.) canillero; ovillador; mechón.

sludge [slʌdž], *s.* lodo, cieno; sedimento.

slue [slju]. **I.** *va.* y *vn.* (a menudo con **round**) revirar, volver, girar. **II.** *s.* giro, vuelta.

slug [slʌg]. **I.** *s.* cualquier cosa, animal o persona de movimiento(s) lento(s) o tardo(s); (zool.) babosa, babaza; (arti.) posta; bala; (impr.) lingote. **II.** *va.* (arti.) cargar con posta; (fam.) aporrear.

sluggard [-ǎrd], *s.* haragán, holgazán, pelmazo.

sluggish [slʌgiš], *a.* perezoso, tardo, pesado; inactivo.—**sluggishly** [-li], *adv.* perezosamente, lentamente.—**sluggishness** [-nis], *s.* lentitud, pesadez, (fam.) pachorra, cachaza, pelmacería; inactividad.

sluice [sljus]. **I.** *s.* acequia, saetín, boquera, bocacaz; esclusa; compuerta; canal; (fig.) salida.—**s. gate,** compuerta.—**s. post,** brenca.—**s. valve,** compuerta; válvula compuerta, llave compuerta, llave de corredera. **II.** *va.* mojar, regar; (min.) lavar; soltar la presa de agua.

sluiceway [-wei], *s.* saetín; canal, conducto; abertura de presa.

slum [slʌm]. **I.** *s.* barrio bajo, de gentes escuálidas o disolutas (ú. a menudo en *pl.*). **II.** *vn.* visitar los barrios bajos y lugares escuálidos o disolutos.—**slumdom** [-dǫm], *s.* los barrios y lugares de la baja vida.—**slumming** [-iŋ], *s.* visita a los barrios de la baja vida.—**to go slumming,** recorrer los barrios o lugares de la baja vida.

slumber [slʌmbœ(r)]. **I.** *vn.* dormitar, estar medio dormido; dormir; dormirse o descuidarse; estar latente. **II.** *s.* sueño ligero y tranquilo.—**s. song,** canción de cuna, nana.

slumberous [-ʌs], *a.* soñoliento, soporífero; dormido; tranquilo.

slump [slʌmp]. **I.** *vn.* hundirse el pie en una materia blanda; apalastarse, rebajarse; caer, bajar. *V.* SLOUCH. **II.** *va.* arrojar violentamente; hacer bajar (precios) súbitamente. **III.** *s.* hundimiento (rompiendo una costra); aplastamiento, rebajamiento (de una masa húmeda por su propio peso); disminución de actividad o vigor; (com.) baja repentina en los valores.

slung [slʌŋ], *pret.* y *pp.* de TO SLING.—**s. shot,** rompecabezas, arma ofensiva.

slunk [slʌŋk], *pret.* y *pp.* de TO SLINK.

slur [slœr]. **I.** *va.* menospreciar, rebajar, amancillar, desdorar; pasar por encima, suprimir, ocultar; farfullar (fam.), comerse sílabas o letras; (mús.) ligar las notas; (impr.) repintar. **II.** *s.* reparo, pulla, observación en desdoro; estigma, *m.;* mancilla, borrón o mancha ligera en la reputación; (mús.) ligadura (⌒ o ⌣); (impr.) trozo repintado.

slush [slʌš]. **I.** *va.* ensebar, engrasar, embarrar; (con **up**) (alb.) rellenar; lavar echando agua. **II.** *s.* cieno, lodo blando; fango; agua nieve fangosa; grasa lubricante; pintura para evitar el enmohecimiento; desperdicios crasos de cocina; (fam.) tonterías sentimentales.—**s. fund,** (fam., pol.) fondos para corrupción política.

slushy [-i], *a.* fangoso; que abunda en o es como agua nieve fangosa; (fam.) sentimental en exceso.

slut [slʌt], *s.* perra; mujer sucia.

sluttish [-iš], *a.* puerco, sucio, desaliñado.—**sluttishness** [-nis], *s.* porquería, suciedad, desaseo.—**sluttishly** [-li], *adv.* asquerosamente.

sly [slái], *a.* astuto, taimado, socarrón, disimulado.—**on the s.,** a hurtadillas, a la chiticallando.—**slyboots** [-buts], *s.* camastrón, mátalas callando.

slyly [-lị], *adv.* astutamente, disimuladamente; a hurtadillas, callandito.

slyness [-nịs], *s.* socarronería, astucia, disimulo.

smack [smǽk]. **I.** *va.* y *vn.* manotear, golpear; besar ruidosamente; hacer sonar o chasquear (un beso, golpe, latigazo, etc.); rechuparse, saborear; saborearse. **II.** *vn.* (con *of*) saber (a), tener gusto, dejo (de); oler (a). **III.** *s.* sabor, gusto, gustillo; olor; tintura, conocimiento ligero o superficial; beso sonado; rechupete; manotada; chasquido de látigo; (mar.) queche. **IV.** *adv.* (fam.) de golpe.—**s. on the lips,** de lleno en los labios.—**s. on the nose,** en las mismas narices.—**to fall s. on the face,** caer de bruces.—**to run s. into,** dar de narices en o contra.

smacking [-iŋ]. **I.** *s.* ruido agudo. *V.* SMACK. **II.** *a.* chasqueador, que chasquea; bueno, medianamente fuerte (*smacking breeze*, buena brisa).—**s. noise,** o **sound,** chasquido.

small [smɔl]. **I.** *a.* pequeño, menudo, diminuto, chico; menor; bajo de estatura; corto, exiguo, escaso, reducido; poco; insignificante; despreciable, mezquino; débil, flojo; tierno, blando; fino, delgado, de poco bulto o volumen; obscuro, bajo, vulgar, plebeyo.—**s. ale, s. beer,** cerveza débil o floja; vaso pequeño de cerveza; bagatela.—**s. arms,** armas ligeras o manuales (rifles, pistolas, espadas, etc.).—**s. cattle,** ganado menor.—**s. change,** calderilla, menudo, suelto, moneda suelta.—**s. coal,** cisco, carbón menudo.—**s. craft,** embarcaciones menores; cosas o personas de poca importancia.—**s. fry,** pececillos; gente menuda; cosas pequeñas.—**s. game,** caza menor.—**s. hours,** primeras horas (de la mañana).—**s. intestine,** (anat.) intestino delgado.—**s. letter,** letra minúscula.—**s. matters,** menudencias.—**s. nettle,** (bot.) ortiga menor, cania.—**s. pica,** (impr.) lecturita (tipo de 11 puntos).—**s. potatoes,** (fam.) persona o cosa de poca monta.—**s. print,** letra menuda. —(to) **s. purpose,** (para) bien poco.—**s. talk,** chismografía, vulgaridades, frivolidades.—**s. voice,** vocecita, voz delgada.—**s. wares,** mercería, artículos menudos.—**s. wood,** brusca, verdasca, leña menuda.—**in a s. way,** modestamente; (com.) con pequeño capital o existencias. **II.** *s.* parte estrecha de cualquier cosa y en particular del lomo, canto o filo; cosa o cantidad pequeña.—*pl.* (com.) artículos menudos; mineral menudo. *V.* SMALLCLOTHES. **III.** *adv.* en tono bajo o suave; menudamente; en miniatura; desdeñosamente.

smallage [smɔ́lịdž], *s.* (bot.) apio silvestre.

smallclothes [smɔ́lklouŏz], *s. pl.* calzones cortos; ropa para niños; ropa interior.

smaller [smɔ́lœ(r)], *a. comp.* de SMALL: menor, más chico, más pequeño, más bajo, más corto. —**smallest** [-ịst], *a. superl.* de SMALL: mínimo, menor, más chico, más pequeño, el más bajo, más corto.—**smallish** [-ịš], *a.* pequeñito.— **smallness** [-nịs], *s.* pequeñez; bajeza, ruindad; exigüidad; insignificancia.

smallpox [smɔ́lpaks], *s.* (med.) viruela(s).—**s. pit,** cacaraña.

smalt [smɔlt], *s.* esmalte, esmaltín.

smart [smárt]. **I.** *a.* vivo, listo, hábil, ingenioso, activo; despejado, despabilado, astuto, ladino; inteligente, talentoso; agudo, sutil; acerbo, punzante, mordaz; elegante, a la moda, de buen tono; galano.—**s. aleck,** tipo engreído o petulante.—**s. set,** gente (*f.*) de buen tono. **II.** *s.* escozor; dolor, aflicción. **III.** *vn.* escocer, picar; requemar; mordicar; dolerse.

smarten [-n], *va.* hermosear, embellecer.

smartly [-lị], *adv.* hábilmente; elegantemente; con despejo.—**smartness** [-nịs], *s.* agudeza, vivacidad, viveza; ingenio, habilidad, talento; astucia; elegancia, buen tono.—**smarty** [-ị], *s.* (fam.) persona que se pasa de listo.

smash [smǽš]. **I.** *va.* y *vn.* romper, quebrar, aplastar, destrozar o hacer pedazos; (fam.) fracasar, quebrar, hacer bancarrota. **II.** *s.* rotura, destrozo; fracaso; ruina, quiebra; bebida de coñac, hierbabuena y azúcar.—**s. hit,** (fam., teat., etc.) exitazo.—**to go to s.,** arruinarse; hacerse añicos.

smashing [-iŋ]. **I.** *s.* rompimiento, aplastamiento, quebrantamiento. **II.** *a.* que rompe, destroza, etc.; extraordinario, triunfante o quebrantante.

smash-up [-ʌp], *s.* desastre; bancarrota, quiebra; desbarate; colisión desastrosa.

smatter [smǽtœ(r)]. **I.** *va.* y *vn.* saber o hablar superficialmente. **II.** *s.* = SMATTERING.— **smatterer** [-œ(r)], *s.* el que sabe una cosa superficialmente; erudito a la violeta.—**smattering** [-iŋ], *s.* tintura, conocimiento superficial, barniz, *m.*

smear [smịr]. **I.** *va.* untar, embarrar, tiznar, ensuciar, manchar; difamar, calumniar; (fig.) derrotar por completo. **II.** *s.* embarradura, mancha; calumnia, difamación; (bact.) frotis, *m.*, extensión de sangre, etc., sobre un portaobjetos para examen microscópico.

smeary [-ị], *a.* graso; lardoso.

smegma [smégma], *s.* (med.) esmegma, *m.*

smell [smél]. **I.** *va.* (*pret.* y *pp.* SMELLED o SMELT) oler; olfatear, oliscar, husmear; ventear; (fig.) (con *out*) percibir, descubrir.—**to s. a rat,** haber gato encerrado. **II.** *vn.* oler, exhalar fragancia o hedor.—**to s. of,** oler a. **III.** *s.* olfato; olor (bueno o malo); perfume o aroma, *m.*; traza, vestigio.

smeller [-œ(r)], *s.* oledor, rastreador, husmeador. —*pl.* (fam.) narices, *f. pl.*

smelling [-iŋ], *s.* olfateo; husmeo, acción de oler. —**s. bottle,** vasito o redomilla para olores.— **s. salts,** sales aromáticas, carbonato de amonio.

smelt [smélt]. **I.** *pret.* y *pp.* de TO SMELL. **II.** *va.* (fund.) fundir o derretir (minerales). **III.** *s.* (ict.) eperlano.

smelter [sméltœ(r)], *s.* fundidor.

smeltery [-ị], *s.* fundición, fundería.

smelting [sméltiŋ], *s.* fusión, fundición.—**s. furnace,** alto horno, horno de fundición.—**s. house,** fundición, apartado.—**s. pot,** cubilote. —**s. works** = s. HOUSE.

smew [smju], *s.* (orn.) mergo, mergánsar.

smilacaceous [smạịlkéịšịʌs], *a.* (bot.) esmiláceo.

smilax [smáịlæks], *s.* (bot.) esmiláceo.

smile [smáịl]. **I.** *vn.* sonreír(se); favorecer, ser propicio.—**to s. at, on, upon,** sonreír a; favorecer. **II.** *va.* expresar con una sonrisa (*to smile assent,* consentir con una sonrisa; *to smile one's thanks,* dar las gracias con una sonrisa). **III.** *s.* sonrisa; aspecto agradable o risueño; disposición favorable o propicia.

smiling [-iŋ], *a.* risueño, sonriente.

smilingly [-lị], *adv.* con cara risueña, con sonrisa, sonriendo.

smirch [smœrch]. **I.** *va.* ensuciar, tiznar; mancillar, deslucir. **II.** *s.* tiznón, tiznadura.

smirk [smœrk]. **I.** *vn.* sonreírse estúpida o afectadamente. **II.** *s.* sonrisa boba o afectada; visaje.

smite [smáịt]. **I.** *va.* (*pret.* SMOTE; *pp.* SMITTEN o SMIT) herir, golpear; afligir, castigar; destruir, asolar; encantar, robar el corazón; conmover, enternecer; apenar; aplanar, aplastar; (con **off** o **out**) cortar, partir o romper de un golpe; matar de un golpe. **II.** *vn.* venir con fuerza repentina; chocar.

smith [smịþ], *s.* forjador, herrero; herrador.—**s. and farrier,** herrador, albéitar.—**s.'s hammer,** destajador.—**s.'s parer,** pujavante.

smithereens [smịðœrínz], *s. pl.* (fam.) añicos, trizas.—**to break,** o **smash, to s.,** hacer(se) añicos o trizas.

smithery [smíþœrị], *s.* herrería.

smithy [smíþị], *s.* fragua, forja, hornaza; herrería.

smitten [smítn], *pp.* de to SMITE; profundamente afectado; muy conmovido; muy enamorado.

smock [smak], *s.* bata corta; camisa de mujer.—**s. frock**, blusa de obrero, sayo.

smoke [smóʊk]. I. *s.* humo; sahum(eri)o; (fam.) cigarr(ill)o, pito, etc.—**s. arch**, (locom.) = s. BOX.—**s. black**, negro de humo.—**s. box**, (m. v.) caja o cámara de humos.—**s.-burner, s.-consumer**, aparato fumívoro.—**s.-burning, s.-consuming**, fumívoro.—**s. condenser**, condensador o lavador de humo.—**s.-dried**, curado o ahumado.—(to) **s.-dry**, curar, ahumar.—**s. helmet**, casco o careta de protección contra el humo.—**s. pipe**, humero.—**s. puff** o **whiff**, fumarada.—**s. screen**, (mil.) cortina de humo, humo de protección.—**s. signal**, ahumada.—**s.-tight**, a prueba de humo.—**s. tree**, (bot.) fustete.—**s. washer** = s. CONDENSER.—**to end in s.**, volverse humo o agua de cerrajas. II. *va.* fumar; ahumar, curar al humo; sahumar; (con **out**) ahumar, ahogar con humo; hacer salir con humo; echar fuera.—**to s. the pipe of peace**, fumar la pipa de paz. III. *vn.* humear, echar humo; fumar, pipar (fumar en pipa), (Am.) pitar (cigarrillos).

smokehouse [-haʊs], *s.* cuarto cerrado para ahumar o acecinar carnes, pieles, etc.

smokejack [-dʒæk], *s.* asador movido por el humo.

smokeless [-lɪs], *a.* sin humo; (m. v.) fumívoro.—**s. powder**, pólvora sin humo.

smoker [-œ(r)], *s.* fumador; sahumador; (api.) caja de ahumar abejas; (f. c.) coche fumador, vagón de fumar; (fam.) tertulia en que se fuma.

smokestack [-stæk], *s.* chimenea.

smokiness [-inɪs], *s.* fumosidad.

smoking [-ɪŋ]. I. *s.* acción de fumar.—**no s.** (allowed), se prohíbe fumar. II. *a.* fumante, humeante, fumífero.—**s. car**, (Ingl.) = **s. carriage**, (f. c.) coche fumador, vagón de fumar.—**s. jacket**, batín.—**s. room**, fumadero, cuarto o salón de fumar.—**s. stand** o **table**, mesita de fumar.

smoky [-i], *a.* humeante; humoso, ahumado.

smolder [smóʊldœ(r)], *vn.* y *s.* = SMOULDER.

smolt [smoʊlt], *s.* (ict.) murgón, salmón pequeño.

smooth [smú:ð]. I. *a.* liso, pulido, alisado; parejo, plano, igual; uniforme; fácil, suave, flúido; manso, tranquilo (agua, etc.); meloso, lisonjero; cortés, afable; (gram. griega) no aspirado; suave, que no rasca (v. gr. un licor).—**s.-faced**, barbilampiño, barbilucio; pulido, alisado; cariparejo.—**s.-grained**, de grano o veta lisa.—**s. muscle**, músculo no estriado.—**s.-paced**, que anda con paso igual.—**s.-shaven**, bien afeitado.—**s.-sliding**, que se desliza con suavidad e igualdad.—**s.-spoken, s.-tongued**, meloso, lisonjero o adulador. II. *va.* allanar, aplanar, alisar, suavizar; (a veces con **out**) desarrugar; (carp.) desbastar, acepillar; lijar; facilitar; pacificar, aquietar; calmar, ablandar; (a veces con **away**) quitar; (gen. con **over**) zanjar, atenuar.

smoothbore [-bɔr]. I. *a.* de ánima lisa. II. *s.* arma de ánima lisa.

smoother [-œ(r)], *s.* alisador; planador.

smoothing [-ɪŋ]. I. *a.* de alisar, de allanar, de emparejar; suavizador. II. *s.—**s. iron**, plancha, alisador, raspa.—**s. plane**, cepillo corto. II. *s.* alisadura.

smoothly [-li], *adv.* llanamente; fácilmente; blandamente; con halagos o afablemente.—**smoothness** [-nɪs], *s.* lisura, tersura, igualdad; suavidad, blandura; dulzura.

smote [smoʊt], *pret.* de to SMITE.

smother [smʌðœ(r)]. I. *va.* ahogar; asfixiar, sofocar; apagar; suprimir, ocultar, encubrir; embadurnar, embarrar; (coc.) estofar. II. *vn.* y *vr.* ahogar(se), asfixiar(se); estar latente, oculto o escondido. III. *s.* supresión, ocultación; ahoguío; asfixia, sofocación; humareda, polvareda.

smothering [-ɪŋ]. I. *a.* sofocante, asfixiante. II. *s.* = SMOTHER.—**smotheringly** [-li], *adv.* sofocantemente.

smo(u)lder [smóʊldœ(r)]. I. *vn.* arder humeando, sin llama; arder en rescoldo; estar latente. II. *s.* humo.

smudge [smʌdʒ]. I. *va.* tiznar, ensuciar, manchar con tizne, tinta u hollín; fumigar, ahumar. II. *s.* tiznajo, tiznadura, tiznón; fumigación o ahumadura.—**s. fire**, fuego humoso (para ahuyentar los insectos, impedir la escarcha, etc.).

smudgy [-i], *a.* tiznado, holliniento, ensuciado; humeante.

smug [smʌg], *a.* presumido, relamido, complaciente, pagado (de sí); acicalado, pulido.

smuggle [smʌgl]. I. *va.* pasar o meter de contrabando, alijar. II. *vn.* hacer contrabando, contrabandear, matutear.

smuggler [-lœ(r)], *s.* contrabandista, matutero, alijador, pasador, metedor.

smuggling [-lɪŋ], *s.* contrabando; matute.

smugly [smʌgli], *adv.* pulidamente; afectadamente, con presunción.

smugness [-nɪs], *s.* afectación y nimiedad en el vestir; presunción, complacencia.

smut [smʌt]. I. *s.* tiznón, tiznadura, mancha; obscenidad, indecencia; (bot., agr.) añublo, tizón, tizoncillo; (min.) hulla terrosa. II. *va.* tiznar, manchar; (fig.) mancillar; (bot.) atizonar, añublar; destizonar. III. *vn.* (bot.) añublarse, atizonarse.

smutch [smʌch]. I. *va.* tiznar, manchar, ensuciar. II. *s.* mancha, tiznajo.

smuttily [smʌtili], *adv.* suciamente.—**smuttiness** [-nɪs], *s.* suciedad; obscenidad, indecencia.—**smutty** [-i], *a.* tiznado; humoso; (bot.) añublado, atizonado; obsceno, indecente, verde.

snack [snæk], *s.* parte, *f.*, porción; bocad(ill)o, refrigerio, (fam.) tente(e)mpié, *m.*, piscolabis, *m.*—**s. bar**, bar donde se puede tomar un refrigerio.—**to go snacks**, ir a medias.

snaffle [snæfl]. I. *s.* (equit.) filete, bridón del bocado (ll. t. **s. bit**). II. *va.* (equit.) refrenar; contener, reprimir.

snag [snæg]. I. *s.* gancho, pedazo que queda en el árbol de una rama rota o desgajada; nudo que sobresale en la madera; protuberancia; (dent.) raigón; sobrediente; pitón del asta del ciervo; tronco o tocón sumergido; obstáculo oculto ignorado.—**s. boat**, buque arrancatroncos.—**to strike a s.**, chocar contra un tronco sumergido; hallarse con un obstáculo inesperado. II. *va.* desgajar, dejando ganchos; rasgar o dañar, chocando contra un gancho, clavo, tronco sumergido, etc.; impedir, obstruir; arrancar troncos y tocones (de un río).

snagged [-d], **snaggy** [-i], *a.* ganchoso; nudoso; lleno de troncos o tocones sumergidos (como un río); que abunda en obstáculos o tropiezos.

snaggletooth [snǽgltuθ], *s.* sobrediente.

snail [snelɪl], *s.* (zool.) caracol (de tierra); babosa, babaza (sin concha; *v.* SLUG); posma, persona roncera, lerda y pesada.—**s. clover**, (bot.) alfalfa, mielga.—**s. pace**, paso de tortuga, de caracol.—**s.-shaped**, acaracolado.—**s. shell**, caracola.

snake [snéik]. I. *s.* (zool.) culebra, sierpe, *f.*, serpiente, *f.*; reptil; persona traidora.—**s. in the grass**, (fam.) enemigo secreto o peligroso. II. *va.* (fam.) arrastrar tirando de una cosa; enrollar; (mar.) embutir. III. *vn.* culebrear, serpentear.

snakeroot [-rut], *s.* (bot.) serpentaria.

snakeweed [-wid], *s.* (bot.) bistorta.

snaky [-i], *a.* culebrino, serpentino, tortuoso; astuto, solapado; traidor; lleno de culebras.

snap [snæp]. I. *va.* chasquear, hacer estallar; dar, apretar o cerrar con golpe o estallido; romper con ruido y violencia; atrapar, arrebatar, echar la zarpa a; interrumpir; fotografiar instantáneamente.—**to s. one's fingers**, castañetear con

los dedos; (con **at**) burlarse de.—**to s.
up**, comprar, aceptar, etc., con avidez; cortar, interrumpir (a uno) con una réplica mordaz. **II.
vn.** chasquear, dar un chasquido; estallar,
romperse con estallido; romperse una cosa
tirante; chispear (los ojos); levantar el gallo,
hablar fuerte; fallar un tiro, dar higa.—**to s.
at**, tirar mordiscos a, pegar una dentellada a;
hablar mordazmente o con aspereza (a uno);
aceptar (una oferta) con entusiasmo y de prisa.
—**to s. in two**, romperse en dos pedazos.—**to
s. off**, soltarse, saltar, abrirse de golpe.—**to s.
out of it**, (fam.) animarse, reportarse. **III. s.**
chasquido; castañeteo (con los dedos); estallido; cierre de resorte, corchete, cerrajita,
garra; dentellada, mordiscón, mordedura;
(coc.) galletica (v. GINGERSNAP); (fam.) vigor,
energía; período corto (de frío); (fam.) ganga,
cosa fácil, canonjía (ll. t. **soft s.**). **IV. a.** hecho
de repente, de golpe o instantáneamente.—**s.
fastener**, cierre, corchete, automático.—**s.
judgment**, opinión o decisión mal pensada.
—**s. lock**, cerradura de resorte.—**s. switch**,
(elec.) llave (f.) de interrupción, interruptor
giratorio de resorte.—**not to care a s.**, (fam.)
importarle a uno un bledo o pito.

snapdragon [-drægǫn], s. (bot.) (boca de) dragón,
becerra, antirrino; (vidr.) puntel.

snapper [snǽpœ(r)], s. el que o lo que chasquea,
etc.; tralla, punta del látigo; (piro.) triquitraque, buscapiés; (ict.) pez (m.) comestible del
golfo de México.—pl. castañuelas, castañetas.
V. SNAPPING TURTLE.

snapping [snǽpįŋ], **I.** s. acción del verbo TO
SNAP. **II.** a. chasqueador; crepitante; saltadizo.
V. SNAPPISH.—**s. beetle**, (ent.) escarabajo de
resorte.—**s. turtle**, gran tortuga voraz.

snappish [snǽpįš], a. respondón; regañón, agrio,
arisco.—**snappishly** [-lį], adv. mordazmente;
agriamente, con aspereza.—**snappishness**
[-nįs], s. aspereza, sequedad.

snapshot [snǽpšat], **I.** s. disparo rápido, sin
apuntar; (foto.) instantánea. **II.** va. y vn. sacar
una fotografía instantánea.

snappy [snǽpį], a. = SNAPPISH; (fam.) vivo,
enérgico; elegante, garboso.

snare [sner]. **I.** s. trampa, armadijo, lazo, cepo;
garlito, celada, asechanza, insidia, artimaña,
red; (fam.) gatuperio, petardo; cuerda de tripa
(para tambor); (cir.) lazo.—**s. drum**, pequeño
tambor militar con cuerdas de tripa, para
mayor resonancia. **II.** va. enredar, tender trampas o lazos a. **III.** vn. cazar con trampas o
cepos.

snarl [snárl]. **I.** vn. gruñir, regañar; refunfuñar;
hacer fu (el gato). **II.** va. enredar, enmarañar;
embutir, estampar (artículos huecos de metal).
III. vn. enredarse, enmarañarse. **IV.** s. gruñido,
regañ(amient)o; (fam.) contienda, riña; maraña, hilo enredado; cabellos desgreñados;
complicación, enredo; (carp.) nudo en la
madera.

snarler [-œ(r)], s. regañón, (fam.) perrengue.

snarly [-į], a. regañón, gruñón; malhumorado,
displicente; enredoso, enredado.

snary [snérį], a. tramposo, enredador, insidioso.

snatch [snæch]. **I.** va. arrebatar; arrapar, birlar,
agarrar, (fam.) apercollar; (fam.) raptar (a una
persona).—**to s. off**, arrebatar. **II.** vn. (con **at**)
tratar de agarrar o arrebatar. **III.** s. arrebatamiento; arrebatiña; (fam.) rapto; pedacito;
ratito.—**s. block**, (mar.) pasteca.—**by
snatches**, a ratos.

snatcher [-œ(r)], s. arrebatador, ladrón.

snatchingly [-įŋlį], adv. arrebatadamente, precipitadamente; irregular o espasmódicamente.

snath(e [snæθ, snejð], s. mango de guadaña.

sneak [sník]. **I.** vn. (con **in**) entrarse a hurtadillas; (con **out** o **away**) salirse a hurtadillas,
escurrir el bulto, escabullirse; obrar solapadamente o con bajeza; arrastrarse. **II.** va. sisar,

ratear.—**s. thief**, ratero que se introduce en
las casas sin ser visto.

sneak(er [-œ(r)], s. sujeto ruin y solapado.

sneakers [-œrz], s. pl. (fam.) zapatos silenciosos
(gen. de lona con suela de caucho); zapatos de
gimnasia.

sneakiness [-nįs], s. socarronería; husmeo;
ruindad, bajeza.

sneaking [-įŋ], a. servil, bajo, vil; secreto, oculto.
—**s. fondness**, afición que se guarda secreta.—
sneakingly [-lį], adv. servilmente, con bajeza;
solapadamente, a hurtadillas.—**sneakingness**
[-nįs], s. bajeza, vileza, ruindad.

sneaky [-į], a. husmeador; socarrón, hipócrita;
bajo, ruin.

sneer [snír]. **I.** vn. (gen. con **at**) hacer un gesto de
desprecio; echar una mirada despectiva; mo-
farse de. **II.** va. expresar o decir con un gesto
de desprecio o escarnecedor. **III.** s. gesto, mirada o expresión de desprecio; mofa.—**sneerer**
[-œ(r)], s. mofador, fisgón, escarnecedor.—
sneering [-įŋ]. **I.** a. burlón, despreciativo o
escarnecedor. **II.** s. escarnio, gesto despreciativo, mofa.—**sneeringly** [-lį], adv. despreciati-
vamente; con mofa.

sneeze [sníz]. **I.** vn. estornudar.—**to s. at**, despreciar, menospreciar (gen. en la expresión, **not
to be sneezed at**, no ser de despreciar, no ser
un cualquiera). **II.** s. estornudo.—**s. gas**, gas
estornutatorio.

sneezewort [-wœrt], s. (bot.) cebadilla.

sneezing [-įŋ], s. estornudo.—**s. powder**, cebadilla, estornutatorio.

snell [snel], s. hilo corto de tripa, etc., de que están provistos algunos anzuelos, al cual se ata
el sedal.

snick [snįk]. **I.** va. cortar ligeramente. V. SNIP,
NICK y CLICK. **II.** s. corte pequeño.—**s. and
snee**, riña a navajazos o cuchilladas; (fam.)
cuchillo.

snicker [snįkœ(r)], **snigger** [snígœ(r)]. **I.** vn.
reírse tontamente o con desprecio. V. GIGGLE.
II. s. risita.

sniff [snįf]. **I.** va. husmear, olfatear, oliscar, ventear; inspirar o aspirar audiblemente. **II.** vn.
resollar, oler; sorberse los mocos; (con **at**) desdeñar, mostrar desprecio por una cosa con
resoplidos. **III.** s. olfateo; cosa olfateada.

sniffle [snįfl]. **I.** vn. resollar repetidas veces; aspirar ruidosamente por las narices; moquear;
lloriquear. V. SNIVEL y SNUFFLE. **II.** s. moquita; lloriqueo.

sniffy [snįfį], a. (fam.) desdeñoso, estirado.

sniggle [snįgl], va. y vn. pescar anguilas; entrampar, enmarañar.

snip [snįp]. **I.** va. tijeretear, dar tijeretadas; cortar con tijeras.—**to s. off**, cortar o recortar de
un golpe. **II.** s. tijeretada; recorte, retazo,
pedacito; parte, f.; (fam.) persona pequeña o
insignificante.

snipe [snáįp]. **I.** s. (orn.) agachadiza, becardón.
II. va. y vn. cazar agachadizas; (mil.) hacer
fuego o tirar de un apostadero (apl. a tiradores
apostados).—**sniper** [-œ(r)], s. tirador apostado.

sniperscope [-skoup], s. (mil.) especie de periscopio de rifle, para uso en las trincheras.

snippet [snįpįt], s. recorte, retacito.

snippy [snįpį], a. fragmentario; (fam.) brusco,
rudo, arisco; (fam.) desdeñoso, estirado.

snips [snįps], s. pl. tijeras de latonero.

snipsnap [snįpsnæp], s. diálogo picante.

snitch [snįch]. **I.** va. enlazar, coger en un lazo;
(fam.) hurtar, ratear. **II.** vn. (fam.) hacerse
delator o soplón.

snivel [snívǫl]. **I.** s. moquita. **II.** vn. moquear;
lloriquear, llorar como una criatura; (Am.)
jeremiquear; hacer pucheros.—**snivel(l)er**
[-œ(r)], s. lloraduelos (fam.), llorón; mocoso.—
snivel(l)ing [-įŋ], s. moqueo; lloriqueo.—
snivelly [-į], a. mocoso; llorón.

snob [snáb], s. (e)snob; fachendón, sujeto vulgar

y fachendista, estirado con sus iguales e inferiores pero servil con sus superiores; (Ingl.) rompehuelgas, esquirol.—**snobbery** [-œri], *s.* (e)snobismo; fachenda, (fig.) ínfulas, *f. pl.*; tufos.—**snobbish** [-iš], *a.* (e)snob, fachendoso, estirado.—**snobbishly** [-li], *adv.* fachendosamente, con vulgar presunción.—**snobbishness** [-nis], **snobbism** [-izm], *s.* = SNOBBERY.

snood [snud], *s.* redecilla, prenda de malla, gen. a modo de bolsa, usada para recoger el pelo y adornar la cabeza; cintillo o cinta para el pelo.

snoop [snúp]. **I.** *s.* (fam.) entremetido; curioso. **II.** *vn.* entremeterse, husmear.—**snooper** [-œ(r)], *s.* snoopy [-i], *a.* entremetido, curioso.

snooze [snuz]. **I.** *vn.* (fam.) dormitar, descabezar el sueño. **II.** *s.* (fam.) siestecita, sueño ligero.

snore [snór]. **I.** *vn.* roncar. **II.** *s.* ronquido.

snorer [-œ(r)], *s.* roncador.

snoring [-iŋ], *s.* ronquido.

snort [snɔrt]. **I.** *va.* y *vn.* resoplar, bufar. **II.** *s.* bufido, resoplido.

snot [snat], *s.* (vulg.) moco.

snout [snáut]. **I.** *va.* proveer de hocico, lanza o embocadura. **II.** *s.* hocico, morro, jeta; trompa de elefante; cañón de un fuelle, tobera; lanza de manguera; embocadura de un cañón.—**s. beetle**, (ent.) gorgojo.—**long-snouted**, hocicón, hocicudo, jetudo.

snow [snóu]. **I.** *s.* nieve, *f.*; nevada, nevasca.—**s.-blind(ed**, cegado por el reflejo de la nieve.—**s. blindness**, nifablepsia, ceguera causada por el reflejo de la nieve.—**s.-bound**, sitiado o detenido por la nieve.—**s. broth**, agua con nieve; líquido muy frío.—**s. bunting**, (orn.) pinzón de las nieves.—**s.-capped**, nevado, coronado de nieve.—**s. ice**, hielo de nieve conglomerada.—**s. water**, aguanieve, *f.*—**s. whirl(wind)**, torva.—**s.-white**, níveo, blanco como la nieve. **II.** *vn.* nevar; neviscar; ventiscar o ventisquear. **III.** *va.* (con **in, over, under**, o **up**) cubrir, obstruir, detener o aprisionar con nieve.—**to s. under**, derrotar por completo (como a un candidato o equipo rival).

snowball [-bol]. **I.** *va.* lanzar bolas de nieve a. **II.** *s.* pella o pelota de nieve.

snowbird [-bœrd], *s.* (orn.) pinzón de las nieves.

snowdrift [-drift], *s.* ventisca, ventisquero.

snowdrop [-drap], *s.* (bot.) campanilla blanca.

snowfall [-fol], *s.* nevada, nevasca, nevisca.

snowflake [-flejk], *s.* copo de nieve; (orn.) pinzón de las nieves; (bot.) campanilla.

snowplow [-plau], *s.* quitanieves; (máquina) barredora de nieve.

snowshed [-šed], *s.* guardaaludes.

snowshoe [-šu], *s.* raqueta reticular a la que se afirma el pie para andar sobre la nieve.

snowslide [-slajd], **snowslip** [-slip], *s.* alud, *m.*, avalancha de nieve.

snowstorm [-storm], *s.* nevasca, nevada, ventisca, tormenta de nieve.

snowy [-i], *a.* nevoso; cargado de nieve; níveo; puro, sin mancha.

snub [snʌb]. **I.** *va.* desairar, tratar con desprecio estudiado o con afectada arrogancia; reprender, regañar (fam.); (con **up**) parar de repente. **II.** *s.* desaire, repulsa; (fam.) nariz chata. **III.** *a.* romo, chato.—**s.-nosed**, chato.

snuff [snʌf]. **I.** *s.* moco, pabilo o pavesa de candela; tufo, olor; tabaco en polvo, rapé.—**s. taker**, tomador de rapé.—**up to s.**, (fam.) despabilado. **II.** *va.* olfatear, oliscar, oler, ventear; introducir una cosa en la nariz con el aliento; despabilar (una vela); (gen. con **out**) extinguir, apagar; destruir.—**to s. up**, tomar por la nariz. **III.** *vn.* aspirar; tomar rapé; (con **it** o **out**) (fam.) morirse.

snuffbox [-baks], *s.* caja de rapé; tabaquera.

snuffer [-œ(r)], *s.* despabilador.—*pl.* despabiladeras.

snuffiness [-inis], *s.* tufo o suciedad causada por el rapé.

snuffle [snʌfl]. **I.** *vn.* ganguear. **II.** *s.* gangueo.—*pl.* romadizo, catarro nasal.

snuffling [snʌfliŋ], *a.* gangoso.

snuffy [snʌfi], *a.* manchado de rapé; tabacoso, que huele a rapé.

snug [snʌg]. **I.** *a.* cómodo, abrigado; bien dispuesto, bien aparejado; apañado, ajustado; acomodado.—**as s. as a bug in a rug**, (fam.) con toda comodidad. **II.** *s.* (mec.) tope, reborde. **III.** *va.* acomodar, aparejar, ajustar, apañar, alisar.

snuggery [-œri], *s.* (fam.) aposento cómodo y bien arreglado.

snuggle [snʌgl], *vn.* y *va.* arrimar(se), apretar(se), poner(se) juntitos.

so [sóu]. **I.** *adv.* y *pron.* así (a veces en el sentido de "cierto," "verdad": *that is so*, así es, eso es verdad; *that is not so*, eso no es cierto); de esta manera; pues bien, conque (usado expletivamente); tan; (fam.) tan (*he is so good*, él es tan bueno, o muy bueno); muy bien; sí, pues; (con *or*) poco más o menos, como (*ten years or so*, como diez años, poco más o menos diez años); (antes de adjetivo) así de, de este (antes de substantivo o adjetivo substantivado: *so wide*, así de ancho, de este ancho; *so big*, así de grande, de este tamaño); lo (*he is rich, but I am not so*, él es rico, pero yo no lo soy); también lo (*I am rich, and so is she*, soy rico, y ella también lo es).—**S.-and-S.**, Fulano, Fulano de tal.—**s. as to**, para, a fin de.—**s. be it**, amén, así sea.—**s.-called**, así llamado, llamado, según se llama (*the so-called hero*, el llamado héroe; *the new art, so called*, el llamado nuevo arte; el nuevo arte, según se llama).—**s. far**, hasta aquí, hasta ahí; hasta ahora.—**s. far as**, tan lejos como; hasta, hasta donde (a veces se cambia el giro: *so far as I know*, hasta donde yo sé, que yo sepa).—**s. far, s. good**, hasta aquí (ahí), muy bien; eso está bien.—**s. forth**, etcétera.—**s. long**, hasta luego, hasta más ver, (fam.) abur; hasta aquí (ahí).—**s. long as**, mientras que.—**s. many**, tantos.—**s. much**, tanto.—**s. much a**, tanto por.—**s. much as**, por mucho que; tanto como; siquiera.—**s. much for**, eso en cuanto a, eso basta en cuanto a.—**s. much s., that**, tanto que.—**s. much the better**, tanto mejor.—**s. much the less**, tanto menos.—**s. much the worse**, tanto peor.—**s. s.**, de un modo u otro.—**s. s.**, así así, tal cual, regular, medianamente.—**s. that**, de suerte que, de modo que; para que, a fin de que.—**s. then**, así pues, conque, por tanto.—**s. to say, s. to speak**, por decirlo así.—**and s. forth**, etcétera, y demás, y así sucesivamente.—**be he ever, o never, s. powerful**, por poderoso que sea.—**how s.?** ¿cómo es eso? ¿cómo así?—**if ever s. little**, por poco que.—**if s.**, si así es, si lo fuere, en tal caso.—**I hope s., I think s.**, así lo espero, lo creo.—**is that s.?** ¿así? ¿de veras?—**just s.**, ni más ni menos; exactamente.—**not s.**, no es así, eso no es verdad.—**very much s.**, lo es (dijo, etc.) sin disputa o muy claramente. **II.** *conj.* con tal que; (fam.) para que; (fam.) por lo tanto; de modo que.

soak [sóuk]. **I.** *va.* empapar; remojar; poner a ablandar, abrevar (pieles); (con **in** o **up**) chupar, embeber, absorber; (con **through**) calar, poner hecho una sopa; (fam.) cobrar precios exorbitantes (a uno); (fam.) beber con exceso. **II.** *vn.* estar en remojo; (con **in, into** o **through**) remojarse, esponjarse, calarse; (fam.) beborrotear, empinar el codo.—**to be soaked to the skin**, estar mojado o calado hasta los huesos. **III.** *s.* remojo, calada; líquido en que se empapa alguna cosa; (fam.) bebedor, borrachín; orgía.

soakage [-idž], *s.* remojo; cantidad absorbida.

soaker [-œ(r)], *s.* remojador; (fam.) borrachín.

soaking [-iŋ], *s.* empapada, ensopada, calada.

soakingly [-iŋli], *adv.* empapando.
soaky [-i], *a.* empapado, calado.
soap [sóup]. **I.** *s.* jabón; (fam.) lisonja, adulación; (fam.) dinero. *V.* SLUSH FUND.—**s. bubble**, burbuja o pompa de jabón.—**s. dish**, jabonera. —**s. earth**, (min.) esteatita, jaboncillo de sastre.—**s. maker**, jabonero.—**s. plant**, (bot.) amole. **II.** *va.* enjabonar, lavar con jabón; (fam.) adular.
soapbark [-bark], *s.* quillay, cáscara de quillay.— **s. tree**, (bot.) quillay.
soap(berry) tree [-beri tri], *s.* (bot.) jaboncillo.
soapbox [-baks], *s.* caja para jabón; (fig.) plataforma improvisada al aire libre para oradores populares.—**s. oratory**, oratoria demagógica de las calles.
soapstone [-stoun], *s.* esteatita, jabón de sastre.
soapsuds [-sʌdz], *s. pl.* jabonaduras, bálago.
soapwort [-wœrt], *s.* (bot.) jabonera.
soapy [-i], *a.* jabonoso, saponáceo.
soar [sor]. **I.** *vn.* remontarse, cernerse; encumbrarse, aspirar; (aer.) deslizarse horizontalmente sin motor. **II.** *s.* vuelo o remonte.
sob [sab]. **I.** *s.* sollozo; suspiro (del viento).—**s. sister**, (fam.) escritora lacrimosa o de sentimentalismo cursi; repórter de lloriqueos.—**s. story**, (fam.) historia o reportaje lacrimosos. **II.** *vn.* sollozar. **III.** *va.* decir sollozando; expresar con sollozos.
sober [sóubœr(r)]. **I.** *a.* cuerdo, sano; en su juicio, no borracho; sereno, tranquilo; de sangre fría; grave, serio, modesto; sobrio, templado, moderado; sombrío, de color apagado.—**s.-minded**, desapasionado; sereno.—**s.-mindedness**, *s.* serenidad; espíritu desapasionado.—**in s. earnest**, de veras, con seriedad, formalmente. **II.** *va.* y *vn.* (a veces con **up** u **off**) desemborrachar(se), desembriagar(se); poner grave, serio, o pensativo; volverse sobrio, cuerdo, moderado, sensato.—**to s. down**, serenar(se); hacer volver o volverse cuerdo; sosegar(se).
soberly [-li], *adv.* sobriamente; juiciosamente.— **soberness** [-nis], **sobriety** [sobráieti], *s.* sobriedad; templanza, moderación; cordura; seriedad; calma.
sodriquet [sóubrikei], *s.* apodo.
soccer [sákœr(r)], *s.* juego de fútbol (jugado según las reglas de *Asociación*).
sociable [sóuʃabl]. **I.** *a.* sociable, social, conversable, comunicativo. **II.** *s.* tertulia; coche de asientos opuestos; cierto tipo de sofá o diván.—**sociability** [-bfliti], *s.* sociabilidad.— **sociably** [-bli], *adv.* sociablemente.
social [sóuʃal]. **I.** *a.* social; sociable; socialista; (zool.) social, que vive en comunidad; (bot.) de agrupación densa; que ocupa grandes áreas. —**s. democracy**, democracia socialista.—**s. evil**, prostitución.—**s. gathering**, tertulia, velada.—**s. insurance**, (e. p.) seguro social.— **s. science**, ciencia política; sociología.—*pl.* ciencias sociales.—**s. security**, (e. p.) seguro social.—**s. service**, **s. work**, auxilio, servicio o asistencia social; investigación y mejoramiento de la vida de las clases pobres y obreras (apl. esp. a la visitación de los hogares con el objeto de estudiar las condiciones existentes y ayudar a mejorarlas).—**s. settlement**, centro de asistencia social.—**s. worker**, el que se consagra al auxilio social. **II.** *s.* tertulia, reunión informal.
socialism [-izm], *s.* socialismo.—**socialist** [-ist], *a.* y *s.* socialista.—**socialistic** [-istik], *a.* socialista.
sociality [souʃiéliti], *s.* sociabilidad.
socialization [sóuʃalizéiʃən], *s.* socialización.
socialize [-laiz], *va.* socializar.
societal [sosáietal], *a.* societario.
society [sosáieti], *s.* sociedad; comunidad; asociación, gremio; consorcio; círculos del buen tono; compañía, conversación o trato amenos.
Socinian [sosínian], *a.* y *s.* sociniano.
Socinianism [-izm], *s.* (teol.) socinianismo.

sociological [soʃioládʒikal], *a.* sociológico.
sociologically [-i], *adv.* sociológicamente.
sociologist [soʃálodʒist], *s.* sociólogo.
sociology [-dʒi], *s.* sociología.
sock [sak], *s.* calcetín, media corta; escarpín, zueco; comedia; reja de arado.
socket [sákit], *s.* cuenca, cubo, caja, encaje, cepo, ojo, casquillo, tubo de candelero, campana (de un tubo con junta de enchufe); (elec.) receptáculo, portalámpara, *m.;* cualquier hueco en que encaja alguna cosa.—**s. of a tooth**, alvéolo de un diente.—**s. of the eye**, cuenca del ojo.—**s. wrench**, llave (*f.*) de boca tubular.
socle [sákl], *s.* (arq.) zócalo; rodapié, *m.*
Socratic(al [sokrétik(al], *a.* socrático.
sod [sad]. **I.** *va.* cubrir de césped. **II.** *s.* césped; témpano de tierra vegetal, turba, tepe.—**the old s.**, el terruño, el país natal.—**under the s.**, enterrado.
soda [sóudə], *s.* (quím.) sosa, soda; carbonato u óxido de sodio; sal (*f.*) soda; gaseosa; refresco de gaseosa.—**s. ash**, (quím.) sosa, carbonato sódico anhidro del comercio.—**s. dispenser**, **s. jerk**, (fam.) dependiente de fuente de gaseosa. —**s. fountain**, fuente (*f.*) o sifón de agua de soda, y esp. de bebidas carbónicas, gen. con servicio de helados, etc.—**s. lime**, (quím.) mezcla de cal y soda cáustica.—**s. pop**, (fam.) gaseosa.—**s. water**, agua de soda; (agua) gaseosa.
sodality [sodéliti], *s.* cofradía, hermandad.
sodden [sádn], *va.* y *vn.* empapar(se); mojar(se), saturar(se).
sodden [sádn]. **I.** *pp.* de TO SEETHE. **II.** *a.* mojado, empapado, saturado; ebrio; (coc.) pesado, mal cocido.
sodium [sóudiʌm], *s.* (quím.) sodio.—**s. bicarbonate**, bicarbonato de sodio.—**s. carbonate**, carbonato sódico.—**s. chloride**, cloruro de sodio, sal (*f.*) común.
sodomite [sádomait], *s.* sodomita, *mf.;* maricón.
sodomitical [-mítikal], *a.* sodomita, sodomítico.
sodomy [-mi], *s.* sodomía.
soever [soévœr(r)], *adv.* por mucho o por más que sea (*how great soever*, por grande que sea). *V.* WHENSOEVER, WHERESOEVER, WHOSOEVER, etc.
sofa [sóufə], *s.* sofá, *m.*
soffit [sáfit], *s.* (arq.) sofito, paflón, intradós.
soft [soft]. **I.** *a.* blando, muelle; pastoso, plástico; dulce, dúctil, maleable, flexible (metales, etc.); liso, suave al tacto; dulce, grato al oído; jugoso, mollar (frutas, etc.); blanducho, fofo; alburente (madera); mollino (lluvias); flojo (hilado); tierno, delicado; meloso, mimoso, almibarado, besuqueador; afeminado; apocado, de poco seso; débil de carácter, condescendiente; de matices delicados o apagados; (fon.) sibilante; sonante; (elec.) poco penetrante (apl. a ciertos rayos X).—**s.-boiled eggs**, huevos pasados por agua.—**s. brass**, latón recocido.—**s. bread**, mollete, pan tierno.—**s. coal**, hulla grasa, carbón bituminoso.—**s. drink**, gaseosa, bebida refrescante no alcohólica.—**s. hat**, sombrero flexible.—**s.-headed**, de pocas luces.—**s.-hearted**, bondadoso con extremo.—**s. iron**, hierro dulce o maleable.—**s. palate**, (anat.) velo del paladar.—**s.-shell**, de cáscara o carapacho blando.—**s. skin**, cutis suave.—**s. snap**, ganga, chiripa.—**s. soap**, jabón blando; (fam.) halago, adulación.—**s. solder**, soldadura débil o tierna (de baja temperatura).—**s. steel**, MILD STEEL.—**s. water**, agua no cruda o gorda (que no lleva en disolución muchas sales).—**s. words**, palabras dulces o melosas. **II.** *interj.* (ant.) ¡poco a poco! ¡sin ruido! ¡quedo! ¡callaos! **III.** *adv.* = SOFTLY.
soften [sófn]. **I.** *va.* ablandar, enmollecer, lenificar; reblandecer, molificar; mitigar, atemperar, calmar, amansar, suavizar; enternecer; endulzar; enervar, afeminar; apagar, amortiguar

(colores). **II.** *vn.* ablandarse; reblandecerse; templarse; amansarse; enternecerse.

softener [-œ(r)], *s.* ablandador o suavizador; (pint.) brocha ancha para amortiguar los colores.

softening [-iŋ]. **I.** *a.* suavizador, emoliente, ablandativo, lenificativo.—s. **iron**, (ten.) hierro de ablandar. **II.** *s.* reblandecimiento; ablandamiento; blandura; enternecimiento; suavidad.—s. **of the brain**, reblandecimiento cerebral.

softish [sóftiŝ], *a.* blandito, blanducho.

softly [-li], *adv.* blandamente; callando; suavemente, sin ruido; lentamente, con lentitud, paso a paso, pasito.

softness [-nis], *s.* blandura; suavidad; pastosidad; (metal.) ductilidad, maleabilidad; pastura, ternura; debilidad de carácter; delicadeza, molicie; (med.) morbidez.

soggy [sági], *a.* empapado, mojado.

soil [sóil]. **I.** *va.* ensuciar, manchar, empañar; dar verde (al ganado); engordar o purgar con verde. **II.** *s.* terreno, tierra vegetal, suelo; país, región; suciedad, porquería; mancha; (agr.) abono; pantano en que se refugia la caza.

soilage [-idž], **soiling** [-iŋ], *s.* acción o resultado de ensuciar, etc.; (agr.) verdes, *m. pl.*; alimentación con verdes.

soirée [swaréi], *s.* (fr.) tertulia, sarao, velada.

sojourn [sóudžœrn]. **I.** *vn.* residir, morar, permanecer. **II.** *s.* morada, permanencia, estada, estancia.—**sojourner** [-œ(r)], *s.* transeúnte.

sol [sal], *s.* sueldo, moneda de cobre de Francia; (quím.) sol, coloide en suspensión.—**(S.)** el sol, Febo.

sol [soul], *s.* sol, moneda del Perú; (mús.) sol.

solace [sális]. **I.** *s.* solaz, *m.*, consuelo, alivio. **II.** *va.* solazar, consolar, confortar, alegrar.

solanaceous [salənéiŝas], *a.* (bot.) solanáceo.

solar [sóulá(r)], *a.* solar.—s. **attachment**, (top., astr.) anteojo solar (de un teodolito, tránsito o brújula).—s. **compass**, (top.) brújula de (con) anteojo solar.—s. **cycle**, ciclo solar.—s. **lamp**, quinqué.—s. **microscope**, microscopio solar.—s. **plexus**, (anat.) plexo solar.—s. **print**, (fot.) impresión solar o heliográfica.—s. **salt**, sal obtenida por evaporación al sol.—s. **spot**, mancha del sol.—s. **system**, (astr.) sistema solar o planetario.—s. **telegraph**, telégrafo solar, heliotropo, helióstato.

solarium [solériʌm], *s.* solana, carasol; apartamiento expuesto al sol (apl. esp. a los cuartos de convalescientes en los hospitales). *V.* SUN PARLOR.

sold [sould], *pret.* y *pp.* de TO SELL.—s. **out**, (com.) agotado.—**to be s. on**, (fam.) estar convencido de, o convertido a.

soldan [sáldən], *s.* (hist.) soldán, sultán.

solder [sádœ(r)]. **I.** *va.* soldar. **II.** *s.* soldadura.—**solderer** [-œ(r)], *s.* soldador.—**soldering** [-iŋ]. **I.** *s.* soldadura. **II.** *a.* de soldar.—s. **iron** o **copper**, soldador con puntas de cobre.—s. **lamp**, lámpara de soldar.

soldier [sóuldžœ(r)], *s.* soldado, militar.—*pl.* tropa, fuerzas.—**soldierlike** [-laik], **soldierly** [-li]. **I.** *a.* soldadesco, marcial, militar. **II.** *adv.* militarmente.—**soldiership** [-ŝip], *s.* soldadesca; milicia, talentos militares.—**soldiery** [-i], *s.* soldadesca, tropa; servicio o profesión militar.

sole [soul]. **I.** *va.* (zap.) solar, echar suelas a. **II.** *s.* planta (del pie); suela (del zapato); (ict.) sol, lenguado; dado, tejuelo, base, *f.*, fondo, suelo.—s. **leather**, (ten.) cuero de suela.—s. **of a gun carriage**, solera de cureña. **III.** *a.* único, solo; (for.) soltero; absoluto, exclusivo.—s. **agency** o **right**, (com.) exclusiva, exclusividad.—s. **agent**, único agente, agente exclusivo.

solecism [sáléŝizm], *s.* solecismo; incongruencia.—**solecist** [-sist], *s.* el que comete solecismos.

—**solecistic(al** [-sístik(al], *a.* incongruo o incongruente.—**solecize** [-saiz], *vn.* cometer solecismos.

solely [sóulli], *adv.* únicamente, solamente.

solemn [sálęm], *a.* solemne, serio, grave, formal; augusto.—**solemness** [-nis], *s.* solemnidad.—**solemnity** [solémniti], *s.* solemnidad; gravedad, formalidad; pompa; rito, ceremonia.—**solemnization** [sálęmnizéiŝon], *s.* solemnización, celebración.—**solemnize** [-naiz], *va.* solemnizar, celebrar solemnemente.—**solemnly** [-li], *adv.* solemnemente; con todas las formalidades.

solenoid [sóulęnoid], *s.* (elec.) solenoide.

sol-fa [sóulfá]. **I.** *va.* y *vn.* (mús.) solfear. **II.** *s.* solfa; solfeo.

solfatara [salfatárá], *s.* (geol.) solfatara.

solfeggio [salfédžou], *s.* (mús.) solfeo.

solicit [solsit]. **I.** *va.* solicitar; importunar, rogar, implorar; inducir, incitar, tentar. **II.** *vn.* pretender, agenciar, pedir, hacer una petición o solicitud.—**solicitation** [-éiŝon], *s.* solicitación, cuestación; requerimiento, incitación.—**solicitor** [-ọ(r)], *s.* procurador, agente, solicitador, diligenciero; pretendiente; abogado.—S. **General**, (en los E. U.) subsecretario de justicia; (en Ingl.) subfiscal de la corona.—**solicitorship** [-ŝip], *s.* personería; procuraduría.

solicitous [solsitas], *a.* solícito, cuidadoso.

solicitously [-li], *adv.* solícitamente.

solicitousness [-nis], *s.* (Am.) acomedimiento.

solicitude [solsitiud], *s.* solicitud, cuidado, afán.

solid [sálid]. **I.** *s.* sólido. **II.** *a.* sólido; duro, firme, consistente, compacto; puro (oro, plata, etc.); macizo; cúbico; unánime; (fam.) completo, verdadero.—s. **angle**, (geom.) ángulo sólido.—s. **end**, (mec.) cabeza cerrada (de una biela).—s. **for**, unánimemente en favor de.—s. **geometry**, geometría del espacio.—s. **rock**, roca firme; (fig.) fundamento sólido.—s. **tire**, (aut.) macizo, llanta maciza.—**to be**, o **stand**, **s. with**, (fam.) gozar de la entera confianza o el favor de; estar muy en gracia o valimiento con.

solidarity [salidériti], *s.* solidaridad.

solidary [sálidęri], *a.* (for.) solidario.

solidification [solidifikéiŝon], *s.* solidificación; consolidación.

solidify [-fai], *va.* y *vn.* solidificar(se).

solidity [-ti], **solidness** [sálidnis], *s.* solidez, firmeza, dureza, consistencia, macicez, asiento.

solidly [sálidli], *adv.* sólidamente, firmemente.

solidungulate [salidáŋgiuleit], *a.* y *s.*, **solidungulous** [-ʌs], *a.* (zool.) solípedo.

soliloquize [solílokwaiz], *vn.* soliloquiar, monologar, hablar a solas.

soliloquy [-kwi], *s.* soliloquio, monólogo.

soliped [sáliped], *s.* (zool.) solípedo.

solipsism [sálipsizm], *s.* (fil.) doctrina que sostiene que el yo es lo único cognoscible o lo único existente.

solitaire [sáliter], *s.* (joy.) solitario; solitario (juego de una sola persona).

solitarily [-ili], *adv.* solitariamente.

solitariness [-inis], *s.* soledad, retiro.

solitary [-i]. **I.** *a.* solitario; retirado; solo, único, aislado; incomunicado; (zool. y bot.) solitario; simple, sencillo. **II.** *s.* solitario, ermitaño.

solitude [sálitiud], *s.* soledad; vida solitaria.

solmization [salmizéiŝon], *s.* (mús.) solfa.

solo [sóulou], *s.* (mús.) solo; (aer.) vuelo de un aviador solo (ll. t. **solo flight**).

soloist [-ist], *s.* (mús.) solista.

Solomonic [salománik], *a.* salomónico.

Solomon's seal [sálomonz síl], *s.* (bot.) sello de Salomón.

solstice [sálstis], *s.* (astr.) solsticio.

solstitial [salstíŝal], *a.* (astr.) solsticial.

solubility [sályubíliti], **solubleness** [-blnis], *s.* solubilidad.—**soluble** [-bl], *a.* soluble.

solute [sáliut], *s.* substancia disuelta.

solution [soljúŝon], *s.* (quím.) solución, disolución; (mat.) solución (resultado, raíz de una ecuación, etc.); resolución (procedimiento); arreglo (de disputas).—**s. of continuity,** solución de continuidad.

solutive [sályŭṭịv], *a.* solutivo; soluble; laxativo, laxante.

solvability [sálvạbịlịtị], **solvableness** [-blnịs], *s.* solubilidad.

solvable [-bl], *a.* disoluble; (re)soluble.

solve [salv], *va.* resolver; solucionar, desatar, desentrañar, desenredar, aclarar.

solvency [sálvẹnsị], *s.* solvencia.

solvent [-ẹnt]. **I.** *a.* solvente, resolvente, disolutivo; (com.) solvente. **II.** *s.* (quím.) disolvente, menstruo; (med.) disolvente.

somatic(al [sọmǽtịk(ạl], *a.* somático, corporal, corpóreo, físico.

somatics [sọmǽtịks], *s.* somatología.

somatology [sọumạtálọdǰị], *s.* somatología.

somatome [sóumạtọum], *s.* (zool.) segmento teórico del cuerpo de un articulado. *V.* SOMITE.

somber, sombre [sámbœ(r], *a.* sombrío, lóbrego, lúgubre, o(b)scuro, tétrico, severo, triste.

sombrero [sambréroụ], *s.* sombrero de fieltro de copa alta y alas anchas (el usado por los vaqueros mejicanos).

sombrous [sámbrʌs], *a.* (poét.) = SOMBER.

some [sʌm]. **I.** *a.* algo de, un poco (cantidad indefinida); algún, alguno; unos pocos, varios, ciertos; algunos, unos (número indefinido). Ú. en lenguaje fam. para indicar sumo grado, gran tamaño, excelencia, etc.: *some house,* gran casa, buena casucha (irón.); *he is some man,* es todo un hombre. Cuando es partitivo, se deja a menudo sin traducir: *give me some water,* déme agua.—**s. difficulty,** cierta dificultad.—**s. fine day,** el mejor día, cuando menos se piensa. —**s. . . . or other,** (fam.) alguno, uno . . . u otro *(for some reason or other,* por algún motivo, por un motivo u otro).—**s. people,** algunas personas, algunas gentes. **II.** *pron.* algunos; parte, una parte, una porción, un poco, algo (de). **III.** *adv.* (fam.) cerca de, como, poco más o menos.

somebody [-badị], *s.* alguien, alguna persona, alguno; un personaje.—**s. else,** algún otro.

somehow [-haụ], **s. or other,** *adv.* de algún modo, de un modo u otro, por alguna razón.

someone [-wʌn], *pron.* = SOMEBODY.

somersault, somerset [sámœrsɔlt, -sɛt]. **I.** *s.* salto mortal, tumbo, voltereta. **II.** *vn.* dar un salto mortal.

something [sámθịŋ]. **I.** *s.* alguna cosa, algo; cosa de importancia y suposición.—**s. else,** otra cosa; alguna otra cosa; algo más.—**s. or other,** algo, alguna cosa.—**to be s. of a,** tener algo de; ser de alguna magnitud o importancia, no ser pequeño, fácil, etc. *(he is something of an orator,* tiene algo de orador; *this is something of a problem,* éste no es problema fácil). **II.** *adv.* algo, algún tanto.

sometime [sámtaịm]. **I.** *adv.* algún día, oportunamente, en algún tiempo.—**s. last week,** durante la semana pasada.—**s. soon,** un día de éstos, en breve, sin tardar mucho. **II.** *a.* antiguo, pasado, ex *(sometime deputy,* ex diputado).

sometimes [-z], *adv.* algunas veces, a veces.

somewhat [sámhwat]. **I.** *s.* alguna cosa, algo; un poco; sujeto o cosa de consecuencia. **II.** *adv.* algo, algún tanto, un poco.

somewhere [sámhwer], *adv.* en alguna parte.—**s. else,** en alguna otra parte.

somite [sóumaịt], *s.* (zool.) somito, metámero.

somnambulant [samnǽmbjulạnt], *a.* y *s.* so(m)námbulo.—**somnambulate** [-leịt], *va.* y *vn.* andar, o andar por, en estado so(m)námbulo. —**somnambulism** [-lịzm], *s.* so(m)nambulismo.—**somnambulist** [-lịst], *s.* so(m)námbulo.

somniferous [samnífẹrʌs], *a.* somnífero, somnífico, somnifaciente, soporífero.

somnific [samnífịk], *a.* narcótico, soporífero.

somniloquism, somniloquence [samnílokwịzm, -kwẹns], *s.* somnilocuencia.

somniloquist [-kwịst], *s.* somnílocuo.

somniloquy [-kwị], *s.* somnilocuencia, somniloquia (apl. sobre todo a la hipnótica).

somnolence, somnolency [sámnolẹns, -ị], *s.* soñolencia, somnolencia,—**somnolent** [-ẹnt], *a.* soñoliento; amodorrado; soporífero, adormecedor.

son [sʌn], *s.* hijo (varón).—**s.-in-law,** yerno, hijo político.—**s. of a gun,** (fam.) camastrón, tuno.

sonant [sóụnạnt], *a.* (fon.) sonante; sonoro.

sonata [sonǽtạ], *s.* sonata.

song [sɔŋ], *s.* canción, cantinela, canto, cantar, copla, tonada; balada, poema lírico; poesía, verso; bagatela, nimiedad, poca cosa, bicoca.— **s. bird,** ave canora, pájaro cantor.—**s. writer,** cancionista.—**the S. of Songs, the S. of Solomon,** (bib.) el Cantar de los Cantares.

songbook [-buk], *s.* cancionero, libro de canciones.

songful [-fụl], *a.* melodioso; dado a cantar.

songster [-stœ(r], *s.* cantor, cantante, cancionista; poeta, *m.;* pájaro cantor.—**songstress** [-strịs], *s.* cant(ad)ora, cantatriz, cantante.

soniferous [sonífẹrʌs], *a.* sonante, sonoro.

sonnet [sánịt]. **I.** *va.* y *vn.* celebrar con sonetos; sonetear, componer sonetos. **II.** *s.* (poét.) soneto.

sonneteer [sanẹtír], *s.* compositor de sonetos, sonetista.

sonny [sánị], *s.* hijito.

sonometer [sonámetœ(r], *s.* sonómetro.

sonorous [sonórʌs], *a.* sonoro, (re)sonante, retumbante.—**sonorously** [-lị], *adv.* sonoramente.—**sonorousness, sonority** [-nịs, sonórịtị], *s.* sonoridad.

sonship [sánšịp], *s.* filiación, calidad de hijo.

soon [sún], *adv.* presto, pronto, prontamente, aína; de buena gana.—**s. after,** poco después; poco después de.—**as s. as,** así que, no bien. *V.* AS.—**how s.?** ¿cuándo? ¿cuándo a más tardar?

sooner [-œ(r], *adv. comp.* de SOON: más pronto; primero, antes; mejor.—**s. or later,** tarde o temprano.—**I had,** o **would, s. die,** antes la muerte; preferiría morir.—**no s. . . . than,** apenas . . . , tan pronto como . . . *(no sooner had John entered than she began to speak,* tan pronto como Juan hubo entrado, ella principió a hablar).—**the s. the better,** cuanto antes, o mientras más pronto, mejor.

soonest [-ịst], *adv. superl.* de SOON: (el) más pronto; primero.—**at the s.,** no antes, no antes de, antes no; cuanto antes.

soot [sụt]. **I.** *va.* manchar o cubrir de hollín, tiznar. **II.** *s.* hollín, tizne, *mf.*—**sooted** [-ịd], *a.* holliniento. *V.* SOOTY.

sooth [suθ]. **I.** *a.* (ant.) agradable, delicioso; verdadero, real. **II.** *s.* (ant.) verdad, realidad.

soothe [súð], *va.* calmar, aliviar, mitigar, sedar; consolar; ablandar, apaciguar, desenfadar.

soother [-œ(r], *s.* consolador; aliviador; amansador, apaciguador; adulador.

soothing [-ịŋ], *a.* calmante, sedante, sedativo; confortante, consolador.—**soothingly** [-lị], *adv.* con dulzura, consoladoramente.

soothsayer [súθseịœ(r], *s.* adivino, adivinador.

soothsaying [-ịŋ], *s.* adivinación.

sootiness [sútịnịs], *s.* fuliginosidad.

sooty [sútị], *a.* holliniento; fuliginoso.

sop [sap]. **I.** *s.* sopa, pan o cualquier cosa empapada en un líquido; soborno, regalo, para sobornar o apaciguar a alguien. **II.** *va.* (en)sopar, empapar, sope(te)ar; (con **up**) absorber.

sophism [sáfịzm], *s.* sofisma, *m.*—**sophist** [sáfịst], *s.* sofista; ergotista.—**sophistic(al** [sofịstịk(ạl],

a. sofístico.—**sophistically** [-i], *adv.* sofística-mente.—**sophisticalness** [-nįs], *s.* sofistería.
sophisticate [sofįstįkeįt]. **I.** *va.* sofisticar; falsi-ficar, alterar, adulterar; seducir, descarriar. **II.** *s.* persona corrida, que tiene mucho mundo.—**sophisticated** [-įd], *a.* corrido de mundo, falto de simplicidad, avezado a las cosas del mundo, sabido.—**sophistication** [-kéįṣọn], *s.* sofistica-ción; adulteración; falta de simplicidad.—**sophisticator** [-keįtọ(r)], *s.* falsificador, adul-terador.
sophistry [sáfįstrį], *s.* sofistería; ergotismo.
sophomore [sáfomọr], *s.* estudiante de segundo año.
sopor [sóupọ(r)], *s.* (med.) sopor, letargo.
soporiferous [-ríferʌs], *a.* soporífero, soporoso.
soporiferousness [-nįs], *s.* virtud o calidad so-porífera.
soporific [-rífįk]. **I.** *a.* soporífico, adormecedor, dormitivo. **II.** *s.* (medicamento) soporífero.
soppy [sápį], *a.* mojado, empapado.
soprano [sopránou]. **I.** *s.* (mús.) tiple, soprano (voz).—**s. singer**, tiple, soprano, *mf.* **II.** *a.* de soprano, (fam.) tiplesonante.
sorb [sọrb], *s.* (bot.) serbo o serval.—**s. apple**, sorba o serba.
sorcerer [sọ́rscœrœ(r)], *s.* hechicero, brujo.
sorceress [sọ́rscœrįs], *s.* hechicera, bruja.
sorcery [sọ́rscœrį], *s.* encantamiento, sortilegio, brujería, magia negra, hechicería.
sordes [sọ́rdiz], *s. pl.* (med.) sarro; saburra.
sordid [sọ́rdįd], *a.* mercenario, avariento, codi-cioso, interesado; vil, bajo; sórdido; sucio; (bot., zool.) de color lodoso.—**sordidly** [-lį], *adv.* codiciosamente, vilmente.—**sordidness** [-nįs], *s.* codicia, avaricia; bajeza, vileza; sordidez.
sordine [sọ́rdin], *s.* (mús.) sordina.
sore [sọr]. **I.** *s.* (med.) llaga, úlcera; lastimadura; mal, dolor; (vet.) matadura (del ganado); en-cono; pena, espina, memoria dolorosa; disgusto. **II.** *a.* enconado, dolorido, sensible; apenado, apesarado; (fam.) enojado, sentido, picado, resentido; doloroso, penoso; molesto; vehe-mente.—**s. ears**, mal o dolor de oídos.—**s. eyes**, mal de ojos.—**s. need**, necesidad extrema.—**s. sight**, espectáculo doloroso.—**s. throat**, mal de garganta, angina; carraspera. **III.** *adv.* (ant.) = SORELY.
sorely [-lį], *adv.* penosamente; suma o urgente-mente.
soreness [-nįs], *s.* dolor, mal; calidad de dolorido, enconado o sensible; amargura de una pena.
sorghum [sọ́rgʌm], *s.* (bot.) sorgo, zahína; melaza de sorgo.
sorites [soráįtiz], *s.* (lóg.) sorites.
sororicide [sorárįsaįd], *s.* asesino (o asesinato) de una hermana.
sorority [-įtį], *s.* club u hermandad de mujeres.
sorosis [sorọ́usįs], *s.* (bot.) fruto compuesto y mollar (como la piña); club de mujeres.
sorrel [sáręl]. **I.** *a.* alazán, roano. **II.** *s.* color ala-zán o roano; caballo (u otro animal) alazán; (bot.) acedera, acetosa, romaza.
sorrily [sárįlį], *adv.* mal, malamente, pésima-mente, lastimosamente.
sorriness [sárįnįs], *s.* pesar, pesadumbre.
sorrow [sárou]. **I.** *s.* pesar, dolor, pena, congoja, aflicción, tristeza; duelo, luto; desgracia, infor-tunio.—**s.-stricken**, afligido, agobiado de dolor.—**to my s.**, con gran sentimiento mío. **II.** *vn.* afligirse, apesararse, sentir pena.
sorrowful [-fụl], *a.* pesaroso, afligido, angustiado, doliente, desconsolado; triste, doloroso, lasti-moso.—**sorrowfully** [-į], *adv.* dolorosamente, con pena; luctuosamente, lastimeramente.—**sorrowfulness** [-nįs], *s.* pesar, tristeza, pesa-dumbre; calidad de triste o lastimoso.—**sor-rowing** [-įŋ], *s.* aflicción, tristeza; lamentación.—**sorrowless** [-lįs], *a.* sin pena, sin pesar, libre de pesares.
sorry [sárį], *a.* apesadumbrado, pesaroso; arre-pentido; triste, lamentable, lastimoso; malo, miserable, ruin, vil, de inferior calidad; despre-ciable, ridículo.—**to be s.**, (fuera del significado literal) sentir, lamentar (*I am sorry*, lo siento); arrepentirse; pesar (*you will be sorry*, le pesará).—**to be s. for**, sentir (una cosa), compadecer (a una persona).
sort [sọrt]. **I.** *s.* clase, *f.*, suerte, *f.*, especie, género, jaez, *m.*, calaña; manera, modo, forma.—**s. of** = KIND OF.—**after a s.**, de cierto modo, hasta cierto punto.—**all sorts of**, toda clase de.—**in like s.**, de modo análogo.—**of sorts**, de varias clases; de mala muerte.—**out of sorts**, indispuesto; malhumorado; triste; (impr.) falto de una fundición especial de letra o guarismos.—**they are a bad s.**, son mala gente. **II.** *va.* (a veces con over) separar, dividir, distribuir en grupos, clasificar; (a veces con out) escoger, seleccionar, colocar, ordenar, arreglar. **III.** *vn.* corresponder, ajustar; estar de acuerdo; juntarse, rozarse; adaptarse.
sortable [-ąbl], *a.* separable, clasificable; acomo-dado, conveniente, apto, oportuno.
sorter [-œ(r)], *s.* distribuidor, clasificador.
sortie [sọ́rtį], *s.* (mil.) salida, surtida; cada vuelo de un avión en una misión o ataque.
sortilege [sọ́rtįlįdž], *s.* sortilegio.
sorting [sọ́rtįŋ], *s.* distribución (de correo, etc.).
sortition [sọrtįṣọn], *s.* sorteo.
S O S [és ou és], *s.* (rad.) SOS, llamada o señal (*f.*) internacional de auxilio.
so-so [sóu sou], *a.* y *adv.* así así; regular o medio-cre(mente).
sot [sat], *s.* borrachín, (fam.) zaque, tumbacuarti-llos.
soteriology [sotirįálodžį], *s.* discurso o exposición acerca de la higiene; (teol.) doctrina de la salva-ción por Jesucristo.
sottish [sátįš], *a.* embotado, hecho una uva, em-brutecido.—**sottishly** [-lį], *adv.* torpemente.—**sottishness** [-nįs], *s.* embriaguez, embruteci-miento.
sotto voce [sátou vóuchį], *adv.* a sovoz.
sou [su], *s.* sueldo (moneda).
soubrette [subrét], *s.* (teat.) graciosa.
soubriquet [súbrįkeį], *s.* apodo.
souffle [súfl], *s.* (med.) soplo, sonido suave que se percibe por auscultación.
soufflé [sufléį], *s.* (coc.) manjar delicado y espon-joso cocido al horno, gen. con huevos batidos, queso, etc.
sough [sʌf *o* sau]. **I.** *vn.* suspirar, susurrar, mur-murar. **II.** *s.* susurro, suspiro, murmullo.
sought [sọt], *pret.* y *pp.* de TO SEEK.—**s.-after**, solicitado, pedido, buscado con avidez.
soul [sóul], *s.* alma, ánima; psiquis o psique, *f.*; espíritu; corazón (en sentido metafórico); esen-cia, virtud principal; inspiración; personifica-ción; individuo, persona; vecino, habitante.—**All-Souls' Day**, día (*m.*) de los difuntos.—**every living s.**, todo bicho viviente (fam.).—**not a s.**, nadie.—**on, o upon my s.**, por vida mía, por mi vida.—**to be the s. of honor**, ser la misma honra o el honor mismo. Con *soul y* algunos adjetivos y gerundios se forman varios compuestos, como *s.-sick, s.-thrilling*, etc., cuyo significado puede inferirse por el segundo ele-mento.
souled [-d], *a.* animado, con alma.
soulful [-fụl], *a.* conmovedor, espiritual.—**soulfully** [-lį], *adv.* de un modo que llega hasta el alma.—**soulfulness** [-nįs], *s.* sensibilidad; cali-dad conmovedora o de expresión emotiva.
soulless [-lįs], *a.* desalmado; sin conciencia; sin nobleza; sin grandeza de espíritu; vil, ruin.
sound [sáund]. **I.** *a.* sano, bueno; sólido, firme; ileso, incólume, entero; puro, ortodoxo; cierto, indudable; recto, justo; firme; bueno, completo; profundo, cabal; (com.) solvente.—**s. busi-ness**, negocio seguro.—**s. reasoning**, racio-cinio sólido, seguro.—**s. sleep**, sueño profundo.

—of s. and disposing mind and memory, (for.) de mente y memoria sanas, capaz de hacer testamento.**—of s. mind,** en su cabal juicio. **II.** *adv.* sanamente, vigorosamente. **III.** *s.* (geog.) estrecho; (mar.) sonda, sondaleza; (cir.) tienta, sonda; son, sonido, tañido; ruido; vejiga natatoria (de los peces).**—s. board = SOUNDING BOARD.—s. damper,** (mús.) sordina. **—s. equipment,** (rad., etc.) artefactos de acústica.**—s. film o picture,** (cine) película sonora o parlante.**—s. post,** alma de violín.— **s. wave,** onda sonora. **IV.** *va.* sonar, tocar, tañer; dar el toque de; entonar, cantar; proclamar; celebrar; probar por el sonido; (mar.) sondear, hondear, fondear, escandallar; (a veces con **out**) inquirir, rastrear, tantear, sondear, tentar el pulso de; (cir.) sondar, tentar; (med.) auscultar.**—to s. a note,** dar señal, dar aviso; formular, enunciar (un plan, principio, regla, etc.).**—to s. the horn,** (aut.) tocar la bocina. **V.** *vn.* sonar; resonar, esparcirse, divulgarse; dar toque de aviso o llamada.

sounder [-œ(r)], *s.* (elec.) resonador; receptor acústico; (mar.) sondeador; (cir.) tienta, sonda.

sounding [-iŋ]. **I.** *a.* sonante, sonable, sonoro; retumbante. **II.** *s.* (mar.) sondeo, braceaje, escandallada.**—***pl.* sondas, cantidad de brazas; muestras sacadas del agua por el sondeador.— **s. balloon,** globo sonda, globo suelto de datos meteorológicos.**—s. board,** (mús.) tabla de armonía, caja armónica (de un piano); secreto, cajón de los órganos; tornavoz, *m.,* sombrero de púlpito.**—s. lead,** (mar.) escandallo.**—s. line,** (mar.) sondaleza, bolina.

soundless [-lįs], *a.* sin sonido, sin ruido, silencioso; mudo; insondable.

soundly [-lį], *adv.* sanamente, con salud; firmemente; verdaderamente, seguramente.**—to sleep s.,** dormir profundamente o a pierna suelta.

soundness [-nįs], *s.* sanidad, salud; vigor; firmeza, solidez, estabilidad; verdad, rectitud, pureza; fuerza, validez; rectitud, justicia; pureza de la fe, ortodoxia; (com.) solvencia.

soundproof [-pruf], *a.* a prueba de sonido o ruido.

soup [sup], *s.* sopa.**—s. kitchen,** (mil.) cocina de campaña; dispensario de alimentos para los pobres.**—s. ladle,** cucharón.**—s. plate,** plato hondo o sopero.**—s. spoon,** cuchara sopera o de sopa.**—s. tureen,** sopera.**—in the s.,** (fam.) en apuros, en aprietos.

sour [sáųr]. **I.** *a.* agrio; ácido, avinagrado, fermentado, rancio; acre, áspero, desabrido, huraño.**—s. apple,** manzana agria o verde.**—s. dock,** acedera.**—s. gourd,** (bot.) pan de mico. **—s. grapes!** ¡están verdes!**—s. grass,** acedera pequeña.**—to taste s.,** agrazar, tener sabor agrio.**—to turn s.,** agriarse, volverse agrio. **II.** *va.* agriar, acedar, avinagrar; desabrir, irritar, indisponer (los ánimos); descontentar, desagradar; macerar (la cal); hacer fermentar (la col). **III.** *vn.* agriarse, avinagrarse; volverse torcerse (el vino, etc.); cortarse (la leche); revenirse, fermentar; irritarse, enojarse; corromperse, podrirse; (agr.) malearse (la tierra).

source [sors], *s.* fuente, *f.;* nacimiento; origen, causa, procedencia, germen.**—to have, o to know, from a good s.,** saber de buena tinta.

sourdough [sáųrdoų], *s.* levadura; (fam.) explorador o buscador del Canadá o Alaska.

sourish [sáųrįš], *a.* agrillo, agrete, vinagroso.

sourly [-lį], *adv.* agriamente.

sourness [-nįs], *s.* agrio, agrura, acedía, acidez; acrimonia, acritud.

soursop [-sap], *s.* (bot.) árbol tropical (y su fruta) algo semejante al guanábano o chirimoyo. *V.* SWEETSOP Y CUSTARD APPLE.

souse [saųs]. **I.** *s.* escabeche; cabeza, patas u orejas de cerdo adobadas; zambullida, chapuz, *m.,* (fam.) borrachín; (cetr.) ataque repentino (del

halcón). **II.** *adv.* zas, de cabeza. **III.** *va.* zabullir, chapuzar; arrojar, derramar, verter; (coc.) escabechar, adobar; arrojarse con violencia sobre. **IV.** *vn.* lanzarse de cabeza; (fam.) emborracharse.

soutane [sután], *s.* sotana.

south [saųθ]. **I.** *s.* sud o sur; comarca o región situada al sur.**—the S.,** (E. U.) los estados del Sur. **II.** *a.* meridional, austral, (del) sur.**—S. African,** sudafricano.**—S. American,** sudamericano.**—S. Pole,** polo sur.**—s. wind,** austro, viento del sur. **III.** *adv.* hacia el sur; del sur (viento).

southeast [saųθíst], *s.* y *a.* sudeste.**—s. by east,** sudeste cuarta al este.**—s. by south,** sudeste cuarta al sur.

southeaster [-œ(r)], *s.* temporal o viento de sudeste.**—southeasterly** [-cerlį], *a.* y *adv.* hacia el sudeste, al sudeste.**—southeastern** [-œrn], *a.* y *adv.* del sudeste.

souther [sáųθœ(r)], *s.* viento o borrasca del sur.

southerly [sʌðœrlį], *a.* meridional.

southern [sʌðœrn], *a.* meridional, austral, del sur; situado al sur.**—S. Cross,** (astr.) Cruz del Sur.

southerner [-œ(r)], *s.* habitante del sur; (S.) sudista (E. U.).

southernmost [-moųst], *a.* de más al sur, más meridional.

southernwood [-wųd], *s.* (bot.) abrótano, lombriguera, boja.

southing [sáųðiŋ], *s.* (mar.) derrota hacia el sur; diferencia de latitud sur.

southland [sáųθlænd], *s.* región o distrito meridional o del sur.

southmost [-moųst], *a.* más meridional (*superl.*).

southpaw [-pɔ], *s.* y *a.* (fam.) zurdo (apl. esp. al que tira la pelota en el baseball).

southron [sʌðrọn], *s.* habitante del sur, meridional.

southward [sáųθwърd]. **I.** *a.* situado hacia el sur. **II.** *adv.* hacia el mediodía.**—s. of the line,** al sur de la línea (ecuador).

southwest [-wést], *s.* y *a.* sudoeste.**—s. by south,** sudoeste cuarta al sur.**—s. by west,** sudoeste cuarta al oeste.**—s. wind,** ábrego, áfrico, el viento sudoeste.

southwester [-œ(r)], *s.* vendaval del sudoeste; sudeste; (mar.) sueste, sombrero de lona encerada (ll. t. sou'wester).**—southwesterly** [-lį], *a.* y *adv.* del sudoeste, hacia el sudoeste.— **southwestern** [-œrn], *a.* y *adv.* o del sudoeste.**—southwestward** [-wърd], *adv.* hacia el sudoeste.

souvenir [súveņịr], *s.* memoria, prenda de recuerdo; estrena.

sovereign [sóvrịn o sʌvrịn]. **I.** *s.* soberano, monarca, *m.,* príncipe, potentado; (Ingl.) libra esterlina. **II.** *a.* soberano, independiente; supremo, preeminente; eficacísimo.**—s. pontiff,** sumo pontífice.

sovereignly [-lị], *adv.* soberanamente; supremamente.**—sovereignty** [-tị], *s.* soberanía; estado soberano.

soviet [sóųvịet]. **I.** *s.* soviet. **II.** *a.* soviético, bolchevista.**—sovietdom** [-dọm], *s.* los países soviéticos; bolchevismo.**—sovietism** [-įzm], *s.* sovietismo, bolchevismo.**—sovietist** [-įst], *s.* sovietista, bolchevista.**—sovietize** [-aįz], *va.* y *vn.* sovietizar, convertir al sovietismo o bolchevismo; propagar el sovietismo.

sow [saų], *s.* (zool.) puerca, cerda, cochina, marrana; (fund.) goa, galápago.**—s. bug,** (ent.) cochinilla de tierra.**—s. thistle,** (bot.) cerraja, cardo ajonjero.

sow [soų]. **I.** *va.* y *vn.* (*pret.* SOWED; *pp.* SOWN o SOWED) (agr.) sembrar; desparramar, esparcir, diseminar.**—to s. one's wild oats,** correr sus mocedades, hacer travesuras juveniles.**—to s. to,** sembrar de.**—who sows the wind reaps the whirlwind,** como sembráredes, cogeredes.

sowbread [sáуbred], *s.* (bot.) pamporcino.

sower [sóуœ(r)], *s.* (agr.) sembrador; diseminador, desparramador; sembradera (máquina).

sowing [sóуịŋ]. **I.** *s.* sementera, siembra; sembradura, diseminación. **II.** *a.* de sembrar, sembrador.—**s. machine**, sembradera.—**s. time**, sementera, tiempo de sembrar.

sown [soun], *pp.* de TO SOW.—**s. ground o land**, (agr.) sembrado, (tierra) sembrada.

soy [sóị], **soya** [sóịä], *s.* (bot.) soja, soya, planta gramínea; salsa de soya; soya, fruto de la soya (ll. t. **soybean y s. pea**).

spa [spa], *s.* balneario; manantial de agua mineral; burga; caldas, *f. pl.*

space [spéịs]. **I.** *va.* espaciar; (impr.) interlinear, regletear. **II.** *s.* (leng. ord., mús., impr.) espacio; extensión, trecho; distancia; lugar, cabida, campo; período, intervalo; rato; ocasión, tiempo, sazón, *f.*, oportunidad; intersticio; (mús.) compás (del pentagrama).—**s. band**, (impr.) cuña o placa de espaciar.—**s. bar o key**, tecla de los espacios (de máquina de escribir, etc.).—**s. line**, (impr.) interlínea.—**s. rule**, (impr.) raya fina.

spacer [-œ(r)], *s.* espaciador; separador.

spacious [spéịäs], *a.* espacioso, amplio, grande, extenso.—**spaciously** [-lị], *adv.* espaciosamente.—**spaciousness** [-nịs], *s.* espaciosidad, amplitud.

spade [spéịd]. **I.** *s.* (agr.) laya, pala; (gen. *pl.*) espada(s) (en la baraja); (mil.) zapa.—**to call a s. a s.**, llamar al pan pan y al vino vino, hablar en plata. **II.** *va.* layar, cavar o remover el suelo con la laya o pala.—**spading fork**, horca de cavar.

spadeful [-fụl], *s.* palada.

spadework [-wœrk], *s.* (fig.) trabajo preliminar.

spadiceous [spǎdịsäs], *a.* (bot.) espadíceo.

spadix [spéịdịks], *s.* (bot.) espádice.

spaghetti [spagétị], *s.* fideos largos, macarrones delgados; (elec.) tubería aisladora.

spahee, spahi [spáhị], *s.* espahí, soldado de caballería turco o argeliano.

spake [spéịk], *pret. ant.* de TO SPEAK.

spall [spɔl]. **I.** *s.* astilla. **II.** *va.* y *vn.* (alb. y min.) desastillar(se); descantillar(se); descascarar(se); desbastar, alisar toscamente.

span [spæn]. **I.** *s.* palmo, llave (*f.*) de la mano; lapso, espacio, trecho; (arq.) tramo, luz; (aer.) envergadura, dimensión máxima transversal; ojo, apertura de puente, arco o bóveda; pareja (de caballos); traba; (mar.) eslinga; amante, guía, braga, nervio. **II.** *va.* medir a palmos; atravesar; abrazar, abarcar, llegar de un lado a otro de; echar sobre, extenderse sobre; ligar, atar. **III.** *vn.* emparejarse (caballos); proceder por etapas o jornadas regulares.

span, *pret. ant.* de TO SPIN.

span [spæn], *adv.* enteramente, perfectamente.—**s.-new**, nuevecito, completamente nuevo.

spandrel [spǽndrel], *s.* (arq.) enjuta, embecadura, riñón de bóveda.

spangle [spǽŋgl]. **I.** *s.* lentejuela, bricho. **II.** *va.* adornar con lentejuelas.—**spangled skies**, cielo estrellado.

Spaniard [spǽnyärd], *s.* español, hispano.

spaniel [spǽnyẹl], *s.* perro de aguas, especie de sabueso español.

Spanish [spǽnịš]. **I.** *s.* español, castellano (el idioma); los españoles. **II.** *a.* español, castellano, hispánico, hispano.—**S.-American**, hispanoamericano.—**S. bayonet**, (bot.) yuca.—**S. black**, negro de España; corcho quemado.—**S. broom**, retama.—**S. cedar**, cedro rojo antillano.—**S. chalk**, esteatita de Aragón.—**S. fly**, (ent.) cantárida, cubillo, carraleja (ll. t. **S. blister(ing) beetle**).—**S. grass**, esparto.—**S. leather**, cordobán.—**S.-like**, españolado; a la española.—**S. mackerel**, (ict.) escombro.—**S. Main**, Tierra Firme; mar Caribe (apl. esp. a la parte meridional, que baña las costas

de Tierra Firme).—**S. moss**, musgo negro o de Florida.—**S. oak**, roble español.—**S. puff**, buñuelo.—**S. saying, action**, etc., españolada.—**S. shawl**, mantón de Manila.—**S. sheep**, oveja merina.—**S. soap**, jabón de Castilla.—**S. style**, a la española.—**S. tile**, teja española.—**S. white**, blanco de España, yeso mate.

spank [spæŋk]. **I.** *va.* zurrar, dar una zurra, dar palmadas o nalgadas. **II.** *vn.* correr, ir de prisa. **III.** *s.* nalgada, palmada.

spanker [-œ(r)], *s.* el o lo que da nalgadas; (mar.) maricangalla; (fam.) algo grande y hermoso; el o lo que marcha velozmente.

spanking [-ịŋ]. **I.** *a.* pronto, veloz; fuerte (brisa); (fam.) extraordinariamente grande o hermoso. **II.** *s.* zurra, nalgadas, azotaina.

spanless [spǽnlịs], *a.* que no se puede abarcar, medir, atravesar o colmar.

spanner [spǽnœ(r)], *s.* (mec.) llave (*f.*) de tuercas; (ent.) oruga geómetra (ll. t. **spanworm**).

spar [spar]. **I.** *s.* (min.) espato; (mar.) palo, mástil, verga, barra, cerreta; berlinga, percha, bordón; asna, cabrio (de grúa o cabria); boxeo, pugilato; altercado, riña; pelea con espolones o las patas (gallos); (aer.) larguero.—*pl.* arboladura.—**s. buoy**, (mar.) baliza.—**s. deck**, (mar.) cubierta de guindaste. **II.** *vn.* boxear; pelear con espolones o con las patas; altercar. **III.** *va.* proveer de vergas o mástiles; mover o alzar por medio de mástiles y poleas.

sparable [spǽrabl], *s.* (zap.) puntilla.

spare [spér]. **I.** *va.* ahorrar, economizar; escatimar; pasar o pasarse sin, prescindir de; conceder, dedicar (tiempo); perdonar; hacer gracia de; no abusar de, compadecer; evitar, ahorrar trabajo o molestia a; usar con moderación; ahorrarle a, eximir de, escapar de (en la voz pasiva **to be spared**: *I was spared the labor*, fuí eximido del trabajo, o escapé del trabajo).—**to s. oneself**, cuidarse de sí mismo, ahorrarse trabajo, molestia, etc.—**to have . . . to spare**, tener de sobra.—**and to s.**, y más, de sobra.—**there's no time to s.**, no hay tiempo que perder. **II.** *vn.* tener piedad o misericordia; abstenerse, detenerse, refrenarse, desistir; ser frugal, vivir con economía. **III.** *a.* disponible, sobrante; de reserva, de repuesto; enjuto, descarnado; económico, mezquino; escaso; sobrio.—**s. bed**, cama de repuesto o de sobra.—**s.-built**, flaco, delgado.—**s. hours**, horas de recreo o de ocio.—**s. money**, dinero de reserva, ahorros.—**s. parts**, (mec.) repuestos, piezas de repuesto o de recambio.—**s. rigging**, (mar.) pertrechos o cordaje de respeto.—**s. room**, cuarto de sobra, cuarto para convidados.—**s. stores** = s. RIGGING.—**s. time**, tiempo desocupado, ratos de ocio.

spareness [-nịs], *s.* magrura, flaqueza; escasez; ahorro; economía, frugalidad.

sparerib [-rịb], *s.* costilla de puerco casi descarnada.

sparge [spardź], *va.* regar, rociar.

sparger [spárdźœ(r)], *s.* regadera, rociadera.

sparing [spérịŋ], *a.* escaso, limitado, poco; parco, frugal, económico.—**sparingly** [-lị], *adv.* escasamente; parcamente; económicamente; rara vez; cautamente.—**sparingness** [-nịs], *s.* ahorro; escasez; frugalidad, parsimonia.

spark [spárk]. **I.** *s.* chispa, morcella; (poét.) centella; pizca, jota; (joy.) chispa, diamante pequeño; petimetre o pisaverde.—*pl.* (rad., fam.) radiotelegrafista.—**s. arrester, s. catcher**, (f. c.) chispero, sombrerete; (elec.) amortiguador de chispas, apagachispas.—**s. coil**, (elec.) bobina de inducción, bobina de chispas.—**s. gap**, (elec.) distancia explosiva; (rad.) mecanismo de chispa.—**s. lead**, (m. comb. int.) avance al encendido.—**s. plug**, (m. comb. int.) bujía (de encendido); (fam.) persona de iniciativa y bríos que estimula a sus compañeros. **II.**

va. centellear; (fam.) galantear, enamorar. **III.** *vn.* chispear, echar chispas, centellear; (elec.) producir chispas.

sparker [-œ(r)], *s.* lo que centellea, produce chispas, etc.; (elec.) = SPARK ARRESTER.

sparking [-iŋ]. **I.** *s.* chispeo, chisporroteo; (elec.) producción de chispas; (fam.) galanteo. **II.** *a.* chispeante; (elec.) de chispas; que produce chispas.—**s. distance,** (elec.) distancia explosiva máxima.—**s. plug** = SPARK PLUG.—**s. voltage,** (elec.) tensión (mínima) de descarga, o de chispas.

sparkle [-l]. **I.** *s.* centelleo, destello, chispa. **II.** *vn.* chispear, rutilar, centellear, brillar, relumbrar, relampaguear; ser espumoso (ciertos vinos).

sparkler [-lœ(r)], *s.* (fam.) diamante, brillante.

sparkling [-liŋ], *a.* centelleante, resplandeciente, rutilante, brillante, chispeante, chisposo; espumoso.—**s. eyes,** ojos brillantes, chispeantes.— **s. wine,** vino espumoso.

sparklingly [-lij], *adv.* con brillantez o brillo; con esplendor; brillantemente.

sparrow [spǽrou], *s.* (orn.) gorrión, *m.,* pardal.— **s. hawk,** (orn.) esparaván, gavilán, cernícalo. —**s. shot,** mostacilla.

sparrowgrass [-græs], *s.* (bot., fam.) espárrago (es corrupción de *asparagus*).

sparry [spárj], *a.* (min.) espático.

sparse [spárs], *a.* esparcido, desparramado; claro, ralo.—**sparsely** [-lij], *adv.* aquí y allá, a grandes trechos, no densamente.—**sparsity** [-jtj], *s.* raleza; parquedad.

Spartan [spártǝn], *a.* y *s.* espartano.

spasm [spǽzm], *s.* (med.) espasmo.—**spasmodic** [spæzmádjk], *a.* espasmódico; irregular.— **spasmodically** [-lij], *adv.* espasmódicamente; a ratos, sin regularidad.

spastic [spǽstjk], *a.* (med.) espástico, espasmódico.

spasticity [spæstísjtj], *s.* (med.) espasticidad.

spat [spæt]. **I.** *pret.* y *pp.* de TO SPIT. **II.** *va.* y *vn.* desovar los mariscos o moluscos; dar una palmadita; (fam.) reñir ligeramente; batir (la lluvia); salpicar. **III.** *s.* huevas de los mariscos; palmadita; manotada; sopapo, bofetada; gota grande de lluvia; salpicadura; riña, disputa.— *pl.* spats, botines (de paño), polainas cortas.

spate [speit], *s.* (Ingl.) creciente, *f.,* avenida; chaparrón, aguacero; tropel, montón.

spathe [speið], *s.* (bot.) espata, espádice.

spathic [spǽθjk], *a.* (min.) espático.

spatial [spéjʃǝl], *a.* del espacio, relativo al espacio, de espacio.

spatter [spǽtœ(r)]. **I.** *va.* y *vn.* salpicar; manchar; regar, rociar, esparcir. **II.** *s.* salpicadura; rociamiento, rociada.

spatterdashes [-dæʃjz], *s. pl.* polainas, botines.

spatterdock [-dak], *s.* (bot.) nenúfar amarillo.

spattle [spǽtl], *s.* (cerá.) instrumento para motear la vajilla de loza; espátula.

spatula [spǽtʃulǝ], *s.* espátula.

spatulate [spǽtʃulejt], *a.* espatulado.

spavin [spǽvjn], *s.* (vet.) esparaván.

spawn [spón]. **I.** *s.* (ict.) freza, huevas; pececillos; (desp.) producto, fruto, resultado. **II.** *va.* y *vn.* (ict.) desovar, frezar; (desp.) producir en abundancia.

spawner [-œ(r)], *s.* pez hembra.—**spawning** [-iŋ], *s.* freza, desove.—**s. time,** desove.

spay [spej], *va.* (vet.) castrar, sacar los ovarios a.

speak [spík], *va.* y *vn.* (*pret.* SPOKE; *pp.* SPOKEN) hablar; decir; departir, platicar, conversar; comunicar(se); expresarse (en); recitar; producir con la palabra.—**to s. about,** u of, hablar o tratar de.—**to s. brokenly,** chapurr(e)ar.— **to s. by the book,** hablar con detallada exactitud; hablar como un libro.—**to s. by the card,** hablar con pleno conocimiento de causa. —**to s. daggers,** desatarse en improperios, echar chispas.—**to s. for,** hablar en favor de; hablar en nombre de; ser señal de o recomenda-

ción para; solicitar; apalabrar, hacer guardar o reservar.—**to s. for itself,** hablar por sí mismo, ser evidente por sí mismo, ser claro y suficiente.—**to s. one's mind,** decir uno lo que piensa, hablar en plata.—**to s. out,** decir, hablar claro.—**to s. thick,** hablar con media lengua, hablar tartajoso.—**to s. through the nose,** ganguear, hablar gangoso.—**to s. to,** hablar a; (fam.) reprender.—**to s. to the point,** ir al grano, dejarse de rodeos.—**to s. up,** hablar en alta voz; interponer; decir claridades. —**to s. volumes,** encerrar muchísimo, ser de suma significación.—**to s. well for,** ser recomendación para, dar prestigio, honrar, demostrar el valor o el mérito de.—**so to s.,** por decirlo así.

speakable [-ǝbl], *a.* decible.

speakeasy [-izj], *s.* (fam.) taberna clandestina.

speaker [-œ(r)], *s.* el que habla; orador, conferenciante; preopinante (en un debate); presidente de un cuerpo legislativo (en los E. U., de la cámara de representantes); libro de declamación; (rad.) = LOUD-SPEAKER.—**speakership** [-ʃjp], *s.* presidencia (de cuerpo legislativo).

speaking [-iŋ]. **I.** *a.* parlante, hablante; para hablar.—**s. arc,** (elec.) arco cantante.—**s. likeness,** retrato muy parecido o (fam.) que está hablando.—**s. machine,** máquina parlante (fonógrafo, etc.)—**s. rod,** (top.) mira parlante.—**s. trumpet,** bocina, portavoz, *m.*—**s. tube,** tubo acústico.—**English (Spanish, etc.)-s.,** de habla inglesa (española, etc.).— **to be on s. terms,** hablarse, tener conocimiento superficial (con). **II.** *s.* habla, discurso, declamación; oratoria.

spear [spír]. **I.** *s.* lanza; venablo; arpón de pesca; (poét.) lancero; (bot.) brizna; (bot.) hierba de los prados, espiguilla.—**s. grass,** (bot.) hierba de los prados, espiguilla.—**s. side,** línea paterna, lado masculino de una familia. **II.** *va.* alancear. **III.** *vn.* (bot.) brotar.

spearhead [-hed]. **I.** *s.* punta de lanza; vanguardia; ataque de vanguardia; arma de entrada (fig.), cosa con que se abre brecha o se inicia algo. **II.** *va.* abrir la brecha (para un ataque).

spearmint [-mjnt], *s.* (bot.) hierbabuena puntiaguda, menta verde.

spearwood [-wud], *s.* (bot.) eucalipto; acacia.

spearwort [-wœrt], *s.* (bot.) ranúnculo.

special [spéʃǝl]. **I.** *a.* especial; extraordinario, particular, privativo, peculiar; diferencial; hecho especialmente o a propósito.—**s. delivery,** entrega inmediata (de correo).—**s. edition,** edición extra.—**s. warrant,** orden (*f.*) de arresto. **II.** *s.* persona o cosa especial; carta enviada para entrega inmediata; (fam., com.) ganga, saldo.

specialism [-jzm], *s.* consagración a una especialidad; carácter de especialista.—**specialist** [-jst], *s.* y *a.* especialista, especializado.—**specialize, specialise** [-ajz], *va.* y *vn.* especializar(se); tener por especialidad.—**specialization** [-jzéjʃǝn], *s.* especialización.—**specially** [-jl], *adv.* especialmente; sobre todo.—**specialness** [-njs], *s.* especialidad.

speciality [speʃjǽljtj], *s.* especialidad, peculiaridad, rasgo característico; caballo de batalla.

specialty [spéʃǝltj], *s.* especialidad; (for.) obligación firmada formalmente.

specie [spíʃj], *s.* efectivo, metálico, numerario.

species [spíʃjz], *s.* (biol., lóg.) especie; clase, *f.,* género, suerte, *f.,* variedad; forma, naturaleza; (farm.) simple; polvos compuestos.

specific(al [spjsífjk(ǝl]. **I.** *a.* específico, preciso; especificativo, determinado, distinto; peculiar; (med.) específico.—**s. gravity,** (fís.) gravedad específica, peso específico.—**s. name,** nombre específico, el de la especie. **II.** *s.* (med.) específico.

specifically [-j], *adv.* específicamente; especificadamente.—**specific(al)ness** [-nis], *s.* calidad de específico.

specification [spésifikéisǫn], *s.* especificación, mención.—*pl.* descripción detallada de un plan o aparato; presupuesto detallado; datos fundamentales; especificaciones; pliego de condiciones.

specificity [-físiti], *s.* especificidad, determinación, carácter de específico.

specify [-fai], *va.* especificar; estipular, prescribir.

specimen [spésimen], *s.* espécimen, muestra; ejemplar.—**s. book,** muestrario.

specious [spíʃʌs], *a.* especioso, aparentemente plausible.—**speciously** [-li], *adv.* especiosamente.—**speciousness** [-nis], *s.* plausibilidad aparente.

speck, speckle [spék, -l]. **I.** *s.* manchita, mácula, motita; nube (*f.*) en un ojo; lunar, señal, *f.*, peca; punto, pizca, átomo. **II.** *va.* abigarrar, manchar, jaspear, espolvorear, motear.

spectacle [spéktąkl], *s.* espectáculo, ostentación, exhibición.—*pl.* (ópt.) espejuelos, gafas, anteojos, lentes, (fam.) antiparras.

spectacled [-d], *a.* que lleva anteojos.

spectacular [spɛktækyūlǫ(r), *a.* espectacular, de espectáculo; aparatoso.

spectator [spékteitǫ(r)], *s.* espectador; mirón.

specter, spectre [spéktœ(r)], *s.* espectro, visión.

spectra [spéktrą], *s. pl.* de SPECTRUM.

spectral [spéktrąl], *a.* espectral.

spectrograph [spéktrogræf], *s.* (fís.) espectrógrafo, aparato para obtener una fotografía o representación de un espectro.—**spectrohelio-graph** [-hílįogræf], *s.* (fís.) espectroheliógrafo.—**spectrometer** [spɛktrámetœ(r)], *s.* espectrómetro, refractómetro, instrumento para medir el índice de refracción.

spectroscope [spéktroskoup], *s.* (ópt.) espectroscopio.—**spectroscopic(al** [-skápik(ąl], *a.* espectroscópico.—**spectroscopy** [spɛktráskopi], *s.* espectroscopia.

spectrum [spéktrʌm], *s.* (ópt.) espectro; imagen o espectro ocular.—**s. analysis,** análisis espectral.

specular [spékyūlǫ(r)], *a.* especular.—**s. iron,** (min.) hierro especular, hematites (*f.*) brillante.—**s. stone,** (min.) mica.

speculate [-leit], *va.* y *vn.* especular, meditar; (com.) especular.—**speculation** [-léiʃǫn], *s.* especulación, teoría; especulativa, teórica; meditación; (com.) especulación.

speculative [-leitiv], *a.* especulativo, contemplativo; teórico; (com.) especulador.—**speculatively** [-li], *adv.* especulativamente; teóricamente; (com.) por especulación.—**speculativeness** [-nis], *s.* carácter especulativo.

speculator [-leitǫ(r)], *s.* teórico; (com.) especulador; bolsista, jugador (de bolsa); (teat.) revendedor de billetes.

speculum [-lʌm], *s.* (cir.) espéculo; (ópt.) espejo.

sped [sped], *pret.* y *pp.* de TO SPEED.

speech [spích], *s.* palabra, habla, oración; lenguaje, idioma, *m.*; voz; discurso, arenga, alocución, perorata, oración; disertación; (teat.) parlamento.—**s. from the throne,** discurso de la Corona.—**s. reading** = LIP READING.—**free s.,** (pol.) libertad de palabra.—**to make a s.,** pronunciar un discurso; echar perorata.

speechcraft [-kræft], *s.* arte de bien decir, don de la oratoria; lingüística; gramática.

speechify [-ifai], *vn.* (fam.) arengar, perorar.

speechless [-lis], *a.* mudo; callado; cortado, sobrecogido, sin habla.—**speechlessness** [-nis], *s.* mudez, falta de habla.

speechmaker [-meikœ(r)], *s.* orador; perorador.

speed [spíd]. **I.** *va.* (*pret.* y *pp.* SPED o SPEEDED) ayudar, favorecer; acompañar, despedir; despachar, expedir; (gen. con *up*) acelerar, apresurar, dar prisa, avivar. **II.** *vn.* correr, apresurarse, darse prisa; andar o moverse con presteza; (aut.) exceder la velocidad permitida; progresar,

adelantar, prosperar, tener buen éxito. **III.** *s.* velocidad; rapidez; prontitud, presteza; progreso, éxito, suceso.—**s. counter,** (mec.) contador de vueltas (de una rueda), cuentavueltas.—**s. ga(u)ge, s. indicator, s. recorder,** cuentavueltas, cuenta-revoluciones, velocímetro; (f. c.) cursómetro; (aut.) taquímetro, contador de velocidad.—**s. gear,** (aut.) cambio de velocidades.—**s. limit,** velocidad máxima permitida; límite de velocidad.—**s. scout,** (aer. mil.) avión reconocedor rápido.—**s. trap,** (aut.) trampa para descubrir a los que exceden la velocidad permitida. Consiste en dos estaciones ocultas a lo largo de la vía, comunicadas por teléfono.—**at full s.,** a toda velocidad; a toda máquina; a carrera tendida; a escape, a rienda suelta; a todo correr o andar.—**with all s.,** a toda prisa, con toda la celeridad posible.

speedboat [-bout], *s.* canoa automóvil.

speeder [-œ(r)], *s.* el o lo que anda a gran velocidad o a revienta cinchas (apl. esp. al automovilista que excede la velocidad permitida).—**speeding** [-iŋ]. **I.** *s.* (aut.) exceder la velocidad permitida. **II.** *a.* veloz, rápido.

speedily [-ili], *adv.* rápidamente, velozmente; de prisa, pronto.—**speediness** [-inis], *s.* celeridad, rapidez; prontitud, prisa, diligencia.

speedometer [-ámetœ(r)], *s.* velocímetro, taquímetro o taquímetro, indicador o marcador de velocidad.

speedster [-stœ(r)], *s.* = SPEEDER; (aut.) róadster rápido de dos asientos.

speed-up [-ʌp], *s.* aceleración; aumento de velocidad, producción, etc.

speedway [-wei], *s.* autoestrada, autopista.

speedwell [-wel], *s.* (bot.) verónica.

speedy [-i], *a.* veloz, rápido; pronto, vivo.

speiss [spais], *s.* (metal.) compuesto de arseniuros y sulfuros de ciertos metales.

spell [spél]. **I.** *s.* hechizo, encanto, ensalmo; fascinación, arrobamiento; turno, tanda, revezo; (fam.) poco tiempo, rato, período, temporada, trecho.—**by spells,** por turnos; a ratos.—**under a s.,** fascinado. **II.** *va.* (*pret.* y *pp.* SPELLED o SPELT) deletrear; descifrar, leer con dificultad; indicar, significar; estudiar (a veces con over o out); hechizar, encantar; (fam.) revezar, relevar, reemplazar.—**to s. the watch,** (mil., mar.) relevar a la guardia. **III.** *vn.* deletrear; (fam.) descansar por un rato.

spellbind [-baind], *va.* (*pret.* y *pp.* SPELLBOUND) encantar, hechizar; fascinar, embelesar.

spellbinder [-baindœ(r)], *s.* arengador, orador popular impetuoso y arrebatador.—**spellbound** [-baund], *a.* arrebatado, embelesado, fascinado.

speller [-œ(r)], *s.* deletreador; libro de deletrear.

spelling [-iŋ], *s.* deletreo; ortografía, grafía.—**s. bee,** concurso o certamen de deletreo.—**s. book,** cartilla de deletrear, abecedario.

spelt [-t]. **I.** *pret.* y *pp.* de TO SPELL. **II.** *s.* (bot.) espelta, farro, escanda.

spelter [spéltœ(r)], *s.* cinc del comercio; peltre.

Spencerian [spensíriąn], *a.* (fil.) spenceriano, de Spencer.—**Spencerism** [spénsœrizm], *s.* spencerismo, filosofía de Spencer.

spend [spénd]. **I.** *va.* (*pret.* y *pp.* SPENT) gastar, expender; consumir, agotar; pasar, emplear (tiempo, etc.).—**to s. a mast,** (mar.) perder un palo. **II.** *vn.* gastar dinero, hacer gastos; gastarse, consumirse; (ict.) echar o poner huevas (los peces), frezar, desovar.

spender [-œ(r)], *s.* gastador.

spendthrift [-θrift], *s.* pródigo, manirroto, despilfarrador, derrochador, malgastador.

Spenserian [spensíriąn], *a.* (poét.) spenseriano, de Spenser.

spent [spent]. **I.** *pret.* y *pp.* de TO SPEND. **II.** *a.* agotado, rendido.—**s. ball, s. bullet,** bala fría o cansada.

sperm [spœrm], *s.* (biol.) esperma, semen, simiente, *f.;* esperma de ballena; aceite de ballena.

—s. oil, cetina, aceite de ballena.—s. sac, (anat., zool.) vesícula seminal.—s. whale, (zool.) cachalote.

spermaceti [-əsɛ́tiˌ], s. espermaceti o esperma de ballena.—s. oil, aceite de esperma.

spermary [-əriˌ], s. (anat., zool.) glándula espermática; testículo.

spermatheca [-əθíkəˌ], s. (zool.) vesícula seminal.

spermatic(al [-ǽtikˌ(əlˌ], a. (anat., zool.) espermático.—s. cord, cordón espermático.—s. duct, espermiducto, conductos deferente y eyaculador juntos.

spermatocyst [spə́rmətosiˌst], s. (zool.) vesícula seminal.—spermatocyte [-saiˌt], s. (biol.) espermatocito, célula generatriz de células espermáticas o espermatozoos.

spermatogenesis [-dʒénisiˌs], s. (biol.) espermatogenia, espermatogénesis, desarrollo de los espermatozoides.

sperm(at)ology [-(ətˌ)álodʒiˌ], s. (biol., bot.) espermatología.

Spermatophyta [-táfitəˌ], s. pl. plantas que producen semillas.—spermatophyte [-tofaiˌt], s. planta que produce semillas.

spermatorrhœa [-toríəˌ], s. (med.) espermatorrea.

spermatozoon [-tozóuˌan], s. (biol.) espermatozoo, espermatozoide, zoospermo.

spew [spiˌú], va. y vn. vomitar, arrojar.

spewer [-œ(r)ˌ], s. el que vomita.

spewing [-iŋ], s. vómito; espadañada.

sphacelate [sfǽselejt]. I. va. y vn. (med.) esfacelar(se), gangrenarse, mortificar(se). II. a. esfacelado, gangrenoso, necrosado; (bot.) marchito.

sphacelus [-ʌs], s. (med.) esfacelo.

sphagnous [sfǽgnʌs], a. (bot.) esfagníneo.

sphagnum [-nʌm], s. (bot.) esfagnínea.

sphalerite [sfǽlerajt], s. (min.) esfalerita, blenda.

sphenoid [sfínojd]. I. a. (anat.) esfenoidal. II. s. (hueso) esfenoides.

spheral [sfíɹəl], a. esférico, redondeado, simétrico; armonioso.

sphere [sfiˌr]. I. s. esfera, globo; orbe; astro; esfera o círculo de acción. II. va. colocar en una esfera; redondear; rodear, abarcar.

spheric [sférikˌ], a. celestial; exaltado; esférico.

spherical [-əlˌ], a. esférico, esferal, globular.

spherically [-liˌ], adv. esféricamente.

sphericalness [-əlnisˌ], sphericity [sfiɹísitiˌ], s. esfericidad.

spherics [sfériksˌ], s. (mat.) teoría o estudio de las propiedades de la esfera.

spheroid [sfíɹojdˌ], s. esferoide.

spheroidal [sfiɹójdəlˌ], a. esferoidal, esferoídico.

spherometer [sfiɹámetœ(r)ˌ], s. esferómetro.

spherule [sférulˌ], s. glóbulo.

sphincter [sfíŋktœ(r)ˌ], s. (anat.) esfínter.

sphinx [sfiŋksˌ], s. esfinge, f.; (ent.) esfinge (mariposa); persona misteriosa o enigmática.—s.-like, (ent.) esfíngido; (fig.) enigmático.

sphygmic [sfígmikˌ], a. (fisiol.) esfígmico; pulsátil.

sphygmograph [sfígmogræfˌ], s. esfigmógrafo.

sphygmomanometer [sfigmomənámetœ(r)ˌ], s. esfigmomanómetro, instrumento para medir la presión de la sangre arterial.

sphygmometer [sfigmámetœ(r)ˌ], s. esfigmómetro.

sphygmus [sfígmʌs], s. (fisiol.) pulso.

spical, spicat(ed [spáikˌəl, spáikejt(idˌ], a. (bot.) espigado, espiciforme; (orn.) espolonado.

spice [spáisˌ]. I. s. especia; (fig.) saborete, sainete, picante, interés; (poét.) aroma, m., fragancia.—pl. especiería, especias.—s. bag, churla, churlo.—s. box, s. dealer, especiero. II. va. (coc.) especiar, condimentar con especias; (fig.) dar gusto o picante a.

spicebush [-bušˌ], s. (bot.) benjuí.

spicery [-œriˌ], s. especiería, especias; picante.—spicily [-iliˌ], adv. de modo picante.—spiciness [-inisˌ], s. sabor de especias; carácter picante, aromático, etc. V. SPICY.

spick-and-span [spíkˌ ənˌ spǽnˌ], a. flamante, muy bien arregladito, fresco, nuevecito.

spicula [spíkjuləˌ], s. (bot.) espiguita.

spicular [-(r)ˌ], a. agudo, puntiagudo.

spicule [spíkjulˌ], s. espiguilla o espina; (zool.) espícula; púa; (bot.) espiguita, espiguilla.—pl. agujas de la escarcha o hielo.

spicy [spáisiˌ], a. que contiene o sabe a especias; aromático, especiado; (fig.) sabroso, picante.

spider [spáidœ(r)ˌ], s. (zool.) araña, arácnido; (coc.) sartén; trébedes, f. pl., cazo con pies; cubo y rayos (de una rueda).—s. crab, (zool.) meya, cangrejo marino.—s.-like, parecido a una araña.—s. line, s. thread, hilo de tela de araña de un instrumento (ll. gen. hilo).—s. monkey, (zool.) aracnoide.—s. web, s.'s web, telaraña.

spiegel [spígelˌ], spiegeleisen [-aizenˌ], s. (metal.) fundición especular (apl. hoy gen. a la mangánica).

spiel [spilˌ]. I. s. (fam.) habla, arenga. II. vn. (fam.) arengar, hablar.

spiffy [spífiˌ], a. (fam.) elegante, bien parecido, de buen talante; excelente, magnífico.

spigot [spígotˌ], s. espiche, espita, canilla; tapón de espita; llave, f., grifo; macho, espiga (de un tubo).

spike [spáikˌ]. I. s. (bot.) espiga de grano; alcayata, escarpia, espigón, clavo largo, perno; (bot.) espiga de gramínea; alhucema, espliego. II. va. clavar con alcayatas, empernar, enclavijar; clavetear; anular, poner fin a; (mil.) clavar (un cañón).

spikelet [-litˌ], s. (bot.) espiguita, espiguilla; espiga secundaria.

spikenard [-nardˌ], s. (bot.) espicanardo, nardo; aceite vegetal.

spiker [spáikœ(r)ˌ], s. clavador.

spiky [spáikiˌ], a. erizado, puntiagudo; armado de púas; claveteado.

spile [spáilˌ]. I. va. horadar un barril y ponerle espita, tapón o espiche; clavar estacas o pilotes. II. s. pilote (estaca); tarugo; clavija, espiche; llave (f.) de sangrar el arce azucarero.

spiling [-iŋ], s. pilotaje.

spill [spílˌ]. I. s. astilla; clavija; mecha, pajuela, fósforo de cartón; (fam.) vuelco, caída (del caballo o de un vehículo); derramamiento. II. va. (pret. y pp. SPILLED o SPILT) derramar, verter; desparramar, esparcir; (fam.) divulgar; (fam.) volcar. III. vn. derramarse; rebosar.

spillway [-wej], s. (hidr.) aliviadero (de una presa); vertedero, bocacaz, m.

spin [spinˌ]. I. va. (pret. SPUN, ant. SPAN; pp. SPUN) hilar; (mec.) tornear; (con oud) alargar, prolongar; retorcer, hacer girar (una peonza).—to s. a yarn, hilar; contar un cuento increíble. II. vn. hilar; girar, rodar rápidamente; (aut., etc.) girar sin avanzar (las ruedas); bailar (una peonza). III. s. giro, vuelta; (fam.) paseo en coche o bicicleta; (aer.) barrena, picado muy pronunciado.

spinach [spínich o spínidʒ], s. (bot.) espinaca.

spinal [spáinəl], a. (anat.) espinal.—s. canal, conducto vertebral.—s. column, espina dorsal o columna vertebral.—s. cord, medula espinal.—s. curvature, (med.) cifosis, encorvadura anormal de la columna vertebral.

spindle [spíndl]. I. s. huso, broca; (mec.) gorrón; eje; carretel; árbol; mandril, torno, astil, aguja, peón; (mar.) pínola.—s.-legged, s.-shanked, zanquilargo, zanquivano.—s.-shaped, ahusado, fusiforme.—s. side, línea materna.—s. tree, (bot.) bonetero. II. va. ahusar, hacer fusiforme. III. vn. (bot.) espigar, crecer un tallo muy alto y delgado.

spindleful [-fulˌ], s. mazorca, husada.

spindlelegs [-legz], s. pl. = SPINDLESHANKS.

spindleshanks [-šæŋks], s. pl. zancas largas y flacas; (sing.) persona zanquivana.

spindling [spíndliŋ]. I. *a.* largo y delgado. II. *s.* persona o cosa larga y delgada.

spine [spaiŋ], *s.* (anat.) espinazo, raquis, *m.*, columna o espina dorsal; (bot.) espina; (zool.) púa (del puerco espín, etc.); (ict.) raspa, esquena.

spinel [spiɲél], *s.* (min.) cierto mineral cristalino de varios colores.—**s. ruby**, (joy.) espinela, balaj(e), alabandina.

spineless [spáiɲlis], *a.* invertebrado (literal y fig.); pusilánime; sin espinazo, sin energía, sin nervio; servil.

spinet [spíɲit], *s.* (mús.) espineta.

spiniferous [spaiɲíferas], *a.* espíneo, espinoso.

spinnaker [spíɲkœ(r)], *s.* (mar.) vela grande triangular o en forma de foque para yates de regata.

spinner [spíɲœ(r)], *s.* hilador, hilandero; hiladora, máquina de hilar; mosca, cuchara u otro cebo artificial para la pesca. *V.* SPOON.

spinneret [-et], *s.* órgano hilandero de las arañas y gusanos de seda, glándula de la seda.

spinning [spíɲiŋ]. I. *s.* hilandería, arte de hilar; filatura; (aut.) rotación estacionaria de las ruedas. II. *a.* de hilar, hilador.—**s. frame**, hiladora continua de anillo.—**s. gland**, glándula hilandera o de la seda (del gusano o araña).—**s. lathe**, torno de ahuecar metal en lámina.—**s. machine, s. jenny**, hiladora, máquina de hilar; (elec.) máquina para poner aislamiento al alambre.—**s. mill**, hilandería (fábrica).—**s. top**, trompo, peonza.—**s. wheel**, torno de hilar.

spinose [spáiɲous], *a.* espinoso.

spinosity [spaiɲásiti], *s.* calidad de espinoso; dificultad, cosa espinosa, perplejidad, enredo.

spinous [spáiɲas], *a.* espinoso, espíneo.

Spinozism [spiɲóuzizm], *s.* (filos.) espinosismo. —**Spinozist** [-ist], *s.* y *a.* espinosista.

spinster [spíɲstœ(r)], *s.* solter(on)a; hilandera.—**spinsterhood** [-hud], *s.* soltería.

spiny [spáiɲi], *a.* espinoso; penoso, difícil.

spiracle [spáiɾakl], *s.* (zool.) espiráculo, respiradero de un insecto o cetáceo; ventosa.

Spiræa [spaiɾíā], *s.* (bot.) género de las espireas; (s.) espirea, reina de los prados.

spiral [spáiɾal]. I. *s.* espiral; (geom.) hélice, *f.;* (f. c.) curva de transición, curva de enlace entre una recta y una curva circular; (aer.) vuelo en espiral. II. *a.* espiral, helicoidal; en espiral; de caracol.—**s. stairs**, escalera en caracol. III. *va.* formar o torcer en espiral. IV. *vn.* tomar forma o curso espiral; (aer.) volar en espiral.

spirally [-i], *adv.* espiralmente.

spirant [spáiɾant], *s.* (fon.) consonante continua.

spire [spaiɾ]. I. *s.* (arq.) aguja, chapitel; (bot.) brizna de hierba; cúspide, *f.*, cima, ápice; espira, espiral, caracol. II. *vn.* rematar en punta; (bot.) germinar.

spirillum [spaiɾíłʌm], *s.* (biol.) espirilo, bacteria espiral.

spirit [spírit]. I. *s.* espíritu; alma, ánima; aparecido, sombra, espectro; inclinación, vocación; humor, temple; intención; ánimo, aliento, brío, energía, denuedo, valor, arresto; espíritu de vino, alcohol; (fam.) espíritu; extracto, tintura; (ten. y tint.) solución usada como mordente.— *pl.* espíritus, vapores; licores espirit(u)osos; humor (estado del ánimo).—**the S.**, Dios; el Espíritu Santo. *V.* HOLY.—**s. lamp**, lámpara de alcohol.—**s. level**, nivel de burbuja.—**s. of salt**, espíritu de sal, ácido clorhídrico o muriático.—**s. o spirits, of wine**, espíritu de vino, alcohol.—**s. rapping**, (entre espiritistas) comunicación con los espíritus por medio de golpecitos o toques sobre una mesa.—**spirits of turpentine**, aceite de trementina, aguarrás. —**s. varnish**, barniz (*m.*) de alcohol.—**in a friendly s.**, de una manera amistosa.—**in a s. of friendship**, con ánimo amistoso, movido por un sentimiento de amistad. II. *va.* (con *away*) arrebatar, llevarse; alentar, animar.

spirited [-id], *a.* vivo, brioso; espiritoso, varonil, animoso.—**s. horse**, caballo fogoso.

spiritedly [-li], *adv.* animosamente, briosamente. —**spiritedness** [-nis], *s.* calor, vigor, energía; ardor; corazón, valor.

spiritism [-izm], *s.* espiritismo.—**spiritist** [-ist], *s.* espiritista.

spiritless [-lis], *a.* abatido, amilanado; insípido; exánime, muerto.—**spiritlessly** [-li], *adv.* sin vigor, sin espíritu.—**spiritlessness** [-nis], *s.* abatimiento, amilanamiento; falta de vigor.

spiritual [spírichụal]. I. *a.* espiritual; mental, intelectual; santo, puro; místico; eclesiástico; piadoso, religioso; (fil.) espiritualista.—**s. director**, (igl.) director o padre espiritual.—**s. father**, (igl.) confesor.—**s. seance**, sesión espiritista. II. *s.* eclesiástico; canto religioso de los negros del sur de los E. U.—*pl.* asuntos eclesiásticos.

spiritualism [-izm], *s.* espiritismo; (filos.) espiritualismo.—**spiritualist** [-ist], *s.*, **spiritualistic** [-istik], *a.* espiritista; (filos.) espiritualista.

spirituality [-áliti], *s.* espiritualidad; (gen. *pl.*) bienes espirituales o eclesiásticos.

spiritualization [-izéiʃạn], *s.* espiritualización, acto de espiritualizar.—**spiritualize** [-aiz], *va.* espiritualizar.

spiritually [-i], *adv.* espiritualmente.

spirituous [spírichụas], *a.* espirit(u)oso, licoroso, destilado; embriagante, ardiente.—**s. liquors**, licores espirituosos, aguardientes.

spirituousness [-nis], *s.* calidad de espirituoso.

spirobacteria [spaiɾobœktíɾiā], *s. pl.* **de spiro-bacterium** [-Am], (biol.) espirilo, bacteria espiral.

spirochete [spáiɾokit], *s.* (biol.) espiroqueta o espiroqueto.

spirometer [spaiɾámetœ(r)], *s.* espirómetro.

spirt [spœrt], *va., vn.* y *s.* = SPURT.

spiry [spáiɾi], *a.* espiral, caracolado; piramidal, puntiagudo, terminado en punta.

spit [spit]. I. *a.* (*pret.* y *pp.* SPIT, SPAT) escupir; esputar; echar en ráfagas o gotas (nieve o lluvia); (*pret.* y *pp.* SPITTED) (coc.) espetar; ensartar. II. *vn.* escupir, salivar; chisporrotear. III. *s.* (coc.) asador, espetón; (geog.) lengua de tierra; banco de arena; saliva; salivazo, escupitajo; espuma de varios insectos.—**the s. and image**, o **the spitting image**, (fam.) el vivo retrato, la imagen viva.

spitball [-bɔl], *s.* pelotilla o bolita de papel mascado.

spite [spait]. I. *s.* rencor, despecho, ojeriza, encono, mala voluntad.—**(in) s. of**, a pesar de, a despecho de, no obstante.—**s. wall**, pared que por pique se levanta para obstruir la vista de un vecino. II. *va.* mostrar resentimiento, dar pique, mortificar.

spiteful [-ful], *a.* rencoroso; malicioso, malévolo. —**spitefully** [-i], *adv.* por despecho; con rencor, con tirria.—**spitefulness** [-nis], *s.* despecho; malevolencia, malicia, rencor.

spitfire [spítfair], *s.* fierabrás; mujer colérica.

spitter [spítœ(r)], *s.* (coc.) el que espeta; escupidor; (zool.) gamezno.

spitting [spítiŋ], *s.* escupidura, saliveo, salivación. —**no s.**, se prohíbe escupir.

spittle [spítl], *s.* saliva, salivazo, escupido.

spittoon [spitún], *s.* escupidera.

spitz [spits], *s.* (zool.) perro pomerano.

splanchnic [splǽŋkɲik], *a.* esplácnico; visceral.

splanchnology [-nálodʒi] *s.* (anat.) esplacnología.

splash [splǽʃ]. I. *va.* salpicar, rociar, enlodar; chapotear, humedecer. II. *vn.* chapotear, chapalear. III. *s.* salpicadura, rociada; chapoteo, chapaleo.—**s. lubrication**, (m. comb. int.) lubricación por salpicadura.

splashboard [-bɔrd], *s.* guardabarros, guardalodos, parafango, alero (del carruaje); alza (de una presa).

splashy [-į], *a.* cenagoso, lodoso, sucio; salpicado, manchado; (fam.) ostentoso, sensacional.

splatter [splǽtœ(r)]. **I.** *va.* y *vn.* chapotear, guachapear (fam.), chapalear. **II.** *s.* salpicadura, rociada; bulla. *V.* SPATTER y SPLASH.

splay [spléį]. **I.** *va.* (arq.) alfeizar; (carp.) achaflanar, descantear; (vet.) despaldar o despaldillar un caballo. **II.** *a.* extendido, desplegado, ancho; pesado. **III.** *s.* (arq.) alféizar, derrame; (carp.) chaflán, bisel.

splayfoot(ed [-fųt(įd], *a.* que tiene los pies aplastados o achatados.

splaymouth [-mauθ], *a.* boquiancho.

spleen [splín], *s.* (anat.) bazo; rencor; mal humor; tristeza, esplín.—**spleenful** [-fųl], *a.* bilioso; irritable, adusto, irascible, enfadadizo.

spleenwort [-wœrt], *s.* (bot.) escolopendra, culantrillo.

spleeny [-į], *a.* melancólico; bilioso; irritable.

splendent [spléndẹnt], *a.* esplendente; resplandeciente; ilustre.

splendid [spléndįd], *a.* espléndido; esplendente, brillante, resplandeciente; ilustre, glorioso; excelente.—**splendidly** [-lį], *adv.* espléndidamente, brillantemente; excelentemente.

splendiferous [splɛndífẹrʌs], *a.* (fam.) espléndido; magnificentísimo.

splendor [spléndǫ(r)], *s.* esplendor; esplendidez; resplandor, refulgencia, brillantez, luz.

splenetic [splịnétįk], *a.* (anat.) esplénico; (med.) atrabiliario, (atra)bilioso; rencoroso; regañón.

splenic [splénįk], *a.* (anat.) esplénico.—**s. fever**, (med.) ántrax, fiebre esplénica.

splenitis [splịnáįtịs], *s.* (med.) esplenitis, inflamación del bazo.

splenius [splínįʌs], *s.* (anat.) esplenio.

splenotomy [splịnátomį], *s.* (cir.) esplenotomía.

splice [spláįs]. **I.** *va.* (mar.) ayustar; empalmar; empotrar, unir, juntar; (fam.) casar. **II.** *s.* junta; empalme; (mar.) ayuste; gaza.—**s. bar**, (f. c.) eclisa, brida, placa de empalme.—**s. grafting**, (agr.) injerto de cópula.

splicer [-œ(r)], *s.* empalmador; (mar.) pasador.

splicing [-įŋ], *s.* ayuste; empalme, empalmadura.—**s. fid**, (mar.) pasador.

spline [spláįn]. **I.** *s.* ranura para una junta de cuña; la cuña de tal junta; tira o faja flexible para dibujar curvas. **II.** *va.* ranurar; proveer de cuña.

splint [splínt]. **I.** *va.* (cir.) entablillar. **II.** *s.* tira plana y delgada; astilla; (cir.) tablilla; (vet.) sobrehueso.

splinter [-œ(r)]. **I.** *va.* astillar, hacer astillas; (cir.) entablillar. **II.** *vn.* hacerse pedazos, romperse en astillas. **III.** *s.* astilla; esquirla (de hueso); brizna; rancajo o astilla de madera clavada en la carne; astillazo.—**s. bar**, (carr.) balancín.

splintery [-œrį], *a.* que puede astillarse; astilloso, astillado.

split [splít]. **I.** *va.* (*pret.* y *pp.* SPLIT) hender, partir; rajar, cuartear, resquebrar, separar; cachar (un madero); dividir, repartir; (quím.) desdoblar; descomponer (a veces con **off** o **up**); desunir, desamistar.—**to s. hairs**, pararse en pelillos, andarse con quisquillas.—**to s. the difference**, partir la diferencia. **II.** *vn.* henderse, rajarse, romperse a lo largo, cuartearse, abrirse, resquebrajarse; estallar, reventar; dividirse; (fam.) disentir, estar en desacuerdo; (fam.) revelar secretos, ser traidor.—**to s. upon a rock**, estrellarse contra una roca.—**to s. with laughing**, reventar o desternillarse de risa. **III.** *s.* hendidura, grieta, raja, rendija, cuarteadura; división, cisma, *m.*; rompimiento. **IV.** *a.* hendido, partido, rajado, cuarteado; curado (pescado).—**s. ballot**, o **ticket**, papeleta de voto dividido, en que no se vota por todos los candidatos regulares de un partido.—**s. infinitive**, (gram.) infinitivo partido, en que se interponen una o más palabras entre *to* y el verbo (*to clearly see*, en vez de *to see clearly*).

—**s. key** = s. PIN.—**s. nut**, tuerca hendida o partida.—**s. personality**, esquizofrenia.—**s. pin**, chaveta hendida.—**s. pulley**, polea de dos piezas.—**s. ring**, (m. v.) anillo de empaquetadura (del émbolo).—**s. wood**, leña rajada o en astillas.

splitsaw [-sɔ], *s.* sierra para cortar madera longitudinalmente.

splitting [-įŋ]. **I.** *a.* hendedor; agudo; (fam.) rápido, vivo. **II.** *s.* acción de hender, etc.; (quím.) desdoblamiento, hidrólisis.

splotch [splách]. **I.** *va.* manchar, salpicar. **II.** *s.* mancha, borrón.

splotchy [-į], *a.* manchado, salpicado, emborronado.

splurge [splœrdž]. **I.** *vn.* (fam.) fachendear, papelonear, hacer una exhibición o esfuerzo ostentoso; permitirse ciertos gastos o placeres extraordinarios. **II.** *s.* (fam.) fachenda; boato, ostentación; lujo inusitado.

splutter [splʌ́tœ(r)]. **I.** *va.* y *vn.* balbucear, farfullar; chisporrotear. **II.** *s.* balbuceo; barullo; chisporroteo.

spoil [spóįl]. **I.** *va.* (*pp.* SPOILED, SPOILT) echar a perder; dar al traste con; estropear, desgraciar, estragar; deteriorar, dañar, inutilizar; viciar, corromper, podrir; malcriar, consentir, mimar, echar a perder con mimos (a los hijos); despojar, saquear.—**to s. one's fun**, aguarle a uno la fiesta. **II.** *vn.* inutilizarse, dañarse, echarse a perder; podrirse, pasarse; ir al saqueo, robar. **III.** *s.* saqueo, robo; despojo, botín.—*pl.* (E. U. pol.) gajes o beneficios de un cargo público; (fam.) turrón.—**s. system**, (pol.) sistema (*m.*) de premiar servicios de partido con empleos públicos.

spoilage [-įdž], *s.* desperdicio; material o producto que se daña durante o después de su elaboración.

spoiled [-d], *pp.* y *a.* dañado, inutilizado, echado a perder; podrido, rancio, pasado; vicioso, mimado, consentido (niño).

spoiler [-œ(r)], *s.* despojador, saqueador; ladrón; corruptor; consentidor.

spoilsman [-zmạn], *s.* (E. U. pol.) partidario del reparto de los empleos dentro del partido que gana en las elecciones.

spoke [spóųk]. **I.** *s.* rayo (de rueda); galga, retranca; escalón de escalera; (mar.) cabilla de la rueda del timón. **II.** *va.* (carr.) enrayar.

spoke, spoken [-n], *pret.* y *pp.* de *to* SPEAK.

spokeshave [-šẹįv], *s.* (carp.) rebajador de rayos; cuchilla de doble mango.

spokesman [-smạn], *s.* interlocutor; vocero, portavoz, *m.*, el que habla en nombre de otro; el que lleva la palabra.

spoliation [spoụlịéįšǫn], *s.* despojo, rapiña; (for.) expoliación.

spoliator [spóụlịẹįtǫ(r)], *s.* expoliador.

spondaic [spandéįįk], *a.* (poét.) espondaico.

spondee [spándi], *s.* (poét.) espondeo.

spondyl [spándįl], *s.* (anat.) espóndilo, vértebra.

sponge [spʌ́ndž]. **I.** *s.* (zool.) esponja; (arti.) lanada, escobillón; (coc.) masa; (fam.) mogollón, gorrista.—**s. cake**, bizcochuelo.—**s. tree**, (bot.) cují, aromo.—**to throw up**, o **in, the s.**, confesarse vencido. **II.** *va.* mojar o limpiar con esponja; lavar(se) con esponja; borrar; esponjar; (con **up**) absorber; (fam.) comer de gorra, chupar; sablear; sacar (dinero, etc.) por extorsión; (arti.) escobillonar. **III.** *vn.* embeberse; pescar o recoger esponjas; (fam.) vivir o comer de mogollón, darle un sablazo a uno.

sponger [-œ(r)], *s.* (fam.) gorrista, sablista, pegote.

sponginess [-inįs], *s.* esponjosidad.

sponging [-įŋ], *s.* acción de limpiar o lavar con esponja, de pescar esponjas, de sablear, etc. (*V.* SPONGE).

spongy [-į], **spongiose, spongious** [-joụs, -įʌs], *a.* esponjoso, esponjado; fofo; empapado; alburente (madera).

sponsion [spánsǫn], s. acto de salir fiador por otro; fianza u obligación formal.

sponson [spánsǫn], s. (mar.) barbeta lateral saliente de los buques de guerra.

sponsor [spánsǫ(r)]. **I.** s. fiador; persona responsable; padrino o madrina; defensor, apadrinador, fomentador, patrocinador, patrono; (rad.) patrono, quien costea un programa de radio que contiene un anuncio comercial. **II.** va. salir fiador de, ser responsable de; apadrinar, ser padrino de; promover, fomentar, patrocinar; (rad.) presentar, costear (un programa con anuncios comerciales).

sponsorship [-šip], s. patrocinio.

spontaneity [spantǫníti], s. espontaneidad; voluntariedad.

spontaneous [spantéiniʌs], a. espontáneo; voluntario; natural, indígena, silvestre.—**s. combustion**, combustión espontánea.—**s. generation**, (biol.) abiogénesis, generación espontánea.

spontaneously [-li], adv. espontáneamente.

spontaneousness [-nis], s. espontaneidad.

spontoon [spantún], s. (arm.) espontón.

spoof [spuf]. **I.** s. (fam.) timo, engaño. **II.** va. (fam.) timar, engañar, tomarle el pelo a uno.

spook [spúk], s. (fam.) fantasma, m., aparición.

spookish [-iš], **spooky** [-i], a. (fam.) que se parece a un fantasma; visitado por fantasmas; horripilante, de fantasmas, de espantos.

spool [spul]. **I.** s. carrete, canilla, carretel, bobina. —**s. cotton**, hilo de algodón en carreteles. **II.** va. ovillar, encanillar, devanar.

spoon [spún]. **I.** s. cuchara; anzuelo de cebo artificial (ll. t. **s. bait, s. hook**).—**s. chisel**, gubia. **II.** va. sacar con cuchara. **III.** vn. pescar con anzuelo de cebo artificial; (fam.) acariciarse, besarse.

spoonbill [-bil], s. (orn.) espátula.

spoondrift [-drift], s. (mar.) rocío del mar.

spoonful [-fųl], s. cucharada.

spoony [-i]. **I.** a. (fam.) amartelado, acaramelado; besador. **II.** s. galán meloso.

sporadic [sporédik], a. esporádico.

sporangium [sporéndžiʌm], s. (bot.) esporangio.

spore [spor], s. (bot. y biol.) espora, esporo; organismo diminuto, germen.—**s. case**, (biol.) esporangio.

sporidium [sporídiʌm], s. (bot.) esporidio.

sporiferous [sporífęrʌs], a. esporífero, que produce esporas.

sporocarp [spórokarp], s. esporocarpio.—**sporocyte** [-sajt], s. célula madre de las esporas.— **sporogenesis** [-džénisis], s. esporogénesis, reproducción por esporas; formación de esporas. —**sporogonium** [-góuniʌm], s. esporogonio.— **sporophore** [-for], s. esporóforo, rama u órgano productor de esporas.—**sporophyl** [-fil], s. hoja generadora de esporas.—**Sporozoa** [-zóuǎ], s. pl. (zool.) esporozoos.—**sporozoan** [-zóuǎn], s. y a. esporozoario.

sport [spórt]. **I.** s. deporte; juego, diversión, entretenimiento, pasatiempo; deportista; caballero, hidalgo, persona campechana o noble; burla, broma; hazmerreír; (biol.) individuo anormal; monstruo; (fam.) tahúr.—pl. deportismo.—**for o in s.**, de burlas, en broma.— **to make s. of**, burlarse de. **II.** va. (fam.) ostentar, hacer alarde de, lucir. **III.** vn. divertirse, jugar, holgar; bromear, chancearse; (biol.) variar espontáneamente del tipo normal. **IV.** a. deportivo. **V. SPORTS**, a.

sporting [-iŋ]. **I.** s. deportismo, deportes. **II.** a. deportivo; arriesgado.—**s. goods**, artículos deportivos (de juegos, caza, pesca, etc.).—**s. house**, garito, casa de juego; burdel.—**s. man**, deportista; (fam.) tahúr.—**s. woman**, deportista; (fam.) mujer de la vida airada.

sportive [-iv], a. juguetón, retozón; bromista.— **sportively** [-li], adv. de un modo retozón o festivo.—**sportiveness** [-nis], s. carácter retozón.

sports [spórts], a. deportivo; de o para deportes. —**s. clothes**, traje o prenda(s) de deporte o de sport.—**s. writer**, cronista deportivo.

sportsman [-mǎn], s. deportista, sujeto aficionado a los deportes, o que los practica.— **sportsmanlike** [-lajk], a. deportivo, característico de los deportes; caballeroso, leal.—**sportsmanship** [-šip], s. arte y pericia en el deporte; espíritu de equidad, juego limpio, proceder leal; nobleza, magnanimidad.

sportswoman [-wųmǎn], s. deportista (mujer).

sporty [spórti], a. deportivo; (fam.) vistoso, ostentoso, chillón; (fam.) alegre, relajado, disipado.

sporule [spórul], s. dim. (bot. y biol.) espórulo.

spot [spát]. **I.** s. sitio, lugar, paraje, puesto, punto; mancha, borrón, maca, tacha; palo (de baraja).—**s. remover**, sacamanchas.—**s. welding**, soldadura eléctrica por puntos.—**five-s., ten-s.**, etc., (fam.) billete de cinco, diez, etc., dólares; (baraja) cinco, diez, etc. (de un palo). —**in spots**, (fam.) en algunos respectos; aquí y allí.—**on o upon the s.**, ahí mismo, allí mismo, al punto, inmediatamente; puntual, despierto.—**to be on the s.**, (fam.) hallarse en un aprieto o en calzas prietas; estar en peligro de muerte; hallarse en la escena misma o el punto preciso donde ocurre algo. **II.** a. en existencia, listo para entregarse (dicho de mercancías).—**s. cash**, dinero contante; pago al contado. **III.** va. abigarrar, motear; macular; manchar; (fam.) marcar, señalar, distinguir, observar, notar; poner (una bola de billar) en posición. **IV.** vn. salir manchas; mancharse.

spotless [-lis], a. inmaculado, sin mancha, puro.

spotlessness [-nis], s. calidad de inmaculado.

spotlight [-lajt], s. luz concentrada; proyector, reflector móvil; lámpara proyectante de rayos concentrados, para iluminar objetos especiales. —**to be in the s.**, estar en posición conspicua, a vista del público.

spotted [-id], a. manchado, moteado, pintado; apulgarado (ú. de la ropa blanca); esquizado (mármol).—**s. fever**, fiebre, (med.) tabardillo pintado.

spotter [-œ(r)], s. vigilante secreto; observador.

spotty [-i], a. cubierto de manchas; desigual o irregular en carácter o calidad.

spousal [spáuzǎl]. **I.** a. nupcial, conyugal. **II.** s. pl. nupcias, bodas.

spouse [spáus], s. esposo, esposa, cónyuge, mf., consorte, mf.; (fam.) oíslo, media naranja.— **spouseless** [-lis], a. soltero o viudo; sin esposo.

spout [spaut]. **I.** s. caño, pitón, conducto, surtidor; canilla de tonel, espita; (arq.) gárgola, canalón; cuello de vasija; pico de cafetera o de tetera; chorro.—**to go up the s.**, (fam.) fracasar, irse todo en humo. **II.** va. y vn. arrojar o echar (un líquido); surgir, brotar, correr a chorro; soplar (la ballena); (fam.) recitar, declamar.

sprain [sprein]. **I.** va. torcer, producir un esguince. **II.** s. (med.) torcedura, torcimiento, desguince.

sprang [spræŋ], pret. de **TO SPRING**.

sprat [spræt], s. (ict.) sardineta.

sprawl [sprol]. **I.** va. y vn. tender o tenderse, caer o hacer caer o moverse con piernas o brazos extendidos; (agr.) desparramarse. **II.** s. acto de caer o tenderse abierto de brazos y piernas.

spray [spréi]. **I.** va. y vn. rociar, pulverizar un líquido. **II.** s. rociada, rocío; espuma del mar; salpicadura; ducha; rociador, pulverizador; líquido o mixtura de rociar; ramaje.

sprayer [-œ(r)], s. rociador, pulverizador.

spread [spréd]. **I.** va. (pret. y pp. **SPREAD**) tender, extender, abrir, desplegar, desarrollar, desenvolver; desparramar, esparcir; divulgar; difundir, diseminar, propalar; untar con, dar una capa de; poner a la vista; exhibir; poner (la mesa); preparar; apartar, separar; (impr.) espaciar.—**to s. abroad**, esparcir, divulgar, propalar.—**to s. one's self,** (fam.) echar el resto, darse tono. *V.* TO SPLURGE.—**to s. over,** cubrir de o untar con. **II.** *vn.* extenderse, desplegarse; esparcirse; difundirse; desarrollarse, propagarse, cundir; apartarse, separarse; poner la mesa. **III.** *a.* extendido; desparramado; (joy.) de poco brillo.—**s.-eagle,** (E. U. fig.) exageradamente patriótico (discurso).—**s.-eagleism,** oratoria patriotera, en que se extreman los alardes patrióticos. **IV.** *s.* extensión, amplitud; ancho; expansión; desarrollo; propagación, diseminación; cobertor de cama; tapete de mesa, mantel; (fam.) festín, banquete, comil(it)ona; (com.) diferencia; anuncio con encabezamiento a través de dos páginas; *v.* STRADDLE; (aer.) envergadura.

spreader [-œ(r)], *s.* esparcidor; propagador; divulgador; separador; untador; distribuidor.

spree [sprī]. **I.** *vn.* ir de parranda o jarana, correrla; emborracharse. **II.** *s.* borrachera; holgorio, parranda, jarana, juerga.

sprig [sprĭg]. **I.** *s.* (bot.) ramita, mugrón, renuevo, pimpollo; (fam.) vástago; (carp.) puntilla, hita, espiga. **II.** *va.* adornar con ramitas; formar ramajes; asegurar o clavar con puntillas, etc.

spriggy [-ĭ], *a.* lleno de ramitas.

sprightliness [sprájtlĭnĭs], *s.* viveza, despejo, vivacidad, desenvoltura.—**sprightly** [-lĭ], *a.* alegre, despejado, despierto, vivo, garboso.

spring [sprĭŋ]. **I.** *va.* (pret. SPRANG O SPRUNG; pp. SPRUNG) soltar (un resorte o muelle); sacar o presentar de golpe; hacer volar o saltar (una mina); torcer, combar, encorvar; rendir un palo o verga; (arq.) arrancar o vaciar (un arco); insertar o meter doblando o forzando; saltar por encima de; pasar saltando; ojear (la caza); asegurar o montar con resortes.—**to s. a leak,** empezar a salirse o a hacer agua (un buque, una vasija). **II.** *vn.* saltar, brincar; salir, brotar, manar (un líquido); dimanar, provenir, originarse; presentarse súbitamente; alabearse, combarse, torcerse; nacer, brotar, crecer; levantarse, elevarse; arrancar (un arco, etc.).— **to s. at,** abalanzarse o lanzarse sobre; saltar a.—**to s. away,** saltar a un lado; lanzarse de un salto.—**to s. back,** saltar hacia atrás; volver a su estado anterior bajo la acción de un resorte; recular.—**to s. forth,** brotar, crecer; salir; lanzarse, precipitarse.—**to s. forward,** abalanzarse, arrojarse, dispararse.—**to s. up,** nacer, brotar, crecer, desarrollarse; salir a luz, presentarse a la vista; subir, engrandecerse.—**to s. upon** = TO S. AT. **III.** *s.* (mec.) muelle, resorte; (carr.) ballesta; elasticidad, fuerza elástica; blandura o suavidad elástica; salto, brinco, corcovo, bote; vuelta a su posición anterior; motivo, móvil; primavera (estación del año); fuente, *f.,* manantial; origen, nacimiento; surtidor; alabeo, combadura. **IV.** *a.* primaveral, vernal, de primavera; de manantial; de resorte; para resortes. **—s. back,** (enc.) lomo plegado (de un libro de cuentas, etc.).—**s. balance,** balanza de resorte.—**s. catch,** fiador de resorte.—**s. coil,** resorte espiral.—**s. gun,** pistola automática con ladrones, disparada por un resorte.—**s. latch,** s. lock, picaporte, cerradura de golpe.—**s. line,** (arq.) arranque, imposta (de un arco).—**s. mattress,** colchón de muelles.—**s. nut,** piñón.—**s. of action,** móvil, motivo determinante de la voluntad.—**s. steel,** acero de (para) resortes.—**s. tide,** aguas vivas. **—s. valve,** válvula de resorte.—**s. water,** agua de manantial.

springboard [-bɔrd], *s.* trampolín.

springbok [-bak], *s.* (zool.) gacela del Cabo.

springe [sprĭndž], *s.* lazo, trampa (caza).

springer [sprĭŋœ(r)], *s.* saltador, brincador; (arq.) imposta; sillar de arranque; perro ojeador.

springhalt [sprĭŋhɔlt], *s.* (vet.) cojera de caballo.

springiness [sprĭŋĭnĭs], *s.* elasticidad, resorte, fuerza elástica.

springing [sprĭŋĭŋ]. **I.** *s.* acción del verbo TO SPRING; (bot.) retoño, tallo; (arq.) línea de arranque. **II.** *pa.* de TO SPRING.—**s. line** = SPRING LINE.—**s. wall,** (arq.) pared de arranque (de un arco).

springtide [sprĭŋtajd], **springtime** [-tajm], *s.* primavera.

springy [sprĭŋĭ], *a.* muelle, elástico; lleno de manantiales; esponjoso.

sprinkle [sprĭŋkl]. **I.** *va.* asperjar, rociar, esparcir; regar, desparramar; salpicar, polvorear o despolvorear; bautizar rociando. **II.** *vn.* (*impers.*) lloviznar (*it is sprinkling,* está lloviznando). **III.** *s.* rocío, rociada; una pizca, un poco.

sprinkler [-klœ(r)], *s.* rociador, irrigador, regadera; (igl.) aspersorio, hisopo; carricuba, carro de riego.

sprinkling [-klĭŋ]. **I.** *s.* rociada, rociadura, aspersión; una pizca, un poco.—**s. of rain,** llovizna, cernidillo. **II.** *a.* de rociar, de riego.

sprint [sprĭnt]. **I.** *vn.* correr a toda carrera. **II.** *s.* corrida, carrera corta y rápida, cosetada.

sprinter [-œ(r)], *s.* (dep.) el que corre velozmente en carreras cortas.

sprit [sprĭt], *s.* (mar.) botavara.

sprite [sprajt], *s.* duende, trasgo; hada.

spritsail [sprĭtsejl], *s.* (mar.) cebadera.

sprocket [sprákĭt], *s.* (mec.) diente de rueda de cadena.—**s. gear,** engranaje de rueda y cadena. **—s. wheel,** rueda dentada para cadena, piñón.

sprout [sprayt]. **I.** *va.* hacer germinar o brotar; quitar los botones o vástagos. **II.** *vn.* (bot.) brotar o retoñar, echar botones o renuevos; crecer; ramificarse. **III.** *s.* (bot.) renuevo, retoño, tallo, plantón, grillo, serpollo, botón.—*pl.* bretones repolludos.—**a course of sprouts,** (fam.) disciplina severa.

spruce [sprūs]. **I.** *a.* garboso, apuesto, majo, pulido. **II.** *s.* (bot.) abeto, pícea.—**s. beer,** cerveza de abeto.—**s. fir,** (bot.) pinabete. **III.** *va.* y *vn.* (gen. con **up**) vestir(se) con esmero; poner(se) majo.

sprucely [-lĭ], *adv.* garbosamente.

spruceness [-njs], *s.* majeza, garbo.

sprue [sprū], *s.* (fund.) mazarota; bebedero de molde; (med.) psilosis.

sprung [sprʌŋ], *pret.* y *pp.* de TO SPRING.—**s. mast,** (mar.) palo rendido.

spry [sprájī], *a.* vivo, listo, ágil, activo.

spryness [-njs], *s.* agilidad.

spud [spʌd], *s.* (agr.) laya, escarda; escoplo; (cir.) limpiaojos; (fam.) patata, papa.

spue [spjū], *va.* y *vn.* = SPEW.

spume [spjum]. **I.** *s.* espuma; espumarajo. **II.** *vn.* espumar, hacer espuma.

spumescent [spjumésønt], *a.* espumescente.

spumous, spumy [spjúmʌs, spjúmĭ], *a.* espumoso, espumajoso, espumante.

spun [spʌn], *pret.* y *pp.* de TO SPIN.—**s. glass,** lana de vidrio.—**s.-out,** prolongado, prolijo.— **s. sugar,** nieve, *f.*—**s. work,** filigrana.—**s. yarn,** (mar.) meollar.

spunk [spʌŋk], *s.* yesca; (fam.) corazón, genio (violento); coraje, valor; enojo.

spunky [-ĭ], *a.* (fam.) vivo; valiente; enfadadizo, enojadizo.

spur [spœr]. **I.** *s.* espuela, acicate; aguijón, incentivo, estímulo; excitación; corvejón, espolón o navaja del gallo; uña puntiaguda; pincho; (geog.) estribación, estribo; (arq.) riostra, contrafuerte, botarel, machón, puntal.—**s. gear,** (mec.) rueda dentada; engranaje de ruedas dentadas (ll. t. s. gearing).—**s. stone,** guardacantón, recantón.—**s. track,** (f. c.) ramal corto. **—s. wheel** = S. GEAR.—**on the s. of the moment,** impulsivamente, sin pensarlo. **II.** *va.* y *vn.* espolear, acicatear, aguijonear, picar con la espuela; incitar, estimular; calzar o ponerse las espuelas; apretar el paso.—**to s. on,** espolear, aguijar, estimular.

spurgall [-gɔl]. **I.** *va.* herir con la espuela. **II.** *s.* espoleadura.

spurge [spœrdź], *s.* (bot.) lechetrezna, titímalo, tártago.—**s. laurel,** lauréola.

spurious [spiúriʌs], *a.* espurio; bastardo, ilegítimo; apócrifo; (biol.) falso; (bot.) aparente.—**spuriously** [-li], *adv.* espuriamente.—**spuriousness** [-niʂ], *s.* falsedad, bastardía, calidad de espurio.

spurn [spœrn], *va.* y *vn.* despreciar, menospreciar; rechazar a puntapiés; cocear.

spurnwater [-wotœ(r)], *s.* (mar.) guardaaguas.

spurred [spœrd], *a.* con espuelas; con espolones.—**s. rye,** centeno atizonado o afectado de cornezuelo.

spurrer [spœrœ(r)], *s.* el que o lo que espolea.

spurrier [spœrjœ(r)], *s.* el que hace espuelas.

spurry [spœri], *s.* (bot.) espérgula.

spurt [spœrt]. **I.** *va.* y *vn.* arrojar o salir en chorro o chorros; espurrear; brotar, surgir; hacer un esfuerzo supremo. **II.** *s.* chorro; arrebato (de ira, etc.); esfuerzo supremo; rato, momento.

sputter [spátœ(r)]. **I.** *va.* y *vn.* espurrear; chisporrotear; farfullar, barbotar. **II.** *s.* chisporroteo; chispeo de saliva; farfulla.—**sputterer** [-œ(r)], *s.* escupidor, farfullador; el que chisporrotea saliva.

sputum [spiútʌm], *s.* saliva; (med.) esputo.

spy [spái]. **I.** *s.* espía, *mf.*, espión, *m.*—**s. hole,** atisbadero. **II.** *va.* atisbar, divisar, columbrar; espiar, observar; (con **out**) explorar, reconocer (un país). **III.** *vn.* espiar, atalayar; ser espía; meterse secretamente a averiguar.

spyboat [-bout], *s.* barco explorador.

spyglass [-glæs], *s.* anteojo de larga vista.

squab [skwáb]. **I.** *a.* acabado de salir de la cáscara; implume; rechoncho o regordete. **II.** *s.* (orn.) pichón; persona gordiflona; cojín, canapé, otomana. **III.** *adv.* (fam.) de golpe y porrazo.

squabbish [-iʂ], **squabby** [-i], *a.* rechoncho.

squabble [skwábl]. **I.** *va.* (impr.) empastelar. **II.** *vn.* reñir, disputar. **III.** *s.* pendencia, riña, disputa, contienda, trifulca.

squabbler [skwáblœ(r)], *s.* pendenciero.

squad [skwad], *s.* (mil.) escuadra, patrulla, pelotón; partida; equipo.

squadron [skwádrɔn], *s.* (mar.) escuadra, armada, flota; (mil.) escuadrón; cuadro; soldados en formación; (aer.) escuadrilla aérea.

squalid [skwálid], *a.* escuálido.—**squalidness** [-niʂ], **squalidity** [skwaliditi], *s.* = SQUALOR.

squall [skwól]. **I.** *va.* y *vn.* chillar, berrear. **II.** *v. impers.* haber borrasca. **III.** *s.* chillido, berrido; borrasca; (mar.) racha, turbonada, chubasco.

squaller [-œ(r)], *s.* chillador, chillón.

squally [-i], *a.* chubascoso; borrascoso.

squalor [skwálɔ(r)], *s.* escualidez, escualor, suciedad, porquería, mugre, *f.*

squama [skwéjmʌ], *s.* (biol.) escama; laminilla delgada de hueso.—**squamaceous** [skwaméiʂʌs], **squamate** [skwéjmeit], *a.* escamoso; lamelar.—**squamation** [skwaméjʂɔn], *s.* carácter escamoso; disposición de las escamas.

squander [skwándœ(r)], *va.* y *vn.* malgastar, malrotar, despilfarrar, derrochar, dilapidar, desparramar, disipar.—**squanderer** [-œ(r)], *s.* derrochador, disipador, manirroto, malbaratador, malgastador.

square [skwér]. **I.** *a.* cuadrado; en cuadro (*two square feet*, dos pies cuadrados; *two feet square*, dos pies en cuadro); rectangular; a escuadra; perfecto, exacto, justo, cabal; íntegro, honrado, equitativo; (fam.) completo, abundante (*square meal*, comida completa); (com.) saldado, en paz; (mar.) en cruz; (mat.) elevado al cuadrado.—**s. bracket,** (impr.) paréntesis angular.—**s. dance,** contradanza, baile de figuras.—**s. deal, s. dealing,** (fam.) buena fe, equidad, justicia, honradez, juego limpio.—**s. iron,** hierro cuadradillo.—**s. measure,** medida cuadrada o de superficie.—**s. piano,** piano de mesa.—**s. root,**

(mat.) raíz cuadrada.—**s. rigged,** (mar.) aparejo de cruzamen.—**s. screw,** tornillo de filete cuadrado.—**s. shooter,** (fam.) persona honrada.—**s. timber,** madero escuadrado.—**to get s. with,** (fam.) vengarse o desquitarse de, hacérselas pagar a. **II.** *s.* cuadrado; cuadro; (mat.) cuadrado, segunda potencia; plaza (de pueblo o ciudad); cristal de ventana; casilla o escaque (de tablero de damas, etc.); (E. U.) manzana de casas; (dib.) escuadra, cartabón; (carp.) escuadra, codal; proporción debida, orden; exactitud; honradez, equidad; (mil.) cuadro.—**on the s.,** (fam.) honradamente, de buena fe; a escuadra.—**out of s.,** fuera de escuadra, no en ángulo recto o a escuadra. **III.** *va.* cuadrar, formar en cuadro; escuadrar; acodar (madera); (mat.) cuadrar, elevar al cuadrado; (geom.) reducir a un cuadrado equivalente; (b. a.) cuadricular; (carp.) esquinar, cuadrar, escuadrar; (com.) saldar, ajustar, arreglar (cuentas); pasar balance; ajustar, arreglar, justificar, conformar, poner de acuerdo; medir una superficie en metros, pies, etc., cuadrados; (mar.) bracear en cuadro.—**to s. one's self,** sincerarse, justificarse; dar satisfacción. **IV.** *vn.* estar en ángulo recto; cuadrar, encajar, conformarse, ajustarse, convenir, concordarse, estar de acuerdo; (con **off**) tomar una actitud pugilística.

squared [-d], *a.* cuadrado; escuadrado; (mat.) elevado al cuadrado; (dib.) cuadriculado (papel).—**s. stone,** (alb.) mampuesto, piedra toscamente labrada y escuadrada.—**s. timber,** madera escuadrada o esquinada.

squarely [-li], *adv.* en cuadro; a escuadra; de frente; honradamente, con toda equidad.

squareness [-niʂ], *s.* calidad de cuadrado; honradez, equidad, justicia.

squaring [-iŋ], *s.* cuadratura; escuadreo; escuadración; cuadriculación.—**s. of the circle,** cuadratura del círculo.—**s. shears,** cizallas de escuadrar.

squarrose, squarrous [skwárouʂ, -rʌs], *a.* (biol., bot.) áspero, escamoso.

squash [skwaʂ]. **I.** *s.* (bot.) calabaza (apl. gen. a la de cuello corvo); cosa blanda o inmatura; pulpa; aplastamiento, despachurramiento.—**s. beetle, s. borer, s. bug,** nombres de insectos norteamericanos que atacan la calabaza. **II.** *va.* aplastar, (fam.) despachurrar.

squat [skwát]. **I.** *vn.* agacharse, agazaparse, sentarse en cuclillas; establecerse en un local sin derecho. **II.** *a.* agachado, puesto en cuclillas; rechoncho, cachigordete, rehecho. **III.** *s.* posición del que está en cuclillas.—**squatter** [-œ(r)], *s.* advenedizo, intruso, colono usurpador.

squatty [-i], *a.* rechoncho, regordete.

squaw [skwo], *s.* india norteamericana.—**s. man,** hombre blanco casado con india.

squawk [skwok]. **I.** *vn.* graznar; (fam.) protestar o quejarse ruidosamente. **II.** *s.* graznido; (fam.) queja o protesta ruidosa.

squeak [skwik]. **I.** *vn.* chirriar, rechinar; (fam.) delatar. **II.** *s.* chillido, chirrido.—**to have a narrow s.,** (fam.) escapar en una tabla.

squeal [skwil]. **I.** *vn.* chillar, lanzar gritos agudos; (fam.) delatar. **II.** *s.* chillido, grito agudo.

squeamish [skwímiʂ], *a.* delicado, escrupuloso, remilgado; asqueado.—**squeamishly** [-li], *adv.* remilgadamente; con asco.—**squeamishness** [-niʂ], *s.* remilgo, escrúpulo; asco, náusea.

squeegee [skwídźi]. **I.** *s.* rodillo o escobilla de goma para restregar y secar superficies mojadas. **II.** *va.* restregar con *squeegee*.

squeeze [skwíz]. **I.** *va.* apretar, comprimir; estrechar; estrujar, exprimir, prensar; tupir, apretujar; acosar, agobiar; rebajar (jornales); (b. a.) recalcar.—**to s. in,** hacer entrar apretando.—**to s. out,** hacer salir, exprimir.—**to s. through,** forzar al través de.—**to s. to death,**

(fam.) matar a apretones, apretar hasta matar. **II.** *vn.* pasar, entrar o salir apretando.—**to s. in,** meterse por lugar apretado o ponerse en sitio apretado.—**to s. through,** pasar apretadamente a través de, abrirse paso por. **III.** *s.* apretadura, apretón; facsímile recalcado de una moneda, etc.

squeezer [-œ(r)], *s.* exprimidera.

squelch [skwélch]. **I.** *va.* aplastar; sofocar; (fam.) hacer callar, paralizar (fig.), desconcertar. **II.** *vn.* ser vencido, desconcertado; chapotear.— **squelcher** [-œ(r)], *s.* (fam.) cosa, persona o respuesta desconcertante.

squib [skwíb]. **I.** *s.* suelto o articulejo satírico; (piro.) buscapiés, carretilla. **II.** *va.* y *vn.* atacar con sátiras o pullas; soltar carretillas.

squid [skwíd], *s.* (zool.) calamar; cebo artificial.

squilgee [skwíldźi], *va.* y *s.* = SQUEEGEE.

squill [skwíl], *s.* (bot.) escila, cebolla albarrana; (zool.) esquila.

squilla [-ă], *s.* (zool.) esquila, camarón.

squinch [skwinch], *s.* (arq.) pechina.

squint [skwínt]. **I.** *s.* estrabismo; mirada bizca; mirada furtiva; tendencia indirecta. **II.** *va.* y *vn.* bizcar, bizquear, mirar bizco; mirar de través o soslayo.—**squint(-eyed)** [-ájd], *a.* bizco, bisojo, estrábico; avieso, torcido; ambiguo.—**squinting** [-iŋ], *s.* (med.) estrabismo.

squire [skwáir]. **I.** *s.* escudero; acompañante de una dama; (Ingl.) hacendado; (E. U.) alcalde, juez (*m.*) de paz. *V.* ESQUIRE. **II.** *va.* acompañar, escoltar (a una dama).

squirm [skwœrm]. **I.** *vn.* retorcerse, serpear, serpentear; trepar; (con **out**) salir de un aprieto con trabajo. **II.** *s.* retorcimiento.

squirrel [skwérel], *s.* (zool.) ardilla.

squirt [skwœrt]. **I.** *va.* y *vn.* (hacer) salir a chorros; espurrear; jeringar. **II.** *s.* chorretada, chisguete (fam.), chorro, jeringazo; (fam.) pisaverde.— **s. (gun),** jeringa.—**squirter** [-œ(r)], *s.* el que jeringa.

stab [stáb]. **I.** *va.* y *vn.* herir con arma blanca, dar de puñaladas. **II.** *s.* puñalada, estocada.

stabber [-œ(r)], *s.* heridor, apuñalador.

stabile [stéibil], *a.* fijo, sin moverse.

stability [stăbíliti], *s.* estabilidad; firmeza, consistencia, solidez; asiento.

stabilize [stéibilaiz], *va.* estabilizar.—**stabilizer** [-œ(r)], *s.* estabilizador.

stabilization [-izéišǫn], *s.* estabilización.

stable [stéibl]. **I.** *a.* estable, firme, fijo, sólido. **II.** *s.* establo, caballeriza, cuadra; caballos de carrera de un particular. **III.** *va.* y *vn.* poner o estar colocado en establo.

stableboy [-bǫi], **stableman** [-măn], *s.* establero, mozo de cuadra o de caballos.

stableness [-nǫs], *s.* estabilidad.

stabling [stéibliŋ], *s.* estabulación.

staccato [stăkátou], *a.* incisivo; (mús.) staccato.

stack [stǎk]. **I.** *s.* niara, rima o rimero, pila, facina o hacina, montón; (mil.) pabellón de fusiles; cañón de chimenea; (fam.) copia, abundancia. **II.** *va.* hacinar, apilar, amontonar; (mil.) poner las armas en pabellón.

stactometer [stǎktámetœ(r)], *s.* (farm.) cuentagotas.

stadia [stéidiă], *s. pl.* de STADIUM; (sing., top.) taquímetro, estadia.—**s. hairs** o **s. wires.**— **s. rod,** mira taquimétrica.—**s. surveying,** taquimetría.—**s. transit,** taquímetro.—**s. wires,** hilos taquimétricos.

stadiometer [steidiámetœ(r)], *s.* estadiómetro, instrumento para medir líneas en un dibujo.

stadium [stéidiᴧm], *s.* estadio; carrera (lugar para correr); grado de progreso o adelantamiento.

stad(t)holder [stáethouldœ(r)], *s.* estatúder.

staff [stáf]. **I.** *s.* báculo, palo, cayado; apoyo, sostén, alivio, arrimo; palo, porra, garrote; vara, bastón de mando; percha, pértiga; vara de medir; (top.) jalón de mira; asta (de lanza,

pica, bandera, etc.); (mil.) estado mayor, plana mayor; personal; facultad; junta, cuerpo (*editorial* **staff**, redacción, cuerpo de redactores); (arq. y b. a.) cartón piedra; (constr.) yeso mezclado con fibra, cemento, etc., usado en construcciones temporales; (mús.) pentagrama, *m.*; (cir.) guía o sonda acanalada; (igl.) báculo pastoral.—**s. officer,** oficial de estado mayor. **II.** *va.* proveer de personal, funcionarios u oficiales.

stag [stǎg], *s.* (zool.) ciervo, venado; (fam.) hombre, varón.—**s. beetle,** (ent.) ciervo volante.—**s. party,** (fam.) tertulia de hombres solos.

stage [stéidź]. **I.** *s.* (teat.) escenario, escena, tablas; por extensión, teatro (arte y profesión); escena de acción; tablado, entarimado, plataforma, estrado; andamio; parada, descansadero; etapa, jornada; grado, estado; período (de una enfermedad); platina (de microscopio); diligencia, ómnibus; (arq.) escalón, paso de escalera; (rad.) elemento, unidad; (mec.) grado (de una turbina de vapor, etc.).—**s. driver,** mayoral; cochero de ómnibus.—**s. effects,** efectos escénicos.—**s. forceps,** pinzas para microscopio.—**s. fright,** pánico oratorio; nerviosidad al presentarse en público.—**s. hand,** metesillas, tramoyista.—**s. manager,** (teat.) director de escena.—**s. micrometer,** micrómetro del portaobjetos.—**s. name,** nombre de teatro, nombre adoptado por un actor en su profesión.—**s. of growth,** grado de crecimiento. —**s. scenery** o **setting,** decoración, decorado. —**s.-struck,** fascinado por el teatro; que se muere por hacerse actor o actriz.—**s. whisper,** cuchicheo destinado al oído de los espectadores. —**by short stages,** a pequeñas etapas, a cortas jornadas. **II.** *va.* preparar; ejecutar, efectuar; (teat.) poner en escena, montar, escenificar; (re)presentar. **III.** *vn.* viajar en diligencia.

stagecoach [-kouch], *s.* diligencia (vehículo).

stagecraft [-kræft], *s.* arte teatral; arte de escribir dramas o ponerlos en escena.

stager [-œ(r)], *s.* caballo de diligencia; (gen. con **old**) persona de gran experiencia en la vida.

stagger [stǎgœ(r)]. **I.** *vn.* hacer eses, tambalear, bambolear; vacilar, titubear. **II.** *va.* causar vértigos o vahídos; asustar o azarar; hacer vacilar; hacer tambalear; disponer o arreglar (plantas, remaches, etc.) al tresbolillo; alternar; espaciar (horas del trabajo, etc.); escalonar (escobillas en una dínamo, planos en un biplano). **III.** *s.* tambaleo, vacilación; (aer.) decalaje.—**s. wires,** (aer.) alambres entre los planos de un avión, paralelos al plano de simetría.

staggered [-d], *a.* al tresbolillo (remachado, plantas, etc.); escalonado, de planos o alas escalonados (avión).

staggering [-iŋ]. **I.** *a.* tambaleante. **II.** *s.* = STAGGER.

staggers [-z], *s.* (vet.) vértigo de los caballos; modorra; vahído.

staghound [stéghaund], *s.* sabueso.

staging [stéidźiŋ], *s.* andamiaje; tráfico en diligencias; (teat.) representación, puesta en escena.

Stagirite [stédźirait], *s.* y *a.* estagirita, *mf.*

stagnancy [stǎgnǫnsi], *s.* estancación, estancamiento, paralización.—**stagnant** [-ǫnt], *a.* estancado.—**stagnate** [-eit], *vn.* estancarse, estacionarse.—**stagnation** [-éišǫn], *s.* = STAGNANCY.

stagy [stéidźi], *a.* teatral.

staid [stéid]. **I.** *pret.* y *pp.* de TO STAY. **II.** *a.* grave, serio, sosegado, formal, sentado, juicioso. —**staidly** [-li], *adv.* juiciosamente.—**staidness** [-nǫs], *s.* juicio, seriedad.

stain [stéin]. **I.** *va.* y *vn.* manchar, macular; colorar, teñir; tiznar; descolorar; ensuciar; mancillar, desdorar; impregnar de materia colorante.—**stained glass,** vidrio de color.

II. *s.* mancha, mácula; descoloramiento, descoloración; tinte, tintura; solución colorante; borrón, estigma, *m.*

stainer [-œ(r)], *s.* el o lo que mancha, tiñe, etc.; tintorero; ensuciador.

stainless [-ljs], *a.* limpio; inmaculado, acendrado; que no se mancha.—**s. steel,** acero inoxidable.

stair [stér], *s.* escalón, peldaño.—*pl.* escalera.—**s. carpet,** alfombra de escalera.—**s. rod,** varilla para alfombra de escalera.—**s. well,** caja de escalera.

staircase [-kejs], **stairway** [-wej], *s.* escalera; escalinata (exterior).

stake [stejk]. **I.** *s.* estaca; piquete; (agr.) rodrigón; (fig.) hoguera, pira; (carr.) telero; (metal.) tas, bigorneta; en los juegos, apuesta, posta o puesta; azar, riesgo; peligro, contingencia; premio (de contienda); (com.) interés, ganancia o pérdida contingente.—**s. boat,** bote anclado para marcar la dirección y distancias en las regatas.—**at s.,** en juego, envuelto, comprometido, en peligro (*his honor was at stake,* su honor estaba comprometido, le iba en ello el honor). **II.** *va.* estacar; empalar (como suplicio); en los juegos, poner, jugar, apostar; aventurar, arriesgar, exponer; (fam.) establecer a uno en los negocios, etc.; darle o prestarle dinero.—**to s. all,** jugar el todo por el todo, envidar el resto, aventurarlo todo.—**to s. off,** o **out,** (top.) demarcar con estacas.

stalactic(al [stalǽktjk(al], **stalactitic**]-tjtjk], *a.* estalactítico.

stalactite [stalǽktajt], *s.* (geol.) estalactita.

stalagmite [stalǽgmajt], *s.* (geol.) estalagmita.

stalagmitic [-mítjk], *a.* estalagmítico.

stale [stéjl]. **I.** *a.* añejo, viejo; rancio, pasado; viciado (el aire); gastado, antiguado, trillado.—**s. beer,** cerveza pasada.—**s. bread,** pan viejo, duro o seco.—**s. news,** noticia fiambre.—**s. olive,** aceituna zapatera.—**s. wine,** vino picado. **II.** *va.* añejar, enranciar. **III.** *vn.* añejarse, enranciarse, picarse; orinar (el ganado).

stalemate [-mejt]. **I.** *s.* mate ahogado (en el ajedrez); empate; atolladero, dificultad insuperable; estancación. **II.** *va.* dar mate ahogado a; estancar, paralizar.

staleness [-njs], *s.* ranciedad, rancidez, vejez.

stalk [stók]. **I.** *va.* cazar al acecho. **II.** *vn.* andar con paso majestuoso, taconear; acabestrillar, cazar con buey de cabestrillo u ocultándose de otro modo.—**stalking-horse,** [-jŋ hɔrs], boezuelo para la caza; máscara, disfraz, *m.* **III.** *s.* (bot.) tallo, caña, agramiza, cabillo, pedúnculo, pecíolo, rabillo; troncho de hortalizas; raspa de uva; pie (*m.*) de copa; paso majestuoso, taconeo.—**stalky** [-j], *a.* tronchudo.

stall [stɔl]. **I.** *s.* pesebre, casilla de establo; puesto, parada, tabanco; tabla (de carnicero); (teat.) luneta o butaca; (igl.) sitial de coro; (min.) galería, tajo de explotación; (aer.) caída de la velocidad de un avión más allá de la velocidad mínima de vuelo.—**s.-fed,** cebado en establo. **II.** *va.* encerrar o meter en cuadra o establo; poner puestos o casillas; atascar, atollar; poner obstáculos; (con **off**) eludir, evitar, tener a raya. **III.** *vn.* estar atascado, atollado; (aut.) pararse, ahogarse (el motor); (aer.) bajar de la velocidad mínima de vuelo; hacerse ingobernable a causa de esta caída.—**to s. for time,** (fam.) dar largas a un asunto, hacer demora innecesaria para ganar tiempo o para no hacer una cosa.

stallion [stǽljɔn], *s.* caballo padre o semental.

stalwart [stólwart], *a.* y *s.* (sujeto) fornido, forzudo, membrudo; valiente; (pol.) leal, fiel, firme.

stamen [stéjmen], *s.* (*pl.* STAMENS, rara vez STAMINA) (bot.) estambre.

stamina [stǽmjnǝ], *s.* nervio, fibra, vigor; aguante.—**staminal** [-l], *a.* (bot.) estaminal; vital, esencial.

staminate [stǽmjnejt], *a.* (bot.) estaminífero.

stamineous [stǝmínjɐs], *a.* (bot.) estamíneo, estaminoso.

stammer [stǽmœ(r)]. **I.** *va.* y *vn.* tartamudear; balbucear. **II.** *s.* tartamudeo; balbuceo.

stammerer [-œ(r)], *s.* tartamudo, gago.

stamp [stæmp]. **I.** *va.* estampar; marcar, señalar; imprimir; estampillar; sellar; timbrar (papel, cartas); fijar el sello de correo; acuñar (monedas y medallas); patear, golpear con los pies; (min.) triturar, quebrantar, bocartear; apisonar; (fig.) marcar, infamar, estigmatizar.—**to s. out,** extirpar, suprimir. **II.** *vn.* patear, patalear; piafar (el caballo). **III.** *s.* sello, estampilla (de correo); timbre; estampa, sigilación, impresión, marca; estampador, estampilla; cuño, troquel (de monedas, medallas, etc.); mano (*f.*) de mortero; (fig.) temple, suerte, *f.*, clase, *f.*; laya, calaña; (metal.) pisón, bocarte.—*pl.* stamps, timbres de impuesto; (fam.) dinero.—**S. Act,** (hist.) ley (*f.*) del timbre.—**s. duties,** derechos de papel sellado o del timbre.—**s. duty,** impuesto pagado en timbres puestos a ciertos artículos, timbres de contribución.—**s. mill,** (min.) molino de mineral, bocarte, molino de pisones.—**s. office,** oficina de timbres.

stamped [-t], *a.* estampado; sellado.—**s. envelope,** sobre con sello; cubierta de sello estampado.—**s. paper,** papel sellado o timbrado.—**s. weight,** peso marcado (por el contraste).

stampede [stæmpíd]. **I.** *va.* y *vn.* ahuyentar, espantar; huir con pavor; dispersarse en desorden; (pol.) obrar por común impulso, tomar de repente un acuerdo en una asamblea. **II.** *s.* (Am.) estampida; desbocada, huída con terror pánico; tropel; determinación repentina y unánime.

stamper [stǽmpœ(r)], *s.* estampador; impresor; martinete de fragua; pilón, punzón de forja; (metal.) bocarte, pisón; triturador de pólvora; mano (*f.*) de almirez.

stamping [-jŋ], *s.* timbrado, estampa, impresión, estampado; pataleo, pateo; trituración.—**s. machine,** estampador mecánico; máquina de franquear (cartas); máquina de perforar.—**s. mill,** bocarte, molino de pisones.

stance [stæns], *s.* postura, posición (esp. de los pies).

stanch [stanch]. **I.** *va.* restañar; estancar. **II.** *a.* firme, fiel, adicto; constante; sano, fuerte, seguro.—**s. ship,** buque marinero. **III.** *s.* (hidr.) compuerta.

stanchion [stǽnšɔn], *s.* puntal, madrina, asnilla, pie derecho, montante, candelero.

stanchness [stánchnjs], *s.* firmeza, constancia, lealtad, fidelidad.

stand [stænd], *va.* (*pret.* y *pp.* STOOD) poner derecho, colocar o poner de pie; resistir, hacer frente a; aguantar, sufrir, tolerar; someterse a, soportar, pasar por; sostener, defender, conservar; (fam.) sufragar, pagar.—**to s. a chance,** o **a show,** tener probabilidad a.—**to s. against the wall,** fusilar.—**to s. fire,** (mil.) aguantar el fuego; (quím.) resistir al calor.—**to s. off,** tener a raya; contener; salir de.—**to s. on end,** poner de punta, asentar por un extremo.—**to s. one's ground,** resistir, defender su puesto o posición, mantenerse en su puesto.—**to s. the test,** pasar por la prueba, resistir la prueba.—**to s. treat,** (fam.) pagar la convidada.—**to s. up,** (fam.) faltar a una cita, dejar plantado a uno.

stand, *vn.* estar; ponerse o estar de pie, tenerse derecho; sostenerse, resistir; quedarse; pararse, quedar suspenso; mantenerse, durar, perdurar; subsistir; tenerse, ponerse, estar en cierta postura; erguirse, levantarse, enderezarse; ocupar (buena o mala) posición, tener (buena o mala) reputación; poseer rectitud moral; estar situado, hallarse; persistir, perseverar; ser consecuente, acordar, convenir; quedar de acuerdo, quedar corrientes; (mar.) navegar, correr, dirigirse (*to stand on the same tack*, correr la misma bordada).—to s. about, rodear, cercar. —to s. against, resistir, hacer frente a.—to s. alone, estar solo; ser el único.—to s. aloof (from), mantenerse apartado, retraerse (de).— to s. aside, hacerse a un lado, apartarse; estarse alejado.—to s. at attention, (mil.) cuadrarse.—to s. back, retroceder; quedarse atrás.—to s. by, ser o permanecer fiel a; estar listo; sostener, favorecer, ayudar, auxiliar; atenerse a, sostenerse en; someterse a; estar de mirón; estar cerca, quedarse allí; mantenerse listo (para prestar ayuda, etc.).—to s. far off, mantenerse lejos.—to s. fast, no cejar o ceder. —to s. for, estar por, estar en lugar de, representar; significar, querer decir; tolerar, permitir; aprobar, favorecer; solicitar, pretender, presentarse como candidato u opositor; sostener, defender, abogar por; apadrinar; mantener o sostener (una opinión); (mar.) dirigirse o llevar rumbo a o hacia.—to s. forth, adelantarse, avanzar; presentarse.—to s. from under, (fam.) alejarse de alguna cosa que está por caer; retirar uno su apoyo.—to s. . . . high, tener . . . de alto (*the wall stands 20 feet high*, la pared tiene 20 pies de alto).— to s. in, costar, montar, importar; estar en; sentir.—to s. in bold relief, resaltar vigorosamente.—to s. in good stead, servir, ser útil.— to s. in line, hacer cola.—to s. in need, tener necesidad, necesitar.—to s. in one's light, taparle a uno la luz.—to s. in with, juntarse o estar aliado con; estar en gracia de, tener el favor de.—to s. inshore, (mar.) correr hacia la tierra.—to s. in the way, cerrar el paso; estorbar, ser un obstáculo.—to s. off, mantenerse a distancia, apartarse; negar, denegar; desconvenir; no acercarse, mantenerse apartado.—to s. off and on, (mar.) bordear, barloventear.—to s. on o upon, estar colocado sobre, estar en; adherirse a; interesar, concernir, tocar, pertenecer; estimar, valuar; fijarse en; picarse de, tener su orgullo en; insistir en, gastar (ceremonia, etc.).—to s. on end, erizarse; mantenerse derecho; ponerse de punta.— to s. on one's own feet, o legs, valerse a sí mismo.—to s. on tiptoe, ponerse o estar de puntillas.—to s. out, mantenerse firme; resistir; separarse, apartarse; desconvenir; denegar; resalir, resaltar, destacarse, estar en relieve.—to s. out of the way, quitarse de en medio, hacerse o estar a un lado, no estorbar. —to s. out to sea, (mar.) llevar la proa al mar.—to s. over, aplazar; plantarse al lado de para vigilar o apurar.—to s. pat, (fam.) estarse o mantenerse en sus trece; plantarse, oponerse inflexiblemente a todo cambio, marcar el paso (fig.).—to s. still, no moverse; estarse quieto; estancarse.—to s. to, mantenerse al lado de, no abandonar; seguir usando o manejando.—to s. together, mantenerse unidos; mancomunarse.—to s. to lose (win, etc.), tener probabilidad de perder (ganar, etc.).— to s. to one's guns, seguir haciendo fuego; mantenerse firme, no cejar.—to s. to one's word, mantenerse en lo dicho, cumplir (con) la palabra.—to s. to reason, ser lógico; ser justo.—to s. under, sufrir, sostener; estar bajo.—to s. up, levantarse, alzarse; ponerse en pie.—to s. up for, defender, sostener, apoyar; personarse por, sacar la cara por.— to s. up to, cumplir con; hacer resueltamente frente a.—to s. upon ceremony, gastar ceremonia, ser cumplimentero.—to s. with, convenirse; estar conforme con; disputar; irlas con. stand, s. puesto, sitio, lugar, posición, situación, estación; tarima, estrado, plataforma; tribuna (de espectadores); mostrador, puesto en un

mercado; velador, mesita, estante, pie, *m.*, pedestal, descanso, sostén, soporte; actitud, opinión; parada, pausa, alto; término; inactividad, estancamiento; atascamiento; oposición, resistencia; (bot.) herbaje.—to make a s., pararse y resistir.—to take a s. for, declararse a favor de.—to take the s., (for.) declarar, deponer (en el lugar o estrado destinado a los testigos).

standard [stǽndȝrd]. I. *s.* norma, tipo, pauta, medida, patrón, modelo, dechado, ley, *f.*, marco, regla fija; patrón o talón monetario; (joy.) ley del oro o la plata; (mec.) soporte, poste, pilar, punta, madrina, pie, *m.*, montante, árbol; bandera, estandarte, pendón.—s. of living, nivel o norma de vida. II. *a.* normal, de ley; patrón (metro, yarda, libra, etc.); clásico.— s. author, autor clásico.—s.-bearer, (mil.) abanderado, portaestandarte, portaguión, *m.*; (pol.) cacique, jefe político.—s. book, o work, obra de autoridad reconocida; obra clásica.— s. candle, bujía normal.—s. clock, reloj magistral.—s. equipment, equipo corriente o regular.—s. gauge, marca, medida o marco que sirve de norma; (f. c.) entrevía normal, anchura normal (56½ pulgadas).—s. pitch, (mús.) diapasón normal.—s. price, precio corriente o regular.—s. scale, escala normal. —s. solution, (quím.) solución valorada.— s. time, tiempo normal; hora normal.—s. weight, peso legal, peso normal.

standardize [-aįz], *va.* uniformar, normalizar.— standardization [-įzéįṣǫn], *s.* uniformación, normalización.—standardized production, producción en serie.

stand-by [stǽnd baį], *s.* adherente fiel; cosa o persona en que se puede confiar o con que se puede contar.

standee [-í], *s.* (fam.) persona sin asiento, que asiste de pie a una función.

stand-in [-įn], *s.* (fam.) posición favorable; influjo, influencia; (cine y teat.) contrafigura, doble, substituto.

standing [-įŋ]. I. *a.* derecho o en pie; levantado, de pie; erecto; con pedestal, con pie; permanente, fijo, establecido; duradero, estable, constante; parado; estancado, encharcado; (for.) vigente.—s. army, ejército permanente. —s. collar, cuello recto.—s. committee, comisión permanente.—s. place, s. room, sitio para estar de pie.—s. timber, árboles en pie.— s. water, agua estancada. II. *s.* posición, reputación, crédito; categoría; puesto, sitio, paraje; duración, antigüedad; alto, parada.—of long s., (que existe o dura, etc.) desde hace mucho tiempo.

stand-off [-ǫf]. I. *s.* empate, tablas (en el juego); indiferencia, frialdad; alejamiento; compensación, neutralización. II. *a.* reservado, retraído, frío.

standpatter [-pǽtǫ(r)], *s.* (fam.) el que se opone inflexiblemente a cambios.—standpattism [-įzm], *s.* (fam.) oposición a cambios de política, etc.

standpipe [-paįp], *s.* columna o tubo vertical de depósito o de alimentación (de agua).

standpoint [-pǫįnt], *s.* punto de vista.

standstill [-stįl], *s.* parada, detención, alto; pausa, descanso.—at a s., parado, atascado.

stand-up [-ʌp], *a.* recto, derecho, vertical; que se hace u ocupa de pie.—s. collar, cuello recto.

stanhope [stǽnhoųp], *s.* cabriolé ligero.

stank [stæŋk], *pret.* de TO STINK.

stannary [stǽnȝrį], *s.* mina de estaño.

stannate [stǽnęįt], *s.* (quím.) estannato.

stannic [stǽnįk], *a.* (quím.) estánnico.

stanniferous [stænífęrʌs], *a.* (min.) estannífero.

stannous [stǽnʌs], *a.* (quím.) estannoso.

stanza [stǽnzạ], *s.* (poét.) estancia, estrofa.

stapedius [stăpídiʌs], *s.* (anat.) músculo estapedio, o del estribo.

stapes [stéipiz], *s.* (anat.) estribo (del oído).

staphylococcus [stæfilokákʌs], *s.* (biol.) estafilococo.

staple [stéipl]. **I.** *s.* artículo o producto principal; renglón de comercio; elemento o asunto principal; fibra, hebra o filamento; materia prima, materia bruta; emporio de comercio, mercado; (mec.) hembra de cerrojo, picolete, grapa, aro, argolla, armella; (mar.) cíbica, grampa. **II.** *a.* (com.) corriente, de consumo o uso general; principal, prominente; establecido, admitido, reconocido; vendible.—**s. commodities**, artículos corrientes de consumo.—**s. ring**, (mec.) argolla con espiga. **III.** *va.* asegurar (papeles, etc.) con grapas delgadas; coser con alambre; (tej.) clasificar hebras textiles según su longitud.

stapler [stéiplœ(r)], *s.* negociante en los artículos corrientes de consumo; (tej.) clasificador de lanas; abrochador, máquina para asegurar (papeles, etc.) con grapas.

star [star]. **I.** *s.* estrella (astro, figura, hado, actor, mancha en la frente de un animal); cosa o persona principal; (impr.) asterisco; mancha brillante en una superficie metálica.—**s. apple**, (bot.) caimito.—**S. Chamber**, (Ingl.) antiguo tribunal criminal y civil.—**s. connection**, (elec.) conexión de estrella.—**s. dust**, (astr.) cúmulo estelar.—**s.-of-Bethlehem**, (bot.) leche (*f.*) de gallina.—**s. polygon**, (geom.) polígono estrellado.—**s. sapphire**, (min.) zafiro que tiene la propiedad del asterismo. *V.* ASTERIATED y ASTERISM.—**s.-shaped**, estelulado.—**s. shell**, (mil.) bomba luminosa.—**s. shower**, caída de meteoritos.—**s.-spangled**, estrellado, tachonado de estrellas.—**S.-Spangled Banner**, bandera estrellada (nombre dado en los E. U. a la bandera nacional y a un himno patriótico).—**s. switch**, (elec.) estrella de interrupción, interruptor de estrella.—**s. thistle**, (bot.) cardo estrellado, abrojo.—**s. wheel**, (mec.) rueda catalina (de reloj).—**the Stars and Stripes**, las estrellas y listas (nombre de la bandera de los E. U.). **II.** *va.* adornar con estrellas; marcar con asterisco; dividir en líneas divergentes; (teat., cine) introducir como estrella. **III.** *vn.* ser estrella (de teatro, cine, etc.); brillar; figurar como estrella o persona sobresaliente.

starboard [stárbord]. **I.** *s.* (mar.) estribor.—**s. side**, banda de estribor.—**s. watch**, guardia de estribor. **II.** *a.* y *adv.* a estribor.

starch [stárch]. **I.** *s.* almidón, fécula; (fig.) entereza, energía, vigor; rigidez, entonación. **II.** *va.* almidonar, atiesar.

starched [-t], *a.* almidonado; tieso, serio, entonado.—**starcher** [-œ(r)], *s.* almidonador.—**starchmaker** [-meikœ(r)], *s.* almidonero.

starch(ed)ness [-(d)nis], **starchiness** [-inis], *s.* almidonamiento; feculencia, calidad de feculento o harinoso; tesura, gravedad.

starchy [-i], *a.* almidonado, amiláceo, de almidón; feculoso, feculento (ú. de ciertos alimentos); tieso, entonado.

stardom [stárdom], *s.* (fig.) el mundo de las estrellas (del teatro, pantalla, etc.); categoría de estrella.

stare [stér]. **I.** *va.* clavar o fijar la vista en o a; encararse con; mirar de hito en hito o descaradamente.—**to s. one in the face**, dar en cara; estar cerca o a la vista; ser claro. **II.** *vn.* abrir grandes ojos; mirar con fijeza, asombro o insolencia; saltar a la vista; ser muy vivo o chillón (un color); erizarse (el pelo). **III.** *s.* mirada fija o de hito en hito; encaro.

starer [-œ(r)], *s.* el que mira fijamente.

starfish [stárfiʃ], *s.* (zool.) estrellamar, *f.*, estrella de mar, asteria.

stargazer [stárgeizœ(r)], *s.* astrónomo; astrólogo.

stargazing [-iŋ], *s.* observación de las estrellas; distracción de ánimo; absorción en ideas quiméricas.

staring [stériŋ], *a.* que mira fijamente.—**s. colors**, colores llamativos, vivos, chillones.

stark [stárk]. **I.** *a.* tieso, rígido; muerto; (fig.) inflexible, severo; completo, cabal; puro.—**s. and stiff**, rígido, muerto.—**s. madness**, locura completa.—**s. nonsense**, pura tontería. **II.** *adv.* completamente, enteramente.—**s. mad**, rematadamente loco.—**s. naked**, completamente desnudo o en cueros.

starkly [-li], *adv.* tiesamente, totalmente.

starless [stárlis], *a.* sin estrellas.

starlet [-lit], *s. dim.* estrellita.

starlight [-lait]. **I.** *s.* luz de las estrellas. **II.** *a.* estrellado. *V.* STARLIT.—**s. night**, noche estrellada.

starlike [-laik], *a.* estrellado; brillante, radiante, rutilante.

starling [stárliŋ], *s.* (orn.) estornino; (ing.) estacada de protección.

starlit [stárlit], *a.* iluminado por las estrellas.

starred [stard], *a.* estrellado; afortunado o desafortunado (*v.* EVIL, ILL); (teatro, cine) presentado o introducido como estrella.

starriness [stárinis], *s.* abundancia de estrellas.

starry [stári], *a.* estrellado; estrellar; centelleante, rutilante; (poét.) estelífero, astrífero; sideral, sidéreo.

starstone [stárstoun], *s.* (min.) piedra preciosa, esp. el zafiro, que tiene la propiedad del asterismo.

start [stárt], *va.* principiar, comenzar, empezar, iniciar; entablar (una conversación, etc.); poner en marcha o en movimiento, dar impulso, hacer mover, andar o funcionar; (mec.) hacer arrancar; levantar (la caza); aflojar, dislocar; sacar un líquido de.—**to s. a row**, armar una gresca, armar la gorda.—**to s. a train**, (f. c.) dar la señal de salida o partida; poner el tren en marcha.

start, *vn.* comenzar; partir, salir; arrancar (una máquina); sobresaltarse, asustarse; provenir, proceder, derivar; aflojarse; descoyuntarse; alabearse, combarse (como la madera).—**to s. aside**, echarse a un lado, ladearse.—**to s. after**, salir tras o en busca de; seguir a.—**to s. back**, dar un respingo; emprender el viaje de regreso.—**to s. for**, ponerse en camino hacia; presentarse como candidato para.—**to s. off**, partir, ponerse en marcha.—**to s. out**, salir, partir; principiar a.—**to s. to** (cry, etc.), o **to s.** (crying, etc.), echar a (llorar, etc.); empezar, principiar o ponerse a (hacer algo).—**to s. up**, levantarse precipitadamente; salir de repente; ponerse en movimiento, empezar a funcionar, arrancar.

start, *s.* principio, comienzo; salida, partida; arranque (de una máquina); sobresalto, susto; respingo; ímpetu, arranque, pronto; estampida; ventaja, delantera; grieta, raja, abrimiento.—**at the s.**, al primer paso, al principio.—**by starts**, a saltos, por botes.—**by fits and starts**, a saltos y corcovos; a ratos.—**to get the s. of**, coger la delantera a.

starter [-œ(r)], *s.* iniciador; levantador, ojeador (en la caza); el que da la señal de partida; (dep.) juez (*m.*) de salida; cualquiera de los que comienzan una carrera, etc.; principio, comienzo; cosa con que se principia; (m. v.) palanca de marcha; (aut.) arranque, mecanismo de arranque.

starting [-iŋ]. **I.** *s.* principio, comienzo; acción de comenzar, poner en marcha, etc.; arranque; (aer.) lanzamiento. **II.** *a.* que inicia o principia; que pone en movimiento; de salida, de partida; (mec.) de puesta en marcha, de arranque; (aer.) de lanzamiento.—**s. crank**, (aut.) manubrio o manivela de arranque.—**s. gear**, engranaje de arranque.—**s. place** o **point**, lugar o punto de partida o de arranque.—**s. post,** arrancadero, poste de partida (en las carreras).

startle [stártl], *va.* espantar, asustar, dar un susto; sobrecoger; alarmar; ojear.

startling [stártliŋ], *a.* pasmoso, sobrecogiente, alarmante; que causa sobresalto o susto.

starvation [starvéişǫn]. **I.** *a.* que causa hambre o inanición. **II.** *s.* hambre, *f.*, inanición.

starve [stárv]. **I.** *vn.* morir de hambre; hallarse en la inopia. **II.** *va.* matar de hambre, hambrear. —**to s. one's self,** dejarse morir de hambre.— **to s. out,** (mil.) hacer rendirse por hambre.

starveling [-liŋ]. **I.** *s.* persona, animal o planta extenuados por el hambre. **II.** *a.* hambriento, muerto de hambre, famélico.

starver [-œ(r)], *s.* el que está muriendo de hambre; el que mata de hambre.

starving [-iŋ], *a.* famélico, hambriento.

stasis [stéişis], *s.* (med.) estasis, estancamiento de la sangre o de otro líquido en el cuerpo.

state [stéit]. **I.** *s.* estado, situación, condición; (pol.) estado: fausto, pompa, ceremonia; majestad; gobierno civil, en contraposición al eclesiástico.—**s.'s evidence,** testimonio aducido en una causa criminal; cómplice que declara por evitar el castigo.—**States-General,** estados generales.—**in a s. of,** o **to,** en estado de.—**in a s. of nature,** desnudo; en estado de pecado, irregenerado; indomado; incivilizado.—**in s.,** con gran pompa, de gran ceremonia.—**the States,** los Estados Unidos.—**to lie in s.,** *v.* LIE, *vn.* **II.** *a.* de estado; del estado; estatal; político, público; de lujo; de gala; perteneciente a los estados o a cada estado (de una república). —**s. affairs,** negocios o asuntos públicos o de estado.—**S. Department,** (E. U.) Ministerio de Estado.—**S. house,** (E. U.) capitolio, edificio del Estado.—**S. paper,** documento de estado; pliego, documento o tratado político.— **S. prison,** penitenciaría del estado.—**S.** o **States' rights,** soberanía o derechos de los estados. **III.** *va.* y *vn.* decir, expresar, declarar, afirmar; exponer, aseverar; consignar (en un escrito); rezar (un texto); manifestar; enunciar, formular (un principio, ley, etc.); (mat., lóg.) enunciar, plantear.

statecraft [-kræft], *s.* política, arte de gobernar.

stated [-įd], *a.* establecido, regular, fijo, periódico.

statehood [-hųd], *s.* existencia y reconocimiento como estado.

Statehouse [-haųs], *s.* = STATE HOUSE. *V.* STATE, *a.*

stateliness [-lįnįs], *s.* grandeza, majestad, dignidad, pompa, señorío.

stately [-lį], *a.* augusto, sublime, majestuoso, imponente, soberbio, regio, encumbrado.

statement [-męnt], *s.* declaración, exposición, presentación; afirmación, aserto o aseveración; manifestación; cuenta; relato, memoria, informe; planteo, enunciado (de problema, ley, etc.); proposición; (com.) balance, (estado de) cuenta.

stater [-œ(r)], *s.* el que declara, afirma, etc.; antigua moneda griega.

stateroom [-rum], *s.* (mar.) camarote; (f. c.) compartimiento, camarote; salón de recepción de un palacio (ll. t. **state room**).

statesman [stéitsmąn], *s.* estadista, hombre de Estado.—**statesmanlike** [-laįk], *a.* de una manera propia de un estadista, como de estadista.

statesmanship [-šįp], *s.* calidad de estadista; habilidad de estadista.

static [stǽtįk], *s.* (rad.) estática, perturbación eléctrica atmosférica.

static(al [-(ąl], *a.* estático.

statics [-s], *s.* (mec.) estática.

station [stéişǫn]. **I.** *s.* estación (de f. c., de top.); sitio, situación, puesto; rango, condición o posición social; (mar.) apostadero; (mil.) puesto militar; (igl.) estación.—**s. agent** o **master,** jefe de estación.—**s. house,** cuartelillo de la policía; (f. c.) estación o paradero; caseta de

salvamento en la costa. **II.** *va.* estacionar, apostar, colocar, situar, alojar.

stationary [-erį], *a.* estacionario, estantío, fijo; (astr.) estacional.—**s. engine,** máquina fija.— **to remain s.,** estacionarse, quedarse inmóvil.

stationer [-œ(r)], *s.* papelero, papelista.

stationery [-erį], *s.* papelería; papel de cartas; efectos de escritorio.—**s. store,** papelería.

statism [stéįtįzm], *s.* (pol.) estatismo.

statist [stéįtįst], *s.* estadístico; (raro) estadista.

statistic(al [stątístįk(ąl], *a.* estadístico.

statistician [stætįstíšąn], *s.* estadístico, (Am.) estadígrafo.—**statistics** [stątístįks], *s.* estadística; datos estadísticos.

stator [stéįtǫ(r)], *s.* (elec., mec.) estator.

statoscope [stǽtoskoųp], *s.* (fís.) estatoscopio, aneroide de gran precisión.

statuary [stǽchụerį], *s.* estatuaria; estatuario, escultor.

statue [stǽchụ], *s.* estatua, imagen, *f.*

statuesque [-ésk], *a.* escultural, estatuario.

statuette [-ét], *s.* figurilla.

stature [stǽchụ(r)], *s.* estatura, altura, talla, tamaño; alzada (de caballo, etc.); importancia.

status [stéįtⱥs], *s.* estado legal; posición relativa.

statute [stǽchụt], *s.* estatuto, ley, *f.*, ordenanza, decreto, reglamento.—**s. law,** derecho escrito. —**s. mile,** milla ordinaria o terrestre (como 1609 m.), a distinción de la marina.

statutory [-ǫrį], *a.* estatutario, estatuído, establecido por la ley.

staunch [stǫnch], *va.* y *a.* = STANCH.

stave [stéįv]. **I.** *va.* (*pret.* y *pp.* STAVED o STOVE) (a menudo con **in**) romper las duelas; abrir boquete, desfondar; quebrantar, destrozar; (ton.) poner duelas; (con **off**) rechazar, parar; detener, evitar; retardar, diferir. **II.** *vn.* desfondarse, romperse, hacerse pedazos. **III.** *s.* duela de barril; escalón, peldaño (de escala); ladera de un pozo; (mús.) pentagrama, *m.*; (poét.) estrofa.—**staves and heading,** (ton.) duelas y frondas.

staves [-z], *s. pl. reg.* de STAVE; *pl. irreg.* de STAFF.

stavesacre [stéįvzeįkœ(r)], *s.* (bot.) estafisagria.

stay [stéį]. **I.** *va.* (*pret.* y *pp.* STAYED o STAID) parar, detener, impedir, poner freno; sostener, apoyar, reforzar; riostrar; aplazar; (for.) sobreseer.—**to s. the stomach,** tomar un bocado o tentempié, *m.* **II.** *vn.* quedarse, permanecer; estarse quieto; parar o pararse; tardar, detenerse; hospedarse, alojarse.—**to s. away,** no volver.—**to s. in,** quedarse en casa, no salir.— **to s. in bed,** guardar cama.—**to s. out,** quedarse fuera, no entrar.—**to s. put,** (fam.) estarse quieto o en un mismo sitio.—**to s. up,** velar, no acostarse. **III.** *s.* estancia, residencia, estada, permanencia, quedada; suspensión, espera, parada, detención; (for.) sobreseimiento, cesación temporal de un procedimiento judicial; freno, impedimento, obstáculo; refuerzo; sostén, soporte, sustentáculo, apoyo; puntal, entibo, atesador, fiador; (arq.) arbotante, apeo, estribo, tirante, riostra; tentemozo; ballena de corsé; (mar.) estay, nervio, codal, contrete; estabilidad, fijeza; (fam.) perseverancia, persistencia, capacidad de resistencia; inacción.—*pl.* corsé, cotilla. **IV.** *a.* de refuerzo, de sostén.—**s. bar,** montante de ventana.—**s. bolt** = STAYBOLT.— **s. rod,** tirante.

stay-at-home [-æt hoụm], *s.* (fam.) persona casera; el que se está en su casa (a veces por cobardía, como en la guerra).

staybolt [-boụlt], *s.* (mec.) virotillo roscado, tornillo de separación y refuerzo.

staysail [-seįl], *s.* (mar.) vela de estay.

stead [stęd], *s.* (precedido de **in**) lugar, sitio; utilidad, provecho; auxilio, ayuda.—**in his s.,** en su lugar.—**in s. of,** en lugar de, en vez de, haciendo las veces de.—**to stand in (good) s.,** ser útil o de provecho.

ste(a)dfast [stédfæst], *a.* constante, inmutable; resuelto, determinado.—**steadfastly** [-li], *adv.* con constancia, con resolución.—**steadfastness** [-nis], *s.* inmutabilidad, constancia.

steadily [stédili], *adv.* constantemente; con constancia; de firme; regular o progresivamente.

steadiness [-nis], *s.* estabilidad, firmeza; entereza, constancia; sostén (de un buque).

steady [stédi]. **I.** *a.* firme, fijo, seguro, estable; juicioso, formal, (a)sentado; constante, uniforme, continuo.—**s. flow**, flujo o corriente (*f.*) uniforme.—**s.-going**, metódico, constante.—**s. load**, (arq., ing.) = DEAD LOAD.—**s. pin**, (mec.) clavija de fijación (de una polea). **II.** *va.* reforzar; hacer firme, impedir el movimiento de; calmar; fortalecer.

steak [steik], *s.* (coc.) tajada para asar; biftec.

steal [stíl]. **I.** *va.* y *vn.* (*pret.* STOLE; *pp.* STOLEN) hurtar, robar; introducirse clandestinamente, pasar furtivamente o a hurtadillas; colarse, escabullirse, escapar sin ser visto.—**to s. along**, pasar en silencio, deslizarse sin ruido.—**to s. a march on**, ganar por la mano, sorprender; adelantarse o anticiparse (a uno).—**to s. away**, marcharse a hurtadillas; escabullirse.—**to s. down, forth, in, into**, descender, salir, penetrar furtivamente.—**to s. off** = TO S. AWAY.—**to s. over**, ganar insensiblemente.—**to s. the show**, (fig.) ganarse todos los aplausos.—**to s. up**, subir a ocultas.—**to s. upon**, aproximarse sin ruido a; sorprender. **II.** *s.* (fam.) hurto, robo.

stealer [-œ(r)], *s.* ladrón, ratero.

stealing [-iŋ], *s.* hurto, robo, ratería.

stealingly [-li], *adv.* furtivamente, ocultamente, secretamente.

stealth [stélθ], *s.* recato, cautela, reserva.—**by s.**, a hurtadillas, a escondidas.—**stealthily** [-ili], *adv.* clandestinamente.—**stealthy** [-i], *a.* furtivo, escondido, clandestino.

steam [stím]. **I.** *s.* vapor; vaho; humo, sahumm(eri)o. **II.** *a.* de vapor; para vapor; por vapor.—**s. boiler**, caldera de vapor.—**s. chest**, caja o cámara de vapor.—**s. dome**, (m. v.) cúpula o cámara de distribución.—**s. engine**, máquina de vapor.—**s. fitter**, montador de calderas y cañerías de vapor.—**s. ga(u)ge**, manómetro.—**s. hammer**, martinete de vapor.—**s. heat, s. heating**, calefacción por vapor.—**s. jacket**, camisa de vapor.—**s. pipe**, tubo o tubería de vapor.—**s. port**, (m. v.) lumbrera de admisión.—**s. pressure**, presión del vapor.—**s. roller**, rodillo de vapor; (máquina) apisonadora de vapor; (mil. y fig.) fuerza arrolladora e incontrastable; (fam.) opresión, dictadura (de un partido, comité, etc.).—**s. shovel**, pala mecánica o de vapor.—**s.-tight**, a prueba de vapor, hermético.—**s. trap**, purgador de agua de condensación.—**with all s. on**, a todo vapor. **III.** *va.* proveer de vapor; ablandar o preparar (comestibles) con vapor; saturar de o limpiar con vapor; secar (ladrillos o adobes). **IV.** *vn.* generar vapor; emitir vaho o vapor; navegar o funcionar por vapor; evaporarse.

steamboat [-bout], *s.* buque de vapor.

steamer [-œ(r)], *s.* buque de vapor; cualquier máquina o vehículo de vapor; bomba de vapor para incendios; (coc.) marmita al vacío, vasija para cocer, esterilizar, etc., con vapor.—**s. rug**, manta de viaje.—**s. trunk**, baúl de camarote.

steamship [-šip], *s.* buque de vapor.—**s. agency**, agencia de vapores.—**s. line**, línea de vapores, mensajería.

stearate [stíəreit], *s.* (quím.) estearato.

stearic [stiérik], *a.* (quím.) esteárico.

stearin [stíərin], *s.* (quím.) estearina.

steatite [stíətait], *s.* (min.) esteatita.

steed [stid], *s.* caballo de regalo; corcel.

steel [stíl]. **I.** *s.* acero; arma blanca, espada; afilón, chaira de afilar cuchillos); eslabón. **II.** *a.* de acero, acerino, acerado; duro; insensible.—**s. bronze**, bronce Uchatius (92% cobre, 8% estaño).—**s.-clad**, cubierto o revestido de acero, acorazado.—**s. engraving**, grabado en acero.—**s. industry**, industria siderúrgica.—**s. wool**, limaduras finas de acero. **III.** *va.* acerar, cubrir o armar de acero; acorazar; fortalecer; hacer insensible.

steeliness [-inis], *s.* dureza de acero.

steelworks [-wœrks], *s.* fundición (fábrica) de acero.

steely [-i], *a.* acerado, acerino, de acero; fuerte, inflexible, firme, duro.

steelyard [-yard], *s.* romana.—**to weigh with a s.**, romanear.

steep [stíp]. **I.** *a.* empinado, pendiente, acantilado, escarpado; (fam.) excesivo, exorbitante. **II.** *s.* precipicio, despeñadero, derrumbadero. **III.** *va.* empapar, impregnar, remojar, macerar; poner en infusión; enriar (lino o cáñamo); (ten.) apelambrar (pieles).

steeper [-œ(r)], *s.* el que remoja, empapa, etc.; (ten.) pelambrero; remojadero, pelambrera.

steeping [-iŋ], *s.* remojo, empapada, maceración.—**s. trough, tub, o vat**, cuba de remojar, remojadero; (ten.) pelambrera.

steeple [stípl], *s.* espira, aguja, campanario, torre, *f.* (de iglesia).

steeplechase [-cheis], *s.* (dep.) carrera de obstáculos; salto de vallas.

steeplechaser [-cheisœ(r)], *s.* (dep.) caballo o corredor de carreras de obstáculos.

steeplejack [-džæk], *s.* reparador de espiras, chimeneas altas, etc.

steepness [stípnis], *s.* calidad de empinado o pendiente; inclinación.

steepy [stípi], *a.* (poét.) enriscado.

steer [stír]. **I.** *s.* (zool.) novillo, novillejo; buey. **II.** *va.* (leng. ord., aut., etc.) guiar, dirigir, conducir; (mar.) gobernar, patronear (un barco). **III.** *vn.* navegar, timonear; gobernarse, conducirse, dirigirse; obedecer al timón.—**to s. clear of**, navegar a distancia prudente de, o evitando; evitar.

steerage [stíridž], *s.* (mar. y fig.) gobierno, dirección.—**s. (accommodation)**, alojamiento de los pasajeros que viajan en cuarta (o tercera) clase.—**s. passenger**, pasajero de proa, de entrepuentes, de bodega o de combés.

steerageway [-weij], *s.* (mar.) movimiento de una embarcación suficiente para poder gobernarla por el timón.

steering [stíriŋ]. **I.** *s.* dirección, gobierno (de buque, automóvil). **II.** *a.* de timonear; de dirección o gobierno.—**s. column**, (aut.) columna de dirección.—**s. committee**, (pol.) comité o comisión de iniciativas.—**s. gear**, (mecanismo de) dirección.—**s. wheel**, (mar.) rueda del timón; (aut.) volante (de dirección); rueda directriz (de bicicleta, etc.).

steersman [stírzmən], *s.* (mar.) piloto, timonel, timonero.

steeve, steeving [stív-, -iŋ], *s.* (mar.) elevación angular del bauprés; grúa.

stein [stain], *s.* pichel alemán para cerveza.

steinbok [stéinbak], *s.* (zool.) íbice, cabra montés.

stele [stíli], *s.* (arq. y bot.) estela.

stellar [stélə], *a.* astral, estelar; (fig.) sobresaliente, superlativo.

stellate [stéljt], *a.* estrellado, estrellar.

stelliferous [steliˈfərəs], *a.* (poét.) estelífero.

stelliform [stéliform], *a.* estrellado.

stellionate [stéljɔneit], *s.* (for.) estelionato.

stellular [stéljulə(r)], *a.* estrellado; estelulado.

stem [stém]. **I.** *s.* (bot.) tallo, tronco, vástago, caña, varita; rabillo, pecíolo, pedúnculo; estirpe, linaje; (mec. y carp.) vástago, caña, espiga, cabillo; pie, *m.* (de copa); cañón de pluma; (gram.) raíz; rabo o rabito de una nota de música; (mar.) roda, roa, tajamar, branque.—**s.-winder**, (reloj de) remontuar o remontoir.—**s.-winding**, de remontoir.—**from s. to stern**, de proa a popa. **II.** *va.* ir contra, hacer frente a, oponerse a, detener; embestir con la proa; represar, contener; tapar o enlodar (una junta); quitar los pedúnculos; desgranar (uvas, pasas); poner pedúnculos postizos (para hacer ramilletes).—**to s. the tide**, rendir la marea. **III.** *vn.* detenerse, contenerse.—**to s. from**, radicar en, originarse en, emanar de.

stemless [-lįs], *a.* (bot.) acaule.

stempel, stemple [stémpęl], *s.* (min.) estemple, montante, asnado; travesaño.

stemson [stémsǫn], *s.* (mar.) contrabranque, contrarroda.

stench [stench], *s.* hedor, hediondez.

stencil [sténsįl]. **I.** *va.* estarcir. **II.** *s.* patrón para estarcir, estarcidor; estarcido, marca.

stenciler [-œ(r)], *s.* estarcidor.

stenograph [sténǫgræf]. **I.** *s.* escritura taquigráfica; maquinita para taquigrafiar. **II.** *va.* estenografiar, taquigrafiar.

stenographer [stenágrǫfœ(r)], *s.* taquígrafo(-fa), estenógrafo(-fa).

stenographic(al [stenǫgréfįk(ạl], *a.* taquigráfico, estenográfico.

stenography [stenágrǫfį], *s.* taquigrafía, estenografía.

stenosis [stenóusįs], *s.* (med.) estenosis.

Stentor [stén̪tǫr], *s.* (mit.) estentor.—(**s.**) persona de voz muy fuerte.

stentorian [stentóriąn], *a.* estentóreo.

step [stép]. **I.** *va.* (*pret.* y *pp.* STEPPED) poner, sentar, plantar (el pie); (con **off**) medir (a pasos); hacer dientes (en llaves); (mar.) plantar (un mástil); (gen. con **down**) reducir, disminuir; escalonar; hacer escaleras en.—**to s. down**, (elec.) reducir (la tensión de una corriente; de donde **s.-down transformer**, transformador de reducción).—**to s. up**, acelerar (el paso); (elec.) elevar (la tensión de una corriente; de donde **s.-up transformer**, transformador elevador). **II.** *vn.* dar un paso; pisar, andar, caminar.—**to s. after**, seguir o ir detrás.—**to s. aside**, apartarse, hacerse a un lado.—**to s. back**, retroceder, volver atrás.—**to s. down**, bajar, descender.—**to s. forth**, avanzar.—**to s. in**, entrar; intervenir; meterse, entrometerse.—**to s. on**, poner el pie sobre, pisar; andar sobre.—**to s. on it**, o **to s. on the gas**, (fam.) menearse, darse prisa.—**to s. out**, salir; apearse (de un vehículo); apretar el paso; (fam.) divertirse, andar de parranda.—**to s. over**, atravesar.—**to s. short**, (mil.) acortar el paso.—**to s. up**, subir. **III.** *s.* paso; escalón; grada, peldaño (de escalera); barrote (de escalera de mano); (carr.) estribo; umbral (de la puerta de entrada); grado; pisada, huella; medida, diligencia; comportamiento; (mús.) intervalo; pedestal de máquina; quicio de eje vertical; diente de una llave; (mar.) carlinga; (rad.) elemento, unidad.—*pl.* medios, medidas, pasos, diligencias, gestiones; gradería; escalinata (escalera exterior); (danz.) mudanza.—**s. box**, (mec.) rangua.—**s. by s.**, paso a paso; punto por punto.—**by such steps**, por tales medios.—**in s.**, de acorde; a compás; llevando el paso; (elec.) en fase.—**out of s.**, discorde, en desacuerdo; no llevando el paso; (elec.) en discordancia de fase.

stepbrother [-brʌðœ(r)], *s.* medio hermano, o hermanastro.—**stepchild** [-chạild], *s.* hijastro, entenado.—**stepdaughter** [-dótœ(r)], *s.* hijastra, entenada.—**stepfather** [-faðœ(r)], *s.* padrastro.

stephanite [stéfǫnạit], *s.* (min.) plata agria, negrillo.

stepladder [stéplædœ(r)], *s.* escala, escalera de mano.

stepmother [stépmʌðœ(r)], *s.* madrastra.—**stepsister** [-sįstœ(r)], *s.* media hermana, hermanastra.—**stepson** [-sʌn], *s.* hijastro, entenado, alnado.

steppe [stép], *s.* estepa, llanura.

stepped [stɛpt], *a.* escalonado.

stepping-stone [stépįŋ stǫun], *s.* estriberón, pasadera; piedra para apoyar el pie; escalón.

stercoraceous [stœrkoréįṣįʌs], *a.* estercolizo.

stere [stįr], *s.* estéreo (un metro cúbico).

stereobate [stérįǫbeįt], *s.* (arq.) estereóbato.

stereochromy [-krǫumį], *s.* estereocromía.

stereographic(al [-gréfįk(ạl], *a.* estereográfico.

stereography [-ágrǫfį], *s.* (geom.) estereografía.

stereometer [-ámętœ(r)], *s.* (fís.) estereómetro.

stereometry [-ámętrį], *s.* (geom.) estereometría.

stereopticon [-áptįkǫn], *s.* estereóptico, linterna mágica.

stereoscope [-oskǫup], *s.* estereoscopio; óptica.

stereoscopic [-oskápįk], *a.* estereoscópico.

stereotomy [-átomį], *s.* estereotomía.

stereotype [stérįǫtạip]. **I.** *va.* (impr.) estereotipar, clisar. **II.** *s.* estereotipo, clisé.—**s. plate**, plancha estereotípica, estereotipia, clisé.—**s. press**, prensa o molde de estereotipar.

stereotyper [-tạipœ(r)], *s.* (impr.) estereotipador.

stereotypic [-típįk], *a.* estereotípico.

stereotyping [-tạipįŋ], *s.* estereotipia, clisado.

stereotypography [-tạipágrǫfį], *s.* estereotipia.

sterile [stérįl], *a.* estéril, infecundo; improductivo, infructuoso.—**sterility** [sterílįtį], *s.* esterilidad, infecundidad.—**sterilization** [sterįljzéįṣǫn], *s.* esterilización.—**sterilize** [stérįlạiz], *va.* y *vn.* (leng. ord. y med.) esterilizar.—**sterilizer** [-œ(r)], *s.*, **sterilizing** [-įŋ], *a.* esterilizador.

sterling [stœrlįŋ], *a.* esterlina; genuino, puro, verdadero, de ley.—**s. silver**, plata fina (de 0,925).

stern [stœrn]. **I.** *a.* austero, duro, torvo, severo; firme, decidido. **II.** *s.* (mar.) popa; (fam.) rabo, cola.—**s. chase**, caza en que la nave que persigue marcha en la estela de la otra.—**s. chaser**, (arti., mar.) guardatimón.—**s. fast**, codera, tangidera, amarra de popa.—**s. timbers**, gambotas de popa.—**s.-wheeler**, bote de rueda trasera, bote de vapor que tiene a popa una rueda de paletas.

sternly [-lį], *adv.* severamente.

sternmost [-mǫust], *a.* (mar.) popel.

sternness [-nįs], *s.* severidad, rigor.

sternpost [-pǫust], *s.* (mar.) codaste, estambor; (aer.) codaste.

sternson [-sǫn], *s.* (mar.) estrave, talón de quilla (ll. t. **stern knee** o **sternson knee**).

sternum [stœrnʌm], *s.* (anat.) esternón.

sternutation [stœrnįutéįṣǫn], *s.* estornudo.

sternutatory [stœrnįútạtǫrį], *s.* y *a.* estornutatorio.

sternward(s [stœrnwạrd(z], *adv.* (mar.) hacia o por la popa.—**sternway** [-weį], *s.* (mar.) reculada, cía, retroceso.

stertor [stœrtǫ(r)], *s.* (med.) estertor.

stertorous [-ʌs], *a.* estertoroso.

stet [stet], *va.* (impr.) dejar como está, no cambiar.

stethograph [stéθogræf], *s.* (med.) estetógrafo, neumatógrafo.

stethometer [steθámętœ(r)], *s.* estetómetro, instrumento para medir los movimientos del tórax.

stethoscope [stéθoskǫup], *s.* (med.) estetoscopio.

stethoscopic [-kápįk], *a.* estetoscópico.

stethoscopy [steθáskopį], *s.* (med.) estetoscopia.

stevedore [stívędǫr], *s.* estibador, cargador de muelle.

stew [stįu]. **I.** *va.* y *vn.* (coc.) estofar; (fam.) agitarse, inquietarse; achicharrarse. **II.** *s.* estofado, guisado, cocido, puchero, olla; (fam.) ansiedad; agitación mental.—*pl.* burdel, lupanar.

steward [stįúwạrd], *s.* administrador; mayordomo, senescal; despensero, ranchero; camarero (en los vapores).—**s.'s room**, despensa.—**stewardship** [-šįp], *s.* mayordomía.—**stewardess** [-įs], *s.* mayordoma; camarera de a bordo.

stewed [stįud], *a.* estofado; (fam.) borracho.—**s. meat**, estofado.

stewpan [stįúpæn], *s.* cazuela, cacerola, estufador.

stewpot [stįúpat], *s.* olla.

sthenia [sθíniạ], *s.* (med.) estenia.

sthenic [sθénįk], *a.* esténico.

stibial [stíbial], a. estíbico, antimonial.
stibin(e [stíbin], s. (quím.) estibina.
stibium [stíbiʌm], s. (quím.) estibio, antimonio.
stich [stik], s. (poét.) verso. V. HEMISTICH.
stick [stík]. I. s. palo, estaca; garrote, porra; vara, bastón (de mando o autoridad); varilla; palillo (de tambor); barra, barrilla (de lacre, tinta china, etc.); batuta (de director de orquesta); estique de escultor; (mús.) arco de contrabajo; (impr.) componedor; (mar.) palo, verga; hurgonazo, estocada, pinchazo; adhesión, pegadura; parada, demora; duda, escrúpulo, vacilación; (fam.) bodoque; (teat.) mal actor.—pl. **sticks**, támaras o rozo, leña menuda, chabasca, chamarasca.—**s. and stone**, todito, todito.—**s.-lac**, laca en palillos.—**the sticks**, (fam.) las afueras, despoblado. II. va. (pret. y pp. STUCK) pegar; clavar, hincar; prender (con alfiler), fijar (con tachuelas, etc.); meter, introducir; matar o herir de una puñalada o cuchillada; picar, punzar; llenar de puntas; (fam.) confundir, aturrullar; (fam.) embaucar, pegársela a uno; componer (tipo); (agr.) plantar (jalones).—**to s. out**, sacar, asomar, mostrar; perseverar hasta el fin en.—**to s. up**, (fam.) atracar, saltear, parar para robar.—**to s. up one's hands**, alzar uno las manos en señal de entrega o sumisión.—**to s. up one's nose at**, hacer un gesto de desprecio, despreciar, hacer ascos. III. vn. estar clavado o prendido; (con **out, through, from**) salir, resaltar, sobresalir; pegarse, adherirse; permanecer fijo; permanecer, estarse; verse o estar parado o detenido; perseverar, ser constante; dudar, vacilar; atollarse.—**to s. at**, detenerse, sentir escrúpulo de.—**to s. at it**, (fam.) persistir.—**to s. at nothing**, (fam.) no pararse en nada.—**to s. at trifles**, reparar en pelillos.—**to s. by**, sostener, apoyar; pegarse (a alguno).—**to s. close**, mantenerse juntos.—**to s. fast**, pegarse, adherirse fuertemente.—**to s. in the mud**, atascarse en el fango, atollarse.—**to s. to**, pegarse o adherirse tenazmente a; perseverar, persistir en; atenerse a.—**to s. to one's guns**, estarse o seguir uno en sus trece; mantenerse firme.—**to s. to one's last**, meterse uno en lo que le importa.—**to s. up for**, (fam.) volver por, apoyar, salir a la defensa de.—**he sticks at everything**, (fam.) se ahoga en poca agua.
sticker [-œ(r)], s. fijador de carteles; papel engomado por un lado (rótulo, cartel, etc.); (fam.) cuestión batallona, cosa peliaguda; (fam.) tapaboca, m., argumento incontestable; persona perseverante; persona que permanece fiel (a un partido, etc.); cosa que no se vende bien, que no tiene salida o demanda.
stickiness [-inis], s. calidad de pegajoso, glutinosidad, viscosidad.
sticking plaster [stíkiŋ plæstœ(r)], s. (med.) tafetán inglés, esparadrapo.
stick-in-the-mud [stík in ðᵊ mʌd], s. persona tarda, perezosa, rutinaria o ultraconservadora.
stickleback [-bæk], s. (ict.) gasterosteo.
stickler [stíklœ(r)], s. porfiador.
stickpin [stíkpin], s. alfiler de corbata.
stick-up [-ʌp], s. (fam.) atraco, salto, salteamiento, robo por salteadores.
sticky [stíki], a. pegajoso, pegadizo, viscoso.
stiff [stíf]. I. a. tieso; duro, firme; envarado, entorpecido, embotado; yerto, aterido; rígido, inflexible; tenso, tendido; desmañado, chabacano; afectado, estirado, ceremonioso; almidonado; espeso; terco, persistente; difícil, severo; (fam.) peliagudo; fuerte, bravo (viento, etc.); fuerte, obstinado (resistencia, etc.); fuerte, cargado (medicamento, bebida alcohólica); (com.) firme (mercado, precios); (fam.) subido, caro (precio); (mar.) de aguante.—**s.-backed**, testarudo, terco.—**s. collar**, cuello duro o muy almido-

nado.—**s. neck**, (med.) torticolis. m.—**s.-necked**, obstinado, terco, testarudo; cuellierguido.—**to be frightened, o scared, s.**, (fam.) casi morirse de miedo, quedarse yerto. II. s. apresto para entiesar sombreros; (fam.) persona huraña o estirada; (fam.) cadáver.
stiffen [-n]. I. va. atiesar; endurecer; espesar; envarar, aterir o arrecir de frío; dificultar; (elec.) aumentar la inductancia de. II. vn. atiesarse; endurecerse; enderezarse; espesarse; envararse, arrecirse, aterirse; obstinarse.
stiffener [-nœ(r)], s. contrafuerte (del calzado); refuerzo, nervio; lo que sirve para dar tiesura o rigidez a una cosa.
stiffly [-li], adv. tiesamente, obstinadamente, inflexiblemente.
stiffness [-nis], s. tiesura, inflexibilidad; rigidez, envaramiento; aterimiento; (med.) rigor; terquedad, obstinación; dureza de estilo; espesura.
stifle [stáifl]. I. va. sofocar, ahogar, asfixiar; apagar; suprimir, callar, ocultar. II. vn. ahogarse, sofocarse o asfixiarse. III. s. acto o condición de sofocar.—**s.** (**joint**), (vet.) articulación de la pata trasera que corresponde a la rodilla.
stifling [-fliŋ], a. sofocante, ahogado(r).
stigma [stígmᵃ], s.—pl. stígmata, m., baldón, afrenta; (bot.) estigma; (anat. y zool.) marca o poro; (igl.) estigma; (med.) estigma, mancha en la piel.
stigmata [-tᵃ], s. pl. de STIGMA.
stigmatic [stigmǽtik], a. señalado, marcado; ignominioso; deforme.
stigmatize [stígmataiz], va. estigmatizar.
stile [stáil], s. portillo con escalones o con molinete; (carp.) larguero. V. STYLE.
stiletto [stilétou], s. estilete; ojeteador, punzón.
still [stíl]. I. va. acallar, hacer callar; amortiguar; calmar, aquietar, apaciguar; parar, detener; destilar. II. vn. acallarse; calmarse, aquietarse. III. adv. todavía, aún; aun; no obstante, sin embargo, a pesar de eso. IV. a. inmóvil; fijo; tranquilo, silencioso, quieto; apacible, sosegado; suave, sordo (ruido); no espumoso (vino); muerto, inanimado.—**s. life**, (pint.) naturaleza muerta.—**s.-life painting**, (pint.) bodegón.—**s. water**, agua tranquila. V. s. silencio, quietud; alambique, destiladera.
stillage [-idʒ], s. caballete.
stillbirth [-bœrθ], s. (med.) parto muerto.
stillborn [-bɔrn], a. nacido muerto.
still-hunt [-hʌnt]. I. va. y vn. cazar al acecho; (pol.) solicitar votos clandestinamente (v. STALK); buscar o investigar secretamente. II. s. caza al acecho; (fam.) busca, pesquisa, conducta o método callados y cautos.
stilling [-iŋ], s. poíno, codal.
stillness [-nis], s. silencio, quietud, tranquilidad, calma.
stilly [-i]. I. a. (poét.) tranquilo, silencioso. II. [-li], adv. quietamente.
stilt [stílt], s. zanco; soporte; (orn.) ave zancuda.
stilted [-id], a. hinchado, altisonante, pomposo.
stimulant [stímyūlạnt], a. y s. estimulante.—
stimulate [-leit]. I. va. estimular, excitar, incitar; avivar; (med.) estimular. II. vn. servir como estímulo o aguijón; ser estimulante.—
stimulation [-léiʃon], s. estímulo, aguijón o excitación; (med.) estimulación.—**stimulative** [-leitiv]. I. a. estimulante. II. s. estímulo; excitación.—**stimulator** [-leitọ(r)], s. irritador, acuciador.—**stimulus** [-lʌs], s. estímulo, aguijón; incentivo; (med.) estimulante; (bot.) aguijón.
sting [stíŋ]. I. va. y vn. (pret. y pp. STUNG) picar; punzar, pinchar, pungir; estimular, aguijonear; herir, atormentar; remorder la conciencia.—**to s. to the quick**, herir en lo vivo. II. s. aguijón; picadura, picada; picazón; (bot.) púa, aguijón; remordimiento de conciencia; estímulo.—**s. ray**, (ict.) pastinaca.

stinger [-œ(r)], *s.* cosa o animal que punza o pica; aguijón de un insecto.

stingily [stíndʒili], *adv.* cicatera o tacañamente.

stinginess [-nis], *s.* tacañería, cicatería, mezquindad, avaricia, (fam.) roñería.

stingless [stínlis], *a.* sin aguijón; sin púa.

stingy [stíndʒi], *a.* mezquino, tacaño, cicatero, avar(ient)o, (fam.) roñoso; escaso, poco, nimio.

stink [stíŋk]. I. *vn.* (pret. STANK o STUNK; pp. STUNK) heder, oler mal, apestar. II. *s.* hedor, hediondez.

stinkball [-bɔl], *s.* = STINKPOT.

stinker [-œ(r)], *s.* cosa o persona hedionda; (fam.) sujeto vil, tipo despreciable, canalla, *m.;* (orn.) petrel grande que se alimenta de carroña.

stinking [-iŋ], *a.* hediondo, apestoso.—**s. c(h)amomile**, (bot.) magarzuela, manzanilla hedionda.—**s. iris**, (bot.) lirio hediondo.

stinkingly [-lii], *adv.* hediondamente, con hediondez.

stinkpot [-pat], *s.* bomba asfixiante.

stinkweed [-wid], *s.* (bot.) estramonio.

stint [stint]. I. *va.* restringir, escatimar; asignar una tarea. II. *vn.* ser económico o parco, estrecharse. III. *s.* cuota, tarea; límite, restricción.

stipend [stáipend], *s.* estipendio, sueldo.

stipendiary [staipéndieri], *a.* y *s.* estipendiario, soldadero.

stipple [stípl]. I. *va.* (b. a.) picar, puntear, granear. II. *s.* picado, punteado.—**s. graver**, graneador.

stippling [stípliŋ], *s.* (b. a.) graneo.

stiptic(al [stíptik(al], *a.* estíptico.

stipulate [stípyuleit]. I. *va.* estipular, especificar. II. *vn.* estipular, contratar, pactar. III. *a.* (bot.) provisto de estípulas.

stipulation [-léiʃ ɔn], *s.* estipulación, condición; convenio, contrato, pacto.

stipule [stípyul], *s.* (bot.) estípula.

stir [stœr]. I. *va.* agitar, menear, batir; hurgar, remover, revolver; perturbar, excitar, irritar; animar, incitar; conmover; ventilar, discutir.— **to s. the fire**, atizar o avivar el fuego o la lumbre.—**to s. up**, conmover, excitar; aguijonear; poner en movimiento; revolver; despertar, suscitar (interés, etc.).—**to s. up a hornet's nest**, o **storm**, armar cisco, promover desórdenes. II. *vn.* moverse; menearse; rebullir. III. *s.* movimiento, conmoción, excitación, bullicio, alboroto, revuelo.—**to cause**, o **kick up**, **a great s.**, levantar gran polvareda; dar golpe, causar sensación.

stirrer [-œ(r)], *s.* agitador; batidor, molinillo; mecedor (de vinos); meneador.

stirrup [stírap], *s.* estribo; (zap.) tirapié; (mar.) estribo.—**s. bone**, (anat.) estribo (del oído).— **s. cup**, trago o copa de despedida.—**s. leather** o **strap**, ación.—**s. pump**, bomba pequeña de mano.

stitch [stitch]. I. *va.* coser, embastar, bastear, hilvanar, unir, juntar.—**to s. up**, remendar, (cir.) dar puntos. II. *vn.* coser, bordar. III. *s.* (cost.) puntada, punto, baste, basta; (med.) punzada, dolor punzante; (agr.) caballón, surco.

stitcher [-œ(r)], *s.* coseder, cosedora; ribeteadora; (enc.) cosedor; máquina cosedora o de coser.— **stitching** [-iŋ], *s.* puntos, puntadas, costura; (enc.) cosido; pespunte, punto atrás, costura a máquina.

stithy [stíði], *s.* fragua; yunque.

stiver [stáivœ(r)], *s.* moneda holandesa; ardite.

stoat [stout], *s.* (zool.) armiño.

stock [stak]. I. *s.* (bot. o hort.) tronco, cepa; patrón; injerto; (bot.) variedad de alhelí; berza; progenitor; estirpe, *f.,* cepa, raza, linaje; (for.) línea directa de una familia; (com.) capital comercial; acciones, valores; abasto, surtido (de mercancías); mercancías almacenadas, existencias; repuesto, provisión, cantidad de primeras materias; (teat.) repertorio; enseres

muebles; (mec.) mango, manija, cubo, zoquete, leño, tajo; berbiquí de barrena; caja (de fusil, cepillo, etc.); cepo (de ancla, yunque); corbatín, alzacuello; colonia de abejas, colmena; baceta o monte de una baraja; ganado (= LIVE STOCK); (coc.) extracto; (fam.) importancia; confianza, fe, *f.*—*pl.* cepo (castigo); (com.) valores, acciones; (mar.) astillero, gradas de construcción. —**s.-blind**, totalmente ciego.—**s. blocks**, (mar.) polines de la grada.—**s. breeder**, criador de ganado.—**s. company**, (com.) compañía o sociedad anónima; (teat.) compañía de repertorio.—**s. dove**, (orn.) paloma silvestre.—**s. exchange**, (com.) bolsa, lonja (de acciones); asociación de corredores de bolsa.—**s. farm, s. farming**, ganadería.—**s. farmer**, ganadero. —**s. in hand**, mercancías en almacén, existencias.—**s. in trade**, artículos que se venden en una tienda; equipo, útiles (de un artesano, etc.); (fam.) caballo de batalla.—**s. market**, (com.) = s. EXCHANGE; compra y venta de valores; precios y tendencias en la bolsa.— **s. pile**, *s.* depósito de abastecimiento o de reserva; almacenamiento.—**s.-pile**, *va.* acumular, almacenar.—**s. raising**, ganadería, cría de ganado.—**s.-still**, enteramente quieto.—**in s.**, (com.) en existencia.—**on the stocks**, (mar.) en vía de construcción; (fig.) en preparación.— **out of s.**, (com.) agotado.—**to lay in a s. (of)**, almacenar, proveerse (de).—**to take s. (in)**, *v.* TO TAKE, *va.* II. *a.* rel. o pert. a la bolsa, a la ganadería o al teatro de repertorio; normal, usual; muy usado; estereotipado; (com.) de surtido. III. *va.* poner o llevar en surtido; proveer, abastecer, surtir; acumular, juntar, acopiar; encepar (anclas, armas de fuego, etc.).

stockade [stakéid]. I. *va.* empalizar. II. *s.* empalizada, estacada, palanquera; vallado.

stockbroker [stákbroukœ(r)], *s.* corredor de bolsa, bolsista.

stockfish [-fiʃ], *s.* bacalao seco, pejepalo.

stockholder [-houldœ(r)], *s.* accionista, tenedor de títulos o acciones.

stockinet [stakinét], *s.* (tej.) elástica.

stocking [stákiŋ], *s.* media, calceta.—**s. frame**, telar de medias.—**s. weaver**, tejedor de medias.

stockish [stákiʃ], *a.* estúpido.

stockjobber [stákdʒabœ(r)], *s.* (Ingl.) agente de corredores de bolsa; (E. U.) corredor de bolsa (apl. esp. al agiotista).—**stockjobbing** [-dʒabiŋ], *s.* oficio del *stockjobber;* agio(taje).

stockman [-mæn], *s.* ganadero; (com.) el encargado de las existencias.

stockroom [-rum], *s.* (com.) almacén, depósito, cuarto de existencias.

stocktaking [-teikiŋ], *s.* (com. y fig.) inventario, acción de inventariar.

stocky [-i], *a.* rechoncho, fornido.

stockyard [-yard], *s.* corral de ganado.

stodgy [stádʒi], *a.* pesado, indigesto; soso, insípido; regordete; hinchado.

stogy [stóuɡi], *s.* bota burda o basta; cigarro tosco y barato, (fam.) tagarnina (ll. t. **stogie**).

Stoic, stoic [stóuik], *s.* y *a.*, **stoical** [-al], *a.* estoico.—**stoically** [-li], *adv.* estoicamente.— **stoicism** [stóuisizm], *s.* estoicismo; estoicidad.

stoke [stóuk], *va.* y *vn.* (m. v.) atizar el fuego; calentar, alimentar, cargar (un hogar).

stokehold [-hould], *s.* (mar.) puesto de fogonero; cuarto de calderas.

stokehole [-houl], *s.* (m. v.) boca del horno; sitio del fogonero; cuarto de calderas.

stoker [-œ(r)], *s.* fogonero, paleador; alimentador de hogar, cargador (automático).

stole [stóul], *s.* (igl.) estola; estola (de señora).

stole, stolen [-n], *pret.* y *pp.* de TO STEAL.

stolid [stálid], *a.* estólido, impasible.

stolidity [stalíditi], *s.* estolidez, impasibilidad.

stolon [stóulan], *s.* (bot.) estolón.

stoma [stóumä], *s.* (bot., fisiol.) estoma, *m.*

stomach [stámak]. I. *s.* (anat., zool.) estómago;

vientre, barriga; apetito; deseo, afición, inclinación.—**s. ache**, dolor de estómago, gastralgia.
—**s. plaster**, estomaticón.—**s. pump**, bomba estomacal. **II.** *va.* tragar, digerir, sufrir, aguantar.

stomachal [-ạl], *a.* (anat.) estomacal.

stomacher [-œ(r)], *s.* peto (prenda de vestir).

stomachic(al [stomékịk(ạl]. **I.** *a.* estoma(ti)cal, estomáquico. **II.** *s.* medicamento estomacal.

stomachless [stámaklịs], *a.* (fig.) desganado.

stomata [stóụmạtạ̄], *s. pl.* de STOMA.

stomatitis [-tájtịs], *s.* (med.) estomatitis.

stomatology [-tálodžị], *s.* (med.) ciencia de la boca y sus enfermedades.

stomatopod [stóụmạtopad], *s.* y *a.* (zool.) estomápodo, estomatópodo.

stone [stóụn]. **I.** *s.* piedra; canto; roca, peña; piedra de molino, de amolar; piedra sepulcral; (joy.) piedra preciosa; (med.) piedra, cálculo; hueso, cuesco (de las frutas); (Ingl.) peso de 14 libras.—**S. Age**, edad de piedra.—**s.-blind**, enteramente ciego.—**s. bottle** o **jug**, caneca, tarro, botella de greda.—**s. breaker**, bocarte, triturador.—**s.-broke**, (fam.) tronado, arrancado, sin un cuartillo.—**s. coal**, antracita.—**s.-cold**, frío como la piedra, frío helado.—**s. color**, gris azulado.—**s. crusher** = **s.** BREAKER.—**s.-dead**, muerto como una piedra.—**s.-deaf**, enteramente sordo.—**s.-dumb**, enteramente mudo.—**s. fruit**, fruta de hueso.—**s. hammer**, dolobre, almádana, marra.—**s. mason**, albañil.—**s. masonry**, mampostería (de piedra), calicanto, cal (*f.*) y canto.—**s. oil**, petróleo.—**s. pit**, **s. quarry**, pedrera, cantera.—**s.-still**, enteramente quieto.—**s. wall**, vallado.—**s.'s cast**, **s.'s throw**, tiro de piedra, corta distancia.—**s. trough**, pilón. **II.** *va.* apedrear; deshuesar, despepitar, quitar los cuescos o huesos a las frutas; (alb.) revestir de piedras.—**to s. to death**, lapidar, matar a pedradas.

stonebreak [-brejk], *s.* (bot.) quebrantapiedras, *mf.*, saxífraga.

stonecrop [-krap], *s.* (bot.) ombligo de Venus; cualquier planta crasulácea.

stonecutter [-kʌtœ(r)], *s.* picapedrero, cantero, labrador de piedra.—**stonecutting** [-kʌtị̄n], *s.* corte o labra de piedra.

stoner [-œ(r)], *s.* apedreador, lapidador; despepitador(a), deshuesador(a) de frutas.

stoneware [-wer], *s.* cacharros; objetos de barro.

stonework [-wœrk], *s.* obra de sillería; cantería, albañilería, mampostería.

stoneworks [-wœrks], *s.* taller de cantería.

stoniness [-ịnịs], *s.* calidad de pedregoso o pétreo; (fig.) dureza, insensibilidad.

stoning [-ịn], *s.* pedrea, apedre(amient)o, lapidación.

stony [-ị], *a.* pedregoso; (ant. y poét.) de piedra, pétreo, lapídeo, lapidoso; duro, insensible; petrificante.—**s.-hearted**, insensible, cruel.—**s. site**, spot o tract, pedregal, pedriza.

stood [stụd], *pret.* y *pp.* de TO STAND.

stooge [studž], *s.* (fam., teat.) preguntador apostado en el auditorio para que haga preguntas preparadas a un comediante, que las contesta chistosamente; bufón que hace un papel algo semejante en la escena misma; (fam.) paniaguado, esbirro, secuaz servil.

stool [stul]. **I.** *s.* banquillo, taburete, escabel; tarimilla, banqueta; inodoro, sillico; (bot.) planta madre; (hort.) vástago acodado; (caza) señuelo, añagaza; cimillo.—*pl.* cámara, evacuación de vientre, deposiciones.—**s. pigeon**, cimbel, señuelo (en la caza de aves); (fam.) persona que sirve de señuelo, ya como confederado de los tahures, etc., ya como espía al servicio de la policía.—**to go to s.**, hacer del cuerpo. **II.** *va.* atraer con añagazas o señuelos. **III.** *vn.* echar tallos, retoños, etc.; evacuar (el vientre); atraer con señuelos; (fam.) hacer el papel de *stool pigeon*.

stoop [stúp]. **I.** *vn.* agacharse, doblar o inclinar el cuerpo; ir encorvado, ser cargado de espaldas; encorvarse, combarse hacia adelante; ba, jarse, humillarse, rebajarse; condescender; lanzarse, arrojarse sobre la presa. **II.** *va.* rebajar-degradar; (ant.) someter, abatir, hacer bajar. **III.** *s.* inclinación de hombros, cargazón (*f.*) de espaldas; descenso, caída; caimiento, declinación, abatimiento; (E. U.) gradería, escalinata de entrada. *V.* STOUP.

stoopingly [-ịnlị], *adv.* con inclinación hacia abajo; servilmente.

stop [stap]. **I.** *va.* parar; detener, atajar, interceptar; suspender, paralizar; contener, reprimir, refrenar; obstruir, atascar, tapar; estancar, represar.—**to s. one's mouth**, tapar la boca a uno, no dejarle que decir.—**to s. payment**, suspender el pago (de un cheque).—**to s. payments**, suspender pagos.—**to s. short**, detener brusca o repentinamente.—**to s. up**, tapar, cerrar, obstruir, obturar, tupir. **II.** *vn.* parar; pararse; detenerse, hacer alto, demorarse; cesar; acabarse, terminar; (fam.) quedarse algún tiempo, alojarse, hospedarse; (mús.) cambiar el tono por medio de un agujero o un traste.—¡s.!, ¡alto!—**to s. at**, detenerse en, reparar en, pararse en; hacer escala en (un puerto).—**to s. over**, hacer escala (en); hacer tránsito.—**to s. short**, detenerse repentina o bruscamente.—**to s. (working**, etc.), cesar o dejar de (trabajar, etc.). **III.** *s.* parada, detención; cesación; pausa, alto; interrupción; suspensión, paro (de trabajo); obstáculo, impedimento, obstrucción; represión; (mús.) tecla; llave, *f.*; traste de guitarra; registro de órgano; (gram.) punto; (mec.) retén, fiador, seguro, leva, tope, paleta, linguete, trinquete.—**s.-gap**, tapón, relleno; procedimiento o cosa de conveniencia; subterfugio, escapatoria.—**s. light**, luz de parada.—**s.-over**, que permite detenerse en lugares intermedios (apl. a billetes de f. c.).—**s.-over point**, punto de escala, estación de escalas.—**s. sign** o **signal**, señal (*f.*) de parada o de alto.—**s. valve**, válvula reguladora o de cierre.—**s. watch**, cronógrafo, cronómetro, reloj de detención.—**to make a s.**, hacer alto. *V.* MAKE, *va.*

stopcock [stápkak], *s.* llave, *f.*, grifo, espita.

stope [stoụp]. **I.** *va.* (min.) excavar en escalones. **II.** *s.* obra en escalones.

stopover [stápoụvœ(r)], *s.* parada temporal en un lugar.

stoppage [stápịdž], *s.* cesación, interrupción; paro (del trabajo); detención, interceptación; obstrucción, impedimento; represa; retención (sobre un pago); (med.) estrangulación.—**s. in transit**, (for.) embargo de mercancías durante su transporte, por insolvencia del comprador.

stopper [stápœ(r)]. **I.** *va.* entaponar, tapar con tapón; (mar.) bozar. **II.** *s.* tapón; taco, tarugo; tapador, obturador; detenedor; (mar.) boza, estopor.—**s. bolts**, (mar.) argollas de boza.

stopping [stápịn]. **I.** *s.* parada; detención; interrupción. **II.** *a.* de detención, que detiene o para.—**s. place**, escala; lugar de descanso o de detención.

stopple [stápl]. **I.** *va.* entaponar, atarugar. **II.** *s.* tapón, tarugo, taco; bitoque.

storage [stórịdž], *s.* (derechos de) almacenaje.—**s. battery**, (elec.) batería de acumuladores, o acumulador.—**s. reservoir**, **s. tank**, depósito de abastecimiento; tanque o depósito de reserva.

storax [stóụræks], *s.* estoraque.—**s. tree**, (bot.) estoraque.

store [stór]. **I.** *s.* abundancia, acopio; provisión, repuesto; almacén, depósito; tienda.—*pl.* pertrechos, equipos; víveres, provisiones; municiones; bastimentos, provisiones de boca. **II.** *va.* proveer o abastecer; municionar o pertrechar;

guardar; acumular, acopiar, recoger; tener en reserva; almacenar.

storehouse [-haus], *s*. almacén.

storekeeper [-kipœ(r)], *s*. guardaalmacén; jefe de depósito; tendero, comerciante; (mar.) pañolero.

storeroom [-rum], *s*. despensa; bodega; cilla (para granos); almacén, cuarto de almacenar; (mar.) pañol de víveres.

storeship [-šip], *s*. (mar.) urca, navío almacén.

storied [stórid], *a*. historiado; legendario; de (tantos) pisos (un edificio).

storiette [storiét], *s*. cuentecillo, novela corta, historieta.

stork [stork], *s*. (orn.) cigüeña; (fam.) mensajero imaginario que trae los recién nacidos.—**s.'s bill**, (bot.) geranio.

storm [storm]. **I**. *s*. tempestad, temporal, tormenta o borrasca; vendaval; arrebato, frenesí; conmoción, tumulto; (mil.) ataque, asalto; turbonada.—**s. door**, guardapuerta, cancel.—**s. petrel**, (orn.) petrel de la tempestad (así llamado porque diz que la presagia).—**s. troops**, (mil.) tropas escogidas de asalto.—**s.-water sewer**, (ing.) alcantarilla para agua de lluvia. **II**. *va*. (mil.) asaltar, tomar por asalto. **III**. *vn. impers*. haber tormenta; bramar o estallar de cólera.

stormbird [-bœrd], *s*. (orn.) procelario, petrel.

storminess [-inis], *s*. estado borrascoso, tempestuoso.

stormy [-i], *a*. tempestuoso, borrascoso; violento, turbulento.—**s. petrel** = STORM PETREL.

story [stóri]. **I**. *s*. historia; cuento, fábula, conseja; historieta; anécdota; (fam.) cuento de viejas, hablilla; enredo, trama, argumento; (fam.) mentira, embuste; (fam.) artículo (escrito); (arq.) alto, piso, planta.—**s. teller**, decidor de cuentos y anécdotas, narrador, cuentista; chismoso; embustero.—**as the s. goes**, según se dice, según cuenta la historia.—**to make a long s. short**, para abreviar.—**that is quite another s.**, eso es harina de otro costal. **II**. *va*. historiar, narrar; colocar en pisos o rimeros.

stoup, stoop [stup], *s*. copa o frasco para beber; (igl.) pila de agua bendita.

stout [staut]. **I**. *a*. fornido, forzudo; gordo, corpulento; fuerte, sólido, firme; resuelto, intrépido, animoso. **II**. *s*. cerveza fuerte.—**stoutly** [-li], *adv*. vigorosamente; recio; con resolución.—**stoutness** [-nis], *s*. corpulencia, gordura; solidez; fuerza; intrepidez.

stove [stóuv], *s*. estufa, hornillo, cocina o fogón de hierro; (Ingl.) invernadero; horno cerámico.

stove, *pret*. y *pp*. de TO STAVE.

stovepipe [-paip], *s*. tubería del fogón a la chimenea; (fam.) chistera (ll. t. **stovepipe hat**).

stow [stóu], *va*. (a)prensar, atestar, hacinar; colocar, meter, alojar; esconder, ocultar; (mar.) estibar, arrumar, abarrotar; arrizar.—**to s. the hold**, (mar.) estibar, abarrotar.

stowage [-idž], *s*. almacenaje; (mar.) estiba; arrumaje.

stowaway [-awei], *s*. (mar.) polizón, llovido.

stower [-œ(r)], *s*. estibador.

strabismic [strabízmik], *a*. estrábico.

strabismus [-mas], *s*. (med.) estrabismo.

strabotomy [strabátomi], *s*. (cir.) estrabotomía.

straddle [strádl]. **I**. *vn*. esparrancarse; montar a horcajadas; (mec., carr.) tener los extremos alternados o al tresbolillo; (fam.) no tomar partido. **II**. *va*. montar a horcajadas; montarse en; (fam.) no tomar partido en; estar por ambas partes en (un partido, disputa). **III**. *s*. posición del que se esparranca o monta a horcajadas; (fam.) posición equívoca; operación de bolsa con opción de compra o venta.—**s.-legged**, **straddling**, patiabierto.

straddler [strádlœ(r)], *s*. (fam.) el que no se

decide, o está entre dos bandos opuestos inclinándose hacia ambos.

Stradivarius [strædivérias], *s*. (mús.) estradivario, violín, etc.

strafe [streif]. **I**. *s*. bombardeo violento; ametrallamiento aéreo (ll. t. **strafing**). **II**. *va*. bombardear violentamente; (fam.) castigar.

straggle [strǽgl], *vn*. extraviarse; rezagarse; rodar, andorrear; extenderse, desparramarse; estar esparcido.

straggler [-glœ(r)], *s*. rezagado; vagamundo, tunante; rama extendida; objeto aislado.

straggling [-gliŋ], *a*. rezagado; extraviado; disperso.—**s. branches**, ramas dispersas.—**s. soldier**, soldado rezagado.

straight [streit]. **I**. *a*. derecho, recto; directo, en línea recta; lacio (el pelo); erguido, derecho; justo, equitativo; íntegro, honrado; correcto, exacto; franco, o sin estorbos; seguido, no interrumpido.—**s. angle**, ángulo rectilíneo o derecho, ángulo de lados colineares (180°).—**s. face**, cara seria.—**s. line**, línea recta.—**s.-line**, en línea recta; de movimiento en línea recta.—**s.-out**, (fam.) sincero, franco, abierto, sin disfraz; firme, intransigente.—**s.-side tire**, (aut.) neumático sin talón. **II**. *adv*. directamente, en derechura, en línea recta; luego, al punto, inmediatamente.—**s. ahead**, (todo) derecho; enfrente.—**s. away**, en seguida, inmediatamente.—**s. off**, sin vacilar, sin demora. **III**. *s*. runfla de cinco naipes del mismo palo en el juego de *poker* (ll. t. **flush**).

straightedge [-edž], *s*. regla (de trazar líneas).

straighten [-n], *va*. enderezar; poner en orden, arreglar; (con **out**) desenmarañar; (carp.) desalabear.—**straightener** [-œ(r)], *s*. enderezador, el que endereza o pone en orden.—**straightening** [-iŋ], *s*. enderezamiento; (carp.) desalabeo.

straightforward(s [-fórwård(z)]. **I**. *a*. recto, derecho; honrado, íntegro, sincero. **II**. *adv*. de frente.

straightly [-li], *adv*. en línea recta, directamente.

straightness [-nis], *s*. derechura, calidad de recto o derecho; rectitud, probidad, honradez.

straightway [-wei], *adv*. inmediatamente, luego.

strain [strein]. **I**. *va*. hacer fuerza a; poner tirante; poner, consagrar (la atención, etc.); forzar (la vista, los nervios, etc.); someter a esfuerzo; estirar, forzar; extremar; perjudicar por esfuerzo excesivo; colar, cerar, tamizar, cribar; apretar; agarrar; (mec.) someter a esfuerzo; (mec.) deformar.—**to s. a point**, excederse; hacer una concesión; hacer violencia (a la lógica, a la conciencia, etc.).—**to s. to one's breast**, apretar a uno contra sí, abrazándole.—**strained relations**, relaciones tirantes. **II**. *vn*. hacer grande esfuerzo, esforzarse; resistir o estar sometido a esfuerzo; pasar o meterse por (un cedazo, una pared); infiltrarse.—**to s. at**, esforzarse o hacer grandes esfuerzos en o por. **III**. *s*. tensión, tirantez, esfuerzo fuerte o violento; (med.) lesión, relajación, torcedura, o cualquier otro daño debido a esfuerzo excesivo; (mec.) esfuerzo; deformación; huella, vena, indicio; (mús.) aire, melodía; acorde, acentos; parte distintiva de un poema, canto; verso; estilo, tono, modo de hablar o pensar; estirpe, *f.*, descendencia, raza, linaje; clase, *f.*; genio o disposición heredada.

strainer [-œ(r)], *s*. colador, coladera, coladero, filtro, tamiz, *m*.

strait [streit]. **I**. *a*. (ant.) estrecho, angosto, ajustado, apretado; estricto, rigoroso.—**s. jacket**, camisa de fuerza.—**s.-laced**, ceñido; estricto; mojigato. **II**. *s*. (geog.) estrecho; garganta, desfiladero, angostura o paso estrecho; (a menudo *pl.*) apuro, aprieto, estrechez.

straiten [-n], *va*. estrechar, angostar, contraer; constreñir, reducir; embarazar, poner en calzas prietas; estorbar; apenar.—**straitened**, *a*. financieramente embarazado, en circunstancias apremiantes; necesitado, sin recursos.

straitly [-lị], *adv.* estrechamente; estrictamente, rigorosamente.—**straitness** [-nịs], *s.* estrechez, estrechura, angostura; aprieto, apuro; penuria.

strake [streịk], *s.* (mar.) traca, hilada.

stramineous [stramínịas], *a.* pajizo; de o semejante a la paja; de color de paja; sin valor.

stramonium [stramóunịam], *s.* (bot. y farm.) estramonio.

strand [strǽnd]. I. *va. y vn.* (mar. y fig.) encallar, embarrancar, vararse, zabordar; dejar o quedarse desamparado; romper uno de los cabos de una cuerda; romperse en cordones; (re)torcer o trenzar (los cabos de un cordel). II. *s.* costa, marina, playa, ribera; cabo, hebra, hilo; hilo o sarta (de perlas); ramal, cordón (de cable); (aer.) cable de alambre con núcleo, formado arrollando varios alambres juntos al rededor de un alambre central.

stranded [-ịd], *a.* de cabos o cordones retorcidos (cable); (mar. y fig.) varado, zabordado; desamparado, sin recursos.—**s. wire**, alambre retorcido, cable de alambre.

stranding [-ịŋ], *s.* (mar.) encalladura, varada, zaborda(miento); retorcimiento (de cordel).

strange [streịndž]. I. *a.* extraño, singular, extraordinario, inaudito; forastero; ajeno; desconocido; retraído, reservado, esquivo.—**s. face**, cara desconocida.—**s. to say**, lo cual es extraño; (es) cosa extraña. II. *interj.* ¡cosa rara! ¡cáspita!

strangely [-lị], *adv.* extrañamente; extraordinariamente.

strangeness [-nịs], *s.* extranjería; extrañeza, rareza; reserva, esquivez; maravilla.

stranger [-œ(r)], *s.* extranjero, extraño, forastero; desconocido.—**he is a s. to me**, me es desconocido.—**to be a s. to**, desconocer, no conocer; ser desconocido.—**you are a s.**, se vende Vd. muy caro, no se le ve a Vd., milagro es verlo.

strangle [strǽŋgl]. I. *va.* estrangular; agarrotar, dar garrote; ahogar, sofocar. II. *vn.* morir estrangulado, estrangularse.—**s. hold**, (fig.) influencia o acción avasalladora o paralizadora; dominio completo.

strangler [-glœ(r)], *s.* estrangulador.

strangulate [-giuleịt], *va.* estrangular; (med. y cir.) estrangular (cerrar u obstruir por compresión para cortar la circulación).

strangulated [-ịd], *a.* (med. y cir.) estrangulado, sometido a la constricción.

strangulation [-léịšǫn], *s.* estrangulación.

strangury [strǽŋgịurị], *s.* (med.) estangurria.

strap [strǽp]. I. *s.* correa; tira, faja, banda; abrazadera; precinta; (tal.) gamarra; (mec.) cabeza de biela; (mil.) capona o charretera mocha; agarrador (de tranvía, autobús, etc.); (sast.) trabilla de pantalón; (zap.) tirante, tirador; (carr.) correón, sopanda; (mar.) gaza. —**s. brake**, freno de cinta.—**s. hinge**, bisagra de ramales.—**s. iron**, hierro en tiras; tira de hierro. II. *va.* liar, fajar o atar con correas; precintar; asentar (navajas de barba).

strapper [-œ(r)], *s.* el o lo que lía, ata, etc.; (fam.) cosa o persona alta y talluda.

strapping [-ịŋ]. I. *a.* (fam.) robusto, alto y fuerte.—**s. girl, woman**, mocetona, mujerona. —**s. youth**, mocetón. II. *s.* acción de liar, atar, etc.; correaje; (fam.) tunda, azotaina.

strata [streịtā], *s. pl.* de STRATUM.

stratagem [strǽtadžem], *s.* estratagema, artimaña.

strategic(al [stratídžịk (al]), *a.* estratégico; ventajoso, dominante.—**strategics** [-s], *s.* estrategia.—**strategist** [strǽtịdžịst], *s.* estratégico.—**strategy** [-džị], *s.* estrategia.

strath [strǽθ], *s.* (Esco.) valle extenso.

stratification [strǽtịfịkéịšǫn], *s.* (geol.) estratificación.—**stratiform** [-form], *a.* estrati-

forme.—**stratify** [-faị], *va.* estratificar.—

stratigraphic(al [-grǽfịk(al]), *a.* estratigráfico. —**stratigraphy** [stratígrafị], *s.* estratigrafía.

stratocracy [stratákrasị], *s.* despotismo militar.

stratosphere [strǽtosfịr], *s.* estratosfera.

stratum [streịtam], *s.* estrato, lecho, capa, tonga, cama; (geol.) estrato; (anat.) capa de tejido.

stratus [streịtas], *s.* (meteor.) estrato.

straw [stró]. I. *s.* paja; bálago; sombrero de paja; bagatela, fruslería; indicio.—**not to care a s.**, no importarle a uno un comino, no dársele a uno un bledo.—**the last s.**, el golpe de gracia, el acabóse. II. *a.* de paja; pajizo; baladí; falso, ficticio.—**s. bail**, (for.) caución o fianza simulada.—**s. bed**, jergón de paja.—**s. bond**, bono o caución ficticios.—**s.-colored**, de color pajizo.—**s. hat**, sombrero de paja.—**s. loft**, pajar. —**s. man**, nulidad; testaferro; títere.—**s. poll, s. vote**, voto o votación no oficial, votos recogidos por persona o empresa particular (gen. un periódico) para determinar la opinión pública.

strawberry [-berị], *s.* (bot.) fresa, (Am.) fresón, frutilla.—**s. patch**, fresal.—**s. plant**, fresera. —**s. tree**, (bot.) madroño; gayuba.

strawboard [-bord], *s.* cartón de paja.

strawworm [-wœrm], *s.* (ent.) gorgojo.

strawy [-ị], *a.* pajizo; de paja.

stray [streị]. I. *vn.* descarriarse, extraviarse; desman(d)arse (el ganado); errar, desviarse del deber. II. *a.* extraviado, descarriado, perdido. III. *s.* persona o animal descarriado o perdido. —**straying** [-ịŋ], *s.* descarriamiento, descarrío.

streak [strịk]. I. *s.* raya, lista, línea, faja, veta; rayo de luz; vena, rasgo de ingenio; traza, pizca; antojo, capricho; (min.) raspadura; (mar.) costura de tablas, traca, hilada.—**s. of luck**, racha.—**like a s.**, veloz como un relámpago. II. *va.* rayar, listar; abigarrar; gayar. III. *vn.* pasar o viajar con suma rapidez.

streaky [-ị], *a.* rayado, listado, veteado, abigarrado; variado, desigual.

stream [strím]. I. *s.* corriente, *f.*; arroyo; corriente de agua (término que comprende ríos y arroyos); flujo, chorro (de líquido, gas, luz, etc.); curso.—**s. anchor**, (mar.) anclote.—**s. cable**, (mar.) calabrote.—**s. tin**, (min.) estaño de aluvión, en grano.—**against the s.**, contra la corriente.—**down s., up s.**, agua abajo, agua arriba. II. *va. y vn.* correr, manar, fluir, brotar; salir a torrentes; derramar con abundancia; lavar en agua corriente; ondear, flotar, flamear, tremolar (una bandera); pasar dejando un rastro de luz.

streamer [-œ(r)], *s.* (mar.) flámula, gallardete, banderola, grímpola; aurora boreal; encabezamiento al través o del ancho de la página (ll. t. **s. headline**).

streamlet [-lịt], *s.* arroyuelo, riachuelo.

streamline [-laịn]. I. *s.* trayectoria (de una corriente, esp. de las uniformes o que no tienen remolinos); línea de trabajo o trayectoria de la vena líquida; perfil aerodinámico; línea perfilada. II. *a.* continuo y sin remolinos (movimiento); que permite o facilita flujo o corriente continuos, sin remolinos; aerodinámico, de líneas aerodinámicas, perfilado, fuselado, de tipo torpedo (ú. de automóviles, aviones, etc.). III. *va.* dar líneas aerodinámicas, dar forma que permita flujo continuo; (fig.) reducir o simplificar para hacer más efectivo o para obtener mayor rendimiento.

streamlined [-d], *a.* = STREAMLINE.

streamy [strímị], *a.* surcado de arroyos; que mana a chorros; radiante.

street [strít], *s.* calle, *f.*, rúa, vía pública.—**s. Arab**, golfo, pillete.—**s. cleaner o sweeper**, barrendero; barredera (automóvil).—**s. intersection**, bocacalle, *f.*, encrucijada.—**s. lamp**, farol.—**s. porter**, mozo de cuerda o de cordel. —**s. railway**, tranvía, *m.*—**s. railway worker**, tranviario.—s. **scenes**, escenas callejeras.—s. **sprinkler**, carricuba, carro de riego.

streetcar [-kar], s. (coche de) tranvía, m.

streetwalker [-wɔkœ(r)], s. prostituta de calle, nocherniega, andorr(er)a; callejero, andorrero.

strength [stréŋθ], s. fuerza, vigor; reciedumbre, reciura; potencia, pujanza, poder; validez, fuerza legal; (ing.) resistencia; aguante; fortaleza, firmeza, resistencia, solidez; intensidad; vehemencia; (quím.) concentración, grado de potencia o de concentración; cuerpo (del vino); seguridad, confianza; (mil.) número, magnitud (de soldados, de ejército, de fuerzas militares); (ant.) baluarte, plaza fuerte.—s. **of a current**, (elec.) intensidad de una corriente (gen. expresada en amperios).—s. **of a field**, (fís.) intensidad de un campo (magnético, de atracción, etc.).—s. **of materials**, (ing.) resistencia de materiales.—**on**, o **upon, the s. of**, fundándose en, confiando en.

strengthen [-n]. I. va. fortalecer, fortificar, robustecer; consolidar; confirmar, corroborar; reforzar; animar, confortar, alentar. II. vn. fortalecerse; reforzarse; arreciar(se).

strengthener [-œ(r)], s. refuerzo; confortador; corroborante.

strengthening [-iŋ]. I. s. fortalecimiento, robustecimiento; consolidación. II. a. fortalecedor, fortificante, robustecedor, tónico.

strengthless [-ljs], a. débil, sin fuerza(s).

strenuous [strényᴜᴀs], a. estrenuo, fuerte; activo, enérgico; acérrimo, tenaz.

strenuously [-lj], adv. vigorosamente, enérgicamente, con grandes esfuerzos.—**strenuousness** [-njs], s. estrenuidad, energía, fortaleza.

streptococcus [streptokákᴀs], s. (bact.) estreptococo.—**streptococcal infection**, (med.) estreptococia.

stress [stres]. I. s. fuerza, peso, importancia, entidad; (ing., mec.) esfuerzo; violencia, tensión; compulsión, coacción; acento tónico, énfasis.—s. **of weather**, mal tiempo.—**by s. of weather**, (mar.) a causa de un temporal. II. va. someter a esfuerzo; dar importancia o énfasis a, subrayar, poner de relieve; poner en aprieto.

stretch [strétch]. I. va. extender, alargar, tender; estirar, atesar; ensanchar, dilatar; violentar, forzar; (fam.) exagerar, llevar al extremo; (mar.) hacer toda fuerza de vela.—**to s. a point**, excederse, pasarse de los justos límites; hacer alguna concesión, ceder un poco.—**to s. forth**, alargar, extender.—**to s. one's feet**, (d)esperezarse.—**to s. out**, extender, estirar, alargar. II. vn. alargarse, extenderse, dar de sí, dilatarse; estirarse, desplegarse; (fig.) esforzarse; exagerar.—**to s. out**, extenderse, desplegarse, prolongarse, llegar (hasta); echarse en la cama, etc.).—**to s. out to sea**, (mar.) tirar a la mar. III. s. alargamiento; extensión, dilatación; elasticidad; tirantez, esfuerzo; violencia o interpretación forzada; alcance, trecho, distancia, tramo, tracto; lapso, tirada, intervalo; (mar.) bordada.—s. **of the imagination**, esfuerzo de la imaginación.—**at a s.**, de una vez, de un tirón.

stretcher [-œ(r)], s. tendedor; estirador, dilatador, atesador, ensanchador; camilla, andas, f. pl., parihuela; (alb.) soga; ladrillo o losa planos; (carp.) viga, madero largo, tirante; (pint.) bastidor (para lienzo); (mar.) peana o pedestal de bote.—s.-**bearer**, camillero.

stretching [-iŋ], s. tendedura, alargamiento, estiramiento, entesamiento, tensión; dilatación; acostamiento; (d)esperezo.

strew [stru], va. (pp. STREWED o STREWN) regar, esparcir, derramar; rociar, sembrar, salpicar.

stria [stráiᴀ], s. (arq.) estría.—**striate** [stráiejt], va. estriar.—**striate(d** [stráiejt(jd], a. estriado.—**striation, striature** [-éjsᴀn, stráiᴀchᴜr], s. estriación, estriadura.

stricken [stríkn]. I. pp. de TO STRIKE. II. a.

herido (por un proyectil); atacado, agobiado.—s. **in years**, viejo, entrado en años.

strickle [stríkl], s. rasero.

strict [stríkt], a. estricto, rígido; exacto, riguroso, escrupuloso; severo; áspero; estirado, tirante; (zool.) limitado, ceñido, estrecho.

strictly [-lj], adv. estrictamente, exactamente, rigurosamente.—s. **private**, muy reservado.

strictness [-njs], s. exactitud, puntualidad; severidad, rigor; tirantez.

stricture [stríkchᴜ(r)], s. crítica severa, censura; (med.) estrechez, constricción.

stride [straid]. I. s. paso largo, tranco, zancada. II. va. (pret. STRODE; pp. STRIDDEN) cruzar a grandes trancos; montar a horcajadas. III. vn. andar a trancos, (fam.) atrancar.

stridency [stráidensj], s. estridencia.

strident [-ent], a. estridente.

stridor [-ǫ(r)], s. estridor.

stridulate [stríðʒᴜlejt], vn. chirriar.

stridulation [-léjʂǫn], s. chirrido.

stridulous [-lᴀs], a. chirriante, rechinante; (med.) estriduloso.

strife [straif], s. contienda, lucha, refriega; rivalidad, porfía.

strigil [stríðʒjl], s. cepillo fuerte, raspador; (arq.) ondulación.—**strigilation** [-éjʂǫn], s. (med.) estrigilación.

strike [stráik]. I. va. (pret. STRUCK; pp. STRUCK o STRICKEN) golpear, pegar, apuñear; herir; cutir o percutir; batir, tocar; sonar (una campana); chocar con, dar contra; encender (un fósforo); acuñar (monedas); (con **off**) cortar, quitar, cercenar; cerrar (un trato); (con **out** u **off**) borrar, tachar, testar; trazar, dibujar; dar (la hora); ocurrirle a uno (una idea); parecer, causar una impresión; descubrir, hallar, dar con, llegar a; asumir (una postura); (mar.) arriar (una bandera); parar (el trabajo); cerrar (un establecimiento como resultado de una huelga); allanar, nivelar; (com.) pasar o hacer (balance).—**to s. a jury**, elegir jurado.—**to s. a lead** [lid], (min.) hallar una veta.—**to s. an arc**, (elec.) hacer que se forme un arco.—**to s. an average**, formar el promedio, tomar el término medio.—**to s. a snag**, dar contra un tronco sumergido; encontrar un obstáculo.—**to s. blind**, cegar o poner ciego de repente.—**to s. camp**, levantar el campo.—**to s. down**, (mar.) arriar; derribar; matar.—**to s. dumb**, hacer mudo; pasmar, asombrar, dejar atónito.—**to s. fire**, sacar fuego del pedernal, dar lumbre.—**to s. hands**, tocar la mano en señal de cerrar un contrato.—**to s. off**, (impr.) tirar, imprimir.—**to s. oil**, encontrar petróleo; (fam.) hacerse rico de súbito; encontrarse un entierro (fig.).—**to s. root**, echar raíces, arraigarse, acepar.—**to s. sail**, arriar una vela.—**to s. the tents**, plegar tiendas, levantar el campo.—**to s. through**, traspasar, atravesar; calar.—**to s. up**, (mús.) tocar, tañer.—**to s. with admiration**, llenar de admiración.—**to s. work**, hallar trabajo; (rara vez) declararse en huelga. II. vn. golpear, dar golpes; tropezar, dar contra; batir; sonar (una campana); (mar.) varar, encallar, embarrancar; (con **upon**) encontrarse: ir adelante, avanzar; brotar, estallar, manifestarse (una epidemia, etc.); declararse en huelga; rehusar, resistirse, plantarse; arriar el pabellón, rendirse; arraigar, echar raíces; (geol.) inclinarse, yacer; saturarse de sal (el pescado salado); (elec.) formar arco.—**to s. at**, atacar, chocar con, estrellarse contra.—**to s. at**, atacar, acometer.—**to s. back**, dar golpe por golpe.—**to s. for**, (fam.) dirigirse hacia; acometer.—**to s. home**, dar en el vivo; (fam.) meterse; juntarse, unirse; interrumpir; conformarse con.—**to s. into**, comenzar de repente; penetrar.—**to s. on**, dar contra; descubrir.—**to s. out**, tomar una resolución; arrojarse, lanzarse.—**to s. upon** = TO S. AGAINST.—**to s. while the**

iron is hot, hacer (uno) su agosto; aprovechar la ocasión; a hierro candente, batir de repente. **III.** *s.* golpe; ataque rápido e inesperado; huelga, paro del trabajo; (min.) descubrimiento de un filón; (fam.) buen éxito, ganga; rasero, medida. *V.* STRICKLE.—**s. breaker,** esquirol, obrero que reemplaza a los huelguistas.

strikeblock [-blak], *s.* (carp.) cepillo bocel.

striker [-œ(r)], *s.* golpeador, percusor; huelguista.

striking [-iŋ], *a.* sorprendente, notable; llamativo; que llama la atención; vívido; conspicuo; que está en huelga; percuciente.

string [striŋ]. **I.** *s.* cuerda; cuerdecita, cordel; bramante; cuelga, ristra; cinta, presilla; hilera, hilo, retahíla, fila; sarta (de mentiras, perlas, etc.); fibra, nervio, tendón; (mar.) durmiente del alcázar y castillo.—*pl.* (mús.) instrumentos de cuerda; (fam.) condiciones, reservaciones, estipulaciones.—**s. bean,** (bot.) habichuela verde, judía, alubia.—**s. instrument,** instrumento de cuerda.—**to have on a s.,** (fam.) tener (a uno) en un puño. **II.** *va.* (*pret.* y *pp.* STRUNG; (raro) *pp.* STRINGED) encordar; templar (un instrumento); ensartar, enhilar; encordelar; enhebrar; atar con bramante; tender (alambre, etc.); estirar, entesar; quitar las fibras.—**to s. (along),** (fam.) engañar, tomarle el pelo a uno; posponer, hacer esperar a uno.—**to s. out,** extender.—**to s. up,** (fam.) ahorcar. **III.** *vn.* extenderse en línea; parecer hebras o fibras.—**to s. along,** (fam.) quedar acorde o conforme (con otro).

stringboard [-bɔrd], *s.* (arq.) zanca, pieza lateral (de escalera).

stringcourse [-kɔrs], *s.* (arq.) cordón.

stringed [-d], *a.* encordado, encordelado.—**s. instrument,** instrumento de cuerda.

stringency [strindʒənsi], *s.* aprieto, apuro, estrechez.—**stringent** [-ənt], *a.* estricto, riguroso, severo; (com.) tirante.

stringer [striŋœ(r)], *s.* (carp.) zanca; (arq.) riostra; (f. c.) durmiente longitudinal; ensartador; encordador.

stringless [striŋlis], *a.* sin cuerdas; sin fibras.

stringy [striŋi], *a.* fibroso, filamentoso; tenaz, duro, correoso.

strip [strip]. **I.** *va.* (*pret.* y *pp.* STRIPPED, STRIPT) desnudar; despojar, quitar; desvestir, desguarnecer; robar; descortezar; ordeñar hasta agotar; desgarrar o cortar en tiras; desvenar, despalillar (tabaco); (mec.) desmontar.—**to s. a mast,** (mar.) desaparejar un palo.—**to s. off,** desnudar; deshojar (hojas). **II.** *vn.* desnudarse, despojarse (de). **III.** *s.* tira, faja, listón, lista; lonja (de carne).—*pl.* tabaco desvenado (ll. t. **strip o stemmed tobacco**).

stripe [straip]. **I.** *va.* rayar, gayar. **II.** *s.* raya, lista, banda, franja, tira, (mil.) galón, barra; cardenal (en el cuerpo); calaña, clase, *f.*, género.—**striped** [-d], *a.* rayado, listado, a rayas.—**striper** [-œ(r)], *s.* (fam.) hombre de galones (apl. a los militares).—**striping** [-iŋ], *s.* listas, franjas.

stripling [stripliŋ], *s.* mozalbete, mozuelo.

strive [straiv], *vn.* (*pret.* STROVE; *pp.* STRIVEN) esforzarse, hacer lo posible; disputar; oponerse; contrarrestar.

strobilaceous [strəbiléiʃiʌs], *a.* (bot.) estrobiliáceo, conífero; de forma de cono.—**strobilation** [-éiʃən], *s.* reproducción asexual por división.

strobile [strəbil], *s.* (bot.) estróbilo.

strode [stroud], *pret.* de TO STRIDE.

stroke [strouk]. **I.** *s.* golpe; (mec.) golpe (de émbolo), carrera (del émbolo); golpe del remo, boga, remada; (pint.) toque, pincelada; plumada, trazo (de pluma o lápiz), raya, rasgo; (med.) ataque fulminante; rasgo de ingenio; golpe de mano; en el billar, tacada, jugada; proeza; éxito, feliz encuentro; caricia con la

mano.—**s. oar,** (mar.) bogavante, primer remero (ll. t. **stroke** y **stroke oarsman**).—**s. of a bell,** campanada.—**s. of a pen o brush,** plumada, pincelada.—**s. of a piston,** (mec.) embolada.—**s. of fortune, of (good) luck,** golpe de fortuna.—**s. of wit,** chiste, gracia.—**at one s.,** de un golpe, de un tirón.—**at the s. of 12,** al acabar de dar las doce. **II.** *va.* pasar la mano por, acariciar; frotar suavemente; (alb.) ranurar la piedra con cincel; (cost.) alisar un plegado.

strokesman [-smən], *s.* (mar.) bogavante.

stroll [stroul]. **I.** *vn.* vagar, callejear, flanear; pasearse. **II.** *s.* paseo, vuelta.

stroller [-œ(r)], *s.* vagabundo; paseante, paseador; cochecillo o carretilla de nene; (teat.) farandulero, cómico ambulante o de la legua.

strolling [-iŋ], *s.* acción de vagar, pasearse, etc.—**s. troupe,** (teat.) farándula.

stroma [stróumə], *s.* (biol. o anat.) estroma; (bot.) estromo.

strombus [strámbʌs], *s.* (zool.) estrombo.

strong [strɒŋ]. **I.** *a.* fuerte; firme; recio, robusto, fornido, de puños; concentrado, fuerte, espirituoso, de cuerpo (vino); capaz, hábil; violento, impetuoso; enérgico, eficaz; vivo, brillante, subido (colores); intenso, conmovedor; picante; celoso, acérrimo; marcado, pronunciado; numéricamente fuerte; (com.) pujante, con tendencia a la alza.—**s.-arm,** que emplea la fuerza o violencia.—**s. box,** cofre fuerte, caja de caudales.—**s.-bodied,** fornido, membrudo.—**s.-bodied wine,** vino de mucho cuerpo.—**s. drink,** bebida alcohólica.—**s.-handed,** fuerte de manos y puños.—**s.-minded,** de espíritu vigoroso; de ideas ahombradas y hombrunas (apl. a mujeres).—**s. room,** cuarto fuerte para guardar objetos de valor.—**s. water,** agua fuerte.—**s.-willed,** de voluntad recia; resuelto; obstinado.—**an army ten thousand s.,** un ejército de diez mil hombres.—**by, o with, the s. arm,** con mano de hierro, por la fuerza. **II.** *adv.* fuertemente, enérgicamente; con entusiasmo.

stronghold [-hould], *s.* (mil.) plaza fuerte; fuerte, fortificación.

strongly [-li], *adv.* fuertemente; firmemente, sólidamente; acérrimamente; vehementemente.

strongyle [strándʒil], *s.* estróngilo, gusano parásito del hombre y los animales.

strontia [strɒnʃiə], *s.* (quím.) estronciana.

strontianite [-nait], *s.* (min.) estroncianita.

strontium [strɒnʃiʌm], *s.* (quím.) estroncio.

strop [strɒp]. **I.** *va.* asentar o suavizar (navajas). **II.** *s.* asentador o suavizador de navajas; (mar.) estrobo; gaza. *V.* STRAP.

strophe [stróufi], *s.* (poét.) estrofa.

strove [strouv], *pret.* de TO STRIVE.

struck [strʌk], *pret.* y *pp.* de TO STRIKE.—**s. jury,** (for.) jurado especial (escogido por procedimiento especial).—**s. measure,** medida al ras o rabajada (apl. a las de áridos cuando el contenido se empareja con los bordes superiores).—**s. plant,** establecimiento cerrado debido a una huelga.—**to be s. by, o with,** llamar la atención a uno (cambiando el giro), parecerle a uno digno de notar.

structural [strʌkchʊrəl], *a.* estructural; de estructura; relativo a la estructura; (ing.) de construcción, de construcciones.—**s. iron o steel,** hierro o acero de construcciones; hierro o acero en barras de construcción.—**s. resistance,** (aer.) resistencia pasiva.—**s. shape,** barra de construcción (apl. a las que se denotan por su sección transversal—barra en U, de doble T, escuadra, etc.).—**structurally** [-li], *adv.* estructuralmente, en cuanto a la estructura.

structure [strʌkchu(r)], *s.* construcción (edificio, puente, etc.); estructura (disposición de las partes de un todo); (fig.) textura, hechura.

struggle [strʌgl]. **I.** *vn.* luchar, pugnar, bregar,

forcejar; esforzarse; contender; agitarse. **II.** *s.* esfuerzo; disputa, contienda; pugna, forcejeo; lucha, conflicto.

strum [strʌm], *va.* y *vn.* arañar, tocar mal un instrumento de cuerda; rasguear una guitarra, etc.

struma [strúmə̪], *s.* (med.) estruma, escrófula, lamparón; bocio, papera.

strummer [strʌ́mœ(r)], *s.* rascacuerdas (fam.), mal tocador (de piano, guitarra, arpa, etc.).

strumous [strúmʌs], *a.* estrumoso, escrofuloso.

strumpet [strʌ́mpit], *s.* ramera.

strung [strʌŋ], *pret.* y *pp.* de TO STRING.

strut [strʌt]. **I.** *vn.* contonearse, pavonearse, farolear; inflarse, ensoberbecerse. **II.** *va.* (ing., etc.) apuntalar; (ar)riostrar; ademar. **III.** *s.* contoneo, pavonada; (ing.) pieza de compresión, poste, puntal; columna; (carp.) riostra, jabalcón, tornapunta de caballete; (min.) adema.

struthious [strúθi̯ʌs], *a.* (orn.) parecido o perteneciente a los avestruces.

strychnin(e [strík̄nin], *s.* (quím.) estricnina.

stub [stʌb]. **I.** *s.* (agr.) tocón, cepa; zoquete; fragmento, resto; punta, cabo o colilla (de cigarro, etc.); talón.—**s. book**, libro talonario. —**s. iron**, hierro hecho de clavos viejos.—**s. nail**, puntilla, hita.—**s. pen**, pluma de escribir de punta mocha, pluma para letra redonda.—**s. twist**, hierro para cañones de fusil. **II.** *va.* tropezar contra una cosa baja; (agr.) rozar, desarraigar; reducir a tocón.

stubbed [-d], *a.* a modo de tocón; lleno de tocones; rozado; fuerte, vigoroso; grosero.

stubbedness [-i̯dni̯s], *s.* forma parecida a un tocón.

stubble [stʌ́bl], *s.* (agr.) rastrojo; barba cerdosa. —**s. field**, rastrojo, rastrojera.

stubborn [stʌ́bɔrn], *a.* obstinado, terco, tesonero, contumaz, cabezudo, testarudo o porfiado; reñido; inquebrantable.—**stubbornly** [-li̯], *adv.* inflexiblemente, tercamente.—**stubbornness** [-ni̯s], *s.* obstinación, terquedad, porfía, tesonería, testarudez, contumacia.

stubby [stʌ́bi̯], *a.* cachigordete (fam.); gordo, corto y tieso; cerdoso; cubierto de cepas.

stucco [stʌ́koʊ]. **I.** *va.* (alb.) estucar. **II.** *s.* estuco. —**s. plasterer**, estucador, estuquista.—**s. work**, guarnecido, estuco.—**s. worker** = s. PLASTERER.

stuck [stak], *pret.* y *pp.* de TO STICK.—**s. on**, (fam.) enamorado de.—**s.-up**, (fam.) presuntuoso, presumido, encopetado, estirado.—**to get s.**, atascarse.

stud [stʌd]. **I.** *s.* (carp.) poste de tabique, paral, montante, pie derecho; perno, pasador; tachón, clavo de adorno; botón de camisa o cuello, gemelo de puño; refuerzo de eslabón; yeguada, caballada; caballeriza; (elec.) tornillo de contacto.—**s. bolt**, perno trabado o de extremos roscados. **II.** *va.* tachonar.

studbook [-bu̪k], *s.* registro genealógico de caballos.

studding sails [-iŋ sei̯lz], *s. pl.* (mar.) alas o arrastraderas, rastreras.

student [stjúdi̯ent], *s.* estudiante, estudianta; alumno, discípulo, escolar, educando; investigador; observador; persona que estudia o se ocupa en un asunto.—**s. body**, alumnado, estudiantado, el grupo estudiantil.—**s. lamp**, quinqué, lámpara Argand.

studhorse [stʌ́dhɔrs], *s.* caballo padre, semental.

studied [stʌ́di̯d], *a.* estudiado, premeditado.

studio [stjúdjoʊ], *s.* estudio, taller; gabinete.

studious [stjúdjʌs], *a.* estudioso; aplicado, asiduo, solícito; estudiado.—**studiously** [-li̯], *adv.* estudiosamente, asiduamente.—**studiousness** [-ni̯s], *s.* estudiosidad, aplicación al estudio.

studwork [stʌ́dwœrk], *s.* (carp.) entramado.

study [stʌ́di̯]. **I.** *s.* estudio; asignatura, materia que se estudia; estudio, retrete, gabinete, despacho; meditación profunda; solicitud, cuidado; (b. a.) ensayo, bosquejo; (mús.) estudio, ejer-

cicio.—**to be in a brown s.**, estar absorto en sus pensamientos. **II.** *va.* estudiar; cursar (una asignatura, etc.); investigar, contemplar, examinar; (con **out** o **up**) considerar, meditar; idear, proyectar. **III.** *vn.* estudiar; meditar.

stuff [stʌf]. **I.** *s.* material, materia prima; materia, substancia, elemento fundamental; cosa, objeto; cachivaches, chismes, baratijas, mueblaje; desechos, desperdicios; cosas, ideas o sentimientos sin valor; fruslería; género, paño, tela, estofa; (farm.) jarope, mejunje, pócima; (mar.) betún; (carp.) tablas, tablillas. **II.** *interj.* ¡bagatela! ¡niñería! ¡fruslería! **III.** *va.* henchir, llenar; (coc.) rellenar (un pavo, etc.), embutir; hartar; atestar, empaquetar; disecar (un animal); meter (la mano en el bolsillo).—**to s. a ballot box**, (pol.) echar votos fraudulentos en una urna electoral. **IV.** *vn.* y *vr.* atracarse, hartarse, engullir, tupirse.

stuffed [-t], *a.* relleno; hartado; atestado.—**s. figure**, pelele.—**s. shirt**, (fam.) persona pretensiosa y pomposa.

stuffing [-iŋ], *s.* material con que se atesta o rellena una cosa; atestadura, rehenchimiento; (mec.) empaquetado; (coc.) relleno.—**s. box**, (mec.) caja de empaquetado, prensaestopas.

stuffy [-i̯], *a.* mal ventilado, sofocante; obstruído; insípido, de poco interés; (fam.) relamido; (fam.) murrio.

stull [stʌl], *s.* (min.) entablado o andamio de protección contra piedras desprendidas.

stultification [stʌltifi̯kéi̯şǫn], *s.* embobecimiento, aturdimiento.

stultify [-fai̯], *va.* embrutecer, atontar, embobecer; (for.) alegar locura o estupidez.

stum [stʌm], *s.* mosto.

stumble [stʌ́mbl]. **I.** *vn.* tropezar, dar un traspié; (con **on** o **upon**) encontrar o tropezar con. **II.** *s.* traspié, tropiezo, tropezón, desliz, *m.*, desatino.

stumbler [-blœ(r)], *s.* tropezador.

stumbling [-bli̯ŋ], *s.* tropezadura, tropezón.—**s. block**, tropiezo, obstáculo.

stump [stʌmp]. **I.** *s.* tocón, cepa; cabo; troncho (de col); muñón (de brazo o pierna); raigón (de una muela); poste; (b. a.) esfumino, difumino; tope de cerradura; tribuna pública; (pol.) arenga electoral; (fam.) desafío, reto.—**to be up a s.**, (fam.) estar en un brete. **II.** *a.* parecido a un tocón; perteneciente a una arenga política. —**s. speaker**, orador callejero. **III.** *va.* recorrer haciendo discursos políticos; (fam.) desafiar; cachifollar, dejar patidifuso; tropezar; (b. a.) esfumar, difum(in)ar. **IV.** *vn.* renquear; andar sobre los muñones; (fam.) pronunciar discursos políticos.

stumper [-œ(r)], *s.* **stump orator, stump speaker**, arengador político.

stumpy [-i̯], *a.* lleno de tocones; tozo, (fam.) cachigordete.

stun [stʌn]. **I.** *va.* aturdir, atontar; pasmar, privar; atronar, atolondrar, ensordecer, aturullar. **II.** *s.* choque, golpe o sacudimiento que aturde; aturdimiento.

stung [stʌŋ]. **I.** *pret.* y *pp.* de TO STING. **II.** *a.* (fam.) burlado, chasqueado, engañado.

stunk [stʌŋk], *pret.* y *pp.* de TO STINK.

stunner [stʌ́nœ(r)], *s.* el o lo que aturde, atolondra o aturrulla; (fam.) cosa pasmosa.

stunning [stʌ́niŋ], *a.* (fam.) sorprendente; magnífico, excelente; elegante, hermoso.

stunt [stʌnt]. **I.** *va.* impedir el crecimiento o desarrollo de, no dejar medrar. **II.** *vn.* (fam.) hacer ejercicios malabares o gimnásticos; hacer suertes y otras pruebas de agilidad y destreza; hacer maniobras sensacionales; (aer.) hacer acrobacias. **III.** *s.* falta de crecimiento o desarrollo; animal o planta achaparrados; (fam.) suerte, *f.*, ejercicio o acción de habilidad o destreza; maniobra sensacional (sobre todo en el aire); (aer.) acrobacia.—**s. flying**, vuelos acrobáticos.

stunted [-ịd], *a.* mal desarrollado, atrofiado; achaparrado (árbol); enclenque, raquítico.

stupe [stjup]. **I.** *s.* (med.) fomento, compresa. **II.** *va.* fomentar.

stupefacient [stjúpẹféịṣẹnt], **stupefactive** [-fǽktịv], *a.* y *s.* estupefaciente, estupefactivo.

stupefaction [-fǽkṣọn], *s.* estupefacción, pasmo, estupor.—**stupefied** [-fajd], *a.* estupefacto, (fam.) turulato.—**stupefier** [-fajœ(r)], *s.* lo que produce estupor.—**stupefy** [-faị], *va.* causar estupor, dejar estupefacto, entorpecer, atolondrar; pasmar.

stupendous [stjupéndʌs], *a.* estupendo.

stupendously [-lị], *adv.* estupendamente.

stupendousness [-nịs], *s.* calidad de estupendo o maravilloso.

stupid [stjúpịd], *a.* estúpido, tonto, necio, mentecato; aburrido(r); estupefacto, turulato.

stupidity [stjupídịtị], **stupidness** [-nịs], *s.* estupidez; necedad, mentecatada; inepcia.

stupidly [-lị], *adv.* estúpidamente.

stupor [stjúpọ(r)], *s.* estupor; atontamiento, estupidez.

sturdily [stœ́rdịlị], *adv.* robustamente, vigorosamente; tenazmente.—**sturdiness** [-nịs], *s.* robustez, fuerza, vigor; tenacidad.

sturdy [stœ́rdị]. **I.** *a.* fuerte, robusto, vigoroso; firme, tenaz, porfiado. **II.** *s.* (vet.) modorra.

sturgeon [stœ́rdʒọn], *s.* (ict.) esturión, *m.*, sollo, marón.

stutter [stʌ́tœ(r)]. **I.** *vn.* tartamudear; (fam.) tartalear. **II.** *s.* tartamudeo.—**stutterer** [-œ(r)], *s.* tartamudo.—**stuttering** [-ịŋ]. **I.** *s.* tartamudeo. **II.** *a.* tartamudo, tartajoso, balbuciente.

sty [staị], *s.* (*pl.* STIES) zahurda, pocilga; zaquizamí, tabuco, cuchitril; lupanar, burdel; (med.) orzuelo, hordéolo (ll. t. stye).

Stygian [stídʒịạn], *a.* estigio; infernal.

style [staịl]. **I.** *s.* estilo, dicción, lenguaje; modo, uso, manera, moda, tono; género, escuela; (arq.) estilo; título, tratamiento; estilo, punzón para escribir; buril; estilo o gnomon del reloj de sol; (cir.) estilete; (zool.) púa; (bot.) estilo.—**to be in s.**, estilarse, estar de moda. **II.** *va.* (in)titular, nombrar, llamar.

stylet [-et], *s.* estilete, punzón; (zool.) púa.

stylish [-ịṣ], *a.* elegante; a la moda.

stylist [-ịst], *s.* estilista.

stylite [-aịt], *s.* (hist., igl.) estilita.

stylize [-aịz], *va.* estilizar.

stylobate [stáịlobeịt], *s.* (arq.) estilóbato.

stylograph [-grœf], *s.* estilógrafo.

stylographic [-grǽfịk], *a.* estilográfico.—**s. pen**, pluma estilográfica.

styloid [stáịlọịd], *a.* (anat.) estiloideo.

stylus [stáịlʌs], *s.* estilo, punzón.

stymie [stáịmị], *va.* frustrar, obstaculizar.

styptic [stíptịk], *a.* y *s.* (med.) estíptico; astrictivo, astringente.

stypticity [stiptísịtị], *s.* (med.) estipticidad.

styracaceous [staịrạkéịṣʌs], *a.* (bot.) estiracáceo.

styrax [stáịrœks], *s.* (bot.) estoraque.

Styx [stịks], *s.* Estigia.

suable [sịúạbl], *a.* (for.) acusable, demandable; que puede ser perseguido en justicia.

suasion [swéịʒọn], *s.* persuasión.—**moral s.**, influencia moral, medidas morales, sanción moral.

suasive [swéịsịv], *a.* persuasivo, suasorio.

suave [swáv], *a.* suave, afable; urbano.

suavity [-ịtị], *s.* suavidad; afabilidad, dulzura, blandura; urbanidad.

sub [sʌb]. **I.** *s.* (abrev. fam.) subordinado; suplente, reemplazo; submarino. **II.** *vn.* (abrev. fam.) (con **for**) substituir, hacer las veces de.

subacid [sʌbǽsịd], *a.* agrillo; (quím.) subácido.

subacrid [sʌbǽkrịd], *a.* asperillo.

subagent [sʌbéịdʒẹnt], *s.* subejecutor, subagente.

subalpine [sʌbǽlpaịn], *a.* del límite superior de la vegetación forestal en las montañas.

subaltern [sʌbóltœrn]. **I.** *a.* subalterno, subordinado, dependiente. **II.** *s.* oficial subalterno; alférez, *m.*; teniente.

subalternant [sʌbɔltœrnạnt]. **I.** *a.* (lóg.) universal. **II.** *s.* proposición universal.

subalternate [sʌbóltœrnịt], *a.* sucesivo; subalterno o subordinado.

subaqueous [sʌbéịkwịʌs], *a.* subacuático.

subbase [sʌ́bbeịs], *s.* (arq.) miembro más bajo de una base. *V.* SUBBASS.

subbass [sʌ́bbeịs], *s.* (mús.) registro grave del pedal.

subcaliber [sʌbkǽlịbœ(r)], *a.* de menor calibre que el del cañón del arma (apl. a proyectiles).

subcarbonate [sʌbkárbọnịt], *s.* (quím.) subcarbonato.

subchanter [sʌbchǽntœ(r)], *s.* (igl.) sochantre.

subchaser [sʌbcheịsœ(r)], *s.* cazasubmarinos.

subclavian [sʌbkléịvịạn], *a.* (anat.) subclavio.

subcommittee [sʌbkọmịtị], *s.* subcomisión.

subconscious [sʌbkánsʌs], *a.* subconsciente.

subconsciousness [-nịs], *s.* subconsciencia.

subcontract [sʌbkántrœkt], *s.* subcontrato.

subcontractor [-trǽktọ(r)], *s.* subcontratista.

subcutaneous [sʌbkịutéịnịʌs], *a.* subcutáneo, hipodérmico.

subdeacon [sʌbdíkọn], *s.* (igl.) subdiácono.

subdeaconship [-ṣịp], *s.* subdiaconato.

subdean [sʌbdín], *s.* subdecano o vicedecano.

subdeb [sʌbdeb], *s.* (fam.) subdebutante.

subdelegate [sʌbdélégeịt]. **I.** *s.* subdelegado. **II.** *va.* subdelegar.—**subdelegation** [-éịṣọn], *s.* subdelegación.

subdivide [sʌbdịváịd], *va.* subdividir.

subdivision [-víʒọn], *s.* subdivisión.

subdominant [sʌbdámịnạnt], *a.* y *s.* (mús.) subdominante.

subduct [sʌbdʌkt], *va.* substraer, quitar, sacar.

subduction [sʌbdʌ́kṣọn], *s.* substracción.

subdue [sʌbdjú], *va.* subyugar, sojuzgar, someter, vencer, avasallar, humillar, sujetar, dominar; domar o amansar; mejorar (tierras); suavizar.—**subdued tone**, tono sumiso; voz baja; color mortecino, apagado o amortiguado.

subduer [-œ(r)], *s.* sojuzgador, conquistador, avasallador; domador, amansador.

subeditor [sʌbédịtọ(r)], *s.* subdirector de periódico, redactor subordinado.

subequatorial [-ikwạtóriạl], *a.* vecino al ecuador.

suberic [sịubérịk], *a.* (quím.) subérico.

suberin(e [sịúbœrịn], *a.* (bioquím.) suberina.

suberose [súbœrọs], *a.* (bot.) suberoso.

subexhaust [sʌbegzɔst], *s.* (m. comb. int.) escape auxiliar.

subfamily [-fǽmịlị], *s.* (biol.) tribu, *f.*, subfamilia.

subgenus [sʌbdʒínʌs], *s.* (biol.) subgénero.

subhead(ing [sʌbhed(-hédịŋ], *s.* subtítulo; título o encabezamiento secundario.

subindex [sʌbịndeks], *s.* (mat.) subíndice.

subjacent [sʌbdʒéịsẹnt], *a.* subyacente.

subject [sʌbdʒékt]. **I.** *va.* sujetar, someter; sojuzgar, subyugar, avasallar; exponer, presentar; supeditar, subordinar. **II.** [sʌbdʒịkt], *a.* sujeto; expuesto, propenso; sometido, dominado, supeditado.—**s. to**, sujeto a, afecto a. **III.** *s.* súbdito; vasallo; materia, tópico, asunto, tema, *m.*, sujeto; asignatura (de estudios); (gram.) sujeto; (med.) individuo, sujeto; cadáver destinado a la disección.—**s. matter**, asunto, materia de que se trata.

subjection [sʌbdʒékṣọn], *s.* sujeción, supeditación, vasallaje, dependencia, servidumbre; sometimiento; ligadura.

subjective [-tịv], *a.* subjetivo.—**subjectively** [-lị], *adv.* subjetivamente.—**subjectiveness** [-nịs], *s.* subjetividad.—**subjectivism** [-izm], *s.* subjetivismo.—**subjectivist** [-ịst], *s.* subjetivista.—**subjectivity** [-tívịtị], *s.* subjetividad.

subjoin [sʌbdʒóịn], *va.* añadir, adjuntar.

subjugate [sʌ́bdʒugeịt], *va.* subyugar, sojuzgar,

someter.—**subjugation** [-éįşǫn], s. sujeción, subyugación.

subjunctive [sʌbdźʌ́ŋktįv], a. y s. subjuntivo.

subkingdom [sʌ́bkįŋdǫm], s. (biol.) subreino.

sublease [sʌ́blis]. I. s. subarriendo. II. [sʌblís], va. subarrendar.

sublet [sʌblét], va. subarrendar.—**subletter** [-œ(r)], s. subarrendador, subarrendante.—**subletting** [-įŋ], s. subarrendamiento.

sublimate [sʌ́blįmeįt]. I. s. (quím.) sublimado. II. va. (quím.) sublimar; (fig.) refinar, purificar.—**sublimation** [-éįşǫn], s. sublimación; exaltación; refinamiento, perfección.

sublimatory [sʌ́blįmaṭǫrį]. I. a. (quím.) sublimatorio. II. s. vasija para sublimar.

sublime [sʌbláįm]. I. a. sublime, elevado, exaltado, excelso; supremo, extremo. II. s. lo sublime, sublimidad. III. va. y vn. sublimar, exaltar, ensalzar; (quím.) sublimar(se).—**sublimely** [-lį], adv. sublimemente.—**sublimeness** [-nįs], **sublimity** [sʌblímįtį], s. sublimidad.

subliminal [sʌblímįnal], a. subconsciente.

sublingual [sʌblíŋgwal], a. (anat.) sublingual.

sublunar [sʌbljúnar], **sublunary** [-į], a. sublunar, terrestre.

submachine gun [sʌbmaşín gʌn], s. (mil.) ametralladora ligera, arma de fuego automática que puede usarse como fusil.

submarine [sʌ́bmarįn]. I. s. y a. submarino, sumergible. II. va. hundir o atacar con un submarino.—s. **boat**, submarino (barco).—s. **chaser**, cazasubmarinos.—s. **mine**, mina submarina.

submaxilla [sʌbmæksįl̹ə̹], s. (anat.) maxilar inferior.

submaxillary [sʌbmǽksįl̹ə̹rį], a. submaxilar.

submerge [sʌbmœ́rdź], va. y vn. sumergir(se), hundir(se).—**submergence** [-ęns], s. submersion [-şǫn], s. sumersión, sumergimiento, hundimiento.

submergible [-dźįbl]. I. s. submarino. II. a. sumergible.

submersible [-sįbl]. s. y a. sumergible; submarino.

submission [sʌbmíşǫn], s. sumisión, sometimiento, rendimiento; resignación; obediencia, deferencia; (for.) sometimiento a arbitraje.

submissive [-sįv], a. sumiso, obediente, dócil.

submissively [-lį], adv. sumisamente, humildemente, rendidamente.

submissiveness [-nįs], s. calidad de sumiso; obediencia, mansedumbre, docilidad, humildad.

submit [sʌbmít]. I. va. someter, referir, dejar a la decisión (de); presentar, exponer como opinión propia, permitirse decir, proponer. II. vr. y vn. ceder, rendirse, someterse, conformarse, resignarse.

submultiple [sʌbmʌ́ltįpl], s. (mat.) submúltiplo.

subnormal [sʌbnórmal]. I. a. subnormal, deficiente. II. s. (mat.) subnormal.

suborder [sʌbórdœ(r)], s. (bot. y zool.) suborden; (arq.) orden subordinado.

subordinacy [sʌbórdįnąşį], s. subordinación, dependencia, sujeción.

subordinate [sʌbórdįnįt]. I. a. y s. subalterno, subordinado, inferior, dependiente, secundario. II. [-eįt], va. subordinar, someter, sujetar.—**subordinately** [-lį], adv. subordinadamente.—**subordination** [-éįşǫn], s. subordinación, dependencia, sujeción; menoría.

suborn [sʌbórn], va. (for.) sobornar, cohechar.

subornation [-éįşǫn], s. soborno, cohecho.

suborner [-œ(r)], s. sobornador, cohechador.

subpena, subpœna [sʌ(b)pínə̹]. I. s. (for.) citación, comparendo. II. va. citar, emplazar.

subpolar [sʌbpóulə̹(r)], a. subpolar.

subprefect [sʌbprífɛkt], s. subprefecto.

subprefecture [-chu̹(r)], s. subprefectura.

subreption [sʌbrépşǫn], s. (for.) subrepción; juicio erróneo debido a subrepción.

subrogate [sʌ́broųgeįt], va. (for.) subrogar, poner

en lugar de otro, substituir. V. SURROGATE.—**subrogation** [-éįşǫn], s. subrogación, substitución.

sub rosa [sʌb róųzə̹], adv. muy confidencialmente, muy en secreto.

subscapular [sʌbskǽpįul̹ə̹(r)], a. y s. (anat.) sub(e)scapular.

subscribe [sʌbskráįb], va. y vn. subscribir, firmar, rubricar; aprobar, consentir; subscribirse, abonarse.—**to s. for**, subscribirse a.—**subscriber** [-œ(r)], s. infrascrito, firmante, el que subscribe; subscriptor, abonado.

subscription [sʌbskrípşǫn], s. firma; subscripción, abono; cantidad subscrita.

subsection [sʌbsékşǫn], s. subdivisión; párrafo de un artículo de ley.

subsequence, subsequency [sʌ́bsįkwɛns(į], s. calidad de subsiguiente; suceso posterior.

subsequent [-ɛnt], a. subsecuente, subsiguiente.—s. **to**, con posterioridad a, después de.

subsequently [-lį], adv. posteriormente, subsiguientemente, ulteriormente.

subserve [sʌbsœ́rv]. I. va. servir, ayudar. II. vn. servir como subordinado.—**subservience, subserviency** [-ięns, -į], s. servicio, ayuda; subordinación.—**subservient** [-įęnt], a. útil o servicial; subordinado.—**subserviently** [-lį], adv. subordinadamente; útilmente.

subside [sʌbsáįd], vn. apaciguarse, calmarse; bajar (un flúido); hundirse, irse a fondo.—**subsidence, subsidency** [-ęns, -į], s. apaciguamiento, calma; desplome, sumersión, asiento.

subsidiary [sʌbsídįerį]. I. a. subsidiario; secundario, incidental, auxiliar, dependiente, subordinado; (com.) sucursal. II. s. auxiliar; (com.) dependencia, compañía dependiente, sucursal, f.

subsidize [sʌ́bsįdaįz], va. subvencionar.

subsidy [sʌ́bsįdį], s. subvención, subsidio.

subsist [sʌbsíst]. I. vn. subsistir, existir; permanecer, perdurar, conservarse; sustentarse, mantenerse. II. va. alimentar o mantener.

subsistence [-ęns], s. existencia, subsistencia; sostenimiento o mantenimiento, manutención, cualidad inherente.—s. **department**, (mil.) comisaría general.

subsistent [-ęnt], a. subsistente; inherente.

subsoil [sʌ́bsoįl]. I. va. (agr.) arar, labrar, desfondar la tierra. II. s. subsuelo.

subsolar [sʌbsóųl̹ə̹(r)], a. subsolar, que está debajo del sol; terrestre; intertropical.

substage [sʌ́bsteįdź], s. (fís.) disposición para los accesorios que van bajo la platina del microscopio; (geol.) subpiso, subdivisión de un sistema estratificado.

substance [sʌ́bstąns], s. substancia; esencia, alma; realidad; miga, enjundia, jugo, fuste; hacienda, caudal o bienes.—**in s.**, en substancia, en el fondo.

substantial [sʌbstǽnşal], a. sólido, fuerte, resistente; importante, valioso; cuantioso, considerable; seguro; responsable; real, existente, verdadero; duradero; esencial; corpóreo, material; substancial, substancioso; enjundioso. II. s. realidad; parte (f.) esencial.

substantiality [-şįélįtį], s. realidad; corporeidad; materialidad; solidez.

substantially [-şalį], adv. substancialmente; sólidamente.

substantialness [-şalnįs], s. calidad de substancial; firmeza, fuerza, duración.

substantiate [-şįeįt], va. verificar, establecer, comprobar, justificar.

substantiation [-şįéįşǫn], s. substanciación; comprobación, verificación, (gal.) constatación.

substantival [sʌbstąntáįval], a. (gram.) substantivo.

substantive [sʌ́bstąntįv]. I. a. substantivo; real, esencial, duradero; explícito; que tiene individualidad distinta, o recursos propios.—s. **dye**, tinte que no requiere mordente. II. s. (gram.) substantivo; el o lo que es independiente.

substantively [-li], *adv.* substancialmente; (gram.) substantiv(ad)amente.

substantiveness [-nis], *s.* substantividad.

substantivize, substantize [-(i̯v)ai̯z], *va.* (gram.) substantivar.

substation [sÁbstei̯s̯on], *s.* subestación.

substitute [sÁbstitiu̯t]. **I.** *va.* substituir, reemplazar, suplir; (for.) subrogar. **II.** *s.* substituto, suplente, reemplazo; sobresaliente. **III.** *a.* substitutivo, reemplazante.

substitution [-tiu̯s̯on], *s.* substitución; reemplazo; delegación; (for.) subrogación.

substratum [sÁbstréi̯tÁm], *s.* capa inferior; (agr.) subsuelo; (fil.) substrato.

substructure [sÁbstrÁkchu̯(r)], *s.* subestructura, substrucción; (neol.) infraestructura, cimientos, *m. pl.*

subsume [sÁbsiu̯m], *va.* incluir (en una clase o categoría mayor); (lóg.) clasificar (dentro de una premisa mayor).—**subsumption** [sÁbsÁmps̯on], *s.* inclusión; cosa o asunto incluídos; (lóg.) premisa menor.

subtangent [sÁbtǽndz̯ent], *s.* (geom.) subtangente.

subtend [sÁbténd], *va.* (geom.) subtender; (bot.) encerrar en la axila.

subtense [sÁbténs], *s.* (geom.) subtensa.

subterfuge [sÁbtœrfiu̯dz̯], *s.* subterfugio, evasiva.

subterranean, subterraneous [sÁbtǝréi̯ni̯an, -i̯as], *a.* subterráneo.

subtile [sÁ(b)til], *a.* sutil, delicado, tenue; refinado; penetrante.—**subtilely** [-li], *adv.* sutilmente.—**subtileness** [-nis], **subtility** [sÁbtíliti], *s.* sutileza, sutilidad; delgadez, tenuidad.—**subtilization** [-izéi̯s̯on], *s.* sutilización.—**subtilize** [sÁ(b)tilai̯z], *va.* y *vn.* sutilizar, adelgazar, refinar.

subtilty [sÁ(b)tílti], *s.* sutileza, alambicamiento, agudeza, argucia.

subtitle [sÁbtai̯tl], *s.* subtítulo; título de escena cinematográfica.

subtle [sÁtl], *a.* sutil, astuto, artero; perspicaz, penetrante; apto, perito; ingenioso, primoroso.

subtleness, subtlety [-nis, -ti], *s.* sutileza; astucia, artificio.

subtly [sÁtli], *adv.* sutilmente, delicadamente, artificiosamente.

subtract [sÁbtrékt], *va.* y *vn.* substraer, quitar; (mat.) restar, substraer.—**subtraction** [-s̯on], *s.* substracción; (mat.) resta, substracción.

subtractive [-tiv], *a.* rel. a la substracción; que puede o tiende a substraer; (mat.) negativo; que lleva el signo menos (−).

subtrahend [sÁbtrahend], *s.* (mat.) substraendo.

subtreasury [sÁbtréz̯uri], *s.* subtesorería.

subtreasurer [-u̯rœ(r)], *s.* subtesorero.

subtropic(al [sÁbtrápik(al], *a.* subtropical.

suburb [sÁbœrb], *s.* suburbio, arrabal.—*pl.* afueras, inmediaciones.—**suburban** [sÁbœrban], *s.* y *a.*, **suburbanite** [-ai̯t], *s.* suburbano, arrabalero.

suburbicarian [-bi̯kéi̯ri̯an], *a.* suburbicario.

subvene [sÁbvín], *vn.* subvenir.

subvention [sÁbvéns̯on], *s.* subvención, subsidio, ayuda. *V.* SUBSIDY.

subversion [sÁbvœ́rs̯on], *s.* subversión, ruina, trastorno.—**subversive** [-si̯v], *a.* subversivo.—**subvert** [sÁbvœ́rt], *va.* subvertir, destruir, trastornar.—**subverter** [-œ(r)], *s.* subversor, destructor, trastornador.—**subvertible** [-ibl], *a.* subvertible, trastornable, destruíble.

subway [sÁbwei̯], *s.* camino artificial subterráneo; mina; (ferrocarril) subterráneo, metropolitano, (fam.) el metro, de subte.

succedaneous [sÁksidéi̯ni̯as], *a.* sucedáneo.

succedaneum [-ni̯Ám], *s.* substituto; (med.) sucedáneo.

succeed [sÁksíd]. **I.** *va.* suceder o seguir a. **II.** *vn.* salir bien, tener buen éxito.—**to s. in,** tener buen éxito en; lograr, conseguir, acertar a.

succeeder [-œ(r)], *s.* sucesor.—**succeeding** [-iŋ]. *a.* subsiguiente, sucediente, futuro, venidero.

succentor [sÁksénto̯(r)], *s.* (igl.) sochantre.

success [sÁksés], *s.* buen éxito, buen resultado, logro, fortuna, prosperidad, medro; triunfo; persona o asunto que tiene buen éxito.—**successful** [-fu̯l], *a.* próspero, afortunado, airoso, venturoso; fructuoso, productivo, satisfactorio.—**successfully** [-i], *adv.* con buen resultado, prósperamente, con buen éxito.—**successfulness** [-nis], *s.* feliz éxito, buen resultado.

succession [sÁksés̯on], *s.* sucesión, serie; seguida, continuación; linaje, descendencia; herencia.

successive [sÁksésiv], *a.* sucesivo.—**successively** [-li], *adv.* sucesivamente.

successor [sÁkséso̯(r)], *s.* sucesor; heredero.

succinate [sÁksinei̯t], *s.* (quím.) succinato.

succinct [sÁksiŋkt], *a.* sucinto, breve; (ent.) enfaldado.—**succinctly** [-li], *adv.* sucintamente.—**succinctness** [-nis], *s.* brevedad, concisión.

succinic [sÁksinik], *a.* (quím.) succínico.

succinite [sÁksinai̯t], *s.* (min.) succino, ámbar.

succor [sÁko̯(r)]. **I.** *va.* socorrer. **II.** *s.* socorro; (mil.) refuerzo; socorredor, auxiliador.

succory [sÁkori], *s.* (bot.) achicoria.

succotash [sÁko̯tæš], *s.* (E. U.) potaje de maíz tierno y habas.

succubus [sÁki̯u̯bÁs], *s.* súcubo (demonio).

succulence, succulency [sÁki̯u̯ʟ̯ens(i], *s.* suculencia, jugosidad.

succulent [-ent], *a.* suculento, jugoso.

succumb [sÁkÁm], *vn.* sucumbir, rendirse; morir.

succumbent [-bent], *a.* sucumbiente.

succuss [sÁkÁs], *va.* sacudir; (med.) practicar la sucusión.—**succussion** [sÁkÁs̯on], *s.* sacudimiento; (med.) sucusión.

such [sÁch]. **I.** *a.* tal; semejante; dicho, mencionado. Generalmente va seguido del *art. indef.* (*v.* A, *art indef.*) (*such a man,* tal hombre, semejante hombre; *such a case,* tal caso).—**s.** **a,** (fam.) tan (*such a bad man,* un hombre tan malo).—**s. and s.,** o **s. or s.,** tal(es) y tal(es), tal o cual (*he did such and such things in such and such a place,* hizo tales y tales cosas en tal y tal sitio).—**s. as,** (tal) como (*a house such as this,* una casa (tal) como ésta).—**s. . . . as,** como el que, de la clase del que; el . . . que (*such books as he reads,* libros como los que él lee, los libros que él lee).—**s. as it is** (they are, etc.), tal cual es, por poco(s), pequeño(s), etc., que sea(n) (*the house, such as it is, suits me,* la casa, tal cual es, me conviene; *these advantages, such as they are,* estas ventajas, por pequeñas que sean; *his argument, such as it is,* su argumento, por débil que sea).—**no s.** (a) **thing,** no hay tal.—**there is s. a thing as,** hay algo que se llama, existe (*there is such a thing as honesty,* hay algo que se llama honradez, la honradez existe). A veces conviene cambiar el giro: *there is such a thing as losing patience,* hay casos en que se pierde la paciencia, la paciencia no es inagotable, o tiene sus límites. **II.** *pron.* tal.—**s. as,** los que, quienes (*such as come here,* los que vienen aquí; *such as wish to come,* los que, o quienes, deseen venir).—**s. is life,** tal (o así) es la vida.

suck [sÁk]. **I.** *va.* y *vn.* chupar, libar; mamar; amamantar; (mec.) aspirar.—**to s. in,** embeber, absorber, chupar.—**to s. out,** o **up,** chupar, extraer o sacar chupando o por succión. **II.** *s.* succión; chupada; mamada.—**to give s.,** amamantar, dar de mamar, lactar.

sucker [-œ(r)], *s.* lechón, gorrinillo, cochinillo que todavía mama; chupador; mamador; mamón, chupón; chupadero (para niños); (mec.) émbolo, chupón, sopapo de bomba; tubo de aspiración; (bot.) pimpollo, chupón, vástago, retoño, serpollo, barbado; (ict.) rémora; nombre que se da a peces de varias especies; (zool.) ventosa (órgano); (fam.) gorrista, chupón, gorrero; pelele, primo, persona fácil de engañar.

sucking [-iŋ]. **I.** *s.* chupadura. **II.** *a.* mamante, chupadero; lechal, recental (apl. al animal de cría que mama).—**s. fish,** rémora, pega, guaicán.—**s. pig,** corezuelo, cochinillo, lechoncillo.

suckle [-l]. **I.** *va.* amamantar, dar de mamar, criar, lactar, tetar. **II.** *vn.* lactar, mamar.

suckling [-liŋ]. **I.** *s.* lactación, lactancia, acción de mamar. **II.** *s. y a.* mamón, mamantón; recental. **III.** *a.* lactante, de teta, de cría. —**s. pig** = SUCKING PIG.

sucrose [sjúkrous], *s.* (quím.) sucrosa.

suction [sʌ́kʃən], *s.* succión.—**s. hose,** manguera de alimentación.—**s. pipe,** tubo aspirante o de succión.—**s. pump,** bomba aspirante.—**s. tube,** chupadero, chupador.

suctorial [sʌktórial], *a.* chupador, chupadero o chupón.

Sudanese [sudaníz], *a. y s.* sudanés.

sudatory [sjúdatori]. **I.** *a.* sudorífero. **II.** *s.* sudorífico; sudadero, estufa.

sudden [sʌ́dn], *a.* repentino, súbito; apresurado, precipitado; (med.) fulminante.—**all of a s., of a s., on a s.,** de repente, de pronto.

suddenly [-li], *adv.* de repente, repentinamente.

suddenness [-njs], *s.* calidad de repentino, impensado, inesperado o imprevisto; brusquedad.

sudor [sjúdor], *s.* sudor.

sudoriferous [sjudoríferʌs], *a.* sudorífero.

sudorific [-fįk], *a. y s.* sudorífico.

Sudra [súdrạ], *s.* zudra, *m.,* miembro de la cuarta casta de la India.

suds [sʌdz], *s. pl.* jabonaduras; espuma.—**in the s.,** (fam.) en apuros.

sue [sju], *va. y vn.* (for.) demandar, poner pleito, entablar juicio; (con **to** or **for**) rogar, pedir, suplicar, tratar de persuadir; (ant.) galantear. —**to s. for damages,** (for.) demandar por daños y perjuicios.—**to s. for divorce,** (for.) solicitar el divorcio.—**to s. out,** (for.) solicitar y obtener.

suède [sweid], *s.* gamuza, ante (piel); cierto tejido o género a imitación de esta piel.

suet [sjúįt], *s.* sebo en rama; grasa, gordo.

suety [-i], *a.* seboso.

suffer [sʌ́fœ(r)], *va. y vn.* sufrir, padecer, sentir; soportar, tolerar, conllevar; permitir, consentir, pasar; (con **from**) adolecer de.

sufferable [-ạbl], *a.* sufrible, soportable, aguantable, tolerable, pasadero.

sufferably [-ạbli], *adv.* sufriblemente.

sufferance [sʌ́f(œ)rạns], *s.* tolerancia, consentimiento tácito; sufrimiento; conformidad, resignación; (com., Ingl.) permiso especial de la aduana.

sufferer [sʌ́fœrœ(r)], *s.* sufridor, paciente; víctima; perjudicado, damnificado; el que tolera tácitamente.

suffering [-iŋ]. **I.** *s.* sufrimiento, padecimiento, pena, dolor, suplicio. **II.** *a.* sufriente, sufridor, paciente, penante.—**s. humanity,** la doliente, o pobre, humanidad.

suffice [sʌfáis], *va. y vn.* bastar, ser suficiente, alcanzar, satisfacer.—**s. it to say,** baste decir.

sufficiency [sʌfíʃensi], *s.* suficiencia; lo suficiente; eficacia; presunción.

sufficient [-ent], *a.* suficiente, bastante.—**sufficiently** [-li], *adv.* suficientemente; asaz, bastante(mente).

suffix [sʌfįks]. **I.** *va.* añadir como sufijo. **II.** [sʌfįks] *s.* (gram.) sufijo, afijo.

suffocate [sʌ́fokeit]. **I.** *va.* sofocar, asfixiar, ahogar; apagar (un fuego). **II.** *vn.* sofocarse, asfixiarse, ahogarse.—**suffocating** [-iŋ], *a.* sofocante, asfixiante.—**suffocation** [-éiʃon], *s.* sofocación, asfixia, ahog(amiento)o.

suffocative [-iv], *a.* sofocante, sofocador, asfixiante.

suffragan [sʌ́fragạn], *a. y s.* (igl.) sufragáneo.

suffrage [sʌ́frįdʒ], *s.* sufragio, voto; aprobación, consentimiento; (igl.) sufragio.—**suffragette** [sʌfrạdʒét], *s.* sufragista (mujer).—**suffragism**

[sʌ́frạdʒįzm], *s.* sufragismo.—**suffragist** [-dʒįst], *s.* sufragista.

suffruticose [sʌfrútįkous], *a.* (bot.) sufruticoso, sufrutescente, leñoso y herbáceo.

suffuse [sʌfiúz], *va.* difundir, bañar, cubrir.

suffusion [sʌfiúʒọn], *s.* difusión, baño; (med.) sufusión.

Sufi [súfi], *s.* sufí, sofí, místico mahometano. —**Sufism** [-fįzm], *s.* sufismo.

sugar [ʃúgạ(r)]. **I.** *s.* azúcar; (fig.) agasajo, lisonja. —**s. almond,** almendra garapiñada.—**s. beet,** (bot.) remolacha.—**s. bowl,** azucarero.—**s. cane,** (bot.) caña de azúcar.—**s.-cane grinding,** molienda de caña de azúcar.—**s. candy,** azúcar cande.—**s.-coated,** confitado, garapiñado; azucarado.—**s.-coated pill,** píldora azucarada.—**s. crop,** zafra.—**s. loaf,** pan de azúcar.—**s. making (season),** zafra.—**s. maple,** (bot.) arce de azúcar.—**s. mill,** trapiche, central azucarera.—**s. of lead,** (quím.) azúcar de plomo o sal de Saturno.—**s. of milk,** azúcar de leche, lactina, lactosa.—**s. paste,** alfeñique.—**s. plantation,** ingenio de azúcar, cañaveral, plantación azucarera.—**s. refinery,** refinería.—**s. syrup,** miel, *f.,* melado.—**s. tongs,** tenacillas para azúcar. **II.** *va.* azucarar, endulzar; confitar, garapiñar.—**to s. -coat,** confitar, garapiñar; (fig.) dorar la píldora, ocultar la verdad desagradable. **III.** *vn.* (E. U. y Canadá) (con **off**) hacer el azúcar de arce.

sugared [-d], *a.* azucarado, endulzado, dulce; garapiñado.

sugarplum [-plʌm], *s.* confite, dulce.

sugary [-i], *a.* azucarado, dulce; meloso.

suggest [sʌgdʒést], *va.* sugestionar; sugerir, insinuar, indicar, intimar, proponer; evocar (un recuerdo).

suggestion [-chọn], *s.* sugestión; sugerencia, insinuación, indicación.

suggestive [-tįv], *a.* sugestivo; sugerente.

suicidal [sjuįsáidạl], *a.* suicida.

suicide [sjúisaid], *s.* suicidio (el acto); suicida, *mf.*—**to commit s.,** suicidarse.

sui juris [sjúį dʒúrįs], de completa capacidad legal.

suing [sjúiŋ], *s.* (for.) solicitación, procesamiento, presentación de demanda; galanteo.

suit [sjút]. **I.** *s.* petición, súplica, solicitación; galanteo, cortejo; (for.) pleito; litigio, juicio; colección, serie, juego, surtido; (sast.) traje completo, terno, (Am.) flux o flus; (en la baraja) palo. **II.** *va. y vn.* cuadrar, convenir, acomodar, adaptar(se), ser apropiado o a propósito; ir o venir bien, sentar, encajar; agradar, contentar, satisfacer; ajustarse, acomodarse, casar, hermanarse.—**to s. (down) to a T,** sentar al dedillo, venir pintiparado o de perilla.—**to s. one's self,** hacer uno lo que guste.

suitable [-ạbl], *a.* adecuado, apropiado, conveniente, satisfactorio, adaptable, a propósito.

suitability [-ạbílįti], **suitableness** [-ạblnįs], *s.* adaptabilidad, conveniencia, adecuación.—**suitably** [-ạbli], *adv.* adecuada o convenientemente, propiamente, debidamente, en conformidad.

suitcase [-keis], *s.* maleta.

suite [swit], *s.* serie, juego; séquito, tren, acompañamiento, comitiva.—**s. of rooms,** serie o crujía de piezas, apartamiento o departamento.

suitor [sjútọ(r)], *s.* (for.) demandante, parte actora; pretendiente, cortejo, requebrador, novio; suplicante, aspirante; postulante.

sulcate(d [sʌ́lkeįt(įd], *a.* surcado, acanalado.

sulcus [sʌ́lkʌs], *s.* (anat.) surco.

sulfa, sulpha drug [sʌ́lfạ], *s.* (farm. y quím.) una de varias drogas relacionadas con la sulfanilamida (*sulfanilamide*).

sulfate, sulfid, sulfur, sulfuric, etc. = SULPHATE, SULPHUR, etc.

sulk [sʌlk]. **I.** *vn.* (fam.) amorrar(se), enfurru-

ñarse, ponerse de mal humor. **II.** *s.* murria, (fam.) fanfurriña.
sulkiness [-iɲis], *s.* ceño; murria.
sulky [-i]. **I.** *a.* murrio, malhumorado. **II.** *s.* (carr.) solitaria, calesín de un solo asiento.
sullen [sʌlɛn], *a.* hosco, adusto, murrio, arisco, huraño; lento (río); sombrío, tétrico.—**sullenly** [-li], *adv.* con murria, de mal humor.—**sullenness** [-nis], *s.* murria, malhumor; enfado, ceño.
sully [sʌli]. **I.** *va.* manchar, empañar, ensuciar; desdorar, mancillar. **II.** *vn.* empañarse. **III.** *s.* mancha; mancilla.
sulphacid [sʌlfæsid], *s.* (quím.) sulfácido.
sulphate [sʌlfeit]. **I.** *s.* (quím.) sulfato. **II.** *va.* sulfatar.
sulphatize [-aiz], *va.* convertir en sulfato.
sulphid(e [sʌlfid], *s.* (quím.) sulfuro.
sulphite [sʌlfait], *s.* (quím.) sulfito; (fam.) persona original y despreocupada.
sulphonal [sʌlfonal], *s.* (quím. y farm.) sulfonal.
sulphonic [sʌlfánik], *a.* (quím.) sulfónico.
sulphovinic [sʌlfováinik], *a.* (quím.) sulfovínico.
sulphur [sʌlfœ(r)]. **I.** *s.* (quím.) azufre.—**s. dioxide**, anhídrido sulfuroso.—**s. trioxide**, anhídrido sulfúrico. **II.** *va.* azufrar; sulfurar.
sulphurate [-eit]. **I.** *va.* sulfurar; azufrar. **II.** [-it], *a.* sulfúreo.
sulphuration [-éiʃọn], *s.* sulfuración.
sulphurator [-eitọ(r)], *s.* sulfurador.
sulphuret [sʌlfyūrit], *s.* (quím.) sulfuro.
sulphureous [sʌlfjúriʌs], **sulphurous** [sʌlfūrʌs], *a.* sulfúreo, azufroso, azufrado.
sulphureousness [-nis], *s.* calidad de sulfúreo.
sulphuric [sʌlfjúrik], *a.* sulfúrico.
sulphurize [sʌlfjuraiz], *va.* sulfurar.
sulphurwort [sʌlfœrwœrt], *s.* (bot.) servato.
sulphury [sʌlfœri], *a.* sulfúreo, azufroso.
sulphydrate [sʌlfájdreit], *s.* (quím.) sulfhidrato.
sulphydric [sʌlfájdrik], *a.* sulfhídrico.
sultan [sʌltan], *s.* sultán, soldán.
sultana [sʌltǽnạ], *s.* sultana.
sultriness [sʌltriɲis], *s.* bochorno.
sultry [sʌltri], *a.* bochornoso, sofocante.
sum [sʌm]. **I.** *s.* suma, tanto, cantidad de dinero; substancia, esencia; cima, máximo, lo sumo; (fam.) problema (*m.*) de aritmética.—**s. and substance**, substancia.—**s. total**, total, cifra, monta o monto.—**in s.**, en suma, en resumen. **II.** *va.* y *vn.* sumar; (gen. con **up**) recapitular o resumir, sintetizar, compendiar; (for.) presentar o exponer su alegato (un abogado).
sumac(h [sjúmæk, śúmæk], *s.* (bot.) zumaque.
sumless [sʌmlis], *a.* innumerable.
summarily [sʌmạrili], *adv.* sumariamente.
summarize [sʌmạraiz], *va.* epitomar, resumir.
summary [sʌmạri]. **I.** *a.* sumario, compendioso, breve, sucinto; pronto, sin demora. **II.** *s.* sumario, resumen, recopilación, compendio, reseña (de un libro).
summation [sʌméiʃọn], *s.* (mat.) suma, total; (for., etc.) recapitulación, resumen (de los argumentos, etc.).
summer [sʌmœ(r)]. **I.** *a.* estival, veraniego, de verano. **II.** *s.* verano, estío; (arq.) viga maestra; dintel; sotabanco; manto de chimenea.—**s. beam**, (arq.) travesero de viga maestra.—**s. boarder**, veraneante.—**s. camp**, campo de verano; colonia juvenil de verano.—**s. house**, casa de verano.—**s. pasture**, veranadero.—**s. resident** o **vacationist**, veraneante.—**s. resort**, lugar de veraneo.—**s. solstice**, solsticio vernal o de verano.—**s. time**, hora de verano.—**s. wheat**, (bot.) trigo candeal.—**to s.-fallow**, (agr.) arar en verano y dejar en barbecho. **III.** *vn.* veranear, pasar el verano.
summerhouse [-haus], *s.* cenador, glorieta, lonjeta, pabellón, quiosco (de jardín).
summersault, summerset [-solt, -set], *s.* salto mortal.
summertide [-taid], *s.* = SUMMERTIME. *V.* SUMMER.

summertime [-taim], *s.* verano, estío.
summertree [-tri], *s.* = SUMMER BEAM.
summit [sʌmit], *s.* cima, cumbre, cúspide, *f.*, ápice.
summon [sʌmọn], *va.* (for.) citar, emplazar, apercibir; llamar, convocar; mandar, requerir; (mil.) intimar; (con **up**) evocar; reunir, despertar, espolear, excitar (valor, bríos, fuerza, etc.).—**summoner** [-œ(r)], *s.* (for.) citador, emplazador.
summons [-z], *s.* (for.) citación, comparendo, emplazamiento, requerimiento, apercibimiento; (mil.) intimación (de rendición).
sump [sʌmp], *s.* (min.) sumidero; (m. comb. int.) colector de aceite; pozo colector; pantano.
sumpter [sʌmptœ(r)], *s.* acémila, cabalgadura.
sumption [sʌmpśọn], *s.* (lóg.) premisa mayor.
sumptuary [sʌmpch ueri], *a.* suntuario.—**s. laws**, leyes suntuarias.
sumptuous [sʌmpchuʌs], *a.* suntuoso, magnífico, lujoso, ostentoso, regio, espléndido.—**sumptuously** [-li], *adv.* suntuosamente.—**sumptuousness** [-nis], *s.* suntuosidad, pompa.
sun [sʌn]. **I.** *s.* sol; luz de sol, solana.—**s. bath**, baño de sol, solana.—**s.-bathed, s.-beat**, asoleado.—**s. bittern**, (orn.) alcaraván.—**s.-bright**, resplandeciente como el sol.—**s. dance**, danza del sol.—**s.-dried brick** = ADOBE.—**s. god**, (mit.) dios del sol.—**s. lamp**, (med.) lámpara de radiación o de cuarzo.—**s. parlor, s. porch**, solana, carasol.—**s. valve**, (mec.) válvula solar, actuada por el sol.—**in the s.**, al sol.—**to have a place in the s.**, ocupar su puesto en el mundo; hacerse conocer o sentir; tener importancia.—**under the s.**, en el mundo. **II.** *va.* (a)solear.—**to s. one's self**, tomar el sol.
sunbeam [-bim], *s.* rayo de sol.
sunbonnet [-banit], *s.* papalina.
sunburn [-bœrn]. **I.** *va.* y *vn.* quemar(se) o tostar(se) con el sol. **II.** *s.* quemadura de sol.—**sunburning** [-iŋ], *s.* quemadura del sol, solanera.
sunburnt [-bœrnt], *a.* quemado, tostado o bronceado por el sol, requemado.
sundae [sʌndi], *s.* refresco de helado con frutas o nueces molidas.
Sunday [sʌndi]. **I.** *s.* domingo. **II.** *a.* dominical, del domingo, dominguero.—**S. clothes**, (fam.) trapitos de cristianar.—**S. law**, ley (*f.*) sobre la observancia del domingo.—**S. letter**, carta dominical.—**S. school**, escuela dominical de iglesia, doctrina dominical.
sunder [sʌndœ(r)]. **I.** *s.* separación.—**in s.**, en dos. **II.** *va.* y *vn.* separar, apartar, dividir; romper o romperse; separarse.
sundial [sʌndaial], *s.* reloj de sol, cuadrante solar, gnomon.
sundown [-daun], *s.* puesta del sol.
sundries [sʌndriz], *s. pl.* (com.) géneros varios.
sundry [sʌndri], *a.* varios, diversos.—**all and s.**, todos y cada uno.
sunfish [sʌnfiś], *s.* (ict.) rueda.
sunflower [-flauœ(r)], *s.* (bot.) girasol.
sung [sʌŋ], *pret.* y *pp.* de TO SING.
sunglow [sʌnglou], *s.* arrebol.
sunk [sʌŋk], *pret.* y *pp.* de TO SINK.
sunken [-n], *a.* sumido, hundido.
sunless [sʌnlis], *a.* sombrío; sin luz; sin sol, nublado.
sunlight [-lait], *s.* luz del sol.
sunlike [-laik], *a.* semejante o parecido al sol; resplandeciente.
sunn [sʌn], **sunn hemp** [-hemp], *s.* (bot.) cáñamo de Bengala.
Sunna, Sunnah [súnạ], *s.* Zuna, cuerpo de tradiciones musulmanas.
Sunnite [súnait], *s.* zunita, *mf.*, miembro de cierta secta musulmana.
sunny [sʌni], *a.* de sol (día); asoleado, resolano; resplandeciente; alegre, risueño; halagüeño.—

s. side, lado del sol; lado bueno, aspecto favorable.

sunproof [sʌ́npruf], *a.* a prueba de sol.

sunrise [-raɪz], *s.* salida del sol, amanecer; (poét.) Oriente.

sunscald [-skold], **sunscorch** [-skorʧ], *s.* (bot.) enfermedad causada por exceso de sol.

sunset [-sɛt], *s.* puesta del sol, ocaso; anochecida.

sunshade [-ʃeɪd], *s.* quitasol, parasol, guardasol, sombrilla; sombrero; pantalla.

sunshine [-ʃaɪn], *s.* solana, luz del sol; claridad del sol; día, *m.*—**in the s.,** al sol.

sunshiny [-ʃaɪnɪ], *a.* lleno de sol; risueño.

sunspot [-spat], *s.* (astr.) mácula, mancha solar.

sunstroke [-stroʊk], *s.* (med.) insolación.

sunstruck [-strʌk], *a.* atacado de insolación.

sunup [-ʌp], *s.* salida del sol.

sunward [-wɑrd], *adv.* hacia el sol.

sunwise [-waɪz], *adv.* con el sol.

sup [sʌp]. **I.** *va.* sorber. **II.** *vn.* cenar. **III.** *s.* sorbo.

super [sjúpœ(r)]. **I.** *s.* (com.) cosa excelente; excelencia, alta calidad; (abrev. fam.) = SUPERNUMERARY; SUPERINTENDENT. **II.** *a.* (fam.) excelente, de más de marca, de marca mayor.

superable [-əbl], *a.* superable, vencible.

superableness [-nɪs], *s.* calidad de superable.

superabound [-əbáʊnd], *vn.* superabundar, sobreabundar.

superabundance [-əbʌ́ndəns], *s.* superabundancia, sobreabundancia, plétora; redundancia.—**superabundant** [-ənt], *a.* superabundante.—**superabundantly** [-lɪ], *adv.* superabundantemente.

superadd [-ǽd], *va.* sobreañadir, requintar.

superaddition [-ǽdɪʃən], *s.* sobreañadidura.

superannuate [-ǽnjueɪt], *va.* y *vn.* jubilar(se); inhabilitar(se), imposibilitar(se) (por edad, vejez, etc.).—**superannuation** [-éɪʃən], *s.* inhabilitación; jubilación.

superb [sjupǿrb], *a.* soberbio, grandioso, magnífico, espléndido; (fam.) de primera.—**superbly** [-lɪ], *adv.* soberbiamente, grandiosamente.

supercargo [sjupœrkárgoʊ], *s.* (mar.) sobrecargo.

supercharge [-ʧárdʒ], *va.* sobrecargar; (m. comb. int.) sobrealimentar.—**supercharged engine,** motor de alimentación adicional por presión.

supercharger [-ʧardʒœ(r)], *s.* (m. comb. int.) compresor para alimentación adicional forzada.

superciliary [-sílɪerɪ], *a.* (anat., zool.) superciliar.

supercilious [-sílɪəs], *a.* ceñudo; arrogante, altanero.—**superciliously** [-lɪ], *adv.* arrogantemente.—**superciliousness** [-nɪs], *s.* arrogancia, altanería.

supercooling [-kúlɪŋ], *s.* (quím., fís.) sobrefusión.

superdominant [-dámɪnənt], *s.* (mús.) superdominante, *f.*

superdreadnought [-drɛ́dnɔt], *s.* (mar.) acorazado mayor.

superelevation [-ɛlɛvéɪʃən], *s.* (f. c.) peralte (del riel exterior).

supereminence, supereminency [-ɛ́mɪnəns, -ɪ], *s.* supereminencia.—**supereminent** [-ənt], *a.* supereminente, eminentísimo.

supererogate [-ɛ́rogeɪt], *vn.* hacer más de lo obligatorio.—**supererogation** [-éɪʃən], *s.* supererogación.—**supererogatory** [-ágətorɪ], *a.* supererogatorio.

superexcellent [-ɛ́ksɛlɛnt], *a.* sobreexcelente, muy excelente.

superfetation [-fɪtéɪʃən], *s.* (fisiol.) superfetación.

superficial [-fíʃəl], *a.* superficial, somero.

superficiality [-fɪʃɪǽlɪtɪ], **superficialness** [-fíʃəlnɪs], *s.* superficialidad.

superficially [-fíʃəlɪ], *adv.* superficialmente.

superficiary [-fíʃɪerɪ], *a.* (for.) superficiario.

superficies [-fíʃɪɪz], *s.* superficie.

superfine [-fáɪn], *a.* superfino, sobrefino; florete.

superfineness [-nɪs], *s.* calidad de superfino.

superfluous [supœ́rflʊəs], *a.* superfluo, sobrado.

superfluousness [-nɪs], **superfluity** [sjupœrflúɪtɪ], *s.* superfluidad, demasía, nimiedad.

superfluously [-lɪ], *adv.* superfluamente.

superfortress [-fɔrtrɪs], *s.* (aer., mil.) superfortaleza (es nombre de fábrica).

superheat [-hít], *va.* recalentar.—**superheated steam,** vapor recalentado.—**superheater** [-œ(r)], *s.* recalentador (de vapor).—**superheating** [-ɪŋ], *s.* recalentamiento.

superheterodyne [-hɛ́tɛrodaɪn], *a.* (rad.) superheterodino.

superhuman [-hjúmən], *a.* sobrehumano.

superimpose [-ɪmpóʊz], *va.* superponer, sobreponer.—**superimposition** [-ɪmpozíʃən], *s.* superposición.

superincumbent [-ɪnkʌ́mbɛnt], *a.* superyacente, sobrepuesto.

superinduce [-ɪndjús], *va.* sobreañadir, promover.

superinduction [-ɪndʌ́kʃən], *s.* sobreañadidura.

superintend [-ɪnténd], *va.* superentender, vigilar, dirigir.—**superintendence,** *o* **superintendency** [-əns, -ɪ], *s.* superintendencia, inspección, dirección.—**superintendent** [-ənt], *s.* superintendente, inspector, interventor; capataz, *m.*

superior [supírɪo(r)], *a.* y *s.* superior (en todas sus acepciones).—**S. Court,** Audiencia.

superiority [supɪrɪárɪtɪ], *s.* superioridad.

superlative [sjupœ́rlatɪv], *a.* y *s.* superlativo.

superlatively [-lɪ], *adv.* superlativamente, en sumo grado.—**superlativeness** [-nɪs], *s.* excelencia, grado superlativo.

superman [sjúpœrmæn], *s.* superhombre.

supernal [sjupǿrnəl], *a.* superno o supremo; celeste.

supernatant [sjupœrnéɪtənt], *a.* flotante.

supernatural [-nǽchʊrəl]. **I.** *a.* sobrenatural. **II.** *s.* lo sobrenatural.—**supernaturally** [-ɪ], *adv.* sobrenaturalmente.—**supernaturalism** [-ɪzm], *s.* calidad de sobrenatural; creencia en lo sobrenatural.

supernumerary [-njúmɛrerɪ]. **I.** *a.* supernumerario, suplementario, agregado. **II.** *s.* supernumerario; (teat.) figurante, comparsa, *mf.*

superorganic [-orgǽnɪk], *a.* sobreorgánico, fuera del organismo; mental; sobreindividual, superior al individuo.

superphosphate [-fásfeɪt], *s.* (quím.) superfosfato.

superphysical [-fízɪkəl], *a.* más allá de lo físico, inmaterial.

superpose [-póʊz], *va.* sobreponer, superponer.

superposition [-pozíʃən], *s.* superposición.

superscribe [-skráɪb], *va.* sobrescribir, poner un sobrescrito a.—**superscription** [-skrípʃən], *s.* sobrescrito.

supersede [-síd], *va.* reemplazar; desalojar; invalidar; (for.) sobreseer.

supersedeas [-sídɪæs], *s.* (for.) auto de sobreseimiento.

supersedure, supersession [-sídʒʊ(r), -séʃən], *s.* (for.) sobreseimiento.

supersensible, supersensual [-sénsɪbl, -sénsjuəl], *a.* más allá de los sentidos, inaccesible a los sentidos; espiritual.

superserviceable [-sœ́rvɪsəbl], *a.* demasiado servicial u oficioso.

supersonic [-sánɪk], *a.* supersónico (ú. de velocidades que superan la del sonido).

superstition [-stíʃən], *s.* superstición.

superstitious [-stíʃəs], *a.* supersticioso.

superstitiously [-lɪ], *adv.* supersticiosamente.

superstructure [-strʌ́kchʊ(r)], *s.* superestructura, la parte superior de una construcción, o la obra propiamente, a distinción de los cimientos.

supertax [-tæks], *s.* (e. p.) sobreimpuesto, impuesto adicional (impuesto sobre capitales o rentas que exceden cierto límite fijado por la ley). *V.* SURTAX.

supervene [-vín], *vn.* sobrevenir, supervenir; suceder, acaecer.

supervenient [-víni̯ent], *a.* superveniente.
supervention [-vénʃǫn], *s.* superveniencia, supervención, sobrevenida.
supervise [-vái̯z], *va.* supervisar, superentender, inspeccionar, intervenir.—**supervision** [-víʒǫn], *s.* supervisión, superintendencia, intervención o inspección.—**supervisor** [-vái̯zǫ(r)], *s.* supervisor, superintendente, inspector, interventor, sobrestante, veedor.
supination [si̯upinéi̯ʃǫn], *s.* supinación.
supinator [-éi̯tǫ(r)], *a.* y *s.* (anat.) supinador (músculo).
supine [si̯upái̯n]. **I.** *a.* supino, boca arriba; inclinado, pendiente; negligente, indolente, descuidado. **II.** [sjúpai̯n], *s.* (gram.) supino.—**supinely** [si̯upái̯nli̯], *adv.* boca arriba; descuidadamente, con negligencia.—**supineness** [-nis], *s.* posición supina; descuido, negligencia, dejadez.
supper [sʌ́pǫ(r)], *s.* cena.—**s. time**, hora de cenar.
supperless [-lis], *a.* sin cenar.
supplant [sʌplǽnt], *va.* suplantar, desbancar; reemplazar, desalojar.
supplanter [-œ(r)], *s.* suplantador, el que suplanta a otro.
supplanting [-iŋ], *s.* suplantación.
supple [sʌ́pl]. **I.** *a.* flexible; dócil, obediente, deferente; servil. **II.** *va.* y *vn.* hacer o volverse flexible, dócil u obediente.
supplement [sʌ́plęmęnt]. **I.** *s.* suplemento; alcance; apéndice. **II.** [sʌ́plęmęnt], *va.* suplementar, completar; reforzar, ayudar.
supplemental, supplementary [sʌplęmę́ntal, -tari̯], *a.* suplementario, suplemental; supletorio.—**s. angles**, (geom.) ángulos suplementarios.
suppleness [sʌ́plnis], *s.* flexibilidad; docilidad, condescendencia.
suppletory [sʌ́plitǫri̯], *a.* supletorio.
suppliance [sʌ́pli̯ans], *s.* ruego, súplica.
suppliant [-ant], **supplicant** [-kant], *s.* y *a.* suplicante.—**supplicate** [-kei̯t], *va.* y *vn.* suplicar, deprecar, implorar, impetrar.—**supplication** [-kéi̯ʃǫn], *s.* súplica, deprecación, ruego; (igl.) preces, *f. pl.*, rogativa.—**supplicating** [-kei̯tiŋ], **supplicatory** [-kątǫri̯], *a.* suplicante, deprecante, deprecatorio, rogativo.
supplier [sʌplái̯œ(r)], *s.* suministrador, proveedor, abastecedor.
supply [sʌplái̯]. **I.** *va.* surtir, abastecer, proveer (de); suministrar, proporcionar, habilitar; suplir, reemplazar. **II.** *s.* (*pl.* SUPPLIES) suministro, provisión, abastecimiento, surtimiento; substituto, suplente; (com.) abasto, oferta; repuesto, surtido.—*pl.* (mil.) pertrechos; materiales, artículos, efectos; víveres, subsistencias, provisiones; enseres.—**s. and demand**, la oferta y la demanda.—**s. line**, (mil.) vía de abastecimiento.—**s. of provisions**, prevención, bastimento.—**s. pipe**, (hidr.) caño o cañería de abastecimiento.—**s. price**, precio mínimo.
support [sʌpórt]. **I.** *va.* sostener, aguantar, sustentar; mantener (a una persona, etc.), proveer para; sostener (un trato o diálogo); resistir, sufrir, tolerar; asistir, amparar; abogar por, apoyar; defender, atestiguar, probar, confirmar, justificar, vindicar; acompañar en público; (teatro) hacer un papel subordinado a otro; desempeñar un papel.—**to s. one's self**, mantenerse, ganarse la vida. **II.** *s.* sostén, apoyo, soporte; respaldo, puntal, apoyadero, pedestal, sustentáculo; sustentación, sostenimiento; ayuda, protección; sufragio; prueba, justificación; sustento, manutención.—**in s. of**, en favor de, en apoyo de, en defensa de.
supportable [-ạbl], *a.* soportable, llevadero, pasadero, tolerable; sostenible.—**supportably** [-ạbli̯], *adv.* soportable o llevaderamente.
supporter [-œ(r)], *s.* mantenedor; defensor, sostenedor; partidario; fautor; sostén, soporte,

sustentáculo; (arq.) atlante o telamón; (blas.) tenante.
supposable [sʌpóu̯zạbl], *a.* que puede suponerse; presumible, imaginable.
suppose [sʌpóu̯z], *va.* suponer; dar por sentado o existente; poner por caso, dar de barato; presuponer; creer, imaginar, hacer (*I supposed he was in Paris*, le hacía en París).
supposed [-d], *a.* supuesto; hipotético; presunt(iv)o, pretendido, pretenso, fingido.
supposedly [-idli̯], *adv.* supuestamente, que se supone (suponía, etc.).
supposer [-œ(r)], *s.* suponedor.
supposing [-iŋ], *conj.* dado (caso) que.—**s. he did it?**, ¿y si lo hiciera?
supposition [sʌpozíʃǫn], *s.* suposición, supuesto, hipótesis.
suppositional [-ạl], *a.* hipotético, supositivo.
supposititious [sʌpazi̯tíʃạs], *a.* supositicio, hipotético, supuesto; falso, fingido.
suppositive [sʌpázitiv], *a.* supositivo.
suppository [sʌpázitǫri̯], *s.* supositorio, cala.
suppress [sʌprés], *va.* suprimir, sofocar, extinguir, acabar con; reprimir, contener; ocultar, omitir, eliminar; parar, detener.
suppressible [-ibl], *a.* suprimible; reprimible.
suppression [-ʃǫn], *s.* supresión, extinción, represión; (med.) suspensión.—**suppressive** [-siv], *a.* supresivo o represivo.—**suppressor** [-sǫ(r)], *s.* supresor.
suppurate [sʌ́pyu̯rei̯t], *vn.* (med.) supurar.
suppuration [-éi̯ʃǫn], *s.* supuración; pus.
suppurative [-ạtiv], *a.* y *s.* supurativo.
supramaxillary [si̯uprạmǽksilạri̯], *a.* y *s.* (anat.) supramaxilar.
supramundane [-mʌ́ndei̯n], *a.* sobrenatural.
suprarenal [-rínạl], *a.* y *s.* (anat.) suprarrenal.—**s. body, capsule,** o **gland,** cápsula suprarrenal.
supremacy [si̯uprémạsi̯], *s.* supremacía.
supreme [si̯uprím], *a.* supremo, sumo, soberano, superno.—**S. Being,** Ser Supremo.—**s. commander,** (mil.) generalísimo.—**S. Court,** Corte Suprema, consejo o tribunal supremo.—**s. work,** obra cumbre.
supremely [-li̯], *adv.* supremamente; soberanamente, sumamente.
sural [si̯úrạl], *a.* (anat.) sural.
surbase [sœ́rbei̯s], *s.* (arq.) cornisa de pedestal; moldura o vuelo en la parte superior.—**surbased** [-t], *a.* provisto de cornisa o moldura superior; rebajado (arco).
surcease [sœrsís]. **I.** *vn.* (ant.) cesar, acabarse. **II.** *va.* (ant.) dejar de. **III.** *s.* (ant.) cesación.
surcharge [sœ́rchardʒ]. **I.** *s.* sobrecarga, sobrepeso; recargo; resello. **II.** [sœrchárdʒ], *va.* sobrecargar, recargar; resellar.
surcingle [sœ́rsiŋgl], *s.* (tal.) sobrecincha; (igl.) cíngulo, ceñidor.
surcoat [sœ́rkou̯t], *s.* (sast.) sobretodo, gabán; (arm.) sobreveste, sobrevesta.
surd [sœrd]. **I.** *a.* (mat.) irracional; (fon.) sordo (no sonoro). **II.** *s.* (mat.) cantidad irracional; (fon.) consonante sorda.
sure [ʃúr]. **I.** *a.* seguro, cierto, indudable, infalible; firme, sentado; certero; puntual; constante, estable.—**be s. to,** o **be s. and,** (seguido de imperativo), no deje(n de, . . . sin falta (*be sure to come*, no deje de venir, venga sin falta).—**for s.,** de fijo, con seguridad, con certidumbre.—**to be s.,** estar seguro; seguramente, sin duda; ya se ve. **II.** *adv.* (fam.) ciertamente, indudablemente, sin duda alguna.—**s. enough,** a buen seguro, con certeza; efectivamente, en efecto, en realidad de verdad.—**s.-footed,** de pie firme, seguro.
surely [-li̯], *adv.* ciertamente, seguramente, sin duda; indudablemente.
sureness [-nis], *s.* certeza, seguridad.
surety [ʃúrti̯], *s.* (for., com.) fiador, dita, garante; fianza, garantía, caución; seguridad, fieldad,

certeza.—**of a s.**, de seguro, como cosa cierta.
—**to be**, o **go, s. for**, ser fiador, salir garante de.

suretyship [-ŝip], *s.* (for.) seguridad, fianza.

surf [sœrf], *s.* (mar.) oleaje, oleada, marejada.

surface [sœrfis]. I. *va.* allanar, alisar, igualar. II. *va.* y *vn.* (hacer) emerger, surgir o salir a la superficie (submarino, etc.). III. *s.* superficie, cara, sobrefaz.—**s. plate**, (mec.) tabla rasa de comprobación de superficies planas.—**s. speed**, o **velocity**, velocidad superficial, o periférica.—**s. tension**, (fís.) tensión superficial.—**s. water**, agua superficial (a distinción de la subterránea).

surfacer [-œ(r)], *s.* máquina de alisar o cepillar madera, metal, piedra, etc.

surfacing [-iŋ], *s.* alisamiento, aplanamiento; arreglo de la superficie; material de revestimiento o coronamiento; (min.) extracción (de mineral) cerca de la superficie; (f. c.) alineación (de los rieles entre sí); emergencia o salida a la superficie del mar.

surfboard [sœrfbɔrd], *s.* (dep.) tabla larga y angosta para flotar sobre las olas.

surfboat [-bout], *s.* (mar.) lancha salvavidas o de auxilio, capaz de resistir a las marejadas.

surfeit [sœrfit]. I. *va.* ahitar, hartar, saciar; (vet.) encebadar. II. *vn.* ahitarse, hartarse. III. *s.* ahíto, empacho, indigestión; (vet.) encebadamiento; empalagamiento; exceso.

surge [sœrdʒ]. I. *s.* (mar.) oleaje, oleada, mareta; (fig.) ola, onda. II. *vn.* agitarse o embravecerse (el mar); romper (las olas). III. *va.* hacer undular; (mar.) largar, lascar (un cable o maroma).

surgeon [sœrdʒon], *s.* cirujano, quirurgo; (mil., mar.) médico (de ejército, de un buque).—**s. dentist**, cirujano dentista.—**s. fish**, (ict.) barbero.—**s.-general**, (E. U.) médico mayor, jefe de sanidad militar o naval.

surgery [sœrdʒœri], *s.* cirugía.

surgical [sœrdʒikal], *a.* quirúrgico.

surgy [sœrdʒi], *a.* (mar.) agitado, de leva, ondeante.

surlily [sœrlili], *adv.* ásperamente, con mal humor, de mal modo.—**surliness** [-nis], *s.* mal genio, mal humor, displicencia; murria.

surly [sœrli], *a.* áspero, rudo, insolente, arisco, displicente; furioso, tempestuoso.

surmise [sœrmáiz]. I. *va.* conjeturar, suponer, presumir, barruntar, vislumbrar. II. *s.* conjetura, suposición, barrunto, vislumbre.

surmount [sœrmáunt], *va.* vencer, superar, salvar; pasar; coronar, poner (algo) sobre.

surmountable [-əbl], *a.* vencible, superable.

surmullet [sœrmʌlit], *s.* (ict.) mullo, salmonete.

surname [sœrneim]. I. *s.* apellido, sobrenombre, apodo. II. *va.* apellidar, denominar, llamar.

surpass [sœrpǽs], *va.* sobrepasar, sobrepujar, superar, aventajar, ganar, exceder, campar.—**surpassing** [-iŋ], *a.* sobresaliente, superior, excelente.

surplice [sœrplis], *s.* (igl.) sobrepelliz.

surpliced [-t], *a.* con sobrepelliz.

surplus [sœrplʌs]. I. *s.* sobra(nte), demasía, excedente, exceso; (com.) superávit. II. *a.* excedente, sobrante, que sobra, de sobra.

surplusage [-idʒ], *s.* = SURPLUS.

surprise [sœrpráiz]. I. *s.* sorpresa; novedad; extrañeza, asombro.—**by s.**, de sorpresa.—**to my great s.**, con grande sorpresa mía. II. *va.* sorprender, asombrar, sobrecoger.—**to be surprised (at)**, admirarse (de).—**surprising** [-iŋ], *a.* sorprendente.—**surprisingly** [-li], *adv.* sorprendentemente.

surrealism [sœriǽlizm], *s.* surrealismo.

surrebut [sœrribʌt], *vn.* (for.) triplicar.

surrebutter [-œ(r)], *s.* (for.) tríplica.

surrejoinder [-dʒóindœ(r)], *s.* (for.) contrarréplica.

surrender [sʌréndœ(r)]. I. *va.* rendir, entregar; ceder, renunciar a, abandonar. II. *vn.* rendirse,

entregarse; (mil.) capitular. III. *s.* rendición, entrega; (mil.) capitulación; renuncia, dejación, abandono; sumisión; (for.) cesión.—**s. value**, valor de rescate (de un seguro, etc.).

surreptitious [sœreptiŝʌs], *a.* subrepticio.

surreptitiously [-li], *adv.* subrepticiamente.

surrey [sœri], *s.* (carr.) especie de birlocho.

surrogate [sœrogeit]. I. *va.* subrogar, substituir, reemplazar. II. *s.* substituto; (igl.) vicario; (for.) juez (*m.*) de testamentarias.

surround [sʌráund], *va.* circundar, cercar, rodear, ceñir, circuir, envolver.—**surrounding** [-iŋ]. I. *a.* circunstante, circunvecino, circumambiente. II. *s. pl.* alrededores, contornos, cercanías, inmediaciones; medio, circunstancias rodeantes.

surtax [sœrtæks], *s.* recargo; impuesto adicional (sobre rentas que pasan de cierto límite).

surtout [sœrtút], *s.* (sast.) levitón, sobretodo.

surveillance [sœrvéiləns], *s.* vigilancia.

survey [sœrvéi]. I. *va.* examinar, estudiar; reconocer, inspeccionar; (top.) apear, medir o deslindar terrenos. II. *vn.* ejecutar operaciones topográficas. III. *s.* examen, estudio; escrutinio, reconocimiento; vista panorámica (de una materia); encuesta (de la opinión pública); (top.) medida, medición, deslinde (de un terreno).

surveying [-iŋ]. I. *s.* topografía, agrimensura. II. *a.* de o para topografía.

surveyor [-ǫ(r)], *s.* topógrafo; agrimensor; investigador, examinador; medidor de licores gravados (en la aduana); vista, *m.*, inspector de aduana.—**s.'s chain**, cadena de agrimensor (gen. GUNTER'S CHAIN).—**s.'s compass**, brújula de agrimensor.—**s.'s level**, nivel de topografía.—**surveyorship** [-ŝip], *s.* empleo de topógrafo o inspector.

survival [sœrváival], *s.* supervivencia; sobreviviente; reliquia.—**s. of the fittest**, (biol.) supervivencia del más apto.

survive [sœrváiv], *va.* y *vn.* sobrevivir (a); salir o quedar vivo.—**surviving** [-iŋ], *a.*, **survivor** [-ǫ(r)], *s.* sobreviviente, superviviente.—**survivorship** [-ŝip], *s.* supervivencia.

susceptibility [sʌseptibíliti], *s.* susceptibilidad; delicadeza.—**susceptible** [-tibl], *a.* susceptible; sensible o delicado; capaz; impresionable; enamoradizo.—**susceptibly** [-tibli], *adv.* de manera susceptible.—**susceptive** [-tiv], *a.* susceptivo.

suspect [sʌspékt]. I. *va.* y *vn.* sospechar (de), tener sospecha (de), desconfiar (de); imaginar, barruntar, maliciar. II. [sʌspekt]. *s.* persona sospechosa. III. *a.* sospechoso.

suspend [sʌspénd]. I. *va.* suspender; colgar; so(s)pesar; mantener suspenso; interrumpir, descontinuar, aplazar, diferir, remitir. II. *vn.* (com.) suspender pagos; dejar de funcionar u obrar.

suspender [-œ(r)], *s.* suspendedor.—*pl.* elásticos, tirantes del pantalón.

suspense [sʌspéns], *s.* suspensión, duda, incertidumbre; impaciencia; ansiedad; (for.) entredicho.—**in s.**, en suspenso.

suspension [-ŝǫn], *s.* suspensión (en todas sus acepciones).—**s. bridge**, (ing.) puente colgante.

suspensive [-siv], *a.* suspensivo.

suspensory [-sori], *a.* y *s.* (anat., med.) suspensorio (ll. t. s. **bandage**).

suspicion [sʌspíŝǫn], *s.* sospecha, recelo, malicia, aprensión, cavilación; (fam.) pizca, sombra.

suspicious [sʌspíŝʌs], *a.* sospechoso; suspicaz, desconfiado, malicioso, receloso, caviloso, escamado.—**suspiciously** [-li], *adv.* sospechosamente; suspicazmente.

suspiciousness [-nis], *s.* calidad de sospechoso; suspicacia, recelo, desconfianza.

sustain [sʌstéin], *va.* sostener, aguantar, sustentar; tener, mantener; sufrir (como pérdida, desgracia, daño); (mús.) prolongar, sostener;

apoyar, afianzar; animar, confortar; alimentar; defender; establecer, probar.

sustainable [-ąbl], *a.* sostenible; sustentable; defendible.

sustainer [-œ(r)], *s.* sostenedor, defensor; protector, sustentador.

sustenance [sástęnąns], *s.* sustento, mantenimiento, subsistencia; alimentos, *m. pl.*

sustentation [sʌstentéįšǫn], *s.* sostenimiento, sustentación, sustentamiento, sustento.

sutler [sátlœ(r)], *s.* vivandero, cantinero.

Sutra [sútrą̆], *s.* precepto o colección de preceptos budistas o brahmanistas.

suttee [sʌtí], *s.* costumbre india de inmolar a la viuda en la hoguera funeraria de su marido; la viuda así inmolada.

suttle [sátl], *a.* y *s.* (com.) neto; peso limpio.

sutural [sįúchŭrąl], *a.* sutural.

suture [sįúchŭ(r)]. **I.** *va.* (cir.) suturar. **II.** *s.* (anat.) sutura, comisura; (bot.) rafe, *mf.;* (cir.) sutura, costura.

suzerain [sįúzęrįn], *s.* soberano.

suzerainty [-tį], *s.* soberanía.

svelte [svelt], *a.* esbelto; flexible.

swab [swáb]. **I.** *s.* escobón, estropajo, fregajo; (cir.) esponja de hilas; (arti.) escobillón; (mar.) lampazo. **II.** *va.* fregar, limpiar; (mar.) lampacear.

swabber [-œ(r)], *s.* (mar.) lampacero, galopín.

Swabian [swéįbįan], *s.* y *a.* suabo.

swaddle [swádl], *va.* fajar, empañar.—**swaddling** [-lįŋ], *s.* fajadura, fajamiento.—**s. band,** o **cloth, faja,** pañal, envoltura de niños.—**s. clothes,** *pl.* pañales, empañadura.

swag [swǽg]. **I.** *vn.* = SWAY O SAG. **II.** *s.* (fam.) robo, hurto; (b. a.) guirnalda.—**swagbellied** [-belįd], *a.* ventrudo, panzudo.

swage [swejdž]. **I.** *s.* estampa, tas, yunque de estampar; herramienta o artificio para dar forma al metal al forjarlo.—**s. block,** matriz o bloque de estampar o modelar. **II.** *va.* forjar en estampa, estampar, dar forma a en el yunque de estampar.

swagger [swǽgœ(r)]. **I.** *vn.* fanfarr(on)ear. **II.** *s.* jactancia, (fam.) fanfarria, baladronada.—**swaggerer** [-œ(r)], *s.* jaque, baladrón, matasiete.

swain [swejn], *s.* zagal; enamorado.

swale [swejl], *s.* terreno pantanoso.

swallow [swáloų]. **I.** *va.* tragar(se); deglutir, ingurgitar; engullir; retractar, retirar, desdecir; aguantar (un insulto, etc.); (fam.) tragar el anzuelo, creer a ciegas.—**to s. up,** tragar(se); absorber. **II.** *vn.* deglutir. **III.** *s.* bocado, trago; deglución; (anat.) tragadero, esófago; (ant.) abismo, sima; sumidero; (orn.) golondrina; (orn.) vencejo, avión, *m.*—**s. dive** = SWAN DIVE.—**s. fish,** (ict.) golondrina.—**s.-tailed coat,** frac.

swallowtail [-tejl], *s.* (carp.) cola de milano.

swallowwort [-wœrt], *s.* (bot.) golondrinera, asclepiada, celidonia.

swam [swǽm], *pret.* de TO SWIM.

swamp [swámp]. **I.** *s.* pantano, marisma, ciénaga, fangal.—**s. oak,** (bot.) carrasco. **II.** *va.* sumergir, echar a pique, hacer zozobrar; empantanar, encenagar, encharcar; arruinar, hundir; abrumar, recargar; inundar (fig.). **III.** *vn.* empantanarse; irse a pique, zozobrar.

swampy [-į], *a.* pantanoso, cenagoso.

swan [swan], *s.* (orn.) cisne.—**s. dive,** salto de ángel (natación).—**s.-like,** semejante al cisne; como de cisne.—**s.'s-down,** plumón de cisne; (tej.) (gen. **swansdown**) muletón o moletón; paño de vicuña.—**s. song,** último canto del cisne moribundo; obra última.

swank [swǽŋk]. **I.** *s.* (fam.) ostentación, boato, elegancia, baladronada. **II.** *a.* (fam.) elegante, ostentoso; jactancioso. **III.** *vn.* (fam.) alardear, fachendear.

swankiness [-įnįs], *s.* (fam.) = SWANK.

swanky [-į], *a.* (fam.) = SWANK.

swanneck [swánnek], *s.* nombre dado a varios artificios en que la parte más conspicua (brazos, soporte, etc.) tiene forma de U; (hidr.) pestaña saliente de paleta de una rueda.

swanskin [swánskįn], *s.* piel (*f.*) de cisne; (tej.) lanilla, bayeta fina.

swap [swap]. **I.** *va.* cambiar, cambalachear (fam.), permutar. **II.** *vn.* hacer cambalaches o trueques. **III.** *s.* cambalache (fam.), trueque, cambio.

swaraj [swąrádž], *s.* (India) autonomía, independencia.

sward [sword]. **I.** *va.* encespedar. **II.** *vn.* cubrirse de hierbas. **III.** *s.* césped, céspede. *V.* TURF.

swarm [swórm]. **I.** *s.* enjambre, jabardo (de abejas); (fig.) hormiguero, multitud. **II.** *va.* y *vn.* enjambrar, jabardear, desahijarse (abejas); arrebozarse; pulular, hervir, bullir, hormiguear; (fam.) trepar.

swarmer [-œ(r)], *s.* enjambrador; insecto que vive o anda en enjambres.

swart [swort], *a.* prieto, moreno, atezado.

swarthily [swórθįlį], *adv.* morenamente.

swarthiness [-įnįs], *s.* color moreno, atezamiento, tez morena.

swarthy [-į], *a.* atezado, prieto, moreno, trigueño.

swash [swáš]. **I.** *s.* ruido o golpe de agua, chorretada; (mar.) canalizo.—**s. plate,** (mec.) placa motriz. **II.** *va.* lanzar una chorretada. **III.** *vn.* batir o hacer ruido el agua; baladronear; meter bulla.—**swashbuckle** [-bʌkl], *vn.* fanfarronear.—**swashbuckler** [-bʌklœ(r)], *s.* matasiete, espadachín, fanfarrón.—**swasher** [-œ(r)], *s.* jaque, fanfarrón.—**swashing** [-įŋ], *a.* fanfarrónico; violento, batiente, abrumador.

swastika [swástįką̆], *s.* svástica, signo simbólico en forma de cruz griega con los cuatro extremos volteados en ángulo recto en un mismo sentido.

swat [swat]. **I.** *s.* (fam.) golpazo. **II.** *va.* (fam.) golpear súbita y violentamente.

swath [swaθ], *s.* (agr.) ringla o ringlera de mies segada; guadañada (ll. t. **swathe**).—**to cut a wide s.,** hacer alarde u ostentación. *V.* SPLURGE y SWANK.

swathe [swejð]. **I.** *va.* fajar (una criatura); enrollar, vendar. *V.* SWADDLE. **II.** *s.* faja, pañal; venda.

sway [swej]. **I.** *va.* inclinar, ladear; influir en el ánimo de (alguno), inducir; blandir, cimbrar, mover; mandar, dominar, gobernar, regir; (mar.) izar, guindar.—**to s. up,** guindar. **II.** *vn.* ladearse, inclinarse, torcerse; oscilar, mecerse; ondular, undular; tambalear, flaquear. **III.** *s.* poder, imperio, predominio, preponderancia, influjo; vaivén, oscilación, ondulación, balanceo, bamboleo.—**to give full s. to,** dar ancho campo a.

swear [swér], *va.* y *vn.* (*pret.* SWORE, y ant. SWARE; *pp.* SWORN) jurar; (gen. con **to**) declarar bajo juramento; renegar, blasfemar, echar votos o ternos; juramentar, tomar o prestar juramento.—**to s. by,** jurar por; (fam.) poner confianza implícita en.—**to s. in,** juramentar, tomar juramento a.—**to s. off,** jurar o resolverse a abandonar (una costumbre).—**to s. up and down,** (fam.) jurar y perjurar, jurar por todos los santos.

swearer [-œ(r)], *s.* jurador; renegador.

sweat [swét]. **I.** *va.* y *vn.* (*pret.* y *pp.* SWEAT o SWEATED) sudar; trasudar; resudar; hacer sudar; trabajar duro; (fam.) arrancar informes o confesión a (un preso) con preguntas continuas, someter a interrogatorio persistente y minucioso; secar en horno; apelambrar o calentar (pieles); soldar; recortar o cercenar monedas.—**to s. it out,** (fam.) aguantarlo lo mejor posible. **II.** *s.* sudor; trabajo, fatiga; exudación.—**s. gland,** (anat.) glándula sudorípara.

sweatband [-bænd], *s.* tira de cuero del forro del sombrero, badana; (Am.) tafilete.

sweatbox [-baks], *s.* sudadero; tina de apelambrar; aparato secador.

sweater [-œ(r)], *s.* el que suda; patrón que impone trabajo excesivo por poco jornal; *swéter, sueter* o *jersey,* chaqueta elástica de punto de lana.

sweating [-iŋ], *s.* y *ger.* de TO SWEAT: transpiración, exudación, sudación; sudante.—**s. fever,** fiebre palúdica.—**s. iron,** raspador de sudor, cuchillo para raspar el sudor de los caballos.—**s. room,** sudadero, cuarto de sudar.—**s. sickness,** peste negra, muerte negra (de los siglos XV, XVI).—**s. system,** sistema opresivo que se aprovecha de la pobreza del obrero para forzarlo a trabajar sin tregua en cuartos apiñados (*v.* SWEATSHOP) por la mera subsistencia.

sweatshop [-šap], *s.* taller donde se impone un trabajo excesivo por paga que escasamente alcanza para la vida.

sweaty [-i], *a.* sudado, sudoso.

Swede [swid], *s.* sueco; (bot.) nabo sueco, naba.

Swedish [-iš]. **I.** *a.* sueco.—**S. turnip,** (bot.) naba. **II.** *s.* idioma sueco.

sweep [swip]. **I.** *va.* (*pret.* y *pp.* SWEPT) barrer, escobar; deshollinar (chimeneas); arrastrar; repasar, pasar rápidamente por; recorrer, pasar la vista por; cubrir, abarcar.—**to s. away,** robar sin dejar nada; arrollar, arrastrar con todo.—**to s. the bottom,** (mar.) rastrear, dragar. **II.** *vn.* barrer; pasar o deslizarse rápidamente; pasar arrasando; (a veces con *along*) pasar con paso o ademán majestuoso.—**to s. down,** descender precipitadamente. **III.** *s.* barredura, barrido; escobada; movimiento de abarque o comprensión (como ojeada, vistazo); alcance, abarque, extensión; curva, comba; barrendero; deshollinador; pieza de una máquina a lo largo de la cual se efectúa un rozamiento; remo largo y pesado; cigoñal de pozo; aspa de molino; guimbalete de bomba; (mar.) cuerda dragaminas. *V.* SWEEPSTAKES.—*pl.* barreduras.—**s. net,** o **seine,** (mar.) jábeca, jábega, red barredera.

sweeper [-œ(r)], *s.* barrendero, barredor; basurero; barredera doméstica (ll. t. **carpet sweeper**) o automóvil (para barrer las calles); (mar.) barco barredor de minas; cable barredor.

sweeping [-iŋ]. **I.** *a.* que barre; arrastrador, arrebatador; arrollador; absoluto, vasto, comprehensivo. **II.** *s.* barrido.—*pl.* barreduras, basura.

sweepstakes [-steiks], *s. sing.* y *pl.* (dep.) carrera (esp. de caballos) o a veces una especie de lotería en que una sola persona puede ganar todas las apuestas, o en que éstas suelen dividirse entre varios individuos.

sweet [swit]. **I.** *a.* dulce; sabroso, rico, gustoso; oloroso, fragante; (mús.) melodioso, grato al oído; bello, bonito, lindo; amable, afable, agradable; fresco; (mec.) suave y sin ruido; (agr.) bueno, fértil (tierra).—**s. alyssum,** (bot.) alhelí dulce.—**s. apple,** (bot.) manzana dulce; anona, chirimoya.—**s. basil,** (bot.) albahaca. —**s. cicely,** (bot.) perifollo.—**s. corn,** (bot.) variedad de maíz tierno cuyas mazorcas se cuecen para comer.—**s. fern,** helecho miricáceo. —**s. flag,** (bot.) cálamo aromático, ácoro.—**s. gale** = **s.** WILLOW.—**s. gum,** (bot.) ocozol.—**s. herbs,** (coc.) hierbas olorosas.—**s. marjoram,** (bot.) mejorana.—**s. oil,** aceite de oliva. —**s. pea,** (bot.) guisante de olor.—**s. pepper,** (bot.) pimiento dulce, morrón o de bonete.—**s. potato,** (bot.) batata, patata dulce, buniato, (Am.) camote.—**s. rush** = **s.** FLAG.—**s. scented,** perfumado.—**s.-smelling,** odorífero, fragante, oloroso.—**s.-spoken,** melifluo.—**s.-tempered,** de carácter dulce, complaciente.— **s.-toned,** (poét.) dulcísono.—**s.-tongued,** melifluo, (de) pico de oro.—**(to have a) s. tooth,** (tener) gusto por, o gustar de, dulces; (ser) goloso.—**s.-toothed,** goloso, aficionado a los dulces.—**s. william,** (bot.) clavel barbado, minutisa, clavel de China.—**s. willow,** (bot.)

mirto holandés o de Brabante. **II.** *s.* dulzura; deleite; persona querida.—*pl.* dulces, golosinas.

sweetbread [-bred], *s.* lechecillas o mollejas (*f. pl.*) de ternera.

sweetbrier [-braiœ(r)], *s.* (bot.) escaramujo oloroso, agavanzo.

sweeten [-n]. **I.** *va.* endulzar, dulcificar, azucarar; (farm.) edulcorar; suavizar, mitigar, aplacar; embalsamar; purificar; hacer salubre. **II.** *vn.* endulzarse.—**sweetener** [-œ(r)], *s.* dulcificante.

sweetheart [-hart], *s.* dulce amiga; querida, amante, *mf.*; amador, galán, galanteador, cortejo.

sweeting [-iŋ], *s.* (bot.) camuesa.

sweetish [-iš], *a.* algo dulce.

sweetly [-li], *adv.* dulcemente.

sweetmeat [-mit], *s.* dulce, confitura, golosina.

sweetness [-nis], *s.* dulzura, melosidad, suavidad, delicadeza, apacibilidad, bondad.

sweetsop [-sap], *s.* (bot.) anona, chirimoya.

swell [swél]. **I.** *va.* (*pp.* SWELLED o SWOLLEN) hinchar, engrosar, inflar, entumecer, henchir, abultar, agravar; engreír, envanecer. **II.** *vn.* hincharse, engrosarse, entumecerse, abotagarse, inflarse; henchirse; crecer, subir; dilatarse, esponjarse; hincharse, engreírse; embravecerse (el mar).—**to s. out,** arrojar (el árbol) sus hojas; espetarse, ampollarse, bufar. **III.** *a.* (fam.) elegante, del buen tono; magnífico, de órdago.—**to have a s. head,** (fam.) estar engreído. **IV.** *s.* entumecencia, hinchazón, *f.,* bulto; aumento de volumen; (mar.) oleada, marejada; ondulación del terreno; prominencia, protuberancia; (mús.) unión de crescendo y diminuendo, y los signos (<>); (fam.) petimetre, persona que sigue las modas con exageración.— **s. box,** (mús.) caja de expresión (de un órgano). —**s. organ,** órgano de expresión.—**s. pedal,** pedal de expresión.

swelling [-iŋ]. **I.** *s.* hinchazón, *f.,* inflación; (med.) tumefacción, entumescencia, turgencia, abotagamiento; bulto, chichón, protuberancia. **II.** *a.* que se hincha o infla; turgente.—**s. breast,** seno agitado; pecho turgente.—**s. sea,** mar agitado.

swelter [swéltœ(r)]. **I.** *va.* sofocar, achicharrar, abrumar de calor. **II.** *vn.* abrasarse, achicharrarse; sudar la gota gorda.

swept [swept], *pret.* y *pp.* de TO SWEEP.

swerve [swœrv]. **I.** *va.* desviar, apartar, torcer. **II.** *vn.* desviarse, apartarse, extraviarse, virar. **III.** *s.* desviación, viraje.

swift [swift]. **I.** *a.* rápido, ligero, raudo, pronto, presto; veloz, volador; vivo, diligente, activo; sumarísimo, repentino; (mar.) velero. **II.** *adv.* = SWIFTLY.—**s.-footed, s. of foot,** de paso rápido, ligero, alípedo. **II.** *s.* (orn.) vencejo, arrejaque; (zool.) lagartija; (mec.) carrete, devanadera.

swifter [-œ(r)], *s.* (mar.) tortor, andarivel.

swiftly [-li], *adv.* velozmente, prontamente, aprisa.—**swiftness** [-nis], *s.* velocidad, rapidez, prontitud.

swig [swig]. **I.** *va.* y *vn.* (fam.) beber a grandes tragos. **II.** *s.* (fam.) trago.

swill [swil]. **I.** *va.* lavar, inundar (con agua); (a menudo con **down**) tragar o engullir vorazmente. **II.** *vn.* emborracharse. **III.** *s.* bazofia; tragantada.

swim [swim]. **I.** *vn.* (*pret.* SWAM; *pp.* SWUM) nadar; flotar, sobrenadar; dejarse ir o llevar; resbalar o deslizarse suavemente; tener la cabeza ida o desvanecida; tener vértigo; padecer vahídos.— **to s. with the tide,** seguir la corriente o ir con la corriente. **II.** *va.* pasar a nado; hacer nadar o flotar. **III.** *s.* natación, nado; nadadera de pez; movimiento de deslizarse; mundo, corriente de las cosas; sociedad, vida social; vida de tono; clases influyentes.—**to be in the s.,** estar en la corriente o a la marcha de las cosas.—**to go for,** o **take, a s.,** ir a nadar, meterse al agua.

swimmer [-œ(r)], *s.* nadador.
swimming [-in]. **I.** *a.* nadador, nadante, natatorio; aguado; lleno de lágrimas.—**s. bladder**, vejiga natatoria de pez.—**s. place**, nadadero.—**s. pool**, piscina natatoria.—**by s.**, a nado. **II.** *s.* natación, nado; vértigo, vahído.
swimmingly [-lī], *adv.* fácilmente, rápidamente, lisamente, sin tropiezo.
swindle [swíndl]. **I.** *va.* petardear, estafar, (fam.) timar, trampear. **II.** *s.* estafa, (fam.) timo, petardo.—**swindler** [-dlœ(r)], *s.* estafador, timador, trampeador.
swine [swáin], *s. sing.* y *pl.* marrano(s), puerco(s), cerdo(s); persona bruta y soez.—**s. plague**, (vet.) peste (*f.*) de los puercos.—**s. pox**, (med. y vet.) variedad de viruelas locas.—**s. thistle** = SOW THISTLE.
swinebread [-bred], *s.* (bot.) trufa, criadilla de tierra; pan de puerco.
swineherd [-hœrd], *s.* porquero, porquerizo.
swing [swin]. **I.** *va.* (*pret.* y *pp.* SWUNG) columpiar, mecer, cunear, hacer oscilar; balancear, bambolear; blandir (arma); hacer girar; engoznar; controlar, influir en (las elecciones, etc.). **II.** *vn.* oscilar, columpiarse, mecerse, balancearse; girar, volverse, dar vueltas; (mar.) bornear; (fam.) ser ahorcado.—**to s. about**, dar una vuelta.—**to s. clear**, evitar un choque. **III.** *s.* vibración, oscilación, vaivén, balanceo, bamboleo, balance; columpio, mecedor; libertad de acción, libre curso; autoridad, control; (mec.) juego, carrera, movimiento, recorrido, alcance.—**s. back**, respaldo de articulación de una cámara fotográfica.—**s. block**, (mec.) gorrón.—**s. bridge**, puente giratorio.—**s. door**, puerta giratoria de soporte central y varias alas.—**s. lamp**, lámpara colgante.—**s. plow**, arado de reja reversible.—**in full s.**, en plena operación, en su apogeo. **IV.** *a.* giratorio; engoznado.
swingbar [-bar], *s.* (carr.) balancín.
swingeing [swíndźiŋ], *a.* (fam.) grande, enérgico; magnífico, estupendo, de primera.
swinger [swíŋœ(r)], *s.* oscilador; columpiador.
swinging [swíŋiŋ]. **I.** *s.* oscilación, vibración; balanceo; (mar. y danz.) borneo. **II.** *a.* oscilante, mecedor; colgante; giratorio.
swingle [swíŋgl]. **I.** *va.* espad(ill)ar (el lino). **II.** *s.* espadilla; (agr.) brazo corto del mayal.
swingletree [-tri], **swingtree** [swíŋtri], *s.* (carr.) balancín, volea; barra articulada de tiro.
swinish [swáinish], *a.* porcuno; cochino, grosero, sucio.—**swinishly** [-lī], *adv.* cochinamente.—**swinishness** [-nis], *s.* calidad de cochino; (fam.) marranada, cochinada.
swipe [swaip]. **I.** *va.* (fam.) dar o golpear duro; robar. **II.** *s.* (fam.) golpe fuerte; cigüeñal de pozo.
swirl [swœrl]. **I.** *va.* y *vn.* arremolinar(se). **II.** *s.* remolino, torbellino.
swish [swish]. **I.** *va.* y *vn.* blandir, dar un latigazo, bastonazo, etc.; zurriagar. **II.** *s.* movimiento o silbido del látigo o bastón al cortar el aire.
Swiss [swis], *a.* y *s.* suizo, helvecio, helvético.—**S. chard**, (bot.) acelga.
switch [swich]. **I.** *s.* varilla, bastoncillo, latiguillo; trenza postiza; (f. c.) cambiavía, *m.*, agujas, *f. pl.*, cambio; (elec.) interruptor, conmutador; acción u operación de desviar un tren o una corriente eléctrica mediante un *switch;* (mil.) sistema (*m.*) de trincheras de comunicación (ll. t. **switch line**).—**s. engine**, locomotora de maniobras.—**s. lever**, (f. c.) palanca de maniobra (de las agujas).—**s. rail**, (f. c.) aguja (de cambio).—**s. stand**, (f. c.) plataforma de maniobra (de las agujas).—**s. tender**, (f. c.) guardagujas, cambiavía, *m.*—**s. tower**, caballete de maniobras. **II.** *va.* azotar, fustigar, dar latigazos; (f. c.) desviar, apartar; (elec.) cambiar.—**to s. off**, desconectar, cortar (la corriente); apagar (las luces).—**to s. on**,

conectar; encender (las luces). **III.** *vn.* (a veces con **off**) desviarse, cambiarse.
switchback [-bæk]. **I.** *s.* (f. c.) desarrollo o construcción (de una vía inclinada) en zigzag; montaña rusa. **II.** *a.* (f. c.) (de desarrollo) en zigzag.
switchboard [-bord], *s.* (elec.) cuadro de distribución; (tlf.) cuadro conmutador.
switcher [-œ(r)], *s.* (f. c.) guardagujas; locomotora de maniobras.
switchman [-man], *s.* (f. c.) guardagujas.
swivel [swívl]. **I.** *va.* y *vn.* girar o hacer girar sobre un eje. **II.** *s.* (mec.) alacrán, torniquete, eslabón giratorio; articulación giratoria; lanzadera (de un telar de cintas; (arti.) colisa (ll. t. **s. gun**).—**s. chair**, silla giratoria.
swob [swab], *s.* y *va.* = SWAB.
swollen [swóuln]. **I.** *pp.* de TO SWELL. **II.** *a.* hinchado, entumecido; henchido; crecido; turgente.—**s. with pride**, inflado, hinchado de orgullo.
swoon [swun]. **I.** *vn.* desmayarse, desvanecerse, desfallecer. **II.** *s.* desmayo, síncope, desfallecimiento, soponcio, deliquio.
swoop [swup]. **I.** *va.* descender y agarrar la presa al vuelo; coger, arrebatar. **II.** *vn.* caer, calarse (las aves), precipitarse sobre algo. **III.** *s.* descenso rápido y cogida al vuelo; calada.
sword [sord], *s.* espada.—**s. arm**, brazo derecho.—**s. belt**, talabarte, biricú, cinturón.—**s. cane**, bastón de estoque.—**s. guard**, **s. hilt**, empuñadura, puño, guarda de la espada.—**s. law**, ley (*f.*) marcial; ley del más fuerte.—**s. lily**, (bot.) estoque.—**s.-shaped**, ensiforme.—**to be at swords' points**, estar de punta, estar a matar, estar como perros y gatos.
swordfish [-fiš], *s.* (ict.) pez espada, *m.*, jifia.
swordplay [-plei], *s.* esgrima, manejo de la espada.
swordsman [-zman], *s.* (*pl.* SWORDSMEN) espadachín, esgrimista, espada, *m.*; militar.
swore, **sworn** [swor(n], *pret.* y *pp.* de TO SWEAR.
swum [swʌm], *pret.* y *pp.* de TO SWIM.
swung [swʌŋ], *pret.* y *pp.* de TO SWING.
Sybarite [síbarait], *s.* sibarita, *mf.*—**sybaritic(al** [sibarítik(al], *a.* sibarítico, sibarita.
sybaritism [síbaraitizm], *s.* sibaritismo.
sycamore [síkamor], *s.* (bot.) sicómoro; (E. U.) plátano falso.
syconium [saikóuniam], *s.* (bot.) siconio.
sycophancy [síkofansi], *s.* adulación, servilismo; parasitismo.—**sycophant** [-ant], *s.* adulador; parásito; (hist.) sicofanta, *m.* sicofante.—**sycophantic** [-ǽntik], *a.* adulatorio; lisonjero; chismoso.
syenite [sáienait], *s.* (min.) sienita.
syenitic [saienítik], *a.* (min.) sienítico.
syllabary [sílabari], *s.* silabario.
syllabic(al [silǽbik(al], *a.* silábico.—**syllabically** [-lī], *adv.* por sílabas.—**syllabicate** [-keit], *va.* silabear.—**syllabication** [-kéišon], *s.* silabeo.
syllable [sílabl], *s.* sílaba; (poét.) pie, *m.*
syllabus [sílabas], *s.* sílabo, sumario, extracto, resumen, compendio.
syllepsis [silépsis], *s.* (gram. y ret.) silepsis.
sylleptic(al [-tik(al], *a.* que envuelve silepsis.
syllogism [sílodźizm], *s.* (lóg.) silogismo.
syllogistic(al [silodźístik(al], *a.* silogístico.
syllogistically [-lī], *adv.* silogísticamente.
syllogize [sílodźaiz], *vn.* silogizar.
sylph [silf], *s.* (mit.) silfo, sílfide, *f.;* (fig.) sílfide, mujer esbelta y graciosa; (orn.) colibrí.
sylva [sílvä], *s.* selva.—**sylvan** [-n], *a.* selvático, silvático; rústico, rural.
sylvanite [-nait], *s.* (min.) telururo de oro y plata.
symbiosis [simbióusis], *s.* (biol.) simbiosis.
symbol [símbol], *s.* símbolo; emblema, *m.;* (teol.) credo.
symbolic(al [simbálik(al], *a.* simbólico.
symbolically [-ali], *adv.* simbólicamente.
symbolics [-s], *s.* ciencia de los símbolos.
symbolism [símbolizm], *s.* simbolismo.
symbolist [-ist], *s.* simbolista.

symbolistic [-ístịk], *a.* simbolista.
symbolization [-izéịsǫn], *s.* simbolización.
symbolize [-aịz], *va.* y *vn.* simbolizar.
symbology [sịmbálodźị], *s.* arte o tratado de los símbolos; simbología.
symmetalism [sịmmétẹlịzm], *s.* (e. p.) sistema monetario en que la moneda patrón consta de dos o más metales.
symmetrical [sịmétrịkạl], *a.* simétrico.
symmetrically [-ị], *adv.* simétricamente.
symmetrize [sịmịtraịz], *va.* simetrizar.
symmetry [sịmịtrị], *s.* simetría.
sympathetic(al [sịmpạθétịk(ạl], *a.* simpático; que simpatiza; simpatizador, simpatizante; afín; benévolo, compasivo.—**s. ink**, tinta simpática o invisible.—**s. nervous system**, (anat.) gran simpático.
sympathetically [-ị], *adv.* simpáticamente, con simpatía, benévolamente.
sympathize [sịmpạθaịz], *vn.* simpatizar, compadecerse, condolerse; doler, padecer o sentir por simpatía; convenir, armonizarse, ajustarse, congeniar.—**sympathizer** [-œ(r)], *s.* simpatizante, el que simpatiza con otro; aprobador, partidario, seguidor.
sympathy [sịmpạθị], *s.* simpatía, afinidad; benevolencia; conmiseración, compasión, lástima; pésame; (med.) simpatía.
symphonic [sịmfánịk], *a.* sinfónico; homónimo.
symphonious [sịmfóụnịạs], *a.* armonioso.—**symphonist** [sịmfonịst], *s.* sinfonista.—**symphony** [sịmfonị], *s.* sinfonía.
symphysis [sịmfịsịs], *s.* (anat.) sínfisis.
symposiac [sịmpóụzịæk], *a.* perteneciente a los banquetes o convites.—**symposium** [-ʌm], *s.* (hist. griega) simposia, festín, banquete; (hoy) reunión, debate o conferencia para tratar algún tema; colección de artículos o comentarios.
symptom [sịmptǫm], *s.* (med. y fig.) síntoma, *m.*
symptomatic(al [-ætịk(ạl], *a.* sintomático.
symptomatically [-ị], *adv.* sintomáticamente.
symptomatology [-ạtálodźị], *s.* (med.) sintomatología, semiología, semiótica.
synæresis [sịnérịsịs], *s.* = SYNERESIS.
synagogue [sịnạgạg], *s.* sinagoga.
synalepha [sịnạlífạ], *s.* (gram.) sinalefa.
synalgia [sịnáldźạ], *s.* (med.) dolor proveniente de acción simpática.
synantherous [sịnǽnθẹrʌs], *a.* (bot.) sinantéreo.
synarthrosis [sịnarθróụsịs], *s.* (anat.) sinartrosis, articulación no movible.
synchromesh [sịnkromeś], *s.* (aut.) engranaje sincrónico.
synchronal [sịnkronạl], **synchronic(al** [sịnkránịk(ạl], *a.* sincrónico.
synchronism [sịnkronịzm], *s.* sincronismo.
synchronization [-ịzéịsǫn], *s.* sincronización.
synchronize [-aịz], *va.* y *vn.* sincronizar.
synchronizer [-œ(r)], *s.* sincronizador.
synchronous [sịnkronạs], *a.* sincrónico.—**synchronously** [-ị], *adv.* sincrónicamente.
synclinal [sịnkláịnạl], *a.* y *s.* (geol.) sinclinal.
syncopate [sịnkopeịt], *va.* (gram., mús.) sincopar.
syncopation [-éịsǫn], *s.* (gram. y mús.) síncopa.
syncope [sịnkopị], *s.* (med.) síncope; (gram., mús.) síncopa.
syncretic [sịnkrétịk], *a.* sincrético.
syncretism [sịnkrịtịzm], *s.* sincretismo.—**syncretist** [-ịst], *s.* y *s.* sincretista.—**syncretize** [-aịz], *va.* conciliar o tratar de conciliar o armonizar (doctrinas distintas).
syndactyl [sịndǽktịl], *s.* y *a.*, **syndactylous** [-ʌs], *a.* (zool.) sindáctilo, que tiene dos o más dedos soldados o unidos entre sí.
syndic [sịndịk], *s.* (com. y for.) síndico.
syndical [sịndịkạl], *a.* sindical.
syndicalism [-ịzm], *s.* (e. p.) sindicalismo.—**syndicalist** [-ịst], *va.* y *s.* sindicalista.—**syndicalize** [-aịz], *va.* sindicalizar, poner bajo dominio sindicalista, u organizar según el sistema sindicalista.

syndicate [sịndịkeịt]. **I.** *va.* y *vn.* (com.) sindicar(se); publicar o vender (artículos, etc.) por medio de un sindicato. **II.** *s.* (for.) sindicado; sindicatura; (com.) sindicato, asociación de capitalistas para emprender un negocio magno; (e. p.) sindicato, asociación de obreros; grupo de periódicos, revistas, etc., bajo una misma dirección; empresa que compra artículos manuscritos, fotografías, etc., y los vende para su publicación simultánea en varios periódicos o revistas.
syndication [-éịsǫn], *s.* sindicación.
synecdoche [sịnékdokị], *s.* (ret.) sinécdoque, *f.*
syneresis [sịnérịsịs], *s.* (gram.) sinéresis.
synergism [sịnœrdźịzm], *s.* (teol.) doctrina según la cual el alma coopera con la gracia divina.
synergy [sịnœrdźị], *s.* (fisiol.) sinergia.
synesthesia [sịnesθíźạ], *s.* (fisiol.) sinestesia; sensación en una parte del cuerpo diferente de la afectada directamente por el estímulo que la produce; sensación asociada o concomitante.
syngenesis [sịndźénịsịs], *s.* (biol.) concurrencia de los gérmenes masculino y femenino en la formación del feto; generación o reproducción sexual.
synod [sịnǫd], *s.* (igl., astr.) sínodo.
synodal [-ạl], **synodic(al** [sịnádịk(ạl], *a.* (igl.) sinodal; (igl., astr.) sinódico.
synonym [sịnonịm], *s.* sinónimo.
synonymize [sịnánịmaịz], *va.* usar sinónimos.
synonymous [-mʌs], *a.* sinónimo.
synonymy [-mị], *s.* sinonimia.
synopsis [sịnápsịs], *s.* sinopsis.
synoptic(al [sịnáptịk(ạl], *a.* sinóptico.
synovia [sịnóụvịạ], *s.* (anat.) sinovia.—**synovial** [-l], *a.* sinovial.—**synovitis** [sịnováịtịs], *s.* sinovitis.
syntactic(al [sịntæktịk(ạl], *a.* sintáctico.
syntax [sịntæks], *s.* (gram.) sintaxis.
synthesis [sịnθesịs], *s.* síntesis; (cir.) reunión de partes divididas.—**synthesize** [-aịz], *va.* y *vn.* sintetizar; producir por síntesis.
synthetic(al [sịnθétịk(ạl], *a.* sintético; fabricado.
synthetically [-ị], *adv.* sintéticamente.
syntonic [sịntánịk], *a.* sintónico, sintonizado.
syntonin [sịntonịn], *s.* (bioquím.) sintonina.
syntonization [sịntonịzéịsǫn], *s.* (rad.) sintonización.—**syntonize** [sịntonaịz], *va.* sintonizar.—**syntonizer** [-œ(r)], *s.* sintonizador.—**syntony** [sịntonị], *s.* sintonía, sintonismo.
syphilis [sịfịlịs], *s.* (med.) sífilis.—**syphilitic** [-ítịk], *a.* sifilítico.—**syphilologist** [-álodźịst], *s.* sifilógrafo.—**syphilology** [-álodźị], *s.* sifilología, sifilografía.
syphon [sáịfǫn], *s.* y *va.* = SIPHON.
Syriac [sịrịæk], *a.* y *s.* siríaco.
Syrian [sịrịạn], *s.* sirio.
syringa [sịrịngạ], *s.* (bot.) jeringuilla; lila.
syringe [sịrịndź]. **I.** *s.* (med.) jeringa. **II.** *va.* jeringar, dar una lavativa o inyección.
syringotomy [sịrịngátomị], *s.* (cir.) siringotomía.
syrinx [sịrịnks], *s.* (anat.) trompa de Eustaquio; (orn.) siringe, *f.*, segunda laringe de las aves; (S., mit.) Siringe, flauta de Pan.
syrtis [sœrtịs], *s.* sirte, *f.*, banco de arena.
syrup [sịrạp], *s.* jarabe, jarope; almíbar.
system [sịstẹm], *s.* sistema, *m.*, método; clasificación ordenada; (fisiol. y biol.) sistema, *m.*; (geol.) formación; instalación (de gas, etc.).
systematic(al [sịstẹmætịk(ạl], *a.* sistemático, metódico.
systematically [-ị], *adv.* sistemáticamente.
systematization [-izéịsǫn], *s.* sistematización.
systematize [sịstẹmạtaịz], *va.* sistematizar; metodizar.
systemic [sịstémịk], *a.* sistemático; (fisiol. y anat.) relativo a todo el sistema o cuerpo.
systole [sịstolị], *s.* (fisiol. y ret.) sístole, *f.*
systolic [sịstálịk], *a.* sistólico.
systyle [sịstaịl], *s.* (arq.) sístilo.
syzygy [sịzịdźị], *s.* (astr.) sicigia.

TAB 595 TAI

T

t [ti], *s.* t.

T [ti]. **I.** *s.* objeto en forma de T; pieza (tubo, viga, etc.) en T. **II.** *a.* de T, de forma de T.—**T iron,** hierro en T.—**T rail,** riel en T, o de hongo.—**T square,** (dib.) regla T.—**to a T,** exactamente, perfectamente.

tab [tæb], *s.* proyección, apéndice; oreja de zapato; herrete de cordón; (fam.) cuenta; vigilia.

tabard [tǽbắrd], *s.* tabardo; cota.

Tabasco (sauce) [tặbǽskou (sọs)], *s.* la marca de fábrica de una salsa hecha de chiles (ajíes) selectos, sujetos a fermentación natural, y condimentados con vinagre y sal.

tab(b)inet [tǽbịnịt], *s.* (tej.) tabinete.

tabby [tǽbị]. **I.** *s.* (tej.) tabí; gato romano; gata; solterona chismosa. **II.** *a.* ondeado, moteado, mosqueado, que hace aguas.

tabefaction [tæbịfǽkṣọn], *s.* (med.) tabefacción, extenuación, emaciación, atrofia, marasmo. *V.* TABES.

tabernacle [tǽbœrnækl], *s.* tabernáculo.

tabes [téjbiz], *s.* (med.) tabes, *f.,* consunción.

tabetic [tặbétịk]. **I.** *a.* (med.) tabético. **II.** *s.* tísico.

tabid [tǽbịd], *a.* (med.) tábido.

tablature [tǽblặchụr], *s.* (anat.) tablatura, pared del cráneo; (b. a.) pintura mural.

table [téjbl]. **I.** *s.* mesa; comida, manjares; tabla (matemática, de la ley, de materias, etc.), cuadro; losa, plancha; tarima; tablero; banco; (geog.) meseta; (b. a.) tabla, pintura en tabla o piedra; (arq.) entablamento; palma de la mano; faceta superior de un diamante; piedra preciosa de dos facetas.—**t. boarder,** pupilo, pensionista.—**t. cover,** carpeta, sobremesa.—**t. d'hôte,** mesa redonda de una fonda; comida de varios platos, o a la francesa; comida corrida.—**t. knife,** cuchillo de mesa.—**t.-land,** (alti)planicie, altiplano, mesa, meseta.—**t. linen,** mantelería.—**t. of contents,** tabla de materias, índice.—**t. runner,** camino de mesa.—**t. service, o set,** vajilla.—**t. wine,** vino de pasto o de mesa. **II.** *va.* y *vn.* dar carpetazo, encarpetar; poner (un naipe) sobre la mesa; (impr.) catalogar; poner índice; (carp.) ensamblar, acoplar.

tableau [tǽblou], *s.* (*pl.* TABLEAUX) cuadro (al vivo).

tablecloth [téjblkloθ], *s.* mantel; tela para manteles, alemanisco.

tablespoon [-spun], *s.* cuchara ordinaria de mesa.—**tablespoonful** [-fụl], *s.* cucharada.

tablet [tǽblịt], *s.* tabla, tableta, tablilla; bloc de papel; plancha, lápida; (farm.) tableta, pastilla, comprimido.

tableware [téjblwer], *s.* servicio de mesa, artículos para la mesa.

tabloid [tǽblojd]. **I.** *s.* (farm.) tabloide; comprimido; periódico de noticias concisas o condensadas (apl. esp. a los chismosos y sensacionales). **II.** *a.* condensado, breve, conciso; de noticias breves (apl. esp. a periódicos populares ilustrados).

taboo, tabu [tặbú]. **I.** *va.* declarar tabú, (fig.) prohibir, excluir, desterrar. **II.** *s.* tabú; preocupación, ostracismo. **III.** *a.* proscri(p)to, prohibido.

tabo(u)r [téjbọ(r)], *s.* tamboril.—**taborer** [-œ(r)], *s.* tamborilero.

tabo(u)ret [tæborét], *s.* tamborilete; taburete; bastidor de bordar.

tabo(u)rine [tæbọrín], **tabret** [tǽbrịt], *s.* tamborilete; pandereta, adufe. *V.* TAMBOURINE.

tabular [tǽbyụlắ(r)], *a.* tabular.—**tabulate** [-lejt], *va.* poner o arreglar en forma de tabla.—**tabulated** [-jd], *a.* liso, plano.—**tabulation** [-léjṣọn], *s.* reducción a forma tabular.—**tabulator** [-lejtọ(r)], *s.* constructor de tablas; tabu-

---

lador (de máquina de escribir).—**t. key,** tecla del tabulador (ll. t. **tabular key**).

tacamahac [tǽkặmặhæk], *s.* (bot.) tacamaca; álamo balsámico.

tacheometer [tækịámetœ(r)], *s.* = TACHYMETER.

tachograph [tǽkogræf], *s.* tacógrafo, registrador de velocidad; registro gráfico hecho con este instrumento o con el tacómetro (ll. t. TACHOGRAM).

tachometer [tækámetœ(r)], *s.* tacómetro, contador de velocidad.

tachygraphy [tækígrặfị], *s.* taquigrafía.—**tachygrapher** [-fœ(r)], *s.* taquígrafo.—**tachygraphic(al** [-grǽfịk(ặl], *a.* taquigráfico.—**tachygraphist** [tækígrặfịst], *s.* taquígrafo, taquígrafa.

tachymeter [tækímetœ(r)], *s.* contador de velocidad; (top.) taquímetro.—**tachymetric** [-métrịk], *a.* taquimétrico.—**tachymetry** [tækímetrị], *s.* (top.) taquimetría.

tacit [tǽsịt], *a.* tácito.

tacitly [-lị], *adv.* tácitamente.

taciturn [tǽsịtœrn], *a.* taciturno.

taciturnity [-tœrnịtị], *s.* taciturnidad.

tack [tæk]. **I.** *va.* clavar con tachuelas; (cost.) puntear, pegar, coser, hilvanar; unir, añadir o anexar. **II.** *vn.* (mar.) virar, cambiar de bordada, voltejear. **III.** *s.* tachuela, puntilla; (cost.) hilván; (mar.) amura; bordada, viraje, virada; cambio de política; nuevo plan de acción.—**t. claw,** sacatachuelas.—**t. hammer,** martillo para tachuelas.

tackle [tǽkl]. **I.** *va.* agarrar, asir; atacar, abordar (un problema, etc.), luchar con; (football) atajar a un adversario. **II.** *s.* (mar.) aparejo, poleame, maniobra, motonería, cuadernal, jarcia; equipo, (fam.) avíos, enseres (vg. *fishing tackle,* avíos de pescar); (football) atajo y agarrada; atajador.—**t. block,** (mar.) motón de aparejo.—**t. fall,** tira de aparejo.—**t. hooks,** ganchos de aparejo.

tact [tækt], *s.* tacto; tino, tiento, tacto, maña, ten con ten, (don de) acierto.

tactful [-fụl], *a.* discreto, cauto, mañoso.

tactfully [-ị], *adv.* discreta, cauta, mañosamente.

tactic(al [tǽktịk(ặl], *a.* táctico.

tactician [tæktíṣặn], *s.* táctico.

tactics [tǽktịks], *s. pl.* (mil.) táctica.

tactile [tǽktịl], *a.* tangible, palpable; táctil, del tacto, relativo al tacto.

tactility [tæktịlịtị], *s.* calidad de tangible.

tactless [tǽktlịs], *a.* falto de tacto o de tino, impolítico.

tactual [tǽkchụạl], *a.* relativo a, o causado por, el tacto.

tadpole [tǽdpoul], *s.* (zool.) renacuajo.

ta'en [tejn], *contr. poét.* de TAKEN.

tænia, tenia [tínịặ], *s.* (antig. gr.) banda, faja, cinta; (arq.) filete, cinta; (zool.) tenia, solitaria.

taffeta, taffety [tǽfịtặ, -tị], *s.* (tej.) tafetán.

taffrail [tǽfrejl], *s.* (mar.) coronamiento.

taffy [tǽfị], *s.* melcocha, arropía; (fam.) lisonja, halago.

tag [tæg]. **I.** *s.* herrete; marbete, marca, rótulo, tejuelo; cartela; apéndice, extremo del rabo; tirador de una bota; (fam.) pingajo, arrapiezo; muchedumbre, populacho; juego de muchachos.—**t. day,** *día de cartelas,* en que se solicitan en las calles contribuciones para obras de caridad, etc., colgando una cartelilla o flor en el pecho o el ojal del contribuyente.—**the t. and rag, o the t., rag and bobtail,** el populacho, la canalla. **II.** *va.* clavetear o poner herretes; marcar con marbete o rótulo; pisar los talones, alcanzar y tocar.

Tagala [tagála], *s.* tagalo.

tagrag [tǽgræg], *s.* (fam.) chusma.

tagtail [tǽgtejl], *s.* (zool.) lombriz; sicofante.

Tahitian [tahítịan], *s.* y *a.* tahitiano, de Tahití.

tail [téjl]. **I.** *s.* cola, rabo; cabo, extremidad; apéndice; (astr.) cola (de cometa); (mús.) rabito

---

de una nota; pie (*m.*) de página; reverso o cruz de una moneda; (sast.) faldón; (alb.) cola o entrega de un sillar; acompañamiento, escolta; fila o hilera de gente; (for.) limitación de propiedad; (aer.) planos de cola, planos estabilizadores traseros.—*pl.* (fam.) frac; cruz (de una moneda).—**t. coat,** frac, saco de faldas sesgadas.—**t. end,** extremo trasero, parte (*f.*) de atrás; lo último.—**t. fin,** (aer.) plano de deriva de cola.—**t. gunner,** (aer.) artillero de cola.—**t. lamp, t. light,** farol trasero.—**t. plane,** (aer.) plano fijo de cola, estabilizador de cola.—**t. rod,** (m. v.) prolongación del vástago del émbolo.—**t. skid,** (aer.) patín de cola.—**t. spin,** (aer.) barrena.—**t. unit,** (aer.) conjunto de cola.—**t. wind,** (aer.) viento de cola. II. *va.* proveer de cola; (vet.) cortar la cola; desrab(ot)ar; (a veces con **on, in** o **into**) añadir, agregar, juntar, unir, empatar; tirar de (la cola); (fam.) espiar, seguir muy de cerca (a uno).

tailage [-idź], *s.* derecho, tributo. *V.* TALLAGE.

tailblock [-blak], *s.* (mar.) motón de rabiza.

tailed [-d], *a.* rabudo; de rabo; con cola.

tailing [-iŋ], *s.* (alb.) cola, entrega.—*pl.* restos, desechos.

tailless [-lis], *a.* sin cola; desrab(ot)ado.

tailor [téilǫ(r)]. I. *s.* sastre.—**t.-made,** de sastrería, hecho por sastres; hecho sobre medidas o a la medida.—**t.-made suit,** traje sastre.—**t.'s shop,** o **trade,** sastrería. II. *va.* vestir, proveer de ropa. III. *vn.* ser sastre; ser (bueno o malo) para hacer ropa (ú. de telas).—**tailored** [-d], *a.* (de) sastre; sencillo, de corte algo severo (ú. de ropas para señoras).—**tailoress** [-is], *s.* sastra.—**tailoring** [-iŋ], *s.* sastrería (arte); corte y confección de vestidos.

tailpiece [téilpis], *s.* apéndice; (impr.) florón; culo de lámpara; cola de violín o guitarra.

tailrace [-reis], *s.* (hidr.) canal o conducto de salida o escape (del agua de una rueda); agua de salida.

tailspin [-spin], *vn.* (aer.) descender en barrena.

taint [téint]. I. *va.* manchar, inficionar, corromper. II. *vn.* inficionarse, corromperse, podrirse. III. *s.* mácula, mancha, corrupción.—**taintless** [-lis], *a.* incorrupto, puro.

take [teik], *va.* (*pret.* TOOK; *pp.* TAKEN) tomar; coger, asir, agarrar; recibir, aceptar; apropiarse, apoderarse de; percibir o cobrar; quitar, hurtar, llevarse; quedarse con (una compra); llevar, conducir, acompañar; restar, deducir; prender, hacer prisionero; escoger; usar, emplear, adoptar; empuñar, tener por; asumir, aceptar; admitir; adaptarse o hacerse a; tomar, emplear o necesitar (tiempo); coger, contraer (una enfermedad); coger, sorprender; sacar (un retrato, una copia); dar (un paseo); hacer (ejercicio); saltar (una barrera).—**to t. aback,** desconcertar.—**to t. a back seat,** ceder su puesto, perder influencia.—**to t. a bath,** bañarse.—**to t. a bite,** comer algo.—**to t. account of,** tener en cuenta, hacer caso de.—**to t. a chance (on** o **with)** arriesgar(se); probar.—**to t. action,** actuar, hacer diligencia, tomar medidas; (for., etc.) proceder (contra).—**to t. a different,** o **another, turn,** cambiar de aspecto.—**to t. advantage of,** aprovecharse de, sacarle partido a (una persona) o de (una situación); abusar de.—**to t. advice,** a onsejarse, tomar consejo.—**to t. a fancy to,** prendarse de; antojarse de.—**to t. a header,** irse de cabeza.—**to t. aim,** apuntar, tomar puntería.—**to t. a journey,** hacer un viaje.—**to t. a leap,** dar un salto o brinco.—**to t. a liking to,** aficionarse a, coger cariño a.—**to t. a look at,** echar una ojeada a, mirar.—**to t. amiss,** tomar en mala parte, ofenderse de—**to t. an examination,** sufrir un examen.—**to t. an oath,** prestar juramento.—**to t. a notion to,** aficionarse a; coger cariño a; metérsele a uno (algo) en la cabeza.—**to t. apart,** desarmar, desmontar (una máquina).—

to t. a rest, descansar.—**to t. arms,** tomar las armas; principiar la guerra.—**to t. asunder,** separar, desunir.—**to t. a short cut,** atajar.—**to t. a shot at,** hacer un tiro a; (fig.) echar una pulla a.—**to t. a step,** dar un paso; tomar una medida.—**to t. a turn,** o **a walk,** dar una vuelta, un paseo.—**to t. away,** quitar, sacar; llevarse.—**to t. back,** retractar, desdecirse de; recibir (algo) devuelto; devolver; llevar a, o hacer pensar en (tiempos pasados, etc.).—**to t. breakfast,** desayunarse.—**to t. breath,** descansar; tomar aliento.—**to t. by storm,** tomar por asalto.—**to t. care,** tener cuidado.—**to t. care of,** cuidar de, atender a.—**to t. chances,** correr el riesgo, arriesgar; confiar en la suerte.—**to t. charge of,** hacerse cargo de, encargarse de, ocuparse de, tomar por su cuenta.—**to t. cold,** resfriarse.—**to t. counsel,** deliberar; consultar.—**to t. cover,** buscar abrigo, abrigarse.—**to t. down,** asentar, tomar nota de; bajar o poner más bajo; descolgar; derribar; quitar los humos a; tragar.—**to t. effect,** surtir efecto; entrar en vigencia; poner en, o llevar a, efecto.—**to t. exception to,** oponerse a, no conceder o aceptar (una proposición, aserción, etc.).—**to t. fire,** encenderse; incendiarse.—**to t. for,** tomar o tener por.—**to t. for granted,** dar por sentado.—**to t. French leave,** despedirse a la francesa, escabullirse, irse callandito.—**to t. fright,** atemorizarse, sobresaltarse.—**to t. from,** despojar a, privar a, quitar a; restar o substraer de.—**to t. heart,** tomar o cobrar aliento, no desalentar.—**to t. heed,** hacer caso, poner atención.—**to t. hold (of** u **on),** asir, coger, agarrar; tomar posesión, apoderarse; encargarse; aprender, comprender; ponerse al corriente.—**to t. horse,** cabalgar, pasear a caballo.—**to t. in,** hacer entrar, dar ingreso; admitir, recibir (en su casa, en la sociedad, etc.); acomodar; tomar; cobrar; recibir (dinero); entender; abarcar, comprender, incluir; observar, notar; (cost.) sisar; contraer, encoger; cercar; (fam.) creer, tragar; estafar, embaucar, engañar.—**to t. (in) a reef,** (mar.) tomar un rizo.—**to t. in hand,** emprender; tomar por su cuenta, hacerse cargo de.—**to t. into account,** o **consideration,** tener o llevar en cuenta, hacerse cargo de.—**to t. into one's head,** metérsele a uno en la cabeza.—**to t. in tow,** tomar a remolque.—**to t. issue with,** oponerse a; disputar.—**to t. it easy,** ir despacio, no afanarse; descansar.—**to t. it or leave it,** aceptar o rechazar sin discusión (gen. en forma imperativa, y puede traducirse por *sí* o *no*).—**to t. it out of,** u **on,** (fam.) desquitarse a costa de, hacer pagar el pato a.—**to t. it that,** entender que, inferir que.—**to t. leave,** despedirse.—**to t. leg bail,** (fam.) tomar las de Villadiego.—**to t. lunch,** almorzar.—**to t. note,** tomar nota, apuntar; notar, advertir.—**to t. notice,** darse por avisado; notar.—**to t. notice of,** hacer caso de; notar, observar, advertir, fijarse en; cuidarse de.—**to t. oath,** prestar juramento.—**to t. occasion,** aprovechar la oportunidad.—**to t. off,** separar, quitar; rebajar; cercenar, amputar; llevarse; arrebatar; causar la muerte a, matar; destruir; (fam.) imitar, remedar, ridiculizar; copiar; despegar; embotar; quitarse (el sombrero, etc.).—**to t. offense,** ofenderse, darse por sentido.—**to t. offense at,** agraviarse u ofenderse de.—**to t. office,** ocupar el poder.—**to t. on,** recibir a bordo; asumir (una actitud, etc.); emprender, asumir (un cargo, etc.).—**to t. one at his word,** fiarse de la palabra de uno.—**to t. one down a peg,** (fam.) bajarle a uno los humos.—**to t. one's breath (away),** dejar a uno sin resuello, pasmado o turulato.—**to t. one's death of (cold, fever),** (fam.) exponerse a morir de (catarro, fiebre).—**to t. one's head off,** (fam.) echar a uno un sermón, ponerlo como nuevo.—**to t. one's life in one's hand,**

arriesgar, o jugarse, la vida.—to t. one's time, ir despacio, no darse prisa.—to t. out, llevar o poner fuera; sacar, obtener; omitir; quitar; arrancar; extraer.—to t. over, tomar posesión de; hacerse cargo de.—to t. (great) pains, afanarse, empeñarse, esmerarse.—to t. part in, participar en, intervenir en.—to t. part with one, tomar la defensa o el partido de uno. —to t. pity on, apiadarse o compadecerse de. —to t. place, tener lugar, suceder, ocurrir.— to t. possession (of), apoderarse (de), posesionarse (de); ocupar (el poder, etc.).—to t. pot luck, hacer penitencia.—to t. precedence over, privar sobre, tener la prioridad a.—to t. pride in, gloriarse en.—to t. refuge o shelter, refugiarse, abrigarse, guarecerse.—to t. root, echar raíces, arraigarse, radicar, prenderse.— to t. sanctuary, acogerse a sagrado.—to t. sides, tomar partido; (con with) ponerse de parte de, apoyar a.—to t. steps, dar pasos, tomar medidas.—to t. (account of) stock, hacer inventario.—to t. stock in, creer; tener confianza en, dar importancia a.—to t. the cake, (fam.) llevarse la palma; ser el mejor (o el peor).—to t. the chair, presidir.—to t. the field, (dep.) entrar (en la cancha, etc.); (mil.) salir a campaña.—to t. the floor, tomar la palabra.—to t. the heart out of, (fam.) desalentar, quitar los bríos a.—to t. the law in(to) one's own hands, hacerse justicia por sí mismo.—to t. the stand, (for.) V. STAND, s. —to t. the wall, tomarse la acera; tomar la mayor parte.—to t. the wind out of one's sails, (fig.) desarmar a uno, apagarle los fuegos, bajarle los humos.—to t. to heart, tomar a pechos.—to t. to pieces, hacer pedazos; desarmar; refutar punto por punto.—to t. to task, reprender, regañar; censurar, criticar.—to t. up, alzar, levantar; arrestar, poner preso; tomar, recibir, admitir; ocupar o llenar (espacio); comprender o incluir; quitar, rebajar o reducir; recoger; empezar o comenzar; atender a, emprender; dedicarse a; tomar posesión; (com.) pagar al vencimiento; aceptar; reprochar, censurar; (fam.) comprar o tomar al fiado, tomar prestado (dinero, etc.); (mec.) sostener, resistir (el peso, etc.); absorber, amortiguar.— to t. upon one's self, tomar a su cargo, encargarse de, asumir.—to t. up quarters at, alojarse en.—to t. up the gauntlet, o glove, aceptar un desafío.—to t. up the hatchet = TO DIG UP THE HATCHET.—to t. warning, estar alerta, tener cuidado.—to t. water, (mar.) hacer agua.—take my word for it, créame Vd., bajo mi palabra.—take notice, aviso, advertencia.—to be taken with, prendarse o estar prendado de.

take, vn. ser poseedor, adquirir propiedad; pegar bien, tener éxito, dar golpe, (fam.) cuajar; prender (la vacuna, el fuego, etc.); hacer su efecto, ser eficaz; (fam.) picar (el pez); sacar bueno o mal retrato; pegar, adherirse; arraigar (las plantas).—to t. after, parecerse a, salir a; imitar a, seguir el ejemplo de; ser como.—to t. ill, caer enfermo.—to t. off, partir, salir; (aer.) despegar, levantar el vuelo, hacerse al aire.— to t. on, (fam.) echarse a morir, lamentarse con vehemencia; hacer grande alharaca.—to t. on with, juntarse con; prendarse de.—to t. to, dedicarse a; recurrir a; irse a; tomar afición a; ponerse a.—to t. to one's heels, apretar los talones, huir.—to t. up with, resignarse a; adoptar, aceptar; entrar en relaciones con.

take, s. toma; cogida, redada; entrada, producto, ingresos (de una función, etc.); (impr.) toma; (cine) porción de una película filmada de una vez.—t.-in, (fam.) fraude, engaño; (fam.) estafador; (fam.) entrada, ingresos.—t.-off, (fam.) sátira; caricatura, remedo; (aer.) despegue; (dep., gimn.) trampolín, raya de donde se salta.—t.-up, (mec.) atesador; (tej.) enjullo.

takedown [téjkdaun]. I. s. rifle desmontable; mecanismo de desmontar o desarmar. II. a. desarmable.

taken [téjkn], pp. de TO TAKE.—to be t. ill, o sick, caer enfermo, enfermar.—to be t. off, o away, morir.

taker [téjkœ(r)], s. tomador.

taking [téjkiŋ]. I. a. encantador, seductor, atractivo; (fam.) contagioso. II. s. toma; (for.) secuestro, embargo; (con for) afición, inclinación, afecto; (fam.) arrebato, agitación; (fam.) brete, trance apurado.—pl. ingresos.

talaria [taléiriä], s. pl. (mit.) talares.

talbot [tólbot], s. perro de San Huberto.

talc [télk]. I. s. (min.) talco.—t. powder, talco en polvo.—t. schist, talquita. II. va. tratar con talco, aplicar talco a.

talcose, talcous, talcky, talcoid [-ous, -as, -i, -ojd], a. talcoso.

talcum [-am], s. (min.) talco.—t. powder, (farm.) polvos de talco.

tale [téjl], s. cuento; novela; narración, relato; fábula, conseja; embuste, filfa; hablilla, chisme; cuenta, número.

talebearer [-bɛrœ(r)], **taleteller** [-telœ(r)], s. chismoso, cuentista, (fam.) correve(i)dile, enredador, soplón.—**talebearing, taletelling** [-bɛriŋ, -teliŋ]. I. a. chismoso, (fam.) soplón. II. s. hablilla, (fam.) chismografía.

talent [télent], s. talento, capacidad, ingenio; aptitud; personas que tienen alguna habilidad; artistas; talento (peso o valor de moneda).

talented [-jd], a. talentoso; hábil.

taler [tálœ(r)], s. tálero (moneda alemana).

tales [téjliz], s. (for.) auto para la citación de jurados suplentes; lista de jurados suplentes.

talesman [téjl(i)zmən], s. (pl. TALESMEN) (for.) jurado suplente.

taleteller [téjltelœ(r)], s. V. TALEBEARER.

talion [téljon], s. talión, m.

talipes [télipiz], s. talipes, m., pie (m.) de piña.— **taliped** [-ped], a. talipédico, de pie contrahecho.

talipot [télipot], s. (bot.) gran palma de Ceilán.

talisman [télismən], s. talismán.

talismanic [-mænjk], a. talismánico.

talk [tók]. I. va. hablar o tratar de (to talk business, hablar de negocios); hablar (en) (they talk German, hablan (en) alemán); decir (he talks nonsense, dice disparates).—to t. a blue streak, (fam.), hablar por los codos.—to t. away, malgastar (el tiempo) hablando; disipar con la palabra.—to t. into, convencer de, inducir a.—to t. out of, disuadir; sonsacar.—to t. over, discutir, conferenciar acerca de.—to t. shop, hablar de negocios o de la propia profesión sin necesidad o fuera de tiempo.—to t. up, alabar, ensalzar. II. vn. hablar; conversar, charlar, platicar.—to t. away, to t. on, hablar sin parar.—to t. to, hablar a; reprender.— to t. to the purpose, hablar al alma.—to t. up, (fam.) hablar claro. III. s. plática, conversación; habla; discurso (apl. gen. al sencillo), conferencia, plática; charla; voz común, fama, rumor; tema (m.) de una conversación; comidilla (objeto de chismes, etc.).

talkative [-ətjv], a. gárrulo, locuaz, hablador, parlero, charlatán.

talkativeness [-njs], s. locuacidad, garrulidad.

talker [-œ(r)], s. conversador, charlador; decidor; discursista; orador; charlatán, fanfarrón.

talkie [-j], s. película sonora o de cine parlante.— pl. **talkies,** cine parlante.

talking [-jŋ], a. parlante, hablante.—t. doll, muñeca parlante.—t. machine, máquina parlante (fonógrafo, etc.).—t. picture, película de cine parlante.—t. point, argumento, razón, f., aliciente (para inducir a la compra de algo).

talking-to [-tu], s. reprensión, regaño, rapapolvo.

tall [tól], a. alto, elevado; espigado; (fam.)

grande; (fam.) altisonante, exagerado, increíble.
—t. hat, sombrero de copa, chistera.

tallage [tǽlidž], *s.* (hist., Ingl.) alcabala; impuesto.

tallboy [tólboi], *s.* cajonería.

tallish [tóliš], *a.* un poco alto.

tallness [tólnis], *s.* altura, estatura, talla.

tallow [tǽlou]. **I.** *va.* ensebar. **II.** *s.* sebo.—t. **chandler,** velero.—t.-**chandler's shop,** velería.—t. **dip,** vela de sebo.—t. **tree,** (bot.) árbol del sebo.

tallowy [-i], *a.* seboso, sebáceo.

tally [tǽli]. **I.** *s.* tarja, taja, tara, cuenta.—t. **sheet,** hoja de cuentas o apuntes.—t. **stick,** tarja. **II.** *va.* tarjar, llevar la cuenta. **III.** *vn.* cuadrar, concordar, estar conforme.

tallyho [-hóu]. **I.** *interj.* grito del cazador. **II.** [tǽlihou], *s.* coche de cuatro caballos.

tallyman [-man], *s.* tendero que vende a tarja.—
tallywoman [-wuman], *s.* tendera que vende a tarja.

Talmud [tǽlmʌd], *s.* Talmud, *m.*—**Talmudic(al** [-mádik(al], *a.* talmúdico.—**Talmudist** [tǽlmʌdist], *s.* talmudista.

talon [tǽlon], *s.* (zool.) garra; (dent.) talón: monte de la baraja; talón de hoja de espada.

talus [téilʌs], *s.* (anat.) astrágalo, tobillo; (arq.) talud, *m.*

tamable [téimabl], *a.* domable, domesticable.

tamal(e [tamál(i], *s.* (Am.) tamal.

tamandua [tamandwá], *s.* (Am., zool.) tamanduá, especie de oso hormiguero.

tamarack [tǽmaræk], *s.* (bot.) alerce.

tamarind [tǽmarind], *s.* (bot.) tamarindo.

tamarisk [tǽmarisk], *s.* (bot.) tamarisco, tamariz, *m.*, taraje, taray.

tambac [tǽmbæk], *s.* = TOMBAC.

tambour [tǽmbur]. **I.** *s.* (mús., fort.) tambor; (arq.) cancel; tambor.—t. **(frame,** (cost.) tambor, bastidor para bordar. **II.** *va.* bordar a tambor.

tambourine [tæmborín], *s.* pandero, pandereta.

tame [téim]. **I.** *a.* amansado, domado, domesticado, manso; dócil, tratable, manso, sumiso; insubstancial, insípido; (fam.) moderado. **II.** *va.* domar, desbravar, domeñar, domesticar, amansar; avasallar, abatir; suavizar; represar (un río).—**tameable** [-abl], *a.* domable.—
tameless [-lis], *a.* indomado, indomable.—
tamely [-li], *adv.* mansamente, dócilmente, sumisamente.—**tameness** [-nis], *s.* domesticidad; mansedumbre; sumisión; docilidad.—
tamer [-œ(r)], *s.* domador, amansador.—**taming** [-in], *s.* amansamiento, domadura.

tamis [tǽmis], *s.* tamiz, *m.*, cedazo.

tam-o'shanter [tæm ošǽntœ(r)], *s.* boina escocesa.

tamp [tǽmp], *va.* atacar (un barreno); apisonar.

tamper [-œ(r)]. **I.** *vn.* (con **with)** entremeterse en, tocar lo que no se debe, meterse en o con; sobornar, corromper (a un testigo, etc.). **II.** *s.* pisón.—**tamping** [-in], *s.* apisonamiento.—t. **bar,** t. **iron,** pisón metálico.

tampion [-ion], *s.* (arti.) tapabocas.

tampon [-an]. **I.** *s.* (cir.) tapón. **II.** *va.* taponar.

tam-tam [tám tam], *s.* tam-tam o tantán; gongom, batintín. *V.* TOM-TOM.

tan [tæn]. **I.** *va.* (ten.) curtir, zurrar, adobar, aderezar; tostar, quemar; (fam.) zurrar la badana (a uno). **II.** *a.* tostado, de color de canela. **III.** *s.* (ten.) casca, corteza de curtir (ll. t. tan-bark); color de canela; tostadura del sol.—t. **liquor,** baño de casca.—t. **mill,** molino de corteza de roble.—t. **pit,** o **vat,** noque, tina de curtir.

tanager [tǽnidžœ(r)], *s.* (orn.) tanagra, (Arg.) tangará.

tanbark [tǽnbark], *s.* (ten.) casca, corteza curtiente.

tandem [tǽndem]. **I.** *a.* tándem, con cilindros, planos, etc., uno tras otro (apl. a máquinas,

aeroplanos, etc.); (elec.) de cascada. **II.** *s.* dos o más caballos enganchados uno tras otro; coche tirado en esa forma; tándem, bicicleta para dos ciclistas; (aer.) avión (*m.*) con alas en tándem (una tras otra). **III.** *adv.* en tándem, uno delante de otro; (elec.) en cascada.

tang [tæŋ]. **I.** *s.* dejo, gustillo, sabor; sonido, retintín; (mec.) cola, espiga, rabera. **II.** *va.* hacer retiñir. **III.** *vn.* retiñir.

tangency [tǽndžensi], *s.* tangencia.

tangent [tǽndžent]. **I.** *s.* (geom., trig.) tangente, *f.*; (f. c.) (fam.) recta, vía recta.—**to fly off,** o **go off, at a t.,** tomar súbitamente otro rumbo, pensamiento, etc. **II.** *a.* tangente; tangencial; de tangentes.—t. **distance,** (f. c.) tangente (distancia de la intersección de dos tangentes al punto de tangencia).—t. **galvanometer,** (elec.) galvanómetro de tangentes.—t. **point,** punto de tangencia.—t. **screw,** tornillo de aproximación (de un instrumento de precisión); (mec.) tornillo sin fin.—t. **spoke,** rayo tangencial, o tangente al cubo (de una rueda).—t. **wheel,** rueda de rayos tangenciales; rueda de engranaje con tornillo sin fin.

tangential [tændžénšal], *a.* tangencial.—t. **stress,** esfuerzo cortante.—**tangentially** [-i], *adv.* tangencialmente.

Tangerine [tændžerín]. **I.** *a.* y *s.* tangerino, natural de Tánger. **II.** *a.* y *s.* (t., bot.) (naranja) tangerina o mandarina.

tangibility [tændžibíliti], *s.* calidad de tangible.

tangible [tǽndžibl], *a.* tangible, palpable.

tangle [tǽŋgl]. **I.** *va.* y *vn.* enredar(se), enmarañar(se), embrollar(se); confundir(se).—**to t. (with),** venir a las manos (con). **II.** *s.* enredo, embrollo, maraña; confusión; (bot.) alga marina.

tango [tǽŋgou], *s.* (danz.) tango.

tank [tæŋk]. **I.** *s.* tanque, depósito, cuba; aljibe, arca (para agua); (mil.) tanque, tractor blindado.—t. **car,** (f. c.) vagón tanque.—t. **engine,** t. **locomotive,** locomotora ténder, que lleva sus propios depósitos de agua y carbón.—
t. **ship,** o **steamer,** (mar.) aljibe, barco tanque.—t. **tender,** (locom.) ténder para agua.—
t. **truck,** camión (*m.*) tanque. **II.** *va.* almacenar o poner en depósitos o tanques.

tankage [-idž], *s.* acto de poner en tanques; precio que se paga por guardar algo en tanques; cabida o capacidad de un tanque; (agr.) residuo de las grasas.

tankard [tǽŋkard], *s.* taza grande para beber, pichel, cangilón.

tanker [tǽŋkœ(r)], *s.* (mar.) barco tanque, aljibe.

tannate [tǽneit], *s.* (quím.) tanato.

tanned [tænd], *pp.* y *a.* (ten.) curtido, curado; tostado del sol, bronceado.—t. **leather(s),** curtidos.

tanner [tǽnœ(r)], *s.* curtidor, noquero.

tannery [-i], *s.* tenería o curtiduría.

tannic [tǽnik], *a.* (quím.) tánico.

tannin [tǽnin], *s.* (quím.) tanino.

tanning [tǽniŋ], *s.* curtimiento, curtido, curtiembre, *f.* **II.** *a.* curtiente.

tansy [tǽnzi], *s.* (bot.) tanaceto, balsamita menor, hierba lombriguera, pazote.

tantalize [tǽntalaiz], *va.* atormentar mostrando lo inasequible; atormentar, molestar.

tantalizing [-iŋ], *a.* atormentador.

tantalum [tǽntalʌm], *s.* (quím.) tantalio.

tantamount [tǽntamaunt], *a.* equivalente.

tantivy [tæntívi]. **I.** *a.* veloz, rápido. **II.** *adv.* (ant.) velozmente, de galope. **III.** *s.* galope; prisa; grito de caza.

tantrum [tǽntrʌm], *s.* (fam.) berrinche, pataleta.

tap [tæp]. **I.** *va.* decentar (un barril); espitar (una cuba, etc.); horadar, taladrar, perforar (para sacar líquido); hacer incisión a un árbol (para extraer el jugo); unir o conectar con (para tomar agua, corriente, gas, etc.); hacer una unión de toma o derivación en; hacer conexión con (líneas telefónicas o telegráficas, para interceptar o transmitir mensajes); sacar de, tomar de; (mec.) aterrajar, roscar (tuerca o hembra de tornillo); (cir.) hacer una puntura en (un absceso); golpear ligeramente, dar una palmadita; poner (media) suela o tacón a (un zapato). **II.** *vn.* tocar o golpear ligeramente.—**to t. at the door**, llamar a la puerta. **III.** *s.* canilla, espita, tubo o llave (*f.*) para sacar vino de un barril; tapón, tarugo; (mec.) macho de terraja; toma (de agua, etc.); (elec.) derivación; colada (de un alto horno); calidad o clase (*f.*) de vino; (fam.) bar; mostrador de taberna; golpecito, golpe ligero; remiendo echado a la suela de un zapato.—*pl.* (mil.) toque de apagar las luces.—**t. dance**, baile zapateado.—**t. hole**, (metal.) piquera, orificio de colada (de un alto horno).—**t. water**, agua corriente.—**on t.**, sacado del barril, por vaso (cerveza, vino, etc.).

tape [téip]. **I.** *s.* cinta, cintilla, listón, galoncillo, trencilla, bocadillo; cinta de papel o de metal; (top.) cinta.—**t. measure**, cinta para medir, metro, cinta métrica (ll. t. **tapeline**). **II.** *va.* proveer de cinta, etc.; atar o arrollar con cinta; vendar; medir con el metro.

taper [-œ(r)]. **I.** *s.* bujía, cerilla, candela, vela pequeña; cirio (de iglesia); hacha, blandón; ahusamiento de un objeto. **II.** *a.* cónico, piramidal, ahusado; (fam.) menguante, que disminuye. **III.** *va.* afilar, adelgazar, ahusar. **IV.** *vn.* rematar en punta, tener forma ahusada; (a veces con **off**) ahusarse; (fam.) menguar; ir disminuyendo; cesar poco a poco.

tapestry [tǽpistri]. **I.** *va.* entapizar; adornar con colgaduras. **II.** *s.* tapiz, *m.*; tapicería, colgadura. —**t. maker**, tapicero.—**t. shop**, tapicería.

tapeworm [téipwœrm], *s.* (zool.) tenia, solitaria.

taphouse [tǽphaus], *s.* taberna; bar.

tapioca [tæpióukǎ], *s.* tapioca, mandioca.

tapir [téipœ(r)], *s.* (zool.) tapir, danta.

tapis [tǽpi(s)], *s.* tapete.—**on the t.**, sobre el tapete.

tapper [tǽpœ(r)], *s.* el o lo que golpea; (tlg.) manipulador; (radtlg.) descohesor; (mec.) máquina de roscar tuercas o hembras de tornillo.

tappet [tǽpit], *s.* (mec.) brazo, aleta; leva.—**t. gear**, (aut.) mando de levas.

tapping [tǽpiŋ], *s.* (cir.) paracentesis.

taproom [tǽprum], *s.* taberna, bar.

tapster [tǽpstœ(r)], *s.* mozo de taberna.

tar [tar]. **I.** *s.* alquitrán, brea o pez líquida; (fam.) marinero.—**t. paper**, papel alquitranado, cartón embreado.—**t. soap**, jabón de brea.—**t. water**, (farm.) agua de alquitrán. **II.** *va.* alquitranar, embrear, embetunar.—**to t. and feather**, embrear y emplumar.

tarantella [tærǎntélǎ], *s.* (danz. y mús.) tarantela.

tarantula [tærénchŭlǎ], *s.* (ent.) tarántula.

tarboosh [tarbúš], *s.* fez, *m.*

tarbrush [tárbraš], *s.* (mar.) escopero.

tardigrade [tárdigreid], *a.* (zool.) tardígrado, lento.

tardily [tárdili], *adv.* morosamente, tardíamente; fuera de tiempo.—**tardiness** [-nis], *s.* lentitud, tardanza, morosidad, demora; cachaza, flema.

tardo [tárdou], *a.* (mús.) lento.

tardy [tárdi], *a.* tardío, moroso, tardo, lento.

tare [ter]. **I.** *s.* (bot.) cizaña; veza, algarroba, vicia, arveja; lenteja; (com.) tara, merma. **II.** *va.* destarar, restar la tara al pesar una cosa.

target [tárgit], *s.* (arti. y fig.) blanco a que se tira, terrero; (top.) tablilla, corredera (de mira de nivelar); (hist.) tarja, escudo, rodela; (fis.) foco, o superficie de emisión, de rayos X.—**t. practice** o **shooting**, tiro al blanco.—**t. (leveling) rod**, mira de tablilla o de corredera (para nivelación).—**to be on**, u **over, the t.**, (aer.) estar sobre el objetivo.

tariff [tǽrif]. **I.** *s.* tarifa; arancel; impuesto; ley

(*f.*) de impuestos (apl. esp. a los de aduana). **II.** *a.* arancelario, aduanero.—**t. protection**, (e. p.) protección arancelaria. **III.** *va.* tarifar; hacer una tarifa (lista) de; afectar por razón de impuestos.

tarlatan, tarletan [tárlatan], *s.* (tej.) tarlatana.

tarn [tarn], *s.* lago pequeño entre montañas.

tarnish [tárniš]. **I.** *va.* deslustrar, empañar, deslucir; manchar, mancillar. **II.** *vn.* deslustrarse, perder el lustre; enmohecerse. **III.** *s.* deslustre, empañadura, mancha.

tarpaulin [tarpólin], *s.* lienzo empegado o alquitranado; encerado; sombrero encerado; (fam.) marinero.

Tarpeian rock [tarpían rak], *s.* roca Tarpeya.

tarragon [tǽragan], *s.* (bot.) estragón.

tarred [tard], *a.* embreado, alquitranado.

tarry [tǽri], *vn.* tardar, demorarse, detenerse, quedarse.

tarry [tári], *a.* embreado, alquitranado; píceo.—**t.-fingered**, aficionado al hurto.

tarsal [társal], *a.* (anat.) tarsal, tarsiano, del tarso.

tarsus [társas], *s.* (anat.) tarso.

tart [tart]. **I.** *a.* acre, ácido, acídulo, picante, acedo; agridulce; mordaz. **II.** *s.* tarta; pastelillo de fruta.

tartan [tártan], *s.* (tej.) tartán; (mar.) tartana.

tartar [tártǎ(r)], *s.* (quím.) tártaro (*v.* ARGOL); (dent.) tártaro, sarro, toba.—**t. emetic**, (quím.) tártaro emético.—**t. sauce**, (coc.) salsa tártara (ll. t. **tartare sauce**).

Tartar, *s.* y *a.* tártaro; (t.) persona de mal genio; arpía.—**to catch a t.**, hallar uno la horma de su zapato.

Tartarean [tartérian], *a.* (poét.) tartáreo; infernal.

tartareous [tartérias], *a.* (quím.) compuesto de, o semejante al, tártaro; tártrico.

tartaric [tartérik], *a.* tártrico, tartárico.

tartarize [tártǎraiz], *va.* (quím., farm.) tartarizar.

tartarous [tártǎras], *a.* (quím.) = TARTAREOUS.

Tartarus [tártǎras], *s.* (mit.) tártaro, el infierno.

tartly [tártli], *adv.* agriamente.—**tartness** [-nis], *s.* acidez, agrura, acedía; acrimonia.

tartrate [tártreit], *s.* (quím.) tartrato.

tasco [tǽskou], *s.* talque.

task [tæsk]. **I.** *s.* tarea, faena, labor, *f.*—**t. force**, (mil., mar.) contingente naval reunida para una misión específica.—**to take to t.**, *v.* TAKE. **II.** *va.* atarear, señalar tarea; exigir esfuerzo de o someter a esfuerzo; poner a prueba; acusar o tachar de.—**tasker** [-œ(r)], **taskmaster** [-mæstœ(r)], *s.* el que da o señala tareas; capataz, *m.*

taskwork [-wœrk], *s.* destajo. *V.* PIECEWORK.

Tasmanian [tæzméinian], *s.* y *a.* tasmanio.

tassel [tǽsɛl]. **I.** *s.* borla, campanilla. **II.** *va.* adornar con borlas.—**tassel(l)ed** [-d], *a.* adornado con borlas o campanillas.

tasse [tæs], **tasset** [tǽsit], *s.* (gen. *pl.*) (arm.) escarcela; faldar.

tastable [téistabl], *a.* sabroso, gustable.

taste [téist]. **I.** *va.* gustar; saborear; paladear; probar, catar; experimentar, ensayar. **II.** *vn.* (a menudo con **of**) saber a, tener sabor o gusto. **III.** *s.* gusto; sabor, (fig.) paladar; gustadura; paladeo, saboreo; cata, sorbo, trago; ligera cantidad, un poco, muy poco; muestra, ejemplar; ensayo, prueba, experimento; gusto, discernimiento; afición, inclinación.—**t. bud**, (anat.) papila del gusto.—**in bad t.**, de mal gusto.—**in good t.**, de buen gusto.—**in poor t.** = IN BAD T.—**to have a t. for**, tener gusto por, gustar de.

tasteful [-ful], *a.* elegante, de buen gusto; (raro) sabroso.—**tastefully** [-i], *adv.* elegantemente, con gusto.—**tastefulness** [-nis], *s.* gusto, discernimiento; gracia, elegancia.

tasteless [-lis], *a.* insípido, insulso; desabrido, falto de gracia; de mal gusto.—**tastelessly** [-li], *cdv.* insípidamente; sin gusto, sin gracia.—

tastelessness [-nĭs], s. insipidez, falta de gusto o de gracia.

taster [-œ(r)], s. catador, probador; catavinos; probeta, catavino.

tasting [-ĭŋ], s. degustación; acto de gustar, etc.

tasty [-ĭ], a. sabroso, gustoso; embocado (vino).

tat [tæt], va. y vn. hacer encaje de frivolité.

Tatar [tátŭr], s. = TARTAR.

tatou [tatú], s. (zool.) tato, tatú, armadillo grande americano.

tatter [tǽtœ(r)], s. andrajo, pingajo, harapo, guiñapo, trapajo, jirón.

tatterdemalion [-dĭméĭlyǫn], s. zarrapastrón.

tattered [-d], a. andrajoso, harapiento.

tatting [tǽtĭŋ], s. encaje de hilo, frivolité, f.

tattle [tǽtl]. I. va. charlar, chacharear. II. vn. chismear, comadrear. III. s. charla, cháchara; chismografía.—**tattler** [tǽtlœ(r)], s. charlador, chacharero; chismoso; (orn.) agachadiza.

tattoo [tætú]. I. s. (mil.) retreta; tatuaje. II. va. tatuar.

tau [tau], s. tau (letra griega).

taught [tot], pret. y pp. de TO TEACH.

taunt [tónt]. I. va. vilipendiar, vituperar; mofarse de; reprender. II. s. vituperio; dicterio, mofa, sarcasmo. III. a. (mar.) altísimo.—t.-masted, (mar.) de mucha guinda.—**taunter** [-œ(r)], s. vituperador; mofador.—**taunting** [-ĭŋ], a. insultante.—**tauntingly** [-lĭ], adv. con vituperio; en tono insultante.

taupe [toup], s. y a. gris oscuro de varios matices.

tauriform [tórĭfǫrm], a. de forma de toro; (astr.) referente a Tauro.

taurine [tórĭn], a. taurino, de toro; (astr.) relativo a Tauro.

Taurus [tóɾʌs], s. (astr.) Tauro.

taut [tót], a. tieso, tirante, tenso; listo, preparado, en regla.—**to haul, o pull, t.,** (a)tesar.

tauten [-n], va. y vn. (mar.) tesar; entesar, atiesar(se).

tautness [-nĭs], s. calidad de tieso; tensión.

tautog [totág], s. (ict.) pez negruzco.

tautologic(al [totoládʒĭk(ǫl], a. tautológico.

tautologist [totálodʒĭst], s. tautologista.

tautologize [-dʒaĭz], vn. repetir en diferentes palabras.

tautology [-dʒĭ], s. tautología.

tavern [tǽvœrn], s. taberna; mesón, posada, figón.—t. keeper, tabernero; posadero.

taw [tǫ]. I. va. (ten.) curtir (ciertas pieles) en alumbre, sal, etc., para hacer baldés. II. s. bolita de mármol con que juegan los niños; línea desde donde se lanzan las bolas.

tawdrily [tódrĭlĭ], adv. charramente.

tawdriness [-nĭs], s. charrería.

tawdry [tódrĭ], a. charro, chillón, curro.

tawny [tónĭ], a. (a)leonado, atezado, tostado.

tax [tæks]. I. s. impuesto, tributo, contribución, gabela; carga, exacción.—t. collector, recaudador de contribuciones, exactor; alcabalero.—t.-exempt, t.-free, exento de contribución, libre de impuestos.—t. list, lista de contribuyentes.—t. rate, cupo.—t. system, sistema tributario; tributación. II. va. imponer contribuciones a; (for.) tasar; acensuar; cargar, abrumar; abusar de; someter a esfuerzo o exigir esfuerzo de; (fam.) pedir como precio; (con of o with) acusar, tachar, imputar.

taxable [-ǎbl], a. tributable, sujeto a impuesto o tributación; pechero.

Taxaceæ [tækséĭšĭĭ], s. pl. (bot.) taxáceas, taxíneas.—**taxaceous** [-šĭʌs], a. taxáceo.

taxation [tækséĭšǫn], s. tributación; imposición o repartimiento de contribuciones o impuestos.

taxer [tæksœ(r)], s. exactor; acusador.

taxgatherer [tǽksgœðœrœ(r)], s. = TAX COLLECTOR.

taxi [tǽksĭ]. I. s. taxi, taxímetro (coche).—t. driver, chófer de taxi. II. va. y vn. llevar, andar o ir en taxímetro; (aer.) (hacer) correr por tierra

o sobre el agua (un avión).—**taxicab** [-kæb], s. taxímetro (coche).

taxidermal, taxidermic [tæksĭdœrmǫl], -mĭk], a. taxidérmico.—**taxidermist** [tæksĭdœrmĭst], s. taxidermista, disecador.—**taxidermy** [-mĭ], s. taxidermia.

taximeter [tǽksĭmitœ(r)], s. taxímetro (coche o instrumento).

taxonomic [tæksonámĭk], a. taxonómico.

taxonomy [tæksánomĭ], s. taxonomía.

taxpayer [tǽkspeĭœ(r)], s. contribuyente, pechero, tributario.

taxying [tǽksĭĭŋ], s. (aer.) corrida.

tazza [tátsǎ], s. (arq.) pila, tazón (receptáculo sostenido por un pie o pedestal).

tea [ti], s. té; cualquier cocimiento, infusión o decocción medicinal; colación o refección de la tarde o prima noche; reunión en que se sirve té.—t. ball, bolsita de tela o papel, o bola metálica perforada, para hacer té.—t. canister, caja para té.—t. dance, té bailable.—t. rose, o t.-scented rose, (bot.) rosa té.—t. service, t. set, juego de té, servicio para té.—t. wagon, mesa rodadiza para té, carrito del té.

teach [tích]. I. va. (pret. y pp. TAUGHT) enseñar, instruir, profesar; aleccionar. II. vn. ejercer el magisterio, enseñar, ser maestro.

teachable [-ǎbl], a. dócil; susceptible de enseñanza, educable.

teache [tich], s. (Am.) tacho, paila evaporadora.

teacher [tíchœ(r)], s. maestro, maestra, preceptor, instructor, profesor.—**teachers' institute,** congreso o instituto pedagógico.

teaching [tíchĭŋ]. I. a. docente, enseñante, enseñador. II. s. enseñanza, instrucción, docencia, adiestramiento, aleccionamiento, magisterio; doctrina.

teacup [tíkʌp], s. taza para té.—**teacupful** [-fŭl], s. taza llena.

teak [tik], s. (bot.) teca.

teakettle [tíkɛtl], s. marmita, olla de calentar agua.

teakwood [tíkwŭd], s. (bot.) (madera de) teca.

teal [til], s. (orn.) cerceta; trullo; verde azulado.

team [tím]. I. s. tronco, tiro, par, yunta (de animales de tiro); atelaje; pareja; (dep.) equipo, cuadro (grupo de jugadores); partido; cuadrilla (de toreros); bandada de pájaros. II. vn. guiar un tronco o yunta; (con up) asociarse (con). III. va. uncir, enganchar, enyugar; transportar (con carro y animales de tiro).

teamster [-stœ(r)], s. tronquista.

teamwork [-wœrk], s. trabajo aunado o colectivo, ejecutado por varias personas con cooperación mutua.

teapot [típat], s. tetera.

teapoy [típoĭ], s. mesita de adorno (para té, etc.).

tear [tĭr]. I. s. lágrima; gota; (fig.) llanto, aflicción.—t. bomb o shell, (mil.) bomba lacrimógena, granada cargada con gas lacrimoso.—t. gas, gas lacrimógeno o lacrimoso, que afecta los ojos.—t. sac, (anat.) saco lacrimal.—in tears, llorando. II. vn. llorar, derramar lágrimas.

tear [ter]. I. va. (pret. TORE; pp. TORN) desgarrar, romper, rasgar, lacerar; rasguñar, arañar, arpar; arrancar, separar con violencia; atormentar.—to t. asunder, separar con violencia.—to t. away, arrancar; desmembrar.—to t. down, derribar, demoler.—to t. (in)to pieces, despedazar, hacer añicos.—to t. off = TO T. AWAY.—to t. one's hair, arrancarse uno los cabellos.—to t. one's self away, arrancarse o desprenderse de un lugar, partir uno contra su voluntad.—to t. out, arrancar; separar con violencia.—to t. to tatters, hacer jirones.—to t. up, arrancar, desarraigar; deshacer, desbaratar. II. vn. rasgarse; andar precipitadamente.—to t. away, u off, irse precipitadamente. III. s. rasgón, rasgadura; desgarradura; precipitación; raja; (fam.) borrachera, jarana.

teardrop [tírdrɑp], *s.* lágrima.

tearful [-fu̥l], *a.* lloroso, lagrimoso, lacrimoso.

tearing [térin], *a.* (fam.) con furia o precipitación, frenético.

tearless [tírli̥s], *a.* sin lágrimas.

tearoom [tírum], *s.* salón de té; restaurante de comidas ligeras.

tease [tíz]. **I.** *va.* molestar, atormentar, fastidiar; embromar, torear; (tej.) cardar, rastrillar, despinzar, carduzar (*v.* TEASEL); despedazar, desgarrar. **II.** *s.* broma continua; acción de embromar; (fam.) atormentador, embromador, cócora, *mf.*

teasel, teazel [tízel]. **I.** *s.* (bot. y tej.) cardencha, carda. **II.** *va.* (tej.) carmenar, cardar paño.— **teaseler** [tíz(e)lœ(r)], *s.* pelaire, cardador, carmenador.

teaser [tízœ(r)], *s.* (tej.) = TEASELER; (fam.) cócora, *mf.*, persona molesta o fastidiosa; cosa tentadora; (elec.) excitador de una dínamo.

teaspoon [tíspun], *s.* cucharita, cucharilla.—**teaspoonful** [-fu̥l], *s.* cucharadita.

teat [tit], *s.* pezón; teta; tetilla; ubre, *f.*

technical [téknikal], *a.* técnico, tecnológico; literal, aparente.—**t. term** *o* **vocabulary**, tecnicismo.—**technicality** [-kǽliti], *s.* cosa técnica; argucia o sutileza; tecnicismo.—**technically** [-kali], *adv.* técnicamente.—**technician** [teknísan], **technicist** [-si̥st], *s.* técnico, experto.—**technicism** [-si̥zm], *s.* tecnicismo.—**technics** [téknik̥s], *s.* técnica.

Technicolor [-kʌlo(r)], *s.* (foto., cine) tecnicolor.

technique [tekník], *s.* técnica, ejecución.

technocracy [teknákrasi], *s.* tecnocracia.

technological [teknoládžikal], *a.* tecnológico.

technologist [teknálodži̥st], *s.* tecnólogo.

technology [-dži], *s.* tecnología, politecnia.

techy [téchi], *a.* cosquilloso, quisquilloso.

tectonic [tektánik], *a.* arquitectónico; (geol.) tectónico, relativo a la estructura.—**tectonics**, *s.* arquitectura, arte de la construcción.

ted [téd], *va.* (agr.) henear.—**tedder** [-œ(r)], *s.* heneador; máquina para volver el heno.— **tedding** [-in], *s.* henaje.

Teddy bear [tédi bér], *s.* osito, juguete en forma de oso.

Te Deum [ti díʌm], *s.* (igl.) tedéum.

tedious [tídi̥ʌs], *a.* tedioso, fastidioso, pesado, prolijo, aburrido(r).—**tediously** [-li], *adv.* tediosamente, aburridamente.—**tediousness** [-ni̥s], *s.* tedio, aburrimiento, pesadez.

tee [ti]. **I.** *s.* (dep.) meta; en el golf, montoncillo donde se coloca la pelota que hay que lanzar; te, letra *t*; cosa en T (*v.* **T**); tubo en T; viga en T; barra atada por el centro a una cuerda o cadena. **II.** *va.* y *vn.* (a veces con **up**) (golf) colocar la pelota en el *tee*; (con **off**) dar el golpe a la pelota o bola; (fig.) comenzar.

teem [tím]. **I.** *va.* (ant.) parir; producir. **II.** *vn.* (gen. con **with**) rebosar (de), abundar (en); estar lleno (de).—**teeming** [-in], *a.* prolífico, fecundo; lleno; abundante.

teens [tinz], *s. pl.* los números cuyos nombres terminan en **-teen**; edad de trece a diecinueve años.

teeny [tíni], *a.* (fam.) chiquitico, diminuto. *V.* TINY.

teepee [típi], *s.* = TEPEE.

teeter [títœ(r)]. **I.** *va.* y *vn.* balancear(se), columpiar(se). **II.** *s.* balanceo, vaivén; columpio. *V.* SEESAW.

teeth [tiθ], *s. pl.* de TOOTH.—**in the t. of**, contra; en presencia de; a despecho de.—**to cast, to throw, in one's t.**, echar en cara a uno, arrojarle a la cara, en señal de insulto o desafío.

teethe [tíð], *vn.* endentecer, dentar, echar los dientes.—**teething** [-in], *s.* dentición.—**t. ring**, chupador, chupadero, (Am.) chupete.

teetotal [títóu̥tal], *a.* (fam.) entero, completo, total; referente a, o que favorece y practica,

la abstinencia completa de bebidas alcohólicas. —**teetotaler** [-œ(r)], *s.* abstemio, nefalista, el que se abstiene por completo de bebidas alcohólicas.—**teetotalism** [-i̥zm], *s.* nefalismo, abstinencia completa de bebidas alcohólicas.

teetotum [titóu̥tʌm], *s.* perinola (juguete).

tegmen [tégmi̥n], *s.* (anat.) placa de hueso; (ent.) élitro; (bot.) túnica interior.

tegument [tégyu̥ment], *s.* tegumento.

tegumentary [-méntari], *a.* tegumentario.

teil (**tree** [tíl (tri], *s.* (bot.) tilo.

telamon [télamon], *s.* (arq.) telamón, atlante.

telautograph [telótograef], *s.* telautógrafo.

telecast [télěkæst]. **I.** *va.* transmitir (imágenes) por televisión. **II.** *s.* transmisión por televisión.

telecommunication [telěkomi̥unikéi̥sǫn], *s.* telecomunicación.

telectroscope [teléktroskoṷp], *s.* telectroscopio, aparato para transmitir imágenes eléctricamente.

telega [telégǝ], *s.* telega, especie de carro tosco usado en Rusia.

telegram [télěgræm], *s.* telegrama, *m.*

telegraph [-graef]. **I.** *va.* y *vn.* telegrafiar; enviar por telégrafo. **II.** *s.* telégrafo; tablero de noticias telegráficas, en el cual se escriben éstas para el público (ll. t. t. **board**).—**t. cable**, cable telegráfico.—**t. money order**, giro telegráfico.—**t. operator**, telegrafista.—**t. wire**, alambre de telégrafos.

telegrapher, telegraphist [télégrafœ(r), -fi̥st], *s.* telegrafista.

telegraphic [telěgræfi̥k], *a.* telegráfico.

telegraphically [-li], *adv.* telegráficamente.

telegraphone [telégrafou̥n], *s.* telegráfono, especie de telégrafo magnético.

telegraphy [-fi], *s.* telegrafía.

telelectric [telěléktri̥k], *a.* teleléctrico, transmitido eléctricamente a distancia.

telemechanics [-mekéni̥ks], *s.* telemecánica.

telemeter [telémetœ(r)], *s.* telémetro.—**telemetric** [telěmétri̥k], *a.* telemétrico.—**telemetry** [telémetri], *s.* telemetría.

telengiscope [telěndžiskou̥p], *s.* (ópt.) telengiscopio, combinación del telescopio y el microscopio.

teleologic(al [tiliolǽdžik(al], *a.* teleológico.

teleology [tiljálodži], *s.* (filos.) teleología.

teleost [téliḁst], *s.* y *a.* (ict.) teleósteo.

telepathy [télěpaθi], *s.* telepatía.—**telepathic** [telěpǽθi̥k], *a.* telepático.—**telepathically** [-li], *adv.* telepáticamente.

telephone [télěfou̥n]. **I.** *va.* y *vn.* telefon(e)ar. **II.** *s.* teléfono.—**t. booth**, cabina o casilla de teléfonos.—**t. call**, llamada o golpe de teléfono; telefonazo.—**t. directory**, guía de teléfonos.— **t. exchange**, central telefónica.—**t. girl**, (fam.) chica telefonista.—**t. message**, telefonema, *m.*, despacho telefónico.—**t. operator**, telefonista.

telephonic(al [-fáni̥k(al], *a.* telefónico.

telephonist [télěfou̥ni̥st], *s.* telefonista.

telephony [télěfoni], *s.* telefonía.

telephote [télěfou̥t], *s.* telefoto, aparato para reproducir eléctricamente imágenes a distancia.

telephotograph [-fóu̥tograef], *s.* telefotografía, imagen fotográfica hecha a distancia.—**telephotography** [-fótágrafi], *s.* telefotografía, procedimiento de fotografiar a distancia.

telergy [télœrdži], *s.* telepatía.

telescope [télěskou̥p]. **I.** *s.* telescopio; catalejo; (top.) anteojo (de teodolito, nivel, etc.). **II.** *va.* y *vn.* enchufar(se), meter(se) uno entre otro; meter(se) en uno.

telescopic(al [-skápi̥k(al], *a.* telescópico; de larga vista; de enchufe, de secciones enchufadas.

telespectroscope [-spéktroskou̥p], *s.* telespectroscopio; espectroscopio para telescopio.

telethermograph [-θœ́rmograef], *s.* teletermómetro registrador; registro gráfico hecho con este instrumento.

telethermometer [-θœrmámɛtœ(r)], s. tele-termómetro, instrumento para medir temperaturas a distancia.

teletype [-taip], s. teletipo.

teletypewriter [-tájpraitœ(r)], s. máquina de escribir telegráfica.

teleview [-vịu[, va. y vn. ver por televisión.

televise [-vaiz], va. televisionar, transmitir o recibir imágenes por televisión.

television [-vịʒɒn], s. televisión, radiovisión.

telford pavement [tɛ́lfɒrd péivmɛnt], s. pavimento compuesto de mezcla de piedras grandes y pequeñas y una capa superficial de grava.—**telfordize** [-aiz], va. poner pavimento télford.

telic [tɛ́lik], a. referente a un designio o intento.

tell [tɛ́l]. I. va. y vn. (pret. y pp. TOLD) decir; expresar; contar, relatar; explicar; descubrir, revelar. II. va. decidir, determinar; saber; descifrar, distinguir, ver (la diferencia, etc.); adivinar, predecir; mandar, disponer, ordenar; contar, numerar.—**to t. off**, contar, recontar; (mil.) designar.—**to t. one (where to get) off**, (fam.) decir a uno cuántas son cinco, cantárselas claras, soltarle cuatro frescas.—**to t. one's, o its, own tale**, contar por sí mismo el cuento, hacer ver por sí mismo lo que hay.—**to t. tales out of school**, revelar secretos.—**to t. the story**, contar el cuento, poner a las claras lo que hay.—**to t. volumes**, ser sumamente significativo.—**tell that to the marines**, (fam.) cuéntaselo a tu abuela; a otro perro con ese hueso. III. vn. saber, juzgar, predecir; producir efecto; acertar (un tiro).—**to t. on**, descubrir, delatar a; dejarse ver en, afectar a.

teller [-œ(r)], s. relat(ad)or, narrador; escrutador de votos; computista; pagador o cobrador (de un banco).—**t.'s window**, taquilla.

telling [-iŋ]. I. a. eficaz, notable. II. s. manera de decir o de contar.—**there is no t.**, no es posible decir, no puede preverse, ¡quién sabe!

telltale [-teil]. I. s. soplón, chismoso; indicador, contador, reloj de vigilancia; (mar.) axiómetro. II. a. delator, denunciador, revelante.

tellurian [tɛljúriạn]. I. s. morador de la tierra. II. a. telúrico, terrestre.

telluric [tɛljúrik], a. (quím.) telúrico.

tellurid(e [tɛ́ljurid, -aid], s. (quím.) telururo.

tellurium [tɛljúriʌm], s. (quím.) telurio.

tellurous [tɛ́ljurʌs], a. (quím.) teluroso.

telodynamic [tɛlodainǽmik], a. teledinámico.

telpher, telfer [tɛ́lfœ(r)]. I. s. carro, cubo, etc., de un sistema de teleferaje. II. va. teleferar.

telpherage, telferage [-idʒ], s. teleferaje, transporte automático aéreo.

temerity [tɛmɛ́riti], s. temeridad.

temper [tɛ́mpœ(r)]. I. va. moderar, mitigar, calmar; (pint.) mezclar; modificar, ajustar; (a)temperar, ablandar; (metal.) templar. II. s. mal genio o carácter irascible; índole, f., humor, disposición, natural, genio, condición; calma, ecuanimidad, sangre fría; (metal.) temple, templadura; punto (grado de densidad de una mezcla); cal (f.) de defecación (para el azúcar); (ant.) temperamento.—**to lose one's t.**, perder la paciencia, enojarse.

tempera [tɛ́mperạ], s. (pint.) templa.

temperament [tɛ́mp(œ)ramɛnt], s. temperamento; (fisiol.) complexión, constitución, naturaleza; composición; disposición; genialidad; (mús.) temple.

temperamental [-mɛ́ntạl], a. extremadamente sensible, emocional o irascible; complexional; genial.

temperamentally [-i], adv. por naturaleza, por índole, genialmente.

temperance [tɛ́mp(œ)rạns], s. templanza, temperancia, sobriedad.—**temperate** [tɛ́mp(œ)rịt], a. sobrio, abstemio; templado, benigno; moderado.—**T. Zone**, (geog.) zona templada.—**temperately** [-li], adv. sobriamente.—**tem-**

perateness [-nịs], s. templanza, moderación; serenidad.

temperature [tɛ́mp(œ)raçhū(r)], s. temperatura; exceso de temperatura, fiebre, f.

tempered [tɛ́mpœrd], a. templado, moderado; templado (cristal, metal); dispuesto, inclinado.

tempering [tɛ́mp(œ)riŋ]. I. a. atemperante, templador. II. s. temple; temperación; templadura.

tempest [tɛ́mpịst]. I. s. tempestad, borrasca. II. va. agitar, conmover violentamente.

tempestuous [tɛmpɛ́schuạs], a. tempestuoso, borrascoso; impetuoso.—**tempestuously** [-li], adv. tempestuosamente.—**tempestuousness** [-nịs], s. calidad de tempestuoso, impetuosidad.

Templar [tɛ́mplạ(r)], s. (hist., igl.) Templario.

template, templet [tɛ́mplịt], s. (tec.) plantilla, patrón, modelo; (mar.) gálibo; (constr.) solera, piedra o madero para distribuir la carga; cuña.

temple [tɛ́mpl], s. (igl.) templo; (anat.) sien, f.; (tej.) encuentro, vara de telar.

tempo [tɛ́mpoṷ], s. (mús.) tiempo, movimiento.

temporal [tɛ́mpɒrạl]. I. a. temporal, secular, profano; civil; transitorio, pasajero; (anat.) temporal. II. s. (anat.) hueso temporal.

temporality [-rǽlịti], s. calidad de temporal o secular, temporalidad; (igl.) (gen. pl.) temporalidad(es).—**temporally** [tɛ́mpɒrạli], adv. temporalmente, transitoriamente.—**temporariness** [-rɛrịnịs], s. calidad de transitorio o provisional; interinidad.—**temporary** [-rɛri], a. temporal, temporáneo o temporario, provisional, provisorio, interino.

temporize [-raiz], vn. (con)temporizar; (fam.) pastelear; andar al uso; ganar tiempo.

temporizer [-œ(r)], s. (con)temporizador; (fam.) pastelero.

tempt [tɛ́mpt], va. tentar, incitar, instigar, solicitar; seducir; poner a prueba; provocar, desafiar.—**temptable** [-ạbl], a. capaz de dejarse tentar.—**temptation** [-éịʃɒn], s. tentación, aliciente; solicitación; prueba.—**tempter** [-œ(r)], s. tentador.—**tempting** [-iŋ], a. tentador, seductor, atractivo.—**temptingly** [-li], adv. de modo atractivo, tentador, etc.—**temptress** [-rịs], s. tentadora.

ten [tɛn], a. y s. diez, m.; decena.—**t.-strike**, jugada en que se derriban los diez bolos con una sola bocha; (Méx.) chufa.

tenable [tɛ́nạbl], a. defendible, sostenible.

tenacious [tịnéịʃạs], a. tenaz; pegajoso, adhesivo; cohesivo; porfiado, terco, testarudo; firme.—**tenaciously** [-li], adv. tenazmente, con firmeza.—**tenaciousness** [-nịs], s. tenacidad; tesón, pertinacia; firmeza.

tenacity [tịnǽsịti], s. tenacidad; tesón; terquedad, porfía; cohesión; adhesión.

tenaculum [tịnǽkjulʌm], s. (cir.) tenáculo.

tenail(le [tịnéịl], s. (fort.) tenaza.

tenancy [tɛ́nạnsị], s. (for.) tenencia, posesión; inquilinato.

tenant [tɛ́nạnt]. I. s. (for.) arrendatario, inquilino; residente, morador, inquilino.—**t. for life**, residente, usufructuario o inquilino vitalicio. II. va. y vn. arrendar; tener en arriendo.

tenantable [-ạbl], a. habitable.

tenantless [-lịs], a. desarrendado, sin inquilinos; deshabitado.—**tenantry** [-ri], s. inquilinato; inquilinos en general.

tench [tench], s. (ict.) tenca.

tend [tɛ́nd]. I. va. guardar, vigilar, cuidar; atender. II. vn. tender, propender; dirigirse; atender; (con **on** o **upon**) asistir, servir a.

tendance [tɛ́ndạns], s. atención, cuidado.

tendency [-ɛnsị], s. tendencia, propensión; dirección, inclinación.—**to have a t.**, propender (a).

tendentious [tɛndɛ́nʃạs], a. tendencioso.

tender [tɛ́ndœ(r)]. I. a. tierno; delicado; muelle, mollar; benigno, benévolo, compasivo; sensible; afectuoso, amoroso; adolorido; dulce, ameno; frágil; cosquilloso, difícil.—**t.-hearted**, tierno de corazón, compasivo.—**t. of**, u **over**, cuidadoso de, solícito de los sentimientos de otros. **II.** *s.* oferta, ofrecimiento, propuesta; (for.) oferta formal de pago; lo que se ofrece en pago de una deuda; (mar.) escampavía, patache, falúa; guarda, *mf.*, servidor; (f. c.) ténder. **III.** *va.* ofrecer, presentar, proponer; (for.) ofrecer en pago sin condiciones; enternecer, ablandar. **IV.** *vn.* hacer una oferta o propuesta; enternecerse.

tenderfoot [-fụt], *s.* (fam.) apodo que dan los mineros al recién llegado; inexperto, novato.

tenderling [-lịŋ], *s.* persona consentida o enfermiza; criatura; (zool.) pitón de asta de venado.

tenderloin [-lọịn], *s.* filete.—**T.**, o **t. district**, barrio de una ciudad (originalmente de Nueva York) donde se vive la vida alegre y corrupta.

tenderly [-lị], *adv.* tiernamente.—**tenderness** [-nịs], *s.* terneza, ternura; sensibilidad; delicadeza; benignidad, benevolencia.

tending [téndịŋ], *a.* tend(i)ente.

tendinous [téndịnʌs], *a.* (anat.) tendinoso.

tendon [téndọn], *s.* (anat.) tendón.

tendril [téndrịl], *s.* (bot.) zarcillo, tijereta.

tenebræ [ténẹbri], *s. pl.* (igl.) tinieblas, maitines del jueves, viernes y sábado santos.

tenebrous [ténẹbrʌs], *a.* tenebroso.

tenement [ténẹmẹnt], *s.* habitación, vivienda, alojamiento (apl. gen. a los de la gente pobre); (for.) heredamiento.—**t. (house)**, casa de vecindad, (Am.) conventillo.

tenementary [tenẹméntạrị], *a.* (for.) arrendable.

tenesmus [tẹnézmʌs], *s.* (med.) tenesmo, pujo(s).

tenet [ténịt], *s.* dogma, *m.*; principio; credo.

tenfold [ténfọụld], **I.** *a.* décuplo. **II.** *adv.* diez veces.

tennis [ténịs], *s.* ten(n)is (juego).—**t. ball**, pelota de tenis.—**t. court**, campo, pista o cancha de tenis.—**t. player**, ten(n)ista.

tenon [ténọn]. **I.** *va.* (carp.) espigar, despatillar, desquijerar; juntar a espiga y mortaja. **II.** *s.* (carp.) espiga, almilla.—**t. saw**, sierra de ingletes, sierra de trasdós.

tenonitis [tenọnáịtịs], *s.* (med.) tenon(t)itis, inflamación de un tendón.

tenor [ténọ(r)]. **I.** *s.* tenor, curso, método; tendencia; texto, contenido, substancia de un escrito; (mús.) tenor; alto; viola. **II.** *a.* (mús.) de tenor.

tenotomy [tịnátọmị], *s.* (cir.) tenotomía.

tenpenny [ténpẹnị]. **I.** *a.* de diez peniques. **II.** *s.* clavo de cierto tamaño; moneda de diez peniques.

tenpins [ténpịnz], *s.* juego con diez bolos de madera.

tenrec [ténrek], *s.* (zool.) mamífero insectívoro de Madagascar.

tense [téns]. **I.** *a.* tieso, estirado, tenso, tirante. **II.** *s.* (gram.) tiempo (del verbo).

tenseness [-nịs], *s.* tirantez, tensión.

tensibility [tensịbíḷịtị], *s.* facilidad en ponerse tenso.

tensible [ténsịbl], *a.* capaz de tensión, extensible.

tensile [ténsịl], *a.* tensor; extensible; de tensión. —**t. strength**, resistencia de tensión, o a la tracción.—**t. stress**, esfuerzo de tensión o de tracción.

tensimeter [tensímẹtœ(r)], *s.* (fís.) manómetro.

tension [ténʃọn], *s.* tensión, tirantez; esfuerzo mental o emocional; ansiedad, nerviosidad; (mec.) tensión, tracción; (fís.) fuerza expansiva de un gas; regulador del hilo en una máquina de coser; (elec., med.) tensión; (dipl.) tirantez de relaciones.

tensive [ténsịv], *a.* tensivo, tirante, tensor.

tensor [ténsọ(r)], *s.* (anat.) músculo extensor; (mat.) tensor.

tent [tent]. **I.** *s.* toldo; (mil.) tienda de campaña, pabellón, alfaneque, (Am.) carpa; (cir.) lechino, tapón.—**t. bed**, catre de tijera.—**t. cloth**, terliz, *m.*—**t. pole**, mástil; montante de tienda. **II.** *vn.* acampar bajo tiendas. **III.** *va.* (cir.) mantener abierta (una herida, etc.) con lechino.

tentacle [téntạkl], *s.* (zool. y bot.) tentáculo.

tentacular [tentǽkịulǎ(r)], *a.* tentacular.

tentative [téntạtịv]. **I.** *a.* tentativo, de ensayo. **II.** *s.* tentativa, ensayo, prueba, tanteo.

tentatively [-lị], *adv.* tentativamente, etc.; de primera intención.

tented [téntịd], *a.* entoldado.

tenter [téntœ(r)]. **I.** *s.* (tej.) tendedor, rambla (máquina o bastidor). **II.** *va.* y *vn.* (tej.) estirar(se) (el paño).

tenterhook [-hụk], *s.* (tej.) escarpia, alcayata; (fig.) causa de ansiedad o tensión.—**to be on tenterhooks**, estar en ascuas o en un potro.

tenth [ténθ]. **I.** *a.* décimo, deceno; diez (ordinal). **II.** *s.* décima parte, décimo; (igl.) diezmo.

tenthly [-lị], *adv.* en décimo lugar.

tentmaker [téntmeịkœ(r)], *s.* tendero.

tentwort [téntwœrt], *s.* (bot.) culantrillo.

tenuirostral [tenyụịrástrạl], *a.* (orn.) tenuirrostro.

tenuity [tịnjúịtị], *s.* tenuidad, delicadeza; delgadez, sutileza; raridad, rarefacción.

tenuous [tényụạs], *a.* tenue, delgado, sutil; raro.

tenuousness [-nịs], *s.* tenuidad. *V.* TENUITY.

tenure [tényụ(r)], *s.* (for.) (per)tenencia, posesión.—**t. of office**, tenencia de un cargo o puesto.—**t. rights, o right of t.**, inamovilidad (de un cargo, etc.).

teocalli [tiokǽlị], *s.* (Méx.) teocali, teucali.

tepee [típí], *s.* tienda o vivienda de los indios de los E. U.

tepefaction [tepịfǽkʃọn], *s.* templadura.

tepefy [tépịfaị], *va.* y *vn.* entibiar(se), poner(se) tibio.

tepid [tépịd], *a.* tibio, templado.—**tepidity** [tịpídịtị], *s.* tibieza.—**tepidly** [tépịdlị], *adv.* tibiamente.

teratogeny [teratádženị], *s.* teratogenia, producción de monstruos.—**teratoid** [tératọịd], *a.* monstruoso, anormal.—**teratologic** [-tǒládžịk], *a.* teratológico.—**teratology** [-tálodžị], *s.* (biol.) teratología, estudio de las monstruosidades.

terbium [tœrbịʌm], *s.* (quím.) terbio.

tercentenary [tœrséntenạrị], **tercentennial** [-téniạl]. **I.** *a.* de tres siglos. **II.** *s.* tricentenario, tercer centenario; aniversario tricentésimo.

tercet [tœrsịt o tœrsét], *s.* (poét., mús.) terceto.

terebinth [térẹbịnθ], *s.* (bot.) terebinto.

terebinthic [terẹbínθịk], *a.* relativo a o del carácter de la trementina.

terebinthin(e [terẹbínθịn], *a.* terebintáceo.

teredo [terídoụ], *s.* (zool.) broma.

terete [tẹrít], *a.* cilíndrico, redondo.

tergal [tœrgạl], *a.* (zool.) tergal, dorsal.

tergiversate [tœrdžívœrseịt], *vn.* tergiversar.

tergiversating [-ịŋ], *a.* tergiversador.

tergiversation [-séịʃọn], *s.* tergiversación, efugio, evasión.

tergiversator [-seịtọ(r)], *s.* tergiversador.

term [tœrm]. **I.** *s.* término, vocablo, palabra, voz, denominación, calificativo; plazo; término, período; semestre (de la escuela); (for.) tiempo en que un tribunal está en sesión; (ant.) límite, confín, fin; (lóg., arq. y mat.) término.—*pl.* términos, palabras, expresiones; condiciones, estipulaciones, obligaciones impuestas; relaciones mutuas; precio; (com.) facilidades de pago.—**in set terms**, en términos escogidos.— **in terms of**, (mat.) en función de.—**not on any terms**, por ningún concepto, a ningún precio.—**to be on good (bad) terms with**, llevarse bien (mal) con; estar en buenas (malas) relaciones con.—**to bring to terms**, imponer condiciones a, hacer arreglos con.—**to come to terms**, arreglarse, convenirse.—**upon what terms?**, ¿en qué términos? **II.** *va.* nombrar, llamar, calificar (de).

termagancy [tœrmạgạnsị], *s.* carácter pendenciero.

termagant [tœrmạgạnt]. **I.** *a.* turbulento; pendenciero. **II.** *s.* (fig.) sierpe, *f.*, fiera, arpía, marimacho.

terminability [tœrminabíliti], s. terminabilidad.
terminable [-bl], a. terminable, limitable.—**terminably** [-bli], adv. terminablemente.
terminal [tœrminal]. I. a. terminal, último, extremo, final. II. s. término, final; (arq.) término; (f. c.) estación terminal o extrema; (elec.) terminal, borne.
terminate [-eit], va. y vn. terminar.
termination [-éişon], s. terminación o fin; (gram.) terminación, desinencia.
terminative [-ativ], a. terminativo.
terminator [-eitọ(r)], s. el o lo que termina; (astr.) límite de iluminación (de la luna o un planeta).
terminer [-œ(r)], s. (for.) = OYER.
terminology [-álodżi], s. terminología.
terminus [tœrminʌs], s. término, fin; (f. c.) estación terminal; (top.) límite, mojón; (arq.) término, remate; (T., mit.) el dios Término.
termite [tœrmait], s. (ent.) termita, termes, comején, hormiga blanca.—**t. nest**, termitero, comejenera.
termless [tœrmlis], a. ilimitado.
tern [tœrn]. I. s. terno; (orn.) golondrina de mar. II. a. ternario.
terna [tœrnä], s. (igl.) terna.
ternary [tœrnari]. I. a. ternario, trino. II. s. terno, trinca; terna.
ternate [tœrneit], a. ternario; (bot.) ternario.
terne [tœrn]. I. s. aleación de estaño y plomo. II. va. revestir con esta aleación.—**terneplate** [-pleit], s. lámina con revestimiento de *terne*.
terpene [tœrpin], s. (quím.) terpeno.—**terpin** [tœrpin], s. (quím.) terpina.—**terpinol** [-al], s. (quím.) terpinol.
Terpsichorean [tœrpsikorían]. I. a. de Terpsícore, del baile. II. s. (t., fam.) bailador, bailarina.
terra [tœrä], s. tierra.—**t. alba**, tierra de pipa.—**t. cotta**, terracota, figulino.—**t. cotta lumber**, objetos de barro en que pueden clavarse clavos.—**t. firma**, tierra firme.—**t. incognita**, tierra desconocida.
terrace [tœris]. I. va. terraplenar. II. s. terraplén, bancal, balate, parata; terraza, terrero, terrado; azotea; balcón, galería abierta.
terrain [teréin], s. campo; ambiente, medio; (mil.) campo, terreno; (geol.) V. TERRANE.
terrane [teréin], s. (geol.) serie continua de rocas.
terrapin [tœrapin], s. (zool.) émido (variedad de tortuga).
terraqueous [teréikwiʌs], a. terráqueo.
terrazzo [terátso], s. piso veneciano, pavimento de cemento con astillas o fragmentos irregulares de piedra ornamental (mármol, etc.).—**t. tile**, mosaico de terrazo, mosaico granítico.
terrene [terín], a. térreo, terreno, terrenal.
terreplein [tœrplein], s. (fort.) plataforma; (ing.) terraplén.
terrestrial [teréstrial], a. terrestre, terreno.
terret [tœrit], s. (tal.) portarriendas.
terre-tenant, tertenant [tœrtenant], s. (for.) terrateniente.
terre-verte [tœr vœrt], s. (min., b. a.) tierra verde, verdacho; color verde azulado.
terrible [tœribl], a. terrible o espantoso; (fam.) tremendo, extremado.
terribleness [-nis], s. terriblez.—**terribly** [tœribli], adv. terriblemente, espantosamente.
terrier [tœriœ(r)], s. perro de busca; zorrero.
terrific [terífik], a. terrífico, espantoso; (fam.) tremendo, extremado, sobresaliente.
terrify [tœrifai], va. aterrar, aterrorizar, espantar.
terrigenous [terídżenʌs], a. terrígeno.
territorial [teritórial], a. territorial.—**t. waters**, aguas jurisdiccionales.
territoriality [-iéliti], s. territorialidad.
territory [tœritori], s. territorio, región, distrito, comarca; (geog.) territorio (división política).
terror [tœrọ(r)], s. espanto, terror.—**terrorism** [-izm], s. terrorismo.—**terrorist** [-ist], s. terrorista, partidario del terrorismo.—**terrorize**

[-aiz], va. aterrorizar.—**terrorizer** [-aizœ(r)], s. aterrorizador.
terse [tœrs], a. sucinto, breve, conciso; (ant.) terso, liso, pulido.—**tersely** [-li], adv. concisamente.—**terseness** [-nis], s. concisión.
tertian [tœrşan]. I. a. tercianario. II. s. (med.) terciana.
tertiary [tœrşieri]. I. a. terciario, tercero; (T., geol.) terciario. II. s. (T., geol.) terreno terciario; (orn.) pluma terciaria de un ave.
tertiate [tœrşieit], va. (arti.) medir el espesor de.
terzet [tœrtset, tœrtsét], s. (poét., mús.) terceto.
terzetto [tœrtsétou], s. (mús.) terceto.
tessellate [tœseleit], va. taracear, poner teselas.
tessellate(d [-(id], a. teselado.
tessellation [-léişon], s. mosaico.
tessera [tœserä], s. tesela; (antig. rom.) tésera.
tessitura [tesitúrä], s. (mús.) tesitura.
test [test]. I. s. prueba, ensayo, experimento; examen; piedra de toque, criterio; (quím.) análisis, mf.; resultado positivo de un análisis, reacción; reactivo; (zool.) concha; (bot.) tegumento de una semilla.—**T. Act**, (Ingl.) ley (f.) que imponía cierto juramento de prueba a los empleados públicos.—**t. case**, (for.) acción o causa de ensayo, para determinar la interpretación de una ley.—**t. flight**, (aer.) vuelo experimental o de prueba.—**t. meal**, (fisiol.) comida de prueba, para analizar el contenido o condición del estómago.—**t. paper**, (quím.) papel reactivo.—**t. pilot**, (aer.) piloto ensayador o probador.—**t. tube**, (quím.) probeta, tubo de ensayo.—**t. type**, (ópt.) serie de letras para probar la vista.—**the acid t.**, la prueba suprema, decisiva. II. va. probar, ensayar, comprobar, hacer la prueba de, poner o someter a prueba; examinar (a un estudiante, etc.); (for.) atestiguar.—**to t.-fly**, (aer.) comprobar mediante el vuelo.
testable [téstabl], a. que puede probarse; (for.) que puede legarse, atestiguar(se), o hacer testamento.
testacean [testéişan], a. y s. (zool.) testáceo.
testaceous [testéişʌs], a. (zool.) testáceo.
testacy [tœstạsi], s. estado o hecho de haber testado.
testament [téstạment], s. (for.) testamento; (T.), el Viejo y el Nuevo Testamento.—**testamental, testamentary** [-méntal, -méntari], a. (for.) testamentario.—**testate** [tésteit], a. (for.) testado.
testator, testatrix [testéitọ(r), -triks], s. (for.) testador(a).
tested [téstid], a. ensayado, probado.
tester [téstœ(r)], s. probador, ensayador; (quím.) reactivo; pabellón (de cama); baldaquín (de altar).
testes [téstiz], s. pl. de TESTIS.
testicle [téstikl], s. (anat., zool.) testículo.—**testicular** [testíkiulạ(r)], a. testicular.—**testiculate** [-leit], a. en forma de testículo; que tiene testículos u órganos parecidos a ellos.
testification [téstifikéişon], s. testificación.
testifier [-faiœ(r)], s. testigo, testificador.
testify [-fai], va. y vn. (for.) testificar, atestiguar, declarar, atestar, rendir declaración; aseverar.
testily [téstili], adv. con mal humor o displicencia.
testimonial [testimóuniạl]. I. a. testimonial, testificativo. II. s. certificación o certificado, fe, f., atestado, testimoniales; recomendación; encomio.
testimony [téstimoni], s. (for.) testimonio, atestación, declaración, fe, f.; Tablas de la Ley, el decálogo; Libro de la Ley, Antiguo Testamento.—**in t. whereof**, en fe de lo cual.
testiness [téstinis], s. quisquillosidad, mal humor, mal genio.
testis [téstis], s. (anat., zool.) teste, testículo; testigo.
testudinal [testiúdinạl], a. (zool.) testudíneo.
testudo [testiúdou], s. (mil. ant.) testudo; (zool.) tortuga; (med.) testudo (tumor).

testy [tésti], *a.* enojadizo, quisquilloso.

tetanic [titǽnik]. **I.** *a.* (med.) tetánico. **II.** *s.* (med.) droga o substancia que causa tétano(s).

tetanus [tétanʌs], *s.* (med.) tétano(s), pasmo.

tetany [tétani], *s.* (med.) tétano(s) intermitente.

tête-à-tête [téjt a téjt]. **I.** *adv.* (fr.) cara a cara, a solas. **II.** *a.* confidencial; privado. **III.** *s.* conversación íntima entre dos personas; confidente (mueble).

tether [téðœ(r)]. **I.** *s.* traba, maniota, correa, atadura.—**to be at the end of one's t.**, estar sin recursos, estar en las últimas. **II.** *va.* estacar, trabar, atar (con maniota, etc.); (Am.) apersogar.

tetrachloride [tɛtrǝklóraid], *s.* (quím.) tetracloruro.

tetrachord [tétrǝkord], *s.* (mús.) tetracordio.

tetracid [tetrǽsid], *a.* (quím.) tetrácido.

tetrad [tétrǽd], *s.* grupo de cuatro; (quím.) átomo o elemento tetravalente.

tetradynamous [tɛtrǝdínǝmʌs], *a.* (bot.) tetradínamo.

tetragon [tétrǝgan], *s.* (geom.) tetrágono.

tetragonal [tɛtrǽgonǝl], *a.* (geom.) tetragonal, cuadrangular.

tetragram [tétrǝgrǽm], *s.* (geom., mús.) tetragrama, *m.;* tetragrámaton.

Tetragrammaton [-grǽmǝtan], *s.* tetragrámaton.

tetrahedral [-hídrǝl], *a.* (geom.) tetraédrico.

tetrahedron [-hídrǝn], *s.* (geom.) tetraedro.

tetralogy [tetrǽlodʒi], *s.* (teat., mús.) tetralogía.

tetrameter [tetrǽmetœ(r)], *s.* y *a.* (pros.) tetrámetro.

Tetrao [tétraou], *s.* tetrao, género de gallináceas cuyo tipo es el urogallo.—**Tetraonidæ** [tetrǝánidi], *s. pl.* tetraónidas.

tetrarch [títrark], *s.* tetrarca, *m.*—**tetrarchate** [-ejt], **tetrarchy** [-i], *s.* tetrarquía.

tetrastyle [tétrǝstajl]. **I.** *s.* (arq.) tetrastilo. **II.** *a.* de cuatro columnas o pilastras.

tetrasyllable [-sílǝbl], *s.*, **tetrasyllabic(al)** [-silǽbik(ǝl], *a.* (pros.) tetrasílabo.

tetratomic [-támik], *a.* (quím.) tetratómico.

tetrode [tétroud], *s.* (elec.) tubo de vacío de cuatro electrodos.

tetter [tétœ(r)], *s.* (med.) herpe, *mf.*, empeiné, serpigo, culebrilla.

Teuton [tjútǝn], *a.* y *s.* teutón; tudesco, alemán.—**Teutonic** [tjutánik]. **I.** *a.* teutónico. **II.** *s.* teutónico (idioma).—**T. Knights,** Caballeros Teutónicos.

tewel [tjúel], *s.* tobera, alcribís, *m.* (de forja).

Texan [téksan], *a.* y *s.* tejano, de Tejas.

text [tékst], *s.* texto; lema, *m.*, tema, *m.*, tesis; (impr.) tipo.—**t. hand**, carácter de letra muy grueso.

textbook [-buk], *s.* texto, libro de texto; libreto de ópera.

textile [tékstil]. **I.** *a.* textil, tejido; de tejer o de tejidos. **II.** *s.* tejido; material textil.

textual [tékschuǝl], *a.* textual.—**textualist** [-ist], *s.* textualista.—**textually** [-i], *adv.* textualmente.

textural [tékschurǝl], *a.* de textura, relativo a la textura o contextura.

texture [tékschur], *s.* textura, contextura; tejido, obra tejida; (biol.) tejido.

thalamus [θǽlǝmʌs], *s.* (bot.) tálamo; (anat.) tálamo óptico (ll. t. **optic t.**).

thalassography [θǝlǝságrǝfi], *s.* oceanografía, ciencia de la vida y otros fenómenos del mar.

thaler [tálœ(r)], *s.* tálero (moneda alemana).

thallic [θǽlik], *a.* (quím.) tálico.

thallium [θǽlʌm], *s.* (quím.) talio.

thallophyte [θǽlofajt], *s.*, **thallophytic** [-fítik], *a.* (bot.) talofita.—**thallus** [θǽlʌs], *s.* (bot.) talo, aparato vegetativo de la planta talofita.

than [ðæn], *conj.* que (comparativo: *I am taller than he*, soy más alto que él); de (cuando va delante de números: *fewer than ten*, menos de diez;

more than two, más de dos; *more than once*, más de una vez); del que, de la que, etc., de lo que (*less time than they expected*, menos tiempo del que esperaban; *easier than you think*, más fácil de lo que Vd. cree). Las frases **t. whom**, **t. which**, se traducen cambiando el giro: *Shakespeare, than whom there is no greater poet*, Shakespeare, que como poeta no tiene superior, o S., poeta de grandeza nunca sobrepasada. Lo mejor es traducir primero la expresión a manera de paréntesis, y luego darle forma más apropiada: Shakespeare (no hay poeta más grande que él); *this book, than which I know few more useful*, este libro (conozco pocos más útiles); este libro, cuya utilidad, que yo sepa, hay pocos que la sobrepasen.

thanage [θéinidʒ], *s.* dignidad o dominio del *thane.*

thane [θejn], *s.* (hist.) caballero, gentilhombre.

thank [θǽŋk]. **I.** *va.* agradecer, dar gracias a.—**t. God,** a Dios gracias.—**t. you,** gracias. **II.** *s. pl.* **thanks,** gracias.—**t. to,** gracias a, debido a.

thankful [-ful], *a.* agradecido.—**thankfully** [-i], *adv.* con agradecimiento.—**thankfulness** [-nis], *s.* agradecimiento, gratitud.—**thankless** [-lis], *a.* desagradecido; ingrato, infructuoso.—**thanklessness** [-nis], *s.* ingratitud.

thanksgiving [-sgívij], *s.* acción de gracias.—**T. Day,** día (*m.*) de acción de gracias.

thankworthy [-wœrði], *a.* digno de reconocimiento; meritorio.

that [ðæt]. **I.** *a.* (*pl.* THOSE [ðouz]) ese, esa, aquel, aquella.—**t. way,** por aquel camino, por allí; de ese modo. **II.** *pron. dem.* ése, ésa, eso; aquél, aquélla, aquello; *pron. rel.* que, quien, el que, la que, lo que; el cual, la cual, lo cual; el, la, lo (substantivados: *that of John*, el de Juan; *that of yesterday*, el o lo de ayer).—**t. is, o t. is to say,** es decir.—**t. is how,** así es como se hace.—**t. is t.,** eso es lo que hay, es asunto concluído, no hay más que hablar; y sanseacabó.—**t. may be,** eso puede ser, es posible.—**t. which,** el que, la que, lo que; lo cual.—**all t.,** cuanto(s), todo(s) lo(s) que.—**and all t.,** (fam.) y cosas por ese estilo.—**at t.,** (fam.) así; aun así, aunque sea así; sin embargo, a pesar de eso.—**for all t.,** a pesar de eso.—**to put this and t. together,** atar cabos.—**upon t.,** sobre esto; luego. **III.** *conj.* que; para que, a fin de que, con el objeto de.—**in t.,** en que; a causa de que, por cuanto.—**not but t.,** no es decir que.—**save t.,** salvo que.—**so t.,** para que; con tal que; de modo que, de suerte que. **IV.** *adv.* (fam.) tan; tan . . . así, así de, de este tamaño, etc. (*that large*, tan grande así, así de grande, de este tamaño; *not that far*, no tan lejos).—**t. many,** tantos.—**t. much,** tanto.

thatch [θǽch]. **I.** *s.* barda; tejado de paja u hojas. **II.** *va.* bardar; empajar, techar con paja.—**thatched roof,** techumbre de paja.—**thatcher** [-œ(r)], *s.* bardador, empajador.—**thatching** [-iŋ], *s.* (acción de) empajar; material de empajar.

thaumaturge [θómǝtœrdʒ], *s.* taumaturgo.—**thaumaturgic(al** [-tœrdʒik(ǝl], *a.* taumatúrgico.—**thaumaturgist** [θómǝtœrdʒist], *s.* taumaturgo.—**thaumaturgy** [-dʒi], *s.* taumaturgia.

thaw [θo]. **I.** *va.* y *vn.* deshelar(se), derretir(se).—**to t. out,** hacer(se) más tratable, menos reservado o ceremonioso, abrirse.—**it thaws,** deshiela. **II.** *s.* deshielo, derretimiento.

the [ði o ðə]. **I.** *art.* el, la, lo, los, las. **II.** *adv.* Cuando precede a un comparativo, se traduce en español por cuanto . . . tanto, mientras más . . . tanto más, o expresiones análogas: *the more he spoke, the more we admired him*, mientras más hablaba, más lo admirábamos; *the less you say, the better*, cuanto menos diga Vd., tanto mejor; *the sooner the better*, mientras más pronto, tanto mejor.

theater, theatre [θíatœ(r)]. *s.* teatro, coliseo; arte dramático; drama, *m.*, comedia, teatro (literatura); asunto o composición teatral, o para las tablas; teatro o escena de algún suceso.—**theatergoer, theatregoer** [-goụœ(r)], *s.* el que frecuenta el teatro o la comedia.

theatric(al [θịátrịk(ạl], *a.* teatral, teátrico; artificial, extravagante.

theatrically [-lị], *adv.* teatralmente.

theatricals [-ạls], *s. pl.* funciones teatrales; asuntos del teatro; acciones teatrales o de carácter artificial.

theatrics [-s], *s. pl.* arte dramático.

Theban [θíbạn], *a.* y *s.* tebano, tebeo.

thee [ðị], *pron.* caso oblicuo de THOU: te, a ti.—**for t.**, para o por ti.—**with t.**, contigo.

theft [θeft], *s.* hurto, robo, ladronicio, latrocinio.

thein(e [θíịn, θíin], *s.* (quím.) teína, alcaloide del té, idéntico a la cafeína.

their [ðer], *pron. pos.* su, suyo, suya, de ellos, de ellas.—**theirs**, el suyo, la suya, los suyos, las suyas, de ellos o de ellas.

theism [θíịzm], *s.* teísmo.—**theist** [θíịst], *s.*, **theistic(al** [θíịstịk(ạl], *a.* teísta.

them [ðem], *pron.* caso oblicuo de THEY: los, las, les; (con *prep.*) ellos, ellas.—**t. that, t. who** (después de preposición) los que, aquellos que, quienes (*this is for them who wish to learn*, esto es para los que, o para quienes, deseen aprender).

thematic [θimétịk], *a.* temático.

theme [θim], *s.* tema, *m.*, asunto; tesis, disertación; (mús.) tema, *m.*, motivo.

themselves [ðemsélvz], *pron. pl.* ellos mismos, ellas mismas; sí mismos. Es el caso oblicuo del pronombre recíproco, y a veces se usa enfáticamente como nominativo. *V.* HIMSELF.

then [ðen], I. *adv.* entonces, en aquel tiempo, a la sazón; luego, después, en seguida; en otro tiempo; además; entonces, en tal caso; por consiguiente, pues, luego, por esta razón.—**t. and there**, allí mismo, al punto.—**but t.**, por otra parte, sin embargo, si bien es cierto que.—**by t.**, para entonces.—**now and t.**, de cuando en cuando; de vez en cuando.—**now . . . t. . . .**, ya . . . ya . . .; ora . . . ora . . .—**now t.**, ahora bien; tenemos pues.—**until t.**, hasta entonces; hasta luego.—**what t.?** ¿qué más? ¿qué resultó, o qué resultará? ¿qué vendrá (vino) luego? ¿qué se hará (se hizo) luego? II. *a.* entonces, de esos días, de aquella época, etc. (*the then President*, el entonces Presidente). III. *s.* entonces (*by then*, para entonces; *until then*, hasta entonces).

thenar [θínar], *s. y a.* (anat.) tenar.

thence [ðens], *adv.* (de lugar) de allí, desde allí; (de tiempo) desde entonces, desde aquel momento, de allí en adelante; (de modo) de ahí, por eso, por esa razón, por ese motivo.—**thenceforth** [-fórθ], *adv.* desde entonces, de allí en adelante.—**thenceforward** [-fórwạrd], *adv.* desde entonces; desde allí hacia adelante.

Theobroma [θiobróụmạ], *s.* (bot.) teobroma, *m.*, género cuyo tipo es el cacao.—**theobromin(e** [-mịn, min], *s.* (quím.) teobromina.

theocentric [θioséntrịk], *a.* (teol.) teocéntrico.

theocracy [θiákrạsị], *s.* (pol.) teocracia.

theocrat [θíokræt], *s.* (pol.) teócrata, *mf.*

theocratic(al [θiokrátịk(ạl], *a.* teocrático.

theodicy [θiádịsị], *s.* (teol.) teodicea.

theodolite [θiádolạịt], *s.* (top.) teodolito.

theogony [θiágonị], *s.* (mit., teol.) teogonía.

theologian [θiolóụdżạn], *s.* teólogo.

theological [θiolɑ́dżịkạl], *a.* teológico, teologal.—**t. seminary**, seminario eclesiástico.—**t. virtues**, virtudes teologales.

theologically [-lị], *adv.* teológicamente.—**theologism** [θiálodżizm], *s.* teologismo.—**theologize** [-dżaịz], I. *va.* hacer teológico; tratar teológicamente. II. *vn.* teologizar.—**theologue** [θíolag],

theology

s. (fam.) seminarista; (raro) teólogo.—**theology** [θiálodżị], *s.* teología.

theorbo [θiórboụ], *s.* (mús.) tiorba.

theorem [θíorem], *s.* teorema, *m.*; (mat.) serie; ecuación. *V.* BINOMIAL THEOREM, TAYLOR'S THEOREM.

theoretic(al [θiorétịk(ạl], *a.* teórico, especulativo.—**theoretically** [-ịl], *adv.* teóricamente.—**theoretician** [-tíṣạn], *s.* teórico.—**theorist** [θíorịst], *s.* teórico.—**theorize** [-rajz], *vn.* y *va.* exponer o formar teorías (sobre); teorizar.—**theorizer** [-œ(r)], *s.* teórico.—**theorizing** [-ịŋ]. I. *a.* teorizante. II. *s.* especulación.—**theory** [θíorị], *s.* teoría; teórica, especulación.

theosophic(al [θiosáfịk(ạl], *a.* teosófico.

theosophism [θiásofịzm], *s.* teosofismo.

theosophist [-fịst], *s.* teósofo.

theosophy [-fị], *s.* teosofía.

Therapeutæ [θerạpjútị], *s. pl.* (hist.) terapeutas, *mf.*—**therapeutic(al** [θerạpjútịk(ạl], *a.* (med.) terapéutico.

therapeutics [-tịks], *s.* (med.) terapéutica.

therapeutist [-tịst], *s.* (med.) terapeuta, *mf.*

therapy [θérạpị], *s.* terapia, terapéutica.

there [ðer]. I. *adv.* ahí, allí, allá; en eso, en cuanto a eso. Ú. como expletivo, sobre todo antes del verbo cuando el sujeto va después: *there came a man*, vino un hombre; *lives there a man so cruel?* ¿vive hombre tan cruel?—**t. is, t. are**, hay. *V.* BE.—**t. you are**, (fam.) eso es todo; ahí nos (me, etc.) tiene; ahí está el busilis. II. *interj.* ¡eso es! ¡toma! ¡vaya! ¡mira!

thereabout(s [-ạbáụt(s], *adv.* por ahí, por allí, cerca; acerca de eso; aproximadamente.

thereafter [-áftœ(r)]. I. *s.* tiempo después. II. *adv.* después, después de eso; conforme.

thereat [-ét], *adv.* en eso, entonces, en aquel punto o lugar; por eso; allí, ahí.

thereby [-bái], *adv.* con eso, con lo cual; de tal modo, así; allí, por allí cerca; acerca de eso.

therefor [-fór], *adv.* por es(t)o; para es(t)o.

therefore [ðérfor], *adv.* por es(t)o, por (lo) tanto, por ende, por consiguiente, en consecuencia, luego.

therefrom [-frám], *adv.* de allí, de ahí; de eso.

therein [-ín], *adv.* allí dentro; en esto, en eso.—**thereinafter** [-áftœ(r)], *adv.* (for.) posteriormente, después, adelante.—**thereinbefore** [-bịfór], *adv.* (for.) anteriormente, antes, más arriba.

thereinto [-íntụ], *adv.* dentro de eso o de esto.

thereof [-áv], *adv.* de esto, de eso.

thereon [-án], *adv.* sobre o encima de él, ella, etc.; por encima; por lo tanto; luego, al punto.

thereto [-tú], **thereunto** [-Antụ], *adv.* a eso, a ello; además.

theretofore [-tufór], *adv.* antes de eso, hasta entonces.

thereunder [-Andœ(r)], *adv.* debajo (de eso), bajo eso; menos de o que; en posición subordinada.

thereupon [-Apán], *adv.* sobre o encima de él, ella, etc.; por lo tanto, por consiguiente; sobre lo cual, luego, al punto.

therewith [-wịð], *adv.* con eso, con esto; en eso, entonces, luego, inmediatamente.

therewithal [-wịðɔ́l], *adv.* a más, además; con todo; en eso, inmediatamente; con es(t)o.

theriaca [θịrájạkạ], *s.* (ant. farm.) triaca, teriaca.

theriac(al [θírjæk(ạl], *a.* teriacal, triacal.

therm [θœrm], *s.* (fís.) unidad térmica (el término se aplica a varias de ellas).

thermæ [-ị], *s. pl.* termas (de los romanos).

thermal [θœrmạl], *a.* termal, térmico.—**t. alarm**, alarma automática de calentamiento.—**t. unit**, unidad térmica.—**t. waters**, aguas termales.

thermesthesia [θœrmesθíżạ], *s.* (fisiol.) sentido de la temperatura, capacidad de sentir cambios de temperatura.

thermic [θœrmịk], *a.* termal, térmico, calorífico.

thermion [θœrmịọn], *s.* termión, *m.*, ión (*m.*)

o electrón emitido por una substancia incandescente.

thermionic [θœrmiánįk], a. (fís.) termiónico, relativo a los termiones.—**t. valve**, (rad.) tubo termiónico, lámpara termiónica.

thermionics [-s], s. (fís.) termiónica, ciencia de los fenómenos termiónicos.

thermit(e [θœrmit o -maįt], s. (quím.) (nombre de fábrica), termita, mezcla de aluminio pulverizado y un óxido metálico, gen. de hierro.— **t. welding process**, soldadura con termita.

thermobattery [θœrmobǽtœrį], s. pila termoeléctrica.

thermocautery [-kótœrį], s. (cir.) termocauterio.

thermochemical [-kémįkạl], a. termoquímico.

thermochemistry [-kémįstrį], s. termoquímica.

thermocouple [θœrmoκʌpl], s. par termoeléctrico.

thermodynamic [-daįnǽmįk], a. termodinámico. —**thermodynamics**, s. (fís.) termodinámica.

thermoelectric [-ịléktrįk], a. termoeléctrico.

thermoelectricity [-ịlɛktrísįtį], s. termoelectricidad.

thermogenesis [-dʒénįsįs], s. termogénesis, producción de calor (apl. esp. al de las funciones orgánicas); combustión espontánea.

thermograph [-græf], s. termógrafo, termómetro registrador automático.

thermolabile [-léįbịl], a. (bioquím.) termolábil.

thermometer [θœrmámɛtœ(r)], s. termómetro.

thermometric(al [-métrįk(ạl], a. termométrico.

thermometry [θœrmámɛtrį], s. termometría.

thermopenetration [-penįtréįʃɔn], s. (med.) termopenetración; diatermia.

thermopile [-paįl], s. pila termoeléctrica.

thermos [θœrmos], **thermos bottle o flask**, s. termos (es nombre de fábrica).

thermoscope [-skoup], s. (fís.) termoscopio.

thermosiphon [-sáįfɔn], s. termosifón.

thermostat [-stæt], s. termóstato.

thermostatic [-stǽtįk], a. termostático.

thermotank [-tæŋk], s. caja de calefacción (o de enfriamiento), que contiene tubos por los cuales circula vapor, agua, etc. (puede llamarse *caja térmica*).

thermotherapy [-θérapį], s. (med.) termoterapia.

thesaurus [θįsóras], s. tesauro, tesoro.

these [ðiz]. I. a. pl. de THIS: estos, estas. II. pron. éstos, éstas.

thesis [θísįs], s. tesis; disertación.

Thespian [θéspįan], a. trágico, dramático.

Thessalian [θeséįlįan], s. y a. tesaliense.

Thessalonian [θesạlóųnįan], s. tesalonicense.

theurgy [θíœrdʒį], s. teurgia.—**theurgic(al** [θíœrdʒįk(ạl], a. teúrgico.—**theurgist** [θíœrdʒįst], s. teurgo.

thew [θįu], s. (anat.) tendón, músculo.—*pl.* (fig.) fuerza muscular, vigor.

they [ðeį], *pron. pl.* de HE, SHE o IT; ellos, ellas.

thick [θįk]. I. a. grueso; espeso; tupido, denso; de espesor (2 *inches thick*, de 2 pulgadas de espesor); continuado, repetido; basto, grosero, tosco; nebuloso, brumoso, sombrío; estúpido, torpe; apagado (la voz, etc.); borroso; oscuro, impenetrable, profundo (la sombra, etc.); (fam.) íntimo.—**t.-and-thin**, cabal, a toda prueba.—**t. of hearing**, teniente de oído, duro de oído.—**t. stuff**, (mar.) tablones, palmejares. II. s. grueso, espesor; lo más denso, nutrido, tupido o recio.—**the t. of the fight**, lo más reñido del combate.—**through t. and thin**, por sobre todo; a toda costa, a despecho de todo. III. adv. frecuentemente, continuadamente; densa o tupidamente.—**t.-headed**, espeso, torpe.—**t.-lipped**, bezudo, jetudo.—**t.-necked**, cervigudo.—**t.-set**, rechoncho, grueso; (agr.) plantado muy espeso.—**t.-skinned**, de pellejo espeso; sin vergüenza; indiferente; (zool.) paquidermo.—**t.-skulled**, lerdo, torpe.

thicken [-n], *va.* y *vn.* espesar(se), condensar(se),

engrosar(se), aumentar; reforzar(se); enturbiar(se); cerrarse; complicar(se).

thickening [-nįŋ]. I. s. espesamiento. II. a. espesativo.

thicket [-įt], s. maleza, soto, espesura, matorral, broza, (Cuba) manigua.

thickhead [-hed], s. estúpido.

thickish [-įʃ], a. algo espeso o denso.

thickly [-lį], adv. espesamente; densa o tupidamente; repetidamente.—**t. settled**, muy poblado.

thickness [-nįs], s. espesor; densidad; grueso, grosor; cuerpo, consistencia; capa (superpuesta); (fam.) estupidez.

thickskin [-skįn], s. persona sin vergüenza.

thickskull [-skʌl], s. estúpido.

thief [θif], s. ladrón, hurtador, caco, estafador.— **t. tube**, pipeta, bombillo, catavino.

thieve [θiv], *va.* y *vn.* hurtar, robar.—**thievery** [-œrį], s. latrocinio o robo.—**thievish** [-įʃ], a. rapaz, ladrón, hurtador.—**thievishly** [-lį], adv. ladronamente, a modo de ladrones.—**thievishness** [-nįs], s. latrocinio; rapacidad.

thigh [θaį], s. (anat.) muslo.—**t. bone**, fémur.

thill [θįl], s. (carr.) limonera, limón, vara.

thimble [θímbl], s. (cost.) dedal; (mec.) manguito; (mar.) guardacabo.

thimbleberry [-berį], s. (bot.) frambuesa negra.

thin [θįn]. I. a. delgado, fino, tenue; flaco, descarnado; raro, ralo, claro (el aire, etc.); ligero, transparente; seroso, aguado (un líquido); (mús.) poco resonante, débil; apagado (color); poco, corto, ligero, escaso; pequeño; (fam.) transparente, débil, artificial, inverosímil (apl. a excusas, etc.). II. *va.* y *vn.* enrarecer(se), poner(se) ralo; adelgazar(se), enflaquecer(se); fluidificar(se) (la sangre, etc.); (gen. con *out*) aclarar, entresacar (el monte, etc.); (con *out*, *off* o *away*) esparcir(se), hacer o ponerse menos denso, tupido, etc.

thine [ðaįn], *pron.* y a. tuyo, el tuyo; tu, tus.

thing [θįŋ], s. cosa, objeto; asunto, acontecimiento, hecho.—*pl.* cosas, efectos, bártulos. En lenguaje familiar, se aplica a veces a personas, sobre todo para expresar desprecio, compasión, etc.: *the young thing*, la chica, la pobre chica; *the mean thing*, el malvado, el ruin, el maldito, el sinvergüenza, el desconsiderado, etc.—**t.-in-itself**, (filos.) una realidad final o metafísica; las cosas en sí mismas, el mundo objetivo en sí mismo.—**above all things**, sobre todas las cosas, sobre todo, muy especialmente.—**as things stand**, como están las cosas.—**for one t.**, entre otras cosas.—**no such (a) t.**, no hay tal (cosa); nada de eso.—**poor (little) t.**, ¡pobrecito!—**the t.**, lo conveniente, lo que está de moda, lo necesario o lo que se desea.

think [θįŋk], *va.* y *vn.* (pret. y pp. THOUGHT) pensar; proponerse, tener intención de; creer, juzgar, conjeturar, considerar; (con *of*, *on* o *upon*) acordarse de, recordar; pensar en; reflexionar acerca de, meditar, considerar.—**to t. better of**, cambiar de opinión acerca de; formar mejor opinión de.—**to t. it over**, pensarlo, meditarlo.—**to t. nothing of**, mirar con desprecio, tener en poco; creer fácil, considerar como cosa común y corriente, no dar importancia a.—**to t. twice**, reflexionar mucho, andar con tiento.—**to t. well (ill) of**, tener buen (mal) concepto de.—**as you t. fit**, como a Vd. le parezca mejor, como Vd. quiera.—**I don't t. so, I t. not**, creo que no.

thinkable [-ạbl], a. concebible.

thinker [-œ(r)], s. pensador.

thinking [-įŋ], s. pensamiento, meditación, reflexión; juicio, concepto, opinión.—**to my t.**, en mi opinión, en mi concepto.—**to put on, o have on, one's t. cap**, poner las mientes, avivar el seso.—**way of t.**, modo de pensar, opinión, parecer.

thinly [θínli], *adv.* delgadamente; esparcidamente. etc. (*V.* THIN); poco, en corto número.

thinness [θínnis], *s.* tenuidad, delgadez; flacura. magrez, escasez; raleza; raridad; poca consistencia; falta de resonancia; debilidad.

thioaldehyde [θaιοǽldęhaịd], *s.* (quím.) aldehido sulfúrico.

thionic [θaịánịk], *a.* (quím.) tiónico.

thiosulphuric [θaịosʌlfịúrịk], *a.* tiosulfúrico.

third [θǽrd]. **I.** *a.* tercero, tercio, terciario.— **t. boiler**, meladora de azúcar.—**t.-class**, de tercera clase.—**t. degree**, grado tres (en la masonería); (fam.) interrogatorio severo de un preso, gen. con crueldad o mal tratamiento.— **t. estate**, estado llano o común.—**t. eyelid**, (anat.) membrana nictitante.—**t. house**, (fam., pol.) camarilla de cabilderos.—**t. person**, tercero; (gram.) tercera persona.—**t. rail**, (elec.) tercer riel, riel conductor.—**t.-rate**, de calidad muy inferior.—**t. service**, (E. U., mil.) servicio de aviación, fuerzas aéreas. **II.** *s.* tercio, tercero, terzuelo, tercera parte; (mús.) tercera. **III.** *va.* terciar.

thirdly [-li], *adv.* en tercer lugar.

thirst [θǽrst]. **I.** *s.* sed; ansia, anhelo. **II.** *vn.* tener o padecer sed; ansiar, anhelar.—**to t. for**, tener sed de; anhelar.

thirstiness [-inis], *s.* sed; ansia.

thirsty [-i], *a.* sediento.—**to be t.**, tener sed.

thirteen [θǽrtín], *s. y a.* trece.—**t. hundred**, mil trescientos.—**thirteenth** [-θ]. **I.** *a.* décimotercio, trece (ordinal). **II.** *s. y a.* trezavo.

thirtieth [θǽrtiiθ]. **I.** *a.* trigésimo, treinta (ordinal). **II.** *s. y a.* treintavo.

thirty [θǽrti], *s. y a.* treinta.

this [δis]. **I.** *a.* (*pl.* THESE) este, esta. **II.** *pron.* éste, ésta, esto.

thistle [θísl], *s.* (bot.) cardo, abrojo.—**t. bird**, **t. finch**, (orn.) jilguero, pintacilgo.

thistledown [-daụn], *s.* (bot.) papo, vilano, milano o escardillo del cardo.

thistly [-i], *a.* lleno de cardos.

thither [θíðœ(r)]. **I.** *adv.* allá, hacia allá; a ese fin, punto o resultado. **II.** *a.* ulterior, situado de la parte de allá.—**on the t. side of**, allende, del otro lado de.

tho' [δoụ], *conj. contr.* de THOUGH.

thole [θóụl], *s.* (mar.) tolete, escálamo; (agr.) asidero del mango de la guadaña; (arq.) tambor. *V.* THOLOS.—**tholepin** [-pịn], *s.* (mar.) tolete, escálamo.

tholos, tholus [θálʌs], *s.* (arq.) tambor, cúpula.

Thomism [tóụmịzm], *s.* (filos.) tomismo.— **Thomist** [-ịst], *s. y a.* tomista.

thong [θaŋ], *s.* correa, correhuela, tira, zurriaga, (Am.) guasca.

thoracic [θorǽsịk], *a.* (anat. y zool.) torácico.

thorax [θóræks], *s.* (anat. y zool.) tórax, pecho, (ent.) coselete; (ant. arm.) coselete.

thoria [θóriạ], *s.* (quím.) torina, óxido de torio.— **thorianite** [-naịt], *s.* torianita, mineral de óxidos de torio, cerio, etc.—**thorite** [θóraịt], *s.* torita, mineral de silicato de torio.

thorium [θóriʌm], *s.* (quím.) torio.

thorn [θórn]. **I.** *va.* pinchar, traspasar o asegurar con una espina. **II.** *s.* (bot.) espina, púa; espino, abrojo; pincho; (fig.) llaga, pesadumbre, zozobra.—**t. apple**, (bot.) estramonio.—**t. in the side**, (fig.) molestia.—**t. prickle**, abrojo, púa. —**to be upon thorns**, estar en ascuas.

thornback [-bæk], *s.* (ict.) raya espinosa.

thornless [-lis], *a.* sin espinas.

thorny [-i], *a.* espinoso; arduo.

thorough [θǽroụ], *a.* cabal, completo, cumplido, acabado; consumado, perfecto; cuidadoso, concienzudo.—**t. bass**, (mús.) contrapunto.

thoroughbred [-bred]. **I.** *a.* de pura raza, casta o sangre; bien nacido. **II.** *s.* (un) pura sangre (caballo, etc.).

thoroughfare [-fęr], *s.* vía pública; paso, tránsito. —**no t.**, no se pasa; calle cerrada.

thoroughgoing [-goụiŋ], *a.* cabal, completo, esmerado, minucioso; pronunciado, intransigente.

thoroughly [-li], *adv.* enteramente, cabalmente; a fondo; concienzudamente, detenidamente.

thoroughness [-nis], *s.* entereza, calidad de cabal o completo; minuciosidad; escrupulosidad, detenimiento.

thoroughpaced [-peịst], *a.* (equit.) instruído en todos los pasos; cabal, completo, perfecto; intransigente.

thoroughwax [-wæks], *s.* (bot.) perfoliada.

thoroughwort [-wœrt], *s.* (bot.) eupatorio.

thorp(e [θórp], *s.* (ant.) lugar, villorrio, caserío.

those [δoụz]. **I.** *a. pl.* de THAT: aquellos, aquellas; esos, esas. **II.** *pron. pl.* ésos, ésas; aquéllos, aquéllas.—**t. that, t. which, t. who**, los que, aquellos que, quienes.

thou [δaụ]. **I.** *pron.* tú. **II.** *va. y vn.* tutear.

though [δoụ]. **I.** *conj.* aunque, bien que, si bien, aun cuando.—**as t.**, como si.—**what t.**, aunque, ¿qué importa que . . .? **II.** *adv.* (fam.) sin embargo, a pesar de eso. En lenguaje familiar, ú. a menudo adverbialmente, sobre todo en oraciones de forma interrogativa, con un expletivo enfático de encarecimiento: *isn't she pretty, though?* ¡y qué bonita que es! *aren't you smart, though?* ¡qué vivo que eres!

thought [θót]. **I.** *pret. y pp.* de TO THINK.—**to be well t. of**, ser tenido en buen concepto, ser estimado. **II.** *s.* pensamiento; meditación, reflexión, consideración; idea; intención, propósito; memoria, recuerdo; cuidado, solicitud, atención; poquito, migaja, pizca.—**to give (a) t. to**, pensar en, acordarse de.—**to take t. of**, o for, pensar en, proveer para.

thoughtful [-fụl], *a.* pensativo, meditabundo; considerado; precavido.—**thoughtfully** [-i], *adv.* meditativamente, con reflexión; con previsión; con consideración.—**thoughtfulness** [-nis], *s.* calidad de meditativo, precavido o considerado; consideración; cuidado, atención; previsión.

thoughtless [-lịs], *a.* atolondrado, descuidado; irreflexivo; inconsiderado.—**thoughtlessly** [-li], *adv.* descuidadamente; irreflexivamente; sin consideración.—**thoughtlessness** [-nis], *s.* descuido o inadvertencia; falta de consideración; ligereza o indiscreción; atolondramiento.

thousand [θáụzạnd]. **I.** *a.* mil. **II.** *s.* mil; millar.— **t. and one**, mil y un(o); innumerables.— **t.-legs**, (ent.) cientopiés, escolopendra.—**a t., one t.**, mil.—**two t.**, dos mil.—**by the t.**, por millar; por millares; a o por miles.

thousandfold [-foụld], *a. y adv.* mil veces más.

thousandth [-θ]. **I.** *a.* milésimo. **II.** *s.* milésimo, milésima.

Thracian [θréịʃạn], *s. y a.* tracio.

thrall [θról], *s.* esclavo, siervo.—**thral(l)dom** [-dọm], *s.* esclavitud, servidumbre.

thrash [θræʃ]. **I.** *va.* (agr.) trillar, desgranar; batanear; batir; sacudir; apalear, azotar, zurrar; (fam.) vencer o derrotar de modo decisivo. **II.** *vn.* trillar el grano; arrojarse, agitarse; (con at) asestar golpes, etc., a.—**thrasher** [-œ(r)], *s.* (agr.) trillador, desgranador; trilladora mecánica, (máquina) trilladora; (orn.) malviz, *m.*, malvís.—**t. shark**, (ict.) tiburón.

thrashing [-iŋ], *s.* (agr.) trilla, trilladura, desgranamiento; zurra, paliza, azotaina; (fam.) derrota.—**t. floor**, era.—**t. machine**, trillo, trilladora.

thrasonical [θreịsánịkạl], *a.* jactancioso, fachendoso.—**thrasonically** [-li], *adv.* con jactancia.

thread [θréd]. **I.** *s.* hilo; fibra, hebra, filamento; filete (de un tornillo).—**t. lace**, encaje de hilo.—**t.-like**, filiforme. **II.** *va.* enhebrar, enhilar, ensartar; colarse a través de, pasar por; (mec.) roscar, labrar un filete en, aterrajar (un tornillo). **III.** *vn.* colarse en, llegar hasta; (coc.) formar hilos (jarabe).

threadbare [-ber], *a.* raído, muy usado, gastado.

threadfish [-fiʃ], s. (ict.) zapatero.

threadworm [-wœrm], s. (zool.) lombricilla filiforme, nemátodo, ascáride, f.

threat [θret], s. amenaza.—**threaten** [θrétn], va. y vn. amenazar, amagar.—**threatener** [-œ(r)], s. amenazador.—**threatening** [-iŋ]. I. s. amenaza. II. a. amenazador, amenazante.—**threateningly** [-li], adv. con amenazas.

three [θrí], s. y a. tres.—**t.-cleft**, (bot.) trífido.—**t.-color**, tricolor; tricromo (estampado).—**t.-cornered**, triangular; de tres picos.—**t.-decker**, navío de tres puentes; edificio de tres pisos; etc.—**t. deep**, en tres hileras o filas.—**t. hundred(th)**, trescientos; tricentésimo.—**t.-leaved**, (bot.) trifolio.—**t.-legged**, de tres pies.—**t.-lobed**, trilobulado.—**t.-parted**, tripartito.—**t.-phase**, (elec.) trifásico.—**t.-piece suit**, traje de tres prendas (vg. pantalón, chaleco y chaqueta).—**t.-ply**, triple; de tres capas.—**t. R's**. V. **R**.—**t.-square file**, (mec.) lima triangular.—**t.-stringed**, de tres cuerdas.—**t.-toed**, de tres dedos (del pie.).—**t.-way cock**, llave (f.) o grifo de tres vías.—**t.-way switch**, (elec.) interruptor de tres direcciones.—**t.-way valve**, válvula de paso triple.

threefold [-foṵld]. I. a. triple, tríplice, tresdoble; tres veces más. II. adv. tres veces; triplicadamente.

threepence [θrépens], s. (Ingl.) tres peniques; moneda de tres peniques.

threepenny [θrépeni], a. que vale tres peniques; barato, despreciable.

threescore [θrískór], a. y s. tres veintenas, sesenta.—**t. and ten**, setenta.

threnody [θrénodi], s. treno.

thresh [θréʃ]. I. va. (agr.) trillar, desgranar (el grano); batanear, batir; (con out) discutir a fondo (un problema, etc.); (con over) decir, cantar, etc., repetidas veces. II. vn. trillar el grano; asestar golpes; agitarse. V. **THRASH**.

thresher [-œ(r)], s. (agr.) trillador; (máquina) trilladora; (ict.) tiburón. V. **THRASHER**.

threshold [θréʃoṵld], s. (arq.) umbral, tranco; entrada; (fig.) comienzo.

threw [θru], pret. de TO THROW.

thrice [θrais], adv. tres veces.

thrift [θríft], s. economía, frugalidad, ahorro; crecimiento o desarrollo vigoroso (de una planta, etc.).

thriftily [-ili], adv. frugalmente, económicamente.—**thriftiness** [-inis], s. frugalidad; parsimonia.—**thriftless** [-lis], a. manirroto, pródigo; extravagante.—**thrifty** [-i], a. frugal, económico, ahorrativo; próspero, floreciente, vigoroso.

thrill [θríl]. I. va. causar una emoción viva, hacer estremecerse. II. vn. emocionarse, conmoverse. III. s. emoción, estremecimiento.

thriller [-œ(r)], s. cosa, persona o historia conmovedora, entusiasmadora, espeluznante, etc.

thrilling [-iŋ], a. conmovedor; espeluznante.

thrive [θráiv], vn. (pret. THROVE o THRIVED; pp. THRIVED o THRIVEN) medrar, prosperar, adelantar, tener buen éxito.—**thriving** [-iŋ], a. próspero, floreciente.—**thrivingly** [-li], adv. prósperamente.

thro' [θru], a., adv. y prep. abrev. de THROUGH.

throat [θróṵt], s. (anat.) garganta, cuello, gola, gaznate; paso, entrada, orificio; tragante (de alto horno).

throatband [-bænd], **throatlatch** [-læch], s. (tal.) ahogadero (de la cabezada).

throating [-iŋ], s. (arq.) goterón.

throb [θrab]. I. vn. latir, palpitar, pulsar; vibrar. II. s. latido, pulsación, palpitación.

throe [θroṵ], s. angustia, dolor, agonía.

thrombosis [θrambóṵsis], s. (med.) trombosis, coagulación en los vasos sanguíneos.—**thrombus** [θrámbʌs], s. coágulo que forma la trombosis.

throne [θroṵn]. I. s. trono; poder o dignidad soberanos.—pl. (igl.) tronos. II. va. entronizar, elevar al trono, exaltar. III. vn. ocupar el trono.

throng [θraŋ]. I. s. tropel de gente, multitud, muchedumbre, caterva. II. va. apretar, atestar, llenar de bote en bote; estrujar. III. vn. venir en tropel, amontonarse, apiñarse.

throstle [θrásl], s. (orn.) zorzal, malvís, m., tordo; (tej.) telar continuo.

throttle [θrátl]. I. s. (anat. y zool.) gaznate, gorja, gargüero, gollete, traquearteria; gollete o cuello (de botella, etc.).—**t. valve**, (m. v.) válvula de estrangulación, válvula reguladora; (locom.) regulador; (aut.) acelerador. II. va. ahogar, estrangular; (a veces con down) interrumpir, cortar, reducir (el vapor, etc.). III. vn. ahogarse, asfixiarse.

through [θru]. I. a. continuo, que va hasta el fin.—**t. bridge**, puente de tablero inferior.—**t. ticket**, (f. c.) billete para determinado punto pasando por varias líneas.—**t. train**, tren directo o terminal. II. adv. de o al través, de parte a parte, de un lado a otro; desde el principio hasta el fin; enteramente, completamente.—**t. and t.**, enteramente; en todo; hasta los tuétanos.—**to be t.**, haber terminado; (fam.) no poder más.—**to be t. with**, haber terminado con; no tener más que ver con; no ocuparse ya en. III. prep. por; a través de; de un extremo (o de un lado) a otro de; por conducto o por medio de, mediante; por entre; por causa de, gracias a, por mediación de.

throughout [-áṵt]. I. prep. por todo, en todo; a lo largo de; durante todo. II. adv. de todas partes; desde el principio hasta el fin; de parte a parte; en todo respecto.

throve [θroṵv], pret. de TO THRIVE.

throw [θróṵ]. I. va. y vn. (pret. THREW; pp. THROWN) arrojar, tirar, disparar, lanzar; echar (suertes, f. pl., dados).—**to t. up**, (fam.) vomitar. II. va. derribar, echar por tierra; desmontar, apear; despojarse de; mudar (la piel); dirigir (la mirada); torcer (hilo); mover rápidamente; dar vuelta a; (vet.) parir; (fam.) perder con premeditación (una carrera, un juego); dar forma a los objetos de alfarería.—**to t. about**, esparcir.—**to t. aside**, desechar, poner de lado.—**to t. away**, arrojar; desperdiciar, malgastar; desechar, arrinconar.—**to t. back**, rechazar, devolver.—**to t. by**, arrinconar.—**to t. cold water, o a wet blanket on**, (fam.) aguar (la fiesta, un plan, etc.). V. **WET BLANKET**.—**to t. down**, derribar, echar por tierra; trastornar.—**to t. down the gauntlet**, echar el guante, retar.—**to t. in**, echar dentro; intercalar, insertar; añadir, dar de más, dar además de lo convenido.—**to t. light on**, esclarecer.—**to t. off**, echar fuera; expeler, hacer salir; quitarse; sacudir; renunciar.—**to t. oneself away**, sacrificarse tontamente, rebajarse, echarse a pique.—**to t. open**, abrir de par en par.—**to t. out**, proferir, insinuar; expeler, excluir; esparcir, exhalar, despedir, emitir.—**to t. out of gear**, (mec.) desengranar, desconectar; (fig.) trastornar.—**to t. overboard**, (mar.) echar a la mar, echar al agua; (fig.) desechar, tirar.—**to t. silk**, torcer seda.—**to t. to the wind(s)**, descartar, no hacer caso de.—**to t. up**, echar al aire; elevar, levantar; renunciar a, abandonar.—**to t. up the heels of**, echar a tierra de una zancadilla; frustrar.—**to t. up the sponge**, (fam.) darse por vencido, desistir, rendirse, cantar el kirieleisón. III. s. tiro, echada, tirada; (elec.) dirección (**two-t.**, **three-t.**, de dos, tres direcciones); (min.) desviación; (geol.) falla; (mec.) golpe o carrera; (mec.) radio (de la excéntrica, manivela); lance de dados.—**within a stone's t.**, a tiro de piedra.

throwback [-bæk], s. vuelta atrás, retroceso; (biol.) reversión, atavismo; (cine) escena retrospectiva, que enseña acontecimientos pasados relacionados con el drama que se representa (ll. t. **flashback**).

thrower [-œ(r)], *s.* tirador, lanzador, arrojador; (tej.) torcedor de seda.

throwing [-iŋ], *s.* lanzamiento; acción de arrojar, tirar, echar, etc.

throwster [-stœ(r)], *s.* (tej.) torcedor de seda; jugador de dados.

thrum [θrʌm]. I. *s.* cadillos, *pl.*; hilo basto; borla; sonido de rascar una guitarra, etc. II. *va.* adornar con borlas; rascar las cuerdas de un instrumento.

thrush [θrʌš], *s.* (orn.) tordo, zorzal, malvís, *m.;* (med.) afta.

thrust [θrʌst]. I. *vn.* (*pret.* y *pp.* THRUST) acometer, embestir (con espada, estoque, etc.); tirar una estocada (con); meterse, pasar abriéndose campo. II. *va.* meter; empujar, impeler; forzar; atravesar; clavar, hincar; (*vr.* gen. con **on** o **upon**) entremeterse, meterse, tratar de hacerse recibir o aceptar; lanzarse.— **to t. aside**, rechazar; empujar a un lado.—**to t. forward**, empujar, echar adelante.—**to t. in**, meter, introducir.—**to t. on**, incitar, empujar.—**to t. out**, echar fuera; sacar (la lengua, etc.).—**to t. the**, **o one's**, **nose into**, entremeterse, meter las narices en, curiosear.—**to t. through**, apuñalar, atravesar de parte a parte. —**to t. upon**, imponer, hacer aceptar. III. *s.* empuje, empujón; (esgr.) cornada, pase; bote, estocada; lanzada; cornada (de un animal astado); aguijonazo; arremetida, ataque; (mec., ing.) empuje, presión (de un eje, de un arco, etc.); (min.) derrumbe.—**t. bearing, t. block**, cojinete de empuje (apl. esp. al de anillos).— **t. collar**, anillo de empuje.—**t. shaft**, (mar.) extremo del eje del motor provisto de anillos de empuje.

thud [θʌd]. I. *s.* baque, golpe o sonido sordo de un objeto duro que choca con otro blando. II. *vn.* hacer ese ruido.

thug [θʌg], *s.* miembro de una secta de asesinos fanáticos de la India; por extensión, asesino.

thuja [θúhjạ], *s.* (bot.) tuya.

thulium [θjúljạm], *s.* (quím.) tulio.

thumb [θʌm]. I. *s.* (anat.) pulgar.—**t. nut**, (mec.) tuerca de orejetas.—**thumbs down (up)**, señal (*f.*) de desaprobación (aprobación).— **under the t. of**, dominado por, bajo el talón de. II. *va.* manosear con poca destreza; emporcar con los dedos; hojear (un libro, etc.).

thumbnail [-neịl]. I. *s.* uña del pulgar. II. *a.* pequeño, en miniatura.

thumbscrew [-skru], *s.* (mec.) tornillo de mano (gen. de orejas); empulgueras, *f. pl.* (antiguo instrumento de tormento).

thumbstall [-stɔl], *s.* dedal, dedil.

thumbtack [-tæk], *s.* chinche, *f.* (de dibujo).

thump [θʌmp]. I. *s.* baque; porrazo, remoquete, (fam.) trastazo. II. *va.* y *vn.* aporrear, acachetear, (fam.) cascar, apuñear; latir con violencia (el corazón).

thunder [θʌ́ndœ(r)]. I. *s.* trueno; tronido, estruendo, estrépito, estampido. II. *vn.* tronar, (poét.) tonar; retumbar. III. *va.* pronunciar en tono amenazador, fulminante, etc.; fulminar. —**it thunders**, truena.—**thunderbolt** [-boult], *s.* rayo, centella.—**thunderclap** [-klæp], *s.* trueno.—**thundercloud** [-klaụd], *s.* nube cargada de electricidad; cosa amenazadora.— **thunderer** [-œ(r)], *s.* tronador, fulminador; (T.) Júpiter.—**thundering** [-iŋ], *a.* atronador, fulminante, tonante; (fam.) extraordinario.— **thunderous** [-ʌs], *a.* tronador, atronador, tonante.—**thundershower** [-šaụœ(r)], *s.* tronada con chubascos.—**thunderstorm** [-storm], *s.* tronada.—**thunderstrike** [-straịk], *va.* fulminar, herir con rayo o centella: aturdir. —**thunderstruck** [-strak], *a.* estupefacto, turulato.—**to be t.**, atronarse.

thurible [θiúrịbl], *s.* (igl.) turíbulo, incensario.— **thurifer** [θiúrịfœ(r)], *s.* (igl.) turibulario.— **thuriferous** [θiụrífœrʌs], *a.* turífero.—**thurification** [-fikéịšọn], *s.* turificación.

Thursday [θœ́rzdiị], *s.* jueves.

thus [ðʌs], *adv.* así, de este modo; por eso, por lo tanto; en estos términos, *sic;* hasta ese punto, tanto; a ese grado; siendo así, en este caso.— **t. and so**, tal y tal cosa; de tal y tal modo.— **t. far**, hasta ahora; hasta aquí.—**t. it is that**, así es que; así es como.

thus [θʌs], *s.* trementina cruda; incienso.

thuya [θúyạ], *s.* (bot.) tuya.

thwack [θwæk]. I. *va.* aporrear, pegar, golpear, (fam.) zurrar. II. *s.* golpe, sequete, porrazo.

thwart [θwort]. I. *va.* impedir, desbaratar, frustrar. II. *a.* transversal, oblicuo, atravesado. III. *s.* banco de remeros, banco de bogar.

thy [ðaị], *a. pos.* tu, tus.

thyme [taịm], *s.* (bot.) tomillo.

thymeiæaceous [θịmelịéịšʌs], *a.* (bot.) timeleáceo.

thymol [θáịmoụl], *s.* (quím.) timol.

thymus [θáịmʌs], *s.* (anat.) timo.

thymy [táịmị], *a.* oliente a tomillo.

thyroid [θáịroịd], *a.* en forma de escudo; (anat.) tiroideo.—**t. body, t. gland**, (cuerpo o glándula) tiroides.—**t. cartilage**, nuez de la garganta; (en pájaros) cartílago laríngeo.

thyroiditis [-áịtịs], *s.* (med.) tiroiditis.

thyroxin(e [θaịráksịn], *s.* (bioquím.) tiroxina.

thyrse, thyrsus [θœrs, -ʌs], *s.* (bot.) tirso.

thyself [ðaịsélf], *pron. refl.* tú mismo, ti mismo.— **love thy neighbor as t.**, ama a tu prójimo como a ti mismo.

tiara [tiárạ], *s.* tiara; diadema.

Tibetan [tịbétạn], *s.* y *a.* tibetano.

tibia [tíbịạ], *s.* (anat.) tibia; (ent.) cuarta articulación; (mús.) tibia.

tibial [-l], *a.* tibial, de la tibia.

tic [tịk], *s.* (med.) tic, contracción nerviosa.

tick [tịk]. I. *s.* tictac, sonido acompasado; pipecito; contramarca, contraseña; (ent.) garrapata, rezno, pito, ácaro; funda de colchón; (tej.) terliz, *m.*, cotí, cutí; (fam.) crédito, fiado. II. *va.* sonar produciendo tictac; contramarcar. III. *vn.* hacer sonido de tictac, batir; (fam.) vender o comprar al fiado; (fam.) tener éxito.

tick(en [-ẹn], *s.* (tej.) terliz, *m.*, cotí. V. TICKING.

ticker [-œ(r)], *s.* (tlg.) indicador eléctrico automático de cotizaciones y noticias (esp. de la bolsa); (fam.) reloj de bolsillo.—**t. tape**, (tlg.) cinta del indicador automático.

ticket [tịkit]. I. *s.* (f. c., etc., teat.) billete, (Am.) boleto; pase, entrada; rótulo, marbete; marca; (pol.) balota; por extensión, candidatura (de un partido).—**t. agent**, taquillero, (Am.) boletero. —**t. holder**, tenedor de un billete.—**t. office**, taquilla o despacho de billetes; (teat.) taquilla. —**t. of leave**, (Ingl.) licencia que se da a un penado para salir de la cárcel.—**t. punch**, sacabocados.—**t. speculator** o **scalper**, revendedor de billetes (a precios exorbitantes). II. *va.* rotular, marcar.

ticking [tịkịŋ], *s.* tictac (de reloj, etc.); (tej.) terliz, *m.*, cotí; marga, márraga. V. TICK(EN.

tickle [tịkl]. I. *va.* hacer cosquillas; halagar, lisonjear, agradar a los oídos; agradar; divertir.— **tickled to death**, (fam.) contentísimo. II. *vn.* hacer, tener o sentir cosquillas.—**tickler** [tịklœ(r)], *s.* el que hace cosquillas; libro borrador o diario.—**tickling** [tịklịŋ], *s.* cosquillas, *f. pl.*, cosquilleo.—**ticklish** [tịklịš], *a.* cosquilloso; inseguro, incierto; arduo, delicado, difícil. —**ticklishness** [-nịs], *s.* calidad de cosquilloso o delicado.

ticktack [tịktæck], *s.* tictac; chaquete (juego).

tick-tack-toe [tịk tæk tóụ], *s.* juego del tres en raya.

tidal [táịdạl], *a.* de marea; periódico.—**t. basin**, dique de marea.—**t. harbor**, puerto de grandes mareas.—**t. wave**, aguaje; ola enorme que acompaña un terremoto o viento violento; gran conmoción, ola popular.

tidbit [tídbit], *s.* bocado regalado o predilecto, golosina, sainete, cotufa; trozo escogido.

tide [táid]. **I.** *s.* marea; corriente, *f.;* curso, marcha; flujo; tiempo, estación, sazón, *f.*—**t. gate**, compuerta de marea; (mar.) angostura.— **t. wave**, aguaje.—**to go against the t.**, ir contra la corriente.—**to go with the t.**, seguir la corriente. **II.** *va.* llevar, conducir (la marea); (con **over**) ayudar a superar una dificultad; aguardar la oportunidad. **III.** *vn.* navegar o flotar con la marea.—**tideless** [-lis], *a.* sin marea.—**tidesman** [-zman], **tidewaiter** [-weitœ(r)], *s.* vista (*m.*) o empleado de aduanas.

tidily [táidili], *adv.* aseadamente.—**tidiness** [-nis], *s.* aseo, pulcritud, atildamiento.

tidings [táidiŋz], *s. pl.* nuevas, noticias.

tidewater [táidwotœ(r)], *s.* agua afectada por la marea; costa del mar; (com.) puerto, embarcadero.

tideway [táidwei], *s.* canal de marea.

tidy [táidi]. **I.** *a.* limpio, aseado, pulcro, ordenado; (fam.) considerable. **II.** *s.* cubierta de respaldar. **III.** *va.* y *vn.* asear, poner en orden.

tie [tai]. **I.** *va.* (*pret.* y *pp.* TIED; *pa.* TYING) atar, amarrar, liar, trincar; unir, enlazar, encadenar, vincular; restringir, limitar; (pol., dep.) empatar.—**to t. the knot**, (fam.) casar(se).—**to t. tight**, apretar.—**to t. up**, atar, amarrar, asegurar; recoger; impedir, obstruir, paralizar (el tráfico, la industria, etc. *V.* TIE-UP); envolver (un paquete, etc.); vincular (con). **II.** *vn.* liarse; relacionarse; empatarse. **III.** *s.* lazo, nudo, atadura, ligadura; vínculo, conexión, ligazón, *f.;* parentesco; apego, adhesión, unión; (dep.) empate; corbata; (mús.) ligadura; (mar.) maroma, ostaga; (carp., ing.) tirante; (f. c.) traviesa.— *pl.* zapatos bajos.—**t. bar**, *s.* (ing.) tirante; (f. c.) barra transversal de las agujas de un cambio.—**t. beam**, *s.* (arq.) tirante, viga de tensión (apl. esp. a la que sostiene la parte superior de una armadura).—**t. plate**, (f. c.) placa de asiento del riel; (mar.) cuerda.—**t. rod**, (ing.) tirante; riostra.

tier [tir], *s.* fila, hilera, andana, ringlera, tonga; (teat.) fila de palcos.

tierce [tirs], *s.* tercerola (medida para líquidos), barril de mediana cabida; tercera o tercerola (en los naipes); (mús.) tercera; (igl.) tercia, hora canónica; (esgr.) parada y posición de mano en tercera.

tiercet [-et], *s.* (poét.) terceto.

tie-up [tái ʌp], *s.* paro o paralización (de la industria, el tráfico, etc.) debida a trastornos imprevistos, sobre todo a las huelgas; enlace, conexión; contubernio, alianza subrepticia.

tiff [tif]. **I.** *s.* pique, disgusto, desavenencia; traguito, sorbo. **II.** *vn.* picarse, atufarse, reñir.

tiffany [tífani], *s.* (tej.) gasa de muselina.

tiffin [tífin], *s.* merienda.

tiger [táigœ(r)], *s.* (zool.) tigre; persona o animal de carácter feroz; (fam.) rufián farandulero; un viva (vítor) más, el último viva.—**t. beetle**, (ent.) cicindela.—**t. cat**, (zool.) gato cerval o gato montés; gato doméstico atigrado.—**t. flower**, **t. lily**, (bot.) tigridia.

tigerish [-iš], *a.* como de tigre, feroz; atigrado.

tight [táit], *a.* bien cerrado, hermético; (mar.) estanco; tirante, tieso; apretado, estrecho; compacto; muy ajustado; (com.) escaso, difícil de obtener; (fam.) apurado, difícil, grave (situación, etc.); (fam.) cicatero, tacaño; (fam.) embriagado, encandilado.—**t.-fisted**, tacaño.— **t. fit**, empalme muy ajustado.—**t.-fitting**, muy ajustado.—**t.-laced**, (fam.) severo, estricto, formal(ote).—**t. lacing**, hábito de apretarse el corsé.—**t.-lipped**, callado, taciturno.—**t. rope**, cuerda tesa, cuerda de volatinero.—**t. squeeze**, (fam.) aprieto.

tighten [-n], *va.* y *vn.* estrechar(se), apretar(se); estirar(se), at(i)esar(se).—**to t. one's belt**, hacer economías o sacrificios, aguantar privaciones.—**tightener** [-nœ(r)], *s.* tensor.—**tightening** [-niŋ], *s.* apretamiento, estrechamiento.

tightly [-li], *adv.* estrechamente; apretadamente; ajustadamente.—**tightness** [-nis], *s.* tensión, tirantez; estrechez; apretadura; impermeabilidad; (fam.) tacañería.

tights [-s], *s. pl.* calzas atacadas; traje de malla (de los gimnastas, etc.); taparrabo (para nadar).

tightwad [táitwad], *s.* (fam.) tacaño, cicatero.

tigress [táigris], *s.* (zool.) hembra del tigre.

tigrine [táigrin], *a.* rel. al tigre; atigrado.

tigrish [táigriš], *a.* = TIGERISH.

tilbury [tílberi], *s.* (carr.) tílburi.

tile [táil]. **I.** *s.* azulejo, losa, baldosa (de suelo, etc.); teja (de techo); mosaico, baldosín; bloque hueco de hormigón o de arcilla; (hidr.) tubo de barro cocido, atanor; (fam.) sombrero de copa, chistera.—**t. floor** o **pavement**, embaldosado. —**t. kiln**, tejar, tejera.—**t. maker**, tejero.—**t. roof**, techo de tejas. **II.** *va.* tejar, trastejar, (en)losar; poner desagüe de atanores en.—**tiler** [-œ(r)], *s.* trastejador; tejero; solador; tejar, tejera.

tiliaceous [tiliéišʌs], *a.* (bot.) tiliáceo.

tiling [táiliŋ], *s.* trastejadura, trastejo; azulejos, tejas en general; tejado; cubierta de tejas.

till [til]. **I.** *s.* caja, cajón o gaveta para guardar dinero. **II.** *prep.* hasta.—**t. further orders**, hasta nueva orden. **III.** *conj.* hasta que. **IV.** *va.* (agr.) cultivar, laborar, labrar.

tillable [-ʌbl], *a.* (agr.) labrantío, laborable.—**t. land**, tierra labrantía o de pan llevar.

tillage [-idž], *s.* labranza, labor, *f.,* cultivo, reja.

tiller [-œ(r)]. **I.** *s.* agricultor, labrador, cultivador; (mar.) caña del timón; (bot.) retoño, gamonito, vástago, renuevo.—**t. chain** o **rope**, (mar.) guardín. **II.** *vn.* echar retoños de la raíz.

tilt [tilt]. **I.** *s.* inclinación, declive; justa, torneo; lanzada; toldillo, toldo, tendal.—**t. cart**, volquete, carro de vuelco o volteo.—**t. hammer**, martinete de báscula.—**t. table**, mesa vocable. **II.** *va.* ladear, inclinar, volcar, voltear; martillar, forjar con martinete; dar una lanzada; entoldar. **III.** *vn.* inclinarse, reclinarse, ladearse; justar, tornear.—**to t. at windmills**, atacar molinos de viento (enemigos o abusos imaginarios).

tilter [-œ(r)], *s.* justador, torneador.

tilth [tilθ], *s.* labranza, cultivo, labor, *f.;* tierra cultivada; capa de cultivo del suelo.

tilting [tíltiŋ]. **I.** *s.* inclinación; vuelco, volteo; forjadura con martinete basculante; acción de justar o tornear. **II.** *a.* inclinado; ladeado; de vuelco, de volteo.—**t. car**, carro o vagón de vuelco.—**t. hammer**, martinete basculante.

timbal, **tymbal** [tímbal], *s.* (mús.) timbal.

timber [tímbœ(r)]. **I.** *s.* madera o materiales de construcción; palo, fuste; maderamen, maderaje; monte, bosque, árboles de monte; viga, madero; (mar.) cuaderna; armazón; mango de madera; (fig.) cualidades.—**t. forest**, bosque maderable.—**t. line**, límite de la vegetación selvática.—**t. merchant**, maderero.—**t. saw**, sierra bracera.—**t. wolf**, (zool.) lobo gris del Canadá y E. U.—**t. yard**, maderería, taller de maderas. **II.** *va.* enmaderar.

timbered [-d], *a.* enmaderado; arbolado.

timbering [-iŋ], *s.* (min.) entibación.

timberland [-lænd], *s.* tierras maderables.

timberwork [-wœrk], *s.* maderaje, maderamen.

timbre [tέmbœ(r)], *s.* (blas., mús., fon.) timbre.

timbrel [tímbrel], *s.* (mús.) pandereta, adufe.

time [táim]. **I.** *s.* tiempo; época, edad; plazo; período, estación; vez, turno; intervalo; oportunidad o coyuntura, sazón, *f.,* ocasión, lugar; (com.) prórroga, respiro, espera; plazo; (mús.) compás, tiempo; (gram.) tiempo; hora (*what time is it?* ¿qué hora es?; *tell me the time*, dígame la hora; *my time has come*, me ha llegado la hora).—*pl.* (mat.) veces (*six times two*, seis veces dos, o seis por dos).—**t. about**, alternadamente; por turnos.—**t. and tide**, oportunidad; tiempo y sazón.—**t. and (t.) again**, una y otra vez, repetidamente.—**t. bomb**, bomba de explosión demorada.—**t. clock**, reloj registrador (de la entrada y salida de los empleados); reloj fechador.—**t. exposure**, (foto.) exposición de tiempo. —**t. fuse**, espoleta graduada o de tiempo.—**t.-honored**, de antigua reputación, consagrado por el tiempo, tradicional.—**t. out of mind**, tiempo inmemorial.—**t. switch**, interruptor horario.—**t. to come**, lo futuro, lo venidero.— **t. was when**, en otro tiempo, tiempos hubo en que.—**t. will tell**, ello dirá.—**t. work**, trabajo a jornal o pagado por tiempo.—**a short t.**, un rato.—**any t.**, a cualquier hora; en cualquier tiempo u ocasión; cuando Vd. guste.—**at a t.**, a la vez.—**at no t.**, jamás, nunca.—**at that t.**, en aquel entonces.—**at the proper t.**, en su día, a su tiempo.—**at the same t.**, a la vez; al mismo tiempo; sin embargo.—**at the same t. as, o that**, a medida que.—**at the t.**, en ese tiempo, entonces.—**at this t.**, al presente, ahora.—**at this t. of day**, a la hora de ésta, a estas horas.—**at times**, a veces.— **behind the times**, atrasado de noticias; anticuado; fuera de moda.—**behind t.**, atrasado, retardado.—**between times**, en los intervalos. —**by that t.**, para entonces.—**each t.**, cada vez.—**for all t.**, para siempre, por siempre.— **for the t. being**, por ahora, de momento, por de pronto.—**from this t. forth**, desde ahora, de hoy en adelante, en lo futuro.—**from t. to t.**, de cuando en cuando.—**in an hour's t.**, en una hora.—**in no t.**, en un instante, en un abrir y cerrar de ojos.—**in old times, in times of yore**, antiguamente, en otros tiempos, en tiempos de Maricastaña.—**in these times**, hoy (en) día, hoy por hoy.—**in t.**, a tiempo; con o andando el tiempo.—**on t.**, a la hora debida, con puntualidad; (com.) a plazos.—**the t. is not yet**, todavía no es tiempo, aún no ha llegado la hora.—**this t. a twelvemonth**, de aquí a un año.—**to be on t.**, ser puntual; llegar con puntualidad.—**to have a good t.**, pasar un buen rato; pasar un día (unos días, una noche, etc.) agradable; divertirse. II. *va.* adaptar al tiempo, hacer con oportunidad; regular, poner a la hora; contar o medir el tiempo de; (mús.) llevar el compás.

timekeeper [-kipœ(r)], *s.* reloj; cronómetro; marcador de tiempo; listero; (dep.) cronometrista.

timeless [-lịs], *a.* eterno; independiente del tiempo; intempestivo, inoportuno.

timeliness [-lịnịs], *s.* oportunidad.

timely [-lị]. I. *adv.* oportunamente; a tiempo. II. *a.* oportuno, conveniente.

timepiece [-pis], *s.* reloj.

timer [-œ r], *s.* cronómetro; marcador de tiempo; (dep.) cronometrista.

timesaver [-seịvœ(r)], *s.*, **timesaving** [-seịvịŋ], *a.* economizador de tiempo.

timeserver [-sœrvœ(r)], *s.*, **timeserving** [-sœrvịŋ], *a.*, contemporizador, esclavo de las cosas del día, (persona) servil.

timetable [-teịbl], *s.* horario, itinerario de trenes, etc.

timeworn [-worn], *a.* usado, gastado por el tiempo; traqueado, viejo.

timid [tịmịd], *a.* tímido.—**timidity** [tịmịdịtị], **timidness** [tịmịdnịs], *s.* timidez.—**timidly** [-lị], *adv.* tímidamente.

timing [taịmịŋ]. I. *a.* de regulación de tiempo; registrador de tiempo. II. *s.* medida o cuenta del tiempo; (el) llevar cuenta del tiempo; (m. comb. int.) regulación o distribución del encendido; (mús.) sentido del compás; (teat., etc.) habilidad de escoger el momento oportuno para producir mayor efecto.

timocracy [taịmákrasị], *s.* (pol.) timocracia. **timocratic** [taịmokrætịk], *a.* timocrático.

timorous [tịmoras], *a.* miedoso, timorato; tímido.—**timorously** [-lị], *adv.* miedosamente; tímidamente.—**timorousness** [-nịs], *s.* timidez; temor, miedo.

timothy [tịmoθị], *s.* (bot.) cierta hierba forrajera.

timpani [tịmpạnị], *s. pl.* (mús.) timbales, tímpanos.

timpanist [tịmpạnịst], *s.* (mús.) timbalero.

tin [tịn]. I. *s.* estaño; (hoja de) lata, hojalata; objeto de hojalatería; (fam.) dinero, moneda, plata.—**t. can**, lata, bote o caja de lata.—**t. foil**, hoja o papel de estaño.—**t. hat**, (fam.) yelmo de acero.—**t. opener**, (Ingl.) abrelatas. —**t. ore**, (min.) casiterita.—**t. plate**, hoja de lata, hojalata.—**t. shop**, hojalatería.—**t. wedding**, décimo aniversario. II. *va.* estañar; cubrir con hoja de lata; (Ingl.) envasar en lata (*v.* CAN); dar una capa (de soldadura, etc.) a. *V.* TINNED GOODS.

tinamou [tịnạmu], *s.* (Am.) (orn.) tinamú.

tincal [tịŋkạl], *s.* atíncar, bórax.

tinctorial [tịŋktórịạl], *a.* tintóreo.

tincture [tịŋkchụ(r)]. I. *s.* tintura, tinte; (farm.) tintura; (fig.) baño, gusto, gustillo.—**t. of iron, u of steel**, solución alcohólica de cloruro de hierro. II. *va.* teñir, colorar, tinturar; impregnar, imbuir.

tinder [tịndœ(r)], *s.* yesca; mecha.

tinderbox [-baks], *s.* yesquero.

tine [taịn], *s.* púa, punta; diente (de tenedor).

tinea [tịnịạ], *s.* (med.) tiña. *V.* RINGWORM.

ting [tịŋ]. I. *va. y vn.* retiñir. II. *s.* retintín.— **t.-a-ling**, tilín tilín.

tinge [tịndž]. I. *va.* colorar, teñir, matizar. II. *s.* tinte, matiz, *m.*; gustillo, dejo.

tingle [tịŋgl]. I. *vn. y va.* sentir o producir hormigueo o picazón; zumbar los oídos. II. *s.* picazón, *f.*, hormigueo, comezón, *f.*; retintín.

tinker [tịŋkœ(r)]. I. *va. y vn.* desabollar; chafallar (fam.), remendar chapuceramente. II. *s.* latonero; calderero remendón; desabollador.—**not to be worth, o care, a tinker's dam(n)**, no valer, o importarle a uno, un pito.

tinkle [tịŋkl]. I. *va.* hacer retiñir. II. *vn.* retiñir, tintin(e)ar; campanillear; (fam.) cencerrear (esp. en la guitarra); (raro) zumbar los oídos. III. *s.* = TINKLING.

tinkling [tịŋklịŋ], *s.* (re)tintín, tintineo.

tinman [tịnmæn], *s.* hojalatero, estañero.

tinned [tịnd], *pp. y a.* cubierto o bañado con estaño.—**t. goods**, conservas alimenticias en latas.

tinner [tịnœ(r)], *s.* minero de estaño; hojalatero, estañero; (Ingl.) el que envasa o enlata conservas.

tinny [tịnị], *a.* de estaño.

tinsel [tịnsẹl]. I. *s.* oropel, relumbrón; talco; lentejuelas; (tej.) lama de oro o plata, brocadillo; restaño. II. *a.* de oropel; de relumbrón. III. *va.* adornar con oropel.

tinsmith [tịnsmịθ], *s.* hojalatero, estañero.

tint [tịnt]. I. *va.* teñir, colorar, matizar. II. *s.* tinte, color, matiz, *m.*; (b. a.) media tinta.

tintinnabulation [tịntịnæbyụléịṣọn], *s.* retintín, campanilleo.—**tintinnabulum** [-næbyụlᴧm], *s.* campanilla.

tintype [tịntaịp], *s.* (foto.) ferrotipo.

tinware [tịnwer], *s.* efectos de hojalata.

tinwork [tịnwœrk], *s.* hojalatería.

tiny [taịnị], *a.* chiquitico, menudo, minúsculo.

tip [tịp]. I. *s.* punta, extremidad, cabo; casquillo, regatón, virola, contera (de bastón, etc.); yema (del dedo); (zap.) puntera, bigotera; propina, gratificación; aviso confidencial, informe dado a veces anónimamente o por debajo de cuerda; palmadita, golpecito.—**from t. to t.**, de extremo a extremo.—**from t. to toe**, de pies a cabeza.—**on the t. of one's tongue**, en la punta de la lengua.—**to have at the tips of one's fingers**, saber al dedillo. II. *va.* ladear, inclinar, voltear; dar un golpecito a; dar propina a; informar por debajo de cuerda; guarnecer; poner regatón a.—**to t. off,** (fam.) advertir en confianza o en secreto.—**to t. over,** volcar. **III.** *vn.* ladearse, inclinarse; dar propina.

tipcart [-kart], *s.* carro de vuelco, volquete.

tip-off [típ ɔf], *s.* (fam.) advertencia secreta.

tippet [típit], *s.* palatina, esclavina; boa, *m.*

tipple [típl]. **I.** *va.* y *vn.* beber con exceso, empinar el codo. **II.** *va.* (mec.) volcar, vaciar. **III.** *s.* bebida, licor; mecanismo de vuelco.—**tippling house,** taberna, bodegón.

tippler [típlœ(r)], *s.* bebedor, borrachón.

tipsily [típsịlị], *adv.* como borracho.—**tipsiness** [-nịs], *s.* borrachera, embriaguez, chispa.

tipstaff [típstæf], *s.* alguacil de vara, ministril; vara de justicia.

tipsy [típsị], *a.* achispado, calamocano; vacilante.

tiptoe [típtou]. **I.** *s.* punta del pie.—**on t.,** de o en puntillas; ansioso. **II.** *vn.* andar de puntillas.

tiptop [típtáp]. **I.** *a.* (fam.) lo mejor de su clase, de primera, excelente. **II.** *s.* cumbre, cima.

tirade [tájreịd], *s.* diatriba, andanada, invectiva.

tire [tájr]. **I.** *s.* (carr.) llanta; calce; (aut.) neumático, llanta, goma, bandaje.—**t.** chain = SKID CHAIN.—**t. pump,** (Am.) inflador. **II.** *va.* cansar, fatigar; aburrir, fastidiar; (carr.) poner llantas.—**to t. out,** rendir de cansancio. **III.** *vn.* cansarse; aburrirse, fastidiarse.

tired [-d], *pp.* y *a.* provisto de llantas; cansado, fatigado; aburrido.—**t. feeling,** lasitud, flojedad.—**t. out,** agotado, rendido de cansancio.

tiredness [-dnịs], *s.* cansancio, fatiga, lasitud.

tireless [-lịs], *a.* infatigable, incansable; sin llanta. —**tiresome** [-sʌm], **tiring** [-iŋ], *a.* tedioso, cansado, pesado, aburrido(r).—**tiresomeness** [-nịs], *s.* tedio, fastidio, aburrimiento.

'tis [tịz], *abreviatura de* IT IS.

tisane [tizán], *s.* (farm.) tisana.

tissue [tíšụ]. **I.** *s.* (biol.) tejido; (tej.) gasa, tisú, gloria, lama; (fig.) serie conexa, encadenamiento.—**t. paper,** papel de seda.—**a t. of lies,** un tejido de mentiras. **II.** *va.* entretejer.

tit [tịt], *s.* (orn.) paro; pezón, teta; jaca, caballito; golpecito.—**t. for tat,** taz a taz, taz por taz; tal para cual; pata es la traviesa.—**to give t. for tat,** rechazar o volver la pelota.

Titan [tájṭan], *s.* (mit.) titán; (t.) gigante.

titanate [tájṭaneịt], *s.* (quím.) titanato.

titanic [tajtǽnịk], *a.* titánico, gigantesco; (quím.) titánico; (T.) titánico, titanio.

titanium [tajtéịnịʌm], *s.* (quím.) titanio.

titbit [títbịt], *s.* = TIDBIT.

titer, titre [tájtœ(r)], *s.* (quím., fisiol.) concentración de una solución, determinada por análisis volumétrico; temperatura de solidificación.—**t. test,** determinación de la temperatura de solidificación.

tithable [tájðạbl], *a.* diezmable.—**tithe** [tájð]. **I.** *s.* diezmo; décima parte; minucia, chispa; pizca.—**t. free,** exento de diezmo. **II.** *va.* diezmar.—**tither** [-œ(r)], *s.* diezmero.—**tithing** [-iŋ], *s.* diezmo; (Ingl., for.) decena de vecinos.—**tithingman** [-man], *s.* (Ingl.) cabeza del *tithing.*

titi [títị], *s.* (zool.) tití.

titillate [títịleịt], **I.** *va.* cosquillear, hacer cosquillas; causar placer, dar gusto. **II.** *vn.* titilar.

titillation [-léịšọn], *s.* titilación; cosquilleo; sensación agradable.

titlark [títlark], *s.* (orn.) especie de alondra.

title [tájtl]. **I.** *s.* título; calificativo; tratamiento; rótulo, inscripción; (for.) título, derecho.—**t. by occupancy,** derecho del primer ocupante.— **t. deed,** (for.) título.—**t. page,** portada. **II.** *va.* (in)titular; conferir título a; rotular.—**titled** [-d], *a.* de título, que tiene título.—**t. person,** título.—**titleless** [-lịs], *a.* sin título.

titling [tájtlịŋ], *s.* acción de (in)titular, etc.

titmouse [títmaµs], *s.* (orn.) paro.

titrate [tájtreịt], *va.* (quím.) graduar o determinar por análisis volumétrico; titular, dosificar.—**to**

t. against, analizar volumétricamente, o dosificar, por comparación con.—**titration** [tajtréịšọn], *s.* análisis volumétrico, titulación.

titrimetry [tajtrímetrị], *s.* (quím.) análisis volumétrico.

titter [tíṭœ(r)], *vn.* reír entre dientes. *V.* GIGGLE y SNICKER.—**titter(ing** [-iŋ], *s.* risita entre dientes; retozo de la risa.—**titterer** [-œ(r)], *s.* el que ríe entre dientes.

tittle [títl], *s.* tilde, vírgula; ápice, jota.

tittle-tattle [-tǽtl]. **I.** *s.* charla ociosa o chismera; chisme, chismografía, murmuración; chismoso. **II.** *vn.* chacharear; chismear, comadrear. *V.* TATTLE.

tittle-tattler [-tǽtlœ(r)], *s.* chacharero; chismoso.

tit(t)up [títʌp]. **I.** *vn.* corvetear, cabriolar. **II.** *s.* cabriola, brinco de contento.

titubation [tịchubéịšọn], *s.* (med.) titubeo, tambaleo, andar vacilante, inestabilidad.

titular [tíchụlá(r)]. **I.** *a.* titular; nominal. **II.** *s.* titular.—**titularly** [-lị], *adv.* con sólo el título. —**titulary** [-ị]. **I.** *a.* titular. **II.** *s.* el que tiene título o derecho a alguna cosa.

to [tu]. **I.** *adv.* hacia el fin que se persigue; en la posición o dirección que conviene (*to lie to,* (mar.) ponerse a la capa); en o al estado normal (*he came to,* volvió en sí).—**t. and fro,** de un lado a otro, de acá para allá.—**t.-and-fro motion,** vaivén. **II.** *prep.* a, en dirección a; hasta, hacia; para. Antepuesto al nombre o pronombre después de verbos de movimiento, dirección, unión, pertenencia, preferencia o atención, se traduce por "a" (*give it to him,* dáselo a él; *I go to London,* voy a Londres; *it belongs to Peter,* pertenece a Pedro; *I prefer this book to mine,* prefiero este libro al mío). Cuando denota la intención o fin con que se ejecuta algo, o después de un participio pasivo o de un adjetivo, corresponde a "para," "por" o "a" en castellano (*he came only to see me,* vino sólo por verme, a verme, o para verme; *born to die,* nacido para morir; *ready to go out,* dispuesto para salir). Cuando expresa obligación o acción futura, se traduce por "que," "por" o "de" (*I have to go,* tengo que irme; *I have much to do,* tengo mucho que hacer; *much remains to be done,* queda mucho por hacer; *he is to come,* ha de venir). En otros casos se traduce de varios modos difíciles de clasificar, como en los siguientes ejemplos: *to my great surprise,* con gran sorpresa mía; *from door to door,* de puerta en puerta; *ten minutes to nine,* las nueve menos diez minutos; *he is a friend to the poor,* es amigo de los pobres; *King Philip II was son and successor to Charles V,* el rey Felipe II fué hijo y sucesor de Carlos V. **III.** partícula que sirve para indicar el infinitivo, y cuando no se traduce (*he wishes to go,* desea ir; *the verb "to go,"* el verbo "ir"; *to be or not to be,* ser o no ser).

toad [tóµd], *s.* (zool.) sapo, escuerzo.

toadeater [-itœ(r)], *s.* parásito adulador y servil, sicofante; (fam.) pegote.—**toadeating** [-itịŋ]. **I.** *s.* parasitismo servil. **II.** *a.* adulador, servil y parásito.

toadflax [-flæks], *s.* (bot.) linaria, lino bastardo.

toadstone [-stoµn], *s.* (min.) estel(i)ón, *m.*

toadstool [-stul], *s.* (bot.) hongo; seta venenosa (gen. se usa en el segundo sentido).

toady [-ị]. **I.** *va.* y *vn.* adular servilmente; ser zalamero. **II.** *s.* adulador, (fam.) quitamotas.

toast [tóµst]. **I.** *va.* tostar; brindar por. **II.** *vn.* tostarse; calentarse; brindar, beber a la salud de. **III.** *s.* tostada; brindis, *m.*—**t. water,** agua panada.—**to return a t.,** hacer la razón.

toasted [-ịd], *a.* tostado.—**t. bread,** tostada.

toaster [-œ(r)], *s.* brindador, el que brinda; tostador; tostadera, parrilla.

toasting [-iŋ]. **I.** *a.* de tostar.—**t. fork,** horquilla de tostar; (fam.) espada. **II.** *s.* tostadura, tostado, tueste.

toastmaster [-mæstœ(r)], *s.* el que propone los

brindis en un banquete, o que presenta a los oradores de sobremesa; maestro de ceremonias.

tobacco [tobǽkou], s. (bot.) tabaco.—**t. box**, tabaquera.—**t. field**, tabacal.—**t. heart**, (med.) afección cardíaca debida al abuso del tabaco.—**t.-pipe clay**, tierra de pipa.—**t. plantation**, vega de tabaco, tabacal.—**t. pouch**, bolsa para tabaco, (Am.) tabaquera.—**t. shop** o **store**, tabaquería, estanco, estanquillo, expendeduría de tabaco.—**t. worm**, (ent.) oruga del tabaco.

tobaccoism [-iẓm], s. (med.) tabaquismo.

tobacconist [-oniṣt], s. fabricante de tabaco; tabaquero, estanquero.

tobacconize [-onaiẓ], va. fumigar con tabaco.

toboggan [tobǽgan]. **I.** s. (dep.) tobogán, especie de trineo plano y sin rieles.—**t. slide**, tobogán, pendiente (f.) natural o artificial para deslizarse. **II.** vn. deslizarse en tobogán; bajar rápidamente (los valores).

toby [tóubi], s. pichel, vaso grande, gen. en forma de hombre; (fam.) cigarro delgado y barato.

tocsin [táksin], s. rebato; toque a rebato.

today, to-day [tudéi], s. y adv. hoy; hoy (en) día.

toddle [tádl]. **I.** vn. hacer pinitos. **II.** s. pinitos.—**toddler** [tádlœr], s. el que hace pinitos.

toddy [tádi], s. ponche; vino de palmera.

to-do [tudú], s. (fam.) baraúnda, alharaca.

tody [tóudi], s. (orn.) pajarillo verde antillano.

toe [tóu]. **I.** s. dedo del pie; uña o pezuña; punta del pie (de media, del calzado); pie, base, f. (de un terraplén, etc.); (mec.) saliente, f., brazo.—**t. cap**, o **piece**, (zap.) puntera.—**t. clip**, estribo de bicicleta.—**toe-in**, (mec.) convergencia (de una rueda).—**toes up**, muerto.—**great t.**, dedo gordo del pie.—**five-toed**, que tiene cinco dedos.—**to be on one's toes**, estar alerta, activo o despabilado.—**to turn up one's toes**, morir. **II.** va. tocar con la punta del pie; dar un puntapié; (zap.) poner punteras; (carp.) clavar oblicuamente; asegurar con clavos un puntal.—**to t. the line** o **mark**, estar o ponerse en la raya o punto de partida; obrar como se debe; hacerlo bien. **III.** vn. **to t. in**, andar con las puntas de los pies hacia adentro; (mec.) convergir (una rueda).

toenail [-neil], s. uña de los dedos del pie.

toffee, toffy [tɔfi o táfi], s. = **TAFFY**.

tog [tag]. **I.** s. (fam.) trapo, prenda de vestir.—pl. ropa, trapos. **II.** va., vn., y vr. (gen. con **out** o **up**) (fam.) acicalar(se), poner(se) majo, engalanar(se).

toga [tóugǝ], s. toga.—**t. virilis**, toga viril.

togaed [-d], **togated** [-tid], a. togado.

together [tugéðœr)]. **I.** adv. juntamente, de consuno; a un tiempo, simultáneamente; de continuo, de seguida, sin interrupción.—**t. with**, a una con, juntos; junto con. **II.** a. juntos.

toggery [tágœri], s. (fam.) ropa, trapos, pl.; arreos.

toggle [tágl], s. (mar.) cazonete; (mec.) palanca acodillada.—**t. bolt**, tornillo con fiador giratorio en T.—**t. joint**, junta de codillo.—**t. switch**, interruptor de presión.

toil [tɔil]. **I.** vn. trabajar asiduamente, afanarse, atrafagar; moverse con dificultad. **II.** va. labrar o conseguir a duras penas. **III.** s. faena, trabajo; pena, fatiga, afán; obra laboriosa; (fig.) (gen. pl.) red, lazo.

toilet [tóilit], s. acto de vestirse; tocado, vestido, atavío; tocador; excusado, retrete; (cir.) limpiadura de una herida.—**t. case**, neceser.—**t. paper** o **tissue**, papel higiénico.—**t. powder**, polvos, m. pl.—**t. room**, tocador; retrete, (lugar) excusado.—**t. set**, juego de tocador.—**t. soap**, jabón de olor, jaboncillo.—**t. water**, (agua de) Colonia.

toilful [tóilful], a. trabajoso, afanoso.

toilsome [tóilsʌm], a. laborioso, trabajoso; penoso.—**toilsomely** [-li], adv. laboriosamente; fatigosamente.—**toilsomeness** [-nis], s. calidad de laborioso o fatigoso; laboriosidad, fatiga.

Tokay [toukéi], s. uva o vino de Tokay.

token [tóukn], s. señal, f., muestra, prueba; prenda, recuerdo; medalla; tanto, ficha (en ciertos juegos); disco metálico (usado en los tranvías, etc.); (hist. rom.) tésera; distintivo, rasgo característico; (impr.) tirada de 250 impresiones.—**t. money**, moneda divisionaria. (En los E. U., monedas inferiores al dólar).—**t. payment**, pago parcial en señal de buena fe y de adeudo.—**as a t. of**, en señal o en prenda de.

told [tould], pret. y pp. de **TO TELL**.

Toledan [tolídan], a. y s. toledano.

tolerable [tálǝrabl], a. tolerable, sufrible, llevadero; mediano, pasadero.—**tolerableness** [-nis], s. calidad de tolerable o mediano.—**tolerably** [-bli], adv. tolerablemente; medianamente.

tolerance [tálǝrans], s. tolerancia; (tecn.) tolerancia, discrepancia permitida.—**tolerant** [-ant], a. tolerante.—**tolerate** [-eit], va. tolerar, sufrir; consentir, permitir.—**toleration** [-éiʃǝn], s. tolerancia, indulgencia; tolerantismo.

tolidin(e [tálidin], s. (quím.) tolidina.

toll [tóul]. **I.** s. peaje, portazgo, pontazgo, pontaje, puerta; derecho de molienda; (fig.) pérdida, sacrificio, número de víctimas (en una batalla, siniestro, etc.); tañido o doble de las campanas.—**t. bridge**, puente de peaje.—**t. call**, llamada telefónica de larga distancia.—**t. collector** = **TOLLMAN**.—**t. corn**, maquila de molinero.—**to take a heavy t.**, (fig.) costar caro (en víctimas, etc.). **II.** va. y vn. cobrar o pagar peaje o portazgo; tañer, tocar o doblar (la campana); atraer.—**to t. the hour**, dar la hora.—**to t. the passing bell**, doblar, tocar a muerto.

tollage [-idʒ], s. peaje.

tollbooth [-buθ], s. caseta de peaje, garita en que se cobra el portazgo; (Esco.) casa consistorial, casa de ayuntamiento; calabozo.

toller [-œr), s. campanero. V. **TOLLMAN**.

tollgate [-geit], s. barrera de peaje.

tollgatherer [-gæðœroœr)], s. = **TOLLMAN**.

tollhouse [-haus], s. oficina de portazgos.

tollkeeper [-kipœr)], s. = **TOLLMAN**.

tollman [-man], s. peajero, portazguero.

Toltec [táltek], a. y s. tolteca, mf.

tolu [tolú], s. bálsamo de tolú.—**t. tree**, (bot.) árbol de tolú.

toluate [tályueit], s. (quím.) toluato.—**toluene** [tályuin], s. tolueno.—**toluic** [tályuik], a. tolúico (ácido).—**toluidin(e** [tolúidin], s. (quím.) toluidina.

tom [tam], s. macho de algunos animales.—**Tom, Dick and Harry**, (fam.) Fulano, Zutano y Mengano.

tomahawk [támahɔk]. **I.** s. (E. U.) hacha de guerra de los indios.—**to bury the t.**, enviar la espada (fig.), hacer la paz.—**to dig up the t.**, desenvainar la espada (fig.), declarar la guerra. **II.** va. herir con tomahawk.

tomato [toméitou], s. (bot.) tomate.—**t. plant**, tomatera.

tomb [tum], s. tumba, sepulcro, sepultura, enterramiento.—**The Tombs**, una cárcel de Nueva York.

tombac [támbæk], s. tombac, latón de 90% de cobre y 10% de cinc; (joy.) tumbaga, liga metálica de oro y de cobre.

tombless [túmlis], a. sin sepulcro.

tomblike [túmlaik], a. sepulcral, como la tumba.

tomboy [támbɔi], s. moza retozona.

tombstone [túmstoun], s. lápida o piedra sepulcral.

tomcat [támkæt], s. gato (macho).

tomcod [támkad], s. (ict.) pez (m.) semejante al bacalao.

tome [toum], s. tomo, volumen.

tomentose [toméntous], a. (bot.) tomentoso.—**tomentum** [toméntʌm], s. (bot.) tomento.

tomfool [tamfúl], s. necio, mentecato; payaso.—**tomfoolery** [-œri], **tomfoolishness** [-iʃnis], s. necedad, mentecatada; payasada.

---

tommy-gun [támiɡʌn], *s.* (mil.) ametralladora ligera.

tommyrot [-rat], *s.* (fam.) tontería, música celestial.

to-morrow, tomorrow [tumárou], *s.* y *adv.* mañana.—**t. afternoon, morning, noon, night,** mañana por la tarde, por la mañana, al mediodía, por la noche.—**day after t.,** pasado mañana.

tompion [támpiọn], *s.* (arti.) tapabocas (*v.* TAMPION); (impr.) rodillo.

tomtit [támtịt], *s.* (orn.) paro. *V.* TIT(MOUSE).

tom-tom [támtam], *s.* especie de tambor indio u oriental; tamtám o tantán, gongo(m), batintín. *V.* TAM-TAM.

ton [tʌn], *s.* tonelada.—**t.-mile,** tonelada-milla, transporte de 1 tonelada a 1 milla de distancia.

tonal [tóunạl], *a.* (mús.) tonal.

tonality [tounélitị], *s.* tonalidad.

tone [toun]. I. *s.* tono; sonido, metal o timbre de la voz; (mús., pint., med.) tono; entonación, tonillo, sonsonete; (gram.) acento, inflexión; carácter, substancia (de un escrito, etc.).—**t. poem,** (mús.) poema sinfónico.—**t. wheel,** (rad.) disco conmutador de audiofrecuencia. II. *va.* dar o modificar el tono, entonar; templar, afinar.—**to t. down,** (pint.) suavizar el tono; (mús.) amortiguar el sonido; modificar la expresión.—**to t. up,** vigorizar, robustecer; subir de tono; (med.) entonar, tonificar. III. *vn.* corresponder en tono o matiz.

tongs [taŋz], *s. pl.* tenazas, tenacillas, mordazas, pinzas, alicates.

tongue [tʌŋ]. I. *s.* (anat.) lengua; lenguaje, lengua, idioma, *m.;* (mús.) lengüeta; (mec. y carp.) espiga, lengüeta; lengüeta de zapato; clavillo de hebilla; lengua de tierra; badajo de campana; (f. c.) carril movible (de un cambio).—**t.-and-groove joint,** (carp.) unión machihembrada.—**t.-and-lip joint,** empalme de espiga.—**t. grafting,** (agr.) injerto de lengüeta.—**t.-tie,** (med.) anquiloglosis, adherencia de la lengua, impedimento en el habla debido esp. a la cortedad anormal del frenillo.—**t.-tied,** que tiene impedimento en el habla; mudo, cortado, tímido.—**t. twister,** trabalenguas.—**t. worm,** (vet.) landrilla.—**to give t.,** ladrar. II. *va.* dar voz o expresión a; (mús.) tomar la embocadura; (carp.) engargolar, machihembrar.—**to t.-tie,** hacer callar.—**to hold one's t.,** callar(se). III. *vn.* (mús.) tener embocadura; usar la lengua, hablar.

tongued [-d], *a.* que tiene lengua o lengüeta.

tongueless [-lịs], *a.* mudo, sin habla; deslenguado; turbado.

tonic [tánịk]. I. *a.* (med.) tónico, tonificador, tonificante; (mús.) tónico; tenso, rígido, tieso.—**t. accent,** (fon., pros.) acento tónico. II. *s.* (med.) tónico, cordial; (mús.) tónica o dominante, *f.*

tonicity [tounísịtị], *s.* (fisiol.) tonicidad.

tonight, to-night [tunáịt], *adv.* y *s.* esta noche; durante esta noche.

toning [tóunịŋ], *s.* entonación.

tonka bean [táŋkạ bín], *s.* (bot.) sarapia, (Am.) cumarú; haba tonca (semilla de la sarapia).

tonnage [tánịdʒ], *s.* tonelaje, porte o arqueo; (com.) derechos de tonelaje.

tonsil [tánsịl], *s.* (anat.) tonsila, amígdala.

tonsil(l)itis [-áịtịs], *s.* (med.) tonsilitis, amigdalitis.

tonsil(l)ectomy [-éktomị], **tonsil(l)otomy** [-átomị], *s.* (cir.) tonsilectomía, amigdalotomía, ablación de las amígdalas.

tonsorial [tansórịạl], *a.* barberil.

tonsure [tánšụ(r)]. I. *s.* (igl.), tonsura, corona. II. *va.* tonsurar.

tontine [tántịn], *s.* tontina.

tonus [tóunʌs], *s.* (fisiol.) tonicidad; tono; (pat.) espasmo muscular.

too [tu], *adv.* demasiado, demasiadamente; además; asimismo, también.—**t. many,** demasiados.—**t. much,** demasiado, excesivo; excesivamente.—**to be t. much for one,** no poder uno con; no poder aguantar más; ser el colmo; no entrarle a uno, parecerle increíble. Como la frase "un poco demasiado" no es usual en español, **a little t., a little t. much,** etc., se traducen cambiando el giro: *he came a little too early,* vino un poco antes de lo que convenía, un poco anticipadamente, un poco temprano, etc.; *you went a little too far,* Vd. se pasó un poco, Vd. se excedió un poco, etc.; *he spoke a little too long,* habló un poco más de lo que convenía, su discurso se pasó un poco de largo, etc.—**(it is) t. bad,** es lástima, es de sentirse.—**t. (funny, strange, etc.) for words,** inmensamente (chistoso, extraño, etc.), lo más . . . del mundo.—**but t.,** desgraciadamente; muy, sumamente.—**none t., not t.,** no muy, que a duras penas puede llamarse (bueno, eficaz, etc.).—**only t.** = BUT T. (*V.* t. ALL TOO.)

took [tuk], *pret.* de TO TAKE.

tool [tul]. I. *va.* y *vn.* labrar con herramienta; filetear; (enc.) relevar. II. *s.* herramienta, utensilio o instrumento; persona que sirve de instrumento a otra;—*pl.* útiles, bártulos, aperos.—**t. bag, t. chest,** barjuleta, herramental, bolsa de herramientas.—**t. steel,** acero de herramientas.

toot [tut]. I. *va.* y *vn.* tocar el cuerno de caza, un instrumento de viento, una bocina o un silbato.—**to t. one's own horn,** alabarse. II. *s.* sonido de trompa, pitazo, bocinazo, etc.—**to go on a t.,** (fam.) ir de parranda.

tooth [tuθ]. I. *s.* (*pl.* TEETH) diente, muela; (mec.) diente de sierra o de rueda; (mec.) leva, cama; púa (de un peine o carda); mella; gusto, paladar.—**t. and nail,** con todo tesón, con empeño.—**t. decay,** caries (*f.*) dental.—**t. extraction,** avulsión dentaria.—**t. paste,** pasta o crema dentífrica.—**t. powder,** polvo dentífrico.—**decayed tooth,** diente cariado.—**to have a sweet t.,** ser muy goloso, gustar de los dulces. II. *va.* (en)dentar; mellar. III. *vn.* (mec.) engranar, endentar, engargantar.

toothache [-eịk], *s.* dolor de diente o de muelas.

toothbrush [-braš], *s.* cepillo de dientes.

toothed [-t], *a.* dentado, serrado, dentellado.—**t. bar,** cremallera.—**t. wheel,** rueda dentada.

toothless [-lịs], *a.* desdentado, edentado.

toothpick [-pịk], *s.* mondadientes, limpiadientes, palillo.—**t. case o holder,** palillero.

toothshell [-šel], *s.* concha parecida a un diente.

toothsome [-sam], *a.* sabroso.—**toothsomeness** [-nịs], *s.* sabor agradable.

toothwort [-wœrt], *s.* (bot.) dentaria.

top [tap]. I. *s.* cima, cumbre, pico, cúspide, *f.,* vértice, cabeza, cresta (de una montaña); ápice, punta, remate; parte (*f.*) superior o parte de arriba; superficie; cabeza (de una página); tabla (de mesa); coronilla (de la cabeza); coronamiento (de pared); copa (de árbol); cielo (de cama, coche, etc.); auge, apogeo; primer puesto, último grado; copete, tupé; trompo, peonza, peón (juguete); (carr.) fuelle; (aut.) capota; (mar.) cofa; tope.—**t.-armor,** (mar.) empavesadas de cofas.—**t. boots,** botas de campaña, botas de librea.—**t. cross,** cruzamiento de una raza inferior con una superior.—**t.-dress,** *va.* (agr.) abonar la superficie del suelo.—**t.-dressing,** abono aplicado a la superficie.—**t. grafting,** (agr.) modo de injertar en que el injerto se introduce en la copa o las ramas del patrón.—**t. hat,** (fam.) sombrero de copa, chistera.—**t.-heavy,** demasiado pesado o grande por arriba; mal proporcionado, organizado o distribuído; que tiene demasiado personal dirigente.—**t. light,** (mar.) farol de la cofa; (arq.) claraboya, tragaluz; luz cenital.—**t. of the skull,** (anat.) tapa de los sesos.—**t. tackle,** (mar.) aparejo de virador.—**t.-timber,**

(mar.) barraganete.—**at, o from, the top,** por arriba.—**from t. to bottom,** de arriba abajo; completamente.—**from t. to toe,** de pies a cabeza, de alto abajo.—**on t.,** con éxito; victorioso.—**on t. of,** encima de, sobre.—**over the t.,** (mil.) a la carga, al ataque, saliendo de las trincheras.—**the t. of the world,** (fam.) "el tejado del mundo," el polo.—**to come out on t.,** (fam.) salir sobresaliente.—**to go over the t.,** (mil.) irrumpir fuera de las trincheras para dar el asalto; (fig.) recaudar todos los fondos asignados en una colecta. **II.** a. superior, más alto; primero, principal.—**t.-flight,** t.-notch, (fam.) de primera fila o línea, preeminente, sobresaliente.—**t.-ranking,** de primer rango. **III.** va. descabezar, desmochar (un árbol, etc.); cubrir, coronar, rematar; llegar a la cima de, coronar; sobrepujar, sobrepasar, aventajar, exceder.—**to t. a yard,** (mar.) embicar, amantillar una verga.—**to t. off,** rematar; terminar. **IV.** vn. erguirse, ser eminente; sobresalir; predominar.—**to t. off with,** terminar con.

topaz [tóupæz], s. (joy.) topacio; (orn.) colibrí.

topcoat [tápkout], s. saco; sobretodo, abrigo ligero, gabán de entretiempo.

tope [toup]. **I.** vn. excederse en la bebida. **II.** s. altar, monumento o bóveda budista.

toper [tóupœ(r)], s. borrachín, bebedor, (fam.) cuba.

topfull [tápfúl], a. lleno hasta los bordes.

topgallant [tapgǽlant], s. (mar.) juanete.

toph(e) [touf], s. (geol.) toba, tosca, tufa.

tophaceous [taféjʃas], a. arenoso, áspero.

tophus [tóufʌs], s. (med.) tofo, nodo; (dent.) sarro.

topic [tápik], s. asunto, materia, tema, m.—pl. (ret.) lugares comunes, tópicos.—**topic**(al [-(al], a. tópico; local, limitado.—**topically** [-li], adv. localmente.

topknot [tápnat], s. moño alto, tupé, copete.

toplofty [táplófti], a. (fam.) pomposo, hinchado.

topman [tápman], s. aserrador de arriba; (mar.) gaviero.

topmast [tápmæst], s. (mar.) mastelero.

topmost [tápmoust], a. el más alto; de la cima o cumbre, de coronamiento.—**to be t.,** o the tops, (fam.) descollar sobre todos los otros; ser flor.

topographer [tapágrafœ(r)], s. topógrafo.—**topographical**(al [tapográfjk(al], a. topográfico.—**topographically** [-i], adv. topográficamente.—**topography** [topágrafi], s. topografía.

toponymy [topánimi], s. toponimia.

topping [tápiŋ]. **I.** a. eminente, distinguido; (fam.) excelente, magnífico; (fam.) empingorotado, empenachado, arrogante; de excelente salud.—**t. lift,** (mar.) perigallo. **II.** s. cubierta; punta, extremidad, cabo.

topple [tápl]. **I.** va. hacer caer, derribar, volcar. **II.** vn. (a veces con **over**) volcarse, venirse abajo.

topsail [tápseil], s. gavia.—**t. sheets,** escotines.

topsoil [tápsoil]. **I.** s. capa superior del suelo (a distinción del subsuelo). **II.** va. quitar la capa superior.

topsy-turvy [tápsitœrvi]. **I.** adv. y a. trastornado, desbarajustado, patas arriba. **II.** s. confusión.

toque [touk], s. cofia, toca.

tor [tɔr], s. tormo.

Torah [tóurǎ], s. Tora, Libro de la Ley (entre los judíos)—es el Pentateuco.

torch [tɔrch], s. tea; antorcha, hacha.—**t. holder,** tedero.—**t. thistle,** (bot.) céreo, cirio.—**torchbearer** [-berœ(r)], s. hachero, portahachón.—**torchlight** [-lait], s. luz de antorcha.

tore [tɔr]. **I.** pret. de TO TEAR. **II.** s. = TORUS.

toreador [tóriadɔr], s. toreador, torero.

torment [tɔrmént]. **I.** va. atormentar, dar tormento, torturar; afligir. **II.** [tɔrment] s. tormento, suplicio, tortura; pena, angustia.

tormenter, o **tormentor** [tɔrméntœ(r)], s. atormentador.

tormentil [tɔrmentil], s. (bot.) tormentila.

tormenting [tɔrmentiŋ], a. atormentador.

tormentingly [-li], adv. atormentadoramente, de modo atormentador.

torn [tɔrn], pp. de TO TEAR: roto, rasgado.

tornado [tɔrnéidou], s. tornado, huracán.

torpedo [tɔrpídou]. **I.** s. (pl. TORPEDOES) torpedo; (ict.) torpedo, tremielga, tembladera; (aut.) torpedo.—**t. boat,** torpedero.—**t.-boat destroyer,** cazatorpedero, contratorpedero.—**t.-plane,** (hidro)avión (m.) torpedero.—**t. tube,** tubo o cañón lanzatorpedos. **II.** va. torpedear. **III.** a. (aut.) torpedo (carrocería).—**torpedoing** [-iŋ], s. torpede(amient)o.

torpid [tɔrpid], a. torpe; entorpecido; adormecido, aletargado.—**torpidity** [tɔrpíditi], **torpidness** [tɔrpidnis], s. entorpecimiento, embotamiento; apatía, pesadez.—**torpor** [tɔrpɔ(r)], s. torpor, torpeza; entorpecimiento; adormecimiento; letargo, apatía, estupor.

torque [tɔrk], s. (joy.) collar; (fís., mec., elec.) momento o fuerza de torsión; impulsivo rotativo.

torrefaction [tarifǽkʃan], s. (farm.) torrefacción.—**torrefy** [tárifai], va. torrar, tostar.

torrent [tárent], s. torrente; raudal, agolpamiento.—**torrential** [tarénʃal], a. torrencial.

torrid [tárid], a. tórrido, tostado; abrasador, ardiente.—**T. Zone,** zona tórrida.

torridness [-nis], **torridity** [taríditi], s. calidad de tórrido o abrasador.

torsade [tɔrséid], s. torzal.

torsion [tɔrʃan], s. torcedura; torsión.—**t. balance,** (fís., elec.) balanza de torsión.—**torsional** [-al], a. de torsión.

torso [tɔrsou], s. torso.

tort [tɔrt], s. (for.) tuerto, agravio, sinrazón, f.

torticollis [tɔrtikális], s. (med.) torticolis, m.

tortile [tɔrtil], a. torcido, doblado.

tortoise [tɔrtis], s. (zool.) tortuga, galápago.—**t. shell,** carey, concha de tortuga.

tortuosity [tɔrchuásiti], **tortuousness** [tɔrchuʌsnis], s. tortuosidad, sinuosidad.—**tortuous** [tɔrchuʌs], a. tortuoso, torcido, sinuoso.

torture [tɔrchu(r)]. **I.** s. tortura, tormento, suplicio. **II.** va. torturar, dar tormento, atormentar; torcer o tergiversar.—**torturer** [-œ(r)], s. atormentador.

torus [tɔras], s. (arq.) torés, toro, bocel, collarino; (geom.) toro; (bot.) receptáculo (de una flor).

Tory [tɔri], s. (Ingl. pol.) tory, conservador.

Toryism [-izm], s. credo político del partido tory en Inglaterra, toryismo.

tosh [taʃ]. **I.** s. (fam. Ingl.) música celestial, tonterías, f. pl.; baño portátil. **II.** vn. bañarse.

toss [tɔs]. **I.** va. tirar, lanzar al aire; menear, agitar, mover, sacudir.—**to t. aside,** echar a un lado.—**to t. in a blanket,** mantear.—**to t. in,** o up, the sponge, darse por vencido; desistir.—**to t. oars,** arbolar los remos.—**to t. off,** tragar de golpe; echar a un lado, no hacer caso de; hacer sin esfuerzo ni esmero.—**to t. out,** derrocar (un gobierno, etc.). **II.** vn. ajetrearse; corcovear; mecerse, ondear.—**to t. for,** o t. up, echar o jugar a cara o cruz. **III.** s. meneo, sacudimiento, sacudida; lanzamiento; ajetreo; cara o cruz.—**t.-up,** cara y cruz; lance de resultado dudoso.

tot [tat], s. chiquitín, nene, nena, niño, niña.

total [tóutal]. **I.** a. total, entero, completo, cabal, global.—**t. abstinence,** abstinencia absoluta de bebidas alcohólicas.—**t. war,** la guerra total. **II.** s. tocal(idad), suma; (arit.) suma. **III.** va. y vn. sumar, ascender a; totalizar.

totalitarian [toutælitérian], s. y a. totalitario.—**totalitarianism** [-izm], s. totalitarismo.

totality [toutǽliti], s. totalidad.

totalize [tóutalaiz], va. totalizar, hacer la suma de.

totalizer [-œ(r)], **totalizator** [-éi̯tǫ(r)], *s.* (aparato) totalizador (ú. esp. para registrar apuestas en las carreras de caballo).

totally [tóu̯t̬ǫli̯], *adv.* totalmente.

tote [tou̯t], *va.* (fam.) cargar, llevar sobre los hombros o en los brazos; transportar.

totem [tóu̯t̬ęm], *s.* totem, objeto o animal reverenciado por algunos salvajes como emblema (*m.*) o progenitor de la tribu.—**t. pole**, o **post**, pilar totémico, erigido por los indios de los E. U. y por otros pueblos primitivos con figuras totémicas pintadas y esculpidas.—**totemism** [-i̯zm], *s.* totemismo.

t'other [tʌ́ðœ(r)], *abrev.* de THE OTHER, el otro.

totter [tát̬œ(r)], *vn.* tambalear, temblar, vacilar.

tottering [-i̯ŋ]. **I.** *a.* vacilante, tambaleante; derruído, ruinoso. **II.** *s.* bamboleo, tambaleo.—**totteringly** [-li̯], *adv.* de modo vacilante, tambaleando.

toucan [túkæn], *s.* (orn.) tucán.

touch [tʌch]. **I.** *va.* tocar; tentar, palpar, manosear; rasar; alcanzar, herir; igualar, aproximarse a; ensayar, probar con la piedra de toque; (b. a.) delinear, esbozar; (mús.) pulsar, tañer o tocar (un instrumento); enternecer, (con)mover, afligir; irritar, aguijonear; tratar (un asunto); influir; tocar a, concernir, importar; (geom.) tocar, ser tangente a; aludir a, tratar por encima; afectar; (fam., a veces con for) dar un sablazo a, pedir prestado a; robar a.—**to t. off**, descargar (arma); hacer o acabar de prisa; bosquejar.—**to t. up**, retocar; corregir. **II.** *vn.* tocar(se); estar en contacto; imponer las manos para curar.—**to t. and go**, tratar de un asunto ligeramente.—**to t. at a port**, hacer escala en un puerto.—**to t. on**, o **upon**, tocar en; tratar ligeramente de; concernir; acercarse a. **III.** *s.* tacto (sentido); toque, tocamiento; tiento; contacto; (b. a.) toque, ejecución, pincelada, rasgo; retoque, última mano; (mús.) pulsación (de un instrumento); dolorcito, punzada; una sombra, un ápice; indirecta; buena inteligencia, armonía o correspondencia; ensayo de metales con la piedra de toque; prueba, examen; corazonada; (fam.) sablazo.—**t.-and-go**, montado al pelo; precario, incierto; ligero de cascos.—**t. paper**, (piro.) papel de salitre para cebo.—**in t. with**, en contacto, en comunicación o relaciones con; al corriente de.

touchable [-abl], *a.* tocable, tangible.

touchback [-bæk], *s.*, **touchdown** [-dau̯n], *s.* diversos lances del juego de football.

touchhole [-hou̯l], *s.* (arti.) fogón, oído del cañón.

touchily [-i̯li̯], *adv.* susceptiblemente.

touchiness [-i̯ni̯s], *s.* susceptibilidad, quisquillosidad.

touching [-i̯ŋ]. **I.** *prep.* tocante a, en cuanto a, acerca de. **II.** *a.* patético, conmovedor. **III.** *s.* toque, palpamiento; tacto; contacto.—**touchingly** [-li̯], *adv.* patéticamente, tiernamente.

touch-me-not [-mi̯ nat], *s.* (bot.) balsamina silvestre o del jardín; (med.) lupus, noli me tángere.

touchstone [-stou̯n], *s.* piedra de toque; examen, prueba; criterio.

touchwood [-wǫd], *s.* yesca; hupe, *f.*

touchy [-i̯], *a.* quisquilloso, susceptible.

tough [tʌf]. **I.** *a.* correoso, duro; vigoroso, de puños, (fam.) de pelo en pecho; resistente; testarudo, tenaz; flexible y fuerte; (metal.) trabajable; (fam.) difícil, penoso, arduo; rudo, vulgar.—**t. break**, **t. luck**, (fam.) mala pata o suerte. **II.** *s.* villano, malvado, rufián, truhán.

toughen [-n], *va.* y *vn.* hacer(se) correoso; endurecer(se).

toughly [-li̯], *adv.* tenazmente, etc.

toughness [-ni̯s], *s.* tenacidad; endurecimiento; tesura, rigidez; flexibilidad; resistencia; rudeza.

toupee, toupet [tupéi̯], *s.* tupé, copete.

tour [tųr]. **I.** *s.* viaje de turismo, excursión, recorrido, peregrinación; (neol.) jira de inspección; vuelta, circuito; turno. **II.** *va.* viajar por, recorrer. **III.** *vn.* viajar por distracción.—**touring** [-i̯ŋ]. **I.** *a.* turístico; de turismo (apl. esp. a coches automóviles). **II.** *s.* turismo.—**tourist** [-i̯st]. **I.** *a.* turístico, de turismo. **II.** *s.* turista, viajero.—**t. trade** o **traffic**, turismo.—**tourism** [-i̯zm], *s.* turismo.

tourmalin(e [tų́rmǝli̯n], *s.* turmalina, chorlo.

tournament [tų́rnǝmęnt], *s.* torneo, justa.

tourney [tų́rni̯]. **I.** *s.* torneo, justa. **II.** *vn.* justar.

tourniquet [tų́rnị̄kęt], *s.* (cir.) torniquete.

tousle [táu̯zl]. **I.** *va.* despeinar, desgreñar, alborotar (los cabellos). **II.** *s.* greña. *V.* TUSSLE.

tout [tau̯t]. **I.** *va.* y *vn.* espiar (apl. esp. a la observación clandestina de caballos de carrera, su manejo, etc.); solicitar parroquianos; dar bombo, bombear o elogiar con exageración. **II.** *s.* espía, *mf.*, acecho (espía que obtiene y vende informes relativos a carreras de caballos).

tow [tóu̯]. **I.** *s.* estopa; remolque; lo que va remolcado; atoaje.—**to take in t.**, atoar; encargarse de (algo o alguien), manejar. **II.** *va.* remolcar, atoar.

towage [-i̯dž], *s.* remolque, atoaje; derechos de remolque.

toward(s [tǫrd(z o tuwɔ́rd(z], *prep.* hacia; con, para con; cosa de, alrededor de; tocante a.

toward, towardly [tɔ́rd(li̯], *a.* que promete o da esperanza; apto; propicio; dócil, complaciente, deferente.—**toward(li)ness** [tɔ́rd(li̯)ni̯s], *s.* aptitud; calidad de propicio; docilidad, complacencia, deferencia.

towboat [tóu̯bou̯t], *s.* remolcador.

towel [táu̯l], *s.* toalla, paño de manos.—**t. rack**, toallero, colgador de toallas.

towel(l)ing [-i̯ŋ], *s.* género para toallas.

tower [táu̯œ(r)]. **I.** *s.* torre, *f.*, campanario; (mil.) torreón; ciudadela, fortaleza. **II.** *vn.* elevarse, remontarse; descollar, sobresalir, destacarse.—**towered** [-d], *a.* torreado, guarnecido de torres.—**towering** [-i̯ŋ], *a.* elevado; descollante, sobresaliente; dominante; violento.

towhead [tóu̯hęd], *s.* el que tiene los cabellos muy rubios, amarillentos o blanquecinos.—**towheaded** [-i̯d], *a.* pelirrubio.

towhee [táu̯hi̯ o tóu̯hi̯], *s.* (orn.) variedad de pinzón.

towing [tóu̯i̯ŋ], *s.* remolque, atoaje.

towline [tóu̯lai̯n], *s.* cable de remolque; (mar.) sirga; estacha, cable de arpón ballenero.

town [tau̯n], *s.* ciudad; villa; pueblo, aldea, lugar, poblado, población; municipio; la ciudad, el pueblo (*he is in town*, está en la ciudad).—**t. clerk**, secretario de ayuntamiento.—**t. crier**, pregonero.—**t. hall**, **t. house**, casa consistorial, casa de ayuntamiento, concejo.—**t. planning**, urbanismo.—**t. talk**, comidilla o habilla(s) de un pueblo.

town(s)folk [-(z)fou̯k], **townspeople** [-pipl], *s. pl.* vecinos, ciudadanos, de un pueblo.

township [-ši̯p], *s.* (E. U.) municipio, sexmo; extensión de terrenos públicos de seis millas en cuadro.

townsman [-zmæn], *s.* vecino; conciudadano, paisano; miembro del ayuntamiento.

towpath [tóu̯pæθ], *s.* camino de sirga.

towrope [tóu̯rou̯p], *s.* = TOWLINE.

tox(a)emia [taksímị̄ǝ], *s.* (med.) toxemia.

toxic(al [táksi̯k(ǝl], *a.*, **toxicant** [-kǝnt], *s.* y *a.* tóxico.—**toxication** [-kéi̯šǫn], *s.* (med.) toxicación, envenenamiento.—**toxicity** [taksí̯si̯ti̯], *s.* toxicidad.—**toxicological** [-kǒlǝdžị̄kǝl], *a.* toxicológico.—**toxicologist** [-kálǒdžị̄st], *s.* toxicólogo.—**toxicology** [-dži̯], *s.* toxicología.

toxin(e [táksi̯n], *s.* (bioquím.) toxina.

toy [tói̯]. **I.** *s.* juguete; retozo, capricho; fruslería, bagatela; perrillo diminuto (ll. t. t. **dog**).—**t. dealer**, juguetero.—**t. store**, juguetería (tienda). **II.** *a.* de juego; diminuto. **III.** *vn.* jugar, retozar, juguetear, estar de chacota.—**toyish** [-iš], *a.* menudo, de juguete; juguetón; frívolo.—**toyishness** [-niš], *s.* puerilidad, muchachada, fruslería, niñería.—**toyman** [-mæn], *s.* juguetero.—**toyshop** [-šap], *s.* juguetería.

trace [tréįs]. **I.** *s.* rastro, huella, pisada, pista; vestigio, señal, *f.,* indicio; una sombra, un ápice, una pizca; tirante o tiradera (de carruaje).—*pl.* (quím.) indicios. **II.** *va.* trazar, delinear; calcar; rastrear, seguir la pista; trazar, señalar, plantear, indicar; reconstruir, determinar el origen o la forma primitiva de, investigar, descubrir, escudriñar; (tal.) enjaezar, enganchar (caballo); (mar.) galibar.—**to t. (back) to,** derivar de; demostrar que (algo) proviene de; seguir, llevar o hacer remontar hasta.

traceable [-əbl], *a.* que se puede trazar, rastrear, o descubrir; atribuible.

tracer [-œ(r)], *s.* trazador; rastreador; (dib.) tiralíneas (instrumento); calcador; puntero, punzón; cédula de investigación para averiguar el paradero de cartas o bultos extraviados; averiguación o averiguador de cosas perdidas (en los trenes, el correo, etc.); (arti.) artificio luminoso unido a un proyectil para determinar su trayectoria.—**t. bullet,** bala trazante o trazadera.

tracery [-œrį], *s.* (arq.) tracería.

trachea [trékiä], *s.* (anat.) tráquea, traquearteria; (bot.) tráquea, ducto.—**tracheal** [-l], *a.* traqueal.

tracheotomy [-átomį], *s.* (cir.) traqueotomía.

trachoma [trəkóumä], *s.* (med.) tracoma, *m.*

trachyte [trékaįt], *s.* (min.) traquita.

trachytic [trəkítįk], *a.* traquítico.

tracing [tréįsiŋ]. **I.** *s.* trazo; calc(ad)o, copia; vía, pista; acción de trazar, calcar, etc. *V.* TRACE, *va.* **II.** *a.* que traza; de trazar; de calcar.—**t. cloth,** tela de calcar.—**t. line,** (mar.) perigallo.—**t. paper,** papel de calcar, papel tela.—**t. point,** aguja recorredora o estilete recorredor (de un planímetro, etc.).

track [trék]. **I.** *s.* vestigio, rastro, pista, huella, pisada, estampa; rodada, carril (de carro, etc.); rumbo, ruta; curso (de cometa, etc.); camino trillado, senda, vereda; (f. c.) vía; rieles o carriles (*pl.*) de la vía; banda o cadena (de tractor oruga); (equit.) pista; (mar.) derrota, estela.—**t. ga(u)ge,** calibre de entrevía.—**t. meet,** (dep.) concurso o competencia de juegos atléticos de pista y campo.—**off the t.,** descarrilado; desviado, extraviado; (fam.) por los cerros de Úbeda.—**on the t.,** en la pista, en el rastro. **II.** *va.* rastrear, seguir la pista a; (con **down**) lograr descubrir (el origen, escondite, etc., de); (mar.) sirgar.

trackage [-įdž], *s.* remolque; (mar.) sirgadura; (f. c.) el conjunto de rieles de un sistema ferroviario.—**tracker** [-œ(r)], *s.* el que rastrea, etc.; (mar.) sirgador.

tracklayer [-leįœ(r)], *s.* (f. c.) tendedor o instalador de carriles.—**tracklaying** [-leįiŋ], *s.* tendido, instalación o asiento de carriles.

trackless [-lįs], *a.* que no presenta ni deja rastro ni huellas; sin caminos; cerrado; intransitado.

trackman [-mən], **trackwalker** [-wɔkœ(r)], *s.* (f. c.) recorredor de la vía, guardavía, *m.*

trackwork [-wœrk], *s.* cálculo y construcción del sistema de carriles de las vías férreas.

tract [trékt], *s.* trecho, tracto; región, comarca, terreno; (anat.) área, región, canal, sistema, *m.;* (igl.) tracto; folleto, tratadico, opúsculo.

tractable [-əbl], *a.* tratable, manejable, dócil; afable.—**tractableness** [-nįs], *s.* afabilidad; docilidad.—**tractably** [-əblį], *adv.* afablemente; dócilmente.

tractate [-eįt], *s.* opúsculo, ensayo.

traction [trékšǝn], *s.* tracción, arrastre; acarreamiento; transporte (por ferrocarriles, tran-

vías, etc.): fricción; (fisiol.) contracción.—**t. engine,** tractor, locomotora o máquina de arrastre.

tractive [tréktįv], *a.* de tracción.

tractor [tréktǝ(r)], *s.* tractor; máquina de arrastre; automóvil tractor; (aer.) aeroplano de tracción o de hélice delantera (ll. t. t. air-plane).—**t. engine,** motor tractor o delantero.—**t. plough,** (agr.) arado mecánico.—**t. propeller,** (aer.) hélice de tracción, hélice delantera.

trade [tréjd]. **I.** *s.* comercio; industria; ramo (vg. the building trade, el ramo de la construcción); movimiento mercantil; oficio; contratación, negocio, trato; gremio; (pol.) convenio de mala ley.—**t. acceptance,** (com.) giro del vendedor contra el comprador que una vez aceptado por este último se convierte en papel negociable.—**t. agreement,** tratado o convenio comercial (entre naciones); pacto entre patronos y gremios obreros.—**t. discount,** (com.) descuento usual del giro o ramo.—**t.-mark,** marca de fábrica.—**t. name,** razón (*f.*) social; nombre comercial; nombre de fábrica (el especial o arbitrario dado por un fabricante a un producto).—**t. price,** precio con rebaja o descuento.—**t. school,** escuela de artes y oficios, escuela industrial.—**t.(s)-union,** gremio de obreros, sindicato.—**t.(s)-unionism,** gremialismo, sindicalismo.—**t.(s)-unionist,** sindicalista, miembro de un gremio obrero; partidario de los gremios obreros.—**t. winds,** vientos alisios. **II.** *va.* y *vn.* negociar, comerciar, tratar, traficar; cambiar.—**to t. in,** negociar en; entregar un objeto (auto, radio, etc.) en pago entero o parcial de otro objeto semejante o de otras mercancías.—**to t. off,** cambalachear.—**to t. on,** aprovecharse de.

trader [-œ(r)], *s.* negociante, comerciante, traficante, mercante, mercader; buque mercante.

tradesfolk, tradespeople [-zfoųk, -zpipl], *s. pl.* comerciantes; gentes (*f. pl.*) del oficio o ramo.

tradesman [-zmən], *s.* tendero, mercader; artesano, menestral.—**tradeswoman** [-zwųmən], *s.* mujer comerciante o de negocios.

trading [-įŋ]. **I.** *s.* comercio, trato. **II.** *a.* mercantil, comercial; venal, corrompido, prostituído.—**t. account,** (com.) cuenta de compraventa.—**t. post,** factoría.—**t. stamp,** billete de premio que se dá al comprador como aliciente.—**t. vessel,** buque mercante.

tradition [trǝdíšǝn], *s.* tradición; (for.) tradición, entrega.—**traditional** [-ǝl], *a.* tradicional.—**traditionalism** [-ǝlįzm], *s.* tradicionalismo.—**traditionalist** [-ǝlįst], *s.* tradicionalista.—**traditionally** [-ǝlį], *adv.* tradicionalmente.—**traditionary** [-ǝrį]. **I.** *a.* tradicional. **II.** *s.* tradicionalista.

traduce [trǝdįús], *va.* calumniar.—**traducer** [-œ(r)], *s.* calumniador.

traducianism [trǝdįúšǝnįzm], *s.* (teol.) traducianismo, doctrina según la cual tanto el alma como el cuerpo son engendrados por los padres.

traffic [tréfįk]. **I.** *s.* tráfico, tráfago, comercio, negocio; transporte, acarreo; tránsito, movimiento; circulación, tráfico o tránsito (en las calles, etc.); mercancías, artículos.—**t. control,** regulación del tráfico.—**t. light,** luz, semáforo o señal (*f.*) de circulación.—**t. policeman** o **cop** (fam.), agente de tráfico o tránsito.—**t. sign,** señal (*f.*) de tránsito.—**t. violation,** infracción del reglamento del tráfico. **II.** *va.* y *vn.* negociar, comerciar, traficar.—**trafficker** [-œ(r)], *s.* traficante.

tragacanth [trégǝkænθ], *s.* (bot.) tragacanto, adraganto, alquitira (arbusto y goma).

tragedian [trǝdžídįǝn], *s.* (actor) trágico; escritor de tragedias.—**tragedienne** [trǝdžidįén], *s.* (actriz) trágica.

tragedy [trédžįdį], *s.* tragedia.

tragic(al [-k(ǝl], *a.* trágico.—**tragically** [-lį]

adv. trágicamente.—**tragicalness** [-kạlnịs], *s.* calidad de trágico, carácter trágico o calamitoso.

tragicomedy [-kámẹdị], *s.* tragicomedia.

tragicomic(al [-kámịk(ạl], *a.* tragicómico, jocoserio.

tragus [tréjgʌs], *s.* (anat.) trago.

trail [tréjl]. **I.** *va.* arrastrar; remolcar; traer, llevar (barro, etc.) en los pies, zapatos, etc.; asentar (la yerba) con el andar, hasta formar vereda; rastrear, seguir el rastro o la pista; (f. c.) agregar (vagones) a un tren. **II.** *vn.* arrastrar, ir arrastrando; dejar rastro; rezagarse; seguir el rastro o la pista; arrastrarse, trepar (una planta). **III.** *s.* rastro, pisada, pista, huella; cola (de vestido, de cometa, etc.); trocha, sendero, vereda; carretera; indicio; (arti.) gualdera.—**t. bridge,** andarivel.—**t. car,** coche de habitación remolcado por un vehículo automóvil (ll. **t. trailer**).—**t. rope,** (aer.) sonda, cuerda freno (cable colgante o de arrastre de un globo, que sirve de lastre variable para regular la altura). *V.* TOWROPE.

trailer [-œ(r)], *s.* el o lo que sigue el rastro o la pista; rezagado; carro o coche remolcado; remolque, acoplado.—**t. truck,** camión (*m.*) con remolque.

trailing [-ịŋ], *a.* rastrero; remolcado; trasero; colgante.—**t. aerial,** (rad.) antena colgante.— **t. arbutus,** (bot.) epigea.—**t. edge,** (aer.) borde de salida.—**t. wheel,** (f. c., carr.) rueda trasera.

train [tréjn]. **I.** *va.* y *vn.* disciplinar, adiestrar, amaestrar; preparar, educar, enseñar; domar y manejar (un caballo, etc.); (dep.) entrenar; (agr.) poner en espaldera; (arti.) apuntar (un cañón); enfocar (un anteojo). **II.** *s.* (f. c.) tren; séquito, comitiva (de rey, etc.); cabalgata; recua; (arti., min.) reguero de pólvora; serie, sucesión, orden, curso (de ideas, acontecimientos, etc.); cola (de ave, de vestido, de cometa), cauda (de la capa magna); (mec.) tren, juego, movimiento; artimaña; lazo, celada, trampa.—**t. dispatcher,** (f. c.) director del movimiento de trenes.—**t.-mile,** tren-milla, milla por tren.—**t. mileage,** kilometraje por tren, total de tren-millas (tren-kilómetros).— **t. oil,** aceite de ballena o de pescado.

trainband [-bænd], *s.* (hist. Ingl.) milicia.

trainbearer [-bércœ(r)], *s.* (igl.) caudatario.

trained [-d], *a.* adiestrado, amaestrado, enseñado; educado, preparado.—**t. nurse,** enfermera o enfermero graduados.

trainee [-í], *s.* persona que se entrena o que se adiestra; (mil.) soldado bisoño, recluta, *m.*

trainer [-œ(r)], *s.* domador (de animales); amaestrador; (dep.) entrenador; (agr.) espaldera; (aer.) entrenador, avión (*m.*) de entrenamiento.

training [-ịŋ]. **I.** *s.* disciplina, adiestramiento, formación, enseñanza, educación, instrucción, preparación; (dep.) entrenamiento. **II.** *a.* de instrucción; (dep.) de entrenamiento.—**t. school,** plantel, escuela práctica.—**t. ship,** buque-escuela, barco de instrucción marina.

trainman [-mạn], *s.* empleado ferroviario.

trait [tréjt], *s.* rasgo, cualidad; golpe, toque.

traitor [tréjtọ(r)], *s.* traidor.—**traitorous** [-ʌs], *a.* pérfido, aleve, alevoso, traidor.—**traitorously** [-lị], *adv.* alevosamente, pérfidamente.—**traitorousness** [-njs], *s.* alevosía, perfidia, traición. —**traitress** [tréjtrịs], *s.* traidora.

traject [trạdžékt], *va.* tirar, arrojar.

trajection [-šọn], *s.* trayecto, travesía.

trajectory [-torị], *s.* trayectoria.

tram [trém], *s.* (Ingl.) tranvía, *m.;* carril, riel plano; (mec.) calibre de alineación; compás de barra o de vara(s).

tramcar [-kar], *s.* (Ingl.) coche de tranvía; (min.) carreta de carbón, mineral, etc.

trammel [trémẹl]. **I.** *s.* impedimento, obstáculo, estorbo; traba, manea; llares, *f. pl.,* garabato

de chimenea; (mec.) compás de barra o de vara(s); calibre de alineación; red de pescar; red para coger pájaros. **II.** *va.* trabar, poner trabas; estorbar, impedir.

tramontane [trạmántejn]. **I.** *a.* tramontano, ultramontano. **II.** *s.* extranjero.

tramp [trémp]. **I.** *va.* y *vn.* patullar, patear, pernear, pisar con fuerza; corretear, vagabundear. **II.** *s.* marcha pesada; ruido de pisadas; caminata, paseo largo; vago, vagabundo, guitón.— **t. steamer,** vapor volandero.

trample [-l]. **I.** *va.* hollar, pisar, pisotear, conculcar. **II.** *vn.* patullar, pisar fuerte; (con **on)** ajar, atropellar, hollar, pisotear. **III.** *s.* pisoteo; atropello.

trampler [-lœ(r)], *s.* pisador, conculcador.

tramroad [trémroụd], **tramway** [-wei], *s.* (Ingl.) tranvía, *m.;* (min.) ferrocarril o cable aéreo para transporte de mineral, etc.—**t. worker,** tranviario.

trance [træns], *s.* rapto, arrobamiento; (med.) síncope, *f.,* catalepsia; estado hipnótico.

tranquil [trǽŋkwịl], *a.* tranquilo, sosegado, sereno.—**tranquil(l)ity** [trǽŋkwílịtị], *s.* tranquilidad, paz, sosiego, serenidad, calma.— **tranquil(l)ize, tranquil(l)ise** [trǽŋkwịlajz], *va.* y *vn.* tranquilizar(se).—**tranquil.ly** [trǽŋkwịlị], *adv.* tranquilamente.

transact [trænzǽkt], *va.* negociar, desempeñar, gestionar, tramitar, hacer, ejecutar, despachar.

transaction [-ǽkšọn], *s.* desempeño, gestión, negociación; operación, transacción, negocio.— *pl.* trabajos de una sociedad docta; memorias; actas.

transactor [-ǽktọ(r)], *s.* negociador, gestor.

transalpine [-ǽlpajn], *a.* transalpino.

transatlantic [-ætlǽntịk], *a.* transatlántico.—**t. liner,** (vapor o buque) transatlántico.

transcend [trænsénd]. **I.** *va.* sobrepujar, superar, propasar(se). **II.** *vn.* tra(n)scender.—**transcendence, transcendency** [-ẹns, -ị], *s.* tra(n)scendencia; excelencia; superioridad; (teol.) doctrina de que Dios es anterior al universo.—**transcendent** [-ẹnt], *a.* sobresaliente, excelente; (filos.) incognoscible; (teol.) no inmanente, sino anterior al universo.

transcendental [-déntạl], *a.* trascendental; eminente, sobresaliente; vago, indefinido; (mat.) transcendental, no algébrico; (filos.) transcendental.—**transcendentalism** [-ịzm], *s.* (filos.) transcendentalismo.—**transcendentally** [-ị], *adv.* de modo tra(n)scendental.

transcendingly [trænséndẹntlị], *adv.* excelente o superlativamente; de modo trascendental.

transcontinental [trænskạntịnéntạl], *a.* transcontinental.

transcribe [trænskrájb], *va.* transcribir, copiar, trasladar; (mús.) transcribir, adaptar; (rad.) grabar (música, discursos, etc.) en un disco fonográfico para la radiodifusión.—**transcriber** [-œ(r)], *s.* copiador, copista; adaptador.

transcript [trénskrịpt], *s.* trasunto, copia, traslado.

transcription [trænskrípšọn], *s.* transcripción, trasunto, traslado; (mús.) adaptación; (rad.) perifonía de un programa preparado de antemano en discos fonográficos.—**transcriptive** [-tịv], *a.* perteneciente al traslado.

transept [trénsẹpt], *s.* (arq.) crucero.

transfer [trænsfœr]. **I.** *va.* transferir, trasladar, transponer, pasar, transbordar; (for.) transferir, traspasar, transmitir, ceder. **II.** [tréns-fœ(r)], *s.* traspaso, transferencia; transbordo, traslado, transporte; (for.) traspaso, cesión.— **t. paper,** papel de calcar.—**transferable** [-fœrạbl], *a.* transferible, cesible; convertible.— **transferee** [-fẹrí], *s.* cesionario; persona transferida de un puesto o empleo a otro.—**transference** [trénsfẹrẹns], *s.* transferencia.—**transferrer, transferror** [-fœrœ(r)], *s.* (for.) transferidor, cesionista, cedente.

transfiguration [-fįgyūréįṣǫn], s. transfiguración.—**transfigure** [-fįgyū(r)], va. transfigurar.

transfix [-fíks], va. traspasar, atravesar.

transfixion [-fíkṣǫn], s. transfixión.

transform [-fórm], va. y vn. transformar(se), convertir(se), alterar(se).

transformable [-ạbl], a. transformable.

transformation [-forméįṣǫn], s. transformación, conversión.—**transformative** [-fórmạtįv], a. transformativo.

transformer [-fórmœ(r)], s. transformador; (elec.) transformador.

transformism [-fórmįzm], s. (biol.) transformismo.

transfuse [-fjúz], va. transfundir, transvasar, decantar.—**transfusion** [-fjúżǫn], s. transfusión.

transgress [-grés]. I. va. transgredir, violar, quebrantar, infringir. II. vn. propasarse, excederse, pecar.—**transgression** [-gréṣǫn], s. transgresión, delito, ofensa, atentado; traspaso, extralimitación.—**transgressor** [-gréṣǫ(r)], s. transgresor, infractor.—**transgressible** [-grésįbl], a. violable.—**transgressing** [-grésįṇ], a. transgresor.—**transgressingly** [-lį], adv. transgresoramente, cometiendo transgresión.—**transgressive** [-grésįv], a. transgresor, culpable.

tranship [trænṣíp], va. = TRANSSHIP.

transcience, transiency [trénṣęns, -įl], s. calidad o estado de pasajero o transitorio.

transient [trénṣęnt]. I. a. pasajero, transitorio; de tránsito, que está de paso; transeúnte. II. s. transeúnte, viajero de paso, persona de tránsito.—**transiently** [-lį], adv. temporalmente, de paso, de tránsito.—**transientness** [-nįs], s. brevedad; naturaleza pasajera o transitoria.

transit [trénṣįt]. I. s. tránsito, paso, pasaje, trámite; (astr.) tránsito; (top.) tránsito (teodolito de anteojo invertible sobre el eje horizontal).—**t. instrument**, (top.) = TRANSIT; (astr.) anteojo meridiano. II. va. y vn. (astr., top.) pasar por; invertir(se) (el anteojo del tránsito) en el plano vertical.

transition [trænżíṣǫn], s. tránsito, paso, mudanza; transición; (mús.) transición.

transitional, transitionary [-ạl, -ạrį], a. transitorio.

transitive [trénṣįtįv], a. (gram.) transitivo, activo.—**transitively** [-lį], adv. transitivamente.

transitman [trénṣįtman], s. (top., f. c.) encargado del tránsito (instrumento).

transitorily [trénṣįtǫrįlį], adv. transitoriamente; provisionalmente.—**transitoriness** [-ǫrįnįs], s. carácter transitorio.—**transitory** [-ǫrį], a. transitorio, pasajero, transeúnte; provisional.

translatable [trænsléįtạbl], a. traducible.

translate [-léįt], va. traducir, verter; descifrar, interpretar; transformar, cambiar; (tlg.) transmitir por relevador; (igl.) trasladar de una silla episcopal a otra; transformar, cambiar.—**to t. from . . . into**, traducir del . . . al.

translation [-léįṣǫn], s. traducción, traslación, versión; interpretación; traslación, remoción; (ret.) traslación.—**motion of t.**, (mec.) movimiento de traslación.

translator [-léįtǫ(r)], s. traductor, intérprete.

transliterate [-lítęreįt], va. representar las letras o sonidos de una lengua por las letras de otra.

translucency [-ljúṣęnṣį], s. translucidez.

translucent, translucid [-ęnt, -įd], a. translúcido, transluciente; transparente.

transmarine [-mạrín], a. ultramarino o transmarino.

transmigrate [-máįgreįt], vn. transmigrar.

transmigration [-éįṣǫn], s. transmigración.

transmigrator [-máįgreįtǫ(r)], s., **transmigratory** [-máįgrạtǫrį], a. transmigrador.

transmissibility [-mįṣįbílįtį], s. transmisibilidad.—**transmissible** [-m[s]įbl], a. transmisible.—**transmission** [-mįṣǫn], s. transmisión; (aut.) cambio de velocidades (ll. t. **transmission**

gear y **gear box**).—**transmissive** [-mísįv], a. transmisible; transmisor.

transmit [-mít], va. transmitir.—**transmittal** [-ạl], s. transmisión.—**transmittance** [-ạnṣ], s. transmisión.—**transmitter** [-œ(r)], s. remitente; (tlg., tlf., elec.) transmisor; (rad.) emisora, transmisor.—**transmitting** [-įṇ], a. transmisor, de transmisión.—**t. set** [-įṇ sęt], (rad.) radiotransmisor, aparato de transmisión.—**t. station**, (rad.) estación emisora.

transmutability [-mįutạbílįtį], s. transmutabilidad.

transmutable [-mįútạbl], a. transmutable.

transmutably [-blį], adv. transmutablemente.

transmutation [-éįṣǫn], s. transmutación.

transmute [-mįút], va. transmutar.

transmuter [-œ(r)], s. transmutador.

transom [trénṣǫm], s. (carp.) travesaño, durmiente; (arq.) montante, lumbre, claraboya; (carr.) telera; (mar.) yugo (de popa).

transpacific [trænṣpạsífįk], a. transpacífico, allende el Pacífico.

transpadane [-péįdeįn], a. transpadano.

transparency [-péręnṣį], s. transparencia, diafanidad; transparente; (foto.) diapositiva.—**transparent** [-ęnt], a. transparente, diáfano, hialino; (fig.) franco, sincero.

transpiration [-pįréįṣǫn], s. transpiración.

transpire [-páįr]. I. va. transpirar, exhalar, sudar. II. vn. rezumarse; traslucirse, trascender; (fam.) acontecer, suceder.

transplant [-plént], va. trasplantar.

transplantation [-éįṣǫn], **transplanting** [-įṇ], s. (agr.) trasplante.

transport [-pórt]. I. va. transportar, acarrear; transponer; deportar, desterrar; arrebatar, enajenar, conmover. II. [trénṣpǫrt], s. transporte, transportación, acarreo; buque o avión transporte; arrobamiento, rapto; paroxismo, acceso.

transportable [-pórtạbl], a. transportable.

transportation [-portéįṣǫn], s. transportación, transporte, acarreo; pasaje, billete; extrañamiento, deportación, destierro; coste del transporte.

transporter [-pórtœ(r)], s. transportador, porteador.

transporting [-įṇ], a. transportador, de transporte; arrobador, arrebatador.

transposal [-póużạl], s. transposición.

transpose [-póuz], va. transponer; (mús.) transportar.

transposition [-pozíṣǫn], s. transposición, trastrueque; (mús.) transportación.

transship [-ṣíp], va. transbordar.

transshipment [-męnt], s. transbordo.

transubstantiate [trænsạbsténṣįeįt], va. transubstanciar.—**transubstantiation** [-éįṣǫn], s. transubstanciación.

transudation [trænsįudéįṣǫn], s. transudación; diapédesis; endosmosis.

transude [trænsįúd], vn. trasudar, trazumarse.

transvase [trænsvéįs], va. transvasar, trasegar (licores, etc.).

transversal [-vœrsạl]. I. a. transversal. II. s. (geom.) (línea) transversal.

transverse [-vœrs], a. transversal, transverso.

transverse(ly) [-lį], adv. transversalmente.

trap [trép]. I. s. trampa, artimaña, ardid, m.; armadijo, garlito, red, lazo; tranquilla; (mec.) sifón, tubo en U para obturación hidráulica; bombillo de retrete, válvula de inodoro; carruaje ligero; juego del palo corvo (ll. t. **trapball**); (teat., etc.) escotillón.—pl. (fam.) equipaje, bártulos; (mús.) instrumentos del redoblante (en una orquesta).—**t.** (rock), roca ígnea o volcánica, basalto.—**t. shooting**, tiro al vuelo o a blanco que se mueve, tiro de pichón.—**to be caught in the t.**, caer en el garlito, en la trampa o en la ratonera. II. va. coger con trampa; atrapar; proveer de escotillones, sifones, etc.; hacer caer en el lazo o en el garlito;

enjaezar (caballos, etc.). **III.** *vn.* armar lazos o asechanzas.

trapdoor [-dɔːr], *s.* (teat. y uso ord.) escotillón; trampa; (min.) puerta de ventilación.

trapeze [trəpíz], *s.* trapecio de gimnasia o circo.

trapezing [-iŋ], *s.* ejercicio o suertes (*f. pl.*) de trapecio.—**trapezist** [-ist], *s.* gimnasta (*mf.*) de trapecio, trapecista.

trapezium [-iʌm], *s.* (geom.) trapezoide: (anat.) trapecio, hueso radial del carpo.

trapezoid [trǽpēzɔid], *s.* (geom.) trapecio.

trapezoidal [-zɔ́idəl], *a.* (geom.) trapecial.

trappean [trǽpiən], *a.* (geol.) de o rel. a cierta roca volcánica. *V.* TRAP(ROCK).

trapper [trǽpœ(r)], *s.* trampero, cazador de pieles.

trappings [trǽpiŋz], *s. pl.* jaeces, arreos, aderezos (de caballo, etc.); adornos.

Trappist [trǽpist], *s.* (igl.) trapense.

trash [trǽʃ]. **I.** *s.* hojarasca, paja, basura, desperdicio, escombro, desecho; bagazo; cachivache, trasto, patarata; escamonda; quídam, un cualquiera; trabanco, trangallo. **II.** *va.* podar, escamondar; poner trabanco (a un perro).

trashy [-i], *a.* hojarascoso; baladí, despreciable.

trauma [trómə̯], *s.* (med.) trauma, *m.*, lesión, herida.

traumatic [trɔmǽtik], *a.* traumático.

traumatism [trómə̯tizm], **traumatosis** [-tóu̯sis], *s.* (med.) traumatismo, traumatosis.

travail [trǽvei̯l]. **I.** *vn.* trabajar, afanarse; estar de parto. **II.** *s.* afán, fatiga, trabajo; dolores de parto.

travel [trǽvel]. **I.** *va.* y *vn.* viajar; navegar; andar, correr; (with **over**) recorrer. **II.** *s.* viaje; excursión; jornada; (mec.) golpe, curso, carrera, recorrido.—*pl.* correrías; relación de un viaje.—**t. agency, t. agent**, agencia, agente, de viajes o pasajes.—**t.-soiled, t.-stained**, manchado o sucio a causa del viaje.—**t.-worn**, fatigado por el viaje.

travel(l)ed [-d], *a.* que ha viajado mucho; experimentado, versado; trillado, frecuentado (camino).

travel(l)er [-œ(r)], *s.* viajero, viajador; viajante (comercial); (mar.) raca, arracada; (mec.) artefacto movible, como carretilla, corredera, etc.—**t.'s check**, cheque para viajeros.

travel(l)ing [-iŋ], *a.* de viaje, para viajar, viajero, viajante.—**t. crane**, puente grúa o grúa puente, grúa corredera.—**t. salesman**, viajante (de comercio), agente viajero.

travelog(ue [-ag], *s.* descripción o representación de un viaje, o de objetos interesantes para viajeros.

traversable [trǽvœrsə̯bl], *a.* atravesable; (for.) negable, contestable.

traverse [trǽvœrs]. **I.** *a.* transversal, atravesado, cruzado.—**t. board**, (mar.) rosa náutica o de los vientos.—**t. circle**, (arti.) círculo en que se mueve la cureña.—**t. jury** (for.) = PETTY JURY.—**t. line**, (top.) poligonal, *f.*, línea quebrada.—**t. survey**, (top.) trazado de una poligonal o línea quebrada.—**t. table**, (top., mar.) tabla de coordenadas de latitud y longitud; (f. c.) plataforma corrediza con rieles para pasar vehículos de una vía a otra. **II.** *adv.* de través, en sentido transversal. **III.** *s.* (carp.) travesaño, travesero; traviesa, cerco travesero; obstáculo, revés; (fort.) través; (top.) trazado de una poligonal, o línea quebrada; línea transversal; viaje, pasaje; (for.) negación, contradicción, objeción legal; (mar.) bordada, ruta oblicua. **IV.** *va.* atravesar, cruzar, recorrer; examinar o escudriñar con cuidado; mover lateral o transversalmente; (carp.) (a)cepillar de través; (for.) negar, oponerse; estorbar, impedir; contrariar, frustrar. **V.** *vn.* atravesarse; hacer vaivén, moverse de un lado a otro; dar vueltas, girar; (top.) trazar una poligonal, o línea quebrada.

travertin(e [trǽvœrtin], *s.* (geol., min.) travertino.

travesty [trǽvisti]. **I.** *va.* disfrazar; parodiar. **II.** *s.* parodia, farsa, imitación burlesca.

trawl [trɔːl]. **I.** *va.* arrastrar o rastrear (un arte de pesca). **II.** *vn.* pescar a la rastra o rastreando. **III.** *s.* cuerda larga y gruesa a la cual se atan otras provistas de anzuelos (ll. t. **t. line**). *V.* TRAWLNET.

trawler [-œ(r)], *s.* pescador rastreador, que pesca a la rastra; barco rastreador, o de pesca a la rastra; barco dragaminas.

trawling [-iŋ], *s.* pesca a la rastra.

trawlnet [-net], *s.* especie de jábega o red barredera en forma de bolsa; red rastrera.

tray [trei̯], *s.* bandeja, salvilla, batea, platillo; cajón (de baúl, etc.); cualquier vasija casi plana o de bordes bajos; (foto.) cubeta de revelar.

treacherous [trǽtʃœrʌs], *a.* traidor, traicionero, alevoso, pérfido.—**t. memory**, memoria infiel. —**treacherously** [-li], *adv.* traidoramente, alevosamente, a traición.—**treacherousness** [-nis], *s.* calidad de traidor o pérfido; perfidia.

treachery [trǽtʃœri], *s.* traición, felonía, perfidia, falsedad, falsía, deslealtad.

treacle [tríːkl], *s.* melado, meladura; (farm.) triaca.

tread [trɛd]. **I.** *va.* y *vn.* (*pret.* TROD; *pp.* TRODDEN o TROD) pisar, hollar; andar, caminar; pisotear; pat(al)ear; pisar (las aves); gallear, cubrir (el gallo a las gallinas).—**to t. back**, desandar, volver atrás.—**to t. in the footsteps of**, seguir las pisadas de, imitar.—**to t. on air**, estar alegre, o como una pascua.—**to t. on eggs**, (fam.) andar pisando huevos.—**to t. on one's heels**, pisarle a uno los talones, seguirle de cerca.—**to t. on one's toes o corns**, (fam.) ofender o vejar a uno. **II.** *s.* pisa; paso; pisada, huella, pisadura; escalón o peldaño de escalera; galladura, cicatrícula (del huevo); chalaza (del huevo); superficie de rodadura (de rueda, neumático, riel, etc.); banda o cadena (de tractor oruga); distancia entre los centros de las superficies de rodadura de dos ruedas opuestas.

treadle [-l], *s.* (mec.) cárcola, pedal; galladura (del huevo); chalaza (del huevo).

treadmill [-mil], *s.* molino de rueda de andar; (fig.) tráfago.

treason [tríːzən], *s.* traición.—**treasonable** [-əbl], *a.* pérfido, desleal, traidor.—**treasonableness** [-nis], *s.* calidad de traidor; traición.—**treasonably** [-əbli], *adv.* traidoramente, a traición.

treasure [trɛ́ʒü(r)]. **I.** *s.* tesoro, caudal, riqueza; preciosidad, prenda.—**t. house**, tesorería.—**t. ship**, barco que lleva fondos o riquezas.—**t.-trove**, tesoro hallado. **II.** *va.* atesorar; acumular riquezas; guardar o recordar como un tesoro.

treasurer [-œ(r)], *s.* tesorero.—**treasurership** [-ṣ̌ip], *s.* dignidad o puesto de tesorero.

treasury [-i], *s.* tesorería; erario, tesoro, hacienda; (com.) caja; (T.) ministerio de hacienda o del tesoro (ll. t. **T. Department**).—**T. note**, bono (a la vista) de la tesorería.

treat [trit]. **I.** *va.* tratar; dar (buen o mal) trato; tratar o atender (a los enfermos); escribir o discurrir sobre alguna materia; convidar, invitar, obsequiar, agasajar. **II.** *vn.* (with **of**) tratar de, versar sobre; negociar un tratado; convidar. **III.** *s.* solaz, *m.*, placer, deleite; obsequio, agasajo, convite, convidada.—**to stand t.**, pagar la convidada.

treatise [-is], *s.* tratado (libro, escrito).

treatment [-mənt], *s.* trat(amient)o; manera de tratar; (med.) tratamiento, régimen; terapéutica.

treaty [-i], *s.* tratado, pacto, convenio.—**t. port**, puerto o ciudad abiertos al comercio extranjero.

treble [trɛbl]. **I.** *a.* triple, triplo; (mús.) atiplado, sobreagudo. **II.** *s.* tresdoble; (mús.) tiple. **III.** *va.* triplicar, tresdoblar. **IV.** *vn.* triplicarse.

trebling [trɛbliŋ], *s.* triplicación.

trebly [trɛbli], *adv.* triplicadamente.

trecentist [treitʃéntist], *s.* trecentista.—**tre-**

cento [-toṷ], *s.* el siglo XIV del arte y de la literatura italianos.

tree [trí]. **I.** *s.* (bot.) árbol; palo, madero; horca; cruz.—**t. cactus,** pitahaya.—**t. fern,** helecho arborescente.—**t. frog** o **toad,** (zool.) calamite, rana arbórea.—**t. of life,** (bib. y bot.) árbol de la vida, tuya.—**t. of the knowledge of good and evil,** (bib.) árbol de la ciencia del bien y del mal.—**t. pruner,** descocador.—**t. stump,** tocón.—**t. trunk,** tronco.—**t. worship,** culto de los árboles.—**up a t.,** (fam.) puesto entre la espada y la pared. **II.** *va.* hacer refugiarse (a una persona o animal) en un árbol; (fam.) poner en aprieto.

treeless [-lịs], *a.* pelado, sin árboles.

treenail [-neịl], *s.* (carp.) espiga, cabilla, clavija.

treetop [-tap], *s.* copa.

trefoil [trífoịl], *s.* (bot.) trébol, trifolio.

treillage [tréịlịdẓ], *s.* varaseto.

trek [trek]. **I.** *vn.* (*pret.* y *pp.* TREKKED) viajar en carromato; emigrar; tirar de una carga. **II.** *s.* emigración; incursión; jornada.

trellis, trelliswork [trélịs, -wœrk], *s.* enrejado; espaldera, espaldar, arriate, varaseto.

trematode [trématoṷd], *s.* y *a.* (zool.) tremátodo.

tremble [trémbl]. **I.** *vn.* temblar, tremer; estremecerse; tiritar (de frío); trinar (la voz). **II.** *s.* temblor, estremecimiento.—**trembler** [-blœ(r)], *s.* el o lo que tiembla; (elec.) interruptor intermitente.—**trembling** [-blịŋ], *a.* temblante, tembloroso, trémulo, tremente.—**t. poplar, t. tree,** álamo temblón.—**tremblingly** [-lị], *adv.* trémulamente.

tremendous [trịméndʌs], *a.* tremendo, formidable, terrible; inmenso, grande.—**tremendously** [-lị], *adv.* tremendamente.

tremolo [trémoloṷ], *s.* (mús.) trémolo.

tremor [trémọ(r)], *s.* tremor, temblor, estremecimiento; vibración, trepidación.

tremulous [trémyṵlʌs], *a.* trémulo, tembloroso.—**tremulously** [-lị], *adv.* trémulamente.

trench [trench]. **I.** *va.* y *vn.* surcar, hacer surcos; hacer zanjas o fosos; (mil.) atrincherar. **II.** *s.* foso, zanja; tajo; agüera, presa (de riego); (mil.) trinchera.—**t. back,** dolor de espalda acompañado de rigidez.—**t. coat,** trinchera (abrigo impermeable).—**t. fever,** especie de fiebre remitente, común en las trincheras, transmitida por los piojos.—**t. foot, t. feet,** enfermedad de los pies semejante a los sabañones, causada por el frío y la humedad, como en las trincheras.—**t. gun,** cañón de trinchera, usado en las trincheras.—**t. mouth,** inflamación de la boca; angina diftérica.—**t. nephritis,** nefritis aguda causada por la intemperie, como en las trincheras.—**t. warfare,** guerra de trincheras.

trenchant [trénchạnt], *a.* afilado, cortante; mordaz, picante; vigoroso, eficaz.

trencher [trénchœ(r)], *s.* el que abre zanjas o fosos; trinchador; (coc.) trinchero, tajadero; (ant.) comida; placeres de la mesa.—**trencherman** [-mạn], *s.* comedor, glotón, goloso; parásito, gorrista.

trend [trend]. **I.** *vn.* dirigirse, tender, inclinarse. **II.** *s.* dirección, rumbo, curso, giro, tendencia.

Trentine [tréntịn], *s.* y *a.* tridentino.

trepan [trịpǽn]. **I.** *s.* (cir.) trépano; (mec.) taladro. **II.** *va.* (cir.) trepanar; (mec.) taladrar.—**trepanation** [trepạnéịṣọn], *s.* (cir.) trepanación.

trephine [trịfáịn]. **I.** *va.* (cir.) trepanar. **II.** *s.* (cir.) trépano.

trepidation [trepịdéịṣọn], *s.* trepidación, azoramiento, alarma, ansiedad nerviosa.

Treponema [trepọnímạ], *s.* (biol.) treponema, género de bacterias a que pertenece el espiroqueto, bacteria de la sífilis.

trespass [tréspạs]. **I.** *vn.* (con **on** o **upon**) violar, quebrantar, infringir; invadir, rebasar o traspasar los límites; (con **against**) pecar, faltar.—**to t. on one's patience,** abusar de la paciencia de uno. **II.** *s.* transgresión, translimitación, in-

vasión; infracción, violación; culpa, pecado; deuda (en el padrenuestro).

trespasser [-œ(r)], *s.* transgresor, violador de una ley; pecador; deudor (en el padrenuestro).

tress [tres], *s.* trenza; rizo, bucle.—*pl.* cabellera, cabellos abundantes.—**tressed** [trest], *a.* trenzado.

trestle [trésl], *s.* (carp.) bastidor (*v.* T. HORSE); armadura; armazón de soporte o refuerzo; (ing.) caballete, viaducto sostenido por armaduras transversales reticuladas.—**t. bridge,** puente de caballetes.—**t. horse,** (carp.) borriquete, caballete.

trestletree [-tri], *s.* (mar.) bao del palo.

trestlework [-wœrk], **trestling** [-ịŋ], *s.* (ing.) caballete, sistema (*m.*) o serie de caballetes; obra de celosía y caballete; obra sobre pilares.

tret [tret], *s.* (com.) deducción por merma, rebaja.

trey [treị], *s.* el tres (en dados o naipes).

triable [tráịạbl], *a.* que se puede probar, ensayar, adjudicar, etc.

triad [tráịæd]. **I.** *s.* tríada, tríade, *f.,* terno, terna, trinca; (mús.) acorde. **II.** *a.* (quím.) trivalente.

triadic [traịædịk], *a.* trino; (quím.) trivalente.

trial [tráịạl]. **I.** *s.* prueba, esfuerzo, ensayo, experimento, tanteo; toque, ensay(e) (de metales); desgracia, aflicción; (for.) proceso, juicio, vista de una causa. **II.** *a.* de prueba; hecho por vía de experimento.—**t. and error,** ensayo, experimento, prueba.—**t. balance,** (com.) balance de comprobación.—**t. balloon,** globo de prueba; artificio para probar la opinión pública, etc.—**t. by jury,** juicio por jurado.—**t. jury,** jurado procesal.—**t. pit,** (min.) calicata.—**t. trip,** viaje de prueba.—**by t.,** al tanteo.—**on t.,** (com.) a prueba; (for.) enjuiciado.

triangle [tráịæŋgl], *s.* (geom.) triángulo; (mús.) triángulo; (dib.) escuadra, cartabón; conjunto de tres cosas o personas; enredo amoroso en que están envueltas tres personas.

triangular [traịæŋgyṵlạ(r)], *a.* triangular, **triangled** [tráịæŋgld], *a.* triangular, triangulado, deltoideo; de tres (cosas, personas, etc.)—**triangularly** [-lị], *adv.* triangularmente.

triangulate [traịæŋgyṵleịt], *va.* (top.) triangular.

triangulation [-éịṣọn], *s.* (top.) triangulación.

Triassic [traịǽsịk], *a.* y *s.* (geol.) triásico.

triatomic [traịạtámịk], *a.* triatómico; trivalente.

tribal [tráịbạl], *a.* tribal, de tribu, relativo a la tribu o a las tribus; descendiente de una misma hembra por la línea materna (apl. al ganado).

tribalism [-ịzm], *s.* vida o sociedad tribal, o de tribu; espíritu tribal, o de tribu.

tribasic [traịbéịsịk], *a.* (quím.) tribásico.

tribe [tráịb], *s.* tribu, *f.;* (biol.) tribu, grupo.

tribesman [-zmạn], *s.* miembro de una tribu.

tribrach [tráịbræk], *s.* (pros.) tribraquio.

tribulation [trịbyṵléịṣọn], *s.* tribulación, congoja, duelo, pena, aflicción.

tribunal [trịbiúnạl], *s.* (for.) sala, juzgado; tribunal; foro.

tribune [tríbiun], *s.* tribuno, defensor del pueblo; tribuna.—**tribuneship** [-ṣịp], *s.* tribunado.

tribunicial, tribunitial [trịbiunịṣạl], *a.* tribunicio.

tributary [tríbyṵterị], *a.* y *s.* tributario (río, estado); subalterno, subordinado.

tribute [tríbịut], *s.* tributo; contribución, impuesto; homenaje.

trice [traịs]. **I.** *s.* momento, instante, tris.—**in a t.,** en un abrir y cerrar de ojos. **II.** *va.* (mar.) izar; amarrar, ligar.

tricennial [traịsénịạl], *a.* tricenal.

tricentennial [-ténịạl], *a.* y *s.* = TERCENTENARY.

triceps [tráịseps], *a.* y *s.* (anat.) triceps o tríceps.

trichina [trịkáịnạ], *s.* (zool.) triquina.

trichinization [trịkịnịzéịṣọn], **trichinosis** [-nóṵsịs], *s.* (med.) triquinosis.—**trichinous** [trịkịnạs], *a.* triquinoso; triquinado.

trichloride [traịklórạịd], *s.* (quím.) tricloruro.

trichotomic [trįkotámįk], **trichotomous** [trįkátomʌs], *a.* tricotómico, tricótomo.

trichotomy [trįkátomį], *s.* tricotomía.

trichroic [traįkróuįk], *a.* tricroico.—**trichroism** [tráįkrouįzm], *s.* tricroísmo.

trichromatic [traįkromǽtįk], *a.* tricromático.—**trichromatism** [traįkróųmątįzm], *s.* tricromatismo.

trick [trįk]. **I.** *s.* treta, petardo, timo, engaño, socaliña; artería, ardid, *m.*, truco, artificio, arte; trampa, tramoya, manganilla; juego de manos; chasco, burla; travesura; jugarreta, (fam.) parchazo, (Am.) volada; destreza, maña; marrullería; costumbre, vicio, muletilla; baza, en el juego de naipes; (mar.) guardia del timonel.—**to do the t.**, resolver el problema, dar en el busilis. **II.** *va.* engañar, embaucar, timar, burlar, petardear, estafar; (con **out**) ataviar, componer, asear. **III.** *vn.* trampear (fam.), vivir de trampas.

tricker, trickster [-œ(r), -stœ(r)], *s.* trampista, embustero, embaucador, (fam.) engañabobos.

trickery [-œrį], *s.* tramperia, ardid, *m.*, embrollo.

trickish [-įš], *a.* falso, trapacero; mañoso.

trickle [-l], *va.* y *vn.* (hacer) gotear; escurrir.

tricksy [-sį], *a.* juguetón, retozón, travieso; artificioso, embustero; ilusorio, engañoso.

tricky [-į], *a.* falso, tramposo, marrullero; vicioso (el animal).

triclinium [traįklínįʌm], *s.* (hist. rom.) triclinio.

tricolor [tráįkʌlo(r)]. **I.** *a.* tricolor. **II.** *s.* bandera tricolor (apl. gen. a la francesa).

tricot [tríkou], *s.* tricot, tejido de punto.

tricuspid [traįkáspįd], *a.* tricúspide.—**t. valve**, (anat.) válvula tricúspide.

tricycle [tráįsįkl], *s.* triciclo, velocípedo.

trident [tráįdent]. **I.** *s.* arrejaque (de pescar). **II.** *a.* tridente.

tridentate [traįdénteįt], *a.* tridente.

Tridentine [traįdéntįn]. **I.** *a.* tridentino. **II.** *s.* católico romano.

tried [traįd]. **I.** *pret.* y *pp.* de TO TRY. **II.** *a.* probado, experimentado; leal, fidedigno.

triennial [traįénįal], *a.* trienal.—**triennium** [-įʌm], *s.* trienio, período de tres años.

trier [tráįœ(r)], *s.* experimentador, ensayador; juez, *m.*, censor; examinador; ensayo, prueba.

trierarch [tráįerark], *s.* (hist. gr.) trierarca, *m.*, capitán de trirreme.

trifacial [traįféįšal], *s.* y *a.* trifacial.—**t. nerve**, (anat.) trigémino.

trifid [tráįfįd], *a.* trífido.

trifle [tráįfl]. **I.** *s.* bagatela, fruslería, friolera, baratija, menudencia, pequeñez, chuchería, chisme.—**a t.**, (como *adv.*) un poco, un poquito.—**to stop at trifles**, (fam.) pararse en pelillos. **II.** *va.* (gen. con **away**) malgastar (el tiempo, etc.). **III.** *vn.* bromear, chancearse, guasearse; holgar(se); (con **with**) jugar; tratar sin seriedad; burlarse de, engañar.

trifler [tráįflœ(r)], *s.* persona frívola.

trifling [-flįŋ], *a.* frívolo; fútil, insignificante.

trifoliate(d [traįfóųlieįt(įd], *a.* (bot.) trifoliáceo.

trifoliolate [-ljoleįt], *a.* (bot.) trifoliado.

triforium [traįfórįʌm], *s.* (arq.) triforio.

triform(ed [tráįform(d], *a.* triforme.

trifurcate(d [traįfœrkeįt(įd], *a.* trifurcado.

trifurcation [-éįšon], *s.* trifurcación.

trig [trįg]. **I.** *va.* calzar, atar o trabar las ruedas; (gen. con **up** o **out**) acicalar, ataviar. **II.** *s.* calzo, galga. **III.** *a.* peripuesto, acicalado; sano, firme.

trigeminal [traįdžéminal], *a.* y *s.* (anat.) (relativo al) trigémino (nervio).—**trigeminous** [-ʌs], *a.* trigémino; triple.

trigger [trígœ(r)], *s.* (arm.) gatillo, disparador; (mec.) fiador; (carr.) pararruedas, calzo, galga. *V.* TRIG.—**t. guard**, (arm.) guardamonte.

triglyph [tráįglįf], *s.* (arq.) triglifo.

trigon [tráįgan], *s.* (geom., astr.) trígono.

trigonal [trígonal], *a.* triangular.

trigonometric(al [trįgonométrįk(al], *a.* trigonométrico.—**t. function**, función o razón trigonométrica.—**trigonometrically** [-į], *adv.* trigonométricamente.

trigonometry [-námetrį], *s.* trigonometría.

trihedral [traįhídrạl], *a.* (geom.) triedro.—**t. angle**, (ángulo) triedro.—**trihedron** [-drọn], *s.* triedro.

trilateral [-lǽterạl], *a.* trilátero, trilateral.

trilingual [-lịŋgwạl], *a.* trilingüe.

triliteral [-líterạl], *a.* trilítero.

trill [trįl]. **I.** *s.* trino, gorjeo, (fam.) gorgorito(s); (fon.) vibración. **II.** *va.* (fon.) vibrar (la *r*). **III.** *vn.* trinar, gorjear, (fam.) gorgoritear; gotear.

trillion [trílyọn], *s.* trillón (en Ingl. y Esp., la tercera potencia de un millón; en Fr. y E. U., un millón de millones).

trilobate(d [traįlóųbeįt(įd], **trilobed** [tráįloųbd], *a.* trilobulado, de tres lobos o lóbulos.

trilobite [tráįlobaįt], *s.* (pal.) trilobites.

trilocular [traįlákįųlą(r)], *a.* trilocular, de tres células o tres cavidades.

trilogy [trílodžį], *s.* trilogía.

trim [trįm]. **I.** *a.* ajustado, bien acondicionado; ataviado, acicalado. **II.** *va.* componer, arreglar, pulir, ajustar, adaptar; (carp.) alisar, desbastar, acepillar; (agr.) podar, mondar, recortar; cortar ligeramente o un poco (cabellos, barba); despabilar (lámpara o vela); reponer (los carbones de una lámpara de arco); (cost.) adornar, guarnecer, franjear, ribetear, pasamanar; (enc.) afinar; igualar o equilibrar; (fam.) reprender; (fam.) zurrar; (fam.) derrotar; sacar ventaja a.—**to t. a ship**, (mar.) orientar o equilibrar un buque.—**to t. off**, recortar; atusar.—**to t. the hold**, (mar.) estibar, abarrotar.—**to t. the sails**, orientar las velas.—**to t. up**, adornar, hermosear, componer. **III.** *vn.* vacilar, titubear entre dos partidos; nadar entre dos aguas; (mar.) estar bien orientado o equilibrado (buque). **IV.** *s.* atavío, adorno, aderezo, compostura; traje, vestido; estilo; condición, estado; buena condición, buen estado; (cost.) franja, ribete, guarnición; (arq.) enmaderamiento, molduras, *f. pl.*; disposición marinera de un buque, asiento.—**t. of the hold**, (mar.) disposición de la estiba.—**t. of the sails**, (mar.) orientación de las velas.—**in (good) t.**, en buena condición, en buen estado; listo, preparado.

trimester [traįméstœ(r)], *s.* trimestre.—**trimestr(i)al** [-tr(į)ạl], *a.* trimestral, de cada tres meses.

trimeter [trímetœ(r)], *a.* y *s.* (poét.) trímetro.

trimly [trímlį], *adv.* en regla.

trimmed [trįmd], *a.* ataviado, adornado, guarnecido; (mar.) equilibrado; (fam.) derrotado;

trimmer [trímœ(r)], *s.* guarnecedor; contemporizador, pastelero; (cost.) ribeteador.

trimming [trímįŋ], *s.* (cost.) guarnición, cenefa, galoneadura, galón, alamar, franja, orla, adorno, pasamanería; (carp.) desbastadura; ajuste, arreglo; (agr.) poda; recorte (del pelo, barba); (fam.) derrota.—*pl.* accesorios, piezas de adorno; arrequives; recortes.

trinal [tráįnal], *a.* triple: trino.—**trinary** [tráįnarį], *a.* ternario.—**trine** [traįn]. **I.** *a.* triple; (astr.) trino. **II.** *s.* compuesto o reunión de tres elementos; (T., igl.) Trinidad; (astr.) aspecto trino.

tringle [trįŋgl], *s.* vara de cortina; (arq.) listel.

trinitarian [trįnįtérįan], *s.* y *a.* (t. T., igl.) trinitario.

trinitrocresol [traįnaįtrokrísoųl], *s.* trinitrocresol.

trinitrophenol [-fínoųl], *s.* (quím.) ácido pícrico.

trinitrotoluene [-tályuįn], *s.* (quím.) trinitrotolueno.

trinity [trínįtį], *s.* (t. T., teol.) trinidad.

trinket [trínkįt], *s.* dije, bujería, chuchería.

trinomial [traįnóųmįạl]. **I.** *a.* (biol.) que tiene tres nombres; (álg.) trinomio. **II.** *s.* trinomio.

trio [tríoų], *s.* terno, terna; (mús.) trío, terceto.

triode [trájoud], *s.* (elec.) tubo de vacío con tres electrodos.

trioxid(e [traiáksaid], *s.* (quím.) trióxido.

trip [trip]. **I.** *va.* hacer caer a uno echándole la zancadilla; trompicar; armar un lazo o zancadilla; coger a uno en falta o cogerle un renuncio; bailar, mover los pies con ritmo; (mec.) soltar, disparar; desatar; (mar.) zarpar, levar anclas. **II.** *vn.* tropezar; equivocarse, cometer un desliz o descuido; (mar.) zarpar; correr, ir aprisa. **III.** *s.* viaje corto, excursión; tropiezo, traspié, *m.;* desliz, *m.,* paso falso; zancadilla; paso o movimiento ágil.—**t. hammer,** martinete de fragua.

tripartite [traipártait], *a.* tripartito.

tripe [traip], *s.* (coc.) callos, *m. pl.,* mondongo; (fam.) cosa sin valor; necedad(es).—**honeycomb t.,** callos de redecilla.—**plain t.,** callos de panza.

tripetalous [traipétalʌs], *a.* (bot.) tripétalo.

triphthong [trífθaŋ], *s.* (fon.) triptongo.

triplane [tráiplein], *s.* (aer.) triplano.

triple [trípl]. **I.** *a.* triple, triplo, tríplice, tresdoble. —**t. crown,** (igl.) tiara.—**t.-expansion,** de triple expansión. **II.** *va.* triplicar, tresdoblar.

triplet [tríplit], *s.* terno; cada uno de tres hermanos nacidos de un parto; (poét.) terceto, tercerilla; (mús.) tresillo.

triplex [trípleks], *a.* tríplice.

triplicate [tríplikit]. **I.** *a.* triplicado, triplo. **II.** *s.* tercera copia.—**in t.,** por triplicado. **III.** [-eit], *va.* triplicar.

triplication [-éişon], *s.* triplicación.

triplicity [triplísiti], *s.* triplicidad.

triply [trípli], *adv.* por triplicado.

tripod [tráipad], *s.* trípode, *mf.*

tripoli [trípoli], *s.* (min.) trípol(i) (ll. t. **t. stone**).

Tripolitan [tripálitan], *s.* y *a.* tripolitano.

tripper [trípœ(r)], *s.* saltarín; excursionista; (mec.) disparador.

trippet [trípit], *s.* brazo, saliente, *f.,* leva, uña.

tripping [trípiŋ]. **I.** *s.* tropezón, traspié, *m.;* baile ligero. **II.** *a.* veloz, ágil, ligero.—**trippingly** [-li], *adv.* velozmente, con agilidad y ligereza.

triptych [tríptik], *s.* (b. a.) tríptico.

triptyque [triptík], *s.* (aut.) pase de aduana.

trireme [tráirim], *s.* (hist. rom. y gr.) trirreme.

Trisagion [triséigion], *s.* (igl.) trisagio.

trisect [traisékt], *va.* trisecar.

trisection [-sékşon], *s.* trisección.

trismus [trízmʌs], *s.* (med.) trismo, tétano de la mandíbula inferior.

trisulphid(e [traisʌlfid], *s.* (quím.) trisulfuro.

trisyllabic(al [traisilébik(al], *a.,* **trisyllable** [traisílabl], *s.* trisílabo.

trite [trait], *a.* traqueado, gastado, trillado; trivial, vulgar.—**tritely** [-li], *adv.* vulgarmente; trilladamente.—**triteness** [-nis], *s.* vulgaridad; trivialidad; calidad de gastado o trillado.

tritheism [tráiθiizm], *s.* (teol.) triteísmo.

triton [tráiton], *s.* (zool.) tritón (gasterópodo y lagartija acuática); (T., mit.) Tritón, tritón.

tritone [tráitoun], *s.* (mús.) trítono.

triturable [tríchŭrabl], *a.* triturable.—**triturate** [-eit], *va.* triturar.—**trituration** [-éişon], *s.* trituración.

triumph [tráiʌmf]. **I.** *s.* triunfo, victoria. **II.** *vn.* triunfar; vencer; salir victorioso.

triumphal [traiʌmfal], *a.* triunfal.—**t. arch,** arco de triunfo.—**t. crown,** lauro.

triumphant [-ant], *a.* triunfante, victorioso.

triumphantly [-li], *adv.* triunfalmente, triunfantemente, en triunfo.

triumpher [tráiʌmfœ(r)], *s.* triunfador.

triumvir [traiʌmvœ(r)], *s.* (hist. rom.) triunviro.

triumvirate [-eit], *s.* triunvirato.

triune [tráiyun]. **I.** *a.* (teol.) trino y uno. **II.** *s.* (T.) Trinidad.

trivet [trívit], *s.* trébedes, *f. pl.,* trípode, *mf.*

trivial [tríviəl], *a.* trivial, frívolo, fútil.—**trivially** [-i], *adv.* frívola o trivialmente.—**triviality**

trivialness [trívialnis], *s.* trivialidad.

trivium [tríviʌm], *s.* trivio, las tres artes liberales (la gramática, la retórica y la dialéctica).

triweekly [traiwíkli], *a.* que sucede tres veces por semana, o cada tres semanas.

trocar [tróukar], *s.* (cir.) trocar.

trochaic(al [trokéiik(al], *a.* (poét.) trocaico.

trochanter [trokæntœ(r)], *s.* (anat.) trocánter; (ent.) segunda articulación de la pierna de un insecto.

troche [tróuki], *s.* (farm.) trocisco, rótula, pastilla.

trochee [tróuki], *s.* (poét.) troqueo (— ⌣).

trochlea [tráklia], *s.* (anat.) troclea.

trochoid [tróukoid]. **I.** *a.* que gira sobre su propio eje. **II.** *s.* (geom.) trocoide, *f.*

trod, trodden [trad, -n], *pret.* y *pp.* de **TO TREAD.** —**trodden path,** camino trillado.

troglodyte [tráglodait], *s.* troglodita, *m.;* (fig.) ermitaño; hombre bárbaro y cruel; (zool.) mono antropoide, chimpancé; (orn.) troglodita, *m.*—**troglodytic** [-dítik], *a.* troglodita; troglodítico.

trogon [tróugan], *s.* (orn.) quetzal.

Trojan [tróudʒan], *a.* y *s.* troyano; valiente, enérgico.

troll [troul]. **I.** *va.* y *vn.* cantar alegre y briosamente; cantar en sucesión (las partes de una canción o rondó); pescar de un bote en movimiento, arrastrando el anzuelo; voltear, girar, rodar. **II.** *s.* rondó, cantar que se entona en partes sucesivas; repetición, rutina; carrete de la caña de pescar (*v.* **TROLLING**); (mit.) gnomo, enano.

trolley, trolly [tráli], *s.* (elec.) polea del trole; coche o tranvía (*m.*) de trole; vagoneta de volquete; carretilla; carro de grúa (ll. t. **crane t.**). —**t. bus** o **coach,** ómnibus eléctrico (es de trole, pero no necesita rieles).—**t. car,** (coche de) tranvía, *m.*—**t. line** o **system,** línea o sistema (*m.*) de tranvías de trole.—**t. wire,** conductor o alimentador del trole; alambre de o para troles.

troll(e)yman [-man], *s.* conductor de tranvía de trole, motorista.

trolling [tróuliŋ], *s.* modo de pescar arrastrando el sedal y anzuelo casi a flor de agua desde un bote en movimiento.

trollop [tráləp], *s.* mujer sucia y desaseada, (fam.) zangarilleja; gorrona, ramera.

trombone [trámboun], *s.* (mús.) trombón.

trompe [tramp], *s.* (fund.) trompa.

troop [trup]. **I.** *s.* tropa, cuadrilla, turba, caterva; compañía (de actores); (mil.) escuadrón de caballería.—*pl.* tropas, ejército.—**t. carrier** = **TROOPSHIP. II.** *vn.* atroparse, apiñarse, agavillarse, ir en tropel.—**to t. away,** u **off,** retirarse, marcharse en tropel.

trooper [-œr], *s.* soldado de caballería; policía montado; corcel de guerra; (Ingl.) = **TROOPSHIP.**

troopial [-ial], *s.* (orn.) turpial, trupial.

troopship [-şip], *s.* buque de transporte de tropas.

tropæolum [tropíolʌm], *s.,* **tropæolaceous** [tropioléişas], *a.* (bot.) tropeoleo.

trope [troup], *s.* (ret.) tropo (metáfora, sinécdoque, metonimia, ironía).

tropein(e [tróupiin], *s.* (quím.) tropeína.

trophic(al [tráfik(al], *a.* trófico, relativo a la nutrición.

trophied [tróufid], *a.* adornado de trofeos.

trophy [tróufi], *s.* trofeo.

tropic [trápik], *s.* (geog. y astr.) trópico.—**T. of Cancer,** trópico de Cáncer.—**T. of Capricorn,** trópico de Capricornio.

tropic(al [-al], *a.* tropical; (ret.) trópico, figurado.

tropically [-li], *adv.* (ret.) metafóricamente, etc.

tropine [tróupin], *s.* (quím.) tropina.

tropism [tróupizm], *s.* (biol.) tropismo.

tropological [trapolódʒikal], *a.* (ret.) tropológico.

tropology [tropálodʒi], *s.* (ret.) tropología.

troposphere [tráposfir], *s.* troposfera, región de la atmósfera situada bajo la estratosfera.

trot [trat]. **I.** *va.* (equit.) hacer trotar; pasar al trote; (con **out**) (fam.) sacar a exhibir. **II.** *vn.* trotar, ir al trote. **III.** *s.* trote.—**at a t.**, al trote.

troth [troθ], *s.* verdad, fe, *f.*, fidelidad; esponsales, *m. pl.*—**in t.**, en verdad.—**to plight one's t.**, desposarse.

trotol [tróʊtoʊl], **trotyl** [-tịl], *s.* (quím.) trinitrotolueno.

trotter [trátœ(r)], *s.* trotón, trotador.—*pl.* (coc.) manos (*f. pl.*) o pies (*m. pl.*) de carnero o cerdo.

trotting [-ɪŋ], *a.* trotón, trotador.

troubadour [trúbạdọr], *s.* trovador.

trouble [trʌbl]. **I.** *va.* (per)turbar, disturbar; revolver, enturbiar; enfadar, hostigar; atribular, preocupar; incomodar, molestar, importunar.—**to t. oneself**, molestarse, tomarse la molestia; inquietarse. **II.** *vn.* incomodarse, darse molestia, apurarse. **III.** *s.* (per)turbación; disturbio, inquietud; enfermedad, mal (*stomach trouble*, mal de estómago; *throat trouble*, enfermedad de la garganta); (mec.) avería (*engine trouble*, avería del motor); cuita, pena, congoja; disgusto, desavenencia; dificultad; molestia, incomodidad, inconveniencia; impertinencia, engorro.—**to be in t.**, estar afligido; hallarse en un apuro.—**to be looking for t.**, (fam.) buscar tres pies al gato. —**not to be worth the t.**, no valer la pena.

troubled [-d], *a.* afligido; inquieto, agitado; preocupado; en dificultades.—**t. waters**, aguas revueltas o agitadas.—**to be t. with**, sufrir de.

troublemaker [-mejkœ(r)], *s.* = TROUBLER.

troubler [trʌblœ(r)], *s.* alborotador, perturbador.

troublesome [trʌblsam], *a.* penoso, pesado, gravoso; importuno, enfadoso, impertinente; incómodo, fastidioso, dificultoso, molesto; querelloso, camorrista, pendenciero.

troublesomely [-lị], *adv.* molestamente, enfadosamente.—**troublesomeness** [-nịs], *s.* calidad de molesto, pesado, dificultoso.

troublous [trʌblʌs], *a.* turbulento, confuso; inquietante; inquieto, agitado. *V.* TROUBLESOME.

trough [trof], *s.* artesa, gamella, dornajo, cubeta, pila, batea; gamellón (para pisar uvas); seno de dos olas; canal, *mf.*; (meteor.) mínimo (de una depresión).

trounce [traʊns], *va.* (fam.) zurrar; derrotar.

troupe [trúp], *s.* (teat.) compañía.

trouper [-œ(r)], *s.* actor (apl. esp. al veterano).

trousers [tráʊzœrz], *s. pl.* pantalón(es), calzón(es).

trousseau [trúsoʊ], *s.* ajuar de novia.

trout [traʊt], *s.* (ict.) trucha.

trover [tróʊvœ(r)], *s.* (for.) repetición.

trowel [tráʊẹl]. **I.** *s.* (alb.) llana, paleta, fratás, palustre; (agr.) desplantador. **II.** *va.* allanar, emparejar con la llana, fratasar.

trowelful [-fʊl], *s.* paletada.

troy (**weight** [tró̞i(wejt], *s.* sistema (*m.*) de pesos cuya unidad es la libra de 12 onzas (5760 granos).

truancy [trúạnsị], *s.* briba, tuna; ausencia sin permiso de la escuela o del deber.—**truant** [trúạnt]. **I.** *s.* novillero; tunante.—**t. officer**, vigilante escolar.—**to play t.**, hacer novillos (fam.). **II.** *a.* que hace novillos; holgazán, tunante. **III.** *vn.* hacer novillos (fam.); correr la tuna, andar a la briba.

truce [trus], *s.* (mil.) tregua; suspensión, cesación.

truck [trʌk]. **I.** *va.* y *vn.* trocar, permutar, cambiar, traficar; acarrear, transportar en camión (*m.*) o carretón. **II.** *s.* carro, carretón; (auto)camión, *m.*; carretilla de mano; (f. c.) bog(g)ie, truc(k); (Ingl.) furgón de plataforma; (mar.) vertellos, bolas; efectos para vender o trocar; hortalizas para el mercado; (fam.) cosas sin valor, hojarasca, basura; cambio, permuta, trueque; (fam.) trato.—**t. driver**, camionero; carret(on)ero.—**t. farm** o **garden**, huerta.— **t. farmer**, hortelano.—**t. horse**, caballo de tiro.—**t. system**, sistema (*m.*) de pago de salarios en especie.—**t. tractor**, camión remolcador que lleva parte del peso del remolque.

truckage [-ịdʒ], *s.* camionaje; carreteo, acarreo.

trucker [-œ(r)], *s.* = TRUCKMAN.

truckle [trʌkl]. **I.** *vn.* someterse servilmente; servir para ganar favores. **II.** *s.* ruedecilla.—**t. bed**, carriola.

truckman [trʌkmạn], *s.* camionero; carret(o)n)ero; traficante; hortelano, el que cultiva hortalizas para el mercado.

truculence [-ạns], *s.* fiereza, crueldad.

truculent [-ẹnt], *a.* truculento, feroz, cruel.

trudge [trʌdʒ]. **I.** *vn.* andar a pie; caminar con trabajo. **II.** *s.* caminata (fam.), paseo largo y difícil.

true [trú]. **I.** *a.* verdadero, cierto, real, efectivo; ingenuo, sincero; verídico; exacto; justo, a plomo, a nivel, alineado, bien arreglado; legítimo, genuino, puro, propio, natural; fiel, constante, leal.—**t. bearing**, (top., mar.) rumbo relativo al meridiano astronómico.— **t.-blue**, leal, fiel.—**t.-born**, legítimo, verdadero; de nacimiento legítimo.—**t.-bred**, de casta o raza legítima.—**t. copy**, copia fiel.— **t. course**, (mar.) rumbo astronómico, o relativo al meridiano astronómico.—**t.-hearted**, leal, sincero.—**t.-heartedness**, fidelidad, sinceridad.—**t.-lover's knot**, nudo o lazo de perfecto amor.—**t. meridian**, meridiano astronómico (a distinción del magnético).—**t. time**, tiempo (solar) verdadero.—**t. to life**, ajustado a la vida real, que pinta la vida al natural.— **in t.**, alineado, exacto, bien arreglado.—**out of t.**, desarreglado, desalineado, mal dispuesto. **II.** *adv.* exactamente, con verdad. **III.** *va.* (a veces con **up**) pulir, alisar, acabar; arreglar, corregir, rectificar.

trueness [-nịs], *s.* fidelidad; sinceridad; verdad; exactitud, arreglo perfecto.

truffle [trʌfl], *s.* (bot.) criadilla de tierra, trufa.

truism [trújzm], *s.* axioma, *m.*, verdad trillada, vejez, (fam.) perogrullada.

trull [trʌl], *s.* perendeca, prostituta, ramera.

truly [trúlị], *adv.* verdaderamente, en verdad; realmente, exactamente, con precisión; sinceramente, de buena fe.—**yours (very) t.**, su afectísimo, su seguro servidor.

trump [trʌmp]. **I.** *s.* triunfo, en juegos de naipes; (fam.) real mozo, excelente persona; (ant. y poét.) trompeta; trompetazo.—**t. card**, naipe de triunfo (en el juego y tg.).—**no t.**, sin-triunfo. **II.** *va.* (en los naipes) matar con un triunfo; engañar.—**to t. up**, forjar; inventar. **III.** *vn.* (en los naipes) triunfar, jugar (del palo del) triunfo, matar.

trumpery [-œrị], *s.* hojarasca, oropel, relumbrón; cachivache, bujería, baratija; (ant.) engaño, fraude.

trumpet [-ịt]. **I.** *s.* (mús.) trompa, trompeta, clarín (instrumento y músico); trompetilla acústica; bocina, portavoz, *m.*; (bot.) serracenia.—**t. blast**, trompetazo.—**t. creeper** o **vine**, (bot.) planta bignoniácea norteamericana.—**t. daffodil** o **narcissus**, (bot.) narciso atrompetado.—**t.-shaped**, atrompetado, abocinado, abocardado.—**t. shell**, trompa o bocina marina.—**t.-tongued**, vocinglero. **II.** *va.* pregonar a son de trompeta. **III.** *vn.* tocar la trompeta o el clarín, (fam.) trompetear.

trumpeter [-œ(r)], *s.* (mús. y mil.) trompetero, trompeta, *m.*, clarín; pregonero; (orn.) agamí; cisne blanco norteamericano de voz sonora.

truncate [trʌŋkejt], *va.* truncar, troncar.— **truncate(d** [-ịd], *a.* truncado, trunco.—**truncation** [-kéjʃọn], *s.* truncamiento, tronca.

truncheon [trʌnchọn]. **I.** *s.* tranca, garrote, (cachi)porra; bastón de mando. **II.** *va.* golpear con tranca, etc.

trundle [trʌndl]. **I.** *s.* rodaja, rodillo.—**t. bed**, carriola. **II.** *va.* y *vn.* (hacer) rodar.

trundleshot [-šat], s. (arti.) palanqueta.

trunk [trʌ́ŋk]. **I.** s. tronco (de árbol, del cuerpo, arterial); baúl, (baúl) mundo, cofre; trompa (de elefante); (ing.) línea principal (de un ferrocarril); tubería maestra o principal de abastecimiento, de alcantarillas, etc. (en los dos últimos sentidos se dice gen. **t. line**, y en español se dice también *tronco* y *línea troncal*); (arq.) fuste (de columna); tolva (para el grano, etc.); pozo, conducto (de ventilación, descarga, etc.); (m. v.) vástago tubular de émbolo.—*pl.* taparrabo, calzones cortos usados para baño, gimnasia, etc. **II.** a. troncal, del tronco; de la parte (vía, tubería, etc.) principal.—**t. dealer** o **maker**, baulero, cofrero.—**t. engine**, (m. v.) máquina de vástago tubular.—**t. hose**, (hist., sast.) gregüescos, trusas.—**t. sleeve**, (hist., sast.) manga corta y ancha.

trunnel [trʌ́nẹl], s. = TREENAIL.

trunnion [trʌ́nyọn], s. (arti.) muñón.—**t. plates**, muñoneras, contramuñones.

truss [trʌs]. **I.** s. (cir.) braguero; (constr.) armazón, f.; armadura (de techo o tejado); viga de celosía o reticulada (de puente); (mar.) troza; (bot.) mazorca, racimo; haz, m., atado, lío, paquete; (Ingl.) 36 libras de paja o 60 de heno.—**t. beam**, viga armada o reforzada.—**t. bridge**, puente de vigas de celosía.—**t. girder**, viga de celosía.—**t. rod**, tirante. **II.** va. (constr.) atirantar, apuntalar, armar; (mar.) atrozar; (coc.) espetar.—**to t. up**, sofaldar; empaquetar, liar; (ant.) ahorcar.

trussing [-iŋ], s. (constr.) refuerzo, armadura; viga de celosía; piezas de una viga de celosía.

trusswork [-wœrk], s. (constr.) armazón, f.

trust [trʌst]. **I.** s. confianza, fe, f. (en una persona); esperanza, expectación, creencia; (com.) crédito; (for.) fideicomiso, cargo, depósito; (com.) trust, asociación de compañías industriales para fijar la producción, precio, etc., de un artículo, o para asumir la dirección y las ganancias de un negocio; monopolio.—**t. buster**, (fam.) fiscal u otro funcionario público que busca (a veces por motivos políticos) la disolución de los trusts o monopolios.—**T. Company**, banco de depósito; compañía fiduciaria o fideicomisaria.—**t. deed of sale**, (for.) escritura de venta condicionada.—**t. territory**, (dipl.) territorio fideicometido.—**in t.**, en confianza; en depósito; en administración.—**on t.**, al fiado. **II.** va. y vn. confiar (en), contar con; esperar (con confianza); tener confianza en o hacer confianza de; encargar y fiar; confiarse, fiarse (de); creer, dar crédito a; vender al fiado.—**to t. to**, o **unto**, confiar en.

trustee [trʌstí], s. (for.) síndico, fideicomisario, fiduciario, depositario; director de una compañía.

trusteeship [-šip], s. cargo de fideicomisario; (dipl.) administración fiduciaria (de un territorio).

truster [trʌ́stœ(r)], s. fiador.

trustful [trʌ́stfụl], a. confiado.—**trustfully** [-i], adv. confiadamente.—**trustfulness** [-nịs], s. confianza plena.

trustification [trʌstịfịkéišọn], s. (fam.) *trustificación*, reducción a, o incorporación en, un trust.

trustily [trʌ́stịli], adv. fielmente, lealmente, honradamente.—**trustiness** [-ịnịs], s. fidelidad, probidad, integridad.

trustless [-lịs], a. pérfido, que no merece confianza o crédito.

trustworthiness [-wœrðịnịs], s. confiabilidad, integridad, honradez.—**trustworthy** [-wœrðị], a. fiable, confiable; fidedigno, seguro.

trusty [-i], a. fiel, leal; íntegro, confiable; firme, fuerte, seguro.

truth [trúθ], s. verdad, realidad; veracidad; exactitud; (ant.) fidelidad, constancia.—**in t.**,

a la verdad, en verdad; en realidad, seriamente.—**of a t.**, de veras, por supuesto.

truthful [-fụl], a. verídico, veraz; verdadero, exacto.—**truthfully** [-li], adv. con verdad, con certeza.—**truthfulness** [-nịs], s. veracidad; exactitud; verismo, realismo.

truthless [-lịs], a. falso; fementido, desleal.

try [tráj]. **I.** va. (pret. y pp. TRIED) probar, ensayar, tantear; procurar, tratar de; intentar, pretender, querer; poner a prueba; exasperar, irritar, cansar; comprobar, (for.) procesar; ver (una causa o litigio); (metal.) purificar, refinar, afinar.—**to t. on**, probarse (ropa).—**to t. one's hand**, hacer uno la prueba.—**to t. one's luck**, probar fortuna.—**to t. out**, probar, someter a prueba; derretir y clarificar (grasas). **II.** vn. probar, ensayar; procurar, hacer lo posible; (mar.) capear.—**to t. and, to t. to**, tratar de, hacer lo posible por. **III.** s. prueba, ensayo.—**t. cock**, (m. v.) llave (f.) de nivel; llave de purga.—**t. square**, (carp.) escuadra de comprobación.

trying [-iŋ], a. de prueba; molesto, exasperador, irritante; angustioso, de tribulación, penoso.

tryout [-aụt], s. prueba de la capacidad, eficacia o competencia de una persona o cosa.

trysail [-sẹịl], s. (mar.) vela cangreja.

tryst [trịst]. **I.** s. cita o lugar de cita. **II.** va. y vn. dar una cita; acudir a una cita.

tsar [tsar], **tsarina** [tsaríŋä], s. = CZAR, CZARINA.

tsetse (**fly**) [tsétsị (flaị], s. (ent.) tsetsé, f.

tub [tʌb]. **I.** s. cuba, artesón; batea, artes(ill)a; tina; cubeta, tonel pequeño; baño, bañera, tina; (fam.) baño (el acto); (fam.) buque viejo y lento. **II.** va. encubar; entinar; lavar (ropa) en cuba, tina, etc.; (fam.) bañar (a uno) en bañera. **III.** vn. (fam.) bañarse en bañera; lavarse (un tejido) sin daño.

tuba [tjúbä], s. (mús.) tuba.

tubage [tjúbịdẓ], s. (cir.) intubación. V. TUBING.

tubbing [tʌ́bịŋ], s. baño; lavado, lavamiento.

tubby [tʌ́bị], a. de forma de un cubo; (fam.) rechoncho.

tube [tjub]. **I.** s. tubo, caño, cañón, cañuto; (anat.) conducto, tubo; cámara (de llanta o neumático); (rad.) válvula o lámpara de radio; tubo termiónico o al vacío; bombillo, bulbo; túnel; (fam.) ferrocarril subterráneo (ll. t. **t. railway**).—**t. saw**, sierra tubular.—**t.-shaped**, tubular.—**t. transmitter**, (rad.) radiotransmisor de tubos termiónicos. **II.** va. entubar; proveer de tubos, etc.

tuber [tjúbœ(r)], s. (bot.) tubérculo; (anat.) tubérculo, tuberosidad, hinchazón, f., prominencia.

tubercle [-kl], s. (bot., anat., med.) tubérculo.

tubercular [tjubœrkyụlä(r)]. **I.** a. tubercular, tuberculoso; rel. o parecido a tubérculos o nódulos. **II.** s. (med.) víctima de la tuberculosis.

tuberculate(d [-lẹịt(ịd], a. tuberculado; cubierto o afecto de tubérculos.

tuberculation [-léišọn], s. tuberculización.

tubercule [tjúbœrkjul], s. = TUBERCLE.

tuberculin [tjubœrkyụlịn], s. (med.) tuberculina.

tuberculose [-loụs], a. tuberculoso.

tuberculosis [-lóụsịs], s. (med.) tuberculosis.

tuberculous [-lʌs], a. (med.) tuberculoso, referente a la tuberculosis o afecto de ella.

tuberose [tjúbroụz], s. (bot.) tuberosa, nardo.

tuberosity [tjubœrásịtị], s. (anat., zool.) tuberosidad; tubérculo.—**tuberous** [tjúbœrʌs], a. tuberoso.

tubiform [tjúbịfọrm], a. tubiforme.

tubing [tjúbịŋ], s. tubería; cañería; instalación de tubos, canalización; material para tubos.

tubular [tjúbyụlä(r)], a. tubular.—**t. boiler**, caldera de tubos de humos, caldera multitubular.

tubulate [-lẹịt], va. poner en tubos; dar forma de tubo a.—**tubulate(d** [-ịd], a. tubular, tubulado, tubiforme.—**t. retort**, retorta tubulada.

---

tubule [tjúbjul], *s.* túbulo, tubito.

tubuliflorous [-líflórʌs], *a.* (bot.) tubulifloro.

tubulose [-loʊs], **tubulous** [-lʌs], *a.* tubuloso; tubular.

tubulure [tjúbjuljur], *s.* (quím.) tubo corto abierto de una retorta, recipiente, etc.

tuck [tʌk]. **I.** *s.* (cost.) alforza, recogido; (enc.) tapa con cartera; (mar.) falda, arca de popa. **II.** *va.* (cost.) alforzar, hacer alforzas; arropar; doblar, apretar; (gen. con **up**) arremangar, recoger, asobarcar, sofaldar (la ropa); (con **away**) guardar, esconder; (con **in**) remeter bien (la ropa de cama, etc.); acostar o meter en cama (a una criatura, etc.) arropándola bien.—**to t. up one's clothes**, arremangarse, sofaldar.

tucker [-œ(r)]. **I.** *s.* (cost.) alforzador; camisolín, escote. **II.** *va.* (fam.) (con **out**) cansar, fatigar.

Tuesday [tjúzdi], *s.* martes.

tufa [tjúfä], *s.* (geol.) tufo, toba.—**tufaceous** [tjuféiʃʌs], *a.* tobáceo.—**tuff** [taf], *s.* = TUFA. (Ú. t. de cierta roca de origen volcánico).

tuft [tʌft]. **I.** *s.* copete, penacho, cresta; borla; manojo, ramillete; topé, moño; (bot.) ramillete, mata espesa. **II.** *va.* empenachar; adornar con borlas; (tapicería) fijar a intervalos regulares con copetes, borlas o botones.

tufted [-id], *a.* copetudo, penachudo; cespitoso.

tufthunter [-hʌntœ(r)], *s.* zalamero, adulón.

tufty [-i], *a.* = TUFTED.

tug [tʌg]. **I.** *va.* tirar de, arrastrar; (mar.) halar, remolcar. **II.** *vn.* luchar, esforzarse, tirar con fuerza. **III.** *s.* tirón, estirón; (mar.) remolcador. —**t. of war**, contienda de tiro de cuerda, en que los contrincantes tiran de los extremos de una cuerda en direcciones opuestas; esfuerzo supremo; lucha crítica.

tugboat [-boʊt], *s.* remolcador.

tugger [-œ(r)], *s.* el que da tirones.

tuille [twil], *s.* (arm.) faldar.

tuition [tjuíʃon], *s.* instrucción o enseñanza; precio de la enseñanza (gen. el que se paga por semestre, año, etc.).

tularemia [tulärímiä], *s.* (med. y vet.) tularemia.

tulip [tjúlip], *s.* (bot.) tulipán, tulipa.—**t. tree**, (bot.) tulipero, tulipanero.

tulipwood [-wud], *s.* (bot.) madera del tulipero o tulipanero; estos mismos árboles.

tulle [tul], *s.* (tej.) tul.

tumble [tʌmbl]. **I.** *vn.* caer, dar en tierra, tumbar; (gen. con **down**) desplomarse, venirse abajo; voltear, rodar, dar vueltas; dar saltos, brincar; volquearse, revolverse, revolcarse; (fam.) comprender, entender, caer en ello.—**to t. in o into bed**, (fam.) tumbarse, acostarse.— **to t. out**, (fam.) levantarse. **II.** *va.* revolver; tirar, arrojar; (gen. con **over o about**) tumbar, derribar; volcar; desarreglar, trastornar; ajar o arrugar (la ropa); cazar al vuelo; (fund., mec.) pulir por fricción. **III.** *s.* tumbo, caída; vuelco, voltereta, tumba, trepa; desorden, confusión.

tumblebug [-bʌg], *s.* (ent.) escarabajo pelotero.

tumble-down [-daʊn], *a.* destartalado.

tumbler [tʌmblœ(r)], *s.* vaso para beber, cortadillo; cubilete; volteador, saltabanco, titiritero; tentemozo, dominguillo (juguete); (mec.) tambor; seguro, fiador (de cerradura); (orn.) paloma volteadora.

tumbrel o **tumbril**, [tʌmbrel, -bril], *s.* chirrión, *m.*, carreta; (arti.) carro de artillería.

tumefacient [tjuméféiʃent], **tumescent** [tjuméseent], *a.* (med.) tumescente, hinchado.

tumefaction [tjuméfækʃon], *s.* (med.) tumefacción, hinchazón, *f.*—**tumefy** [tjúmeˌfai], *va.* y *vn.* entumecer(se), hinchar(se).

tumescence [tjuméssens], *s.* (med.) tumescencia; tumefacción, hinchazón, *f.*

tumid [tjúmid], *a.* (med.) túmido, turgente, hinchado; prominente, (poét.) turgente; inflado, rimbombante (estilo, lenguaje, etc.).

tumidity, **tumidness** [tjumíditi, tjúmidnis], *s.* hinchazón, *f.*; turgencia; calidad de inflado.

tummy [tʌmi], *s.* (fam.) estómago, panza.

tumor [tjúmo(r)], *s.* (med.) tumor, dureza.

tumular [tjúmjulä(r)], *a.* tumulario; abultado.

tumult [tjúmʌlt], *s.* tumulto, alboroto, escándalo, barullo, motín, conmoción; agitación.

tumultuarily [tjumʌlchuerili], *adv.* tumultuariamente, desordenadamente.—**tumultuariness** [-erinis], *s.* turbulencia.—**tumultuary** [-eri], *a.* tumultuario.

tumultuous [-ʌs], *a.* tumultuoso, alborotado.

tumultuously [-li], *adv.* tumultuosamente.

tumultuousness [-nis], *s.* turbulencia, tumulto.

tumulus [tjúmjulʌs], *s.* túmulo.

tun [tʌn], *s.* tonel, cuba; tanque de fermentación; cantidad de cerveza fermentada de una vez; medida indeterminada de líquidos.—**t. belly**, gran barriga. **II.** *va.* entonelar, envasar, embarrilar.

tuna [túnä], *s.* (bot.) tuna, higo de tuna; nopal (árbol); (ict.) atún (ll. t. **t. fish**).

tunable [tjúnäbl], *a.* acordable, que se puede templar; cantable, armonioso, musical.

tundra [tʌndrä], *s.* tundra, llanura árida musgosa de las regiones árticas.

tune [tjun]. **I.** *s.* (mús.) tonada, son, tañido, tono; afinación, concordancia, armonía.—**in t.**, templado, afinado.—**out of t.**, destemplado, desafinado, desentonado.—**to the t. of**, al son de, tocando o entonando (tal o cual tonada). **II.** *va.* templar, afinar, acordar, entonar; ajustar, adaptar; (rad.) sintonizar.—**to t. out**, (rad.) excluir (señales, etc.) por sintonización apropiada.—**to t. up**, (mec.) hacer funcionar por corto tiempo (una máquina, un automóvil) para poner en punto. **III.** *vn.* armonizar, modular; (rad.) (a veces con **in**) sintonizar el aparato receptor.

tuneful [-ful], *a.* armonioso, melodioso.

tuneless [-lis], *a.* desentonado, disonante; mudo.

tuner [-œ(r)], *s.* afinador, templador; (rad.) sintonizador; circuito de sintonización.

tung oil [tʌŋ ɔil], *s.* tung.—**t. tree**, (bot.) aleurita.

tungstate [tʌŋsteit], *s.* tungstato, volframiato.

tungsten [-sten], *s.* (quím.) tungsteno, volframio. —**t. steel**, acero tungsteno.

tungstic [-stik], *a.* (quím.) túngstico.

tungstite [-stait], *s.* (min.) tungstita, volframina.

tunic [tjúnik], *s.* túnica, blusa, ropón; (hist.) túnica; (igl.) túnica, tunicela; (mil.) casaca; (bot. y anat.) túnica.

Tunicata [tjunikéitä], *s. pl.* (zool.) tunicados.

tunicate(d [tjúnikeit(id], **I.** *a.* (bot.) tunicado (bulbo). **II.** *a.* y *s.* (zool.) tunicado.

tunicle [tjúnikl], *s.* (bot. anat. zool.) túnica, tegumento; (igl.) tunicela, túnica.

tuning [tjúnin]. **I.** *s.* (mús.) afinación, templadura; (rad.) sintonización. **II.** *a.* de templar, de afinar; (rad.) sintonizador, de sintonización.— **t. coil**, (rad.) bobina de sintonización.—**t. dial**, (rad.) cuadrante graduado.—**t. fork**, (mús.) diapasón.—**t. hammer**, **t. key**, (mús.) (llave (*f.*) de) afinador, templador, martillo.

Tunisian [tjunísän], *a.* y *s.* tunecí, tunecino.

tunnage [tʌnidž], *s.* tonelaje.

tunnel [tʌnel]. **I.** *s.* túnel; (min.) socavón; (aer.) túnel de pruebas.—**t. net**, red abocinada. **II.** *va.* atravesar por túnel, construir un túnel a través de; horadar. **III.** *vn.* construir o abrir un túnel.—**tunnel(l)ing** [-iŋ], *s.* perforación; construcción de túneles o de un túnel o socavón.

tunny [tʌni], *s.* (ict.) atún.—**t. fishery**, almadraba.—**striped t.**, bonito.

tup [tʌp], *s.* (zool.) morueco, carnero padre; (mec.) martillo, (cabeza o mazo de) martinete.

tuppence [tʌpens], *s.* moneda de dos peniques.

Turanian [tyuréinän], *s.* y *a.* turanio.

turban [tœrban], *s.* turbante.

turbellarian [tœrbɛléįrįan], *a.* y *s.* (zool.) turbelario.

turbid [tœrbįd], *a.* turbio, túrbido, espeso; zurrapiento, zurraposo; turbulento.

turbidity [tœrbídįtį], **turbidness** [tœrbįdnįs], *s.* turbieza, turbiedad; turbulencia.

turbinal [tœrbįnal], **turbinate(d** [-eįt(id]. I. *a.* (bot., anat., etc.) turbinado, en forma de peonza; espiral. II. *s.* (anat., zool.) cornete de la nariz.

turbine [tœrbįn], *s.* (hidr.) turbina (ll. t. t. **wheel**).

turbot [tœrbǫt], *s.* (ict.) rodaballo, rombo.

turbulence, turbulency [tœrbyǫḷęns, -į], *s.* turbulencia, tumulto, alboroto, agitación.—**turbulent** [-ęnt], *a.* turbulento; levantisco, revoltoso.—**turbulently** [-lį], *adv.* turbulentamente.

Turcoman [tœrkǫman], *s.* = TURKOMAN.

Turdidæ [tœrdįdį], *s. pl.* (orn.) túrdidos.

Turdus [tœrdʌs], *s.* (orn.) género de los tordos.

tureen [tųrín], *s.* sopera, salsera.

turf [tœrf]. I. *s.* césped(e), *m.*, tepe; turba; (con **the**) las carreras de caballos, el hipódromo.—**t. parlance**, el tecnicismo hípico. II. *va.* encespedar.

turfiness [-įnįs], *s.* abundancia de césped o de turba.—**turfman** [-man], *s.* aficionado a las carreras de caballos.—**turfy** [-į], *a.* encespedado; rel. a las carreras de caballos.—**t. ground**, cespedera.

turgescence, turgescency [tœrdźéşęns, -į], *s.* (med.) turgencia, hinchazón, *f.*; ostentación.

turgescent [-ęnt], *a.* turgente, hinchado. V. TURGID.

turgid [tœrdźįd], *a.* turgente, hinchado; ampuloso, pomposo.—**turgidity** [tœrdźídįtį], *o* **turgidness** [tœrdźįdnįs], *s.* turgencia, hinchazón, *f.*; ampulosidad.

Turk [tœrk], *s.* turco.—**T.'s-cap (lily)**, (bot.) martagón.—**T.'s-head**, escobón, deshollinador; (*v.* POPE'S HEAD); (mar.) cierto nudo en forma de turbante.

turkey [tœrkį], *s.* (orn.) pavo.—**t. buzzard**, aura, gallinazo.—**t. cock o gobbler**, (galli)pavo, (Am.) guanajo; (fig.) persona engreída que se pavonea.—**t. hen**, pava.—**T. red**, carmesí.—**t. trot**, cierto baile popular.

Turkish [tœrkįš]. I. *a.* turco, turquesco.—**T. bath**, baño turco.—**T. tobacco**, tabaco turco.—**T. towel**, toalla de baño, toalla rusa o peluda.—**T. towel(l)ing**, género de algodón grueso y velludo para toallas ásperas de baño.—**in the T. fashion**, a la turquesca. II. *s.* turco (idioma).

Turkoman [tœrkǫman], *s.* (*pl.*-MANS) turcomano.

turmeric [tœrmęrįk], *s.* (bot.) cúrcuma.—**t. paper**, (quím.) papel de cúrcuma.

turmoil [tœrmǫįl], *s.* disturbio, tumulto, baraúnda, alboroto, desorden, agitación.

turn [tœrn], *va.* volver, voltear; dar vueltas a, hacer girar; cambiar, transformar, convertir; (mec.) tornear; volver del revés al derecho; revolver (en la mente); desviar; traducir, verter; rechazar; doblar, dar la vuelta a (una esquina, etc.); aplicar, destinar, adaptar; transferir; dar náusea; echar (una llave); cumplir (años); expresar o crear de modo artístico.—**to t. a deaf ear to**, no dar oídos a, no hacer caso a o de, hacer oídos de mercader, hacerse el sordo.—**to t. adrift**, soltar o abandonar.—**to t. against**, predisponer en contra de; causar aversión a o contra.—**to t. an honest penny**, (fam.) ganar el dinero honradamente.—**to t. around**, voltear, dar vuelta a.—**to t. (a person) around one's fingers**, tener (a una persona) de la ternilla, dominarla.—**to t. aside**, desviar; hacer a un lado.—**to t. away**, despedir, echar; desviar.—**to t. back**, volver atrás; devolver, restituir.—**to t. down**, plegar, doblar; poner boca abajo; bajar (el gas); (fam.)

abandonar; rechazar, rehusar.—**to t. from**, desviar o alejar de.—**to t. in**, replegar; doblar hacia adentro; entregar.—**to t. into**, convertir en, cambiar en.—**to t. off**, despachar, rechazar, despedir; desviar, apartar; (mec.) reducir torneando o en el torno; tornear; cortar (el agua, el vapor); cerrar (la radio o la llave del gas, del agua, etc.); desconectar (el encendido, la lámpara, etc.); apagar (la luz), volteando una llave.—**to t. on** (*water, steam*), abrir la llave (del agua, vapor); dar (vapor); echar (el agua); establecer (la corriente eléctrica); encender (la luz); poner (la radio).—**to t. one's back on**, volver la(s) espalda(s) a.—**to t. one's coat**, cambiar de uniforme; pasarse al partido opuesto.—**to t. one's hand to**, dedicarse a, meter el hombro a.—**to t. out**, echar, expeler, arrojar; sacar hacia afuera; apagar (la luz, etc.); producir; volver al revés; doblar, torcer; echar al campo (los animales).—**to t. over**, transferir, pasar, trasladar; volver, invertir, volcar; revolver; doblar; abuñuelar (huevos).—**to t. over a new leaf**, enmendarse, empezar vida nueva.—**to t. over in one's mind**, pensar con detenimiento, meditar sobre.—**to t. tail**, volver la espalda, mostrar los talones.—**to t. the brain o the head of**, trastornar la cabeza o el juicio a; volver loco.—**to t. the cold shoulder to**, desairar, tratar con desprecio.—**to t. the flank of**, (mil.) flanquear.—**to t. the scale(s)**, cambiar el orden de las cosas; determinar, decidir.—**to t. the stomach**, causar asco.—**to t. the tables**, cambiar la suerte; devolver la pelota, (fam.) volver la tortilla.—**to t. thumbs down on**, condenar a; rechazar.—**to t. to account, advantage, o profit**, sacar partido de, aprovechar.—**to t. up**, voltear, volver; levantar; cavar (el suelo); arremangar (la manga, la ropa); subir (el cuello).—**to t. up one's nose at**, mirar con desprecio, desdeñar; (fam.) respingar.—**to t. up one's toes**, (fam.) lanzar el último suspiro, marcharse al otro mundo.—**to t. upside down**, trastornar; volver lo de arriba abajo, poner patas arriba; volcar.

turn, *vn.* girar, rodar, voltear, dar vueltas; torcer, seguir otra dirección; (mar.) virar, bornear; volverse, voltearse; convertirse en; hacerse, ponerse, volverse (a menudo se expresa usando el verbo indicado por un adjetivo: *to turn pale*, palidecer; *to turn red*, enrojecerse); mudar de posición, estado u opinión; desdecirse, cambiar de casaca o de religión; avinagrarse (vino), agriarse (leche).—**to t. about o around**, volverse, volver la cara; voltearse.—**to t. against**, volverse contra; coger aversión a.—**to t. aside**, desviarse, torcer.—**to t. away**, desviarse, alejarse, apartarse; volver la cara o espalda.—**to t. back**, retroceder; volverse.—**to t. down a street**, torcer por una calle.—**to t. from**, apartarse de; huir de.—**to t. in**, guarecerse; entrar; llegar a casa; (fam.) irse a la cama, acostarse.—**to t. into**, entrar en; transformarse, convertirse en; volverse.—**to t. off**, torcer, desviarse.—**to t. on**, depender de; volverse contra; acometer a.—**to t. out**, resultar; asistir, acudir; volverse o estar vuelto o dirigido hacia fuera; salir de casa; (fam.) levantarse.—**to t. over**, dar vueltas, revolverse, voltearse; volcar (un coche, etc.).—**to t. round**, cambiar de frente; voltearse, volverse; cambiar de opinión o partido.—**to t. short**, dar media vuelta.—**to t. state's evidence**, confesar su delito y declarar contra sus cómplices (dicho de un reo).—**to t. to**, recurrir o acudir a; dirigirse hacia o a; convertirse o transformarse en; redundar en.—**to t. turtle**, voltearse patas arriba; (mar.) zozobrar.—**to t. up**, acontecer, suceder; aparecer; tirar hacia arriba (la nariz).—**to t. upon**, estribar, depender de; recaer sobre.—**to t. upside down**, voltearse patas arriba; (mar.) zozobrar.—**my head turns (round)**, se me va la cabeza.—**not to t. a hair**, quedar impávido, no pestañear.—**please t. over** (**p. t. o.** en abreviatura), a la vuelta (de la página).

turn [tǽrn], s. vuelta, revolución, giro, rotación; rodeo, (re)vuelta, recodo; turno, revezo, tanda; lance (en un juego); ocasión, oportunidad; mudanza, cambio; torcimiento, torcedura; curso, marcha, dirección; fase, f., faz, aspecto, sesgo, cariz, m.; proceder, procedimiento, comportamiento; partida o pasada (buena o mala) hecha a alguno; genio, inclinación, propensión, aptitud, carácter; provecho, utilidad; forma, figura, hechura; giro de frase; vuelta, paseo corto, caminata; (teat.) pieza u acto cortos; (dep.) contienda, partido; (com.) transacción. —**t. indicator**, (aer.) indicador de giro.—**t. of life**, (med.) menopausia.—**a friendly t.**, un favor.—**an ill t.**, una partida serrana.—**at every t.**, a cada instante, a cada momento.—**by turns**, por turnos.—**in t.**, a su turno, a su vez.—**to a t.**, exactamente, con absoluta perfección.—**to have a t. for**, ser aficionado a, tener aptitud para.—**to take a t.**, dar un paseo. —**to take a t. for the better o worse**, mejorarse, empeorarse.—**to take another t.**, cambiar de aspecto, tomar otro sesgo o cariz.—**to take turns**, turnarse, alternar.

turnbuckle [-bʌkl], s. torniquete; tensor, templador; tarabilla.

turncoat [-kout]. **I.** s. (pol.) desertor, renegado, apóstata, mf., tránsfuga, mf. **II.** vn. volver (la) casaca.

turndown [-daun], a. doblado hacia abajo, caído (cuello, etc.).

turned-up [-d-ʌp], a. vuelto o doblado hacia arriba; respingada o respingona (la nariz).

turner [-œ(r)], s. (mec.) tornero, fustero; gimnasta, m., volteador.—**t.'s lathe**, torno.

turnery [-œri], s. (mec.) tornería.

turning [-iŋ]. **I.** s. vuelta, rodeo; recodo, ángulo; (mec.) tornería; gimnasia.—pl. virutas que se hacen torneando. **II.** a. giratorio; de giro; de rotación.—**t. point**, punto decisivo, crisis; (top.) punto de cambio (en nivelación).—**t. radius**, radio de giro.

turnip [tǽrnip], s. (bot.) nabo.—**t. greens o tops**, nabizas.

turnkey [tǽrnki], s. llavero de una cárcel.

turnout [-aut], s. salida de personas a paseo; concurrencia; huelga de obreros; tren, séquito; carruaje de lujo; andén; (f. c.) apartadero, desviadero; producción de una fábrica en un tiempo determinado.

turnover [-ouvœ(r)]. **I.** a. doblado o vuelto hacia abajo. **II.** s. vuelco; vuelta, voltereta; (coc.) pastelillo con repulgo; (coc.) estrelladera, pala; (com.) cambio (de personal); reorganización; número de transacciones comerciales; compras y ventas; período de venta y repuesto de un surtido de mercancías, o tiempo en que se les da salida o en que hay que reponerlas; número de empleados que se cambian o reemplazan en un tiempo dado; (e. p.) capital invertido transitoriamente, que debe reintegrarse antes de empezar a contar ganancias; cada una de las personas que se emplean durante períodos cortos para mantener un número constante de empleados; empleo parcial turnado.

turnpike [-paik], s. camino o barrera de portazgo. —**t. duty**, portazgo.—**t. road**, camino de portazgo.

turnplate [-pleit], s. (f. c., Ingl.) = TURNTABLE.

turnscrew [-skru], s. destornillador.

turnsole [-soul], s. (bot.) heliotropo; tornasol, girasol, mirasol.

turnspit [-spit], s. galopillo o perro que voltea el asador.

turnstile [-stail], s. torniquete.

turnstone [-stoun], s. (orn.) revuelvepiedras.

turntable [-teibl], s. (f. c.) placa giratoria; disco giratorio del fonógrafo o microscopio.

turpentine [tǽrpǝntain], s. trementina.—**t. tree**, (bot.) terebinto.—**oil of t.**, aguarrás.

turpeth [tǽrpɛθ], s. (bot.) turbit.—**t. mineral**, (farm.) turbit mineral.

turpitude [tǽrpitjud], s. vileza, infamia; depravación.

turquoise [tǽrkwojz], s. (min.) turquesa.

turret [tǽrit], s. torre(cilla); (fort.) roqueta; (mar.) torre blindada, cúpula; (aer.) torre blindada.

turreted [-id], a. que tiene torre o figura de torre.

turtle [tǽrtl], s. (zool.) tortuga de mar, carey; (impr.) bastidor cilindrado que sostiene el tipo en una prensa rotatoria.—**t. shell**, carey.

turtledove [-dʌv], s. (orn.) tórtola.

Tuscan [tʌ́skǝn], a. y s. toscano.

tush [tʌʃ]. **I.** s. = TUSK. **II.** interj. ¡bah!

tusk [tʌsk], s. colmillo, diente incisivo o canino, navaja, presa (de elefante, jabalí, foca, etc.).

tusked, tusky [-t, -i], a. (zool.) colmilludo, que tiene colmillos, etc.

tussis [tʌ́sis], s. (med.) tos, f.

tussive [tʌ́siv], a. (med.) tusivo.

tussle [tʌ́sl]. **I.** vn. forcejear, (fam.) tener una agarrada (con). **II.** s. sarracina, agarrada, pelea.

tussock [tʌ́sɔk], s. montecillo de hierbas crecientes; penacho, copete.

tut [tʌt], interj. ¡tate! ¡basta! ¡bah!

tutelage [tjútelidʒ], s. tutela, tutoría, curaduría.

tutelar, tutelary [tjútelǝ(r), -ɛri], a. tutelar.—**t. angel**, ángel de la guardia.—**t. saint**, santo patrón.

tutor [tjútǝ(r)]. **I.** s. tutor, ayo, preceptor; (for.) curador. **II.** va. enseñar, instruir; (for.) ser curador de.

tutorage [-idʒ], s. tutoría, tutela; (for.) curaduría.

tutoress [-is], s. tutora, tutriz, aya.

tutorial [tjutórial], a. relativo a preceptores, curadores o curaduría.

tutorship [tjútǝrʃip], s. curaduría, oficio de curador.

tutti-frutti [túti frúti]. **I.** s. tutifruti, dulce o confitura de varias clases de frutas. **II.** a. compuesto de frutas de varias clases.

tutty [tʌ́ti], s. (quím.) tucía, (a)tutía, cadmía.

tu-whit, tu-whoo [tu hwit, tu hwú]. **I.** vn. gritar (el buho). **II.** s. grito del buho.

tuxedo [tʌksídou], s. smoking, saco de ceremonia.

tuyère [twiɛ́r], s. (metal.) alcribís, tobera.

twaddle [twádl]. **I.** vn. disparatar, decir tonterías, charlar, parlotear. **II.** s. habladuría, charla; tonterías, f. pl., disparates, m. pl.; charlatán.

twain [twein]. **I.** a. (poét.) dos. **II.** s. un par.

twang [twæŋ]. **I.** va. y vn. producir un sonido vibrante; puntear las cuerdas de un instrumento; hablar por la nariz. **II.** s. punteado de una cuerda; tonillo nasal, gangueo, dejo.

'twas [twaz], contr. de IT WAS.

tweak [twik]. **I.** va. pellizcar retorciendo. **II.** s. pellizco retorcido.

tweed [twid]. **I.** s. (tej.) paño de lana de dos colores. **II.** a. hecho de este paño.

tweedle [twídl]. **I.** va. y vn. cantar o silbar; tocar un instrumento. **II.** s. sonido agudo del violín, etc.—**tweedledum** [-dʌm] **and tweedledee** [-dí], fo o fa.

'tween [twin], prep. contr. de BETWEEN, entre.

tweet [twit]. **I.** s. gorjeo. **II.** vn. gorjear, piar.

tweezers [twízœrz], s. pl. tenacillas, tenazuelas, pinzas; despinzas, despinces (para el paño).

twelfth [twélfθ]. **I.** a. duodécimo, doceno, dozavo; doce (ordinal).—**T.-day** = TWELFTHTIDE.—**T.-night**, víspera del día de los Reyes. **II.** s. dozavo; (mús.) duodécima.—**Twelfthtide** [-taid], s. día (m.) de los Reyes, Epifanía.

twelve [twélv], a. y s. doce.

twelvemo [-mou], a. y s. (enc.) duodécimo, en dozavo (libro).

twelvemonth [-mʌnθ], *s.* un año, o doce meses.
twentieth [twéntjiθ]. **I.** *a.* vigésimo, vicésimo, veintavo; veinte (ordinal). **II.** *s.* veintavo.
twenty [twénti], *a.* y *s.* veinte; una veintena.
—**t. odd**, veintitantos.—**t.-one**, veintiuna (juego de naipes o dados).
'twere [twœr], *contr.* de IT WERE.
twibil(l [twáibil], *s.* (hist.) hacha de dos filos.
twice [twais], *adv.* dos veces; al doble.—**t. as much o as many**, el doble, otros tantos.—**t.-told**, repetido; trillado.
twiddle [twídl]. **I.** *va.* y *vn.* jugar con algo (ociosa o distraídamente); (hacer) girar (los pulgares, etc.); estar mano sobre mano; entretenerse con menudencias. **II.** *s.* vuelta, movimiento giratorio u ocioso.
twig [twig], *s.* (bot.) ram(it)a, vástago; varilla.
twilight [twáilait]. **I.** *s.* crepúsculo, nochecita.—**by t.**, entre dos luces. **II.** *a.* obscuro, sombrío, crepuscular.—**t. sleep**, (med.) narcosis parcial obstétrica, producida para mitigar los dolores del parto.
twill [twil]. **I.** *va.* (tej.) cruzar, asargar.—**twilled silk**, tela cruzada de seda, sarga. **II.** *s.* tela cruzada o asargada.
'twill [twil], *contr.* de IT WILL.
twin [twin]. **I.** *s.* y *a.* gemelo, mellizo.—**t. brother, sister**, hermano, hermana gemelos. —**T. Brothers, o Brethren**, (mit., astr.) Cástor y Pólux.—**t.-cylinder**, (m. v.) de cilindros gemelos.—**t. engine**, (m. v.) máquina de cilindros gemelos.—**t.-engine(d)**, **t. motor(ed)**, (aer.) bimotor, provisto de dos motores.—**Twins**, (astr.) Géminis, *m.*—**t.-screw**, (mar.) de doble hélice, *f.*, de dos hélices.—**t.-six**, de doce cilindros (motor, coche). **II.** *vn.* nacer mellizo; aparearse; parir mellizos.
twinborn [-bɔrn], *a.* mellizo, gemelo.
twine [twain]. **I.** *va.* (re)torcer; enroscar, acordonar. **II.** *vn.* enroscarse; ensortijarse; caracolear. —**to t. about**, abrazar. **III.** *s.* (hilo de) bramante, guita; enroscadura; abrazo.
twinge [twindʒ]. **I.** *va.* y *vn.* causar o sentir un dolor agudo; atormentar; sufrir. **II.** *s.* dolor agudo, punzada; remordimiento.
twining [twáinin], *a.* que se enrosca, etc.; (bot.) voluble.
twinkle [twínkl], *va.* y *vn.* destellar, (hacer) centellear, chispear, rutilar, titilar; (hacer) parpadear, pestañear.
twinkle, twinkling [twínkl, -klin], *s.* destello, titilación, centelleo; pestañeo, guiñada; momento, instante.—**in the twinkling of an eye**, en un abrir y cerrar de ojos.
twirl [twœrl]. **I.** *va.* y *vn.* (hacer) girar; dar vueltas. **II.** *s.* rotación, vuelta, giro; rasgueo.
twist [twist]. **I.** *va.* (re)torcer, enroscar, entrelazar, entretejer, arrollar, enrollar; doblar, doblegar; trenzar; ceñir, bornear, rodear; (mar.) virar. **II.** *vn.* enroscarse, envolverse, torcerse; virar; encarrujarse, ensortijarse; serpentear; caracolear. **III.** *s.* torsión, torcedura, enroscadura; tirón, sacudida; cordoncillo, torzal; peculiaridad, rasgo característico; contorsión, quiebro; rosca de pan, pan retorcido; rollo de tabaco; en baseball, efecto dado a la pelota.—**t. drill**, barrena o broca espiral.
twister [-œr)], *s.* torcedor; cordelero, soguero, cabestrero, guitero; torcedero (instrumento); torbellino, viento giratorio; ciclón.
twisting [-iŋ], *s.* torcedura, torsión, retorcimiento.—**t. machine**, torcedor, torcedero.
twit [twit]. **I.** *va.* fisgar, escarnecer, dar matraca a; reprender. **II.** *s.* escarnio, mofa, fisga; reprensión.
twitch [twitʃ]. **I.** *va.* tirar o sacudir bruscamente. **II.** *vn.* crisparse, convelerse, contorcerse. **III.** *s.* tirón, sacudida; crispatura, contracción nerviosa o espasmódica; (vet. y herr.) acial.—**t. grass**, (bot.) grama.
twitter [twítœ(r)]. **I.** *vn.* gorjear los pájaros; temblar de agitación. *V.* TITTER y GIGGLE. **II.** *s.* gorjeo (de los pájaros); agitación, inquietud, emoción.
'twixt [twikst], *prep. contr.* de BETWIXT (poét.)
two [tú]. **I.** *s.* y *a.* dos.—**t. abreast**, de dos en dos. —**t. bits**, (fam.) 25 centavos (*v.* TWO-BIT).— **t. by t.**, by twos, in twos, dos a dos, de dos en dos, a pares.—**t. hundred(th)**, doscientos. —**in t.**, en dos (partes o pedazos).—**to put t. and t. together**, atar cabos. **II.** *a.* de dos. En esta acepción modifica a muchos substantivos y adjetivos y participios derivados de substantivos, indicando siempre la existencia de dos de las partes que el substantivo denota, como en *two-volume*, de dos volúmenes; *two-cylinder*, de dos cilindros; *two-barreled*, de dos cañones.—**t.-bit**, (fam.) del valor de 25 centavos; pequeño, estrecho, de poco valor.—**t.-by-four**, madera o cualquier objeto que mide cuatro pulgadas (o pies) por dos; (fam.) pequeño, insignificante. —**t.-cleft**, (bot.) bífido, hendido en dos.—**t.-color**, bicromático, relativo a la bicromía; de dos colores.—**t.-cycle engine**, motor de dos tiempos; bifásico.—**t.-decker**, barco de dos puentes.—**t.-edged**, de dos filos.—**t.-faced**, de dos caras; doble, falso, disimulado.—**t.-fisted**, (fam.) viril, vigoroso.—**t.-foot rule**, regla de dos pies de largo.—**t.-handed**, de o para dos manos; ambidextro.—**t.-handed saw**, tronzador.—**t.-handed sword**, espadón. —**t.-headed**, bicéfalo, bicípite, de dos cabezas. —**t.-horse**, de dos caballos.—**t.-leaf**, **t.-leaved**, difilo o difilo.—**t.-legged**, de dos patas o pies; bípedo.—**t.-masted**, de dos palos o mástiles.—**t.-motor**, bimotor.—**t.-phase**, (elec.) bifásico.—**t.-ply**, de dos tramas, capas, o hilos.—**t.-seater**, coche, avión, *m.*, etc., de dos asientos.—**t.-sided**, de dos lados; de dos caras, falso.—**t.-step**, (mús. y danz.) cierto baile de salón; (mús.) paso doble.—**t.-throw**, de dos direcciones (interruptor, etc.).—**t.-tongued**, falso, doble.—**t.-way**, de dos direcciones; de dos conductos; de tránsito en ambas direcciones (calle, vía).—**t.-wheeler**, (fam.) vehículo de dos ruedas.—**t.-wire** (elec.) bifilar (sistema, distribución, etc.); de o para dos conductores.
twofold [-fóuld]. **I.** *a.* doble; duplicado; de dos clases o aspectos. **II.** *adv.* duplicadamente, al doble.
twopence [tʌpɛns], *s.* moneda de dos peniques.
twopenny [tʌpeni], *a.* del valor de dos peniques; despreciable.—**twosome** [túsʌm], *s.* grupo de dos personas; juego en que toman parte dos personas.
tycoon [taikún], *s.* taicún (*v.* SHOGUN); (fam.) magnate industrial.
tying [táiin]. **I.** *ger.* de TO TIE. **II.** *s.* acción de atar, ligar, amarrar, etc.; ligamiento, ligadura, (mar.) ligada.
tympan [tímpan], *s.* membrana tensa; (impr.) tímpano; (mús., ant.) tímpano, timbal; (arq.) = TYMPANUM.
tympanic [timpénik], *a.* timpánico.—**t. membrane**, (anat., zool.) tímpano.
tympanist [tímpanist], *s.* (mús.) timbalero, el que toca el timbal u otros instrumentos de percusión.
tympanites [timpanáitiz], *s.* (med.) timpanitis, distensión o enfisema (*m.*) abdominal.
tympanitis [timpanáitis], *s.* (med.) inflamación del tímpano, otitis media.
tympanum [tímpanʌm], *s.* (anat., zool.) tímpano; (arq.) tímpano, témpano, faldón.
type [taip]. **I.** *s.* tipo, género; símbolo, signo, emblema, *m.*; ejemplar distintivo; (impr.) tipo, letra; (biol.) tipo, modelo.—**t. bar**, línea de tipos que se funde en una sola pieza; palanca que sostiene el tipo (de una máquina de escribir).—**t. founder**, fundidor de letras de imprenta.—**t. foundry**, fundición de tipos.—**t.-measure**,

regla, tipómetro.—t. **metal**, metal de imprenta. **II.** va. y vn. mecanografiar, escribir en máquina; (bioquím.) clasificar, determinar el tipo de (la sangre, el suero, etc.).

typescript [-skrípt], s. material escrito a máquina; tipo de imprenta o de máquina que imita la letra de mano.

typesetter [-sɛtœ(r)], s. máquina para componer tipos; (impr.) cajista, tipógrafo, componedor.—**typesetting** [-sɛtiŋ], s. (impr.) composición (de tipo); tipografía.

typewrite [-raịt], va. y vn. (pret. TYPEWROTE; pp. TYPEWRITTEN) mecanografiar, escribir a máquina.

typewriter [-raịtœ(r)], s. máquina de escribir, tipiadora. V. TYPIST.

typewriting [-raịtiŋ], s. acción o arte de usar una máquina de escribir; trabajo hecho con dicha máquina; mecanografía, dactilografía. **II.** a. mecanográfico.

typewritten [-rịtn], a. escrito con o a máquina.

typhlitis [tịfláịtịs], s. (med.) tiflitis, inflamación del intestino ciego.

typhlology [tịfláloḍʒị], s. (med.) ciencia de la ceguera.

typhoid [táịfoịd]. **I.** a. (med.) tifoideo, parecido al tifo.—t. **fever**, fiebre tifoidea. **II.** s. fiebre tifoidea.

typhoon [taịfún], s. tifón.

typhous [táịfʌs], a. (med.) tifoso, tífico.

typhus [táịfʌs], s. (med.) tifus, tifo (ll. t. t. **fever**).

typical [tịpịkạl], a. típico; característico, regular.

typically [-ị], adv. de modo típico o característico.

typicalness [-nịs], s. calidad de típico, etc.; representación figurativa o simbólica.

typify [tịpịfaị], va. representar, simbolizar, ser ejemplo de.

typist [táịpịst], s. mecanógrafo (-fa), dactilógrafo (-fa), dactilografista, tipiadora, escribiente a máquina; (Am. fam.) tiperrita.

typographer [taịpágrạfœ(r)], s. tipógrafo.

typographic(al [taịpográfịk(ạl], a. tipográfico.—t. **error**, errata (de impresión).

typographically [-ị], adv. tipográficamente.

typography [taịpágrạfị], s. tipografía.

typoscript [táịposkrịpt], s. trabajo mecanográfico.

tyrannic(al [tịrɛ́nịk(ạl], **tyrannous** [tírạnʌs], a. tiránico, tirano.—**tyrannically** [-ạlị], **tyrannously** [-lị], adv. tiránicamente, tiranamente, tiranizadamente.—**tyrannicide** [tịrɛ́nịsaịd], s. tiranicidio; tiranicida, mf. (persona).—**tyrannize** [tírạnaịz], va. y vn. tiranizar.

tyranny [tírạnị], s. tiranía.

tyrant [táịrạnt], s. tirano.

Tyrian [tírịạn], a. y s. tirio.—**T. dye**, púrpura de Tiro, múrice.

tyro [táịroụ], s. tirón, bisoño, novicio, novato.

Tyrolese [tịrolíz], **Tyrolian** [tịróụlịạn], a. y s. tirolés, del Tirol.

Tyrrhenian [tịrínịạn], a. tirreno, etrusco.

tythe [taịð], s. y v. = TITHE.

tzar, tzarina [tsar, -ínậ], s. = CZAR, CZARINA.

tzetze [tsɛ́tsị], s. = TSETSE.

U

u [yú], s. u.

U [yú], **U-shaped** [-šeịpt], a. en U, en forma de U (U iron, hierro en U; U tube, tubo en U).—**U-boat** [-boụt], s. submarino.

Ubiquitarian [yubịkwịtérịạn], a. y s. ubiquitario.

ubiquitous, ubiquitary [yubíkwịtʌs, -terị], a. ubicuo, omnipresente.

ubiquity [-tị], s. ubicuidad, omnipresencia.

udder [ádœ(r)], s. (zool.) ubre, f., teta.

udometer [yụdámɛtœ(r)], s. udómetro o pluviómetro.

ugh! [uk, ʌk, u, ʌ], interj. ¡puf! ¡uf! ¡fo!

uglily [ágḷịlị], adv. feamente; perversamente; con mal genio.—**ugliness** [-nịs], s. fealdad; fiereza; perversidad; mal genio.

ugly [ágḷị], a. feo, malparecido; asqueroso, repugnante; perverso, endiablado; fiero, feroz; malcarado, insolente, de mal genio, rudo.

uhlan, ulan [úlạn], s. (mil.) ulano.

uinta(h)ite [yụíntạạịt], s. asfalto de Utah.

ukase [yụkéịs], s. ucase.

Ukrainian [yukréịnịạn], s. y a. ucranio.

ulcer [Álsœ(r)], s. (med. y fig.) úlcera, llaga.—**ulcerate** [-eịt], va. y vn. ulcerar(se).—**ulceration** [-éịšọn], s. ulceración.—**ulcerous** [-ʌs], a. ulceroso.

ulema [uḷemá], s. concilio de los ulemas.

ullage [Álịḍʒ], s. merma de un tonel.

ulmaceous [ʌlméịšʌs], a. (bot.) ulmáceo.

ulna [Álnậ], s. (anat.) cúbito.—**ulnar** [-r], a. cubital.

ulster [Álstœ(r)], s. levitón ruso.

ulterior [ʌltírịọ(r)], a. ulterior.

ultima [Áltịmậ], s. última sílaba.

ultimate [Áltịmịt], a. último, final; fundamental, esencial; primario.—**ultimately** [-lị], adv. últimamente, en su esencia; finalmente, al fin.

ultimatum [ʌltịméịtạm], s. ultimátum.

ultimo [Áltịmoụ], adv. del mes próximo pasado (abrev. ult., ppdo.).

ultimogeniture [-dʒénịchụr], s. ultimogenitura, precedencia del hijo menor (opuesto a primogenitura).

ultra- [Áltrậ]. **I.** prefijo (lat.) más allá o además. **II.** a. exagerado, extremo. **III.** s. V. ULTRAIST.

ultraism [-ịzm], s. ultraísmo, extremismo, exageración en las opiniones o creencias.

ultraist [-ịst], s. ultraísta, extremista, exaltado.

ultramarine [-marín]. **I.** a. ultramarino. **II.** s. azul de ultramar(ino), formado del lapislázuli.

ultramicroscope [-máịkroskoụp], s. ultramicroscopio.

ultramicroscopic [-kápịk], a. ultramicroscópico, invisible con el microscopio ordinario; relativo al ultramicroscopio.

ultramontane [-mánteịn], s. y a. ultramontano; ultracatólico.—**ultramontanism** [-mántạnịzm], s. ultramontanismo.

ultramundane [-mándeịn], a. ultramundano.

ultraviolet [-vájoḷịt], a. (fís.) ultraviolado.

ululant [Áḷụlạnt], a. ululante.—**ululate** [-eịt], vn. ulular.—**ululation** [-éịšọn], s. ululato.

umbel [Ámbel], s. (bot.) umbela.

umbellate(d [-eịt(ịd], **umbelliferous** [-ịfɛ́rʌs], a. (bot.) umbelífero, aparasolado.

umber [Ámbœ(r)]. **I.** s. (pint.) tierra de sombra; sombra. **II.** a. pardo obscuro. **III.** va. sombrear.

umbilic(al [ʌmbịlịk(ạl], a. (anat.) umbilical; central; descendiente por parte de madre.—**u. cord**, (anat.) cordón umbilical, ombligo.

umbilicus [-ʌs], s. (anat.) ombligo.

umbo [Ámboụ], s. cazoleta de broquel.

umbra [Ámbrậ], s. (astr.) sombra.

umbrage [Ámbrịḍʒ], s. pique, resentimiento; sombra, umbría; sombrajo.

umbrageous [ʌmbréịḍʒʌs], a. sombrío, umbroso, umbrío, umbrático.—**umbrageousness** [-nịs], s. umbría, sombra; calidad de umbroso.

umbrella [ʌmbréḷậ], s. paraguas; parasol, sombrilla; (zool.) concha de los umbrélidos; (**U.**, zool.) umbrela.—**u. shell**, (zool.) umbrélido y su concha.—**u. shop**, paragüería.—**u. stand**, paragüero.

umlaut [úmlaụt], s. (filol.) diéresis; cambio de sonido indicado por la diéresis.

umpirage [Ámpaịrịḍʒ], s. arbitraje; (for.) arbitramento, tercería.

umpire [Ámpaịr]. **I.** s. (dep. y for.) árbitro; (juez) arbitrador; tercero en discordia; compromisario o secuestro. **II.** va. y vn. arbitrar.

un- [ʌn], prefijo que denota negación, oposición, contrariedad o privación, y corresponde gen. a no, sin, des-, o in-. Anteponiéndolo a un infinitivo, participio, gerundio, substantivo, adjetivo o adverbio, se forman gran número de voces, muchas de las cuales no están en los diccionarios, por ser obvio su significado, dado el carácter negativo del prefijo.

unabased [ʌnᴧbéjst], a. no envilecido.

unabashed [ʌnᴧbǽʃt], a. desenvuelto, desenfadado; descarado, (fam.) descocado.

unabated [ʌnᴧbéjtid], a. no disminuído; cabal.

unabbreviated [ʌnᴧbríyiejtid], **unabridged** [ʌnᴧbríʤd], a. íntegro, completo, sin abreviar.

unable [ʌnéjbl], a. inhábil, incapaz, impotente; imposibilitado.—**to be u.,** no poder, serle a uno imposible.

unabsolved [ʌnᴧbzálvd], a. no absuelto.

unaccented [ʌnᴧkséntid], a. sin acento; átono.

unacceptable [ʌnᴧkséptᴧbl], a. inaceptable.

unaccessible [ʌnᴧksésjbl], a. inaccesible.

unaccompanied [ʌnᴧkámpᴧnid], a. solo, sin acompañamiento.

unaccomplished [ʌnᴧkámpliʃt], a. incompleto, no acabado; falto de prendas o gracias.

unaccountable [ʌnᴧkáuntᴧbl], a. inexplicable, extraño; irresponsable.—**unaccountably** [-bli], adv. extraña o inexplicablemente; irresponsablemente.

unaccustomed [ʌnᴧkʌ́stomd], a. desacostumbrado, insólito, inhabituado.

unacknowledged [ʌnᴧknálidʒd], a. no reconocido; no declarado; por contestar (una carta).

unacquainted [ʌnᴧkwéjntid], a. inexperto; (con **with**) ignorante de.—**to be u. with**, no conocer; ignorar.

unadjusted [ʌnᴧdʒʌ́stid], a. no ajustado; no regulado o arreglado.

unadorned [ʌnᴧdórnd], a. llano, liso, simple, sin adorno.

unadulterated [ʌnᴧdʌ́ltœrejtid], a. genuino, puro, neto; natural, sin mezcla.

unadvisable [ʌnᴧdváizᴧbl], a. poco cuerdo, no prudente o conveniente.—**unadvised** [-d], a. inconsiderado; desatentado.—**unadvisedly** [-idli], adv. imprudentemente, desacordadamente.

unaffected [ʌnᴧféktid], a. inafectado; franco, natural; impasible.—**unaffectedly** [-li], adv. naturalmente, sin afectación.—**unaffectedness** [-nis], s. sencillez, lisura, naturalidad; impasibilidad.

unaided [ʌnéjdid], a. sin ayuda.

unallowable [ʌnᴧláuᴧbl], a. inadmisible; no permisible.

unalloyed [ʌnᴧlójd], a. puro, sin mezcla.

unalterable [ʌnóltœrᴧbl], a. inalterable; invariable, inmutable.—**unalterably** [-bli], adv. inalterablemente.

un-American [ʌnᴧmérikᴧn], a. contrario al espíritu o a las instituciones norteamericanos.

unanimity [yunᴧnímiti], s. unanimidad.

unanimous [yunǽnimᴧs], a. unánime.

unanimously [-li], adv. unánimemente, por unanimidad, de común acuerdo, al unísono, a una.

unanimousness [-nis], s. unanimidad.

unannealed [ʌnᴧníld], a. (cerá., etc.) no recocido.

unanswerable [ʌnǽnsœrᴧbl], a. incontrovertible, incontestable, indisputable.

unanswerably [-bli], adv. indisputablemente.

unanswered [ʌnǽnsœrd], a. por contestar, no contestado; no correspondido.

unappealable [ʌnᴧpílᴧbl], a. (for.) inapelable.

unapprehensive [ʌnǽprihénsiv], a. inaprensivo; impertérrito; lerdo, torpe.

unapproachable [ʌnᴧpróuchᴧbl], a. inaccesible.

unapproachableness [-nis], s. inaccesibilidad.

unappropriate(d [ʌnᴧprópriejt(id], a. no concedido o designado (fondos, etc.); libre; baldío, realengo (terrenos).

unapproved [ʌnᴧprúvd], a. desaprobado.

unapt [ʌnǽpt], a. poco inclinado, poco propenso; inepto, inhábil; lerdo.—**unaptly** [-li], adv. ineptamente.—**unaptness** [-nis], s. ineptitud.

unarmed [ʌnármd], a. desarmado, indefenso, inerme; (zool. y bot.) inerme.

unartistic [ʌnartístik], a. inartístico.

unasked [ʌnǽskt], a. no solicitado, espontáneo; no llamado; no convidado, sin convidar.

unaspirated [ʌnǽspirejtid], a. (fon.) no aspirado.

unassailable [ʌnᴧséjlᴧbl], a. inexpugnable.

unassembled [ʌnᴧsémbld], a. (mec., etc.) sin montar, desarmado, en piezas.

unassignable [ʌnᴧsájnᴧbl], a. intransferible.

unassuming [ʌnᴧsjúmiŋ], a. modesto.

unattached [ʌnᴧtǽcht], a. suelto, despegado; libre; (for.) no embargado; (mil.) de reemplazo.

unattainable [ʌnᴧtéjnᴧbl], a. inasequible, inalcanzable, irrealizable.

unattempted [ʌnᴧtémptid], a. no experimentado, no ensayado, no intentado.

unattended [ʌnᴧténdid], a. solo.

unattractive [ʌnᴧtrǽktiv], a. inatractivo.

unau [yunóu], s. (zool.) perezoso del Brasil.

unauthorized [ʌnóθᴧraizd], a. sin autorización, no autorizado, desautorizado.

unavailable [ʌnᴧvéjlᴧbl], a. inasequible, inaprovechable; inadaptable.

unavailing [-iŋ], a. inútil, vano, infructuoso.

unavoidable [ʌnᴧvójdᴧbl], a. inevitable, ineludible, inclutable, fatal.

unavoidableness [-nis], s. inevitabilidad.

unavoidably [-bli], adv. inevitablemente.

unaware [ʌnᴧwér], a. ignorante o inconsciente de, ajeno a.—**to be u. of**, no percatarse de, no tener conocimiento de.

unaware(s [-(z], adv. inopinadamente, repentinamente, de improviso, de golpe y porrazo; sin pensar, inadvertidamente.—**to take u.,** coger desprevenido.

unawareness [-nis], s. inconsciencia.

unbacked [ʌnbǽkt], a. sin ayuda, sin apoyo (financiero, etc.); sin respaldo; cerril (caballo).

unbalance [ʌnbǽlᴧns], va. desequilibrar; trastornar.—**unbalanced** [-t], a. desequilibrado; (fam.) chiflado, destornillado; (com.) no balanceado.

unballast [ʌnbǽlᴧst], va. (mar.) deslastrar.

unbaptized [ʌnbᴧptájzd], a. no bautizado; gentílico, pagano.

unbar [ʌnbár], va. desatrancar, desbarretar.

unbarrel [ʌnbǽrᴧl], va. desembarrilar.

unbearable [ʌnbérᴧbl], a. intolerable, insoportable, insufrible, inaguantable.

unbeaten [ʌnbítn], a. no pisado, no frecuentado; no batido; invicto.

unbecoming [ʌnbikámiŋ], a. indecoroso; impropio, indigno; que sienta mal (vestido, etc.). —**unbecomingly** [-li], adv. indecorosamente, etc.

unbeknown [ʌnbinóun], **I.** a. (fam.) no conocido, no sabido. **II.** adv. (fam.) sin conocimiento (de otro), por o de sorpresa.

unbelief [ʌnbilíf], s. incredulidad, descreimiento; irreligión, infidelidad.

unbeliever [ʌnbilívœ(r)], s. incrédulo, descreído; infiel, irreligioso.

unbend [ʌnbénd]. **I.** va. (pret. y pp. **UNBENT** o **UNBENDED**) enderezar, desencorvar; aflojar, relajar, zafar, soltar; (mar.) desenvergar (las velas). **II.** vn. enderezarse; condescender, ceder; ponerse afable; descansar, solazarse.

unbending [-iŋ], a. inflexible.

unbias(s)ed [ʌnbájᴧst], a. imparcial.

unbid(den [ʌnbíd(n], a. no invitado; espontáneo, no pedido o solicitado.

unbind [ʌnbájnd], va. (pret. y pp. **UNBOUND**) desligar, desatar, desamarrar; desvendar.

unbleached [ʌnblícht], a. crudo, sin blanquear.

unblemished [ʌnblémiʃt], a. puro, sin mancha.

unbolt [ʌnbóult], va. desbarretar, desempernar. —**unbolted** [-id], a. desempernado; sin cerner.

unborn [ʌnbórn], a. no nacido aún; venidero.

unbosom [ʌnbúzᴧm], va., vn. y vr. mostrar (uno) su corazón; desahogarse (de), confesar, (fam.) desembuchar.

unbottomed [ʌnbátɔmd], a. insondable; infundado; sin fondo.
unbound [ʌnbáund], a. **I.** pret. y pp. de to UNBIND. **II.** a. no encuadernado, sin encuadernar, en rústica; suelto, desatado.
unbounded [-íd], a. infinito, ilimitado.
unbrace [ʌnbréis], va. aflojar, soltar, desabrochar; desasegurar.
unbraid [ʌnbréid], va. destejer, destrenzar.
unbreakable [ʌnbréikabl], a. irrompible; impenetrable.—**u. glass,** cristal o vidrio irrompible.
unbreathed [ʌnbríðd], a. no comunicado a nadie.
unbred [ʌnbréd], a. malcriado.
unbridled [ʌnbráidld], a. desenfrenado, licencioso, irrefrenable.
unbroken [ʌnbróukn], a. intacto, entero; inviolado; continuo, no interrumpido; invicto; indómito, cerril (caballo).
unbuckle [ʌnbʌkl], va. deshebillar.
unburden [ʌnbɶrdn], va. descargar; aliviar.
unburied [ʌnbérid], a. insepulto.
unburned, unburnt [ʌnbɶrnd, ʌnbɶrnt], a. no cocido; incombusto.—**u. brick,** adobe.
unbury [ʌnbéri], va. desenterrar, exhumar.
unbusinesslike [ʌnbíznislaik], a. contrario a la práctica mercantil; informal; inexperto en los negocios.
unbutton [ʌnbʌtn], va. desabotonar, desabrochar.
uncalled [ʌnkóld], a. no llamado, no pedido.—**u.-for,** inmerecido, innecesario, gratuito; no reclamado.
uncancelled [ʌnkǽnseld], a. sin cancelar; no anulado, no rescindido.
uncanny [ʌnkǽni], a. misterioso, pavoroso.
uncap [ʌnkǽp], **I.** va. destapar. **II.** vn. desgorrarse, descubrirse para saludar.
uncared [ʌnkérd], a. (con **for**) desamparado, descuidado, abandonado.
uncase [ʌnkéis], va. desenvainar; (mil.) desplegar (la bandera); revelar.
unceasing [ʌnsísin], a. incesante.
unceasingly [-li], adv. sin cesar, incesantemente.
unceremonious [ʌnserɛmóuniʌs], a. familiar, llano, de confianza, inceremonioso.
uncertain [ʌnsɶrtǎn], a. incierto; perplejo, irresoluto, indeciso.—**uncertainly** [-li], adv. inciertamente.—**uncertainty** [-ti], s. incertidumbre; (lo) incierto; irresolución; instabilidad, inseguridad.
unchain [ʌnchéin], va. desencadenar.
unchangeable [ʌnchéindʒabl], a. inalterable, invariable, inmutable; igual.—**unchangeableness** [-nis], s. inmutabilidad o invariabilidad.—**unchangeably** [-abli], adv. inmutablemente, invariablemente.—**unchanged** [-d], a. inalterado.—**unchanging** [-iŋ], a. inalterable, inmutable, uniforme.
uncharitable [ʌnchǽritabl], a. no caritativo, falto de benevolencia, duro.—**uncharitableness** [-nis], s. falta de benevolencia, dureza.—**uncharitably** [-bli], adv. sin benevolencia o caridad, duramente.
unchaste [ʌnchéist], a. incasto.—**unchastity** [ʌnchǽstiti], s. incontinencia, falta de castidad.
unchecked [ʌnchékt], a. desenfrenado, inestorbado; no confrontado, cotejado o comprobado.
unchristian [ʌnkríschan], a. no cristiano; pagano, anticristiano.
unchurch [ʌnchɶrch], va. expulsar o excluir de la iglesia; excomulgar.—**unchurched** [-t], a. no perteneciente a, o miembro de, ninguna iglesia.
uncial [ʌnsial], a. y s. uncial (letra).
unciform [ʌnsiform], s. y a. (anat.) unciforme.
uncinariasis [-naráiasis], s. (med.) uncinariasis.
uncircumcised [ʌnsɶrkʌmsaizd], a. y s. incircunciso.
uncivil [ʌnsívil], a. incivil, descortés, grosero.
uncivilized [-aizd], a. incivilizado, bárbaro.

uncivilly [-i], adv. incivilmente, descortésmente.
unclad [ʌnklǽd], a. desnudo, sin vestir.
unclaimed [ʌnkléimd], a. no reclamado (correo, etc.).
unclasp [ʌnklǽsp], va. desabrochar.
unclassifiable [ʌnklǽsifaiabl], a. inclasificable.
uncle [ʌŋkl], s. tío; anciano; (fam.) prestamista, usurero.—**U. Sam,** el tío Sam (los E. U.).
unclean [ʌnklín], a. sucio, inmundo, desaseado; impuro; obsceno.
uncleanliness [ʌnklénlinis], s. suciedad, desaseo, falta de limpieza.
uncleanly [-li], a. sucio, desaseado, inmundo; impuro; indecente.
uncleanness [ʌnklínnis], s. suciedad; impureza, obscenidad.
uncloak [ʌnklóuk], va. quitar la capa o el abrigo a; (fig.) desembozar, desenmascarar.
unclog [ʌnklág], va. desembarazar, exonerar.
uncloister [ʌnklóistɶr(r)], va. exclaustrar.
unclose [ʌnklóuz], va. abrir; revelar.
unclothe [ʌnklóuð], va. quitar la ropa a, desnudar.
unclouded [ʌnkláudid], a. claro, despejado.
uncock [ʌnkák], va. desmontar (arma de fuego).
uncoil [ʌnkóil], va. desarrollar, desenrollar.
uncoined [ʌnkóind], a. no acuñado, sin acuñar.
uncollectable [ʌnkɔléktabl], a. incobrable.
uncollected [-tid], a. disperso; no cobrado.
uncolored [ʌnkʌlɔrd], a. descolorido; incoloro; imparcial.
uncombed [ʌnkóumd], a. despeinado.
uncomfortable [ʌnkʌmfɔrtabl], a. incómodo, penoso, desagradable, molesto; embarazado, intranquilo; indispuesto, con malestar.—**uncomfortableness** [-nis], s. incomodidad, penalidad; malestar; molestia, desagrado.—**uncomfortably** [-bli], adv. incómodamente; molestamente; etc.
uncommerical [ʌnkɔmɶršal], a. poco versado o interesado en el comercio; impropio de comerciantes o de los métodos comerciales.
uncommitted [ʌnkɔmítid], a. no cometido; no cumplido, no hecho; no comprometido, sin compromiso.
uncommon [ʌnkámɔn], a. poco común, excepcional, extraordinario, infrecuente, raro, extraño.
uncommonly [-li], adv. raramente, infrecuentemente; excepcionalmente.
uncompleted [ʌnkɔmplítid], a. inacabado, incompleto.
uncomplimentary [ʌnkampliméntari], a. poco halagüeño; desfavorable, ofensivo.
uncompromising [ʌnkámpromaiziŋ], a. inflexible, firme, intransigente; irreconciliable.
uncompromisingly [-li], adv. inflexiblemente, firmemente; de manera intransigente, sin concesión alguna.
unconcern [ʌnkɔnsɶrn], s. indiferencia, frialdad.
unconcerned [-d], a. indiferente, frío, impasible.
unconcernedly [-idli], adv. indiferentemente, sin inmutarse.
unconditional [ʌnkɔndíšɔnal], a. absoluto, incondicional; a discreción.—**unconditionally** [-i], adv. incondicionalmente; a discreción.
unconditioned [ʌnkɔndíšɔnd], a. libre, exento de condiciones, no limitado ni restringido; (filos.) incondicional, absoluto; (psic.) espontáneo, no aprendido.
unconfined [ʌnkɔnfáind], a. libre, ilimitado, sin trabas, sin obstáculos.
unconfirmed [ʌnkɔnfɶrmd], a. no confirmado.
unconformable [ʌnkɔnfórmabl], a. desconforme, diferente; (geol.) discordante.—**unconformableness** [-nis], **unconformity** [-iti], s. desconformidad; (geol.) discordancia.
uncongenial [ʌnkɔndʒínial], a. incongenial, incompatible.—**uncongeniality** [-éliti], s. incongenialidad, incompatibilidad.

unconnected [Ʌnkǫnéktįd], *a.* inconexo, irrelacionado.

unconquerable [Ʌnkáŋkœrąbl], *a.* invencible, insuperable, inconquistable.

unconscionable [Ʌnkánŝǫnąbl], *a.* exorbitante, desmedido, injusto; sin conciencia.

unconscionably [-blį], *adv.* sin razón, sin conciencia.

unconscious [Ʌnkánŝʌs], *a.* inconsciente; privado, insensible, desmayado, sin conocimiento; no sabedor, que ignora; desconocido, involuntario.—**the u.,** (psic.) lo inconsciente.—**unconsciously** [-lį], *adv.* inconscientemente, sin saberlo.—**unconsciousness** [-nįs], *s.* insensibilidad; falta de conocimiento, privación, inconsciencia.

unconstitutional [Ʌnkanstįtįúŝǫnąl], *a.* inconstitucional.—**unconstitutionality** [-élįtį], *s.* carácter inconstitucional.—**unconstitutionally** [-ąlį], *adv.* inconstitucionalmente.

uncontrollable [ankǫntróulạbl], *a.* ingobernable; indomable, irrefrenable.

uncontrolled [-d], *a.* sin freno, libre.

unconventional [Ʌnkǫnvénŝǫnąl], *a.* despreocupado, informal, libre.—**unconventionality** [-élįtį], *s.* despreocupación, informalidad, libertad de acción.

unconverted [Ʌnkǫnvœ́rtįd], *a.* no convertido.

uncork [Ʌnkórk], *va.* destapar, descorchar.

uncorrected [Ʌnkǫréktįd], *a.* sin corregir, no corregido.

uncorrupted [Ʌnkǫrʌ́ptįd], *a.* incorrupto.

uncounted [Ʌnkáuntįd], *a.* no contado, sin contar; innumerable.

uncouple [Ʌnkʌ́pl], *va.* desconectar, desengranar, zafar, soltar.—**uncoupled** [-d], *a.* suelto; soltero.

uncouth [Ʌnkúθ], *a.* tosco, rústico, desgarbado; extraño.—**uncouthly** [-lį], *adv.* rústicamente, toscamente; singularmente.—**uncouthness** [-nįs], *s.* tosquedad, rusticidad; extrañeza, rareza.

uncover [Ʌnkávœ(r)], **I.** *va.* destapar, descubrir; desabrigar, desarropar; revelar, poner al descubierto. **II.** *vn.* descubrirse; desembozarse.

uncowl [Ʌnkául], *va.* quitar la capucha de o a.

uncreated [Ʌnkrįéitįd], *a.* increado, sin crear.

uncrown [Ʌnkráun], *va.* destronar.

unction [Ʌ́ŋkŝǫn], *s.* unción, ungimiento; untura, untamiento; ungüento; (igl.) extremaunción; fervor, unción; divina gracia.

unctuous [Ʌ́ŋkchʌạs], *a.* untuoso, craso; zalamero.—**unctuousness** [-nįs], *s.* untuosidad.

uncultivated [Ʌnkʌ́ltįveįtįd], *a.* yermo, baldío, inculto; rústico, grosero.

uncurl [Ʌnkœ́rl], *va.* desrizar, desencrespar, destorcer.

uncut [Ʌnkʌ́t], *a.* sin cortar; sin tallar, sin labrar (apl. a piedras preciosas).

undamaged [Ʌndǽmįdžd], *a.* ileso, indemne.

undaunted [Ʌndóntįd], *a.* impávido, denodado, intrépido, impertérrito.—**undauntedly** [-lį], *adv.* intrépidamente, impávidamente.—**undauntedness** [-nįs], *s.* intrepidez, impavidez.

undeceive [Ʌndįsív], *va.* desengañar, desilusionar.

undecided [Ʌndįsáįdįd], *a.* indeciso; irresoluto.

undecipherable [Ʌndįsáįfœrąbl], *a.* indescifrable.

undeclinable [Ʌndįkláįnąbl], *a.* indeclinable.

undefiled [Ʌndįfáįld], *a.* impoluto, puro, limpio, inmaculado.

undefinable [Ʌndįfáįnąbl], *a.* indefinible.

undefined [Ʌndįfáįnd], *a.* indefinido.

undeniable [Ʌndįnáįąbl], *a.* innegable.

undeniably [-blį], *adv.* innegablemente.

under [Ʌ́ndœ(r)], **I.** *a.* inferior, bajero; subalterno, subordinado; bajo (de tono). **II.** *adv.* debajo; más abajo; menos. **III.** *prep.* debajo de, bajo; so; menos de o que; a (*under sail,* a la vela; *under steam,* al vapor); en; en tiempo de, en la época de; conforme a, según.—**u. a cloud,** en aprietos.—**u. arms,** bajo las armas.—**u. color of,** so color de.—**u. consideration,** en consi-

deración.—**u. contract,** bajo contrato; conforme al contrato.—**u. cover,** al abrigo, a cubierto.—**u. fire,** en combate; bajo el fuego del enemigo; (fig.) atacado, criticado, en aprietos.—**u. one's nose,** en las barbas de uno, en su presencia.—**u. pain of,** bajo o so pena de.—**u. separate cover,** por separado, bajo cubierta.—**u. the care of,** al cuidado de.—**u. the circumstances,** en las circunstancias.—**u. the command of,** al mando de.—**u. the rose,** en secreto.—**u. this act,** (for.) con arreglo a esta ley.—**u. way,** en camino, en marcha; andando; principiando.—**to be u. an obligation,** deber favores. *Under* se usa en composición para denotar inferioridad de categoría o de lugar, o bien falta o escasez.

underage [-éįdž], *a.* menor de edad.

underbid [-bíd], *va.* (pret. y pp. UNDERBID) rebajar; ofrecer o pedir (según el caso) menos que otro.

underbred [-bréd], *a.* de raza impura (caballo, etc.); sin urbanidad, rudo.

underbrush [-brʌŝ], *s.* maleza, broza.

underbuy [-báį], *va.* comprar a menor precio que; pagar por (algo) menos de lo que vale.

undercarriage [-kærįdž], *s.* (aer.) tren de aterrizaje. *V.* UNDERFRAME.—**u. skid,** patín de cola.

undercharge [-chárdž], *va.* cargar por (algo) menos de lo que conviene; (arti.) cargar insuficientemente.

underclassman [-klǽsmąn], *s.* estudiante del primero o segundo año.

underclerk [-klœrk], *s.* subsecretario; escribiente.

underclothes [-klouðz], *s. pl.,* **underclothing** [-klouðįŋ], *s.* ropa interior.

undercover [-kávœ(r)], *a.* secreto, clandestino; escondido.—**u. agent,** agente secreto de la policía, etc.; espía.

undercurrent [-kœ́rǫnt], *s.* corriente submarina; tendencia oculta.

undercut [-kʌ́t], **I.** *va.* (min.) socavar; en pugilismo, dar una puñada de abajo arriba; (b. a.) formar (obra de relieve, etc.) con base adelgazada o rebajada (menor que la parte superior); vender, o trabajar, a menor precio que (un competidor). **II.** [-kʌt], *s.* (min.) socava(ción); (coc.) solomillo (de carne); puñada pugilística de abajo arriba; corte sesgado; muesca hecha en un árbol para que caiga por ella al cortarlo. **III.** *a.* de base rebajada o entallada, más angosto en la base que arriba.

underdevelopment [-dįvélǫpmǫnt], *s.* desarrollo defectuoso; (foto.) revelamiento insuficiente.

underdo [-dú], *va.* (pret. UNDERDID; pp. UNDERDONE) (coc.) soasar, medio asar.—**underdone** [-dʌ́n], *a.* soasado, a medio asar.

underdog [-dǫg], *s.* el perdidoso; el más débil.—**the underdogs,** los de abajo.

underdrain [-dreįn], *s.* (hidr., agr.) desagüe o avenamiento subterráneo.

underdrawers [-drǫœrz], *s. pl.* calzoncillos.

underestimate [-éstįmeįt], *va.* menospreciar, desestimar, subestimar, apreciar en menos de lo que merece; no dar suficiente importancia a.

underexposure [-ekspóužṳ(r)], *s.* (foto.) insuficiente exposición.

underfeed [-fíd], *va.* (pret. y pp. UNDERFED) desnutrir, no alimentar suficientemente.—**underfeeding** [-įŋ], *s.* desnutrición, alimentación deficiente.

underfilling [-fílįŋ], *s.* cimiento de un edificio.

underfoot [-fút], **I.** *adv.* bajo los pies; en el piso, en el suelo. **II.** *a.* pisoteado, oprimido; abyecto.

underframe [-freįm], *s.* armazón (*f.*) de sustentación.

undergarment [-gármǫnt], *s.* prenda de ropa interior.

undergo [-góu], *va.* (pret. UNDERWENT; pp. UNDERGONE) sufrir, padecer; aguantar, sobrellevar; pasar por, ser sometido a; arrostrar.

undergraduate [-grǽdźu̯i̯t], *s.* estudiante no graduado aún.

underground [-gráu̯nd]. **I.** *a.* subterráneo; secreto.—**u. movement,** (pol.) movimiento de resistencia.—**u. trolley,** tranvía (*m.*) de canalización subterránea. **II.** *s.* sótano, subterráneo; ferrocarril subterráneo; (fam.) el subte; (fam.) modo secreto de permitir escapar a los esclavos, fugitivos, etc. **III.** *adv.* bajo tierra; ocultamente.

undergrown [-gróu̯n], *a.* de pequeña estatura, de desarrollo incompleto; (bot.) achaparrado; (agr.) cubierto de malezas.

undergrowth [-grou̯θ], *s.* maleza; baja estatura, desarrollo imperfecto.

underhand [-hǽnd]. **I.** *adv.* bajo mano, por debajo de cuerda, clandestinamente. **II.** *a.* secreto, clandestino, solapado.

underhanded [-i̯d], *a.* disimulado, clandestino.

underhandedly [-li̯], *adv.* por debajo de cuerda.

underlay [-léi̯]. **I.** *va.* (*pret.* y *pp.* UNDERLAID) reforzar; (impr.) calzar, realzar. **II.** *vn.* (min.) inclinarse (un filón). **III.** [-lei̯], *s.* (impr.) calzo, realce; (min.) buzamiento.

underlease [-lis], *s.* (for.) subarriendo.

underlet [-lét], *va.* (*pret.* y *pp.* UNDERLET) (for.) arrendar a menor precio que el valor verdadero; subarrendar.

underlie [-lái̯], *va.* (*pret.* UNDERLAY; *pp.* UNDERLAIN) estar debajo de; ser la razón fundamental o sostén de; sustentar, sostener.

underline [-lái̯n], *va.* subrayar.

underling [-li̯ŋ], *s.* subordinado.

underlying [-lái̯i̯ŋ], *a.* subyacente; fundamental.

undermine [-mái̯n], *va.* socavar, minar, descalzar, zapar; trasminar; debilitar, arruinar subrepticiamente.—**underminer** [-œ(r)], *s.* minador, zapador; enemigo oculto.

undermost [-mou̯st]. **I.** *a.* ínfimo, el más bajo. **II.** *adv.* debajo de todo.

underneath [-ní̱θ]. **I.** *adv.* debajo. **II.** *prep.* debajo de, bajo.

undernourish [-nœ́ri̯š], *va.*, **undernourishment** [-mẹnt], *s.* = UNDERFEED(ING).

underpaid [-péi̯d], *pp.* y *a.* mal pagado, insuficientemente retribuído.

underpass [-pǽs], *s.* paso inferior.

underpay [-péi̯]. **I.** *va.* pagar insuficientemente. **II.** *s.* retribución insuficiente.

underpin [-pín], *va.* (alb., constr.) socalzar, apuntalar, poner puntales; apoyar, mantener.—**underpinning** [-pi̯ni̯ŋ], *s.* apuntalamiento por la base.

underplot [-plat], *s.* acción secundaria en un drama o novela; trama secreta.

underprivileged [-prívi̯li̯dźd], *a.* menesteroso; que no goza de las ventajas de la mayoría.

underprize [-prái̯z], *va.* desapreciar, desestimar.

underproduction [-prodʌ́kšọn], *s.* baja producción, producción insuficiente.

underprop [-práp], *va.* apuntalar. *V.* UNDERPIN.

underrate [-réi̯t], *va.* menospreciar, desestimar, adocenar, rebajar.

underrun [-rʌ́n], *va.* correr por debajo de; (mar.) resacar; recorrer (los cables).

underscore [-skór]. **I.** *va.* subrayar. **II.** *s.* línea de subrayar o que subraya.

undersea [-sí], *a.* submarino.—**undersea(s)** [-z], *adv.* bajo la superficie del mar.

undersecretary [-sékrẹteri̯], *s.* subsecretario.

undersell [-sél], *va.* vender a bajo precio, malbaratar; vender a menor precio que.

undershirt [-šœrt], *s.* elástica, camiseta.

undershot [-šat], *a.* (hidr.) de alimentación o impulsión por abajo (apl. a ruedas).

undersign [-sái̯n], *va.* su(b)scribir.—**the undersigned,** el infrascrito, el suscrito, el abajo firmado.

undersized [-sái̯zd], *a.* de tamaño o estatura menor que lo normal.

underskirt [-skœrt], *s.* enagua(s); faldellín, refajo, zagalejo, (Cuba) sayuela.

underslung [-slʌ́ŋ], *a.* (aut.) aplícase a carrocerías suspendidas de las ballestas de tal modo que el bastidor del chasis queda más bajo que los ejes.

undersold [-sóu̯ld], *pret.* y *pp.* de TO UNDERSELL.

understand [-stǽnd], *va.* y *vn.* (*pret.* y *pp.* UNDERSTOOD) entender, comprender; saber, ser sabedor, hacerse cargo, tener conocimiento de, tener entendido; conocer, penetrar; sobrentender.

understandable [-ạbl], *a.* comprensible.

understanding [-i̯ŋ]. **I.** *s.* entendimiento, inteligencia; modo de ver o entender; comprensión; acuerdo, arreglo; armonía, mutua comprensión. **II.** *a.* entendedor, inteligente, comprensivo.

understandingly [-li̯], *adv.* de manera inteligente, con conocimiento (de causa, de los hechos).

understate [-stéi̯t], *va.* decir menos de lo que es.

understatement [-mẹnt], *s.* proposición en que no se dice todo, en que se dice menos de lo que realmente hay; exposición incompleta.

understood [-stúd], *pret.* y *pp.* de TO UNDERSTAND; sobrentendido, subentendido; convenido.—**to be u.,** sobrentenderse, subentenderse.—**be it u.,** entiéndase.—**it being u.,** bien entendido.—**that is u.,** está entendido; por supuesto, eso se entiende.—**to make one's self u.,** hacerse comprender.

understratum [-strei̯tʌm], *s.* estrato subyacente.

understudy [-stadi̯], *s.* (teat.) sobresaliente, suplente, substituto.

undertake [-téi̯k], *va.* y *vn.* (*pret.* UNDERTOOK; *pp.* UNDERTAKEN) emprender, acometer, intentar; comprometerse a, responder de, encargarse de.

undertaker [-tei̯kœ(r)], *s.* empresario de pompas fúnebres, (Am.) muñidor, zacateca, *m.*; contratista.—**u.'s establishment,** funeraria, casa mortuoria.

undertaking [-tei̯ki̯ŋ], *s.* empresa; contratación; empresa funeraria; (for.) compromiso, promesa; empeño o garantía.

undertenant [-tenạnt], *s.* (for.) subarrendatario, subinquilino.

undertone [-tou̯n], *s.* voz baja; color apagado; sentido que se implica pero no se expresa.

undertook [-túk], *pret.* de TO UNDERTAKE.

undertow [-tou̯], *s.* resaca, corriente submarina.

undervaluation [-vælyu̯éi̯šọn], *s.* menosprecio, estimación baja, avalúo inferior al verdadero.

undervalue [-víe̯lyu̯], *va.* des(a)preciar, desestimar, menospreciar; tasar en menos del valor real.

underwater [-wótœ(r)], *a.* que está (o sirve para uso) debajo de la superficie del agua.

underwear [-wɛr], *s.* ropa interior.

underweight [-wéi̯t], *a.* que no tiene el peso justo o normal.

underwent [-wént], *pret.* de TO UNDERGO.

underwood [-wu̯d], *s.* maleza.

underwork [-wœrk]. **I.** *va.* trabajar por menos jornal que otro. **II.** *vn.* trabajar menos de lo que se debe. **III.** *s.* trabajo de rutina.

underworld [-wœrld], *s.* averno, infierno; los antípodas; mundo terrenal, la tierra; hampa, vida del vicio, clases depravadas.

underwrite [-rái̯t], *va.* (*pret.* UNDERWROTE; *pp.* UNDERWRITTEN) su(b)scribir; (com.) asegurar (contra riesgos); subscribir una emisión de valores.—**underwritten** [-rítn], *a.* infrascripto; asegurado (por); subscrito; garantizado.

underwriter [-rai̯tœ(r)], *s.* el que firma o suscribe un documento; (com.) asegurador; suscriptor de una emisión de bonos, etc.

undeserved [ʌndi̯zœ́rvd], *a.* inmerecido.

undeservedly [-vidli̯], *adv.* inmerecidamente, injustamente.—**undeserving** [-vi̯ŋ], *a.* desmerecedor, inmeritorio, indigno.

undesignedly [ʌndizáinidli], adv. involuntariamente, sin intención.—**undesigning** [-iŋ], a. sincero, sencillo; de buena fe.

undesirable [ʌndizáirabl], a. que no es de desearse, indeseable; inconveniente, desventajoso; nocivo, pernicioso.

undetected [ʌndité̃ktid], a. no descubierto.

undetermined [ʌnditœ́rmind], a. indeterminado; indeciso, incierto.—**u. coefficients,** (mat.) coeficientes indeterminados.

undeveloped [ʌndivélopt], a. rudimentario, sin desarrollo; inexplotado (tierras, etc.); (foto.) sin revelar, no revelado.

undeviating [ʌndívieitiŋ], a. regular, directo; sin rodeo, siempre igual.

undid [ʌndíd], pret. de TO UNDO.

undies [ʌ́ndiz], s. pl. (fam.) prendas íntimas.

undigested [ʌndaidʒéstid], a. indigesto, no digerido; mal ordenado.

undignified [ʌndígnifaid], a. indecoroso, falto de dignidad; falto de seriedad o de gravedad.

undiminished [ʌndimíniʃt], a. sin disminución, sin merma, no disminuído.

undine [ʌndín], s. (mit.) ondina.

undirected [ʌndiréktid], a. sin dirección, sin señas.

undiscernible [ʌndizœ́rnabl], a. invisible, imperceptible.

undisciplined [ʌndísiplind], a. indisciplinado, falto de corrección; sin instrucción.

undiscovered [ʌndiskʌ́vœrd], a. ignoto, oculto, por descubrir.

undisguised [ʌndisgáizd], a. sin disfraz; cándido, franco, abierto, sencillo.

undismayed [ʌndisméid], a. perseverante, que no ha perdido el ánimo o valor; firme.

undisputed [ʌndispiútid], a. que no se disputa; indisputable, incontestable.

undistinguishable [ʌndistíŋgwiŝabl], a. indistinguible.

undisturbed [ʌndistœ́rbd], a. imperturbable, impasible, sereno; sin molestar, sin cambiar, sin mover, como está (estaba).

undivided [ʌndiváidid], a. indiviso, íntegro.

undo [ʌndú], va. (pret. UNDID; pp. UNDONE) anular, desvirtuar, contrarrestar; reparar (un daño); arruinar, perder; causar pesadumbre a; deshacer; desatar, desliar; (mec.) desarmar, desmontar.

undoing [-iŋ], s. anulación; ruina, pérdida.

undone [ʌndʌ́n], pp. de TO UNDO; sin terminar; sin hacer; deshecho.—**to be u.,** estar perdido o arruinado.—**to come u.,** deshacerse; desatarse.—**to leave nothing u.,** no dejar nada por hacer.

undoubted [ʌndáutid], a. indudable, seguro.

undoubtedly [-li], adv. indudablemente.

undraw [ʌndró], va. (pret. UNDREW; pp. UNDRAWN) abrir, tirar hacia fuera; tirar (una cortina).—**undrawn** [-n], pp. y a. no sacado; no extraído; no sorteado (billete de lotería); (com.) no girado.

undreamed, undreamt [ʌndrímd, -drémt], a. (a menudo con of) no soñado; inopinado.

undress [ʌndrés]. I. va. desnudar, desvestir, quitar la ropa; (cir.) desvendar, quitar el vendaje. II. vn. desnudarse. III. [ʌ́ndres], a. desabillé, paños menores; ropa de casa; (mil.) traje de cuartel.—**to be in u.,** estar de trapillo. IV. a. de trapillo; de confianza.

undressed [-t], a. desnudo; de trapillo; (com.) en rama o en bruto.—**u. sheepskin,** zalea, vellón, zamarra.—**u. skin,** cuero sin curtir o al pelo.

undried [ʌndráid], a. húmedo, sin secar; verde (frutos, etc.).

undue [ʌndjú], a. indebido, excesivo, desmedido; ilícito, injusto; (com.) por vencer.

undulant [ʌ́ndjulant], a. undulante, ondulante. —**u. fever,** (med.) fiebre de Malta o mediterránea.

undulate [ʌ́ndjuleit]. I. vn. undular, ondular, ondear, fluctuar. II. va. hacer ondear. III. a. ondeado, ondulado.—**undulating** [-iŋ], a. ondulante, undoso.—**undulation** [-éiŝon], s. ondulación, onda, ondeo.

undulatory [ʌ́ndjulatori], a. undulatorio, undoso. —**u. theory,** (fís.) teoría de las ondulaciones.

unduly [ʌndjúli], adv. indebidamente; irregularmente, ilícitamente.

undutiful [ʌndjútiful], a. desobediente, que falta a sus deberes.—**undutifulness** [-nis], s. desobediencia; falta de respeto; falta de cumplimiento del deber.

undying [ʌndáiiŋ], a. imperecedero.

unearned [ʌnœ́rnd], a. no ganado; inmerecido. —**u. increment,** plusvalía.

unearth [ʌnœ́rθ], va. desenterrar.

unearthly [-li], a. sobrenatural; aterrador, espantoso.

uneasily [ʌnízili], adv. inquietamente, desasosegadamente; incómodamente, penosamente.— **uneasiness** [-nis], s. inquietud, desasosiego, ansiedad; incomodidad, disgusto, malestar.— **uneasy** [ʌnízi], a. inquieto, intranquilo, ansioso, desasosegado; molesto, incómodo; desgarbado; difícil, pesado.—**to be u.,** no tenerlas todas consigo.

uneducated [ʌnédʒukeitid], a. falto de educación, indocto, ignorante.

unemployed [ʌnimplóid], a. sin empleo, desocupado, desempleado, cesante, parado; ocioso, inactivo.—**the u.,** los cesantes o sin trabajo.— **unemployment** [-ment], s. falta de empleo o colocación, cesantía, desempleo, paro forzoso; ociosidad.—**u. insurance,** seguro contra cesantía.

unencumbered [ʌninkʌ́mbœrd], a. (for.) libre de gravamen; saneado; sin trabas.

unending [ʌnéndiŋ], a. inacabable, sin fin, eterno.

unendowed [ʌnindáud], a. indotado, no dotado.

unendurable [ʌnindjúrabl], a. insufrible, inaguantable, insoportable.

unengaged [ʌniŋgéidʒd], a. desocupado, libre; no comprometido.

unenviable [ʌnénviabl], a. inenvidiable.

unenvied [ʌnénvid], a. no envidiado.

unequal [ʌníkwal], a. desigual, dispar; ineficaz, insuficiente, inferior; desproporcionado; injusto, parcial; falto de uniformidad.—**to be u. to,** no tener fuerzas para, ser incapaz de.—**unequalled** [-d], a. sin igual, sin par, incomparable.—**unequally** [-i], adv. desigualmente.

unequipped [ʌnikwípt], a. desprovisto, no preparado.

unequivocal [ʌnikwívokal], a. inequívoco.

unerring [ʌnœ́riŋ], a. infalible.—**unerringly** [-li], adv. infaliblemente.

unessayed [ʌneséid], a. no ensayado.

unessential [ʌnesénŝal]. I. a. que no es esencial o indispensable; de poca importancia, que no importa. II. s. cosa accesoria o no esencial.

uneven [ʌnívn], a. desigual; escabroso, quebrado, accidentado, fragoso; irregular, poco uniforme; non, impar (número).—**unevenly** [-li], adv. desigualmente.—**unevenness** [-nis], s. desigualdad; escabrosidad, aspereza; abolladura; desnivel; irregularidad, intercadencia.

uneventful [ʌnivéntful], a. exento de acontecimientos notables; sin peripecias, sin novedad; tranquilo, quieto.

unexamined [ʌnigzǽmind], a. no examinado.

unexampled [ʌnigzǽmpld], a. que no tiene igual, sin ejemplo, único.

unexceptionable [ʌniksépŝonabl], a. intachable, irrecusable.—**unexceptional** [-al], a. ordinario, usual y corriente; que no admite excepción.

unexpected [ʌnikspéktid], a. inesperado, impensado; repentino.—**unexpectedly** [-li], adv. de repente o inesperadamente.—**unexpected-**

ness [-nis], *s.* calidad de inesperado; (lo) inesperado.

unexperienced [-spírienst], *a.* inexperto, novel.

unexploited [-splóitid], *a.* inexplotado.

unexplored [-splórd], *a.* inexplorado.

unexposed [-spóuzd], *a.* (foto.) no expuesto.

unexpressive [-sprésiv], *a.* sin expresión, poco expresivo, inexpresivo.

unfading [ʌnféidiŋ], *a.* inmarcesible.

unfailing [ʌnféiliŋ], *a.* inagotable; indefectible; seguro, cierto, infalible.

unfair [ʌnfér], *a.* doble, falso, desleal; injusto; (for.) leonino (pacto).—**unfairly** [-li], *adv.* de mala fe; injustamente; con doblez.—**unfairness** [-nis], *s.* falta de equidad; deslealtad, mala fe.

unfaithful [ʌnféiθful], *a.* infiel; infidente, fementido, desleal, pérfido; inexacto.—**the u.**, los infieles.—**unfaithfully** [-i], *adv.* infielmente, deslealmente.—**unfaithfulness** [-nis], *s.* infidelidad, perfidia, infidencia, deslealtad.

unfaltering [ʌnfóltœriŋ], *a.* firme, resuelto, inquebrantable.—**unfalteringly** [-li], *adv.* sin vacilar, resueltamente.

unfamiliar [ʌnfamílyə(r)], *a.* poco familiar, poco común; no conocido; ignorante, poco conocedor.

unfasten [ʌnfésn], *va.* desatar, desligar, desabrochar, desenganchar, desprender, soltar, aflojar, zafar.

unfathomable [ʌnfáðǫmabl], *a.* insondable; sin fondo; impenetrable, inescrutable.

unfavorable [ʌnféivǫrabl], *a.* desfavorable, desventajoso, contrario, adverso.—**unfavorably** [-bli], *adv.* desfavorable o desventajosamente.

unfeathered [ʌnféðœrd], *a.* (orn.) implume.

unfed [ʌnféd], *a.* falto de alimento; sin comer.

unfeeling [ʌnfíliŋ], *a.* insensible, impasible, empedernido.—**unfeelingly** [-li], *adv.* cruelmente; insensiblemente.

unfeigned [ʌnféind], *a.* verdadero, genuino; sincero, ingenuo.—**unfeignedly** [ʌnféinidli], *adv.* ingenuamente, sinceramente; sin fingimiento.

unfelt [ʌnfélt], *a.* no percibido, sin sentido.

unfermented [ʌnfœrméntid], *a.* no fermentado.

unfetter [ʌnfétœ(r)], *va.* desencadenar; desmanear, destrabar (bestias).—**unfettered** [-d], *a.* libre, sin cadenas; sin trabas.

unfinished [ʌnfíniʃt], *a.* sin o por acabar, inacabado, incompleto; imperfecto, crudo.

unfit [ʌnfít]. **I.** *a.* inepto, incapaz, incompetente; impropio, inoportuno; inadaptable, inadecuado, inservible. **II.** *va.* inhabilitar.—**unfitly** [-li], *adv.* ineptamente; impropiamente.—**unfitness** [-nis], *s.* ineptitud, incompetencia; inadaptabilidad.

unfixed [ʌnfíkst], *a.* suelto, desprendido; errante, voluble; desarreglado.

unflagging [ʌnflégiŋ], *a.* persistente, incansable.

unfledged [ʌnflédźd], *a.* (orn.) sin empollar, implume; (fig.) inmaturo, novel.

unflinching [ʌnflínchiŋ], *a.* firme, resuelto.

unfold [ʌnfóuld]. **I.** *va.* desplegar, desdoblar, desenvolver, desarrollar, abrir; extender; descifrar, revelar, descubrir, poner en claro; manifestar, explicar. **II.** *vn.* abrirse, desenvolverse, desarrollarse.

unfolding [-iŋ], *s.* despliegue; desarrollo.

unforeseeable [ʌnfǫrsíabl], *a.* imprevisible.

unforeseen [-sín], *a.* imprevisto, impensado, inesperado, inopinable.

unforgettable [ʌnfǫrgétabl], *a.* inolvidable.

unforgiving [ʌnfǫrgíviŋ], *a.* duro, inexorable, implacable, que no perdona.

unformed [ʌnfórmd], *a.* informe; amorfo; embrionario; crudo.

unfortunate [ʌnfórchûnit]. **I.** *a.* desafortunado, infortunado, desgraciado, desventurado, desdichado; infausto, aciago. **II.** *s.* infortunado, desgraciado; prostituta.—**unfortunately** [-li], *adv.* por desgracia, desgraciadamente.—**unfortunateness** [-nis], *s.* desventura; calidad de desafortunado, desdichado o aciago.

unfounded [ʌnfáundid], *a.* infundado, sin fundamento; (for.) improcedente.

unfrequented [ʌnfrikwéntid], *a.* solitario, poco frecuentado.

unfriendliness [ʌnfréndlinis], *s.* falta de amistad, hostilidad, malevolencia.—**unfriendly** [-li], *a.* poco amistoso; hostil, enemigo; desfavorable, perjudicial.—**an u. act**, un acto hostil.

unfrock [ʌnfrák], *va.* expulsar, deponer, degradar (a un monje, ministro del culto, etc.).

unfruitful [ʌnfrútful], *a.* estéril, infecundo; improductivo, infructuoso, vano.—**unfruitfully** [-i], *adv.* infructuosamente.—**unfruitfulness** [-nis], *s.* esterilidad, infecundidad; infructuosidad.

unfulfilled [ʌnfulfíld], *a.* incumplido.

unfurl [ʌnfœrl], *va.* desplegar, desarrollar, desdoblar, extender; (mar.) desaferrar.

unfurnished [ʌnfœrniʃt], *a.* desamueblado; sin muebles, sin amueblar (piso, etc.); desprovisto.

ungainliness [ʌngéinlinis], *s.* falta de gracia, desgarbo, mala apariencia.—**ungainly** [-li], *a.* desmañado, desgarbado, torpe.

ungear [ʌngír], *va.* desengranar, desembragar.

ungenerous [ʌndźénœrʌs], *a.* poco generoso, ajeno o contrario a la generosidad.—**ungenerously** [-li], *adv.* sin generosidad; indignamente.

ungentlemanly, *o* **ungentlemanlike** [ʌndźéntlmanli, -laik], *a.* indigno de un caballero.

ungird [ʌngœrd], *va.* desceñir, desfajar; descinchar (bestias).

unglazed [ʌngléizd], *a.* sin vidrios; sin vidriar; deslustrado; sin satinar (papel).

ungloved [ʌnglávd], *a.* sin guantes.

unglued [ʌngljúd], *a.* despegado, desencolado.

ungodliness [ʌngádlinis], *s.* impiedad, irreligión.

ungodly [-li], *a.* impío, irreligioso; malvado.

ungovernable [ʌngávœrnabl], *a.* indomable, ingobernable, díscolo.

ungraceful [ʌngréisful], *a.* desagraciado, desgarbado.

ungracefully [-i], *adv.* sin gracia, deslucidamente.

ungracious [ʌngréiʃʌs], *a.* poco afable, rudo, descortés; desagradable, ofensivo.—**ungraciously** [-li], *adv.* rudamente, ásperamente.—**ungraciousness** [-nis], *s.* aspereza, descortesía.

ungrammatical [ʌngramétikal], *a.* ingramatical, incorrecto.

ungrateful [ʌngréitful], *a.* desagradecido, ingrato, desconocido; desagradable.—**ungratefully** [-i], *adv.* ingratamente, desagradecidamente; desagradablemente, de mala gana.—**ungratefulness** [-nis], *s.* ingratitud, desagradecimiento.

ungratified [ʌngrétifaid], *a.* no satisfecho.

ungrounded [ʌngráundid], *a.* infundado, inmotivado, gratuito.

ungrudgingly [ʌngrʌdźiŋli], *adv.* de buena gana, sin quejarse.

ungual [ʌŋgwal], *a.* (zool.) unguinal, unguiculado.

unguarded [ʌngárdid], *a.* sin guardia; desguarnecido, indefenso; descuidado, desprevenido; incauto, indiscreto.

unguent [ʌŋgwent], *s.* (farm.) ungüento.

unguicular [ʌŋgwíkiulǝ(r)], *a.* unguiculado.

unguiculate [-eit], *a.* y *s.* (zool.) unguiculado.

unguided [ʌngáidid], *a.* no dirigido, no gobernado, sin guía.

unguinous [ʌŋgwinʌs], *a.* oleoso, aceitoso.

unguis [ʌŋgwis], *s.* (zool.) uña, pezuña, garra, zarpa; (anat.) unguis, *m.*, hueso lagrimal.

ungula [ʌŋgiulǝ], *s.* (zool.) = UNGUIS; (geom.) cilindro o cono cortados por un plano oblicuo a la base.

ungulate [ʌŋgiuleit], *a.* y *s.* ungulado.

ungum [ʌngʌm], *va.* desengomar.

unhair [ʌnhér], *va.* (ten.) apelambrar.

unhallowed [ʌnhéloud], *a.* no consagrado; profano, impío; profanado.

unhand [ʌnhǽnd], va. soltar (de las manos), desasir.

unhandy [-i], a. desmanotado (fam.), desmañado, torpe; incómodo, inconveniente.

unhang [ʌnhǽŋ], va. (*pret.* y *pp.* UNHUNG) descolgar, desprender, desmontar, desarmar.

unhappily [ʌnhǽpili], adv. desgraciadamente, por desgracia.—**unhappiness** [-ṇis], s. infelicidad, desgracia, desdicha.—**unhappy** [ʌnhǽpi], a. infeliz, desgraciado, desdichado, desventurado; infausto, aciago, malhadado.

unharmed [ʌnhármd], a. ileso, incólume, sano y salvo; sin daño, a salvo.

unharness [ʌnhárnis], va. desenjaezar, desguarnecer, desaparejar, desenganchar.

unhealthful [ʌnhélθful], a. malsano, insalubre.

unhealthfulness [-nis], s. insalubridad.

unhealthiness [-ṇis], s. falta de salud.

unhealthy [-i], a. enfermizo, achacoso; insalubre, malsano.

unheard [ʌnhérd], a. que no se ha oído; (con of) desconocido, sin ejemplo, inaudito, extraño.

unheeded [ʌnhídid], a. desatendido, despreciado.

unheeding [-iŋ], a. desatento, descuidado, distraído.

unhesitating [ʌnhéziteitiŋ], a. que no vacila; resuelto; pronto, listo.—**unhesitatingly** [-li], adv. sin vacilar; prontamente.

unhewn [ʌnhjún], a. en bruto.

unhinge [ʌnhíndʒ], va. desgoznar, desgonzar; desquiciar, sacar de quicio; desequilibrar, trastornar (el juicio).

unhitch [ʌnhích], va. descolgar, desatar; desenganchar, desaparejar (bestias).

unholily [ʌnhóuḷiḷi], adv. impíamente.

unholiness [-ṇis], s. impiedad.

unholy [ʌnhóuḷi], a. profano, impío.

unhonored [ʌnánọrd], a. despreciado.

unhook [ʌnhúk], va. desenganchar, desabrochar, desaferrar; descolgar.

unhoped-for [ʌnhóupt fọr], a. inesperado.

unhorse [ʌnhórs], va. desarzonar, desmontar.

unhung [ʌnhʌ́ŋ], pp. y pret. de TO UNHANG.

unhurt [ʌnhért], a. ileso, indemne.

unhygienic [ʌnhaidʒiénik], a. antihigiénico.

uniaxial [juniǽksjal], a. uniaxil, de un solo eje.

unicellular [juniséljulā(r)], a. (biol.) unicelular.

unicolor [júnikaḷọ(r)], a. unicolor.

unicorn [júnikọrn], s. (mit.) unicornio.

unidirectional [junidirékṣọnal], a. de una sola o misma dirección.—**u. current**, (elec.) corriente continua de dirección constante.

unification [junifikéiṣọn], s. unificación.

uniflorous [juniflóras], a. (bot.) unifloro.

uniflow [júniflou], a. (hidr.) de corrientes paralelas.

unifoliate [junifóuljeit], a. (bot.) unifoliado.

uniform [júnifọrm]. I. a. uniforme; semejante; acorde, armonioso; consistente, constante. II. s. uniforme.—**in full u.**, de gran uniforme, de gala. III. va. uniformar; hacer uniforme; vestir de uniforme.

uniformity, uniformness [junifórmiti, júnifọrmnis], s. uniformidad, uniformación.—**uniformly** [-li], adv. uniformemente.

unify [júnifai], va. unificar, unir.

unifying [-iŋ], a. unificador, unidor.

unigenital [junidʒénital], a. unigénito.

unilateral [juniléteral], a. unilateral.

unimaginable [ʌnimǽdʒiṇabl], a. inimaginable.

unimpaired [ʌnimpérd], a. intacto, ileso, inalterado, incólume.

unimpeachable [ʌnimpíchạbl], a. intachable, irreprensible; irrecusable.

unimportant [ʌnimpórtạnt], a. de poca o ninguna importancia, insignificante.

unimproved [ʌnimprúvd], a. no adelantado; yermo, baldío, inculto; sin urbanizar.

uninfluenced [ʌnínfljuenst], a. no predispuesto, no afectado; exento de preocupaciones.

uninformed [ʌninfórmd], a. inculto, ignorante; mal informado.

uninhabitable [ʌninhǽbitạbl], a. inhabitable.

uninhabited [-id], a. inhabitado; deshabitado.

uninjured [ʌníndʒurd], a. ileso, incólume; sin daño.

uninstructed [ʌninstrʌ́ktid], a. indocto; que no ha recibido aviso o instrucciones.

uninsured [ʌninṣúrd], a. no asegurado.

unintelligible [ʌnintéḷidʒibl], a. ininteligible.

unintelligibility [-ibíḷiti], o **unintelligibleness** [-iblnis], s. calidad de ininteligible.

unintelligibly [-iblij], adv. ininteligiblemente.

unintentional [ʌninténṣọnal], a. hecho sin intención, involuntario, no intencional.

unintentionally [-i], adv. sin intención, involuntariamente.

uninterested [ʌníntristid], a. no interesado.

uninteresting [-iŋ], a. falto de interés, poco interesante, soso, insípido.

uninterrupted [ʌnintęrʌ́ptid], a. continuo, ininterrumpido, no interrumpido.—**uninterruptedly** [-li], adv. sin interrupción, continuamente.

union [júnyọn]. I. s. unión; conformidad, concordia, armonía; mancomunidad, fusión; estado matrimonial; emblema (m.) de unión representado en un pabellón; (E. U.) las estrellas (de la bandera nacional); (e. p.) sindicato, gremio de obreros.—**u. card**, matrícula gremial o de sindicato, expedida a los miembros de un gremio; certificado gremial o sindicalista, en que consta que un patrón o fábrica emplean sólo obreros agremiados.—**u.-made**, hecho por obreros agremiados.—**u. shop**, fábrica o taller que reconoce los derechos colectivos sindicalistas, o que emplea sólo obreros agremiados.—**u. suit**, traje interior de una sola pieza.—**U. Jack**, pabellón militar de la Gran Bretaña.—**the U.**, (E. U.) la Unión Norteamericana. II. a. de o relativo al unionismo o a los gremios obreros; perteneciente a un gremio obrero.

unionism [-jzm], s. unionismo; (e. p.) sindicalismo, gremialismo.—**unionist** [-ist], s. unionista; (e. p.) sindicalista.

unionization [-izéiṣọn], s. (e. p.) agremiación, sindicalización.

unionize [-aiz], va. (e. p.) reducir a gremio obrero; hacer entrar en un gremio, agremiar, sindicar; establecer el sistema unionista en.

uniparous [juníparas], a. unípara.

unipersonal [junipérsọnal], a. unipersonal.

unipolar [junipóulā(r)], a. (elec.) unipolar.

unique [juník], a. único en su género, singular, señero, raro, original.

unisexual [juniséksḳ̣al], a. unisexual.

unison [júnisọn]. I. s. (mús.) unisonancia; unisón; (fig.) concordancia, armonía.—**in u.**, todos juntos, a una. II. a. al unísono, unísono.—**unisonal** [junísọnal], **unisonant** [-ạnt], **unisonous** [-ʌs], a. unísono; concordante, armonioso; unisonante, que suena solo.

unit [júnit]. I. s. unidad. II. a. individual; unitario; unidad (en expresiones como *unit force*, fuerza unidad; *unit volume*, volumen unidad); igual a la unidad; (arit.) de las unidades (*unit figure*, cifra de las unidades).

Unitarian [junitérian], a. y s. (igl.) unitario.

Unitarianism [-jzm], s. (igl.) unitarismo.

unitary [júniteri], a. unitario.

unite [junáit]. I. va. unir, juntar, reunir, enlazar, adunar, mancomunar; avenir, concordar. II. vn. unirse, juntarse; concertarse.

united [-id], a. unido; conexo; de acuerdo.—**U. States**, Estados Unidos.

unitedly [-li], adv. unidamente, de acuerdo; a una.

unitive [júnitiv], a. unitivo.

unity [júniti], s. unidad; unión, concordia; (mat.) la unidad.

univalence [junívalens], s. (quím.) univalencia.

univalent [-ẹnt], a. (quím.) univalente.

univalve [yúnįvælv]. **I.** *a.* univalvo. **II.** *s.* (zool.) molusco univalvo, gasterópodo.

univalvate, univalved [yunįvælveįt, yúnįvælvd], *a.* *V.* UNIVALVE.

universal [yunįvœrsąl], *a.* universal.—**u. chuck,** (mec.) mandril universal de torno.—**u. coupling, o joint,** (mec.) junta universal; cardán, junta cardánica.

Universalism [-įzm], *s.* (igl.) universalismo.— **Universalist** [-įst], *a.* y *s.* universalista.

universality [-sǽlįtį], *s.* universalidad, generalidad.—**universalize** [-vœrsąlaįz], *va.* universalizar.—**universally** [-vœrsąlį], *adv.* universalmente, generalmente.

universe [yúnįvœrs], *s.* universo, mundo.—**u. of discourse,** (lóg.) extensión de una idea o concepto, o conjunto de cosas o ideas que abarca.

university [yunįvœrsįtį]. **I.** *s.* universidad. **II.** *a.* universitario.

univocal [yunįvokąl], *a.* unívoco.—**univocally** [-į], *adv.* unívocamente.

unjointed [ʌndžóįntįd], *a.* desunido; desencajado, desarticulado.

unjust [ʌndžʌst], *a.* injusto; pecador.—**the just and the u.,** justos y pecadores.

unjustifiable [ʌndžʌstįfáįąbl], *a.* injustificable, inexcusable.—**unjustifiableness** [-nįs], *s.* falta de justificación o razón.—**unjustifiably** [-blį], *adv.* injustificadamente.

unjustly [ʌndžʌstlį], *adv.* injustamente.

unkempt [ʌnkémpt], *a.* despeinado, desgreñado; desarreglado, desaseado; sin pulimento, tosco.

unkind [ʌnkáįnd], *a.* desprovisto de bondad o benevolencia, des(a)piadado, poco amable; duro, hiriente, áspero.

unkindliness [-lįnįs], *s.* aspereza, dureza, falta de benevolencia o amabilidad.

unkindly [-lį], *adv.* duramente, despiadadamente.

unkindness [-nįs], *s.* falta de bondad, dureza; acción cruel, tratamiento duro o des(a)piadado.

unknown [ʌnnóųn]. **I.** *a.* desconocido, ignoto.— **u. quantity,** (mat.) incógnita.—**u. to one,** sin saberlo uno. **II.** *s.* cosa o persona desconocida; (mat.) incógnita.

unlace [ʌnléįs], *va.* desenlazar; desatar.

unlade [ʌnléįd], *va.* descargar. *V.* UNLOAD.

unladylike [ʌnléįdįlaįk], *a.* impropio de una dama; poco femenino.

unlaid [ʌnléįd], *a.* y *pp.* de TO UNLAY; que no está colocado o puesto; no apaciguado ni aquietado.

unlawful [ʌnlófųl], *a.* ilegal, ilícito, ilegítimo.— **u. interest,** usura.—**unlawfully** [-į], *adv.* ilegalmente, ilegítimamente, ilícitamente.—**u. born,** ilegítimo, bastardo.—**unlawfulness** [-nįs], *s.* ilegalidad, ilegitimidad.

unlay [ʌnléį], *va.* (mar.) destorcer (un cable).

unlearn [ʌnlœrn], *va.* desaprender, olvidar.

unlearned [-d], *pp.* y *a.* indocto, ignorante, ignaro; ignorado, no aprendido.

unleavened [ʌnlévnd], *a.* ázimo, cenceño (pan).

unless [ʌnlés], *conj.* a menos que, a no ser que, como no sea, no siendo; salvo, con excepción de que, excepto, si no, si no es que.

unlettered [ʌnlétœrd], *a.* iletrado, iliterado.

unlevelled [ʌnlévęld], *a.* desnivelado.

unlicensed [ʌnláįsęnst], *a.* no autorizado, sin permiso o licencia.

unlike [ʌnláįk]. **I.** *a.* desemejante, diferente, distinto, dispar. **II.** *adv.* otramente, de otro modo; a diferencia de.—**unlikelihood, unlikeliness** [-lįhųd, -nįs], *s.* improbabilidad, inverisimilitud. —**unlikely** [-lį]. **I.** *a.* inverosímil, improbable, difícil. **II.** *adv.* improbablemente.—**unlikeness** [-nįs], *s.* disimilitud, desemejanza.

unlimber [ʌnlímbœr]. **I.** *va.* (arti.) quitar el avantrén (a un cañón). **II.** *va.* y *vn.* alistar(se), preparar(se).

unlimited [ʌnlímįtįd], *a.* ilimitado; sin restricción, sin trabas.

unlink [ʌnlíŋk], *va.* deseslabonar.

unliquidated [ʌnlíkwįdeįtįd], *a.* (com.) ilíquido, no liquidado, por liquidar, pendiente de pago.

unload [ʌnlóųd]. **I.** *va.* descargar; exonerar, aligerar; (arti.) descargar; (fam., com.) deshacerse de una mercancía. **II.** *vn.* descargar.—**unloader** [-œr)], *s.* descargador.—**unloading** [-įŋ], *s.* descarga, descargo, descargue.

unlock [ʌnlák], *va.* abrir (una cerradura, etc.); (impr.) desapretar (las formas); dar libre acceso; revelar (secretos).

unlooked-for [ʌnlúkt fǫr], *a.* inesperado, imprevisto, inopinado.

unloose(n) [ʌnlús(n)]. **I.** *va.* desatar, aflojar; desencadenar. **II.** *vn.* deshacerse, aflojarse.

unluckily [ʌnlʌkįlį], *adv.* desgraciadamente, por desgracia.—**unluckiness** [-nįs], *s.* mala suerte.

unlucky [ʌnlʌkį], *a.* de mala suerte; desgraciado, desafortunado; funesto, infausto, aciago, de mal agüero.

unmade [ʌnméįd], *a.* y *pp.* increado; deshecho.

unmaidenly [ʌnméįdęnlį], *a.* impropio de una doncella.

unmake [ʌnméįk], *va.* (*pret.* y *pp.* UNMADE) deshacer, destruir, aniquilar; deponer, destituir.

unman [ʌnmǽn], *va.* acobardar, desanimar; castrar, capar; (mil.) desguarnecer.

unmanageable [ʌnmǽnįdžąbl], *a.* inmanejable, ingobernable, indomable.

unmanlike, unmanly [ʌnmǽnlaįk, -lį], *a.* indigno de un hombre; afeminado, enervado.

unmannered [ʌnmǽnœrd], *a.* rudo, incivil, grosero.—**unmannerliness** [-lįnįs], *s.* rudeza, grosería, mala crianza.—**unmannerly** [-lį]. **I.** *a.* malcriado, mal educado, grosero. **II.** *adv.* descortésmente, groseramente.

unmarked [ʌnmárkt], *a.* sin marca; inadvertido.

unmarketable [ʌnmárkįtąbl], *a.* invendible, incomerciable.

unmarriageable [ʌnmǽrįdžąbl], *a.* incasable.

unmarried [ʌnmǽrįd], *a.* soltero, célibe, mozo, libre.—**u. man, woman,** soltero, soltera.

unmask [ʌnmǽsk]. **I.** *va.* desenmascarar, quitar la careta a; descubrir. **II.** *vn.* desenmascararse.

unmast [ʌnmǽst], *va.* (mar.) desarbolar.

unmatched [ʌnmǽcht], *a.* único, sin par; desapareado, dispar.

unmeaning [ʌnmínįŋ], *a.* sin significación, vacío o falto de sentido.

unmeasurable [ʌnméžŭrąbl], *a.* ilimitado, inmensurable, inmenso.

unmeasured [ʌnméžŭrd], *a.* desmedido; infinito, ilimitado.

unmentionable [ʌnménšǫnąbl]. **I.** *a.* infando, que no debe mencionarse. **II.** *s.* *pl.* (fam.) prendas íntimas, calzones, pantalones.

unmerchantable [ʌnmœrchąntąbl], *a.* invendible, incomerciable.

unmerciful [ʌnmœrsįfųl], *a.* inclemente, riguroso; cruel, desapiadado.—**unmercifully** [-į], *adv.* cruelmente, desapiadadamente, sin misericordia.—**unmercifulness** [-nįs], *s.* inclemencia, crueldad.

unmerited [ʌnmérįtįd], *a.* desmerecido, inmerecido, inmérito.

unmindful [ʌnmáįndfųl], *a.* olvidadizo, desatento, desentendido.—**to be u. of, o that,** olvidar, olvidar que; desconocer.

unmindfulness [-nįs], *s.* desatención, descuido, negligencia.

unmistakable [ʌnmįstéįkąbl], *a.* inequívoco, inconfundible, inerrable, evidente.

unmitigated [ʌnmítįgeįtįd], *a.* duro, no mitigado; redomado, absoluto.

unmixed, unmixt [ʌnmíkst], *a.* puro, sin mezcla; simple, sencillo.

unmolested [ʌnmoléstįd], *a.* quieto, tranquilo, sin ser molestado.

unmoor [ʌnmúr], *va.* (mar.) desamarrar, desaferrar.

unmoral [ʌnmárąl], *a.* amoral, ajeno a la moral o independiente de ella.

unmounted [ʌnmáuntid], *a.* desmontado.
unmoved [ʌnmúvd], *a.* inmoble, inmovible, fijo; inmutable, impasible, frío; inflexible, inexorable.
unnamed [ʌnnéimd], *a.* innominado, sin nombre.
unnatural [ʌnnǽchŷrạl], *a.* contranatural, monstruoso, inhumano; desnaturalizado; forzado, artificial o afectado.—**unnaturally** [-i], *adv.* contra la naturaleza; afectada o forzadamente.—**unnaturalness** [-nịs], *s.* calidad de desnaturalizado o afectado.
unnavigable [ʌnnǽvigạbl], *a.* innavegable.
unnecessarily [ʌnnéseserịlị], *adv.* sin necesidad, inútilmente.—**unnecessariness** [-inịs], *s.* superfluidad; inutilidad.—**unnecessary** [-i], *a.* innecesario, inútil, superfluo, excusado.
unnerve [ʌnnérv], *va.* enervar, acobardar, quitar el valor, desalentar.
unnoticed [ʌnnóutịst], *a.* inadvertido, desadvertido, no observado.
unnumbered [ʌnnʌ́mbœrd], *a.* no numerado o contado; innumerable.
unobjectionable [ʌnọbdʑéksǫnạbl], *a.* exento de objeciones o inconvenientes.
unobservant, unobserving [ʌnọbzœ́rvạnt, -iŋ], *a.* inobservante.
unobserved [-d], *a.* inadvertido.
unobstructed [ʌnọbstrʌ́ktịd], *a.* libre, no obstruido, despejado, raso.
unobtainable [ʌnọbtéinạbl], *a.* inalcanzable.
unobtrusive [ʌnọbtrúsịv], *a.* discreto, modesto, moderado, recatado.
unoccupied [ʌnákịupạid], *a.* desocupado o vacante.
unoffending [ʌnọféndiŋ], *a.* inofensivo.
unofficial [ʌnọfíšạl], *a.* no oficial, oficioso, extraoficial.
unopened [ʌnóupnd], *a.* cerrado, sin abrir.
unorganized [ʌnórgạnạizd], *a.* inorganizado; inorgánico.
unorthodox [ʌnórθodaks], *a.* no ortodoxo, heterodoxo; herético.
unostentatious [ʌnastẹntéišʌs], *a.* sencillo, llano, modesto.—**unostentatiously** [-lị], *adv.* sin ostentación.
unowned [ʌnóund], *a.* sin dueño; mostrenco.
unoxidizable [ʌnáksịdạizạbl], *a.* inoxidable.
unpack [ʌnpǽk], *va.* desempaquetar, desembalar, desenfardar; abrir, vaciar (un baúl, etc., para sacar lo que en él se ha transportado).
unpaid [ʌnpéịd], *a.* no pagado, sin pagar o por pagar.
unpalatable [ʌnpǽlạtạbl], *a.* ingustable, de mal sabor.
unparalleled [ʌnpǽrạleld], *a.* único, sin igual.
unpardonable [ʌnpárdọnạbl], *a.* imperdonable, inexcusable.
unpardonably [-blị], *adv.* imperdonablemente.
unparliamentary [ʌnparlịméntạrị], *a.* contrario a las reglas parlamentarias.
unpatriotic [ʌnpeịtríǽtịk], *a.* antipatriótico.
unpaved [ʌnpéịvd], *a.* sin pavimentar, sin empedrar, desempedrado.
unpeg [ʌnpég], *va.* desenclavijar.
unpen [ʌnpén], *va.* soltar del redil.
unpeople [ʌnpípl], *va.* despoblar.
unperceived [ʌnpœrsívd], *a.* inadvertido.
unpin [ʌnpín], *va.* quitar los alfileres, desprender; desenclavijar.
unpleasant [ʌnplézạnt], *a.* desagradable.
unpleasantly [-lị], *adv.* desagradablemente.
unpleasantness [-nịs], *s.* calidad de desagradable; (lo) desagradable; desagrado o desazón, *f.*; (fam.) riña, desavenencia.
unpleasing [ʌnplízịŋ], *a.* desagradable.
unploughed, unplowed [ʌnplúyd], *a.* (agr.) inculto.—**u. land**, erial.
unpolished [ʌnpálịšt], *a.* áspero, tosco, sin pulir, mate; rudo, grosero; impolítico, zafio.—**u. diamond**, diamante en bruto.
unpolluted [ʌnpọlútịd], *a.* impoluto, puro, limpio; inmaculado, sin mancha.

unpopular [ʌnpápyūlậ(r)], *a.* impopular.
unpopularity [-lǽrịtị], *s.* impopularidad.
unpractical [ʌnprǽktịkạl], *a.* impráctico.
unpracticed, unpractised [ʌnprǽktịst], *a.* inexperto, imperito; no practicado.
unprecedented [ʌnprésédentịd], *a.* inaudito, nunca visto, sin precedente, sin ejemplar.
unprecise [ʌnprịsáịs], *a.* impreciso, vago, indefinido.
unprejudiced [ʌnprédʑudịst], *a.* sin prejuicios, imparcial, despreocupado.
unpremeditated [ʌnprịmédịteịtịd], *a.* impremeditado.—**unpremeditation** [-éịšǫn], *s.* ausencia o falta de premeditación.
unprepared [ʌnprịpérd], *a.* desprevenido, desapercibido, desproveído.
unpreparedness [-pérịdnịs], *s.* falta de preparación.
unprepossessing [ʌnprịpǫzésịŋ], *a.* poco atractivo, poco insinuante.
unpretending [ʌnprịténdịŋ], **unpretentious** [-šʌs], *a.* modesto, sencillo, sin pretensiones.
unprincipled [ʌnprịnsịpld], *a.* sin conciencia.
unproductive [ʌnprodʌ́ktịv], *a.* improductivo.
unprofessional [ʌnproféšǫnạl], *a.* que no tiene profesión; extraño a una profesión o contrario a sus reglas.
unprofitable [ʌnpráfịtạbl], *a.* improductivo, inútil, infructuoso.—**unprofitableness** [-nịs], *s.* inutilidad.—**unprofitably** [-blị], *adv.* inútilmente, sin provecho, sin beneficio.
unpromising [ʌnprámịsịŋ], *a.* que no promete, que da poca esperanza.
unpronounceable [ʌnpronáụnsạbl], *a.* impronunciable.
unpropitious [ʌnpropíšʌs], *a.* desfavorable, impropicio.
unprosperous [ʌnpráspœrʌs], *a.* impróspero.
unprotected [ʌnprotéktịd], *a.* sin protección, sin defensa, desamparado.
unproved, unproven [ʌnprúvd, ʌnprúvn], *a.* sin demostrar, no probado, no demostrado.
unprovided [ʌnprovájdịd], *a.* desproveído, desprovisto, desabastecido, desprevenido.—**u. for**, (for.) no proveído.—**u. with**, desprovisto de.
unprovoked [ʌnprovóụkt], *a.* no provocado; sin motivo, sin provocación; infundado.
unpublished [ʌnpʌ́blịšt], *a.* no publicado; inédito.
unpunished [ʌnpʌ́nịšt], *a.* impune.
unqualified [ʌnkwálịfạịd], *a.* inhábil, inepto, incompetente; desautorizado; inhabilitado; absoluto, ilimitado, incondicional, omnímodo, sin restricción; completo, entero.
unquenchable [ʌnkwénchạbl], *a.* inextinguible.
unquestionable [ʌnkwéšchǫnạbl], *a.* incuestionable, indisputable, indiscutible.—**unquestionably** [-blị], *adv.* incuestionablemente, sin disputa.
unquestioned [-d], *a.* incontestable, indisputable, no examinado, no preguntado.
unquiet [ʌnkwáịet], *a.* inquieto, desasosegado; agitado, turbado.—**unquietly** [-i], *adv.* inquietamente.—**unquietness** [-nịs], *s.* inquietud, desasosiego.
unracked [ʌnrǽkt], *a.* no trasegado (el vino).
unraked [ʌnréịkt], *a.* no rastrillado.
unravel [ʌnrǽvl]. **I.** *va.* desenredar, desenmarañar; deshilar; desembrollar, aclarar; descifrar; desatar o desenredar el nudo de un drama. **II.** *vn.* desenredarse; desenlazarse.
unread [ʌnréd], *a.* no leído, sin leer; iliterato, indocto.
unreadiness [ʌnrédịnịs], *s.* desprevención, falta de preparación; lentitud.—**unready** [-i], *a.* lento, lerdo; desprevenido.
unreal [ʌnríạl], *a.* no real; quimérico, ilusorio, imaginario, inmaterial, incorpóreo; insincero.
unreality [ʌnrịǽlịtị], *s.* irrealidad.
unrealizable [ʌnríạlạizạbl], *a.* irrealizable.

unreasonable [ʌnrízọnạbl], *a.* desrazonable, irrazonable; irracional; inmoderado, exorbitante.

unreasonableness [-nịs], *s.* sinrazón, *f.*, falta de razón.

unreasonably [-blị], *adv.* desrazonablemente.

unreclaimed [ʌnrịkléịmd], *a.* no reclamado; sin mejorar; no aprovechado; incorregible.

unrecognizable [ʌnrékǫgnaịzạbl], *a.* que no puede reconocerse.

unreconcilable [ʌnrékǫnsaịlạbl], *a.* incompatible; irreconciliable; intransigente (en pol. ú. a veces como *s.*).

unreconciled [ʌnrékǫnsaịld], *a.* no reconciliado, no resignado.

unrecoverable [ʌnrịkávœrạbl], *a.* irrecuperable; irreparable; incurable.

unrecovered [ʌnrịkávœrd], *a.* no recobrado.

unreeve [ʌnrív], *va.* (mar.) despasar.

unrefined [ʌnrịfáịnd], *a.* no refinado, impuro; en bruto; inculto, rudo, grosero, ordinario.

unregenerate [ʌnrịdźénẹrịt], *a.* irregenerado, no regenerado.

unrelenting [ʌnrịléntịŋ], *a.* inexorable, inflexible; tenaz.—**unrelentingly** [-lị], *adv.* inexorablemente; sin tregua.

unreliable [ʌnrịláịạbl], *a.* indigno de confianza.

unrepentant, unrepented, unrepenting [ʌnrịpéntạnt, -ịd, -ịŋ], *a.* impenitente.

unreserved [ʌnrịźœrvd], *a.* que no es reservado; sin restricción; franco, libre; comunicativo, abierto.—**u. seat**, (teat., etc.) entrada general.—**unreservedly** [-vịdlị], *adv.* sin reserva; francamente.—**unreservedness** [-vịdnịs], *s.* candor, franqueza, ingenuidad.

unresisted [ʌnrịzístịd], *a.* sin resistencia.

unresisting [-ịŋ], *a.* que no ofrece resistencia.

unrest [ʌnrést], *s.* inquietud, desasosiego.

unrestrained [ʌnrịstréịnd], *a.* desenfrenado, licencioso; suelto, desembarazado; ilimitado.

unrestricted [ʌnrịstríktịd], *a.* ilimitado; libre, sin trabas.

unriddle [ʌnrịdl], *va.* descifrar, resolver.

unrifled [ʌnráịfld], *a.* no pillado ni saqueado; (arti.) no rayado, de ánima lisa.

unrig [ʌnríg], *va.* (mar.) desaparejar.

unrighteous [ʌnráịchʌs], *a.* inicuo, malo, perverso; injusto.—**unrighteously** [-lị], *adv.* inicuamente, perversamente.—**unrighteousness** [-nịs], *s.* iniquidad, perversidad; injusticia.

unripe [ʌnráịp], *a.* verde, agraz, inmaturo; crudo, prematuro.

unripeness [-nịs], *s.* falta de madurez; crudeza.

unrivalled [ʌnráịvạld], *a.* sin rival, sin igual.

unrivet [ʌnríyịt], *va.* quitar los remaches a.

unrobe [ʌnróụb], *va.* y *vn.* desnudar(se), desvestir(se).

unroll [ʌnróụl], I. *va.* desarrollar, desenrollar, desenvolver, desplegar. II. *vn.* abrirse, desarrollarse.

unroof [ʌnrúf], *va.* destechar.

unroot [ʌnrút], *va.* desarraigar, extirpar.

unruffled [ʌnrʌfld], *a.* tranquilo, sereno.

unruled [ʌnrúld], *a.* sin rayar (papel).

unruliness [ʌnrúlịnịs], *s.* turbulencia, inquietud; desenfreno.

unruly [ʌnrúlị], *a.* indócil, inmanejable; ingobernable; indómito; revoltoso, levantisco; intratable; desarreglado.

unsaddle [ʌnsædl], *va.* desensillar (bestias); sacar de la silla, derribar (a una persona).

unsafe [ʌnséịf], *a.* peligroso, inseguro.—**unsafely** [-lị], *adv.* insegura o peligrosamente.

unsaid [ʌnséd], *a.* no proferido, no dicho.

unsal(e)able [ʌnséịlạbl], *a.* invendible.

unsalted [ʌnsóltịd], *a.* no salado, sin salar.

unsatisfactoriness [ʌnsætịsfæktọrịnịs], *s.* calidad de insatisfactorio o defectuoso.

unsatisfactory [-orị], *a.* insatisfactorio, que no satisface; malo, inaceptable.

unsatisfied [ʌnsætịsfaịd], *a.* no satisfecho, insa-

tisfecho; descontento; no convencido; (com.) no saldado (cuenta, etc.).

unsatisfying [-faịịŋ], *a.* que no satisface.

unsaturated [ʌnsæchụreịtịd], *a.* no saturado.

unsavorily [ʌnséịvọrịlị], *adv.* desabridamente, con sabor soso.—**unsavoriness** [-ịnịs], *s.* insipidez; mal sabor; mal olor.—**unsavory** [-ị], *a.* insípido, soso; desabrido; hediondo; desagradable, ofensivo (moralmente); de mala conducta.

unsay [ʌnséị], *va.* (*pret.* y *pp.* UNSAID) retractar (lo dicho).

unscathed [ʌnskéịðd], *a.* ileso, sin daño, incólume.

unscrew [ʌnskrú], *va.* des(a)tornillar, desenroscar; desenganchar, separar.

unscrupulous [ʌnskrúpyụlʌs], *a.* inescrupuloso, falto de escrúpulo.

unscrupulously [-lị], *adv.* sin escrúpulo, sin conciencia.

unseal [ʌnsíl], *va.* desellar, abrir.

unsearchable [ʌnsœrchạbl], *a.* inescrutable.

unseasonable [ʌnsízọnạbl], *a.* intempestivo, inoportuno; fuera de tiempo; prematuro; indebido, inconveniente.—**at u. hours**, a deshora.

unseasonableness [-nịs], *s.* inoportunidad.

unseasonably [-blị], *adv.* intempestivamente, fuera de tiempo o sazón.

unseasoned [ʌnsízọnd], *a.* sin sazonar, no sazonado; soso, insípido; verde (madera).

unseat [ʌnsít], *va.* quitar de un asiento; (equit.) desarzonar; privar del derecho de tomar asiento (como legislador, etc.); echar abajo (a un ministerio).

unseaworthy [ʌnsíwœrðị], *a.* innavegable, sin condiciones marineras.

unseemly [ʌnsímlị], *a.* indecoroso, impropio, indigno.

unseen [ʌnsín], *a.* no visto, inadvertido; oculto; invisible.

unselfish [ʌnsélfịš], *a.* desinteresado, generoso, abnegado, no egoísta, desprendido.—**unselfishness** [-nịs], *s.* desinterés, generosidad, abnegación.

unsensitized [ʌnsénsịtaịzd], *a.* (foto.) no sensibilizado, sin sensibilizar.

unserviceable [ʌnsœrvịsạbl], *a.* inútil o inservible.

unserviceableness [-nịs], *s.* inutilidad.

unsettle [ʌnsétl], *va.* alterar, perturbar, desarreglar, trastornar, conmover.

unsettled [-d], *a.* instable, variable, inconstante; desarreglado, descompuesto; no establecido, no instalado, vago, errante, sin residencia fija; indeciso; incierto; (com.) por pagar, no liquidado, pendiente; turbio, revuelto; inhabitado, despoblado; lunático.

unsex [ʌnséks], *va.* quitar (esp. a una mujer) los atributos y condiciones propios de su sexo.

unshackle [ʌnšékl], *va.* destrabar, desencadenar, desaherrojar, libertar.

unshaken [ʌnšéịkn], *a.* firme, inmovible.

unshapely [ʌnšéịplị], *a.* desproporcionado.

unshapen [ʌnšéịpn], *a.* disforme.

unshaven [ʌnšéịvn], *a.* sin afeitar.

unsheathe [ʌnšíð], *va.* desenvainar.

unsheltered [ʌnséltœrd], *a.* desabrigado; sin asilo, sin casa.

unship [ʌnšíp], *va.* desembarcar.—**to u. the oars**, desarmar los remos.—**to u. the rudder**, desmontar el timón.

unshod [ʌnšád], *a.* descalzo; sin herrar, sin herraduras (caballos).

unshorn [ʌnšórn], *a.* intonso.—**u. sheep**, ovejas sin esquilar.

unsightliness [ʌnsáịtlịnịs], *s.* fealdad, deformidad.—**unsightly** [-lị], *a.* feo, repugnante.

unsized [ʌnsáịzd], *a.* desencolado; sin apresto (apl. al papel).

unskilful [ʌnskílfụl], *o* **unskilled** [ʌnskíld], *a.* inexperto, imperito.—**unskilfully** [-ị], *adv.* sin arte, torpemente, sin pericia.—**unskilfulness**

[-nịs], *s.* impericia, inhabilidad, desmaña, torpeza.

unsociable [ʌnsóuṣ̌ạbl], *a.* insociable, intratable, huraño.—**unsociableness** [-nịs], *s.* insociabilidad.—**unsociably** [-blị], *adv.* insociablemente.

unsold [ʌnsóuld], *a.* no vendido, sin o por vender.

unsolder [ʌnsádœ(r)], *va.* desoldar, desestañar.

unsoldierlike, unsoldierly [ʌnsóuldœ̌erlajk, -lị], *a.* indigno de un soldado, poco marcial.

unsolicited [ʌnsolísịtịd], *a.* no solicitado, no buscado, sin solicitar.

unsolved [ʌnsálvd], *a.* sin solución, sin resolver.

unsophisticated [ʌnsof[stịkejtịd], *a.* puro, sin adulteración; sencillo, cándido; inexperto.

unsound [ʌnsáụnd], *a.* defectuoso; falto de vigor, de fuerza, de solidez; poco firme; falto de salud, enfermizo; erróneo, falso; (rel.) heterodoxo; podrido, corrompido.

unsoundness [-nịs], *s.* calidad de defectuoso; mal estado; (rel.) heterodoxia; falta de solidez o de fuerza; corrupción.

unsparing [ʌnspériŋ], *a.* liberal, generoso, pródigo; inhumano, cruel.—**unsparingly** [-lị], *adv.* liberalmente, pródigamente; sin piedad.

unspeakable [ʌnspíkạbl], *a.* indecible; inefable; execrable, atroz.—**unspeakably** [-blị], *adv.* indeciblemente; execrablemente, atrozmente.

unspecialized [ʌnspéṣ̌ạlajzd], *a.* general(izado); (biol.) no específico.

unspent [ʌnspént], *a.* inexhausto; no gastado.

unspotted [ʌnspátịd], *a.* inmaculado, sin mancha.

unstable [ʌnstéjbl], *a.* instable, inestable; no fijo.

unstamped [ʌnstǽmpt], *a.* no sellado.—**u. letter,** carta sin sello o sin franquear.

unsteadily [ʌnstédịlị], *adv.* instablemente; inconstantemente.—**unsteadiness** [-nịs], *s.* instabilidad, falta de firmeza o equilibrio, inconstancia.—**unsteady** [-ị], *a.* instable, inseguro, no firme; vacilante, tambaleante; inconstante, veleidoso.

unstinted [ʌnstíntịd], *a.* liberal, no escatimado.

unstop [ʌnstáp], *va.* destapar; abrir, dar paso.

unstratified [ʌnstrǽtịfajd], *a.* no estratificado.

unstring [ʌnstríŋ], *va.* (*pret.* y *pp.* UNSTRUNG) desencordar; desensartar; desliar, desatar, aflojar; debilitar, trastornar (los nervios).

unstudied [ʌnstádịd], *a.* no estudiado; impensado, natural; desaplicado.

unsubstantial [ʌnsʌbstǽnṣạl], *a.* insubstancial, poco sólido; inconsistente.

unsuccessful [ʌnsʌksésfụl], *a.* infructuoso, sin éxito; desafortunado; que no logra buen éxito, impróspero.—**unsuccessfully** [-ị], *adv.* sin buen éxito, infelizmente.—**unsuccessfulness** [-nịs], *s.* falta de buen éxito, infructuosidad; infortunio.

unsuitable [ʌnsjútạbl], *a.* inadecuado, no apropiado, impropio, inadaptable; incompetente.

unsung [ʌnsáŋ], *a.* no cantado o; (fig.) olvidado.

unsupported [ʌnsʌpórtịd], *a.* sin apoyo; sin sostén.

unsurmountable [ʌnsœrmáụntạbl], *a.* insuperable, invencible, infranqueable.

unsurpassable [-pǽsạbl], *a.* insuperable, inmejorable.—**unsurpassed** [-pǽst], *a.* excelente, insuperado.

unsuspected [ʌnsʌspéktịd], *a.* insospechado.

unsuspecting, unsuspicious [-iŋ, -píṣ̌ʌs], *a.* confiado, cándido, poco receloso o sospechoso.

unswear [ʌnswér], *va.* (*pret.* UNSWORE; *pp.* UN-SWORN) abjurar, retractar.

unsworn [ʌnswórn], *a.* no juramentado.

unsymmetrical [ʌnsịmétrịkạl], *a.* asimétrico.

unsympathetic [ʌnsịmpaθétịk], *a.* indiferente, frío, falto de conmiseración.

unsystematic(al [ʌnsịstemǽtịk(ạl], *a.* falto de sistema, inmetódico.

untainted [ʌntéjntịd], *a.* incorrupto.

untamable [ʌntéjmạbl], *a.* indomable.

untamed [ʌntéjmd], *a.* indomado, bravío, cerril.

untarnished [ʌntárnịṣ̌t], *a.* limpio, sin mancha.

untaught [ʌntót]. **I.** *pret.* y *pp.* de TO UNTEACH. **II.** *a.* no enseñado, sin instrucción, ignorante.

unteach [ʌntích], *va.* hacer desaprender; hacer olvidar o abandonar (una creencia, etc.).

untenable [ʌnténạbl], *a.* insostenible.

untenanted [ʌnténạntịd], *a.* desarrendado, desalquilado, vacío, desocupado, deshabitado.

unthankful [ʌnθǽŋkfụl], *a.* ingrato; mal recibido.—**unthankfully** [-ị], *adv.* ingratamente.—**unthankfulness** [-nịs], *s.* ingratitud.

unthinking [ʌnθíŋkịŋ], *a.* descuidado, desatento, indiscreto; irreflexivo.

unthought-of [ʌnθót ǫv], *a.* impensado; inesperado; olvidado.

unthread [ʌnθréd], *va.* desenhebrar, desensartar; deshilachar.

untidily [ʌntájḍịlị], *adv.* desaseadamente; sin pulcritud.—**untidiness** [-nịs], *s.* desaliño, desaseo, falta de pulcritud.—**untidy** [-ị], *a.* desaliñado, desarreglado, falto de pulcritud.

untie [ʌntáị], *va.* desatar, desprender, desligar; deshacer (un nudo); aflojar, soltar, zafar.

until [ʌntíl]. **I.** *prep.* hasta. **II.** *conj.* hasta que.

untile [ʌntájl], *va.* destejar; desembaldosar.

untilled [ʌntíld], *a.* (agr.) inculto, baldío.

untimely [ʌntájmlị]. **I.** *a.* intempestivo, extemporal, inoportuno, prematuro.—**to have an u. end,** malograrse. **II.** *adv.* intempestivamente, sin sazón; a deshora, a destiempo; abortivamente.

unto [ʌntụ], *prep.* (poét., ant.) hasta; a, hacia.

untold [ʌntóụld], *a.* nunca dicho, no narrado; sin decir; indecible, incalculable.

untouchable [ʌntáchạbl], *a.* intocable, intangible.

untouched [ʌntácht], *a.* intacto, ileso; insensible, impasible.

untoward [ʌntórd], *a.* adverso, desfavorable; embarazoso; indócil, testarudo, refractario.

untowardness [-nịs], *s.* calidad de adverso o embarazoso; testarudez, terquedad.

untraceable [ʌntréjsạbl], *a.* que no se puede rastrear, inquirir o averiguar.

untractable [ʌntrǽktạbl], *a.* intratable.

untrained [ʌntréjnd], *a.* indisciplinado, indócil; inexperto, imperito.

untrammelled [ʌntrǽmęld], *a.* libre, sin trabas; desembarazado.

untransferable [ʌntrǽnsfœrạbl], *a.* intransferible, que no se puede traspasar o ceder.

untranslatable [-léjtạbl], *a.* intraducible.

untravelled [ʌntrǽvęld], *a.* inexplorado, intransitado; que no ha recorrido mundo, provinciano.

untried [ʌntrájd], *a.* no probado o ensayado; no experimentado; novel.

untrimmed [ʌntrímd], *a.* sin adornos, sin guarniciones; sin cortar.

untrod(den [ʌntrád(n], *a.* no pisado ni hollado; no frecuentado.

untroubled [ʌntrʌ́bld], *a.* no molestado o perturbado; quieto, tranquilo; claro, transparente.

untrue [ʌntrú], *a.* falso; mendaz, falsario; engañoso, pérfido.—**untruly** [-lị], *adv.* falsamente.

untrustworthy [ʌntrʌ́stwœrŏ̌ị], *a.* indigno de confianza.

untrusty [ʌntrʌ́stị], *a.* infiel, pérfido.

untruth [ʌntrú́θ], *s.* falsedad, mentira; infidelidad, traición.

untruthful [-fụl], *a.* mendaz, inverídico, falto de veracidad; falso, no verdadero.—**untruthfully** [-ị], *adv.* falsamente; mendazmente, faltando a la verdad.—**untruthfulness** [-nịs], *s.* mendacidad, falta de veracidad; falsedad.

untutored [ʌntjútǫrd], *a.* inculto, que no ha recibido educación.

untwine [ʌntwájn], **untwist** [ʌntwíst], *va.* destorcer, desenrollar, desarrollar, desenroscar.

unused [ʌnyúzd], *a.* inusitado, insólito; no usado, nuevo; desacostumbrado.

unusual [ʌnyúźụ̌ạl], *a.* raro, extraordinario, extraño; excepcional; insólito; inusitado; desacostumbrado.—**unusually** [-į], *adv.* excepcionalmente; raramente.

unutterable [ʌnʌ́tœɹəbl], *a.* inenarrable, indecible, inexpresable, inefable.

unutterably [-blį], *adv.* indeciblemente.

unvalued [ʌnvǽlyud], *a.* desestimado, menospreciado; inapreciable.

unvanquished [ʌnvǽŋkwįšt], *a.* invicto.

unvarnished [ʌnvárnįšt], *a.* sin barnizar; sin adorno, sencillo.

unvarying [ʌnvériįŋ], *a.* invariable, constante, uniforme.

unveil [ʌnvéįl]. I. *va.* quitar el velo a, descubrir. II. *vn.* descubrirse, quitarse el velo.

unventilated [ʌnvéntįleįtįd], *a.* ahogado, falto de ventilación.

unwalled [ʌnwóld], *a.* sin murallas, sin muros; abierto; sin paredes.

unwarily [ʌnwérįlį], *adv.* incautamente, imprudentemente.—**unwariness** [-įnįs], *s.* imprevisión, falta de precaución.

unwarlike [ʌnwórlaįk], *a.* pacífico.

unwarned [ʌnwórnd], *a.* desprevenido.

unwarrantable [ʌnwárəntəbl], *a.* indisculpable, injustificable, insostenible; no garantizable.

unwarrantably [-əblį], *adv.* injustamente; injustificablemente, indefensiblemente.

unwarranted [-įd], *a.* injustificable, indefensible, inexcusable; sin garantía.

unwary [ʌnwérį], *a.* incauto, imprudente, irreflexivo.

unwashed [ʌnwášt], *a.* sin lavar; puerco, sucio.— **the great u.**, (fam.) el populacho, la canalla.

unwavering [ʌnwéįvœrįŋ], *a.* firme, determinado, resuelto.

unwearied [ʌnwírįd], *a.* infatigable.

unweave [ʌnwív], *va.* (*pret.* UNWOVE o UNWOVEN) destejer, destramar.

unwed(ded [ʌnwéd(įd], *a.* soltero, soltera, célibe.

unwelcome [ʌnwélkʌm], *a.* mal recibido, mal acogido; desagradable, incómodo, importuno.

unwell [ʌnwél], *a.* indispuesto, enfermizo, malo; menstruante.

unwept [ʌnwépt], *a.* no llorado, no lamentado; no vertidas (lágrimas).

unwholesome [ʌnhóųlsʌm], *a.* dañino, nocivo, malo para la salud, malsano, insalubre.

unwieldily [ʌnwíldįlį], *adv.* pesadamente.

unwieldiness [-įnįs], *s.* pesadez, incomodidad.

unwieldy [-į], *a.* pesado, ponderoso, difícil de manejar.

unwilling [ʌnwílįŋ], *a.* desinclinado, renuente, maldispuesto.—**unwillingly** [-lį], *adv.* de mala gana o voluntad, con repugnancia.—**unwillingness** [-nįs], *s.* mala gana, repugnancia, renuencia.

unwind [ʌnwáįnd]. I. *va.* (*pret.* y *pp.* UNWOUND) devanar (hilo, etc.); desenredar, desenrollar, desenvolver. II. *vn.* devanarse; desarrollarse.

unwise [ʌnwáįz], *a.* imprudente, no cuerdo, indiscreto; ignorante, tonto, necio.—**unwisely** [-lį], *adv.* neciamente; imprudentemente, sin cordura.

unwitting [ʌnwítįŋ], *a.* inconsciente.

unwittingly [-lį], *adv.* inconscientemente, sin saberlo.

unwomanly [ʌnwúmənlį], *a.* indigno de una mujer.

unwonted [ʌnwʌ́ntįd], *a.* no acostumbrado, poco común, inusitado.

unwooded [ʌnwúdįd], *a.* sin árboles, pelado.

unworkmanlike [ʌnwœ́rkmənlaįk], *a.* desmañado, sin maña, chapucero.

unworldly [ʌnwœ́rldlį], *a.* espiritual, no terrenal.

unworthily [ʌnwœ́rðįlį], *adv.* indignamente.

unworthiness [-įnįs], *s.* indignidad, desmerecimiento.—**unworthy** [-į], *a.* indigno, desmerecedor.

unwound [ʌnwáųnd], *pret.* y *pp.* de TO UNWIND; sin cuerda (reloj).

unwounded [ʌnwúndįd], *a.* ileso, sin herida.

unwove(n [ʌnwóųv(n], *pret.* y *pp.* de TO UNWEAVE.

unwrap [ʌnrǽp], *va.* desenvolver.

unwrinkle [ʌnríŋkl], *va.* desarrugar.

unwritten [ʌnrítn], *a.* no escrito; en blanco; tradicional.—**u. law**, derecho consuetudinario; derecho no escrito (apl. esp. a lo que muchos consideran el derecho natural de un cónyuge de vengar personalmente la afrenta del adulterio del otro).

unwrought [ʌnrót], *a.* en bruto; no elaborado o manufacturado.—**u. wax**, cera virgen.

unyielding [ʌnyíldįŋ], *a.* inflexible, inexorable, inconmovible, firme; reacio, terco.

unyoke [ʌnyóųk]. I. *va.* desuncir; separar, desunir. II. *vn.* libertar(se) de un yugo.

up [ʌp]. I. *a.* que va hacia arriba; levantado (de la cama); empinado; erecto; ascendente (tren, etc.). II. *s.* tierra elevada; prosperidad.—**ups and downs**, altibajos, vaivenes.—**on the u. and u.**, (fam.) sin fraude o dolo. III. *adv.* arriba, en lo alto, hacia arriba; para arriba (*from three dollars up*, de tres dólares para arriba); en pie, derecho; de pie, levantado; (fam.) bien enterado, adelantado, competente, capaz, a la altura de, a la par de; llegado, acabado, concluido; enteramente, totalmente, completamente.—**u. above**, arriba, más arriba.— **u.-and-aboveboard**, legítimo, legal; honrado; sincero.—**u.-and-doing**, *a.* que se menea, enérgico, emprendedor.—**u. and down**, acá y allá; por todas partes; de arriba abajo; por todos lados; de un lado a otro.—**u.-and-down**, *a.* vertical, de vaivén (movimiento); (fam.) franco, claro, abierto.—**u. and u.**, subiendo más y más; progresando.—**u. to**, hasta; capaz de; tramando, proyectando, haciendo (gen. algo reprensible); al corriente de, sabedor de. *V.* TO BE UP TO.—**u. to anything**, dispuesto para cualquier travesura.—**u. to date**, hasta la fecha.—**u.-to-date**, *a.* moderno, al día.—**u. to the minute**, hasta este momento, hasta la fecha.—**u.-to-the-minute**, *a.* que llega hasta el último momento o hasta la fecha; que está enteramente al día, de actualidad.—**it is all u.**, todo se acabó.—**the hour is u.**, ha llegado la hora.—**time is u.**, ha expirado el plazo, se ha cumplido el tiempo; ha llegado la hora.—**to be u. against it**, (fam.) hallarse en apuros; tener que luchar con.—**to be u. in**, u on, estar al corriente de, al día de, o versado en.—**to be u. in arms**, estar sublevado; haber tomado las armas; estar alborotado o excitado.—**to be u. to**, ser suficiente o competente para; estar al nivel o a la altura de; estar haciendo u ordiendo, andar en (travesuras, intrigas, etc.).—**to be u. to one**, (fam.) depender de, ser asunto de, o tocarle a uno.—**what's u.?** (fam.) ¿qué hay? ¿qué pasa? ¿de qué se trata?—El adverbio *up* se usa a menudo como expletivo enfático para indicar acción completa, y o no se traduce o se traduce cambiando algo el giro: *they ate up all they found*, se comieron cuanto encontraron (sin dejar nada); *the enemy burned up the village*, el enemigo quemó la aldea por completo. IV. *prep.* hacia arriba de; a lo largo de; en lo alto de.—**u. one's sleeve**, en secreto, para sí.—**u. the river**, río arriba; (fam.) en o a la cárcel. V. *interj.* ¡arriba! ¡aupa! ¡sus! ¡levántese Vd.! VI. *va.* (fam.) subir, elevar; aumentar (precios, etc.).

upas [yúpəs], *s.* (bot.) antiar; (fig.) ponzoña.

upbraid [ʌpbréįd], *va.* echar en cara, vituperar, afear; reconvenir.

upbringing [ʌ́pbrįŋįŋ], *s.* crianza, educación.

upcast [ʌ́pkæst]. I. *a.* tirado o arrojado a lo alto. II. *s.* tiro por alto; (min.) pozo de ventilación ascendente.

upcountry [ʌ́pkʌntrį]. I. *s.* tierra adentro, lo interior (de un país). II. *a.* de tierra adentro, del interior.

upgrade [ʌ́pgreįd]. I. *a.* ascendente. II. *adv.* hacia arriba. **III.** *s.* pendiente (*f.*) o cuesta arriba; ascensión, ascenso.

upgrowth [Λpɡroυθ], *s.* crecimiento; lo que crece o ha crecido.

upheaval [Λphívạl], *s.* solevantamiento; trastorno, cataclismo.

upheave [Λphív]. **I.** *va.* solevantar. **II.** *vn.* levantarse, alzarse.

upheld [Λphéld], *pret.* y *pp.* de TO UPHOLD.

uphill [Λphíl]. **I.** *adv.* cuesta arriba. **II.** *a.* ascendente; penoso, dificultoso.

uphold [Λphóuld], *va.* (*pret.* y *pp.* UPHELD) sostener, apoyar; defender.—**upholder** [-œ(r)], *s.* defensor, sostenedor; sustentáculo, apoyo.

upholster [Λphóulstœ(r)], *va.* rellenar y cubrir muebles; tapizar o entapizar; poner colgaduras, cortinas, etc.—**upholsterer** [-œ(r)], *s.* tapicero. —**upholstery** [-į], *s.* tapicería.

upkeep [Λpkip], *s.* conservación; mantenimiento.

upland [Λplænd]. **I.** *s.* terreno elevado, tierra alta. **II.** *a.* alto, elevado.—**u. cotton, uplands,** algodón superfino.—**uplander** [-œ(r)], *s.* montañés.

uplift [Λplíft]. **I.** *va.* levantar, elevar, alzar. **II.** [Λplíft], *s.* levantamiento, elevación.

upmost [Λpmoųst], *a.* = UPPERMOST.

upon [Λpán], *prep.* = ON, pero hay frases en que gen. se prefiere.—**u. my honor,** a fe mía, por mi (palabra de) honor.—**u. my word,** por mi palabra; (fam., *interj.*) ¡qué cosa! ¿habráse visto?

upper [Λpœ(r)]. **I.** *a.* superior, de encima o de arriba, encimero; (más) alto.—**u. case,** (impr.) caja alta (mayúsculas y versalitas).—**u.-case,** *a.* mayúscula (letra).—**U. Egypt,** Alto Egipto. —**u. hand,** ventaja, dominio.—**U. House,** cámara alta; senado.—**u. leather,** pala de zapato.—**u. millstone,** muela, volandera, corredera.—**u. transit,** (astr.) tránsito superior, culminación.—**u. works,** (mar.) obra muerta. —**the u. regions,** las regiones etéreas.—**the u. ten (thousand),** las clases de tono, la nata social. **II.** *s.* (zap.) caña y pala del zapato. —*pl.* botines.—**on one's uppers,** (fam.) en aprietos, sin blanca, tronado.

upperclassman [-klésmạn], *s.* estudiante del tercero o cuarto año.

uppercut [-kΛt], *s.* (dep.) golpe de abajo arriba con el brazo encogido.

uppermost [-moųst]. **I.** *a.* más alto, supremo, más elevado, de encima de todo; principal, predominante. **II.** *adv.* en lo más alto; en primer lugar.

uppish [Λpįš], *a.* (fam.) arrogante, encopetado.

uppishness [-nįs], *s.* (fam.) altivez, arrogancia.

upright [Λprait]. **I.** *a.* derecho, vertical, recto, enhiesto; recto, probo, honrado, equitativo.— **u. piano,** piano recto o vertical.—**u. projection,** alzado, proyección vertical. **II.** *s.* montante, pieza vertical; soporte, apoyo.—**uprightly** [-lį], *adv.* verticalmente; rectamente, con justicia.—**uprightness** [-nįs], *s.* calidad de vertical; rectitud, probidad.

uprise [Λpráįz], *vn.* (*pret.* UPROSE; *pp.* UPRISEN) levantarse; alzarse; sublevarse, rebelarse.

uprising [-įŋ], *s.* levantamiento; solevantamiento; alzamiento; insurrección, sublevación; subida, cuesta, pendiente, *f.*

uproar [Λproɹ], *s.* grita, bulla, bullicio, alboroto, conmoción; (fig.) rugido.—**uproarious** [Λprór-įΛs], *a.* ruidoso, tumultuoso; bullanguero.

uproot [Λprút], *va.* desarraigar, descuajar.

upset [Λpsét]. **I.** *va.* trastornar, desbaratar, desbarajustar, desarreglar, trasegar; volcar, tumbar, derribar; desconcertar, inquietar, agitar, turbar; (metal.) acortar a macha martillo; recalcar; triscar los dientes de una sierra; (mar.) zozobrar. **II.** *vn.* volcarse; (mar.) zozobrar. **III.** *a.* trastornado; volcado, turbado, inquieto; erigido; fijo, determinado.—**u. price,** precio

mínimo fijado en una subasta. **IV.** [Λpsɛt], *s.* vuelco; trastorno.

upsetter [Λpsétœ(r)], *s.* (mec.) prensa de acortar llantas.

upsetting [-įŋ]. **I.** *s.* trastorno, desbarajuste; vuelco; (mec.) acortamiento. **II.** *a.* desconcertante.

upshot [Λpšat], *s.* secuela, resultado final; total.

upside [Λpsaįd], *s.* parte (*f.*) superior, lo de arriba. —**u. down,** lo de arriba abajo, al revés, invertido; (fam.) patas arriba; en confusión, trastornado.

upstairs [Λpstérz]. **I.** *adv.* arriba, en la (o un) piso de arriba. **II.** [Λpsterz], *a.* de arriba (de las escaleras); alto (piso, etc.).

upstanding [Λpstándįŋ], *a.* de pie; erguido; honrado.

upstart [Λpstart], *a.* y *s.* advenedizo; encumbrado, presuntuoso.

upstream [Λpstrím], *adv.* agua(s) o río arriba.

upswing [Λpswįŋ], *s.* vuelta hacia arriba; (com., etc.) mejora, alza.

uptake [Λpteįk], *s.* acción de alzar o levantar; compresión; tubo o conducto ascendente; (m. v.) canal de salida a la chimenea.

upthrow [Λpθroų], *s.* = UPHEAVAL y UPTHRUST.

upthrust [ΛpθrΛst], *s.* (geol.) solevantamiento.

uptown [Λptáųn]. **I.** *adv.* en o a la parte alta de la ciudad, arriba (hablando de dicha parte). **II.** [Λptaųn], *a.* de arriba, de la parte alta de la ciudad.

upturn [Λptœrn]. **I.** *s.* vuelta hacia arriba; alza. **II.** [Λptœrn], *va.* volver hacia arriba; trastornar; volcar.—**upturned** [-d], *a.* respingada (nariz).

upward [Λpwạrd], *a.* vuelto hacia arriba; ascendente.—**u. moving o pulling,** ascensional.

upward(s [-(z], *adv.* hacia arriba; más.—**u. and downwards,** por arriba y por abajo.—**u. of,** más de, arriba de (una suma o cantidad indicada).—**from ten cents u.,** de diez centavos en adelante.

uralite [yúrạlaįt], *s.* (min.) uralita.

uranic [yųrénįk], *a.* celeste, astronómico; (quím.) uránico.

uraninite [yųrénįnaįt], *s.* (min.) uranina, uraninita, pechurana, mineral de uranio que contiene helio, radio, etc.

uranism [yúrạnįzm], *s.* uranismo.

uranite [yúrạnaįt], *s.* (min.) uranita.

uranium [yųréįnįΛm], *s.* (quím.) uranio.

uranometry [yųrạnámétrį], *s.* (astr.) uranometría.

Uranus [yúrạnΛs], *s.* (astr.) Urano.

urate [yúreįt], *s.* (quím.) urato.

urban [œrbạn], *a.* urbano.

urbane [œrbéįn], *a.* fino, cortés.

urbanity [œrbénįtį], *s.* urbanidad, cultura.

urbanize [œrbạnaįz], *va.* urbanizar.

urceolate [œrsįoleįt], *a.* (bot.) urceolado.

urchin [œrchįn], *s.* rapacejo, (fam.) granuja, *m.*, pilluelo, golfillo, bribonzuelo; (zool.) erizo.

urea [yúrįạ], *s.* (quím.) urea.

uredo [yųrídoų], *s.* (med.) urticaria.

uremia [yųrímįạ], *s.* (med.) uremia.—**uremic** [yųrímįk], *a.* urémico.

ureter [yųrítœ(r)], *s.* (anat.) uréter.

urethra [yųríθrạ], *s.* (anat.) uretra.—**urethral** [-l], *a.* urético, uretral.—**urethritis** [yųrįθráįtįs], *s.* (med.) uretritis.—**urethroscope** [yųríθroskoųp], *s.* (cir.) uretroscopio.—**urethrotome** [-toųm], *s.* (cir.) uretrótomo.—**urethrotomy** [yųríθrátomį], *s.* (cir.) uretrotomía.

urge [œrdž]. **I.** *va.* impeler, empujar; incitar, impulsar; instar, apremiar; apresurar, acuciar, acelerar; acosar, seguir de cerca; solicitar, importunar; pedir, recomendar con ahinco.—**to u. upon,** instigar; pedir o manifestar vehementemente a; empeñarse con, esforzarse por convencer a. **II.** *vn.* presentar argumentos o pretensiones; perorar; estimular, animar. **III.** *s.* impulso, instinto.

urgency [-ęnsị], *s.* urgencia.—**urgent** [-ęnt], *a.* urgente, apremiante.—**to be u.,** urgir.—**urgently** [-lị], *adv.* urgentemente.

urger [-œ(r)], *s.* acuciador.—**urging** [-iŋ], *s.* acuciamiento, incitación, apremio, instancia.

uric [yúrịk], *a.* (quím.) úrico.

Urim [yúrịm], *s. pl.* (igl.) adornos del pectoral del gran sacerdote de los judíos.

urinal [yúrịnạl], *s.* orinal; urinario, meadero.—**urinanalysis** [-ǽlịsịs], *s.* (med.) uroscopia, análisis urinario.—**urinary** [-erị], *a.* urinario.—**urinate** [-eịt], *va. y vn.* orinar.—**urination** [-éịṣǫn], *s.* urinación, micción.—**urinative** [-ǻtịv], *a.* (med.) diurético.

urine [yúrịn], *s.* orina, orines, *m. pl.*

uriniferous [-ífęrAs], *a.* urinífero.

urinology [-álǫdżị], *s.* (med.) ur(in)ología.

urinoscopy [-áskǫpị], *s.* = UROSCOPY.

urinose [-oụs], **urinous** [-As], *a.* urinoso; urinario.

urn [œrn], *s.* urna; jarrón.

urobilin [yụrǫbílịn], *s.* (quím.) urobilina.

Urodela [yụrǫdilǽ], *s. pl.* (zool.) urodelos.

urogenital [yụrǫdżénịtạl], *a.* (anat.) genitourinario.

urolith [yúrǫlịθ], *s.* (med.) urolito, cálculo urinario.

urology [yụrálǫdżị], *s.* (med.) ur(in)ología.

uropygium [yụrǫpídżịAm], *s.* (orn.) rabadilla.

uroscopy [yụráskǫpị], *s.* (med.) uroscopia.

ursa [œrsǽ], *s.* (zool.) osa.—**U. Major,** (astr.) Osa Mayor.—**U. Minor,** Osa Menor.

Ursidæ [œrsịdi], *s. pl.* (zool.) úrsidos.

ursiform [œrsịform], *a.* de figura de oso.

ursine [œrsịn], *a.* ursino, relativo al oso.

Ursuline [œrsyụlịn], *a. y s.* (igl.) ursulina.

urticaceous [œrtịkéịṣịAs], *a.* (bot.) urticáceo.

urticaria [œrtịkérịǽ], *s.* (med.) urticaria.

urticate [œrtịkeịt], *va.* flagelar con ortigas.

urtication [-éịṣǫn], *s.* (med.) urticación.

us [As], *pron.* nos; nosotros (caso oblicuo de WE).

us(e)able [yúzạbl], *a.* que se puede usar; utilizable, practicable.

usage [yúsịdż], *s.* trato, tratamiento; uso, usanza.

usance [yúzạns], *s.* (com.) usanza.

use [yus]. **I.** *s.* uso; aprovechamiento; aplicación; servicio, utilidad, provecho, ventaja; necesidad; ocasión de usar; costumbre, uso.—**uses of the sea,** usos de la mar.—**in u.,** en uso; usándose.—**no u.** (of) talking, es inútil discutirlo, eso no tiene discusión; sin duda, es claro que.—(of) **no u.,** inútil.—**out of u.,** inusitado, olvidado o fuera de moda.—**to be of no u.,** no servir; ser inútil.—**to have no u. for,** no necesitar; no servirse de; (fam.) no tener muy buena opinión de, tener en poco, no tener en mucho.—**what is the u.** (of)?, ¿de qué sirve? ¿para qué?, es inútil. **II.** [yuz], *va.* usar, utilizar, emplear, gastar; hacer uso, servirse o valerse de; usar de; practicar; tratar; acostumbrar, habituar (gen. en la voz pasiva **to be used,** estar acostumbrado).—**to u. one's** (own) judgment, obrar uno como le parezca.—**to u. one's** (own) way, obrar uno, o hacer (algo), a su modo.—**to u. up,** gastar, consumir, agotar; (fam.) rendir, agotar de cansancio o fatiga. **III.** *vn.* soler, acostumbrar. Ú. gen. en *pret.* para indicar acción, condición o costumbre pasadas y casi siempre equivale al pretérito imperfecto o de coexistencia con negación implícita, la cual puede hacerse explícita mediante un adverbio, como *antes: he used to come every day,* él solía venir todos los días, él venía todos los días; *the city used to be smaller,* antes (en otro tiempo) la ciudad era más pequeña; *slaves used to be sold,* antes (en otro tiempo) se vendían esclavos.

useful [yúsfụl], *a.* útil; provechoso.—**u. load,** (aer.) carga útil.—**usefully** [-ị], *adv.* útilmente;

provechosamente.—**usefulness** [-nịs], *s.* utilidad.

useless [yúslịs], *a.* inútil; ocioso; inservible; inepto.—**to be** (wholly) **u.,** no servir (para nada).—**uselessly** [-lị], *adv.* inútilmente.—**uselessness** [-nịs], *s.* inutilidad.

user [yúzœ(r)], *s.* el que usa, se sirve o se vale de alguna cosa; consumidor, comprador; dueño.

usher [Áṣœ(r)]. **I.** *s.* ujier, conserje, aposentador: (igl. y teat.) acomodador; (Ingl.) sotamaestro. **II.** *va.* (a menudo con **in**) introducir, aposentar, acomodar; anunciar.

ustulation [Aschụléịṣǫn], *s.* quemadura; (farm.) ustulación, desecación o calcinación; (quím.) volatilización, expulsión por el calor.

usual [yúżuạl], *a.* usual, acostumbrado, ordinario, común.—**as u.,** como de costumbre, como siempre.—**usually** [-ị], *adv.* usualmente, por lo general, por regla general, ordinariamente, de ordinario.—**usualness** [-nịs], *s.* calidad de común u ordinario; (lo) común.

usucapt [yúzịụkæpt], *va.* (for.) usucapir.

usucap(t)ion [-kéịpịǫn, -kǽpṣǫn], *s.* (for.) usucapión.

usufruct [-frʌkt], *s.* (for.) usufructo.—**usufructuary** [-frákchụạrị], *a. y s.* usufructuario.

usurer [yúżụrœ(r)], *s.* usurero, logrero, lechero.

usurious [yużúrịAs], *a.* usurario.—**usuriously** [-lị], *adv.* usurariamente.—**usuriousness** [-nịs], *s.* calidad de usurario.

usurp [yuzœrp], *va.* usurpar; arrogarse.

usurpation [yuzœrpéịṣǫn], *s.* usurpación.

usurpatory [yuzœrpạtǫrị], *a.* usurpatorio.

usurper [yuzœrpœ(r)], *s.*, **usurping** [-iŋ] *a.* usurpador.

usurpingly [-lị], *adv.* por usurpación.

usury [yúżụrị], *s.* usura.—**to practice u.,** usurear.

ut [ut], *s.* (mús.) do; (ant.) ut.

utensil [yuténṣịl], *s.* utensilio.—*pl.* útiles.

uterine [yútęrịn], *a.* (anat.) uterino.—**uteritis** [-rǻịtịs], *s.* (med.) uteritis, *m.,* metritis.—**uteromania** [-roméịnịǽ], *s.* uteromanía, ninfomanía.

uterus [yútęrạs], *s.* (anat.) útero, matriz.

utilitarian [yutịlịtérịạn], *s. y a.* utilitario; (filos.) utilitarista.—**utilitarianism** [-ịzm], *s.* (filos.) utilitarismo.

utility [yutílịtị], *s.* utilidad; servicio; empresa de servicio público.—**u. man,** criado o mozo para todo; (teat.) racionista, suplente.

utilizable [yútịlaịzạbl], *a.* utilizable, aprovechable.—**utilization** [-ịzéịṣǫn], *s.* utilización, aprovechamiento.

utilize, utilise [yútịlaịz], *va.* utilizar, hacer uso de, aprovechar.

utmost [Átmoụst]. **I.** *a.* extremo, sumo; mayor, más grande; más posible; más distante; último, postrero. **II.** *s.* lo sumo, lo mayor, lo más.—**to do one's u.,** hacer uno lo sumo posible o cuanto pueda.—**to the u.,** hasta no más.

Utopia [yutóụpịǽ], *s.* Utopía; (u.) utopía.

utopian [-n]. **I.** *a.* utópico. **II.** *s. y a.* utopista.

utricle [yútrịkl], *s.* (anat.) cavidad en el laberinto del oído; (bot.) utrículo.

utricular [yutríkịụlǽ(r)], *a.* utricular.

utter [Átœ(r)]. **I.** *a.* total, entero, cabal, completo; absoluto, perentorio, terminante. **II.** *va.* proferir, pronunciar, articular; decir, expresar; dar (un grito, etc.); descubrir, publicar, revelar; engañar, defraudar con (moneda falsa); hacer pasar fraudulentamente; emitir, poner en circulación.

utterable [-ạbl], *a.* articulable, decible.

utterance [-ạns], *s.* pronunciación; expresión, lenguaje; aserción, declaración.

utterer [-œ(r)], *s.* el que pronuncia o profiere; divulgador.

utterly [-lị], *adv.* totalmente, completamente, enteramente, absolutamente.

uttermost [-moụst], *a. y s.* = UTMOST.

utterness [-nịs], *s.* extremidad; calidad de completo o absoluto.
uvate [yúveịt], *s.* (coc.) uvate.
uvea [yúvịạ], *s.* (anat.) úvea, túnica del ojo.
uvula [yúvyŭlạ], *s.* (anat.) úvula, campanilla, galillo.—**uvular** [-(r)], *a.* (anat.) uvular.
uxorial [ʌksórịạl], *a.* perteneciente a la esposa.
uxoricide [ʌksórịsaịd], *s.* uxoricida, *m.* (persona); uxoricidio (crimen).
uxorious [ʌksórịʌs], *a.* gurrumino (fam.).—**uxoriously** [-lị], *adv.* con gurrumina.—**uxoriousness** [-nịs], *s.* gurrumina (fam.).

V

v [vi], *s.* v.
V [vi]. **I.** *s.* (mec.) apoyo o guía en V; (fam.) billete de 5 dólares. **II.** *a.* en V, de forma de V; triangular.—**V engine** = V motor.—**V gear**, rueda de dientes en hélice.—**V motor**, (aut.) motor de cilindros convergentes o en V.—**V-threaded**, de filete triangular.—**V. tool**, cincel para ranuras triangulares.
vacancy [véịkạnsị], *s.* vacuidad; vacío; vacancia, vacante, *f.*—**to fill a v.**, proveer o cubrir una vacante.—**vacant** [-ạnt], *a.* vacío, desocupado; descargado; libre, desembarazado; vacante; vago; estúpido, estólido; (for.) ocioso, abandonado.
vacate [véịkeịt]. **I.** *va.* evacuar, dejar vacío; desocupar; abandonar; dejar vacante; (for.) anular, rescindir, revocar. **II.** *vn.* salir, irse, marcharse; desalojar; vacar; desocupar.
vacation [veịkéịȿọn], *s.* vacación, días feriados, asueto; (igl.) recle; (for.) anulación, revocación.—**vacationist** [-ịst], *s.* persona que está de vacaciones (veraneante, *si se trata del verano*).
vaccinal [væksịnạl], *a.* (med.) vacunal.
vaccinate [væksịneịt], *va.* (med.) vacunar.—**vaccination** [-éịȿọn], *s.* vacunación, inoculación.—**vaccinator** [-eịtọ(r)], *s.* vacunador.
vaccine [væksịn]. **I.** *a.* vacuno. **II.** *s.* (med.) vacuna, vaccino.—**v. point**, lanceta o aguja de vacunar.
vaccineaceous [væksịnịéịȧʌs], *a.* (bot.) vaccinieo.
vaccinia [væksịnịạ], *s.* (med.) vacuna.
vacillate [væsịleịt], *vn.* vacilar.
vacillating [-ịn], *a.* vacilante, remiso.
vacillation [-éịȿọn], *s.* vacilación.
vacuity [vækịúịtị], *s.* vacuidad, vacío; hueco, laguna; ociosidad; estupidez; inanidad.
vacuo [vækyọụl], *s.* el vacío (en la expresión **in v.**, en el vacío).
vacuole [-yọụl], *s.* (biol.) vacuola.
vacuous [-yụʌs], *a.* vacío, desocupado; fatuo, mentecato.
vacuum [-yụʌm]. **I.** *s.* vacío. **II.** *a.* de vacío; (mec.) aspirante.—**v. bottle**, termos.—**v. brake**, freno de vacío.—**v. cleaner**, aspirador (de polvo), limpiador o barredera aspirante.—**v. ga(u)ge**, vacuómetro, indicador de vacío.—**v. pan**, (azú.) tacho de vacío.—**v. pump**, bomba aspirante o de vacío; (hidr.) pulsómetro.—**v. tube**, (elec.) tubo de vacío; (rad.) audión, *m.*, tubo termiónico.—**v. valve**, (m. v.) válvula de admisión de aire; (rad.) = v. TUBE.—**in a v.**, en el vacío.
vade mecum [véịdị mík ʌm], *s.* (lat.) vademécum.
vagabond [vǽgạband]. **I.** *a.* vagabundo, vagamundo, errático, errante; fluctuante. **II.** *s.* vag(amund)o, (fam.) pelafustán.—**vagabondage**, **vagabondism** [-ịdź, -ịzm], *s.* vagancia.—**vagabondize** [-aịz], *vn.* vagabundear, vagamundear.
vagary [vạgéịrị], *s.* capricho, extravagancia, humorada, antojo.
vagina [vạdźáịnạ], *s.* (anat.) vagina; (bot.) vaina.—**vaginal** [vǽdźịnạl], *a.* (anat.) vaginal; (bot.) rel. o semejante a una vaina.—**v. process**, apófisis vaginal (del temporal).—**v. tunic**, túnica vaginal —**vaginate** [-neịt], *a.* (bot.)

vaginado, provisto de una vaina.—**vaginitis** [-náịtịs], *s.* (med.) vaginitis, inflamación de la vagina.
vaginula [vadźínyŭlạ], *s.* (bot., zool.) vagínula.
vagitus [vædźáịtʌs], *s.* primer grito de la criatura recién nacida.
vagrancy [véịgrạnsị], *s.* vagancia.—**vagrant** [-ạnt]. **I.** *a.* vagabundo, vagamundo, vagante, vag(aros)o, errante. **II.** *s.* vago, vagabundo, golfo.—**vagrantly** [-lị], *adv.* vagarosamente.
vague [véịg], *a.* vago, indefinido, impreciso; incierto, dudoso.—**vaguely** [-lị], *adv.* vagamente.—**vagueness** [-nịs], *s.* vaguedad.
vagus [véịgʌs], *s.* (anat.) nervio neumogástrico.
vain [véịn], *a.* vano, vanidoso; inútil, vano; fútil, hueco, insubstancial.—**in v.**, en vano.
vainglorious [-glórịʌs], *a.* vanaglorioso, jactancioso.—**vaingloriously** [-lị], *adv.* jactanciosamente.—**vainglory**, **vaingloriousness** [-glórị, -ʌsnịs], *s.* vanagloria, jactancia.
vainly [-lị], *adv.* vanamente, arrogantemente, inútilmente.—**vainness** [-nịs], *s.* vanidad, envanecimiento; inutilidad.
vair [ver], *s.* (blas.) veros (*pl.*); cierta piel.
valance [vǽlạns], *s.* cenefa, doselera, gotera del dosel.
vale [véịl], *s.* (poét.) val o valle; cañada.
vale [-i], *interj.* (lat.) ¡adiós!
valediction [vælịdíkȿọn], *s.* vale, despedida.
valedictorian [-dịktórịạn], *s.* alumno que hace el discurso de despedida a fin de curso.
valedictory [-díktorị]. **I.** *a.* de despedida. **II.** *s.* discurso de despedida en los colegios.
valence [véịlẹns], **valency** [-ị], *s.* (quím.) valencia.
Valenciennes [vạlensịénz], *s.* puntas (*pl.*) de Valenciennes (ll. t. **V. lace**).
valentine [vǽlẹntaịn], *s.* misiva o regalo que se suele enviar a una persona amada el día de San Valentín (14 de febrero); a veces, misiva anónima, jocosa o satírica.
valerian [vạlírịạn], *s.* (bot.) valeriana.
valerianaceous [-éịȧʌs], *a.* (bot.) valerianáceo.—**valerianate** [-eịt], *s.* (quím.) valerianato.—**valerianic** [-ǽnịk], **valeric** [vạlírịk], *a.* (quím.) valeriánico, valérico.
valet [vǽlịt *o* vǽleị], *s.* criado, camarero, paje; aguijón para adiestrar caballos.—**v. de chambre**, (fr.) ayuda (*m.*) de cámara.
valetudinarian [vælẹtỵudịnérịạn], *a.* y *s.* valetudinario.—**valetudinary** [-tịúdịnerị], *a.* valetudinario, enfermizo, delicado, impedido.
Valhalla [vælhǽlạ], *s.* Valhala (Campos Elíseos de los escandinavos); sala o templo de héroes.
valiant [vǽlyạnt], *a.* valiente, valeroso, bravo, (fam.) de puños.—**valiantly** [-lị], *adv.* valerosamente.—**valiantness** [-nịs], *s.* valentía, valor.
valid [vǽlịd], *a.* válido, justo; valedero; fuerte.
validate [-eịt], *va.* validar, hacer válido; legalizar.—**validation** [-éịȿọn], *s.* validación.
validity [vạlídịtị], **validness** [vǽlịdnịs], *s.* validez, valor; fuerza legal.
validly [vǽlịdlị], *adv.* válidamente.
valise [vạlís], *s.* maleta, valija, saco de viaje.
Valkyr(ie [vælkír(ị], *s.* (mit. escand.) valquiria.
valley [vǽlị], *s.* valle, cuenca; (arq.) lima hoya.
valor [vǽlọ(r)], *s.* valor, valentía, ánimo, aliento, brío, fuerza, fortaleza.
valorization [-ịzéịȿọn], *s.* fijación arbitraria oficial de precios.—**valorize** [-aịz], *va.* y *vn.* fijar o tratar de fijar precios arbitrarios oficialmente.
valorous [-ʌs], *a.* valeroso, valiente, intrépido.—**valorously** [-lị], *adv.* valerosamente.
valuable [vǽlyụạbl]. **I.** *a.* valioso; precioso, apreciable, estimable, preciado. **II.** *s. pl.* joyas u otros objetos de valor.—**valuably** [-blị], *adv.* valiosamente.—**valuation** [-éịȿọn], *s.* justiprecio, aprecio, tasa(ción), (a)valuación, valoración, avalúo.—**valuator** [-eịtọ(r)], *s.* tasador, avaluador.
value [vǽlyụ]. **I.** *s.* valor, mérito, valía; precio, justiprecio, valuación, monta, importe; aprecio,

estimación; entidad, importancia; (mús.) valor de una nota.—**v. received**, (com.) valor recibido.—**to the v. of**, por valor de. **II.** *va.* (a)valuar, (a)valorar, tasar, (a)preciar; hacer caso de, tener en mucho; considerar.—**valueless** [-ljs], *a.* sin valor, despreciable.—**valuer** [-œ(r)], *s.* tasador, (a)valuador.

valval, valvar [válval, -ä(r)], *a.* (biol.) valvar, valvular, relativo a las valvas o válvulas.

valvate [válvejt], *a.* valvulado, valvular.

valve [vælv], *s.* (mec.) válvula, ventalla; (anat.) válvula; (zool.) valva de los moluscos; (bot.) ventalla; (rad.) válvula, tubo termiónico.—**v. box, v. chest**, (m. v.) caja de válvula.—**v. face**, cara, superficie de trabajo de la válvula.—**v. gear**, (m. v.) distribución, mecanismo de distribución.—**v. lift**, alza de la válvula.—**v. rod**, varilla de la válvula.—**v. seat**, asiento de la válvula.—**v. stem**, vástago de la válvula.—**v. travel**, carrera de la válvula.

valvular [válvyülä(r)], *a.* valvular.—**v. heart disease**, enfermedad orgánica de las válvulas del corazón.

valvule [válvjul], *s.* valvulilla.

vamoos [vamús], *vn.* (fam.) marcharse, largarse.

vamp [væmp]. **I.** *s.* (zap.) pala, empella; capellada; remiendo, remonta; acompañamiento músico improvisado; (fam.) coqueta; aventurera poco escrupulosa; (fam.) bombero voluntario. **II.** *va.* (zap.) poner pala, empella, o capellada; remontar, remendar; (mús.) improvisar (acompañamiento); (fam.) embaucar (una mujer a un hombre). **III.** *vn.* (fam.) coquetear; hacer el papel de *vamp* o *vampire*.

vamper [-œ(r)], *s.* remendón.

vampire [vámpajr], *s.* (zool. y fig.) vampiro; chupador de sangre; concusionario; parásito; estafador, aventurero (apl. esp. a mujeres).

vampirism [-jzm], *s.* vampirismo.

van [væn], *s.* camión, *m.*, carromato, galera, conductora de muebles; (Ingl., f. c.) furgón de equipajes; (mil., etc.) vanguardia; jefes (*pl.*) de una empresa.

vanadate [vánadejt], *s.* (quím.) vanadato.

vanadic [vánédik], *a.* (quím.) vanádico.

vanadium [vanéjdjam], *s.* (quím.) vanadio.

vandal [vándal], *a. y s.* vándalo.—**vandalism** [-jzm], *s.* vandalismo.

Vandyke [vændájk]. **I.** *a.* de Van Dyck, a la Van Dyck.—**V. beard**, barba corta y puntiaguda.—**V. collar**, cuello ancho de lienzo y encaje. **II.** *s.* (b. a.) cuadro pintado por Van Dyck.

vane [vejn], *s.* veleta; (mar.) grímpola; aspa (de molino); paleta (de hélice); (orn.) barbas (*pl.*) (de pluma); pínula (de instrumentos matemáticos); (top.) tablilla, corredera (de una mira).

vanguard [vángard], *s.* vanguardia.—**Vanguardism** [-jzm], *s.* (lit., b. a.) vanguardismo.—**Vanguardist** [-jst], *a. y s.* vanguardista.

vanilla [vánjla], *s.* (bot.) vainilla.

vanillin [vánjljn], *s.* (quím.) va(i)nil(l)ina.

vanish [vénjš], *vn.* desvanecerse, desaparecer, esfumarse.—**vanishing** [-jŋ]. **I.** *s.* desaparición. **II.** *a.* que desaparece, etc.—**v. point**, (dib.) punto de la vista.

vanity [vánjti], *s.* vanidad.—**v. bag, v. box, v. case**, neceser, cajita de polvo y afeites.—**v. dresser**, tocador.

vanquish [vánkwjš], *va. y vn.* vencer.—**vanquishable** [-ạbl], *a.* vencible.—**vanquisher** [-œ(r)], *s.* vencedor.

vantage [vántjdž], *s.* ventaja, superioridad.—**v. ground**, posición ventajosa.

vapid [vápjd], *a.* insípido, soso, insulso.—**vapidity** [væpjditj], **vapidness** [vápjdnjs], *s.* insipidez.

vapor [véjpọ(r)]. **I.** *s.* vapor; niebla, bruma; vaho, exhalación; hálito; humo, cosa insubstancial; (med.) remedio inhalado.—*pl.* (ant.) vapores, melancolía.—**v. bath**, baño de vapor. **II.** *vn.*

exhalar vapor, avahar; evaporarse; alardear, baladronear. **III.** *va.* evaporar; reducir a vapor; exhalar. *V.* VAPORIZE.

vaporish [-jš], *a.* vaporoso; hipocondríaco.—**vaporizable** [-ajzạbl], *a.* vaporizable.—**vaporization** [-jzéjšọn], *s.* vaporización.—**vaporize** [-ajz], *va. y vn.* (e)vaporizar(se), vapor(e)ar(se), volatilizar(se).—**vaporizer** [-œ(r)], *s.* vaporizador.—**vaporous** [-ʌs], *a.* vaporoso, nebuloso; vano, quimérico; caprichudo.—**vapory** [-j], *a.* vaporoso; melancólico, hipocondríaco.

Varanidæ [vaŕénjdj], *s. pl.* (zool.) varánidos.—**varanus** [véranʌs], *s.* (zool.) varano, monitor.

variability [veŗjabjljtj], *s.* variabilidad.

variable [véŗjabl], *s. y a.* (leng. ord., mec. y mat.) variable, *f.*—**v. condenser**, (elec.) condensador de capacidad graduable continuamente.—**v. gear**, (ing.) engranaje de relación de multiplicación variable.—**v. inductor**, (elec.) inductor de inductancia graduable continuamente.—**v.-speed gear**, (aut.) cambio de velocidades.

variableness [-njs], *s.* variabilidad, inconstancia.—**variably** [-blj], *adv.* variablemente.

variance [véŗjans], *s.* variación, cambio, mudanza; discordia, desavenencia, desacuerdo; discrepancia.—**to be at v.**, estar discorde(s) o en desacuerdo, estar de punta o reñido (con); discrepar.

variant [-ạnt]. **I.** *a.* variante, vario; variable; mudable, inquieto, indeciso. **II.** *s.* variante, *f.*

variation [-éjšọn], *s.* variación; variedad; (gram.) (in)flexión; (mús., astr., biol.) variación.

varicella [veŗjsélạ], *s.* (med.) varicela.

varicocele [véŗjkousjl], *s.* (med.) varicocele.

varicolored [véŗjkalọrd], *a.* abigarrado.

varicose [véŗjkous], *a.* (med.) varicoso.

varied [véŗjd], *a.* variado, vario; cambiado, alterado; (zool., orn.) abigarrado, multicolor.

variegate [véŗjgejt], *va.* jaspear, vetear, varetear, matizar, gayar; (pint.) abigarrar, (fam.) pintorrear, pintarrajar; (fig.) diversificar, diferenciar.—**variegated** [-jd], *a.* abigarrado, jaspeado, veteado; divers(ificad)o.—**variegation** [-éjšọn], *s.* jaspeadura, abigarramiento; variedad de colores; diversificación; veteado, jaspeado.

variety [váŗájetj], *s.* variedad, diversidad; surtido; tipo, clase, *f.*, especie.—**v. is the spice of life**, en la variedad está el placer.—**v. show**, (teat.) función de variedades.

variola [váŗájolạ], *s.* (med.) viruela.

varioloid [véŗjolojd], *s.* (med.) varioloide, *f.*

variolous [váŗájolʌs], *a.* varioloso, variólico.

variometer [veŗjámetœ(r)], *s.* (rad.) variómetro.

variorum [veŗjóram], *s. y a.* (texto) con variantes o anotado por varios críticos o expertos.

various [véŗjʌs], *a.* varios, algunos, unos cuantos, *pl.*; vario, desemejante, distinto, diverso, diferente; inconstante, mudable; veteado, abigarrado.

variously [-lj], *adv.* variamente.

varix [véŗjks], *s.* (med.) varice, várice, *f.* o variz.

varlet [várljt], *s.* (ant.) lacayo; paje. *V.* KNAVE.

varletry [-rj], *s.* (ant.) chusma, canalla.

varnish [várnjš]. **I.** *s.* barniz, *m.*, charol; (cerá.) mogate. **II.** *va.* barnizar, charolar; (cerá.) vidriar; paliar, disimular, encubrir.—**varnisher** [-œ(r)], *s.* barnizador, charolista; encubridor.

varsity [vársjtj], *s.* (abrev. fam. de **university**) universidad; (dep.) equipo de primera categoría que representa a una universidad o colegio.

vary [véŗj], *va. y vn.* variar, cambiar; diversificar(se); desviar(se).—**varying** [-jŋ], *a.* variante, variable.

vas [væs], *s.* (anat.) conducto, vaso.—**v. deferens**, conducto deferente.

vascular [véskyülä(r)], *a.* (zool., bot.) vascular, vasculoso.—**vascularity** [-ǽŗitj], *s.* vascularidad, calidad de vascular.—**vasculose** [-ous], **vasculous** [-ʌs], *a.* = VASCULAR.

vase [veis], s. jarrón, vaso; florero.
vasomotor [væsomóutǫ(r)]. I. a. (anat.) vasomotor. II. s. (med.) estimulante que produce acción vascular.
vassal [væsǫl]. I. s. vasallo, siervo. II. a. tributario, servil.—**vassalage** [-idǯ], s. vasallaje.
vast [væst]. I. a. vasto, dilatado; inmenso, enorme, grandísimo. II. s. (poét.) inmensidad, infinito.—**vastly** [-li], adv. en sumo grado, muy, muchísimo, sumamente.—**vastness** [-nis], s. vastedad, inmensidad.—**vasty** [-i], a. (poét.) vasto, inmenso.
vat [væt], s. tina, tanque, cuba; (ten.) noque.
vatic(al [vætik(ǫl], a. vaticinante, profético.
Vatican [vætikǫn], s. Vaticano.
vaticide [vætisaid], s. asesino o asesinato de un profeta.
vaticinate [vǫtísineit], vn. y va. vaticinar.
vaticination [-éiṣǫn], s. vaticinio.
vaudeville [vóudvil], s. (teat.) función de variedades; jácara, romance, canción.
vaudevillian [voudvílyǫn], a. de, o relativo a, un teatro de variedades.
vault [vǫlt]. I. s. (arq.) bóveda, cúpula, cimbor(r)io; cueva, bodega, subterráneo, sibil; tumba; (igl.) cripta; (fig.) cielo, firmamento; (dep.) voltereta, salto con garrocha o pértiga. II. va. (arq.) abovedar, voltear. III. va. y vn. (dep.) voltear, saltar por encima con garrocha o pértiga, o apoyando las manos en potro de madera, etc.
vaulted [-id], a. abovedado, arqueado.
vaulter [-œ(r), s. (dep.) volteador, saltador.
vaulting [-iŋ], s. abovedado, bóvedas, f. pl.; construcción de bóvedas; (dep.) acto de saltar con garrocha, etc.—**v. horse**, (gimn.) caballo o potro de madera.
vaunt [vǫnt]. I. va. y vn. ostentar, alardear, jactarse, vanagloriarse (de), decantar, blasonar, hacer alarde o gala (de). II. s. jactancia, gala, (fam.) fachenda.—**vaunter** [-œ(r)], s. blasonador, (fam.) fanfarrón, fachendista.—**vaunting** [-iŋ], a. jactancioso.—**vauntingly** [-li], adv. con jactancia.
veal [vil], s. (carne (f.) de) ternera.—**v. cutlet**, chuleta de ternera.—**v. pie**, pastel de ternera.
vector [vɛ́ktǫ(r), s. (mat.) vector.—**v. quantity**, cantidad vectorial.—**vectorial** [vɛktórjǫl], a. vectorial.
Veda [véidǫ], s. Veda, m., libro sagrado de la India.
vedette [vedét], s. (mil.) centinela (m.) o escucha de caballería; lancha naval de reconocimiento.
Vedic [véidik], a. védico, rel. a o de los Vedas.
veer [vír]. I. vn. desviarse; cambiar, variar (el viento, etc.); (mar.) virar, rolar. II. va. virar, dirigir el buque a otro rumbo; arriar, aflojar, largar.—**to v. and haul**, lascar y halar; largar y escasear.—**to v. away the cable**, soltar cable.
veery [-i], s. (orn.) tordo canoro.
vegetable [védǯtǫbl]. I. s. vegetable, planta vegetal.—pl. verduras, hortalizas, legumbres. II. a. vegetable, vegetal; de hortalizas.—**v. garden**, huerta (de legumbres).—**v. ivory**, tagua.—**v. kingdom**, reino vegetal.—**v. market**, verdulería.—**v. marrow**, (bot.) calabacín, especie de calabaza.—**v. stew**, potaje, menestra.—**v. sulphur**, azufre vegetal, licopodio en polvo.
vegetal [védǯetǫl], a. vegetal.
vegetarian [vedǯetérjǫn], a. y s. vegetariano, vegetalista.—**vegetarianism** [-izm], s. vegetarianismo.
vegetate [védǯeteit], vn. vegetar.—**vegetating** [-iŋ], a. vegetante.—**vegetation** [-éiṣǫn], s. vegetación.—**vegetative** [-eitiv], a. vegetativo, vegetante.—**vegetativeness** [-nis], s. potencia vegetativa.
vehemence, vehemency [víhimǫns, -i], s. vehemencia, viveza.—**vehement** [-ǫnt], a. vehemente, impetuoso, intensivo, extremoso.—

vehemently [-li], adv. vehementemente, impetuosamente.
vehicle [víhikl], s. vehículo, carruaje; medio; (farm.) excipiente.—**v. road**, camino carretero.
vehicular [vihíkyǫlǫ(r)], a. perteneciente o relativo al vehículo; de o para vehículos.
veil [veil]. I. va. velar, cubrir con velo; encubrir, disimular, disfrazar, tapar. II. s. velo; cortina; disfraz, m., máscara, pretexto.—**to take the v.**, (igl.) profesar.—**veiled** [-d], a. velado, encubierto, indirecto, disfrazado.
vein [véin]. I. s. (anat.) vena; (ent.) nervio del ala de un insecto; (bot.) vena, nervio; (min.) venero, vena, veta, capa, filón; (carp.) vena, veta, hebra, trepa (de la madera); (fig.) humor, genio. II. va. jaspear, vetear.
veined [-d], a. venoso, que tiene venas; veteado, avetado.—**veinless** [-lis], a. sin venas, desprovisto de venas.—**veinlet** [-lit], s. venilla.
veinstone [-stoun], s. (min.) ganga.
veiny [-i], a. = VEINED.
velar [vílǫ(r)], a. (fon.) velar.
veld, veldt [velt], s. veldt, tierra abierta; sabana, tierras ganaderas o de pastos.
vellication [velikéiṣǫn], s. (med.) sacudimiento muscular espasmódico.
vellum [vélʌm], s. vitela, pergamino.—**v. paper**, papel vitela o avitelado.
velocimeter [velosímetǫ(r)], s. velocímetro.
velocipede [vilásipid], s. velocípedo.
velocity [vilásiti], s. velocidad.
velodrome [vílodroum], s. velódromo, lugar de carreras (apl. esp. a las de bicicleta).
velour(s [velúr], s. (tej.) terciopelado.
velum [vílam], s. (anat.) cubierta membranosa; velo del paladar.
velure [veliúr]. I. s. (tej.) terciopelado; cepillo de pana (para sombreros de copa). II. va. cepillar o limpiar con cepillo de pana.
velvet [vélvit]. I. s. (tej.) terciopelo, velludo; (zool.) vello.—**v.-like**, terciopelado.—**v. weaver**, terciopelero. II. a. de terciopelo, terciopelado.
velveteen [velvetín], s. (tej.) pana, velludillo.
velvety [vélviti], a. (a)terciopelado.
vena [vínǫ], s. (pl. **venæ** [víni] (anat., hidr.) vena. —**v. cava**, (anat.) vena cava.—**v. contracta**, (hidr.) contracción de la vena flúida.—**v. portæ**, (anat.) vena porta.
venal [vínǫl], a. venal, mercenario.
venality [vinǽliti], s. venalidad.
venatic [vinǽtik], a. venatorio.
venation [vinéiṣǫn], s. (ent., bot.) venación.
vend [vend]. I. va. vender (esp. en carretón, o como buhonero); divulgar, decir públicamente. II. vn. vender(se).
vendee [vendí], s. (for.) comprador; cesionario.
vender [véndœ(r)], s. vendedor (esp. el ambulante), buhonero. V. VENDING MACHINE.
vendetta [vendétǫ], s. vendetta, venganza particular ejecutada por familias.
vendible [véndibl]. I. a. vendible; venal, mercenario. II. s. (gen. pl.) artículos o géneros de venta.—**vendibleness** [-nis], s. calidad de vendible.
vending [véndiŋ], s. acción de vender.—**v. machine**, máquina vendedora o expendedora (de confituras, cigarillos, sellos, etc.).
vendor [véndo(r)], s. (for.) vendedor; cedente.
vendue [vendiú], s. almoneda, subasta, venta pública, (Am.) venduta.
veneer [venír]. I. va. chapear, enchapar; revestir; tapar, ocultar, disfrazar. II. s. hoja para chapear, chapa; capa exterior, apariencia.
veneering [-iŋ], s. chapeado, enchapado; material para chapas; chapería.
venerability [venerabíliti], s. venerabilidad.
venerable [vénerabl], a. venerable, venerando, reverenciable; sagrado; antiguo.—**venerableness** [-nis], s. venerabilidad.—**venerably** [-bli], adv. venerablemente, con veneración o reve-

rencia.—**venerate** [vénereit], va. venerar, reverenciar.—**veneration** [-éiŝǫn], s. veneración, reverencia.—**venerator** [-eitǫ(r)], s. venerador.

venereal [vęnírial], a. venéreo.

venery [véneri], s. venus, f., acto venéreo; (ant.) montería o caza mayor.

venesection [vinįsékŝǫn], s. flebotomía, sangría.

Venetian [vęníŝąn], a. y s. veneciano.—**V. blind**, persiana, celosía.—**V. chalk**, jabón de sastre, esteatita blanca, talco gráfico.—**V. sumac**, (bot.) fustete.

vengeance [véndźąns], s. venganza.—**with a v.**, con violencia, con toda su alma; con creces, extremamente.

vengeful [véndźful], a. vengativo.

venial [vínial], a. venial; perdonable.—**v. sin**, pecado venial.—**venially** [-i], adv. venialmente, levemente, ligeramente.—**veniality, venialness** [vinįéliti, vínialnįs], s. venialidad.

venire (facias [vįnáįri (féiŝąs], s. (for.) auto de convocación del jurado; (Ingl.) orden (f.) o requerimiento de comparecencia.

venireman [-mąn], s. jurado (persona).

venison [vénįzǫn], s. carne (f.) de venado.

venom [vénǫm], s. veneno, tósigo, ponzoña; rencor, malicia, malignidad.

venomous [-ʌs], a. venenoso, ponzoñoso; dañoso; maligno.—**venomously** [-li], adv. venenosamente.—**venomousness** [-nįs], s. venenosidad.

venosity [vįnásiti], s. (anat.) venosidad.

venous [vínʌs], a. venoso; veteado.—**v. blood**, sangre venosa.

vent [vent], I. s. respiradero, resolladero, tronera, lumbrera, ventosa; salida, paso, abertura, pasaje; (arti.) oído, fogón (de arma de fuego); (fund.) bravera; (zool.) ano; expresión; emisión; desahogo.—**v. searcher**, (arti.) gubia. II. va. expresar, desembuchar (fam.), desahogar, desfogar, dar salida.—**to v. one's spleen**, descargar uno la bilis.

venter [véntœ(r)], s. (anat.) vientre; (con)cavidad; (for.) matriz.

venthole [vénthoul], s. orificio de escape; (arti.) oído, fogón; (ton.) venteo; atabe de cañería.

ventiduct [véntįdʌkt], s. conducto de ventilación.

ventilate [véntileit], va. ventilar; proveer de respiradero; (ant.) aechar.—**ventilation** [-éiŝǫn], s. ventilación.—**ventilator** [-eitǫ(r)], s. ventilador.

ventral [véntrąl], a. (anat.) ventral, abdominal. —**v. hernia**, (med.) eventración, hernia abdominal.

ventricle [véntrįkl], s. (anat.) ventrículo.

ventricular [ventríkįulą(r)], a. ventricular.

ventriloquism [ventrílokwįzm], s. ventriloquia. —**ventriloquist** [-ist], s. ventrílocuo.—**ventriloquize** [-aįz], vn. hablar como ventrílocuo, ser ventrílocuo.—**ventriloquy** [-i], s. = VENTRILOQUISM.

venture [vénchṷ(r)], I. s. riesgo, ventura, albur; (com.) pacotilla, ancheta; operación o empresa arriesgada; especulación.—**at a v.**, a la ventura, al azar. II. va. aventurar, arriesgar. III. vn. osar, atreverse; aventurarse, arriesgarse.—**to v. abroad**, o **out**, atreverse a salir, arriesgarse fuera.—**to v. at**, o **(up)on**, probar ventura en.

venturer [-œ(r)], s. aventurero.

venturesome [-sʌm], a. atrevido, emprendedor; aventurado, azaroso.—**venturesomely** [-li], adv. atrevidamente.—**venturesomeness** [-nįs], s. arrojo, temeridad, carácter aventurero.

venturous [-ʌs], a. osado, atrevido.—**venturously** [-li], adv. osadamente.—**venturousness** [-nįs], s. arrojo, temeridad.

venue [vénįu], s. (for.) jurisdicción en que se ha cometido un crimen o en que está sita la cosa litigiosa.—**change of v.**, cambio de tribunal en un pleito.

venule [vénįul], s. (anat., zool.) venilla.

Venus [vínʌs], s. Venus; (astr.) Venus.—**V.'s-comb**, (bot.) peine de pastor o de Venus.—**V.'s-fan**, especie de zoófito.—**V.'s-flytrap**, (bot.) atrapamoscas, f., dionea.—**V.'s-looking-glass**, (bot.) espejo de Venus, especularia. —**V.'s navelwort**, (bot.) ombligo de Venus.

veracity [vįrésiti], s. veracidad.

veracious [vįréiŝʌs], a. veraz, verídico.

veranda(h [vįrándą], s. pórtico, galería, balcón largo.

veratrin(e [vérątrin], s. (quím.) veratrina.

Veratrum [vįréįtrʌm], s. veratro, eléboro blanco.

verb [vœrb], s. (gram.) verbo.

verbal [-ąl], I. a. verbal; oral, de viva voz; literal; (gram.) verbal.—**v. contract**, contrato verbal, de palabra.—**v. noun**, substantivo verbal. II. s. substantivo verbal.

verbalism [-įzm], s. expresión oral; palabrería.

verbally [-i], adv. verbalmente.

verbatim [vœrbéįtįm], adv. al pie de la letra, palabra por palabra.

verbena [vœrbíną], s. (bot.) verbena.

verbenaceous [vœrbįnéįŝʌs], a. (bot.) verbenáceo.

verbiage [vœrbiidź], s. verbosidad; ripio.

verbose [vœrbóṷs], a. verboso, difuso, prolijo.

verboseness [-nįs], **verbosity** [vœrbásįti], s. verbosidad, ampulosidad, filatería; palabrería.

verdancy [vœrdąnsi], s. verdor, verdín.

verdant [vœrdąnt], a. verde, verdoso, fresco; inocente, sencillo.

verd antique [vœrd æntík], s. verde antiguo; variedad de serpentina (mármol).

verdict [vœrdįkt], s. (for.) veredicto, fallo; opinión, dictamen.—**v. of guilty**, fallo condenatorio.

verdigris [vœrdigris], s. verdete, cardenillo, verdín, pátina verdosa o azulada.

verdin [vœrdįn], s. (orn.) especie de paro.

verditer [vœrdįtœ(r)], s. (pint.) verdete.

verdure [vœrdźúr], s. verde, verdor; frondas, f. pl.

verdurous [-ʌs], a. verdoso.

Verein [feráįn], s. (alem.) sociedad, asociación.

verge [vœrdź], I. s. borde, margen, mf.; vera; círculo, anillo; alcance, esfera; vara, varilla, báculo; (arq.) fuste de columna; árbol de volante de un reloj; (Ingl., for.) jurisdicción del mayordomo de palacio.—**on**, o **upon, the v. of**, al borde de; a punto de, al a dos dedos de. II. vn. acercarse a, tender.—**to v. on**, o **upon**, llegar casi hasta, acercarse a, rayar en.

verger [-œ(r)], s. alguacil de vara; macero; aposentador, pertiguero.

veridical [vįrídįkąl], a. verídico.—**veridically** [-i], adv. verídicamente.

verifiable [vérįfaiąbl], a. verificable.

verification [-fįkéįŝǫn], s. verificación, comprobación, constatación.

verify [-faį], va. verificar, justificar, comprobar, constatar, demostrar; cerciorarse de; cumplir, ejecutar (una promesa); (for.) afirmar bajo juramento; acreditar.

verily [vérįli], adv. en verdad.

verisimilar [verįsímįlą(r)], a. verosímil.

verisimilitude [-sįmílįtiud], s. verosimilitud.

veritable [vérįtąbl], a. verdadero.

verity [vérįti], s. verdad, realidad; hecho; axioma, m.

verjuice [vœrdźus], s. agraz, m.; agrazada; aspereza, mordacidad.

vermeil [vœrmįl], s. plata o bronce sobredorados; barniz (m.) transparente de agua; (poét.) bermellón; granate rojo anaranjado.

Vermes [vœrmįz], s. pl. (zool.) vermes, gusanos.

vermicelli [vœrmįséli o -chéli], s. fideos, m. pl.

vermicide [vœrmįsaid], s. (med.) vermicida, m.

vermicular [vœrmíkįulą(r)], a. vermicular.—**v. work**, (arq.) ornamentación vermiforme.

vermiculate [-eit], I. va. poner adornos vermiformes. II. a. vermiforme, vermicular.—**vermiculation** [-éiŝǫn], s. ornamentación vermiforme; (fisiol.) vermiculación, peristalsis, movimiento vermicular de los intestinos.—**vermiculose, vermiculous** [-ous, -as], *a.* vermicular.

vermiform [vœrmiform], *a.* vermiforme, vermicular.—**v. appendix,** apéndice vermiforme.

vermifuge [-fjudʒ], *a.* y *s.* (med.) vermífugo.

vermilion [vœrmilyǫn]. **I.** *s.* bermellón, cinabrio. **II.** *va.* enrojar, teñir de rojo.

vermin [vœrmin], *s.* (*sing.* y *pl.*) bichos asquerosos, sabandijas (gusanos, chinches, piojos, etc.).

vermination [-éiʃǫn], *s.* generación de bichos.

verminous [-as], *a.* verminoso.

vermivorous [vœrmivǫras], *a.* vermívoro.

vermouth [vœrmúθ], *s.* vermut (licor).

vernacular [vœrnǽkyǫlǎ(r)]. **I.** *a.* vernáculo, nativo; local. **II.** *s.* idioma vernáculo.

vernacularism [-izm], *s.* modismo.

vernal [vœrnǎl], *a.* vernal; primaveral.—**v. equinox,** (astr.) equinoccio vernal.

vernation [vœrnéiʃǫn], *s.* (bot.) prefoliación.

vernier [vœrniǫ(r)], *s.* nonio, vernier; aparato o instrumento auxiliar de regulación o graduación.

Veronese [veronís], *a.* y *s.* veronés, veronense.

veronica [vęrǎníkǎ], *s.* (bot.) verónica; lienzo de la Verónica.

verruca [verúkǎ], *s.* (med., zool.) verruga.

verrucose, verrucous [vérukous, vérukas], *a.* verrugoso, cubierto de verrugas.

versatile [vœrsǎtil], *a.* versátil, de conocimientos muy variados; adaptable, que se adapta fácilmente a varias ocupaciones o situaciones; giratorio; inconstante, voluble.—**versatility** [-tʃiliti], *s.* versatilidad, adaptabilidad; variedad de conocimientos; veleidad, inconstancia.

verse [vœrs]. **I.** *s.* verso; estrofa, copla, poesía; (igl.) versículo.—**v. maker,** versificador.—**v. making,** versificación, metrificación. **II.** *va.* y *vn.* rimar, metrificar, versificar, hacer versos.

versed [-t], *a.* versado, perito.

versed sine [-sain], *s.* (mat.) seno verso.

verseman [-man], *s.* poeta, *m.*, versista; poetastro.

versemonger [-mʌngœ(r)], *s.* poetastro.

versicle [-ikǎl], *s.* verso corto; (igl.) versículo.

versification [-ifikéiʃǫn], *s.* versificación, metrificación.—**versifier** [-faiœ(r)], *s.* versificador, metrista.—**versify** [-fai], *va.* y *vn.* versificar. *V.* VERSE.

version [vœrʃǫn], *s.* versión; exposición, interpretación; traducción; (cir.) versión.

verso [vœrsou], *s.* reverso; (impr.) página par.

versus [vœrsas], *prep.* (for., dep., etc.) contra.

vert [vœrt], *s.* (Ingl., for.) árbol o arbusto con hojas en un bosque; derecho de tala; (blas.) sinople.

vertebra [vœrtębrǎ], *s.* (*pl.* **vertebræ** [-bri]), (anat., zool.) vértebra.—**vertebral** [-brǎl], *a.* vertebral; vertebrado.—**Vertebrata** [-bréitǎ], *s. pl.* vertebrados.—**vertebrate** [-breit], *s.* y *a.* vertebrado.

vertex [vœrteks], *s.* vértice; cima, cumbre, cúspide, *f.*, ápice.

vertical [vœrtikǎl], *a.* vertical; (e. p.) por industrias, de cada industria por separado.—**v. angles,** ángulos opuestos por el vértice.—**v. circle,** (astr.) vertical, *m.*—**v. line, plane,** etc., (geom.) vertical, *f.*—**verticality** [-éliti], *s.* verticalidad.—**vertically** [-li], *adv.* verticalmente.

vertices [vœrtisiz], *s. pl.* de VERTEX.

verticil [vœrtisil], *s.* (bot.) verticilo.

verticillate [vœrtísileit], *a.* (bot.) verticilado.

verticity [vœrtísiti], *s.* verticidad, giro.

vertiginous [vœrtídʒinas], *a.* vertiginoso.

vertigo [vœrtigou], *s.* (med.) vértigo, vahído.

vervain [vœrvein], *s.* (bot.) verbena.

verve [vœrv], *s.* estro, numen, entusiasmo, energía, vigor; (teat.) vis cómica.

very [véri]. **I.** *a.* mismo, propio, idéntico; verdadero, real; mismísimo.—**for that v. reason,** por lo mismo.—**the v. idea of doing it,** sólo la idea, o la mera idea de hacerlo.—**this v. day,** hoy mismo.—**this v. night,** esta misma noche.

—**to conceal his v. name,** ocultar aun (o hasta) su nombre.—**to weep for v. joy,** llorar de pura alegría. **II.** *adv.* muy; mucho, muchísimo.—**v. much,** mucho, muchísimo; sumamente, muy (antes de un participio).—**v. many,** muchísimos.—**v. much so,** muy mucho, muchísimo, en sumo grado.

vesania [viséiniǎ], *s.* (med.) vesania, locura.

vesica [visáikǎ], *s.* (anat.) vejiga.—**v. piscis** [písis], (b. a.) aureola.

vesical [vésikǎl], *a.* vesical.—**vesicant** [-kǎnt]. **I.** *a.* (med.) vesicante. **II.** *s.* vejigatorio.—**vesicate** [-keit], *va.* avejigar.—**vesication** [-kéiʃǫn], *s.* acción de producir vejigas o ampollas.—**vesicatory** [-kǎtori], *s.* y *a.* vesicante, vejigatorio.—**vesicle** [-kl], *s.* (anat., bot., med.) vesícula, vejiguilla.

vesicula [visíkjulǎ], *s.* (anat., med.) vesícula.—**v. seminalis,** (anat.) vesícula seminal.

vesicular [-(r)], *a.* **vesiculate** [-eit], *a.* vesicular; vesiculoso.

vesper [véspœ(r)]. **I.** *s.* tarde, caída de la tarde, el anochecer; campana que llama a vísperas; (V., astr.) Véspero, estrella vespertina.—*pl.* (igl.) vísperas. **II.** *a.* vespertino.—**vespertine** [-tin], *a.* vespertino.

vespid [véspid], *s.* y *a.* (zool.) véspido.—**Vespidæ** [-i], *s. pl.* véspidos.

vessel [vésęl], *s.* vasija, vaso; (anat.) vaso; (mar.) barco, buque, bajel, embarcación; (bot.) *V.* DUCT.

vest [vest]. **I.** *s.* chaleco; chaqueta antigua; (Ingl.) elástica, camiseta interior; (poét.) vestido, vestidura.—**v.-pocket,** (de tamaño) propio para el bolsillo del chaleco; en miniatura. **II.** *va.* vestir; revestir (de autoridad), investir; (for.) hacer entrega, dar posesión.—**to v. in,** revestir de, investir de, poner en posesión de.—**to v. with,** (re)vestir de. **III.** *vn.* vestirse; tener validez, ser válido; (con **in**) pasar (un título o derecho) a.

vestal [véstǎl], *s.* y *a.* vestal, *f.*; virgen, *f.*

vested [véstid], *a.* (re)vestido; (igl.) que lleva vestimentas; cabal y completo, absoluto; establecido o protegido por la ley.—**v. interests,** intereses creados.

vestibule [véstibjul], *s.* vestíbulo, recibimiento, portal, zaguán; (anat.) vestíbulo (del oído); (f. c.) pasillo cubierto entre dos coches ferroviarios.—**v. car,** (f. c.) coche de un tren de pasillos cubiertos de comunicación (llamado **v. train**).

vestige [véstidʒ], *s.* vestigio, huella, señal, *f.*; reliquia; (biol.) rudimento.—**vestigial** [vestídʒiǎl], *a.* (biol.) atrofiado, degenerado, rudimentario.

vesting [véstiŋ], *s.* corte de chaleco.

vestment [véstmęnt], *s.* prenda de vestir; ropa, vestidura; (igl.) vestimenta; sabanilla (de altar).

vestry [véstri], *s.* (igl.) vestuario, sacristía; junta que administra los asuntos de una iglesia episcopal protestante.—**vestryman** [-mǎn], *s.* miembro de dicha junta.

vesture [véschŭ(r)], *s.* vestidura, vestuario; traje, hábito; (Ingl., for. ant.) todo lo que cubre el terreno excepto los árboles.

vetch [véch], *s.* (bot.) arveja, veza, yer(v)o, algarroba, almorta.

vetchling [-liŋ], *s.* (bot.) arveja, áfaca.

veteran [vétęrǎn], *s.* y *a.* veterano.

veterinarian [vetęrinérięn], *s.* albéitar, veterinario.

veterinary [vétęrinęri], *a.* y *s.* veterinario.—**v. science,** veterinaria, albeitería.—**v. surgeon,** albéitar.

veto [vítou]. **I.** *va.* poner el veto; vedar, prohibir; rehusar la aprobación de, (Am.) vetar. **II.** *s.* veto; prohibición hecha con autoridad.

vex [veks], *va.* vejar, molestar, hostigar, acosar, irritar, enfadar; afligir, desazonar, acongojar; agitar, turbar, perturbar.

vexation [-éįṣǫn], *s.* vejación, vejamen, molestia, maltrato, provocación; enojo, enfado; disgusto, (fam.) chinchorrería.—**vexatious** [-éįṣʌs], *a.* vejatorio, molesto, enfadoso, provocativo.—**vexatiously** [-lį], *adv.* enfadosamente, con molestia.—**vexatiousness** [-nįs], *s.* vejamen, molestia, vejación.

vexed [vɛkst], *a.* vejado, enfadado; discutido, debatido.—**v. question**, cuestión batallona.—**to be v.**, incomodarse, enojarse, picarse, (fam.) amostazarse.

via [váįạ]. **I.** *prep.* por (la vía de). **II.** *s.* vía.

viability [vaįạḅílįtį], *s.* viabilidad.

viable [váįạbl], *a.* viable, capaz de vivir.

viaduct [váįạdʌkt], *s.* viaducto.

vial [váįạl], *s.* redoma, frasco, ampolleta, pomo.

viand [váįạnd], *s.* vianda.—*pl.* comida, alimentos, provisiones, vitualla.

viatic [vaįétįk], *a.* de viaje, de viático.

viaticum [-ʌm], *s.* viático; (igl.) Viático.

vibrant [váįbrạnt], *a.* vibrante.

vibrate [-reįt]. **I.** *va.* vibrar, blandir. **II.** *vn.* vibrar, oscilar, cimbrarse.—**vibratile** [-rạtįl], *a.* vibrátil, vibratorio.—**vibrating** [-reįtįn], *a.* vibrador, vibrante, oscilante, trepidante.—**vibration** [-réįṣǫn], *s.* vibración, oscilación.—**vibrative** [-rạtįv], *a.* vibratorio.—**vibrator** [-reįtǫ(r)], *s.* (elec.) interruptor intermitente, vibrador; (rad.) oscilador, interruptor de la bobina de inducción; (impr.) cilindro oscilante.—**vibratory** [-rạtǫrį], *a.* = VIBRATIVE.

vibrio(n [víbrįǫụ(n], *s.* vibrión, *m.*, especie de bacteria.

viburnum [vaįbœ̆rnʌm], *s.* (bot.) viburno, mundillo.

vicar [víḳạ(r)], *s.* (igl.) vicario.—**v. forane**, vicario foráneo.—**v. general**, vicario general.—**vicarage** [-įdž], *s.* vicaría.—**vicarial** [vįḳérįạl], *a.* vicarial.—**vicariate** [vįḳérįeįt]. **I.** *s.* vicariato. **II.** *a.* vicario.—**vicarious** [vaįḳérįʌs], *a.* vicario; (fisiol.) sustitutivo.—**vicariously** [-lį], *adv.* substitutivamente, por substitución.—**vicarship** [víḳạ̄rṣịp], *s.* vicaría.

vice [vaįs], *s.* vicio, inmoralidad; defecto, falta; vicio o resabio del caballo; (fam.) substituto, suplente. *V.* VISE.

vice [váįs], *prep.* en lugar de, en vez de.

vice- [váįs], *prefijo* que corresponde a "vice-" en español.—**v.-admiral**, vicealmirante.—**v.-admiralty**, vicealmirantazgo.—**v.-chancellor**, (pol., igl.) vicecanciller; vicecancelario (de universidad).—**v.-consul**, vicecónsul.—**v.-consulate, v.-consulship**, viceconsulado.—**v.-presidency**, vicepresidencia.—**v.-president**, vicepresidente.

vicegerent [-džérẹnt], *s.* vicegerente, teniente, diputado, substituto.—**vicegerency** [-ẹnsį], *s.* vicegerencia, agencia, tenencia, substitución.

vicennial [vaįsénįạl], *a.* vicenal.

viceregal [-rígạl], *a.* de virrey.

viceroy [-rǫį], *s.* virrey.—**viceroyalty** [-rǫįạltį], **viceroyship** [-rǫįṣịp], *s.* virreinato.

vice versa [váįsį vœ̆rṣạ], *adv.* viceversa.

vicinage [vísįnįdž], *s.* vecindad.—**vicinal** [-ạl], *a.* vecino, vecinal.

vicinity [vįsínịtį], *s.* vecindad, cercanía, proximidad, alrededores, *pl.*, contornos, *pl.*, inmediaciones, *pl.*

vicious [víṣʌs], *a.* vicioso, depravado; defectuoso, imperfecto; (fam.) maligno, rencoroso.—**v. circle**, círculo vicioso.—**viciously** [-lį], *adv.* viciosamente.—**viciousness** [-nįs], *s.* vicio; depravación; resabio, lacra; malignidad.

vicissitude [vįsísįtįud], *s.* vicisitud, alternativa.

victim [víḳtịm], *s.* víctima; (for.) interfecto.

victimize [-aįz], *va.* hacer víctima; estafar, embaucar; sacrificar.

victor [víḳtǫ(r)], *s.* vencedor, triunfador.

victoria [vįḳtórįạ], *s.* (bot.) victoria, ninfea gigantea; (carr.) victoria.

Victorian [-n], *a.* victoriano, perteneciente a la reina Victoria o a su época.

victorious [-s], *a.* victorioso.—**victoriously** [-lį], *adv.* victoriosamente.—**victoriousness** [-nįs], *s.* calidad de victorioso.

victory [víḳtǫrį], *s.* victoria, triunfo.

victress [víḳtrįs], *s.* vencedora.

victual [vítạl]. **I.** *va.* abastecer, bastimentar, avituallar. **II.** *s. pl.* (fam. o dial.) vitualla, víveres, provisiones, comestibles.

victual(l)er [-œ(r)], *s.* abastecedor, proveedor; vivandero; (Ingl.) hostelero.

vicugna, vicuña [vįkúnyạ], *s.* (zool.) vicuña.

vide [váįdį], *v.* (lat.) véase, véanse, *vide.*—**v. ante**, véase lo anterior.—**v. infra**, véase más abajo.—**v. supra**, véase más arriba.—**quod v.**, véase (esto, esta palabra, etc.).

videlicet [vįdélįsịt], *adv.* (lat.) a saber. *V.* VIZ.

video [vídįoụ], *a.* y *s.* (de o rel. a la) televisión.

vie [vaį], *vn.* competir, rivalizar, disputar(se).

Viennese [vįeníz], *a.* y *s.* vienés.

view [vįú]. **I.** *va.* mirar, ver; contemplar; examinar, inspeccionar, reconocer; considerar, especular. **II.** *s.* vista, mirada; inspección; contemplación; visión; escena, panorama, *m.*, paisaje, perspectiva; alcance de la vista; modo de ver, criterio; opinión, parecer; fase, *f.*, aspecto; mira, intento, propósito; (for.) inspección judicial de una propiedad o paraje.—**v. finder**, (foto.) visor.—**at first v.**, a primera vista.—**at one v.**, de una ojeada, de una mirada.—**in v.**, en mira.—**in v. of**, en vista de; respecto de.—**on v.**, en exhibición.—**with a v. to**, con miras a, a fin de, con el propósito de.—**with this v.**, con esta mira, con este intento.

viewer [-œ(r)], *s.* veedor, mirador.

viewless [-lįs], *a.* invisible; sin opiniones.

viewpoint [-pǫįnt], *s.* punto de vista.

viewy [-į], *a.* (fam.) destornillado; visionario; teorizante; espectacular, vistoso.

vigesimal [vaįdžésịmạl], *a.* vigésimo.

vigil [vídžįl], *s.* vela, velación, vigilia, desvelo; vigilancia; (igl.) vigilia.

vigilance [-ạns], *s.* desvelo; vigilancia, cuidado.—**v. committee**, junta de vigilancia.—**vigilant** [-ạnt], *a.* vigilante, atento, alerto.—**vigilante** [-ántį], *s.* vigilante, miembro de una junta vigilante.—**vigilantly** [-lį], *adv.* vigilantemente, alertamente.

vignette [vįnyét]. **I.** *va.* (foto.) hacer un retrato en viñeta; aviñetar, adornar con viñetas. **II.** *s.* (arq.) ramaje; (impr.) viñeta, marmosete; (foto. y grab.) viñeta; corto bosquejo literario.

vigor [vígǫ(r)], *s.* vigor; fuerza, fortaleza, reciedumbre, tesón, energía; verdor, lozanía.—**vigorous** [-ʌs], *a.* vigoroso, fuerte, robusto, esforzado.—**vigorously** [-lį], *adv.* vigorosamente, enérgicamente, con fuerza o con tesón.—**vigorousness** [-nįs], *s.* vigorosidad, robustez; actividad.

viking [váįkịn], *s.* antiguo pirata escandinavo.

vilayet [vilayét], *s.* vilayato, provincia (de Turquía).

vile [váįl], *a.* vil, bajo, soez, despreciable; malvado, ruin; malísimo, detestable (dicho de las cosas).—**vilely** [-lį], *adv.* vilmente, bajamente, ruinmente.—**vileness** [-nįs], *s.* vileza, ruindad.

vilification [vįlįfịkéįṣǫn], *s.* vilipendio, difamación; (raro) envilecimiento.

vilifier [-faįœ(r)], *s.* difamador.—**vilify** [-faį], *va.* difamar, vilipendiar; envilecer.

vilipend [-pɛnd], *va.* vilipendiar; difamar.

villa [vílạ], *s.* villa, quinta, casa de campo.

village [vílįdž], *s.* aldea, pueblo, lugar, caserío.—**villager** [-œ(r)], *s.* aldeano.

villain [vílạn], *s.* villano, bellaco, malvado, maleante, infame; pechero. *V.* VILLEIN.

villa(i)nous [-ʌs], *a.* villano, bellaco, ruin, malvado; asqueroso, repugnante.

villainously [-lį], *adv.* vilmente, villanamente.

villainousness [-nįs], *s.* ruindad, villanía.

villa(i)ny [-i], s. villanía, vileza, infamia.
villa(i)nage, ville(i)nage [vílinidž], s. villanaje, servidumbre; feudo.
villose [víloųs], **villous** [vílʌs], a. (anat., bot.) velludo, velloso; felpudo.
villosity [vilásiti], s. vellosidad.
villus [vílʌs], s. (pl. villi) (anat., bot.) vello.
vim [vim], s. fuerza, vigor; energía, espíritu, brío.
vimineous [vimínias], a. mimbreño; mimbroso.
vinaceous [vainéiŝʌs], a. vinario; vinoso.
vinaigrette [vinȧgrét], s. redomilla para vinagre o sales aromáticos; (coc.) salsa de vinagre, aceite, etc.
vinca [vínkȧ], s. (bot.) (vinca)pervinca.
vincible [vínsibl], a. vencible.
vinculum [vínkiųlʌm], s. vínculo.
vindicable [víndikȧbl], a. vindicable.
vindicate [víndikeit], va. vindicar.—**vindication** [-éiŝon], s. vindicación.—**vindicative** [víndikȧtiv], a. vindicativo, justificativo.—**vindicator** [víndikéito(r)], s. defensor, vindicador.—**vindicatory** [-kȧtori], a. vindicatorio.
vindictive [víndíktiv], a. vindicativo, vengativo. —**vindictively** [-li], adv. vengativamente, por venganza.—**vindictiveness** [-nis], s. carácter vengativo.
vine [vain], s. (bot.) enredadera; vid, parra.—**v. arbor**, emparrado.—**v. beetle**, (ent.) escarabajuelo.—**v. branch**, sarmiento.—**v. bud**, brota, botón.—**v.-clad**, cubierto de enredaderas, de vides o de viñas.—**v. fretter, v. grub**, (ent.) pulgón de las viñas, brugo, (gusano) revoltón.—**v. grower**, vitícola, mf.; viticultor.—**v. growing**, viticultura.—**v. leaf**, hoja de vid o de parra.—**v.-like**, aparrado.—**v.-moth**, (ent.) piral de la vid.—**v. pest**, (ent.) filoxera.—**v. shoot**, sarmiento.—**v. stock**, cepa.
vinedresser [-dresœ(r)], s. viñador, deslechugador.
vinegar [vínigȧ(r)], s. vinagre.—**v. aspect**, cara de vinagre.—**v. cruet**, vinagrera.—**v. sauce**, (coc.) vinagreta.—**vinegarish, vinegary** [-iŝ, -i], a. vinagroso, avinagrado, agrio.
vinery [váinœri], s. invernadero para las uvas; emparrado.
vineyard [vínyard], s. viña, viñedo.—**v. keeper**, viñadero, viñador, (Am.) viñatero.
vinic [váinik], a. vínico.
viniculture [vínikʌlchų(r)], s. vinicultura.—**vinicultural** [-kʌlchųrȧl], a. vinícola.—**viniculturist** [-ist], s. vinicultor, viñero.
viniferous [viníferʌs], a. vinífero.
vinification [vinifikéiŝon], s. vinificación.
vinosity [vainásiti], s. vinosidad.
vinous [váinʌs], **vinose** [váinoųs], a. vinoso; de color de vino.
vintage [víntidž], s. vendimia.—**vintager** [-œ(r)], s. vendimiador, vinícola, mf., vinariego.
vintner [víntnœ(r)], s. vinatero, tratante en vinos.
viny [váini], a. perteneciente a las vides, parras o enredaderas; productor de vides.
viol [váiol], s. (mús.) violón; (mar.) virador.—**double-base v.**, (mús.) contrabajo.
viola [vióųlȧ], s. (mús.) viola, alto; (V., bot.) género que incluye las violetas y los pensamientos.
violable [váiolȧbl], a. violable.
violaceous [vaioléiŝʌs], a. violado, de color de violeta; (bot.) violáceo.
violate [váioleit], va. violar, infringir (una ley); atropellar; violar o deshonrar (a una mujer).—**violation** [-éiŝon], s. violación, infracción (de una ley); violación, deshonra (de una mujer). —**violator** [-ọ(r)], s. violador.
violence [váiolęns], s. violencia.—**violent** [-ęnt], a. violento.—**violently** [-li], adv. violentamente.
violet [váiolit], **I.** s. (bot.) violeta; color violado. **II.** a. violado, violáceo.
violin [vaiolín], s. (mús.) violín; violinista.—**violinist** [-ist], s. violinista.
violoncellist [víolanchélist], s. (mús.) violon-

celista.—**violoncello** [-chéloų], s. violoncelo o violonchelo.
viper [váipœ(r)], s. (zool.) víbora.—**vipergrass** [-græs], s. (bot.) escorzonera.—**viperine, viperish, viperous** [-in, -iŝ, -ʌs], a. viperino, vipéreo.
virago [viréigoų], s. arpía, mujer regañona o pendenciera; (ant.) virago, f., marimacho.
vireo [vírioų], s. (orn.) víreo, virio, oropéndola.
virescent [vairésęnt], a. verdoso.
Virgilian [vœrdžílian], a. virgiliano.
virgin [vœrdžin], **I.** s. virgen, f., doncella; religiosa que ha hecho voto de virginidad; (V., astr.) Virgo.—**the V.**, (igl.) la Virgen. **II.** a. virginal, virgen.—**v. birth**, (biol.) partenogénesis; (teol.) parto virginal de María, virginidad de María.—**v. forest**, selva virgen.—**v. metal**, metal nativo.—**v. queen**, (Ingl.) la reina virgen (Isabel).—**v.'s bower**, (bot.) clemátide, f.—**v. soil**, tierra virgen.
virginal [-ȧl], **I.** a. virginal, virgíneo. **II.** s. (mús.) especie de clavicordio o espineta.
Virginian [vœrdžínian], a. y s. virginiano (de Virginia).
virginity [vœrdžíniti], s. virginidad, virgo.
virginium [vœrdžíniʌm], s. (quím.) virginio.
Virgo [vœrgoų], s. (astr.) Virgo.
viridescent [viridésęnt], a. verdoso.
viridity [viríditi], s. verdor.
virile [víril], a. viril.
virility [viríliti], s. virilidad.
virose [váiroųs], a. viroso, ponzoñoso.
virtu [vœrtú], s. objetos curiosos o raros; valor, mérito o excelencia de tales objetos; afición a, o conocimiento de, dichos objetos.
virtual [vœrchuȧl], a. virtual.—**v. amperes**, (elec.) amperaje efectivo, intensidad efectiva. —**v. axis**, (mec.) eje instantáneo de rotación.— **v. displacement**, (mec.) desalojamiento virtual.—**v. focus**, (fís.) foco virtual.—**v. volts**, (elec.) voltaje efectivo.
virtuality [-ǽliti], s. virtualidad.
virtually [-i], adv. virtualmente.
virtue [vœrchu], s. virtud (en todas sus acepciones).—**virtues**, virtudes (quinto coro celestial).—**by** o **in v. of**, en virtud de.
virtuosity [-ásiti], s. (b. a.) maestría, habilidad técnica, esp. en la música; afición a los objetos curiosos o raros; los maestros, los técnicos.
virtuoso [-óųsoų], s. artista eximio; músico muy hábil; el aficionado a los objetos curiosos o raros.
virtuous [vœrchųʌs], a. virtuoso, honesto, santo; pura, casta (mujer); (ant.) eficaz.—**virtuously** [-li], adv. virtuosamente.—**virtuousness** [-nis], s. virtud, calidad de virtuoso.
virulence [víryulęns], s. virulencia; malignidad, acrimonia.—**virulent** [-ęnt], a. virulento, ponzoñoso; maligno, cáustico.—**virulently** [-li], adv. virulentamente, malignamente.
virus [váirʌs], s. (med.) virus; linfa vacunal; virulencia, influencia maligna.
vis [vis], s. (lat.) fuerza.
visa [vízȧ], s. y va. = visé.
visage [vízidž], s. rostro, cara, semblante, faz, aspecto distintivo.
visaged [-d], a. de cara, de rostro, de semblante.
vis-à-vis [ví zȧ vi], **I.** s. (fr.) el o lo que está enfrente; confidente (mueble). **II.** adv. y a. cara a cara, frente a frente, vis a vis. **III.** prep. comparado, o por comparación con; acerca de; en presencia de.
viscacha [viskáchȧ], s. (zool.) vizcacha.
viscera [vísęrȧ], s. pl. (anat.) vísceras, entrañas.
visceral [-l], a. visceral; ventral, abdominal.
viscid [vísid], a. viscoso, pegajoso.—**viscidity** [visíditi], **viscosity** [viskásiti], s. viscosidad.
viscount [váikaųnt], s. vizconde.—**viscountess** [-is], s. vizcondesa.—**viscountship** [-ŝip], s. vizcondado.
viscous [vískʌs], a. viscoso, glutinoso, pegajoso.

vise [vaịs], *s.* tornillo de carpintero o de banco.

visé [vízeị]. **I.** *va.* (*pret.* viséed; *pa.* viséing) visar (un pasaporte), refrendar. **II.** *s.* visto bueno, refrendación, refrendo.

visibility [vízibílịtị], **visibleness** [-blnịs], *s.* visibilidad.—**visible** [-bl], *a.* visible; notorio, manifiesto; externo.—**visibly** [-blị], *adv.* visiblemente; manifiestamente.

Visigoth [vízigaθ], *a.* y *s.* visigodo.—**Visigothic** [-gáọịk], *a.* visigodo, visigótico.

vision [vízọn], *s.* visión, vista; clarividencia, perspicacia, previsión; fantasma, *m.;* fantasía; revelación inspirada y profética; (cine) representación de los pensamientos o sueños de un actor. (Podría llamarse *psicograma, m.*)

visionary [-erị]. **I.** *a.* visionario, imaginario, quimérico; impracticable, infactible. **II.** *s.* visionario, soñador.

visit [vízịt]. **I.** *va.* visitar; hacer visita a; hacer un reconocimiento o registro de; (teol.) visitar. **II.** *vn.* visitarse; hacer visitas, ir de visita. **III.** *s.* visita, visitación; reconocimiento, registro, inspección; visita de médico; visitación de un obispo, etc.—**visitable** [-ạbl], *a.* visitable, sujeto a inspección.

visitant [-ạnt], *s.* visitador, visitante.

visitation [-éịọn], *s.* visitación, visita; inspección, registro, reconocimiento; gracia o castigo del cielo.—**visitatorial** [-ạtórịạl], *a.* perteneciente a la visitación.

visiting [-ịŋ]. **I.** *a.* visitador, visitante; de visita. —v. card, tarjeta de visita. **II.** *s.* visita(ción).

visitor [-ọ(r)], *s.* visita, visitador, visitante.

visor, visored [vájzọ(r), -d] = vizor, vizored.

vista [vístạ], *s.* vista, perspectiva.

visual [vízụạl], *a.* visual.—v. angle, line, ángulo, línea visual.

visuality [-ǽlịtị], *s.* calidad de visual; visibilidad.

visualization [-izéịọn], *s.* representación, formación de una imagen mental clara; imagen mental; descripción vívida o gráfica.—**visualize** [-aịz], *va.* y *vn.* representar(se) vívidamente en la mente.

visually [-ị], *adv.* visualmente; visiblemente.

vital [vájtạl], *a.* vital, esencial, cardinal, fundamental; fatal, mortal.—v. statistics, estadística demográfica.—**vitalism** [-izm], *s.* (biol.) vitalismo.—**vitalist** [-ịst], *s.* y *a.* vitalista.

vitality [-ǽlịtị], *s.* vitalidad, energía vital.

vitalize [-ajz], *va.* vitalizar, vivificar, dar vida; animar, reanimar.

vitally [-ị], *adv.* vitalmente, fundamentalmente.

vitals [-z], *s. pl.* (anat., etc.) partes (*f.*) vitales.

vitamin(e [vájtạmịn], *s.* (quím.) vitamina.—**vitaminic** [vajtạmínịk], *a.* vitamínico.

vitascope [vájtạskoụp], *s.* proyector cinematográfico.

vitellin [vịtélịn], *s.* (bioquím.) vitelina.

vitelline [vịtélịn], *a.* (biol.) vitelina (bilis, etc.).

vitellus [vịtélʌs], *s.* (biol.) vitelo, yema del huevo.

vitiate [víṣịeịt], *va.* viciar; inficionar, infectar, corromper; (for.) viciar, invalidar.—**vitiation** [-éịọn], *s.* depravación, corrupción; (for.) invalidación.

viticulture [vítịkʌlchụr], *s.* viticultura.

viticultural [-kʌlchụrạl], *a.* vitícola.—**viticulturist** [-ịst], *s.* viticultor, vitícola, *mf.*, viñero, viñador.

vitreous [vítrịʌs], *a.* vítreo; vidrioso.—v. body, o humor, (anat.) humor vítreo (del ojo), vitrina.—**vitreousness** [-nịs], *s.* vidriosidad.

vitrescent [vịtrésẹnt], *a.* vitrescible, vitrificable.

vitrifiable [vítrifaịạbl], *a.* vitrificable.

vitrification [-fịkéịọn], *s.* vitrificación.

vitriform [-fọrm], *a.* vítreo.

vitrify [-faị], *va.* y *vn.* vitrificar(se).

vitriol [vítrịọl], *s.* (quím.) vitriolo; ácido sulfúrico; sulfato; crítica cáustica.—**vitriolate(d** [-eịt(ịd], *a.* vitriolado.—**vitriolic** [vịtrịálịk], *a.* vitriólico; mordaz, sumamente hiriente, feroz.

vituline [víchụlịn], *a.* becerril.

vituperable [vaịtịúpœrạbl], *a.* vituperable.

vituperate [-eịt], *va.* vituperar.—**vituperation** [-éịọn], *s.* vituperación, vituperio.—**vituperator** [-eịtọ(r)], *s.* vituperador.

vivacious [vịvéịṣʌs], *a.* vivo, vivaracho, vivaz.

vivaciousness [-nịs], **vivacity** [vịvǽsịtị], *s.* vivacidad, viveza.

vivandier [vivandyéị], *s.* (mil.) vivandero.

vivandière [vivandyér], *s.* cantinera, vivandera.

vivarium [vaịvérịʌm], **vivary** [vájvạrị], *s.* vivar, vivero.

viva voce [vájvạ vóụsị], *adv.* y *a.* de viva voz, de palabra.

Viverridæ [vaịvérịdi], *s. pl.* (zool.) vivérridos.—**viverrine** [vaịvérịn], *s.* y *a.* (zool.) vivérrido.

vives [vájvz], *s. pl.* (vet.) adivas.

vivid [vívịd], *a.* vivo, vívido, gráfico; intenso; subido, brillante (color); animado, enérgico, activo.—**vividly** [-lị], *adv.* vivamente; vívidamente; a lo vivo, al vivo.—**vividness** [-nịs], *s.* vivacidad; intensidad, fuerza, brillo.

vivification [vịvịfịkéịọn], *s.* vivificación.

vivify [vívịfaị], *va.* vivificar, avivar, dar vida.

vivifying [-ị], *a.* vivificador, vivificante.

viviparous [vaịvípạrʌs], *a.* (zool.) vivíparo.

vivisect [vịvịsékt], *va.* y *vn.* disecar un animal vivo.

vivisection [-sékṣọn], *s.* vivisección.

vixen [víksn], *s.* (zool.) zorra o raposa; mujer regañona o colérica, arpía.

viz [vịz], *abrev.* de **videlicet** (se lee generalmente namely o to wit), a saber, o sea.

vizier, vizir [vịzír], *s.* visir.—**vizierate** [-eịt], **viziership** [-ṣịp], *s.* visirato, oficio o dignidad de visir.

vizor [vájzọ(r)], *s.* visera.—**vizored** [-d], *a.* con visera, provisto de visera.

vocable [vóụkạbl], *s.* voz, vocablo.

vocabulary [vokǽbyụlẹrị], *s.* vocabulario; nomenclador; léxico.

vocal [vóụkạl]. **I.** *s.* (fon.) vocal, *f.;* diptongo; consonante líquida (*l, r*). **II.** *a.* vocal; oral; vocinglero, voceador.—v. bands = v. cords. —v. chink, (anat.) glotis.—v. cords v. lips, (anat.) cuerdas vocales.—v. music, canto.

vocalic [vokǽlịk], *a.* vocálico.

vocalist [vóụkạlịst], *s.* cantor, cantora, cantatriz.

vocality [vokǽlịtị], *s.* calidad de vocal.

vocalization [voụkạlịzéịọn], *s.* vocalización.

vocalize [-aịz], *va.* y *vn.* (mús.) vocalizar; articular; cantar; marcar los puntos vocales.

vocally [-ị], *adv.* vocalmente; verbalmente.

vocation [vokéịọn], *s.* vocación; oficio, profesión, carrera.

vocational [-ạl], *a.* profesional; práctico; de artes y oficios.—v. school, escuela práctica (apl. esp. a las de artes y oficios).—v. training, instrucción práctica, enseñanza de oficios.

vocative [vákạtịv], *a.* y *s.* (gram.) vocativo.

vociferate [vosíferẹịt], *va.* y *vn.* vociferar, vocear.

vociferation [-éịọn], *s.* vociferación; vocería.

vociferator [-ọ(r)], *s.* vociferador, voceador.

vociferous [vosífẹrʌs], *a.* vocinglero, clamoroso. —**vociferously** [-lị], *adv.* vocingleramente, a gritos.

vodka [vádkạ], *s.* vodca, bebida alcohólica rusa.

vogue [voụg], *s.* moda.—in v., en boga, de moda.

voice [vóịs]. **I.** *s.* voz; habla, palabra; el que habla en nombre de otro; opinión; voto, sufragio; (gram.) voz (del verbo).—with one v., por unanimidad. **II.** *va.* expresar, proclamar, decir su parecer; interpretar; hacerse eco de; (mús.) dar el tono; acordar o templar (un instrumento); escribir la parte vocal de; (fon.) vocalizar, hacer sonoro.

voiced [-t], *a.* que tiene voz; dicho, expresado, hablado; (fon.) sonoro.

voiceless [-lịs], *a.* mudo; que no tiene voz ni voto; (fon.) sordo, no sonoro.

void [vóịd]. **I.** *a.* vacío, desocupado, hueco; vacante; vano, ilusorio; (for.) nulo, inválido,

Írrito, sin valor ni fuerza; (con **of**) falto, privado, desprovisto de. **II.** *s.* vacuo, vacío; claro, laguna. **III.** *va.* (for.) anular, invalidar, irritar; vaciar, desocupar, evacuar. **IV.** *vn.* vaciarse, evacuarse.

voidable [-əbl], *a.* anulable; que se puede evacuar o vaciar.—**voidance** [-əns], *s.* vaciamiento, evacuación; vacancia; (for.) anulación.—**voider** [-œ(r)], *s.* vaciador; anulador.—**voidness** [-nis], *s.* vacío, vacuidad; invalidez.

voile [vɔil], *s.* (tej.) espumilla.

volant [vóulənt]. **I.** *a.* volante; ligero. **II.** *s.* volante.

Volapük [válapŭk], *s.* volapuk, una de las lenguas artificiales universales.

volatile [válətil], *a.* volátil, vaporable; sutil, fugaz; voluble; pasajero, transitorio.—**v. oil**, aceite esencial o volátil.

volatileness [-nis], **volatility** [-ĭliti], *s.* volatilidad; fugacidad; voltariedad, volubilidad.—**volatilization** [-izéişən], *s.* volatilización.—**volatilize** [-aiz], *va.* y *vn.* volatilizar(se).

vol-au-vent [val o ván], *s.* (fr.) (coc.) una especie de fajardo.

volcanic [valkánik], *a.* volcánico.—**v. glass**, (min.) obsidiana.

volcano [valkéinou], *s.* volcán.

vole [voul], *s.* (zool.) ratón campestre.

volition [volíşən], *s.* voluntad; (filos.) volición.

volitional [-əl], **volitive** [válitiv], *a.* volitivo.

volley [váli]. **I.** *s.* (mil.) descarga cerrada, andanada; salva; (dep.) voleo de la pelota. **II.** *va.* y *vn.* lanzar una descarga; (dep.) volear.

volleyball [-bɔl], *s.* (dep.) pelota de voleo.

volplane [válplein], *vn.* (aer.) planear, deslizarse en aeroplano.

Volsci [válsai], *s. pl.* (hist.) volscos.—**Volscian** [válşən], *s.* y *a.* volsco.

volt [vóult], *s.* (elec.) volt, voltio; (equit.) vuelta.—**v.-ampere**, (en corriente continua) vatio; (en corriente alterna) voltamperio, vatio aparente.

voltage [-idž], *s.* (elec.) voltaje, tensión.

voltaic [valtéik], *a.* (elec.) voltaico, galvánico.—**v. arc**, arco voltaico.—**v. battery**, pila voltaica.—**v. cell**, elemento de una pila.—**v. electricity**, electricidad dinámica.

Voltairian [valtériən], *a.* y *s.* volteriano.

Voltairianism [-izm], *s.* volterianismo.

voltaism [váltaizm], *s.* voltaísmo, galvanismo.

voltameter [valtémetœ(r)], *s.* (fís.) voltámetro.

voltammeter [vóultǽmmitœ(r)], *s.* voltamperímetro (si se trata de corriente alterna); voltímetro (si de corriente continua).

voltmeter [vóultmitœ(r)], *s.* (elec.) voltímetro.

volubility [vályŭbíliti], *s.* volubilidad; verbosidad.—**voluble** [-bl], *a.* voluble, suelto, flúido, facundo.—**volubly** [-bli], *adv.* volublemente.

volume [vályŭm], *s.* tomo, volumen, obra; (hist.) rollo de vitela; volumen, bulto; caudal de río; importe, suma, gran cantidad; (mat. y mús.) volumen; (fís.) masa.

volumetric [-étrik], *a.* (fís. y quím.) volumétrico.

voluminous [volúminǝs], *a.* voluminoso, abultado; prolijo, copioso.—**voluminously** [-li], *adv.* voluminosa o copiosamente.—**voluminousness** [-nis], *s.* calidad de voluminoso; prolijidad.

voluntarily [válʌnterili], *adv.* voluntariamente.

voluntariness [-nis], *s.* voluntariedad.

voluntary [válʌnteri]. **I.** *a.* voluntario. **II.** *s.* voluntario; cualquier acción voluntaria; (igl.) solo de órgano.

volunteer [valʌntír]. **I.** *s.* voluntario. **II.** *va.* contribuir u ofrecer voluntariamente. **III.** *vn.* ofrecerse a hacer algo; servir como voluntario.

voluptuary [volʌpchueri]. **I.** *s.* sibarita, *mf.*, voluptuoso. **II.** *a.* sibarítico, voluptuoso, sensual.

voluptuous [-chuʌs], *a.* voluptuoso.

voluptuously [-li], *adv.* voluptuosamente.

voluptuousness [-nis], *s.* voluptuosidad.

volute [voljút], *s.* (arq.) voluta; (zool.) voluta (molusco).—**v. spring**, (mec.) resorte de espiral.

volvulus [válvjulʌs], *s.* (med.) volvo, vólvulo, íleo.

vomer [vóumœ(r)], *s.* (anat.) vómer.—**vomerine** [-in], *a.* del vómer.

vomica [vámikǝ], *s.* (med.) vómica.

vomit [vámit]. **I.** *va.* y *vn.* vomitar, arrojar, (fam.) provocar. **II.** *s.* vómito; vomitivo, emético.—**vomiting** [-iŋ], *s.* vómito.—**vomitive** [-iv], *a.* vomitivo, emético.—**vomitory** [-ori]. **I.** *a.* y *s.* vomitorio, vomitivo. **II.** *s.* (arq.) vomitorio.

voodoo [vúdu]. **I.** *s.* vudú, brujería de los negros de los E. U. y las Antillas. **II.** *a.* vuduísta, relativo al vudú. **III.** *va.* hechizar, conjurar según las prácticas vuduístas.—**voodooism** [-izm], *s.* vuduísmo, creencias y prácticas vuduístas.

voracious [voréişʌs], *a.* voraz, devorador; rapaz.—**voraciously** [-li], *adv.* vorazmente.—**voraciousness** [-nis], **voracity** [voréusiti], *s.* voracidad.

vortex [vórteks], *s.* (*pl.* VORTICES O VORTEXES) vórtice, vorágine, *f.*, remolino, torbellino.

vortical [vórtikəl], **vortiginous** [vortídžinʌs], *a.* vortiginoso.

votaress [vóutaris], **votress** [vóutris], *s.* mujer que ha hecho y cumple un voto.

votary [vóutari]. **I.** *a.* votivo, consagrado al cumplimiento de un voto. **II.** *s.* el que se consagra a cumplir un voto; adorador; seguidor, partidario, adepto.

vote [vóut]. **I.** *s.* voto; votación; sufragio.—**v. by show of hands**, votación que se efectúa levantando las manos.—**v. of confidence**, voto de confianza. **II.** *va.* votar por; (fam.) declarar por consentimiento general; (fam.) dominar el voto de.—**to v. down**, rechazar por votación. **III.** *vn.* votar, dar voto.

voter [-œ(r)], *s.* votante, voto, votador, elector.

voting [-iŋ]. **I.** *s.* votación. **II.** *a.* votador; de votación; de votar; electoral.—**v. precinct**, distrito electoral.—**v. trust**, (com.) fideicomiso para la votación.

votive [-iv], *a.* votivo.—**v. mass**, (igl.) misa votiva.—**v. offering**, (igl.) exvoto, presentalla.

vouch [váuch]. **I.** *va.* atestiguar, certificar, atestar, testificar, afirmar; garantizar, responder de o por. **II.** *vn.* salir fiador.—**to v. for**, responder de; confirmar.

voucher [-œ(r)]. **I.** *s.* comprobante, resguardo, recibo, descargo, cualquier documento justificativo; fiador. **II.** *va.* atestar, confirmar, certificar.

vouchsafe [-séif]. **I.** *va.* conceder, permitir, otorgar. **II.** *vn.* dignarse, condescender.

voussoir [vuswár], *s.* (arq.) dovela, piedra de arco.

vow [vau]. **I.** *s.* voto, promesa solemne. **II.** *va.* hacer promesa solemne de, votar, hacer voto de, jurar. **III.** *vn.* hacer un voto.

vowel [váuel]. **I.** *s.* (fon., gram.) vocal, *f.* **II.** *a.* vocal; vocálico. **III.** *va.* poner vocales.

vowellike [-laik], *a.* (fon.) vocálico.

vox [vaks], *s.* (mús.) voz.—**v. humana**, registro del órgano que imita la voz humana.

voyage [vóidž]. **I.** *s.* viaje por mar, travesía; viaje redondo de un buque. **II.** *vn.* navegar, viajar.—**voyager** [-œ(r)], *s.* viajero.

Vulcanian [vʌlkéiniən], *a.* (geol.) vulcanio; (v.) volcánico; metalúrgico.

Vulcanism [válkǝnizm], *s.* (geol.) vulcanismo.

Vulcanist [-ist], *s.* vulcanista.

vulcanite [-ait], *s.* vulcanita.

vulcanization [-izéişən], *s.* vulcanización.

vulcanize [-aiz], *va.* vulcanizar.—**vulcanizer** [-œ(r)], *s.* vulcanizador.—**vulcanizing** [-iŋ]. **I.** *a.* vulcanizador, de vulcanizar. **II.** *s.* vulcanización.

vulgar [válgǝ(r)]. **I.** *a.* vulgar; común, ordinario, adocenado, cursi; vernáculo; público, generalmente sabido.—**v. fraction**, (mat.) fracción común, quebrado.—**V. Latin**, latín rústico o vulgar. **II.** *s.* (ant.) vulgo, plebe, *f.;* (ant.) idioma vernáculo.

vulgarism [-ĭzm], *s.* vulgarismo.

vulgarity [vʌlgǽrĭtĭ], *s.* vulgaridad; trivialidad; bajeza, grosería; mal tono.

vulgarization [-ĭzéĭȿọn], *s.* vulgarización.

vulgarize [-aĭz], *va.* vulgarizar; adocenar.

vulgarly [-lĭ], *adv.* vulgarmente.

vulgarness [-nȷ̣s], *s.* = VULGARITY.

Vulgate [vʌ́lgeĭt], *s.* (igl.) Vulgata.

vulnerability [vʌlnẹrạbĭlĭtĭ], *s.* vulnerabilidad. —**vulnerable** [-bl], *a.* vulnerable.—**vulnerableness** [-nȷ̣s], *s.* = VULNERABILITY.

vulnerary [vʌ́lnẹrạrĭ]. **I.** *a.* vulnerario. **II.** *s.* medicamento vulnerario.

vulpine [vʌ́lpaĭn], *a.* zorruno, raposuno, vulpino; astuto, ladino.

vulture [vʌ́lchŭ(r)], *s.* (orn.) buitre.—**vulturine, vulturous** [-ĭn, -ʌs], *a.* buitrero; rapaz.

vulva [vʌ́lvạ], *s.* (anat.) vulva.

vulval [-l], **vulvar** [-(r)], *a.* vulvario.

vying [váĭĭŋ] (*ger.* de TO VIE), *a.* rival, emulador. —**vyingly** [-lĭ], *adv.* con emulación, rivalizando, a cuál más.

W

w [dʌ́blyu *o* dʌ́b(l)ĭu], *s.* w.

wabble [wábl], *v. y s.* = WOBBLE.

wabbly [wáblĭ], *a.* = WOBBLY.

wacke [wǽkœ], *s.* roca parda arenisca o basáltica.

wad [wád]. **I.** *s.* borra o pelote para rehenchir muebles; (cost.) guata; (arti.) taco; mineral de manganeso y cobalto; rollo (de papeles, billetes de banco, etc.); (fam.) dinero, dineral, ahorros, *pl.*—**w. hook,** (arti.) sacatrapos, descargador. **II.** *va.* (cost.) acolchar, enguatar; emborrar (muebles); (arti.) atacar.

wadding [-ĭŋ], *s.* (sast.) entretela, entreforro, relleno; guata, algodón en rama; pelotes, *pl.;* (arti.) taco.

waddle [wádl]. **I.** *vn.* anadear, nanear, (fam.) nalguear, columpiarse. **II.** *s.* anadeo, meneo, tambaleo.

wade [wéĭd], *va. y vn.* vadear; meterse en agua baja y andar en ella (como hacen los niños); (gen. con **in** o **through**) andar con dificultad en (el lodo, etc.); terminar con dificultad o con tedio; (con **into**) (fam.) atacar resueltamente. —**wader** [-œ(r)], *s.* el que vadea.—**w.,** o **wading bird,** (orn.) ave zancuda.

wadi, wady [wádĭ], *s.* uadi, valle (el primer término es árabe, y se aplica gen. a un valle atravesado por el cauce de un arroyo que se seca en tiempo seco).

wafer [wéĭfœ(r)]. **I.** *va.* pegar o cerrar con oblea. **II.** *s.* oblea; (igl.) hostia; (coc.) barquillo; (farm.) sello.—**w. holder,** obleera.—**w. iron,** o **mold,** (coc.) barquilla, barquillero (molde).— **w. man,** obleero; barquillero.

waffle [wáfl], *s.* (coc., E. U.) especie de barquillo plano; suplicación.—**w. iron,** barquilla, molde para hacer tales barquillos.

waft [wáft]. **I.** *vn.* mecer, flotar, sobrenadar. **II.** *va.* llevar por el aire o por encima del agua. **III.** *s.* mecedura, fluctuación; bationdeo; ráfaga de aire o de olor; (mar.) señal hecha con bandera; banderín de señales.

waftage [-ĭdž], *s.* acción de mecer, etc.; conducción por el aire o por el agua.

wafture [wáfchŭ(r)], *s.* fluctuación. *V.* WAFTAGE.

wag [wǽg]. **I.** *va.* sacudir, mover o menear ligeramente.—**to w. the tail,** rabear, colear. **II.** *vn.* oscilar, tambalear, balancearse; ir pasando, deslizarse; (fam.) irse. **III.** *s.* meneo; coleada, coleo; movimiento de cabeza; burlador, matraquista, bromista.

wage [wéĭdž]. **I.** *va.* emprender, sostener, empeñar; (cerá.) hacer la masa.—**to w. war,** hacer guerra. **II.** *s.* (gen. en *pl.*, **wages**) (ant.) premio,

galardón; (e. p.) gaje, paga, jornal, sueldo, salario.—**w. earner,** trabajador, obrero; asalariado.

wager [-œ(r)]. **I.** *va.* apostar, poner (apuesta). **II.** *s.* apuesta, postura; competidor; (ant.) gaje, palabra, empeño; (hist.) prueba.—**w. of battle,** prueba del duelo, juicio de Dios determinado por el duelo.—**w. of law,** prueba de la compurgación, juicio de Dios determinado por el juramento del acusado y sus compurgadores.

waggery [wǽgœrĭ], *s.* jocosidad, chocarrería, bufonada; travesura.—**waggish** [wǽgĭȿ], *a.* juguetón, retozón, (fam.) chacotero, zumbón.— **waggishness** [-nȷ̣s], *s.* retozo, chacota, chocarrería.

waggle [wǽgl]. **I.** *va.* menear ligeramente. **II.** *vn.* anadear; menearse; tambalear(se); bullir. **III.** *s.* meneo, anadeo, tambaleo.

Wagnerian [vagnĭ́rĭạn], *a.* vagneriano.

wag(g)on [wǽgọn], *s.* carro, carretón, carreta, carromato, galera; vehículo, coche; (mil., f. c., etc.) furgón; vagón; (Ingl., f. c.) furgón.—**w.-lit** [-lĭ́], *s.* (f. c.) vagón-cama, coche cama o dormitorio.—**w. maker** = WAGONWRIGHT.— **wagonage** [-ĭdž], *s.* porte, carretaje.—**wagoner** [-œ(r)], *s.* carret(on)ero, carromatero; (W., astr.) Carro, Osa Mayor.—**wagonet(te** [-ét], *s.* carricoche, birlocho.—**wagonful** [-fụl], *s.* furgón; vagón; (Ingl., f. c.) furgón.—**wagonload** [-loụd], *s.* galerada, carretada.— **wagonwright** [-raĭt], *s.* carretero.

wagtail [wǽgteĭl], *s.* (orn.) aguzanieve(s), *f.,* nevatilla, motacila, herreruelo.

waif [weĭf], *s.* granuja, *m.;* niño, animalito u objeto extraviado o abandonado; (for.) cosa robada y soltada por el ladrón; bienes mostrencos; (mar.) *V.* WAFT.

wail [wéĭl], *va. y vn.* deplorar, llorar, lamentar o lamentarse, gemir.—**wail(ing** [-ĭŋ], *s.* lamentación, lamento, gemido.

wain [weĭn], *s.* (ant. o poét.) carreta, carruaje.— **the W.,** (astr.) Carro, Osa Mayor.

wainscot [wéĭnskọt]. **I.** *s.* (arq. y carp.) enmaderamiento, friso inferior, arrimadillo. **II.** *va.* entablar, enmaderar; poner friso de madera.— **wainscoting** [-ĭŋ], *s.* entablamento, entabladura.

wainwright [-raĭt], *s.* carretero.

waist [wéĭst], *s.* (anat.) cintura, talle, cinto; (cost.) talle, corpiño, corpecico, jubón; (mar.) combés de una nave.—**w. board,** (mar.) falca.

waistband [-bænd], *s.* pretina, cinto, cinturón.

waistcloth [-klọθ], *s.* pampanilla.

waistcoat [-koụt *o* wéstkọt], *s.* (sast.) chaleco; (ant.) chupa; (cost.) justillo, ajustador, monillo.

waistline [-laĭn], *s.* cintura.

wait [wéĭt]. **I.** *va.* esperar, aguardar; (fam.) dilatar, diferir. **II.** *vn.* estar aguardando o esperando, estar en expectativa; atender; estar listo; ⏤rvir; ser criado, sirviente o mozo (de fonda). —**to w. at table,** servir a la mesa.—**to w. for,** esperar.—**to w. on,** o **upon,** ir a ver o presentar sus respetos a; servir a; atender a, despachar (en una tienda); seguirse, inferirse; (fam.) acompañar. **III.** *s.* espera; (fam.) plantón; pausa, dilación, demora; (ant.) asechanza, celada;—*pl.* murga (fam.) de nochebuena.—**in w.,** al o en acecho. *V.* LIE IN WAIT.

waiter [-œ(r)], *s.* mozo de café o restaurante, camarero, sirviente, criado; azafate o bandeja.

waiting [-ĭŋ]. **I.** *s.* espera; demora; servicio. **II.** *a.* que espera; que sirve; de o en espera.—**w. (gentle)woman,** w. **maid,** doncella, camarera.—**w. room,** antesala; sala de espera.

waitress [-rȷ̣s], *s.* criada, moza, camarera.

waive [wéĭv], *va.* renunciar a; desistir de; diferir, posponer; repudiar.—**waiver** [-œ(r)], *s.* renuncia (de un derecho, etc.); repudio.—**w. of notice,** (for.) renuncia de citación.

wake [wéĭk]. **I.** *va.* (*pret. y pp.* WAKED O WOKE) despertar; resucitar; excitar, animar; (dial.) velar un muerto.—**to w. up,** llamar o despertar. **II.** *vn.* despertar(se) (a veces con **up**); (fig.) recordar; velar, pasar la noche en vela; despabilarse; estar de velorio. **III.** *s.* vela o velación de un muerto, vel(at)orio; (Ingl., igl.) vela; fiesta nocturna o verbena; (mar.) estela, aguaje. —**in the w. of,** tras; inmediatamente después de; a raíz de.

wakeful [-fųl], *a.* vigilante, en vela, alerto; desvelado.—**wakefully** [-į]. *adv.* alerta; desveladamente.—**wakefulness** [-nįs], *s.* vigilia, pervigilio, desvelo, falta de sueño, insomnio.

waken [-n], *va.* y *vn.* despertar(se).

wake-robin [-rabįn], *s.* (bot.) aro o yaro; (E. U.) hierba liliácea.

waking [-įŋ]. **I.** *s.* vela; acto de despertar(se). **II.** *a.* que despierta; despierto; de vela o vigilia.—**w. hours,** horas de vela o de estar despierto.

Walachian [waléįkįąn], *a.* y *s.* valaco.

Waldenses [waldénsiz], *s. pl.* (igl.) valdenses.—**Waldensian** [-śąn], *s.* y *a.* valdense.

wale [weįl]. **I.** *va.* levantar roncha; azotar; (tej.) cruzar, tejer con relieve. **II.** *s.* roncha, cardenal, verdugo; (tej.) relieve; (mar.) cinta.

Walhalla [welhǽlą], *s.* = VALHALLA.

walk [wók]. **I.** *vn.* andar, caminar, marchar, ir a pie; pasear(se); (equit.) ir al paso; obrar, conducirse, portarse; aparecer (fantasmas, espectros o duendes); (fam.) liar el petate, ser despedido.—**to w. after,** seguir a, ir tras.—**to w. away,** irse, marcharse.—**to w. back,** volver atrás, regresar.—**to w. down,** bajar (a pie).—**to w. forth,** salir.—**to w. in,** entrar, pasar adelante; pasearse en.—**to w. off,** disipar, quitarse (una jaqueca, etc.) a fuerza de andar mucho.—**to w. off with,** ganar, llevarse; robar.—**to w. on air,** estar muy gozoso o ufano. —**to w. out,** salir, irse; (e. p.) declararse en huelga.—**to w. over,** ir al paso (caballo); (fam.) ganar fácilmente; dominar a, abusar de.—**to w. up,** subir (a pie); acercarse.—**to w. up and down,** pasearse, ir y venir. **II.** *va.* hacer andar, (sacar a) pasear; recorrer, andar o pasar de una parte a otra de; andar por; hollar; conducir; hacer ir al paso (un caballo).—**to w. Spanish,** entrar por el aro (fam.); someterse, ceder; ser despedido.—**to w. the hospitals,** estudiar clínica en los hospitales.—**to w. the plank,** ser echado al mar (por los piratas, que hacían andar la víctima por una tabla oscilante hasta volcarla); ser echado o despedido.—**to w. the streets,** andar por las calles, andorrear. **III.** *s.* paseo, caminata; modo de andar; paso del caballo; paseo, alameda; andador; plantación de árboles en hileras; acera; carrera, oficio, empleo, estado, condición; método de vida, conducta, porte.—**w. of life,** clase (*f.*) social; oficio, ocupación.

walkaway [-ąweį], *s.* triunfo fácil, ganga.

walker [-œ(r)], *s.* paseante, caminante; peatón.

walkie-talkie [-į tókį] *s.* (rad.) transmisor portátil.

walking [-įŋ]. **I.** *s.* paseo; piso (estado de los caminos para andar).—**to go w.,** ir de paseo, dar un paseo. **II.** *a.* de andar, para andar; que anda; andador, ambulante.—**w. beam,** balancín de máquina vertical de vapor).—**w. cane,** bastón.—**w. delegate,** visitador y representante o delegado de un gremio obrero.—**gentleman, w. lady,** (teat.) segundo galán, segunda dama.—**w. pace,** paso de andadura. —**w. staff,** o **stick** = w. CANE.—**to give one his w. papers,** o **ticket,** (fam.) despedir a uno, darle calabazas.

walkout [-aųt], *s.* (fam.) paro, huelga de obreros.

walkover [-oųvœ(r)], *s.* (fam.) triunfo fácil, ganga.

wall [wol]. **I.** *s.* pared; tabique; muro o tapia; (fort.) muralla; (geol.) banco de roca natural. —**w. bracket,** palomilla.—**w. clock,** reloj de pared.—**w. creeper,** (orn.) pico murario.—**w. fence,** tapia.—**w. fruit,** fruta de espal(d)era.—

—**w. louse,** (ent.) chinche. *V.* WOOD LOUSE.— **w. paper,** empapelado, papel de empapelar.— **w. pepper,** (bot.) siempreviva.—**w. plate,** (arq.) solera, viga de apoyo.—**w. rock,** (geol. y min.) roca estéril, roca circundante de una veta.—**w. rue,** (bot.) ruda muraria.—**w. saltpetre,** afronitro, espuma de nitro.—**w. tile,** azulejo.—**w. tree,** (hort.) árbol frutal de espaldera.—**to drive, push,** o **thrust, to the w.,** acosar; poner entre la espada y la pared.— **to go to the w.,** verse o hallarse acosado, o en calzas prietas; verse obligado a ceder; (com.) quebrar. **II.** *va.* emparedar, tapiar; tabicar; murar, cercar; (fort.) amurallar.

wallaby [wáląbi], *s.* (zool.) especie de canguro.

Wallachian [waléįkįąn], *s.* y *a.* valaco.

wallboard [wólbord], *s.* tabla de fibra comprimida para revestir paredes.

wallet [wálįt], *s.* cartera; bolsa de cuero; mochila; zurrón o alforja.

walleye [wólaį], *s.* (med.) estrabismo divergente; leucoma, *m.*—**walleyed** [-d], *a.* que padece leucoma, etc.; de ojos saltones o reventones; (oji)zarco, o de ojos casi blancos.

wallflower [wólflaųœ(r)], *s.* (bot.) al(h)elí doble; (fam.) mujer que en un baile "come pavo."

Walloon [walún], *s.* y *a.* valón.

wallop [wálǫp]. **I.** *va.* (fam.) zurrar, tundir; vencer decisivamente. **II.** *s.* (fam.) golpe rudo; capacidad de asestar tales golpes.

walloping [-įŋ]. **I.** *s.* (fam.) tunda, zurra; derrota decisiva. **II.** *a.* (fam.) ingente, tremendo.

wallow [wáloų]. **I.** *vn.* revolcarse, chapalear, estar encenagado en algún vicio.—**to w. in riches,** nadar en la opulencia. **II.** *s.* revuelco, revolcadura.

wallower [-œ(r)], *s.* el que se revuelca en el fango.

wallwort [wólwœrt], *s.* (bot.) cañarroya.

walnut [wólnat], *s.* (bot.) nogal; nuez de nogal.— **w. color** o **stain,** nogalina.—**w.-colored,** noguerado.—**w. tree, w. wood,** nogal, noguera.

walrus [wólrʌs], *s.* (zool.) morsa.

waltz [wólts]. **I.** *vn.* valsar, bailar el vals. **II.** *s.* (mús. y danz.) vals.

waltzer [-œ(r)], *s.* valsador, valsadora.

wampum [wámpʌm], *s.* cuentas o cañutillos de madreperla que usaban los indios americanos como dinero y como adorno; abalorio; (fam.) dinero.

wan [wan], *a.* pálido, descolorido.

wand [wand], *s.* vara; varilla de virtudes; batuta.

wander [wándœ(r)]. **I.** *vn.* errar, vagar, rodar, andorrear; delirar; perderse, extraviarse; desviarse, apartarse. **II.** *va.* recorrer, andar por.—

wanderer [-œ(r)], *s.* vagamundo, andorrero; persona errante o extraviada; transgresor.— **wandering** [-įŋ]. **I.** *s.* viaje; divagación; aberración; extravío; delirio. **II.** *a.* errante, errabundo; vago, vagamundo; descaminado, descarriado; delirante.—**w. cell,** (anat.) leucocito.—**W. Jew,** judío errante.—**w. kidney,** (anat.) riñón flotante.

wanderlust [-lʌst], *s.* impulso hacia la vida errante, pasión de viajar.

wanderoo [wanderú], *s.* (zool.) macaco con crin, mono grande.

wane [weįn]. **I.** *vn.* menguar, disminuir; decaer. **II.** *s.* mengua, disminución; decadencia, decremento, declinación; menguante, *f.* (de la luna); (carp.) bisel.

wangle [wǽŋgl], *va.* (fam.) sacar (dinero, etc.) con engañifas, obtener (algo) por astucia y engatusamiento.

waning [wéįnįŋ]. **I.** *a.* menguante. **II.** *s.* = WANE.

wanness [wánnįs], *s.* palidez; descaecimiento, languidez.

want [wánt]. **I.** *va.* necesitar, tener necesidad de; estar desprovisto de, carecer de; querer, desear; clamar, pedir con urgencia; exigir, requerir; dispensarse de, pasarse sin. **II.** *vn.* estar necesitado o indigente, carecer, pasar necesidades;

faltar. **III.** *s.* necesidad, falta, carencia; privación, necesidad, indigencia; exigencia; solicitud, demanda.—**for w. of,** a o por falta de.—**to be in w.,** estar necesitado, sufrir necesidad.

wantage [-idž], *s.* deficiencia, merma, déficit.

wanted [-id], *pp.* de TO WANT. Ú. elípticamente en anuncios en el sentido de "se solicita," "se necesita," "se desea," "se busca."

wanting [-iŋ]. *a.* falto, defectuoso, deficiente; menguado; necesitado, escaso.—**to be w.,** faltar.

wanton [wántǫn]. **I.** *a.* desenfrenado; protervo; (poét.) juguetón, travieso; extravagante; suelto, libre; lascivo, salaz; licencioso, disoluto; desconsiderado; imperdonable; injustificable. **II.** *s.* libertino; ramera; persona frívola. **III.** *va.* malgastar; echar a perder. **IV.** *vn.* retozar, juguetear; hacer picardías; pasar el tiempo en liviandades.—**wantonly** [-li], *adv.* desenfrenada o licenciosamente; protervamente.

wantonness [-nis], *s.* desenfreno, licencia; protervia; (poét.) retozo; picardía; desgarro.

wapiti [wápiti], *s.* (zool.) uapití, gran ciervo de la América del Norte.

war [wor]. **I.** *s.* guerra; estrategia, arte militar; lucha, disensión. **II.** *a.* de o rel. a la guerra; bélico, guerrero, militar, marcial.—**w. baby,** hijo natural de un soldado; (fam.) ganga debida a la guerra.—**w. bonnet,** (E. U.) casco de plumas que usa(ba)n los indios en sus ritos y cuando guerreaban.—**w. bride,** novia (esposa reciente) de un soldado en servicio de guerra; (fam.) ganga de guerra; empresa industrial o comercial que prospera con la guerra.—**w. club,** maza.—**w. cry,** grito de guerra.—**w. dance,** danza bélica de los salvajes.—**W. Department,** ministerio de la guerra.—**w. flail,** mangual.—**w. head,** (mil.) punta o cabeza de un torpedo, en la cual van los explosivos.—**w. horse,** corcel de guerra; (fam.) veterano.—**w. lord,** señor de los ejércitos; jefe guerrero.—**W. of Secession,** (E. U.) guerra de secesión (de 1861 a 1865).—**w. paint,** pintura con que se embadurnaban los indios para guerrear; (fam.) los trapitos de cristianar.—**w. tax,** impuesto de guerra.—**w. to the death,** o **knife,** guerra a muerte.—**w. whoop,** alarido de guerra (de los indios americanos).—**on a w. footing,** en pie de guerra. **III.** *vn.* guerrear, estar en guerra.—**to w. on,** hacer la guerra a.

warble [wórbl]. **I.** *va.* y *vn.* cantar con quiebros y trinos; trinar, gorjear, gargantear; murmurar (un arroyo). **II.** *s.* canto, gorjeo.—**warbler** [-blœ(r)], *s.* cantor, gorjeador; pájaro cantor; (orn.) cerrojillo.—**warbling** [-bliŋ]. **I.** *a.* canoro, melodioso; susurrante. **II.** *s.* garganteo; canto, gorjeo.

ward [word]. **I.** *va.* (ant.) guardar, defender, proteger, poner a buen recaudo; (con **off**) parar, detener, evitar, desviar. **II.** *s.* pupilo o menor en tutela; barriada, barrio, cuartel o distrito de ciudad; sala, división, cuadra de hospital, etc.; pupilaje, tutela; guarda, custodia, protección; guarda de llave o cerradura; defensa, posición defensiva.—**w. chief** o **leader,** (pol.) alcalde o cacique de barrio.—**w. heeler,** (fam.) ayudante de cacique político.

warden [wórdęn], *s.* custodio, guardián, celador, capataz, *m.*; castellán o castellano (de un castillo); alcaide, carcelero, conserje; bedel; (en Ingl.) director de ciertos colegios; (igl.) *V.* CHURCHWARDEN.—**w. of a port,** capitán de un puerto.—*pl.* maestros o jurados en algún oficio.—**wardens and vestry,** (igl.) mayordomos y junta parroquial.

wardenry [-ri], **wardenship** [-šip], *s.* conserjería; bedelía; alcaidía; celaduría.

warder [wórdœ(r)], *s.* guarda, *mf.*; guardia, *m.*; alcaide; bastón de mando; (fig.) baluarte, fuerte.

wardrobe [-roub], *s.* guardarropa, *mf.*, armario, ropero, (Am.) escaparate; ropería; (teat.) guardarropía; vestuario, ropa.—**w. trunk,** baúl ropero, baúl cuelgarropa.

wardroom [-rum], *s.* (mar. mil.) cuarto de los oficiales; (pol.) sala de reunión de un barrio.

wardship [-šip], *s.* tutela, tutoría, pupilaje.

ware [wér], *s.* (gen. *pl.*) mercancías, mercaderías, efectos, géneros o artículos de comercio. *V.* HARDWARE, TINWARE, POTTER'S WARE.

ware. I. *a.* (ant.) = AWARE. **II.** *va.* y *vn.* (ant.) = BEWARE.

warehouse [-haus]. **I.** *s.* almacén, depósito.—**w. keeper,** guarda(a)lmacén.—**w. rent,** almacenaje. **II.** *va.* almacenar.—**warehouseman** [-mąn], *s.* almacenero, almacenador.

warehousing system [-hauziŋ sĺstįm], *s.* sistema (*m.*) de almacenaje o de depósitos.

wareroom [-rum], *s.* pieza para almacenaje o venta de géneros.

warfare [wórfęr], *s.* guerra; milicia, arte militar; operaciones militares; lucha, combate.

warily [wériļi], *adv.* cautelosamente; astutamente.—**wariness** [-nis], *s.* cautela, precaución.

warlike [wórlaik], *a.* bélico, belicoso, marcial.

warlock [wórlak], *s.* brujo, hechicero, mago.

warm [wórm]. **I.** *a.* caloroso, cálido, caliente; ardiente, acalorado; fogoso, furioso, violento, celoso; conmovido, arrebatado, apasionado; expresivo; afectuoso; (pint.) caliente, que tira a rojo o amarillo; reciente, fresco; (fam.) cercano al objeto buscado; molesto, fastidioso; peligroso.—**w.-blooded,** de sangre caliente; entusiasta, ardiente.—**w.-hearted,** de buen corazón; afectuoso; simpático.—**w. temper,** genio vivo, ardiente.—**to be w.,** tener calor; estar o ser caliente (una cosa); (con **it** por sujeto) hacer calor. **II.** *va.* calentar; caldear; abrigar; entusiasmar, encender, enfervorizar; (fam.) azotar, zurrar.—**to w. over,** o **up,** (re)calentar (comida fría). **III.** *vn.* calentarse; (gen. con **up**) entusiasmarse; acalorarse; tomar bríos.—**to w. to(ward),** simpatizar con; cobrar cariño o afición a.

warming [-iŋ]. **I.** *s.* calentamiento; calefacción. **II.** *a.* de calentar, para calentar; calentador.—**w. pan,** calentador (de cama); mundillo.

warmly [-li], *adv.* acaloradamente; con entusiasmo, ardientemente; afectuosamente.

warmonger [wórmʌŋgœ(r)], *s.* atizador de la guerra.

warmth [wormθ], *s.* calor (moderado); celo, entusiasmo, ardor, viveza, animación; cordialidad, irritación, enojo, resentimiento.

warn [wórn]. **I.** *va.* avisar, prevenir, advertir, poner en guardia o sobre aviso; aconsejar, amonestar; (for.) apercibir. **II.** *vn.* servir de escarmiento.—**warner** [-œ(r)], *s.* amonestador.—**warning** [-iŋ], *s.* amonestación; advertencia, aviso, admonición; (for.) apercibimiento; lección, escarmiento, gobierno.

warp [worp]. **I.** *s.* torcedura, torcimiento, alabeo, comba; (tej.) urdi(e)mbre, *f.*; (mar.) espía, calabrote, estacha, remolque.—**w. and woof,** (tej.) trama y urdimbre.—**w. beam,** (tej.) enjullo, plegador.—**w. thread,** lizo. **II.** *va.* torcer, retorcer; encorvar, empandar; combar, alabear; prevenir el ánimo; (tej.) urdir; (mar.) remolcar. **III.** *vn.* torcerse; combarse, alabearse; desviarse, alejarse, apartarse del camino recto; (tej.) urdir; (mar.) ir a remolque, espiarse.

warpath [wórpæθ], *s.* senda que siguen los indios para atacar al enemigo.—**to be on the w.,** (fam.) estar en guerra; buscar pendencia, pelear.

warped [worpt], *a.* con comba, combado, adunco.—**w. surface,** (geom.) superficie alabeada.

warper [wórpœ(r)], *s.* (tej.) urdidor(a).

warping [wórpiŋ], *pa.* y *s.* alabeo, combadura; (tej.) urdidura; (mar.) remolque, atoaje.—**w. machine, frame** o **mill,** (tej.) urdidera, urdidora.

warplane [wórplejn], s. avión (m.) de guerra.
warrant [wárant]. I. va. garantir, garantizar, abonar; responder por; asegurar, fiar, certificar, aseverar; justificar; autorizar. II. s. (for.) auto, decreto, libramiento, mandamiento, cédula, patente, despacho; orden (f.) de prisión; autorización, poder; documento justificativo, comprobante, garantía; (com.) certificado de depósito; autoridad, apoyo, testimonio; sanción; justificación, apología, razón, f., motivo.—w. **officer**, (E. U.) oficial subalterno del ejército o de la marina.
warrantable [-abl], a. que se puede abonar, garantizar o justificar.—**warrantableness** [-nis], s. calidad de justificable; certeza, seguridad.—**warrantably** [-abli], adv. justificadamente.
warrantee [warantí], s. (for.) afianzado.
warranter, warrantor [wárantœ(r), -ǫ(r)], s. (for.) garante, fiador.
warranty [wáranti], s. (for.) garantía; seguridad; autoridad, autorización.—w. **clause**, cláusula de evicción y saneamiento.—w. **of title**, (for.) saneamiento, garantía de título.
warren [wárjn], s. conejera, conejar; vivar, vivero; vedado.—**warrener** [-œ(r)], s. conejero.
warrior [wórjǫ(r)], s. guerrero.
warship [wórṣip], s. navío o buque de guerra.
wart [wórt], s. verruga; espejuelo en la cuartilla del caballo; (bot.) verruga.—w. **hog**, (zool.) facóquero, especie de jabalí sudafricano.—**warty** [-i], a. verrugoso, averrugado.
wartime [wórtajm], s. I. s. período o tiempo de guerra. II. a. rel. a dicho período; de guerra.
warworn [wórworn], a. agotado por el servicio militar.
wary [wérj], a. cauto, cauteloso, prudente, avisado, precavido, astuto, sagaz.
was [waz], pret. del verbo TO BE.
wash [wáś]. I. va. lavar; bañar, regar; fregar (la loza, los platos); dar un baño o capa de metal; dar una mano o capa de color; (min.) lavar el mineral; (alb.) deslavar; (mar.) baldear.—to **w. away, off,** o **out**, lavar, borrar, hacer desaparecer; quitar lavando; llevarse (el agua o un golpe de mar).—to **w. one's hands of**, lavarse las manos en cuanto a, no tomar parte en. II. vn. lavarse; lavar ropa, hacer la colada; no perder el color al lavarse, no desteñir; (fam.) colar, ser creído, soportar examen o prueba; gastarse por la acción del agua; mecerse (las olas). III. s. lavado, lavadura; colada; ropa lavada o para lavar (ropa sucia); lavación, ablución; lavatorio; loción, agua de tocador, cosmético; (min.) baño, capa; batiente del mar; chapaleo; (geol.) aluvión, m., depósito; bazofia, lavazas, f. pl.; aguachirle, f.; (mar.) pala de remo; (aer.) perturbación aerodinámica, conmoción del aire. IV. a. de o para lavar; lavable, que puede lavarse (apl. esp. a géneros que no destiñen).—w. **ball**, bola de jabón, jaboncillo de olor.—w. **leather**, gamuza.—w.-**off**, fugitivo, que se destiñe.—w. **sale**, (com.) venta ficticia.
washable [-abl], a. lavable, que puede lavarse.
washbasin [-bejsin], s. lavamanos. V. WASH-BOWL.
washboard [-bord], s. tablilla de lavandera; (carp.) rodapié; (mar.) falca, batemar, batidero.
washbowl [-boul], s. jofaina, palangana.
washcloth [-klɔθ], s. paño (para lavarse).
washed-out [wáśt áut], a. descolorido, desteñido; (fam.) agotado, rendido.
washed-up [wáśt áp], a. (fam.) agotado; descartado, rechazado, fracasado.
washer [wáśœ(r)], s. lavador; máquina de lavar; (mec.) arandela, volandera, estornija, disco de cuero o de goma, (prov.) alfardón.
washerman [-man], s. lavandero.
washerwoman [-wuman], s. lavandera.

washery [-i], s. (min.) lavadero (apl. esp. a los de hulla).
washhouse [wáśhaus], s. lavadero.
washin [wáśin], s. (aer.) alabeo que aumenta el ángulo de ataque; dicho aumento.
washing [wáśiŋ], s. lavado, lavadura, lavamiento; colada, ropa lavada o para el lavado; loción, lavatorio; blanqueadura; (mar.) baldeo; (min.) lave.—w. **machine**, máquina de lavar, lavadora mecánica.—w. **soda**, sosa para blanquear.
washout [wáśaut], s. hundimiento o derrumbe causado por el arrastre del agua; (aer.) alabeo que disminuye el ángulo de ataque; disminución del ángulo de ataque; (fam.) fracaso; chasco; persona o cosa sosa, inútil, etc.
washpot [-pat], s. bacía; paila de lavar.
washrag [-ræg], s. = WASHCLOTH.
washroom [-rum], s. cuarto de aseo; retrete, excusado (en un restaurante, etc.).
washstand [-stænd], s. palanganero, lavabo, lavamanos, aguamanil.
washtub [-tab], s. cuba de lavar o de colada; artesa, gamella, tina de lavar.
washwoman [-wuman], s. lavandera.
washy [-i], a. aguado; mojado; débil, flojo; insulso.
wasp [wásp], s. (ent.) avispa.—w.('s) **nest**, avispero.—w. **waist**, w.-**waisted**, (de) cintura de avispa; muy ceñido.
waspish [-iś], a. enojadizo, irascible; de cintura de avispa.—**waspishly** [-lj], adv. ásperamente, con mal humor.—**waspishness** [-nis], s. mal genio, mal humor, irritabilidad.
wassail [wásal], s. francachela, gaudeamus (fam.), borrachera, orgía; bebida compuesta de vino, cerveza y especias; brindis, m.—w. **bowl**, ponchera.
wast [wast], (poét.) 2d pers. sing. (pret.) de TO BE.
wastage [wéjstidʒ], s. merma, desgaste; desperdicio; material desechado.
waste [wéjst]. I. va. malgastar, derrochar, desperdiciar, malbaratar, disipar, dilapidar; gastar, consumir; comer, mermar, agotar; desgastar, arruinar, talar. II. vn. gastarse, consumirse; desgastarse, alterarse, dañarse.—to **w. away**, demacrarse, descaecer, consumirse; ir a menos, menguar. III. a. desechado, inútil; yermo, baldío, desierto, inculto; desolado; arruinado; superfluo, sobrante.—w. **iron**, chatarra.—w. **matter**, o **products**, residuos, desperdicios.—w. **mold**, (esc.) molde transitorio, gen. de yeso, que se usa una vez y luego se rompe.—w. **paper**, papel de desecho.—w. **silk**, borra de seda.—w. **steam**, vapor de escape o de educción; vapor que se fuga. IV. s. despilfarro, derroche, disipación, desperdicio; decadencia, consunción; merma, pérdida; borra, restos, despojos, desperdicio(s); erial, desierto; extensión, inmensidad; estrago, devastación, destrozo, ruina; (min.) escombros.—w. **heap**, o **pile**, (min.) escombrera.—w. **pipe**, tubo de desagüe, desaguadero.
wastebasket [-bæskit], s. cesto para papeles y desechos.
wasteful [-ful], a. manirroto, malgastador, disipador, despilfarrado(r), pródigo; destructivo, ruinoso; antieconómico.—**wastefully** [-lj], adv. pródigamente, despilfarradamente; antieconómicamente.—**wastefulness** [-nis], s. prodigalidad; calidad de antieconómico; gasto inútil.
waster [-œ(r)], s. disipador, (mal)gastador, derrochador; devastador; objeto imperfecto.
wasting [-iŋ]. I. a. que usa, agota o consume. II. s. derramamiento; desgaste; agotamiento; (med.) extenuación, consunción, marasmo.
wastrel [-rel], s. desperdicios, pl.; objeto imperfecto o inútil; pródigo, manirroto; (fam.) botarate; libertino, perdido, holgazán.
watch [wách]. I. s. reloj de bolsillo; vela, velación, desvelo o vigilia; velorio; vigilancia, cuidado, observación; centinela, mf., vigía, m.,

atalaya, *m.*, guardia, *m.*, sereno, vigilante; (mar.) cuarto, servicio, guardia, *f.*—w. **and ward**, patrulla, ronda.—w. **case**, caja de reloj, relojera.—w. **chain**, cadena o cinta de reloj, leontina.—w. **charm**, dije.—w. **glass**, cristal de reloj; (mar.) ampolleta de media hora.—w. **guard** = w. CHAIN.—w. **house**, cas(it)a de guarda; cuerpo de guardia.—w. **night**, víspera de año nuevo.—w. **spring**, muelle de reloj.— w. **stand**, relojera, portarreloj.—**to be on the w.**, estar alerta o a quién vive. II. *va.* vigilar, observar; contemplar; espiar, atisbar, (Am.) aguaitar; cuidar, guardar; tener cuidado de o con.—**to w. one's step**, tener cuidado, andarse con tiento. III. *vn.* vigilar, estar alerta; hacer centinela o guardia; velar.—w. **out!** ¡cuidado! ¡ojo!—**to w. for**, esperar; buscar.—**to w. out for**, tener cuidado con.—**to w. over**, guardar, vigilar; velar por, cuidar de; inspeccionar, superentender.

watchdog [-dɔg], *s.* perro de guarda, perro guardián; (fig.) guardián fiel.

watcher [-œ(r)], *s.* vigilante, velador; el que vela a un enfermo.

watchful [-fṵl], *a.* despierto, vigilante, observador, que está alerta; desvelado.—w. **waiting**, (pol.) espera vigilante, paciencia vigilante.

watchfully [-i], *adv.* desveladamente; atentamente, vigilando.—**watchfulness** [-nĭs], *s.* vigilia, vigilancia, cuidado; desvel(amient)o.

watching [-iŋ], *s.* observación, vigía; desvelo.

watchmaker [-mejkœ(r)], *s.* relojero.— w.'s **shop**, relojería.

watchman [-mạn], *s.* sereno, guardián, vigilante, salvaguardia, *m.*

watchtower [-tạŭœ(r)], *s.* (mil.) atalaya, torre, torre albarrana; mira(dero).

watchword [-wœrd], *s.* (mil.) santo y seña, (contra)seña, nombre; lema, *m.*

watchwork [-wœrk], *s.* mecanismo de un reloj de bolsillo.

water [wótœ(r)], *s.* agua; cualquier extensión de agua (lago, río, mar); (fisiol.) linfa; orina, orines, *m. pl.*; (joy.) aguas (de las piedras preciosas); (tej.) viso (de los géneros); (com.) acciones emitidas sin aumento de capital que la represente. Se emplea en palabras compuestas y en frases para denotar que el segundo elemento crece en el agua, es movido por agua, la contiene o sirve para contenerla o ir por ella.— w. **back**, caja de agua caliente en una estufa. —w. **bag**, bolsa para agua; (zool.) redecilla, segundo estómago.—w. **ballast**, lastre de agua. —w. **bar**, (arq.) plancha o barra obturadora, para impedir la entrada del agua; (ing.) caballón, lomo de desviación.—w. **bath**, baño de María.—w. **battery**, (elec.) pila de agua.—w. **bearing**, cojinete lubricado por agua.—w. **bed**, (med.) colchón de agua.—w. **bird**, ave acuática.—w. **boatman** = w. BUG.—w.-**borne**, llevado por las aguas.—w. **bottle**, botella o bolsa para agua, calientapiés; vasija para recoger muestras acuáticas.—w. **brash**, (med.) pirosis, acedía.—w. **bubble**, ampolla. —w. **bucket**, cubo, balde.—w. **buffalo**, carabao.—w. **bug**, (ent.) chinche de agua.—w. **butt**, bota de agua, pipa.—w. **carriage**, transporte para agua; conducción de aguas por cañerías, etc.—w. **carrier**, aguador, azacán; barco u otro artificio para transporte por agua; tubería o depósito de abastecimiento de agua.—w. **cask** = w. BUTT.—w. **cell**, bolsa o celda de agua (del camello).—w. **clock**, clepsidra, reloj de agua.—w. **closet**, inodoro, excusado, retrete, letrina, común.—w. **cock**, grifo, espita. —w. **color**, (pint.) color para acuarela; acuarela, pintura a la aguada.—w. **colorist**, acuarelista.—w. **column**, columna de agua; indicador del nivel del agua; (f. c.) depósito de alimentación del ténder.—w.-**cooled**, enfriado por

agua.—w. **cooler**, cantimplora, cubilla refrigeradora de agua.—w. **cooling**, enfriamiento por agua.—w. **cress**, (bot.) berro.—w. **cure**, (med.) hidroterapia; (fam.) tormento del agua que consiste en repletar de agua el estómago de la víctima.—w. **curtain**, cortina de agua contra incendios.—w. **dog**, perro de aguas; (fam.) marinero viejo; buen nadador.—w. **engine**, máquina hidráulica; máquina de apagar incendios. —w. **faucet**, grifo.—w. **front**, tierra ribereña; barrio o distrito contiguos a los muelles, etc.— w. **ga(u)ge**, indicador de nivel de agua.—w. **gap**, boquete o puerto de montaña por donde pasa una corriente de agua.—w. **gas**, gas de agua.—w. **gate**, abertura para el agua; compuerta.—w. **germander**, (bot.) escordio, ajote. —w. **gilding**, dorado al destemple.—w. **glass**, vaso para beber; vidrio soluble, silicato de sodio o de potasio; (m. v.) indicador de nivel. V. w. CLOCK.—w. **head**, (hidr.) carga hidrostática, diferencia de nivel.—w. **heater**, calentador de agua; aparato de calefacción por agua.—w. **hemlock**, (bot.) cicuta.—w. **hole**, aguadero, bebedero; charco, charca; manantial (en el desierto).—w. **ice**, sorbete, (Am.) granizada.— w.-**inch**, especie de paja de agua, cuyo valor varía, siendo poco más o menos 7 cuartos (*quarts*), o 6.6 litros, por minuto.—w. **jacket**, (m. v.) camisa de agua.—w. **jug**, aguamanil, jarro.—w.-**laid**, torcido hacia la izquierda (cable).—w. **level**, nivel de agua.—w. **lily**, (bot.) ninfea, nenúfar.—w. **line**, (mar.) línea de agua, línea de flotación; orilla del agua.—w.- **logged**, anegado en agua.—w. **main**, (hidr.) cañería maestra de agua.—w. **meter**, contador de agua.—w. **mill**, aceña, molino de agua. w. **mint**, (bot.) hierbabuena acuática.—w. **mite**, (ent.) ácaro acuático.—w. **moccasin**, (zool.) mocasín, culebra venenosa de agua.—w. **nymph**, náyade, *f.*—w. **ordeal**, prueba del agua.—w. **pail**, cubo, balde.—w. **pipe**, cañería de abastecimiento o conducción de agua; caño o tubo para conducción de agua.— w. **pitcher**, jarro.—w. **plane**, (aer.) hidroavión, *m.*—w. **plantain**, (bot.) alisma, llantén de agua.—w. **polo**, (dep.) polo acuático.—w. **power**, fuerza o energía hidráulica.—w. **purification**, (ing.) depuración de agua.—w. **rate**, cupo del consumo de agua.—w. **seal**, cierre hidráulico, agua de obturación.—w. **skater**, (ent.) tejedera.—w. **skipper** o **strider**, (ent.) tejedor.—w. **snake**, (zool.) culebra de agua.— w. **softener**, generador de agua dulce.—w. **spider**, (ent.) esquila.—w. **spring**, manantial, ojo de agua.—w. **sprite**, ondina.—w. **supply**, abastecimiento de agua.—w. **table**, (arq.) retallo de derrame.—w. **tank**, aljibe, tanque o depósito para agua.—w. **tax**, contribución de aguas.—w. **tower**, torre (*f.*) de elevación de aguas; torre de agua para incendios; arca de agua, cambija.—w. **trough**, abrevadero.—w.- **tube boiler**, caldera acuatubular.—w. **wave**, onda de agua; especie de rizo u ondulación por vía húmeda, formado metiendo peinetas en el pelo humedecido.—w. **wheel**, rueda hidráulica. —w. **wings**, nadaderas.—**above w.**, fuera de la dificultad o del aprieto, salvo.—**in deep w.**, en dificultades, en aprietos.—**like w.**, en gran abundancia; muy libremente.—**of the first w.**, de la mejor calidad o clase.—**to be**, o **go**, **on the w. wagon**, (fam.) abstenerse del licor, no beber.—**to go by w.**, ir por mar.

water [wótœ(r)]. I. *va.* regar; humedecer, mojar; bañar; aguar, echar agua a, diluir con agua; dar aguas o visos a (una tela).—**to w. cattle**, abrevar, dar de beber al ganado.—**to w. ships**, (mar.) hacer aguada.—**to w. the stock**, *diluir* o *aguar* las acciones, aumentar su número sin aumentar el capital.—**to w. wine**, aguar o bautizar el vino. II. *vn.* chorrear agua o humedad; tomar agua (para una locomotora, etc.); beber agua (ú. de animales).—**my mouth waters**, se me hace la boca agua.

waterage [-iʤ], s. (Ingl.) barcaje.

watercourse [-kɔrs], s. corriente (f.) de agua; vaguada; río, arroyo; madre (f.) o lecho de un río; (for.) derecho de aguas.

watercraft [-kræft], s. destreza en la navegación, natación o en los deportes acuáticos; cualquier buque; barcos, embarcaciones en general.

watered [-d], a. aguado, diluído; regado, abundante en agua.—**w. silk**, (tej.) muaré.

waterer [-œ(r)], s. regador; aguador de noria; abrevador (de ganado, etc.).

waterfall [-fɔl], s. cascada, catarata, salto o caída de agua. Ú. gen. en pl.

waterfowl [-fa̩ul], s. sing. y pl. ave(s) acuática(s).

wateriness [-inịs], s. acuosidad, humedad.

watering [-iŋ]. I. s. riego, regadura; irrigación; (mar.) aguada. II. a. de regar; de beber; de aguas.—**w. boat**, barco aguador.—**w. cart**, carro de regar.—**w. place**, aguadero o abrevadero; balneario, lugar de baños; fuentes (f. pl.) de aguas minerales; (mar.) aguada.—**w. pot**, regadera, hurtagua.—**w. trough**, abrevadero.

waterish [-ịʃ], a. = WATERY.

waterishness [-nịs], s. acuosidad.

waterman [-mạn], s. barquero; remero.

watermark [-mark], s. (pap.) marca de agua, filigrana, corondeles, m. pl.; (mar.) nivel del agua.

watermelon [-melọn], s. (bot.) sandía, badea, melón de agua.

waterpot [-pat], s. aguamanil; regadera.

waterproof [-pruf]. I. a. a prueba de agua, impermeable. II. va. impermeabilizar, hacer impermeable.—**waterproofing** [-iŋ]. I. s. impermeabilización; material impermeable o de impermeabilizar. II. a. impermeable; de impermeabilizar.

watershed [-ʃed], s. hoya, cuenca; vertiente, f., divisoria de aguas.

waterside [-sa̩id], s. borde u orilla del agua.

waterspout [-spa̩ut], s. tromba, prester, manga o bomba marina, surtidor; remolino.

watertight [-ta̩it], a. impermeable, a prueba de agua, hermético, estanco.

waterway [-weị], s. vía acuática, fluvial o de agua; canal o río navegable; (mar.) trancanil.

waterworks [-wœrks], s. instalación de abastecimiento de agua.

watery [-i], a. acuoso, ácueo, aguajoso, aguanoso, aguado; seroso; insípido, insulso, soso; lloroso.

watt [wạt], s. (elec.) vatio.—**w. hour**, vatio-hora. —**w.-hour meter**, contador de vatio-horas; contador de energía eléctrica.

wattage [-iʤ], s. (elec.) vatiaje, potencia en vatios.

wattle [wátl]. I. s. zarzo; sebe, f.; barba de gallo, pavo, etc.; barba de pez. II. va. enzarzar, tejer, entretejer, entrelazar.

wattless [wátlịs], a. (elec.) sin energía o vatios; desvat(i)ada (corriente).

wattmeter [wátmitœ(r)], s. vatiómetro; (errónea pero frecuentemente) contador de vatio-horas.

waul [wɔl], vn. maullar.

wave [weịv]. I. s. ola; onda, ondulación; movimiento de la mano, ademán; (tej. y joy.) aguas, pl., visos, pl.—**w. band**, (rad.) escala de longitudes de onda dentro de ciertos límites.—**w. detector**, (rad.) detector de ondas.—**w. length**, (rad.) longitud de onda.—**w. meter**, (rad.) ondómetro.—**w. train**, (fís.) tren de ondas, serie o sucesión de ondas.—**w. winding**, (elec.) arrollamiento ondulado. II. va. y vn. (hacer) ondear o flamear, tremolar, blandir(se), agitar(se); ondular (el pelo, etc.); hacer señas o señales.

waved [-d], a. ondeado, ondulado.

waveless [-lịs], a. sin olas, tranquilo, calmado; sin ondas.

wavelet [-lịt], s. olita, cabrilla.

waver [-œ(r)], vn. ondear, oscilar; tambalear, balancearse; vacilar, titubear, fluctuar.—**waverer** [-œ(r)], mf., persona mudable o irresoluta.—**wavering** [-iŋ]. I. a. irresoluto, inconstante, fluctuante. II. s. irresolución, vacilación, titubeo, fluctuación.—**waveringly** [-lị], adv. con incertidumbre y vacilación.

wavy, waving [-i, -iŋ], a. ondeado, ondulado, undoso, ondeante, ondulante, (poét.) undante.

wawl [wɔl], vn. = WAUL.

wax [wǽks]. I. s. cera; cerumen, cer(ill)a (del oído); parafina. II. a. de cera, céreo, ceroso.— **w. bean**, (bot.) variedad de judía amarilla.— **w.-bearing**, cerífero.—**w. cake**, pan o marqueta de cera.—**w. candle**, vela de cera.—**w. chandler**, cerero.—**w. end**, (zap.) hilo encerado.—**w. engraving, w. etching**, electrotipia en cera.—**w. match**, cerilla, fósforo de cera.—**w. model(l)ing**, modelado en cera.—**w. myrtle**, (bot.) mírica cerífera.—**w. painting**, encausto a la cera.—**w. paper**, papel encerado. —**w. plant**, (bot.) ceriflor, f.; especie de begonia de follaje lustroso; mírica cerífera.—**w. pocket**, cavidad secretora (de la abeja).—**w. process** = W. ETCHING.—**w. taper**, cerilla; cirio, blandón, hacha de cera.—**w. tree**, (bot.) árbol de la cera. III. va. encerar; encerotar (hilo). IV. vn. aumentarse, crecer (la luna, etc.); hacerse, ponerse (he waxed angry, se puso colérico, se encolerizó; I am waxing old, me estoy haciendo viejo, me estoy envejeciendo).

waxen [-n], a. de cera; plástico. V. WAXY.

waxer [-œ(r)], s. encerador.

waxflower [-fla̩uœ(r)], s. = WAX PLANT.

waxing [-iŋ], s. enceramiento; creciente, f. (de la luna).

waxwing [-wiŋ], s. (orn.) picotero.

waxwork [-wœrk], s. objeto o figura de cera.—pl. figuras de cera.—**waxworker** [-œ(r)], s. cerero; (ent.) abeja obrera.

waxy [-i], a. ceroso, céreo; ceráceo; de cera; encerado; plástico.

way [weị], s. vía; camino, senda, derrota; conducto, paso, pasaje; canal, mf.; distancia, espacio recorrido; rumbo, curso, dirección; (mar.) ruta, rota, derrota; marcha, andar, velocidad de un buque, etc.; modo, medio, manera, expediente, derrotero; uso, costumbre, hábito; modo de obrar, sistema, m., línea de conducta, comportamiento; avance, progreso, adelantamiento; (fam.) situación, estado.—pl. (mar.) anguilas de grada.—**w. in**, entrada.—**w. out**, salida.—**w. station**, (f. c.) estación intermediaria.—**w. through**, pasaje.—**w. train**, tren de escala. —**ways and means**, medios y arbitrios.— **across the w.**, al otro lado, en el otro lado, en frente.—**all the w.**, en todo el camino; en todo; del todo; hasta el fin; (gen. con **in, out, to**) hasta.—**a long w. off**, muy lejos.—**any w.** (no ANYWAY) de cualquier modo, de cualquiera manera, como se quiera.— **by w. of**, por la vía de, pasando por; por vía de, a modo de; a título de.—**by the w.**, a propósito, entre paréntesis; de paso.—**by the w. of**, por la vía de.—**every w.**, por todas partes, de todos lados; de todos modos.—**in the w. of**, para impedir o estorbar; que impide o estorba.—**no w.**, de ningún modo, de ninguna manera.—**on the w.**, en camino; de paso.—**on the w. to**, (en) camino de, con rumbo a.—**out of the w.**, fuera de camino; extraviado; escondido; fuera de orden; donde no estorba o estorbe; a un lado; poco común, extraordinario, original.—**that w.**, por ahí, por allí; de ese modo, así.—**the other w. around**, al contrario, al revés.—**this w.**, por aquí; de este modo, así.—**to be in the w.**, estar en el camino o en la vía; incomodar, estorbar.—**to go one's w.**, seguir su camino.—**to have a w. with one**, tener don de gentes; saber congraciarse.—**to have one's (own) w.**, hacer uno lo que quiera; salirse con la suya.—

under w., en camino, en marcha; empezado, haciéndose.

waybill [-bil], *s.* hoja de ruta; itinerario.

wayfarer [-fɛrœ(r)], *s.* pasajero, viajador, viajante, caminante.

wayfaring [-fɛriŋ], *a.* que va de viaje o de camino. —**w. man** = WAYFARER.—**w. tree**, (bot.) viburno.

waylay [-léi], *va.* (*pret.* y *pp.* WAYLAID) insidiar, asechar o acechar para asaltar o robar.—**way-layer** [-œ(r)], *s.* asechador, insidiador.—**way-laying** [-iŋ]. I. *s.* asechanza, asechamiento, acecho. II. *a.* asechoso.

waymark [-mark], **waypost** [-poust], *s.* hito, mojón, poste indicador.

wayside [-said]. I. *s.* orilla o borde del camino. II. *a.* que está junto al camino.

wayward [-wǝrd], *a.* descarriado; díscolo, voluntarioso, avieso; vacilante.—**waywardly** [-li], *adv.* voluntariosa o aviesamente.—**wayward-ness** [-nis], *s.* indocilidad, voluntariedad.

we [wi], *pron. pers.* (*pl.* de I) nosotros, nosotras.

weak [wik], *a.* débil, endeble, enclenque; delez-nable, frágil; poco fuerte, poco resistente; inse-guro; ineficaz; impotente; escaso; (com.) flojo (precio o mercado); (gram. ingl.) regular (verbo o nombre) en sus desinencias o (adjetivo) en la formación del comparativo.—**w.-eyed**, de vista débil.—**w.-handed**, escaso de braceros; de manos débiles.—**w.-headed**, de inteligencia menguada.—**w.-kneed**, débil de rodillas; (fig.) falto de energía; servil.—**w.-minded**, pobre de espíritu; simple, mentecato, pusilánime.—**w. point**, **w. side**, el flaco, el lado débil.—**w.-sighted** = W.-EYED.

weaken [-n]. I. *va.* debilitar, enflaquecer, enervar; relajar; quebrantar; disminuir, atenuar. II. *vn.* debilitarse, flaquear, desfallecer, resentirse; per-der resolución, enervarse; ahilarse.

weakening [-iŋ]. I. *a.* debilitante, enervante. II. *s.* debilitación, enervamiento.

weakfish [-fiš], *s.* (ict.) nombre de un pez nor-teamericano de boca muy delicada.

weakling [-liŋ]. I. *a.* = WEAKLY. II. *s.* criatura débil (física, mental o moralmente); (fam.) canijo, alfeñique.

weakly [-li]. I. *adv.* débilmente, sin vigor, sin fuerzas. II. *a.* enfermizo, achacoso, enclenque, (fam.) canijo, alfeñicado.

weakness [-nis], *s.* debilidad, debilitamiento; de-caimiento; poca consistencia; fragilidad; fla-queza, desliz, *m.*; (fam.) el flaco o lado débil.

weal [wil], *s.* (ant.) bienandanza, bienestar o felicidad, prosperidad; cardenal, verdugón.

weald [wild], *s.* (poét.) campiña, campo abierto.

wealth [wélθ], *s.* riqueza, opulencia; lujo; caudal, abundancia.

wealthily [-ili], *adv.* rica u opulentamente.

wealthiness [-inis], *s.* riqueza, opulencia.

wealthy [-i], *a.* rico, adinerado, acaudalado.

wean [win], *va.* destetar, ablactar; desahijar; des-becerrar; descorderar; enajenar el afecto de.

weaning [-iŋ], *s.* destete, ablactación.

weanling [-liŋ], *s.* niño o animal recién destetado o desmamado.—*pl.* desteto.

weapon [wépǝn], *s.* arma.—*pl.* (biol.) púas, espi-nas; aguijones, garras, etc.; medios de defensa de vegetales o animales.—**weaponed** [-d], *a.* armado.—**weaponless** [-lis], *a.* desarmado.

wear [wɛr]. I. *va.* (*pret.* WORE; *pp.* WORN) usar; vestir, llevar o traer puesto (un traje, etc.); gastar (sombrero, corsé, bigote, etc., habitual-mente); mostrar, tener aspecto o apariencia de, exhibir; gastar, consumir; desgastar, deteriorar; apurar, agotar; cansar, aburrir, enfadar; (mar.) virar.—**to w. away**, mermar, gastar o consu-mir.—**to w. down**, gastar, consumir; desgastar por rozamiento.—**to w. one's heart on one's sleeve**, andar con la cara descubierta, llevar el corazón en la mano.—**to w. out**, gastar, des-gastar; acabar con, agotar; cansar, fastidiar.—

to w. the breeches, o **the pants**, (fam.) llevar o haberse puesto los calzones, mandar. II. *vn.* gastarse, consumirse; durar, perdurar; pasar, correr (el tiempo); (mar.) virar.—**to w. away**, decaer; gastarse, consumirse, mermarse.—**to w. off**, usarse, gastarse; borrarse; pasarse, disi-parse, desaparecer.—**to w. on**, pasarse lenta-mente.—**to w. on one's nerves**, cansar, en-fadar, fastidiar.—**to w. out**, gastarse; inutili-zarse.—**to w. well**, durar largo tiempo, ser duradero. III. *s.* uso, gasto, deterioro; moda, boga; prendas (*f. pl.*) de vestir; durabilidad.— **w. and tear**, uso; desgaste o deterioro natural (debido al uso).—**little the worse for w.**, casi nuevo, casi sin usar; como nuevo.

wearable [-ǝbl], *a.* que se puede llevar, usar o gastar.

wearer [-œ(r)], *s.* el que lleva, gasta o usa algo.

wearied [wírid], *a.* cansado, fatigado; aburrido, fastidiado.—**weariness** [wírinis], *s.* lasitud, cansancio; aburrimiento, fastidio.

wearing [wériŋ]. I. *s.* uso; desgaste, deterioro; pérdida, decaimiento. II. *a.* de uso; desgasta-dor; agotador, fatigoso.—**w. apparel**, ropa, ropaje, indumentaria, prendas (*f. pl.*) de vestir.

wearisome [wírisʌm], *a.* fatigoso; tedioso, fasti-dioso, pesado, cansado, aburrido(r).—**weari-somely** [-li], *adv.* fatigosa o pesadamente.— **wearisomeness** [-nis], *s.* tedio, fastidio, can-sancio, hastío.

weary [wíri]. I. *va.* cansar, fatigar; hastiar, abu-rrir, enfadar, molestar.—**to w. out**, moler, cansar la paciencia. II. *vn.* fatigarse, cansarse, aburrirse. III. *a.* cansado, fatigado, rendido, molido; aburrido, hastiado; tedioso, fastidioso.

weasand [wízǝnd], *s.* (anat.) gaznate.

weasel [wízęl], *s.* (zool.) comadreja.

weather [wɛðœ(r)]. I. *s.* tiempo (estado atmosfé-rico); (gen. *pl.*) vicisitudes de la suerte.—**to be bad**, **good w.** (con *it* por sujeto), hacer mal, buen tiempo. II. *a.* del tiempo, relativo al tiempo; (mar.) de barlovento, del lado del viento.—**w.-beaten**, trabajado por la tor-menta; curtido por la intemperie.—**w.-bound**, detenido por el mal tiempo.—**W. Bureau**, (E. U.) Oficina Meteorológica (en el Ministerio de Agricultura de Wáshington).—**w. changes**, cambios atmosféricos.—**w. chart**, o **map**, mapa meteorológico.—**w. forecast(ing)**, pre-dicción o pronóstico del tiempo.—**w. prophet**, pronosticador del tiempo.—**w. report**, boletín meteorológico.—**w. sheets**, (mar.) escotas de barlovento.—**w. side**, costado de barlovento.— **w. signal**, señal, *f.* (bandera, etc.) para indicar las variaciones del tiempo.—**w. strip**, burlete. —**w. vane**, veleta, giraldilla, (mar.) cataviento, grímpola.—**w.-worn**, gastado o deteriorado por la intemperie, o por los agentes atmosféri-cos. III. *va.* aguantar (el temporal); resistir a, sobrevivir (a la adversidad); orear, airear, poner al aire; secar al aire; (mar.) ganar (el barlo-vento); doblar o montar (un cabo).—**to w. a point**, ganar alguna ventaja.—**to w. out**, vencer (obstáculos). IV. *vn.* curtirse en la intemperie.

weatherboard [-bǝrd], *s.* (carp.) tabla solapada; (mar.) lado del viento.—**weatherboarding** [-iŋ], *s.* solapadura de tablas; (mar.) falcas, *f. pl.*

weathercock [-kak], *s.* veleta, giraldilla, (mar.) cataviento; persona inconstante o mudable.

weatherglass [-glæs], *s.* instrumento indicador del tiempo (barómetro, etc.).

weathering [-iŋ], *s.* desgaste o alteración debida a los agentes atmosféricos; (arq.) declive de derrame.

weatherly [-li], *a.* (mar.) de bolina, de barlovento.

weatherman [-mæn], *s.* (fam.) meteorologista.

weatherproof [-pruf], *a.* a prueba de mal tiempo, a prueba de intemperie, inatacable por los agentes atmosféricos.

weatherwise [-waįz], *a.* perito en pronosticar las mudanzas del tiempo.

weave [wív]. **I.** *va.* (*pret.* WOVE; *pp.* WOVEN, WOVE) tejer, tramar; trenzar; entrelazar, entretejer; urdir, forjar (cuentos). **II.** *vn.* tejer, trabajar en telar. **III.** *s.* tejido; textura.

weaver [-œ(r)], *s.* tejedor(a), tejedera; tramador; (ent.) araña tejedora.—**w. bird**, (orn.) tejedor.

weaving [-įŋ], *s.* tejido, tejedur(í)a; textura.

web [wéb], *s.* tela, tejido, obra tejida; bobina o rollo de papel continuo; trama, lazo; artificio engañoso, trampa; (orn.) membrana que une los dedos de los palmípedos; tela de araña; barba o pelo de pluma; (ing.) alma (de viga, de riel); hoja de sierra.—**w.-footed**, palm(e)ado, palmípedo.

webbed [-d], *a.* unido por una telilla o membrana; (orn.) palm(e)ado, palmípedo.

webbing [-įŋ], *s.* tejedura; tejido; cincha, pretal.

webfoot [-fųt], *s.* (orn.) pie palm(e)ado.

wed [wéd]. **I.** *va.* casarse con; casar, unir en matrimonio. **II.** *vn.* casarse, contraer matrimonio.

wedded [-įd], *pp.* y *a.* casado.—**w. to**, (fig.) empeñado en, declarado por, aferrado en.

wedding [-įŋ]. **I.** *s.* boda, nupcias, *f. pl.*, casamiento; unión, enlace. **II.** *a.* de boda, nupcial, de casamiento; de novia.—**w. cake**, torta o pan de boda.—**w. dress**, traje nupcial, o de boda.— **w. ring**, anillo nupcial, sortija de matrimonio. —**w. trip**, viaje de novios.

wedge [wedž]. **I.** *s.* cuña, calza, calce, alzaprima; (geom.) prisma (*m.*) triangular.—**w.-shaped**, cuneiforme, (anat.) esfenoidal.—**entering w.**, comienzo, entrada; (cambiando el giro) para abrir brecha. **II.** *va.* acuñar, meter cuñas, calzar; (cerá.) hacer la masa.

wedlock [wédlak], *s.* matrimonio, himeneo, (poét.) connubio.

Wednesday [wénzdį], *s.* miércoles.

wee [wi], *a.* pequeñito, chiquito.—**a w. bit**, un poquit(ill)o.

weed [wíd]. **I.** *s.* maleza, mala hierba o yerba, cizaña; lo que crece en abundancia dañosa o inútil; (fam.) tabaco; (gen. *pl.*) ropa o gasa de luto. **II.** *va.* desyerbar, escardar, sachar, sallar, arrancar las malas hierbas; (a veces con **out**) quitar, extirpar, suprimir; entresacar, segregar. —**weeder** [-œ(r)], *s.* desyerbador, desmalezador, escardador; escarda, sacho, sallete.—**weedhook** [-hųk], *s.* escarda, escardillo, azadilla.— **weeding** [-įŋ], *s.* deshierba o desyerba, escarda(dura), sachadura, salladura.

weedy [-į], *a.* enmalezado; herboso; que abunda en malas hierbas; flacucho; malhecho, inservible.

week [wík], *s.* semana, hebdómada.—**w. about**, una semana sí y otra no.—**w.-end**, *vn.* pasar el fin de la semana; salir de vacación o ir a descansar durante el fin de la semana.—**w.-ender**, *s.* el que sale, o tiene costumbre de salir, de vacación durante el fin de la semana.—**w. end**, fin de semana.—**w. in, w. out**, semana tras semana.—**this day w.**, de hoy en ocho días; hoy hace ocho días.

weekday [-deį], *s.* día (*m.*) de trabajo.—*pl.* los días laborables o de entre semana.

weekly [-lį]. **I.** *a.* semanal, hebdomadario.—**w. paper**, semanario, periódico semanal. **II.** *adv.* semanalmente, por semana.

ween [win], *va.* y *vn.* (ant.) imaginar, pensar, creer.

weep [wíp], *va.* y *vn.* (*pret.* y *pp.* WEPT) llorar; deplorar, lamentar, condolerse de; (bot.) llorar, destilar; estar pendiente, inclinarse hacia el suelo.—**to w. for**, llorar a; llorar por; llorar de (tristeza, alegría, etc.).

weeper [-œ(r)], *s.* llorador, plañidero, (fam.) lloraduelos; llorón; gasa o señal (*f.*) de luto; (gen. *pl.*) velo de viuda; festón de musgo que pende de algunos árboles.

weeping [-įŋ]. **I.** *s.* llanto, lloro, lágrimas, *f. pl.* **II.** *a.* plañidero, llorón.—**w. ash**, (bot.) fresno llorón.—**w. willow**, (bot.) sauce llorón.

weepingly [-lį], *adv.* llorosamente, con lágrimas con llanto.

weevil [wívįl], *s.* (ent.) gorgojo, calapatillo, mordihuí, gusano del trigo.

weft [weft], *s.* (tej.) trama. *V.* WOOF, (mar.) WAFT

weigh [wéį]. **I.** *va.* pesar; considerar, reflexionar acerca de.—**to w. anchor**, (mar.) levar anclas, desancorar, zarpar.—**to w. down**, exceder en peso; sobrepujar; sobrecargar, agobiar, abrumar, oprimir.—**to w. out**, pesar, sacar o separar por peso. **II.** *vn.* pesar, ser pesado; ser digno de mucho aprecio, ser de importancia; (gen. con **on**) gravar, pesar sobre, ser opresivo o gravoso; (mar.) levar anclas; hacerse a la vela.—**to w. down**, hundirse por su propio peso.

weighable [-ạbl], *a.* capaz de ser pesado o vendido al peso.

weighed [-d], *a.* pesado; experimentado, probado.

weigher [-œ(r)], *s.* pesador.—**public w.**, almotacén, pesador público.

weighing [-įŋ]. **I.** *s.* peso; pesada. **II.** *a.* de pesar, para pesar; pesante.—**w. machine, w. scale**, balanza; báscula.

weight [wéįt]. **I.** *va.* cargar, gravar; aumentar el peso de; poner un peso o una pesa a. **II.** *s.* peso, pesantez; pesa; carga, gravamen; cargo, lastre; importancia, autoridad.—**weights and measures**, pesas y medidas.—**by w.**, por peso.—**to be worth its w. in gold**, valer su peso en oro.

weightily [-lį], *adv.* pesadamente; con mucho peso, con gran fuerza.

weightiness [-įnįs], *s.* ponderosidad, pesadez; solidez, fuerza; importancia, momento.

weightless [-lįs], *a.* ligero, leve; sin peso; imponderable.

weighty [-į], *a.* ponderoso, pesado; grave, serio, importante; de peso.

weir [wir], *s.* (hidr.) vertedero, vertedor, azud, presa de aforo; presa, cañal (para pescar).

weird [wírd]. **I.** *a.* misterioso, horripilante, fantástico, sobrenatural, como del otro mundo.—**the W. Sisters**, (Esco.) las Parcas. **II.** *s.* (ant. o Esco.) destino; pronóstico; encantamiento.— **weirdness** [-nįs], *s.* calidad de horripilante y misterioso.

welcome [wélkʌm]. **I.** *a.* bienvenido, bien llegado; grato, agradable.—**you are w.**, sea Vd. bienvenido; de nada, no hay de qué (cuando se dan las gracias).—**you are w. to it**, está a la disposición de Vd.; tengo mucho gusto en dárselo (prestárselo) a Vd.; (irónico) con gusto se lo dejo, buen provecho le haga. **II.** *interj.* ¡bien venido! **III.** *s.* bienvenida, buena acogida. **IV.** *va.* dar la bienvenida a, recibir con agasajo o regocijo.

welcomeness [-nįs], *s.* calidad de ser bienvenido; buena acogida.—**welcomer** [-œ(r)], *s.* el que acoge o da la bienvenida.

weld [wéld]. **I.** *va.* soldar; unir; unificar. **II.** *vn.* ser soldable, soldarse. **III.** *s.* soldadura (procedimiento y resultado); (bot., tint.) gualda. **IV.** *a.* gualdo.—**w.-colored**, gualdado.—**weldable** [-ạbl], *a.* soldable.—**welder** [-œ(r)], *s.* soldador; (elec.) transformador de soldar.—**welding** [-įŋ]. **I.** *s.* soldadura. **II.** *a.* de soldar, para soldar.— **w. blowpipe**, soplete de soldar.—**w. rod**, varilla de soldar, o de soldadura.—**w. torch**, lámpara de soldar; soplete de soldar.

welfare [wélfer], *s.* bien, bienestar, bienandanza, felicidad, prosperidad.—**w. society**, sociedad benéfica.—**w. work**, obra social o de beneficencia.

welkin [wélkįn], *s.* (poét.) firmamento, cielo.—**to make the w. ring**, atronar el espacio.

well [wel]. **I.** *va.* verter, derramar, arrojar, vaciar. **II.** *vn.* manar, brotar, fluir. **III.** *s.* pozo (de agua, petróleo, etc.); fuente, *f.*, manantial, ojo de agua; venero, origen; aljibe, cisterna; cavidad; vaso o copa de tintero; receptáculo; cañón (de pluma fuente); (arq.) caja o pozo de escalera; vivar (de pesca); (mar.) caja de bombas o sentina.—**w. borer, digger** o **sinker**, pocero.—**w. curb**, brocal (de pozo).—**w. of a fishing boat**, pozo de barco pescador.—**w. sweep**, cigüeñal o cigoñal de pozo.—**w. water**, agua de pozo.

well, *a.* bueno, bien, en buena salud, alentado; bien, satisfactorio; salvo, sano; grato, agradable, conveniente; ventajoso; bueno, provechoso.—**w. and good**, enhorabuena, bien está. **w.-being**, bienandanza, felicidad, bien, bienestar.—**w.-doer**, persona virtuosa; bienhechor.— **w.-doing**, *a.* benéfico; *s.* beneficencia, buenas obras.—**w.-wisher**, bienqueriente.—**all is w.**, todo va bien.—**very w.**, está bien, bien está.

well, *adv.* bien; muy; favorablemente; suficientemente; convenientemente; con propiedad, razonablemente; con razón; en sumo grado, considerablemente.—**w.-accomplished**, lleno de dotes o buenas cualidades; bien educado.—**w.-affected**, bien intencionado.—**w.-aged**, añejo (vino, etc.).—**w.-aimed**, acertado, certero.— **w.-appointed**, bien provisto; bien amueblado; bien equipado.—**w.-behaved**, de buena conducta; cortés.—**w.-bred**, bien criado o bien educado.—**w.-browned**, (coc.) bien dorado.— **w.-disposed**, bien dispuesto, favorable.—**w. done**, bien hecho; (coc.) bien cocido, bien asado.—**w. done!** ¡bravo! ¡bien hecho!—**w. enough**, bastante bien.—**w.-favored**, agraciado, bien parecido.—**w.-founded**, fundado, fundamentado.—**w.-gowned**, bien vestida.— **w.-informed**, instruído.—**w.-meaning**, bien intencionado; honrado, sincero.—**w.-meant**, hecho con buena intención.—**w.-nigh**, casi; poco menos que.—**w.-off**, acomodado, bien de fortuna.—**w.-read**, leído, instruído, ilustrado. —**w.-reputed**, prestigioso.—**w.-spoken**, que habla bien; bien dicho; urbano.—**w.-spoken of**, de buena reputación.—**w.-stocked**, bien abastecido.—**w.-suited**, apropiado, adecuado. —**w. then**, conque, pues bien.—**w.-thought of**, bien mirado.—**w.-timed**, oportuno.—**w.-to-do**, acomodado.—**w.-worn**, usado, gastado. —**and w. he** (we, etc) may, o **might** (be), y con razón.—**it is all very w. to** (antes de infinitivo), fácil es.

well, *interj.* ¡vaya! ¡vamos! ¡toma! ¡bueno!—**w., w.!**, ¡vaya, vaya! ¡qué cosa!

welladay [wéladéj], *interj.* (ant.) ¡ay de mí!

wellborn [wélbórn], *a.* bien nacido.

wellhead [wélhed], *s.* fuente, *f.*, manantial.

wellhole [-houl], *s.* caja de escalera; boca de pozo.

wellspring [-spriŋ], *s.* manantial, fuente, *f.*

welsh [welš], *va.* y *vn.* (fam.) no cumplir; no pagar; alzarse con el santo y la limosna; engañar, estafar.—**welsher** [-œ(r)], *s.* (fam.) estafador, pícaro.

Welsh. I. *a.* galés, de Gales.—**W. rabbit**, o **rarebit**, tostada cubierta de queso derretido con cerveza.—**the W.**, los galeses. II. *s.* idioma galés.

Welshman [-man], *s.* galés.

welt [welt]. I. *s.* (cost.) ribete, vivo; (zap.) vira, cerquillo; (carp.) refuerzo; (fam.) costurón, roncha, verdugo; (fam.) azotaina, tunda. II. *va.* (cost.) ribetear; (zap.) poner viras; (fam.) azotar levantando ronchas.

welter [wéltœ(r)]. I. *vn.* encenagarse; revolcarse en agua, cieno o lodo; hincharse (las olas). II. *s.* oleaje; conmoción, agitación, tumulto; cenagal, revolcadero.

welterweight [-wejt], *s.* (dep.) peso *welter;* púgil o luchador que pesa 60 a 68 kilos.

wen [wen], *s.* (med., vet.) lobanillo, lupia, quiste sebáceo, talpa(ria).

wench [wench], *s.* moza; criada; (desp.) ramera.

wend [wend]. I. *va.* dirigir, encaminar. II. *vn.* andar, ir, seguir camino, pasar.

wennish [wénniš], **wenny** [wénni], *a.* (med.) que parece un lobanillo o lo tiene.

went [went], *pret.* de TO GO.

wept [wept], *pret.* y *pp.* de TO WEEP.

were [wœr], *pret. pl.* de *indic.* y *sing.* y *pl.* de *subj.* de TO BE: *we were*, nosotros éramos o estábamos, fuimos o estuvimos; *if I were*, si yo fuera o fuese, estuviera o estuviese; *if they were*, si ellos fueran, fuesen, estuvieran o estuviesen; *there were*, había, hubo.—**as it w.**, por decirlo así; como si fuese.

wer(e)wolf [wírwulf, o wœrwulf], *s.* persona que, según la superstición, se convertía en lobo y devoraba a otras personas; licántropo.

wergild [wœrgild], *s.* (hist.) multa o indemnización impuesta a un asesino y sus parientes entre los antiguos teutones y anglosajones.

wert [wœrt], (poét.) *2a. pers. sing. pret.* de TO BE.

Wesleyan [wéslian], *s.* y *a.* wesleyano, de Wesley.

west [wést]. I. *s.* oeste, poniente, occidente, ocaso. —**w. northwest**, oesnorueste.—**w. southwest**, oessudueste. II. *a.* occidental, del oeste. —**W. End**, barrio aristocrático de Londres, al oeste de Charing Cross.—**W. Indies**, Antillas. —**W. Indian**, antillano.—**W. Pointer**, (E. U.) cadete o graduado de West Point (escuela militar nacional).—**W. wind**, poniente, favonio, céfiro. III. *adv.* a poniente o hacia el poniente; hacia el occidente.

westerly [-œrli]. I. *a.* occidental; del oeste; al oeste; hacia el oeste. II. *adv.* hacia el oeste.

western [-œrn]. I. *a.* occidental, ponentino. II. *s.* novela o película de la vida (esp. la de los vaqueros o *cowboys*) del oeste de los E. U.

westerner [-œ(r)n], *s.* natural o habitante del oeste.

westernmost [-moust], *a.* más occidental, del extremo occidental.

Westphalian [-féjlian], *s.* y *a.* vestfaliano.

westward [-wárd], *a.* que tiende o está al oeste.

westward(s, westwardly [-(z, -li], *adv.* a poniente, hacia occidente, hacia el ocaso.

wet [wet]. I. *a.* mojado; húmedo; lluvioso; (E. U.) antiprohibicionista.—**w. blanket**, (fam.) aguafiestas, paño frío (fig.), el o lo que echa a perder o apaga el entusiasmo, la alegría, etc.—**w. bulb**, ampolla humedecida del psicrómetro.— **w.-bulb thermometer**, psicrómetro.—**w. cell**, (elec.) pila hidroeléctrica.—**w. cupping**, (med.) ventosa escarificada o sajada.—**w. goods**, (com.) líquidos envasados; (fam.) aguardiente, licor, vino.—**w. nurse**, ama de leche, nodriza.—**w. pack**, (med.) tratamiento con sábanas mojadas.—**w. plate**, (fot.) placa de colodión.—**w. process**, (quím.) vía húmeda. —**w. through**, empapado, hecho una sopa.— **to get w. (through)**, mojarse, calarse. II. *s.* humedad, agua; lluvia; (E. U.) antiprohibicionista, antinefalista. III. *va.* mojar, humedecer, humectar.—**to w. one's whistle**, (fam.) mojar el gaznate, beber.

wether [wéðœ(r)], *s.* carnero castrado; eunuco.

wetness [wétnis], *s.* humedad.

wetted [wétid], *pret.* y *pp.* de TO WET.—**w. perimeter**, (hidr.) perímetro mojado.

wetting [wétiŋ], *s.* mojada, (re)mojadura, remojo, calada.

whack [hwæk]. I. *va.* (fam.) pegar, golpear, vapulear. II. *vn.* (fam.) dar una tunda; ajustar cuentas; participar de. III. *s.* (fam.) golpe, trastazo; participación; porción; prueba, tentativa.—**whacker** [-œ(r)], *s.* (fam.) vapuleador. —**whacking** [-iŋ], *a.* (fam.) grueso, desmesurado, enorme.

whale [hwéjl]. I. *va.* (fam.) vapulear, dar una tunda. II. *vn.* dedicarse a la pesca de la ballena. III. *s.* (zool.) ballena; cachalote; (fam.) cosa enorme o descomunal.—**w. fin**, (com.) = WHALEBONE.—**w. fishing** = WHALING.—**w. oil**, grasa de ballena.

whaleback [-bæk], *s.* (mar.) buque de cubierta cerrada y redondeada que se usa en aguas turbulentas.—**whaleboat** [-bout], *s.* buque ballenero.—**whalebone** [-boun], *s.* ballena o barba de ballena.—**whaler** [-œ(r)], *s.* ballenero, pescador de ballenas; buque ballenero.—**whaling**

[-iŋ], *s.* pesca de ballenas; (fam.) tunda, zurra, vapuleo.

wham [hwæm], **whang** [hwæŋ], *interj.* ¡zas! ¡cataplum! ¡pum!

whang [hwæŋ]. **I.** *va.* y *vn.* (fam.) dar tundas; golpetear. **II.** *s.* (Esco.) cuero fuerte; (fam.) tunda, paliza; golpazo.

wharf [hwórf], *s.* (*pl.* WHARFS o WHARVES) muelle, (des)embarcadero, descargadero. —**wharfage** [-idź], *s.* muellaje.

wharfinger [-indźœ(r)], *s.* fiel de muelle.

what [hwát]. **I.** *a. interr.* y *rel.* qué (*what train?* ¿qué tren?; *what a pity!* ¡qué lástima!); el, la, los o las . . . que (*give me what books you can,* déme Vd. los libros que pueda). **II.** *pron.* qué, qué cosa; cuál; el que, lo que, aquello que.—**w. about,** qué diremos de, qué opina Vd. de, qué le parece, qué hay de, qué hay en cuanto a, etc. (Gen. se cambia el giro.)—**w. about it?** = w. OF IT?—**w. else?** ¿qué más?—**w. for?** ¿para qué?—**w. ho!** ¡hola!—**w. if,** qué será si, y si, qué se hará o sucederá si (en interrogaciones problemáticas: *what if he should refuse?* ¿y si él rehusa?); y qué importa que, aunque (*what if he is a doctor?* ¿y qué importa que él sea médico? aunque sea médico).—**w. is w.,** (fam.) lo que hay; cuántas son cinco.—**w. of it?** ¿y qué?, ¿y eso qué importa?—**w. though,** aun cuando; ¿qué importa que?—**and w. not,** o **w. all,** y qué sé yo qué más.—**but w.,** que no (*he is not so rich but what he needs assistance,* él no es tan rico que no necesite ayuda). **III.** *adv.* cuán, cuánto; cómo (*what do you call it?* ¿cómo se llama?).—**w. with,** tanto, sea, en parte, entre (*what with hunger and what with weariness,* parte por hambre, parte por cansancio; entre el hambre y el cansancio).

whate'er [-ér], **whatever** [-évœ(r)]. **I.** *pron.* cuanto, cualquier cosa que, todo lo que; sea lo que fuere, que sea. **II.** *a.* cualquier(a), *pl.* cualesquiera.

whatnot [-nat], *s.* rinconera, estante, juguetero; (fam.) lo que Vd. guste; cualquier cosa.

whatsoever [-soévœ(r)], *pron.* y *a.* = WHATEVER.

wheal [hwil], *s.* cardenal, roncha.

wheat [hwit], *s.* (bot.) trigo.—**w. field,** trigal, sembrado de trigo.—**w.-growing,** triguero.

wheatear [-ir], *s.* (orn.) triguero.

wheaten [-n], *a.* de trigo.

wheedle [hwídl], *va.* y *vn.* halagar, engatusar, sonsacar, hacer zalamerías, (fam.) engaitar, lagotear.

wheedler [hwídlœ(r)], *s.* zalamero, engatusador, (fam.) engaitador, lagotero.

wheedling [-iŋ], *s.* engatusamiento, zalamería.

wheel [hwil]. **I.** *s.* rueda; torno; disco, roldana, rodete, rodaja; polea; (fam.) bicicleta; rueda de fuegos artificiales; (mar.) rueda del timón; (aut.) volante (de dirección); (fig.) timón; muela o rodezno del molino; noria; rueda, instrumento de tortura.—**w. and axle,** cabria.— **w. animal,** o **animalcule,** (zool.) rotífero.— **w. barometer,** barómetro de cuadrante.—**w. base,** (f. c., aut.) distancia entre ejes.—**w. boss,** cubo de rueda.—**w. chair,** silla de ruedas. —**w. horse,** caballo de varas.—**w. rope,** (mar.) guardín del timón.—**w. track,** carril. **II.** *va.* (hacer) rodar; acarrear, transportar o llevar sobre ruedas; volver, (hacer) girar, dar vueltas a; poner ruedas; labrar con rueda de alfarero. **III.** *vn.* rodar, girar, dar vueltas; (fam.) ir en bicicleta; (a veces con *about* o *around*) cambiar de rumbo o de opinión.

wheelbarrow [-bærou], *s.* carretilla.

wheeler [-œ(r)], *s.* rodador, girador; caballo de varas; el o lo que rueda o da vueltas; vapor de rueda.

wheelhouse [-haus], *s.* (mar.) timonera.

wheeling [-iŋ], *s.* transporte sobre ruedas; (fam.) ciclismo, paseo en bicicleta; estado de un ca-

mino carretero; rotación; (mil.) vuelta, conversión.

wheelman [-man], *s.* (mar.) timonero, timonel; (dep.) biciclista, ciclista.

wheelwork [-wœrk], *s.* rodaje, conjunto de ruedas de una máquina.

wheelwright [-rait], *s.* carretero, aperador, carpintero de carretas.

wheeze [hwiz]. **I.** *vn.* resollar con dificultad y ronquera o ruido silbante. **II.** *s.* resuello difícil y ronco (ll. t. **wheeziness, wheezing** [-inis, -iŋ]); (fam.) chiste viejo, cuento viejo.—**wheezy** [-i], *a.* que resuella con dificultad.

whelk [hwɛlk], *s.* (zool.) buccino, caracol de mar; (med.) pápula, roncha, pústula.

whelm [hwɛlm], *va.* sumergir, anegar; sobrepujar, subyugar; destruir.

whelp [hwɛlp]. **I.** *s.* (zool.) cachorro, perrezno; osezno (de oso); (despec.) mozalbete; (mar.) guardainfante; (mec.) diente de engranaje. **II.** *vn.* parir (la hembra de animal carnívoro).

when [hwɛn], *adv.* y *conj.* cuando, al tiempo que, mientras que; que, en que (*the day when he arrived,* el día (en) que llegó); en cuanto, así que, tan pronto como; y entonces (*I waited till noon, when I went home,* esperé hasta mediodía, y entonces me fui a casa).—**since w.?** ¿desde cuándo? ¿de cuándo acá?

whence [hwɛns], *adv.* de donde o desde donde, de que o quien; de qué causa; de ahí que, por eso es por lo que; por consiguiente.

whencesoever [-soévœ(r)], *adv.* de dondequiera, de cualquier paraje que sea.

whene'er, when(so)ever [hwɛnér, hwɛn(so)-évœ(r)], *adv.* cuando quiera que, siempre que, en cualquier tiempo que sea, todas las veces que.

where [hwér], *adv.* donde, dónde; en donde, por donde, adonde.

whereabout(s [-abaut(s]. **I.** *s.* paradero. **II.** *adv.* donde, dónde, en qué lugar.

whereas [-éz], *conj.* considerando; por cuanto, visto que, en vista de que, puesto que, siendo así que; mientras que, al paso que.

whereat [-ét], *adv.* a lo cual, con lo cual; en qué, por qué, de qué. *V.* WHEREUPON.

whereby [-bái], *adv.* por lo cual, con lo cual, por donde, de que; por medio del cual; ¿por qué? ¿cómo?

where'er [-ér], *contr.* de WHEREVER.

wherefore [-for]. **I.** *adv.* por lo cual; por qué; por eso. **II.** *s.* porqué, causa, motivo.

wherefrom [-frám], *adv.* de donde.

wherein [-in], *adv.* donde, en donde, en lo cual; en qué, (en) dónde.

whereinto [-intu], *adv.* en donde, dentro de lo que o dentro de lo cual, en lo cual.

whereof [-áv], *adv.* de lo cual, de (lo) que; cuyo; de qué, de quién.

whereon [-án], *adv.* en que; sobre lo cual, sobre que; en qué.

wheresoe'er, wheresoever [-soé(v)œ(r)], *adv.* y *conj.* dondequiera (que), en cualquier parte que, en cualquier sitio que sea.

whereto [-tú], (ant.) **whereunto** [-Λntu], *adv.* a lo que, a que; donde, adónde; a qué.

whereupon [-Λpán], *adv.* sobre lo cual, después de lo cual, con lo cual; entonces; en qué sobre qué.

wherever [-évœ(r)], *adv.* dondequiera que o por dondequiera que, adondequiera que.

wherewith [-wiθ], **wherewithal** [-wiθál]. **I.** *adv.* con que, con lo cual; ¿con qué? **II.** [hwér-wiθal], *s.* dinero necesario, (fam.) cumquibus.

wherry [hwéri]. **I.** *s.* barquilla, chalana; botiquín. **II.** *va.* y *vn.* pasar, llevar o ir en barco, chalana, etc. —**wherryman** [-man], *s.* barquero.

whet [hwét], *va.* afilar, amolar; (con **on** o **forward**) estimular, incitar; aguzar o abrir el apetito.

whet(ting [-iŋ], *s.* afiladura, aguzadura, amoladura; aperitivo.

whether [hwéðœ(r)]. **I.** *conj.* si; sea, sea que, ora, ya.—**w. or no, o w. or not,** de un modo u otro; sea que . . . o que no . . .; tanto si . . . como si no (*whether you will or not,* que quieras, que no quieras). **II.** *pron.* (ant.) cual o cuál (de los dos).

whetstone [hwétstoun], *s.* aguzadera, amoladera, afiladera, piedra de afilar, eslabón, mollejón.

whetter [hwétœ(r)], *s.* amolador. *V.* WHETSTONE.

whew [hwju], *interj.* ¡cáspita! ¡zambomba! ¡sopla!

whey [hwéj], *s.* suero.

wheyey, wheyish [-į, -įŝ], *a.* seroso.

which [hwįch]. **I.** *a. interr.* y *rel.* qué, cuál (*which book have you?* ¿qué libro tiene Vd.?; *which sister did he marry?* ¿con cuál de las hermanas se casó?); cuyo, el cual, la cual, etc. (*for which reason,* por cuya razón, por la cual razón). **II.** *pron. rel.* e *interr.* que, el cual, la cual, lo cual, los cuales, las cuales; el que, la que, lo que, etc.; qué, cuál.—**w. is w.?** ¿cuál es cuál?—**w. of them?** ¿cuál de ellos?—**w. way?** ¿por dónde? ¿por qué camino?—**all of w., all w.,** todo lo cual.—**both of w.,** que . . . ambos, que (*the book and the hat, both of which are on the table,* el libro y el sombrero, que están [ambos] sobre la mesa).

whichever, whichsoever [-(so)évœ(r)], *pron.* y *a.* cualquiera (que), *pl.* cualesquiera; el que.

whidah bird [hwįḍạ̈ bœrd], *s.* (orn.) viuda (ll. t. **widow bird**).

whiff [hwįf]. **I.** *s.* vaharada; fumada, fumarada, bocanada; soplo de viento; olor, sabor. **II.** *va.* soplar; fumar (cigarro, pipa, etc.). **III.** *va.* y *vn.* echar bocanadas o vaharadas; (fam.) oler (mal).

whiffet [-įt], *s.* pelagatos, nulidad.

whiffle [-l]. **I.** *va.* hacer bambolearse, sacudir; soplar, disipar, desvanecer; tremolar. **II.** *vn.* vacilar, cambiar de rumbo o de opinión; soplar a ráfagas ligeras; revolotear; revolverse; echar bocanadas.—**whiffler** [-lœ(r)], *s.* veleta (persona); fumador que echa bocanadas de humo.

whiffletree [-ltri], *s.* (carr.) balancín, volea. *V.* SWINGLETREE.

Whig [hwíg]. **I.** *s.* (Ingl., pol.) partido liberal; liberal; (E. U., pol.) partidario de la independencia en 1776; partido centralista, predecesor del actual partido republicano. **II.** *a.* pert. a dicho partido.

Whiggery [-œrį], **Whiggism** [-įzm], *s.* credo del partido *whig.*

while [hwájl]. **I.** *s.* rato; tiempo.—**a (little) w. ago,** hace poco rato, no hace mucho.—**all this w.,** en todo este tiempo.—**at whiles,** a ratos; de cuando en cuando.—**a w. after,** poco después, a poco.—**between whiles,** de cuando en cuando, a intervalos.—**for a w.,** por algún tiempo.—**little w.,** ratito.—**the w.,** mientras tanto, entre tanto.—**to be worth w.,** valer la pena. **II.** *conj.* mientras (que), en tanto que, al mismo tiempo que; aun cuando, si bien. **III.** *va.* (gen. con **away**) pasar, entretener (el tiempo).

whilom [-ọm]. **I.** *a.* (poét.) antiguo, que fué. **II.** *adv.* antiguamente, en otro tiempo; a veces.

whilst [-st], *conj.* = WHILE.

whim [hwím], **whims(e)y** [-zį], *s.* antojo, capricho, fantasía; (min.) malacate, cabria, trucha (ll. t. **w. gin**).

whimper [hwímpœ(r)]. **I.** *vn.* sollozar, plañir, quejarse; lloriquear, (fam.) gimotear. **II.** *va.* decir lloriqueando, etc. **III.** *s.* plañido, quejido; lloriqueo, (fam.) gimoteo.

whimsical [hwímzįḳạl], *a.* caprichoso, caprichudo.

whimsicality [-kélįtį], *s.* extravagancia, capricho, ridiculez.—**whimsically** [-į], *adv.* caprichosamente, de un modo raro.—**whimsicalness** [-nįs], *s.* rareza, singularidad, extravagancia.

whin [hwįn], *s.* (bot.) aliaga, aulaga, tojo, retama.

whine [hwajn]. **I.** *vn.* gemir, plañir, quejarse, la-

mentarse; lloriquear, (fam.) gimotear. **II.** *s.* quejido, plañido, lamento; lloriqueo, (fam.) gimoteo.

whinny [hwínį]. **I.** *vn.* relinchar. **II.** *s.* hin; relincho.

whip [hwíp]. **I.** *va.* azotar, fustigar, flagelar; zurrar, vapular, tundir; (fam.) vencer, batir, ganar a; (agr.) trillar; (coc.) batir (huevos, crema); (cost.) sobrecoser; enrollar, envolver un cabo, soga, palo, etc., con cuerdecilla; (mar.) izar con candaliza.—**to w. away,** arrebatar, llevarse.—**to w. in,** meter con violencia; reunir, hacer juntar; mantener juntos.—**to w. into shape,** poner en debida forma o en forma final.—**to w. off,** ahuyentar a latigazos; sacar, quitar de repente; despachar prontamente.—**to w. on,** poner(se) rápidamente.—**to w. out,** arrebatar; sacar prontamente.—**to w. up,** agarrar, coger de repente; arreglar o preparar al instante; (mar.) izar con la candaliza.—**whipped cream,** nata o crema batida. **II.** *vn.* (gen. con **away, off,** etc.) echar a correr, marcharse de prisa; obrar con ligereza; echar repetidas veces el anzuelo al agua.—**to w. down,** bajar corriendo o volando.—**to w. out,** zafarse, escaparse.—**to w. up,** subir corriendo. **III.** *s.* azote; látigo, zurriago, fusta, (Am.) fuete; latigazo; cochero, mayoral; vibración; movimiento circular de vaivén; aspa de molino de viento; (coc.) huevos batidos con leche, etc., (Am.) caspiroleta; (pol.) diputado encargado de velar por los intereses de su partido en el Parlamento o Congreso; exhortador, llamador; (caz.) perrero, el encargado de mantener juntos los perros; (mec.) malacate, izador.—**w. and spur,** a uña de caballo.—**w. graft, graftage,** o **grafting,** (hort.) injerto machihembrado o de lengüeta.—**w. hand,** mano (*f.*) del látigo; mano derecha; (fig.) ventaja.—**w. money,** aguijetas.

whipcord [-kọrd], *s.* mecha o tralla del látigo; (tej.) cierto paño fuerte. *V.* CATGUT.

whipgraft [-græft], *va.* (hort.) injertar a lengüeta y ranura, o por unión machihembrada.

whiplash [-læŝ], *s.* fusta del látigo.

whipper [-œ(r)], *s.* azotador; batidor.

whippersnapper [-œrsnæpœ(r)], *s.* títere, (fam.) mequetrefe, ñiquiñaque.

whippet [-įt], *s.* especie de perro lebrero; (mil.) tanque ligero (ll. t. **w. tank**).

whipping [-įŋ]. **I.** *s.* azotamiento, flagelación, vapuleo, zurriazgo. **II.** *a.* de azotar, para azotar; azotador.—**w. boy** = SCAPEGOAT.—**w. post,** poste de flagelación, al cual se ata a los reos para azotarlos.—**w. top,** trompo, peonza.

whippletree [hwípltri], *s.* (carr.) volea, balancín.

whippoorwill [hwįpurwíl], *s.* (orn.) chotacabras americana.

whipsaw [hwípso], *s.* sierra larga y angosta de bastidor para cortes longitudinales.

whipstaff [-stæf], *s.* (mar.) pinzote; puño del látigo.

whipster [-stœ(r)], *s.* mequetrefe (fam.); azotador.

whipstitch [-stįch]. **I.** *va.* (cost.) sobrecoser. **II.** *s.* sobrecostura.

whir(r [hwœr]. **I.** *va.* y *vn.* girar; zumbar; (hacer) rehilar. **II.** *s.* zumbido, aleteo.

whirl [hwœrl]. **I.** *va.* y *vn.* girar, rodar, voltejear, dar vueltas, remolin(e)ar, danzar. **II.** *s.* giro, vuelta, rotación, volteo, remolino.

whirlbone [-boụn], *s.* (anat.) rótula, choquezuela.

whirligig [-įgįg], *s.* perinola; tiovivo; (ent.) girino.

whirlpool [-pul], *s.* vórtice, vorágine, *f.,* remolino.

whirlwind [-wįnd], *s.* torbellino, remolino de viento, tifón.

whirr [hwœr], *v.* y *s.* = WHIR.

whish [hwįŝ]. **I.** *s.* zumbido de una varita que corta el aire. **II.** *vn.* = WHIZ y SWISH.

whisk [hwįsk]. **I.** *s.* escobilla, cepillo (ll. t. **w.**

broom); movimiento rápido; (coc.) batidor; manojo de heno o paja. **II.** *va.* cepillar, barrer, arrastrar; (con **away, off**) arrebatar, llevarse. **III.** *vn.* hopear, menear la cola; moverse con velocidad; marcharse de prisa.

whisker [hwískœ(r)], *s.* (gen. *pl.*) patilla; barba; bigotes del gato, de la rata, etc.

whiskered [-d], *a.* patilludo, barbudo.

whisk(e)y [hwíski], *s.* whisk(e)y, wiski, aguardiente de semillas.

whisper [hwíspœ(r)]. **I.** *va.* y *vn.* cuchichear, secretear, decir al oído; murmurar, susurrar; apuntar, soplar o sugerir. **II.** *s.* cuchicheo; susurro, murmullo.—**whisperer** [-œ(r)], *s.* cuchicheador; susurrador.—**whispering** [-iŋ]. **I.** *s.* cuchicheo; susurro o murmullo. **II.** *a.* de cuchicheo, baja (la voz); murmurante, susurrante.

whist [hwist]. **I.** *a.* (ant.) silencioso, mudo, callado. **II.** *interj.* ¡chitón! ¡punto en boca! **III.** *s.* whist (juego de naipes).

whistle [hwísl]. **I.** *va.* y *vn.* silbar; chiflar.—**to w. for**, llamar silbando; (fam.) buscar en vano. **II.** *s.* silbo, silbido, (re)chifla (sonido); silbato, pito, chifl(at)o (instrumento); silbido del viento; (fam.) gaznate.—**to pay (too) dear for one's w.**, pagar demasiado cara una chuchería.—**to wet one's w.**, (fam.) remojar el gaznate.—**whistling** [-iŋ]. **I.** *s.* silb(id)o, chiflido. **II.** *a.* silbante, silbador, silboso.—**w. buoy**, (mar.) boya de silbato.

whistler [hwíslœ(r)], *s.* silbador.

whit [hwit], *s.* ápice, jota, punto, (fam.) pizca.

white [hwájt]. **I.** *a.* blanco, (poét.) cano, albo; cano (pelo, barba); candeal (trigo, pan); puro, inmaculado; inocente; feliz, propicio; de plata; de vestiduras o hábitos blancos; (blas.) argén; (pol.) monarquista; antirrevolucionario.—**w. alkali**, (agr.) depósito blanco de sales de sodio y magnesio; (com.) carbonato sódico calcinado y refinado.—**w. ant**, (ent.) comején, hormiga blanca, termita.—**w.-breasted**, pechiblanco.—**w. bronze**, bronce claro, rico en estaño.—**w. city**, (fam.) lugar de diversiones.—**w. coal** = WATER POWER.—**w.-collar**, de o pert. a los dependientes, empleados de oficina, hombres profesionales, etc.—**w. corpuscle**, (anat.) leucocito.—**w. crop**, cereal (apl. esp. al ya maduro en la planta).—**w. damp**, gas venenoso de las minas de carbón (se cree ser óxido de carbono).—**w. elephant**, (zool. y fam.) elefante blanco; carga, fardo, posesión estorbosa o gravosa.—**w.-eyed**, ojiblanco.—**w.-faced**, pálido; cariblanco.—**w. feather**, (fig.) cobardía o señal (*f.*) de cobardía.—**w. flag**, (mil.) bandera de parlamento o de rendición.—**w. flux**, (metal.) castina blanca de carbonato potásico.—**w.-footed**, patiblanco, patialbo, maniblanco, manialbo.—**W. Friar**, (igl.) carmelita, *m.*—**w.-fronted**, cariblanco.—**w. gold**, aleación blanquizca de oro.—**w.-handed**, maniblanco; puro, inocente, de manos limpias (fig.); (zool.) = W.-FOOTED.—**w. heat**, rojo blanco, candencia, incandescencia; (fig.) fiebre, *f.*, sumo acaloramiento, exacerbación.—**w.-hot**, calentado al (rojo) blanco.—**W. House**, Casa Blanca, palacio presidencial de los E. U.—**w. iron**, fundición blanca; hierro estañado, hojalata.—**w. lead**, albayalde, cerusa.—**w. lie**, mentirilla, mentira oficiosa.—**w. lily**, azucena.—**w. list**, lista de gente favorecida, digna de confianza, etc.; (com., E. U.) lista de las transacciones de la bolsa.—**w.-livered**, pálido, débil; cobarde.—**w. magic**, magia blanca.—**w. matter**, (anat.) substancia blanca, tejido nervioso (del cerebro y medula espinal).—**w. meat**, pechuga; carne (*f.*) de ternera o cerdo.—**w. metal**, régulo como de 78% de cobre; (com., ind.) maillechort y otras aleaciones blancas semejantes.—**w. oak**, roble blanco.—**w. paper**, papel blanco; informe oficial.—**w. plague**, (med.) tisis.—**w. poplar**, álamo blanco.—**w.**

sauce, (coc.) salsa blanca.—**w. slave**, víctima de la trata blanca, mujer forzada a vivir en la prostitución.—**w. slaver**, traficante en mujeres para la prostitución.—**w. slavery**, trata de blancas.—**w. sugar**, azúcar blanco, refino o de flor.—**w. vitriol**, (quím.) vitriolo blanco, sulfato de cinc. **II.** *s.* blanco (color); pintura blanca; blanco, persona blanca; (ant.) blanco, o centro del blanco (a que se tira); clara (del huevo); (anat.) lo blanco de los ojos, esclerótica; (impr.) espacio en blanco; (pol.) monarquista; reaccionario, antirrevolucionario.—*pl.* **whites**, (med.) flores blancas, leucorrea; flor de harina. **III.** *va.* y *vn.* = WHITEN.

whitebait [-bejt], *s.* (ict.) sardineta; arenques o boquerones pequeños.

whitecap [-kæp], *s.* (mar.) cabrilla; (**W.**, E. U.) miembro de una sociedad secreta de hombres enmascarados que castigan cruelmente a los vecinos que faltan a la moral.

whitefish]-fíʃ], *s.* (ict.) pez parecido al salmón.

whiten [-n], *va.* y *vn.* blanquear(se), emblanquecer(se).—**whitener** [-œ(r)], *s.* blanqueador.

whiteness [-nis], *s.* blancura, albura, albor; palidez; pureza, candor.

whitening [-niŋ], *s.* blanqueo, emblanquecimiento; enjalbegadura; lechada.

whitewash [-waʃ]. **I.** *s.* (alb.) jalbegue, lechada, blanqueo; blanquete (afeite); informe en que se encubren las faltas de alguno.—**w. brush**, brochón. **II.** *va.* (alb.) blanquear, enlucir, encalar; encubrir (las faltas o defectos de alguno); (fam., Ingl.) poner a un deudor insolvente al abrigo de procedimientos ulteriores; (fam.) en el juego y en varios deportes, dejar al contrario zapatero o sin ganar un solo tanto.

whitewasher [-œ(r)], *s.* enjalbegador, blanqueador.

whitewashing [-iŋ], *s.* blanqueo, encaladura, jalbegue, enlucido; (fig.) cohonestación.

whitewood [-wud], *s.* (bot.) tulípero.

whither [hwíδœ(r)], *adv.* (poét.) adonde; adónde, a qué parte.—**whithersoever** [-soévœ(r)], *adv.* adondequiera, al lugar que fuere.

whiting [hwájtiŋ], *s.* blanco de España, yeso blanco, tiza; (ict.) fice, romero, especie de merluza o pescadilla.

whitish [hwájtiʃ], *a.* blanquizco, blanquecino.

whitishness [-niʃ], *s.* color blanquizco.

whitleather [hwítleδœ(r)], *s.* (ten.) baldés; (zool.) ligamento de la nuca (ll. t. **white leather**).

whitlow [hwítlou], *s.* (med.) panadizo.

whitlowwort [-wœrt], *s.* (bot.) nevadilla.

Whitsunday [hwítsʌndej], *s.* (igl.) domingo de Pentecostés.—**Whitsuntide** [-tajd], *s.* pascua de Pentecostés.

whittle [hwítl]. **I.** *va.* cortar, tallar, cercenar, mondar; aguzar, sacar punta. **II.** *vn.* cortar un pedazo de madera con cuchillo.

whiz(z) [hwiz]. **I.** *vn.* zumbar o silbar; rehilar (flecha, etc.); pasar o ir muy a prisa. **II.** *s.* sonido entre zumbido y silbido; (fam.) perito; persona muy experta en cierta materia o especialización; cosa excelente.

who [hu], *pron.*, *interr.* y *rel.* quién(es); quien(es), que, el, la, los, las que, el, la, los, las cual(es).—**as w. should say**, (ant.) como quien dice, como si dijéramos.

whoa [hwou], *interj.* ¡so! ¡cho! ¡jo!

whoever [huévœ(r)], *pron.* quienquiera que, cualquiera que; quien, el que, la que, etc.

whole [hóul]. **I.** *a.* todo; entero, completo, total; íntegro, intacto; enterizo, continuo; sano; ileso.—**w. brother, w. sister**, hermano, hermana carnal.—**w.-hearted**, sincero; enérgico, activo.—**w.-heartedly**, sinceramente, de todo corazón; con tesón.—**w. note**, (mús.) semibreve, *f.*, redonda.—**w. number**, (arit.) número entero.—**w.-wheat bread**, morena, pan íntegro, pan moreno de trigo entero.—**of w. cloth**, sin fundamento, por invención.—**the w.** (seguido de substantivo), todo el (the whole country, todo el país). **II.** s. total, totalidad, conjunto, todo.—**as a w.**, en conjunto.—**on, o upon, the w.**, en conjunto; en general.

wholeness [-njs], s. todo, integridad, totalidad; calidad de entero.

wholesale [-seįl]. **I.** a. y adv. (com.) (al) por mayor; en grande.—**w. house,** (Am.) casa mayorista. **II.** s. venta o comercio (al) por mayor.—**by w.**, (al) por mayor. **III.** va. y vn. vender (al) por mayor.

wholesaler [-œ(r)], s. comerciante (al) por mayor; (Am.) mayorista.

wholesome [-sam], a. sano, saludable, salutífero; edificante.—**wholesomely** [-lį], adv. saludablemente.—**wholesomeness** [-njs], s. calidad de saludable o sano; sanidad, salubridad.

wholly [-į], adv. totalmente, enteramente, del todo, por completo.

whom [hum], pron. (caso oblicuo de WHO) a quién(es); a quien(es), que, al que o al cual, etc.—**by w.**, por quien, por el que o el cual, etc.—**than w.** V. THAN.

whom(so)ever [-(so)éνœ(r)], pron. (caso oblicuo de WHOSOEVER) a quienquiera o cualquiera que.

whoop [hup]. **I.** s. grito; alarido; estertor de la tos ferina; chillido del buho. **II.** va. expresar, alentar, vitorear, incitar, insultar, etc., a gritos. —**to w. it up,** (fam.) jaranear, armarla. **III.** vn. huchear, chiflar, gritar, vocear; respirar ruidosa y convulsivamente, como después de un paroxismo de tos.—**whooping cough,** (med.) tos ferina, coqueluche, f.

whoopee [hwúpi], s. (fam.) gran parranda, holgorio o jolgorio, diversión bulliciosa.

whopper [hwápœ(r)], s. (fam.) mentira o bola colosal; cosa extraordinaria, non plus ultra.

whopping [-iŋ], a. (fam.) colosal, ingente.

whore [hôr]. **I.** s. prostituta, ramera, puta. **II.** va. prostituir. **III.** vn. prostituirse, hacer de prostituta; (fam.) put(añ)ear; (bib.) adorar dioses falsos.—**whoredom** [-dǫm], s. prostitución; clase (f.) de las prostitutas; (bib.) idolatría.—**whorish** [-įš], a. lascivo, putesco.

whorl [hwœrl], s. (tej.) tortera o tortero, volante (de la rueca), nuez (del huso); (bot.) verticilo; (zool.) espira del caracol marino.

whorled [-d], a. verticilado.

whortleberry [hwœrtlberį], s. (bot.) variedad de arándano, planta vacciniea.

whose [huz], pron. y a. rel. e interr. (genitivo de WHO y WHICH) cuyo, cuya, cuyos, cuyas, de quien(es) (the author whose name I recall, el autor cuyo nombre recuerdo, o de quien recuerdo el nombre); de quién(es) (whose hat is this? ¿de quién es este sombrero?).

whoso(ever) [huso(éνœ(r)], pron. V. WHOEVER.

why [hwaį]. **I.** adv. ¿por qué? ¿para qué? ¿a qué?; por qué, por el cual, etc. (vg.: the reason why, la razón por la cual; we don't know why, no sabemos por qué). A veces se cambia el giro (that is why, es por eso que). **II.** interj. ¡cómo! ¡toma! ¡qué! ¡ca! A veces se traduce por si: why, I just saw it, si lo acabo de ver; why, he must be crazy, si debe de estar loco. Se usa a menudo para dar énfasis, y no se traduce: why, certainly, por supuesto, ciertamente. **III.** s. el porqué, la causa.—**the w. and wherefore,** el porqué y la razón.

wick [wįk], s. mecha, pabilo, torcida.

wicked [wįkįd], a. malo, malvado, perverso, inicuo; travieso, picaresco.—**wickedly** [-lį], adv. inicuamente, perversamente.—**wickedness** [-njs], s. maldad, iniquidad, perversidad; impiedad.

wicker [wįkœ(r)]. **I.** a. mimbroso, tejido de mimbres. **II.** s. mimbre.—**wickerwork** [-wœrk], s. cestería, artículos de mimbre.

wicket [wįkįt], s. portillo, postigo, portezuela; meta (en el juego de criquet).

wicking [wįkįŋ], s. mechas, f. pl.; material para mechas; material fibroso trenzado o torcido.

wide [wáįd]. **I.** a. ancho, anchuroso; holgado; vasto, dilatado; extenso, amplio, espacioso; del ancho de, de ancho (five inches wide, cinco pulgadas de ancho); remoto, apartado, lejano; comprensivo; muy abierto.—**w. ga(u)ge =** BROAD GA(U)GE. **II.** adv. lejos, a gran distancia; anchamente; extensamente; descaminadamente; fuera de lugar o del caso.—**w.-awake,** muy despierto, vigilante.—**w.-mouthed,** boquiancho; abocardado o bocudo.—**w.-open,** abierto de par en par.

widely [-lį], adv. lejos, a gran distancia; extensivamente; muy, mucho; ancha u holgadamente.

widen [-n]. **I.** va. ensanchar, extender, ampliar, dilatar; abocardar. **II.** vn. ensancharse, dilatarse.

wideness [-njs], s. anchura.

widespread [-spréd], a. esparcido, difuso, diseminado; general, extenso.

widgeon [wídžǫn], s. (orn.) cerceta, zarceta.

widow [wídoų]. **I.** s. viuda.—**w.'s pension,** viudedad.—**w.'s weed,** luto de una viuda. **II.** va. dejar viuda; privar de una cosa muy útil.—**widowed** [-d], a. enviudado, -da; privado.—**widower** [-œ(r)], s. viudo.—**widowhood** [-hųd], s. viudez.

width [wįdθ], s. anchura, ancho.

wield [wįld], va. esgrimir; manejar; (fig.) empuñar (el cetro); mandar, gobernar.—**wielder** [-œ(r)], s. esgrimidor.—**wieldy** [-į], a. manejable.

wiener(wurst [wínœr(wœrst], s. especie de salchicha.

wife [wáįf], s. (pl. WIVES) esposa, mujer, señora, (fam.) costilla, media naranja, oíslo.

wifehood [-hųd], s. estado de la mujer casada.

wifeless [-lįs], a. sin mujer; soltero o viudo.

wifely [-lį], adv. como mujer casada.

wig [wįg], s. peluca; (fam.) juez, m.; regaño.

wigged [-d], a. con peluca, de peluca.

wiggle [wígl]. **I.** va. y vn. menear(se) rápidamente; culebrear. V. WRIGGLE. **II.** s. culebreo; meneo.—**to get a w. on,** (fam.) apresurarse. —**wiggler** [wíglœ(r)], s. el o lo que se menea o culebrea; (ent.) larva de mosquito.

wight [waįt], s. (ant. o despec.) tipo, sujeto.

wigmaker [wígmejkœ(r)], s. peluquero, fabricante de pelucas.

wigwag [wígwæg]. **I.** va. y vn. mover(se) rápidamente de un lado a otro; menear(se); (hacer) ondear; (mil. y mar.) comunicar(se) por señales, banderolas, etc. **II.** s. comunicación por señales.

wigwam [wígwam], s. tienda o vivienda de los indios norteamericanos; (fam., E. U.) gran edificio público para reuniones políticas, etc.

wild [wáįld]. **I.** a. silvestre (ú. de plantas, aves y animales); rusticano (ú. de plantas); salvaje; selvático, montés, montaraz; cerril, indómito, fiero, feroz, bravo, (Am.) bagual, cimarrón (ú. de animales); inculto, desierto, despoblado; turbulento, alborotado, borrascoso; atronado, alocado; descabellado o disparatado; desenfrenado, libre, desarreglado o desordenado; extravagante, estrafalario o insensato; impetuoso, violento, fogoso.—**w. ass,** (zool.) onagro.—**w. beast,** fiera.—**w. boar,** jabalí.—**w. carrot,** (bot.) dauco.—**w. fowl,** aves (f. pl.) de caza.— **w. game,** caza mayor y menor.—**w. goat,** cabra montés.—**w. goose,** (orn.) ganso silvestre.—**w.-goose chase,** (fig.) caza infructuosa; empresa quimérica.—**w. marjoram,** (bot.) orégano silvestre.—**w. mustard,** ajenabo.—**w. oat,** avena loca o silvestre.—**w. oats,** (fig.) excesos de la juventud.—**w. olive,** acebuche.—**w.-olive tree,** (bot.) oleastro, acebuche.—**w. rye,** (bot.) ballico o vallico.— **w. service,** (bot.) serbal silvestre.—**w. sow,** jabalina o puerca montés.—**w. swine,** jabalí.— **w. vine,** vid silvestre. **II.** adv. = WILDLY. **III.** s. desierto, yermo, selva o tierra virgen.

wildcat [-kæt]. **I.** *s.* (zool.) gato montés; negocio arriesgado; pozo (de petróleo) de prueba o de exploración; (fam.) locomotora sin vehículos. **II.** *a.* atolondrado, descabellado; quimérico, sin fundamento; ilícito, no autorizado.—**w. bank**, (E. U., fam.) banco que emitía billetes sin valor.—**w. strike**, (e. p.) huelga no autorizada por el sindicato obrero.

wildebeest [wíldəbist], *s.* (zool.) gnú.

wilder [wíldœ(r)]. **I.** *va.* (poét.) despistar, confundir. **II.** *vn.* (poét.) extraviarse; confundirse.

wilderness [wíldœrnəs], *s.* desierto, yermo; soledad; multitud confusa, (fam.) mezcolanza; la inmensidad del mar.

wildfire [wáildfair], *s.* fuego griego; fuego fatuo; fucilazo; (ant., med.) erisipela; sarpullido.—**like w.**, muy rápidamente, como un relámpago.

wilding [-iŋ]. **I.** *s.* planta o animal silvestre. **II.** *a.* inculto; indómito.

wildly [-li], *adv.* sin cultivo; salvajemente; desatinadamente.

wildness [-nəs], *s.* selvatiquez; tosquedad, rusticidad; rudeza, brutalidad, ferocidad; travesura; desvarío, locura.

wile [wail]. **I.** *va.* engañar, sonsacar, (fam.) engatusar, embaucar; (con **away**) pasar (el rato). **II.** *s.* ardid, *m.*, red, superchería, treta, fraude, engaño; astucia, artería.

wilful [wílful], *a.* voluntarioso, testarudo; voluntario, premeditado.—**wilfully** [-i], *adv.* voluntariosamente; voluntariamente, intencionadamente.—**wilfulness** [-nəs], *s.* terquedad, obstinación, voluntariedad; intención, premeditación.

wilily [wáilili], *adv.* astutamente, arteramente, con astucia.—**wiliness** [wáilinəs], *s.* artería, astucia.

will [wil], *va.* y *vn.* Debe considerarse bajo tres aspectos: 1. *defectivo;* 2. *auxiliar;* 3. *regular.*— 1. Como defectivo, no tiene más tiempos que el indicativo presente (WILL en todas las personas, menos la 2a. del singular, que es [ant. o poét.] WILT), el pretérito y el subjuntivo (WOULD para todas las personas menos la 2a. del singular, que es [ant. o poét.] WOULDST), y significa desear: *what wilt thou?* ¿qué deseas? *come when you will,* venga Vd. cuando guste: *would God it were daylight,* pluguiera a Dios (u ojalá) que fuese de día.—2. Como auxiliar, tiene igualmente los tres tiempos citados, que se anteponen a un infinitivo (sin la partícula *to*) para formar el futuro de indicativo o de subjuntivo del segundo verbo, con la particularidad de que en las primeras personas significa determinación, voluntad, promesa, o amenaza, por parte del que habla, mientras que en las otras personas sólo indica tiempo futuro (véase SHALL): *I will go by all means,* iré a todo trance; *I suppose he will go too,* supongo que él irá también. A menudo el infinitivo se subentiende: *he will not go, but she will (go),* él no irá, pero ella sí. A veces se usa enfáticamente en las segundas y terceras personas para denotar voluntad o determinación: *if you will go, then go,* si quieres ir, vé. Otras veces indica costumbre o persistencia: *he will sit for hours by the fire,* se pasa las horas junto a la lumbre; *he would get up early,* se levantaba, o acostumbraba o solía levantarse temprano. Ú. t. para indicar propiedades físicas: *platinum will not rust,* el platino no se enmohece. En preguntas de cortesía, se usa en el sentido de "¿me hace Vd. el favor?" etc.: *will you tell me the time?* ¿me hace Vd. el favor de decirme la hora? —3. Como verbo regular (*pret.* y *pp.* WILLED, *ger.* WILLING; *pres. ind. I* WILL, *thou* WILT, *he* WILLS; *we, you, they,* WILL), significa: querer, estar resuelto a, resolver, determinar, tener o determinar la voluntad; disponer, mandar, ordenar; (for.) legar, dejar en testamento; sugestionar, hipnotizar. Cuando va seguido de infinitivo, éste

retiene la partícula *to: I will to raise my arm but cannot,* tengo la voluntad de levantar e brazo, pero no puedo; *I will my estate to b distributed,* dispongo que mis bienes se repartan —**w. I, nill I; w. he, nill he,** quiera o no quiera. *V.* WILLY-NILLY.

will, *s.* voluntad, facultad de querer; albedrío discreción; volición; decisión; intención, resolu ción, determinación; gana, inclinación, deseo precepto, mandato; (for.) testamento.—**w.-o' the-wisp,** fuego fatuo.—**w. power,** fuerza d voluntad.—**at w.,** a gusto, a voluntad, a dis creción.—**thy w. be done,** hágase tu voluntad —**to have one's w.,** salirse uno con la suya hacer lo que quiera.—**to make one's w.,** hace testamento, disponerse.—**with a w.,** con tod el alma, con todo el corazón.

willful, *a.,* **willfully,** *adv.,* etc. = WILFUL, etc

willies [wíliz], *s. pl.* (fam.) ataque de nervios pavor, miedo pánico.

willing [wíliŋ], *a.* gustoso, dispuesto, pronto, complaciente; espontáneo, voluntario.

willingly [-li], *adv.* voluntariamente; de buena gana, con gusto.—**willingness** [-nəs], *s.* buena voluntad, buena gana, gusto, complacencia.

willow [wílou]. **I.** *s.* (bot.) sauce, salce, mimbrera bardaguera; (mec.) diablo, máquina para lim piar el algodón.—**w. oak,** (E. U.) roble con hojas parecidas a las del sauce.—**w. plot,** saucedal, salceda. **II.** *va.* limpiar (fibras).— **willowish** [-iʃ], *a.* parecido al sauce.—**willowy** [-i], *a.* mimbreño, sarguero; lleno de sauces; que se cimbrea, esbelto.

willy [wíli], *va.* limpiar (algodón, etc.).

willy-nilly [-níli]. **I.** *a.* irresoluto. **II.** *adv.* quieras o no quieras, de grado o por fuerza, de buen o mal grado, (fam.) velis nolis.

wilt [wilt]. **I.** *va.* marchitar, ajar. **II.** *vn.* agostarse, marchitarse, secarse; descaecer; (fam.) aman sarse; irse con el rabo entre piernas. **III.** *s.* (agr.) enfermedad hongosa que causa marchitamiento.

wilt, (poét.) 2a. *pers. sing. pres. ind.* de WILL.

wily [wáili], *a.* astuto, marrullero.

wimble [wímbl], *s.* barrena, taladro.

wimple [wímpl], *s.* toca, griñón.

win [win], *va.* y *vn.* (*pret.* y *pp.* WON) ganar, vencer; lograr, conquistar, obtener, alcanzar; persuadir, atraer, arrastrar tras sí; prevalecer.—**to w. one's spurs,** ganar la dignidad de caballero; llevarse la palma; hacerse una reputación.—**to w. out,** triunfar, salir bien, lograr buen éxito.— **to w. the favor of,** caer en gracia a.

wince [wins]. **I.** *vn.* retroceder, recular; respingar. **II.** *s.* respingo; devanadera de tintorero.

winch [winch], *s.* (mec.) montacargas, malacate, torno, cabria, cabrestante; manubrio, cigüeña.

wind [wind; wajnd *en poesía*]. **I.** *s.* viento, aire; resuello, aliento, respiración; flatulencia, flato, ventosidad; palabrería; presunción, vanidad.— *pl.* (mús.) instrumentos de viento; los músicos que los tocan.—**w. aft,** (mar.) viento en popa. —**w. ahead,** viento por la proa o a fil de roda. —**w.-blown,** soplado o desarreglado por el viento.—**w.-borne,** llevado por el viento (polen, etc.).—**w.-bound,** detenido por vientos contrarios.—**w. brace,** contraviento, pieza de refuerzo contra el viento.—**w. bracing,** contravientos, *pl.*—**w. ga(u)ge,** anemómetro.—**w. instrument,** (mús.) instrumento de viento.— **w. on end = w. ahead.**—**w. on the beam,** (mar.) viento derrotero.—**w. sail,** aspa (de molino); (mar.) mang(uer)a de ventilación.—**w. tunnel,** (aer.) túnel de prueba, cámara de corriente de aire para probar aviones.—**between w. and water,** a flor del agua.—**in the teeth of the w., in the w.'s eye,** de cara al viento.— **something is in the w.,** se trama algo, algo pasa, algo se prepara.—**to catch, o get, one's w.,** recobrar el aliento.—**to get w. of,** husmear, descubrir.—**to have the w. up,** (fam.) estar ansioso o alarmado; enojarse. **II.** *va.* dejar recobrar el aliento; ventear, husmear u olfatear; quitar el resuello a; airear, orear. **III.** [wạịnd], *va.* (*pret.* y *pp.* WOUND) soplar; tocar un instrumento de viento (ú. esp. del cuerno).

wind [waịnd]. **I.** *va.* (*pret.* y *pp.* WOUND [waụnd] *o* WINDED [wạịndịd]) devanar, ovillar, encanillar (hilo, etc.); enrollar, arrollar; tejer; (re)torcer; dar cuerda a; manejar, dirigir, gobernar; perseguir, seguir las vueltas o los rodeos de; (mar.) virar; levantar o izar con torno.—**to w. a ship,** virar en redondo.—**to w. off,** desdevanar; desenrollar.—**to w. out,** desenmarañar, desenredar; salir de un enredo o laberinto.—**to w. up,** concluir, acabar, finalizar; devanar, ovillar; montar, excitar; dar cuerda a (un reloj). **II.** *vn.* enrollarse, arrollarse; (a veces con **up**) enroscarse; serpear, culebrear, serpentear; rodear, ir con rodeos, insinuarse; (re)torcerse, ensortijarse, retortijarse.—**to w. about,** enrollarse.—**to w. along,** serpentear, culebrear.—**to w. up,** (fam.) terminar, acabar; ir o dar a (la cárcel, etc.).

windage [wịndịdź], *s.* (arti.) viento o huelgo de la bala.

windbag [wịndbæg], *s.* (fam.) palabrero vano.

windbreak [-breịk], *s.* árboles o estructuras que sirven de abrigo contra el viento.

winded [-ịd], *a.* falto de aliento, sin resuello.

winder [wạịndœ(r)], *s.* el o lo que devana, etc.; argadillo, devanador, devanadera, carretel, canilla; (bot.) enredadera; (arq.) escalón de abanico.

windfall [wịndfol], *s.* fruta caída del árbol; ganga, ganancia inesperada, (fam.) chiripa.

windflower [-flaụœ(r)], *s.* (bot.) anemone, *f.,* anemona.

windgall [-gol], *s.* (vet.) aventadura, vejiga, agalla.

windhover [-hʌvœ(r)], *s.* (orn.) cernícalo.

windiness [-ịnịs], *s.* ventolera; ventosidad, flatulencia, flato; hinchazón, *f.,* verbosidad, vanidad, presunción.

winding [wạịndịŋ]. **I.** *s.* vuelta, revuelta, giro, rodeo; recodo, recoveco, tortuosidad; alabeo, comba, combadura; (elec., etc.) arrollamiento; (min.) extracción del mineral; (mar.) pitazo del contramaestre.—**w. engine,** (Ingl.) cabria; (min.) máquina de extracción.—**w. frame,** (tej.) devanadera, argadillo.—**windings and turnings,** vueltas y revueltas, recovecos.—**w. up,** acto de dar cuerda (a un reloj); liquidación; conclusión; desenlace. **II.** *a.* sinuoso, tortuoso; serpentino; enrollado: en espiral; de caracol (escalera, etc.).—**w. sheet,** mortaja, sudario; ladrón de vela o bujía.

windjammer [wịnddźæmœ(r)], *s.* (mar., fam.) buque de vela; miembro de la tripulación.

windlass [wịndlạs], *s.* (mec.) argüe, árgana, árgano, torno, cabria, montacargas; (min.) malacate; (mar.) cabrestante pequeño o molinete.

windless [wịndlịs], *a.* sin viento, encalmado; sin resuello.

windmill [wịndmịl], *s.* molino de viento; (aer.) turbina de aire.

window [wịndoụ], *s.* ventana; ventanilla (de coche, etc.); vidriera, escaparate (de tienda).—**w. blind,** persiana, celosía (en el interior); postigo, contraventana, puertaventana (en el exterior).—**w. case,** o **frame,** cuadro, bastidor o marco de ventana.—**w. curtain** = **w.** SHADE.—**w. dresser,** (com.) el que arregla los escaparates.—**w. fastener,** pasador.—**w. glass,** cristal o vidrio para ventanas.—**w. post,** jamba de ventana.—**w. sash,** bastidor o marco de vidriera.—**w. seat,** asiento o banco interior al pie de una ventana.—**w. shade,** transparente, visillo, (gal.) estor.—**w. shutter** = **w.** BLIND.—**w. sill,** antepecho o mesilla de ventana.—**w. stud,** montante o jamba de ventana.

windowed [-d], *a.* fenestrado.

windowpane [-peịn], *s.* cristal o vidrio de ventana.

windpipe [wịndpaịp], *s.* (anat.) tráquea; gaznate.

windrow [wịndroụ]. **I.** *s.* (agr.) hilera de heno amontonado con el rastrillo; hilera doble de maíz para secar; hilera de árboles, yerba, etc., formada por el viento. **II.** *va.* arrollar (heno) en una hilera, rastrillar.

windscreen [wịndskrin], **windshield** [-śild], *s.* (aut.) parabrisa(s), *m.,* guardabrisa, *m.*—**w. wiper,** limpiavidrios del parabrisa.

windstorm [-storm], *s.* ventarrón, vendaval, huracán.

wind-up [wạịnd ʌp], *s.* conclusión, final, fin, desenlace.

windward [wịndwạrd]. **I.** *a.* (mar.) de barlovento.—**W. Islands,** Islas de Barlovento.—**w. tide,** marea contraria al viento. **II.** *s.* barlovento.—**to lie to w.,** barloventear. **III.** *adv.* a barlovento.

windy [wịndị], *a.* ventoso; ventiscoso; borrascoso; expuesto al viento; vano, hinchado, pomposo; flatulento.—**it is w.,** hace viento.

wine [waịn]. **I.** *s.* vino; licor; zumo fermentado de algunas frutas; color de vino, rojo oscuro; embriaguez; (Ingl.) holgorio o parranda en que se bebe.—**w. bag** = WINESKIN.—**w. bottle,** botella para vino.—**w. cellar,** bodega, cueva.—**w. cooler,** garapiñera.—**w. decanter,** garrafa para vino.—**w. grower,** vinariego, viñero, viticultor.—**w. industry,** industria vinícola.—**w. merchant,** vinatero.—**w. palm,** (bot.) palma de vino, de que se hace vino.—**w. press,** lagar, trujal, prensa de lagar.—**w. shop,** vinatería, taberna.—**w. vault,** candiotera, cueva, bodega.—**to be in w.,** estar ebrio. **II.** *va.* convidar u obsequiar con vino; proveer de vino. **III.** *vn.* beber vino.

winebibber [-bịbœ(r)], *s.* borrachín, bebedor.—**winebibbing** [-bịbịŋ]. **I.** *s.* beber en demasía, ser borracho. **II.** *a.* borracho, bebedor.

wineglass [-glæs], *s.* copa para vino.

winery [-œrị], *s.* fábrica vinícola; bodega de vino, candiotera.

winesap [-sæp], *s.* (E. U., bot.) manzana roja de invierno.

wineskin [-skịn], *s.* odre, boto, cuero, pellejo.

winetaster [-teịstœ(r)], *s.* catavinos, mojón.

wing [wịŋ]. **I.** *s.* ala; vuelo; (arq.) ala; (mil.) ala, flanco; costado, lado; apéndice; aspa o vela (de molino de viento); (teat.) bastidor; bambalina; (bot.) apéndice foliáceo; (aer.) ala; (pol.) facción (dentro de un partido).—**w. case,** **w. cover,** (ent.) élitro.—**w. chair,** sillón de respaldo alado.—**w. collar,** cuello doblado, o de pajarita.—**w. flap,** (aer.) alerón engoznado.—**w.-footed,** (poét.) alípede, rápido.—**w. loading,** (aer.) intensidad de la carga, carga por unidad de superficie de sustentación.—**w. nut,** (mec.) tuerca de orejas.—**w. rail,** (f. c.) guardarriel.—**w. resistance,** (aer.) resistencia activa.—**w. screw** = **w.** NUT.—**w.-shaped,** aliforme.—**w. transom,** (mar.) yugo principal.—**w. wall,** (ing.) ala (de alcantarilla, etc.).—**on,** o **upon, the w.,** al vuelo; con un pie en el estribo; en marcha.—**to take w.,** alzar el vuelo, irse volando.—**under one's w.,** bajo la protección de uno. **II.** *va.* llevar, transportar sobre las alas; ejecutar por medio de las alas; hender (volando); dar o prestar alas a, impeler; añadir una ala (a un edificio, etc.); herir en el ala; dañar, incapacitar, inhabilitar. **III.** *vn.* alear; volar.

winged [-d *o* -ịd], *a.* alado, alífero, (poét.) alígero; que vuela; elevado.—**w. ant,** (ent.) aluda, aladica.

wingless [-lịs], *a.* sin alas; áptero.

wingspread [-spred], *s.* (aer., orn.) extensión máxima de las alas.

wink [wịŋk]. **I.** *vn.* pestañear, parpadear; guiñar (esp. a otra persona); centellear, dar luz trémula; (con **at**) tolerar, disimular; hacer la vista gorda. **II.** *s.* pestañeo, parpadeo; un abrir y cerrar de ojos; guiño, guiñada; siestecita.—**to**

take forty winks, (fam.) descabezar el sueño.—**not to sleep a w.,** no pegar o cerrar los ojos.

winker [-œ(r)], *s.* guiñador; anteojera (de caballo); músculo que produce el pestañeo; (fam.) pestaña u ojo.

winkle [-l], *s.* (zool.) caracol marino.

winner [wínœ(r)], *s.* ganador, vencedor.

winning [wíniŋ]. **I.** *s.* triunfo; (gen. *pl.*) ganancia, lucro. **II.** *a.* victorioso, triunfante, ganador, vencedor; ganancioso; que gana; afortunado; atractivo, encantador; persuasivo.—**w. back,** desquite.—**w. manners,** don de gente.—**w. post,** poste o pilar que marca el fin de una carrera.—**w. side,** partido triunfante.

winnow [wínou]. **I.** *va.* (agr.) aventar, ventilar, bieldar, despajar; (fig.) zarandar, cerner, analizar, entresacar, escoger; (poét.) batir el aire (como con alas); soplar. **II.** *vn.* aventar o ventilar el grano.

winnower [-œ(r)], *s.* aventador.

winnowing [-iŋ], *s.* aventamiento, despajadura; zarandeo.—**w. fork,** bieldo.—**w. machine,** aventadora, aventador mecánico.—**winnowings** [-iŋz], *s. pl.* tamo.

winrace [wínreis], *s.* velocidad máxima de trote de un caballo victorioso.

winsome [wínsəm], *a.* atractivo, simpático.

winter [wíntœ(r)]. **I.** *s.* invierno.—**w.-beaten,** invernizo.—**W.'s bark,** (bot.) magnolia magallánica. **II.** *a.* hibernal, hiemal, invernal, de invierno.—**w. cherry,** (bot.) alquequenje.—**w. clothes,** ropa de invierno.—**w. pasture,** invernadero.—**w. quarters,** invernadero; (mil.) cuarteles de invierno.—**w. resort,** lugar invernal.—**w. season,** invierno, invernada.—**w. solstice,** solsticio de invierno.—**w. wheat,** (bot.) trigo otoñal, o de invierno. **III.** *va.* hacer invernar, guardar durante el invierno. **IV.** *vn.* invernar, pasar el invierno.

winterberry [-beri], *s.* (bot.) apalachina; especie de acebo o agrifolio norteamericano, planta ilínica.

wintergreen [-grin], *s.* (bot.) pirola; gaulteria.

wintering [-iŋ], *s.* invernada.

winterish [-iš], *a.* invernizo.

winterless [-lis], *a.* sin invierno.

wintertide, wintertime [-taid, -taim], *s.* (tiempo o estación de) invierno.

wint(e)ry [wínt(œ)ri], *a.* invernal, invernizo; como de invierno.

wintriness [wíntrinis], *s.* invernada.

winy [wáiŋi], *a.* vinoso; avinado.

wipe [wáip]. **I.** *va.* limpiar frotando (con un trapo, etc.); enjugar, secar; frotar, restregar; cepillar; aplicar soldadura a; soldar.—**to w. away,** secar (frotando).—**to w. off,** borrar, cancelar; limpiar, lavar.—**to w. off the slate,** o **to w. the slate clean,** cancelar la cuenta; cancelar los planes o el programa anteriores para empezar de nuevo; mudar la hoja, cambiar de plan o de intento.—**to w. one's boots on,** (fam.) abusar de, tratar de una manera ofensiva.—**to w. out,** borrar, cancelar, testar, suprimir; destruir, extirpar, aniquilar, exterminar; agotar. **II.** *s.* limpión, *m.,* limpiadura; (fam.) revés, manotada.

wiper [-œ(r)], *s.* persona que enjuga o restrega; limpiador, trapo, paño, toalla, (cualquier objeto que sirve para limpiar frotando); (mec.) leva, álabe; (aut.) limpiavidrios del guardabrisa.

wire [wáir]. **I.** *s.* alambre; hilo o cuerda metálicos; cuerda de piano o arpa; telégrafo eléctrico, sistema telegráfico; (fam.) telegrama, *m.,* parte; hilo (del retículo de un teodolito, etc.); (gen. *pl.*) (fam.) medios subrepticios de controlar ciertos actos, cargos, etc.—**w. brush,** cepillo metálico.—**w. cloth,** tela o gasa de alambre.—**w. coil,** carrete.—**w. cover, netting, screen,** etc., alambrera, alambrado.—**w. edge,** filván (de una navaja, etc.).—**w. entanglement,** (mil.) alambrada, defensa de alambres trabados.—**w.**

fence, alambrado, cerca de alambre.—**w. ga(u)ge,** calibrador para alambre; escala de calibres o diámetros de alambre.—**w. gauze,** gasa de alambre, tela metálica.—**w. glass,** vidrio armado con tela de alambre, la cual va encajada en el vidrio para reforzarlo e impedir que los fragmentos se caigan si el vidrio se rompe.—**w.-haired terrier,** foxterrier de pelo áspero.—**w. nail,** alfiler o punta de París.—**w. plate,** hilera de estirar alambre.—**w. rod,** varilla para alambre.—**w. rope,** cable de alambres.—**w. screening,** tela metálica.—**w. stretcher,** estirador de alambre.—**w. tapper,** quien forma subrepticiamente conexión con una línea telefónica o telegráfica para interceptar mensajes u obtener informes.—**w. tapping,** interceptación de mensajes telefónicos o telegráficos.—**w. wheel,** pulidor o limpiador giratorio de alambre. **II.** *va.* proveer de alambre; atar o liar con hilo metálico; (elec.) instalar alambres o conductores eléctricos en, hacer una canalización en; (caz.) coger con lazo de alambre. **III.** *va.* y *vn.* (com.) telegrafiar.

wiredraw [-dro], *va.* (*pret.* WIREDREW; *pp.* -DRAWN) estirar (metal); alargar, prolongar; sutilizar; desfigurar; (m. v.) estrangular (el vapor).—**wiredrawer** [-œ(r)], *s.* hilera; estirador de metales.

wireless [-lis]. **I.** *s.* radiocomunicación; telégrafo o teléfono sin hilos. **II.** *va.* y *vn.* comunicar por radiotelegrafía o radiotelefonía (gen. lo primero). **III.** *a.* inalámbrico, sin hilos (telégrafo, teléfono); de o por radiocomunicación.—**w. compass** = RADIOCOMPASS.—**w. telegraphy,** radiotelegrafía.—**w. telephony,** radiotelefonía.

wireman [-mən], **wirer** [-œ(r)], *s.* alambrero; (elec.) montador o tendedor de alambres de distribución; (caz.) armador de trampas de alambre.

wirephoto [-fóutou], *s.* teléfoto. *V.* TELEPHOTE.

wirepuller [-pulœ(r)], *s.* titiritero; (fam.) intrigante político.—**wirepulling** [-iŋ], *s.* (fam.) maquinaciones secretas; intrigas políticas.

wirework [-wœrk], *s.* enrejado, alambrado.

wireworm [-wœrm], *s.* (ent.) larva de escarabajo.

wiring [-iŋ], *s.* acción del verbo TO WIRE; (elec.) alambrado (sistema (*m.*) o distribución); instalación de alambres o cables de distribución; canalización (eléctrica); (cir.) costura con alambre; (aer.) alambrado.

wiry [-i], *a.* de alambre; alambrino, semejante a un alambre; tieso, tenso; flaco pero fuerte y nervioso.—**w.-coated, w.-haired,** de pelo áspero.

wisdom [wízdəm], *s.* sabiduría; sapiencia; discernimiento, juicio, buen criterio; cordura, prudencia, sentido común; buena conducta; erudición; máxima, apotegma, *m.*—**w. tooth,** muela cordal o del juicio.

wise [wáiz]. **I.** *a.* sabio, docto, ilustrado, erudito; cuerdo, juicioso, prudente, sensato, discreto, sesudo; atinado.—**w. move,** paso acertado.—**the w. men,** los tres reyes magos; los siete sabios de Grecia.—**to put one w.,** (fam.) advertir a uno lo que hay o lo que pasa, ponerlo al tanto. **II.** *s.* modo, manera.—**in any w.,** de cualquier modo.—**in no w.,** de ningún modo, absolutamente.

wiseacre [-eikœ(r)], *s.* sabihondo (fam.), el que presume de sabio.

wisecrack [-kræk]. **I.** *s.* (fam.) agudeza, chiste, dicho u observación agudos. **II.** *vn.* (fam.) chancear(se), decir agudezas.

wisecracker [-œ(r)], *s.* (fam.) decidor de agudezas.

wisely [-li], *adv.* sabiamente; cuerdamente.

wish [wiš]. **I.** *va.* y *vn.* (a menudo con **for**) desear, querer, apetecer, ansiar, anhelar; hacer votos por; pedir. **II.** *s.* deseo, anhelo; cosa deseada; voto; súplica.—**to make a w.,** formar un deseo, pensar algo que se quiere.

wishbone [-boṇn], s. espoleta de la pechuga de las aves.

wisher [-œ(r)], s. persona que desea, deseador.

wishful [-fụl], a. deseoso, ganoso; ansioso, anheloso, ávido.—**w. thinking**, creencia deseada, o movida por el deseo; creer en lo que se desea; racionalización de la esperanza.—**wishfully** [-i], adv. ansiosamente, ardientemente, con anhelo.

wishy-washy [wíṣi waṣi], a. (fam.) débil, ligero, diluído, aguado, flojo.

wisp [wịsp]. I. va. cepillar; hacer un manojo. II. s. manojito, mechón, puñado; trozo; bandada de pájaros; escobilla; fuego fatuo.

wist [wịst], (ant.) pret. y pp. de TO WIT.

wistaria, wisteria [wịstériạ, wịstíriạ], s. (bot.) vistaria.

wistful [wístfụl], a. anhelante, ansioso, ávido; pensativo.—**wistfully** [-i], adv. ansiosamente, ávidamente; pensativamente.—**wistfulness** [-nịs], s. avidez, anhelo; estado pensativo.

wit [wịt]. I. va. y vn. (pret. y pp. WIST) (ant.) saber, tener noticia.—**to w.**, a saber, o sea. II. s. rasgo de ingenio, agudeza, sal, f.; ingenio, decidor (persona); talento, ingenio; imaginación, inventiva.—pl. juicio, sentido, razón, f.; industria.—**the five wits**, los cinco sentidos.—**to be at one's w.'s end**, no saber uno qué hacer o decir, (fam.) perder la chaveta.—**to be out of one's wits**, estar fuera de juicio o fuera de sí; no saber uno lo que hace.—**to live by one's wits**, vivir de gorra, ser caballero de industria.

witch [wịch]. I. s. bruja, hechicera; (fam.) vejarrona; (fam.) mujer encantadora; niña traviesa.—**w. doctor**, exorcista, hechizador.—**w. hazel**, (bot.) carpe; hamamelis; (med.) hamamelina (loción).—**witches' Sabbath**, aquelarre. II. va. encantar, maleficiar, hechizar, embrujar.

witchcraft, witchery [-kræft, -œri], s. brujería, hechicería, sortilegio, aojadura; fascinación.

witch-elm [-ɛlm], s. (bot.) = WYCH-ELM.

witching [-iŋ], a. encantador, hechicero.

with [wịð], prep. con; en compañía de; de (to fill with, llenar de; to part with, separarse de; smitten with, enamorado de; a man with good sense, un hombre de juicio; the lady with the camellias, la dama de las camelias; the boy with a straw hat, el niño del sombrero de paja). A veces queda mejor traducida por: contra, en, entre, a, hacia, con respecto a, para con, concerniente (with all speed, a toda prisa; to struggle with need, luchar contra la necesidad; deal not harshly with me, no sea Vd. duro para conmigo; this happens with students, esto sucede entre estudiantes; identical with, idéntico a; that country abounds with oil, ese país abunda en petróleo).

withal [-ól], adv. además, a más de esto; también; por otra parte; con todo; al mismo tiempo.

withdraw [wịðdró]. I. va. (pret. WITHDREW; pp. WITHDRAWN) retirar; apartar, separar, quitar, sacar, privar de; distraer, remover; desdecirse de, retractar o retractarse de. II. vn. retirarse, apartarse, separarse; irse, salir.

withdrawal [-ạl], s. retiro, retirada; recogida.

withdrawing room [-iŋ rum], s. retrete, gabinete. V. DRAWING ROOM.

withe [wại ð]. I. s. mimbre, junco; vencejo; (mec.) mango flexible. II. va. atar con juncos o mimbres.

wither [wịðœ(r)]. I. va. marchitar; ajar, deslucir, poner mustio; debilitar; avergonzar, sonrojar. II. vn. (a veces con away) marchitarse, secarse.

witherband [-bænd], s. (tal.) pieza que sujeta los fustes de la silla de montar.

withered [-d], a. mustio, marchito, seco, lacio, maciento.—**witheredness** [-nịs], s. marchitez, marchitamiento, sequedad.

withers [wíðœrz], s. pl. cruz o crucera del caballo, etc.—**wither-wrung**, herido en la cruz.

withhold [wịθhóụld]. I. va. (pret. y pp. WITHHELD) detener, impedir; retener; apartar, con-

tener; negar, rehusar. II. vn. reprimirse, contenerse.

within [wịðín]. I. prep. dentro de, en lo interior de; dentro de, en el espacio de; a la distancia de; al alcance de; a; a poco de; casi a, cerca de.—**w. an inch**, pulgada más o menos; (fig.) a dos dedos (de).—**w. bounds**, a raya.—**w. a short distance**, a poca distancia.—**w. four months**, dentro de cuatro meses.—**w. hearing**, al alcance de la voz.—**he was w. a little of being killed**, por poco lo matan. II. adv. dentro, adentro, en el interior; dentro de uno, en el corazón o en la mente; en casa, en la habitación.—**from w.**, de adentro.

without [wịðáụt]. I. prep. sin; falto de; fuera de, más allá de.—**w. prejudice**, (for.) sin prejuicio o menoscabo. II. adv. fuera, afuera, por fuera, hacia fuera, de la parte de afuera; exteriormente, en lo exterior. III. conj. (fam. o dial.) si no, a menos que.

withstand [wịθstǽnd], va. (pret. y pp. WITHSTOOD) resistir, contrarrestar; sufrir, soportar.

withy [wíði]. I. a. de mimbre; delgado; flexible. II. s. mimbre.

witless [wítlịs], a. necio, tonto; ignorante (de).

witling [wítliŋ], s. presumido de ingenioso; pelele.

witness [wítnịs]. I. s. testigo; espectador; testimonio, atestación, prueba; (for.) testigo, declarante.—**in w. whereof**, en fe de lo cual.—**to be a w. of**, ser testigo de, presenciar.—**to take the w. stand**, (for.) subir al estrado o a la tribuna de testigos. II. va. presenciar, ver, ser espectador de o concurrir a; (for.) atestar, atestiguar, testificar, declarar (como testigo); dar fe; mostrar.—**witnessed before me**, atestado ante mí. III. vn. dar testimonio; servir de testigo.

witted [wítịd], a. ingenioso.

witticism [wítịsịzm], s. rasgo de ingenio, dicho agudo, chiste, gracia, donaire, aticismo.

wittily [wítịli], adv. ingeniosamente, agudamente, donosamente.

wittiness [-nịs], s. donosura, ingenio, sal, f., gracia.

wittingly [wítịŋli], adv. a sabiendas, ex profeso, adrede, de propósito.

witty [wíti], a. satírico, sarcástico; ingenioso, agudo; chistoso, gracioso, ocurrente.—**w. saying**, chiste, agudeza, ocurrencia.

wive [wại v]. I. va. tomar por esposa, casarse con; casar a o con. II. vn. casarse, tomar esposa.

wives [-z], s. pl. de WIFE.

wizard [wízạrd]. I. a. hechicero, mágico. II. s. brujo, hechicero; mago; adivino.

wizardry [-ri], s. hechicería, magia.

wizen [wízṇ], va. y vn. marchitar(se), secar(se).—**wizen(ed** [-(d], a. marchito, mustio.

woad [wóụd], s. (bot., tint.) (hierba) pastel, glasto.

woaded [-id], a. teñido con glasto.

wobble [wábl]. I. vn. balancear(se), tambalear(se), bambolear(se); (fam.) vacilar. II. va. hacer tambalear(se) o vacilar. III. s. bamboleo, tambaleo.

wobbly [wáblị], a. que se bambolea; instable.

wo(e [wóụ]. I. s. dolor, pena, angustia, pesar, calamidad, infortunio, miseria. II. interj. **w. is me!** ¡desgraciado de mí! ¡pobre de mí!—**w. to!** ¡guay de! ¡ay de! ¡desdichado el que!

wo(e)begone [-bịgon], a. angustiado, desdichado, abrumado de pesares.

wo(e)ful [-fụl], a. calamitoso, funesto, desastroso; triste, afligido, angustiado; lastimero, doloroso; ruin, vituperable.—**wo(e)fully** [-i], adv. funestamente, desastrosamente; tristemente; ruinemente.

wold [wóụld], s. campiña undulada; (bot.) gualda.

wolf [wụlf]. I. s. (pl. WOLVES) (zool.) lobo; persona cruel o rapaz; (fam.) libertino o faldero; (ent.) larva destructora de varios escarabajos y mariposas nocturnas; (med.) = LUPUS.—**w. cub**, lobezno, lobato.—**w. dog**, perro lobero o de cazar lobos; híbrido de perro y lobo.—**w. fish**, (ict.) cierto pez muy feroz.—**w.'s milk**, (bot.)

titímalo, lechetrezna.—**to cry w.**, gritar "¡el lobo!", dar falsa alarma.—**to have a w. by the ears,** ver las orejas al lobo.—**to have a w. in the stomach,** tener apetito voraz.—**to keep the w. from the door,** ponerse a cubierto del hambre. **II.** *va.* (fam.) engullir.

wolfhound [-haund], *s.* mastín, perro lobero ruso.

wolfish [-iš], *a.* lobero, lobuno, lupino.

wolfram [wúlfram], *s.* (quím.) volframio, tungsteno.—**wolframite** [-(ait], *s.* (min.) volfram(ita).

wolfsbane [wúlfsbejn], *s.* (bot.) acónito, napelo.

wolverene, wolverine [wulvęrín], *s.* (zool.) especie de glotón americano; (**W.,** E. U.) habitante del Estado de Míchigan.

wolves [wulvz], *s. pl.* de WOLF.

woman [wúman], *s.* (*pl.* **women** [wímin]) mujer; (fam.) hembra; las mujeres; criada, sirvienta. Ú. adjetivamente para denotar sexo femenino, v. gr.: *woman writer,* escritora; *woman voter,* electora; *woman witness,* testigo mujer, o mujer testigo.—**w. hater,** misógino, aborrecedor de las mujeres.—**w. of the street,** prostituta, mujer de mala vida.—**w. of the town,** dama cortesana.—**w. of the world,** mujer de mundo.—**w. servant** = SERVANT GIRL.—**w. suffragist,** sufragista.

womanhood [-hud], *s.* estado o condición de mujer; sexo femenino.

womanish [-iš], *a.* mujeril, femenil, femenino, afeminado.

womankind [-kajnd], *s.* la mujer (en general), las mujeres; el sexo femenino.

womanliness [-linis], *s.* naturaleza o carácter femenil.

womanly, womanlike [-li, -lajk]. **I.** *a.* mujeril; de mujer, femenil, femenino. **II.** *adv.* mujerilmente; femeninamente.

womb [wum], *s.* (anat.) útero, matriz; (fig.) madre, *f.*; caverna; seno, entrañas, *f. pl.*

women [wímin], *s. pl.* de WOMAN.

womenfolk [-fouk], *s.* las mujeres.

won [wAn], *pret.* y *pp.* de TO WIN.

wonder [wándœ(r)]. **I.** *va.* desear saber; sorprenderse, maravillarse de; preguntarse (con una cláusula como complemento). Ú. a menudo para indicar incertidumbre o curiosidad, y puede traducirse por el futuro del verbo que le sigue: *I wonder if it will rain tomorrow,* ¿si lloverá mañana? *I wonder what he wants,* ¿qué querrá? **II.** *vn.* admirarse, asombrarse, pasmarse.—**to w. at,** extrañar, maravillarse de. **III.** *s.* admiración, pasmo; maravilla, prodigio, portento, milagro; enigma, *m.*, misterio, cosa extraña o inexplicable.—**w.-worker,** fabricador de prodigios o milagros.—**no w.,** no es extraño, no es mucho.—**the seven wonders of the world,** las siete maravillas del mundo.

wonderer [-œ(r)], *s.* el que se admira de algo o lo extraña; el que se pregunta, o desea saber algo.

wonderful [-ful], *a.* maravilloso, portentoso, pasmoso, asombroso; admirable, excelente.

wonderfully [-i], *adv.* maravillosamente, prodigiosamente, a las mil maravillas; admirablemente, sumamente.

wonderland [-lænd], *s.* mundo fantástico; reino de las hadas o de los duendes.

wonderment [-ment], *s.* admiración, asombro, extrañeza, maravilla.

wonderstricken [-strikn], **wonderstruck** [-strAk], *a.* atónito, pasmado, asombrado.

wondrous [wándrAs], *a.* (poét.) extraño, maravilloso, pasmoso, asombroso.—**wondrously** [-li], *adv.* pasmosamente, maravillosamente.

wont [wAnt]. **I.** *a.* acostumbrado, sólito.—**to be w.,** soler, tener la costumbre. **II.** *s.* uso, costumbre, hábito. **III.** *vn.* soler, acostumbrar. **IV.** *va.* habituar, acostumbrar.

won't [wount], *contr.* de **will not.**

wonted [wántid], *a.* acostumbrado, usual, habitual, ordinario.

woo [wu], *va.* y *vn.* cortejar, galantear, enamorar pretender a una mujer; solicitar, importunar buscar, esforzarse por obtener (fama, etc.).

wood [wud]. **I.** *va.* proveer de leña; cubrir cor bosques; convertir en selva. **II.** *vn.* proveerse de leña. **III.** *s.* madera; leña; bosque, selva, monte (en este sentido ú. gen. en *pl.,* **woods**); madero palo. **IV.** *a.* de o para madera; de o para almacenar, transportar o labrar madera; de monte que vive o crece en la selva.—**w. acid,** vinagre de madera, ácido piroleñoso, ácido acético.—**w. alcohol,** alcohol metílico.—**w. ant,** (ent.) hormiga leonada.—**w.-block pavement,** pavimento de bloques de madera.—**w. borer,** xilófago, insecto u otro animal horadador (de los árboles y la madera); broma (molusco horadador).—**w. carver,** tallador en madera.—**w. carving,** talla en madera.—**w. cement,** cola de alcohol (aglutinante disuelto en alcohol) para madera.—**w. dealer,** leñero.—**w. engraver,** grabador en madera.—**w. engraving,** grabado en madera.—**w. fiber,** fibra de la madera; célula de los tejidos vegetales; madera molida.—**w. grouse,** (orn.) urogallo.—**w. ibis,** (orn.) tántalo, ave zancuda americana.—**w. lark,** (orn.) alondra, calandria.—**w. louse,** (ent.) porqueta, cochinilla, milpiés.—**w. nymph,** orea, napea. —**w. pigeon,** (orn.) paloma torcaz.—**w. pulp,** pulpa de madera (para papel).—**w. rasp,** escofina.—**w. screw,** tirafondo, tornillo de metal para madera (evítese el disparate "tornillo de madera").—**w. sorrel,** (bot.) aleluya, acederilla.—**w. thrush,** (orn.) tordo pardo.—**w. tick,** (ent.) carcoma.—**w. turner,** torneador. —**w. turning,** arte de tornear.—**w. vinegar** = w. ACID.—**w. yard,** depósito de maderas maderería.—**to be out of the wood**(s), haber salido de la dificultad, estar a salvo.

woodbin [-bin], **woodbox** [-baks], *s.* leñera.

woodbine [-bajn], *s.* (bot.) madreselva; especie de enredadera norteamericana.

woodchopper [-chapœ(r)], *s.* leñador.

woodchuck [-chAk], *s.* (zool.) marmota.

woodcock [-kak], *s.* (orn.) chocha, pitorra, chochaperdiz o becada.

woodcraft [-kræft], *s.* conocimientos relativos a los bosques o a los trabajos en madera.

woodcut [-kAt], *s.* grabado en madera.

woodcutter [-œ(r)], *s.* leñador, hachero; grabador en madera.—**woodcutting** [-iŋ], *s.* tala; corte de leña.

wooded [-id], *a.* provisto de madera; arbolado, plantado de árboles; boscoso, cubierto de bosques.

wooden [-n], *a.* de palo o madera; grosero, rudo; torpe, estúpido.—**w. bowl,** dornillo, hortera, cuenca.—**w.-headed,** (fam.) zote, zopenco, bolo.—**w. horse,** potro de madera (para gimnasia).—**w. leg,** pierna o pata de palo.—**w. shoes,** zuecos, chanclos, almadreñas.—**w. spoon,** cuchara de palo.—**w. wedding,** quinto aniversario.

woodenhead [-hed], *s.* (fam.) zopenco, imbécil.

woodenware [-wer], *s.* vasijas y utensilios de madera.

woodhouse [-haus], *s.* leñera.

woodiness [-inis], *s.* calidad de leñoso.

woodland [-lænd]. **I.** *s.* arbolado, monte, bosque, selva. **II.** *a.* de bosque, selvático.

woodless [-lis], *a.* sin bosques.

woodman [-man], *s.* leñador, hachero; (Ingl.) guardabosque; habitante de los bosques.

woodpecker [-pekœ(r)], *s.* (orn.) pico, picaposte, picamaderos, pájaro carpintero.

woodpile [-pajl], *s.* pila de leña, tinada; hoguera.

woodruff [-rAf], *s.* (bot.) aspérula, asperilla.

woodshed [-šed], *s.* leñera.

woodsman [-zman], *s.* leñador, hachero; cazador o habitante del bosque. *V.* WOODWORKER.

woodwork [-wœrk], *s.* enmaderamiento, maderaje, maderamen; obra de carpintería; ebanistería.

woodworker [-œ(r)], *s.* carpintero, ebanista; artífice que labra madera.

woodsy [-zi], *a.* selvático.

woody [-i], *a.* leñoso; de madera; arbolado, selvoso.—**w. tissue**, tejido leñoso.

wooer [wúœ(r)], *s.* cortejador, pretendiente.

woof [wuf], *s.* (tej.) trama; textura. *V.* WEFT.

wooing [wúiŋ], *s.* galanteo.

wool [wul]. **I.** *s.* lana, vellón; pasa (cabello de los negros). **II.** *a.* lanar, de lana; para lana; relativo o perteneciente a la lana.—**w. ball**, pelotón de lana.—**w.-bearing**, lanar.—**w. card**, carda.—**w. comber**, o **dresser**, cardador, pelaire.—**w. combing**, cardadura; pelairía.—**w. fat**, **w. grease**, lanolina.—**w. gatherer**, vellonero.—**w. stapler**, lanero, comerciante en lanas. *V.* WOOLSORTER.

woold [wuld], *va.* (mar.) trincar, reatar, encarcelar.

wooled [wuld], *a.* que tiene lana, con lana.

wool(l)en [wuljn]. **I.** *a.* de lana; lanoso, lanudo; lanero.—**w. draper**, (Ingl.), o **merchant**, pañero, comerciante en paños.—**w. dyer**, tintorero de lana.—**w. yarn**, estambre, *mf.* **II.** *s.* paño o tejido de lana.—*pl.* ropa o prendas de lana, lanificio.

woolfell [wúlfɛl], *s.* piel (*f.*) con su lana.

woolgathering [-gæðœriŋ]. **I.** *s.* acción de recoger los vellones; (fig.) distracción, ensimismamiento. **II.** *a.* distraído, ensimismado, visionario.

woolgrower [-grouœ(r)], *s.* criador de ganado lanar.

woolgrowing [-iŋ], *s.* cría de ganado lanar.

woolliness [-iniš], *s.* calidad de lanudo; lanosidad, vellosidad; pelaje.

wool(l)y [-i], *a.* lanudo, lanoso; lanar, lanífero; de lana; crespo, (Am.) pasudo (cabello); (b. a.) falto de detalles, vago y borroso; aborregado (cielo); (bot.) lanoso, lanuginoso; velludo.

woolman [-man], *s.* lanero.

woolpack [-pæk], *s.* paca o fardo de lana; cúmulo (nube).

woolsack [-sæk], *s.* saco de o para lana; asiento del gran canciller en la Cámara de los Lores; por extensión, dignidad de gran canciller.

woolsorter [-sortœ(r)], *s.* escogedor de lana.

woozy [wúzi], *a.* (fam.) confuso, ofuscado, vaguido.

word [wœrd]. **I.** *s.* palabra; vocablo, voz; habla; conversación breve, dos palabras; palabra de honor, promesa; (ant.) dicho, sentencia, apotegma, *m.;* aviso, recado, mensaje; noticia, noticias; santo y seña; voz de mando, orden, *f.,* mandato.—*pl.* palabras mayores; disputa, contienda verbal; (desp.) frases; (mús.) letra (de una canción).—**w. square**, cuadrado de palabras que pueden leerse en varios sentidos.—**by w. of mouth**, verbalmente, de palabra.—**in a w.**, en una palabra, en resumidas cuentas.—**in other words**, en otros términos.—**in so many words**, en esas mismas palabras, exactamente así; claramente, sin ambages.—**in the words of**, según las palabras de, como dice.—**in w.**, de palabra.—**on my w.**, bajo mi palabra, a fe mía.—**the W.**, (bib.) el Verbo; la Escritura.—**to have a w. with**, hablar con.—**to have words**, (fam.) tener palabras, reñir de palabra.—**to leave w.**, dejar dicho.—**too . . . for words**. (*V.* TOO). **II.** *va.* expresar; enunciar; formular; redactar.

wordbook [-buk], *s.* vocabulario; diccionario; léxico; (mús.) libro, libreto (de ópera).

wordiness [-iniš], *s.* verbosidad; palabrería.

wording [-iŋ], *s.* dicción, estilo; redacción, fraseología; expresión, términos, *m. pl.*

wordless [-liš], *a.* falto de palabras, mudo.

wordy [-i], *a.* verbal; verboso, difuso.

wore [wor], *pret.* de TO WEAR.

work [wœrk]. **I.** *va.* trabajar; lab(o)rar, explotar (una mina, un privilegio, etc.); (cost.) bordar; tallar (una piedra); fabricar, elaborar, manufacturar; producir, preparar; formar, componer; obrar sobre, influir en, impeler, excitar, inducir; investigar o resolver (un problema); hacer trabajar (a persona o bestia) o funcionar (máquina, etc.); hacer mover o andar, poner en movimiento; manejar, manipular; mover nerviosamente (los dedos); hacer fermentar; causar, efectuar, producir, surtir (algún efecto); pagar (algo) con o en trabajo; (mar.) maniobrar.—**to w.!** ¡manos a la obra!—**to w. a pump**, dar a una bomba.—**to w. down**, hacer bajar.—**to w. in**, hacer entrar, meter.—**to w. it**, manejar las cosas, darse trazas.—**to w. off**, deshacerse de; satisfacer, desempeñar, pagar trabajando o con el trabajo (una deuda, etc.).—**to w. one's head off**, (fam.) trabajar duro o hasta más no poder.—**to w. one's way through**, abrirse cámino por o en; pagar uno con su trabajo los gastos de.—**to w. out**, resolver (un problema); borrar o expiar (culpas, etc.); acabar, lograr o conseguir a fuerza de trabajo; ejecutar, llevar a cabo, efectuar; agotar (una mina); labrarse, determinar (su destino, etc.).—**to w. over**, alterar, rehacer.—**to w. through**, penetrar; atravesar a fuerza de trabajo.—**to w. up**, elaborar, labrar, dar forma a; amasar; agotar, consumir; excitar, inflamar.—**to w. water**, (m. v.) hacer o arrastrar espuma. **II.** *vn.* trabajar, estar empleado u ocupado; obrar, surtir efecto, tener buen éxito; ser eficaz; funcionar, marchar, ir (bien o mal); obrar u operar (un remedio); fermentar; (mec.) efectuar trabajo.—**to w. against**, trabajar contra; oponerse a.—**to w. at**, trabajar en; ocuparse en o de.—**to w. down**, descender, bajarse.—**to w. free**, aflojarse o soltarse con el movimiento o el uso.—**to w. in**, trabajar en; insinuarse en; entrar poco a poco.—**to w. into**, entrar en, penetrar en.—**to w. loose** = TO W. FREE.—**to w. out**, tener éxito (bueno o malo); surtir o no efecto; resultar.—**to w. round**, volverse lentamente o con esfuerzo.—**to w. to windward**, (mar.) barloventear, ceñir el viento.—**to w. upon**, obrar sobre; trabajar en, estar ocupado en; sublevar, excitar, mover a compasión. **III.** *s.* trabajo; tarea, empresa, labor, *f.,* faena, fajina; obra (construcción, libro, producción, etc.); (cost.) labor, costura; bordado; obra, acción; empleo u ocupación; (mec.) trabajo (de una fuerza); obra (cosa en que se trabaja).—*pl.* fábrica, taller, establecimiento; rodaje, engranaje motor; mecanismo, maquinaria; (reloj) movimiento.—**out of w.**, sin trabajo, sin empleo, cesante.—**(to be) at w.**, (estar) ocupado, trabajando o funcionando.—**to be hard at w.**, estar muy afanado o atareado.

workable [-abl], *a.* (min.) explotable; practicable; trabajable, laborable, labradero; labrantío, labradío (campo o tierra); factible, viable; que puede trabajar, trabajarse o funcionar.—**workableness** [-niš], **workability** [-abiliti], *s.* aplicabilidad, practicabilidad, viabilidad; calidad de trabajable, explotable o manejable.

workaday [-adei], *a.* laborable (día); práctico; ordinario, cuotidiano, de cada día; prosaico, árido, escueto.

workbag [-bæg], *s.* saco de labor.

workbasket [-bæskit], **workbox** [-baks], *s.* caja o estuche de labor, costurero, neceser de costura, tabaque.

workbench [-bench], *s.* banco de taller.

workday [-dei]. **I.** *s.* día (*m.*) útil, laborable, o de trabajo. **II.** *a.* = WORKADAY.

worker [-œ(r)], *s.* trabajador, obrero, operario; (ent.) abeja u hormiga obrera.

workfellow [-fɛlou], *s.* compañero de trabajo; obrero.

workfolk(s [-fouk(s], *s.* = WORKPEOPLE.

workhouse [-haus], *s.* (Ingl.) hospicio, casa de

misericordia; (E. U.) casa de corrección; presidio.

working [-iŋ]. **I.** *s.* obra, trabajo; (mec., etc.) actuación, juego, funcionamiento, operación; (min.) explotación, laboreo; (mar.) maniobra. **II.** *a.* que trabaja, laborante; obrero, trabajador; de trabajo; fundamental, que sirve de base, guía o regla.—**w. ant, w. bee,** hormiga, abeja obrera o neutra.—**w. barrel,** cuerpo o cilindro (de bomba).—**w. capital,** capital circulante o de explotación.—**w. class,** clase obrera o proletaria; obrerismo.—**w. cylinder,** (m. comb. int.) cilindro motor.—**w. day,** día (*m.*) de trabajo, día útil o laborable; jornada.—**w. drawing,** (ing.) plano, dibujo de guía; (arq.) montea. —**w. fluid,** (mec.) flúido de trabajo.—**w. hypothesis,** postulado.—**w. load,** (ing.) carga (máxima) normal, carga de trabajo.—**w. model,** modelo de guía.—**w. plan** = W. DRAWING; plan, sistema, *m.*—**w. steam,** (m. v.) vapor vivo.—**w. strength, w. stress,** (mec.) coeficiente de trabajo; esfuerzo de trabajo.—**w. theory,** postulado.

workingman [-man], *s.* obrero, operario, jornalero, trabajador.—**workingwoman** [-wuman], *s.* obrera.

workman [-man], *s.* trabajador, obrero, operario. —**workmen's compensation law (insurance),** ley, *f.* (seguro) de accidentes del trabajo.

workmanlike, workmanly [-lajk, -lij]. **I.** *a.* primoroso, bien acabado. **II.** *adv.* primorosamente.

workmanship [-šip], *s.* hechura, mano (*f.*) de obra; artificio; primor o destreza del artífice.

workmaster [-mæstœ(r)], *s.* oficial, maestro de taller.

workout [-aut], *s.* prueba, ensayo; (dep.) ejercicio de entrenamiento.

workpeople [-pipl], *s. pl.* obreros, operarios.

workroom [-rum], *s.* taller.

workshop [-šap], *s.* taller, obrador.

worktable [-tejbl], *s.* costurero.

workwoman [-wuman], *s.* obrera.

world [wœrld], *s.* mundo.—**w. history,** historia mundial.—**w. power,** (pol. int.) gran potencia. —**w.'s end,** cabo del mundo.—**w. soul,** alma del universo.—**w. spirit,** espíritu del universo; Dios.—**W. War,** guerra mundial, gran guerra (la de 1914 a 1918, o la de 1939-1945).—**w.-weary,** cansado o hastiado del mundo.—**w.-wide,** mundial, global, de alcance mundial.—**w. without end,** para siempre jamás; por los siglos de los siglos.—**for all the w.,** exactamente, cabalmente; bajo todos conceptos; por nada del mundo.—**the other w.,** el otro mundo, la vida futura.

worldliness [-linis], *s.* mundanalidad.

worldling [-liŋ], *s.* persona mundana.

worldly [-lij]. **I.** *a.* mundano, mundanal, carnal, terreno, terrenal, terrestre; seglar, profano. **II.** *adv.* mundana(l)mente, profanamente.—**w.-minded,** mundano, carnal, entregado a las cosas de este mundo.—**w.-mindedness,** mundanalidad, carnalidad.

worm [wœrm]. **I.** (zool.) *s.* gusano; lombriz; oruga; polilla, carcoma; coco; gorgojo; (fig.) gusano roedor, remordimiento; persona vil o despreciable; (mec.) tornillo sin fin; (arti.) sacatrapos; (quím.) serpentín.—**w. drive,** (mec.) transmisión de tornillo sin fin.—**w.-eaten,** agusanado, carcomido, apolillado, abromado, picado o comido de gusanos.—**w. fence,** cercado en zigzag.—**w. gear,** (mec.) rueda para tornillo sin fin.—**w. gear, w. gearing,** engranaje de tornillo sin fin.—**w. in the conscience,** gusano de la conciencia, remordimiento.—**w. tea,** tisana vermífuga.—**w. wheel,** rueda para engranaje de tornillo sin fin. **II.** *va.* y *vr.* insinuarse, introducirse o arrastrarse (como un gusano); (arti.) sacar con sacatrapos; (fig.) (con **from** o **out of**) arrancar mañosamente un secreto; quitar gusanos o lombrices.—**to w. a**

cable, (mar.) embutir un cable. **III.** *vn.* trabajar u obrar lentamente y por bajo mano.

wormer [-œ(r)], *s.* (arti.) sacatrapos.

wormhole [-houl], *s.* agujero o picadura de gusano.

wormlike [-lajk], *a.* vermicular, vermiforme.

wormseed [-sid], *s.* (bot.) santónico.

wormwood [-wud], *s.* (bot.) ajenjo; amargura.

wormy [-i], *a.* gusarapiento, agusanado.

worn [worn], *pp.* de TO WEAR.—**w.-out,** gastado, raído; estropeado; cansado, rendido; agotado.

worried [wœrid], *a.* angustiado; intranquilo, preocupado; vejado, incomodado.—**to be w.,** estar con cuidado; no tenerlas todas consigo.

worriment [wœrimənt], *s.* (fam.) = WORRY.

worrisome [-sam], *a.* angustioso, inquietante; molesto, vejatorio.

worry [wœri]. **I.** *va.* acosar, vejar; atormentar, angustiar; inquietar, preocupar; lacerar, desgarrar o matar mordiendo o sacudiendo. **II.** *vn.* estar intranquilo, inquietarse, apurarse; morderse (los perros que riñen). **III.** *s.* cuidado, ansiedad, inquietud, apuro, preocupación, quebradero de cabeza, zozobra; mordedura, desgarro, laceración.

worse [wœrs]. **I.** *a. comp.* de BAD, ILL, EVIL: más malo; inferior; en peor situación.—**w. and w.,** de mal en peor, peor que nunca; cada vez más malo (o peor).—**w. than ever,** peor que nunca.—**to be w. off,** estar en peores circunstancias, o quedar peor.—**to make, o render, w.,** empeorar. **II.** *adv.* peor; menos. **III.** *s.* peoría, menoscabo, detrimento; lo peor.—**for the w.,** en mal (gen. se traduce por *empeorar,* cambiando un poco el giro: *there has been a change for the worse,* la situación ha empeorado). —**to have the w. of it (of the fight,** etc.), llevar la peor parte, salir perdiendo.

worsen [-n], *va.* y *vn.* empeorar(se), agravar(se).

worsening [-iŋ], *s.* empeoramiento.

worship [wœršip]. **I.** *s.* culto, adoración; reverencia, respeto.—**your w.,** usía; vuestra merced. **II.** *va.* adorar; reverenciar, honrar. **III.** *vn.* adorar; profesar culto o religión.—**worship-(p)er** [-œ(r)], *s.* adorador, devoto, cultor.

worshipful [-ful], *a.* adorable, venerable; (como tratamiento) honorable, respetable (*the worshipful president,* el respetable presidente).—**w. master** (entre los francmasones), el Venerable.—**worshipfully** [-fuli], *adv.* venerablemente, con adoración.

worship(p)ing [-iŋ]. **I.** *s.* adoración, culto. **II.** *a.* adorador, cultor, devoto; venerador.

worst [wœrst]. **I.** *a. superl.* de BAD, ILL, EVIL: pésimo, malísimo, más malo, peor. **II.** *adv.* del peor modo posible; pésimamente. **III.** *s.* lo peor, lo más malo.—**at the w.,** a peor andar; en el peor estado posible; en las peores circunstancias.—**if (the) w. comes to the w.,** si sucede lo peor.—**the w. is yet to come,** aún falta lo peor, (fam.) falta el rabo por desollar. —**to get the w. of,** llevar la peor parte en.—**to want the w. way,** (fam.) desear muchísimo. **IV.** *va.* vencer, rendir o derrotar a; triunfar de.

worsted [-id], *a.* vencido.

worsted [wuštid], *s.* estambre.—**w. stockings,** medias de estambre o de lana.—**w. work,** (cost.) labor hecha con estambre.—**w. yarn,** estambre.

wort [wœrt], *s.* (bot.) planta, hierba (en composición); mosto de cerveza, jugo de lúpulo, repollo; cerveza nueva que no ha fermentado.

worth [wœrθ]. **I.** *s.* mérito; consideración, importancia, entidad; valor, valía; monta; precio; nobleza, excelencia, dignidad.—**a dollar's w. of,** un dólar de (lo que se compra). **II.** *a.* que vale o posee; equivalente a; de precio o valor de; (antes de gerundio) digno de, que vale la pena, que merece (*he is a man worth knowing,* es hombre digno de conocerse; *the change is not worth making,* el cambio no vale la pena [de hacerse]).—**to be w.**, valer, costar; merecer; (hablando de riqueza) tener (*Jones is worth a million dollars*, Jones tiene un millón de dólares).—**to be w. while**, valer la pena.

worthily [wǿrðili], *adv.* dignamente, honorablemente.—**worthiness** [-nis], *s.* dignidad, mérito, valía.

worthless [wǿrθlis], *a.* inútil, inservible; sin valor; indigno, despreciable.—**worthlessness** [-nis], *s.* falta de mérito o de valor; inutilidad.

worthy [wǿrði]. **I.** *a.* digno; apreciable, benemérito; merecedor, acreedor, meritorio.—**w. of notice**, digno de atención o de mención. **II.** *s.* notable, ilustre, benemérito, prócer, primate.

would [wúd], *pret. y subj.* de WILL. La distinción que se hace en el empleo de *would* y *should* es la misma que existe entre *will* y *shall*. (*V.* WILL, SHALL, SHOULD.) *Would* se usa a veces en el sentido de *querer* y equivale al presente, futuro o pretérito de subjuntivo, según las circunstancias: *those that would prosper*, los que quieran (o quisieren) prosperar; *I would I were there*, yo quisiera estar allá; *would (to) God*, quiera (o quisiera) Dios, plegue (o pluguiera) a Dios.—**it w. seem**, parecería; parece, según parece.

would-be [-bi], *a.* pretendiente, aspirante, seudo, supuesto: *would-be poet*, presumido de poeta.

wound [waund], *pret. y pp.* de TO WIND.

wound [wúnd], (poét.) waund]. **I.** *s.* herida; llaga, lesión; ofensa, golpe, daño. **II.** *va. y vn.* herir, lesionar, llagar, lastimar; ofender, agraviar.

wounded [-id], *a.* herido, leso; descalabrado.

woundwort [-wœrt], *s.* (bot.) vulneraria.

wove(n [wóuv(n], *pret. y pp.* de TO WEAVE.—**w. paper**, papel avitelado.

wowser [wáuzœ(r)], *s.* puritano quisquilloso; fariseo, formalista.

wrack [ræk], *s.* (bot.) fuco, ova; naufragio, ruina; pecio; nubes (*f. pl.*) sutiles, celajes (*pl.*).—**to go to w. (and ruin)**, arruinarse; correr a su perdición.

wraith [reiθ], *s.* fantasma, *m.*, espectro, aparecido, ánima en pena.

wrangle [rǽŋgl]. **I.** *vn.* reñir; disputar, contender, altercar. **II.** *s.* pelotera, pendencia, riña; disputa, altercado.—**wrangler** [-glœ(r)], *s.* pendenciero, camorrista (fam.); disputador, argumentador.

wrangling [-gliŋ], *s.* camorra (fam.), reyerta, riña; disputa, altercación.

wrap [ræp]. **I.** *va.* (*pret. y pp.* WRAPPED O WRAPT) arrollar o enrollar; envolver.—**to w. up**, rollar, arrollar; envolver; apañar, arropar; embozar; cubrir, ocultar.—**to be wrapped up in**, estar envuelto o enrollado en; estar demasiado prendado de o embebido en. **II.** *vn.* arrollarse; envolverse.—**to w. up (in)**, envolverse (en). **III.** *s.* bata; abrigo.—*pl.* abrigos y mantas (de viaje, etc.).—**to put on w.**, abrigarse.

wrapper [-œ(r)], *s.* envolvedor; funda, cubierta, cobertura, carpeta, papel; faja de periódico; capa de tabaco; bata, peinador, abrigo holgado; envoltura o pañal de niño; (fam.) elástica, camiseta.

wrapping [-iŋ]. **I.** *a.* de envolver, de estraza (apl. esp. al papel). **II.** *s.* envoltura, cubierta.

wrath [ræθ], *s.* ira, cólera.—**wrathful** [-ful], *a.* airado, colérico.—**wrathfully** [-i], *adv.* airada o coléricamente.

wreak [rik], *va.* descargar (la cólera); tomar (venganza).

wreath [riθ], *s.* corona, guirnalda; festón; trenza; espiral, *f.*

wreathe [ríð]. **I.** *va.* enroscar, entrelazar, tejer (coronas o guirnaldas), enguirnaldar; ceñir, rodear. **II.** *vn.* enroscarse, ensortijarse.

wreathy [-i], *a.* coronado; enroscado, ensortijado; en espiral.

wreck [rék]. **I.** *s.* naufragio; ruina, destrozo, destrucción; buque naufragado, barco perdido; restos (*pl.*) de un naufragio, pecios (*pl.*). **II.** *va.*

hacer naufragar; arruinar, echar a pique; demoler, desbaratar. **III.** *vn.* naufragar, zozobrar, irse a pique; fracasar.

wreckage [-idžl, *s.* naufragio; restos (*pl.*) de naufragio, pecios (*pl.*); despojos, ruinas (*pl.*).

wrecker [-œ(r)], *s.* raquero; destructor; demoledor. *V.* WRECKING CAR.

wrecking [-iŋ], *a.* de o relativo a naufragios; demoledor; que hace naufragar; ruinoso, desastroso.—**w. car**, (f. c., aut.) furgón, carro o automóvil de auxilio (en accidentes).

wren [ren], *s.* (orn.) reyezuelo, abadejo, régulo.

wrench [rench]. **I.** *va.* arrancar, arrebatar; (re)torcer; dislocar, desencajar, sacar de quicio.—**to w. one's foot**, torcerse el pie. **II.** *s.* arranque; tirón; torcedura, arrancamiento; (mec.) llave (*f.*) de tuerca; sistema (*m.*) compuesto de un par y una fuerza.

wrest [rést]. **I.** *va.* arrancar; torcer; desvirtuar, pervertir.—**to w. from**, arrebatar. **II.** *s.* violencia; torsión, torcimiento; dislocación; arranque; (mús.) llave (*f.*) de afinar.—**w. pin**, clavija de piano.

wrested [-id], *a.* torcido; forzado.

wrester [-œ(r)], *s.* violador, infractor.

wrestle [résl]. **I.** *va.* luchar con; forcejear contra). **II.** *vn.* luchar a brazo partido; esforzarse; disputar.—**wrestler** [réslœ(r)], *s.* luchador.—**wrestling** [résliŋ], *s.* lucha.

wretch [réch], *s.* infeliz, desventurado, miserable; ente vil, despreciable.

wretched [-id], *a.* infeliz, cuitado, desdichado, miserable, desgraciado; calamitoso, lastimero; vil, despreciable; perverso; mezquino; malísimo, detestable.—**wretchedly** [-li], *adv.* míseramente, desastradamente; ruinmente, vilmente.

wretchedness [-nis], *s.* desdicha, miseria, desgracia; escualidez, lacería; vileza, ruindad, bajeza.

wriggle [rígl]. **I.** *va.* menear, retorcer, hacer colear. **II.** *vn.* colear, culebrear, serpentear, undular; retorcerse.—**to w. away**, escaparse culebreando.—**to w. into**, insinuarse en.—**to w. off**, escaparse culebreando o retorciéndose.—**to w. out**, escaparse, deslizarse.

wriggling [rígliŋ], *s.* enroscadura, coleadura, ondulación, meneo serpentino.

wright [rait], *s.* artífice, artesano, obrero.

wring [riŋ], *va.* (*pret. y pp.* WRUNG) torcer, retorcer; arrancar; estrujar, exprimir, escurrir; forzar; atormentar, aquejar.—**to w. off**, arrancar retorciendo.—**to w. out**, exprimir.

wringbolt [-boult], *s.* perno de atraca, clavija de apretar, argolla.

wringer [-œ(r)], *s.* torcedor, torcedora; exprimidor (de ropa mojada).

wrinkle [ríŋkl]. **I.** *s.* arruga; surco, buche; (fam.) capricho, maña; artificio; idea, ocurrencia; indicio, insinuación. **II.** *va.* arrugar, hacer arrugas.—**to w. one's brow**, fruncir o arrugar las cejas.—**to w. up**, arrugar, plegar. **III.** *vn.* arrugarse; encarrujarse.

wrinkled [-d], *a.* arrugado, rugoso; encarrujado; (cost.) fruncido, plegado.

wrinkly [ríŋkli], *a.* arrugado.

wrist [ríst], *s.* (anat.) muñeca, carpo; (mec.) muñón; (m. comb. int.) muñón del pie de la biela, o eje del émbolo (ll. t. **w. pin**); (m. v.) pasador de la cruceta.—**w. bandage**, pulsera.—**w. watch**, reloj de pulsera.

wristband [-bænd], *s.* puño de camisa.

wristdrop [-drap], *s.* (med.) parálisis de los músculos de la mano debida a envenenamiento plúmbico.

wristfall [-fol], *s.* (cost.) vuelo, vuelillo.

wristlet [-lit], *s.* manguito elástico, pulsera.

writ [rit], *s.* escritura; (for.) escrito; orden, *f.*, auto, mandamiento, decreto judicial, provisión, ejecutoria.—**w. of privilege**, auto de excarcelación.—**Holy W.**, Sagrada Escritura.

write [rait]. **I.** *va.* (*pret.* WROTE; *pp.* WRITTEN) escribir; describir.—**to w. after**, copiar de.—

to w. a good hand, hacer o tener buena letra. **—to w. down,** poner por escrito; redactar; apuntar; vilipendiar por escrito.—**to w. in,** o **into,** insertar o incorporar en.—**to w. off,** (com.) cancelar, saldar.—**to w. one's self,** calificarse, tomar algún título, calidad, honor, etc.—**to w. out,** redactar; copiar, trasladar, transcribir; escribir entero (sin abreviar).—**to w. over again,** volver a escribir.—**to w. up,** narrar, relatar; describir; (fam.) ensalzar por escrito, alabar, bombear, dar bombo; (com.) poner al día (el libro mayor); valorar en demasía una partida del activo. **II. vn.** escribir; tener correspondencia epistolar; ser escritor o autor.—**to w. back,** contestar a una carta.—**to w. on,** continuar escribiendo; escribir acerca de.

writer [-œ(r)], *s.* escritor; literato, hombre de letras, autor; pendolista.—**w.'s cramp,** (med.) mogigrafía; calambre del escribiente.—**the w.** (usado por modestia fingida para no decir *yo*) el que esto escribe; el infrascrito; nosotros (cambiando el verbo).

write-up [-ʌp], *s.* (fam.) bombo, escrito encomiástico; descripción o narración escrita; crónica de prensa.

writhe [ráið]. **I.** *va.* (re)torcer. **II.** *vn.* retorcerse; contorcerse (por algún dolor).

writhing [-iŋ], *s.* retorcimiento, contorsión.

writing [ráitiŋ]. **I.** *s.* escritura; letra; escrito; el (arte de) escribir. **II.** *a.* de o para escribir.—**w. book,** cuaderno de escritura.—**w. desk,** escritorio, mesa de escribir, pupitre, buró.—**w. machine,** máquina de escribir.—**w. master,** maestro de escritura.—**w. materials** = w. set. —**w. pad,** bloc de papel.—**w. paper,** papel de escribir (gen. se subentiende que es de cartas). —**w. set,** recado de escribir.—**at the present,** o **at this, w.,** al tiempo que esto se escribe, ahora mismo.—**in one's own w.,** de su puño y letra.—**(to put) in w.,** (poner) por escrito.

written [rítn], *pp.* de TO WRITE.

wrong [róŋ]. **I.** *s.* injuria, injusticia, sinrazón, *f.,* agravio, tuerto, entuerto; mal (*knowledge of right and wrong,* conocimiento del bien y el mal); daño, perjuicio; culpa; error, extravío; falsedad. —**to be in the w.,** no tener razón.—**to do w.,** obrar o hacer mal; hacer daño, causar perjuicio. **II.** *a.* injusto; censurable, repre(he)nsible; inicuo; desacertado, erróneo, incorrecto; falso; irregular; equivocado; inconveniente o inoportuno; mal hecho, mal escrito, etc.; que no es (era, etc.) (*he brought the wrong book,* trajo el libro que no era, *u* otro libro que el que debía haber traído, etc.).—**w.-headedness,** terquedad, obstinación (en el error).—**w. side,** envés, revés; lado malo.—**w. side out**(**ward**), al envés, al revés.—**to be w.,** ser malo; no ser justo; estar mal hecho (dicho, escrito, etc.); no tener razón, equivocarse. **III.** *adv.* mal; sin razón, sin causa; injustamente; al revés. **IV.** *va.* causar perjuicio a; hacer mal a; ofender; agraviar, injuriar; ser injusto con.

wrongdoer [-dúœ(r)], *s.* injuriador; malvado, perverso; pecador.—**wrongdoing** [-dúiŋ], *s.* maldad; perversidad, iniquidad.

wrongful [-ful], *a.* injusto; inicuo.

wrongfully [-li], *adv.* injustamente, sin razón, sin causa ni motivo.—**wrongly** [-li], *adv.* injustamente; mal; equivocadamente.

wrongness [-njs], *s.* injusticia, maldad, iniquidad; falsedad, error, inexactitud.

wrote [rout], *pret.* de TO WRITE.

wroth [roθ], *a.* airado, enojado.

wrought [rot]. **I.** *pret.* y *pp. irreg.* de TO WORK. **II.** *a.* forjado, labrado, trabajado.—**w. iron,** hierro forjado.—**w.-up,** (sobre)excitado; perturbado.

wrung [rʌŋ], *pret.* y *pp.* de TO WRING.

wry [rái], *a.* torcido, doblado, sesg(ad)o; pervertido, tergiversado.—**w. face,** gesto, visaje,

mueca, mohín.—**w.-mouthed,** boquitorcido, boquituerto.—**to make a w. face,** hacer visajes, etc.—**wryly** [-li], *adv.* torcidamente.

wryneck [-nɛk], *s.* (orn.) torcecuello; (med.) torticolis, *m.*

wryness [-njs], *s.* torcedura.

wych-elm [wɥch ɛlm], *s.* (bot.) olmo escocés.

wych-hazel, *s.* = WITCH HAZEL.

Wyclif(f)ite [wɥklífait], *s.* y *a.* wiclefista, vielefista, seguidor de o relativo a Wiclef.

wye [wai], *s.* la letra Y; horquilla, cualquier cosa en forma de Y. *V.* Y.

X

x [eks], *s.* x.

X [eks]. **I.** *s.* cruz; cualquier cosa de forma de X; (fam.) billete de 10 dólares. **II.** *a.* en cruz; en X, de forma de X.—**X-ray,** rayo X, catódico o Roentgen.—**X-ray film,** película radiográfica. —**X-ray picture,** radi(o)grafía.—**X-ray room, table,** sala, mesa, de radiaciones.—**X-ray tube,** tubo de rayos X, tubo de vacío para la producción de rayos X.—**X-ray,** *va.* radiografiar.

xanthate [zǽnθeit], *s.* (quím.) jantato, xantato.

xanthein(**e** [zǽnθiin], *s.* (quím.) xanteína.

xanthic [zǽnθik], *a.* (quím.) jántico, xántico.

xanthine [zǽnθin], *s.* (quím.) xantina, jantina.

Xanthochroi [zænθokrói], *s. pl.* caucasianos rubios.—**xanthocroid** [-króid], *a.* y *s.* rubio.

xanthophyl(**l** [zǽnθofil], *s.* (bioquím.) jantofila, xantofila, pigmento amarillo de las hojas.

xanthous [zǽnθʌs], *a.* mogol; rubio, blondo.

Xanthoxylum [zænθáksilʌm], *s.* (bot.) jantoxilo, xantoxilo o zantoxilo; fresno espinoso.

xebec [zíbɛk], *s.* (mar.) jabeque.

xenogenesis [zenodʒénjsis], *s.* (biol.) xenogénesis.

xenon [zénan], *s.* (quím.) xenón.

xenophobia [zenofóybiǎ], *s.* xenofobia, odio o antipatía hacia los extraños.

xerophagy [zjráfadʒi], *s.* xerofagia.

xerophthalmia [zirafθélmiǎ], *s.* (med.) xeroftalmia.

xerophyte [zírofait], *s.* (bot.) planta xerófila, planta de climas y suelos secos.

xerosis [zjróysjs], *s.* (med.) xerodermia.

xiphias [zífias], *s.* (ict.) jifia.

xiphisternum [zifjstœrnʌm], *s.* (anat., zool.) xifisternón, cartílago o apófisis xifoides.

xiphoid [zífoid], *a.* (anat., zool.) xifoideo, xifoides, ensiforme.—**x. cartilage,** (anat.) xifoides.

xiphosuran [zifosúran], *a.* y *s.* (zool.) xifosuro.

Xmas [krísmas], *s.* = CHRISTMAS.

xylem [záilem], *s.* (bot.) parte leñosa de las plantas.

xylene [záilin], *s.* (quím.) xileno.—**xylic** [záilik], *a.* xílico.—**xylidin**(**e** [záilidin], *s.* xilidina.

xylocarpous [zailokárpʌs], *a.* (bot.) de fruto duro y leñoso.

xylograph [záilogræf], *s.* grabado en madera.— **xylographer** [zailágrafœ(r)], *s.* xilógrafo, grabador en madera.—**xylographic**(**al** [zailográfik(al], *a.* xilográfico.—**xylography** [zailágrafi], *s.* xilografía (arte).

xyloid [záiloid], *a.* xiloide, semejante o relativo a la madera.

xylol [záilal], *s.* (quím.) xileno.

xylophagous [zailáfagʌs], *a.* (ent., zool.) xilófago.

xylophone [záilofoun], *s.* (mús.) xilórgano o xilófono; (Am.) especie de marimba.

xyster [zístœ(r)], *s.* (cir.) raspador de huesos.

xyst(**us** [zíst(ʌs], *s.* (arq.) pórtico, galería, terrado.

Y

y [wai], *s.* y.

Y [wai]. **I.** *s.* horquilla; Y, cualquier cosa en forma de Y; (f. c.) cambio en Y, triángulo de cambio de marcha; (hidr.) tubo bifurcado, horquilla, tubo en Y; (quím.) itrio; (fam.) Asociación

Cristiana de los Jóvenes. **II.** *a.* en Y. de forma de Y; de horquilla; bifurcado.—**Y box,** (elec.) caja bifurcada.—**Y connection,** (elec.) conexión de estrella.—**Y gun,** cañón doble antisubmarino en Y.—**Y. level,** (top.) nivel de apoyos en Y, nivel invertible en los apoyos (ll. a veces *nivel norteamericano*, por ser el más usado en los E. U.).—**Y track,** (f. c.) triángulo de inversión de marcha.

yacht [yát]. **I.** *s.* (mar.) yate.—**y. race,** regata de yates. **II.** *vn.* ir, viajar o pasear en yate; manejar un yate.—**yachting** [-iŋ], *s.* deporte de los yates; paseo o navegación en yate.—**yachtsman** [-smạn], *s.* dueño o timonel de yate; deportista de yates.—**yachtsmanship** [-ṣip], *s.* arte del conductor de yates; habilidad en la conducción de yates.

yak [yæk], *s.* (zool.) yack o yak (del Tíbet).

yam [yæm], *s.* (bot.) ñame; especie de batata.

yank [yæŋk]. **I.** *va. y vn.* (fam.) sacar de un tirón; dar un tirón. **II.** *s.* (fam.) tirón, estirón.

Yankee [yǽŋki], *a. y s.* (fam.) yanqui, natural de la Nueva Inglaterra.—**Y. Doodle,** canción popular de los norteamericanos.—**Yankeedom** [-dọm], *s.* tierra de los yanquis; los yanquis.—**Yankeeism** [-izm], *s.* yanquismo.—**Yankeeland** [-lænd], *s.* Yanquilandia (apl. a la Nueva Inglaterra y a los E. U.).

yap [yæp]. **I.** *vn.* (fam.) ladrar, (re)gañir (el perro); charlar agria o ruidosamente; parlotear. **II.** *s.* (fam.) ladrido, gañido; charla o charlador displicentes, ruidosos u ociosos.

yard [yárd]. **I.** *va.* acorralar, apriscar. **II.** *s.* corral; patio; cercado; yarda (medida); (mar.) verga.

yardarm [-arm], *s.* (mar.) penol de la verga.

yardstick, yardwand [-stịk, -wand], *s.* yarda graduada de medir; patrón, modelo; criterio.

yarn [yarn], *s.* hilaza; hilo, hilado; estambre; (fam.) cuento chino o increíble, andaluzada.

yarrow [yǽroụ], *s.* (bot.) milenrama, milhojas, *f.*

yashmak [yǽ̂ŝmæk], *s.* velo de las musulmanas.

yataghan [yǽtagæn], *s.* yatagán.

yaw [yó]. **I.** *s.* (mar.) guiñada; (aer.) derrape, desviación lateral con respecto a la línea regular de vuelo. **II.** *va. y vn.* (mar.) guiñar; (aer.) desviar(se) de la línea regular de vuelo por rotación alrededor del eje vertical.

yawing [-iŋ], *s.* (aer.) derrape, movimiento alrededor del eje vertical.

yawl [yọl], *s.* (mar.) bote, yola; serení; balandra.

yawmeter [yómitœ(r)], *s.* (aer.) goniómetro de derrape, medidor de ángulos de derrape.

yawn [yón]. **I.** *vn.* bostezar; quedarse con la boca abierta; anhelar; abrirse. **II.** *s.* bostezo; abrimiento; abertura.—**yawner** [-œ(r)], *s.* bostezador.—**yawning** [-iŋ]. **I.** *a.* bostezante; abierto. **II.** *s.* bostezo.

yaws [yoʒ], *s. pl.* (med.) frambesia, pian, enfermedad contagiosa de la piel en países tropicales.

ye [yi]. **I.** *pron. ant.* (*pl.* de THOU) vosotros, (v)os. **II.** [ði], *art.* (contr. ant. de THE), el, la, los, las.

yea [yei]. **I.** *adv.* sí, ciertamente, verdaderamente; y aún, más aún, no solamente . . . sino.—**y. or nay,** sí o no. **II.** *s.* sí, voto afirmativo.—**the yeas and nays,** los votos en pro y en contra.

yean [yín], *va. y vn.* parir la oveja o cabra.

yeanling [-liŋ], *s.* cordero o cabrito mamantón.

year [yír], *s.* año.—*pl.* años, edad; vejez.—**y. of grace, y. of our Lord,** año de gracia.—**y.'s purchase,** renta anual.—**by the y.,** por año.—**in years,** de edad.—**of late years,** en los últimos años, en años recientes.—**once a y.,** una vez al año, cada año.—**to grow in years,** envejecer.

yearbook [-buk], *s.* anuario.

yearling [-liŋ], *s.* primal, añojo, añal, borro.

yearlong [-loŋ], *a.* que dura un año, o años.

yearly [-li]. **I.** *a.* anual. **II.** *adv.* anualmente, cada año; una vez al año; al año.

yearn [yǿrn], *vn.* anhelar, desear vivamente,

suspirar por; añorarse.—**yearning** [-iŋ], *s.* anhelo.

yeast [yíst], *s.* levadura, fermento, ludia; giste, espuma.—**y. cake,** pastilla o tortita de levadura.

yeasty [-ị], *a.* de o semejante a levadura; espumoso; ligero; frívolo, trivial.

yegg(man [yég(mạn], *s.* (fam.) ladrón.

yelk [yelk], *s.* (dialecto) *V.* YOLK.

yell [yel]. **I.** *va. y vn.* dar alaridos, vociferar, gritar, aullar; decir a gritos. **II.** *s.* alarido, grito, aullido; grito salvaje o de guerra.—**college y.,** grito peculiar que sirve de distintivo a los estudiantes de cada colegio.

yellow [yélou]. **I.** *a.* amarillo, gualdo; rubio; sensacional, escandaloso (periódico, etc.); (fam.) cobarde, gallina, medroso.—**y. berries,** bayas persas, semillas de cambrón.—**Y. Book,** Libro Amarillo (de Francia).—**y. brass,** latón ordinario.—**y.-dog money,** (hist., E. U.) moneda sin valor; billetes de un *wildcat bank.* (*V.* WILDCAT.)—**y. fever,** (med.) fiebre amarilla.—**y. flag,** bandera amarilla (la insignia de cuarentena).—**y. iris,** (bot.) ácaro falso, bastardo o palustre.—**y. jack** = Y. FEVER; Y. FLAG.—**y. jacket,** especie de avispa con pintas amarillas.—**y. journalism,** periodismo sensacional.—**y. lead,** albayalde calcinado.—**y. metal,** oro; metal Muntz (aleación como de 60% de cobre y 40% de cinc).—**y. ocher,** anorca, ocre amarillo.—**y. sapphire,** (min.) topacio oriental, especie de zafiro amarillo.—**y. spot,** (anat.) mácula amarillenta en la retina de los vertebrados; (ent.) mariposa de mancha amarilla.—**y. water lily,** (bot.) nenúfar amarillo. **II.** *s.* amarillo (color). **III.** *vn.* ponerse amarillo, enmarillecerse, amarillear.

yellowbird [-bœrd], *s.* (orn.) jilguero, pintacilgo; oropéndola.

yellowhammer [-hæmœ(r)], *s.* (orn.) emberizo, verderol, verderón; (E. U.) picamaderos.

yellowish [-iŝ], *a.* amarillento, amarillazo, gualdado.—**yellowishness** [-iŝnịs], *s.* color amarillento.—**yellowness** [-nịs], *s.* amarillez.

yellowwood [-wụd], *s.* (bot.) fustete.

yelp [yélp]. **I.** *vn.* latir, (re)gañir (el perro). **II.** *s.* latido, gañido del perro.—**yelping** [-iŋ], *s.* gañido.

yen [yen], *s.* yen, moneda japonesa.

yeoman [yóumạn], *s.* (*pl.* YEOMEN) (Ingl., hist.) hacendado, labrador acomodado; (mar.) pañolero; (E. U.) subalterno de marina.—**y. of the guard,** (Ingl.) alabardero de palacio.—**y. ('s) service,** servicio leal o notable.—**yeomanry** [-rị], *s.* (hist.) burguesía; cuerpo de los *yeomen;* (Ingl.) cuerpo de guardia del rey.

yes [yes]. **I.** *adv.* sí.—**y. indeed,** sí por cierto, ya lo creo. **II.** *s.* respuesta afirmativa o favorable. —**y. man,** (fam.) hombre servil, que obedece ciegamente.

yesterday [yéstœrdị], *s. y adv.* ayer.—**y. morning,** ayer por la mañana.—**yesternight** [-nájt], *s. y adv.* (poét.) anoche, la noche pasada.—**yesteryear** [-yír], *s. y adv.* (poét.) el año pasado; antaño.

yet [yet]. **I.** *conj.* con todo, sin embargo, no obstante; mas, pero, empero; aun así. **II.** *adv.* aún, todavía, hasta ahora; a lo menos; más, además, más que.—**as y.,** hasta ahora, hasta aquí, todavía.—**not y.,** todavía no, aún no.

yew [yu], *s.* (bot.) tejo.

yield [yíld]. **I.** *va.* producir; redituar, rendir, rentar, dar, dejar; dar de sí, ceder; deferir, condescender; devolver, restituir; admitir, pasar por, conceder; otorgar.—**to y. consent,** dar consentimiento, consentir.—**to y. up,** ceder, entregar; devolver; abandonar. **II.** *vn.* producir; dar utilidad; ceder, caer, sucumbir, rendirse o someterse; consentir; flaquear, ceder, doblegarse; mollearse, blandear, ceder.—**to y. to,** ceder a, rendirse a; acceder a, consentir en; someterse a.

III. *s.* rendición; producción; rédito, rendimiento, renta, beneficio; cosecha.—**y. point,** (ing.) límite elástico aparente, esfuerzo mínimo de deformación permanente.

yielding [-iŋ], *a.* dócil, complaciente; flojo; condescendiente; dúctil.—**yieldingly** [-liɟ], *adv.* libremente; flojamente.—**yieldingness** [-nis], *s.* facilidad en ceder o en condescender.

yodel [yóudel]. **I.** *va.* y *vn.* cantar modulando la voz rápidamente desde el tono natural al falsete, y viceversa. **II.** *s.* manera de cantar de los tiroleses.

yoga [yóugə̄], *s.* yoga, *m.*

yogi [yóugi], *s.* yogi, asceta (*m.*) de la India.

yogurt [yóugurt], *s.* yogurt, yogh(o)urt.

yoke [yóuk]. **I.** *s.* yugo; (fig.) férula, esclavitud, opresión, servidumbre; horcajo, camella; horquilla; guía; (arq.) tirante; (elec.) culata (de imán); (mec.) garra de fijación (de taladro); (mar.) barra de timón; balancín o pinga (para llevar pesos); (cost.) canesú, hombrillo de la camisa; (aer.) palanca de mando.—*sing.* y *pl.* yunta de bueyes; par de otros animales de tiro.—**y. elm,** (bot.) carpe.—**y. of land,** yugada.—**y. pad,** frontil, rollo.—**y. ring,** barzón.—**to throw off the y.,** sacudir el yugo. **II.** *va.* uncir, acoyundar, acollarar, acoplar; (raro) sojuzgar, sujetar; oprimir.

yokefellow [-felou], **yokemate** [-meit], *s.* compañero de fatigas; socio; esposo o esposa.

yokel [yóukel], *s.* campesino, patán, paleto.

yolk [youk], *s.* yema (de huevo); exudación de las ovejas.

yon, yond [yan(d], *adv.* y *a.* (ant. o dial.) = YONDER.

yonder [yándœ(r)]. **I.** *adv.* allí, allá, acullá. **II.** *a.* aquel, aquella, aquellos, aquellas.

yore [yor], *s.* (con of) de otro tiempo; de antaño.

you [yu], *pron. pers. sing.* y *pl.* (nominativo y caso oblicuo) tú, usted, vosotros, ustedes; te, a ti, le, la, a usted, os, a vosotros, les, a ustedes. Se usa indefinidamente, y entonces se traduce por *uno* o haciendo refleja la construcción: *as you come near it, you see nothing,* cuando uno se acerca, no ve nada; *you cannot enter without permission,* no se puede entrar sin permiso.—**y. thief!** ¡so (o don) ladrón!

young [yʌŋ]. **I.** *a.* joven; mozo; nuevo; tierno, verde; fresco, reciente; novicio, inexperto.—**y. ass,** pollino, asnico.—**y. face,** cara remozada.—**y. fellow,** joven, mozo.—**y. girl,** chica, mozuela (apl. gen. a jóvenes no mayores de 20 años).—**y. goat,** cabrito, chivo, choto.—**y. hare,** lebrat(ill)o.—**y. lady,** señorita.—**y. man,** joven (hombre).—**Y. Men's Christian Association,** Asociación de los Jóvenes Cristianos (más propiamente, Asociación Cristiana de los Jóvenes).—**Y. Men's Hebrew Association,** Asociación Hebrea de los Jóvenes.—**y. one,** mozo; hijuelo; (fam.) niño, chiquillo.—**y. partridge,** perdigón.—**y. people,** la juventud, los jóvenes.—**y. rabbit,** gazap(ill)o.—**y. woman,** joven, mujer joven.—**Y. Women's Christian Association,** Asociación de las Jóvenes Cristianas (es la expresión usual, aunque la traducción propia es Asociación Cristiana de las Jóvenes).—**to grow y. again,** remozarse, rejuvenecer(se). **II.** *s. pl.* hijuelos, la cría de los animales.—**with y.,** preñada, encinta.

younger [-gœ(r)], *a.* más joven.—**y. brother,** hermano menor.—**Pliny the Y.,** Plinio el Joven.—**to be the y. hand,** ser pie (en el juego).

youngish [-iš], *a.* mozuelo, jovencillo, tierno.

youngling [-liŋ], *s.* pequeñuelo, joven.

youngster [-stœ(r)], *s.* jovencito, mocito, mozalbete, rapaz, *mf.*; niño, chiquillo, pequeñuelo.

your [yur], *a. pos.* tu(s), vuestro(s), vuestra(s); su(s), de usted(es).

yours [-z], *pron. pos.* (*sing.* y *pl.*) el tuyo, la tuya,

los tuyos, las tuyas; el vuestro, etc.; el, la, lo, los o las de usted(es); el suyo, etc. (de usted(es)).—**y. affectionately,** su afectísimo.—**y. (very) cordially,** su afectísimo servidor.—**y. (very) faithfully,** su seguro servidor (o su afmo. y atto. S. S.).—**y. sincerely, y. (very) truly =** Y. FAITHFULLY. (Estas son formas convencionales de significado más o menos vago, y a veces se usan las unas por las otras.)

yourself [-sélf], *pron. pers.* tú mismo, Vd. mismo.—*pl.* **yourselves** [-sélvz], vosotros o Vds. mismos.

youth [yúθ], *s.* juventud, mocedad; mozalbete, joven; la juventud, los jóvenes.

youthful [-ful], *a.* juvenil; joven, mozo; fresco, vigoroso; juguetón.—**y. exploits,** mocedades.—**youthfully** [-i], *adv.* de un modo juvenil, como muchacho.—**youthfulness** [-nis], *s.* mocedad, juventud; frescura.

yowl [yaul]. **I.** *vn.* aullar, ladrar; gritar. **II.** *s.* aullido; alarido.

yperite [ípœrait], *s.* yperita, gas mostaza.

ytterbia [itœrbiə̄], *s.* iterbina, óxido de iterbio.

ytterbium [itœrbiʌm], *s.* (quím.) iterbio.

yttria [ítriə̄], *s.* (quím.) itria.

yttrium [-ʌm], *s.* (quím.) itrio.

yuca [yiúkə̄], *s.* (bot.) mandioca.

yucca [yʌ́kə̄], *s.* (bot.) yuca.

Yugoslav [yúgouslav], etc. = JUGOSLAV, etc.

Yule [yúl], **Yuletide** [-taid], *s.* pascua de Navidad, natividad.—**yule log,** nochebueno.

Z

z [zi], *s.* z.

Z [zi]. **I.** *s.* hierro en Z; cosa de forma de Z. **II.** *a.* en Z, en forma de Z.—**Z bar,** barra en Z.

zaffer, zaffre [zǽfœ(r)], *s.* (min.) zafre.

Zanthoxylum [zænθáksilʌm], *s.* (bot.) jantoxilo.

zany [zéini]. **I.** *s.* (ant.) bufón, truhán; simplón. **II.** *a.* (fam.) tonto, estúpido, alocado.

zeal [zil], *s.* celo, fervor, ardor, ahinco; acucia.

zealot [zélot], *s.* entusiasta, *mf.*, partidario acérrimo, fanático.—**zealotry** [-ri], *s.* fanatismo.—**zealous** [zélʌs], *a.* celoso, entusiasta, fervoroso, acucioso.—**zealously** [-li], *adv.* apasionadamente, con pasión y celo; con ardor.

zebec [zíbek], *s.* V. XEBEC.

zebra [zíbrə̄], *s.* (zool.) cebra.

zebrass [zíbræs], *s.* (zool.) híbrido nacido de cebra macho y burra.

zebu [zíbju], *s.* (zool.) cebú.

zed [zed], *s.* zeda, zeta, ceda, ceta (la letra *z*).

zedoary [zédoə̄ri], *s.* (bot.) cedoaria.

Zeitgeist [tsáitgaist], *s.* espíritu u orientaciones de la época.

zenana [zenánə̄], *s.* harén indio.

Zend [zend], *s.* zendo.—**Z.-Avesta,** Zendavesta, *m.*

zenith [zíniθ], *s.* (astr.) cenit; (fig.) apogeo.—**z. distance,** distancia cenital.

zephyr [zéfœ(r)], *s.* céfiro, (poét.) favonio; hilaza muy ligera para bordar; (tej.) céfiro, tela ligera o diáfana; prenda de vestir de dicha tela.

Zeppelin [zépelin]. **I.** *s.* (aer.) zepelín. **II.** *va.* (z.) bombardear desde un zepelín.

zero [zírou], *s.* cero.—**z. hour,** (mil.) hora de ataque; hora o momento críticos.—**z. lift,** (aer.) resistencia nula.—**z. weather,** tiempo de cero grados (de temperatura).—**below z.,** bajo cero.

zest [zest]. **I.** *s.* deleite, gusto; sainete, sabor; luquete (que se echa a una bebida). **II.** *va.* dar gusto o sabor.

zeta [zéita o zítə̄], *s.* = ZED.

zeugma [ziúgmə̄], *s.* (gram. y ret.) zeu(g)ma.

Zeus [zius], *s.* (mit.) Júpiter griego.

zibel(l)ine [zíbelin], *a.* cebellino, de marta; de piel de marta. **II.** *s.* piel (*f.*) de marta.

zibet [zíbit], *s.* (zool.) gato de algalia.

zigzag [zígzæg]. **I.** *va.* y *vn.* ir o pasar en zigzags, hacer zigzags, zigzaguear. **II.** *a.* serpentino, en zigzag. **III.** *s.* zigzag, ziszás, (Am.) quingos.

zinc [zíŋk]. **I.** *s.* (quím. y com.) cinc o zinc.—**z. blende,** (min.) esfalerita, blenda.—**z. bloom,** (min.) flor (*f.*) de cinc.—**z. oxide,** óxido de cinc.—**z. white,** blanco u óxido de cinc. **II.** *va.* plaquear con cinc, galvanizar.

zincate [-eit], *s.* (quím.) cincato.—**zincic** [-ik], *a.* cíncico.—**zinciferous, zinkiferous** [ziŋkí-feras], *a.* cincífero.—**zincite** [zíŋkait], *s.* (min.) cincita, óxido natural de cinc.

zincograph [zíŋkogræf], *s.* cincograbado, grabado en cinc.—**zincography** [ziŋkágrafi], *s.* cincografía, arte de grabar en cinc.

zincous [zíŋkʌs], *a.* cíncico, de cinc; del cinc, electropositivo (en una pila eléctrica).

Zion [záion], *s.* Sión; cielo.—**Zionism** [-izm], *s.* sionismo, movimiento en favor de reestablecer a los judíos en Palestina.—**Zionist** [-ist], *s.* y *a.* sionista.

zip [zip]. **I.** *s.* zumbido de, o como de, bala; (fam.) energía, vigor. **II.** *vn.* zumbar como una bala.

zipper [-œ(r)], *s.* cierre (de) cremallera, cierre (automático, metálico o relámpago); abrochador o apretador de corredera; bota o zapato que lo lleva. (Es nombre de fábrica).

zircon [zǽrkan], *s.* (min.) circón.

zirconium [zœrkóuniʌm], *s.* (quím.) circonio, zirconio.—**z. oxide,** circona.

zither(n [zíθœr(n], *s.* (mús.) cítara.

zoanthropy [zoǽnθroupi], *s.* (med.) zoantropía.

zodiac [zóudiæk], *s.* (astr.) zodíaco; circuito.

zodiacal [zodáiakal], *a.* zodiacal.—**z. light,** luz zodiacal.

zoea [zoíạ], *s.* forma larval de algunos crustáceos.

zoetic [zoétik], *a.* (biol.) zoético.

zoic [zóuik], *a.* (zool.) zoico.

Zollverein [tsólfrain], *s.* unión aduanera.

zonal [zóunal], *a.* perteneciente a una zona; que tiene bandas o zonas.

zone [zóun]. **I.** *s.* zona; distrito, sección, territorio; zona, división, sección de una ciudad; banda circular, faja; (poét.) cinturón o cíngulo. **II.** *va.* dividir en zonas o secciones.

zoned [-d], *a.* zonal; dividido en zonas; (poét.) que lleva cinturón; marcado con fajas.

zoneless [-lis], *a.* que no tiene zona, etc.

zonule [-iul], *s.* zona pequeña; faja, anillo, aro pequeño.

zoo [zu], *s.* (*contr.* de ZOOLOGICAL) jardín o parque zoológico.

zoochemistry [zouokémistri], *s.* zooquímica.

zoogeny [zouádʒeni], *s.* zoogenia, zoogonía.

zoogloea [zouoglíạ], *s.* (bacter.) zooglea, aglomerado gelatinoso de bacterias.

zoographer [zouágrafœ(r)], *s.* zoógrafo.

zoographic(al [zouográfik(al], *a.* zoográfico.

zoography [zouágrafi], *s.* zoografía.

zooid [zóuoid]. **I.** *a.* zooideo; de carácter animal. **II.** *s.* (biol.) zooide.

zooidal [zouóidal], *a.* (biol.) zooideo.

zoolater [zouálatœ(r)], *s.*, **zoolatrous** [-trʌs], *a.* zoólatra.

zoolatry [-tri], *s.* zoolatría.

zoolite [zóuolait], **zoolith** [-liθ], *s.* (geol.) zoolito.

zoolit(h)ic [-lítik o líθik], *a.* zoolítico.

zoologic(al [zouoládʒik(al], *a.* zoológico.

zoologist [zouálodʒist], *s.* zoólogo.

zoology [zouálodʒi], *s.* zoología.

zoom [zum], *vn.* (aer.) subir de pronto, levantar el vuelo rápidamente; empinarse.

zoomorphic [zouomórfik], *a.* zoomorfo, de forma de animal; que representa animales.—**zoomorphism** [-izm], *s.* representación de o por medio de animales; culto de animales.

zoonomy [zouánomi], *s.* zoonomía.

zoophagan [zouáfagan], *s.* zoófago, carnívoro.

zoophagous [zouáfagas], *a.* zoófago.

zoophoros [zouáforas], *s.* (arq.) zoóforo.

zoophyte [zóuofait], *s.* (zool.) zoófito.

zoophytic(al [-fítik(al], *a.* zoofítico.

zoosperm [-spœrm], *s.* (biol.) zoospermo.

zoosporangium [-sporéndʒiʌm], *s.* zoosporangio.

zoospore [-spor], *s.* (bot.) zoospora, zoósporo.

zootechnic(al [-téknik(al], *a.* zootécnico.—**zootechnics, zootechny** [-tékniks, zóuotekni], *s.* zootecnia.

zootomist [zouátomist], *s.* zootomista.

zootomy [zouátomi], *s.* zootomía.

Zoroastrian [zouroǽstrian], *a.* parsi, zoroástrico.

Zoroastrianism [-izm], *s.* zoroastrismo.

zoster [zástœ(r)], *s.* cíngulo; (med.) zoster, *f.*, zona.

Zouave [zuáv], *s.* (mil.) zuavo.

zounds [zaundz], *interj.* ¡voto al chápiro! ¡cáspita!

Zulu, Zooloo [zúlu], *a.* y *s.* zulú.

zwieback [swíbak], *s.* especie de pan retostado.

Zwinglian [zwíŋlian]. **I.** *s.* zuingliano o zwingliano, partidario de Zuinglio. **II.** *a.* zuingliano, relativo a Zuinglio o a sus doctrinas.

Zwinglianism [-izm], *s.* (teol.) zuinglianismo.

zygoma [zaigóumạ], *s.* (anat.) cigoma, *m.*, arco cigomático; apófisis cigomática del temporal.

zygomatic [zaigomǽtik], *a.* (anat.) cigomático.—**z. bone,** hueso malar, pómulo.—**z. process,** apófisis cigomática del temporal.

zygomorphic, zygomorphous [-mórfik,-fʌs], *a.* (bot.) cigomorfo, en forma de yugo.—**zygomorphism** [-fizm], *s.* cigomorfismo.

zygophyllaceous [-filéisʌs], *a.* (bot.) cigofíleo.

zyme [zaim], *s.* (biol.) zimo o cimo; un fermento; germen de enfermedad cimótica.

zymogen [záimodʒen], *s.* (bioquím.) cimógeno; (bact.) organismo productor de fermentos.

zymogenesis [-dʒénisis], *s.* (bioquím.) cimogénesis, fermentación.

zymogenic [-dʒénik], *a.* (bioquím.) cimógeno o zimógeno, que produce fermentación.

zymology [zaimálodʒi], *s.* cimología, zimología.

zymosis [zaimóusis], *s.* cimosis o zimosis, fermentación morbífica; enfermedad cimótica.

zymotic [zaimátik], *a.* cimótico, zimótico.

Para la pronunciación véase la clave al principio del libro.

APENDICE

NOMBRES GEOGRAFICOS QUE SE ESCRIBEN DE DISTINTO MODO EN INGLES Y EN ESPAÑOL

A

Aachen [áken], Aquisgrán, Aix-la-Chapelle.
Abydos [abáidas], Abidos.
Abyssinia [æbisíniā], Abisinia.
Achaia [akéiyā], Achæa [akíā], Acaya.
Actium [ǽkšiᴧm o ǽktiᴧm], Accio.
Adelaide [ǽdeleid], Adelaida.
Admiralty Islands, Islas del Almirante.
Adrianople [eidrianóupl], Adri(a)nópolis.
Adriatic [eidriǽtik] Sea, Mar Adriático.
Ægean [idžían] Sea, Mar Egeo.
Ægina [idžáinā], Egina.
Æolis [íolis], Eólida.
Ætna [étnā], Etna.
Ætolia [itóuliā], Etolia.
Afghanistan [æfgǽnistæn], Afganistán.
Aix-la-Chapelle [eks la šapél], Aquisgrán.
Aleppo [alépou], Alepo.
Alessandria [alesándriā], Alejandría (Italia).
Aleutian [aliúšan] Islands, Islas Aleutas o Aleutianas.
Alexandria [ælegzǽndriā], Alejandría (Egipto).
Algeria [ældžíriā], Argelia.
Algiers [ældžírz], Argel.
Allegheny [ælegéini] Mountains, Montes Alleghanys.
Alps [ælps], Alpes.
Alsace [ælséis o ælsǽs], Alsacia.
Alsace-Lorraine, Alsacia-Lorena.
Amazon [ǽmazan], (Río de las) Amazonas.
Andalusia [ændalúžā], Andalucía.
Angouleme [angulém], Angulema.
Annam [ænǽm], Anam.
Antilles [æntíliz], Antillas.
Antioch [ǽntiak], Antioquía.
Antwerp [ǽntwœrp], Amberes.
Apennines [ǽpenainz], Apeninos.
Appalachian [æpalǽchian] Mountains, Montes Apalaches.
Apulia [apiúlyā], Pulla, Apulia.
Aquitaine [ǽkwitein], Aquitania.
Arabia Deserta [aréibiā dizœrtā], Arabia Desierta.—A. Felix [fíliks], Arabia Feliz.—A. Petræa [pœtríā], Arabia Petrea.
Archipelago [arkipélagou], Archipiélago, Mar Egeo.
Ardennes [ardén], Ardenas.
Asia Minor [éižā máino(r)], Asia Menor.
Assisi [asízi], Asís.
Assyria [asíriā], Asiria.
Astrakhan [ǽstrakæn], Astracán.
Athens [ǽθinz], Atenas.
Attica [ǽtikā], Atica.
Augsburg [ɔ́gzbœrg], Augsburgo.
Austria-Hungary [ɔ́striā hᴧ́ŋgari]. Austria-Hungría.
Auvergne [ouvérn], Auvernia.
Avignon [avinyán], Aviñón.

B

Babylon [bǽbilan], Babylonia [-lóuniā], Babilonia.

Bactra [bǽktrā], Bactria.—Bactria [-triā], Bactriana.
Baku [bakú], Bakú.
Bâle [bal], Basel [bázel], Basle [bal], Basilea.
Balearic [bæliǽrik] Islands, Islas Baleares.
Balkan [bɔ́lkan] Mountains, Montes Balcanes.
Balkans [-z], Balcanes.
Baltic [bɔ́ltik] Sea, Mar Báltico.
Baluchistan [balúchistæn], Beluchistán, Baluchistán.
Banat [banát], Banato.
Barbados [barbéidouz], Barbada, Barbados.
Barbary [bárbari], Berbería.
Basque [bæsk] Provinces, Provincias Vascongadas.
Bavaria [bavériā], Baviera.
Bayonne [beiyóun], Bayona.
Bayreuth [bajrɔ́it], Baireut.
Bearn [beár], Bearne.
Beaucaire [boukér], Belcaire.
Bechuanaland [bechuánalænd], Bechuanalandia.
Beirut, Beyrouth [béirut], Beirut.
Belgium [béldž(i)ᴧm], Bélgica.
Belgrade [belgréid], Belgrado.
Belize [beliz], Belice.
Belleisle [beláil], Strait of, Estrecho de Bella Isla.
Bengal [bengɔ́l], Bengala.
Bern o Berne [bœrn], Berna.
Bethany [béθani], Betania.
Bethlehem [béθli(h)em], Belén.
Bethsaida [beθséiadā], Betsaida.
Biscay [bískei], Vizcaya.
Bithynia [biθíniā], Bitinia.
Black Sea, Mar Negro, Ponto Euxino.
Bœotia [bióušā], Beocia.
Bokhara [boukárā], Bojara, Bokhara, Bujara.
Bologna [boulóunyā], Bolonia.
Bordeaux [bɔrdóu], Burdeos.
Bosporus [básporas], Bósforo.
Bothnia [báθniā], Botnia.
Boulogne [bulóun], Boloña.
Brabant [brabǽnt], Brabante.
Brandenburg [brǽndenbœrg], Brandeburgo.
Brazil [brazíl], Brasil.
Bretagne [bretány], Brittany [brítani], Bretaña.
British Columbia [kolᴧ́mbiā], Columbia Británica.
British Honduras [handúras], Belice, Honduras Británica.
British Isles, Islas Británicas.
Bruges [brúdžiz o brué], Brujas.
Brussels [bráselz], Bruselas.
Bucharest [biukarést], Bucarest.
Bukhara [buhárā] = BOKHARA.
Bucovina, Bukovina, Bukowina [bukovínā], Bucovina.
Burgundy [bœ́rgandi], Borgoña.
Byzantium [bizænšiᴧm], Bizancio.

C

Cæsarea [sesaríā], Cesarea.
Calcutta [kælkátā], Calcuta.
Cameroon [kæmerún], Camerún.

Canaan [kéinan], Canaán.
Canary Islands, Islas Canarias.
Canossa [kanásä], Canosa.
Canterbury [kǽntœrb(e)ri], Cantórbery.
Cape Breton [keip brítǫn o brétǫn] **Island**, Isla Real o del Cabo Bretón.
Cape Colony, Colonia del Cabo.
Cape Haitien [héitien], Cabo Haitiano.
Cape of Good Hope, Cabo de Buena Esperanza.
Capernaum [kapœrneiam], Cafarnaúm.
Cape Verde [vœrd] **Islands**, Islas del Cabo Verde.
Carcassonne [karkasón], Carcasona.
Caribbean [kæríbïan o kâríbïan] **Sea**, Mar Caribe, Mar de las Antillas.
Caroline [kǽrolain] **Islands**, Islas Carolinas.
Carpathian [karpéiþïan] **Mountains**, Montes Cárpatos.
Carthage [kárθïdž], Cartago.
Caspian [kǽspian] **Sea**, Mar Caspio.
Castile [kæstíl], Castilla.
Catalonia [kætalóuniä], Cataluña.
Caucasus [kókasás], Cáucaso.
Cayenne [kaién o keién], Cayena.
Ceylon [silán], Ceilán.
Chæronea [keroníä], Queronea.
Chalcedon [kǽlsidan], Calcedonia.
Chaldea [kældíä], Caldea.
Champagne [šæmpéin], Champaña.
Chefoo [chifú], Chifú.
Cherbourg [šérburg o šerbúr], Cherburgo.
Chersonese [kœrsoníz], Quersoneso.
China [cháinä] **Sea**, Mar de la China.
Christiania [krischiǽnïä], Cristianía, Oslo.
Circassia [sœrkǽš(i)ä], Circasia.
Coblenz [kóublents], Coblenza.
Coburg [kóubœrg], Coburgo.
Cochin China [kóuchin cháinä], Cochinchina.
Cologne [kolóun], Colonia.
Constance [kánstans], **Lake of**, (lago de) Constanza.
Constantine [kánstantin], Constantina.
Constantinople [kanstæntinóupl], Constantinopla, (ant.) Bizancio.
Copenhagen [koupenhéigen], Copenhague.
Corinth [kórinθ], Corinto.
Cornwall [kórnwol], Cornualles.
Corsica [kórsikä], Córcega.
Corunna [kǫránä], **Coruña** [kǫrúnyä], la Coruña.
Côte d'Or [kout dór], Costa de Oro.
Cracow [krǽkau o kréikou], Cracovia.
Crete [krit], Creta.
Croatia [kroéišä], Croacia.
Curaçao [kyurasóu], Curazao.
Cyclades [síkladiz], Cíclades.
Cydnus [sídnas], Cidno.
Cyprus [sáipras], Chipre.
Czecho-Slovakia, Czechoslovakia [chekoslovékiä], Checo(e)slovaquia.
Czernowitz [chérnovits], Cernaut(z)i.

D

Damascus [damǽskas], Damasco.
Dalmatia [dælméišä], Dalmacia.
Danube [dǽnjub], Danubio.
Dardanelles [dardanélz], Dardanelos.
Dauphiné [doufinéi], Delfinado.
Dead Sea, Mar Muerto.
Deccan [dékan], Decán.
Delphi [délfai], Delfos.
Denmark [dénmark], Dinamarca.
Dnieper [nípœ(r)], Dniéper.
Dordogne [dordórny], Dordoña.
Douro [dóuru], Duero.
Dover, Dóver.
Dover [dóuvœ(r)], **Strait of**, Paso de Calais.
Dresden [drézdęn], Dresde.

Dunkirk, Dunkerque [dánkœrk], Dunkerque, Dunquerque.
Dvina [dvjná], Duina.

E

Easter Island, Isla de Pascua, Rapanuí.
East Indies [índiz], Indias Orientales.
Edinburgh [édinbœrou], Edimburgo.
Egypt [ídžipt], Egipto.
Elbe [élbä], Elba.
England [íngland], Inglaterra.
English Channel, Paso de Calais.
Ephesus [éfęsas], Éfeso.
Epirus [ipáiras], Epiro.
Erin [érin], (poét.) Erín (Irlanda).
Escurial [eskyúriäl], Escorial.
Esthonia [estóuniä o esθóuniä], Estonia.
Ethiopia [iθïóupiä], Etiopía, Abisinia.
Eubœa [yubíä], Eubea.
Euphrates [yufréitiz], Eufrates.
Europe [yúrǫp], Europa.

F

Falkland Islands [fóklánd], Islas Malvinas o Falkland.
Finland [fínland], Finlandia.
Flanders [flǽndœrz], Flandes.
Florence [flórens], Florencia.
Florida [flóridä] **Keys**, Cayos de la Florida.
Flushing [flásin], Flesinga.
France [fræns o frans], Francia.
Franche-Comté [fráns konté], Franco-Condado.
Franz Josef [fránts yóuzef] **Land**, Archipiélago o Tierra de Francisco José.
Freiburg, Fribourg [fráiburk o fribúr], Friburgo.
Friesland [frízland], Frisia.

G

Galilee [gǽlili], Galilea.
Gallipoli [galípoli], Gal(l)ípoli.
Gand [gan], Gante.
Garonne [garón], Garona.
Gascony [gǽskoni], Gascuña.
Gaul [gol], Galia.
Gelderland [géldœrlænd], Güeldres.
Geneva [dženívä], Ginebra.
Genoa [dženowä], Génova.
Germany [džœrmani], Alemania; (hist. ant.) Germania.
Ghent [gent], Gante.
Gironde [džjránd o žjrónd], Gironda.
Giza [gizä], Guidsé.
Glarus [glárus], Glaris.
Gold Coast, Costa de Oro.
Good Hope (Cape of), Cabo de Buena Esperanza.
Göteborg [yétębary], **Gothenburg** [gátęnbœrg], Göteborg, Gotemburgo.
Göttingen [gétinen], Got(t)inga, Gottingen.
Græcia Magna [gríšä mǽgnä], Magna Grecia.
Granicus [granáikas], Gránico.
Great Britain [brítn], Gran Bretaña.
Greece [gris], Grecia.
Greenland [grínland], Groenlandia.
Guadaloupe [gwadalúp], Guadalupe.
Guam [gwam], Guaján, o Guam.
Guelderland [géldœrlænd], Güeldres.
Guernsey [gœrnzi], Guernesey.
Guiana [giǽnä o giánä], Guayana.
Guienne [gwiyén], Guiena.

H

Hague [héig], **The**, La Haya.
Hainaut [enóu], Henao.
Haiti [héiti], Haití, Isla Española.
Halicarnassus [hælikarnǽsas], Halicarnaso.
Hamburg [hǽmbœrg], Hamburgo.

Hankow [hǽnkáu], Hankao, Hankow.
Hanse [hǽns] **Towns, Hanseatic** [-iǽtik] **Towns,** ciudades hanseáticas.
Harbin [hárbín], Jarbín o Karbín.
Havana [hǝvǽnǝ], La Habana.
Hawaii [hǝwáii], Hawaii, Hawái, Hauái.
Hawaiian [hǝwáiyǝn] **Islands,** Islas Hawái.
Hebrides [hébridiz], Hébridas.
Hejaz [hidžǽz], Heyaz.
Hellas [hélǝs], Hélada.
Helvetia [helvíšǝ], Helvecia.
Herculaneum [hœrkyūléiniʌm], Herculano.
Hindustan [hindustán], Indostán.
Hispaniola [hispǝnyóulǝ], la Española.
Holland [hálǝnd], Holanda.
Holy Land, Tierra Santa.
Horn [hórn] **(Cape),** Cabo de Hornos.
Hungary [hʌ́ŋgǝri], Hungría.
Hymettus [haimétʌs], Himeto.

I

Iceland [áislǝnd], Islandia.
Ilion [ílion], **Ilium** [íliʌm], Ilión (Troya).
Illyria [ilíriǝ], Iliria.
India [índiǝ], India, Indostán.
Indian Ocean, Mar de las Indias, Océano Índico.
Indus [índʌs], Indo.
Ionia [aióuniǝ], Jonia.
Ionian [aióuniǝn] **Sea,** Mar Jónico.
Ireland [áirlǝnd], Irlanda.
Iron Gates, Puertas de Hierro.
Issus [ísʌs], Iso.
Italy [ítǝli], Italia.
Ithaca [íθǝkǝ], Itaca.
Ivory Coast, Costa del Marfil.

J

Japan [džǝpǽn], Japón.
Jericho [džérikou], Jericó.
Jerusalem [džirúsǝlem], Jerusalén.
Judah [džúdǝ], Judá.
Jugoslavia [yúgoslávjǝ], Yugoeslavia.
Julian Alps [džúljǝn ǽlps], Alpes Julianos.
Jutland [džʌ́tlǝnd], Jutlandia.

K

Kaffraria [kǝfrériǝ], Cafrería.
Karelia [kǝrílyǝ], Carelia.
Kashmir [kæšmír], Cachemira.
Key West, Cayohueso, Cayo Hueso.
Khartoum [kartúm], Jartum o Kartum.
Khiva [hívǝ], Jiva.
Kiaochow [kyáucháu], Kiao-Cheu.
Korea [kouríǝ], Corea.
Kronstadt [kranštát], Cronstadt.
Kurdistan [kérdistæn], Curdistán o Kurdistán.
Kurland [kúrlǝnd], Curlandia.

L

Labrador [lǽbrǝdor], Tierra del Labrador.
Lacedæmon [lǽsǝdímon], Lacedemonia.
Lapland [lǽplǝnd], Laponia.
Lassa [lásǝ], Lasa.
Latium [léišiʌm], Lacio.
Lausanne [louzǽn], Lausana.
Lebanon [lébǝnon], Líbano.
Leeward Islands, Islas de Sotavento.
Leghorn [léghorn], Liorna.
Leningrad [léningræd], Leningrado.
Lesser Antilles, Las Pequeñas Antillas.
Lhasa [lásǝ], Lasa.
Libya [líbiǝ], Libia.
Liége [liéž o liéiž], Lieja.
Lille [líl], Lila.
Limburg [límbœrg], Limburgo.
Limousin [limuzén], Lemosín.

Lisbon [lízbon], Lisboa.
Lisle [láil o líl], Lila.
Lithuania [liθuéiniǝ], Lituania.
Loire [lwar], Loira.
Lombardy [lámbǝrdi], Lombardía.
London [lʌ́ndon], Londres.
Lorraine [loréin], Lorena.
Louisiana [luiziǽnǝ], Luisiana.
Louvain [luvǽn], Lovaina.
Low Countries, Países Bajos.
Lower California [kælifórnyǝ], Baja California.
Lower Egypt [ídžipt], Bajo Egipto.
Lower Rhine [rain], Bajo Rin.
Lucerne [lusœrn], Lucerna.
Luxemburg [lʌ́ksembœrg], Luxemburgo.
Lyons [láionz], Lión, Lyón, León de Francia.

M

Maas [mas], Mosa.
Macedon(ia [mǽsǝdǝn, -dóuniǝ], Macedonia.
Madeira [mǝdírǝ], Madera.
Magellan [mǝdžélǝn], **Strait of,** Estrecho de Magallanes.
Magna Græcia [mǽgnǝ grísiǝ], Magna Grecia.
Mainz [máints], Maguncia.
Majorca [mǝdžórkǝ], Mallorca.
Malay [méilei o mǝléi] **Archipelago,** Malasia, Archipiélago Malayo.
Malay Peninsula, Península de Malaca.
Malay States, Federated, Estados Federados de Malaca.
Malines [mǝlínz o malín], Malinas.
Marathon [mǽrǝθan], Maratón.
Marseilles [marséi(lz], Marsella.
Martinique [martiník], Martinica.
Maskat, Masqat [mæskǽt] = MUSCAT.
Mauritius [morís(i)ʌs], Isla de Francia, o Mauricio.
Mayence [mayáns], Maguncia.
Mecca [mékǝ], Meca.
Mechlin [méklin], Malinas.
Mediterranean [mediteréiniǝn] **Sea, Mar** Mediterráneo.
Memphis [mémfis], Menfis.
Metaurus [metórʌs], Metauro.
Meuse [miuz], Mosa.
Mexico [méksikou], México, Méjico.
Middleburg [mídelbœrg], Middelburgo.
Milanese [milǝníz], Milanesado.
Minho [mínyu], Miño.
Minorca [minórkǝ], Menorca.
Mississippi [misisípi], Misisipí.
Missouri [misúri], Misurí.
Mobile [moubíl], Mobila.
Mœsia [míšiǝ], Mesia.
Montpellier [monpelyé], Mompeller.
Montserrat [montserát], Mon(t)serrat(e).
Morocco [morákou], Marruecos.
Moscow [máskau o máskou], Moscú.
Moselle [mouzél], Mosela.
Muscat [mʌskǽt], Mascate (y Omán).
Muscovy [mʌ́skovi], Moscovia.
Mycenæ [maisíni], Micenas.
Mysore [maisóur], Maisur o Misora.

N

Naples [néiplz], Nápoles.
Narbonne [narbón], Narbona.
Navarre [nǝvár], Navarra.
Nazareth [nǽzǝreθ o nǽzriθ], Nazaret.
Nejd [nɛžd o neid], Neyed.
Netherlands [néðœrlǝndz], Países Bajos, Holanda.
New England [íŋglǝnd], Nueva Inglaterra.
Newfoundland [niúfʌndlænd], Terranova.
New Orleans [órliǝnz o orlínz], Nueva Orleáns.
New South Wales [wéilz], Nueva Gales del Sur.
New York [york], Nueva York.
New Zealand [zílǝnd], Nueva Zelandia.

Nicæa [naiṣíǎ], Nicea.
Nice [nis], Niza.
Nile [naĭl], Nilo.
Nineveh [nínevę], Nínive.
Nippon [nipán o nípan], Nipón.
Normandy [nórmandi], Normandía.
North America [amérikǎ], América del Norte.
North Carolina [kærolájnǎ], Carolina del Norte.
North Sea, Mar del Norte.
Norway [nórwei], Noruega.
Nova Scotia [nóuvǎ skóuṣǎ], Nueva Escocia.
Nova Zembla [nóvǎ zemblá], Nueva Zembla.
Numantia [n(i)umǽnṣǎ], Numancia.

O

Oceania [oṣiǽnǎ], **Oceanica** [-ǽnikǎ], Oceanía.
Odessa [oudésǎ o adésa], Odesa.
Old Castile [kæstíl], Castilla la Vieja.
Olives (Mount of), Olivet [álĭvet], Monte Olivete, o de los Olivos.
Olympia [oulímpĭǎ], Olimpia.
Olympus [oulímpʌs], Olimpo.
Olynthus [oulínθʌs], Olinto.
Ophir [óufi(r)], Ofir.
Orange Free State, Estado Libre de Orange.
Ostend [asténd], Ostende.
Ottoman [átomǎn] **Empire**, Imperio Otomano.
Oxus [áksʌs], Oxo, Oxus.

P

Pacific Ocean, Océano Pacífico.
Palatinate [palǽtĭneit], Palatinado.
Palestine [pǽlestaĭn], Palestina.
Palmyra [pǽlmáirǎ], Palmira.
Pamphylia [pǽmfílĭǎ], Panfilia.
Parnassus [parnǽsʌs], Parnaso.
Parthia [párθĭǎ], Partia.
Peiping [béipíŋ], Peiping, Pei-Ping, Pekín.
Pekin(g [pikín o pikíŋ], Pekín.
Pella [pélǎ], Pela.
Peloponnesus [pélopanísʌs], Peloponeso.
Pennine Alps [pénaĭn ǽlps], Alpes Peninos.
Pennsylvania [pensĭlvéinĭǎ], Pensilvania.
Pergamum [pǿrgamʌm], Pérgamo.
Perpignan [perpinyán], Perpiñán.
Persian Gulf, Golfo Pérsico.
Perugia [perúža], Perusa.
Petrograd [pétrogræd], Petrogrado.
Pharsalia [farséilĭǎ], Farsalia.
Philadelphia [fĭladélfĭǎ], Filadelfia.
Philippi [fĭlípaĭ], Filipos.
Philippines [fĭlipinz], Filipinas.
Philippopolis [filĭpápolĭs], Filipópolis.
Phocis [fóuṣĭs], Fócida, Fócide.
Phœnicia, Phenicia [fĭníṣǎ], Fenicia.
Phrygia [frídžĭǎ], Frigia.
Picardy [píkǎrdĭ], Picardía.
Piedmont [pídmant], Piamonte.
Pillars of Hercules [hǿrkyŭliz], Columnas de Hércules.
Piræus [paĭríʌs], Pireo.
Platæa [plǎtĭǎ], Platea.
Poland [póulǎnd], Polonia.
Polynesia [palĭníṣǎ], Polinesia.
Pompeii [pampéji], Pompeya.
Pontus [pántʌs], Ponto.
Port Arthur [árθœr], Puerto Arturo.
Port-au-Prince [port o príns], Puerto Príncipe.
Port of Spain [spéin], Puerto (de) España.
Porto Rico [pórtou ríkou], Puerto Rico.
Prague [prag o préig], Praga.
Pressburg [présburk], Presburgo.
Prince Edward Island, Isla del Príncipe Eduardo.
Provence [provÁns], Provenza.
Providence [právidens], Providencia.
Prussia [prÁṣǎ], Prusia.
Pyrenees [píreniz], Pireneos.

R

R(h)ætia [ríṣǎ], Retia.
Ratisbon [rǽtisban], **Regensberg** [réigensburk], Ratisbona (ciudad de Alemania).
Red Sea, Mar Rojo.
Rheims [rimz o ræns], Reims.
Rhine [ráĭn], Rin o Rhin.
Rhineland [-lænd], Provincias Renanas.
Rhodes [roudz], Rodas.
Rhodesia [roudížǎ], R(h)odesia.
Rhone [roun], Ródano.
Rif, Riff [rĭf], (el) Rif.
River Plate [pléit], Río de la Plata.
Rochelle (La) [roṣél], La Rochela.
Rocky [rákĭ] **Mountains**, Montes Rocosos o Rocallosos.
Romagna [románya], Romaña.
Rome [roum], Roma.
Rouen [ruán o rwan], Ruán.
Roumania [ruméinĭǎ], Rumania.
Roussillon [rusiyón], Rosellón.
Russia [rÁṣǎ], Rusia.

S

Saint-Quentin [sæn kantǽn], San Quintín.
Salamis [sǽlamĭs], Salamina.
Salonika [saloníka], Salónica.
Salt Lake, Lago Salado.
Samothrace [sǽmoθreis], Samotracia.
Sandwich Islands, Islas Sándwich (Hawaii).
Saragossa [særagásǎ], Zaragoza.
Sardinia [sardínĭǎ], Cerdeña.
Sarmatia [sarméiṣĭǎ], Sarmacia.
St. Gothard [seĭnt gátǎrd o sæn gotár], San Gotardo.
St. Helena [helínǎ], Santa Elena.
St. Kitts [kĭts], San Kitts o San Cristóbal.
St. Lucia [lúṣĭǎ], Santa Lucía.
St. Petersburg [pítœrzbœrg], San Petersburgo.
Savoy [savóĭ], Saboya.
Saxe-Coburg [sæks kóubœrg], Sajonia-Coburgo. **—S.-Gotha** [góuθǎ], Sajonia-Gotha.**—S.-Weimar** [vájmar], Sajonia-Wéimar.
Saxony [sæksonĭ], Sajonia.
Scamander [skamǽndœ(r)], Escamandro.
Scandinavia [skændĭnéĭvĭǎ], Escandinavia.
Scania [skéinĭǎ], Escania.
Schaffhausen [ṣáfhauzen], Escafusa.
Scheldt [skelt], Escalda.
Scotland [skátland], Escocia.
Scutari [skútari], Escútari.
Seine [sein o sen], Sena.
Seoul [sáŭl], Seúl.
Serb-Croat-Slovene State [sœrb krouæt slouvín], Servia-Croacia-Eslovenia.
Serbia [sœrbĭǎ], (antes) **Servia**, Servia.
Seville [sevíl o sévĭl], Sevilla.
Shantung [ṣǽntʌŋ], Chantung.
Sheba [ṣíbǎ], Saba o Sabá.
Sicily [sĭsĭlĭ], Sicilia.
Siena [syénǎ], Sena.
Slavonia [slǎvóunĭǎ], Eslavonia.
Slovakia [slouvákĭǎ], Eslovaquia.
Slovenia [slouvínĭǎ], Eslovenia.
Smyrna [smœrnǎ], Esmirna.
Society Islands, Islas de la Sociedad, Tahití.
Somaliland [soumálĭlænd], Somalia.
Soudan [sudán], Sudán.
Sound [saund], Sund.
South Africa, Union of, Unión Sudafricana.
South America, América del Sur, Sud-América.
South Carolina, Carolina del Sur.
South Dakota [dakóutǎ], Dakota del Sur.
Spain [spein], España.
Spanish America, Hispano-América, América Española.
Sparta [spártǎ], Esparta.
Spitzbergen [spítsbœrgen], Spítzberg.
Spoleto [spoléĭtou], Espoleto.

Sporades [spóradiz], Espórades.
Stalingrad [stálingræd], Stalingrado.
Stambul [stambúl], Estambul, Istanbul.
Stockholm [stákhou(l)m], Estocolmo.
Straits Settlements, Establecimientos del Estrecho (de Malaca).
Strasbourg [stræsbœrg, strázbyrg], Estrasburgo.
Stromboli [strómboli], Estrómboli.
Styria [stíriá], Estiria.
Sudan [sudǽn], Sudán.
Sunda [sándá, súnda] Isles, Islas de la Sonda.
Swabia [swéibiá], Suabia.
Sweden [swíden], Suecia.
Switzerland [swítscœrland], Suiza.
Syracuse [síraḳjus], Siracusa.
Syria [síriá], Siria.

T

Tagus [téigas], Tajo.
Tahiti [tahíti o táiti], Tahití.
Tanganyika [tænganyíká], Tangañica, Tanganyka.
Tangier [tændźír], Tánger.
Tartary [tártári], Tatary [tátári], Tartaria.
Taurus [tóras], Tauro.
Texas [téksas], Tejas.
Thailand [táiland], Thailandia (Siam).
Thames [temz], Támesis.
Thapsus [θǽpsas], Tapso.
Thebes [θibz], Tebas.
Thermopylæ [θœrmápili], Termópilas.
Thessalonica [θesalonáiká], Tesalónica, Salónica.
Thessaly [θésali], Tesalia.
T(h)ibet [tiḅét], Tibet.
Thrace [θreis], Tracia.
Tiberias [taiḅíriǎs], Tiberíades.
Ticino [tichínou], Tesino.
Tobago [touḅéigou], Tabago.
Tokio, Tokyo [tóuḳjou], Tokio.
Toulon [tulán], Tolón.
Toulouse [tulúz], Tolosa.
Touraine [turén], Turena.
Trebizond [tréḅizand], Trebisonda.
Trent [trent], Trento.
Treves [trivz], Tréveris.
Troy [troi], Troya.
Tunis [tiúnis o túnis], Túnez.
Tunisia [t(i)unísá], Túnez (región).
Turkestan [tœrkistǽen], Turquestán.
Turkey [tœrki], Turquía.
Tuscany [táskani], Toscana.
Tusculum [táskyulam], Túsculo.
Tyre [tair], Tiro.

Tyrol [tíral o tiróul], Tirol.
Tyrrhenian [tirínian] Sea, Mar Tirreno.

U

Ukraine [yúkrein o yukréin], Ucrania.
United States of America, Estados Unidos de América.
Upper Egypt, Alto Egipto.
Ural [yúral] Mountains, Montes Urales.

V

Valence [valáns], Valencia de Francia.
Veii [víyai], Veyos.
Venetia [veníšiá], Véneto.
Venice [vénis], Venecia.
Versailles [vœrséilz o versáy], Versalles.
Vesuvius [vesúvias], Vesubio.
Vienna [viénǎ], Viena (de Austria).
Vienne [vyén], Viena (de Francia).
Villefranche [vilfránš], Villafranca.
Virgin Islands, Islas Vírgenes.
Vosges [vouž], Vosgos.

W

Wales [weilz], Gales.
Wal(l)achia [waléikiá], Valaquia.
Warsaw [wórsó], Varsovia.
Wartburg [vártḅyrk], Wartburgo.
Watling [wátlin] Island, Isla de Guanahaní o San Salvador.
West Indies, Antillas.
Westphalia [westféiliá], Westfalia, Vestfalia.
West Virginia [vœrdźínyá], Virginia Occidental.
White Sea, Mar Blanco.
Windward Islands, Islas de Barlovento.
Würtemburg [wœrtęmḅœrg], Wurtemberg.

Y

Yan(n)ina [yánjná], Janina, Yanina.
Yeddo [yédó], Yedo.
Yellow River, Río Amarillo.
Yellow Sea, Mar Amarillo.
Yugoslavia [yúgouslávjá], Yugo(e)slavia.

Z

Zambesi [zæmbízi], Zambese, Zambeze.
Zanzibar [zénzibar], Zanguebar (costa); Zanzíbar o Zanzibar (isla).
Zealand [zíland], Zelandia.
Zion [záion], Sión.
Zululand [zúlulænd], Zululand(ia).

NOMBRES PROPIOS ORDINARIOS DE PERSONAS Y NOMBRES DE PERSONAJES NOTABLES

[Se dan sólo los que se escriben de distinto modo en inglés y en español.]

A

Abélard [ǽbelard], Abelardo.
Abraham [éiḅrahæm], Abrahán.
Absalom [ǽbsalom], Absalón.
Abu-Bekr [abú békœ(r)], Abubéker.
Achilles [aḳíliz], Aquiles.
Ada [éidá], Edita.
Adam [ǽdam], Adán.
Adelaide [ǽdeleid], Adelaida.
Adeline [ǽdelain], Adelina.
Adolph [ǽdalf o éidolf], Adolphus [aḍálfas], Adolfo.
Adrian [éidrian], Adriano, Adrián.
Æmilius [imílias], Emilio.

Æneas [iníǎs], Eneas.
Æschines [éskiniz], Esquines.
Æschylus [éskilas], Esquilo.
Æsop [ísop o ísap], Esopo.
Agatha [égaθá], Águeda, Agata.
Agnes [ǽgnis], Inés.
Aileen [eilín o ailín] = HELEN.
Alan, Allen [ǽlan, ǽlen], Alano.
Alaric [ǽlarik], Alarico.
Albert [ǽlbœrt], Alberto.
Albertus Magnus [ælbœrtas mǽgnas], Alberto Magno.
Alcæus [ælsíǎs], Alceo.
Alexander [æligzǽndœ(r)], Alejandro.
Alexandra [-drá], Alejandra.

Para la pronunciación véase la clave al principio del libro.

Alfred [ǽlfrid], Alfredo.
Alice [ǽlis], Alicia.
Alison [ǽlison], Eloísa.
Allan, Allen [ǽlan, ǽlen], Alano.
Alphonso [ælfánsou], Alfonso, Alonso, Ildefonso.
Alwin [ǽlwin], Aluino.
Amadeus [æmǽdiʌs], Amadeo.
Ambrose [ǽmbrouz], Ambrosio.
Amy [éimi], Amata.
Anacreon [anǽkrion], Anacreonte.
Andrew [ǽndru], Andrés.
Ann, Anna [æn, ǽnɐ], **Anne** [æn], Ana.—**Anne Boleyn** [búlin], Ana Bolena.
Anselm [ǽnselm], Anselmo.
Anthony [ǽntoni] *o* ǽnθoni], Antonio.
Antigonus [æntígonʌs], Antígono.
Antiochus [æntáiokʌs], Antíoco.
Antoinette [æntwanét], Antonia.
Antoninus [æntonáinʌs], Antonino.
Antony [ǽntoni], Antonio.
Apuleius [æpyūlíʌs], Apuleyo.
Archibald [árchibold], Archibaldo.
Archimedes [arkimídiz], Arquímedes.
Aristophanes [æristáfaniz], Aristófanes.
Aristotle [ǽristatl], Aristóteles.
Arius [aráiʌs *o* ǽriʌs], Arrio.
Arnold [árnold], Arnaldo.
Arrian [ǽrian], Arriano.
Artaxerxes [artazǽrksiz], Artajerjes.
Arthur [árθœr], Arturo.
Ashurbanipal [ásurbanipál], Asurbanipal.
Athanasius [æθanéiṣʌs], Atanasio.
Attila [ǽtilā], Atila.
Augustine [ɔ́gʌstin *u* ogʌ́stin], Agustín.
Augustus [ogʌ́stʌs], Augusto.
Aurelian [ɔríliạn], Aureliano.
Aurelius [ɔríliʌs], Aurelio.
Austin [ɔ́stin], Agustín.

B

Bacchus [bǽkʌs], Baco.
Baldwin [bɔ́ldwin], Balduino, Baldovino(s).
Baptist [bǽptist], Bautista.
Barnabas, Barnaby [bárnabas, -bi], Bernabé.
Bartholomew [barθálomiu], Bartolomé.
Basil [bǽzil *o* bǽsil], Basilio.
Bayard [béiārd], Bayardo.
Beatrice, Beatrix [bíatris, -triks], Beatriz.
Bede [bid], **Bæda** [bídā], Beda.
Belisarius [beliṣériʌs], Belisario.
Benedict [bénẹdikt], Benito, Benedicto.
Benedicta [benẹdíktā], Benita, Benedicta.
Benjamin [béndẓamin], Benjamín.
Bernard [bœrnārd *o* bernárd], Bernardo.
Bertha [bœ́rθā], Berta.
Bertram [bœ́rtram], Beltrán.
Blaise [blez], Blas.
Boccaccio [bokách(i)o], **Boccace** [bokás], Bocacio, Boccaccio.
Bonaventura [bánavenchū̄rā], Buenaventura, Ventura.
Boniface [bánifeis], Bonifacio.
Bourbon [búrbon], Borbón.
Bridget [brídẓit], Brígida.
Brutus [brútʌs], Bruto.
Buddha [búdā], Buda.

C

Cæsar [síẓā(r)], César.
Calvin [kǽlvin], Calvino.
Cambyses [kæmbáisiz], Cambises.
Camilla, Camille [kamílā, kamíl], Camila.
Camillus [kamílʌs], Camilo.
Caracalla [kærakǽlā], Caracal(l)a.
Caroline [kǽrolain], Carolina.
Casimir [kǽsimir], Casimiro.
Caspar, Casper [kǽspā(r),-œ(r)], Gaspar.
Cassandra [kaṣǽndrā], Casandra.
Cassius [kǽṣiʌs], Casio.

Catharine [kǽθarin], **Catherine** [kǽθerin], Catalina.
Catiline [kǽtilain], Catilina.
Cato [kéitou], Catón.
Catullus [katʌ́lʌs], Catulo.
Cecil [sísil *o* sésil], Cecilio.
Cecile [sisíl], **Cecily** [sésili], Cecilia.
Charlemagne [sárlẹmein], Carlomagno.
Charles [charlz], Carlos.
Charlotte [ṣárlot, -lot], Carlota.
Charon [kéron], Caronte.
Christ [kraist], Cristo.
Christian [kríschan], Cristiano.
Christine [kristín], Cristina.
Christopher [krístofœ(r)], Cristóbal.
Chrysostom [kríṣostom], Crisóstomo.
Ciceley [síṣẹli], Cecilia.
Cicero [síṣẹrou], Cicerón.   1
Cincinnatus [sinṣinéitʌs], Cincinato.
Claude [klod], Claudio.
Claudia [klɔ́diā], Claudia, Claudina.
Claudine [klodín], Claudina.
Claudius [klɔ́diʌs], Claudio.
Cleanthes [kliǽnθiz], Cleanto.
Clement [klément], Clemente.
Cleobulus [klióubulʌs], Cleóbulo.
Clotilda [kloutíldā], Clotilde.
Clovis [klóuvis], Clodoveo.
Columbus [kolʌ́mbʌs], Colón.
Commodus [kámodʌs], Cómodo.
Confucius [konfjúṣʌs], Confucio.
Conrad [kánræd], Conrado.
Constance [kánstans], Constanza, Constancia.
Constantine [kánstantain *o* -tin], Constantino.
Cornelius [kornílyʌs], Cornelio.
Crœsus [krísʌs], Creso.
Cyprian [síprian], Cipriano.
Cyril [síril], Cirilo.
Cyrus [sáirʌs], Ciro.

D

Dagobert [dǽgobert, dagobér], Dagoberto.
Daisy [déizi], Margarita.
Darius [daráius], Darío.
Democritus [dimákritʌs], Demócrito.
Demosthenes [dimásθeniz], Demóstenes.
Dennis [dénis], Dionisio.
Diogenes [daiádẓeniz], Diógenes.
Dionysius [daioníṣiʌs], Dionisio.
Dominic [dáminik], Domingo.
Domitian [domíṣan], Domiciano.
Dorothy [dóroθi *o* dároθi], Dorotea.

E

Edith [ídiθ], Edita.
Edmund [édmʌnd], Edmundo.
Edward [édwārd], Eduardo.
Elagabalus [elagǽbalʌs], Elagábalo, Heliogábalo (hoy se prefiere el primero).
Eleanor, Elinor [élino(r)], Leonor.
Elias [iláias], **Elijah** [iláidẓā], Elías.
Elisha [iláiṣā], Eliseo.
Eliza [iláizā], Elisa.
Elizabeth [ilízabẹθ], Isabel.
Ellen [élen], Elena.
Elsa [élsā], Alicia.
Em(m)anuel [imǽnyuel], Manuel.
Emma [émā], Ema *o* Manuela.
Emily [émili], Emilia.
Epictetus [epiktítʌs], Epicteto.
Epicurus [epikyúrʌs], Epicuro.
Erasmus [irǽzmʌs], Erasmo.
Eratosthenes [eratásθeniz], Eratóstenes.
Ernest [œ́rnist], Ernesto.
Ernestine [œ́rnestin], Ernestina.
Esther [éstœ(r)], Ester.
Euclid [yúklid], Euclides.
Eugene [yudẓin *o* yúdẓin], Eugenio.
Eugénie [œẓení], Eugenia.

Euphemia [yufímiǎ], Eufemia.
Euphrosyne [yufrásini], Eufrosina.
Eusebius [yusíbiʌs], Eusebio.
Eustace [yústis], Eustacio; Eustaquio.
Evangeline [ivǽndźelin, -lain], Evangelina.
Eve [iv], Eva.
Ezekiel [izíkiel], Ezequiel.

F

Fabius [féibiʌs], Fabio.
Faustine [fostín], Faustina.
Felicia [filíśiǎ], Felisa, Felicia.
Ferdinand [férdinænd], Fernando.
Florence [flórens], Florencio, Florencia.
Frances [frǽnsis], Francisca.
Francis [frǽnsis], Francisco.
Frédégonde [fredegónd], Fredegunda.
Frederica [frederíkǎ], Federica.
Frederick [fréderik], Federico.

G

Gabrielle [geibriél o gæbriél], Gabriela.
Gaius [géiʌs], Gayo.
Galen [géilen], Galeno.
Gallienus [galyéinʌs], Galieno.
Genevieve [dźenevív], Genoveva.
Genseric [dźénserik], Genserico.
Geoffrey [dźéfri], Geofredo.
George [dźordź], Jorge.
Geraldine [dźéraldin], Gerarda.
Gerard [dźirárd o dźérard], Gerardo.
Germanicus [dźœrmǽnikʌs], Germánico.
Gertrude [gœrtrud], Gertrudis.
Gideon [gídion], Gedeón.
Gilbert [gílbœrt], Gilberto.
Giles [dźailz], Gil, Egidio.
Godfrey [gádfri], Godofredo.
Gracchii [grékai], Gracos.
Gracchus [grékʌs], Graco.
Grace [greis], Engracia.
Gregory [grégori], Gregorio.
Gustavus [gʌstéivʌs], Gustavo.
Guy [gai], Guido.
Gwendolyn [gwéndolin], Genoveva.

H

Hadrian [héidrian], Adriano.
Hannah [hǽnǎ], Ana.
Hannibal [hǽnibal], Aníbal.
Harold [hérold], Haraldo.
Helen [hélin], Elena.
Héloïse [eloíz], Eloísa.
Helvetius [helvíšʌs], Helvecio.
Henrietta [henriétǎ], Enriqueta.
Henry [hénri], Enrique.
Heraclitus [hérʌklaitʌs], Heráclito.
Herbert [hœrbœrt], Heriberto.
Herman [hœrman], Arminio.
Herod [hérod], Herodes.
Herodotus [hirádotʌs], Herodoto.
Hesiod [hísiod o hésiod], Hesíodo.
Hester [héstœ(r)], Ester.
Hezekiah [hezekáiǎ], Ezequías.
Hiero [háijrou], Herón.
Hieronymus [haieránimʌs], Jerónimo.
Hilary [hílari], Hilario.
Hildebrand [híldebrænd], Hildebrando.
Hipparchus [hipárkʌs], Hiparco.
Hippocrates [hipákratiz], Hipócrates.
Hippolytus [hipálitas], Hipólito.
Homer [hóymœ(r)], Homero.
Honorius [honóriʌs], Honorio.
Horace, Horatio [hóris, hóréiśjou], Horacio.
Hortense [horténs o hórtens], Hortensia.
Hosea [hoziǎ o hozéiǎ], Oseas.
Hubert [hjúbœrt], Huberto.
Hugh [hju], Hugo.—**H. Capet** [kéipit], Hugo Capeto.

Humbert [hʌmbœrt], Humberto.
Humphrey [hʌmfri], Hunfredo.

I

Ignatius [ignéiśjʌs], Ignacio.
Immanuel [imǽnyuel], Manuel.
Inez [áinez o ínez], Inés.
Innocent [ínosent], Inocencio.
Irenæus [airinʌs], Ireneo.
Isabella [izabélǎ], Isabel.
Isidore [ízidor], Isidro o Isidoro.

J

James [dźeimz], Jaime, Jacobo, Santiago.
Jane [dźein], Juana.
Jansen, Jansenius [dźǽnsen, -sínjʌs], Jansenio.
Jasper [dźǽspœ(r)], Gaspar.
Jehovah [dźihóuvǎ], Jehová.
Jeremiah [dźeremáiǎ], **Jeremy** [dźéremi], Jeremías.
Jerome [dźiróum o dźérom], Jerónimo, Gerónimo.
Jesus Christ [dźízʌs kráist], Jesucristo.
Joachim [yóuǎkim], Joaquín.
Joan [dźoun], **Joanna** [dźoǽnǎ], Juana.
Joan of Arc [dźoun ov ark], Juana de Arco.
John [dźan], Juan.
Jonah [dźóunǎ], Jonás.
Jonathan [dźánǎθan], Jonatán, Jonatás.
Joseph [dźóuzef], José.
Josephine [dźóuzefin], Josefina.
Josephus [dźosífʌs], Josefo.
Joshua [dźáśuǎ], Josué.
Josiah [dźosáiǎ], Josías.
Jovian [dźóuvian], Joviano.
Judith [dźúdiθ], Judit.
Jugurtha [dźugœrθǎ], Yugurta.
Julia [dźúlyǎ], Julia.
Julian [dźúlyan], Julián; Juliano (emperador).
Juliet [dźúlyet o dźuliét], Julia.
Julius [dźúlyʌs], Julio.
Justinian [dźʌstínian], Justiniano.
Justin Martyr [dźʌstin mártœ(r)], Justino Mártir.

K

Katharine, Katherine [kǽtharin, kǽθerin], **Kathleen** [kǽθlin o kæθlín] = CATHERINE.
Kempis, a [ǎ kémpis], de Kempis.

L

Ladislas [lǽdislas], Ladislao.
Lambert [lǽmbœrt], Lamberto.
Lawrence, Laurence [lórens], Lorenzo.
Lazarus [lǽzʌrʌs], Lázaro.
Leander [liǽndœ(r)], Leandro.
Leo [líou], León.
Leonard [lénǎrd], Leonardo.
Leonora, Lenore [lionórǎ, linór], Leonor.
Leopold [líopould], Leopoldo.
Lepidus [lépidʌs], Lépido.
Letitia [litíśǎ], Leticia.
Lewis [lúis], Luis.
Livy [lívi], Livio.
Longinus [landźáinʌs], Longino.
Lothaire [lotér], Lotario.
Louis [lúis o lúi], Luis.
Louisa [luízǎ], **Louise** [luíz], Luisa, Eloísa.
Lucan [lúkan], Lucano.
Lucia [lúśǎ], Lucía.
Lucian [lúśan], Luciano.
Lucius [lúśʌs], Lucio.
Lucretia [lukríśǎ], Lucrecia.
Lucretius [lukríśʌs], Lucrecio.
Lucullus [lukálʌs], Luculo.
Lucy [lúsi], Lucía.
Luke [luk], Lucas.
Luther [lúθœ(r)], Lutero.
Lycurgus [laikœrgʌs], Licurgo.

Lysander [lajséndœ(r)], Lisandro.
Lysias [lísjas], Lisias.
Lysimachus [lajsímakʌs], Lisímaco.
Lysippus [lajsípʌs], Lísipo.

M

Mæcenas [misínas], Mecenas.
Magdalen [mǽgdalen], Magdalena.
Magellan [madʒélan], Magallanes.
Mahomet [mahámit], Mahoma.
Malachi, Malachy [mǽlakaj], Malaquías.
Marcel [marsél], Marcellus [-ʌs], Marcelo.
Margaret [márgarit], Margery, Marjorie [márdʒori], Margarita.
Marian, Marion [mérjan], Mariana.
Marie Louise [marí luíz], María Luisa.
Marion [mérjon], Mariano.
Marius [mérjʌs], Mario.
Mark [mark], Marco, Marcos.
Martha [márθa], Marta.
Martial [márśal], Marcial.
Mary [méri], María.
Masinissa [mæsinísa], Masinisa.
Matilda, Mathilda [matíldä], Matilde.
Matthew [mǽθju], Mateo.
Matthias [maθájas], Matías.
Maurice [mórjs o márjs], Mauricio.
Maximilian [mæksimílyan], Maximiliano.
Messalina [mesaláinä], Mesalina.
Michael [májkel], Miguel.
Michelangelo [majkelǽndʒelou], Miguel Ángel.
Millicent [mílisent], Melisenda.
Miriam [mírjam], María.
Mithridates [míθradéjtiz], Mitrídates.
Mohammed [mouhǽmid], Mahoma.
Moses [móuzjz], Moisés.

N

Napier [néjpjœ(r) o napír], Néper, Nápier.
Nathan [néjθan], Natán.
Nathaniel [naθǽnyel], Nataniel.
Nebuchadnezzar [nebyukadnézä(r)], Nabucodonosor.
Nehemiah [niemájä], Nehemías.
Nepos [nípas o népas], Nepote.
Nero [nírou], Nerón.
Nestorius [nestórjʌs], Nestorio.
Nicholas [níkolas], Nicolás.
Nimrod [nímrad], Nemrod.
Noah [nóuä], Noé.

O

Octavius [aktéjvjʌs], Octavio.
Odoacer [odoéjsœ(r)], Odoacro.
Oliver [álivœ(r)], Oliverio.
Origen [órjdʒen], Orígenes.
Othman [áθman], Otmán.
Otho [óuθou], Otto [átou], Otón.
Ovid [ávjd], Ovidio.

P

Patrick [pǽtrik], Patricio.
Paul [pol], Pablo.
Paulina, Pauline [polínä, polín], Paula, Paulina.
Pepin [pépjn], Pepino.—P. the Short, Pepino el Breve.
Perseus [pérsus o pérsjʌs], Perseo.
Peter [pítœ(r)], Pedro.
Phædrus [fídrʌs], Fedro.
Philemon [filímon], Filemón.
Philip [fílip], Felipe; Filipo (de Macedonia).
Philippa [filípä], Felipa.
Philippus [filípʌs], Filipo.
Philo Judæus [fájlou dʒudíʌs], Filo el Judío.
Phineas [fínjas], Fineas.
Phocion [fóuśjon], Foción.
Pilate [pájlät], Pilatos.

Pindar [píndä(r)], Píndaro.
Pius [pájʌs], Pío.
Plato [pléjtou], Platón.
Plautus [plótʌs], Plauto.
Pliny [plíni], Plinio.
Plotinus [plotájnʌs], Plotino.
Plutarch [plútark], Plutarco.
Polybius [políbjʌs], Polibio.
Polycarp [pálikarp], Policarpo.
Polycletus [paliklítʌs], Policleto.
Polycrates [políkratiz], Polícrates.
Pompey [pámpj], Pompeyo.
Pretorius [pritórjʌs], Pretorio.
Proclus [próuklʌs], Proclo.
Procopius [prokóupjas], Procopio.
Prometheus [promíθus, -θjʌs], Prometeo.
Prudence [prúdens], Prudencia.
Ptolemy [tálemj], Tolomeo, Ptolomeo.
Pyrrhus [pírʌs], Pirro.
Pythagoras [piθǽgoras], Pitágoras.

Q

Quentin [kwéntjn], Quintín.
Quintilian [kwjntílyan], Quintiliano.

R

Rachel [réjchel], Raquel.
Ralph [rælf], Rodolfo.
Randall, Randolph [rǽndal, -dalf], Randolfo.
Raphael [réjfjel], Rafael.
Raymond [réjmond], Raimundo, Ramón.
Rebecca, Rebekah [rjbékä], Rebeca.
Reginald [rédʒinald], Reinaldo(s), Reginaldo.
Regulus [régyûlʌs], Régulo.
René [renéj], Renato.
Reuben [rúbjn], Rubén.
Reynold [rénold], Reinaldo(s), Reginaldo.
Rhodes [roudz], Rodas.
Richard [ríchard], Ricardo.
Robert [rábœrt], Roberto.
Roderic(k [ráderjk], Rodrigo.
Rodolphus [rodálfas], Rodolfo.
Roger [rádʒœ(r)], Rogerio.
Roland [róuland], Rolando, Orlando, Roldán.
Rollo [rálou], Rollón, Rolón.
Romulus [rámyûlʌs], Rómulo.
Ronald [ránald], Renaldo.
Rosalie [rázali o róuzalj], Rosalía.
Rosamond [rázamond o róuzamond], Rosamunda.
Rosary [róuzarj], Rosario.
Rose [rouz], Rosa.
Rowland [róuland], Rolando.
Rudolph [rúdalf], Rodolfo.
Rufus [rúfʌs], Rufo.
Rupert [rúpœrt], Ruperto.

S

Saladin [sǽladjn], Saladino.
Sallust [sǽlʌst], Salustio.
Salome [salóumj], Salomé.
Sam(p)son [sǽm(p)son], Sansón.
Sardanapalus [sardanapéjlas], Sardanápalo.
Scaliger [skǽljdʒœ(r)], Escalígero.
Scipio [sípjou], Escipión.—S. Africanus, [æfrikéjnas], Escipión el Africano.
Sennacherib [senǽkerjb], Senaquerib.
Sertorius [scertórjas], Sertorio.
Severus [sevírʌs], Severo.
Sigismund [sídʒjsmʌnd], Segismundo.
Silvanus, Silvan [silvéjnʌs, sílvan], Silvano, Silvio.
Silvester, Sylvester [silvéstœ(r)], Silvestre.
Solomon [sálomon], Salomón.
Solyman [sáliman], Solimán.
Sophia [sóufjä o sofájä], Sofía.
Sophocles [sáfokliz], Sófocles.
Spartacus [spártakʌs], Espartaco.

Stephen [stívɐn], Esteban.
Strabo [stréjboų], Estrabón.
Stradivarius [strædjvériʌs], Estradivario.
Suetonius [swjtóųnjʌs], Suetonio.
Suleiman [suleįmán], Solimán.
Sulla [sʌ́lə], Sila.
Susan, Susanna [súzən, suzǽnə], Susana.

T

Tacitus [tǽsjtʌs], Tácito.
Tamerlane [tǽmœrleįn], Tamerlán.
Tantalus [tǽntalʌs], Tántalo.
Terence [térɐns], Terencio.
Tertullian [tœrtʌ́ljan], Tertuliano.
Thaddeus [θǽdjʌs o θadíʌs], Tadeo.
Thales [θéįliz], Tales.
Themistocles [θemístokliz], Temístocles.
Theobald [θíobɔld], Teobaldo.
Theocritus [θiákrjtʌs], Teócrito.
Theodore [θíodɔr], Teodoro.
Theodoric [θiádorjk], Teodorico.
Theodosius [θiodóųsʌs], Teodosio.
Theophilus [θiáfjlʌs], Teófilo.
Theophrastus [θiofrǽstʌs], Teofrasto.
Theresa [tjrísə], Teresa.
Thomas [táməs], Tomás.
Thrasybulus [θræsjbjúlʌs], Trasíbulo.
Thucydides [θusídjdiz], Tucídides.
Tiberius [tajbírjʌs], Tiberio.
Timothy [tímoθj], Timoteo.
Timour [tjmúr], Timur, Tamerlán.
Titian [tíšən], el Ticiano.
Titus [táįtʌs], Tito.
Tobias [tobáįəs], Toby [tóųbj], Tobías.
Trajan [tréįdžan], Trajano.
Tribonian [trjbóųnjan], Triboniano.
Tristram [trístram], Tristán.
Turenne [tųrén], Turena.
Tybald [táįbɔld], Teobaldo.

U

Ulpian [ʌ́lpjan], Ulpiano.
Ulysses [yulísiz], Ulises.

Urban [œ́rban], Urbano.
Uriah [yųráįə], Urías.

V

Valens [véįlɐnz], Valente.
Valentine [vǽlɐntaįn], Valentín.
Valentinian [vælɐntínįan], Valentiniano.
Valerian [valírjan], Valeriano.
Vergil [vœ́rdžjl], Virgilio.
Veronese [veronése], el Veronés
Vespasian [vɛspéįžįan], Vespasiano.
Vespucci [vɛspútchi], Vespucio.
Vincent [vínsɐnt], Vicente.
Viola, Violet [vaįóųlə, vájoljt], Violante.
Virgil [vœ́rdžjl], Virgilio.
Vitruvius [vįtrúvįʌs], Vitruvio.
Vivian [vívįan], Bibiana.

W

Walter [wɔ́ltœ(r)], Gutierre (ant.), Gualterio.
Wilhelmina [wjlhɛlmínə], Guillermina.
William [wílyəm], Guillermo, Guillén.
Winifred [wínjfred], Genoveva.

X

Xavier [zéįvįœ(r) o zǽvįœ(r)], Javier.
Xenocrates [zenákrʌtjz], Jenócrates.
Xenophanes [zenáfanįz], Jenófanes.
Xenophon [zénofan], Jenofonte.
Xerxes [zœ́rksiz], Jerjes.

Y

Yahveh [yáwɛ], Jehová.

Z

Zachary [zǽkarį], Zacarías.
Zeno [zínoų], Zenón, Cenón.
Zoroaster [zɔ́roœstœ(r)], Zoroastro.
Zwingli [tsvíŋli], Zuinglio.

NOMBRES DIMINUTIVOS Y ABREVIADOS DE PERSONAS USADOS FAMILIARMENTE EN INGLES

Abe [eįb] por Abraham.
Al [æl] por Albert, Alfred o Alexander.
Alec(k [ǽljk] por Alexander, Alejandro.

Bab(s [bæb(z] por Barbara, Barbarita.
Becky [bɛ́kį] por Rebecca, Rebeca.
Bel, Belle [bel] por Isabella, Bela, Belita.
Ben, Benny [bén(į] por Benjamin, Benjamín.
Bert, Bertie [bœrt(į] por Herbert o Albert, Heriberto o Alberto.
Bess, Bet, Betsy, Bessy, Betty, Lizzie por Elizabeth, Belita, Belica.
Biddy [bídį] por Bridget, Brígida.
Bob, Rob [bab, rab] por Robert, Roberto.
Bill, Billy [bįl(į] por William, Guillermito.

Carrie [kérį] por Caroline, Carolina.
Charley, Charlie, Charly [chárlį] por Charles, Carlitos.
Chris [krįs] por Christine o Christopher.
Cis [sįs] por Cicely, Cecilia.
Clare [kler] por Clara, Clarita.

Dan, Danny [dén(į] por Daniel, Daniel.
Dave, Davy [déįv(į] por David, David.
Dick, Dicky [dík(į] por Richard, Ricardito.

Doll, Dolly [dál(į] Dora [dórə], Dot, Dotty [dát(į], por Dorothy, Dorotea.
Don [dan] por Donald.

Ed, Eddie [éd(į] por Edward, Edwin, Edgar o Edmund.
Effie [éfį] por Euphemia, Eufemia.
Etta [étə] por Henrietta, Enriqueta.

Fan, Fannie, Fanny [fǽn(į] por Frances, Francisca, Frasquita, Paquita, Panchita, Currita, Paca, Farruca.
Flo [floų] por Florence.
Fred [fred] por Frederick, Federiquito.

Hal, Harry [hæl, hǽrį] por Henry, Enriquito.
Harriet, Hatty [hǽrįet, hǽtį] por Henrietta, Enriqueta.
Hetty [hétį] por Hester, Ester.
Hodge [hadž] por Roger, Rogerio.

Jack [džæk] por John, Juanito.
Janet [džǽnet o džǽnįt] por Jane, Juanita.
Jeff [džɛf] por Geoffrey o Jefferson.
Jennie, Jenny [džénį] por Jane, Juanita.
Jerry [džérį] por Jeremiah, Jerónimo, Geromo.

Jim, Jimmie [džím(i] *por* **James,** Santiago, Jaimito, Jacobo.
Joe, Josy [džoụ, džóụzi] *por* **Joseph,** Pepe, Pepito, Pepillo.
Johnny [džáni] *por* **John,** Juanito, Juanch(it)o.
Josie [džóụzi] *por* **Josephine,** Pepa, Pepita, Pepilla.

Kate, Kitty *por* **Catharine,** Catuca, Catujita.
Kit [kịt] *por* **Christopher,** Tobalito.

Larry, Laurie, Lawrie *por* **Lawrence,** Lorenzo.
Len [lεn] *por* **Leonard,** Leonardo.
Letty [léti] *por* **Letitia,** Leticia.
Libby, Lib, Lizzie, Liz *por* **Eliza,** Elisa.
Lottie, Lotty [láti] *por* **Charlotte,** Carlota.
Lulu [lúlu] *por* **Lucy** *y* **Louisa,** Lucía, Luisita.

Madge, Maggie, Mag, Meg, Maisie, Mamie, Margot, Margery *por* **Margaret,** Margarita.
Magda *por* **Magdalen.**
Mae, May [mei] *por* **Mary,** Mariquita, Maruja.
Mat *por* **Matthew,** Mateo.
Mat, Mattie, Matty *por* **Martha** *y* **Mathilda.**
Maud [mɔd] *por* **Mathilda,** Matilde.
Mike [maik] *por* **Michael,** Miguelito.
Moll, Mollie, Molly [mál(i] *por* **Mary,** Mariquita, Maruja.

Nan, Nancy [nǽn(si] *por* **Ann,** Anita.
Ned, Neddy [néd(i] *por* **Edward** *o* **Edwin,** Eduardo.
Nell, Nelly [nél(i] *por* **Ellen** *y* **Eleanor,** Elenita y Leonorcita.
Netty [néti] *por* **Janet,** Juanita.

Nick [nịk] *por* **Nicholas,** Nicolasito.

Pam *por* **Pamela,** Pamela.
Patty [pǽti] *por* **Martha,** Marta y **Patricia.**
Peg, Peggy [pég(i] *por* **Margaret,** Margarita.
Pen, Penny [pén(i] *por* **Penelope,** Penélope.
Phil [fịl] *por* **Philip,** Felipe.
Polly [páli] *por* **Mary,** Mariquita, Maruja.
Prue [pru] *por* **Prudence,** Prudencia.

Rita [rítạ] *por* **Margaret,** Margarita.

Sadie [séidi], **Sal, Sally** [sǽl(i] *por* **Sarah,** Sara.
Sam [sæm] *por* **Samuel,** Samuel.
Sil *por* **Silvester,** Silvestre.
Sim *por* **Simon,** Simón, Simoncito.
Sue [su] **Susie** [súzi] *por* **Susan,** Susana.

Ted, Teddy, Theo *por* **Theodore,** Teodoro.
Tess, Tessie *por* **Theresa,** Teresa.
Tilda, Tillie, Tilly *por* **Mathilda,** Matilde.
Tim *por* **Timothy,** Timoteo.
Tom, Tommy *por* **Thomas,** Tomás.
Tony *por* **Anthony,** Toño, Toñico, Antoñito.
Tracy *por* **Theresa,** Teresita.
Trudy *por* **Gertrude,** Gertrudis.

Val *por* **Valentine,** Valentín.
Vicky *por* **Victoria,** Victorina.
Vin *por* **Vincent,** Vicente.

Walt *por* **Walter,** Gualterio.
Will, Willie *por* **William,** Guillermito.

Zach [zæk] *por* **Zachary,** Zacarías.

Para la pronunciación véase la clave al principio del libro.

ABREVIATURAS MAS USUALES

[La abreviatura *sq.* significa *símbolo químico*]

A

A, *sq.* argon.
A. Academician; Academy; America; American; acre(s).
a. accepted; acre(s); alto; are (área); at.
aa. (med.) ana (de cada cosa).
A. A. A. Automobile Association of America, American Automobile Association; Amateur Athletic Association.
A. A. A. S. American Association for the Advancement of Science.
A. A. C. *Anno ante Christum* (año a. de J. C.).
A. B. Bachelor of Arts.
A. B. C. Argentina, Brazil, and Chile (el A. B. C.).
abr. abridged; abridgment.
abs. re. *absente reo* (en la ausencia del acusado).
Ac, *sq.* actinium; acetyl.
A. C. Alpine Club; alternating current; *Ante Christum* (antes de J. C.); Army Corps; Air Corps; Ambulance Corps.
acad. academy; academic.
acct., a/c. account (cuenta).
A. D. *Anno domini* (año de Cristo).
a. d. after date; *ante diem* (antes del día).
ad. advertisement (anuncio).
ad fin. *ad finem* (al fin).
ad inf. *ad infinitum* (hasta el infinito).
ad lib. *ad libitum* (a voluntad).
Adm. Admiral; Admiralty.
Adm. Co. Admiralty Court.
adv. ad valorem; *adversus* (contra); advertisement; advocate.
A. E. F. American Expeditionary Forces.
ae., aet., aetat. *ætatis* (de edad).
A. F. of L. American Federation of Labor.
aft. afternoon (tarde).
Ag, *sq., argentum* (plata).
agcy. agency (agencia).
agr., agric. agriculture; agricultural.
agt. agent.
Al, *sq.* alumin(i)um.
Ala. Alabama.
Alas. Alaska.
a. m. *ante meridiem* (a. m., antes del mediodía).
A. M. *Anno mundi* (año del mundo); *artium magister* (Master of Arts); *ante meridiem* (antes del mediodía); Ave María.
amp. ampere (amperio); amperage (amperaje).
amt. amount.
an. *anno* (año); anonymous.
anat. anatomical; anatomy.
anon. anonymous.
ans. answer (respuesta; resultado—de un problema).
A. N. Z. A. C., *o* **Anzac.** Australian and New Zealand Army Corps (ll. gen. *Anzac*, como palabra completa).
A. O., a/o, account of.
A. P., AP. Associated Press.
app. appendix; appointed.
Apr. April.
Apt. apartment.
aq., Aq. *aqua* (agua).—**AQ,** achievement quotient.
Ar, argon.—**Ar.** Arabic; Aramaic; argentum.
A. R. *Anno Regni* (año del reinado).
A. R. A. Associate of the Royal Academy; American Railway Association.
arith. arithmetic.
Ariz. Arizona.
Ark. Arkansas.

A. R. R. *Anno regni Regis, Reginæ* (en el año del reinado del rey, de la reina).
art. article; artillery.
As, *sq.* arsenic.
A. S. C. E. American Society of Civil Engineers.
A. S. M. E. American Society of Mechanical Engineers.
A. S. P. C. A. American Society for the Prevention of Cruelty to Animals.
assn., assoc. association.
Asst. assistant.
A. S. T. M. American Society for Testing Materials.
A. T. S. American Temperance Society; American Tract Society.
att., atty. attorney.
Att. Gen. Attorney General.
Au, *sq., aurum* (oro).
A. U. C. *ab urbe condita* (de la fundación de Roma).
aug. augmentative; augmented.
Aug. August.
Auth. Ver. Authorized Version (de la Biblia).
auto. automatic; automotive.
aux., auxil. auxiliary.
a. v. *annos vixit* (vivió . . . años).
Av., ave. avenue.
av., avdp. avoirdupois.

B

B, *sq.* boron.
b. base; bass; book; born; brother.
B. British.
B. A. Bachelor of Arts; British Academy; British America; Buenos Aires.
Ba, *sq.* barium.
Bact. bacteriology.
B. Agr. Bachelor of Agriculture.
bal. balance.
B. Arch. Bachelor of Architecture.
barr. barrister.
Bart., Baronet.
bbl. (*pl.* **bbls.**) barrel(s).
B. C. before Christ; British Columbia.
B. C. E. Bachelor of Civil Engineering.
B. C. L. Bachelor of Civil Law.
bd. board; bond; bound.
bdl. (*pl.* **bdls.**) bundle(s).
bds. boards (pasta).
Be, *sq.* beryllium.
Bé. Baumé (grados Baumé).
b. e. bill of exchange.
bet. between.
b. h. p. brake horsepower (potencia al freno).
Bi, *sq.* bismuth.
B. I. British India.
Bibl., bibl. Biblical; bibliographical.
biog. biographical; biography.
bkpt. bankrupt.
bl. (*pl.* **bls.**) bale(s); barrel(s).
B. L. Bachelor of Laws.
B/L. bill of lading.
b. l. bill of lading (conocimiento); breechloader; breechloading.
bldg. building (edificio).
B. L. E. Brotherhood of Locomotive Engineers.
blvd. boulevard.
b. m. board measure.
B. M. E. Bachelor of Mining Engineering.
B. O. T. Board of Trade.
b. p. below proof; bill of parcels; bills payable.

Para la pronunciación véase la clave al principio del libro.

B. P. O. E. Benevolent and Protective Order of Elks.
Br. Breton; British.
Br, *sq.* bromine.
Br. Am. British America.
b. rec. bills receivable.
brl. barrel.
Bros. brothers.
b. s. balance sheet; bill of sale.
B. S. Bachelor of Science; Bachelor of Surgery.
B. Sc. Bachelor of Science.
Bt., bt. Baronet; bought.
B. T. U. British thermal units.
bu., bus. bushel, bushels.
bull. bulletin.
bx. box.

C

C, *sq.* carbon.
C. Cæsar; Caius; Cape; Catholic; centigrade; Chancellor; Chancery; Congress; Consul; Court.
c. cent; centime; chapter; cubic; current; center. —**c. to c.** center to center (de centro a centro).
Ca, *sq.* calcium.
C. A. Chartered Accountant; Chief Accountant; Confederate Army; Court of Appeal; Central America.
ca. case; cathode; centare; circa.
cal. calendar; calends; calorie; calibre.
Cal., Calif. California.
Cam., Camb. Cambridge.
Can. Canada; Canadian.
cap. capital (mayúscula); capitalize; captain; *caput* (capítulo).
Capt. Captain.
catal. catalogue.
Cath. Catholic; Catherine.
cath. cathedral.
C. B. Cape Breton; Companion of the Bath; Common Bench.
Cb, *sq.* columbium.
cc., cc, c. c. cubic centimeter(s).
C. C. C. Christ's College, Cambridge; Corpus Christi College.
Cd, *sq.* cadmium.
Ce, *sq.* cerium.
C. E. Civil Engineer; Chemical Engineer; Church of England.
cent. centigrade; central; *centum* (ciento); century.
cert. certificate; certify.
cf. *confer* (cotéjese); calf binding.
c. f. & i. cost, freight, and insurance.
C. G. Consul-general; Captain-general; Coast Guard; center of gravity.
cg. centigram(me.
C. G. S., o c. g. s. centimeter-gram-second (C. G. S., centímetro-gramo-segundo).
Ch. Chancery; Charles; China; Church.
ch. chapter; child, children; church.
chap. chapter.
Chas. Charles.
chem. chemical, chemistry.
c. i. f. cost, insurance and freight (c. i. f., *o* c. s. f. costo, seguro y flete).
C. I. O. Congress of Industrial Organizations.
ck. cask; check.
Cl, *sq.* chlorine.
cl. centiliter; clause; cloth (pasta de libros).
cm. centimeter.—**cm.²** square centimeter.—**cm.³** cubic centimeter.
c. m. circular measure (radianes).
Co, *sq.* cobalt.
Co. company; county.
c. o., c/o care of; carried over.
C. O. Commanding Officer; Colonial Office.
C. O. D. collect (*o* cash) on delivery (cóbrese a la entrega).

Col. Colonel; Colorado; Columbia; Colossians.
Colo. Colorado.
com. commentary; commerce; commercial.
Com. Commander; Commission; Commissioner; Committee; Commodore.
comp. comparative; compare; composer; compound.
Com. Ver. Common Version (de la Biblia).
con. conclusion; contra.
Cong. Congregational; Congress; Congressional.
Conn. Connecticut.
Cont. Continental.
cont. containing; contents; continent; continue(d); contra; contract.
co-op. co-operative.
cop. copper; copyrighted.
Cor. Corinthians; coroner.
cor. corpus; corrected; correction; correspondent; corner; cornet.
corol., coroll. corollary.
corpn. corporation.
cos, cosine.
cot, cotangent.
c. p. candle power; (gen. **C. P.**) chemically pure.
cp. compare (cotéjese, véase).
C. P. A. Certified Public Accountant.
cpd. compound.
Cr, *sq.* chromium.
cr. credit; creditor; center; crown.
cres., cresc. crescendo.
Cs, *sq.* cæsium.
C. S. Christian Science; Civil Service; Court of Sessions.
cs. cases (cajas).
C. S. A. Confederate States Army; Confederate States of America.
C. S. I. Companion of the Star of India.
Ct. Connecticut; court; Count.—**Ct,** *sq.* celtium.
ct. cent; county.
ctf. certificate.
c. to c. center to center.
cts. cents; centimes; certificates.
Cu, *sq., cuprum* (cobre).—**Cu.** cumulus.
cu., cub. cubic.
C. V. Common Version (versión corriente—de la Biblia).
c. w. o. cash with order.
cwt. hundredweight(s.
cyl. cylinder; cylindrical.

D

d. day; denarius (penique); died; dime; dollar.
d/a. days after acceptance.
D/A. deposit account.—**D. A.** District Attorney.
Dan. Daniel; Danish.
D. A. R. Daughters of the American Revolution.
D. C. *da capo* (desde el principio); direct current; District of Columbia; District Court.
D. C. L. Doctor of Civil Law.
D. D. Doctor of Divinity.
d. d. days after date; day's date.
D. D. S. Doctor of Dental Surgery.
deb., deben. debenture.
Dec. December.
deg. degree.
Del. Delaware.
Dem. Democrat, Democratic.
Dep., Dept. department; deponent; deputy.
der., deriv. derivation; derivative.
dft. defendant; draft.
D. G. *Dei gratia* (por la gracia de Dios); Director-General.
dg. decigram.
dial. dialect, dialectical.
diam. diameter.
diff. difference; different; differs.
dim. diminuendo; diminutive; dimension.

dioc. diocese; diocesan.
dipl. diplomatic; diplomatist.
disc. discount; discovered.
dist. distance; district.
Div. Divinity.
div. divergence; divide; dividend; division; divorced.
dkl. dekaliter(s).
dkm. dekameter(s).
dl. deciliter.
D. Lit(t). Doctor of Letters, *or* of Literature.
D. L. O. Dead Letter Office.
dm. decimeter; decameter.
D. Mus. Doctor of Music.
D. O. Doctor of Osteopathy.
do. ditto (ídem, lo mismo).
dol., doll. (*pl.* **dols.**) dollar.
doz. dozen, dozens.
Dr. debtor; doctor.
dr. dram; drawer.
dram. pers. *dramatis personæ* (personajes dramáticos).
D. Sc. Doctor of Science.
dup. duplicate.
D. V. *Deo volente* (Dios mediante).
D. V. M. Doctor of Veterinary Medicine.
dwt. pennyweight.
Dy, *sq.* dysprosium.
D. Z. Doctor of Zoology.
dz. dozen.

E

E. Earl; earth; east; eastern; engineer; English.
ea. each.
E. & O. E. errors and omissions excepted.
E. C. Eastern Central (distrito postal de Londres); Established Church; Engineering Corps.
Eccl., Eccles. Ecclesiastes.
eccl., eccles. ecclesiastic.
econ. economic(s); economy.
ed. edition; editor (redactor).
Ed., Edin. Edinburgh.
edit. edited; edition.
educ. education(al).
E. E. Electrical Engineer; errors excepted.
E. E. & M. P. Envoy Extraordinary and Minister Plenipotentiary.
Eg. Egypt.
e. g., *exempli gratia* (v. g.).
E. I., E. Ind. East India; East Indies.
elec., elect. electrical; electricity.
Eliz. Elizabeth; Elizabethan.
E. lon., E. long. east longitude.
E. M. F. electromotive force.
E. N. E. east-northeast.
Eng. England; English.
eng., engin. engineer; engineering.
Epis(c). Episcopal.
Erb, *sq.* erbium.
E. S. E. east-southeast.
esp., espec. especially.
Esq., Esqr. (*pl.* con s) esquire.
est., estab. established.
E. T., e. t. electric telegraph; English translation.
et al. *et alibi* (y en otra parte); *et alii* (y otros).
etc. et cetera.
et seq. *et sequentia* (y que sigue).
etym(ol). etymology.
Eu, *sq.* europium.
Eur. Europe; European.
ex. example; exception; excursion; executive.
Ex., Exod. Exodus.
Exc. Excellency.
exc. excellent; except; excepted; exception.
Exch. exchange; exchequer.
ex div. without dividend.
Exec., Exr. executor.
Execx., Exrx., Exx. executrix.

exp. export, exported; express; expenses.
Ezek. Ezekiel.

F

F, *sq.* fluorine.
F. Fahrenheit; Father; Fellow; Friday.
f. farthing; fathom; folio; forte (en la música); franc.
F. A. G. S. Fellow of the American Geographical Society.
Fah., Fahr. Fahrenheit.
fam. familiar; family.
F. A. M. Free and Accepted Masons.
far. farad; farthing; farriery.
F. A. S. Fellow of the Antiquarian Society.
FBI, Federal Bureau of Investigation.
F. B. S. Fellow of the Botanical Society.
fcp., fcap. foolscap.
F. D. Defender of the Faith.
Fe, *sq., ferrum* (hierro).
Feb. February.
Fed. Federal.
ff. folios; following; fortissimo.
F. G. S. Fellow of the Geological Society.
fid. fiduciary.
fig. figurative(ly); figure(s).
fin. *ad finem* (al fin); financial.
Fin. Sec. financial secretary.
Fla. Florida.
F. M. Field Marshal; Foreign Mission.
fo. folio.
f. o. b. free on board (libre a bordo).
fol. folio.
fol., foll. following.
for. foreign; forestry.
f. o. r. free on rail (libre en la estación ferroviaria).
F. P. fire-plug.
Fr. France; Francis; French; Friday.
fr. fragments; francs; from.
F. R. A. S. Fellow of the Royal Astronomical Society.
F. R. C. P. Fellow of the Royal College of Physicians (Londres).
F. R. C. S. Fellow of the Royal College of Surgeons (Londres).
Fred., Fredk. Frederick.
F. R. G. S. Fellow of the Royal Geographical Society.
Fri. Friday.
F. R. I. B. A. Fellow of the Royal Institute of British Architects.
F. R. S. Fellow of the Royal Society.
F. S. A. Fellow of the Society of Antiquities (o of Arts).
Ft. fort.—ft. feet, foot.
FTC, Federal Trade Commission.
F. Z. S. Fellow of the Zoological Society.

G

G., German; Germany.
g. genitive; gram(me; guide; gauge; guinea.
Ga. Georgia.
Ga, *sq.* gallium.
Gal. Galatians; Galen.
gal., gall. (*pl.* **gals.**) gallon(s).
G. A. R. Grand Army of the Republic.
gaz. gazette; gazeteer.
G. B. Great Britain.
G. B. & I. Great Britain and Ireland.
g. c. d. greatest common divisor.
g. c. m. greatest common measure.
Gd, *sq.* gadolinium.
G. D. Grand Duchess, Grand Duke.
Ge, *sq.* germanium.
gen. gender; general(ly; genus.
Gen. General; Genesis; Geneva.

Geo. George; Georgia.
geog. geography, -phic(al).
Ger., Germ. German; Germany.
g. gr. great gross.
G. H. Q. General Headquarters.
Gl, *sq.* glucinum.
G. M. Grand Master; general manager.
G. M. T. Greenwich mean time.
G. O. P. Grand Old Party (Republican).
Gov. Government; Governor.
Gov. Ptg. Off. Government Printing Office.
Govt. Government.
G. Ph. Graduate in Pharmacy.
G. P. O. General Post Office.
gr. grain; gram(me.
gs. guineas.
G. T. Good Templar; Grand Tiler; gross ton.
gt. *gutta* (gota).—*pl.* **gtt.**
Gt. Br., Gt. Brit. Great Britain.
gu. güinea.
guar. guaranteed.

H

H, *sq.* hydrogen.
h. hardness; height; hour; hundred.
H. B. M. Her (*o* His) Britannic Majesty.
H. C. Herald's College; House of Commons.
h. c. f. highest common factor.
hdkf. handkerchief.
hdqrs. headquarters.
H. E. His Eminence, His Excellency.
He, *sq.* helium.
hf. half.—**hf. cf.** half-calf.
Hg, *sq., hydrargyrum* (mercurio).
hg. hektogram(me.
H. H. His (*o* Her) Highness; His Holiness.
hhd. hogshead.
H. I. Hawaiian Islands.
H. I. H. His (*o* Her) Imperial Highness.
H. I. M. His (*o* Her) Imperial Majesty.
H. L. House of Lords.
H. M. His (*o* Her) Majesty.
H. M. S. His (*o* Her) Majesty's service, ship *o* steamer.
Ho, *sq.* holmium.
Hon. Honorable.
hort., hortic. horticulture.
h. p. horse power; high pressure; half pay.
H. Q. Headquarters.
H. R. Home Rule; House of Representatives.
hr. (*pl.* **hrs.**) hour(s).
H. R. E. Holy Roman Empire (*o* Emperor).
H. R. H. His (*o* Her) Royal Highness.
H. T. Hawaii Territory.
ht. height; heat.

I

I, *sq.* iodine.
I. Idaho; Iowa; Imperator; island.
Ia. Iowa.
ib., ibid. *ibidem* (ibídem).
I. C. C. Interstate Commerce Commission.
Ice., Icel. Iceland, Icelandic.
id. *idem* (ídem).
Id(a). Idaho.
i. e. *id est* (esto es, es decir).
i. h. p. indicated horsepower.
Ill., Ills. Illinois.
imp. imperial; imported; importer; imperative; imperfect; imprimatur.
in. inch(es).
In, *sq.* indium.
inc. including; incorporated; increase.
incl. including; inclusive; inclosure.
incog. incognito.
incor(p). incorporated.
Ind. India; Indian; Indies; Indiana.
init. *initio* (al principio).

in loc. cit. in the place cited.
I. N. R. I. Iesus Nazarenus, Rex Iudæorum (Inri—Jesús Nazareno, Rey de los Judíos).
I. N. S. International News Service.
ins. inches; insurance.
inst. instant; institute; installment.
int. interest; interior; international.
in trans. *in transitu* (en el tránsito).
Int. Rev. Internal Revenue.
inv. invented; inventor; invoice.
Io. Iowa.—**Io,** *sq.* Ionium.
I. O. O. F. Independent Order of Odd Fellows.
I. O. U. I owe you (abonaré).
i. q. *idem quod* (lo mismo que).
I. Q. intelligence quotient.
Ir, *sq.* iridium.—**Ir.** Ireland; Irish.
Is. Island, Isle.
Is., Isa. Isaiah.
Isl(s). Island(s).
It., Ital. Italian; Italic; Italy.
ital. italic (bastardilla).
I. W. Isle of Wight.
I. W. W. Industrial Workers of the World.

J

Jam. Jamaica.
Jan. January.
Jap. Japan; Japanese.
Jas. James.
J. C. Jesus Christ; Julius Cæsar; Justice Clerk.
jc., jct., jctn. junction.
J. D. *Jurum Doctor* (doctor en Jurisprudencia).
Jer. Jeremiah.
j. g., jg, junior grade (*U. S. Navy*).
Jno. John.
Jon(a). Jonathan.
Jos. Joseph; Josiah.
Josh. Joshua.
J. P. Justice of the Peace.
Jr. junior; juror.
Judg. Judges.
Jul. Julian; Julius; July; julep.
Jun. June; Junius, Junior.
Junc. junction (empalme, f. c.).
Junr. junior.

K

K, *sq.,* kalium (potasio).
K. King; Knight(s).
K., Ki. Kings (Libro de los Reyes).
K., Kal. *Kalendæ,* kalends.
Kan., Kans., Kas. Kansas.
K. B. King's Bench; Knight of the Bath.
K. C. King's Counsel; Knights of Columbus.
K. C. B. Knight Commander of the Bath.
Ken. Kentucky.
K. G. Knight of the Garter.
kg. keg; kilogram(s).—**kgs.** kegs.
kgm., kilo., kilog. kilogram(me.
kilom. kilometer.
K. K. K. Ku-Klux-Klan.
km. kingdom.
km. kilometer(s)—**km.²** square kilometer(s).
Knt. Knight.
k. o. knockout (boxeo).
K. O. Commanding Officer (fam.).
K. of C. Knights of Columbus.
Kr, *sq.* krypton.
Kt. Knight.—**kt.** carat.
kw. kilowatt.
Ky. Kentucky.

L

L. lady; lake; Latin; *libra;* London; Lord.
l. latitude; league; length; line; liter.
La. Louisiana.

La, *sq.* lanthanum.
Lab. Labrador.
Lat. Latin.—**lat.** latitude.
lb. (lbs. *pl.*) *libra*, pound(s).
L. C. Lower Canada; Library of Congress; Lord Chamberlain; Lord Chancellor.
l. c. lower case; left center; letter of credit.
L/C. Letter of Credit.
l. c. d. lowest common denominator.
l. c. m. least common multiple.
Ld., ld. Lord; limited.
Leg., Legis. legislature; legislative.
Lev., Levit. Leviticus.
L. G. Life Guards; Low German.
l. h. left hand.
Li, *sq.* lithium.
lib. *liber* (libro).—**Lib.** Liberal.
Lieut. Lieutenant.
Linn. Linnæus; Linnean.
liq. liquid; liquor.
Lit. D., Litt. D. *Literarum Doctor* (doctor en letras).
LL. B. *Legum Baccalaureus* (bachiller en leyes).
LL. D. *Legum Doctor* (doctor en leyes).
loc. cit. *loco citato.*
log, logarithm.
lon., long. longitude.
Lon., Lond. London.
L. S. Linnean Society; *locus sigilli* (lugar del sello).—**l. s.** left side.
L. (*o* £) **s. d.** *Libræ, solidi, denarii*, pounds, shillings, pence.
Lt. Lieutenant.
Ltd., ltd. limited.
Lu, *sq.* lutecium.
Luth. Lutheran.

M

M. Monsieur; Member.
m. married; *meridiem* (mediodía); meter(s); mile; minim; month; moon.—**m.²** square meter(s).—**m.³** cubic meter(s).
M. A. *Magister artium*, Master of Arts.
Mad. Madam.
mag. magazine; magnet(ism).
Maj. Major.
Mal. Malachi; Malayan.
man. manual (teclado).
Manit. Manitoba.
manuf. manufactory; manufacturer.
Mar. March.—**mar.** maritime.
M. Ar., M. Arch. Master of Architecture.
Mass. Massachusetts.
math. mathematics.
Matt. Matthew; Matthias.
M. B. *Medicinæ baccalaureus*, Bachelor of Medicine; Bachelor of Music.
M. C. Member of Congress; Member of Council; Master Commandant; Master of Ceremonies.
Mch. March.
M. D. *Medicinæ doctor*, Doctor of Medicine.
Md. Maryland.
Mdlle. Mademoiselle.
Mdm. Madam.
M. D. S. Master of Dental Surgery.
mdse. merchandise.
M. E. Methodist Episcopal; Mining Engineer; Mechanical Engineer.
Me. Maine.—**Me,** *sq.* methyl.
meas. measure.
mech. mechanic; mechanical.
med. medical; medicine; medieval; medium.
mem. memorandum; memoir; member.
Messrs., MM. Messieurs.
metal., metall. metallurgy.
Meth. Methodist.
Mex. Mexican; Mexico.
mf. mezzo forte (algo fuerte).
mfd. manufactured; microfarad.
mfg. manufacturing.

mfs. manufactures.
Mg, *sq.* magnesium.—**mg.** milligram.
Mgr. manager; Monseigneur; Monsignor(e).
mi. mile(s); mill(s); minute; minor.
Mic. Micah.
M. I. C. E. Member Institute of Civil Engineers.
Mich. Michigan; Michaelmas; Michael.
mil., milit. military.
mim. mimeograph.
min. mining; minute.
Minn. Minnesota.
Min. Plen. Minister Plenipotentiary.
misc. miscellaneous; miscellany.
Miss. Mississippi; mission; missionary.
ml. millilitre.
Mlle. (*pl.* **Mlles.**) Mademoiselle.
mm. millimeter(s).—**m.²** square millimeter(s).—**m.³** cubic millimeter(s).
Mme. (*pl.* **Mmes.**) Madame.
Mn, *sq.* manganese.
Mo, *sq.* molybdenum.
Mo. Missouri; Monday.
M. O. Money Order.
mo. (*pl.* **mos.**) month(s).
mod. moderato; modern.
Mon. Monday.
Mons. Monsieur.
Monsig. Monsignor; Monseigneur.
Mont. Montana.
morn. morning.
M. P. Member of Parliament; Military Police.
M. P. C. Member of Parliament, Canada.
m. p. h. miles per hour.
Mr. Mister, Master (señor).
Mrs. Mistress (señora).
MS. (*pl.* **MSS.**) manuscript(s).
M. S. Master of Science; Master of Surgery.
M. Sc. Master of Science.
m. s. l. mean sea level.
Mt. (*pl.* **Mts.**) mount, mountain.
mun. municipal.
Mus. Doc. Doctor of Music.
m. v. *mezza voce* (a media voz); mean variation.
myth(ol). mythological; mythology.

N

N, *sq.* nitrogen.
N. north; Norse; Nero.
n. name; *natus* (nacido); neuter; noon; number.
Na, *sq., natrium* (sodio).
N. A. A. National Aeronautic Association.
N. A., N. Am. North America.
N. A. S. National Academy of Sciences.
nat., natl. national.
naut. nautical.
nav. naval; navigation.
Nb, *sq.* niobium.
N. B. New Brunswick; North Britain; North British; *nota bene* (nótese bien).
N. C. North Carolina; New Church.
Nd, *sq.* neodymium.
n. d. no date.
N. Dak. North Dakota.
Ne, *sq.* neon.
N. E. northeast, northeastern; New England.
Neb., Nebr. Nebraska.
neg. negative(ly).
n. e. i. *non est inventus* (no ha sido hallado).
nem. con. *nemine contradicente* (némine discrepante).
N. Eng. New England.
Neth. Netherlands.
Nev. Nevada.
New Test. New Testament.
N. F. Newfoundland.
N. G. National Guard; (fam.) no good (que no sirve para nada; malo).
Ng. Norwegian.—**n. g.** (fam.) no good (no sirve).
N. H. New Hampshire.
Ni, *sq.* nickel.

N. J. New Jersey.
N. L. north latitude.
N. M., N. Mex. New Mexico.
N. N. E. north-northeast.
N. N. W. north-northwest.
No. number (*pl.* **nos.**); north.
N. O. New Orleans.
nol. pros. *nolle prosequi.*
noncom. noncommissioned officer.
non seq. *non sequitur* (no sigue).
Norw. Norway, Norwegian.
Nos. numbers.
Nov. November.
N. P. New Providence; Notary Public.
N. S. Nova Scotia; North Sea; New School (teol.); New Style.
n..s. not specified; nickel steel.
N/S not sufficient (funds).
N. S. W. New South Wales.
Nt, *sq.* niton.
N. T. New Testament; new translation.
nt. wt. net weight.
n. u. name unknown.
Num., Numb. Numbers (Biblia).
N. V. New Version (de la Biblia).
N. W. northwest (N. O.).
N. Y. New York.—**N. Y. C.** New York City.
N. Z., N. Zeal. New Zealand.

O

O, *sq.* oxygen.
O. Ohio; Ontario; Ocean; October; Ossa.
o/a. on account (of); our account.
ob. *obiit* (murió); *obiter* (de paso).
obdt., obt. obedient.
obs. observation; observatory; obsolete.
o. c. on centers (entre centros).
Oct. October.—**oct.** octavo.
O. D., o. d. Officer of the Day; Old Dutch; ordinary seaman; overdraft, overdrawn; outside diameter; olive drab (uniform).
o/d, o/d. on demand.
O. E. Old English.—**o.e.** omissions excepted.
O. F. Odd Fellows; Old French.
O. K. all correct (visto bueno, V.° B.°).
Okla. Oklahoma.
Old Test. Old Testament.
Ont. Ontario.
op. opposite; opus (obra); opera; operation.
op. cit. *opere citado,* in the work cited.
Or. Oregon; Oriental.
ord. ordained; order; ordinance.
Ore., Oreg. Oregon.
Os, *sq.* osmium.
O. S. Old Saxon; Old School; Old Style (calendario); Old Series; Outside Sentinel.
O. T. Old Testament.
oz. (*pl.* **oz.** *u* **ozs.**) ounce.

P

P, *sq.* phosphorus.
p. page; part; particle; piano (suave); pint; pipe.
Pa. Pennsylvania.
P/A power of attorney; private account.
Pac. Pacific.
Pat. Off. Patent Office.
P. A. U. Pan American Union.
paym't, payt. payment.
Pb, *sq.,* *plumbum* (plomo).
P. B. British Pharmacopœia.
pc. piece; prices.
p. c. per cent; post card.
p/c petty cash; prices current.
Pd, *sq.* palladium.
pd. paid.
P. E. Presiding Elder; Protestant Episcopal.
P. E. I. Prince Edward Island.
Penn. Pennsylvania.
per an. *per annum* (por año).

per ct. *per centum,* percent (porcentaje).
pert. pertaining.
Peruv. Peruvian.
pes. peseta.
pf. perfect; preferred.
p. f. *più forte* (un poco más fuerte).
Pg. Portugal; Portuguese.
Phar., Pharm. pharmacy; pharmacopœia; pharmaceutical.
Ph. C. Pharmaceutical Chemist.
Ph. D. Doctor of Philosophy.
Ph. G. Graduate in Pharmacy.
Phil., Phila. Philadelphia.
phot., photog. photographic; photography.
phys. physician; physics.
Phys. Sci. physical science.
P. I. Philippine Islands.
pil. *pilula* (píldora).
pkg. (**pkgs.** *pl.*) package(s).
pl. place; plate; plural.
plf., plff., pltff. plaintiff.
P. M. postmaster; *post meridiem* (tarde); paymaster; Past Master.—**pm.** premium.
P. O. post office; Province of Ontario.
p. o. postal order; post office.
P. O. B. post-office box.
P. O. D. pay on delivery; Post-Office Department.
P. O. O. postoffice order.
pop. population.
pos. positive; possession; possessive.
pot. potential.
pp. pages; pianissimo; past participle.
ppd. prepaid.
p. p. i. policy proof of interest.
p. q. previous question.—**P. Q.** Province of Quebec.
Pr, *sq.* praseodymium; propyl.
Pr. preferred (stock).
pr. pair; price; pronoun; proper; present.
P. R. Porto Rico *o* Puerto Rico.
Pres. President.—**pres.** present; presidency.
Presb(yt). Presbyterian.
prin. principal(ly); principles.
priv. privative.
Prof. Professor.
Prot. Protestant.
pro tem. *pro tempore.*
Prov. Proverbs.—**prov.** province; provincial.
prox. proximo (el mes que viene).
prs. pairs.
Prus. Prussia; Prussian.
Ps., Psa. Psalm; Psalms.
P. S. postscript; Privy Seal.
ps. pieces; pseudonym.
pt. part; payment; pint; port; point.
Pt, *sq.* platinum.
Ptg. Portugal; Portuguese.
P. T. O. please turn over.
pub. public; published; publisher.
Pub. Doc. public documents.
pwt. pennyweight.
P. X. please exchange.
PX, Post Exchange (military).

Q

Q. Quebec; queen; Quintus.
q. quasi; query; quintal; quarto; quire.
Q. B. Queen's Bench.
Q. C. Queen's Counsel.
Q. E. D. *quod erat demonstrandum* (L. C. D. D., lo cual debíamos demostrar).
Q. E. F. *quod erat faciendum* (que era lo que se trataba de hacer).
q. l. *quantum libet* (tanto como se desee).—**ql.** quintal.
Q. M. C., QMC, Quartermaster Corps.
q. s. *quantum sufficit* (lo que baste); quarter section.

qt. quantity; quart.—qts. quarts.
qu. question; query; quart(er); queen.
Que. Quebec.
ques. question.
quot. quotation.
q. v. *quantum vis* (cuanto se quiera); *quod vide* (véase).
qy. query.

R

R. Réaumur; radical; railway; recipe; river; Republican; Royal.
r. rod; rood; rupee.
Ra, *sq.* radium.
R. A. Rear Admiral; right ascension (astr.); Royal Academy; Royal Arch.
Rad. Radical.—rad. radix (raíz).
R. A. F. Royal Air Force.
Rb, *sq.* rubidium.
R. C. Roman Catholic; Red Cross; Reserve Corps.
R. C. Ch. Roman Catholic Church.
R. C. S. Royal College of Surgeons.
Rd. road
R. E. Reformed Episcopal; Right Excellent; Royal Engineers; Royal Exchange.
rec., recpt., rect. receipt.
rec'd., recd. received.
Rec. Sec. recording secretary.
ref. reference; referred; reformed; reformer.
reg. registry; regular.—Reg. *regina* (reina).
Reg., Regt. regent; regiment.
rep. report; reporter; representative.
Rep., Repub. Republic; Republican.
Rev., rev. Revelation (Apocalipsis); revenue; Reverend (Revs. *pl.*); review; revolution.
Rev. Stat. Revised Statutes.
Rev. Ver. Revised Version (de la Biblia).
R. F. A. Royal Field Artillery.
RFC, Reconstruction Finance Corporation.
R. F. D. Rural Free Delivery.
R. G. S. Royal Geographical Society (Londres).
Rh, *sq.* rhodium.
R. H. Royal Highness.—r. h. right hand.
R. I. Rhode Island; Rex Imperator.
Rich., Rich'd. Richard.
R. I. P. *requiescat in pace* (en paz descanse).
R. M. S. Royal Mail Steamer.
R. N. Royal Navy; registered nurse.
R. N. R. Royal Naval Reserve.
Robt. Robert.
Rom. Cath. Roman Catholic.
R. P. Reformed Presbyterian; Regius Professor.
r. p. m. revolutions per minute.
r. p. s. revolutions per second.
R. R. railroad.
R. S. recording secretary; Revised Statutes.—r. s. right side.
R. S. V. P. *Répondez s'il vous plaît* (Sírvase contestar).
Rt. Hon. Right Honorable.
Rt. Rev. Right Reverend.
Ru, *sq.* ruthenium.
R. V. Revised Version (versión corregida—de la Biblia).
R. W., Rw., Rwy., Ry. railway.

S

S, *sq.* sulphur.
S. Saxon; Servius; Sextus; scribe; sign; society; south; Sunday; Sabbath.
s. second; section (SS., *pl.*); series; shilling.
Sa, *sq.* samarium.
S. A. South Africa; South America; South Australia; Salvation Army.
s. a. *secundum artem* (según arte); *sine anno* (sin fecha).

Sab. Sabbath.
S. Am. South America.
Sam., Saml. Samuel.
S. A. R. Sons of the American Revolution; South African Republic.
Sat. Saturday.
Sb, *sq. stibium* (antimonio).
S. B., Sc. B. Bachelor of Science.
Sc, *sq.* scandium.
S. C. South Carolina; Supreme Court.
s. c., s. caps., sm. caps. small capitals (versalitas).
sc. scene; *scilicet* (a saber).
Scot. Scotch; Scotland; Scottish.
scr. scruple (peso).
sculp., sculpt. *sculpsit* (lo esculpió); sculptor; sculptural; sculpture.
s. d. *sine die.*
S. D., s. d. sight draft.
S. D., S. Dak. South Dakota.
Se, *sq.* selenium.
S. E. southeast; southeastern.
sec. secant; secretary; section; security.
Sec. secretary.—sec. second; secondary.
SEC, Securities and Exchange Commission.
Sen. Senate; Senator.
Sen. Doc. Senate Document.
sep. separate.
Sep., Sept. September; Septuagint.
seq. sequel; sequens.
Serg., Sergt., Sgt. Sergeant.
serv., servt. servant (= S. S. S.).
S. G. Solicitor General; Surgeon General.
s. g. specific gravity.
Sh., sh. shilling.
Shak., Shaks. Shakespeare.
Si, *sq.* silicon.
S. I. Staten Island; Sandwich Islands.
S. J. Society of Jesus.
S. l., S. lat. south latitude.
Sm, *sq.* samarium.
S. M. short meter; Sons of Malta.
Smith. Inst. Smithsonian Institution.
Sn, *sq., stannum* (estaño).
So. south.
Soc. Society; Socrates.
Soc. Isl. Society Islands.
sop. soprano.
sov. sovereign (moneda de oro).
Sp. Spain; Spanish.
S. P. C. A. Society for the Prevention of Cruelty to Animals.
S. P. C. C. Society for the Prevention of Cruelty to Children.
sp. gr. specific gravity.
spt. seaport.
sq. square; *sequentes-tia* (siguiente(s).
sqq. *sequentes* (siguientes).
Sr, *sq.* strontium.
Sr. senior; sir.
SS. saints.—ss. *scilicet* (es decir).
S. S. Sunday School; Sabbath School; Steamship.
s. s. screw steamer; steamship.
S. S. E. south-southeast.
S. S. W. south-southwest.
St. Saint; strait; street.
st. stanza; stet; strophe.
ster., stg. sterling.
str. steamer.
sub. subject; substitute; suburb; suburban.
subj. subject(ive); subjunctive.
Sun., Sund. Sunday.
sup., super. superior; superfine.
Sup., Supp. supplement.
Supt. superintendent.
Surg., surg. surgeon; surgery; surgical.
Surv. surveying; surveyor.
s. v. *sub verbo o voce* (en la palabra).
S. W. southwest; southwestern; South Wales.

T

T. Territory; Testament; Titus; ton(s); Tuesday; Tullius.
t. tenor; ton; town; township; *tempore* (en el tiempo de).
Ta, *sq.* tantalum.
tan., tan, tangent.
Tb, *sq.* terbium.
tbs. tablespoon(s).
Te, *sq.* tellurium.
tel. telegram; telegraph(ic); telephone.
teleg. telegram; telegraph.
Tenn. Tennessee.
Ter., Terr. Territory.
Test. Testament (Biblia).
Tex. Texas.
tf. till forbidden.
Th, *sq.* thorium.
Th. Thursday.
Tho., Thos. Thomas.
Thu., Thur., Thurs. Thursday.
Ti, *sq.* titanium.
t. i. d. *ter in die* (3 veces al día).
Tim. Timothy.
Tit. Titus.
Tl, *sq.* thallium.
Tm, *sq.* thulium.
Tn, *sq.* thoron.
t. o. turn over; turnover.
T. O. Telegraph Office; Transport Officer.
tp. township.—**t. p.** title page.
Tr, *sq.* terbium.
tr. transpose; trill; trustee.
tr., trans. transitive; translation; translated; transaction; transportation.
treas. treasurer; treasury.
ts. till sale.
T. T. L. to take leave.
T. U. Trade Union.—**Tu,** thulium.
Tu., Tues. Tuesday.

U

U, *sq.* uranium.
U. C. Upper Canada.
U. K. United Kingdom.
ult., ulto. ultimate; ultimo (el mes pasado).
um., unm. unmarried.
Unit. Unitarian.
Univ. Universalist; University.
U. of S. A. Union of South Africa.
U. S. United States; Uncle Sam.
U. S. A. United States of America; United States Army; Union of South Africa.
U. S. M. United States Mail; United States Marines.
U. S. M. A. United States Military Academy.
U. S. N. United States Navy.
U. S. N. A. United States Naval Academy.
U. S. P., U. S. Pharm. United States Pharmacopœia.
U. S. S. United States Senate; United States Steamer.
U. S. S. R., USSR, Union of Soviet Socialist Republics.
usu. usual, usually.
Ut. Utah.
ut sup. *ut supra* (como arriba o antes).
ux. *uxor* (esposa).

V

V, *sq.* vanadium.
V. venerable; Victoria; violin; volunteers.
v. verse; versus (contra); volume; volt.
v. *vide* (véase).
Va. Virginia.
V. A., VA, Veterans' Administration.
val. value.
var. variant; variation; variety; various.

Vat. Vatican.
Vd, *sq.* vanadium.
Ven. Venerable.
vet., veter. veteran; veterinary.
v. g., vg., v. gr., *verbi gratia.*
Vice Pres. Vice President.
vid. *vide* (véa(n)se).
Vis., Visc., Visct. Viscount.
viz. *videlicet* (a saber).
voc. vocabulary; vocative.
vol. volume (*pl.* **vols.**); volunteer.
V. P. Vice President.
V. Rev. Very Reverend.
V. S. Veterinary Surgeon.
vs. *versus* (contra).
Vt. Vermont.
Vul., Vulg. Vulgate (Biblia).

W

W, *sq.* *wolframium* (volframio, tungsteno).
W. warden; Welsh; west; western; William; Wednesday.
w. week; wife; with; watt; weight.
W. A. West Africa; West Australia.
W. Afr. West Africa.
Wash. Washington (Estado).
w. c. water-closet; without charge.
W. C. Western Central (distrito postal); Wesleyan Chapel.
W. C. A. Women's Christian Association.
W. C. T. U. Women's Christian Temperance Union.
We., Wed. Wednesday.
w. f., wf. wrong font.
W. G. wire gauge.
wh., whr. watt-hour.
whf. wharf.
W. I. West India; West Indies.
Wis., Wisc. Wisconsin.
Wisd. Wisdom (Biblia).
wk. week.—**wk., w'k,** work.
W. lon. west longitude.
Wm. William.
W. N. W. west-northwest.
wp. worship.
wpful. worshipful.
W. S. W. west-southwest.
wt. weight.
W. Va. West Virginia.
Wy., Wyo. Wyoming.

X

X, Xe, *sq.* xenon.
x-cp. without coupon.
x-d., x-div. without dividend.
Xm., Xmas. Christmas.
Xn., Xtian. Christian.

Y

Y, *sq.* yttrium.
y. yard; year.
Yb, *sq.* ytterbium.
Y. B., Yr. B. Year-book.
yd. (*pl.* **yds.**) yard (medida).
Y. M. C. A. Young Men's Christian Association.
Y. M. Cath. A. Young Men's Catholic Association.
Y. M. H. A. Young Men's Hebrew Association.
yr. (*pl.* **yrs.**) year; younger; your.
Yt, *sq.* yttrium.
Y. W. C. A. Young Women's Christian Association.

Z

z. zone; zero; zinc.
Zach. Zacharias; Zachary.
Zn, *sq.* zinc.
zool. zoology; zoological.
Zr, *sq.* zirconium.

Para la pronunciación véase la clave al principio del libro.

APPLETON'S REVISED

English-Spanish AND *Spanish-English*

DICTIONARY

CONTAINING MORE THAN ONE HUNDRED AND TWENTY
THOUSAND PRINCIPAL AND SUBSIDIARY TERMS,
WITH IDIOMS AND TECHNICAL USAGES;
NEW PRONOUNCING KEYS AND THE
FUNDAMENTAL FORMS OF THE
IRREGULAR VERBS

By

ARTURO CUYAS

Revised and enlarged by

Lewis E. Brett (Part I)
and
**Helen S. Eaton, with the assistance of
Walter Beveraggi-Allende (Part II)**

FOURTH EDITION

APPLETON-CENTURY-CROFTS, INC.

NEW YORK

1953

PART II

SPANISH–ENGLISH

PARTE II

ESPAÑOL–INGLES

PREFACE TO THE FIRST EDITION

In the compilation of this work the endeavor has been to produce in a compact volume that may be conveniently used by students, travelers, and business men a complete and accurate vocabulary of the Spanish language.

With this end in view, and for the purpose of including all the modern words with which the language has been enriched through a general advancement in human knowledge and activity, the thirteenth edition (1899) of the Dictionary of the Royal Spanish Academy—which is the latest and highest authority in Spanish lexicography—has been adopted as a groundwork, and every word, every acceptation, every idiom contained in that dictionary, with the exception of those that have become archaic, is defined in this volume.

Furthermore, many words and acceptations have been added which, while not purely Castilian, are in general use in Spanish-American countries and in the Philippine Islands, and also a great number of technical terms that are frequently used in commercial intercourse between Spanish- and English-speaking countries. Indeed, this rapidly increasing intercourse, and the ties that now bind to the United States several million people whose vernacular is the Spanish language, have been kept steadily in view during the preparation of the work, which is intended to be as helpful to the American or English student of Spanish as to the great number of Spaniards who are now studying English.

To accomplish this purpose, a radical departure has been made from the practice adopted in many dictionaries of giving long explanations in English of the meaning of a Spanish word, instead of supplying the student with the English equivalents. A bilingual dictionary, like a good rule, should work both ways, and to do this it should give equivalents rather than definitions.

Numberless examples might be cited here to show the laborious task implied in the search for correct equivalents, especially as regards technical terms, many of which are either omitted or erroneously translated in other dictionaries.

All the dictionaries of the Spanish and English languages, and especially those by Velázquez, Gray and Iribas, Lopes and Bensley, Ponce de León, Bustamente, Tolhausen, Wellesley and Gironés, have

been frequently consulted and compared in the course of compilation
and acknowledgment is hereby made for valuable suggestions found
in them.

Many new features, however, and thousands of words and acceptations not found in any similar work, have been introduced here
as any one may verify by careful comparison of a single page of this
book with the corresponding page in any other dictionary. As illustrative examples of the exhaustiveness of this compilation, the reader
is referred to such words as *a, de, con, por, que, le, se, nos, ese, uno; dar,
hacer, coger, estar, correr, echar, ser, salir, seguir, poner, tirar, ver, venir,
llave, medio, fuerza, ropa, tiro, título, viga, vida.*

One special feature will no doubt commend itself to students as a
help toward the proper use of irregular verbs. The fundamental tenses
of such verbs, from which other modes are formed, are given with
each infinitive, as well as the literal mutations that some regular verbs
undergo in some tenses.

In order to save space for more important matter, the pronunciation
usually given for each word has been dispensed with, except in a few
cases where some difficult word occurs; but as the Spanish pronunciation is simple, the few rules given in the following pages, explanatory
of a comprehensive key placed at the foot of each page, should enable
the student to pronounce any word correctly.

ARTURO CUYÁS.

NEW YORK, *July,* 1903.

PREFACE TO THE NEW EDITION

The original English-Spanish, Spanish-English Dictionary compiled y Arturo Cuyás and published in 1903 was based on the then latest dition of the Dictionary of the Royal Spanish Academy but also conained many words and meanings that, while not purely Castilian, were a general use in Latin-American countries.

A new edition contained a Supplement compiled by Antonio Llano hich supplied corrections and additional entries of words added to the urrent language during the years following the publication of the first dition.

In the present edition the original Cuyás is preserved almost intact ut the material of the Supplement is incorporated into the main work nd many additions have been made. The 1947 edition of the Diconary of the Royal Spanish Academy was consulted in preparing this ew edition.

The aim of the present revision is to bring the Cuyás Dictionary up o date. And, since the Dictionary is used extensively in the United tates and the Spanish contacts in this country are increasingly with atin America, the feature of including words peculiar to Latin-American ountries mentioned by Cuyás has been appreciably expanded.

The difficulty of finding new material for a dictionary is obvious. Iodern newspapers, periodicals, Bulletins of the United Nations, etc. a Spanish have been searched for new words, phrases, and meanings. erhaps the largest number of these entered in the new edition of the ictionary has been culled from consultations and discussions with ative Latin-American speakers.

HELEN S. EATON.

EW YORK, 1953.

SPANISH PRONUNCIATION

The only way of learning the exact sounds in a foreign language is by hearing them spoken by a native speaker. English equivalents given below must, therefore, be looked on as only the nearest approximation possible in written letters.

Vowels

Vowels in Spanish are always pronounced (with one exception mentioned below under **u**). Accent marks over vowels are only to indicate stress or to distinguish between words spelled alike and make no difference in the pronunciation of the vowel.

The Spanish vowels are **a, e, i, o, u,** and **y** when it stands alone as the conjunction *and,* or is at the end of a word. In some parts of Spanish America, notably in Chile, **y** is not used in these cases which are spelled with **i.** The vowels *a, e, o,* are called strong vowels while *i* and *u* are called weak vowels.

The sound of **a** is full, open, as in *far, father, farm, alarm.*

The sound of **e** is between the English *a* in *mate* and the *e* in *met,* like the initial part of *e* in *they.* At the end of a word and not stressed, it becomes shorter. Before *n* or *r* at the end of a syllable, it is like the English *ai* in *fair:* see Spanish ard*e*r.

The sound of **i** is like the English *i* in *machine, ee* in *teeth.*

The sound of **o,** in open syllables, is like the English *o* in *note.* In closed syllables, as before *n* or *r* at the end of a syllable, it is like the English *o* in *nor:* see Spanish señ*o*r.

The sound of **u** is like the English *oo* in *moon, food.* It is silent in the syllables *que, qui;* also in the syllables *gue, gui,* unless marked with a dieresis (*güe, güi*).

The sound of **y** when a vowel is like the Spanish **i** (above).

Diphthongs

A diphthong in Spanish is a combination of a strong and a weak vowel or of two weak vowels in the same syllable.

When **a, e,** or **o,** is followed in the same syllable by an unstressed **i,** or **u,** the two vowels form a single syllable. The two vowels are both pronounced but the strong vowel is prolonged a bit more than the following weak one, as in b*ai*le, tr*ai*dor, p*ei*nar, *oi*go, c*au*sa, de*u*da. At the end of a word such an **i** is written **y**, as in h*a*y, r*e*y, s*o*y.

When unstressed **i** or **u** precedes another vowel in the same syllable, the two vowels form a single syllable. In such cases the **i** is pronounced like English *y* in *y*es; and the **u** is like English *w*. In this situation the second vowel is the prolonged one, as in graci*a*, di*a*blo, bi*e*n, ci*e*lo, medi*o*, atenci*ó*n, vi*u*da, cu*a*ndo, igu*a*l, bu*e*no, pu*e*rta, lu*i*r (lweer), fu*í* (fwee), antigu*o*. At the end of a word such an **i** is written *y*, as in m*u*y (mwee).

CONSONANTS

(Consonants that are pronounced approximately the
same as in English are not listed.)

Contrary to the indication for vowels in Spanish, the consonants are pronounced much less emphatically than in English and in some cases are rather slurred.

B, b, has a softer sound than in English, produced by joining the lips, without pressure.

C, c, before *a, o, u,* or before another consonant, has the sound of the English *k*, as in *carro* (car), *costo* (cost), *cubo* (cube), *clase* (class), *crema* (cream), *acto* (act).

C, c, before *e, i,* has the sound of English *th* in *theft, thin,* as in **cinc,** which is pronounced *theenk.* However, in many parts of Spain and in Spanish America, **c** in these cases is pronounced like Spanish *s* (*seenk*).

Ch, ch, like English *ch* in *cheese, riches.* In Mexico it is often softened to a sound nearly like English *sh,* like *ch* in *machine.*

D, d, is softer than in English. It is sounded by touching the edge of the upper teeth with the tip of the tongue. In Spanish America *d* is always like this. Between two vowels (**todo,** *all*) and at the end of a word (**usted,** *you*) it has the sound of English *th* in *weather, with, although.*

G, g, before *a, o, u,* or another consonant, at the beginning of a syllable or after an *n,* has the sound of English *g* in *gas, go, gun, grand, ignorant.*

G, g, before *e* or *i* is like strongly aspirated English *h,* like *ch* in Scotch *loch.*

H, h, is *always* silent.

J, j, is like Spanish **g** before *e* or *i.*

Ll, ll, is a special letter, which sounds very much like English *lli* in *million, brilliant,* or, more exactly, like the combination *ll-y* in *all year.* In Spanish America it has only the English *y* sound.

Ñ, ñ, like *ny* in *canyon, ronyon.*

R, r, at the beginning of a word or preceded by *l, n,* or *s,* is pronounced with a trill produced by vibrating the tip of the tongue with a strong expulsion of breath; elsewhere it is pronounced with a touch of the tongue against the roof of the mouth.

Rr, rr, is always trilled like the first indication of **r** above.

S, s, has the sound of English *s* in *sassafras,* and no other.

T, t, differs from English *t* in that it is sounded by placing the tip of the tongue between the teeth.

V, v, as in English, but in Spanish-American countries it is quite commonly pronounced like the Spanish *b.*

X, x, sounds like *ks* or *gs,* never like *sh.* In **México, mexicano** (written *Méjico, mejicano* in nearly all places outside of Mexico) and a few other words of Mexican origin, it is pronounced like Spanish *j.*

Y, y, when a consonant, between vowels, sounds like English *y* in *year, young.*

Z, z, has the sound of English *th* in *thick, thatch, thought.* However, in some parts of Spain and throughout Spanish America it is pronounced like Spanish *s* (English *s* in *less*).

Rules of Accentuation

1. Words that end in a consonant, except *n* or *s,* have the stress on the last syllable, *ciudad, animar, cruel.* If this rule is not to be followed, then an accent mark (´) is written in over the vowel to be stressed, as in *capitán, interés, ángel.*

2. Words that end in a vowel or a diphthong have the stress on the next-to-the-last syllable, *acto, arriba, casi, cuello, comedia, corte, edificio.* If this rule is not to be followed, then an accent mark (´) is written in over the vowel to be stressed, *médico, música, bahía, héroe, cámara, allí, acá, mamá.*

3. Final *y* as part of a diphthong is actually the vowel *i* but in accentuation is taken as a consonant, as in *Paraguay.*

4. With the exception of adverbs ending in -*mente,* no Spanish word has more than one emphatic vowel. In adverbs in -*mente,* the adjectives from which they are formed preserve their original emphatic syllable, and the first *e* of the ending is also emphasized. Thus, **tristemente** (from *triste*), **útilmente** (from *útil*), are accented thus: *tris'temen'te, u'tilmen'te.*

Bear in Mind—

1. That **ch, ll** and **ñ** are independent letters, coming after **c, l** and **n** respectively. Therefore, all words or syllables beginning with **ch** come after all words or syllables beginning with **c,** and similarly for words and syllables beginning with **ll** or **ñ.**

2. That in some parts of Latin-America, mainly in Chile, **i** is used instead of **y,** both as a conjunction (*and*) and at the end of words (**rei** for **rey, voi** for **voy**).

3. That in order to preserve the sound of the stem of certain words, the final consonant is necessarily changed in certain forms. Such forms, then, are in a different alphabetical position in the dictionary.

Examples of Consonant Changes:

nouns & adjs. ending in **-z**	change the **-z** to **-ces** in the plural	so **rapaces, voces,** etc. are to be found under **rapaz, voz,** etc.
regular verbs ending in **-car**	change the **-c-** to **-qu-** before **e**	so **saqué, saquemos,** etc. belong with the infinitive **sacar,** etc.
regular verbs ending in **-cer, -cir,** preceded by a consonant	change the **-c-** to **-z-** before **o** or **a**	so **venzo, esparzo,** etc. belong with infinitives **vencer, esparcir,** etc.
most irregular verbs ending in **-cer, -cir,** preceded by a vowel	change the **-c-** to **-zc-** before **o** or **a**	so **conozco, luzca,** etc. belong with infinitives **conocer, lucir,** etc.

(Some notable exceptions to this rule are: **cocer** and its compounds, and **mecer,** in which the **-c-** changes to **-z-,** and **hacer,** and **decir,** which are highly irregular.)

regular verbs ending in **-gar**	change the **-g-** to **-gu-** before **e**	so **pagué, paguen,** etc. belong with the infinitive **pagar,** etc.

regular verbs ending in **-ger, gir**	change the **-g̣-** to **-j-** before **o** or **a**	so **cojo, dirijo,** etc. belong with infinitives **coger, dirigir,** etc.
regular verbs ending in **-guar**	change the **-gu-** to **-gü-** before **e**	so **averigüé,** etc. belong with infinitive **averiguar** etc.
regular verbs ending in **-guir**	change **-gu-** to **-g-** before **o** or **a**	so **distingo,** etc. belong with infinitive **distinguir,** etc.
regular verbs ending **-zar**	change **-z-** to **-c-** before **e**	so **lancé, lancemos,** etc. belong with infinitive **lanzar,** etc.

4. That in order to conform to Spanish rules of orthography, in some cases vowels are affected. Such affected forms are, then, in a different alphabetical position in the dictionary.

Examples of Vowel Changes:

| regular verbs ending in **-eer** | change the **-i-** of diphthongal conjugational endings to **-y-** | so **creyó, leyendo,** etc. belong with the infinitives **creer, leer,** etc. |

(This happens also to irregular verbs ending in **-uir**, as **atribuyo** from **atribuir**, etc.)

| regular verbs ending in **-iar, -uar** | change the **-i-** to **-í-** and the **-u-** to **-ú-** when these vowels have the tonic accent | so **guío, continúo,** etc. belong with the infinitives **guiar, continuar,** etc. |

5. That short **e** and **o** within a Latin stem taken into Spanish become diphthongized to **ie** and **ue** in Spanish when they receive the stress. Such forms are, then, in a different alphabetical position in the dictionary.

| regular verbs having forms with **-e-** or **-o-** stressed | change **-e-** to **-ie-** and **-o-** to **-ue-** when these vowels have the stress | so **pienso, suenan,** etc. belong with the infinitives **pensar, sonar,** etc. |

Irregular and Radical-Changing Verbs

The fundamental forms of irregular verbs are given both with their infinitives and, unless they are in the immediate vicinity of their infinitive, also in their proper alphabetical position in the dictionary. The same applies to the main forms of verbs changed in spelling to preserve the pronunciation of the radical or to conform to certain rules in Spanish (see 3, 4, and 5 above).

ABBREVIATIONS

a.	adjective.
abbr.	abbreviation.
acc.	accusative.
adv.	adverb.
(aer.)	aeronautics.
(agr.)	agriculture.
(alg.)	algebra.
(Am.)	Spanish America(n).
(anat.)	anatomy.
(anc.)	ancient.
(Angl.)	Anglicism.
(app.)	applied.
(arch.)	architecture.
(archeol.)	archeology.
(Arg.)	Argentina(-ian).
(arith.)	arithmetic.
art.	article.
(artil.)	artillery.
(astr.)	astronomy.
(astrol.)	astrology.
aug.	augmentative.
(auto)	automobiles(-ism).
aux.	auxiliary verb.
(bacteriol.)	bacteriology.
(bib.)	Biblical.
(biol.)	biology.
(Bol.)	Bolivia(n).
(bot.)	botany.
(build.)	building.
(bus.)	business.
(C.A.)	Central America(n).
(Carib.)	Caribbean countries.
(carp.)	carpentry.
cf.	compare.
(chem.)	chemistry.
(chron.)	chronology(-ical).
(coll.)	colloquial.
(collect.)	collectively.
(Colomb.)	Colombia.
(com.)	commerce(-ial).
comp.	comparative.
conj.	conjunction.
(constr.)	construction.
(contempt.)	contemptuous.
contr.	contraction.
(cook.)	cooking.
dat.	dative.
def.	definite.
defect.	defective.
(dent.)	dentistry.
(diff.)	different.
dim.	diminutive.
(eccl.)	ecclesiastic.
(econ.)	economics, economy.
(Ecua.)	Ecuador(-ian).
(elec.)	electricity.
(Engl.)	English.
(eng.)	engine(-eering).
(entom.)	entomology.
(esp.)	especially.
(ethnol.)	ethnology.
(ext.)	extension.
f.	feminine.
(fig.)	figurative(-ly).
(foll.)	followed.
(fort.)	fortifications.
fut.	future.
(Gal.)	Gallicism.
(gen.)	generally.
(geog.)	geography.
(geol.)	geology.

(geom.)	geometry.
ger.	gerund.
(Gk.)	Greek.
(gram.)	grammar.
(Guat.)	Guatemala.
(her.)	heraldry.
(hist.)	history.
(Hond.)	Honduras.
(hort.)	horticulture.
(humor.)	humorous.
(hydraul.)	hydraulics.
(ichth.)	ichthyology, fish.
imp.	imperfect.
imper.	imperative.
impers.	impersonal.
ind.	indicative.
(Ind.)	Indian.
indef.	indefinite.
indir. obj.	indirect object.
inf.	infinitive.
(int. combust.)	internal-combustion.
(int.)	international.
interj.	interjection.
interrog.	interrogative.
irreg.	irregular.
(jewel.)	jewelry.
(lang.)	language.
(Lat.)	Latin.
(ling.)	linguistics.
(lit.)	literally.
(lith.)	lithography.
m.	masculine.
(mason.)	masonry.
(math.)	mathematics.
(mech.)	mechanics.
(med.)	medical, pathological
(metal.)	metallurgy, metal wo
(meteorol.)	meteorology.
(Mex.)	Mexico(-an).
(mil.)	military.
(min.)	mining, mineralogy.
(mov. pict.)	moving pictures.
(mus.)	music.
(mut.)	mutation(s).
(myth.)	mythology.
n.	noun.
(nat. hist.)	natural history.
(naut)	nautical.
neut.	neuter.
nom.	nominative case.
(numis.)	numismatics.
obj.	object (gram.)
(obs.)	obsolete.
(opt.)	optics.
(ornith.)	ornithology, birds.
(paleontol.)	paleontology.
(parl.)	parliamentary.
pers.	person or personal.
(pert.)	pertaining.
(pharm.)	pharmaceutical.
(philos.)	philosophy.
(phon.)	phonetics; phonogra
(photog.)	photography.
(phys.)	physics.
(physiol.)	physiology.
(P.I.)	Philippine Islands.
pl.	plural.
(poet.)	poetry.
(pol.)	politics(-al).
(Port.)	Portugal, Portugues
poss.	possessive.

.	past participle.
.R.)	Puerto Rico.
ep.	preposition.
es.p.	present participle.
et.	preterit.
rint.)	printing.
on.	pronoun.
rov.)	provincial.
sych.)	psychology.
ef.)	referring to.
fl.	reflexive (pronoun).
j.	regular.
het.)	rhetoric.
tom. Cath.)	Roman Catholic.
tom. Hist.)	Roman History.
Ry.)	railway, railroad.
.A.)	South America(-n).
ew.)	sewing.
p.)	Spain, Spanish.
bj.	subject (gram.), subjunctive.

super.	superlative.
(surg.)	surgery.
(surv.)	surveying.
(tech.)	technology.
(tel.)	telegraph(y), telephone.
(theat.)	theatre.
(theol.)	theology(-ical).
(topog.)	topography(-ical).
(Uru.)	Uruguay(-an).
V.	Vide, see.
v.	verb.
va.	active, transitive verb.
(Venez.)	Venezuela(-n).
(vet.)	veterinary.
vn.	intransitive verb.
vr.	reflexive verb.
(vulg.)	vulgar, low.
(W.I.)	West Indies(-ian).
(zool.)	zoölogy.

A NEW BILINGUAL DICTIONARY

OF THE

SPANISH AND ENGLISH LANGUAGES

SPANISH-ENGLISH PART

Abbreviations and proper names are given at the end.

a, *f.* a (letter *a*).—**a por a y be por be,** point by point, minutely.

a, *prep.* (1) to, to indicate (a) a noun indirect object, when it follows the direct object: *di el libro a Juan,* I gave the book to John; (b) direction, purpose, destination, limit, in place, time, movement, or activity: *voy a Madrid,* I am going to Madrid; *él me enseñó a leer,* he taught me to read; *vine a verle,* I came to see him; *de once a doce,* from eleven to twelve; *con el agua a la cintura,* with water (up) to the waist; *echó a correr,* he started to run; (c) accord: *a mi gusto,* to my taste; *a mi pesar,* to my regret; *cara a cara,* face to face. (2) at, to indicate (a) location: *a la puerta,* at the door; *a la mesa,* at table; *a la derecha,* at the right; *a lo lejos,* at a (great) distance; *con el termómetro a 30°,* with the thermometer at 30°; *a dos millas de Lima,* (at) two miles from Lima; (b) rate, price: *a dos pesos por kilo,* at two dollars a kilo; *a la vez,* at a time; (c) time (when): *a mediodía,* at noon; *a las dos y media,* at half past two; *al fin* or *al cabo,* at last; *al principio* or *a los principios,* at the beginning, or, at first; *a la vista,* at sight; (d) accord: *a instancias de Vd.,* at your request; *a su disposición,* at your disposal; *a voluntad,* at will; *a lo menos* or *al menos,* at least. (3) by, to indicate (a) instrument, means: *a máquina,* by machine; *a mano,* by hand; *a fuerza bruta,* by brute force; (b) manner: *a pedazos,* by pieces; *a súplicas,* by entreaties; *paso a paso,* step by step; *poco a poco,* little by little; *al año,* by the year. (4) on, to indicate (a) simultaneity: *a mi llegada,* on my arrival; *al entrar,* on entering; (b) position in place or time: *a bordo,* on board; *al otro lado,* on the other side; *a la mañana siguiente,* on the next morning; (c) manner: *a caballo,* on horseback; *a pie,* on foot; (d) in many idioms such as: *al contrario,* on the contrary; *a causa de,* on account of; *a condición de que,* on condition that. (5) in, to indicate (a) style, manner: *a la francesa,* in the French style, à la française; *a lo marinero,* in a seamanlike manner (or, like a seaman); *a lo caballero,* in a gentlemanly manner (or, like a gentleman); *a lo filósofo,* in the manner of philosophers (or, like a philosopher); *a lo bobo,* in the manner of a fool (or, like a fool); (b) time (within which): *a poco,* in a little while (or, presently); *a últimos de octubre,* in the latter part of Octo-

ber. (6) after, at the end of: *a la semana,* at the end of a week, a week after; *a los dos meses,* two months after; *a los pocos años,* a few years after (or, later). (7) not translated, to indicate (a) a direct object of a verb when denoting a specific and known person, or a thing when the subject also denotes a thing, or a geographical name not preceded by a definite article, etc.: *amo a mi madre,* I love my mother; *oigo a Juan,* I hear John; *esta línea encuentra a la otra,* this line meets the other; *veo a Nueva York,* I see New York; (b) a noun indirect object when it precedes the direct object: *di el libro a Juan,* I gave John the book. (8) not translated, often to indicate the addition of, or treatment with, a material or substance, or a distinguishing ingredient (the corresponding English noun is used adjectively): *acero al carbono,* carbon steel; *papel al bromuro,* bromide paper, paper treated with bromide; *cuadro al óleo,* oil painting; *dibujo a lápiz,* pencil drawing. —This construction is commonly but improperly applied to denote the natural agent moving a machine, or some characteristic feature of an apparatus or another object: *máquina a* (properly, *de*) *vapor,* steam engine; *tubo al* (properly, *de*) *vacío,* vacuum tube; *motor a* (properly, *de*) *ocho cilindros,* eight-cylinder motor.—Followed by an infinitive, **a** forms implicitly negative phrases rendered by *if* and the subjunctive: *a estar él aquí,* if he were here, were he here. If, in such phrases, the infinitive is preceded by *no,* the translation may be made by using "but for": *a no venir Juan,* but for John's coming, had not John come; *a no ser por Vd.,* but for you; *a no ser que,* unless.—This preposition is used in many idioms such as: *a lo que,* from what; *a lo que veo,* from what I see; *a lo que parece,* as it seems; *a qué,* what for, what is the use; *a que,* I bet that. Most of the frequently used idioms will be found in the regular alphabetical position in the dictionary under the main word of a phrase.

aarónico, aaronita, *a.* Aaronic, pertaining to or descended from Aaron.

aba, *m.* aba, a coarse woolen fabric.

ababa, *f.* **ababol,** *m.* = AMAPOLA, *f.* poppy.

ab absurdo, *adv.* (math. & logic) ad absurdum.

abacá, *m.* (bot.) abaca; manila hemp; manilahemp fabric.

abacería, *f.* grocery.

For pronunciation, see the rules at the beginning of the book.

abacero, ra, *n.* grocer.
abacial, *a.* abbatial, pertaining to an abbot, abbess, or abbey.
ábaco, *m.* abacus, calculating frame; (arch.) abacus; (min.) washing trough.
abacómite, *m.* one belonging to a ruler's train or retinue.
abactor, ra, *n.* (Arg.) horse thief.
abad, *m.* abbot.
abada, *f.* rhinoceros.
abadanar, *va.* to dress or finish like sheepskin.
abadejo, *m.* = BACALAO, codfish; pollack. Spanish fly or blistering beetle; (ornith.) kinglet or golden-crested wren.
abadengo, ga, *a.* = ABACIAL.
abadernar, *va.* (naut.) to fasten with short ropes.
abadesa, *f.* abbess.
abadía, *f.* abbey.
abadiato, *m.* abbotship.
abajadero, *m.* slope, incline.
abajador, *m.* (min.) stable man; helper.
abajeño, ña, *a.* (Am.) lowlander.
abajo, *adv.* under, underneath, below, down.—**a. de,** *prep.* beneath.—**boca a.,** face down.—**de a.,** lower (*a.*).—**de arriba a.,** from top to bottom.—**por a.,** at the bottom; down there.—**venirse a.,** to fall.—**¡a. N.!** down with N.!
abalanzar. I. *va.* (*pret.* ABALANCÉ; *subj.* ABALANCE) to balance; to throw suddenly with force. **II.** *vr.* to rush impetuously; to venture.
abalaustrado, da, *a.* balustered.
abaleador, ra, *n.* grain cleaner or separator.
abalear, *va.* to clean or separate (grain) from chaff after winnowing.
abaleo, *m.* (agr.) cleaning or separating grain.
abalizar. I. *va.* (*pret.* ABALICÉ; *subj.* ABALICE) (naut.) to lay buoys in. **II.** *vr.* (naut.) to take bearings.
abalorio, *m.* glass bead; beadwork.
aballestar, *va.* (naut.) to haul a cable.
abámeas, *f. pl.* (bot.) Abama (lily family).
abanar, *va.* to ventilate with fans.
abanderado, *m.* standard-bearer.
abanderar, *va.* to register (a ship).
abandericé, abanderice, *v.* V. ABANDERIZAR.
abanderizador, ra, *n.* ringleader.
abanderizar. I. *va.* (*pret.* ABANDERICÉ; *subj.* ABANDERICE) to organize in bands. **II.** *vr.* to band together.
abandonado, da, *a.* negligent, shiftless; slovenly.
abandonamiento, *m.* forlornness; slovenliness; lewdness, debauchery.
abandonar. I. *va.* to leave; to forsake; to give up. **II.** *vr.* to despair; to give oneself up to.
abandono, m. = ABANDONAMIENTO.
abanicar, *va.* (*pret.* ABANIQUÉ; *subj.* ABANIQUE) to fan.
abanicazo, *m.* blow with a fan.
abanico, *m.* fan; anything fan-shaped; (coll.) sword; (naut.) derrick; crane.—**en a.,** fan-shaped.
abaniqué, abanique, *v.* V. ABANICAR.
abaniqueo, *m.* fanning; swinging motion; excessive gesturing in speaking.
abaniquería, *f.* fan factory or shop.
abaniquero, ra, *n.* fan maker or dealer.
abano, *m.* fan; hanging fan; ventilator.
abanto, *m.* (ornith.) African vulture.
abaratar. I. *va.* to cheapen; to abate. **II.** *vr.* to fall in price.
abarca, *f.* sandal worn by peasants and muleteers.
abarcado, da, *a.* sandaled; embraced, contained.
abarcador, ra, *n.* clasper; monopolist.
abarcadura, *f.*, **abarcamiento,** *m.* embracing, comprising.
abarcar, *va.* (*pret.* ABARQUÉ; *subj.* ABARQUE) to clasp, embrace, contain; to comprise; to monopolize; (com.) to corner, control (the market). —**quien mucho abarca poco aprieta,** one shouldn't bite off more than one can chew.

abarcón, *m.* a pole-ring in carriages; large iron clamp.
abarloar, *va.* (naut.) to bring alongside a ship or wharf.
abarqué, abarque, *v.* V. ABARCAR.
abarquero, ra, *n.* maker or seller of *abarcas.*
abarquillado, da, *a.* rolled up; curled up.
abarquillamiento, *m.* curling up into a roll.
abarquillar, *va.* to curl up; to form into a roll.
abarracarse, *vr.* to go into barracks.
abarraganarse, *vr.* to live in concubinage.
abarrancadero, *m.* heavy road; precipice; difficult business.
abarrancamiento, *m.* fall into a pit; embarrassment.
abarrancar. I. *va.* (*pret.* ABARRANQUÉ; *subj.* ABARRANQUE) to ditch; to form a ravine. **II.** *vr.* to fall into a pit; to become embarrassed.
abarredera, *f.* broom, carpet sweeper; anything that sweeps and cleans.
abarrotar, *va.* to bar; to strengthen with bars; (naut.) to stow; to overstock.
abarrote, *m.* (naut.) a small package for filling up; stop-gap; (Mex.) retail grocery.—*pl.* (Am.) goods; foodstuffs.
abarrotero, ra, *n.* (Mex.) retail grocer.
abarse, *vr.* (*defect., used only in imper.:* ÁBATE ABAOS) to move aside; to get out of the way.
abastamiento, *m.* providing; supplying with provisions, stores, etc.
abastar, va. = ABASTECER.
abastecedor, ra, *n.* caterer, provider, purveyor.
abastecer, *va.* (*ind.* ABASTEZCO; *subj.* ABASTEZCA) to purvey; supply.—**abastecimiento,** *m.* providing; supply; provisions, supplies.—**el a. y la demanda,** supply and demand.
abastionar, *va.* (fort.) to protect or fortify with bastions.
abasto, *m.* supply of provisions; (fig.) anything abundant; (com.) supply.—**dar a. (a),** to be sufficient (for); to provide, furnish (to).
abate, *m.* abbé.
abatidamente, *adv.* dejectedly.
abatido, da, *a.* dejected; discouraged; crestfallen; abject, mean; (com.) depreciated, fallen in price or demand.
abatimiento, *m.* depression, low spirits; lowering, falling; taking apart; (naut., aer.) drift, leeway.—**a. de costado,** (aer.) side drift.
abatir. I. *va.* to throw down, overthrow, knock down; to bring down, shoot down; to fold down; to humble, debase; to discourage, dishearten; to lower, strike (a flag, etc.); to dismount, take apart. **II.** *vn.* to descend; to stoop. **III.** *vr.* to be disheartened or depressed; (naut.) to have leeway; (aer.) to drift.
abazón, *m.* cheek pouch (of monkeys, etc.).
abdicación, *f.* abdication.
abdicar, *va.* (*pret.* ABDIQUÉ; *subj.* ABDIQUE) to abdicate.
abdomen, *m.* abdomen.
abdominal, *a.* abdominal.
abducción, *f.* (logic & math.) abduction.
abductor, *m.* (anat.) abducent muscle.
abecé, *m.* a-b-c, alphabet; rudiments.
abecedario, *m.* alphabet; primer.
abedul, *m.* (bot.) birch.
abeja, *f.* bee.—**a. machiega, maesa,** *or* **maestra,** queen bee.—**a. neutra,** *or* **obrera,** working bee, worker.—**a. reina,** queen bee.
abejar, *m.* place for beehives. Also COLMENAR.
abejarrón, abejorro, *m.* bumblebee.
abejaruco, abejeruco, *m.* (ornith.) bee eater.
abejera, *f.* ABEJAR; (bot.) balmmint or beewort.
abejero, *m.* beekeeper.
abejón, *m.* drone.
abejorro, *m.* bumblebee.
abejuno, na, *a.* pertaining to the bee.
abelmosco, *m.* (bot.) abelmosk.

---

abellacado, da, *a.* mean-spirited.

abellacarse, *vr.* to degrade oneself.

abellotado, da, *a.* acorn-shaped.

abencerraje, *n.* one of a famous Moorish family.

aberenjenado, da, *a.* eggplant-shaped or -colored.

aberración, *f.* aberration, error, mania; (phys., opt. & astr.) aberration.

aberrugado, da, *a.* warty.

abertal. I. *s.* crack; small opening. **II.** *a.* easily cracked or cleft.

abertura, *f.* aperture; opening; cleft, crevice, fissure; gap.

abestiado, da, *a.* beast-like.

abetal, *m.* fir wood or grove.

abete, *m.* hook for holding cloth in shearing it.

abete, *m.* (bot.) = ABETO.

abetina, *f.* (chem.) abietin.

abetinote, *m.* fir-tree rosin.

abeto, *m.* (bot.) silver tree; yew-leaved fir; spruce; hemlock.—*a.* **del norte, falso,** or **rojo,** spruce.

abetuna, *f.* fir-tree sprout.

abetunado, da, *a.* bitumen-like.

abetunar, *va.* = EMBETUNAR, to bituminize.

abey, *m.* (bot.) jacaranda; W. I. mahogany.

abiertamente, *adv.* frankly, openly.

abierto, ta. I. *pp. irreg.* of ABRIR. **II.** *a.* open, clear; candid, frank, outspoken; full-blown.

abietina, *f.* = ABETINA.

abietíneas, *f. pl.* (bot.) trees of the fir family.

abigarrado, da, *a.* variegated, motley.

abigarrar, *va.* to paint with various ill-matched colors; to fleck.

abigeato, *m.* (law) cattle stealing.

abigeo, *m.* (law) cattle thief.

abigotado, da, *a.* having a heavy mustache.

abinicio, ab initio, from the beginning.

ab intestato. I. *adv.* intestate. **II.** *a.* neglected, unprotected.—**abintestato,** *m.* legal adjudication of an intestate estate.

abiótico, ca, *a.* not life-producing or life-supporting.

abiselar, biselar, *va.* to bevel.

abisinio, a, *n.* & *a.* Abyssinian.

abismado, da, *a.* dejected, depressed; absorbed in profound meditation.

abismal. I. *a.* abysmal. **II.** *m.* clasp nail, shingle nail.

abismar. I. *va.* to depress, humble, destroy. **II.** *vr.* to think or feel deeply.

abismo, *m.* abyss; gulf; chasm; hell.

abitadura, *f.* (naut.) a turn of the cable around the bitts.

abitaque, *m.* joist.

abitar, *va.* (naut.) to bitt.

abitas, *m. pl.* (naut.) bitts.—*a.* **del molinete,** carrick bitts.

abitones, *m. pl.* (naut.) topsail sheet bitts.

abizcochado, da, *a.* biscuit-shaped.

abjuración, *f.* abjuration, recantation.

abjurar, *va.* to abjure, retract under oath.

ablación, *f.* ablation.

ablactación, *f.* weaning.

ablactar, *va.* to wean.

ablandabrevas, *m.* & *f.* (coll.) good-for-nothing.

ablandador, ra, *m.* & *f.* mollifier.

ablandahigos, *m.* & *f.* (coll.) good-for-nothing.

ablandamiento, *m.* softening, mollification.

ablandar, *va.* & *vn.* to soften, mellow, relent; to loosen; to assuage, mitigate, melt, soothe.

ablandativo, va, *a.* mollifying.

ablanedo, *m.* = AVELLANEDO, filbert plantation.

ablano, *m.* = AVELLANO, filbert.

ablativo, *m.* & *a.* (gram.) ablative.

ablepsia, *f.* ablepsy, blindness; lack or loss of mental powers.

ablución, *f.* ablution.

abnegación, *f.* abnegation, self-denial.

abnegar, *va.* (*ind.* ABNIEGO; *subj.* ABNIEGUE) to renounce; to deny oneself.

abobado, da, *a.* stultified, silly.

abobamiento, *m.* stupefaction, stupidity.

abobar. I. *va.* to stupefy. **II.** *vr.* to grow stupid.

abocado, *a.* (of wine) mild, agreeable.

abocamiento, *m.* approach; meeting, interview.

abocar (*pret.* ABOQUÉ; *subj.* ABOQUE). **I.** *va.* to bring near; to draw in place (as cannon); to open the mouth of (a bag); to decant; to seize with the mouth. **II.** *vr.* to meet by appointment. **III.** *vn.* (naut.) to occupy the mouth of, or enter, a channel, strait, etc.

abocardado, da, *a.* bell-mouthed (esp. of fire-arms).

abocardar, *va.* to widen or expand (the opening of a tube, hole, etc.); to ream.

abocardo, *m.* large drill.

abocetado, da, *a.* (of pictures) roughly sketched in, unfinished.

abocinado, da, *a.* funnel- or trumpet-shaped; (of horses) with drooping head.

abocinar. I. *va.* to shape like a trumpet. **II.** *vn.* to fall on one's face.

abochornado, da, *a.* out of countenance, flushed, mortified.

abochornar. I. *va.* to overheat; to shame; to embarrass. **II.** *vr.* to blush; to become embarrassed; (agr.) to wilt from excessive heat.

abofeteador, ra, *m.* & *f.* buffeter; one who insults or slaps.

abofetear, *va.* to slap; to insult.

abogacía, *f.* law (as a subject or profession).

abogada, *f.* woman lawyer or mediator; lawyer's wife.

abogado, *m.* lawyer, barrister; mediator.—*a.* **de secano,** quack lawyer; charlatan.

abogar, *vn.* (*pret.* ABOGUÉ; *subj.* ABOGUE) to advocate, plead (as a lawyer); to intercede.

abolengo, *m.* ancestry, lineage; inheritance.

abolición, *f.* abolition, abrogation, extinction.

abolicionista, *m.* abolitionist.

abolir, *va. and defective* (*only those modes and persons are used having the letter i in their terminations*) to abolish; to revoke, repeal.

abolsado, da, *a.* puckered, purse-shaped; having or forming pockets.

abollado, *a.* & *m.* pleat(ed); fluted(-ing).

abolladura, *f.* unevenness, dent, embossment; bruise.

abollar, *va.* to emboss; to dent; to stun and confound; to bruise.

abollonar, *va.* to emboss.

abombar. I. *va.* to give a convex form to; to deafen; to confuse. **II.** *vr.* (Am.) (of meat, fluids, etc.) to begin to spoil.

abominable, *a.* abominable, execrable.

abominación, *f.* abomination, detestation, execration.

abominar, *va.* to abominate, abhor.

¹abonado, da. I. *m.* & *f.* subscriber; commuter. **II.** *a.* reliable; apt, inclined.

²abonado, da, *a.* (of soil) rich.

abonador, ra, *m.* & *f.* (com.) surety or security for a principal, person responsible for one who himself acts as surety; barrel maker's augur.

abonamiento, *m.* = ¹ABONO; bail, security.

abonanzar, *vn.* (*impersonal verb: subj.* ABONANCE) to grow calm, clear up.

¹abonar. I. *va.* to bail; to guarantee, indorse, answer for; to give credit; (com.) to credit with, put to the credit of. **II.** *vr.* to subscribe; to buy a season or commutation ticket.

²abonar. I. *va.* to improve; to enrich, manure (soil). **II.** *vn.* = ABONANZAR.

abonaré, *m.* promissory note; due-bill.

¹abono, *m.* security, guarantee; subscription; allowance, discount; receipt, voucher.

²abono, *m.* manure, fertilizer.

aboqué, aboque, *v. V.* ABOCAR.

abordador, *m.* (naut.) boarder; intruder.

abordaje, *m.* (naut.) the act of boarding a ship.

abordar. I. *va.* (naut.) to board a ship; to run foul of a ship; to attack (a subject), enter upon (a matter). II. *vn.* to put into a port.

abordo, *m.* = ABORDAJE.

aborigen. I. *a.* aboriginal. II. *m.* *pl.* (**aborígenes**) aborigines.

aborrachado, da, *a.* bright red.

aborrascarse, *vr.* to become stormy.

aborrecedor, ra, *m.* & *f.* detester, hater.

aborrecer, *va.* (*ind.* ABORREZCO; *subj.* ABORREZCA) to hate, abhor; (of birds) to desert.—**aborrecible,** *a.* hateful; abhorrent.—**aborrecimiento,** *m.* abhorrence, hate; dislike, grudge.

aborrezco, aborrezca, *v.* *V.* ABORRECER.

abortamiento, *m.* abortion.

abortar, *vn.* to miscarry, abort; to fail; (med.) to abort (a foetus or a disease).

abortivamente, *adv.* abortively; inopportunely.

abortivo, va, *a.* abortive; producing abortion.

aborto, *m.* miscarriage, abortion; monstrosity.

abortón, *m.* the abortion of a quadruped; unborn lamb's skin.

aborujar, aburujar. I. *va.* to make lumps. II. *vr.* to muffle up, wrap oneself up.

abotagarse, *vr.* to become bloated.

abotinado, da, *a.* shaped like a gaiter.

abotonador, *m.* button-hook.

abotonar. I. *va.* to button. II. *vn.* (of plants) to bud.

abovedado, da, *a.* arched, vaulted.

abovedar, *va.* to arch, vault.

aboyado, da, *a.* (tilled) with oxen.

aboyar, *va.* (naut.) to lay buoys.

abozalar, *va.* to muzzle.

abra, *f.* bay, haven; cove, creek; dale, valley; fissure, gorge.

abracadabra, *m.* abracadabra.

abracé, abrace, *v.* *V.* ABRAZAR.

abracijo, *m.* *dim.* (coll.) an embrace, a hug.

abrahonar, *va.* (coll.) to hold one fast by the garment.

abrasador, ra, *a.* burning, exceedingly hot.

abrasamiento, *m.* taking fire, burning; excess of passion.

abrasar. I. *va.* to burn; to fire; to squander; to dry up; to provoke; to shame, humiliate. II. *vr.* (**en** or **de**) to burn (with); to boil (with) (any violent passion); to burn up, down.

abrasión, *f.* (geol. & med.) abrasion.

abrazadera. I. *f.* clasp, clamp, band, cleat; (print.) brace or bracket { . II. *a.* **sierra a.,** lumberman's saw.

abrazador, ra, *n.* embracer; bolster used in P. I.

abrazamiento, *m.* embracing.

abrazar, *va.* (*pret.* ABRACÉ; *subj.* ABRACE) to embrace, hug; to clamp, cleat; to contain, comprise; to surround; to accept, follow; to embrace, adopt (a religion, etc.); to take charge of.

abrazo, *m.* hug, embrace.

ábrego, áfrico, *m.* southwest wind.

abrelata, abrelatas, *m.* (Am.) can opener.

abrenuncio, (Lat.) far be it from me; fie!

abrevadero, *m.* watering place for cattle; drinking trough.

abrevador, *m.* one who waters cattle; waterer.

abrevar, *va.* to water cattle; to irrigate; to soak skins.

abreviación, *f.* abbreviation; abridgment; shortening; contraction; reduction; acceleration; hastening.

abreviadamente, *adv.* briefly, summarily.

abreviador, ra. I. *m.* & *f.* one who abridges or shortens. II. *m.* (eccl.) abbreviator (Vatican officer).

abreviaduría, *f.* (eccl.) office of abbreviator.

abreviamiento, *m.* = ABREVIACIÓN.

abreviar, *va.* to abridge, abbreviate; to hasten.

abreviatura, *f.* abbreviation; contraction; shorthand.—**en a.,** in abbreviation; (coll.) hastily

abreviaturía, *f.* = ABREVIADURÍA.

abribonado, da, *a.* rascally, knavish.

abribonarse, *vr.* to become lazy; to loaf; to become a rascal.

abridero. I. *m.* a variety of freestone peach II. *a.* easily opened; freestone, freeshell.

abridor, *m.* (bot.) nectarine, peach tree; opener grafting knife; eardrop or wire to keep the ears pierced.—**a. de guantes,** glove stretcher —**a. de láminas,** engraver.—**a. de latas,** car opener.—**a. en hueco,** die sinker.

abrigadero, *m.* sheltered place, shelter.

abrigador, ra. (Am.) I. *a.* protecting; (of clothing) warm. II *n.* & *a.* concealer(-ing).

abrigaño, *m.* a place sheltered from the wind.

abrigar. I. *va.* (*pret.* ABRIGUÉ; *subj.* ABRIGUE) to shelter, protect; to cover, to warm; to lodge to patronize; (fig.) to nourish; to cherish. II *vr.* to take shelter; to cover oneself; to put or a wrap.

abrigo, *m.* shelter; protection; overcoat; wrap aid, support; cover; (naut.) harbor, haven.—**al a. de,** sheltered from; under protection of shielded by.

abrigué, abrigue, *v.* *V.* ABRIGAR.

abril, *m.* April.—*pl.* (fig.) (years of) youth.—**estar hecho,** or **parecer, un a.,** to be dressed up; to look very smart, or very smartly dressed —**los dieciséis abriles,** sweet sixteen.

abrileño, ña, *a.* April (as *a.*), pert. to, or like April.

abrillantar, *va.* to cut a diamond into facets to make sparkle; to impart brilliance; to glaze polish, brighten.

abrimiento, *m.* opening; cracking.

abrir. I. *va.* (*pp.* ABIERTO) to open, unlock, unfasten, uncover, unseal; to engrave; to expand separate, distend; to cut open, cleave; to rend to dig.—**a. los cimientos,** to dig the foundation trenches.—**a. paso,** to make way; to clea the way. II. *vn.* to open; to unfold; to extend to display; (Am.) to back out, withdraw. III *vr.* to open, expand; to crack; to yawn; (fig.) to unbosom oneself; to burst open; to fall out become estranged.

abrochador, *m.* buttoner; buttonhook.

abrochadura, *f.,* **abrochamiento,** *m.* lacing fastening, buttoning.

abrochar, *va.* to clasp, buckle, button, faster with hooks and eyes.

abrogación, *f.* abrogation, repeal.

abrogar, *va.* (*pret.* ABROGUÉ; *subj.* ABROGUE) t abrogate, annul, repeal.

abrojal, *m.* thistly ground.

abrojín, *m.* murex, a mollusk or its purple shell

abrojo, *m.* (bot.) thistle, thorn, prickle; (mil. caltrop; crowfoot; sharp metal ends of a lash —*pl.* hidden rocks in the sea.

¹abromado, da, *a.* (naut.) hazy, foggy.

²abromado, da, *a.* worm-eaten; barnacled.

abromarse, *vr.* (naut.) to be worm-eaten.

abroquelar. I. *va.* (naut.) to boxhaul. II. *vr* to shield oneself.

abrótano, *m.* (bot.) southernwood.

abrumador, ra, *a.* overwhelming, crushing wearisome.

abrumar. I. *va.* to crush, overwhelm, oppress to weary, annoy. II. *vr.* to worry.

abrumarse, *vr.* to become foggy.

abrupto, ta, *a.* abrupt; craggy, rugged.

abrutado, da, *a.* brutish, bestial.

abruzo, za, *a.* & *n.* Abruzzian.

absceso, *m.* abscess.

abscisa, *f.* abscissa.

abscisión, *f.* (med.) incision.

absentismo, *m.* absenteeism (app. **to landlords)**

ábside, *m.* or *f.* (arch.) presbytery.

absintemia, *f.* (med.) presence of absinthe in the blood.

absintina, *f.* (chem.) absinthin.

absintismo, *m.* (med.) absinthism.

absit, *interj.* (Lat.) God forbid!

absolución, *f.* absolution; pardon, acquittal.—**a. de la demanda**, finding for the defendant.—**a. libre**, verdict of not guilty, acquittal.

absoluta, *f.* dogmatic assertion, dictum.

absolutamente, *adv.* absolutely.

absolutismo, *m.* despotism, absolutism.

absolutista, *n.* absolutist.

absoluto, ta, *a.* absolute, unconditional; imperious, despotic.—**en a.**, unqualifiedly, peremptorily; absolutely; (in negative sentences) at all.—**lo a.**, *n.* the absolute.

absolutorio, a, *a.* absolutory, absolving.

absolver, *va.* (*pp.* ABSUELTO; *ind.* ABSUELVO; *subj.* ABSUELVA) to absolve; to acquit.

absorbencia, *f.* absorbing, absorption; absorbency.

absorbente, *m. & a.* absorbent(-ing).

absorber, *va.* (*pp.* ABSORBIDO, ABSORTO) to absorb; to imbibe.

absorción, *f.* absorption.

absorto, ta. I. *pp. irreg.* of ABSORBER. II. *a.* amazed; absorbed in thought.

abstemio, mia, *a.* abstemious.

abstención, *f.* forbearance; abstention (as from voting).

abstenerse, *vr.* (*ind. pres.* ME ABSTENGO, *pret.* ME ABSTUVE; *subj.* ME ABSTENGA) to abstain, forbear.—**a. de**, to abstain from, forbear.

abstergente, *a.* detergent; cleansing; abstergent.

absterger, *va.* to cleanse; to sterilize.

abstersión, *f.* abstersion, purification.

abstersivo, va, *a.* = ABSTERGENTE.

abstinencia, *f.* abstinence, temperance; fasting.

abstinente, *a.* abstinent, abstemious.

abstracción, *f.* abstraction; concentration.

abstractivo, va, *a.* abstractive.

abstracto, ta. I. *pp. irreg.* of ABSTRAER. II. *a.* abstract. III. *m.* abstract.—**en a.**, in the abstract.

abstraer. I. *va.* (*pp.* ABSTRAÍDO, ABSTRACTO) *ind. pres.* ABSTRAIGO, *pret.* ABSTRAJE; *subj.* ABSTRAIGA) to abstract. II. *vn.* **a. de**, to do without; to leave aside. III. *vr.* to be withdrawn mentally.

abstraído, da. I. *pp.* of ABSTRAER. II. *a.* retired; absent-minded.

abstraigo, abstraje, *v. V.* ABSTRAER.

abstruso, sa, *a.* abstruse, difficult.

abstuve, *pret. irreg.* of ABSTENERSE.

absuelto, ta. I. *pp. irreg.* of ABSOLVER. II. *a.* acquitted.

absuelvo, absuelva, *v. V.* ABSOLVER.

absurdidad, *f.* absurdity.

absurdo, da. I. *a.* absurd, nonsensical. II. *m.* absurdity, nonsense.—**reducción al a.**, reductio ad absurdum.

abubilla, *f.* (ornith.) hoopoe.

abuela, *f.* grandmother.

abuelo, *m.* grandfather; elderly man; ancestor.

abuje, *m.* (zool.) (Cuba) a parasitic mite in plants and man, causing the itch.

abulia, *f.* (med.) abulia, a mental derangement.

abultado, da. I. *pp.* of ABULTAR. II. *a.* bulky, massive, big.

abultar. I. *va.* to augment; to enlarge. II. *vn.* to be bulky or large.

abundamiento, *m.* = ABUNDANCIA.—**a mayor a.**, furthermore; with greater reason.

abundancia, *f.* abundance.

abundante, *a.* abundant.—**abundantemente**, *adv.* abundantly.

abundar, *vn.* to abound.—**lo que abunda no daña**, better too much than too little; you can't have too much of a good thing.

abundosamente, *adv.* abundantly.

abundoso, sa, *a.* abundant.

abuñolado, da, abuñuelado, da, *a.* turned over (eggs); shaped like a fritter.

abuñuelar, *va.* to turn (eggs) over in frying; to shape like a fritter.

abur, *interj.* (coll.) = AGUR, good-bye.

aburar, *va.* to burn; scorch.

aburelado, da, *a.* dark red.

aburrición, *f.* = ABURRIMIENTO.

aburrido, da. I. *pp.* of ABURRIR. II. *a.* weary; tiresome, boresome.

aburrimiento, *m.* tediousness, weariness, ennui; annoyance.

¹**aburrir**. I. *va.* to vex, annoy; to tire, weary, bore. II. *vr.* to grow tired, weary; to be bored.

²**aburrir**, *va.* to risk, spend (money, time).

aburujado, da. I. *pp.* of ABURUJAR. II. *a.* pressed together; perplexed.

aburujar, aborujar, *va. & vr.* to form lumps; to clot.—**aburujarse**, *vr.* to wrap oneself up.

abusar, *vn.* to exceed, go too far; to take undue advantage.—**a. de**, to abuse, use wrongly; to betray (a confidence); to take undue advantage of; to impose upon.

abusión, *f.* abuse; superstition.

abusionero, ra, *a.* superstitious; fortune-telling.

abusivamente, *adv.* abusively.

abusivo, va, *a.* abusive.

abuso, *m.* misuse, abuse.—**a. de confianza**, betrayal of confidence.

abyección, *f.* abjection, abjectness.

abyecto, ta, *a.* abject, servile, slavish.

acá, *adv.* here; hither.—**a. y acullá, or a. y allá**, here and there.—**de ayer a.**, at present.—**¿de cuándo a.?** since when?—**desde entonces a.**, = DE AYER A.—**para a.**, hither, here.—**por a.**, here, hereabouts; this way.

acabable, *a.* that can be finished; achievable.

acabadamente, *adv.* completely, perfectly.

acabado, da. I. *pp.* of ACABAR. II. *a.* perfect, faultless; consummate; wasted, emaciated; worn out; dilapidated. III. *m.* (art) finish.

acabador, ra, *m. & f.* finisher.

acabalar, *va.* to complete, finish.

acaballadero, *m.* time and place at which horses cover mares.

acaballado, da. I. *pp.* of ACABALLAR. II. *a.* horselike.

acaballar, *va.* to cover (a mare).

acaballerado, da. I. *pp.* of ACABALLERAR. II. *a.* gentlemanlike.

acaballerar, *va.* to render genteel; to make a gentleman of.

acabamiento, *m.* completion, finishing; emaciation; death; end.

acabar. I. *va.* and *vn.* to finish; to complete; to end.—**a. con**, to finish, destroy; to use up, exhaust; to get rid of, extirpate.—**a. de** (foll. by *inf.*), to have just (foll. by *pp.*): *él acaba de llegar*, he has just arrived.—**a. por**, to end by, to . . . finally (*Juan acabá por decir*, John ended by saying, John finally said). II. *vr.* to be finished; to end, be over; to grow feeble or wasted; (foll. by *dat.*) to be or run out of, become exhausted (diff. constr.: *se me acabó el pan*, I ran out of bread: *se me ha acabado la paciencia*, my patience is exhausted).

acabellado, da, *a.* light chestnut colored.

acabestrillar, *vn.* to go shooting (birds) with a stalking horse or ox.

acabildar, *va.* to unite persons by persuasion to do something.

acabóse, *m.* (coll.) end (usually disastrous).

acacia, *f.* (bot.) acacia.

academia, *f.* academy; university; literary society or contest; (fine arts) academy figure.

académicamente, *adv.* academically.

académico, ca, *a. & n.* academic(-ian).

acaecedero, ra, *a.* eventual, contingent.

acaecer, *vn. defect. (subj.* ACAEZCA) to happen, come to pass.

acaecimiento, *m.* event, incident.

acahual, *m.* (bot.) sunflower; (Mex.) weeds; stubble.

acal, *m.* (Mex.) canoe; craft, vessel.

acalabrotar, *va.* (naut.) to make a cable by intertwining three ropes of three strands each.

acalefo, fa, *n. & a.* (zool.) acalephan.—*m. pl.* Acalephæ, Acalepha.

acalenturarse, *vr.* to become feverish.

acalia, *f.* (bot.) marsh mallow.

acaloradamente, *adv.* heatedly, excitedly.

acalorado, da. I. *pp.* of ACALORAR. **II.** *a.* heated, fiery, excited, angry. **III.** *n.* (fig.) hothead.

acaloramiento, *m.* ardor, heat, excitement.

acalorar. I. *va.* to warm; to inflame, excite; to move, arouse enthusiasm in; to urge on; to further, promote. **II.** *vr.* to grow warm; to get overheated; to get excited.

acallar, *va.* to quiet, hush; to mitigate, assuage.

acamar, *va.* (of wind, rain) to beat down (plants).

acambrayado, da, *a.* cambric-like.

acamellado, da, *a.* camel-like.

acampamento, *m.* (mil.) encampment, camp.

acampanado, a, *a.* bell-shaped.

acampanar, *va.* to shape like a bell.

acampar, *va., vn. & vr.* to encamp.

acampo, *m.* common pasture.

ácana, *f.* a hard reddish Cuban wood.

acanalada, da. I. *pp.* of ACANALAR. **II.** *a.* striated, fluted, corrugated, grooved. **III.** *m. pl.* ridge of a horse's back.

acanalador, *m.* (mech.) grooving plane.

acanaladura, *f.* groove, stria, striation.

acanalar, *va.* to make a channel in; to flute, corrugate, groove.

acandilado, da, *a.* shaped like a three-cornered hat; dazzled.

acanelado, da, *a.* cinnamon-colored.

acanillado, da, *a.* ribbed, striped (cloth).

acantáceas, *f. pl.* (bot.) Acanthaceæ.

acantáceo, a, a. (bot.) acanthaceous.

acantalear, *vn.* to hail large hailstones.

acantilado, da. I. *a.* (of sea bottom) stepped; steep. **II.** *m.* scarp, escarpment.

acanto, *m.* (bot.) prickly thistle; (arch.) acanthus leaf.

acantocéfalo, la, *n. & a.* (zool.) acanthocephalan.

acantonamiento, *m.* cantonment.

acantonar, *va.* to quarter (troops).

acantopterigio, gia, *n. & a.* (zool.) acanthopterygian.

acañaverear, *va.* to wound with sharp-pointed canes.

acañonear, *va.* to cannonade.

acaparador, ra, *n.* monopolizer.

acaparar, *va.* to monopolize; to corner, control (the market).

acaparrarse, *vr.* to close a bargain.

acaparrosado, da, *a.* copperas-hued.

acapizarse, *vr.* (coll.) to grapple, clinch.

acaponado, da, *a.* capon-like.

acaracolado, da, *a.* spiral-shaped, winding.

acaramelado, da. I. *pp.* of ACARAMELAR. **II.** *a.* (coll.) overpolite, disgustingly attentive.

acaramelar, *va.* to cover with caramel.

acarar, *va.* to confront; to face; to brave.

acardenalar. I. *va.* to beat black and blue. **II.** *vr.* to be covered with welts.

acareamiento, *m.* facing; confronting.

acarear, *va.* = ACARAR.

acariciador, ra, *m. & f.* one who fondles and caresses.

acariciar, *va.* to fondle, caress; to cherish.

acarnerado, da, *a.* having a sheeplike head.

ácaro, *m.* (zool.) acarus.—**a. de queso,** cheese mite.

acarralar, *va.* to skip a thread in weaving.

acarrarse, *vr.* to seek the shade (app. to sheep).

acarreadizo, za, *a.* portable.

acarreador, ra, *m. & f.* carrier; porter.

acarreamiento, *m.* carrying, transportation; cartage.—*pl.* supplies.

acarrear. I. *va.* to carry, cart, transport, convey; to occasion, cause. **II.** *vr.* to bring upon oneself.

acarreo, *m.* = ACARREAMIENTO.

acartonado, a, *a.* pasteboardlike.

acartonar. I. *va.* to give the appearance or consistence of pasteboard. **II.** *vr.* (coll.) to become dried up by age.

acasamatado, da, *a.* (fort.) having or resembling a casemate.

acaso. I. *m.* chance; accident. **II.** *adv.* by chance, by accident; maybe, perhaps.—**por si a.,** in case, if it should happen.

acastorado, da, *a.* like beaver skin.

acatable, *a.* worthy of respect.

acatadamente, *adv.* respectfully.

acatamiento, *m.* esteem, respect; obeisance.

acatante, *n. & a.* respecter(-ing).

acatar, *va.* to hold in high esteem; to respect, revere, do homage to; to treat with great deference or respect.

acatarrarse, *vr.* to catch cold.

acato, *m.* = ACATAMIENTO.

acatólico, ca, *n. & a.* noncatholic.

acaudalado, da. I. *pp.* of ACAUDALAR. **II.** *a.* rich, opulent, well-to-do.

acaudalar, *va.* to hoard up riches; (fig.) to acquire a reputation.

acáudeo, a, *a.* (zool.) acaudal, tailless.

acaudillador, *m.* commander of troops; leader.

acaudillamiento, *m.* leading, command.

acaudillar, *va.* to command, lead (esp. troops).

acaule, *a.* (bot.) short-stemmed.

accedente, *a.* acceding.

acceder, *vn.* to accede, agree, consent.

accesible, *a.* accessible, approachable; attainable.

accesión, *f.* accession; accessory; (med.) periodic attack of fever; (law) accession.

acceso, *m.* access; carnal intercourse; accession; (med.) access, attack.—**a. del sol,** (astr.) apparent motion of sun towards the equator.

accesoria, *f.* outbuilding.

accesoriamente, *adv.* accessorily.

accesorio, a, *a.* accessory, additional.

accessit, *m.* (Lat.) second prize or award.

accidentado, da. I. *pp.* of ACCIDENTARSE. **II.** *a.* troubled, agitated; undulating, rolling (ground).

accidental. I. *a.* accidental, contingent. **II.** *m.* (mus.) = ACCIDENTE.

accidentalmente, *adv.* accidentally.

accidentarse, *vr.* to be seized with a fit.

accidente, *m.* accident; chance; sudden fit; (mus.) accidental; (gram.) inflexion.—**a. del trabajo,** work accident, occupational accident.—**de,** or **por, a.,** accidentally, by chance.

acción, *f.* action; feat; lawsuit; gesticulation, gesture; battle; action in drama, plot; (art) posture; (com.) stock, share.—**a. de gracias,** thanksgiving.—**a. de guerra,** battle.—**a. de presencia,** (chem.) catalysis.—**en a.,** in action, at work.—**accionar,** *va.* to gesticulate; (mech.) to operate, move.—**accionista,** *m.* stockholder, shareholder.

accípitre, *m.* bird of prey.—**accipitrino, na,** *a.* like a bird of prey, accipitral.

acebadamiento, *m.* (vet.) disease of animals surfeited with barley.

acebadar, *va.* = ENCEBADAR, to overfeed.

acebal, *m.*, **acebeda,** *f.*, **acebedo,** *m.* plantation of holly trees.

acebo, *m.* (bot.) holly tree.

acebollado, da, *a.* damaged by *acebolladura.*

acebolladura, *f.* damage (to a tree) from separation of the woody layers.

acebuchal. I. *m.* grove or wood of wild olive trees. **II.** *a.* pertaining to wild olives.

acebuche, *m.* (bot.) wild olive tree.—**acebucheno, na,** *a.* = ACEBUCHAL, *a.*

acebuchina, *f.* wild olive.

acecé, acece, *v.* V. ACEZAR.

acecinar. I. *va.* to salt and dry (meat.) **II.** *vr.* to grow old, dry, withered.

acechador, ra, *m.* & *f.* ambusher; observer, lookout; intruder, prier.

acechar, *va.* to lie in ambush for; to spy on.

acecho, *m.* waylaying, lying in ambush.—**al a.,** or **en a.,** *a.* in wait, in ambush.

acechón, na, *m.* & *f.* (coll.) = ACECHADOR.

acedamente, *adv.* sourly, bitterly.

acedar, *va.* to sour; to displease, vex.

acedera, *f.* (bot.) sorrel.

acederaque, *m.* (bot.) bead tree.

acederilla, *f.* (bot.) wood sorrel.

acederón, *m.* (bot.) a variety of sorrel.

acedía, *f.* acidity, heart-burn, sourness; roughness; asperity of address.

acedo, da, *a.* acid, sour; harsh, unpleasant.

acefalía, *f.* **acefalismo,** *m.* sect and doctrine of the Acephali.

acéfalo, la, *a.* acephalous.—*pl.* Acephali, members of a religious sect that recognized no head or hierarchy.

aceitada, *f.* spilled oil; cake kneaded with oil.

aceitar, *va.* to oil; to rub with oil.

aceitazo, *m.* *aug.* = ACEITÓN.

aceite, *m.* oil; essential oil.—**a. de ballena,** whale oil.—**a. de comer,** olive, sweet oil.—**a. de hígado de bacalao,** cod-liver oil.—**a. de palo,** balsam of copaiba.—**a. de vitriolo,** vitriol, oil of vitriol (sulphuric acid).—**a. lubricante,** lubricating oil.—**a. secante,** linseed oil.

aceitera, *f.* woman who sells oil; oil jar, oil cruet; oil can; (mech.) oil cup.—*pl.* **aceiteras,** casters (for oil, etc.).

aceitería, *f.* oil shop.

aceitero, ra, *m.* & *f.* oiler; oil seller.

aceitillo, *m.* (bot.) satinwood.

aceitón, *m.* lubricating oil.

aceitoso, sa, *a.* oily, greasy.

aceituna, *f.* olive.—**a. de la reina,** or **gordal,** queen olive.—**a. manzanilla,** manzanilla olive.—**a. picudilla** = A. ZORZALEÑA.—**a. zapatera,** stale olive.—**a. zofairón,** baby queen olive.—**a. zorzaleña,** crescent olive.

aceitunado, da, *a.* olive-colored.

aceitunero, ra, *n.* olive dealer.

aceituní, *m.* arabesque work.

aceitunil, *a.* olive-colored.

aceitunillo, *m.* (bot.) satinwood.

aceituno, *m.* (bot.) olive tree.

acelajado, da, *a.* showing clouds of various hues.

aceleración, *f.* acceleration; haste.

aceleradamente, *adv.* speedily, swiftly; hastily; at an accelerated speed.

acelerador, ra. I. *a.* accelerating. **II.** *m.* accelerator; (auto) accelerator; (med.) accelerator.

aceleramiento, *m.* = ACELERACIÓN.

acelerar. I. *va.* to accelerate; to hasten, hurry, rush. **II.** *vr.* to move fast; to make haste.

aceleratriz, *f.* *a.* (of force) accelerating.

acelerómetro, *m.* (aer.) accelerometer.

acelga, *f.* (bot.) salt-wort.

acémila, *f.* beast of burden; pack animal.—**acemilar,** *a.* pert. to mules and muleteers.

acemilería, *f.* mule stable.

acemilero, ra. I. *a.* pert. to ACEMILERÍA. **II.** *m.* muleteer.

acemita, *f.* bran bread, graham bread.

acemite, *m.* fine bran, middlings; pottage.

acendrado, da. I. *pp.* of ACENDRAR. **II.** *a.* purified, refined; unspotted, stainless.

acendrar, *va.* to purify or refine (metals); to free from stain or blemish.

acensuar, *va.* to tax (a property).

acento, *m.* accent, stress; accent, way of speaking.—**a. ortográfico,** written accent.—**a. prosódico,** or **tónico,** tonic accent, emphasis.

acentuación, *f.* accentuation.

acentuar, *va.* to accentuate; to emphasize.

aceña, *f.* water mill.—**aceñero,** *m.* water-mill keeper.

acepar, *vn.* to take root. Also ENCEPAR.

acepción, *f.* acceptation, meaning.—**a. de personas,** unfair discrimination among persons.

acepilladura, *f.* planing; wood shavings.

acepillar, *va.* to plane; to brush; to polish.

aceptabilidad, *f.* acceptability.

aceptable, *a.* acceptable, admissible.—**aceptablemente,** *adv.* acceptably.

aceptación, *f.* acceptation; (formal) acceptance; approbation; (com.) acceptance.—**a. de personas** = ACEPCIÓN DE PERSONAS.

aceptador, ra, *m.* & *f.* acceptor.

aceptante, I. *m.* & *f.* accepter. **II.** *a.* accepting.

aceptar, *va.* to accept; (com.) to accept or honor.

acepto, ta, *a.* acceptable, agreeable.

acequia, *f.* trench; drain; channel; irrigation ditch.

acequiado, da. I. *pp.* of ACEQUIAR. **II.** *a.* intersected by canals.

acequiador, *m.* canal or dike maker.

acequiar, *va.* to construct ditches, channels, flumes in or for.

acequiero, *m.* canal or dike keeper.

ácer, *m.* (bot.) maple tree.

acera, *f.* sidewalk; row of houses on either side of a street; (arch.) face or facing stone (of a wall).

acerado, da. I. *pp.* of ¹ACERAR. **II.** *a.* made of steel; steel (as *a.*); strong; biting, acrimonious.

¹acerar, *va.* to steel; to impregnate (liquids) with steel; to strengthen; to convert (iron) into steel; to cover with steel.

²acerar, *va.* (arch.) to lay the facing stones of (a wall).

acerbamente, *adv.* cruelly, severely, harshly.

acerbidad, *f.* acerbity, harshness; rigor, cruelty.

acerbo, ba, *a.* tart; harsh, severe, cruel.

acerca de, *prep.* about, with regard to.

acercamiento, *m.* approximation, approaching; rapprochement.

acercar. I. *va.* (*pret.* ACERQUÉ; *subj.* ACERQUE) to bring or place near, or nearer. **II.** *vr.* (a) to draw near (to), approach.

ácere, *m.* maple tree.

acerico, acerillo, *m.* pincushion; small pillow.

aceríneo, a. I. *a.* (bot.) aceraceous. **II.** *f.* *pl.* Aceraceæ.

acerino, na, *a.* (poet.) steel-like; of steel.

acero, *m.* steel; sword; pointed or edged arm.—*pl.* (fig.) arms; spirit, courage; appetite.—**a. colado,** or **fundido,** cast steel.—**a. al carbono,** etc. V. A *prep.* for usage.

acerola, *f.* haw, fruit of the hawthorn.

acerolo, *m.* (bot.) hawthorn.

acerque, acerquo, *v.* V. ACERCAR.

acérrimamente, *adv.* vigorously; strongly.

acérrimo, ma, *a.* *super.* very strong (taste, odor); very harsh; very vigorous; very stanch or stalwart.

acerrojar, *va.* to bolt; to lock.

acertadamente, *adv.* opportunely, fitly, wisely.

acertado, da. I. *pp.* of ACERTAR. **II.** *a.* fit, proper; wise.

acertador, ra, *m.* & *f.* good guesser.

acertar. I. *va.* (*ind.* ACIERTO; *subj.* ACIERTE) to hit the mark; to hit by chance; to succeed in; to guess (something). **II.** *vn.* to guess right; to succeed; (agr.) to thrive.—**a. a,** to happen.—**a. con,** to find, come across.

acertijo, *m.* riddle, conundrum.

aceruelo, *m.* small packsaddle.

acervo, *m.* a heap; undivided estate; common property.

acescencia, *f.* acescence, slight sourness.

acescente, *a.* acescent, turning or slightly sour.

acetábulo, *m.* cruet; acetabulum (small cup); (anat.) acetabulum, socket (esp. for hip bone).

acetal, *m.* (chem.) acetal.

acetámida, *f.* (chem.) acetamide.

acetanilida, *f.* (chem.) acetanilide.

acetato, *m.* (chem.) acetate.

acético, ca, *a.* acetic.

acetificar, *va.* to acetify, convert into acetic acid.

acetileno, *m.* acetylene.

acetílico, ca, *a.* (chem.) acetylic.

acetilo, *m.* (chem.) acetyl.

acetímetro, *m.* acetimeter.

acetín, *m.* (bot.) satinwood.

acetona, *f.* (chem.) acetone.

acetosa, *f.* (bot.) sorrel.

acetosidad, *f.* acetosity.

acetosilla, *f.* = ACEDERILLA, (bot.) wood sorrel.

acetoso, sa, *a.* acetous, containing acetic acid.

acetre, *m.* small bucket; holy-water font.

acezar, *vn.* (*pret.* ACECÉ; *subj.* ACECE) to pant.

acezo, *m.* pant, panting.—**acezoso, sa,** *a.* panting.

aciago, ga, *a.* unfortunate, sad, fateful.

acial, *m.* barnacle, twitch, (for horses).

aciano, *m.* (bot.) cornflower.

aciar, *m.* = ACIAL.

acíbar, *m.* aloes; aloe tree; bitterness; displeasure. —**acibarar,** *va.* to put aloes into; to embitter.

aciberar, *va.* to grind very fine, pulverize.

acicalado, *m.* act of polishing a weapon; polish.

acicalador, ra. I. *a.* polishing; embellishing; attiring. **II.** *m.* burnishing tool.

acicaladura, *f.,* **acicalamiento,** *m.* burnishing; polish, glossiness; adornment; dressing.

acicalar. I. *va.* to polish, burnish; to dress, adorn, embellish. **II.** *vr.* (fig.) to dress in style, make an elaborate toilet.

acicate, *m.* long-pointed Moorish spur; inducement; goad.

acíclico, ca, *a.* (elec.) acyclic, out of phase.

aciclo, cla, *a.* (bot.) acyclic.

acicular, *a.* aciculate; needle-shaped.

aciche, *m.* paving hammer; brick hammer.

acidez, *f.* acidity, tartness.

acidia, *f.* laziness; weakness.

acidificación, *f.* (chem.) acidification.

acidificar, *va.* to acidify.

acidimetría, *f.* acidimetry.

acidímetro, *m.* acidimeter.

acidioso, sa, *a.* lazy; weak; lax.

ácido, da. I. *m.* (chem.) acid. **II.** *a.* acid; sour, tart; harsh.

acidular, *va.* to acidulate.

acídulo, la, *a.* (chem.) acidulous, tart.

¹acierto, *m.* a good hit, good shot; ability; tact; knack; dexterity.

²acierto, acierte, *v.* V. ACERTAR.

aciguatado, da. I. *pp.* of ACIGUATARSE. **II.** *a.* jaundiced.

aciguatarse, *vr.* to become ill with jaundice.

acijado, da, *a.* copper- or copperas-colored.

acije, *m.* copperas.—**acijoso, sa,** *a.* containing copperas; brownish.

acimboga, *f.* = AZAMBOA, citron (the fruit).

ácimo, ma, *a.* = ÁZIMO, unleavened.

acimut, *m.* azimuth.—**acimutal,** *a.* azimuthal, azimuth (as *a.*).

acinesia, *f.* (med.) akinesia, paralysis of the motor nerves.

acino, *m.* (bot., anat.) acinus.

ación, *f.* stirrup strap.—**acionera,** *f.* piece of saddle from which stirrup strap hangs.—**acionero,** *m.* maker of stirrup straps.

acipado, da, *a.* well-milled (woolens).

acirate, *m.* landmark, boundary.

acitara, *f.* partition wall; rail of bridge; chair or saddle cover. Also CITARA.

acitrón, *m.* candied citron.

aclamación, *f.* acclamation.

aclamador, ra, *m. & f.* applauder.

aclamar, *va.* to shout, applaud, acclaim.

aclaración, *f.* explanation.

aclarador, ra. I. *a.* explanatory. **II.** *m.* comb in looms.

aclarar. I. *va.* to make clear; to explain; to thin; to clarify; to rinse. **II.** *vn.* to clear up; to recover brightness; CLAREAR, to dawn.

aclaratorio, ria, *a.* explanatory.

aclasto, ta, *a.* (opt.) aclastic, not refracting.

acleido, da, *a.* (zool.) with no clavicles.

aclimatación, *f.* acclimatization, acclimatation.

aclimatar, *va. & vr.* to acclimatize, acclimate.

aclínico, ca. I. *a.* (phys.) aclinic. **II.** *m.* opera glasses.

aclocar I. *vn.* (*ind. pres.* ACLUECO, *pret.* ACLOQUÉ; *subj.* ACLUEQUE) (of hens) to brood, be broody. **II.** *vr.* to stretch out, lie down; (of hens) to become broody.

acobardar, *va.* to daunt, intimidate, frighten.

acobijar, *va.* (agr.) to mulch.—**acobijo,** *m.* mulch.

acobrado, da, *a.* copper-hued.

acoceador, ra, *a.* that kicks, kicking.

acoceamiento, *m.* kicking.

acocear, *va.* to kick; to humiliate; to ill-treat.

acocotar, *va.* = ACOGOTAR.

acocote, *m.* long gourd used in Mexico for extracting the juice of the maguey.

acocharse, *vr.* to squat, stoop down.

acochinar, *va.* (coll.) to murder; to humble; (checkers game) to corner (a checker).

acodado, da, *a.* elbowed; cranked (axle); toggled.

acodadura, *f.* bending the elbow; (hort.) layering.

acodalamiento, *m.* (arch.) propping; staying.

acodalar, *va.* (arch.) to prop; to shore; to stay.

acodar, *va.* to lean the elbow upon; (hort.) to layer (cuttings); (arch.) = ACODALAR; (carp.) to square (timber).

acoderamiento, *m.* (naut.) bringing the broadside to bear.

acoderar, *va.* (naut.) to put a spring on a cable; to bring the broadside to bear.

acodiciar. I. *va.* to long for, covet. **II.** *vr.* to become covetous.

acodillar. I. *va.* to bend into an elbow or angle. **II.** *vr.* to sink down under a burden.

acodo, *m.* (agr.) shoot, scion.

acogedizo, za, *a.* collected promiscuously.

acogedor, ra, *m. & f.* harborer, protector.

acoger. I. *va.* (*ind.* ACOJO; *subj.* ACOJA) to receive; (fig.) to protect, shelter. **II.** *vr.* (**a**) to take refuge (in); to resort (to).

acogeta, *f.* shelter, cover, place of safety.

acogida, *f.* reception; place of meeting, confluence; asylum.—**dar a. a una letra,** (com.) to honor a draft.—**tener buena, mala a.,** to be well, unfavorably received.

acogido, *m.* collection of brood mares given to owner of principal steed, to keep them at a certain price; letting out of pasture for flocks.

acogimiento, *m.* = ACOGIDA.

¹acogollar, *va.* to cover up (plants).

²acogollar, *vn.* to bud.

acogombradura, *f.* banking of plants.

acogombrar, *va.* = APORCAR, to cover (plants) with earth, to bank.

acogotar, *va.* to kill by a blow on the back of the neck.

acohombrar, *va.* (agr.) = ACOGOMBRAR.

acojinamiento, *m.* (mech.) cushioning.

acojinar, *va.* to quilt; (mech.) to cushion.

acojo, acoja, *v.* V. ACOGER.

acolar, *va.* (her.) to unite (two coats of arms) under the same crown, shield, etc.

acolchado, *m.* (hydraul. eng.) mattress.

¹acolchar, acolchonar, *va.* to quilt.

²acolchar, *va.* (naut.) to intertwine (cords).

acolia, *f.* (med.) acholia.

acólito, *m.* acolyte, assistant.

acología, *f.* (med.) acology.

acolladores, *m. pl.* (naut.) lanyards.

acollar, *va.* (*ind.* ACUELLO; *subj.* ACUELLE) (agr.) to cover with earth the base of a trunk; (naut.) to caulk.

acollarado, da, *a.* ring-necked.

acollarar, *va.* to yoke or harness (horses, oxen, etc.); to couple (hounds); to put a collar on.

acollonar, *va.* (coll.) = ACOBARDAR, to frighten.

acombar, *va.* to bend; to warp.

acomedirse, *vr.* to offer oneself, volunteer.

acometedor, ra, *n. & a.* aggressor(-ive); enterpriser(-ing).

acometer, *va.* to attack, rush on, (coll.) go for; to undertake; (of sleep, an illness) to overtake.

acometida, *f.,* **acometimiento,** *m.* attack, assault; branch or outlet (in a sewer).

acometividad, *f.* combativeness.

acomodable, *a.* easily arranged.

acomodación, *f.* accommodation.

acomodadamente, *adv.* commodiously, comfortably.

acomodadizo, za, *a.* accommodating.

acomodado, da. I. *pp.* of ACOMODAR. **II.** *a.* convenient, fit; well-to-do, wealthy; fond of comfort; moderate, reasonable.

acomodador, ra, *n.* one who accommodates; usher in a theatre.

acomodamiento, *m.* accommodation.

acomodar. I. *va.* to arrange; to accommodate; to set to rights; to place; to reconcile, compound, compromise; to furnish, supply; to take in, shelter, lodge. **II.** *vn.* to fit; to suit. **III.** *vr.* to condescend; to adapt oneself; to put up with; to settle, agree.

acomodaticio, cia, *a.* accommodating.

acomodo, *m.* employment, situation; lodgings.

acompañado, da. I. *pp.* of ACOMPAÑAR. **II.** *a.* frequented. **III.** *n.* assistant.

acompañador, ra. I. *n.* chaperon, attendant; companion; (mus.) accompanist. **II.** *a.* accompanying.

acompañamiento, *m.* attendance; retinue; (mus.) accompaniment; supernumeraries in a theatre; (her.) ornament around an escutcheon.

acompañante, ta, *n. & a.* = ACOMPAÑADOR.

acompañar. I. *va.* to accompany; to attend, escort; to enclose; (mus.) to accompany. **II.** *vr.* to hold a consultation.

acompasadamente, *adv.* rhythmically.

acompasado, da, *a.* measured, rhythmic; (coll.) monotonous and slow in speech or unhurried in gait; of fixed, regular habits.

acompasar, compasar, *va.* to measure with a compass; to arrange in order.

acomplexionado, da, *a.* of (good, bad) complexion.

acomunarse, *vr.* to unite, combine.

aconchabarse, conchabarse, *vr.* (coll.) to unite (esp. for evil purpose).

aconchar, *va.* to push to a place of shelter; (naut.) to run aground.

acondicionado, da. I. *pp.* of ACONDICIONAR. **II.** *a.* (of persons) of (good, bad) disposition; (of things) in (good, bad) condition; of (good, bad) quality.—**con aire a.,** air-conditioned.

acondicionamiento, *m.* conditioning; drying (of silk, etc.).

acondicionar. I. *va.* to prepare, arrange; to repair; to condition. **II.** *vr.* to acquire a quality or condition; to qualify (for a position).

acongojadamente, *adv.* sorrowfully, sadly.

acongojar. I. *va.* to afflict, grieve. **II.** *vr.* to become sad; to grieve.

aconitina, *f.* (chem.) aconitine.

acónito, *m.* (bot.) aconite.

aconsejable, *a.* advisable.

aconsejador, ra, *n.* adviser, counsellor.

aconsejante, *n. & a.* adviser(-ing).

aconsejar. I. *va.* to advise, counsel. **II.** *vr.* (con) to advise (with); to consult.

aconsonantar. I. *va.* to make (a word) rhyme with another; to use rhymes in prose. **II.** *vn.* to rhyme.

acontecedero, ra, *a.* possible, that may happen.

acontecer, *v. impers.* (*subj.* ACONTEZCA) to happen, come about.—**acontecido, a. I.** *pp.* of ACONTECER. **II.** *a.* sad, despondent.

acontecimiento, *m.* event, happening.

acontezca, *v. V.* ACONTECER.

acopado, da. I. *pp.* of ACOPAR. **II.** *a.* cuplike, cupped.

acopar, *vn.* to trim to shape; to cup, hollow.

acopetado, da, *a.* tufted.

acopiador, ra, *n.* one who stores or collects.

acopiamiento, *m.* gathering, collecting; collection; supply, stock.

acopiar, *va.* to gather, store, collect, garner.

acopio, *m.* gathering, storing; assortment; collection, quantity.

acoplado, da. I. *pp.* of ACOPLAR. **II.** *a.* fitted, adjusted; coupled; (carp.) scarfed.—**a. directamente,** (mech.) direct-connected.

acopladura, *f.* = ACOPLAMIENTO.

acoplamiento, *m.* coupling; joint; scarfing.

acoplar. I. *va.* to couple, join, connect; to hitch, yoke; to scarf (timber); to reconcile; to settle (differences); to pair, mate (animals). **II.** *vr.* to make up a difference; to settle, come to an agreement; (coll.) to become intimate.

acoquinamiento, *m.* intimidation.

acoquinar. I. *va.* to intimidate; frighten. **II.** *vr.* to be afraid.

acoracé, acorace, *v. V.* ACORAZAR.

acorar, *va.* to afflict; to cause grief.

acorazado, da. I. *a.* ironclad; shell (app. to transformers, as shell core). **II.** *m.* armored ship, ironclad.

acorazamiento, *m.* armoring; armor.

acorazar, *va.* (*pret.* ACORACÉ; *subj.* ACORACE) to armor.

acorazonado, da, *a.* heart-shaped.

acorchamiento, *m.* shrivelling.

acorcharse, *vr.* to shrivel; (of fruits) to get stale; to become torpid; (of arm, leg, etc.) to go to sleep.

acordada, *f.* (law) resolution, decision.

acordadamente, *adv.* by common consent, jointly; with mature deliberation.

acordado, da. I. *pp.* of ACORDAR. **II.** *a.* done with mature deliberation.

acordar. I. *va.* (*ind.* ACUERDO; *subj.* ACUERDE) to resolve; to agree; to remind; (mus.) (reg. conj. in this meaning) to tune; to dispose (figures) in a picture; to make flush, level, smooth. **II.** *vn.* to agree. **III.** *vr.* (de) to remember, recollect (*no me acuerdo de eso,* I do not remember that); to come to an agreement.—**si mal no me acuerdo,** if I remember rightly, if my memory does not fail me.

acorde. I. *a.* agreed; in tune; in accord. **II.** *m.* chord; harmony of sounds or colors.

acordelar, *va.* to measure with a cord.

acordemente, *adv.* by common consent; harmoniously; consistently.

acordeón, *m.* accordion.

acordonado, da. I. *pp.* of ACORDONAR. **II.** *a.* surrounded; in the form of a cord.

acordonamiento, *m.* act of lacing; milling (coins); cording; shirring.

acordonar, *va.* to lace; to mill (a coin); to cord, shirr, twine; to surround (with a cordon of troops, etc.).

acores, *m. pl.* (med.) achor, scald head.

acornar, *va.* (*ind.* ACUERNO; *subj.* ACUERNE) = ACORNEAR.

acornear, *va.* to butt (with the head).

acorneador, ra, *n. & a.;* butter(-ing).

ácoro, *m.* (bot.) sweet flag.

acorralamiento, *m.* corralling.

acorralar, *va.* to corral; to surround; to intimidate; to silence.

acorrer. I. *va.* to help, succor. **II.** *vn.* to run to the aid (of someone). **III.** *vr.* to take shelter.

acorrucarse, accurrucarse, *vr.* to huddle up.

acortamiento, *m.* shortening; (astr.) difference between the distance from the sun or a planet to the earth and the projection of that distance on the plane of the ecliptic.

a cortar. I. *va.* to shorten, lessen, reduce; to obstruct.—**a. la marcha,** to slow down.—**a. la vela,** (naut.) to shorten sail. **II.** *vr.* to shrivel, contract, shrink; to be bashful; to fall back.

acorullar, *va.* (naut.) to bridle (the oars).

acosador, ra, *n.* pursuer, persecutor.

acosamiento, *m.* relentless persecution.

acosar, *va.* to pursue relentlessly; to vex, harass.

acosmismo, *m.* (philos.) acosmism.

acostado, da. I. *pp.* of ACOSTAR. **II.** *a.* stretched out, lying down; laid down; in bed.

¹acostamiento, *m.* stretching or laying down.

²acostamiento, *m.* stipend, emolument.

acostar. I. *va.* (*ind.* ACUESTO; *subj.* ACUESTE) to lay down; to put to bed; to bring (a vessel) alongside the shore. **II.** *vn.* to tilt, have a list. **III.** *vr.* to lie down; to go to bed.—**a. con las gallinas,** (coll.) to go to bed with the chickens.

acostumbradamente, *adv.* customarily.

acostumbrado, da, *a.* accustomed, used.

acostumbrar. I. *va.* to accustom. **II.** *vn.* to be accustomed, be in the habit (*acostumbro comer temprano,* I am in the habit of dining early). **III.** *vr.* to get used, or become accustomed.

acotación, f., acotamiento, *m.* boundary mark or monument; directions (for a theatrical performance); marginal note; (surv.) elevation marked on a map.

¹acotar. I. *va.* to set boundary marks on; to mark out. **II.** *vr.* to seek refuge outside the boundary line.

²acotar, *va.* to annotate; to accept; to select; to witness, vouch for; (surv.) to put the elevation figures on (a map).

³acotar, *va.* to prune (a tree).

acotiledóneo, ea. I. *a.* (bot.) acotyledonous. **II.** *f. pl.* (bot.) Acotyledons.

acotillo, *m.* sledgehammer.

acoyundar, *va.* to yoke (oxen).

¹acre, *a.* sour; acrimonious; tart; mordant; keen.

²acre, *m.* acre.

acrecencia, *f.* increase; growth.

acrecentador, ra, *n. & a.* increaser(-ing).

acrecentamiento, *m.* = ACRECENCIA.

acrecentar (*ind.* ACRECIENTO; *subj.* ACRECIENTE), **acrecer** (*ind.* ACREZCO; *subj.* ACREZCA), *va.* to increase; to promote, advance.

acreditado, da. I. *pp.* of ACREDITAR. **II.** *a.* well reputed, of good repute.

acreditar, *va.* to assure, affirm; to verify, prove; (com.) to recommend, answer for, guarantee; to accredit, authorize; to prove.

acreedor, ra. I. *a.* meritorious, deserving; creditor (as *a.*).—**a. a,** deserving or worthy of. **II.** *n.* creditor.—**a. hipotecario,** mortgagee.

acreencia, *f.* (Am.) debt claimed; balance in favor of creditor.

acremente, *adv.* sourly, bitterly.

acrezca, acrezco, *v.* V. ACRECER.

acribador, ra, *n. & a.* one who sifts; sifting.

acribadura, *f.* sifting.—*pl.* siftings.

acribar, *va.* to sift; to perforate like a sieve.

acribillar, *va.* to pierce, perforate; to torment; to cover with wounds.

acriminación, *f.* crimination, accusation.

acriminador, ra, *n.* accuser, informer.

acriminar, *va.* to accuse, charge; to impeach; (law) to aggravate.

acrimonia, *f.* acrimony; tartness; sourness.

acriollarse, *vr.* (Am.) (of Europeans, Anglo-Americans) to adopt native ways, get to be like a creole.

acrisoladamente, *adv.* honestly.

acrisolado, da, *a.* honest, virtuous, upright.

acrisolar, *va.* to assay; to refine; to purify, cleanse; to prove.

aristianar, *va.* (coll.) to baptize, christen.

acritud, *f.* = ACRIMONIA.

acrobacia, *f.* (aer.) fancy air maneuver, stunt.

acróbata, *n.* acrobat.

acrobático, ca, *a.* acrobatic.

acrocéfalo, la, *a.* acrocephalous, with a lofty skull.

acromático, ca, *a.* (opt.) achromatic, free from color.

acromatismo, *m.* achromatism.

acromatizar, *va.* (opt.) to make achromatic (lenses, etc.).

acromatopsia, *f.* color blindness.

acromial, acromiano, na, *a.* (anat.) acromial.

acrómico, ca, *a.* achromic.

acromio, *m.* (anat.) acromion.

acrónico, ca, *a.* (astr.) acronical.

acrópolis, *m.* (mil.) acropolis.

acróstico, ca, *a.* acrostic.

acrostolio, *m.* (naut.) acrostolium.

ac:otera, *f.* (arch.) acroterium.

acta, *f.* act or record of proceedings; certificate of election.—*pl.* acts or records of communities, chapters, councils; proceedings; transactions, minutes; papers, file, etc.—**a. notarial,** notarial certificate.—**tomar a.,** (Am.) to note, set down; to bear in mind.

actínico, ca, *a.* actinic.

actinio, *m.* actinium.

actinismo, *m.* actinism.

actinométrico, ca, *a.* (opt.) actinometric.

actinómetro, *m.* (opt.) actinometer.

actitud, *f.* attitude, position, posture.

activamente, *adv.* actively.

activar, *va.* to make active; to expedite, hasten.

actividad, *f.* activity, energy.—**en a.,** in operation.

activo, va. I. *a.* active. **II.** *m.* (com.) assets.

acto, *m.* act, action; public function; commencement in colleges, etc.; act (of a play); thesis defended in universities; carnal intercourse.—**a. continuo,** (*adv.*) immediately afterward.—**en el a.,** (*adv.*) at once.

actor, ra. I. *a.* acting, that acts.—**parte actora,** (law) prosecution; plaintiff. **II.** *m.* actor, player; (law) plaintiff, claimant.

actriz, *f.* actress.

actuación, *f.* actuation; action.—*pl.* (law) proceedings.

actuado, da. I. *pp.* of ACTUAR. **II.** *a.* actuated; skilled, experienced.

actual, *a.* present, of the present time (not *actual*).—**actualidad,** *f.* present time (never *actuality*).—**en la a.,** at the present time, at present, nowadays.—**actualmente,** *adv.* at present, at the present time (never *actually*).

actuante, *a. & n.* defender of a thesis in colleges.

actuar. I. *vn.* to act; to perform judicial acts; to take the affirmative side in a university debate. **II.** *va.* to put in action, actuate.

actuario, *m.* clerk of a court of justice.—**a. de seguros,** actuary, expert on insurance.

acuadrillar, *va.* to collect or head (a band of armed men).

acuantiar, *va.* to determine the quantity of.

acuapuntura, *f.* (med.) acupuncture.

acuarela, *f.* water-color painting.

acuarelista, *m.* water-color painter.

acuario, *m.* Aquarius (in zodiac); aquarium.

acuartelado, da. I. *pp.* of ACUARTELAR. **II.** *a.* (her.) quartered, divided into quarters.

acuartelamiento, *m.* quartering or billeting (of troops); troops; quarters.

For pronunciation, see the rules at the beginning of the book.

acuartelar, *va.* to quarter, billet.—**a. las velas,** (naut.) to flat in the sails.

acuartillar, *vn.* (of pack animals) to bend in the quarters under a heavy load.

acuático, ca, acuátil, *a.* aquatic, water (as *a.*).

acuatizaje, *m.* (aer.) alighting on the water; place for alighting on the water.

acuatizar, *vn.* (aer.) to alight on the water.

acuatubular, *a.* water-tube (boiler).

acubado, da, *a.* resembling a pail or bucket.

acucia, *f.* zeal, diligence; longing.

acuciamiento, *m.* urging, hastening.

acuciar, *va.* to urge, hasten; to covet.

acuciosamente, *adv.* actively, diligently; eagerly.

acucioso, sa, *a.* zealous, hasty, eager.

acuclillado, da, *a.* cowering, squatting.

acuclillarse, *vr.* to crouch, squat.

acucharado, da, *a.* spoonlike.

acuchillado, da. I. *pp.* of ACUCHILLAR. **II.** *a.* schooled by experience; slashed (app. to garments).

acuchillador, ra, *n.* slasher; bully.

acuchillar. I. *va.* to cut, hack; to slash, cut open; to knife; to put to the sword. **II.** *vr.* to fight with knives or swords.

acudimiento, *m.* aid, assistance.

acudir, *vn.* to be present frequently; to attend; to go, come; to respond (to a call); to go or come to the rescue; to resort; to have recourse; to keep (an appointment).

acueducto, *m.* aqueduct; water-supply line, main.

acuello, acuelle, *v.* V. ACOLLAR.

ácueo, a, *a.* watery; aqueous.

acuerdado, da, *a.* aligned.

¹acuerdo, *m.* resolution; determination; opinion; report, advice; remembrance, recollection; concurrence, accord; agreement, convention, pact; body of the members of a tribunal; harmony.—**de a.,** in agreement; unanimously; of the same opinion; complying, in accordance.—**de común a.,** unanimously; by mutual agreement.

²acuerdo, acuerde, *v.* V. ACORDAR.

acuerno, acuerne, *v.* V. ACORNAR.

acuesto, acueste, *v.* V. ACOSTAR.

acuitar. I. *va.* to afflict. **II.** *vr.* to grieve.

acular, *va.* (coll.) to make (a horse) back up.

aculebrinado, da, *a.* in the form of a culverin.

acúleo, a, *a.* (zool.) aculeate, armed with a sting.

acullá, *adv.* on the other side, opposite; yonder.

acumen, *m.* acumen, quick discernment.

acuminado, da, *a.* (bot.) acuminate.

acumulación, *f.* accumulation; gathering.

acumulador, ra, *n.* accumulator; (elec.) storage battery, accumulator.

acumular, *va.* to accumulate; to impute to, charge with; (law) to try or dispose of jointly.

acumulativamente, *adv.* cumulatively; (law) by way of prevention or precaution; jointly.

acumulativo, va, *a.* cumulative; joint.

acuñación, *f.* coining, minting; wedging.

acuñador, ra, *n.* coiner; wedge; (print.) shooting stick.

acuñar, *va.* to coin, mint; to wedge; (print.) to key, lock; to quoin.

acuosidad, *f.* wateriness.

acuoso, sa, aguoso, sa, *a.* watery, aqueous.

acupuntura, *f.* (surg.) acupuncture.

acure, *m.* (Venez.) Guinea pig.

acurrucarse, acorrucarse, *vr.* to huddle up.

acusación, *f.* accusation.

acusado, da, *n. & a.* defendant, accused.

acusador, ra, *n.* accuser; informer; prosecutor.

acusante, *a.* accusing, prosecuting.

acusar. I. *va.* to accuse; to prosecute; to indict; to acknowledge (receipt); at cards, to announce in due time that one holds certain cards that count so many points.—**a. las cuarenta,** to call out the forty honor points (at cards); (coll.) to

give a piece of one's mind. **II.** *vr.* (**de**), to confess (to).

acusativo, *m.* & *a.* accusative.

acusatorio, ria, *a.* accusatory.

acuse, *m.* at cards, each of the cards duly announced in certain games.—**a. de recibo,** acknowledgment of receipt.

acusiador, ra, *n.* & *a.* hastener(-ing), urger(-ing).

acusón, na, *a.* & *n.* (coll.) telltale, talebearer.

acústica, *f.* acoustics.

acústico, ca, *a.* acoustic; speaking (tube).

acutángulo, *a.* (geom.) acute-angled.

acutí, *m.* (Arg.) agouti.

achacar, *va.* to impute.

achacosamente, *adv.* sickly.

achacoso, sa, *a.* siekly, ailing.

achaflanar, chaflanar, *va.* to chamfer, bevel.

achantarse, *vr.* (coll.) to hide during danger.

achaparrado, da, *a.* shrub-sized (tree).

achaparrarse, *vr.* (agr.) not to grow or thrive, to become stunted.

achaque, *m.* habitual indisposition; monthly courses; pregnancy; subject matter; excuse, pretext; frequent lapse or failing.—*pl.* matters.

achaquiento, ta, *a.* = ACHACOSO.

acharolado, da, *a.* japanned; japanlike.

acharolar, *va.* to japan; to enamel.

achatado, da, *a.* flattened.

achatamiento, *m.* flattening.

achatar, *va.* to flatten.

achicado, da, *a.* childish.

achicador, ra, *m.* & *f.* diminisher; reducer; (naut.) scoop for bailing boats.

achicadura, *f.* diminution; (naut.) bailing.

achicamiento, *m.* = ACHICADURA.

achicar. I. *va.* to diminish, lessen; to humble, belittle; to bail, drain.—**a. el agua del navío,** to free the ship.—**a. un cabo,** to shorten a rope. **II.** *vr.* to humble oneself; to feel small.

achicoria, *f.* (bot.) chicory.

achicharrar, *va.* to fry too much; to overheat.

achichinque, *m.* (min.) scooper.

achilenado, da, *a.* (Peru) pro-Chilean.

achinado, da, *a.* (Arg.) plebeian; of dark reddish color.

achinar, *va.* (coll.) to intimidate, frighten.

achinelado, da, *a.* slipper-shaped.

achiote, *m.* (bot.) annatto tree; annatto (a dye).

achique, *m.* scooping, bailing, draining.

achispar. I. *va.* (coll.) to make tipsy. **II.** *vr.* to get tipsy.

achocadura, *f.* knock against an object.

achocar, *va.* to throw one against the wall; to knock asunder; (coll.) to hoard money.

acholado, da, *a.* half Indian; half-breed.

achorizado, da, *a.* slashed; made into sausages.

achote, *m.* = ACHIOTE.

achubascarse, *vr.* (naut.) to become squally.

achucutarse, *vr.* (Am.) to become downhearted; to lose courage; to wither.

achuchar, achuchurrar, *va.* (coll.) to crush with a blow; to thrust; to push roughly, jostle.

achuchón, *m.* (coll.) push, squeeze.

achulado, da, *a.* (coll.) rough; tough.

achunchar, *va.* (Chile) to foil, frustrate.

achura, *f.* (Am.) gut (of cattle).

adafina, *f.* stew eaten by the Jews in Spain.

¹adagio, *m.* proverb, adage.

²adagio, *m.* (mus.) adagio.

adala, *f.* (naut.) pump dale.

adalid, *m.* chief, chieftain, leader.

adamado, da, *a.* effeminate, womanish.

adamantino, na, *a.* adamantine.

adamarse, *vr.* to become effeminate.

adamascado, da, *a.* damasklike.

adamascar, *va.* to damask.

adámico, ca, *a.* (geol.) (of sand or other deposit) accumulated by the tide.

adamita, *m.* Adamite, a nudist.

Adán, *m.* Adam; slovenly man.

adaptabilidad, *f.* adaptability, suitability.
adaptable, *a.* adaptable.
adaptación, *f.* adaptation.
adaptado, da, *a.* adapted, suited.
adaptador, ra, *n.* & *a.* adapter(-ing).
adaptante, *a.* adapting.
adaptar. I. *va.* to adapt, fit. **II.** *vr.* to adapt oneself.
adaraja, *f.* (arch.) toothing.
adarce, *m.* dry sea froth.
adarga, *f.* oval leather shield.—**adargar,** *va.* to shield, defend.—**adarguilla,** *f.* small shield.
adarme, *m.* half a drachm, ⅟₁₆ ounce (179 centigrams).—**por adarmes,** in driblets, stingily.
adarvar, *va.* to stun; to bewilder.
adarve, *m.* flat top of a wall.
adatar, *va.* to open an account; to credit.
adaza, *f.* (bot.) panic grass.
ad calendas graecas, at the time of the Greek kalends (never).
adecenamiento, *m.* formation with ten abreast.
adecenar, *va.* to form with ten abreast; to count by tens.
adecuación, *f.* fitness; adequateness.
adecuadamente, *adv.* adequately, fitly.
adecuado, da. I. *pp.* of ADECUAR. **II.** *a.* adequate.
adecuar, *va.* to fit; to adapt.
adefagia, *f.* voracity.
adéfago, ga, *a.* voracious; (entom.) of the Adephaga, a beetle family.
adefesio, *m.* (coll.) nonsense, absurdity; blunder; queer person; ridiculous attire.
adefina, adafina, *f.* stew eaten by Spanish Jews.
adehala, *f.* gratuity, perquisite, tip.
adehesado, *m.* pasture land.
adehesamiento, *m.* pasturage; turning into pasture.
adehesar, *va.* to convert land into pasture.
adelantadamente, *adv.* beforehand.
adelantado, da. I. *pp.* of ADELANTAR. **II.** *a.* anticipated; advanced; far ahead; proficient; precocious; bold, forward; (of a timepiece) fast; early (fruit, plants).—**por a.,** in advance. **III.** *m.* governor of a province.
adelantador, ra, *n.* one that advances, extends, or amplifies.
adelantamiento, *m.* progress; improvement, increase; furtherance; cultivation; anticipation; betterment, promotion.
adelantar. I. *va.* & *vn.* to progress, advance; to grow; to keep on; to anticipate; to pay beforehand; to improve; to go fast; (of a timepiece) to gain; to be fast; to set ahead. **II.** *vr.* to take the lead; to come forward;—**a. a,** to excel, outdo.
adelante, *adv.* ahead; farther on; forward, onward.—**¡a!** forward! go on! let's go! come in!—**de a.,** ahead, in the front; forward, head (as a.). —**de aquí en a., de hoy en a.,** or **en a.,** henceforth, from now on, in the future.—**llevar a.,** to go ahead with, carry on.—**más a.,** farther on.—**salir a.,** to come through, come out well or ahead.
adelanto, *m.* advance, progress; improvement; (com.) advanced payment.
adelfa, *f.* (bot.) rosebay.—**adelfal,** *m.* rosebay field.
adelgacé, adelgace, *v.* V. ADELGAZAR.
adelgazado, da. I. *pp.* of ADELGAZAR. **II.** *a.* made slender or thin.
adelgazador, ra, *n.* one that makes thin or slender.
adelgazamiento, *m.* slenderness, thinness.
adelgazar. I. *va.* (*pret.* ADELGACÉ; *subj.* ADELGACE) to attenuate, make thin, slender; to lessen; to taper; to split hairs. **II.** *vr.* to become thin or slender.
adema, *f.* (min.) shore; strut; prop.
ademador, ra, *n.* (min.) one who props.

ademán, *m.* gesture, look, manner; attitude.— *pl.* manners.—**en a. de,** as if getting ready, or going, to, showing an intention of.
ademar, *va.* (min.) to shore.
además, *adv.* moreover, furthermore, besides; exceedingly, too.—**a. de,** besides, in addition to.
ademe, *m.* = ADEMA.
adenia, *f.* (med.) adenia.
adenitis, *f.* (med.) adenitis, gland inflammation.
adenoídeo, dea, *a.* adenoid.—**tumor a., vegetación a.,** adenoids.
adenología, *f.* (anat.) adenology.
adenoma, *m.* (med.) adenoma.
adenopatía, *f.* adenopathy.
adenoso, sa, *a.* glandular.
adentellar, *va.* to bite, catch with the teeth.— **a. una pared,** to leave toothing stones or bricks in a wall to continue it.
adentro. I. *adv.* within, inside. **II.** *interj.* come in!, let's go in! **III.** *m.* (in the *pl.*) the innermost thoughts.
adepto, ta, *a.* adept; initiated.
aderecé, aderece, *v.* V. ADEREZAR.
aderezamiento, *m.* embellishment; dressing.
aderezar, *va.* (*pret.* ADERECÉ; *subj.* ADERECE) to dress, embellish, adorn; to prepare; to cook, season; to clean; to repair; to mix (drinks); to blend (wines); to gum (silk); to size (goods).
aderezo, *m.* dressing; adorning; finery; gum, starch, used to stiffen cloth; set of jewelry; trappings of a saddle horse; furniture; hilt, hook, and other appendages of a sword.
aderra, *f.* rush rope.
adestrado, da. I. *pp.* of ADESTRAR. **II.** *a.* (her.) on the dexter side of the escutcheon.
adestrador, ra, *n.* teacher, trainer; censor, critic.
adestramiento, *m.* = ADIESTRAMIENTO.
adestrar. I. *va.* (*ind.* ADIESTRO; *subj.* ADIESTRE) to guide, lead; to teach, train. **II.** *vr.* to practice, train.
adeudado, da. I. *pp.* of ADEUDAR. **II.** *a.* indebted; in debt.
adeudar. I. *va.* to owe; to be dutiable; (com.) to charge, debit. **II.** *vr.* to run into debt.
adeudo, *m.* indebtedness; custom house duty; (com.) debit; charge.
adherencia, *f.* adhesion; adherence; relationship; bond.
adherente. I. *a.* adhesive, adhering; attached. **II.** *n.* follower, adherent. **III.** *m.* (gen. *pl.*) accessory; equipment.
adherir, *va.* & *vr.* (*ind.* ADHIERO; *subj.* ADHIERA) to adhere; to stick.
adhesión, *f.* adhesion; following, adherence.
adhesividad, *f.* concentration of mind; love of one's fellow beings.
adhesivo, va, *a.* adhesive.
adhiero, adhiera, *v.* V. ADHERIR.
ad hoc, ad hoc, expressly.
adiabático, ca, *a.* adiabatic.
adiafa, *f.* tip given to seamen at end of a voyage.
adiamantado, da, *a.* adamantine.
adicción a díe, or **in díe,** (law) addictio in diem.
adición, *f.* addition; remark or note put to accounts.—**a. de la herencia,** acceptance of an inheritance.—**adicional,** *a.* additional.
adicionar, *va.* to make additions in, add to; to extend, prolong.
adicto, ta, *n.* & *a.* addicted, devoted; follower, supporter.
adiestrador, ra, *a.* = ADESTRADOR.
adiestramiento, *m.* guiding; teaching, training; practice.
adiestrar, *va.* = ADESTRAR.
adiestro, adiestre, *v.* V. ADESTRAR.
adietar, *va.* to put on a diet.
adifés, *adv.* (Venez.) on purpose.
adinamia, *f.* adynamia, debility, prostration.
adinerado, da, *a.* rich, wealthy.

adinerar. I. *va.* to convert into cash, realize. **II.** *vr.* to get rich.

adintelado, da, *a.* (arch.) falling from an arch gradually into a straight line.

au interin, ad interim, provisional(ly), in the meantime.

adiós, *interj.* good-bye, adieu.

adipocira, *f.* adipocere; waxy substance from buried animals.

adiposidad, *f.* adiposity.

adiposo, sa, *a.* adipose.

adir, *va.* to accept (an inheritance).

aditamento, *m.* addition.—**por a.,** in addition, into the bargain.

adiva, *f.* **adive,** *m.* jackal.

adivas, *m. pl.* (vet.) vives, fives, the strangles.

adivinación, *f.* divination.

adivinador, ra, *n.* & *a.* diviner, soothsayer.

adivinaja, *f.* puzzle, conundrum.

adivinanza, *f.* prophecy; riddle; guess.

adivinar, *va.* to foretell; to divine, guess; to solve (a riddle).

adivino, na, *n.* soothsayer; fortune teller; wizard; guesser.

adjetivación, *f.* adjectival use or function; (gram.) agreement.

adjetivadamente, *adv.* adjectively.

adjetival, *a.* adjectival.

adjetivar, *va.* & *vr.* to use, or be used, adjectively; (gram.) to make agree.

adjetivo, va, *n.* & *a.* adjective.—**a. calificativo,** qualifying adjective.—**a. comparativo,** comparative adjective.—**a. determinativo,** limiting adjective.—**a. gentilicio,** proper adjective.

adjudicación, *f.* adjudgment, adjudication.

adjudicador, ra, *n.* & *a.* adjudicator(-ing).

adjudicar. I. *va.* to adjudge, adjudicate. **II.** *vr.* to appropriate.—**adjudicativo, va,** *a.* adjudicative.—**adjudicatario, ria,** *n.* grantee.

adjunción, *f.* (law) adjunction.

adjunta, *f.* (com.) letter enclosed in another.

adjuntar, *va.* (Am.) to enclose, send enclosed or with something else.

adjunto, ta. I. *a.* joined, annexed, enclosed, attached, adjunct. **II.** *m.* adjective; addition.

adjutor, ra, *a.* & *n.* helper(-ing), assistant(-ing).

ad líbitum, ad libitum, at will, optional(ly).

adminicular, *va.* to strengthen, reinforce, corroborate.

adminículo, *m.* auxiliary; helper.—*pl.* small things carried for emergencies.

administración, *f.* administration, management; office of an administrator.—**a. activa,** executive action.—**a. económica,** treasury department.—**a. militar,** commissariat.—**a. pública,** public administration.—**en a.,** in trust.—**por a.,** by the government; officially; by the management, company, firm, etc.

administrador, ra, *n.* administrator, manager; director, trustee.—**a. de aduanas,** collector of customs.—**a. de correos,** postmaster.

administrar, *va.* to administer.

administrativamente, *adv.* administratively.

administrativo, va, *a.* administrative.

administratorio, ria, *a.* (law) pertaining to an administration or administrator.

admirable, *a.* admirable, excellent.

admirablemente, *adv.* admirably.

admiración, *f.* admiration, wonder; exclamation point (! ¡).

admirador, ra, *n.* admirer.

admirar. I. *va.* to admire. **II.** *vr.* to wonder; to be surprised, amazed.—**a. de,** to be surprised at; to regard with admiration, wonder at.

admirativamente, *adv.* admiringly.

admirativo, va, *a.* admiring; admirable; filled with admiration.

admisible, *a.* admissible.

admisión, *f.* admission, acceptance.

admitir, *va.* to receive; to admit, grant; to accept; to permit.

admonición, *f.* admonition, warning, advice.

admonitor, *m.* monitor (esp. in some religious communities).

adnata, *f.* (anat.) conjunctiva, the external white membrane of the eye.

adnato, ta, *a.* adnate.

adobado, da. I. *pp.* of ADOBAR. **II.** *m.* pickled pork.

adobador, ra, *n.* dresser, preparer.

adobar, *va.* to dress, prepare or cook (food); to pickle (meat); to tan or dress (hides).

adobe, *m.* adobe, unburnt sun-dried brick.

adobera, *f.* mold for adobe; brick-shaped cheese, and mold for it.

adobería, *f.* brickyard; tannery.

adobío, *m.* front wall of a blast furnace.

adobo, *m.* repairing, mending; pickle sauce; dressing for seasoning; ingredients for dressing leather or cloth; pomade.

adocenado, da. I. *pp.* of ADOCENAR. **II.** *a.* common, ordinary, vulgar.

adocenamiento, *m.* counting or arranging by, or dividing into, dozens.

adocenar, *va.* to count or sell by dozens; to depreciate, underrate.

adoctrinar, *va.* to instruct, indoctrinate.

adolecente, *n.* sufferer; patient.

adolecer. I. *vn.* (*ind.* ADOLEZCO; *subj.* ADOLEZCA) to become ill.—**a. de,** to suffer from, be ill with; to be subject to. **II.** *vr.* to condole.

adoleciente, *n.* & *a.* = ADOLECENTE.

adolescencia, *f.* adolescence.

adolescente, *n.* & *a.* adolescent.

adolezco, adolezca, *v.* V. ADOLECER.

adolorido, da, dolorido, da, *a.* painful; doleful.

Adonaí, *n.* one of the names of Deity.

adonde (adónde, when interr.), *adv.* where, whither.—**adondequiera,** *adv.* wherever.

adopción, *f.* adoption.—**adopcionismo,** *m.* adoptionism, an ancient Spanish sect.—**adopcionista,** *a.* adhering or pert. to adoptionism.

adoptable, *a.* adoptable.

adoptador, ra, *n.* adopter.

adoptante, *n.* & *a.* adopter(-ing).

adoptar, *va.* to adopt; to embrace (an opinion).

adoptivo, va, *a.* adoptive.

adoquín, *m.* paving stone or tile.—**adoquinado,** *m.* pavement.—**adoquinar,** *va.* to pave.

ador, *m.* time for watering land, where water is officially distributed.

adorable, *a.* adorable.

adoración, *f.* adoration, worship.

adorador, ra; adorante, *n.* adorer, worshipper.

adorar, *va.* to adore, worship.

adoratorio, *m.* Am. Indian temple for an idol.

adormecedor, ra, *a.* soporific, sleep-inducing.

adormecer. I. *va.* (*ind.* ADORMEZCO; *subj.* ADORMEZCA) to cause drowsiness or sleep; to lull to sleep; to calm, lull. **II.** *vr.* to fall asleep; to grow benumbed; to persist in vice.

adormecido, da. I. *pp.* of ADORMECER. **II.** *a.* langorous, sluggish; drowsy.

adormecimiento, *m.* drowsiness, sleepiness, numbness.

adormezco, adormezca, *v.* V. ADORMECER.

adormidera, *f.* (bot.) poppy.

adormir, *va.* & *vr.* (*ind. pres.* ADUERMO, *pret.* él ADURMIÓ; *subj.* ADUERMA) = ADORMECER.

adormitarse, *vr.* to doze, drowse.

adornado, da, *a.* ornamented, adorned.

adornador, ra, *n.* adorner, decorator.

adornamiento, *m.* embellishment, decoration.

adornante, *n.* & *a.* adorner (-ing).

adornar, *va.* to adorn, embellish, decorate, ornament, trim; to furnish, garnish; to be a gift or an accomplishment of.—**a. de,** to adorn with.

adornista, *m.* painter, decorator.

adorno, *m.* adornment; ornament; trimming; accomplishment.

adosar, *va.* to put on or near (something); to paste (as on a wall).

adqülero, adquiera, *v.* V. ADQUIRIR.

adquirente, adquiriente, *n.* acquirer.

adqulridor, ra, *n.* acquirer.

adquirir, *va.* (*ind.* ADQUIERO; *subj.* ADQUIERA) to acquire, obtain, get.

adquisición, *f.* acquisition; attainment.

adquisidor, ra, *n.* = ADQUIRIDOR.

adquisitivo, va, *a.* that helps to acquire.

adra, *f.* turn (in succession); portion of the population of a town.

adraganto, *m.* tragacanth, a gummy substance.

adrales, *m. pl.* hurdles, side boards (of a wagon).

adrazo, *m.* sea-water distiller.

adrede, adredemente, *adv.* purposely.

adrenalina, *f.* (chem.) adrenaline.

adrián, *m.* bunion: a magpie's nest.

adrizar, *va.* (naut.) to right.

adrubado, da, *a.* deformed.

adscribir, *va.* (*pp. irreg.* ADSCRIPTO, ADSCRITO) to inscribe; to add as an employee.

adscripción, *f.* inscription; appointment; adscription.

adscripto, ta, adscrito, ta. I. *irreg. pp.* of ADSCRIBIR. **II.** *a.* adscript, written after.

aduana, *f.* custom house.

aduanar, *va.* to pass or put through (goods) at the custom house; to pay duty on.

aduanero, ra. I. *a.* custom house, customs (as *a.*). **II.** *m.* custom house officer; revenue officer.

aduanilla, *f.* food store.

aduar, *m.* Arab village or settlement; gipsy camp.

adúcar, *m.* coarse silk from outer part of cocoon; the stuff made from that silk.

aducción, *f.* adduction.

aducir, *va.* (*ind. pres.* ADUZCO, *pret.* ADUJE; *subj.* ADUZCA) to adduce, bring up in argument.

aductor, *m.* (anat.) adductor (muscle).

aduendado, da, *a.* fairylike.

adueñarse, *vr.* to take possession.

aduermo, aduerma, *v.* V. ADORMIR.

adufe, *m.* timbrel or tambourine.

adufero, ra, *n.* tambourine player.

adujadas, adujas, *f. pl.* (naut.) coil, coiled cable.

adujar, *va.* (naut.) to coil (a cable).

aduje, adujo, *v.* V. ADUCIR.

adula, dula, *f.* common pasture.

adulación, *f.* fawning, adulation.

adulador, ra, *n.* fawner, adulator, cringer.

adular, *va.* & *vn.* to adulate, flatter fawningly; to cringe to; to fawn, creep, crouch, grovel.

adulatorio, ria, *a.* flattering, honey-mouthed.

adulero, dulero, *m.* shepherd; guardian of common pasture.

adulón, na, *n.* & *a.* toady, cringer(-ing).

adúltera, *f.* adulteress.

adulteración, *f.* adulteration.

adulterador, ra, adulterante, *n.* & *a.* adulterator(-ing), adulterant; falsifier.

adulterar. I. *va.* to adulterate; to corrupt. **II.** *vn.* to commit adultery.

adulterinamente, *adv.* adulterously.

adulterino, na, *a.* adulterous; begotten in adultery; adulterated, falsified, forged.

adulterio, *m.* adultery.

adúltero, ra, *n.* adulterer(-ess).

adulto, ta, *n.* & *a.* adult.

adulzar, *va.* to render (metals) more ductile.

adumbración, *f.* adumbration, shade in a picture.

adunar, *va.* to unite, join; to unify.

adunco, ca, *a.* aduncous; curved; warped.

adunia, *adv.* abundantly.

adusto, ta, *a.* austere, stern, sullen.

aduzco, aduzca, *v.* V. ADUCIR.

ad valórem, ad valorem.

advenedizo, za, *n.* & *a.* foreign(-er), newly arrived, immigrant; upstart, parvenu.

advenimiento, *m.* arrival; advent.

advenir, *vn.* to come; to arrive.

adventicio, cia, *a.* adventitious, accidental; (law) acquired by industry, (law) adventitious.

adverbial, *a.* adverbial.—**adverbialmente,** *adv.* adverbially.

adverbio, *m.* adverb.

adversamente, *adv.* adversely.

adversario, *m.* adversary, opponent; foe.

adversativo, va, *a.* (gram.) adversative.

adversidad, *f.* adversity, misfortune.

adverso, sa, *a.* adverse; calamitous; opposite, facing.

advertencia, *f.* admonition, warning; remark, notice; foreword.

advertidamente, *adv.* advisedly, deliberately.

advertido, da. I. *pp.* of ADVERTIR. **II.** *a.* noticed; skilful; intelligent; expert; clever.

advertir, *va.* (*ind. pres.* ADVIERTO, *pret.* él ADVIRTIÓ; *subj.* ADVIERTA) to take notice of; to observe; to instruct, advise, give notice or warning; to acquaint; to mark, note.

adviento, *m.* Advent, the four weeks before Christmas.

advierto, advierta, advirtió, *v.* V. ADVERTIR.

advocación, *f.* appellation given to a church, chapel, or altar, dedicated to the Virgin or a saint.

adyacencia, *f.* adjacency, contiguity.

adyacente, *a.* adjacent.

aechadero, aechar, etc. = AHECHADERO, AHECHAR, etc.

aeración, *f.* aeration, charging with gas or with air; (med.) action of atmospheric air in the treatment of disease.

aéreo, rea, *a.* aerial; overhead; elevated; air (as *a.*, as in **fuerzas aéreas,** air forces); (fig.) airy, fantastic.—**por correo a.,** by airmail.

aerífero, ra, *a.* aeriferous, conveying air.

aerificar, *va.* to gasify; to aerify, aerate.

aeriforme, *a.* aeriform, gaseous.

aerobio. I. *a.* aerobic. **II.** *m.* aerobe.

aerodinámica, *f.* aerodynamics.

aerodinámico, ca, *a.* streamline(d).

aeródromo, *m.* airdrome, aerodrome.

aerofobia, *f.* aerophobia, morbid dread of air.

aeróforo, a, *a.* aeriferous.

aerografía, *f.* aerography.

aerograma, *m.* wireless message, radiogram.

aerolito, *m.* aerolite, meteoric stone.

aerología, *f.* aerology.

aeromancia, *f.* aeromancy.

aerometría, *f.* aerometry, pneumatics.

aerómetro, *m.* aerometer.

aeronauta, *m.* aeronaut.

aeronáutica, *f.* aeronautics.

aeronáutico, ca, *a.* aeronautic.

aeronave, *f.* airship, dirigible.

aeroplano, *m.* aeroplane, airplane.

aeropuerto, *m.* airport.

aeroscopia, *f.* aeroscopy.

aeroscopio, *m.* aeroscope.

aerostación, *f.* aerostation, air navigation.

aerostática, *f.* aerostatics.

aerostático, ca, *a.* aerostatic.

aeróstato, *m.* aerostat, dirigible.

aerostero, rá, *a.* aviation (as *a.*), aeronautic.

aeroterapia, *f.* aerotherapeutics.

aeta, *m.* mountain tribe in P. I.; their language.

afabilidad, *f.* affability.

afable, *a.* affable, pleasant.—**afablemente,** *adv.* affably.

áfaca, *f.* (bot.) yellow vetch.

afamado, da, *a.* celebrated, noted, famous.

afamar, *va.* to make famous, give fame to.

afán, *m.* anxiety, solicitude, eagerness.

afanadamente, *adv.* anxiously, laboriously, eagerly.

afanador, ra, *n.* & *a.* eager; painstaker(-ing); hustler(-ing); hurrier(-ying); laborious. toilsome.

afanar. I. *va.* to press, urge, hurry. **II.** *vn.* & *vr.* to act or work eagerly or anxiously; to toil.

afaníptero, ra. I. *a.* (entom.) aphanipterous. **II.** *m. pl.* Aphaniptera.

afanita, *f.* (min.) amphibolite, kind of rock.

afanosamente, *adv.* = AFANADAMENTE.

afanoso, sa, *a.* solicitous; laborious, painstaking; arduous, hard, difficult.

afararlarse, *vr.* (Am., coll.) to become unduly excited, (coll.) to make a fuss; to lose one's temper, (coll.) to get hot under the collar.

afarollonado, da, *a.* steep, cliffy.

afasia, *f.* aphasia.

afeador, ra, *n.* & *a.* (something or someone) deforming, distorting or making ugly.

afeamiento, *m.* defacing; ugliness.

afear, *va.* to deform, deface; to make ugly or faulty; to impair; to decry; to condemn.

afeblecerse, *vr.* to grow feeble or delicate.

afección, *f.* affection, fondness; (med.) affection.

afectación, *f.* affectation.

afectadamente, *adv.* affectedly.

afectado, da. I. *pp.* of AFECTAR. **II.** *a.* affected.

afectador, ra, *n.* one who acts affectedly.

afectar. I. *va.* to affect, have an effect on; to affect, feign, put on; (law) to charge, impose, encumber. **II.** *vr.* to be moved; to be shocked.

afectividad, *f.* affection; (psych.) affectivity.

afectivo, va, *a.* affective.

afecto. I. *m.* affection, love, fondness. **II.** *a.* affectionate: (a) fond (of), inclined (to); (law) subject to charge or encumbrance.

afectuosamente, *adv.* fondly, affectionately.

afectuosidad, *f.* fondness, affection.

afectuoso, sa, *a.* affectionate.

afeitada, *f.* (Am.) shave, shaving.

afeitar. I. *va.* to shave; to beautify, embellish, make up; to trim (a tree, the tail, mane of a horse). **II.** *vr.* to shave (oneself); to make up.

afeite, *m.* paint, rouge, cosmetic; make-up.

afelio, *m.* (astr.) aphelion.

afelpado, da, *a.* plushlike or velvetlike.

afeminación, *f.* effeminacy; emasculation.

afeminadamente, *adv.* effeminately.

afeminado, da. I. *pp.* of AFEMINAR. **II.** *a.* effeminate.

afeminamiento, *m.* = AFEMINACIÓN.

afeminar, *va.* to make effeminate; to unman.

aferente, *a.* afferent.

aféresis, *f.* (gram.) aphæresis, omission of one or more initial letters of a word.

aferrado, da. I. *pp.* of AFERRAR. **II.** *a.* headstrong.

aferrador, ra, *n.* one that grapples or grasps.

aferramiento, *m.* grasping, grappling, seizing or binding; obstinacy.—**a. de las velas,** (naut.) furling of the sails.

aferrar. I. *va.* to grasp, seize; (naut.) to furl; to moor; to anchor. **II.** *vr.* to fasten to each other; to interlock; (**a** or **en**) to persist obstinately or persistently (in).

aferruzado, da, *a.* angry, irate.

afestonado, a, *a.* festooned.

afgano, na, *n.* & *a.* Afghan.

afiancé, afiance, *v.* V. AFIANZAR.

afianzamiento, *m.* security, guarantee, bail; prop, support; fastening, securing.

afianzar, *va.* (*pret.* AFIANCÉ; *subj.* AFIANCE) to become bail or security for; to guarantee; to prop; to make fast, clinch.

afición, *f.* affection, fondness; taste, inclination; eagerness, enthusiasm.—**tomar a. a,** to take a liking to, become fond of.

aficionadamente, *adv.* fondly; amateurishly.

aficionado, da. I. *pp.* of AFICIONAR. **II.** (sport) *n.* & *a.* amateur; fan.—**a. a,** fond of, having a taste for.

aficionar. I. *va.* to cause or inspire affection, fondness or liking. **II.** *vr.* (**a**) to fancy; to become fond of.

afijo, ja. (gram.) **I.** *a.* affixal. **II.** *m.* affix.

afiladera, *f.* whetstone.

afilado. I. *pp.* of AFILAR. **II.** *a.* sharp, keen.

afiladura, *f.* sharpening, whetting.

afilamiento, *m.* slenderness of the face, nose, or fingers.

afilar. I. *va.* to whet, grind, sharpen; to render keen. **II.** *vr.* to grow thin.

afiliado, da, *a.* affiliated; adopted.

afiliar. I. *va.* (a) to affiliate (with). **II.** *vr.* (a) to join, affiliate oneself (with).

afiligranado, da, *a.* filigree, filigreed; slender, thin; delicate, neat; dainty.

afiligranar, *va.* to make filigree work; to polish, embellish.

áfilo, la, *a.* (bot.) leafless.

afilón, *m.* steel, knife sharpener; razor strop.

afilosofado, da, *a.* putting on airs of a philosopher.

afín. I. *a.* close by, contiguous; related. **II.** *m.* relation by affinity.

afinación, *f.* completion, finishing touch, refining; tuning.

afinadamente, *adv.* perfectly; delicately.

afinado, da. I. *pp.* of AFINAR. **II.** *a.* well-finished, refined; well tuned.

afinador, ra, *n.* finisher; piano tuner; tuning key.

afinadura, *m.* = AFINACIÓN.

afinamiento, *m.* AFINACIÓN; refinement.

afinar. I. *va.* to complete; to polish; to refine (metals); to trim (binding); to tune. **II.** *vr.* to become polished.

afincar, fincar, *vn.* & *vr.* to acquire real estate.

afine, *a.* = AFÍN.

afinidad, *f.* analogy, resemblance; relationship by marriage; (chem.) affinity.

afino, *m.* refinement (of metals).

afirmación, *f.* affirmation.

afirmadamente, *adv.* firmly.

afirmador, ra, afirmante, *n.* & *a.* affirmer(-ing).

afirmar. I. *va.* to make fast, secure, fasten; to affirm, assert, contend. **II.** *vr.* to hold fast; to steady oneself or make oneself firm; to maintain firmly.

afirmativa, *f.* = AFIRMACIÓN.

afirmativamente, *adv.* affirmatively.

afirmativo, va, *a.* affirmative.

afistular, *va.* (med.) to render fistulous.

aflato, *m.* afflatus, inspiration.

aflechada, *a.* arrow-shaped (leaf).

aflicción, *f.* affliction, sorrow, grief.

aflictivo, va, *a.* afflictive, distressing.

aflicto, ta, *pp. irreg.* of AFLIGIR.

afligidamente, *adv.* sorrowfully, sadly.

afligir. I. *va.* (*pp. irreg.* AFLICTO; *ind.* AFLIJO; *subj.* AFLIJA) to afflict, cause pain. **II.** *vr.* to grieve, languish, become despondent, lose heart.

aflijón, na, *a.* (Am., coll.) gloomy-tempered, ever-weeping.

aflojadura, *f.,* **aflojamiento,** *m.* relaxation; loosening, slackening.

aflojar. I. *va.* to loosen, slacken, relax, let loose; to relent; to debilitate.—**a. los obenques,** (naut.) to ease the shrouds. **II.** *vn.* to grow weak; to abate. **III.** *vr.* to grow cool in fervor or zeal; to lose courage.

aflorado, *a.* FLOREADO, (of bread) made of the finest flour; flowered, figured.

afloramiento, *m.* (min.) outcrop.

aflorar, *vn.* to crop out.

afluencia, *f.* plenty, abundance; fluency.

afluente. I. *a.* affluent, copious, abundant; loquacious. **II.** *m.* affluent, tributary.

afluir, *vn.* (*ind.* AFLUYO; *subj.* AFLUYA) (**a**) to congregate, assemble (in); to flow (into).

¹aflujo, *m.* (med.) afflux, affluxion.

²**afluyo, afluya,** v. V. AFLUIR.

afofar, va. & vr. to make (become) spongy or light.

afogarar, va. = ASURAR, to burn, scorch.

afolador, ra. I. n. & a. calker(-ing). II. calking iron.

afolar, va. to calk, caulk.

afollar, va. (ind. AFUELLO; subj. AFUELLE) to blow with bellows.

afondar, va., vn., vr. to submerge; (naut.) to sink, founder.

afonía, f. (med.) aphonia.

afónico, ca, áfono, na, a. aphonic.

aforado. I. pp. of AFORAR. II. a. privileged, favored.

aforador, m. gauger; appraiser.

aforamiento, m. the giving of privileges.

aforar, va. to gauge, measure; to appraise; to give privileges (in this meaning: ind. AFUERO; subj. AFUERE).

aforisma, f. (vet.) swelling in the arteries.

aforismo, m. aphorism, maxim.

aforístico, ca, a. aphoristical.

aforo, m. gauging; appraisal.

aforrador, ra, n. one who lines clothes.

aforrar. I. va. to line (clothes, vessels, tubes, etc.); (naut.) to sheathe.—**a. un cabo,** (naut.) to serve a cable. II. vr. to put on heavy underclothing; to gorge.—**aforro,** m. lining; (naut.) sheathing; (naut.) waist of a ship.

afortunadamente, adv. luckily, fortunately.

afortunado, da. I. pp. of AFORTUNAR. II. a. fortunate, lucky.

afortunar, va. to make happy.

afosarse, vr. (mil.) to entrench, "to dig in."

afoscarse, vr. to become hazy.

afrailar, va. (agr.) to prune (trees).

afrancesado, da. a. Frenchified, Frenchlike.

afrancesar. I. va. to Gallicize; to give a French termination to (words). II. vr. to be or become Frenchified; to be naturalized in France.

afrecho, m. bran.

afrenillar, vn. (naut.) to bridle (the oars).

afrenta, f. affront, outrage; disgrace.

afrentar. I. va. to affront; to insult. II. vr. to be ashamed; to blush.

afrentosamente, adv. ignominiously.

afrentoso, sa, a. ignominious.

afretar, va. to scrub and clean.

africano, na, n. & a. African.

áfrico, ábrego, m. southwest wind.

afrodisíaco, ca, n. & a. aphrodisiac.

afrontar, va. to confront; to face.

afta, f. (med.) aphthæ, thrush.

aftoso, sa, a. (med.) aphthous.

afuello, afuelle, v. V. AFOLLAR.

afuera. I. adv. out; outside; in public.—¡**a.!** one side! clear the way! II. f. pl. suburbs, outskirts.

afuero, afuere, v. V. AFORAR.

afuetear, va. (Am.) to horsewhip.

afufa, f. (coll.) flight.—**afufar,** vn. & vr. (coll.) to run away; to escape.

afusión, f. affusion, shower bath.

afuste, m. (milit.) gun carriage.—**a. de mortero,** mortar bed.

agachadiza, f. (ornith.) snipe.—**hacer la a.,** (coll.) to hide (oneself).

agachar. I. va. to lower, bow down. II. vr. to stoop, squat, crouch, cower.—**a. las orejas,** (coll.) to humble oneself, bend the knee; to be dejected or crestfallen.

agalbanado, da, a. = GALBANOSO, indolent.

agalerar, va. (naut.) to tip (an awning).

agáloco, m. (bot.) aloes wood.

agalla, f. (bot.) gallnut; (anat.) tonsil; (vet.) windgalls of a horse; beaks of a shuttle; ear lobe (of a bird); gill (of a fish);—pl. (coll.) courage; cheek, gall.—**a. de ciprés,** cypress gall.—**tener a.,** to have vim, be enterprising;

(Am.) to be greedy; (Colomb. & Ecua.) to be stingy; (Peru) to be shrewd, cunning, wily.

agallado, da, a. steeped in an infusion of gall.

agallato, m. gallate.—**agállico,** a. gallic.

agallón, m. large gallnut.—**agallones,** pl. strings of hollow silver beads; wooden rosary beads.

agalludo, da, a. (Am.) stingy; cunning, foxy; brave.

agalluela, f. dim. of AGALLA.

agamí, m. (Am.) (ornith.) trumpeter.

ágamo, ma, a. (biol.) agamic, asexual.

agamuzado, da, a. chamois-colored.

agangrenarse, gangrenarse, vr. to gangrene.

ágape, m. agape, love feast of early Christians; banquet.

agarbado, da, a. = GARBOSO, graceful, airy.

agarbarse, vr. to bend, stoop down, crouch.

agarbillar, v. = AGAVILLAR.

agareno, na, a. Mohammedan.

agárico, m. (bot.) agaric.

agarrada, f. (coll.) wrangle, scrap, scuffle.

agarradero, m. holder, handle; (coll.) protection, patronage; (naut.) anchorage.

agarrado, da. I. pp. of AGARRAR. II. a. stingy, close-fisted.

agarrador, ra, n. one that grasps or seizes; flatiron-holder; catch-pole; bailiff.

agarrafar, va. (coll.) to grab hard in a scuffle.

agarrama, garrama, f. Moslem tax: imposition.

agarrar. I. va. to grasp, seize; (coll.) to obtain; to come upon. II. vr. to clinch, grapple, hold on.—**agarro,** m. grasp.

agarrochador, m. pricker, goader.

agarrochar, agarrochear, va. to prick with a pike or spear; to goad.

agarrón, m. fight, scrap, scuffle, encounter.

agarrotar, va. to compress with ropes; to garrote, execute with the garrote; to strangle.

agasajador, ra, a. kind, obliging.

agasajar, va. to receive and treat kindly; to fondle; to regale; to entertain.—**agasajo,** m. friendly treatment, kindness; consideration, regard; friendly present; afternoon refreshment.

ágata, f. agate.

agavanzo, m., **agavanza,** f. (bot.) dog-rose.

agave, m. (bot.) agave; (commonly but erroneously) pita.

agavillar. I. va. to bind or tie in sheaves. II. vr. (coll.) to associate with a gang of sharpers.

agazapar. I. va. (coll.) to nab a person. II. vr. to hide oneself; to crouch.

agencia, f. agency; ministration, commission; agent's bureau, office; diligence.

agenciar, va. to solicit, promote, negotiate.

agencioso, sa, a. diligent, active.

agenda, f. notebook, memorandum book.

agenesia, f. (med.) impotence, agenesis.

agente, m. agent; solicitor, attorney.—**a. de bolsa, de cambio,** or **de cambio y bolsa,** exchange notary.—**a. de cambios,** bill broker. —**a. de negocios,** promoter.—**a. de policía,** policeman.—**a. fiscal,** assistant attorney.— **a. provocador,** (Gal.) agent provocateur.

agerasia, f. old age free from ailments.

agérato, m. (bot.) sweet milfoil or maudlin.

agestado, da (bien, mal), a. (well-, ill-) featured.

agibílibus, m. (coll.) cleverness, slickness; clever or slick person.

agible, a. feasible, practicable.

agigantado, da, a. gigantic; extraordinary.

ágil, a. nimble, fast, light.—**agilidad,** f. agility, nimbleness, sprightliness.—**agilitar,** va. to render nimble; to make active.—**ágilmente,** adv. nimbly, sprightly.

agio, agiotaje, m. (com.) exchange of paper money for coin, or coin for bills; premium; stockjobbing; usury; jobbing.

agiotador, ra; agiotista, n. money changer; bill broker; stockjobber; usurer.

agitable, *a.* agitable; that can be shaken.

agitación, *f.* agitation; excitement.

agitador, ra, *n.* & *a.* agitator(-ing), stirrer(-ing).

agitanado, da, *a.* gipsylike; bewitching.

agitar. I. *va.* to agitate; to stir, shake up; to ruffle. **II.** *vr.* to flutter; to become excited.

aglobar, *va.* to pile, put together.

aglomeración, *f.* agglomeration.

aglomerado, *m.* coal brick, made with coal dust and tar.

aglomerar, *va.* to agglomerate.

aglutición, *f.* (med.) aglutition, inability to swallow.

aglutinación, *f.* agglutination.

aglutinante. I. *a.* agglutinating, cementing. **II.** *m.* cementing material; (med.) sticking plaster.

aglutinar, *va.* to stick, cement, agglutinate.

aglutinativo, va, *a.* agglutinative.

agnación, *f.* (law) agnation.

agnado, da, *n.* & *a.* agnate.

agnaticio, cia, *a.* agnatic.

agnición, *f.* (rhet.) recognition of a person in a poem or drama.

agnocasto, *m.* = SAUZGATILLO, chaste-tree.

agnosticismo, *m.* agnosticism.

agnóstico, ca, *n.* & *a.* agnostic.

agnus, agnusdéi, *m.* Agnus Dei; ancient Spanish coin, of smallest value.

agobiar. I. *va.* to bend the body down; to overwhelm; to oppress. **II.** *vr.* to bow; to crouch.

agobio, *m.* bending down; oppression, burden.

agojía, *f.* water outlet in mines, drain.

agolar, *va.* (naut.) to furl (the sails).

agolpamiento, *m.* crowding, rush.

agolparse, *vr.* to crowd.

agonal, *a.* agonistic (esp. of the Janus games).

agonía, *f.* agony.

agónico, ca, *a.* agony (as *a.*), pertaining to the death struggle.

agonioso, sa, *a.* eager, persistent.

agonística, *f.* art of athletic contests.

agonizante. I. *a.* dying. **II.** *m.* a monk who assists a dying person; in some universities, one who assists students in their examinations.

agonizar. I. *va.* to assist (a dying person); to annoy, importune. **II.** *vn.* estar agonizando, to be dying.

ágora, *f.* agora, public place in Greek cities.

agorar, *va.* (*ind.* AGÜERO; *subj.* AGÜERE) to divine, prognosticate.

agorero, ra, *n.* diviner, augur, fortune teller.

agorgojarse, *vr.* to be infested with grubs (app. to corn).

agostadero, *m.* summer pasture.

agostamiento, *m.* parching, drying up.

agostar. I. *va.* to parch. **II.** *vn.* to pasture cattle on stubbles in summer.

agostero, *m.* harvestman; religious mendicant who begs corn in August.

agostizo, za, *a.* born in August; (of animals) weak.

agosto, *m.* August; harvest time; harvest.— **hacer su a.,** to improve the opportunity, make hay while the sun shines.

agotable, *a.* exhaustible.

agotamiento, *m.* draining; exhaustion.

agotar. I. *va.* to drain off (water); to beat out one's brains; to run through (a fortune); to exhaust. **II.** *vr.* to become exhausted; to give out; to wear oneself out; to be out of print.

¹agracejo, *m.* unripened grape; unripe olive that falls.

²agracejo, *m.* a kind of shrub.

agraceño, ña, *a.* as bitter as verjuice.

agracera. I. *f.* verjuice cruet. **II.** *a.* vine yielding unripening fruit.

agraciado, da. I. *pp.* of AGRACIAR. **II.** *a.* graceful, gracious. **III.** *m.* grantee.

agraciar, *va.* to adorn, embellish; to favor; to grace; to give employment to.

agracillo, agrecillo, *m.* = ²AGRACEJO.

agradable, *a.* agreeable, pleasing, pleasant.

agradablemente, *adv.* agreeably, pleasantly.

agradar. I. *vn.* to be pleasing; to please, like (diff. const.: *esto le agrada*, this pleases him, he likes this. Here *le* is dative, not accusative.)

agradecer, *va.* (*ind.* AGRADEZCO; *subj.* AGRADEZCA) to thank for; to be grateful for.—**agradecido, da. I.** *pp.* of AGRADECER. **II.** *a.* grateful; thankful.

agradecimiento, *m.* gratefulness, gratitude.

agradezco, agradezca, *v.* *V.* AGRADECER.

agrado, *m.* affability, agreeableness; pleasure, liking.—**esto no es de mi a.,** this is not to my liking.—**ser del a. de uno,** to be to one's taste, have one's approval.

agramadera, *f.* brake; scutch, instrument for dressing flax.

agramador, ra, *n.* flax or hemp breaker.

agramar, *va.* to dress (flax, hemp) with a brake.

agramilar, *va.* to point and color (a brick wall).

agramiza, *f.* the stalk of hemp; hemp, tow.

agrandamiento, *m.* enlargement.

agrandar, *va.* to enlarge, increase; let out (dress).

agranujado, da, *a.* grain-shaped; filled with grain.

agrario, ria, *a.* agrarian, rustic.

agravación, *f.* aggravation.

agravador, ra, *n.* aggravator; oppressor.

agravamiento, *m.* aggravating.

agravantemente, *adv.* aggravatingly; burdensomely.

agravar. I. *va.* to aggravate; to add to a burden; to oppress; to aggrieve; to exaggerate. **II.** *vr.* to become grave or worse.

agravatorio, ria, *a.* aggravating; (law) confirmatory and compulsory.

agraviadamente, *adv.* in an offended manner.

agraviador, ra, *n.* injurer, offender.

agraviamiento, *m.* wrong, offense, injury.

agraviante, *a.* offending.

agraviar. I. *va.* to wrong, offend, injure, harm. **II.** *vr.* to be piqued, take offense.

agravio, *m.* offense, insult, affront; injury, damage, harm.—**agravioso, sa,** *a.* offensive, insulting; injurious.

¹agraz, *m.* unripe grape; grape verjuice; (coll.) displeasure.—**en a.,** unseasonably.

²agraz, *m.* (bot.) red-berried mistletoe.

agrazada, *f.* verjuice water with sugar.

agrazar. I. *vn.* to taste sour. **II.** *va.* to vex.

agrazón, *m.* wild grape; (bot.) gooseberry bush; (coll.) displeasure, resentment.

agrecillo, *m.* = AGRACILLO, a kind of shrub.

agredir, *va.* (*defect.*) to attack, assault.

agregación, *f.* aggregation; aggregate, collection.

agregado, m. aggregate; congregation; assistant; attaché; farmhand living on another's farm or ranch; (eng.) aggregate (of concrete).

agregar, *va.* (*pret.* AGREGUÉ; *subj.* AGREGUE) to add; to collect, gather, heap; to nominate, appoint.

agremiar, *va.* & *vr.* to form into a guild or union; to unionize.

agresión, *f.* aggression.

agresivamente, *adv.* aggressively.

agresivo, va, *a.* aggressive, offensive.

agresor, ra, *n.* aggressor, assaulter; (law) one who violates another's rights.

agreste, *a.* rustic, countrylike, wild; rude, uncultured, uncouth.

agrete, *a.* sourish, tartish.

agriamente, *adv.* sourly; harshly, tartly, bitterly, severely.

agriar. I. *va.* to make sour or tart; to irritate, exasperate. **II.** *vr.* to sour, turn acid.

agriaz, *m.* (bot.) bead tree.

agrícola, *a.* & *n.* agricultural; agriculturist.

agricultor, ra, *n.* husbandman, farmer, agriculturist.
agricultura, *f.* agriculture.
agridulce, *a.* bittersweet.
agrietado, da, *a.* cracked.
agrietamiento, *m.* cracking; crack, fissure.
agrietarse, *vr.* to crack.
agrifolio, *m.* (bot.) holly tree.
agrilla, *f.* (bot.) = ACEDERA, sorrel.
agrillarse, grillarse, *vr.* to sprout.
agrillo, lla, *a. dim.* sourish, tartish.
agrimensor, *m.* land surveyor.
agrimensura, *f.* land surveying.
agrimonia, *f.* (bot.) agrimony, liverwort.
agrio, ria. I. *a.* sour, acrid; rough (app. to a surface); rude, disagreeable; brittle, unmalleable. **II.** *m.* acidity.—*pl.* **agrios,** sour-fruit trees.
agrión, *m.* (vet.) callosity in a horse's knee.
agrisado, da, *a.* grayish.
agrisetado, da, *a.* flowered or small-figured (silk).
agronometría, *f.* (agr.) science of soils.
agronomía, *f.* agronomy, science of agriculture.
agrónomo, *m.* agronomist, agricultural scientist.
agropecuario, ria, *a.* agriculture and cattle (as *a.*).
agropila, *m.* German bezoar.
agrupación, *f.* cluster; crowd; group; grouping; gathering.
agrupar, *va.* to group; to cluster.
agrura, *f.* acidity, acerbity; orchard of sour-fruit trees.
agua, *f.* water; liquid; rain; (chem.) liquor distilled from herbs, flowers, or fruit; lustre of diamonds; (naut.) leak; (arch.) slope (of a roof). *pl.* mineral waters in general; clouds (in silk, etc.); gloss (in feathers, stones, etc.); urine; tide.—**a. abajo** or **aguas abajo,** downstream.—**a. angélica,** manna water.—**a. arriba** or **aguas arriba,** upstream; (fig.) uphill.—**a. bendita,** holy water.—**a. cruda,** hard water.—**a. de azahar,** orange-flower water.—**a. de cal,** lime water.—**a. de cepas,** (coll.) wine.—**a. de cerrajas,** (coll.) worthless thing, truck, rubbish.—**a. de coco,** cocoanut milk.—**a. de Colonia,** Cologne water.—**a. del pantoque,** (naut.) bilge water.—**a. del timón,** wake of a ship.—**a. de manantial,** spring water.—**a. de nafa,** = A. DE AZAHAR.—**a. de nieve,** melted snow water.—**a. de olor,** perfume.—**a. de pie,** (of springs, streams) running water. —**a. de pozo,** well water.—**a. dulce,** fresh water.—**a. fresca,** cold water.—**a. fuerte,** aqua fortis, nitric acid.—**a. gorda,** hard water. —**a. llovediza, a. lluvia,** rain water.—**a. manantial,** = A. DE MANANTIAL.—**a. muerta,** stagnant water.—**a. nieve,** sleet.—**a. pesada,** (chem.) heavy water.—**a. regia,** aqua regia.— **a. rica,** scented water.—**a. sal,** salt and water. —**a. termal,** hot-spring water.—**a. tofana,** aqua tofana.—**a. viento,** wind-and-rain storm. —**a. viva,** surface water, running water.—**estar con el a. hasta la boca,** to be in a fix, in difficulties.—**¡hombre al a.!,** man overboard!— **nadie diga,** or **no hay que decir, de esta a. no beberé,** don't be too sure the same thing won't happen to you, or, that you won't do that very thing.—**aguas jurisdiccionales,** (int. law) territorial waters.—**aguas madres,** (chem.) mother liquor.—**aguas mayores,** stools (evacuation).—**aguas menores,** urine, urinating.—**aguas vertientes,** drainage, drain water, flowoff; water shed, basin.—**estar entre dos aguas,** to be undecided, be on the fence.— **hacer aguas,** make water, urinate.
aguacatal, *m.* avocado plantation or grove.
aguacate, *m.* avocado, alligator pear; pear-shaped emerald.
aguacatillo, *m.* (bot.) a kind of avocado.
aguacero, *m.* heavy shower.

aguacibera, *f.* water used to irrigate ground sowed when dry.
aguachar. I. *va.* to load (a thing) with water; (Am.) to tame, break (a horse); to win the good will of with gifts. **II.** *vr.* to fatten in idleness (app. to horses). **III.** *m.* pool, puddle.
aguacharnar, *va.* = ENAGUAZAR, to flood.
aguachento, ta, *a.* (Am.) watery.
aguachinar, *va.* = AGUACHARNAR.
aguachirle, *f.* inferior wine; slipslop; any weak or stale liquor; trifle; frivolity.
aguada, *f.* watering station; flood in a mine; (naut.) ship's drinking-water supply; (art) water color.—**a la a.,** water color (picture).— **hacer a.,** (naut.) to take water.
aguaderas, *f. pl.* frames for jars of water carried by horses.
aguadero, *m.* watering place; water station.
aguadija, *f.* serum in pimples or sores.
aguado, da. I. *pp.* of AGUAR. **II.** *a.* watery; abstemious.—**manos aguadas,** butterfingers.
aguador, ra, *n.* water carrier; (mech.) sprocket. —**a. del real,** (mil.) sutler.
aguaducho, *m.* water course; stall for selling water.
aguadura, *f.* surfeit of water (in cattle).
aguafiestas, *n.* (coll.) wet blanket.
aguafuerte, *f.* etching; etched plate.
aguagoma, *f.* (painting) gum water.
aguaitamiento, *m.* watching, spying, lying for some one.
aguaitar, *va.* to spy, watch.
aguajaque, *m.* fennel gum.
aguajas, *f. pl.* (Chile) ulcers above the hoofs.
aguaje, *m.* tidal wave; (naut.) whirlpool or eddy at the rudder; sea current; wake of a ship.
agualluvia, *f.* = AGUA LLUVIA, rain water.
aguamanil, *m.* water jug; washstand.
aguamanos, *m.* water for washing the hands; washstand.
aguamarina, *f.* aquamarine.
aguamasa, *f.* (Am.) crushed-corn washings.
aguamelado, da, *a.* washed over with water and honey.
aguamiel, *f.* hydromel, honey and water, mead; unfermented juice of the maguey.
aguana, *f.* wood used in canoe making in S. A.
aguanieve, *f.* = AGUA NIEVE, sleet.
aguanieves, *f.* = AGUZANIEVES, *f.* magpie.
aguanosidad, *f.* aqueous substances.
aguanoso, sa, *a.* very wet; very watery.
aguantable, *a.* bearable, tolerable.
aguantar. I. *va.* to bear, endure; to resist; to maintain; (naut.) to carry a stiff sail. **II.** *vr.* to forbear.—**aguante,** *m.* strength, resistance; patience, tolerance.
aguañón, *m.* constructor of hydraulic works.
aguapié, *m.* weak, watered wine.
aguar. I. *va.* to dilute with water; to mar (pleasure). **II.** *vr.* to fill with water; to become thin (app. to liquids); (vet.) to become constipated from drinking water at the wrong time.
aguardar, *va.* to expect; to wait for; to grant time to.
aguardentado, da, *a.* containing aguardiente; tipsy, drunk.
aguardentera, *f.* liquor flask.
aguardentería, *f.* liquor shop; saloon.
aguardentero, ra, *n.* maker or seller of aguardiente.
aguardentoso, sa, *a.* mixed with aguardiente; harsh (app. to the voice).
aguardiente, *m.* aguardiente, brandy.—**a. de cabeza,** the first spirits drawn from the still.— **a. anisado,** anisette.—**a. de caña,** rum.
aguardo, *m.* hiding place for a hunter, blind.
aguarrás, *m.* oil of turpentine.
aguatero, ra, *n.* water carrier.
aguatocha, *f.* pump.
aguaturma, *f.* (bot.) Jerusalem artichoke.

aguavientos, *m.* (bot.) yellow sage tree.
aguaza, *f.* watery serum; sap from trees.
aguazal, *m.* marsh, fen.
aguazarse, *vr.* to become marshy.
aguazo, *m.* painting in gouache.
aguazoso, sa, *a.* = AGUANOSO.
agucé, aguce, *v.* V. AGUZAR.
agudeza, *f.* sharpness; fineness; witty saying; repartee; wit.
agudo, da, *a.* sharp; sharp-pointed; keen-edged; high-pitched; witty; clever(minded); brisk, ready, active or lively; (med., geom.) acute.
agüera, *f.* trench for irrigation.
¹agüero, *m.* augury, prognostication; omen, sign, indication.
²agüero, agüere, *v.* V. AGORAR.
aguerrido, da. I. *pp.* of AGUERRIR. **II.** *a.* inured to war; veteran.
aguerrir. I. *va.* & *vr.* (*defect.*) to accustom to war.
aguijada, *f.* spur, goad.
aguijador, ra, *n.* one that goads, spurs, or urges.
aguijadura, *f.* spurring, urging, egging on.
aguijar. I. *va.* to prick, spur, goad; to incite, egg on. **II.** *m.* to march fast; to hurry.
aguijatorio, ria, *a.* (law) re-mandatory.
aguijón, *m.* sting (of insect); prick; spur, goad.—**cocear, or dar coces, contra el a.,** to kick against the pricks.
aguijonazo, *m.* thrust with a goad.
aguijoneador, ra, *n.* one who pricks or goads.
aguijonear, *va.* to prick, goad; push, urge, egg on.
águila, *f.* eagle; eagle ray (fish).—**a. barbuda,** lammergeir, bearded vulture.—**a. blanca,** a variety of Andine vulture.—**a. cabdal,** or **caudal,** royal or golden, eagle—**a. de mar,** eagle ray.—**a. imperial,** imperial eagle.—**a. real** = A. CAUDAL.
aguileño, na, *a.* aquiline; hawknosed.
aguililla, *f.* *dim.*—**caballo a.,** (Am.) swift, pacing horse.
aguilón. I. *m.* boom of a crane. **II.** *n. aug.* of ÁGUILA.
aguilucho, *m.* young eagle, eaglet.
aguinaldo, *m.* New Year's or Christmas present; (Cuba) wild convolvulus that blossoms at Christmas.
aguja, *f.* needle; bodkin; hatpin; spire, steeple; obelisk; needlefish, hornfish; needle shell; hand of a watch; style of a dial; needle, magnetic compass; (Ry.) switch rail; (Ry., gen. *pl.*) switch; spindle; pin (in typography and artil.); brad; graft.—*pl.* ribs of an animal; (Ry.) switch, (Brit.) points.—**a. capotera,** darning needle. —**a. colchonera,** tufting needle.—**a. de arria, a. de enjalmar,** pack-needle.—**a. de marear,** binnacle, marine compass.—**a. espartera** = A. DE ENJALMAR.
agujazo, *m.* prick with a needle.
agujerear, *va.* to pierce, perforate.
agujero, *m.* hole; needlemaker or seller; dugout.
agujeta, *f.* lace, string or latchet with metal tips. —*pl.* tip, gratuity; pains from overexercise.
agujetar, *va.* to lace, sew with strips.
agujetería, *f.* shop where *agujetas* are made or sold.
agujetero, ra, *n.* maker or seller of *agujetas;* ALFILETERO, (Am.) pin or needle case or cushion.
agujón, *m. aug.* large needle.
agujuela, *f.* brad.
aguosidad, *f.* lymph.
aguoso, sa, acuoso, sa, *a.* aqueous, watery.
agur, *adv.* (coll.) adieu, farewell, good-bye.
agusanarse, *vr.* to become infested with worms.
agustiniano, na; agustino, na, *n.* & *a.* Augustinian (monk, nun).
agutí, acutí, *m.* agouti.
agúzadera, *f.* whetstone.
aguzadero, *m.* haunt of wild boars.
aguzado, da. I. *pp.* AGUZAR. **II.** *a.* sharp; keen.
aguzador, n. & *a.* sharpener(-ing).

aguzadura, *f.* whetting, sharpening.
aguzanieve, *f.* wagtail, a small bird.
aguzar, *va.* (*pret.* AGUCÉ; *subj.* AGUCE) to whet, sharpen; to urge, excite.—**a. el ingenio,** to sharpen the wits.—**a. las orejas,** to prick up the ears.—**a. la vista,** to sharpen the sight.
aguzonazo, *m.* blow with a poker.
¡ah!, *interj.* ah!
ahebrado, da, *a.* threadlike, fibrous.
ahechadero, *m.* place where grain is sifted.
ahechador, ra, *a.* & *n.* sifter(-ing).
ahechaduras, *f. pl.* refuse of grain, chaff.
ahechar, *va.* to sift (grain).—**ahecho,** *m.* sifting.
ahelear. I. *va.* to gall, embitter. **II.** *vn.* to taste bitter.
aherrojamiento, *m.* putting in irons, shackling.
aherrojar, *va.* to chain, put in irons, shackle.
aherrumbrar. I. *va.* to impart the taste and color of iron to. **II.** *vr.* to have the taste and color of iron (as water); to become ferruginous; to rust.
ahervorarse, *vr.* (of grain in a granary) to become heated.
ahí, *adv.* there; yonder.—**de a.,** hence.—**de por a.,** insignificant, nothing much.—**por a.,** somewhere around here; that way; over there. —**por a., por a.,** about, more or less.—**a. donde lo (la) ve,** although he (she) doesn't look it, although you wouldn't expect it.
ahidalgado, da, *a.* gentlemanly(-womanly).
ahijadero, *m.* breeding place for sheep.
ahijado, da, *n.* godchild; protegé.
ahijador, ra, *n.* shepherd in charge of a sheep breeding place.
ahijar. I. *va.* to adopt; to impute. **II.** *vn.* to bring forth young; to bud, shoot out.
ahilarse, *vr.* to become faint, weak; to grow sour; to grow thin.—**ahilo,** *m.* faintness, weakness.
ahinco, *m.* earnestness, eagerness, ardor.
ahitar, *va.* & *vr.* to surfeit, cloy, stuff.
ahitera, *f.* (coll.) violent or continued indigestion.
ahito, ta. I. *a.* gorged, surfeited; stuffed; full; disgusted, bored. **II.** *m.* indigestion; surfeit.
ahocicar, *vn.* (naut.) to pitch or plunge.
ahocinarse, *vr.* to run in deep and narrow ravines.
ahogadero, *m.* hangman's rope; stifling place; throatband, halter.
ahogadizo, za, *a.* easily drowned; (of fruit) harsh, rough; (of wood) heavier than water, non-floating.
ahogado, da. I. *pp.* of AHOGAR. **II.** *a.* close, unventilated.—**estar, or verse, a.,** to be overwhelmed or swamped. **III.** *n.* suffocated or drowned person.
ahogador, ra, *n.* hangman.
ahogamiento, *m.* suffocation; drowning.
ahogar. I. *va.* (*pret.* AHOGUÉ; *subj.* AHOGUE) to drown; to choke, throttle, smother; to oppress; to quench, extinguish; to water (plants) to excess. **II.** *vr.* to drown; to be suffocated; (naut.) to founder.—**ahogo,** *m.* oppression, tightness (of the chest, etc.); suffocation; pain; severe affliction; embarrassment.
ahogué, ahogue, *v.* V. AHOGAR.
ahoguijo, *m.* (vet.) quinsy, swollen throat.
ahoguío, *m.* oppression in the chest.
ahombrado, da, *a.* (coll.) mannish.
ahondar. I. *va.* to deepen; to dig; to go deep into. **II.** *vn.* to go deep, penetrate; to advance in knowledge; to investigate.
ahonde, *m.* act of sinking or digging; depth to which a mine should reach to acquire title.
ahora. I. *adv.* now.—**a. mismo,** just now; right now; at once.—**hasta a.,** hitherto, until now; so far.—**por a.,** for the present. **II.** *conj.* now; whether . . . or (*ahora hable, ahora escriba, lo hace bien,* whether he speaks or writes, he does it well).—**a. bien,** now, now then.
ahorcadura, *f.* (act of) hanging.

ahorcajarse, *vr.* to sit astride.

ahorcar, *va.* (*pret.* AHORQUÉ; *subj.* AHORQUE) to hang (kill by hanging).

ahorita, *adv.* (Am. coll.) just now.—**a. mismo,** just now, this very moment; right away, at once.

ahormar, *va.* to fit, shape, adjust; to break in (shoes); to bring to reason.

ahornagarse, *vr.* (of lands, plants, etc.) to become parched or burned.

ahornar. **I.** *va.* to put in an oven. **II.** *vr.* to be scorched in the oven without being baked.

ahorqué, ahorque, *v.* V. AHORCAR.

ahorquillado, da. **I.** *a.* forked.

ahorquillar. **I.** *va.* to stay, prop up with forks. **II.** *vr.* to become forked.

ahorrado, da. **I.** *pp.* of AHORRAR. **II.** *a.* unencumbered.

ahorrador, ra. **I.** *n.* emancipator; saver, economizer. **II.** *a.* saving.

ahorramiento, *m.* emancipation, enfranchisement; saving.

ahorrar, *va.* to save, economize; to spare; to enfranchise, emancipate.—**no ahorrarse,** or **no ahorrárselas, con nadie,** to be afraid of nobody, not to mince words with anybody.

ahorrativa, *f.* (coll.) = AHORRO.

ahorrativo, va, *a.* frugal, thrifty, saving.

ahorro, *m.* economy.—*pl.* savings.

ahoyadura, *f.* hole; digging.

ahoyar, *vn.* to dig holes.

ahuate, *m.* (Mex.) prickly hair (of sugar cane, etc.).

ahuchador, ra, *n.* hoarder, miser.

ahuchar, *va.* to hoard.

ahuecamiento, *m.* hollowing.

ahuecar. **I.** *va.* (*pret.* AHUEQUÉ; *subj.* AHUEQUE) to make hollow, scoop out; to loosen; to give (to the voice) a tone of solemnity. **II.** *vr.* to become hollow; to puff up, swell, put on airs.

ahuehué, ahuehuete, *m.* a Mexican coniferous tree like a cypress.

ahuequé, ahueque, *v.* V. AHUECAR.

ahumado, da. **I.** *a.* smoky; smoked. **II.** *f.* smoke signal from the coast.

ahumar. **I.** *va.* to smoke; to cure in smoke. **II.** *vn.* to fume; to emit smoke. **III.** *vr.* to be smoked; to look smoky.

ahusado, da. **I.** *pp.* of AHUSAR. **II.** *a.* spindle-shaped, tapered.

ahusar, *va.* & *vr.* to taper.

ahuyentador, ra, *n.* one that drives or scares away; scarecrow.

ahuyentar, *va.* to drive away, put to flight; to frighten away; to overcome (a passion), banish (care).

aijada, *f.* = AGUIJADA, goad.

aína, aínas, *adv.* soon; easily; almost.

aindiado, da, *a.* Indianlike.

airadamente, *adv.* angrily.

airado, da, *a.* angry, wrathful.

airamiento, *m.* wrath, anger.

airar. **I.** *va.* to anger; to irritate. **II.** *vr.* to grow angry.

aire, *m.* air; atmosphere; wind; pace (of a horse); air, carriage, gait; aspect, countenance, look; musical composition; frivolity.—**a. colado,** cold draught.—**al aire libre,** in the open air, outdoors.—**(con) a. acondicionado,** air-conditioned.—**en el a.,** in suspense, in the air.—**por a.,** by air.—**por el a.,** or **por los aires,** very rapidly, posthaste, like lightning.—**hablar al a.,** to make empty talk.—**¿qué aires lo traen a Vd. por acá?** what good wind brings you here?—**tomar el a.,** to take a walk.

airear. **I.** *va.* to give air to, ventilate; to aerate; to charge with gas. **II.** *vr.* to take the air; to cool oneself.

airecico, llo, to, *m. dim.* gentle breeze.

¹airón, *m. aug.* violent gale.

²airón, *m.* crested heron; egret; crest; ornament of plumes.

³airón, *m.* deep Moorish well.

airosamente, *adv.* gracefully, lightly.

airosidad, *f.* graceful deportment.

airoso, sa, *a.* airy, windy; graceful, gracious; lively; successful.

aisladamente, *adv.* in isolation, apart.

aislado, da, *a.* isolated; (elec., phys.) insulated.

aislador, ra, *n.* & *a.* isolator(-ing); (elec., phys.) insulator(-ing).

aislamiento, *m.* isolation; (elec., phys.) insulation; insulating material.

aislar. **I.** *va.* to isolate; (elec., phys.) to insulate. **II.** *vr.* to become isolated; to seclude oneself.

¡aja! *interj.* aha! (denoting approval).

ajada, *f.* garlic sauce.

ajado, da, *a.* garlicky.

ajamiento, *m.* disfiguring; crumpling, rumpling.

ajaquecarse, *vr.* to have a headache.

¹ajar, *m.* garlic field.

²ajar, *va.* to crumple, rumple.—**a. la vanidad a uno,** to pull down one's pride.

ajarafe, *m.* table-land; terrace; flat roof.

aje, *m.* chronic complaint.

ajea, *f.* brushwood for fuel.

ajear, *vn.* to cry (app. to a pursued partridge).

ajedrea, *f.* (bot.) winter savory.

ajedrecista, *n.* chess player.

ajedrez, *m.* chess; (naut.) netting, grating.

ajedrezado, da, *a.* checkered.

ajedrista, *n.* chess player.

ajenabe, ajenabo, *m.* (bot.) wild mustard.

ajenable, *a.* alienable.

ajengibre, jengibre, *m.* ginger.

ajenjo, *m.* (bot.) wormwood; absinth.

ajeno, na, *a.* another's; foreign; abhorrent, contrary; ignorant; improper; unsuited.—**a. a,** foreign to: free from.—**a. de,** devoid of, lacking; ignorant of; indifferent to.

ajenuz, *m.* (bot.) field fennel-flower.

ajeo, *m.*—**perro de a.,** setter.

ajero, ra, *n.* garlic dealer or vender.

ajesuitado, da, *a.* Jesuitical, Jesuit-like.

ajete, *m.* young garlic; leek; garlic sauce.

ajetrearse, *vr.* to tire; to fidget.—**ajetreo,** *m.* fatigue; agitation.

ají, *m.* chili, capsicum; chili sauce.

ajiaceite, *m.* mixture of garlic and oil.

ajiaco, *m.* dish made of boiled meat and vegetables; chili sauce.

ajicola, *f.* glue made of kidskin boiled with garlic.

ajilimoje, ajilimójili, *m.* pepper-and-garlic sauce.

ajillo, *m.* tender young garlic.

ajimez, *m.* arched window with pillar in centre.

ajipuerro, *m.* wild leek.

ajironar, *va.* to put colored pieces in (a dress, etc.).

¹ajo, *m.* (bot.) garlic; garlic sauce; (coll.) rouge.

²ajo, *m.* (coll.) oath, swear word; shady business.—**echar ajos (y cebollas),** to swear, curse.

ajobar, *va.* to carry on the back.

ajobilla, *f.* common sea shell.

ajobo, *m.* a heavy load or burden.

ajofaina, aljofaina, *f.* wash bowl, basin.

ajolote, *m.* axolotl, a Mexican salamander.

ajomate, *m.* (bot.) a variety of seaweed.

ajonje, *m.* bird lime.

ajonjera, *f.*; **ajonjero,** *m.* (bot.) the low carline thistle.

ajonjolí, *m.* (bot.) benne, sesame.

ajoqueso, *m.* dish made of garlic and cheese.

ajorca, *f.* Moorish bracelet or anklet.

ajornalar, *va.* to hire by the day.

ajuagas, *f. pl.* (vet.) ulcers over the hoofs.

ajuanetado, da, *a.* bunionlike; having bunions.

ajuar, *m.* bridal apparel and furniture; trousseau; household furniture.

ajudiado, da, *a.* Jewish; Jewlike.

ajuiciado, da, *a.* wise, sensible

ajuiciar, *vn.* & *vr.* to become wise; to reform, mend one's ways.

ajustadamente, *adv.* tightly; justly, rightly.

ajustado, da. I. *pp.* of AJUSTAR. **II.** *a.* exact, right; stingy; adapted; tight; fitted.

ajustador, ra. I. *n.* fitter, adjuster. **II.** *m.* close waistcoat, jacket; (print.), justifier; (mech.) adapter; adjusting tool.

ajustamiento, *m.* agreement; fitting; settling of accounts; receipts.

ajustar. I. *va.* to regulate; to adapt, adjust, fit; to justify (type); to agree about; to settle (an account, a controversy, etc.); to reconcile; to press close, oppress; to size, make true; to trim; to engage, hire. **II.** *vr.* to settle; to conform; to engage oneself; to be engaged or hired. **III.** *vn.* to fit.—**ajuste,** *m.* proportion of the constituent parts of a thing; adjustment, fitting; agreement, contract, covenant; engagement; settlement.—*pl.* couplings.

ajusticiar, *va.* to execute, put to death.

al (contraction of a and **el**) to the (foll. by a masc. noun); used also with the *inf.* of verbs to indicate coexistence or immediate anteriority, and often equivalent to "on" (foll. by *pres. p.*), "about," "on the point of": *al llegar,* on arriving; *al amanecer,* at daybreak; *estoy al partir,* I am about to leave; *Juan estuvo al perder su empleo,* John was on the point of losing (or, came very near losing) his position.

ala, *f.* wing; row, file; (mil., aer.) wing; wing (of a building); brim (of hat); (anat.) auricle; fin (of fish); leaf (of a door, table); (naut.) blade (of a propeller).—*pl.* **alas,** upper studding sails.—**a. de gavia,** maintop studding sail.—**a. de mesana,** (naut.) driver.—**a. de proa,** head of a ship.—**a. de sobremesana,** mizzentop studding sail.—**a. de velacho,** fore studding sail.—**cortar,** or **quebrantar, las alas a uno,** to discourage one or throw a wet blanket on one's plans; to deprive one of means or elements; to clip one's wings.

Alá, *m.* Allah, Arabic name of God.

alabado, *m.* hymn in praise of the sacrament.

alabador, ra, *n.* praiser.

alabamiento, *m.* praise.

alabancioso, sa, *a.* (coll.) boastful, ostentatious.

alabandina, *f.* manganese sulphide; alabandine, spinel ruby.

alabanza, *f.* praise, commendation.

alabar, *va.* & *vr.* to praise, commend.—**a. uno sus agujas,** (coll.) to blow one's own horn.

alabarda, *f.* halberd.—**alabardado, da,** *a.* halberd-shaped.—**alabardazo,** *m.* a blow with a halberd.—**alabardero,** *m.* halberdier; one of a theatre claque.

alabastrado, da, *a.* alabasterlike.

alabastrina, *f.* thin sheet of alabaster.

alabastrino, na, *a.* alabastrine.

alabastro, *m.* alabaster.

álabe, *m.* drooping branch of a tree; bucket (of a water wheel); mat used in carts; cam.

alabear, *va.* & *vr.* to warp.

alabega, *f.* (bot.) sweet basil.

alabeo, *m.* warping.

alabiado, da, *a.* lipped or ragged (coins).

alacena, *f.* cupboard; closet; (naut.) locker.

alaciar, *vn.* = ENLACIAR, to lose vigor; to wilt.

alacrán, *m.* scorpion; ring of the bit of a bridle; stop or hook in organ bellows; chain or link of a sleeve button; swivel.—**alacranado, da,** *a.* scorpion-bitten; vice- or disease-ridden.

alacranera, *f.* (bot.) scorpion grass.

alacranídeo, a; alacránido, da, *a.* scorpionlike.

alacranino, na, *a.* pertaining to scorpions.

alacridad, *f.* alacrity.

alacha, alache, *f.* anchovy.

alada, *f.* fluttering of the wings.

aladares, *m. pl.* forelocks over the temples.

aladierna, alaterno, *m.* mock privet.

alado, da, *a.* winged.

aladrada, *f.* (prov.) furrow (from ploughing).

aladrar, *va.* to plow.

aladro, *m.* plow; plowed land.

aladroque, *m.* unsalted anchovy.

alafia, *f.*—**pedir a.,** (coll.) to beg pardon.

álaga, *f.* a species of yellow wheat.

alagar, *va.* to make ponds or lakes in.

alagartado, da, *a.* variegated, motley.

alajú, *m.* paste made of nuts and honey.

alamar, *m.* frog and braid trimming.

alambicadamente, *adv.* pedantically.

alambicado, da. I. *pp.* of ALAMBICAR. **II.** *a.* pedantic, euphuistic; given with a sparing hand.

alambicamiento, *m.* distillation; pedantry, affected language.

alambicar, *va.* to distil; to scrutinize; to use affected language.

alambique, *m.* still.—**por a.,** sparingly.

alambor, *m.* (arch.) face of a hewn stone; (fort.) inside slope.

alambrada, *f.* (mil.) wire entanglements.

alambrado, *m.* wire netting, wire screen; wire cover; electric wiring; wire fence; wire entanglements.

alambrar, *va.* to put a wire fence round.

alambre, *m.* wire; (anc.) copper, bronze, brass; sheep bells.—**a. conejo,** rabbit wire (used for rabbit-catching nets).—**a. de púas,** barbed wire.—**alambrera,** *f.* wire netting; wire screen; wire cover; (agr.) wire trellis.

alameda, *f.* poplar grove; public walk.

alamín, *m.* clerk appointed to inspect weights and measures; surveyor of buildings; (prov.) farmer appointed to superintend irrigation.

alamina, *f.* fine paid by potters.

alaminazgo, *m.* office of the *alamín.*

alamirré, *m.* musical chord.

álamo, *m.* (bot.) poplar.—**a. blanco,** white poplar.—**a. temblón,** aspen tree.

alampar, *va.* & *vr.* (por) (coll.) to long (for); to crave.

alamud, *m.* square bolt for a door.

alanceador, *m.* lancer.

alancear, *va.* to spear.

alandrearse, *vr.* (of silkworms) to become dry, stiff, and blanched.

alanés, *m.* a large Mexican deer.

alano, na. I. *a.* pert. to the Alani, barbarian invaders of Spain. **II.** *m.* large mastiff.

alanzar, *va.* to spear.

alaqueca, *f.* bloodstone.

¹alar, *m.* overhanging roof; (hunting) snare made with horsehair.

²alar, halar, *va.* (naut.) to haul.

alárabe, alarbe. I. *n.* & *a.* Arabian. **II.** *n.* unmannerly person.

alarde, *m.* review of soldiers, parade; ostentation, boasting, vanity.—**hacer a.,** to boast, brag; to show off.—**alardear,** *m.* to boast.

alardoso, sa, *a.* boastful, bragging; ostentatious.

alargadera, *f.* lengthening bar (of compasses, etc.); (chem.) adapter, lengthening tube.

alargador, ra, *n.* stretcher; one that lengthens or stretches.

alargamiento, *m.* lengthening; (eng.) elongation.

alargar. I. *va.* (*pret.* ALARGUÉ; *subj.* ALARGUE) to lengthen; to extend; to stretch; to protract, prolong; to increase; to hand (a thing to another).—**a. un cabo,** (naut.) to pay out a cable. **II.** *vr.* to be prolonged; to drag; to become longer; to go or move away; to deviate; to expatiate, enlarge.

alarguez, *m.* (bot.) dog-rose.

alaria, *f.* potters' finishing tool.

alarida, *f.* hue and cry.

alarido, *m.* howl, outcry, shout, scream.

alarije, arije, *f.* name of a large grape.

alarma, *f.* alarm.

alarmante, *a.* alarming.

alarmar. I. *va.* to alarm. **II.** *vr.* to become alarmed.

alarmista, *n.* alarmist.

alastrar. I. *va.* (of animals) to throw back the ears; (of persons) to squint (to see better); (naut.) to ballast. **II.** *vr.* (of a bird in hiding) to lie flat.

alátere, *n.* (coll.) constant companion, shadow.

alaterno, *m.* (bot.) mock privet.

alatinado, da, *a.* (of language) Latinlike, puristic.

alatrón, *m.* froth of saltpetre.

alavanco, lavanco, *m.* a kind of wild duck.

alavense, alavés, *a.* Alavese, of Alava.

alazán, na, *a.* sorrel-colored.

alazo, *m.* a blow with the wings.

alazor, *m.* (bot.) bastard saffron.

alba, *f.* dawn of day; alb, white gown worn by priests.—**al a., al rayar del a.,** at daybreak.— **quebrar, rayar, or reír, el alba,** to dawn.

albacara, *f.* (fort.) round tower.

albacea, *m.* & *f.* (law) executor, executrix.

albaceazgo, *m.* (law) executorship.

albacora, *f.* fish resembling a tunny; a large fig.

albada, *f.* dawn; (Mex.) attack at daybreak.

albahaca, *f.* (bot.) sweet basil.

albahaquero, *m.* flowerpot; sweet-basil vender.

albahaquilla (de río), *f.* (bot.) pellitory.

albaida, *f.* (bot.) the shrubby gypsophila.

albalá, *m.* or *f.* (obs.) royal letter patent; a public instrument.

albanega, *f.* hair net; net for catching partridges or rabbits.

albanés, esa, *n.* & *a.* Albanian.

albañal, albañar, *m.* common sewer; dirty water sink.

albañil, *m.* mason, builder.

albañilería, *f.* masonry (occupation or work).

albaquía, *f.* remnant.

albar, *a.* white.

albarán, *m.* "to-let" sign; royal grant or cedula; letter patent.

albarazada, *f.* marble-colored grape.

albarazado, da, *a.* affected with white leprosy; pale, whitish; (Mex.) cross between Chinese and half-breed parents.

albarazo, *m.* white leprosy.

albarca, abarca, *f.* peasant's sandal.

albarcoque, *m.* = ALBARICOQUE.

albarcoquero, *m.* apricot tree.

albarda, *f.* packsaddle.

albardado, da. I. *pp.* of ALBARDAR. **II.** *a.* (of animals) different-colored skin at the loins.

albardar, *va.* to put a packsaddle on; to lard (fowls).

albardela, *f.* small saddle.

albardería, *f.* packsaddle making or shop.

albardero, ra, *n.* packsaddle maker.

albardilla, *f.* small packsaddle; coping; border of a garden bed; wool tuft; bard.

albardín, *m.* (bot.) matweed.

albardón, *m.* large packsaddle.

albardoncillo, *m. dim.* small packsaddle.

albarejo, *m.* a variety of wheat.

albareque, *m.* fishing net.

albaricoque, *m.* apricot.—**albaricoquero,** *m.* apricot tree.

¹albarillo, *m.* a tune on the guitar.

²albarillo, *m.* white apricot.

albarino, *m.* white cosmetic.

albarrada, *f.* dry wall; earth fence; wall for defense.

albarranilla, *f.* blue-flowered onion.

¹albarraz, *m.* (bot.) lousewort.

²albarraz, *m.* = ALBARAZO.

albatoza, *f.* small covered boat.

albatros, *m.* albatross.

albayaldado, da, *a.* covered with white lead.

albayaldar, *va.* & *vr.* to cover with white lead.

albayalde, *m.* white lead, ceruse.

albazano, na, *a.* of dark chestnut color.

albear, *va.* to whiten. Also BLANQUEAR.

albedrío, *m.* will; free will; impulsiveness, wilfullness; (law) precedent; judgment.—**al a. de uno,** to, or according to, one's judgment or pleasure; as one likes.

albéitar, *m.* veterinarian.

albeitería, *f.* veterinary science.

albellón, *m.* = ALBAÑAL, sewer.

albenda, *f.* ornamented white-linen hangings.

albendera, *f.* woman who makes hangings; gadding woman.

albengala, *f.* gauze worn in turbans.

albéntola, *f.* fine fishing net.

alberca, *f.* pool; reservoir, tank; pond.—**a. natatoria, de natación,** swimming pool.— **en a.,** roofless.

albérchiga, *f.,* **albérchigo,** *m.* a variety of peach.

alberchiguero, *m.* variety of peach tree.

albergador, ra, *n.* one who shelters.

albergar. I. *va.* (*pret.* ALBERGUÉ; *subj.* ALBERGUE) to lodge, shelter, harbor; to take (lodgers). **II.** *vr.* to lodge; to find shelter or lodging.

albergue, *m.* lodging; shelter; (animal) den.

alberguería, *f.* inn; poorhouse.

albericoque, *m.* = ALBARICOQUE, apricot.

albero, *m.* whitish earth; dishcloth.

alberquero, *m.* tender of pools or tanks.

alberquilla, *f. dim.* little pool.

albicante, *a.* whitening, bleaching.

albicaudo, da, *a.* white-tailed.

albicaulo, la, *a.* (bot.) white-stemmed.

albiceps, *a.* white-headed, white-faced.

albiense, *n.* & *a.* (geol.) Albian.

albigense, *n.* & *a.* Albigensian.

albihar, *m.* (bot.) oxeye.

albillo, lla. I. *a.*—**uva a.,** early white grape.— **vino a.,** white grape wine. **II.** *m.* = UVA A.

albín, *m.* bloodstone; carmine pigment.

albina, *f.* salt-water marsh.

albino, na, *a.* albino.—**albinismo,** *m.* albinism.

Albión, *f.* Albion (England).

albita, *f.* (min.) albite, white feldspar.

albitana, *f.* fence to inclose plants; (naut.) an apron.—**a. del codaste,** (naut.) inner post.

albo, ba, *a.* (poet.) snow-white.

alboaire, *m.* glazed tile work.

albogalla, *f.* a kind of gallnut.

albogue, *m.* pastoral flute; martial music.

alboguero, ra, *n.* player of or composer for the *albogue.*

albohol, *m.* (bot.) red poppy.

albollón, *m.* gutter (on road), drain; sewer.

albóndiga, almóndiga, *f.* ball of forcemeat with eggs and spice.—**albondiguilla, almondiguilla,** *f. dim.* small ball of forcemeat.

albor, *m.* dawn; whiteness; beginning.—**a., or albores, de la vida,** childhood, youth.

alborada, *f.* dawn; (mil.) battle at dawn; reveille; morning watch; musical piece celebrating dawn.

albórbola, *f.* shouting and yelling (gen. for joy).

alborear, *vn.* to dawn.

alborga, *f.* matweed sandal.

albornía, *f.* large glazed jug.

alborno, alburno, *m.* (bot.) alburnum.

albornoz, *m.* coarse woollen stuff; Moorish cloak; burnoose.

alborocé, alboroce, *v.* V. ALBOROZAR.

alboronía, almoronía, *f.* dish of eggplant, tomatoes, pumpkins, and pimento.

aloroque, *m.* treat to seal a bargain.

alborotadamente, *adv.* noisily, confusedly.

alborotadizo, za; alborotado, da, *a.* restive; excitable; turbulent.

alborotador, ra, *n.* agitator, rioter.

alborotapueblos, *m.* rioter, agitator; (coll.) good-natured person; promoter of gaieties.

alborotar. I. *va.* to disturb, agitate, excite; to

make a noise; to start (the game). **II.** *vr.* to become excited; to fuss; to riot.

alboroto, *m.* disturbance, tumult; hubbub, fuss; (C. A.) (gen. *pl.*) pop corn.

alborozador, ra, *n.* promoter of mirth.

alborozar, *va.* (*pret.* ALBOROCÉ; *subj.* ALBOROCE) to exhilarate, gladden.

alborozo, *m.* merriment, gaiety, joy.

albotín, *m.* = TEREBINTO, turpentine tree.

albricias, *f. pl.* reward for good news; (Mex.) top holes in casting moulds.—¡**albricias!** joy! joy!

albudeca, *f.* (bot.) watermelon.

albufera, *f.* large lagoon by the sea.

albugíneo, a., *a.* entirely white; albuminous.

albugo, *m.* leucoma, a disease of the eye.

albuhera, *f.* lake or reservoir.

álbum, *m.* album.

albumen, *m.* albumen.—**albúmina**, *f.* albumin.

albumina, *f.* (chem.) albuminin.

albuminoideo, a, *adj.* albuminoid.

albuminoso, sa, *adj.* albuminous.

albuminuria, *f.* (med.) albuminuria.

albumosa, *f.* (chem.) albumose.

¹albur, *m.* dace, river fish.

²albur, *m.* first draw at "monte"; risk, chance.—**correr un a.**, to venture, chance, risk.—*pl.* **albures**, a card game.

albura, *f.* whiteness; (bot.) = ALBURNO.

alburero, *m.* *albures* player.

alburno, *m.* (bot.) = ALBORNO, alburnum.

alca, *f.* razorbill (a bird).

alcabala, *f.* sales tax.—**a. del viento**, duty paid by a visiting merchant.—**alcabalatorio**, *m.* book of alcabala rates; tax register.—**alcabalero**, *m.* taxgatherer, revenue officer.

alcacel, alcacer, *m.* green barley.

alcachofa, *f.* (bot.) artichoke; instrument to stop blood; fluted mallets.—**alcachofado, da. I.** *a.* artichokelike. **II.** *m.* artichoke dish.—**alcachofal**, *m.* artichoke bed.—**alcachofera**, *f.* artichoke plant.—**alcachofero, ra**, *a.* producing or selling artichokes.

alcahaz, *m.* large bird cage.—**alcahazada**, *f.* collection of birds in a cage.—**alcahazar**, *va.* to cage (birds).

alcahueto, ta, *n.* procurer; abettor; gossip.—**alcahuetear**, *va. & vn.* to aid, abet; to pander.

alcahuetería, *f.* pandering; (coll.) trick.

alcaicería, *f.* raw-silk exchange.

alcaico, *a.* (poet.) Alcaic verse in Latin.

alcaide, *m.* governor of a castle; jailer, warden.

alcaidesa, *f.* wife of an *alcaide*.

²alcaidía, *f.* office of an *alcaide*; duty on cattle.

alcalaíno, na, *n. & a.* (one) from Alcalá.

alcaldada, *f.* abusive action of an *alcalde*.

alcalde, *m.* mayor; justice of the peace; leader; name of a card game.—**a. de barrio**, selectman to whom the mayor delegates his function in a section of a city.—**alcaldear**, *vn.* (coll.) to play the *alcalde*.—**alcaldesa**, *f.* wife of an *alcalde*; mayoress.—**alcaldía**, *f.* office and jurisdiction of an *alcalde*.

alcalescencia, *f.* (chem.) alkalescence.

alcalescente, *a.* (chem.) alkalescent.

álcali, *m.* (chem.) alkali.—**alcalificable**, *a.* alkalifiable.—**alcalígeno, na**, *a.* alkaligenous.—**alcalimetría**, alkalimetry.—**alcalimétrico**, alkalimetric.—**alcalímetro**, *m.* alkalimeter.—**alcalinidad**, *f.* alkalinity.—**alcalino, na**; **alcalizado, da**, *a.* alkaline.—**alcalización**, *f.* (chem.) alkalization.—**alcalizar**, *va.* (*pret.* ALCALICÉ; *subj.* ALCALICE) (chem.) to alkalize.—**alcaloide**, *m.* alkaloid.

alcaller, *m.* potter.

alcam, *m.* (bot.) bitter apple.

alcamonías. I. *f. pl.* various aromatic seeds for seasoning. **II.** *m.* (Venez.) go-between.

alcana, *f.* ALHEÑA, privet.

alcance, *m.* reach; overtaking; balance; arm's length; scope, extent; range (of fire arms, etc.);

capacity, ability; fathom; compass; supplement, extra edition; postscript; (print.) copy; importance; last-minute news; (com.) deficit; *pl.* understanding, grasp, mental powers.—**al a. de**, within reach of.—**a largo a.**, long-term (as *a.*).—**dar a. a**, to overtake.—**irle a uno a**, or **en, los alcances**, to watch, or spy on, one.—**seguir los alcances a**, to pursue.

alcancé, alcance, *v. V.* ALCANZAR.

alcancía, *f.* bank, money box; earthen balls stuffed with flowers for missiles; (mil.) explosive bullet.

alcandía, *f.* (bot.) Turkey millet; sorghum.

alcandial, *m.* millet field.

alcandora, *f.* beacon; bonfire; white tunic.

alcanfor, *m.* camphor.—**alcanforada**, *f.* (bot.) a camphor-smelling shrub.—**alcanforar**, *va.* to camphorate.—**alcanforero**, *m.* camphor tree.

alcántara, *f.* cover for velvet in the loom.

alcantarilla, *f.* small bridge; culvert; drain; sewer.—**alcantarillado**, *m.* sewerage, sewerage system; providing with sewers.

alcantarillar, *va.* to make or install sewers.

alcanzadizo, za, *a.* easily reached or obtainable.

alcanzado, da. I. *pp.* of ALCANZAR. **II.** *a.* needy; short of money; in arrears; impecunious.

alcanzadura, *f.* (vet.) tumor in the pastern.

alcanzar. I. *va.* (*pret.* ALCANCÉ; *subj.* ALCANCE) to follow; to overtake, come up to; to reach; to acquire, obtain, attain; to comprehend; to be creditor of a balance; to be contemporaneous. **II.** *vn.* to share; to suffice, be enough; to reach.—**a. a** (*inf.*), to succeed in (*pres. p.*). **III.** *vr.* (of horses and cattle) to wound the pasterns with the feet.

alcaparra, *f.* **alcaparro**, *m.* (bot.) caper bush; caper.—**alcaparrado, da**, *a.* dressed with capers.—**alcaparral**, *m.* caper field.—**alcaparrón**, *m. aug.* large caper.

alcaparrosa, *f.* = CAPARROSA, copperas.

alcaraván, *m.* (ornith.) bittern.—**alcaravanero**, *m.* bittern hawk.

alcaravea, *f.* (bot.) caraway seed.

alcarceña, *f.* (bot.) bitter vetch.

alcarceñal, *m.* field sown with vetch.

alcarracero, ra, *n.* potter; shelf for earthenware.

alcarraza, *f.* unglazed and porous jar.

alcartaz, *m.* = CUCURUCHO, cornucopia.

alcatifa, *f.* fine carpet or rug; layer of earth.

¹alcatraz, *m.* (ornith.) pelican.

²alcatraz, *m.* = ALCARTAZ.

alcaucil, *m.* wild artichoke.

alcayata, *f.* spike.

alcázar, *m.* castle; fortress; (naut.) quarterdeck

alcazuz, *m.* licorice.

¹alce, *m.* (zool.) elk; moose.

²alce, *m.* cut (at cards).

alcino, *m.* (bot.) wild basil.

alción, *m.* (ornith.) Chinese swallow; kingfisher.

alcista, *f.* bull (stock speculator).

alcoba, *f.* alcove; bedroom; case for the tongue of a balance; place for public weighing.

alcocarra, *f.* gesture, grimace.

alcohol, *m.* alcohol; antimony; galena; spirit of wine; cosmetic for pencilling eyebrows; liquor.—**a. amílico**, amyl alcohol.—**a. metílico**, methyl alcohol, wood alcohol.

alcoholado, da. I. *pp.* of ALCOHOLAR. **II.** *a.* (of animals) of a darker color round the eyes. **III.** *m.* medication composed with alcohol.

alcoholador, ra, *n.* rectifier of spirits.

alcoholar, *va.* to paint or dye with antimony; to distil alcohol from; (pharm.) to pulverize.

alcoholato, *m.* alcoholate.

alcoholera, *f.* vessel for antimony or alcohol.

alcoholicé, alcoholice, *v. V.* ALCOHOLIZAR.

alcohólico, ca, *a.* alcoholic.

alcoholimetría, *f.* alcoholometry.

alcoholímetro, *m.* alcoholometer.

alcoholismo, *m.* alcoholism.

alcoholización, *f.* (chem.) alcoholization.
alcoholizado, da, *a.* affected by alcoholism.
alcoholizar, *va.* (*pret.* ALCOHOLICÉ; *subj.* ALCO-HOLICE) to alcoholize.
alcor, *m.* hill.
Alcorán, Corán, *m.* Koran.—**alcoranista,** *m.* Koran expounder; Koran scholar.
alcornocal, *m.* plantation of cork trees.
alcornoque, *m.* (bot.) cork tree; blockhead.
alcornoqueño, ña, *a.* pertaining to the cork tree.
¹alcorque, *m.* corkwood clogs or soles.
²alcorque, *m.* ditch for water round trees.
alcorza, *f.* sugar paste for frosting.
alcorzar, *va.* to frost with sugar.
alcotán, *m.* (ornith.) lanner, bird of prey.
alcotana, *f.* pickaxe.
alcotancillo, *m. dim.* young lanner.
alcrebite, *m.* sulphur. Also AZUFRE.
alcribis, *m.* (metal.) tuyere.
alcubilla, *f.* reservoir; basin, mill pond.
alcucero, ra. I. *n.* maker or seller of ALCUZAS. **II.** *a.* pertaining to an ALCUZA.
alcucilla, *f. dim.* small oil can.
alcuña, alcurnia, *f.* ancestry, lineage.
alcuza, *f.* oil bottle or cruet; oil can, oiler.
alcuzada, *f.* cruetful of oil.
alcuzcuz, *m.* ball of flour, water, and honey.
alcuzón, *m. aug.* large oil can.
aldaba, *f.* knocker (of a door); latch; sliding crossbar to secure doors and windows.—**tener buena a.,** or **buenas aldabas,** to be well protected, be pretty safe.—**aldabada,** *f.* rap with the knocker; sudden fear; pangs of conscience.—**aldabazo, aldabonazo,** *m.* knocking.—**aldabear,** *vn.* to rap or knock at the door.—**aldabía,** *f.* horizontal crossbeam.—**aldabilla,** *f. dim.* small knocker; latch.—**aldabón,** *m. aug.* large knocker; iron trunk handle.
aldea, *f.* village, hamlet.
aldeanamente, *adv.* in village style, countrylike.
aldeaniego, ga, *a.* pertaining to a hamlet.
aldeano, na. I. *n.* villager, peasant. **II.** *a.* rustic, uncultured.
Aldebarán, *m.* (astr.) Bull's Eye.
aldehido, *m.* aldehyde.
aldehuela, aldeilla, *f. dim.* little village.
aldeorrio, *m.* small, insignificant village.
aldiza, *f.* small reed without knots.
aldrán, *m.* one who sells wine to shepherds.
aleación, *f.* alloying; alloy.
aleador, *m.* alloyer.
¹alear, *vn.* to flutter; to move the arms quickly up and down; to recover from sickness or fatigue.
²alear, *va.* to alloy.
aleatorio, ria, *a.* pertaining to games of chance; (law) aleatory; fortuitous.
alebrado, da. I. *pp.* of ALEBRARSE. **II.** *a.* timid as a hare, chicken-hearted.
alebrarse, *vr.* (*ind.* ALIEBRO; *subj.* ALIEBRE) to squat; to cower (from fear).
alebrastarse, alebrestarse, *vr.* to cut capers; to become frightened or excited; to get puffed up.
alebronarse, *vr.* to lose heart; to take fright.
aleccionamiento, *m.* instruction, coaching.
aleccionar, *va.* to teach, instruct, coach.
alece, *m.* ragout of fish liver.
alecrín, *m.* a Cuban fish of the shark family.
alectórico, ca, *a.* pertaining to cocks; cocklike.
alechigar. I. *va.* to soften. **II.** *vr.* to turn milky.
alechugado, da. I. *pp.* of ALECHUGAR. **II.** *a.* curled, wrinkled; fluted, plaited.
alechugar, *va.* to curl like lettuce; to flute.
aledaño, ña. I. *a.* bounding, bordering. **II.** *m.* boundary, border.
alefanginas, *f. pl.* purgative pills from spices.
alefricé, alefrice, *v.* V. ALEFRIZAR.
alefris, alefriz, *m.* mortise, rabbet.
alefrizar, *va.* (*pret.* ALEFRICÉ; *subj.* ALEFRICE) to rabbet, mortise.

alegación, *f.* allegation, argument.
alegar, *va.* (*pret.* ALEGUÉ; *subj.* ALEGUE) to allege, affirm; to quote; to adduce.
alegato, *m.* allegation; (law) summing-up.
alegoría, *f.* allegory.
alegóricamente, *adv.* allegorically.
alegórico, ca, *a.* allegorical.
alegorista, *m.* allegorist.
alegorizar, *va.* (*pret.* ALEGORICÉ; *subj.* ALEGO-RICE) to turn into allegory.
¹alegrador, *m. & a.* (one) causing merriment.
²alegrador, *m.* paper spill; (mech.) reamer.
¹alegrar. I. *va.* to make merry, gladden, comfort, exhilarate; to enliven; to beautify. **II.** *vr.* (**de**), to rejoice (at); to be glad (of, *foll. by noun*; to, *foll. by verb*); to exult (in, over); to get tipsy.
²alegrar, *va.* (mech.) to round, bore, ream, widen.
alegre, *a.* merry, joyful; light-hearted, full of gaiety, lively; cheerful; funny, comic, facetious; gay; showy, fine; brilliant, (of colors) bright; lucky, fortunate; (coll.) off-color (story); reckless, careless; optimistic; tipsy.—**a. de cascos,** featherbrained.—**alegremente,** *adv.* merrily, gaily; gladly, cheerfully; facetiously.
alegreto, *m. adv.* (mus.) allegretto.
alegría, *f.* mirth, merriment, gaiety; rejoicing, joy; (bot.) sesame; oily grain; sesame and honey paste.—*pl.* rejoicings, public festival.
alegrillo, *a.* sprightly, gay.
alegro, *m.* (mus.) allegro, fast and brisk.
alegrón. I. *m.* (coll.) sudden, unexpected joy; a flash. **II.** *a.,* **na,** *a.* tipsy; lively (from liquor).
alegué, alegue, *v.* V. ALEGAR.
alejamiento, *m.* removal to a distance; receding; retiring, withdrawal; estrangement.
¹alejandrino, na, *n. & a.* Alexandrian (from Alexandria).
²alejandrino, *n. & a.* Alexandrine (verse).
alejar. I. *va.* to remove to a distance; to separate; to withdraw; to estrange. **II.** *vr.* to recede; to draw or move away.
alejijas, *f. pl.* barley porridge.
alelarse, *vr.* to become stupified.
alelí, alhelí, *m.* (bot.) winter gilliflower.
aleluya, *f.* hallelujah; joy, merriment; Easter time; (bot.) wood-sorrel.—*pl.* small prints thrown among the people on Easter eve; dull, poor verses, doggerel.
alema, *f.* allotted quantity of irrigation water.
alemán, na, *n. & a.* German.—**alemana, ale-manda,** *f.* anc. Sp. dance of German origin.
alemanisco, ca, *a.* Germanic; cloth made in Germany; huckaback; damask table linen.
alenguamiento, *m.* agreement relative to pasture lands.
alenguar, *va.* to make a pact about pasture lands.
alentada, *f.* a long breath.
alentadamente, *adv.* bravely, gallantly.
alentado, da. I. *pp.* of ALENTAR. **II.** *a.* spirited, courageous; well, in good health.
alentador, ra. I. *n.* one who inspires courage. **II.** *a.* encouraging, cheering.
alentar. I. *vn.* (*ind.* ALIENTO; *subj.* ALIENTE) to breathe. **II.** *va.* to encourage, cheer; to inspire.
aleonado, leonado, da, *a.* lionlike; lion-colored.
alepín, *m.* a kind of bombazine.
alerce, *m.* (bot.) larch tree.
alergia, *f.* allergy.
alérgico, ca, *a.* allergic.
alero, *m.* projecting part of a roof; eaves; gable end, corona; hood moulding; water table; splashboard of a carriage.—*pl.* snares for partridges.
alerón, *m.* (aer.) aileron.
alerta. I. *adv.* vigilantly, carefully.—**estar a.,** to be on the alert. **II.** *interj.* look out! watch out! **III.** *m.* (mil.) alarm, alert.
alertamente, *adv.* = ALERTA, *adv.*
alertar, *va.* to render vigilant; to put on guard.
alerto, ta, *a.* vigilant, alert, guarded.

alesna, lesna, lezna, *f.* awl.—**alesnado, da,** *a.* awl-shaped, pointed.

aleta, *f. dim.* small wing; fin (of a fish); (arch.) alette; (mech.) leaf of a hinge; teeth of a pinion; blade (of a screw propeller).

aletada, *f.* motion of the wings.

aletargado, da. I. *pp.* of ALETARGARSE. **II.** *a.* lethargic.

aletargamiento, *m.* lethargy.

aletargarse, *vr.* to fall into a lethargy.

aletazo, *m.* blow with the wing; flapping.

aleteado, da, *a.* finlike; finned.

aletear, *vn.* to flutter (wings or fins).

aleteo, *m.* fluttering (of wings or fins); palpitation (of heart).

aleto, halieto, *m.* (ornith.) sea eagle; (Peru) falcon.

aletón, *m. aug.* large wing.

aletría, *f.* vermicelli.

aleudarse, leudarse, *vr.* to become fermented.

aleve, *a.* treacherous, perfidious.

alevilla, *a.* (entom.) white moth resembling the silkworm's moth.

alevosa, *f.* (vet.) tumor under the tongue.

alevosamente, *adv.* treacherously.

alevosia, *f.* perfidy, treachery.

alevoso, sa, *a.* treacherous.

alexifármaco, ca, *a.* (med.) alexipharmic, antidotal, prophylactic.

alfa, *f.* alpha (Greek letter); beginning.

alfábega, *f.* = ALBAHACA, (bot.) sweet basil.

alfabéticamente, *adv.* alphabetically.

alfabético, ca, *a.* alphabetical.

alfabeto, *m.* alphabet.

alfaguara, *f.* copious stream.

alfajía, *f.* wood frame for windows and doors.

alfajor, *m.* = ALAJÚ, nut and honey confection.

alfalfa, *f.* (bot.) lucern, alfalfa.—**alfalfal, alfalfar,** *m.* alfalfa field.—**alfalfe,** *m.* = ALFALFA.

alfana, *f.* strong and spirited horse.

alfandoque, *m.* candy made with molasses, cheese and ginger, or of thickened brown-sugar syrup.

alfaneque, *m.* white eagle; tent, booth.

alfanjado, da, *a.* cutlass-shaped.

alfanje, *m.* hanger, cutlass.—**alfanjete,** *m. dim.* small cutlass.—**alfanjazo,** *m.* wound with a cutlass.—**alfanjón,** *m. aug.* large hanger or cutlass.—**alfanjonazo,** *m.* cut with a large hanger.

alfaque, *m.* shoal or bar.

alfaquí, *m.* alfaqui, a Mussulman expounder and teacher of the Koran.

¹alfar, *m.* pottery; ARCILLA, clay.

²alfar, *vn.* (of horses), to raise the head too much.

³alfar, *a.* (of a horse), that raises the head too much.

alfaraz, *m.* Moorish horse for light cavalry.

¹alfarda, *f.* tax paid for land irrigation.

²alfarda, *f.* (arch.) light wooden beam.

alfardero, *m.* (prov.) collector of irrigation taxes.

¹alfardilla, *f.* tax for cleaning water-supply ditches.

²alfardilla, *f.* galloon; gold or silver braid.

¹alfardón, *m.* washer of a wheel.

²alfardón, *m.* = ¹ALFARDA.

alfarería, *f.* pottery; potter's art, workshop or store.

alfarero, ra, *n.* potter.

¹alfarje, *m.* lower stone of an oil mill.

²alfarje, *m.* ceiling with carved wood; wainscot.

alfarjía, *f.* = ALFAJÍA.

alféizar, *m.* (arch.) splay of a door or window; embrasure.

alfeñicado, da, *a.* weakly, delicate.

alfeñicar, *va.* to frost with sugar.

alfeñicarse, *vr.* to become thin; (coll.) to affect delicateness.

alfeñique, *m.* sugar paste; (coll.) delicate person.

alferazgo, *m.* second lieutenancy.

alferecía, *f.* epilepsy.

alférez, *m.* ensign; second lieutenant.

alficoz, alpicoz, *m.* cucumber (plant & fruit).

alfil, *m.* bishop (in chess).

alfiler, *m.* pin; scarf-pin; brooch; tip, gift.—*pl.* **alfileres,** pin money.—**a. de París,** wire nail.— **a. de seguridad,** safety pin (more generally called IMPERDIBLE).—**con todos sus alfileres,** or, **de veinticinco alfileres,** dressed up in high style.—**no estar con sus alfileres,** not to be in a good mood.—**pedir para alfileres,** to ask for a tip.—**pegar,** or **prender, con alfileres,** to do in a slipshod way; (fig.) to build on sand.

alfilerazo, *m.* prick with a pin; large pin.

alfilerera, *f.* alfilaria, seed of the geranium.

alfilerero, ra, *n.* maker or seller of pins.

alfiletero, *m.* pin case, needlecase; pincushion.

alfitete, *m.* paste made of coarse wheat flour.

alfolí, *m.* granary; salt depot.—**alfoliero, alfolinero,** *m.* keeper of a granary or depot.

¹alfombra, *f.* = ²ALFOMBRILLA.

²alfombra, *f.* floor carpet.

alfombrar, *va.* to carpet.

alfombrero, ra, *n.* carpet maker.

¹alfombrilla, *f.* small carpet, rug.

²alfombrilla, *f.* (med.) measles.

alfóncigo, *m.* pistachio; pistachio tree.

alfonsearse, *vr.* (coll.) to mock, banter.

alfónsigo, *m.* = ALFÓNCIGO.

alfonsina, *f.* solemn act held in the Alphonsine college of Alcalá.

alfonsino, na, *a.* pertaining to the Alphonsos (Spanish kings).

alforfón, *m.* buckwheat.

alforja, *f.* saddlebag; knapsack.

alforjero, *m.* maker or seller of saddlebags; lay brother who begs alms; one who carries the bag with provisions.—**perro a.,** watchdog.

alforjilla, ita, uela, *f. dim.* small saddlebag; small knapsack.

alforza, *f.* plait, tuck; (coll.) scar.

alfoz, *m.* & *f.* district, borough, neighboring district or dependency.

alga, *f.* (bot.) alga, seaweed.

algadonera, *f.* (bot.) cudweed.

¹algaida, *f.* ridge of shifting sand; sand dune.

²algaida, *f.* jungle, brush.

¹algaído, da, *a.* (prov.) thatched.

¹algalia, *f.* civet, substance used in perfume; *m.* civet cat.—**algaliar,** *va.* to perfume with civet.

²algalia, *f.* (surg.) catheter.

¹algara, *f.* skin (of an egg, onion, etc.)

²algara, *f.* foraging party of cavalry.

algarabía, *f.* Arabic (language); (fig.) gabble, jargon; din, clamor; (bot.) centaury.

¹algarada, *f.* loud cry, din; ²ALGARA.

²algarada, *f.* (mil.) ancient catapult.

algarero, ra, *a.* prating, chattering, talkative.

¹algarrada, *f.* driving bulls into the pen; bull baiting.

²algarrada, *f.* = ²ALGARADA.

algarroba, *f.* (bot.) carob bean; honey mesquite.

algarrobal, *m.* carob tree plantation or grove.

algarrobera, *f.,* **algarrobo,** *m.* (bot.) carob tree.

algazara, *f.* huzza; din, clamor.

algazul, *m.* seaweed producing barilla.

álgebra, *f.* algebra; (anc. surg.) art of setting joints.

algebraico, ca; algébrico, ca, *a.* algebraic.

algebrista, *m.* algebraist; (anc. surg.) bonesetter.

algecireño, ña, *n.* & *a.* Algecirian, from, or pertaining to, Algeciras.

algidez, *f.* (med.) icy coldness.

álgido, da, *a.* algid, icy.

algo. I. *n.* some, something, aught.—**a. de nuevo,** something new.—**a. es a.,** or, **más vale algo que nada,** something is better than nothing, every little bit counts. **II.** *adv.* somewhat, a little, rather.

algodón, *m.* cotton (substance, cloth, thread); cotton plant.—**a. en rama,** raw cotton.—**a. pólvora, pólvora de a.,** guncotton.—*pl.* CENDALES, cotton put in bottom of inkwells.

algodonado, da, *a.* filled with cotton.

algodonal, *m.* cotton plantation.

algodonar, *va.* to cover or fill with cotton.

algodonería, *f.* cotton factory; cotton trade.

algodonero, ra. I. *a.* pertaining to cotton. **II.** *m.* cotton plant; cotton dealer; cottonwood poplar.

algodonoso, sa, *a.* cottony; covered with thick down; woolly; (of fruit) tasteless.

algonquín, na, *n.* & *a.* Algonquin.

algorín, *m.* place in oil mills for receiving olives.

algoritmo, *m.* algorithm; algorism; arithmetical or algebraic computation.

algoso, sa, *a.* full of algæ.

alguacil, *m.* constable, peace officer, bumbailiff; short-legged spider.

alguacilazgo, *m.* office of an *alguacil.*

alguarín, *m.* storeroom; flour-mill bucket.

alguaza, *f.* (prov.) hinge.

alguien, *pron.* somebody, someone.

algún, *a. contr.* of ALGUNO.—**a. tanto,** a little, somewhat.

alguno, a. I. *a.* (**algún,** before *m. n.*) some, any. —**a. que otro,** a few, some.—**alguna que otra vez,** sometimes, once in a while.—**a. vez,** sometime; sometimes, now and then. **II.** *n.* somebody, someone.—*pl.* some, some people.

alhábega, *f.* (prov.) = ALBAHACA, sweet basil.

alhadida, *f.* (chem.) saffron or burnt copper.

alhaja, *f.* jewel, gem; showy furniture; highly prized thing; an excellent person; (ironic) a bad one, a tough one (of persons, often in the form, ¡buena a.!).

alhajar, *va.* to adorn; to furnish, fit up.

alhajuela, *f. dim.* little jewel.

alhamel, *m.* (prov.) beast of burden; porter; muleteer.

alhandal, *m.* (pharm.) colocynth, plant with purgative properties.

alharaca, *f.* clamor, fuss, ado.

alharaquiento, ta, *a.* fussy, grumbling.

alhárgama, alharma, *f.* (bot.) wild rue.

alhasa, *f.* hydroa, a skin disease.

alhelí, alelí, *m.* (bot.) gilliflower.

alheña, *f.* (bot.) privet; powder from privet leaves used in dyeing; rust, mildew, blight (on corn).—**alheñar. I.** *va.* to dye with privet. **II.** *vr.* to become mildewed (app. to corn.)

alhoja, *f.* a bird resembling a lark.

alholva, *f.* (bot.) fenugreek, plant used for forage.

alhóndiga, *f.* public granary; wheat exchange.— **alhondiguero,** *m.* keeper of a public granary.

alhorma, *f.* Moorish camp or royal tent.

alhorre, *m.* (med.) meconium, first discharge from infant's bowels; skin eruption (on baby).

alhoz, *m.* = ALFOZ.

alhucema, *f.* (bot.) lavender.

alhumajo, *m.* pine needles.

aliabierto, ta, *a.* open-winged.

aliacán, *m.* (med.) jaundice.

aliacanado, da, *a.* jaundiced.

aliáceo, a, *a.* pertaining to or like garlic.

aliado, da. I. *pp.* of ALIARSE. **II.** *a.* & *n.* ally, allied.

aliaga, aulaga, *f.* (bot.) furze, whin.—**aliagar, aulagar,** *m.* furze field.

alianza, *f.* alliance; agreement, pact; (Bib.) covenant; alliance by marriage.

aliara, *f.* drinking horn.

aliaria, *f.* (bot.) garlic mustard.

aliarse, *vr.* to become allied; to form an alliance.

alias, *adv.* (Lat.) otherwise, alias.

alible, *a.* nutritive, nourishing.

alica, ta, *f. dim.* small wing.

álica, *f.* porridge of corn, wheat, and pulse.

alicaído, da, *a.* drooping, weak, extenuated; discouraged, depressed, downhearted.

alicántara, *f.,* **alicante,** *m.* a poisonous snake.

alicantina, *f.* (coll.) artifice, stratagem, trap.

alicantino, na, *n.* & *a.* (one) from Alicante.

alicatado, *m.* work inlaid with tiles in Arab style.

alicates, *m. pl.* pliers.

aliciente, *m.* attraction, inducement.

alicuanta, *a.* (math.) aliquant.

alícuota, *f. a.* (math.) aliquot; proportional.— **partes alícuotas,** (arith.) aliquot parts.

alidada, *f.* alidade, surveyor's telescope.

aliebro, aliebre, *v. V.* ALEBRARSE.

alienación, *f.* (law and med.) alienation.

alienado, da, *a.* insane.

alienar, *va.* (law) to alienate (property); to estrange; to numb.

alienista, *n.* alienist.

¹aliento, *m.* breath; breathing; vigor; bravery; enterprise, activity.—**dar a.,** to encourage; to further; to cheer.—**de un a.,** in a single breath; without stopping.—**sin a.,** out of breath.

²aliento, aliente, *v. V.* ALENTAR

alier, *m.* (naut.) rower; sailor on watch.

¹alifafe, *m.* callous tumor on a horse's hock.

²alifafe, *m.* (coll.) chronic complaint.

alifar, *va.* (prov.) to polish, burnish.

alifara, *f.* (prov.) collation, luncheon.

alífero, ra, *a.* having wings, winged.

aliforme, *a.* aliform, wing-shaped.

aligación, *f.* binding together; (math.) alligation.

aligamiento, *m.* = ALIGACIÓN.

aligar, *va.* (*pret.* ALIGUÉ; *subj.* ALIGUE) = LIGAR, to bind, join.

aliger, *m.* cross guard (of a sword).

aligeramiento, *m.* alleviation, lightening.

aligerar, *va.* to lighten; to alleviate; to ease; to hasten, hurry (up); to shorten.

alígero, ra, *a.* (poet.) winged, fast, fleet.

aligue, aligüe, *v. V.* ALIGAR.

alijador, ra, *n.* smuggler; (naut.) one who lightens (ship's cargo); (naut.) lighter; one who clears cotton of seeds.

¹alijar, *va.* (naut.) to lighten (cargo); to clear (cotton) of seeds, to gin; to smuggle.

²alijar, *m.* waste, stony ground.—**alijarar,** *va.* to divide (waste lands) for cultivation.

alijarero, *m.* sharer of waste lands to till.

alijares, *m. pl.* royal pleasure resort in Granada.

alijariego, ga, *a.* pertaining to waste lands.

alijo, *m.* (naut.) lightening of a ship's cargo; ginning (cotton); smuggling or smuggled goods.

alilla, *f. dim.* small wing; fin of a fish.

alimaña, *f.* animal (gen. destructive ones).

alimentación, *f.* feeding; meals, board; nutrition.—**de a.,** feeding, feed (as *a.,* as in *agua de alimentación,* feed water).

alimentar, *va.* to feed, nourish; to feed (a machine); to support, supply with the necessaries of life; to nurture, fondle, encourage, further; to cherish, have (hope).

alimentario, ria, *n.* one who enjoys a maintenance.

alimenticio, cia, *a.* nourishing; feeding, food (as *a.*).

alimentista, *n.* = ALIMENTARIO.

alimento, *m.* nourishment, food, nutriment; anything furnished to keep something going, as a fire; encouragement, incentive.—*pl.* allowance, pension, alimony; meals, board.—**a. combustible,** (of foods) carbohydrate or fat.— **a. plástico,** protein, nitrogenous food.—**a. respiratorio** = A. COMBUSTIBLE.

alimentoso, sa, *a.* nourishing, nutritious.

alimo, *m.* (bot.) = ORZAGA, mountain spinach.

alimoche, *m.* a bird of prey, a kind of vulture.

alimonarse, *vr.* to turn yellowish from disease (said of tree leaves).

alindado, da, *a.* affectedly nice or elegant.

¹alindar, *va.* to mark the limits of.

²alindar, *va.* to embellish, make beautiful.

alinde, *m.* (obs.) quicksilver for mirrors.

alineación, *f.* alinement.
alinear. I. *va.* to aline. **II.** *vr.* to aline itself; to fall in line; to form a line.
aliñador, ra, *n.* one who embellishes; one who seasons or dresses food.
aliñar, *va.* to adorn; to dress or season (food).
aliño, *m.* ornament, decoration; cleanliness; dressing or seasoning.—**aliñoso, sa,** *a.* dressed up, decked out; decorated.
alioli, *m.* (prov.) mixture of garlic and oil.
alionín, *m.* (ornith.) the blue-feathered duck.
alipata, *m.* a Philippine poison tree.
alípede, *a.* (poet.) winged, swift, nimble.
alípedo, da, *a.* (zool.) aliped, with toes connected by winglike skin.
aliquebrado, da, *a.* broken-winged; dejected.
alisador, ra, *n.* polisher, smoothing iron; silk stick; tool to shape wax candles.
alisadura, *f.* planing, smoothing, polishing.
alisaduras, *f. pl.* shavings, cuttings.
¹alisar, *va.* to plane, smooth, polish, burnish.
²alisar, *m.* **aliseda,** *f.* alder-tree plantation.
alisios, *m. pl.* trade winds.
alisma, *f.* (bot.) water plantain.
aliso, *m.* (bot.) alder tree.
alistado, da, listado, da, *a.* listed; enlisted.
alistador, ra, *n.* one who enrolls or lists.
alistamiento, *m.* enrollment; conscription, levy.
¹alistar, *va. & vr.* to enlist, enroll.
²alistar, *va.* to get or make ready.
aliteración, *f.* alliteration.
aliviadero, *m.* (eng.) relief, outlet; spillway.
aliviador, ra, *n.* assistant; helper; spindle to raise or lower a running millstone.
aliviar, *va.* to lighten; to loosen; to alleviate, assuage, soothe, relieve; to hasten, speed up.
alivio, *m.* alleviation, easement; mitigation; relief; improvement, betterment.
alizace, *m.* trench for foundation of a building.
alizar, *m.* dado or wainscoting of tiles.
aljaba, *f.* quiver (for arrows).
aljafana, *f.* = ALJOFAINA.
aljama, *f.* assembly of Moors or Jews; synagogue.
aljamía, *f.* (obs.) corrupted Arabic spoken by Moors; Moorish name of the Spanish language.
aljarafe, *m.* roof; terrace.
aljarfa, *f.,* **aljarfe,** *m.,* **aljerife,** *m.* tarred fishing net with small meshes.
aljévena, *f.* (prov.) = ALJOFAINA.
aljez, *m.* gypsum; plaster of Paris.—**aljezar,** *m.* gypsum pit.—**aljezón,** *m.* plaster rubbish; ALJEZ.
aljibe, *m.* cistern; reservoir, pool; (naut.) tank boat for supplying vessels with water.
aljibero, *m.* one who takes care of cisterns.
aljimierado, *a.* shaved, trimmed.
aljofaina, jofaina, *f.* washbowl, basin.
aljófar, *m.* misshapen pearl; (poet.) **water or** dewdrops.
aljofarado, da. I. *pp.* of ALJOFARAR. **II.** *a.* (poet.) full of little drops or pearls.
aljofarar, *va.* to adorn with pearls.
aljofifa, *f.* mop.—**aljofifar,** *va.* to clean with a cloth; to mop.
aljonje, *m.* = AJONJE, bird lime.
aljonjera, *f.* **aljonjero,** *m.* = AJONJERA, (bot.) a kind of thistle.
aljonjolí, *m.* = AJONJOLÍ, (bot.) sesame.
aljor, *m.* crude gypsum.
aljorozar, *va.* to level, render smooth; to plaster.
aljorra, *m.* (Cuba) a very small insect which, carried by the wind, destroys plantations.
aljuba, *f.* a Moorish garment.
alma, *f.* soul; ghost; phantom; human being; vigor, strength; substance, main point; staff; (arch.) scaffolding pole; web (of a beam, rail, etc.) (gun) bore; core (of rope, of a casting); (naut.) body of a mast; sounding-post in a fiddle, etc.—**a. atravesada, de Caín, or de Judas,** devilish or heartless person.—**a. de**

cántaro, fool.—**a. de Dios,** harmless, inoffensive person; simple, kind-hearted person.—**a. en pena,** soul in purgatory.—**a. mía, mi a.,** my dearest; my love.—**a., vida y corazón,** heart and soul.—**con toda el a.,** with all one's heart and soul.—**dar, entregar, exhalar, or rendir, el a.,** to give up the ghost, die.—**del a., de mi a.,** dearest.—**en el a.,** keenly, deeply; with all one's heart.—**tener el a. bien puesta,** to have courage and energy.
almacén, *m.* store, shop; warehouse; storage house, depot; (Arg. & Cuba) grocery store; naval arsenal, dockyard.—**a. de agua,** (naut.) water cask.—**a. de una bomba de agua,** (naut.) chamber of a pump.—**almacenado, da,** *a.* stored, bonded.—**almacenador,** *m.* warehouseman.—**almacenaje,** *m.* storage.—**almacenar,** *va.* to lay up, hoard; to store.—**almacenero,** *m.* shopkeeper.—**almacenista,** *m.* shop owner; salesman; (Cuba) wholesale grocer.
¹almáciga, *f.* mastic; resin from certain trees.
²almáciga, *f.* tree nursery.
almacigado, da, *a.* perfumed with mastic.
almacigar, *va.* to perfume with mastic.
¹almácigo, *m.* mastic tree.
²almácigo, *m.* = ²ALMÁCIGA.
almaciguero, ra, *a.* pertaining to mastic.
almádana, almadaneta, *f.* sledge-hammer.
almadén, *m.* (anc.) mine.
almádena, *f.* = ALMÁDANA.
almadía, *f.* canoe used in India; raft.
almadiero, *m.* a raft pilot.
almadraba, *f.* tunny fishing or fishery; tunny-fish net.—**almadrabero, ra,** *n.* tunny fisher.
almadreña, *f.* wooden shoe or sabot.
almaganeta, *f.* = ALMÁDANA.
almagesto, *m.* Almagest, anc. book on astronomy.
almagra, *f.* = ALMAGRE.
almagral, *m.* place abounding in ochre.
almagrar, *va.* to color with red ochre; (vulg.) to draw blood.
almagre, *m.* red ochre, red earth, Indian red.
almaizal, almaizar, *m.* gauze veil worn by Moors; sash worn by priests.
almajaneque, *m.* (mil.) battering ram.
almajara, *f.* (prov.) forcing bed, hotbed.
almajo, *m.* (bot.) plant yielding barilla.
almaleque, *f.* long robe worn by Moors.
almanac, almanaque, *m.* almanac, calendar.—**hacer almanaques,** (fig.) to muse, be pensive.
almanaquero, ra, *n.* maker or vender of almanacs.
almancebe, *m.* fishing net.
almandina, *f.* (min.) red garnet; almandine.
almanguena, *f.* = ALMAGRE.
almanta, *f.* space between rows of vines and olive trees; ridge between two furrows.
almarada, *f.* triangular poniard; needle for making rope sandals.
almarcha, *f.* town on marshy ground or lowland.
¹almarjal, *m.* glasswort field.
²almarjal, marjal, *m.* marshy ground.
almarjo, *m.* (bot.) glasswort.
almaro, *m.* (bot.) common clary.
almarrá, *m.* cotton gin.
almarraja, almarraza, *f.* perforated glass bottle used for sprinkling or watering.
¹almártaga, almártega, *f.* (chem.) massicot; litharge.
²almártaga, almártiga, *f.* halter; (Colomb.) sluggard; good-for-nothing.
almartigón, *m.* rough halter.
almástiga, *f.* mastic.—**almastigado, da,** *a.* containing mastic.
almatrero, *m.* one fishing with shad nets.
almatriche, *m.* irrigation canal.
almazara, *f.* (prov.) oil mill.—**almazarero,** *m.* oil miller.
almazarrón, *m.* = ALMAGRE.
¹almea, *f.* Oriental poetess and dancer.

²**almea,** *f.* (bot.) dried bark of the storax tree.
almear, *m.* stack of hay, corn, or straw.
almeja, *f.* clam.—**almejar,** *m.* clam bed.
almejía, *f.* small cloak used by poor Moors.
almena, *f.* merlon of a battlement.
almenado, da. I. *pp.* of ALMENAR. **II.** *a.* having battlements. **III.** *m.* = ALMENAJE.
almenaje, *m.* series of merlons; battlement.
¹**almenar,** *va.* to crown with merlons.
²**almenar,** *m.* cresset, cuplike metal torch.
¹**almenara,** *f.* beacon; large candelabra.
²**almenara,** *f.* outlet channel for irrigation water.
almendra, *f.* almond; kernel; bean; almond-shaped diamond; cut glass drop; fine cocoon.—**a. confitada,** praline.—**a. de cacao,** cocoa bean; chocolate nut.—**a. garapiñada,** sugar almond, praline.
almendrada, *f.* almond milk.
almendrado, da. I. *a.* almondlike. **II.** *m.* macaroon.
almendral, *m.* almond-tree plantation.
almendrera, *f.* = ALMENDRO.
almendrero, *m.* dish for almonds; ALMENDRO.
almendrilla, *f.* almond-shaped file.—**almendrillas,** almond-shaped diamond earrings.
almendro, *m.* almond tree.
almendrón, *m.* Jamaican myrtle tree and its fruit.
almendruco, *m.* green almond.
almenilla, *f. dim.* small merlon; merlon-shaped fringe.
almete, *m.* helmet; soldier wearing a helmet.
almez, *m.* lotus tree.—**almeza,** *f.* fruit of the lotus tree.—**almezo,** *m.* = ALMEZ.
almiar, *m.* haystack.
almíbar, *m.* sugar sirup.—**almíbares,** preserved fruit.
almibarado, da. I. *pp.* of ALMIBARAR. **II.** *a.* (fig.) honeyed (language); sweet (person); endearing.
almibarar, *va.* to preserve (fruit) in sugar; (fig.) to conciliate with soft words.
almicantarada, *f.,* **almicantarat,** *f.* (astr.) almucantar, small circle parallel to the horizon to determine the height of stars.
almidón, *m.* starch; fecula.
almidonado, da. I. *pp.* of ALMIDONAR. **II.** *a.* starched; (fig.) dressed with affected nicety; spruce; stiff.
almidonar, *va.* to starch.
almidonería, *f.* starch factory.
almiforero, ra, *n.* horse thief.
almijara, *f.* oil tank (in the Almadén mines).
almijarero, *m.* keeper of oil tanks.
almilla, *f.* under waistcoat; short military jacket; (carp.) tenon; breast of pork.
almimbar, *m.* pulpit of a mosque.
alminar, *m.* minaret, turret of a mosque.
almiranta, *f.* (naut.) vice admiral's ship, flagship; admiral's wife.
almirantazgo, *m.* (naut.) board of admiralty; admiralty court; admiral's dues; admiralship.
almirante, *m.* admiral, commander of a fleet; head ornament for women; swimming master; a kind of shell.
almirez, *m.* brass mortar; wood engraver's tool.
almirón, *m.* wild chicory.
almizclar, *va.* to perfume with musk.
almizcle, *m.* musk.—**almizcleña,** *f.* (bot.) musk, grape hyacinth.—**almizcleño, ña,** *a.* musky.
almizclero, ra. I. *a.* musky. **II.** *m.* muskdeer. **III.** *f.* muskrat.
almo, ma, *a.* (poet.) creating; animating, fostering (*cf.* alma mater); venerable.
almocadén, *m.* (anc.) infantry commander; cavalry officer commanding part of a platoon; delegated mayor of part of a city (in Morocco).
almocafrar, *va.* (garden.) to dibble.
almocafre, *m.* gardener's hoe, dibble.

almocárabes, almocarbes, *m. pl.* (arch. and carp.) bow-shaped ornaments.
almocatracía, *f.* duty on broadcloths and woollens.
almoceda, *f.* tax on water for irrigation; right of irrigation upon fixed days.
almocela, *f.* ancient hood.
almocrate, *m.* sal ammoniac.
almocrí, *m.* reader of the Koran in a mosque.
almodí, *m.* = ALMUDÍ, a dry measure.
almodón, *m.* baking flour.
almodrote, *m.* sauce for eggplant; hodgepodge.
almófar, *m.* mail head cover under helmet.
almofía, *f.* = ALJOFAINA, washbowl, basin.
almofrej, almofrez, *m.* travelling bag for bedding.
almogama, *f.* (naut.) sternpost of a ship.
almogávar, *m.* soldier of raiding troops sent to enemy's territory; raider.—**almogavarear,** *va.* to raid.—**almogavaría, almogavería,** *f.* body of raiding troops.
almohada, *f.* pillow; bolster; pillowcase; (naut.) piece of timber on which the bowsprit rests.—**aconsejarse, or consultar, con la a.,** (coll.) to sleep on the matter, think it over carefully.—**dar a.,** to raise to the nobility (a ceremony in which the queen raises a lady to nobility by having her sit beside her on a cushion).
almohadilla, *f. dim.* small bolster or pillow; sewing cushion; pads of a harness; (arch.) projecting wall stone; (vet.) callous excrescence on the back of mules.
almohadillado, da, *a.* quilted; (arch.) with projecting wall stones.
almohadón, *m. aug.* large cushion or pillow.
almohatre, *m.* = ALMOCRATE, sal ammoniac.
almohaza, *f.* currycomb.
almohazador, *m.* groom.
almohazar, *va.* to curry with a currycomb.
almojábana, *f.* cake made of cheese and flour; cruller.
almojarifadgo, almojarifalgo, almojarifazgo, *m.* ancient duty on imports or exports.
almojarife, *m.* the king's taxgatherer; custom house officer.
almojatre, *m.* = ALMOHATRE.
almojaya, *f.* (build.) putlog.
almona, *f.* public stores; shad fishery; soap manufactory.
almóndiga, almondiguilla, *f.* = ALBÓNDIGA, etc., ball of forcemeat with eggs and spice.
almoneda, *f.* auction.—**almonedear,** *va.* to auction.
almoradux, *m.* (bot.) sweet marjoram.
almorávide, *n. & a.* Almoravide (name of an ancient Moorish tribe).
almorcé, *pret.* of ALMORZAR.
almorejo, *m.* (bot.) a species of grass.
almorí, almurí, *m.* sweetmeat or cake.
almoronía, *f.* = ALBORONÍA, eggplant, tomato dish.
almorranas, *f. pl.* (med.) piles, hemorrhoids.
almorraniento, ta, *a.* suffering from piles.
almorrefa, *f.* triangular tile.
almorta, *f.* (bot.) blue vetch.
¹**almorzada,** *f.* as much as can be held in the hollow of both hands.
²**almorzada,** *f.* (Mex.) = ²ALMUERZO.
almorzado, da. I. *pp.* of ALMORZAR. **II.** *a.* having already breakfasted.
almorzar. I. *vn.* (*ind. pres.* ALMUERZO, *pret.* ALMORCÉ; *subj.* ALMUERCE) to breakfast; (more often) to lunch. **II.** *va.* to eat (at or for breakfast or lunch).
almotacén, *m.* inspector of weights and measures; inspector's office or function.
almotacenazgo, *m.* office of ALMOTACÉN.
almotacenía, *f.* fee paid to ALMOTACÉN.
almozárabe, *m.* Christian subject to the Moors.

almud, *m.* a dry measure, about 0.8 of a liter.—**a. de tierra,** about ½ acre.—**almudada,** *f.* ground sufficient for one *almud* of seed.—**almudejo,** *m.* each of the weights kept by the *almudero.*—**almudero,** *m.* keeper of dry measures.

almudí, almudín, *m.* (prov.) measure containing six *cahices.*

almuecín, almuédano, *m.* muezzin.

almuérdago, *m.* birdlime.

almuertas, *f. pl.* tax on cereals sold.

almuerza, *f.* = ¹ALMORZADA.

¹almuerzo, almuerce, *v. V.* ALMORZAR.

²almuerzo, *m.* breakfast; (more often) lunch; breakfast cover.

almunia, *f.* orchard; vegetable garden.

almurí, *m.* = ALMORÍ.

almutazafe, *m.* (prov.) = ALMOTACÉN.

alnabi, *m.* Moorish prophet.

alnado, da, *n.* = HIJASTRO, stepchild.

alo, *m.* (Mex.) a large cockatoo.

aloaria, *f.* (arch.) vault.

alobadado, da, *a.* bitten by a wolf; (vet.) laboring under morbid swellings.

alóbroge, *a.* Allobrogic.—**alóbroges,** *m. pl.* Allobroges, inhabitants of an ancient town in Gaul.

alobunado, da, *a.* wolf-colored.

alocadamente, *adv.* rashly, recklessly.

alocado, da, *a.* half-witted; wild, reckless.

alocroísmo, *m.* property of being allochroic, changeable in color.

alocroíta, *m.* (min.) allochroite, iron-garnet.

alocución, *f.* allocution, address, speech.

alodial, *a.* (law) allodial.—**alodio,** *m.* alodium.

áloe, *m.* (bot.) aloe tree, aloes.—**aloético, ca,** *a.* aloetic.—**aloína,** *f.* aloin, active principle of aloes.

alogamia, *f.* allogamy, cross fertilization in plants.

aloja, *f.* mead, drink made with honey and spices.

alojamiento, *m.* lodging; quartering of soldiers; (naut.) steerage.—*pl.* (mil.) camp, quarters.

alojar. I. *va.* to lodge; to quarter (troops). **II.** *vr.* to take lodgings; to lodge; to dwell; to go (into), be contained or work (in).

alojería, *f.* mead shop.

alojero, ra, *n.* mead mixer and seller; *m.* (theat.) box near the pit.

alomado, da, *a.* (of animals) having a curved back.

alomar. I. *va.* to distribute equally (the load on a horse); to plow in furrows. **II.** *vr.* (of horses) to become strong and vigorous.

alón, *m.* plucked wing of any fowl.

alondra, *f.* (ornith.) lark.

alongadero, *a.* dilatory.

alongamiento, *m.* delay; distance (separating points or things).

alongar, *va.* (*ind.* ALUENGO; *subj.* ALUENGUE) to enlarge; to extend; to prolong; to separate.

alópata, *m.* allopath.—**alopatía,** *f.* allopathy.—**alopático, ca,** *a.* allopathic.

alopecia, *f.* (med.) alopecia, baldness.

alopiado, da, *a.* opiate.

aloque, *a.* clear white or red and white (wine).

aloquín, *m.* stone inclosure in a wax bleachery.

alosa, *f.* (ichth.) = SÁBALO, shad.

alosna, *f.* (bot., prov.) wormwood.

alotar, *va.* (naut.) ARRIZAR, to reef, stow, lash.—**a. las anclas,** (naut.) to stow the anchors.

alotropia, *f.* (chem.) allotropy.

alotrópico, ca, *a.* (chem.) allotropic.

¹alpaca, alpaga, *f.* alpaca (animal and fabric).

²alpaca, *f.* German silver.

alpañata, *f.* piece of chamois skin.

alpargata, *f.,* **alpargate,** *m.* fiber sandal.

alpargatado, da, *a.* wearing *alpargatas.*

alpargatar, *vn.* to make *alpargatas.*

alpargatería, *f.* *alpargata* shop or factory.

alpargatero, ra, *n.* maker or seller of *alpargatas.*

alpargatilla, *f. dim.* small *alpargata;* crafty, designing fellow.

alpechín, *m.* juice oozing from a heap of olives.

alpende, *m.* tool shed (esp. in mines).

alpestre, *a.* Alpine.

alpícola, *a.* growing in the Alps.

alpicoz, *m.* (prov.) = ALFICOZ, cucumber.

alpinismo, *m.* mountain climbing, Alpinism.

alpinista, *n.* mountain climber, Alpinist.

alpino, na, *a.* Alpine.

alpiste, *m.* birdseed.—**dejar a uno a.,** (coll.) to leave one out (of a business, etc.).—**quedarse a.,** (coll.) to be disappointed or to get left.—**alpistela, alpistera,** *f.* cake made of flour, eggs, sesame, and honey.—**alpistero,** *m.* sieve for canary seed.

alquequenje, *m.* Barbadoes winter cherry, used as a diuretic.

alquería, *f.* farmhouse.

alquermes, *m.* kermes, a cordial; (pharm.) medicinal sirup.

alquerque, *m.* place in oil mills for olives after the first pressing.

alquez, *m.* wine measure containing twelve *cántaras.*

alquibla, *f.* point toward which Mohammedans look when praying.

alquicel, alquicer, *m.* Moorish cloak; cover for benches, tables, etc.

alquifol, *m.* (min.) alquifou, potter's ore.

alquiladizo, za, *a.* that can be let or hired.

alquilador, ra, *n.* hirer.

alquilamiento, *m.* hiring or letting.

alquilar. I. *va.* to let, rent; to hire; to fee. **II.** *vr.* to serve for wages; to hire out.

alquilate, *m.* sales tax in Murcia.

alquiler, *m.* wages; rent, rental; the act of hiring or letting.—**de a.,** for hire, for rent; that may be hired or rented.

alquilón, na, *a.* (of person, disparaging) that can be hired.

alquilona, *f.* charwoman.

alquimia, *f.* alchemy.

alquímico, ca, *a.* alchemistic.

alquimila, *f.* (bot.) ladies' mantle.

alquimista, *m.* alchemist.

alquinal, *m.* veil or headdress for women.

alquitara, *f.* = ALAMBIQUE, a still.

alquitarar, *va.* to distil.

alquitira, *f.* (bot.) tragacanth.

alquitrán, *m.* tar, pitch; (naut.) stuff made of pitch, grease, etc.—**a. mineral,** coal tar.

alquitranado, *m.* (naut.) tarpaulin, tarred cloth.

alquitranar, *va.* to tar.

alrededor, *adv.* around.—**a. de,** about, around, (coll.) approximately.—**alrededores,** *m. pl.* environs.

alrota, arlota, *f.* coarse tow.

alsaciano, na, *n. & a.* Alsatian.

álsine, *m.* (bot.) scorpion grass.

alta, *f.* a kind of court dance; dancing exercise; fencing bout; certificate of discharge from a hospital, as being cured; (mil.) record or statement of the entrance of a man into active service; the man so entering.—**dar de a.,** to enroll (in the army); to discharge as cured, or declare fit.—**darse de a.,** to be admitted (in a profession, etc.), to join, become a member.

altabaque, tabaque, *m.* needlework basket.

altabaquillo, *m.* (bot.) small bindweed.

altamente, *adv.* highly, exceedingly; (fig.) in a distinguished manner.

altanería, *f.* haughtiness, loftiness, insolence; hunting with hawks.

altanero, ra, *a.* soaring, towering; haughty, arrogant, insolent.

altar, *m.* altar; the church; bridge (in a furnace, etc.).—**a. mayor,** high altar.—**el A.,** (astr.) the Altar, Ara.

altarero, ra, *n.* altar maker or dresser.

altarreina, *f.* (bot.) milfoil, yarrow.

altavoz, *m.* (radio) loudspeaker.

altea, *f.* (bot.) marsh mallow.

altearse, *vr.* (of land) to rise above the surrounding land.

alterabilidad, *f.* alterability.

alterable, *a.* changeable, alterable.

alteración, *f.* alteration; unevenness of the pulse; strong emotion; tumult, commotion.

alterado, da. I. *pp.* of ALTERAR. **II.** *a.* disturbed, agitated.

**alterador, ra,] ** *n.* & *a.* alterer(-ing), disturber (-ing).

alterante, *a.* (med.) alterative.

alterar. I. *va.* to alter, change, transform; to disturb, stir up. **II.** *vr.* to become altered, disturbed, agitated; to become angry.

alterativo, va, *a.* alterative.

altercación, *f.*, **altercado,** *m.* altercation, controversy, quarrel, wrangle.

altercador, ra, *n.* arguer, wrangler, quarreler.

altercar, *va.* to dispute obstinately; to quarrel, bicker, wrangle.

álter ego, alter ego, second self.

alternación, *f.* alternation.

alternadamente, *adv.* = ALTERNATIVAMENTE.

alternador, *m.* (elec.) alternator.

alternar, *va., vn.* & *vr.* to alternate.

alternativa, *f.* alternative; service by turn.

alternativamente, *adv.* alternatively.

alternativo, va, *a.* alternate, alternating.

alterno, na, *a.* = ALTERNATIVO.—**corriente alterna,** (elec.) alternating current.

alteza, *f.* elevation, sublimity, highness, height; (A-) Highness (title).

altibajo, *m.* embossed velvet; downright blow in fencing.—*pl.* uneven ground; ups and downs.

altillo, lla. I. *a. dim.* rather high. **II.** *m.* hillock.

altilocuencia, *f.* grandiloquence.

altilocuente (poet.), **altílocuo, cua,** *a.* grandiloquent.

altimetría, *f.* altimetry; leveling.

altímetro, tra. I. *a.* pertaining to altimetry. **II.** *m.* altimeter, altitude indicator.

altiplanicie, *f.*, **altiplano,** *m.* plateau, tableland.

altísimo, ma. I. *a. aug.* exceedingly high, most high. **II.** *m.* (A-), Most High.

altisonante, altísono, na, *a.* high-sounding.

altitonante, *a.* (poet.) thundering.

altitud, *f.* altitude, elevation.

altivamente, *adv.* loftily, haughtily.

altivarse, *vr.* to put on airs.

altivez, altiveza, *f.* haughtiness, arrogance, insolence; pride.

altivo, va, *a.* haughty, proud, lofty; high-handed; overbearing, arrogant.

¹alto, ta. I. *a.* (of a building, hill, price, etc.) high; elevated; tall; arduous, difficult; eminent; enormous; deep.—**a a bajo, (de)** downward; from the top down; from top to bottom.—**a. horno,** blast furnace.—**alta mar,** (naut.) high seas.—**a. relieve,** high relief.—**altas horas,** late hours.—**de a. bordo,** large seagoing (vessel).—**de lo a.,** from above.—**en a.,** up high. **II.** *m.* height, elevation; hill; top; story, floor; (naut.) depth or height of a ship; summit, mountain top, crest; top floor; heap, pile.—**pasar por a.,** to overlook, forget.—**altos y bajos,** ups and downs, vicissitudes. **III.** *adv.* (of tone of voice) loud, high.

²alto. I. *m.* (mil.) halt; place or time of rest.—**hacer a.,** to halt. **II.** (*interj.*) (mil. command) halt!—**¡a. ahí!** halt! stop there!—**¡a. de aquí!** move off!

altoparlante, *m.* (radio) loudspeaker.

altozano, *m.* hillock, knoll; height; paved terrace or platform in front of a building (gen. a church).

altramuz, *m.* (bot.) lupine *altramuces;* black voting balls.

altruísmo, *m.* altruism.

altruísta, *n.* & *a.* altruist(-ic).

altura, *f.* height, altitude; tallness, stature; summit, top; (naut.) the latitude; (geom.) altitude (of a plane figure), height (of a solid); (astr.) altitude.—**estar a la a. de (su) tarea,** to be equal to (his) task.—*pl.* **alturas,** the heavens, Heaven.

alúa, *f.* (Arg.) glowworm.

alubia, *f.* (bot.) French bean.

aluciar, *va.* to polish, burnish, brighten.

alucinación, *f.* hallucination.

alucinadamente, *adv.* erroneously.

alucinamiento, *m.* = ALUCINACIÓN.

alucinar, *va.* & *vr.* to dazzle, fascinate, delude.

alucón, *m.* barn owl.

alud, *m.* avalanche.

aluda, *f.* (entom.) winged ant or emmet.

aludel, *m.* (chem.) sublimating pots.

aludir, *vn.* to allude, refer.

aludo, da, *a.* winged, large-winged.

aluengar, *va.* = ALONGAR.

aluengo, aluengue, *v. V.* ALONGAR.

¹alumbrado, da. I. *pp.* of ALUMBRAR. **II.** *a.* (coll.) flustered with wine, tipsy. **III.** *m.* lighting.—*pl.* illuminati.—**de a.,** illuminating (gas, etc.).

²alumbrado, da, *a.* aluminous, pert. to alum.

alumbrador, ra, *n.* lighter; linkboy.

alumbramiento, *m.* supplying with light; childbirth.

¹alumbrar. I. *va.* to light, illuminate; to enlighten, instruct; to dig about the roots of (vines). **II.** *vn.* to give, or shed, light; to be delivered of, give birth to (a child). **III.** *vr.* to get tipsy; to become lively (from liquor).

²alumbrar, *va.* to dip (cloth) in alum water.

alumbre, *m.* alum.—**a. catino,** alkali from glasswort.—**a. de rasuras,** salt of tartar.—**a. sacarino,** alum medicinal mixture.

alumbrera, *f.* alum mine.—**a. artificial,** alum works.

alumbroso, sa, *a.* containing alum.

alúmina, *f.* (chem.) alumina.

aluminado, da, *a.* (chem.) mixed with alum.

aluminato, *m.* aluminate.

alumínico, ca, a., **aluminífero, ra,** *a.* aluminous.

aluminio, *m.* aluminium, aluminum.

aluminita, *f.* aluminite.

aluminoso, sa, *a.* aluminous.

alumno, na, *n.* foster child; pupil, student.

alunado, da, *a.* lunatic; (of horses) jerky from constipation; long-tusked (boar); tainted (meat).

alunita, *f.* (min.) alunite.

alusión, *f.* allusion, reference, hint.

alusivamente, *adv.* allusively.

alusivo, va, *a.* allusive, hinting.

alustrar, lustrar, *va.* to give luster to.

alutación, *f.* (min.) gold dust bearing stratum.

alutrado, da, *a.* otter-colored.

aluvial, *a.* alluvial.

aluvión, *f.* alluvium.

alveario, *m.* (anat.) alveary, hollow of outer ear.

álveo, *m.* bed (of a river).

alveolar, *a.* alveolar.

alvéolo, *m.* alveolus, alveole, small cavity.

alverja, alverjana, *f.* (bot.) common vetch; (Am.) (also ARVEJA), green pea.

alvino, na, *a.* (med.) alvine, intestinal.

alza, *f.* piece of leather put round the last to make the shoe wider; instrument used in ropewalks; advance, rise (in price); (print.) overlay; (artil.) front sight (gen. app. to the notched-slide sight).

alzacuello, *m.* neck stock.

alzada, *f.* height, stature (of horses); appeal (to a higher governmental body).

alzadamente, *adv.* for a lump sum.

alzado, da. I. *pp.* of ALZAR. II. *a.* & *m.* (of) a lump sum; (of a) fraudulent bankrupt; *m.* (arch.) front elevation.

alzadura, *f.* elevation.

alzamiento, *m.* lifting, raising; higher bid (at an auction); rising (in arms), insurrection.

alzapaño, *m.* curtain holder.

alzapié, *m.* snare (for birds or animals).

alzaprima, *f.* lever; wedge; (naut.) heaver.—**dar a.,** to ruin or damage by treacherous cunning.—**alzaprimar,** *va.* to raise with a lever; (naut.) to move with handspikes; to incite, spur on.

alzapuertas, *m.* (theat.) supernumerary.

alzar. I. *va.* (*pret.* ALCÉ; *subj.* ALCE) to raise (a load, price, siege, building, penalty); to lift, heave; to pick up; to carry off; to hide, lock up; to cut (the cards); to gather up and arrange in order (printed sheets) for the binder; (eccl.) to elevate (the host); (naut.) to heave.—**a. cabeza,** to recover from a calamity or disease.—**a. el codo,** to be a toper.—**a. la casa,** to break up house.—**a. velas,** (naut.) to set the sails; to raise camp (fig.), to move. II. *vr.* to rise in rebellion; to rise; to make a fraudulent bankruptcy; to appeal (to a higher court).—**a. con,** to run away with; to embezzle; to steal; to usurp.—**a. con el santo y la limosna,** to carry away, or appropriate, everything.

alzatirantes, *m. pl.* harness straps to suspend the traces.

allá, *adv.* there; thither, or to that place; (with a modifying *adv.*) far, beyond (*más allá,* farther; *muy allá,* much beyond, far beyond). Applied to time, it indicates remoteness, and either is not translated, or is rendered by "in the old times," "in times of old," "in the far-off time," etc.: *allá en mi niñez,* in the old times of my childhood; *allá en tiempo de Salomón,* in the far-off time of Solomon.—**a. por el año de 1900,** about 1900.—**a. arriba,** up there.—**a. veremos,** we shall see.—**a. voy,** I am coming.—**el más a.,** the beyond.—**por a.,** there, thereabouts, through there, that way.

allanador, *m.* leveller; gold-beater's book.

allanamiento, *m.* levelling; smoothing; acceptance of a judicial finding; affability, suavity.

allanar. I. *va.* to level, smooth; to flatten; to remove or overcome (difficulties); to pacify, subdue; to break into (a house). II. *vr.* to abide (by), acquiesce.

allegadizo, za, *a.* collected without selection.

allegado, da. I. *pp.* of ALLEGAR. II. *a.* near; related. III. *n.* relative; friend; ally.

allegador, ra, *n.* reaper; gatherer; board for gathering thrashed wheat; (fire) poker.

allegamiento, *m.* collecting; reaping, gathering; close friendship; union; relationship.

allegar. I. *va.* (*pret.* ALLEGUÉ; *subj.* ALLEGUE) to reap; to collect; to solicit, procure. II. *vr.* to come near, approach; to adhere (to a sect, etc.).

allende, *adv.* beyond, on the other side.—**a. el mar,** overseas.

allí, *adv.* there, in that place; thereto.—¡**a. fué Troya!** there the trouble began, then came the crash!—**de a.,** from there; thence.—**por a.,** that way; through there; there, thereabouts.

alloza, *f.* = ALMENDRUCO, green almond.

allozo, *m.* (bot.) wild almond tree.

alludel, *m.* earthen water pipe; ALUDEL.

ama, *f.* mistress of the house; landlady; (woman) owner; housekeeper; wet nurse; (anc.) governess.—**a. de cría** = A. DE LECHE.—**a. de gobierno** = A. DE LLAVES.—**a. de huéspedes,** boarding-house keeper.—**a. de leche,** wet nurse.—**a. de llaves,** housekeeper.

amabilidad, *f.* amiability, affability; kindness.

amable, *a.* amiable, affable; kind.—**amablemente,** *adv.* amiably; kindly; courteously.

amacayo, *m.* (Am.) fleur-de-lis, iris.

amaceno, na. I. *a.* Damascene. II. *f.* (bot.) damson plum.

amacollarse, *vr.* (of plants) to throw out shoots.

amacrático, ca, *a.* amacratic, focussing actinic rays.

amachetear, *va.* to strike with a machete.

amador, ra, *n.* & *a.* lover (-ing).

amadrigar. I. *va.* (*pret.* AMADRIGUÉ; *subj.* AMADRIGUE) to receive well, esp. one not deserving. II. *vr.* to burrow; to seclude oneself.

amadrinar, *va.* to couple, yoke together; (naut.) to join (one thing to another for reinforcement); to act as godmother or bridesmaid to; to uphold.

amadroñadc, da, *a.* resembling *madroños.*

amaestrado, da. I. *pp.* of AMAESTRAR. II. *a.* taught, schooled; trained, experienced.

amaestrar, *va.* to instruct, train, coach.

amagar. I. *va.* to threaten; to show signs of; to hint. II. *vn.* to threaten; to be impending; to feign. III. *vr.* (coll.) to hide.

amago, *m.* threatening; hint; empty promise; symptom of disease which does not develop.

ámago, *m.* bitter stuff found in some bee cells; nausea, loathing.

amainar. I. *va.* (naut.) to lower or shorten (sail); to relax. II. *vn.* to subside, lessen, moderate. III. *vr.* to give in, yield, desist.

amaitinar, *va.* to observe attentively.

amajadar. I. *va.* to keep (sheep) in a field to fertilize it. II. *vr.* (of sheep) to be in, or go to, the fold.

amalecita, *n.* & *a.* (Bible) Amalekite.

amalgama, *f.* amalgam.

amalgamación, *f.* amalgamation.

amalgamar, *va.* to amalgamate.

amamantar, *va.* to nurse, suckle.

amán, *m.* amnesty.

amancebamiento, *m.* concubinage.

amancebarse, *vr.* to live in concubinage.

amancillar, *va.* to stain, pollute; to defame, tarnish one's reputation.

amanecer, *vn. defect.* (*ind.* AMANEZCO; *subj.* AMANEZCA) to dawn; to arrive, be or appear at daybreak or in the morning (often diff. constr.: *amanecimos en la costa,* we were on shore, we reached the shore at daybreak, it was daybreak when we arrived at the shore; *amaneció la noticia en los periódicos,* the news appeared in the papers in the morning). Often used with *Dios* as subject: *amaneció Dios,* it dawned (literally, God sent forth the dawn).—**amanecerá y veremos,** we shall see. II. *m.* dawn, daybreak.—**al a.,** at dawn, at daybreak.

amanecida, *f.* dawn, daybreak.

amanerado, da, *a.* full of mannerisms.

amanerarse, *vr.* to adopt mannerisms; to become affected.

amanezco, amanezca, *v.* V. AMANECER.

amanojar, *va.* to gather by handfuls.

amansador, ra, *n.* tamer; horse breaker; soother, appeaser.

amansamiento, *m.* taming; breaking (horses).

amansar, *va.* to tame, domesticate; to break (a horse); to soften, pacify.

amantar, *va.* (coll.) to cloak.

¹amante, *n.* & *a.* lover(-ing); sweetheart.

²amante, *m.* (naut.) rope, part of the running rigging.

amantillar, *va.* (naut.) to top the lifts.

amantillo, *m.* (naut.) lift.

amanuense, *m.* amanuensis, clerk.

amañar. I. *va.* to do cleverly. II. *vr.* to be handy; to adapt oneself.

amaño, *m.* cleverness, neatness.—*pl.* tools or implements; intrigue or machinations.

amapola, *f.* (bot.) poppy.

amar, *va.* to love.

amáraco, *m.* (bot.) = MEJORANA, marjoram.
amarantáceo, a. I. *a.* (bot.) amaranthaceous. **II.** *f. pl.* (bot.) Amaranthaceæ.
amaranto, *m.* (bot.) amaranth.
amarar, *vn.* (aer.) to alight on the water.
amargado, da. I. *pp.* of AMARGAR. **II.** *a.* embittered.
amargaleja, *f.* bitter or wild plum.
amargamente, *adv.* bitterly.
amargar. I. *va.* (*pret.* AMARGUÉ; *subj.* AMARGUE) to make bitter; to exasperate, offend. **II.** *vn.* to be bitter. **III.** *vr.* to become bitter.
amargo, ga. I. *a.* bitter. **II.** *m.* bitterness; sweetmeat made of bitter almonds.—*pl.* bitters.
amargón, *m.* (bot.) dandelion.
amargor, *m.* bitterness.
amargosamente, *adv.* bitterly.
amargoso, sa, *a.* bitter.
amargué, amargue, *v.* V. AMARGAR.
amarguillo, lla, *a. dim.* somewhat bitter.
amargura, *f.* bitterness.
amaricado, a, a. (coll.) effeminate.
amarilídeo, a. I. *a.* (bot.) amarylidaceous. **II.** *f. pl.* (bot.) Amarylidaceæ.
amarilis, *f.* amaryllis.
amarilla, *f.* gold coin, especially the *onza*; (vet.) a liver disease of sheep.
amarillazo, za, *a.* pale-yellow.
amarillear, *vn.* to incline to yellow.
amarillejo, ja; amarillento, ta, *a.* yellowish.
amarillez, *f.* yellowness.
amarillo, lla. I. *a.* yellow. **II.** *m.* jaundice; a disease of silkworms.
amarinar, marinar, *va.* to salt (fish); (naut.) to man (a ship).
amariposado, da, *a.* (bot.) butterflylike.
amaro, *m.* (bot.) common clary.
amarra, *f.* cable; rope; martingale.
amarradero, *m.* hitching post; tying or fastening place or object; (naut.) mooring berth.
amarraje, *m.* moorage (charge for mooring).
amarrar, *va.* to tie, fasten; to lash, belay.
amarrazones, *pl.* (naut.) ground tackle.
amarre, *m.* tying; mooring; mooring line or cable. —**a. de retenida,** mooring guy (of a dirigible).
amarrido, da, *a.* dejected, gloomy.
amartelar. I. *va.* to court, make love to; to love devotedly. **II.** *vr.* to fall in love.
amartillar, *va.* to hammer; to cock (gun, pistol).
amasadera, *f.* kneading bowl.
amasador, ra, *n.* kneader.
amasadura, *f.* kneading.
amasamiento, *m.* uniting; (med.) massage; AMASADURA.
amasar, *va.* to knead; to mold; to arrange for a purpose; (med.) to massage.
amasijo, *m.* dough; (act of) kneading; quantity of mortar or plaster; medley; plot; place where dough is made; (coll.) work, task.
amate, *m.* (Mex.) a fig tree the milky juice of which is used medically as a resolvent.
amatista, ametista, *f.* (min.) amethyst.
amatividad, *f.* amativeness.
amatorio, ria, *a.* amatory.
amaurosis, *f.* (med.) amaurosis, loss of sight.
amaurótico, ca, *n.* & *a.* amaurotic.
amauta, *m.* safe (among ancient Peruvians).
amayorazgado, da, *a.* (law) entailed.
amayorazgar, *va.* (law) to entail.
amazacotado, da, *a.* heavy, thick; (of writings) jumbled, incoherent, clumsy.
amazona, *f.* Amazon; amazon; riding habit; horsewoman; (Am.) a large parrot of Brazil.
amazónico, ca, *a.* Amazonian.
amba, *f.* (bot.) fruit of the mangrove.
ambages, *m. pl.* maze; circumlocutions, beating about the bush.—**sin a.,** in plain language, without mincing words.
ambagioso, sa, *a.* ambiguous; circumlocutory.

ámbar, *m.* amber.—**a. gris,** ambergris.—**a. negro,** jet.—**a. pardillo** = A. GRIS.
ambarar, *va.* to scent with amber.
ambariba, *f.* (bot.) sweet centaury.
ambarilla, *f.* (bot.) amber seed.
ambarina, *f.* (bot.) scabious.
ambarino, na, *a.* pert. to amber; amberlike.
ambición, *f.* ambition; aspiration; covetousness.
ambicionar, *va.* to seek eagerly; to aspire to; to covet.
ambiciosamente, *adv.* ambitiously.
ambicioso, sa, *a.* ambitious, aspiring; covetous, greedy.
ambidextro, tra, *a.* ambidextrous.
ambiente, *m.* atmosphere, ambient air.
ambigú, *m.* luncheon; collation.
ambiguamente, *adv.* ambiguously.
ambigüedad, *f.* ambiguity.
ambiguo, gua, *a.* ambiguous.
ámbito, *m.* contour, boundary line; limit; compass, scope.
amblar, *va.* to amble; (of quadrupeds) to pace.
ambleo, *m.* short, thick wax candle; candlestick for the same.
ambliopía, *f.* (med.) amblyopia, dimness of vision.
ambo, *m.* combination of two numbers in lotto.
ambón, *m.* pulpit on each side of the high altar.
ambos, bas, *a.* both.—**a. a dos,** both, or both together.
ambrosía, *f.* ambrosia; (fig.) any delicious viand or liquor.—**a. campestre,** (bot.) buckthorn.
ambrosiano, na, *a.* pertaining to St. Ambrose.
ambuesta, *f.* = ALMORZADA, a double handful.
ambulancia, *f.* field hospital; ambulance.
ambulante, *a.* ambulant; shifting; roving.
ambulativo, va, *a.* of a roving disposition; shifting; ambulatory.
ambulatorio, a, *a.* ambulatory, adapted for walking.
ameba, *f.* = AMIBA.
amebeo, *a.* & *m.* (pert. to) dialogue in verse.
amechar, *va.* to put a wick in; (cook.) (also **mechar**) to lard (meat).
amedrentador, ra, *n.* & *a.* threatener(-ing); discourager(-ing); frightener(-ing).
amedrentar, *va.* to frighten, discourage, intimidate.
amelga, *f.* ridge between two furrows.
amelgado. I. *pp.* of AMELGAR. **II.** *m.* (prov.) boundary mound.
amelgar, *va.* to cut even furrows in for planting; to mark the boundaries of with mounds.
amelo, *m.* (bot.) golden starwort.
amelonado, da, *a.* melon-shaped.
[1]**amén,** *m.* amen, so be it.—**llevarle a uno el amén,** to agree to, or approve, everything one says, be one's echo.
[2]**amén,** *adv.* **a. de,** besides; aside from, except for.
amenacé, amenace, *v.* V. AMENAZAR.
amenaza, *f.* threat, menace.
amenazador, ra, *n.* & *a.* threatener(-ing).
amenazante, *a.* menacing, threatening.
amenazar, *va.* & *vn.* (*pret.* AMENACÉ; *subj.* AMENACE) to threaten, menace; be impending.
amencia, *f.* dementia.
amenguamiento, *m.* diminution, lessening, abatement.
amenguar, *va.* to diminish; to defame.
amenice, amenice, *v.* V. AMENIZAR.
amenidad, *f.* amenity.
amenizar, *va.* (*pret.* AMENICÉ; *subj.* AMENICE) to render pleasant or agreeable.
ameno, na, *a.* pleasant, agreeable, pleasing.
amenorrea, *f.* (med.) amenorrhea.
amentáceo, cea, *a.* (bot.) amentaceous.
amentar, *va.* to lace (shoes).
amento, *m.* (bot.) ament; AMIENTO.
amerar, merar. I. *va.* to mix (wine or liquor) with water. **II.** *vr.* to percolate; to soak.

amerengado, da, *a.* like, or having, meringue; (coll.) prudish.

americana, *f.* coat (of a man's suit).

americanismo, *m.* Americanism (esp. app. to Lat. Am. Span.).

americanista, *n.* student of Lat. Am. languages, cultures, etc.

americano, na, *a.* American (app. to Lat. Am.; for U. S. *V.* NORTEAMERICANO).

amestizado, da, *a.* mestizolike.

ametalado, da, *a.* brass-colored.

ametista, *f.,* **ametisto,** *m.* = AMATISTA.

ametralladora, *f.* rapid-fire gun, machine gun.

ametrallar, *va.* to shoot with grapeshot; to shell; to machine-gun.

amia, lamia, *f.* (ichth.) white shark.

amianto, *m.* (min.) amianthus; asbestos.

amiba, *f.,* **amibo,** *m.* (zool.) amœba.

amiboideo, a, *a.* amœboid, amœbic.

amicísimo, ma, *a. super.* most friendly, being, or like, a very good friend.

amida, *f.* (chem.) amide.

amidina, amidinas, *f.* (chem.) amidine, soluble matter in starch.

amidógeno, *m.* (chem.) amidogen.

amiento, *m.* leather strap to secure helmet; shoe lace; leather string.

amiga, *f.* female friend; schoolmistress; kindergarten; concubine, mistress.

amigable, *a.* friendly; fit, suitable.

amigablemente, *adv.* amicably.

amígdala, *f.* tonsil.

amigdaláceo, a, *a.* (bot.) amygdalaceous.— *f. pl.* Amygdalaceæ.

amigdalina, *f.* (chem.) amygdalin.

amigdalitis, *f.* tonsilitis.

amigdalotomía, *f.* (med.) tonsilectomy.

amigo, ga. I. *n.* friend.—**ser a. de,** to be a friend of; to have a taste for. **II.** *m.* a man living in concubinage. **III.** *a.* friendly; fond.—**ser muy amigos,** to be very good friends.

amigote, *m. aug.* (coll.) dear old friend.

amiláceo, a, *a.* starchy.

amilanamiento, *m.* terror, abject fear; terrifying; cowing.

amilanar. I. *va.* to frighten, terrify; to stupefy; to cow. **II.** *vr.* to become terrified; to cower, quail; to flag.

amílico, ca, *a.* amyl (alcohol).

amillaramiento, *m.* assessment of a tax.

amillarar, *va.* to assess a tax on.

amillonado, da, *a. & n.* very rich (person).

amimar, mimar, *va.* to fondle; to indulge.

amina, *f.* (chem.) amine.

aminorar, minorar, *va.* to lessen; to enfeeble.

amir, *m.* ameer.

amistad, *f.* friendship; concubinage.—**hacer amistad,** or **amistades,** to become acquainted; to make friends.—**hacer las amistades,** to make up, become reconciled.

amistar. I. *va.* to make (others) friends; to make acquainted. **II.** *vr.* to become acquainted; to become reconciled, make up.

amistosamente, *adv.* amicably, in a friendly manner.

amistoso, sa, *a.* friendly, amicable.

amito, *m.* amice, part of a priest's garment.

amnesia, *f.* amnesia, loss of memory.

amnios, *f.* (zool.) amnion, fœtal envelope.

amniótico, ca, *a.* (zool.) amniotic.

amnistía, *f.* amnesty.—**amnistiar. I.** *va.* to pardon, grant amnesty to. **II.** *vr.* to receive amnesty.

amo, *m.* master, head (of household or family); owner; foster father; overseer; (coll.) boss.

amoblar, *va.* (*ind.* AMUEBLO; *subj.* AMUEBLE) = AMUEBLAR, to furnish, provide with furniture.

amodita, *f.* = ALICANTE, a horned serpent.

amodorrado, da. I. *pp.* of AMODORRARSE. **II.** *a.* drowsy, sleepy.

amodorrarse, *vr.* to become drowsy.

amodorrido, da, *a.* = AMODORRADO.

amogotado, da, *a.* knoll-like.

amohecerse, *vr.* (*ind.* AMOHEZCO; *subj.* AMOHEZCA) to mold or rust.

amohinar, *va.* to irritate, annoy.

amojamado, da, *a.* tasting like tunny fish.

amojamar, *va.* to dry and smoke (tunny fish).

amojonador, *m.* one who sets landmarks.

amojonamiento, *m.* setting of landmarks.

amojonar, *va.* to set landmarks on (for marking boundaries).

amoladera, *f.* whetstone, grindstone.

amolador, *n. & a.* grinder(-ing); whetter(-ing); sharpener(-ing).

amoladura, *f.* whetting, grinding.

amolar, *va.* (*ind.* AMUELO; *subj.* AMUELE) to whet, grind, sharpen.

amoldar, *va.* to mold, fashion, figure; to adjust; to brand (cattle); to adapt.

amole, *m.* root of a plant used as soap.

amollador, ra, *n.* one who plays an inferior card, having a winning one.

amollar. I. *va.* (naut.) to slacken (a rope). **II.** *vn.* to play an inferior card, having a winning one.

amolletado, da, *a.* oblong, oval.

amomo, *m.* (bot.) plant producing seeds called grains of paradise, used medicinally.

amondongado, da, *a.* (coll.) coarse and fat.

amonedación, *f.* coining (money).

amonedar, *va.* to coin (money).

amonestación, *f.* admonition, warning; marriage banns.—**correr las amonestaciones,** to publish the banns.

amonestador, ra, *n. & a.* admonisher(-ing).

amonestar, *va.* to admonish, warn, advise; to publish (banns).

amoniacal, *a.* ammoniacal.

amoníaco, *m.* ammonia; ammoniac, gum resin.

amónico, ca, *a.* ammonic, ammonium (as *a.*).

amonio, *m.* ammonium.

¹**amonita,** *f.* (zool.) ammonite, spiral fossil shell.

²**amonita,** *n. & a.* (pertaining to) Ammon (the people or their founder).

amontarse, *vr.* to flee to the mountains.

amontonador, ra, *n.* heaper, accumulator.

amontonamiento, *m.* heaping, accumulating; hoarding; gathering; crowding (of people).

amontonar. I. *va.* to heap, pile up; to accumulate indiscriminately; to hoard, lay up. **II.** *vr.* (coll.) to crowd; to pile up; to fly into a passion.

amor, *m.* love; the object of love.—*pl.* love affairs, amours.—**a. con a. se paga,** the punishment should fit the crime.—**a. patrio,** love of country, patriotism.—**a. propio,** self-esteem, amour propre.—**por a. de,** for the sake of; on account of.—**con** or **de mil amores,** with all one's heart, with the greatest pleasure.

amoral, *a.* amoral.—**amoralidad,** *f.* amorality. —**amoralismo,** *m.* amoralism.

amoratado, da, *a.* livid.

amorcillo, *m. dim.* slight love; (figure of) Cupid.

amordazar, *va.* (*pret.* AMORDACÉ; *subj.* AMORDACE) to gag, muzzle; (naut.) to fasten with bitts.

amores, *m.* (bot.) red valerian.

amorfia, *f.* organic deformity.

amorfo, fa, *a.* amorphous.

amorgado, da, *a.* filled with *morga* or *alpechín.*

amorgar, *va.* to stupefy (fish) with *morga* or *alpechín,* fetid olive juice.

amoricones, *m. pl.* (coll.) love looks, flirtations.

amorío, *m.* love making; love, amour.

amoriscado, da, *a.* Moorlike.

amormado, da, *a.* (vet.) having the glanders.

amorosamente, *adv.* lovingly, with love.

amoroso, sa, *a.* affectionate, loving; pleasing, gentle; mild.

amorrar. I. *vn.* (coll.) to be sullen; to muse; (naut.) (of a ship) to pitch. **II.** *vr.* to sulk.

amortajar, *va.* to shroud (a corpse).

amortecer. I. *va.* (*ind.* AMORTEZCO; *subj.* AMORTEZCA) to deaden. **II.** *vr.* to faint, swoon.

amortecimiento, *m.* swoon, fainting.

amortezco, amortezca, *v.* V. AMORTECER.

amorticé, amortice, *v.* V. AMORTIZAR.

amortiguación, *f.,* **amortiguamiento,** *m.* softening, mitigation, lessening.

amortiguador, ra. I. *n.* & *a.* reducer(-ing). damper(-ing), softener(-ing). **II.** *m.* (mech.) dashpot; shock absorber.

amortiguar, *va.* to lessen, mitigate, deaden; to temper; to soften (colors); to absorb, take up (shocks); (radio) to damp (waves).

amortizable, *a.* amortizable.

amortización, *f.* amortization.

amortizar, *va.* (*pret.* AMORTICÉ; *subj.* AMORTICE) to amortize; to recoup, recover; to abolish (offices, etc.); to refund; to redeem (debt, etc.).

amoscar, *va.* & *vr.* (*pret.* AMOSQUÉ; *subj.* AMOSQUE) to shake off the flies; (coll.) to get peeved.

amosquilado, da, *a.* tormented with flies.

amostacé, amostace, *v.* V. AMOSTAZAR.

amostachado, *a.* having a mustache.

amostazar. I. *va.* (*pret.* AMOSTACÉ; *subj.* AMOSTACE) (coll.) to exasperate, provoke. **II.** *vr.* to be vexed, angry.

amotinadamente, *adv.* mutinously.

amotinado, da. I. *pp.* of AMOTINAR. **II.** *a.* mutinous. **III.** *n.* mutineer.

amotinador, ra, *n.* mutineer.

amotinamiento, *m.* mutiny.

amotinar. I. *va.* to excite to rebellion; to disorder (the mind). **II.** *vr.* to mutiny, rebel.

amover, *va.* (*ind.* AMUEVO; *subj.* AMUEVE) to discharge (from an employment).

amovible, *a.* removable.

amovilidad, *f.* quality of being removable.

ampac, *m.* (bot.) champak.

ampara, *f.* (law) seizure of chattels.

amparador, ra, *n.* protector; shelterer.

amparar. I. *va.* to shelter; to protect, help, assist; to comply with the requirements for working (a mine). **II.** *vr.* to claim or enjoy protection; to defend oneself; to seek shelter.

amparo, *m.* favor, aid; protection; shelter, refuge, asylum.

ampelita, *f.* soft sandy slate.

ampelografía, *f.* viticulture, science of vine growing.

ampelográfico, ca, *a.* pert. to viticulture.

ampelógrafo, fa, *n.* one versed in viticulture.

amper, *m.* = AMPERIO.

amperaje, *m.* (elec.) amperage.

amperímetro, *m.* (elec.) amperometer, ammeter.

amperio, *m.* (elec.) ampere.—**a.-hora,** amperehour.—**a.-vuelta,** ampere turn.

amperómetro, *m.* = AMPERÍMETRO.

amplexicaulo, la, *a.* (bot.) amplexicaul.

amplexo, xa, *a.* (bot.) clasped by amplexicaul organs.

ampliación, *f.* enlargement (gen. & photog.).

ampliador, ra, *n.* & *a.* amplifier(-ying).

ampliamente, *adv.* largely, copiously, plentifully, amply.

ampliar, *va.* to amplify, extend; (photog.) to enlarge.

ampliativo, va, *a.* amplifying, enlarging.

amplificación, *f.* enlargement; (rhet.) amplification.

amplificador, ra, *n.* & *a.* amplifier(-ying), enlarger(-ing).—*m.* (radio) amplifier.

amplificar, *va.* to amplify, enlarge, extend, expand; to dilate, expatiate.

amplio, lia, *a.* ample, roomy, extensive, large; full, bold (e.g. of a drawing).

amplitud, *f.* extent, largeness, fullness; (phys., astr.) amplitude.

ampo (de la nieve), *m.* pure, shining whiteness; snowflake.

ampolla, *f.* blister; decanter, cruet; water bubble; bulb (of a lamp).—**ampollar. I.** *va.* to blister; to make hollow. **II.** *vr.* to bubble up.—**ampollar,** *a.* blisterlike, bubblelike.—**ampolleta,** *f. dim.* small vial; cruet; sandglass or time taken for sand to run through; bulb; (naut.) watch glass.

amprar, *vn.* (prov.) to borrow.

ampulosidad, *f.* verbosity.

ampuloso, sa, *a.* pompous, bombastic.

amputación, *f.* amputation.

amputar, *va.* to amputate.

amuchachado, da, *a.* boyish, childish.

amueblar, *va.* to furnish (a house, etc.).

amueblo, amueble, *v.* V. AMOBLAR.

amuelo, amuele, etc. *v.* V. AMOLAR.

amuevo, amueve, *v.* V. AMOVER.

amugamiento, *m.* setting out boundary marks.

amugronador, ra, *a.* (of one) planting vines.

amugronar, *va.* to plant the shoot of a vine.

amujerado, da, *a.* effeminate.

amujeramiento, *m.* effeminacy.

amularse, *vr.* (of mares) to become sterile.

amulatado, da, *a.* mulattolike.

amuleto, *m.* amulet.

amunicionar, *va.* to supply with ammunition.

amuñecado, da, *a.* puppetlike.

amura, *f.* (naut.) beam of a ship at one-eighth of its length from the bow; part on each side of the ship that corresponds to that section; tack (rope) of a sail.

amurada, *f.* (naut.) interior side of a ship.

amurallar, *va.* = MURAR. to wall.

amurar, *va.* (naut.) to haul (the tack) aboard.

amurcar, *va.* (of a bull) to gore with the horns.

amurco, *m.* (of a bull) blow with the horns.

amurillar, *va.* (agr.) to earth up.

amusco, ca, musco, ca, *a.* brown.

amusgar, *va.* (of an animal about to kick, bite, etc.) to throw back (the ears); to squint to see better.

ana, *f.* ell, a measure.

anabaptismo, *m.* Anabaptism.

anabaptista, *n.* & *a.* Anabaptist.

anábasis, *f.* (med.) anabasis, course of a disease to its climax.

anacarado, nacarado, da, *a.* like mother-of-pearl.

anacardina, *f.* (pharm.) anacardic preparation.

anacardino, na, *a.* anacardic, made of cashews.

anacardo, *m.* (bot.) cashew (tree or fruit).

anaco, *m.* (Peru, Bol.) Indian women's dress; (Ecua.) Indian women's hair-do, a single braid.

anaconda, *f.* anaconda, a South-American boa.

anacoreta, *m.* anchorite, hermit.

anacorético, ca, *a.* anchoretic.

anacreóntico, ca, *a.* pertaining to or like the poet Anacreon or his poetry.

anacrónico, ca, *a.* anachronistic.

anacronismo, *m.* anachronism.

ánade, *m.* & *f.* (ornith.) duck; by extension, goose.—**anadear,** *vn.* to waddle.—**anadeja,** *f. dim.* duckling.—**anadino, na,** *n.* young duck.—**anadón,** *m.* mallard.

anaerobio, *n.* & *a.* (biol.) anaerobe (-ic).

anafalla, anafaya, *f.* thick corded silk.

anafe, *m.* portable furnace.

anáfora, *f.* (rhet.) anaphora.

anafre, *m.* portable furnace.

anafrodisia, *f.* (med.) diminution of sexual desire.—**anafrodisíaco, ca,** *a.* anaphrodisiac.

anafrodita, *n.* abstainer from sexual intercourse.

anáglifo, *m.* anaglyph.

anagnórisis, *f.* (poet.) = AGNICIÓN.

anagoge, *m.,* **anagogia,** *f.* anagoge, spiritual interpretation or application.

For pronunciation, see the rules at the beginning of the book.

anagógico, ca, *a.* anagogical.

anagrama, *f.* anagram.

anagramatizador, ra, *n.* anagrammatist.

anal, *a.* anal.

analectas, *f. pl.* analects.

analéctico, ca, *a.* analectic.

analéptico, ca, *a.* (med.) restorative.

analepsia, *f.* (med.) convalescence.

anales, *m. pl.* annals.

analfabetismo, *m.* illiteracy.

analfabeto, ta, *a. & n.* illiterate (person).

analgesia, *f.* (med.) analgesia, insensibility to pain.—**analgésico, ca,** *n. & a.* analgesic.

analgesina, *f.* antipyrine.

analicé, analice, *v. V.* ANALIZAR.

análisis, *m.* or *f.* analysis; (gram.) parsing; (math.) analysis (gen. app. to infinitesimal calculus and the theory of functions).—**a. cualitativo,** qualitative analysis.—**a. cuantitativo,** quantitative analysis.—**a. espectral,** spectrum analysis.—**a. volumétrico,** volumetric analysis, titration (gen. in latter sense).

analista, *m.* annalist.

analítica, *f.* (philos.) analytics; (math.) analytic geometry.

analíticamente, *adv.* analytically.

analítico, ca, *a.* analytical.

analizable, *a.* capable of analysis.

analizador, *m.* analyzer.

analizar, *va.* (*pret.* ANALICÉ; *subj.* ANALICE) to analyze; (gram.) to parse.

análogamente, *adv.* analogously; in like manner, likewise.

analogía, *f.* analogy; resemblance; (biol., linguistics) analogy.

analógicamente, *adv.* analogically.

analógico, ca; análogo, ga, *a.* analogous.

anamorfosis, *f.* anamorphosis.

ananá, ananás, *f.* (bot.) pineapple.

anapelo, *m.* (bot.) wolfsbane.

anapesto, *m.* anapæst, a Latin verse, ᴗ ᴗ —.

anaquel, *m.* shelf.

anaquelería, *f.* shelving, case of shelves.

anaranjado, da. I. *a.* orange-colored. **II.** *n.* orange (color).—**a. de metilo,** methyl orange.

anarquía, *f.* anarchy.

anárquico, ca, *a.* anarchical.

anarquismo, *m.* anarchism.

anarquista, *n. & a.* anarchist(-ic).

anasarca, *f.* (med.) general dropsy.

anascote, *m.* woollen stuff like serge.

anastasia, *f.* = ARTEMISA, (bot.) mugwort.

anastomosis, *f.* (anat.) anastomosis, communication between blood vessels through channels.

anástrofe, *m.* (rhet.) anastrophe, inversion of the usual order of words.

anata, *f.* yearly income.—**media a.,** tax paid on assuming office (eccl. & secular).

anatema, *m.* or *f.* **anatematismo,** *m.* anathema.

anatematizar, *va.* (*pret.* ANATEMATICÉ; *subj.* ANATEMATICE) to anathematize.

anatista, *m.* official in charge of MEDIAS ANATAS.

anatomía, *f.* anatomy; dissection.

anatómicamente, *adv.* anatomically.

anatomicé, anatomice, *v. V.* ANATOMIZAR.

anatómico, ca, *a.* anatomical; dissecting.

anatomista, *m.* anatomist.

anatomizar, *va.* (*pret.* ANATOMICÉ; *subj.* ANATOMICE) to anatomize or dissect; (art) to draw or carve the bones and muscles of.

anavajado, da, *a.* knife-scarred.

anca, *f.* croup (of animals); (coll.) buttock.

ancado, *m.* (vet.) contraction of muscles of the hind legs.

ancianidad, *f.* old age; antiquity.

anciano, na, *n. & a.* old (man, woman); ancient.

ancla, *f.* anchor.—**a. de la esperanza,** sheet anchor.—**a. flotante,** (aer.) drogue, sea anchor.—**al a.,** at anchor.—**el a. agarra,** the anchor bites.—**echar anclas,** to anchor.—

levar el a., levar anclas, to weigh anchor.—**sobre el a., sobre las anclas,** at anchor, anchored.

ancladero, *m.* (naut.) anchorage, anchoring place.

anclaje, *m.* casting anchor; anchoring ground.

anclar, *vn.* to anchor.

anclote, *m.* stream anchor, kedge.

anclotillo, *m.* kedge anchor.

ancón, *m.* corner; (arch.) bracket; cove, bay.

áncora, *f.* = ANCLA.

ancoraje, *m.* = ANCLAJE.

ancorar, *vn.* = ANCLAR.

ancorca, *f.* yellow ochre.

ancorel, *m.* large stone to secure fish-nets.

ancorería, *f.* anchor forge, workshop.

ancorero, *m.* anchor smith, maker.

ancusa, *f.* (bot.) common alkanet.

anchamente, *adv.* widely, largely.

ancheta, *f.* small amount of goods ventured in trade; profit in a bargain.

anchicorto, ta, *a.* wider than long.

ancho, cha. I. *a.* broad, wide.—**ancha Castilla,** (coll.) as you please; without hindrance. —**a. de conciencia,** not overscrupulous, not too conscientious. **II.** *m.* width, breadth.—**a sus anchas,** with absolute freedom, unrestricted(ly), as one pleases; at ease.

anchoa, anchova, *f.* anchovy.

anchor, *m.* = ANCHURA.

anchuelo, la, *a. dim.* somewhat wide.

anchura, *f.* width, breadth; extent; laxity.

anchuroso, sa, *a.* large, spacious, extensive, vast, ample.

anchusa, *f.* (bot.) alkanet.

andábata, *m.* gladiator fighting blindfold.

andada, *f.* track trail; "hike"; thin, crisp, waferlike cake.—*pl.* **andadas,** trail, tracks (esp. of birds or small animals).—**volver a las andadas,** to backslide; to go back to one's old tricks.

andaderas, *f. pl.* gocart (for learning to walk).

andadero, ra. I. *n.* runner. **II.** *m.* easy ground.

¹andado, da, *m.* (coll.) (for *adnado*) stepchild.

²andado, da. I. *pp.* of ANDAR. **II.** *a.* beaten, trodden (path, etc.); busy, thronged (street); worse for wear, threadbare; common, ordinary; elapsed.

andador, ra. I. *a.* fast walking or running, swift; that walks. **II.** *m.* messenger of a court; (naut.) fine sailer; leading string; garden walk.

andadura, *f.* gait; amble.

andalón, *m.* (Am.) gadabout; wanderer.

andaluz, za, *n. & a.* Andalusian.—**andaluzada,** *f.* boasting; exaggeration; (coll.) fish story, yarn.

andamiada, *f.,* **andamiaje,** *m.* scaffolding.

andamio, *m.* scaffold, platform, grandstand; (naut.) gangboard.

¹andana, *f.* row, line, tier.

²andana, *f.*—**llamarse a.,** (coll.) not to fulfill a promise.

andanada, *f.* (naut.) broadside; grandstand for spectators; reproof, reprimand; tirade.

andaniño, *m.* gocart in which children learn to walk. Also ANDADERAS, POLLERA.

¹andante, *a.* walking; (knight) errant.

²andante, *m.* (mus.) andante.

andantesco, ca, *a.* pert. to knights-errant.

andantino, *m.* (mus.) andantino.

andanza, *f.* (obs.) occurrence, event.—**buena** or **mala a.,** good or bad fortune.—*pl.* running about.

andar. I. *vn.* (*pret.* ANDUVE, *fut.* ANDUVIERE) (of a person) to walk, go; (of a watch, machine, etc.) to go, run, move; to act, behave; to elapse, pass; to be (esp. as *aux.* with *ger.* as *a. escribiendo,* to be writing); to get along, be going (*¿cómo anda el negocio?* how is the business going?).—**a. andando,** (Mex. C. A.) to roam about, "chase round."—**a. en,** to be attending to, or engaged in; to be going on, be near (*Juan anda en los veinte años*, John is going on twenty).—**a. en coche, automóvil**, etc., to go, ride in a carriage, automobile, etc.— **andarse por las ramas**, to beat about the bush.—**¡anda!** gracious! move on! get up! all right! go ahead! let it go! **II.** *m.* = ANDADURA, gait, pace.—**a largo a.**, in the long run.— **a más**, or **a todo, a.**, at full speed, quickly.— **a. un a.**, on the same level.

andaraje, *m.* wheel of a wheel and axle; frame of a garden roller.

andariego, ga, *a.* restless, roving; fast walker, runner.

andarín, *m.* professional walker, runner.

andarina, *f.* (ornith.) = GOLONDRINA, swallow.

andarivel, *m.* ferry cable; (naut.) safety ropes.

andarrío, *m.* (ornith.) white wagtail.

andas, *f. pl.* stretcher; litter; bier with shafts.

andén, *m.* bridle path; sidewalk by a road, wharf, or bridge; platform (of a railway station).

andero, ra, *n.* litter bearer; bier bearer.

andesita, *f.* (geol.) andesite, a volcanic rock.

andilú, *m.* shoemaker's burnishing stick.

andino, na, *a.* Andean.

ándito, *m.* gallery or path around a building.

andolina, *f.* (ornith.) = GOLONDRINA, swallow.

andón, na, *a.* roving, that walks a great deal; (of horses) ambling.—**andonear**, *vn.* to amble.

andorga, *f.* (coll.) belly.—**llenar la a.**, to gorge, stuff oneself.

andorina, *f.* = ANDOLINA.

andorra, *f.* street walker.

andorrear, *vn.* to gad about.

andorrero, ra. I. *a.* prone to walk or loiter about the streets. **II.** *m.* gadder, rover, tramp, *f.* street walker.

andosco, ca, *a.* two-year old (sheep).

andrajero, ra, *n.* ragpicker.

andrajo, *m.* rag, tatter; despicable person.

andrajosamente, *adv.* raggedly.

andrajoso, sa, *a.* ragged, in tatters.

andrina, endrina, *f.* (bot.) *f.* sloe.

andrino, *m.* (bot.) sloe tree, blackthorn.

androfobia, *f.* (med.) dread of, or aversion to, men.

andrógino, *m.* androgyne, being both male and female.

androide, *m.* automaton shaped like a man.

andrómina, *f.* (coll.) trick, fraud, fib.

androsemo, *m.* (bot.) parkleaves.

andularios, *m. pl.* (coll.) long wide gown.

andullo, *m.* (naut.) canvas shield on harpings and blocks; plug tobacco.

andurriales, *m. pl.* byroads, lonely places.

anduve, anduviera, etc. *v.* V. ANDAR.

anea, *f.* (bot.) cattail; rush (used for chair seats).

aneaje, *m.* measuring by ells.

anear, *va.* to measure by ells.

aneblar. I. *va.* (*ind.* ANIEBLO; *subj.* ANIEBLE) to cloud, darken. **II.** *vr.* to become cloudy.

anécdota, *f.* anecdote.—**anecdótico, ca**, *a.* anecdotic.—**anecdotista**, *n.* anecdotist.

anegación, *f.* overflowing, inundation.

anegadizo, za, *a.* liable to be inundated.

anegado, da. I. *pp.* of ANEGAR. **II.** *a.* overflowed; wet, soaked.

anegamiento, *m.* = ANEGACIÓN.

anegar. I. *va.* to inundate, flood; to submerge; to flush; to drown. **II.** *vr.* to drown, sink; to become wet or soaked; to be flooded.

anegociado, da, *a.* full of business.

anejín, anejir, *m.* popular proverb which can be sung.

anejo. I. *m.* church depending on another. **II. a., ja, anexo, xa**, *a.* annexed, joined.

aneléctrico, ca, *a.* not susceptible to electrification.

anélido, da, *n.* & *a.* (zool.) annelid.—*m. pl.* Annelida.

anemia, *f.* (med.) anæmia.—**a. tropical**, uncinariasis, hookworm disease.

anémico, ca, *a.* anæmic.

anemografía, *f.* (meteorol.) anemography, science treating of winds.

anemográfico, ca, *a.* (meteorol.) anemographic.

anemógrafo, *m.* one who studies anemography; anemoscope.

anemometría, *f.* (meteorol.) anemometry.

anemómetro, *m.* anemometer, wind gauge.

anemometrógrafo, *m.* anemometrograph.

anémona, anémone, *f.* (bot.) anemone, windflower.—**a. de mar**, sea anemone.

anemoscopio, *m.* (meteorol.) anemoscope.

anepigráfico, ca, *a.* without title or inscription.

anequín, *adv.*—**a**, or **de, a.**, at so much a head (in shearing of sheep).

anerobio, a, *a.* anaerobe(-ic).

aneroide, *a.* & *m.* aneroid (barometer).

anestesia, *f.* anæsthesia.—**anestesiar**, *va.* to anæsthetize.

anestésico, ca, *m.* & *a.*, anæsthetic.

aneurisma, *m.* & *f.* (med.) aneurism.

anexar, *va.* to annex.

anexidades, *f. pl.* annexes, appurtenances.

anexión, *f.* annexation.—**anexionismo**, *m.* annexationism.—**anexionista**, *m.* annexationist.

anexo, xa, *a.* = ANEJO, JA.

anfibio, a, *n.* & *a.* (zool. & aer.) amphibian (-bious).

anfíbol, *m.* (min.) amphibole.—**anfibolita**, *f.* (min.) amphibolite.

anfibología, *f.* amphibology.

anfibológicamente, *adv.* amphibologically.

anfibológico, ca, *a.* amphibological.

anfíbraco, *m.* (poet.) amphibrach, ⌣ — ⌣.

anfictión, *m.* amphictyon.—**anfictionía**, *f.* amphictyony.—**anfictiónico, ca**, *a.* amphictyonic.

anfímacro, *m.* (poet.) amphimacer, — ⌣ —.

anfión, *m.* opium.

anfioxo, *m.* (zool.) amphioxus, lancelet.

anfípodo, da, *n.* & *a.* amphipod.—*m. pl.* Amphipoda.

anfiprostilo, *m.* (arch.) amphiprostyle.

anfisbena, *f.* amphisbæna, a kind of lizard.

anfiscios, *m. pl.* inhabitants of the torrid zone.

anfisibena, *f.* amphisbæna.

anfiteatro, *m.* amphitheatre.—**a. (anatómico)**, dissecting room (of hospital or medical school).

anfitrión, *m.* host entertaining guests.

anfitrite, *f.* (poet. and zool.) amphitrite.

ánfora, *f.* amphora, two-handled narrow-necked jar; (Mex.) ballot box.—*pl.* cruets.

anfractuosidad, *f.* crookedness; anfractuosity.

anfractuoso, sa, *a.* anfractuous, winding.

angaria, *f.* ancient servitude; forced delay in sailing of ship (to use it for public service).

angarillas, *f. pl.* handbarrow; panniers; cruet stands; frames for things carried by horses.

angarillón, *m.* large wicker basket; large handbarrow.

angaripola, *f.* calico.—*pl.* gaudy ornaments.

ángaro, *m.* beacon.

angas, (Am.)—**por a. o por mangas**, in any case, some way or other, anyhow.

ángel, *m.* angel; a raylike fish.—**a. custodio**, or **de la guarda**, guardian angel.

angélica, *f.* (bot.) garden angelica.—**a. carlina**, (bot.) carline thistle.—**a. palustra**, wild angelica; (pharm.) purgative mixture.

angelical, *a.* angelic.

angelicalmente, *adv.* angelically.

angélico, ca, *a.* angelic.

angelico, ito, *m. dim.* little angel.

angelón, angelonazo, angelote, *m. aug.* large figure of an angel placed on altars; fat child.

ángelus, *m.* Angelus.

angina, *f.* angina.—**a. de pecho**, angina pectoris.

angiología, *f.* angiology, part of anatomy dealing with blood vessels and lymphatics.

---

angiospermo, ma, *n.* & *a.* (bot.) angiosperm (-ous).—*f. pl.* Angiospermæ.

angla, *f.* cape (of land).

anglesita, *f.* (min.) anglesite, a lead ore

anglicanismo, *m.* Anglicanism.

anglicano, na, *a.* Anglican.

anglicismo, *m.* Anglicism.

anglo, gla, *a.* Angle; English.

angloamericano, na, *n.* & *a.* Anglo-American.

anglomanía, *f.* Anglomania.

anglómano, na, *n.* Anglomaniac.

anglosajón, na, *a.* & *n.* Anglo-Saxon.

angolán, *m.* (bot.) alangium, East India tree.

angostamente, *adv.* narrowly.

angostar, *va.* & *vr.* to narrow; to contract.

angosto, ta, *a.* narrow, close; insufficient.

angostura, *f.* narrowness; strait; distress; narrows (in a river, etc.).

angra, *f.* small bay, cove.

angrelado, da, *a.* (her., arch.) serrated.

anguarina, *f.* loose coat with long sleeves.

anguila, *f.* (zool.) eel.—**a. de cabo,** (naut.) rope to flog sailors.—**anguilas,** launching ways.

anguilazo, *m.* stroke with an ANGUILA DE CABO.

anguilero, *a.* (basket) for eels.

anguina, *f.* (vet.) the vein of the groins.

angula, *f.* the brood of eels.

angular, *a.* angular.

angularmente, *adv.* angularly.

angulema, *f.* hemp stuff.—*pl.* (coll.) foolish flattery. Also ZALAMERÍA.

ángulo, *m.* angle; angle iron.—**á. acimutal,** azimuth.—**á. de ataque,** (aer.) angle of attack.—**á. de balance,** (aer.) angle of bank or of roll.—**á. de contingencia,** (Ry.) (*interior*) intersection angle (of two tangents).—**á. de derrape,** (aer.) angle of yaw.—**á. de incidencia,** (phys.) angle of incidence; (aer.) angle of attack.—**á. de incidencia creciente, decreciente,** (aer.) washin, washout.—**á. de planeo,** (aer.) gliding angle.—**á. de resistencia nula,** (aer.) angle of zero lift.—**á. entrante,** reëntrant angle, convex angle.—**á. externo,** (geom.) exterior angle.—**á. horario,** (astr.) hour angle.—**á. interno,** (geom.) interior angle.—**á. recto,** right angle.—**á. tangencial,** (Ry.) deflection angle (from a tangent to a curve).—**ángulos alternos externos,** alternate exterior angles.—**ángulos correspondientes,** corresponding, or interior-exterior, angles.—**ángulos opuestos por el vértice,** vertical angles.—**anguloso, sa,** *a.* angular, cornered; (of sand, etc.) sharp.

angustia, *f.* anguish, affliction, pang.

angustiadamente, *adv.* painfully.

angustiado, da. I. *pp.* of ANGUSTIAR. **II.** *a.* sorrowful; anxious; narrow-minded.

angustiar, *va.* to cause anguish to, afflict, worry.

angustioso, sa, *a.* full of, or causing, anguish.

anhelación, *f.* panting; longing.

anhelante, *a.* eager, deeply desirous, longing.

anhelar, *vn.* to breathe with difficulty; to desire anxiously, long for, covet.

anhélito, *m.* difficult respiration.

anhelo, *m.* strong desire; eagerness.—**anheloso, sa,** *a.* difficult (breathing); anxiously desirous.

anhídrico, ca, *a.* = ANHIDRO.

anhídrido, *m.* (chem.) anhydride.—**a. carbónico,** carbon dioxide, carbonic-acid gas.—**a. sulfúrico,** sulphur trioxide.

anhidrita, *f.* (min.) anhydrite.

anhidro, dra, *a.* anhydrous.

aní, *m.* (ornith.) (S. A.) a pretty creeping bird.

anidar, *vn.* to nest; to nestle; (fig.) to dwell, reside; to cherish; to shelter.

anieblar, *va.* to darken, obscure; to mystify.

anieblo, anieble, *v. V.* ANEBLAR.

anilina, *f.* (chem.) aniline.

anilismo, *m.* aniline poisoning.

anilla, *f.* ring; curtain ring; hoop.

anillado, da, *a.* in the form of a ring, annulated.—*m.* (zool.) Annelida.

anillar, *va.* to form rings or hoops with; to fasten with rings.

anillejo, anillete, *m. dim.* small ring.

anillo, *m.* small hoop; finger ring; circlet; ring of a turbine; circular band; (naut.) hank or grommet; (arch.) astragal.—**a. de boda,** wedding ring.—**a. de matrimonio,** engagement ring.—**de a.,** honorary.—**venir como a. al dedo,** to fit like a glove; to come in the nick of time.

ánima, *f.* soul; (mech.) bore of a gun.—**ánimas,** ringing of church bells at sunset.

animable, *a.* susceptible of animation.

animación, *f.* animation, liveliness; bustle.

animado, da. I. *pp.* of ANIMAR. **II.** *a.* lively, animated; manful.

animador, ra, *n.* one who animates or enlivens.

animadversión, *f.* animadversion; enmity.

animal. I. *m.* animal; dunce, blockhead. **II.** *a.* animal; stupid.—**animalejo, ico, illo,** *m. dim.* small or little animal, animalcule.

animalización, *f.* animalization.

animalizar, *va.* to animalize.

animalote, *m. aug.* big animal.

animalucho, *m.* ugly, hideous animal.

animar. I. *va.* to animate, enliven, comfort; to encourage; to revive; to incite, excite; to give power or vigor to. **II.** *vr.* to become lively; to feel encouraged, energetic; to cheer up.

anime, *f.* a myrrhlike resin.

animero, *m.* one who begs for souls in purgatory.

animismo, *m.* animism.

ánimo, *m.* spirit, soul, mind; courage, valor, fortitude, manfulness; hardiness; mind, intention, will; thought; attention.—**hacer,** or **tener, a. de,** to intend to, make up one's mind to.

animosamente, *adv.* courageously.

animosidad, *f.* animosity; courage.

animoso, sa, *a.* brave, spirited, courageous.

aniñadamente, *adv.* childishly.

aniñado, da, *a.* childish.

aniñarse, *vr.* to become childish.

aniquilable, *a.* destructible.

aniquilación, *f.* annihilation.

aniquilador, ra, *n.* & *a.* annihilator(-ing).

aniquilamiento, *m.* destruction, annihilation; decay, wasting away.

aniquilar. I. *va.* to annihilate; to consume, waste away. **II.** *vr.* to decline; to decay; to waste away, become emaciated.

anís, *m.* (bot.) anise, aniseed; sugar-coated aniseed.

anisado, da. I. *a.* made of or flavored with anise. **II.** *m.* anisating; AGUARDIENTE ANISADO, a liquor flavored with anise.

¹anisar, *va.* to tincture with anise.

²anisar, *m.* patch sowed with aniseed.

anisete, *m.* anisette.

anisidina, *f.* (chem.) a substance used in dyeing.

aniversario, ria. I. *a.* annual, yearly. **II.** *m.* anniversary; holiday; annual memorial service.

anjeo, *m.* coarse linen.

ano, *m.* anus.

anoche, *adv.* last night.

anochecedor, ra, *n.* person who retires late at night; (coll.) night hawk.

anochecer. I. *vn.* (*ind.* ANOCHEZCO; *subj.* ANOCHEZCA) to grow dark (at the approach of night); to be or reach (somewhere) at nightfall (*anochecimos en París,* we reached Paris at nightfall. The construction of this verb is similar to that of AMANECER). **II.** *vr.* to become dark (at nightfall). **III.** *m.* nightfall, dusk.—**al a.,** at nightfall, at dusk.

anochecida, *f.* nightfall, dusk.

anochezco, anochezca, *v. V.* ANOCHECER.

anodinar, *va.* to use, or put under the influence of, anodynes.

For pronunciation, see the rules at the beginning of the book.

anodinia, *f.* (med.) anodynia, absence of pain.
anodino, na, *n.* & *a.* (med.) anodyne.
ánodo, *m.* (elec.) anode.
anomalía, *f.* anomaly; (astr.) anomaly.
anómalo, la, *a.* anomalous.
anón, *m.* (bot.) custard apple tree.
¹**anona,** *f.* annona or custard apple.
²**anona,** *f.* store of provisions.
anonáceo, a. I. *a.* (bot.) annonaceous. **II.** *m. pl.* Annonaceæ.
anonadación, *f.*; **anonadamiento,** *m.* annihilation; overwhelming, crushing.
anonadar. I. *va.* to annihilate; to diminish. **II.** *vr.* to humble oneself.
anónimamente, *adv.* anonymously.
anónimo, ma, *a.* anonymous.
anormal, *a.* abnormal.—**anormalmente,** *adv.* abnormally.
anotación, *f.* annotation, note.
anotador, ra, *n.* commentator.
anotar, *va.* to make notes; to comment, annotate.
anquera, *f.* (Mex.) round covering for the hind quarters of a horse.
anqueta.—estar de media a., to be uncomfortably seated.
anquialmendrado, da, *a.* (of a horse) having a narrow croup.
anquiboyuno, na, *a.* having a croup like an ox.
anquilosis, *f.* (med.) ankylosis.
anquirredondo, da, *a.* having a rounded croup.
anquiseco, ca, *a.* lean-crouped.
ansa, hansa, *f.* commercial league among the free cities of Germany.
ánsar, *m.* goose.—**a. macho,** gander.
ansarería, *f.* goose farm.
ansarero, ra, *n.* gooseherd.
ansarino, na. I. *a.* (poet.) pert. to geese. **II.** *m.* gosling.
ansarón, *m.* = ÁNSAR.
anseático, ca, *a.* Hanseatic.
ansí, (obs.) = ASÍ, so, thus.
ansia, *f.* anxiety; eagerness, ardent desire; longing, hankering; greediness.
ansiadamente, *adv.* anxiously; earnestly.
ansiar, *va.* to desire anxiously; to long for; to hanker for; to covet.
ansiedad, *f.* anxiety; (med.) pain accompanying illness.
ansiosamente, *adv.* anxiously; eagerly.
ansioso, sa, *a.* anxious; eager; greedy; hot.
¹**anta,** *f.* elk.
²**anta,** *f.* obelisk, needle.—*pl.* (arch.) pillars of a building.
antagallas, *f. pl.* (naut.) spritsail reef bands.
antagónico, ca, *a.* antagonistic.
antagonismo, *m.* antagonism.
antagonista, *m.* antagonist; competitor.
antañazo, *adv.* (coll.) a long time ago.
antaño, *adv.* last year; long ago; yore.
antártico, ca, *a.* antarctic.
¹**ante. I.** *prep.* before; in the presence of.—**representante, delgado, miembro, a.,** representative at, delegate to, member of, (an organization, as the U. N.).—**a. todo,** above all, first of all. **II.** *m.* first dinner course; (Peru) drink made of wine, sugar, cinnamon, nutmeg, etc.
²**ante,** *m.* elk; buffalo; buffalo skin.
anteado, da, *a.* buff-colored.
antealtar, *m.* chancel.
anteanoche, antenoche, *adv.* night before last.
anteayer, *adv.* day before yesterday.
antebrazo, *m.* forearm.
antecama, *f.* carpet laid in front of a bed.
antecámara, *f.* antechamber; lobby; hall.
antecapilla, *f.* anteroom to a chapel.
antecedente, *a.* & *m.* antecedent.—**antecedentemente,** *adv.* previously, beforehand.
anteceder, *va.* to precede, go before.
antecesor, ra, *n.* predecessor, forefather.—*pl.* ancestors.

antecoger, *va.* (ind. ANTECOJO; subj. ANTECOJA) to forereach; to gather in (thing), receive (person), too soon.
antecolumna, *f.* (arch.) column of a porch.
antecoro, *m.* entrance leading to the choir.
antecos, cas, *n.* & *a. pl.* (those) living on same meridian but on opposite sides of equator.
Antecristo, *m.* Antichrist.
antedata, *f.* antedate.—**antedatar,** *va.* to antedate.
antedecir, *va.* (ger. ANTEDICIENDO; *pp.* ANTEDICHO; ind. pres. ANTEDIGO, pret. ANTEDIJE, fut. ANTEDIRÉ; subj. ANTEDIGA) to foretell.
antedicho, cha, *a.* aforesaid.
ante diem, (Lat.) the preceding day.
antediluviano, na, *a.* antediluvian.
antefirma, *f.* closing phrases (of a letter) or denomination of the signer, put before the signature.
anteiglesia, *f.* porch of a church; parochial church and district in Biscay.
antelación, *f.* precedence in order of time.
antemano.—de a., beforehand.
antemeridiano, na, *a.* of the forenoon (a. m.).
ante merídiem, in the forenoon (a. m.).
antemural, *m.* **antemuralla,** *f.*, **antemuro,** *m.* fort, rock or mountain serving for the defense of a fortress; safeguard.
antena, *f.* (naut.) lateen yard; (zool., radio) antenna.—*pl.* antennæ.
antenallas, *f. pl.* pincers.
antenatal, *a.* prenatal.
antenoche, anteanoche, *adv.* night before last.
antenombre, *m.* title before a proper name.
anténula, *f.* (zool.) antennule, small antenna.
antenupcial, *a.* before marriage, prenuptial.
anteojera, *f.* spectacle case; blinker (for horse).
anteojero, ra, *n.* spectacle maker or seller.
anteojo, *m.* spyglass; eyeglass; telescope (of a surveying instrument); opera glass; blinker (for horse);—*pl.* spectacles; goggles.—**a. de larga vista,** field glass.
antepagar, *va.* to pay beforehand.
antepasado, da. I. *a.* (of time) passed, elapsed. **II.** *n.* ancestor, predecessor.
antepecho, *m.* balcony, bridge rail; window sill railing; breastwork, parapet; footstep of a coach; poitrel (harness); breast roller of a loom.
antepenúltimo, ma, *a.* antepenultimate.
anteponer, *va.* (*pp.* ANTEPUESTO; ind. pres. ANTEPONGO, pret. ANTEPUSE, fut. ANTEPONDRÉ; subj. ANTEPONGA) to prefer.—**a. a,** to prefer (one thing) to (another); to place before.
anteportada, *f.* front page (of a book) bearing the title only.
anteportal, antepórtico, *m.* vestibule, porch.
anteproyecto, *m.* preliminary plans for an architectural or engineering work.
antepuerta, *f.* portier; (fort.) inner gate.
antepuerto, *m.* (naut.) anteport.
antera, *f.* (bot.) anther.
anterior, *a.* anterior; former; above, preceding.
anterioridad, *f.* anteriority; priority; preference.—**con a.,** previously, beforehand.
anteriormente, *adv.* previously.
antero, *m.* worker in buckskin.
antes, *adv.* before; formerly; first; rather; on the contrary.—**a. bien,** on the contrary; rather.—**a. de,** before.—**a. de anoche** = ANTENOCHE.—**a. de ayer** = ANTEAYER.—**a. de que,** before.—**a. que,** before; rather than.
antesacristía, *f.* anteroom of a sacristy.
antesala, *f.* antechamber.—**hacer a.,** to be kept waiting, dance attendance.
antestatura, *f.* (mil.) improvised intrenchment of palisades and sandbags.
antetemplo, *m.* portico of a church.
antever, *va.* (*pp.* ANTEVISTO; ger. ANTEVIENDO; ind. ANTEVEO; subj. ANTEVEA) to foresee.
antevíspera, *f.* two days before.

For pronunciation, see the rules at the beginning of the book.

antiaéreo, a, *a.* anti-aircraft (as *a.*).
antiafrodisíaco, ca, *a.* anaphrodisiac.
antialcohólico, ca, *a.* (Am.) antialcoholic.
antiapopléctico, ca, *a.* antiapoplectic.
antiapóstol, *m.* & *f.* antiapostle.
antiarina, *f.* (chem.) antiarin.
antiaro, *m.* upas tree.
antiartístico, ca, *a.* unartistic.
antiartrítico, ca, *a.* (med.) antiarthritic.
antiasmático, ca, *a.* (med.) antiasthmatic.
antibaquio, *m.* antibacchius, foot in poetry.
antibilioso, sa, *a.* antibilious.
anticiclón, *m.* (meteorol.) anticyclone.
anticipación, *f.* anticipation; foretaste.
anticipada, *f.* (fencing) unexpected thrust.
anticipadamente, *adv.* prematurely; in advance, beforehand.
anticipado, da, *a.* advanced (money); in advance (payment).
anticipador, ra, *n.* & *a.* anticipator(-ing).
anticipamiento, *m.* = ANTICIPACIÓN.
anticipante, *n.* & *a.* forestalling(-er).
anticipar. I. *va.* to anticipate (in the sense of to do, bring to happen, etc. before the regular time); to advance (money, payment); to lend. **II.** *vr.* (a) to anticipate, act ahead (of); to act or occur before the regular or expected time.
anticipo, *m.* advance; money lent; advance payment.
anticlerical, *a.* anticlerical.
anticlímax, *m.* or *f.* (rhet.) anticlimax.
anticlinal, *m.* (geol.) anticline.
anticonstitucional, *a.* unconstitutional.
anticosmético, ca, *a.* anticosmetic.
anticresis, *f.* (law) antichresis.
anticresista, *m.* the creditor in antichresis.
anticristiano, na, *a.* antichristian.
anticristo, *m.* Antichrist.
anticrítico, *m.* opponent to a critic.
anticuado, da. I. *pp.* of ANTICUAR. **II.** *a.* antiquated.
anticuar. I. *va.* to antiquate, outdate. **II.** *vr.* to become antiquated.
anticuario, ria, *n.* antiquarian.
anticuerpo, *m.* antibody.
antideslizante, *a.* nonskidding (esp. auto tires).
antidisentérico, ca, *a.* antidysenteric.
antidoral, *a.* (law) remunerative.
antidotario, *m.* pharmacology; place in a pharmacy for antidotes.
antídoto, *m.* antidote.
antiemético, ca, *a.* (med.) antiemetic.
antiepiléptico, ca, *a.* (med.) antiepileptic.
antier, *adv.* (coll.) day before yesterday.
antiesclavista, *a.* (Am.) antislavery.
antiescorbútico, ca, *a.* antiscorbutic.
antiescrofuloso, sa, *a.* antiscrofulous.
antiespasmódico, ca, *a.* antispasmodic.
antifaz, *m.* veil that covers the face; mask.
antifebril, *a.* (med.) antifebrile.
antiflogístico, ca, *a.* & *m.* (med.) antiphlogistic.
antífona, *f.* (eccl.) antiphony, responsive singing.
antifonal, antifonario, *m.* antiphonal.
antifonero, *m.* precentor.
antífrasis, *f.* (rhet.) antiphrasis.
antigobiernista, *n.* & *a.* oppositionist, antigovernment (person).
antigramatical, *a.* ungrammatical.
antigualla, *f.* object of remote antiquity; antique; out-of-date custom or object.
antiguamente, *adv.* formerly, in antiquity.
antiguar, *vn.* to attain seniority (in a position).
antigüedad, *f.* antiquity; ancient times; antique.
antiguo, gua. I. *a.* antique; ancient, old.—**A. Testamento,** Old Testament.—**a la antigua, a lo antiguo,** after the manner of the ancients, in an old-fashion manner.—**de antiguo,** from times of yore, since old times.—**lo antiguo,** ancient things; antiquity. **II.** *m.* aged member

of a community; veteran (in an occupation); senior of a college.—**los antiguos,** the ancients.
antihelmíntico, ca, *a.* (med.) anthelmintic.
antiherpético, ca, *a.* (med.) antiherpetic.
antihistérico, ca, *a.* (med.) antihysteric.
antiinflacionista, *a.* anti-inflationary.
antilogía, *f.* antilogy, contradiction in terms.
antilógico, ca, *a.* illogical.
antílope, *m.* antelope.
antillano, na, *n.* & *a.* West-Indian.
Antillas, *f. pl.* West Indies, Antilles.
antiministerial. I. *a.* opposed to the Administration. **II.** *n.* member of the opposition (to the government).
antimonárquico, ca, *a.* antimonarchical.
antimonial, *a.* (chem.) antimonial.
antimoniato, *m.* antimonate.
antimónico, ca, *a.* antimonic.
antimonio, *m.* antimony.
antinacional, *a.* antinational.
antinatural, *a.* unnatural.
antinefrítico, ca, *a.* (med.) antinephritic.
antineurálgico, ca, *n.* & *a.* antineuralgic.
antinomia, *f.* (law) antinomy.
antioqueno, *n.* & *a.* Antiochian.
antipalúdico, ca, *a.* antimalarial.
antipapa, *m.* antipope.—**antipapado,** *m.* antipapacy.—**antipapal,** *a.* antipapal.
antipara, *f.* screen; legging covering the front part of leg and foot.
antiparras, *f. pl.* (coll.) spectacles.
antipatía, *f.* antipathy; dislike, aversion.
antipático, ca, *a.* uncongenial, disagreeable.
antipatizar, *vn.* not to be congenial.—**a. con,** to dislike, not to be congenial with.
antipatriótico, ca, *a.* unpatriotic.
antiperistáltico, ca, *a.* antiperistaltic.
antiperistasis, *f.* antiperistasis.
antiperistático, ca, *a.* antiperistatic.
antipestilencial, *a.* (med.) antipestilential.
antipirina, *f.* antipyrine.
antipoca, *f.* (law, prov.) agreement to lease.
antipocar, *va.* (law) to execute (a lease).
antipoda. I. *a.* antipodal. **II.** *m.* (in *pl.*) antipodes.
antipolítico, ca, *a.* impolitic.
antipútrido, da, *a.* antiseptic.
antiquísimo, ma, *a.* *super.* very ancient.
antirreglamentario, ria, *a.* against the rules.
antirreligioso, sa, *a.* irreligious.
antirrevolucionario, ria, *a.* antirevolutionary.
antirrino, *m.* (bot.) snapdragon.
antisemita I. *a.* anti-Semitic. **II.** *n.* anti-Semite.
antisepsia, *f.* (med.) antisepsis.
antiséptico, ca, *n.* & *a.* antiseptic.
antisifilítico, ca, *a.* antisyphilitic.
antisocial, *a.* antisocial.
antístrofa, *f.* antistrophe.
antisubstancia, *f.* antibody. Also ANTICUERPO.
antitanque, *a.*—**cañon a.,** antitank gun.
antitérmico, ca, *a.* heat-resisting.
antítesis, *f.* antithesis.
antitético, ca, *a.* antithetical.
antitóxico, ca, *a.* antitoxic.
antitoxina, *f.* antitoxin.
antitrago, *m.* (anat.) antitragus.
antitrinitario, *m.* antitrinitarian.
antituberculoso, sa, *a.* antitubercular.
antivenenoso, sa, *a.* antitoxic.
antófago, ga; *a.* (zool.) anthophagous.
antojadizo, za; antojado, da, *a.* capriciously desirous, having whimsical desires for trifles; wishing, or taking a notion to, everything (gen. said of children and women).
antojarse, *vr.* to be desired capriciously or on the spur of the moment, to arouse a whimsical desire, or a fancy (diff. constr.: *se me antojó ese sombrero,* I took a fancy to (buy) that hat, (coll.) I fell in love with that hat and longed for it: *no hago eso porque no se me antoja,*

I don't do that because it doesn't appeal to me, or, because I won't; *se nos antojó ir a París,* we took a notion to go to Paris); to occur (to the mind), seem probable (diff. constr.: *se me antojó que Juan no sabía,* it occurred to me, *or,* I suspected, that John did not know).— **a. de,** to take a fancy to, to desire capriciously.

antojo, *m.* whim, capricious desire, fancy; will.— **a su a.,** as one pleases; arbitrarily.

antojuelo, *m. dim.* slight desire.

antología, *f.* anthology.

antónimo, ma, *a. & m.* (pert. to) antonym.

antonomasia, *f.* (rhet.) antonomasia.

antonomástico, ca, *a.* antonomastic.

antor, ra, *n.* (law) vender of stolen goods he acquired in good faith.

antorcha, *f.* torch, flambeau, taper; cresset.

antorchero, *m.* cresset.

antoría, *f.* (law, prov.) right of reclaim from the seller of stolen goods.

antracita, *f.* anthracite coal.

ántrax, *m.* (med.) anthrax.

antro, *m.* cavern, grotto; (anat.) antrum.

antropofagía, *f.* anthropophagy, cannibalism.

antropófago, ga, *n. & a.* cannibal.

antropofobia, *f.* anthropophobia.

antropografía, *f.* anthropography.

antropoide, *n. & a.* anthropoid.

antropología, *f.* anthropology.

antropológico, ca, *a.* anthropological.

antropólogo, *m.* anthropologist.

antropómetra, *n.* anthropometrist.—**antropometría,** *f.* anthropometry.—**antropométrico, ca,** *a.* anthropometric.

antropomorfismo, *m.* anthropomorphism.

antropomorfita, *n.* anthropomorphite.

antropomorfo, fa, *a.* anthropomorphous.

antroposofía, *f.* anthroposophy.

antruejar, *va.* to play carnival tricks on.

antruejo, *m.* the three days of carnival before Ash Wednesday.

antuviada, *f.* (coll.) unexpected blow or stroke.

antuviar, *va.* to forestall, anticipate; (coll.) to be first in striking.—**antuvión,** *m.* (coll.) sudden blow or attack.—**de a.,** unexpectedly.

anual, *a.* annual, yearly.—**anualidad,** *f.* annual recurrence; annuity.—**anualmente,** *adv.* annually, yearly.

anuario, *m.* yearbook; trade or professional directory.

anúbada, *f.* = ANÚTEBA, a call to war.

anubarrado, da, *a.* clouded.

anublado, da, *a.* overcast, clouded, cloudy.

anublar. I. *va.* to cloud, darken; to obscure. **II.** *vr.* to be blasted, withered, mildewed; to fail, fall through, fall off; to become cloudy.

anublo, *m.* = AÑUBLO, mildew (of grain).

anudar. I. *va.* to knot; to join, unite. **II.** *vn.* to wither, fade, pine away.—**anudarse la voz a uno,** (fig.) to become speechless.

anuencia, *f.* compliance, consent.

anuente, *a.* complying, consenting.

anulable, *a.* voidable.

anulación, *f.* abrogation, voiding, nullification.

anulador, ra, *n.* repealer.

¹**anular,** *va.* to annul, make void; to frustrate.

²**anular,** *a.* ring-shaped.—**dedo a.,** ring finger.

anulativo, va, *a.* voiding.

anuloso, sa, *a.* annular, ring-shaped.

anunciación, *f.* announcement; Annunciation.

anunciador, ra. I. *n. & a.* announcer(-ing); advertiser(-ing). **II.** *m.* (elec.) annunciator; (radio) announcer (Arg. also SPEAKER).

anunciante, *n.* announcer; advertiser.

anunciar, *va.* to announce, proclaim; to foretell; to advertise.

anuncio, *m.* announcement, notice; omen, forerunner; advertisement; (com.) advice.

anuo, nua, *a.* = ANUAL, annual.

anuria, *f.* (med.) anuria.

anuro, *n.* (zool.) anuran.

anúteba, *f.* a call to war.

anverso, *m.* observe (of coin, medal, etc.).

anvir, *m.* liquor from fermented tobacco leaves.

anzolero, *m.* fishhook maker or dealer.

anzuelo, *m.* fishhook; fritters.—**caer en el a., tragar el a.,** to be gullible, swallow the hook.

aña, *f.* (Peru) a kind of small fox.

añacal, *m.* wheat carrier to mills; baker's board to carry bread.

añada, *f.* good or bad season in a year; pasture or arable land lying fallow alternate years.

añadido, *m.* hair switch.

añadidura, *f.* addition, increase; extra, over.— **por a.,** in addition, into the bargain, (often in the sense of "to make matters worse"); over, to boot.

añadir, *va.* to add, join; to exaggerate.

añafil, *m.* a Moorish musical pipe.

añafilero, *m.* player on the *añafil.*

añagaza, *f.* call, lure, or decoy; allurement, enticement.

añal. I. *a.* annual; yearling. **II.** *m.* offering in memory of a person one year after his death.

añalejo, *m.* ecclesiastical almanac.

añascar, *va.* (*pret.* AÑASQUÉ; *subj.* AÑASQUE) (coll.) to collect (small trinkets).

añejar. I. *va.* to make old. **II.** *vr.* to age (of things, either deteriorating or improving).

añejo, ja, *a.* old; aged (improved); stale, musty.

añicos, *n. pl.* fragments, "smithereens."—**hacer a.,** to break to smithereens.—**hacerse a.,** to take great pains, exert oneself to the utmost.

añil, *m.* (bot.) indigo; indigo blue.—**añilar,** *va.* to blue (clothes).—**añilería,** *f.* indigo farm.

añinero, *m.* dealer in lambskins.

añinos, *m. pl.* the fleecy skins of yearling lambs; lamb's wool.

año, *m.* year; cavalier; valentine drawn by lot on New Year's day; crop.—*pl.* birthday; long ago; old age.—**a. anomalístico,** anomalistic year. —**a. antepasado,** year before last.—**a. bisiesto,** leap-year.—**a. civil,** civil year.—**a. climatérico,** grand climacteric.—**a. de gracia,** year of grace.—**a. económico,** fiscal year.— **a. en curso,** current year.—**a. escolar,** school year.—**a. intercalar,** leap-year.—**a. nuevo,** New Year.—**a. platónico,** Platonic year.—**a. sideral,** sidereal year.—**a. sinódico,** synodic period of the earth and another planet.—**a. tras a.,** year after year.—**a. tropical,** tropical or solar year.—**al a.,** by the year.—**entrado en años,** of mature age, of uncertain age (not young).—**entre a.,** during the year.—**estar de buen a.,** to be in good health.—**por los años de . . . ,** about the year . . .—**tener . . . años,** to be . . . years old (*tengo 20 años,* I am 20 years old; *¿cuántos años tiene Vd.?* how old are you?)

añojal, *m.* fallow land.

añojo, ja, *n.* yearling calf.

añoranza, *f.* nostalgia; loneliness (through bereavement).

añorar, *vn.* to suffer from nostalgia; to recall old times.

añoso, sa, *a.* old, aged, stricken in years.

añublado, da. I. *pp.* of AÑUBLAR. **II.** *a.* blindfolded.

añublar, añublarse, = ANUBLAR.

añublo, *m.* mildew (on grain). Also TIZÓN.

añusgar, *vn.* to choke; to become angry.

aojador, ra, *n.* hoodoo, evil-eyed person.

aojadura, *f.* **aojamiento,** *m.* witchcraft, fascination, evil eye.

aojar, *va.* to charm, bewitch, hoodoo.

aojo, *m.* bewitching, fascination, evil eye.

aonio, nia, *a.* pertaining to the Muses.

aorta, *f.* (anat.) aorta.—**aórtico, ca,** *a.* aortic.

aovado, da, *a.* oviform, egg-shaped.

aovar, *vn.* to lay eggs.

aovillarse, *vr.* to crumple, shrink.
apabilar, *va.* to trim (a wick).
apabullar, *va.* (coll.) to flatten, crush.
apacentadero, *m.* grazing field, pasture.
apacentador, *m.* herdsman.
apacentamiento, *m.* grazing; pasturage.
apacentar, *va.* (*ind.* APACIENTO; *subj.* APACIENTE) to graze (cattle); to graze, feed on (grass, etc.); to teach, instruct spiritually; to incite.
apacibilidad, *f.* peaceableness, mildness.
apacible, *a.* peaceable, peaceful, gentle, placid, calm.—**apaciblemente,** *adv.* peacefully, gently.
apaciento, apaciente, *v. V.* APACENTAR.
apaciguador, ra, *n. & a.* pacifier(-fying).
apaciguamiento, *m.* pacification, appeasement.
apaciguar. I. *va.* to appease, pacify, calm. II. *vn.* (naut.) to abate. III. *vr.* to calm down.
apache, *m.* Apache, gangster, gunman.
apacheta, *f.* (Am.) devotional heap of stones on hills.
apachurrar, *va.* (Am.) to crush, flatten.
apadrinador, ra, *n.* patron, defender, protector; second (in a duel).
apadrinar, *va.* to act as second of, in a duel; to act as godfather to; to uphold, approve, favor.
apagable, *a.* extinguishable, quenchable.
apagadizo, za, *a.* poorly burning, of difficult combustion.
apagado, da, *a.* humble-minded, submissive, pusillanimous; dull (color).
apagador, *m.* one that extinguishes; damper, extinguisher; damper (in pianos).
apagaincendios, *m.* fire engine; fire extinguisher.
apagamiento, *m.* extinguishment.
apagapenoles, *m. pl.* (naut.) leech ropes, lines.
apagar. I. *va.* (*pret.* APAGUÉ; *subj.* APAGUE) to quench, put out, extinguish; to efface, destroy; (art) to soften (colors); (mech.) to deaden.— **a. cal,** to slake lime.—**a. la voz,** to put a mute on musical instruments.—**a. los fuegos,** or **el fuego, del enemigo,** to silence the enemy's guns. II. *vr.* to become extinguished, go out, die out.
apagógico, ca, *a.* apagogical.
apagón, *m.* blackout (as when electricity fails).
apainelado, da, *a.* elliptic (arch).
apaisado, da, *a.* of greater width than depth.
apalabrar, *va.* to make an engagement with; to speak about, discuss; to bespeak, engage.
apalancar, *va.* (*pret.* APALANQUÉ; *subj.* APALANQUE) to move with a lever.
apaleador, ra, *n.* cudgeller.
apaleamiento, *m.* drubbing, beating.
apalear, *va.* to cane, cudgel; to horsewhip.
apaleo, *m.* moving or shovelling grain.
apanalado, da, *a.* honeycombed.
apancora, *f.* sea hedgehog.
apandar, *va.* (coll.) to pilfer, steal.
apandillar, *va. & vr.* to form a gang or faction.
apanojado, da, *a.* (bot.) paniculate.
apantanar, *va.* to flood; to inundate.
apantuflado, da, *a.* slipper-shaped.
¹apañado, da, *a.* resembling woollen cloth in body.
²apañado, da, *a.* dexterous, skillful; (coll.) suitable.
apañador, ra, *n.* one that seizes; pilferer.
apañadura, *f.* act of seizing, snatching; trimming (on counterpanes).
apañamiento, *m.* act of seizing, snatching.
apañar. I. *va.* to grasp, seize; to carry away; to pilfer; to dress, clothe; to fit close, wrap; to patch, mend. II. *vr.* (coll.) to be handy, to be skillful; to contrive, manage.—**apaño,** *m.* a seizing, grasping; knack; patch, repair.
apañuscar, *va.* (*pret.* APAÑUSQUÉ; *subj.* APAÑUSQUE) to rumple, crush, crumple.
apapagayado, da, *a.* parrotlike; aquiline (nose).
aparador, *m.* sideboard, cupboard; workshop of an artisan; show window.

aparadura, *f.* (naut.) garbel, garboard plank.
aparar, *va.* to stretch out the hands or skirts for catching; (agr.) to dress (plants); (shoemaking) to close (the uppers); to prepare, arrange; to dress with an adze, dub.—**a. un navio,** (naut.) to dub a ship.
aparasolado, da, *a.* (bot.) umbelliferous.
aparatado, da, *a.* prepared, disposed.
aparatero, ra, *a.* = APARATOSO.
aparato, *m.* apparatus; preparation; pomp, show; circumstance; signs, symptoms; elaborate scenic display; collection of surgical instruments; system, associated organs.—**a. de radio,** radio set.—**aparatoso, sa,** *a.* pompous, showy.
aparcería, *f.* partnership.
aparcero, ra, *n.* partner.
apareamiento, *m.* matching, mating, pairing.
aparear. I. *va.* to match, mate; to pair. II. *vr.* to be paired, matched, mated.
aparecer, *vn. & vr.* (*ind.* APAREZCO; *subj.* APAREZCA) to appear, show up, turn up.
aparecido, da. I. *pp.* of APARECER. II. *m.* ghost.
aparecimiento, *m.* appearing, appearing.
aparejado, da. I. *pp.* of APAREJAR. II. *a.* fit; ready.
aparejador, ra, *n.* one who prepares or gets ready; overseer of a building; (naut.) rigger.
aparejar. I. *va.* to get ready; to prepare; to saddle or harness; (naut.) to rig; to furnish; to size (work before painting or gilding). II. *vr.* to get ready; to equip oneself.
aparejo, *m.* preparation, disposition; harness, gear; packsaddle; (mech.) tackle; (art) sizing canvas or board; (mason.) bond; (naut.) tackle and rigging on a ship; furniture.—*pl.* equipment, trappings.—**a. real,** main tackle.
aparentar, *va.* to feign, pretend.
aparente, *a.* apparent, not real; fit, suited; evident, manifest.
aparentemente, *adv.* apparently, outwardly.
aparezco, aparezca, *v. V.* APARECER.
aparición, *f.* apparition; appearance (coming in sight).
apariencia, *f.* appearance, aspect, looks; likeness, resemblance; vestige; outward show; pageant; probability, conjecture.—*pl.* scenic effects.
aparrado, da, *a.* shrubby, vinelike.
aparroquiado, da, *a.* established in a parish.
aparroquiar, *va.* to bring customers to.
apartadamente, *adv.* privately, apart.
apartadero, *m.* sidetrack, siding; free space (beside a road, etc.); sorting room.
apartadijo, *m.* small part, share, or portion.
apartadizo, *m.* recluse; small room; partition.
apartado, da. I. *pp.* of APARTAR. II. *a.* distant, retired; aloof; out-of-the-way, remote; distinct, different. III. *m.* room separated from others; smelting house; mail separated for early or special delivery; P. O. letter box; separation of cattle; board of cattle ranchers.
apartador, ra, *n.* one that divides or separates; sorter; separator.—**a. de metales,** smelter.
apartamiento, *m.* separation; retirement; secluded place; apartment, flat; waiver, relinquishment.
apartar. I. *va.* to part off; to separate, divide; to dissuade; to remove, dislodge; to sort. II. *vr.* to withdraw; to hold off; to desist; to retire.
aparte. I. *m.* paragraph; (theat.) aside. II. *adv.* separately; aside (on the stage); different, another, other (*ésta es cuestión aparte,* this is another matter).
aparvar, *va.* to heap (grain for thrashing).
apasionadamente, *adv.* passionately; unfairly, in a biassed way.
apasionado, da. I. *pp.* of APASIONAR. II. *a.* passionate; impassioned; intolerant; (of a part of the body) affected with pain; devoted, passionately fond. III. *m.* admirer.
apasionamiento, *m.* passion.

apasionar. I. *va.* to impassion; to afflict, torment. **II.** *vr.* to become passionately fond.

apasturar, *va.* to pasture, forage.

apatán, *m.* (P. I.) a dry measure (.094 litre).

apatía, *f.* apathy.—**apático, ca,** *a.* apathetic.

apátrida, *a.* & *n.* stateless (person).

apatusco, *m.* (coll.) ornament, dress.

apea, *f.* rope fetter for horses.

apeadero, *m.* landing, horseblock; Ry. station.

apeador, *m.* land surveyor.

apeamiento, *m.* = APEO.

apear. I. *va.* to dismount; to get out (of a carriage, etc.); to bring down; to survey; to set landmarks to; to fell; to block or scotch (a wheel); (arch.) to prop; (artil.) to dismount (a gun); to dissuade; to remove (difficulties); to shackle (a horse). **II.** *vr.* to alight.

apechugar, *va.* (*pret.* APECHUGUÉ; *subj.* APECHUGUE) to push with the breast; (fig.) to face with courage (something distasteful).

apedazar, *va.* (*pret.* APEDACÉ; *subj.* APEDACE) to patch, mend, repair.

apedernalado, da, *a.* (fig.) flinty.

apedreado, da. I. *pp.* of APEDREAR. **II.** *a.* variegated; pitted with the smallpox.

apedreador, ra, *n.* stoner, stone thrower.

apedreamiento, *m.* lapidation, stoning.

apedrear. I. *va.* to stone; to kill with stones. **II.** *vn.* to hail. **III.** *vr.* to be injured by hail.

apedreo, *m.* stoning.

apegadamente, *adv.* devotedly.

apegarse, *vr.* to become attached.—**apego,** *m.* attachment, fondness.

apelable, *a.* (law) appealable.

apelación, *f.* (law) appeal; (coll.) consultation (of doctors); (coll.) remedy, help.

¹apelado, da. I. *a.* (law) successful in an appeal.

²apelado, da, *a.* (of horses) of the same coat or color.

apelambrar, *va.* to steep (hides) in limewater.

apelante, *n.* & *a.* (law) appellant.

¹apelar, *vn.* (law) to appeal; have recourse to.

²apelar, *vn.* (of horses) to be of the same color.

apeldar, *vn.* (coll.) to flee, run away.

apelde, *m.* (coll.) flight, escape.

apelmacé, apelmace, *v. V.* APELMAZAR.

apelmazado, da, *a.* compressed, compact.

apelmazamiento, *m.* compactness.

apelmazar, *va.* (*pret.* APELMACÉ; *subj.* APELMACE) to compress; to render less spongy.

apelotonar, *va.* & *vr.* to form into balls.

apellar, *va.* to dress (leather).

apellidado, da. I. *pp.* of APELLIDAR. **II.** *a.* named, by the name of.

apellidamiento, *m.* naming.

apellidar. I. *va.* to name; to proclaim; to call to arms. **II.** *vr.* to be called (have the name).

apellido, *m.* surname, family name; nickname; forces called to arms.

apenar. I. *va.* to cause pain, sorrow. **II.** *vr.* to grieve.

apenas, *adv.* scarcely, hardly; only; with trouble; no sooner than, as soon as.

apencar, *vn.* (*pret.* APENQUÉ; *subj.* APENQUE) to accept with reluctance.

apéndice, *m.* appendix.—**a. cecal, vermicular,** or **vermiforme,** vermiform appendix.

apendicitis, *f.* appendicitis.

apendicitomía, *f.* (surg.) appendectomy.

apendicular, *a.* pertaining to appendix.

apenino, na, *a.* Apennine.

apenqué, apenque, *v. V.* APENCAR.

apeo, *m.* survey; prop, propping.

apeonar, *va.* to walk or run swiftly (birds).

apepsia, *f.* (med.) apepsy, indigestion.

aperador, *m.* farmer; wheelwright; foreman.

aperar, *va.* to make, repair, equip.

apercibimiento, *m.* preparation, preparedness; order, advice, warning; summons.

apercibir, *va.* to provide; to get ready; to warn, advise; (law) to summon.

aperción, *f.* = ABERTURA, opening.

apercollar, *va.* (*ind.* APERCUELLO; *subj.* APERCUELLE) (coll.) to collar; to snatch.

aperdigar, *va.* to parboil, roast slightly.

apergaminado, da, *a.* parchmentlike.

aperitivo, va, *a.* that stimulates appetite.

apernador, *m.* dog that seizes game by the legs.

apernar, *va.* (*ind.* APIERNO; *subj.* APIERNE) to seize by the leg.

apero, *m.* farm implements; tools, outfit; sheepfold; (often *pl.*) equipment (for an activity); (Am.) luxurious riding equipment.

aperreado, da. I. *pp.* of APERREAR. **II.** *a.* harassed.

aperreador, ra, *n.* (coll.) importunate person, nuisance; intruder.

aperrear. I. *va.* to throw to the dogs; to annoy, bother. **II.** *vr.* to toil, overwork.

apersogar, *va.* (Mex.) to tether.

apersonarse, *vr.* (law) to appear (in court).

apertura, *f.* opening (of a convention, etc.); reading (of a will).

apesadumbrar, *va.* & *vr.* to grieve; to make (become) sad, grief-stricken.

apesaradamente, *adv.* mournfully, sadly.

apesarar, *va.* & *vr.* = APESADUMBRAR.

apesgamiento, *m.* sinking under a burden.

apesgar. I. *va.* (*pret.* APESGUÉ; *subj.* APESGUE) to overwhelm with a load. **II.** *vr.* to be aggrieved.

apestado, da. I. *pp.* of APESTAR. **II.** *a.* pestered, annoyed; satiated; full, overstocked.

apestar. I. *va.* to infect with the plague; to corrupt, turn putrid; to annoy, bother; to sicken, nauseate. **II.** *vn.* to stink.

apestoso, sa, *a.* foul-smelling, sickening, nauseating, offensive.

apétalo, la, *a.* (bot.) apetalous.

apetecedor, ra, *n.* one that longs or desires.

apetecer, *va.* (*ind.* APETEZCO; *subj.* APETEZCA) to like (a food or drink); to desire.—**apetecible,** *a.* appetizing; desirable.

apetencia, *f.* appetite, hunger; desire.

apetezco, apetezca, *v. V.* APETECER.

apetite, *m.* sauce, appetizer; inducement.

apetitivo, va, *a.* appetitive.

apetito, *m.* appetite; appetence.—**abrir el a.,** to stimulate appetite.

apetitoso, sa, *a.* appetizing, savory, palatable.

apezonado, da, *a.* nipple-shaped.

apezuñar, *vn.* to climb laboriously, sinking the edge of the hoof into the ground.

apiadarse. I. *va.* to inspire pity. **II.** *vr.* (de) pity, take pity (on).

apiaradero, *m.* shepherd's account of the sheep.

apiario, a, *a.* beelike.

apicarado, da, *a.* roguish, knavish; impudent.

apicararse, *vr.* to become roguish.

ápice, *m.* apex, summit, top, pinnacle; trifle; whit, iota; written accent; most intricate and pointed part of a question.

apículo, *m.* (bot.) small, keen point.

apicultor, ra, *n.* apiculturist, beekeeper.

apicultura, *f.* apiculture, beekeeping.

ápidos, *m. pl.* (zool.) Apidæ.

apierno, apierne, *v. V.* APERNAR.

apilador, *m.* piler (esp. of wool).

apilamiento, *m.* piling up; crowding.

apilar, *va.* to heap, pile up.

apimpollarse, *vr.* to germinate, sprout.

apiñado, da. I. *pp.* of APIÑAR. **II.** *a.* pyramidal, pine-shaped; crowded, close together.

apiñadura, *f.,* **apiñamiento,** *m.* pressing together; crowd, jam, congestion.

apiñar, *va.* & *vr.* to press together, crowd.

apio, *m.* (bot.) celery.

apiolar, *va.* to gyve (a hawk); to tie by the legs; (coll.) to seize, apprehend; to kill, murder.

apiparse, *vr.* (coll.) to gorge.

apirético, ca, *a.* (med.) apyretic, free from fever.

apirexia, *f.* (med.) apyrexia.

apisonamiento, *m.* tamping.

apisonar, *va.* to tamp.

apitonamiento, *m.* (of deer, etc.) initial growing of horns; passion, anger.

apitonar. I. *vn.* (of deer, etc.) to begin to grow horns; to bud, germinate. II. *va.* to break with bill or horn; to shell. III. *vr.* to abuse each other.

apizarrado, da, *a.* slate-colored.

aplacable, *a.* placable.

aplacación, *f.* appeasement.

aplacador, ra, *n.* & *a.* appeaser(-ing).

aplacamiento, *m.* stay of execution.

aplacar, *va.* (*pret.* APLAQUÉ; *subj.* APLAQUE) to appease, pacify, calm.

aplacé, aplace, *v.* V. APLAZAR.

aplacer, *va.* to please.

aplacerado, da, *a.* (naut.) level and not very deep; (Am.) open, cleared of trees.

aplacible, *a.* pleasant.

aplaciente, *a.* pleasing, agreeable.

aplacimiento, *m.* pleasure.

aplanadera, *f.* levelling board, float; rammer.

aplanador, *m.* leveller; (mech.) battledore, brusher, riveter; ingot hammer; cylinder roller; (print.) planishing mallet.

aplanamiento, *m.* levelling, flattening.

aplanar. I. *va.* to smooth, make even; to flatten; to terrify or astonish. II. *vr.* to tumble down; to weaken; to dismay; to get depressed.

aplanchado, planchado, *m.* ironing (act or collection of clothes ironed or to be ironed).

aplanchador, planchador, ra, *n.* ironer.

aplanchar, *va.* to iron (clothes).

aplanético, ca, *a.* (optics) aplanatic.

aplantillar, *va.* to adjust or fit (stones).

aplaqué, aplaque, *v.* V. APLACAR.

aplastado, da. I. *pp.* of APLASTAR. II. *a.* caked; dispirited.

aplastar. I. *va.* to flatten, crush, smash; to floor (an opponent). II. *vr.* to flatten; to collapse.

aplaudidor, ra, *n.* & *a.* applauder(-ing).

aplaudir, *va.* to applaud.

aplauso, *m.* applause; approbation, praise.

aplayar, *vr.* (of a river) to overflow the banks.

aplazamiento, *m.* convocation; summons; postponement.

aplazar, *va.* (*pret.* APLACÉ; *subj.* APLACE) to convene; to summon; to adjourn; to postpone.

aplebeyar. I. *va.* to make plebeian; to degrade. II. *vr.* to lower oneself; to become mean.

aplegar, *va.* (*pret.* APLEGUÉ; *subj.* APLEGUE) (prov.) to join, unite.

aplicable, *a.* applicable.

aplicación, *f.* application.

aplicado, da. I. *pp.* of APLICAR. II. *a.* studious, industrious, assiduous.

aplicar. I. *va.* (*pret.* APLIQUÉ; *subj.* APLIQUE) to apply; to put on; to clap; to attribute or impute; (law) to adjudge. II. *vr.* to apply oneself.

aplomado, da. I. *pp.* of APLOMAR. II. *a.* lead-colored; calm, grave; heavy, dull, lazy.

aplomar. I. *va.* to overload, crush. II. *vn.* to plumb. III. *vr.* to tumble, fall to the ground.

aplomo. I. *m.* tact, prudence; self-possession, poise; (mus.) exactness in time; (art) due proportion. II. *a.* plumb, vertical.

apnea, *f.* (med.) apnea, suspension of respiration.

apocado, da. I. *pp.* of APOCAR. II. *a.* pusillanimous, cowardly; of low extraction.

apocador, ra, *n.* lessener, diminisher.

Apocalipsis, *m.* Apocalypse, Revelation.

apocalíptico, ca, *a.* apocalyptical.

apocamiento, *m.* bashfulness; diffidence; pusillanimity, incapacity.

apocar. I. *va.* (*pret.* APOQUÉ; *subj.* APOQUE) to lessen; to cramp, contract. II. *vr.* to humble, belittle oneself.

apócema, apócima, *f.* (med.) apozem.

apocináceo, a. I. *a.* (bot.) apocynaceous, of the dogbane family. II. *f. pl.* Apocynaceæ.

apocopar, *va.* to apocopate.

apócope, *f.* (gram.) apocope; apocopation.

apócrifamente, *adv.* apocryphally.

apócrifo, fa, *a.* apocryphal.—Apócrifos, (Bib.) Apocrypha.

apocrisiario, *m.* Byzantine envoy; (eccl.) apocrisiary, envoy of the pope.

apodador, *m.* wag, scoffer.

apodar, *va.* to give nicknames to, scoff at.

apoderado, da. I. *pp.* of APODERAR. II. *m.* proxy; attorney.

apoderar. I. *va.* to empower; to grant power of attorney to. II. *vr.* to take possession.

apodíctico, ca, *a.* apodictic; indisputable.

apodo, *m.* nickname.

ápodo, da, *a.* (zool.) apodal, without feet.

apódosis, *f.* (rhet.) apodosis.

apófige, *f.* (arch.) apophyge.

apófise, apófisis, *f.* (anat.) apophysis, process.

apoflegmático, ca, *a.* (med.) apophlegmatic.

apogamia, *f.* (bot.) apogamy.

apogeo, *m.* apogee; height (of fame, etc.).

apógrafo, *m.* apograph, transcript.

apolillado, da. I. *pp.* of APOLILLAR. II. *a.* motheaten, worm-eaten.

apolilladura, *f.* moth hole.

apolillar. I. *va.* (of moths) to eat (clothes). II. *vr.* to become moth-eaten.

apolinar, *a.* (poet.) pertaining to Apollo.

apolinarista, *n.* & *a.* Apollinarian.

apolíneo, a, *a.* = APOLINAR.

apologético, ca, *a.* apologetic.

apologia, *f.* apologia, defense, eulogy.

apológico, ca, *a.* pertaining to fables.

apologista, *n.* apologist.

apólogo, *m.* apologue, fable.

apoltronarse, *vr.* to grow lazy; to loiter.

apomazar, *va.* (*pret.* APOMACÉ; *subj.* APOMACE) to glaze; to burnish with pumice stone.

aponeurosis, *f.* (anat.) aponeurosis.

aponeurótico, ca, *a.* (anat.) aponeurotic.

apoplejía, *f.* apoplexy.

apoplético, ca, *a.* apoplectic.

apoqué, apoque, *v.* V. APOCAR.

aporcadura, *f.* hilling around plants.

aporcar, *va.* (*ind. pres.* APUERCO, *pret.* APORQUÉ; *subj.* APUERQUE) to hill (plants).

aporisma, *m.* (med.) ecchymosis.

aporismarse, *vr.* to become an ecchymosis.

aporqué, aporque, *v.* V. APORCAR.

aporracear, *va.* (prov.) to pommel.

aporrar. I. *vn.* (coll.) to stand mute. II. *vr.* (coll.) to become importunate.

aporreado, da. I. *pp.* of APORREAR. II. *a.* cudgelled; miserable, dragged out. III. *m.* name of a Cuban dish made of highly seasoned beef.

aporreamiento, *m.* beating or pommelling.

aporreante, *n.* (coll.) cudgeller.

aporrear. I. *va.* to beat, cudgel, knock, maul. II. *vr.* to study with intense application.

aporreo, *m.* beating, pommelling, cudgelling.

aporrillarse, *vr.* to swell in the joints.

aportadera, *f.* pannier; large, long box for the side of a pack animal (used in pairs); wooden tub with handles to carry grapes from the vineyard.

aportadero, *m.* stopping place.

¹aportar, *vn.* to make a port; to arrive; to reach an unexpected place.

²aportar, *va.* to cause, bring; (law) to contribute.

aportillar. I. *va.* to break down, break open. II. *vr.* to tumble down.

aposentador, ra, *n.* one that lets lodgings; usher.

aposentamiento, *m.* lodging.

aposentar. I. *va.* to lodge. II. *vr.* to take lodging.—aposento, *m.* room or apartment; temporary habitation; inn; (theat.) box.

aposesionar, posesionar. I. *va.* to give possession. **II.** *vr.* to take possession.

aposición, *f.* (gram.) apposition.

apósito, *m.* external medicinal application.

aposta, apostadamente, *adv.* designedly, on purpose.

apostadero, *m.* station for soldiers; (naut.) naval station.

apostador, ra, *n.* (Am.) better, one who bets.

apostal, *m.* good fishing place in a river.

apostáleos, *m. pl.* (naut.) thick planks for gun platforms.

apostar. I. *va.* (*ind.* APUESTO; *subj.* APUESTE) to bet; (reg. conj. in the next two meanings) to place (relays); to post (soldiers).—**apostar a que,** to bet that. **II.** *vr.* to station oneself.

apostasía, *f.* apostasy.

apóstata, *m.* apostate.—**apostatar,** *vn.* to apostatize.

apostema, postema, *f.* abscess, tumor.

apostemación, *f.* (med.) formation of an abscess.

apostemar. I. *va.* to form an abscess in, fester. **II.** *vr.* to become abscessed.

apostemilla, *f. dim.* small abscess; gumboil.

apostemoso, sa, *a.* apostematous.

aposteriori, *adv.* (philos.) a posteriori.

apostilla, *f.* marginal note, annotation.

¹apostillar, *va.* to annotate on the margin.

²apostillar, *vr.* to break out in pimples.

apóstol, *m.* apostle.—*pl.* (naut.) hawse pieces.

apostolado, *m.* apostleship; the twelve Apostles.

apostólicamente, *adv.* apostolically.

apostólico, ca, *a.* apostolic.

apostrofar, *va.* to apostrophize.

apóstrofe, *f.* (rhet.) apostrophe.

apóstrofo, *m.* apostrophe (written sign).

apostura, *f.* gentleness; neatness.

apotegma, *m.* apothegm, maxim.

apoteosis, *f.* apotheosis, deification.

apotrerar, *va.* to take (horses) to pasture.

apoyadero, *m.* prop, support.

apoyadura, *f.* flow of milk in nursing.

apoyar. I. *va.* (**en**) to rest or lean (on); to favor, advocate, support; to back, defend; to aid; to abet; to bear out, confirm; (of horses) to droop (the head).—**a. la proposición,** to second the motion. **II.** *vn.* (**en** or **sobre**) to rest (on). **III.** *vr.* (**en**), to depend (on); to be based (on); to rest (on); to lean (on or against); to be supported (by).

apoyatura, *f.* (mus.) appoggiatura.

apoyo, *m.* prop, stay; support; fulcrum; protection, help, aid; approval, support, backing.

apreciable, *a.* appreciable, noticeable; worthy of esteem; (coll.) nice, fine; valuable; that can be priced; salable.

apreciación, *f.* estimation, valuation; appreciation; (tech.) least reading (of a vernier).

apreciadamente, *adv.* appreciatively.

apreciador, ra, *n.* estimator, appraiser.

apreciar, *va.* to appreciate; to appraise, estimate, price, value; to esteem.—**apreciativo, va,** *a.* appreciative.—**aprecio,** *m.* appraisement, valuation; esteem, regard, liking.

aprehender, *va.* to apprehend, seize; to conceive, think.—**aprehensión,** *f.* seizure, capture; apprehension, acuteness; fear.—**aprehensivo, va,** *a.* apprehensive.—**aprehensor, ra,** *n.* one that apprehends.

apremiador, ra, *n.* compeller.

apremiante, *a.* urgent, pressing.

apremiar, *va.* to press, urge; to compel, oblige.

apremio, *m.* pressure, constraint; (law) judicial compulsion.

aprendedor, ra, *n.* learner.

aprender, *va.* & *vn.* to learn.

aprendiz, za, *n.* apprentice.—**aprendizaje,** *m.* apprenticeship; (act of) learning.

aprensador, *m.* presser, calenderer.

aprensar, *va.* to dress, press, calender; to crush, oppress; (naut.) to stow.

aprensión, *f.* apprehension, scruple; fear; distrust, suspicion.

aprensivo, va, *a.* apprehensive, fearing.

apresador, ra, *n.* privateer; captor.

apresamiento, *m.* capture; clutch, hold.

apresar, *va.* to seize, grasp; to capture.

aprestar, *va.* to prepare, make ready; to size (cloth).—**apresto,** *m.* preparation; accoutrement; sizing (for cloth).

apresuración, *f.* haste.

apresuradamente, *adv.* hastily.

apresurado, da. I. *pp.* of APRESURAR. **II.** *a.* hasty, quick.

apresuramiento, *m.* hastiness, quickness.

apresurar. I. *va.* to hasten. **II.** *vr.* to make haste.

apretadamente, *adv.* tightly, closely, fast.

apretadera, *f.* strap or rope to tie with.—*pl.* pressing remonstrances.

apretador, *m.* truss for ruptures.

apretadizo, za, *a.* easily compressible.

apretado, da. I. *pp.* of APRETAR. **II.** *a.* tight, compact; difficult, dangerous; stingy, tight.

apretador, *m.* one who presses; tightener; presser, rammer, quoin wedge; waistcoat; soft stays for children; broad bandage for infants; hair net.

apretadura, *f.* compression.

apretamiento, *m.* tightening; crowding, jamming; conflict; closeness.

apretar. I. *va.* (*ind.* APRIETO; *subj.* APRIETE) to tighten; to press down, compress; to clench (teeth, fist); to grip (hand in greeting); to squeeze; to vex, distress; to urge, press, drive. **II.** *vn.* (of shoes, etc.) to pinch.—**a. a** (foll. by *inf.*) to start to, (foll. by *pres. p.*) to start, with the implication of haste, effort, etc. (*apretamos a correr,* we started to run for all we were worth).—**¡aprieta!** gracious! nonsense!

apretazón, *f.* (Am.) crowd; congestion.

apretón, *m.* pressure (esp. strong and quick); struggle, conflict; short run, spurt.—**a. de manos,** handshake.

apretujar, *va.* (coll.) to squeeze, press hard.

apretujón, *m.* tight squeezing.

apretura, *f.* jamming, crush; narrowness; distress, anguish; straits, difficulties.

apriesa, *adv.* fast, rapidly.

¹aprieto, *m.* jamming, crush; stringency, scrape, difficulty; cramp, gripe.

²aprieto, apriete, *v.* V. APRETAR.

apriori, a priori, *a.* & *adv.* a priori.

apriorismo, *m.* method of a priori reasoning.

apriorístico, ca, *a.* pert. to a priori reasoning.

aprisa, *adv.* swiftly, promptly, fast.

apriscar, *va.* to gather (the sheep) in the fold.

aprisco, *m.* sheepfold.

aprisionar, *va.* to imprison.

aproar, *vn.* (naut.) to turn the prow.

aprobación, *f.* approval.

aprobador, ra, *n.* & *a.* approver(-ing).

aprobante, *n.* approver; examiner.

aprobar, *va.* (*ind.* APRUEBO; *subj.* APRUEBE) to approve; to pass (in an examination).

aprobatorio, ria, *a.* approbative, approving.

aproches, *m. pl.* (mil., eng.) approaches.

aprontar, *va.* to prepare quickly; to deliver at once; (P. R.) to advance (money).

apropiación, *f.* appropriation, giving or taking possession; adaptation; (act of) fitting.

apropiadamente, *adv.* fitly, appropriately.

apropiado, da. I. *pp.* of APROPIAR. **II.** *a.* appropriate, fit.

apropiador, ra, *n.* appropriator.

apropiar. I. *va.* to give possession of; to apply, adapt, fit. **II.** *vr.* to appropriate, take possession of.

apropincuación, *f.* approach.

apropincuarse, *vr.* (coll.) to approach.

aprovechable, *a.* available; that can be used.

aprovechado, da. I. *pp.* of APROVECHAR. **II.** *a.* advanced, proficient; economical, saving.

aprovechamiento, *m.* utilization, use; exploitation, development; progress, proficiency.—**a. forestal,** forest products.

aprovechar. I. *vn.* to be useful, profitable or beneficial, to avail; to progress. **II.** *va.* to profit by, make use of. **III.** *vr.* to avail oneself.

aprovisionar, *va.* (Am.) to supply.

aproximación, *f.* approximation.

aproximadamente, *adv.* approximately.

aproximado, da. I. *pp.* of APROXIMAR. **II.** *a.* approximate.—**a. hasta,** (arith.) approximate to.

aproximar, *va.* & *vr.* to approach, move near; to determine approximately; to be about.—**aproximarse a,** to move near to, approach.

aproximativo, *va, a.* approximate; approaching.

apruebo, apruebe, *v.* V. APROBAR.

ápside, *m.* (astr.) apsis.

aptamente, *adv.* fitly, aptly.

áptero, ra, *a.* (entom.) apterous, wingless.

aptitud, *f.* aptitude, fitness, ability.

apto, ta, *a.* apt, fit, competent.

apuerco, apuerque, *v.* V. APORCAR.

apuesta, *f.* bet, wager.

¹**apuesto, ta,** *a.* elegant, stylish, spruce.

¹**apuesto, apueste,** *v.* V. APOSTAR.

apulgarar, *vn.* to press, push with the thumb.

apulgararse, *vr.* (of white cloth) to mildew (from moisture).

apulso, *m.* (astr.) passing of the edge of a heavenly body over the vertical wire of the telescope; appulse, coming together of two heavenly bodies.

apunarse, *vr.* (Am.) to get ill from altitude.

apunchar, *va.* to cut out the teeth of (a comb).

apuntación, *f.* note; memorandum; musical notation.

apuntado, da. I. *pp.* of APUNTAR. **II.** *a.* pointed at both ends.

apuntador, ra, *n.* observer; one that takes or keeps notes; (theat.) prompter; (naut.) gunner.

apuntalamiento, *m.* propping.

apuntalar, *va.* to prop; to shore (a vessel).

apuntamiento, *m.* note, abstract, summary; judicial report.

apuntar. I. *va.* to aim, level; to point out, mark; to note, make a note of; to hint; to sketch; (sew.) to baste, tack; to sharpen; (theat.) to prompt. **II.** *vn.* to begin to appear; (of wine) to begin to turn.

apunte, *m.* APUNTAMIENTO; annotation, memorandum; rough sketch; prompt-book; stake (in games).

apuñadar, *va.* (prov.) to strike with the fist.

apuñalado, da, *a.* dagger-shaped.

apuñalar, *va.* to stab.

apuñar. I. *va.* to seize with the fist. **II.** *vn.* to tighten the fist.

apuñear, *va.* (coll.) to strike with the fist.

apuracabos, *m.* candle holder with a sharp point for the butt of the candle; catchall.

apuración, *f.* investigation; trouble, misfortune.

apuradamente, *adv.* punctually, exactly; with difficulty.

apurado, da. I. *pp.* of APURAR. **II.** *a.* needy; exhausted; difficult; conscientious.

apurador, *m.* refiner, purifier; APURACABOS.

apuramiento, *m.* research; exhaustion, consumption; pressing, urging; purification.

apurar. I. *va.* to purify; to clear up, verify, scrutinize; to consume, drain, exhaust; to push, hurry; to annoy. **II.** *vr.* to worry, fret, grieve; to exert oneself.

apurativo, *a.* (med.) detersive, cleansing.

apuro, *m.* want, strait; scrape, tight spot, "jam."

aquejar, *va.* to grieve, sadden; to fatigue.

aquel (*f. sing.* **aquella;** *pl.* **aquellos, llas**). **I.** *a.* that, those, yonder. **II.** *pron. m.* & *f.* he, she (*pl.*

they, those, such as) (*aquellos que deseen venir,* those who, or such as, wish to come); those (ones). **III. aquél, aquélla,** *n.* that one; the former, the first mentioned. **IV. aquello,** *pron. neut.* that; the former, the first-mentioned (fact, statement, etc.); that thing, that matter, the matter we spoke about, etc. (used with reference to something known to the listener or reader but that it is not desired to mention); attractiveness, appeal, "a certain something."—**a. de,** that matter of.—**a. de (que),** the common saying, notion, belief, rule (that) (*no creo en aquello de que el comercio es la base del progreso,* I do not believe in the common saying that commerce is the 'oundation of progress).

aquellare, *m.* witches' Sabbath.

aquende, *adv.* on this side of.

aqueo, a, *n.* & *a.* Achæan.

aquerenciarse, *vr.* (esp. of animals) to become attached to (a place).

aquese, *m.,* **aquesa,** *f.,* **aqueso,** *neut.* = ESE, etc.

aqueste, *m.,* **aquesta,** *f.,* **aquesto,** *neut.* = ESTE, ESTA, etc.

aquí, *adv.* here; hither; then; now.—**de a.,** from here, from this place; hence.—**de a. en adelante,** from now on, hereafter.—**por a.,** here, hereabouts; this way, through here.

aquiescencia, *f.* (law) acquiescence, consent.

aquietar. I. *va.* to quiet, lull, pacify, hush, allay. **II.** *vr.* to become calm; to quiet down.

aquilatar, *va.* to assay; to examine closely.

aquilea, *f.* (bot.) milfoil, yarrow.

aquileña, *f.* (bot.) columbine.

aquilífero, *m.* Roman standard bearer.

aquilino, na, *a.* (poet.) = AGUILEÑO, aquiline.

aquilón, *m.* north wind; north point.

aquilonal, aquilonar, *a.* northern, northerly.

aquillado, da, *a.* keel-shaped.

aquistar, *va.* to acquire.

ara, *f.* altar; communion table; altar slab, mensa.

árabe, *n.* & *a.* Arab(-ic).—**árabesco,** *m.* arabesque, moresque work.—**arábico, ca,** or **arábigo, ga,** *a.* Arabian, Arabic.—**arábiga,** *f.* a stone similar to spotted ivory.—**arabismo,** *m.* Arabicism.—**arabista,** *n.* Arabist.

arácnido, da. I. *n.* & *a.* (zool.) arachnidian. **II.** *m. pl.* Arachnida.

aracnoides, *f.* (anat.) arachnoid membrane.

aracnoiditis, *f.* (med.) arachnitis.

arada, *f.* (agr.) plowed ground; land plowed in a day; husbandry.

arado, *m.* plow.

arador, *m.* plowman; (entom.) harvest mite.

aradura, *f.* plowing; land plowed in a day.

aragonés, esa, *n.* & *a.* Aragonese.

aragonita, *m.* (min.) aragonite.

araguato, *m.* (zool.) ursine howler, howling monkey, howler.

arambel, *m.* rag, tatter.

arameo, a, *n.* & *a.* Aramean.

arana, *f.* imposition, trick; Cuban grass.

aranata, *f.* prairie dog.

arancel, *m.* tariff.—**a. de aduanas,** customs, duty.

arancelario, ria, *a.* tariff, customs (as *a.*).

arandanedo, *m.* cranberry patch.

arándano, *m.* (bot.) cranberry.

arandela, *f.* the socket pan of a candlestick; (mech.) washer; axleguard; rivet plate, collar plate; guard around the staff of a lance; nave box of a gun carriage; (naut.) half-ports; glass candelabrum.

arandillo, *m.* a kind of bird; (prov.) hip pad.

aranero, ra, *a.* deceitful, tricky.

aranzada, *f.* a land measure (about .5 hectare).

araña, *f.* (entom.) spider; chandelier; (zool.) common weaver; (bot.) crowfoot; (fig.) hustler, go-getter; disreputable woman, whore.—**a. de mar,** sea spider, spider crab.

arañador, ra, *n.* scratcher, scraper.
arañamiento, *m.* (act of) scratching.
arañar, *va.* to scratch; to scrape up (as money).
arañazo, *m. aug.* a scratch (on the skin).
araño, *m.* scratch, nipping.
arañuela, *f. dim.* small spider; a flower plant.
arañuelo, *m.* small spider; net (for bird-catching).
arapenne, *m.* ancient measure (120 sq. ft.).
¹arar, *va.* to plow, to work the soil.
²arar, *m.* an African coniferous tree.
araucano, na, *n. & a.* Araucanian.
araucaria, *f.* araucaria, a tall pine.
arauja, *f.* (Brazil) a creeping plant.
araza, *m.* a Uruguayan fruit tree.
arbalestrilla, *f.* an old surveying instrument.
arbellon, *m.* (prov.) gutter to drain roads.
arbitrable, *a.* arbitrable.
arbitración, *f.* arbitration.
arbitrador, ra, *n.* arbitrator; umpire, referee.
arbitraje, *m.* (com.) arbitrage; ARBITRAMENTO.
arbitral, *a.* arbitral.
arbitramento, arbitramiento, *m.* arbitration, arbitrament.
arbitrar, *va.* to arbitrate; to act unhampered; to contrive.
arbitrariamente, *adv.* arbitrarily.
arbitrariedad, *f.* arbitrariness; arbitrary act.
arbitrario, ria; arbitrativo, va, *a.* arbitrary; (law) arbitral.
arbitratorio, ria; *a.* arbitral.
arbitrio, *m.* free will; means, expedient; arbitration; bond, compromise; discretion, judgment.—*pl.* excise taxes.
arbitrista, *m.* schemer, contriver.
árbitro, *m.* arbitrator, arbiter, umpire, referee.
árbol, *m.* (bot.) tree; (naut.) mast; in machines, upright post; (mech.) axle or shaft; arbor; spindle; drill; body of shirt; crown post of winding stairs.—**a. de Diana,** (chem.) arbor Dianæ.—**a. de la ciencia del bien y del mal,** (Bib.) tree of knowledge of good and evil.—**a. de la vida,** (Bib.) tree of life.—**a. del pan,** breadfruit tree.—**a. de María,** tolu-balsam tree.—**a. de pie,** seed-grown tree.—**a. de Saturno,** (chem.) arbor Saturni.—**a. de transmisión,** transmission shaft, belt shaft.—**a. motor,** driving shaft or axle.
arbolado, da. I. *pp.* of ARBOLAR. II. *a.* wooded; masted. III. *m.* woodland.
arboladura, *f.* (naut.) masts and spars.
arbolar, I. *va.* to hoist; to set upright.—**a. un navío,** (naut.) to mast a ship. II. *vr.* (of horses) to rear on the hind feet.
arbolario, *m.* = HERBOLARIO, madcap.
arbolecico, cillo, arbolico, ito, *m. dim.* small tree.
arboleda, *f.* grove.
arbolejo, *m. dim.* small tree.
arbolete, *m.* branch to fasten lime twigs on (for catching birds).
arbolillo, *m.* side of a blast furnace; small tree.
arbolista, *m.* arborist.
arbollón, albollón, *m.* floodgate, sluice, outlet.
arbóreo, rea, *a.* pertaining to trees.
arborescencia, *f.* arborescence.
arborescente, *a.* arborescent.
arboricultor, ra, *n.* arboriculturist.
arboricultura, *f.* arboriculture.
arboriforme, *a.* arboriform, tree-shaped.
arborizado, *a.* foliagelike.
arbotante, *m.* vault-supporting arch.
arbusto, *m.* shrub.—**arbustillo,** *m. dim.* small shrub.
arca, *f.* chest, coffer; reservoir, tank; ark; tempering oven for blown glass.—**a. cerrada,** extremely reticent person.—**a. de la Alianza,** Ark of the Covenant.
arcabucear, *va.* to shoot with a harquebus.
arcabucería, *f.* body of harquebusiers; collection

of harquebuses; fusillade of harquebuses; harquebus factory.
arcabucero, *m.* harquebus maker or user.
arcabuco, *m.* (Am.) craggy spot.
arcabuz, *m.* harquebuse.—**arcabuzazo,** *m.* harquebus shot; wound inflicted by a harquebus.
arcacil, *m.* (bot.) a kind of wild artichoke.
arcada, *f.* retching; (arch.) row of arches.
árcade, *n. & a., arcadio, dia, a.* Arcadian.
arcaduz, *m.* conduit; bucket; means, way.
arcaico, ca, *a.* archaic.
arcaísmo, *m.* archaism.
arcaizar, *vr.* to use archaisms.
arcángel, *m.* archangel.
arcangélico, ca, *a.* archangelical.
arcano, I. *m.* arcanum. II. *a.* secret, recondite.
arcaza, *f. aug.* large chest.
arcazón, *m.* arbuscle, osier, willow plot.
arce, *m.* (bot.) maple tree.
arcedianato, *m.* archdeaconship.
arcediano, *m.* archdeacon.
arcedo, *m.* maple grove.
arcén, *m.* border, brim, edge.
arcilla, argila, argilla, *f.* clay.—**arcilloso, sa,** *a.* clayey, argillaceous.
arciprestazgo, *m.* archpriesthood.
arcipreste, *m.* archpriest.
arco, *m.* arc; (arch.) arch; bow; fiddle bow; hoop; (geom.) arc.—**a. apainelado,** three-center arch.—**a. de medio punto,** round, or semicircular, arch.—**a. iris,** rainbow.—**a. ojival,** equilateral arch.—**a. peraltado,** horseshoe arch.—**a. rebajado,** segmental arch.
arcón, *m. aug.* large chest; bin, bunker.
arcontado, *m.* archontate.
arconte, *m.* archon.
archicofradía, *f.* privileged brotherhood.
archidiácono, *m.* archdeacon.
archiducado, *m.* archdukedom, archduchy.
archiducal, *a.* archducal.
archiduque, *m.* archduke.—**archiduquesa,** *f.* archduchess.
archilaúd, *m.* large lute.
archimandrita, *m.* (Gr. ch.) archimandrite, abbot.
archimillonario, ria, *a.* multimillionaire.
archipámpano, *m.* very dignified person with imaginary authority.
archipiélago, *m.* archipelago.
archivar, *va.* to file; to deposit in archives; (fig.) to put on the shelf, pigeonhole, forget.
archivero, archivista, *m.* archivist.
archivo, *m.* archives; file, files.
arda, *f.* = ARDILLA, (zool.) squirrel.
ardalear, *vn.* (of vine roots) to grow sparse.
ardea, *f.* (ornith.) bittern.
ardentía, *f.* heat; phosphorescence; blink.
ardeola, *f.* (Am.) small kind of heron.
arder, I. *vn.* to burn; (of war, etc.) to rage. II. *vr.* (of fruit, grain, etc.) to spoil from heat.
ardero, ra, *a.* squirrel dog.
ardid, *m.* stratagem, artifice, cunning.
ardido, da, I. *pp.* of ARDER. II. *a.* heated; burning; (Am.) "burned up," angry.
ardiente, *a.* ardent, burning; passionate, fervent; fiery.—**ardientemente,** *adv.* ardently, fervidly; fearlessly.
ardilla, *f.* (zool.) squirrel.
¹ardimiento, *m.* conflagration.
²ardimiento, *m.* undaunted courage, hardihood.
ardínculo, *m.* (vet.) inflamed swelling on the back.
ardita, *f.* (Colomb. & Venez.) squirrel.
ardite, *m.* ancient coin of little value; trifle; (fig.) straw, farthing.—**no importar un a.,** not to matter a particle.—**no se me da un a.,** I don't care a straw, or a rap.—**no valer un a.,** not to be worth a straw, not to amount to a hill of beans.
ardor, *m.* ardor; hotness, heat; dash, valor.

ardoroso, sa, *a.* fiery; ardent, vigorous.

arduamente, *adv.* arduously.

arduo, dua, *a.* arduous.

área, *f.* area; are, square decameter.

areca, *f.* palm tree of the Philippine Islands.

arefacción, *f.* drying out; emaciation.

arel, *m.* large sieve.—**arelar,** *va.* to sift.

arena, *f.* sand, grit; arena.—**arenáceo, ea,** *a.* arenaceous, sandy.—**arenal,** *m.* sandy ground, sand pit.—**arenalejo,** *m. dim.* small sandy place.—**arenar,** *va.* to sand; to rub with sand.

arencar, *va.* (*pret.* ARENQUÉ; *subj.* ARENQUE) to salt and dry (fish).

arencón, *m. aug.* large herring.

arenero, *m.* sand dealer; sand box.

arenga, *f.* harangue, speech.

arengador, ra, *n.* speech maker.

arengar, *vn.* (*pret.* ARENGUÉ; *subj.* ARENGUE) to harangue, deliver a speech.

arenilla, *f.* molding sand; sand to dry writing.—*pl.* granulated saltpeter.

arenisca, *f.* (min.) sandstone.

arenisco, ca; arenoso, sa, *a.* sandy, gravelly, gritty; sand (as *a.*).

arenque, *m.* herring.

arenqué, arenque, *v. V.* ARENCAR.

aréola, *f.* areola, circle around the nipple.

areómetro, *m.* hydrometer.

areopagita, *m.* Areopagite.

areópago, *m.* Areopagus.

areóstilo, *m.* (arch.) aræostyle.

areotectónica, *f.* areotectonics.

arepa, *f.* corn griddle cake.

arequipa, *f.,* **arequipe, ariquipe,** *m.* (Am.) a kind of jelly made with rice, milk and sugar.

arestín, *m.* (vet.) frush.

arestinado, da, *a.* afflicted with frush.

arete, *m.* eardrop, earring.

arfada, *f.* (naut.) pitching of a ship.

arfar, *vn.* (naut.) (of a ship) to pitch.

arfil, *m.* = ALFIL, (chess) bishop.

argadijo, argadillo, *m.* reel, bobbin, winder; blustering, noisy, restless person; large wicker basket.

argado, *m.* prank, trick.

argal, *m.* argol, crude tartar.

argalia, *f.* = ²ALGALIA, (surg.) catheter.

argallera, *f.* saw for cutting grooves; forkstaff plane, reed plane.

argamandel, *m.* rag, tatter.

argamandijo, *m.* collection of trifling implements.

argamasa, *f.* mortar.—**argamasar. I.** *vn.* to make mortar. **II.** *va.* to cement with mortar.

argamasón, *m.* large dry piece of mortar.

argamula, *f.* (bot., prov.) golden starwort.

árgana, *f.* (mech.) crane.

árganas, *f. pl.* wicker baskets on a horse.

arganel, *m.* ring in an astrolabe.

arganeo, *m.* (naut.) anchor ring.

árgano, *m.* = ÁRGANA.

argel, *a.* (horse) whose right hind foot is white.

argelino, na, *a.* Algerine.

argema, argemón, *m.* (med.) argema.

argemone, *f.* (bot.) prickly or horned poppy.

argén, *m.* (her.) white or silver color, argent.

argentada, *f.* ladies' cosmetic.

argentado, da. I. *pp.* of ARGENTAR. **II.** *a.* silvered, silver-plated; silvery; slashed (shoes).

argentador, *n.* silversmith.

argentar, *va.* to plate or adorn with silver; to polish like silver.

argentario, *m.* silversmith; master of the mint.

argénteo, a, *a.* silvery; silver-plated.

argentería, *f.* embroidery in gold or silver.

argentero, *m.* = ARGENTARIO.

argentífero, ra, *a.* silver-bearing.

argentina, *f.* (bot.) satin cinquefoil.

argentinismo, *m.* word or expression peculiar to Argentina.

argentino, na. I. *a.* silvery, argentine; Argentine, Argentinian. **II.** *m.* Argentine gold coin.

argento, *m.* (poet.) silver.

argentoso, sa, *a.* mixed with silver.

argila, argilla, *f.* clay.

argiritas, *m. pl.* marcasite, white pyrites.

argivo, va, *n.* & *a.* (person) of Argos.

argo, *m.* (chem.) argon.

argolla, *f.* ring; collar; staple; hoop; ring (in bowling); pillory.—**argolleta, ica, ita,** *f. dim.* small staple or ring.—**argollón,** *m. aug.* very large ring or staple.

árgoma, *f.* (bot.) furze.—**argomal,** *m.* furze plantation.—**argomón,** *m. aug.* large prickly furze, gorse.

argonauta, *m.* one of the Argonauts; (zool.) paper nautilus.

Argos, *m.* (myth.) Argus; very observant person.

argot, *m.* (Gal.) cant; French jargon.

argucia, *f.* subtilty, sophistry; trick, scheme.

argüe, *m.* windlass, capstan.

argüellarse, *vr.* (prov.) to become emaciated.

argüello, *m.* lack of health.

árguenas, árgueñas, *f. pl.* handbarrow.

arguerita, *f.* (min.) argyrite or argentite.

argüir. I. *vn.* (*ind.* ARGUYO; *subj.* ARGUYA) to argue, dispute. **II.** *va.* to infer; to imply.

argumentación, *f.* argumentation.

argumentador, ra, *n.* arguer, reasoner.

argumentar, *vn.* to argue, dispute.

argumentativo, va, *a.* argumentative.

argumentillo, *m. dim.* argument of no account.

argumento, *m.* (logic, math.) argument; summary; plot (of a play, etc.); indication, sign.

arguyente, *n.* arguer; opponent.

arguyo, arguya, *v. V.* ARGÜIR.

aria, *f.* (mus.) aria, song for a single voice.

aribar, *va.* to reel into skeins.

aribo, *m.* reel for making skeins.

aricar, *va.* to plow across.

aridecer, *va., vn.* & *vr.* (*ind.* ARIDEZCO; *subj.* ARIDEZCA) to render or become arid.

aridez, *f.* drought; barrenness, aridity.

árido, da. I. *a.* arid, dry, barren. **II.** *m. pl.* dry articles, esp. grains and vegetables, measured with dry measure.

Aries, *m.* Aries, sign of the zodiac.

arieta, *f. dim.* (mus.) arietta, short tune.

ariete, *m.* battering ram.—**a. hidráulico,** hydraulic ram.

arietino, na, *a.* like a ram's head.

arigue, *m.* Philippine timber.

arije, *f.* = ALARIJE, name of a large grape.

arijo, ja, *a.* (agr.) light, easily tilled.

arillo, *m. dim.* earring; neck-stock frame.

arimez, *m.* projection in a building.

arindajo, *m.* (ornith.) jay.

ario, ia, *n.* & *a.* Aryan.

arisblanco, ca, *a.* white-bearded (wheat).

arisaro, *m.* (bot.) wake-robin.

arisco, ca, *a.* churlish, shy, cross, surly.

arisnegro, arisprieto, *a.* (of wheat) having blackish beard.

arista, *f.* beard or awn grains; (geom.) edge.—*pl.* (mil.) salient angles.

aristado, da, *a.* awned, bearded.

aristarco, ca, *n.* severe censurer.

aristocracia, *f.* aristocracy.

aristócrata, *m.* & *f.* aristocrat.

aristocrático, ca, *a.* aristocratic.

aristoloquia, *f.* (bot.) birthwort.

aristoloquiáceo, a, *a.* (bot.) of the aristolochia. —*f. pl.* Aristolochiæ.

aristón, *m.* (arch.) edge, corner; groin rib.

aristoso, sa, *a.* having many beards or awns.

aristotélico, ca, *a.* Aristotelian.

aristotelismo, *m.* Aristotelianism

aritmancia, *f.* arithmancy.

aritmética, *f.* arithmetic.

aritméticamente, *adv.* arithmetically.

aritmético, ca. I. *a.* arithmetical. **II.** *m.* & *f.* arithmetician; accountant.

aritmo, *a.* (med.) arrhythmic.

aritmómetro, *m.* calculating machine.

arjorán, *m.* (bot.) an ornamental tree.

arlequín, *m.* harlequin, buffoon; mixed ice cream, Neapolitan.

arlequinada, *f.* harlequin's trick or joke.

arlo, *m.* (bot.) barberry.

arlota, alrota, *f.* tow of flax or hemp.

arma, *f.* weapon, arm; (mil.) technical division of military forces; (fig.) means, power, reason.— *pl.* troops, armies; armorial ensigns, coat of arms.—**a. arrojadiza,** missile weapon.—**a. blanca,** steel arm.—**a. de caballería,** cavalry. —**a. de fuego,** firearm.—**a. de infantería,** infantry.—**a. de puño,** hand steel arm (sword, etc.).—**a. falsa,** trial, or test, attack.—**armas de agua,** (Mex.) waterproof skins for riding.— **¡a las armas!** to arms!—**de armas tomar,** resolute; capable.—**sobre las armas,** under arms.

armada, *f.* navy; fleet; squadron; armada.— **a. naval,** royal navy, royal fleet.

armadera, *f.* (naut.) main timber of a ship.

armadía, *f.* raft, float.

armadijo, *m.* trap, snare for game.

armadillo, *m.* (zool.) armadillo.

armado, da. I. *pp.* of ARMAR. **II.** *a.* (mech.) mounted, assembled. **III.** *m.* man in armor in processions.

armador, *m.* outfitter, ship owner; privateer, cruiser; one who outfits whaleboats; (mech.) adjuster, fitter, assembler; jacket.

armadura, *f.* armor; framework, shell of a building; (mech.) setting, fitting; truss; (elec.) armature, yoke (of a magnet); framing, mounting; trestle; reinforcement (of concrete); armature (of a dynamo).

armajal, marjal, *m.* moor, bog.

armamentisto, ta, *a.* armaments (as *a.*).

armamento, *m.* armament, accoutrements.

armar. I. *va.* to arm; to man; (carp.) to bind; to assemble, mount; (mech.) to adjust, set, frame, piece, mount, make true, rig up; to reinforce (concrete, etc.); to form, prepare; to start, cause; (naut.) to equip, fit out, put in commission.—**a. caballero,** to knight.—**a. en corso,** to privateer.—**a. en guerra,** (naut.) to fit or equip (a ship) for war.—**a. un lío, or líos,** to make a mess of something, or of things. **II.** *vr.* to prepare oneself; to arm oneself.— **armarse de,** to arm oneself with, put on; (Am.) to build up (a business).

armario, *m.* clothespress; cabinet; bookcase; wardrobe; closet.

armatoste, *m.* hulk; unwieldly machine; cumbersome piece of furniture; fat, clumsy fellow.

armazón, *f.* framework, skeleton, frame; hulk (of a ship)—*m.* skeleton of body.

armelina, *f.* ermine skin.

armella, *f.* staple, box staple, screw eye.

armelluela, *f. dim.* small staple or ring.

armenio, nia, *n.* & *a.* Armenian.

armería, *f.* armory, arsenal; gunsmith trade or shop.

armero, *m.* armorer, gunsmith; keeper of arms; (mil.) rack or stand for firearms.

armífero, ra; armígero, ra, *a.* (poet.) warlike.

armilla, *f.* part of the base of a column.

armiñado, da, *a.* trimmed or lined with ermine fur; ermine-white.

armiño, *m.* (zool.) ermine.

armipotente, *a.* (poet.) mighty in war.

armisticio, *m.* (mil.) armistice.

armoisín, *m.* thin silk or taffeta.

armón, *m.* (artil.) limber.

armonía, *f.* harmony.

armonicé, armonice, *v.* *V.* ARMONIZAR.

armónico, ca, *a.* harmonious; musical.

armonio, *m.* harmonium, reed organ.

armoniosamente, *adv.* harmoniously.

armonioso, sa, *a.* harmonious.

armonista, *f.* harmonist.

armonización, *f.* harmonization.

armonizar, *va.* (*pret.* ARMONICÉ; *subj.* ARMONICE) to harmonize.

armuelle, *m.* (bot.) orach.

arna, *f.* (prov.) beehive.

arnacho, *m.* (bot.) rest-harrow. Also GATUÑA.

arnés, *m.* harness; coat of mail, armor.—*pl.* harness, trappings; tools, outfit, equipment.

árnica, *f.* arnica.

arnilla, *f. dim.* (prov.) small beehive.

¹aro, *m.* hoop, rim; staple; hoop pole.—**entrar por el a.,** (coll.) to be forced to yield.

²aro, yaro, *m.* (bot.) arum.

aroma. I. *f.* flower of the aromatic myrrh tree. **II.** *m.* aroma; perfume, fragrance.

aromar, *va.* to give aroma to, perfume.

aromaticé, aromatice, *v.* *V.* AROMATIZAR.

aromaticidad, *f.* aromatic quality, perfume.

aromático, ca, *a.* aromatic, fragrant.

aromatización, *f.* aromatization.

aromatizador, *m.* (perfume) atomizer.

aromatizar, *va.* (*pret.* AROMATICÉ; *subj.* AROMATICE) to aromatize, perfume.

aromo, *m.* (bot.) aromatic myrrh tree.

aromoso, sa, *a.* aromatic, fragrant.

aroza, *m.* foreman in ironworks.

arpa, *f.* (mus.) harp.

¹arpado, da. I. *pp.* of ARPAR. **II.** *a.* serrated, toothed.

²arpado, da, *a.* (poet.) (of a bird) singing.

arpadura, *f.* = ARAÑO, a scratch.

arpar, *va.* to tear to pieces, rend, claw.

arpegio, *m.* (mus.) arpeggio.

arpella, *f.* (ornith.) eagle; harpy.

arpende, *m.* ancient measure (120 sq. ft.).

arpeo, *m.* (naut.) grappling iron.

arpía, harpía, *f.* harpy; fiend; ugly shrew.

arpillador, *m.* (Mex.) packer.

arpilladura, *f.* packing with sackcloth.

arpillar, *va.* (Mex.) to pack with sackcloth.

arpillera, *f.* sackcloth, burlap.

arpista, *m.* (mus.) harper, harpist.

arpón, *m.* harpoon.—**arponado, da,** *a.* harpoonlike.—**arponear,** *va.* to harpoon.—**arponero,** *m.* harpooner; harpoon maker.

arqueada, *f.* drawing of bow across fiddle.

¹arqueador, *m.* ship gauger.

²arqueador, *m.* wool beater.

arqueaje, *m.* gauging of a ship.

arqueamiento, *m.* = ²ARQUEO.

¹arquear, *va.* to arch; to beat (wool).

²arquear, *va.* to gauge (ships).

¹arqueo, *m.* arching.

²arqueo, *m.* (naut.) tonnage.

³arqueo, *m.* (com.) checking of effects in a safe; balance (in accounting).

arqueología, *f.* archæology.

arqueológico, ca, *a.* archæological.

arqueólogo, *m.* archæologist.

arquería, *f.* series of arches; (Mex.) aqueduct.

¹arquero, ra, *n.* treasurer, cashier.

²arquero, ra. I. *a.* pert. to bows. **II.** *m.* archer; bow maker.

arqueta, *f. dim.* small chest.

arquetipo, *m.* archetype.

arquetón, *m. aug.* large chest.

arquibanco, *m.* bench with drawers.

arquidiócesis, *f.* archiepiscopal diocese.

arquiepiscopal, *a.* archiepiscopal.

arquifilósofo, *m.* archphilosopher.

arquilla, ita, *f. dim.* little chest.

arquillo, *m. dim.* small bow.

arquimesa, *f.* (prov.) writing desk.

arquisinagogo, *m.* ruler of a synagogue.

arquitecto, *m.* architect.

arquitectónica, *f.* (philos.) architectonics.

arquitectónico, ca, *a.* architectural.

arquitectura, *f.* architecture.

arquitrabe, *m.* architrave.

arrabal, *m.* suburb.—*pl.* environs, outskirts.

arrabalero, ra, *a.* suburban; ill-bred.

arrabio, *m.* cast iron melted for making steel.

arracachá, *f.* (bot.) arracacha.

arracada, *f.* earring with pendant.

arracimado, da. I. *pp.* of ARRACIMARSE. **II.** *a.* in clusters.

arracimarse, *vr.* to cluster.

arraclán, *m.* alder tree.

arráez, *m.* chief; captain or master of a ship.

arraigadamente, *adv.* fixedly, securely.

arraigadas, *f. pl.* (naut.) futtock shrouds.

arraigado, da. I. *pp.* of ARRAIGAR. **II.** *a.* owning real estate; fixed, inveterate.

arraigar. I. *vn.* to take root. **II.** *vr.* to settle, establish oneself; to take root.

arraigo, *m.* settling in a place; landed property.

arralar, *vn.* to become thin or sparse; (agr.) to give a poor yield.

arramblar, *va.* (of rushing rivers, etc.) to cover with sand and gravel; (fig.) to sweep away.

arrancaclavos, *m.* nail puller.

arrancada, *f.* (coll.) sudden departure; violent sally.

arrancadera, *f.* leading bell for cattle.

arrancadero, *m.* starting point; thickest part of a gun barrel.

arrancado, da. I. *pp.* of ARRANCAR. **II.** *a.* (coll.) "broke," poor, penniless.

arrancador, ra, *n.* extirpator; extractor, puller.

arrancadura, *f.,* **arrancamiento,** *m.* extirpation; pulling out.

arrancapinos, *n.* small person, (fig.) dwarf.

arrancar. I. *va.*(*pret.* ARRANQUÉ; *subj.* ARRANQUE) to root out, extirpate; to pull out, tear off. **II.** *vn.* (of train, etc.) to start, (ship) set sail.

arrancasiega, *f.* poor grain half mowed, half pulled up; quarrel, dispute.

arranciarse, *vr.* to grow or become rancid.

arrancharse, *vr.* to mess, take meals, together.

arranque, *m.* extirpation; impulse, fit (of passion, charity, love, etc.); sudden start, sudden impulse; (arch.) springer (of an arch); (mech.) start; starter.—**a. automático,** self-starter.

arranqué, arranque, *v. V.* ARRANCAR.

arrapar, *va.* (low) to snatch away, carry off.

arrapiezo, arrapo, *m.* tatter, rag; worthless youngster.

arras, *f. pl.* consideration of a contract; coins the bridegroom gives to the bride at the wedding; dowry; earnest money, pledge.—**a. de la bodega,** (naut.) wings of the hold.

arrasado, da. I. *pp.* of ARRASAR. **II.** *a.* like satin. **III.** *m.* satin-faced stuff.

arrasadura, rasadura, *f.* levelling.

arrasamiento, *m.* razing, demolition.

arrasar. I. *va.* to level, raze, demolish; to obliterate; to fill up to the brim. **II.** *vn., vr.* to clear up.

arrastradamente, *adv.* imperfectly; painfully, wretchedly.

arrastraderas, *f. pl.* (naut.) lower studding sails.

arrastradero, *m.* (naut.) careening place; log path, a path over which logs are dragged; (bullfighting) spot whence dead bulls are carried off.

arrastrado, da. I. *pp.* of ARRASTRAR. **II.** *a.* dragged along; (of life, etc.) dragging out; (coll.) knavish; destitute; (coll.) contemptible.

arrastramiento, *m.* dragging.

arrastrante, *n.* applicant for a scholarship.

arrastrar. I. *va.* to drag; to drag down, degrade; to wash down, carry away (sand, stones, etc.); to haul; to attract; to prompt, move, urge.— **a. bayeta,** to perform the ceremonies required of applicants for a scholarship.—**a. el ala a,** (coll.) to make up to; to make love to. **II.** *vn.* (of one's coat, etc.) to drag, touch the floor or

ground; (in cards) to play a trump. **III.** *vr.* to crawl, creep (literally and fig.).

arrastre, *m.* dragging; haulage; drayage; leading a trump; slope or grade in a mining shaft; applicant for a scholarship; (Mex.) mining mill.

arrate, *m.* pound of sixteen ounces.

arratonado, da, *a.* gnawed by mice.

arrayán, *m.* (bot.) myrtle.

arrayanal, *m.* myrtle field or plantation.

¡arre! *interj.* gee, get up!

arreador, *m.* muleteer; driving whip.

arreala, *f.* herding the grazing flock.

arrear, *va.* to drive (horses, mules, etc.).

arrebañador, ra, *n.* gleaner, gatherer.

arrebañadura, *f.* gleaning, picking up.

arrebañar, *va.* to glean, gather.

arrebatadamente, *adv.* precipitately, headlong, recklessly; violently.

arrebatado, da. I. *pp.* of ARREBATAR. **II.** *a.* rapid, violent; precipitate, rash, impetuous.

arrebatador, ra. I. *n.* one that snatches or carries away. **II.** *a.* that snatches or carries away; captivating, charming; violent; stirring.

arrebatamiento, *m.* carrying away by violence; fury, rage; rapture; ecstasy.

arrebatar. I. *va.* to carry off; to snatch; to attract, hold (the attention, etc.); to charm; to move, stir. **II.** *vr.* to be led away by passion.

arrebatiña, *f.* struggle, scramble, scuffle.

arrebato, *m.* surprise; sudden attack; fit, rage; rapture.

arrebocé, arreboce, *v. V.* ARREBOZAR.

arrebol, *m.* red sky or clouds; rouge.

arrebolar. I. *va.* to paint red. **II.** *vr.* to rouge.

arrebolera, *f.* rouge box; rouge seller; (bot.) four-o'clock or marvel of Peru.

arrebollarse, *vr.* to precipitate; to fall headlong.

arrebozar. I. *va.* (*pret.* ARREBOCÉ; *subj.* ARREBOCE) to overlay (meat) with jelly. **II.** *vr.* to wrap oneself up; (of insects) to swarm.

arrebujadamente, *adv.* confusedly.

arrebujar. I. *va.* to jumble together; to huddle. **II.** *vr.* to wrap oneself up.

arreciar. I. *vn.* to increase in strength or intensity. **II.** *vr.* to become stronger.

arrecife, *m.* stone-paved road; (naut.) reef.

arrecirse, *vr.* (defect.) to grow stiff with cold.

arrechucho, *m.* fit of anger; sudden and passing indisposition.

arredilar, *va.* to fold (sheep).

arredomado, redomado, da, *a.* artful, sly.

arredondar, redondear, *va.* to round off.

arredramiento, *m.* removing to a greater distance; backing out; fear.

arredrar. I. *va.* to remove, separate; to terrify, scare. **II.** *vr.* to be or become afraid; to fear.

arregacé, arregace, *v. V.* ARREGAZAR.

arregazado, da. I. *pp.* of ARREGAZAR. **II.** *a.* with the point turned up.

arregazar, *va.* (*pret.* ARREGACÉ; *subj.* ARREGACE) to tuck up (the skirts).

arregladamente, *adv.* regularly, orderly.

arreglado, da. I. *pp.* of ARREGLAR. **II.** *a.* regular, moderate.

arreglador, *m.* (com.) surveyor, valuer (of averages).

arreglar. I. *va.* to regulate, guide; to frame; to arrange; to settle, adjust; (Chile) to castrate. **II.** *vr.* to conform; to settle, come to an agreement; to compromise.

arreglo, *m.* rule; order; disposition, arrangement; adjustment; (com.) agreement; compromise, settlement.—**con a. a,** according to; in accordance with, pursuant to.

arregostarse, *vr.* to relish.

arrejaca, *f.* = ARREJAQUE.

arrejacar, *va.* (*pret.* ARREJAQUÉ; *subj.* ARREJAQUE) to plow across for clearing weeds.

arrejaco, *m.* (ornith.) swift, martin.

arrejada, *f.* (agr.) paddle of a plow.

arrejaque, *m.* fishing fork with three prongs.
arrejaqué, arrejaque, *v.* V. ARREJACAR.
arrejerar, *va.* (naut.) to make (a ship) fast by casting two anchors fore and one aft.
arrel, arrelde, *m.* weight of four pounds.
arrellanarse, *vr.* to sit at ease; to be satisfied with one's situation.
arremangado, da. I. *pp.* of ARREMANGAR. **II.** *a.* turned upward.
arremangar. I. *va.* (*pret.* ARREMANGUÉ; *subj.* ARREMANGUE) to tuck up (the sleeves, etc.). **II.** *vr.* to be determined.
arremango, *m.* tucking up.
arremetedero, *m.* place through which a fortress can be attacked.
arremetedor, ra, *m.* assailant, aggressor.
arremeter. I. *va.* to assail, attack. **II.** *vn.* to launch forth; to attack.—**arremetida,** *f.* attack, assault; start of horses.
arremolinado, da, *a.* whirling, in a whirl.
arremolinarse, *vr.* to form a crowd.
arrendable, *a.* rentable; farmable; tenantable.
arrendación, *f.* renting, lease.
arrendadero, *m.* ring to tie horses to.
¹arrendado, da, *a.* obedient to the reins.
²arrendado, da. I. *pp.* of ²ARRENDAR. **II.** *a.* rented, leased.
arrendador, *m.* landlord; lessor; hirer; tenant, lessee, holder; farmer.
arrendadorcillo, *m. dim.* petty tenant.
arrendajo, *m.* mocking bird; (coll.) mimic.
arrendamiento, *m.* renting, letting; lease; rent.
arrendante, *n.* lessor, renter.
¹arrendar, *va.* (*ind.* ARRIENDO; *subj.* ARRIENDE) to bridle; to tie (a horse); to train (a horse).
²arrendar, *va.* (*ind.* ARRIENDO; *subj.* ARRIENDE) to rent, let, lease, hire.
³arrendar, *va.* to mimic.
arrendatario, ria, *n.* lessee, tenant.
arrentado, da, *a.* receiving a large rental.
¹arreo, *m.* dress, ornament, decoration.—*pl.* appurtenances, accessories; harness, trappings.
²arreo, *adv.* successively, uninterruptedly.
arrepápalo, *m.* a kind of fritter.
arrepentido, da. I. *pp.* of ARREPENTIRSE. **II.** *a.* repentant. **III.** *n.* penitent.
arrepentimiento, *m.* repentance.
arrepentirse, *vr.* (*ind. pres.* me ARREPIENTO, *pret.* él se ARREPINTIÓ; *subj.* me ARREPIENTA) to repent.
arrepistar, *va.* to grind (rags) into pulp.
arrepisto, *m.* grinding or pounding (of rags).
arrepollado, da, *a.* cabbagelike.
arrepticio, cia, *a.* possessed by the devil.
arrequesonarse, *vr.* to curdle.
arrequife, *m.* singeing iron in cotton gins.
arrequives, *m. pl.* dress trimmings; ornaments; adornments; circumstances; requirements.
arrestado, da. I. *pp.* of ARRESTAR. **II.** *a.* bold, audacious.
arrestar. I. *va.* to arrest, imprison. **II.** *vr.* to be bold and enterprising; to dare.—**arresto,** *m.* imprisonment, arrest; spirit, enterprise.
arretín, *m.* = FILIPICHÍN, a kind of woolen cloth.
arretranca, *f.* (Am.) crupper of a packsaddle.
arrevesado, da, *a.* difficult, intricate.
arrezafe, *m.* place full of brambles.
arrezagar, *va.* to raise; to tuck up (sleeves, etc.).
arria, *f.* drove of beasts.—**aguja de a.,** packneedle.
arriada, riada, *f.* (prov.) flood, washout.
arrial, *m.* = ARRIAZ.
arrianismo, *m.* Arianism.
arriano, na, *n. & a.* Arian.
¹arriar, *va.* (naut.) to lower, strike.—**a. la bandera,** to strike the colors.
²arriar. I. *va.* to flood. **II.** *vr.* to be flooded.
arriata, *f.* **arriate,** *m.* border, edge (in gardens); trellis; causeway.
arriaz, *m.* hilt-bar of a sword.

arriba, *adv.* above, high, on high, overhead; upstairs; (naut.) aloft.—**a. de,** above; higher up than; beyond (in an upward direction).—**de a. abajo,** from the top down; from top to bottom; from beginning to end; from head to foot.—**más a.,** higher up.—**para a.,** up, upwards (e.g. *de cuatro pesos para arriba,* from four pesos up).—**por a.,** at, or from, the top.—**por a. de,** above, over. **II.** *interj.* long live!
arribada, *f.* **arribaje,** *m.* (naut.) arrival.—**de arribada,** (naut.) putting into a port by stress.
arribar, *vn.* to arrive; (naut.) to put into a harbor in distress; (naut.) to fall off to leeward; to reach; to recover, convalesce.
arribeño, ña, *n.* (Mex.) highlander.
arribo, *m.* arrival.
arricé, arrice, *v.* V. ARRIZAR.
arricés, *m.* buckle of a stirrup strap.
arricete, *m.* shoal, sand bank.
¹arriendo, *m.* renting; lease; rent.
²arriendo, arriende, *v.* V. ARRENDAR.
arrieraje, *m.* (Am.) (collect.) muleteers; ARRIERÍA.
arriería, *f.* driving of mules.
arrierico, illo, ito, *m. dim.* of ARRIERO.
arriero, *m.* muleteer.
arriesgadamente, *adv.* dangerously, hazardously.
arriesgado, da, *a.* dangerous, risky; daring.
arriesgar. I. *va.* (*pret.* ARRIESGUÉ; *subj.* ARRIESGUE) to risk, hazard, jeopardize. **II.** *vr.* to expose oneself to danger; to dare.
arrimadero, *m.* support; stopping or landing place; shelter.
arrimadillo, *m.* mat, wainscot, dado.
arrimadizo, za, *a.* designed to be placed against or joined to a thing; parasitic, sycophantic, sponging.
arrimador, *m.* backlog in a fireplace.
arrimadura, *f.* act of ARRIMAR or ARRIMARSE.
arrimar. I. *va.* to place near; (naut.) to stow; to put beside or against; to put by; to give up, abandon; to lay down; to fling, dismiss; to discard.—**a. el hombro,** to work with a will; to lend a hand. **II.** *vr.* (**a**) to go near (to); to seek the protection (of); to seek shelter (in or under); to lean (on or against); to join.
arrime, *m.* proximity to the goal (in bowling).
arrimo, *m.* putting near, beside or against (some person or thing); abandonment, relinquishment, giving up; support, protection; staff, cane, crutch; (arch.) idle wall, wall bearing no load.—**al a. de,** protected or shielded by.
arrimón, *m.* loafer, idler.—**estar de a.,** to keep watch.
arrinconado, da. I. *pp.* of ARRINCONAR. **II.** *a.* distant, out of the way; neglected, put away, forgotten.
arrinconar. I. *va.* to lay aside, put away; to pigeonhole; to remove, dismiss; to neglect, forsake. **II.** *vr.* to live secluded.
arriñonado, da, *a.* kidney-shaped.
arriostrar, riostrar, *va.* to brace, stay.
arriscadamente, *adv.* boldly, audaciously.
arriscado, da. I. *pp.* of ARRISCARSE. **II.** *a.* forward, bold; brisk, easy, free; craggy.
arriscador, ra, *n.* (prov.) olive gleaner.
arriscar. I. *va.* (*pret.* ARRISQUÉ; *subj.* ARRISQUE) to risk. **II.** *vr.* to be vain, conceited; (of sheep, etc.) to plunge over a cliff.
arritmia, *f.* arrhythmy, lack of rhythm (esp. med. app. to pulse).—**arrítmico, ca,** *a.* arrhythmic (esp. med.).
arritranca, *f.* crupper of a packsaddle.
arrizafa, *f.* = RUZAFA, garden, park.
arrizar, *va.* (*pret.* ARRICÉ; *subj.* ARRICE) (naut.) to reef, stow, lash.
arroba, *f.* weight of twenty-five pounds (about 11½ kg.); name of a variable liquid measure.
arrobadizo, za, *a.* (coll.) feigning ecstasy.

arrobador, ra, *a.* enchanting, entrancing.
arrobamiento, *m.* ecstatic rapture, bliss, trance.
arrobarse, *vr.* to be enraptured, entranced.
arrobero, ra. I. *a.* weighing an arroba. **II.** baker for a community.
arrobo, *m.* = ARROBAMIENTO.
arrocabe, *m.* wooden frieze.
arrocé, arroce, *v. V.* ARROZAR.
arrocero, ra, *n.* rice planter or dealer.
arrocinado, da. I. *pp.* of ARROCINARSE. **II.** *a.* jaded, worn-out (horse).
arrocinar. I. *va.* to brutalize. **II.** *vr.* to become foolishly enamored; to become stupid.
arrodajarse, *vr.* (Costa Rica) to sit on the ground with the legs crossed.
arrodelarse, *vr.* to be armed with a buckler.
arrodilladura, *f.,* **arrodillamiento,** *m.* kneeling.
arrodillar. I. *va.* to make kneel down. **II.** *vr.* to kneel down.
arrodrigar, arrodrigonar, *va.* to prop (vines).
arrogación, *f.* arrogation; child adoption.
arrogador, ra, *n.* one who claims arrogantly.
arrogancia, *a.* arrogance; haughtiness; bravery, courage; stately carriage.
arrogante, *a.* arrogant; haughty, proud.
arrogantemente, *adv.* arrogantly; proudly.
arrogar. I. *va.* (*pret.* ARROGUÉ; *subj.* ARROGUE) to adopt; to arrogate. **II.** *vr.* to usurp.
arrojadamente, *adv.* audaciously, boldly.
arrojadizo, za, *a.* easily thrown or darted; missile that can be, or is intended to be, thrown.
arrojado, da. I. *pp.* of ARROJAR. **II.** *a.* rash, dashing, fearless.
arrojador, ra, *n.* thrower, flinger.
¹arrojar, *va.* to make red-hot (a furnace, etc.).
²arrojar. I. *va.* to throw, fling, hurl; to cast out; to shed, emit; to bring forth (shoots, sprouts); (naut.) to drive or cast on rocks; to leave, show (a certain figure, as a balance, etc.); to turn away, dismiss. **II.** *vr.* to throw oneself (lit. from a height & fig.); to venture.
arroje, *m.* man who drops as counterweight to raise the curtain in a theater.
arrojo, *m.* fearlessness, dash, boldness.
arrollador, ra. I. *a.* (of waves, wind) violent, sweeping; winding, that winds or serves to wind. **II.** *n.* one that winds.
¹arrollamiento, *m.* (elec.) winding.
²arrollamiento, *m.* = ARRULLO.
arrollar, *va.* to roll; to wrap; to twist; to carry off, sweep away; (Am.) to trample, run over; to defeat, rout, confound; to wind.
arromadizarse, *vr.* to catch cold.
arromar, *va.* to blunt; to dull.
¹arropado, da. I. *pp.* of ¹ARROPAR. **II.** *a.* mixed with must.
²arropado, da, *pp.* of ²ARROPAR.
arropamiento, *m.* wrapping, covering.
¹arropar, *va.* to mix with boiled wine.—**arrope,** *m.* grape juice boiled to a syrup; boiled honey.
²arropar, *va.* to cover, wrap.
arropea, *f.* irons, fetters, shackles.
arropera, *f.* vessel for boiled must, etc.
arropía, *f.* taffy.—**arropiero, ra,** *n.* maker or seller of ARROPÍA.
arrostrar. I. *va.* to set about dauntlessly; to defy, face. **II.** *vr.* to fight face to face.
arroyada, *f.,* **arroyadero,** *m.* channel of a stream; gully; flood, freshet.
¹arroyar, *vr.* to form, or run in, gullies.
²arroyar, *vr.* (agr.) to blight.
arroyuelo, *m. dim.* rill, brook.
arroyo, *m.* rivulet, small stream, brook.
arroz, *m.* rice.—**arrozal,** *m.* rice field.—**arrozar,** *va.* (*pret.* ARROCÉ; *subj.* ARROCE) to sow rice.
arruar, *vn.* to grunt like a wild boar.
arrufadura, *f.* (naut.) sheer of a ship.
arrufaldado, da, *a.* with clothes tucked up.
arrufar. I. *va.* (naut.) to incurvate, to form the sheer. **II.** *vr.* (of dogs) to snarl.

arrufianado, da, *a.* ruffianly, impudent.
arrufo, *m.* = ARRUFADURA.
arruga, *f.* wrinkle (in face, clothes, etc.).
arrugación, *f.,* **arrugamiento,** *m.* corrugation, wrinkling, wrinkle.
arrugar, *va.* (*pret.* ARRUGUÉ; *subj.* ARRUGUE) to wrinkle, corrugate; to crumple, rumple; to fold, gather, crease, pleat.—**a. el entrecejo,** to knit the brow.—**a. la frente,** to frown.
arrugia, *f.* (min.) gold mine.
arrugón, *m.* decoration of carved work.
arruinador, ra, *n.* & *a.* ruiner(-ing), demolisher (-ing), destroyer(-ing).
arruinamiento, *m.* destruction, ruin.
arruinar, *va.* to demolish, ruin, destroy.
arrullador, ra, *n.* luller, rocker; flatterer.
arrullar, *va.* to lull; to court; to bill and coo.
arrullo, *m.* billing and cooing; lullaby.
arrumaco, *m.* caress, fondling.
arrumaje, *m.* (naut.) stowage.
arrumar, *va.* to stow.
arrumazón, *f.* (naut.) stowing; overcast horizon.
arrumbadas, *f. pl.* (naut.) wales of a row galley.
¹arrumbador, ra, *n.* heaper, piler.
²arrumbador, *m.* (naut.) steersman, helmsman.
arrumbamiento, *m.* (naut.) bearing.
¹arrumbar, *va.* to put away; to range (casks of wine) in a cellar; to silence; to remove from a trust.
²arrumbar. I. *va.* (naut.) to determine the direction of. **II.** *vn., vr.* (naut.) to take bearings.
arrunflarse, *vr.* to have a flush in cards.
arrurruz, *m.* arrowroot.
arsáfraga, *f.* = BERRERA, (bot.) parsnip.
arsenal, *m.* shipyard, dockyard, navy yard; arsenal; (fig.) depository; collection of data.
arseniato, *m.* (chem.) arseniate.
arsenical, *a.* (chem.) arsenical.
arsénico. I. *m.* (chem.) arsenic; ratsbane. **II.** *a.* arsenic.
arsenioso, *a.* arsenious.
arsenito, *m.* arsenite.
arseniuro, *m.* arsenide.
arsolla, arzolla, *f.* (bot.) milk thistle.
arta, *f.* (bot.) English plantain; ribwort.
artalejo, artalete, *m.* a sort of tart; meat pie.
artanica, artanita, *f.* (bot.) sow bread.
arte, *m.* or *f.* art; skill, craft, cunning; trade, profession; artifice, device; intrigue; fishing net.—**a. bella, liberal,** one of the fine, liberal arts.—**artes y oficios,** arts and crafts.—**no tener a. ni parte en,** to have nothing to do with.
artefacto, *m.* manufacture, handiwork, contrivance, appliance, device.
artejo, *m.* joint or knuckle of the fingers.
artemisa, artemisia, *f.* (bot.) mugwort.
artena, *f.* name of a water bird.
artera, *f.* iron stamp (for marking bread).
arteramente, *adv.* craftily, cunningly, artfully.
artería, *f.* cunning, trick, artfulness.
arteria, *f.* artery; (Ry., etc.) trunk or main line; main highway; (elec.) feeder.—**arterial,** *a.* arterial.—**arteriografía,** arteriography.—**arteriola,** *f.* arteriole, small artery.—**artereología,** arteriology.—**arteriosclerosis,** *f.* arteriosclerosis.—**arterioso, sa,** *a.* arterial; abounding in arteries.—**arteriotomía,** *f.* arteriotomy.—**arteritis,** *f.* arteritis.
artero, ra, *a.* cunning, artful.
artesa, *f.* trough; bowl; canoe.
artesano, na, *n.* artisan, mechanic.
artesiano, a. Artesian.
artesilla, *f.* trough.
artesón, *m.* kitchen tub; (arch.) carved panel on ceiling.—**artesonado, da,** *a.* panelled (ceiling).
artesuela.—*f. dim.* small trough or bowl.
artético, ca, *a.* arthritic, gouty. Also ARTRÍTICO.
ártico, ca, *a.* arctic.
articulación, *f.* articulation, joint; pronunciation; (bot.) geniculation.

For pronunciation, see the rules at the beginning of the book.

articuladamente, *adv.* distinctly, articulately.
articulado, da. I. *pp.* of ¹ARTICULAR. **II.** *a.* jointed. **III.** *m.* (zool.) articulate.—*m. pl.* Articulata.
¹articular, *va.* to unite, join; to articulate; (law) to question, interrogate.
²articular; articulario, ria, *a.* articular.
articulista, *n.* writer of articles.
artículo, *m.* article; (law) plea; (bot.) geniculation; (anat.) joint.—**a. de fondo,** leader, editorial.—*pl.* articles, things, goods, products.—**a. de consumo,** consumer goods.—**a. de primera necesidad,** basic commodities.
artifice, *n.* artificer, artisan, maker.
artificial, *a.* artificial.—**artificialmente,** *adv.* artificially.
artificio, *m.* workmanship, craft; artifice; cunning; trick, ruse; contrivance, device, appliance.
artificiosamente, *adv.* craftily, artfully.
artificioso, sa, *a.* skilful, ingenious; artful, crafty, cunning.
artiga, *f.* land newly broken up.
artigar, *va.* to break and level (land).
artillar, *va.* to mount (cannon).
artillería, *f.* gunnery, artillery; ordnance.—**a. de a lomo** = A. DE MONTAÑA.—**a. de avancarga,** muzzle-loading artillery.—**a. de campaña,** field artillery.—**a. de costa,** coast artillery.—**a. de montaña,** light mountain artillery.—**a. de plaza,** siege artillery.—**a. de retrocarga,** breech-loading artillery.
artillero, *m.* gunner, artilleryman.
artimaña, *f.* trap, snare, stratagem.
artimón, *m.* (naut.) mizzenmast.
artina, *f.* fruit of the boxthorn.
artista, *m.* artist.
artísticamente, *adv.* artistically.
artístico, ca, *a.* artistic.
artocárpeo, a, *a.* (bot.) artocarpous.
artolas, *f. pl.* set of two back-to-back seats (put on a horse like saddle-bags).
artos, *m.* a kind of thistle; boxthorn.
artralgia, *f.* (med.) arthralgia, pain in a joint.
artrítico, ca, *a.* arthritic, gouty, rheumatic.
artritis, *m.* (med.) arthritis, gout.—**artritismo,** *m.* arthritism, disposition to joint affections.
artrografía, *f.* arthrography.
artrología, *f.* (anat.) arthrology.
artrópodo, da. I. *n.* & *a.* arthropod. **II.** *m. pl.* Arthropoda.
artrotomía, *f.* arthrotomy.
Arturo, *m.* (astr.) Arcturus.
arugas, *f.* (bot.) = MATRICARIA, feverfew.
árula, *f. dim.* small altar.
aruñar, *va.*, **aruñazo,** *m.*, etc. (coll.) = ARAÑAR, to scratch, etc.
arúspice, *m.* augur, soothsayer.
aruspicina, *f.* art of divining from animals' entrails.
arveja, *f.* (bot.) carob tree and its fruit; (S. A.) green pea.—**arvejal, arvejar,** *m.* field of carob trees; (S. A.) greenpea garden.
arvejo, *m.* (bot.) bastard chickpea.
arvejón, *m.* (bot.) chickling vetch.
arvejona, *f.* = ARVEJA.
arvense, *a.* growing in sown fields.
arza, *f.* (naut.) fall of a tackle.
arzobispado, *m.* archbishopric.
arzobispal, *a.* archiepiscopal.
arzobispo, *m.* archbishop.
arzolla, *f.* (bot.) lesser burdock; milk thistle.
arzón, *m.* saddletree.
as, *m.* (cards, dice, aer.) ace; Roman copper coin.
¹asa, *f.* handle, haft.
²asa, *f.* juice of certain plants.—**a. dulce,** gum benzoin.
asación, *f.* (pharm.) decoction.
asadero, ra. I. *a.* fit for roasting. **II.** *m.* (Mex.), small flat cheese.
asado, da. I. *pp.* of ASAR. **II.** *m.* roast.

asador, *m.* spit, roasting jack.
asadura, *f.* entrails.—**a. de puerco,** haslet.
asaeteador, *m.* archer, bowman.
asaetear, *va.* to attack, kill with arrows.
asaetinado, da, *a.* satinlike.
asafétida, *f.* asafœtida, a resinous gum.
asainetado, da, *a.* farcical.
asalariado, da. I. *pp.* of ASALARIAR. **II.** *a.* working for a salary or wages; (contempt.) serving for hire. **III.** *n.* salaried person, wage earner; hireling.
asalariar, *va.* to fix a salary for; to hire.
asalmonado, da, *a.* tasting like salmon.
asaltador, *m.* assailant, assaulter; highwayman.
asaltar, *va.* to assault, storm, assail; to surprise; to occur or come suddenly (to one).
asalto, *m.* assault; attack.—**a. de armas,** fencing bout.—**por a.,** by storm.
asamblea, *f.* assembly; legislature; meeting; junta; (mil.) assembly (bugle call).—**asambleísta,** *n.* assemblyman, member of an assembly.
asar. I. *va.* to roast. **II.** *vr.* (fig.) to be roasting, be very hot.
asarbácara, asáraca, *f.* (bot.) asarabacca.
asarero, *m.* (bot.) = ENDRINO, blackthorn, sloe.
asargado, da, *a.* sergelike, twilled.
asarina, *f.* (bot.) bastard asarum.
ásaro, *m.* (bot.) asarum.
asativo, va, *a.* (pharm.) dressed or boiled in its own juice.
asaz, *adv.* enough, abundantly; greatly, very.
asbestino, na, *a.* pertaining to asbestos.
asbesto, *m.* asbestos.
ascalonia, *f.* (bot.) shallot.
áscar, *m.* army (in Morocco).—**áscari,** *m.* Moroccan infantryman.
ascárides, *f. pl.* ascarides, intestinal worms.
ascendencia, *f.* line of ancestors; origin.
ascendente, *a.* ascendant, ascending.
ascender, *vn.* (*ind.* ASCIENDO; *subj.* ASCIENDA) to ascend, mount, climb; to be promoted.—**a. a,** to amount to, add up to.
ascendiente, *m.* ancestor; influence, power.
ascensión, *f.* ascension; exaltation.—**a. recta,** (astr.) right ascension.
ascensional, *a.* (astr.) ascensional.
ascenso, *m.* promotion.
ascensor, *m.* lift, elevator.
asceta, *m.* ascetic, hermit.—**asceticismo, ascetismo,** *m.* asceticism.—**ascético, ca,** *n.* & *a.* ascetic.
ascidia, *f.* (bot.) ascidium; (zool.) Ascidium, ascidian.—*pl.* (zool.) Ascidian.—**ascidiáceo, a,** *a.* ascidiaceous.
asciendo, ascienda, *v. V.* ASCENDER.
ascios, *m. pl.* (geog.) Ascians.
asciro, *m.* (bot.) St. Andrew's cross.
ascitis, *f.* (med.) ascites, abdominal dropsy.—**ascítico, ca,** *a.* ascitic.
asclepiada, *f.* (bot.) swallowwort.
asco, *m.* nausea, loathing; despicable thing.—**estar hecho un a.,** to be very dirty.—**hacer ascos,** to turn up one's nose.
ascosidad, *f.* loathsomeness.
ascoso, sa, *a.* loathsome.
ascua, *f.* red-hot, or live, coal.—**¡ascuas!** how it hurts!—**en a.,** red hot.—**estar en ascuas,** to be greatly agitated.—**sacar el a. con la mano del gato, or con mano ajena,** (coll.) to get some one to pull one's chestnuts out of the fire.
aseadamente, *adv.* cleanly, neatly.
aseado, da. I. *pp.* of ASEAR. **II.** *a.* clean, neat.
asear, *va.* to adorn, embellish, polish; to clean.
asechador, ra, *a.* ensnarer, waylayer.
asechamiento, *m.*, **asechanza,** *f.* waylaying, snare, trap, stratagem.
asechar, *va.* to waylay; to ambush.
asechoso, sa, *a.* waylaying; intriguing.
asedado, da. I. *pp.* of ASEDAR. **II.** *a.* silky.

asedar, *va.* to work (esp. flax) soft as silk.

asediador, ra, *n.* besieger.

asediar, *va.* to besiege, blockade.—**asedio,** *m.* siege, blockade.

aseglararse, *vr.* (of a religious) to secularize oneself.

asegundar, *va.* to repeat.

asegurable, *a.* insurable.

aseguración, *f.* insurance.

asegurado, da. I. *pp.* of ASEGURAR. **II.** *n.* & *a.* insured (person).

asegurador, ra, *n.* & *a.* insurer(-ing), underwriter(-ing).

aseguramiento, *m.* securing; security; insurance.

asegurar. I. *va.* to secure, fasten, fix; to affirm, assert; (com.) to insure. **II.** *vr.* to make sure; hold fast; to get insured, take out insurance.

aseidad, *f.* self-existence (as of God).

asemejar. I. *va.* to make, or represent as, similar; to copy. **II.** *vr.* (a) to look like, resemble.

asendereado, da. I. *pp.* of ASENDEREAR. **II.** *a.* (of a road, path) beaten; frequented; worn out by trouble.

asenderear, *va.* to open a path in or through; to persecute.

asenso, *m.* assent, consent; credence.

asentada, *f.* session; sitting.

asentaderas, *f. pl.* (coll.) = NALGAS, buttocks.

asentadillas.—**a a.,** *adv.* woman-fashion.

asentado, da. I. *pp.* of ASENTAR. **II.** *a.* seated; settled; permanent.

asentador, *m.* razor strop; turning chisel.

asentadura, *f.,* **asentamiento,** *m.* (law) possession of goods given by default; establishment, settlement.

asentar. I. *va.* (*ind.* ASIENTO; *subj.* ASIENTE) to place, fix, seat; to adjust; to stop at; to note down; to enter (an account, etc.); to strike; to found, establish; to hone; to estimate. **II.** *vn.* to fit; to sit down; to settle. **III.** *vr.* (arch.) to sink, settle.

asentimiento, *m.* assent.

asentir, *vn.* (*ind.* ASIENTO; *subj.* ASIENTA) to agree, to assent, acquiesce.

asentista, *m.* contractor.

aseo, *m.* cleanliness, neatness, tidiness.

asépalo, la, *a.* (bot.) without sepals.

asepsia, *f.* (med.) asepsis.

aséptico, ca, *a.* aseptic.

asequible, *a.* attainable, obtainable, available.

aserción, *f.* assertion, affirmation.

aserradero, *m.* sawmill; sawpit, sawhorse.

aserradizo, za, *a.* fit to be sawed.

aserrado, da. I. *pp.* of ASERRAR. **II.** *a.* serrate, serrated, dentate.

aserrador, *m.* sawer or sawyer.

aserradura, *f.* sawing, kerf.—*pl.* sawdust.

aserrar, *va.* (*ind.* ASIERRO; *subj.* ASIERRE) to saw.

aserrín, serrín, *m.* sawdust.

asertivamente, *adv.* affirmatively.

asertivo, va, *a.* assertive.

aserto, *m.* assertion, affirmation.

asertorio, *a.* (logic) affirmatory.

asesar, *vn.* to become wise.

asesinar, *va.* to assassinate.—**asesinato,** *m.* assassination.

asesino, na, *n.* assassin, murderer(-ess).

asesor, ra, *n.* consultant, adviser.—**asesorar. I.** *va.* to give legal advice to. **II.** *vr.* to take advice.—**asesoría,** *f.* office, pay and fees of a consultant.

asestador, *m.* gunner.

asestadura, *f.* taking aim.

asestar, *va.* to aim, point; to deal (a blow); to discharge, fire.

aseveración, *f.* asseveration, assertion.

aseveradamente, *adv.* affirmatively.

aseverar, *va.* to asseverate, affirm, assert.

asexual, *a.* asexual.

asfaltado, *m.* asphalt pavement; asphalt paving, paving with asphalt.

asfaltar, *va.* to asphalt.

asfáltico, ca, *a.* asphaltic; asphalt (as *a.*); bituminous.

asfalto, *m.* asphalt, asphaltum.

asfíctico, ca, *a.* asphyxial.

asfixia, *f.* (med.) asphyxia.

asfixiante, *a.* asphyxiating.

asfixiar. I. *va.* to asphyxiate, suffocate. **II.** *vr.* to be asphyxiated.

asfódelo, *m.* asphodel, day lily.

asgo, asga, *v.* V. ASIR.

así, *adv.* so, thus, in this manner; therefore. Foll. by verb in *subj.,* it is translated by "would that."—**a., a.,** so so, middling.—**a. como,** as soon as, just as.—**a. como a.,** anyway, anyhow.—**a. (los fijos) como (las fijas),** both (sons) and daughters, (sons) as well as (daughters).—**a. es,** that, or it, is so.—**a. es (son),** such is (are).—**a. es que,** and so; (improper but common) that is the way to, that is how.—**a. no,** not that way, not so.—**a. que,** as soon as, after.—**a. y todo,** and yet; just the same.—**ponerse a.,** to take on so; to act like that.

asiático, ca, *n.* & *a.* Asiatic.

asidera, *f.* (S. A.) (harness) strap with rings.

asidero, *m.* handle; occasion, pretext.—**asideros,** (naut.) towropes.

asido, da. I. *pp.* of ASIR. **II.** *a.* fastened, tied, attached.

asiduamente, *adv.* assiduously.

asiduidad, *f.* assiduity.

asiduo, dua, *a.* assiduous.

¹**asiento,** *m.* seat; site; solidity; settling; bottom; sediment, settlings; treaty; contract; entry; registry; judgment, wisdom; stability; permanence; mining district; list, roll; collar band; indigestion.

²**asiento, asienta,** *v.* V. ASENTIR.

³**asiento, asiente,** *v.* V. ASENTAR.

asierro, asierre, *v.* V. ASERRAR.

asignable, *a.* assignable.

asignación, *f.* assignment; distribution, partition; destination.

asignado, *m.* assignat.

asignar, *va.* to assign; to devote; to appoint; to ascribe, attribute.

asignatura, *f.* subject (of study).

asilar, *va.* to shelter; to place in an asylum.

asilo, *m.* asylum; refuge; shelter.—**a. de huérfanos,** orphan asylum.—**a. de locos,** insane asylum.

¹**asilla,** *f. dim.* small handle; slight pretext.

²**asilla,** *f.* (anat.) clavicle, collarbone.

asimiento, *m.* grasp; attachment, affection.

asimilable, *a.* assimilable.

asimilación, *f.* assimilation.

asimilar. I. *vn.* to resemble. **II.** *va.* to assimilate.

asimilativo, va, *a.* assimilating.

asimismo, *adv.* likewise, so too, in like manner.

asimplado, da, *a.* like a simple, ingenuous person.

asincrónico, ca, *a.* asynchronous.

asincronismo, *m.* asynchronism.

asíndeton, *m.* (rhet.) asyndeton.

asinino, na, *a.* asinine; like a donkey.

asíntota, *f.* (geom.) asymptote.

asir. I. *va.* & *vn.* (*ind.* ASGO; *subj.* ASGA) to grasp or seize; to hold; to take root. **II.** *vr.* (**de**); to avail oneself (of); to hold (to), to take hold (of); to take advantage (of); to dispute (with) each other.—**a. a las ramas,** to give foolish excuses.

asiriano, na; asirio, ria, *n.* & *a.* Assyrian.

asiriología, *f.* Assyriology.

asiriólogo, *n.* Assyriologist.

asistencia, *f.* attendance, presence; assistance, aid; reward; board, meals.—*pl.* allowance; alimony.

For pronunciation, see the rules at the beginning of the book.

asistenta, *f.* handmaid; waiting maid; attendant.
asistente, *m.* assistant, helper; chief officer of justice at Seville; orderly.
asistir. I. *vn.* **(a)** to attend, be present (at); to follow suit. **II.** *va.* to lend; to attend, take care of; to assist, help, serve; to accompany.
asma, *f.* asthma.—**asmático, ca,** *a.* asthmatic.
asna, *f.* female donkey.—*pl.* (carp.) rafters.
asnacho, *m.* (bot.) = GATUÑA, cammock.
asnada, *f.* foolish action.
asnado, *m.* side-wall timber in mines.
asnal, *a.* asinine, stupid, idiotic.
asnalmente, *adv.* foolishly, idiotically.
asnallo, *m.* (bot.) = ASNACHO.
asnería, *f.* collection of donkeys; idiotic action.
asnico, ca, *n. dim.* little donkey.
asnilla, *f.* stanchion or prop.
asnillo, lla, *n. dim.* little donkey; (zool.) field cricket.
asnino, na, *a.* = ASININO.
asno, *m.* donkey, ass.
asobarcar, (coll. for) **sobarcar,** *va.* (*pret.* ASO-BARQUÉ; *subj.* ASOBARQUE) to take under the arm; to lift up (the skirts).
asocarronado, da, *a.* crafty, cunning.
asociación, *f.*, **asociamiento,** *m.* association; fellowship; partnership, union.
asociacionismo, *m.* associationism.
asociado, *m.* associate, partner.
asociar. I. *va.* to associate. **II.** *vr.* to associate; to form a partnership; to join.
asolación, *f.* desolation, devastation.
asolador, ra, *n.* & *a.* destroyer(-ing), ruiner(-ing).
asoladura, *f.* = ASOLACIÓN.
asolamiento, *m.* destruction, havoc.
asolanar, *va.* (of the east wind) to damage (fruit, etc.).
¹asolar. I. *va.* (*ind.* ASUELO; *subj.* ASUELE) to raze, devastate. **II.** *vr.* to settle, get clear (wine).
²asolar. I. *va.* (of the sun) to burn, parch. **II.** *vr.* (of soil) to become parched, dry up.
asoldar (*ind.* ASUELDO; *subj.* ASUELDE), **asoldadar,** *va.* to hire.
asolear. I. *va.* to sun; (Am.) to dry in the sun. **II.** *vr.* to be sunburnt; (Am.) to take a sun bath.
asomada, *f.* appearance; point from which something is first seen.
asomado, da. I. *pp.* of ASOMAR. **II.** *a.* fuddled.
asomar. I. *vn.* to begin to appear. **II.** *va.* to show, put out (as one's head out the window). **III.** *vr.* to become flustered with wine; to peep.
—**a. a,** to look out of; to peep into.
asombradizo, za, *a.* timid, shy.
asombrador, ra, *a.* astonishing.
asombramiento, *m.* = ASOMBRO.
asombrar. I. *va.* to shade, darken; to frighten; to astonish, amaze. **II.** *vr.* (**de**) to wonder, be astonished (at).—**asombro,** *m.* dread, fear; amazement or astonishment.
asombrosamente, *adv.* amazingly, wonderfully.
asombroso, sa, *a.* wonderful, astonishing.
asomo, *m.* indication, sign; conjecture.
asonada, *f.* riotous crowd; mobbing, attack of a mob.
asonancia, *f.* consonance, harmony; (poet.) assonance.
asonantar, *va.* (poet.) to make assonant.
asonante, *n.* & *a.* assonant.
asonar, *vn.* (*ind.* ASUENO; *subj.* ASUENE) to be assonant; to accord.
asordar, *va.* to deafen.
asotanar, *va.* to excavate for a cellar.
aspa, *f.* cross; reel; wings of a windmill; cross stud.—**aspadera,** *f.* (mech.) reel.
aspado, da. I. *pp.* of ASPAR. **II.** *a.* having both arms extended.
aspador, ra. I. *n.* reeler; winder. **II.** *m.* reel.
aspalato, *m.* (bot.) rosewood.
aspalto, *m.* = ESPALTO, dark, clear paint.
aspar, *va.* to reel, wind; to crucify; to vex.

aspaviento, *m.* exaggerated wonder or fear; fuss.
aspecto, *m.* aspect, look; (arch.) outlook; (astr.) aspect.
ásperamente, *adv.* rudely, harshly, gruffly.
asperear, *vn.* to taste acrid.
asperete, *m.* = ¹ASPERILLO.
aspereza, *f.* asperity; roughness; keenness; harshness, snappishness; rough place.
asperges, *m.* sprinkling.
asperidad, *f.* = ASPEREZA.
asperiego, ga, *a.* sour (pippin).
¹asperillo, *m.* sourish taste of unripe fruit.
²asperillo, lla, *a. dim.* tart, sourish.
asperjar, *va.* to sprinkle.
áspero, ra, *a.* rough; knotty; harsh, gruff.
asperón, *m.* grindstone; flagstone.
aspérrimo, ma, *a. super.* of ÁSPERO.
aspersión, *f.* aspersion; sprinkling.
aspersorio, *m.* water sprinkler.
áspid, áspide, *m.* asp.
aspillera, *f.* loophole, embrasure, crenel.
aspiración, *f.* aspiration; (mus.) short pause.
aspiradamente, *adv.* with aspiration.
aspirador, *m.* vacuum cleaner.
aspirante. I. *a.* **bomba a.,** suction pump. **II.** *m.* & *f.* aspirant, neophyte.
aspirar. I. *va.* to inhale; to aspire; to covet; to aspirate; to suck. **II.** *vn.* to aspire; to draw breath in, inhale.
aspirina, *f.* aspirin.
asquear. I. *va.* to loathe. **II.** *vn.* to be nauseated.
asquerosamente, *adv.* loathsomely; basely.
asquerosidad, *f.* filthiness, foulness; vileness, baseness.
asqueroso, sa, *a.* filthy, loathsome; vile, base.
asta, *f.* lance; staff, pole, flagstaff; horn, antler; shank; shaft, spindle.—**a media a.,** at half mast.
ástaco, *m.* crawfish.
astado, astero, *m.* Roman pikeman.
astático, ca, *a.* astatic.
astenia, *f.* (med.) asthenia, debility.
asténico, ca, *a.* (med.) asthenic.
asteria, *f.* starstone; cat's-eye.
asterisco, *m.* asterisk (*); (bot.) oxeye.
asteroide, *m.* asteroid.—**asteroideo. I.** *n.* & *a.* (zool.) asteroidean. **II.** *n. pl.* Asteroidea.
astigmatismo, *m.* (med.) astigmatism.
astigmómetro, *m.* (med.) instrument for measuring astigmatism.
astil, *m.* handle; shaft; beam of a balance.
astilejos, *m. pl.* = ASTILLEJOS.
astilla, *f.* chip, splinter.—**astillar,** *va.* to chip.
astillazo, *m.* blow from a flying chip.
Astillejos, *m. pl.* (astr.) Castor and Pollux.
astillero, *m.* rack for lances, spears, pikes, etc.; shipyard, dockyard.
astilloso, sa, *a.* easily splintered.
astracán, *m.* astrakhan (cloth).
astrágalo, *m.* (arch.) astragal; (mil.) molding on a cannon; (bot.) milk vetch; (anat.) astragalus, anklebone; round molding; beads.
astral, *a.* astral.
astrancia, *f.* (bot.) masterwort.
astricción, *f.* astriction, binding.
astrictivo, va, *a.* astrictive, styptic.
astricto, ta, *a.* contracted; determined.
astrífero, ra, *a.* (poet.) starry.
astringencia, *f.* astringency.
astringente, *a.* astringent.
astringir, *va.* (*ind.* ASTRINJO; *subj.* ASTRINJA) to astringe, contract, compress.
astro, *m.* heavenly body.
astrofísica, *f.* astrophysics.
astrografía, *f.* astrography.
astroite, *m.* astroite, star-shaped fossil.
astrolabio, *m.* astrolabe.
astrólatra, *n.* astrolater.
astrolatría, *f.* astrolatry, star worship.
astrología, *f.* astrology.

astrológico, ca, *a.* astrological.
astrólogo, *m.* astrologer.
astronomía, *f.* astronomy.
astronómicamente, *adv.* astronomically.
astronómico, ca, *a.* astronomical.
astrónomo, *m.* astronomer.
astroquímica, *f.* astrochemistry.
astrosamente, *adv.* meanly, basely.
astroso, sa, *a.* vile, loathsome.
astucia, *f.* cunning, slyness.
astur, ra, asturiano, na, *n.* & *a.* Asturian.
asturión, *m.* pony; (ichth.) sturgeon.
astutamente, *adv.* cunningly, craftily.
astuto, ta, *a.* astute, cunning, sly, crafty.
asueldo, asuelde, *v.* V. ASOLDAR.
asuelo, asuele, *v.* V. ASOLAR.
asueno, asuene, *v.* V. ASONAR.
asueto, *m.* school holiday, vacation.
asumir, *va.* to assume; to raise, elevate.
asunción, *f.* assumption; elevation, ascent.
asunto, *m.* subject, matter; affair, business.
asuramiento, *m.* (of cooking food) burning.
asurarse, *vr.* to burn; to become parched.
asurcano, na, *a.* (of land or those working it) neighboring.
asurcar, surcar, *va.* (*pret.* ASURQUÉ; *subj.* ASUR-QUE) to furrow; to plow.
asustadizo, za, *a.* easily frightened; shy.
asustar. I. *va.* to frighten, scare. **II.** *vr.* to be frightened.
atabaca, *f.* (bot.) groundsel.
atabacado, da, *a.* tobacco-colored.
atabal, *m.* kettledrum.—**atabalear,** *vn.* (of horses' hooves) to clatter; to drum (with the fingers).—**atabalero, ra,** *n.* kettledrummer.
atabanado, da, *a.* (of a horse) spotted white.
atabardillado, da, *a.* resembling spotted fever.
atabe, *m.* small vent in water pipes.
atabernado, da, *a.* (of wine) sold by the glass.
atabillar, *va.* to fold (cloth) with selvages out.
atabladera, *f.* roller.
atablar, *va.* to level, roll (ground already sown).
atacadera, *f.* blaster's rammer.
atacado, da. I. *pp.* of ATACAR. **II.** *a.* (fig.) irresolute, undecided; stingy, close.
atacador, *m.* aggressor; ramrod, rammer.
atacadura, *f.,* **atacamiento,** *m.* ramming.
atacamita, *f.* (min.) atacamite.
atacar, *va.* (*pret.* ATAQUÉ; *subj.* ATAQUE) to attack; to button; to fit; to ram; to corner.
atacir, *m.* (astrol.) division of the celestial arch into twelve parts.
ataderas, *f. pl.,* (Mex.) garters.
atadero, *m.* cord, rope; tying place or thing.
atadijo, ito, *m. dim.* (coll.) ill-shaped parcel.
atado, da. I. *pp.* of ATAR. **II.** *a.* pusillanimous, good-for-nothing. **III.** *m.* bundle, parcel.
atador, ra. I. *n.* tier, binder. **II.** *m.* bonnet-string.
atadura, *f.* fastening, binding; connection; knot.
atafagar, *va.* to stifle, stupefy; to tease, bother.
atafetanado, da, *a.* taffetalike.
ataguía, *f.* cofferdam.
ataharre, *m.* broad crupper of a packsaddle.
atahorma, *f.* (ornith.) osprey.
ataifor, *m.* deep dish; Moorish round table.
atairar, *va.* to mold (panels and frames of doors or windows).
ataire, *m.* molding in panels and frames.
atajadero, *m.* sluice gate.
atajadizo, *m.* partition.
atajador, *m.* one that stops or intercepts; (mil.) scout; (min.) boy who tends the horses.
atajar. I. *va.* to intercept, stop; to partition off. **II.** *vr.* to be confounded with shame or fear.
atajea, atajía, *f.* = ATARJEA.
atajo, *m.* short cut; interception, stopping.—**echar por el a.,** (fig.) to escape through a loop-hole.
atalajar, *va.* to harness and hitch.

ataleje, *m.* breast harness; draft.
atalantar, = ATARANTAR.
atalaya. I. *f.* watchtower; height. **II.** *m.* guard; lookout.
atalayador, ra, *n.* sentry, lookout; prier.
atalayar, *va.* to watch, guard; to spy on, pry into.—**atalayero,** *m.* advance scout.
atalvina, talvina, *f.* porridge of almond meal.
atamiento, *m.* pusillanimity, meekness.
¹atanasia, *f.* (bot.) costmary or alecost.
²atanasia, *f.* (print.) English type (14-point).
atanor, *m.* tile water pipe; tile (clay or concrete tube or pipe).
atanquía, *f.* depilatory; silk refuse.
atañer, *v. impers.* to belong appertain, concern.
ataque, *m.* attack; (mil.) offensive works; (med.) fit (of illness); wrangle.
ataqué, ataque, *v.* V. ATACAR.
ataquiza, *f.* laying (a vine).
ataquizar, *va.* to lay (a vine).
atar. I. *va.* to tie, bind; to lace; to deprive of motion, stop.—**a. cabos,** to put two and two together, draw one's own conclusions. **II.** *vr.* to become embarrassed.
ataracea, taracea, *f.* marquetry, inlaid work.
ataracear, taracear, *va.* to checker; to inlay.
atarantado, da, *a.* bitten by a tarantula: restless, wild; astonished, amazed; dizzy.
atarantar. I. *va.* to astound, dumbfound. **II.** *vr.* to be or become dumbfounded; to rush, dash.
atarazana, *f.* arsenal; spinner's shed.
atarazar, *va.* to bite.
atareado, da. I. *pp.* of ATAREAR. **II.** *a.* busy.
atarear. I. *va.* to give or assign work to. **II.** *vr.* to be exceedingly busy.
atarjea, *f.* culvert; conduit; drain pipe.
atarquinar. I. *va.* to cover with mud. **II.** *vr.* to be covered with mud.
atarraga, *f.* (bot.) = OLIVARDA, elecampane.
atarrajar, *va.* = ATERRAJAR, to thread (a screw).
atarraya, *f.* casting net.
atarugamiento, *m.* wedging; stuffing.
atarugar, *va.* (*pret.* ATARUGUÉ; *subj.* ATARUGUE) to fasten; to wedge, plug, bung; to stuff, fill; (coll.) to silence.
atasajado, da, *a.* (coll.) stretched across a horse.
atasajar, *va.* to jerk (beef).
atascadero, atascamiento, *m.* deep miry place; obstruction; impediment.
atascar. I. *va.* (*pret.* ATASQUÉ; *subj.* ATASQUE) to stop (a leak); to obstruct. **II.** *vr.* to stick in mire; to get stopped up; to be nonplussed, (coll.) to get stuck.—**atasco,** *m.* obstruction.
atasqué, atasque, *v.* V. ATASCAR.
ataúd, *m.* coffin, casket· anc. grain measure.
ataujía, *f.* damaskeening.
ataujiado, da, *a.* damaskeened.
ataurique, *m.* (arch.) ornamented plasterwork.
ataviar, *va.* to deck out, trim, adorn.
atávico, ca, *a.* atavistic.
atavío, *m.* dress; finery, gear.
atavismo, m. atavism.
ataxia, *f.* (med.) ataxia.—**a. locomotriz,** loco-motor ataxia.—**atáxico, ca,** *a.* ataxic.
atecé, atece, *v.* V. ATEZAR.
atediar. I. *va.* to bore, tire. **II.** *vr.* to be bored.
ateísmo, *m.* atheism.
ateísta; ateo, a, *n.* & *a.* atheist(-ic).
ateje, *m.* a kind of hardwood tree (Cuba).
atelaje, *m.* ATALAJE, harness; team.
atemorizar, *va.* (*pret.* ATEMORICÉ; *subj.* ATEMO-RICE) to cause fear to, frighten.
atemperación, *f.* tempering, moderating.
atemperante, *a.* tempering, soothing, cooling.
atemperar, *va.* to temper, soften, assuage, cool; to accommodate (one thing to another).
atenacear, atenazar, *va.* to tear off the flesh of with nippers; to torture.
atención, *f.* attention; civility; kindness; deal in

wool.—*pl.* affairs, business.—**en a. a,** considering, in view of.—*interj.* Attention! Look out!

atender. I. *vn.* (*pp.* ATENDIDO and ATENTO; *ind.* ATIENDO; *subj.* ATIENDA) to attend; to pay attention; to wait. **II.** *va.* to take care of (a person); to wait on; to show courtesy to; to treat.

ateneo, *m.* athenæum.

atenerse (a), *vr.* (*ind. pres.* me ATENGO, *pret.* me ATUVE; *subj.* me ATENGA) to depend or rely (on); to abide (by), stick (to).

atengo, atenga, *v.* **V.** ATENERSE.

ateniense, *n.* & *a.* Athenian.

atenta, *f.*—**su a.,** (bus.) your favor (i.e. letter).

atentación, *f.* (law) illegal procedure.

atentadamente, *adv.* contrary to law.

¹**atentado, da. I.** *pp.* of ATENTAR. **II.** *m.* (law) transgression, offense, violation; crime.

²**atentado, da,** *a.* discreet, moderate; noiseless.

atentamente, *adv.* attentively; politely.—**att^e,** used abbrev. in ending to business letters.

atentar, *va.* (*ind.* ATIENTO; *subj.* ATIENTE) to attempt; to attempt (a crime) (reg. conj. in this meaning).

atentatorio, ria, *a.* tending to unlawful acts; leading to criminal act; with criminal or unlawful intent.

atento, ta. I. *pp. irr.* of ATENDER. **II.** *a.* attentive, heedful; polite, courteous.—**su a. seguro servidor,** (ending formal or business letter) very truly yours; (anc.) your obedient servant.

atenuación, *f.* extenuation, diminution; (rhet.) litotes.

atenuante, *a.* attenuating; extenuating (circumstances).

atenuar, *va.* to attenuate, diminish, lessen; to tone down (as angry speaking).

ateo, a, *n.* & *a.* atheist (-ic).

atepocate, *m.* (Mex.) frog spawn.

atercianado, da, *a.* afflicted with tertian fever.

aterciopelado, da, *a.* velvety.

aterido, da, *a.* stiff with cold.

aterimiento, *m.* stiffness from cold.

aterino, *m.* atherine, sand smelt.

aterirse, *vr. defect.* (*ind.* me ATIERO; *subj.* me ATIERA) to become stiff with cold.

atermal, *a.* (of mineral waters) cold.

atérmano, na, *a.* (phys.) athermanous.

atérmico, ca, *a.* = ATÉRMANO.

ateroma, *f.* (med.) atheroma, a kind of tumor.

aterrador, ra, *a.* frightful, terrible, dreadful.

aterrajar, *va.* to thread, tap (a screw).

aterramiento, *m.* terror; humiliation.

¹**aterrar. I.** *va.* (*ind.* ATIERRO; *subj.* ATIERRE) to destroy, pull down, demolish. **II.** *vn.* (aer.) to land. **III.** *vr.* (naut.) to stand inshore.

²**aterrar. I.** *va.* (*this verb is regular*) to terrify; to awe; to appal. **II.** *vr.* to be filled with terror, to be awed or appalled.

aterrizaje, *m.* (aer.) landing, alighting.—**pista de a.,** runway; landing field.—**técnicos de a.,** landing experts.

aterrizar, *vn.* (aer.) to land.

aterronar. I. *va.* to clot; to make bumpy. **II.** *vr.* to become lumpy; to cake.

aterrorizar, *va.* to frighten, terrify.

atesador, *m.* (mech.) stretcher, tightener; brace pin.

atesar, *va.* (*ind.* ATIESO; *subj.* ATIESE) to pull tight, to tighten; (naut.) = TESAR, to haul taut.

atesorador, ra, *n.* hoarder.

atesorar, *va.* to treasure, hoard up.

atestación, *f.* attestation, testimony, affidavit.

atestado, da, *a.* attested, witnessed.

atestados, *m. pl.* certificates, testimonials.

atestadura, *f.* cramming or stuffing; must for soaking casks.

atestamiento, *m.* cramming, stuffing.

¹**atestar,** *va.* (*ind.* ATIESTO; *subj.* ATIESTE) to cram, stuff, crowd; to fill up wine casks.

²**atestar,** *va.* (*reg. conj.*) to attest, witness.

atestiguación, *f.,* **atestiguamiento,** *m.* affidavit.

atestiguar, *va.* to depose, witness, attest; to give evidence; to prove.

atetado, da, *a.* mammilliform, teat-shaped.

atetar, *va.* to suckle.

atetillar, *va.* to trench around roots.

atezado, da. I. *pp.* of ATEZAR. **II.** *a.* black.

atezamiento, *m.* blackening.

atezar. I. *va.* (*pret.* ATECÉ; *subj.* ATECE) to blacken. **II.** *vr.* to become or get black.

atibar, *va.* (min.) to fill up (excavations).

atiborrar, *va.* to stuff with coarse wool.

aticé, atice, *v.* **V.** ATIZAR.

aticismo, *m.* Atticism; elegant, delicate diction.

ático, ca. I. *a.* Attic; elegant. **II.** *m.* Attic (arch.) attic.

atiendo, atienda, *v.* **V.** ATENDER.

atiento, atiente, *v.* **V.** ATENTAR.

atiero, atiera, *v.* **V.** ATERIRSE.

atierre, *m.* deals; caving in; ruin; (mining) attle, heap of waste ore.

atierro, atierre, *v.* **V.** ¹ATERRAR.

atiesar, *va.* to stiffen.

atieso, atiese, *v.* **V.** ATESAR.

atiesto, atieste, *v.* **V.** ¹ATESTAR.

atifle, *m.* potter's trivet.

atigrado, da, *a.* marked like tiger skin.

atildadura, *f.,* **atildamiento,** *m.* punctuation; censure; tidiness, nicety.

atildar, *va.* to put a dash or TILDE over; to censure; to adorn.

atinadamente, *adv.* cautiously; wisely; judiciously.

atinar, *vn.* to hit the mark; to guess; to find out. —**a. a** (*inf.*), to succeed in (*pres. p.*).

atíncar, *m.* tincal, borax.

atinconar, *va.* (min.) to prop the side walls of.

atiplar. I. *va.* to raise the pitch of (a musical instrument). **II.** *vr.* to become sharp (in tone).

atirantar, *va.* (arch.) to stay, brace with ties.

atiriciarse, *vr.* (med.) to become jaundiced.

atisbadero, *m.* (Am.) peephole.

atisbador, ra, *n.* prier, observer.

atisbadura, *f.* prying, observing cautiously.

atisbar, *va.* to scrutinize; to pry, watch.

atisbo, *m.* = ATISBADURA.

atisuado, da, *a.* tissuelike.

atizador, *m.,* **atizador, ra,** *n.* inciter; (fire) poker; (candle) snuffer; feeder.

atizar, *va.* (*pret.* ATICÉ; *subj.* ATICE) to poke (the fire); to snuff or trim (a candle, etc.); to rouse, stir.

atizonar. I. *va.* to bond (a wall) with headers; to embed (a beam in a wall). **II.** *vr.* (agr.) to become blighted.

atlantes, *m.* (arch.) atlantes.

atlántico, ca, *n.* & *a.* Atlantic.

atlas, *m.* atlas; (anat.) atlas; (com.) atlas (satin).

atleta, *m.* athlete.—**atlético, ca,** *a.* athletic.—**atletismo,** *m.* athletics.

atmósfera, *f.* atmosphere; sphere of influence.

atmosférico, ca, *a.* atmospheric.

atoar, *va.* (naut.) to tow.

atocinado, da. I. *pp.* of ATOCINAR. **II.** *a.* fat, fleshy.

atocinar. I. *va.* to cut up (a pig); to convert into bacon; (coll.) to assassinate. **II.** *vr.* to swell with anger; to fall desperately in love.

atocha, *f.* tough feather grass, bassweed.

atochal, ¹**atochar,** *m.* bassweed field.

²**atochar,** *va.* to fill with bassweed.

atochón, *m.* panicle of tough feather grass.

atol, atole, *m.* non-alcoholic corn-flour drink.

atolería, *f.* place where ATOLE is sold.

atolero, ra, *n.* maker and vender of ATOLE.

atolondrado, da. I. *pp.* of ATOLONDRAR. **II.** *a.* hare-brained, thoughtless, giddy, careless.

atolondramiento, *m.* confusion, perplexity, amazement; giddiness; recklessness.

atolondrar. I. *va.* to confound, amaze, perplex, rattle. **II.** *vr.* to become confused, rattled.

atolladero, *m.* deep miry place; difficulty, stumbling block.

atollar, *vn. & vr.* to fall into the mire; to stick in the mud; to be involved in difficulties, (coll.) to get stuck.

atomicidad, *f.* atomicity.

atómico, ca, *a.* atomic.—**bomba a.,** atom bomb. —**peso a.,** atomic weight.

atomismo, *m.* atomism.

atomista, *m.* atomist.

atomístico, ca, *a.* atomistic.

átomo, *m.* atom.—**exponente de un a.,** atomic number.

atonal, *a.* (mus.) atonal.

atondar, *va.* to spur (a horse).

atonía, *f.* (med.) atony; debility.

atónito, ta, *a.* astonished, amazed, aghast.

átono, na, *a.* unaccented; atonic.

atontadamente, *adv.* foolishly, stupidly.

atontado, da. I. *pp.* of ATONTAR. **II.** *a.* foolish, stupid; stunned.

atontamiento, *m.* stupefaction, stunning.

atontar. I. *va.* to stun, stupefy; to confound, confuse. **II.** *vr.* to become stupid, dull, stunned.

¹atorar. I. *va.* to obstruct; to jam, choke. **II.** *vr.* to stick in the mire; to fit the bore closely; to choke; to stuff oneself.

²atorar, *va.* to cut (wood) into logs.

atormentadamente, *adv.* anxiously, tormentedly.

atormentador, ra, *n. & a.* tormentor(-ing).

atormentar, *va.* to torment, torture.

atornillar, *va.* to screw; to turn a screw.

atorozonarse, *vr.* (vet.) (of horses) to suffer colic.

atortolar. I. *va.* to confound; to intimidate. **II.** *vr.* to be intimidated.

atortorar, *va.* (naut.) to frap (a ship).

atortujar, *va.* to squeeze, make flat.

atosigador, ra, *n. & a.* poisoner(-ing).

atosigamiento, *m.* poisoning.

atosigar, *va.* (*pret.* ATOSIGUÉ; *subj.* ATOSIGUE) to poison; to harass, press.

atoxicar, *va.* to poison.

atóxico, ca, *a.* nonpoisonous.

atrabancar, *va.* (*pret.* ATRABANQUÉ; *subj.* ATRABANQUE) to huddle; to perform in a hurry.

atrabanco, *m.* huddling, acting hurriedly.

atrabiliario, ria; atrabilioso, sa, *a.* atrabilious.

atrabilis, *f.* black bile.

atracable, *a.* approachable.

atracadero, *m.* (naut.) landing place.

atracar. I. *va.* (*pret.* ATRAQUÉ; *subj.* ATRAQUE) (naut.) to overtake; to approach; to cram; to pamper; (Am.) (of robbers) to assault, attack, or hold up. **II.** *vn.* (naut.) to make the shore; to stop, moor. **III.** *vr.* to be pampered.

atracción, *f.* attraction.

atracón, *m.* overeating, gluttony; push.

atractivo, va. I. *a.* attractive. **II.** *m.* charm, grace; inducement.

atraer, *va.* (*ind. pres.* ATRAIGO, *pret.* ATRAJE; *subj.* ATRAIGA) to attract; to allure, charm.

atrafagado, da, *a.* very busy; laborious; fidgety.

atrafagar. I. *vn.* to toil, work hard. **II.** *vr.* to fidget, fuss.

atragantarse, *vr.* to choke; to become confused in conversation.

atraíble, *a.* attractable.

atraidorado, da, *a.* traitorlike, peculiar to traitors.

atraigo, atraje, atraiga, *v. V.* ATRAER.

atraillar, *va.* to leash; to follow (game) guided by a dog on a leash.

atramento, *m.* black color.

atramparse, *vr.* to be trapped; to be locked out; to be blocked up; to be involved in difficulties.

atramuz, *m.* (bot.) lupine.

atrancar, *va.* (*pret.* ATRANQUÉ; *subj.* ATRANQUE) to bar (a door); to obstruct; to stride; to read hurriedly.

atranque, *m.* difficulty, tight box, fix.

atrapamoscas, *f.* (bot.) Venus's flytrap.

atrapar, *va.* to overtake; to catch, grab; to trap, ensnare, deceive.

atraqué, atraque, *v. V.* ATRACAR.

atrás, *adv.* backward, behind, back; past.—**a. de,** behind, back of.—**dar marcha a.,** (auto) to back up, go into reverse.—**de a.,** back (as *a.*).—**hacerse a.,** to fall back.

atrasado, da. I. *pp.* of ATRASAR. **II.** *a.* short of funds, poor; backward; behind the times; late, tardy; (of timepiece) slow; back (number of a periodical).

atrasar. I. *va.* to retard, delay, detain; to set, put back (timepiece). **II.** *vn.* (of timepiece) to go or be slow. **III.** *vr.* to remain or be left behind; (of timepiece) to lose time; to be in arrears; to be late.

atraso, *m.* tardiness; backwardness.—*pl.* arrears.

atravesado, da. I. *pp.* of ATRAVESAR. **II.** *a.* squint-eyed; perverse; mestizo, crossbred, mongrel.

atravesaño, *m.* crosstimber; crosspiece.

atravesar. I. *va.* (*ind.* ATRAVIESO; *subj.* ATRAVIESE) to place across, lay athwart; to run through, pierce; to cross; to go through; to wager; (naut.) to lie to; to monopolize, corner (the market). **II.** *vr.* (en) to be, come or lie across or in the way (of); to break in, interrupt, (coll.) intrude (in); to meddle; to spring up, arise (as an obstacle); (con) to meet; to have an encounter or fight (with).

atravieso, *v. V.* ATRAVESAR.

atrayente, *a.* attractive.

atreguado, da, *a.* foolish; deranged; under truce.

atreguar. I. *va.* to give a truce to; to give an extension. **II.** *vr.* to agree to a truce.

atrenzo, *m.* conflict, difficulty.

atresia, *f.* (med.) atresia, occlusion of a channel.

atresnalar, *va.* to collect (grain) into shocks.

atreverse, *vr.* to dare; to venture.

atrevidamente, *adv.* daringly, boldly.

atrevido, da. I. *pp.* of ATREVERSE. **II.** *a.* bold, daring, fearless; forward, insolent.

atrevimiento, *m.* boldness, audacity; effrontery, impudence.

atribución, *f.* attribution; attribute.

atribuir. I. *va.* (*ind. pres.* ATRIBUYO, *pret.* él ATRIBUYÓ; *subj.* ATRIBUYA) to attribute, ascribe, impute. **II.** *vr.* to assume, take to oneself.

atribular. I. *va.* to grieve, afflict. **II.** *vr.* to be or become sad or despondent; to lose heart.

atributivo, va, *a.* attributive.

atributo, *m.* attribute; (logic) predicate.

atribuyo, atribuya, *v. V.* ATRIBUIR.

atrición, *f.* contrition; (vet.) contraction.

atril, *m.* lectern; music stand; easel.

atrilera, *f.* ornamental cover for a lectern.

atrincheramiento, *m.* (mil.) entrenchment; trenches (collect.).

atrincherar, *va. & vr.* (mil.) to entrench.

atrio, *m.* atrium; paved terrace or raised platform in front of a building (gen. a church).

atrípedo, da, *a.* (zool.) black-footed.

atrirrostro, tra, *a.* (ornith.) black-beaked.

atrito, ta, *a.* contrite.

atro, ra, *a.* (poet.) dark, black, obscure.

atrocidad, *f.* atrocity.

atrochar, *vn.* to go by cross-paths.

atrofia, *f.* atrophy.—**atrofiar,** *va. & vr.* to atrophy.—**atrófico, ca,** *a.* atrophic.

atrojarse, *vr.* (Mex., coll.) to be nonplussed.

atrompetado, da, *a.* trumpetlike.

atronadamente, *adv.* recklessly, hastily.

atronado, da. I. *pp.* of ATRONAR. **II.** *a.* reckless, thoughtless.

atronador, ra, *n. & a.* thunderer(-ing).

atronadura, *f.* crack or split (in trees); (vet.) tumor in the pastern.

atronamiento, *m.* thundering; stupefaction; (vet.) crepance, wound or chap in the hoof.

atronar. I. *va.* (ind. ATRUENO: *subj.* ATRUENE) to deafen; to stun, stupefy; to stop (the ears of horses so they won't take fright); to kill (a bull). II. *vr.* to be thunderstruck.

atronerar, *va.* to make embrasures in.

atropar, *va.* to assemble in groups.

atropelladamente, *adv.* tumultuously, helter-skelter; unscrupulously.

atropellado, da. I. *pp.* of ATROPELLAR. II. *a.* hasty; precipitate.

atropellador, ra, *n.* trampler; transgressor, violator.

atropellamiento, *m.* trampling under foot; confusion.

atropellar. I. *va.* to trample under foot; to knock down; to run over, hit, injure; to push through; to insult. II. *vr.* to move or act hastily or recklessly; to rush (through a job).

atropello, *m.* trampling, upsetting; running over, injuring (a pedestrian); abuse, insult, outrage.

atropina, *f.* atropine.

atroz, *a.* atrocious; (coll.) huge, vast, enormous.

atrozar, *va.* (naut.) to truss (a yard).

atrozmente, *adv.* atrociously; enormously.

atruendo, *m.* pomp, ostentation.

atrueno, atruene, *v. V.* ATRONAR.

atruhanado, da, *a.* scurrilous, rascally.

atuendo, *m.* = ATRUENDO.

atufadamente, *adv.* peevishly.

atufar. I. *va.* to vex, irritate, plague. II. *vr.* to fret (liquors); to become angry.

atufo, *m.* vexation, annoyance.

atún, *m.* tunny fish.—**atunara,** *f.* place to catch tunny fish.—**atunera,** *f.* tunny-fish hook.

atunero, *m.* tunny fisherman or dealer.

¹aturar, *va.* to close tight.

²aturar, *vn.* to act wisely, with good judgment.

aturdido, da. I. *pp.* of ATURDIR. II. *a.* harebrained, giddy, rattled.

aturdimiento, *m.* bewilderment; confusion.

aturdir. I. *va.* to bewilder, amaze; to rattle, perplex; to stun. II. *vr.* to become dazed, bewildered, rattled, stunned.

aturrullar, *va.* to confound, perplex, bewilder.

atusador, ra, *n.* hairdresser; plant trimmer.

atusar. I. *va.* to trim; to comb and smooth (the hair). II. *vr.* to overdress.

atutía, *f.* tutty.

atuve, *v. V.* ATENERSE.

auca, oca, *f.* goose.

audacia, *f.* audacity, boldness.

audaz, *a.* bold, fearless, audacious.

audible, *a.* audible.

audiencia, *f.* audience, hearing; audience chamber; court of oyer and terminer; audiencia (a kind of high court and its jurisdiction).

audiofrecuencia, *f.* (radio) audio frequency.

audiómetro, *m.* audiometer.

audión, *m.* (radio) audion.

auditivo, va, *a.* auditory.

auditor, *m.* judge.—**a. de guerra,** Judge Advocate (army).—**a. de la Rota,** member or auditor of the Rota.—**a. de marina,** Judge Advocate (navy).

auditoría, *f.* office of an AUDITOR.

auditorio, ria. I. *a.* auditory. II. *m.* audience, assembly of listeners.

auge, *m.* culmination, supreme height; (astr.) apogee.

augita, *f.* (min.) augite.

augur, *m.* augur, augurer.

auguración, *f.* augury.

augural, *a.* augurial.

augurar, *va.* to augur.

augurio, *m.* = AGÜERO, augury; omen.

augusto, ta, *a.* august, magnificent.

aula, *f.* lecture hall; class room; (poet.) palace.

aulaga, *f.* furze, whin, gorse.

áulico, ca, *a.* aulic, pertaining to a royal court.

aulladero, *m.* place where wolves congregate and howl.

aullador, ra, *n.* & *a.* howler(-ing); *n.* (zool.) howling monkey, howler.

aullar, *vn.* to howl, yell, cry.

aullido, aúllo, *m.* howl (of animals).

aumentable, *a.* that can be increased.

aumentación, *f.* increase; (rhet.) climax.

aumentado, da. I. *pp.* of AUMENTAR. II. *a.* increased, augmented; magnified.—**a. de,** or **en,** increased by.

aumentador, ra, *n.* & *a.* enlarger(-ing), amplifier(-ing).

aumentar, *va.* & *vr.* to augment, increase, enlarge, magnify.

aumentativo, va, *a.* increasing, enlarging; (gram.) augmentative.

aumento, *m.* augmentation, increase; enlargement; access, accession; growth.—*pl.* **aumentos,** promotion, advancement.

aun, *adv.* & *conj.* even; still; AÚN.—**a. cuando,** even if, even though, notwithstanding.

aún, *adv.* yet, still; as yet.—**a. no,** not yet, not as yet.—**más a.,** still more; nay; what is more; furthermore.

aunar. I. *va.* to unite, join; to combine, assemble; to unify. II. *vr.* to be united or confederated; to combine.

aunque, *conj.* though, although, notwithstanding, even if.

¡aúpa! ¡upa! *interj.* up, up! (to children).—**aupar,** *va.* to help (a person) get up.

¹aura, *f.* gentle breeze; (med.) aura.—**a. popular,** popularity; popular acclamation.

²aura, *f.* (Am.) (zool.) turkey buzzard.

auranciáceo, *a.* aurantiaceous, orangelike.

áureo, rea. I. *a.* golden, gilt, gold.—**a. número,** golden number. II. *m.* ancient gold coin; weight of four scruples.

aureola, auréola, *f.* aureola; lunar corona.

auricalco, *m.* brass, bronze or copper.

aurícula, *f.* (anat.) auricle; (bot.) primrose.

auricular. I. *a.* auricular. II. *m.* (tel.) receiver; (radio) earphone.

auriculato, ta, *a.* auriculate.

aurífero, ra, *a.* auriferous, gold-bearing.

auriga, *m.* coachman; (astr.) Auriga, Charioteer.

aurígero, ra, *a.* = AURÍFERO.

aurista, *m.* aurist, ear specialist.

aurívoro, ra, *a.* (poet.) avaricious of gold.

aurora, *f.* dawn; first appearance; a beverage made from almonds and cinnamon; roseate hue; (naut.) morning watch gun.—**a. austral,** aurora australis.—**a. boreal,** aurora borealis.

aurragado, da, *a.* badly tilled and cultivated.

auscultación, *f.* (med.) auscultation.

auscultar, *va.* (med.) to auscultate.

ausencia, *f.* absence.

ausentarse, *vr.* to absent oneself.

ausente, *a.* absent.—**ausentismo,** *m.* = ABSENTISMO, absenteeism (app. to landlords).

auspiciar, *va.* (Am.) to sponsor, promote.—**auspiciado por,** under the auspices of, sponsored by.

auspicio, *m.* presage, prediction; protection; patronage; auspices.

austeramente, *adv.* austerely.

austeridad, *f.* austerity.

austero, ra, *a.* austere; astringent, acrid.

austral, *a.* austral.

australiano, na, *n.* & *a.* Australian.

austríaco, ca, *n.* & *a.* Austrian.

austrino, na, *a.* austral.

austro, *m.* south wind; notus.

autarquía, *f.* autarchy.

auténtica, *f.* certificate, attestation.

autenticación, *f.* authentication.

For pronunciation, see the rules at the beginning of the book.

auténticamente, *adv.* authentically.

autenticar, *va.* (*pret.* AUTENTIQUÉ; *subj.* AUTENTIQUE) to authenticate; to attest.

autenticidad, *f.* authenticity.

auténtico, ca, *a.* authentic.

autentiqué, autentique, *v.* V. AUTENTICAR.

¹autillo, *m.* a particular decree of the Inquisition.

²autillo, *m.* (ornith.) barn owl.

¹auto, *m.* judicial decree or sentence; writ, warrant; edict, ordinance.—*pl.* proceedings.—**a. de fe,** auto-da-fé.—**a. sacramental,** allegorical or religious play.—**en autos,** informed.

²auto, *m.* (coll.) auto (automobile).

autobiografía, *f.* autobiography.

autobiográfico, ca, *a.* autobiographical.

autobús, *m.* autobus.

autocamión, *m.* autotruck.

autocracia, *f.* autocracy.

autócrata, *m.* & *f.* autocrat.

autocrático, ca, *a.* autocratical.

autóctono, na, *a.* autochthonous, aboriginal.

autógamo, ma, *a.* (bot.) autogamous.

autogénesis, *f.* autogenesis, spontaneous generation.

autógeno, na, *a.* autogenous.

autografía, *f.* autography.

autográfico, ca, *a.* autographical.

autógrafo, *m.* autograph.

autoinducción, *f.* (elec.) self-induction.

autointoxicación, *f.* autointoxication, autotoxemia.

autómata, *m.* automaton.

automático, ca, *a.* automatic.

automotor, ra, triz, *n.* & *a.* automotor(-tive).

automóvil, *m.* automobile.—**automovilismo,** *m.* motoring as an amusement.—**automovilista.** I. *n.* devotee of motoring as an amusement; automobilist. II. *a.* automotive; automobile (as *a.*).

autonomía, *f.* autonomy; home rule; self-determination.

autonómico, ca, *a.* pert. to self-government.

autónomo, ma, *a.* autonomous, self-governing.

autoplastia, *f.* (surg.) autoplasty.

autopropagado, da, *a.* self-propagating.

autopsia, *f.* autopsy.

autópsido, da, *a.* having a metallic lustre.

autor, *m.* author; theatrical manager; (law) perpetrator or abettor of a crime.—**autores clásicos,** or **príncipes,** classical authors, old masters.—**autora,** *f.* authoress.

autorcillo, *m.* *dim.* writer of no account.

autoría, *f.* business management of a theater.

autoricé, autorice, *v.* V. AUTORIZAR.

autoridad, *f.* authority; ostentation, display.

autoritario, ria. I. *a.* authoritative; overbearing. II. *n.* & *a.* authoritarian.

autoritarismo, *m.* authoritarianism.

autoritarista, *n.* & *a.* authoritarian.

autoritativo, va, *a.* authoritative.

autorizable, *a.* that can be authorized.

autorización, *f.* authorization.

autorizadamente, *adv.* authoritatively, with authorization.

autorizado, da. I. *pp.* of AUTORIZAR. II. *a.* respectable, responsible.

autorizador, ra, *n.* & *a.* authorizer(-ing).

autorizamiento, *m.* = AUTORIZACIÓN.

autorizar, *va.* (*pret.* AUTORICÉ; *subj.* AUTORICE) to authorize, empower; to attest, legalize; to prove by quotation; to approve, exalt.

autorretrato, *m.* self-portrait.

autorzuelo, *m.* = AUTORCILLO.

autosugestión, *f.* (psych.) autosuggestion.

autumnal, otoñal, *a.* autumnal.

auxiliador, ra, *n.* & *a.* helper(-ing); abettor (-ing), saver(-ing).

auxiliante, *a.* helping, aiding.

¹auxiliar, *va.* to aid, help, assist; to attend (a dying person).

²auxiliar, *a.* auxiliary; helping; (gram.) auxiliary.

auxiliatorio, ria, *a.* (law) auxiliary.

auxilio, *m.* aid, help, assistance.—*pl.* **primeros auxilios,** first aid.

ava-ava, *f.* (bot.) kava.

avacado, da, *a.* (of a horse) cowlike.

avadarse, *vr.* to become fordable.

avahar. I. *va.* to warm with breath or vapor. II. *vn.* to fume, give out vapor.

aval, *m.* (com.) indorsement.

avalentado, da, *a.* bragging, boasting.

avalentonado, da, *n.* & *a.* braggart(-ing).

avalo, *m.* slight movement; earthquake.

avalorar, *va.* to estimate, value, price; to inspirit, encourage.

avaluación, valuación, *f.* valuation, appraisal.

avaluar, *va.* to value, appraise, estimate.

avalúo, *m.* valuation, appraisal.

avambrazo, *m.* armlet, armor for the arm.

avampiés, *m.* leggings; vamp (of a shoe).

avancarga, *f.*—**de a.,** muzzle loading.

avance, *m.* advance; attack, assault; (com.) payment in advance; balance sheet.

avancé, avance, *v.* V. AVANZAR.

avante, *adv.* ahead, forward.—**sacar a.,** to carry out, make a success of.—**salir a.,** to succeed.

avantrén, *m.* (mil.) limbers of a gun carriage.

avanzada, *f.* (mil.) outpost, advance guard.

avanzado, da, *a.* advanced (in age; in ideas).

avanzar. I. *vn.* (*pret.* AVANCÉ; *subj.* AVANCE) to advance; (Cuba) (vulg.) to vomit; (com.) to have a balance in one's favor. II. *va.* to advance, push forward.

avanzo, *m.* (com.) balance sheet.

avaramente, *adv.* avariciously.

avaricia, *f.* avarice.

avariciosamente, *adv.* greedily or covetously.

avaricioso, sa, *a.* = AVARIENTO.

avariento, ta, *a.* avaricious, miserly.

avaro, ra, *a.* = AVARIENTO.

avasallar. I. *va.* to subdue, subject, enslave. II. *vr.* to become a subject, vassal.

ave, *f.* bird; fowl.—**a. acuática,** water bird.—**aves de corral,** domestic fowl.—**a. del Paraíso,** bird of Paradise.—**a. de paso,** bird of passage, migratory bird.—**a. de rapiña,** bird of prey.—**a. lira,** lyre bird.—**a. pasajera** = A. DE PASO.—**a. rapaz** = A. DE RAPIÑA.

avecé, avece, *v.* V. AVEZAR.

avecica, illa, ita, *f.* *dim.* little bird.

avecinar, *va.* & *vr.* to get near, approach.

avecindamiento, *m.* citizenship.

avecindar. I. *va.* to admit as a citizen. II. *vr.* to establish a domicile.

avechucho, *m.* ugly bird; ragamuffin.

avejentado, da, *a.* old in appearance.

avejentar, *va.* & *vr.* to make (or become) old looking before one's time.

avejigar, *va.* to produce pimples; to blister.

avellana, *f.* filbert, hazelnut.

avellanado, da, *a.* nut-brown.

avellanador, *m.* countersink bit, rose bit; rimer.

avellanal, ¹avellanar, *m.* hazel plantation.

²avellanar. I. *va.* to countersink. II. *vr.* to shrivel.

avellaneda, *f.,* **avellanedo,** *m.* = AVELLANAL.

avellanera, *f.* = AVELLANO.

avellanero, ra, *n.* dealer in filberts.

avellánica, *f.* *dim.* small filbert.

avellano, *m.* hazelnut tree; filbert tree.

avemaría, *f.* Hail Mary; rosary bead.—**al a.,** at dusk.—**en un a.,** in the twinkling of an eye.

¡Ave María! *interj.* Good Heavens!

avena, *f.* oats; (poet.) pastoral pipe.

avenáceo, a, *a.* oatlike.

¹avenado, da, *a.* pertaining to oats.

²avenado, da, *a.* lunatic.

avenal, *m.* oatfield.

avenamiento, *m.* draining, drainage.

avenar, *va.* to drain.

¹avenate, *m.* oatmeal gruel.

²**avenate,** *m.* fit of madness.

avenencia, *f.* agreement; compact; bargain; conformity; compromise.

avengo, avenga, *v. V.* AVENIR.

aveníceo, cea, *a.* oaten.

avenida, *f.* flood, freshet; avenue; gathering; agreement; approach, way of access.

avenidor, *ra, n.* mediator.

avenimiento, *m.* convention; agreement.

avenir. I. *va.* (*ind. pres.* AVENGO, *pret.* AVINE; *subj.* AVENGA) to reconcile. **II.** *vr.* to settle differences; to compromise; to agree.

aventadero, *m.* winnowing place.

aventador, *m.* blowing fan; (arch.) scutcher; (gas) batwing; (agr.) winnower; pitchfork.

aventadura, *f.* (vet.) wind-gall.—**a. de estopa,** (naut.) leak.

aventajadamente, *adv.* advantageously; exceedingly well.

aventajado, da, *a.* advantageous; superior, excelling.

aventajar. I. *va.* to advance, raise, better; to prefer; to be above or superior to. **II.** *vr.* (a) to be ahead (of); to advance, rise; to excel.

aventamiento, *m.* winnowing; fanning.

aventar. I. *va.* (*ind.* AVIENTO; *subj.* AVIENTE) to fan; to winnow, expel. **II.** *vn.* to breathe hard. **III.** *vr.* to be inflated or puffed up; to escape, run away; (of meat) to be tainted.

aventura, *f.* adventure; contingency, chance, event; risk.

aventurado, da, *a.* risky; uncertain.

aventurar, *va.* to venture, hazard, risk.

aventureramente, *adv.* adventurously.

aventurero, ra. I. *n.* (gen. *m.*) adventurer; knight-errant; free lance. **II.** *a.* adventurous; undisciplined.

avergoncé, *pret.* of AVERGONZAR.

avergonzar (*ind. pres.* AVERGÜENZO, *pret.* AVERGONCÉ; *subj.* AVERGÜENCE), **avergoñar. I.** *va.* to shame, abash, confound. **II.** *vr.* to be ashamed.

¹**avería,** *f.* aviary; poultry yard; AVERÍO.

²**avería,** *f.* damage; (com.) average.—**a. gruesa,** (com.) general average.

averiado, da. I. *pp.* of AVERIARSE. **II.** *a.* damaged.

averiarse, *vr.* to be damaged.

averiguable, *a.* investigable.

averiguación, *f.* investigation, inquiry, inquest.

averiguadamente, *adv.* certainly, surely.

averiguador, ra, *n.* & *a.* investigator(-ing), inquirer(-ing).

averiguar, *va.* to inquire, investigate, ascertain, find out.

averío, *m.* flock of birds.

averno, *m.* Avernus.

averroísmo, *m.* Averroism.

averroísta, *n.* & *a.* Averroist(-ic).

averrugado, da, *a.* having warts.

averrugarse, *vr.* to develop warts.

aversión, *f.* aversion, dislike, loathing.

Avesta, *m.* Avesta, sacred writings of Zoroaster.

avestruz, *m.* (ornith.) ostrich; (fig.) blockhead.

avetado, da, *a.* veined, streaked.

avezar, *va.* (*pret.* AVECÉ; *subj.* AVECE) to accustom, inure.

aviación, *f.* aviation.

aviado, *m.* (Am.) one supplied with money to work a mine.

¹**aviador,** *m.* provider; calking auger; one who supplies money to work mines.

²**aviador,** *m.* (aer.) aviator.

aviar. I. *va.* to equip; to lend, advance money to; to supply; to prepare. **II.** *vr.* to prepare; to equip oneself; to go, get on the way.

aviciar, *va.* to give bloom (to plants).

avicultor, ra, *n.* aviculturist, bird keeper.

avicultura, *f.* aviculture, bird keeping.

avidez, *f.* covetousness, avidity.

ávido, da, (de), *a.* eager, anxious (for); covetous (of).

aviejarse, *vr.* to grow old.

¹**aviento,** *m.* pitchfork; BIELDO, winnowing fork.

²**aviento, aviente,** *v. V.* AVENTAR.

aviesamente, *adv.* perversely.

avieso, sa, *a.* crooked, irregular; mischievous, perverse.

avigorar, *va.* to invigorate; to revive.

avilantez, avilanteza, *f.* forwardness, boldness, audacity; insolence.

avillanado, da, *a.* rustic; clownish; mean.

avillanar. I. *va.* to debase. **II.** *vr.* to become mean; to degenerate.

avinado, da, *a.* wine-colored; bibulous.

avinagradamente, *adv.* harshly.

avinagrado, da. I. *pp.* of AVINAGRAR. **II.** *a.* harsh, crabbed, peevish.

avinagrar. I. *va.* to sour, acidulate. **II.** *vr.* to become sour.

avine, *pret.* of AVENIR.

avío, *m.* preparation, provision; money advanced. —*pl.* equipment.—**avíos de pescar,** fishing tackle.—**¡al a.!** make ready! hurry up!

¹**avión,** *m.* (aer.) airplane.—**a. de caza,** pursuit plane.—**a. de cubierta,** ship plane.—**a. de chorro,** jet plane.

²**avión,** *m.* (ornith.) martin, martlet.

avisadamente, *adv.* prudently.

avisado, da. I. *pp.* of AVISAR. **II.** *a.* cautious, sagacious, clear-sighted.—**mal a.,** ill-advised.

avisador, ra, *n.,* adviser, admonisher; announcer, informer.

avisar, *va.* to inform, announce, give notice of; to warn, advise, counsel, admonish.

aviso, *m.* information, notice, announcement; advertisement; advice, warning; prudence, care, attention; (naut.) advice boat.—**a. luminoso,** illuminated (advertising) sign; flashing signal. —**andar,** or **estar, sobre a.,** to be prepared; to be warned and take precautions.

avispa, *f.* wasp.

avispado, da, *a.* lively, brisk, clever.

avispar. I. *va.* to spur, incite, rouse. **II.** *vr.* to fret, worry.

avispero, *m.* wasp's nest; (med.) carbuncle.

avispón, *m.* hornet.

avistar. I. *va.* to descry at a distance. **II.** *vr.* to have an interview.

avitar, *va.* (naut.) to bitt (the cable).

avitelado, da, *a.* vellumlike.

avituallar, *va.* (mil.) to victual, provide food.

avivadamente, *adv.* lively, briskly.

avivador, ra. I. *n.* enlivener; hastener. **II.** *m.* rabbet plane; fluting plane; perforated paper for raising silkworms; (arch.) quirk.

avivamiento, *m.* enlivening, quickness.

avivar. I. *va.* to quicken, enliven; to encourage; (fig.) to heat, inflame; to revive; to make (fire, light) burn more brightly; to heighten (colors); to rabbet.—**a. el ojo,** to be watchful, look sharp. **II.** *vr.* to revive; cheer up.

avizor, *m.* one who watches.

avizorador, ra, *n.* & *a.* watcher(-ing).

avizorar, *va.* to watch; to keep a sharp lookout.

avocación, *f.,* **avocamiento,** *m.* (law) removing a lawsuit to a superior court.

avocar, *va.* (*pret.* AVOQUÉ; *subj.* AVOQUE) (law) to remove to a superior court.

avoceta, *f.* (ornith.) avocet, a wading bird.

avolcanado, da, *a.* volcanic.

avoqué, avoque, *v. V.* AVOCAR.

avora, *f.* (Cuba) oil palm.

avucasta, *f.* (ornith.) widgeon, wild duck.

avugo, *m.* very small early pear.

avuguero, *m.* a kind of pear tree.

avulsión, *f.* (surg.) extirpation.

avutarda, *f.* bustard, wild turkey.

avutardado, da, *a.* bustardlike.

axial, *a.* axial.

axil, *a.* axial.

axila, *f.* armpit; (bot.) axilla.

axilar, *a.* axillar; (bot.. anat.) axillary.

axinita, *f.* (min.) axinite.

axioma, *m.* axiom; maxim.

axiomático, ca, *a.* axiomatic.

axiómetro, *m.* (naut.) axiometer.

axis, *m.* (anat.) axis, second vertebra; (zool.) axis deer.

axo, *m.* a woolen garment of Peruvian Indians.

axoideo, a, *a.* (anat.) axoid, axoidean.

axon, *m.* (anat.) axon, nerve cell process.

ay. I. *m.* moan, lament. **II.** *interj.* oh!, ouch!, alas!—**a. de,** woe to.—**¡a. de mí!** woe is me! wretched that I am! poor me!

aya, *f.* governess, instructress.

ayate, *m.* cloth made of maguey fiber or sisal.

aye-aye, *m.* (zool.) aye-aye, kind of lemur.

ayer, *adv.* yesterday.—**a. tarde,** yesterday afternoon.—**tarde a.,** late yesterday.

¡aymé! *interj.* = ¡AY DE MÍ!

ayo, *m.* tutor or guardian; teacher.

ayocote, (Mex.) kidney bean.

ayocuantoto, *m.* a Mexican mountain bird.

ayuda, *f.* help, aid, assistance, support; (med.) injection, enema, or clyster; syringe; (naut.) preventer rope.—**a. de cámara,** valet.—**a. de parroquia,** chapel for parishioners living far from the parish church.

ayudador, ra, *n.* & *a.* helper(-ing).

ayudante, *m.* assistant; (mil.) adjutant, aide-de-camp.

ayudar, *va.* to aid, help, assist.

ayuga, *f.* (bot.) ground-pine.

ayunador, ra, ayunante, *n.* one who fasts.

ayunar, *vn.* to fast.

ayunas.—en a., fasting before breakfast; on an empty stomach; without knowledge.—**quedarse en a.,** not to understand, (fig.) be left at sea, know nothing at all (about something).

¹ayuno, *m.* fast, abstinence.

²ayuno, na, *a.* fasting, abstemious; uninformed; uncomprehending.

ayunque, yunque, *m.* anvil.

ayuntable, *a.* that can be joined.

ayuntamiento, *m.* municipal government; sexual intercourse.

ayustar, *va.* (naut.) to splice.

ayuste, *m.* (naut.) splicing; scarf, scarfing.

azabachado, da, *a.* jetlike, jet-colored.

azabache, *m.* jet.—*pl.* jet trinkets.

azábara, *f.* (bot.) common aloe.

azacán, *m.* water carrier.

azacaya, *f.* (prov.) water pipe.

azache, *a.* inferior (silk), from the outside of the cocoon.

azada, *f.* (agr.) hoe; spade.—**azadica, illa, ita,** *f. dim.* small hoe.

azadón, *m.* hoe.—**a. de peto, or de pico,** pickaxe.—**azadonada,** *f.* blow with a hoe.—**azadonar,** *va.* to hoe, dig with a hoe.—**azadonazo,** *m.* blow with a hoe.—**azadoncillo,** *m. dim.* small hoe.—**azadonero,** *m.* hoer.

azafata, *f.* lady of the queen's wardrobe.

azafate, *m.* low, flat basket; (Am.) tray.

azafrán, *m.* (bot.) saffron; (naut.) afterpiece (of the rudder).

azafranado, da. I. *a.* saffronlike.

azafranal, *m.* saffron plantation.

azafranar, *va.* to dye with saffron.

azafranero, *m.* saffron dealer.

azagador, *m.* path for cattle.

azagaya, *f.* javelin, spear.—**azagayada,** *f.* cast of a javelin.

azahar, *m.* orange or lemon blossom.

azainadamente, *adv.* perfidiously.

azalá, *m.* Mohammedan prayer.

azalea, *f.* (bot.) azalea.

azamboa, *f.* a kind of citron.

azamboero, azamboo, *m.* zamboa tree.

azanahoriate, *m.* preserved carrot.

azanca, *f.* subterranean spring.

azanoria, zanoria, *f.* carrot.

azar, *m.* unforeseen disaster; accident; disappointment; losing card or throw at dice; impediment; hazard, chance; cushion sides of a billiard pocket.—**al a.,** at random.—**correr (ese) a.,** to take (that) chance, run the risk.

azarar. I. *va.* to confuse, stagger, bewilder. **II.** *vr.* to get bewildered; to be frustrated, go wrong.

azarbe, *m.* irrigation ditch.

azarbeta, *f. dim.* small irrigation ditch.

azarcón, *m.* minium, red lead; orange (color).

azaría, *f.* a kind of coral.

azarja, *f.* instrument for winding raw silk.

azarolla, *f.* (bot.) fruit of the hawthorn.

azarollo, *m.* (bot.) true service tree.

azarosamente, *adv.* unfortunately.

azaroso, sa, *a.* unlucky, unfortunate.

azcón, *m.* **azcona,** *f.* dart, javelin.

azenoria, *f.* = AZANORIA.

ázimo, ma, ácimo, ma, *a.* unleavened.

azimut, acimut, *m.* (astr.) azimuth.

azimutal, acimutal, *a.* pert. to the azimuth.

aznacho, aznallo, *m.* Scotch fir; a species of rest harrow.

azoado, da, *a.* nitrogenous.

azoar. I. *va.* to treat with nitrogen, make nitrogenous. **II.** *vr.* to absorb nitrogen, become nitrogenous.

azoato, *m.* nitrate.

ázoe, *m.* (chem.) nitrogen.

azofaifa, *f.* = AZUFAIFA, jujube.

azófar, *m.* brass, latten.

azogadamente, *adv.* quickly; restlessly.

azogado, da, *a.* restless; trembling.

azogamiento, *m.* overlaying with quicksilver; restlessness.

azogar. I. *va.* (*pret.* AZOGUÉ; *subj.* AZOGUE) to overlay, coat with quicksilver; to silver (a mirror, etc.); to slake (lime). **II.** *vr.* to be affected by mercury vapors; to get agitated.

¹azogue, *m.* quicksilver; ship carrying quicksilver.

²azogue, *m.* market place.—**azoguejo,** *m.* small market place.

azoguería, *f.* amalgamation works.

azoguero, *m.* dealer in quicksilver; amalgamator.

¹azoico, ca, *a.* (chem.) nitric.

²azoico, ca, *a.* (geol.) azoic, of time before life appeared.

azolar, *va.* (*ind.* AZUELO; *subj.* AZUELE) to dress or hew (timber).

azolvar, *va.* to obstruct.—**azolve,** *m.* (Mex.) obstruction.

azomar, *va.* to bait, goad, madden (animals).

azor, *m.* (ornith.) goshawk.

azoramiento, *m.* confusion.

azorar. I. *va.* to terrify; to confound; to excite; to prompt. **II.** *vr.* to become restless.

azorrado, da, *a.* drowsy; (naut.) waterlogged.

azorramiento, *m.* heaviness of the head.

azorrarse, *vr.* to be drowsy from heaviness.

azotacalles, *n.* street lounger, idler.

azotado. I. *pp.* of AZOTAR. **II.** *a.* variegated. **III.** *n.* criminal publicly whipped; penitent.

azotador, ra, *n.* & *a.* whipper(-ing).

azotaina, *f.* drubbing, flogging, spanking.

azotalengua, *f.* goose grass.

azotamiento, *m.* whipping, flogging.

azotar, *va.* to whip, horsewhip; to flagellate, strike repeatedly; to scourge.

azotazo, *m. aug.* severe lashing or spanking.

azote, *m.* whip; lashing; spanking; scourge.—**el a. de Dios,** the Scourge of God (Attila).

azotea, *f.* flat roof.

azotera, *f.* multithonged whip; end of a long whip.

azótico, ca, *a.* (chem.) nitric.

azotina, *f.* = AZOTAINA.
azteca, *n.* & *a.* Aztec.
azúcar, *m.* sugar.—**a. blanco,** refined sugar (app. to the highest quality).—**a. cande,** or **candi,** rock candy.—**a. de flor** = A. BLANCO.—**a. de leche,** sugar of milk.—**a. de pilón,** loaf sugar. —**a. de plomo,** calcined sugar of lead.—**a. de Saturno,** sal Saturni.—**a. moscobado,** muscovado.—**a. moreno,** brown sugar.—**a. negro,** or **prieto,** coarse brown sugar.—**a. quebrado,** brown sugar.—**a. refino** = A. BLANCO.—**a. terciado,** brown sugar.—**a. y canela,** sorrel gray.
azucarado, da. I. *pp.* of AZUCARAR. **II.** *a.* sugary; affable, pleasing. **III.** *m.* cosmetic.
azucarar, *va.* to sugar; to sweeten; to soften; to coat or ice with sugar.
azucarera, *f.* sugar bowl; sugar refinery.
azucarería, *f.* retail sugar shop.
azucarero. I. *m.* sugar master; sugar bowl; sugar producer or dealer; confectioner. **II.** *a.* pertaining to sugar; sugar (as *a.*).
azucarillo, *m.* fondant.
azucé, azuce, *v.* V. AZUZAR.
azucena, *f.* white lily.
azuche, *m.* pile shoe, pile ferrule.
azud, azuda, *f.* dam with a sluice; irrigation water wheel.
azuela, *f.* adze.—**a. curva,** hollow adze.—**a. de construcción,** shipwright's adze.
azuelo, azuele, *v.* V. AZOLAR.
azufaifa, *f.* jujube or jujubes.
azufaifo, azufeifo, *m.* jujube tree.
azufrado, da. I. *pp.* of AZUFRAR. **II.** *a.* fumigated with sulphur; sulphureous; sulphur-hued.
azufrador, *m.* machine for drying linen; instrument for sulphuring vines.
azufral, *m.* = AZUFRERA.
azufrar, *va.* to bleach; to sulphur.
azufre, *m.* sulphur; brimstone.—**azufrera,** *f.* sulphur mine.—**azufrón,** *m.* pyrites powder.—**azufroso, sa,** *a.* sulphureous.
azul, *n.* & *a.* blue.—**a. celeste,** sky-blue.—**a. de mar,** or **marino,** navy blue.—**a. de Prusia,** Prussian blue.—**a. de ultramar,** or **ultramarino,** ultramarine.—**a. turquí,** indigo.
azulado, da, *a.* azure, bluish.
azulaque, *m.* (hydraul.) packing stuff.
azular, *va.* to dye or color blue.
azulear, *vn.* to have a bluish cast.
azulejado, da, *a.* tiled.
azulejo, *m.* little bluebird; glazed tile; (bot.) blue-bottle.
azulenco, ca, *a.* = AZULADO.
azulete, *m.* blue lining.
azulino, na, *a.* bluish.
azumar, *va.* to dye (the hair).
azumbrado, da, *a.* measured by AZUMBRES; (coll.) tipsy.
azumbre, *f.* a liquid measure (about 2 liters).
azur, *a.* (her.) azure.
azurita, *f.* (min.) azurite.
azutero, *m.* sluice master.
azuzador, ra, *n.* & *a.* instigator (-ing).
azuzar, *va.* (*pret.* AZUCÉ; *subj.* AZUCE) to urge, set (dogs) on; to incite.
azuzón, na, *n.* gossiping trouble maker.

B

baba, *f.* drivel, slaver, spittle; viscous substance. —**caérsela a uno la b., echar la b.,** to be a silly; to be delighted, tickled to death.
bababuí, *m.* mocking bird.
babada, *f.* = BABILLA.
babadero, babador, *m.* bib, chin cloth.
babaza, *f.* slime; BABOSA, slug.
babazorro, *m.* clown, ill-bred man.
babear, *vn.* to drivel; slaver; to court, woo with excessive demonstrations.

Babel, *f.* Babel, bedlam.
babeo, *m.* driveling, slavering.
babera, *f.* beaver of a helmet; bib.
babero, *m.* = BABADERO.
baberol, *m.* beaver of a helmet.
Babia, *f.*—**estar en B.,** to be absent-minded, or absorbed in other thoughts.
babieca, *m.* ignorant, stupid fellow; idiot.
babilla, *f.* muscles about the flank of a horse.
Babilonia, *f.* crowd, uproar, confusion, bedlam.
babilónico, ca, *or* **onio, nia,** *a.* Babylonian.
babirusa, *f.* (zool.) babiroussa, a wild hog.
bable, *m.* Asturian dialect.
babor, *m.* (naut.) port, larboard.—**a b. todo,** hard a-port.—**de b. a estribor,** athwart ship.
babosa, *f.* (zool.), slug; young onion.
babosear, *va.* to drivel, slaver.
babosilla, *f.* *dim.* small slug.
babosillo, illa, uelo, uela, *a.* *dim.* somewhat driveling or slavering; spoony.
baboso, sa, *a.* driveling, slavering, silly; spoony, over-affectionate.
babucha, *f.* slipper, babouche.
baca, *f.* top of a stagecoach; leather cover for a stagecoach.
bacalao, *or* **bacallao,** *m.* (ichth.) codfish.
bacanales, *f.* *pl.* Bacchanalia.
bacante, *f.* bacchante.
bácara, bácaris, *f.* (bot.) great fleabane.
bacelar, *m.* arbor with grapevines.
bacera, *f.* (vet.) swelling of the belly.
baceta, *f.* stock (card playing).
bacía, *f.* metal basin, washpot; shaving dish.
báciga, *f.* game played with three cards.
bacilar, *a.* (min.) of coarse fiber; (biol.) bacillar.
bacilo, *m.* bacillus.
bacillar, *m.* new vineyard.
bacín, *m.* high chamber pot; despicable man.
bacina, *f.* poor box; BACÍA.
bacinada, *f.* filth thrown from a close-stool; despicable action.
bacinejo, *m.* *dim.* small chamber pot.
bacinero, ra, *n.* person who carries about the poor box in a church.
bacineta, *f.* small poor box; pan (of a gun-lock).
bacinete, *m.* headpiece worn by warriors; cuirassier; (anat.) pelvis.
bacinica, *f.* small chamber pot.
bacinilla, *f.* chamber pot; alms basin.
baconiano, na, *a.* Baconian.
bacteria, *f.* bacterium.—**bacteriano, na,** *a.* bacterial.
bacteriología, *f.* bacteriology.
bacteriológico, ca, *a.* bacteriological.
bacteriólogo, ga, *n.* bacteriologist.
báctris, *m.* bactris, a South American palm.
báculo, *m.* walking stick, staff; support, relief, aid.—**b. pastoral,** bishop's crosier.
bache, *m.* deep hole, rut; sweating place for sheep.
¹bachiller, ra, *n.* bachelor (degree).
²bachiller, ra, *n.* babbler, prater.
bachilleramiento, *m.* conferring or obtaining the degree of bachelor.
bachillerar. I. *va.* to confer the degree of bachelor on. **II.** *vr.* to be graduated as a bachelor.
bachillerato, *m.* baccalaureate, B. A. degree.
bachillerear, *vn.* to babble, prattle.
bachillerejo, ja, *n.* *dim.* talkative little person.
bachillería, *f.* babble, prattle.
badajada, *f.* stroke of a clapper; idle talk.
badajazo, *m.* *aug.* large clapper.
badajear, *vn.* to talk nonsense.
badajo, *m.* clapper of a bell; idle talker.
badajuelo, *m.* *dim.* small clapper.
¹badal, *m.* muzzle (for dogs, etc.); (surg.) mouth opener.
²badal, *m.* shoulder and ribs of butcher's meat.
badán, *m.* trunk of a body.
badana, *f.* dressed sheepskin.

badazas, *f. pl.* (naut.) keys of the bonnets.

badea, *f.* watermelon; insipid muskmelon; dull, insipid fellow.

badén, *m.* channel made by rainfall; catchwater conduit.

badiana, *f.* (bot.) Indian aniseed, badian.

badil, *m.,* **badila,** *f.* fire shovel.

badina, *f.* puddle.

badomía, *f.* nonsense, absurdity.

badulacada, *f.* (Peru) foolishness.

badulaque, *m.* cosmetic; ragout of stewed livers; unreliable or good-for-nothing person.

¹**baga,** *f.* rope to tie packs on the back of animals.

²**baga,** *f.* little head of flax.

bagaje, *m.* beast of burden; baggage of an army; horse appropriated by an army, or given to an officer.—**bagajero,** *m.* driver of military baggage.

bagar, *vn.* (of flax) to yield the seed.

bagasa, *f.* prostitute, harlot.

bagatela, *f.* bagatelle, trifle.

bagazo, *m.* bagasse; oil cake.

bagre, *m.* a Sp. Am. fish; (Am.) ugly low woman, baggage; (Am.) smart, alert person.

baguío, *m.* (P. I.) hurricane.

¡**bah!** *interj.* bah!

baharí, *m.* sparrow hawk.

bahía, *f.* bay, harbor.

bahorrina, *f.* slops; rabble.

bahuno, na, bajuno, na, *a.* base, vile.

baila, *f.* (ichth.) sea trout.

bailable. I. *a.* (of music) composed for dancing.—**té b.,** tea with dancing, tea dance. **II.** *m.* ballet.

bailadero, *m.* public dancing place.

bailador, ra, *n.* dancer.

bailar, *vn.* to dance, spin.—**b. como un trompo,** (S. A.) to dance well, be light on one's feet.

bailarín, na, *n.* dancer; caperer.

¹**baile,** *m.* dance, ballet; ball, rout.—**b. casero,** family, informal dance.—**b. de figuras,** square dance.—**b. de máscaras,** masquerade.—**b. de San Vito,** St. Vitus' dance.—**b. de trajes,** fancy-dress ball.—**b. serio,** formal dance.

²**baile,** *m.* bailiff.

bailete, *m.* short ballet.

bailía, f., bailiazgo, *m.* bailiwick.

bailiaje, *m.* commandery in the order of Malta.

bailío, *m.* knight commander of Malta.

bailotear, *vn.* (coll.) to dance frequently; to dance clumsily.—**bailoteo,** *m.* ungraceful dancing.

baivel, *m.* bevel with a curved leg.

bajá, *m.* pasha, bashaw.

baja, *f.* fall in price; (mil.) casualty; vacancy.—**dar de b.,** to drop (person from a list, etc.)—**darse de b.,** to drop out (as a member, etc.).

bajada, *f.* descent; slope; inclination of an arch.—**b. de aguas,** rainwater pipe, leader.

bajalato, *m.* office of a pasha.

bajamar, *f.* low water, low tide.

bajamente, *adv.* basely, meanly.

bajar. I. *vn.* to descend, come or go down; to fall; to drop, lessen, diminish.—**b. de,** to be less than. **II.** *va.* to lower, reduce; to bring or take down, let down; to humble. **III.** *vr.* to bend over, stoop, to crouch, grovel; to alight, get out (ot a vehicle); to get down, dismount.

bajel, *m.* (naut.) ship, boat, vessel.

bajelero, *m.* owner or master of a vessel.

bajero, ra, *a.* lower, under (as, *sábana bajera,* under sheet).

bajete, *m. dim.* (contempt.) short person; (mus.) baritone; (mus.) counterpoint exercise.

bajeza, *f.* meanness; lowliness; low action.

bajial, *m.* marsh.

bajillo, *m.* stand cask for wine.

bajío, *m.* shoal, sand bank, flat; obstacle.

bajista, *m.* (com.) bear (in stocks); (mus.) (Arg.) bassoon player.

bajo, ja. I. *a.* low, shallow; short; abject, despic-

able; common, humble; (of color) dull, faint; (of sound) low, soft, coarse, vulgar; downcast. —**b.** relieve, bas-relief.—**por lo b.,** on the sly, unobservedly; in an undertone. **II. bajo,** *adv.* underneath, below. **III.** *prep.* under.—**b. mano,** underhandedly, secretly. **IV.** *m.* (mus.) bass (voice, score, singer, player, instrument); ground floor; shoal; sand bank.—*pl.* underskirts; hoofs (of a horse).

bajoca, *f.* string bean; dead silkworm.

bajón, *m.* (mus.) bassoon; bassoon player.

bajoncillo, *m.* treble bassoon.

bajonista, *m.* bassoon player.

bajorrelieve, bajo relieve, *m.* bas-relief.

bajoventre, *m.* (anat.) hypogastrium.

bajuno, na, *a.* vile, low, contemptible.

bala, *f.* ball, bullet, shot; bale; wax ball; printer's inking ball.—**b. de cadena,** or **encadenada,** chain shot.—**b. enramada,** bar shot.—**b. fría,** spent bullet.—**b. perdida,** stray bullet.—**b. rasa,** solid cannonball.—**b. roja,** red-hot incendiary ball.

balada, balata, *f.* ballad.

baladí, *a.* frivolous, trivial.

balador, ra, *n.* bleating animal.

baladrar, *vn.* to cry out, shout.

baladre, *m.* (bot.) rosebay.

baladrero, ra, *n.* shouter.

baladro, *m.* shout, outcry.

baladrón, na, *n.* boaster, bragger, bully.

baladronada, *f.* boast, bravado; rodomontade.

baladronear, *vn.* to boast, brag, bully.

balagar, *m.* haystack, hayrick.

bálago, *m.* grain stalk, straw; soap ball.—**balaguero,** *m.* rick of straw.

balaj, *m.* balas, spinel ruby.

balance, *m.* oscillation, rolling, rocking, swinging; (fig.) vacillation; (com.) balancing; balance; balance sheet; (Cuba) rocking chair; (aer.) rolling.

balancear. I. *va.* to balance; to put into equilibrium. **II.** *vn. & vr.* to roll, rock; to hesitate, waver.

balanceo, *m.* rocking, rolling; wobbling.

balancero, *m.* = BALANZARIO.

balancín, *m.* splinter bar, swing bar; whippletree, singletree, whiffletree; (mech.) walking beam, balancebeam; oscillating beam (as that of a beam engine); mincing knife; tightrope-walker's pole.—**balancines,** (naut.) lifts.—**balancines de la brújula,** (naut.) brass rings of the compass.

balandra, *f.* (naut.) sloop.

balandrán, *m.* cassock.

balandro, *m.* (Cuba) fishing smack.

balanitis, *f.* (med.) balanitis.

bálano, *m.* (anat.) balanus.

balante, *a.* (poet.) bleating.

balanza, *f.* scales; balance; tightrope-walker's pole; comparative estimate, judgment.—**b. de comercio,** balance of trade.—**en b.,** undecided; in danger, at stake.—**poner a uno en b.,** to cause one to doubt or hesitate.

balanzario, *m.* weighmaster (in the mint).

balanzón, *m.* (jewel.) cleaning pan.

balar, *vn.* to bleat.—**b. por,** to crave.

balastar, *va.* (Ry.) to ballast.

balasto, *m.* (Ry.) ballast.

balata, *f.* dancing song; ballad; (bot.) balata.

¹**balate,** *m.* terrace; border of a trench.

²**balate,** *m.* (zool.) snail.

balausta, -tra, *f.* varieties of pomegranate.

balaustrada, *f.* balustrade.

balaustrado, da, balaustral, *a.* balustered.

balaústre, *m.* baluster.

balaustrería, *f.* = BALAUSTRADA.

balay, *m.* wicker basket.

balazo, *m.* shot; bullet wound.

balbucear, *vn.* to hesitate in speech, stammer.

balbucencia, *f.* stammering.

---

balbuciente. I. *pres.p.* of BALBUCIR. **II.** *a.* stammering.
balbucir, *vn.* (*defect.*) = BALBUCEAR.
balcánico, ca, *n.* & *a.* Balkan.
balcón, *m.* balcony; porch.—**balconaje,** *m.*, range of balconies.—**balconcillo,** *m.* *dim.* small balcony.—**balconería,** *f.* = BALCONAJE.
balda, *f.* trifle.
baldadura, *f.,* **baldamiento,** *m.* a physical disability.
baldaquín, baldaquino, *m.* canopy, dais.
baldar, *va.* to cripple; (cards) to trump; obstruct.
¹**balde,** *m.* bucket, pail.
²**balde.—de b.,** gratis; free; idle; in vain.—**en b.,** in vain, with no result.
baldear, *vn.* (naut.) to wash (the deck).
baldeo, *m.* (naut.) washing the decks.
baldés, *m.* soft dressed skin for gloves, etc.
baldíamente, *adv.* vainly, in vain; idly.
baldío, día, *a.* untilled, uncultivated; public (lands); idle, lazy; vagabond.—*m.* *pl.* public lands; common.
baldón, *m.* affront, insult.
baldonar, baldonear, *va.* to insult, affront.
¹**baldosa,** *f.* ancient string instrument.
²**baldosa,** *f.* paving tile; flat paving stone, flag.—**baldosado,** *m.* tile pavement.—**baldosín,** *m.* small square tile; paving tile.
balduque, *m.* narrow red tape (used in offices to tie up packages of business papers).
balear, *va.* (Am.) to shoot (wound or kill).
baleárico, ca; baleario, ia, *a.* Balearic.
baleo, *m.* round mat.
balería, *f.* (artil.) pile of balls or shot.
balero, *m.* ball mold.
baleta, *f.* *dim.* small bale of goods.
balido, *m.* bleating, bleat.
balín, *m.* small bullet.—*pl.* mold shot, buckshot.
balista, *f.* ballista.
balística, *f.* (artil.) ballistics.
balitadera, *f.* call, a reed pipe for calling fawns.
baliza, *f.* buoy.
balneario, ria. I. *a.* pertaining to baths. **II.** *m.* bathing resort; watering place.
balompié, *m.* football. (Formerly) FÚTBOL.
balón, *m.* football; game of football; large bale; bale of paper (24 reams); (auto) balloon tire.
baloncesto, *m.* basketball. Also BASKETBOL.
balota, *f.* ballot.
balotada, *f.* balotade, leap of a horse.
balotar, *vn.* to ballot.
¹**balsa,** *f.* pool; pond; half a butt of wine.
²**balsa,** *f.* (naut.) raft.
balsadera, *f.,* **balsadero,** *m.* ferry.
balsamera, *f.* flask for balsam.
balsamerita, *f.* small flask for balsam.
balsámico, ca, *a.* balsamic, balmy.
balsamina, *f.* (bot.) balsam apple.
balsamita mayor, (bot.) = ATANASIA, costmary.
—**b. menor,** (bot.) maudlin, tansy.
bálsamo, *m.* balsam, balm; (med. & fig.) balm.
—**b. de copaiba,** balsam of copaiba.—**b. de calaba,** calaba balsam.—**b. de Judea, or de la Meca,** balsam of Mecca.—**b. del Canadá,** balsam of fir, Canada balsam.—**b. del Perú,** balsam of Peru.—**b. de María** = B. DE CALABA.
—**b. de Tolú,** balsam of Tolu.
balsar, *m.* marshy ground with brambles.
balsear, *va.* to ferry on rafts.
balsero, ra, *n.* ferryman(-woman).
balso, *m.* rope with loops for raising men or goods on board ship; sling; a S.A. tree of very light wood used for rafts, balsa, corkwood.
balsopeto, *m.* large pouch carried near the breast; (fig. coll.) bosom.
bálteo, *m.* officer's belt.
báltico, ca, *a.* Baltic.
baluarte, *m.* bastion; bulwark; defense.
balumba, *f.* bundle of many miscellaneous things.

balumbo, balume, *m.* bulky thing.
ballena, *f.* whale; train oil; whalebone; (B-, astr.) Whale, Cetus.—**ballenato,** *m.* young whale.
ballener, *m.* an ancient vessel.
ballenera, *f.* whaleboat.
ballenero, ra. I. *a.* whaling, whale (as *a.*). **II.** *n.* whaler, whale fisherman.
ballesta, *f.* crossbow; ballista; spring (of a carriage).—**ballestada,** *f.* shot from a crossbow.
ballestazo, *m.* blow with a crossbow.
ballesteador, *m.* crossbowman, arbalister.
ballestear, *va.* to shoot with a crossbow.
ballestera, *f.* loopholes for crossbows.
ballestería, *f.* archery; collection of crossbows or bowmen; armory for crossbows.
ballestero, *m.* archer, crossbowman; crossbow maker; king's armorer or porter; mace bearer.
ballestilla, *f.* crossbow; small whiffletree; fleam; cross-staff; (naut.) forestaff.
ballestón, *m.* *aug.* large crossbow, arbalest.
ballestrinque, *m.* (naut.) clove hitch.
ballico, *m.* (bot.) rye grass.
ballueca, *f.* wild oats.
bambalear, *vn.* = BAMBOLEAR.
bambalina, *f.* fly in theatrical scenery.
bambarria, *m.* lucky shot at billiards, fluke; fool, idiot.
bambochada, *f.* painting representing a spree.
bamboche, *n.* (coll.) plump, red-faced person.
bambolear, *vn.* & *vr.* to swing, sway.
bamboleo, *m.* swinging, swaying.
bambolla, *f.* (coll.) boast, humbug, sham.
bamboneo, *m.* = BAMBOLEO.
bambú, bambuc, *m.* bamboo.
bambuco, *m.* a Colombian popular air.
banana, *f.,* **banano,** *m.* banana. Also CAMBUR.
banas, *f.* *pl.* (Mex.) matrimonial banns.
banasta, *f.* large basket.—**banastero,** *m.* basket maker or dealer.—**banasto,** *m.* large round basket.
banca, *f.* bench; stand; washing box; Philippine canoe; name of a card game; (com.) banking.
bancada, *f.* bench; portion of masonry.
bancal, *m.* oblong orchard or garden plot; terrace; bench cover.
bancalero, *m.* weaver of bench covers.
bancario, ria, *a.* banking; financial.
bancarrota, *f.* bankruptcy; failure.—**hacer b.,** (com.) to fail.
banco, *m.* form, bench; settee; pew; (mech.) bed, table, horse; planing bench; bench for rowers; cheeks (of the bit); pedestal; school of fish, shoal; (com.) bank.—**b. de ahorros,** savings bank.—**b. de emisión,** bank of issue.—**b. de hielo,** iceberg.—**b. de liquidación,** clearing-house.—**b. del tundidor,** shearing board.
banda, *f.* sash; scarf; ribbon; band, strip (of material); band, gang; party; crew; brass band; covey; bank, border, edge; side of a ship; felloe (of wheel); cushion (of a billiard table).
bandada, *f.* covey; flock of birds.
bandaje, *m.* (Gal.) (auto) tire.
bandarria, *f.* (naut.) iron maul.
bandazo, *m.* (naut.) (of ship) violent roll to side.
bandeado, da, *a.* striped.
¹**bandear. I.** *va.* to conduct. **II.** *vn.* to band.
²**bandear,** *vr.* to shift for oneself.
bandeja, *f.* tray.
bandera, *f.* flag, banner; colors; infantry.—**b. blanca, b. de paz,** white flag, flag of truce.—**b. de popa,** (naut.) ensign.—**b. de proa,** (naut.) jack.—**a, or con, banderas desplegadas,** with flying colors; openly, in broad daylight (fig.); freely.—**bandereta,** *f.* *dim.* banneret, small flag.—*pl.* (mil.) camp colors.—**bandería,** *f.* band, faction.—**banderica, illa,** *dim.* banneret, small flag.
banderilla, *f.* banderilla, a small dart with a bannerol for baiting bulls.—**poner a uno una b.,** to taunt or provoke one.—**banderillear,**

va. to thrust banderillas in (a bull).—**bande-rillero,** *m.* banderillero, banderilla man.

banderín, *m.* camp colors; flag; railway signal; recruiting post.

banderizar, *va.* to band together.

banderizo, za, *a.* partisan, party (as *a.*); fiery, agitating, strenuous.

banderola, *f.* bannerol; camp colors; streamer, pennant; signal flag.

bandidaje, *m.* brigandage, banditry; gang, ring of bandits.

bandido, da. I. *a.* fugitive from justice. **II.** *m.* bandit.

bandín, *m.* (naut.) seat in a row galley.

¹bando, *m.* proclamation, edict.

²bando, *m.* faction, party.

bandola, *f.* mandolin; (naut.) jury mast.

¹bandolera, *f.* bandoleer, shoulder belt.

²bandolera, *f.* bandit's wife; woman bandit.

bandolerismo, *m.* banditry, brigandage.

bandolero, *m.* highwayman, robber.

bandolín, *m.* = BANDOLA.

bandolina, *f.* bandoline.

bandolón, *m.* mandola, large mandolin.

bandullo, *m.* (vulg.) belly; the bowels.

bandurria, *f.* bandore, musical instrument like a guitar.

banjo, *m.* banjo.

bánova, *f.* bedquilt, bedcover.

banquera, *f.* (prov.) open beehive; frame for beehives.

banquero, ra, *n.* (com. & gambling games) banker.

banqueta, *f.* three-legged stool; footstool; (mil.) banquette or footbank; (Mex.) sidewalk.—**b. de calafate,** (naut.) calking stool.—**b. de cureña,** (artil.) gun, carriage bed.

banquete, *m.* banquet.

banquetear, *vn.* to banquet, feast.

banquillo, *m. dim.* little stool; prisoner's or defendant's seat; (Am.) scaffold; gallows.

banquito, *m. dim.* stool, footstool.

banzo, *m.* cheek of an embroidering frame.

bañadera, *f.* (Am.) bathtub.

bañadero, *m.* puddle; bathing place (for animals).

bañado, *m.* BACÍN, chamber pot.

bañador, ra, *n.* one who bathes; (*m.*) dipping tub for candle makers.

bañar. I. *va.* to bathe, wash, lave; to water; to dip; to coat, apply a coating or layer to. **II.** *vr.* to take a bath.

bañera, *f.* bathtub.

bañero, ra, *n.* bathhouse owner or keeper.

bañil, *m.* pool in which cattle bathe.

bañista, *m.* bather.

baño, *m.* bath; bathing; bathing place; bathtub; bathroom; foot tub; coat, coating (of paint, etc.); (chem.) bath.—**b. de María,** double boiler.—**b. de vapor,** (med.) vapor bath.—*pl.* bathhouse; watering place, spa.

bañuelo, *m. dim.* little bath.

bao, *m.* (naut.) beam, cross timber.

baobab, *m.* (bot.) baobab.

baptisterio, bautisterio, *m.* baptistery.

baque, *m.* blow in falling; thud.

baqueta, *f.* ramrod; switch used in breaking in young horses.—*pl.* drumsticks; (punishment) gantlet.—**a b., a la b.,** harshly, despotically, without consideration.

baquetazo, *m.* blow with a ramrod.

baqueteado, da. I. *pp.* of BAQUETEAR. **II.** *a.* inured (to hard work).

baquetear, *va.* to inflict the punishment of the gantlet on; to vex.

baquía, *f.* familiarity with a region (app. esp. to roads, forests, etc.); skill.

baquiano, na. I. *n.* guide. **II.** *a.* skilful, expert.

báquico, ca, *a.* Bacchic.

baquio, *m.* (poet.) a metrical foot.

bar, *m.* bar (for drinks).

baraja, *f.* pack of cards; game of cards.

barajadura, *f.* shuffling of cards; dispute.

barajar, *va.* to shuffle (the cards); to jumble together; to entangle; to stop; to trick out of.

baranda, *f.* railing; bannister; cushion (of a billiard table).—**barandado, barandaje,** *m.* balustrade.—**barandal,** *m.* upper and under piece of a balustrade; railing.—**barandilla,** *f. dim.* balustrade, railing.

barangay, *m.* (P. I.) a kind of rowboat; a native village.

barangayán, *m.* (P. I.) = GUBÁN, a large canoe.

barata, *f.* barter; reduction sale; bargain.

baratador, ra, *n.* barterer.

baratar, *va.* to barter, traffic.

baratear, *va.* to sell cheap; to sell under price.

baratería, *f.* barratry, fraud, deception.

baratero, ra, *n.* one who exacts money from winning gamblers; one who sells cheap; haggler.

baratijas, *f. pl.* trifles, trinkets, notions.

baratillero, ra, *n.* peddler; seller of second-hand goods or articles.

baratillo, *m.* second-hand shop; bargain counter; heap of trifling articles.

baratista, *n.* barterer, trafficker.

barato, ta. I. *a.* cheap.—**dar de b.,** to grant for the sake of argument.—**de b.,** gratis.—**echar,** or **meter, a b.,** to mix up or confuse things by too much fuss.—**lo b. es,** or **siempre es, caro,** cheap things are always dear. **II.** *m.* reduction sale; bargain sale; money given by winning gamblers to the bystanders. **III.** **barato,** *adv.* cheaply.

báratro, *m.* (poet.) hell; abyss.

baratura, *f.* cheapness.

baraúnda, *f.* noise, hurly-burly, confusion.

barba, *f.* chin; beard; whiskers; wattle; first swarm of bees; top of beehive; player who acts old men's parts.—*pl.* head of a comet; slender roots; fibers; rough edges of paper; (ornith.) vanes of a quill.—**b. a b.,** face to face.—**b. cabruna,** (bot.) yellow goat's beard.—**b. cerrada,** heavy, thick beard.—**b. de Aarón,** (bot.) Aaron's beard.—**b. de ballena,** whalebone.—**en sus barbas,** to his face.—**por b.,** a head, apiece.—**tener pocas barbas,** to be young or inexperienced.

barbacana, *f.* (mil.) barbican, outwork of fortified place; churchyard wall.

barbacoa, *f.* (Am.) barbecue; (Am.) stretcher; elevated board bed supported on sticks; rough sleeping or storage loft or attic, usually of boards or canes; trellis; greenwood broiler used by Indians, or the meat thus broiled.

barbada, *f.* jaw of a horse; bridle curb; dab, small flat fish.

barbadamente, *adv.* strongly, vigorously.

barbado, da. I. *a.* bearded; barbed, barbated. **II.** *m.* full-grown man; vine or tree transplanted; shoot; sucker.

barbaja, *f.* (bot.) cut-leaved viper's grass.—*pl.* (agr.) first roots.

barbar, *vn.* to grow a beard; to rear bees; (of plants) to strike root.

bárbaramente, *adv.* barbarously, savagely; atrociously; rudely, coarsely.

barbáricamente, *adv.* like barbarians.

barbaricé, barbarice, *v. V.* BARBARIZAR.

barbárico, ca, *a.* barbarous, barbarian.

barbaridad, *f.* barbarity, barbarous deed, atrocity; cruelty; rashness; rudeness; (Am.) excess (in anything); wild statement or action; nonsense; blunder.

barbarie, *f.* fierceness; cruelty; barbarity; lack of culture, rusticity.

barbarismo, *m.* barbarism; barbarousness; barbarous deed; barbarians.

barbarizar. I. *va.* (*pret.* BARBARICÉ; *subj.* BAR-

BARICE) to barbarize. II. *vn.* to make wild statements.

bárbaro, ra. I. *a.* barbarous; barbarian; rude, crude, unpolished. II. *n.* barbarian.

barbarote, *m. aug.* great barbarian.

barbato, ta, *a.* (astr.) (of comets) having the tail before the head.

barbear, *va.* to reach with the chin; to be almost as high as; to fell (cattle) by twisting the neck; to shave.

barbechar, *va.* to plough for seeding; to fallow.

barbechera, *f.* series of plowings; fallowing season; plowing.

barbecho, *m.* fallow.

barbera, *f.* barber's wife.

barbería, *f.* barber's shop or trade.

barberil, *a.* pertaining to a barber; barberlike.

barbero, *m.* barber; (ichth.) mutton fish.

barbeta, *f.* (naut.) rackline, gasket; (artil.) barbette.—**a b.,** en barbette.

barbibermejo, ja, *a.* red-bearded.

barbiblanco, ca, *a.* gray- or white-bearded.

barbicacho, *m.* ribbon tied under the chin.

barbicano, na, *a.* gray-bearded.

barbiespeso, sa, *a.* having a thick beard.

barbihecho, cha, *a.* fresh-shaved.

barbilampiño, ña, *a.* smooth-faced, beardless.

barbilindo, barbilucio, *a.* small, good-looking (*rather*, pretty) and effeminate; dandy.

barbilla, *f.* point of the chin; (carp.) rabbet; (vet.) tumor under the tongue.

barbillera, *f.* tuft of tow; chin bandage.

barbinegro, gra, *a.* black-bearded.

barbiponiente, *a.* beginning to grow a beard; apprenticed.

barbiquejo, *m.* bonnet string; guard ribbon for a hat; curb chain; (naut.) bobstay.

barbirrubio, bia, *a.* blond-bearded.

barbirrucio, cia, *a.* having a black beard sprinkled with gray.

barbitaheño, ña, *a.* having a red beard.

barbiteñido, da, *a.* having a dyed beard.

barbo, *m.* (ichth.) barbel, a river fish.

barbón, *m.* long-bearded man; Carthusian lay brother; buck.

barboquejo, *m.* chin strap; hat guard.

barbotar, *vn.* to mumble, mutter.

barbote, *m.* beaver of a helmet.

barbudo, da. I. *a.* having a long beard. II. *m.* vine transplanted with the roots.

barbulla, *f.* loud prattling noise.

barbullar, *vn.* to talk loud and fast.

barbullón, na, *a. & n.* loud, fast prattler.

barca, *f.* (naut.) boat, barge, bark.—**b. chata, b. de pasaje,** ferryboat.—**barcada,** *f.* passage in a ferryboat; boatload.—**barcaje,** *m.* ferriage. —**barcal,** *m.* wooden vessel.

barcarola, *f.* barcarole.

barcaza, *f.* barge, lighter; privilege of loading and unloading.

barcelonés, sa, *a.* from, or of, Barcelona.

barceno, na, *a.* = BARCINO.

barceo, *m.* dry bass or sedge for mats, ropes, etc.

barcia, *f.* chaff (from grain).

barcina, *f.* (Am.) grass net; large bundle of straw.

barcinar, *va.* (Am.) to load with sheaves.

barcino, na, *a.* (of animals) red-brown and white.

barco, *m.* boat, barge, vessel, ship; bottom.

barcolongo, barcoluengo, *m.* oblong boat with a round bow.

barcón, barcote, *m. aug.* large boat.

barchilón, *m.* (Am.) hospital nurse.

barda, *f.* bard, horse armor; thatch; reed.

bardado, da, *a.* barded, caparisoned.

bárdago, *m.* (naut.) pendant.

bardaguera, *f.* (bot.) willow.

bardal, *m.* thatched wall or fence.

bardana, *f.* burdock.

bardar, *va.* to thatch (fences).

bardilla, *f. dim.* small brushwood.

bardiota, *m.* Byzantine soldier.

bardo, *m.* bard, poet.

bardoma, *f.* (Am.) filth, mud.

bardomera, *f.* brush carried off by a stream.

bargueño, *m.* gilt and painted desk.

bario, *m.* (chem.) barium.

barita, *f.* (chem.) baryta or barytes.

baritel, *m.* = MALACATE, hoisting machine.

baritina, *f.* barium sulphate.

barítono, *m.* (mus.) baritone.

barjuleta, *f.* knapsack, haversack; tool bag.

barloar, *va., vn. & vr.* (naut.) to grapple in order to board; ABARLOAR, to bring alongside.

barloas, *f. pl.* (naut.) relieving tackles.

barloventear, *vn.* (naut.) to ply to windward; to beat about.

barlovento, *m.* (naut.) windward.—**ganar el b.,** to get to windward.

barnacla, *m.* barnacle, sea goose.

barnicé, barnice, *v.* V. BARNIZAR.

barniz, *m.* varnish; cosmetic; printer's ink.— **b. del Japón,** japan.

barnizador, ra, *n. & a.* varnisher(-ing).

barnizar, *va.* (*pret.* BARNICÉ; *subj.* BARNICE) to varnish.

barógrafo, *m.* (meteorol.) barograph.

barología, *f.* barology.

barométrico, ca, *a.* barometric.

barómetro, *m.* barometer.—**b. aneroide,** aneroid barometer.—**b. metálico,** Bourdon gauge.

barometrógrafo, *m.* barometrograph.

barón, *m.* baron.—**barones del timón,** (naut.) rudder pendants and chains.—**baronesa,** *f.* baroness.—**baronía,** *f.* barony; baronage.

baroscopio, *m.* baroscope.

barotermógrafo, barotermómetro, *m.* instrument for measuring both atmospheric pressure and temperature.

baroto, *m.* small boat in the Philippines.

barquear, *vn.* to go about in a boat; to cross (a river, lake) in a boat.

barquero, *m.* bargeman, boatman, ferryman.

barqueta, *f.,* **barquete,** *m.,* **barquichuelo,** *m. dim.* small barge or boat.

barquilla, *f.* conical mold for wafers; little boat, wherry; (aer.) car, basket (of a dirigible).— **b. de la corredera,** (naut.) the log.

barquillero, ra. I. *n.* maker or seller of rolled wafers. II. *m.* wafer mold.

barquillo, *m.* cockboat; thin rolled wafer.

barquin, m., barquinera, *f.* large bellows.

barquinazo, *m.* fall from a vehicle; tumble, fall.

barquinero, *m.* bellows maker.

barquino, *m.* wine skin. Also ODRE.

barra, *f.* (mech., eng.) bar, beam, rod; stripe; sandbar; gross-spun thread in cloth; mold for small candles; chase bar; shaft of a carriage; thill; (her.) third part of a shield; a country game in Spain; railing in a court room; visitors' gallery (in a parliamentary hall, etc.); (Am.) "fans" (at a game), supporters, (theat.) claque; (Arg.) "gang" (of boys); (naut.) spar.—*pl.* mining shares; stripes, bars (on a shield, etc.).—**b. colectora,** (elec.) busbar.—**b. de la excéntrica,** (steam eng.) eccentric rod.—**en barra,** or en barras, in bars, bar (as *a.*).

Barrabás, *m.* devil (fig.).—**barrabasada,** *f.* serious mischief; bold action.

barraca, *f.* barrack, cabin, hut; storage shed.

barraco, *m.* (Am. coll.) = VERRACO, boar; foam of fermenting must.

barrado, da. I. *pp.* of BARRAR. II. *a.* corded; ribbed; striped; (her.) barred.

barragán, *m.* barracan, camlet; waterproof woollen stuff; waterproof overcoat.

barragana, *f.* concubine; morganatic wife.

barraganería, *f.* concubinage.

barraganete, *m.* (naut.) top-timber, futtock.

barral, *m.* (Am.) demijohn of about 25 pints.

barranca, *f.,* **barrancal,** *m.* deep hollow; gorge, ravine; cliff; precipice.
barranco, *m.* BARRANCA; great difficulty.
barrancoso, sa, *a.* uneven, rough.
barranquera, *f.* BARRANCA; obstruction, difficulty.
barraquillo, *m.* (artil.) short light gun.
¹barrar, *va.* to daub, smear.
²barrar, *va.* to bar, barricade.
barrate, *m.* little joist or rafter.
barrear. II. *va.* to bar, barricade; to cancel, cross off. **II.** *vn.* to graze a knight's armor with a lance. **III.** *vr.* to intrench.
barrederas, *f. pl.* (naut.) studding sails.
barredero, ra. I. *a.* that drags along; sweeping. **II.** *f.* sweeper (machine), cleaner (esp. for cleaning streets). **III.** *f.* baker's mop.
barredura, *f.* sweeping.—*pl.* sweepings, refuse, chaff.
barreminas, *m.* mine sweeper (ship).
barrena, *f.* drill; auger; gimlet; (aer.) spin; spinning dive.—**b. de diminución,** taper auger.—**b. de guía,** centerbit.—**b. de gusano,** wimble; rock drill.—**b. grande,** auger, borer.— **b. pequeña,** gimlet.
barrenado, da. I. *pp.* of BARRENAR. **II.** *a.* bored, drilled. **III.** *m.* boring, drilling.
barrenador, *m.* (naut.) auger or borer.
barrenar, *va.* to bore, drill; to foil; to infringe (a law).—**b. un navío,** (naut.) to scuttle a ship.— **b. una roca,** or **mina,** to blast a rock, or a mine.
barrendero, ra, *n.* sweeper, dustman(-woman).
barrenero, *m.* maker or seller of augers and drills; blaster, driller.
barrenillo, *m.* insect that bores into trees.
barreno, *m.* large borer, drill or auger; bored hole, blast hole; vanity.—**dar b.** (naut.) to sink (a ship).
barreña, *f.,* **barreño,** *m.* earthen pan; tub.
barrer, *va.* to sweep; (naut.) to rake.—**al b.** (com.) on an average.
¹barrera, *f.* barricade, barrier, parapet, fence; bar, tollgate, turnpike.
²barrera, *f.* clay pit; mound of earth; cupboard for crockery.
barrero, *m.* potter; marshy ground; salty soil.
barreta, *f.* small bar; shoe lining.
barretear, *va.* to fasten with bars; line (a shoe).
barretero, *m.* in mining, one who works with a crowbar, wedge, or pick.
barretón, *m.* miner's pickaxe, bede.
barriada, *f.* city ward, district, precinct, quarter.
barrial, *m.* mire.
barrica, *f.* cask containing about 60 gallons.
barricada, *f.* barricade.
barrido, *m.* sweeping.
barriga, *f.* belly; pregnancy.
barrigón, na, barrigudo, da, *a.* big-bellied.
barriguilla, *f. dim.* little belly.
barril, *m.* barrel; (naut.) water cask.
barrilaje, *m.* (Mex.) barrels collectively; BARRILAME.
barrilame, barrilamen, *m.* stock of casks or barrels; barrel factory.
barrilejo, *m. dim.* rundlet, small barrel.
barrilería, *f.* = BARRILAME.
barrilero, ra, *n.* barrel maker, cooper.
barrilete, *m.* holdfast, dog, clamp; (naut.) mouse; (zool.) crab covered with prickles; keg; kite; upper joint of a clarinet.
barrilico, illo, ito, *m. dim.* keg, rundlet, small barrel, firkin.
barrilla, *f.* little bar; rod; (bot.) saltwort.
barrillar, *m.* barilla plantation; barilla pits.
barrio, *m.* city district, ward, precinct, quarter; suburb.—**el otro b.,** the other world; eternity.
barrizal, *m.* clay pit; mire.
¹barro, *m.* clay; mud; earthenware; drinking vessel made of sugar clay.—**hacer un b.,** (Arg.) to make a break, put one's foot in it.
²barro, *m.* (gen. *pl.*) pimples on the face; (vet.) fleshy tumors.
barrocho, *m.* two-seat light wagon without top.
¹barroso, sa, *a.* muddy, miry.
²barroso, sa, *a.* pimpled; reddish.
barrote, *m.* short and thick iron bar; round rung (of a ladder); (carp.) brace.—**barrotes,** (naut.) battens, scantlings.
barrueco, *m.* pearl of irregular form.
barrumbada, *f.* extravagant expense; boast.
barruntador, ra, *n.* conjecturer.
barruntamiento, *m.* conjecturing, guessing.
barruntar, *va.* to conjecture, guess.
barrunto, *m.* conjecture.
bartola, *f.*—**a la b.,** carelessly.
bartolillo, *m.* three-cornered little meat pie.
bártulos, *m. pl.* household goods; tools; means, measures, way (to do something).
baruca, *f.* cunning, deceit, trickery.
barulé, *m.* upper part of the stockings rolled over the knee.
barullo, *m.* confusion, disorder, tumult.
barzón, *m.* idle walk; ring of a yoke.
barzonear, *vn.* to loiter, stroll about.
basa, *f.* pedestal, base; basis.
basácula, *f.* locker of the thumb plate in a stocking frame.
basada, *f.* stocks for ship building.
basáltico, ca, *a.* basaltic.
basalto, *m.* basalt.
basamento, *m.* (arch.) base and pedestal.
basar. I. *va.* to support, give a base to; to base, found; (surv.) to refer (operation, etc.) to a base line. **II.** *vr.* (en) to base one's opinion (on).
basáride, *f.* (Mex.) bassaris, a species of racoon.
basca, *f.* squeamishness, nausea; swoon.
bascosidad, *f.* nastiness; filth.
báscula, *f.* platform scales.
base, *f.* base, basis; (mil., chem., alg., geom.) base; (surv.) base (line).
basicidad, *f.* (chem.) basicity.
básico, ca, *a.* basic.
basificar, *va.* (chem.) to basify.
basílica, *f.* royal palace; public hall; basilica, privileged church; (arch.) basilica; (anat.) basilic vein.
basilicón, *m.* (med.) basilicon, ointment.
basilio, lia, *n. & a.* Basilian (monk, nun).
basilisco, *m.* basilisk (animal, cannon).—**estar hecho un b.,** to be furious, (coll.) to be hot under the collar.
basketbol, *m.* basketball.—**basketbolista. I.** *n.* basketball player. **II.** *a.* basketball (as *a.*).— **basketbolero, ra,** *a.* basketball (as *a.*).
basketero, ra, *n.* basketball player.
basquear, *vn.* to be squeamish or nauseated.
basquetbol, etc. = BASKETBOL, etc.
basquilla, *f.* a disease of sheep.
basquiña, *f.* outer skirt.
basta, *f.* coarse stitch; basting.
bastaje, *m.* porter; carrier.
bastante. I. *a.* sufficient, enough. **II.** *adv.* enough; rather, fairly, pretty.—**bastantear,** *va.* (law) to acknowledge the validity of (a power of attorney).—**bastantemente,** *adv.* sufficiently.
bastanteo, *m.* acknowledging a power of attorney.
bastantero, *m.* (law) officer who examines powers of attorney.
bastar, *vn.* to suffice; to be enough.—**¡basta!** that will do; stop!
bastarda, *f.* bastard file; piece of ordnance.
bastardear, *vn.* to degenerate; to bastardize.
bastardelo, *m.* notary's draft book; blotter, record book.
bastardía, *f.* bastardy; meanness.
bastardilla, *f.* a kind of flute; (print.) italic.

bastardo, da. I. *a.* bastard; (print.) bastard (type). **II.** *n.* bastard. **III.** *m.* boa (snake); a kind of saddle; (naut.) parrel rope.

¹baste, *m.* = BASTA.

²baste, *m.* saddle pad.

bastear, *va.* (sewing) to baste.

bastero, *m.* maker or seller of packsaddles.

bastida, *f.* an ancient war engine.

bastidor, *m.* frame; easel; embroidery frame; stretcher for canvas; wing of stage scenery; window sash; frame of a screw propeller; (photog.) plate holder.—*pl.* (naut.) frames for canvas bulkheads.—**entre bastidores,** behind the scenes.

bastilla, *f.* hem.—**bastillar,** *va.* to hem.

bastimentar, *va.* to victual; to provision.

¹bastimento, *m.* supply of provisions; building, structure; (naut.) vessel.

²bastimento, *m.* mattress tufting.

bastión, *m.* = BALUARTE, bastion.

¹basto, *m.* packsaddle; pad; (cards) ace of clubs. —*pl.* clubs (cards).

²basto, ta, *a.* coarse; rude; gross; homespun.

bastón, *m.* walking cane; gad, truncheon; baton; roller of a silk frame.—**bastonada,** *f.*, **bastonazo,** *m.* bastinado.—**bastoncillo,** *m.* small cane or stick; narrow trimming lace.—**bastonear,** *va.* to cane.—**bastonero,** *m.* cane maker or seller; manager of a ball; cotillon leader; assistant jailer.

basura, *f.* sweepings, rubbish; garbage, refuse.

basurero, *m.* dustman; dustpan; dunghill.

basuriento, ta, *a.* (Am.) full of rubbish.

¹bata, *f.* dressing gown; smoking jacket; wrapper; woman's frock; silk refuse.

²bata, *n.* (P. I.) native child or half-breed minor.

batacazo, *m.* violent bump from a fall.

batahola, *f.* hurly-burly, bustle, hubbub.

batalla, *f.* battle; fencing bout; joust, tournament; (artil.) battle piece.—**b. campal,** pitched battle.

batallador, ra, *n.* & *a.* battler(-ing), fighter (-ing).

batallar, *vn.* to battle, fight, struggle; to fence.

batallola, *f.* (naut.) rail.

batallón, *m.* battalion.

batallona, *a.*—**cuestión b.,** vexed question, hard nut to crack.

batán, *m.* fulling mill.—*pl.* batanes, a boys' game.—**batanar,** *va.* to full (cloth).—**batanear,** *va.* to drub, thrash, beat.—**batanero,** *m.* fuller, clothier.

batanga, *f.* (P. I.) bamboo outrigger in boats.

batata, *f.* sweet potato.—**batatal, batatar,** *m.* sweet-potato field.

batatazo, *m.* (Am. coll.).—**dar b.,** (of horses) to win against all expectations.

bátavo, va, *a.* Batavian.

batayola, *f.* (naut.) rail.

bate, *m.* (Angl.) (Am.) baseball bat.

batea, *f.* painted tray; foot tub; flat-bottomed boat, punt; large wash tray or trough.

batear, *va.* & *vn.* (in baseball) to bat.

batehuela, *f. dim.* small hamper or tray.

batel, *m.* small vessel.

batería, *f.* (artil., elec.) battery; (naut.) range of guns, broadside; repeated importunities; battering; (mus.) aggregate of percussion instruments in a band or orchestra.—**b. a rebote,** ricochet battery.—**b. cruzante,** cross battery. —**b. de acumuladores,** (elec.) storage battery.—**b. de cocina,** kitchen metal utensils.— **b. enterrada,** sunk battery.

batero, ra, *n.* dressmaker; ladies' tailor.

batey, *m.* (Cuba) sugar plant (factory).

batiborrillo, *m.* = BATURRILLO, hodgepodge.

baticola, *f.* crupper.

batida, *f.* hunting party; battue.

batidera, *f.* beater (in masonry); stirrer (in glass-making); batlet; batting arm; scutcher; flap of a churn; instrument for cutting honeycombs.

batidero, *m.* continuous striking or beating; collision; craggy ground; (naut.) washboard.

batido, da. I. *pp.* of BATIR. **II.** *a.* shot, chatoyant (silks); beaten, trodden, as roads. **III.** *m.* batter of flour, eggs, etc.

batidor, *m.* beater; scout; ranger; lifeguard rider before a royal coach; outrider; leather beater; stirring rod; haircomb; hemp dresser.

batiente, *m.* jamb (of a door); leaf (of a door); port-sill; damper (of a piano); spot where the sea beats against the shore.—**b. de la bandera,** (naut.) fly of the ensign.—**b. de un dique,** apron of a dock.

batifulla, *m.*, **batihoja,** *m.* gold beater; sheet-metal worker; warp.

batimiento, *m.* beating.

batín, *m.* smoking jacket.

batintín, *m.* Chinese gong.

bationdeo, *m.* fluttering of a banner or curtain.

batiportar, *va.* (naut.) to house (a gun).

batiportes, *m. pl.* (naut.) port-sills.

batir. I. *va.* to beat, pound; to strike; to demolish; to flap; to stir; to comb; to adjust (reams of paper); to vanquish; to reconnoiter; to beat (a drum).—**b. banderas,** to salute with colors. —**b. el campo,** to reconnoiter the enemy's camp; to investigate.—**b. el record,** to beat the record.—**b. hoja,** to foliate.—**b. las olas,** to ply the seas.—**b. moneda,** to coin money. —**b. palmas,** to clap the hands.—**b. una catarata,** (med.) to couch a cataract. **II.** *vr.* to fight; to duel; to lose courage; to decline in health.

batista, *f.* batiste, finest cambric.

bato, *m.* rustic, simpleton.

batojar, *va.* to gather (fruit from a tree) by knocking it down with a stick.

batología, *f.* battology, needless repetition.

batómetro, *m.* bathometer, bathymeter, an instrument used for determining depths at sea.

batracio, cia. (zool.) **I.** *n.* & *a.* batrachian. **II.** *m. pl.* Batrachia.

batuda, *f.* springboard jumping contest.

baturrillo, *m.* hodgepodge, mash, salmagundi; potpourri; medley.

batuta, *f.* conductor's wand; baton.—**llevar la b.,** to lead; to preside; to manage.

baúl, *m.* trunk, chest; belly.—**b. escaparate,** wardrobe trunk.—**b. mundo,** Saratoga trunk. —**b. ropero,** = B. ESCAPARATE.—**baulito,** *m. dim.* small trunk.

bauprés, *m.* (naut.) bowsprit.

bausán, na, *m.* manikin, effigy; fool, idiot.

bauticé, bautice, *v. V.* BAUTIZAR.

bautismal, *a.* baptismal.

bautismo, *m.* baptism, christening.

bautista, *n.* baptizer; Baptist.—**el B.,** the Baptist (John).

bautisterio, *m.* baptistery.

bautizante, *n.* baptizer, christener.

bautizar, *va.* (*pret.* BAUTICÉ: *subj.* BAUTICE) to baptize, christen; to name, call; to mix (wine) with water.

bautizo, *m.* baptism; christening party.

bávaro, ra, *n.* & *a.* Bavarian.

baya, *f.* berry, any small globular fruit.

bayadera, *f.* Oriental dancer.

¹bayal, *a.* long-stem autumn (flax).

²bayal, *m.* lever used in raising millstones.

bayeta, *f.* baize, thick flannel; (print.) blanket.

bayetón, *m.* coating, cloth for coats; (Am.) long baize poncho.

¹bayo, ya. I. *a.* bay (color). **II.** *m.* bay horse; silkworm moth used as bait in fishing.—**uno piensa el b. y otro quien lo ensilla,** it is one thing to command and another to obey, it all depends on who is master and who servant.

²bayo, *m.* (Chile) poor man's bier.

¹bayoco, *m.* Italian copper coin.

²bayoco, *m.* unripe or withered fig.

bayón, *m.* (P. I.) sack of matting for baling.

bayoneta, *f.* bayonet.—**bayonetazo,** *m.* bayonet thrust or wound.

bayoque, *m.* = ¹BAYOCO.

bayuca, *f.* tippling house, tavern.

baza, *f.* trick (at cards).—**no dejar meter b.,** not to let one put in a single word.

bazar, *m.* bazaar, market place; department store; fair.

bazo, za. I. *n.* & *a.* yellowish brown. II. *m.* (anat.) spleen.

bazofia, *f.* offal, waste meat, refuse, remnants.

bazucar, *va.* (*pret.* BAZUQUÉ; *subj.* BAZUQUE) to stir (liquids) by shaking; to dash.

bazuqueo, *m.* shaking (a liquid); jumble.

¹be, *m.* baa, cry of sheep.

²be, *f.* b (the letter).—**b. por b.,** with all particulars, minutely.

beata, *f.* woman engaged in works of charity; overpious woman, one that devotes much of her time to praying and church going (gen. with the implication of prudery and bigotry).

beatería, *f.* affected piety; bigotry.

beaterío, *m.* pious women's house or institution.

beatificación, *f.* beatification.

beatíficamente, *adv.* beatifically.

beatificar, *va.* to beatify; to render respectable; to make happy.

beatífico, ca, *a.* (theol.) beatific.

beatilla, *f.* a kind of fine linen.

beatísimo, ma, *a. super.* of BEATO.—**b. padre,** Most Holy Father (the Pope).

beatitud, *f.* beatitude, blessedness, holiness.

beato, ta. I. *a.* happy, blessed; beatified; devout; overpious, prudish, bigoted. II. *n.* pious person; one who lives in pious retirement; overpious, prudish person.

beatón, na, *n.* hypocrite, bigot.

bebedero, ra. I. *a.* drinkable. II. *m.* drinking place or trough; spout.—*pl.* strips for lining clothes; facing.

bebedizo, za. I. *a.* drinkable. II. *m.* medicinal potion; draught; philter or love potion; poisonous draught.

bebedo, da, bebido, da, *a.* drunk.

bebedor, ra, *n.* tippler, toper.

beber. I. *va.* & *vn.* to drink; to swallow; to pledge, toast.—**b. a la salud de alguno,** to drink some one's health.—**b. como una cuba,** to drink like a fish.—**b. en,** to drink from, out of.—**b. los pensamientos a alguno,** to anticipate one's thoughts.—**b. los vientos,** to solicit with much eagerness. II. *m.* drinking; a drink.

bebible, *a.* pleasant to drink, drinkable.

bebida, *f.* drink, beverage; potion; time allowed to workmen for drinks.

bebido, da. I. *pp.* of BEBER. II. *a.* intoxicated.

bebirina, *f.* (chem.) bebeerine.

bebistrajo, *m.* mixture of drinks; a nasty drink.

beborrotear, *vn.* to sip often.

beca, *f.* collegian's sash worn over the gown; fellowship; pension; fellow, alumnus, collegian; tippet worn by dignitaries of the church.—*pl.* velvet or satin facings of cloaks.—**b. de merced,** scholarship.

becabunga, *f.* (Am.) (bot.) brooklime; veronica.

becada, *f.* (ornith.) woodcock. Also CHOCHA.

becafigo, *m.* (ornith.) figpecker.—**b. raro,** (ornith.) red-headed linnet.

becardón, *m.* (ornith.) snipe.

becerra, *f.* (bot.) snapdragon.

becerril, *a.* bovine; calf (as *a.*).

becerro, ra, *n.* yearling calf; calfskin; church register; book bound in calfskin.—**b. de oro,** golden calf; mammon, riches.—**b. marino,** sea calf, seal.

becoquín, *m.* cap tied under the chin.

becuadrado, *m.* first property in plain song, or Gregorian mode.—**becuadro,** *m.* (mus.) the sign ♮, denoting a return to the natural tone.

bedel, *m.* beadle, warden.

bedelía, *f.* beadleship, wardenship.

bedelio, *m.* bdellium, an aromatic gum.

beduino, na, *a.* Bedouin; harsh, uncivil.

befa, *f.* jeer, scoff, mock, taunt.

befabemí, *m.* a musical sign.

befar. I. *va.* to mock, scoff, ridicule. II. *vn.* (of horses) to move the lips trying to catch the chain of the bit.

befo, fa. I. *a.* having a thick lower lip; knock-kneed. II. *m.* lip of an animal; a kind of monkey.

begonia, *f.* (bot.) begonia.—**begoniáceo, ea.** I. *a.* (bot.) begoniaceous. II. *f. pl.* Begoniaceæ.

behén, *m.* = BEN, a small, oil-bearing fruit.

behetría, *f.* free, independent town; confusion, disorder.

beisbol, *m.* (Angl.) (Am.) baseball (game).—**beisbolero, ra,** *n.* & *a.* (Am.) baseball (player).—**beisbolista,** *m.* = BEISBOLERO.

bejín, *m.* (bot.) common puffball, fuzzball; whining, peevish child.

bejinero, *m.* one who extracts oil from the lees.

bejucal, *m.* place where BEJUCOS grow.

bejuco, *m.* large creeping or climbing wild plant; rattan.

bejuquillo, *m.* gold chain made in China; (bot.) ipecacuanha; thin BEJUCO.

belcho, *m.* (bot.) horsetail tree.

beldad, *f.* beauty, belle.

belemnita, *f.* (paleontol.) belemnite.

belemnoide, belemnoideo, a, *a.* belemnoid.

Belén, *m.* Bethlehem; a Christmas crèche; confusion, bedlam.

beleño, *m.* (bot.) henbane, poison.

belérico, *m.* (bot.) a kind of myrobalan.

belez, *f.,* **belezo,** *m.* jar for oil or wine; furniture.

belfo, fa. I. *a.* having a thick lower lip. II. *m.* lip of an animal.

belga, *n.* & *a.* Belgian.—**bélgico, ca,** *a.* Belgian, Belgic.

bélico, ca, *a.* warlike, martial.

belicosidad, *f.* warlikeness.

belicoso, sa, *a.* warlike, bellicose; quarrelsome.

beligerancia, *f.* belligerency.

beligerante, *n.* & *a.* belligerent.

belígero, ra, *a.* (poet.) warlike, belligerent.

belísono, na, *a.* with martial, warlike sound.

belitre, *a.* low, mean, vile, vulgar; roguish.

bellacada, *f.* nest of rogues; knavish act.

bellacamente, *adv.* knavishly, roguishly.

bellaco, ca. I. *a.* artful, sly, cunning, roguish, deceitful. II. *m.* rogue, villain, knave.

bellacón, na; bellaconazo, za, *n. aug.* great knave, arrant rogue.

bellacuelo, *m. dim.* tricky, cunning little fellow.

belladona, *f.* (bot.) belladonna.

bellamente, *adv.* prettily, gracefully, fairly.

bellaquear, *vn.* to cheat, swindle; to play knavish, roguish tricks; (Arg.) (of horse) to buck.

bellaquería, *f.* knavery, roguery, cunning; vile act or expression.

belleza, *f.* beauty.

bello, lla, *a.* beautiful, fair.—**bello sexo, fair sex.—bellas artes,** fine arts.—**las bellas,** the fair ones.

bellorio, ria, *a.* mouse-colored.

bellorita, *f.* (Am.) (bot.) primrose, cowslip.

bellota, *f.* acorn; carnation bud; perfume box.

bellote, *m.* large round-headed nail.

bellotear, *vn.* to feed on acorns.

bellotera, *f.* acorn season.

bellotero, ra. I. *n.* one who gathers or sells acorns. II. *m.* oak forest.

bembo, ba. I. *n.* & *a.* thick-lipped. II. *m.* thick lip, esp. Negro's lip.—**bembón, na,** *a.* (of persons) thick-lipped.

bemol, *m.* (mus.) flat.—**tener bemoles,** (coll.) to be very difficult, a tough job.

bemolado, *a.* flat(ted), lowered a semitone.

bemolar, *va.* (mus.) to flat.

ben, *m.* behen, a small oil-producing fruit.

benarriza, *f.* (ornith.) ortolan.

bencénico, ca, *a.* pertaining to benzene.

benceno, *m.* (chem.) benzene.

bencilato, *va.* a sal of benzilic acid.

bencílico, ca, *a.* benzilic.

bencina, *f.* benzine.

bendecidor, ra, *n.* & *a.* blesser(-ing).

bendecir, *va.* (*pp.* BENDITO and BENDECIDO; *ind.* *pres.* BENDIGO, *pret.* BENDIJE; *imper.* BENDICE; *subj.* BENDIGA) to bless; to consecrate.

bendición, *f.* benediction, blessing.—*pl.* or **bene-diciones nupciales,** marriage ceremony.

bendigo, bendije, bendiga, *v.* V. BENDECIR.

bendito, ta. I. *pp. irreg.* of BENDECIR. II. *a.* sainted, blessed; simple, silly.—**es un b.,** he is a simpleton.

benedícite, *m.* (Lat.) permission solicited by ecclesiastics; grace before meals.

benedicta, *f.* (med.) benedict, electuary.

benedictino, na. I. *a.* Benedictine. II. *m.* bene-dictine.

benefactor, *m.* benefactor.

beneficencia, *f.* beneficence, charity; department of public welfare.

beneficiación, *f.* benefaction.

beneficiado, *m.* curate; beneficiary.

beneficiador, ra, *n.* benefactor; improver, de-veloper, exploiter (of a mine, etc.).

beneficial, *a.* pertaining to benefices or ecclesi-astical livings.

beneficiar. I. *va.* to benefit; to cultivate, develop, exploit; to confer a sinecure on; to purchase. II. *vr.* to profit.

beneficiario, ria, *n.* beneficiary.

beneficio, *m.* benefit; profits; favor, kindness, benefaction; benefit, ecclesiastical living; right belonging to one either by law or charter; working, development (of a mine); (com.) premium.—**b. bruto,** gross profit.—**b. neto,** clear profit.—**b. simple,** sinecure.—**bene-ficioso, sa,** *a.* beneficial, profitable.

benéfico, ca, *a.* beneficent, charitable; beneficial.

benemérito, ta, *a.* meritorious, worthy.

beneplácito, *m.* approval, consent.

benevolencia, *f.* benevolence, kindness

benévolo, la, *a.* benevolent, kind.

bengala, *f.* a kind of muslin; cane.

bengalí, *n.* & *a.* Bengalese.

benignamente, *adv.* kindly, benevolently.

benignidad, *f.* benignity, kindness; mildness.

benigno, na, *a.* benign, kind; mild.

benito, ta, *n.* & *a.* Benedictine (friar or nun).

Benjamín, *m.* youngest son or daughter, "the baby."

benjamita, *a.* descending from, or pertaining to, Benjamin or the tribe of Benjamin.

benjuí, *m.* benzoin.

benzoato, *m.* benzoate.—**benzoico, ca,** *a.* ben-zoic.—**benzol,** *m.* benzol.

beocio, cia, *n.* & *a.* Bœotian.

beodez, *f.* drunkenness.

beodo, da, *a.* drunk.

beorí, *m.* an American tapir.

beque, *m.* (naut.) head of the ship.

berberí, *n.* & *a.* Berber.

berberídeo, a. I. *a.* (bot.) berberidaceous. II. *m.* *pl.* Berberidaceæ.

berberina, *f.* (chem.) berberine.

berberís, *m.* (bot.) barberry, piperidge bush.

berberisco, ca, *n.* & *a.* Berber.

bérbero, *m.* barberry; a barberry confection.

berbí, *m.* a kind of woollen cloth.

berbiquí, *m.* drill brace, bitstock; wimble.

bercería, *f.* greengrocer's shop.

bercero, ra, *n.* greengrocer.

bereber = BERBERISCO.

berenjena, *f.* eggplant.—**berenjenado, da,** *a.* eggplant-colored.—**berenjenal,** *m.* bed of egg-plants; difficulties, troubles.

bergamota, *m.* bergamot (fruit, essence, snuff).

bergamote, bergamoto, *m.* bergamot tree.

bergante, *m.* brazen-faced villain, ruffian, rascal.

bergantín, *m.* (naut.) brig, brigantine.

bergantinejo, *m. dim.* small brig.

bergantón, na, *n. aug.* brazen-faced person.

bergantonazo, *m. aug.* most impudent ruffian.

beriberi, *m.* beriberi.

berilio, *m.* beryllium. Also GLUCINIO.

berilo, *m.* beryl.

¹**berlina,** *f.*—**en b.,** in a ridiculous position, ex-posed to ridicule; (diff. constr.) laughingstock.

²**berlina,** *f.* berlin (carriage); front compartment of a stagecoach or a railway carriage.

berlinés, sa, *a.* of or from Berlin.

berlinga, *f.* clothesline post; round timber.

berma, *f.* (mil.) berm, ground at the foot of a rampart.

bermejear, bermejecer, *vn.* to have a reddish color.

bermejizo, za. I. *a.* reddish. II. *m.* (zool.) red bat.

bermejo, ja, *a.* bright reddish.—**bermejón, na,** *a.* reddish.—**bermejuela,** *f.* (zool.) red gur-nard; (bot.) heather.—**bermejuelo, la,** *a. dim.* somewhat reddish.—**bermejura,** *f.* reddish-ness, ruddy color.

bermellón, bermillón, *m.* vermilion.—**berme-llonar,** *va.* to paint with vermilion.

bermudiana, *f.* (bot.) grassflower.

bernardina, *f.* fanfaronade; boast.

bernardo, da, *n.* & *a.* Bernardine (monk, nun).

bernegal, *m.* cup with scalloped edges.

bernés, sa, *n.* & *a.* Bernese.

bernia, *f.* rug; cloak made of rug.

berra, *f.* strong watercress plant.

berraza, *f.* water parsnip.

berrear, *vn.* to cry like a calf, low, bellow.

berrenchín, *m.* foaming, grunting of a wild boar; cry of wayward children.

berrendearse, *vr.* (of wheat) to grow yellow.

berrendo, da, *a.* two-colored; spotted; (of silk-worm) dark brown (from a disease).

berrera, *f.* (bot.) = BERRAZA.

berrido, *m.* bellowing.

berrín, *m.* child in a violent passion.

berrinche, *m.* anger, passion; sulkiness.

berrinchudo, *a.* (Am.) irritable, sulky.

berrizal, *m.* place full of watercress.

berro, *m.* (bot.) watercress.

berrocal, *m.* craggy or rocky place.

berrueco, *m.* rock; pin; a disease of the eye.

berza, *f.* (bot.) cabbage.—**b. común,** common cabbage.—**b. de perro,** dog's cabbage.—**b. lombarda,** red cabbage.—**berzaza,** *f. aug.* large cabbage.

besador, ra, *n.* & *a.* kisser(-ing).

besalamano, *m.* unsigned note in the third per-son beginning with the abbreviation B.L.M.

besamanos, *m.* reception at court; raising the hand to the lips in greeting.

besana, *f.* first furrow with a plow; series of parallel furrows.

besar. I. *va.* to kiss; (of inanimate things) to touch closely.—**b. la mano,** or **los pies,** ex-pressions of courtesy and respect. II. *vr.* to strike heads or faces together accidentally.

besico, sillo, sito, *m. dim.* little kiss.—**besicos de monja,** (bot.) FAROLILLO, Indian heartseed.

beso, *m.* kiss; collision of persons or things; (among bakers) kissing crust.

bestezuela, *f. dim.* little beast.

bestia, *f.* beast, quadruped; (fig.) dunce, idiot; ill-bred fellow.—**b. de carga,** beast of burden.

bestiaje, bestiame, *m.* group of beasts of bur-den.

bestial, *a.* bestial, brutal.—**bestialidad,** *f.* brutality; stupid notion.—**bestialmente,** *adv.* bestially, brutally.

bestiaza, *m. aug.* great beast; big idiot.

bestiecica, cilla, cita; bestiezuela, *f. dim.* little beast; ignorant person.

bestión, *m. aug.* large beast.

béstola, bístola, *f.* paddle for cleaning the coulter of the plow.

besucador, ra, *n.* (coll.) kisser, spooner.

besucar. I. *va.* (*pret.* BESUQUÉ; *subj.* BESUQUE) to kiss repeatedly. **II.** *vn.* to spoon.

besucón, na, *n.* & *a.* spooner(-ing).

besugada, *f.* luncheon of sea breams.

besugo, *m.* (ichth.) sea bream, red gilthead.

besuguera, *f.* pan for dressing BESUGOS.

besuguero, ra. I. *n.* fishmonger who sells breams. **II.** *m.* fishing tackle for breams.

besuguete, *m.* (ichth.) red sea bream.

besuqué, besuque, *v. V.* BESUCAR.

besuqueador, ra, *n.* = BESUCADOR.

besuquear, *va.* & *vn.* = BESUCAR.—**besuqueo,** *m.,* (coll.) spooning.

¹**beta,** *f.* bit or line of thread, tape.—**betas,** (naut.) pieces of cordage for all kinds of tackle.

²**beta,** *f.* beta (Greek letter).

betabel, *f.* (Mex.) = BETARRAGA.

betarraga, betarrata, *f.* (bot.) beet, beetroot.

betel, *m.* betel, an Indian shrub.

bético, ca, *a.* Andalusian.

betlemita, *n.* & *a.* Bethlehemite.

betlemítico, ca, *a.* from, or pertaining to, Bethlehem or the Bethlehemites.

betol, *m.* (chem.) betol.

betónica, *f.* (bot.) betony.

betuláceo, cea. I. *a.* (bot.) betulaceous. **II.** *f. pl.* Betulaceæ.

betulina, *f.* (chem.) betulin.

betún, *m.* bitumen, pitch; shoeblacking; coarse wax.—**b. judaico,** asphalt.—**betunar,** *va.* to pitch, tar.

beuna, *f.* a red grape or red wine made from it.

bey, *m.* bey, Turkish governor.

bezaar, bezar, *m.* = BEZOAR.

bezante, *m.* (her.) bezant.

bezo, *m.* thick underlip; (med.) proud flesh in a wound.

bezoar, *m.* bezoar.—**b. occidental, b. oriental,** Occidental, Oriental bezoar.—**bezoárico, ca,** *a.* bezoardic.

bezote, *m.* ring worn by Indians in under lip.

bezudo, da, *a.* thick lipped.

biangular, *a.* biangulated, biangulous.

biazas, bizazas, *f. pl.* saddlebags.

bíbaro, *m.* (zool.) = CASTOR, beaver.

bibero, *m.* a kind of linen from Galicia.

biberón, *m.* nursing bottle.

Biblia, *f.* Bible.—**bíblico, ca,** *a.* Biblical.

bibliófilo, la, *n.* book lover, bibliophile.

bibliografía, *f.* bibliography.

bibliográfico, ca, *a.* bibliographical.

bibliógrafo, fa, *n.* bibliographer.

bibliomanía, *f.* bibliomania.

bibliómano, na, *n.* bibliomaniac.

biblioteca, *f.* library.

bibliotecario, ria, *n.* librarian.

bica, *f.* unleavened cake of maize.

bicapsular, *a.* (bot.) having two carpels.

bicarbonato, *m.* bicarbonate.

biceps, *m.* (anat.) biceps.

bicerra, *f.* wild or mountain goat.

bicicleta, *f.* bicycle.—**bicicletista,** *n.* cyclist.

biciclo, *m.* large bicycle.—**biciclista,** *n.* = BICICLETISTA.

bicípite, *a.* bicipital, two-headed.

bicoca, *f.* small fort; trifle, bagatelle.

bicolor, *a.* two-colored.

bicóncavo, va, *a.* biconcave, double-concave.

biconvexo, a, *a.* double-convex.

bicoquete, *m.* **bicoquín,** *m.* double-pointed skullcap.

bicorne, *a.* (poet.) bicorn, having two horns.

bicorpóreo, rea, *a.* bicorporal.

bicos, *m. pl.* gold trimmings on skullcaps.

bicromato, *m.* bichromate.

bicromía, *f.* two-color print.

bicuadrado, da, *a.* (of biquadratics having only even powers of x) raised to the fourth power; in the quadratic form.

bicuento, *m.* (arith.) billion.

bicha, *f.* snake; (arch.) fantastic caryatid.

bichero, *m.* (naut.) boat hook.

bicho, *m.* small grubs or insects; (coll.) beast (often app. to bulls); ridiculous fellow.

bidé, *m.* bidet, washtub.

bidente. I. *a.* having two teeth or prongs. **II.** *m.* two-pronged spade.

biela, *f.* (mech.) connecting rod.

bielda, *f.* pitchfork with six or seven prongs, and a rack.—**bieldar,** *va.* to winnow corn with a BIELDO.—**bieldo, bielgo,** *m.* winnowing fork.

biempareciente, *a.* good-looking.

bien. I. *m.* good; benefit; righteousness.—**mi b.,** my dearest, my darling.—**en,** or **por, b. de,** for the sake, good, or benefit of.—*pl.* property; possessions; estate.—**bienes de fortuna,** worldly possessions.—**bienes dotales,** dower. —**bienes forales,** leasehold estate.—**bienes gananciales,** property acquired during married life.—**bienes inmuebles** = BIENES RAÍCES.— **bienes monstrencos,** goods having no known owner.—**bienes muebles,** goods and chattels. —**bienes raíces,** real estate.—**bienes sedientes,** real estate.—**bienes semovientes,** cattle.—**de b.,** honest. **II.** *adv.* well; all right; right, uprightly; happily, prosperously; willingly, readily, heartily; very; perfectly, fully.— **b. a b.,** willingly.—**b. así como,** just as.— **b. que,** although.—**ahora b.,** now then.— **de b. en mejor,** better and better.—**encontrar,** or **hallar b.,** to find satisfactory, approve.—**más b.,** rather; somewhat.—**no b.,** as soon as, just as.—**o b.,** or else; otherwise.— **por b.,** willingly.—**si b.,** while, though.—**y b.,** well, now then.—**¿y b.?** well? what of that?

bienal, *a.* biennial.

bienamado, da, *a.* dearly beloved.

bienandante, *a.* happy, prosperous.

bienandanza, *f.* happiness, welfare, prosperity.

bienaventuradamente, *adv.* luckily, happily.

bienaventurado, da, *a.* blessed; happy; fortunate; (ironic) simple, harmless.

bienaventuranza, *f.* beatitude; bliss; well-being. —*pl.* beatitudes.

bienestar, *m.* well-being, comfort.

bienfortunado, da, *a.* fortunate, successful.

biengranada, *f.* (bot.) curl-leaved goosefoot.

bienhablado, da, *a.* well and civilly spoken.

bienhadado, da, *a.* lucky, fortunate, happy.

bienhecho, cha, *a.* well-shaped; well-done.

bienhechor, ra, *n.* benefactor.

bienintencionado, da, *a.* well-meaning.

bienio, *m.* term or space of two years.

bienmandado, da, *a.* obedient, submissive.

bienmesabe, *m.* meringue batter.

bienquerencia, *f.* good will, affection, esteem.

bienquerer. I. *va.* (*ind. pres.* BIENQUIERO, *pret.* BIENQUISE, *fut.* BIENQUERRÉ; *subj.* BIENQUIERA) to esteem, to like. **II.** *m.* esteem, good will.

bienqueriente, *n.* well-wisher.

bienquistar, *va.* to reconcile.

bienquisto, ta. I. *pp. irreg. of* BIENQUERER. **II.** *a.* esteemed and respected.

bienteveo, *m.* = CANDELECHO, raised hut.

bienvenida, *f.* safe arrival; welcome.

bienvenido, da, *a.* welcome.

bienvivir, *vn.* to live in comfort; live uprightly.

bifásico, ca, *a.* (elec.) two-phase.

bífido, da, *a.* (bot.) bifid.

bifilar, *a.* bifilar; (elec.) two-wire.

bifloro, ra, *a.* (bot.) biflorous.

biforme, *a.* biformed, biform.
bifronte, *a.* (poet.) double-fronted or -faced.
biftec, *m.* beefsteak. Also BISTEC.
biftequera, *f.* (Chile) beefsteak broiler.
bifurcación, *f.* branch railroad; junction; bifurcation or forking.
bifurcado, da, *a.* forked or branched, bifurcate.
bifurcarse, *vr.* to branch off; to divide in two.
biga, *f.* (poet.) team (of two horses).
bigamia, *f.* bigamy.
bígamo, ma, *a. & n.* bigamist.
bigardear, *vn.* to live licentiously; to gad.
bigardía, *f.* jest; fiction; dissimulation.
bigardo, *m.* licentious friar; lubber.
bígaro, bigarro, *m.* large sea snail.
bigarrado, da, *a.* = ABIGARRADO, variegated.
bignoniáceo, cea. I. *a.* (bot.) bignoniaceous.
II. *f. pl.* Bignoniaceæ.
bigorneta, *f. dim.* small anvil.
bigornia, *f.* anvil.
bigotazo, *m. aug.* large mustache.
bigote, *m.* mustache; block; (print.) dash rule.
bigotera, *f.* leather cover for mustachios; ribbon ornament worn by women on the breast; folding seat in front of a chariot; bow compass.
bigotudo, *a.* having a large mustache.
bija, *f.* (bot.) arnotto tree; (com.) annatto dye.
bilateral, *a.* bilateral.
bilbaíno, na, *a.* of or from Bilbao.
biliario, ria, *a.* (physiol.) biliary.
bilingüe, *a.* bilingual.
bilioso, sa, *a.* bilious.
bilis, *f.* bile.
bilocarse, *vr.* (*pret.* BILOQUÉ; *subj.* BILOQUE) to be simultaneously in two different places.
biltrotear, *vn.* (coll.) to gad.
biltrotera, *f.* (coll.) gadder, gossiping woman.
billa, *f.* (billiards) pocketing a ball after it has struck another.
billalda, billarda, *f.* a children's game.
billar, *m.* billiards, pool; billiard, pool, table.
billarista, *n.* billiard player.
billete, *m.* an order of the king; note, brief letter; love letter; ticket.—**b. de banco,** bank-note.—**b. de abonado,** commutation ticket.—**b. de ida y vuelta,** round-trip ticket.—**b. kilométrico,** mileage ticket.—**billetera,** *f.* (Am.) pocketbook, wallet.
billetico, *m. dim.* billet, love letter.
billón, *m.* billion (gen. one million millions).
billonésimo, ma, *n. & a.* billionth (gen. one millionth of one millionth).
bimano, na. I. *a.* (zool.) bimanous. **II.** *m.* bimane.—*pl.* Bimana.
bimembre, *a.* having two members.
bimensual, *a.* occurring twice a month.
bimestral, *a.* bimonthly.
bimestre. I. *a.* bimonthly. **II.** *n.* bimonthly rent, salary, subscription, pension, etc.
bimetalismo, *m.* bimetallism.
bimetalista, *n.* bimetallist.
bimotor, ra, *a.* two-motor.
bina, *f.* second plowing or digging.
binador, *m.* he who re-digs ground; weeding fork.
binar, *va.* to dig or plow the second time.
binario, ria, *a.* binary.
binazón, *f.* digging or plowing a second time.
binocular, *a.* binocular.
binóculo, *m.* binocle, dioptric telescope; marine or field glasses; opera glasses.
binomio, a. I. *a.* binomial. **II.** *m.* binomial.—**b. de Newton,** (alg.) binomial theorem.
binza, *f.* pellicle, lining of the shell of an egg; any thin membrane.
biodinámica, *f.* biodynamics.
biofísica, *f.* biophysics.
biogénesis, *f.* biogenesis.
biografía, *f.* biography.
biográfico, ca, *a.* biographical.
biógrafo, *m.* biographer.

biología, *f.* biology.
biólogo, ga, *n.* biologist.
biombo, *m.* folding screen.
bioquímica, *f.* biochemistry.
biótico, ca, *a.* biotic.
biotita, *f.* (min.) biotite.
bióxido, *m.* dioxide.
bipartido, da, *a.* (poet.) divided in two.
bipedal, *a.* bipedal.
bípede, bipedo, da, *n. & a.* biped.
bipétalo, la, *a.* (bot.) bipetalous.
biplano, *m.* (aer.) biplane.
bipolar, *a.* bipolar, two-pole.
biribís, *m.* = BISBÍS.
biricú, *m.* sword belt.
birimbao, *m.* (mus.) Jew's harp.
birla, *f.,* **birlo,** *m.* bowling pin.
birlador, ra, *n.* one who bowls a second time from the place where the ball stopped the first time.
birlar, *va.* to bowl a second time from the same place; to knock down at one blow; to kill with one shot; to snatch away; to rob, pilfer.
birlibirloque, *m.*—**por arte de b.,** (coll.) by occult and extraordinary means.
birlocha, *f.* paper kite.
birlocho, *m.* two-seat light wagon without top.
birlón, *m.* jack pin (in bowling).
birlonga, *f.* a card game.—**a la b.,** carelessly.
birmano, na, *n. & a.* Burman.
birrectángulo, la, *a.* (geom.) birectangular, having two right angles.
birrefringencia, *f.* double refraction of light rays.
birrefringente, *a.* producing double refraction.
birreme, *n. & a.* bireme.
birreta, *f.* biretta.
birrete, *m.* cap.—**birretina,** *f.* grenadier's and hussar's cap; small cap.
bis, bis, Latin word used in the sense of "twice," "repeated" or "second."
bisabuela, *f.* great-grandmother.
bisabuelo, *m.* great-grandfather.
bisagra, *f.* hinge; shoemaker's boxwood polisher.
bisanuo, nua, *a.* (bot.) biennial.
bisayo, ya, *a.* native of or pertaining to the Bisayas Islands in the Philippines.
bisbís, *m.* a game resembling baccarat.
bisbisar, *va.* to mutter.—**bisbiseo,** *m.* muttering.
bisecar, *va.* to bisect.
bisección, *f.* bisection.
bisector, triz, *a. & n.* (geom.) bisector.
bisel, *m.* bevel, bevel edge, chamfer; (cooperage) sloping tool.
biselado, *m.* beveling; bevel.
biselar, *va.* to bevel.
bisextil, *a.* bissextile.
bisexual, *a.* (bot.) bisexual.
bisiesto, *a.* leap (year).
bisílabo, ba, *a.* disyllabic.
bislingua, *f.* (bot.) butcher's-broom.
bismuto, *m.* bismuth.
bisnieta, biznieta, *f.* great-granddaughter.
bisnieto, biznieto, *m.* great-grandson.
bisojo, ja, bizco, ca, *a.* squint-eyed, cross-eyed.
bisonte, *m.* bison.
bisoñada, bisoñería, *f.* act of a novice.
bisoño, ña, *n. & a.* novice, tyro, greenhorn; inexperienced, new.
bispón, *m.* roll of oilcloth.
bistec, *m.* beefsteak. Also BIFTEC.
bístola, *f.* paddle for cleaning plow.
bistorta, *f.* (bot.) great bistort, snakeweed.
bisturí, *m.* (surg.) bistoury, surgical knife.
bisulco, ca, *a.* bisulcous, cloven-footed.
bisulfato, *m.* bisulphate.
bisulfito, *m.* (chem.) bisulfite.
bisulfuro, *m.* disulphide.
bisunto, ta, *a.* dirty, greasy.
bitácora, *f.* (naut.) binnacle.
bitadura, *f.* (naut.) cable bitt; a turn of the cable.

For pronunciation, see the rules at the beginning of the book.

bitas, *f. pl.* (naut.) bitts.
bitones, *m. pl.* (naut.) pins of the capstan.
bitongo, ga, *a.* (of children) like an overgrown baby.
bitoque, *m.* bung, stopple.
bitor, *m.* (ornith.) rail, king of the quails.
bitubulado, da, *a.* two-tube.
bituminoso, sa, *a.* bituminous.
bivalente, *a.* (chem.) bivalent.
bivalvo, va, *a.* bivalve, bivalvular.
biza, *f.* (ichth.) = BONITO, striped tunny.
bizantino, na, *a.* Byzantine.
bizarramente, *adv.* courageously, gallantly.
bizarrear, *vn.* to act spiritedly, gallantly.
bizarría, *f.* bravery, gallantry; generosity, magnanimity.
bizarro, rra, *a.* gallant, brave; generous, liberal.
bizaza, *f.* saddle-bag.
bizcacha, *f.* viscacha, a South Am. rodent.
bizcar, *vn.* (*pret.* BIZQUÉ; *subj.* BIZQUE) to squint.
bizco, ca, *a.* = BISOJO, squint- or cross-eyed.
bizcochada, *f.* biscuit boiled in milk; French bread.
bizcochar, *va.* to bake a second time.
bizcochero, *m.* biscuit cask; one who makes or sells biscuits.
bizcochito, *m. dim.* small biscuit.
bizcocho, *m.* biscuit; hard-tack; sponge cake; whiting made of old plaster; bisque.
bizcochuelo, *m. dim.* sponge cake.
bizcorneto, ta, *a.* (Am.) = BIZCO.
bizcotela, *f.* light biscuit with sugar icing.
bizma, *f.* poultice.—**bizmar,** *va.* to poultice.
bizna, *f.* membrane dividing walnut kernel.
biznaga, *f.* (bot.) carrotlike ammi with sprigs used as toothpicks; useless, worthless thing.
biznieta, bisnieta, *f.* great-granddaughter.
biznieto, bisnieto, *m.* great-grandson.
bizqué, bizque, *v. V.* BIZCAR.
bizquear, *vn.* to squint.
blanca, *f.* old copper coin; mite; (coll.) money, funds.—**b. morfea,** (vet.) alphos, white scurf, tetter, or ringworm.
blancazo, za, *a.* whitish.
blanco, ca. I. *a.* white; (of the complexion) fair; (coll.) cowardly; light-colored; blank (page). **II.** *n.* white person. **III.** *m.* white (color); white star or spot in horses; target; blank; gap left in writing; aim, goal; (print.) blank form; interlude, interval; white page; (her.) argent; sizing.—**b. de ballena,** spermaceti.—**b. de la uña,** half-moon of the nail.—**b. de plomo,** white lead.—**dar en el b.,** to hit the mark.—**en b.,** blank (space, book).—**quedarse en b.,** to be frustrated, disappointed.—**blancor,** *m.* whiteness; fairness (of skin).—**blancote,** *n. & a.* (coll.) coward(-ly).
blancura, *f.* = BLANCOR.—**b. del ojo,** (vet.) white film on the eye.
blancuzco, ca, *a.* whitish.
blandamente, *adv.* softly, mildly, smoothly.
blandeador, ra, *n. & a.* softener(-ing).
¹blandear. I. *va.* to soften, render mild; to persuade, convince. **II.** *vn.* to slacken; to yield, give in. **III.** *vr.* to soften, yield, change one's mind.
²blandear, *va.* = BLANDIR.
blandengue. I. *m.* Argentine lancer. **II.** *a.* exceedingly kind, bland.
blandiente, *a.* swaying, brandishing.
blandir, *va. & vr.* to brandish, flourish, swing.
blando, da. I. *a.* soft (to the touch); pliant; tender, kindly, mild, bland; delicate; pusillanimous, cowardly. **II.** *m. adv.* = BLANDAMENTE.
blandón, *m.* wax taper; large church candlestick.—**blandoncillo,** *m. dim.* small candlestick for wax tapers.
blandujo, ja, *a.* (coll.), rather soft.
blandura, *f.* softness; litheness, daintiness, delicacy; gentleness; emollient application; soft,

endearing language; blandishing; white cosmetic; mild temperature.
blanduzco, ca, (Am.) = BLANDUJO.
blanqueación, *f.* blanching (metals); bleaching; whitewashing.
blanqueador, ra, *n.* blancher, whitener, whitewasher, kalsominer; bleacher.
blanqueadura, *f., or* **blanqueamiento,** *m.* = BLANQUEO.
blanquear. I. *va.* to whiten; to whitewash; to bleach; (of bees) to wax (the honeycomb) after winter to begin work; to give coarse wax to bees in winter. **II.** *vn.* to show white; to whiten.
blanquecedor, *m.* coin polisher (in the mint).
blanquecer, *va.* (*ind.* BLANQUEZCO; *subj.* BLANQUEZCA) to blanch (coin).
blanquecimiento, *m.* blanching.
blanquecino, na, *a.* whitish.
blanqueo, *m.* whitening, bleaching, whitewashing.
blanquería, *f.* bleaching place, bleach field.
blanqueta, *f.* coarse blanket.
blanquete, *m.* whitewash; white cosmetic.
blanquezco, blanquezca, *v. V.* BLANQUECER.
blanquición, *f.* blanching of metals.
blanquilla, *f.* doit, small coin; a long yellowish plum; white grape.
blanquillo, lla. I. *a. dim.* whitish. **II.** *m.* a S.A. fish; (Peru, Chile) white peach; (Mex.) egg.
blanquimiento, *m.* bleaching solution.
blanquinoso, sa, *a.* = BLANQUECINO, whitish.
blanquizal, blanquizar, *m.* clay pit.
blanquizco, ca, *a.* whitish.
blao, *a.* (her.) azure.
blasfemador, ra, *n. & a.* blasphemer(-ing).
blasfemamente, *adv.* blasphemously.
blasfemante, *n. & a.* = BLASFEMADOR.
blasfemar, *vn.* to blaspheme; to curse.
blasfematorio, ria, *a.* blasphemous.
blasfemia, *f.* blasphemy; grave insult.
blasfemo, ma, *n. & a.* blasphemer(-ing).
blasón, *m.* heraldry, blazon, blazonry; armorial bearing; honor, glory.
blasonador, ra; blasonante, *n. & a.* boaster (-ing).
blasonar. I. *va.* to design or emblazon (a heraldic shield). **II.** *vn.* to boast, brag.
blasonería, *f.* boast, bravado.
blastema, *m.* (biol.) blastema.
blastodermo, *m.* (biol.) blastoderm.
blastogénesis, *f.* (biol.) blastogenesis.
blavo, va, *a.* yellowish gray and reddish.
bledo, *m.* (bot.) wild amaranth.—**no me importa un b.,** I don't care a straw.
blefaritis, *f.* (med.) blepharitis.
blefaroplastia, *f.* (med.) blepharoplasty.
blefaróstato, *m.* (surg.) blepharostat.
blenda, *f.* (min.) blende.
bleno, *m.* (ichth.) hake, blenny.
blenorragia, *f.* (med.) blennorrhea.
blenorrea, *f.* (med.) chronic blennorrhea.
blinda, *f.,* **blindas,** *pl.* (fort.) blindage.
blindado, da, *n. & a.* iron-clad.
blindaje, *m.* (mil.) blindage; (naut.) armor.
blindar, *va.* to armor; to protect with blindage.
blino, *m.* = BLENO.
blocao, *m.* (mil.) portable blockhouse.
blonda, *f.* broad silk lace, blond lace.
blondina, *f.* narrow silk lace, narrow blond lace.
blondo, da, *a.* blond, fair; flaxen, light.
bloque, *m.* block (of stone, etc.).
bloqueador, ra, *n. & a.* blockader(-ing).
bloquear, *va.* to blockade.—**bloqueo,** *m.* blockade.—**b. efectivo,** (int. law) effective blockade.—**b. en el papel,** (int. law) paper blockade.
blusa, *f.* blouse.
boa, *f.* (zool.) boa; boa, neckpiece.
boardilla, buhardilla, *f.* garret; skylight.
boato, *m.* ostentation, pomp; acclamation.
bobada, *m.* = BOBERÍA.

bobalías, *n.* very stupid person, dolt.

bobalicón, ona; bobazo, za, *n.* blockhead; simpleton.

bobamente, *adv.* foolishly, stupidly; easily, without any trouble.

bobarrón, na; bobatel, *n.* simpleton.

bobático, ca, *a.* silly, foolish, stupid.

bobear, *vn.* to act or talk foolishly; to dally, fribble, fritter away (time).

bobería, *f.* foolish speech or action; trifle; folly, foolishness.—*pl.* idle conceits.

bóbilis.—de b. b., easily, with no effort; for nothing.

¹**bobillo, illa, ito, ita,** *n. dim.* little fool.

²**bobillo,** *m.* big-bellied jug with one handle; modesty piece, a frill or lace formerly worn by women around the tucker.

bobina, *f.* bobbin; (elec.) coil.—**b. apagachispas,** blow-out coil.—**b. de inducción,** induction coil.—**b. de reacción,** or **de reactancia,** choking, kicking, or reactance, coil.—**b. de sintonización,** tuning coil.

bobo, ba, *n.* dolt, fool, simpleton, ninny; ruff formerly worn by women; (ornith.) booby.—**b. de Coria,** great fool; fools in general.—**a bobas,** foolishly.—**bobón, na,** (Am.), **bobote, ta,** (coll.) *n. aug.* big dolt, great fool.

boca, *f.* mouth; entrance, opening; nozzle: muzzle; bunghole; pincers of crayfish; cutting part of edge tools; taste, flavor, relish; approach (to a tunnel, etc.).—**b. abajo,** flat on one's face, prone.—**b. a b.** = A B.—**b. arriba,** flat on one's back, supine.—**b. de agua,** hydrant.—**b. de dragón,** (bot.) snap dragon.—**b. de fuego,** firearm (esp. artillery).—**b. del estómago,** pit of the stomach.—**b. del metro,** subway entrance.—**b. de riego,** faucet (for a watering hose).—**a b.,** verbally, by word of mouth.—**a b. de,** at the beginning of.—**a b. de jarro,** drinking without measure; very near; at close range.—**a b. llena,** perspicuously, openly.—**andar de b. en b.,** to be the talk of the town.—**como b. de lobo,** pitch black.—**de b.,** A B.; boastingly.—**en b. cerrada no entra mosca,** (coll.) silence is golden, it pays to hold one's tongue.—**no decir esta b. es mía,** to keep a profound silence, not to say boo.

bocabarra, *f.* (naut.) barhole in a capstan.

bocacalle, *f.* opening of a street (into another); street intersection.

bocacaz, *m.* (hydraul.) spillway.

bocací, bocacín, *m.* fine glazed buckram.

bocadear, *va.* to divide into bits or morsels.

bocadico, illo, ito, *m. dim.* morsel, bit.

bocadillo, *m.* thin, middling sort of linen; narrow ribbon or tape, gimp; mid-morning luncheon given to laborers in the field; guava paste.

bocado, *m.* morsel, mouthful, bite, bit; modicum; bit of a bridle.—*pl.* preserved cut fruit.—**con el b. en la boca,** right after eating.—**no tener para un b.,** to be in absolute destitution.

¹**bocal,** *m.* narrow-mouthed pitcher.

²**bocal,** *m.* (naut.) narrows (of a harbor); mouthpiece (of musical instrument).

bocamanga, *f.* part of a sleeve near the wrist.

bocamina, *f.* entrance to a mine.

bocanada, *f.* mouthful (of liquor); whiff, puff (of smoke).—**b. de gente,** crowd, rush, jam.—**b. de viento,** sudden gust of wind.

bocarón, *m.* wind chest of an organ; wind trunk.

bocarte, *m.* ore crusher, stamp mill.

bocateja, *f.* front tile of each line of tiling.

bocatijera, *f.* socket for a carriage pole.

bocaza, *f. aug.* large wide mouth.

bocazo, *m.* fizzle (in blasting).

bocear, *va.* (vet.) = BOCEZAR.

bocel, *m.* (arch.) bowtel, solid cylindrical molding; tool for making bowtels.

bocelar, *va.* to make cylindrical moldings on.

bocelete, *m. dim.* small molding plane.

bocelón, *m. aug.* large molding plane.

bocera, *f.* something sticking to the lip after eating or drinking.

boceto, *m.* sketch.

bocezar, *vn.* (vet.) (of horses) to move the lips from side to side.

bocín, *m.* round piece of bass mat put about the nave of a cart, as a cap of defense; feed pipe of an overshot wheel.

bocina, *f.* large trumpet, buglehorn, megaphone, foghorn, huntsman's horn; (Mex.) mouthpiece (of a telephone); horn (of a phonograph or of an automobile); shell used as a horn; speaking or hearing trumpet; blowgun; (B-, astr.) Ursa Minor; (mech.) bushing; wheel hoop.

bocinar, *vn.* to sound the trumpet or horn.

bocinero, *m.* trumpeter, hornblower.

bocón, na, *n.* wide-mouthed person; braggart.

bocoy, *m.* hogshead, large barrel or cask.—**bocoyes abatidos,** shooks of hogsheads.

bocudo, da, *a.* large-mouthed.

bocha, *f.* bowl, ball for playing at bowls; fold or bag in ill-fitting clothes.—**bochar,** *va.* to dislodge (a ball).—**bochazo,** *m.* stroke of one bowl against another.

¹**boche,** *m.* chuck hole (boys' game).

²**boche,** *m.* (Venez. coll.) disappointment; quarrel, row, riot; slight, contemptuous treatment.—**dar b.,** or **un b.,** to slight, turn the cold shoulder on.

bochinche, *m.* (Am.) tumult, uproar, riot.

bochinchero, ra, *n.* (Am.) rioter; disturber.

bochista, *m.* good bowler.

bochorno, *m.* hot, sultry weather, scorching heat; rush of blood to the head; blush, flushing; humiliation, embarrassment.—**bochornoso, sa,** *a.* humiliating; embarrassing; sultry.

boda, *f.* nuptials, wedding.—**b. de negros,** (coll.) riotous carousal, orgy.—**bodas de diamante, de oro, de plata,** diamond, golden, silver wedding.

bode, *m.* (zool.) buck.

bodega, *f.* wine vault, cellar; abundant vintage; storeroom, warehouse; (Cuba, Mex.) retail grocery; (naut.) hold of a ship.

bodegaje, *m.* (Am.) storage (charges).

bodegón, *m.* low-class chophouse; alehouse; still life painting, esp. of edibles.—**bodegoncillo,** *m. dim.* low-class chophouse.—**bodegonear,** *vn.* to run from one alehouse to another.—**bodegonero, ra,** *n.* keeper of a BODEGÓN.

bodeguero, ra, *n.* butler, one in charge of a winecellar; (Cuba) retail grocer.

bodeguilla, *f. dim.* small cellar or vault.

bodigo, *m.* small loaf of fine white bread presented as an offering in the church.

bodijo, *m.* mésalliance; marriage with little ceremony.

bodocal, *n.* a kind of black grape.

bodocazo, *m.* blow from a pellet shot from a crossbow.

bodollo, *m.* pruning knife, pruning hook.

bodoque, *m.* pellet, ball of clay shot from a crossbow; dunce, idiot.

bodoquera, *f.* blowgun; mold for clay pellets; cradle of a crossbow; pea-shooter.

bodoquillo, *m. dim.* clay pellet.

bodorrio, *m.* (Am.) = BODIJO.

bodrio, *m.* soup formerly given to the poor; hodgepodge; mixture of hog's blood and onions for sausages.

bóer, *n.* & *a.* Boer.

boezuelo, *m.* stalking ox, or figure representing one, which serves to screen fowlers.

bofe, *m.* lung.—**echar los bofes,** to toil; (Am.) to pant, be out of breath.

bófeta, *f.* thin, stiff cotton stuff.

bofetada, *f.* slap in the face, buffet.

bofetón, *m.* slap in the face, buffet; (theat.) revolving-door trick.

¹boga. I. *f.* vogue, popularity; rowing; rowing stroke. **II.** *m.* & *f.* rower.

²boga, *f.* small two-edged knife.

³boga, *f.* (ichth.) ox-eyed cackerel, mendole.

¹bogada, *f.* space covered by a stroke of oars.

²bogada, *f.* bucking of clothes with lye.

bogador, *m.* rower (of a boat).

bogante, *n.* & *a.* rower(-ing) (a boat).

bogar, *vn.* (*pret.* BOGUÉ; *subj.* BOGUE) to row (a boat).

bogavante, *m.* (naut.) stroke oar; large lobster.

bogotano, na, *a.* of or from Bogotá.

bogué, bogue, *v. V.* BOGAR.

bohardilla, *f.* = BUHARDILLA, garret; skylight.

bohemiano, na, *n.* & *a.* Bohemian (person).

bohémico, ca, *a.* Bohemian (of Bohemia).

bohemio, mia. I. *n.* & *a.* Bohemian (of Bohemia); (pertaining to) a bohemian life or person; gypsy. **II.** *m.* short cloak formerly worn by the guard of archers; Czech (language).

bohemo, ma, *a.* of Bohemia.

bohena, boheña, *f.* pork sausage.

bohío, buhío, *m.* (Am.) Indian hut, hovel, cabin.

bohordar, *vn.* to throw BOHORDOS in tournaments.

bohordo, *m.* short spear; dart; (bot.) scape.

boicot, *m.* boycott.

boicoteador, ra, *n.* & *a.* boycotter(-ing).

boicotear, *va.* & *vn.* to boycott.—**boicoteo,** *m.* boycott, boycotting.

boíl, *m.* ox stall.

boina, *f.* beret.

boj, *m.* box tree, boxwood; shoemaker's boxwood tool.

boja, *f.* southernwood. Also ABRÓTANO.

¹bojar, bojear. I. *va.* (naut.) to sail round and measure (an island or cape). **II.** *vn.* to measure.

²bojar, *va.* to scrape off the stains from (leather).

bojedal, *m.* plantation of box trees.

bojeo, *m.* (naut.) sailing round and measuring an island or headland.

bojeta, *f.* (ichth.) a kind of herring.

bojete, *m.* (Venez.) parcel, package.

bojiganga, *f.* company of strolling players.

bojo, *m.* = BOJEO.

¹bol, *m.* punch bowl.

²bol, *m.* Armenian bole, red earth.

bola, *f.* ball; marble; bolus; game of bowling; (coll.) lie, falsehood, humbug, hoax, fib; (Mex.) crowd; disturbance, tumult, riotous meeting; (naut.) truck, ball for signals; shoe blacking.— **b. de jabón,** wash ball.—**b. pampa, b. perdida,** (Arg.) a kind of Indian sling.—**dejar rodar la b.,** to let things run their natural course, keep hands off; to look on with indifference.

bolada, *f.* stroke (in billiards).

bolado, *m.* a sweetmeat; fondant.

bolandista, *n.* Bollandist.

bolazo, *m.* blow with a ball.—**de b.,** hurriedly.

bolchevique, *n.* & *a.* Bolshevik(-ist).

bolchevismo, *m.* Bolshevism.

bolchevista, *n.* & *a.* = BOLCHEVIQUE.

boleada, *f.* (Mex.) shoeshine.

boleador, *m.* (Mex.) bootblack.

boleadoras, *f. pl.* (Arg.) lariat with balls on one end, thrown so to twist round animal's legs.

¹bolear. I. *vn.* to play billiards for pleasure; to bowl; to boast; to lie, fib. **II.** *va.* to throw; (Arg.) to throw BOLEADORAS at, or catch with them; (Arg.) to confuse.

²bolear, *va.* (Am.) to fail, not to pass (in an exam.); to reject, turn down (in an election).

boleo, *m.* bowling; bowling green, place where balls are thrown.

¹bolera, *f.* bowling alley.

²bolera, *f.* woman dancer of the BOLERO.

¹bolero, *m.* bolero, Andalusian dance; bolero dancer.

²bolero, ra, *a.* truant; fibbing, lying.

boleta, *f.* admission ticket; lodging billet; pay order; small package of tobacco; (Am.) ballot. —**b. de guardarropa,** (hat, baggage, etc.) check.

boletar, *va.* to put up (tobacco) in packages.

boletería, *f.* (Am.) box, or ticket, office.

boletero, ra, *n.* ticket agent.

boletín, *m.* pay warrant; pay bill; lodging billet; admission ticket; bulletin; (com.) price list; price current.

boleto, *m.* (Am.) ticket; (Am.) ballot; (Am.) lottery ticket.

bolichada, *f.* casting (a fish net); fish caught in a net.—**de una b.,** at one throw, at the same time.

¹boliche, *m.* jack; small bowling ball; a gambling game; furnace for lead smelting; cup and ball (toy).

²boliche, *m.* small dragnet; small fish caught in a dragnet near the shore.—*pl.* (naut.) foretop bowlines and top-gallant bowlines.

¹bolichero, *m.* seller of BOLICHES, fish.

²bolichero, ra, *n.* one who runs a ¹BOLICHE, gambling table.

bólido, *m.* shooting star.

bolilla, *f. dim.* small ball; marble (ball).

bolillo, *m.* bobbin for lace making; iron pin in the game of trucks; mold for stiffening lace cuffs; bone joined to skull of horses.—*pl.* paste nuts; starched lace cuffs.

bolín, *m.* jack; small bowl.—**de b., de bolán,** at random, carelessly.—**bolines,** (Am.) mold shot.

bolina, *f.* sounding line; punishment on shipboard; noise, turmoil; (naut.) bowline.—**echar de b.,** to boast.—**navegar de b.,** or **bolinear,** *vn.* to sail with bowlines hauled.

bolisa, *f.* embers, hot cinders.

bolívar, *m.* bolivar, monetary unit of Venezuela (about 20 cents, or one franc).

bolivariano, na, *a.* Bolivarian, pert. to Bolívar.

boliviano, na. I. *n.* & *a.* Bolivian. **II.** *m.* monetary unit of Bolivia (about 40 cts.).

¹bolo, *m.* (bowling, etc.) a ninepin; game of ninepins; large pill; cushion for lacemaking; axis or core of winding staircase; dunce, blockhead.

²bolo, *m.* (P. I.) large knife like a machete.

³bolo, la, *a.* & *n.* (Am.) drunk (person).

bolones, *m. pl.* (naut.) square bolts or mortarbed pintles.

bolonio, *n.* & *a.* ignorant (person).

boloñés, esa, *a.* Bolognese; Bologna (as *a.*).

bolsa, *f.* purse; pouch, bag; wrinkle, pucker (in cloth); (anat.) scrotum; (min.) pocket; (med.) sac; exchange center.—**b. de comercio,** stock exchange.—**b. de pastor,** (bot.) shepherd's purse.—**b. de trabajo,** employment bureau, or exchange.

bolsear, *vn.* to wrinkle, pucker.

bolsera, *f.* woman's hair bag or net.

bolsería, *f.* purse or bag shop or factory.

bolsero, ra, *n.* manufacturer or seller of purses.

bolsica, ita, illa, *f. dim.* small purse.

bolsico, *m.* (Chile) poke, pocket.

bolsicón, *m.* (Am.) baize skirt of poor women.

bolsillo, *m.* pocket; (woman's) handbag, purse; money (belonging to a person).—**rascarse el b.,** to put one's hand in one's pocket (fig., in the sense of spending or paying), (slang) to come across.—**tener a una persona en el b.,** (coll.) to have a person in the palm of one's hand, or under one's thumb.

bolsín, *m.* gathering of brokers out of exchange hours.

bolsista, *m.* stockbroker; speculator.

bolso, *m.* purse of money, moneybag.

For pronunciation, see the rules at the beginning of the book.

bolsón, *m. aug.* of BOLSO; large purse; large iron ring to hold braces of arches; board lining.

bolla, *f.* duty on woollens and silks formerly levied in Catalonia; tax on the manufacture of playing cards; in S. A., great richness of an ore.

bolladura, *f.* = ABOLLADURA, unevenness; dent.

¹bollar, *va.* to mark (goods) with a lead seal.

²bollar, *va.* to emboss.

bollería, *f.* bakery, pastry shop.

bollero, ra, *n.* pastry cook; cake seller.

bollico, ito, *m. dim.* small loaf or roll.

bollo, *m.* small loaf or roll, penny loaf; small biscuit or cake; puff in dress; tuft in upholstery; bruise made in metal; morbid swelling; lump; in Peru, bars of silver.—**bollos de relieve,** embossed or raised work.—**bollón,** *m.* brassheaded nail; bud on a plant; button earring.

bollonado, da, *a.* having brass-headed nails.

bolluelo, *m. dim.* of BOLLO.

¹bomba, *f.* pump; pumping engine; fire engine; carcass; piece of wind instruments; lamp globe; earthen jar or firkin for skimming oil from water; high hat.—**¡b.!** listen! (calling attention to a toast).—**b. alimenticia,** feed pump.— **b. aspirante,** lift pump; suction pump.—**b. aspirante-impelente,** lift-and-force pump.— **b. centrífuga,** centrifugal pump.—**b. de aire comprimido,** air lift.—**b. de alimentación** = B. ALIMENTICIA.—**b. de carena,** bilge pump. —**b. de doble efecto,** double-acting pump.— **b. de émbolo buzo,** plunger pump.—**b. impelente,** force pump.—**b. marina,** waterspout.—**b. rotatoria,** rotary pump.—**dar a la b.,** to pump.

²bomba, *f.* bomb, shell.—**b. atómica,** atom(ic) bomb.

bombáceo, a. I. *a.* (bot.) bombaceous. **II.** *f. pl.* Bombaceæ.

bombachas, *f. pl.* (Arg.) loose trousers fastened at the bottom.

bombacho, cha, *a.* (of trousers) loose, loosefitting.

¹bombarda, *f.* bombard, ancient thick piece of ordnance; (naut.) bomb ketch or bomb vessel.

²bombarda, *f.* ancient wind instrument; stop of a pipe organ.

bombardear, *va.* to bombard.—**bombardeo,** *m.* bombardment.—**b. de precisión, de saturación,** precision, saturation, bombing.—**bombardero,** *m.* bombardier; bomber (airplane).

bombasí, *m.* bombazine, dimity.

bombástico, ca, *a.* bombastic, high-sounding.

bombazo, *m.* explosion or noise of a bursting bomb; throwing of a bomb; bomb hit; damage caused by a bomb.

bombé, *m.* light two-wheeled carriage open in front.

¹bombear, *va.* (Am.) to pump; to praise, write up; (Am.) to watch, spy; (Peru, Arg.) to reconnoiter.

²bombear, *va.* to bomb, bombard; (Colomb.) to dismiss, "fire."

bombeo, *m.* pumping; curving, bulging.

¹bombero, *m.* fireman; pumper.

²bombero, *m.* howitzer.

bombilla, *f.* (Am.) small tube for drinking MATE; (naut.) hand lantern; electric light bulb.

bombillo, *m.* lamp chimney; water-closet trap; small pump; sample or thief tube.

bombista, *n.* pump maker; lamp-chimney maker; praiser, writer of write-ups.

bombo, ba. I. *a.* bewildered; astonished; (Am.) tepid. **II.** *m.* large drum; player on bass drum; (naut.) barge or lighter; leather pouch in billiards, for numbered balls.—**dar b.,** to praise excessively; to write up.

¹bombón, *m.* bonbon, candy.

²bombón, *m.* (P. I.) vase made of cane; carboy.

bombonaje, *m.* screw pine.

bombonera, *f.* box for bonbons.

bonachón, na, *a.* good-natured, kind.

bonaerense, *a.* of or from Buenos Aires.

bonancible, *a.* moderate, calm, fair.

bonanza, *f.* fair weather; prosperity, success.— **ir en b.,** to be prosperous.

bonapartismo, *m.* Bonapartism.

bonapartista, *n. & a.* Bonapartist.

bonarense, *n. & a.* = BONAERENSE.

bonazo, za, *a.* good-natured, kind-hearted.

bondad, *f.* goodness, excellence; kindness, kindliness.—**tener la b.** (de), please (*inf.*).

bondadosamente, *adv.* kindly.

bondadoso, sa, *a.* kind, good.

bonetada, *f.* salutation by taking off the hat.

bonetas, *f. pl.* (naut.) bonnets.

bonete, *m.* bonnet, college cap; secular clergyman; bonnet of a fortress; preserve jar; second stomach of ruminants.

bonetería, *f.* bonnet factory or shop.

bonetero, ra, *n.* bonnet maker or seller; (bot.) prickwood, gatheridge.

bonetillo, *m.* small bonnet; hair ornament.

bonga, *f.* a Philippine palm. Also ARECA.

bongo, *m.* (Am.) a large, rough canoe or boat.

bonhomía, *f.* honesty; naïveté, simplicity, ingenuousness.

boniato, buniato, *m.* sweet potato.

bonicamente, *adv.* prettily, neatly, slyly.

bonico, ca, *a. dim.* fairly good.

bonificación, *f.* allowance, discount; bonus.

bonificar, *va.* (*pret.* BONIFIQUÉ; *subj.* BONIFIQUE) to credit; to improve.

bonina, *f.* (bot.) oxeye chamomile.

bonísimo, ma, *a. super.* of BUENO: very good.

bonítalo, *m.* (ichth.) = ¹BONITO.

bonitamente, *adv.* prettily, neatly.

bonitillo, illa, *a. dim.* somewhat pretty.

¹bonito, *m.* (ichth.) striped tunny.

²bonito, ta, *a.* pretty.

bonizal, *m.* cornfield.

bonizo, *m.* corn grown wild in Asturias.

bono, *m.* (com.) bond; certificate; duebill.

bonote, *m.* cocoanut fiber; (naut.) coir.

bonzo, *m.* bonze, a priest of Buddha.

boñiga, *f.* cow dung; castings.

boñigar, *a.* app. to a kind of round white fig.

Bootes, *m.* Bootes, a northern constellation.

boqueada, *f.* gasp, gasping.

boquear. I. *vn.* to gape to gasp; to breathe one's last; to end, terminate. **II.** *va.* to pronounce; to utter.

boquera, *f.* sluice in an irrigation canal; door; opening; cesspool; crack in the corner of the mouth; (vet.) ulcer in the mouth.—**boquerón,** *m.* wide opening, large hole; (ichth.) anchovy.

boquete, *m.* gap, narrow entrance.

boquiabierto, ta, *a.* open-mouthed; gaping.

boquiancho, cha, *a.* wide-mouthed.

boquiangosto, ta, *a.* narrow-mouthed.

boquiconejuno, na, *a.* rabbit-mouthed; (of horses) hare-lipped.

boquiduro, ra, *a.* (of horses, etc.) hard-mouthed.

boquifresco, ca, *a.* (of horses) tender-mouthed; frank, outspoken (esp. in disagreeable utterances).

boquifruncido, da, *a.* (of horses) puckermouthed.

boquihendido, da, *a.* (esp. of horses) largemouthed.

boquihundido, da, *a.* (of horses) having a sunken mouth.

boquilla, *f. dim.* little mouth; opening of bottom of trouser leg; opening in an irrigation canal; chisel for mortising; mouthpiece of a wind instrument; cigar- or cigarette-holder; (mason.) verge, course; (mech.) nozzle; bushing, bush; gas burner; mouth of a scabbard.

boquimuelle, *a.* (of horses) sensitive-mouthed; unwary, easily imposed upon.

boquín, *m.* a kind of coarse baize.
boquinatural, *a.* (of horses) with a normally sensitive mouth.
boquinegro, gra. I. *a.* (of animals) black-mouthed. **II.** *m.* or *f.* a blackish snail.
boquirrasgado, da, *a.* deep-mouthed.
boquirroto, ta, *a.* loquacious, garrulous.
boquirrubio, bia, *a.* blabbing; simple, artless.
boquiseco, ca, *a.* dry-mouthed.
boquisumido, da, *a.* = BOQUIHUNDIDO.
boquita, *f. dim.* small or little mouth.
boquitorcido; da; boquituerto, ta, *a.* wry-mouthed, having a crooked mouth.
boquiverde, *a.* plain-spoken about off-color matters.
borácico, ca, *a.* boracic.
boracita, *f.* (min.) boracite.
borato, *m.* borate.
bórax, *m.* borax. Also ²BORRA, BORRAJ.
borbollar, *vn.* to bubble out, gush out.
borbollón, borbotón, *m.* bubbling, gushing up of water; flash.—**a borbollones,** impetuously.
borbollonear, *vn* = BORBOLLAR.
borbónico, ca, *a.* pertaining to the Bourbons.
borbonismo, *m.* Bourbonism.
borborigmo, *m.* rumbling in the bowels.
borbotar, *vn.* to gush out; to boil over.
borbotón, *m.* = BORBOLLÓN.—**a borbotones = a borbollones.—hablar a borbotones,** to speak in torrents.
borceguí, *m.* buskin, half-boot; lace shoe.
borceguinería, *f.* lace-shoe factory or shop.
borceguinero, ra, *n.* lace-shoe maker or retailer.
borcellar, *m.* brim of a vessel.
¹borda, *f.* hut, cottage.
²borda, *f.* (naut.) gunwale.
bordada, *f.* (naut.) tack; pacing to and fro.—**dar una b.,** or, **dar bordadas,** (naut.) to tack; to promenade.
bordadillo, *m.* double-flowered taffeta.
bordado, *m.* embroidery; embroidering.
bordador, ra, *n.* embroiderer.
bordadura, *f.* embroidery; (her.) border of an escutcheon.
bordaje, *m.* (naut.) side planks of a ship.
bordar, *va.* to embroider; to perform prettily and artistically.—**b. a tambor,** to tambour.
¹borde, *m.* border, edge, verge, fringe, ledge; hem of a garment; brim of a vessel; (naut.) board, the side of a ship.—**b. de ataque,** (aer.) leading edge.—**b. de salida,** (aer.) trailing edge.—**a b.,** on the brink; on the eve.
²borde, *a.* (of plants, trees) wild, uncultivated; (of persons) bastard.
bordear, *vn.* (naut.) to ply to windward.
bordelés, sa, *a.* of or from Bordeaux.
bordo, *m.* board, the side of a ship; border, outer edge; tack.—**a b.,** on board, aboard.—**al b.,** alongside the ship.—**dar bordos,** (naut.) to tack.—**de alto b.,** (of ships) sea-going, major; (fig.) of importance, of heavy caliber, first rank; (of persons) high-up.
bordón, *m.* Jacob's staff, pilgrim's staff; bass-string; bass of an organ, iteration of words· refrain, burden of a song; staff, guide, or support of another.—*pl.* (naut.) shores, outriggers.
bordoncico, illo, *m. dim.* small staff.
bordoneado, da, *a.* (her.) pommelled.
bordonear. I. *vn.* to try the ground with a stick; to rove about. **II.** *va.* to beat, cudgel.
bordonería, *f.* wandering idly about, on pretense of religious pilgrimage.
bordonero, ra, *n.* vagabond, roamer, tramp.
bordura, *f.* (her.) = BORDADURA.
boreal, *a.* boreal, northern.
bóreas, *m.* Boreas, the north wind.
borgoña, *m.* Burgundy wine.
borgoñón, na, *a.* of or from Burgundy.—**a la borgoñona,** in Burgundy fashion.

borgoñota, *f.* a sort of ancient helmet.—**a la b.,** in the Burgundy fashion.
bórico, ca, *a.* boric.
borinqueño, ña, *n. & a.* Porto-Rican.
borla, *f.* tassel, tuft, lock, flaunt; in universities, doctor's hood; doctorship.—**tomar la b.,** to graduate.
borlica, illa, ita, *f. dim.* small tassel.
borlilla, *f.* (bot.) anther.
borlón, *m. aug.* large tassel; napped stuff, made of thread and cotton yarn.
¹borne, *m.* end of a lance; (elec.) binding post, binding screw; terminal.
²borne, *m.* (bot.) cytissus.
borneadero, *m.* (naut.) berth of a ship at anchor; swinging berth.
borneadizo, za, *a.* pliant, easily warped.
bornear. I. *va.* to bend, turn, twist; (arch.) to model and cut (pillars); to hoist and place (building stones, etc.). **II.** *vn.* (naut.) to swing around the anchor. **III.** *vr.* to warp, bulge.
borneo, *m.* turning or winding; swinging motion in dancing; (naut.) swinging round the anchor.
borneol, *m.* (chem.) borneol.
bornera, *f.* blackish millstone.
bornero, ra, *a.* ground by a BORNERA.
borní, *m.* (ornith.) lanner, a kind of falcon.
boro, *m.* (chem.) boron.
borona, *f.* Indian corn; cornbread; crumb.
boronía, *f.* eggplant and tomato dish.
¹borra, *f.* yearling ewe; thick wool; goat's hair; nap; floss, burl; tax on sheep; lees, sediment, waste, idle talk.—**b. de lana,** flock wool.—**b. de seda,** floss silk.
²borra, *f.* borax.
borracha, *f.* (coll.) a leather bottle for wine.
borrachear, *vn.* to get intoxicated often.
borrachera, borrachería, *f.* drunkenness; carousal, drunken feast, orgy; drunken condition, (coll.) drunk; (fig.) madness, great folly.
borrachero, *m.* a South American shrub, whose seed, when eaten, causes delirium.
borrachez, *f.* intoxication; perturbation of the judgment or reason.
borrachín, *m.* drunkard.
borracho, cha. I. *n.* drunkard. **II.** *a.* habitually drunk; violet-colored.—**borrachón, borrachonazo,** *m. aug.* great drunkard, toper.
borrachuela, *f.* (bot.) bearded darnel.
borrachuelo, la, *n. dim.* tippler.
borrador, *m.* rough draft; (com., etc.) record book.
borradura, *f.* erasure, scratching out.
borragíneo. I. *a.* (bot.) boraginaceous. **II.** *f. pl.* Boraginaceæ.
borraj, *m.* borax.
borraja, *f.* (bot.) borage.
borrajear, *vn.* to scribble, scrawl.
borrajo, *m.* = RESCOLDO, embers, hot ashes.
borrar, *va.* to cross out; to efface, erase, rub out, obliterate; (fig.) to cloud, darken, obscure.
borrasca, *f.* storm, tempest, squall; (Mex.) (min.) barren rock; (fig.) hazard, danger; obstruction.—**b. deshecha,** violent tempest.
borrascoso, sa, *a.* stormy, tempestuous.
borrasquero, ra, *n. & a.* reveller(-ing).
borregada, *f.* large flock of sheep or lambs.
borrego, ga, *n.* lamb not yet a year old; (fig.) simpleton.—**borreguero,** *m.* shepherd who tends lambs.—**borreguito,** *m. dim.* little lamb.
borrén, *m.* saddle-tree.
borrica, *f.* female donkey; ignorant woman.
borricada, *f.* drove of donkeys; cavalcade on donkeys; asinine word or action.
borrico, *m.* ass, donkey; (carp.) sawhorse.
borricón, borricote, *m. aug.* large jackass; plodder, laborious man; sawyer's horse.
borrilla, *f.* downy matter enveloping fruits.
borriqueño, ña, *a.* asinine.
borriquero, *m.* one who keeps or tends donkeys.

For pronunciation, see the rules at the beginning of the book.

borriquete, *m.* (carp.) sawhorse.—**b. de proa,** (naut.) fore-topmast.

borriquillo, illa, ito, ita, *n. dim.* little donkey.

borriquillos, *m. pl.* crossbars of a table frame.

borro, *m.* male lamb not two years old; (coll.) dolt; duty on sheep.

borrón, *m.* blot; blur; rough draft; blemish, stigma, stain.—**borroncillo,** *m. dim.* small blot or stain.—**borronear,** *va.* to sketch; to waste (paper) by scribbling on it.

borroso, sa, *a.* full of dregs, thick, muddy; blurred, faded.

borrufalla, *f.* empty sounds or words.

borrumbada, *f.* boast; extravagant expense.

boruca, *f.* noise, hubbub, uproar

borujo, *m.* pack, bundle; refuse of olive pits; oil cake.—**borujón,** *m.* = BURUJÓN, lump; badly wrapped parcel.

borusca, *f.* withered leaf. Also SEROJA.

boscaje, *m.* cluster of trees, grove; (art) boscage, landscape.

Bósforo, *m.* Bosporus.

bosnio, nia, *n. & a.* Bosnian.

bosque, *m.* wood, forest; grove.

bosquecillo, *m. dim.* small wood, coppice.

bosquejar, *va.* to sketch, outline; to plan, design; to explain vaguely; to make a rough model of.

bosquejo, *m.* sketch; any unfinished work, writing or composition.—**en b.,** unfinished.

bosquete, *m.* wood; forest; artificial forest.

bosta, *f.* dung, manure.

bostecé, bostece, *v. V.* BOSTEZAR.

bostezante, *a.* gaping, yawning.

bostezar, *vn.* (*pret.* BOSTECÉ; *subj.* BOSTECE) to yawn, gape.—**bostezo,** *m.* yawn, yawning.

bota, *f.* boot; small leather wine bag; butt or pipe for liquids; liquid measure equal to about 125 gallons; (naut.) water cask.—**b. de montar,** riding boot.—**ponerse las botas,** to become rich or prosperous, (fig.) strike oil.

botado, da. I. *pp.* of BOTAR. **II.** *a.* (Am.) cheap, inexpensive; (Am.) (of person) lying down.

botador, *m.* thrower, pitcher; punch; instrument for pulling out nails; nail set; dentist's crow's bill or pelican; (naut.) starting pole, boat hook; (mech.) furnace bar, fire iron; bolt driver; (med.) refractor.

botafuego, *m.* (artil.) linstock, match staff; irritable, quick-tempered person.

botagueña, *f.* pig-haslets sausage.

botalón, *m.* (naut.) boom (of a crane or derrick). —**b. del foque,** jib-boom.

botamen, *m.* (naut.) collection of water casks on board a ship; collection of pots and jars in a drug store.

botana, *f.* plug; plaster on a wound; scar.

botánica, *f.* botany.

botánico, ca. I. *a.* botanical. **II.** *n.* botanist.

botanista, *n.* botanist.

botanomancia, *f.* divination by herbs.

botantes, *m. pl.* (naut.) shores, outriggers.

botar. I. *va.* to cast, pitch, throw, fling; (Am.) to throw out (of a job), "fire"; (Am.) to squander, misspend; to throw away; (naut.) to shift (the helm).—**b. al agua,** (naut.) to launch. **II.** *vn.* to bound; rebound. **III.** *vn. & vr.* (of unbroken horse) to jump and kick, caper. *vr.* (Cuba) to carry to excess, overdo (something).

botaratada, *f.* rash, thoughtless action.

botarate, *m.* (coll.) madcap, thoughtless, blustering person; (Am.) spendthrift.

botarel, *m.* (arch.) buttress, abutment, spur, counter pillar.

botarga, *f.* loose breeches, galligaskins; motley dress; harlequin, buffoon; a kind of large sausage; DOMINGUILLO, tumbler (toy).

botasilla, *f.* (mil.) bugle signal for the cavalry to saddle.

botavante, *m.* (naut.) boarding pike.

botavara, *f.* (naut.) small boom or pole, gaff,

sprit; boat hook.—**b. de cangreja,** gaffsail boom.

¹bote, *m.* thrust with a weapon; rebound; frolicsome bound of a horse; chuck-farthing (boys' game).—**de b. y voleo,** instantly.

²bote, *m.* druggist's pot for medicine; can or jar.— **b. de tabaco,** snuff canister.

³bote, *m.* boat.—**b. de lastre,** ballast lighter.— **b. de salvamento,** (aer.) crash boat.—**b. salvavidas,** lifeboat.

⁴bote, *m.*—**de b. en b.,** crowded, jammed.

botella, *f.* bottle.—**b. de Leiden,** Leyden jar.

botellazo, *m.* blow with a bottle.

botellería, *f.* bottle factory; (Am.) BOTILLERÍA.

botellón, *m.* demijohn.

botequín, *m.* (naut.) cog, scull.

botería, *f.* (naut.) collection of casks of wine.

¹botero, *m.* maker of wine bags and bottles.

²botero, ra, *n.* boatman, ferryman (-woman).

botica, *f.* apothecary's shop, drug store; medicines; (Arg.) shop, store.—**de todo, como en b.,** everything under the sun.

boticaria, *f.* apothecary's wife.

boticario, ria, *n.* apothecary.

botiga, *f.* (prov.) shop.—**botiguero,** *m.* shopkeeper.—**botiguilla,** *f. dim.* of BOTIGA.

botija, *f.* earthen round, short-necked jug; fat person.—**botijero,** *m.* one who makes or sells jars.—**botijilla, juela,** *f. dim.* small jar.

botijo, *m.* round earthen jar with a spout and handle; plump child.

botijón, *m. aug.* large earthen jar; fat child.

botilla, *f. dim.* small wine bag; woman's shoe.

botiller, *m.* = BOTILLERO.

botillería, *f.* ice-cream parlor; (naut.) steward's room and stores.

botillero, ra, *n.* one who prepares or sells ice cream and refreshments.

botillo, *m. dim.* small leather wine bag.

¹botín, *m.* buskin, half-boot; high shoe; leggings.

²botín, *m.* booty, spoils of war.

botina, *f.* modern gaiter; a woman's boot.

botinería, *f.* shoe shop or factory.

¹botinero, ra. I. *a.* (of cattle) black-foot. **II.** *n.* shoemaker.

²botinero, *m.* soldier who took care of and sold the booty.

botinico, illo, ito, *m. dim.* little gaiter.

botiquín, *m.* medicine chest.

botito, *m.* man's gaiter with elastics or buttons.

botivoleo, *m.* recovering a ball on the rebound.

boto, ta. I. *a.* blunt; dull of understanding. **II.** *m.* wine skin; large gut filled with butter.

botón, *m.* button; sprout, bud; (fencing) tip of a foil; knob (of door or window); bead (in assaying); annulet of balusters, and of keys; piece of wood which fastens a fowling net; crankpin; dowel; handle.—**b. de fuego,** cautery in the form of a button.—**b. de oro,** (bot.) creeping double-flowered crowfoot.

botonadura, *f.* set of buttons.

botonazo, *m.* (fencing) thrust with a foil.

botoncito, *m. dim.* small button.

botonería, *f.* button maker's shop.

botonero, ra, *n.* button maker; button seller.

botones, *m. sing.* (*pl.* of BOTÓN) bellboy.

bototo, *m.* (Am.) gourd or calabash for water.

botuto, *m.* stem of the papaw fruit; war trumpet of the Orinoco Indians.

bou, *m.* joint casting of a fish net by two boats.

bovaje, bovático, *m.* ancient duty on cattle.

bóveda, *f.* arch; vault; cave, cavern; vault for the dead.—**b. celeste,** firmament.—**b. craneal,** cranial cavity.—**b. palatina,** (anat.) palate.

bovedilla, *f.* (arch.) small vault, cove.—*pl.* (naut.) counters.

bóvido, da. I. *a.* (zool.) bovine. **II.** *m. pl.* Bovidæ.

bovino, na, *a.* bovine.

For pronunciation, see the rules at the beginning of the book.

BOX 79 BRA

box, *m.* (bot.) = BOJ, box tree.
boxeador, ra, *n.* (sports) boxer.
boxear, *vn.* to box.—**boxeo,** *m.* boxing.
bóxer, *m.* Boxer,member of Chinese Boxer Assn.
boya, *f.* (naut.) beacon; buoy; net float.
boyada, *f.* drove of oxen.
boyal, *a.* pertaining to cattle.
boyante. I. *a.* buoyant, floating. **II.** *a.* (naut.) light, sailing well; prosperous, successful.
boyar, *vn.* (naut.) to buoy; to float.
boyazo, *m.* *aug.* large ox.
boycot, etc. = BOICOT, etc., boycott.
boyera, boyeriza, *f.* ox stall, cow house.
boyero, boyerizo, *m.* ox driver; cowherd.
boyezuelo, *m.* *dim.* young or small ox.
boyuno, na, *a.* bovine.
boza, *f.* (naut.) rope with one end fast in a bolt ring.—**bozas,** (naut.) stoppers.
bozal. I. *m.* muzzle (for dogs, etc.); bells on a harness. **II.** *a.* (of Negroes) pure, unmixed; (of Negroes) newly immigrating; novice, inexperienced, greenhorn; stupid, foolish; wild, not broken in, untamed.
bozalejo, *m.* small muzzle.
bozo, *m.* down that precedes the beard; mustache; mouth around the lips; headstall of a horse.
brabante, *m.* Brabant or Flemish linen.
brabantés, brabanzón, *n.* & *a.* Brabantine.
braceada, *f.* violent stretching out of the arms.
¹braceaje, *m.* coinage; beating metal for coining.
²braceaje, *m.* (naut.) bracing of yards; depth of water.
¹bracear, *vn.* to move or swing the arms.
²bracear, *va.* (naut.) to brace; to fathom; (foundry) to tap (a furnace).
braceo, *m.* repeated swinging of the arms.
bracero. I. *m.* one who offers his arm to a lady; day laborer; strong-armed man.—**de b.,** arm in arm. **II.** *a.* (weapon) thrown with the hand.
bracete.—**de b.,** arm in arm.
bracillo, *m.* *dim.* branch of the bit of a horse's bridle; little arm
bracmán, *m.* Brahman; Brahmin.
bracmánico, ca, *a.* Brahmanic.
braco, ca, *a.* pug-nosed.
bráctea, *f.* (bot.) bract.
bractéola, *f.* (bot.) bractlet.
bradipepsia, *f.* bradypepsia, slow digestion.
bradiuria, (med.) (Am.) difficulty in urinating.
brafonera, *f.* brassart, armor for the arm.
braga, *f.* breeches, knickerbockers; child's diaper; hoisting rope; (mil.) breeching, lashing rope.
bragada, *f.* flat of the thigh in animals.
bragado, da, *a.* with flanks of different color from the rest of the body; (fig.) ill-disposed, of depraved sentiments; energetic, firm.
bragadura, *f.* crotch (of the body, of trousers, etc.); flat of the thigh in beasts.
bragazas, *m.* & *a.* (coll.) (man) easily ruled or henpecked.
braguero, *m.* truss, bandage for a rupture, brace; (Peru) martingale.—**b. de cañón,** (artil.) breeching of a gun.
bragueta, *f.* fly (of trousers).
braguetero. I. *m.* (low) lecher. **II.** *a.* lecherous.
braguillas, *f.* *pl.* *dim.* little breeches; child wearing his first breeches; small, ugly child.
Brahma = **Brahma,** *f.* Brahma, deity of the Hindus.
brahmán = BRACMÁN.—**brahmanismo,** *m.* Brahmanism.—**brahmín** = BRAHMÁN.
brahón, *m.* fold which, in ancient apparel, surrounded the upper part of the arm.
brama, *f.* rut, mating season.
bramadera, *f.* rattle; horn call.
bramadero, *m.* rutting place; (Am.) tethering post.
bramador, ra, *n.* & *a.* roarer(-ing).
¹bramante, *m.* packthread, hempcord, twine; Brabant linen.

²bramante, *a.* roaring.
bramar, *vn.* to roar, bellow; to storm, bluster; to rage, cry.—**bramido,** *m.* cry uttered by wild beasts, howl; roaring of the elements.
bramil, *m.* chalkline used by sawyers.
bramín, *m.* = BRACMÁN.
bran de Inglaterra, *m.* an old Spanish dance.
branca, *f.* point of a horn.—**b. ursina** (bot.) = ACANTO, thistle.
brancada, *f.* dragnet or sweep net.
brancaursina, *f.* (bot.) bear's breech.
branchas, *f.* *pl.* gills of a fish.
brandal, *m.* (naut.) backstay, ladder rope.
brandís, *m.* greatcoat formerly worn.
brandy, *m.* (Angl.) brandy.
branque, *m.* (naut.) stem.
branquia, *f.* gill of a fish.
branquiado, da, *a.* (ichth.) branchiate.
branquial, *a.* (ichth.) branchial, pert. to gills.
branquífero, ra, *a.* gill-bearing.
braña, *f.* summer pasture; brushwood.
braquial, *a.* brachial, pertaining to the arm.
braquicéfalo, la, *a.* (ethnol.) brachycephalous.
braquiópodo, da. (zool.) **I.** *n.* & *a.* brachiopod. **II.** *m.* *pl.* Brachiopodæ.
brasa, *f.* live coal; red-hot coal or wood.—**estar en brasas,** to be on pins and needles.—**estar hecho unas brasas,** to be red in the face, flushed.
braserito, *m.* *dim.* small pan to hold coals.
brasero, *m.* brazier; fire pan; place where criminals were burnt; (Mex.) hearth, fireplace.
brasil, *m.* (bot.) braziletto; brazilwood; rouge.
brasilado, da, *a.* of a red color; ruddy.
brasileño, ña, *n.* & *a.* Brazilian.
brasilero, ra, *n.* & *a.* = BRASILEÑO.
brasilete, *m.* Jamaica wood, braziletto.
brasilina, *f.* brazilin, red coloring-matter of brazilwood.
brasmología, *f.* science of the tides.
bravamente, *adv.* bravely, gallantly; cruelly, barbarously; finely, extremely well; copiously.
bravata, *f.* bravado, boast, brag.
braveador, ra, *n.* bully, hector.
bravear, *vn.* to bully, hector, menace.
bravera, *f.* vent, chimney.
braveza, *f.* bravery; vigor; ferocity; fury (esp. of sea, wind, etc.).
bravillo, illa, *a.* *dim.* rather wild, not yet tamed.
bravío, vía. I. *a.* ferocious, wild, untamed; uncultivated; coarse, unpolished. **II.** *m.* fierceness (esp. of a bull).
bravo, va, *a.* brave, manly, fearless; angry; pungent, hot; bullying, hectoring; savage, wild, fierce; severe, untractable; rude, unpolished; rough (land); sumptuous, expensive; excellent, fine.—¡**bravo!** bravo!
bravonel, *m.* brave; hector, braggart.
bravosidad, *f.* = GALLARDÍA, bravery; gallantry.
bravucón, na, *n.* & *a.* boaster(-ing), braggart.
bravura, *f.* ferocity, fierceness; courage, manliness; bravado, boast, brag.
braza, *f.* fathom (measure).
brazada, *f.* uplifting of the arms; armful.
brazado, *m.* armful.
brazaje, braceaje, *m.* (naut.) depth of water.
brazal, *m.* bracer, brassart; bracelet; irrigation ditch from a river or canal; mourning band around the arm; (naut.) rail.—**brazalete,** *m.* armlet, bracelet.—*pl.* (naut.) brace pendants.
brazazo, *m.* *aug.* large or long arm.
brazo, *m.* arm (of the body, a chair, a lever, the sea); upper half of the arm; foreleg; branch (of a tree, a chandelier); bravery, energy, enterprise. —*pl.* hands, laborers; assistance, protection, backing; protectors, backers.—**b. a b.,** hand to hand.—**b. de palanca,** lever arm.—**a b.,** by hand; swimming.—**a b. partido** = B. A B. —**con los brazos abiertos,** with open arms.— **con los brazos cruzados,** with folded arms.

—de b., arm in arm.—**hecho un b. de mar,** gorgeously attired.—**no dar el b. a torcer,** to be stubborn.—**ser el b. derecho de alguien,** to be somebody's righthand man.

brazolas, *f. pl.* (naut.) coamings of the hatchways.

brazuelo, *m. dim.* small arm; shoulder or fore thigh of beasts; branch of the bit of a bridle.

brea, *f.* pitch, tar; coarse canvas; sackcloth.

¹**brear,** *va.* to pitch, tar.

²**brear,** *va.* to vex; thwart; (fig.) to play a joke on.

brebaje, *m.* beverage, potion; (naut.) grog.

breca, *f.* (ichth.) bleak or blay; dace.

brécol, bróculi, *m.,* **brecolera,** *f.* (bot.) broccoli.

brecha, *f.* breach, opening; (fig.) impression (on the mind).—**abrir b.,** to make a breach; to create an impression; to make progress.—**batir en b.,** (fort.) to batter, breach; to persecute.

brega, *f.* struggle; scrap, fight.—**andar a la b.,** to work hard.—**dar b. (a),** to be hard or laborious.—**dar b. (a),** to play a trick or joke (on).

bregar. I. *vn.* (*pret.* BREGUÉ; *subj.* BREGUE) to contend, struggle. **II.** *va.* to roll (dough).

bren, *m.* bran. Also SALVADO.

brenca, *f.* (bot.) maidenhair; sluice post.

brenga, *f.* filament, one of the three cristated anthers of saffron.

breña, *f.,* **breñal, breñar,** *m.* craggy and brambled ground.

breñoso, sa, *a.* craggy and brambled.

breque, *m.* (ichth.) = BRECA.

bresca, *f.* honeycomb.—**brescar,** *va.* (*pret.* BRESQUÉ; *subj.* BRESQUE) to take combs from (a beehive).

bretador, *m.* call or whistle to attract birds.

bretaña, *f.* fine linen made in Brittany; (bot.) hyacinth.

¹**brete,** *m.* fetters, shackles; perplexity, difficulties.—**estar en un b.,** to be in difficulties.

²**brete,** *m.* (P. I.) a food made of betel leaves.

bretón, na. I. *n. & a.* Breton. **II.** *m.* (bot.) borecole, kale.

breva, *f.* early fruit of a fig tree; early large acorn; choice cigar, rather flat; (coll.) any valuable thing obtained easily, (coll.) snap, cinch.

breval, *m.* (bot.) early fig tree.

breve. I. *a.* brief, short, concise; (phon.) short.—**en b.,** shortly, in a little while. **II.** *m.* apostolic brief. **III.** *f.* (mus.) breve, longest note.

brevedad, *f.* briefness, conciseness.

brevemente, *adv.* briefly, concisely.

brevete, *m.* = MEMBRETE, memorandum.

breviario, *m.* breviary; abridgement, epitome; (print.) brevier, small size of type.

brevipenne, *a.* (zool.) brevipennate.

brezal, *m.* heath, place planted with heaths.

brezo, *m.* (bot.) heath, heather.

briaga, *f.* bass-weed rope.

brial, *m.* rich silken skirt.

briba, *f.* truantship, idleness.

bribar, *vn.* to lead a vagabond life.

bribia, *f.* beggar's tale of woe.—**echar la b.,** to go a-begging.

bribón, na, *n.* vagrant; impostor; knave, scoundrel, rascal.—**bribonada,** *f.* knavery, petty villainy, mischief.—**bribonazo,** *m.. aug.* great cheat, big rascal.—**briboncillo,** *m dim.* little rascal.—**bribonear,** *vn.* to loiter about; to loaf.

bribonería, *f.* life of a vagabond; rascality.

bribonzuelo, *m. dim.* little rascal.

bricho, *m.* spangle, used in embroidery.

brida, *f.* bridle; rein; horsemanship, curb, restraint, check; rail coupling; fishplate; flange; clamp, staple (watchmaking).

bridecú, *m.* sword belt.

bridón, *m.* horseman riding a bur saddle; horse accoutred with a bur saddle; small bridle; (poet.) fine horse.

brigada, *f.* brigade; group of people doing a task together; beasts of burden for an army.—

brigadero, *m.* man who tends beasts of burden in the army.

brigadier, *m.* (mil.) brigadier general; navy officer commanding a division of a fleet.

brigola, *f.* (mil.) battering ram.

Briján, *m.*—**saber más que B.,** to be very wise and cautious.

brillador, ra, *a.* sparkling, glittering.

brillante. I. *a.* brilliant, bright; shining, sparkling, glittering; glossy, lustrous; excellent, magnificent. **II.** *m.* brilliant, diamond.—**brillantemente,** *adv.* brilliantly; brightly, resplendently; splendidly.—**brillantez,** *f.* brilliance.—**brillantina,** *f.* brillantine; polishing powder (for metals).

brillar, *vn.* to shine, sparkle, glitter.

brillo, *m.* brilliance, brightness, lustre; splendor, magnificence.

brincador, ra, *n. & a.* leaper(-ing), jumper(-ing).

brincar. I. *vn.* (*pret.* BRINQUÉ; *subj.* BRINQUE) to leap, jump; to frisk, skip; to fly into a passion, become excited, (coll.) complain. **II.** *va.* to omit, skip; to throw (a child) up and down.

brinco, *m.* leap, jump; hop, bounce; small jewel worn in the hair.

brindar. I. *vn.*—**b. por,** to drink a person's health, toast. **II.** *va.* to offer, present, afford.

brindis, *m.* drinking the health of another; toast.

brinqué, brinque, *v. V.* BRINCAR.

brinquillo, brinquiño, *m.* gewgaw, small trinket; sweetmeat from Portugal.

brinza, *f.* blade, slip, sprig, shoot.

brío, *m.* vigor, enterprise, courage.

briol, *m.* (naut.) bunt line.

briolín, *m.* (naut.) slab line.

brionia, *f.* (bot.) bryony.—**brionina,** *f.* (chem.) bryonin.

briós.—¡voto a b.! *interj.* by the Almighty!

briosamente, *adv.* spiritedly, courageously, vigorously.

brioso, sa, *a.* vigorous, enterprising, courageous; lively, spirited.

¹**brisa,** *f.* breeze.

²**brisa,** *f.* residue of pressed grapes.

brisca, *f.* a card game.

briscado, da. I. *pp.* of BRISCAR. **II.** *a.* mixed with silk (app. to gold and silver twist).

briscar, *va.* to embroider with gold or silver twist.

brisera, *f.,* **brisero,** *m.* glass screen for a candle.

bristol, *m.* Bristol board, Bristol paper.

británica, *f.* (bot.) great water dock.

británico, ca, *a.* British.

britano, na., *n. & a.* Briton.

brizar, *va.* to rock (a cradle).

brizna, *f.* fragment; splinter or chip; string (of beans, etc.).

briznoso, sa, *a.* full of fragments or scraps.

brizo, *m.* cradle.

¹**broa,** *f.* (P. I.) a kind of biscuit or cracker.

²**broa,** *f.* (naut.) shallow cove.

broca, *f.* reel for twist, silk, or thread; conical drill for boring in iron; shoemaker's tack.

brocadillo, *m.* brocade of inferior quality.

brocado, da. I. *a.* embroidered like brocade. **II.** *m.* gold or silver brocade.

brocal, *m.* curbstone of a well; metal ring of the scabbard of a sword.—**b. de bota,** mouthpiece of a leathern wine bottle.

brocamantón, *m.* diamond brooch.

brocatel, *m.* stuff made of hemp and silk; whitestreaked Spanish marble.

bróculi, *m.* broccoli.

brocha, *f.* painter's or shaving brush; loaded dice.—**de b. gorda,** (art) poorly done; (painter) of doors and windows; crude, badly done or written.

brochada, *f.* stroke of the brush.

brochado, da, *a.* pertaining to brocade.

brochadura, *f.* set of hooks and eyes.

For pronunciation, see the rules at the beginning of the book.

brochazo, *m.* = BROCHADA.

broche, *m.* clasp; hook and eye; locket; fastener; hasp; brooch.—*pl.* cuff buttons.

brocheta, broqueta, *f.* (cook.) skewer.

brochón, *m. aug.* large brush; whitewash brush.

brochuela, *f. dim.* small brush.

brodio, *m.* hodge-podge (of food); mixture of hog's blood and onions for sausages.

brodista, *m.* poor student who exists on charity.

¹broma, *f.* gaiety, merriment; noisy gathering; jest, joke.—**dar b.,** or **bromas,** to jest; to tease.—**por b.,** in jest, for fun.

²broma, *f.* shipworm; teredo.

³broma, *f.* (mason.) riprap; (Am.) (fig.) oatmeal gruel.

bromado, da, *a.* worm-eaten.

bromar, *va.* (of insects) to bore.

bromato, *m.* (chem.) bromate.

bromatología, *f.* bromatology, science of foods.

bromear, *vn.* to joke, jest, make fun.

bromeliaceo, cea. I. *a.* (bot.) bromeliaceous. **II.** *f. pl.* Bromeliaceæ.

bromhidrato, *m.* (chem.) hydrobromide.

bromhídrico, ca, *a.* (chem.) hydrobromic.

bromhidrosis, *f.* (med.) fetid sweating.

brómico, ca, *a.* (chem.) bromic.

bromista, *n.,* merry person; practical joker.

¹bromo, *m.* (chem.) bromine.

²bromo, *m.* (bot.) brome grass.

bromurado, da, *a.* containing bromine; bromine (as *a.,* as in *agua bromurada,* bromine water).

bromuro, *m.* (chem.) bromide.

bronca, *f.* practical joke; wrangle, quarrel.

broncamente, *adv.* peevishly, morosely.

bronce, *m.* bronze; brass; (poet.) trumpet, bell, or cannon.—**b. de aluminio,** aluminum bronze.—**b. de campanas,** bell metal.—**b. de cañón,** gun metal.—**b. fosforado,** phosphor bronze.

bronceado, da. I. *pp.* of BRONCEAR. **II.** *a.* bronze-colored; tanned, sunburnt. **III.** *m.* bronze-color finish(-ing).

bronceadura, *f.* = BRONCEADO, *m.*

broncear, *va.* to bronze; to adorn with brass.

broncería, *f.* collection of bronzes.

broncíneo, a, *a.* bronzelike.

broncista, *n.* worker in bronze.

bronco, ca, *a.* rough, coarse, unpolished; crusty; sturdy; morose, crabbed; rude; hard; abrupt, harsh; hoarse.

bronconeumonía, *f.* broncho-pneumonia.

broncopulmonía, *f.* bronchial pneumonia.

broncorrea, *f.* bronchorrhoea, chronic bronchitis.

broncotomía, *f.* (surg.) bronchotomy.

broncha, *f.* short poniard; jewel; whitewashing brush.

bronquedad, *f.* harshness, roughness, rudeness; brittleness.

bronquial, *a.* (anat.) bronchial.

bronquina, *f.* dispute, quarrel, scrap.

bronquio, *m.* (anat.) bronchus, bronchial tube.

bronquíolo, *m.* (anat.) bronchiol.

bronquitis, *f.* bronchitis.

broquel, *m.* shield, buckler; support, protection.—**broquelazo,** *m. aug.* blow with a shield or buckler; large shield or buckler.—**broquelero,** *m.* one who makes or wears shields or bucklers; wrangler, disputer.—**broquelete,** *m. dim.* small buckler.—**broquelillo,** *m. dim.* small shield; small earring.

broqueta, *f.* = BROCHETA, skewer.

brosquil, *m.* sheepfold, sheepcote.

brota, *f.* vine bud.

brotadura, *f.* budding.

brótano, *m.* (bot.) southernwood.

brotar. I. *vn.* to bud, germinate, put forth shoots; to gush, rush out; to issue, appear. **II.** *va.* (of the earth & fig.) to bring forth, produce.

brote, *m.* germ of vines; bud of trees; outbreak (of a disease); fragment, crumb, bit.

broto, *m.* = BROTE, bud.

brotón, *m.* large clasp; shoot, tender twig.

broza, *f.* rotten branches, leaves, etc., on the ground; weeds, underbrush; chaff, rubbish; BRUZA, (print.) brush.

brozar, bruzar, *va.* (print.) to brush (type).

brozoso, sa, *a.* full of rubbish.

brucero, *m.* brush and broom maker or seller.

bruces.—a, or **de, b.,** forward, headlong; face downward; on one's stomach.

brucita, *f.* (min.) brucite.

brugo, *m.* vine grub, plant louse.

bruja, *f.* witch, hag; owl.—**brujear,** *vn.* to practice witchcraft.—**brujería,** *f.* witchcraft, sorcery.

brujidor, *m.* glaziers' nippers. Also GRUJIDOR.

brujidura, *f.* bewitching, casting spells.

brujir, *va.* (of glaziers) to trim. Also GRUJIR.

brujo, *m.* sorcerer, conjurer, wizard.

brújula, *f.* magnetic needle; compass; sight, small hole to point a gun, peephole.

brujulear, *va.* at cards, to examine (one's cards) by slowly uncovering the tops; to discover by guess.—**brujuleo,** *m.* examining one's cards by slowly uncovering the tops; close examination; guess.

brulote, *m.* fire ship; an ancient engine of war.

bruma, *f.* mist, fog.

brumador, ra, *a.* = ABRUMADOR, overwhelming.

brumal, *a.* misty, foggy.

brumamiento, *m.* weariness, lassitude.

brumar, *va.* = ABRUMAR, to crush; to weary.

brumario, *m.* Brumaire (month in calendar of early French republic).

brumazón, *m.* thick fog or mist.

brumo, *m.* refined wax, for polishing tapers.

brumoso, sa, *a.* foggy, hazy, misty.

¹bruno, *m.* black plum; plum tree.

²bruno, na, *a.* dark brown, blackish.

bruñido, *m.* polish, burnish.

bruñidor, ra. I. *n.* & *a.* burnisher(-ing), polisher(-ing). **II.** *m.* burnisher.

bruñimiento, *m.* polishing, burnishing; polish.

bruñir, *va.* to burnish, polish; (coll.) to put on rouge.

brusca, *f.* (naut.) bevel, sweep, or rounding of masts; brushwood.

bruscamente, *adv.* rudely, harshly.

bruscate, *m.* stew made of milt and lambs' livers.

brusco, ca. I. *a.* rude, rough, crude. **II.** *m.* (bot.) kneeholly, butcher's broom; trifling remains; refuse shearings.

brusela, *f.* (bot.) lesser periwinkle.

bruselense, *a.* & *n.* (native) of Brussels.

brusquedad, *f.* rudeness; rude action or treatment.

brutal. I. *a.* brutal; brutish. **II.** *m.* animal (esp. quadruped).—**brutalidad,** *f.* brutality; brutishness; stupidity; brutal or stupid action.—**brutalizar. I.** *va.* to brutalize. **II.** *vr.* to become brutalized.—**brutalmente,** *adv.* brutally.

brutesco, ca, *a.* = GRUTESCO, grotesque.

bruteza, *f.* roughness, want of polish; brutality.

bruto, ta. I. *a.* beastly, brutish, brutal; crude (ore, oil, etc.); gross (profits, etc.); unpolished, rough.—**en b.,** in a rough state, in the rough. **II.** *m.* brute, beast; ignoramus; blockhead.

bruza, *f.* horse brush; stove brush; scrubbing brush; printer's brush.—**bruzar,** *va.* to brush, bu, *m.* bugaboo, bugbear.—**hacer el b.,** to scare, frighten.

búa, *f.* = BUBA, pustule.

buaro, buarillo, *m.* (ornith.) buzzard.

buba, *f.* pustule, small tumor.—*pl.* buboes.

búbalo, *m.* African antelope.

bubático, ca, *a.* having glandular tumors.

bubilla, *f. dim.* small pustule, pimple.

bubón, *m.* bubo.—**bubónico, ca,** *a.* bubonic.

buboso, sa, *a.* having pustules or buboes.

bucal, *a.* pertaining to the mouth; buccal.

bucanero, *m.* buccaneer.

bucaral, *m.* plantation of BÚCARES.

bucarán, *m.* buckram. Also BOCACÍ.

búcare, *m.* a South American shade tree.

bucarito, *m. dim.* small earthen vessel of fragrant earth.

búcaro, *m.* vessel made of a fragrant earth of the same name; (Colomb.) BÚCARE.

buccino, *m.* (zool.) whelk, a marine gastropod.

buceador, ra, *n.* diver.

bucear, *vn.* to dive.

bucéfalo, *m.* bucephalus; blockhead, jackass.

bucentauro, *m.* bucentaur.

buceo, *m.* diving; searching under water.

bucero, ra, *a.* (of dogs) black-nosed.

bucle, *m.* ringlet, curl, lock of hair; loop.

¹buco, *m.* opening, aperture, gap.

²buco, *m.* (zool.) buck.

¹bucólica, *f.* (coll.) food; meal.

²bucólica, *f.* bucolic, pastoral poetry.

bucólico, ca, *a.* bucolic.

buchada, *f.* mouthful. Also BOCANADA.

¹buche, *m.* craw or crop; maw; belly; (coll.) bosom; mouthful; bag, pucker in clothes.

²buche, *m.* young suckling donkey; foal.

buchete, *m.* cheek puffed with wind.

buchón, ona, *a.* of a pouter (pigeon).

budare, *m.* (Venez.) large baking pan.

búdico, ca, *a.* Buddhic, Buddhistic.

budín, *m.* (Angl.) pudding.

budión, *m.* (ichth.) peacock fish.

budismo, *m.* Buddhism.

budista, *n. & a.* Buddhist(-ic).

buega, *f.* landmark; boundary marker.

buen, *a. contr.* of **bueno,** good. Used only before a masculine substantive, as *buen hombre,* good man, and before an infinitive used as a substantive, as *el buen decir,* correct speaking.

buenaboya, *m.* volunteer galley seaman.

buenamente, *adv.* freely, spontaneously; conveniently, easily.

buenandanza, *f.* = BIENANDANZA, prosperity.

buenaventura, *f.* fortune, good luck; fortune (as told by a fortune teller).

bueno [**buen** (*v.* BUEN)], **na. I.** *a.* good; kind; suited, fit; appropriate; well, in good health (*estoy bueno,* I am well); in good condition; great; high (excitement, fever, etc.); advisable, desirable; strange (often with *lo* in the expression **lo bueno es,** the strange thing is); simple, too good, (coll.) easy, soft.—**¡buena es ésa!** (coll.) that's strange; that is a pretty how-de-do, a pretty fix.—**bueno está lo bueno,** let good enough alone.—**buenas noches,** good night.—**buenas tardes,** good afternoon.—**buenos días,** good day, good morning.—**a buenas,** willingly, without compulsion.—**¿a dónde bueno?** where are you going?—**de buenas,** in good luck, lucky.—**de buenas a primeras,** all of a sudden, without warning. —**¿de dónde bueno?** where do you come from?—**por buenas, por las buenas** = A BUENAS. **II.** *adv.* well, very well, all right; that is enough.

buenparecer, *m.* good looks or appearance.

buera, *f.* pustule or pimple in the mouth.

buey, *m.* ox, bullock.—**b. de caza,** stalking ox.— **b. marino,** sea calf.—**bueyazo,** *m. aug.* big ox.—**bueyecillo, -zuelo,** *m. dim.* little ox.— **bueyuno, na,** *a.* bovine; oxlike.

bufado, da. I. *pp.* of BUFAR. **II.** *a.* blown (app. to glass drops blown very thin).

bufalino, na, *a.* pertaining to buffaloes.

búfalo, *m.* buffalo.

bufanda, *f.* muffler (for the neck); scarf.

bufar, *vn.* to puff and blow with anger; to snort.

bufete, *m.* desk or writing table; lawyer's office or clientele; bureau; sideboard.

bufetillo, *m. dim.* small desk or writing table.

bufido, *m.* bellow, roar, snort.

bufo, fa, *a. & n.* comic (singer).

¹bufón, *m.* peddler, street vender.

²bufón, na. I. *a.* funny, comical. **II.** *m.* buffoon, merry andrew; fool, clown, jester.—**bufonada,** *f.* buffoonery, jest.—**bufonazo,** *m. aug.* great buffoon.—**bufoncillo,** *m. dim.* little merry andrew.—**bufonearse,** *vr.* to jest.—**bufonería,** *f.* = BUFONADA.

bugada, *f.* = BOGADA, space covered by one stroke of the oars.

bugalla, *f.* gallnut growing on oak leaves.

buglosa, *f.* (bot.) alkanet; bugloss.

buharda, *f.* dormer window, skylight; garret.

buhardilla, *f.* garret; skylight.

buharro, *m.* (ornith.) eagle owl.

buhedera, *f.* embrasure, loophole.

buhedo, *m.* temporarily dried-out marsh.

buhero, *ra, n.* owl keeper.

buhío, *m.* = BOHÍO, Indian hut, hovel, cabin.

buho, *m.* (ornith.) owl; (fig.) unsociable person.

buhonería, *f.* peddler's box; peddlery.

buhonero, *m.* peddler, hawker.

buir, *va.* to polish, burnish.

buitre, *m.* vulture.—**buitrera,** *f.* place to catch vultures.—**buitrero, ra. I.** *a.* vulturine. **II.** *m.* vulture fowler.

buitrón, *m.* osier basket to catch fish; partridge net; furnace where silver ores are smelted; snare for game.

buja, *f.* chuck (in watchmaking).

bujarasol, *m.* fig with reddish pulp.

buje, *m.* axle box, bush box; pillow of a shaft.

bujeda, *f.,* **bujedal, bujedo,** *m.* = BOJEDAL, plantation of box trees.

bujería, *f.* gewgaw, bauble, toy, knickknack.

bujeta, *f.* boxwood box; perfume box; case for smelling bottle.

bujía, *f.* candle; candlestick; (physics) candle, candlepower; (int. combust. eng.) spark plug (called also **b. del encendido**); (surg.) solid probe.—**b. normal,** standard candle.

bujiería, *f.* office where wax candles are kept.

bula, *f.* papal bull.

bulario, *m.* collection of papal bulls.

bulbo, *m.* (bot.) bulb.—**bulboso, sa,** *a.* bulbous.

buleto, *m.* brief granted by the Pope or by his legate.

bulevar, *m.* (Gal.) boulevard.

búlgaro, ra, *n. & a.* Bulgarian.

bulí, burí, *m.* (P. I.) a palm tree.

bulimia, *f.* (med.) bulimia, excessive appetite.

bultito, *m. dim.* little lump; small bundle.

bulto, *m.* bulk, anything which appears bulky; form, object not clearly discerned; protuberance; tumor, swelling; massiness; bust; bundle, parcel, package; pillowcase.—**a b.,** wholesale; as a whole; broadly.—**de b.,** obvious, manifest, striking.—**escurrir, huir,** or **sacar, el b.,** to sneak out.

bululú, *m.* strolling player (actor).

bulla, *f.* noise, bustle, fuss; noisy stir, crowd, mob.—**armar b.,** to make a racket.—**bullaje,** *m.* noisy crowd.—**bullanga,** *f.* tumult, riot.— **bullanguero, ra,** *n.* rioter, turbulent person.

bullar, *va.* to mark (goods) with a seal.

bullebulle, *m.* busybody, bustler, hustler.

bullicio, *m.* bustle, noise, uproar; sedition; heat.

bulliciosamente, *adv.* noisily.

bullicioso, sa, noisy; lively, merry; (of the sea) turbulent, boisterous.

bullidor, ra, *a.* = BULLICIOSO.

bullir. I. *vn.* to boil, bubble up; to move about, bustle, hustle. **II.** *va.* to move, stir.

¹bullón, *m.* dye bubbling up in a boiler.

²bullón, *m.* metallic ornament for large books; puff (in sewing).

bumerang, *m.* boomerang.

bunde, *m.* (Am.) a Negro dance; rough, low dance.

buneto, *m.* (ornith.) hedge sparrow.

For pronunciation, see the rules at the beginning of the book.

bungo, *m.* a Nicaraguan flatboat.
buniato, *m.* = BONIATO, sweet potato.
bunio, *m.* sort of earthnut or pignut.
buñolada, *f.* platter of buns or waffles; botch work.
buñolería, *f.* bun shop.
buñolero, ra, *n.* maker or seller of crullers or waffles.
buñuelo, *m.* fritter, bun, cruller; anything poorly done or spoiled; failure.
buque, *m.* vessel, ship; steamer; bulk, capacity (of a ship); hull (of ship).—**b. de guerra,** man-of-war.—**b. de torres,** turreted man-of-war.—**b. de vapor,** steamer.—**b. de vela,** sailing vessel.—**b. mercante,** merchant vessel.
burato, *m.* Canton crêpe; cypress (fabric); transparent veil of light silk.
burba, *f.* an African coin of small value.
burbuja, *f.* bubble.
burbujear, *vn.* to bubble.—**burbujeo,** *m.* bubbling.
burchaca, *f.* = BURJACA.
burche, *m.* tower.
burda, *f.* (naut.) backstay.
burdégano, *m.* hinny, mule.
burdel. I. *m.* brothel. **II.** *a.* libidinous.
burdinalla, *f.* (naut.) sprit-topsail stay.
burdo, da, *a.* coarse; common, ordinary.
burel, *m.* (her.) bar, the ninth part of a shield; (naut.) marlinespike.
bureles, *m. pl.* (naut.) pointed wooden rollers.
burengue, *m.* mulatto slave.
bureo, *m.* court of justice; entertainment, amusement, diversion, spree.
bureta, *f.* (chem.) burette, a glass tube.
burga, *f.* spa, hot springs.
burgalés, *m.* native of Burgos.
burgués, sa, *a.* bourgeois (*f.* bourgeoise).
burguesía, *f.* bourgeoisie.
buri, *m.* (bot.) buri, talipot palm.
buriel. I. *a.* reddish, dark red. **II.** *m.* kersey, coarse cloth; ropewalk.
buril, *m.* burin, engraver's chisel; graver.
burilada, *f.* line or stroke of a burin; silver taken by an assayer for testing.
buriladura, *f.* engraving with a burin.
burilar, *va.* to engrave with a graver.
burjaca, *f.* pilgrim's leather bag.
burla, *f.* scoff, flout, mockery, sneer; jest, fun, trick; jeer, gibe; hoax, deceit, cheat.—**b. burlando,** in an easy way, without effort.—**b. pesada,** biting jest.—**burlas aparte,** joking aside.—**de burlas,** in jest.—**hacer b.,** to make fun of, or a fool of.
burladero, *m.* refuge or covert in a bull ring.
burlador, ra. I. *n.* wag, jester, scoffer, practical joker; seducer. **II.** *m.* seducer, Don Juan; conjurer's cup.
burlar. I. *va.* to ridicule, mock, scoff; to abuse; to deceive, frustrate, disappoint, evade. **II.** *vr.* (de) to mock, laugh (at), make fun (of); to gibe, banter.
burlería, *f.* fun, mockery, scoffing; drolling; fish story, yarn, fairy tale; deceit, illusion; derision, banter, ridicule.
burlescamente, *adv.* comically, ludicrously.
burlesco, ca, *a.* burlesque, ludicrous, comical.
burleta, *f. dim.* little trick, fun, or joke.
burlete, *m.* weather strip.
burlón, na, *n. & a.* banterer(-ing), jester(-ing), scoffer(-ing).
buro, *m.* (prov.) chalk, marl.
buró, *m.* bureau; writing desk.
burocracia, *f.* bureaucracy.
burocrático, ca, *a.* bureaucratic.
burra, *f.* female donkey; ignorant, unrefined woman; industrious, strong woman.
burrada, *f.* drove of donkeys; stupid or foolish action or expression; play contrary to rule in the game of BURRO.

burrajo, *m.* dry stable dung for fuel.
burrazo, za, *n. aug.* big donkey.
burrero, *m.* ass keeper who sells asses' milk.
burrillo, *m.* (coll.) = AÑALEJO, church almanac.
burrito, ta, *n. dim.* little donkey.
burro, *m.* ass, donkey; sawyer's jack or horse; wheel of a reel; a game at cards; windlass.—**burros de la mesana,** (naut.) mizzen-bowlines.
burrumbada, *f.* = BARRUMBADA, extravagant outlay of money; boast.
bursátil, *a.* (com.) pert. to the stock exchange.
burujo, *m.* lump of pressed wool or other matter; parcel, package; bagasse.
burujón, *m.* lump, badly made parcel.
burujoncillo, *m. dim.* little lump or bundle.
bus, *m.* motorbus, bus.
busaca, *f.* (Am.) pocket (of a pool table); bag.
busardas, *f. pl.* (naut.) breasthooks, compass timbers.
busca, *f.* search, research; pursuit; terrier; hunting party.—*pl.* (Mex.) perquisites.
buscada, *f.* search, research.
buscador, ra. I. *n. & a.* searcher(-ing), investigator(-ing). **II.** *m.* finder (optical appliance).
buscaniguas, *m.* (Am.) (coll.) = BUSCAPIÉS.
buscapié, *m.* hint.
buscapiés, *m. sing.* squib cracker; serpent firecracker.
buscapleitos, *n.* (Am.) quarrelsome person, trouble maker.
buscar. I. *va.* (*pret.* BUSQUÉ; *subj.* BUSQUE) to seek, look for.—**b. tres pies al gato,** to pick a quarrel. **II.** *vr.* to bring upon oneself.
buscarruidos, *n.* (coll.) quarrelsome person.
buscavidas, *n.* busybody, gossip monger; hustler; thrifty person.
busco, *m.* base of a sluice gate.
buscón, na, *n. & a.* searcher(-ing); cheat; pilferer(-ing), filcher(-ing).
busilis, *m.* (coll.) difficulty, difficult point.—**dar en el b.,** to hit the bull's eye.
busqué, busque, *v. V.* BUSCAR.
búsqueda, *f.* search.
busto, *m.* bust (statue); torso.
bustrófedon, *m.* boustrophedon, writing lines alternately from left to right and right to left.
butaca, *f.* armchair; easy-chair; orchestra seat in a theater.
butifarra, *f.* a sort of sausage made in Catalonia; (fig.) wide or badly fitting stockings or trousers; (Peru) ham sandwich.—**butifarrero, ra,** *n.* maker and seller of BUTIFARRAS.
butilo, *m.* (chem.) butyl.
butiondo, a. *a.* fetid; goatish; lustful.
butírico, ca, *a.* (chem.) butyric.
butirilo, *m.* butyryl.
butirina, *f.* butyrin.
butirómetro, *m.* (chem.) butyrometer.
butomeo, a. I. *a.* (bot.) butomaceous. **II.** *f. pl.* Butomaceæ.
butrino, butrón, *m.* fowling net.
butuco, ca, *a.* (Hond.) thick, stumpy.
buyador, *m.* brazier.
buyo, *m.* (P. I.) chewing paste of bonga fruit and leaves, and lime.
buz, *m.* kiss of respect and reverent regard.—**hacer b.,** to do homage or pay respect.
buzamiento, *m.* (geol.) dip of a stratum.
búzano, *m.* diver; a kind of culverin.
buzar, *va.* (geol.) to dip downward.
buzardas, *f. pl.* (naut.) breasthooks, forehooks.
buzcorona, *f.* blow on the head in fun while kissing the hand.
buzo, *m.* diver; a kind of ancient ship.
buzón, *m.* conduit, canal; letter drop, letter box, drop box; lid, cover; hook to take off the lids of melting pots; sluice of a mill.
buzonera, *f.* drain or gutter in a courtyard.

C

ca, *conj.* (obs.) because, for.

¡ca! *interj.* oh, no! no, indeed! Also ¡QUIÁ!

cabal, *a.* just, exact; perfect, complete, thorough; full; faultless, consummate.—**por sus cabales,** exactly, perfectly, according to rule and order.

cábala, *f.* cabala, superstitious divination; secret science of Hebrew rabbis; cabal, intrigue, plot.

cabalgada, *f.* cavalcade; booty.

cabalgadero, *m.* mounting block.

cabalgador, ra. I. *n.* rider, horseman(-woman). II. *m.* horse block.

cabalgadura, *f.* beast of burden; riding horse or mule; stirrup strap.

cabalgar. I. *vn.* (*pret.* CABALGUÉ; *subj.* CABALGUE) to ride on horseback; to parade on horseback; to go in a cavalcade. II. *va.* (of a horse) to cover (a mare); to ride.

cabalgata, *f.* cavalcade.

cabalgué, cabalgue, *v.* V. CABALGAR.

cabalhuste, *m.* ancient saddle with high semicircular pommel and cantle.

cabalista, *m.* cabalist.

cabalístico, ca, *a.* cabalistic.

cabalmente, *adv.* exactly, completely, perfectly, fully, precisely.

caballa, *f.* horse mackerel.

caballaje, *m.* place where mares and she-asses are served by stallions or jackasses; money paid for that service.

caballar, *a.* pert. to or like horses, equine.

caballear, *vn.* to ride horseback frequently.

caballejo, *m. dim.* little horse, nag; (vet.) shoeing-frame.

caballerato, *m.* ecclesiastical benefice granted by the Pope to a married layman; privilege of gentleman or esquire, in Catalonia.

caballerear, *vn.* to set up for a gentleman.

caballerescamente, *adv.* knightly, cavalierly.

caballeresco, ca, *a.* knightly, chivalrous; gentlemanly.

caballerete, *m. dim.* (coll.) spruce young gentleman.

caballería, *f.* riding animal; cavalry; art of riding, horsemanship; knight-errantry; chivalry; order of knights; knighthood; share of spoils given to a knight; (W.I.) a land measure (about 33½ acres).—**c. andante,** knight-errantry.—**c. mayor,** saddle horse or mule.—**c. menor,** ass, donkey.

caballerito, *m. dim.* young gentleman.

caballeriza, *f.* stable; number of horses, mules. etc., in a stable; stud of horses; staff of grooms, hostlers, etc.; wife of a CABALLERIZO.

caballerizo, *m.* head groom of a stable.—**c. del rey,** equerry to the king.—**c. mayor del rey,** master of the horse to the king.

caballero, ra. I. *a.* riding. II. *m.* knight; cavalier; gentleman; rider, horseman; a sort of fortification; old Spanish dance; (ornith.) red-legged horseman; gambet.—**c. andante,** knight-errant.—**c. de industria,** defrauder, knave, one who lives by his wits, sponger.—**c. del hábito de Santiago,** knight of the military order of St. James.

caballerosamente, *adv.* generously, nobly; like a gentleman.

caballerosidad, *f.* condition, quality of a gentleman; nobleness, honorable behavior.

caballeroso, sa, *a.* noble, generous; gentlemanlike, gentlemanly.

caballerote, *m.* (coll.) uncouth or unpolished gentleman.

caballeta, *f.* (entom.) field cricket.

caballete, *m.* ridge of a roof; carpenter's horse, sawhorse; trestle; easel; horse (instrument of torture); brake, for dressing hemp and flax; ridge between furrows; cap of a chimney; bridge of the nose; gallows of a printing press.

—c. de aserrar, sawbuck, sawhorse.—**c. de colchar cabos,** (naut.) rope-laying truss, stakehead.

caballico, ito, *m. dim.* little horse, pony; hobby- or rocking-horse.—**c. del diablo,** dragon fly.

caballista, *m.* horseman; good rider; horse connoisseur.

caballo, *m.* horse; (cards) the queen; (chess) knight; (med.) bubo.—*pl.* (mil.) horse, cavalry.—**c. aguililla,** (Am.), a very swift pacing horse.—**c. amaestrado,** horse completely broken in.—**c. blanco,** a person who finances a doubtful enterprise.—**c. castizo,** blood horse.—**c. de agua** = C. MARINO.—**c. de aldaba** = C. DE REGALO.—**c. de batalla,** battle horse, charger; hobby, favorite idea; specialty, forte; main or crucial point.—**c. de carga,** pack horse.—**c. de carrera,** or **corredor,** race horse.—**c. de caza,** hunter.—**c. de Frisia,** (mil.) chevaux-de-frise.—**c. de fuerza,** = C. DE VAPOR.—**c. de mar** = C. MARINO.— **c. de montar,** saddle horse.—**c. de palo,** any vessel fit for sea; rack for criminals; (tannery) tanner's beam.—**c. de posta,** post horse.—**c. de regalo,** gala horse, handsome horse kept for special occasions.—**c. de silla,** saddle horse.—**c. de tiro,** draught horse.—**c. de vapor,** horsepower.—**c. entero,** stallion. —**c. marino,** sea horse; hippopotamus.—**c. padre,** stallion.—**c. rabón,** docked horse.— **—a c.,** on horseback.—**a c. regalado no hay que mirarle el diente,** or **no se le mira el colmillo,** you should not look a gift horse in the mouth.—**a mata c.,** at breakneck speed. —**caballón,** *m.* large, clumsy horse; ridge between two furrows.

caballuelo, *m. dim.* little horse.

caballuno, na, *a.* pertaining to horses; horselike.

cabaña, *f.* hut, cottage, cabin; hovel, mean dwelling; flock of ewes or breeding sheep; drove of mules; balk line in billiards.

cabañal. I. *a.* sheep-and-cattle (roads). II. *m.* village or settlement of huts.

cabañería, *f.* a shepherd's rations for a week.

cabañero, ra. I. *a.* pertaining to a CABAÑA in any of its meanings. II. *n.* keeper of a CABAÑA (of sheep or mules).

cabañil. I. *a.* pertaining to a shepherd's hut. II. *m.* man in charge of a drove of mules.

cabañuela. I. *f. dim.* small hut or cottage.—*pl.* weather forecast made in August for the following year; festival of Jews in Toledo.

cabaret, *m.* (Am.) cabaret, night club (gen. low-class).

¹cabe, *m.* stroke on a ball in game of ARGOLLA. —**dar un c. al bolsillo,** or **a la hacienda,** (fig.) to hurt one in one's business, fortune, etc.

²cabe, *prep.* (poet.) near, nigh, by.

cabeceamiento, *m.* = CABECEO.

cabecear. I. *vn.* to nod; to shake the head in disapproval; to raise or lower the head (app. to horses); to incline to one side, to hang over (app. to a load); (naut., aer.) to pitch; (of carriages) to lurch. II. *va.* in writing, to give (the letters) a thick loop; among bookbinders, to put (the head-band) to (a book); to bind (cloth or rugs); to close by cauterization; to head (wine).—**cabeceo,** *m.* nod of the head; (naut., aer.) pitching.

cabecera, *f.* beginning or principal part; upper end; head or head-board of a bed; seat of honor; headwaters; capital of a province, district, nation; fortified point of a bridge; head piece or vignette; each extremity of the back of a book; pillow or bolster.—**c. de puente,** bridgehead.

cabeciancho, cha, *a.* broad-headed.

cabecica, ita, *f. dim.* small head.

cabeciduro, ra, *a.* (Am.) stubborn.

---

cabecilla, *m.* wrong-headed person; leader, ringleader.

cabellar, *vn.* to put on false hair.

cabellejo, *m. dim.* little hair.

cabellera, *f.* hair (collect.), head of hair; switch of hair; tail (of a comet).

cabello, *m.* a hair; hair of the head (collect.), also *pl.*; large sinews (in mutton); corn silk.—**cabellos de ángel,** sweetmeat made with CIDRACAYOTE.—**asirse de un cabello,** to resort to trivial pretexts or flimsy arguments, catch at trifles.—**traer por los cabellos,** to drag in irrelevantly, resort to or introduce far-fetched (arguments, facts, etc.).

cabelludo, da, *a.* hairy; fibrous.

cabelluelo, *m. dim.* thin and short hair.

caber, *vn.* (*ind. pres.* QUEPO, *pret.* CUPE, *fut.* CABRÉ; *subj.* QUEPA) to go in or into (*la clavija no cabe en el agujero,* the peg does not go in the hole, the peg is too large for the hole); to have enough room, to be able to go through (often diff. constr.: *yo no quepo aquí,* I have not enough room here, this place is too small for me; *el elefante cabe por esta puerta,* the elephant can go through this door, this door is large enough for the elephant); to fall (to one), to befall, to have (often diff. constr.: *me ha cabido buena suerte,* good luck has befallen me, I have been fortunate; *me ha cabido el honor de ser nombrado,* the honor of being appointed has fallen to me, I have had the honor to be appointed); to be possible or natural (*todo cabe en la naturaleza,* in nature everything is possible); to be pertinent, appropriate or applicable.—**no cabe duda (de que),** there is no doubt (that).—**no cabe más,** that is the worst (or the best), that is the limit.—**no c. de,** to overflow, or be filled, with.—**no c. en sí,** to be puffed up with conceit, (coll.) to have a swelled head.

cabero, *m.* maker of handles for tools.

cabestraje, *m.* halter; fee paid to a drover.

cabestrante, *m.* (naut.) capstan.

cabestrar, *va.* to put on or lead by the halter.

cabestrear, *vn.* to be led by a halter.

cabestrería, *f.* shop where halters and collars are made and sold.

cabestrero, ra. I. *a.* that can be led by a halter. **II.** *n.* maker or seller of horse collars and halters.

cabestrillo, *m.* sling (for injured arm, etc.); gold or silver chain, necklace.

cabestro, *m.* halter; leading ox.—**llevar, or traer, de c.,** to lead by the halter; (fig.) to lead by the nose.

cabeza, *f.* head; chief, leader; understanding, mind, judgment, brains; beginning; end; forward, front end; big end; top or upper part; capital, seat of a province, district, etc. (also **c. de partido**); head of cattle.—**c. a c.** (horse racing) neck and neck.—**c. de biela,** big end of connecting rod.—**c. de chorlito,** hare-brained.—**c. de hierro,** stubborn, stiff-necked person.—**c. de puente,** bridgehead.—**c. mayor,** head of neat cattle.—**c. menor,** head of sheep, goats, etc.—**c. redonda,** blockhead.—**a la c.,** at the head.—**alzar c.,** to get better; to get on one's feet.—**de c.,** head first, headlong; by heart; *a.* brainy, smart.—**de pies a c.,** from head to foot, all over.—**hacer c.,** to lead.—**levantar c.,** to be restored in health or fortune.—**no tener pies ni c.,** to have neither head nor tail, neither rhyme nor reason.—**poner las cosas pies con c.,** to jumble things up; to put topsy-turvy.

cabezada, *f.* headshake; blow or butt given with the head, or on it; nod; headgear (of harness); headstall of a bridle; (naut., aer.) pitch, pitching, plunge; headband of a book;

instep of a boot.—**dar cabezadas,** to nod (when napping).

cabezal, *m.* small pillow; (med.) compress; long round bolster; post of a door; fore part of a carriage; narrow mattress used by laborers.

cabezalejo, ico, illo, ito, *m. dim.* little pillow or bolster; small compress.

cabezalero, ra, *n.* executor of a will.

cabezazo, *m.* blow with the head.

cabezo, *m.* summit; reef; collar band.

cabezón, na. I. *a.* big-headed; obstinate. **II.** *m.* tax register; collar band; head; opening of a garment; cavesson or nose band, used in breaking in a horse.

cabezorro, *m. aug.* large, disproportioned head.

cabezota, *m. & f. aug.* (coll.) big-headed or obstinate person.

cabezudo, da. I. *a.* large-headed; headstrong; (of wine) heady. **II.** *m.* (ichth.) chub, mullet.

cabezuela, *f. dim.* small head; coarse flour; rose bud from which rose water is distilled; hare-brained fellow, simpleton; (bot.) eryngo, rag-wort-leaved centaury.

cabezuelo, *m. dim.* of CABEZA: little head.

cabida, *f.* content, capacity; space, room; influence.—**tener c.,** to be appropriate; to apply, be applicable.

cabila, *f.* (in Morocco) tribe.

cabildada, *f.* hasty, ill-advised proceeding.

cabildante, *m.* councilman, member of CABILDO.

cabildear, *vn.* to lobby; to influence or win votes in a corporation.—**cabildeo,** *m.* lobbying.

cabildero, *ra,* *n.* lobbyist.

cabildo, *m.* chapter of a cathedral or collegiate church; meeting of a chapter or place where held; municipal council; (in some places) city hall.

cabilla, *f.* (naut.) dowel; treenail; belaying pin.

cabillejo, *m. dim.* (bot.) partial flower stalk.

cabillo, *m.* (bot.) stalk; stem; small end of a rope.

cabio, *m.* joist; breastsummer of a chimney; top or bottom piece of window or door frame.

cabito, *m. dim.* small end; butt.

cabizbajo, ja, *a.* crestfallen; thoughtful, pensive; melancholy.

cable, *m.* cable; cable's length, measure of 120 fathoms.—**c. de cizalla,** (aer.) shear wire (of a dirigible).—**c. de sustentación,** (aer.) light wire.

cablear, cablegrafiar, *va.* to cable.

cablegráfico, ca, *a.* pertaining to submarine telegraphy; cable (as *a.*).

cablegrama, *m.* cablegram.

cabo, *m.* extreme, extremity; tip; bit; stub, stump; cape, headland, foreland; handle, haft, holder; rope, cord; thread; chief, leader; (mil.) corporal; end, termination, finish; parcel or package smaller than a bale.—*pl.* tail and mane (of a horse); loose pieces of apparel, as stockings, shoes, hats, etc.; divisions, sections, headings.—**c. de año,** anniversary funeral.—**c. de desgarro,** (aer.) rip cord, ripline.—**c. de escuadra,** (mil.) corporal.—**c. de maestranza,** foreman of a workmen's brigade.—**c. de presa,** prizemaster.—**cabos negros,** black hair, eyes, and eye-brows.—**al c.,** at last.—**al c. de,** at the end of, after.—**dar c. a,** to finish, end.—**de c. a c.,** or **de c. a rabo,** from head to tail, from beginning to end.—**estar al c. de,** to be conversant with, or informed about.—**llevar a c.,** to carry out; to accomplish.—**llevar hasta el c.,** to carry to the end, see (something) through.

cabotaje, *m.* (naut.) coasting trade; pilotage.

cabra, *f.* goat; engine formerly used to throw stones.—*pl.* (Am.) little clouds; (Arg.) wavelets.

cabrahigadura, *f.* a fig-ripening process.

cabrahigal, **¹cabrahigar,** *m.* wild-fig field.

²cabrahigar, *va.* to ripen figs artificially.

cabrahigo, *m.* wild fig tree; its fruit.
cabrería, *f.* herd of goats; goat's milk dairy.
cabreriza, *f.* goatherds' hut; woman goat tender.
cabrerizo, za. I. *a.* goatish, hircine. **II.** *n.* goatherd.
cabrero, ra, *n.* goatherd.
cabrestante, *m.* (naut.) capstan, winch.
cabresto, *m.* = CABESTRO, halter.
cabria, *f.* crane; wheel and axle; winch; windlass; hoist; axletree; (naut.) sheers.
cabrilla, *f. dim.* little goat; (ichth.) a kind of fish; sawhorse; sawbuck.—*pl.* (astr.) Pleiades; marks on the legs, produced by being continually too near the fire; (naut.) whitecaps.
cabrillear, *vn.* to form whitecaps.
cabrilleo, *m.* the forming of whitecaps.
cabrio, *m.* (carp.) joist.
cabrío. I. *a.* goatish, hircine. **II.** *m.* herd of goats.
cabriola, *f.* caper; gambol, skip; nimble leap.
cabriolar, *vn.* to caper or cut capers; to jump, curvet, frisk.
cabriolé, *m.* a kind of sleeveless cloak; cabriolet.
cabriolear, *vn.* = CABRIOLAR.
cabrita, *f. dim.* little she-kid.
cabritero, *m.* dealer in kids.
cabritilla, *f.* kid, dressed kidskin.
cabritillo, cabrito, *m. dim.* kid.
cabrón, *m.* buck, he-goat; (fig.) acquiescing cuckold.
cabronada, *f.* (low) infamous action which a man permits against his own honor; great annoyance or nuisance.
cabruno, na, *a.* goatish, goatlike.
cabruñar, *va.* to sharpen by hammering.
cabruño, *m.* sharpening the scythe.
cabujón, *m.* rough, unpolished ruby.
cábula, *f.* (Am.) trick, cunning scheme to get or accomplish something.
cabuya, *f.* (bot.) common American agave; sisal; sisal or hemp cord.—**dar c.,** (Am.) to tie, or bind.—**ponerse en la c.,** (Am.) to catch the drift; to become informed.
cabuyero, *m.* (Am.) ship chandler.
cabuyería, *f.* (Am.) ship chandlery.
cacahual, *m.* cacao plantation.
cacahuate, cacahué, cacahuete, cacahuey, *m.* (bot.) peanut.
cacalote, *m.* (Mex.) raven; (Am.) cracked corn and syrup; mistake, blunder.
¹**cacao,** *m.* (bot.) cacao; cacao tree; cacao seed; chocolate.
²**cacao,** *m.*—**pedir c.,** (coll.) to beg for quarter, throw up the sponge.—(Am.) **tener c.,** to have vim, energy, courage.
cacaotal, *m.* cacao plantation.
cacaraña, *f.* pit caused by the smallpox.
cacarañado, da, *a.* pitted.
cacaraquear, *vn.* = CACAREAR.
cacareador, ra, *n.* cackler; boaster, braggart.
cacarear, *vn.* to cackle; (coll.) to brag, boast.
cacareo, *m.,* cackling; boast, brag.
cacarizo, za, *a.* (Mex.) pock-marked.
cacatúa, *f.* (ornith.) cockatoo.
cacaxtle, *m.* (Mex.) crate to carry fruit.
cacaxtlero, *m.* (Mex.) Indian who carries a CACAXTLE on his shoulders.
cacé, cace, *v. V.* CAZAR.
cacear, *va.* to stir with a dipper or ladle.
cacera, *f.* irrigating canal; channel, conduit.
cacería, *f.* hunt, hunting.
cacerilla, *f. dim.* small drain or canal.
cacerina, *f.* cartridge box or pouch.
cacerola, *f.* casserole.
caceta, *f. dim.* small pan.
cacica, *f.* wife or daughter of a cacique.
cacicato, cacicazgo, *m.* dignity and territory of a cacique.
cacillo, ito, *m. dim.* small dipper or ladle.
cacimba, *f.* hole dug on the sea shore for drinking water.

cacique, *m.* cacique, Indian chief; (coll.) boss; (ornith. Mex.) cacique.
caciquil, *a.* pert. to or like caciques; boss (as *a.*).
caciquismo, *m.* caciquism, bossism.
cacle, *m.* (Mex.) leather sandal.
caco, *m.* pickpocket; thief; coward.
cacodilato, *m.* (chem.) cacodylate.
cacodílico, ca, *a.* (chem.) cacodylic.
cacodilo, *m.* (chem.) cacodyl.
cacófago, ga, *a.* cacophagous.
cacofonía, *f.* cacophony, harsh sound.
cacofónico, ca, *a.* cacophonous, ill-sounding.
cacografía, *f.* defective orthography.
cacomite, *m.* a Mexican flower plant.
cacomixtle, *m.* (Mex.) (zool.) cacomistle.
cacoquimia, *f.* (med.) cacochymy.
cacoquímico, ca, *a.* (med.) cacochymical.
cacoquimio, *m.* one suffering from cacochymia.
cácteo, a, *a.* (bot.) cactaceous.
cacto, (Am.) **cactus,** *m.* (bot.) cactus.
cacumen, *m.* top, height; head, acumen.
cacha, *f.* each of the two leaves of a razor or knife handle; (Am., coll.) handle.—**hasta las cachas,** (coll.) up to the hilt, as much as one can manage.—**hacer la c.,** to try, do what one can; **(a),** to make fun (of).
cachaco, *m.* (Am.) dandy, fop.
cachada, *f.* thrust or wound with the horns.
cachalote, *m.* sperm whale.
cachamarín, *n.* coasting lugger.
cachapa, *f.* (Venez.) corn bread with sugar.
cachar, *va.* to break in pieces; to split.
cacharpari, *m.* (Peru) farewell supper.
cacharrería, *f.* crockery store; collection or stock of earthen pots.
cacharrero, ra, *n.* maker or seller of crockery; (Am.) notion dealer; peddler.
cacharro, *m.* coarse earthen pot, or a piece of it; useless, worthless thing, truck; (Am.) notion, trinket.
cachava, *f.* children's sport resembling hockey or golf; stick for driving the ball.
cachavazo, *m.* stroke with the CACHAVA.
cachaza, *f.* slowness, tardiness; forbearance; (Am.) rum; first froth on cane juice when boiled.
cachazudo, da. I. *a.* slow, calm, phlegmatic. **II.** *m.* sluggard; (Am.) tobacco worm.
cache, *a.* (Arg.) uncouth.
cachemarín, *m.* = CACHAMARÍN.
cachemir, *m.,* **cachemira,** *f.* cashmere.
cacheo, *m.* search for hidden arms.
cachera, *f.* coarse shagged cloth or baize.
cachería, *f.* (Am.) small business; uncouthness.
cachetas, *f. pl.* teeth or wards in a lock.
cachete, *m.* punch in the face or head; cheek.
cachetero, *m.* short poniard; bullfighter who kills the bull with the poniard.
cachetina, *f.* hand-to-hand fight.
cachetudo, da, *a.* plump-cheeked, fleshy.
cachicamo, *m.* (Am.) armadillo.
cachicán, *m.* overseer of a farm; cunning, clever man.
cahicuerno, na, *a.* having a horn handle or haft.
cachidiablo, *m.* hobgoblin; one disguised in a devil's mask.
cachifo, fa, *n.* (Colomb., coll.) boy, girl.
cachifollar, *va.* (coll.) to disappoint; to vex, humble, banter, sit upon.
cachigordete, eta, ito, ita, *a.* squat, plump.
cachillada, *f.* litter (of animals).
cachimba, *f.* low well; (water) spring; (Cuba) disreputable woman; CACHIMBO.
cachimbo, *m.* (Am.) smoking pipe.—**chupar c.,** (Venez.) to smoke a pipe; to suck one's thumb.
cachipolla, *f.* (entom.) dayfly or May fly.
cachiporra, *f.* stick with a big knob; bludgeon, billy.

cachiporrazo, *m.* blow with a bludgeon.

cachiporro, *m.* = CACHIPORRA.

cachirulo, *m.* earthen, glass, or tin pot for preserving liquor; head ornament formerly worn by women; (Mex.) reinforcing chamois skin patches on riding breeches; small three-masted vessel.

cachivache, *m.* pot, utensil; stuff, trash; broken crockery; trumpery; worthless fellow; (Am.) notion, trinket.

cachizo, *a.*—**madero c.,** thick, heavy log.

¹cacho, *m.* slice, piece; a card game; bunch; (C. A.) joke, fun; (Chile, com.) left-over, goods unsold.

²cacho, *m.* (ichth.) surmullet.

³cacho, cha. I. *a.* bent, crooked. **II.** *m.* (Am.) horn.—**echar c.,** (Colomb.) to excel, get ahead.—**empinar el c.,** = EMPINAR EL CODO, to drink to excess, be a toper.

cacholas, *f. pl.* (naut.) cheeks of the masts.

cachón, *m.* breaker; small waterfall, cascade.

cachondez, *f.* sexual appetite.

cachondo, da, *a.* in heat, rutting.

cachones, *m. pl.* breakers (waves).

cachopo, *m.* (naut.) gulf; dry trunk, stump.

cachorrillo, ito. I. *n.* little cub or whelp. **II.** *m.* pocket pistol.

cachorro, rra. I. *n.* whelp, puppy, cub. **II.** *m.* pocket pistol.

cachú, *m.* catechu, astringent from plants.

cachúa, *f.* Indian dance in Peru, Bolivia, etc.

cachucha, *f.* rowboat; man's cloth or fur cap; Andalusian dance in three-quarter time with castanets.

cachuchero, ra, *n.* maker or seller of caps; maker or seller of pin or needle cases.

cachucho, *m.* oil measure, containing the sixth part of a pound; pin or needle case; clumsy earthen pot.

cachuela, *f.* fricassee of rabbits' livers and lights; gizzard.

cachuelo, *m.* (ichth.) small river fish like anchovy.

cachulera, *f.* cavern; hiding place.

cachumbo, *m.* hard shell of cocoanut and other fruit.

cachunde, *f.* aromatic paste munched to sweeten the breath; cachou.

cachupín, *m.* Spaniard who settles in Spanish America.

cada, *a.* every, each.—**c. cual,** each; every one, everybody.—**c. que** = C. VEZ QUE.—**c. uno** = C. CUAL.—**c. vez que, c. y cuando,** every time, whenever; as soon as.

cadahalso, *m.* shed, cabin, shanty.

cadalecho, *m.* bed made of branches of trees.

cadalso, *m.* platform, stage, stand; scaffold for capital punishment.

cadañal, ñego, ga, *a.* annual, yearly.

cadañero, ra, *a.* lasting a year; CADAÑAL.—**mujer c.,** woman who bears a child every year.

cadarzo, *m.* coarse, entangled silk which can not be spun; cover of the cocoon; narrow silk ribbon.

cádava, *f.* burnt stump of furze.—**cadaval,** *m.* place where many CÁDAVAS remain standing.

cadáver, *m.* corpse, cadaver.

cadavérico, ca, *a.* cadaverous.

cadejo, *m.* tangled hair; small skein; threads put together to make tassels.

cadena, *f.* chain; bond, tie; series; range (of mountains); malefactors chained together to be led to the galleys; imprisonment for life; (arch.) buttress.—**c. de puerto,** boom of a harbor.—**c. radial,** radio network, broadcasting system.—**c. de rocas,** ledge or ridge of rocks.—**c. sin fin,** endless chain.

cadencia, *f.* cadence; fall of the voice; rhythm;

measure; flow of verses or periods; in dancing, harmony of motion and music; (mus.) cadenza.

cadencioso, sa, *a.* rhythmical.

cadenear, *va. & vn.* (surv.) to chain.

cadenero, *m.* (surv.) chainman.

cadeneta, *f.* lace or needlework worked in form of a chain; chain stitch; work put upon the heads of books to reinforce the sewing.

cadenilla, ita, *f. dim.* small chain; pearls of a certain size.

cadente, *a.* decaying, declining; going to ruin; rhythmical.

cadera, *f.* hip, the joint of the thigh.

caderillas, *f. pl.* bustle (garment).

cadetada, *f.* injudicious, thoughtless action.

cadete, *m.* (mil.) cadet.

cadí, *m.* cadi, magistrate among Mohammedans.

cadillar, *m.* place where bur parsley grows.

cadillo, *m.* (bot.) great bur parsley; prickly bur weed; common burdock.

cadillos, *m. pl.* thrum; warp ends.

cadmía, *f.* (min.) calamine; tutty.

cadmio, *m.* (chem.) cadmium.

cado, *m.* ferret hole.

cadoso, cadozo, *m.* deep place in a river.

caducamente, *adv.* weakly, feebly.

caducante, *n. & a.* dotard, in one's dotage.

caducar, *vn.* (*pret.* CADUQUÉ; *subj.* CADUQUE) to dote (from old age); to be worn out by service; to fall into disuse; to become superannuated or extinct; (law, com.) to lapse.

caduceador, *m.* king at arms, who proclaims war and peace.

caduceo, *m.* caduceus, Mercury's staff.

caducidad, *f.* (law) caducity; decrepitude.

caduco, ca, *a.* worn out; senile; decrepit; perishable; frail.—**caduquez,** *f.* caducity; senility.

caedizo, za, *a.* ready to fall; (bot.) deciduous.

caedura, *f.* loose threads dropping from the loom.

caer. I. *vn.* (*ind. pres.* CAIGO, *pret.* él CAYÓ; *subj.* CAIGA) to fall, drop, tumble down; lighten; fall off; hang down, droop; fit; be becoming; deviate from the right path; fall due; decrease, decline, drop, fall; fall to one's lot; befall, happen to; come to pass; to understand, see; (of color) to become faint; to be included, fall (within certain limits, etc.).—**c. a,** to be (located) on (this or that side, etc.); to look out on, overlook (*la ventana cae a la playa,* the window overlooks the beach).—**c. bien (mal),** to create a good (bad) impression, to be well (unfavorably) received; to fit (not to fit); to be (not to be) becoming.—**c. de,** to fall on (*caer de espaldas,* to fall on one's back, or backwards).—**c. de plano,** to fall flat (stretched). —**c. en cama,** or **enfermo,** to be taken ill. —**c. en la cuenta,** to understand the situation; to realize.—**c. en la cuenta de,** to think, or take note, of—**c. en gracia,** to arouse liking, to become a subject of affection or esteem, to please.—**c. redondo,** to drop unconscious. —**al c. de la noche,** at nightfall;—**dejar c.,** to drop, let fall. **II.** *vr.* **caerse,** to fall; to lose heart, to become downcast.—**c. de su peso,** or **c. de suyo,** to be self-evident, to be obvious; to fall, or fall, by itself.—**c. redondo** = CAER REDONDO.—**caérsele a uno la cara de vergüenza,** to be deeply ashamed, to feel like hiding one's face.

café, *m.* coffee (tree, berry, beverage); coffeehouse; café.—**c. retinto,** very strong, black coffee.—**c. tinto,** strong black coffee.— **cafeína,** *f.* caffein.—**cafeona,** *f.* the aromatic oil of coffee.—**cafetal,** *m.* coffee plantation.— **cafetera,** *f.* coffee pot; woman who gathers coffee berries; woman who makes and serves coffee.—**cafetería,** *f.* (Mex.) retail coffee shop. —**cafetero, ra. I.** *a.* coffee (as *a a.*). **II.** *m.* one who raises, makes or sells coffee; (bot.) coffee tree.—**cafetín,** *m.* small café.—**cafeto,** *m.* coffee tree.—**cafetucho,** *m.* small and untidy café.

cáfila, *m.* multitude, large number; caravan.

cafre, *n. & a.* Kaffrarian; savage, inhuman; rude, uncivil.

cagachín, *m.* small reddish mosquito.

cagafierro, *m.* scoria, dross of iron.

cagajón, *m.* horse dung; dung of mules or asses.

cagalaolla, *m.* masquerader who dances in processions.

cagarrache, *m.* one who washes the olive pits in an oil mill.

cagarria, *f.* St. George's-mushroom.

cagarropa, *m.* = CAGACHÍN, small mosquito.

cagarruta, *f.* dung of sheep, goats, mice, etc.

cagatinta, *m.* (contempt.) minor office workers.

cahiz, *m.* nominal measure of twelve bushels.

cahizada, *f.* land sufficient for one CAHIZ of seed.

caída, *f.* fall; falling; tumble; downfall; lapse; drop; falling off; droop; diminution, drop; descent; (geol.) dip; landslip; interior gallery in houses of Manila, with views upon the courtyard.—*pl.* coarse wool cut off the skirts of a fleece; witty remarks, repartee; (sew.) reverse.—**c. de una vela,** depth or drop of a sail.—**a la c. de la tarde,** at the close of the afternoon.—**a la c. del sol,** at sunset.

caído, da. I. *pp.* of CAER. **II.** *a.* languid; downfallen. **III.** *m. pl.* arrears of taxes or rents; slanting lines to show the proper slant in writing.

caigo, caiga, *v. V.* CAER.

caimacán, *m.* kaimakam, assistant grand vizier; (coll.) big gun, person of importance.

caimán, *m.* cayman, alligator; sharp, exploiter.

caimiento, *m.* fall, drop; droop, languidness.

caimito, caimo, *m.* star apple.

caique, *m.* (naut.) skiff, small boat.

cairel, *m.* false hair or switch worn by women to embellish their head dress; fringe trimming; silk threads to which the hair of wigs is fastened.

cairelar, *va.* to trim with fringe.

caja, *f.* box; case; coffin; chest; cash box or safe; sheath; body (of a carriage, truck, etc.); stock (of firearm); cavity, hole; distributing or central post office; (com.) cash, funds; cashier's office; socket; frame; drum; printer's case; portable writing desk; well or cavity in which a staircase is raised; wooden case of an organ; (mil.) drum; drum case, or frame; (mech.) shell, block (of a pulley); (Chile) bed (of a river); (min.) barren rock.—**c. alta,** (print.) upper case.—**c. baja,** (print.) lower case.—**c. capilla,** (naut.) chest for chapel ornaments.—**c. de ahorros,** savings bank.—**c. de amortización,** Department of Public Debts (an old branch of the Spanish administration); sinking fund.—**c. de caudales,** (Am.) c. **de hierro,** strong box, safe.—**c. de las muelas,** (coll.) gums (of the mouth); mouth.—**c. del cuerpo,** thorax, thoracic cavity.—**c. de música,** music box.—**c. de reclutamiento,** (mil.) recruiting branch (of the army or navy).—**c. de seguridad,** safe-deposit box.—**c. fuerte,** (Am.) = C. DE CAUDALES.—**c. registradora,** cash register.—**con cajas destempladas,** roughly, without ceremony; coldly, slightingly.—**en c.,** cash, cash on hand (kept in the safe); (fig.) in good condition.

cajeras, *f. pl.* (naut.) cavities in blocks which contain the sheaves.

cajero, ra. I. *n.* box maker; cashier. **II.** *m.* reservoir.

cajeta, *f.* little box; poor-box; (Mex.) box of jelly; (Cuba) tobacco box; cigar case; (Am.) puffed up townsman (so called by farmers).

cajete, *m.* (Mex.) flat earthen pulque bowl.

cajetilla, *f.* package (of cigarettes).

cajetín, *m. dim.* very small box; (print.) fount case. letter case.

cajiga, *f.* = QUEJIGO, *m.* a kind of oak.

cajigal, *m.* = QUEJIGAL, plantation of CAJIGAS.

cajilla, ita, *f. dim.* small box; (bot.) capsule.

cajista, *n.* compositor (in printing).

cajo, *m.* bookbinder's groove.

cajón, *m.* box, case, chest, (Am.) coffin; drawer, till, locker, mold for casting; space between the shelves of a bookcase; wooden stand or shed for selling provisions; (Mex.) dry-goods store; crib, caisson.—**c. de sastre,** confused mass; odds and ends.—**ser de c.,** to be a matter of course, go without saying.—**cajonada,** *f.* (naut.) lockers.—**cajoncito,** *m. dim.* small box or drawer.—**cajonera,** *f.* chest of drawers in a vestry.—**cajonería,** *f.* set of drawers; tallboy or chiffonier.

cajuela, *f. dim.* small box.

cal, *f.* lime.—**c. hidráulica,** hydraulic lime.—**c. muerta,** slaked lime.—**c. viva,** quicklime, unslaked lime.—**c. y canto** = CALICANTO, stone masonry.—**de c. y canto,** (fig.) firm, solid.

¹**cala,** *f.* cove, small bay; fishing ground.

²**cala,** *f.* sample slice cut out of a fruit to try its flavor; hole made in a wall to try its thickness; (med.) suppository; (naut.) hold.

³**cala,** *f.* (bot.) calla lily.

calaba, *m.* calaba tree. Also CALAMBUCO.

calabacear, *va.* = DAR CALABAZAS.

calabacera, *f.* (bot.) pumpkin, gourd or squash plant. Also CALABAZA.

calabacero, ra. I. *n.* retailer of pumpkins. **II.** *m.* calabash tree.

calabacica, illa, ita, *f. dim.* small pumpkin.

calabacilla, *f.* core of gourd-shaped tassel; earring made of pearls in the shape of a gourd.

calabacín, *m.* small, young, tender pumpkin; silly person.—**calabacinate,** *m.* fried pumpkins.

calabacino, *m.* dry gourd, calabash bottle.

calabaza, *f.* (bot.) pumpkin; squash; gourd; (fig.) stupid, ignorant person.—**c. confitera,** or **totanera,** pumpkin.—**c. vinatera,** bottle gourd.—**dar calabazas,** to fail in examination; to refuse (a lover), give the mitten.—**calabazada,** *f.* knock with the head against something.—**darse de calabazadas,** (fig.) to labor in vain.—**calabazar,** *m.* pumpkin orchard.—**calabazate,** *m.* preserved pumpkin candied; piece of pumpkin steeped in honey.

calabazo, *m.* gourd.

calabazón, *m. aug.* large winter pumpkin.

calabobos, *m.* drizzle; mizzle.

calabocero, *m.* jailer; warden.

calabozaje, *m.* fee paid by prisoners to the jailer.

¹**calabozo,** *m.* dungeon; cell; calaboose; jail.

²**calabozo,** *m.* curved pruning and weed-cutting knife.

calabrés, sa, *a.* Calabrian.

calabriada, *f.* mixture of different things; mixture of white and red wine; balderdash.

calabrote, *m.* (naut.) stream cable.

calacanto, *m.* (bot.) flea bane.

calacuerda, *f.* (mil.) drum call to attack.

calada, *f.* soaking; wetting through; rapid flight of birds of prey; reprimand.

caladio, *m.* (bot.) caladium.

calado, da. I. *pp.* of CALAR. **II.** *m.* open work in metal, stone, wood, or linen; fretwork; (naut.) draught of a vessel.—*pl.* calados, lace.

calador, *m.* perforator; borer; one who makes open work; (naut.) calking iron; surgeon's probe.

caladre, *f.* (ornith.) a bird of the lark family.

calafate, calafateador, *m.* calker.

calafateadura, *f.* calking.

calafatear, *va.* to calk.

calafateo, *m.,* **calafatería,** *f.* calking.

For pronunciation, see the rules at the beginning of the book.

calafatín, *m.* calker's boy or mate.
calafetear, *va.* = CALAFATEAR.
calafraga, *f.* (bot.) saxifrage.
calagozo, *m.* bill or hedging hook.
calagraña, *f.* table grape, not fit for wine.
calaguala, *f.* (Peru, bot.) calaguala.
calahorra, *f.* public office where bread is distributed in times of scarcity.
calaíta, *f.* turquoise.
calaje, *m.* chest, trunk, coffer.
calaluz, *m.* (naut., P.I.) a kind of vessel.
calamaco, *m.* calamanco, a woolen fabric.
calamar, *m.* (zool.) calamary, squid.
calambac, *m.* (bot.) calamba; eaglewood.
calambre, *m.* cramp (of muscles).
calambuco. I. *m.* (bot.) calaba tree. **II.** *a.* (Am.) pious, devout; (Cuba) pharisaical, hypocritical.
calamento, *m.* (bot.) mountain balm or calamint.
calamidad, *f.* calamity.
calamillera, caramillera, *f.* pothook of a crane.
calamina, *f.* calamine.
calaminta, *f.* = CALAMENTO.
calamita, *f.* loadstone; magnetic needle.
calamite, *m.* a little green tree toad.
calamitosamente, *adv.* calamitously.
calamitoso, sa, *a.* calamitous, unfortunate.
cálamo, *m.* (bot.) sweet flag; (poet.) pen; ancient flute.
calamocano, *a.* fuddled; tipsy; unsteady.
calamoco, *m.* icicle.
calamón, *m.* (ornith.) purple water hen or gallinule; round-headed nail; stay supporting the beam of an oil mill.
calamorra, *f.* (coll.) head, (vulg.) block.
calamorrada, *f.* butt of horned cattle.
calamorrar, *va.* to butt.
calandraca, *f.* (naut.) mess of hard-tack.
calandrajo, *m.* rag hanging from a garment; ragamuffin.
¹calandria, *f.* (ornith.) bunting, calendar lark.
²calandria, *f.* mangle; clothier's press; beetle mill; rolling press.
cálanis, *m.* (bot.) sweet flag.
calaña, *f.* pattern; sample; model, form; character; quality, kind, sort.
calañés, *a.* native of Calañas.—**sombrero c.,** Andalusian hat.
cálao, *m.* a large P.I. bird with serrated bill.
calapatillo, *m.* (zool.) weevil, ant grub.
calapé, *m.* turtle roasted in its shell.
¹calar. I. *va.* to penetrate, soak through, permeate, drench; to go through, pierce, perforate; to make open work in (metal, wood, linen, or paper); (mech.) to wedge; to let down (a drawbridge); to fix (the bayonet); to pull down (the hat); to pick (a pocket); to see through (a person), understand; to sample, take or cut out a sample of. **II.** *vn.* (naut.) (of ships) to draw. **III.** *vr.* to put on; to get drenched; (of birds of prey) to rush, dart down, descend; to get in, squeeze in; to sneak in, enter clandestinely.
²calar, *a.* calcareous.
calato, ta, *a.* (Peru) nude, naked.
calavera, *f.* skull; madcap, wild fellow, daredevil.—**calaverada,** *f.* foolishness, tomfoolery.
calaverear, *vn.* to act foolishly and recklessly.
calaverilla, ita. I. *f. dim.* little skull. **II.** *m.* youth who sows his wild oats.
calaverón, *m. aug.* rake, debauchee.
calcado, *m.* tracing.
calcamar, *m.* a Brazilian sea bird.
calcáneo, *m.* (anat.) calcaneum.
calcañal, calcañar, *m.* heel, heel bone.
calcañuelo, *m.* a disease of bees.
calcar, *va.* (*pret.* CALQUÉ; *subj.* CALQUE) to trace; to trample on.
calcáreo, rea, *a.* calcareous.

calce, *m.* tire of a wheel; piece of iron or steel added to the coulter of a plow when it is worn; wedge; wheel shoe, a form of brake; (Am.) bottom (of a writing); (naut.) top.
calcé, calce, *v. V.* CALZAR.
calcedonia, *f.* chalcedony.
calcés, *m.* (naut.) masthead.
calceta, *f.* hose, stocking; fetters worn by criminals.—**hacer c.,** to knit.
calcetería, *f.* hosier's shop and trade; hosiery.
calcetero, ra, *n.* one who makes, mends, or sells thread stockings; hosier.
calcetín, *m.* sock.
calcetón, *m. aug.* cloth stocking worn under boots.
cálcico, ca, *a.* (chem.) calcic.
calcídico, *m.* (archeol.) perpendicular gallery.
calcificación, *f.* calcification.
calcificar, *va.* to calcify.
calcímetro, *m.* lime meter, an instrument to determine the lime in soils.
calcina, *f.* mortar.
calcinación, *f.* (chem.) calcination.
calcinar, *va. & vr.* to calcine.
calcinatorio, *m.* calcinatory, calcining vessel.
calcio, *m.* calcium.
calcita, *f.* (min.) calcite.
calco, *m.* tracing.
calcografía, *f.* chalcography, engraving on copper; place where engravings are made.
calcógrafo, *m.* engraver.
calcomanía, *f.* decalcomania.
calcopirita, *f.* (min.) chalcopyrite.
calculable, *a.* calculable.
calculador, ra. I. *n.* calculator, computer. **II.** *m.* calculating machine.
calcular, *va.* to calculate, compute; to estimate.
calculista, *n.* calculator, computer; designer.
cálculo, *m.* calculation, computation; estimate; conjecture; (math.) calculus (differential, integral, etc.); (med.) calculus, (kidney, etc.) stone.—**c. prudencial,** approximate calculation, estimate.
calculoso, sa, *a.* (med.) calculous.
calcha, *f.* (Chile) workman's clothing and bedding.
calchona, *f.* (Am.) bogey, goblin.
calda, *f.* warming or heating.—*pl.* **caldas,** hot mineral-water baths.—**dar calda a,** to heat, reheat.
caldaico, ca, *a.* = ¹CALDEO.
caldario, *m.* calderium.
caldarium, *m.* hot-water room in Roman baths.
caldear, *va.* to warm, heat; to weld.
¹caldeo, a, *n. & a.* Chaldean, Chaldaic.
²caldeo, *m.* heating.
caldera, *f.* caldron; sugar kettle, boiling pan; teakettle; (Am.) coffeepot; teapot; shell of kettle drum; (steam eng.) boiler.—**c. acuatubular,** water-tube boiler.—**c. de hogar interior,** flue boiler.—**c. de tubos de humos,** fire-tube boiler.—**c. de vapor,** steam boiler.—**c. fija,** stationary boiler.—**c. locomóvil,** portable boiler.—**c. marina,** or **marítima,** marine boiler.—**c. tubular,** tubular boiler.
calderada, *f.* caldronful.
calderería, *f.* brazier's or boiler maker's shop and trade.
calderero, *m.* brazier; coppersmith; boiler maker.
caldereta, *f. dim.* small caldron, kettle, pot; holy-water pot; fish stew; lamb stew; (Mex.) chocolate pot; (C. A.) thunderstorm.
calderilla, *f.* holy-water pot; any copper coin.
caldero, *m.* semispherical caldron or boiler; a copper; caldronful; ladle.
calderón, *m.* large caldron or kettle; mark for a thousand (Ↄ); (print.) paragraph (¶); (mus.) sign (⌒) denoting a pause; hold.

calderoniano, na, *a.* Calderonian, pertaining to, or like, Calderón or his style.

calderuela, *f. dim.* small kettle; dark lantern used to drive partridges into the net.

caldillo, caldito, *m.* sauce of a ragout or fricassee; light broth.

caldo, *m.* broth; beef tea; bouillon; salad dressing; sauce; gravy.—*pl.* (com.) wine, oil and liquors.—**c. alterado,** medicinal broth.—**c. de carne,** consommé; beef tea.

caldoso, sa, *a.* having plenty of broth.

calducho, *m.* badly seasoned broth; hog wash.

calecer, *va.* to become heated.

calecico, *m. dim.* small chalice.

calefacción, *f.* heating; heating system.

calefaciente, *a.* (med.) heating.

calefactorio, *m.* calefactory, heated sitting-room (in convents).

caleidoscopio, *m.* (Am.) = CALIDOSCOPIO.

calenda, *f.* part of the martyrology which treats of the acts of the saints of the day.—*pl.* **calendas,** calends.—**calendas griegas,** Greek calends (a time that will never come, as there were no Greek calends).

calendario, *m.* almanac; calendar.—**hacer calendarios,** (fig.) to muse; to make hasty prophecies.—**calendarista,** *n.* calendar maker.

caléndula, *f.* (bot.) marigold.

calentador, *m.* heater; warming pan; (coll.) large, clumsy watch.

calentamiento, *m.* warming, heating; a horse disease.

calentano, na, *n.* (Am.) lowlander, native of a hot climate.

calentar. I. *va.* (*ind.* CALIENTO; *subj.* CALIENTE) to heat, warm; to roll and heat (a ball) in one's hand before it is played; to urge; press forward; despatch speedily. **II.** *vr.* to be in heat, rut; to get hot; become excited or angry.

calentón, *m.*—**darse un c.,** to take a bit of a warming.

calentura, *f.* fever.—**calenturiento, ta,** *a.* feverish.—**calenturilla,** *f. dim.* slight fever.—**calenturón,** *m. aug.* high fever.—**calenturoso, sa,** *a.* feverish.

calepino, *m.* (coll.) Latin dictionary.

¹**calera,** *f.* lime kiln; lime pit.

²**calera,** *f.* fishing smack.

calería, *f.* place where lime is burnt and sold.

calero, ra. I. *a.* calcareous. **II.** *m.* lime burner, lime maker or seller.

calesa, *f.* two-wheeled calash, chaise.

calesera, *f.* bolero jacket.

calesero, *m.* driver of a calash.

calesín, *m.* light chaise.—**calesinero,** *m.* owner or driver of a light chaise.

caleta, *f.* (naut.) cove, creek, small bay; (Venez.) trade of carriers.—**caletero,** *m.* (Venez.) carrier.

caletre, *m.* (coll.) judgment, acumen.

calibeado, da, *a.* (med.) chalybean; chalybeate.

calibración, *f.* calibration; gaging.

calibrador, *m.* gage (instrument); calipers.

calibrar, *va.* to calibrate (a ball, a firearm); to gage, measure.

calibre, *m.* caliber; diameter; bore (of a cylinder, pipe, etc.); gage (instrument); calipers; gage, diameter (of wire).

¹**calicanto,** *m.* stone masonry.—**de c.,** (fig.) strong, firm, solid.

²**calicanto,** *m.* (Am.) (bot.) allspice.

calicata, *f.* (min.) trial pit.

caliciforme, *a.* (bot.) chaliced, chalice-shaped.

calicó, *m.* calico.

calicud, *f.* silk stuff from India.

calicular, *a.* (bot.) calycular.

calículo, *m.* (bot.) calycle.

calicut, *f.* = CALICUD.

caliche, *m.* pebble burnt in a brick; crust of lime which flakes from a wall; (Peru and Chile) native saltpetre.

calidad, *f.* quality; grade; nobility; rank.—*pl.* conditions, terms, stipulations; personal qualifications; gifts, parts.—**en c. de,** as; in one's capacity as.

¹**cálido, da,** *a.* warm; hot; piquant.

²**cálido, da,** *a.* crafty, artful.

calidoscópico, ca, *a.* kaleidoscopic.

calidoscopio, *m.* kaleidoscope.

calientapiés, *m.* foot warmer.

calientaplatos, *m.* plate warmer.

caliente, *a.* warm, hot; fiery.—**en c.,** while hot; at once.—**estar c.,** to be in heat, rut.

caliento, caliente, *v. V.* CALENTAR.

califa, *m.* caliph.—**califato,** *m.* caliphate.

calificable, *a.* qualifiable.

calificación, *f.* qualification; judgment, censure; proof; mark (in an examination).

calificado, da. I. *pp.* of CALIFICAR. **II.** *a.* qualified, authorized, competent.

calificador, ra, *n.* qualifier; censor.

calificar. I. *va.* (*pret.* CALIFIQUÉ; *subj.* CALIFIQUE) to qualify; rate, class; to pass on, judge; to authorize; to certify, attest; ennoble.—**c. de,** to call, declare. **II.** *vr.* to prove one's noble birth and descent according to law.

calificativo, va, *a.* (gram.) qualifying.

californiano, na, *n. & a.* Californian.

califórnico, ca, *a.*; **californio, ia,** *n. & a.* Californian.

cáliga, *f.* caliga, a Roman soldier's sandal.

caligine, *f.* mist, obscurity, darkness.

caliginoso, sa, *a.* caliginous, dark, dim.

caligrafía, *f.* calligraphy, penmanship.

caligráfico, ca, *a.* calligraphic.

calígrafo, *m.* expert penman.

calilla, *f. dim.* a small suppository.

calima, calina, *f.* thick vapor; light mist, haze.

calinda, *f.* (Cuba) a popular creole dance.

calinoso, sa, *a.* vapory, misty, hazy.

calípedes, *m.* (zool.) a kind of sloth.

calípico, ca, *a.* (astr.) callippic.

calisaya, *f.* (bot.) calisaya.

calistenia, *f.* calisthenics.—**calisténico, ca,** *a.* calisthenic.

cáliz, *m.* chalice; communion cup; bitter cup of grief and affliction; (bot.) calyz.

caliza, *f.* limestone (called also **piedra c.**).

calizo, za, *a.* calcareous; limy; calc (spar).

calma, *f.* calm; calmness, tranquillity; slowness; suspension of business; cessation of pain.—**c. chicha, c. muerta,** (naut.) dead calm.—**con c.,** calmly, quietly.—**en c.,** (of the sea) calm, smooth.

calmadamente, *adv.* quietly, calmly.

calmado, da. I. *pp.* of CALMAR. **II.** *a.* quiet, calm, still.

calmante. I. *a.* mitigating; quieting, soothing. **II.** *m. & a.* (med.) narcotic, anodyne, sedative.

calmar. I. *va.* to calm, quiet, pacify; to allay, mitigate, soothe. **II.** *vn.* to abate; to be becalmed. **III.** *vr.* to quiet down, abate; to calm oneself, be pacified.

calmo, ma, *a.* uncultivated, untilled; treeless; barren.

calmoso, sa, *a.* (of the sea) calm; slow, tardy.

calmuco, ca, *n. & a.* Kalmuck.

caló, *m.* cant; slang of gipsies and ruffians.

calocéfalo, la, *a.* (zool.) having a beautiful head.

calofilo, la, *a.* (bot.) having handsome leaves.

calofriado, da. I. *pp.* of CALOFRIARSE. **II.** *a.* chilly, shivering with cold.

calofriarse, *vr.* to have a chill.

calofrío, *m.* chill, shiver. Also ESCALOFRÍO.

calomel, *m.*, **calomelanos,** *m. pl.* calomel.

caloña, *f.* fine or damages for slander.

calóptero, ra, *a.* (zool.) handsome-winged.

calor, *m.* heat; glow; warmth, ardor; brunt of a battle; favor, kind reception.—**hacer c.,** (of weather) to be warm.—**tener c.**, (of person) to be, feel, warm.

caloría, *f.* calorie.

caloricidad, *f.* (physiol.) caloricity.

calórico, *m.* (chem.) caloric.

calorífero, ra. I. *a.* giving out heat. **II.** *m.* heater, radiator.—**c. de aire**, hot-air register. —**c. de vapor**, steam radiator.

calorificación, *f.* (physiol.) calorification.

calorífico, ca, *a.* calorific.

calorífugo, ga, *a.* non-conductor of heat; fire-proof, non-combustible.

calorimetría, *f.* calorimetry.

calorimétrico, ca, *a.* calorimetric.

calorímetro, *m.* (chem.) calorimeter.

calorimotor, *m.* (phys.) calorimotor.

calorosamente, *adv.* = CALUROSAMENTE.

caloroso, sa, *a.* = CALUROSO.

calostro, *m.* colostrum, first milk secreted after childbirth.

caloyo, *m.* new-born lamb or kid.

calpamulo, la, *a.* (Mex.) half-breed, mestizo.

calpisque, calpixque, calpizque, *m.* (Mex.) tax collector, steward.

calpul, *m.* (Guat.) gathering, meeting; (Hond.) Indian mound.

calqué, calque, *v.* V. CALCAR.

calseco, ca, *a.* cured with lime.

calta, *f.* caltha, marsh marigold.

calumbarse, *vr.* to plunge, dive.

calumbo, *m.* plunge, diving.

calumnia, *f.* calumny, slander.

calumniador, ra, *n. & a.* slanderer(-ing).

calumniar, *va.* to slander.

calumniosamente, *adv.* slanderingly.

calumnioso, sa, *a.* calumnious, slanderous.

calurosamente, *adv.* warmly; ardently; hotly; passionately.

caluroso, sa, *a.* warm, hot; heating; excited; vehement, enthusiastic.

calva, *f.* bald head; bald pate; clearing, open space.—**c. de almete**, crest of a helmet.

calvar. I. *va.* to cheat, deceive. **II.** *vn.* to become bald.

calvario, *m.* Calvary; debts; tally; score.

calvatrueno, *m.* baldness of the whole head; a wild person.

calvaza, *f. aug.* large bald pate.

calverizo, za, *a.* having many barren or bare spots.

calvero, *m.* barren spot; clearing, open space.

calvete, *m. dim.* little bald pate, when only part of the head is bald.

calvez, calvicie, *f.* baldness.

calvijar, *m.* = CALVERO.

calvilla, *f. dim.* slight baldness.

calvinismo, *m.* Calvinism.

calvinista, *n. & a.* Calvinist(-ic).

calvo, va, *a.* bald; bare; barren.

calza, *f.* loose breeches; trousers; hose, stockings; garter or ribbon tied on some animals; wedge.— *pl.* fetters.—**c. de arena**, sandbag.—**calzas acuchilladas**, slashed trousers.—**echarle una c. a**, to size up (a person).—**en calzas prietas**, in an embarrassing or difficult position, in a tight fix.—**medias calzas**, stockings reaching to the knees.—**tomar las calzas de Villa-diego**, to make a precipitate flight or escape, to bolt.

calzacalzón, *m.* galligaskins, loose breeches.

calzada, *f.* paved highway; (Am.) sidewalk.

calzadera, *f.* hempen cord; net twine.

calzadillo, ito, *m. dim.* small shoe.

calzado, da. I. *a.* (of monks, etc. who are not barefoot) shod; (of a horse) with white feet; (of birds) having feathers on the legs and feet. **II.** *m.* footwear.

calzador, *m.* shoeing leather; shoehorn.

calzadura, *f.* act of putting on the shoes; tip for this service; felloe, outer rim of a wheel.

calzar. I. *va.* (*pret.* CALCÉ; *subj.* CALCE) to put on (shoes, gloves, spurs, etc.); to scot or scotch (a wheel); (of firearms) to carry (a ball) of a certain size; to underlay, chock, key; (Am.) to fill (teeth); (Am.) to hill (plants); (print.) to overlay, raise, underlay; to shoe (an anchor); to put a steel edge on (an iron tool); to block (a wheel, carriage, to place something under the wheels to prevent sliding); to have (aptitudes, skill, ability, etc.).—**c. muchos (pocos) puntos en**, to be well (poorly) posted on, have a good (poor) knowledge of. **II.** *vr.* to put on; to control, dominate; to get, obtain.

calzo, *m.* (print.) frisket sheet, overlay; (Ry.) block, brake shoe; (mech.) wedge, quoin; shoe of a felloe; (naut.) skid, chock, bed, shoe.

calzón, *m.* ombre, a card game; (Mex.) a disease of the sugar cane from lack of irrigation.—*pl.* breeches; trousers; (naut.) goosewing.—**c. corto**, knee breeches.—**calzonarias**, *f. pl.* (Colomb.) suspenders (for trousers).—**calzonazos**, *m. aug.*—**ser un calzonazos**, to be a weak, soft fellow.—**calzoncillos**, *m. pl.* drawers, underdrawers.—**calzoneras**, *f. pl.* (Mex.) trousers buttoned down both sides.

calzorras, *m.* = CALZONAZOS.

¹callada, *f.* a dish of tripe.

²callada, *f.* silence (only in certain phrases).—**a las calladas**, or **de callada**, privately, on the quiet.—**dar la c. por respuesta**, to answer by silence.

calladamente, *adv.* silently, secretly.

callado, da. I. *pp.* of CALLAR. **II.** *a.* silent; quiet; reticent.

callana, *f.* (Am.) an almost flat earthen bowl used as a baking griddle.

callandico, ito, *adv.* in a low voice; silently, without noise, slyly, softly.

callar, *vn., va. & vr.* to keep silent; to stop talking (playing, singing, etc.); to shut up; to hush, conceal, keep from being known; to dissemble; (poet.) to abate, moderate, grow calm.—**c. su pico**, to hold one's tongue.—**¡calla!** or **¡calle!** you don't mean it! is it possible?—**quien calla, otorga**, silence gives consent.

calle. I. *f.* street; walk in a garden; passage, way.—**c. abajo**, down the street.—**c. de árboles**, path or space between two rows of trees; the rows themselves.—**c. hita**, from house to house.—**abrir c.**, to clear the way.—**azotar calles**, to loiter about, loaf.—**dejar en la c.**, to leave penniless, or in destitution.—**echar a la c.**, to put on the street, to put out of the house; to make public.—**hacer c.** = ABRIR C.—**llevar**, or **llevarse, de c.**, to sweep away; to overmaster; to confound, silence. **II.** *interj.* make way! move aside!

callear, *va.* to clear (walks) in a vineyard.

Calleja, *proper n.*—**ya se verá**, or **ya verán, quién es C.**, you shall see what I can do.

calleja, *f.* = CALLEJUELA.—**callejear**, *vn.* to walk or loiter about the streets; to gad; to ramble.—**callejero, ra**, *n.* loiterer, gadder.

callejo, *m.* pit into which game falls when pursued.

callejón, *m.* lane, alley.—**c. sin salida**, a blind alley.—**callejoncillo**, *m. dim.* little, narrow passage or lane.

callejuca, *f. dim.* small, narrow street.

callejuela, *f. dim.* small street, lane, or narrow passage; shift, subterfuge, evasion.

calleyo, *m.* = CALLEJO.

callialto, ta, *a.* pert. to horseshoe with thick borders.

callicida, *m.* corn eradicator.

callista, *n.* corn doctor, chiropodist.

callizo, *m.* = CALLEJÓN and CALLEJUELA, lane.

callo, *m.* corn, callous on foot; wen; (surg.) callus; extremity of a horseshoe.—*pl.* tripe.

callosidad, *f.* callosity, callousness.

calloso, sa, *a.* callous; corneous, horny.

¹cama, *f.* bed; couch; bed hangings and furniture; seat or couch of wild animals; floor or body of a cart; part of a melon resting on the ground; straw laid under animals or on plants; slice of meat put upon another when cooking; garden bed; (mech.) bedplate; base; (geol.) layer, stratum.—**c. de tijera,** folding bed, cot. —**guardar,** or **hacer, c.,** to be confined to one's bed.—**hacer la c.,** to make the bed.— **hacerle la c. a uno,** to injure one secretly.

²cama, *f.* part of a plow that connects the share with the beam, the sheathe; felloe of a wheel; check of a bridle; V-shaped piece in a cloak; (mech.) cam, cog, catch, tooth.

camada, *f.* brood of young animals, litter; band of thieves.

camafeo, *m.* cameo.

camal, *m.* hempen halter; camail.

camaleón, *m.* chameleon; person who changes his opinions to suit his interest.

Camaleopardo, *m.* (astr.) Camelopard.

camalote, *m.* a South Am. river plant resembling a floating island.

camama, *f.* (coll.) sham, humbug.

camamila, camomilla, *f.* (bot.) common camomile.

camándula, *f.* chaplet or rosary of one or three decades.—**tener muchas camándulas,** to be very tricky.

camandulense, *n.* & *a.* Camaldolite, order of Camandula or reformed Benedictines.

camandulería, *f.* prudery; hypocrisy.

camandulero, ra, *a.* & *n.* hypocrite(-ic), dissembler(-ing).

cámara, *f.* hall; parlor; chamber; each of the two houses of a legislative body; chamber (of a firearm, a mine); cabin of a ship; (aer.) cockpit; granary; mow; (physiol.) stool; evacuation by stool; laxity; (photog.) camera.—**c. alta,** senate; House of Lords, upper house.—**c. ardiente,** = **c. mortuoria.**—**c. baja,** House of Commons, lower house, chamber of deputies.—**c. clara,** = **c. lúcida.**—**c. de comercio,** chamber of commerce.—**c. de diputados,** Chamber of Deputies; House of Representatives.—**c. lúcida,** (opt.) camera lucida.—**c. mortuoria,** funeral chamber.—**c. obscura,** camera obscura.—**c. plegadiza,** folding camera.

camarada, *n.* comrade, companion, crony, pal, or chum.—**camaradería,** *f.* (Gal.) comradeship, camaraderie.

camaraje, *m.* rent for a granary.

camaranchon, *m.* garret; attic.

camarera, *f.* head waiting maid; keeper of the queen's wardrobe; chambermaid; waitress.

camarería, *f.* employment of a waiting maid; ancient perquisite of the lord chamberlain.

camarero, *m.* chamberlain; steward or keeper of stores; waiter; valet.

camareta, *f. dim.* (naut.) small cabin; deck cabin; midshipman's cabin.

camariento, ta, *a.* having diarrhœa.

camarilla, *f. dim.* small room; coterie of private advisers of the king; coterie or ring of influential persons; clique.

camarín, *m.* place behind an altar where the images are dressed and the ornaments kept; closet; car (of elevator); (theat.) dressing room.

camarista. I. *m.* member of the supreme council; (Mex.) valet. **II.** *f.* maid of honor to the queen and princesses.

camarita, *f. dim.* small chamber or room.

camarlengo, *m.* lord of the bedchamber of the kings of Aragon; camerlengo.

cámaro, camarón, *m.* (zool.) shrimp.

camaronero, ra, *n.* shrimp seller.

camarote, *m.* (naut.) stateroom, cabin.

camasquince, *n.* meddlesome person.

camastra, *n.* (Chile) cunning, trickery.

camastrear, *vn.* (Chile) to dissemble, act cunningly.

camastro, *m.* poor, miserable bed.

camastrón, na, *n.* sly, artful, cunning person.

camastronazo, *m. aug.* great impostor, humbug.

camastronería, *f.* cunning, humbug, trickery.

camatones, *m. pl.* (naut.) iron fastenings of the shrouds.

camba, *f.* check of a bridle; felloe, outer rim of a wheel; a V-shaped piece in garments.

cambalache, *m.* (coll.) barter, swap; swapping. —**cambalachear,** *va.* to barter, to swap.— **cambalachero, ra,** *n.* barterer.

cambaleo, *m.* strolling troupe of players.

cámbaro, *m.* crawfish.

cambiable, *a.* exchangeable; changeable; changing.

cambiador, ra, *n.* barterer; money changer; (Chile, Mex.) (Ry.) switchman.

cambial, *m.* bill of exchange.

cambiamano, *f.* railroad switch.

cambiamiento, *m.* change, alteration.

cambiante. I. *a.* bartering, exchanging; changing. **II.** *m.* banker, exchanger; iridescence; iridescent fabric.

cambiar. I. *va.* to change; to barter; to exchange. **II.** *vn.* to change, shift.—**c. de opinión,** to change one's mind.—**c. de traje,** to change (one's) clothes.

cambiavía, *m.* (Am.) (Ry.) switch; switch tender.

cámbija, *f.* reservoir.

cambio, *m.* change; barter; exchange; premium paid or received for negotiating bills; rate of exchange (of money); rise and fall of the course of exchange; public or private bank; return of a favor; recompense.—**c. minuto,** small change.—**a c. de,** in exchange for.—**en c.,** in return; on the other hand.—**en c. de,** in lieu of, instead of; in return for.

cambista, *m.* banker, money broker; (Arg.) (Ry.) switchman.

cambray, *m.* cambric, fine linen.—**cambrayado, acambrayado, da,** *a.* cambriclike.—**cambrayón,** *m.* coarse cambric.

cambriano, na; cámbrico, ca, *a.* (geol.) Cambrian.

cambrón, *m.* (bot.) buckthorn; bramble.

cambronal, *m.* brambled ground or place.

cambronera, *f.* (bot.) boxthorn.

cambuj, *m.* child's cap tied close to keep its head straight; mask.

cambujo, ja, *n.* & *a.* Indian mestizo; half-breed.

cambullón, *m.* (Peru) imposition, swindle.

cambur, *m.* a kind of plantain or banana.—**c. amarillo,** or **criollo,** yellow or Johnson banana.—**c. higo,** or **titiaro,** very small and fine variety of banana.—**c. manzano,** small banana with apple flavor.—**c. morado,** red banana.

cambuy, *m.* an American myrtle tree.

camedafne, *f.* (bot.) dwarf bay.

camedrio, camedris, *m.* (bot.) wall germander.

camelar, *va.* to flirt; court; woo; seduce, deceive.

camelea, *f.* (bot.) widowwail.

camelete, *m.* (obs.) a kind of large gun.

camelia, *f.* (bot.) camellia.

camelo, *m.* flirtation; courtship; joke; jest.

¹camelote, *m.* camlet, a waterproof garment.

²camelote, *m.* (bot.) a tropical weed.

camelotillos, *m. pl.* light or thin camlets.

¹camella, ¹gamella, *f.* curve in each end of yoke (for animals).

²camella, ²gamella, *f.* pail for feeding animals; milk pail.

³camella, *f.* she-camel; ridge in plowed land.

camellejo, *m. dim.* small camel.

camellería, *f.* stable or stand for camels; employment of a camel driver.

camellero, *m.* keeper or driver of camels.

camello, *m.* camel; an ancient gun; engine for setting ships afloat in shoal water.—**c. pardal,** giraffe.

¹camellón, *m.* ridge turned up by plow or spade; bed of flowers; camlet; (Am.) avenue, boulevard; cultivated lands in the islets of the Valley of Mexico.

²camellón, *m.* drinking trough; carpenter's horse.

camero, ra. I. *n.* upholsterer; one who lets beds. **II.** *a.* pertaining to beds.

camilla, *f. dim.* small bed, pallet, cot; litter, stretcher; clothes horse; shearer's frame.

caminador, ra, *n.* good walker.

caminante, *m.* traveler, walker.

caminar, *vn.* to walk, travel, go, move along.— **c. con pies de plomo,** to act cautiously, go slowly.—**c. derecho,** to act uprightly.

caminata, *f.* long walk for exercise; "hike"; promenade; excursion, jaunt, outing.

caminero, ra, *a.* road, highway (as *a.*).

camino, *m.* road; highway; path, pass; passage, trip, journey; profession, station, calling; way; manner, method; (min.) drift, gait; (naut.) ship's way, rate of sailing.—**c. carretero,** vehicle road, drive.—**c. cubierto,** (mil.) covert way.—**c. de herradura,** bridle road.—**c. de hierro,** railroad.—**c. de ruedas = c. CARRETERO.—c. de sirga,** tow path.—**c. real,** highway.—**c. trillado,** thoroughfare; routine; commonplace.—**c. vecinal,** municipal road, cared for by a municipality.—**abrir c.,** to open the way, find the means.—**de c.,** stopping on the way; traveling (as *a.*).—**de un c. dos mandados,** to kill two birds with one stone.—**en c. (de),** on the way (to), on one's way (to).—**fuera de c.,** off the road; unreasonable; astray.—**no llevar c.,** to be wrong, not to be cogent, not to lead anywhere.—**partir el c. con,** to meet half way.—**ponerse en c.,** to set out, start.— **traer a buen c.,** to disabuse, open the eyes of (one who is in error).

camión, *m.* dray, truck; (Mex.) bus.—**c. automóvil,** autotruck.—**camionaje,** *m.* truckage.

camisa, *f.* shirt; chemise; thin skin (of fruit); coat of whitewash; slough of a serpent; (mil.) chemise; (obs.) catamenia; jacket, case, casing; lining (of a furnace).—**c. alquitranada,** **embreada,** or **de fuego,** (naut.) fire chemise. —**c. de fuerza,** strait jacket.—**c. de una vela,** (naut.) body of a sail.—**c. de vapor,** steam jacket.—**meterse en c. de once varas,** to interfere in other people's affairs.—**no llegarle a uno la c. al cuerpo,** to be frightened; to be anxious.

camisería, *f.* shirt store, haberdashery.

camisero, ra, *n.* shirt maker, haberdasher.

camiseta, *f.* undershirt; short shirt with wide sleeves; chemisette.

camisilla, *f. dim.* small shirt.

camisola, *f.* ruffled shirt; dicky.

camisolín, *m.* shirt front; tucker; wimple.

camisón, *m. aug.* long and wide shirt; nightshirt; (Am.) (woman's) gown; (Cuba) chemise.

camisote, *m.* hauberk, long coat of mail.

camita, *n. & a.* Hamite(-tic).—**camítico, ca,** *a.* Hamitic.

camomila, *f.* chamomile.

¹camón, *m. aug.* large bed; portable throne; glass partition; oriel window.

²camón, *m. aug.* each one of the round pieces forming the frame of a water wheel; oak tires of cart wheels; lath frame of an arch.

camoncillo, *m.* seat in a drawing-room.

camorra, *f.* quarrel.—**camorrear,** *vn.* to quarrel.

camorrista, *n.* noisy, quarrelsome person.

camote, *m.* (Am.) sweet potato; infatuation; love; lie, fib; lover; fool.—**tragar c.,** to hesitate in speaking, become confused, get rattled.

campal, *a.* field, camp (as *a.*).

campamento, *m.* encampment; camp.

campana, *f.* bell; anything bell-shaped; (fig.) parish church, parish; bell-shaped bottom of a well; (arch.) drum, corbel.—**c. de chimenea,** mantel of a chimney.—**c. de buzo,** diving bell. —**c. de rebato,** alarm bell.—**oír campanas y no saber dónde,** to have heard of a fact, but not to be well informed of its true nature.— **campanada,** *f.* stroke of a bell; scandal; sensational report.—**campanario,** *m.* belfry; noddle, head; rack (in looms).

campanear. I. *vn.* to ring the bells frequently. **II.** *va.* to divulge; to noise about.

campanela, *f.* a fancy step in dancing.

campaneo, *m.* bell ringing; chime; affected sway in walking.

campanero, *m.* bell founder; bellman; (ornith.) bellbird.

campaneta, *f. dim.* small bell.

campanil, *m.* small belfry.

campanilla, *f. dim.* small bell; hand bell; small bubble; (anat.) uvula; little tassel for ladies' gowns; (naut.) cabin bell; (bot.) bellflower.

campanillazo, *m.* violent ringing of a bell; signal given with a bell.

campanillear, *vn.* to keep ringing a small bell.

campanillero, *m.* bellman; public crier.

campanología, *f.* campanology.

campanólogo, ga, *n.* campanologist.

campante, *a.* surpassing; buoyant, cheerful.

campanudo, da, *a.* puffed up; bell-shaped; (bot.) campanulate; pompous, high-sounding.

campánula, *f.* (bot.) bellflower.

campanuláceo, a. I. *a.* (bot.) campanulaceous. **II.** *f. pl.* Campanulaceæ.

campanulado, da, *a.* campanulate, bell-shaped.

campaña, *f.* campaign; level country.—**c. naval,** (naut.) cruise.—**batir,** or **correr, la c.,** to reconnoiter.

campañol, *m.* water rat.

campar, *vn.* to excel; ACAMPAR, to encamp

campeador, ra, *a.* surpassing in bravery.

campear, *vn.* to be in the field; to pasture; frisk about; crop out; grow; be prominent, excel.

campecico, illo, ito, *m. dim.* small field.

campechana, *f.* (Cuba & Mex.) a kind of cocktail or mixed drink; (Venez.) hammock.

¹campechano, na, *a.* frank; hearty; cheerful; generous.

²campechano, na, *n. & a.* native of or pert. to Campeche.

campeche, *m.* campeche wood, logwood.

campeón, *m.* champion; combatant; defender.

campeonato, *m.* championship.

campero, ra. I. *a.* exposed to the weather in the open field; unsheltered, unhoused; good at farming; (Mex.) having a gait like gentle trotting; pacing. **II.** *m.* friar who superintends a farm; field guard.

campesino, na; campestre. I. *a.* rural; country (as *a.*), rustic. **II.** *n.* countryman(-woman).

campilán, *m.* long, straight sabre used in P. I.

campillo, *m. dim.* small field.

campiña, *f.* flat tract of arable land; field; country; landscape.

campo, *m.* country; field; space, room; ground of silks and other stuffs; (mil.) field, camp; ground of a painting.—**c. de Agramonte,** bedlam.—**c. de batalla,** battle field.—**c. de golfo,** golf course.—**c. de labor,** cultivated ground; farm.—**c. del honor,** field of honor. —**c. de puna,** (Arg.) sandy, clayey grounds not suitable for cattle raising.—**c. magnético,** magnetic field.—**c. raso,** flat, open field (mainly in the phrase **a c. raso,** in the open air, in the open, without shelter).—**c. santo,** or **camposanto,** cemetery.—**c. visual,** field of vision.—**a c. traviesa,** or **travieso,** *adv.* crosscountry.—**dar c. a la fantasía,** to give free range to one's fancy.—**quedar en el c.**, to be killed.—**salir al c.**, to go out to fight a duel.

camuatí, *m.* (Am.) hut, rough cabin.

camuesa, *f.* (bot.) pippin (apple).

camueso, *m.* (bot.) pippin tree; dunce, fool.

camuñas, *f. pl.* all seeds, except wheat, barley, and rye.

camuza, gamuza, *f.* chamois goat.

camuzón, gamuzón, *m. aug.* large chamois skin.

can, *m.* dog; (arch.) bracket; shoulder; modillion; corbel; trigger; an ancient piece of ordnance.—**C. Mayor,** (astr.) Canis Major.—**C. Menor,** (astr.) Canis Minor.—**el C.**, the Dog Star.

¹**cana,** *f.* gray hair.—**echar una c. al aíre,** to go on a lark.

²**cana,** *f.* long measure, about two ells.

canabíneo, a. I. *a.* (bot.) pertaining to the hemp family. **II.** *f. pl.* the hemp family.

canáceo, a. I. *a.* (bot.) cannaceous. **II.** *f. pl.* Cannaceæ.

canadense, canadiense, *n.* & *a.* Canadian.

canal. I. *m.* channel; strait; canal; duct.—**abrir en c.**, to cut from top to bottom. **II.** *f.* natural underground waterway; long and narrow dell; any open conduit; groove; gutter; carcass, body of an animal killed and dressed for food; comb of the loom; hemp once hackled; front edge of a book; drinking trough; crease, slot in metalwork; bed of a hot press; (tel.) copper pole; well (of the rim of a wheel).—**c. maestra,** (arch.) main valley drain, or gutter (of a tiled roof).—**sombrero de c.**, priest's hat.

canalado, da, *a.* = ACANALADO, fluted; grooved.

canaladura, *f.* (arch.) hollow molding; groove.

canaleja, *f. dim.* small drinking trough; mill spout; SOMBRERO DE CANAL, priest's hat.

canalera, *f.* roof gutter.

canalete, *m.* bladed paddle for canoeing.

canalita, *f. dim.* small channel, gutter or groove.

canalización, *f.* canalization; (elec.) wiring.

canalizar, *va.* to construct channels or canals in or for; to improve the channel of (a river, etc.); to canalize; (elec.) to wire.

canalizo, *m.* (naut.) narrow channel.

canalón, *m. aug.* gutter, leader, spout; gargoyle.

canalla. I. *f.* rabble, canaille. **II.** *m.* mean, despicable fellow, cur.—**canallada,** *f.* base, despicable act.—**canallesco, ca,** *a.* base, currish.

canameño, *m.* (Am.) traveling hammock.

canana, *f.* cartridge belt.

cananeo, a, *n.* & *a.* Canaanite (-ish).

canapé, *m.* couch; settee; lounge.

canard, *m.* (Am., Gal.) canard, a false report.

canaria, *f.* female canary bird.

canariense, *n.* & *a.* (person) of the Canary Islands.

canario, ria. I. *a.* CANARIENSE. **II.** *m.* canary bird; a dance introduced into Spain by natives of the Canaries; (naut.) a barge used in the Canary Islands; (Chile) generous patron (of hotel or restaurant), good tipper. **III.** *interj.* zounds!

canasta, *f.* basket, hamper; crate.

canastero, ra, *n.* basket maker.

canastilla, *f. dim.* small basket; gift to ladies of the court; an infant's basket; layette.

canastillo, *m.* small tray; pannier; small basket.

canasto, canastro, *m.* large basket.—**¡canastos!** *interj.* gracious! confound it!

¹**cáncamo,** *m.* a rare gum resembling myrrh.

²**cáncamo,** *m.* (naut.) ringbolt.—**c. de argolla,** ringbolt.—**c. de ojo,** eyebolt.

cancamurria, *f.* (coll.) sadness, melancholy.

cancamusa, *f.* (coll.) trick to deceive.

cancán, *m.* cancan (dance).

¹**cáncana,** *f.* cricket, stool for punishing children.

²**cáncana,** *f.* a kind of spider.

cancanear, *vn.* to loiter about, loaf; (Am.) to stammer.

cancaneo, *m.* (Am.) stammering.

cáncano, *m.* (coll.) louse.

cancel, *m.* wooden screen; glass partition in chapel for the king incognito.

cancela, *f.* front door grating or screen.

cancelación, canceladura, *f.* cancellation, expunging, obliteration.

cancelar, *va.* to annul; to dispel.

cancelaría, cancelería, *f.* papal chancery.

cancelario, *m.* chancellor in universities who grants degrees.

cáncer, *m.* (med.) cancer; (C-, astr.) Cancer.

cancerarse, *vr.* to develop a cancer; to become cancerous.

Cancerbero, *m.* (myth.) Cerberus; strict and incorruptible guard.

canceroso, sa, *a.* cancerous.

cancilla, *f.* wicker door or gate.

canciller, *m.* chancellor.

cancilleresco, ca, *a.* pert. to or like a chancery.

cancillería, *f.* chancery, chancellery.

canción, *f.* song, lay, ballad.—**c. vernácula,** folk song.—**cancioncica, illa, ita,** *f. dim.* canzonet.—**cancionero,** *m.* song book; song writer.—**cancioneta,** *f. dim.* little song, canzonet.—**cancionista,** *n.* author or singer of songs, songster, ballad singer.

cancriforme, *a.* cancriform.

cancrinita, *f.* (min.) cancrinite.

cancro, *m.* (bot.) sore spot in trees, canker.

cancrófago, ga, *a.* crab-eating.

cancroide, *m.* (med.) cancroid tumor.

cancroideo, ea, *a.* cancroid, cancriform.

cancha, *f.* roasted corn or beans; (Am.) popcorn; cockpit; game grounds; (tennis) court.

canchal, *m.* ground full of boulders.

canchalagua, canchelagua, canchilagua, *f.* (Peru) a medicinal herb.

canchear, *vn.* (S. A.) to shirk, evade doing one's duty.

canchero, ra, *n.* (Am.) owner or keeper of game grounds; (S. A.) shirker; (Peru) (of some priests) extortioner, bleeder.

cancho, *m.* big boulder or rock.

candado, *m.* padlock; pendant; earring.—*pl.* cavities around the frog of a horse's feet.

candamo, *m.* an old rustic dance.

candar, *va.* to lock, shut.

cándara, *f.* sifting screen, sieve.

candela, *f.* fire; light; candle, taper; flower or blossom of the chestnut tree; inclination of the balance needle towards the thing weighed.—**en c.**, (of a mast) vertical.

candelabro, *m.* candelabrum; bracket.

candelada, *f.* = HOGUERA, bonfire; blaze.

candelaria, *f.* Candlemas; (bot.) mullen.

candelecho, *m.* hut built on piles for watching a vineyard.

candelerazo, *m.* blow with a candlestick.

candelero, *m.* candlestick; student's lamp; fishing torch.—*pl.* (naut.) stanchions or crotches.—**estar en c.**, (fig.) to be high in office; to hold an exalted station.

candelica, illa, ita, *f. dim.* small candle.

candelilla, *f.* (surg.) bougie, catheter; blossom; will-o'-the-wisp; firefly; catkin, ament.—**le hacen candelillas los ojos,** (coll.) his eyes sparkle with the fumes of wine.

candelizas, *f. pl.* (naut.) brails.

candelizo, *m.* (coll.) = CARÁMBANO, icicle.

candencia, *f.* incandescence.

candente, *a.* incandescent, red-hot.

cándidamente, *adv.* candidly.

candidato, *m.* candidate.

candidatura, *f.* candidacy; list of candidates; (U. S. pol.) slate.

candidez, *f.* ingenuousness; whiteness.

cándido, da, *a.* simple, guileless; white, snowy.

---

candiel, *m.* sweetmeat of white wine, egg yolks, sugar, etc.

candil, *m.* kitchen or stable oil lamp; Greek lamp; (coll.) cock of a hat; (coll.) long irregular fold in petticoats; (Mex.) chandelier; top of a stag's horn.—**candilada,** *f.* (coll.) oil spilt from a lamp.—**candileja,** *f.* oil receptacle of a lamp.—*pl.* footlights of a theater; (bot.) willow-herb.—**candilejo,** *m. dim.* small kitchen lamp; (bot.) lucern.—**candilera,** *f.* (bot.) campion; lamp wick made from campion leaves. —**candilón,** *m. aug.* large open lamp.

candiota. I. *n.* & *a.* of the island of Candía. **II.** *f.* barrel; cask; large earthen jar for wine.— **candiotera,** *f.* wine cellar; storage place for casks.—**candiotero,** *m.* CANDIOTA maker.

candonga, *f.* (coll.) cunning; (coll.) merry, playful trick; practical joke; (coll.) draught mule.

candongo, ga, *a.* (coll.) cunning, artful.—**candonguear,** *va.* (coll.) to joke with; play a joke on; (coll.) to shirk.—**candonguero, ra,** *n.* (coll.) joker.

candor, *m.* pure whiteness; candor.

candorosamente, *adv.* candidly.

candoroso, sa, *a.* candid, ingenuous.

cané, *m.* a card game of chance.

caneca, *f.* glazed stone bottle for liquor and cordials.

canecillo, *m.* (arch.) corbel, modillion; truss; cantilever; console.

canéfora, *f.* canephore.

canela, *f.* (bot.) cinnamon; (coll.) anything exquisitely fine; (Colomb.) vim, energy.

canelado, da, acanelado, da, *a.* = CANELO, *a.*

canelo, la. I. *a.* cinnamon-colored. **II.** *m.* cinnamon tree.

canelón, *m.* gargoyle; CANALÓN, gutter, spout; icicle; tubular fringe; cinnamon candy.—*pl.* end of a cat-o'-nine-tails.

canequí, caniquí, *m.* fine muslin.

canesú, *m.* corset cover; yoke of a shirt.

caney, *m.* (Venez.) log cabin; (Cuba) bend of a river; bight.

canfol, *m.* (chem.) camphol, borneol.—**canfolato,** *m.* (chem.) campholate.—**canfólico, ca,** *a.* (chem.) campholic.

canfor, alcanfor, *m.* camphor.

canforato, *m.* (chem.) camphorate.

canfórico, ca, *a.* (chem.) camphoric.

cangilón, *m.* earthen jar or pitcher; metal tankard for wine; bucket (of a water wheel); fold of a frilled collar; (Am.) hole, pit; ditch; (Peru) wrinkle (in a poorly made garment).

cangrejal, *m.* place frequented by crabs.

cangrejero, ra, *n.* crab seller.

cangrejo, *m.* (zool.) crab; crawfish.

cangrejuelo, *m. dim.* small crab.

cangrena, gangrena, *f.* gangrene.—**cangrenarse, gangrenarse,** *vr.* to get gangrenous. —**cangrenoso, sa, gangrenoso, sa,** *a.* gangrenous.

canguelo, *m.* (coll.) fear.—**tener c.,** to show the white feather.

cangüeso, *m.* (ichth.) a sea fish.

canguro, *m.* (zool.) kangaroo.

cania, *f.* (bot.) small nettle.

caníbal, *m.* cannibal, man-eater.

canibalismo, *m.* cannibalism.

canica, *f.* wild cinnamon.

canicie, *f.* whiteness of the hair.

canícula, *f.* dog days; (C-, astr.) Dog Star.

canicular, I. *a.* canicular, pert. to CANÍCULA. **II.** *m. pl.* dog days.—**caniculario,** *m.* beadle who keeps dogs out of church.

canido, *m.* a kind of parrot.

cánidos, *m. pl.* (zool.) Canidæ, the dog family.

canijo, ja, *a.* (coll.) weak, infirm, sickly.

canil, *m.* coarse bread, dogs' bread.

canilla, *f.* long bone of leg or arm; any of the principal bones of the wing of a fowl; stop-

cock, faucet; reel, bobbin, spool; unevenness of the woof in thickness or color.—**c. de la pierna,** tibia, shin bone.—**c. del brazo,** ulna, arm bone.

canillado, da, *a.* ribbed, striped (cloth).

canillaire, *m.* = CANILLERO.

canillera, *f.* ancient leg armor; (Am.) fear.

canillero, ra. I. *n.* one who makes reels. **II.** *m.* small tap in a cask or vat; weaver's quill winder.

canime, *m.* (bot.) a Colombian tree producing a medicinal oil.

canina, *f.* excrement of dogs.

caninamente, *adv.* furiously, snarling.

caninero, *m.* collector of dogs dung for tanyards.

caninez, *f.* inordinate appetite.

canino, na, *a.* canine.

caniquí, *m.* cannequin, Indian fine muslin.

canje, *m.* (mil., dipl., com., journ.) exchange.

canjeable, *a.* that can be exchanged.

canjear, *va.* to exchange (prisoners, treaties, credentials, newspapers).

cano, na, *a.* gray-haired; hoary, hoar; frosty; ancient; (poet.) white.

canoa, *f.* canoe; (Am.) conduit; (Am.) trough (esp. for feeding animals).—**canoero,** *m.* canoeman.

canoi, *m.* (Am.) basket used by Indians in a fishing party.

canoíta, *m. dim.* small canoe.

canon, *m.* canon, rule, precept; catalogue of the books composing the Bible; catalogue, list; part of the mass; (law) fee paid in acknowledgment of superiority in a higher lord; (mus.) canon; (print.) canon type.—*pl.* canons canonical law.

canonesa, *f.* canoness.

canónica, *f.* canonic life in a convent.

canonical, *a.* canonical, pertaining to canons.

canónicamente, *adv.* canonically.

canonicato, *m.* = CANONJÍA.

canónico, ca, *a.* canonical, canonic.

canóniga, *f.* (coll.) nap taken before dinner.

canónigo, *m.* canon, prebendary.

canonista, *m.* canonist.

canonizable, *a.* worthy of canonization.

canonización, *f.* canonization.

canonizar, *va.* to canonize; consecrate; (fig.) to applaud or praise.

canonjía, *f.* canonship, canonicate; sinecure.

canoro, ra, *a.* canorous, musical, melodious.

canoso, sa, *a.* gray-haired, hoary, hoar, frosty.

canquén, *m.* (zool.) Chilean wild goose.

cansadamente, *adv.* botheringly, importunely.

cansado, da. I. *pp.* of CANSAR. **II.** *a.* tired; weary; tedious, tiresome, dry. **III.** *m.* bore.

cansancio, *m.* tiredness, weariness, fatigue.

cansar. I. *va.* to weary, tire, fatigue; to tease, harass; to bore; (agr.) to exhaust (the soil.) **II.** *vr.* to become tired or weary. **III.** *vn.* to be tiring or tiresome.

cansera, *f.* (coll.) fatigue; boredom.

cansino, na, *a.* (of animals) worn out by work.

cantable. I. *a.* that can be sung; (mus.) to be sung slowly. **II.** *m.* (mus.) passage in a simple, even tempo.

cantábrico, ca; cántabro, bra, *n.* & *a.* Cantabrian, of or from Cantabria.

cantada, *f.* = CANTATA.

cantador, *n.* singer (gen. of popular songs).

cantal, *m.* stone block.

cantaleta, *f.* charivari; tin-pan serenade.—**dar c.,** (coll.) to deride; laugh at; turn into ridicule; sermonize.—**estar con la misma c.,** to harp on the same string.—**cantaletear,** *va.* (Am.) to lecture, scold; to keep repeating ad nauseam.

cantante, *n.* & *a.* singer(-ing).

¹cantar, *m.* song set to music.—**C. de los Cantares,** Song of Songs.—**cantares de gesta,** old legendary romances.—**ése, or eso, es otro**

c., (coll.) that is another story, that is a horse of another color.

²**cantar. I.** *va.* to sing.—**cantarlas claras,** to speak in plain language, to make no bones about, to call a spade a spade. **II.** *vn.* to sing; to speak out; (coll.) to creak, make a harsh, grinding noise; (coll.) to divulge or give away a secret; at cards, to call out the trump.—**c. de piano,** to make a full confession.

cántara, *f.* large, narrow-mouthed pitcher; a liquid measure (32 pints).

cantarcico, illo, ito, *m. dim.* little song.

cantarera, *f.* shelf for jars, pitchers, etc.

cantarería, *f.* earthenware shop.

cantarero, ra, *n.* dealer in earthenware.

cantárida, *f.* Spanish fly; cantharides, Spanish fly blistering plaster; blister raised by the blistering plaster.

cantarillo, *m. dim.* small jar or pitcher.

cantarín, ina, *m. & f.* (coll.) songster(-tress); professional singer.

cántaro, *m.* large, narrow-mouthed pitcher, and the liquid contained in it; a wine measure; vessel into which votes are put.—**llover a cántaros,** to rain pitchforks, to pour.

cantata, *f.* (mus.) cantata, choral composition.

cantatriz, *f.* (woman) singer.

canteles, *m. pl.* (naut.) ends of old ropes put under casks to keep them steady.

cantera, *f.* (stone) quarry; talent, genius.

cantería, *f.* art of hewing stone; building made of hewn stone; parcel of hewn stone.

cantero, *m.* stonecutter; extremity of a hard substance that can be easily separated from the rest.—**c. de heredad,** piece of ground.—**c. de pan,** crust of bread.

canticio, *m.* (coll.) constant or frequent singing.

cántico, *m.* canticle.

cantidad, *f.* quantity; amount; (phonet.) quantity; sum of money; large portion.—**c. de movimiento,** (mech.) momentum.

cantiga, *f.* poetical composition to be put to music.

cantil, *m.* steep rock.

cantilena, *f.* = CANTINELA.

cantimplora, *f.* siphon; water cooler; (Chile, Mex.) canteen, water bottle; (Colomb.) powder flask; (Guat.) mumps.

cantina, *f.* wine cellar; (Am.) bar room, saloon, public house; canteen; restaurant (esp. in Ry. station); case used to cool wine on a journey.

cantinela, *f.* ballad; irksome repetition of a subject.

cantinera, *f.* vivandière.

cantinero, *m.* one in charge of drinks; saloon keeper, bartender.

cantiña, *f.* (coll.) a popular song.

cantizal, *m.* stony ground.

¹**canto,** *m.* singing; short heroic poem; canto, division of a long poem; chant or canticle.—**c. tradicional,** folk song.—**al c. del gallo,** at cock's crow, at dawn.—**con un c. a los pechos,** with pleasure, alacrity.

²**canto,** *m.* end, edge, border; crust (of a loaf); thickness; back of a knife; front edge of a book; stone, pebble; game of throwing the stone (duck on a rock); quarry stone, block; ashlar stone.—**c. rodado,** boulder.—**a c.,** very near.—**al c.,** by the side of.—**de c.,** on edge.

cantón, *m.* corner; canton, region.—**cantonada,** *f.* corner.—**dar c.,** to disappoint or evade.

cantonal, *a.* cantonal.

cantonalismo, *m.* (pol.) a cantonal system.

cantonar, *va.* to quarter (troops).

cantonearse, *vr.* = CONTONEARSE, (coll.) to strut.

cantoneo, *m.* = CONTONEO, a strut.

cantonera, *f.* plate nailed to the corners of a chest, etc.; corner plate, clip; angle iron; corner bracket; wench; street walker.

cantonero, ra, *n.* loafer.

cantor, ra. I. *n.* singer; minstrel; one who composes hymns or psalms; small singing bird. **II.** *a.* that sings.—**ave cantora,** song bird.

cantorcillo, *m. dim.* worthless singer.

cantorral, *m.* = CANTIZAL, stony ground.

cantoso, sa, *a.* stony.

cantuariense, *a.* of or pert. to Canterbury.

cantueso, *m.* (bot.) French lavender, spike.

canturía, *f.* vocal music; musical composition; monotonous singing; method of performing musical compositions.

canturrear, canturriar, *va. & vn.* to hum, sing in a low voice.

cánula, *f.* canula, short tube used in surgery.

canutero, *m.* = CAÑUTERO.

canutillo, *m.* = CAÑUTILLO.

canuto, *m.* = CAÑUTO.

caña, *f.* cane; reed; reed spear; stem, stalk; walking stick; bone of arm or leg; leg, upper part of boot or stocking; chase (of a gun); groove (for the barrel of a firearm); subterranean passage in mines; shaft of a column; marrow; (naut.) helm, tiller; drill; ratchet drill; a long and narrow wine tumbler; an Andalusian song; crack in a sword's blade; glass blower's pipe; (carp.) shank; reed of wind instruments.—**c. brava,** (Am.) bamboo.—**c. de azúcar,** sugar cane.—**c. de Bengala,** rattan.—**c. de cuentas,** (bot.) Indian shot, Indian reed.—**c. de Indias,** rattan.—**c. de la India** = C. DE CUENTAS.—**c. del pulmón,** (anat.) trachea.—**c. de pescar,** fishing pole or rod.—**c. de vaca,** bone of a cow's leg.—**c. dulce,** sugar cane.—**correr cañas,** to engage in equestrian exercises with reed spears.

cañacoro, *m.* (bot.) Indian shot, Indian reed.

cañada, *f.* dell, ravine; cattle path.

cañadilla, *f.* a kind of murex, an edible mollusk.

cañaduzal, *m.* = CAÑAMELAR.

cañafístola, cañafístula, *f.* (bot.) a tropical tree with long pods, Cassia fistula; the pods.

cañaheja, cañaherla, *f.* (bot.) fennel-giant.

cañahuate, *m.* (bot.) a species of lignum-vitæ.

cañajelga, *f.* = CAÑAHEJA.

cañal, *m.* cane or reed plantation or field; reed weir for fishing; small channel for catching fish.

cáñama, *f.* assessment of taxes.

cañamar, *m.* hemp field.

cañamazo, *m.* coarse canvas; canvas for embroidery; embroidered canvas; burlap.

cañamelar, *m.* sugar-cane plantation.

cañameño, ña, *a.* hempen, made of hemp.

cañamiel, *f.* (bot.) sugar cane.

cañamiza, *f.* hemp bagasse; bun.

cáñamo, *m.* (bot.) hemp; cloth made of hemp.—**c. en rama,** undressed hemp.—**cañamón,** *m.* hemp seed.

cañar, *m.* = CAÑAL.

cañareja, *f.* = CAÑAHEJA.

cañariego, ga, *a.*—**pellejos cañariegos,** skins of sheep that die on the road.

cañarroya, *f.* (bot.) pellitory, wallwort.

cañavera, *f.* (bot.) reed grass.—**cañaveral,** *m.* cane or reed field; (Colomb.) bamboo field.

cañaverear, *va.* to wound with sharp-pointed canes.

cañaverería, *f.* place where reed grass, reeds or bamboo are sold.

cañaverero, ra, *n.* cane, reed or bamboo seller.

cañedo, *m.* = CAÑAVERAL.

cañería, *f.* conduit; water or gas pipe line.

¹**cañero, ra.** *n.* conduit maker; pipe layer.

²**cañero, ra. I.** *n.* (Am.) sugar-cane dealer; owner or manager of sugar-cane plantation. **II.** *m.* (Mex.) store room in a sugar mill.

cañete, *m. dim.* small tube.

cañilavado, da, *a.* (of horses, mules) small-limbed.

cañilla, ita, *f. dim.* small cane or reed.

For pronunciation, see the rules at the beginning of the book.

cañillera, *f.* = CANILLERA, ancient leg armor.

cañiza, *f.* coarse linen.

cañizal, cañizar, *m.* = CAÑAVERAL.

cañizo, *m.* hurdle, frame for rearing silkworms; hurdle used by hatters for shearing hats; (naut.) flake.

caño, *m.* tube, pipe; open sewer, ditch; gutter; spout; conduit; cellar or other place for cooling water; organ tube or pipe; (naut.) channel at the entrance to seaports.

cañón, *m.* any cylindrical tube or pipe; tube or pipe for blowing glass; quill; down, soft feathers; leg or sleeve of a garment; part of the beard next to the root; (Colomb.) trunk (of tree); cannon, gun; (min.) gallery; (mech.) socket; (Mex., P. R., Peru) gorge, ravine, canyon; bit of a bridle; flue (of a chimney); well (of a staircase).—**c. antiaéreo,** anti-aircraft gun.—**c. antitanque,** antitank gun.—**c. obús,** howitzer.—**c. rayado,** rifled gun.

cañonazo, *m.* cannon shot; report of a gun.

cañoncico, illo, ito, *m. dim.* small cannon; small tube or pipe.

cañonear. I. *va.* to cannonade, bombard. **II.** *vr.* to cannonade each other.—**cañoneo,** *m.* cannonade; bombardment.—**cañonera,** *f.* embrasure for cannon; large tent; holster; gunboat.—**cañonería,** *f.* set of organ pipes; (mil.) number of cannons collectively.—**cañonero, ra. I.** *a.* (naut.) carrying guns. **II.** *f.* gunboat.

cañota, *f.* (bot.) paniculate sorghum.

cañucela, *f.* slender cane or reed.

cañuela, *f. dim.* small reed; (bot.) fescue grass.

cañutazo, *m.* (coll.) information, gossip, tale.

cañutería, *f.* set of organ pipes.

cañutero, *m.* pin or needle case.

cañutillo, *m. dim.* small tube or pipe; bugle for fringes, tassels, etc.; quill of gold or silver twist for embroidery.

cañuto, *m.* internode of a cane; small pipe or tube; informer, talebearer.—**cañutos helados,** (Mex.) small ice-cream cylinders.

caoba, caobana, *f.* (bot.) mahogany.

caobo, *m.* (bot.) mahogany (tree).

caolín, *m.* fine white clay used in pottery making.

caos, *m.* chaos.—**caótico, ca,** *a.* chaotic.

capa, *f.* cloak, mantle, cape; layer; coat, coating; lamina; cover; (fig.) cloak, mask, cover; color of an animal; hider, harborer; property; fortune; (com.) primage; an American rodent; the spotted cavy; third mold used in casting bells; coat of paint; bed, stratum, vein, seam; (mas.) bed, course; wrapper for tobacco.—**c. del cielo,** canopy of heaven.—**c. del timón,** rudder coat.—**c. magna,** pontifical cope worn by officiating bishops.—**c. pluvial,** pluvial or choir cope.—**c. rota,** secret emissary.—**a c. y espada,** at any cost; through thick and thin. —**andar,** or **ir, de c. caída,** to be down in the mouth, seedy, crestfallen.—**de c. y gorra,** informal, informally.—**echar la c. al toro,** to risk all on a last effort, to play one's last trump. —**estar,** or **estarse, a la c.,** (naut.) to lie to.— **hacer de su c. un sayo,** to go one's way, to follow one's own judgment.

capá, *m.* capa, W. I. tree used for shipbuilding.

capacete, *m.* helmet, casque.

capacidad, *f.* capacity; contents; ability, capability; talent.

capacitación, *f.* training.

capacitar, *va. & vr.* to enable, qualify, prepare; to commission, empower, delegate.

capacha, *f.* fruit basket, hamper.

capachazo, *m.* blow with a basket.

capachero, *m.* one who carries things in baskets.

capacho, *m.* fruit basket; hamper, large basket; hempen pressing bag; leaf wrapper (for salt, etc.); bundle (of salt) done up in leaves; (Peru)

bag, pocket; (Bol.) old hat; (ornith.) common barn owl.—**c. de albañil,** bricklayer's hod.

capada, *f.* (coll.) anything carried in a person's cloak; cloakful.

capadocio, cia, *n. & a.* Cappadocian.

capador, *m.* gelder, castrator; gelder's whistle.

capadura, *f.* castration; scar from castration; leaf of second cut tobacco, used for filling or wrappers.

capar, *va.* to geld, castrate; (coll.) to curtail, cut down, reduce.

caparazón, *m.* caparison; saddle cover; oil-cloth carriage cover; piano cover; hempen feed bag, nose bag; carcass of a fowl; shell of insects and crustaceans.

caparídeo. I. *a.* (bot.) caparidaceous. **II.** *f. pl.* Caparidaceæ.

caparra, *f.* sheep louse.

caparrilla, *f. dim.* small tick that infests bees.

caparrós, *m.,* **caparrosa,** *f.* copperas.—**c. azul,** blue vitriol.—**c. blanca,** white vitriol.—**c. verde,** green vitriol.

capataz, *m.* overseer, foreman, steward, warden, conductor; leader.—**c. de cultivo,** practical agriculturist or forester.

capaz, *a.* capacious, ample, roomy, large; capable, able, competent.

capaza, *f.* (prov.) = CAPACHO.

capazmente, *adv.* capaciously, amply; ably.

¹capazo, *m.* large basket; hamper; esparto mat.

²capazo, *m.* blow with a cloak.

capazón, *m. aug.* very large esparto basket.

capciosamente, *adv.* insidiously, captiously, artfully, cunningly.

capcioso, sa, *a.* captious, insidious, artful.

capeador, *m.* bull fighter who challenges the bull with his cloak; cloak stealer.

capear, *va.* to strip or rob (one) of one's cloak; to challenge (a bull) with the cloak; (naut.) to lay to; (fig.) to evade (in discussion).

capeja, *f. dim.* small shabby cloak or cape.

capelina, *f.* (surg.) capeline, caplike bandage.

capelo, *m.* dues to bishops from their clergy; cardinal's hat or office; (Am.) glass bell.

capellada, *f.* toe piece of a shoe.

capellán, *m.* chaplain; clergyman.—**c. castrense,** army chaplain.—**c. de altar,** priest who assists at the mass.—**c. de honor,** the king's private chaplain.—**c. de navío,** navy chaplain.—**c. mayor de los ejércitos,** vicar-general of the army.

capellanía, *f.* chaplaincy.

capellar, *m.* a Moorish cloak.

capellina, *f.* headpiece of a helmet or casque; hood worn by country people; trooper wearing a helmet; (surg.) = CAPELINA.

capeo, *m.* challenging a bull with a cloak.

capeón, *m.* young bull challenged with a cloak.

capero, *m.* priest who carries the cope, or pluvial, in churches; cloak rack.

caperuceta, illa, ita, *f. dim.* small hood.— **Caperucita Roja,** or **Encarnada,** Little Red Ridinghood.

caperuza, *f.* pointed hood or cap; ulster cap.—**c. de chimenea,** chimney cap.—**dar en c.,** (coll.) to frustrate one's views and designs.

caperuzón, *m. aug.* large hood.

capeta, *f.* short cape.

capialzado, *a.* (arch.) arched cap piece; back (arch).

capibara, *m.* (Am.) capybara, a large S. A. rodent.

capichola, *f.* ribbed silk stuff.

capicholado, da, *a.* resembling CAPICHOLA.

capidengue, *m.* small cloak worn by women.

capigorrista; capigorrón, na, *n.* (coll.) vagabond; slovenly person; student who never takes a high degree.

capilar, *n. & a.* capillary.

capilaridad, *f.* capillarity; capillary attraction.

capilla, *f.* hood; cowl; chapel; small church;

priests and others employed in chapel service; choir (musicians and singers) of a church; chapter or assembly of collegians; (print.) author's proof sheet; (mil.) portable chapel; death house.—**c. ardiente,** chapelle ardente, a hall or chamber where a dead body lies in state.—**estar en c.,** to be in the death house, to be sentenced to death and awaiting execution; (coll.) to be on pins and needles.

capillada, *f.* hoodful; blow with a hood.

capilleja, ita, *f. dim.* small chapel.

capillejo, *m. dim.* small hood; skein of sewing silk.

capiller, capillero, *m.* sexton; churchwarden.

capilleta, ita, *f. dim.* small chapel; shrine.

capillo, *m.* child's cap; christening fee; baptismal cap; ancient hood for women; bud of a rose; toe-piece lining; cap of a distaff; net for catching rabbits; colander for wax; silk cocoon; cloth that covered church offering; (anat.) foreskin.

capilludo, da, *a.* resembling a hood or cowl.

capincho, carpincho, *m.* (zool.) = CAPIBARA.

capirotada, *f.* a batter made of herbs, eggs, etc.

capirotazo, *m.* fillip on the nose.

capirote. I. *a.* (of cattle) having the head of a different color from that of the body. **II.** *m.* hood; half-gown worn by collegians; sharp-pointed cap worn in processions; hood of a hawk.—**c. de colmena,** cover of a beehive.

capirotero, *a.* (hawk) used to wearing a hood.

capirucho, *m.* (coll.) = CAPIROTE.

capisayo, *m.* cloaklike garment; bishop's vestment.

capiscol, *m.* precentor, leader of church choir.

capiscolía, *f.* office and dignity of a precentor.

capita, *f. dim.* small cloak.

capitación, *f.* capitation, head or poll tax.

capital. I. *m.* capital; estate of a husband at his marriage; principal (money placed at interest, invested, etc.); (com.) capital, capital stock; (mil.) capital of a bastion. **II.** *f.* capital city. **III.** *a.* capital, pertaining to the head; main, principal; leading; essential; great; excellent, unsurpassed.

capitalicé, capitalice, *v. V.* CAPITALIZAR.

capitalino, na, *a. & n.* (Am.) from or pertaining to the capital (city).

capitalismo, *m.* capitalism.

capitalista, *n. & a.* capitalist(-ic).

capitalización, *f.* capitalization.

capitalizar, *va.* (*pret.* CAPITALICÉ; *subj.* CAPITALICE) to capitalize, add interest to principal.

capitalmente, *adv.* fatally; seriously.

capitán, *m.* captain; ringleader; leader, commander.—**c. de bandera,** (naut.) captain of the admiral's ship.—**c. de fragata,** navy officer ranking as lieutenant colonel.—**c. del puerto,** (naut.) port captain; harbor master. —**c. de navío,** navy officer ranking as a colonel.—**c. general,** captain general.—**c. general de ejército,** field marshal.—**c. general de provincia,** commander-in-chief of a military district.—**capitana,** *f.* admiral's ship; captain's wife.—**capitanear,** *va.* to command; to head, lead.

capitanía, *f.* captainship; captaincy; company commanded by a captain; tax paid to the port captain by ships anchored in the harbor.—**c. del puerto,** harbor master's position.—**c. general,** captaincy general.

capitel, *m.* (arch.) capital of a column or pilaster; spire over the dome of a church.

capitolino, na, *a.* pertaining to the capitol; Capitoline.

capitolio, *m.* capitol; any lofty or majestic public building.

capitón, *m.* (zool.) pollard, chub.

capítula, *f.* lesson, Bible passage read at divine service.

capitulación, *f.* capitulation; stipulation, agreement.—**c. de matrimonio,** articles of marriage.

capitulante, *n. & a.* capitulator(-ing).

¹**capitular. I.** *m.* capitular, member of a chapter. **II.** *a.* capitulary, pertaining to a chapter.

²**capitular. I.** *vn.* to enter into agreement; draw up the articles of a contract; to compound; to sing prayers at divine service; to capitulate. **II.** *va.* (law) to impeach.

capitulario, *m.* prayer book for divine service.

capitularmente, *adv.* according to the rules of a chapter.

capitulear, *vn.* (Am.) to lobby.—**capituleo,** *m.* lobbying.

capítulo, *m.* chapter; meeting of the prelates of religious orders, and place where they meet; meeting; charge, reproof, reprimand.—**capítulos matrimoniales,** articles of marriage.— **llamar a c.,** to call to account, to take to task.

capnomancia, *f.* divination by smoke.

capolado, *n.* hash, minced meat.

capolar, *va.* to hash, mince, or chop; to behead.

¹**capón. I.** *a.* castrated, gelded. **II.** *m.* eunuch; capon; fagot, bundle of brushwood; (naut.) anchor stopper at the cathead.

²**capón,** *m.* (coll.) fillip on the head.

capona, *f.* epaulet without fringe.

caponado, da. I. *pp.* of CAPONAR. **II.** *a.* tied together, as branches of vines.

caponar, *va.* to tie up (the branches of vines).

caponera, *f.* coop, inclosure to fatten poultry; (coll.) place where one lives well at other people's expense; (coll.) jail; (mil.) caponier.

caporal, *m.* chief, ringleader; (Mex.) keeper of horned cattle.

capot, *m.* (aer.) cowl, cowling, engine cover.

¹**capota,** *f.* head of the teasel or fuller's thistle; light bonnet; leather top of some vehicles.

²**capota,** *f.* cape without a hood.

capote, *m.* raglan or cloak with sleeves to keep off rain; short cloak of bright color, used by bullfighters; browbeating; (coll.) thick cloud or mist.—**dar c.,** to leave a guest without dinner, for coming late; to win all the tricks at cards. —**dije para mí c.,** I said to myself.

capotear, *va.* to trick (a bull) with a CAPOTE; to wheedle, bamboozle; to evade cleverly.

capotera, *f.* (Am.) hat, or clothes, rack.

capotero, ra, *n.* cloak maker or dealer.

capotillo, *m.* cape, mantelet.—**c. de dos faldas,** a loose jacket.

capotín, *m. dim.* small cloak or CAPOTE.

capotudo, da, *a.* frowning.

caprario, ria, *a.* pertaining to the goat.

Capricornio, *m.* (astr.) Capricorn.

capricho, *m.* caprice, whim, fancy; great desire; (mus.) caprice, capriccio; (art) original work that ignores accepted rules.

caprichosamente, *adv.* capriciously.

caprichoso, sa, *a.* capricious; stubborn.

caprichudo, da, *a.* stubborn; whimsical.

caprifoliáceo, a. I. (bot.) caprifoliaceous. **II.** *f. pl.* Caprifoliaceæ.

caprino, na, *a.* caprine, goatlike.

caprípedo, da, *a.* (zool.) capriped, goat-footed.

cápsula, *f.* metal cap on bottles; cartridge shell; (bot., anat., chem., pharm.) capsule.

capsular, *a.* capsular, capsulary.

captar, *va.* to captivate, attract, win.

captura, *f.* (law) capture, seizure.

capturar, *va.* (law) to apprehend; to arrest.

capuana, *f.* (coll.) spanking.

capucha, *f.* hood; cowl; capuche; (print.) circumflex accent.

capuchina, *f.* (bot.) nasturtium; small lamp with extinguisher; confection of egg yolks.— *pl.* (naut.) crotches and knees.

capuchino, na, *n. & a.* Capuchin (monk, nun).

capucho, *m.* cowl, hood.—**capuchón,** *m. aug.*

---

of CAPUCHO; lady's cloak with hood; short domino.

capulí, capulín, *m.* capulin, a kind of cherry.

capullito, *m. dim.* small cocoon; small bud.

capullo, *m.* cocoon; flax knotted at the end; (com.) bunch of boiled flax; flower bud; coarse stuff of spun silk; acorn cup; chestnut bur; (anat.) foreskin.

capuz, *m.* ancient hooded cloak; CHAPUZ, ducking (a person).

capuzar, *va.* (naut.) to sink (a ship) by the head.

caquéctico, ca, *a.* (med.) cachectic.

caquexia, *f.* (med.) cachexia, emaciation and failing health.

caqui, *n.* & *a.* khaki.

car, *m.* (naut.) larger end of the mizzenyard.

cara, *f.* face; visage, mien, countenance; base of a sugar loaf; façade, front, surface, facing.—**c. a c.,** face to face.—**c. apedreada** = C. EM-PEDRADA.—**c. de acelga,** pale, sallow face.—**c. de aleluya** = C. DE PASCUA.—**c. de bronce,** brazen face.—**c. de cartón,** wrinkled face.—**c. de hereje,** harried face.—**c. de Pascua,** smiling, cheerful face.—**c. de perro,** ugly (angry) face, bearish face.—**c. de pocos amigos,** churlish look, froward countenance.—**c. de vaqueta** = C. DE BRONCE.—**c. de viernes,** sad, lean, meagre face.—**c. empedrada,** face pitted by the smallpox.—**c. y cruz,** heads or tails.—**a c. descubierta,** openly.—**buena c.,** good appearance; promising or encouraging appearance.—**de c.,** opposite, facing.—**dar a uno con las puertas en la c.,** to shut the door in one's face.—**dar el sol de c.,** to have the sun in one's face.—**dar en c.,** to call to task, to throw in one's face.—**decírselo en su c.,** to tell one to one's face.—**de dos caras,** double-faced, false.—**no volver la c. atrás,** not to flinch.

carabao, *m.* (zool.) carabao.

cárabe, *m.* amber. Also ÁMBAR.

carabela, *f.* (naut.) caravel; large provision basket.—**carabelón,** *m.* (naut.) brig, brigantine.

carabido, da. I. *a.* (entom.) carabideous. **II.** *m. pl.* Carabidæ, large carnivorous beetles.

carabina, *f.* fowling piece; carbine.—**c. rayada,** rifle carbine.—**la c. de Ambrosio,** a harmless weapon; a worthless thing; bluff.—**carabinazo,** *m.* report or firing of a carbine; carbine wound.—**carabinero, ra,** *n.* carabineer; internal-revenue guard.

¹cárabo, *m.* a small Moorish vessel; (zool.) a kind of crab or cockle.

²cárabo, *m.* (ornith.) a large horned owl.

caracal, *m.* (zool.) a kind of lynx.

caracará, *m.* (ornith.) caracara, a kind of hawk.

caracoa, *f.* (P. I.) small oared barge.

caracol, *m.* (zool.) snail; winding staircase (also ESCALERA DE C.); prancing of a horse; night-dress used by women in Mexico; cochlea of the ear.—**c. marino,** periwinkle.—**caracola,** *f.* small snail with a whitish shell; shell used as a horn.—**caracolear,** *vn.* (of horses) to caracole, wheel.—**caracolejo,** *m. dim.* small snail or snail shell.—**¡caracoles!** *interj.* = ¡CARAMBA!

caracoleo, *m.* caracoling.

caracolero, ra, *n.* snail gatherer or dealer.

caracolilla, *f. dim.* small snail shell.

caracolillo, *m. dim.* small snail; (bot.) snail-flowered kidney bean; veined mahogany.—*pl.* trimmings, fringes.—**café c.,** pea-bean coffee.

caracolito, *m. dim.* small snail.

carácter, *m.* character; brand on cattle; temper, nature, disposition; loftiness of soul, firmness, energy; style of speaking or writing.—**caracteres de imprenta,** printing types.

caractericé, caractérice, *v.* V. CARACTERIZAR.

característica, *f.* characteristic; feature, fundamental property; (math.) characteristic.

característicamente, *adv.* characteristically.

característico, ca. I. *a.* characteristic, typical, distinctive, distinguishing. **II.** *m.* & *f.* actor or actress who plays the part of an old person.

caracterizado, da, *a.* characterized, distinguished; apt, competent; reliable, responsible.

caracterizar, *va.* (*pret.* CARACTERICÉ; *subj.* CA-RACTERICE) to characterize, distinguish by peculiar qualities; to confer a distinguished employment, dignity, or office on; to mark, point out; to act (a part) properly.

caracha, *f.*, **carache,** *m.* itch, mange (esp. of llamas).

caracho, cha, *a.* violet-colored.

caraguata, *f.* a kind of Paraguayan sisal.

caraja, *f.* sail used by Vera Cruz fishermen.

caramanchel, *m.* fixed or movable shed over the hatchways of ships.

caramanchón, *m.* = CAMARANCHÓN, garret.

¹caramba, *interj.* (coll.) gracious! confound it!

²caramba, *f.* ancient headgear for women.

carámbano, *m.* icicle, a shoot of ice.

carambanado, da, *a.* forming icicles.

carambillo, *m.* (bot.) saltwort.

¹carambola, *f.* carom, in billiards; a method of playing the card game called *revesino*; (coll.) device or trick to deceive.—**por c.,** (coll.) indirectly.

²carambola, *f.* (bot.) fruit of the carambola tree.

carambolo, *m.* (bot.) carambola tree.

carambolear, *va.* (billiards) to carom.

carambolero, *m.* carom player; *revesino* player.

carambú, *m.* (bot.) willow herb.

caramel, *m.* (ichth.) a kind of pilchard or sardine.

caramelización, *f.* caramelization.

caramelizar, *va.* to caramelize.

caramelo, *m.* caramel; (P. I.) fondant.

caramente, *adv.* dearly; exceedingly, highly; rigorously; solemnly (swear, entrust, etc.).

caramiello, *m.* a kind of hat worn by women.

caramillar, *m.* saltwort field.

caramilleras, *f. pl.* pothook.

caramillo, *m.* flageolet; small flute; (bot.) saltwort; confused heap of things; deceit; tricks; gossip; tale-carrying.

caramuzal, *m.* vessel used by the Moors.

caranga, *f.* (Am.), **carángano,** *m.* (Colomb., C. R., Cuba), louse.

carantamaula, *f.* (coll.) hideous mask or visor; ugly, hard-featured person.

carantoña, *f.* (coll.) ugly old woman who makes up and dresses stylishly.—*pl.* caresses, soft words and acts of endearment.—**carantoñera,** *f.* coquette.—**carantoñero,** *m.* flatterer, cajoler.

caraña, *f.* a kind of resinous American gum.

caráota, *f.* (Venez.) bean.

carapa, *f.* (bot.) carapa, carap.

carapacho, *m.* shell (cover of certain animals).

carapato, *m.* castor oil.

caraqueño, ña, *a.* of Caracas.

carasol, *m.* sun parlor, solarium.

carate, *m.* brown spots on the skin, similar to "liver spots"—common in the lowlands of S. A.—**caratejo, ja, caratoso, sa,** *a.* (Am.) having CARATE.

carátula, *f.* pasteboard or wire mask; (Am.) title page of a book; (fig.) the histrionic art.

caratulero, ra, *n.* mask maker or dealer.

carava, *f.* holiday meeting of country people.

caravana, *f.* caravan; company of traders, pilgrims, etc.

¹caray, carey, *m.* tortoise; tortoise shell.

²caray, *interj.* (Am.) = ¹[CARAMBA!

caraza, *f. aug.* big face.

cárbaso, *m.* a kind of fine flax; (poet.) sail of a ship; an ancient tunic.

carbinol, *m.* (chem.) carbinol.

carbólico, ca, *a.* carbolic.

carbolíneo, *m.* (chem.) carbolineum.

carbón, *m.* coal; charcoal; carbon (of an arc lamp).—**c. animal,** bone black, animal charcoal.—**c. de arranque,** root charcoal (made from roots).—**c. de leña,** charcoal.—**c. de piedra,** or **mineral,** coal.—**c. vegetal** = c. DE LEÑA.

carbonada, *f.* coal charge of a furnace; broiled chop or steak; grillade; a kind of pancake.

carbonario, *m.* Carbonaro, member of a secret pol. party.—**carbonarismo,** *m.* Carbonarism.

carbonatado, da, *a.* (chem.) carbonated.

carbonatar, *va.* (chem.) to carbonate.

carbonato, *m.* (chem.) carbonate.

carboncillo, *m. dim.* small coal; black crayon; carbon pencil.

carbonear, *vn.* & *va.* to make charcoal (of).

carboneo, *m.* carbonization; charring.

carbonera, *f.* wood prepared for burning into charcoal; place where charcoal is made; coalhouse, coal hole, coal cellar, coal bin; coal pit, colliery, coal mine; woman who sells charcoal.

carbonería, *f.* coal yard, coal shed; coal mine.

carbonero, ra. I. *a.* pert. to coal or charcoal. **II.** *m.* & *f.* coal or charcoal seller. **III.** *m.* charcoal maker; collier, coal miner; coal merchant; (naut.) coal ship, collier.

carbonicé, carbonice, *v. V.* CARBONIZAR.

carbónico, ca, *a.* (chem.) carbonic.

carbónidos, *m. pl.* (chem.) carbon and its compounds.

carbonífero, ra, *a.* carboniferous.

carbonita, *f.* carbonite.

carbonización, *f.* carbonization.

carbonizado, da, *a.* carbonized.

carbonizar, *va.* (*pret.* CARBONICÉ; *subj.* CARBONICE) to carbonize; to char.

carbono, *m.* (chem.) carbon.

carbonoso, sa, *a.* carbonaceous, coaly, charry.

carborundo, *m.* carborundum.

carboxilo, *m.* (chem.) carboxyl.

carbuncal, *a.* carbuncular.

carbunclo, *m.* carbuncle, garnet; sometimes used for ruby (also CARBÚNCULO); CARBUNCO.

carbunco, *m.* gangrenous tumor.

carbuncoso, sa, *a.* = CARBUNCAL.

carbúnculo, *m. V.* CARBUNCLO.

carburación, *f.* carburation.

carburador, *m.* (auto, etc.) carburetor.

carburante, *n.* & *a.* containing hydrocarbons.

carburar, carburizar, *va.* to carburize, carburet.

carburo, *m.* (chem.) carbide.

carcaj, *m.* = ¹CARCAX.

carcajada, *f.* outburst of laughter.

carcajear(se), *vn.* & *vr.* (coll.) to laugh boisterously or heartily.

carcamal, *n.* (coll.) old, decrepit person.

carcamán, *m.* tub; heavy, unseaworthy vessel.

cárcamo, *m.* (Am.) riffle, a cleated trough.

carcañal, calcañal, *m.* heel bone, calcaneum.

cárcava, *f.* gully; (mil.) inclosure; mound; hedge; ditch; grave.

carcavina, *f.* = CÁRCAVA.

cárcavo, *m.* hollow in which a water wheel turns.

carcavón, *m.* large and deep ditch.

carcavuezo, *m.* deep pit.

¹carcax, *m.,* **carcaza,** *f.* quiver; sash with a case in which the cross is borne in a procession; (Am.) leathern case for a rifle at the saddle bow.

²carcax, *m.* Moorish anklet.

cárcel, *f.* jail; prison; groove of a sluice gate; (carp.) clamp, clasp, cramp; (mech.) holder; cheek; collar; (print.) cheek of a printing press; (weaving) reed of a loom.—**carcelaje,** *m.* jailer's fees.—**carcelario, ria,** *a.* pert. to a jail.

carcelería, *f.* imprisonment; bail given for the appearance of a prisoner.

carcelero, ra. I. *a.* = CARCELARIO. **II.** *m.* jailer, warden.

carceraje, *m.* = CARCELAJE.

carcinoma, *m.* (med.) carcinoma, cancer.

carcinomatoso, sa, *a.* (med.) carcinomatous.

cárcola, *f.* treadle of a loom.

carcoma, *f.* wood borer; woodlouse; wood tick; gribble; dust made by the wood borer; grief, anxiety; spendthrift.

carcomer. I. *va.* to gnaw; (of wood borers) to destroy; to consume or impair by degrees, to undermine. **II.** *vr.* to decay, decline; become worm- or insect-eaten.—**carcomido, da,** *a.* worm-eaten; consumed; decayed; impaired.

carda, *f.* act of carding; teasel; card; hatter's jack; severe reprimand or censure; (naut.) a small vessel like a galley.

cardador, ra, *n.* carder, comber; (entom.) myriapod.

cardadura, *f.* carding, combing (wool).

cardamomo, *m.* (bot.) cardamomum.

cardar, *va.* to card or comb (wool); to raise (the nap on cloth) with a teasel.

cardelina, *f.* (ornith.) goldfinch, thistle finch.

¹cardenal, *m.* wale, welt.

²cardenal, *m.* (eccl.) cardinal; (ornith.) Virginian nightingale; cardinal bird.

cardenalato, *m.* cardinalate, cardinalship.

cardenalicio, cia, *a.* pert. to a cardinal.

cardencha, *f.* (bot.) teasel; card, comb.—**c. cardadora,** fuller's teasel.—**c. silvestre,** wild teasel.

cardenchal, *m.* place where teasels grow.

cardenillo, *m.* verdigris; (art) verditer, Paris green.

cárdeno, na, *a.* livid.

cardería, *f.* place where wool is carded.

cardero, ra, *n.* maker of cards (for wool).

cardíaca, *f.* (bot.) common motherwort.

cardíaceo, a, *a.* heart-shaped.

cardíaco, ca, *a.* (med.) cardiac.

cardialgia, *f.* (med.) cardialgia, heartburn.

cardiálgico, ca, *a.* pert. to cardialgia.

cardias, *m.* cardiac orifice of the stomach.

cardico, illo, ito, *m. dim.* small thistle.

cardílico, ca, *a.* cardiac, pert. to the heart.

cardillo, *m.* (bot.) golden thistle.

cardinal, *a.* cardinal (point); main, fundamental.

cardiografía, *f.* cardiography.

cardiógrafo, *m.* cardiograph.

cardiología, *f.* cardiology.

cardiópata, *n.* (med.) person with heart disease.

cardipatía, *f.* (med.) cardiopathy, heart disease.

cardioscopio, *m.* (med.) cardiometer.

carditis, *f.* (med.) carditis.

cardizal, *m.* land full of thistles and weeds.

cardo, *m.* (bot.) thistle.—**c. alcachofero,** garden artichoke.—**c. aljonjero,** stemless, carline thistle.—**c. arrocife,** cardoon artichoke.—**c. bendito,** blessed thistle, centaury, holy thistle.—**c. borriqueño,** (bot.) spear-plume thistle.—**c. corredor,** sea holly, field eringo.—**c. de comer, c. hortense** = c. ARROCIFE.—**c. huso,** wooly carthamus.—**c. lechero,** or **mariano,** milk thistle.—**c. santo** = c. BENDITO.—**c. setero** = c. CORREDOR.—**c. silvestre** = c. BORRIQUEÑO.

cardón, *m.* act and effect of carding; (bot.) CARDENCHA, teasel.

Cardona, *m.*—**más listo que C.,** very smart, clever fellow, sharp as a needle.

cardoncillo, *m.* (bot.) mountain carthamus.

carducé, carduce, *v. V.* CARDUZAR.

carducha, *f.* large iron comb for wool.

cardume, cardumen, *m.* school of fish; (Chile) multitude of things.

carduzador, *m.* carder.

carduzal, *m.* = CARDIZAL.

carduzar, *va.* (*pret.* CARDUCÉ; *subj.* CARDUCE) to card or comb (wool).

carear, *va.* (law) to confront (criminals); (coll.)

to compare; to tend (cattle, sheep).—*vr.* to assemble or meet; to meet face to face.

carecer, *vn.* (*ind.* CAREZCO; *subj.* CAREZCA) (**de**) to lack, not to have.

carena, *f.* (naut.) careening, repairing; (poet.) ship.—**dar c.,** (coll.) to reprimand in a jocular way; to banter.—**carenar,** *va.* (naut.) to careen, repair.

carencia, *f.* lack; scarcity, deficiency.

carenero, *m.* careening place.

carente, *pres.p. irreg.* of CARECER.—**c. de,** in need of.

careo, *m.* (law) confrontation of criminals or witnesses; comparison; act of placing or meeting face to face; (fort.) front of a bastion or fortress.

carero, ra, *a.* (coll.) selling things dear.

carestía, *f.* scarcity, dearth; lack; famine; dearness, high price.

careta, *f.* mask.—**quitar la c.,** to tear off the mask, to unmask.

careto, ta, *a.* (of horses) having the forehead marked with a white spot or stripe.

carey, *m.* (zool.) tortoise; tortoise shell.

carezco, carezca, *v.* V. CARECER.

carga, *f.* load; burden; freight; cargo; loading; charge (of a cannon, furnace, etc.); nozzle of the flask which measures the powder for a charge; corn measure containing 4 FANEGAS; a preparation to cure sprains and inflammation in horses and mules; impost, duty, tax; (hydraul.) head; (mil.) charge, attack.—**c. concejil,** municipal obligatory service.—**c. de rotura,** or **de fractura,** breaking load.—**c. fija,** (eng.) dead load.—**c. hidrostática,** (hydraul.) head.—**c. móvil,** (eng.) live load.—**c. personal,** obligatory personal service.—**a cargas,** abundantly, in great plenty.—**volver a la c.,** to insist; to harp on a subject; to keep at it.

cargadas, *f. pl.* a card game.

cargadera, *f.* (naut.) downhauls, brails.—*pl.* (Colomb.) (trousers) suspenders.

cargadero, *m.* place where goods are loaded or unloaded; freight station.

cargadilla, *f.* (coll.) increase of a debt through the accumulation of interest.

cargado, da. I. *pp.* of CARGAR. **II.** *a.* full; fraught. —**c. de espaldas,** round-shouldered, stooping. —**c. de vino,** full, tipsy. **III.** *m.* Spanish step in dancing.

cargador, *m.* shipper; freighter; expressman, carrier; porter; rammer, ramrod; large pitchfork for straw; (arch.) post put in a doorway or window; (naut.) tackle; plate used in gilding.

cargamento, *m.* (naut.) cargo; shipment.

cargar. I. *va. & vn.* (*pret.* CARGUÉ; *subj.* CARGUE) to load; burden; to carry (a load); to charge (a furnace, battery, etc.); to attack; to ship; to overload, overburden; to clog; to lay in, collect; to charge on account; to book; to impose or lay (taxes); to impute, charge (one) with; to crowd; (coll.) to vex, annoy, pester; in cards, to take (a card with a higher one); (gram.) to put more stress or inflection on one letter or syllable.—**c. la mano,** to pursue with eagerness; to reproach with severity; to overcharge; to be too exacting. **II.** *vn.* to incline, tip; (**en** or **sobre**) to rest (on), be supported (by), lean (against); (of trees) to bear abundantly; (**con**) to assume (responsibility); bear (the blame); carry away; (**sobre**) to urge, press. **III.** *vr.* (**sobre**) to rest (on); (**contra**) to lean (against, on); (of clouds or sky) to gather, become denser, heavier or darker; (**de**) to have or obtain a large number or quantity (of); to load oneself (with); to become tired, peeved or vexed (about); to trouble oneself (with).—**c. de razón,** to strengthen one's position, find greater justification.

cargareme, *m.* receipt, voucher.

cargazón, *f.* cargo; abundance; clumsy, badly made thing.—**c. de cabeza,** heaviness of the head.—**c. de tiempo,** cloudy, thick weather.

cargo, *m.* act of loading; burden, load, weight; load of stones weighing 40 *arrobas* (1000 lb.); number of baskets piled one on the other and put in the oil press; load of pressed grapes to be re-pressed; total amount of what has been received, in a general account; post, dignity, office, ministry; charge, keeping, care; duty, obligation; command or management; fault or inefficiency in the performance of duty; charge, accusation; (law) count.—**c. concejil,** compulsory public office or function.—**c. de conciencia,** remorse, sense of guilt.—**c. y data,** (com.) creditor and debtor (Cr. and Dr.). —**a c. de,** in charge of, under the direction of. —**hacer c. a uno de,** to charge one with.— **hacerse c. de,** to take charge of, be responsible for; to take into consideration; to make oneself acquainted with; to understand.

cargoso, sa, *a.* burdensome, onerous.

cargué, cargue, *v.* V. CARGAR.

carguera, *f.* (Colomb.) nursemaid.

carguero, ra. I. *a.* (beast) of burden; freight-carrying, freight (as *a.*). **II.** *n.* beast of burden.

carguío, *m.* cargo, freight; load.

cariacontecido, da, *a.* sad, mournful.

cariacuchillado, da, *a.* scar-faced.

cariado, da, *a.* (of bone, teeth) carious, decayed.

cariadura, *f.* (med.) caries, bone ulcer.

cariagüileño, ña, *a.* (coll.) aquiline-nosed and pointed-faced.

carialegre, *a.* smiling, cheerful.

cariampollado, da, *or* **cariampollar,** *a.* round-faced, plump-cheeked.

cariancho, cha, *a.* broad-faced, chubby, chub-faced, bull-faced.

cariarse, *vr.* (med.) to become carious.

cariátide, *f.* (arch.) caryatides.

caribe, *m.* cannibal, man-eater, savage; Carib, Antilles Indian; (Venez.) a man-eating fish.

caribito, *m.* (Am.) a river fish of the bream species.

cariblanco, *m.* a C. A. small wild boar.

caribobo, *a.* stupid- or dumb-looking.

caribú, *m.* (zool.) caribou.

carica, *f.* a kind of spotted kidney bean.

caricatura, *f.* caricature; cartoon.—**caricaturar,** *va.* to caricature.—**caricaturesco, ca,** *a.* caricaturish.—**caricaturista,** *m.* caricaturist. —**caricaturizar,** *va.* = CARICATURAR.

caricia, *f.* caress; petting; endearing expression.

cariciosamente, *adv.* fondlingly, caressingly.

caricioso, sa, *a.* fondling, endearing, caressing.

caricuerdo, da, *a.* wise-looking.

caridad, *f.* charity, charitableness; refreshment given to travelers at the church door.—**la c. empieza por uno mismo,** charity begins at home.

caridelantero, ra, *a.* (coll.) brazen-faced, bold-looking.

caridoliente, *a.* mournful-looking.

caries, *f.* (med., bot.) caries.

carifruncido, da, *a.* (coll.) wrinkle-faced; frowning, cross-looking.

carigordo, da, *a.* (coll.) full-faced.

cariharto, ta, *a.* round-faced.

carilampiño, ña, *a.* (Am.) smooth-faced, beardless.

carilargo, ga, *a.* long-visaged.

carilucio, cia, *a.* (coll.) having a shining face.

carilla, *f. dim.* little or small face; face guard; silver coin in Aragon worth eighteen CINEROS, or deniers; page (of a book).

carilleno, na, *a.* (coll.) plump-faced.

carillo, lla, *a. dim.* rather dear or expensive.

carillón, *m.* carillon.

carimba, *f.* (Peru) brand on slaves.

For pronunciation, see the rules at the beginning of the book.

carincho, *m.* a dish resembling chile con carne.

carinegro, gra, *a.* of a swarthy complexion; black-faced.

cariñana, *f.* ancient headdress like a nun's veil.

cariño, *m.* love, fondness, affection; endearing expression.—**tener c.** (*indir. obj.*), to be fond of.

cariñosamente, *adv.* fondly, kindly.

cariñoso, sa, *a.* affectionate, loving; affable.

cariocinesis, *f.* (biol.) mitosis.

cariofileo, a. I. (bot.) caryophyllaceous. **II.** *f. pl.* Caryophyllaceæ.

cariofilina, *f.* (chem.) cariophyllene.

cariópsida, *f.* (bot.) caryopsis.

carioquinesis, *f.* (incorrect for) CARIOCINESIS.

cariparejo, ja, *a.* (coll.) having an impassive countenance, "poker face."

carirraído, da, *a.* (coll.) brazen-faced, impudent.

carirredondo, da, *a.* round-faced.

carisma, *m.* divine gift or favor, charism.

carita, *f. dim.* little or small face.

caritán, *m.* (P. I.) gatherer of tuba (liquor from certain plants).

caritativamente, *adv.* charitably.

caritativo, va, *a.* charitable.

cariucho, *m.* (Ecua.) dish of meat, potatoes and garlic.

cariz, *m.* aspect.

carlán, *m.* a person having certain rights and jurisdiction in a district.

carlanca, *f.* mastiff's collar.—**tener muchas carlancas,** to be very cunning or crafty.

carlancón, *m.* (coll.) very sharp or crafty person.

carlanía, *f.* dignity and district of a CARLÁN.

carlear, *vn.* to pant.

carlín, *m.* an ancient silver coin.

carlina, *f.* (bot.) carline thistle.

carlinga, *f.* (naut.) step of a mast.

carlismo, *m.* Carlism.—**carlista,** *n., a.* Carlist.

carlita, *f.* reading eyeglasses.

carlovingio, gia, *a.* Carlovingian.

carmañola, *f.* carmagnole.

carmelita. I. *n. & a. f.* Carmelite. **II.** *f.* flower of Ind. cress.—**carmelitano, na,** *a.* Carmelite.

¹carmen, *m.* country house and garden; villa.

²carmen, *m.* Carmelite religious order.

³carmen, *m.* verse; poem.

carmenador, *m.* teasler (man or machine).

carmenadura, *f.* teaseling (woolen cloth, etc.)

carmenar, *va.* to teasel; to disentangle, unravel; to comb (the hair); (coll.) to pull (the hair); to cheat.

carmes, *m.* kermes, the cochineal insect.

carmesí. I. *m.* cochineal powder. **II.** *n. & a.* crimson, bright red.

carmín, *m.* coloring matter of cochineal; carmine color; (bot.) pokeweed, phytolacca.—**c. bajo,** pale rose color.

carminativo, *m.* (med.) carminative.

carnada, *f.* bait.

carnadura, *f.* muscularity; flesh, fleshiness.

carnaje, *m.* salt beef.

carnal. I. *a.* carnal, sensual; related by blood; full (as in *hermano carnal*, full brother). **II.** *m.* time of the year when meat may be eaten (opposed to Lent and other fast days).

carnalidad, *f.* carnality, lustfulness.

carnalmente, *adv.* carnally, sensually.

carnaval, *m.* carnival.—**carnavalesco, ca,** *a.* pertaining to or resembling a carnival.

carnaza, *f.* fleshy side of a hide or skin; (coll.) abundance of meat; bait.

carne, *f.* flesh; meat; pulp (of fruit); flesh, one of the evil temptations; kin; name of a children's game with a hollow bone.—**c. ahogadiza,** meat from a drowned animal.—**c. asada en horno,** baked meat.—**c. asada en parrillas,** broiled meat.—**c. bien cocida,** well-done meat.—**c. cediza,** tainted meat.—**c. de cañón,** cannon fodder; inferior person or peo-

ple.—**c. de gallina,** (fig.) goose flesh.—**c. de membrillo,** preserved quinces.—**c. de pelo,** meat of small quadrupeds (hares, rabbits, etc.).—**c. de pluma,** flesh of fowls.—**c. de res,** (Am.) beef.—**c. fiambre,** cold meat.—**c. magra, c. mollar,** lean meat.—**c. nomia,** (coll.) choice meat without bones.—**c. sin hueso,** (fig.) much profit and little trouble.—**c. viva,** quick or raw flesh in a wound.—**c. y hueso,** flesh and blood.—**c. y sangre,** flesh and blood, near kindred.—**cobrar carnes,** to recover one's flesh or weight, to pick up.—**echar carnes,** (coll.) to grow fat, put on flesh.—**en carnes,** naked.—**en c. viva,** raw, with the flesh exposed.—**envuelto en carnes,** fleshy, fat.—**ni c. ni pescado,** neither flesh nor fish; nondescript; insipid.—**ser c. y hueso de,** to be flesh and blood of, to be part and parcel of.—**ser uña y carne,** (fig.) to be hand and glove, to be one, to be intimate.—**tener c. de perro,** to have an iron constitution.

carnecilla, *f.* small excrescence on the body.

carnerada, *f.* flock of sheep.

carneraje, *m.* tax or duty on sheep.

carnerario, *m.* (prov.) charnel house.

carnereamiento, *m.* poundage, penalty for the trespass of sheep.

carnerear, *va.* to fine for damage done by sheep.

carnerero, ra, *n.* shepherd(-ess).

carneril, *m.* sheepwalk; pasture for sheep.

¹carnero, *m.* family vault, burying place; charnel house.

²carnero, *m.* sheep; mutton; sheepskin.—**c. ahogado,** stewed mutton.—**c. ciclán,** ridgil or ridgeling.—**c. de simiente,** ram kept for breeding.—**c. manso para guía,** bellwether.—**c. marino,** seal.—**no hay tales carneros,** (coll.) there is no such a thing.

carneruno, na, *a.* pert. to, or like, sheep.

carnestolendas, *f. pl.* carnival (the three carnival days before Ash Wednesday).

carnet, *m.* (Gal.) bank book; memorandum book.

carnicería, *f.* meat market, butcher's shop; slaughter house; carnage, slaughter.

carnicero, ra. I. *a.* (zool.) carnivorous; blood-thirsty, sanguinary; (of pasture) fattening; (coll.) meat fiend; (one) eating much meat; pertaining to shambles. **II.** *n.* butcher, one who sells meat. **III.** *m. pl.* (zool.) Carnivora.

carnicol, *m.* hoof of cloven-footed animals.

carnificación, *f.* carnification.

carnificarse, *vr.* to carnify, convert into flesh.

carnina, *f.* (chem.) carnine.

carnívoro, ra. I. *n. & a.* carnivore (-vorous). **II.** *m. pl.* Carnivora.

carniza, *f.* (coll.) refuse of meat; cat or dog meat; decayed flesh.

carnosidad, *f.* (med.) proud flesh; fatness, fleshiness.

carnoso, sa, *a.* fleshy; full of marrow; meaty; (of fruit) pulpy.

carnudo, da, *a.* = CARNOSO.

carnuza, *f.* disgusting coarse or heaped meat.

caro, ra. I. *a.* dear, costly; dear, beloved.—**c. mitad,** better half. **II.** *adv. m.* dearly, at a high price or cost.

caroca, *f.* decoration in public festivities; farcical piece; (coll.) caress, endearing action or expression made with a selfish purpose.

carocha, carrocha, *f.* insect eggs.—**carochar, carrochar,** *va.* (of insects) to lay eggs.

carolingio, a, *n. & a.* Carolingian, Carlovingian.

cárolus, *m.* an anc. Flemish coin used in Spain.

caromomia, *f.* the dry flesh of a mummy.

carona, *f.* padding of saddle next to animal's back; part of animal's back on which saddle lies.—**caroñoso, sa,** *a.* (of horses) old, galled.

caroquero, ra. I. *n.* wheedler, flatterer. **II.** *a.* honey-worded, fondling.

carosis, *f.* (med.) complete stupor.

carótida, f. & a. (anat.) carotid.

carozo, m. core of an apple, pear, etc.; corn cob.

¹carpa, f. (ichth.) carp.

²carpa, f. part of bunch of grapes torn off.

³carpa, f. (Peru) canvas tent.

carpanel, m. (arch.) basket-handle arch.

carpanta, f. (coll.) keen appetite, hunger.

carpe, m. common hornbeam tree; witch-hazel.

carpedal, m. hornbeam plantation.

carpelo, m. (bot.) carpel.

carpeta, f. table cover; portfolio; (Am.) brief-case; letter file; folder; docket; writing desk; small curtain or screen before tavern door.

carpetazo, m.—**dar c.,** to lay aside; to table; to pigeonhole.

carpintear, vn. to do carpenter's work.

carpintería, f. carpentry; carpenter's shop.

carpintero, m. carpenter, joiner; (ornith.) wood-pecker.—**c. de blanco,** joiner.—**c. de carretas,** cartwright.—**c. de navío,** shipwright.—**c. de obras de afuera,** carpenter who timbers or roofs houses.—**c. de prieto** = c. DE CARRETAS.—**c. de ribera** = c. DE NAVÍO.—**c. real,** (ornith.) ivory-billed woodpecker.

carpir, vn. to quarrel, wrangle; (Am.) to scratch (ground for clearing).

carpo, m. (anat.) carpus, wrist.

carpobálsamo, m. (bot.) balm of Gilead.

carpóforo, m. (bot.) carpophore.

carpología, f. (bot.) carpology.

carquesa, f. in glassworks, annealing furnace.

carquexia, f. (bot.) a species of broom plant.

¹carraca, f. carack, large and slow-sailing ship; the Cadiz navy yard.

²carraca, f. rattle; ratchet brace.

carraco, ca, a. old, withered, decrepit.

carral, m. barrel, vat.

carraleja, f. black beetle with yellow stripes; oil beetle; Spanish blistering beetle.

carralero, m. cooper.

carramplón, m. (Colomb.) flintlock musket.

carranque, m. a Peruvian cranelike bird.

carraón, m. short-stemmed wheat.

carrasca, f., **carrasco,** m. (bot.) pin oak, swamp oak.—**carrascal, carrascalejo,** m. pin-oak field.—**carrascón,** m. aug. large pin oak.

carraspada, f. negus (beverage).

carraspera, f. (coll.) hoarseness; frog-in-the-throat; sore throat.

carraspique, m. (bot.) candytuft.

carrasposo, sa, a. suffering from chronic hoarse-ness or sore throat; (Colomb., Venez.) rough (to the touch).

carrasqueño, ña, a. pertaining to the pin oak; (coll.) harsh, sharp.

carrera, f. run; race; course; racetrack; high-road; avenue, broad street; row; stroke (of a piston); travel (of a valve); range of iron teeth in combing cards; line, parting of the hair; girder, joist; broken stitch in a stocking; course and duration of life; career; course, method of life; conduct, mode of action; route of a line of steamers; coach or stage line; Spanish step in dancing.—**c. armamentista,** armaments race.—**c. de baquetas,** gantlet, a military punishment.—**c. de Indias,** trade from Spain to South America.—**a c. abierta,** at full speed.—**a la c., de c.,** hastily, hurriedly.—**no poder hacer c. con,** not to be able to bring (one) to reason.—**partir de c.,** to act in a rash and inconsiderate manner.—**poner en c.,** to give employment (to), to procure em-ployment (for).—**carrerilla, ta,** f. dim. small race, sprint or course; rapid motion in a Span-ish dance; (mus.) run up or down an octave.—**carrerista,** n. race fan.

carrero, m. = CARRETERO, carter, driver.

carreta, f. long narrow cart, wagon.

carretada, f. cartful, cart load; (Mex.) measure for lime, = 3,000 pounds.—**pl.** great quantity.

—a carretadas, (coll.) copiously, in abun-dance, in heaps.

carretaje, m. cartage; trade with carts.

carretal, m. rough, ragged building stone.

carrete, m. spool, bobbin, reel; reel of a fishing rod; (elec.) bobbin, coil.

carretear, I. va. to cart, to convey in a cart or wagon; to drive (a cart). II. vr. (of oxen or mules) to draw unevenly.

carretel, m. spool, reel, bobbin; fishing reel, line reel; (naut.) log reel; spunyarn winch; rope-walk reel.—**c. de carpintero,** carpenter's marking line.

carretela, f. calèche, calash.

carretera, f. wide, public road, highway; drive.

carretería, f. number of carts; trade of a car-man; cartwright's yard; wheelwright's shop.

carretero, a. I. a. for vehicles, vehicle (as a.). **II.** m. cartwright; carter, driver, truckman.

carretil, a. pertaining to a cart or truck.

carretilla, f. dim. small cart; wheelbarrow, push-cart, trolley cart, handcart; (Ry.) truck; go-cart; squib, firecracker; small wheel.—**c. de equipaje,** baggage truck or car.—**de c.,** me-chanically, unconsciously, by rote.

carretón, m. cart; truck; go-cart.—**c. de lám-para,** pulley for raising or lowering lamps.

carretonada, f. wagonload, truckload.

carretoncillo, m. dim. small go-cart.

carretonero, m. truckman, truck driver.

carricoche, m. ancient cart with a coachlike body; wagonette; muck cart, dung cart.

carricuba, m. watering or sprinkling cart.

carricureña, f. (mil.) carriage of a light gun.

carriego, m. osier fishing basket; rough basket for bleaching flax yarn.

carriel, m. (C. A.) traveling bag for papers and money; (Colomb.) GUARNIEL, pouch carried by strapping across shoulders and chest.

carril, m. rut, cartway; narrow road; furrow; (Ry.) rail.—**carrilera,** f. rut (in road); (Am. Ry.) siding; track.

carrillada, f. oily or medullar substance of a hog.

carrillera, f. jaw; chin strap (of helmet).

carrillo, m. dim. cheek; (naut.) hoisting tackle.

carrilludo, da, a. plump or round-cheeked.

carriola, f. trundle bed; small chariot, curricle.

carrizal, m. (bot.) reed-grass, -field.

carrizo, m. (bot.) common reed-grass.

carro, m. cart; car; (Am.) automobile; running gear of a carriage without the body; (C-, astr.) Great Bear, Dipper; (naut.) manufactory for cables and other ship cordage; measure for wood; cartload; bed of a printing press.—**c. de colchar,** rope maker's sledge.—**c. de riego,** sprinkling car.—**c. de volteo,** tip car, tilt car, dump car.—**C. Mayor,** Great Bear.—**C. Menor,** Little Bear, Ursa Minor.—**c. tranvía,** or **urbano,** street car.—**untar el c.,** (fig.) to grease the palm, to bribe.

carrocería, f. shop where carriages are made, repaired, or sold; (auto) body.

carrocilla, f. dim. small carriage.

carrocín, m. chaise, curricle.

carrocha, f. insect eggs.

carrochar, vn. (of insects) to lay eggs.

carromatero, m. carter; charioteer; carman.

carromato, m. long, narrow cart with two wheels and tilt.

carronada, f. (artil.) short gun of large calibre.

carroña, f. carrion, putrid flesh.

carroñar, va. to infect (sheep) with the scab.

carroño, ña. I. a. putrefied, putrid, rotten. **II.** n. & a. (Am.) coward(ly).—**carroñoso, sa,** a. rotting; ill-smelling.

carroza, f. large coach; superb state coach; ca-roche; (naut.) awning.

carruaje, m. vehicle; carriage; car.

carruajero, m. carter, wagon or coach driver.

carruco, m. small cart used in mountains.

carrucha, *f.* = GARRUCHA, pulley.
carrujado, da, *a.* corrugated, wrinkled.
carta, *f.* letter, epistle; royal ordinance; map, chart; playing card; written constitution, charter.—**c. blanca,** carte blanche, full powers.—**c. certificada,** registered letter.—**c. credencial,** credentials.—**c. cuenta,** bill or account of sale.—**c. de amparo,** safe-conduct.—**c. de contramarca,** letter of reprisal (against those having letters of marque).—**c. de crédito,** letter of credit.—**c. de creencia** = c. CREDENCIAL.—**c. de dote,** articles of marriage.—**c. de encomienda,** letter of safe-conduct.—**c. de espera,** (law) moratory permit, moratorium.—**c. de examen,** license to practice a trade or profession.—**c. de fletamento,** (com.) charter party.—**c. de guía,** safe-conduct, passport.—**c. de horro,** letter of enfranchisement.—**c. de libre,** (law) guardian's discharge.—**c. de marear,** sea chart.—**c. de moratoria** = C. DE ESPERA.—**c. de naturaleza,** naturalization papers.—**c. de pago,** acquittance, receipt, discharge in full.—**c. de presentación, c. de recomendación,** letter of introduction.—**c. de sanidad,** bill of health.—**c. de seguridad,** safe-conduct.—**c. de Urías,** trap, snare, traitorous scheme.—**c. de vecindad,** burgher brief.—**c. de venta,** bill of sale.—**c. de vuelta,** dead letter.—**c. en lista,** letter "to be kept till called for"; general-delivery letter.—**c. orden,** mandatory letter.—**c. receptoria,** warrant, voucher.—**c. requisitoria,** letter requisitorial.—**c. viva,** messenger who delivers his message verbally.—**a c. cabal,** thorough, in every respect, every inch.—**a la carta,** (Am.) à la carte.—**enseñar las cartas,** to show one's hand.—**pecar por c. de más o de menos,** to have either too much or too little.—**tomar cartas,** to take part; to be (in something); to take sides.
cartabón, *m.* carpenter's square; drawing triangle; rule; shoemaker's slide, size stick; quadrant, gunner's square.
cartagenero, ra, *a.* of or from Cartagena.
cartaginense; cartaginés, esa, *n.* & *a.* Carthaginian.
cártama, *f.,* **cártamo,** *m.* (bot.) saffron.
cartapacio, *m.* memorandum book; student's notebook; book satchel; batch or pile of papers.
cartapel, *m.* memorandum filled with useless matter.
cartear. I. *vn.* to play low cards as feelers; to falsecard. **II.** *va.* & *vn.* (naut.) to steer by the chart. **III.** *vr.* to write to each other, correspond.
cartel, *m.* placard, handbill, poster; cartel.
cartela, *f.* slip of paper, piece of wood, or other materials on which a memorandum is made; (arch.) modillion, console, bracket; iron stay supporting a balcony.
cartelera, *f.* billboard.
cartelón, *m. aug.* long edict; show bill.
carteo, *m.* intercourse by letters.
cartera, *f.* portfolio; writing case; briefcase; pocketbook; wallet; notebook; letter case, letter box; portfolio, office of a cabinet minister; pocket flap; (com.) securities forming part of the assets.
cartería, *f.* employment of letter carrier; sorting room in a post office.
carterista, *m.* pickpocket.
cartero, *m.* letter carrier, postman.
cartesianismo, *m.* Cartesianism.
cartesiano, na, *n.* & *a.* Cartesian.
carteta, *f.* a card game.
cartica, ita, *f.* short letter, note.
cartilagíneo, a; cartilaginoso, sa, *a.* (zool.) cartilaginous.
cartílago, *m.* (anat.) cartilage; parchment.
cartilla, *f. dim.* short letter, note; primer; certificate of a clergyman duly ordained.—**leerle a uno la c.** (fig.) to give one a lecture.—**no saber la c.,** to be extremely ignorant, know nothing.
cartografía, *f.* cartography.
cartográfico, ca, *a.* cartographic.
cartógrafo, *m.* cartographer.
cartomancía, *f.* cartomancy, fortune telling by playing cards.
cartómetro, *m.* curvometer.
cartón, *m.* pasteboard; cardboard; binders' board; metal ornament imitating the leaves of plants; cartoon, painting, or drawing on strong paper.—**c. piedra,** (art) staff; papier-maché.
cartonero, ra, *n.* pasteboard maker.
cartuchera, *f.* cartridge box or pouch.
cartucho, *m.* cartouch; cartridge; metallic cartridge; roll of coins; (Am.) paper cornet.
cartuja, *f.* Carthusian order or monastery.—**cartujano, na,** *a.* Carthusian.—**cartujo,** *m.* Carthusian monk; (coll.) taciturn man; recluse.
cartulario, *m.* archives or registry; archivist; coucher, register book in monasteries.
cartulina, *f.* bristol board, cardboard.—**c. común,** millboard.—**c. de porcelana,** enameled card.—**c. en hojas,** sheet card.
carúncula, *f.* (zool.) caruncle.—**c. lagrimal,** lachrymal caruncle.
caruto, *m.* (bot.) caruto, genipap.
carvajal, carvallar, carvalledo, *m.* oak field.
carvajo, carvallo, *m.* (bot.) common British oak.
carvi, *m.* (bot.) common caraway; caraway seed.
casa, *f.* house; dwelling; home; household; family residing in a house; firm, commercial house; square of a chess or draught board.—**c. consistorial, c. de ayuntamiento,** city hall, town hall.—**c. de banca,** banking house.—**c. de beneficencia,** asylum, poorhouse.—**c. de campo,** country house.—**c. de comercio,** commercial house, firm.—**c. de Dios,** house of God, church.—**c. de empeño,** pawnshop.—**c. de expósitos,** foundling home.—**c. de huéspedes,** boarding house.—**c. de juego,** gambling house.—**c. de locos,** madhouse; noisy place, bedlam.—**c. de maternidad,** lying-in hospital, maternity hospital.—**c. de moneda,** mint.—**c. de orates,** madhouse.—**c. de placer** = C. DE CAMPO.—**c. de posada, c. de pupilos** = C. DE HUÉSPEDES.—**c. de sanidad,** health office.—**c. de socorro,** emergency hospital.—**c. de tía,** (coll.) jail.—**c. de tócame Roque,** a house where many live, not well directed, and in consequent disorder.—**c. de vacas,** dairy farm.—**c. de vecindad,** tenement house.—**c. mortuoria,** house of the deceased.—**c. pública,** brothel.—**c. real,** royal palace.—**c. solar,** or **solariega,** manor, old homestead, ancient mansion of a family.—**a,** or **en c.,** at home.—**en c. de (los Martínez),** at the (Martínez').—**los de c.,** the family.—**no tener c. ni hogar,** to have neither house nor home.—**su c.** (often abbreviated to **s. c.**), a polite form of giving one's address, saying "your house" instead of "my house," the implication being that "my house" is yours or at your disposal: it simply means "my address is."
casabe, *m.* cassava.
casaca, *f.* dress coat; (coll.) marriage, wedding.—**volver c.,** to become a turncoat.
casación, *f.* (law) cassation, abrogation, repeal.
casacón, *m.* greatcoat; cassock.
casadero, ra, *a.* marriageable.
casado, da. I. *pp.* of CASAR. **II.** *a.* married. **III.** *m.* (print.) imposition.
casalicio, *m.* house, edifice.
casamata, *f.* (mil.) casemate.
casamentero, ra, *n.* match or marriage maker; marriage broker.
casamiento, *m.* marriage, matrimony; wedding.

casamuro, *m.* (mil.) single wall without a terreplein.

casapuerta, *f.* vestibule, entrance hall.

casaquilla, *f.* short jacket.

¹casar. I. *vn.* & *vr.* to marry, get married.—**c. con,** to marry, be married to (Shakespeare says "to marry *with*," as in Spanish).—**antes que te cases, mira lo que haces,** look before you leap. **II.** *va.* to marry, join in wedlock; to couple, pair; to match; to suit; (painting) to blend; (print.) to impose.

²casar, *va.* (law) to repeal, annul.

³casar, *m.* hamlet, small village.

casarón, *m. aug.* large old house.

casatienda, *f.* tradesman's shop and dwelling combined.

casca, *f.* grape skins; tanning bark; a kind of fruit cake.

cascabel, *m.* bell, jingle; rattle; cascabel, knob at the end of the breech of a cannon.—**poner el c. al gato,** to bell the cat, undertake a risky thing.—**ser un c.,** to be a rattlebrain.

cascabelada, *f.* jingling with small bells; (coll.) thoughtless or indiscreet speech or action, break.

cascabelear. I. *va.* to feed with vain hopes; to bamboozle. **II.** *vn.* to act with levity or recklessly.—**cascabeleo,** *m.* jingling of bells.

cascabelero, ra, *a.* light-witted.

cascabelillo, *m. dim.* small black plum.

cascabillo, *m.* hawk's bell; glume of cereals, chaff, husk; cup of an acorn.

cascaciruelas, *n.* (coll.) mean, base person.

cascada, *f.* waterfall, cataract, cascade.

cascado, da. I. *pp.* of CASCAR. **II.** *a.* broken, burst; decayed; infirm; crazy.

cascadura, *f.* bursting or breaking asunder.

cascajal, cascajar, *m.* gravel pit; gravelly place; place where grape husks are thrown.

cascajero, *m.* (Colomb.) CASCAJAL; old mine still containing some ore.

cascajo, *m.* gravel; fragments; rubbish; (coll.) old and useless furniture, junk; dry fruit.—**estar hecho un c.,** to be old and infirm, to be a total wreck.—**cascajoso, sa,** *a.* gravelly.

cascamajar, *va.* to break, crush slightly.

cascamiento, *m.* breaking, bruising.

cascanueces, *m.* nutcracker.

cascapiñones, *m.* one who shells hot pine nuts and cleans the seed; pine-nut cracker.

cascar. I. *va.* (*pret.* CASQUÉ; *subj.* CASQUE) to crack, burst, break into pieces; to crunch; (coll.) to lick, beat, strike. **II.** *vn.* (coll.) to talk too much. **III.** *vr.* to break open.

cáscara, *f.* rind, peel, shell, hull, husk; shell; bark (of trees); lansquenet, a card game.—**c. sagrada,** (med.) cascara sagrada, bark of the Californian buckthorn.—**de la c. amarga,** mischievous; rash; sporty; ultraradical, extremist.—*pl. interj.* by Jove!

cascarela, *f.* a card game.

cascarilla, *f. dim.* small thin shell, skin or bark; Peruvian bark; thin metal shell; powdered egg shell for cosmetic.

cascarillero, ra, *n.* gatherer of Peruvian bark.

cascarón, *m. aug.* eggshell; (arch.) arch, vault; calotte; niche for the sacrament; a trick in CASCARELA; (Mex.) eggshell filled with confetti.

cascarrabias, *m.* & *f.* (coll.) testy, irritable person.

cascarrón, na, *a.* (coll.) rough, harsh, rude.

cascarudo, da, *a.* with a thick rind or shell.

cascaruleta, *f.* (coll.) noise made by the teeth when chucked under the chin.

casco, *m.* skull, cranium; potsherd; fragments of an earthen vessel; quarter of a fruit; coat or tegument (of an onion); crown (of a hat); helmet; hull (of a ship); head (of a barrel); casque, headpiece; tree of a saddle; (com.) cask, pipe, vat, tank; printers' inking ball; sheepskin stripped of the wool; hoof.—*pl.* heads of sheep or bullocks without the tongues and brains.—**c. y quilla,** (naut.) bottomry, borrowing money for a trip with ship as security.

cascol, *m.* resin of a Guayaquil tree.

cascolote, *m.* (Mex.) thick bark of a tree.

cascote, *m.* rubbish, debris.

cascudo, da, *a.* large-hoofed.

caseación, *f.* coagulation of milk to make cheese.

caseato, *m.* (chem.) caseate.

caseico, ca, *a.* (chem.) lactic.

caseificar, *va.* (chem.) to change into casein; to separate the casein from (milk).

caseína, *f.* casein.

caseoso, sa, *a.* caseous, cheesy.

casera, *f.* housekeeper.

caseramente, *adv.* informally.

casería, *f.* manor's lodge; outbuilding for farm hands.

caserío, *m.* group of houses; small village, settlement.

caserna, *f.* (mil.) casern; barracks.

casero, ra. I. *a.* domestic; homemade; house (as *a.*); familiar; housekeeping. **II.** *n.* landlord (-lady); tenant; house agent; caretaker.

caserón, *m. aug.* big house.

caseta, *f. dim.* small house, cottage, hut.—**c. de baños,** bathhouse (at seaside or spa).

casi, *adv.* almost, nearly.—**c. que,** or **c. c., very nearly.**

casia, *f.* (bot.) bastard cinnamon, cassia.

casica, illa, ita, *f. dim.* small house, cabin.

casicontrato, cuasicontrato, *m.* (law) quasi contract.

casilla, *f.* ticket office; hut of a railway guard or flagman; cabin; booth; keeper's lodge; pigeonhole; square (of chessboard); (Cuba) bird trap; (Ecua.) privy; watercloset.—*pl.* ruled columns in accounts; points of a backgammon table.—**sacar a uno de sus casillas,** (coll.) to make one change one's habits; to vex one beyond patience.—**salir de sus casillas,** to lose self-control (esp. from anger, etc.).

casiller, ra, *n.* servant who empties slops etc.

casillero, *m.* desk or board with pigeonholes.

casillo, *m. dim.* trifling or slight case.

casimbas, *f. pl.* (naut.) buckets for baling.

casimir, *m.*, **casimira,** *f.*, cashmere.

casino, *m.* casino, dancing hall, public resort, clubhouse; social or political club.

Casiopea, *f.* (astr.) Cassiopeia.

casiterita, *f.* (min.) cassiterite.

caso, *m.* case; occurrence, event; (law, med., gram.) case.—**c. de conciencia, de honra,** a question of conscience, of honor.—**c. fortuito,** unexpected circumstances; (law) force majeure. —**c. que,** in case.—**dado c., or demos c.,** supposing that.—**de c. pensado,** deliberately. —**el c. es que,** the fact is that.—**en c. de que** = c. QUE.—**en c. necesario,** in case of necessity.—**en tal c.,** in such a case.—**en todo c.,** at all events anyway.—**hacer c.,** to mind, obey.—**hacer c. de,** to take notice of; to mind; to take into account; to esteem.—**no hacer, or no venir, al c.,** to be irrelevant, to have nothing to do with the case.—**poner por c.,** to assume, suppose.—**vamos al c.,** let us come to the point.—**verse en el c. de,** to be obliged to, have to, must.

casón, *m. aug.* large house.

casorio, *m.* (coll.) hasty or unwise marriage; informal wedding.

caspa, *f.* dandruff, scurf.

caspera, *f.* fine comb for dandruff.

caspia, *f.* core of an apple.

caspio, ia, *a.* Caspian.

caspiroleta, *f.* (Am.) eggnog.

¡cáspita! *interj.* gracious! confound it! by Jove!

casposo, sa, *a.* full of dandruff; lentiginous.

casqué, casque, *v.* V. CASCAR.

casquetazo, *m.* blow with the head.

casquete, *m.* helmet, skullcap, cap; skull; wig, periwig; (mech.) cap; (arch.) calotte; helmet shell; plaster to remove the scurf.—**c. esférico,** (geom.) spherical sector.

casquiacopado, da, *a.* cup-hoofed (horse).

casquiblando, da, *a.* soft-hoofed.

casquiderramado, da, *a.* wide-hoofed.

casquijo, *m.* gravel; ballasting material.

casquilla, *f.* cell of the queen bee.

casquillo, *m. dim.* little helm; tip, cap; ferrule; socket; iron arrowhead; (Am.) horseshoe.

casquimuleño, ña, *a.* (of horses) having narrow hoofs like a mule.

casquitos, *m. pl.*—**c. de guayaba,** guava preserve.

casquivano, na, *a.* feather-brained; ridiculously conceited.

casta, *f.* caste, race, breed; clan; offspring; kind or quality.—**hacer c.,** to get a particular breed.

Castálidas, *f. pl.* the Muses.

castalio, lia, *a.* belonging or pert. to Castalia.

castamente, *adv.* chastely.

castaña, *f.* (bot.) chestnut; bottle, jug, jar; knot of hair, chignon; abandoned mine; (Mex.) valise, satchel.—**c. apilada,** or **pilonga,** dried chestnut.—**c. regoldana,** wild or horse-chestnut.—**dar a uno la c.,** to play a trick on one.

castañal, *m.,* **castañar,** *m.,* **castañeda,** *f.,* **castañedo,** *m.* chestnut grove or plantation.

castañera, *f.* country abounding with chestnut trees.

castañero, ra, *n.* chestnut dealer or seller.

castañeta, *f.* castanet; snapping of the fingers.

castañetazo, *m.* blow with a castanet; cracking a chestnut in the fire; cracking of the joints.

castañete, *m. dim.* small chestnut tree.

castañeteado, *m.* sound of castanets.

castañetear. I. *va.* to rattle the castanets. **II.** *vn.* (of teeth) to chatter; (of knees) to creak; (of partridges) to cry.

castañeteo, *m.* sound of castanets; rattling the castanets; clattering; rattling noise.

castaño, ña. I. *a.* hazel, brown. **II.** *m.* (bot.) common chestnut tree; chestnut wood.—**c. de Indias,** horse-chestnut tree.—**c. regoldano,** wild chestnut tree.—**pasar de c. oscuro,** (coll.) to be beyond reason or endurance.

castañola, *f.* a large Mediterranean sea fish.

castañuela, *f.* castanet; (bot.) round tuberous-rooted cyperus.—*pl.* (naut.) cleats fastened to the yardarms.—**estar como unas castañuelas,** (coll.) to be very gay.

castañuelo, la, *a. dim.* of a light chestnut color.

castellán, *m.* castellan, governor of a castle.

castellana, *f.* mistress of a castle; wife of a CASTELLÁN; stanza in old Spanish poetry.

castellanía, *f.* independent district.

castellanizar, *va.* to make (a word) Spanish.

castellano, na. I. *a.* Castilian; Spanish (lang., gram., etc.). **II.** *m.* Sp. language; anc. Sp. coin, fiftieth part of gold mark; CASTELLÁN.

castellar, *m.* (bot.) St. John's-wort, tutsan.

casticidad, *f.* correctness, quality of being good Spanish.

castidad, *f.* chastity.

castigación, *f.* castigation, punishment; revision and correction.

castigadera, *f.* strap or rope for tying the clapper of a wether's bell; small cord with which the ring of a stirrup is tied to the girth.

castigador, ra, *n. & a.* punisher(-ing), chastiser (-ing), castigator(-ing).

castigar, *va.* (*pret.* CASTIGUÉ; *subj.* CASTIGUE) to chastise, punish, castigate; to afflict, put to pain, grieve; to revise and correct (proof sheets or writings).—**castigo,** *m.* chastisement, punishment; penalty; penance; censure, animadversion, reproach; alteration or correction.

castigué, castigue, *v. V.* CASTIGAR.

castillaje, *m.* = CASTILLERÍA.

castillejo, *m.* small castle; go-cart; scaffolding.

castillería, *f.* transit toll over castle property.

castillo, *m.* castle; wooden tower on the back of an elephant; mounting of a velvet loom; cell of the queen bee.—**c. de fuego,** fireworks.—**c. de naipes,** house of cards, flimsy structure; air castles.—**c. de proa,** (naut.) forecastle.—**c. roquero,** castle built on a rock.—**hacer castillos en el aire,** to build air castles.

castilluelo, *m. dim.* castlet, small castle.

castina, *f.* (chem. and metal.) flux.

castizo, za, *a.* of noble descent; of good breed; pure-blooded; pure, correct (language).

casto, ta, *a.* chaste.

castor, *m.* (zool.) beaver; beaver cloth; (Mex.) fine red baize.

Cástor, *m.* (astr.) Castor (a star).—**C. y Pólux,** (naut.) corposant, St. Elmo's fire.

castorcillo, *m.* a kind of rough sergelike cloth.

castoreño, ña, *a.* made of beaver.

castóreo, *m.* (med.) castoreum.

castorina, *f.* a kind of cloth similar to castor cloth; (chem.) castorin.

castra, *f.* pruning; pruning season.

castración, *f.* castration, gelding.

castradera, *f.* iron instrument with which honey is taken from a hive.

castrado, *m.* eunuch.

castrador, ra, *n.* gelder, castrator.

castradura, *f.* castration; scar from castration.

castrametación, *f.* (mil.) castrametation, laying out of camps.

castrapuercas, *m.* gelder's whistle.

castrar, *va.* to geld, castrate; (surg.) to cut away the proud flesh of (a wound); to prune; to cut the honeycombs from (beehives).

castrazón, *f.* act of cutting honeycombs out of hives; season when it is done.

castrense, *a.* military.

¹**castro,** *m.* game played by boys; headland; hilltop with castle in ruins.

²**castro,** *m.* = CASTRAZÓN.

castrón, *m.* castrated goat.

casual, *a.* accidental, occasional, chance (as *a.*).

casualidad, *f.* chance; chance event; hazard; accident; coincidence.—**por c.,** by chance.

casualmente, *adv.* accidentally; by chance.

casuáridos, *m. pl.* (zool.) family of the cassowaries.

casuario, *m.* (zool.) cassowary.

casuca, casucha, *f.;* **casucho,** *m.* (coll.) miserable hut or cottage; crib.

casuísta, *n.* casuist.—**casuística,** *f.* casuistry.

casuístico, ca, *a.* casuistical.

casulla, *f.* chasuble, vestment worn by priests.

casullero, ra, *n.* one who makes chasubles and other vestments for priests.

casus belli, casus belli, incident leading to war.

cata, *f.* act of trying a thing by the taste; sample, trial; plummet for measuring heights; (Am.) buried treasure; trial excavation (of prospective mine); hidden thing (esp. if valuable).

catabre, *m.* (naut.) sheep-shank.

catacaldos, *m.* taster of wine, soup, etc.; sampler.

cataclismo, *m.* cataclysm; catastrophe.

catacresis, *f.* (rhet.) catachresis.

catacumbas, *f. pl.* catacombs.

catacústica, *f.* (phys.) catacoustics.

catadióptrica, *f.* (phys.) catadioptrics.

catadióptrico, ca, *a.* (phys.) catadioptric.

catador, *m.* taster, sampler.

catadura, *f.* act of tasting; (coll.) gesture, face.

catafalco, *m.* catafalque.

catalán, na, *n. & a.* Catalan, Catalonian.

cataléctico, ca; **catalecto, ta,** *a.* (poet.) catalectic.

catalejo, *m.* telescope.

catalepsia, *f.* (med.) catalepsis.

cataléptico, ca, *a.* cataleptic.

catalicón, catolicón, *m.* (pharm.), a purgative.
catalina, *f.*—**rueda c.,** Catherine wheel.
catálisis, *f.* (chem.) catalysis.
catalítico, ca, *a.* catalytic.
catalizador, *m.* catalyser; catalytic.
catalogar, *va.* to catalogue, list.
catálogo, *m.* catalogue, table, list.
catalpa, *f.* (bot.) catalpa.
catalufa, *f.* a kind of floor carpet.
catán, *m.* Indian sabre or cutlass.
catante, *n.* one who tastes or looks.
cataplasma, *f.* poultice; (Am. fig.) nuisance, vexer.
cataplexia, *f.* catalepsy; apoplexy.
catapulta, *f.* catapult.
catar, *va.* to sample, try by tasting; to investigate; to judge, pass on; to esteem; to bear in mind; to cut the combs out of (beehives).
cataraña, *f.* (ornith.) sheldrake.
catarata, *f.* cataract, waterfall, cascade; cataract of the eye.—**abrirse las cataratas del cielo,** to rain heavily, to pour.—**tener cataratas,** (coll.) not to understand clearly.
catarral, *a.* catarrhal.
catarribera, *m.* falconer; (humor.) lawyer appointed to examine into the proceedings of magistrates.
catarro, *m.* catarrh; head cold.
catarroso, sa, *a.* catarrhal; subject to colds.
catártico, ca, *a.* (med.) cathartic.
catastral, *a.* pertaining to the census.
catastro, *m.* former royal tax on real estate; census or list of real property of a county or state.
catástrofe, *f.* catastrophe; dénouement, winding up (esp. when sad or tragic).
cataviento, *m.* (naut.) dogvane; weathercock.
catavino, *m.* small jug or cup for tasting wine; small hole at top of wine vessels for tasting wine.
catavinos, *m.* winetaster, expert sampler; (fig.) one going the rounds of taverns; drunkard.
cate, *m.* (P. I.) a weight, equal to 0.633 kg.
cateador, ra, *n.* (Am.) mine prospector; tester.
catear, *va.* (S. A.) to prospect (for minerals); (Am.) to raze.
catecismo, *m.* catechism.
catecú, *m.* = CATO, astringent from plants.
catecuménico, ca, *a.* catechumenical.
catecúmeno, na, *n.* catechumen.
cátedra, *f.* seat or chair of a professor; professorship; subject taught by a professor; lecture room in a university.—**c. del Espíritu Santo,** pulpit.—**c. de San Pedro,** Holy See.
catedral, *n. & a.* cathedral.
catedralidad, *f.* dignity of a cathedral church.
catedrático, *m.* professor; contribution paid to bishops and prelates.
catedrilla, *f. dim.* small or poor professor's chair; in some universities, lecture by an aspirant to a professorship.
categorema, *f.* (logic) quality of being assignable to a category.
categoría, *f.* (philos.) category; class, condition; rank; character, quality.—**de c.,** of importance; of high rank, prominent.
categóricamente, *adv.* categorically.
categórico, ca, *a.* categorical, categoric.
catenaria, *n. & a.* catenary.
cateo, *m.* (Am.) testing, sampling; (Am.) prospecting.
catequesis, *f.* catechesis.
catequicé, catequice, *v.* V. CATEQUIZAR.
catequismo, *m.* catechesis, religious instruction; art of teaching by questions and answers.
catequista, *m.* catechist.
catequístico, ca, *a.* catechetical, catechetic.
catequizante, *n. & a.* catechiser(-ing).
catequizar, *va.* (*pret.* CATEQUICÉ; *subj.* CATE-

QUICE) to catechise; to instruct in the Christian faith; to persuade, induce.
caterético, ca, *a.* (med.) corrosive, catheretic.
caterva, *f.* multitude; throng, crowd.
catéter, *m.* (surg.) catheter.—**cateterismo,** *m.* catheterization.—**cateterizar,** *va.* to catheterize.
cateto, *m.* (arch.) cathetus; (geom.) leg (of a right-angled triangle).
catetómetro, *m.* cathetometer.
catilinaria, *f.* one of Cicero's orations against Catiline; severe criticism or denunciation.
catimbao, *m.* (Chile, Peru) clown; ridiculously dressed person; short and fat person.
catín, *m.* copper-refining crucible.
catinga, *f.* (Am.) bad smell (esp. that of sweating Negroes).—**catingoso, sa; catingudo, da,** *a.* (Am.) ill-smelling.
catión, *m.* (phys.) cation, kation.
catire, *n. & a.* (Am.) blond, light-haired.
catirrino, na. I. *n. & a.* (zool.) catarrhine. **II.** *m. pl.* Catarrhina, a division of the primates.
catite, *m.* loaf of the best refined sugar.
cato, *m.* astringent from plants.
catoche, *m.* (Mex. coll.) bad humor.
catódico, ca, *a.* (elec.) cathodic.
cátodo, *m.* (elec.) cathode.
católicamente, *adv.* conforming to Catholicism.
catolicismo, *m.* Catholicism.
católico, ca. I. *a.* catholic, general or universal; true, infallible. **II.** *n. & a.* (Roman) Catholic. **no estar muy c.,** (coll.) to feel under the weather.
catolicón, *m.* (pharm.) a purgative.
catolizar, *va.* (*pret.* CATOLICÉ; *subj.* CATOLICE) to convert to Catholicism; to preach, propagate Catholicism.
catón, *m.* reading book for children.
catoniano, na, *a.* Catonian.
catóptrica, *f.* (opt.) catoptrics.
catóptrico, ca, *a.* catoptrical.
catorce, *n. & a.* fourteen; fourteenth.—**catorcena,** *f.* group of fourteen.—**catorceno, na,** *a.* fourteenth.
catorzavo, va, *n. & a.* fourteenth.
catre, *m.* small bedstead; cot.—**c. de mar,** hammock or cot.—**c. de tijera,** field bed.
catrecillo, *m.* camp canvas chair.
catricofre, *m.* folding bed, bed lounge.
catrín, catrina, *a.* (Mex.) dandyish, foppish.
caucáseo, a; caucásico, ca, *a.* Caucasian.
cauce, *m.* bed of a river; trench, ditch.
caución, *f.* caution, precaution; pledge, surety, guarantee.—**c. de indemnidad,** or **personal,** (law) bond given by another for person in custody.—**c. juratoria,** parole given by person in custody but not yet tried and sentenced.—**c. real,** bail.
caucionar, *va.* (law) to guard against an evil or loss; to bail.
cauchal, *m.* rubber plantation or patch.
cauchero, ra. I. *a.* (India) rubber (as *a.*). **II.** *n.* rubber man, one engaged in the rubber industry or trade.
cauchil, *m.* small basin or reservoir of water.
caucho, *m.* India rubber (material), gum elastic.
cauda, *f.* train or tail of a bishop's robe.
¹**caudal,** *a.* (zool.) caudal, pert. to the tail.
²**caudal,** *m.* fortune, wealth, means; volume (of water); plenty, abundance.—**hacer c. de,** to value highly.—**caudalejo,** *m. dim.* middling fortune.
caudalosamente, *adv.* copiously, abundantly.
caudaloso, sa, *a.* of great volume, carrying much water; copious, abundant; rich, wealthy.
caudatario, *m.* clergyman who carries the train of an officiating bishop's robe.
caudato, ta, *a.* (astr. of a comet) having a tail.
caudatrémula, *f.* (ornith.) wagtail.
caudillaje, *m.* leadership; tyranny; bossism.

caudillismo, *m.* (Am.) = CAUDILLAJE.

caudillo, *m.* commander, chief, leader.

caudimano, na, *a.* (zool.) having a prehensile tail.

caudón, *m.* a bird of prey.

caulescente, *a.* (bot.) caulescent.

caulículo, caulículo, *m.* (arch.) ornament of the capital of columns.

caulífero, a, *a.* (bot.) cauline.

cauro, *m.* northwest wind.

causa, *f.* cause; motive, reason; lawsuit, case; trial (at law).—**c. célebre,** famous (criminal) case, cause célèbre.—**c. final,** (philos.) final cause.—**c. impulsiva,** or **motiva,** prompting motive.—**c. primaria,** or **primera,** first cause.—**c. pública,** public welfare, commonweal.—**a,** or **por, c. de,** on account of, because, due to.—**formar c. a,** to sue, bring suit against.

causador, a, *n.* originator.

causahabiente, *m.* & *f.* (law) person holding a right from others.

causal, *a.* causal.—**causalidad,** *f.* causality.

causante. I. *a.* causing, originating, causative. **II.** *n.* originator; (law) the person from whom a right is derived; constituent, principal.

causar, *va.* to cause, occasion; to sue.

causeo, *m.* (Am.) light lunch between meals, snack.

causídico, ca. I. *n.* advocate, counsellor. **II.** *a.* (law) causidical, forensic.

causón, *m.* burning fever of short duration.

causticidad, *f.* causticity.

cáustico, ca. I. *a.* caustic, burning; biting, aggressive. **II.** *m.* (med.) caustic.

cautamente, *adv.* cautiously.

cautela, *f.* caution, prudence; craft, cunning.

cautelar, *va.* & *vr.* (de) to guard (against).

cautelosamente, *adv.* cautiously, warily.

cauteloso, sa, *a.* cautious, wary.

cautericé, cauterice, *v. V.* CAUTERIZAR.

cauterio, *m.* (med.) cautery.—**c. actual,** actual cautery, burning with hot iron.—**c. potencial,** potential cautery, produced by chemicals.

cauterización, *f.* cauterization, cauterizing.

cauterizador, *m.* he who or that which cauterizes.

cauterizante, *a.* cauterizing.

cauterizar, *va.* (*pret.* CAUTERICÉ; *subj.* CAUTERICE) to cauterize; to reproach with severity; to blame.

cautivador, ra, cautivante, *a.* captivating, charming.

cautivar, *va.* to take prisoner, carry into captivity; to captivate, charm.

cautiverio, *m.,* **cautividad,** *f.* captivity.

cautivo, va, *n.* captive.

cauto, ta, *a.* cautious, wary, prudent.

cava, *f.* digging and earthing of vines; wine cellar in the royal palace.

cavacote, *m.* mound made with the hoe.

cavadiza, *a.* dug out of a pit (as sand).

cavador, ra, *n.* digger.

cavadura, *f.* digging.

caván, *m.* (P. I.) a measure equivalent to seventy-five quarts.

cavar. I. *va.* to dig, excavate; (of horses) to paw. **II.** *vn.* to dig; to think carefully or intently; to go to the bottom (of a subject, etc.)

cavatina, *f.* (mus.) cavatina.

cavazón, *f.* digging.

cávea, *f.* (archeol.) cage or cave.

caverna, *f.* cavern, cave; (med.) hollow from a wound.

cavernilla, *f. dim.* small cavern.

cavernoso, sa, *a.* cavernous, caverned.

caveto, *m.* (arch.) cavetto.

caví, *m.* oca, a South-American tuber.

cavia, *f.* circular excavation at the foot of a tree to collect water.

cavial, caviar, *m.* caviar.

cavicornio, nia. I. *a.* (zool.) cavicorn. **II.** *m. pl.* Cavicornia.

cavidad, *f.* cavity.

cavilación, *f.* cavilling.

cavilar, *va.* to cavil; to criticize.

cavilosamente, *adv.* captiously.

cavilosidad, *f.* captiousness, cavilling.

caviloso, sa, *a.* captious, overparticular; fault-finding.

cayada, *f.,* **cayado,** *m.* shepherd's hook, crook; crozier of a bishop; walking staff.

cayán, *m.* (P. I.) awning of matting in boats.

cayente, *a.* falling.

cayeputi, *m.* cajuput tree; cajuput oil.

cayo, *m.* rock, shoal, islet; key.

cayó, *v. V.* CAER.

cayote, *m.* (bot.) = CIDRACAYOTE, gourd.

cayuca, *f.* (Cuba, coll.) head (of person), "bean."

cayuco, *m.* (W. I., Venez., Mex.) dugout canoe.

caz, *m.* trench, ditch; mill race, flume.

caza, *f.* hunting, chase; game; pursuit.—**c. mayor,** big game.—**c. menor,** small game.—**andar a c. de,** to be, or go, hunting for, or in search of.—**dar c.,** to pursue.—**de c.,** (as *a.*) hunting; pursuit (plane, boat, etc.).

cazabe, *m.* (bot.) manioc, cassava; flour of the cassava plant; bread made with it.

cazadero, *m.* chase; hunting grounds.

cazador, ra. I. *a.* hunting. **II.** *n.* hunter.—**c. de alforja,** one who sports with dogs, snares, and other devices. **III.** *f.* huntress; hunting jacket.

cazamoscas, *m.* (ornith.) flycatcher.

cazar, *va.* (*pret.* CACÉ; *subj.* CACE) to chase, hunt; (coll.) to attain by skill; (coll.) to charm and captivate by caresses and deceitful tricks; to chase, pursue.—**c. una vela,** (naut.) to tally a sail; haul the sheet aft.

cazasubmarino, *m.* submarine chaser.

cazatorpedero, *m.* torpedo-boat destroyer.

cazcalear, *vn.* (coll.) to fidget and fuss.

cazcarria, *f.* mud splashings on clothes; (Am.) sheep dung.—**cazcarriento, ta,** *a.* (coll.) splashed.

cazo, *m.* dipper, ladle; founders' scoop; size kettle; glue pot; melting pan.

cazoleja, eta, *f. dim.* small saucepan; pan of a musket lock; perfuming pan.

cazolero, *m.* (coll.) man who does women's work in the kitchen.

cazoleta, *f.* pan of a musket lock; boss or defence of a shield; hand guard or languet of a sword; a kind of perfume.

cazolón, *m. aug.* large earthen pot or stewpan.

cazón, *m.* (ichth.) dogfish or small shark.

cazonal, *m.* tackle for shark fishing.

cazonete, *m.* (naut.) toggle.

cazudo, da, *a.* (of knives) with a thick back.

cazuela, *f.* earthen cooking pan; stewing pan, crock; meat dressed in an earthen pan; (theat.) gallery reserved for women; (theat.) top gallery.

cazumbrar, *va.* to join (staves) with hempen cords.

cazumbre, *m.* hempen cord used to join staves.

cazumbrón, *m.* cooper.

cazurro, ra, *a.* (coll.) taciturn, sulky, sullen.

cazuz, *m.* (bot.) ivy.

¹ce, *f.* cee, name of the letter *c.*—**c. por be, or c. por c.,** minutely, circumstantially.—**por c. o por be,** somehow or other.

²¡ce!, *interj.* hark! listen! come here! see here!

cea, cía, *f.* thigh bone.

ceanoto, *m.* (bot.) New Jersey tea, redroot.

ceática, ciática, *f.* (med.) sciatica.

ceático, ciático, ca, *a.* (med.) sciatical.

ceba, *f.* fattening of domestic animals.

cebada, *f.* barley.—**c. perlada,** pearl barley.

For pronunciation, see the rules at the beginning of the book.

cebadal, *m.* barley field.

cebadazo, za, *a.* pertaining to barley.

¹**cebadera,** *f.* nose bag; barley bin.

²**cebadera,** *f.* (naut.) spritsail; (metal.) furnace charger.

cebadería, *f.* barley market.

¹**cebadero,** *m.* place where game or fowls are fed; breeder and feeder of hawks; (metal.) mouth for feeding a furnace.

²**cebadero,** *m.* barley dealer; mule carrying the feed; bell mule.

cebadilla, *f.* (bot.) Indian caustic barley; (bot.) sneeze-wort; (bot., prov.) prickly oxeye; hellebore snuff.

cebado, da, *a.* (her.) ravening; (Am. of animals) haunting a place where they find food or prey; ferocious.

cebador, *m.* one who fattens animals; priming horn, powder horn; (int. combust. eng.) primer.

cebadura, *f.* fattening of domestic animals.

cebar. I. *va. & vn.* to fatten (animals); to stuff, cram; to feed (a furnace, fire, lamp); to prime (a firearm); to start (a machine or apparatus); to light (a rocket or pyrotechnic piece); to re-magnetize; to excite and cherish (a passion); to bait (a fishhook). **II.** *vn.* to penetrate; to take hold of; to stick fast. **III.** *vr.* to be firmly bent upon a thing; to prey upon; to gloat over (a victim).

cebellina, *f.* (zool.) sable; sable fur.

cebero, *m.* feed bag, nose bag.

cébido, da. I. *n. & a.* (zool.) cebid. **II.** *m. pl.* Cebidæ.

¹**cebo,** *m.* food given to animals, fodder; fattening of animals; bait; incentive; (artil.) priming of guns.—**c. fulminante,** percussion cap.

²**cebo,** *m.* a kind of monkey.

cebolla, *f.* (bot.) onion; onion bulb; any bulbous root; oil receptacle of a lamp; spherical screen in a water pipe.—**c. albarrana,** (bot.) squill.—**c. ascalonia,** (bot.) shallot garlic.—**cebollana,** *f.* (bot.) three-toothed globularia; chives.—**cebollar,** *m.* onion patch.—**cebollero, ra,** *n.* onion seller.—**cebolleta,** *f. dim.* tender onion.—**cebollino,** *m.* young onion fit to be transplanted; onion seeds; (bot.) chive.—**cebollón,** *m. aug.* large onion.—**cebolludo, da,** *a.* bulbous, having a big bulb.

cebón, *m.* fattened bullock or hog.

ceboncillo, *m. dim.* fatling.

cebra, *f.* (zool.) zebra.—**cebrado, da,** *a.* having stripes like the zebra.

cebratana, *f.* = CERBATANA, blowgun; ear trumpet.

cebruno, cervuno, na, *a.* deer-colored.

cebú, *m.* (zool.) zebu; (Arg.) a variety of monkey.

ceca, *f.* mint (for coining).

Ceca, *m.* name of the mosque that the Arabs had in Cordova, the most venerated after Mecca.—**de C. en Meca,** or **de la C. a la Meca,** to and fro, hither and thither.

cecear. I. *vn.* to lisp. **II.** *va.* to call, hail; to lisp.—**ceceo,** *m.* lisping, lisp; calling, hailing.

ceceoso, sa. I. *a.* lisping. **II.** *n.* lisper.

cecial, *m.* fish cured and dried.

cecina, *f.* corned, dried, jerked, or hung beef.

ecografía, *f.* writing of the blind.

ecógrafo, *m.* a writing apparatus for the blind.

ceda, zeda, *f.* zee, last letter of the alphabet.

cedacería, *f.* shop where sieves or cribs are made or sold.

cedacero, *m.* maker or seller of sieves, cribs, etc.

cedacillo, ito, *m. dim.* small sieve.

cedazo, *m.* sieve, screen, strainer.

cedazuelo, *m. dim.* small sieve or strainer.

cedente. I. *a.* ceding, granting. **II.** *n.* conveyer, assigner, transferrer.

ceder. I. *va.* to transfer, cede, convey, yield, deliver up. **II.** *vn.* to yield, submit, comply, give in; to give out, slacken, fail; to happen turn out ill or well; to abate, diminish.

cedilla, *f.* cedilla.

cedizo, za, *a.* (of food) tainted.

cedoria, *f.* (bot.) zedoary.

cedral, *m.* cedar field or forest.

cedras, *f. pl.* skin saddlebags.

cedria, *f.* resin from the cedar.

cédride, *m.* fruit of the cedar tree.

cedrino, na, *a.* pertaining to the cedar.

cedrio, *m.* = CÉDRIDE.

cedro, *m.* (bot.) cedar; Spanish juniper.—**c. colorado,** red cedar.—**c. de la India,** deodar.—**c. de las Antillas,** Spanish cedar.—**c. del Líbano,** cedar of Lebanon.—**c. de Misiones,** an Argentine cedar, producing fine wood and a valuable febrifuge.—**c. dulce,** red cedar.

cédula, *f.* cedula, slip of parchment or paper written or to write upon; order, bill, decree; cedule, a scroll or writing.—**c. ante diem,** secretary's summons of meeting to the members of a society.—**c. de abono,** order to remit a task.—**c. de aduana,** permit.—**c. de cambio,** (com.) draft.—**c. personal, or de vecindad,** official document declaring the name, occupation, domicile, etc. of the bearer, and to serve for identification.—**c. real,** royal letter patent.—**echar cédulas,** (coll.) to draw or cast lots.—**cedulaje,** *m.* fees or dues paid for a cedula.—**cedulilla, ita,** *f. dim.* small slip of paper.—**cedulón,** *m. aug.* large bill; long edict; proclamation; public notice.

cefalalgia, *f.* (med.) cephalalgia, headache.

cefalea, *f.* violent headache, migraine.

cefálico, ca, *a.* cephalic.

cefalitis, *f.* (med.) encephalitis.

céfalo, *m.* (ichth.) mullet, a kind of perch.

cefalópodo, da. I. *n. & a.* (zool.) cephalopod. **II.** *m. pl.* Cephalopoda.

cefalotomía, *f.* cephalotomy.

cefalotórax, *m.* (anat.) cephalothorax.

Cefeo, *m.* (astr.) Cepheus, a constellation.

céfiro, *m.* zephyr.

cefo, *m.* (zool.) a large African monkey.

cegajo, *m.* two-year-old he-goat.

cegajoso, sa, *a.* blear-eyed.

cegar. I. *vn.* (*ind. pres.* CIEGO, *pret.* CEGUÉ; *subj.* CIEGUE) to grow blind. **II.** *va.* to blind; to wall up (a door or window); to close up (a well); to stop up, close (a channel, road).—**c. una vía de agua,** (naut.) to fother a leak. **III.** *vr.* to become or be blinded (by passion, etc.).

cegarra, *a.* (coll.) CEGATO.—**cegarrita,** *n.* (coll.) one who contracts the eye to see at a distance.

cegato, ta, *a.* (coll.) short-sighted.

cegatoso, sa, *a.* = CEGAJOSO.

cegesimal, *a.* (phys.) C. G. S. (app. to the system of units in which the fundamental units are the centimeter, gram and second).

cegué, *pret.* of CEGAR.

ceguecillo, lla, *n. dim.* little blind person.

ceguedad, *f.* blindness; ignorance, intellectual darkness; obfuscation.

ceguera, *f.* disorder in the eye; absolute blindness; obfuscation.

ceguezuelo, la, *n.* = CEGUECILLO.

ceiba, *f.* (bot.) sea moss, alga; *also* **ceibo,** *m.* ceiba, God tree, W. I. silkcotton tree.

ceja, *f.* eyebrow; edging of clothes; projecting part, as in the binding of books; bridge of a string instrument; summit; circle of clouds round a hill; cloud cap; (arch.) weather molding; rim; (carp.) rabbet; (naut.) opening in the clouds.—**dar entre ceja y ceja,** to tell one unpleasant truths to one's face.—**hasta las cejas,** to the utmost, to the extreme.—**quemarse las cejas,** to burn the midnight oil.—**tener entre c. y c.,** to dislike, have a grudge against; to have on one's brain, to think constantly about.

cejadero, *m.* hold-back strap of a harness.

cejar, *vn.* to go backward; to hold back; to hesitate; to slacken, relax.

cejijunto, ta, *a.* having eyebrows that meet.

¹cejo, *m.* fog from rivers.

²cejo, *m.* esparto cord tied round a bundle of esparto grass.

cejudo, da, *a.* having heavy and long eyebrows.

cejuela, *f. dim.* small eyebrow.

¹celada, *f.* ambuscade, ambush; snare; lurch; artful trick.

²celada, *f.* sallet; helmet without visor; part of the key of the crossbow; horse soldier with helmet.—**c. borgoñota,** visorless helmet.

celadilla, *f. dim.* small helmet.

celador, ra, *n.* watchman(-woman), caretaker; curator; monitor in a school; warden.

celaje, *m.* aspect of the sky with clouds of varied hues; cloud scenery; cloud effect; painting representing the rays of the sun breaking through clouds; presage, prognostic; skylight; sky of a picture.—*pl.* light, swiftly moving clouds; scud.

celandés, sa, *n.* & *a.* New Zealander.

¹celar, *vn.* & *va.* to fulfil (duties) with care; to watch (any person's motions) from suspicion.

²celar, *va.* to cover, conceal.

³celar, *va.* to engrave; to carve.

celda, *f.* cell (in a convent, beehive, prison).

celdica, illa, ita, *f. dim.* cellule.

celdilla, *f.* cell in beehives; (bot.) cell; capsule.

celebérrimo, ma, *a. super.* most (very) famous.

celebración, *f.* celebration; praise, applause.

celebrado, da, *pp.* of **CELEBRAR.**—**la reunión c. en—,** the meeting held in—.

celebrador, ra, *n.* applauder, praiser, approver; celebrator.

celebrante, *n.* & *a.* celebrator(-ing); celebrant (officiating).

celebrar, *va.* to celebrate; to praise, applaud, approve; to revere, respect, venerate; to be glad of, rejoice at; to say (mass); to hold (formal meeting).

célebre, *a.* famous, renowned; (coll.) facetious, witty, funny.—**célebremente,** *adv.* with pomp; facetiously, humorously.—**celebridad,** *f.* celebrity, renown, fame; pomp, magnificence; public demonstration, celebration, pageant.

celebro, cerebro, *m.* skull; brain; judgment.

celemín, *m.* a dry measure (about a peck).

celeminada, *f.* quantity contained in a CELEMÍN.

celenterado, da; celenterio, ria. I. *n.* & *a.* (zool.) cœlenterate. II. *m. pl.* Cœlenterata.

célere. I. *a.* quick, rapid. II. *m.* one of the select three hundred knights of ancient Roman nobility.—**celeridad,** *f.* celerity, quickness.—**celerífero, ra,** *a.* rapid-transit.—**celerímetro,** *m.* speedometer.

celeste, *a.* celestial, heavenly; sky-blue.

celestial, *a.* celestial, heavenly; agreeable, delightful, excellent; (ironic) silly, sottish.

celestialmente, *adv.* celestially, heavenly.

¹celestina, *f.* (min.) celestite.

²celestina, *f.* procuress.

celfo, *m.* = **CEFO,** an African monkey.

celia, *f.* beer made from wheat.

celíaca, *f.* (med.) a kind of diarrhea.

celíaco, ca, *a.* (anat.) celiac, pertaining to the abdominal cavity.

celibato, *m.* celibacy; (coll.) bachelor.

célibe, *a.* & *n.* unmarried (person).

célico, ca, *a.* (poet.) celestial, heavenly.

celidonia, *f.* (bot.) celandine, swallow-wort.

celindrate, *m.* ragout made with coriander seed.

celo, *m.* zeal, ardor, fervor; piety, devotion; heat, rut.—*pl.* jealousy; suspicions.—**dar celos,** to excite suspicions.

celosamente, *adv.* with zeal; jealously.

celosía, *f.* lattice; Venetian blind; jealousy.

celoso, sa, *a.* zealous; jealous; suspicious; (naut.) light and swift-sailing.

celotipia, *f.* jealousy.

celsitud, *f.* celsitude, elevation, grandeur; (obs.) highness, a title, now expressed by **alteza.**

celta, *n.* & *a.* Celt(ic).

celtibérico, ca; celtiberio, ria; celtíbero, ra, *n.* & *a.* Celtiberian.

celticismo, *m.* Celticism.

céltico, ca, *a.* Celtic.

celtista, *n.* Celtist.

celtohispánico, ca; celtohispano, na, *a.* Celtic-Spanish, Celto-Spanish (remains of the old Celtic civilization in Spain).

célula, *f.* cell.—**celular, celulario, ia,** *a.* cellular.

celulilla, *f. dim.* very small cell or cavity.

celuloide, *m.* celluloid.

celulosa, *f.* cellulose, woody fibre.

celuloso, sa, *a.* cellulose, containing cells.

cellenco, ca, *a.* (coll.) decrepit.

cellisca, *f.* fine rain, snow, or sleet driven by a heavy wind.—**cellisquear,** *vn.* to sleet; to be squally with fine snow or rain.

cello, *m.* hoop used in cooperage.

cementación, *f.* cementation.

cementar, *va.* (metal.) to cement; to convert (metals); to subject to the process of cementation.

cementerio, *m.* cemetery, graveyard.

cemento, *m.* cement; (metal.) cement, substance used in converting metals; cementing material.—**c. armado,** reinforced concrete.—**c. de Pórtland** (more commonly **c. pórtland**), Portland cement.—**cementoso, sa,** *a.* cement-like.

cena, *f.* supper; by extension, the Last Supper.

cenaaoscuras, *n.* recluse; miser.

cenáculo, *m.* cenacle, room where Last Supper was held.

cenacho, *m.* basket for fruit and greens.

cenadero, *m.* supper room; summerhouse.

cenador, *m.* one fond of suppers; summerhouse in a garden; arbor, bower; gallery around a courtyard.

cenaduría, *f.* (Mex.) supper room, supper inn.

cenagal, *m.* slough, quagmire; arduous, unpleasant affair.

cenagoso, sa, *a.* muddy, miry, marshy.

cenar. I. *vn.* to sup. II. *va.* to have for supper.

cenceño, ña, *a.* lean, thin, slender.

cencerra, *f.* = **CENCERRO.**

cencerrada, *f.* charivari; tin-pan serenade.

cencerrear, *vn.* to jingle continually; to play on an untuned guitar; to make a din or rattling noise.

cencerreo, *m.* noise made by mule or cow bells.

cencerro, *m.* bell worn by the leading wether or cow; ill-tuned guitar.—**c. zumbón,** bell borne by the leading horse or mule.—**a cencerros tapados,** on the sly, quietly, by stealth.

cencerrón, *m.* small bunch of grapes unpicked.

cencido, da, *a.* untilled, uncultivated.

cencro, *m.* a Brazilian serpent.

cendal, *m.* light thin stuff of silk or thread; gauze; scarf used by priests in consecrating the host; barbs of a feather.—*pl.* cotton for an inkstand.

cendea, *f.* (prov.) in Navarre, municipal borough composed of several villages.

cendra, cendrada, *f.* bone-dust paste used for cupels.—**ser una c.,** (fig.) to be lively as a cricket.

cenefa, *f.* border; band or stripe on the edge of a stuff; middle piece of a priest's chasuble; rim, hangings, flounce, trimming; (naut.) top rim; paddle-box rim; awning.

cení, *m.* fine brass or bronze.

cenia, *f.* water-raising machine; noria, well wheel and axle; garden watered from a noria.

For pronunciation, see the rules at the beginning of the book.

cenicero, *m.* ash hole, ash pit, ash pan.

cenicienta, *f.* thing or person unjustly despised or ill treated.—la C., Cinderella.

ceniciento, ta, *a.* ash-color red.

cenicilla, *f.* (bot.) oidium.

cenit, *m.* (astr.) zenith.—cenital, *a.* zenith (as *a.*).

ceniza, *f.* ashes, cinders.—cenizas azules, blue paint; lapis lazuli.—cenizas de estaño, putty. —cenizas de vegetales, potash.—cenizas graveladas, weed ashes.

cenizal, *m.* heap of ashes.

cenizo, za. I. *a.* ash-colored. II. *m.* (bot.) white goosefoot.

cenizoso, sa, *a.* ashy; covered with ashes.

cenobial, *a.* pert. to a convent or monastery.

cenobio, *m.* cenoby, convent or monastery.

cenobita, *m.* Cenobite, monk.

cenobítico, ca, *a.* cenobitic.

cenojil, *m.* garter.

cenopegias, *f. pl.* Jewish feast of tabernacles.

cenotafio, *m.* cenotaph.

cenote, *m.* cenote, a water reservoir in a cave.

cenozoico, ca, *a.* (geol.) Cenozoic.

censal, *a.* = CENSUAL. *n.* = CENSO.

censalista, *m.* = CENSUALISTA, lessor.

censatario, ria; censero, ra, *n.* one who pays an annuity out of his estate; lessee.

censo, *m.* census; agreement for settling an annuity on a person; annual rent; lease; rental; income; polltax among the Romans.—c. al quitar, or redimible, quit rent or annuity that can be paid at once by a certain sum.—c. de agua, water tax.—c. de por vida, life annuity.

censontli, censontle, *m.* (Mex.) mocking bird.

censor, *m.* censor, critic; censorious person.

censoría, *f.* censorship; censor's office.

censorio, ria, *a.* censorial.

censual, *a.* pertaining to a lease, annuity, or rent; rental; pertaining to lawful interest.

censualista, *m.* lessor; annuitant.

censura, *f.* censorship; office of a censor; act of censoring; review (of a book); censure, blame, reproach; gossiping; spiritual punishment.

censurable, *a.* reprehensible, blameworthy.

censurador, ra; censurante, *n. & a.* critic(-al); faultfinder(-ing), censor(-ing).

censurar, *va.* to review, criticize, judge; to censure, blame; to accuse; to find fault with.

centaura, centaurea, *f.* (bot.) centaury.—c. mayor, great centaury.—c. menor, common erythræa.

centauro, *m.* (myth.) centaur; (C-, astr.) Centaur.

centavo, *m.* hundredth (part); cent.

centella, *f.* lightning; thunderbolt; flash of a flint struck with steel; flake of fire; (fig.) remaining spark of passion, smoldering fire.

centellador, ra, *a.* brilliant, flashing.

centellante, *a.* sparkling, flashing.

centellar, *or* centellear, *vn.* to sparkle, scintillate; to twinkle.—centelleo, *m.* sparkling; twinkling.

centellica, ita, *f. dim.* small flash or spark.

centellón, *m. aug.* large spark or flash.

centén, *m.* an old Spanish gold coin worth about 25 pesetas.

centena, *f.* a hundred (collect.).

centenadas.—a c., by hundreds.

¹centenal, ¹centenar, *m.* = CENTENA.—a centenares, by hundreds.

²centenal, ²centenar, *m.* rye field.

centenario, ria. I. *a.* centenary; secular. II. *m.* centennial.

centenaza, za, *a.* pertaining to rye.

centenero, ra, *a.* (of land, soil) good for rye.

¹centeno, na, *a.* hundredth.

²centeno, *m.* (bot.) rye.

centenoso, sa, *a.* mixed with rye.

centesimal, *a.* (of a number) between one and one hundred.

centésimo, ma, *n. & a.* hundredth.

centiárea, *f.* centiare (square meter).

centígrado, da, *a.* centigrade.

centígramo, *m.* centigram.

centilitro, *m.* centiliter.

centiloquio, *m.* a work divided into a hundred parts.

centímano, na, *a.* (poet.) hundred-handed, having a hundred hands.

centímetro, *m.* centimeter.

céntimo. I. *m.* centime; hundredth part of a monetary unit. II. *n. & a.* hundredth.

centinela, *m. & f.* (mil.) sentry, sentinel; person on watch.—c. a caballo, vidette, sentinel on horseback.—c. avanzado, advance guard.— c. de vista, prisoner's guard.—c. perdida, forlorn hope.—estar de c., or hacer c., to be on sentry duty.

centinodia, *f.* (bot.) knot grass, persicaria.

centípedo, *m.* centipede.

centiplicado, da, *a.* centuple, hundredfold.

centola, centolla, *f.* center fish, a marine crab with spotted scales.

centón, *m.* crazy quilt; coarse covering of war engine in old times; cento, a literary composition.

centrado, da, *a.* centered.

central. I. *a.* central. II. *f.* main office of a public service; (Am.) sugar mill, refinery.—c. eléctrica, powerhouse.

centralicé, centralice, *v.* V. CENTRALIZAR.

centralismo, *m.* centralism.

centralista, *n. & a.* centralist (-ic).

centralización, *f.* centralization.

centralizar, *va.* (*pret.* CENTRALICÉ; *subj.* CENTRALICE) to centralize.

centralmente, *adv.* centrally.

centrar, *va.* to center.

céntrico, ca, *a.* central.

centrifugar, *va.* (Am.) to put (sugar) through a centrifuge.

centrífugo, ga. I. *a.* centrifugal. II. *f.* centrifugal machine.

centrípeto, ta, *a.* centripetal.

centro, *m.* center; middle, midst; innermost part, core; (mil.) center of an army; height and depth of a thing; main office, headquarters; (pol.) center; principal object of desire and exertion; social circle in which a person moves; club, social meeting place; (bot.) disk of flowers; short flannel dress worn by Indian women in Ecuador.—c. de gravedad, center of gravity.—c. de mesa, (flower) centerpiece (for table).—centros nerviosos, nerve centers. —estar en su c., to be in one's element.

centroamericano, na, *n. & a.* Central-American.

centrobárico, ca, *a.* centrobaric.

centunviral, *a.* centumviral.

centunvirato, *m.* centumvirate.

centunviro, *m.* centumvir.

centuplicar, *va.* to centuplicate.

céntuplo, pla, *a.* centuple.

centuria, *f.* century (period of time; division of Roman army).

centurión, *m.* centurion.

centurionazgo, *m.* office of a centurion.

cenzalino, na, *a.* pertaining to mosquitoes.

cénzalo, *m.* (entom.) mosquito.

ceñido, da. I. *pp.* of CEÑIR. II. *a.* moderate in pleasure or expense; (of insects) narrow-waisted; beelike-waisted.

ceñidor, *m.* belt, girdle, cestus, sash.

ceñidura, *f.* act of girding.

ceñiglo, *m.* (bot.) white goosefoot, summer cypress.

ceñir. I. *va.* (*ind.* CIÑO; *subj.* CIÑA) to gird, surround, girdle; to hem in; to fit tight; to condense, abbreviate.—**c. el viento,** (naut.) to haul the wind.—**c. espada,** to wear a sword. II. *vr.* to reduce one's expenses; to confine or limit oneself; (of auto) to hug (as the inside of a curve).

¹**ceño,** *m.* ring, hoop, band; (vet.) circle round upper part of horse's hoof.

²**ceño,** *m.* frown; browbeating; supercilious look; (poet.) gloomy aspect.—**ceñoso, sa;** **ceñudo, da,** *a.* frowning; browbeating; supercilious; grim, gruff.

ceo, *m.* (ichth.) doree, dory.

cepa, *f.* underground butt end of a tree stem; stump, stub; vinestock; stock or origin of a family; bud or root of the horns and tails of animals; (Mex.) hole, pit (dug for planting); (Am.) group of banana plants with common root; (arch.) pier of an arch; (agr.) sole of a plow; (carriage) tongue of a pole.—**de buena c.,** of acknowledged good quality; on good authority.—**de c.** blue-blood; thoroughbred.

cepacaballo, *m.* (bot.) cardoon.

cepeda, *f.* land overgrown with heath.

cepejón, *m.* butt end of tree branch torn off.

cepellón, *m.* ball of earth left around the roots of a plant for transplanting.

cepera, *f.* inflammation of the hoofs: CEPEDA.

cepilladura, *f.* wood shavings.

cepillar, *va.* to plane; to brush; to polish.

cepillo, *m.* brush; (carp.) plane; charity box, poor-box corban.—**c. bocel,** fluting plane; modelling plane.—**c. de cabeza,** hairbrush.—**c. de dientes,** toothbrush.—**c. de ropa,** clothesbrush.—**c. para la cabeza,** hairbrush.—**c. para ropa,** clothesbrush.

¹**cepo,** *m.* bough or branch off a tree; stock of an anvil; stocks, for punishment; (naut.) bilboes; stock (of an anchor); reel for winding silk; trap, snare; charity box; (mil.) stocks of a gun carriage; (mech.) block; socket; clasp, clamp; joining press; shoemaker's horse.—*pl.* notch cleats.—**c. colombiano,** or **c. de campaña,** (Am.) an old form of military punishment in which the thumbs were tied together, the knees put between the arms, and one or two rifles placed on the arms between these and the legs.—**c. de maniguetes,** (naut.) crosspiece of the kevel.—**c. de molinete,** (naut.) knighthead of the windlass.—**¡cepos quedos!** keep still! keep quiet! stop that!

²**cepo,** *m.* = CEFO, an African monkey.

cepón, *m.* *aug.* large stub of a tree or vinestock.

ceporro, *m.* old vine pulled up for fuel.

cequí, *m.* an ancient gold coin.

cequión, *m.* (Chile) large ditch or channel.

cera, *f.* wax; beeswax; wax tapers and candles.—*pl.* honeycomb.—**c. aleda,** propolis, bee glue.—**c. de dorar,** gold size.—**c. de higos,** drum of figs.—**c. de los oídos,** earwax, cerumen.—**c. virgen,** virgin wax.—**no hay más c. que la que arde,** there is nothing more than what you see.—**ser como una c., ser una c., estar hecho de c.,** to be very condescending, very docile, very "easy."

ceráceo, ea, *a.* ceraceous, waxy.

cerachates, *f. pl.* wax stones.

cerafolio, *m.* (bot.) common chervil.

cerambícido, da. I. *n. & a.* (zool.) cerambycid. II. *m. pl.* Cerambycidæ.

cerámica, *f.* ceramic art; ceramics.

cerámico, ca, *a.* ceramic, pertaining to pottery.

ceramista, *m.* ceramist.

ceramita, *f.* a precious stone; a kind of brick of exceedingly high strength.

cerapez, *f.* plaster of wax and pitch.

cerasina, *f.* cerasin.

cerasta, *f.,* **ceraste, cerastes,** *m.* cerastes, a horned serpent.

cerastio de granada, *m.* (bot.) white mouse-ear chickweed.

ceratias, *m.* double-tailed comet.

cerato, *m.* (pharm.) ointment containing wax.

cerbatana, *f.* blowgun, popgun, pea-shooter; ear trumpet for the deaf; small culverin.

cerbero, *m.* = CANCERBERO, Cerberus.

¹**cerca,** *f.* fence; hedge.

²**cerca,** *adv.* near, close by, nigh. (Before a noun, pron., or adv., it requires **de:** *cerca de París, near Paris; cerca de aquí,* near here; but *aquí cerca,* near here).—**c. de** (when not used as explained), nearly, about.—**de c.,** closely; close at hand.—**por aquí c.,** somewhere near here.

cercado, da. I. *pp.* of CERCAR. II. *a.* inclosed, fenced in, walled in. III. *m.* garden or field fenced in; inclosure; fence; lock; (Peru) territorial division comprising state-capital and towns within its jurisdiction.

cercador, *m.* hedger, fencer; iron graver; marking iron; blunt chisel for repoussé work.

cercanamente, *adv.* near, nearly.

cercanía, *f.* proximity; (gen. *pl.*) neighborhood, vicinity, surroundings.

cercano, na (de) *a.* near (to); neighboring.

cercar, *va.* (*pret.* CERQUÉ; *subj.* CERQUE) to hem, circle, compass, gird; to surround; to fence in, hedge in, wall in; to pale; (mil.) to invest, lay siege to; to crowd about.

cercén.—**a c.,** all around.

cercenadamente, *adv.* with retrenchment.

cercenadera, *f.* waxchandler's clipping knife.

cercenador, *m.* clipper.

cercenadura, *f.* clipping, retrenchment.—*pl.* cuttings.

cercenar, *va.* to pare, clip; to lop off the ends of; to lessen, reduce, curtail, cut down.

cercera, *f.* air tube of a vault.

cerceta, *f.* (ornith.) widgeon, garganey, a species of duck.—*pl.* first growth of a deer's antlers.

cercillo, *m.* tendril of a vine.

cerciorar. I. *va.* to assure, affirm. II. *vr.* to make sure.

cerco, *m.* fence; hoop, ring; encirclement; rim, border, edge; halo; (mil.) blockade, siege; circular motion; circle of people; frame or case of a door or window.—**alzar,** or **levantar, el c.,** to raise a blockade.—**poner c. a,** to lay siege to, to blockade.

cercopiteco, *m.* (zool.) cercopithecus, an African monkey.

cercha, *f.* flexible wooden rule for measuring curved objects; (arch.) form or center for building arches; (carp.) segment of a rim.

cerchar, *va.* = ACODAR, to plant cuttings.

cerchón, *m.* = CIMBRA, (carp.) form; center.

cerda, *f.* horse's hair; bristle; (zool.) sow; new-mown cereals; bundle of flax broken but not yet hackled.—*pl.* snares for birds.—**c. de puerco,** hog's bristle.

cerdamen, *m.* bristles prepared for brushes.

cerdear, *vn.* (of animals, esp. bulls) to be weak in the fore quarter; to emit a harsh and inharmonious sound (on string instrument); (coll.) to decline a request or demand; to look for excuses.

cerdito, *m.* *dim.* little pig.

cerdo, *m.* hog.—**c. de muerte,** pig old enough to be slaughtered.—**c. de vida,** pig not old enough to be slaughtered.—**chuleta de c.,** pork chop.

cerdoso, sa; cerdudo, da, *a.* bristly; hairy.

cereal, *n. & a.* cereal.

cerebelitis, *f.* (med.) inflammation of the cerebellum.

cerebelo, *m.* (anat.) cerebellum.

cerebral, *a.* cerebral.

cerebrina, *f.* (chem.) cerebrin.

cerebritis, *f.* (med.) inflammation of the cerebrum.

cerebro, *m.* cerebrum; brain; judgment.

cerebroespinal, *a.* cerebrospinal.

cereceda, *f.* = CEREZAL.

cerecilla, *f. dim.* = GUINDILLA, red pepper pod.

cerecita, *f. dim.* small cherry.

ceremonia, *f.* ceremony; pomp, display; formality; ceremoniousness; compliment.—**de c.,** with all due ceremony; formal; (of dress) full, evening.—**guardar c.,** to comply with the formalities; to be formal.—**por c.,** simply as a matter of form or of etiquette.

ceremonial. I. *m.* book of ceremonies for public occasions. **II.** *a.* ceremonial, ceremonious.

ceremonialmente, *adv.* with all ceremony.

ceremoniáticamente, *adv.* ceremoniously.

ceremoniático, ca, *a.* ceremonious.

ceremoniosamente, *adv.* ceremoniously.

ceremonioso, sa, *a.* ceremonious, formal.

céreo, *m.* (bot.) torch thistle.

cereolita, *f.* soft, waxlike lava.

cerería, *f.* wax chandler's shop; chandlery in the royal palace.

cerero, ra, *n.* wax chandler.—**c. mayor,** royal chandler.

cereza, *f.* cherry.—**c. garrafal,** large white-heart cherry, bigaroon.

cerezal, *m.* cherry orchard.

cerezo, *m.* (bot.) cherry tree; cherry wood.—**c. silvestre,** dog-cherry tree.

cergazo, *m.* (bot.) rockrose, cistus.

cérico, ca, *a.* ceric, pertaining to cerium.

céridos, *m. pl.* (chem.) cerium metals.

cerífero, ra, *a.* wax-producing.

ceriflor, *f.* (bot.) honeywort, honeyflower.

cerilla, *f.* wax taper in rolls; wax match; a kind of cosmetic; cold cream; wax tablet; earwax.

cerillera, *f.* lamplighter with a taper.

cerillo, *m.* (Mex.) wax match.

cerina, *f.* a variety of wax or waxlike material extracted from the cork tree.

cerinto, *m.* (bot.) wax flower, honeywort.

cerio, *m.* (chem.) cerium.

cerita, *f.* (min.) cerite.

cermeña, *f.* small early pear; muscadine.

cermeño, *m.* (bot.) muscadine pear tree.

cernada, *f.* cinder; leached ashes; (art) size on canvas; (vet.) plaster of ashes and other ingredients.—**cernadero,** *m.* coarse linen strainer for lye; linen or silk-and-linen fabric for collars.

cernedero, *m.* apron worn in sifting flour; place for sifting flour.

cernedor, *m.* sifter.

cerneja, *f.* fetlock of a horse.

cernejudo, da, *a.* having large fetlocks.

cerner. I. *va.* (*ind.* CIERNO; *subj.* CIERNA) to sift; to bolt. **II.** *vn.* to bud and blossom; to drizzle. **III.** *vr.* to waggle, wiggle, waddle; to soar.

cernícalo, *m.* (ornith.) kestrel; sparrow-hawk; person of scanty abilities.—**coger,** or **pillar, un c.,** (coll.) to get drunk.

cernidillo, *m.* drizzle; short and waddling gait.

cernido, *n.* sifting; the flour sifted.

cernidura, *f.* sifting.

cernir, *va.* = CERNER.

cero, *m.* zero; cipher; naught.—**ser un c.,** or **un c. a la izquierda,** to be a mere cipher, to be insignificant or of no account, not to count.

ceroferario, *m.* acolyte bearing a candelabrum.

cerografía, *f.* cerography.

cerográfo, *m.* (archeol.) wax seal used by the Romans.

ceroleína, *f.* cerolein, a constituent of beeswax.

cerollo, lla, *a.* reaped when green and soft.

ceroma, *f.* ointment used by Roman athletes.

ceromancía, *f.* divination from melted wax in water.

ceromiel, *m.* wax and honey ointment.

cerón, *m.* dross of wax.

ceroplástica, *f.* ceroplastics, modelling in wax.

cerotato, *m.* (chem.) cerotate.

cerótico, ca, *a.* cerotic.

cerote, *m.* shoemaker's wax; shoeblacking; (coll.) panic; fear.

ceroto, *m.* (pharm.) soft cerate of oil and wax.

cerqué, cerque, *v.* V. CERCAR.

cerquillo, *m. dim.* small circle or hoop; seam or welt of a shoe; ring of hair or tonsure; hair bangs.

cerquita, *adv.* at a short distance; very near.—**aquí c.,** close by, very near here.

cerrada, *f.* hide or skin covering the backbone.

cerradera, *f.,* **cerradero,** *m.* bolt staple; catch of a lock; catch, clasp; purse strings.—**echar la cerradera,** to turn a deaf ear; to refuse point-blank.

cerradero, ra, *n.* & *a.* locked (place); locking (device).

cerradizo, za, *a.* that may be locked or fastened.

cerrado, da. I. *pp.* of CERRAR.—**c. por reformas,** closed for alterations. **II.** *a.* incomprehensible, obscure; close, reserved; dissembling; secreted, concealed; obstinate; inflexible; cloudy, overcast; stupid, thick; dense.—**a puerta c.,** closed (meeting, etc.). **III.** *m.* fenced in field or garden.

cerrador, *m.* shutter; locker; lock; any contrivance that shuts or locks.

cerradura, *f.* lock; closure; act of shutting or locking.—**c. de golpe,** or **de muelle,** spring lock.—**c. embutida,** mortise lock.

¹**cerraja,** *f.* lock of a door; bolt.

²**cerraja,** *f.* (bot.) common sow-thistle.

cerrajear, *vn.* to work as, or to be, a locksmith.

cerrajería, *f.* trade of a locksmith; locksmith's shop or forge.

cerrajero, *m.* locksmith.

cerrajón, *m.* steep, craggy cliff.

cerramiento, *m.* closure, occlusion; act of shutting or locking; costiveness; inclosure; (arch.) roof; (mason.) partition wall.

cerrar. I. *va.* & *vn.* (*ind.* CIERRO; *subj.* CIERRE) to close, shut, fasten, lock; to close, conclude (as an interview); to stop up, obstruct, block up; to inclose, include, contain; fence in; to fold and seal (a letter).—**c. la boca,** to be silent, shut up.—**c. los oídos,** to turn a deaf ear.—**c. los ojos,** to close one's eyes; die; sleep; to be stubborn.—**al c. del día,** at the close of day, at nightfall. **II.** *vr.* to close; to remain firm in one's opinion; to become cloudy and overcast; to close up, get close to each other.—**cerrársele a uno todas las puertas,** to find all avenues closed.

cerrazón, *f.* dark and cloudy weather preceding a storm.

cerrejón, *m.* hillock.

cerrero, ra, *a.* wild; untamed; unbroken (horse).

cerreta, *f.* (naut.) spar; rough tree.

cerril, *a.* mountainous; rough, uneven; wild, untamed, unbroken; (coll.) unpolished, rough, boorish.

cerrilla, *f.* die for milling.—**cerrillar,** *va.* to mill (coined metal).

cerrillo, *m. dim.*—*pl.* milling dies.

cerrión, *m.* icicle.

cerro, *m.* hill; peak; neck of an animal; backbone; hackled and cleaned flax or hemp.—**c. enriscado,** steep, rugged hill.—**en c.,** bareback; nakedly, without the proper or usual trappings.—**por los cerros de Ubeda,** (coll.) foreign to the purpose, irrelevant, (coll.) off the track.

cerrojillo, *m.* (ornith.) wagtail, warbler.

cerrojo, *m.* bolt, latch.

cerrón, *m.* a kind of coarse fabric made in Galicia.

cerruma, *f.* weak or defective quarter in horses.

certamen, *m.* literary contest; disputation; competition; (obs.) duel, battle.

certero, ra, *a.* well-aimed; good shot (shooter); sure; well-informed; skillful.

certeza, *f.* certainty, assurance.

For pronunciation, see the rules at the beginning of the book.

certidumbre, f. certainty, conviction.

certificación, f. certificate, affidavit.

certificado, n. certificate, attestation; testimonial; piece of registered mail.

certificador, ra, n. & a. certifier(-ying).

certificar, va. (pret. CERTIFIQUÉ; subj. CERTIFIQUE) to certify, attest; to register (a letter); (law) to prove by a public instrument.

certificatorio, ria, a. that serves to certify.

certifiqué, certifique, v. V. CERTIFICAR.

certísimo, a. super. of CIERTO: most certain.

cerúleo, lea, a. cerulean, sky-blue.

ceruma, f. (vet.) = CERRUMA.

cerumen, m. earwax, cerumen.

cerusa, f. ceruse, white lead.

cerval, a. pertaining to deer.

cervantesco, ca; cervántico, ca; cervantino, na, a. like, or in the style of, Cervantes; pertaining or peculiar to Cervantes.

cervantista, n. expert in matters relating to Cervantes; Cervantes scholar.

cervario, ria, a. = CERVAL.

cervatica, f. (ichth.) = LANGOSTÓN, crawfish.

cervatico, illo, m. dim. small deer.

cervato, m. fawn.

cervecería, f. brewery; alehouse, beer-saloon.

cervecero, ra. I. a. beer (as a.). II. n. brewer; beer seller. III. m. set of beer jugs, mugs, etc.

cerveza, f. beer, ale.

cervicabra, f. gazelle.

cervical; cérvico, ca, a. (anat.) cervical.

cérvido, da. I. a. (zool.) cervine, pertaining to deer or cervids. II. n. cervid. III. m. pl. Cervidæ.

cervigudo, da, a. high- or thick-necked.

cerviguillo, m. thick nape of the neck.

cervillera, f. helmet.

cervino, na, a. deerlike.

cerviz, f. cervix, nape of the neck.—**bajar, or doblar, la c.,** to humble oneself.—**levantar la c.,** to be elated; to grow proud.—**ser de dura c.,** to be incorrigible or stubborn.

cervuno, na, a. resembling or pertaining to deer; deer-colored.

cesación, f., **cesamiento,** m. cessation, discontinuance, stopping, pause.—**cesación a divinis,** suspension from religious functions.

cesante. I. a. ceasing. II. n. dismissed or retired public officer, in some cases with a pension.

cesantía, f. state or pension of a retired official.

cesar, vn. to cease, stop; to desist; to retire; to leave a post or employment.—**c. de** (inf.), to stop (pres. p.).

cesáreo, rea, a. Cæsarean, pert. to imperial matters; (surg.) Cæsarean.

cesariano, na, a. Cæsarean, pert. to Cæsar.

cesarismo, m. Cæsarism.

cesarista, n. & a. Cæsarist(-ic).

cese, m. cease; stop of pension.

cesible, a. (law) transferable.

cesio, m. (chem.) cæsium.

cesión, f. cession, transfer, conveyance; resignation; concession.—**c. de bienes,** surrender of property.—**cesionario, ria,** n. cessironay, grantee, assignee, transferee.—**cesionista,** n. transferrer, assigner, grantor.

cesonario, ria, n. = CESIONARIO.

césped, céspede, m. turf, sod, clod, sward, grass; grass plot, lawn; rind of a vine where it has been pruned.—**cespedera,** f. field where turf is cut.

cespitar, vn. to hesitate, vacillate.

cesta, f. basket, pannier, hamper; scoop or racket fastened to the arm for playing ball.—**cestada,** f. basketful.—**cestería,** f. basket factory or shop.—**cestero, ra,** n. basket maker or seller.

cestiaro, m. Roman pugilist who fought with the cestus.

cestica, illa, ita, f. dim.; **cestico, illo, ito,** m. dim. small basket; hand basket.

¹**cesto,** m. hand basket, maund, hutch.—**coger agua en c.,** to labor in vain.—**estar hecho un c.,** (coll.) to be overcome by sleep or liquor.—**quien hace un c. hará ciento,** he that steals a penny will steal a pound.—**ser un c.,** (coll.) to be ignorant and rude.

²**cesto,** m. cestus used by Roman boxers.

céstodo. I. n. & a. (zool.) cestode, tapeworm. II. m. pl. Cestoda.

cestón, m. aug. large pannier or basket; (mil.) gabion.—pl. (mil.) corbeils.

cestonada, f. range of gabions.

cesura, f. cæsura, pause in poetry.

cetáceo, cea. I. n. & a. cetacean. II. n. pl. Cetaceæ.

cetilo, m. (chem.) cetyl.

cetina, f. whale oil, sperm oil.

cetís, m. an old Portuguese coin.

cetra, f. leather shield formerly used.

cetre, m. assistant acolyte.

cetrería, f. falconry, hawking; fowling with falcons.

¹**cetrero,** m. verger.

²**cetrero,** m. falconer; sportsman.

cetrino, na, a. citrine, lemon-colored; jaundiced, melancholy; pertaining to citron.

cetro, m. sceptre; reign of a prince; verge borne by canons on solemn occasions; wand or staff; perch or roost for birds.—**empuñar el c.,** to ascend the throne, to begin to reign.

ceugma, zeugma, f. (rhet.) zeugma.

ceutí. I. n. & a. of, from, or pertaining to Ceuta. II. m. a very fragrant lemon.

C. G. S., m. (phys.) C. G. S. (centimeter-gram-second system of units).

cía, f. hip bone, huckle bone.

ciaboga, f. (naut.) putting a row galley about with the oars.—**hacer c.,** to turn the back, to flee.

cianato, m. (chem.) cyanate.

cianhídrico, ca, a. hydrocyanic.

ciánico, ca, a. cyanic (acid).

cianógeno, m. cyanogen.

cianosis, f. (med.) cyanosis.

cianuración, f. (metal.) cyaniding.

cianuro, m. (chem.) cyanide.

ciar, vn. to back up, retrograde; (naut.) to back water; to go astern; to slacken, slow down.

ciática, f. (med.) sciatica.

ciático, ca, a. sciatic, sciatical.

ciato, m. (bot.) a tropical tree fern.

cibario, ria, a. cibarious, pertaining to food.

cibéleo, lea, a. pert. to the goddess Cybele.

cibera, f. quantity of wheat put at once in the hopper; all seeds or grains fit for food; bagasse of grain, fruit, husks, etc.; hopper in a corn-mill.

cibica, f. clout; hurter of a wooden axle tree; (naut.) staple, cramp.

cibicón, m. large clout (for axle tree).

cíbolo, la, n. bison.

cibuí, m. (Peru) a variety of cedar.

cicadáceo, a; cicádido, da. I. n. & a. (bot.) cycad. II. f. pl. Cycadaceæ.

cicatear, vn. (coll.) to be sordidly parsimonious.

cicatería, f. niggardliness, stinginess.

cicatero, ra, a. niggardly, stingy.

cicateruelo, la, n. dim. stingy little person; little miser; curmudgeon.

cicatricé, cicatrice, v. V. CICATRIZAR.

cicatricera, f. a woman who used to follow troops and tend the wounded.

cicatricilla, f. dim. small scar.

cicatriz, f. cicatrice, scar.

cicatrización, f. cicatrization.

cicatrizal, a. cicatricial.

cicatrizante, n. & a. cicatrizant.

cicatrizar, va. & vn. (pret. CICATRICÉ; subj. CICATRICE) to cicatrize; to heal.

cicatrizativo, va, a. cicatrisive.

CIC 115 CIL

icércula, cicercha, *f.* (bot.) = ALMORTA, vetch.
ícero, *m.* (print.) pica; (print.) unit of measurement for type bodies, equivalent to 12 points.
icerone, *n.* cicerone, guide.
iceroniano, na, *a.* Ciceronian.
iclamor, *m.* an ornamental tree.
iclatón, *m.* tunic formerly worn by women.
íclico, ca, *a.* cyclical.
iclismo, *m.* bicycling as a sport.
iclista, *n.* cyclist, rider on a bicycle.
iclo, *m.* cycle.
icloidal, *a.* cycloidal.
icloide, *f.* (geom.) cycloid.
iclometría, *f.* cyclometry.
iclométrico, ca, *a.* cyclometric.
iclómetro, *m.* cyclometer.
iclón, *m.* cyclone.—**ciclonal,** *a.* cyclonic.
íclope, *m.* Cyclops.—**ciclópeo, a,** *a.* Cyclopean.
iclorama, *m.* cyclorama.
iclóstilo, *m.* cyclostyle.
iclóstomas, *m.* *pl.* (zool.) Cyclostomata.
iclotrón, *m.* (phys.) cyclotron.
icuta (bot.) hemlock, cicuta; water hemlock; spotted cowbane.
id, *m.* brave, valiant man; leader, chief.—**el C.,** or **el C. Campeador,** El Cid, a title of the Spanish hero Rodrigo Díaz de Vivar.
idra, *f.* (bot.) citron.
idracayote, *f.* (bot.) American gourd or calabash.
idrada, *f.* preserve made with citrons.
idral, *m.* plantation of citron trees.
idria, *m.* = CEDRIA, resin from the cedar.
idro, *m.* (bot.) citron tree.
idronela, *f.* citronella, common balm.
ciegamente, *adv.* blindly.
ciegayernos, *m.* showy, worthless thing; humbug.
ciego, ga. I. *a.* blind; choked or closed; blinded.—**c. de,** blind with, blinded by.—**a ciegas,** blindly, in the dark; thoughtlessly. **II.** *n.* blind person; (anat.) cæcum or blind gut; large black pudding; (Cuba) isolated farm, ranch; hilly woodland.
ciego, ciegue, *v. V.* CEGAR.
cieguecico, ica; illo, illa; ito, ita; cieguezuelo, ela, *n. dim.* little blind person.
cielito, *m.* S. A. tune and dance; darling, dearest, dearie.
cielo, *m.* sky, firmament; heaven(s); atmosphere; climate; ceiling; glory, felicity; paradise; roof; cover; canopy (of a bed).—**c. raso,** flat ceiling; clear sky.—**c. de la boca,** roof of the mouth.—**a c. descubierto,** in the open air; in the open, openly.—**a c. raso,** in the open air.—**escupir al c.,** to do bad deeds that turn against the doer, to throw a boomerang (fig.).—**estar hecho un c.,** to be splendid, brilliant.—**llovido del c.,** godsend.—**poner en,** or **por, el c.,** to praise to the utmost, to lionize.—**tomar el c. con las manos,** to be carried away with joy, grief, etc.—**un c. alegre,** a clear, beautiful sky.—**venirse el c. abajo,** to pour, rain pitchforks.—**ver el c. abierto,** to find an unforeseen opportunity.—**ver el c. por embudo,** not to know the world.
ciempiés, *m.* CIENTOPIÉS, (zool.) centipede; mediocre literary work.
cien, *a.* one hundred (used before nouns instead of **ciento,** as, *cien hombres,* a hundred men; *cien mujeres,* a hundred women). *V.* CIENTO.
ciénaga, *f.* marsh, moor, miry place.
ciencia, *f.* science; knowledge; certainty.—**ciencias exactas,** exact sciences.—**ciencias naturales,** natural science.—**a c. cierta,** with certainty, knowingly.—**a c. y paciencia de,** with the knowledge and connivance of.
cienmilésimo, ma, *n.* & *a.* hundred-thousandth.
cienmilmillonésimo, ma, *n.* & *a.* hundred-thousand millionth.

cienmillonésimo, ma, *n., a.* hundred-millionth.
cieno, *m.* mud, mire, slime; slough, bog.
científicamente, *adv.* scientifically.
científico, ca. I. *a.* scientific. **II.** *n.* scientist.
ciento. I. *a.* (*V.* CIEN) one hundred; one hundredth (*calle ciento,* One-hundredth Street). **II.** *m.* a hundred. (Gen. without the article: *tengo ciento,* I have a hundred; *somos ciento,* we are a hundred. When used with the article before a noun, it is followed by **de:** *un ciento de libros,* a hundred books).—*pl.* tax assessed at so much per cent; piquet, a card game.—**por c.,** per cent; by the hundred.—**por cientos,** by hundreds, by the hundred; in large number.
cientopiés, *m.* (zool.) centipede.
cierna, *f.* the staminate blossom of vines, corn, and some other plants.
cierne.—en c., in blossom; in its infancy.
cierno, cierne, *v. V.* CERNER.
¡cierra España! *interj.* war cry of the ancient Spaniards.
cierre, *m.* act and mode of closing; shutting, locking, fastening; snap; clasp; plug of a valve.—**c. hidráulico,** hydraulic seal, water seal.
cierro, *m.* inclosure.—**c. de cristales,** glass-covered balcony or veranda.
cierro, cierre, *v. V.* CERRAR.
ciertamente, *adv.* certainly, surely.
cierto, ta. I. *a.* certain, doubtless; sure, positive; true. (Used indefinitely, gen. without an article: *cierto lugar,* a certain place).—**ciertas hierbas, ciertos lienzos,** (coll.) certain people.—**de c.,** certainly, surely; in earnest.—**lo c. es que,** the fact is that.—**no por c.,** certainly not.—**por c., sí por c.,** certainly, surely, yes indeed.—**por c. que,** indeed. **II.** *adv.* certainly.
cierva, *f.* hind, female stag.
ciervo, *m.* deer, stag.—**c. volante,** stag beetle.
cierzo, *m.* cold northerly wind.
cifosis, *f.* (med.) outward bending of the spine.
cifra, *f.* figure, number, numerical character; cipher, code, cryptogram; monogram, device, emblem; sum total; contraction, abbreviation; music written with numbers.—**en c.,** secretly, mysteriously; briefly, concisely.
cifrar, *va.* to write in cipher; to abridge.—**c. en,** to place (one's hopes, etc.) on; to make (a thing) depend on.
cigarra, *f.* (entom.) cicada, harvest fly.
cigarral, *m.* in Toledo, orchard or fruit garden.
cigarrera, *f.* cigar cabinet or showcase; pocket cigarcase; woman cigar maker or dealer.
cigarrero, ra, *n.* cigar maker or dealer.
cigarrería, *f.* cigar shop.
cigarrillo, *m.* cigarette.
cigarrista, *n.* heavy smoker.
cigarro, *m.* cigar; (in some places) **cigarette.—c. de papel,** cigarette.—**c. puro,** cigar.
cigarrón, *m. aug.* large cicada.
cigomático, ca, *a.* (anat.) zygomatic.
cigoñal, *m.* well sweep.
cigoñino, *m.* (ornith.) young stork.
cigoñuela, *f.* (ornith.) small storklike bird.
cigua, *f.* (bot.) a tropical tree.
ciguatarse, *vr.* to have jaundice.
ciguatera, *f.* (Mex.) a kind of jaundice, from eating diseased fish.
ciguato, ta, *a.* suffering from CIGUATERA.
cigüeña, *f.* (ornith.) white stork; crane; bell crank; (mech.) crank, winch.—**cigüeñal,** *m.* CIGOÑAL; (int. combust. eng.) crankshaft.
cigüeñuela, *f. dim.* small crank or winch.—**c. de la caña del timón,** (naut.) gooseneck of the tiller.
cigüete, *f.* a variety of white grape.
cija, *f.* building for sheltering sheep; dungeon; granary.
cilanco, *m.* pool left by a river on the bank.
cilantro, *m.* (bot.) coriander.
ciliado, da, *a.* (zool.) ciliated.

For pronunciation, see the rules at the beginning of the book.

ciliar, *a.* pert. to eyebrows or eyelashes.
cilicio, *m.* haircloth; hair shirt.
cilindrado, *m.* rolling; calendering.
cilindrar, *va.* to roll; calendar; to bore; rebore.
cilindricidad, *f.* cylindricity.
cilíndrico, ca, *a.* cylindrical.
cilindro, *m.* cylinder; (print.) roller; press roll; (mech.) chamber.
cilindroeje, *m.* (anat.) axis cylinder, axon.
cilindroide, *m.* (geom.) cylindroid.
cilindroideo, a, *a.* cylindroid, cylinderlike.
cilla, *f.* granary; tithe.
cillazgo, *m.* storehouse fees paid on tithes.
cillerero, *m.* cellarist or butler of a monastery.
cilleriza, *f.* nun who directs the domestic affairs of a convent.
cillerizo, za, *n.* keeper of a granary.
cillero, *m.* keeper of a granary or storehouse for tithes; granary; vault; cellar; storeroom.
cima, *f.* summit, peak; top; cap, head; finish, completion; heart and tender sprouts of cardoons.—dar c., to conclude happily.—por c., in the uppermost part, at the very top.
cimacio, *m.* (arch.) cymatium, gola, ogee
cimarrón, na. I. *a.* (Am.) wild, unruly. II. *n.* runaway slave; maroon; (Arg.) black maté; (naut.) lazy sailor.
cimarronear, *vn.* (Am.) to run away; (Arg.) to drink black maté.
cimbalaria, *f.* (bot.) ivywort.
cimbalillo, *m. dim.* small bell.
címbalo, *m.* small bell; cymbal.
cimbanillo, *m.* = CIMBALILLO.
címbara, *f.* large sickle.
cimbel, *m.* decoy pigeon; rope used to tie decoy pigeons.
cimborio, cimborrio, *m.* (arch.) dome.
cimbra, *f.* (carp.) form, center (for an arch, etc.); (naut.) curvature; bending of a board.
cimbrado, *m.* quick bending movement in a Spanish dance.
cimbrar. I. *va.* to brandish; to shake; to sway, to bend; (carp.) to place cradlings in; (arch.) to arch; (coll.) to give a drubbing to. II. *vr.* to bend; to vibrate; to shake, tremble.
cimbre, *m.* subterranean gallery or passage.
cimbrear, *va. & vr.* = CIMBRAR.
cimbreño, ña, *a.* pliant, flexible.
cimbreo, *m.* act of bending, brandishing, swaying, vibrating.
címbrico, ca, *a.* Cimbrian.
cimbro, bra, *n. & a.* Cimbrian.
cimbronazo, *m.* blow with flat of sword (also CINTARAZO); (Am.) jerk, sudden shaking.
cimentación, *f.* foundation; laying of a foundation.
cimentado, *m.* refining of gold.
cimentador, *m.* one that lays the foundation.
cimentar, *va.* (*ind.* CIMIENTO; *subj.* CIMIENTE) to lay the foundation of; to found; to ground; to establish the fundamental principles of; to refine (metals).
cimenterio, *m.* = CEMENTERIO, cemetery.
cimento, *m.* = CEMENTO, cement.
cimera, *f.* crest of a helmet or coat of arms.
cimerio, ria, *a.* Cimmerian.
cimero, ra, *a.* placed at the height of some elevated spot; apical.
¹cimiento, *m.* foundation; groundwork, bed; base; root, origin.
²cimiento, cimiente, *v. V.* CIMENTAR.
cimillo, *m.* flexible twig on which a decoy pigeon is tied.
cimitarra, *f.* scimitar, falchion.
cimófana, *f.* cymofane, cat's-eye.
cimorra, *f.* (vet.) glanders.
cinabrio, *m.* (min.) cinnabar; vermilion.
cinamato, *m.* (chem.) cinnamate.
cinámico, *a.* (chem.) cinnamic.
cinamomo, *m.* (bot.) bead tree; (P. I.) privet.

cinc, *m.* zinc.
cinca, *f.* infraction of the rules of the game ninepins (tenpins).
cincel, *m.* chisel; engraver; scorper; burin; drov
cincelador, *m.* engraver; sculptor; stonecutte
cincelar, *va.* to chisel, engrave, carve.
cincelito, *m. dim.* small chisel.
cinco, *n. & a.* five; fifth (app. specially to dates five-spot card; (Venez.) five-string guitar.—decir cuántas son c., to threaten with r proof or punishment; to tell (one) what what.—no saber cuántas son c., (coll.) n to know beans.
cincoenrama, *f.* (bot.) common cinquefoil.
cincograbado, *m.* zinc etching.
cincografía, *f.* zincography.
cincomesino, na, *a.* five-month old.
cincona, *f.* (bot.) cinchona.—cinconina, (chem.) cinchonine.
cincuenta, *n. & a.* fifty; fiftieth (*calle cincuent* Fiftieth Street).
cincuentavo, *n. & a.* fiftieth.
cincuentén, *m.* piece of timber fifty palms i length (50 x 3 x 2).
cincuentena, *f.* group of fifty.—una c. de, fift
cincuenteno, na, *a.* fiftieth.
cincuentón, na. I. *a.* fifty-year-old. II. *n.* fift year old person.
cincha, *f.* girth, cinch.—a revienta cincha at breakneck speed; (Am.) grudgingly, u willingly.
cinchadura, *f.* cinching, girthing.
cinchar, *va.* to girt, cinch up.
cinchera, *f.* girth place; (vet.) sore from girth.
cincho, *m.* belt, girdle, sash or bellyband; iro hoop; tire of a wheel; cheese mold; (Mex cinch; (arch.) transverse rib; (vet.) growth i horse's hoof.
cinchón, *m. aug.* broad cinch or girth.
cinchuela, *f. dim.* small cinch or girth; narro ribbon.
cine, *m.*, cinema, *m.* (coll.) moving picture "movie"; movie theatre.—estrella de cine movie star.
cinegética, *f.* cynegetics, hunting with dogs.
cinegético, ca, *a.* cynegetic.
cinemadrama, *m.* photoplay.
cinemática, *f.* kinematics.
cinemático, ca, *a.* kinematic.
cinematográfico, ca, *a.* cinematographic.
cinematografía, *f.* cinematography.
cinematógrafo, *m.* cinematograph; moving picture; movie house.
cineración, = INCINERACíON, incineration.
cinerario, ia, *a.* cinerary.
cinéreo, a; cinericio, cia, *a.* ashy; ash-colored
cinética, *f.* kinetics.—cinético, ca, *a.* kinetic.
cingalés, sa, *n. & a.* Singhalese.
cíngaro, ra, *n.* gipsy.
cinglar, *va.* (metal.) to shingle, expel impuritie of (iron) by hammering.
cinglador, *m.* (metal.) shingler.
cingleta, *f.* rope with a cork to buoy up a net.
cíngulo, *m.* priest's girdle; ancient militar. badge.
cínicamente, *adv.* cynically.
cínico, ca. I. *a.* cynic, cynical; satirical; impu dent, barefaced. II. *n.* cynic.
cínife, *m.* mosquito.
cinismo, *m.* cynicism; shamelessness, barefaced ness, impudence.
cinocéfalo, *m.* (zool.) dog-headed.
cinógeno, *m.* (auto) starter.
cinoglosa, *f.* (bot.) hound's-tongue.
Cinosura, *f.* (astr.) Cynosure, Little Bear.
cinquén, *m.* an ancient Spanish coin.
cinqueño, cinquillo, *m.* game of ombre, playe by five persons.
cinta, *f.* ribbon; tape, band, strip, sash; (surv. tape; strong net for tunny fishing; lowest par

of the pastern of a horse; (arch.) fillet, belt; scroll; sidewalk curb; first course of floor tiles; moving-picture film (also **c. cinematográfica**). **—cintas de navío,** (naut.) wales.—**cintas galimas,** bow wales or harpings.—**en c.,** under subjection.—**cintadero,** *m.* part of a crossbow to which the string is fastened.

cintagorda, *f.* coarse fishing net.

cintajos, *m. pl.* knot or bunch of tumbled ribbons; tawdry ornaments in female dress.

cintarazo, *m.* slap with a sword or something flat.

cintarear, *va.* (coll.) to slap with a sword.

cinteado, da, *a.* adorned with ribbons.

cintería, *f.* ribbon trade; ribbon shop; collection or heap of ribbons.

cintero, ra. I. *n.* ribbon weaver or dealer. **II.** *m.* belt, girdle; hoisting rope.

cintilla, *f. dim.* small ribbon, narrow tape.

cintillo, *m.* hatband; ring set with precious stones.

cinto, ta. I. *pp. irreg.* of CEÑIR. **II.** *m.* belt, girdle.

cintra, *f.* (arch.) curvature (of an arch).

cintrel, *m.* (arch.) guide rule or line for arching.

cintura, *f.* waist; (woman's) girdle, belt; (arch.) throat of a chimney.—**meter en c.,** (coll.) to discipline, restrain, control.

cinturica, illa, ita, *f. dim.* small girdle; small or delicate waist.

cinturón, *m. aug.* large waist; belt, girdle, cest; that which encircles or surrounds.

ciño, ciña, ciñé, ciñera, *v. V* CEÑIR.

cipariso, *m.* (poet.) cypress.

cipayo, *m.* Sepoy.

ciperáceo, a. I. *a.* (bot.) cyperaceous. **II.** *f. pl.* Cyperaceæ.

cipo, *m.* milestone; signpost; boundary, or memorial, monument; large piece or fragment.

cipolino, na, *a.* cipoline, a kind of marble.

cipote, *n.* fool, blockhead, idiot; little one, youngster; short and fat person.

ciprés, *m.* cypress.—**cipresal,** *m.* cypress grove.

cipresino, na, *a.* pert. to or like cypress.

ciprino, na; ciprio, ia, *n. & a.* Cyprian.

ciquiricata, *f.* (coll.) caress; flattery.

circasiano, na, *n. & a.* Circassian.

circe, *f.* Circe; artful, deceitful woman.

circense, *a.* Circensian, pert. to Roman Circus.

circo, *m.* circus; amphitheatre,

circón, *m.* zircon.—**circonia,** *f.* zirconium oxide.

circonio, *m.* (chem.) zirconium.

circución, *f.* act of surrounding or encircling.

circuir, *va.* (*ind.* CIRCUYO; *subj.* CIRCUYA) to surround, compass, encircle.

circuito, *m.* circuit; contour, periphery; enclosure, field; (elect.) circuit.—**corto c.,** short circuit.

circulación, *f.* circulation; currency; traffic; movement.

circulante, *a.* circulatory, circulating.

¹circular. I. *vn.* to circulate; travel, move; (of vehicles, traffic, etc.) to run. **II.** *va.* to circulate, pass round.

²circular. I. *a.* circular; circulatory; circling. **II.** *f.* circular, letter.

circularmente, *adv.* circularly.

circulatorio, ria, *a.* circulatory.

círculo, *m.* circle; circumference; ring; circuit, district; social circle, club, casino.—**c. acimutal,** (naut.) azimuth circle.—**c. horario,** (astr.) hour circle.—**c. mamario,** (anat.) areola of the nipple.—**c. máximo,** (geom.) great circle.—**c. polar,** (astr.) polar circle.—**c. repetidor,** (surv., etc.) repeating circle.—**c. vicioso,** vicious circle, reasoning in a circle.

circumambiente, *a.* surrounding.

circumcirca, *adv.* about, thereabout; almost.

circumpolar, *a.* circumpolar.

circuncidante, *n. & a.* circumciser(-ing).

circuncidar, *va.* to circumcise; to diminish, curtail, clip.

circuncisión, *f.* circumcision.

circunsiso, sa, *a.* circumcised.

circundar, *va.* to surround, circle, compass.

circunferencia, *f.* circumference.

circunferencial, *a.* circumferential.—**circunferencialmente,** *adv.* in a circular manner.

circunflejo, ja, *a.* circumflex.

circunlocución, *f.,* **circunloquio,** *m.* circumlocution.

circunnavegación, *f.* circumnavigation.

circunnavegar, *va.* to circumnavigate, sail round.

circunscribir, *va.* (*pp.* CIRCUNSCRIPTO and CIRCUNSCRITO) to circumscribe; enclose, encircle.

circunscripción, *f.* circumscription.

circunscriptible, *a.* circumscribable.

circunscriptivo, va, *a.* circumscribing, limiting.

circunscripto, ta; circunscrito, ta, *a.* circumscribed.

circunspeción, *f.* circumspection, prudence; decorum, dignity.

circunspectamente, *adv.* circumspectly.

circunspecto, ta, *a.* circumspect, cautious.

circunstancia, *f.* circumstance, incident; condition, state; particular, detail.—**c. agravante,** aggravating circumstance.—**c. atenuante,** extenuating circumstance.—**en las circunstancias presentes,** in, or under, the circumstances.

circunstanciadamente, *adv.* circumstantially, minutely, in detail.

circunstanciado, da, *a.* with all particulars, in detail.

circunstancial, *a.* circumstantial.

circunstante. I. *a.* surrounding; present, attending. **II.** *m. pl.* bystanders, persons present; audience.

circunvalación, *f.* (mil.) circumvallation.

circunvalar, *va.* to surround, encircle; (mil.) to circumvallate, surround with trenches.

circunvecino, na, *a.* neighboring, adjacent, contiguous, surrounding.

circunvolución, *f.* convolution.

circuyo, circuya, *v. V.* CIRCUIR.

cirial, *m.* (eccl.) processional candleholder.

cirigaña, *f.* flattery.

cirineo, *m.* (coll.) mate, assistant.

cirio, *m.* thick and long wax taper.—**c. pascual,** paschal, or Easter, candle.

cirolero, *m.* (bot.) = CIRUELO.

¹cirro, *m.* (med.) scirrhus, a kind of tumor.

²cirro, *m.* (bot.) short rootlets of creepers; (meteorol.) cirrus.

cirrosis, *f.* (med.) cirrhosis.

cirroso, sa, *a.* (bot.) fibrous; (meteorol.) cirrose.

ciruela, *f.* plum; prune.—**c. de fraile,** long green plum.—**c. de yema,** yellow plum.—**c. pasa,** dried plum, prune.—**c. verdal,** greengage.

ciruelar, *m.* plantation of plum trees.

ciruelica, illa, ita, *f. dim.* small plum.

ciruelico, illo, ito, *m. dim.* dwarf plum tree.

ciruelo, *m.* (bot.) plum tree.

cirugía, *f.* surgery.

cirujano, na, *n.* surgeon.

cisalpino, na, *a.* cisalpine, on Roman side of Alps.

cisca, *f.* reed for roofing huts and cottages.

ciscar. I. *va.* (*pret.* CISQUÉ; *subj.* CISQUE) (coll.) to smear, dirty. **II.** *vr.* to evacuate (bowels).

cisco, *m.* coal dust, culm, slack; breeze; (coll.) noisy wrangle, hubbub, hue and cry.

cisión, *f.* incision.

cisípedo, da, *a.* finger-footed.

cisma, *m.* schism; disturbance in a community; discord.—**cismático, ca,** *n. & a.* schismatic; disturber(-ing); (Am.) finicky, prudish.

cismontano, na, *a.* from or on this side of the mountains.

cismoso, sa, *n. & a.* troublemaker(-making).

cisne, *m.* (ornith.) swan; (C-, astr.) Cygnus, Swan; good poet or musician.

cispadano, na, *a.* on Roman side of the Po.

cisqué, cisque, *v.* V. CISCAR.

cisquero, *m.* coal-dust seller; pounce bag.

cistel, cister, *m.* Cistercian order of St. Bernard.

cisterciense, *n.* & *a.* Cistercian.

cisterna, *f.* cistern; reservoir; water tank.

cístico, ca. I. *a.* (med., anat.) cystic. II. *m.* (anat.) bladder duct.

cistitis, *f.* (med.) cystitis.

cisto, *m.* (bot.) cistus, rockrose.

cistocele, *f.* (med.) cystocele.

cistoma, *m.* (med.) cystoma.

cistoscopio, *m.* (med.) cystoscope.

cistotomía, *f.* (surg.) cystotomy.

cistótomo, *m.* (surg.) lithotrite.

cisura, *f.* incision.

cita, *f.* appointment, engagement; summons; citation, quotation; (Mex.) (also) assignation.

citable, *a.* worthy of being cited, quotable.

citación, *f.* citation, quotation; summons, judicial notice.

Citano, na, *n.* = ZUTANO, (Mr.) So-and-So.

citar, *va.* to make an appointment with; to convoke, convene; to quote; to summon; to give judicial notice.—c. a junta, to call a meeting.

citara, *f.* (mason.) partition wall of the thickness of a brick.—citarilla, *f. dim.* (mason.) thin partition wall.

cítara, *f.* cithara, zither, musical instrument.

citarista, *n.* zither player.

citatorio, ria, *a.* (law) (of a summons) citatory.

citerior, *a.* hither, nearer, toward this part.—España c., the higher or northeastern part of Spain.

cítiso, *m.* (bot.) shrub trefoil, cytisus.

cítola, *f.* in corn mills, clack or clapper.

citolegia, *f.* primer (for learning to read).

citoplasma, *m.* (biol.) cytoplasm.

citote, *m.* (coll.) summons, citation.

citramontano, na, *a.* = CISMONTANO.

citrato, *m.* (chem.) citrate.

cítrico, ca, *a.* (chem.) citric.

citrina, *f.* lemon oil.

citrón, *m.* lemon; (P. R., bot.) lime.

ciudad, *f.* city; civic body.

ciudadanía, *f.* citizenship.

ciudadano, na. I. *a.* pertaining to a city; civil; citylike. II. *n.* citizen.

ciudadela, *f.* (mil.) citadel, fortress; (Am.) tenement house.

civeta, *f.* civet cat.

civeto, *m.* civet, the perfume.

cívico, ca, *a.* civic; domestic.

civil, *a.* civil; polite, courteous; (law) civil, not criminal.—derechos civiles, civil rights.

civilicé, civilice, *v.* V. CIVILIZAR.

civilidad, *f.* civility, politeness, urbanity.

civilista, *n.* attorney skilled in the civil law, especially the Roman law; (Am.) partisan of civil government, opponent of militarism.

civilización, *f.* civilization.

civilizador, ra, *a.* civilizing.

civilizar, *va.* (*pret.* CIVILICÉ; *subj.* CIVILICE) to civilize.

cívilmente, *adv.* civilly, courteously, politely; according to the civil law.

civismo, *m.* civism; patriotism.

cizalla, *f.* shears, plateshears; fillings, metal clippings.—cizallar, *va.* to shear.

cizaña, *f.* (bot.) darnel; weed; corrupting vice; discord, disagreement; pollution.

cizañador, ra, *n.* one who sows discord or enmity, troublemaker.

cizañar, *vn.* to sow discord; to provoke enmity.

cizañero, ra, *n.* = CIZAÑADOR.

clac, *m.* collapsible hat, opera hat.

clamar, *vn.* to utter loud outcries; to whine; to

clamor, vociferate.—c. por, to want, require demand, cry out for.

clámide, *f.* short cape, the chlamys of the Greeks.

clamor, *m.* clamor, outcry; whine, plaint; toll of bells, knell.

clamoreada, *f.* outcry, clamor; whine, plaint.

clamorear, *vn.* to clamor; to implore assistance appeal; to toll.

clamoreo, *m.* repeated or prolonged clamor knell; (coll.) importunate appeal.

clamorosamente, *adv.* clamorously.

clamoroso, sa, *a.* clamorous, loud, noisy.

clan, *m.* clan.

clandestinamente, *adv.* clandestinely.

clandestinidad, *f.* clandestineness, secrecy.

clandestinista, *m.* & *f.* (Am.) smuggler of liquor.

clandestino, na, *a.* clandestine, secret.

clanga, *f.* (ornith.) = PLANGA, a kind of eagle.

clangor, *m.* (poet.) sound of a trumpet.

clara, *f.* white of an egg; piece of ill-woven cloth; bald spot; (coll.) short interval of fair weather on a rainy day.

claraboya, *f.* skylight; bull's-eye; transom.

claramente, *adv.* clearly; openly, frankly.

clarar, *va.* = ACLARAR, to clarify; to clear up.

clarea, *f.* mulled wine, mulse.

clarear. I. *va.* to give light to. II. *vn.* to dawn, to grow light, to clear up. III. *vr.* to be transparent, translucent; to give oneself away.

clarecer, *vn.* (*subj.* CLAREZCA) to dawn, to grow or become light.

clarete, *m.* claret.

claridad, *f.* brightness, splendor, light; clearness, distinctness; glory of the blessed; celebrity, fame.—*pl.* plain truths, plain language.

clarificación, *f.* clarification, refining.

clarificadora, *f.* clarifying pan, evaporator.

clarificar, *va.* (*pret.* CLARIFIQUÉ; *subj.* CLARIFIQUE) to brighten; to illuminate; to clarify, purify, refine.

clarificativo, va, *a.* purifying; lightening.

clarilla, *f.* lye of ashes.

clarimente, *m.* an ancient lotion used by women.

clarín, *m.* bugle, clarion; organ stop; bugler; fine cambric; (ornith.) an American song bird.

clarinada, *f.* (coll.) uncalled-for, tart remark.

clarinado, da, *a.* (her.) bell-bearing.

clarinero, *m.* bugler.

clarinete, *m.* clarinet; clarinet player.

clarión, *m.* white crayon, chalk.

clarisa, *f.* Clare, nun of the order of St. Clare.

clarísimo, ma, *a.* (*super.* of CLARO) very clear, perfectly clear; most illustrious.

clarividencia, *f.* clairvoyance; clear-sightedness.

clarividente, *a.* clairvoyant; clear-sighted, sagacious.

claro, ra, I. *a.* clear; bright, light, nitid; neat; thin, rare, sparse; cloudless, fair; light, not deeply tinged; plain, clear; obvious, evident, indisputable; open, frank, ingenuous; celebrated, illustrious; sagacious, quick of thought.—c. está, of course; evidently.—c. intervalo, remission of madness; lucid interval.—c. oscuro, chiaroscuro.—c. que no, of course not.—a la clara, a las claras, in the open, openly. II. *adv.* = CLARAMENTE, clearly. III. *m.* skylight; break in a discourse; gap, lacuna, interval; bald spot; glade; clearing; light spot; (arch.) space between columns; (naut.) clear spot in the sky.—de c. en c., evidently, manifestly.—pasar la noche de c., or en c., not to sleep a wink.—poner en c., to make plain.—por lo c., clearly, manifestly, conspicuously.—sacar en c. = PONER EN C.; to conclude, arrive at a conclusion.

claror, *m.* = RESPLANDOR, light; brilliance.

claroscuro, *m.* combination of fine and heavy strokes in penmanship; monochrome, painting in one color; chiaroscuro, light and shade.

clarucho, cha, *a.* (coll.) too watery, too thin.

clase, *f.* class; class in school; lecture; classroom; order; (eccl.) classis; kind, kin.—**de c.,** of distinction, of high standing.—**toda c. de,** all kinds of.

clásicamente, *adv.* classically.

clasicismo, *m.* classic style, classicism.

clásico, ca, *a.* classical, classic; principal; remarkable.

clasificación, *f.* classification.

clasificar, *va.* (*pret.* CLASIFIQUÉ; *subj.* CLASIFIQUE) to classify, to class; to sort (as mail).

claudicación, *f.* claudication, limp; crookedness.

claudicante, *a.* halting, limping.

claudicar, *vn.* (*pret.* CLAUDIQUÉ; *subj.* CLAUDIQUE) to halt, limp; to proceed in a bungling manner, without rule or order.

claustral, *a.* claustral, cloistral.

claustro, *m.* cloister; piazza; gallery around a court; faculty of a university; monastic state.

cláusula, *f.* (gram.) period, sentence; clause of a discourse; (law) clause, article.

clausulado, da, I. *a.* (rhet.) written in short sentences. **II.** *m.* (collect.) clauses or articles of a writing.

clausular, *va.* to close (a period), terminate (a speech).

clausulilla, *f. dim.* short or little clause.

clausura, *f.* cloister; inner recess of a convent, sanctum; clausure, confinement, retirement; cloture, closure.—**vivir en c.,** to lead a monastic or retired life.—**clausurar,** *va.* to bring to a close, conclude (as a meeting).

clava, *f.* club, cudgel; (naut.) scupper.

clavadizo, za, *a.* adorned with nails.

clavado, da. I. *pp.* of CLAVAR. **II.** *a.* nailed, adorned with nails, hobnailed; exact, precise.—**venir c.,** to fit exactly.

clavador, *m.* nail driver.

clavadura, *f.* wound made by driving a nail to the quick in horseshoeing.

clavar, *va.* to nail, fasten with nails; to fasten in, drive in, stick in, force in; to stick, prick, gore, pin, pierce; to set in gold or silver; (coll.) to cheat, to deceive.—**c. a un caballo,** to prick a horse in shoeing.—**c. la artillería,** to spike, to nail up the guns.—**c. las armas,** to ground the arms.—**c. los ojos, or la vista, en,** to stare or look with fixed eyes at.

clavaria, *f.* = CLAVERA, nail mold; nail hole.

clavario, *m.* = ¹CLAVERO, keeper of the keys.

clavazón, *f.* set of nails.

clave. I. *m.* clavichord. **II.** *f.* key of a code; (arch.) keystone of an arch; (mus.) clef, key.—**echar la c.,** to close (a speech, an affair).

clavel, *m.* (bot.) pink, carnation.—**c. reventón,** large carnation.—**clavelito,** *m. dim.* (bot.) a plant bearing a small variety of pink.—**clavelón,** *m. aug.* (bot.) marigold.—**clavellina,** *f.* (bot.) pink, carnation; (mil.) vent stopple.

claveque, *m.* rock crystal cut like a diamond.

clavera, *f.* nail mold; heading stamp; nail hole; nail bore; screw hole; boundary where landmarks are set up.

clavería, *f.* office and dignity of the keybearer in military orders; (Mex.) treasury of a cathedral.

¹clavero, ra, *n.* keeper of the keys; treasurer, cashier; key bearer of some military orders.

²clavero, *m.* aromatic clove tree.

clavete, *m. dim.* tack, small nail.—**clavetear,** *va.* to nail; to garnish with nails; to point or tag (a lace); (fig.) to finish up, put in final form.

clavicordio, *m.* clavichord, harpsichord.

clavicornio, nia. I. *n.* & *a.* (zool.) clavicorn. **II.** *m. pl.* Clavicornia.

clavícula, *f.* (anat.) clavicle, collar bone.

clavicular, *a.* (anat.) clavicular.

clavija, *f.* pin, peg; frenail, pintle, peg of a string instrument.—**c. maestra,** fore-axletree pintle.—**apretar las clavijas,** to push home an argument; to put on the thumb screws.

clavijera, *f.* water hole in walls.

clavijero, *m.* bridge of a clavichord.

clavillo, ito, *m. dim.* small nail, spill, brad, tack, pin.—**c. de hebilla,** rivet of a buckle.—*pl.* cloves.

claviórgano, *m.* clavichord, instrument having strings and pipes.

clavo, *m.* nail; spike; (naut.) rudder of a ship; severe grief or pain; (vet.) tumor between the hair and the hoof of a horse; (min.) bunch of rich ore; corn (on the feet); (surg.) lint; tent.—**c. de especia,** clove.—**c. de gota de sebo,** semispherical-headed nail.—**c. de herradura,** hobnail.—**c. de rosca,** screw nail.—**c. romano,** (Am.) curtain knob, picture nail.—**c. tachuela,** tack.—**c. trabadero,** keyed bolt.—**c. trabal,** clasp nail.—**dar en el c.,** to hit the nail on the head.—**de c. pasado,** self-evident, well-known; easy (a "cinch").—**sacarse el c.,** to get even.—**un c. saca otro c.,** one grief cures another.

clazol, *m.* (Mex.) residue of sugar cane, etc.

clemátide, *f.* (bot.) traveller's-joy, virgin's-bower, clematis.

clemencia, *f.* mercy, clemency, forbearance.

clemente, *a.* merciful.—**clementemente,** *adv.* mercifully.—**clementísimo, ma,** *a. super.* of CLEMENTE.

clepsidra, *f.* clepsydra, water clock.

cleptomanía, *f.* kleptomania.

cleptomaníaco, ca; cleptómano, na, *n.* & *a.* kleptomaniac.

clerecía, *f.* clergy.

clerical. I. *a.* clerical, pert. to the clergy. **II.** *n.* (pol.) Clerical, belonging to the Clerical party.—**clericalismo,** *m.* clericalism.—**clericalmente,** *adv.* in a clerical manner.

clericato, *m.* state and dignity of a clergyman.

clericatura, *f.* clergy, ecclesiastical state.

clerigalla, *f.* (collect.) (contempt.) priests.

clérigo, *m.* clergyman.—**c. de misa,** presbyter.—**c. de misa y olla,** ignorant priest.—**c. suelto,** one fighting with an army but not belonging to it and not subject to orders.

cleriguillo, *m. dim.* petty clergyman (a term of contempt).

clerizón, *m.* chorister.

clerizonte, *m.* layman who wears a clerical dress; ill-dressed or ill-mannered clergyman.

clero, *m.* clergy.

clerofobia, *f.* hatred of priests.

clerófobo, ba, *n.* & *a.* priest hater(-ing).

cliente, *n.* client; customer.

clientela, *f.* protection or patronage; following, clientele; state of being a client.

clima, *m.* climate, clime.

climatérico, ca, *a.* climacteric; (coll.) ill-humored; (Am.) wrongly used for CLIMÁTICO.

climático, ca, *a.* climatic, pert. to climate.

climatología, *f.* climatology.

climatológico, ca, *a.* climatological.

climatoterapia, *f.* (med.) climatotherapy.

clímax, *m.* (rhet.) climax.

clin, *f.* = CRIN, mane.

clínica, *f.* clinic (instruction and place); private hospital.

clínico, ca. I. *a.* clinic, clinical. **II.** *m.* & *f.* (eccl.) one asking for baptism on his deathbed.

clinométrico, ca, *a.* clinometric.

clinómetro, *m.* clinometer.

clinopodio, *m.* (bot.) calamint.

clíper, *m.* (naut.) clipper.

clisado, *m.* (print.) stereotyping.

clisar, *va.* (print.) to stereotype; to make a cliché or stereotype plate of.

clisé, *m.* (print.) stereotype plate; (print.) cut.

clistel, clister, *m.* (med.) clyster, enema.

clitómetro, *m.* (surv.) clinometer.

clítoris, *m.* (anat.) clitoris.

clivoso, sa, *a.* (poet.) sloping.

clo, clo, *m.* cackle of a hen.
cloaca, *f.* sewer; (zool.) cloaca, large intestine of fowls.
clocar, *va.* to cluck.
cloque, *m.* (naut.) grapnel; grappling iron, harpoon.
¹cloquear, *va.* to angle; to hook fish (gen. tunny).
²cloquear, *vn.* to cluck, cackle.
cloqueo, *m.* cluck, chuck, cackle.
cloquera, *f.* (of birds) broodiness.
cloquero, *m.* tunny harpooner.
cloración, *f.* (chem.) chlorination.
clorador, *m.* (chem.) chlorinator.
cloral, *m.* (chem.) chloral.
clorar, *va.* (chem.) to chlorinate.
clorato, *m.* (chem.) chlorate.
clorhidrato, *m.* (chem.) hydrochlorate.
clorhídrico, *m.* (chem.) hydrochloric.
clórico, ca, *a.* chloric.
cloris, *f.* (ornith.) greenfinch.
clorita, *f.* (min.) chlorite.
cloro, *m.* (chem.) chlorine.
clorófila, *f.* chlorophyll, green coloring-matter of plants.—**clorofílico, ca,** *a.* chlorophyllous.
clorofórmico, ca, *a.* pertaining to chloroform.
cloroformización, *f.* chloroforming.
cloroformizar, *va.* (*pret.* CLOROFORMICÉ; *subj.* CLOROFORMICE) to chloroform.
cloroformo, *m.* chloroform.
clorosis, *f.* (med.) chlorosis, greensickness.
cloroso, sa, *a.* chlorous.
clorótico, ca, *a.* (med.) chlorotic.
clorurar, *va.* to transform into chloride.
cloruro, *m.* chloride.
club, *m.* club, social or political association.—**clubista,** *m. & f.* clubman(-woman).
clueco, ca. I. *a.* (of birds) broody; (coll.) decrepit. **II.** *f.* brooding hen.
coa, *f.* sharp stick used by Indians to till the land; (Mex.) a kind of hoe.
coacción, *f.* coaction; compulsion, coercion.
coacervar, *va.* to heap together.
coactivo, va, *a.* coactive, coercive, compulsory.
coacusado, da, *n.* (law) co-defendant.
coacusar, *va.* (law) to accuse jointly.
coadjutor, *m.* coadjutor, assistant, associate, co-worker.—**coadjutora,** *f.* coadjutrix.—**coadjutoría,** *f.* help, assistance; coadjutorship.
coadministrador, *m.* co-administrator.
coadunación, *f.,* **coadunamiento,** *m.* coadunation.
coadunar, *va.* to join closely together.
coadyutor, *m.* = COADJUTOR.
coadyutorio, ria, *a.* cooperative.
coadyuvador, *m.* fellow helper, assistant.
coadyuvante. I. *n.* helper, assistant. **II.** *a.* co-operative, auxiliary.
coadyuvar, *va.* to help, assist, aid.
coagente, *m.* co-agent, associate.
coagulable, *a.* coagulable.
coagulación, *f.* coagulation.
coagulador, ra, *n. & a.* coagulator (-ing,-ive).
coagulante, *n. & a.* coagulant.
coagular. I. *va.* to coagulate, to curd. **II.** *vr.* to coagulate, condense, clod, curdle.
coagulativo, va, *a.* coagulative.
coágulo, *m.* coagulated blood, clot, coagulation; body formed by coagulation.
coairón, *m.* piece of timber.
coalescencia, *f.* (med.) coalescence.
coalescente, *a.* coalescent.
coalición, *f.* coalition.
coalla, *f.* (ornith.) woodcock.
coapóstol, *m.* co-apostle.
coaptación, *f.* (surg.) coaptation.
coarmador, *m.* part owner of a vessel.
coarrendador, *m.* joint lessor.
coarrendatario, ria, *n.* joint tenant.
coartación, *f.* limitation, restriction; obligation to be ordained within a certain time.

coartada, *f.* (law) alibi.—**probar la c.,** to prove an alibi.
coartado, da, *a.* (slave) who has paid his master a partial sum to obtain freedom.
coartar, *va.* to limit, restrain.
coate, ta, *a.* (Mex.) = CUATE, twin.
coatí, *m.* (zool.) coati.
coautor, ra, *n.* coauthor, joint author.
coba, *f.* (coll.) funny yarn.
cobaltífero, ra, *a.* cobalt-bearing, cobaltic.
cobaltina, *f.* (min.) cobaltite.
cobalto, *m.* cobalt.
cobarde, *a.* cowardly; faint-hearted.—**cobardear,** *vn.* to be a coward; to be faint-hearted.—**cobardemente,** *adv.* cowardly.
cobardía, *f.* cowardice.
cobertera, *f.* cover, potlid; bawd; procuress; white water lily.—*pl.* the two middle feathers of a hawk's tail.
cobertizo, *m.* shed, hut.
cobertor, *m.* coverlet, bedspread, quilt.
cobertura, *f.* cover, wrapper, covering, coverlet; ceremony of a grandee of Spain keeping his hat on for the first time in the presence of the king.
cobija, *f.* imbrex tile; short mantilla; small feather (of bird); cover; (Am.) blanket; (Mex.) shawl.—*pl.* (Mex.) bedclothes.
cobijador, ra, *a.* covering, protective.
cobijamiento, *m.* act of covering; lodging.
cobijar, *va.* to cover; shelter, protect; to lodge.
cobijo, *m.* = COBIJAMIENTO.
¹cobra, *f.* rope for yoking oxen; number of mares (not less than five) for treading out corn.
²cobra, *f.* (zool.) cobra.
cobrable, *a.* = COBRADERO.
cobracapelo, *f.* (zool.) cobra.
cobradero, ra, *a.* that may be recovered or collected.
cobrador, ra. I. *a.* collecting.—**perro c.,** retriever. **II.** *m.* collector, receiving teller; (Ry., bus, etc.) conductor.
cobranza, *f.* recovery or collection of money; retrieval of game.
cobrar. I. *va.* to collect, receive (what is due); to recover (something lost); (of dog) to retrieve (shot game); to recuperate, regain; to gain; to charge (price, fee); to cash (check); to pull, draw in; to win, obtain.—**c. ánimo,** or **corazón,** to take courage.—**c. carnes,** to become fat, put on flesh.—**c. fuerzas,** to gather strength. **II.** *vr.* to recover; to come to.
cobratorio, ia, *a.* pertaining to collection of money; collectible.
¹cobre, *m.* or, **c. de cecial,** pair of dried hake or haddock.
²cobre, *m.* copper; kitchen brass utensils; (mus.) brass instruments of an orchestra.—**c. quemado,** copper sulphate.—**c. verde,** malachite.—**batir el c.,** to pursue with spirit and vigor, to hustle.
cobreño, ña, *a.* made of copper.
cobrizo, za, *a.* coppery, cupreous; copper-colored.
cobro, *m.* COBRANZA; receptacle; place of safety.
¹coca, *f.* (bot.) coca; coca leaves; juice from coca leaves, coca tea.
²coca, *f.* (prov.) ugly woman; bugbear.
³coca, *f.* (naut.) a kind of small vessel; side hair of women put back from the face; (coll.) head; (coll.) rap with knuckles on head.
⁴coca, *f.* cake.
⁵coca, *f.* a small berry.—**c. de Levante,** moonseed yielding India fishberries.
cocada, *f.* coconut candy or preserve.
cocador, ra, *a.* wheedling, coaxing, flattering.
cocaína, *f.* cocaine.
cocal, *m.* coca; (Peru & Bol.) coca plantation; (Am.) coconut or coconut tree plantation.
cocán, *m.* (Peru) breast of a fowl.

cocar, *va.* (coll.) to coax; to gain by wheedling and flattering; to flirt with; to make faces at.

cocarar, *va.* to supply coca leaves to.

cocaví, *m.* (Am.) coca and other provisions for a journey.

coccíneo, nea, *a.* of a purple color.

cocción, *f.* cooking, baking, calcining.

cóccix, *m.* (anat.) coccyx.

coceador, ra, *n. & a.* (of animals) kicker(-ing).

coceadura, *f.*, coceamiento, *m.* kicking.

cocear, *va. & vn.* to kick.—c. contra el aguijón, to kick against the pricks.

cocedero, ra. I. *a.* easily boiled. II. *m.* place where anything is cooked or baked.

cocedizo, za, *a.* = COCEDERO.

cocedura, *f.* act of boiling; cooking.

cocer. I. *va.* (*ind.* CUEZO; *subj.* CUEZA) to boil; to bake; to cook; to burn, bake, calcine (brick, etc.); to digest. II. *vn.* to boil, cook, ferment; to seethe, ferment without fire, as wine. III. *vr.* to suffer intense and continued pain.

coces, *pl.* of COZ, kick.—dar c., to kick.

cocido, da. I. *pp.* of COCER. II. *a.* boiled, baked, cooked; skilled, experienced. III. *m.* a Spanish dish of boiled meat and vegetables.

cociente, *m.* (math.) quotient.

cocimiento, *m.* cooking, decoction; bath or mordant for dyeing.

cocina, *f.* kitchen; cuisine, cookery; pottage of greens.—c. de hierro or c. económica, cooking range.—cocinar, *va. & vn.* to cook; (coll.) to meddle in other people's affairs.—cocinero, ra, *n.* cook; chef.—cocinilla. I. *f. dim.* small kitchen; alcohol stove; fireplace. II. *m. & f.* meddler.

cocktail, *m.* (Angl.) cocktail. Also COTEL.

cóclea, *f.* ancient machine for raising water; endless screw.

coclearia, *f.* (bot.) common scurvy grass.

¹coco, *m.* (bot.) coconut (tree, shell, fruit); vessel made of coconut shell.—c. avellanado, dry coconut.—c. de embarque, select coconut.—c. nacido, sprout.—c. pequeño, cull.—c. vano, dry.—c. zarazo, rot.

²coco, *m.* worm or grub of seeds and fruit; scale insect; coccus (bacterium).

³coco, *m.* bugbear; phantasm; gesture, grimace; flattering gesture.—hacer cocos, (coll.) to flatter, wheedle; to flirt.

⁴coco, *m.* India berries from which rosaries are made.

cocobacilo, *m.* bubonic-plague bacillus.

cocobálsamo, *m.* fruit of the balm of Gilead.

cocobolo, *m.* (bot.) a hardwood tree; cocobolo.

cocodrillo, *m.* (zool.) crocodile.—*pl.* Crocodilia.

cocol, *m.* (Mex.) (bread) roll.—cocolero, ra, *n.* roll baker.

cocoliste, *m.* (Mex.) an epidemic fever.

cócora, *f.* annoying person, bore.

cocoso, sa, *a.* worm-eaten; gnawed by grubs.

cocotal, *m.* clump of coconut trees; coconut plantation or field.

cocote, cogote, *m.* (anat.) occiput.

cocotero, *m.* (bot.) coconut tree.

coctel, *m.* (Angl.) cocktail.—coctelera, *f.* (Am.) cocktail shaker.

cocuyo, *m.* glowworm.

cocha, *f.* (min.) small water reservoir.

cochambre, *m.* (coll.) greasy, dirty thing.

cochambrería, *f.* (coll.) heap of filthy things.

cochambrero, ra; cochambroso, sa, *a.* (coll.) nasty, filthy, stinking.

cocharro, *m.* wooden or stone dish, cup, platter.

cochastro, *m.* little, sucking wild boar.

coche, *m.* carriage, coach; car.—c. cama, sleeping-car, Pullman.—c. comedor, dining car.—c. de alquiler, hack or hackney coach.—c. de plaza, or de punto, hack licensed at a customary stand.—c. de tranvía, street car.—c. dormitorio, sleeping car.—c. parado,

balcony.—c. salón, parlor car.—c. simón = C. DE ALQUILER.

cochear, *vn.* to drive a carriage.

cochera, *f.* carriage house; (Ry.) car house, roundhouse, barn; garage; coachman's wife.—puerta c., carriage porch; porte-cochère.

cocheril, *a.* (coll.) pert. to coachmen.

¹cochero, *m.* coachman; C. (astr.) Charioteer.

²cochero, ra, *a.* easily boiled.

cocherón, *m. aug.* large coach house; engine house; roundhouse.

cochevira, *f.* lard.

cochevís, *m.* (ornith.) crested shore lark.

cochifrito, *m.* fricassee of lamb, mutton, etc.

cochigato, *m.* a Mexican bird.

cochina, *f.* sow.

cochinada, *f.* herd of swine; (coll.) hoggishness; mean, dirty action, dirty trick.

cochinamente, *adv.* hoggishly, filthily; meanly, basely.

cochinata, *f.* (naut.) rider.

cochinería, *f.* foulness, filthiness; meanness, niggardliness, baseness.

cochinero, ra, *a.* (of poor fruit) for hogs.

¹cochinilla, *f.* woodlouse.

²cochinilla, *f.* cochineal.

cochinillo, illa, *n. dim.* pig.—c. de Indias, guinea pig.—c. de leche, sucking pig.

cochino, na, *n.* I. hog (sow). II. *a. & n.* dirty, filthy, vile (person).

cochiquera, *f.* (coll.) hogsty, pigpen; small and filthy room.

cochite hervite, (coll.) helter-skelter.

cochitril, *m.* (coll.) pigsty; filthy room.

cochura, *f.* cooking; dough for a batch of bread.

coda, *f.* = COLA, tail; (mus.) coda, ending, finale.

codadura, *f.* layer of an old vine.

codal, I. *a.* one cubit long. II. *m.* elbow piece of ancient armor; short and thick wax candle; shoot of vine; frame of a handsaw; carpenter's square; prop, shore, stay, strut; stay bolt.

codaste, *m.* (naut., aer.) sternpost.

codazo, *m.* blow with the elbow; (Mex.) hunch.

codear. I. *vn.* to elbow. II. *va.* to nudge.

codeína, *f.* codein.

codelincuencia, *f.* joint delinquency, complicity.

codelincuente, *n.* partner in crime, accomplice.

codera, *f.* itch or scabbiness on the elbow; piece reinforcing the elbows of jackets; elbow rail; (naut.) breastfast.

codesera, *f.* spot grown over with hairy Cytisus.

codeso, *m.* (bot.) hairy Cytisus.

codeudor, ra, *n.* joint debtor.

códice, *m.* old manuscript; codex.

codicia, *f.* covetousness, cupidity, greediness.—la c. rompe el saco, covetousness is self-defeating.

codiciable, *a.* covetable.

codiciador, ra, *n. & a.* coveter(-ing).

codiciante, *a.* coveting.

codiciar, *va. & vn.* to covet.

codicilar, *a.* pertaining to a codicil.

codicilo, *m.* codicil.

codiciosamente, *adv.* covetously, greedily.

codicioso, sa, *a.* greedy, covetous, grasping; ambitious; (coll.) diligent; laborious; thrifty.

codificar, *va.* (*pret.* CODIFIQUÉ) *subj.* CODIFIQUE) to codify.

código, *m.* code (of laws).—c. del honor, code of honor.—c. de minas, mining code.—c. de señales, signal code.—c. mercantil, mercantile, or commerce, code.—c. militar, military law.—c. penal, penal, or criminal, code.

codillera, *f.* (vet.) tumor on the knee of a horse.

codillo, *m.* knee of quadrupeds; bend; elbow; knee; breech; angle; codille, a term at ombre; part of a branch of a tree which joins the trunk; foot rule; stirrup of a saddle.—codillos, file used by silversmiths.

codito, ta, *a.* (Mex.) stingy.

codo, *m.* elbow; cubit; (mech.) angle, elbow, knee (of quadruped); foot rule.—**c. real,** royal cubit.—**alzar el c.,** to drink too much.—**comerse los codos de hambre,** to be starving to death.—**hablar por los codos,** to chatter, to be a chatterbox.—**levantar el c.** = ALZAR EL CODO.

codón, *m.* leather dock of a horse's tail.

codorniz, *f.* (ornith.) quail.

coeducación, *f.* coeducation.

coeducar, *va.* to coeducate.

coeficiencia, *f.* coefficiency.

coeficiente, *a.* coefficient.—**c. de seguridad,** safety factor.—**c. de trabajo,** working stress.

coepíscopo, *m.* contemporary bishop.

coercer, *va.* (*ind.* COERZO; *subj.* COERZA) to coerce, check, restrain.

coercibilidad, *f.* coercibility, liability to restraint.

coercible, *a.* coercible, subject to check; (phys.) compressible.

coerción, *f.* coercion, restraint, check.

coercitivo, va, *a.* coercive, restraining.

coerzo, coerza, *v.* V. COERCER.

coetáneo, a, *a.* contemporary.

coeterno, na, *a.* coeternal.

coevo, va, *a.* coeval.

coexistencia, *f.* coexistence.

coexistente, *a.* coexistent.

coexistir, *vn.* to coexist.

coextenderse, *vr.* to be coextensive, coextend.

cofa, *f.* (naut.) top of the lower masts.

cofia, *f.* hair net, cowl, headdress, coif; die case in coining—**cofiezuela,** *f. dim.* small hair net or coif.

cofín, *m.* small basket for fruit; fruit box.

cofosis, *f.* complete deafness.

cofrade, da, *n.* member (of a confraternity or brotherhood).—**cofradía,** *f.* confraternity, brotherhood, sisterhood; trades union; association.

cofre, *m.* trunk for clothes; coffer; box, case; (print.) coffin of the imposing stone.

cofrecico, illo, ito, *m. dim.* small trunk or box.

cofrero, ra, *n.* trunk maker or seller.

cofto, ta, *a.* = COPTO, Coptic.

cogedera, *f.* rod for gathering grass hemp; box for catching swarming bees; pole for gathering fruit; handle.

cogedero, ra. I. *a.* ready to be gathered. **II.** *n.* handle.

cogedizo, za, *a.* that can be easily collected or gathered.

cogedor, *m.* collector, gatherer; dust box or dust pan; coal or ash shovel; box for the woven velvet.

cogedura, *f.* act of gathering or collecting.

coger. I. *va.* (*ind.* COJO; *subj.* COJA) to catch; to seize, grasp, take hold of; to fetch; gather, pick (fruit, etc.); to collect, take; to imbibe, soak; to have room or capacity for; to occupy, take up; to find, procure; to surprise, catch; to attack unexpectedly; to intercept, obstruct.—**c. la delantera,** to get the start. **II.** *vn.* to fit, have room, reach.

cogida, *f.* (coll.) gathering or harvesting of fruits; (coll.) yield of fruits; (coll.) act of the bull's catching the bullfighter; (fish) catch.

cogido, da. I. *pp.* of COGER. **II.** *m.* gather, fold in clothing, curtains, etc.; pleat.

cogitabundo, da, *a.* pensive, thoughtful.

cogitación, *f.* (obs.) meditation, cogitation.

cogitativo, va, *a.* cogitative; given to meditation.

cognación, *f.* cognation; kindred, relationship.

cognado, da, *a.* cognate; related by blood.

cognaticio, ia, *a.* cognatic.

cognición, *f.* cognition.

cognomento, *m.* cognomen, surname.

cognoscible, conocible, *a.* cognoscible, knowable.

cognoscitivo, va, *a.* cognitive.

cogollico, ito, *m. dim.* small heart of garden plants.

cogollo, *m.* heart of garden plants; shoot of a plant; top, summit; (Cuba & Mex.) sugarcane top, used as forage.

cogombro, *m.* = COHOMBRO, cucumber.

cogón, *m.* (bot.) bamboo used in the Philippines for thatching.

cogonal, *m.* COGÓN plantation.

cogotazo, *m.* slap on the back of the neck.

cogote, *m.* occiput, back of the neck; crest at the back of the helmet.—**ser tieso de c.,** (coll.) to be haughty, conceited, airy, stiff.—**cogotera,** *f.* neckprotector put round ox's neck.—**cogotudo, da,** *a.* thicknecked.

cogucho, *m.* sugar of coarse quality.

cogujada, *f.* (ornith.) crested lark.

cogujón, *m.* corner of a mattress or bolster.

cogujonero, ra, *a.* pointed, as the corners of mattresses or bolsters.

cogulla, *f.* cowl, monk's habit.—**cogullada,** *f.* = PAPADA DEL PUERCO, hog's dewlap.

cohabitación, *f.* cohabitation.

cohabitar, *vn.* to cohabit.

conecha, *f.* (agr.) last tillage before sowing the crop.

cohechador, *m.* briber, suborner.

¹cohechar, *va.* to bribe, suborn.

²cohechar, *va.* (agr.) to plow the last time before sowing.

¹cohecho, *m.* bribery.

²cohecho, *m.* (agr.) plowing season.

cohén, *n.* soothsayer; procurer, pimp.

coheredera, *f.* coheiress, joint heiress.

coheredero, *m.* coheir, joint heir.

coherencia, *f.* coherence; connection.

coherente, *a.* coherent; connected; consistent; cohesive.

coherentemente, *adv.* cohesively; connectedly.

cohesión, *f.* cohesion.

cohesivo, va, *a.* cohesive.

cohesor, *m.* (radio) coherer.

cohete, *m.* skyrocket.—**cohetear,** *va.* (Mex.) to blast (a rock).

cohetería, *f.* fireworks shop.

cohetero, *m.* maker or seller of fireworks.

cohibición, *f.* cohibition, prohibition.

cohibir, *va.* to cohibit, prohibit, restrain.

cohobación, *f.* (chem.) cohobation.

cohobar, *va.* to redistil, cohobate.

cohobo, *m.* stag skin; (Am.) stag, deer.

cohombral, *m.* cucumber bed.

cohombrillo, *m. dim.* gherkin.

cohombro, *m.* cucumber; fritter cut into pieces like a cucumber.

cohonestación, *f.* specious justification (of an action), "whitewashing."

cohonestar, *va.* to give an honest appearance to (an action).

cohorte, *f.* cohort.

coima, *f.* perquisite received by the keeper of a gaming table.

coime, coimero, *m.* keeper of a gaming table; scorer at billiards.

coincidencia, *f.* coincidence.

coincidente, *a.* coincident.

coincidir, *vn.* to coincide.

coinquinarse, *vr.* to become stained.

cointeresado, da. I. *a.* jointly interested. **II.** *n.* joint party in interest.

coipo, coipú, *m.* coypu, a S. A. amphibious mammal similar to the beaver.

coirón, *m.* (S. A.) a kind of thatching grass.

coironal, *m.* COIRÓN field.

coito, *m.* coition, carnal copulation.

coja, *f.* (coll.) lewd woman.

cojear, *vn.* to limp, hobble; (of an unsteady table, etc.) to tilt; to deviate from virtue.—**c. de,** to limp with; to have the defect of.

For pronunciation, see the rules at the beginning of the book.

cojera, *f.* lameness, hobble, limp.

cojijo, *m.* complaint of some slight injury; grub or insect.

cojijoso, sa, *a.* peevish, irritable.

cojín, *m.* cushion, pillow; saddle pad.

cojinete, *m. dim.* cushionet, small cushion, small pillow, pad; rail chair; (mech.) journal bearing, shaft bearing; pillow block.

cojitranco, ca, *a.* an epithet applied to evil-disposed lame persons.

¹cojo, coja, *v. V.* COGER.

²cojo, ja, *a.* (of table, etc.) unsteady, tilting; *n.* & *a.* lame, cripple, halt.

cojudo, da, *a.* entire, not gelt or castrated.

cojuelo, ela, *a. dim.* a small cripple.

cok, coque, *m.* coke.

col, *f.* cabbage (this name is given to several varieties).—**c. común,** Savoy cabbage.

¹cola, *f.* tail; cue; tail end; hind portion of anything; extremity; appendage; line of people awaiting turn; end seat in a row; lowest place in a school class; (arch.) inside joint; train of a dress; (mus.) prolonged note at the end of a song.—**c. de caballo,** (bot.) horsetail.—**c. de golondrino,** (fort.) hornwork.—**(a) c. de milano,** tongue-and-groove, dovetailed.—**de c.,** rear, last.—**hacer c.,** to stand in line.—**tener, or traer, c.,** (coll.) to be followed by serious consequences.

²cola, *f.* glue.—**c. clara,** transparent glue.—**c. de boca,** glue on stamp, envelope flap, etc.—**c. de pescado,** isinglass.—**c. de retazo,** or **retal,** size used by painters.

³cola, *f.* (bot.) cola, Kola; (pharm.) kola.

colaboración, *f.* collaboration, working together; contribution (to a periodical, etc.).

colaborador, ra, *n.* collaborator, co-worker; contributor (to a periodical, etc.).

colaborar, *vn.* to collaborate; to contribute.

colación, *f.* collation, critical comparison; act of bestowing an ecclesiastical benefice, or conferring degrees in universities; conference on spiritual affairs; appendage; slight repast, luncheon; sweetmeats given to servants on Christmas eve; precinct or district of a parish.—**sacar a c.,** to make mention of.—**traer a c.,** (coll.) to produce proofs or reasons; to introduce something irrelevant in conversation; to bring up for discussion.

colacionar, *va.* to collate.

colactáneo, a, *n.* foster brother or sister.

¹colada, *f.* wash, buck, bucking; common, an open ground; road for cattle over a common; tap (of a furnace).

²colada, *f.* (coll.) good sword.

coladera, *f.* strainer, colander; wax-chandler's sieve; (Mex.) perforated sink cover.

coladero, *m.* colander, strainer, filtering bag; narrow passage; (min.) hole for dumping ore.

colador, *m.* colander; (print.) leach tub.

coladora, *f.* woman who bucks clothes.

coladura, *f.* straining, filtering.—*pl.* wax dregs.

colagogo, ga, *a.* (med.) stimulating bile secretion.

colaire, *m.* place through which a current of air passes.

colambre, *f.* (tanning) = CORAMBRE, pelts.

colanilla, *f.* small sliding bolt; sash bolt.

colaña, *f.* low partition in stairs or granaries; joist about twenty palms long and six inches broad.

colapez, colapiscis, *f.* isinglass. Also COLA DE PESCADO.

colapso, *m.* (med.) collapse, prostration.

colar. I. *va.* & *vn.* (*ind.* CUELO; *subj.* CUELE) to strain, drain, pass through, percolate, filter; to bleach clothing after washing; (coll.) to spread false news; to pass counterfeit money; to pass through a narrow place; (coll.) to pass muster; (coll.) to drink wine. **II.** *vr.* to strain, be filtered; to steal or squeeze into a place; (coll.) to be displeased with a jest.

colateral, *a.* collateral.

colateralmente, *adv.* collaterally.

colativo, va, *a.* filtering.

colbac, *m.* calpack, Turkish cap.

colcótar, *m.* (chem.) colcothar; rouge; jewellers' red.

colcha, *f.* coverlet, quilt, bedspread.

¹colchadura, *f.* quilting.

²colchadura, *f.* (naut.) laying or twisting ropes.

¹colchar, *va.* = ACOLCHAR, to quilt.

²colchar, *va.*—**c. cabos,** (naut.) to lay or twist ropes.

colchero, *n.* quilt maker.

cólchico, *m.* (bot.) colchicum, meadow saffron.

colchón, *n.* mattress.—**c. de muelles,** spring mattress.—**c. de pluma,** feather bed.—**c. de viento,** air cushion, air bed.

colchoncico, illo, ito, *m. dim.* small mattress.

colchonero, ra, *n.* mattress maker.

colchoneta, *f.* quilted covering for a lounge.

coleada, *f.* wag of the tail; (S. A.) act of felling a bull by a twist of the tail.

coleador, *m.* (S. A.) man who fells a bull by twisting its tail.

coleadura, *f.* wagging of the tail; wriggling.

colear. I. *vn.* to wag (the tail). **II.** *va.* (Mex.) in bullfights, to take (the bull) by the tail, while on horseback, and, by suddenly starting the horse, to overturn him; (Am.) to pull down (cattle) by the tail; (fig.) to refuse, turn down.

colección, *f.* collection, aggregation, accumulation; set; array; gathering.

coleccionador, ra, *n.* collector (of stamps, birds, etc.).

coleccionar, *va.* to collect, form a collection of.

coleccionista, *n.* = COLECCIONADOR.

colecta, *f.* assessment; collect, a prayer; collection for charity.

colectación, *f.* levy; collecting rents, taxes, etc.

colectar, *va.* to collect (taxes, etc.).

colecticio, cia, *a.* untrained; (of soldiers) raw; compilatory, of the nature of a compilation.

colectivamente, *adv.* collectively.

colectividad, *f.* collectivity; mass of people; community.

colectivismo, *m.* collectivism.

colectivista, *n.* & *a.* collectivist(-ic).

colectivo, va, *a.* aggregated, collective; (gram.) collective.

colector, *m.* collector, gatherer; tax or rent collector; water conduit; (elec.) commutator.

colecturía, *f.* collectorship; office of the collector; tax office.

colega, *m.* colleague; contemporary (newspaper).

colegatario, ra, *n.* collegatary, co-legatee.

colegiado, da, *a.* collegiate.

colegial. I. *a.* collegiate; college (as *a.*). **II.** *m.* collegian.—**colegiala,** *f.* college woman.

colegialmente, *adv.* in a collegial manner.

colegiarse, *vr.* to form an association.

colegiata, *f.* collegiate church.

colegiatura, *f.* fellowship in a college.

colegio, *m.* college; school, academy, seminary; body of students, students collectively; association; college, body of dignitaries, electors, etc.

colegir, *va.* (*ind. pres.* COLIJO, *pret.* el COLIGIÓ; *subj.* COLIJA) to collect or gather; to deduce, infer, conclude.

colegislador, ra, *a.* co-legislative (body).

coleo, *m.* = COLEADURA, tail wagging.

coleóptero, ra. I. *a.* coleopterous. **II.** *m. pl.* Coleoptera.

coleorriza, *f.* (bot.) coleorhiza.

cólera. I. *f.* anger, rage, fury. **II.** *m.* cholera.—**c. asiático,** Asiatic cholera.—**c. morbo,** cholera morbus.

colera, *f.* ornament for the tail of a horse.

coléricamente, *adv.* angrily, wrathfully.

colérico, ca, *a.* angry, wrathful; irascible, irritable.

coleriforme, *a.* (med.) resembling cholera.

colerina, *f.* cholerine, a mild diarrhoea.

colesterina, *f.* (chem.) cholesterol, cholesterin.

coleta, *f.* cue or queue of the hair; (coll.) short addition to a discourse or writing; postscript; (Am.) burlap.—**cortarse la c.,** to quit the (bull) ring.

coletero, ra, *n.* maker or seller of buff doublets and breeches.

coletilla, *f. dim.* small cue (hair); postscript.

coletillo, *m. dim.* small buff doublet.

coleto, *m.* buff doublet or jacket; (coll.) body of a man; interior of a person.—**decir para su c.,** to say to oneself.—**echarse al c.,** (coll.) to read through; to eat or drink.

colgadero, ra. I. *a.* fit to be hung up, taken care of. **II.** *m.* hook or peg to hang things on; hat or coat rack; hanger.

colgadizo, za. I. *a.* hanging, suspended. **II.** *m.* shed roof; (Cuba) shed.

colgado, da, *a.* suspended, hanging; (coll.) disappointed, left (as in **dejar c.,** to disappoint, to fail; **quedarse c.,** to be foiled, to get left).

colgador, *m.* (print.) peel hanger; Y-lintel.

colgadura, *f.* tapestry, hanging or drapery; bunting.—**c. de cama,** bed hangings.

colgajo, *m.* tatter or rag hanging from clothes; bunch of grapes or fruit hung up to be preserved.—*pl.* the fleshy tissues left in some amputations to cover the wound.

colgandejo, *m.* (Colomb.) = COLGAJO.

colgandero, ra, *a.* = COLGANTE.

colgante. I. *a.* hanging, pending, clinging. **II.** *m.* (arch.) drop, pendent; (mech.) hanger; (carp.) king-post.

colgar. I. *va.* (*ind. pres.* CUELGO, *pret.* COLGUÉ; *subj.* CUELGUE) to hang up, suspend; to adorn with hangings; to attribute, charge with, make responsible for; (coll.) to kill by hanging.—**c. los hábitos,** to doff the cassock. **II.** *vn.* to hang, be suspended; to dangle; to flag, droop.

colgué, *v. V.* COLGAR.

colibacilo, *m.* intestinal microbe.

coliblanca, *f.* (ornith.) white-tailed S. A. eagle.

coliblanco, ca, *a.* (ornith.) white-tailed.

colibre, colibrí, *m.* (ornith.) humming bird.

cólica, *f.* colic.

colicano, na, *a.* gray-tailed.

cólico, ca. I. *a.* (med.) pertaining to the colon. **II.** *m.* colic.—**c. hepático,** hepatic colic.—**c. miserere,** ileus.—**c. nefrítico,** or **c. renal,** renal colic.

colicuación, *f.* colliquation.

colicuante, *a.* colliquant; colliquative.

colicuar. I. *va.* to colliquate, melt, dissolve. **II.** *vr.* to colliquate; to become liquid.—**colicuativo, va,** *a.* colliquative.

colicuecer, *va.* (*ind.* COLICUEZCO; *subj.* COLICUEZCA) to fuse or melt.

coliflor, *f.* (bot.) cauliflower.

coligación, *f.* colligation; binding of things together; connection, union; alliance.

coligado, da. I. *pp.* of COLIGARSE. **II.** *a.* allied, associate, associated. **III.** *n.* leaguer, covenanter.

coligadura, *f.* **coligamiento,** *m.* = COLIGACIÓN.

coligarse, *vr.* to colligate, confederate, unite, become allies.

coligió, colijo, colija, *v. V.* COLEGIR.

colilla, *f. dim.* stub of a cigar or cigarette.—**colillero, ra,** *n.* person who gathers cigar stubs as a trade.

colimación, *f.* (opt.) collimation.

colimador, *m.* (opt.) collimator.

colín, *a.* short-tailed (horse).

¹colina, *f.* hill, hillock, knoll.

²colina, *f.* seed of cabbage.

colinabo, *m.* (bot.) turnip; young cabbage.

colindante, *a.* contiguous, adjacent, abutting.

colindar, *vn.* (con) to be contiguous, or adjacent (to), to abut (on).

colino, *m.* small cabbage not transplanted.

colirio, *m.* (med.) collyrium, eyewash.

colirrábano, *m.* (bot.) kohlrabi.

colisa, *f.* (artil.) swivel gun.

coliseo, *m.* theatre, opera house, playhouse; coliseum, colosseum.

colisión, *f.* collision, crush, clash; bruise, chafe, soreness from rubbing; opposition, clash of ideas.

colitigante, *m.* co-litigant, one who carries on a lawsuit with another.

colitis, *f.* (med.) colitis.

colmadamente, *adv.* abundantly, plentifully.

colmado, da. I. *pp.* of COLMAR. **II.** *a.* (de) abundant, copious; full (of), filled (with). **III.** *m.* specialty eating house (gen. for sea food).

colmar, *va.* (de) to heap up, fill to the brim (with); to fulfil, make up; to bestow liberally.

colmena, *f.* beehive.—**colmenar,** *f.* apiary.

colmenero, ra, *n.* beekeeper, beemaster.

colmenilla, *f.* (bot.) morel, an edible mushroom.

colmillada, *f.* attack, or wound, with tusks or fangs.

colmillar, *a.* pert. to eyetooth, fang or tusk.

colmillazo, *m. aug.* large eyetooth; COLMILLADA.

colmillejo, *m. dim.* small eyetooth, fang or tusk.

colmillo, *m.* eyetooth, canine tooth; fang; tusk.—**escupir por el c.,** (coll.) to brag, boast.—**mostrar los colmillos,** (coll.) to show spirit and resolution.—**tener colmillos,** (coll.) to be quick-sighted, not easily imposed upon.

colmilludo, da, *a.* having long eyeteeth, fangs, or tusks; sagacious, quick-sighted.

¹colmo, *m.* heap; finishing, completion, crowning; overmeasure; fill; thatched roof; height (of folly, etc.); acme, extreme.—**a c.,** abundantly, plentifully.—**llegar a c.,** to reach perfection.—**ser el c.,** (coll.) to be the limit.

²colmo, ma, *a.* heaping full.

colocación, *f.* place, situation, position, employment, job; laying, putting in place; placement; distribution of parts.

colocar. I. *va.* (*pret.* COLOQUÉ; *subj.* COLOQUE) to arrange, put in due place or order; to place, provide with employment, take on (in a job). **II.** *vr.* to take (a job).

colocasia, *f.* (bot.) Egyptian bean.

colocolo, *m.* a handsome S. A. wild cat; (Chile) an imaginary monster hatched from a rotten egg.

colocutor, ra, *n.* one taking part in a conversation.

colodión, *m.* collodion.

colodra, *f.* milk pail; kit; pailful; wooden can for measuring wine; drinking can with a handle; drinking horn with a cork bottom; whetstone case.—**ser una c.,** (coll.) to be a toper.

colodrazgo, *m.* tax on wine sold at retail.

colodrillo, *m.* occiput, nape of the neck.

colofón, *m.* (print.) colophon.

colofonia, *f.* colophony; resin.—**colofonita,** *f.* garnet of a light green or rosy red color.

coloidal, *a.* (chem.) colloidal.

coloide, *m.* colloid.—**coloideo, a,** *a.* colloidal.

colombiano, na, *n. & a.* Colombian.

colombino, na, *a.* Columbian, pertaining to Columbus.

¹colon, *m.* (gram.) principal part of a period.

²colon, *m.* (anat.) colon.

colonato, *m.* system of colonization.

colonche, *m.* (Mex.) an intoxicating drink from the sap of the cactus and sugar.

colonia, *f.* colony; plantation; silk ribbon two fingers wide; (Mex.) extension, development, new quarter (of a town).

colonial, *a.* colonial.

colonicé, colonice, *v. V.* COLONIZAR.

olonización, *f.* colonization.

olonizador, ra, *n. & a.* colonizer(-ing).

olonizar, *va.* (*pret.* COLONICÉ; *subj.* COLONICE) to colonize, settle.

olono, *m.* colonist, settler; tenant farmer.

oloño, *m.* load of wood carried on the back.

oloqué, coloque, *v. V.* COLOCAR.

oloquíntida, *f.* (bot.) colocynth; bitter apple or gourd.

oloquio, *m.* colloquy, talk.

olor, *m.* color; dye, paint; rouge; pretext, pretense, false show or appearance; coloring, tint; complexion; flush, blush; aspect.—**c. muerto,** or **quebrado,** wan or faded color.—**c. vivo,** bright color.—**de c.,** colored.—**sacarle los colores a uno,** to make one blush.—**so c.,** on pretense, under pretext.

oloración, *f.* coloring, coloration, painting.

olorado, da. I. *pp.* of COLORAR. **II.** *a.* ruddy; red; indelicate, smutty; colored; specious.—**poner a uno c.,** to put one to the blush.—**ponerse c.,** to blush.

olorante, *a.* coloring.

olorar, *va.* to dye; to paint, stain, tint, color.

olorativo, va, *a.* coloring, giving color to.

olorear. I. *va.* to make plausible, palliate, excuse. **II.** *vn.* to redden, grow red.

olorete, *m.* rouge.

olorido, da. I. *pp.* of COLORIR. **II.** *a.* colored. **III.** *m.* coloring or color; pretext, pretense.

oloridor, ra, *n.* = COLORISTA.

olorimetría, *f.* colorimetry.

olorimétrico, ca, colorimetric.

olorímetro, *m.* colorimeter.

olorín, *m.* (ornith.) linnet; bright, vivid, loud color.

olorir, *va.* to color artistically; make plausible.

olorista, *m.* (painting) colorist.

olosal, *a.* colossal, huge, gigantic.

olosense, *n. & a.* Colossian.

oloso, *m.* colossus.

olotipia, *f.* collotype; collotypy.

olpa, *f.* whitish sort of copperas.

olpotomía, *f.* (surg.) colpotomy, incision of the vagina.

ólquico, *m.* (bot.) colchicum, meadow saffron.

olúbridos, *m. pl.* (zool.) Colubridae, a snake family.

olumbino, na, *a.* dovelike, innocent, candid.

olumbio, *m.* (chem.) columbium, niobium.

olumbrar, *va.* to espy, perceive, discern at a distance; to trace by conjectures.

olumelar, *m.* incisor.

olumna, *f.* (arch., eng., mil., print.) column, supporter, protector; pile of things; column of air or water.—**c. dorsal,** spine.—**c. miliaria,** milestone.—**c. salomónica,** (arch.) twisted column.—**c. vertebral,** spine.—**columnario, ria,** *a.* columnar (app. to money coined in Sp. Am., with the impressions of two columns).

olumnata, *f.* colonnade.

olumpiar. I. *va.* to swing. **II.** *vr.* to swing; (coll.) to waddle.

olumpio, *m.* swing; seesaw.

oluna, *f.* = COLUMNA.

olunita, *f. dim.* small column.

olurión, *m.* (ornith.) butcher bird, flusher.

oluro, *m.* (astr.) colure.

olusión, *f.* collusion.

olusoriamente, *adv.* collusively, fraudulently.

olusorio, ria, *a.* collusive.

olutorio, *m.* (pharm.) gargle.

oluvie, *f.* gang of rascals; sewer, sink.

olza, *f.* (bot.) colza, summer rape.

colla, *f.* (P. I.) continuous squalls preceding the monsoons; last oakum placed in a seam.

colla, *f.* collet, piece of ancient armor; channel of an auger.

ollado, *m.* height, fell, hillock.

collar, *m.* necklace; chain or cord from which hang certain insignia of honor; collar, collet.

collareja, *f.* (C. A.) wild pigeon.

collarejo, *m. dim.* small collar or necklace.

collarín, *m.* black neck stock edged with white, worn by the Roman Catholic clergy; collar of a coat; (mech.) tube, sleeve.

collarino, *m.* (arch.) half round, torus.

collazo, *m.* plowman, farmhand, laborer.

colleja, *f.* (bot.) lamb's-lettuce or corn salad.

collejas, *f. pl.* slender nerves in sheep's neck.

collera, *f.* collar, breast harness for draught cattle; horse collar; (naut.) stay of the dead blocks.—*pl.* (Am.) cuff buttons.

collerón, *m.* harness collar, hame.

colleta, *f.* (bot.) a kind of small cabbage.

collón, *m.* (coll.) coward, poltroon, base fellow.

collonada, *f.,* **collonería,** *f.* (coll.) cowardice.

¹coma, *f.* comma(,); (mus.) each of the parts into which a tone is divided.

²coma, *m.* (med.) coma, profound insensibility.

comadre, *f.* midwife; mother or godmother with respect to each other; (coll.) gossip; pal, intimate friend; go-between.

comadrear, *vn.* to gossip, tattle.

comadreja, *f.* weasel.

comadreo, *m.* **comadrería,** *f.* gossip, gossipping.

comadrero, ra, *n. & a.* gossip (person), gossipping (person).

comadrón, *m.* obstetrician, accoucheur.

comal, *m.* (Mex.) flat earthenware pan for cooking maize cake.

comalía, comalición, *f.* an epizoötic disease of sheep.

comandado, da, *a.* (mil.) officered.

comandancia, *f.* command; office of a commander; province or district of a commander.—**C. general de Marina,** High Court of Admiralty.

comandanta, *f.* commander's wife.

comandante, *n.* commander, commandant, leader; major, (Colomb.) lieutenant colonel.

comandar, *va.* (mil.) to command, govern.

comandita, *f.* (com.) silent partnership.

comanditario, a. I. *a.* (com.) pertaining to a silent partnership; silent (partner, partnership). **II.** *n.* (com.) silent partner.

comando, *m.* (mil.) command.—*pl.* controls (of an airplane).

comarca, *f.* territory, region; border, boundary, limit.

comarcano, na, *a.* neighboring, near, bordering.

comarcar. I. *va.* (*pret.* COMARQUÉ; *subj.* COMARQUE) to plant (trees) in a straight line, so as to form walks. **II.** *vn.* to border, to abut (on).

comatoso, sa, *a.* (med.) comatose.

comba, *f.* curvature, warp, bend, bulge; game of jumping or skipping rope; skipping rope.

combadura, *f.* bending, bend, bulging, belly; sag.

combar. I. *va.* to bend, to curve. **II.** *vr.* to warp, bulge, sag.

combate, *m.* combat, fight, battle; agitation of the mind; struggle.

combatible, *a.* combatable, conquerable.

combatidor, ra, *n.* combatant.

combatiente, *n. & a.* combatant, fighter(-ing).

combatir, *va. & vn.* to combat, fight; to contest, attack, oppose; to struggle.

combatividad, *f.* combativeness.

combeneficiado, *m.* prebendary of the same church as another.

combés, *m.* open space; (naut.) waist of a ship; upper deck.

combinable, *a.* combinable.

combinación, *f.* combination; aggregate of words beginning with the same syllable; concurrence; (chem.) compound; (woman's) slip.

combinador, ra. I. *n. & a.* combiner(-ing). **II.** *m.* (elec.) controller (of electric car).

combinar, *va. & vr.* to combine, join, unite.

combinatorio, ria, *a.* combining, uniting; combinative; (math.) combinatorial.

combleza, *f.* concubine of a married man.

comblezo, *m.* one who lives in concubinage with a married woman.

combo, ba. I. *a.* bent, crooked, warped. **II.** *m.* stand or frame for casks.

comburente, *a.* producing combustion.

combustibilidad, *f.* combustibility.

combustible. I. *a.* combustible. **II.** *m.* fuel.

combustión, *f.* combustion.

combusto, ta, *a.* burnt.

comedero, ra. I. *a.* eatable, edible. **II.** *m.* feeding trough; dining room, eating place; (Am.) haunt, place frequented by a person.

comedia, *f.* comedy; play, drama; farce; theater.—**c. de capa y espada,** costume play of the seventeenth century.—**c. de costumbres,** drawing-room comedy.—**c. de enredo,** play with a complicated plot.—**c. togada,** ancient Latin play; Grecian or Roman costume play.

comedianta, *f.* comedienne.

comediante, *m.* player, actor, comedian.

comediar, *va.* to divide into equal shares or parts; to average.

comedidamente, *adv.* courteously, civilly; with moderation.

comedido, da. I. *pp.* of COMEDIRSE. **II.** *a.* civil, polite, courteous; prudent, moderate.

comedimiento, *m.* civility, politeness, kindness; moderation, prudency.

comedio, *m.* center of a realm or place; intermediate time between epochs.

comedión, *m.* long and tedious comedy.

comedirse, *vr.* (*ind.* me COMIDO; *subj.* me COMIDA) to govern oneself; to be moderate, civil, obliging, kind.

comedor, ra. I. *n.* & *a.* eater(-ing), feeder(-ing). **II.** *m.* dining room.

comején, *m.* (entom.) termite, white ant.

comejenera, *f.* nest of COMEJÉN; (Venez.) disreputable resort.

comencé, *pret.* of COMENZAR.

comendador, *m.* knight commander of a military order; prefect of religious houses.

comendadora, *f.* superior of a nunnery.

comendatario, *m.* (eccl.) one holding a benefice.

comendaticio, cia, *a.* commendatory (letter).

comendatorio, ria, *a.* pertaining to letters of introduction or recommendation.

comendero, *m.* beneficiary of the crown.

comensal, *n.* commensal; member of a household; table companion.

comensalía, *f.* fellowship of house and table.

comentador, ra, *n.* commenter, commentator.

comentar, *va.* to comment.

comentario, *m.* commentary.

comentarista, *n.* commentator.

comento, *m.* comment.

comenzante, *n.* & *a.* beginner(-ing).

comenzar, *va.* & *vn.* (*ind. pres.* COMIENZO, *pret.* COMENCÉ; *subj.* COMIENCE) to commence, begin.

comer. I. *vn.* to eat; to feed; to dine.—**c. a dos carrillos,** to enjoy two places or benefices at the same time.—**c. como un sabañón,** (coll.) to eat excessively, to stuff oneself.—**c. de mogollón,** to live at other people's expense; to sponge.—**c.,** or **comerse, vivo,** to devour(fig.); to scalp (fig.); to be very painful or troublesome.—**tener que c.,** to have a competence. **II.** *va.* to eat; to have (an income); to spend, waste, exhaust; to corrode, consume; (of sun) to fade (colors); to take (a piece or checker in a game). **III.** *vr.* to omit, skip; to eat up.—**comerse a uno con los ojos,** to look daggers at one.—**comerse los codos de hambre,** (coll.) to be starved to death.—**comerse unos a otros,** to live like cats and dogs. **IV.** *m.* eating.—**ganar de c.,** to earn a living.

comerciable, *a.* merchantable, marketable; sociable, social, affable.

comercial, *a.* commercial, mercantile.—**comercialmente,** *adv.* commercially.

comerciante, *n.* trader, merchant.—**c. comisionista,** commission merchant.

comerciar, *vn.* to trade, deal; to commerce, have intercourse.

comercio, *m.* trade, commerce, communication; intercourse; unlawful sexual intercourse; tradesmen, body of merchants; business section of a town; store, shop; a card game.—**c. exterior,** foreign trade.—**c. interior,** domestic trade.—**bolsa de c.,** stock exchange.

comestible. I. *a.* eatable, edible. **II.** *m. pl.* foodstuffs, provisions.

cometa. I. *m.* (astr.) comet.—**c. crinito,** long bearded comet. **II.** *f.* kite; a card game.

cometedor, ra, *n.* offender, perpetrator.

cometer, *va.* to commit, charge, intrust; to commit, perpetrate; (com.) to order.—**cometido,** *m.* commission; charge, trust; task, duty.

comezón, *f.* itch, itching; longing desire.

comible, *a.* (coll.) eatable, fit to eat.

cómicamente, *adv.* comically.

comicastro, *n. m.* mediocre or poor actor.

comicial, *a.* comitial.

comicios, *m. pl.* (anc. Rome) comitia; (pol.) primaries, district assemblies.

cómico, ca. I. *a.* comic, dramatic, pertaining to the stage; comical, ludicrous, funny. **II.** *n.* player, actor(-tress); writer of comedies.—**c. de la legua,** small-town touring actor, strolling player.

comida, *f.* eating; food, dressed victuals; dinner, meal, fare; feed.—**c. corrida** (Am.) table d'hôte.

comidilla, *f. dim.* slight repast; peculiar fancy, fad, or favorite amusement; hobby.

¹comido, da, *a.* fed; having eaten.—**c. de,** eaten by, -eaten (*comido de gusanos,* worm-eaten).—**c. por servido,** hand-to-mouth wages.

²comido, comida, *v. V.* COMEDIRSE.

¹comienzo, *m.* beginning, initiation, start.—**dar c.,** to make a beginning, a start.

²comienzo, comience, *v. V.* COMENZAR.

comilitón, *m.* parasite; fellow soldier.

comilitona, comilona, *f.* (coll.) splendid and plentiful repast.

comilón, na, *n.* great eater, glutton.

comilla, *f. dim.* of ¹COMA.—*pl.* quotation marks (" ").

cominear, *vn.* (coll.) to indulge in trifles or occupations belonging to women.

cominero. I. *a.* meddlesome, officious. **II.** *n.* cotquean, man meddling with women's affairs.

cominillo, *m.* (bot.) darnel. Also JOYO.

comino, *m.* (bot.) cumin plant, cumin seed; a Colombian tree producing very valuable construction and cabinet wood.—**no valer un c.,** not to be worth a rush.

comisar, *va.* to confiscate, sequestrate, attach.

comisaría, *f.,* commissaryship, commissariat.

comisariato, *m.* COMISARÍA; (Am.) police station.

comisario, *m.* commissary; delegate, deputy manager.—**c. de barrio,** or **cuartel,** justice of the peace of a ward.—**c. de entradas,** in hospitals, the person that keeps an account of the patients who enter.—**c. de guerra,** (mil.) reviewing officer.—**c. de policía,** (Mex., Cuba, Arg.) chief of police.—**c. ordenador,** (mil.) assistant quartermaster.

comisión, *f.* trust; commission, assignment; mandate, charge; precept, order; ministration; ministry; committee; commission, perpetration.

comisionado, da. I. *pp.* of COMISIONAR. **II.** *a.* commissional or commissionary; commissioned deputed, empowered. **III.** *n.* commissioner; (com.) agent; proxy, attorney.

comisionar, *va.* to commission, depute, empower, appoint.

comisionista, *m.* commissioner; commission merchant; commission agent.

comiso, *m.* (law) confiscation of prohibited goods; the goods when confiscated; (law) seizure, attachment.

comisorio, ria. *a.* obligatory for a time or valid for a fixed day.

comistión, *f.* = COMMISTIÓN, commixture.

comistrajo, *m.* (coll.) hodge-podge, mess.

comisura, *f.* (anat.) commissure; suture.

comital, *a.* = CONDAL, of an earldom.

comité, *m.* committee; commission.

comitiva, *f.* suite, retinue; party, group.

cómitre, *m.* (naut.) boatswain on board a galley; sea captain under orders of the admiral of the fleet.

comiza, *f.* (ichth.) a kind of barbel.

como. I. *adv.* how; in what manner; to what degree; as; like; about, approximately, a sort of; if; as soon as; in the same manner as; so that; such as; that; inasmuch as.—**c. que**, apparently, it seems that.—**c. quien no quiere la cosa**, unconcernedly.—**c. quiera que**, although; since. **II.** *interrog.* **cómo,** what? how? why?—**¿cómo?** what is it? what did you say? —**¿cómo así?** how? how so?—**¿cómo no?** why not? of course, naturally.—**¿a c.,** how much?—**¿a c. estamos?** what is the date? **III.** *interj.* why, is it possible?

cómoda, *f.* chest of drawers; bureau.

comodable, *a.* (law) that can be lent or borrowed.

cómodamente, *adv.* conveniently; comfortably.

comodante, *n.* (law) one who lends gratuitously for a limited time.

comodatario, ria, *n.* (law) borrower; pawnbroker.

comodato, *m.* loan; (law) contract of loan and restitution.

comodidad, *f.* comfort, convenience; ease, freedom from want; leisure; opportunity; profit, interest, advantage.

comodín, *m.* (coll.) something of general utility; in cards, a card that has different values.

cómodo, da. I. *a.* convenient, handy, suitable; comfortable. **II.** *m.* utility, profit; convenience.

comodoro, *m.* (naut.) commodore.

compactibilidad, *f.* compactness.

compacto, ta, *a.* compact, close, dense.

compadecer. I. *va.* (ind. COMPADEZCO; subj. COMPADEZCA) to pity, sympathize with. **II.** *vr.* to agree with each other, accord, conform; (de) to pity, sympathize (with).

compadraje, *m.* confederacy or alliance for mutual protection and advancement (gen. used in a bad sense); ring, clique.

compadrar, *vn.* to become a godfather or -mother; to contract a spiritual affinity.

compadrazgo, *m.* COMPADRAJE; state of being COMPADRES.

compadre, *m.* godfather and father of a child, each with respect to the other; protector, benefactor; (coll.) friend, old chap (an expression of familiarity).—**compadrear,** *vn.* (coll.) to be on familiar terms.—**compadrería,** *f.* friendship between COMPADRES, companions, pals.—**compadrito,** *m.* dim. of COMPADRE; (Am.) boaster.

compaginación, *f.* arrangement, connection.

compaginador, ra, *n.* arranger, adjuster.

compaginar, *va.* to arrange in proper order; to unite, join.

companage, compango, *m.* cold cuts or lunch.

compaña, *f.* (obs.) family; company.

compañerismo, *m.* good fellowship, comradeship.

compañero, ra, *n.* companion, friend, pal, comrade, chum; fellow member; partner or associate; one of a pair, mate.

compañía, *f.* company; society; partnership; co-partnership; (mil.) company; theatrical company.—**c. de Jesús,** Society of Jesus.—**c. de la legua,** strolling company of players.—**c. de seguros,** insurance company.—**hacer c. a,** to keep (someone) company. (For **c. anónima, c. comanditaria,** etc. V. SOCIEDAD.)

comparable, *a.* comparable.

comparación, *f.* comparison.

comparador, *m.* comparing rule; comparer.

comparar, *va.* to compare; to confront, collate.

comparativamente, *adv.* comparatively.

comparativo, va, *a.* comparative.

comparecencia, *f.* (law) appearance (in court).

comparecer, *vn.* (ind. COMPAREZCO; subj. COMPAREZCA) (law) to appear (before a judge, etc.)

compareciente, *n. & a.* (law) (one) that appears (before a judge, etc.)

comparendo, *m.* summons, citation.

comparezco, comparezca, *v. V.* COMPARECER.

comparición, *f.* (law) appearance.

comparsa. I. *f.* (theat.) retinue of personages; masquerade in carnival. **II.** *m. & f.* (theat.) supernumerary.

comparte, *n.* (law) joint party; accomplice.

compartimiento, *m.* compartment; division of a whole into parts; inclosure, department; (aer.) curtain (of a dirigible).

compartir, *va.* to divide into equal parts; to share.

comparto, *m.* (Colomb.) tax, contribution.

compás, *m.* compasses; dividers; calipers; territory and district assigned to a monastery; (mus.) measure, time, motion of the baton of a conductor; space on the staff between two bars; size, compass; rule of life, standard, pattern; springs of a coach roof.—**c. de barra,** beam compass.—**c. de calibres,** calipers.—**c. de división,** dividers.—**c. de espesores, or de gruesos,** spring calipers; thickness gage.—**c. de mar, or de marear,** mariner's compass.—**c. de proporción,** proportional dividers.—**c. de puntas secas, or de punta fija,** dividers.—**c. de regla** = C. DE BARRA.—**a c.,** in right musical time.—**a c. con,** keeping time with; in line or harmony with.—**llevar el c.,** (mus.) to keep, beat time.

compasadamente, *adv.* by rule and measure.

compasar, *va.* to measure with a rule and compass; to arrange properly; (mus.) to divide (a score) into equal bars.—**c. la carta de marear,** (naut.) to prick the chart.

compasible, *a.* pitiful; compassionate.

compasillo, *m.* (mus.) quadruple, or ⅜ time.

compasión, *f.* compassion, pity, sympathy.—**tener c. de,** to take pity on, show mercy to.

compasivamente, *adv.* compassionately.

compasivo, va, *a.* compassionate, merciful, tender-hearted.

compaternidad, *f.* = COMPADRAZGO, relationship between father and godfather of a child.

compatibilidad, *f.* compatibility.

compatible, *a.* compatible, suitable, consistent.

compatricio, cia; compatriota, *n.* countryman (countrywoman), compatriot, fellow citizen.

compatrón, *m.* = COMPATRONO.

compatronato, *m.* common right of patronage.

compatrono, na, *n.* fellow patron or patroness, joint patron.

compeler, *va.* to compel, force, constrain.

compendiador, ra, *n.* epitomizer, abridger.

compendiar, *va.* to abridge, condense.

compendiariamente, *adv.* briefly.

compendio, *m.* compendium, epitome, abridgment, summary, abstract.

compendiosamente, *adv.* briefly, concisely.

compendioso, sa, *a.* brief; abridged, concise; compact.

compendizar, *va.* = COMPENDIAR.

compenetración, *f.* compenetration.

compenetrarse, *vr.* to pervade, intermix; to harmonize, be in full agreement.—**c. de,** to be thoroughly informed about; to be fully convinced of.

compensable, *a.* compensable.

compensación, *f.* compensation; recompense, reward.—**de c.,** compensating.

compensador, ra. I. *a.* compensated; balanced. **II.** *m.* compensator; compensating pendulum.

compensar, *va. & vn.* to compensate, recompense; to counterbalance; to balance, equilibrate; to make amends for, indemnify.

compensativo, va. I. *a.* compensating. **II.** *m.* (chem.) compensation.

compensatorio, ria, *a.* compensating.

competencia, *f.* competition, rivalry; competence; cognizance.—**a c.,** competitively.

competente, *a.* competent, apt, able; consistent (with); applicable (to); adequate.

competentemente, *adv.* competently.

competer, *vn.* to be one's business or concern, to be incumbent on.

competición, *f.* competition.

competidor, ra. I. *n.* competitor, rival, opponent. **II.** *a.* competing.

competir, *vn.* (*ind.* COMPITO; *subj.* COMPITA) to vie, contest, contend, compete; to be on a level or par with another.

compilación, *f.* compilation; compilement.

compilador, ra, *n.* compiler; collector.

compilar, *va.* to compile.

compinche, *m.* (coll.) bosom friend, comrade, chum, crony, pal.

compito, compita, *v. V.* COMPETIR.

complacedero, ra, *a.* = COMPLACIENTE.

complacencia, *f.* pleasure, satisfaction; complacency, compliance, condescension.

complacer. I. *va.* (*ind.* COMPLAZCO; *subj.* COMPLAZCA) to please, humor, accommodate. **II.** *vr.* (**en**) to be pleased (with or to), to delight (in), to take pleasure (in).—**complaciente,** *a.* pleasing, accommodating, kind, agreeable.

complazco, complazca, *v. V.* COMPLACER.

complejo, ja, *a.* = COMPLEXO.

complejidad, *f.* = COMPLEXIDAD.

complementario, ia, *a.* complementary; completing, perfecting.

complemento, *m.* complement; perfection; completion; (gram.) complement, object.

completamente, *adv.* completely, entirely; absolutely.

completar, *va.* to complete, perfect, finish.

completas, *f. pl.* (eccl.) compline.

completivamente, *adv.* completively.

completivo, va, *a.* completive, completing, finishing.

completo, ta, *a.* complete, perfect; finished, completed; full; absolute.—**por c.,** completely.

complexidad, *f.* complexity, intricacy.

complexión, *f.* constitution, temperament, habit, nature.—**complexionado, da,** *a.* constituted.—**bien, mal complexionado, da,** of a good, bad, constitution.—**complexional,** *a.* constitutional, temperamental.

complexo. I. *a.* complex; intricate, arduous, difficult. **II.** *m.* complex.

complicación, *f.* complication.

complicadamente, *adv.* complicatedly.

complicado, da, *a.* complicated.

complicar, *va.* (*pret.* COMPLIQUÉ; *subj.* COMPLIQUE) to complicate; to jumble together.

cómplice, *m. & f.* accomplice.

complicidad, *f.* complicity.

compliqué, complique, *v. V.* COMPLICAR.

complot, *m.* plot, conspiracy.

complutense, *n. & a.* Complutensian.

compluvio, *m.* (archeol.) compluvium.

componedor, ra. I. *n.* compositor, typesetter; writer, author; composer; contriver; repairer; arbitrator. **II.** *m.* (print.) composing stick.

componenda, *f.* fees paid for documents and licenses; arbitration; compromise; settlement.

componente, *n. & a.* component.

componer. I. *va.* (*pp.* COMPUESTO; *ind. pres.* COMPONGO, *fut.* COMPONDRÉ, *pret.* COMPUSE; *subj.* COMPONGA) to compose; compound; construct; prepare; amount to; devise, invent; to mend, repair; heal, restore; to strengthen, brace, fortify; to trim, fit up, garnish; to compose (differences), reconcile, adjust, settle; to ward off; to compose (music); to write (poetry, etc.); (print.) to compose.—**c. el semblante,** to put on a calm appearance.—**c. tanto de renta,** to have so much a year. **II.** *vr.* to prink, "doll up"; to compose, calm, quiet oneself.—**componérselas,** to shift for oneself.

compongo, componga, *v. V.* COMPONER.

componible, *a.* mendable, capable of repair; adjustable, that may be settled or compounded.

comporta, *f.* large basket for grape gathering.

comportable, *a.* bearable, endurable.

comportamiento, *m.* behavior, deportment.

comportar. I. *va.* to suffer, tolerate. **II.** *vr.* to comport, behave oneself.—**comporte,** *m.* behaviour, conduct; air, manner, carriage.

comportería, *f.* trade and shop of a COMPORTERO.

comportero, ra, *n.* maker or seller of COMPORTAS.

comportilla, *f. dim.* small basket.

composición, *f.* composition; repair, mending; making up, compromise, adjustment; (print.) composition; (fig.) composure; calm, modest, or sedate appearance.

compositivo, va, *a.* compositive, synthetic.

compositor, ra, *n.* composer (of music).

compostura, *f.* composure; mending, repair, repairing; cleanliness, neatness of dress; adjustment, settlement, compromise; modesty, circumspection, sedateness; adulterating compound.

compota, *f.* compote, stewed fruit; preserves.

compotera, *f.* compotier.

compra, *f.* purchase; buying, shopping.—**hacer compras,** to shop.—**ir de compras,** to go shopping.

comprable; compradero, ra; compradizo, za, *a.* purchasable.

comprado, compradillo, *m.* play in the game of ombre.

comprador, ra; comprante, *n.* buyer; purchaser; shopper; caterer.

comprar, *va.* to buy, purchase; to shop.

compraventa.—contrato de c., contract of sale.

comprehensivo, va, *a.* comprehensive.

comprendedor, ra, *a.* including; understanding.

comprender, *va.* to embrace, comprise, include, cover; to understand, comprehend.

comprensibilidad, *f.* intelligibility, comprehensibility.

comprensible, *a.* comprehensible, understandable.

comprensión, *f.* comprehension, understanding; comprehensiveness; act of comprising or containing.

comprensividad, *f.* understandability, quality of being understandable; understanding.

comprensivo, va, *a.* comprehensive; capable of understanding; comprising, containing.

comprensor, ra, *a. & n.* (one) that understands, attains or embraces; (theol.) blessed (one).

compresa, *f.* (surg.) compress.

compresbítero, *m.* fellow presbyter or priest.

compresibilidad, *f.* compressibility.

compresible, *a.* compressible.

compresión, *f.* compression; (gram.) synizesis.

compresivo, va, *a.* compressive, compressing, reducing, compacting.

compreso, *pp. irreg.* of COMPRIMIR.

compresor, ra, *n. & a.* compressor(-ing).—**c. de aire,** air compressor.

comprimente, *a.* compressing; restraining.

comprimible, *a.* compressible; repressible.

comprimir. I. *va.* (*pp.* COMPRIMIDO, COMPRESO) to compress, condense; to repress, restrain. **II.** *vr.* to become compact; to control oneself.

comprobación, *f.* verification, checking; proof, substantiation; (print.) checking up of proof corrections.

comprobante. I. *a.* proving, evidential. **II.** *m.* proof, evidence; voucher.

comprobar, *va.* (*ind.* COMPRUEBO; *subj.* COMPRUEBE) to verify, confirm, check; to compare; to prove, substantiate, evidence.

comprofesor, *m.* colleague in a profession.

comprometedor, ra. I. *a.* compromising, jeopardizing. **II.** *n.* one that jeopardizes.

comprometer. I. *va.* to compromise, arbitrate; to engage, bind; to render accountable or answerable; to risk; to expose, jeopardize, endanger. **II.** *vr.* to commit oneself; to undertake; to become liable; to bind oneself; to expose oneself; to become engaged, betrothed; to become involved.

comprometimiento, *m.* pledge, promise; adjustment; jeopardy, embarrassment, predicament.

compromisario, ria, *n.* arbitrator, umpire, referee; presidential elector.

compromiso, *m.* compromise, arbitration; pledge, obligation; commitment; jeopardy, embarrassment, predicament; engagement, betrothal; engagement, appointment.

compromisorio, ria, *a.* pertaining to an agreement, promise, or pledge.

compropietario, ia, *n.* joint owner.

comprovincial, *a.* comprovincial, of the same metropolitan church.

comprovinciano, na, *a.* from the same province.

compruebo, compruebe, *v.* V. COMPROBAR.

compuerta, *f.* hatch or half-door; lock, sluice, floodgate; door curtain of an old-fashioned coach; piece of cloth bearing a knight's badge. —**c. de marea,** (naut.) tide gate, tiderace.

compuestamente, *adv.* regularly, orderly.

compuesto, a. I. *pp.* of COMPONER. **II.** *a.* compound; composed, consisting, made up; repaired; arranged. **III.** *m.* compound, preparation, mixture; (gram.) compound.

compulsa, *f.* (law) authentic or attested copy of an instrument or writing duly compared.

compulsar, *va.* (law) to make an authentic copy or transcript of; to compare, collate.

compulsión, *f.* compulsion.

compulsivo, va, *a.* compulsive.

compulsorio, ria, *n.* compulsory decree of a court, ordering an authentic copy to be made.

compunción, *f.* compunction, repentance.

compungido, da, *a.* compunctious, repentant.

compungirse, *vr.* (*ind.* COMPUNJO; *subj.* COMPUNJA) to feel compunction or remorse.

compungivo, va, *a.* pricking, stinging.

compurgación, *f.* (law) compurgation.

compurgador, ra, *n.* (law) compurgator.

compurgar, *va.* (law) to prove (one's veracity or innocence) by the oath of another.

compuse, *pret.* of COMPONER.

computación, *f.* computation, calculation.

computador, ra, *n.* computer.

computar, *va.* to compute, calculate.

computista, *m.* computist, computer.

cómputo, *m.* computation, calculation.

comulación, *f.* cumulation.

comulgante, *n.* (eccl.) communicant.

comulgar. I. *va.* (*pret.* COMULGUÉ; *subj.* COMULGUE) to administer communion.—**c. con ruedas de molino,** to fool, bamboozle, humbug.

II. *vn.* to commune, communicate; to take communion.

comulgatorio, *m.* communion altar.

común. I. *a.* common, public; common, usual, customary, ordinary, generally or extensively used; current; vulgar, mean, low.—**c. de dos,** (gram.) that applies to both genders.—**c. de tres,** (gram.) that applies to masculine, feminine, and neuter.—**en c.,** in common.—**por lo c.,** in general, generally. **II.** *m.* community; toilet, water closet.—**c. de las gentes,** the general public, the average person, the man in the street.

comuna, *f.* main irrigation channel; Commune (of Paris); (Am.) municipality.

comunal. I. *m.* commonalty, common people. **II.** *a.* common, commonable.

comunero. I. *a.* popular, common, pleasing to the people. **II.** *n.* commoner, one of the common people; joint holder of a tenure of lands; member of the party that upheld liberty against the encroachments of Charles V.; (Colomb.) member of the body of first patriots that rose against Spanish rule.

comunicabilidad, *f.* communicability.

comunicable, *a.* communicable; communicative.

comunicación, *f.* communication, intercourse; communiqué, official statement.—*pl.* means of communication.

comunicado, *m.* article of a personal nature sent to a periodical for publication.

comunicante, *n.* one who communicates (something).

comunicar. I. *va.* (*pret.* COMUNIQUÉ; *subj.* COMUNIQUE) to communicate, impart, make known; to announce; to transmit, send. **II.** *vr.* to communicate; to connect.—**c. entre sí,** to communicate with each other; to correspond, exchange correspondence; to be in mutual communication.

comunicativo, va, *a.* communicative; unreserved, informative.

comunidad, *f.* commonness; commonalty, the common people; community; corporation, guild, society.—*pl.* the cities of Castile which rose in support of Spanish liberty against the government of Charles V.—**de c.,** conjointly.

comunión, *f.* communion; fellowship; familiar intercourse; congregation; political party.

comuniqué, comunique, *v.* V. COMUNICAR.

comunismo, *m.* communism.

comunista, *n. & a.* communist(-ic).

comunizante, *n. & a.* communizer(-ing).

comunizar, *va. & vn.* to teach communism to, or make a communist of; to become a communist.

comúnmente, *adv.* commonly, usually, generally; frequently, often.

comuña, *f.* mixed wheat and rye, maslin, or meslin.—**comuñas,** seeds.

con, *prep.* with; by (when followed by infinitive: *con confesar se salvó,* by confessing, he saved himself); in other infinitive phrases, it simply indicates action, and the phrase is translated by Eng. *pres.p.* or *inf.* used as a noun (*con escribir basta,* writing is enough); notwithstanding, despite (also in infinitive phrases: *con ser muy enérgico, nada pudo hacer,* notwithstanding his being very energetic, he could do nothing); in (*con dolor,* in pain). With the pronouns *mi, sí, ti,* it forms the single words **conmigo,** with me, **consigo,** with himself, **contigo,** with thee.—**c. tal que,** provided that.—**c. que,** and so, then, so then.—**c. todo,** nevertheless, notwithstanding.—**para c.,** towards, in (one's) relations with.

conato, *m.* endeavour, effort, exertion; (law) crime attempted but not committed, attempt.

concadenar, *va.* to concatenate; to chain or link together.

concambio, *m.* exchange.

concanónigo, *m.* fellow canon.

concatedralidad, *f.* union of two cathedral churches.

concatenación, *f.* concatenation.

concausa, *f.* concause, joint cause.

cóncava, *f.* a hollow, cavity.

concavidad, *f.* concavity, hollowness; CÓNCAVA.

cóncavo, va. **I.** *a.* concave. **II.** *m.* concavity.

concebible, *a.* mentally conceivable.

concebir, *va.* & *vn.* (*ind.* CONCIBO; *subj.* CONCIBA) to conceive, become pregnant; to conceive, have an idea of; to comprehend, understand.

concedente, *n., a.* granter(-ing), conceder(-ing).

conceder, *va.* to give, bestow, grant; to concede, admit.

concedido, da, *a.* conceded, granted.

concejal, *m.* councilman.

concejil, *a.* pertaining to the municipal council; common, public, belonging to the public.

concejo, *m.* civic body of a small town; board of aldermen; municipal council; town hall; in Asturias, a district composed of several parishes with one common jurisdiction; foundling.

concento, *m.* concert of voices, harmony.

concentración, *f.* concentration.

concentrado, da. **I.** *pp.* of CONCENTRAR. **II.** *a.* concentered, concentrate.

concentrar. **I.** *va.* to concentrate; to concenter. **II.** *vr.* to concentrate (mentally).

concéntrico, ca, *a.* concentric.

concepción, *f.* conception, act of conceiving; idea; immaculate conception of the Virgin; feast of the Immaculate Conception; Madonna, picture of the Virgin.

conceptear, *vn.* to give smart repartees.

conceptible, *a.* conceivable.

conceptismo, *m.* exaggerated witticism.

conceptista, *m.* one who overdoes witticism.

concepto, *m.* concept, thought, idea; pithy sentence, epigram, flash of wit; judgment, opinion; expression of opinion; (com.) item, article; account.—**por c. de,** resulting from.

conceptualismo, *m.* conceptualism.

conceptualista, *a.* conceptualistic.

conceptuar, *va.* to conceive; to judge, think, form an opinion of.

conceptuosamente, *adv.* ingeniously, wittily, pithily.

conceptuoso, sa, *a.* witty, sententious, epigrammatic.

concernencia, *f.* respect, concernment, relation.

concerniente, *a.* (a) concerning, relating (to); applicable.—**en lo c. a,** with regard to, as for. —**lo c.,** what concerns the matter, the proper action, consideration, etc.

concernir, *v. defect.* (*ind.* ello CONCIERNE; *subj.* ello[CONCIERNA) (a) to concern, belong, appertain, be the business (of).

concertadamente, *adv.* regularly, orderly, methodically, concertedly; by agreement or appointment.

concertado, da, *pp.* of CONCERTAR.—**mampostería c.,** (mason.) rubble work.

concertador, *m.* regulator, adjuster, expediter.

concertante, *a.* (mus.) concerted, arranged for two or more voices or instruments.

concertar. **I.** *va.* (*ind.* CONCIERTO; *subj.* CONCIERTE) to arrange by agreement, adjust, harmonize, to agree on; to bargain, covenant, conclude (an agreement); close (a deal); to put in tune (musical instruments); to compare, estimate the relative qualities of; (shooting) to start or rouse (the game). **II.** *vn.* to agree, accord, suit one another; (gram.) to agree. **III.** *vr.* to go hand in hand; to covenant; to contrive, design.

concertina, *f.* concertina, a musical instrument similar to the accordion.

concertista, *n.* person who manages or performs in concerts.

concesible, *a.* grantable.

concesión, *f.* concession, grant.

concesionario, *m.* (law) grantee, concessionary.

concesivo, va, *a.* that may be granted.

concia, *f.* prohibited part of a forest.

concibo, conciba, *v.* *V.* CONCEBIR.

conciencia, *f.* conscience; conscientiousness; scruples; consciousness.—**a c.,** conscientiously; painstakingly.—**en c.,** in good faith, in truth. —**libertad de c.,** freedom of worship.

concienzudamente, *adv.* conscientiously, scrupulously, thoroughly.

concienzudo, da, *a.* conscientious, scrupulous, thorough.

concierne, concierna, *v.* *V.* CONCERNIR.

¹concierto, *m.* good order and arrangement; concert; bargain; agreement; contract; act of beating the wood with hounds to start the game; musical concert; concerto, a musical composition.—**de c.,** by agreement.

²concierto, concierte, *v.* *V.* CONCERTAR.

conciliable, *a.* reconcilable, capable of conciliation.

conciliábulo, *m.* conventicle; unlawful assembly or meeting.

conciliación, *f.* conciliation; settlement (of disputes); affinity; winning (esteem, favor, etc.).

conciliador, ra, *n.* & *a.* conciliator(-ing), peacemaker(-ing), reconciler(-ing).

¹conciliar, *va.* to conciliate, compose, reconcile; to gain, win (affection, esteem).—**c. el sueño,** to induce sleep.—**c. las amistades,** to make friends.

²conciliar. **I.** *a.* conciliar, pertaining to councils. **II.** *n.* member of a council.

conciliativo, va, *a.* conciliating.

conciliatorio, ria, *a.* conciliatory.

concilio, *m.* council; collection of decrees.

concisamente, *adv.* concisely.

concisión, *f.* conciseness.

conciso, sa, *a.* concise.

concitación, *f.* instigation, stirring up.

concitador, ra, *n.* instigator, incitor, agitator.

concitar, *va.* to excite, stir up, agitate.

concitativo, va, *a.* inciting; stirring.

conciudadano, *m.* fellow citizen, countryman.

conclave, cónclave, *m.* conclave; place for a conclave; meeting, convention.—**conclavista,** *m.* conclavist; domestic of a cardinal.

concluir, *va.* (*ind.* CONCLUYO; *subj.* CONCLUYA) to conclude, end, finish, close; to convince with reason, make evident, silence by argument; to decide finally, determine; to infer, deduce; to close (judicial proceedings); to submit to a final decision; (fencing) to disarm (an adversary) by engaging the guard of his sword.

conclusión, *f.* conclusion, end; winding up, denouement; close or closure; date; issue; conclusion of the proceedings in a lawsuit; conclusion, inference, deduction, consequence; thesis in schools.—**en c.,** finally, in conclusion; in closing.

conclusivo, va, *a.* conclusive, final.

concluso, sa, *a.* concluded, closed, terminated.

concluyente, *a.* concluding, conclusive; unanswerable.—**concluyentemente,** *adv.* conclusively.

concluyo, concluya, *v.* *V.* CONCLUIR.

concofrade, *m.* fellow member, brother (of a brotherhood).

concoide, *f.* (geom.) conchoid.

concoideo, a, *a.* (min.) conchoidal, shell-like.

concolega, *m.* fellow collegian.

concomerse, *vr.* (coll.) to shrug the shoulders.

concomido, concomimiento, *m.* (coll.) shrugging of the shoulders.

concomitancia, *f.* concomitance.

concomitante, *a.* concomitant, accompanying.

concomitar, *va.* to accompany, be a concomitant of, go with.

concordable, *a.* concordant, conformable, agreeable, consistent.

concordación, *f.* coördination, conformity.

concordador, **ra**, *n.* conciliator, peacemaker, moderator.

concordancia, *f.* concordance, conformity; harmony, concord of sounds; concordance of text or words; (gram.) concord, agreement.—*pl.* concordance (of a book, an author).

concordante, *a.* concordant, agreeing.

concordar. **I.** *va.* (*ind.* CONCUERDO; *subj.* CONCUERDE) to accord, regulate; to make agree. **II.** *vn.* to accord, agree, tally; to be congenial; to be in accord; (gram.) to agree.

concordata, *f.*, **concordato**, *m.* concordat, covenant made by a government with the Pope.

concordatorio, **ria**, *a.* concordat (as *a.*); of a, or the, concordat.

concorde, *a.* concordant, agreeing, tallying, in agreement.—**concordemente**, *adv.* with one accord, in agreement, concordably.

concordia, *f.* concord, conformity, harmony; agreement, settlement out of court; peace, good will.—**de c.**, jointly, by common consent.

concorpóreo, **rea**, *a.* (eccl.) becoming (through the Eucharist) of the same body with Christ.

concreción, *f.* concretion.

concrecionar, *vn.* & *vr.* to form concretions.

concretamente, *adv.* concretely.

concretar. **I.** *va.* to unite, harmonize, bring into conformity; to reduce to its simplest form; to express concretely. **II.** *vr.* to limit or confine oneself (to a subject).

concreto, **ta**. **I.** *a.* concrete, not abstract; definite.—**en c.**, concretely; in brief, in so many words. **II.** *m.* concretion; (erroneously but commonly) concrete (building material) (properly, HORMIGÓN).

concubina, *f.* concubine, mistress.

concubinario, *m.* one who keeps a mistress.

concubinato, *m.* concubinage.

concúbito, *m.* coition.

concuerdo, **concuerde**, *v. V.* CONCORDAR.

conculcación, *f.* violation (of rights).

conculcador, **ra**, *n.* violator (of rights), oppressor.

conculcar, *va.* (*pret.* CONCULQUÉ; *subj.* CONCULQUE) to trample underfoot; to violate, infringe.

concuñado, **da**, *n.* brother- or sister-in-law, term confined to persons who are married to two brothers or sisters.

concupiscencia, *f.* concupiscence, lust, cupidity.

concupiscible, *a.* concupiscible, exciting desire.

concurrencia, *f.* audience; attendance; concurrence, coincidence; competition.

concurrente, *a.* concurrent; coincident.

concurrido, **da**. **I.** *pp.* of CONCURRIR. **II.** *a.* frequented; (of a meeting, etc.) attended.

concurrir, *vn.* to concur; to meet in one point, time, or place; to attend; to contribute; to coincide, agree; to compete (in an examination, etc.)

concursar, *va.* (law) to declare insolvent.

concurso, *m.* concourse, confluence of persons; conflux, crowd, congregation, assembly; aid, assistance; call for bids (on a piece of work, a service, etc.); competitive contest between candidates for a professorship, curacy, etc.—**c. de acreedores**, meeting of creditors.

concusión, *f.* concussion, shaking, shock; exaction, extortion.

concusionario, **ia**. **I.** *a.* concussive, shaking. **II.** *n.* extortioner.

concha, *f.* shell, case, carapace; mollusk, shell-fish; tortoise shell; any object that has the shape of a shell; prompter's box; bay in the shape of a horseshoe; basin; fixed grindstone in mills; ancient copper coin, worth about three

farthings; (arch.) volute; conch; the external ear; shell of a dagger or cutlass; shell-shaped covering of the spike of Indian corn.—**c. de cabrestante**, (naut.) socket of the capstan.—**c. de nácar**, mother-of-pearl shell.—**conchas de escobenes**, (naut.) navel woods or navel hoods.—**meterse en su c.**, to become a recluse; to shut up like a clam.—**tener muchas conchas**, to be very reserved, artful, cunning.

conchabanza, *f.* manner of making oneself easy and comfortable; (coll.) plotting, conspiracy.

conchabar. **I.** *va.* to join, unite; to mix (inferior wool with superior); (Am.) to employ (gen. in domestic service). **II.** *vr.* to unite for some evil purpose; to plot, conspire.—**conchabo**, *m.* (Am.) work, job (gen. in domestic service).

conchado, **da**, *a.* scaly, shelly.

conchal, *a.*—**seda c.**, finest silk from choice cocoons.

conchífero, **ra**, *a.* conchiferous, shell-bearing.

conchil, *m.* rock shell; murex.

conchilla, **ita**, *f. dim.* small shell.

conchudo, **da**, *a.* shelly, scaly; cunning, crafty, reserved; cautious.

conchuela, *f. dim.* = CONCHILLA.

condado, *m.* earldom, county; dignity of a count or earl.

condal, *a.* pert. to the dignity of an earl or count.

conde, *m.* earl, count; overseer; elected head or chief of the gipsies.

condecente, *a.* convenient, fit, proper.

condecoración, *f.* decoration, embellishing or decorating; jewelled insignia of knighthood; medal; badge.

condecorar, *va.* to decorate, adorn, embellish; to bestow honors on; to bestow a medal or insignia on; to knight.

condena, *f.* court clerk's attestation of sentence imposed; sentence, term of imprisonment.

condenable, *a.* condemnable, blamable, damnable.

condenación, *f.* condemnation; sentence to penalty; conviction (of a criminal); punishment; damnation.

condenado, **da**, *a.* damned, condemned to eternal punishment; condemned; convicted.

condenador, **ra**, *n.* & *a.* condemner(-ing), blamer(-ing), incriminator(-ing).

condenar. **I.** *va.* to prove, find or declare guilty, convict; to sentence; to damn; to condemn, censure, blame; to disapprove; to nail or wall up (a door, window, passage); to condemn as unsafe. **II.** *vr.* to condemn oneself, acknowledge one's fault; to be damned (to hell).

condenatorio, **ria**, *a.* condemnatory, damnatory.

condensabilidad, *f.* condensability.

condensable, *a.* condensable.

condensación, *f.* condensation.

condensador, **ra**. **I.** *a.* condensing. **II.** *m.* (steam eng., elec.) condenser.—**c. de chorro**, (steam eng.) jet condenser.—**c. de mezcla**, (steam eng.) mixing condenser.—**c. de placas**, (elec.) plate condenser.—**c. de superficie**, (steam eng.) surface condenser.

condensante, *a.* condensing.

condensar. **I.** *va.* to thicken, condense, compress. **II.** *vr.* to be condensed; to gather.

condensativo, **va**, *a.* condensative.

condesa, *f.* countess.

condescendencia, *f.* compliance.

condescender, *vn.* (*ind.* CONDESCIENDO; *subj.* CONDESCIENDA) to yield, submit, comply.

condescendiente, *a.* agreeable, complaisant.

condesciendo, **condescienda**. *v. V.* CONDESCENDER.

condesita, *f. dim.* little or young countess.

condesito, *m. dim.* little earl; little count.

condesil, *a.* (coll.) pert. to counts or countesses.

condestable, *m.* constable; lord high constable; (naut.) master gunner.

condestablía, *f.* constableship.

condición, *f.* condition, quality, state; footing; habit, disposition, temper; constitution; quality; rank, class; fashion; clause, stipulation, specification.—**c. callada**, tacit condition, condition understood.—**c. imposible de derecho**, provision or stipulation contrary to the law.—**c. imposible de hecho**, physically impossible provision, provision impossible per se, or de facto.—**c. sine qua non**, condition sine qua non, or absolutely indispensable.—**a c. de que, or con la c. de que**, on condition that.—**de c.**, of importance, of high rank.—**de c. que**, so as to.—**estar en condiciones de**, to be in condition to.—**tener c.**, to be rude or ill-tempered.

condicionado, da. I. *pp.* of CONDICIONAR. II. *a.* conditioned; conditional.

condicional, *a.* conditional.—**condicionalmente**, *adv.* conditionally; hypothetically.

condicionar, *vn.* to agree, accord; to impose conditions.

condicioncilla, ita, *f. dim.* hasty temper; small clause or stipulation.

condignamente, *adv.* deservedly, duly.

condigno, na, *a.* condign, suitable, deserved, due, merited.

cóndilo, *m.* (anat.) condyle.

condimentar, *va.* to dress or season (foods).

condimento, *m.* condiment, seasoning.

condiscípulo, *m.* schoolmate, fellow student.

condolerse, *vr.* (*ind.* CONDUELO; *subj.* CONDUELA) (de) to condole (with), to be sorry (for), to sympathize (with); to regret.

condominio, *m.* joint ownership.

condómino, *m.* joint owner.

condonación, *f.* condonation, pardoning.

condonante, *a.* condoning, forgiving, remitting.

condonar, *va.* to pardon, forgive, remit.

cóndor, *m.* Chilean and Colombian gold coin worth ten dollars; (ornith.) condor.

condotiero, condottiere, *m.* condottiere. (English *pl.* condottieri, as in Italian).

condrila, *f.* (bot.) common gum succory.

condrín, *m.* (P. I.) weight for precious metals = 0.3768 gram.

condrografía, *f.* (zool.) description of cartilages.

condrográfico, ca, *a.* pert. to CONDROGRAFÍA.

condrología, *f.* treatise on cartilages.

condropterigio, gia. I. *n.* & *a.* (ichth.) chondropterygian. II. *m. pl.* Chondropterygii.

conducción, *f.*, conducencia, *f.* conveyance; carriage; cartage, transportation; act of conveying or conducting, leading, guiding; conduct; stipulated rate or charge for transportation; (auto) driving.

conducente, *a.* conducive, conducent; official.

conducir. I. *va.* & *vn.* (*ind. pres.* CONDUZCO, *pret.* CONDUJE; *subj.* CONDUZCA) to convey, carry; to take, accompany; to direct, lead; to direct, manage, conduct; (auto) to drive. II. *vn.* (a) to conduce, contribute (to); to be suitable (for); to lead, tend (to). III. *vr.* to behave, act, conduct oneself.

conducta, *f.* conduct, behavior; conveyance, convoy; property convoyed; conduct, government, command, direction, management; party of recruits conducted to the regiment; contract made by a town or village with a physician to attend its sick.

conductero, *m.* one in charge of a convoy.

conductibilidad, *f.* conductibility.

conductible, *a.* conveyable, conductible.

conductividad, *f.* conductivity.

conductivo, va, *a.* conductive, conducting.

conducto, *m.* duct, conduit; channel through which any business is conducted or managed; means; mediator; person through whom any-

thing is accomplished.—**por c. de**, by means of; through.

conductor, ra. I. *a.* conducting. II. *m.* conductor; leader; usher; guide; conveyer; (phys. & elec.) conductor; (auto) driver; (Mex.) (Ry. & street car) conductor. III. *f.* woman conductor or director.

conduelo, conduela, *v.* V. CONDOLER.

condueño, *m.* (com.) joint owner.

conduje, *pret.* of CONDUCIR.

condumio, *m.* (coll.) meat dressed to be eaten with bread plenty of food.

conduplicación, *f.* (rhet.) reduplication.

condutal, *m.* (mason.) leader; gutter.

conduzco, conduzca, *v.* V. CONDUCIR.

conectador, *m.* (mech.) connector.

conectar, *va.* to connect.

conectivo, va, *a.* connective, connecting.

coneja, *f.* female rabbit.

conejal, conejar, *m.* rabbit warren.

conejera, *f.* warren for breeding rabbits; burrow; brothel; (coll.) den or cavern inhabited by poor people or frequented by bad characters, joint.

conejero. I. *m.* warrener, keeper of a rabbit warren. II. *a.* rabbit (as *a.*), for rabbits.

conejillo, lla; conejito, ta, *n. dim.* little rabbit. —**conejillo de Indias**, guinea pig.

conejo, ja, *n.* (zool.) rabbit.—**conejuna**, *f.* rabbit down or fur.—**conejuno, na**, *a.* pertaining to rabbits, rabbit (as *a.*)

conexidades, *f. pl.* rights annexed to the principal.

conexión, *f.* connection, union; joint; coherence; (mech.) coupling.—*pl.* connections (social, commercial).—**conexionarse**, *vr.* to make (social, commercial) connections, to get in touch.

conexivo, va, *a.* connective.

conexo, xa, *a.* connected, united, related.

confabulación, *f.* confabulation, easy conversation, chat; leaguing, conspiracy, plot, collusion.

confabulador, ra, *n.* gossip; schemer, plotter.

confabular. I. *vn.* to confabulate; to talk informally, chat. II. *vr.* to league, conspire.

confalón, *m.* gonfalon, standard, ensign.

confalonier, confaloniero, *m.* gonfalonier, chief standard-bearer.

confarreación, *f.* (anc. Rome) confarreation.

confección, *f.* any handwork; workmanship; fancy work, ready made article; (pharm.) confection, compound remedy, concoction.

confeccionador, ra, *n.* one who makes articles of dress or any handwork.

confeccionar, *va.* to make, prepare; put together; to compound, put up (medicines, prescriptions).

confederación, *f.* confederacy, confederation; federation, coalition; international treaty or convention.

confederado, da. I. *pp.* of CONFEDERAR. II. *n.* & *a.* confederate, convenanter(-ing), associate.

confederar, *va.* & *vr.* to confederate, join, form a confederacy.

conferencia, *f.* conference, meeting, conversation, interview; congress; daily lecture in universities; public lecture.

conferenciante, *n.* lecturer.

conferenciar, *vn.* to confer, consult together, hold an interview; to lecture.

conferencista, *n.* (Am.) = CONFERENCIANTE.

conferir. I. *va.* (*ind.* CONFIERO; *subj.* CONFIERA) to confer; to give, bestow, award; to compare. II. *vn.* to confer; to lecture.

confesa, *f.* widow who has become a nun.

confesado, da, *n.* (coll.) penitent.

confesante, *n.* one who confesses before a judge.

confesar. I. *va.* (*ind.* CONFIESO; *subj.* CONFIESE) to confess, acknowledge, own, avow, grant; to confess, hear or receive confessions; to confess to a priest.—**c. de plano**, to confess plainly or openly. **II.** *vr.* to confess or make confession; to shrive.

confesión, *f.* confession, avowal, acknowledgment; confession to a priest.—**c. auricular,** auricular confession.—**confesionario,** *m.* treatise with rules for confessing; confessional.—**confesionista,** *n.* Lutheran.

confeso, sa. I. *a. & n.* (one) confessing a crime; converted Jew. **II.** *m.* lay-brother.

confesonario, *m.* confessional.

confesor, *m.* father confessor; title given to holy men by the Roman Catholic Church.

confetti, *m. pl.* confetti.

confiable, *a.* trusty, reliable.

confiadamente, *adv.* trustingly, with confidence.

confiado, da. I. *pp.* of CONFIAR. **II.** *a.* confident, unsuspicious, trusting; presumptuous, arrogant or forward.

confiador, *m.* (law) joint surety, fellow bondsman.

confianza, *f.* confidence, trust, reliance, faith; courage, firmness of opinion; presumptuousness, forwardness, assurance; familiarity, intimacy.—**de c.,** informal, unceremonious.—**en c.,** confidentially.—**confianzudo, da,** *a.* presumptuous, bold, "fresh."

confiar. I. *vn.* (**en**) to rely (on), to trust (in). **II.** *va.* to confide, intrust, credit; to commit to the care of another.

confidencia, *f.* trust, confidence; secret or confidential information.—**hacer confidencias a,** to confide in, tell secrets to.

confidencial, *a.* confidential.—**confidencialmente,** *adv.* confidentially.

confidente. I. *n.* confidant, intimate, counsellor; detective, secret agent, spy; settee for two persons, tête-à-tête. **II.** *a.* true, faithful, trusty.

confidentemente, *adv.* confidently, faithfully.

confiero, confiera, *v. V.* CONFERIR.

confieso, confiese, *v. V.* CONFESAR.

configuración, *f.* configuration.

configurar, *va.* to form, shape.

confín. I. *a.* bordering, abutting, conterminous; limiting, boundary (as *a.*) **II.** *m.* limit, boundary, confine, border.

confinación, *f.* = CONFINAMIENTO.

confinado, da, *n.* one confined to a place or region under surveillance.

confinamiento, *m.* confinement; banishment to a definite place; (law) confinement within certain bounds under surveillance.

confinante, *a.* = CONFÍN, *a.*

confinar, *va. & vn.* to banish to a definite place; to confine, imprison; to border on, abut.—**c. con,** to abut on, be bounded by.

confingir, *va.* (*ind.* CONFINJO; *subj.* CONFINJA) (pharm.) to mix into one mass.

confirmación, *f.* confirmation, corroboration, attestation; (eccl.) confirmation.

confirmadamente, *adv.* firmly, assuredly.

confirmador, ra, *n.* attester, confirmer.

confirmante, *n. & a.* confirmer(-ing).

confirmar, *va.* to confirm, corroborate, verify; to strengthen, support, ratify; (eccl.) to confirm.

confirmativamente, *adv.* confirmingly.

confirmatorio, ria, *a.* confirmatory, confirmative.

confiscable, *a.* confiscable, forfeitable.

confiscación, *f.* confiscation, forfeiture.

confiscado, da, *a.* confiscate, confiscated.

confiscar, *va.* (*pret.* CONFISQUÉ; *subj.* CONFISQUE) to confiscate.

confitar, *va.* to confect, to candy with melted sugar; to make into sweetmeats or into preserves; to dulcify, to sweeten.

confite, *m.* (gen. *pl.*) bonbon; sweets.—**estar a partir de un c.,** or **morder en un c.,** to be hand and glove, to be intimate.

confitente, *a.* (one) confessing a crime.

confíteor, *m.* (Rom. Cath.) confiteor.

confitera, *f.* bonbon container; candy box.

confitería, *f.* confectionery; confectioner's shop.

confitero, ra, *n.* confectioner; tray for sweets.

confítico, illo, ito, *m. dim.* small cookie or cake; caraway cookie.—*pl.* ornaments in the shape of cookies wrought on coverlets.

confitura, *f.* confection, sweetmeat, preserve.

conflación, *f.* fusion, melting of metals, smelting.

conflagración, *f.* conflagration; sudden and violent perturbation of towns and nations.

conflátil, *a.* fusible.

conflictivo, va, *a.* conflicting.

conflicto, *m.* conflict, struggle, strife, combat; (fig.) agony, pang.

confluencia, *f.* confluence.

confluente, *a.* confluent.

confluir, *vn.* (*ind. pres.* él CONFLUYE, *pret.* CONFLUYÓ; *subj.* CONFLUYA) to join (app. to rivers and sea currents); to assemble in one place.

conformación, *f.* conformation.

conformador, *m.* shaper; hat block; boot crimper.

conformar. I. *va.* to conform, adjust, fit. **II.** *vn.* to suit, fit, conform; to cohere; to level. **III.** *vr.* to comply; to yield, submit; to resign oneself.

conforme. I. *a.* alike, corresponding, suitable, congruent, consonant, accordant; correct, acceptable, O. K.; consistent; agreed; as (as in *todo queda c. estaba,* everything remains as it was); compliant, resigned.—**c. a,** consistent with, agreeable to.—**c. con,** resigned to; in agreement with. **II.** *adv.* in due proportion; agreeably, accordingly.

conformemente, *adv.* conformably, unanimously; correctly; agreeably.

conformidad, *f.* resemblance, likeness; conformity; agreement, consistence, consonance, congruence; concord, concordance; symmetry; close attachment of one person to another; affinity; submission, patience, resignation.—**de c.,** by common consent; correctly.—**en c.,** agreeably, suitably, accordingly.

conformismo, *n.* conformism.

conformista, *m.* conformist.

confortable, *a.* that comforts, consoles; comfortable.

confortablemente, *adv.* comfortably.

confortación, *f.* comfort, consolation; encouragement.

confortador, ra, *n. & a.* comforter(-ing), consoler(-ing), strengthener(-ing).

confortamiento, *m.* comfort, consolation; encouragement.

confortante. I. *a. & n.* comforting, soothing (thing or person). **II.** *m. pl.* mitts.

confortar, *va.* to comfort, strengthen, enliven, invigorate; to encourage, console, cheer, solace.

confortativo, va, *a.* comforting; encouraging, cheering, strengthening.

conforte, *m.* = CONFORTACIÓN.

confracción, *f.* fracture, breaking.

confraternidad, *f.* confraternity, brotherhood.

confricación, *f.* rubbing, friction.

confricar, *va.* to rub.

confrontación, *f.* confrontation, confronting; comparison, comparing; sympathy, natural congeniality (between persons).

confrontante, *n. & a.* confronter(-ing).

confrontar. I. *va.* to collate, confront; to compare. **II.** *vn.* to agree in sentiments and opinion. —**c. con,** to border on.

confucianismo, *m.* Confucianism.

confucianista, *n. & a.* Confucian.

confuciano, na, *n. & a.* = CONFUCIANISTA.

confundir. I. *va.* (*pp.* CONFUNDIDO and CONFUSO) to confound, jumble; to perplex, confuse, darken, throw into disorder; to convince by argument; to abase, humiliate.—**c. con,** to confuse with, mistake for. **II.** *vr.* to be bewildered, perplexed, confounded, rattled, mixed up; to be ashamed and humbled.

confusamente, *adv.* confusedly; helter-skelter.

confusión, *f.* confusion, disorder; perplexity; embarrassment, entanglement, confusedness; obscurity; humiliation, shame, ignominy.

confuso, sa. I. *pp. irreg.* of CONFUNDIR. **II.** *a.* confused, mixed, confounded, jumbled together; obscure, doubtful, unintelligible; blurred, indistinct; fearful, timorous, perplexed.—**en c.,** confusedly.

confutación, *f.* confutation, disproof.

confutar, *va.* to confute, disprove, refute.

congelable, *a.* congealable.

congelación, *f.* solidification, freezing, congealing; congealment.

congelador, *m.* freezer.

congelamiento, *m.* = CONGELACIÓN.

congelar, *va. & vr.* to congeal, freeze.—**congelativo, va,** *a.* having the power of congealing.

congénere, congenérico, ca, *a.* congeneric, of like kind.

congenial, *a.* congenial; analogous.

congeniar, *vn.* to be congenial.

congénito, *a.* congenital, connate.

congerie, *f.* congeries, heap, mass.

congestión, *f.* (med.) congestion; (sun, etc.) stroke.—**congestionar. I.** *va.* to congest. **II.** *vr.* (of the blood) to accumulate; (Am.) (of traffic) to get congested.

congiario, *m.* (anc. Rome) congiary, gift to the people.

congio, *m.* congius, an ancient liquid measure.

conglobación, *f.* being made into a ball; mixture and union of immaterial things; (rhet.) accumulation of proofs.

conglobar, *va.* to form into a ball; heap together.

conglomeración, *f.* conglomeration, heterogeneous mixture.

conglomerado, da, *a. & a.* conglomerate.

conglomerar, *va.* to conglomerate.

conglutinación, *f.* conglutination, glutination, cementing, sticking.

conglutinar. I. *va.* to conglutinate, cement, unite. **II.** *vr.* to conglutinate, stick together.

conglutinativo, va; conglutinoso, sa, *a.* viscous, glutinous, cementing.

congo, *m.* (Mex. & Cuba) pig's foot; (Cuba) hog's hind leg, ham; (Am.) howling monkey; (Colomb.) iron ore mixed with gold ore.

congoja, *f.* anguish, dismay, anxiety, grief, sorrow.—**congojar,** *va.* to afflict, grieve.

congojosamente, *adv.* anxiously, sorrowfully.

congojoso, sa, *a.* afflictive, distressing; afflicted.

congoleño, ña, *a.* of or pertaining to the Congo.

congosto, *m.* narrow pass, defile.

congraciador, ra, *n.* flatterer, fawner, wheedler; congratulator.

congraciamiento, *m.* flattery, fawning.

congraciar. I. *va.* to adulate, flatter. **II.** *vr.* (con) to get into the good graces (of).

congratulación, *f.* congratulation.

congratular. I. *va.* to congratulate, compliment. **II.** *vr.* to congratulate oneself, rejoice.

congratulatorio, ria, *a.* congratulatory, congratulating.

congregación, *f.* congregation; meeting, assembly; fraternity, brotherhood.

congregacionalismo, *m.* Congregationalism.

congregacionalista, *n. & a.* Congregationalist.

congregante, ta, *n.* member of a congregation, fraternity, or brotherhood.

congregar, *va. & vr.* (*pret.* CONGREGUÉ; *subj.* CONGREGUE) to assemble, meet, congregate, gather.

congresista, *n.* congressman(-woman).

congreso, *m.* congress, consistory, convention, assembly; sexual intercourse.—**C. de los Diputados,** House of Representatives.

congrio, *m.* (zool.) conger eel, sea eel.

congrua, *f.* competent sustenance to one who is to be ordained a priest.

congruamente, *adv.* conveniently; becomingly.

congruencia, *f.* convenience; fitness; congruence.

congruente, *a.* congruent, corresponding.

congruentemente, *adv.* suitably, congruously.

congruísmo, *m.* congruism, a religious doctrine.

congruísta, *n.* supporter of congruism.

congruo, grua, *a.* congruous, apt, fit, suitable.

cónica, *f.* (math.) conic, conic section.

conicidad, *f.* conicity.

cónico, ca, *a.* conical, conic.

conidio, *m.* (bot.) conidium.

conífero, ra. I. *a.* (bot.) coniferous. **II.** *f. pl.* Coniferæ.

coniforme, *a.* coniform, cone-shaped.

conivalvo, va, *a.* (zool.) having a conical shell.

coniza, *f.* (bot.) great fleabane.

conjetura, *f.* conjecture, surmise, guess.

conjeturable, *a.* conjecturable.

conjeturador, ra, *n.* conjecturer, guesser.

conjetural, *a.* conjectural.

conjeturalmente, *adv.* conjecturally, by guess.

conjeturar, *va.* to conjecture, guess.

conjuez, *m.* cojudge.

conjugación, *f.* conjugation.

conjugado, da. I. *pp.* of CONJUGAR. **II.** *a.* (math.) conjugate.

conjugar, *va.* (*pret.* CONJUGUÉ; *subj.* CONJUGUE) (gram.) to conjugate.

conjunción, *f.* conjunction, union, association, league; conjugation; copulation; act of coupling or joining together; consolidation; (gram., astr.) conjunction.

conjuntamente, *adv.* in all, all together, jointly.

conjuntiva, *f.* (anat.) conjunctiva.

conjuntivitis, *f.* (med.) conjunctivitis.

conjuntivo, va, *a.* conjunctive.

conjunto, ta. I. *a.* united, connected; contiguous; allied by kindred or friendship; mixed or incorporated with another thing. **II.** *m.* whole, aggregate, entirety; (sport) team; unit, system of parts (as *c. de cola*, tail unit of an airplane).—**en c.,** as a whole; in all, totally.

conjura, conjuración, *f.* conspiracy, conjuration, plot, machination.

conjurado, da. I. *pp.* of CONJURAR. **II.** *n.* conspirator.

conjurador, ra, *n.* conspirator; exorcist.

conjuramentar. I. *va.* to administer an oath to, swear in. **II.** *vr.* to bind oneself by oath, take an oath.

conjurante, *a.* conjuring; conspiring.

conjurar. I. *vn.* to conspire, plot; to join in a conspiracy. **II.** *va.* to exorcise; to entreat, implore; to avert, ward off.

conjuro, *m.* conjuration; exorcism; entreaty.

conllevador, ra, *n.* helper, assistant.

conllevar, *va.* to aid; to bear with patience.

conmemoración, *f.* remembrance; commemoration; anniversary.

conmemorar, *va.* to commemorate.—**conmemorativo, va,** or **conmemoratorio, ria,** *a.* commemorative, memorial (as a).

conmensal, *m.* messmate, fellow boarder.

conmensalía, *f.* eating together.

conmensurabilidad, *f.* commensurability.

conmensurable, *a.* commensurable.

conmensuración, *f.* commensuration.

conmensurar, *va.* to make commensurate.

conmensurativo, va, *a.* that makes commensurate.

conmigo, with me, with myself. *V.* CON.

conmilitón, *m.* comrade, companion; fellow soldier.

conminación, *f.* commination, threat.

conminar, *va.* to threaten; (law) to denounce punishment.—**conminatorio, ria,** *a.* comminatory, denunciatory, threatening.

conminuta, *a.* (surg.).—**fractura c.,** comminuted.

conmiseración, *f.* commisseration, pity, sympathy.

conmistión, *f.* commixture.

conmisto, ta, *a.* mixed, mingled, incorporated.

conmistura, *f.* = CONMISTIÓN.

conmixto, ta, *a.* = CONMISTO.

conmoción, *f.* commotion, excitement, stirring up, flurry, disturbance.

conmonitorio, *m.* written narrative of an event; (law) reminder from a superior to an inferior judge.

conmovedor, ra. I. *a.* touching; sad, pathetic; exciting, stirring. II. *n.* disturber, agitator.

conmover, *va.* (*ind.* CONMUEVO; *subj.* CONMUEVA) to touch, appeal to; to disturb, agitate, stir up.

conmutabilidad, *f.* commutability.

conmutable, *a.* commutable.

conmutación, *f.* commutation, exchange.

conmutador, *m.* electric switch; telegraph key.

conmutar, *va.* to exchange, barter.

conmutativo, va, *a.* commutative.

connatural, *a.* connatural, inborn.

connaturalización, *f.* naturalization, adaptation to new conditions, acclimatization.

connaturalizarse, *vr.* to accustom oneself; to become inured or acclimated.

connaturalmente, *adv.* connaturally.

connivencia, *f.* connivance; plotting.

connotación, *f.* (gram.) connotation; distant relationship.

connotado, *m.* remote relationship.

connotante, *a.* connotative.

connotar, *va.* to connote, imply.

connotativo, va, *a.* (gram.) connotative.

connovicio, cia, *n.* fellow novice.

connubial, *a.* connubial, matrimonial, conjugal.

connubio, *m.* matrimony, marriage, wedlock.

connumerar, *va.* to enumerate, include in a number.

cono, *m.* (geom.) cone; (bot.) cone, fruit of the pine family.

conocedor, ra. I. *a.* (**de**) familiar (with), expert (in). II. *n.* connoisseur, expert; chief herdsman.

conocer. I. *va.* (*ind.* CONOZCO; *subj.* CONOZCA) to know; to experience, observe, perceive, comprehend; to be, or become, acquainted with; to know carnally. II. *vn.* to know.—**c. de una causa,** or **pleito,** (law) to try a case (app. to a judge). III. *vr.* to know each other; to meet, get acquainted; to know oneself.

conocible, *a.* cognoscible, knowable.

conocidamente, *adv.* in a known manner.

conocido, da. I. *pp.* of CONOCER. II. *a.* prominent, well known. III. *n.* acquaintance.

conocimiento, *m.* knowledge, understanding; consciousness; skill, ability; acquaintance, slight friendship; (com.) (or **c. de embarque**) bill of lading; note of identification, voucher; (Am.) check for baggage.—*pl.* learning, erudition.—**poner en c. de,** to inform, notify.—**venir en c. de,** to learn of.

conoidal, *a.* conoidal.

conoide, *m.* (geom.) conoid.

conopial, conopio, *m.* (arch.) ogee arch.

conozco, conozca, *v.* V. CONOCER.

conque. I. *conj.* so then; now then; and so; well then. II. *m.* (coll.) wherewithal.

conquiforme, *a.* conchiform, shell-shaped.

conquiliología, *f.* (zool.) conchology.

conquista, *f.* conquest, subjugation; conquered territory or thing; winning another's affections.

conquistable, *a.* conquerable; attainable, accessible.

conquistador, ra, *n.* & *a.* conqueror(-ing).

conquistar, *va.* to conquer, overcome, subdue; to win (another's affections).

conrear, *va.* to grease (wool); (agr.) to hoe.

conregnante, *a.* reigning with another.

conreinar, *vn.* to reign with another.

consabido, da, *a.* already known, alluded to, in question, before-mentioned, aforesaid.

consabidor, ra, *n.* one who possesses knowledge jointly with others.

consagración, *f.* consecration.

consagrado, da. I. *pp.* of CONSAGRAR. II. *a.* sacred; devoted, given (to study, sports, etc.).

consagrante, *n.* consecrator.

consagrar. I. *va.* to consecrate, hallow, make sacred; to deify; to consecrate, devote, dedicate; to erect (a monument). II. *vr.* to devote or give oneself (to study, work, etc.)

consanguíneo, nea, *a.* consanguineous, cognate, kindred.—**consanguinidad,** *f.* consanguinity.

consciente, *a.* conscious; aware; of sound mind, sane; (law) compos mentis.

conscientemente, *adv.* consciously.

conscripción, *f.* (mil.) conscription.

conscripto, a.—**padre c.,** senator of anc. Rome.

consectario, ria. I. *a.* consequent; annexed. II. *m.* corollary.

consecución, *f.* attainment, obtaining, acquisition.

consecuencia, *f.* consequence, conclusion, inference; issue; consistence, firmness, coherence; consequence, importance, moment, concern.—**a c. de,** because of.—**en c.,** consequently, therefore.—**guardar c.,** to be consistent.—**por c.** = EN C.—**ser de c.,** to be important.—**traer a c.,** to adduce, bring to bear, or as corroborative evidence.

consecuente. I. *m.* effect, issue, consequence; (math.) consequent. II. *a.* consequent, following; consistent, logical.

consecuentemente, *adv.* consequently.

consecutivamente, *adv.* consecutively.

consecutivo, va, *a.* consecutive.

conseguimiento, *m.* attainment, obtainment, acquisition.

conseguir, *va.* (*ind.* CONSIGO; *subj.* CONSIGA) to attain, get, obtain (*consigue que venga,* he gets him to come); to succeed in.

conseja, *f.* story, fairy tale, fable.

consejera, *f.* counsellor's wife; woman adviser.

consejero, *m.* counsellor, member of a council; adviser; anything that gives warning.—**c. de la corona,** crown minister.

consejo, *m.* counsel, advice; council, court, assembly of magistrates, advisory board, consulting body; council house.—**c. de guerra,** court-martial; council of war.—**c. de ministros,** cabinet.—**seguir c. de guerra a,** to court-martial.

consenciente, *a.* consenting; conniving.

consenso, *m.* general assent; agreement of opinion, consensus.

consensual, *a.* (law) consensual.

consentido, da. I. *pp.* of CONSENTIR. II. *a.* spoiled (child), coddled.

consentidor, ra, *n.* complier, conniver; coddler.

consentimiento, *m.* consent; coddling; compliance, acquiescence; (med.) consent.

consentir. I. *va.* (*ind.* CONSIENTO; *subj.* CONSIENTA) to allow, permit, tolerate, acquiesce in, condescend to; to believe; to accept, admit; to admit of; to coddle, spoil, overindulge. II. *vn.* (mech.) to flag, give way, weaken, become loose. —**c. en** (foll. by inf.), to consent to (inf.). III. *vr.* to spring, crack, begin to break.

conserje, *m.* keeper or warden of a royal palace, castle, or public building; janitor, concierge.

conserjería, *f.* wardenship of a royal palace or castle; warden's dwelling; janitor's office, conciergerie.

conserva, *f.* conserve, preserve, jam; pickles; fleet of merchantmen under convoy of a ship of war.—**c. trojezada,** preserve of minced fruit.—**conservas alimenticias,** canned goods.—**en c.,** canned, preserved.

conservación, *f.* conservation; maintenance, up-keep.

conservador, ra. I. *n.* conservator, preserver; curator. **II.** *n.* & *a.* conserver(-ing); (pol.) Conservative.—**juez c.** person appointed to guard the rights of a community.

conservaduría, *f.* dignity in the order of Malta.

conservante, *n.* & *a.* conserver (-ing).

conservar. I. *va.* to conserve, maintain, preserve, keep; to guard; to preserve or pickle (fruit), to can. **II.** *vr.* to keep young, be well preserved.

conservativo, va, *a.* conservative, preservative.

conservatoría, *f.* place and office of a JUEZ CON-SERVADOR; grant to communities to choose their own conservators.—*pl.* letters patent granted by conservators.

conservatorio, ria. I. *a.* conservatory; having a preservative quality. **II.** *m.* conservatory, place for instruction in the fine arts.

conservero, ra, *n.* preparer of conserves.

considerable, *a.* considerable, great, large.

considerablemente, *adv.* considerably.

consideración, *f.* consideration, regard; notice; sake, account; reflection, contemplation, meditation; importance; urbanity, respect.—**en c.,** considering, in, or into, consideration, in proportion.—**guardar,** or **tener, consideraciones a,** to show consideration to.—**ser de c.,** to be of importance or moment.

consideradamente, *adv.* considerately; calmly.

considerado, da, *a.* prudent; considerate; thoughtful, tactful; esteemed, distinguished.

considerador, ra, *n.* one who considers or who shows consideration.

considerando. I. *ger.* of CONSIDERAR. **II.** *conj.* whereas (as used in enumerating reasons or circumstances in legal language). **III.** *m.* introductory clause, introduced with "whereas."

considerante, *a.* considering.

considerar, *va.* to consider, meditate, think over; to treat with respect, show consideration to.

consiento, consienta, *v. V.* CONSENTIR.

consiervo, *m.* fellow serf.

consigna, *f.* (mil.) watchword, countersign.

consignación, *f.* consignation, assignation, apportionment; (com.) consignment, shipment.

consignador, ra, *n.* (com.) consignor.

consignar, *va.* to consign, assign, make over; to set apart, devote; to yield, intrust; to state in writing; to lay by, to deposit; (com.) to consign (goods); (law) to deposit in trust.

consignatario, *m.* trustee; (law) mortgagee who enjoys the property mortgaged until the debt be paid out of the proceeds; (com.) consignee.

¹**consigo,** with oneself, himself, herself, themselves, yourself, yourselves. *V.* CON.—**c. mismo, c. propio,** or **c. solo,** alone, by oneself.

²**consigo, consiga,** *v. V.* CONSEGUIR.

consiguiente. I. *m.* consequence, result, effect.—**de c., por c., por el c.,** consequently, therefore. **II.** *a.* consequent, resulting, following; consistent, logical.—**consiguientemente,** *adv.* consequently.

consiliario, *m.* counsellor; assistant to head of a corporation.

consintiente, *a.* consenting, agreeing.

consistencia, *f.* consistence, consistency; stability; duration; coherence; conformity; firmness, solidity.

consistente, *a.* consistent, firm, solid.

consistir, *vn.* to consist, subsist, continue fixed; to be comprised, contained.—**c. en,** to lie, to be a matter of, consist in (*never* to consist *of,* in the sense of "to be composed of").

consistorial, *a.* consistorial, belonging or relating to an ecclesiastical court.

consistorialmente, *adv.* in or by a consistory.

consistorio, *m.* consistory, ecclesiastical court; pontifical senate; in some Spanish towns, the municipal council and the townhouse or town hall.—**c. divino,** tribunal of God.

consocio, *m.* partner, associate; companion, fellow, comrade.

consol, *m.* (Peru) = CONSOLA.

consola, *f.* console, pier table; bracket shelf.

consolable, *a.* consolable, relievable.—**consolablemente,** *adv.* consolably, comfortingly.

consolación, *f.* consolation, comfort; (in some card games) forfeit.

consolado, da. I. *pp.* of CONSOLAR. **II.** *a.* consoled, comforted.

consolador, ra, *n.* & *a.* comforter(-ing), consoler(-ing), soother(-ing).

consolante, *a.* comforting, consoling, soothing.

consolar, *va.* (*ind.* CONSUELO; *subj.* CONSUELE) to console, comfort, cheer, soothe.

consolativo, va; consolatorio, ria, *a.* consolatory, consoling, comforting.

consólida, *f.* (bot.) = CONSUELDA.—**c. real,** larkspur.

consolidación, *f.* consolidation.

consolidado, da, *a.* consolidated; (of debts) funded.—*pl.* consolidated annuities, consols, government securities.

consolidar. I. *va.* to consolidate, compact; to harden, strengthen; to fund (debts). **II.** *vr.* to consolidate, grow firm, hard, or solid; (law) to unite.

consolidativo, va, *a.* consolidant, consolidative.

consonancia, *f.* consonance, harmony, rime; consistency, congruence; consent; conformity.

consonante. I. *m.* riming word, rime; (mus.) consonous or corresponding sound. **II.** *f.* & *a.* (gram.) consonant. **III.** *a.* consonant, consistent, concordant.

consonantemente, *adv.* consonantly, fittingly.

consonar, *vn.* (*ind.* CONSUENO; *subj.* CONSUENE) (mus.) to make harmonious sounds; (poet.) to rime; to agree, harmonize, become, fit.

cónsones, *m. pl.* (mus.) harmonious chord.

cónsono, na, *a.* consonous, harmonious, consonant.

consorcio, *m.* consortium, partnership, society; marital union; friendly intercourse; mutual affection.

consorte, *n.* consort; companion, partner, mate; one who enters or defends an action jointly with another.

conspicuo, cua, *a.* conspicuous; prominent, distinguished.

conspiración, *f.* conspiracy, plot.

conspirado, da; conspirador, ra; conspirante, *n.* & *a.* conspirator(-ing).

conspirar, *vn.* to conspire, plot; to agree together, coöperate, combine.

constancia, *f.* constancy, perseverance; (Am.) record, written evidence.

constante. I. *a.* constant; continual, uninterrupted; firm, unalterable, immutable; loyal, constant; manifest, apparent, clear; composed, consisting. **II.** *f.* & *a.* (math.) constant.

constantemente, *adv.* constantly; firmly, unalterably; evidently, undoubtedly.

constantinopolitano, na, *a.* of or pertaining to Constantinople.

constar, *v. impers.* to be clear, evident, certain (with diff. constr. as *le consta que,* he is certain that); to be recorded, registered; (**de**) to be composed (of), consist (of); (of verses) to have the proper measure and accent.

constatación, *f.* (Gal.) substantiation, verification.

constatar, *va.* (Gal.) to verify, confirm; to record.

constelación, *f.* constellation; climate, temperature; (with **correr**) epidemic.—**una c. corre,** an epidemic is raging.

consternación, *f.* consternation, distress; horror, panic.

consternar, *va.* to terrify, strike with horror or amazement; to cause a panic to or in; to distress, grieve.

constipación, *f.* constipation; cold in the head.

constipado, da. I. *pp.* of CONSTIPAR. II. *a.* suffering from a cold. III. *m.* head cold.

constipante, *a.* constipating, binding.

constipar. I. *va.* to constipate, bind; to cause a cold. II. *vr.* to become costive; to catch cold.

constipativo, va, *a.* = CONSTIPANTE.

constitución, *f.* constitution (in all its meanings); rules and by-laws.

constitucional. I. *m.* constitutionalist. II. *a.* constitutional.

constitucionalidad, *f.* constitutionality.

constitucionalismo, *m.* constitutionalism.

constitucionalmente, *adv.* constitutionally.

constituir. I. *va.* (*ind.* CONSTITUYO; *subj.* CONSTITUYA) to constitute; erect, establish, make, create; appoint, depute. II. *vr.* **constituirse en obligación de,** to bind oneself to perform.

constitutivo, va. I. *a.* constitutive, essential. II. *n.* constituent.

constituyente, *n.* & *a.* constituent.

constituyo, constituya, *v.* V. CONSTITUIR.

constreñidamente, *adv.* compulsively.

constreñimiento, *m.* constraint compulsion.

constreñir, *va.* (*ind.* CONSTRIÑO; *subj.* CONSTRIÑA) to constrain, compel, force; (med.) to bind or make costive; to contract.

constricción, *f.* contraction.

constrictivo, va, *a.* binding, constricting, astringent; compelling, forcing.

constrictor, ra, *a.* constrictor.

constringente, *a.* constringent.

constriño, constriña, *v.* V. CONSTREÑIR.

construcción, *f.* construction; act and art of constructing; architecture; structure; building; (gram.) construction.—**de c.,** *a.* building (as *a.*), structural.

constructor, ra, *n.* builder; maker.—**c. de buques,** shipbuilder.

construir, *va.* (*ind. pres.* CONSTRUYO, *pret.* él CONSTRUYÓ; *subj.* CONSTRUYA) to form, build, construct; to translate literally; (gram.) to construct.

constuprador, *m.* debaucher, defiler, corrupter.

constuprar, *va.* to defile, debauch, corrupt.

consubstanciación, *f.* (theol.) consubstantiation.

consubstancial, *a.* (theol.) consubstantial.

consubstancialidad, *f.* consubstantiality.

consuegrar, *vn.* to become joint fathers- or mothers-in-law.

consuegro, gra, *n.* parent-in-law with respect to the parent of one's son- or daughter-in-law.

consuelda, *f.* (bot.) comfrey.

¹consuelo, *m.* consolation, comfort; joy, merriment.—**sin c.,** (coll.) without stint, to excess.

²consuelo, consuele, *v.* V. CONSOLAR.

consueno, consuene, *v.* V. CONSONAR.

consueta, *n.* stage prompter; (prov.) directory for divine service.—*pl.* short prayers.

consuetudinario, ria, *a.* customary, generally practised; common (law); (theol.) in the habit of sinning.

cónsul, *n.* consul.—**c. general,** consul general.

consulado, *m.* consulate; consulship; tribunal or court of commerce.—**c. general,** consulate general.

consular, *a.* consular.

consulta, *f.* question proposed, or the answer given in writing; consultation, conference; office hours (of a doctor); report made and advice given to the king in council.

consultable, *a.* worthy or necessary to be deliberated upon.

consultación, *f.* consultation, conference, meeting.

consultante, *n.* & *a.* consulter(-ing).

consultar, *va.* to consult, ask advice of; to advise; to deliberate about, discuss.—**c. con la almohada,** (coll.) to sleep on, think over.

consultivo, va, *a.* consultative, conciliary, advisory.

consultor, ra, *n.* & *a.* consulter(-ing), adviser (-ing), counsel, counsellor.

consultorio, *m.* bureau of information; (med.) consulting institution, clinic.

consumación, *f.* consummation, end, completion; destruction, suppression, total extinction.—**c. de los siglos,** end of the world.

consumadamente, *adv.* perfectly, completely, consummately.

consumado, da. I. *pp.* of CONSUMAR. II. *a.* consummate, complete, perfect. III. *m.* jelly broth; consommé.

consumador, ra, *n.* finisher; one who consummates, perfects, or finishes.

consumar, *va.* to consummate, finish, perfect, complete; to commit (a crime).

consumativo, va, *a.* consummate; (of the sacrament) that consummates or completes.

consumido, da, *a.* (coll.) thin, exhausted, emaciated, wasted away; easily afflicted.

consumidor, ra, *n.* & *a.* consumer(-ing); -eating (as **países consumidores de arroz,** rice-eating countries).

consumimiento, *m.* consumption.

consumir. I. *va.* (*pp.* CONSUMIDO and CONSUNTO) to consume; to waste away; to destroy, extirpate; to wear out, exhaust; to afflict, grieve; to take (the Eucharist) in the mass (used also as *vn.*). II. *vr.* to be spent, exhausted, run out; to fret; to be uneasy, vexed; to waste away, pine, languish.—**c. de,** to be consumed by, or with.

consumo, *m.* consumption (of provisions, fuel, merchandise).—*pl.* excise tax.

consunción, *f.* consumption, waste, decline; (med.) consumption, tuberculosis.

consuno, na.—de c., jointly, together, in accord.

consuntivo, va, *a.* consuming.

consunto, ta, *pp. irreg.* of CONSUMIR.

consustanciación, *f.* = CONSUBSTANCIACIÓN.

consustancial, *a.* = CONSUBSTANCIAL.

contabilidad, *f.* bookkeeping, accounting; calculability.

contabilista, *n.* (Am.) bookkeeper, accountant.

contacto, *m.* contact; (elec.) contact; terminal, binding post; (auto) ignition.

contadero, ra. I. *a.* countable, numerable. II. *m.* narrow passage where sheep or cattle are counted.—**entrar,** or **salir, por c.,** to go in or out through a narrow passage.

contado, da. I. *pp.* of CONTAR. II. *a.* scarce, rare, uncommon; few (as *son contadas las personas que,* there are very few people that).—**al c.,** (for) cash.—**de c.,** cash; instantly, immediately; in hand.—**por de c.,** of course, as a matter of course.

contador, ra, *n.* purser, paymaster, cashier; computer; accountant, bookkeeper; numberer; automatic counter; telltale; meter for gas, water, or electricity; cash register, counter; table or bench in a business office, desk; (law) auditor; receiver.—**c. de Geiger,** Geiger counter.

contaduría, *f.* accountant's or auditor's office at the exchequer; auditorship; office of a cashier, paymaster or treasurer; box office, in a theater.

contagiar. I. *va.* to infect, communicate, spread by contagion; to corrupt, pervert. II. *vr.* (de) to become infected (with), take by contagion.

contagio, *m.* contagion; contagious disease; corruption of morals.

contagión, *f.* progressive malignity of a disease, as cancer; propagation of vice and evil habits.

contagiosidad, _f._ contagiousness.

contagioso, sa, _a._ contagious; perverting.

contal, _m._ string of beads for counting.

contaminación, _f._ contamination, pollution; defilement; stain, blot.

contaminado, da. I. _pp._ of CONTAMINAR. **II.** _a._ contaminated, corrupted, polluted.

contaminar, _va._ to contaminate, defile, pollute; pervert, corrupt; to infect by contagion; to corrupt, vitiate, or destroy the integrity of (a text or original); to profane.

contante.—dinero c., or **dinero c. y sonante,** ready money, cash.

contar. I. _va._ (_ind._ CUENTO; _subj._ CUENTE) to count, reckon, number; to relate, tell; to book; to place to account; to class; to rate; to consider, look upon. **II.** _vn._ to compute, figure.—**c. con,** to depend on, rely on; to reckon with, take into account.

contemperar, _va._ to temper, moderate.

contemplación, _f._ contemplation, meditation; compliance, complaisance.

contemplador, ra, _n._ contemplator.

contemplar, _va._ to contemplate, examine, study; to view, behold, look upon; to meditate, muse over; to be lenient or complaisant with; to coddle, overindulge, spoil (a child).

contemplativamente, _adv._ attentively, thoughtfully, contemplatively.

contemplativo, va. I. _a._ contemplative; studious; lenient; complaisant. **II.** _m._ contemplator; pious devotee.

contemporáneamente, _adv._ contemporaneously, simultaneously.

contemporaneidad, _f._ contemporaneousness.

contemporáneo, nea, _n._ & _a._ contemporary, coetaneous, coeval.

contemporicé, contemporice, _v._ V. CONTEMPORIZAR.

contemporización, _f._ temporizing, compliance.

contemporizador, ra, _n._ temporizer; complier.

contemporizar, _vn._ (_pret._ CONTEMPORICÉ; _subj._ CONTEMPORICE) to temporize; to comply; to adapt oneself.

contención, _f._ contention; emulation; contest, dispute, strife.

contencioso, sa, _a._ contentious; quarrelsome, disputatious; (law) being the object of strife or dispute; litigious.

contendedor, _m._ = CONTENDOR.

contender, _vn._ (_ind._ CONTIENDO; _subj._ CONTIENDA) to fight, combat; contend, debate; dispute; litigate; to argue, discuss, expostulate. —**contendiente,** _n._ & _a._ fighter(-ing), disputant, litigant.—**contendor,** _m._ fighter, contender, antagonist, opponent.

contenedor, ra, _n._ holder, tenant.

contenencia, _f._ suspension in the flight of birds; a peculiar movement in Spanish dancing; (law) demurrer.

contener. I. _va._ (_ind. pres._ CONTENGO, _pret._ CONTUVE; _subj._ CONTENGA) to contain, hold; to comprise, include, embrace; to check, curb, restrain, stop. **II.** _vr._ to control oneself, to refrain.

contenido, da. I. _pp._ of CONTENER. **II.** _a._ moderate, prudent, temperate, modest. **III.** _m._ contents; inclosure.

conteniente, _a._ containing, comprising.

contenta, _f._ (com.) indorsement (also ENDOSO); satisfactory treat or present; (mil.) certificate of good conduct; (law) acknowledgment of payment, release.

contentadizo, za, _a._ (sometimes preceded by **bien**) easily pleased.—**mal c.,** hard to please.

contentamiento, _m._ contentment, joy, satisfaction, content.

contentar. I. _va._ to satisfy, gratify, please; (com.) to indorse (also ENDORSAR).—**ser de buen (mal) c.,** to be easy (hard) to please. **II.**

vr. to be contented, satisfied; (Am.) to become reconciled, make up.

contentible, _a._ contemptible.

contentivo, va, _a._ containing, comprising.

contento, ta. I. _a._ glad, pleased, contented, satisfied, content. **II.** _m._ contentment, joy, satisfaction, mirth; (law) release, discharge.—**a c.,** to one's satisfaction.

contera, _f._ shoe (of cane, umbrella, etc.); chape of a scabbard; button of the cascabel of a gun; refrain of a song.—**por c.,** at the end, as a finish.

contérmino, na, _a._ contiguous, abutting.

conterráneo, nea, _n._ countryman(-woman), fellow citizen.

contertuliano, na; contertulio, lia, _a._ belonging to the same social circle, of the same set.

contestable, _a._ contestable, disputable.

contestación, _f._ answer, reply; contestation, the act of contesting; debate, altercation, dispute.

contestar. I. _va._ to answer, reply; to confirm (the deposition of another); to prove; to attest. **II.** _vn._ to agree, to accord.

conteste, _a._ (law) confirming the evidence of another.

contexto, _m._ intertexture; context.

contextuar, _va._ to prove by quoting authorities.

contextura, _f._ contexture, texture; context; frame and structure of the human body.

conticinio, _m._ dead of night.

contienda, _f._ contest, dispute, debate; strife, fray, struggle.

contiendo, contienda, _v._ V. CONTENDER.

contignación, _f._ (arch.) contignation.

contigo, with thee, you (intimate). V. CON.

contiguamente, _adv._ contiguously, closely.

contigüidad, _f._ contiguity, closeness.

contiguo, gua, _a._ contiguous, close, adjacent.

continencia, _f._ continence, self-control; abstinence, moderation; graceful bow in a dance; act of containing.—**c. de la causa,** (law) unity which should exist in every judgment or sentence.

continental, _a._ continental.

continente. I. _m._ continent; container; countenance, mien. **II.** _a._ continent, abstemious, sober, moderate.—**continentemente,** _adv._ moderately, abstemiously, chastely.

contingencia, _f._ contingency, emergency, possibility, risk.

contingente. I. _a._ contingent, accidental. **II.** _m._ contingent, share.—**contingentemente,** _adv._ casually, accidentally, contingently.

contingible, _a._ that may happen, possible.

continuación, _f._ continuation; prolongation, lengthening; continuance, stay.—**a c.,** immediately (afterwards).

continuadamente, _adv._ continuedly.

continuador, ra, _n._ continuer, continuator.

continuamente, _adv._ continually; continuously.

continuar, _va._ & _vn._ to continue, pursue, carry on; to remain, or still be, in the same state, hold; to last, endure; to prolong.

continuativo, va, _a._ continuative.

continuidad, _f._ continuity.

continuo, nua. I. _a._ continuous, uninterrupted; prolonged; continual, constant, lasting; assiduous, steady, persevering; (mech.) endless.—**a la continua,** de _or_ **de continuo,** continually, constantly.—**corriente c.,** (elec.) direct current. **II.** _m._ continuous whole; yeoman of the crown; (math., phil.) continuum.

contonearse, _vr._ to walk with an affected air or manner, to strut.—**contoneo,** _m._ affected gait or manner of walking, strut.

contorcerse, _vr._ (_ind._ CONTUERZO; _subj._ CONTUERZA) to distort, twist one's body, writhe.

contorción, _f._ contortion.

contornado, _a._ (her.) (of animals' heads) turned toward the left side of the shield.

contornar, contornear, *va.* to trace the contour or outline of.—**contorneo,** *m.* = RODEO, a turn (round a place).

contorno, *m.* environs of a place; neighborhood; contour, outline.—**en c.,** round about.

contorsión, *f.* contortion, twist, wry motion, grotesque gesture.

contra. I. *prep.* against, across, athwart, in opposition to, counter, contrary to, opposite to; (in composition, gen.) counter.—**c. viento y marea,** against all odds. **II.** *m.* opposite sense; opposite opinion; pedal of an organ.—*pl.* (mus.) organ pipes forming the lowest bass.— **el pro y el c.,** the pros and cons. **III.** *f.* difficulty, obstacle; counter, in fencing; (Am.) ÑAPA, extra, something thrown in.—**en c., en c. de,** against, in opposition to.—**hacer la c., llevar la c.,** to oppose, to contradict.

contraabertura, *f.* (surg.) contrafissure.

contraábside, *n.* western absis.

contraaletas, *f. pl.* (naut.) counter-fashion pieces.

contraalmirante, *m.* rear admiral.

contraamantillos, *f. pl.* (naut.) preventer lifts, counterbraces.

contraamura, *f.* (naut.) preventer tack.

contraaproches, *m. pl.* (fort.) counterapproaches.

contraarmiños, *m. pl.* (her.) black field and white spots.

contraataque, *m.* (mil.) counter attack.—*pl.* fortified lines of defense.

contraaviso, *m.* counterinformation, counterorder.

contrabajo, *m.* (mus.) contrabass; contrabass viol; contrabassist, contrabasso.

contrabalancear, *va.* to counterbalance, counterpoise.

contrabalanza, *f.* CONTRAPESO, counterweight; counterbalance; CONTRAPOSICIÓN, contrast.

contrabandear, *vn.* to smuggle.

contrabandista, *m.* smuggler, contrabandist.

contrabando, *m.* contraband; smuggling; unlawful action.—**c. de guerra,** contraband of war.—**ir,** or **venir, de c.,** to go, or come, by stealth; to sneak out, or in.

contrabarrado, da, *a.* (her.) counterbarred.

contrabarrera, *f.* inner barrier in a bull ring.

contrabasa, *f.* (arch.) = PEDESTAL, pedestal.

contrabatería, *f.* counterbattery.

contrabatir, *va.* to fire upon (the enemy's artillery).

contrabitas, *f. pl.* (naut.) standards of the bitts.

contrabolina, *f.* (naut.) preventer bowline.

contrabovedilla, *f.* (naut.) second counter, upper counter.

contrabracear, *va.* (naut.) to counterbrace.

contrabraceo, *m.* (naut.) counterbracing.

contrabranque, *m.* (naut.) stemson, apron.

contrabraza, *f.* (naut.) preventer brace.

contrabrazola, *f.* (naut.) headledge.

contracalcar, *va.* to trace from the back, so as to obtain a back view of the original drawing.

contracambiada, *f.* changing of the forefoot by a horse.

contracambio, *m.* (com.) re-exchange; (fig.) = EQUIVALENTE, equivalent; compensation.

contracanal, *m.* counterchannel.

contracandela, *f.* (Am.) back fire, fire made to create a gap between part of a burning field and the rest, in order to prevent the spread of the conflagration.

contracarril, *m.* check rail, guard rail, safety rail; wing rail.

contracción, *f.* contraction, shrinking, shriveling; corrugation; abbreviation; abridgment.

contracebadera, *f.* (naut.) sprit-topsail.

contracédula, *f.* counterdecree.

contracifra, *f.* countercipher.

contraclave, *f.* (arch.) voussoir next to the keystone.

contracodaste interior, *m.* (naut.) inner sternpost.—**c. exterior,** (naut.) back of the sternpost.

contracorriente, *f.* countercurrent, reverse current; stopwater.

contracosta, *f.* coast, shore opposite another.

contráctil, *a.* contractile, contractible.

contractilidad, *f.* contractility, contractibility.

contracto, ta, *pp. irreg.* of CONTRAER.

contractual, *a.* contractual.

contractura, *f.* (med.) contracture.

contracuartelado, da, *a.* (her.) having the quarters opposed in metal or color.

contracuerdas, *f. pl.* (naut.) outward deck planks or platforms.

contracurva, *f.* (Ry.) reversed curve.

contradancista, *m.* leader of a cotillon.

contradanza, *f.* contredanse, quadrille, cotillon.

contradecir, *va.* (*pp.* CONTRADICHO; *ind. pres.* CONTRADIGO, *pret.* CONTRADIJE, *fut.* CONTRADIRÉ; *subj.* CONTRADIGA) to contradict, gainsay.

contradicción, *f.* contradiction; opposition; gainsaying.

contradictor, ra, *n.* contradictor, gainsayer.

contradictoria, *f.* (logic) contradictory.

contradictoriamente, *adv.* contradictorily, inconsistently.

contradictorio, ria, *a.* contradictory.

contradicho, cha, *pp. irreg.* of CONTRADECIR.

contradigo, contradije, contradiga, *v. V.* CONTRADECIR.

contradique, *m.* counterdock, counterdike.

contradriza, *f.* (naut.) second halliard.

contradurmente, contradurmiente, *m.* (naut.) clamp.

contraeje, *m.* countershaft.

contraelectromotriz, *a.* (elec.) counter electromotive.

contraemboscada, *f.* counterambuscade.

contraemergente, *a.* (her.) countersalient.

contraempuñadura, *f.* (naut.) preventer earring.

contraendosar, *va.* to reindorse, indorse back.

contraer. I. *va. & vn.* (*pp.* CONTRAÍDO and CONTRACTO; *ind. pres.* CONTRAIGO, *pret.* CONTRAJE; *subj.* CONTRAIGA) to contract (an obligation); to catch (a disease); to tighten, join, unite; to incur; to acquire; to reduce.—**c. matrimonio,** to marry (get married). **II.** *vr.* to contract, diminish; to shrink.

contraescarpa, *f.* (mil.) counterscarp.

contraescota, *f.* (naut.) preventer sheet.

contraescotín, *m.* (naut.) preventer topsail sheet.

contraescritura, *f.* counterdeed.

contraestay, *m.* (naut.) preventer stay.

contrafajado, da, *a.* (her.) (of shields) having faces opposed in metal or color.

contrafallar, *va.* at cards, to overtrump.

contrafallo, *m.* overtrump at cards.

contrafianza, *f.* indemnity bond.

contrafigura, *f.* person or dummy that imitates a personage in the theater.

contrafilo, *m.* (armor) back edge (near point).

contraflorado, da, *a.* (her.) having flowers opposed in color and metal.

contrafoque, *m.* (naut.) foretop staysail.

contrafoso, *m.* (fort.) avantfosse or outer ditch.

contrafuero, *m.* infringement or violation of a charter or privilege.

contrafuerte, *m.* strap of leather to secure the girths on a saddletree; spur, counterfort (of a mountain); stiffener of a shoe; (fort.) counterfort; (arch.) abutment, buttress, spur.

contragolpe, *m.* (med.) effect of a blow on a part not actually struck; (eng.) back or reverse stroke (of a piston).

contraguardia, *f.* (fort.) counterguard.

contraguía, *f.* in a team, the near or left-hand animal.

contrahacedor, ra, *n.* imitator, impersonator.

contrahacer, *va.* (*pp.* CONTRAHECHO; *ind. pres.* CONTRAHAGO, *pret.* CONTRAHICE; *subj.* CONTRAHAGA) to counterfeit, falsify, forge; to imitate, copy; to pirate (the works of an author); to mimic, impersonate.

contrahaz, *m.* wrong side (of cloth).

contrahecho, cha. I. *pp. irreg.* of CONTRAHACER. **II.** *a.* humpbacked; deformed; counterfeit; spurious.

contrahice, *pret.* of CONTRAHACER.

contrahierba, *f.* (bot.) contrayerva, a South American medicinal plant; antidote.

contrahilera, *f.* line of defense that defends another.

contrahilo, *m.*—**a c.,** across the grain.

contrahoradar, *va.* to bore on the opposite side.

contrahuella, *f.* (arch.) riser of a stair.

contraigo, contraje, etc., *v.* *V.* CONTRAER.

contraindicación, *f.* (med.) contraindication.

contraindicante, *m.* (med.) contraindicant.

contraindicar, *va.* (*pret.* CONTRAINDIQUÉ; *subj.* CONTRAINDIQUE) (med.) to contraindicate.

contralecho, *m.*—**a c.,** (arch.) crossbond.

contralizo, *m.* (weaving) back leash.

contralmirante, *m.* rear admiral.

contralor, *m.* comptroller, inspector.

contraloría, *f.* comptrollership.

contralto, *m.* contralto (voice), *m. & f.* (person).

contraluz, *f.* view (of thing) seen against the light.

contramaestre, *m.* overseer, foreman; (naut.) boatswain.

contramalla, contramalladura, *f.* double net for catching fish.

contramallar, *va.* to make CONTRAMALLAS.

contramandar, *va.* to countermand.

contramangas, *f. pl.* oversleeves.

contramaniobra, *f.* countermanœuvre.

contramarca, *f.* countermark; duty to be paid on goods which have no customhouse mark.

contramarcar, *va.* (*pret.* CONTRAMARQUÉ; *subj.* CONTRAMARQUE) to countermark.

contramarco, *m.* (carp.) counterframe.

contramarcha, *f.* countermarch, retrocession; part of a weaver's loom; (mil. and naut.) evolution.—**de c.,** reverse (lever, etc.).

contramarchar, *vn.* to countermarch; to go backwards.

contramarea, *f.* (naut.) countertide.

contramarqué, contramarque, *v.* *V.* CONTRAMARCAR.

contramesana, *f.* (naut.) mizzenmast.

contramina, *f.* countermine; (min.) driftway, heading.

contraminar, *va.* to countermine.

contramolde, *m.* countermold.

contramotivo, *m.* (mus.) countersubject.

contramuelle, *m.* (mech.) duplicate spring.

contramuralla, *f.,* **contramuro,** *m.* (mil.) countermure, low rampart.

contranatural, *a.* contranatural, unnatural.

contraorden, *f.* countermand.

contrapalanquín, *m.* (naut.) preventer clew garnet.

contrapares, *m. pl.* (arch.) counterrafters.

contrapartida, *f.* (in bookkeeping) emendatory or corrective entry.

contrapás, *m.* a step in dancing.

contrapasamiento, *m.* act and effect of passing to the opposite side or party.

contrapasar, *vn.* to join the opposite party.

contrapaso, *m.* back step; (mus.) second part.

contrapelo.—**a c.,** *adv.* against the grain.

contrapesar, *va.* to counterbalance; to countervail, offset.

contrapeso, *m.* counterweight; counterpoise, counterbalance, countervail; plummet; balancing weight; ropedancer's pole; equipollence, equivalence of power; something thrown in to make up the weight of meat, fish, etc.

contrapeste, *m.* remedy against pestilence or epidemic.

contrapilastra, *f.* (arch.) counterpilaster; (carp.) weatherstrip.

contrapolicía, *f.* police that secretly watches the ordinary police.

contrapóliza, *f.* insurance policy that annuls a previous one.

contraponedor, ra, *n.* one who compares.

contraponer, *va.* (*pp.* CONTRAPUESTO; *ind. pres.* CONTRAPONGO, *pret.* CONTRAPUSE; *subj.* CONTRAPONGA) to oppose; to compare.

contraposición, *f.* contraposition; counterview; contrast.

contrapozo, *m.* (fort.) counterblast.

contrapresión, *f.* back pressure.

contraprincipio, *m.* opposite principle, statement contrary to a principle known as such.

contraproducente, contraproducéntem, *a.* self-defeating, producing the opposite of the desired effect.

contrapromesa, *f.* withdrawal of a promise; promise opposed to another.

contraproposición, *f.* counterproposition.

contrapropósito, *m.* change of purpose; purpose opposed to another.

contraprueba, *f.* (print.) second proof.

contrapuerta, *f.* inner large door after the street door.

contrapuesto, ta, *pp. irreg.* of CONTRAPONER; (a) compared, contrasted (with); opposed (to).

contrapuntante, *n.* counterpoint singer.

contrapuntear. I. *va.* (mus.) to sing in counterpoint; to taunt; to revile. **II.** *vr.* to abuse one another; to wrangle, dispute.

contrapuntista, *m.* (mus.) contrapuntist, one skilled in counterpoint.

contrapunto, *m.* (mus.) counterpoint, harmony.

contrapunzón, *m.* puncheon for driving in a nail; counterpunch; gunsmith's mark on guns.

contrapuse, *pret.* of CONTRAPONER.

contraquerella, *f.* cross-complaint.

contraquilla, *f.* (naut.) false keel.

contrariamente, *adv.* contrarily.

contrariar, *va.* to contradict, oppose, counteract, thwart, run counter to; to disappoint; vex, upset, annoy.

contrariedad, *f.* contrariety, contrariness; opposition, contradiction; disappointment, impediment, obstacle; trouble, vexation.

contrario, ria. I. *a.* contrary, opposite, contradictory; opposed, adverse; abhorrent; unfavorable, antagonistic. **II.** *m.* opponent, antagonist, competitor, rival.—**al c.,** on the contrary.—**de lo c.,** otherwise, if not.—**en c.,** against, in opposition to.—**por el c.,** or **por lo c.,** on the contrary. **III.** *f.*—**llevar la c.,** to contradict; to oppose.

contrarregistro, *m.* control register.

contrarreguera, *f.* lateral drain.

contrarréplica, *f.* rejoinder, reply to an answer; rebutter.

contrarrestar, *va.* to resist, oppose, check; to counteract, offset; to return (a ball).

contrarresto, *m.* check; opposition, contradiction; player who strikes back the ball.

contrarrevolución, *f.* counter-revolution.

contrarrevolucionario, ria, *n. & a.* counterrevolutionist, counter-revolutionary.

contrarriel, *m.* (Ry.) guard rail, wing rail.

contrarroda, *f.* (naut.) stemson.

contrarronda, *f.* (mil.) counterround.

contrarrotura, *f.* (vet.) plaster or poultice applied to fractures or wounds.

contrasalida, *f.* (mil.) countersally.

contrasalva, *f.* (mil.) countersalute.

contraseguro, *m.* a contract by which an underwriter agrees to return to the insured, under specified conditions, all premiums previously paid.

contrasellar, *va.* to counterseal.

contrasello, *m.* counterseal, small seal superimposed on another seal.

contrasentido, *m.* countersense, opposite sense; conclusion contrary to premises; (Gal.) nonsense.

contraseña, *f.* countersign, countermark; (Cuba) check (for hat, baggage, etc.); (mil.) watchword.—**c. de salida,** (theat.) check (to re-admit one who goes out).

contrasol, *m.* sunshade.

contrastable, *a.* contrastable.

contrastar. I. *va.* to contrast, place in opposition, oppose; to resist; contradict; to assay and stamp (metals); **II.** *vn.* to contrast, be different.—**c. bien,** (of colors, etc.) to go well together.—**c. mal,** (of colors, etc.) to clash.

contraste, *m.* contrast; opposition; strife, contest; assayer of the mint; assayer's office; assay; mark of assay; inspector of weights and measures; public office where raw silk is weighed; (naut.) sudden change of the wind, by which it becomes foul or contrary.

contrata, *f.* contract.

contratación, *f.* trade, commerce; enterprise, undertaking; business transaction.

contratante, *n.* & *a.* contractor(-ing).

contratar, *va.* to enter into an agreement about; to contract for; to engage, hire; to make a deal or bargain about.

contratela, *f.* among hunters, second inclosure of canvas to shut up game.

contratiempo, *m.* disappointment; misfortune, mishap.

contratista, *m.* contractor; lessee; patentee; grantee; covenanter.

contrato, *m.* contract.—**c. a la gruesa, or a riesgo marítimo,** respondentia.—**c. aleatorio,** aleatory contract.—**c. consensual,** consensual contract.—**c. de compraventa, or de compra y venta,** contract of bargain and sale.—**c. de locación y conducción,** agreement to let one enjoy the use of property for a price or service.—**c. de retrovendendo,** reversion clause of bargain and sale.—**c. enfitéutico,** emphyteusis.—**c. perfecto,** contract of record.

contratorpedero, *m.* torpedo-boat destroyer.

contratrancaniles, *m. pl.* (naut.) inner waterways.

contratreta, *f.* counterplot.

contratrinchera, *f.* (mil.) countertrench.

contratuerca, *f.* check nut, lock nut.

contravalación, *f.* (mil.) contravallation.

contravalar, *va.* to form a contravallation about.

contravalor, *m.* (com.) countervalue, equivalent.

contravapor, *m.* (steam eng.) back steam.

contravención, *f.* contravention, violation (of a law).

contraveneno, *m.* counterpoison, antidote; precaution taken to avoid some infamy or mischief.

contravenir, *va.* (*ind. pres.* CONTRAVENGO, *pret.* CONTRAVINE; *subj.* CONTRAVENGA) to contravene, transgress, violate; to oppose, obstruct, baffle, countermine.

contraventana, *f.* window shutter.

contraventor, ra, *n.* transgressor, offender.

contravidriera, *f.* storm window.

contravine, *pret.* of CONTRAVENIR.

contravisita, *f.* second visit, made to verify the results of a previous one.

contravoluta, *f.* (arch.) inner volute.

contray, *m.* a sort of fine cloth.

contrayente, *a.* engaged (to be married).

contrecho, cha, *a.* crippled, maimed.

contrete, *m.* (Am.) (naut.) breastshore; crochet; angle iron; stay; gusset, face wheel in watches.

contribución, *f.* contribution; tax, impost.—**c. de sangre,** military service.—**c. territorial,** land tax.

contribuidor, ra, *n.* & *a.* contributor(-ing).

contribuir, *va.* & *vn.* (*ind.* CONTRIBUYO; *subj.* CONTRIBUYA) to contribute; (fig.) to help.

contribulado, da, *a.* grieved, afflicted.

contributario, *m.* contributor, taxpayer.

contribuyente. I. *a.* contributing; contributory. **II.** *n.* contributor; taxpayer.

contribuyo, contribuya, *v. V.* CONTRIBUIR.

contrición, *f.* contrition, compunction, repentance.

contrín, *m.* (P.I.) weight of 0.39 gramme, or 6½ grains.

contrincante, *m.* competitor, rival, opponent.

contristar, *va.* to sadden, grieve.

contrito, ta, *a.* contrite, repentant, penitent.

control, *m.* (Gal.) control, checking, verifying.—**controlar,** *va.* (Gal.) to control, check, verify (esp. in technical lang.).

contróler, *m.* (elec.) controller, esp. on elec. car or locomotive (better COMBINADOR).

controversia, *f.* controversy, debate.

controversista, *m.* controversialist, debater.

controvertible, *a.* controvertible, disputable.

controvertir, *va.* (*ind.* CONTROVIERTO; *subj.* CONTROVIERTA) to controvert, dispute, argue against.

contubernio, *m.* cohabitation, concubinage; base or infamous alliance.

contuerzo, contuerza, *v. V.* CONTORCERSE.

contumacia, *f.* obstinacy, stubbornness; (law) contumacy, non-appearance, contempt of court; default.

contumaz, *a.* obstinate, stubborn; contumacious, disobedient; guilty of contempt of court.

contumazmente, *adv.* contumaciously; obstinately, stubbornly.

contumelia, *f.* contumely, insult, abuse; contumeliousness.

contumeliosamente, *adv.* contumeliously, insultingly.

contumelioso, sa, *a.* contumelious, insulting.

contundente, *a.* (of a weapon or an act) producing contusion; impressing the mind deeply, forceful.

contundir, *va.* to contuse, bruise, pound.

conturbación, *f.* perturbation, uneasiness, anxiety.

conturbado, da. I. *pp.* of CONTURBAR. **II.** *a.* turbulent, troublesome.

conturbador, *m.* perturber, disturber.

conturbar. I. *va.* to perturb, disturb, trouble. **II.** *vr.* to become uneasy, agitated, anxious.

conturbativo, va, *a.* disquieting, disturbing.

contusión, *f.* contusion, bruise.

contuso, sa, *a.* bruised.

contutor, *m.* assistant tutor, fellow tutor.

contuve, *pret.* of CONTENER.

conuco, conusco, *m.* (Am.) patch of ground given to slaves; maize field.

convalecencia, *f.* convalescence.

convalecer, *vn.* (*ind.* CONVALEZCO; *subj.* CONVALEZCA) to recover from sickness; to recover lost prosperity, influence, etc.; (coll.) to come back.—**convaleciente,** *n.* & *a.* convalescent.

convalidar, *va.* (law) to confirm.

convecino, na, *a.* neighboring.

convelerse, *vr.* (med.) to twitch; to be contracted.

convencedor, ra, *n.* & *a.* convincer(-ing).

convencer. I. *va.* (*pp.* CONVENCIDO and CONVICTO; *ind.* CONVENZO; *subj.* CONVENZA) to convince; to prove irrefutably to (a person). **II.** *vr.* to become convinced.

convencible, *a.* convincible.

convencimiento, *m.* conviction, belief; (act of)

convincing.—**en el c. de que,** being convinced that, believing that.

convención, *f.* convention; contract, agreement, pact; conformity.—**convencional,** *a.* conventional.

convencionalismo, *m.* conventionalism, conventionality.

convencionalmente, *adv.* conventionally.

convengo, convenga, *v. V.* CONVENIR.

convenible, *a.* docile, tractable, compliant; (of prices) reasonable, moderate.

convenido, da. I. *pp.* of CONVENIR. **II.** *a.* settled by consent; agreed.

conveniencia, *f.* conformity, congruity, consistence; suitability, fitness; desirability, expedience, advantage; self-interest; agreement, adjustment; employ, service; servant's place in a house or family; convenience, ease.—*pl.* emoluments, perquisites; income, property.

conveniente, *a.* useful, advantageous, good; conformable; fit, suitable; desirable, advisable; expedient, opportune, timely; decent, discreet.—**convenientemente,** *adv.* fitly, appropriately, suitably; expediently.

convenio, *m.* convention, agreement, pact; consent; contrivance.

convenir. I. *vn.* (*ind. pres.* CONVENGO, *pret.* CONVINE; *subj.* CONVENGA) to agree; coincide, cohere; to fit, harmonize, comport, suit; to correspond, belong; to assemble, convene.—**c. en,** to agree to. **II.** *v. impers.* to be to the purpose; (foll. by inf.) to be a good thing to (inf.).—**conviene a saber,** namely, to wit.—**según convenga,** according to circumstances, according to what seems best. **III.** *vr.* to agree, make a deal; to suit one's interests.

conventazo, *m. aug.* large convent.

conventico, illo, ito, *m. dim.* (coll.) tenement inhabited by persons of ill repute.

conventícula, *f.,* **conventículo,** *m.* conventicle.

convento, *m.* convent; monastery; nunnery; community of religious men or women.

conventual. I. *a.* conventual, monastic. **II.** *m.* conventual, a monk; Conventual, a member of the Conventual Franciscan order.—**conventualidad,** *f.* state of living in a convent or monastery; assignment of a monk to a convent.—**conventualmente,** *adv.* monastically.

convenzo, convenza, *v. V.* CONVENCER.

convergencia, *f.* convergence.

convergente, *a.* convergent, converging.

converger, convergir, *vn.* to converge; to agree in opinion.

conversa, *f.* chat, talk.

conversable, *a.* sociable, tractable.

conversación, *f.* conversation, talk; conference; commerce, intercourse, society, company; illicit intercourse.

conversador, ra, *n. & a.* (Am.) talker(-ative); good conversationalist.

conversar, *vn.* to converse, talk; to chat; to live in the company of others; to have social intercourse; (mil.) to change front, wheel.

conversión, *f.* conversion; change, transformation; (rhet.) apostrophe; (mil.) wheel, wheeling.

conversivo, va, *a.* having the power of converting or changing.

converso, sa. I. *pp. irreg.* of CONVERTIR. **II.** *m.* convert; lay brother.

conversón, na, *a.* (Colomb. coll.) garrulous, talkative.

convertibilidad, *f.* convertibility.

convertible. I. *a.* convertible; movable, transferable. **II.** *m.* (auto) convertible.

convertido, da. I. *pp.* of CONVERTIR. **II.** *n. & a.* (one) converted.

convertidor, *m.* (elec., metal.) converter.

convertir. I. *va.* (*pp.* CONVERTIDO and CONVERSO; *ind.* CONVIERTO; *subj.* CONVIERTA) to convert;

reform; change; transform. **II.** *vr.* to be converted, reformed.

convexidad, *f.* convexity.

convexo, xa, *a.* convex.

convicción, *f.* conviction, certainty, certitude.

convicto, ta, *pp. irreg.* of CONVENCER; (law) convicted, guilty.

convictor, *m.* (prov.) boarder; person living in a college without being a member or student.

convictorio, *m.* among the Jesuits, living quarters of students.

convidada, *f.* invitation to drink, treat.

convidado, da. I. *pp.* of CONVIDAR. **II.** *a. & n.* invited (guest).

convidador, ra, *n.* inviter.

convidante, *n.* inviter, one who invites; host.

convidar. I. *va.* to invite; to treat; to allure, entice, induce. **II.** *vr.* to offer one's services spontaneously; to invite oneself, come uninvited.

convierto, convierta, *v. V.* CONVERTIR.

convincente, *a.* convincing; convincible

convincentemente, *adv.* convincingly.

convine, *pret.* of CONVENIR.

convite, *m.* invitation; banquet; treat.

convivencia, *f.* act of living together.

conviviente, *a.* living together.

convivir, *vn.* to live together.

convocación, *f.* convocation, calling.

convocador, ra, *n.* convener, convoker.

convocar, *va.* (*pret.* CONVOQUÉ; *subj.* CONVOQUE) to convene, convoke, call together, summon; to acclaim.

convocatoria, *f.* letter of convocation, edict, summons; notice of meeting.

convocatorio, ria, *a.* that convokes.

convóluto, ta, *a.* convolute.

convoluláceo, cea, *a.* convolvulaceous.

convólvulo, *m.* (zool.) vine inchworm; (bot.) convolvulus.

convoqué, convoque, *v. V.* CONVOCAR.

convoy, *m.* convoy, conduct, escort, guard; property under convoy; (coll.) retinue; railway train.

convoyante, *a.* convoying.

convoyar, *va.* to convoy, escort, guard.

convulsión, *f.* convulsion.

convulsivamente, *adv.* convulsively.

convulsivo, va, *a.* convulsive.

convulso, sa, *a.* convulsed.

conyugal, *a.* conjugal, connubial.

conyugalmente, *adv.* conjugally, matrimonially.

cónyuge, *n.* spouse, husband or wife.

coñac, *m.* cognac, brandy.

cooperación, *f.* coöperation.

cooperador, ra; cooperante, *n. & a.* coöperator (-ing, -ive); contributor(-ing).

cooperar, *vn.* to coöperate.

cooperario, ria, *n. =* COOPERADOR.

cooperativa, *f.* coöperative (ass'n or soc'y).

cooperativamente, *adv.* coöperatively, coöperatingly.

cooperativo, va, *a.* coöperative, coöperating.

coopositor, *m.* one of two candidates for a professorship, etc., to be obtained by competition.

coordenado, a. I. *a.* coördinate. **II.** *f.* (math.) coördinate.—**c. cartesiana,** Cartesian coördinate.—**c. polar,** polar coördinate.

coordinación, *f.* coördination.

coordinadamente, *adv.* coördinately.

coordinado, da. I. *pp.* of COORDINAR. **II.** *a.* = COORDENADO.

coordinamiento, *m. =* COORDINACIÓN.

coordinar, *va.* to coördinate.

copa, *f.* goblet, wineglass, cup; liquid contained in a glass; drink (of liquor); treetop; bower; crown of a hat; brasier, fire pan; roof or vault of an oven or furnace; gill, liquid measure; teacupful; (in cards) a card of heart suit.—**sombrero de c.,** top hat.—*pl.* (cards) hearts; bosses of a bridle.

copada, *f.* (ornith.) = COGUJADA, crested lark.

copado, da, *a.* tufted, abundant in foliage.

copaiba, *f.* (bot.) copaiba.

copal, *m.* copal, a transparent resin.

copaljocol, copaljocote, *m.* a Mexican tree resembling a cherry tree.

copanete, cópano, *m.* an ancient small boat.

copaquira, *f.* (Am.) copperas.

copar, *va.* in monte, to put on a card a sum equal to what there is in the bank; (coll.) to corner; (mil.) to surprise; cut off the retreat of; to corner; to grab.

copartícipe, *n.* participant, copartner.

copayero, *m.* copaiba tree.

copaza, *f.* *aug.* large cup or glass with a stem.

copazo, *m.* *aug.* large fleece of wool; large flake of snow.

copec, *m.* kopeck (Russian coin).

copela, *f.* (metal.) cupel.

copelación, *f.* (metal.) cupellation.

copelar, *va.* (metal.) to cupel.

copépodo. I. *n.* & *a.* (zool.) copepod. **II.** *m. pl.* Copepoda.

copera, *f.* cupboard, sideboard; china closet.

coperillo, *m.* *dim.* little cupbearer.

copernicano, na, *a.* Copernican.

copero, *m.* cupbearer; sideboard, buffet; glass rack.

copeta, *f.* *dim.* small cup or drinking vessel.

copete, *m.* toupee, tuft, pompadour, aigret; forelock of a horse; crownwork of a piece of furniture; top of the shoe that rises over the buckle; top, summit; projecting top or cop of sherbet or ice cream.—**asir la ocasión por el c.,** to profit by, or improve, the opportunity.—**de c.,** or **de alto c.,** of (the) blood, of the nobility; aristocratic, high-rank.—**tener mucho c.,** to put on airs, to be haughty or stuck up.

copetudo, da, *a.* copped, tufted; rising to a top or head; high, lofty.

copey, *m.* an American tree of excellent wood for engraving; bitumen found in Ecuador.

copia, *f.* copiousness, plenty, abundance; fertility; copy (of a letter, picture, person, etc.); "living image" (of another person); imitation; taking up; rate or valuation of tithe; (gram.) list of nouns and verbs, and the cases they govern; (poet.) couple.—**c. verbal,** literal, verbatim copy.

copiador, *m.* copyist, copier, transcriber.—**c. de cartas,** (copying) letter book.

copiante, *n.* copyist; imitator.

copiar, *va.* to copy; to imitate; to mimic, take up; ape; (poet.) to describe, depict.—**c. del natural,** to copy from life.

copilador, *m.* = COMPILADOR, compiler, collector.

copilar, *va.* = COMPILAR, to compile, collect.

copilla, *f.* *dim.* of COPA; cigarlighter.

copín, *m.* in Asturias, a grain measure equal to half a CELEMÍN.

copina, *f.* (Mex.) skin taken off whole.

copinar, *va.* to remove (a skin) entire.

copiosamente, *adv.* copiously, abundantly.

copiosidad, *f.* copiousness, abundance.

copioso, sa, *a.* copious, abundant.

copista. I. *m.* & *f.* copyist, transcriber. **II.** *m.* copying machine.

copita, *f.* *dim.* small glass or cup.

copito, *m.* *dim.* small fleece or flake.

copla, *f.* couplet; popular song, ballad; sarcastic hint or remark; lampoon.

coplear, *vn.* to compose or sing ballads.

copleja, *f.* *dim.* little ballad.

coplero, ra, *n.* ballad seller; poetaster.

coplica, illa, ita, *f.* *dim.* little ballad.

coplista, *n.* = COPLERO, poetaster.

coplón, *m.* *aug.* low, vile poetry (gen. used in the plural, **coplones**).

¹copo, *m.* small bundle of cotton, hemp, flax, or silk, put on the distaff to be spun; snowflake; soap flake; cornering, surprise; grab; (Colomb.) = COPA, treetop.

²copo, *m.* bottom of a purse seine; hauling with a purse seine.

copón, *m.* *aug.* large cup or drinking vessel; ciborium.

coposo, sa, *a.* = COPADO.

copra, *f.* copra, dried kernel of the coconut.

coprolito, *m.* (paleontol.) coprolite; (med.) intestinal calculus.

copropiedad, *f.* joint ownership; property held in common.

copropietario, ia, *n.* joint owner, co-proprietor.

cóptico, ca, *a.* Coptic.

copto, *m.* Coptic, the language of the Copts.

copudo, da, *a.* tufted, bushy, thick-topped (tree).

¹cópula, *f.* joining, coupling two things together; connection; copulation, carnal union; (logic) copula.

²cópula, *f.* = CÚPULA, (arch.) cupola.

copularse, *vr.* to copulate.

copulativamente, *adv.* jointly.

copulativo, va, *a.* joining or uniting together; (gram.) copulative.

coque, *m.* coke.

coqueluche, *f.* (Gal. for TOS FERINA), whooping cough.

¹coquera, *f.* head or handle of a top.

²coquera, *f.* small hollow in a stone.

³coquera, *f.* coke scuttle or box.

⁴coquera, *f.* (Am.) a place for coca.

coquero, *m.* (Am.) dealer in coconuts.

¹coqueta, *f.* feruling (esp. of schoolchildren); small loaf or roll (of bread).

²coqueta, *f.* coquette, flirt.—**coquetamente,** *adv.* coquettishly, flirtatiously.

coquetear, *vn.* to flirt, coquet.

coqueteo, *m.* coquetting, flirting; flirtation.

coquetería, *f.* coquetry; flirtation; affectation.

coquetón, *m.* male flirt, lady-killer.—**coquetonamente,** *adv.* = COQUETAMENTE.

coquimbo, *m.* (Am.) burrowing owl.

coquina, *f.* cockle, an edible bivalve; cockle shell; soft shelly stone.—**coquinero, ra,** *n.* cockleseller.

¹coquito, *m.* *dim.* grimace to amuse children.

²coquito, *m.* turtledove of Mexico.

³coquito, *m.* a tall Chilean palm tree.

coráceo, a, *a.* = CORIÁCEO, leathery.

coracero, *m.* cuirassier; (coll.) poor cigar.

coracilla, *f.* *dim.* small coat of mail.

coracina, *f.* small breastplate.

coracora, *f.* (P.I.) coasting vessel.

coracha, *f.* leather bag.

corachín, *m.* *dim.* small leather bag.

coraje, *m.* courage, bravery; fortitude, mettle; anger, passion.—**corajoso, sa,** *a.* brave, dashing.—**corajudo, da,** *a.* angry, ill-tempered.

¹coral, *m.* coral; (Venez., Colomb.) a white-and-red poisonous snake.—*pl.* string of corals.

²coral, *a.* choral, pert. to choir.

coralero, ra, *n.* worker or dealer in corals.

coralífero, ra, *a.* coral-bearing.

coralillo, *m.* a venomous coral-color snake.

coralina, *f.* coral insect, sea coralline; any sea animal resembling coral.

coralino, na, *a.* coralline, of or resembling coral.

corambre, *f.* hides, skins, dressed or undressed; pelts.—**corambrero,** *m.* dealer in hides and skins.

Corán, *m.* Koran.—**coránico, ca,** *a.* Koranic.

coranvobis, *m.* (coll.) corpulent person strutting about with affected gravity.

coraza, *f.* cuirass, armor plating; shell or carapace of a turtle, etc.; armor (of a vessel, cable, etc.)

coraznada, *f.* pith of a pine tree; fricassee of the hearts of animals.

corazón, *m.* heart; core, pith; love, benevolence,

affection; spirit, courage, will, mind; middle or centre of anything; in a loom, cam.—**c. de un cabo,** (naut.) heart strand.—**anunciar,** or **decir, el c.,** to have a presentiment.—**arrancársele a uno el c.,** to be heartbroken, to bleed at the heart (diff. constr.: *se me arranca el corazón al ver su desgracia,* my heart bleeds at his misfortune).—**de c.,** heartily, sincerely; courageous, enterprising.—**llevar,** or **traer, el c. en la mano,** to wear one's heart upon one's sleeve.—**corazonada,** *f.* impulse of the heart; presentiment, foreboding; (coll.) entrails.—**corazonazo,** *m. aug.* great heart.—**corazoncico, illo, ito,** *m. dim.* little heart; faint-hearted person.—**corazoncillo,** *m.* (bot.) perforated St.-John's-wort.

corbachada, *f.* lash with a CORBACHO.
corbacho, *m.* cowhide whip.
corbata. I. *f.* cravat, necktie; scarf, neckcloth; sash or ribbon badge tied to banners; ribbon, insignia of an order.—**c. de lazo,** or de **mariposa,** bow tie.—**c. de nudo,** four-in-hand tie. **II.** *m.* magistrate not trained in law, so without a vote in certain cases.
corbatería, *f.* necktie shop.
corbatero, ra, *n.* necktie maker or dealer.
corbatín, *m.* cravat, tie; stock.
corbato, *m.* cooler, worm tub of a still.
corbatón, *m.* small knee, bracket.
corbe, *m.* an ancient measure for baskets.
corbeta, *f.* (naut.) corvette.—**c. de guerra,** sloop of war.
corcel, *m.* steady horse, charger.
corcesca, *f.* ancient barbed spear.
corcino, *m.* small deer.
corcova, *f.* hump, crooked back; hunch, protuberance, curvature.
corcovado, da. I. *pp.* of CORCOVAR. **II.** *a.* humpbacked, gibbous; crooked.
corcovar, *va.* to crook.
corcovear, *vn.* (of horse) to cut capers; to buck.
corcoveta, *f. dim.* small hump; (coll.) crookbacked person.
corcovo, *m.* spring, curvet made by a horse on the point of leaping; (coll.) crookedness, wrong step, unfair proceeding.
corcusido, da. I. *pp.* of CORCUSIR. **II.** *a.* clumsily mended or sewed on.
corcusir, *va.* (coll.) to darn clumsily.
¹**corcha,** *f.* cork bark; wine cooler.
²**corcha,** *f.* (naut.) laying of a rope.
corchar. I. *va.* (naut.) to lay (strands of ropes); to accept (a challenge). **II.** *vn.* (Colomb.) not to pass an examination, "flunk."
corche, *m.* cork-soled sandal or clog.
corchea, *f.* (mus.) quaver, an eighth note.
corchear, *va.* to grain (leather) with a cork.
corchera, *f.* wine cooler made of cork.
corcheta, *f.* eye of a hook or clasp; (carp.) rabbet in a door or window frame.
corchete, *m.* clasp, hook, hook and eye (*pl.* **corchetes,** hooks and eyes); crotch; snaplock, catch; (coll.) constable; brace to connect lines in writing or printing (⁓⁓); (carp.) bench hook.
corcho, *m.* cork; bark of the cork tree; wine cooler; beehive; cork box for carrying eatables; cork mat; cork-soled sandal or clog; float of a fishing line; (mil.) tampion.
corchoso, sa, *a.* corklike.
corda, *f.*—**estar a la c.,** (naut.) to be close-hauled or lying to.
cordaje, *m.* rigging; cordage.
¹**cordal,** *m.* string bar at the bottom of stringed instruments.
²**cordal,** *a. & f.* = MUELA C., double tooth; wisdom tooth.—*pl.* grinders.
cordato, ta, *a.* prudent, discreet, judicious.
cordel, *m.* cord, thin rope; (naut.) line; length of five steps; land measure in Cuba equal to about 1 sq. ch.—**c. de corredera,** log line.—**a c.,** in

a straight line.—**cordelado, da,** *a.* twisted silk for ribbons or garters.—**cordelazo,** *m.* stroke or lash with a rope.—**cordelejo,** *m. dim.* small rope; fun, jest.—**dar c.,** to banter.
cordelería, *f.* cordage; ropewalk; (naut.) rigging.
cordelero, ra, *n.* ropemaker, cordmaker.
cordelito, *m. dim.* small rope, cord, or line.
cordellate, *m.* grosgrain, a kind of ribbed fabric.
cordera, *f.* ewe lamb; meek, gentle woman.
cordería, *f.* cordage; place where cordage is kept.
corderica, illa, ita, *f. dim.* little ewe lamb.
corderico, illo, ito, *m. dim.* little lamb.
corderillo, *m.* lambskin dressed with the fleece.
corderina, *f.* lambskin.
corderino, na, *a.* pertaining to lambs.
cordero, *m.* lamb; dressed lambskin; meek, gentle, or mild man.—**c. añal,** yearling lamb. —**c. de Dios,** Lamb of God (Christ).—**c. pascual,** paschal lamb.—**c. recental,** suckling lamb.
corderuela, *f. dim.* little ewe lamb.
corderuelo, *m. dim.* little or young lamb.
corderuna, *f.* lambskin.
cordeta, *f.* small bassweed rope.
cordezuela, *f. dim.* small rope.
cordíaco, ca, *a.* (med.) = CARDÍACO, cardiac.
cordial. I. *a.* cordial, hearty; sincere; invigorating. **II.** *m.* cordial; tonic.
cordialidad, *f.* cordiality, heartiness, sincerity.
cordialmente, *adv.* cordially, sincerely, affectionately, heartily.
cordiforme, *a.* heart-shaped.
cordila, *f.* spawn of tunny fish.
cordilo, *m.* an amphibious animal resembling a crocodile.
cordilla, *f.* guts of sheep given to cats to eat.
cordillera, *f.* cordillera, mountain range.
cordita, *f.* cordite (explosive).
corditis, *f.* inflammation of the vocal cords.
cordobán, *m.* cordovan, Spanish leather; tanned goatskin.—**cordobana,** *f.* nakedness, nudity.— **andar a la c.,** (coll.) to go stark naked.
cordobanero, ra, *n.* cordovan tanner.
cordobés, sa, *f.* of or pertaining to Cordova.
cordón, *m.* cord, round cord, twine; (shoe) lace; monk's rope belt; (mil.) cordon; strand of a "cable or rope; (arch.) torus molding; string course; milled edge of a coin.—*pl.* (mil.) aglets or aiguillettes; harness cords of a velvet loom. —**c. umbilical,** umbilical cord.
cordonazo, *m. aug.* large cord; blow with a cord or rope.—**c. de San Francisco,** first equinoctial storm in the autumn.
cordoncico, illo, ito, *m. dim.* small cord.
cordoncillo, *m.* twisted cord; round lace, lacing, braid; milling on edge of a coin.
cordonería, *f.* work of twisters or lace makers; lace maker's shop.
cordonero, ra, *n.* lace maker; ropemaker.
cordula, *f.* = CORDILO.
cordura, *f.* prudence, practical wisdom, sanity.
corea, *f.* dance accompanied by a chorus; (med.) chorea, St. Vitus's dance.
corear, *vn.* to compose chorus music.
corecico, illo, *m. dim.* of CUERO, pelt.
¹**coreo,** *m.* foot in Latin verse; trochee.
²**coreo,** *m.* connected harmony of a chorus.
coreografía, *f.* art of dancing; choreography, writing dance music.
coreográfico, ca, *a.* choreographic.
coreógrafo, *m.* choreograph.
corezuelo, *m. dim.* small hide; suckling pig; small roasted pig.
cori, *m.* (bot.) Montpellier coris, St.-John's-wort.
coriáceo, a, *a.* coriaceous, leathery.
coriámbico, ca, *n. & a.*; **coriambo,** *m.* (poet.) choriambic, foot of two short between two long syllables.
coriandro, *m.* (bot.) coriander.
coribante, *m.* Corybantes, priest of Cybele.

coribantismo, *m.* corybantiasm, a kind of frenzy accompanied by many contortions.

corifeo, *m.* coryphæus, leader of anc. dramatic chorus; leader or member of a sect or party.

corimbo, *m.* (bot.) corymb.

corindón, *m.* corundum.

corintio, tia, *n. & a.* Corinthian.

corión, *m.* (zool.) chorion.

corista, *n.* chorister, chorus singer.

corito, ta. I. *a.* naked; timid, pusillanimous. **II.** *n.* person who treads grapes in the wine press.

¹coriza, *f.* leather sandal worn by peasants in some parts of Spain.

²coriza, *f.* (med.) coryza, head-cold.

corladura, *f.* gold varnish.

corlar, corlear, *va.* to cover with gold varnish.

corma, *f.* (restraining) stocks; trouble, uneasiness.

cornac, cornaca, *m.* keeper of tame elephants.

cornada, *f.* thrust with the horns; upward thrust with a foil, in fencing.

cornadillo, *m. dim.* small coin.

cornado, *m.* old copper coin mixed with silver.

cornadura, *f.* = CORNAMENTA.

cornal, *m.* strap or thong with which oxen are tied to the yoke by the horns.

cornalina, *f.* (min.) cornelian, carnelian.

cornamenta, *f.* the horns of any animal.

cornamusa, *f.* cornemuse, a bagpipe; (mus.) a sort of brass horn; (naut.) belaying cleat.

cornatillo, *m.* a kind of olive.

córnea, *f.* (anat.) cornea.—**c. opaca,** sclera.

corneador, ra, *n. & a.* butting (animal).

cornear, *va.* = ACORNEAR, to butt.

cornecico, illo, ito, *m. dim.* cornicle, small horn.

corneja, *f.* (ornith.) crow; fetlock; dow.

cornejal, *m.* dogwood field.

cornejalejo, *m.* (bot.) pod.

cornejo, *m.* (bot.) hound tree or cornel tree, dogwood.

cornelina, *f.* = CORNALINA.

córneo, a. I. *a.* horny, callous; (bot.) cornaceous. **II.** *f. pl.* (bot.) Cornaceae.

cornerina, *f.* = CORNALINA.

cornero, *m.*—**c. de pan,** crust (of bread).

corneta. I. *f.* bugle; horn used by swineherds; cornet, ensign of horse; flag carried by horse troops; troop of horse; (naut.) broad pennant; rear admiral's flag.—**c. de llaves,** cornet.—**c. de monte,** huntsman's horn.—**c. de posta,** post's horn. **II.** *n.* bugler.

cornete, *m. dim.* small bugle horn.

cornetín, *m.* cornet; cornettist.

cornezuelo, *m.* ergot of rye; (vet.) instrument for bleeding horses; (bot.) CORNICABRA.

corniabierto, ta, *a.* having wide-spread horns.

cornial, *a.* horn-shaped.

corniapretado, da, *a.* having horns close-set.

cornicabra, *f.* (bot.) turpentine tree, pistachio tree, wild fig tree; a kind of crescent olive.

cornidelantero, ra, *a.* (Mex.) with horns turned forward.

corniforme, *a.* horn-shaped.

cornigacho, cha, *a.* having the horns turned slightly downward.

cornígero, ra, *a.* (poet.) horned, cornigerous.

cornija, *f.* (arch.) = CORNISA.

cornijal, *m.* angle or corner of a mattress, building, etc.

cornijamento, cornijamiento, *m.* (arch.) = CORNISAMENTO.

cornijón, *m.* (arch.) entablature; street corner of a building.

cornil, *m.* = CORNAL.

corniola, *f.* = CORNALINA.

cornisa, *f.* (arch.) cornice.—**cornisamento, cornisamiento,** *m.* (arch.) entablature.

cornisica, illa, ita, *f. dim.* small cornice.

cornisón, *m.* = CORNIJÓN.

corniveleto, ta, *a.* having horns turned strongly upward.

cornizo, corno, *m.* = CORNEJO.

cornucopia, *f.* cornucopia; sconce; pier glass.

cornudo, da. I. *a.* horned. **II.** *m.* cuckold.

cornúpeta, *a.* (poet.) attacking with the horns.

¹coro, *m.* choir; chorus; singing chorus; assembly unanimous in sentiment; choir loft; choir of angels.—**hablar a coros,** to speak alternately. —**hacer c. a,** to follow, support; to play second fiddle to.

²coro, *m.* memory.—**de c.,** from memory, by rote.

¹corocha, *f.* an ancient loose coat.

²corocha, *f.* vine fretter or vine grub.

corografía, *f.* chorography.

corográficamente, *adv.* chorographically.

corográfico, ca, *a.* chorographical.

corógrafo, fa, *n.* chorographer.

coroideo, a, *a.* (anat.) choroid.

coroides, *f.* (anat.) choroid, choroid coat of the eye.

corojo, *m.* a tropical palm bearing an oily nut; the nut itself.

corola, *f.* (bot.) corolla.

corolario, *m.* corollary.

corolífloro, ra. I. *a.* (bot.) corollifloral. **II.** *f. pl.* Corollifloræ.

corología, *f.* chorology, science of the distribution of organisms on the earth's surface.

corona, *f.* crown; wreath, garland; halo, aureola; coronet; top of the head; clerical tonsure; an old Spanish gold-and-silver coin; crown, English silver coin; Portuguese coin; reward, distinction, honor; splendor, ornament, decoration; end or crowning of a work; glory, triumph; rosary of seven decades; (astr.) corona; (naut.) pendant; (bot.) corona, crown; (mil.) crownwork; (arch.) corona, crown; (vet.) pastern of horses.—**C. austral,** (astr.) Corona Australis. —**C. boreal,** Corona Borealis.—**c. circular,** (geom.) circular ring, space between two concentric circles.—**c. de casco,** skin surrounding the top of hoof.—**c. de fraile,** three-toothed globularia.—**c. de rey,** (bot.) melilot.—**c. mural,** mural crown.—**c. real,** (bot.) annual sunflower.

coronación, *f.* coronation; crowning, completion; (arch.) crown.

coronado, *m.* tonsured Catholic clergyman.

coronador, ra, *n.* crowner, finisher.

coronal. I. *m.* (anat.) frontal bone. **II.** *a.* frontal; pert. to frontal bone or forehead.

coronamiento, *m.* end of a work; (arch.) top ornament; capping; (naut.) taffrail.

coronar, *va.* to crown; to cap, to top; to complete, perfect; to decorate the top of; to crowd on a roof or on the top of a hill.

coronaria, *f.* crown wheel of a watch.

coronario, ria, *a.* (anat.) coronary; (bot.) coronary; extremely refined (gold).

corondel, *m.* (print.) column rule; reglet; watermark in paper.

¹coronel, *m.* (arch.) top molding; (her.) crown.

²coronel, *m.* colonel.—**coronela. I.** *f.* colonel's wife. **II.** *a.* applied to the company, flag, etc., supposed to belong to the colonel of a regiment. —**coronelato,** (Am.) *m.*, **coronelía,** *f.* colonelship.

coronilla, *f. dim.* small crown; top of the head; cock's comb; cap; chaplet; ear of a bell; (bot.) coronilla.—**c. de fraile,** French daisy.—**c. de rey,** nine-leaved coronilla.—**c. juncal,** rush coronilla.

corotos, *m. pl.* (Am.) belongings; outfit.

coroza, *f.* cone hood of pasteboard worn as a mark of infamy; straw cape or cloak worn by farmers.

corozal, *m.* field or plantation of COROZO.

corozo, *m.* = COROJO, tropical palm.

corpanchón, corpazo, *m. aug.* very big body or carcass.—**c. de ave,** carcass of a fowl.

corpecico, illo, ito; corpezuelo, *m. dim.* little or small body, or carcass; underdoublet; waist; corset cover.

corpiño, corpiñejo, *m. dim.* = CORPECICO.

corporación, *f.* corporation, guild; community; institution, organization.

corporal. I. *a.* corporal, bodily, pert. to the body. **II.** *m.* (eccl.) corporal cloth.—**corporalidad,** *f.* corporality; any corporeal substance.—**corporalmente,** *adv.* corporally, bodily.

corporativo, va, *a.* corporate.

corpóreo, rea, *a.* corporeal, corporeous.

corpudo, da, *a.* corpulent, bulky.

corpulencia, *f.* corpulence, corpulency.

corpulento, ta, *a.* corpulent, fleshy, fat.

Corpus, *m.* Corpus Christi, religious festival and procession.

corpuscular, *a.* corpuscular; (philos.) atomistic.

corpusculista, *n.* (philos.) atomist.

corpúsculo, *m.* corpuscle.

corpus delicti, (law) corpus delicti.

corral, *m.* corral; yard; poultry yard; fold, stockyard; fishpond; ancient playhouse; blank left by students in writing the lectures.—**c. de madera,** timber yard.—**c. de vacas,** mean hovel, (fig.) pigsty.—**c. de vecindad,** tenement house.—**aves de c.,** domestic fowl.

corralera, *f.* an Andalusian song and dance; brazen-faced, impudent woman.

corralero, *m.* keeper of a dung yard.

corralillo, ito, *m. dim.* small corral or yard.

corraliza, *f.* yard, corral, court.

corralón, *m. aug.* large corral or yard.

correa, *f.* leather strap; tether, leash; toughness, flexibility; (mech.) belt, belting; hand strap.— *pl.* duster made of straps.—**c. de zapatos,** shoe string, lace, latchet.—**besar la c.,** (coll.) to be obliged to humble oneself to another.— **tener c.,** to bear wit or raillery without irritation; to be strong and hardy.—**correaje,** *m.* heap of leather straps or thongs; belting.— **correal,** *m.* reddish dressed deerskin.—**correar,** *va.* to draw out (wool) and prepare for use.—**correazo,** *m.* blow with a strap.

correcalles, *n.* loiterer.

corrección, *f.* correction; adjustment (of an instrument); correctness; proper demeanor; decorum.

correccional, *a.* correctional, corrective.

correccionalismo, *m.* system of eliminating criminal tendencies by education and correctional treatment in adequate institutions.

correccionalista, *n.* follower of, or believer in, CORRECCIONALISMO.

correccionalmente, *adv.* correctively.

correctamente, *adv.* correctly.

correctivo, va. I. *a.* corrective. **II.** *m.* corrective, corrective agent or measure.

correcto, ta, *a.* correct; conformable to the rules; irreproachable.

corrector, *m.* corrector, amender; (print.) proofreader; superior, or abbot, in the convent of St. Francis of Paula.

corredentor, ra, *n.* one who redeems from captivity jointly with another.

corredera, *f.* race ground; small wicket or back door; runner or upper grinding stone in a corn mill; street; procuress; (naut.) log or log line; roller, metal cylinder for rolling plate glass; cockroach; (steam eng.) slide valve; (print.) track, slide, rail; (mech.) tongue, rail, guide (of piston rod, etc.), runner; (mint) milling machine.—**c. de aire,** (aer.) air log.

corredizo, za, *a.* running; sliding; easy to be untied, like a running knot.

corredor, ra. I. *m.* runner; race horse; corridor, gallery; porch; (fort.) covert way; (mil.) scout, forerunner; broker; (Am.) travelling salesman.

—**c. de aduana,** customhouse broker.—**c. de cambios, or de oreja,** exchange broker; (coll.) talebearer; procurer, procuress. **II.** *a.* running; (zool.) ratite, flightless, non-flying (birds that do not fly, like the ostrich). **III.** *f. pl.* (zool.) Ratitæ, flightless birds.—**corredorcillo,** *m. dim.* small corridor; petty broker.

corredura, *f.* overflow (of liquid).

correduría, *f.* broker's office; brokerage.

correería, *f.* trade and shop of a strap maker.

correero, ra, *n.* strap maker or seller.

corregencia, *f.* co-regency.

corregente, *m.* co-regent.

corregibilidad, *f.* corrigibility.

corregible, *a.* corrigible.

corregidor, *m.* corrector; corregidor, Sp. magistrate; mayor.—**corregidora,** *f.* CORREGIDOR'S wife.

corregimiento, *m.* office or district of a CORREGIDOR.

corregir. I. *va.* (*ind.* CORRIJO; *subj.* CORRIJA) to correct; to adjust (an instrument); to remove, destroy; remedy; to reprehend, admonish; to punish; to temper, mitigate.—**c. el cuerpo,** (coll.) to go to stool.—**c. pruebas,** (print.) to read proofs. **II.** *vr.* to mend, reform.

corregüela, correhüela, *f. dim.* small strap; child's play with stick and strap; (bot.) bindweed.

correinante, *a.* reigning jointly with another.

correjel, *m.* sole leather.

correlación, correlation.—correlacionar, *va.* to correlate.

correlativamente, *adv.* correlatively.

correlativo, va, *a.* correlative.

correligionario, ia, *a. & n.* (person) of the same religion or political views.

correncia, *f.* (coll.) looseness, diarrhœa.

correndilla, *f.* (coll.) short run.

correntía, *f.* artificial irrigation of stubbly ground.

correntiar, *va.* to irrigate (stubble ground).

correntío, tía, *a.* current; (of liquids) running; (coll.) light, free, unembarrassed.

correntón, na. I. *n.* gadder, man about town. **II.** *a.* gay, pleasant, cheerful.

correntoso, sa, *a.* (Am.) (of streams) swift, rapid, having a strong current.

¹**correo,** *m.* (law) accomplice.

²**correo,** *m.* post, mail; courier; letter carrier; post office.—**c. aéreo,** airmail.—**c. certificado,** registered mail.—**c. marítimo,** packet boat. —**echar al correo,** to post, mail.—**lista de correos,** general delivery.

correón, *m. aug.* large leather strap.

correoso, sa, *a.* flexible, easily bent; (of food) tough, leathery.

correr. I. *vn.* to run; to race; to flow; (of wind) to blow; to pass away; to take the proper course; to extend, expand; to arrive; become due; to go on, continue; to prevail, be current or common; to pass, be accepted or admitted, be current; to be said; be common talk; (followed by **con**) to charge oneself with a matter, take care of.—**c. a cargo de,** to be the concern of.—**c. a rienda suelta,** to ride full speed; to give loose rein to passion.—**c. a uno,** to be one's concern, to be incumbent on one.— **c. la voz,** to be reported, to be said or rumored. —**c. por cuenta de uno,** to be one's affair, be "up to" one.—**a más c., a todo c.,** at full speed; swiftly.—**el que menos corre, vuela,** artful unconcern succeeds quickest. **II.** *va.* to cause to run or move swiftly; to race (a horse); to pursue; to move, push, draw aside, draw, slide; to meet with; to go over, travel; to sell at auction; (coll.) to snatch away; to disconcert, rattle, make blush.—**c. baquetas,** to run the gantlet.—**c. el gallo,** (Mex.) to pass the night carousing in the streets.—**correrla,** to go on a spree.—**c. la cortina**, to draw the curtain; to discover anything; to conceal, quash. —**c. monte**, to go hunting.—**c. mundo**, to travel.—**c. un velo**, to draw a veil. III. *vr.* to file right or left; to slide, go through easily; to slide, slip; to spread itself; to melt, run out, run over; (coll.) to be very generous; to become confused; to run away, to flee.

correría, *f.* hostile incursion, foray, raid; pleasure trip, excursion.—*pl.* youthful escapades.

correspondencia, *f.* correspondence, relation, fitness, agreement; commerce, intercourse; correspondence (mail, writing); friendship, interchange; consent.—**en justa c.**, in retaliation, to get even.

corresponder. I. *vn.* (a) to return (a favor, love); to match, correspond; respond (to); fit, suit; pertain (to); to regard, concern; to agree. II. *vr.* to correspond, keep up intercourse by mail; to respect or esteem each other.

correspondiente. I. *a.* corresponding, respective; conformable, agreeable, suitable. II. *m.* correspondent.

correspondientemente, *adv.* correspondingly.

corresponsal, *m.* correspondent; agent; corresponding clerk.—**c. de prensa**, newspaper correspondent.

corretaje, *m.* brokerage.

corretear, *vn.* to walk the streets, rove, ramble.

corretora, *f.* nun who directs the choir.

correvedile, correveidile, *m.* (coll.) talebearer; mischief maker; procurer, go-between.

correverás, *m.* spring or mechanical toy.

corrida, *f.* course, run, sprint, race; career; row, series; (Am.) (min.) bearing or direction of a lode; (Am.) (min.) outcrop; (aer.) taxying.—**c. de toros**, bull baiting, bullfight.—**de c.**, at full speed, swiftly; in haste; fast, without stopping.

corridamente, *adv.* currently, plainly; easily.

corrido, da. I. *pp.* of CORRER. II. *a.* exceeding in weight or measure; expert, experienced; abashed, confused, ashamed; continuous, unbroken.—**comida c.**, (Am.) table d'hôte.—**de c.** = DE CORRIDA. III. *m.* shed along the walls of a corral.

corriente. I. *a.* current; running; flowing; present (month or year), instant; plain, easy; generally received, admitted; ordinary, common, general; regular, standard; fluent (app. to style); marketable, merchantable; correct, acceptable.—**al c.**, posted, informed; punctually. II. *f.* current (of a river, of electricity, etc.); tendency; course.—**c. alterna**, or **alternativa**, alternating current.—**c. avatia**, or **devatiada**, (elec.) wattless current.—**c. continua**, (elec.) direct current.—**c. de aire**, draught (of air).—**c. del Golfo**, Gulf Stream. —**c. y moliente**, commonplace.—**contra la c.**, against the tide (fig.).—**dejarse llevar de la c.**, to follow the current, follow the crowd. III. *adv.* all right.

corrientemente, *adv.* currently.

corrigendo, da, *n.* inmate of a reformatory.

corrijo, corrija, *v. V.* CORREGIR.

corrillero, *m.* idler, lounger, loafer.

corrillo, *m.* group of talkers (gen. app. to gossips or loungers).

corrimiento, *m.* act of running; melting; (med.) running sore; gumboil; landslide; shyness.

corrincho, *m.* meeting of low, vulgar people.

corrivación, *f.* impounding of brooks and streams.

corro, *m.* group of gossipers or spectators; circular space.—**hacer c.**, to clear the way.

corroboración, *f.* corroboration.

corroborante, *n. & a.* corroborator(-ing, -ive).

corroborar, *va.* to corroborate.

corroborativo, va, *a.* corroborative.

corrobra, *f.* treat to close a bargain. Also ROBRA.

corroer, *va.* to corrode.

corrompedor, ra, *n. & a.* corrupter(-ing).

corromper. I. *va.* (*pp.* CORROMPIDO and CORRUPTO) to corrupt; vitiate, mar; seduce, debauch; to bribe. II. *vn.* to stink. III. *vr.* to rot, get putrid; to become corrupt(ed).

corrompidamente, *adv.* corruptly.

corrompido, da. I. *pp.* of CORROMPER. II. *a.* corrupt; spoiled, unsound; depraved, degenerate.

corrosible, *a.* corrosible.

corrosión, *f.* corrosion.

corrosivo, va, *a.* corrosive.

corroyente, *a.* corroding, corrosive; abrasive.

corroyera, *f.* a kind of sumac used in tanning.

corrugación, *f.* corrugation, contraction into wrinkles.

corrugado, da, *a.* corrugated.

corrugador, m. (anat.) corrugator.

corrulla, *f.* (naut.) room under deck in a row galley.

corrumpente, *a.* corrupting, vitiating; (coll.) teasing, vexatious, wayward.

corrupción, *f.* corruption, putrefaction; decay; pollution, filth; stench; corruptness; perversion, distortion (of a writing); depravity, immorality.

corruptamente, *adv.* corruptly.

corruptela, *f.* corruption; depravation, corruptness; (law) bad habit or practice contrary to law; abuse.

corruptibilidad, *f.* corruptibility.

corruptible, *a.* corruptible.

corruptivo, va, *a.* corruptive.

corrupto, ta. I. *pp. irreg.* of CORROMPER. II. *a.* corrupt.

corruptor, ra, *n. & a.* corrupter(-ing).

corrusco, *m.* (coll.) broken or dried bread.

corsario, ria, *n. & a.* privateer; corsair, pirate.

corsé, *m.* corset.

corsear, *vn.* to cruise against the enemy.

corsetería, *f.* corset factory or shop.

corsetero, ra, *n.* corset maker or dealer.

¹corso, *m.* privateering.—**a c.**, posthaste, with post horses.

²corso, sa, *n. & a.* Corsican.

corta, *f.* felling of wood; cutting.

cortabolsas, *n.* (coll.) pickpocket, filcher.

cortacallos, *m.* corn cutter.

cortacigarros, *m.* cigar cutter.

cortacircuitos, *m.* (elec.) circuit breaker.

cortada, *f.* (Am.) cut, slash, gash.

cortadera, *f.* chisel for cutting hot iron; knife used by beekeepers.

cortadero, ra, *a.* cutting readily; easily cut.

cortadillo, *m.* small drinking glass; a liquid measure, about a gill; clipped piece of money. —**echar cortadillos**, to speak in an affected manner; to drink wine.

cortado, da. I. *pp.* of CORTAR. II. *a.* adapted, proportioned, fit, exact; (of hands) chapped; (her.) parted in the middle; confused, abashed; written in short sentences; (Chile, Arg.) short of funds. III. *m.* (dance) caper, cabriole.

cortador, ra. I. *n.* (tailoring, boot-making, etc.) cutter; that which, or one who, cuts; splitter. II. *m.* butcher; slicing machine, cutter; (tel.) interrupter; (zool.) scissorbill.—*pl.* incisor teeth. III. *f.* cutting board in a velvet loom.

cortadura, *f.* cut; cutting, incision; slit, slash; (fort.) parapet with embrasures and merlons; work raised in narrow passes.—*pl.* shreds.

cortafrío, *m.* cold chisel; cutting iron.

cortafuego, *m.* (agr.) clear space to prevent fire from spreading; (arch.) fire wall.

cortalápices, cortalápiz, *m.* pencil sharpener.

cortamente, *adv.* sparingly, scantily; curtly.

cortante. I. *a.* cutting, sharp. II. *m.* butcher.

cortapapel, *m.* paper cutter, paper knife.

cortapiés, *m.* (coll.) thrust at the legs in fencing.

cortapisa, *f.* obstacle, hindrance; elegance and grace in speaking; restriction with which a thing is given, "strings."

cortaplumas, *m.* penknife, pocketknife.

cortapuros, *m.* cigar cutter.

cortar. I. *va.* to cut, cup up, cut off, cut out; curtail; to disjoin, separate, hew, cleave, chop, hack, carve, fell; whittle; to shut or cut off (steam, water, etc.); dock; pare, prune; interrupt, stop, cut short; to abridge; to take a short cut; to suspend, restrain, keep back; to pronounce or enunciate; to read; to arbitrate or decide; (Am.) to speak ill of, criticize.—**c. a uno,** (fig.) to put one to the blush.—**c. la corriente,** (elec.) to break the circuit, cut off the current. **II.** *vr.* to be daunted, ashamed, confused; to curdle; to chap; to fret; to fray; (geom.) to intersect, cut each other.

cortavapor, *m.* cut-off of a steam engine.

cortavidrios, *m.* glazier's diamond.

cortaviento, *m.* windshield.

¹corte, *m.* cutting edge; cutting; cut; felling of trees; arbitration, compromise or settlement; measure, expedient, step; notch, hack, slot; in tailoring, cut, fit, also length (of material) necessary for a garment (*un corte de chaleco,* length for a vest; *un corte de pantalón,* length for a pair of trousers; *un corte de vestido,* a dress length); edge of a book; (min.) shaft; cross opening; (in drawing) section, sectional view.

²corte, *f.* (royal) court; city where the court resides (*la C.,* in Spain, Madrid); (Am.) (law) court; levee; retinue, suite; yard; courtship; civility, politeness; stable for cattle; sheepfold; ancient tribunal of chancery.—*pl.* Cortes, Spanish parliament.—**c. celestial,** heaven.—**c. suprema,** Supreme Court.

cortedad, *f.* smallness, littleness, minuteness; dulness, stupidity; pusillanimity; timidity, bashfulness.—**c. de medios,** poverty, indigence.

cortejador, *m.* suitor; wooer.

cortejante. I. *a.* courting. **II.** *m.* gallant, beau.

cortejar, *va.* to accompany, escort, attend; to court, woo, make love to.

cortejo, *m.* court; homage paid to another; courtship; gift, present; gallant, beau; lover, sweetheart; paramour.

cortés, *a.* courteous, civil, gracious, polite.

cortesanamente, *adv.* courteously, politely.

cortesanazo, za, *a. aug.* awkwardly or fulsomely polite.

cortesanía, *f.* courtesy, civility, politeness.

cortesano, na. I. *a.* courtlike; courteous, obliging; courtly. **II.** *n.* courtier.

cortesía, *f.* courtesy; civility or courteousness; compliment; attention; gift, present; days of grace for payment; mercy, favor.

cortésmente, *adv.* courteously, politely.

¹corteza, *f.* bark of a tree; peel, skin, rind; crust of bread, pies, etc.; outward appearance; rusticity, want of politeness, crustiness.

²corteza, *f.* wild fowl of widgeon family.

cortezón, *m. aug.* thick bark, rind, or crust.

cortezudo, da, *a.* corticose, barky; rustic, unmannerly, unpolished.

cortezuela, *f. dim.* thin bark, skin, or rind.

cortical, *a.* cortical.

cortijada, *f.* collection of houses about a grange.

cortijo, *m.* farmhouse, grange, manse.—**alborotar el c.,** (coll.) to stir up a hornets' nest.

cortil, *m.* = CORRAL, corral; yard.

cortina, *f.* curtain; shade; portière; (fort.) curtain.—**cortinaje,** *m.* curtains, hangings.

cortinal, *m.* fenced-in land near a village or farmhouse.

cortinilla, *f.* small screen, shade; carriage curtain.

cortinón, *m. aug.* large heavy curtain.

cortiña, *f.* garden plot.

cortisona, *f.* cortisone.

corto, ta, *a.* short; dull, stupid; pusillanimous; shy, bashful, backward; imperfect, defective.—**c. circuito,** (elec.) short circuit.—**c. de alcances,** stupid.—**c. de genio,** diffident.—**c. de oído,** hard of hearing.—**c. de vista,** nearsighted.—**a la corta o a la larga,** sooner or later.

cortocircuito, *m.* = CORTO CIRCUITO.

cortón, *m.* (entom.) mantis, an orthopterous insect.

corulla, *f.* in galleys, place for the stoppers of cables.

corundo, *m.* corundum. Also CORINDÓN.

coruñés, sa, *a.* of or pertaining to Corunna.

coruscación, *f.* coruscation, brilliancy, flashing.

coruscante, *a.* coruscant, glittering, brilliant.

coruscar, *va.* (poet.) to shine, sparkle.

corusco, ca, *a.* = CORUSCANTE.

corva, *f.* back of the knee, ham, hock; CORVAZA.

corvadura, *f.* curvature, crookedness, bend; humped-back state; (arch.) bend of an arch or vault.

corvato, *m.* young crow or rook.

corvaza, *f.* (vet.) curb, tumor on the hock.

corvecito, *m. dim.* little crow or rook.

¹corvejón, *m.* hock joint of a quadruped.

²corvejón, *m.* (zool.) cormorant.

corveta, *f.* curvet; leap or bound of a horse.

corvetear, *vn.* to curvet, bound, leap.

córvidos, *m. pl.* (zool.) Corvidæ.

corvillo, *m.* hooked bill; pruning knife; shoemaker's paring knife; small sickle in velvet looms.

corvina, *f.* a variety of conger eel in the Mediterranean; corvina, a Californian fish.

corvino, na, *a.* corvine, rooklike; pertaining to rooks, crows, ravens.

corvo, va. I. *a.* bent, crooked; arched; stingy, mean. **II.** *m.* (ichth.) a variety of mullet; pothook.

corzo, za, *n.* roe deer, fallow deer.

corzuelo, *m.* wheat left in the husks by the thrashers.

cosa, *f.* thing; matter, affair.—**c. así,** the like, something like it.—**c. de,** about, more or less.—**c. del otro jueves,** (coll.) a marvellous thing; something out of date.—**c. de oír,** a thing worth hearing.—**c. de risa,** laughable thing, a thing to laugh at.—**c. de ver,** a thing worth seeing.—**c. no vista,** or **nunca vista,** unheard-of thing.—**c. rara,** a strange thing; strange to say.—**c. hecha,** surely, as good as done (diff. constr.).—**cada c. para su c.,** everything in its place, or where it belongs.—**como quien no quiere la c.,** unconcernedly, in a go-as-you-please way.—**como si tal c.,** as if nothing had happened.—**cosas de,** doi gs, or tricks of (diff. constr.: *esas son cosas de Juan,* that is one of John's tricks; that is just like John).—**cosas del otro jueves,** something very unusual.—**fuerte c.,** nuisance.—**ni c. parecida, ni c. que lo parezca,** nor anything like it.—**no es c.,** it is nothing, it is but a trifle; no matter.—**no hay tal c.,** no such thing.—**no ser,** or **no valer, c.,** not to be worth a cent, to be of little account.—**otra c.,** something else.—**poquita c.,** (coll.) a pusillanimous person.—**¿qué c.?** (coll.) how goes it? what's the news?

cosaco, ca, *n. & a.* Cossack.

cosario, ria. I. *a.* pert. to carriers; (of roads) frequented, having much traffic. **II.** *m.* carrier, expressman; huntsman, hunter.

coscarana, *f.* (prov.) cracknel, crisp cake.

coscarse, *vr.* (coll.) = CONCOMERSE, to shrug.

coscoja, *f.* (bot.) kermes, or scarlet, oak; dry leaves of the kermes oak; ring or knob on the bit of a bridle.

coscojal, coscojar, *m.* plantation or field of kermes.

coscojo, *m.* kermes berry.—*pl.* chain of a horse's bridle.

coscomate, *m.* (Mex.) corn barn.

coscón, na, *a.* crafty, sly.

coscoroba, *f.* a South-American variety of swan.

coscorrón, *m.* blow on the head.

cosecante, *m.* (geom.) cosecant.

cosecha, *f.* harvest, crop; yield; harvest time; harvesting; reaping; aggregate of immaterial things, as virtues, vices, etc.—**de su c.,** of one's own invention.—**cosechar,** *va.* to reap, gather (the harvest).—**cosechero, ra,** *n.* owner or reaper of a crop, harvester.

coselete, *m.* corselet, ancient coat of armor; pikeman; (entom.) thorax of insects.

coseno, *m.* (math.) cosine.—**c. verso,** coversed sine.

coser, *va.* to sew; to join, unite; to rivet (as a boiler); (naut.) to lash, nail, fix, frap, seize.—**c. a puñaladas,** (coll.) to stab repeatedly.—**c. un motón,** (naut.) to lash a block.—**c. y cantar,** to offer no difficulties; to be very easy, child's play.—**coserse con la pared,** to stick close to a wall.—**coserse la boca,** not to speak a word, to shut up like a clam.

cosera, *f.* piece of land that can be irrigated at one time.

cosetada, *f.* race, quick run, sprint.

cosible, *a.* that can be sewed.

cosicosa, *f.* = QUISICOSA, (coll.) enigma, puzzle.

cosido, da. I. *pp.* of COSER. II. *a.* (a) devoted (to), wedded (to). III. *m.* sewing; needlework.—**c. de cama,** quilt and blankets stitched together.

cosiduras, *f. pl.* (naut.) lashings.

cosita, *f. dim.* small thing, trifle; (Cuba) luncheon.

cosmético, *m.* cosmetic.

cósmico, ca, *a.* cosmic.

cosmogonía, *f.* cosmogony.

cosmogónico, ca, *a.* cosmogonic.

cosmografía, *f.* cosmography, descriptive astronomy.

cosmográfico, ca, *a.* cosmographic.

cosmógrafo, fa, *n.* cosmographer.

cosmología, *f.* cosmology.

cosmológico, ca, *a.* cosmological.

cosmopolita, *n. & a.* cosmopolite, cosmopolitan.

cosmopolitismo, *m.* cosmopolitanism.

cosmorama, *m.* cosmorama.

cosmos, *m.* cosmos.

¹coso, *m.* place or enclosure for bullfights or other public spectacles; main street.

²coso, *m.* timber worm.

cospel, *m.* coin blank, in the mint.

cospillo, *m.* refuse of the olive.

cosquillar, cosquillear. I. *va.* to tickle; to arouse the curiosity of. II. *vr.* to become disturbed or upset.

cosquillas, *f. pl.* tickling; ticklishness.—**buscarle a uno las c.,** (coll.) to tease, pick on one.—**hacer c.,** to tickle; to excite, disturb; to incite.—**tener c.,** to be ticklish.—**tener malas c.,** (coll.) to be easily offended; to be ill-tempered; to be overparticular.—**cosquillejas,** *f. pl. dim.* little tickling.

cosquilleo, *m.* tickling sensation.

cosquilloso, sa, *a.* ticklish; susceptible, easily offended.

¹costa, *f.* cost, price, charge; expense, expensiveness.—*pl.* costs of a lawsuit.—**a c. de,** at the expense of; by dint of.—**a mi c.,** at my expense.—**a poca c.,** with little effort.—**a toda c.,** at any price; at all hazards.—**condenar en c.,** (law) to sentence to pay the costs.

²costa, *f.* coast, shore; beach, seashore, seaboard; cobbler's tool for polishing edges of soles.—**c.**

de barlovento, (naut.) weather shore.—**dar a la c.,** (naut.) to be blown or driven to shore, to be beached.

costado, *m.* side; (mil.) flank.—*pl.* race, lineage, succession of ancestors.—**c. de barlovento,** (naut.) weather side.

costal. I. *m.* sack or large bag; brace of frame for making adobe walls. II. *a.* costal, pert. to the ribs.—**costalada,** *f.,* **costalazo,** *m.* bump one gets when falling flat on the ground.—**costalejo,** *m. dim.* small sack.—**costalero,** *m.* porter who carries goods.—**costalito,** *m. dim.* small sack.

costanera, *f.* slope.—*pl.* (carp.) rafters.

costanero, ra, *a.* pert. to a coast; declivous, sloping.—**buque c.,** coaster, coasting vessel.

costanilla, *f. dim.* gentle slope; steep street.

costar, *vn.* (*ind.* CUESTO; *subj.* CUESTE) to cost; to cause or occasion detriment or loss.—**c. la torta un pan,** (coll.) to pay dear for one's whistle.—**cuesta trabajo creerlo,** it's hard to believe.

costarricense; costarriqueño, ña, *n. & a.* Costa-Rican.

coste, *m.* = ¹COSTA.—**a c. y costas,** at cost.

¹costear. I. *va.* to pay the cost of. II. *vr.* to pay; to produce sufficient to repay its cost.

²costear, *vr.* (naut.) to sail along the coast.

costeño, ña, *a.* from, or pertaining to, the coast or seashore; coasting (vessel).

costera, *f.* side of a bale of goods; surmullet, fishing season; outside quire of a ream; slope of a hill.

costero, ra. I. *a.* pertaining to the coast; outward. II. *m.* first plank cut from a pine tree.

costezuela, *f. dim.* slight declivity or slope.

costilla, *f.* rib; chop; cutlet; (coll.) wife, better half; rung of a chair; stave of a barrel; (carp.) fur; (arch.) rib of a cupola; springer; (coll.) property, wealth; (bot.) rib of a leaf.—*pl.* (coll.) shoulders, back; (agr.) wooden strips to which horses are tied in plowing; (mech.) cramp-irons, chimney ties.—**c. falsa,** false rib.—**c. flotante,** floating rib.—**costillas de un navío,** (naut.) ribs of a ship.—**medirle a uno las costillas,** to cudgel one.

costillaje, costillar, *m.* (anat.) the ribs, or rib system; (naut.) frame of a ship.

costilludo, da, *a.* (coll.) broad-shouldered.

¹costino, na, *a.* pertaining to the costus root.

²costino, na, *a.* (Chile, Arg.) = COSTEÑO.

¹costo, *m.* (bot.) sweet and bitter costus; costus root.

²costo, *m.* cost, price; charges, expense; labor, fatigue.—**a c. y costas,** at cost.—**c. de la vida,** cost of living.

costosamente, *adv.* expensively, extravagantly.

costoso, sa, *a.* costly, dear, expensive; difficult to be obtained; sad, grievous.

costra, *f.* crust, scab; broken biscuit; incrusted part of a wick; crust of casting.

costrada, *f.* candied seedcake.

costroso, sa, *a.* crusty, having crusts or scabs.

costumbre, *f.* custom; habit; catamenia, courses.—**de c.,** usual, customary.—**tener por c.,** to be in the habit of.—*pl.* customs, ways.

costumbrista, *n.* genre writer, one who portrays everyday life and prevailing customs.

costura, *f.* sewing, needlework; seam, stitching; (surg.) suture; (mech.) crease, ridge; joint; riveting; (naut.) splicing of a rope; (carp.) joint.—**c. sobrecargada,** felting.—**sin c.,** seamless (esp. app. to tubes).—**costurera,** *f.* seamstress.—**costurero,** *m.* sewing box, table, or room.—**costurón,** *m. aug.* big seam; coarse suture; large scar.

¹cota, *f.* coat of mail (called also **c. de malla**); coat of arms, tabard coat; back and callous part of a boar's hide.

²cota, *f.* (topog.) number indicating elevation

above sea level or some other fixed level; quota, share.

cotana, *f.* mortise, mortise hole.

cotangente, *f.* (geom.) cotangent.

cotanza, *f.* a kind of medium-fine linen.

cotarrera, *f.* (coll.) gadding woman.

cotarro, *m.* charity hut to shelter beggars; side of a pit.—**alborotar el c.,** to cause disturbance. —**andar de c. en c.,** to go sauntering about.

cotejar, *va.* to compare, confront.

cotejo, *m.* comparison, collation.

cotel, *m.* cocktail. Also COCKTAIL.

cotense, *m.* (Mex.) coarse brown linen wrapper.

coterráneo, *a.* fellow (citizen).

cotí, cutí, *m.* ticking for mattresses.

coticé, cotice, *v. V.* COTIZAR.

cotidianamente, *adv.* daily.

cotidiano, na, *a.* daily, everyday; quotidian.

cotiledón, *m.* (bot.) cotyledon.

cotiledóneo, ea, *a.* (bot.) cotyledonous.

cotilla, *f.* stays, corsets.

cotillero, ra, *n.* stay maker.

cotillo, *m.* face or flat surface of a hammer.

cotillón, *m.* cotillion.

cotín, *m.* back stroke given to a ball.

¹**cotiza,** *f.* (her.) cotise.

²**cotiza,** *f.* (S. A.) an Indian sandal.

cotizable, *a.* quotable; valued (at).

cotización, *f.* (com.) quotation; price current, price list.

¹**cotizado, da,** *a.* (com.) quoted, listed.

²**cotizado, da,** *a.* (her.) cotised.

cotizar, *va.* (*pret.* COTICÉ; *subj.* COTICE) (com.) to quote (prices); to call out (current prices) in the stock exchange.

¹**coto,** *m.* (com.) combination among merchants; rate or price limitation; measure of a handbreadth; billiard contest.

²**coto,** *m.* inclosure of pasture ground; landmark, boundary; (money) fine.—**poner c. a,** to put a stop to, check.

³**coto,** *m.* (ichth.) chub.

⁴**coto,** *m.* (Am.) (med.) goiter.

cotobelo, *m.* opening in the branch of a bridle.

cotón, *m.* printed cotton.

cotona, *f.* (Mex.) chamois jacket.

cotonada, *f.* print; printed linen or cotton.

cotoncillo, *m.* button of a painter's maulstick.

cotonía, *f.* dimity, fine fustian.

cotorra, *f.* a kind of parrot; magpie; (coll.) loquacious woman.

cotorrear, *vn.* to chatter; to gossip.

cotorreo, *m.* chattering; gossiping.

cotorrera, *f.* hen parrot; (coll.) prattling woman.

cotorrón, ona, *f.* *I.* *a.* (of old persons) affecting youth, or acting silly like young people. *II.* *m.* (Am.) bachelor.

cotral, cutral, *m.* old worn-out ox.

cotudo, da, *a.* hairy, cottony; (Am.) having a goiter.

cotufa, *f.* (bot.) Jerusalem artichoke; tidbits; delicate food.—**pedir cotufas en el golfo,** to expect impossibilities.

cotufero, ra, *a.* producing tidbits or delicate food.

cotunto, *m.* (Cuba) a kind of night bird.

coturno, *m.* cothurnus, buskin.

covacha, *f.* small cave or hollow underground; grotto.—**covachuela,** *f.* *dim.* small cave or grotto; (coll.) office of a crown minister, formerly in vaulted corridors of royal palace.

covachuelista *or* **covachuelo,** *m.* (coll.) clerk in one of the COVACHUELAS.

covadera, *f.* (Peru) guano bed.

covanilla, *f.,* **covanillo,** *m.* *dim.* basket for gathering grapes.

covezuela, *f.* *dim.* small cave.

coxal, *a.* hip (as *a.*), pert. to hip or hip joint.

coxalgia, *f.* hip-joint disease, coxalgia.

coxcojilla, ita, *f.* children's game; hopscotch.—**a. c.,** lamely, haltingly, hippety-hoppety.

coxis, *m.* (anat.) coccyx.

coy, *m.* (naut.) hammock, cot, sailor's bed.—**afuera coys,** all hammocks up.

coya, *f.* (Peru) queen, wife and sister of the Inca.

coyabra *f.* (Am.) = CUYABRA, bowl made from a gourd.

coyote. I. *a.* (Am.) native, domestic. **II.** *m.* (Mex.) coyote; (Mex.) (coll.) curbstone broker.

coyunda, *f.* strap for yoking oxen; shoestring; dominion, tyranny; matrimonial union.

coyuntura, *f.* joint, articulation; occasion, juncture, opportunity; nick of time.

coz, *f.* kick; drawback; recoil of a gun; flowing back of a flood; butt of a pistol; (coll.) churlishness, unprovoked brusqueness.—**c. de mastelero,** (naut.) heel of a mast.—**dar coces,** to kick.—**dar coces contra el aguijón,** to kick against the pricks.—**soltar una c.,** to answer rudely.—**tirar coces,** to kick.

cozcojilla, *f.* = COXCOJILLA.

crabrón, *m.* hornet.

crac, *m.* failure, bankruptcy.

crameria, *f.* krameria, rhatany.

cran, *m.* (print.) nick of a type.

craneal; craneano, na, *a.* cranial.

cráneo, *m.* skull, cranium.

craneología, *f.* craniology.

craneometría, *f.* craniometry.

craneómetro, *m.* craniometer.

craneoscopía, *f.* cranioscopy.

craniano, na, *a.* cranial.

crápula, *f.* intoxication; crapulence, debauchery.

crapuloso, sa, *a.* drunken; dissolute, dissipated.

crasamente, *adv.* crassly; grossly; rudely.

crascitar, *vn.* to crow; to croak.

crasiento, grasiento, ta, *a.* greasy.

crasitud, *f.* fatness, corpulency, obesity; ignorance, stupidity, dulness.

craso, sa, *a.* fat, greasy; thick, gross, crass.

crasuláceo, a. I. *a.* (bot.) crasulaceous. **II.** *f.* *pl.* Crasulaceæ.

cráter, *m.* crater of a volcano.

crátera, *f.* (archeol.) crater.

cratícula, *f.* small wicket through which nuns receive the communion.

craza, *f.* crucible.

crea, *f.* a kind of linen stuff.

creable, *a.* creatable.

creación, *f.* creation.

creado, da. I. *pp.* of CREAR. **II.** *a.* created, begotten, made.

creador, ra, I. *n.* & *a.* creator(-ing, -ive); originator(-ing). **II. C.** *m.* Creator.

crear, *va.* to create; to institute, establish; to appoint, be made; to invent, design.

crébol, *m.* (bot.) holly tree.

crecedero, ra, *a.* able to grow; increasable.

crecer. I. *vn.* (*ind.* CREZCO; *subj.* CREZCA) to grow; to bud forth; to increase; to swell; to augment in extrinsic value (app. to money).—**c. como la mala hierba,** to grow like weeds. **II.** *vr.* to swell with pride or with authority.

creces, *f.* *pl.* augmentation, increase, excess; additional quantity of corn paid by a farmer to a public granary, besides what he borrowed from it.—**con c.,** amply.

crecida, *f.* freshet.

crecidamente, *adv.* plentifully, copiously, abundantly.

crecidito, ta, *a.* *dim.* somewhat grown.

crecido, da. I. *pp.* of CRECER. **II.** *a.* grown, increased; grave, important; large, swollen.

crecidos, *m.* *pl.* widening stitches in knitting.

creciente. I. *a.* growing, increasing; crescent; susceptible of increase. **II.** *m.* (her.) half-moon with points upward. **III.** *f.* swell, freshet of waters; leaven; crescent (of the moon).—**c. de la marea,** (naut.) flood tide, flow, flowing.

crecimiento, *m.* growth; growing; increase, increment.—**c. de la marejada,** (naut.) swell of the sea.

credencia, *f.* sideboard of an altar.—**credencial,** *f.* credential, accreditation.—*pl.* credentials.

credibilidad, *f.* credibility.

crédito, *m.* credit; acquiescence, assent; belief, faith; reputation, character, name, standing; note, bill, order for payment.—**créditos activos,** assets.—**créditos pasivos,** liabilities.—**a c.,** on credit.—**dar c.,** to believe.

credo, *m.* creed, articles of faith.—**c. político,** political creed, platform.—**en un c.,** in a trice.

crédulamente, *adv.* credulously, unsuspectingly.

credulidad, *f.* credulity.

crédulo, la, *a.* credulous.

creedero, ra, *a.* credible.—**tener buenas creederas,** to be easy of belief.

creedor, ra, *a.* credulous.

creencia, *f.* belief; creed, persuasion.

creer, *va.* (*pret.* él CREYÓ) to believe; to credit; to think, think it probable.—**creerse del aire,** to be credulous.—**ver y c.,** seeing is believing.—**¡ya lo creo!** (coll.) of course, undoubtedly.

crehuela, *f.* Osnaburg, a sort of linen.

creíble, *a.* credible, likely, believable.

creíblemente, *adv.* credibly, possibly.

¹crema, *f.* cream of milk; custard; cream, select society; cold cream; cosmetic.

²crema, *f.* (gram.) diaeresis.

cremación, *f.* cremation, incineration.

cremallera, *f.* ratch, rack; toothed bar.

cremar, *va.* to cremate.

crematística, *f.* political economy.

crematología, *f.* political economy.

crematológico, ca, *a.* pert. to political economy.

crematólogo, ga, *n.* political economist.

crematorio, ria. I. *a.* burning, cremating. II. *m.* or **horno c.,** crematory, incinerator.

cremómetro, *m.* instrument to measure fat content of milk.

cremonés, sa, *a.* of or pert. to Cremona.

crémor, *m.*—**c. tártaro,** cream of tartar.

crencha, *f.* parting of the hair into two parts; each of these parts.

creosota, *f.,* **creosoto,** *m.* (chem.) creosote.

crepitación, *f.* crepitation, crackling; (surg.) crepitation of fractures.

crepitante, *a.* crackling, crepitant.

crepitar, *vn.* to crackle, crepitate.

crepuscular; crepusculino, na, *a.* crepuscular.

crepúsculo, *m.* crepuscule, twilight; dawn; dusk.

cresa, *f.* egg or larva of the queen bee; flyblow, egg of a fly; maggot.

crescendo, *m.* (mus.) crescendo.

crespilla, *f.* (bot.) agaric, a fungus.

crespina, *f.* hair net.

crespo, pa. I. *a.* curly; crispy; (bot.) crisp-leaved; obscure and bombastic; (Am.); angry, displeased, vexed. II. *m.* (Am.) curl.

crespón, *m.* crape.

cresta, *f.* comb (of a bird); cock's comb, aigrette, tuft; crest of a helmet; wave crest; top, brow; crost or summit of a mountain; (min.) crop; (mil.) cramp iron.—**c. de la explanada,** (fort.) crest of the glacis.—**alzar, or levantar, la c.,** to be elated with pride.

crestado, da, *a.* crested.

crestería, *f.* (arch.) cresting; (fort.) battlement.

crestomatía, *f.* chrestomathy.

crestón, *m. aug.* large crest; crest of a helmet; (min.) outcrop.

creta, *f.* chalk.

cretáceo, cea, *a.* cretaceous; chalky.

cretense; crético, ca, *n.* & *a.* Cretan.

crético, *m.* verse of three syllables.

cretinismo, *m.* cretinism.

cretino, na, *n.* & *a.* cretin.

cretona, *f.* cretonne.

creyente, *n.* & *a.* believer(-ing).

creyó, *pret.* of CREER.

creyón, *m.* (Gal.) crayon; charcoal pencil.

crezco, crezca, *v.* V. CRECER.

crezneja, crizneja, *f.* braid of hair; streak of bleached bassweed.

cría, *f.* act of nursing; breeding; rearing, bringing up; keeping (as bees); litter of animals; suckling; (coll.) child reared by a nurse.

criada, *f.* female servant; maid, maid servant.—**c. de mano,** (Cuba) housemaid; bat for beating clothes in washing.

criadero, ra. I. *a.* fruitful, prolific. II. *m.* nursery, plantation of young trees; breeding place; fish hatchery; (min.) seam; cocoon bed; hotbed.

criadilla, *f.* testicle of an animal; lamb fry; mountain oyster; small loaf or roll; potato; (bot.) truffle.

criado, da. I. *pp.* of CRIAR. II. *a.* bred. III. *m,* servant, menial, groom, valet.

criador, ra. I. *a.* creating creative; fruitful, fecund. II. *n.* rearer, raiser, breeder, keeper (as of bees); creator. III. *f.* wet nurse.

criaduelo, la, *n. dim.* little or young servant.

criamiento, *m.* renovation and preservation.

criandera, *f.* (Am.) wet nurse.

crianza, *f.* nursing; lactation; breeding; manners, education; nursery.—**dar c.,** to breed; to rear, educate, bring up.

criar, *va.* to create; to breed, procreate; to raise, rear, bring up; to nurse, nourish; to fatten (animals).—**c. carnes,** to grow fat.—**c. molleja,** to grow lazy.

criatura, *f.* creature; fœtus; baby, infant; child; being, man.—**es una c.,** he is but an infant, or like an infant.

criba, *f.* cribble, sieve, crib, screen.

cribado, da, *a.* sifted, screened.

cribador, ra, *n.* sifter.

cribar, *va.* to sift, sieve, screen.

cribo, *m.* = CRIBA.

cric, *m.* jackscrew, lifting jack. Also GATO.

crica, *f.* trench, fissure; (anat.) female pudenda.

crimen, *m.* a serious crime; (theol.) mortal sin.

criminación, *f.* incrimination.

criminal, *n.* & *a.* criminal.

criminalidad, *f.* criminality, guilt.

criminalista, *m.* criminalist.

criminalmente, *adv.* criminally.

criminar, *va.* to accuse, incriminate.

criminología, *f.* criminology.

criminoso, sa. I. *n.* delinquent, criminal. II. *a.* criminal, guilty.

crimno, *m.* coarse flour meal.

crin, *f.* mane, horsehair.

crinado, da, *a.* (poet.) maned, having long hair.

crinífero, ra, *a.* mane-bearing.

crinito, ta, *a.* = CRINADO.

crinolina, *f.* (Mex.) crinoline.

crío, *m.* nursing baby.

criolita, *f.* (min.) cryolite.

criollo, lla. I. *n.* creole. II. *a.* indigenous, domestic; (of negroes) native (to Am.); (of Europeans) naturalized (in Am.).

cripta, *f.* crypt.

criptógamo, ma. I. *a.* (bot.) cryptogamous. II. *f. pl.* Cryptogamia.

criptografía, *f.* cryptography.

criptograma, *m.* cryptogram, a writing in cipher.

criquet, *m.* (Angl.) (sport) cricket.

cris, *m.* creese or kris, a Malayan dagger.

crisálida, *f.* (entom.) pupa, chrysalis.

crisantema, *f.,* **crisantemo,** *m.* (bot.) chrysanthemum.

crisis, *f.* crisis; judgment passed after mature deliberation; criterion; decisive moment.—**c. ministerial,** resignation or dismissal of the cabinet.

crisma. I. *m.* (eccl.) chrism. II. *f.* (coll.) head,

"block."—**romperse la c. con**, to come to blows with.

crismera, *f.* chrismatory.

crisneja, *f.* = CRIZNEJA.

crisoberilo, *m.* (min.) chrysoberyl.

crisocola, *f.* (min.) chrysocola.

crisol, *m.* crucible; croslet or crosslet; cruset; hearth of a furnace.

crisolada, *f.* charge of a crucible.

crisolito, *m.* (min.) chrysolite.—**c. oriental**, yellow topaz.

crisopacio, *m.* = CRISOPRASA.

crisopeya, *f.* alchemy.

crisoprasa, *f.* (min.) chrysoprase.

crispamiento, *m.* contraction, twitching.

crispar. I. *va.* to cause (muscles) to contract convulsively. II. *vn.* to twitch.

crispatura, *f.* spasmodic contraction, twitching.

crispir, *va.* to marble, marbleize.

crista, *f.* (her.) crest.

cristal, *m.* (min. and chem.) crystal; flint glass; (window) pane (also **c. de ventana**); (watch) crystal (also **c. de reloj**); looking-glass; a fine shiny woollen stuff.—**c. de roca**, rock crystal. —**c. tallado**, cut glass.—**c. tártaro**, cream of tartar.

cristalería, *f.* glassware; glass store.

cristalicé, cristalice, *v.* V. CRISTALIZAR.

cristalino, na. I. *a.* crystalline, clear. II. *m.* (anat.) crystalline of the eye.

cristalizable, *a.* crystallizable.

cristalización, *f.* crystallization.

cristalizador, *m.* (chem.) vessel in which crystals are made.

cristalizar, *va. & vr.* (*pret.* CRISTALICÉ; *subj.* CRISTALICE) to crystallize.

cristalografía, *f.* crystallography.

cristalográfico, ca, *a.* crystallographical.

cristaloide, *m.* (chem.) crystalloid.

cristel, clister, *m.* (med.) clyster, enema.

cristianamente, *adv.* Christianly.

cristianar, *va.* (coll.) to baptize, to christen.

cristiandad, *f.* Christendom; observance of the law of Christ; missionary's flock.

cristianesco, ca, *a.* applied to Moorish forms which imitate the Christian manner.

cristianicé, cristianice, *v.* V. CRISTIANIZAR.

cristianillo, illa, *n.* contemptible Christian; (app. to Spaniards by the Moors).

cristianísimo, *a. super.* most Christian (app. to certain sovereigns as a title).

cristianismo, *m.* Christianity; the body of Christians; christening.

cristianizar, *va.* (*pret.* CRISTIANICÉ; *subj.* CRISTIANICE) to christianize.

cristiano, na. I. *a.* Christian. II. *n.* Christian; (coll.) the Spanish language, opposed to Arabic or other foreign tongues; (coll.) living soul, person; (coll.) watered wine.

cristino, na, *a.* supporting Queen Regent María Cristina against pretender Don Carlos.

Cristo, *m.* Christ; image of Christ crucified.— **estar sin c.**, to be penniless, "broke."—**haber la de Dios es C.**, to have a grand dispute or quarrel.—**ni por un c.**, by no means, not for the world.—**poner como un c.**, to abuse, ill-treat.—**¡voto a C.!**, by the Almighty!

cristofué, *m.* (Venez.) a bird.

cristus, *m.* christcross, a cross formerly printed at the beginning of the alphabet; the alphabet.— **estar en el c.**, to be in the rudiments, or learning the A B C.—**no saber el c.**, to be very ignorant, not to know one's A B C.

crisuela, *f.* dripping pan of a lamp.

criterio, *m.* criterion; judgment, discernment.

crítica, *f.* criticism, critique; censure.

criticable, *a.* that may be criticized; blameworthy.

criticador, ra, *n. & a.* critic(-izing).

criticar, *va.* (*pret.* CRITIQUÉ; *subj.* CRITIQUE) to criticize; to judge; to blame, find fault with.

criticastro, *m.* criticaster, incompetent critic.

criticismo, *m.* critical, or Kantian, philosophy.

crítico, ca. I. *a.* critical, decisive; hypercritical; (med.) critical. II. *n.* critic; (coll.) affected writer or speaker; censurer, faultfinder.

criticón, na, *n. & a.* faultfinder(-ing).

critiqué, critique, *v.* V. CRITICAR.

critiquizar, *va.* to overcriticize, criticize for the sake of criticizing.

crizneja, *f.* braid of hair; rope of osiers or rushes.

croar, *vn.* to croak like a frog.

croata, *n. & a.* Croatian.

crocante, *m.* almond or peanut brittle.

crocino, na, *a.* of crocus, saffron.

crocitar, *vn.* to crow.

crocodilo, *m.* crocodile.

croché, crochet, *m.* (Gal.) crochet.

cromático, ca. I. *a.* (mus. and opt.) chromatic. II. *f.* (phys.) chromatics.

cromatismo, *m.* (opt.) chromatic aberration.

cromato, *m.* (chem.) chromate.

cromatología, *f.* chromatics, the science of colors.

crómico, ca, *a.* (chem.) chromic.

cromo, *m.* chromium; chromo, a chromolithograph.

cromolitografía, *f.* chromolithograph, colored lithograph; chromolithography.

cromolitografiar, *va.* to chromolithograph.

cromolitográfico, ca, *a.* chromolithographic; lithographed in colors.

cromolitógrafo, fa, *n.* chromolithographer.

cromoso, sa, *a.* (chem.) chromous.

cromosfera, *f.* (astr.) chromosphere.

cromotipia, *f.* color printing.

cromotipografía, *f.* art of color printing.

crónica, *f.* chronicle.

crónico, ca, *a.* chronic.

cronicón, *m.* brief chronicle.

cronista, *m.* chronicler, annalist.

crónlech, *m.* (archeol.) cromlech.

cronografía, *f.* = CRONOLOGÍA.

cronógrafo, *m.* annalist; chronograph.

cronograma, *f.* chronogram.

cronología, *f.* chronology.

cronológicamente, *adv.* chronologically.

cronológico, ca, *a.* chronological, chronologic.

cronologista; cronólogo, ga, *n.* chronologist.

cronometría, *f.* chronometry.

cronométrico, ca, *a.* chronometric.

cronometrista, *n.* chronometer maker.

cronómetro, *m.* chronometer.

croquet, *m.* (Angl.) (sport) croquet.

croqueta, *f.* croquette, fritter.

croquis, *m.* sketch, rough draft.

croscitar, *vn.* to crow.

crótalo, *m.* castanet; rattlesnake (crotalus).

croton, crotontiglio, *m.* castor-oil plant.

crotorar, *vn.* to cry like a crane or stork.

cruce, *m.* crossing; crossroads.

crucé, cruce, *v.* V. CRUZAR.

crucera, *f.* withers of a horse.—*pl.* bolting pins.

crucería, *f.* Gothic architecture.

crucero, *m.* crucifer, cross-bearer; crossing of two streets or roads; railway crossing; (arch.) transept; (print.) crossbar of a chase; (carp.) crosspiece; binding beam; (naut.) cruising station; cruiser; (S. A.) (pleasure) cruise; (astr.) Cross, a constellation; (min.) cleavage plane.

cruceta, *f.* crosspiece; headstick; crosshead (of connecting rod); crosstail; (naut.) crosstree; trelliswork.

crucial, *a.* cross-shaped, cruciform.

cruciata, *f.* (bot.) crosswort.

cruciferario, *m.* crucifer, cross-bearer.

crucífero, ra. I. *a.* cruciferous; cross-shaped; bearing a cross; (bot.) cruciate. II. *m.* crucifer.

cross-bearer; crutched friar. **III.** *f. pl.* (bot.) Cruciferæ.

crucificado, da. I. *pp.* of CRUCIFICAR. **II.** *a.* crucified.—**el C.,** the Crucified, Jesus Christ.

crucificar, *va.* (*pret.* CRUCIFIQUÉ; *subj.* CRUCIFIQUE) to crucify; to vex, torment, torture; to sacrifice; to ruin.

crucifijo, *m.* crucifix.

crucifiqué, crucifique, *v.* **V.** CRUCIFICAR.

crucifixión, *f.* crucifixion.

cruciforme, *a.* cruciform.

crucífero, ra, *a.* cruciferous.

crucigrama, *m.* crossword puzzle.

crucillo, *m.* pushpin, a game.

crudamente, *adv.* rudely, crudely.

crudelísimo, ma, *a. super.* most cruel.

crudeza, *f.* crudity, crudeness; unripeness; rawness; (of water) hardness; rudeness; severity, rigor; (coll.) vapor, vain boasting.—**crudezas del estómago,** undigested food.

crudo, da, *a.* raw; crude; green, unripe; rude; cruel, pitiless; rough, unfinished; immature; hard of digestion; blustering, hectoring person; (of water) hard; (med.) unripe, not mature.

cruel, *a.* cruel.—**crueldad,** *f.* cruelty; cruel action or treatment.

cruelmente, *adv.* cruelly, with cruelty.

cruentamente, *adv.* bloodily, with effusion of blood; cruelly.

cruento, ta, *a.* bloody; cruel, inhuman.

crujía, *f.* (naut.) midship gangway of a galley; large open hall, corridor or passage in a building, with rooms on either side; great hall of a hospital; aisle of a ward; in cathedrals, passage between rails from choir to altar.—**c. de piezas,** suite of rooms.—**pasar c.,** to run the gantlet; to suffer great troubles.

crujidero, ra, *a.* creaking, crackling, rustling.

crujido, *m.* crack, creak, crackling, creaking; rustle; (metal.) flaw in a blade.

crujidor, ra. I. *a.* cracking, creaking. **II.** *n.* glass trimmer.

crujiente, *a.* cracking, creaking; rustling.

crujir, *vn.* to crackle, creak; rustle.

cruor, *m.* cruor, blood clot; hemoglobin, coloring matter of the blood.—**cruórico, ca,** *a.* bloody.

crup, *m.* (med.) croup, membranous or true croup.—**crupal,** *a.* (med.) croupous; croupy.

crural, *a.* crural, pertaining to the leg.

crustáceo, cea. I. *n.* & *a.* crustacean(-ceous). **II.** *m. pl.* Crustacea.

crústula, *f.* thin bark or rind.

cruz, *f.* cross; tail (of a coin); upper end of a tree trunk, where the branches begin; (vet.) withers; (print.) dagger, obelisk.—*pl.* wings of a reel.— **c. ancorada,** or **de Jerusalén,** anchor cross. —**c. de las bitas,** (naut.) crosstree of the bitts. —**C. del Sur,** (astr.) Southern Cross.—**c. de Malta,** Maltese cross.—**c. de San Andrés,** St. Andrew's cross.—**c. gamada,** swastika.— **c. griega,** Greek cross.—**c. latina,** Latin cross. —**c. potenzada,** potent cross.—**c. trebolada,** trefoil cross.—**c. y raya,** no more of this.—**de la c. a la fecha,** from beginning to end.—**en c.,** crosswise, crossing each other; cross-shaped.

cruzada, *f.* crusade; tribunal of the crusade; crossroads.

cruzado, da. I. *a.* crossed; cross (breed, etc.); crosswise, transverse, twilled.—**estarse con los brazos cruzados,** to be idle. **II.** *m.* an old Spanish coin; Portuguese coin; crusader; knight of a military order; manner of playing on the guitar; figure in dancing.

cruzamen, *m.* (naut.) square or width (of a sail).

cruzamiento, *m.* crossing.

cruzar. I. *va.* (*pret.* CRUCÉ; *subj.* CRUCE) to cross; to lay, place, pass, or go across; to honor with a cross or medal; to cruise; to cross (the breed); to twill.—**c. los brazos,** to fold the arms. **II.** *vr.* to be knighted; (of affairs) to accumulate.—

c. (**con**), to pass (as on the street).—**c. de brazos,** to fold the arms; to be indolent; to be unmoved.

¹**cu,** *m.* name of the letter q.

²**cu,** *m.* ancient Mexican temple.

cuácara, *f.* (Chile) work blouse or coat; (Colomb. coll.) frock coat.

cuaderna, *f.* double fours, in backgammon; fourth part of anything; (naut.) frame.—**c. maestra,** (naut.) midship frame.

cuadernal, *m.* (naut.) block, tackle.

cuadernalete, *m.* (naut.) short double block.

cuadernillo, *m.* quire of paper; clerical directory.

cuaderno, *m.* writing book, memorandum book, composition book; (print.) four printed sheets placed within each other; an ancient form of punishment for students; (coll.) pack of cards. —**c. de bitácora,** (naut.) log book.

cuadra, *f.* large hall; stable; ward in hospital, barracks, or prison; quarter of a mile; (S. A.) unit of length, about 275 ft.; (Am.) block of houses; (naut.) quarter of a ship.

cuadradamente, *adv.* exactly, completely.

cuadradillo, *m. dim.* little cube; block of sugar; cross-section paper, plotting paper.

cuadrado, da. I. *pp.* of CUADRAR. **II.** *a.* square; perfect. **III.** *m.* square; square ruler; clock, in stockings; gusset of a shirt sleeve; die; (arith., alg.) square; (astr.) quadrate; (carp.) square; (print.) quadrat, quad.—**de c.,** face to face; perfectly.

cuadragenario, ria. *a.* forty-year old.

cuadragésima, *f.* Lent.

cuadragesimal, *a.* Lenten.

cuadragésimo, ma, *a.* fortieth.

cuadral, *m.* (carp.) angle brace, truss; shoulder tie.

cuadrangular, *a.* quadrangular.

cuadrángulo, la, *m.* & *a.* quadrangle(-gular).

cuadrantal, *a.* (math.) quadrantal.

cuadrante, *m.* (geom., astr.) quadrant; sundial; face of clock or watch; (law) fourth part of an inheritance; ancient copper coin.

cuadrar. I. *va.* & *vn.* to square; to form into or reduce to a square; (arith.) to square; (art) ¹CUADRICULAR; to square, fit, suit, adjust; to please. **II.** *vr.* (mil.) to stand at attention; (coll.) to assume a very serious attitude; (Am.) to acquit oneself well, do well; (Chile) to be or get ready.

cuadratín, *m.* (print.) quadrant.

cuadratura, *f.* squaring, square; (math., astr.) quadrature.

cuadrete, *m. dim.* small square.

cuadricenal, *a.* done every forty years.

cuadrícula, *f.* (collect.) squares (as on squared paper).

cuadriculado, da, *a.* cross-section, squared (paper).

¹**cuadricular,** *va.* (art) to divide (design) into squares.

²**cuadricular,** *a.* squared, in squares.

cuadrienal, *a.* quadrennial, comprising four years.

cuadrienio, *m.* time and space of four years.

cuadrífido, da, *a.* (bot.) quadrifid.

cuadrifoliado, da, *a.* (bot.) quadrifoliated.

cuadriforme, *a.* four-faced.

cuadriga, *f.* quadriga.

cuadril, *m.* haunch bone; haunch; hip.

cuadrilátero, ra. I. *a.* quadrilateral, four-sided. **II.** *m.* (geom.) quadrilateral.

cuadriliteral, *a.* consisting of four letters.

cuadrilongo, ga. I. *a.* rectangular. **II.** *m.* rectangle; (mil.) rectangular formation.

cuadrilla, *f.* meeting of four or more persons; gang; party; crew; herd; troop; band of armed men; patrol of the Inquisition.

cuadrillero, *m.* chief of a band; patrolman of the Inquisition; (P. I.) rural guard.

cuadrillo, *m. dim.* small square; Moorish dart.

cuadrimestre, *m.* period of four months.

cuadringentésimo, ma, *a.* four-hundredth.

cuadrinieto, ta, *n.* great-grandchild.

cuadripartido, *a.* quadripartite, divided in four.

cuadriplicado, da, *a.* quadrupled.

cuadrisílabo, ba, *a.* quadrisyllabic.

cuadrivio, *m.* a quadrivial place; quadrivium, in the Pythagorean system.

cuadrivista, *m.* expert in the quadrivium.

cuadríyugo, *m.* cart with four horses; quadriga.

cuadro, *m.* square; picture, painting; picture frame; window frame; flower bed: (sport) team; (Am.) blackboard; (Am.) slaughter-house; (mil.) square body of troops; (print.) platen; scene, tableau, division of a play; impressive spectacle; vivid description.—**c. de café,** (Cuba) 10,000-tree coffee plantation.—**c. de distribución,** (elec., tel.) switchboard.—**c. de servicio,** (Ry.) train schedule.—**cuadros de costumbres,** genre writings, on everyday life.—**c. vivo,** living picture, tableau vivant.—**en c.,** on each side, square (*tres pies en cuadro,* three feet square).—**estar,** or **quedarse, en c.,** to be bereft of either relatives or means; (mil.) to be reduced to the officers (of a body of troops having lost its soldiers).—**un traje a cuadros,** a checked dress.

cuadrúmano, na. (zool.) I. *a.* quadrumanous, four-handed. II. *m. pl.* Quadrumana.

cuadrupedal, *a.* quadruped.

cuadrupedante, *a.* (poet.) four-footed.

cuadrúpede, cuadrúpedo, da, *n. & a.* quadruped.

cuádruple, *a.* quadruple, fourfold.

cuádruplex, *a.* (tel.) quadruplex.

cuadruplicación, *f.* quadruplication.

cuadruplicar, *va.* to quadruplicate.

cuádruplo, pla, *a.* quadruple, fourfold.—**al c.,** fourfold.

cuaga, *m.* (zool.) quagga, a South-African wild ass, similar to the zebra.

cuaima, *f.* (Venez.) a very poisonous snake; wily, cruel person.

cuajada, *f.* curd of milk separated from whey.

cuajadillo, *m.* fine heavy flower embroidery on silk.

cuajado, da. I. *pp.* of CUAJAR.—**leche cuajada,** junket. II. *a.* (coll.) dumfounded. III. *m.* a sort of mince pie.

cuajaleche, *f.* (bot.) yellow bedstraw; cheese rennet.

cuajamiento, *m.* coagulation.

¹cuajar. I. *va.* to coagulate, curd, curdle; to ornament or decorate with too many ornaments. II. *vn.* (coll.) to succeed, materialize; to please, be well received. III. *vr.* to coagulate; to curdle; (coll.) to fill, become full (of people).

²cuajar, *m.* rennet bag, maw; stomach of a sucking animal; crop of a fowl; the fourth stomach, or abomasum, of a ruminant.

cuajarón, *m.* clot (of blood or other liquid).

cuajo, *m.* rennet, runnet, maw; curdling, bonnyclabber; concretion, coagulation; (sugar manufact.) thickening of the cane juice; (Mex.) idle chat; (Mex.) recess (in school).—**arrancar de c.,** to eradicate, to tear up by the roots.—**tener buen c.,** to be too dull and patient.

cuakerismo, cuaquerismo, *m.* Quakerism.

cuákero, cuáquero, ra, *n. & a.* Quaker.

cual (*pl.* cuales). I. *rel. pron.* which, such as, as. —**cada c.** *V.* CADA.—**el c., la c., los cuales, las cuales,** which, who.—**lo c.,** which.—**por lo c.,** for which reason, for that reason, whence. II. *adv.* as, like.—**c.** (**el padre**), **tal** (**el hijo**), like, as (father), like, so (son).—**c. si,** as if. III. (**cuál**) *interr. pron.* which, what.—**a c.** **más,** vyingly. IV. (**cuál**) *interjectional pron.* how. V. (**cuál**) *distributive or disjunctive pron.* some (*cuál más, cuál menos,* more or less).

cualesquier, *pl.* of CUALQUIER.

cualesquiera, *pl.* of CUALQUIERA.

cualidad, *f.* quality.

cualitativo, va, *a.* qualitative.

cualquier, *a. contr.* of CUALQUIERA (before noun).

cualquiera, I. *a.* any. II. *pron.* any one, some one, either one or the other, whichsoever, whoever.—**ser un c.,** to be of no account, a nobody.

cuan, *adv. contr.* of CUANTO, how, as: used only before adjectives and adverbs.

cuando (*interr.* **cuándo**), *adv.* when; at, or during, the time of (**cuando la guerra,** at the time of the war); in case that, if; though, although, even; sometimes.—**c. más,** or **c. mucho,** at most, at best.—**c. menos,** at least. —**c. quiera** (**que**), when you please; whenever. —**de c. en c.** or **de vez en c.,** once in a while, from time to time, now and then.—**¿hasta c.?** when shall I see you again?

cuantía, *f.* amount, quantity; rank, distinction, importance, degree.

cuantiar, *va.* to estimate; appraise.

cuantidad, *f.* quantity.

cuantimás, (coll.) = CUANTO MÁS.

cuantiosamente, *adv.* copiously.

cuantioso, sa, *a.* numerous, copious, abundant.

cuantitativo, va, *a.* quantitative.

cuanto, ta. I. *a.* as much as, all the (in the *pl.,* as many as, all the: *cuantos libros halle,* all the books, or as many books as, you find). II. **cuánto, ta,** *a. interj.* (*jc. dolor!* what suffering!). III. **cuánto, ta,** *a. interrog.* how much (many). —**c. tiempo,** how long (a time). IV. *m. adv.* as, the more (*cuanto más habla, menos dice,* the more he talks, the less he says. *cuanto más tiene, tanto más quiere,* the more he has, the more he wants).—**c. más c. antes,** immediately, without delay.—**c. más** (**que**), the more; all the more because. V. **cuánto,** *m. adv. interj.* how! VI. *neut. pron.* all (that), as much as (*cuanto Vd. quiera,* all you wish).— **en c.,** as soon as.—**en c. a,** as for, with regard to.—**por c.** inasmuch as.—**unos cuantos,** a few. VII. **cuánto,** *interrog. pron.* how much; how long; how far.

cuaquerismo, cuakerismo, *m.* Quakerism.

cuáquero, cuákero, ra, *n. & a.* Quaker.

cuarango, *m.* Peruvian-bark tree.

cuarcita, *f.,* (min.) quartzite.

cuarenta, *a. & n.* forty; fortieth.

cuarentavo, va, *n. & a.* fortieth.

cuarentena, *f.* quarantine; period of forty days, months, or years; fortieth part; Lent; suspension of assent to anything; the number 40 in general, two score.—**hacer c.,** to be in quarantine.

cuarentón, na, *n. & a.* (person) forty years old.

cuaresma, *f.* Lent; collection of Lent sermons.— **cuaresmal,** *a.* Lenten.—**cuaresmero, ra,** *n.* (Chile) one who fasts every day in Lent.

cuarta, *f.* fourth, fourth part. quarter; quadrant, fourth part of a circle; (naut.) quarter, point of the compass; quart, sequence of four cards in piquet; (fencing) carte; span (of the hand); a lineal measure (¼ vara); quart, liquid measure; (mil.) quarter of a company of soldiers; (mus.) fourth; (carp.) square timber; section; (prov.) guide mule; (Mex.) short whip, riding crop.

cuartago, *m.* nag, pony, hack.

cuartal, *m.* bread weighing one quarter of a loaf; quarter, dry measure, fourth part of a fanega.

cuartán, *m.* grain measure (18 liters 8 centi-liters); oil measure (4 liters 15 centiliters).

cuartana, *f.* (med.) quartan, an ague recurring every four days.

cuartanal, *a.* quartan.

cuartanario, ria, *a.* afflicted with a quartan.

cuartar, *va.* to plow for the fourth time.

cuartazo, *m.* (Mex.) blow with a whip.

cuartazos, *m. pl. aug.* coarse, corpulent person.

cuartear. I. *va.* to quarter, divide into four equal parts; to bid a fourth more on, at public sales; to make a fourth person at (a game); to zigzag up steep places; (Mex.) to whip. **II.** *vr.* to split, crack, rift.

cuartel, *m.* quarter, fourth part; district; ward of a city; barracks; duty imposed on villages for the quartering of soldiers; (coll.) dwelling, habitation; quarter, remission of life granted by victorious troops; flower bed; (poet.) quatrain; (her.) quarter; (naut.) hatch.—**c. de la salud,** safe place, shelter.—**c. general,** general headquarters.—**c. maestre general,** (mil.) quartermaster-general.—**estar de c.,** to be off active service with reduced pay.

cuartelada, *f.* military coup d'état, sedition of soldiers to carry out a coup d'état.

cuartelar, *va.* (her.) to quarter.

cuartelero, ra. I. *a.* pertaining to soldiers. **II.** *m.* (mil.) soldier who keeps the ward clean.

cuartelesco, ca, *a.* (Am.) = CUARTELERO.

cuarteo, *m.* act of dodging; crack, rift, fissure.

cuartera, *f.* dry measure (about 70 liters); land measure (about 36 acres); square timber.

cuarterada, *f.* land measure (about 8 sq. yds.).

cuartero, ra, *n.* collector of grain taxes.

cuarterola, *f.* quarter cask.

cuarterón, na. I. *n.* & *a.* quadroon. **II.** *m.* quartern, quarter, fourth part; quarter of a pound; upper shutter of windows; (carp.) door or wainscot panel.

cuarteta, *f.* (poet.) quatrain.

cuartete, cuarteto, *m.* (poet.) quatrain; (mus.) quartet.

cuartilla, *f.* fourth part of an ARROBA (about 6 lbs.); grain measure (about 1.38 liters); liquid measure (about 4 qts.); fourth part of a large sheet of paper; sheet of paper; (print.) sheet of copy; pastern of horses.

cuartillo, *m.* pint, in liquid or dry measure; fourth part of a REAL (about 1¢).

cuartilludo, da, *a.* (horse) having long pasterns.

cuartito, *m. dim.* small room, hall room.

cuarto, ta. I. *n.* & *a.* fourth, fourth part, quarter. **II.** *m.* room, chamber, hall; copper coin worth four MARAVEDÍS; series of paternal or maternal ancestors; crack in horses' hoofs; quarter of clothes; quarter of animals or of criminals whose body is quartered; quarter of an hour; (astr.) quarter (of the moon); service in the royal palace.—*pl.* cash, money; well-proportioned members of an animal's body.—**c. a c.,** in a mean, stingy manner.—**c. bocel,** astragal. —**c. de baño,** bathroom.—**c. de conversión,** quarter wheeling.—**c. de costura,** sewing room.—**c. de dormir,** bedroom.—**de tres al c.,** of little moment.—**en c.,** (print.) quarto.— **no tener un c.,** (fig.) not to be worth a cent.— **tener cuartos,** or **cuatro cuartos,** to be well off, to have money.

cuartogénito, ta, *a.* fourth-born.

cuartón, *m.* quarter; large joist or girder; beam sixteen feet long; oblong patch of farming land; a liquid measure.

cuarzo, *m.* quartz.—**c. citrino,** Occidental topaz.

cuarzoso, sa, *a.* quartziferous, containing quartz.

cuasi, *adv.* almost.

cuasia, *f.* (bot.) quassia.

cuasicontrato, *m.* (law) quasi contract.

cuasidelito, *m.* (law) unintentional wrong.

cuasimodo, *m.* Quasimodo, first Sunday after Easter.

cuate, *m.* (Mex.) twin.—**eso no tiene c.,** (coll.) that has no match.

cuaterna, *f.* union of four things; four points in the game of lotto.

cuaternario, ria, *a.* consisting of 4 units.

cuaternidad, *f.* quaternity, quaternary.

cuaternio, *m.* (math.) quaternion, set of 4.

cuaterno, na, *a.* consisting of four numbers.

cuatezón, na, *a.* (Mex.) hornless ox or sheep.

cuatí, *m.* a South-American monkey.

cuatralbo, ba. I. *a.* having four white feet. **II.** *m.* commander of four galleys.

cuatratuo, tua, *a.* quadroon.

cuatrero, *m.* horse thief, cattle thief.

cuatriduano, na, *a.* lasting four days.

cuatrienio, *m.* = CUADRIENIO, 4 yrs. time.

cuatrillo, *m.* a card game.

cuatrillón, *m.* quadrillion.

cuatrimestre. I. *a.* lasting four months. **II.** *m.* period of four months.

cuatrín, *m.* an ancient small coin.—*pl.* (coll.) cash in general.

cuatrinca, *f.* union of four persons or things; four cards of a kind.

cuatrisílabo, ba, *a.* = CUADRISÍLABO.

cuatro. I. *n.* & *a.* four; fourth.—**c. gatos,** (contempt.) just a few people.—**c. letras,** a few lines.—**más de c.,** (coll.) a great many. **II.** *m.* figure 4; one delegated to vote for four absent persons; (mus.) quatuor, quartet; four, four-spot card; small four-string guitar; (Mex.) blunder. **III.** *pl. f.* **las cuatro,** four o'clock.

cuatrocientos, tas, *n.* & *a.* four hundred.

cuatrodoblar, *va.* to quadruple.

cuatropea, *f.* sales tax on horses.

cuatropeado, *m.* step in dancing.

cuatrotanto, *m.* (coll.) quadruple.

cuba, *f.* cask; big-bellied person; (coll.) toper, drunkard; tub, coop, vat, trough.

cubano, na, *n.* & *a.* Cuban.

cubeba, *f.* (bot.) cubeb.

cubería, *f.* cooperage, cooper's shop.

cubero, *m.* cooper.

cubertura, *f.* cover, covering.

cubeta, *f. dim.* of CUBA; small barrel or cask, keg; tub, pail, bucket; trough; basin, cup or cistern (of a barometer); (photog.) developing tray; (Mex.) high hat.

cubetilla, ita, *f. dim.* small bucket.

cubeto, *m. dim.* of ²CUBO; small pail, tub, etc.

cúbica, *f.* cubica, fine worsted fabric.

cubicación, *f.* measurement of solids; calculation of volumes; cubing.

cúbicamente, *adv.* cubically.

cubicar, *va.* (math.) to cube; to determine the volume of.

cúbico, ca, *a.* cubical, cubic.

cubiculario, *m.* valet-de-chambre.

cubichete, *m.* (naut.) waterboards or weatherboards; (mil.) gun apron.

cubierta, *f.* cover, covering; envelope; wrapping; book cover; casing; coat, facing; roof; top of a carriage; pretext, pretense; deck (of ship).— **c. del motor,** (auto) hood.

cubiertamente, *adv.* secretly, under cover.

cubierto, ta. I. *pp. irreg.* of CUBRIR. **II.** *m.* cover, place for one at the table; roof; shed; covert, coverture, cover; allowance of a soldier; plate dinner; refreshment tray or plate.

cubil, *m.* lair or couch of wild beasts.

cubilar, *vn.* to take shelter.

cubilete, *m.* copper pan or mold for kitchen use; pastry made in it; dicebox, juggler's goblet; tumbler, mug; (Colomb., coll.) high hat; (Am.) political intrigue, wirepulling; (Am.) clique.

cubiletero, *m.* juggler; paste mold.

cubilote, *m.* cupola smelting furnace or pot.

cubilla, *f.*, **cubillo,** *m.* Spanish fly, blister beetle; water cooler; (theat.) small box near the stage; (naut.) socket for flagpole; bucket or scoop of a water-raising wheel.

cubismo, *m.* (art) cubism.

cubista, *a.* & *n.* (art) cubist.

cubital, *a.* cubital.

cúbito, *m.* (anat.) ulna, larger bone of forearm.

¹cubo, *m.* (geom., alg.) cube; (arch.) dado, die.

²cubo, *m.* wooden pail, bucket; tub, vat; mill

pond; barrel of a watch or clock; fort, small tower; nave or hub of a wheel; bayonet socket; (mason.) hodful of mixed mortar; (mech.) tongue way, socket, shaft case; (carp.) stock.

cuboide, *m.* (anat.) cuboid bone.

cubrecama, *f.* coverlet, counterpane, bedspread.

cubrecorsé, *m.* corset cover.

cubrepán, *m.* fire shovel used by shepherds.

cubreplatos, *m.* wire-net cover for food in dishes.

cubriente, *a.* covering, hiding.

cubrimiento, *m.* covering; roofing.

cubrir. I. *va.* (*pp.* CUBIERTO) to cover; spread over; face; coat; envelop; veil; shroud; screen, hide, palliate; disguise, mask, dissemble, cloak; hood, drape, clothe; box up; case, incase; (mil.) to cover or protect; (arch.) to roof; (of male animals) to cover; (com.) to meet (a draft); to cover (a shortage or expenses); to compensate; to include, comprise.—**c. la cuenta,** to balance an account.—**c. la mesa,** to lay the table. —**c. los gastos,** to pay expenses. II. *vr.* to cover oneself; to protect oneself against loss, damage or attack; to hedge; to be covered; to put on one's hat; in fencing, to be well guarded.— **cubrírsele a uno el corazón,** to feel deep grief.

cuca, *f.* root tubercle of a sedge; a Peruvian plant; coca; sort of caterpillar; (coll.) gambling woman.—**c. y matacán,** a card game.—**mala c.,** (coll.) wicked person.

cucamonas, *f. pl.* (coll.) caresses, soft words.

cucaña, *f.* greased pole to climb for a prize; the sport itself; anything acquired with little trouble at other people's expense; easy thing, "child's play."

cucañero, *m.* (coll.) parasite, hanger-on.

cucaracha, *f.* cockroach, croton bug; cochineal; snuff.—**cucarachera,** *f.* cockroach nest.

cucarda, *f.* = ESCARAPELA, cockade.

cucarrón, *m.* (Colomb.) beetle.

cuclillas.—en c., in a crouching or squatting position.—**sentarse en c.,** to squat.

cuclillo, *m.* (ornith.) cuckoo.

cuco, ca. I. *a.* (coll.) prim, dainty; cunning, crafty, astute; alert for one's own advantage. II. *m.* a kind of caterpillar; cuckoo; a card game; (coll.) gambler.

cucuiza, *f.* (Am.) thread of the agave.

cuculí, *m.* a handsome wild pigeon of S. A.

cuculla, *f.* cowl, old-fashioned hood.

cucuma, *f.* bread made in Colombia from a root like yucca.

cucúrbita, *f.* distilling retort.

cucurbitáceo, a. I. *a.* (bot.) cucurbitaceous. II. *f. pl.* Cucurbitaceæ.

cucurucho, *m.* paper cone; cornucopia.

cucuy, cucuyo, *m.* = COCUYO, glow-worm.

cucha, *f.* (Peru) = LAGUNA, lagoon.

¹cuchar, *va.* to fertilize with CUCHO.

²cuchar, *f.* spoon; old corn measure, twelfth part of a peck; tax or duty on grain.—**c. herrera,** iron spoon.

cuchara, *f.* spoon; ladle; (mason.) trowel; (naut.) pitch ladle; (mil.) gunner's ladle; (naut.) scoop for baling boats; bucket, scoop (of dredging machine, excavator, etc.); (Am.) pickpocket, thief.—**c. cafetera,** teaspoon.—**c. de aire,** (aer.) air scoop.—**meter c.,** or **su c.,** to meddle, intrude; to put in one's oar.

cucharada, *f.* spoonful; ladleful.—**meter c.,** or **su c.** = METER CUCHARA. *V.* CUCHARA.

cucharadita, *f.* teaspoonful.

cucharal, *m.* spoon bag used by shepherds.

cucharero, ra, *n.* spoon maker or dealer.

cuchareta, *f. dim.* small spoon; a variety of wheat; inflammation of the liver in sheep.

cucharetear, *vn.* (coll.) to stir with a spoon; to busy oneself with other people's affairs.

cucharetero, *m.* maker or retailer of wooden spoons; spoon rack; petticoat fringe.

cucharilla, *f. dim.* small spoon, teaspoon, coffee spoon; (vet.) liver disease in swine; (surg.) scoop.—**c. de barrenero,** (min.) scraper.

cucharón, *m. aug.* large spoon; soup ladle, kitchen ladle; dipper; scoop, bucket (of a dredge, excavator, etc.)

cucharro, *m.* (naut.) harping; watering vessel made from a gourd.

cuchi, cuchí, *m.* (Am.) hog.

cuchichear, *vn.* to whisper.

cuchicheo, *m.* whisper, whispering.

cuchichiar, *vn.* to call like a partridge.

cuchilla, *f.* large chopping knife; cleaver; any knife; blade of a knife or sword; razor blade; ancient poniard; (poet.) sword; mountain ridge; knife edge.

cuchillada, *f.* cut or slash with a knife; gash, deep wound.—**dar c.,** (of competing actors) to win the preference of the public.—*pl.* fight, row.—**andar a c.,** to come to blows.

cuchillar, *a.* pertaining to knives.

cuchilleja, *f.,* **cuchillejo,** *m. dim.* small knife; paring knife used by horseshoers.

cuchillera, *f.* knife case or scabbard.

cuchillería, *f.* cutler's shop; cutlery.

cuchillero, *m.* cutler.

cuchillo, *m.* knife; knife edge; gore, triangular piece in a garment; right of governing; any object or place ending in a point or acute angle; (arch.) gable frame; (naut.) cant piece; triangular sail; goring of a sail; (carp.) beam, girder. —*pl.* chief feathers in a hawk's wing.—**c. de monte,** hunter's cutlass.

cuchillón, *m. aug.* large knife.

cuchipanda, *f.* (coll.) cheerful dinner shared by several persons.

cuchitril, *m.* narrow hole or corner; very small room, "den"; hut.

cucho, *m.* fertilizer of manure and compost.

cuchuco, *m.* (Colomb.) pork-and-barley soup.

cuchuchear, *vn.* = CUCHICHEAR, to whisper.

cuchufleta, *f.* joke, jest, fun.

cuchufletero, ra, *n.* jester, tease.

cuchuvo, *m.* (S. A.) saddle bag.

cudria, *f.* flat woven bast rope.

cudú, *m.* koodoo, an African antelope.

cuébano, *m.* = CUÉVANO, basket, hamper.

cuélebre, *m.* = DRAGÓN, dragon.

cuelga, *f.* bunch of grapes or other fruit hung up for use during the winter; (coll.) birthday present.—**c. de cebollas,** bunch of onions.

cuelgacapas, *m.* cloak hanger, rack.

cuelgo, cuelgue, *v. V.* COLGAR.

cuelmo, *m.* candlewood.

cuelo, cuele, *v. V.* COLAR.

cuellicorto, ta, *a.* short-necked.

cuellierguido, da, *a.* stiffnecked; swelled up with pride.

cuellilargo, ga, *a.* long-necked.

cuello, *m.* neck; throat; collar (of garments); neck of a bottle; neck stock; small end of a wax candle; thinnest part of a mast, pole, cane, etc.; collar of a beam in oil mills.—**c. duro,** stiff collar.—**levantar el c.,** to be prosperous.

cuenca, *f.* wooden bowl; socket of the eye; basin of a river; deep valley.

cuenco, *m.* earthen bowl; sifting basket.

cuenda, *f.* end of packthread; tie of a skein; end of a skein.

cuenta. I. *f.* computation, calculation, count, reckoning; account; bill; note; statement (of accounts); narrative, report; obligation, care, duty; bead (of a rosary, etc.); accountability; reason, satisfaction; consideration; merit, importance.—**c. corriente,** (com.) account current.—**c. de venta,** (com.) account sales.—**c. en participación,** joint account.—**c. pendiente,** unsettled account.—**c. simulada,** pro forma account.—**c. y mitad,** (com.) joint account.—**cuentas del Gran Capitán,** account overcharged.—**a c.**, or **a buena c.**, on account, in part payment.—**a esa c.**, at that rate.—**a fin de cuentas**, in the end.—**caer en la c.**, (fig.) to see, make out, "catch on."—**dar c.**, to answer, report, give an account.—**dar c. de algo**, (coll., ironic) to use up, waste, destroy.—**darse c. de**, to realize; to notice.—**de c. y riesgo de**, for account and risk of.—**en resumidas cuentas**, (coll.) in short, in a word; after all.—**estemos a cuentas**, let us settle this, let us come to an understanding.—**hacer cuentas**, to figure, reckon.—**hacer cuentas alegres**, or **galanas**, to build air castles.—**hacer de c. (que)**, to pretend, act (as if).—**hacer la c.**, to figure out.—**hacer**, or **hacerse, la c.**, to imagine, take for granted.—**la c. es c.**, business is business.—**llevar c.**, or **la c.**, to keep account; to count, reckon.—**por c. de**, to the account of.—**por c. y mitad**, joint account.—**por c. y riesgo de uno**, at one's expense and risk; on one's own responsibility.—**por la c.**, as far as one can judge, judging from the facts known, stated, etc.—**rendir cuentas**, (lit. & fig.) to give, render an account.—**tener c.**, to answer the purpose; to be profitable or advantageous; (**con**) to be concerned (with), have a part (in).—**tener en c.**, to take into account, remember, bear in mind.—**tomar en c.**, to take under advisement, consider.—**tomar por su c.**, to take upon oneself.—**vamos a cuentas** = ESTEMOS A CUENTAS. **II.** *interj.* take care, look out!

cuentadante, *m.* one who renders an account of moneys received.

cuentagotas, *m.* dropper (for counting or measuring drops).

cuentahilos, *m.* thread counter; linen prover; weaver's glass.

cuentapasos, *m.* odometer.

cuentero, ra, *n. & a.* = CUENTISTA.

cuentezuela, *f. dim.* small account.

cuentista, *m.* talebearer, informer.

¹cuento, *m.* tale, story; narrative; fable, fairy tale; gossip; million; million of millions; account; number;—**c. del tío**, (Am.) (coll.) confidence game, trick.—**c. de viejas**, old women's stories, notion, superstition.—**andar en cuentos**, to be at loggerheads; to carry tales; to gossip.—**dejarse de cuentos**, to stop beating about the bush, to come to the point.—**estar en el c.**, to be informed, to be on the inside.—**sin c.**, numberless.—**traer a c.**, to bring to bear upon the subject; to drag into the subject.—**venir a c.**, to be pertinent, to be to the point.

²cuento, *m.* articulation of a wing; ferrule of a pike; cane, or tool; prop, shore, support.

³cuento, cuente, *v. V.* CONTAR.

cuentón, na, *n.* story-teller, talebearer.

cuera, *f.* leather jacket.

cuerda, *f.* cord, rope, string; (fishing) line; string for musical instruments; compass of a voice; (geom.) chord; match for firing a gun; spring, mainspring of a watch or clock; a West-Indian land measure (3240 centiares); number of galley slaves tied together.—*pl.* human nerves.—**c. floja**, or **tesa**, tight rope, ropedancing rope.—**c. freno**, (aer.) dragrope.—**cuerdas de las cubiertas**, (naut.) deck streaks or strakes.—**cuerdas vocales**, vocal chords.—**bajo c.**, or **por debajo de c.**, underhandedly, deceitfully.—**dar c. a**, to wind up (a watch, clock).

cuerdamente, *adv.* prudently, wisely.

cuerdecica, illa, ita, or **cuerdezuela**, *f. dim.* funicle, small cord.

cuerdo, da, *a.* prudent, discreet, sensible, wise, judicious; in his senses, not mad.

cuerecico, ito, *m. dim.* small hide or skin.

cuerezuelo, corezuelo, *m.* suckling pig.

cuerna, *f.* horn vessel; stag's or deer's horn; sportsman's horn.

cuernecico, illo, ito, *m.* cornicle, small horn.

cuernezuelo, *m. dim.* cornicle, small horn; farrier's paring knife.

cuerno, *m.* horn; feeler, antenna of insect; horn of the moon; button of a manuscript roll; huntsman's horn; (bot.) horn; (naut.) outrigger; (vet.) a disease of horses; callosity.—**c. de abundancia**, cornucopia, horn of plenty.

cuero, *m.* pelt, fell, rawhide; tanned skin, leather; goatskin dressed entire, which serves as a bag to carry wine or oil; toper, drinker.—*pl.* hangings or drapery of gilded or painted leather.—**c. cabelludo**, scalp.—**c. de suela**, sole leather.—**c. exterior**, cuticle.—**c. interior**, skin.—**cueros al pelo**, raw hides, undressed hides.—**de cuero**, leathern, leather (as *a.*).—**en cueros**, or **en cueros vivos**, stark naked.—**entre c. y carne**, between the skin and the flesh.

cuerpecico, illo, ito; cuerpezuelo, *m. dim.* small body; small carcass.

cuerpo, *m.* body, matter (opposed to spirit); (chem.) body, element; body of an animal; also, more narrowly, the trunk; figure and build of a person; corpse; body, assembly, corporation, guild; (geom.) body, solid; body, thickness (of oil, etc.); (arch.) entire part of a building up to a cornice or entablature; volume, book, whole of a book, except preface and index; (law) body, collection of laws; degree of thickness of silks, woolens, or cottons; strength, thickness of liquids; collective mass; body in several other senses, as a body of a musical instrument, of ore, of scientific or diplomatic persons, etc.—**c. a c.**, hand to hand; in single combat.—**c. de batalla de una escuadra**, the entire division of a fleet.—**c. de bomba**, barrel of a pump.—**c. de caldera**, boiler shell.—**c. de ejército**, army corps.—**c. de guardia**, guard; guarded place, post of a guard.—**c. del cabrestante**, (naut.) barrel of the capstan.—**c. del delito**, corpus delicti.—**c. sin alma**, dull person.—**c. tiroides**, (anat.) thyroid gland.—**c. volante**, (mil.) flying column.—**a c. de rey**, royally, like a king.—**a c. descubierto**, without cover or shelter; manifestly.—**de c. entero**, full-length (picture).—**en c.**, without cloak or wrap.—**en c. de camisa**, in shirt sleeves.—**en c. y alma**, (coll.) body and soul, wholly.—**estar de c. presente**, to be actually present; to lie in state.—**hacer del c.**, to go to stool.—**tomar c.**, to take shape; to increase, enlarge, grow.

cuerria, *f.* circular space fenced in where chestnuts are thrown to ripen.

cuerva, *f.* (ornith.) crow, rook; jay.

cuervecico, illo, ito, *m. dim.* little rook.

cuervo, *m.* (ornith.) raven; crow; rook.—**c. marino**, cormorant; (C., astr.) Corvus, a southern constellation.

cuesco, *m.* stone (of fruit); millstone of an oil mill; (coll.) noise from breaking wind; fisticuff; (Chile) man in love.

cuesquillo, *m. dim.* small stone of fruit.

¹cuesta, *f.* = CUESTACIÓN.

²cuesta, *v.*—**c. trabajo creerlo**, it's hard to believe. *V.* COSTAR.

³cuesta, *f.* slope, grade.—**c. abajo**, down hill.—**c. arriba**, up hill; painfully, with great trouble and difficulty.—**a cuestas**, on one's shoulders or back; to one's charge or care.

cuestación, *f.* petition, solicitation or collection for a charitable purpose.

cuestero, ra, *n.* alms collector.

cuestezuela, *f. dim.* easy slope, light grade.

cuestión, *f.* question, dispute, quarrel; matter, problem, affair, business.—**c. batallona**, much-debated, or vexed, question.—**c. candente**, burning question.—**c. de gabinete**, state affair that may cause a change in the cabinet; serious matter.—**c. de tormento**, torture.

cuestionable, *a.* questionable, doubtful.

cuestionar, *va.* to dispute, discuss, argue.

cuestionario, *m.* questionnaire.

cuesto, cueste, *v. V.* COSTAR.

cuestor, *m.* questor; solicitor of alms.

cuestuario, ria; cuestuoso, sa, *a.* lucrative, productive.

cuestura, *f.* questorship.

cuete, *m.* firecracker; skyrocket.

cueto, *m.* (fort.) rocky peak; defended tor.

cuetzale, *m.* (ornith.) quetzal, a large Mexican bird of golden green plumage.

cueva, *f.* cave, grotto; cellar.—**c. de fieras,** den of wild beasts.—**c. de ladrones,** den of thieves.

cuévano, *m.* basket, hamper; (min.) sump basket.

cuevero, *m.* maker of caves and grottoes.

cueza, *f.,* **cuezo,** *m.* mortar hod.

cuezo, cueza, *v. V.* COCER.

cugujada, *f.* (ornith.) common field lark, skylark.

cugulla, cogulla, *f.* cowl.

cuicacoche, *f.* a Mexican song bird.

cuico, ca, *m.* (Mex.) policeman; *m.* & *f.* (Am.) gossip.

cuida, *f.* in ladies' seminaries, young lady who takes care of a young girl.

cuidado. I. *m.* care, solicitude; attention, heed; keeping, custody, charge, trust; carefulness, caution; fear, apprehension, anxiety.—**estar con c.,** to be anxious or apprehensive.—**estar de c.,** to be seriously ill.—**no hay c. (de que),** there is no danger (that).—**no pasar c.,** or **perder c.,** not to worry.—**tener cuidado (de),** to be careful (to); to be worried or anxious. **II.** *interj.* look out! beware!—¡**c. con él!** look out for him!—¡**c. con perderlo!** take care not to lose it!

cuidadosamente, *adv.* carefully.

cuidadoso, sa, *a.* careful; solicitous; painstaking; curious, observing.

cuidante, *n.* caretaker.

cuidar. I. *va.* to care for, look after, keep; to execute with care, diligence, and attention; take care of. **II.** *vn.* **c. de,** to take care of. **III.** *vr.* to take care of oneself.—**c. de,** to look out for, to be on guard against; to avoid; to pay attention to.—**cuido,** *m.* caretaking.

cuita, *f.* care, grief, affliction, trouble.—**contar sus cuitas,** to tell one's troubles.

cuitadamente, *adv.* afflictedly, sorrowfully.

cuitado, da, *a.* unfortunate, wretched; timid.

cuitamiento, *m.* bashfulness, timidity.

cuja, *f.* lance bucket; bedstead.

cuje, *m.* withe; pole supported by two vertical ones for hanging tobacco.—*pl.* hop poles.

cují, *m.* (bot.) sponge tree.

cujisal, *m.* plantation of sponge trees.

culantrillo, *m.* (bot.) maidenhair fern.

culantro, *m.* (bot.) coriander.

culata, *f.* buttock, haunch; butt of a firearm; screw pin which fastens the breech of a gun to the stock; rear part; (int. combust. eng.) cylinder head; (elec.) yoke (of an electromagnet).

culatada, *f.,* **culatazo,** *m.* kick; recoil of a firearm; blow with the butt of a firearm.

culcusido, corcusido, *m.* botch work.

culebra, *f.* snake; trick, fun, joke; hazing; distil worm; cock of a firearm; sudden disorder in a peaceful assembly.—**c. de cascabel,** rattlesnake.—**saber más que las culebras,** (coll.) to be very crafty and cunning.—**culebrazo,** *m. aug.* big snake; whipping given by jail prisoners to newcomers; hazing.—**culebrear,** *vn.* to wriggle (as a snake); to wind (as a rivulet). —**culebrilla,** *f.* tetter, ringworm; a skin disease; rocking staff of a loom; fissure in a gun barrel.—**culebrina,** *f.* (mil.) culverin; undulated meteor.—**culebrino, na,** *a.* snaky.—

culebrón, na, *n. aug.* big snake; crafty fellow, double-dealer; intriguing woman.

culera, *f.* stain of urine in swaddling clothes; patch on the seat of trousers.

culero, ra. I. *a.* slothful, lazy. **II.** *m.* baby's diaper.

culinario, ia, *a.* culinary.

culminación, *f.* culmination; high tide.

culminante, *a.* culminating.

culminar, *vn.* to culminate.

culo, *m.* breech, backside, rump, buttock; bottom; socket; anus; bottom of anything.

culombio, *m.* (elec.) coulomb.

culón, *m.* (coll.) retired soldier.

culpa, *f.* fault; guilt; sin.—**echar la c. a,** to blame.—**no por (su) c.,** through no fault of (his) own.—**tener la c. de,** to be to blame, or responsible, for.

culpabilidad, *f.* culpability, guilt.

culpabilísimo, *ma, a. super.* guilty or culpable in the highest degree.

culpable, *a.* culpable, guilty; blamable, blameworthy.—**culpablemente,** *adv.* culpably.

culpación, *f.* inculpation, blame.

culpadamente, *adv.* culpably.

culpado, da. I. *pp.* of CULPAR. **II.** *a.* guilty.

culpar, *va.* to blame, accuse; condemn.

cultamente, *adv.* neatly, politely, in a refined manner; affectedly, in a showy manner.

cultedad, *f.* (humor.) affected elegance and purity of style; fustian.

culteranismo, *m.* high-flown style; fustian.

culterano, na. I. *n.* purist with affectation; fustianist. **II.** *a.* pertaining to fustian.

cultero, ra, *a.* (humor.) using high-flown style.

cultiparlar, *vn.* to speak with affected elegance.

cultiparlista, *a.* speaking with affected elegance and correctness.

cultipicaño, ña, *a.* (humor.) speaking with affected elegance and in a jeering manner.

cultivable, *a.* cultivable, arable.

cultivación, *f.* cultivation, culture.

cultivador, ra, *a.* & *n.* cultivator (person or machine).

cultivar, *va.* to cultivate; to farm, develop, husband, till; to dress (a garden); to nurse (a plant); to preserve.

cultivo, *m.* cultivation; farming, tillage; culture of the mind; elegance of manners; (bacteriol.) culture.—*pl.* crops.

culto, ta. I. *a.* improved, cultivated; nursed (plants); pure, elegant, correct (style and language); cultured, educated; enlightened, civilized.—**II.** *m.* worship; religion; cult; respect or veneration for superior men; homage to lofty ideals.—**c. de dulía,** worship of saints and angels.—**c. de hiperdulía,** adoration of the Virgin.—**c. de latría,** worship of God.—**c. divino,** public worship in churches.—**c. externo,** external religious ceremonies.

cultura, *f.* cultivation of the soil or of the mind; urbanity, politeness; culture.

cultural, *a.* cultural.

culturar, *va.* to cultivate.

cuma, *f.* (Am.) godmother; crony.

cumárico, ca, *a.* (chem.) coumaric.

cumarina, *f.* (chem.) coumarin.

cumarú, *m.* Tonka bean, coumaron.

cumbé, *m.* a negro dance.

cumbre, cumbrera, *f.* top, summit, crest; peak of a mountain; acme; greatest height of favor, fortune, science, etc.; (carp.) ridgepole, tie beam, rooftree.

cúmplase, *m.* be it carried out—a term used by the executive of Spanish-American republics over his signature in approving an act of Congress; also, as a confirmation of an appointment.

cumpleaños, *m.* birthday.

cumplidamente, *adv.* completely.

cumplidero, ra, *a.* that must be fulfilled or executed; convenient, fit, suitable; accomplishable.

cumplido, da. I. *pp.* of CUMPLIR. **II.** *a.* full, complete, thorough; accomplished, perfect; large; plentiful, ample; fulfilled, lapsed, passed; due; polished, courteous. **III.** *m.* compliment; attention, courtesy; present; ceremony, formality.

cumplidor, ra. I. *n.* one who executes a commission. **II.** *a.* true to one's word, reliable.

cumplimentar, *va.* to compliment, congratulate; to show courtesy to; to fulfil, carry out.

cumplimentero, ra, *a.* (coll.) giving fulsome compliments; excessively courteous or formal; officious; ceremonious.

cumplimiento, *m.* completion, performance, fulfilment; lapse, expiration; compliment; civility, courtesy; formality, ceremony; complement.—**con c., con cumplimientos,** formally, ceremoniously.—**de c.,** formal.

cumplir. I. *va.* to execute, discharge, perform, obey, fulfil; keep (a promise).—**c. años,** to reach one's birthday (*hoy cumplo veinte años,* I am twenty years old to-day). **II.** *vn.* to perform one's duty; to fulfil a social engagement; to perform a duty in the name of another; to have served the time required in the militia; to mature, expire, fall due; to behoove; to be fit.—**c. con,** to fulfil, do, perform.—**c. por otro,** to perform in another's name.—**por c.,** as a matter of form. **III.** *vr.* to be realized or fulfilled; to come true; (of a period of time) to expire, be up; (com.) to mature, fall due.

cumquibus, *m.* (coll.) money, wherewithal.

cumulador, *m.* = ACUMULADOR, accumulator.

cumular, acumular, *va.* to accumulate.

cumulativamente, *adv.* cumulatively.

cumulativo, acumulativo, va, *a.* cumulative.

cúmulo, *m.* heap, pile; congeries; large quantity or number, lot; cumulus (clouds).

cuna, *f.* cradle; foundling hospital; place of birth; family, lineage; origin, source.

cunasirí, *m.* a Peruvian aromatic tree.

cuncuna, *f.,* a Chilean caterpillar; (Colomb.) wild pigeon.

cunchos, *m. pl.* an indigenous independent race in Chile.

cundido, *m.* provision of oil, vinegar, and salt given to shepherds; honey or cheese given to boys.

cundir, *vn.* to spread (app. to liquids or news); to yield abundantly; to grow, expand, propagate.

cunear. I. *va.* to rock (a cradle). **II.** *vr.* to swing; to rock.

cuneiforme, *a.* cuneiform, wedge-shaped.

cúneo, *m.* (mil.) triangular formation of troops; space between the passages in ancient theatres.

cuneo, *m.* rocking motion; (naut.) rolling, pitching.

cunera, *f.* cradle rocker, woman appointed to rock the infantas in the royal palace.

cunero, ra, *m.* foundling.

cuneta, *f.* (mil.) small trench; side ditch; gutter, road drain.

cuña, *f.* wedge, quoin; paving stone.

cuñada, *f.* sister-in-law.

cuñadía, *f.* relationship by marriage.

cuñado, *m.* brother-in-law.

cuñar, *va.* = ACUÑAR, to coin, mint; to wedge.

cuñete, *m.* keg; firkin.

cuño, *m.* coin; die for stamping money; the device stamped; mark on silver; (mil.) triangular formation of troops.

cuociente, *m.* quotient.

cuodlibetal, cuodlibético, ca, *a.* pert. to CUODLIBETO.

cuodlibeto, *m.* argument; debatable point; thesis; subtilty; pungent saying; quodlibet.

cuota, *f.* quota, share.

cupano, *m.* (P. I.) a large tree, the bark yielding a dyestuff and the wood being used for building.

cupe, cupiera, *v.* V. CABER.

cupé, *m.* coupé, cab; banquette of a coach.

cupido, *m.* gallant, lover.

cupitel.—tirar de c., (in game of bowls) to throw a bowl with a curve.

cupo, *m.* quota; tax rate; (Mex.) contents, capacity.

cupón, *m.* (com.) coupon.

cupresino, na, *a.* (poet.) made of or pertaining to the cypress tree.

cúprico, ca, *a.* (chem.) cupric.

cuprífero, ra, *a.* (chem.) cupriferous.

cuproso, sa, *a.* (chem.) cuprous.

cúpula, *f.* cupola, dome, vault; turret of a monitor; (bot.) cupule, cup.

cupulífero, ra, *a.* (bot.) cupuliferous, cup-bearing.

cupulino, *m.* (arch.) sky lantern.

cuquillo, *m.* (ornith.) cuckoo.

cura. I. *m.* parish priest, rector, curate; any clergyman. **II.** *f.* CURACIÓN; curing, seasoning (of timber, etc.); parsonage.—**c. de almas,** cure, or care, of souls.—**c. de misa y olla,** ignorant priest.—**c. de urgencia,** PRIMEROS AUXILIOS, first aid; emergency measure.

curable, *a.* curable.

curaca, *m.* (Peru) governor, potentate; master, boss.

curación, *f.* cure, healing; (surg.) dressing, care (of a wound).

curadero, *m.* bleaching place.

curadillo, *m.* (ichth.) codfish, ling fish.

curado, da. I. *pp.* of CURAR. **II.** *a.* hardened; tanned.

curador, ra, *n.* overseer, caretaker; healer; (law) guardian, administrator(-trix).—**c. de bacalao,** cod salter.—**c. de lienzo,** bleacher of linen cloth.

curaduría, *f.* guardianship.

curandero, *m.* quack, medicaster.

curar. I. *vn.* to recover from sickness; (de), to take care (of). **II.** *va.* to cure, heal, restore to health; to administer (medicines), prescribe; (surg.) to dress (a wound); to salt, cure, preserve; to bleach (fabrics); to cure, season (timber); to soothe, subdue. **III.** *vr.* to recover from sickness.

curare, *m.* curare.—**curarina,** *f.* (chem.) curarine.

curasao, *m.* curaçao.

curatela, *f.* (law) = CURADURÍA.

curativo, va, *a.* curative.

curato, *m.* curacy, parish.

curazao, *m.* curaçao.

curbaril, *m.* (bot.) W.I. locust tree; courbaril.

curculiónido, da, *a.* curculionid.

cúrcuma, *f.* (bot.) curcuma, turmeric.

curcusilla, *f.* = RABADILLA, coccyx; rump.

curdo, da, *n.* & *a.* Kurd(-ish).

cureña, *f.* gun carriage; stay of a crossbow; gunstock in the rough.—**a c. rasa,** (mil.) without a parapet or breastwork; (coll.) without shelter or defense.—**cureñaje,** *m.* (collect.) gun carriages.

curesca, *f.* shear wool from the cloth.

curí, *m.* (Am.) guinea pig; (bot.) a S. A. coniferous tree, whose cones are used as food.

curia, *f.* ecclesiastical tribunal; bar, the legal profession; care, skill, nice attention; (old Roman) curia.—**c. romana,** pontifical court, aggregate of tribunals and congregations forming the Pope's court.—**curial. I.** *a.* curial. **II.** *m.* curialistic agent; officer of a court; attorney; (Roman) curial, member of a curia.

curialesco, ca, *a.* clerical, priestlike.

curiana, *f.* = CUCARACHA, cockroach.

curiara, *f.* (Am.) a long canoe.

curiel, *m.* (Cuba) guinea pig.

curiosamente, *adv.* curiously; neatly, cleanly; in a diligent, careful manner.

curiosear, *vn.* to act from curiosity; to pry into others' affairs; (coll.) to be a busybody.

curiosidad, *f.* curiosity, inquisitiveness; neatness, cleanliness; curious thing; rare object or person; curio.

curioso, sa, *a.* curious, inquisitive, prying; neat, clean; careful, attentive, diligent; quaint, rare.

curricán, *m.* spinning tackle.

curro, rra, *a.* (coll.) showy, tawdry, loud; (Mex., Cuba) (coll.) native of Cadiz.

curruca, *f.* (ornith.) linnet, babbling warbler.

currutaco, ca. I. *a.* ultra-fashionable, dudish, exquisite. **II.** *n.* dude, fop, dandy.

cursado, da. I. *pp.* of CURSAR. **II.** *a.* accustomed, habituated, inured.

cursante. I. *a.* frequenting; assiduous. **II.** *n.* student, pupil.

cursar, *va.* to frequent, to do repeatedly; to study; to take action on, attend to. **II.** *vn.* (incorrectly used for CORRER) to circulate, be current.

cursi, *a.* vulgar, shoddy, in bad taste; clumsy.

cursillo, *m. dim.* short course of lectures in a university.

cursivo, va, *a.* (print.) cursive, script.

curso, *m.* course, direction, career, progress; run, route, current; course of study; term of tuition in schools; collection of the principal treatises used in instruction in some branch; lapse; succession; (com.) current rate.—*pl.* laxity or looseness of the bowels.—**c. de la corriente,** (naut.) current's way.—**ser de c.,** or **tener c. forzoso,** to be legal tender.

cursor, *m.* (mech.) slider, slide.

curtación, *f.* (astr.) curtation.

curtido, da. I. *pp.* of CURTIR. **II.** *a.* tanned, curried; accustomed, experienced, expert; weather-beaten. **III.** *m.* leather; tanning. **IV.** *m. pl.* tanned leather.

curtidor, *m.* tanner, currier, leather dresser.

curtiduría, *f.* tanyard; tannery.

curtiente, *n.* tanning material or substance.

curtimiento, *m.* tanning.

curtir. I. *va.* to tan (hides, the complexion); to inure to hardships, to harden.—**estar curtido,** (coll.) to be used or inured. **II.** *vr.* to become tanned, sunburned, weather-beaten.

curto, corto, ta, *a.* short, dock-tailed.

curú, *m.* (Peru) a clothes moth.

curuca, *f.* (ornith.) eagle owl.

curucucú, *m.* a disease caused by the bite of a South American snake.

curuja, *f.* (ornith.) eagle owl.

curul, *a.* (anc. Rome) curule; edile.

curva, *f.* curve; curvature; bend; (naut.) knee.—**c. de bao,** (naut.) spur.—**c. de enlace,** (Ry.) connecting curve.—**c. de nivel,** (surv.) contour line.

curvatón, *m.* (naut.) small knee, bracket.

curvatura, *f.* curvature; curving.

curvilíneo, a, *a.* (geom.) curvilinear.

curvímetro, *m.* instrument for measuring curves.

curvo, va. I. *a.* curve, curved; crooked, bent. **II.** *m.* inclosed pasture ground.

cusculia, *f.* (bot.) = COSCOJA, scarlet oak.

cuscurro, *m.* end piece of bread, heel.

cuscuta, *f.* (bot.) common dodder.

cusir, *va.* (coll.) = CORCUSIR, to sew clumsily.

cúspide, *f.* cusp, apex, top, summit, peak.

cuspídeo, dea, *a.* (bot.) cuspidate.

custodia, *f.* custody, safe-keeping; monstrance; shrine; guardian, custodian; tabernacle.

custodiar, *va.* to guard; to convoy; take care of.

custodio, *m.* guard, watchman; custodian.

cutáneo, nea, *a.* cutaneous, of the skin.

cúter, *m.* (naut.) cutter.

cutí, *m.* bedticking, crash.

cutícula, *f.* pellicle, cuticle, epidermis.

cuticular, *a.* cuticular.

cutio, *m.* labor, work.

cutir, *va.* to knock, strike, pound, beat, hammer.

cutis, *m.* or *f.* skin of the human body (esp. that of the face); complexion.

cutó, *m.* (naut.) dirk.

cutral, *n.* old worn-out ox or cow.

cutre, *m.* miser.

cuyabra, coyabra, *f.* (Colomb.) bowl or receptacle formed by halving a gourd lengthwise.

cuyo, ya, (*pl.* **cuyos, cuyas**). **I.** *pron. poss.* of which, of whom, whose, whereof. **II.** *a.* which, this, that (*por cuya razón,* for which reason; *en cuyo caso,* in that case). **III.** *m.* (coll.) beau, lover, suitor.

cuzma, *f.* (Peru) sleeveless shirt.

czar, *m.*; **czarevitz,** *m.*; **czariano, na,** *a.*; **czarina,** *f.* = ZAR, ZAREVITZ, etc., czar, etc.

CH

cha, *f.* (P. I.) tea.

chabacanamente, *adv.* bunglingly, clumsily.

chabacanería, *f.* bungle, muddle; vulgar expression or action.

¹**chabacano, na,** *a.* awkward, clumsy.

²**chabacano,** *m.* (Mex.) a variety of apricot.

chacal, *m.* jackal.

¹**chácara,** *f.* = CHACRA.

²**chácara,** *f.* (Venez.) large leather bag strapped across the back and chest over one shoulder.

chacarero, ra, *n.* (Am.) field laborer.

chacarrachaca, *f.* loud wrangle.

chacina, *f.* spiced pork for sausages and balls.

chaco, *m.* (Am.) hunt, hunting.

chacó, *m.* shako, military cap.

chacolí, *m.* chacoli, a light red wine made in Vizcaya, Spain.

chacolotear, *vn.* (of loose horseshoe) to clatter.

chacoloteo, *m.* clatter of a loose horseshoe.

chacón, *m.* (P. I.) a large lizard.

chacona, *f.* chaconne, an old Spanish dance.

chaconada, *f.* jaconet, a fine cotton material.

chacota, *f.* noisy mirth.—**echar a ch.,** (coll.) to carry off with a joke.—**hacer ch. de,** (coll.) to turn into ridicule, make fun of.—**chacotear,** *vn.* to indulge in noisy mirth.—**chacotero, ra,** *a.* (coll.) waggish, acting the merry-andrew.

chacra, *f.* (Am.) a small isolated farm.

chacuaco. I. *m.* (Mex., min.) small smelting furnace. **II.** *a.* (coll.) rustic, boorish.

chachalaca. I. *f.* (Mex.) a gallinaceous bird that cries continually while flying; (coll.) chatterbox. **II.** *a.* chattering, talkative.

cháchara, *f.* (coll.) prate, chitchat, idle talk.

chacharear, *vn.* (coll.) to prate, chatter, prattle.

chacharero, ra; chacharón, na, *n. & a.* prater (-ing), prattler(-ing).

chacho, *m.* (coll.) little boy (short for MUCHACHO); stake at the game of ombre.

chafaldetes, *m.* (naut.) clew lines.

chafaldita, *f.* (coll.) chaff, raillery, banter.

chafalditero, ra, *n.* (coll.) chaffer, person given to banter.

chafalmejas, *n.* (coll.) (painting) dauber.

chafalonía, *f.* (Peru) old plate.

chafallar, *va.* to botch, to mend clumsily.

chafallo, *m.* coarse patch, clumsy mending.

chafallón, na, *n.* (coll.) botcher.

chafar, *va.* to flatten; to crease, rumple, crumple; (coll.) to cut short.

chafarote, *m.* cutlass; (coll.) broadsword; (fig.) sword, military force.

chafarrinada, *f.* blot, spot, stain.

chafarrinar, *va.* to blot, stain.

chafarrinón, *m.* blot, stain.—**echar un ch. a,** (coll.) to disgrace; to defame, throw mud at.

chaflán, *m.* bevel, chamfer.

chaflanar, *va.* to bevel, chamfer; (carp.) to cant.

chagra, *m.* a rustic in Ecuador.

chagrín, *m.* (Am.) grained morocco.

chaguarama, *f.* a Central-American palm.

chair, *m.* (tanning) inner side of a skin.

chaira, *f.* steel for sharpening knives, etc.

chal, *m.* shawl.

chala, *f.* (Peru) green corn husk.

chalado, da, *a.* addle-pated, light-witted.

chalán, na, *n.* hawker, huckster; horsedealer; horse breaker.

chalana, *f.* scow, lighter, wherry.

chalanear. I. *va.* to buy or sell cleverly; (Am.) to break (horses). II. *vn.* to deal in horses.

chalanería, *f.* artifice and cunning used by dealers in buying and selling.

chalate, *m.* (Mex.) small, lean horse.

chaleco, *m.* waistcoat, vest.

chalequero, ra, *n.* vest maker.

chalet, *m.* chalet, hut; cottage like a Swiss chalet.

chalí, *m.* mohair; challis, shalli; delaine.

chalina, *f.* cravat, scarf.

chalote, *m.* (bot.) shallot.

chalupa, *f.* (naut.) sloop, launch, small light vessel; long boat; (Mex.) a small canoe; (Mex.) corn pancake.**—chalupero,** *m.* boatman, canoeman.

chama, *f.* (low) barter, trade.

chamaco, *m.* (Am. esp. Mex.) youngster.

chamada, *f.* chips, brushwood, brush fire.

chamagoso, sa, *a.* (Mex.) greasy, filthy; ill-performed; low, vulgar.

chamar, *va.* (vulg.) to barter, trade off.

chamarasca, *f.* brushwood, brush fire.

chamarillero, ra, *n.* gambler; dealer in second-hand goods.

chamarillón, *m.* bad player at cards.

chamariz, *m.* (ornith.) blue titmouse.

chamarón, *m.* (ornith.) long-tailed titmouse.

chamarra, *f.* a garment of very coarse frieze.

chamarreta, *f.* a short, loose jacket.

chamba, *f.* (coll.) (billiards) fluke; (coll.) piece of good luck; (Colomb.) wide, deep ditch.

chambelán, *m.* chamberlain.

chamberga, *f.* long and wide cassock.

chambergo, ga. I. *a.* belonging or pert. to the Chamberga regiment, serving as a guard to Charles II of Spain. II. *m.* (Arg.) soft hat.

chambilla, *f.* stone wall topped by iron railing.

chambón, na. I. *a.* (coll.) awkward, unhandy; bungling. II. *n.* botcher, bungler, greenhorn.

chambonada, *f.* (coll.) blunder.

chambra, *f.* dressing sack or jacket.

chambrana, *f.* doorcase, jamb dressing.

chamelote, camelote, *m.* camlet, waterproof material or garment.**—ch. de aguas,** shiny camlet.

chamelotón, *m.* coarse camlet.

chamicera, *f.* half-burnt woodland.

chamicero, ra, *a.* pertaining to scorched wood.

chamiza, *f.* (bot.) chamiso; brush used as kindling wood.**—chamizal,** *m.* chamiso thicket.

chamizo, *m.* half-burnt stick of kindling wood.

chamorra, *f.* (coll.) a shorn head.

chamorro, ra, *a.* shorn, with hair cropped.

champán, *m.* (naut.) pink stern; sampan.

champaña, *m.* champagne.

champola, *f.* (Cuba) refreshment made from GUANÁBANA, custard apple.

champú, *m.* shampoo.

champurrado. I. *pp.* of CHAMPURRAR. II. *m.* mixture of liquors; (Mex.) chocolate made with ATOLE instead of water.

champurrar, *va.* (coll.) to mix (liquors).

chamuchina, *f.* (Peru) populace, rabble.

chamuscado, da. I. *pp.* of CHAMUSCAR. II. *a.* (coll.) tipsy; addicted to vice; singed, scorched.

chamuscar, *va.* (*pret.* CHAMUSQUÉ; *subj.* CHAMUSQUE) to singe or scorch; to sear.**—chamusco,**

m. = CHAMUSQUINA.**—chamuscón,** *m.* *aug.* bad singe or scorch.

chamusqué, chamusque, *v.* *V.* CHAMUSCAR.

chamusquina, *f.* scorching or singeing; (coll.) scolding, wrangling, high words.**—oler a ch.,** to look like (show signs of) a fight.

chanada, *f.* (coll.) trick, joke; deceit.

chanate, *m.* (Mex.) blackbird.

chancaco, ca. I. *a.* brown. II. *f.* (Am.) raw brown sugar; molasses cake.

chancear, *vn.* & *vr.* to jest, joke, fool.

chancero, ra, *a.* jocose, sportful, merry.

chanciller, *m.* chancellor.

chancillería, *f.* chancery; right and fees of a chancellor.

chancla, *f.* old shoe with worn-down heel.

chancleta, *f.* slipper.**—en ch.,** (of shoes) having no back.**—chancletear,** *vn.* to go in slippers.

chancleteo, *m.* clatter of slippers.

chanclo, *m.* patten; rubber, galosh, overshoe.

chancro, *m.* chancre, syphilitic ulcer.

chancha, *f.* (Arg.) pod; string bean.

chanchira, *f.* (Colomb.) rag, ragged clothes.

chanchiriento, ta, *a.* (Colomb.) ragged.

chancho, cha. I. *a.* (Am.) dirty, unclean; mean; stingy. II. *n.* dirty person; pig; hog.**—ch. de monte,** (Peru) agouti.

chanchullero, ra, *n.* trickster, sharper; smuggler.

chanchullo, *m.* unlawful conduct; sharp practice, vile trick; "racket"; (Am.) contraband.

chanfaina, *f.* ragout of livers and lights.

chanflón, na. I. *a.* awkward, coarse, gawky. II. *m.* ancient copper coin beaten out.

changa, *f.* (Cuba) jest.

changador, *m.* (Am.) porter, carrier.

changamé, *m.* (ornith.) thrush of Panama.

chango, a. *n.* (Am.) monkey.

changote, *m.* (metal.) bloom, billet.

changuear, *vn.* to be sporty or jesting.

changuí, *m.* (coll.) jest, trick (used with DAR); (Cuba) a country dance.

changuito, ta, *n.* *dim.* little monkey.

chantado, *m.* wall or fence of upright flags.

chantaje, *m.* blackmail; blackmailing.

chantajista, *n.* blackmailer.

chantar. I. *va.* to put on (as clothes); to tell to one's face; to give a piece of one's mind to (diff. constr.); to build (a fence) with upright flagstones; to pave with flagstones. II. *vr.* to put on (clothes).

chanto, *m.* flagstone.

chantre, *m.* precentor.

chantría, *f.* precentorship.

chanza, *f.* joke, jest, fun.**—ch. pesada,** offensive or serious joke.

¹chanzoneta, *f.* (coll.) joke, jest.

²chanzoneta, *f.* ballad, chansonette.

chanzonetero, ra, *n.* ballad writer; petty poet.

chapa, *f.* veneer; plate, sheet (of metal); (Am.) doorlock; foil; cap (of compass); leather chape; (Ecua.) policeman; rosy spot on the cheek, flush; rouge; transom and trunnion plates in gun carriages; judgment, good sense.**—***pl.* game of tossing up coins; (Am.) rosy cheeks.

chapado, da, *a.* having red cheeks.**—ch. a la antigua,** old-fashioned.

chapalear, *vn.* = CHAPOTEAR; CHACOLOTEAR.

chapaleo, *m.* splash, splatter.

chapaleta, *f.* flap valve, clack valve; cap; clapper.

chapaleteo, *m.* continuous splashing of the waters on the shore.

chapapote, *m.* (Cuba) mineral tar, variety of asphalt.

chaparra, *f.* a kind of oak; ancient low-roofed carriage; bramble bush.

chaparrada, *f.* shower (of rain).

chaparral, *m.* (Am.) chaparral; plantation of evergreen oaks.

For pronunciation, see the rules at the beginning of the book.

chaparrear, *vn.* to shower, to pour.

chaparreras, *f. pl.* chaps, chaparejos.

chaparro, *m.* (bot.) evergreen oak.—**c., ra,** *a. & n.* (Am.) short, stocky (person).

chaparrón, *m.* violent shower, downpour.

chapatal, *m.* mire; muddy place.

chapear. I. *va.* to veneer; inlay; cover with metal plate. **II.** *vn.* to splash, splatter.

chapelete, *m.* an ancient cover for the head.

chapeo, *m.* hat.

chapera, *f.* inclined plane.

chapería, *f.* ornament of metal plates.

chaperón, *m.* chaperon (ancient hood or cap).

chapeta, *f.* small metal plate; red spot on the cheek.

¹chapetón, na. I. *n. & a.* (Am.) Spaniard (recently arrived in Am.), Spanish. **II.** *m.* CHAPETONADA.

²chapetón, *m.* (Mex.) silver plate on a riding harness.

chapetonada, *f.* (Peru) illness of Europeans due to change of climate; act or conduct worthy of a ¹CHAPETÓN.

chapín. I. *m.* woman's clog with a cork sole. **II.** *n. & a.* (Am.) (one) having defective feet; (Am.) bowlegged (person).

chapinazo, *m.* blow with a clog or patten.

chapinería, *f.* shop where clogs and pattens are made and sold; art of making them.

chapinero, ra, *n.* clog maker or seller.

chápiro, *m.* a word used only in the phrases, *¡por vida del chápiro verde!* good gracious! *¡voto al chápiro!* by Jove! by thunder!

chapitel, *m.* (arch.) spire; capital of a column; (naut.) agate socket of the needle.

chaple, *m.* graver.

chapó, *m.* four-handed billiard game.

chapodar, *va.* to lop (branches of a tree).

chapodo, *m.* lopping; branch lopped off.

chapola, *f.* (Am.) butterfly; moth.

chapón, *m.* large blot of ink.

chapona, *f.* = CHAMBRA, dressing jacket, sack.

chapote, *m.* black wax for cleaning the teeth.

chapotear. I. *va.* to wet with a sponge or wet cloth. **II.** *vn.* to paddle in the water, to dabble.

chapoteo, *m.* splash, splatter.

chapucé, chapuce, *v. V.* CHAPUZAR.

chapucear, *va.* to botch, bungle, cobble.

chapuceramente, *adv.* fumblingly, clumsily, bunglingly.

chapucería, *f.* bungle, botch; clumsy fib.

chapucero, ra. I. *a.* rough, unpolished; clumsy, bungling; rude. **II.** *m.* blacksmith who makes nails, trivets, shovels, etc.; nailer; junk dealer.

chapurrar, *va.* to jabber (a language); to speak brokenly; to mix (app. to liquors).

chapurrear, *va.* to jabber (a language).

¹chapuz, *m.* ducking.

²chapuz, *m.* unimportant work; clumsy performance.—*pl.* **chapuces,** (naut.) mast spars.

chapuzar. I. *va.* (*pret.* CHAPUCÉ; *subj.* CHAPUCE) to duck. **II.** *vn. & vr.* to dive, draggle, duck.

chaqué, chaquet, *m.* cut-away coat.

chaqueta, *f.* jacket; sack coat; (mech.) case, casing, jacket.

chaquete, *m.* the game of checkers.

chaquetear, *vn.* (Cuba) to run away with fright.

chaquetón, *m. aug.* pea-jacket; (Cuba) overcoat.

chaquira, *f.* (Peru) fine mock pearl or glass colored bead; (Colomb.) bead.

charada, *f.* word charade.

charadrio, *m.* (ornith.) common roller.

charal, *m.* (Mex.) a lake fish.

charamusca, *f.* (Mex.) twisted candy; (Peru) brushwood.

charamusquero, ra, *n.* (Mex.) seller of twisted candy.

charanga, *f.* military brass band; fanfare.

charango, *m.* (Peru) a kind of bandore or small guitar.

charanguero, ra. I. *a.* clumsy, unpolished. **II.** *m.* bungler, botcher; peddler, hawker; small coast-trading ship.

charca, *f.* pool, basin, pond.

charco, *m.* pool, puddle.—**pasar el ch.,** (coll.) to cross the big pond (the sea).

charla, *f.* prattle, chat, talk; loquaciousness; (ornith.) Bohemian chatterer, silktail.

charlador, ra, *n. & a.* prater(-ing), talker(-ative), chatterbox.

charladuría, *f.* garrulity, gossip, prattle.

charlante, *n.* gabbler, chatterer.

charlantín, na, *n.* (coll.) mean prattler, gossip.

charlar, *vn.* to chat, prattle, prate.

charlatán, na, *n.* prater, babbler; charlatan, quack, humbug.

charlatanear, *vn.* = CHARLAR.

charlatanería, *f.* garrulity, verbosity; charlatanry, quackery, humbug.

charlatanismo, *m.* charlatanry, quackery; verbosity, loquaciousness.

charlotear, *vn.* = CHARLAR.

charneca, *f.* (bot.) mastic tree.

charnecal, *m.* plantation of mastic trees.

charnela, *f.* hinge, chape of a buckle, hinge joint, knuckle.

charneta, *f.* (coll.) hinge joint.

charol, *m.* varnish, japan; patent leather.—**darse ch.,** to blow one's own horn, to brag.

charolar, *va.* to varnish, polish, enamel; japan.

charolista, *n.* gilder, varnisher.

charpa, *f.* leather belt with compartments for pistols; sling for a broken arm; (naut.) sling.

charpar, *va.* to scarp; to lap.

charque, *m.* (Am.) jerked beef.

charquear, *va.* (Am.) to jerk or dry (beef).

charqueo, *m.* (min.) cleaning of the drains; cleaning holy-water fonts.

charquí, *m.* = CHARQUE.

charquillo, *m. dim.* small pool or puddle.

charrada, *f.* speech or action of a peasant; country dance; (coll.) tawdriness, tinsel, gaudiness.

charramente, *adv.* tawdrily, gaudily, tastelessly.

charrán, *a.* rascally, knavish.—**charranada,** *f.* knavish, roguish action.—**charranear,** *vn.* to play the knave.—**charranería,** *f.* rascality, knavery.

charrasca, *f.* folding knife; (coll., humor.) dangling sword.

charrería, *f.* tawdriness, gaudiness.

charretera, *f.* strap on the bottom of trousers; the buckle of the strap; (mil.) the lower part of trousers to fasten them with a buckle; the buckle; epaulet.—**ch. mocha,** shoulder knot; (coll.) shoulder pad for carrying loads.

charro, ra. I. *n.* churl; coarse, ill-bred person; (Mex.) cowboy. **II.** *a.* tawdry, showy, flashy, loud.

chascar, *vn.* to crackle, crack, sputter.

chascarrillo, *m.* (coll.) spicy anecdote.

chasco, *m.* practical joke, jest, trick; failure, disappointment.—**dar ch.,** to disappoint.—**dar un ch.,** to play a joke, trick.—**llevarse ch.** (con), to be disappointed (in), to get left.

chasí, *m.* photographic plate holder.

chasis, *m.* (auto) chassis.

chasponazo, *m.* mark made by a spent bullet.

¹chasquear. I. *va.* to crack or snap (a whip). **II.** *vn.* to crack, snap; crepitate.

²chasquear, *va.* to fool; to play a trick on; to disappoint, fail; to cheat.

chasqui, *m.* (Peru) postboy, foot messenger.

chasquido, *m.* crack of a whip or lash; crack, noise made by timber when it breaks or splits.

chata, *f.* bedpan; (naut.) flat-bottomed boat.—**ch. alijadora,** lighter.—**ch. de arbolar,** sheer-hulk.—**ch. de carenar,** careening hulk.

chatedad, *f.* flatness.

chato, ta, *a.* flat; flat- or pug-nosed; flattened.

chatón, *m.* bezel holding a gem; large gem set in.

chatre, *a.* (Ecua.). richly decked out.
chaucha, *f.* (Arg.) pod; string bean.
chaúl, *m.* blue Chinese silk.
chauvinismo, *m.* chauvinism.
chauvinista, *n. & a.* chauvinist(-ic).
chaval, la, *n.* lad, lass.
chaveta, *f.* bolt, forelock, pin, key, wedge; cotter, cotter pin.—**perder la ch.**, to become rattled.
chaya, *f.* (Chile) amusement consisting in throwing water on passers-by during carnivals; confetti; spray of a watering pot.
chayote, *m.* (Mex.) pear-shaped fruit with a large stone.—**chayotera**, *f.* (Mex.) a climbing plant yielding the CHAYOTE.
chaza, *f.* point where the ball is driven back or where it stops, in the game of PELOTA; mark where the ball stops; (naut.) space between ports.—**hacer chazas**, (of horses) to walk on the hind feet.
chazador, *m.* (in PELOTA) person employed to stop the ball and mark the game.
chazar, *va.* (in PELOTA) to stop (the ball) before it reaches the winning point; to mark the point whence the ball was driven back.
checo, ca, *n. & a.* Czech.
checoslovaco, ca, *n. & a.* Czecho-Slovak, Czecho-Slovakian.
chécheres, *m. pl.* (Colomb.) small things, notions.
cheira, *f.* = CHAIRA, steel for sharpening.
chelín, *m.* shilling.
chepa, *f.* (coll.) hump, hunch.
cheque, *m.* (com.) check, sight draft.
chequear, *va.* (Angl.) (Am.) to check, verify; to check (mark).
cherna, *f.* (ichth.) ruffle, a salmonlike fish.
cherva, *f.* (bot.) castor-oil plant.
cheurón, *m.* (her.) chevron.
¹chía, *f.* short black mantle, cowl.
²chía, *f.* white medicinal earth; (bot.) lime-leaved sage.
chibalete, *m.* (print.) cabinet, composing frame.
chibcha. I. *a.* pert. to the Chibchas. **II.** *m.* one of the aborigines of the Bogotá plateau.
chibuquí, *m.* Turkish chibouk, smoking pipe.
chica, *f.* girl. *V.* CHICO.
cicada, *f.* herd of sickly kids; childish action.
chicalote, *m.* (bot.) Mexican argemone.
chicana, *f.* (Am.) chicanery.
chicanero, ra, *a.* (Am.) tricky, cunning.
chicle, *m.* chicle.
chico. ca. I. *a.* little, small. **II.** *n.* little boy, little chap; little girl or lass; dear boy, dear fellow; dear girl; (coll. familiar) boy, old chap.
chicolear, *va.* (coll.) to pay compliments to (a woman).
chicoleo, *m.* (coll.) flattering compliment.
chicoria, *f.* (bot.) = ACHICORIA, chicory.
chicorrotico, ca, llo, lla, to, ta, *a.* dim. (coll.) very little or small, tiny (child).
chicorrotín, *a.* (coll.) very small, tiny.
chicotazo, *m.* (Mex.) blow with a whip.
chicote, ta. I. *n.* (coll.) fat strong boy or girl. **II.** *m.* (naut.) end of a rope or cable; junk; (Mex.) whip; (coll.) cigar.
chicotear, *va.* (Mex.) to whip.
chicozapote, *m.* (bot.) sapodilla.
chicuelo, la, *n. dim.* little boy; little girl.
¹chicha, *f.* chicha, a popular fermented beverage, variously made from maize, pineapple, etc.
²chicha, *f.* children's term for meat.
chícharo, *f.* (bot.) pea.
chicharra, *f.* harvest fly, jarfly, cicada; talkative woman; kazoo, a plaything.—**cantar la ch.**, (coll.) to be scorching hot.
chicharrar, *va.* = ACHICHARRAR, to overheat.
chicharrear, *vn.* to creak; to chirp (said of the cicada).

chicharrero, ra. I. *n.* maker or seller of kazoos. **II.** *m.* (coll.) very hot place or climate.
chicharro, *m.* young tunny fish; horse-mackerel.
chicharrón, *m.* crackling, fried scrap, cracknel; (Mex.) thick, crisp bacon; overroasted meat; (coll.) person sunburnt or tanned.
chiche, *m.* (Am.) potted and devilled fish.
chichear, *va.* to hiss as a sign of displeasure.
chicheo, *m.* act of hissing.
chichería, *f.* tavern where ¹CHICHA is sold.
chichero, ra, *n.* seller or drinker of ¹CHICHA.
chichigua, *f.* (Mex., vulg.) wet nurse.
chichimeco, ca, *n. & a.* Chichimec(-an).
chichisbeador, *m.* gallant, wooer.
chichisbear, *va.* to woo, court.
chichisbeo, *m.* court paid to a lady; cicisbeo, gallant who trails a married woman.
chichón, *m.* bump; bruise.
chichoncillo, cito, *m. dim.* small bump.
chichonera, *f.* tumbling cap; child's wadded hood.
chichota, *f.*—**sin faltar ch.**, without lacking one iota.
¹chifla, *f.* whistling, hissing.
²chifla, *f.* paring knife.
chiflacayote, *m.* a large kind of pumpkin.
chifladera, *f.* whistle.
chiflado, da, *a.* (Am.) (fig.) crazy, crackbrained.
chifladura, *f.* hissing, whistling; (coll.) crankiness; eccentricity; whim, fad; hobby.
¹chiflar. I. *vn.* to hiss, whistle; (coll.) to tipple. **II.** *vr.* (coll.) to become mentally unbalanced; to lose one's head.
²chiflar, *va.* to pare (leather).
chiflato, *m.* whistle.
chifle, *m.* whistle; call; instrument to decoy birds; (naut.) priming horn; powderflask.
chiflete, *m.* whistle.
chiflido, *m.* shrill whistling sound.
chiflo, *m.* whistling.
chiflón, *m.* (Am.) draught (of air); (Mex.) waterspout; (min.) caving of loose stone.
chilaba, *f.* Moorish hooded garment.
chilacayote, *m.* (bot.) bottle gourd.
chilanco, *m.* = CILANCO, pool (of water).
chilar, *m.* field planted with chillies.
chile, *f.* (bot.) chilli, red pepper.
chileno, na; chileño, ña, *n. & a.* Chilean.
chilindrina, *f.* (coll.) trifle, thing of little value; (coll.) joke, fun, witticism, anecdote.
chilindrinero, ra, *n. & a.* (coll.) trifler(-ing).
chilindrón, *m.* a card game.
chilote, *m.* (Am.) = JILOTE, ear of green corn; (Mex.) liqueur-like drink.
chiltipiquín, *m.* (Mex.) small hot chilli.
¹chilla, *f.* call for foxes, hares, or rabbits.
²chilla, *f.* (carp.) clapboard.—**chillado**, *m.* clapboard roof.
chillador, ra, *n. & a.* screamer(-ing); screecher (-ing); creaking.
chillante, *a.* shrieking, screeching.
chillar, *vn.* to screech, scream, shriek; to crackle, creak; to imitate the notes of birds; (of something frying) to hiss, sizzle.
chilleras, *f. pl.* (naut.) shot lockers for balls; rowlocks.
chillido, *m.* screech, scream, shriek, shrill sound; bawling of a woman or child.—**dar un ch.**, to utter a scream.
chillo, *m.* call.
¹chillón, *m.* lath nail.—**ch. real**, spike.
²chillón, na. I. *n.* (coll.) screamer, bawler; whiner. **II.** *a.* whining; screechy, shrill, harsh; showy, tawdry, loud; (of colors) loud.
chimachima, chimango, *m.* (Chile, Peru), a species of caracara, a vulture-like bird.
chimenea, *f.* chimney, smokestack; hearth, fireplace; kitchen range, cooking stove.—**ch. francesa**, fireplace with mantelpiece.
chimpancé, *m.* chimpanzee.

---

¹**china,** *f.* pebble, small stone; game of shutting the hands, and guessing which contains the pebble.

²**china,** *f.* (bot.) Chinaroot; china, porcelain; China silk or cotton stuff; (P. R., Cuba) sweet orange.

³**china,** *f.* (Am.) maid servant; (C. A.) children's nurse; (Colomb.) little or young girl.

chinampa, *f.* small garden tract in lakes near Mex.—**chinampero,** *m.* tiller of a CHINAMPA.

chinanta, *f.* (P. I.) a unit of weight (about 14 lbs.)

chinarro, *m.* large pebble.

chinateado, *m.* stratum or layer of pebbles.

chinazo, *m.* *aug.* blow with a pebble.

chincharrazo, *m.* (coll.) = CINTARAZO, slap.

chincharrero, *m.* place swarming with bedbugs; fishing smack.

chinche, *m.* or *f.* bedbug; thumb tack; (coll.) tedious person, bore.—**chinchero,** *m.* bug trap made of twigs; place full of bedbugs.

chinchilla, *f.* (zool.) chinchilla; its fur.

chinchín, *m.* (Cuba, Carib.) drizzling rain.

chinchorrería, *f.* (coll.) nuisance, vexation; (coll.) mischievous tale.

chinchorrero, ra, *n.* insidious and pestering taleteller.

chinchorro, *m.* small dragnet; smallest rowboat on board a ship.

chinchoso, sa, *a.* (coll.) querulous, tiresome.

chinela, *f.* slipper; pattens, chopines, or clogs worn by women in bad weather.

chinero, *m.* china closet, cupboard.

chinesco, ca, *a.* Chinese.—*m. pl.* (mus.) bells.

chingar. I. *va.* (Am.) to annoy, bother; (C. A.) to cut off the tail of, bob. **II.** *va. & vn.* to drink to excess. **III.** *vr.* to get drunk; (S. A.) to be fooled, "get left."

chinguirito, *m.* (Mex.) rum from lees of sugar.

chinito, ta, *n.* (Am.) dearie, dearest.

chino, na. I. *a. & n.* Chinese. **II.** *m.* Chinese (language); (Colomb.) boy (esp. a newsboy, gamin, etc.); (Am.) crossbred (app. to offspring of non-white parents).

chipichipi, *m.* (Mex.) mist; drizzle.

chipirón, *m.* calamary, a kind of cuttle-fish.

chiprio, pria; chipriota, chipriote, *n. & a.* Cyprian (from Cyprus).

chiqueadores, *m. pl.* disks of tortoise shell formerly used in Mexico as a feminine ornament; small plasters for headache.

chiquero, *m.* pigpen; hut for goats; place where bulls are shut up.

chiquichaque, *m.* (coll.) sawyer; noise of things rubbing against each other.

chiquigüite, chiquihuite, *m.* (Mex.) willow basket.

chiquilicuatro, *m.* (coll.) dabbler, meddler.

chiquilín, na, *n.* (Mex. & C. A.) = CHIQUILLO.

chiquillada, *f.* childish speech or action.

chiquillería, *f.* (coll.) a great number of small children.

chiquillo, illa, *n.* small child, little one.

chiquirritico, ica, illo, illa, ito, ita, *a.* *dim.* very small, tiny.

chiquirritín, na, *n.* (coll.) baby boy; baby girl; very little child.

chiquitico, ca; lio, lla, *a.* *dim.* very small, tiny.

chiquitín, na, *n.* = CHIQUIRRITÍN.

chiquito, ta. I. *a.* small, little; very small, very little, tiny.—**andarse en chiquitas,** to be lenient, condescending.—**hacerse chiquito,** to be modest, to conceal one's accomplishments. **II.** *n.* little boy (girl), little one.

chiribitas, *f. pl.* (coll.) particles that float in the eyes and obscure the sight.

chiribitil, *m.* crib, narrow and low hole or corner; small room, "den."

chirigaita, *f.* a kind of gourd.

chirigota, *f.* (coll.) jest, joke, fun.

chirimbolos, *m. pl.* (coll.) odds and ends; utensils, traps.

chirimía. I. *f.* (mus.) flageolet. **II.** *n.* flageolet player.

chirimoya, *f.* (bot.) cherimoya, a tropical fruit.

chirimoyo, *m.* cherimoya tree.

chirinola, *f.* bowling, boys' game; trifle.—**estar de ch.** (coll.) to be in good spirits.

chiripa, *f.* in billiards, fluke; (coll.) stroke of good luck; chance or unexpected event.—**de ch.,** by chance, unexpectedly.—**chiripear,** *vn.* to make flukes at bililards.—**chiripero, ra,** *n.* poor player who wins by fluke; lucky person.

chirivía, *f.* (bot.) parsnip; (ornith.) wagtail.

chirla, *f.* mussel.

chirlador, ra, *n.* (coll.) clamorous prattler.

chirlar, *vn.* to talk fast and loud.

chirle. I. *a.* (coll.) insipid, tasteless. **II.** *m.* = SIRLE, dung of sheep and goats.

chirlo, *m.* large wound in the face and its scar.

chirona, *f.* (coll.) prison.

chirriadero, |ra; chirriador, ra, *a.* hissing; sizzling, when frying; creaking, as a hinge; chirping.

chirriar, *vn.* to hiss; sizzle; creak, squeak; (coll.) to sing out of tune or time.

chirrido, *m.* chirping of birds; chattering; creaking; any shrill sound.

chirrío, *m.* creaking noise made by carts.

chirrión, *m.* tumbrel, creaking muck or dung cart; (Am.) heavy horsewhip.

chirrionero, *m.* scavenger, dung-cart driver.

chirumen, *m.* (coll.) common sense.

¡chis! *interj.* sh! hush! silence!

chisgarabís, *n.* (coll.) meddler, dabbler; insignificant, noisy person.

chisguete, *m.* (coll.) small draft of wine; small spout of any liquid, squirt.—**echar un ch.,** to drink.

chisme, *m.* tale of a gossip monger; gossip; (coll.) jigger, any household gadget.—**chismear,** *va.* to tattle, gossip.—**chismero, ra,** *n. & a.* talebearer(-ing), gossip(-ing).

chismografía, *f.* (coll.) gossip, tattle.

chismoso, sa, *n. & a.* = CHISMERO, RA.

chispa, *f.* spark; ember; sparkle; flake; very small diamond; small particle; little bit; state of drunkenness; cleverness, wit; rumor.—**coger una ch.,** (coll.) to get drunk.—**de ch.,** flintlock.—**echar chispas,** (coll.) to rave, be in a passion.—**ser ch.,** to be very lively.

chisparse, *vr.* (Am.) to get tipsy.

¡chispas! *interj.* fire and tow! blazes!

chispazo, *m.* flying off of a spark; damage it does; (coll.) tale mischievously circulated.

chispeante, *a.* sparking, sparkling.

chispear, *vn.* to spark; sparkle; to scintillate; to rain gently.

chispero, ra. I. *a.* sparkling. **II.** *m.* blacksmith; spark catcher; (coll.) Madrilenian ruffian.

chispo. I. *a.* (coll.) tipsy. **II.** *m.* short drink.

chisporrotear, *vn.* (coll.) to sputter sparks.

chisporroteo, *m.* (coll.) sputtering sparks.

chisposo, sa, *a.* sputtering, sparkling.

chistar, *vn.* to mumble, mutter; answer back.—**sin ch. ni mistar,** without (saying) a word.

chiste, *m.* witty saying; joke, jest.—**ch. verde,** off-color, risqué joke.—**dar en el ch.,** to guess right.

chistera, *f.* hand fish basket; (coll.) silk hat.

chistosamente, *adv.* facetiously, humorously.

chistoso, sa, *a.* funny, witty.

chita, *f.* ankle bone in sheep and bullocks; a game with this bone.—**a la ch. callando,** on the quiet, by stealth.

chiticalla, *m.* (coll.) discreet person; secret.

chiticallando, *adv.* (coll.) quietly, on the quiet.—**a la ch.,** noiselessly, quietly.—**andar, or ir, ch.,** to go on tiptoes, to go very quietly.

¹**chito,** *m.* piece of wood or bone on which money

is put in the game of CHITA.—**irse a chitos**, (coll.) to lead a debauched life, to go to the dogs.

²¡chito! ¡¹chitón! *interj.* hush! not a word!

²chitón, *m.* mollusk with coat-of-mail shell.

chiva, *f.* kid; female goat.

chivata, *f.* shepherd's staff.

chivato, *m.* kid between six and twelve months old; (Colomb.) rascal, knave.

chivero, *m.* (Am.) puma.

chivetero, chivital, chivitil, *m.* fold for kids.

¹chivo, va, *n.* kid; goat.

²chivo, *m.* pit for the lees of oil; (Colomb.) anger, angry spell.

¡cho! *interj.* whoa!

¹choca, *f.* part of the game given to a hawk.

²choca, *f.* soap-boiler's paddle.

chocador, ra. I. *n.* & *a.* provoker(-ing). **II.** *a.* repulsive, disagreeable.

chocante, *a.* (Mex.) provoking; disagreeable; strange, surprising.

chocar. I. *vn.* (*pret.* CHOQUÉ; *subj.* CHOQUE) to strike, collide, hit, clash; to meet, fight, combat. **II.** *va.* to provoke; to displease, be disliked; to surprise.

chocarrear, *vn.* to joke, act the buffoon.

chocarrería, *f.* buffoonery, coarse jest.

chocarrero, ra, *a.* scurrilous, vulgar.

chocilla, *f. dim.* hut, low cottage.

choclar, *vn.* in the game of ARGOLLA, to drive the ball through the rings.

¹choclo, *m.* clog, galosh.

²choclo, chócolo, *m.* (Am.) green ear of corn.

choclón, *m.* in the game of ARGOLLA, the driving of a ball through the rings.

choco, *m.* small cuttlefish.

chocolate, *m.* chocolate.

chocolatear, *vn.* (Am.) to drink chocolate.

chocolatera, *f.* chocolate pot; woman who makes or sells chocolate.

chocolatería, *f.* shop where chocolate is sold.

chocolatero, ra. I. *a.* fond of chocolate. **II.** *n.* chocolate maker or dealer. **III.** *m.* (Mex.) stiff north wind.

chocha, chochaperdiz, *f.* (ornith.) woodcock.

chochear, *vn.* to dote.

chochera, chochez, *f.* dotage.

¹chocho, cha, *n.* & *q.* dotard(-ing).

²chocho, *m.* (bot.) lupine; cinnamon candy stick. —*pl.* sweetmeats, dainties.

chofer, chófer, *n.* chauffeur.

chofes, *m. pl.* livers and lights; lungs.

chofeta, *f.* chafing dish; fire pan; foot stove.

chofista, *n.* one living on livers and lights.

cholo, la, *n.* (Am.) a term applied by whites to Indians and servants; half-breed.

cholla, *f.* (coll.) skull, head, noddle; faculty.

chonta, *f.* a hardwood palm tree.

¹chontal, *m.* CHONTA field or grove.

²chontal, *m.* one of the Chontal tribe of Nicaragua; (coll.) uncivilized Indian; uncultured person.

¹chopa, *f.* (ichth.) a kind of sea bream.

²chopa, *f.* (naut.) top-gallant poop.

chopera, *f.* black-poplar grove.

¹chopo, *m.* (bot.) black-poplar tree.

²chopo, *m.* (coll.) musket, gun.

choqué, choque, *v. V.* CHOCAR.

choque, *m.* impact; collision; clash; (mil.) skirmish; (naut.) chock, fur, rush; (Angl.) (elec.) shock.

choquezuela, *f.* (anat.) kneecap.

chordón, churdón, *m.* raspberry jam.

choricera, *f.* woman who makes or sells sausages; (mech.) sausage stuffer.

choricería, *f.* = SALCHICHERÍA, sausage shop.

choricero, ra, *n.* sausage maker or seller.

chorillo, *m.* (Peru) mill for coarse fabrics.

chorizo. I. *m.* pork sausage; tightrope walker's pole. **II. chorizo, za,** *n.* & *a.* (Colomb., Ecua.) fool(-ish), (fig.) idiot(-ic).

chorlito, *m.* (ornith.) curlew or gray plover; (ornith.) red shank.

chorlo, *m.* (min.) schorl, tourmalin.

chorote, *m.* (Venez.) poor-quality chocolate; (Colomb.) chocolate pot; (Cuba) any thick beverage.

chorreado, da. I. *pp.* of CHORREAR. **II.** *a.* (of cows) striped.

chorreadura, *f.* dripping, welling; stain from drippings.

chorrear, *vn.* to spout; to drip; to be dripping wet; to come out little by little or one by one.

chorreo, *m.* spouting, dripping.

chorrera, *f.* spout or place whence liquids drip; mark left by dripping or running water; ornament formerly appended to badges; shirt frill; (Am.) (coll.) string (of things), stream (of things, people), lot (in the sense of great quantity or number).

chorretada, *f.* (coll.) squirt, spurt, jet.

chorrillo, *m. dim.* small spout; (coll.) continual coming in and outgoing of money, etc.

chorrito, *m. dim.* small spout.

chorro, *m.* jet, spurt; stream; anything issuing, entering, flowing, or passing.—**ch. de voz,** voice of large volume.—**a chorros,** (coll.) abundantly.—**de ch.,** jet (as *a.*)

chorroborro, *m.* (coll.) flood, inundation.

chorrón, *m.* dressed hemp.

chortal, *m.* fountain or spring.

chota, *f.* suckling kid; heifer calf.

chotacabras, *f.* (ornith.) goat-sucker, churn owl.

chote, *m.* (Cuba) = CHAYOTE, a kind of fruit.

chotear, *va.* (Cuba, coll.) to banter, gibe.

choteo, *m.* (Cuba, coll.) chaffing, jeering.

choto, *m.* suckling kid, calf.

chotuno, na, *a.* suckling (young goats or kids); poor, starved (lambs); goatish.—**oler a ch., to** smell like a goat.

chova, *f.* (ornith.) jay, chough; jackdaw, crow.

choz, *f.* stroke, blow; suddenness.

choza, *f.* hut, hovel, cabin, shanty.

chozno, na, *m., f.* great-grandson(-daughter).

chozo, *m.* small hut or cabin.

chozpar, *vn.* to gambol, caper.

chozpo, *m.* gambol, leap.—**chozpón, na,** *a.* frisky, capering.

chozuela, *f. dim.* small hut or shanty.

chual, *m.* (bot.) pigweed or goosefoot.

chualar, *m.* place abounding in pigweed.

chubarba, *f.* (bot.) stonecrop.

chubasco, *m.* squall, shower.—**ch. de nieve,** blizzard.

chubascoso, sa, *a.* squally, gusty.

chúcaro, ra, *a.* (Am.) (of horses) shy; (of cattle) wild.

chucero, *m.* (mil.) pikeman.

chucha, *f.* female dog; (Am.) opossum.

chuchear. I. *va.* to fowl with calls, gins, and nets. **II.** *vn.* to whisper.

¹chuchería, *f.* gewgaw, trinket, notion, titbit.

²chuchería, *f.* fowling with calls, gins, and nets.

chuchero, ra, *n.* birdcatcher; (Cuba) (Ry.) switch tender.

chucho. I. *m.* (coll.) dog; (Cuba) whip; (Cuba) railway switch; (Chile, Arg.) chill; malaria. **II.** *interj.* used to curb or scare off a dog.

chuchumeco, *m.* contemptible little fellow.

chueca, *f.* head of a bone; hockey; small hockey ball; (coll.) joke, trick; soap maker's paddle.

chuecazo, *m.* stroke given to a ball at hockey.

chueco, ca, *a.* (Am.) crooked, bent, out of shape.

chufa, *f.* (bot.) chufa, edible tuber of a sedge.

chufar, *vn.* & *vr.* to mock, to scoff.

chufería, *f.* place where chufa orgeat and sherbet are made or served.

chufero, ra, *n.* seller of chufas.

¹chufeta, chofeta, *f.* chafing dish; fire pan.

²**chufeta,** *f.* (coll.) jest.

chufleta, *f.* (coll.) taunt, scoff.

chufletear, *vn.* (coll.) to show contempt.

chufletero, ra, *a.* (coll.) taunting, sneering.

chulada, *f.* droll speech or action; pleasant conversation; breach of manners.

chulear, *va.* to jest with, to poke fun at; (Mex.) to court, make love to.

chulería, *f.* pleasing manner.

chuleta, *f.* chop; cutlet; (carp.) chips for filling joints; (coll.) slap, blow with the fist.

chulillo, illa, ito, ita, *m. & f. dim.* little wag.

¹**chulo, la. I.** *n.* punster, jester; funny person; sly, deceitful person. **II.** *m.* rascal, knave; pimp, man kept by a woman; bullfighter's assistant; butcher's mate. **III.** *f.* woman of low class loud in dress and manners.

²**chulo, la,** *a.* (Am.) pretty, nice, graceful, attractive.

chulla, *f.* slice of bacon.

chumacera, *f.* (mech.) journal bearing; (naut.) rowlock.

chumbe, *m.* (Am.) band to hold dress at waist.

chumbera, *f.* (bot.) opuntia, prickly pear.

chumbo, ba, *a.* prickly (pear); Indian (fig).

chumpipe, *m.* (C. A.) turkey.

chuncaca, *f.* (C. A.) = CHANCACA, brown sugar.

¹**chunga,** *f.* (coll.) jest, fun, banter.—**estar de ch.,** to be in good humor.

²**chunga, chuña,** *f.* (ornith.) S. A. wading bird.

chungón, ona, *n.* jester.

chunguearse, *vr.* (coll.) to chaff, gibe, jest.

chuña, *f.* CHUNGA; (Chile) scramble, scuffle.

¹**chupa,** *f.* (P. I.) liquid measure (0.735 liter); dry measure (0.37 liter).

²**chupa,** *f.* waistcoat; undercoat with sleeves.—**poner a uno como ch. de dómine,** (coll.) to wipe the floor with one.

chupada, *f.* suck, suction.

chupaderito, *m. dim.*—**andarse con,** or **en, chupaderitos,** to use ineffective means for difficult tasks.

chupadero, ra, dor, ra. I. *a.* sucking, absorbent. **II.** *m.* baby's coral or teething ring; (mech.) suction tube; (Am.) tippler.

chupado, da, *a.* (coll.) lean, emaciated.

chupadorcito, *m. dim.* of CHUPADOR; CHUPADERITO.

chupadura, *f.* act and effect of sucking.

chupaflores, *m.* (ornith.) humming bird.

chupalandero, *m.* snail that lives on plants.

chupamiel, chupamirtos, *m.* humming bird.

chupar, *va.* to suck; to draw, sip; to absorb; to imbibe; (coll.) to hang upon (others) for subsistence; to fool.—**ch. la sangre** (coll.) to stick like a leech.—**chuparse los dedos,** to eat with pleasure; to be overjoyed.

chupativo, va, *a.* of a sucking nature.

¹**chupeta,** *f.* (naut.) roundhouse.

²**chupeta, illa, ita,** *f. dim.* short waistcoat.

chupetear, *va.* to suck gently and by starts.

chupeteo, *m.* gentle sucking.

chupetín, *m.* man's inner garment.

chupetón, *m.* violent suction.

chupón, na. I. *n. & a.* (coll.) sponge, parasite. **II.** *m.* (bot.) sucker, shoot; (mech.) sucker, plunger piston, valve bucket.

churdón, *m.* raspberry jam.

churla, *f.*, **churlo,** *m.* seroon, spicebag.

churra, *f.* little pin-tailed grouse; heifer one year old.

churrasco, *m.* (Am.) piece of broiled meat.

churrascón, *m.* scorching.

churre, *m.* (coll.) thick, dirty, oozing or dripping grease; anything dirty and greasy.

churrea, *f.* Californian grouse.

churriburri, *m.* = ZURRIBURRI, ragamuffin.

churriento, ta, *a.* greasy.

churrigueresco, ca, *a.* (arch.) overloaded, tawdry, loud.

churreguerismo, *m.* (arch.) overornamentation, tawdriness.

¹**churro, ra,** *a.* (of wool) coarse; (of sheep) having coarse wool.

²**churro,** *m.* a sort of fritter, cruller.

churrullero, ra, *n.* tattler, gossip.

churrupear, *vn.* to sip wine.

churruscarse, *vr.* to be scorched.

churrusco, *m.* bread toasted too much.

churumbela, *f.* reed instrument resembling a flageolet; (Am.) small cup for maté.

churumen, *m.* (coll.) = CHIRUMEN, common sense.

churumo, *m.* (coll.) juice or substance.

chus ni mus.—(coll.) **no decir chus ni mus,** not to say a word, not to open one's mouth.

chuscada, *f.* pleasantry, joke.

chuscamente, *adv.* in a droll manner.

chusco, ca, *a.* droll, merry, funny.

chusma, *f.* crew and slaves of a row galley; rabble, mob, crowd.

chuspa, *f.* (Am.) bag.

chute, *m.* (C. A.) prick.

chuza, *f.* (Mex.) (bowling) a strike.

chuzar, *va.* (Colomb.) to prick.

chuzazo, *m.* large pike; prick; thrust with a prick or pointed weapon.

chuzo, *m.* pike; prick; anything pointed; (naut.) boarding pike.—**a. chuzos,** abundantly, impetuously.—**echar chuzos,** (coll.) to brag.

¹**chuzón, na,** *n.* crafty, artful person; wag, punster, jester.

²**chuzón,** *m. aug.* = CHUZAZO.

D

da, *v. V.* DAR.—**¡lo mismo da!** it amounts to the same thing!—**da lástima,** it's a pity, pitiful.

dable, *a.* possible, practicable.

daca (word formed by the verb **da** and the adv. **acá**), give me, give it me.—**andar d. y toma,** to dispute.—**toma y d.,** give-and-take.

da capo, (mus.) da capo.

¹**dacio, cia,** *n. & a.* Dacian.

²**dacio,** *m.* tribute, tax.

dación, *f.* (law) ceding, yielding or giving up.

dactílico, ca, *a.* dactylic.—**dáctilo,** *m.* dactyl.

dactilografía, *f.* typewriting.

dactilografiar, *n.* typist.

dactilógrafo, *m.* typewriter (machine); typist.

dactilología, *f.* dactylology, talking with fingers.

dactiloscopia, *f.* study of finger prints.

dactiloscópico, ca, *a.* pert. to finger prints.

dádiva, *f.* gift, gratification, grant, keepsake.

dadivosamente, *adv.* liberally, bountifully.

dadivosidad, *f.* liberality, bounty.

dadivoso, sa, *a.* bountiful, liberal.

¹**dado,** *m.* die; block, bushing; pivot collar; coin; (arch.) dado.—*pl.* (naut.) case shot or grapeshot.—**d. falso,** false die.—**dados de las velas,** (naut.) tablings of the bowling cringles.—**correr el d.,** (coll.) to be in good luck.—**estar como un d.,** to fit exactly.

²**dado, da,** *pp.* of DAR.—**d. que,** provided; so long as; assuming that.

dador, ra, *n.* giver; (com.) drawer of a bill of exchange; bearer (of a letter).

¹**daga,** *f.* dagger.—**llegar a las dagas,** (coll.) to reach the most difficult point.

²**daga,** *f.* line of bricks in a kiln.

dagoba, *f.* (arch.) dagoba, an East-Indian shrine.

dagón, *m. aug.* large dagger.

daguerrotipar, *va.* to daguerreotype.

daguerrotipia, *f.* the making of daguerreotypes.

daguerrotipo, *m.* daguerreotype.

daguilla, *f. dim.* small dagger.

daifa, *f.* mistress, concubine.

dala, *f.* (naut.) pump dale of a ship.

¡dale! or ¡dale que dale! *interj.* expressive of displeasure at obstinacy.

dalia, *f.* (bot.) dahlia.

dálmata; dalmático, ca, *n.* & *a.* Dalmatian.

dalmática, *f.* dalmatica, wide-sleeve tunic.

daltoniano, na, *a.* color-blind.

daltonismo, *m.* color blindness, daltonism.

dallador, *m.* grass mower.

dallar, *va.* to mow.

dalle, *m.* scythe, sickle.

¹**dama,** *f.* lady, dame; noble or distinguished woman; lady courted by a gentleman; lady of honor at court; mistress or concubine; king in checkers; an old Spanish dance.—**d. cortesana,** courtesan.—**segunda d.,** (theat.) woman who has a walk-on part.—**soplar la d.,** to huff a king in the game of draughts; (coll.) to carry off and marry a woman who was courted by another man.

²**dama,** *f.* (metal.) dam of a blast furnace.

damajuana, *f.* demijohn.

damascado, da, *a.* damasklike.

damascena, *f.* damson, plum.

damasceno, na, *a.* Damascene.

damasco, *m.* damask, figured silk stuff; Brussels apricot; damson, plum.

damasina, *f.* silk stuff resembling damask.

damasquillo, *m.* silk or woollen stuff resembling damask; apricot.

damasquinado, da, *a.* damaskeened.

damasquino, na, *a.* damaskeened; Damascene.—**a la d.,** Damascus fashion.

damería, *f.* excessive nicety in conduct, prudery.

damisela, *f.* young woman; (coll.) courtesan.

damnificar, *va.* (*pret.* DAMNIFIQUÉ; *subj.* DAMNIFIQUE) to hurt, to damage, to injure.

dancé, dance, *v. V.* DANZAR.

danchado, da, *a.* (her.) dentate, indented.

dandismo, *m.* dandies (collect.); dandylike behavior or speech.

danés, sa. I. *a.* Danish. II. *n.* Dane. III. *m.* Danish (language).

dánico, ca, *a.* Dane, Danish.

dango, *m.* (ornith.) a species of eagle.

danta, *f.* (zool.) tapir.

dante. I. *a.* giving. II. *n.* giver.

dantellado, da, *a.* dentated, serrated.

dantesco, ca, *a.* Dantesque.

danubiano, na, *a.* Danubian.

danza, *f.* dance; set or number of dancers; entangled affair; (Cuba and P. Rico) a slow dance and its tune.—**d. de espadas,** (coll.) quarrel, fight.—**meter en la d.,** (coll.) to draw into the fray, to involve.

danzador, ra, *n.* dancer.

danzante, ta, *n.* dancer; (coll.) active person, hustler; (coll.) fickle, airy person.

danzar, *vn.* (*pret.* DANCÉ; *subj.* DANCE) to dance; to whirl; (coll.) to introduce oneself into any business.

danzarín, na, *n.* dancer; (coll.) giddy, meddling person.

danzón, *m.* (Cuba) slow dance and its tune.

dañable, *a.* prejudicial, condemnable.

dañado, da. I. *pp.* of DAÑAR. II. *a.* spoiled, tainted, bad, wicked; damned.

dañador, ra. I. *a.* injurious. II. *n.* one who harms.

dañar. I. *va.* to hurt, damage, impair; to harm, injure; to spoil; to weaken. II. *vr.* to spoil; to be damaged; to get hurt, hurt oneself.

dañino, na, *a.* mischievous, destructive; harmful, hurtful, injurious.

daño, *m.* damage, hurt, loss, nuisance, hindrance; (com.) discount.—**d. emergente,** (law) damage caused by non-payment.—**daños y perjuicios,** damages.—**en daño de,** with damage to, to the injury of, to the detriment of.—**hacerse d.,** to get hurt, hurt oneself.

dañosamente, *adv.* harmfully, injuriously; mischievously.

dañoso, sa, *a.* harmful, noxious, injurious.

dar. I. *va.* (*ind. pres.* DOY, *pret.* DI; *subj.* DÉ) to give; to hand, to deliver; to confer, grant; to inspire, suggest; to represent (as a play); to emit (as heat, light); to return, to render (as thanks); to proffer, to extend (as the hand); to suppose, to assume, to consider; to allow, admit, concede (a proposition); yield (as fruit, crops, income, etc.); to surrender, submit; to excite, to cause (as pain, sorrow); to strike (the hour); to hold, maintain; to deal (cards); to manifest, show (as signals); to enable, to allow; to apply, put on (as paint, a coating). When joined to some nouns, it expresses the action implied by the noun, as *dar saltos,* to jump; *dar golpes,* to strike (blows).—**d. a conocer,** to make known.—**d. a entender,** to insinuate.—**d. a luz,** to be delivered of, give birth to; to issue, publish.—**d. cabezadas,** to nod.—**d. caza,** to give chase to, pursue.—**d. calle,** to clear the way.—**d. comienzo,** to make a start, beginning.—**d. cuenta de,** to account for; to report on.—**d. cuerda a,** to wind up (clock, watch).—**d. culadas,** (naut.) to strike repeatedly.—**d. de baja,** to dismiss (from a team), muster out (from the army).—**d. de barato,** to grant, take for granted.—**d. de mano,** to depreciate or despise.—**d. diente con diente,** to shiver with cold.—**d. el espíritu,** to give up the ghost.—**d. el nombre, or el santo,** (mil.) to give the watchword.—**d. el sí,** to grant; to consent to marry.—**d. en cara, or en rostro,** to reproach, upbraid, throw in one's face.—**d. fiado,** to give on credit.—**d. fiador, or fianza,** to find bail, give security.—**d. fin a,** to complete, finish.—**d. fin de,** to destroy.—**d. fondo,** (naut.) to cast anchor.—**d. frente a,** to face, be facing.—**d. fruto,** to yield, bear fruit.—**d. gana, or ganas, de,** to excite a desire to, make one feel like (doing something); to have a mind to.—**d. garrote,** to garrote, strangle.—**d. golpe,** to astonish; to create a sensation, make a "hit."—**d. golpes a,** to beat, thrash.—**d. grima,** to strike with despair, terror, pity.—**d. gritos,** to shout.—**d. guerra,** to wage war; to torment.—**d. higa,** to miss fire.—**d. la cara por,** to go to the defense of.—**d. la ley,** to lay down the law, dictate.—**d. la razón a,** to say (a person) is right, agree with.—**d. largas,** to prolong an affair.—**d. las dos, tres,** etc., to strike two, three, o'clock.—**d. las espaldas a,** to turn one's back on.—**d. las gracias,** to thank.—**d. los buenos días,** to pass the time of day.—**d. los días a uno,** to congratulate one on one's birthday.—**d. lugar a,** to give rise to.—**d. memorias,** to give regards.—**d. pábulo a,** to substantiate.—**d. parte (de),** to report (about), communicate; to announce.—**d. pasos,** to take steps.—**d. pena a,** to grieve.—**d. poder,** to empower, authorize; to give power of attorney.—**d. por** (foll. by *pp.*), to take for, consider as.—**d. prestado,** to lend.—**d. principio,** to begin.—**d. punto,** (com.) to become insolvent.—**d. que decir,** to give occasion for censure or criticism.—**d. que hacer,** to give trouble.—**d. que pensar,** to arouse suspicions.—**d. que sentir,** to hurt others' feelings; to give occasion for regret.—**d. razón de,** to give information about.—**d. saltos,** to jump.—**d. satisfacción,** to apologize.—**d. suspiros,** to sigh.—**d. un abrazo,** to embrace.—**d. un grito,** to scream.—**d. un paseo,** to take a walk.—**d. un paso,** to take a step.—**d. una vuelta,** to take a turn, a stroll.—**d. voces,** to call out or scream.—**d. zapatetas,** to leap with joy.—**darla de,** (coll.) to brag of being, to set up for.—**no d. pie con bola,** not to do a thing right, to make a mess of it. **II.** *vn.* to give; to yield, stretch; to set in, come on (diff. constr.: *me dió fiebre,* I was taken with fever; *me dió catarro,* I took cold, or was taken with a cold).—**d. a,** to overlook, open on (*mi ventana da al parque,* my window overlooks the park).—**d. a la bomba,** to pump. —**d. al traste** (often with **con**), to give up; to spoil, destroy; to set aside, ignore.—**d. con,** to meet, to find (*por fin di con él,* at last I found him); to apply, cover with (paint, stucco, etc.). —**d. contra,** to knock or hit against.—**d. de,** to fall down, to fall on (*dar de espaldas,* to fall on one's back); to deal (blows, etc.).—**d. de beber,** to give a drink, water (animals).—**d. de codo,** to elbow; to treat with contempt.—**d. de comer,** to serve food, give meals; to feed (animals).—**d. de sí,** to give, stretch, extend. —**d. en,** to persist in; to fall into (as an error); to land on; to take to (as a hobby); to contract, acquire (as a custom); to guess, find out (as a joke, puzzle); to hit, to strike.—**d. en el clavo,** to hit the nail on the head.—**d. en que pensar,** to arouse suspicion; to set one to thinking.— **d. en un bajío** (naut.) to strike ground, to get on shore.—**d. en vacío,** or **en vago,** to fail.— darle a uno por, to take it into one's head to; to take to.—**d. mal,** to have poor luck at cards.—**d. sobre,** to rush on, to attack.—**d. tras,** to pursue, follow with hostility.—**dé donde diere,** inconsiderately, heedlessly. **III.** *vr.* (**darse**) to yield, surrender, submit; to devote oneself.—**d. a la vela,** to set sail.—**d. a merced,** to surrender at discretion; (hunting) to halt exhausted.—**d. cuenta de,** to realize.—**d. la mano,** or **las manos,** to shake hands.—**d. maña,** to manage ably.—**d. por** (followed by *pp.*), to consider oneself as.—**d. por sentido,** to show resentment, to take offense.—**d. por vencido,** to acknowledge defeat; to surrender; to give up.—**d. priesa,** or **prisa,** to make haste, hurry.—**d. tono,** to put on airs.—**d. una panzada,** (coll.) to eat to satiety, to stuff oneself.—**no se me da nada,** I don't care.—**no se me da un bledo,** I don't care a straw.

dardabasí, *m.* (ornith.) hawk, kite.

dardada, *f.* blow of a dart.

dárdano, na, *a.* Trojan, Dardanian.

dardo, *m.* dart, arrow; light lance; fresh-water fish, dartfish, dace.—**d. de pescador,** harpoon.

dares y tomares, *m. pl.* (coll.) give and take; disputes.—**andar en dares y tomares,** to dispute.

dársena, *f.* inner harbor; dock.

dartros, *m. pl.* (med.) dartre, herpes.—**dartroso, sa,** *a.* dartrous.

darviniano, na; darwiniano, na, *n. & a.* Darwinian.

darvinismo, darwinismo, *m.* Darwinism.

darvinista, darwinista, *n. & a.* Darwinian.

dasocracia, *f.* forestry.

dasocrático, ca, *a.* forest (as *a.*), pertaining to forestry.

dasonomía, *f.* = DASOCRACIA.

dasonómico, ca, *a.* = DASOCRÁTICO.

data, *f.* date, day of month and year; item in an account; outlet of a reservoir.—**estar de mala d.,** to be in bad humor.

datar. I. *va.* to date; (com.) to credit on account. **II.** *vn.* to take origin, date.

dataría, *f.* (Rom. Cath.) datary.

datario, *m.* datary, a papal officer.

dátil, *m.* (bot.) date; (zool.) date shell.—**datilado, da,** *a.* datelike.—**datilera,** *f.* common date palm.—**datilillo,** *m. dim.* small date.

datismo, *m.* (rhet.) use of redundant synonyms.

dativo, *m. & a.* (gram.) dative.

¹dato, *m.* datum.—*pl.* data.

²dato, *m.* title of dignity in Oriental countries.

daturina, *f.* (chem., med.) daturine, atropine.

dauco, *m.* (bot.) wild carrot.

davalar, *vn.* (naut.) to drift.

davídico, ca, *a.* Davidic, of David.

daza, *f.* (bot.) lucern; (bot.) panic grass.

de, *prep.* of; from (*soy de Boston,* I am from Boston); from, because of, out of (*confesó de miedo,* he confessed from fear; sometimes foll. by adj. translated by corresponding noun in Eng. *lloré de alegre,* I wept from joy); for, to (*hora de partir,* time to leave; *tiempo de arar,* time for plowing); with (*la dama de las camelias,* the lady with the camellias; *el señor de los guantes,* the gentleman with the gloves; *casa de tres pisos,* three-story house); on, at (*la casa de la derecha,* the house on the right); in (*dos pies de diámetro,* two feet in diameter); by, on the part of (*temido de sus enemigos,* feared by his enemies; *abandonado de Dios,* forsaken by God, God-forsaken); by, as (*médico de profesión,* a physician by profession). Sign of possessive: *la ley de Dios,* the law of God; *la casa de mi padre,* my father's house. Denotes the manner in which a thing is done: *comer de pie,* to eat standing; *se vistió de prisa,* he dressed in haste; *se bebió el vino de un trago,* he drank the wine at a gulp. Denotes the object or purpose to which a thing is put: *escopeta de caza,* fowling gun; *cuarto de fumar,* smoking room; *máquina de coser,* sewing machine. Indicates the material of which a thing is made: *vaso de plata,* silver cup. Is used by women before their husbands' family name: *doña Isabel Pérez de González.* Mrs. Isabel Pérez-González (née Pérez.) Indicates the moving power of a machine; *máquina de vapor,* steam engine; *molino de viento,* windmill. Sometimes used as an emphatic expletive after an adjective: *el pícaro del muchacho,* the rogue of a boy.—**d. a,** foll. by numerical expression, translated in Eng. by qualifying phrase: *billete de a cinco pesos,* a five-peso bill. —**d. . . . en,** by, after, in serial order (*de día en día,* day by day; *de grano en grano,* grain by grain; *de calle en calle,* from street to street.

dé, *irreg. imper. & pres. subj.* of DAR.

dea, *f.* (poet.) goddess.

deán, *m.* dean.

deanato, deanazgo, *m.* deanship.

debajo, *adv.* beneath, underneath.—**d. de,** under, beneath.—**por d.,** from below; underneath.— **por d. de,** under; below.

debate, *m.* debate; altercation.

debatir, *va.* to argue, discuss, debate.

debe, *m.* (com.) debtor side of an account, debit (Dr. in bookkeeping).

debelación, *f.* conquering in war; conquest.

debelador, ra, *n.* conqueror, victor.

debelar, *va.* to conquer; subdue, put down.

deber. I. *va.* to owe; must, ought, have to.—**d. de,** must have, must be (indicating probability): *él debe de haber salido,* he must have (I think he has) gone out. **II.** *m.* duty, obligation.

debidamente, *adv.* justly, duly, exactly.

debido, da, *pp.* of DEBER.—**d. a,** owing to, on account of.

debiente. I. *a.* owing. **II.** *n.* debtor.

débil, *a.* weak; feeble.—**debilidad,** *f.* weakness.

debilitación, *f.* debilitation, weakness.

debilitadamente, *adv.* feebly, weakly.

debilitante, *a.* weakening, debilitating.

debilitar. I. *va.* to weaken; to debilitate, enfeeble, enervate. **II.** *vr.* to become feeble.

débilmente, *adv.* weakly, lamely.

débito, *m.* debt; (or **d. conyugal**), conjugal duty.

debitorio, *m.* contract of bargain and sale upon credit, by virtue of a partial payment.

debó, *m.* scraper (for skins).

debut, *m.* (Gal.) debut.

debutante, *n.* (Gal.) debutant, debutante.

debutar, *vn.* (Gal.) to make one's debut.

década, *f.* decade, ten.
decadencia, *f.* decadence, decay, decline.—**ir en d.,** to be on the decline.
decadente, *a.* decaying, declining, decadent.
decaedro, *m.* (geom.) decahedron.
decaer, *vn.* (*ind.* DECAIGO; *subj.* DECAIGA) to decay, fail, languish, fade; to fall off, lessen; (naut.) to fall to leeward.
decágono, *m.* (geom.) decagon.
decagramo, *m.* decagram.
decaigo, decaiga, *v.* V. *decaer.*
decaimiento, *m.* decay, decline; weakness.
decalaje, *m.* (aer.) stagger.
decalitro, *m.* decaliter.
decálogo, *m.* decalogue.
decamerón, *m.* narrative of the events of ten days; D., Decameron.
decámetro, *m.* decameter.
decampar, *vn.* to decamp.
decanato, *m.* deanship; deanery.
decano, *m.* senior, dean; oldest member of a community or corporation.
decantación, *f.* pouring off, decantation.
decantado, da, *a.* boasted, exalted.
¹decantar, *va.* to cry up, to exaggerate, to puff.
²decantar, *va.* to decant, to draw off.
decapitación, *f.* beheading.
decapitar, *va.* to behead, decapitate.
decápodo, da. I. *n.* & *a.* (zool.) decapod. **II.** *m. pl.* Decapoda.
decárea, *f.* decare, ten ares.
decasílabo, ba, *a.* ten-syllable.
decena, *f.* ten; (mus.) tenth; (arith.) ten (figure in second place from the right).
decenal, *a.* decennial, lasting ten years.
decenar, *m.* group of ten.
decenario, ria. I. *a.* decennary, decennial. **II.** *m.* ten-bead rosary; decennial.
decencia, *f.* decency, propriety; cleanliness, tidiness; honesty, modesty.
decenio, *m.* decade, ten years, decennial.
deceno, na, *a.* tenth.
decentar. I. *va.* (*ind.* DECIENTO; *subj.* DECIENTE) to cut off the first slice of; to begin to lose, as the health. **II.** *vr.* to have bedsores.
decente, *a.* decent; honest; kind, "nice"; tidy; well-behaved.—**decentemente,** *adv.* decently; fairly, honorably; modestly; (ironic) excessively.
decenvirato, *m.* decemvirate.
decenviro, *m.* decemvir.
decepción, *f.* disappointment, disillusionment; humbug.—**decepcionar,** *va.* (Am.) to disappoint.
deciárea, *f.* deciare, one-tenth of an are.
decible, *a.* that may be expressed, speakable.
decidero, ra, *a.* that may be said without difficulty or impropriety.
decididamente, *adv.* decidedly.
decidido, da, *a.* decided, determined; devoted.
decidir. I. *va.* to decide, determine, resolve. **II.** *vr.* to decide, make up one's mind; to be determined.
decidor, ra. I. *n.* one who speaks with fluency and elegance; a wit. **II.** *a.* of pleasant speech, being a good talker.
deciento, deciente, *v.* V. DECENTAR.
decigramo, *m.* decigram.
decilitro, *m.* deciliter.
décima, *f.* (poet.) ten-line stanza; tenth stanza.
decimal. I. *a.* decimal; pertaining to tithes. **II.** *n.* decimal.
decimanovena, *f.* a register of a pipe-organ.
decímetro, *m.* decimeter.
décimo, ma, *n.* & *a.* tenth.
decimoctavo, va, *a.* eighteenth.
decimocuarto, ta, *a.* fourteenth.
decimonono, na, *a.* nineteenth.
decimonoveno, na, *a.* nineteenth.
decimoquinto, ta, *a.* fifteenth.

decimoséptimo, ma, *a.* seventeenth.
decimosexto, ta, *a.* sixteenth.
decimotercero, ra, *a.* thirteenth.
decimotercio, cia, *a.* thirteenth.
deciocheno, na, *n.* & *a.* eighteenth.
decir. I. *va.* & *vn.* (*ger.* DICIENDO; *pp.* DICHO; *ind. pres.* DIGO, *pret.* DIJE, *fut.* DIRÉ; *imper.* DI; *subj.* DIGA) to say, tell; speak; to name, call; to denote, bespeak, indicate, show, be a sign of.—**d. bien,** to be right, to speak true.—**d. mal,** to misspeak; to be mistaken.—**d. para sí, or para su capote,** to say to oneself.—**d. por d.,** to talk for the sake of talking.—**bien d.,** to be right in saying.—**como quien dice,** as who should say, as if to say, as if meaning.—**como quien no dice nada,** unconcernedly; and this is, or which is, no small matter.—**¡digo!,** I say!, listen!—**el qué dirán,** what people will say, gossip.—**ello dirá,** we shall see, time will tell.—**es d.,** that is to say, that is.—**por decirlo así,** so to speak.—**por mejor d.,** more properly speaking; rather.—**querer d.,** to mean, signify.—**se dice,** they say, it is said. **II.** *m.* a saw, proverbial or familiar saying; witty remark; language.—**el bien d.,** elegant style of language.—**el d. de las gentes,** the opinion of the people.—**es un d.,** it is a mere saying.
decisión, *f.* decision, determination, resolution, issue; decision, judgment by court of justice; verdict by a jury.
decisivamente, *adv.* decisively.
decisivo, va, *a.* decisive, final, conclusive.
declamación, *f.* declamation, harangue, oration, speech; oratorical invective; reading, recitation; delivery in reciting.
declamador, ra, *n.* orator; reciter.
declamar, *vn.* to declaim; recite; harangue; rant.
declamatorio, ria, *a.* declamatory.
declaración, *f.* declaration; statement; interpretation, exposition; avowal; manifestation; account; overture, proposal; (law) deposition.
declaradamente, *adv.* declaredly, avowedly.
declarado, da, *a.* declared; stanch; firm.
declarador, ra, *n.* & *a.* declarer(-ing); deponent.
declarante. I. *a.* declaring, expounding. **II.** *n.* declarer, deponent; witness.
declarar. I. *va.* to declare, manifest, make known, state; to expound, explain; (law) to determine and decide, to find; (law) to testify. **II.** *vr.* to declare one's opinion, to explain one's mind; (coll.) to make a declaration of love.
declarativo, va, *a.* declarative, assertive.
declaratorio, ria, *a.* declaratory, explanatory.
declinable, *a.* (gram.) declinable.
declinación, *f.* declination, descent, decay, fall, decline, falling; (gram.) declension, inflection; (astr.) declination; (arch.) deviation.—**d. de la aguja,** magnetic declination.
declinante, *a.* declining; bending down.
declinar. I. *vn.* to decline; to lean downward or to either side, to bend, slope; to descend; (of illness) abate, diminish; to approach the end; (naut.) to vary from the true magnetic meridian. **II.** *va.* (gram.) to decline; (law) to challenge (a judge); to transfer to another tribunal.
declinatoria, *f.* (law) plea that questions the competency of a judge.
declinatorio, *m.* declinator (instrument).
declive, *m.* declivity, dip; descent, slope, fall; (Ry.) gradient, grade.—**en d.,** slanting, sloping.—**declividad,** *f.* declivity.—**declivio,** *m.* = DECLIVE.
decocción, *f.* decoction.
decomisar, *va.* to confiscate, seize, forfeit.
decomiso, *m.* confiscation, forfeiture, seizure.
¹decoración, *f.* decoration; ornament; (theat.) setting, props.
²decoración, *f.* act of committing to memory.
¹decorado, *m.* decoration, ornamentation.

²**decorado**, *m.* thing committed to memory.

decorador, ra, *n.* & *a.* decorator(-ing).

¹**decorar**, *va.* to decorate; to adorn, embellish.

²**decorar**, *va.* to learn by heart; to recite; to repeat.

decorativo, va, *a.* decorative.

decoro, *m.* honor, respect, reverence due to any person; circumspection, gravity; integrity, purity, honesty; decorum, decency, civility; fitness, propriety.

decorosamente, *adv.* decently, decorously.

decoroso, sa, *a.* decorous, decent.

decrecer, *vn.* (*ind.* DECREZCO; *subj.* DECREZCA) to decrease, diminish.

decreciente, *a.* diminishing, decreasing.

decremento, *m.* decrement, decrease.

decrepitación, *f.* (chem.) decrepitation.

decrepitante, *a.* (chem.) decrepitant.

decrepitar. I. *va.* to decrepitate, to expose to a high heat. **II.** *vn.* to decrepitate, to crackle.

decrépito, ta, *a.* decrepit.—**decrepitud,** *f.* decrepitude.

decretal, *f.* & *a.* decretal.

decretalista, *m.* interpreter of papal decrees.

decretar, *va.* to decree, resolve; decide.

decretero, *m.* list of the names and offenses of criminals; decretal, collection of decrees.

decretista, *m.* propounder of Decretals.

decreto, *m.* decree; judicial decree or decision.

decretorio, ria, *a.* (med.) critical.

decrezco, decrezca, *v.* *V.* DECRECER.

decúbito, *m.* (med.) decubitus.

decuplar, decuplicar, *va.* to multiply by ten.

décuplo, pla, *n.* & *a.* decuple, tenfold.

decuria, *f.* decury; class of ten students.

decuriato, *m.* student belonging to a class of ten.

decurión, *m.* decurion, commander of a decury; in schools, monitor having the care of ten pupils.—**decurionato,** *m.* decurionship.

decurrente, *a.* (bot.) decurrent.

decursas, *f. pl.* (law) arrears of rent.

decurso, *m.* course, lapse of time.

decusado, da, *a.* (bot.) decussate, decussated.

dechado, *m.* model; sample, pattern, standard; linen on which young girls learn needlework.

dedada, *f.* portion of some substance, like honey, that can be taken up with the top of the finger.—**dar una d. de miel,** (fig.) to feed one's hopes.

dedal, *m.* thimble; leather finger stall used by calkers.

dedalera, *f.* (bot.) foxglove.

dédalo, *m.* labyrinth; entanglement.

dedicación, *f.* dedication; consecration; inscription.

dedicante, *n.* & *a.* dedicator(-ing).

dedicar. I. *va.* (*pret.* DEDIQUÉ; *subj.* DEDIQUE) to dedicate, devote; to inscribe, autograph (a literary work). **II.** *vr.* (a) to devote oneself (to), to make a specialty (of), to interest oneself (in).

dedicativo, va, *a.* = DEDICATORIO.

dedicatoria, *f.* dedication; dedicatory inscription of a book or work of art.

dedicatorio, ria, *a.* dedicatory.

dedición, *f.* unconditional surrender.

dedil, *m.* thumbstall of rubber, linen, or leather.

dedillo, ito, *m. dim.* little finger.—**saber al d.,** to have at one's finger tips, know perfectly.

dediqué, dedique, *v.* *V.* DEDICAR.

dedo, *m.* finger; toe; forty-eighth part of a Spanish vara; finger's breadth, small bit.—**d. anular,** ring, or fourth, finger.—**d. auricular** = DEDO MEÑIQUE.—**d. del corazón,** cordial, or de enmedio, middle finger.—**dedos de manteca,** (Arg.) butterfingers.—**d. gordo, d. grande,** thumb; big toe.—**d. índice,** index finger, forefinger.—**d. meñique,** little finger; little toe.—**d. pulgar,** thumb; big toe.—**d. saludador** = D. ÍNDICE.—**a dos dedos,** within

an inch (fig.).—**alzar el d.,** to raise one's hand (in taking an oath, etc.).

deducción, *f.* derivation, origin; deduction, inference, conclusion; (mus.) natural progression of sounds; (math.) derivation (of a formula).

deducible, *a.* deducible, inferable.

deduciente, *a.* deducing, inferring.

deducir, *va.* (*ind. pres.* DEDUZCO, *pret.* DEDUJE; *subj.* DEDUZCA) to deduce, infer; to fetch, to devise, to draw; (law) to allege in pleading, to offer as a plea; (com.) to subtract, deduct; (math.) to derive (a formula).

deductivo, va, *a.* deductive.

deduje, deduzco, deduzca, *v.* *V.* DEDUCIR.

defácile, *adv.* easily.

defacto, *adv.* de facto.

defalcar, *va.* to cut off; to embezzle.

defecación, *f.* purification; voiding of excrement.

defecadora, *f.* defecator (in sugar refining).

defecar. I. *va.* (*pret.* DEFEQUÉ; *subj.* DEFEQUE) to defecate, purify, clarify. **II.** *vn.* to defecate, void excrement; to remove impurities.

defección, *f.* defection, apostasy, desertion.

defectible, *a.* that may be faulty or lacking.

defectillo, *m. dim.* slight fault or defect.

defectivo, va, *a.* defective, imperfect; (gram.) defective.

defecto, *m.* defect, fault, blemish, imperfection.—*pl.* (print.) sheets lacking, after a day's work, to complete the full number.

defectuosamente, *adv.* defectively, faultily.

defectuoso, sa, *a.* defective, imperfect, faulty.

defendedero, ra, *a.* defensible.

defendedor, ra, *a.* & *n.* = DEFENSOR.

defender, *va.* (*ind.* DEFIENDO; *subj.* DEFIENDA) to defend; protect; to prohibit, forbid; to prevent, retard, delay.—**defendible,** *a.* defensible.

defenecer, *va.* (*ind.* DEFENEZCO; *subj.* DEFENEZCA) (com.) to close (an account).

defenecimiento, *m.* (com.) settlement.

defensa, *f.* defense; protection; shelter; (aer.) bumping bag, bumper.—**de d.,** guard (as *a.*) safety (as *a.*), sheltering.—*pl.* (fort.) defenses, fortifications; (naut.) skids or skeeds, fenders; (mech.) fender, guard, pad.

defensión, *f.* safeguard, defense.

defensiva, *f.* defensive.—**estar, ponerse, a la d.,** to be or stand on the defensive.

defensivo, va. I. *a.* defensive, justificatory, protective. **II.** *m.* defense, safeguard, preservative; (med.) wet compress.

defensor, ra, *n.* defender; supporter; (law) counsel for the defense, defender.

defensoría, *f.* duty and office of a defender.

defensorio, *m.* plea, defense.

defequé, defeque, *v.* *V.* DEFECAR.

deferencia, *f.* deference.

deferente, *a.* assenting, deferring to the opinion of another, deferential.

deferir. I. *vn.* (*ind.* DEFIERO; *subj.* DEFIERA) to yield, submit. **II.** *va.* to communicate; to share in jurisdiction or power.

deficiencia, *f.* deficiency.

deficiente, *a.* deficient, faulty.

déficit, *m.* deficit, shortage.

defiendo, defienda, *v.* *V.* DEFENDER.

defiero, defiera, *v.* *V.* DEFERIR.

definible, *a.* definable.

definición, *f.* definition; decision, determination.—*pl.* statutes of military orders.

definido, da. I. *pp.* of DEFINIR. **II.** *a.* definite.

definidor, ra. I. *n.* & *a.* definer(-ing). **II.** *m.* in some religious orders, member of the governing committee.

definir, *va.* to define; to establish, determine.

definitivamente, *adv.* definitively.

definitivo, va, *a.* definitive.—**en definitiva,** in conclusion; in short.

definitorio, *m.* governing assembly of a religious order; place where it meets.

For pronunciation, see the rules at the beginning of the book.

deflacionista, *a*. deflationary.
deflagración, *f*. deflagration, sudden burning.
deflagrador, *m*. deflagrator, ignitor.
deflagrar, *va*. to deflagrate, burn suddenly.
deflegmar, *va*. (chem.) to dephlegmate.
defoliación, *f*. defoliation, shedding of leaves.
deformación, *f*. deformation; defacing.
deformador, ra, *n. & a*. deformer(-ing); defacer (-ing).
deformar. I. *va*. to deform, disfigure, misshape. II. *vr*. to become deformed, change shape.
deformatorio, ria, *a*. deforming, disfiguring.
deforme, *a*. deformed, disfigured; hideous.
deformemente, *adv*. deformedly.
deformidad, *f*. deformity; hideousness, ugliness; gross error.
defraudación, *f*. defrauding; fraud, deceit.
defraudador, ra, *n*. defrauder, defaulter.
defraudar, *va*. to defraud; to rob of; to intercept (light); to disturb (sleep).
defuera, *adv*. externally, outwardly, on the outside.—**por d.**, outwardly.
defunción, *f*. death, demise.
degeneración, *f*. degeneration, degeneracy.
degenerado, da, *n. & a*. degenerate.
degenerar, *vn*. to degenerate.
deglución, *f*. (physiol.) deglutition, swallowing.
deglutir, *va*. to swallow.
degollación, *f*. decollation, beheading.
degolladero, *m*. throttle, windpipe; slaughterhouse; stand with block where people were beheaded; (anc. theat.) board partitioning the pit.
degollado, *m*. low neck cut in a blouse or dress.
degollador, *m*. headsman, executioner.
degolladura, *f*. cutting of the throat; (mason.) joint; (carp.) slender part of balusters; DEGOLLADO.
degollante, *n*. (coll.) bore, nuisance.
degollar, *va*. (*ind*. DEGÜELLO; *subj*. DEGÜELLE) to behead, decapitate; to cut (a garment) low in the neck; to destroy, ruin; (coll.) to importune.
degollina, *f*. (coll.) slaughter, butchery.
degradación, *f*. degradation, humiliation, debasement; depravity, baseness, degeneracy; (art.) degradation, diminution, blending.
degradante, *a*. degrading.
degradar. I. *va*. to degrade, debase; humiliate, revile. II. *vr*. to degrade or lower oneself.
degu, *m*. a ratlike Chilean rodent.
¹degüello, degüelle, *v*. V. DEGOLLAR.
²degüello, *m*. decollation, act of beheading or cutting the throat; neck or narrow part of many things; destruction, ruin; putting to the sword; attack without quarter.—**tirar al d.**, to endeavor to harm or ruin a person.
degustación, *f*. act of tasting.
dehesa, *f*. pasture ground.
dehesar, *va*. to turn into pasture ground.
dehesero, *m*. keeper of a pasture ground.
dehiscencia, *f*. (bot.) dehiscence.
deicida, *m*. deicide, slayer of a god.—**deicidio**, *m*. deicide, murder of a god; slaying of Jesus.
deidad, *f*. deity, divinity; god, goddess.
deificación, *f*. deification.
deificar, *va*. (*pret*. DEIFIQUÉ; *subj*. DEIFIQUE) to deify; to exalt or praise extravagantly, lionize.
deífico, ca, *a*. deific, deifical, divine.
deifiqué, deifique, *v*. V. DEIFICAR.
deiforme, *a*. deiform, godlike.
Deípara, *f*. Deipara, the Mother of God (app. to the Virgin Mary).
deísmo, *m*. deism.
deísta, *n. & a*. deist(-ic).
deja, *f*. prominence between two fissures or notches.
dejación, *f*. abandonment, relinquishment, giving up; (law) assignment.
dejada, *f*. relinquishment.
dejadez, *f*. slovenliness, neglect.

dejado, da. I. *pp*. of DEJAR. II. *a*. slovenly; indolent, negligent; dejected, low-spirited.
dejamiento, *m*. act of leaving, relinquishing, or giving up; indolence, carelessness; languor, depression of spirits; abdication, resignation; coolness, indifference, estrangement.
dejar. I. *va*. to leave; to let; let go, relinquish; to permit, consent, allow; to leave, abandon; forsake, desert; to yield, produce, bring (as income, profit); to commit, give in charge, intrust; to deliver, deposit (as money); to fling up, to give up; to lay away.—**¡deja!**, let it go, never mind!—**d. caer**, to drop, let fall.—**d. cargado**, to debit.—**d. dicho**, to leave word or orders.—**d. en cueros**, to strip (one) of one's money or property.—**d. escrito**, to leave in writing.—**d. fresco**, to frustrate, to baffle.—**d. mucho que desear**, to leave much to be desired. II. *vr*. not to take care of oneself; to let or allow oneself (to die, be robbed, etc.); to become languid; to abandon oneself.—**d. caer** (con before noun or phrase) to insinuate, bring up as if casually; to drop in, appear unexpectedly; to give up.—**d. de**, to stop, leave off.—**d. ver**, to be seen, to be easy to see; to show; to appear, in public, at friends' homes, etc. III. *vn*. (**de** and *inf*.) to cease, stop (followed by present participle); to fail to.—**d. de ser**, to cease to be, disappear, die, be no longer.—**no d. de**, not to fail to.—**no d. de ser a**, to be, to be rather.—**no d. de tener**, not to be without, not to lack.
dejativo, va, *a*. lazy, slovenly, indolent.
dejillo, *m*. *dim*. slight relish or taste which remains after eating or drinking.
dejo, *m*. abandonment, relinquishment; end, termination; negligence, slovenliness; relish or taste which remains after eating or drinking; effect; peculiar inflection or accent in speaking.
de jure, de jure.
del, *contraction of* DE *and* EL: of the.
delación, *f*. accusation, information.
delantal, *m*. apron; dashboard of a carriage.
delante, *adv*. before, ahead, in front.—**por d.**, in front.—**d. de, por d. de**, *prep*. before, in front of, in the presence of.
delantera, *f*. front, fore end, fore part; front seats in theaters, etc.; front part of garments; boundary line of a town, village, property; lead, advance, advantage.
delantero, ra. I. *a*. foremost, first; front (as *a*.) II. *m*. postilion; front part; (sport) forward.
delatable, *a*. accusable, blamable.
delatante, *n*. informer, accuser.
delatar, *va*. to inform against, accuse, denounce.
delator, ra, *n*. accuser, informer, denouncer.
dele, *m*. (print.) dele, mark of deletion, delete (ϑ).
delectación, *f*. delectation, pleasure, delight.
delegación, *f*. delegation; power conferred; proxy; office of a delegate.
delegado, da, *n*. delegate, proxy.
delegante, *n*. constituent, one that delegates.
delegar, *va*. (*ind*. DELEGUÉ; *subj*. DELEGUE) to delegate.
deleitabilísimo, ma, *a. super*. most delightful.
deleitable, *a*. delectable, delightful.
deleitablemente, *adv*. delightfully.
deleitación, *f*. **deleitamiento**, *m*. delectation, pleasure, delight.
deleitante, *a*. delighting, delightful.
deleitar. I. *va*. to delight, please. II. *vr*. to delight, take delight or pleasure.—**deleite**, *m*. pleasure, delight; lust, carnal appetite.
deleitosamente, *adv*. delightfully; cheerfully.
deleitoso, sa, *a*. delightful, pleasing.
deletéreo, ea, *a*. deleterious, poisonous.
deletreador, *m*. speller.
deletrear, *va*. to spell, to spell out; to decipher or interpret.
deletreo, *m*. spelling; reading by spelling.

deleznable, *a.* crumbly; fragile, frail, perishable; smooth, slippery.

délfico, ca, *a.* Delphian, of Delphi.

¹delfín, *m.* (ichth.) dolphin; (astr.) Dolphin, a northern constellation.

²delfín, *m.* dauphin, formerly title of eldest son of King of France.—**delfina,** *f.* dauphiness, wife of the dauphin.

delgadamente, *adv.* thinly, delicately; acutely, sharply, finely.

delgadez, *f.* thinness, tenuity; acuteness, ingenuity; slenderness, leanness.

delgado, da. I. *a.* thin; lean; lank, slender, slim; light, delicate, tenuous; acute, fine, ingenious, sharp; (agr.) poor, exhausted. **II.** *m.* (naut.) dead rise; flank of an animal.

delgaducho, cha, *a.* thinnish, lanky.

deliberación, *f.* deliberation.

deliberadamente, *adv.* deliberately.

deliberante, *a.* deliberating, deliberative.

deliberar. I. *vn.* to deliberate, ponder; to consult or take counsel together. **II.** *va.* to determine after mature consideration.

deliberativo, va, *a.* deliberative.

delicadamente, *adv.* delicately.

delicadez, *f.* delicateness, weakness of constitution; prudery; overscrupulousness.

delicadeza, *f.* delicacy, fineness, refinement; sensitiveness; daintiness, tenderness, softness; scrupulousness, susceptibility; subtlety, dexterity; acuteness of understanding, refinement of wit; perspicacity.

delicado, da, *a.* delicate; gentle, refined; effeminate, finical, ladylike; sensitive, susceptible; dainty, exquisite, delicious; thin, slender; subtile; fastidious, prudish; scrupulous, honest, upright; arduous, difficult; captious, suspicious.

delicia, *f.* delight, satisfaction; sensual pleasure.

deliciosamente, *adv.* deliciously; delightfully.

delicioso, sa, *a.* delicious; delightful.

delictivo, va, *a.* pertaining to crime or guilt.

delicuescencia, *f.* (chem.) deliquescence.

delicuescente, a. (chem.) deliquescent.

delimitación, *f.* = DEMARCACIÓN, demarcation.

delimitar, *va.* = DEMARCAR, to delimit.

delinco, delinca, *v. V.* DELINQUIR.

delincuencia, *f.* delinquency, guilt.

delincuente. I. *n.* delinquent, offender. **II.** *a.* delinquent, guilty.

delineación, *f.* delineation, draft, sketch.

delineador, ra, *n.* delineator, draftsman, designer.

delineam(i)ento, *m.* = DELINEACIÓN.

delineante. I. *a.* designing. **II.** *n.* draftsman.

delinear, *va.* to delineate, draw, sketch, design.

delinquimiento, *m.* delinquency, guilt.

delinquir, *vn.* (*ind.* DELINCO; *subj.* DELINCA) to transgress, to offend, to be guilty.

delio, a, *a. & n.* Delian, from or of Delos.

deliquio, *m.* swoon, faint; ecstasy, rapture.

delirante, *a.* delirious.

delirar, *vn.* to be delirious; to rave; to rant, talk nonsense.

delirio, *m.* delirium; frenzied rapture; nonsense. **—d. de grandeza,** delusions of grandeur.

delírium tremens, *m.* delirium tremens.

delito, *m.* delict, transgression of a law; crime.

delta. I. *f.* delta (Δ), fourth letter of the Greek alphabet. **II.** *m.* delta (of a river).

deltoideo, a, *a.* deltoid, triangular.

deltoides. I. *a.* deltoid. **II.** *m.* (anat.) deltoid.

delusivo, va, *a.* delusive, fallacious.

delusoriamente, *adv.* delusively, deceitfully.

delusorio, ria, *a.* deceitful, fallacious.

della, dellas, dello, dellos, *contr.* of DE ELLA, etc.

demacración, *f.* (med.) emaciation, marasmus.

demacrar. I. *va.* (of the body) to cause to waste away. **II.** *vr.* to waste away.

demagogia, *f.* demagogism; demagogy.

demagógico, ca, *a.* demagogical.

demagogo, ga, *n.* demagogue.

demanda, *f.* demand, claim, complaint; request; petition, the act of asking charity; gathering, charity-box; image carried about by beggars of alms; question, inquiry; enterprise, endeavor; (com.) demand, call; (law) claim; (naut.) lookout.—**la oferta y la d.,** (com.) supply and demand.

demandadero, ra, *n.* messenger to do errands in convents or prisons.

demandado, da, *n.* (law) defendant.

demandador, ra, *n.* one who claims, asks, or begs; one who solicits charity for pious uses; (law) complainant, plaintiff.

demandante, *n.* (law) complainant, plaintiff.

demandar, *va.* to demand, ask, solicit; to wish for, desire; (law) to enter an action against.

demarcación, *f.* demarcation.

demarcador, *m.* boundary surveyor.

demarcar, *va.* to demarcate, demark, delimit.

demás, *a.* other.—**los d., las d.,** others; the others.—**lo d.,** the rest.—**por lo d.,** aside from this; furthermore; as to the rest.—**todo lo d.,** everything else.—**y d.,** and other things, or persons; and so forth. **II.** *adv.* besides, moreover.—**estar d.,** to be useless or superfluous; to be unwelcome, not wanted.—**por d.,** uselessly, in vain; too much.

demasía, *f.* excess, surplus, superabundance; boldness, audacity, insolence; badness, iniquity; guilt; outrage; affront; (min.) space between two claims.—**en d.,** excessively.

demasiadamente, *adv.* excessively; too.

demasiado, da. I. *a.* too, excessive; too much, too many. **II.** *adv.* too, excessively; too much.

demencia, *f.* dementia, insanity.

dementar. I. *va.* to render demented or insane. **II.** *vr.* to become demented.

demente, *a.* demented, mad, insane.

demérito, *m.* that which renders (something) without merit; being undeserving.

demeritorio, ria, *a.* without merit, undeserving.

demisión, *f.* submission, humility.

democracia, *f.* democracy.

demócrata, *m.* democrat.

democráticamente, *adv.* democratically.

democrático, ca, *a.* democratic.

democratizar, *va.* to democratize.

demografía, *f.* demography, vital statistics.—**demográfico, ca,** *a.* demographic.

demógrafo, fa, *n.* demographist.

demoledor, ra, *n. & a.* demolisher(-ing).

demoler, *va.* (*ind.* DEMUELO; *subj.* DEMUELA) to demolish, tear down, dismantle.

demolición, *f.* demolition, destruction.

demonche, *m.* (coll.) little devil.

demoníaco, ca, *a.* demoniacal, devilish.

demonio. I. *m.* demon; evil spirit; (the) devil. **II.** *interj.* the deuce!

demonolatría, *f.* demonolatry (esp. worship of the devil).

demonología, *f.* demonology.

demonomancia, *f.* divination with the assistance of demons.

demontre. I. *m.* devil. **II.** *interj.* the deuce!

demoñejo, demoñuelo, *m. dim.* little devil, imp.

demora, *f.* delay, procrastination; (naut.) bearing; (com.) demurrage; (Am.) period of work required of Indians in lieu of taxes, esp. eight months' work in the mines.

demorar. I. *va.* to delay. **II.** *vn.* to delay, tarry; (naut.) to bear (*la costa demora norte*, the coast bears north). **III.** *vr.* to delay; to be delayed, tarry, stop (on the way).

demostino, na, *a.* Demosthenic, like, or pertaining to, Demosthenes.

demostrable, *a.* demonstrable.

demostrablemente, *adv.* demonstrably.

demostración, *f.* demonstration; proof; (public) demonstration.

demostrador, ra, *n.* & *a.* demonstrator(-ing); teacher.

demostrar, *va.* (*ind.* DEMUESTRO; *subj.* DEMUESTRE) to demonstrate, show; to prove; to teach.

demostrativamente, *adv.* demonstratively.

demostrativo, va, *a.* demonstrative.

demótico, ca, *a.* (of Egyptian writing) demotic.

demudación, *f.* change, alteration.

demudar. I. *va.* to alter, change, vary; to cloak, disguise. **II.** *vr.* to be changed; to change color or the expression of countenance suddenly.

demuelo, demuela, *v.* V. DEMOLER.

demuestro, demuestre, *v.* V. DEMOSTRAR.

demulcente, *a.* & *m.* demulcent, emollient.

denante, -s, *adv.* (obs.) = ANTES, before.

denario, ria. I. *a.* denary. **II.** *m.* denarius.

dende, *prep.* (obs. or prov.) since.

dendrita, *f.* (geol.) dendrite.

dendrítico, ca, *a.* (geol.) dendritic.

dendrografía, *f.* (bot.) dendrology.

dendrómetro, *m.* (bot.) dendrometer.

denegación, *f.* denial, refusal, denegation.

denegar, *va.* (*ind. pres.* DENIEGO, *pret.* DENEGUÉ; *subj.* DENIEGUE) to deny, refuse, denegate.

denegrecer, *va.* (*ind.* DENEGREZCO; *subj.* DENE-GREZCA) to blacken, darken.

denegrir, *va.* = DENEGRECER.

denegué, *pret.* of DENEGAR.

dengoso, sa, *a.* finicky, fastidious, overnice.

¹dengue, *m.* fastidiousness, prudery; affectation; woman's cape with long points; (med.) dengue, breakbone fever.

²dengue, *m.* boat used in sardine fishing.

denguero, ra, *a.* prudish, affected.

deniego, deniegue, *v.* V. DENEGAR.

denigración, *f.* defamation, stigma, disgrace.

denigrar, *va.* to denigrate, revile, defame.

denigrativamente, *adv.* revilingly, insultingly.

denigrativo, va, *a.* reviling; soiling.

denodadamente, *adv.* bravely, resolutely.

denodado, da, *a.* brave, daring, intrepid.

denominación, *f.* denomination.

denominadamente, *adv.* distinctly, markedly.

denominador, *m.* (arith.) denominator.—**quitar,** or **hacer desaparecer, los denominadores,** (math.) to clear of fractions.

denominar, *va.* to call, give a name to.

denominativo, va, *a.* denominative.

denostadamente, *adv.* ignominiously, insultingly.

denostador, ra, *n.* & *a* vilifier(-ing) or reviler (-ing).

denostar, *va.* (*ind.* DENUESTO; *subj.* DENUESTE) to insult, to revile, abuse (with words).

denotación, *f.* designation, denotation.

denotar, *va.* to denote, express; to explain.

denotativo, va, *a.* denoting, denotative.

densamente, *adv.* closely, densely.

densidad, *f.* density; closeness, compactness; specific gravity; obscurity, darkness; confusion. —**d. de población,** density of population.

densímetro, *m.* densimeter.

denso, sa, *a.* dense, thick; close, compact.

dentado, da. I. *pp.* of DENTAR. **II.** *a.* having teeth; denticulated, dentated, serrated, toothed; crenated, indented; cogged, pronged.

dentadura, *f.* set of teeth, false or natural.

¹dental, *a.* dental, pertaining to the teeth or to dentistry; (phon.) dental.

²dental, *m.* bed to which the plowshare is fixed; (agr.) teeth of a rake; fork used to separate the straw from corn.

dentar. I. *va.* (*ind.* DIENTO; *subj.* DIENTE) to tooth, to furnish with teeth or prongs; to indent; to cut into teeth. **II.** *vn.* to teethe, cut teeth.

dentaria, *f.* (bot.) toothwort.

dentecillo, *m. dim.* small tooth.

dentejón, *m.* yoke for oxen.

dentellada, *f.* gnashing of teeth; bite, nip, seizure with the teeth; mark made by the teeth.—**a dentelladas,** with the teeth.

dentellado, da. I. *pp.* of DENTELLAR. **II.** *a.* having teeth; denticulate; serrated; wounded with the teeth.

dentellar, *vn.* (of the teeth) to chatter.

dentellear, *va.* to bite; to bite on or into.

dentellón, *m.* piece of a door lock; (arch.) dentil.

dentera, *f.* sensation of having the teeth on edge; (coll.) envy.—**dar d.,** to set the teeth on edge; to cause great desire, make one's mouth water.

dentezuelo, *m. dim.* little tooth.

dentición, *f.* dentition, teething.

denticular, *a.* dentiform, toothlike.

dentículo, *m.* (arch.) denticle, dentil.

dentífrico, ca. I. *a.* dentifrice. **II.** *m.* dentifrice.

dentirrostros, *m. pl.* (zool.) Dentirostres.

dentista, *m.* dentist.—**dentistería,** *f.* dentistry.

dentivano, na, *a.* (of horses) having long and large teeth.

dentolabial, *a.* (phon.) dentilabial.

dentón, na. I. *a.* (coll.) having large uneven teeth. **II.** *m.* a sea fish of the Sparus genus.

dentrambos, contraction of DE ENTRAMBOS, of both, from both.

dentro, *adv.* inside, within.—**d. de,** inside of.— **d. del año,** in the course of the year.—**d. de poco,** shortly, presently, soon.—**d. en,** in the interior of.—**a d.,** inside.—**de d.,** from inside. —**hacia d.,** towards the interior, inwards.— **por d.,** inside, on the inside; inwardly.

dentudo, da, *a.* having large uneven teeth.

denudación, *f.* (geol.) denudation.

denudar, *va.* (geol.) to denude.

denuedo, *m.* daring, bravery, intrepidity.

¹denuesto, *m.* affront, insult, abuse.

²denuesto, denueste, *v.* V. DENOSTAR.

denuncia, *f.* denunciation; (law) arraignment, accusation; announcement, proclamation; (min.) application for a concession.

denunciable, *a.* that may be denounced.

denunciación, *f.* denunciation, denouncement.

denunciador, ra, *n.* denunciator, accuser; announcer; denouncer.

denunciante, *n.* & *a.* denouncer(-ing); informer (-ing); accuser(-ing).

denunciar, *va.* to advise, give notice; to denounce; to prognosticate, foretell; to pronounce, proclaim solemnly; (min.) to apply for a concession (to own or work).

denunciatorio, ria, *a.* denunciatory.

denuncio, *m.* (min.) DENUNCIA; (Am.) = DE-NUNCIA, DENUNCIACIÓN.

Deo gracias, *m.* Deo gratias (thanks be to God), a greeting; submissive, humble attitude.

deontología, *f.* deontology, ethics.

Deo volente, God willing.

deparar, *va.* to offer, afford, furnish, present.

departamental, *a.* departmental.

departamento, *m.* department; compartment, section; political division within a sovereign state or its autonomous provinces; extent of country under the jurisdiction of the admiral commanding in chief any of the four arsenals in Spain; apartment (dwelling).

departidor, ra, *n.* converser, interlocutor.

departir, *vn.* to chat, talk, converse.

depauperación, *f.* impoverishment; (med.) weakness, exhaustion.

depauperar, *va.* to depauperate, impoverish; (med.) to weaken, exhaust.

dependencia, *f.* dependence, dependency; subordination; branch office; business, affair; trust, charge; dependence, relation; (arch.) outbuildings; relation by blood or marriage.— *pl.* accessories.

depender, *vn.* (de) to depend, rely (on).

dependiente. I. *a.* dependent, subordinate. **II.** *m.* clerk, salesman.

dependientemente, *adv.* dependently.

depilatorio, a, *a.* & *n.* depilatory.

deplorable, *a.* deplorable, lamentable, pitiful.

deplorablemente, *adv.* deplorably, sadly.

deplorar, *va.* to deplore, lament, regret.

depondré, *fut.* of DEPONER.

deponente, *n.* & *a.* deposer(-ing), deponent; (gram.) deponent.

deponer. I. *va.* (*pp.* DEPUESTO; *ind. pres.* DE-PONGO, *pret.* DEPUSE, *fut.* DEPONDRÉ; *subj.* DEPONGA) to lay by, put aside; to depose, remove from office; (law) to attest, depose; to take down, remove. **II.** *vn.* to evacuate the bowels.

depongo, deponga, *v.* V. DEPONER.

depopulador, ra, *n.* & *a.* depopulator(-ing); devastator(-ing).

deportación, *f.* deportation, banishment.

deportar, *va.* to deport, exile, banish.

deporte, *m.* sport; amusement, recreation.

deportismo, *m.* sports, sporting.

deportista, *n.* sportsman(-woman).

deportivo, va, *a.* athletic, sport (as *a.*).

deposición, *f.* assertion, affirmation; deposition from a position or station; (law) deposition, testimony; evacuation (of the bowels).

depositador, ra, *n.* depositor.

depositante, *n.* & *a.* depositor(-ing).

depositar. I. *va.* to deposit; to intrust, confide; to put (a person) in safety, to bring (a person) out of danger of violence or intimidation; to inclose; to place (a corpse) in a receiving vault; to lay aside, put away. **II.** *vr.* (chem.) to settle.

depositaria, *f.* depository; subtreasury; dignity and office of a depositary; trust.

depositario, ria. I. *a.* pertaining to a depository. **II.** *n.* depositary, trustee, receiver.

depósito, *m.* deposit, trust, depository; (com.) store, warehouse, depot; (mech.) chamber; (chem.) deposit, precipitate, sediment; (geol.) deposition.—**d. de agua,** tank, reservoir.—**en d.,** deposited; on deposit; in bond.

depravación, *f.* depravation, depravity.

depravadamente, *adv.* depravedly.

depravada, da, *a.* depraved, lewd.

depravador, ra, *n.* depraver, corrupter.

depravar, *va.* to deprave, corrupt.

deprecación, *f.* petition, prayer, entreaty.

deprecante, *a.* supplicating, pleading.

deprecar, *va.* (*pret.* DEPREQUÉ; *subj.* DEPREQUE) to entreat, implore.

deprecativa, va; deprecatorio, ria, *a.* = DE-PRECANTE.

depreciación, *f.* depreciation.

depreciar. I. *va.* to depreciate, to reduce the price of; to undervalue. **II.** *vr.* to depreciate.

depredación, *f.* depredation, plundering; malversation committed by guardians or trustees.

depredador, ra, *n.* & *a.* depredator(-ing), marauder(-ing).

depredar, *va.* to depredate, maraude, pillage.

depreque, depreque, *v.* V. DEPRECAR.

depresión, *f.* depression; pressing down; (astr., com., meteorol.) depression.—**d. de horizonte,** (naut.) dip of the horizon.

depresivo, va, *a.* depressive, depressing.

depresor, ra, *n.* & *a.* depressor(-ing); oppressor (-ing).

deprimente, *a.* = DEPRESIVO.

deprimir. I. *va.* to depress, compress; to humiliate; to belittle, make light of. **II.** *vr.* to become depressed or compressed; to be or seem lower.

de profundis, *m.* De Profundis, the 130th psalm, sung at funerals.

depuesto, *pp. irreg.* of DEPONER.

depurable, *a.* purifiable.

depuración, *f.* purification.

depurar, *va.* to depurate, purify.—**depurativo, va. I.** *a.* purifying. **II.** *m.* (med.) depurative.

depuse, *pret.* of DEPONER.

deputar, *va.* = DIPUTAR, to depute.

deque, *adv.* (coll.) since.

derecera, *f.* = DERECHERA.

derecha, *f.* right hand; right side; (pol.) right, moderate or conservative party.—**a la d.,** to the right, on the right-hand side; right-handed (screw, key, etc.); (mil.) right about.—**a. derechas,** or **a las derechas,** right, well done; honestly, rightly, justly.—**a tuertas o dere-chas,** right or wrong; inconsiderately.

derechamente, *adv.* directly, straight; wisely; honestly, justly.

derechera, *f.* direct or straight road; short cut.

derechero, *m.* clerk who collects fees.

derechista, *m.* & *f.* (pol.) rightist; reactionary.

derechito, *dim. adv.* right straight (ahead, etc.)

derecho, cha. I. *a.* straight; right, (opposite to left); right-handed; just, lawful, reasonable, legitimate; (mech.) standing, upright.—**d. la caña,** (naut.) right the helm.—**hecho y d.,** perfect, complete; in all respects; grown up; true, certain; without doubt.—**ponerse d.,** to stand up straight. **II.** *adv.* = DERECHAMENTE. **III.** *m.* right; law (body of laws); equity; exemption, frank, grant, privilege; road, path; right side of cloth, etc.).—*pl.* fees, dues, taxes, duties.—**d. administrativo,** administrative law; collection of ordinances, regulations, etc.—**d. canónico,** canon law.—**d. civil,** or **común,** civil law.—**d. consuetudinario,** common law, law established by custom and precedent.—**d. de gentes,** international law; jus gentium (among the Romans).—**d. de visita,** right of search.—**d. diferencial de bandera,** differential duties.—**d. divino,** divine right.—**d. internacional,** international law.—**d. mercantil,** commercial law.—**d. municipal,** municipal law.—**d. natural,** natural right.—**d. no escrito** = D. CONSUETUDINA-RIO.—**d. penal,** criminal law.—**d. positivo,** positive law.—**de d.,** de jure.—**del d.,** right-side out.—*pl.* **derechos.—d. civiles,** civil rights.—**d. consulares,** consular fees.—**d. de aduana,** customs duties.—**d. de almacenaje,** storage.—**d. de anclaje,** anchorage dues.—**d. de autor,** copyright; royalties (on printed works).—**d. de depósito** = DERECHOS DE ALMACENAJE.—**d. de entrada,** import duties.—**d. del hombre,** rights of man.—**d. de in-ventor,** patent.—**d. de muelle,** wharfage, pierage.—**d. de puerto,** harbor dues, port dues.—**d. de remolque,** towage.—**d. huma-nos,** human rights.—**d. reales,** inheritance tax; duty on transfer of real estate.

derechuelo, *m.* first sewing taught to little girls.

derechura, *f.* straightness.—**en d.,** by the most direct road; as the crow flies.

deriva, *f.* (naut.) ship's course; deviation, drift; (aer.) drift; drifting.

derivación, *f.* derivation, descent; deduction, inference; draining of water, turning of its course; (gram.) derivation; (elec.) branch, tap (of a wire, current, etc.); shunt.—**en d.,** (elec.) shunt (as *a.*); shunted.

derivada, *f.* (math.) derivative.

derivado, da, *a.* (gram.) derivative.

derivar. I. *vn.* & *vr.* to derive, proceed, descend **II.** *vn.* (naut., aer.) to drift. **III.** *va.* to guide, lead, conduct; to derive, trace to its origin (elec.) to tap; to shunt.

derivativo, va, *a.* & *n.* derivative.

derivómetro, *m.* (aer.) drift meter.

dermalgia, *f.* (med.) neuralgia of the skin.

dermatitis, *f.* (med.) dermatitis.

dermatología, *f.* dermatology.

dermatológico, ca, *a.* dermatological.

dermatólogo, ga, *n.* dermatologist.

dermatosis, *f.* (med.) dermatosis.

dermesto, *m.* (zool.) larder beetle.

dermis, *f.* derm, dermis, skin.

derogación, *f.* derogation, repeal; deterioration, diminution.

derogar, *va.* (*pret.* DEROGUÉ; *subj.* DEROGUE) to derogate, annul, revoke, repeal; to reform; to remove.

derogatorio, ria, *a.* annulling, repealing.

derogué, derogue, *v.* V. DEROGAR.

derrabadura, *f.* wound made in docking the tail of an animal.

derrabar, *va.* to dock the tail of.

derrama, *f.* apportionment of an assessment, tax, or contribution.

derramadamente, *adv.* profusely, lavishly; disorderly, confusedly.

derramadero, ra, *a.* = VERTEDERO, sink, dump.

derramado, da; derramador, ra, *a.* prodigal, extravagant.

derramamiento, *m.* pouring out; spilling, shedding; overflow; dispersion, scattering; lavishing, wasting.—**d. de sangre,** bloodshed.

derramar. I. *va.* to pour out; to spill; shed; scatter; to apportion (taxes); to publish, spread; to lavish, give freely; to waste. **II.** *vr.* to overflow, run over; to be scattered or spread.

derrame, *m.* overflow, running over; spread, scattering; shedding; portion of liquor or seed lost in measuring; leakage; waste; (arch.) chamfering, splay; declivity, slope; (naut.) draft of a sail; outlet of a ravine, driftway; (med.) effusion, discharge.

derramo, *m.* (arch.) chamfering, splay, flare, bevel, flanging of a door or window.

derrape, *m.* (aer.) yawing.

derraspado, *a.* beardless (wheat).

derredor, *m.* circumference, circuit.—**al d., or en d.,** round about.—**al d. de, en d. de,** about, around.

derrelicto, a. I. *pp. irreg.* of DERRELINQUIR. **II.** *a.* derelict. **III.** *m.* (naut.) derelict.

derrelinquir, *va.* (*pp.* DERRELICTO; *ind.* DERRELINCO; *subj.* DERRELINCA) to abandon, forsake.

derrenegar, *vn.* (*ind. pres.* DERRENIEGO, *pret.* DERRENEGUÉ; *subj.* DERRENIEGUE).—**d. de,** (coll.) to hate, detest, loathe, abhor.

derrengada, *f.* (prov.) a step in dancing.

derrengado, da. I. *pp.* of DERRENGAR. **II.** *a.* bent, crooked; lame, crippled.

derrengadura, *f.* dislocation of the hip; lameness.

derrengar, *va.* (*ind.* DERRIENGO; *subj.* DERRIENGUE) to sprain or dislocate the hip of; to break or injure the spine of; to cripple; to bend, make crooked; to knock (fruit) off a tree.—**derrengo,** *m.* stick with which fruit is knocked down.

¹derreniego, *m.* (coll.) curse.

²derreniego, derreniegue, *v.* V. DERRENEGAR.

derretido, da. I. *pp.* of DERRETIR. **II.** *a.* enamored, deeply in love.

derretimiento, *m.* thaw, liquefaction, fusion, melting; consuming love or passion.

derretir. I. *va.* (*ind.* DERRITO; *subj.* DERRITA) to liquefy, melt, fuse; (coll.) to change (money); to consume, expend, waste, exhaust. **II.** *vr.* to fuse, melt, thaw; to be deeply in love; to fall in love very easily; to grow tender; to be impatient.

derribado, da. I. *pp.* of DERRIBAR. **II.** *a.* (of horses) having a round and low rump.

derribador, *m.* slaughterer (in slaughterhouse).

derribar. I. *va.* to throw down, knock down; overthrow; fell; to demolish, tear down; to strike down (a bull) with a pike on horseback; to subdue (a passion). **II.** *vr.* to tumble down, to throw oneself on the ground.—**derribo,** *m.* demolition, pulling down; debris, ruins.

derriengo, derriengue, *v.* V. DERRENGAR.

derrito, derrita, *v.* V. DERRETIR.

derrocadero, *m.* rocky precipice.

derrocamiento, *m.* throwing down, overthrow.

derrocar, *va.* (*ind.* DERRUECO; *subj.* DERRUEQUE) to precipitate or fling down from a rock; to pull down, demolish; to pull down (from office, position, etc.), put down; to oust; to dethrone, overthrow.

derrochador, ra, *n.* prodigal, spendthrift, squanderer.

derrochar, *va.* to waste, squander.

derroche, *m.* waste, squandering.

derrota, *f.* defeat, rout; overthrow; route, road, path, track; (naut.) ship's course.

derrotar, *va.* to defeat; to waste away, wear away; to ruin; (naut.) to cause to drift.

derrote, *m.* thrust of a bull's horn.

derrotero, *m.* (naut.) collection of seacharts; ship's course; navigation track or route; course, way or plan of life, conduct, or action.

derrotismo, *m.* defeatism.

derrotista, *m. & f.* defeatist.

derrubiar, *va.* to undermine or wash away.

derrubio, *m.* alluvion, alluvium.

derrueco, derrueque, *v.* V. DERROCAR.

derruir, *va.* (*ind.* DERRUYO; *subj.* DERRUYA) to demolish, tear down, raze, destroy.

derrumbadero, *m.* precipice; craggy, steep, and broken ground; arduous affair.

derrumbamiento, *m.* landslide; collapse; downfall.

derrumbar. I. *va.* to throw down headlong. **II.** *vr.* to throw oneself headlong; to sink down, crumble away, tumble down.—**derrumbe,** *m.* tumbling down, collapse; landslide.

derruyo, derruya, *v.* V. DERRUIR.

derviche, *m.* dervish.

desabarrancar, *va.* (*pret.* DESABARRANQUÉ; *subj.* DESABARRANQUE) to drag, draw, or pull out of a ditch; to disentangle, extricate.

desabastecer, *va.* (*ind.* DESABASTEZCO; *subj.* DESABASTEZCA) to neglect to supply with, or impede the supply of, provisions.

desabejar, *va.* to remove bees from.

desabillé, *m.* dishabille; house or morning gown.

desabitar, *va.* (naut.) to unbitt.

desabollador, *m.* tinworker's instrument.

desabollar, *va.* to tinker.

desabonarse, *vr.* to discontinue a subscription.

¹desabono, *m.* discontinuance of a subscription.

²desabono, *m.* prejudice, injury.

desabor, *m.* insipidity, tastelessness.

desabordarse, *vr.* (naut.) to get clear of a ship which has run foul of one's vessel.

desaborido, da, *a.* tasteless, insipid; without substance; (coll.) dull, witless.

desabotonar. I. *va.* to unbutton. **II.** *vn.* to blow, bloom, blossom.

desabozar, *va.* (naut.) to unstopper.

desabridamente, *adv.* without taste or flavor; rudely, disagreeably.

desabrido, da, *a.* tasteless, insipid; rude, disagreeable, peevish; kicking (gun); bleak, sharp.

desabrigadamente, *adv.* without covering; without shelter.

desabrigado, da, *a.* uncovered; shelterless; harborless; without support.

desabrigar. I. *va.* (*pret.* DESABRIGUÉ; *subj.* DESABRIGUE) to uncover; to strip; to deprive of shelter or harbor. **II.** *va. & vr.* to take off outer clothing.

desabrigo, *m.* lack of covering, clothing, shelter or harbor; destitution.

desabrillantar, *va. & vr.* to (make) lose luster.

desabrimiento, *m.* insipidity, flatness; rudeness, disagreeableness; despondency, lowness of spirits; recoil of firearms.

desabrir, *va.* to impart a bad taste to; to vex, plague, torment, harass.

desabrochar. I. *va.* to unclasp, unbutton, unfasten; burst open. II. *vr.* to unbosom oneself, to open one's heart.

desacalorarse, *vr.* to cool off.

desacatadamente, *adv.* disrespectfully.

desacatado, da. I. *pp.* of DESACATAR. **II.** *a.* disrespectful.

desacatador, ra, *a.* & *n.* irreverent, uncivil, or disrespectful (person).

desacatamiento, *m.* disrespect.

desacatar, *va.* to treat disrespectfully; to dishonor.—**desacato,** *m.* disrespect, incivility; lack of reverence; desecration, profanation.

desaceitado, da, *a.* lacking oil.

desaceitar, *va.* to take off oil or grease from.

desacerar, *va.* to unsteel.

desacerbar, *va.* to temper, sweeten, take away harshness and bitterness from.

desacertadamente, *adv.* unwisely; wrongly or erroneously.

desacertado, da, *a.* wrong, mistaken; unwise.

desacertar, *vn.* (*ind.* DESACIERTO; *subj.* DESACIERTE) to err, make a mistake; act unwisely.

desacidificar, *va.* to remove acidity from; to neutralize (an acid).

¹desacierto, *m.* error, mistake, blunder.

²desacierto, desacierte, *v.* *V.* DESACERTAR.

desacobardar, *va.* to remove fear from; to encourage, reassure.

desacollar, *va.* (*ind.* DESACUELLO; *subj.* DESACUELLE) to dig up the ground about (vines).

desacomodadamente, *adv.* incommodiously, inconveniently.

desacomodado, da. I. *pp.* of DESACOMODAR. **II.** *a.* destitute of conveniences; out of service; troublesome.

desacomodamiento, *m.* inconvenience, trouble.

desacomodar. I. *va.* to inconvenience; to trouble, discommode; to discharge, dismiss. **II.** *vr.* (of servants) to lose one's place.

desacomodo, *m.* discharge; loss of a position.

desacompañamiento, *m.* lack of company or society.

desacompañar, *va.* to leave the company of.

desaconsejado, da. I. *pp.* of DESACONSEJAR. **II.** *a.* ill-advised, imprudent; capricious.

desaconsejar, *va.* to dissuade.

desacoplar, *va.* to unfasten, disconnect.

desacordadamente, *adv.* unwisely, unadvisedly.

desacordado, da; desacordante, *a.* discordant.

desacordar. I. *va.* (mus.) (*reg. conj.* in this meaning) to put out of tune. **II.** *vr.* (*ind.* DESACUERDO; *subj.* DESACUERDE) to be forgetful.

desacorde, *a.* discordant; inharmonious, incongruous.

desacorralar, *va.* to let out of the corral; to bring (a bull) into the ring or open field.

desacostumbradamente, *adv.* unusually.

desacostumbrado, da. I. *pp.* of DESACOSTUMBRAR. **II.** *a.* unaccustomed; unusual.

desacostumbrar, *va.* to disaccustom, break of a habit.

¹desacotar, *va.* to lay open (a pasture); to take down (fences).

²desacotar, *va.* to raise or withdraw (a prohibition); to withdraw from (an agreement); among boys, to play without conditions or rules; to reject, refuse.

desacoto, *m.* taking fences off a pasture-ground.

desacreditar, *va.* to discredit; bring discredit on, injure the credit or reputation of.

desacuello, desacuelle, *v.* *V.* DESACOLLAR.

¹desacuerdo, *m.* discordance, disagreement; error, mistake, blunder; forgetfulness; mental derangement.

²desacuerdo, desacuerde, *v.* *V.* DESACORDAR.

desacuñador, *m.* (print.) shooting stick.

desacuñar, *va.* (print.) to unwedge, loosen.

desaderezar, *va.* to ruffle, disarrange.

desadeudar, *va.* & *vr.* to free from debt.

desadorar, *va.* to cease to worship or love.

desadormecer, *va.* (*ind.* DESADORMEZCO; *subj.* DESADORMEZCA) to wake, to rouse.

desadornar, *va.* to divest of ornaments.—**desadorno,** *m.* want of embellishments and charms.

desadvertidamente, *adv.* inadvertently.

desadvertido, da. I. *pp.* of DESADVERTIR. **II.** *a.* unwise, imprudent; unnoticed.

desadvertimiento, *m.* unwisdom; lack of reflection, thoughtlessness.

desadvertir, *va.* (*ind.* DESADVIERTO; *subj.* DESADVIERTA) to give no heed to, not to notice.

desafear, *va.* to remove or lessen the blemishes of.

desafección, *f.* disaffection.

desafecto, ta. I. *a.* disaffected; opposed. **II.** *m.* disaffection, discontent.

desaferrar, *va.* (*ind.* DESAFIERRO; *subj.* DESAFIERRE) (naut.) to unmoor, weigh anchor; to convince, bring to a change of opinion.

desafiadero, *m.* private dwelling ground.

desafiador, ra, *n.* challenger, duellist; one who dares or defies.

desafianzar, *va.* (Am.) to withdraw security.

desafiar, *va.* to challenge, dare; to defy; to rival, oppose, compete with.

desafición, *f.* disaffection.

desaficionar, *va.* & *vr.* to destroy or lose the desire, wish, or affection of.

desafierro, desafierre, *v.* *V.* DESAFERRAR.

desafijar, *va.* to disown as a son.

desafinación, *f.* discordance, being out of tune.

desafinadamente, *adv.* dissonantly or discordantly.

desafinar. I. *vn.* (mus.) to be out of tune; to speak irrelevantly. **II.** *vr.* to get out of tune.

desafío, *m.* challenge; duel; struggle, contest, rivalry, competition.

desaforadamente, *adv.* disorderly, excessively, outrageously, impudently.

desaforado, da. I. *pp.* of DESAFORAR. **II.** *a.* disorderly, lawless; impudent, outrageous; huge, uncommonly large.

desaforar. I. *va.* (*ind.* DESAFUERO; *subj.* DESAFUERE) to encroach upon the rights of; (mil.) to cashier. **II.** *vr.* to be outrageous or disorderly.

desaforrar, *va.* to take out the lining of; (naut.) to unserve, unsheath.

desafortunado, da, *a.* unfortunate, unlucky.

¹desafuero, *m.* excess, outrage, open violence.

²desafuero, desafuere, *v.* *V.* DESAFORAR.

desagarrar, *va.* (coll.) to unfasten, loosen.

desagitadera, *f.* instrument used in removing honeycomb.

desagitar, *va.* to remove honeycombs from.

desagraciado, da, *a.* ungraceful.

desagraciar, *va.* to disfigure, make ungraceful.

desagradable, *a.* disagreeable, unpleasant.

desagradablemente, *adv.* disagreeably.

desagradar, *va.* to displease, offend.

desagradecer, *va.* (*ind.* DESAGRADEZCO; *subj.* DESAGRADEZCA) to be ungrateful.

desagradecidamente, *adv.* ungratefully.

desagradecido, da, *a.* ungrateful.

desagradecimiento, *m.* ingratitude.

desagradezco, desagradezca, *v.* *V.* DESAGRADECER.

desagrado, *m.* discontent, displeasure.

desagraviar, *va.* to right a wrong to, to apologize to; to indemnify.

desagravio, *m.* satisfaction for an injury; compensation for damages; vindication.

desagregación, *f.* separation, segregation.

desagregar, *va.* (*pret.* DESAGREGUÉ; *subj.* DESAGREGUE) to disjoin, separate, segregate.

desaguadero, *m.* drain, waste pipe, outlet; drain of money.

desaguador, *m.* small drain for irrigation.

desaguar. I. *va.* to drain (of liquid), empty; to squander, waste. **II.** *vn.* (of rivers) to empty. **III.** *vr.* to discharge by vomit or stools.

desaguazar, *va.* to drain.

desagüe, *m.* drainage; drain, outlet; waste.

desaguisado, da. I. *a.* lawless, illegal, unjust. **II.** *m.* offense, injury, wrong, outrage.

desaherrojar, *va.* to unchain, unshackle.

desahijar. I. *va.* to wean; to separate (the young) from the dams. **II.** *vr.* (of bees) to breed swarms.

desahitarse, *vr.* to relieve indigestion.

desahogadamente, *adv.* comfortably, easily; freely, unobstructedly; in a brazen-faced or unconcerned manner, brazenly.

desahogado, da. I. *pp.* of DESAHOGAR. **II.** *a.* petulant, impudent, brazen-faced; clear, free, unencumbered; in comfortable circumstances; (naut.) having sea room.

desahogar. I. *va.* (*pret.* DESAHOGUÉ; *subj.* DESAHOGUE) to ease the pain of, alleviate, relieve. **II.** *vr.* to recover from fatigue or disease; to unbosom oneself, to disclose one's grief; to give a piece of one's mind; to express one's feelings; to extricate oneself from debt.

desahogo, *m.* ease, relief from pain or affliction; rest or respite from work; unbosoming oneself or disclosing one's troubles or grief; laxity; comfort, ease; comfortable circumstances.

desahogué, desahogue, *v.* *V.* DESAHOGAR.

desahuciadamente, *adv.* hopelessly.

desahuciado, da. I. *pp.* of DESAHUCIAR. **II.** *a.* despaired of, hopeless.

desahuciar, *va.* to take away all hope from; to give over; to declare (a patient) past recovery; to dispossess or oust (a tenant).

desahucio, *m.* dispossession of a tenant.

desahumado, da. I. *pp.* of DESAHUMAR. **II.** *a.* (of liquor) weakened (from standing open).

desahumar, *va.* to free from smoke.

desainadura, *f.* a disease of horses caused by their fat being consumed through overwork.

desainar. I. *va.* to take off the fat of (an animal); to lessen or diminish the thickness or substance of. **II.** *vr.* to lose fat.

desairadamente, *adv.* unhandsomely, clumsily, gracelessly.

desairado, da. I. *pp.* of DESAIRAR. **II.** *a.* unhandsome, graceless; unrewarded, unsuccessful.

desairar, *va.* to disregard, to slight, to ignore; to scorn; to rebuff.—**desaire,** *m.* slight, rebuff, disdain, disrespect; awkwardness, clumsiness.

desaislarse, *vr.* to cease to be insulated or isolated; to leave one's seclusion.

desajustar. I. *va.* to disarrange, disadjust. **II.** *vr.* to disagree, to withdraw from an agreement; to get out of order or adjustment.

desajuste, *m.* disarrangement, lack of adjustment; disagreement; maladjustment.

desalabanza, *f.* vituperation, disparagement.

desalabar, *va.* to dispraise, belittle, disparage.

desalabear, *va.* (carp.) to straighten.

desalabeo, *m.* (carp.) straightening.

desaladamente, *adv.* anxiously, swiftly, eagerly; greedily; hurriedly.

desalado, da, *a.* hasty, impatient, disordinate.

desaladura, *f.* (chem.) = DESALAZÓN.

¹desalar. I. *va.* to cut off the wings of. **II.** *vr.* to run or walk swiftly; to be in great haste; to long for, to crave.

²desalar. I. *va.* to remove the salt from. **II.** *vr.* (of fish, meat, etc.) to lose its salt.

desalazón, *f.* (chem.) removing the salt from a liquid.

desalbardar, *va.* to take off the packsaddle from.

desalentadamente, *adv.* faintly, feebly.

desalentador, ra, *a.* dispiriting, discouraging.

desalentar. I. *va.* (*ind.* DESALIENTO; *subj.* DESALIENTE) to put out of breath by labor; to discourage, to dismay. **II.** *vr.* to jade, become exhausted.

desalfombrar, *va.* to take up the carpets from.

desalforjar. I. *va.* to take out of a saddlebag. **II.**

vr. (coll.) to loosen one's garments; to make oneself easy.

desalhajar, *va.* to strip of fine furniture.

¹desaliento, *m.* dismay, depression of spirits, discouragement, dejection; faintness, languor.

²desaliento, desaliente, *v.* *V.* DESALENTAR.

desalineación, *f.* lack of alinement; getting or putting out of alinement.

desalinear, *va.* to throw out of alinement.

desaliñadamente, *adv.* slovenly, uncleanly.

desaliñar, *va.* & *vr.* to disarrange, disorder, ruffle; to make slovenly or dirty.

desaliño, *m.* slovenliness, negligence of dress; disarray; neglect.—*pl.* very long earrings.

desalivación, *f.* salivation.

desalivar, *vn.* to salivate.

desalmadamente, *adv.* soullessly, inhumanly.

desalmado, da. I. *pp.* of DESALMAR. **II.** *a.* soulless, inhuman, merciless; impious, profligate.

desalmamiento, *m.* inhumanity; perversity.

desalmar, *va.* & *vr.* to long for eagerly, to crave.

desalmenado, da, *a.* stripped of battlements.

desalmidonar, *va.* to take the starch out of.

desalojado, da. I. *pp.* of DESALOJAR. **II.** *a.*— **personas desalojadas,** displaced persons.

desalojamiento, *m.* dislodging; displacing.

desalojar. I. *va.* to dislodge, dispossess, oust, evict, eject; to displace. **II.** *vn.* to quit one's lodgings; to move out.

desalquilado, da, *a.* unrented, vacant.

desalquilar, *va.* & *vr.* to leave or cause to leave (a rented room or house); to become vacant.

desalterar, *va.* to allay, assuage, calm down.

desalumbradamente, *adv.* blindly, erroneously.

desalumbrado, da, *a.* dazzled, rattled, dazed; groping in the dark.

desalumbramiento, *m.* blindness, want of judgment, foresight, or knowledge.

desamable, *a.* unlovable.

desamador, ra, *n.* one who has ceased loving; one who dislikes persons or things.

desamar, *va.* to love no more; to dislike, hate.

desamarrar. I. *va.* to untie, unbind, unlash; to separate; (naut.) to unmoor; to unbend (a rope). **II.** *vr.* to get loose; to part.

desamasado, da, *a.* dissolved, disunited.

desamigado, da, *a.* unfriendly; estranged.

desamistarse, *vr.* to fall out, to quarrel.

desamoblar, *va.* = DESAMUEBLAR.

desamoldar, *va.* to change the form, proportion, or symmetry of; to disfigure.

desamor, *m.* disaffection; lack of sentiment and love; enmity, hatred.

desamorado, da. I. *pp.* of DESAMORAR. **II.** *a.* unloving, cold-hearted.

desamorar. I. *va.* to kill the love of. **II.** *vr.* to cease loving.

desamoroso, sa, *a.* unloving.

desamorrar, *va.* (coll.) to make lively, make (a person) talk.

desamortajar, *va.* to disenshroud.

desamortización, *f.* disentail.

desamortizador, ra, *a.* disentailing.

desamortizar, *va.* (*pret.* DESAMORTICÉ; *subj.* DESAMORTICE) to disentail.

desamotinarse, *vr.* to withdraw from a mutiny.

desamparadamente, *adv.* helplessly.

desamparado, da. I. *pp.* of DESAMPARAR. **II.** *a.* forsaken; needy, helpless.

desamparador, ra, *n.* & *a.* forsaker(-ing).

desamparar, *va.* to forsake, abandon, leave; to quit; (naut.) to dismantle, dismast.

desamparo, *m.* abandonment, desertion; want of protection, helplessness, neediness; dereliction.

desamueblado, da, *a.* unfurnished.

desamueblar, *va.* to strip of furniture.

desanclar, desancorar, *va.* (naut.) to weigh the anchor of.

desandadura, *f.* going back over the same road.

desandar, *va.* (*pret.* DESANDUVE) to retrace

(steps).—**d. lo andado**, to undo what has been done.

desandrajado, da, *a.* ragged, in tatters.

desanduve, *pret.* of DESANDAR.

desangramiento, *m.* bleeding to excess.

desangrar. I. *va.* to bleed to excess; to drain (a lake, etc.); to exhaust the means of, to make poor. **II.** *vr.* to lose blood, to bleed.

desanidar. I. *vn.* (of birds) to leave the nest. **II.** *va.* to dislodge from a post.

desanimación, *f.* (Am.) lack of enthusiasm; dullness.

desanimadamente, *adv.* spiritlessly, faintly, with discouragement.

desanimado, da, *a.* dull, flat; discouraged; (Am.) (of a party, etc.) poorly attended.

desanimar. I. *va.* to dishearten, discourage. **II.** *vr.* to get discouraged; to jade.

desánimo, *m.* discouragement, downheartedness.

desanublar. I. *va.* & *vr.* to calm down, cool off. **II.** *va.* to elucidate, make clear.

desanudar, *va.* to untie, loosen; to extricate, disentangle.

desañudadura, *f.* untying; disentanglement.

desañudar, *va.* = DESANUDAR.

desaojadera, *f.* woman supposed to dispel charms.

desaojar, *va.* to cure of the effects of the evil eye.

desapacibilidad, *f.* disagreeableness.

desapacible, *a.* disagreeable, unpleasant.

desapaciblemente, *adv.* disagreeably.

desapadrinar, *va.* to disapprove, disavow.

desaparear, *va.* to separate (two of a pair).

desaparecer. I. *va.* (*ind.* DESAPAREZCO; *subj.* DESAPAREZCA) to cause to disappear. **II.** *vn.* & *vr.* to disappear.

desaparecimiento, *m.* disappearance.

desaparejar, *va.* to unharness, unhitch; (naut.) to unrig (a ship).

desaparezco, desaparezca, *v.* V. DESAPARECER.

desaparición, *f.* disappearance; (astr.) occultation.

desaparroquiar. I. *va.* to remove from a parish. **II.** *vr.* to remove from one parish to another; (com.) to cease to be a customer.

desapasionadamente, *adv.* dispassionately.

desapasionarse, *vr.* to root out love or fondness.

desapegarse, *vr.* to lose liking or love (for a person or thing).—**desapego**, *m.* loss of love, affection, or liking; coolness; impartiality, disinterestedness; indifference.

desapercibidamente, *adv.* inadvertently, unpreparedly.

desapercibido, da, *a.* unprovided; unprepared, unguarded.

desapercibimiento, *m.* unpreparedness.

desapestar, *va.* to disinfect.

desapiadadamente, *adv.* unmercifully.

desapiadado, da, *a.* merciless.

desaplicación, *f.* lack of application, indolence.

desaplicadamente, *adv.* indolently, without application.

desaplicado, da, *a.* indolent, careless, neglectful.

desaplomar, *va.* to put out of plumb.

desapoderadamente, *adv.* hastily, impetuously.

desapoderado, da. I. *pp.* of DESAPODERAR. **II.** *a.* impetuous, unruly.

desapoderamiento, *m.* seizure of another's possessions; depriving of power or authority.

desapoderar, *va.* to dispossess; to rob; to repeal or revoke the power of attorney of.

desapolillar. I. *va.* to free and clear of moths. **II.** *vr.* (coll.) to take the air when it is cold or after a long confinement.

desaporcar, *va.* (*ind. pres.* DESAPUERCO, *pret.* DESAPORQUÉ; *subj.* DESAPUERCA) to take away (from plants) earth which had been heaped about them.

desaposentar, *va.* to dispossess, oust, evict; to drive out of one's mind.

desaposesionar, *va.* to deprive of holdings.

desapoyar, *va.* to withdraw support of or from.

desapreciar, *va.* to undervalue, belittle.

desaprecio, *m.* depreciation, belittling, undervaluation.

desaprender, *va.* to forget what one has learned.

desaprensar. I. *va.* to take away the gloss of (clothes). **II.** *vr.* to extricate oneself.

desapretar, *va.* (*ind.* DESAPRIETO; *subj.* DESAPRIETE) to slacken, loosen, loose; to ease, free from anxiety.

desaprisionar. I. *va.* to release, to set at liberty. **II.** *vr.* to extricate oneself.

desaprobación, *f.* disapprobation, disapproval.

desaprobar, *va.* (*ind.* DESAPRUEBO; *subj.* DESAPRUEBE) to disapprove of, condemn.

desapropiamiento, *m.* = DESAPROPIO.

desapropiarse, *vr.* (**de**) to divest oneself (of), surrender, transfer (one's property).

desapropio, *m.* surrender or transfer of property.

desaprovechadamente, *adv.* unprofitably.

desaprovechado, da, *a.* unprofitable; unimproved; backward.

desaprovechamiento, *m.* lack of improvement; backwardness.

desaprovechar. I. *va.* to waste, misspend, make no use of. **II.** *vn.* to be backward, make little or no progress.

desapruebo, desapruebe, *v.* V. DESAPROBAR.

desapuntalar, *va.* to take away the props or supports of or from.

desapuntar, *va.* to rip out the stitching of; to lose the aim of (a gun).

desaquellarse, *vr.* to become disheartened.

desarbolar, *va.* (naut.) to strip (a ship) of masts; (agr.) to clear of trees.

desarbolo, *m.* stripping (a ship) of masts.

desarenar, *va.* to clear of sand.

desareno, *m.* clearing of sand.

desarmado, da, *a.* unarmed.

desarmador, *m.* hammer of a gun.

desarmadura, *f.*, **desarmamiento**, *m.* disarming, disarmament.

desarmar, *va.* to disarm; to prohibit the carrying of arms to; to dismount, take apart; to disband; to make (a bull) butt in the air; (naut.) to lay up.—**desarme**, *m.* disarming, disarmament.

desarraigar, *va.* (*pret.* DESARRAIGUÉ; *subj.* DESARRAIGUE) to eradicate, root out; to dig up (a tree); to extirpate, exterminate; to expel.

desarraigo, *m.* eradication; expulsion.

desarrancarse, *vr.* to desert, to separate from a body or association.

desarrapado, desharrapado, da, *a.* ragged.

desarrebozadamente, *adv.* frankly, clearly.

desarrebozar, *va.* & *vr.* to unmuffle; to lay open, manifest, uncover.

desarrebujar, *va.* to disentangle; to unfold, spread out; to uncover; to explain, clear up.

desarregladamente, *adv.* disorderly.

desarreglado, da, *a.* immoderate, intemperate; extravagant, excessive; slovenly, disorderly; disarranged; lawless, unruly.

desarreglar, *va.* to disarrange, derange, disorder. —**desarreglo**, *m.* disarrangement, disorder, confusion.

¹desarrendar, *va.* (*ind.* DESARRIENDO; *subj.* DESARRIENDE) to break the lease of.

²desarrendar, (*for mut.* V. ¹DESARRENDAR). **I.** *va.* to unbridle (a horse). **II.** *vr.* (of a horse) to shake off the bridle.

desarrimar, *va.* to remove, separate; to dissuade.

desarrimo, *m.* lack of props or support.

desarrinconar, *va.* to bring out, unearth.

desarrollable, *a.* that can be developed.

desarrollado, da. I. *pp.* of DESARROLLAR. **II.** *a.* undeveloped; underdeveloped.—**países poco desarrollados**, underdeveloped countries.

desarrollar. I. *va.* to develop; to unroll, unfold,

unwind, unfurl; to promote, improve; to explain, expound; to work out; (math.) to develop (a surface), to rectify (a curve), to develop or expand (a power, a function); (Ry.) to develop (a line) (*v.* DESARROLLO). **II.** *vr.* to develop; evolve; to unwind, unfold.

desarrollo, *m.* development; unfolding; unwinding; (math.) development (of a surface, a curve); rectification, calculation of the length (of a curve); expansion, development (of a power, a function); (Ry.) development, lengthening of the line by curves to obtain the appropriate grade.

desarropar, *va.* to uncover, to undress.

desarrugadura, *f.* taking out wrinkles.

desarrugar, *va.* (*pret.* DESARRUGUÉ; *subj.* DESARRUGUE) to take wrinkles out of, to smooth out.

desarrumar, *va.* (naut.) to break out (the hold).

desarticulación, *f.* disarticulation.

desarticular, *va.* & *vr.* to disarticulate, take or come apart at the joints; (naut.) to loose, disconnect.

desartillar, *va.* to take the guns out of.

desarzonar, *va.* to throw from the saddle, unhorse.

desasado, da, *a.* without handles.

desaseadamente, *adv.* untidily, slovenly.

desaseado, da, *a.* slovenly, not clean.

desasear, *va.* to make dirty or unclean; to disarrange, to disorder.

desasegurar. I. *va.* to loosen, unbrace, make unsteady. **II.** *vr.* (Am.) to cancel an insurance.

desasentar. I. *va.* (*ind.* DESASIENTO; *subj.* DESASIENTE) to displace, move, remove. **II.** *vn.* to be unbecoming; to be disliked, to displease. **III.** *vr.* to stand up.

desaseo, *m.* uncleanliness, untidiness, slovenliness.

desasgo, desasga, *v.* *V.* DESASIR.

desasiento, desasiente, *v.* *V.* DESASENTAR.

desasimiento, *m.* loosening or letting loose; alienation of affection; lack of interest.

desasimilación, *f.* (physiol.) katabolism.

desasir. I. *va.* (*ind.* DESASGO; *subj.* DESASGA) to loosen, let go, give up. **II.** *vr.* (**de**) to disengage or rid oneself (of); to give away, give up.

desasistir, *va.* to abandon, forsake.

desasnar. I. *va.* (coll.) to polish (one's manners). **II.** *vr.* to grow clever; to become polite.

desasociable, *a.* unsociable.

desasosegadamente, *adv.* uneasily, anxiously.

desasosegar, *va.* (*ind. pres.* DESASOSIEGO, *pret.* DESASOSEGUÉ; *subj.* DESASOSIEGUE) to disquiet, disturb, make uneasy or anxious.

desasosiego, *m.* restlessness, uneasiness.

desastradamente, *adv.* calamitously, unhappily.

desastrado, da, *a.* wretched, unfortunate; shabby, ragged.

desastre, *m.* disaster, catastrophe.

desastrosamente, *adv.* disastrously.

desastroso, sa, *a.* unfortunate, disastrous.

desatacar. I. *va.* (*pret.* DESATAQUÉ; *subj.* DESATAQUE) to loosen, untie, unfasten; to draw (the ramrod from). **II.** *vr.* to unfasten one's trousers.

desatadamente, *adv.* loosely, freely.

desatado, da. I. *pp.* of DESATAR. **II.** *a.* loose, untied.

desatador, ra, *n.* one that unties or unfastens.

desatadura, *f.* untying, loosening.

desatalantado, da, *a.* unwise, injudicious.

desatancar, *va.* (*pret.* DESATANQUÉ; *subj.* DESATANQUE) to clear of obstructions.

desataqué, desataque, *v.* *V.* DESATACAR.

desatar. I. *va.* to untie, undo (a knot), unfasten, unhitch, unloose, loosen, unbind; to separate, detach; to let loose; to liquefy, dissolve; to unriddle, solve, find out, unravel. **II.** *vr.* to give a loose rein to one's tongue; to lose all reserve, fear, or bashfulness; to break loose, break out (as a storm).—**d. en,** to break out into, to let out, to pour out (insult, etc.).

desatascar, *va.* (*pret.* DESATASQUÉ; *subj.* DESATASQUE) to pull or draw out of the mud; to remove an obstruction from; to extricate from difficulties.

desataviar, *va.* to strip of ornaments.

desatavío, *m.* uncleanliness, disarray.

desate, *m.* glibness, excessive talk; disorderly proceeding.—**d. de vientre,** looseness of the bowels.

desatención, *f.* inattention; absent-mindedness; disrespect, slight, discourtesy.

desatender, *va.* (*ind.* DESATIENDO; *subj.* DESATIENDA) to pay no attention to; to be unheedful or unmindful of; to disregard, slight, neglect; to take no notice of.

desatentadamente, *adv.* unwisely, injudiciously.

desatentado, da. I. *pp.* of DESATENTAR. **II.** *a.* unwise, injudicious; excessive, rigorous; disordered.

desatentamente, *adv.* discourteously.

desatentar, *va.* (*ind.* DESATIENTO; *subj.* DESATIENTE) to perturb the mind of, to perplex, confuse, derange.

desatento, ta, *a.* inattentive, careless, heedless, thoughtless; unmannerly, discourteous.

desaterrar, *va.* (*ind.* DESATIERRO; *subj.* DESATIERRE) (Am.) to free (a mine) from rubbish and debris; to remove obstructive earth or mud from.

desatesorar, *va.* to spend the treasure of.

desatibar, *va.* (min.) = DESATOAR.

desatiendo, desatienda, *v.* *V.* DESATENDER.

¹desatiento, *m.* lack of the sense of touch; restlessness, uneasiness, worry.

²desatiento, desatiente, *v.* *V.* DESATENTAR.

desatierre, *m.* (min.) dumping ground; cleaning-up, removal of debris, etc.

desatierro, desatierre, *v.* *V.* DESATERRAR.

desatinadamente, *adv.* unwisely, foolishly, bunglingly; extravagantly, disproportionately.

desatinado, da. I. *pp.* of DESATINAR. **II.** *a.* unwise, ill-advised, foolish, wild. **III.** *n.* idiot, fool.

desatinar. I. *va.* to rattle, to confuse, bewilder. **II.** *vn.* to act or talk foolishly; to get rattled or bewildered; to lose one's bearings.

desatino, *m.* lack of tact, adroitness, or address; unwisdom; foolish act or expression; irrelevancy; nonsense, folly, blunder.

desatolondrar. I. *va.* to bring (a person) to his senses. **II.** *vr.* to recover one's senses (fig.) to wake up, open one's eyes.

desatollar, *va.* = DESATASCAR.

desatontarse, *vr.* to recover from stupefaction.

desatorar, *va.* (naut.) to break out (the hold); (min.) to clear from rubbish.

desatornillar, *va.* to unscrew.

desatracar, *va.* (*pret.* DESATRAQUÉ; *subj.* DESATRAQUE) (naut.) to sheer off, to bear away.

desatraer, *va.* (*ger.* DESATRAYENDO; *ind. pres.* DESATRAIGO, *pret.* DESATRAJE; *subj.* DESATRAIGA) to disjoin, separate.

desatraillar, *va.* to unleash (hounds).

desatrampar, *va.* to clear out (a drain, etc.).

desatrancar, *va.* (*pret.* DESATRANQUÉ; *subj.* DESATRANQUE) to unbar; to clear, remove the obstructions from.

desatraqué, desatraque, *v.* *V.* DESATRACAR.

desatrayendo, *ger.* of DESATRAER.

desatufarse, *vr.* to go out from a close room; to become calm, to calm down, cool off.

desaturdir, *va.* to rouse from dizziness or stupor.

desautoricé, desautorice, *v.* *V.* DESAUTORIZAR.

desautoridad, *f.* want of authority.

desautorización, *f.* withdrawal of authority.

desautorizadamente, *adv.* without authority.

desautorizado, da, *a.* unauthorized; discredited.

desautorizar, *va.* (*pret.* DESAUTORICÉ; *subj.* DESAU-

TORICE) to take authority from, to deprive of authority.

desavahado, da, *a.* clear (weather), free from vapor; bold.

desavahamiento, *m.* uncovering a hot thing to let it cool.

desavahar. I. *va.* to expose to the air, to let cool off; to air, ventilate. **II.** *vr.* to become, or get, lively or sprightly.

desavecindado, da. I. *pp.* of DESAVECINDARSE. **II.** *a.* deserted, unpeopled.

desavecindarse, *vr.* to change one's domicile.

desavendré, *fut.* of DESAVENIR.

desavenencia, *f.* discord, disagreement, misunderstanding; quarrel.

desavengo, desavenga, *v. V.* DESAVENIR.

desavenido, da. I. *pp.* of DESAVENIR. **II.** *a.* discordant, disagreeing.

desavenir. I. *va.* (*ger.* DESAVINIENDO; *ind. pres.* DESAVENGO, *pret.* DESAVINE, *fut.* DESAVENDRÉ; *subj.* DESAVENGA) to disturb, unsettle. **II.** *vr.* to disagree, to quarrel.

desaventajadamente, *adv.* disadvantageously.

desaventajado, da, *a.* disadvantageous; inferior.

desaviar. I. *va.* to mislead, lead astray; to strip of necessaries or conveniences. **II.** *vr.* to go astray; to lose the means of acquiring necessaries.

desavine, desaviniendo, *v. V.* DESAVENIR.

desavío, *m.* leading or going astray; want of necessary means.

desavisado, da. I. *pp.* of DESAVISAR. **II.** *a.* ill-advised, unadvised, misguided.

desavisar, *va.* to contradict (previous advice, news or reports); to countermand.

desayudar, *va.* to prevent from being aided.

desayunado, da. I. *pp.* of DESAYUNAR. **II.** *a.* having breakfasted.

desayunarse, *vr.* to breakfast; to have first intelligence; to be aware of something.

desayuno, *m.* light breakfast, morning meal (usually coffee or chocolate and rolls or bread).

desazogar. I. *va.* (*pret.* DESAZOGUÉ; *subj.* DESAZOGUE) to take off the quicksilver from (a looking-glass). **II.** *vr.* (Peru) to become restless.

desazón, *f.* insipidity, want of taste or flavor; displeasure, vexation; uneasiness, restlessness; unfitness of a soil for agricultural purposes.

desazonado, da, *a.* (agr.) unfit for cultivation; peevish, ill-humored; indisposed.

desazonar. I. *va.* to render tasteless; to vex, ruffle. **II.** *vr.* to become indisposed.

desbabar, *vn.* to drivel, to slaver.

desbagar, *va.* (*pret.* DESBAGUÉ; *subj.* DESBAGUE) to extract (the flaxseed) from the capsule.

desbancar, *va.* (*pret.* DESBANQUÉ; *subj.* DESBANQUE) to clear (a room) of benches, etc.; to win the bank from, to break the bank; to cut out, supplant in the affection of another.

desbandada, *f.* disbandment.—**a la d.,** in great disorder, helter-skelter.

desbandarse, *vr.* to disband; to withdraw (from others); (mil.) to desert.

desbanqué, desbanque, *v. V.* DESBANCAR.

desbarahustar, desbarajustar. I. *va.* to disorder, confuse, disarrange. **II.** *vr.* to get out of order, break down.—**desbarahuste, desbarajuste,** *m.* disorder, confused medley.

desbaratadamente, *adv.* brokenly, dispersedly.

desbaratado, da. I. *pp.* of DESBARATAR. **II.** *a.* (coll.) debauched, corrupted.

desbaratador, ra, *n.* destroyer, confounder, disturber; debaucher.

desbaratamiento, *m.* perturbation, commotion, disarrangement, ruin, downfall.

desbaratar. I. *va.* to destroy, break to pieces, smash, ruin; to waste, misspend, squander; to cross, impede, prevent, thwart; (mil.) to disperse, rout, break up. **II.** *vn.* to talk nonsense.

III. *vr.* to be unbalanced; to get out of order; to fall to pieces; to become, or get, undone.

desbarate, desbarato, *m.* smash, breakage, destruction; (mil.) rout, defeat; waste, squandering.—**d. de vientre,** loose bowels.

desbarbado, da, *a.* beardless.

desbarbar, *va.* to trim, to cut off filaments from; (coll.) to shave.

desbarbillar, *va.* (agr.) to cut out (from young vines) the roots which spring from the stems.

desbardar, *va.* to remove thatch from.

desbarnizar, *va.* to remove the varnish from.

desbarrancadero, *m.* (Am.) precipice.

desbarrar, *vn.* to throw an iron bar without taking aim; to sneak, steal away; to act foolishly; to talk nonsense.

desbarretar, *va.* to unbar, unbolt.

desbarrigado, da, *a.* small-bellied.

desbarrigar, *va.* (*pret.* DESBARRIGUÉ; *subj.* DESBARRIGUE) (coll.) to rip open the belly of.

desbarro, *m.* foolish action; nonsensical talk; aimless throw of the bar (sports).

desbastador, *m.* dressing chisel, paring tool, hewer.

desbastadura, *f.* planing, trimming, hewing.

desbastar, *va.* to hew, pare, dress, trim, plane, smooth; to waste, consume, weaken; to educate and polish.—**desbaste,** *m.* hewing, rough dressing, trimming.

desbastecido, da, *a.* without provisions.

desbautizarse, *vr.* (coll.) to lose one's temper, fly into a passion; (Am.) (coll.) to fracture one's skull.

desbazadero, *m.* humid, slippery place.

desbeber, *va.* (coll.) to urinate.

desbecerrar, *va.* to wean (young animals).

desblanquecido, da; desblanquiñado, da, *a.* blanched, bleached.

desbocadamente, *adv.* impudently, shamelessly, without restraint.

desbocado, da, *a.* (artil.) (of cannon) wide-mouthed; runaway (horse); broken-lipped or -mouthed (as a jar); broken-faced (as a tool); foul-mouthed, indecent.

desbocamiento, *m.* impertinence, impudence; (of a horse) act of running away.

desbocar. I. *va.* (*pret.* DESBOQUÉ; *subj.* DESBOQUE) to break the mouth or spout of. **II.** *vn.* to debouch. **III.** *vr.* to run away; (coll.) to use abusive language, unloosen one's tongue.

desbonetarse, *vr.* (coll.) to take off one's cap.

desboqué, desboque, *v. V.* DESBOCAR.

desboquillar, *va.* to break or remove the mouthpiece or stem of (a pipe, etc.); to break or remove the nozzle of.

desbordamiento, *m.* inundation, overflowing.

desbordar, *vn. & vr.* to overflow; to lose one's temper or self control; to give free rein to one's tongue or passions.

desbornizar, *va.* to strip cork from (tree).

desborrar, *va.* to burl; to lop off the shoots of.

desbragado, da, *a.* (coll.) shabby.

desbravador, *m.* mustang breaker.

desbravar, = DESBRAVECER.

desbravecer. I. *va.* (*ind.* DESBRAVEZCO; *subj.* DESBRAVEZCA) to tame, to break in (horses). **II.** *vn.* to become less fierce; to diminish in force, to moderate, abate.

desbrazarse, *vr.* to stretch out the arms violently.

desbrevarse, *vr.* (of wine) to lose body and strength.

desbridamiento, *m.* (surg.) separation of fibrous tissues with an instrument.

desbridar, *va.* (surg.) to open up, separate the tissues of.

desbriznar, *va.* to chop or mince (meat); to cut or divide into small parts; to pluck the stamens, the filaments of.

desbroce, *m.* clippings, cuttings from pruning trees; clearing of lands or trenches.

For pronunciation, see the rules at the beginning of the book.

desbrozar, *va.* (*pret.* DESBROCÉ; *subj.* DESBROCE) to clear away rubbish from.—**desbrozo**, *m.* = DESBROCE.

desbruar, *va.* to clean (cloth) of grease; to put (cloth) in the fulling mill.

desbrujar, *va.* = DESMORONAR. to abrade.

desbuchar, *va.* to disclose (one's secrets); (of birds) to ease (the stomach).

desbulla, *f.* oyster shell.

desbullar, *va.* to take (oyster) out of shell.

desca, *f.* (naut.) tar pot.

descabal, *a.* imperfect, incomplete.

descabalamiento, *f.* diminution, impairment.

descabalar, *va.* to take away a part of; to chop off, impair, damage, maim, cripple; to pilfer.

descabalgadura, *f.* dismounting or alighting from a horse.

descabalgar. **I.** *vn.* (*pret.* DESCABALGUÉ; *subj.* DESCABALGUE) to dismount, to alight from a horse. **II.** *va.* to dismount (a gun).

descabecé, descabece, *v.* V. DESCABEZAR.

descabelladamente, *adv.* wildly, haphazard, thoughtlessly.

descabellado, da. I. *pp.* of DESCABELLAR. **II.** *a.* dishevelled, disordered, disarranged; out of all reason, illogical, preposterous, absurd.

descabelladura, *f.* dishevelling of the hair.

descabellamiento, *m.* absurdity, nonsense.

descabellar. **I.** *va.* & *vr.* to disarrange (the hair). **II.** *va.* to kill (the bull) by pricking it in the back of the neck with the sword.

descabello, *m.* killing the bull properly.

descabestrar, *va.* to unhalter.

descabezadamente, *adv.* wildly, thoughtlessly.

descabezado, da. I. *pp.* of DESCABEZAR. **II.** *a.* beheaded; light-headed, injudicious, wild, rash.

descabezamiento, *m.* act of beheading; quandary, puzzling predicament.

descabezar. **I.** *va.* (*pret.* DESCABECÉ; *subj.* DESCABECE) to behead; to revoke (an assessment); to cut the upper parts or points of; to head, to top; to poll; to lop off; to overcome; (naut.) to break (a mast) through its neck.—**d. el sueño**, to take a nap. **II.** *vn.* to abut. **III.** *vr.* (coll.) to cudgel one's brains; (of cereals) to shed the grain.

descabritar, *va.* to wean (goats).

descabullirse, *vr.* to sneak off, to steal away, to scamper; to elude the strength of an argument.

descacilar, *va.* to trim (bricks).

descachar. **I.** *va.* (Chile) to cut off the horns of. **II.** *vr.* (billiards) to miscue.

descachazar, *va.* (Am.) to skim (sugar-cane juice).

descaderar, *va.* to sprain or dislocate the hip of.

descadillador, ra, *n.* one who cuts off the fag-end of the warp.

descadillar, *va.* to cut off the loose threads or fag-end of (the warp).

descaecer, *vn.* (*defect. subj.* DESCAEZCA) to decline, droop, languish; decrease; (naut.) to edge away.

descaecido, da. I. *pp.* of DESCAECER. **II.** *a.* weak, feeble, languishing.

descaecimiento, *m.* weakness, debility; despondency, dejection, languor.

descaezca, *v.* V. DESCAECER.

descaimiento, *m.* = DESCAECIMIENTO.

descalabazarse, *vr.* (coll.) to cudgel one's brains in vain.

descalabrado, da. I. *pp.* of DESCALABRAR. **II.** *a.* injured; wounded on the head.—**salir d.**, to be a loser, to fail, to be worsted.

descalabradura, *f.* slight wound in the head; scar remaining after such wound.

descalabrar. **I.** *va.* to wound slightly in the head; to attack or impeach the character of; to hurt, to injure; (naut.) to cause (a ship) considerable damage; to occasion losses to. **II.** *vr.* to fracture one's skull; (Peru) to become ruined or be violently destroyed.

descalabro, *m.* calamity; setback; misfortune.

descalandrajar, *va.* to rend or tear into rags.

descalar, *va.* (naut.) to unship (the helm); to unhang (the rudder).

descalcador, *m.* (carp.) ripping iron, claw; (naut.) ravehook.

descalcar, *va.* (*pret.* DESCALQUÉ; *subj.* DESCALQUE) (naut.) to extract oakum from (seams).

descalce, *m.* undermining, unwedging.

descalcez, *f.* lack of shoes, barefootedness.

descalificación, *f.* disqualification, withdrawal of authority.

descalificar, *va.* to disqualify, to take the power or authority from.

descalostrado, da, *a.* (of a baby) having passed the days of the first milk.

descalzadero, *m.* little door of a pigeonhouse.

descalzador, *m.*, bootjack; crowbar.

descalzar. **I.** *va.* (*pret.* DESCALCÉ; *subj.* DESCALCE) to pull off the shoes and stockings from; to take off wedges or chocks from; to undermine. **II.** *vr.* to take off one's shoes and stockings; (of horses) to lose a shoe.—**d. los guantes**, to take off one's gloves.

descalzo, za, *a.* barefoot, barefooted, shoeless; (of certain friars and nuns) barefooted.

descamación, *f.* (med.) desquamation, (of skin) peeling off in scales.

descambiar, *va.* to cancel an exchange or barter.

descaminadamente, *adv.* absurdly, unreasonably, foolishly.

descaminado, da. I. *pp.* of DESCAMINAR. **II.** *a.* ill-advised, misguided, mistaken.

descaminar. **I.** *va.* to misguide, mislead, lead astray; to seize as contraband; declare contraband; punish for smuggling. **II.** *vr.* to go astray, to lose one's way.

descamino, *m.* leading or going astray; seizure of smuggled goods; the goods thus seized; error, blindness; deviation from justice, truth, reason.

descamisado, da. I. *a.* shirtless, naked, ragged. **II.** *m.* (coll.) ragamuffin.

descampado, da, *a.* disengaged, free, open, clear.—**en d.**, in the open air.

descansadamente, *adv.* easily, without toil or fatigue, leisurely.

descansadero, *m.* resting place.

descansado, da. I. *pp.* of DESCANSAR. **II.** *a.* rested, refreshed.

descansar. **I.** *vn.* to rest, take repose; to be quiet; to rest, lean upon; to be satisfied; to trust or place confidence (in a person); to lie at rest (as lands which lie fallow); to sleep in death. **II.** *va.* to aid or alleviate; to place or set down on a support or base.

descansillo, *m.* landing of a stairway.

descanso, *m.* rest, repose; let-up; relief, aid, help; sleep; landing of stairs; (mech.) seat, bench, support; (mil.) parade rest.

descantar, *va.* to clear of stones.

descantear, *va.* to smooth angles or corners in; to splay, chamfer, edge.

descanterar, *vn.* to take off the corners or ends of.

descantillar, *va.* to pare off, to chip; to subtract from.

descantillón, *m.* = ESCANTILLÓN, pattern.

descantonar, *va.* = DESCANTILLAR.

descañonar, *va.* to pluck out the feathers of; to shave close; (coll.) to trick (one) out of his money.

descaperuzar, *va.* & *vr.* to unhood, uncowl.

descaperuzo, *m.* taking off the cowl, hood, cap.

descapillar, *va.* to take the hood off.

descapirotar, *va.* to take off the CAPIROTE.

descaradamente, *adv.* impudently, barefacedly.

descarado, da. I. *pp.* of DESCARARSE. **II.** *a.* impudent, barefaced, saucy.

descaramiento, *m.* = DESCARO, impudence.

descararse, *vr.* to behave in an impudent or insolent manner, to be saucy.

descarburación, *f.* decarbonization.

descarburar, *va.* to decarbonize.

descarcañalar, *va. & vr.* (of the heel of a shoe) to run down.

descarga, *f.* unburdening, unloading; (mil.) volley, round, discharge; (mason.) easement of a wall; (elec.) discharge.

descargadero, *m.* wharf, unloading place.

descargador, *m.* unloader, lighterman; wad hook.

descargadura, *f.* bone that a butcher takes out of meat.

descargar. I. *va.* (*pret.* DESCARGUÉ; *subj.* DESCARGUE) to unload, disburden; to ease, lighten; to empty, dump; to free or relieve; to take off the flap and bones of (meat); (mil.) to fire, to discharge (firearms); to unload (firearms), to draw out the charge of powder and ball from; (naut.) to brace (a lee), to clear (the sails or yards); (elec.) to discharge; to deal. give, inflict (as blows); to acquit, clear from a charge, exonerate; to free or release from a charge, obligation, or debt. **II.** *vn.* to disembogue or disgorge; to vent fury, to burst, to strike with violence (as a storm). **III.** *vr.* (**de**) to resign (from) (a job); to shirk duty by transferring it to another; to shake off, rid oneself (of); (law) to clear or vindicate oneself (of).

descargo, *m.* unloading, unburdening; exoneration, discharge, acquittal; (com.) acquittance, receipt, release, discharge, voucher; (law) plea or answer to an impeachment or action.

descargue, *m.* unloading: license to unload vessels.

descariñarse, *vr.* to withdraw or lose love or affection; to become cool.

descariño, *m.* coolness, indifference.

descarnada, *f.*—**la d.,** death.

descarnadamente, *adv.* plainly, without trimmings; with effrontery.

descarnado, da, *a.* thin, lean; bare, unadorned.

descarnador, *m.* (dent.) scraper; (tanning) hide scraper.

descarnadura, *f.* divesting of flesh.

descarnar. I. *va.* to clear of flesh; to take or eat away; to corrode, wash away, abrade, denudate; (tanning) to flesh, to scrape; to remove from earthly things. **II.** *vr.* to lose flesh, become emaciated.

descaro, *m.* impudence, barefacedness, effrontery, sauciness, assurance, "nerve," "cheek."

descarriamiento, *m.* going or leading astray.

descarriar. I. *va.* to lead astray, misguide, mislead; to separate (cattle). **II.** *vr.* to be separated; to deviate from justice or reason; to go astray; to lead a dissipated life.

descarrilamiento, *m.* derailment.

descarrilar. I. *va.* to derail. **II.** *vn. & vr.* to run off the track, be derailed.

descarriladura, *f.* act of breaking the jaws.

descarrillar, *va.* to break the jaws of.

descarrío, *m.* going astray, losing the way.

descartar. I. *va.* to discard, throw away; lay aside. **II.** *vr.* to discard (at cards); to excuse oneself; to shirk.

descarte, *m.* cards discarded; act of discarding; act of shirking; evasion, subterfuge.

descasamiento, *m.* annulling (of marriage).

descasar, *va.* to annul the marriage of; to separate, put asunder; (print.) to alter the position of (the pages of a sheet).

descascar. I. *va.* (*pret.* DESCASQUÉ; *subj.* DESCASQUE) to remove the bark, husk, etc. from; to boast; to bluster; to mumble. **II.** *vr.* to break into pieces.

descascarador, ra, *n.* huller, husker, sheller.—**d. de café,** coffee pulper.

descascarar. I. *va.* to peel, shell, hull, husk. **II.** *vr.* to peel off, shell off.

descascarillar, *va.* to peel, husk; to take off the powder from (the face).

descaspar, *va.* to take dandruff from; (tanning) to scrape (a half-dressed hide).

descasque, *m.* removing bark (esp. of the cork tree).

descastado, da, *a.* showing little natural affection to whom it is due.

descastar, *va.* to deprive of caste; to exterminate.

descatolizar, *va.* to cause to abandon Catholicism.

descaudalado, da, *a.* ruined, penniless.

descebar, *va.* to unprime (firearms).

descendencia, *f.* descent, origin; descendants.

descendente, *a.* descending.

descender. I. *vn.* (*pp.* DESCENDIDO; *ind.* DESCIENDO; *subj.* DESCIENDA) to descend; get, come or go down; to flow or run, as liquids; (of temperature) to drop; to descend, be descended, derive; to stoop, lower oneself. **II.** *va.* to let down, lower; to bring down.

descendiente. I. *a.* descending. **II.** *m.* descendant, offspring.

descendimiento, *m.* descent, lowering.

descensión, *f.* descension, descent.

descenso, *m.* descent; lowering; decrease; fall, degradation; (med.) hernia, rupture; prolapse of the womb.

descentrado, da, *a.* out of center; out of plumb.

descentralización, *f.* decentralization.

descentralizador, ra, *n. & a.* decentralizer (-ing).

descentralizar, *va.* (*pret.* DESCENTRALICÉ; *subj.* DESCENTRALICE) to decentralize; to grant local autonomy to.

descentrar. I. *va.* to uncenter. **II.** *vr.* to get out of center or out of plumb.

desceñidura, *f.* ungirding or loosening a belt.

desceñir, *va.* (*ind.* DESCIÑO; *subj.* DESCIÑA) to ungird, to loosen or take off (as a belt, a crown).

¹descepar, *va.* to eradicate, to pull up by the roots; to extirpate.

²descepar, *va.* (naut.) to remove the stocks from (an anchor).

descerar, *va.* to take the empty combs from (a beehive).

descercado, da. I. *pp.* of DESCERCAR. **II.** *a.* open, unfenced, undefended.

descercador, *m.* one who forces the enemy to raise a siege.

descercar, *va.* (*pret.* DESCERQUÉ; *subj.* DESCERQUE) to destroy or pull down a wall, a fence, etc. of; to raise the siege of; to oblige (the enemy) to raise a siege.

descerco, *m.* the act of raising a siege.

descerezar, *va.* to pulp (the coffee berry).

descerqué, descerque, *v. V.* DESCERCAR.

descerrajado, da, *a.* (coll.) corrupt, wicked, ill-disposed.

descerrajadura, *f.* taking off locks or bolts.

descerrajar, *va.* to take the lock off; to discharge (firearms).

descerrumarse, *vr.* (vet.) to be wrenched or distorted at the joints.

descervigamiento, *m.* act of twisting the neck.

descervigar, *va.* to twist the neck of; humiliate.

desciendo, descienda, *v. V.* DESCENDER.

descifrable, *a.* decipherable.

descifrador, ra, *n.* decipherer.

descifrar, *va.* to decipher, make out.

descimbramiento, *m.* (arch.) removing the centers.

descimbrar, *va.* (arch.) to remove the centers of.

descimentar, *va.* to demolish the foundations of.

descinchar, *va.* to ungirt.

desciño, desciña, *v. V.* DESCEÑIR.

descivilizar. I. *va.* to uncivilize. **II.** *vr.* to become uncivilized.

desclavador, *m.* carpenter's chisel; nail puller, claw wrench.

desclavar, *va.* to draw out the nails from, unpeg.

descoagulable, *a.* that can be redissolved after coagulation.

descoagulación, *f.* solution, of a clot or curd.

descoagulante, *a.* that liquefies a clot or curd, clot-dissolving.

descoagular, *va.* to liquefy, dissolve (a clot).

descobajar, *va.* to pull the stem from (a grape).

descobijar, *va.* to uncover.

descocadamente, *adv.* impudently, boldly, brazen-facedly.

descocado, da. I. *pp.* of DESCOCARSE. **II.** *a.* (coll.) bold, excessively free and forward.

descocar. I. *va.* (*pret.* DESCOQUÉ; *subj.* DESCOQUE) to clean insects from (trees).

descocarse, *vr.* (coll.) to be impudent, saucy, or petulant.

descocedura, *f.* digestion.

descocer, *va.* (*ind.* DESCUEZO; *subj.* DESCUEZA) to digest.

descoco, *m.* barefacedness, impudence, sauciness.

descodar, *va.* to rip, to unstitch.

descoger, *va.* (*ind.* DESCOJO; *subj.* DESCOJA) to unfold, extend, spread, expand.

descogollar, *va.* to strip (a tree) of shoots; to take out the heart of (vegetables).

descogotado, da, *a.* (coll.) low-necked.

descogotar, *va.* to cut off the horns of (a stag).

descojo, descoja, *v.* V. DESCOGER.

descolada, *f.* (Mex.) slight, discourtesy.

descolar, *va.* (*ind.* DESCUELO; *subj.* DESCUELE) to dock or crop the tail of; to cut off the fag end of (a piece of cloth); (carp.) to unglue; (Mex.) to ignore, slight; (C. A.) to dismiss, "to fire."

descolchar, *va.* (naut.) to untwist (a cable).

descolgar. I. *va.* (*ind. pres.* DESCUELGO, *pret.* DESCOLGUÉ; *subj.* DESCUELGUE) to take down; to let down. **II.** *vr.* to come down gently, to slip down (by a rope, etc.); to descend; (con) to make an unexpected remark or sally; to come on suddenly (as a cold snap).

descoligado, da, *a.* not belonging to a league, non-union.

descolmar, *va.* to strike off, level off (the heaping corn in a measure); to diminish.

descolmillar, *va.* to pull out or break the fangs or eyeteeth of.

descoloramiento, *m.* discoloration.

descolorante, *m.* & *a.* discolorer(-ing).

descolorar, *va.* & *vr.* to discolor, pale, lose its color, fade.

descolorido, da. I. *pp.* of DESCOLORIR. **II.** *a.* pale, colorless, faded.

descolorimiento, *m.* discoloration, fading.

descolorir, *va.* & *vr.* = DESCOLORAR.

descolladamente, *adv.* loftily, haughtily.

descollamiento, *m.* = DESCUELLO, excessive height; superiority; haughtiness.

descollante, *a.* outstanding, prominent, conspicuous; main, principal.

descollar, *vn.* & *vr.* (*ind.* DESCUELLO; *subj.* DESCUELLE) to tower, stand out, be prominent or conspicuous, excel.

descombrar, *va.* to disencumber, to clear of obstacles, débris, etc.

descombro, *m.* disencumbering.

descomedidamente, *adv.* rudely, disagreeably; excessively, immoderately.

descomedido, da. I. *pp.* of DESCOMEDIRSE. **II.** *a.* excessive, disproportionate, immoderate; rude, impolite, disobliging.

descomedimiento, *m.* rudeness, incivility.

descomedirse, *vr.* (*ger.* DESCOMIDIENDO; *ind. pres.* DESCOMIDO, *pret.* DESCOMIDIÓ; *subj.* DESCOMIDA) to forget oneself; to be rude or disrespectful.

descomer, *vn.* (coll.) to evacuate (bowels).

descomidió, descomido, etc., *v.* V. DESCOMEDIRSE.

descomodidad, *f.* inconvenience, discomfort.

descompadrar. I. *va.* (coll.) to cause estrangement of. **II.** *vn.* (coll.) to disagree, to fall out.

descompaginar, *va.* to disarrange, upset.

descompás, *m.* excess, redundancy, want of measure or proportion.

descompasadamente, *adv.* DESCOMEDIDAMENTE.

descompasado, da. I. *pp.* of DESCOMPASARSE. **II.** *a.* excessive, extravagant, disproportionate; out of tune or time.

descompasarse, *vr.* to exceed all rule and measure; be out of tune or time; forget oneself.

descomponer. I. *va.* (*pp.* DESCOMPUESTO; *ind. pres.* DESCOMPONGO, *pret.* DESCOMPUSE; *subj.* DESCOMPONGA) to disarrange, upset, disturb; to disable; to put out of order; to destroy the harmony of, set at odds; (chem.) to decompose; (mech.) to resolve (forces). **II.** *vr.* to decompose, spoil, rot; to get out of order; (Am.) to dislocate (arm, etc.); to lose one's looks (through illness); to forget oneself, lose one's temper; to change for the worse.

descompongo, descomponga, *v.* V. DESCOMPONER.

descomposición, *f.* discomposure, disagreement; disarrangement; disorder, confusion; decomposition, putrefaction, rotting; (chem.) decomposition, separation of elements; (mech.) resolution (of forces).

descompostura, *f.* disarrangement; disadjustment; slovenliness, uncleanliness, untidiness; forwardness, want of modesty; disrespectful conduct, impudence.

descompuestamente, *adv.* impudently, insolently.

descompuesto, ta. I. *pp. irreg.* of DESCOMPONER. **II.** *a.* impudent, insolent; out of temper; immodest; out of order.

descompuse, *pret.* of DESCOMPONER.

descomulgado, da. I. *pp.* of DESCOMULGAR. **II.** *a.* perverse, nefarious, wicked.

descomulgador, *m.* excommunicator.

descomulgar, *va.* (*pret.* DESCOMULGUÉ; *subj.* DESCOMULGUE) to excommunicate.

descomunal, *a.* extraordinary, monstrous, enormous, huge, colossal.—**descomunalmente,** *asv.* immensely, enormously, extraordinarily.

descomunión, *f.* excommunication.

desconceptuar, *va.* & *vr.* to discredit.

desconcertadamente, *adv.* disorderly, confusedly, disconcertedly.

desconcertado, da. I. *pp.* of DESCONCERTAR. **II.** *a.* disorderly, slovenly.

desconcertador, ra, *n.* disturber, disconcerter.

desconcertadura, *f.* disturbance; confusion.

desconcertante, *a.* disconcerting, baffling.

desconcertar. I. *va.* (*ind.* DESCONCIERTO; *subj.* DESCONCIERTE) to disarrange, disturb, confuse; to disconcert, thwart, baffle; to disjoint, dislocate. **II.** *vr.* to disagree; to act or speak thoughtlessly or recklessly; to become disarranged; (of bones) to be or to become dislocated.

¹desconcierto, *m.* disconcert, disagreement; disorder, confusion; disarrangement (as of machinery); want of prudence and circumspection; maladministration, mismanagement; flux or looseness of the body.

²desconcierto, desconcierte, *v.* V. DESCONCERTAR.

desconcordia, *f.* discord, disarrangement, disunion.

desconchabar, *va.* (Am.) to disarrange, upset.

desconchadura, *f.* removal of varnish, stucco, etc.; peeling, scaling.

desconchar. I. *va.* to strip off a surface (varnish, stucco, plaster, etc.). **II.** *vr.* to peel off, scale off.

desconectar. I. *va.* to disconnect. **II.** *vr.* to become disconnected.

desconfiadamente, *adv.* diffidently; distrustfully, suspiciously.

desconfiado, da. I. *pp.* of DESCONFIAR. **II.** *a.* diffident, distrustful; mistrustful, jealous.

desconfianza, *f.* diffidence; distrust; jealousy, suspicious fear.

desconfiar, *vn.* (**de**) to mistrust, be distrustful (of); to have no confidence (in); to suspect, doubt; to have little hope (of).

desconformar. I. *vn.* to dissent, disagree, differ in opinion. **II.** *vr.* to disagree; not to fit or suit each other.

desconforme, *a.* discordant, disagreeing, contrary.

desconformidad, *f.* disagreement, opposition, nonconformity; inequality, disparity.

descongestión, *f.* relieving of congestion.

descongestionar, *va.* to relieve the congestion of.

desconocer, *va.* (*ind.* DESCONOZCO; *subj.* DESCONOZCA) to fail to recognise; to disregard, ignore; to forget; to deny, disown, disavow; to be unacquainted with; to be ungrateful for.

desconocidamente, *adv.* ignorantly, unknowingly; ungratefully.

desconocido, da. I. *pp.* of DESCONOCER. **II.** *a.* ungrateful, unthankful; unknown. **III.** *n.* unknown person, stranger.

desconocimiento, *m.* ungratefulness, ingratitude; ignorance; disregard.

desconozco, desconozca, *v.* V. DESCONOCER.

desconsentir, *va.* (*ind.* DESCONSIENTO; *subj.* DESCONSIENTA) not to acquiesce in, to disapprove.

desconsideración, *f.* inconsiderateness.

desconsideradamente, *adv.* inconsiderately; rashly, recklessly.

desconsiderado, da, *a.* inconsiderate; imprudent, thoughtless, rash.

desconsiento, desconsienta, *v.* V. DESCONSENTIR.

desconsolación, *f.* disconsolateness, grief.

desconsoladamente, *adv.* disconsolately.

desconsolado, da. I. *pp.* of DESCONSOLAR. **II.** *a.* disconsolate, grief-stricken, dejected, downhearted.

desconsolador, ra, *a.* discouraging; lamentable.

desconsolar. I. *va.* (*ind.* DESCONSUELO; *subj.* DESCONSUELE) to afflict; to treat rudely. **II.** *vr.* to lose one's cheerfulness; to become low-spirited or afflicted.

¹desconsuelo, *m.* affliction, disconsolateness; disorder in the stomach.

²desconsuelo, desconsuele, *v.* V. DESCONSOLAR.

descontagiar, *va.* to purify, to disinfect.

descontar. I. *va.* (*ind.* DESCUENTO; *subj.* DESCUENTE) to discount, deduct, allow, take off; to abate, lessen, diminish; to detract from the merit of; to take for granted. **II.** *vr.* to miscount.

descontentadizo, za, *a.* fastidious, hard to please, overparticular; easily displeased, squeamish.

descontentamiento, *m.* discontentment, displeasure; grief.

descontentar, *va.* to dissatisfy, displease.

descontento, ta. I. *a.* discontented, dissatisfied, displeased; uneasy. **II.** *m.* discontent; uneasiness, dissatisfaction.

descontinuación, *f.* discontinuance, cessation.

descontinuar, *va.* to discontinue, leave off, cease.

descontinuo, nua, *a.* disjoined, discontinued; discontinuous.

desconvengo, desconvenga, *v.* V. DESCONVENIR.

desconvenible, *a.* discordant, disparate, opposed.

desconveniencia, *f.* inconvenience, disadvantage.

desconveniente, *a.* inconvenient; discordant, incongruous.

desconvenir, *vn.* (*ind. pres.* DESCONVENGO, *pret.* DESCONVINE; *subj.* DESCONVENGA) to disagree; to be unlike or dissimilar; not to suit, match, or mate.

desconversable, *a.* unsociable, retiring.

desconvidar, *va.* to recall, take back (as an invitation or a promise).

desconvine, *pret.* of DESCONVENIR.

descopar, *va.* to lop off the top of (a tree).

descoqué, descoque, *v.* V. DESCOCAR.

descorazonadamente, *adv.* dejectedly, spiritlessly, with dismay.

descorazonamiento, *m.* low spirits, depression, dejection.

descorazonar, *va.* to tear out the heart of; to dishearten, discourage.

descorchador, *m.* uncorker, cork drawer.

descorchar, *va.* to bark (a cork tree); to uncork; to break (a beehive) to steal the honey; to break open.

descordar, *va.* to unstring (an instrument).

descorderar, *va.* to wean (lambs).

descornar. I. *va.* (*ind.* DESCUERNO; *subj.* DESCUERNE) to dehorn, to knock off the horns of. **II.** *vr.* to break one's skull by a fall.

descoronar, *va.* to take off the top or crown of.

descorrear, *vn.* & *vr.* to loosen the skin that covers the new horns of a deer.

descorregido, da, *a.* incorrect, disarranged.

descorrer. I. *va.* to run back over (the same ground); to draw (as a curtain); to draw (a bolt, unbolt a door, etc.). **II.** *vn.* to flow.

descorrimiento, *m.* flow.

descortecé, descortece, *v.* V. DESCORTEZAR.

descortés, *a.* impolite, uncivil, discourteous.

descortesía, *f.* incivility, discourtesy.

descortésmente, *adv.* discourteously, rudely.

descortezador, *m.* one who strips off the bark; decorticator.

descortezadura, *f.,* **descortezamiento,** *m.* decortication, excortication; bark taken off.

descortezar. I. *va.* (*pret.* DESCORTECÉ; *subj.* DESCORTECE) to bark, peel; take off the crust of; to hull, shell (as fruits); to rough-hew; to polish or civilize. **II.** *vr.* (coll.) (of a person) to become polished.

descortinar, *va.* (fort.) to demolish or destroy (a curtain).

descosedura, *f.* ripping, unseaming.

descoser. I. *va.* to rip, unstitch; to separate, disjoin; (naut.) to unlash.—**no d. los labios,** to keep a profound silence. **II.** *vr.* to loose one's tongue.

descosidamente, *adv.* immoderately.

descosido, da. I. *pp.* of DESCOSER. **II.** *a.* ripped, unstitched; disjointed, disconnected; deranged. **III.** *n.* babbler, teller of secrets.—**comer or beber como un d.,** to eat or drink immoderately.

descostarse, *vr.* to draw away from an object or a coast.

descostillar. I. *va.* to strike or hit in the ribs; to take out the ribs of; to break the ribs of. **II.** *vr.* to fall flat on the ground.

descostrar, *va.* to take off the crust of.

descotar, *va.* to remove a restriction from.

descotarse, *vr.* to wear a low-neck dress.

descote, *m.* being décolleté, wearing of a low-neck dress.

descoyuntado, da. I. *pp.* of DESCOYUNTAR. **II.** *a.* disjointed, disconnected, out of gear.

descoyuntamiento, *m.* dislocation (of a joint); pain or tiredness from overexertion.

descoyuntar. I. *va.* to dislocate or disjoint; to vex, displease; to upset, disarrange. **II.** *vr.* to become disjointed, get out of joint.—**d. de risa,** to split one's sides with laughter.

descoyunto, *m.* = DESCOYUNTAMIENTO.

descrecencia, *f.* decrement, decreasing.

descrecer, *va. & vn. (ind.* DESCREZCO; *subj.* DESCREZCA) to decrease, diminish; to fall, to subside (tides and rivers); to grow short (days).

descrecimiento, *m.* decrease, diminution.

descrédito, *m.* discredit, loss of reputation.

descreer, *va.* to disbelieve; to deny due credit to; to disown or abjure.

descreídamente, *adv.* incredulously.

descreído, da. I. *pp.* of DESCREER. **II.** *n. & a.* unbeliever(-ing); infidel.

descreimiento, *m.* unbelief, lack of faith.

descrestar, *va.* to take off the crest or comb of; (Am., coll.) to impose upon; to swindle.

descrezco, descrezca, *v.* V. DESCRECER.

descriarse, *vr.* to weaken; to pine with desire or anxiety.

describir, *va. (pp.* DESCRITO) to describe; to sketch, delineate; to relate minutely.

descripción, *f.* description; sketch, delineation; (law) inventory, schedule.

descriptible, *a.* describable.

descriptivo, va, *a.* descriptive.

descriptor, ra, *n. & a.* describer(-ing).

descrismar. I. *va.* (eccl.) to remove the chrism from; (coll.) to hit on the head. **II.** *vr.* (coll.) to lose patience, to lose one's temper.

descristianar, *va.* = DESCRISMAR.

descristianizar, *va.* to dechristianize.

descrito, ta, *pp. irreg.* of DESCRIBIR; described.

descruzar, *va. (pret.* DESCRUCÉ; *subj.* DESCRUCE) to uncross.

descuadernar. I. *va.* to unbind (books); to disarrange, disconcert, disorder. **II.** *vr.* to get disjointed, loose.

descuadrillado, da. I. *pp.* of DESCUADRILLARSE. **II.** *a.* separated from the rank or lines. **III.** *m.* (vet.) sprain in the haunch.

descuadrillarse, *vr.* to sprain the haunches.

descuajado, da. I. *pp.* of DESCUAJAR. **II.** *a.* dispirited, disheartened; liquefied.

descuajar, *va.* to dissolve, liquefy; to eradicate, to grub; to extirpate, uproot; to dishearten.

descuajaringarse, *vr.* (coll.) to be broken down by excessive fatigue; to fall to pieces.

descuaje, descuajo, *m.* (agr.) grubbing up weeds; clearing ground of underbrush.

descuartelar, *va.* to remove from winter quarters; to undo the quartering of (the sails).

descuarticé, descuartice, *v.* V. DESCUARTIZAR.

descuartizamiento, *m.* quartering; breaking or cutting in pieces; carving.

descuartizar, *va. (pret.* DESCUARTICÉ; *subj.* DESCUARTICE) to quarter; to carve.

descubierta, *f.* pie without an upper crust; (mil.) reconnoitering; (naut.) scanning of the horizon at sunrise and sunset.—**a la d.,** openly, in the open.

descubiertamente, *adv.* manifestly, openly.

descubierto, ta. I. *pp.* of DESCUBRIR. **II.** *a.* patent, manifest, exposed, unveiled; bareheaded. **III.** *m.* solemn exposition of the sacrament; shortage, deficiency, overdraft.—**al d.,** openly, manifestly.—**en d.,** (com.) uncovered; overdrawn; owing a balance.—**estar, quedar, en d.,** (com.) to owe a balance; to have overdrawn a bank account. **IV.** *f.* DESTAPADA, open pie.

descubretalles, *m.* small fan.

descubridero, *m.* eminence commanding an extensive view; lookout.

descubridor, ra, *n.* discoverer; finder, descrier; (mil.) scout, spy; vessel on a voyage of discovery.

descubrimiento, *m.* discovery; find; disclosure; country or thing discovered.

descubrir. I. *va. (pp.* DESCUBIERTO) to discover; disclose, show, bring to light; to uncover, make visible, expose to view, lay open; to reveal, communicate, make known; (eccl.) to expose (the sacrament); (mil.) to reconnoiter; to overlook.—**d. la tierra,** (naut.) to make the land. —**d. por la popa** or **por la proa,** (naut.) to descry astern or ahead. **II.** *vr.* to take off one's hat.

descuelgo, descuelgue, *v.* V. DESCOLGAR.

descuelo, descuele, *v.* V. DESCOLAR.

¹descuello, descuelle, *v.* V. DESCOLLAR.

²descuello, *m.* excessive height or tallness; prominence, superiority; loftiness, haughtiness.

¹descuento, *m.* discount; deduction, rebate, allowance; diminution, decrease.

²descuento, descuente, *v.* V. DESCONTAR.

descuernacabras, *m.* cold north wind.

¹descuerno, *m.* (coll.) slight, affront.

²descuerno, descuerne, *v.* V. DESCORNAR.

descuezo, descueza, *v.* V. DESCOCER.

descuida, *imper.* of DESCUIDAR, don't worry.

descuidadamente, *adv.* carelessly, negligently.

descuidado, da. I. *pp.* of DESCUIDAR. **II.** *a.* careless, negligent or thoughtless; unprepared, unaware; slovenly, unclean.

descuidar. I. *va.* to neglect, forget, overlook; to relieve from care; to divert the attention of. **II.** *vn.* to lack attention or diligence; to be careless or neglectful; to take one's ease; not to trouble oneself. **III.** *vr.* to be forgetful of duty, to become negligent.—**descuido,** *m.* carelessness, indolence, negligence, forgetfulness, absent-mindedness; oversight, slip; lack of attention; incivility, coldness; improper or disgraceful action; imprudence; immodesty.—**al d.,** unobserved, on the sly; carelessly; (Am.) when least expected.—**al d.,** or **al d. y con cuidado,** with studied carelessness or naturalness.

descuitado, da, *a.* living without trouble or care.

descular, *va.* to break the bottom of (as of a jar).

deschuponar, *va.* (agr.) to strip (a tree) of its shoots or suckers.

desdar, *va. (ind. pres.* DESDOY, *pret.* DESDI; *subj.* DESDÉ) to turn in the opposite direction so as to untwist or loosen.

desde, *prep.* since, from, after.—**d. ahora,** from now on.—**d. el punto de vista de,** from the point of view of.—**d. entonces,** since then, ever since.—**d. luego,** immediately, whereupon; doubtless, of course.—**d. niño,** from a child, ever since one's childhood.—**d. que,** since, ever since.

desdecir. I. *vn. (ger.* DESDICIENDO; *pp.* DESDICHO; *ind. pres.* DESDIGO, *pret.* DESDIJE, *fut.* DESDIRÉ; *subj.* DESDIGA) **(de)** to degenerate; to differ (from), disagree (with); to be unworthy (of) or unbecoming (to); to detract (from), to impair. **II.** *vr.* to retract, recant.

desdén, *m.* disdain, slight, scorn, contempt.—**al d.,** affectedly careless.

desdentado, da. I. *pp.* of DESDENTAR. **II.** *a.* toothless. **III.** *m. pl.* (zool.) edentates.

desdentar, *va. (ind.* DESDIENTO; *subj.* DESDIENTE) to draw teeth from.

desdeñable, *a.* contemptible, despicable.

desdeñadamente, *adv.* disdainfully, scornfully.

desdeñador, ra, *n. & a.* scorner(-ing), disdainer (-ing, -ful).

desdeñar. I. *va.* to disdain, scorn. **II.** *vr.* **(de)** to be disdainful (of); to loathe.

desdeñosamente, *adv.* disdainfully.

desdeñoso, sa, *a.* disdainful, contemptuous.

desdevanar, *va.* to unwind or unravel (a clue).

desdi, *pret.* of DESDAR.

desdibujado, da, *a.* (art) badly drawn.

desdibujo, *m.* faulty drawing.

desdicha, *f.* misfortune, ill-luck, misery.

desdichadamente, *adv.* unfortunately, unhappily.

desdichado, da. I. *a.* unfortunate; unhappy,

unlucky, wretched. II. *n.* wretch, unfortunate one; good-for-nothing, insignificant person.

desdicho, *pp. irreg.* of DESDECIR.

desdiento, desdiente, *v. V.* DESDENTAR.

desdigo, desdiga, desdije, etc. *v. V.* DESDECIR.

desdinerar, *va.* to impoverish.

desdoblar, *va.* to unfold, to spread open.

desdorar, *va.* & *vr.* to take off the gilding of; to lose its gilding; to tarnish the reputation of.—

desdoro, *m.* dishonor, blemish, stigma.

desdoy, *1st pers. pres. ind.* of DESDAR.

deseable, *a.* desirable.—**deseablemente,** *adv.* desirably.

deseador, ra, *n.* desirer, wisher.

desear, *va.* to desire, wish.

desecación, *f.* desiccation, exsiccation.

desecado, da, *a.* dry, desiccated.

desecador, *m.* drying room; dryer.

desecamiento, *m.* desiccation.

desecante, *a.* & *n.* dryer(-ing), desiccant, desiccative.

desecar, *va.* (*pret.* DESEQUÉ; *subj.* DESEQUE) to dry; to desiccate; to drain, to draw.

desecativo, va. I. *a.* desiccative, exsiccant. II. *m.* healing plaster.

desechable, *a.* disposable (as *d. Kleenex*).

desechadamente, *adv.* vilely, despicably.

desechado, da. I. *pp.* of DESECHAR. II. *a.* refused, excluded, expelled, rejected; outcast.

desechar, *va.* to reject; to exclude; to depreciate, undervalue; decline, refuse; to put or lay aside; dispose of, throw away; cast off; to vote down.

desecho, *m.* residue, surplus, remainder; débris, rubbish, refuse, offal; rejection; disregard, contempt.—**de d.,** cast off, discarded; scrap (iron, etc.).

desedificación, *f.* scandal, bad example.

desedificar, *va.* (*pret.* DESEDIFIQUÉ; *subj.* DESEDIFIQUE) to set a bad example to; to be an evil influence on.

deseguida, *a.* lewd (woman).

deselectrización, *f.* dielectrification.

deselectrizar, *va.* to dielectrify.

deselladura, *f.* unsealing or taking off the seals.

desellar, *va.* to unseal, to take off the seals of.

desembalaje, *m.* unpacking, opening of bales.

desembalar, *va.* to unpack, open.

desembaldosar, *va.* to take up the flagstones or tiles of.

desemballestar, *vn.* (of a falcon) to get ready to come down.

desembanastar. I. *va.* to take out of a basket; (coll.) to draw (the sword). II. *vn.* to talk much and without sense. III. *vr.* to break out or break loose; (coll.) to alight from a carriage.

desembaracé, desembarace, *v. V.* DESEMBARAZAR.

desembarazadamente, *adv.* freely, without embarrassment.

desembarazado, da, *a.* free, disengaged; clear, open; unrestrained, unencumbered.

desembarazar. I. *va.* (*pret.* DESEMBARACÉ; *subj.* DESEMBARACE) to disembarrass, free, ease; to remove an impediment or encumbrance from; to clear; to unburden, disencumber, expedite. II. *vr.* to rid oneself of difficulties or hindrances.

desembarazo, *m.* disembarrassment, disencumbrance; disengagement; freedom, lack of restraint or hindrances; ease, naturalness.

desembarcadero, *m.* landing place; wharf, pier.

desembarcar. I. *va.* (*pret.* DESEMBARQUÉ; *subj.* DESEMBARQUE) to unload, put ashore, debark. II. *vn.* to land, disembark, go ashore; (coll.) to alight (from a vehicle); (coll.) to be delivered of a child; to end (as a staircase).

desembarco, *m.* landing, disembarkation, unloading; landing place at the top of stairs.

desembargadamente, *adv.* freely.

desembargador, *m.* chief magistrate and privy councillor in Portugal.

desembargar, *va.* (*pret.* DESEMBARGUÉ; *subj.* DESEMBARGUE) to remove impediments from; (law) to disembargo, raise an embargo.

desembargo, *m.* (law) raising of an embargo.

desembarque, *m.* landing or debarkation; unloading.

desembarqué, desembarque, *v. V.* DESEMBARCAR.

desembarrancar, *va.* (*pret.* DESEMBARRANQUÉ; *subj.* DESEMBARRANQUE) to extricate.

desembarrar, *va.* to clear of mud.

desembaular, *va.* to take out of a trunk; to empty; (coll.) to speak (one's mind) freely; to disclose (one's thoughts).

desembebecerse, *vr.* (*ind.* DESEMBEBEZCO; *subj.* DESEMBEBEZCA) to recover one's senses, to come to.

desembelesarse, *vr.* to recover from amazement or abstraction.

desembocadero, *m.*, **desembocadura,** *f.* exit, outlet; mouth (of a river, canal, etc.).

desembocar, *vn.* (*pret.* DESEMBOQUÉ; *subj.* DESEMBOQUE) (en) to flow (into); to end (at), lead (to).

desembocé, desemboce, *v. V.* DESEMBOZAR.

desembojadera, *f.* woman who takes the cocoons of silkworms from the southern-wood.

desembojar, *va.* to remove (silk-cocoons) from the southern-wood.

desembolsar, *va.* to empty from a purse; to pay out, disburse.

desembolso, *m.* disbursement, expenditure.

desemboque, *m.* = DESEMBOCADERO.

desemboqué, desemboque, *v. V.* DESEMBOCAR.

desemborrachar. I. *va.* to sober, to make sober, to cure of intoxication. II. *vr.* to sober up, get over one's intoxication.

desemboscarse, *vr.* to get out of the woods; to get clear of an ambuscade.

desembotar, *va.* to remove dulness from (a cutting edge); to sharpen (as wits).

desembozar, *va.* & *vr.* (*pret.* DESEMBOCÉ; *subj.* DESEMBOCE) to unmuffle or uncover; to unmask, show oneself in one's true colors (or others in theirs).

desembozo, *m.* uncovering the face.

desembracé, desembrace, *v. V.* DESEMBRAZAR.

desembragar, *va.* (*pret.* DESEMBRAGUÉ; *subj.* DESEMBRAGUE) to unbind from the cable; (mech.) to ungear, disengage, disconnect.

desembravecer, *va.* (*ind.* DESEMBRAVEZCO; *subj.* DESEMBRAVEZCA) to tame, domesticate; to calm, pacify.

desembravecimiento, *m.* taming or reclaiming from wildness.

desembrazar, *va.* (*pret.* DESEMBRACÉ; *subj.* DESEMBRACE) to take (something) off the arms; to dart or throw (weapons); to throw from the arms.

desembriagar. I. *va.* (*pret.* DESEMBRIAGUÉ; *subj.* DESEMBRIAGUE) to sober, to cure from intoxication. II. *vr.* to become sober, recover from drunkenness.

desembridar, *va.* to unbridle.

desembrollar, *va.* to unravel, disentangle, clear, extricate.

desembrozar, *va.* to clear of rubbish.

desembuchar, *va.* to disgorge, to turn out of the maw (birds); (coll.) to tell all.

desemejante, *a.* dissimilar, unlike.

desemejantemente, *adv.* dissimilarly.

desemejanza, *f.* unlikeness, dissimilarity.

desemejar. I. *vn.* to be dissimilar or unlike. II. *va.* = DESFIGURAR, to disfigure.

desempacar. I. *va.* (*pret.* DESEMPAQUÉ; *subj.* DESEMPAQUE) to unpack. II. *vr.* (coll.) to calm down, cool off.

desempachar. I. *va.* to make (the stomach) discharge undigested food. II. *vr.* (coll.) to grow bold, lose all bashfulness.

desempacho, *m.* ease; forwardness, unconcern.

desempalagar. I. *va. & vr.* (*pret.* DESEMPALAGUÉ; *subj.* DESEMPALAGUE) to remove nausea or loathing (from); to restore the appetite (to). **II.** *va.* to clear (a mill) of stagnant water.

desempañar, *va.* to clean (a glass); to take off the swaddling clothes from (children).

desempapelar, *va.* to unwrap, take out of a package; to take (hangings) off a wall, to take off the paper from.

desempaque, *m.* act of unpacking.

desempaqué, desempaque, *v.* V. DESEMPACAR.

desempaquetar, *va.* to unpack.

desemparejar, *va.* to unmatch, make unequal or uneven.

desemparentado, da, *a.* without relatives.

desemparvar, *va.* to gather in heaps.

desempastado, da, *a.* (Am.) (of books) unbound.

desempastar, *va.* (Am.) to take the cover off (a book); to take the filling out of (a tooth).

desempastelar, *va.* (Am.) (print.) to distribute (mixed letters).

desempatar, *va.* to disjoint, disunite; to make unequal or uneven; to decide (a tie vote); to run, play, or shoot off a tie.

desempedrador, *m.* one who removes paving.

desempedrar, *va.* (*ind.* DESEMPIEDRO; *subj.* DESEMPIEDRE) to remove paving.—**ir desempedrando la calle,** (coll.) to go very rapidly.

desempegar, *va.* (*pret.* DESEMPEGUÉ; *subj.* DESEMPEGUE) to unglue; to take the pitch off.

desempeñado, da. I. *pp.* of DESEMPEÑAR. **II.** *a.* free or clear of debt.

desempeñar. I. *va.* to redeem, to recover (what was pledged); to take out of pawn; to clear or extricate from debt; to perform, discharge (a duty); to play (a part); to fill (an office, a function); to transact; to accomplish, carry out (an undertaking); to act (a part in a play); to acquit, free from an obligation; to disengage from a difficulty. **II.** *vr.* to extricate oneself from debt; in bull fighting, to disengage oneself from the attack of a bull.—**desempeñarse de la tierra,** or **costa,** (naut.) to claw off, to stand off shore.

desempeño, *m.* the act of redeeming a pledge; performance of an obligation or promise; fulfilment, discharge; acting of a part.

desempeorarse, *vr.* to recover from sickness, to regain health.

desemperezar, *vn. & vr.* (*pret.* DESEMPERECÉ; *subj.* DESEMPERECE) to relinquish habits of laziness and indolence; to shake off laziness.

desempernar, *va.* to take the bolts out of.

desempiedro, desempiedre, *v.* V. DESEMPEDRAR.

desempleado, da, *n. & a.* unemployed.

desempleo, *m.* unemployment.

desemplomar, *va.* to remove the leaden seal from.

desemplumar, *va.* to pluck (a bird).

desempobrecer. I. *va.* (*ind.* DESEMPOBREZCO; *subj.* DESEMPOBREZCA) to relieve from poverty. **II.** *vr.* to extricate oneself from poverty.

desempolvar, *va.* to remove dust or powder from, to dust.

desempolvoradura, *f.* dusting.

desempolvorar, *va.* to dust.

desemponzoñar, *va.* to heal from the effects of poison; to free from poison.

desempotrar, *va.* to remove the support of; to take out.

desempulgadura, *f.* unbending of a bow.

desempulgar, *va.* (*pret.* DESEMPULGUÉ; *subj.* DESEMPULGUE) to unbend (a bow).

desenalbardar, *va.* to take a packsaddle off (an animal).

desenamorar. I. *va.* to destroy the love or affection of. **II.** *vr.* to lose love or affection.

desenastar, *va.* to remove the handle or haft from.

desencabalgar, *va.* (*pret.* DESENCABALGUÉ; *subj.* DESEMCABALGUE) (mil.) to dismount (cannon).

desencabestradura, *f.* disentangling (of an animal) from the halter.

desencabestrar, *va.* to disentangle the feet (of an animal) from the halter.

desencadenamiento, *m.* unchaining.

desencadenar. I. *va.* to unchain; to free, liberate. **II.** *vr.* to break loose, free oneself from chains; to become infuriated, lose one's self-control; (of a storm) to break out with fury; (of rain) to come down in torrents.

desencajado, da. I. *pp.* of DESENCAJAR. **II.** *a.* run down, looking bad, rickety; out of kilter; out of joint.

desencajadura, *f.* disjointedness, disconnection.

desencajamiento, *m.* = DESENCAJE.

desencajar. I. *va.* to disjoint, unjoin, disconnect, throw out of gear; to disarticulate; to dislocate. **II.** *vr.* to become rickety; to get disjointed, disconnected, out of gear.

desencaje, *m.* disjointedness; broken-down appearance; rickety appearance.

desencajonar, *va.* to unpack, take out of a box.

desencalabrinar, *va.* to remove dizziness from; to free from stupidity; to remove wrong impressions from.

desencalcar, *va.* (*pret.* DESENCALQUÉ; *subj.* DESENCALQUE) to loosen or dissolve (what was caked or close pressed).

desencallar, *va.* (naut.) to set (a stranded ship) afloat again.

desencaminar, *va.* to mislead, lead astray.

desencantamiento, *m.* = DESENCANTO.

desencantar, *va.* to disenchant; disillusion.

desencantaración, *f.* act and effect of drawing lots or of balloting.

desencantarar, *va.* to draw (lots) for candidates out of a CÁNTARO; to withdraw (a name).

desencanto, *m.* disenchantment, disillusion.

desencapillar, *va.* (naut.) to unrig, to take off the rigging of.

desencapotadura, *f.* stripping off a cloak or a greatcoat.

desencapotar. I. *va.* to strip (one) of his cloak or greatcoat; (coll.) to uncover, to make manifest; to raise and keep up the head of (a horse). **II.** *vr.* (of the sky) to clear up; to put away anger, to smooth one's brow, put on a pleasing countenance.

desencaprichar. I. *va.* to dissuade from error or prejudice; to disabuse, to cure of conceit. **II.** *vr.* to desist, yield, get over a whim, give up a hobby or mania.

desencarcelar, *va.* to set free (from prison).

desencarecer, *va.* (*ind.* DESENCAREZCO; *subj.* DESENCAREZCA) to reduce, to lower the price of.

desencarnar, *va.* to prevent (dogs) from eating game; to lose affection, liking for; to divert the mind from.

desencastillar, *va.* to expel or drive out of a castle; to manifest, make appear, reveal.

desencepar, *va.* (naut.) to clear (the anchor).

desencerrar, *va.* (*ind.* DESENCIERRO; *subj.* DESENCIERRE) to free from confinement; to open; to disclose, make known.

desencintar, *va.* to remove ribbons from (a person or thing); to remove the curb of (a sidewalk).

desenclavar, *va.* to draw out nails from; to put (one) violently out of one's place.

desenclavijar, *va.* to take the pins or pegs out of.

desencoger. I. *va.* (*ind.* DESENCOJO; *subj.* DESENCOJA) to unfold, to spread open. **II.** *vr.* to lay aside bashfulness or reserve, to grow bold.

desencogimiento, *m.* ease, naturalness.

desencojo, desencoja, *v.* V. DESENCOGER.

desencoladura, *f.* act or effect of ungluing.

desencolar, *va.* to unglue, to unsize.

desencolerizarse, *vr.* to grow calm, to cool off.

desenconamiento, *m.* act and effect of allaying an inflammation or appeasing anger.

desenconar. I. *va.* to allay (an inflammation); to calm, appease; to make mild and benign. **II.** *vr.* to become milder; to be appeased, to quiet down, cool off.

desencono, *m.* mitigation of anger or passion.

desencordar, *va.* (*ind.* DESENCUERDO; *subj.* DESENCUERDE) to unstring (a musical instrument).

desencordelar, *va.* to loosen, untie or take off strings or cords from.

desencorvar, *va.* to straighten.

desencrespar, *va.* to uncurl, unfrizzle.

desencrudecer, *va.* (*ind.* DESENCRUDEZCO; *subj.* DESENCRUDEZCA) to prepare (silk or thread) for receiving the dye; to clean (fabrics) with lye.

desencrudecimiento, *m.* cleansing with lye.

desencrudezco, desencrudezca, *v.* V. DESENCRUDECER.

desencuadernar, *va.* to unbind, to take off the binding of (a book).

desencuerdo, desencuerde, *v.* V. DESENCORDAR.

desendemoniar, desendiablar, *va.* to drive an evil spirit out of.

desendiosar, *va.* to humble the vanity of.

desenfadadamente, *adv.* without embarrassment, boldly, unconcernedly.

desenfadaderas, *f. pl.*—**tener d.,** (coll.) to be resourceful.

desenfadado, da. I. *a. pp.* of DESENFADAR. **II.** *a.* unencumbered, free; ample, spacious; bold.

desenfadar. I. *va.* to appease, pacify. **II.** *vr.* to calm down, become calm, cool off.

desenfado, *m.* freedom, ease, naturalness; relaxation, diversion, entertainment.

desenfaldar, *va.* to let fall the train of (a gown).

desenfangar, *va.* to clean the mud out of.

desenfardar, desenfardelar, *va.* to unpack (bales of goods).

desenfilado, da. I. *a.* (mil.) under cover from fire. **II.** *f.* (fort.) defilading.

desenfilar, *va.* to put under cover from flank fire; (fort.) to defilade.

desenfrailar, *vn.* to leave the monastic life, become secularized; (coll.) to come out from subjection; to rest from business for a time.

desenfrenadamente, *adv.* ungovernably, licentiously.

desenfrenado, da. I. *pp.* of DESENFRENAR. **II.** *a.* ungoverned, unbridled, wild, wanton.

desenfrenamiento, *m.* unruliness, rashness, wantonness, licentiousness, boundless liberty or license; libidinousness.

desenfrenar. I. *va.* to unbridle. **II.** *vr.* to give loose rein to one's passions and desires; to fly into a violent passion; to be mad or wild.

desenfreno, *m.* = DESENFRENAMIENTO.—**d. de vientre,** diarrhea.

desenfundar, *va.* to take out of a bag, bolster, pillowcase, sheath, etc.

desenfurecerse, *vr.* (*ind.* DESENFUREZCO; *subj.* DESENFUREZCA) to become calm or appeased.

desengalanar, *va.* to remove trappings or adornments from.

desenganchar, *va.* to unhook, unclasp, unpin, unfasten; to uncouple; to disengage; to unhitch, unharness.

desengañadamente, *adv.* truly, clearly, ingenuously; awkwardly, carelessly, scurvily.

desengañado, da. I. *pp.* of DESENGAÑAR. **II.** *a.* disabused, disillusioned; schooled by experience; despicable; ill-executed.

desengañador, ra, *n.* undeceiver, disabuser.

desengañar. I. *va.* to undeceive, disabuse, set right. **II.** *vr.* to be disillusioned, not to fool oneself.

desengañilar, *va.* to free or disengage (a person or animal held by the throat).

desengaño, *m.* detection or discovery of an error; undeceiving; disillusion, disappointment; censure, reproof, reproach, upbraiding.—*pl.* sad lessons of experience.

desengarrafar, *va.* to unfasten or disengage from claws or clenched fingers.

desengarzar, *va.* to take out of a setting; to loosen from clasps, links or hooks.

desengastar, *va.* to take out of its setting.

desengomar, *va.* to ungum; to unsize (silk).

desengoznar, *va.* to unhinge; to disjoint.

desengranar. I. *va.* to uncouple; to disengage. **II.** *vr.* to get out of gear.

desengrane, *m.* disengaging of gear.

desengrasador, *m.* wringing machine; scourer; wiping cloth.

desengrasar, *va.* to clean from grease; to scour.

desengrase, *m.* removal of grease; cleaning, scouring.

desengraso, *m.* (Chile) dessert.

desengrosar, *va.* (*ind.* DESENGRUESO; *subj.* DESENGRUESE) to extenuate, make lean, weaken; to make thin or fine.

desengrudamiento, *m.* removal of sticking paste.

desengrudar, *va.* to scrape or rub off paste from.

desengrueso, desengruese, *v.* V. DESENGROSAR.

desenguantarse, *vr.* to take off one's gloves.

desenhebrar, *va.* to unthread.

desenhornar, *va.* to take out of the oven.

desenjaezar, *va.* (*pret.* DESENJAECÉ; *subj.* DESENJAECE) to unharness; to unsaddle.

desenjalmar, *va.* to take off a packsaddle from.

desenjaular, *va.* to uncage; (coll.) to remove from or let out of jail.

desenlabonar, *va.* to unlink.

desenlace, *m.* denouement, winding up; conclusion, end.

desenlacé, desenlace, *v.* V. DESENLAZAR.

desenladrillar, *va.* to take off the tiles or bricks of.

desenlazar, *va.* (*pret.* DESENLACÉ; *subj.* DESENLACE) to unlace, untie, loose; to unravel (a dramatic plot).

desenlodar, *va.* to remove, clean off, mud from.

desenlosar, *va.* to take up the flagstones of; to remove paving from.

desenlutar, *va. & vr.* to take off mourning (from); to banish sorrow.

desenmallar, *va.* to take (fish) out of the net.

desenmarañar, *va.* to disentangle; to sleave (as a skein); straighten up; unravel, make clear.

desenmascarar, *va.* to unmask.

desenmohecer, *va.* (*ind.* DESENMOHEZCO; *subj.* DESENMOHEZCA) to clear of rust.

desenmudecer. I. *va.* (*ind.* DESENMUDEZCO; *subj.* DESENMUDEZCA) to remove an impediment of speech from. **II.** *vn. & vr.* to break a long silence.

desenojar. I. *va. & vr.* to appease, pacify, calm, allay the passion of. **II.** *vr.* to amuse oneself.

desenojo, *m.* appeasement, getting over anger.

desenojoso, sa, *a.* appeasing, reconciling.

desenredar. I. *va.* to disentangle; to unravel; to extricate, loose; to clear. **II.** *vr.* to extricate oneself from difficulties.

desenredo, *m.* disentanglement; denouement.

desenrollar, *va.* to unroll, unwind.

desenronar, *va.* to remove débris from.

desenronquecer, *va.* to free from hoarseness.

desenroscar, *va.* (*pret.* DESENROSQUÉ; *subj.* DESENROSQUE) to untwine, untwist; to unscrew.

desensabanar, *va.* (coll.) to change or take off the sheets of.

desensamblar, *va.* to disjoint, separate.

desensañar, *va.* to appease, pacify.

desensartar, *va.* to unthread, unstring.

desensebar. I. *va.* to strip of fat. **II.** *vn.* to change occupation or exercise in order to render one's work more endurable; to draw breath; to take away the taste of fat (with an olive or sweets).

desenseñado, da, *a.* untaught.

desenseñar, *va.* to correct faulty learning.

desensillar, *va.* to unsaddle.

desensoberbecer. I. *va.* (*ind.* DESENSOBERBEZCO; *subj.* DESENSOBERBEZCA) to humble. **II.** *vr.* to become humble, to control one's pride.

desensortijado, da, *a.* dislocated, displaced.

desentablar, *va.* to rip up or off planks or boards from; to disturb, disarrange, confuse; to embroil; to break off (a bargain); to estrange.

desentalingar, *va.* (naut.) to unbend (a cable).

desentarimar, *va.* to remove a platform or stand from.

desentarquinar, *va.* to free from mud.

desentejar, *va.* to take off the tiles of.

desentenderse, *vr.* (*ind.* DESENTIENDO; *subj.* DESENTIENDA) (**de**) to feign not to understand; to ignore; to pay no attention (to); to shirk.

desentendido, da. I. *pp.* of DESENTENDERSE. **II.** *a.* unmindful, showing or feigning ignorance.— **hacerse el d.,** or **darse por d.,** (coll.) to wink at a thing; to pretend not to have noticed.

desenterrador, *m.* one that disinters or digs up.

desenterramiento, *m.* disinterment.

desenterrar, *va.* (*ind.* DESENTIERRO; *subj.* DESENTIERRE) to disinter, dig up, unearth; to recall (to the mind).

desentiendo, desentienda, *v.* V. DESENTENDERSE.

desentierramuertos, *m.* (coll.) calumniator or abuser of the dead.

desentierro, desentierre, *v.* V. DESENTERRAR.

desentoldar, *va.* to take off an awning from; to strip of ornaments.

desentonación, *f.* dissonance.

desentonadamente, *adv.* inharmoniously.

desentonado, da. I. *pp.* of DESENTONAR. **II.** *a.* out of tune; inharmonious, discordant.

desentonamiento, *m.* dissonance.

desentonar. I. *va.* to humble; to wound the pride of. **II.** *vn.* to be out of tune; to be inharmonious. **III.** *vr.* to be rude or uncouth; to raise the voice in disrespect.—**desentono,** *m.* harsh, rude tone of voice; musical discord; false note.

desentornillar, *va.* to unscrew.

desentorpecer. I. *va.* (*ind.* DESENTORPEZCO; *subj.* DESENTORPEZCA) to free from torpor; to restore motion to (torpid limbs). **II.** *vr.* to be freed from torpor; to be restored from numbness; to become lively, smart, or pert.

desentrampar, *va.* to free from debts.

desentrañamiento, *m.* giving away one's belongings as a proof of love.

desentrañar. I. *va.* to eviscerate, disembowel; to penetrate or dive into; to bring out, reveal, dig out; (naut.) to remove loops, twists, from (ropes). **II.** *vr.* to give away one's all out of love.

desentristecer, *va.* (*ind.* DESENTRISTEZCO; *subj.* DESENTRISTEZCA) to soothe the sadness of, to cheer, comfort.

desentronizar, *va.* (*pret.* DESENTRONICÉ; *subj.* DESENTRONICE) to dethrone; to deprive of power or authority.

desentumecer. I. *va.* (*ind.* DESENTUMEZCO; *subj.* DESENTUMEZCA) to free from torpor. **II.** *vr.* to be freed from numbness.

desentumir, *va.* & *vr.* = DESENTUMECER.

desenvainar, *va.* to unsheath (as a sword); (coll.) to expose, uncover; to show (the claws).

desenvelejar, *va.* (naut.) to strip of sails.

desenvendar, *va.* to take off fillets or bands from.

desenvenenar, *va.* to extract, remove poison from; to destroy the poison of, or in.

desenvergar, *va.* (*pret.* DESENVERGUÉ; *subj.* DESENVERGUE) (naut.) to unbend (a sail).

desenviolar, *va.* to bless or purify (a holy place which has been desecrated).

desenvoltura, *f.* sprightliness, ease; impudence, effrontery; lewd posture or gesture in women; graceful and easy delivery in conversation or acting.

desenvolvedor, ra, *n.* unfolder, investigator.

desenvolver. I. *va.* (*pp.* DESENVUELTO; *ind.* DESENVUELVO; *subj.* DESENVUELVA) to unfold, unroll; unwrap; to decipher, discover, unravel; to develop (as a theme); to evolve. **II.** *vr.* to be forward, to behave with too much assurance; to unfold, unroll.

desenvolvimiento, *m.* unfolding, development.

desenvueltamente, *adv.* in a free and easy manner; expeditiously.

desenvuelto, ta. I. *pp. irreg.* of DESENVOLVER. **II.** *a.* forward; free, easy.

desenvuelvo, desenvuelva, *v.* V. DESENVOLVER.

desenyesar. I. *va.* to remove plaster from. **II.** *vr.* (of a plastered surface) to scale off.

desenzarzar, *va.* & *vr.* to disentangle from brambles; to appease, reconcile.

deseo, *m.* desire, wish.—**tener d. de, venir en d. de,** to desire, be eager to.

deseoso, sa, *a.* desirous.

desequé, deseque, *v.* V. DESECAR.

desequido, da, *a.* dry.

desequilibrado, da. I. *pp.* of DESEQUILIBRAR. **II.** *a.* unbalanced, unpoised; of an unbalanced mind; reckless, thoughtless.

desequilibrar, *va.* to put out of balance.

desequilibrio, *m.* lack of equilibrium; an unbalanced condition; disorder, disturbance, confusion.

deserción, *f.* desertion; (law) abandonment of a suit by plaintiff.

deserrado, da, *a.* free from error.

desertar. I. *va.* to desert; to abandon. **II.** *vn.* (**de**) to desert (from).—**d. a,** to go over to.

desertor, ra, *n.* deserter; forsaker.

deservicio, *m.* disservice; fault committed against a person who has a claim to services.

deservidor, *m.* he who fails in serving another.

deservir, *va.* (*ger.* DESIRVIENDO; *ind. pres.* DESIRVO, *pret.* él DESIRVIÓ; *subj.* DESIRVA) not to perform one's duty to; to disserve.

desescamar, *va.* to scale; to remove scales from.

desescombrar, *va.* to clear of rubbish.

deseslabonar, *va.* to cut the links of; to unlink.

desespaldar, *va.* to wound in the shoulder.

desespaldillar. I. *va.* to wound in the shoulder blade. **II.** *vr.* to receive a lesion in the shoulder blade.

desesperación, *f.* despondency, despair, desperation; anger, passion, fury.—**es una d.,** (coll.) it is unbearable.

desesperadamente, *adv.* despairingly, hopelessly; desperately, furiously, madly.

desesperado, da. I. *pp.* of DESESPERAR. **II.** *a.* desperate, hopeless; furious, raving mad.

desesperancé, desesperance, *v.* V. DESESPERANZAR.

desesperante, *a.* causing despair, maddening; hopeless.

desesperanza, *f.* despair, hopelessness.

desesperanzar. I. *va.* (*pret.* DESESPERANCÉ; *subj.* DESESPERANCE) to deprive of hope, to discourage. **II.** *vr.* to lose hope, to despair, become discouraged.

desesperar. I. *vn.* to lose hope, to despair. **II.** *va.* to make (one) despair, to discourage hope; (coll.) (fig.) to drive crazy. **III.** *vr.* to despair, to despond; to fret, to be grievously vexed.— **desespero,** *m.* (Am.) despair; vexation.

desespigar, *va.* (*pret.* DESESPIGUÉ; *subj.* DESESPIGUE) to thrash (grain).

desesponjarse, *vr.* to lose sponginess.

desestancar, *va.* (*pret.* DESESTANQUÉ; *subj.* DESESTANQUE) to take away (a monopoly) from; to declare open to trade, raise the monopoly on.

desestañar, va. & vr. to unsolder.

desesterar, va. to take up the matting (from floors).

desestero, m. act and season of taking up mats.

desestima, desestimación, f. disesteem, disrespect; crying down, rejection.

desestimador, ra, n. & a. contemner(-ing), despiser(-ing).

desestimar, va. to disesteem, undervalue; to reject, deny.

desfacedor, m. (obs.) destroyer.—**d. de entuertos,** undoer of injuries, righter of wrongs.

desfacer, va. (pp. DESFECHO; ind. pres. DESFAGO, pret. YO DESFICE, él DESFIZO, fut. DESFARÉ; subj. DESFAGA) (obs.) = DESHACER.—**d. agravios,** or **d. entuertos,** to right wrongs.

desfacimiento, m. (obs.) destruction, undoing.

desfachatadamente, adv. impudently, with effrontery, brazenly.

desfachatado, da, a. (coll.) impudent, saucy, "nervy," "cheeky," brazen.

desfachatez, f. (coll.) impudence, assurance, effrontery, barefacedness, "nerve," "cheek."

desfago, desfaga, v. V. DESFACER.

desfajar, va. to ungird.

desfalcador, ra, n. embezzler, defaulter.

desfalcar, va. (pret. DESFALQUÉ; subj. DESFALQUE) to take away part of; to cut off, to lop; to defalcate, embezzle.

desfalco, m. diminution, diminishing, detracting; defalcation, embezzlement, peculation.

desfalqué, desfalque, v. V. DESFALCAR.

desfallecer. I. vn. (ind. DESFALLEZCO; subj. DESFALLEZCA) to pine, to fall away; to grow weak; to swoon, faint. II. va. to weaken, debilitate.

desfalleciente, a. pining, languishing.

desfallecimiento, m. languor; dejection; swoon, fainting fit.

desfallezco, desfallezca, v. V. DESFALLECER.

desfavorable, a. unfavorable, contrary.

desfavorablemente, adv. unfavorably.

desfavorecedor, ra, n. one who disfavors.

desfavorecer, va. (ind. DESFAVOREZCO; subj. DESFAVOREZCA) to disfavor, to discountenance; to despise, contemn; to injure, hurt; to contradict, oppose.

desfecho, pp. of DESFACER.

desfibrar, va. to rid of fibers; to extract the fiber from.

desfice, pret. of DESFACER.

desfiguración, f., **desfiguramiento,** m. deformation, disfigurement.

desfigurar. I. va. to disfigure, deform; misshape; to disguise (as the voice); to misrepresent, misstate, distort; to cloud, to darken. II. vr. to become disfigured.

desfijar, va. to take off, pull off, remove.

desfilachar, va. to ravel; to uncord.

desfilada, f. (mil.) single file.

desfiladero, m. defile, narrow passage; road at the side of a precipice.

desfilar, vn. (mil.) to defile, to march off by files, file off; to march in review, parade.

desfile, m. defiling, marching by files; parade.

desfizo, pret. of DESFACER.

desflecar, va. (pret. DESFLEQUÉ; subj. DESFLEQUE) to remove the flakes of (wool) or frettings of (cloth).

desflocar, va. (ind. pres. DESFLUECO, pret. DESFLOQUÉ; subj. DESFLUEQUE) = DESFLECAR.

desfloración, f. defloration.

desfloramiento, m. violation, ravishment.

desflorar, va. to tarnish; to ruffle, discompose; to violate, deflower; to treat superficially, touch upon.

desflorecer, vn. & vr. to lose the flowers.

desflorecimiento, m. falling of flowers.

desflueco, desflueque, v. V. DESFLOCAR.

desfogar. I. va. (pret. DESFOGUÉ; subj. DESFOGUE) to vent, to make an opening in for fire; to give loose rein to (a horse). II. vr. to vent one's anger.

desfogonadura, f. erosion of a cannon.

desfogonar, va. to widen or burst the vent of (a cannon).

desfogue, m. venting or foaming out of passion.

desfogué, desfogue, v. V. DESFOGAR.

desfollonar, va. to strip useless leaves off.

desfondar, va. to break or take off the bottom of; (naut.) to penetrate the bottom of (a ship); (agr.) to cultivate or dig (the soil) to a great depth.

desformar, va. to disfigure, deform.

desfortalecer, va. (ind. DESFORTALEZCO; subj. DESFORTALEZCA) (mil.) to dismantle, to demolish.

desfortificar, va. (pret. DESFORTIFIQUÉ; subj. DESFORTIFIQUE) = DESFORTALECER.

desforzarse, vr. to take revenge.

desfosforar, va. to dephosphorize.

desfrenar, va. to unbridle.

desfrutar, va. to take the green fruit off (a tree).

desgaire, m. graceless mien or deportment; slovenliness; affected carelessness in dress; contemptuous gesture.—**al d.,** affectedly careless; disdainfully.

desgajadura, f. disruption, tearing off the branch of a tree.

desgajar. I. va. to tear off the branches of; to break or tear off. II. vr. to be separated or disjointed; to be torn off; to fall off.

desgaje, m. act of breaking or tearing off.

desgalgadero, m. rugged steep place.

desgalgado, da. I. pp. of DESGALGAR. II. a. precipitated.

desgalgar, va. & vr. (pret. DESGALGUÉ; subj. DESGALGUE) to precipitate, to throw headlong.

desgalichado, da, a. (coll.) ungainly, ungraceful.

desgana, f. lack of appetite; unwillingness, reluctance.—**desganado, da,** having no appetite.

desganar. I. va. to discourage. II. vr. to lose one's appetite; to lose interest; to become reluctant or unwilling.

desganchar, va. to lop off the branches of.

desgano, m. = DESGANA.

desgañifarse, desgañitarse, vr. to shriek, to scream at the top of one's voice.

desgarbado, da, a. ungraceful, uncouth, ungainly, gawky.

desgargantarse, vr. (coll.) to get hoarse from bawling or screaming, to shout oneself hoarse.

desgargolar, va. to ripple (as flax or hemp); to take (a board) out of a groove.

desgaritar. I. vn. (naut.) to lose the course. II. vr. (of sheep) to go astray from a fold; to give up a plan or undertaking.

desgarradamente, adv. impudently, barefacedly, shamelessly.

desgarrado, da, a. licentious, dissolute; impudent, shameless, bold.

desgarrador, ra. I. n. tearer. II. a. tearing; heart-breaking, heart-rending.

desgarradura, f. rent, laceration, break.

desgarrar. I. va. to rend, tear; to claw; (Cuba) to expectorate, cough up (phlegm). II. vr. to withdraw from another's company; to tear oneself away.

desgarro, m. laceration, rent, break, breach; impudence, effrontery; looseness, criminal levity; idle boast, brag.—**desgarrón,** m. aug. large rent or hole; piece of cloth torn off.

desgastamiento, m. prodigality, extravagance.

desgastar. I. va. to wear away, abrade, consume, waste by degrees; to corrode, gnaw, eat away. II. vr. to lose strength and vigor; to debilitate oneself; to wear down or away.

desgaste, m. slow waste; attrition, abrasion; wear and tear; erosion, fray.

desgatar, va. (agr.) to root out the rest-harrow from.

desgaznatarse, *vr.* = DESGAÑITARSE.

desglosar, *va.* to blot out marginal notes from; to take off; to separate sheets from (a book).

desglose, *m.* act of blotting out a comment or gloss.

desgobernado, da. I. *pp.* of DESGOBERNAR. **II.** *a.* ill-governed or ungovernable person.

desgobernadura, *f.* (vet.) confining of a vein.

desgobernar. I. *va.* (*ind.* DESGOBIERNO; *subj.* DESGOBIERNE) to disturb or upset the government of; to misgovern; to dislocate or disjoint (as bones); (vet.) to bar (a vein) on a horse's leg; (naut.) to neglect, not handle right. **II.** *vr.* to affect ridiculous motions in dancing.

¹desgobierno, *m.* mismanagement; misrule; maladministration; (vet.) barring a vein on a horse's leg.

²desgobierno, desgobierne, *v. V.* DESGOBERNAR.

desgolletar, *va.* to break off the neck of (a bottle or other vessel); to uncover the neck of.

desgomar, *va.* to ungum, to unsize (silk).

desgonzar, *va.* = DESGOZNAR.

desgorrarse, *vr.* to pull off one's hat, cap, etc.

desgoznar. I. *va.* to unhinge, disjoint. **II.** *vr.* to be dislocated or disjointed; to be torn in pieces; to distort the body with violent motions.

desgracia, *f.* misfortune, mishap; affliction, sorrow, grief, bereavement; enmity, unfriendly attitude; disgrace, state of being out of favor; lack of grace, ungracefulness; unpleasantness, rudeness of language and address.—**caer en d.,** to lose favor.—**correr d.,** to fail.—**por d.,** unfortunately.

desgraciadamente, *adv.* unfortunately.

desgraciado, da. I. *pp.* of DESGRACIAR. **II.** *a.* unfortunate, unhappy, unlucky; misadventured, luckless, hapless; out of work; disagreeable, ungrateful. **III.** *n.* wretch, unfortunate person.

desgraciar. I. *va.* to displease; maim; to spoil. **II.** *vr.* to disgrace, to lose favor; to fall out (with a person); to become a cripple; to lose the perfection formerly possessed; to degenerate; to die young; to fail, fall through (as a project).

desgramar, *va.* to pull up the grass from.

desgranadera, *f.* grape picker.

desgranador, ra, *n.* sheller, thrasher; flail.

desgranamiento, *m.* (agr.) shaking or beating out grain; thrashing, shelling; (mil.) grooves that the powder forms on the inner orifice of the venthole.

desgranar. I. *va.* to beat or shake out the grain from (cereals); to thrash, flail; to shell (as peas). **II.** *vr.* to shed the grains; to scatter about (as beads); (mil.) to wear away (app. to the vent of firearms).—**desgrane**, *m.* shelling; (of grain) becoming loose; scattering of grain or beads.

desgranzar, *va.* to separate the husks or chaff from; (art) to give the first grinding to (colors).

desgrasar, *va.* to remove the grease from.

desgrase, *m.* removal of grease.

desgreñar. I. *va.* to dishevel. **II.** *vr.* to quarrel; to pull each other's hair.

desguace, *m.* rough dressing (of lumber).

desguarnecer, *va.* (*ind.* DESGUARNEZCO; *subj.* DESGUARNEZCA) to strip of trimmings and ornaments; to deprive of strength; to strip of all accessories; to disarm; to unharness.

desguarnir, *va.* (naut.) to unrig (the capstan).

desguazar, *va.* to rough-dress (timber) with ax; (naut.) to take (ship) to pieces; to break up.

desguince, *m.* knife that cuts rags in paper-mills; dodging, dodge.

desguindar. I. *va.* (naut.) to take and bring down. **II.** *vr.* to slide down a rope.

desguinzar, *va.* to cut (cloth or rags) in paper mills.

deshabitado, da. I. *pp.* of DESHABITAR. **II.** *a.* uninhabited, untenanted, deserted.

deshabitar, *va.* to move out of; to depopulate.

deshabituación, *f.* disuse, disusage, desuetude.

deshabituar, *va.* to disaccustom.

deshacedor, *m.*—**d. c. agravios**, undoer of injuries, righter of wrongs.

deshacer. I. *va.* (*pp.* DESHECHO; *ind. pres.* DESHAGO, *pret.* yo DESHICE, él DESHIZO, *fut.* DESHARÉ; *subj.* DESHAGA) to undo; to destroy; take apart; to unwrap, untie (as a parcel); to upset (plans); to consume, to diminish; to cancel, blot or scratch out; to efface; to cut to pieces, destroy; to put to flight; to melt, dissolve, liquefy; to cut up, divide; to violate (a treaty or agreement); (mil.) to discharge from service. —**d. agravios**, to right wrongs. **II.** *vr.* to be consumed, destroyed; to wear oneself out; to grieve, mourn; to disappear, vanish; to outdo oneself; to grow feeble or meagre; to be crippled, grievously maltreated.—**deshacerse de**, to get rid, or rid oneself, of; to part with.— **deshacerse en lágrimas**, to burst into tears.

deshago, deshaga, *v. V.* DESHACER.

deshaldo, *m.* = MARCEO, trimming honeycombs.

deshambrido, da, *a.* exceedingly hungry, famished, starving.

desharé, *fut.* of DESHACER.

desharrapado, da, *a.* shabby, ragged, in tatters.

desharrapamiento, *m.* misery, meanness.

deshebillar, *va.* to unbuckle.

deshebrar, *va.* to unthread, to ravel into threads to separate into filaments.

deshecha, *f.* simulation, evasion, shift; polite farewell; a step in a Spanish dance.—**a la d.,** dissemblingly; deceitfully.—**hacer la d.,** to dissemble, feign, pretend.

deshechizar, *va.* to disenchant; break a spell in.

deshechizo, *m.* disenchantment, breaking of a magic spell.

deshecho, cha. I. *pp.* of DESHACER. **II.** *a.* undone; exhausted; perfectly mixed (app. to colors).

deshelar. I. *va. & vr.* (*ind.* DESHIELO; *subj.* DESHIELE) to thaw; to melt. **II.** *v. impers.* to thaw.

desherbar, *va.* (*ind.* DESHIERBO; *subj.* DESHIERBE) to pluck up or extirpate herbs from; to weed.

desheredación, *f.*, **desheredamiento**, *m.* disinheriting, disinheritance.

desheredar. I. *va.* to disinherit; to cut out from an hereditary right. **II.** *vr.* to degenerate.

deshermanar. I. *va.* to destroy the similarity of. **II.** *vr.* to violate the love due to a brother.

desherradura, *f.* (vet.) surbating.

desherrar, *va.* (*ind.* DESHIERRO; *subj.* DESHIERRE) to unchain; to rip off the shoes of (horses).

desherrumbrar, *va.* to clean of rust.

deshice, *pret.* of DESHACER.

deshidratación, *f.* dehydration.

deshidratar, *va.* to dehydrate.

deshidrogenar, *va.* to dehydrogenize.

¹deshielo, *m.* thaw, thawing.

²deshielo, deshiele, *v. V.* DESHELAR.

deshierbo, deshierbe, *v. V.* DESHERBAR.

deshierro, deshierre, *v. V.* DESHERRAR.

deshilachar. I. *va.* to ravel, to uncord. **II.** *vr.* to fuzz; to ravel.

deshiladiz, *m.* = FILADIZ, floss silk; tape.

deshilado, da. I. *pp.* of DESHILAR. **II.** *a.* marching in a file.—**a la d.,** in file, one after another; stealthily; deceitfully, dissemblingly. **III.** (embroidery) openwork, drawn work.

deshiladura, *f.* ripping, ravelling out.

deshilar. I. *va.* to ravel; to scrape (lint); to distract (bees); to carve (a fowl) in thin strips. **II.** *vr.* to grow thin; to fuzz.

deshilo, *m.* obstructing the communication of bees, to get them into a new hive.

deshilvanado, da. I. *pp.* of DESHILVANAR. **II.** *a.* disjointed, disconnected; without sequence.

deshilvanar, *va.* to remove basting threads from.

deshincadura, *f.* act of drawing out anything nailed or fixed.

deshincar, *va.* to draw out, pull out, remove.

deshinchadura, *f.* act of reducing a swelling.

deshinchar. I. *va.* to reduce the swelling of, to deflate; to appease the anger or annoyance of. **II.** *vr.* (of anything swollen) to contract, decrease, shrink, shrivel; (coll.) to stop putting on airs.

deshizo, *pret.* of DESHACER.

deshojador, *m.* stripper of leaves.

deshojadura, *f.* stripping a tree of its leaves.

deshojar, *va.* to strip off the leaves of.

deshoje, *m.* falling off of leaves.

deshollejar, *va.* to peel, pare, skin (as grapes); to shell (as beans).

deshollinadera, *f.* chimney-sweeping broom.

deshollinador, *m.* chimney sweeper; any device used for sweeping chimneys; (coll.) one that examines and inspects minutely and curiously.

deshollinar, *va.* to sweep or clean (chimneys); to clean (ceilings and walls) with a turk's head; (coll.) to view and examine minutely.

deshonestamente, *adv.* dishonorably, disgracefully; lewdly, lustily, immodestly.

deshonestarse, *vr.* to be indecorous or lewd.

deshonestidad, *f.* immodesty; indecency; dishonesty; lewdness.

deshonesto, ta, *a.* immodest; lewd, unchaste, lustful; dishonest, dishonorable.

deshonor, *m.* dishonor, disgrace; insult, affront.

deshonorar, *va.* to dishonor, disgrace; to deprive of office or employ.

deshonra, *f.* dishonor, disgrace; seduction or violation (of a woman).—**tener a d.,** to consider dishonorable or disgraceful.

deshonrabuenos, *n.* calumniator; degenerate.

deshonradamente, *adv.* dishonorably, shamefully, disgracefully.

deshonrador, ra, *n.* dishonorer, disgracer.

deshonrar, *va.* to affront, insult, defame; to dishonor, disgrace; to scorn, to despise; to seduce or ruin (a woman).

deshonrible, *a.* (coll.) shameless, despicable.

deshonroso, sa, *a.* dishonorable, disgraceful.

deshora, *f.* unseasonable or inconvenient time.— **a d.,** or **a deshoras,** untimely, unseasonably; extemporary.

deshornar, *va.* to take out of the oven.

deshospedamiento, *m.* inhospitality, act of refusing strangers a lodging.

deshuesar, *va.* to bone (an animal); to take the pits out of (fruits). Also DESOSAR.

deshuevo, deshueve, *v.* V. DESOVAR.

deshumanizar, *va.* to dehumanize.

deshumano, na, *a.* inhuman.

deshumedecer. I. *va.* (*ind.* DESHUMEDEZCO; *subj.* DESHUMEDEZCA) to dry out, to deprive of humidity. **II.** *vr.* to dry, become dry.

desiderable, *a.* desirable.

desiderativo, va, *a.* desirous.

desiderátum, *m.* desideratum.

desidia, *f.* laziness, indolence.

desidiosamente, *adv.* indolently, lazily.

desidioso, sa, *a.* lazy, indolent.

desierto, ta. I. *a.* deserted, uninhabited, lonely. **II.** *m.* desert, waste, wilderness.

designación, *f.* designation.

designar, *va.* to intend; to designate, name, appoint.

designio, *m.* design, purpose, intention.

desigual, *a.* unequal, unlike; uneven, unlevel, rough, broken, craggy; arduous, difficult; perilous; changeable; abrupt; excessive, extreme.

desigualar. I. *va.* to make unequal or dissimilar; to mismatch. **II.** *vr.* to excel, to surpass.

desigualdad, *f.* inequality, difference; changeableness, inconstancy; wrong, injury, injustice; knottiness; unevenness, roughness, cragginess.

desigualmente, *adv.* unequally, unevenly.

desilusión, *f.* disillusion, disillusionment.

desilusionar. I. *va.* to disillusion, disenchant; to

undeceive. **II.** *vr.* to lose an illusion; to be disabused, undeceived; to become disillusioned.

desimaginar, *va.* to blot out of the mind.

desimanación, *f.* demagnetization.

desimanar. I. *va.* to demagnetize. **II.** *vr.* to become demagnetized, lose its magnetism.

desimantación, *f.* = DESIMANACIÓN.

desimantar, *va.* & *vr.* = DESIMANAR.

desimpresionar, *va.* to undeceive.

desinclinar, *va.* to disincline.

desincorporación, *f.* end of corporate existence.

desincorporar, *va.* & *vr.* to dissolve (a corporation).

desincrustante. I. *a.* scale-removing. **II.** *n.* disincrustant, boiler compound.

desincrustar, *va.* to remove incrustations from.

desinencia, *f.* (gram.) declension, inflection, desinence; (rhet.) ending of a sentence.

desinfección, *f.* disinfection; disinfecting.

desinfectante, *n.* & *a.* disinfectant(-ing).

desinfectar, *va.* to disinfect; to sterilize.

desinficionamiento, *m.* disinfection.

desinficionar, *va.* to disinfect.

desinflamar, *va.* to remove the inflammation of.

desinflar, *va.* to deflate.

desinsaculación, *f.* act of drawing lots.

desinsacular, *va.* to draw lots or names from an urn or balloting box.

desinterés, *m.* disinterestedness.

desinteresadamente, *adv.* disinterestedly.

desinteresado, da, *a.* disinterested, impartial.

desinvernar, *vn.* (mil.) to leave winter quarters.

desirvo, etc. *v.* V. DESERVIR.

desistencia, *f.,* **desistimiento,** *m.* desisting, act of desisting.

desistir, *vn.* (de) to desist (from), cease, give up; to flinch (from); (law) to waive (a right).

desjarretadera, *f.* hooked knife for hocking or hamstringing cattle.

desjarretar, *va.* to hock, to hamstring; (coll.) to weaken, to debilitate (as by bleeding a patient).

desjarrete, *m.* act of hamstringing or hocking.

desjugar, *va.* (*ind.* DESJUGUÉ; *subj.* DESJUGUE) to extract the juice from.

desjuiciado, da, *a.* lacking sense or judgment.

desjuntamiento, *m.* separation, disjunction.

desjuntar, *va.* & *vr.* to disjoint, divide; to separate, to part.

deslabonar. I. *va.* to unlink, to disjoin; to destroy. **II.** *vr.* to withdraw, to retire.

desladrillar, *va.* to remove tiles or bricks from.

deslamar, *va.* to clear of mud.

deslastrar, *va.* (naut.) to remove ballast from.

deslatar, *va.* to take off the laths from.

deslavado, da. I. *pp.* of DESLAVAR. **II.** *a.* (fig.) impudent, barefaced.

deslavadura, *f.* washing, rinsing.

deslavar, *va.* to wash or cleanse superficially, to rinse; to wet, spoil by wetting; to take away the color, force, or vigor of.

deslavazar, *va.* = DESLAVAR.

deslavazamiento, *m.* disjunction, dissolution.

deslazar, *va.* to unlace, untie.

desleal, *a.* disloyal; perfidious, faithless.

deslealmente, *adv.* disloyally, treacherously.

deslealtad, *f.* disloyalty, treachery, faithlessness.

deslechar, *va.* to remove the leaves and dirt from (silkworms).

deslecho, *m.* act of cleansing silkworms.

deslechugador, *m.* vinedresser, pruner.

deslechugar, deslechuguillar, *va.* (agr.) to cut and prune the branches of (vines).

desleidura, *f.,* **desleimiento,** *m.* dilution; making thin or weak.

desleír, *va.* (*ind. pres.* yo DESLÍO, *pret.* él DESLIÓ; *subj.* yo DESLÍA) to dilute; dissolve; to make thin or weak.

deslendrar, *va.* (*ind.* DESLIENDRO; *subj.* DESLIENDRE) to clear (hair) of nits, delouse.

deslenguado, da. I. *pp.* of DESLENGUAR. **II.** *a.* loquacious; impudent; foul-mouthed, scurrilous.

deslenguamiento, *m.* loquacity; impudence.

deslenguar. I. *va.* to cut out the tongue of. **II.** *vr.* to speak impudently or recklessly, to unloosen one's tongue.

desliar, *va.* to untie, loose, unpack.

deslicé, deslice, *v.* V. DESLIZAR.

desliendro, desliendre, *v.* V. DESLENDRAR.

desligadura, *f.*, **desligamiento,** *m.* disjunction, untying.

desligar. I. *va.* (*pret.* DESLIGUÉ; *subj.* DESLIGUE) to loosen, untie, unbind; to disentangle, extricate, unravel; to absolve from ecclesiastical censure; excuse from an obligation; to remove (from a ship) part of its knees or futtock-timbers, or the spikes holding them; (med.) to unfasten (bandages or ligatures); (mus.) to play or sing] staccato. **II.** *vr.* to get loose, to give way.

deslindable, *a.* capable of demarcation.

deslindador, *m.* one who sets boundaries.

deslindamiento, *m.* demarcation, determination of boundaries.

deslindar, *va.* to mark the boundaries of; to clear up, to define, circumscribe.

deslinde, *m.* = DESLINDAMIENTO.

desliñar, *va.* to clean (fulled cloth) before sending to the press.

deslío, deslió, etc. *v.* V. DESLEÍR.

desliz, *m.* slip; act of slipping or sliding; false step; frailty, slight fault; (min.) mercury that escapes in smelting silver ore.

deslizable, *a.* that can slip or slide.

deslizadero, ra. I. *a.* slippery. **II.** *m.* slippery place.

deslizadizo, za, *a.* = DESLIZADERO.

deslizador, *m.* (aer.) glider.

deslizamiento, *m.* slip, slipping; skidding.

deslizante, *a.* gliding.

deslizar. I. *vn.* & *vr.* (*pret.* DESLICÉ; *subj.* DESLICE) to slip; to slide; to skid; to glide; to act or speak carelessly. **II.** *vr.* to shirk, to evade.

deslomadura, *f.* act of breaking the back; (vet.) a disease of the muscles of the loins.

deslomar, *va.* to break the back of; to distort or strain the loins of, to chine.

deslucidamente, *adv.* ungracefully, inelegantly; poorly, badly, unsuccessfully.

deslucido, da, *a.* unadorned; ungraceful, awkward; useless, fruitless.—**quedar,** or **salir, d.,** to fail, make or be a failure, to make or be a fizzle.

deslucimiento, *m.* failure, lack of success; awkwardness, uncouthness.

deslucir. I. *va.* (*ind.* DESLUZCO; *subj.* DESLUZCA) to tarnish or impair the lustre and splendor of; to discredit, impair the reputation of. **II.** *vr.* to do poorly, to be a failure; to tarnish one's reputation.

deslumbrador, ra, *a.* dazzling, glaring.

deslumbramiento, *m.* glare, overpowering lustre, dazzling; confusion of sight or mind, hallucination.

deslumbrante, *a.* dazzling.

deslumbrar, *va.* to dazzle; to puzzle, to leave in doubt and uncertainty.

deslustrado, da. I. *pp.* of DESLUSTRAR. **II.** *a.* unglazed.

deslustrador, ra, *n.* & *a.* tarnisher(-ing).

deslustrar, *va.* to tarnish, to take away the lustre of, to dim; to remove the glaze from; to sponge; to make less beautiful or illustrious; to soil, stain, (reputation, etc.).

deslustre, *m.* spot or stain; dimness, dulness; disgrace, ignominy, stigma.

deslustroso, sa, *a.* unbecoming, ugly.

desluzco, desluzca, *v.* V. DESLUCIR.

desmadejamiento, *m.* languishment, languidness.

desmadejar. I. *va.* to enervate, to produce languor in. **II.** *vr.* to languish, to be enervated and weak.

desmadrado, da, *a.* (of animals) separated from the mother.

desmadrar, *va.* to separate (an animal) from the mother.

desmagnetizar, *va.* to demagnetize.

desmajolar, *va.* to pull up (vines) by the roots; to loosen or untie.

desmalezar, *va.* to weed.

desmallador, ra, *n.* one who breaks or cuts meshes.

desmalladura, *f.* act of ripping up or breaking meshes.

desmallar, *va.* to cut and destroy the meshes of.

desmamar, *va.* = DESTETAR, to wean.

desmamonar, *va.* to cut off the young shoots of.

desmán, *m.* misbehavior; excess in actions or words; misfortune, mishap, calamity.

desmanarse, *vr.* to stray from a flock or herd.

desmandado, da. I. *pp.* of DESMANDAR. **II.** *a.* impudent; unbridled, lawless, unruly; disobedient.

desmandamiento, *m.* countermanding of an order; sauciness, impudence.

desmandar. I. *va.* to repeal (an order), to countermand; to revoke. **II.** *vr.* to transgress the bounds of justice and reason; to be impudent; to lose moderation or self-control; to stray from the flock; to go astray.

desmanear, *va.* to unfetter, to take off fetters or shackles from (horses, mules, etc.).

desmangar, *va.* to take off the handle of.

desmanotado, da, *a.* unhandy, awkward.

desmantecar, *va.* to take butter or lard out of.

desmantelado, da. I. *pp.* of DESMANTELAR. **II.** *a.* dismantled, dilapidated.

desmantelamiento, *m.* dismantling; dilapidation, ruined condition.

desmantelar, *va.* to dismantle; to abandon, desert, forsake; (naut.) to unmast.

desmaña, *f.* awkwardness, clumsiness; laziness.

desmañado, da, *a.* unhandy, clumsy, awkward; lazy, indolent.

desmarañar, *va.* to disentangle.

desmarcar, *va.* (*pret.* DESMARQUÉ; *subj.* DESMARQUE) to remove, efface, obliterate (marks).

desmarojador, ra, *n.* one who rids the trees of dead leaves or branches.

desmarojar, *va.* to take dry leaves or branches off (a tree).

desmarrido, da, *a.* sad, dejected; exhausted.

desmatar, *adv.* = DESCUAJAR, to uproot.

desmayadamente, *adv.* weakly, dejectedly.

desmayado, da. I. *pp.* of DESMAYAR. **II.** *a.* pale, wan, faint of lustre; dismayed, discouraged.

desmayar. I. *vn.* to be dispirited, faint-hearted, discouraged. **II.** *va.* to dismay, depress, discourage. **III.** *vr.* to faint, swoon.

desmayo, *m.* swoon, fainting fit; lowering of vigor or strength; dismay, discouragement.

desmazalado, da, *a.* weak, dejected, faint-hearted, spiritless.

desmechado, da, *a.* (Am.) disheveled.

desmedidamente, *adv.* disproportionately, excessively.

desmedido, da. I. *pp.* of DESMEDIRSE. **II.** *a.* excessive, out of proportion or measure.

desmedirse, *vr.* (*ger.* DESMIDIENDO; *ind.* pres. me DESMIDO, *pret.* se DESMIDIÓ; *subj.* me DESMIDA) to forget oneself, to be impudent or saucy; to lose self-control.

desmedrado, da. I. *pp.* of DESMEDRAR. **II.** *a.* damaged, injured; worn out; wasted, emaciated.

desmedrar. I. *vn.* to decrease, decay. **II.** *va.* to impair.

desmedro, *m.* diminution, detriment.

desmedular, *va.* to remove the marrow from.

For pronunciation, see the rules at the beginning of the book.

desmejora, *f.* deterioration, depreciation, impairment; diminution, loss.

desmejorar. I. *va.* to debase, to make worse, impair. **II.** *vn. & vr.* to decline, become worse; to deteriorate.

desmelancolizar, *va.* to cheer, enliven, gladden.

desmelar, *va.* (*ind.* DESMIELO; *subj.* DESMIELE) to take the honey from (a hive).

desmelenar, *va.* to dishevel, to disarrange or muss the hair of.

desmembración, *f.* dismemberment, amputation, division.

desmembrador, ra, *n.* divider; one who dismembers or divides.

desmembrar, *va.* (*ind.* DESMIEMBRO; *subj.* DESMIEMBRE) to dismember, to tear asunder; to curtail; (surg.) to amputate; to separate, divide.

desmemoria, *f.* forgetfulness; lack of memory.

desmemoriado, da. I. *pp.* of DESMEMORIARSE. **II.** *a.* forgetful; devoid of memory.

desmemoriarse, *vr.* to become forgetful, to forget; to lose the memory.

desmenguar, *va.* to lessen; to diminish.

desmentida, *f.* act of giving the lie.

desmentidor, ra. I. *a.* that gives the lie, disproving. **II.** *n.* one who gives the lie; disprover.

desmentir. I. *va.* (*ind.* DESMIENTO; *subj.* DESMIENTA) to give the lie to; to convince of a falsehood; to contradict, disprove; to counterfeit, conceal, dissemble; to do things unworthy of (one's birth, character, profession). **II.** *vn.* to deviate from the right line. **III.** *vr.* to recant, retract, take back.

desmenucé, desmenuce, *v.* V. DESMENUZAR.

desmenuzable, *a.* crisp, crumbly, crimp, easily crumbled.

desmenuzador, ra, *n.* one who crumbles; investigator; purifier.

desmenuzamiento, *m.* crumbling, breaking into small pieces.

desmenuzar. I. *va.* (*pret.* DESMENUCÉ: *subj.* DESMENUCE) to crumble, crumb; to shred; to break or tear into bits; to chip, mill, fritter; to sift, examine minutely. **II.** *vr.* to crumble, to fall into small pieces.

desmeollamiento, *m.* taking out the marrow.

desmeollar, *va.* to take the marrow or pith from.

desmerecedor, ra, *a.* unworthy, undeserving.

desmerecer. I. *va.* (*ind.* DESMEREZCO; *subj.* DESMEREZCA) to become unworthy or undeserving of. **II.** *vn.* to lose worth; to deteriorate; to be comparatively inferior, compare unfavorably.

desmerecimiento, *m.* demerit, unworthiness.

desmerezco, desmerezca, *v.* V. DESMERECER.

desmesura, *f.* excess, lack of measure.

desmesuradamente, *adv.* disproportionately, excessively.

desmesurado, da. I. *pp.* of DESMESURAR. **II.** *a.* disproportionate, excessive.

desmesurar. I. *va.* to disorder, disarrange, disturb. **II.** *vr.* to be forward, impudent, saucy.

desmido, desmida, etc. *v.* V. DESMEDIRSE.

desmielo, desmiele, *v.* V. DESMELAR.

desmiembro, desmiembre, *v.* V. DESMEMBRAR.

desmiento, desmienta, *v.* V. DESMENTIR.

desmigajar. I. *va. & vr.* to crumble; to comminute (as bread). **II.** *vr.* to crumble.

desmigar, *va.* (*pret.* DESMIGUÉ; *subj.* DESMIGUE) to crumble (bread).

desmilitarización, *f.* demilitarization.

desmineralización, *f.* (med.) abnormal loss of mineral substances.

desmirriado, da, *a.* (coll.) lean, emaciated, exhausted; melancholy.

desmocha, desmochadura, *f.* lopping or cutting off; diminution or destruction of part of a thing.

desmochar, *va.* to lop or cut off the top of (a tree, etc.); to dehorn.

desmoche, *m.* = DESMOCHA.

desmocho, *m.* heap of things lopped or cut off.

desmogar, *vn.* to cast the horns, as deer.

desmografía, *f.* desmography.

desmogue, *m.* act of casting the horns.

desmolado, da, *a.* having no molars or grinders.

desmoldamiento, *m.* removal of a casting from the mold.

desmoldar, *va.* to remove from the mold, to "strike the frame."

desmolde, *m.* = DESMOLDAMIENTO.

desmología, *f.* desmology.

desmonetización, *f.* demonetization; conversion of coins into bullion.

desmonetizar. I. *va.* to convert (money) into bullion; to demonetize. **II.** *vr.* (of stocks) to depreciate, lose value.

desmonta, *f.* = DESMONTE.

desmontado, da. I. *pp.* of DESMONTAR. **II.** *a.* unmounted, dismounted; (mech.) knocked down.

desmontador, ra, *n.* one who fells wood; dismounter.

desmontadura, *f.* felling timber, clearing of shrubbery.

desmontar. I. *va.* to clear (a wood); to remove (dirt or rubbish); to grub, to fallow; to uncock (firearms); to take apart (as a machine); to dismount (a troop of horse); to dismount (cannon). —**d. el timón,** (naut.) to unhang the rudder. **II.** *vn., vr.* to dismount, to alight from a horse, mule, etc.

desmonte, *m.* grubbing or clearing of trees and undergrowth; timber remaining on the spot; (Ry.) cut; (min.) discarded ore or rock.

desmoñar, *va.* (coll.) to undo (the hair knot).

desmoralicé, desmoralice, *v.* V. DESMORALIZAR.

desmoralización, *f.* demoralization; corruption.

desmoralizar. I. *va.* (*pret.* DESMORALICÉ; *subj.* DESMORALICE) to demoralize, corrupt, deprave. **II.** *vr.* to become demoralized; (mil.) to lose the morale, to flag in morale.

desmoronadizo, za, *a.* easily crumbled, crumbly; lacking solidity or permanence.

desmoronamiento, *m.* crumbling.

desmoronar. I. *va.* to abrade, to destroy little by little, to ruin by insensible degrees. **II.** *vr.* to fall, decay, crumble.

desmostar. I. *va.* to separate the must from (grapes). **II.** *vn.* to ferment.

desmotadera, *f.* woman who burls cloth; burling iron.

desmotador, ra. I. *n. & a.* burler(-ing). **II.** *f.* cotton opener; (Am.) cotton gin.

desmotar, *va.* to burl; to gin.

desmullir, *va.* to disarrange or impair the softness of.

desmurador, *m.* mouser (cat).

desmurar, *va.* to exterminate rats from.

desnarigado, da. I. *pp.* of DESNARIGAR. **II.** *a.* noseless; having a tiny nose.

desnarigar, *va.* to cut off the nose of.

desnatadora, *f.* skimmer (utensil).

desnatar, *va.* to skim; to take off the flower or choicest part of.

desnaturalicé, desnaturalice, *v.* V. DESNATURALIZAR.

desnaturalización, *f.* expatriation, denaturalization, denationalization.

desnaturalizado, da. I. *pp.* of DESNATURALIZAR. **II.** *a.* denaturalized; denatured; low, base, conscienceless.

desnaturalizar. I. *va.* (*pret.* DESNATURALICÉ; *subj.* DESNATURALICE) to denaturalize, denationalize; to banish, exile; to disfigure, pervert (as a fact); to denature. **II.** *vr.* to abandon one's country.

desnegamiento, *m.* denial; contradiction; retraction, retractation.

desnegar. I. *va.* (*ind. pres.* DESNIEGO, *pret.*

DESNEGUÉ; *subj.* DESNIEGUE) to deny, gainsay, contradict. II. *vr.* to retract, recant.

desnervar, *va.* to enervate.

desnevado, da. I. *pp.* of DESNEVAR. II. *a.* free from snow.

desnevar, *va.* (*ind.* DESNIEVO; *subj.* DESNIEVE) to thaw, dissolve.

desniego, desniegue, *v.* V. DESNEGAR.

desnievo, desnieve, *v.* V. DESNEVAR.

desnivel, *m.*, **desnivelación,** *f.* unevenness, difference of elevation, drop.

desnivelado, da, *a.* unlevel, uneven.

desnivelar. I. *va.* to unlevel, make uneven. II. *vr.* to lose its level.

desnucamiento, *m.* breaking the neck.

desnucar. I. *va.* (*pret.* DESNUQUÉ; *subj.* DESNUQUE) to break the neck of; to kill by a blow on the nape. II. *vr.* to break one's neck.

desnudador, ra, *n.* one that denudes.

desnudamente, *adv.* nakedly; evidently.

desnudar. I. *va.* to strip, undress, denude, uncover; to fleece; (naut.) to unrig. II. *vr.* to undress, to strip, to deprive oneself of; to rid oneself of.

desnudez, *f.* nudity, nakedness.

desnudo, da. I. *a.* nude, naked; bare, uncovered; ill-clothed; plain, evident; empty-handed; destitute of merit, interest, resources, etc. II. *m.* nude figure in art.

desnuqué, desnuque, *v.* V. DESNUCAR.

desnutrición, *f.* malnutrition, underfeeding.

desobedecer, *va. & vn.* (*ind.* DESOBEDEZCO; *subj.* DESOBEDEZCA) to disobey.

desobediencia, *f.* disobedience.

desobediente, *a.* disobedient.

desobedientemente, *adv.* disobediently.

desobligar, *va.* (*pret.* DESOBLIGUÉ; *subj.* DESOBLIGUE) to release from an obligation; to disoblige; to offend; to alienate the good will of.

desobstrucción, *f.* clearing, removal of obstructions or obstacles.

desobstruir, *va.* (*ind.* DESOBSTRUYO; *subj.* DESOBSTRUYA) to remove obstructions from, to clear; (med.) to deobstruct.

desocupación, *f.* leisure; unemployment.

desocupadamente, *adv.* deliberately, leisurely.

desocupado, da. I. *pp.* of DESOCUPAR. II. *a.* idle, without occupation; vacant, unoccupied. III. *n.* unemployed person; (Am.) idler.

desocupar. I. *va.* to vacate; to evacuate; to empty. II. *vr.* to disengage oneself from a business or occupation.

desodorante, *n. & a.* deodorant.

desoír, *va.* (*ger.* DESOYENDO; *ind. pres.* DESOIGO, *pret.* él DESOYÓ; *subj.* DESOIGA) to pretend not to hear; not to heed.

desojar. I. *va. & vr.* to break or burst the eye of (as of a needle). II. *vr.* to strain one's sight; to look intently.

desolación, *f.* desolation, destruction, havoc; fall; intense grief or affliction.

desolado, da. I. *pp.* of DESOLAR. II. *a.* desolate; disconsolate.

desolar. I. *va.* (*ind.* DESUELO; *subj.* DESUELE) to desolate, lay waste; to harass. II. *vr.* to suffer great grief.

desoldar. I. *va.* (*ind.* DESUELDO; *subj.* DESUELDE) to unsolder. II. *vr.* (of soldered pieces) to come unsoldered, break apart.

desolladamente, *adv.* (coll.) impudently, petulantly.

desolladero, *m.* abattoir, slaughterhouse.

desollado, da. I. *pp.* of DESOLLAR. II. *a.* (coll.) forward, impudent, insolent.

desollador, ra. I. *n.* flayer, extortioner. II. *m.* butcher bird.

desolladura, *f.* act and effect of flaying or skinning; excoriation; extortion.

desollar, *va.* (*ind.* DESUELLO; *subj.* DESUELLE) to flay, to skin; to excoriate; to fleece; to cause

great harm or injury to.—**d. vivo,** (coll.) to extort an immoderate price from; to speak ill of.—**falta el rabo por d.,** the worst is yet to come.

desollón, *m.* = DESOLLADURA.

desonce, *m.* discount of a certain number of ounces in each pound.

desonzar, *va.* to discount or deduct a certain number of ounces per pound of; to insult, to defame, revile.

desopilar, *va.* (med.) to clear obstructions from.

desopilativo, va, *a.* (med.) deobstruent.

desopinado, da. I. *pp.* of DESOPINAR. II. *a.* having lost reputation.

desopinar, *va.* to defame.

desoprimir, *va.* to free from oppression.

desorden, *m.* disorder, confusion, mess; lawlessness, excess; turmoil, disturbance, riot.

desordenadamente, *adv.* disorderly, irregularly, confusedly.

desordenado, da. I. *pp.* of DESORDENAR. II. *a.* disorderly, irregular; lawless, licentious.

desordenar. I. *va.* to disorder, disarrange, upset. II. *vr.* to exceed or go beyond all rule; to be out of order, to be irregular; to get unruly, be unmanageable (as a horse).

desorejado, da, *a.* (coll.) licentious, dissolute, degraded.

desorejamiento, *m.* cropping off the ears.

desorejador, ra, *n.* one who crops off the ears.

desorejar, *va.* to crop off the ears of.

desorganicé, desorganice, *v.* V. DESORGANIZAR.

desorganización, *f.* disorganization.

desorganizador, ra, *n. & a.* disorganizer(-ing).

desorganizar. I. *va.* (*pret.* DESORGANICÉ; *subj.* DESORGANICE) to disorganize; to break up, disperse; (chem.) to decompose; (mil.) to disband. II. *vr.* to become disorganized; to disband, disperse; (med.) to be altered, disorganized.

desorientación, *f.* lack of orientation, loss of bearings; confusion, lack of system.

desorientar, *va. & vr.* to disorient; to lose or cause to lose one's bearings; to lose the way; to confuse, to lead into error.

desorillar, *va.* to cut off the selvage of (cloth); to cut the border off.

desortijado, da. I. *pp.* of DESORTIJAR. II. *a.* (vet.) sprained.

desortijar, *va.* to hoe or weed the first time.

desosar, *va.* (*ind.* DESHUESO; *subj.* DESHUESE) = DESHUESAR, to bone (an animal); to pit (fruit).

desovar, *vn.* (*ind.* DESHUEVO; *subj.* DESHUEVE) to spawn.

desove, *m.* spawning; spawning season.

desovillar, *va.* to unwind; to unclew, unravel, disentangle.

desoxidable, *a.* deoxidizable.

desoxidación, *f.* deoxidation.

desoxidante, *n. & a.* deoxidizer(-ing).

desoxidar, *va. & vn.* to deoxidize.

desoxigenación, *f.* deoxidation.

desoxigenante, *n. & a.* = DESOXIDANTE.

desoxigenar, *va.* to deoxidize.

desoyendo, desoyó, *v.* V. DESOÍR.

despabiladeras, *f. pl.* snuffers (for candles).

despabilado, da. I. *pp.* of DESPABILAR. II. *a.* vigilant; wakeful; lively, smart.

despabilador, ra. I. *n. & a.* snuffer(-ing). II. *m.* candle snuffer.

despabiladura, *f.* end of candlewick snuffed or trimmed.

despabilar. I. *va.* to trim or snuff (a candle); to trim, cut off from; to finish briefly or quickly (as a dinner or a fortune); to rouse, to enliven; (coll.) to rob, to plunder; (coll.) to kill.—**d. el ingenio,** to sharpen the wits.—**d. los ojos,** to keep a sharp lookout. II. *vr.* to wake up.

despacio. I. *adv.* slowly; deliberately. II. *interj.* softly, gently. III. *m.* (Am.) slowness.—**con d.,** slowly; carefully.

---

despacioso, sa, *a.* slow, phlegmatic, sluggish.

despacito, *adv.* (coll.) very slowly, gently, softly.

despachaderas, *f. pl.* (coll.) surly rejoinder; quickness, resourcefulness.

despachado, da. I. *pp.* of DESPACHAR. **II.** *a.* (coll.) impudent, bold-faced, brazen.

despachador, ra, *n.* sender, one who despatches.

despachar. I. *va.* to despatch; to expedite, abridge, facilitate; to send; to ship, to express; to perform with despatch; to get out, write and send, attend to (correspondence); to wait on, serve (as in a shop); to dismiss, discharge.—**d. géneros,** or **mercaderías, en la aduana,** to clear or take out goods or merchandise at the customhouse.—**d. un barco,** (com.) to clear a vessel at the customhouse. **II.** *vr.* to make haste. **III.** *vn.* in offices, to carry papers drawn up for the signature of the principal; (com.) to expend, to let goods go for money or barter; (coll.) to wait on customers.

despacho, *m.* expedient, determination; despatch, expedition; shipping, shipment, sending; custom, application from buyers; cabinet, department; office, bureau; countinghouse; depot; sale of goods; trade; demand; commission, warrant, patent; official communication or despatch.—**d. de aduana,** customhouse clearance.—**d. de billetes,** or **boletos,** ticket office.—**d. de localidades,** box office.—**d. telegráfico,** cablegram, telegram.—**d. universal,** state department.—**tener buen d.,** to be quick, to be energetic and prompt.

despachurrado, da. I. *pp.* of DESPACHURRAR. **II.** *a.* smashed, squashed, crushed.—**dejar a uno d.,** (coll.) to leave one dumfounded.

despachurrar, *va.* (coll.) to squash, smash, crush; (coll.) to make a jumble of (an explanation).—**d. el cuento,** to interrupt a story and prevent its conclusion.

despajador, ra, *n.* & *a.* winnower(-ing).

despajadura, *f.* winnowing.

despajar, *va.* to winnow or separate (grain from chaff).—**despajo,** *m.* winnowing or cleaning.

despaldar, *va.* & *vr.* to dislocate or break the shoulder of.

despaldilladura, *f.* breaking or dislocation of an animal's shoulder.

despalillar, *va.* to remove the stems from (raisins); to strip (tobacco, etc.).

despalmador, *m.* (naut.) careening place, dockyard; hoof-paring knife.

despalmadura, *f.* calking, paying the bottom.

despalmar, *va.* (naut.) to grave, to calk; to pare (a horse's hoof).—**despalme,** *m.* = DESPALMADURA.

despampanador, *m.* pruner of vines.

despampanadura, *f.* act of pruning vines.

despampanar. I. *va.* to prune (vines); (coll.) to astound by a piece of news. **II.** *vn.* (coll.) to unbosom oneself, to give vent to one's feelings. **III.** *vr.* (coll.) to be injured by a fall.

despamplonador, ra, *n.* one who separates (vine) stems.

despamplonar. I. *va.* to separate the shoots of. **II.** *vr.* to sprain the hand.

despanar, *va.* to remove (grain) from the field.

despancijar, despanzurrar, *va.* (coll.) to burst the belly of.

despapar, *vn.* (of a horse) to carry the head too high.

desparecer, *vn.* (*ind.* DESPAREZCO; *subj.* DESPAREZCA) = DESAPARECER, to disappear.

desparedar, *va.* to take down the walls of.

desparejar, *va.* to break a pair of, to separate from a pair.

desparpajado, da. I. *pp.* of DESPARPAJAR. **II.** *a.* pert, petulant, garrulous.

desparpajar. I. *va.* to undo in a disorderly manner. **II.** *vn.* & *vr.* (coll.) to rant, to prattle.

desparpajo, *m.* (coll.) pertness of speech or of manner.

desparramado, da. I. *pp.* of DESPARRAMAR. **II.** *a.* wide open; spread, scattered.

desparramador, ra, *n.* disperser; dilapidator; prodigal, waster, spendthrift.

desparramamiento, *m.* spreading, scattering; squandering, extravagance, dissipation.

desparramar. I. *va.* & *vr.* to scatter, disseminate, spread; to squander, dissipate, lavish. **II.** *vr.* to amuse oneself; to be dissipated.

despartidor, *m.* one who separates or divides.

despartimiento, *m.* separation, or division.

despartir, *va.* to part, separate, divide; to reconcile, make peace between.

desparvar, *va.* to undo the sheaves and spread the stalks of (grain) on the floor.

despasar, *va.* (naut.) to unsling, unreeve, shift.

despatarrada, *f.* (coll.) spreading of the legs; a certain change or movement in a Spanish dance.—**hacer la d.,** (coll.) to pretend disease or pain; to feign death.

despatarrarse, *vr.* (coll.) to straddle; to fall with spread legs; to do the splits; to be stupefied or dumfounded; to remain motionless.

despatillar. I. *va.* to tenon; (naut.) to break off the arm of (an anchor). **II.** *vr.* (coll.) to shave off one's whiskers.

despavesaderas, *f. pl.* = DESPABILADERAS.

despavesadura, *f.* act of snuffing a candle.

despavesar, *va.* to snuff (a candle).

despavoridamente, *adv.* terrifiedly, aghast.

despavorido, da, *a.* terrified, aghast.

despavorir, *vn.* & *vr.* (*defect.: it has only the moods and persons having the letter* **i**) to be terrified, to be frightened, to be aghast.

despeadura, *f.*, **despeamiento,** *m.* bruising the feet with travel; (vet.) surbating.

despearse, *vr.* to bruise the feet (or hoofs) or make them sore by much walking.

despectivo, va, *a.* depreciatory; contemptuous.

despechadamente, *adv.* angrily, spitefully.

¹despechar. I. *va.* to enrage, to excite indignation in. **II.** *vr.* to fret; to despair; to be spiteful.

²despechar, *va.* (coll.) to wean.

despecho, *m.* spite; despair; grudge.—**a d. de,** despite, in spite of, in defiance of.

despechugadura, *f.* cutting off the breast of a fowl; uncovering one's breast.

despechugar. I. *va.* (*pret.* DESPECHUGUÉ; *subj.* DESPECHUGUE) to cut off the breast of (a fowl). **II.** *vr.* (coll.) to uncover the breast; to walk with bare breast.

despedacé, despedace, *v.* V. DESPEDAZAR.

despedazador, ra, *n.* & *a.* dissector(-ing); tearer(-ing); lacerator(-ing), mangler(-ing).

despedazamiento, *m.* laceration, dissection, cutting to pieces; mangling.

despedazar, *va.* (*pret.* DESPEDACÉ; *subj.* DESPEDACE) to cut into bits, to tear into pieces; to cut asunder; to limb, to claw; to lacerate, mangle; to torment, to harrow (as the feelings). **II.** *vr.* to break or fall to pieces.—**d. de risa,** to hold one's sides with laughter.

despedida, *f.* leave-taking, farewell; send-off; seeing a person off; discharge, dismissal.

despedimiento, *m.* = DESPEDIDA.

despedir. I. *va.* (*ger.* DESPIDIENDO; *ind. pres.* DESPIDO, *pret.* él DESPIDIÓ; *subj.* DESPIDA) to emit, discharge; fling, throw off or out; to dismiss, discharge; to see (a person) off on a journey; to escort (a guest) to the door; to dismiss (as from the mind). **II.** *vr.* (**de**) to take leave (of), say good-bye (to); to quit; to renounce; to go out from service, to leave one's occupation.—**d. a la francesa,** to take French leave, sneak away.

despedregar, *va.* to clear of stones.

despegable, *a.* that may be unglued or disjoined.

despegadamente, *adv.* unconcernedly, unaffectionately.

despegado, da. I. *pp.* of DESPEGAR. **II.** *a.* unglued; (coll.) sour of temper; unpleasant, harsh; distant, indifferent; unaffectionate, unfeeling.

despegador, ra, *a.* that unglues or detaches.

despegadura, *f.* ungluing, detaching, separating.

despegamiento, *m.* DESAPEGO, indifference.

despegar. I. *va.* (*pret.* DESPEGUÉ; *subj.* DESPEGUE) to unglue, detach, separate, disjoin.—**d. los labios, la boca,** to speak. **II.** *vr.* to come off; to withdraw one's affection; to become indifferent. **III.** *vn.* (aer.) to rise, to take off.—**despego,** *m.* asperity; aversion; coolness, indifference, lack of affection.

despegué, despegue, *v.* V. DESPEGAR.

despegue, *m.* (aer.) take-off.

despeinado, da, *a.* uncombed, unkempt.

despeinar, *va.* to disarrange the hair of.

despejadamente, *adv.* expeditiously, readily, smartly, neatly.

despejado, da. I. *pp.* of DESPEJAR. **II.** *a.* sprightly, smart, vivacious; clear, cloudless; unobstructed, clear.

despejar. I. *va.* to remove impediments from, clear; (math.) to solve for, find the value of. **II.** *vr.* to become bright and smart; to amuse oneself; (of an ill person) to be relieved of pain; (of the weather, sky, etc.) to clear up.

despejo, *m.* removal of obstacles, clearing; sprightliness, smartness, briskness; grace, ease.

despelotar, *va.* to dishevel.

despeluzamiento, *m.* entanglement or disarrangement of the hair; making the hair stand on end; goose flesh.

despeluzar, *va. & vr.* to make (the hair) stand on end; to be horrified.

despeluznante, *a.* horrifying, frightful.

despeluznar, *va. & vr.* = DESPELUZAR.

despellejadura, *f.* scratch, slight wound; skinning.

despellejar, *va.* to flay, to skin, to strip; (fig.) to speak ill of.

despenador, ra, *n.* one that relieves pain.

despenar, *va.* to relieve from pain; (coll.) to kill.

despendedor, ra, *n.* spendthrift, prodigal, lavisher, waster.

despender, *va.* to spend; to waste, squander.

despensa, *f.* pantry, larder; store of provisions for a journey; butlership; provisions for daily use; marketing; contract for a yearly supply of fodder; (naut.) steward's room.

despensería, *f.* office of steward.

despensero, ra, *n.* butler; caterer, dispenser, distributer; (naut.) steward.

despeñadamente, *adv.* precipitately.

despeñadero, ra. I. *a.* steep, precipitous, headlong. **II.** *m.* precipice, crag; dangerous undertaking.

despeñadizo, za, *a.* steep, precipitous; glib, slippery.

despeñamiento, *m.* = DESPEÑO.

despeñar. I. *va.* to precipitate, to fling down a precipice. **II.** *vr.* to throw oneself headlong; to lead a riotous life.—**despeño,** *m.* precipitate fall; loss of fortune and character; diarrhea.

despepitador, *m.* stoner, corer (for fruit).

despepitadora, *f.* stoner, corer; seed separator. —**d. de algodón,** cotton gin.

despepitar, *va.* to remove the seeds from; to gin.

despepitarse, *vr.* to loosen one's tongue; to vociferate; to speak or act rashly or heedlessly.— **d. por,** to long for, to be dying or itching for.

despercudir, *va.* to clean or wash.

desperdiciadamente, *adv.* profusely, wastefully.

desperdiciado, da. I. *pp.* of DESPERDICIAR. **II.** *a.* wasted, destroyed, squandered.

desperdiciador, ra, *n.* spendthrift, squanderer.

desperdiciar, *va.* to waste; to squander, mis-

spend; not to avail oneself of, not to utilize, to lose, miss (an opportunity, etc.).

desperdicio, *m.* waste; prodigality, profusion; (gen. *pl.*) refuse, offal, remains, garbage.

desperdigamiento, *m.* spreading, scattering.

desperdigar, *va.* to separate, disjoin; to scatter.

desperecerse, *vr.* (*ind.* DESPEREZCO; *subj.* DESPEREZCA) to crave, to long, to desire eagerly.

desperezarse, *vr.* to stretch one's limbs; to shake off sloth.

desperezco, desperezca, *v.* V. DESPERECERSE.

desperezo, *m.* = ESPEREZO, stretching (limbs).

desperfecto, *m.* deterioration, wear and tear; slight injury or damage, blemish, imperfection, flaw.

desperfilar, *va.* (art) to soften the lines of.

despernada, *f.* a movement in dancing.

despernado, da. I. *pp.* of DESPERNAR. **II.** *a.* weary, fatigued, tired.

despernar. I. *va.* (*ind.* DESPIERNO; *subj.* DESPIERNE) to injure or cut off the legs of. **II.** *vr.* to injure or lose one's legs.

despertador, ra. I. *n.* awakener. **II.** *m.* alarm bell in clocks; alarm clock; warning, admonition, hint that causes worriment.

despertamiento, *m.* awakening.

despertar. I. *va. & vr.* (*pp.* DESPERTADO, DESPIERTO; *ind.* DESPIERTO; *subj.* DESPIERTE) to wake up, awaken; to enliven; to remind, recall; to excite, sharpen (as the appetite, curiosity). **II.** *vn.* to awake, wake up; to revive.

despesar, *m.* displeasure, aversion, dislike.

despestañar. I. *va.* to pluck out the eyelashes of. **II.** *vr.* to look intently, to study hard.

despezar, *va.* to bevel; to taper.

despezo, *m.* taper; bevel.—*pl.* (arch.) beveled faces of a stone at the joints.

despezonar. I. *va.* to cut off the stem of; to divide, to separate. **II.** *vr.* to break off (as the stalk of fruit or the arm of an axletree).

despezuñar. I. *va.* to cut off the hoof of. **II.** *vr.* (Am.) to rush at breakneck speed.—**d. por,** to long for; to hustle for, set one's heart on.

despiadadamente, *adv.* unmercifully, pitilessly.

despiadado, da, *a.* unmerciful, pitiless.

despicar. I. *va.* (*pret.* DESPIQUÉ; *subj.* DESPIQUE) to satisfy, to gratify. **II.** *vr.* (**de** or **con**) to take revenge (for), get square (with).

despicarazar, *va.* (of birds) to pick (the figs).

despichar. I. *va.* to expel or discharge; to pick; (Am.) to crush, smash. **II.** *vn.* (coll.) to die.

despidida, *f.* gutter, passage for water.

despidiente, *m.* board between a hanging scaffold and the wall.—**d. de agua,** (arch.) flashing.

¹despido, etc., *v.* V. DESPEDIR.

²despido, *m.* discharge, dismissal, layoff.

despierno, despierne, *v.* V. DESPERNAR.

despiertamente, *adv.* ingeniously, cleverly.

¹despierto, ta. I. *pp. irreg.* of DESPERTAR. **II.** *a.* awake; watchful; diligent; lively, smart; clearsighted.

²despierto, despierte, *v.* V. DESPERTAR.

despiezo, *m.* (arch.) = DESPEZO, bevel.

despilar, *va.* (min.) to take away the pillars of.

despilfarradamente, *adv.* wastefully; slovenly.

despilfarrado, da. I. *pp.* of DESPILFARRAR. **II.** *a.* ragged, shabby, in tatters; prodigal, wasteful.

despilfarrador, ra, *a.* spendthrift, wasteful.

despilfarrar, *va.* to waste, squander.

despilfarro, *m.* slovenliness, uncleanliness; waste, lavishness, squandering, extravagance; misgovernment, maladministration.

despimpollar, *va.* to prune away the useless stems of.

despincé, despince, *v.* V. DESPINZAR.

despinces, *m. pl.* tweezers. Also DESPINZAS.

despintar. I. *va.* to blot or efface; to disfigure; to mislead. **II.** *vn.* to degenerate. **III.** *vr.* to fade, wash off, lose color; to forget.

despinte, *m.* (Am.) (min.) low-grade or poor ore.

despinzadera, *f.* woman that burls.—*pl.* burling iron.

despinzar, *va.* (*pret.* DESPINCÉ; *subj.* DESPINCE) to burl.

despinzas, *f. pl.* burling iron; DESPINCES.

despiojar, *va. & vr.* to delouse; (coll.) to relieve from misery.

despique, *m.* VELGEANCE, revenge.

despiqué, despique, *v.* V. DESPICAR.

despistar, *va.* to turn from the trail or course.

despizcar. I. *va.* (*pret.* DESPIZQUÉ; *subj.* DESPIZ-QUE) to triturate, crush; break or cut into small bits. **II.** *vr.* to exert oneself to the utmost.

desplacer. I. *va.* (*ind.* DESPLAZCO; *subj.* DES-PLAZCA) to displease. **II.** *m.* displeasure.

desplanchar, *va.* to wrinkle, rumple, muss.

desplantación, *f.* eradication, uprooting.

desplantador, ra. I. *n.* eradicator, one who pulls up plants. **II.** *m.* trowel, scoop trowel.

desplantar. I. *vr.* to lose one's erect posture in fencing or dancing. **II.** *va.* to uproot; to deviate from the vertical.—**desplante,** *m.* oblique posture in fencing; injudicious action or speech.

desplatar, *va.* to separate silver from.

desplate, *m.* act of separating silver from other metals.

desplayar, *vn.* to recede from the shore (as the tide).

desplazamiento, *m.* displacement.

desplazar, *va.* (naut.) to displace, have a displacement of.

desplazco, desplazca, *v.* V. DESPLACER.

desplegadura, *f.* unfolding, spreading out; elucidation, explanation.

desplegar. I. *va.* (*ind.* DESPLIEGO; *subj.* DES-PLIEGUE) to unfold, display; to spread, lay out; to explain, elucidate; (naut.) to unfurl.—**d. la bandera,** to hoist the flag. **II.** *vr.* to open, unfold (as flowers); to spread out, deploy (as troops).

despleguetear, *va.* (agr.) to remove the folds from the tendrils of (vines).

despliego, despliegue, *v.* V. DESPLEGAR.

despliegue, *m.* unfurling, unfolding; spreading out; (mil.) deployment.

desplomar. I. *va.* (of a wall, etc.) to put out of vertical, to cause to lean. **II.** *vr.* to get out of plumb, to lean over; to tumble down, collapse, topple over; (aer.) to pancake.

desplome, *m.* leaning; collapse, tumbling down, downfall; (aer.) pancaking.

desplomo, *m.* deviation from the vertical.

desplumadura, *f.* plucking (a bird).

desplumar. I. *va. & vr.* to deplume, to pluck (a bird); (coll.) to despoil or strip of property. **II.** *vr.* to moult.

despoblación, *f.* depopulation.

despoblado, *m.* uninhabited place; wilderness.

despoblador, ra, *n. & a.* depopulator(-ing).

despoblar. I. *va.* (*ind.* DESPUEBLO; *subj.* DES-PUEBLE) to depopulate; to despoil or desolate. **II.** *vr.* to become depopulated.

despojador, ra, *n. & a.* despoiler(-ing).

despojar. I. *va.* to despoil, strip of property; to deprive of, to cut off from, judicially; to dismiss, turn out of a place or employment. **II.** *vr.* (de) to take off (as a coat); to undress, to strip; to relinquish; to forsake; to divest oneself (of).

despojo, *m.* spoliation; plunder, spoils; slough, cast-off skin of a serpent; head, pluck, and feet of slaughtered animals.—*pl.* leavings, scraps from the table; giblets of fowls; débris; remains; second-hand building materials.

despolaricé, despolarice, *v.* V. DESPOLARIZAR.

despolarización, *f.* depolarization.

despolarizador, ra, *n. & a.* depolarizer(-ing).

despolarizar, *va.* (*pret.* DESPOLARICÉ; *subj.* DES-POLARICE) to depolarize.

despolvar, *va.* to dust.

despolvorear, *va.* to dust; to cast away, scatter, dissipate; (coll.) to sprinkle.

despopularizar, *va. & vr.* (*pret.* DESPOPULARICÉ; *subj.* DESPOPULARICE) to make or become unpopular.

desportillar, *va.* to chip off the corners or edges of; break the neck of (a bottle, pot, etc.); (arch.) to splay.

desposado, da. I. *pp.* of DESPOSAR. **II.** *a.* newly married; handcuffed.

desposando, da, *n.* person newly married or about to be married; bride; bridegroom.

desposar. I. *va.* to marry (to perform the marriage ceremony for). **II.** *vr.* to be betrothed, engaged or married.

desposeer, *va.* to dispossess, oust.

desposeimiento, *m.* dispossession.

desposorio, *m.* betrothal; (gen. *pl.*) mutual promise to contract marriage, engagement.

déspota, *m.* despot, tyrant.

despóticamente, *adv.* despotically.

despótico, ca, *a.* despotic.

despotismo, *m.* despotism, tyranny.

despotizar, *va. & vn.* to tyrannize, to oppress.

despotricar, *vn. & vr.* (coll.) to talk without restraint.

despreciable, *a.* contemptible, despicable, lowdown; inappreciable, negligible.

despreciador, ra, *n. & a.* despiser(-ing), scorner (-ing), contemner(-ing).

despreciar, *va.* to despise, scorn, look down on; to reject, lay aside; to neglect.—**despreciativo, va,** *a.* depreciative, depreciatory; contemptuous.—**desprecio,** *m.* scorn, contempt; slight; neglect; dispraise.

desprender. I. *va.* to unfasten, loose, separate; to emit, give out. **II.** *vr.* (de) to give way, to fall down; to issue (from), come out (of), break, or fall, off (of); to extricate oneself (from); to dispossess oneself (of), give away; to follow, be a consequence (of); to part (with); to rid oneself (of).

desprendido, da. I. *pp.* of DESPRENDER. **II.** *a.* disinterested, generous; loose.

desprendimiento, *m.* act of loosening; disinterestedness; indifference; landslide, landslip.

desprensar, *va.* to remove from the press.

despreocupación, *f.* freedom from bias, openmindedness; unconventionality.

despreocupado, da. I. *pp.* of DESPREOCUPAR. **II.** *a.* unprejudiced; unconventional; freethinking.

despreocupar. I. *va.* to unbias, free from prejudice. **II.** *vr.* to become unbiased, to shake off prejudice; (de) to ignore; to discard, set aside; to pay no attention (to).

desprestigiado, da. I. *pp.* of DESPRESTIGIAR. **II.** *a.* having lost one's reputation, in bad repute, unpopular.

desprestigiar. I. *va.* to bring into disrepute, to impair the reputation of. **II.** *vr.* to lose reputation or prestige.—**desprestigio,** *m.* loss of reputation or prestige, unpopularity.

desprevención, *f.* improvidence, want of caution.

desprevenidamente, *adv.* improvidently.

desprevenido, da, *a.* unprovided; unprepared.

desproporción, *f.* disproportion; disparity.

desproporcionadamente, *adv.* disproportionately.

desproporcionado, da. I. *pp.* of DESPROPOR-CIONAR. **II.** *a.* disproportionate; out of proportion; unsuitable, unbecoming.

desproporcionar, *va.* to disproportion, to mismatch, to misproportion.

despropositado, da, *a.* absurd.

despropósito, *m.* absurdity, nonsense.

desproveer, *va.* (*pp.* DESPROVEÍDO, DESPROVISTO) to deprive of provisions or the necessaries of life.

desproveídamente, *adv.* improvidently.

desproveído, da. I. *pp.* of DESPROVEER. **II.** *a.* unprepared; unprepared.

desprovisto, ta. I. *pp. irreg.* of DESPROVEER. **II.** *a.* (de) unprovided (with), lacking (in).

despueble, ¹despueblo, *m.* depopulation.

²despueblo, despueble, *v. V.* DESPOBLAR.

después, *adv.* after, afterward, next, then, later. —**d. de,** after; next to.—**d. de que, d. que,** after.

despulir, *va.* to tarnish; to frost, grind (glass).

despulsarse, *vr.* to be violently affected with any passion; (por) to be eagerly desirous (of).

despumación, *f.* despumation, skimming.

despumadera, *f.* = ESPUMADERA, skimmer.

despumar, *va.* = ESPUMAR, to skim.

despuntador, *m.* (min.) ore separator; hammer for breaking ore.

despuntadura, *f.* blunting, taking off the point.

despuntar. I. *va.* to blunt, to crop, cut off, wear out the point of; to cut away the dry combs of (a beehive); (naut.) to double (a cape). **II.** *vn.* to advance in knowledge; to manifest wit and genius; to begin to sprout or bud; to be outstanding; to surpass, excel, morally.—**d. el día, d. el alba, d. la aurora,** to dawn.

desquejar, *va.* to pluck up a shoot near the root of (a plant).—**desqueje,** *m.* pulling up a shoot near the root of a plant.

desquerer, *va.* to lose affection or liking for, to cease to love or like.

desquiciador, ra, *n.* he who or that which unhinges, unsettles or overthrows.

desquiciamiento, *m.* unhinging, disjoining; downfall.

desquiciar. I. *va.* to unhinge, to disjoint; to unsettle, disorder; to deprive of favor or protection; to undermine; to overthrow. **II.** *vr.* to become unhinged; to lose support or backing; to fall down.

desquijaramiento, *m.* act of breaking the jaws.

desquijarar, *va.* to break the jaws of; (naut.) to break the cheek of (a block).

desquijerar, *va.* (carp.) to tenon.

desquilatar, *va.* to diminish the intrinsic value of (gold).

desquitar. I. *va.* to retrieve (a loss). **II.** *vr.* (de) to win one's money back; to retaliate, take revenge (for); to get even.

desquite, *m.* compensation, recovery of a loss; revenge, retaliation.

desrabotar, *va.* to cut off the tail of.

desramar, *va.* to strip of branches.

desramillar, *va.* (agr.) to prune (vines).

desrancharse, *vr.* to leave a mess (eating together).

desrastrojar, *va.* to remove the stubble from.

desrayadura, *f.* last furrow of tillage; deep boundary furrow.

desrayar, *va.* to open furrows in for irrigation; to make a boundary furrow in.

desrazonable, *a.* (coll.) unreasonable.

desregladamente, *adv.*, **desreglado, da,** *a.*, **desreglarse,** *vr.* = DESARREGLADAMENTE, etc.

desrelingar, *va.* (naut.) to take away the boltropes from (the sails).

desreputación, *f.* (coll.) dishonor, disrepute.

desrizar, *va.* (*pret.* DESRICÉ; *subj.* DESRICE) to uncurl.

desroblar, *va.* to take the rivets out of.

desroñar, *va.* to lop off decayed branches from.

destacado, da, I. *pp.* of DESTACAR. **II.** *a.* prominent, outstanding.

destacamento, *m.* (mil.) detachment; station; post.

destacar. I. *va.* (*pret.* DESTAQUÉ; *subj.* DESTAQUE) to bring out, make conspicuous, emphasize; (mil.) to detach. **II.** *vr.* to stand out, be conspicuous; to be prominent, outstanding; to loom.

destaconar, *va.* to wear out the heels of.

destajador, *m.* smith's hammer.

destajar, *va.* to contract for (a job); to do as taskwork; to cut (the cards); to bring out, make stand out. **II.** *vr.* to stand out; to tower, be conspicuous; to project.

destajero, ra, destajista, *n.* person who does taskwork.

destajo, *m.* job, taskwork.—**a d.,** by the job, piece (work); by the lump; earnestly, diligently.

destalonar, *va.* to break or wear out the heels of; to take off coupons from; (vet.) to level the hoofs of.

destallar, *va.* to prune useless branches from.

destapada, *f.* pie without an upper crust.

destapar. I. *va.* to uncover, take off (cover, lid, cap). **II.** *vr.* to become or get uncovered.

destapiado, *m.* place where mud walls have been torn down.

destapiar, *va.* to pull down the mud walls of.

destaponar, *va.* to remove the stopper from.

destarar, *va.* (com.) to diminish the tare of.

destartalado, da, *a.* huddled, jumbled; scantily and poorly furnished.

destazador, ra, *n.* one who cuts up slaughtered animals.

destazar, *va.* to cut up (a carcass).

deste, ta, to, contraction formerly used for **de este, de esta, de esto.**

destechadura, *f.* unroofing.

destechar, *va.* to unroof.

destejar, *va.* to remove tiles; to leave defenseless.

destejer, *va.* to unweave, ravel, unbraid.

destellar. I. *vn.* to twinkle, beam, sparkle, flash. **II.** *va.* to give forth, emit.

destello, *m.* sparkle, beam, flash, scintillation.

destempladamente, *adv.* intemperately; discordantly, inharmoniously.

destemplado, da. I. *pp.* of DESTEMPLAR. **II.** *a.* inharmonious; out of tune; intemperate; (art) inharmonious, incongruous.

destemplanza, *f.* unsteadiness of the weather; disorder, intemperance; excess, abuse; (med.) indisposition, distemper; want of moderation.

destemplar. I. *va.* to disorder, alter; disconcert; to put to confusion; to put out of tune (a musical instrument). **II.** *vr.* to be ruffled, discomposed; to be out of order; to be irregular or abnormal; to get out of tune; to act improperly or rashly; to lose moderation; (of metal) to lose its temper.

destemple, *m.* discordance, disharmony; being out of tune; discomposure, disorder; intemperance, lack of moderation; slight indisposition; (of metals) untempering, lack of temper.

destentar, *va.* (*ind.* DESTIENTO; *subj.* DESTIENTE) to lead out of temptation.

desteñir, *va.* & *vr.* (*pret.* DESTIÑÓ; *subj.* DESTIÑA) to discolor, to change from the natural hue.

desternillarse, *vr.* to break a cartilage.—**d. de risa,** (coll.) to split one's sides with laughter.

desterradero, *m.* retired part of the town.

desterrado, da. I. *pp.* of DESTERRAR. **II.** *n.* exile, outcast.

desterrar, *va.* (*ind.* DESTIERRO; *subj.* DESTIERRE) to banish, exile; to lay or put aside; to take the earth off the roots of.

desterronador, ra, *n.* clod crusher, stubble plow.

desterronar, *va.* & *vr.* to break the clods of.

destetadera, *f.* pointed instrument placed on the teats of cows to prevent the calves from sucking.

destetar. I. *va.* to wean. **II.** *vr.* to wean oneself from an evil habit or custom.

destete, *m.* weaning.

desteto, *m.* number of weanlings; place where newly-weaned mules are kept.

destiempo, *adv.*—**a d.,** unseasonably, untimely.

¹destiento, *m.* surprise; mental commotion.

²destiento, destiente, *v. V.* DESTENTAR.

destierre, *m.* removal of dirt from ore, cleaning.

¹**destierro,** *m.* exile, banishment; place where exile lives; any remote and solitary place.

²**destierro, destierre,** *v.* V. DESTERRAR.

destilable, *a.* distillable.

destilación, *f.* distillation; filtration; flow of serum.—**d. seca,** destructive distillation.

destiladera, *f.* still, alembic, distilling vessel; filter.

destilador, ra. I. *n.* & *a.* distiller(-ing). **II.** *m.* filtering stone; alembic, still.

destilar. I. *va.* to distil; to filter through a stone. **II.** *vn.* to distil, to drop, to fall in drops.

destilatorio, ria. I. *a.* distilatory, distilling. **II.** *m.* distillery; still, alembic.

destilería, *f.* distillery.

destinación, *f.* destination; assignment.

destinado, da. I. *pp.* of DESTINAR.—**estar d. a,** to be bound to (e.g. fail). **II.** *a.* (**a**), (of a letter, etc.) addressed (to).

destinar, *va.* to destine; to appoint; to designate; to allot, assign; (naut.) to station (ships).

destinatario, ria, *n.* addressee; consignee.

destino, *m.* destiny, fate; destination; appointment, job, employment; (naut.) station.—**con d. a,** bound for, going to.

destiño, etc. *v.* V. DESTEÑIR.

destiranizado, da, *a.* freed from tyranny.

destitución, *f.* dismissal from an employment, office, or charge; destitution, dereliction, abandonment.

destituible, *a.* dismissable, removable.

destituído, da. I. *pp.* of DESTITUIR. **II.** *a.* destitute, forsaken, friendless, helpless.

destituir, *va.* (*ger.* DESTITUYENDO; *ind. pres.* DESTITUYO, *pret.* él DESTITUYÓ; *subj.* DESTITUYA) to deprive; to make destitute; to dismiss from office.

destocar, *va.* (*pret.* DESTOQUÉ; *subj.* DESTOQUE) to uncoif, to pull off the cap or headdress from.

destorcedura, *f.* untwisting; uncurling.

destorcer. I. *va.* (*ind.* DESTUERZO; *subj.* DESTUERZA) to undo, untwist, uncurl; to rectify, to straighten out. **II.** *vr.* to become untwisted; to bend, warp; to feaze, to unlay; to deviate; to drift.

destorgar, *va.* (prov.) to break off the branches of (evergreen oaks) when taking off their acorns.

destornillado, da. I. *pp.* of DESTORNILLAR. **II.** *a.* reckless, heedless, rash.

destornillador, *m.* unscrewer; screwdriver.

destornillamiento, *m.* unscrewing; recklessness, rashness, wildness.

destornillar. I. *va.* to unscrew. **II.** *vr.* to act recklessly, or wildly.

destoserse, *vr.* to feign a cough.

destostarse, *vr.* (of the skin) to lose the suntan.

destotro, tra, *a.* (obs.) contraction of **de este otro, de esto otro, de esta otra.**

destrabar, *va.* to unfetter, unbind, to untie, loosen, separate; to break the barriers of.

destraillar, *va.* to unleash.

destral, *m.* small axe or hatchet.—**destraleja,** *f.* very small hatchet.—**destralero, ra,** *n.* axe maker.

destramar, *va.* to unweave, to undo the warp of.

destrejar, *vn.* to work or act with expertness.

destrenzar, *va.* (*pret.* DESTRENCÉ; *subj.* DESTRENCE) to unplait, unbraid, undo a tress of.

destreza, *f.* dexterity, skill; nimbleness.

destricé, destrice, *v.* V. DESTRIZAR.

destrincar, *va.* & *vr.* (naut.) to loose, to unlash.

destripacuentos, *n.* one who interrupts often the person who is talking, one "butting in."

destripamiento, *m.* disembowelment; crushing.

destripar, *va.* to disembowel, gut, eviscerate; to crush, smash; to draw out the inside of; (coll.) to interrupt and spoil (a story).

destripaterrones, *m.* (coll.) harrower, clodbeater; uncultured person.

destripular, *va.* to discharge the crew of.

destrísimo, ma, *a.* *super.* very dexterous or skillful.

destriunfar, *va.* (cards) to draw out the trumps from (the other players).

destrizar. I. *va.* (*pret.* DESTRICÉ; *subj.* DESTRICE) to mince, crumble, break in pieces; to tear in strips. **II.** *vr.* to be heartbroken, to languish with grief.

destrocar, *va.* (*ind.* DESTRUECO; *subj.* DESTRUEQUE) to return (a thing bartered).

destrocé, destroce, *v.* V. DESTROZAR.

destrón, *m.* blind man's guide.

destronamiento, *m.* dethronement.

destronar, *va.* to dethrone, overthrow.

destroncamiento, *m.* detruncation, amputation, lopping of trees; ruination.

destroncar, *va.* (*pret.* DESTRONQUÉ; *subj.* DESTRONQUE) to detruncate, lop, cut short; to maim, dislocate; to cut in pieces; to ruin, destroy; to tire out; (of animals) to overwork.

destróyer, *m.* (Angl.) (naut.) destroyer.

destrozador, ra, *n.* destroyer, mangler.

destrozar, *va.* (*pret.* DESTROCÉ; *subj.* DESTROCE) to destroy, to shatter, to mangle, to break or cut to pieces; to annihilate; to waste, squander.

destrozo, *m.* destruction, havoc, ruin; rout, defeat; massacre.—**destrozón, na,** *a.* destructive of wearing apparel, shoes, etc.

destrucción, *f.* destruction.

destructibilidad, *f.* destructibility.

destructible, *a.* destructible.

destructivamente, *adv.* destructively.

destructividad, *f.* destructiveness.

destructivo, va, *a.* destructive.

destructor, ra, *n.* & *a.* destructor, destroyer (-ive, -ing).

¹**destrueco, destrueque,** *m.* mutual restitution of things bartered.

²**destrueco, destrueque,** *v.* V. DESTROCAR.

destruíble, *a.* destructible.

destruidor, ra, *n.* & *a.* = DESTRUCTOR, RA.

destruir. I. *va.* (*ger.* DESTRUYENDO; *ind. pres.* DESTRUYO, *pret.* él DESTRUYÓ; *subj.* DESTRUYA) to destroy; to ruin; to demolish; to squander; to baffle, thwart; to prevent from earning a living. **II.** *vr.* to destroy one another; (math.) to cancel.

destruyente, *a.* destroying, destructive.

destuerzo, destuerza, *v.* V. DESTORCER.

desubstanciar, *va.* = DESUSTANCIAR.

desucación, *f.* act of extracting the juice.

desudar, *va.* to wipe off the sweat from.

desueldo, desuelde, *v.* V. DESOLDAR.

desuelo, desuele, *v.* V. DESOLAR.

desuellacaras, *m.* (coll.) bad barber; (coll.) impudent, shameless person.

¹**desuello,** *m.* act of flaying, fleecing, or skinning; forwardness, impudence, insolence; (coll.) extortion.

²**desuello, desuelle,** *v.* V. DESOLLAR.

desulfuración, *f.* desulphurization.

desulfurar, *va.* to desulphurize.

desuncir, *va.* (*ind.* DESUNZO; *subj.* DESUNZA) to unyoke.

desunidamente, *adv.* separately, severally; disunitedly.

desunión, *f.* separation, disunion, disjunction; discord, disunion, feud.

desunir. I. *va.* to separate, take apart; to occasion discord between, to estrange. **II.** *vr.* to loosen, to fall or break apart; to become separated.

desuno, *adv.* (obs.) jointly.

desunzo, desunza, *v.* V. DESUNCIR.

desuñar. I. *va.* to tear off the nails of; to pull out the roots of. **II.** *vr.* to plunge into vice and dissipation; to work one's fingers to the bone, work oneself to death.

desurcar, *va.* (*ind.* DESURQUÉ; *subj.* DESURQUE) to remove or undo furrows in.

---

desurdir, *va.* to unweave; to upset, nip in the bud, stop, frustrate.

desurqué, desurque, *v.* *V.* DESURCAR.

desusadamente, *adv.* unusually, contrary to custom.

desusado, da. I. *pp.* of DESUSAR. II. *a.* obsolete, out of date, archaic.

desusar. I. *va.* to discontinue the use of. II. *vr.* to become obsolete; to go out of date.

desuso, *m.* disuse, obsoleteness, desuetude.

desustanciación, *f.* enervation, sapping of vigor.

desustanciar, *va.* to enervate, deprive of strength and substance.

desvahar, *va.* (agr.) to take away the dry or withered part of (a plant).

desvaído, da, *a.* tall and graceless, gaunt; (of colors) dull.

desvainadura, *f.* act of shelling.

desvainar, *va.* to shell, to husk.

desvalido, da, *a.* helpless, destitute, unprotected.

desvalijador, *m.* highwayman.

desvalijamiento, *m.* act of robbing the contents of a valise; robbery.

desvalijar, *va.* to take out the contents of (a valise or gripsack); to rob.

desvalimiento, *m.* dereliction or abandonment; want of favor or protection; want, neediness.

desván, *m.* garret, loft, attic.—**d. gatero,** cockloft, room over the garret.

desvanecer. I. *va.* (*ind.* DESVANEZCO; *subj.* DESVANEZCA) to disintegrate, spread, or divide into minute parts; to cause to vanish or disappear; to take away from the sight; to undo, to remove. II. *vr.* to pall, to grow vapid, to become insipid; to vanish, disappear; to swell with presumption or pride; to faint, swoon.

desvanecidamente, *adv.* haughtily, proudly.

desvanecimiento, *m.* pride, haughtiness, loftiness; giddiness, dizziness.

desvanezco, desvanezca, *v.* *V.* DESVANECER.

desvaporizadero, *m.* place for evaporating.

desvarar, *va.*, *vn.* & *vr.* to slip, skid; (naut.) to set afloat a ship that was aground.

desvariadamente, *adv.* ravingly, foolishly or madly, stupidly.

desvariado, da. I. *pp.* of DESVARIAR. II. *a.* delirious, raving; disorderly, irregular; nonsensical; long, crooked (as branches of trees).

desvariar, *vn.* to rave, rant; to dote; to make extravagant demands.

desvarío, *m.* extravagant action or speech; delirium, raving; inconstancy; caprice, whim; monstrousness, extravagancy; derangement, disunion.

desvedar, *va.* to raise the prohibition of.

desveladamente, *adv.* watchfully, vigilantly.

desvelado, da. I. *pp.* of DESVELAR. II. *a.* watchful, vigilant, careful.

desvelamiento, *m.* watchfulness.

desvelar. I. *va.* to keep awake. II. *vr.* to go without sleep; to pass a sleepless night; be watchful or vigilant; to take great pains.

desvelo, *m.* watching, want or privation of sleep; watchfulness, vigilance; anxiety, uneasiness.

desvenar, *va.* to separate or clear the veins of; to extract from the veins of (mines) or the filaments of (plants); to raise the bit of (a bridle) so as to form an arch.

desvencijado, da, *a.* rickety, loose-jointed.

desvencijar. I. *va.* to disunite, weaken, divide, break. II. *vr.* to be ruptured, disjointed, loose, relaxed; (coll.) to be exhausted.

desvendar, *va.* to take off a bandage from, to unbandage.

desveno, *m.* arch of a horse's bit.

desventaja, *f.* disadvantage.

desventajosamente, *adv.* disadvantageously, unprofitably.

desventajoso, sa, *a.* disadvantageous, unfavorable, unprofitable, detrimental.

desventar, *va.* (*ind.* DESVIENTO; *subj.* DESVIENTE) to vent; to let out the air of.

desventura, *f.* misfortune, mishap; misery.

desventuradamente, *adv.* unhappily, unfortunately.

desventurado, da, *a.* unfortunate, unlucky, wretched; chicken-hearted, pusillanimous.

desvergonéé, *v.* *V.* DESVERGONZAR.

desvergonzadamente, *adv.* shamelessly.

desvergonzado, da, *a.* impudent; shameless.

desvergonzarse, *vr.* (*ind.* *pres.* DESVERGÜENZO, *pret.* DESVERGONCÉ; *subj.* DESVERGÜENCE) to speak or act in an impudent or insolent manner.

desvergüenza, *f.* impudence, effrontery, assurance; shamelessness; shame, disgrace.

desvergüenzo, *v.* *V.* DESVERGONZARSE.

desvestir, *va.* & *vr.* to undress.

desvezar, *va.* (agr.) to cut the young shoots of (vines) near the roots.

desviación, *f.* deviation, deflection; detour; oblique direction; (med.) deviation from natural position (as the bones); (med.) extravasation of fluids; (astr.) deviation from the meridian; variation of the magnetic needle.

desviadero, *m.* (Cuba) railway siding.

desviado, da. I. *pp.* of DESVIAR. II. *a.* devious, out of the common track, askew.

desviar. I. *va.* to deflect; to sway; to dissuade; to put by; (fencing) to ward off; (Ry.) to switch.—**d. la mirada,** to avoid (someone's) eyes. II. *vr.* to deviate (from), wander (away from); to turn off (from); to swerve; (aer.) to drift (away from).

desviejar, *va.* among shepherds, to separate the old ewes or rams from (the flock).

desviento, desviente, *v.* *V.* DESVENTAR.

desvío, *m.* deviation, turning away; going astray; deflection; aversion, displeasure; coldness, indifference; (Ry.) siding, side track; (mason.) steadying board (of a suspended platform).

desvirar, *va.* to pare off the fore part of (a sole); (bookbinding) to trim (a book); (naut.) to reverse (the capstan).

desvirgar, *va.* (low) to deflower.

desvirtuar, *va.* to lessen the value, strength or merit of; to detract from.

desvitrificación, *f.* devitrification.

desvitrificar, *va.* devitrify.

desvivirse, *vr.* (**por**) to have excessive love (for); to show great interest (in behalf of); to long (for), be dying (for, to).

desvolvedor, *m.* nut wrench.

desvolver, *va.* (*pp.* *irreg.* DESVUELTO; *ind.* DESVUELVO; *subj.* DESVUELVA) to alter the shape of; to plow, till.

desvuelto, ta, *pp.* *irreg.* of DESVOLVER.

desvuelvo, desvuelva, *v.* *V.* DESVOLVER.

desyemar, *va.* (agr.) to remove buds from; (Am.) to separate yolk from white of (an egg).

desyerbador, ra, *n.* grubber, weeder.

desyerbar, *va.* to weed, grub.

deszocar, *va.* to disable the foot of.

deszumar, *va.* to extract the juice or substance from.

detallar, *va.* to detail, relate minutely, particularize; to specify; to retail.

detalle, *m.* detail, particular; (com.) retail.

detallista, *n.* one addicted to details (esp. a painter); (com.) retailer.

detasa, *f.* (Ry.) rebate.

detective; detectivo, va, *n.* detective.

detectivismo, *m.* detective force or service.

detector, *m.* (elec., radio) detector.

detención, *f.* delay, stop, stay, halt, standstill, deadlock; (naut.) demurrage, arrest, embargo (of a ship).

detenedor, ra, *n.* detainer, stopper; check, arrester, catch.

detener. I. *va.* (*ind.* *pres.* DETENGO, *pret.* DETUVE, *fut.* DETENDRÉ; *subj.* DETENGA) to stop, detain,

check; arrest; (naut.) to capture, to embargo;
to keep back; to retain, reserve. **II.** *vr.* to tarry,
stay, stop over; to stop halt; to pause.

detengo, detenga, *v.* V. DETENER.

detenidamente, *adv.* dilatorily; carefully, painstakingly, thoroughly.

detenido, da. I. *pp.* of DETENER. **II.** *a.* sparing,
niggardly, parsimonious; dilatory; careful,
thorough, conscientious. **III.** *a.* & *n.* (person)
under arrest.

detenimiento, *m.* care, thoroughness.

detentación, *f.* (law) deforcement.

detentador, *m.* deforciant.

detentar, *va.* to deforce (law), to retain or keep
unlawfully.

detergente, *a.* (med.) detergent, detersive.

deterger, *va.* (med.) to cleanse (a wound, etc.)

deterioración, *f.* = DETERIORO.

deteriorar, *va.* & *vr.* to deteriorate, impair, damage, wear out.—**deterioro,** *m.* deterioration,
impairment, damage, wear and tear.

determinable, *a.* determinable, ascertainable.

determinación, *f.* determination, resolution;
conclusion or final decision; firmness.

determinadamente, *adv.* determinately; resolutely; definitely; expressly, especially.

determinado, da. I. *pp.* of DETERMINAR. **II.** *a.*
determinate, determined, decided; fixed, resolute; settled, definite; (math.) determinate.

determinante. I. *a.* determining, determinate,
determinative. **II.** *m.* (gram.) determining
verb. **III.** *m.* or *f.* (math.) determinant.

determinar. I. *va.* to determine, fix; to limit; to
specify; to distinguish, discern; to appoint, to
assign (as time and place); to decide, resolve;
to conclude (as a lawsuit). **II.** *vr.* to determine,
resolve; to make up one's mind.

determinativo, va, *a.* determinative.

determinismo, *m.* (philos.) determinism.

determinista, *n.* & *a.* (philos.) determinist.

detersión, *f.* (med.) detersion; cleansing.

detersivo, va; detersorio, ria, *a.* detersive,
cleansing, detergent.

detestable, *a.* detestable; hateful.

detestablemente, *adv.* detestably; hatefully.

detestación, *f.* detestation, abhorrence, abomination.

detestar, *va.* to detest, abhor, abominate.

detienebuey, *m.* (bot.) common rest-harrow.

detonación, *f.* detonation, report.

detonante, *a.* detonating.

detonar, *vn.* to detonate; to flash, to explode.

detorsión, *f.* (med.) distortion.

detracción, *f.* detraction, defamation, obloquy;
detraction, withdrawing, taking away.

detractar, *va.* to detract; to defame, slander.

detractor, ra, *n.* & *a.* detractor(-ing), slanderer
(-ing, -ous).

detraer, *va.* (ger. DETRAYENDO; *pp.* DETRAÍDO;
ind. pres. DETRAIGO, *pret.* DETRAJE; *subj.* DE-
TRAIGA) to detract, remove, take away; to defame, slander, villify.

detrás, *adv.* behind, after; back; in the rear.—**d.
de,** behind, in back of.—**por d.,** from the rear,
from behind; behind one's back.

detrimento, *m.* detriment, damage, harm.—
con (sin) d. de, with (without) detriment to.

detrítico, ca, *a.* (geol.) detrital, detritic.

detrito, *m.* detritus.

detuve, *pret.* of DETENER.

deuda, *f.* debt; fault, offence; indebtedness; public debt.—**d. consolidada,** funded debt.—**d.
exterior,** foreign debt.—**d. flotante,** floating
debt.—**d. interior,** internal debt.—**d. pendiente,** unpaid balance.—**deudas activas,**
assets.—**deudas pasivas,** liabilities.—**estar en
d. con,** to be indebted to.

deudo, da, *n.* relative, kindred.

deudor, ra, *n.* & *a.* debtor; indebted.

Deuteronomio, *m.* Deuteronomy.

deutón, *m.* (phys.) deuton.

deutóxido, *m.* (chem.) deutoxide, dioxide.

devalar, *vn.* (naut.) to deviate, to drift.

devanadera, *f.* reel, spool, bobbin, winding
frame.—**d. de golpe,** clock reel, snap reel;
(naut.) log reel.

devanador, ra, *n.* winder, spool, reel; anything
on which another thing is wound.—**d. de lanzadera,** shuttle winder.

devanar. I. *va.* to reel, wind. **II.** *vr.* (Am.) to be
convulsed (with laughter); to writhe (with
pain).—**d. los sesos,** to rack one's brain.

devanear, *vn.* to rave, talk nonsense.

devaneo, *m.* delirium, alienation of mind, giddiness; frenzy; idle or mad pursuit; dissipation;
love affair.

devantal, *m.* apron.

devastación, *f.* devastation, destruction, havoc.

devastador, ra, *n.* & *a.* desolator(-ing), devasta-
tor(-ing).

devastar, *va.* to devastate, lay waste, ruin.

devengar, *va.* (*pret.* DEVENGUÉ; *subj.* DEVENGUE)
to earn, draw (as salary, interest, etc.).

devenir, *vn.* to happen; to become.

deviación, *f.* = DESVIACIÓN.

devisar, *va.* (Am.) to descry; to see vaguely.

devoción, *f.* piety, devoutness; prayer; devotion,
strong affection, faithful attachment.

devocionario, *m.* prayer book.

devocionero, ra, *a.* devotional.

devolución, *f.* (law) devolution, restitution.—**d.
de derechos,** (com.) drawback; debenture.

devolutivo, a, (law) returnable, restorable.

devolver, *va.* (*pp.* DEVUELTO; *ind.* DEVUELVO;
subj. DEVUELVA) to return; to restore; to refund, pay back.

devoniano, na; devónico, ca, *a.* Devonian.

devorador, ra. I. *n.* devourer. **II.** *a.* devouring,
intense, ravenous.

devorante, *a.* = DEVORADOR.

devorar, *va.* to devour, swallow up, consume
ravenously, gobble.

devotamente, *adv.* devoutly, piously.

devotería, *f.* false devoutness, overreligiosity.

devoto, ta, *a.* devout, pious; strongly attached,
devoted.

devuelto, ta, *pp. irreg.* of DEVOLVER.

devuelvo, devuelva, *v.* V. DEVOLVER.

dexiocardia, *f.* (med.) dexiocardia.

dextrina, *f.* (chem.) dextrine.

dextro, *m.* area around a church.

dextrógiro, m. (chem.) dextrorotatory.

dextrórsum, *adv.* towards the right.

dextrosa, *f.* (chem.) dextrose.

dey, *m.* dey (a Moslem ruler).

deyección, *f.* (geol.) débris; (med.) dejection.

dezmable, *a.* subject to tithes.

dezmar, *va.* (*ind.* DIEZMO; *subj.* DIEZME) =
DIEZMAR.

dezmatorio, *m.* place where tithes are collected;
tithing.

dezmeño, ña; dezmero, ra. I. *a.* pertaining to
tithes. **II.** *m.* tither.

dezmería, *f.* tithe land.

¹di, *pret. irreg.* of DAR.

²di, *imper.* of DECIR.

día, *m.* day; daylight, sunshine.—**d. artificial,**
ordinary day, from sunrise to sunset.—**d.
de abstinencia** = D. DE AYUNO.—**d. de año
nuevo,** New Year's day.—**d. de años,** birthday.—**d. de ayuno,** fast day, fasting day.—**d.
de besamanos,** court day.—**d. de carne,**
meat day.—**d. de cumpleaños,** = D. DE
AÑOS.—**d. de cutio,** work day.—**d. de descanso,** day of rest, Sabbath.—**d. de fiesta,**
holiday.—**d. de gala,** court day; holiday; gala
day.—**d. de huelga,** day off (when no work is
done); (med.) intercalary day.—**d. del juicio,**
doomsday.—**d. de los difuntos,** All-Souls'
Day.—**d. de los Inocentes,** Innocents' Day.

—**d. de pescado** = D. DE AYUNO.—**d. de recibo**, reception day, at-home day.—**d. de trabajo**, working day.—**d. de viernes**, Meager Day.—**d. de vigilia** = D. DE AYUNO.—**d. diado**, appointed day.—**d. entre semana**, working day, week day.—**d. festivo** = D. DE FIESTA.—**d. intercalar**, intercalary day of February.—**d. laborable** = D. DE TRABAJO.—**d. medio**, mean day.—**d. natural** = D. ARTIFICIAL.—**d. onomástico**, a person's saint's day.—**d. pesado**, gloomy day.—**d. por medio**, every other day.—**d. quebrado**, half holiday.—**d. sidéreo**, sidereal day.—**d. útil** = D. DE TRABAJO.—**días caniculares**, dog days.—**días de gracia**, (com.) days of grace.—**días ha**, it is a long time since.—**a días**, at times, once in a while.—**al d.**, up to date; per day; by the day.—**al d. siguiente**, on the next day.—**a los pocos días**, a few days later.—**al otro d.**, on the following day.—**buenos días**, good morning.—**cada tercer d.** = UN D. SÍ Y OTRO NO.—**dar los días**, to send birthday congratulations.—**de d.**, by day, in the daytime.—**de d. en d.**, or de un d. para otro, from day to day.—**de hoy en ocho días**, this day week, a week from today.—**el d. de ayer**, yesterday.—**el d. de hoy**, or hoy en d., the present day, today.—**el d. menos pensado**, one of these days, when one least expects.—**el mejor d.**, some fine day.—**el otro d.**, the other day.—**en días de Dios**, en los días de la vida, never.—**en días pasados**, some days ago.—**en estos, or los últimos, días**, recently.—**en mis días**, in my day, in my lifetime.—**en su d.**, at the proper time.—**entre d.**, in the daytime.—**hasta el d. de hoy**, (up) to this day.—**hoy (en) d.**, nowadays.—**los días de uno**, one's saint's day or birthday.—**medio d.**, or mediodía, noon.—**ocho días**, a week.—**quince días**, two weeks, a fortnight.—**ser persona de días**, or tener días, to be of advanced age.—**todos los días**, daily, every day.—**un día sí y otro no**, day about, every other day.

diabasa, *f.* diorite, diabase, a kind of rock.
diabetes, *f.* diabetes.
diabético, ca, *a.* diabetic.
diabla, *f.* (coll.) she-devil.—**a la d.**, carelessly, roughly.—**cosido a la d.**, (bookbinding) bound in paper.
diablazo, *m. aug.* great devil.
diablear, *vn.* (coll.) to commit deviltries, play pranks.
diablejo, *m.* little devil, imp.
diablesa, *f.* (coll.) she-devil.
diablillo, *m. dim.* deviling, devilkin, little devil, imp; (coll.) smart, clever, mischievous fellow.—**d. cartesiano**, or de Descartes, (phys.) Cartesian diver.
diablo, *m.* devil, Satan; devil, a perverse, cunning, subtle or hideous person.—**¡d.!** the devil! the deuce!—**d. cojuelo**, artful devil.—**¡cómo diablos!**—(coll.) how the deuce.—**como un d.**, (coll.) like the deuce, like the devil.—**eso es el d.**, (coll.) that is the trouble.—**haber la de todos los diablos**, there to be (that is, *there* followed by the appropriate tense of *to be*) a great row or commotion.—**llevarse el d.**, to be ruined, fall through, be a fizzle.—**no valer un d.**, (coll.) to be good for nothing.—**pobre d.**, poor devil.—**¡qué d.!** or **¡un d.!** (coll.) the devil!—**ser de la piel del d.**, to be a limb of the devil.
diablura, *f.* diabolical undertaking; deviltry, mischief, wild prank.
diabólicamente, *adv.* diabolically, devilishly.
diabólico, ca, *a.* diabolical, devilish.
diábolo, *m.* diabolo, an old game.
diacatalicón, *m.* (med.) diacatholicon, a laxative.
diacitrón, *m.* lemon peel preserved in sugar.

diaconado, *m.* deaconship.
diaconal, *a.* diaconal.
diaconato, *m.* deaconship.
diaconía, *f.* deaconry.
diaconisa, *f.* deaconess.
diácono, *m.* deacon.
diacrítico, ca, *a.* (gram.) diacritical; (med.) diagnostic.
diacústica, *f.* diacoustics.
diadelfo, fa, *a.* (bot.) diadelphous.
diadema, *f.* diadem, crown; glory, halo.
diademado, da, *a.* (her.) diademed.
diafanidad, *f.* diaphaneity, transparency.
diáfano, na, *a.* transparent, clear, diaphanous.
diáfisis, *f.* (anat.) diaphysis.
diaforesis, *f.* (med.) diaphoresis, perspiration.
diaforético, ca, *a.* (med.) diaphoretic.
diafragma, *m.* (anat., mech., etc.) diaphragm.
diafragmático, ca, *a.* diaphragmatic.
diagnosis, *f.* (med.) diagnostics.
diagnosticar, *va.* (pret. DIAGNOSTIQUÉ; subj. DIAGNOSTIQUE) to diagnose.
diagnóstico, ca. I. *a.* (med.) diagnostic. **II.** *m.* diagnosis.
diagnostiqué, diagnostique, *v. V.* DIAGNOSTICAR.
diagonal. I. *a.* diagonal; oblique. **II.** *f.* (geom.) diagonal.
diagonalmente, *adv.* diagonally, obliquely.
diágrafo, *m.* diagraph.
diagrama, *m.* diagram.
dialage, *f.* (min.) diallage.
dialectal, *a.* dialect (as *a.*), pert. to dialects.
dialéctica, *f.* dialectics.
dialéctico, ca. I. *a.* dialectic, dialectical. **II.** *n.* dialectician, logician.
dialecto, *m.* dialect; derived language.
dialectología, *f.* dialectology, science or study of dialects.
dialisis, *f.* (chem.) dialysis.
dializador, ra, *n. & a.* (chem.) dialyzer(-ing).
dializar, *va.* (chem.) to dialyze.
dialogal, *a.* colloquial, dialogistic.
dialogar, *vn.* to dialogize; to chat, converse.
dialogismo, *m.* (rhet.) dialogism.
dialogístico, ca, *a.* colloquial, dialogistic.
dialogizar, *vn.* = DIALOGAR.
diálogo, *m.* dialogue.—**dialoguista**, *m.* dialogist.
dialtea, *f.* marsh mallow ointment.
diamagnético, ca, *n. & a.* (phys.) diamagnetic.
diamantado, da, *a.* diamondlike.
diamante, *m.* diamond; adamant.—**d. en bruto**, rough or uncut diamond; (coll.) an uncultured person of sterling qualities, "a rough diamond."
diamantífero, ra, *a.* diamantiferous, containing diamonds.
diamantino, na, *a.* adamantine, diamantine.
diamantista, *m.* diamond cutter; jeweller.
diametral, *a.* diametrical.
diametralmente, *adv.* diametrically.
diámetro, *m.* diameter.
diamina, *f.* (chem.) diamin.
diana, *f.* (mil.) reveille; (poet.) the moon.
dianche, *m. & interj.* (coll.) the deuce! the devil!
diandro, dra, *a.* (bot.) diandrous.
diantre, *m.* (coll.) = DIANCHE.
diapasón, *m.* (mus.) tuning fork; diapason; pitch, accord; regular octave.—**d. normal**, standard pitch.
diapédesis, *f.* (med.) diapedesis.
diapente, *m.* (mus.) perfect fifth.
diaplejía, *f.* (med.) general paralysis.
diapositiva, *f.* (photog.) plate; lantern slide.
diaprea, *f.* a sort of round plum.
diaquilón, *m.* (pharm.) diachylon, diachylum.
diariamente, *adv.* daily.
diario, ria. I. *a.* daily. **II.** *m.* journal, diary; daily newspaper; daily household expense.—**a d.**, *adv.* daily, every day.—**d. de navegación**, log

book.—**diarismo**, *m.* journalism.—**diarista**, *n.* journalist, diarist.

diarrea, *f.* diarrhea.

diarreico, ca; diárrico, ca, *a.* diarrheic.

diartrosis, *f.* (anat.) diarthrosis.

diascordio, *m.* (pharm.) diascordium.

diáspero, *m.* jasper.

diásporo, *m.* (min.) diaspore.

diastasa, *f.* (chem.) diastase.

diastasis, *f.* (surg.) diastasis.

diástilo, *a.* (arch.) diastyle.

diástole, *m.* (anat. and rhet.) diastole.

diatérmano, na; diatérmico, ca, *f.* (phys.) diathermanous.

diatermia, *f.* diathermy.

diatesarón, *m.* (mus.) diatessaron.

diatésico, ca, *a.* (med.) diathetic.

diátesis, *f.* (med.) diathesis.

diatómico, ca, *a.* (chem.) diatomic.

diatónicamente, *adv.* (mus.) diatonically.

diatónico, *a.* (mus.) diatonic.

diatriba, *f.* diatribe.

dibujador, ra, *n.* draftsman(-woman).

dibujante. I. *a.* sketching. II. *m.* draftsman.

dibujar. I. *va.* to draw, make a drawing of; to depict, describe vividly. II. *vr.* to throw a shadow upon a surface.

dibujo, *m.* drawing; sketch; portrayal, description.—**d. a pulso**, freehand drawing.—**d. del natural**, drawing from life or from nature.—**d. lineal**, instrumental drawing.

dicacidad, *f.* pertness, sauciness, banter.

dicaz, *a.* (of speech) keen, biting.

dicción, *f.* diction, style, language.

diccionario, *m.* dictionary.

diccionarista, *n.* lexicographer.

dicente, diciente, *a.* saying, talking.

diciembre, *m.* December.

diciendo, *ger.* of DECIR.

diclinismo, *n.* (bot.) diclinism.

diclino, na, *a.* (bot.) diclinous.

dicotiledón; dicotiledóneo, a. I. *a.* (bot.) dicotyledonous. II. *n.* dicotyledon. III. *f. pl.* Dicotyledones.

dicotomía, *f.* dichotomy.

dicotómico, ca; dicótomo, ma, *a.* dichotomic, dichotomous.

dicroico, ca, *a.* (phys.) dichroic.

dicroísmo, *n.* (phys.) dichroism.

dictado, *m.* title of dignity or honor; dictation.—*pl.* dictates, promptings.

dictador, ra, *n.* dictator.

dictadura, *f.* dictatorship.

dictamen, *m.* opinion, judgment; suggestion, insinuation, advice.—**dictaminar**, *vn.* to express an opinion, pass judgment.

dictamo, *m.* (bot.) dittany.—**d. bastardo**, shrubby white horehound.—**d. blanco**, or **real**, white flaxinella.—**d. crético**, marjoram.

dictar, *va.* to dictate; to command, prescribe, direct; to inspire, suggest, prompt.

dictatorial, *a.* dictatorial.

dictatorialmente, *adv.* dictatorially.

dictatorio, ria, *a.* dictatorial.

dicterio, *m.* taunt, keen reproach; insult.

dicha, *f.* happiness, good, luck, good fortune.—**a d.**, or **por d.**, *adv.* by chance.

dicharachero, ra, *a.* (coll.) that uses slang.

dicharacho, *m.* (coll.) vulgar, low, or slang expression.

dichero, ra, *a.* witty.

dicho, cha. I. *pp. irreg.* of DECIR.—**d. se está**, it goes without saying.—**d. y hecho**, no sooner said than done. II. *a.* (the) said, mentioned; this.—**lo d., d.**, I mean what I say, I have said it; it's agreed. III. *m.* saying, saw, proverb; expression, sentence; statement; witty remark, repartee; declaration, deposition; promise of marriage.—**d. de las gentes**, gossip; rumor.—**del d. al hecho hay gran trecho**, it is a long

way from saying to doing; it is one thing to say, and quite another thing to do.

dichosamente, *adv.* happily, fortunately.

dichoso, sa, *a.* happy; fortunate, lucky.

didáctica, *f.* didactics.

didácticamente, *adv.* didactically.

didáctico, ca; didascálico, ca, *a.* didactic, didactical.

didelfo, fa, *n. & a.* (zool.) didelphian (as the kangaroo or the opossum).

didimio, *m.* (chem.) didymium.

dídimo, ma, *a.* (bot.) didymous.

diecinueve, *n. & a.* nineteen; nineteenth.

diecinueveavo, va, *n. & a.* nineteenth.

dieciochavo, va, *n. & a.* eighteenth.

dieciocheno, na. I. *a.* eighteenth. II. *m.* a kind of cloth.

dieciocho, *n. & a.* eighteen; eighteenth.

dieciseis, *n. & a.* sixteen; sixteenth.

dieciseisavo, va, *n. & a.* sixteenth.

dieciseiseno, na, *a.* sixteenth.

diecisiete, *n. & a.* seventeen; seventeenth.

diecisieteavo, va, *n. & a.* seventeenth.

diedro, dra. I. *a.* (math.) dihedral. II. *m.* dihedral angle.

dieléctrico, ca, *a.* dielectric.

diente, *m.* tooth; fang or tusk of wild boars or elephants; tooth (of a saw, comb, rake, file); cog (of a wheel or pinion); tine or prong (of a fork); tongue (of a buckle); clove (of garlic).—*pl.* indented edges of tools or ornaments, indentations.—**d. de leche**, milk, first tooth.—**d. de león**, (bot.) dandelion or lion's tooth.—**d. de lobo**, burnisher, spike.—**d. de perro**, sculptor's dented chisel; (bot.) dog-tooth violet.—**d. incisivo**, incisor, cutting tooth, foretooth.—**d. mamón**, = D. DE LECHE.—**d. molar**, molar tooth, back tooth.—**dientes caninos**, eye teeth, canine teeth.—**dientes postizos**, false teeth.—**aguzar los dientes**, to whet the appetite.—**a regaña dientes**, *adv.* most unwillingly.—**dar d. con d.**, to shiver with cold or fear, to be with teeth chattering.—**decir**, or **hablar, entre dientes**, to mumble, to mutter.—**de dientes afuera**, without sincerity, as mere lip service.—**tener buen d.**, to be a hearty eater.

dientecico, illo, ito, *m. dim.* little tooth.

diento, diente, *v. V.* DENTAR.

diéresis, *f.* diæresis.

diesi, *f.* (mus.) diesis; a sharp.

diestra, *f.* right hand; favor, support.

diestramente, *adv.* skilfully, cleverly, neatly.

diestro, tra. I. *a.* right; dexterous, able, skilful, handy; dexter; sagacious, wise; sly, artful, cunning; favorable, propitious.—**a d. y siniestro**, recklessly; right and left. II. *m.* skilful fencer; bullfighter; halter or bridle.

¹**dieta**, *f.* diet, prescribed or regulated meals.—*pl.* (naut.) provisions for the sick and wounded.

²**dieta**, *f.* diet, legislative assembly; (law) one day's journey of ten leagues by land; daily salary of judges and other officers of the law; daily fees paid a physician.—*pl.* allowance to public functionary while serving away from his residence.

dietario, *m.* family account book; record book, book where notable events are registered.

dietética, *f.* (med.) dietetics.

dietético, ca, *a.* dietetic, dietetical.

diez, *m. & a.* ten; tenth.—**d. de bolos**, pin standing alone in front of the ninepins.—*pl. f.* **las diez**, ten o'clock.

diezmador, *m.* = DIEZMERO.

diezmal, *a.* decimal.

diezmar, *va.* (of war, disease, etc.) to decimate; to tithe; (mil.) to punish one in ten of.

diezmero, *m.* one who pays or receives tithes.

diezmesino, na, *a.* ten months old.

diezmilésimo, ma, *n. & a.* ten-thousandth.

diezmilímetro, *m.* ten-thousandth of a meter.

diezmillonésimo, ma, *n.* & *a.* ten-millionth.

diezmo, *m.* tithe; tenth part; duty of ten per cent; decimation.

difamación, *f.* defamation

difamador, ra, *n.* & *a.* defamer(-ing).

difamar, *va.* to defame, to discredit.—**difamatorio, ria,** *a.* defamatory.

difarreación, *f.* (Rom. hist.) diffarreation.

diferencia, *f.* difference, dissimilarity; disagreement; (math.) difference.—**a d. de,** unlike; as distinguished from.

diferenciación, *f.* (biol., math., etc.) differentiation.

diferencial. I. *a.* differential. **II.** *m.* (auto) differential. **III.** *f.* (math.) differential.

diferenciar. I. *va.* to differentiate, distinguish between; to alter the use or destination of. **II.** *vn.* to differ, dissent, disagree. **III.** *vr.* to differ, to be different; to distinguish oneself.

diferente, *a.* different.

diferentemente, *adv.* differently.

diferido, da. I. *pp.* of DIFERIR. **II.** *a.* deferred (cablegram).

diferir. I. *va.* (*ind.* DIFIERO; *subj.* DIFIERA) to defer, postpone, put off; to adjourn, suspend; to protract, prolong, extend. **II.** *vn.* to differ, be different; (naut.) to remove the gaskets of a sail.

difícil, *a.* difficult, hard.

difícilmente, *adv.* with difficulty.

dificultad, *f.* difficulty; objection.

dificultador, ra. I. *n.* one who raises difficulties. **II.** *a.* causing difficulties.

dificultar, *va.* to make difficult; to impede.

dificultosamente, *adv.* with difficulty.

dificultoso, sa, *a.* difficult, hard; (coll.) ugly, homely.

difidación, *f.* declaration of war.

difidencia, *f.* diffidence; distrust.

difidente, *a.* distrustful; diffident.

difiero, difiera, *v.* V. DIFERIR.

difilo, la, *a.* (bot.) two-leaf.

difluencia, *f.* diffluence.

difluente, *a.* diffluent.

difluir, *vn.* (*ger.* DIFLUYENDO; *ind. pres.* DIFLUYO, *pret.* él DIFLUYÓ; *subj.* DIFLUYA) to be diffused or spread out.

difracción, *f.* diffraction.

difrangente, *a.* diffractive.

difteria, *f.* (med.) diphtheria.

diftérico, ca, *a.* diphtheritic.

difteritis, *f.* (med.) diphtheritic inflammation.

difundido, da. I. *pp.* of DIFUNDIR. **II.** *a.* diffuse, diffused, scattered.

difundir, *va.* to diffuse, spread out; to spread (as news); to divulge, publish; (radio) to broadcast.

difunto, ta. I. *a.* defunct, deceased, dead; late; decayed, withered. **II.** *m.* & *f.* corpse.

difusamente, *adv.* diffusely, diffusedly.

difusible, *a.* diffusible.

difusión, *f.* diffusion; diffusiveness, dispersion; exuberance of style; (radio) broadcasting.

difusivo, va, *a.* diffusive.

difuso, sa, *a.* diffuse; wordy; wide-spread.

difusor, ra. I. *a.* difusing, defusive; (radio) broadcasting. **II.** *m.* (sugar manufact.) diffuser. **III.** *f.* broadcasting station.

diga, digo, *v.* V. DECIR.

digástrico, ca, *a.* (anat.) digastric.

digerible, *a.* digestible.

digerir, *va.* (*ind.* DIGIERO; *subj.* DIGIERA) to digest; to bear; to put up with; (chem.) to digest.

digestibilidad, *f.* digestibility.

digestible, *a.* digestible.

digestión, *f.* (physiol. and chem.) digestion.

digestivo, va. I. *a.* digestive. **II.** *m.* (surg.) suppurative.

digesto, *m.* (law) digest, systematic compilation of laws.

digestor, *m.* digester (apparatus).

digiero, digiera, *v.* V. DIGERIR.

digitación, *f.* fingering.

digitado, da, *a.* (bot. and zool.) digitate.

digital. I. *a.* digital, finger (as *a.* as in *impresión digital,* fingerprint). **II.** *f.* (bot.) digitalis, foxglove.

digitalina, *f.* (chem.) digitalin.

digitígrado, da, *a.* (zool.) digitigrade.

dígito, ta. I. *a.* digital. **II.** *m.* (astr., arith.) digit.

dignación, *f.* condescension, accommodation.

dignamente, *adv.* worthily; with dignity.

dignarse, *vr.* to condescend, deign, vouchsafe.

dignatario, *m.* dignitary.

dignidad, *f.* dignity, high rank, office or position; honor, greatness; dignified bearing; archbishop or bishop.

dignificante, *a.* (theol.) dignifying.

dignificar, *va.* to dignify.

digno, na, *a.* meritorious, worthy, deserving; worthwhile; suitable, fit, fitting, appropriate.

digo, diga, *v.* V. DECIR.—¡**digo**!, listen! say!—**digo,** I mean (clarifying or amending a previous statement).

digresión, *f.* digression; (astr.) digression.

digresivamente, *adv.* digressively.

digresivo, va, *a.* digressive.

dihueñe, dihueñi, *m.* (Chile) an edible fungus growing on trees.

dij, dije, *m.* amulet, charm; trinket; watchcharm; any small piece of jewellery; (coll.) person of sterling qualities; (coll.) one gorgeously attired; (coll.) handy person.

dije, dijo, *v.* V. DECIR.

dilaceración, *f.* dilaceration, tearing apart.

dilacerar, *va.* to dilacerate, tear asunder.

dilación, *f.* delay, procrastination.

dilapidación, *f.* dilapidation.

dilapidador, ra, *n.* dilapidator.

dilapidar, *va.* to dilapidate.

dilatabilidad, *f.* expansibility.

dilatable, *a.* dilatable, expansible.

dilatación, *f.* dilatation, expansion, distention; prolongation; enlargement; diffuseness, prolixity; calmness, serenity in sorrow; (phys., etc.) expansion.—**d. lineal,** linear expansion.

dilatadamente, *adv.* dilatedly; with delay or procrastination.

dilatado, da. I. *pp.* of DILATAR. **II.** *a.* large, extended, extensive, vast; drawn out.

dilatador, ra. I. *a.* dilating, expanding; retarding, causing delay. **II.** *m.* (surg.) dilator.

dilatar. I. *va.* & *vr.* to dilate, widen, expand, enlarge, lengthen, prolong; to swell, spread out; to defer, retard, delay, put off, protract; (fig.) to comfort, to cheer up. **II.** *vr.* to be diffuse, expatiate; to expand; to delay, tarry.

dilatativo, va, *a.* dilative.

dilatoria, *f.* delay, waste of time.

dilatorio, ria, *a.* dilatory, delaying, long.

dilección, *f.* dilection, love, affection.

dilecto, ta, *a.* loved, beloved.

dilema, *m.* dilemma.

dilemático, ca, *a.* dilemmatic.

diligencia, *f.* diligence, assiduity, industriousness; action, measure (to carry out something); speediness, activity, briskness; diligence, stagecoach; (coll.) affair, business, errand; (law) judicial proceeding.—**hacer d.,** or **la d.,** to endeavor, try.—**hacer una d.,** to do an errand; to attend, or go on, some business.

diligenciar, *va.* to conduct, to carry out; to further.

diligenciero, *m.* agent, attorney.

diligente, *a.* diligent, assiduous; prompt, swift.

diligentemente, *adv.* diligently, assiduously.

dilogía, *f.* ambiguity, double sense.

dilucidación, *f.* elucidation, explanation.

dilucidador, ra, *n.* elucidator.

dilucidar, *va.* to elucidate, explain, discuss.

dilucidario, *m.* explanatory writing.

dilución, *f.* dilution.

diluente, *a.* diluent.

diluir, *va.* & *vr.* (*ger.* DILUYENDO; *ind. pres.* DILUYO, *pret.* él DILUYÓ; *subj.* DILUYA) to dilute; to weaken.

diluvial, *a.* (geol.) diluvial.

diluviano, *a.* diluvian.

diluviar, *vn. impers.* to rain heavily.

diluvio, *m.* flood, deluge; overflow, inundation; (coll.) vast abundance, a lot, lots.

diluyendo, diluyó, etc. *v.* V. DILUIR.

diluyente, *n.* & *a.* diluent.

dimanación, *f.* springing or issuing.

dimanante, *a.* springing, originating.

dimanar, *vn.* (**de**) to spring or proceed (from); to originate (in); to be due (to); to follow (from).

dimensión, *f.* dimension; extent, capacity, magnitude, size.—**dimensional,** *a.* dimensional.

dimes, *m. pl.*—**andar en d. y diretes,** to haggle, chaffer, quibble, argue.

dimetilo, *m.* (chem.) dimethyl.

dimidiar, *va.* to dimidiate, to halve.

diminución, *f.* diminution.—**ir en d.,** to taper (as a pole); to be diminishing or becoming less or lower.

diminuir, *va., vn.* & *vr.* = DISMINUIR, diminish.

diminutamente, *adv.* diminutively; minutely; by retail.

diminutivamente, *adv.* (gram.) diminutively.

diminutivo, va. I. *a.* diminishing; diminutive. **II.** *m.* (gram.) diminutive.

diminuto, ta, *a.* diminutive, very little or small.

dimisión, *f.* resignation (of membership, office).

dimisorias, *f. pl.* (eccl.) letters dimissory; (coll.) dismissal or discharge, "firing."

dimitente, *n.* & *a.* (one) resigning.

dimitir, *va.* to resign, give up, relinquish.

dimorfismo, *m.* (min.) dimorphism.

dimorfo, fa, *a.* (min.) dimorphous.

din, *m.* (coll. for DINERO) money, boodle.

dina, *f.* (phys.) dyne.

dinamarques, sa, *n.* & *a.* Dane, Danish.

dinamia, *f.* kilogrammeter per unit of time (a unit of power).

dinámica, *f.* dynamics.

dinámico, ca, *a.* dynamic.

dinamismo, *m.* dynamism.

dinamista, *n.* & *a.* dynamist(-ic).

dinamita, *f.* dynamite.

dinamitero, ra, *n.* dynamiter.

dínamo, *f.* (gen. *m.* in Am.) dynamo.

dinamoeléctrico, ca, *a.* dynamo-electric.

dinamométrico, ca, *a.* dynamometric.

dinamómetro, *m.* dynamometer.

dinasta, *m.* dynast, sovereign, monarch.

dinastía, *f.* dynasty.

dinástico, ca, *a.* dynastic, dynastical.

dinastismo, *m.* fealty to a dynasty.

dinerada, *f.* large sum of money.

dineral, *m.* large sum of money; formerly, a set of weights for gold and silver.

dinerillo, *m.* small copper coin; (coll.) small sum of money.

dinero, *m.* money; currency, coin; gold, coinage; ancient Spanish silver coin; standard of silver, 24 grains; Peruvian silver coin; wealth, fortune.—**d. contante, d. contante y sonante, d. efectivo,** or **d. en tabla,** ready money, cash.—**d. suelto,** small change.—**persona de d.,** person of means, or well off.

dineroso, sa, *a.* moneyed, rich.

dineruelo, *m. dim.* small coin; a little money, some money.

dingo, *m.* dingo, Australian wild dog.

dinornis, *m.* (paleontol.) dinornis, moa.

dinosauro, *m.* (paleontol.) dinosaur.—*pl.* Dinosauria.

dinoterio, *m.* (paleontol.) dinothere, dinotherium.

dintel, *m.* (arch.) lintel, doorhead.

dintelar, *va.* to provide with lintels.

dintorno, *m.* (art) within the contour.

diocesano, na. I. *a.* diocesan. **II.** *m.* diocesan, bishop.

diócesi, diócesis, *f.* diocese.

dioico, ca, *a.* (bot.) diœcious.

dionisia, *f.* bloodstone; hematite.

dionisíaco, ca, *a.* Dionysiac, Bacchic.

dioptria, *f.* (opt.) diopter.

dióptrica, *f.* (opt.) dioptrics.

dióptrico, ca, *a.* (opt.) dioptric.

diorama, *m.* diorama.

diorámico, ca, *a.* dioramic.

diorita, *f.* diorite, a kind of rock.

dios, *m.* god; (D-) God.—D. delante, with God's help.—D. es D., as sure as God lives; by Jupiter!—D. es grande, trust in God; all things are possible.—D. le guarde, God be with you.—D. lo haga, or lo quiera, God grant.—D. los hace y ellos se juntan, birds of a feather flock together.—D. mediante, God willing, with God's help.—D. me (nos) libre, God forbid, God protect or deliver me (us).—¡D. mío! my God! goodness me! oh my!—anda con D., farewell, adieu.—la, or las, de D. es Cristo, turmoil, bedlam, row.—mediante D., God willing.—no lo quiera D., God forbid.—plegue a D., or quiera D., God grant.—¡por D.! for Heaven's sake! goodness!—sabe D., goodness knows, only God knows.—sea como D. quiera, be it as God wishes.—¡válgame D.! bless me!—¡válgate D.! God preserve, or bless, you!—vaya Vd. con D., good-bye; go on; off with you, begone.—¡vive D.! as sure as God lives; by God! by Heaven!

diosa, *f.* goddess.

diostedé, *m.* S. A. bird like the toucan.

diploma, *m.* diploma; bull, patent, license; title, credential.—**diplomacia,** *f.* diplomacy.

diplomática, *f.* diplomacy; (archæol.) diplomatics.

diplomaticamente, *adv.* diplomatically; tactfully.

diplomático, ca. I. *a.* diplomatic; (archæol.) diplomatic. **II.** *m.* diplomatist, diplomat.

diplopia, *f.* (med.) diplopia, seeing double.

dipsáceo, a. I. *a.* (bot.) dipsacaceous. **II.** *f. pl.* Dipsacaceæ.

dipsomanía, *f.* dipsomania, craving for liquor.

dipsomaníaco, ca, *a.* & *n.* dipsomaniac(-al).

díptero, ra. I. *a.* (arch.) having two wings or a double colonnade; (entom.) dipterous. **II.** *m. pl.* Diptera.

dipterocárpeo, a. I. *a.* (bot.) dipterocarpaceous. **II.** *f. pl.* Dipterocarpaceæ.

díptica, f., díptico, *m.* diptych.

diptongación, *f.* (gram.) diphthongization.

diptongar, *va.* to diphthongize.

diptongo, *m.* diphthong.

diputación, *f.* deputation; object of a deputation.

diputado, da. I. *pp.* of DIPUTAR. **II.** *m.* deputy, representative, delegate; (com.) assignee.—**d. a Cortes,** congressman.—**d. cunero,** (coll.) congressman who owes his election to the influence of the government.

diputador, ra, *n.* & *a.* constituent.

diputar, *va.* to depute, delegate, commission; to constitute, empower.

dique, *m.* dike, dam, mole, jetty; (naut.) dry dock; check, bar, stop; (min.) crop.

dirección, *f.* direction, course, tendency, trend, turn; direction, management, administration; order, command, instruction; address (for letters, etc.); board of directors, executive board; editorship of a newspaper; managership of a theater; office of a director.

directamente, *adv.* directly, in a direct manner.

directivo, va. I. *a.* directive, managing. **II.** *f.* governing board, board of directors, management.

directo, ta, *a.* direct; straight.

director, ra. I. *n.* & *a.* director(-ing). **II.** *n.* director, manager; chief; editor (of a newspaper); principal (of a school).—**d. de escena,** stage manager.—**d. de orquesta,** conductor, leader of an orchestra.—**d. espiritual,** father confessor.—**directoral,** *a.* directorial.

directorio, ria. I. *a.* directive, directorial. **II.** *m.* directory; body of directors, directorate.

directriz, *f.* (math.) directrix.

dirigente. I. *a.* directing, leading; ruling. **II.** *m.* & *f.* leader.

dirigible. I. *a.* dirigible; manageable; (aer.) dirigible. **II.** *m.* (aer.) dirigible.

dirigir. I. *va.* (*ind.* DIRIJO; *subj.* DIRIJA) to direct; to dedicate (a work); to address (a letter, etc.); to command, lead, head; to govern, control, manage; (naut.) to steer.—**d. la palabra,** to speak (to), address. **II.** *vr.* (a) to address, speak (to); to apply, resort (to); to go (to or toward).

dirimente, *a.* breaking off, dissolving.

dirimible, *a.* that may be broken off.

dirimir, *va.* to dissolve, disjoin, separate; to annul, to declare void; to adjust, reconcile.

dirruir, *va.* to ruin, destroy.

disanto, *m.* holy day.

discantar, *va.* to chant, sing; to comment; to descant, discourse much about; (mus.) to sing in counterpoint.—**discante,** *m.* small guitar; concert, especially of string instruments.

disceptación, *f.* argument, controversy.

disceptar, *vn.* to dispute, argue.

discernidor, ra, *n.* & *a.* discerner(-ing).

discerniente, *a.* discerning.

discernimiento, *m.* discernment, judgment, discrimination; (law) appointment of a guardian.

discernir, *va.* (*ind.* DISCIERNO; *subj.* DISCIERNA) to discern, judge, discriminate; (law) to appoint (a guardian).

disciplina, *f.* discipline; education, instruction; systematic training; any art or science taught; rule of conduct, order.—*pl.* scourge, cat-of-nine-tails; flagellation.

disciplinable, *a.* disciplinable.

disciplinadamente, *adv.* with discipline.

disciplinado, da. I. *pp.* of DISCIPLINAR. **II.** *a.* disciplined, trained; marbled, variegated (as flowers).

disciplinal, *a.* disciplinal, disciplinary.

disciplinante. I. *a.* disciplinary; Disciplinant. **II.** *n.* Disciplinant.

disciplinar. I. *va.* to discipline, educate, instruct, train; (mil.) to drill. **II.** *vr.* to scourge oneself as penance.

disciplinario, ria, *a.* disciplinary.

disciplinazo, *m.* lashing; whipping.

discipulado, *m.* discipleship; education, instruction; group of pupils.

discipular, *a.* pertaining to a disciple or pupil.

discípulo, la, *n.* disciple; follower; pupil, student.

disco, *m.* disk; a quoit; solid wheel; circular plate (glass, metal, etc.); discus; (astr.) disk.—**d. de señales,** (Ry.) signal disk; semaphore.—**d. (fonográfico),** (phonograph) record.

discóbolo, *m.* discobolus, discus thrower.

discoidal, discoide, discoideo, a, *a.* disk-like, flat and round.

díscolo, la, *a.* ungovernable; wayward, froward.

discoloro, ra, *a.* (bot.) colorless.

disconforme, -midad = DESCONFORME, etc.

discontinuación, *f.* discontinuation.

discontinuar, *va.* to discontinue, to stop.

discontinuo, a, *a.* discontinuous.

disconveniencia, -niente, -nir, = DESCON-VENIENCIA, -NIENTE, -NIR.

discordancia, *f.* disagreement, discordance.

discordante, *a.* dissonant, discordant.

discordar, *vn.* (*ind.* DISCUERDO; *subj.* DISCUERDE) to be in discord, disagree.

discorde, *a.* discordant; (mus.) dissonant.

discordia, *f.* discord, disagreement, discordance, opposition, clash.

discrasia, *f.* (med.) cacochymy.

discreción, *f.* discretion, judgment; acuteness of mind, sagacity; liberty of action and decision. —**a d.,** optional; (mil.) unconditionally.

discrecional, *a.* optional, discretionary.

discrecionalmente, *adv.* optionally, discretionarily.

discrepancia, *f.* discrepancy.

discrepante, *a.* disagreeing, discrepant.

discrepar, *vn.* to differ, to disagree.

discretamente, *adv.* discreetly.

discretear, *vn.* to affect discretion.

discreteo, *m.* affected discretion.

discreto, ta, *a.* discreet, circumspect, prudent; fairly good, not bad; ingenious, sharp, witty; (math.) (of quantity) discrete; (med.) discrete (as smallpox pustules).

discrimen, *m.* hazard, risk, peril; difference.

discriminador, ra, *n.* & *a.* (Am.) discriminator (-ing, -ive).

discriminar, *va.* (Am.) to discriminate.

discuerdo, discuerde, *v.* *V.* DISCORDAR.

disculpa, *f.* apology, excuse; exculpation.

disculpabilidad, *f.* excusability; pardonableness.

disculpable, *a.* excusable; pardonable.

disculpablemente, *adv.* pardonably, excusably.

disculpadamente, *adv.* excusably.

disculpar, *va.* & *vr.* to exculpate; to excuse; to apologize.

discurrir. I. *vn.* to roam, ramble about; to flow (as a river); to reflect, think; to reason; to discourse. **II.** *va.* to invent, plan, contrive; to conjecture, infer.

discursante, *n.* discourser, lecturer.

discursar, *vn.* (**sobre** or **acerca de**) to discourse (on); to treat (of); to lecture (on).

discursear, *vn.* (coll. and contempt.) to harangue, to make a speech.

discursista, *m.* speech maker.

discursivo, va, *a.* discursive; thoughtful, meditative, cogitative.

discurso, *m.* discourse; cogitation, ratiocination, reasoning; speech, lecture, oration; dissertation, treatise, tract; conversation, talk; space of time.

discusión, *f.* discussion.

discutible, *a.* controvertible, disputable.

discutidor, ra, *n.* & *a.* arguer(-ing).

discutir, *va.* & *vn.* to discuss; to argue about.

disecación, *f.* = DISECCIÓN.

disecador, ra, *n.* dissector; taxidermist.

disecar, *va.* (*pret.* DISEQUÉ; *subj.* DISEQUE) to dissect; to do an autopsy on; to stuff (dead animals).

disección, *f.* dissection, anatomy.

disector, ra, *n.* dissector.

diseminación, *f.* dissemination; scattering, spreading.

diseminador, ra, *n.* & *a.* disseminator(-ing); spreader(-ing).

diseminar, *va.* to disseminate; spread, scatter.

disensión, *f.* dissent; contest, strife.

disenso, *m.* dissent, disagreement.

disentería, *f.* (med.) dysentery.

disentérico, ca, *a.* dysenteric.

disentimiento, *m.* dissent, disagreement.

disentir, *vn.* (*ger.* DISINTIENDO; *ind. pres.* DISIENTO, *pret.* él DISINTIÓ; *subj.* DISIENTA) to dissent, to disagree, to differ.

diseñador, ra, *n.* designer, delineator.

diseñar, *va.* to draw; to sketch, outline.

diseño, *m.* sketch, plan, outline; portrayal, description.

disertación, *f.* dissertation, disquisition.

disertador, ra; disertante, *n.* & *a.* discourser (-ing), expounder(-ing).

disertar, *vn.* (**sobre** or **acerca de**) to discourse (on), treat (of), discuss.

diserto, ta, *a.* eloquent, fluent.

disfagia, *f.* (med.) dysphagia.

disfamación, *f.* defamation.

disfamador, ra, *n.* & *a.* defamer(-ing).

disfamar, *va.* to defame.

disfamatorio, ria, *a.* defamatory.

disfasia, *f.* (med.) dysphasia.

disfavor, *m.* disregard, disfavor.

disforme, *a.* deformed, hideous; huge, big.

disformidad, *f.* deformity; excessive bigness.

disfracé, disfrace, *v. V.* DISFRAZAR.

disfraz, *m.* mask, costume, disguise; dissimulation, dissembling.

disfrazar. I. *va.* (*pret.* DISFRACÉ; *subj.* DISFRACE) to disguise; to misrepresent. **II.** *vr.* to disguise oneself; to masquerade; to travesty.

disfrutar. I. *va.* to benefit by; to have the benefit of; to enjoy (good health, etc.). **II.** *vn.* **d. de,** to enjoy, to have.—**disfrute,** *m.* use, benefit.

disgregable, *a.* separable.

disgregación, *f.* separation, disjunction; disintegration, dissociation.

disgregar, *va.* (*pret.* DISGREGUÉ; *subj.* DISGREGUE) to separate, disjoin, disperse.

disgregativo, va, *a.* disjunctive.

disgregué, disgregue, *v. V.* DISGREGAR.

disgustadamente, *adv.* with displeasure.

disgustar. I. *va.* to displease; to dislike (diff. constr.: *esto me disgusta,* I dislike this); to offend; to anger. **II.** *vr.* to be (get) displeased, hurt or angry; to fall out (with each other).

disgustillo, *m. dim.* displeasure, slight unpleasantness or difference.

disgusto, *m.* disgust, loathing; ill humor; displeasure; unpleasantness, quarrel; vexation, annoyance; grief sorrow.—**a d.,** against one's will.—**estar a d.,** to be ill at ease, uncomfortable.

disidencia, *f.* dissidence, nonconformity.

disidente, *a.* & *n.* dissident, dissenter(-ing), nonconformist.

disidir, *vn.* to dissent, disagree.

disiento, disienta, *v. V.* DISENTIR.

disílabo, ba, *a.* & *n.* dissyllable(-ic).

disimetría, *f.* dissymmetry, lack of symmetry.

disimétrico, ca, *a.* dissymmetric, unsymmetric.

disímil, disimilar, *a.* dissimilar.

disimilitud, *f.* unlikeness.

disimulable, *a.* that may be dissembled; excusable.

disimulación, *f.* dissimulation, dissembling.

disimuladamente, *adv.* dissemblingly, on the sly, on the quiet.

disimulado, da. I. *pp.* of DISIMULAR. **II.** *a.* dissembling; reserved, sullen; sly, cunning.—**hacer la d.,** (coll.) to feign ignorance.

disimulador, ra, *n.* & *a.* dissembler(-ing).

disimular, *va.* to dissimulate, dissemble; to feign, pretend; to tolerate, overlook, let pass; to misrepresent.

disimulo, *m.* dissimulation; tolerance.

disintiendo, disintió, *v. V.* DISENTIR.

disipable, *a.* easily scattered; capable of being dissipated.

disipación, *f.* dissipation; dispersion, scattering; evanescence; extravagance, waste.

disipado, da. I. *pp.* of DISIPAR. **II.** *a.* dissipated; prodigal; dissolute.

disipador, ra, *n.* & *a.* squanderer(-ing); spendthrift.

disipar. I. *va.* & *vr.* to dissipate, to disperse, to scatter (as clouds). **II.** *va.* to squander, misspend, lavish; to drive away; to dispel.

dislate, *m.* nonsense, absurdity.

dislocación, dislocadura, *f.* dislocation; sprain; (min.) slide.

dislocar, *va.* & *vr.* (*pret.* DISLOQUÉ; *subj.* DISLOQUE) to dislocate, displace, sprain, disjoint.

dismembración, *f.* = DESMEMBRACIÓN.

dismenorrea, *f.* (med.) dysmenorrhœa.

disminución, *f.* DIMINUCIÓN, diminution; (vet.) a disease in horses' hoofs.

disminuir. I. *va.* (*ger.* DISMINUYENDO; *ind. pres.* DISMINUYO, *pret.* él DISMINUYÓ; *subj.* DISMINUYA) to diminish, lessen, lower, decrease; to detract from. **II.** *vr.* to diminish, decrease.

disnea, *f.* (med.) dyspnœa.—**disneico, ca,** *a.* dyspnœic.

disociación, *f.* separation, dissociation.

disociar, *va.* to dissociate, separate.

disolubilidad, *f.* dissolubility; solubility.

disoluble, *a.* dissoluble.

disolución, *f.* dissolution, disintegration; (chem.) dissolution; solution; dissoluteness, dissipation.—**d. de sociedad,** dissolution of partnership.

disolutamente, *adv.* dissolutely, licentiously.

disolutivo, va, *a.* solvent.

disoluto, ta, *a.* dissolute, loose, dissipated.

disolvente, *m.* dissolvent, dissolver.

disolver. I. *va.* (*pp. irreg.* DISUELTO; *ind.* DISUELVO; *subj.* DISUELVA) to loosen, untie; to dissolve, break up (as a meeting); to separate, disunite; (phys., chem.) to dissolve. **II.** *vr.* to dissolve.

disón, *m.* (mus.) discord.

disonancia, *f.* harsh sound; disagreement, discord; (mus.) dissonance.

disonante, *a.* dissonant, inharmonious; discordant, unsuitable.

disonar, *vn.* (*ind.* DISUENO; *subj.* DISUENE) to disagree in sound, to be inharmonious; to be discordant, to disagree.

dísono, na, *a.* dissonant, inharmonious.

dispar, *a.* unlike, unequal, unmatched.

disparada, *f.* (Am.) sudden and hasty start; flight.—**a la d.,** at full speed; hurriedly and recklessly.—**de una d.,** promptly; at once.

disparadamente, *adv.* hurriedly.

disparadero, *m.* trigger (on firearms).

disparador, *m.* shooter; trigger; ratchet or ratchet wheel, in clockwork; (naut.) anchor tripper.

disparar. I. *va.* & *vn.* to shoot, discharge, fire; let off; to cast or throw with violence. **II.** *vn.* (coll.) to talk nonsense, to blunder. **III.** *vr.* to run headlong, to rush; to run away (as a horse); (naut.) to turn violently (as the capstan); to go off (as a gun).

disparatadamente, *adv.* blunderingly; absurdly, nonsensically.

disparatado, da. I. *pp.* of DISPARATAR. **II.** *a.* absurd, foolish, nonsensical.

disparatador, ra, *n.* nonsensical talker.

disparatar, *vn.* to act absurdly; to talk nonsense; to blunder.—**disparate,** *m.* blunder, mistake; absurdity, nonsense.

disparatero, ra, *n.* (Am.) bungler; one who "talks through his hat."

disparatorio, *m.* nonsensical or blundering act, speech or writing.

disparejo, ja, *a.* uneven.

disparidad, *f.* disparity, inequality.

disparo, *m.* discharge, explosion; nonsense, absurdity.

dispendio, *m.* excessive expense; excessive waste.

dispendiosamente, *adv.* expensively.

dispendioso, sa, *a.* costly, expensive.

dispensa, *f.* dispense, privilege, exemption, dispensation; document granting a dispensation.

dispensable, *a.* dispensable; excusable.

dispensación, *f.* dispensation, exemption.

dispensador, ra, *a.* granting a dispensation; dispensing, distributing.

---

dispensar, *va.* to dispense, deal out, distribute; to exempt; to acquit, absolve; to excuse, pardon.

dispensario, *m.* (incorrectly used for) pharmacopoeia; clinic.

¡dispense! ¡dispénseme!, (*subj.* of DISPENSAR) excuse me! (beg) pardon!

dispepsia, *f.* (med.) dyspepsia.

dispéptico, ca, *a.* dyspeptic.

dispersar, *va.* to disperse, scatter, put to flight; to dissipate.—**dispersión,** *f.* dispersion.

disperso, sa, *a.* dispersed, separated; scattered.

dispertador, ra, *a. & n.* = DESPERTADOR.

dispertar, *va. & vn.* = DESPERTAR.

displacer, *va. & vn.* = DESPLACER.

displicencia, *f.* disagreeableness; lukewarmness.

displicente, *a.* disagreeable, unpleasant; peevish.

disponedor, ra, *n. & a.* disposer(-ing), distributer(-ing).

disponente, *a.* disposing.

disponer. I. *va. & vn.* (*pp.* DISPUESTO; *ind. pres.* DISPONGO, *pret.* DISPUSE, *fut.* DISPONDRÉ; *subj.* DISPONGA) to dispose; arrange, prepare, lay out; to resolve, direct, order, command.—**d. de,** to have at one's disposal. **II.** *vr.* (**para** or **a**) to prepare oneself, to get ready (to); to make one's will.

dispongo, disponga, *v.* V. DISPONER.

disponible, *a.* disposable, available.

disposición, *f.* disposition, arrangement; disposal; aptitude, natural fitness, capacity; inclination; state of health; condition, circumstances; elegance of carriage; temper; ability, expediency; proportion, symmetry, measure; resolution, order, command; specification, requirement; provision, proviso, prescription; power, authority; (naut.) trim of a ship.—**a la d. de usted,** I am (or it is) at your disposal.

dispositivamente, *adv.* dispositively.

dispositivo, va. I. *a.* dispositive. **II.** *m.* device, contrivance; mechanism; appliance.

dispuesto, ta. I. *pp. irreg.* of DISPONER. **II.** *a.* disposed, ready; genteel, graceful.—**bien d.,** quite well; favorably disposed or inclined.—**mal d.,** indisposed, ill; unfavorably disposed.

dispuse, dispuso, *v.* V. DISPONER.

disputa, *f.* dispute, controversy; contest; debate. —**sin d.,** undoubtedly, indisputably.

disputable, *a.* disputable; contestable.

disputador, ra, *n.* disputant, disputer.

disputar, *va. & vn.* to dispute, controvert, contend, debate, contest; to question; to debate, argue; to fight for.

disputativamente, *adv.* disputingly.

disquisición, *f.* disquisition.

distancia, *f.* distance, interval of time or place; range; difference, disparity.—**a d.,** at a distance, far.—**a larga d.,** (Am.) (tel.) long-distance.—**distanciar,** *va.* to place at a distance; to separate, put farther apart.

distante, *a.* distant, far, remote; (naut.) off.

distantemente, *adv.* distantly.

distar, *vn.* to be distant; to be different.—**d. de,** to be far from; to be (a specified distance) from.

distender, *va.* (*ind.* DISTIENDO; *subj.* DISTIENDA) (med.) to distend, to swell.

distensión, *f.* distention, expansion.

dístico, *m.* (poet.) distich, couplet.

distiendo, distienda, *v.* V. DISTENDER.

distinción, *f.* distinction; difference; prerogative, privilege; superiority (in culture); honor, consideration; order, precision.—**a d. de,** in contradistinction to, as distinguished from; unlike.

¹distingo, *m.* restriction, qualification; (logic) distinction.

²distingo, distinga, *v.* V. DISTINGUIR.

distinguible, *a.* distinguishable.

distinguido, da. I. *pp.* of DISTINGUIR. **II.** *a.* distinguished, conspicuous, prominent.

distinguir. I. *va.* (*ind.* DISTINGO; *subj.* DISTINGA) to distinguish, tell apart; to see clearly at a distance, make out; to esteem, show regard for; to clear up, explain. **II.** *vr.* to distinguish oneself, to excel; (**de**) to differ, be distinguished (from).

distintamente, *adv.* distinctly; differently.

distintivo, va. I. *a.* distinctive. **II.** *m.* distinctive mark; distinguishing or peculiar feature or fact.

distinto, ta, *a.* distinct; plain, clear; different (separate, individual).

distocia, *f.* (surg.) dystocia.—**distócico, ca,** *a.* dystocial.

distracción, *f.* heedlessness, absent-mindedness; oversight; diversion, amusement, pastime; licentiousness, want of constraint.—**por d.,** for amusement, as a diversion; through an oversight.

distraer. I. *va.* (*ger.* DISTRAYENDO; *ind. pres.* DISTRAIGO, *pret.* DISTRAJE; *subj.* DISTRAIGA) to distract, to harass the mind; to perplex, bewilder, confuse; to divert, amuse, entertain; to lead astray. **II.** *vr.* to be absent-minded; to be inattentive; to amuse or enjoy oneself.

distraídamente, *adv.* absent-mindedly, without thinking.

distraído, da. I. *pp.* of DISTRAER. **II.** *a.* inattentive, heedless; absent-minded; dissolute, licentious.

distraigo, distraiga, *v.* V. DISTRAER.

distraimiento, *m.* = DISTRACCIÓN.

distraje, distrajo, distrayendo, *v.* V. DISTRAER.

distribución, *f.* distribution; division, apportionment; (print.) distribution of type.

distribuidor, ra. I. *n. & a.* distributer(-ing). **II.** *m.* (hydraul.) guides, guide system (of a turbine); (steam eng.) slide valve; valve gear.

distribuir, *va.* (*ger.* DISTRIBUYENDO; *ind. pres.* DISTRIBUYO, *pret.* él DISTRIBUYÓ; *subj.* DISTRIBUYA) to distribute, divide, deal out; to sort (as mail matter); (print.) to distribute (type).

distributivo, va, *a.* distributive, dissuading.

distributor, ra; distribuyente, *n. & a.* distributer(-ing).

distribuyo, etc. *v.* V. DISTRIBUIR.

distrito, *m.* district, ward, precinct, region.

disturbar, *va.* to disturb.

disturbio, *m.* disturbance, outbreak.

disuadir, *va.* to dissuade, deter.

disuasión, *f.* dissuasion, determent.

disuasivo, va. I. *a.* dissuasive, dissuading. **II.** *m.* deterrent.

disuelto, ta, *pp. irreg.* of DISOLVER.

disuelvo, disuelva, *v.* V. DISOLVER.

disueno, disuene, *v.* V. DISONAR.

disuria, *f.* (med.) dysuria.

disyunción, *f.* disjunction, separation; (gram.) disjunctive particle.

disyunta, *f.* (mus.) change of the voice.

disyuntiva, *f.* alternative.

disyuntivamente, *adv.* disjunctively; singly.

disyuntivo, va. I. *a.* disjunctive. **II.** *f.* disjunctive proposition; dilemma.

disyuntor, *m.* (elec.) circuit breaker.

dita, *f.* surety, bondsman; security, bond.

ditá, *m.* (bot.) dita, a P. I. tree that yields ditamine.

ditaína, *f..* ditamine, a febrifuge extracted from dita bark.

diteísmo, *m.* ditheism.

diteísta, *n. & a.* ditheist(-ic).

ditirámbico, ca, *a.* dithyrambical.

ditirambo, *m.* dithyramb.

dítono, *m.* (mus.) ditone.

diuresis, *f.* (med.) diuresis, excess of urine.

diurético, ca, *a. & m.* diuretic.

diurno, na. I. *a.* diurnal. **II.** *m.* diurnal, prayerbook.—*f. pl.* butterflies, Lepidoptera.—*m. pl.* dayflies.

diuturnidad, *f.* long duration.

diuturno, na, *a.* lasting, of long duration.

diva, *f.* goddess; diva, great singer.

divagación, *f.* wandering, digression.

divagador, ra, *n.* & *a.* roamer(-ing), rambler (-ing); digressor(-ing).

divagar, *vn.* (*pret.* DIVAGUÉ; *subj.* DIVAGUE) to roam, to ramble; to digress.

diván, *m.* divan, supreme council among the Turks; place of its meetings; divan, low cushioned sofa; collection of Oriental poems.

divergencia, *f.* divergence, divergency.

divergente, *a.* divergent; dissenting.

divergir, *vn.* to diverge; to dissent.

diversamente, *adv.* diversely, differently.

diversidad, *f.* diversity, unlikeness; variety, abundance, plenty.

diversificar, *va.* to diversify, vary.

diversiforme, *a.* diversiform, of varied forms.

diversión, *f.* entertainment, amusement.

diversivo, va, *a.* (med.) divertive.

diverso, sa, *a.* diverse, different; various, several.

divertido, da. I. *pp.* of DIVERTIR. **II.** *a.* amusing, entertaining; humorous, funny.

divertimiento, *m.* diversion, amusement.

divertir. I. *va.* (*ind. pres.* DIVIERTO, *pret.* él DIVIRTIÓ; *subj.* DIVIERTA) to turn aside, divert; to amuse, entertain; (mil.) to divert (the enemy). **II.** *vr.* to amuse oneself, to have a good time.

dividendo, *m.* (arith. & com.) dividend.

divididero, ra, *a.* divisible.

dividir. I. *va.* & *vn.* to divide. **II.** *vr.* to divide; to split; to be divided; (de) to separate (from), part company (with).

dividivi, *m.* (bot.) dividivi, a tropical-American tree yielding valuable dyeing and tanning products.

divíduo, dua, *a.* (law) divisible.

divierto, divierta, *v.* V. DIVERTIR.

divieso, *m.* (med.) furuncle, boil.

divinal, *a.* (poet.) = DIVINO.

divinamente, *adv.* divinely; admirably.

divinatorio, ria, *a.* divinatory.

divinicé, divinice, *v.* V. DIVINIZAR.

divinidad, *f.* divinity; god; woman of great beauty.—**la D.,** the Deity.

divinización, *f.* deification.

divinizar, *va.* (*pret.* DIVINICÉ; *subj.* DIVINICE) to deify; (fig.) to sanctify.

divino, na. I. *a.* divine; excellent, admirable; most beautiful. **II.** *n.* diviner.

divirtió, *pret.* of DIVERTIR.

divisa, *f.* badge, emblem, impress; (law) devise. —*pl.* (com.) holdings; (law) devisen.

divisar, *va.* to descry at a distance, to perceive indistinctly; (her.) to vary.

divisibilidad, *f.* divisibility.

divisible, *a.* divisible.

división, *f.* division; distribution; section, quarter, ward, compartment; disunity, discord; hyphen; (mil.) division; (math. etc.) division.

divisional, *a.* divisional.

divisivo, va, *a.* divisible, divisive.

diviso, sa, *a.* divided; disunited.

divisor, ra. I. *n.* & *a.* divider(-ing). **II.** *m.* (math.) divisor.

divisorio, ria. I. *a.* dividing. **II.** *m.* (print.) copyholder. **III.** *f.* (geol.) divide.

divo, va. I. *a.* (poet.) divine, godlike. **II.** *m.* god. **III.** *m.* & *f.* prominent singer.

divorciar. I. *va.* to divorce; to separate, part, divide. **II.** *vr.* to get divorced.

divorcio, *m.* divorce; disunion; breach.

divulgable, *a.* that may be divulged.

divulgación, *f.* publication, spreading abroad.

divulgador, ra, *n.* & *a.* divulger(-ing).

divulgar. I. *va.* (*pret.* DIVULGUÉ; *subj.* DIVULGUE)

to publish, divulge, spread, give out, reveal; to popularize. **II.** *vr.* to become widespread.

diz (contr. of DÍCESE), it is said.—**dizque. I.** = DIZ QUE. **II.** *m.* objection, muttering; rumor.

¹do, *m.* (mus.) first note of a diatonic scale.

²do, dó, *adv.* (poet.) DONDE, DÓNDE.

dobla, *f.* an ancient Spanish gold coin.

dobladamente, *adv.* doubly; deceitfully, artfully.

dobladilla, *f.* an ancient game of cards.—**a la d.,** doubly, repeatedly.

dobladillo, *m.* (sewing) hem, border; strong knitting thread.

doblado, da. I. *pp.* of DOBLAR. **II.** *a.* strong, robust, thick-set; deceitful, dissembling. **III.** *m.* measure of the fold in cloth.

doblador, ra, *n.* doubler, bender, folder.

dobladura, *f.* fold, crease.

doblamiento, *m.* doubling, bending, folding.

doblar. I. *va.* to double, make double; to fold; to crease; to bend; to subdue; to induce or influence.—**d. la esquina,** to turn the corner.—**d. un cabo,** (naut.) to double or round a cape. **II.** *vn.* to toll the passing bell. **III.** *vr.* to bend; bow, stoop; submit, acquiesce, give in, yield.

doble. I. *a.* double, twofold, duplicate; thick, heavy (as cloth); thick-set, robust, strong; two-faced, deceitful; (chem.) binary.—**al d.,** doubly. **II.** *m.* fold, crease; toll of the passing bell; step in a Spanish dance.

doblegable, *a.* pliable, pliant; easily folded.

doblegadizo, za, *a.* easily bent or folded.

doblegar. I. *va.* (*pret.* DOBLEGUÉ; *subj.* DOBLEGUE) to fold; twist; bend; to gain by persuasion, to dissuade. **II.** *vr.* to bend; to yield, submit, acquiesce.

doblemente, *adv.* doubly; deceitfully, artfully.

doblero, *m.* (carp.) piece of timber.

doblete. I. *a.* of medium thickness. **II.** *m.* doublet (gem); a stroke in billiards.

doblez. I. *m.* crease, ply, fold; duplication. **II.** *f.* duplicity, double-dealing.

doblón, *m.* doubloon, old Sp. gold coin.—**doblonada,** *f.* heap of doubloons or money.— echar **doblonadas,** (coll.) to exaggerate one's income.

doce. I. *n.* & *a.* twelve; twelfth. **II.** *f. pl.* las doce, twelve o'clock.

doceañista, *n.* maker or follower of the 1812 Spanish Constitution.

docena, *f.* dozen.—**d. de fraile,** baker's dozen.— **a docenas,** abundantly, in great quantities.

docenal, *a.* sold by dozens.

docenario, ria, *a.* containing a dozen.

doceno, na. I. *a.* twelfth. **II.** *n.* & *a.* (cloth) of twelve hundred threads.

docente, *a.* educational; teaching.

docientos, a, = DOSCIENTOS, two-hundred(-th).

dócil, *a.* docile, yielding, tractable; obedient; pliable, flexible, soft.—**docilidad,** *f.* docility, meekness; flexibility; tractableness.—**dócilmente,** *adv.* mildly, meekly.

docimasia, docimástica, *f.* docimacy.

docimástico, ca, *a.* docimastic.

doctamente, *adv.* learnedly.

docto, ta, *a.* learned, expert, well posted or informed; qualified.

doctor, ra. I. *n.* (academic) doctor; teacher of any art or science; (coll.) physician. **II.** *f.* (coll.) a bluestocking; (coll.) wife of a doctor.

doctorado, *m.* doctorate, doctorship.

doctoral, *a.* doctoral.

doctoramiento, *m.* act of conferring or taking the degree of doctor.

doctorando, *m.* one about to graduate as a doctor.

doctorar, *va.* to confer the degree of doctor on.

doctorcillo, *m. dim.* (coll.) insignificant doctor; quack, petty physician.

doctorzuelo, la, *n.* = DOCTORCILLO, LLA.

doctrina, *f.* doctrine; preaching of the Gospel; Sunday school; catechism; (Am.) curacy.

doctrinador, ra, *n.* instructor, teacher.

doctrinal. I. *m.* catechism. **II.** *a.* doctrinal.

doctrinante, *a.* instructor.

doctrinar, *va.* to teach, to instruct.

doctrinario, ria. I. *a.* doctrinarian; doctrinal; party (as *a.*); pert. to, or following, doctrinairism. **II.** *n.* doctrinaire.

doctrinarismo, *m.* doctrinairism.

doctrinero, *m.* teacher of Christian doctrine; (Am.) curate, parish priest.

doctrino, na, *n.* charity pupil.

documentación, *f.* documentation; documents.

documentado, da, *a.* having the necessary documents or vouchers.

documental, *a.* documentary.

documentalmente, *adv.* with proper documents.

documento, *m.* document; instruction, advice to avoid evil; (com.) collateral security.

dodecaedro, *m.* (geom.) dodecahedron.

dodecágono, *m.* (geom.) dodecagon.

dodecasílabo, ba, *a.* having twelve syllables.

dogal, *m.* halter, noose, slipknot; hangman's rope.

dogma, *m.* dogma.

dogmáticamente, *adv.* dogmatically.

dogmático, ca. I. *a.* dogmatical or dogmatic. **II.** *n.* dogmatist.

dogmatismo, *m.* dogmatism.

dogmatista, *n.* dogmatist.

dogmatizador, dogmatizante, *m.* dogmatizer, dogmatist.

dogmatizar, *va.* to dogmatize.

dogo, ga, *n.* bulldog.

dogre, *m.* dogger, Dutch boat.

doladera, *n.* cooper's adze.

dolador, *m.* joiner; stonecutter.

doladura, *f.* shavings, splinters, chips.

dolaje, *m.* wine absorbed by its container.

dolamas, *f. pl.,* **dolames,** *m. pl.,* (Am.) (vet.) hidden vices and defects (of horses).

dolar, *va.* to hew (wood or stone).

dólar, *m.* dollar (U. S. money).

dolencia, *f.* aching, ache; disease, ailment.

doler. I. *vn.* (*ind.* DUELO; *subj.* DUELA) to pain, ache; (as *me duele la cabeza,* my head aches); to hurt; to cause regret or grief. **II.** *vr.* (de) to repent (of); to regret; to be moved (by), take pity (on), condole (with), feel or express sympathy (for); to complain (of).

dolicocéfalo, la, *a.* dolichocephalous.

doliente. I. *a.* aching, suffering; sorrowful; sick. **II.** *m.* mourner; patient (sick person).

dolmen, *m.* (archeol.) dolmen.

dolo, *m.* fraud, deceit, guile.

dolobre, *m.* stone hammer.

dolomía, *f.* (min.) dolomite.

dolomítico, ca, *a.* dolomitic.

dolor, *m.* pain, aching, ache; sorrow, affliction, grief; regret, repentance, contrition.—*pl.* throes of childbirth.—**d. de cabeza,** headache.—**d. de corazón,** heartache; repentance.—**d. de costado,** pneumonia.—**d. latente,** dull pain, constant but not severe pain.—**dolores del parto,** labor pains.—**estar con dolores,** to be in labor.

dolora, *f.* a short sentimental and philosophic poem.

dolorcillo, ito, *m. dim.* slight pain.

dolorido, da. I. *a.* doleful, afflicted; painful, aching; sore, tender; heartsick. **II.** *m.* chief mourner.

dolorosamente, *adv.* painfully; sorrowfully, regrettably, lamentably, pitifully.

Dolorosa, *f.* (art) Mater Dolorosa, Sorrowing Mary.

doloroso, sa, *a.* painful; regrettable; pitiful.

dolosamente, *adv.* deceitfully.

doloso, sa, *a.* deceitful; fraudulent.

doma, *f.* breaking in of a horse.

domable, *a.* tamable; conquerable.

domador, ra, *n.* tamer; horsebreaker.

domadura, *f.* act of taming or subduing.

domar, *va.* to tame; to break in; to subdue, overcome, master, conquer.

dombo, *m.* dome, cupola.

domeñar, *va.* to reclaim, to make tractable; to tame, domesticate; to master, subdue.

domesticable, *a.* tamable, capable of domestication.

domesticación, *f.* domestication.

domésticamente, *adv.* domestically.

domesticar. I. *va.* (*pret.* DOMESTIQUÉ; *subj.* DOMESTIQUE) to domesticate. **II.** *vr.* to become tame.

domesticidad, *f.* domesticity; domestication.

doméstico, ca. I. *a.* domestic; domesticated, tamed. **II.** *n.* household servant.

domestiquez, *f.* tameness.

domiciliado, da. I. *pp.* of DOMICILIARSE. **II.** *a.* domiciled, residing.

domiciliar. I. *va.* to lodge. **II.** *vr.* to dwell.

domiciliario, ria, *a.* domiciliary.

domicilio, *m.* domicile; home; residence.

dominación, *f.* dominion, domination, authority, rule, command, power; (mil.) commanding ground.—*pl.* dominations, angelic beings.

dominador, ra. I. *a.* dominating, controlling; overbearing. **II.** *n.* dominator.

dominante, *a.* domineering, dictatorial, overbearing; prevailing; excelling; commanding; towering; (mus.) dominant.

dominar. I. *va.* to dominate; to stand out above (as a hill); to master (a subject, language, etc.); to subdue, repress. **II.** *vr.* to control oneself.

dominativo, va, *a.* = DOMINANTE.

dómine, *m.* dominie, teacher; puffed-up fool, pompous, empty-headed fellow.

domingada, *f.* Sunday festival or function.

domingo, *m.* Sunday.—**D. de Cuasimodo,** Low Sunday.—**D. de Ramos,** Palm Sunday.—**D. de Resurrección,** Easter Sunday.

dominguero, ra, *a.* done on Sunday; Sunday (as *a.*), pertaining to Sunday.

dominguillo, *m.* tumbler (a toy).

dominica, *f.* the Sabbath.

dominical. I. *a.* dominical, Sunday (as *a.*). **II.** *f.* Sunday function in universities.

dominicano, na; *n. & a.* Dominican; DOMINICO.

dominicatura, *f.* duty of vassalage.

dominico, *m.* Jacobin, Dominican friar.

dominio, *m.* dominion, control; domination, rule, authority; dominion, domain; (law) fee.—**d. absoluto,** (law) fee simple absolute.—**d. directo,** (law) dominium directum.—**d. eminente,** (law) eminent domain.—**d. público,** public or general knowledge; (law) public domain, government or state property.—**d. útil,** (law) dominium utile.

dómino, *m.* domino (game piece); the game.

dominó, *m.* domino (for masquerade); DÓMINO.

dompedro, *m.* (bot.) morning-glory.

¹don, *m.* Don, title for a gentleman, equivalent to Mr. or Esq. in English, but used only before Christian names, as *Don Juan, Don Alfonso.*

²don, *m.* gift, present, donation; ability, natural gift, faculty, knack.—**d. de acierto,** tact.—**d. de errar,** (coll.) knack for doing things wrong. —**d. de gentes,** winning manners.

¹dona, *f.* woman, dame.

²dona, *f.* (Chile) legacy.—*pl.* wedding presents given by the bridegroom to the bride.

donación, *f.* donation, gift, grant.—**d. piadosa,** donary, pious donation.

donadío, *m.* property derived from royal grants.

donado, da, *n.* lay brother (sister).

donador, ra, *n.* donor, bestower, giver.

donaire, *m.* gracefulness, gentility; witticism.

donairosamente, *adv.* gracefully.

donairoso, sa, *a.* graceful, elegant; witty.

donante, *n.* & *a.* giver(-ing).
donar, *va.* to give, bestow, contribute.
donatario, ria, *n.* donee, grantee.
donatista, *n.* & *a.* Donatist.
donativo, *m.* donative, donation, gift.
doncel. I. *m.* king's page; virgin man. **II.** *a.* mild, mellow in flavor (as wine).
doncella, *f.* maid, servant; virgin; maiden, girl; lady's maid, waiting maid; (ichth.) snakefish.
doncelleja, *f. dim.* little maid.
doncellez, *f.* maidenhood.
doncellica, ita, *f. dim.* young maid, girl.
doncellueca, *f.* (coll.) old maid.
doncelluela, *f. dim.* young maid.
donde (*interr.* **dónde**) *adv.* where; wherein; in which; wherever; (Am.) to, or at, the house, shop, etc. of (*voy donde Juan,* I am going to John's [house]; *esto se vende donde Macy,* this is sold at Macy's).—**d. no,** otherwise.—**a d.,** where, whereto.—**¿de dónde?** where from, whence?; (Am.) how?—**¿en dónde?** where?—**¿por dónde?** whereabouts? by what way or road? by what reason or cause?
dondequiera, *adv.* anywhere; wherever.—**por d.,** everywhere, in every place.
dondiego, dondiego de día, (bot.) morning-glory.—**dondiego de noche,** *m.* (bot.) jalap, marvel of Peru.
dongón, *m.* (P. I.) a tree of very hard wood used in shipbuilding.
donillero, *m.* roper-in, decoy.
donjuán, *m.* (bot.) = DONDIEGO.
donosamente, *adv.* gracefully, pleasingly.
donosidad, *f.* gracefulness; wittiness.
donoso, sa, *a.* gay, witty; graceful.
donosura, *f.* gracefulness, elegance; wittiness.
¹doña, *f.* title given to a lady, equivalent to the English Mrs. or Miss, but used only before Christian names, as *Doña Isabel;* formerly, a duenna or a nun.
²doña, *f. pl.* present made every year to the miners in the iron mines in Spain.
doñear, *vn.* (coll.) to converse much with women.
doñegal, doñigal, *a.* a variety of fig.
doquier, doquiera, *adv.* = DONDEQUIERA.
dorada, doradilla, *f.* (ichth.) gilthead, giltpoll.
doradilla, *f.* (bot.) common ceterach.
doradillo, *m.* fine brass wire; (ornith.) wagtail; (S. A.) satinwood.
dorado, da. I. *pp.* of DORAR. **II.** *a.* gilt. **III.** *m.* (act or operation of) gilding.
dorador, ra, *n.* gilder.
doradura, *f.* gilding.
doral, *m.* (ornith.) flycatcher.
dorar, *va.* to gild; to palliate, excuse; (poet.) to illume (as sunshine).
dórico, ca, *a.* Doric.
dorio, ria, *n.* & *a.* Dorian.
dormán, *m.* dolman, huzzar's jacket.
dormida, *f.* sleep of the silkworm; place where animals repose; (Am.) alcove; bed.
dormidera, *f.* (bot.) garden poppy.—*pl.* (coll.) readiness to sleep.
dormidero, ra. I. *a.* soporiferous, narcotic. **II.** *m.* place where cattle repose.
dormiente, = DURMIENTE, sleeping.
dormilón, na, *n.* (coll.) sleepy head.
dormilona, *f.* screw earring.
dormir. I. *vn.* (*ind. pres.* DUERMO, *pret.* él DUR-MIÓ; *subj.* DUERMA) to sleep; to rest; (naut.) to be calm or still.—**d. a pierna suelta,** (coll.) to be fast asleep; to sleep soundly and peacefully. **II.** *vr.* to go to sleep, fall asleep.
dormirlas, *m.* hide and seek.
dormitar, *vn.* to doze, nap.
dormitivo, *m.* dormitive.
dormitorio, *m.* dormitory; bedroom.
dornajo, *m.* small trough; tray; pan.
dornillo, *m.* small trough, wooden bowl.
dorsal, *a.* dorsal, pertaining to the back.

dorso, *m.* spine, back; dorsum.
dos. I. *n.* & *a.* two; second (of the month); deuce. —**d. a d.,** two to two, or two by two.—**a d. por tres,** suddenly.—**de d. en d.,** two abreast; by twos, in pairs.—**en un d. por tres,** in a twinkling.—**las d.,** two o'clock.—**los d.,** both. —**para entre los d.,** between you and me.
dosalbo, ba, *a.* (of horse) having two white stockings.
dosañal, *a.* biennial, of two years.
doscientos, tas, *n.* & *a.* two hundred; two-hundredth.
dosel, *m.* canopy, dais; portière.
doselera, *f.* valance, drapery of a canopy.
dosificación, *f.* proportioning; determination of the quantity of a substance; (med.) dosage.
dosificar, *va.* to measure out the doses of (a medicine); to proportion (ingredients, etc.); to determine the quantity of; to analyse.
dosimetría, *f.* (med.) dosimetric system.
dosimétrico, ca, *a.* dosimetric.
dosis, *f.* dose (of medicine); quantity.
dotación, *f.* endowment, foundation; allotment; settlement, dowry; equipment; (naut.) complement of a crew; (mil.) munition and garrison of a fortress; (Cuba) workmen on a plantation.
dotado, da, *pp.* of DOTAR.—**d. de,** endowed with, gifted with.
dotador, ra, *n.* endower, donor.
dotal, *a.* dotal, pertaining to a dowry.
dotar, *va.* to portion; to endow; to give a dowry to; to gift, to endow with powers or talents.
dote, *m.* & *f.* dowery, dowry; stock of counters to play with.—*f. pl.* gifts, natural talents.
dovela, *f.* (arch.) voussoir, stone of an arch.
dovelaje, *m.* voussoirs of an arch.
dovelar, *va.* to hew (a stone) for an arch.
doy, *1st pers. sing. pres.* of DAR.
dozavado, da, *a.* twelve-sided.
dozavo, va, *n.* & *a.* twelfth.
dracma, *f.* (pharm.) drachm, dram; Greek coin.
draconiano, na, *a.* Draconian.
draga, *f.* dredge.—**dragado,** *m.* dredging.
dragaminas, *m.* mine sweeper.
dragante, *m.* (naut.) bowsprit pillow.
dragar, *va.* (*pret.* DRAGUÉ; *subj.* DRAGUE) to dredge.
drago, *m.* (bot.) dragon tree.
dragomán, *m.* dragoman, interpreter.
dragón, *m.* dragon; (zool.) dragon; (bot.) dragon; (metal.) feeding opening of a furnace; (mil.) dragoon, a soldier; (vet.) white spots in the pupils of horses' eyes; a kind of exhalation or vapor; (**D-,** astr.) Dragon, Draco.—**dragona,** *f.* (mil.) shoulder knot; female dragon.—**dragoncillo,** *m.* drake, ancient gun; little dragon or dragoon.
dragonear, *vn.* (Am.) (**de**) to pass oneself off (for), to pretend to be, play the; to boast.
dragontea, dragontía, *f.* (bot.) common dragon.
dragontino, na, *a.* dragonish.
drama, *m.* drama; play.
dramática, *f.* dramatic art.
dramáticamente, *adv.* dramatically.
dramático, ca, *a.* dramatic.
dramatismo, *m.* quality of being dramatic.
dramatizable, *a.* dramatizable.
dramatizar, *va.* & *vn.* to dramatize.
dramaturgia, *f.* dramatic art.
dramaturgo, ga, *n.* playwright.
drástico, ca, *a.* (med.) drastic.
drávida, *n.,* **dravidiano, na,** *n.* & *a.* Dravidian.
dravídico, ca, *a.* Dravidian.
drecera, *f.* straight row of houses, trees, etc.
drenaje, *m.* drainage.
dríada, dríade, *f.* dryad.
dril, *m.* drilling, strong cloth, drill.
drino, *m.* a kind of poisonous serpent.
driza, *f.* (naut.) halyard.

drizar, va. (naut.) to hoist up (the yards).

droga, f. drug; medicine; fib; stratagem, artifice, deceit; nuisance.

drogmán, m. = DRAGOMÁN.

droguería, f. drug store; drug trade.

droguero, ra, n. druggist.

droguete, m. drugget, East Indian rug.

droguista, n. druggist; cheat, humbug, impostor.

dromedario, m. dromedary; unwieldy animal.

drope, m. (coll.) vile, despicable man.

druida, m. Druid.—**druídico, ca,** a. Druidic.

druidismo, m. druidism.

drupa, f. (bot.) drupe, stone fruit.

drusa, f. (min.) geode, vug.

dúa, f. (min.) gang of workmen.

dual, a. (gram.) dual.

dualidad, f. duality.

dualismo, m. (philos.) dualism.

dualista, n. & a. dualist(-ic).

dubio, m. (law) doubt.

dubitable, a. doubtful, dubious.

dubitación, f. dubitation, doubt.

dubitativo, va, a. doubtful, dubious.

ducado, m. duchy, dukedom; ducat.

ducal, a. ducal.

ducentésimo, ma, a. two-hundredth.

dúctil, a. ductile; yielding.

ductilidad, f. ductility.

ductivo, va, a. conducive.

ductor, m. guide, conductor; (surg.) probe.

ductriz, f. conductress.

¹ducha, f. douche, shower bath.

²ducha, f. stripe (in cloth); straight piece of land reaped.

ducho, cha, skilful, expert.

duda, f. doubt.—**sin d.,** certainly; doubtless.

dudable, a. dubious, doubtful.

dudar, vn. & va. to doubt; to hesitate (before doing something).—**d. de,** to doubt, distrust, question.

dudosamente, adv. doubtfully, dubiously.

dudoso, sa, a. doubtful, dubious; hazardous.

duela, f. (cooperage) stave.

duelaje, m. wine absorbed by its container.

duelista, m. duellist.

¹duelo, m. duel.

²duelo, m. sorrow, grief, affliction; mourning; mourners; condolement; bereavement.—**duelos y quebrantos,** giblets and haslets, formerly eaten on Saturday.—**sin d.,** abundantly.

³duelo, duela, v. V. DOLER.

duende, m. elf, hobgoblin, ghost.

duendecillo, m. dim. little elf.

duendo, da. a. tame (as doves).

dueña, f. owner, proprietress, mistress, landlady; duenna; married lady.

dueñesco, ca, a. duennalike.

dueño, ña, owner, proprietor, landlord(-lady); master (to a servant).—**d. de sí mismo,** self-controlled.—**hacerse dueño de,** to appropriate to oneself, take possession of; to become familiar with, to master (a subject, a theory, etc.).—**ser d. de,** to own, be master of; to be at liberty to (do, etc.).

duermevela, m. (coll.) dozing, light sleep.

duermo, duerma, v. V. DORMIR.

duerna, f., **duerno,** m. trough; bowl.

dúerno, m. (print.) double sheet.

dúeto, m. duet.—**duetista,** m. & f. duettist.

dugongo, m. (zool.) dugong.

dula, f. common pasture ground.

dulcamara, f. (bot.) bittersweet; (pharm.) dulcamara; nightshade.

dulce. I. a. sweet; (of water) fresh; comfortable, pleasing, pleasant, agreeable; soft, ductile (as metals). **II.** m. sweetmeat, confection, bonbon, piece of candy.—**d. de almíbar,** preserves.

dulcecillo, illa, ito, ita. I. a. dim. sweetish, somewhat sweet. **II.** m. bonbon, candy.

dulcedumbre, f. sweetness.

dulcémele, m. (mus.) dulcimer.

dulcemente, adv. sweetly.

dulcera, f. preserve dish, compotier.

dulcería, f. confectionery shop.

dulcero, ra. I. a. fond of sweets. **II.** n. confectioner.

dulcificación, f. dulcification.

dulcificante, a. dulcifying; sweetening.

dulcificar, va. to sweeten, dulcify.

Dulcinea, f. (coll.) Dulcinea, sweetheart, beloved one.

dulcísono, na, a. sweet-toned.

dulero, m. shepherd; guardian of common pasture.

dulía, f. (Rom. Cath.) dulia, saint worship.

dulimán, m. long Turkish robe.

¹dulzaina, f. (coll.) quantity of sweetmeats.

²dulzaina, f. (mus.) flageolet.

dulzainero, m. flageolet player.

dulzaino, na, a. (coll.) too sweet or rich.

dulzamara, f. (bot.) = DULCAMARA.

dulzarrón, na, a. (coll.) sickening, too sweet.

dulzura, f. sweetness; meekness; gentleness; comfort, pleasure; forbearance; pleasing manner, kindliness.

dulzurar, va. (chem.) to free from salt; sweeten.

duma, f. duma, douma.

duna, f. (geol.) dune.

dúo, m. (mus.) duo, duet.

duodecimal, a. (arith.) duodecimal.

duodécimo, ma, a. twelfth.

duodécuplo, pla, a. duodecuple.

duodenal, a. duodenal.

duodenario, ria, a. lasting twelve days.

duodenitis, f. (med.) duodenitis.

duodeno, na. I. a. twelfth. **II.** m. (anat.) duodenum.

duomesino, na, a. of two months.

dupla, f. in colleges, extra dish.

duplex, dúplex, a. (tel.) duplex.

dúplica, f. (law) answer.

duplicación, f. duplication, doubling.

duplicadamente, adv. doubly.

duplicado, da, I. pp. of DUPLICAR. **II.** m. duplicate; counterpart.—**por d.,** in duplicate.

duplicador, m. duplicator.

duplicar, va. (pret. DUPLIQUÉ; subj. DUPLIQUE) to double, duplicate; to repeat.

duplicatura, f. = DOBLADURA, fold; crease.

dúplice, a. double.—**duplicidad,** f. duplicity, deceit, foul dealing; duplication.

dupliqué, duplique, v. V. DUPLICAR.

duplo, m. double, twice as much.

duque, m. duke; fold in mantillas.—**duquecito,** m. dim. young or little duke.—**duquesa,** f. duchess.

dura, f. (coll.) duration, continuance.

durabilidad, f. durability, permanence.

durable, a. durable, lasting.

duración, f. duration; life.—**ser de d.,** to wear well, last.

duraderamente, adv. durably, lastingly.

duradero, ra, a. lasting, durable.

duramadre, duramáter, f. (anat.) dura mater.

duramen, m. (bot.) duramen.

duramente, adv. rigorously, harshly.

durante, prep. during.

durar, vn. to last; to endure; (of clothes) to wear (well).

duraznero, m. (bot.) peach tree.

duraznilla, f. a variety of peach.

durazno, m. (bot.) peach; peach tree.

dureza, f. hardness, solidity, firmness; sharpness of temper, obduracy; harshness, hardness of heart, cruelty; steadiness, perseverance; obstinacy; (art) crudeness; (med.) tumor or callosity.—**d. de vientre,** costiveness.

durillo, lla. I. a. dim. rather hard. **II.** m. (bot.) common laurestine; (vet.) callosity.

durmiente. I. a. sleeping, dormant. **II.** m.

(arch.) dormer; girder, stringer; crosstie; (Ry.) (Am.) tie, sleeper; (naut.) clamp, shelf.

durmió, *pret.* of DORMIR.

duro, ra. I. *a.* hard; solid, firm; stiff (collar); vexatious, unbearable; unjust, unkind; oppressive, rigorous, cruel; stubborn, obstinate; avaricious, stingy; rude, harsh, rough; (naut.) carrying a stiff sail; (art) harsh, crude; (mus.) harsh, inharmonious.—**a duras penas,** with difficulty; hardly, scarcely. **II.** *m.* dollar, peso; (Am.) low, rough saddle. **III.** *adv.* hard, with exertion; forcibly, violently.

duunvir, duunviro, *m.* duumvir.—**duunviral,** *a.* duumviral.—**duunvirato,** *m.* duumvirate.

dux, *m.* doge.

E

e, *conj.* and (used only before words that begin with *i* or *hi* not followed by *e*).

¡ea! *interj.* (used to attract attention or as an encouragement).

ebanista, *m.* cabinetmaker.—**ebanistería,** *f.* cabinetwork; cabinetmaker's shop.

ébano, *m.* (bot.) ebony.

ebenáceo, a. I. *a.* (bot.) ebenaceous. **II.** *f. pl.* Ebenaceæ.

ebionita, *n. & a.* Ebionite.

ebonita, *f.* ebonite, hard rubber.

ebriedad, *f.* drunkenness, intoxication.

ebrio, bria; ebrioso, sa, *a.* intoxicated, drunk.

ebullición, ebullición, *f.* ebullition; boiling.

ebúrneo, a, *a.* eburnean, ivorylike.

ecarté, *m.* a card game.

Eccehomo, *m.* Ecce Homo; wretched, pity-inspiring person.

eclampsia, *f.* (med.) eclampsia, convulsions.

eclecticismo, *m.* eclecticism.

ecléctico, ca, *n. & a.* eclectic.

Eclesiastés, *m.* Ecclesiastes (one of the books of the Old Testament).

eclesiásticamente, *adv.* ecclesiastically.

eclesiástico, ca. I. *a.* ecclesiastical. **II.** *m.* clergyman, ecclesiastic, priest, minister; Ecclesiasticus.

eclesiastizar, *va.* to spiritualize.

eclímetro, *m.* clinometer.

eclipsable, *a.* that may be eclipsed.

eclipsar. I. *va.* (astr.) to eclipse; to outshine. **II.** *vr.* (astr.) to be eclipsed.

eclipse, *m.* (astr.) eclipse.

eclipsis, *f.* (gram.) = ELIPSIS, ellipsis.

eclíptica, *f.* ecliptic.

eclisa, *f.* (Ry.) fishplate, shin.

écloga, égloga, *f.* eclogue.

eco, *m.* echo; distant sound (as of a drum); repetition of words.—**hacer e.,** to fit, correspond; to become important or famous; to create an impression; to be noised about.

ecoico, ca, *a.* pertaining to echo.

ecometría, *f.* (arch.) echometry.

ecómetro, *m.* echometer.

economato, *m.* guardianship, trusteeship.

economía, *f.* economy.—**e. animal,** (zool.) organism.—**e. política,** political economy, economics.—*pl.* savings.

económicamente, *adv.* economically.

económico, ca, *a.* economical, economic; saving, thrifty; frugal; miserly, niggardly.

economista, *m.* economist.

economizar, *va.* to economize; to save.

ecónomo, *m.* curator or guardian; trustee; ecclesiastical administrator.

éctasis, *f.* (gram.) ectasis.

ectoblasto, ectodermo, *m.* (biol.) ectoblast, ectoderm.

ectopia, *f.* (med.) ectopia, displacement.

ectropión, *m.* (med.) ectropion, eversion of eyelid.

ecuable, *a.* equitable; equable; uniform (motion).

ecuación, *f.* equation.—**e. de tiempo,** (astr.) equation of time.

ecuador, *m.* equator.

ecuánime, *a.* equable, calm, serene.

ecuanimidad, *f.* equanimity.

ecuatorial. I. *a.* equatorial. **II.** *f.* equatorial telescope.

ecuatoriano, na, *n. & a.* Ecuadorian.

ecuestre, *a.* equestrian.

ecuménico, ca, *a.* œcumenical.

ecuóreo, rea, *a.* (poet.) pertaining to the sea.

eczema, *f.* (med.) eczema.—**eczematoso, sa,** *a.* eczematous.

echacantos, *m.* (coll.) rattle-brained fellow.

echacorvear, *vn.* (coll.) to pimp; to procure.

echacorvería, *f.* (coll.) profession of a pimp or procurer.

echacuervos, *m.* (coll.) pimp; procurer; cheat, impostor; a nickname given to some preachers.

echada, *f.* cast, throw; (sport) man's length.

echadero, *m.* place of rest or repose.

echadillo, *m.* foundling.

echadizo, za, *a.* spying; (of propaganda) artfully spread; foundling; rejected, discarded.

echador, ra, *n.* thrower.

echadura, *f.* brooding, hatching; winnowing.

echamiento, *m.* cast, throw; casting or throwing; rejection; ejection, expulsion.

echapellas, *m.* wool soaker.

echar. I. *va.* to cast, throw, fling, hurl, pitch, toss, dart; to turn or drive away, eject, throw out, expel; to discharge, dismiss, (coll.) fire; to emit, give out (as sparks); to pour (as wine); to serve (as food); to put (in, into); to jet (as cargo); to put on (as a cloak); to turn (as a key); to begin to have or grow (as teeth, hair, etc.); to put forth, produce, bear (shoots, fruit); to put on, to apply; to lay on or impose (as a tax); to play (as a game); to lean toward; to move, push, to set (aside); to tell (a fortune); to couple, mate (male and female animals for procreating); to impute, to ascribe; to perform for a wager; to deal (cards), deal out, to distribute; to publish, give out, issue; (with the words rayos, centellas, chispas, fuego, etc.) to show much annoyance, to be very angry; (with the name of a punishment) to condemn to.—**e. a,** to start, begin, to.—**e. abajo,** to overthrow, throw down; to tear down, demolish.—**e. a fondo,** or **a pique,** (naut.) to sink; to ruin, spoil, wreck.—**e. a la cara** = E. EN CARA.—**e. al mundo,** to create; to bring forth.—**e. a pasear,** or **a paseo,** = E. CON CAJAS DESTEMPLADAS.—**e. a perder,** to spoil, ruin.— **e. a pique,** to sink (a ship).—**e. baladronadas,** to boast, brag.—**e. bando,** to publish something through a crier; (coll.) to sermonize, lecture.—**e. boca,** to sharpen; to even the tip of.—**e. bravatas** = E. BALADRONADAS.—**e. carnes,** to put on flesh, gain weight.—**e. carrillos,** to grow plump in the cheeks.—**e. con cajas destempladas,** or **enhoramala,** to dismiss contemptuously; to turn away in a harsh manner.—**e. coche,** to set up a coach.—**e. chufas,** to act the bully.—**e. de menos,** to miss, notice the absence or loss of.—**e. de ver,** to notice, observe; to happen to see.—**e. el bofe,** to work very hard; to solicit anxiously.— **e. el cuerpo fuera,** to withdraw from an affair.—**e. el escandallo,** (naut.) to take soundings.—**e. el guante,** to arrest.—**e. en cara,** or **en la cara,** to throw in one's face.—**e. en tierra** = E. ABAJO.—**e. la cargo a otro,** to throw the blame or responsibility on another. —**e. la corredera,** (naut.) to heave the log.— **e. la cuenta,** to balance the account.—**e. los bofes** = E. EL BOFE.—**e. los hígados,** to be exhausted, dead tired.—**e. los hígados por,** (coll.) to desire anxiously, to itch for (or to).—

e. mano a, to grab, seize.—**e. mano de,** to resort to.—**e. plantas** = E. BALADRONADAS.—
e. por el suelo, or **por tierra** = E. ABAJO.—
e. por en medio, e. por la calle de en medio, to rush recklessly; to take a final resolution.
—**e. raíces,** to put down roots, take root.—**e. suertes,** to draw lots.—**e. tierra a,** (fig.) to bury; to hush up; to drop (a matter).—**e. todo a rodar,** to spoil everything, to make a fizzle.
—**e. un remiendo** (a), to put a patch (on).—
e. un remiendo a la vida, (coll.) to take a little refreshment.—**echarla de,** to pretend or claim to be, to boast of being, to pass oneself off as. **II.** *vn.*—**e. a** (foll. by *inf.*), to begin to, to start (foll. by *pres. p.*: *echar a correr,* to start running).—**e. de baranda,** to exaggerate, boast.—**e. en tierra,** (naut.) to land, to disembark.—**e. por,** to go by, take to, take the way of. **III.** *vr.* to lie down; to stretch oneself at full length; to throw oneself down; to apply oneself; (of a hen) to sit (on her eggs).—**e. a morir,** to give up in despair; to worry oneself to death.—**e. a perder,** (of food or drink) to spoil; to become stale; to become ruined or destroyed; to go down (in prestige, virtue, etc.)—
echárselas de, = ECHARLA DE.—**e. en brazos de,** to throw oneself into the arms of; to trust in; to resort to.—**e. sobre,** to rush at, fall upon.

echazón, *f.* (naut.) jettison or jetsam.

echona, *f.* (Am.) sickle.

edad, *f.* age; epoch, era, time.—**e. crítica,** menopause.—**e. madura,** mature age, maturity.—
e. media, Middle Ages.—**e. provecta,** = E. MADURA.—**de cierta e.,** of uncertain age, of somewhat mature age.—**mayor de e.,** of (legal) age.—**menor de e.,** underage (legally), minor.

edecán, *m.* (mil.) aide-de-camp.

edema, *f.* œdema, edema.

edematoso, sa, *a.* œdematous, edematose.

Edén, *m.* Eden, paradise.—**edénico, ca,** *a.* paradisiacal.

edición, *f.* edition, issue; publication.—**e. príncipe,** first edition.

edicto, *m.* edict, proclamation, placard.

edificación, *f.* construction, building; edification.

edificador, ra, *n. & a.* edifier(-ying); constructor (-ing), builder(-ing).

edificante, *a.* edifying; erecting.

edificar, *va. & vn.* (*pret.* EDIFIQUÉ; *subj.* EDIFIQUE) to edify; to build, construct, erect.

edificativo, va, *a.* edifying.

edificatorio, ria, *a.* pert. to building or making.

edificio, *m.* edifice, building, structure.

edil, *m.* edile, a Roman magistrate.

edilidad, *f.* edileship.

editar, *va.* to publish.

editor, ra, *n. & a.* publisher(-ing).

editorial. I. *n. & a.* editorial. **II.** *a.* publishing.

editorialista, *m.* editorial writer.

edredón, *m.* eider down; feather pillow.

educable, *a.* educable.

educación, *f.* education; good breeding, politeness.—**e. física,** physical culture.

educacional, *a.* educational.

educador, ra, *n. & a.* educator(-ing).

educando, da, *n.* pupil, student.

educar, *va.* (*pret.* EDUQUÉ; *subj.* EDUQUE) to educate, instruct, raise, train.

educativo, va, *a.* educational.

educción, *f.* deduction; eduction; (steam eng.) exhaust.

educir, *va.* to educe, extract, bring out.

edulcoración, *f.* (pharm.) sweetening.

edulcorar, *va.* (pharm.) to sweeten (bad-tasting substance).

eduqué, eduque, *v. V.* EDUCAR.

efe, *f.* Spanish name of the letter *f.*

efectismo, *m.* (art) striving after effect.

efectista, *a.* (art) sensational.

efectivamente, *adv.* effectually; really, actually.

efectivo, va. I. *a.* effective; real, actual.—**hacer e.,** to cash (a check, etc.). **II.** *m.* (com.) cash, specie.—**e. en caja,** cash on hand.—**en e.,** in cash, in coin.

efecto, *m.* effect; impression; end, purpose, meaning; general intent; (in billiards) English.—
pl. assets: merchandise, chattels, goods, movables; (com.) drafts.—**efectos a pagar,** bills payable.—**efectos a recibir,** bills receivable.—
efectos en cartera, securities in hand.—**efectos públicos,** public securities.—**a ese, este,** or **tal, e.,** for that purpose, to that end.—**con,** or **en, e.,** in fact, as a matter of fact, actually; (math., logic) for (in introducing the proof of a proposition).—**tener e.,** to become effective.

efectuación, *f.* accomplishment.

efectuar, *va.* to effect, carry out, do, make.

efémera, *a.*—**fiebre e.,** (med.) a one-day fever.

efemérides, *f. pl.* diary; ephemeris.

efémero, *m.* (bot.) iris.

efendi, *m.* effendi (Turkish title).

eferente, *a.* efferent.

efervescencia, *f.* effervescence; ardor, fervor.

efesio, sia, *n. & a.* Ephesian.

eficacia, *f.* efficacy, efficiency.

eficaz, *a.* efficacious, effective.

eficazmente, *adv.* efficaciously, effectively.

eficiencia, *f.* efficiency, effectiveness.

eficiente, *a.* efficient, effective.

eficientemente, *adv.* efficiently.

efigie, *f.* effigy, image.

efímera, *f.* (med.) EFÉMERA; (entom.) dayfly.

efímero, ra, *a.* ephemeral.

eflorecerse, *vr.* to effloresce.

eflorescencia, *f.* efflorescence.

eflorescente, *a.* efflorescent.

efluvio, *m.* effluvium or effluvia; exhalation, emanation.

efod, *m.* ephod (a Jewish garment).

éforo, *m.* ephor (a Greek magistrate).

efugio, *m.* subterfuge, evasion, shift.

efundir, *va.* to effuse, pour out, spill.

efusión, *f.* effusion, shedding; warmth of manner.
—**e. de sangre,** bloodshed.

efuso, sa, *a.* effused.

égida, egis, *f.* (bot.) wild bastard oat.

egílope, *f.* (bot.) wild bastard oat.

egipcíaco, ca; egipciano, na; egipcio, cia; egiptano, na, *n. & a.* Egyptian.

egiptología, *f.* Egyptology.

egiptólogo, *m.* Egyptologist.

égira, *f.* hegira.

égloga, écloga, *f.* eclogue, pastoral poem.

egoísmo, *m.* selfishness, self-love, egoism.

egoísta. I. *a.* selfish, egoistic. **II.** *m.* egoist.

egolatría, *f.* self-idolatry.

egotismo, *m.* egotism.

egotista, *n. & a.* egotist(-ic).

egregiamente, *adv.* egregiously.

egregio, gia, *a.* egregious, eminent.

egrena, *f.* iron clamp.

egreso, *m.* expense, debit.—*pl.* discharge.

egrisador, *m.* box for diamond dust.

egrisar, *va.* to polish (diamonds).

¡eh! *interj.* eh! here!

eje, *m.* axis; axletree, axle; shaft, spindle, arbor; (fig.) main point, crux.—**e. auxiliar,** countershaft.—**e. conjugado,** minor axis (of an ellipse).—**e. coordenado,** coördinate axis.—
e. de (las) abscisas, axis of abscissæ.—**e. de (las) coordenadas** = E. COORDENADO.—**e. delantero,** front axle (of a vehicle).—**e. de las x, de las y,** *x*-axis, *y*-axis.—**e. del timón,** (aer.) rudder post.—**e. de ordenadas,** axis of ordinates.—**e. secundario,** countershaft.—**e. trasero,** rear axle (of a vehicle).

ejecución, *f.* execution, carrying out; execution,

capital punishment; (law) attachment; (mus.) technique.

ejecutable, *a.* feasible, practicable.

ejecutante, *n.* performer; (law) one who compels another to pay a debt by legal execution.

ejecutar, *va.* to execute, perform, make, do, carry out; to execute (a criminal); to impel, urge, importune, incite; (law) to attach the property of.

ejecutivamente, *adv.* executively; promptly.

ejecutivo, va. I. *a.* executive; active; executory. **II.** *m.* (Am.) executive (power or person).

ejecutor, ra, *n.* executor; executer; (law) officer who attaches property.—**e. de la justicia,** executioner.

ejecutoría, *f.* office of executive or attacher.

ejecutoria, *f.* sentence, judgment; letters patent of nobility, pedigree; executorship.

ejecutorial, *a.* (law) applied to the execution of the sentence of an ecclesiastical tribunal.

ejecutoriar, *va.* to obtain (a judgment) in one's favor; to establish the truth of.

ejecutorio, ria, *a.* (law) executory.

ejemplar. I. *a.* exemplary. **II.** *m.* pattern, model; precedent, example; specimen, sample; copy of a work; example, warning.—**sin e.,** without precedent; exceptional and not a precedent.

ejemplarmente, *adv.* exemplarily; edifyingly.

ejemplificación, *f.* exemplification, illustration.

ejemplificar, *va.* to exemplify, to illustrate.

ejemplo, *m.* example, instance; copy.—**dar e.,** to set an example.—**por e.,** for example.—**sin e.,** without precedent or parallel, unheard-of.

ejercer, *va.* (*ind.* EJERZO; *subj.* EJERZA) to exercise, practise; perform, ply; to exert.

ejercicio, *m.* exercise, exertion; employment, office, task; ministry; practice; fiscal year; military drill.—**e. espiritual,** spiritual retreat.—**hacer e.,** to exercise; (mil.) to drill.

ejercitación, *f.* exercise, practice.

ejercitante. I. *n.* one who is in a spiritual retreat; exerciser. **II.** *m.* exercising, training.

ejercitar. I. *va.* to exercise, to put into practice; to drill (troops); to train. **II.** *vr.* to practice.

ejercitativo, va, *a.* that may be exercised.

ejército, *m.* army.

ejerzo, ejerza, *v.* V. EJERCER.

ejido, *m.* common, public land.

ejión, *m.* (arch.) corbel piece, purlin, bracket.

ejote, *m.* (Mex.) string bean.

el, *art. masc. sing.* (*pl.* **los**) the.

él, *pron. masc. sing.* (*pl.* **ellos**) he.

elaboración, *f.* elaboration, working up (of material).

elaborado, da. I. *pp.* of ELABORAR. **II.** *a.* elaborate; manufactured, wrought.

elaborador, ra, *n.* & *a.* elaborator(-ing); manufacturer(-ing).

elaborar, *va.* to elaborate; to manufacture.

elación, *f.* elation, haughtiness, pride; magnanimity, generosity; inflation of style.

elamita, *n.* & *a.* Elamite(-ic).

elástica, *f.* undershirt.

elasticidad, *f.* elasticity.

elástico, ca. I. *a.* elastic. **II.** *m.* an elastic (webbing); wire spring.—*pl.* suspenders.

elaterina, *f.* (chem.) elaterin.

elaterio, *m.* (bot.) elaterium.

elche, *m.* apostate, renegade.

ele, *f.* Spanish name of the letter *l.*

eleagnáceo, a. I. *a.* (bot.) elæagnaceous. **II.** *f. pl.* Elæagnaceæ.

eleático, ca, *n.* & *a.* (philos.) Eleatic.

eleatismo, *m.* (philos.) Eleaticism.

elebor, eléboro, *m.* (bot.) hellebore.

elección, *f.* election; choice, selection.

electivo, va, *a.* elective.

electo, ta. I. *pp. irreg.* of ELEGIR. **II.** *a.* elect, chosen. **III.** *n.* elect, person chosen or appointed.

elector, ra. I. *n.* & *a.* elector(-ing). **II.** *m.* elector, German prince.—**electorado,** *m.* electorate.—**electoral,** *a.* electoral.

electricé, electrice, *v.* V. ELECTRIZAR.

electricidad, *f.* electricity.

electricista, *m.* electrician.

eléctrico, ca, *a.* electric, electrical.

electrificación, *f.* electrification.

electrificar, *va.* to electrify.

electriz, *f.* electress.

electrización, *f.* electrification, electrization.

electrizador, ra; electrizante, *n.* & *a.* electrifier (-ying).

electrizar. I. *va.* (*pret.* ELECTRICÉ; *subj.* ELECTRICE) to electrify. **II.** *vr.* to become electrified.

electro, *m.* amber; electrum.

electrocución, *f.* electrocution.

electrocutar, *va.* to electrocute.

electrodinámica, *f.* electrodynamics.

electrodinámico, ca, *a.* electrodynamic.

electrodinamómetro, *m.* electrodynamometer.

electrodo, *m.* electrode.

electrofisiología, *f.* electrophysiology.

electróforo, *m.* electrophorus.

electroimán, *m.* electromagnet.

electrólisis, *f.* electrolysis.

electrólito, *m.* electrolyte.

electrolizable, *a.* electrolyzable.

electrolización, *f.* electrolyzation.

electrolizar, *va.* to electrolyze.

electromagnetismo, *m.* electromagnetism.

electrometalurgia, *f.* electrometallurgy.

electrometría, *f.* electrometry.

electrométrico, ca, *a.* electrometric.

electrómetro, *m.* electrometer.

electromotor, ra. I. *a.* electromotor. **II.** *m.* electric motor.

electromotriz, *a.* electromotive (force).

electrón, *m.* (phys.) electron.

electronegativo, va, *a.* electronegative.

electropositivo, va, *a.* electropositive.

electropuntura, *f.* (med.) electropuncturation.

electroquímica, *f.* electrochemistry.

electroquímico, ca, *a.* electrochemical.

electroscopio, *m.* electroscope.

electrostática, *f.* electrostatics.

electrotecnia, *f.* electrical engineering.

electroterapia, *f.* electrotherapy.

electrotipia, *f.* electrotypy.

electrotípico, ca, *a.* pert. to electrotypy.

electuario, *m.* electuary.

elefancía, *f.* (med.) elephantiasis.

elefancíaco, ca, *a.* (med.) elephantiac.

elefante, ta, *n.* elephant.

elefantiasis, *f.* (med.) = ELEFANCÍA.

elefantino, na, *a.* elephantine.

elegancia, *f.* elegance, gracefulness; neatness.

elegante, *a.* elegant, stylish, tasteful, graceful.

elegantemente, *adv.* elegantly, tastefully.

elegía, *f.* elegy.

elegíaco, ca, *a.* elegiac, mournful.

elegibilidad, *f.* eligibility.

elegible, *a.* eligible.

elegido, da. I. *pp.* of ELIGIR. **II.** *a.* elect, chosen.

elegir, *va.* (*pp.* ELEGIDO, ELECTO; *ind.* ELIJO; *subj.* ELIJA) to elect; choose, select, prefer.

élego, ga, *a.* mournful, plaintive.

elemental, *a.* elementary; fundamental.

elementalmente, *adv.* elementarily.

elementar, *a.* elementary.

elemento, *m.* element; constituent, ingredient; (elec.) element.—*pl.* elements, rudiments.

elemí, *m.* elemi, gum resin.

elenco, *m.* catalogue, list, table, index; (theat.) cast; (Am.) personnel, members (of governing body).

eleusino, na, *a.* Eleusinian.

elevación, *f.* elevation; height; rise, ascent; exaltation, dignity; advancement; exaltation of mind, ecstasy, rapture; haughtiness, pride.

elevadamente, *adv.* with elevation, loftily.
elevado, da. I. *pp.* of ELEVAR. **II.** *a.* elevated; high; exalted, grand, lofty.
elevador, *m.* elevator, hoist, lift.
elevamiento, *m.* elevation; ecstasy, rapture.
elevar. I. *va.* to raise, elevate, heave, lift, hoist; exalt. **II.** *vr.* to rise, ascend, soar; to be enraptured; to be elated.
elidir, *va.* to weaken; (gram.) to elide.
elijable, *a.* (pharm.) that can be steeped.
elijación, *f.* (pharm.) steeping.
elijar, *va.* (pharm.) to steep.
elijo, elija, *v.* V. ELEGIR.
eliminación, *f.* elimination.
eliminador, ra, *n.* & *a.* eliminator(-ing).
eliminar, *va.* to eliminate.
elipse, *f.* (geom.) ellipse.
elipsis, *f.* (gram.) ellipsis.
elipsoidal, (geom.) ellipsoidal.
elipsoide, *m.* (geom.) ellipsoid.
elípticamente, *adv.* elliptically.
elipticidad, *f.* ellipticity.
elíptico, ca, *a.* elliptic, elliptical.
Elíseos, Elisios (Campos), *m. pl.* Elysian (fields).
elisión, *f.* (gram.) elision.
élitro, *m.* (entom.) elytron.
elixir, elíxir, *m.* elixir.
elocución, *f.* elocution; effective diction, style.
elocuencia, *f.* eloquence.
elocuente, *a.* eloquent.—**elocuentemente,** *adv.* eloquently.
elogiador, ra, *n.* eulogist, encomiast.
elogiar, *va.* to praise, extol, eulogize, laud.
elogio, *m.* eulogy, praise.
elongación, *f.* (astr.) elongation.
elote, *m.* (Mex., C. A.) ear of green corn.
elucidación, *f.* elucidation.
elucidar, *va.* to elucidate.
eludible, *a.* eludible, avoidable.
eludir, *va.* to elude, to evade, avoid.
elzeviriano, na, *a.* Elzevir.
ella, *pron. fem. sing.* (*pl.* **ellas**) she.
elle, *f.* name of the letter *ll.*
ello, *pron. neuter sing.* it.—**e. dirá,** the event will tell.—**e. es que,** the fact is that (often expletive).
ellos, ellas, *pron. m.* & *f. pl.* they.
emaciación, *f.* (med.) emaciation.
emanación, *f.* emanation; effluvium.
emanante, *a.* emanating, issuing.
emanantismo, *m.* (philos.) emanationism, theory of creation by emanation.
emanar, *vn.* to emanate, issue; to follow, arise (from).
emancipación, *f.* emancipation.
emancipador, ra, *n.* & *a.* emancipator(-ing).
emancipar. I. *va.* to emancipate. **II.** *vr.* to free oneself; to become free or independent.
embabiamiento, *m.* (coll.) open-mouthed wonder.
embacé, embace, *v.* V. EMBAZAR.
embachar, *va.* to pen (sheep to be shorn).
embadurnador, ra, *n.* & *a.* dauber(-ing).
embadurnar, *va.* to besmear, to bedaub.
embaidor, ra, *n.* & *a.* swindler(-ing).
embaimiento, *m.* delusion, illusion; deceit, imposition, imposture.
embair, *va. defect.* (*only in forms having* i *in the ending*) to impose upon, deceive, humbug.
embajada, *f.* embassy, legation; (coll.) message, errand.
embajador, *m.* ambassador.—**e. cerca de,** ambassador to.—**embajadora, embajatriz,** *f.* ambassadress; ambassador's wife.
embalador, *m.* packer.
embalaje, *m.* packing, baling.
embalar, *va.* to bale, pack.
embaldosado, *m.* tile floor; pavement.
embaldosar, *va.* to pave with tiles or flagstones.

embalsadero, *m.* morass, swamp, marsh.
embalsamador, ra, *m.* embalmer.
embalsamamiento, *m.* embalming.
embalsamar, *va.* to embalm; to perfume.
embalsar, *va.* to put on a raft; to impound, dam (water); (naut.) to sling or hoist.
embalse, *m.* act of putting into a pond or on a raft; (naut.) slinging; impounding (of water).
embalumar. I. *va.* to load unequally. **II.** *vr.* to embarrass oneself with business.
emballenador, ra, *n.* corset maker.
emballenar, *va.* to stiffen with whalebones.
emballestado, da. I. *pp.* of EMBALLESTARSE. **II.** *m.* (vet.) contraction of nerves in feet.
emballestarse, *vr.* to get set to discharge a crossbow.
embanastar, *va.* to put into a basket.
embancarse, *vr.* (metal.) to stick to the walls of the furnace.
embanderar, *va.* to decorate with banners.
embanquetar, *va.* (Mex.) to build sidewalks for (a street).
embaracé, embarace, *v.* V. EMBARAZAR.
embarazada, *a. f.* pregnant.
embarazadamente, *adv.* with embarrassment.
embarazador, ra, *n.* & *a.* embarrasser(-ing).
embarazar, *va.* (*pret.* EMBARACÉ; *subj.* EMBARACE) to embarrass; (coll.) to impregnate.
embarazo, *m.* impediment; embarrassment, confusion, awkwardness; perplexity; pregnancy.
embarazosamente, *adv.* cumbersomely; embarrassingly.
embarazoso, sa, *a.* difficult, entangled, cumbersome; vexatious, embarrassing.
embarbascado, da. I. *pp.* of EMBARBASCAR. **II.** *a.* difficult, intricate, involved.
embarbascar. I. *a.* to stupefy (fish) by throwing hellebore, mullein, etc., into the water; to perplex, confound, embarrass. **II.** *vr.* (of a plow) to become entangled among roots.
embarbecer, *vn.* (*ind.* EMBARBEZCO; *subj.* EMBARBEZCA) to have a beard appearing.
embarbillar, *va.* (carp.) to join.
embarcación, *f.* vessel, ship, craft; embarkation; navigation.—**e. de alijo,** (naut.) lighter.—**e. menor,** small craft.
embarcadero, *m.* wharf, quay, pier, ferry; (Ry.) freight station.
embarcador, ra, *n.* shipper.
embarcar. I. *va.* (*pret.* EMBARQUÉ; *subj.* EMBARQUE) to put on board (ship or train); to ship; to embark on an enterprise.—**e. agua,** (naut.) to ship a sea. **II.** *vr.* to embark, to go on board (ship or train).
embarco, *m.* embarkation (of persons).
embardar, *va.* to thatch.
embargador, ra, *n.* one who lays an embargo.
embargante, *a.* arresting, impeding, restraining.—**no e.,** notwithstanding, nevertheless.
embargar, *va.* (*pret.* EMBARGUÉ; *subj.* EMBARGUE) to impede, restrain, suspend; (law) to embargo, to seize, to attach.
embargo, *m.* indigestion; (law) embargo, sequestration, seizure, attachment.—**sin e.,** notwithstanding, however, nevertheless.—**sin e. de (que),** notwithstanding (that), in spite of (the fact that.)
embarnizadura, *f.* varnishing.
embarnizar, *va.* to varnish.
embarque, *m.* shipment (of goods).
embarqué, embarque, *v.* V. EMBARCAR.
embarrador, ra, *n.* plasterer, dauber; fibber, mischief maker.
embarradura, *f.* smear, plastering; mud stain.
embarrancar. I. *vn.* & *vr.* to run aground. **II.** *vr.* to stick in the mud.
¹**embarrar. I.** *va.* to plaster roughly; to stain or smear with mud; to bedaub.
²**embarrar.**—*vr.* to collect on trees (as partridges).

For pronunciation, see the rules at the beginning of the book.

embarrilador, *m.* packer in barrels.

embarrilar, *va.* to barrel.

embarrotar, *va.* (naut.) = ABARROTAR, to stow.

embarrullador, ra, *n.* muddler, one who makes a mess of things.

embarullar, *va.* (coll.) to muddle, make a mess of; to do carelessly or disorderly.

embasamiento, *m.* (arch.) foundation.

embastar, *va.* (sewing) to baste, to stitch.

embaste, *m.* (sewing) basting.

embastecer. I. *vn.* (*ind.* EMBASTEZCO; *subj.* EMBASTEZCA) to grow fleshy. **II.** *vr.* to become gross or coarse.

embate, *m.* dashing of the waves; sudden impetuous attack.—**embates de la fortuna,** sudden reverses of fortune.

embaucador, *m.* sharper, impostor.

embaucamiento, *m.* deception, humbug.

embaucar, *va.* (*pret.* EMBAUQUÉ; *subj.* EMBAUQUE) to deceive, trick, humbug.

embaular, *va.* to pack in a trunk; (coll.) to cram with food.

embausamiento, *m.* amazement, astonishment.

embazador, *m.* one who or that which dyes a thing brown.

¹embazadura, *f.* brown dye or tinge.

²embazadura, *f.* (fig.) amazement, astonishment.

¹embazar, *va.* (*pret.* EMBACÉ; *subj.* EMBACE) to dye, tinge, or shade brown.

²embazar. I. *va.* to astonish; to embarrass. **II.** *vn.* to be dumfounded. **III.** *vr.* to become tired, disgusted, or satiated.

embebecer: I. *va.* (*ind.* EMBEBEZCO; *subj.* EMBEBEZCA) to entertain, amuse. **II.** *vr.* to be struck with amazement.

embebecidamente, *adv.* amazedly.

embebecimiento, *m.* amazement, astonishment.

embebedor, ra, *n.* & *a.* imbiber(-ing).

embeber. I. *va.* to imbibe, drink in, absorb; to soak, saturate; to contain, include; to sink in, introduce, insert; to incorporate; to shrink, shorten, reduce, squeeze. **II.** *vn.* to shrink, to contract. **III.** *vr.* to be enraptured or ravished; to be absorbed in thought; to learn thoroughly, to master.

embebezco, embebezca, *v.* V. EMBEBECER.

embecadura, *f.* (arch.) spandrel.

embelecador, ra, *n.* impostor, sharper.

embelecar, *va.* (*pret.* EMBELEQUÉ; *subj.* EMBELEQUE) to impose upon, deceive, humbug.

embeleco, *m.* fraud, imposition, humbug.

embeleñado, da. I. *pp.* of EMBELEÑAR. **II.** *a.* enraptured, ravished; stupefied, besotted.

embeleñar, *va.* to narcotize with henbane; to charm, fascinate.

embelesamiento, *m.* rapture, ecstasy.

embelesar. I. *va.* to charm, enchant, fascinate. **II.** *vr.* to be charmed, ravished, or delighted.

embeleso, *m.* rapture, ecstasy, fascination, ravishment; charm.

embellaquecerse, *vr.* to become a knave.

embellecer, *va.* (*ind.* EMBELLEZCO; *subj.* EMBELLEZCA) to beautify, embellish.—**embellecimiento,** *m.* embellishment or beautifying.

embermejar, *va.* = EMBERMEJECER.

embermejecer. I. *va.* (*ind.* EMBERMEJEZCO; *subj.* EMBERMEJEZCA) to dye red; to put to blush, to shame. **II.** *vn.* to blush; to turn red.

emberrenchinarse, emberrincharse, *vr.* (coll.) to fly into a violent passion (as children).

embestida, *f.* assault, violent attack, onset, drive; (coll.) importunate demand.

embestidor, ra. I. *n.* & *a.* rusher(-ing). **II.** *n.* importunate solicitor or beggar.

embestidura, *f.* attack, assault, onset.

embestir. I. *va.* (*ind.* EMBISTO; *subj.* EMBISTA) to assail, attack, rush against; (coll.) to importune with unreasonable demands; (mil.) to attack, make a drive on. **II.** *vn.* to attack, rush.

embetunar, *va.* to bituminate; to black.

embicar, *va.* (*pret.* EMBIQUÉ; *subj.* EMBIQUE) (naut.) to top (the yards).

embijar, *va.* to paint with minium.

embisto, embista, *v.* V. EMBESTIR.

embizcar. I. *va.* to make cross-eyed. **II.** *vn.* & *vr.* to become cross-eyed.

emblandecer. I. *va.* (*ind.* EMBLANDEZCO; *subj.* EMBLANDEZCA) to soften, to mollify. **II.** *vr.* to soften, become soft; to be moved to pity.

emblanquecer. I. *va.* (*ind.* EMBLANQUEZCO; *subj.* EMBLANQUEZCA) to bleach or whiten. **II.** *vr.* to become white.

emblanquecimiento, *m.* whitening, bleaching.

emblema, *m.* emblem, symbol.

emblemáticamente, *adv.* emblematically.

emblemático, ca, *a.* emblematic.

embobamiento, *m.* astonishment, enchantment, open-mouthed wonder.

embobar. I. *va.* to amuse, entertain; to enchant, fascinate. **II.** *vr.* to be struck with astonishment, to stand aghast.

embobecer. I. *va.* (*ind.* EMBOBEZCO; *subj.* EMBOBEZCA) to stultify, make foolish, stupefy. **II.** *vr.* to become stupefied or foolish.

embobecimiento, *m.* stultification.

embocadero, *m.* mouth of a channel.

embocado, da, *a.* tasty (wine).

embocador, *m.* = EMBOCADERO.

embocadura, *f.* entrance by a narrow passage; (mus.) embouchure, mouthpiece; mouthpiece of a bridle; taste (of wine); mouth (of a river); (arch.) proscenium arch.

embocar, *va.* (*pret.* EMBOQUÉ; *subj.* EMBOQUE) to put into the mouth; to put through a narrow passage; (coll.) to swallow in haste, to cram; to hoax.

embocé, emboce, *v.* V. EMBOZAR.

embocinado, da, *a.* trumpet-shaped.

embochinchar, *vn.* to raise a row or a riot.

embodegar, *va.* to store.

embojar, *va.* to prepare sheds for (silkworms).

embojo, *m.* shed for silkworms.

embolada, *f.* piston stroke.

¹embolar, *va.* to put balls on the tips of (bulls' horns).

²embolar, *va.* to apply the gilding size to; to shine, polish (shoes).

embolia, *f.* (med.) embolism.

embolismador, ra, *n.* & *a.* detractor(-ing).

embolismal, *a.* embolismic (year).

embolismar, *vn.* (coll.) to gossip, to carry tales.

embolismático, ca, *a.* confused, muddled.

embolismo, *m.* embolism, intercalation; confusion, disorder, maze; (coll.) falsehood.

émbolo, *m.* (mech.) piston; (med.) embolus.—**e. buzo,** plunger (of a pump).

embolsar, *va.* to put into a purse; to reimburse.

embolso, *m.* act of putting (money) into a purse.

embonar, *va.* to make good, improve, repair; (naut.) to sheathe.—**embono,** *m.* (naut.) doubling, lining, stiffening, sheathing.

emboñigar, *va.* to plaster with cow dung.

emboque, *m.* passage through the mouth or a narrow place (as a ring or a channel); (coll.) deception, cheat, fraud.

emboqué, emboque, *v.* V. EMBOCAR.

emboquillar, *va.* to put a tip on (a cigarette); (min.) to make the entrance of (a shaft); to prepare the mouth of (a drill) for blasting.

embornal, *m.* (naut.) scupper hole.

emborracé, emborrace, *v.* V. EMBORRAZAR.

emborrachador, ra, *a.* intoxicating.

emborrachamiento, *m.* (coll.) intoxication.

emborrachar. I. *va.* to intoxicate. **II.** *vr.* to become intoxicated, get drunk.

emborrar, *va.* to stuff, wad, pad; to card a second time; (coll.) to cram (food).

emborrazamiento, *m.* basting a roasting fowl.

emborrazar, *va.* (*pret.* EMBORRACÉ; *subj.* EMBORRACE) to lard (a fowl).

---

emborricarse, *vr.* (coll.) to make a fool of oneself.

emborrizar, *va.* (*pret.* EMBORRICÉ; *subj.* EMBORRICE) to give the first combing to (wool).

emborronar. I. *va.* to blot. **II.** *va.* & *vn.* to scribble.

emborrullarse, *vr.* (coll.) to dispute noisily.

emboscada, *f.*, **emboscadura,** *f.* ambush, ambuscade.

emboscar. I. *va.* (*pret.* EMBOSQUÉ; *subj.* EMBOSQUE) (mil.) to place in ambush. **II.** *vr.* to retire into a forest; to lie in ambush.

embosquecer, *vn.* & *vr.* to become wooded.

embotado, da, *a.* blunt, dull.

embotador, ra, *n.* one who blunts the points or edges of swords, etc.

embotadura, *f.* bluntness or dulness (app. to weapons).

embotamiento, *m.* blunting of weapons; bluntness, obtuseness, dulness.

¹embotar. I. *va.* to blunt, to dull (an edge or point); to enervate, debilitate; to dull, stupefy. **II.** *vr.* to become dull.

²embotar, *va.* to put (tobacco) in a jar.

embotarse, *vr.* (coll.) to put on one's boots.

embotellador, ra, *n.* & *a.* bottler(-ing).

embotellar, *va.* to bottle; to bottle up.

embotijar. I. *va.* to set jars under (a tile floor) for draining; to put into jars or bottles. **II.** *vr.* (coll.) to swell, to expand; to be in a passion.

embovedar, *va.* = ABOVEDAR, to arch, vault.

emboza, *f.* inequalities in the bottom of barrels.

embozadamente, *adv.* dissemblingly.

embozado, da. I. *pp.* of EMBOZAR. **II.** *a.* muffled, with face covered or concealed (esp. with a cloak). **III.** *n.* one with muffled face.

embozar. I. *va.* (*pret.* EMBOCÉ; *subj.* EMBOCE) to muffle; to cloak, to dissemble; to muzzle. **II.** *vr.* to muffle oneself up.

embozo, *m.* muffler; fold in upper part of bedclothing; artful way of expressing one's thoughts.—**quitarse el e.,** to take off one's mask, to show one's real intention, lay one's cards on the table.

embrace, *m.* curtain clasp.

embracé, embrace, *v.* V. EMBRAZAR.

embracilado, da, *a.* (coll.) carried about in the arms, as children.

embragar, *va.* (*pret.* EMBRAGUÉ; *subj.* EMBRAGUE) to throw in the clutch; (naut.) to sling.

embrague, *m.* clutch; coupling.

embravecer. I. *va.* (*ind.* EMBRAVEZCO; *subj.* EMBRAVEZCA) to enrage, to irritate. **II.** *vn.* (of plants) to become strong. **III.** *vr.* to become angry, to be enraged; (of the sea) to swell.

embravecimiento, *m.* fury, rage, passion.

embravezco, embravezca, *v.* V. EMBRAVECER.

embrazadura, *f.* clasp of a shield or buckler; grasp, clasping, embracing.

embrazar. I. *va.* (*pret.* EMBRACÉ; *subj.* EMBRACE) to clasp (a shield); to grasp, buckle. **II** *vn.* to gear, engage.

embreado, *m.*, **embreadura,** *f.* (naut.) paying with pitch, tarring.

embrear, *va.* (naut.) to pay with pitch.

embregarse, *vr.* to quarrel, wrangle.

embreñarse, *vr.* to hide among brambles.

embriagado, da. I. *pp.* of EMBRIAGAR. **II.** *a.* intoxicated, drunk.

embriagador, ra, or **embriagante,** *a.* intoxicating.

embriagar. I. *va.* (*pret.* EMBRIAGUÉ; *subj.* EMBRIAGUE) to intoxicate; to transport, enrapture. **II.** *vr.* to get drunk.—**embriaguez,** *f.* intoxication, drunkenness; rapture.

embridar, *va.* to bridle; to govern, check.

embriogenia, *f.* (biol.) embryogeny.

embriogénico, ca, *a.* (biol.) embryogenic.

embriología, *f.* embryology.

embriológico, ca, *a.* embryologic.

embriólogo, ga, *n.* embryologist.

embrión, *m.* embryo.

embrionario, ria, *a.* embryonal, embryonic.

embroca, embrocación, *f.* (med.) embrocation.

¹embrocar, *va.* (*pret.* EMBROQUÉ; *subj.* EMBROQUE) to pour out of one vessel into another by joining the mouths; to place upside down.

²embrocar, *va.* (*for mut.* V. ¹EMBROCAR) to wind on a bobbin or quill; (shoemaking) to tack to the last; to toss between the horns.

embrochado, da, *a.* embroidered.

embrochalar, *va.* (carp.) to support (a beam) by a crosspiece or a stay.

embrolla, *f.* (coll.) = EMBROLLO.

embrolladamente, *adv.* tangledly; confusedly.

embrollador, ra, *n.* & *a.* entangler(-ing), troublemaker(-ing).

embrollar, *va.* to entangle, muddle, mess up; to insnare, embroil.—**e. la bandera,** (naut.) to wait the ensign.

embrollo, *m.* tangle, muddle, jumble; trickery, deception; embroiling; involved plot or story.

embrollón, na, *n.* liar, talebearer; mischiefmaker; entangler.

embrolloso, sa, *a.* tangled.

embromado, da. I. *pp.* of EMBROMAR. **II.** *a.* vexed, annoyed; (naut.) misty, hazy, foggy.

embromador, ra, *n.* one who is tumultuously merry; banterer, chaffer; wheedler; trickster.

embromar, *va.* to cajole, to wheedle; to chaff, banter; play jokes on; to vex, annoy; to detain, delay; to injure, harm.

embroqué, embroque, *v.* V. ¹ ²EMBROCAR.

embroquelarse, *vr.* to shield oneself.

embroquetar, *va.* to skewer the legs of.

embrosquilar, *va.* to put (cattle) into a fold.

embrujar, *va.* to bewitch.

embrutecer. I. *va.* (*ind.* EMBRUTEZCO; *subj.* EMBRUTEZCA) to brutalize, make irrational. **II.** *vr.* to become brutalized or irrational.

embrutecimiento, *m.* brutalization.

embrutezco, embrutezca, *v.* V. EMBRUTECER.

embuchado, *m.* a kind of sausage.

embuchar, *va.* to stuff with minced meat; to cram the maw of (animals); (coll.) to swallow without chewing.

embudador, *m.* one who funnels.

embudar, *va.* to put a funnel into; to trick; to scheme, to insnare.

embudista, *m.* trickster, intriguer.

embudito, *m.* *dim.* little funnel.

embudo, *m.* funnel; wax candle mold; watercloset basin; trick; fraud.

embullarse, *vr.* (Cuba) to get ready for a ball, sport, etc.; to revel, to be gay.

embullo, *m.* (Cuba) excitement, anticipation; gaiety, revelry.

emburujar, *va.* (coll.) to jumble, muddle.

embuste, *m.* fib, lie; trick, fraud.—*pl.* gew-gaws, baubles, trinkets.

embustear, *vn.* to fib, lie; impose upon, gab.

embustería, *f.* deceit, imposture, trick.

embustero, ra, *n.* liar; talebearer; trickster, cheat; hypocrite; (coll.) cajoler.

embusterón, na, *n.* *aug.* big liar.

embusteruelo, la, *n.* *dim.* little liar, fibber.

embutidera, *f.* rivet knob.

embutido, da. I. *pp.* of EMBUTIR. **II.** *m.* inlaid work, marquetry; sausage.

embutidor, *m.* rivet set, punch.

embutidura, *f.* (naut.) worming.

embutir, *va.* to inlay, to enchase; to insert; to stuff; to pack tight; to force; to imbed; (coll.) to cram, to eat much; (naut.) to worm.

eme, *f.* Spanish name of the letter *m*.

emenagogo, *m.* (med.) emmenagogue.

emendable, *a.* = ENMENDABLE, amendable.

emendación, *f.* = ENMENDACIÓN, emendation, amendment, correction; satisfaction, amends.

emendador, *m.* = ENMENDADOR, corrector.

emendar, *va.* = ENMENDAR, to amend; reform; indemnify.

emergencia, *f.* act of emerging; emergency, accident; (opt.) emergence.

emergente, *a.* emergent, resulting, issuing.

emérito, *a.* emeritus.

emersión, *f.* (astr.) emersion.

emético, ca. I. *n.* & *a.* emetic. **II.** *m.* tartar emetic.

emetocatártico, ca, *n.* & *a.* emeto-cathartic.

emetropía, *f.* (med.) emmetropia, normal vision.

emienda, *f.* = ENMIENDA, correction; indemnity.

emigración, *f.* emigration; group of emigrants; periodical migration of animals.

emigrado, da, *n.* emigrant; émigré.

emigrante, *n.* & *a.* emigrant.

emigrar, *vn.* to emigrate.

emigratorio, ria, *a.* emigration (as *a.*).

eminencia, *f.* eminence, prominence; height, hill; eminence, title of cardinals; outstanding person.—**con e.,** eminently.

eminencial, *a.* (philos.) acting eminently.

eminencialmente, *adv.* eminently.

eminente, *a.* eminent, prominent; high, lofty.

eminentemente, *adv.* eminently.

eminentísimo, ma, *a. super.* most eminent.

emir, *m.* emir, ameer.

emisario, *m.* emissary; spy; outlet, discharge; (physiol.) emunctory.

emisión, *f.* emission, vent; issue (of paper money, bonds, etc.); (med.) emission; (phys.) radiation.—*pl.* **emisiones radiofónicas,** or **radiotelefónicas,** broadcasting.

emisivo, va, *a.* emitting; emission (as *a.*).

emisor, ra. I. *a.* emitting; (radio) broadcasting. **II.** *m.* (radio) transmitter; broadcasting instrument or apparatus. **III.** *f.* (radio) broadcast; broadcasting station.

emitir, *va.* to emit, send forth; to issue (as bonds, etc.); to utter, express; (radio) to broadcast.

emoción, *f.* emotion.

emocional, *a.* emotive; emotional.

emocionante, *a.* touching, causing emotion.

emocionar. I. *va.* to touch, move, shock, arouse emotion in. **II.** *vr.* to be moved.

emoliente, *m.* & *a.* emollient.

emolumento, *m.* emolument, fee, perquisite.

emotive, va, *a.* emotive, pertaining to emotion.

empacar, *va.* (*pret.* EMPAQUÉ; *subj.* EMPAQUE) to pack, to bale.

empacarse, *vr.* to persist, act stubbornly; to become confused or rattled; to balk.

empacón, *a.* (Am.) obstinate, stubborn; balky.

empachado, da. I. *pp.* of EMPACHAR. **II.** *a.* awkward, timid, bashful; surfeited, glutted; (naut.) overloaded.

empachar. I. *va.* to impede, embarrass; to overload, cram, encumber; to cause indigestion; to disguise. **II.** *vr.* to be ashamed, embarrassed, bashful; to surfeit.

empacho, *m.* bashfulness, timidity; embarrassment; obstacle; surfeit, indigestion.—**sin e.,** without ceremony; without blushing; unconcernedly.

empachoso, sa, *a.* embarrassing; disgraceful.

empadronador, *m.* census taker.

empadronamiento, *m.* census; tax list.

empadronar, *va.* to take the census of; to register (taxpayers).

empajada, *f.* hay with bran for horses.

empajar, *va.* to cover or stuff with straw; thatch.

empalagamiento, *m.* surfeit, cloying; boring.

empalagar, *va.* (*pret.* EMPALAGUÉ; *subj.* EMPALAGUE) to pall, cloy; surfeit; to vex, bother.

empalago, *m.* = EMPALAGAMIENTO.

empalagoso, sa, *a.* cloying, too rich or sweet, sickening; wearisome, annoying, boresome.

empalagué, empalague, *v. V.* EMPALAGAR.

empalamiento, *m.* empalement, empaling.

empalar, *va.* to empale.

empaliada, *f.* hangings of bunting.

empaliar, *va.* to adorn with hangings.

empalizada, *f.* palisade, stockade, pale fence.

empalizar, *va.* to palisade, to stockade, fence.

empalmadura, *f.* joint; coupling; splicing.

empalmar. I. *va.* to couple, join; to splice. **II.** *vn.* (Ry.) to branch, to join.

empalme, *m.* scarf, joint, connection; splicing; (Ry.) junction.

empalomado, *m.* (hydraul.) loose-stone damming wall.

empalomar, *va.* (naut.) to sew (the boltrope).

empalletado, *m.* (naut.) mattress barricade.

empamparse, *vr.* (Am.) to get lost in a pampa.

empanada, *f.* meat pie; fraudulent muddle or concealment.—**empanadilla,** *f. dim.* small pie; movable footstep in carriages.

empanado, da. I. *pp.* of EMPANAR. **II.** *a.* & *n.* (room) receiving light only from another room.

empanar. I. *va.* to bake in paste; to sow (grain) **II.** *vr.* (agr.) to be choked by too much seed.

empandar, *va.* to bend, to sag; to warp.

empandillar, *va.* (coll.) to cheat at cards.

empantanar, *va.* to submerge; to swamp; to bemire; to embarrass; to obstruct.

empañadura, *f.* swaddling clothes.

empañar, *va.* to swaddle; to dim, blur, tarnish; to soil, sully (reputation).

empañetar, *va.* (Am.) to plaster.

empañicar, *va.* (naut.) to hand or furl.

empapar. I. *va.* to imbibe, saturate, soak, drench. **II.** *vr.* (en) to imbibe; to be soaked (in); to absorb; to enter into the spirit (of); (coll.) to surfeit.

empapelado, *m.* papering, paper hanging; paper (on a wall); paper lining.

empapelador, ra, *n.* paperhanger.

empapelar, *va.* to wrap up in paper; to paper.

empapirotar, *va.* (coll.) to adorn, to deck.

empapujar, *va.* (coll.) to make (one) eat too much, to stuff.

¹**empaque,** *m.* packing.

²**empaque,** *m.* mien, appearance, looks; affected seriousness; (Chile, Peru, P. R.) boldness, brazenness, impudence.

empaqué, empaque, *v. V.* EMPACAR; EMPACARSE.

empaquetador, ra, *n.* packer.

empaquetadura, *f.* packing, gasket.

empaquetar, *va.* to pack; to stuff.

emparamado, da. (Am.) **I.** *pp.* of EMPARAMARSE. **II.** *a.* shivering with cold; (fig.) frozen.

emparamarse, *vr.* (Am.) to freeze to death; to shiver with cold.

emparamentar, *va.* to adorn, to bedeck.

emparchar, *va.* to cover with plasters.

emparedado, da. I. *pp.* of EMPAREDAR. **II.** *n.* recluse. **III.** *m.* sandwich.

emparedamiento, *m.* confinement, religious retirement; cloister.

emparedar, *va.* to immure, to shut up.

emparejador, ra, *n.* smoother, matcher, fitter.

emparejadura, *f.,* **emparejamiento,** *m.* matching; smoothing; evening up.

emparejar, *va.* & *vn.* to level, make even, smooth; to match, to fit; to put abreast.

emparentado, da. I. *pp.* of EMPARENTAR. **II.** *a.* related by marriage.

emparentar, *vn.* & *vr.* (*ind.* EMPARIENTO; *subj.* EMPARIENTE) to become related by marriage.

emparrado, *m.* vine arbor or bower.

emparrar, *va.* to embower.

emparrillado, *m.* (eng.) grillage; grate.

emparrillar, *va.* to broil on the gridiron.

emparvar, *va.* to lay (grain) for thrashing.

empastado, da, *a.* (bookbinding) bound with a stiff cover (cloth, calf, etc.).

empastador, ra. I. *a.* (painter) who impastes. **II.** *m.* paste brush. **III.** *n.* bookbinder.

empastar, *va.* to fill (a tooth); to paste; (art) to

impaste; (bookbinding) to bind with a stiff cover (cloth, leather, etc.).—**empaste**, *m.* filling (of a tooth); binding; (art) impasto.

empastelar, *va. & vr.* (coll.) to compound, compromise; (print.) to pie.

empatadera, *f.* (coll.) checking, impeding.

empatar, *va.* to equal; to be a tie (in voting or games); to hinder, obstruct; to join.

empate, *m.* tie (in voting or games); hindrance, stopping, checking; joint; joining.

empavesada, *f.* (naut.) waistclothes; armings; hammock cloth; boat's cloth.—**empavesadas de las cofas**, top armor.

empavesado, da. I. *pp.* of EMPAVESAR. **II.** *a.* covered with a large shield. **III.** *m.* soldier with large shield; dressing of a ship.

empavesar, *va.* (naut.) to dress (ships); (naut.) to spread (waistclothes).

empavonar, *va.* to paint (iron) (to preserve it).

empecatado, da, *a.* very wily, evil-minded, incorrigible; ill-starred, unlucky.

empecé, *pret.* of EMPEZAR.

empecer. I. *va.* (*ind.* EMPEZO; *subj.* EMPEZA) to hurt, offend. **II.** *vn.* to prevent.

empecimiento, *m.* damage; obstacle.

¹**empecinado**, *m.* maker or seller of pitch.

²**empecinado, da. I.** *pp.* of EMPECINARSE. **II.** *a.* (Am.) stubborn.

empecinarse, *vr.* (en) (Am.) to persist (in), be stubborn (about), or bound (to).

empechar, *va.* to prevent, hinder.

empedernido, da, *a.* hard-hearted.

empedernir. I. *va.* (*defect., used only in forms with i in their termination*) to indurate, to harden. **II.** *vr.* to be petrified; to become hard-hearted.

empedrado, da. I. *pp.* of EMPEDRAR. **II.** *a.* (of the sky) spotted with clouds; (of the face) pitted from smallpox. **III.** *m.* stone pavement.

empedrador, *m.* stone paver.

empedramiento, *m.* stone paving.

empedrar, *va.* (*ind.* EMPIEDRO; *subj.* EMPIEDRE) to pave with stones.

empega, *f.* pitch varnish; mark with pitch.

empegado, *m.* tarpaulin.

empegadura, *f.* coat of pitch.

empegar, *va.* (*pret.* EMPEGUÉ; *subj.* EMPEGUE) to pay with pitch; to mark (sheep) with pitch.

empego, *m.* marking sheep with pitch; (Am.) pitchy taste.

empegué, empegue, *v. V.* EMPEGAR.

empeguntar, *va.* to mark (sheep) with pitch.

¹**empeine**, *m.* groin; instep; hoof.

²**empeine**, *m.* (med.) tetter, ringworm; (bot.) cotton flower.—**empeinoso, sa,** *a.* full of ringworms.

empelar, *vn.* to grow hair.

empelazgarse, *vr.* (coll.) to become involved.

empelechar, *va.* to cover or line with marble.

empelotarse, *vr.* to get into a wrangle; (Am.) to take off all one's clothes.

empeltre, *m.* small shoot or sapling.

empella, *f.* vamp of a shoe.

empellar, *va.* (*ind.* EMPIELLO; *subj.* EMPIELLE) to push, shove, jostle.

empellejar, *va.* to cover or line with skins.

empeller, *va.* = EMPELLAR.

empellón, *m.* push, shove.—**a empellones**, pushing, by pushing rudely.

empenachado, da, *a.* plumed.

empenachar, *va.* to adorn with plumes.

empenta, *f.* prop, stay, shore.

empeñadamente, *adv.* strenuously; hard; insistently.

empeñado, da. I. *pp.* of EMPEÑAR. **II.** *a.* determined, persisting.

empeñaduría, *f.* (Am.) pawnshop.

empeñar. I. *va.* to pawn; to pledge; to engage, oblige. **II.** *vr.* (en) to bind oneself (to); to per-

sist (in); to insist, be bent (on); to intercede, mediate; (mil.) (of a battle) to begin.

empeñero, ra, *n.* (Mex.) pawnbroker.

empeño, *m.* pledge, pawn; engagement, contract; earnest desire; determination; protection, recommendation; recommender; (Mex.) EMPEÑADURÍA.—**casa de empeños**, pawnshop.—**con e.**, eagerly, persistently.

empeoramiento, *m.* deterioration; making matters worse; becoming worse.

empeorar. I. *va.* to impair, to deteriorate; make worse. **II.** *vn. & vr.* to grow worse.

empequeñecer, *va.* (*ind.* EMPEQUEÑEZCO; *subj.* EMPEQUEÑEZCA) to make smaller, diminish; belittle.

emperador, *m.* emperor.

emperatriz, *f.* empress.

emperchado, *m.* fence formed with interwoven green trees.

emperchar, *va.* to hang on a perch.

emperdigar, *va.* to brown (meat); to prepare.

emperejilar, *va. & vr.* to dress up or elaborately.

emperezar. I. *vn. & vr.* to be lazy, indolent. **II.** *va.* to retard, delay, obstruct.

empergaminado, da, *a.* bound in parchment.

emperifollar, *va. & vr.* = EMPEREJILAR.

empernar, *va.* to bolt, nail, spike, peg.

empero, *conj.* yet, however, notwithstanding.

emperrada, *f.* a card game.

emperramiento, *m.* obstinacy.

emperrarse, *vr.* (en) (coll.) to be obstinate or stubborn (about); to persist (in); (Colomb.) (a llorar) to burst out (crying).

empersonar, *va.* to register in the census.

empesador, *m.* warp evener.

empetro, *m.* (bot.) crowberry.

empezar, *va. & vn.* (*ind. pres.* EMPIEZO; *pret.* EMPECÉ; *subj.* EMPIECE) to begin.—**e. por** (*inf.*), to begin by (*pres. p.*).

empicarse, *vr.* to become too fond or infatuated.

empicotadura, *f.* act of pillorying.

empicotar, *va.* to pillory; to picket.

empiedro, empiedre, *v. V.* EMPEDRAR.

empiello, empielle, *v. V.* EMPELLAR.

empiema, *f.* (med.) empyema.

empiezo, empiece, *v. V.* EMPEZAR.

empilonar, *va.* (Cuba) to pile up (tobacco leaves).

empinada, *f.* (aer.) zooming.

empinado, da, *a.* steep; high, lofty.

empinador, ra, *n.* (coll.) toper.

empinadura, *f.*, **empinamiento**, *m.* erection, elevation, rising.

empinar. I. *va.* to raise; to exalt; to tip, incline. —**e. el codo**, to be a toper, to drink much. **II.** *vr.* to stand on tiptoe; to stand on the hind legs; to tower, rise high; (aer.) to zoom.

empingorotado, da. I. *pp.* of EMPINGOROTAR. **II.** *a.* haughty, stuck-up.

empingorotar, *va.* (coll.) to raise with a wedge or support.

empino, *m.* (arch.) summit of a curve.

empiolar, *va.* to tie by the legs; to arrest.

empíreo, a. I. *a.* empyreal; celestial, divine. **II.** *m.* empyrean.

empireuma, *f.* (chem.) empyreuma.

empireumático, ca, *a.* (chem.) empyreumatic.

empíricamente, *adv.* empirically.

empírico, ca. I. *a.* empirical. **II.** *m.* quack.

empirismo, *m.* empiricism; quackery.

empizarrado, *m.* slate roof.

empizarrar, *va.* to roof with slate.

emplacé, emplace, *v. V.* EMPLAZAR.

emplastadura, *f.*, **emplastamiento**, *m.* plastering, putting plasters on; applying paint or cosmetics (to the face).

emplastar. I. *va.* to apply plasters to; to paint the face of; (coll.) to stop, check, obstruct. **II.** *vr.* to get smeared.

emplastecer, *va.* (*ind.* EMPLASTEZCO; *subj.* EM-
PLASTEZCA) (art) to smooth for painting.
emplástico, ca, *a.* glutinous, sticky.
emplasto, *m.* plaster, poultice.
emplástrico, ca, *a.* glutinous, sticky; (med.)
suppurative, dissolving.
emplazador, ra, *n.* (law) summoner.
emplazamiento, *m.* (law) summons.
emplazar, *va.* (*pret.* EMPLACÉ; *subj.* EMPLACE)
(law) to summon; (sport) to set (the hunting
party).
empleado, da. I. *pp.* of EMPLEAR. **II.** *n.* employee; officeholder.
emplear. I. *va.* to employ; give occupation to;
to engage, hire; to appoint; to invest, to spend
(as money); to use. **II.** *vr.* to be employed, to
be in business.
empleita, *f.* plaited length of bast.—**empleitero,
ra,** *n.* one who plaits and sells bass-weed.
emplenta, *f.* section of mud wall made at once.
empleo, *m.* employ, employment, occupation,
job; public office; calling, profession; use; aim
or object of desire; investment.
empleomanía, *f.* (coll.) mania for public office.
emplomado, *m.* roof covered with lead.
emplomador, ra, *n.* one who leads (covers,
lines, etc. with lead.)
emplomadura, *f.* leading (covering, filling, etc.,
with lead); lead covering, lining, etc.
emplomar, *va.* to lead; to line with sheet lead; to
put lead seals on.
emplumar. I. *va.* to feather; to adorn with
plumes; to tar and feather; (Hond.) to thrash.
II. *vn.* = EMPLUMECER.
emplumecer, *vn.* (*ind.* EMPLUMEZCO; *subj.* EM-
PLUMEZCA) to fledge, grow feathers.
empobrecer. I. *va.* (*ind.* EMPOBREZCO; *subj.*
EMPOBREZCA) to impoverish. **II.** *vn.* to become
poor.
empobrecimiento, *m.* impoverishment.
empocé, empoce, *v.* V. EMPOZAR..
empolvar, *va.*, *vr.* to cover with dust; to powder.
empolvoramiento, *m.* covering with dust or
powder.
empolvorar, empolvorizar, *va.* = EMPOLVAR.
empollador, ra. I. *n.* hatcher. **II.** *m.* incubator.
empolladura, *f.* brood of bees.
empollar. I. *va.* to brood, to hatch. **II.** *vn.* (of
bees) to breed.
emponchado, da, *a.* (Am.) covered with, or
wearing, a poncho.
emponzoñador, ra, *n.* & *a.* poisoner(-ing, -ous).
emponzoñamiento, *m.* poisoning.
emponzoñar, *va.* to poison; to corrupt.
empopar, *va.* (naut.) to poop.
emporcar, *va.* (*ind. pres.* EMPUERCO, *pret.* EM-
PORQUÉ; *subj.* EMPUERQUE) to soil, dirty, foul.
emporio, *m.* emporium, mart.
empotramiento, *m.* (arch.) embedding.
empotrar, *va.* (arch.) to embed, to fix in a wall;
to scarf, to splice; to put (beehives) in a pit;
(naut.) to fasten (cannon).
empotrerar, *va.* (Am.) to convert into pasture;
to put (cattle) in a pasture.
empozar. I. *va.* (*pret.* EMPOCÉ; *subj.* EMPOCE) to
throw into a well; to soak (flax). **II.** *vr.* (coll.)
to be pigeonholed; (Am.) (of water) to collect
in puddles.
empradizar. I. *va.* to turn into a meadow;
(Colomb.) to weed. **II.** *vr.* to become a meadow.
emprendedor, *n.* & *a.* enterpriser(-ing).
emprender, *va.* to undertake, to engage in.—**e.
a,** or **con,** to address, accost.
empreñar, *va.* to impregnate; to beget.
empresa, *f.* enterprise, undertaking; company,
firm; device, motto; intention, purpose; management of a theater.
empresario, *m.* promoter; contractor; theatrical
manager; impresario.

empréstito, *m.* loan.—**e. público,** government
loan.
emprima, *f.* = PRIMICIA, first fruits.
emprimado, *m.* last combing of wool.
emprimar, *va.* to give the last combing **to**
(wool); (coll.) to deceive.
empringar, *va.* = PRINGAR.
empuchar, *va.* to buck (skeins of thread).
empuerco, empuerque, *v.* V. EMPORCAR.
empuesta.—**de e.,** from the rear, from behind.
empujar, *va.* to push, impel, shove.
empuje, empujo, *m.* push, pressure; energy,
enterprise; (eng.) thrust.
empujón, *m.* push, violent shove.—**a empujones,** pushing, jostling.
empulgadura, *f.* drawing the string of a crossbow.
empulgar, *va.* to draw the string of (a crossbow).
empulgueras, *f. pl.* wings of a crossbow; thumb-
screws.
empuñador, ra, *n.* grasper.
empuñadura, *f.* hilt (of a sword); beginning (of
a story).
empuñar, *va.* to clinch, clutch, grip, hold tightly
with the fist.
empuñidura, *f.* (naut.) earing.
emulación, *f.* emulation; envy, jealousy.
emulador, ra, *m.* emulator, rival.
emular, *va.* to emulate, rival, compete with.
emulgente, *a.* (physiol.) emulgent.
émulo, la, *n.* competitor, rival, emulator.
emulsión, *f.* emulsion.—**emulsionar,** *va.* to
emulsify.
emulsivo, va, *a.* emulsive, emulsifying.
emulsor, *m.* grease mixer.
emunción, *f.* (med.) excretion.
emuntorio, *m.* emunctory.—*pl.* emunctory
glands in armpits, groins, and back of the ears.
en, *prep.* in; at; on, upon (*en la mesa,* on the
table; *en domingo,* on Sunday; *en la pared,* on
the wall; *en esa ocasión,* on that occasion); to;
into (*convertir en gas,* to convert into a gas; *convertirse en polvo,* to turn to dust); (before gerund)
on, upon, immediately after (*en llegando,* on
arriving; *en acabando esta carta,* immediately,
or right, after finishing this letter). Foll. by
adj. makes an adverbial phrase (*en alto,* on
high).
enaceitarse, *vr.* to become oily or rancid.
enagua, *f.* gen. in the *pl.*, **enaguas,** underskirt,
petticoat; skirt.
enaguachar, *va.* to load with water.
enaguazar, *va.* to flood.
enagüillas, *f. pl.* short skirt or petticoat; kilt.
enajenable, *a.* alienable.
enajenación, *f.*, **enajenamiento,** *m.* alienation
(of property); absence of mind; rapture, overjoy.—**e. mental,** mental derangement.
enajenar. I. *va.* to alienate, to transfer (property); to transport, enrapture. **II.** *vr.* to be enraptured, ravished.
enálage, *f.* (gram.) enallage.
enalbardar, *va.* to saddle (beasts of burden); to
cover with a batter; to bread.
enalmagrado, da. I. *pp.* of ENALMAGRAR. **II.** *a.*
colored with ochre; vile, despicable.
enalmagrar, *va.* to cover with ochre.
enalmenar, *va.* to provide with battlements.
enaltecer, *va.* (*ind.* ENALTEZCO; *subj.* ENAL-
TEZCA), to extol.
enamarillecer, *va.* & *vr.* (*ind.* ENAMARILLEZCO;
subj. ENAMARILLEZCA) to dye yellow.
enamoradamente, *adv.* lovingly, wooingly.
enamoradizo, za, *a.* inclined to fall in love.
enamorado, da. I. *pp.* of ENAMORAR. **II.** *a.* fond
of love-making; in love, enamored, lovesick.
III. *n.* lover; sweetheart.
enamorador, ra, *n.* & *a.* courter(-ing), wooer
(-ing); love-maker(-ing).

For pronunciation, see the rules at the beginning of the book.

enamoramiento, *m.* love, being in love; courting, love-making.

enamorar. I. *va.* to inspire love in; to make love to, woo. **II.** *vr.* (de) to fall in love (with).

enamoricarse, *vr.* (coll.) to be slightly in love.

enanchar, *va.* (coll.) to widen, enlarge.

enangostar, *va.* to narrow, contract.

enanito, ita. I. *a.* *dim.* little, minute. **II.** *n.* little dwarf; midget.

enano, na. I. *a.* dwarfish, small, little. **II.** *n.* dwarf.

enante, *m.* (bot.) water dropwort.

enantes, *a.* (low) = ANTES, before.

enarbolar. I. *va.* to hoist, raise high, hang out (a flag, etc.). **II.** *vr.* = ENCABRITARSE.

enarcar, *va.* to arch; to hoop (barrels).

enardecer. I. *va.* (*ind.* ENARDEZCO; *subj.* ENARDEZCA) to fire with passion, to inflame. **II.** *vr.* to be kindled, inflamed (with passion).

enardecimiento, *m.* act of inflaming or state of being inflamed with passion; being or becoming fiery or impassioned.

enardezco, enardezca, *v.* *V.* ENARDECER.

enarenación, *f.* plaster for a wall before painting.

enarenar. I. *va.* to sand; to gravel. **II.** *vr.* (naut.) to ground.

enarmonar. I. *va.* to raise, to rear. **II.** *vr.* (of quadrupeds) to rise up on the hind feet.

enarmónico, ca, *a.* (mus.) enharmonic.

enartrosis, *f.* (anat.) enarthrosis.

enastado, da, *a.* horned.

enastar, *va.* to put a haft or handle on.

encabador, *m.* (Colomb.) penholder.

encabalgamiento, *m.* gun carriage.

encabalgar. I. *vn.* (*pret.* ENCABALGUÉ; *subj.* ENCABALGUE) to rest upon (as a beam on a joist). **II.** *va.* to provide horses for.

encaballadura, *f.* (mason.) lapping over.

encaballar, *va.* to lap over, to imbricate (as tiles).

encabar, *va.* (S. A.) to put a handle on.

encabellecerse, *vr.* (*ind.* ENCABELLEZCO; *subj.* ENCABELLEZCA) to grow hair.

encabestrar. I. *va.* to halter; to force to obedience. **II.** *vr.* to become entangled in the halter.

encabezador, *m.* header, reaping machine.

encabezadura, *f.* scarfing, heading.

encabezamiento, *m.* headline, heading, title; census taking; tax roll; act of enrolling taxpayers; tax rate.—**e. de factura,** billhead.

encabezar. I. *va.* to draw up (a tax roll); to put a heading or title to; to head, lead; to strengthen (wine) with alcohol; (carp.) to scarf, to join. **II.** *vr.* to compound for taxes; to compromise.

encabezonamiento, *m.* = ENCABEZAMIENTO.

encabezonar, *va.* = ENCABEZAR.

encabillar, *va.* (naut.) to scotch, pin, bolt.

encabrahigar, *va.* to ripen figs artificially.

encabriar, *va.* (arch.) to place the rafters of.

encabritarse, *vr.* to rise up on the hind feet.

encabuyar, *va.* (Am.) to tie with hemp cord.

encachado, *m.* (hydraul.) concrete lining.

encachar, *va.* (hydraul.) to line with concrete.

encadenación, encadenadura, *f.,* **encadenamiento,** *m.* chaining, enchainment; concatenation, linking, connection.

encadenar, *va.* to chain, fetter, shackle; to enslave; to concatenate, connect, link together (as thoughts); to captivate; to paralyze.

encajador, *m.* one who chases or inserts; chasing tool.

encajadura, *f.* act of chasing, inserting or joining; socket, groove.

encajar. I. *va.* to chase, drive in, fit in, insert; to push or force in; (carp.) to rabbet, join; (mech.) to gear; to fit closely (as a lid); to put in (a remark); to tell (a story); to throw out (a hint); to fire off; to throw, hurl (as a missile); to administer (as a scolding); to pass off (as a spuri-

ous coin). **II.** *vn.* to fit, fit in. **III.** *vr.* to thrust oneself into some narrow place; to intrude.

encaje, *m.* act of adjusting or fitting; socket, cavity, groove; enchasing; joining; lace; inlaid work, mosaic; looks, appearance.

encajera, *f.* woman who makes lace.

encajerado, da, *a.* (naut.) fouled on the sheave.

encajetillar, *va.* to packet (cigarettes, tobacco).

encajonado, da. I. *pp.* of ENCAJONAR. **II.** *a.* (of rivers) narrow, flanked by steep inclines. **III.** *m.* (mason.) packed work; cofferdam.

encajonamiento, *m.* packing in boxes or cases; (of rivers) narrowing between steep banks.

encajonar, *va.* to box; to case; to narrow.

encalabozar, *va.* (coll.) to put into a dungeon.

encalabrinado, da. I. *pp.* of ENCALABRINAR. **II.** *a.* headstrong, stubborn, obstinate.

encalabrinar. I. *va.* to affect the head of with some unpleasant smell or vapor. **II.** *vr.* (coll.) to become stubborn.

encalada, *f.* metal piece of a harness.

encalador, *m.* lime pit or vat.

encaladura, *f.* whitewashing.

encalar, *va.* to whitewash; to lime.

encalmadura, *f.* (vet.) a disease of horses caused by overheating.

encalmarse, *vr.* (vet.) to be overheated; (naut.) to be becalmed.

encalostrarse, *vr.* to become sick by sucking the first milk.

encalvecer, *vn.* (*ind.* ENCALVEZCO; *subj.* ENCALVEZCA) to become bald.

encalladero, *m.* (naut.) shoal, sand bank.

encalladura, *f.* (naut.) grounding, stranding.

encallar, *vn.* (naut.) to run aground; to fail.

encallecer. I. *vn.* (*ind.* ENCALLEZCO; *subj.* ENCALLEZCA) to get corns or callosities. **II.** *vr.* to become hardened or callous.

encallecido, da. I. *pp.* of ENCALLECER. **II.** *a.* hardened; hard-hearted; callous.

encallejonar, *va.* to put in, force into, an alley.

encallezco, encallezca, *v.* *V.* ENCALLECER.

encamación, *f.* (min.) stull.

encamarar, *va.* to store (grain).

encamarse, *vr.* (coll.) to stay in bed; (of game birds) to lie hidden; (of corn, etc.) to be beaten down by rain, wind, etc.

encambijar, *va.* to conduct (water).

encambrar, *va.* = ENCAMARAR.

encambronar, *va.* to hedge with brambles; to strengthen with iron.

encaminadura, *f.,* **encaminamiento,** *m.* act of putting on the right road.

encaminar. I. *va.* to guide, to put on the right road; to direct, to manage; to forward; to aim at, intend. **II.** *vr.* (a) to take the road (to); to be on the way (to); to be intended (for, to).

encamisada, *f.* (mil.) camisado; an ancient night masquerade.

encamisar. I. *va.* to put a shirt or a cover on. **II.** *vr.* to put a shirt over one's clothes for a camisado.

encampanado, da, *a.* bell-shaped.

encanalar, encanalizar, *va.* to convey through pipes or conduits.

encanallamiento, *m.* degeneracy, becoming base and despicable.

encanallarse, *vr.* to become low, base, mean.

encanarse, *vr.* (of infants) to stiffen from rage.

encanastar, *va.* to put in baskets.

encancerarse, *vr.* to become cancerous.

encandecer, *va.* (*ind.* ENCANDEZCO; *subj.* ENCANDEZCA) to make incandescent.

encandelar, *vn.* (agr.) (of trees) to bud.

encandiladera, *f.* (coll.) procuress.

encandilado, da. I. *pp.* of ENCANDILAR. **II.** *a.* (of hats) cocked.

encandiladora, *f.* = ENCANDILADERA.

encandilar. I. *va.* to dazzle; to daze, bewilder;

(coll.) to stir (the fire). **II.** *vr.* to have bloodshot eyes, as from drink; to be dazzled.

encanecer, *vn.* (*ind.* ENCANEZCO; *subj.* ENCANEZCA) to grow gray-haired; to mold; to grow old.

encanijamiento, *m.* weakness, emaciation.

encanijar. I. *va.* to weaken (a baby) by poor nursing. **II.** *vr.* to pine, be emaciated.

encanillar, *va.* to wind on a quill or spool.

encantación, *f.* incantation.

encantado, da. I. *pp.* of ENCANTAR. **II.** *a.* absent-minded; haunted; enchanted, charmed.

encantador, ra. I. *n.* enchanter, sorcerer; charmer. **II.** *a.* charming, delightful.

encantamiento, *m.* enchantment.

encantar, *va.* to enchant, charm; bewitch; to fascinate; to delight.

encantarar, *va.* to put into a jar or ballot box.

encante, *m.* auction, public sale.

encanto, *m.* enchantment, charm, spell; fascination; delight.

encantorio, *m.* (coll.) enchantment.

encantusar, *va.* (coll.) to coax, wheedle.

encañada, *f.* gorge, notch.

encañado, *m.* conduit for water, pipe line; hedge or trellis of reeds.

encañador, ra, *n.* spool winder.

¹**encañar. I.** *va.* to hedge with reeds; to wind (silk). **II.** *vn.* (of cereals) to form stalks.

²**encañar,** *va.* to convey (water) through pipes; to drain.

encañizada, *f.* (fish) weir.

encañonar. I. *va.* to put into pipes; to plait, to fold; to wind on quills. **II.** *vn.* to fledge out.

encañutar, *va.* to flute.

encapacetado, da, *a.* wearing a helmet.

encapachadura, *f.* collection of baskets of olives to be pressed.

encapachar, *va.* to put into a fruit basket; (agr.) to protect (grapes) with the shoots.

encapado, da, *a.* cloaked.

encapazar, *va.* to collect into a basket.

encaperuzado, da, *a.* hooded.

encaperuzarse, *vr.* to put on a hood.

encapillado, *n.* (Am.) clothes on one's back.

encapilladura, *f.* (naut.) top rigging.

encapillar. I. *va.* (naut.) to rig (the yards); (min.) to start a new gallery in. **II.** *vr.* to put clothes on over the head.

encapirotado, da, *a.* wearing a hood.

encapotadura, *f.,* **encapotamiento,** *m.* frown.

encapotar. I. *va.* & *vr.* to cloak; to muffle; to frown. **II.** *vr.* to become cloudy; (of horses) to lower the head too much.

encapricharse, *vr.* to indulge in whims; to become stubborn; (coll.) to be infatuated.

encapuchar, *va.* to cover with a hood.

encapuzar, *va.* to cover with a cowl.

encarado, da. I. *pp.* of ENCARAR. **II.** *a.*—**bien (mal) e.,** well- (ill-) favored (in looks).

encaramar, *va.* & *vr.* to raise; to elevate; to extol; to climb; to reach a high post.

encaramiento, *m.* act of facing or aiming.

encarar. I. *vn.* to face. **II.** *va.* to aim, to point. **III.** *vr.* (con) to face, be face to face (with).

encaratularse, *vr.* to mask.

encarcelación, *f.* incarceration.

encarcelar, *va.* to imprison; (carp.) to clamp, to jam; (mason.) to embed with mortar; (naut.) to woold.

encarecedor, ra, *n.* & *a.* praiser(-ing), extoller (-ing).

encarecer, *va.,* *vn.* & *vr.* (*ind.* ENCAREZCO; *subj.* ENCAREZCA) to raise the price; to overrate; to extol; to enhance; to recommend.

encarecidamente, *adv.* exceedingly, highly; eagerly, earnestly.

encarecimiento, *m.* enhancement, exaggeration.—**con e.,** ardently, earnestly.

encarezco, encarezca, *v.* *V.* ENCARECER.

encargado, da. I. *pp.* of ENCARGAR. **II.** *a.* in charge. **III.** *n.* person in charge; agent, representative.—**e. de negocios,** chargé d'affaires; (Mex.) agent, attorney.

encargar. I. *va.* (*pret.* ENCARGUÉ; *subj.* ENCARGUE) to entrust, put under the care (of a person); to advise, warn; to order (goods, etc.); to ask, request; to urge. **II.** *vr.* to take charge.

encargo, *m.* charge, commission, request; errand; job, assignment; place, employ; (com.) order.

encargué, encargue, *v.* *V.* ENCARGAR.

encariñar. I. *va.* to inspire affection or love, endear. **II.** *vr.* (con) to become fond (of).

encarna, *f.* giving entrails of game to dogs.

encarnación, *f.* incarnation; personification; (art) flesh color.

encarnadino, na, *a.* incarnadine.

encarnado, da. I. *pp.* of ENCARNAR. **II.** *a.* incarnate; flesh-colored; red.

encarnadura, *f.* (surg.) ENCARNAMIENTO; flesh wound made by a sharp weapon.

encarnamiento, *m.* (surg.) natural healing of the flesh.

encarnar. I. *vn.* to incarnate; to penetrate, or lodge in, the flesh; (med.) to granulate (as a wound); to make a strong impression upon the mind. **II.** *va.* to incarnate; to embody; to flesh (hunting dogs); to bait (a fishhook); to paint or make flesh-colored; to cause or produce granulation in (a wound). **III.** *vr.* to unite, mix (with one another).

encarnativo, *m.* & *a.* (surg.) incarnative.

encarne, *m.* entrails given to dogs.

encarnecer, *vn.* (*ind.* ENCARNEZCO; *subj.* ENCARNEZCA) to grow fleshy, put on flesh.

encarnicé, encarnice, *v.* *V.* ENCARNIZAR.

encarnizado, da. I. *pp.* of ENCARNIZAR. **II.** *a.* blood-, or flesh-, colored; cruel, pitiless; bloody, hard-fought.

encarnizamiento, *m.* act of fleshing (dogs); cruelty, rage, fury.

encarnizar. I. *va.* (*pret.* ENCARNICÉ; *subj.* ENCARNICE) to flesh (dogs); to provoke, irritate. **II.** *vr.* (of dogs) to be or become fond of flesh; to be cruelly bent, to gloat over injuring a person.

encaro, *m.* stare; blunderbuss; aim; levelling a musket.

encarpetar, *va.* to keep in a file or portfolio; (Am.) to lay (a motion, bill, etc.) on the table.

encarrilar, *va.* to put on the right track; to set right.

encarrilarse, encarrillarse, *vr.* (naut.) to be fouled on the sheave.

encarroñar. I. *va.* to infect, corrupt. **II.** *vr.* to be infected or corrupted.

encarrujado, da. I. *a.* curled; corrugated; fluted. **II.** *m.* fluting, shirring, gathering.

encarrujarse, *va.* & *vr.* to twist, coil, kink.

encartación, *f.* enrolment under a charter; vassalage, tenure at will; village under vassalage.—*pl.* charter lands, especially those adjoining the province of Vizcaya.

encartamiento, *m.* outlawry, proscription; sentence on an absent defendant; charter.

encartar. I. *va.* to ban, proscribe; to summon; to enrol; to register in a tax list; (in card games) to force to follow suit (when disadvantageous). **II.** *vr.* to have to follow suit so be unable to discard (in card games).

encarte, *m.* fortuitous order in which the cards remain at the close of a hand.

encartonador, ra, *n.* (bookbinding) one who applies boards.

encartonar, *va.* to bind in, or cover with, boards.

encasar, *va.* (surg.) to set (a bone).

encascabelado, da, *a.* adorned with bells.

encasillado, *m.* set of pigeonholes.

encasillar, *va.* to put in pigeonholes; to distribute, assign; to make a list of (candidates).

encasquetar. I. *va.* & *vr.* to pull down (one's hat) tight. **II.** *va.* to convince. **III.** *vr.* to persist in, to be headstrong about; to get a notion.

encasquillador, *m.* (Am.) farrier.

encasquillar, *va.* to shoe (horses).

encastar. I. *va.* to improve (a race of) by cross-breeding. **II.** *vn.* to breed.

encastillado, da, *a.* lofty, haughty.

encastillador, ra, *n.* one who shuts himself up in a castle; headstrong person.

encastillamiento, *m.* act of shutting up in a castle or steadfastly adhering to an opinion.

encastillar. I. *va.* to fortify with castles. **II.** *vn.* to make the cell of the queen bee in beehives. **III.** *vr.* to shut oneself up in a castle; to be unyielding or headstrong.

encastrar, *va.* to chase, embed.

encastre, *m.* fitting in; groove; socket.

encatarrado, da, *a.* having a cold.

encatusar, engatusar, *va.* (coll.) to wheedle.

encauchado, *m.* India-rubber poncho.

encauchar, *va.* to cover with rubber.

encausar, *va.* to prosecute, indict, sue.

encauste, *m.* = ENCAUSTO.

encáustico, ca, *a.* encaustic.

encausto, *m.* (art) encaustic painting.

encauzamiento, *m.* channeling; direction.

encauzar, *va.* to channel; to conduct through channels; to guide, lead, direct.

encavarse, *vr.* to hide in a cave.

encebadamiento, *m.* (vet.) surfeit.

encebadar. I. *va.* (vet.) to surfeit. **II.** *vr.* (of horses) to be surfeited.

encebollado, *m.* beef stew with onions.

encefálico, ca, *a.* encephalic.

encefalitis, *f.* (med.) encephalitis.—**e. letárgica,** encephalitis lethargica, sleeping sickness.

encéfalo, *m.* (physiol.) encephalon, brain.

encelamiento, *m.* jealousy.

encelar. I. *va.* to excite jealousy in, make jealous. **II.** *vr.* to become jealous.

encella, *f.* cheese basket or mold.

encellar, *va.* to mold (curds or cheese).

encenagado, da. I. *pp.* of ENCENAGARSE. **II.** *a.* mixed or filled with mud.

encenagamiento, *m.* wallowing in dirt or vice.

encenagar. I. *va.* (*pret.* ENCENAGUÉ; *subj.* ENCENAGUE) to mud, to mire. **II.** *vr.* to wallow in dirt, mire, or vice.

encencerrado, da, *a.* carrying a wetherbell.

encendedor, ra. I. *n.* & *a.* lighter(ing). **II.** *m.* (cigarette, etc.) lighter.

encender. I. *va.* (*ind.* ENCIENDO; *subj.* ENCIENDA) to kindle, light; to inflame, inspirit, incite. **II.** *vr.* to take fire; to light up; to burn.—**e. en,** to burn with (anger, etc.); to become excited with.

encendidamente, *adv.* ardently.

encendido, da. I. *pp.* of ENCENDER. **II.** *a.* inflamed; red. **III.** *m.* (int. combust. eng.) ignition.

encendimiento, *m.* kindling, lighting; incandescence, glow; ardor, eagerness.

encenizar, *va.* to cover with ashes.

encentador, *m.* one who begins to use a thing.

encentadura, *f.,* **encentamiento,** *m.* act of beginning the use of a thing.

encentar. I. *va.* (*ind.* ENCIENTO; *subj.* ENCIENTE) to begin the use of. **II.** *vr.* to develop bedsores.

encepador, *m.* stocker, gunstocker.

encepadura, *f.* (carp.) tie joint.

encepar. I. *va.* to put in the stocks; to stock (a gun); (naut.) to stock (the anchor); (carp.) to join with ties. **II.** *vr.* to take root; (naut.) (of the anchor) to foul.

encepe, *m.* (agr.) taking firm root.

encerado, da. I. *pp.* of ENCERAR. **II.** *a.* wax-colored; like wax; thick; hard (as a boiled egg). **III.** *m.* oilcloth, oilskin; (naut.) tarpaulin; sticking plaster; blackboard in schools.

enceramiento, *m.* act and effect of waxing.

encerar, *va.* to wax; to inspissate (lime).

encernadar, *va.* to cover with leached ashes.

encerotar, *va.* to wax (thread).

encerradero, *m.* sheepfold; pen.

encerrador, ra, *n.* one who locks up; driver of black cattle.

encerradura, *f.* act of locking up; cloister, retreat; prison, jail, dungeon.

encerramiento, *m.* encirclement; ENCERRADURA.

encerrar. I. *va.* (*ind.* ENCIERRO; *subj.* ENCIERRE) to lock or shut up; to confine; to include, contain, involve. **II.** *vr.* to live in seclusion; to be locked up; to be closeted.

encerrona, *f.* (coll.) voluntary retreat.

encespedar, *va.* to cover with sod.

encestar, *va.* to put in a basket.

encía, *f.* gum (of the mouth).

encíclico, ca. I. *a.* encyclic. **II.** *f.* encyclical.

enciclopedia, *f.* encyclopedia, cyclopedia.

enciclopédico, ca, *a.* encyclopedic.

enciclopedismo, *m.* Encyclopedism.

enciclopedista, *a.* & *n.* encyclopedist.

enciendo, encienda, *v.* *V.* ENCENDER.

enciento, enciente, *v.* *V.* ENCENTAR.

¹encierro, *m.* act of closing or locking up; confinement; inclosure; cloister, religious retreat; prison, lockup; folding (of cattle).

²encierro, encierre, *v.* *V.* ENCERRAR.

encima, *adv.* above; at the top; overhead; over and above, besides; in addition, to boot.—**e. de,** on, upon.—**por e.,** superficially, hastily.—**por e. de,** over, above; regardless of.

encimar. I. *va.* to place on top; to raise high; to throw in (something) to boot. **II.** *vr.* to rise above.

encina, *f.* (bot.) evergreen oak, holm oak.

encinal, encinar, *m.* holm-oak grove.

encinta, *a.* pregnant.

encintado, *m.* curb (of a sidewalk, etc.).

encintar, *va.* to trim with ribbon; (eng.) to put a curb, or curbs, on.

encismar, *va.* (coll.) to sow discord among.

encisto, *m.* encysted tumor.

encizañar, *va.* = CIZAÑAR, to sow discord.

enclaustración, *f.* cloistering.

enclaustrar, *va.* to cloister.

enclavación, *f.* nailing or fixing.

enclavado, da. I. *pp.* of ENCLAVAR. **II.** *a.* enclaved, encircled.

enclavadura, *f.* (carp.) groove; embedding.

enclavar, *va.* to nail; to embed; (vet.) to prick (horses) in shoeing; to pierce through.

enclavijar, *va.* to join, pin; to peg (a guitar).

enclenque, *a.* weak, feeble, sickly.

enclítico, ca, *n.* & *a.* (gram.) enclitic.

enclocar, *vn.* & *vr.* (of hens, etc.) to become broody.

encloquecer, *vn.* = ENCLOCAR.

encobar, *vn.* & *vr.* (of hens) to sit on eggs.

encobijar, *va.* = COBIJAR, to cover; to shelter.

encobrado, da. I. *pp.* of ENCOBRAR. **II.** *a.* containing copper; copper-colored.

encobrar, *va.* to coat or cover with copper.

encoclar = ENCLOCAR.

encocorar, *va.* (coll.) to vex, annoy.

encofrado, *m.* (min.) plank lining, timbering.

encofrar, *va.* (min.) to plank, to timber.

encoger. I. *va.* (*ind.* ENCOJO; *subj.* ENCOJA) to contract, shorten, shrink; to discourage. **II.** *vr.* to be low-spirited, dismayed, or bashful; to shrink, to shrivel.—**e. de hombros,** to shrug the shoulders.

encogidamente, *adv.* abjectly; bashfully, awkwardly.

encogido, da. I. *pp.* of ENCOGER. **II.** *a.* bashful, timid.

encogimiento, *m.* contraction, shrinkage; pusillanimity; bashfulness; awkwardness.

encojar. I. *va.* to cripple, to lame. **II.** *vr.* to become lame; (coll.) to feign sickness.

encojo, encoja, *v. V.* ENCOGER.
encolado, *m.,* **encoladura,** *f.,* **encolamiento,** *m.,* gluing; priming, sizing.
encolar, *va.* to glue; to stick.
encolerizar. I. *va. (pret.* ENCOLERICÉ; *subj.* EN-COLERICE) to anger. **II.** *vr.* to become angry.
encomendable, *a.* commendable.
encomendado. da. I. *pp.* of ENCOMENDAR. **II.** *n.* one under a knight commander.
encomendamiento, *m.* = ENCOMIENDA.
encomendar. I. *va. (ind.* ENCOMIENDO; *subj.* ENCOMIENDE) to recommend, commend; to entrust; to knight. **II.** *vn.* to hold a knight commandery. **III.** *vr.* to put oneself in the hands, under the protection, of another; to send compliments.
encomendero, *m.* agent; commissionaire.
encomiador, ra, *n. & a.* praiser(-ing).
encomiar, *va.* to praise, eulogize, extol.
encomiasta, *m.* eulogizer, panegyrist.
encomiástico, ca, *a.* encomiastic, complimentary.
encomienda, *f.* commission, charge; message, compliment sent; encomienda (certain estates assigned or granted by the Spanish kings); knight commandery; land or rent belonging to a commandery; badge of a knight commander; patronage, protection, recommendation; compliments, respects; (S. A.) parcel-post parcel.
encomiendo, encomiende, *v. V.* ENCOMENDAR.
encomio, *m.* praise, encomium, eulogy.
encompadrar, *vn.* (coll.) to become a COMPADRE; to be close friends.
enconamiento, *m.* inflammation, soreness; infection; animadversion, anger.
enconar. I. *va.* to inflame, irritate, provoke; to increase the inflammation or soreness of; to infect. **II.** *vr.* to rankle; to fester, get infected.
enconcharse, *vr.* (Am.) to withdraw oneself from society; to retire into one's shell.
encono, *m.* rancor, ill-will; soreness; sore spot.
enconoso, sa, *a.* easily festered or infected; rancorous, resentful; irritating, difficult to deal with.
enconrear, *va.* to oil (wool) before carding.
encontradamente, *adv.* contrarily.
encontradizo, za, *a.* met, run across.
encontrado, da. I. *pp.* of ENCONTRAR. **II.** *a.* opposite; in front; hostile, opposed.
encontrar *(ind.* ENCUENTRO; *subj.* ENCUENTRE).
I. *va.* to find; to meet. **II.** *vn.* to meet; to collide. **III.** *vr.* to meet; to collide; to be, find oneself; to feel (app. to health); to oppose, or be opposed to, each other; to conflict; to find; (con) to meet, come across or upon.
encontrón, encontronazo, *m.* collision, bump.
encopetado, da. I. *pp.* of ENCOPETAR. **II.** *a.* presumptuous, haughty, stuck-up; of high social standing or noble descent.
encopetar, I. *va.* to brush the hair up from the forehead. **II.** *vr.* to get well-groomed.
encorachar, *va.* to put in a leather bag.
encorajar. I. *va.* to encourage; to inflame. **II.** *vr.* to be furious, in a rage.
encorar. I. *va. (ind.* ENCUERO; *subj.* ENCUERE) to cover with or wrap up in leather; to cause or help the formation of skin in (a wound). **II.** *vn. & vr.* (of a wound) to heal, develop skin.
encorazado, da, *a.* covered with a cuirass; covered with leather.
encorchar, *va.* to hive (bees); to cork (bottles).
encorchetar, *va.* to put on hooks or clasps; to hook, to clasp.
encordar, *va. (ind.* ENCUERDO; *subj.* ENCUERDE) (mus.) to string (instruments); to lash or bind with ropes.
encordelar, *va.* to string; to bind with strings.
encordonado, da. I. *pp.* of ENCORDONAR. **II.** *a.* corded; adorned with cords.
encordonar, *va.* to cord; to tie with cords.

encorecer. I. *va. (ind.* ENCOREZCO; *subj.* ENCOREZCA) to cause the formation of skin in (a wound). **II.** *vn. & vr.* = ENCORAR.
encoriación, *f.* healing a wound.
encornado, da, *a.* horned.
encornadura, *f.* (of bulls, etc.) set of the horns.
encornudar, *vn.* to begin to grow horns.
encorozar, *va.* to put a COROZA, a kind of hood, on the head of (a criminal).
encorralar, *va.* to corral.
encorrear, *va.* to strap (cattle).
encorsetar, *va. & vr.* to put a corset on.
encortinar, *va.* to put up curtains on or in.
encorvada, *f.* act of bending the body; grotesque manner of dancing; (bot.) hatchet vetch coronilla.—**hacer la e.,** to feign sickness.
encorvadura, *f.,* **encorvamiento,** *m.* bending; curvature, crookedness.
encorvar, *va. & vr.* to bend, curve.
encostillado, *m.* timbering; lathing.
encostradura, *f.* incrustation, crust.
encostrar. I. *va.* to crust, to incrust. **II.** *vr.* to become crusty; to develop a crust or a scab.
encovadura, *f.* act of placing in a cellar.
encovar. I. *va. (ind.* ENCUEVO; *subj.* ENCUEVE) to put in a cellar; to keep, lock up, conceal. **II.** *vr.* to hide oneself.
encrasar, *va.* to fatten; to thicken.
encrespador, *m.* crisping iron, curling tongs.
encrespadura, *f.* act of curling the hair.
encrespamiento, *m.* curling; (of hair) standing on end; fury, roughness (of the sea, the waves, etc.)
encrespar. I. *va.* to curl; to set (the hair) on end; to ruffle (the feathers). **II.** *vr.* (naut.) (of the sea) to become rough and boisterous; to be agitated (by passion); to wrangle; (of affairs) to become entangled.
encrestado, da. I. *pp.* of ENCRESTARSE. **II.** *a.* adorned with a crest or comb; haughty, lofty.
encrestarse, *vr.* to stiffen the crest or comb (as a cock); to be proud or haughty.
encrucijada, *f.* street or road intersection; ambush; opportunity to do harm to another.
encrudecer. I. *va. (ind.* ENCRUDEZCO; *subj.* ENCRUDEZCA) to make (a wound) worse or raw; to exasperate, irritate. **II.** *vr.* to be enraged.
encruelecer. I. *va. (ind.* ENCRUELEZCO; *subj.* ENCRUELEZCA) to excite to cruelty. **II.** *vr.* to become cruel.
encuadernación, *f.* binding (books).
encuadernador, ra, *n.* bookbinder.
encuadernar, *va.* (of books) to bind; to reconcile.—**sin e.,** unbound.
encuadrar, *va.* to frame.
encuarte, *m.* extra horse to draw a coach uphill.
encubar, *va.* to cask (liquids); to put (a ciminal) into a butt.
encubertar. I. *va. (ind.* ENCUBIERTO; *subj.* ENCUBIERTA) to caparison, trap (as a horse) **II.** *vr.* to put on armor.
encubierta, *f.* fraud, deceit, imposition.
encubiertamente, *adv.* hiddenly, secretly; deceitfully, fraudulently.
¹**encubierto, encubierta,** *v. V.* ENCUBERTAR.
²**encubierto, ta,** *pp. irreg.* of ENCUBRIR.
encubridor, ra, *n. & a.* concealer(-ing).
encubrimiento, *m.* concealment.
encubrir, *va. (pp. irreg.* ENCUBIERTO) to hide, conceal, cloak, mask, palliate.
¹**encuentro,** *m.* encounter, meeting; collision; clash; fight, finding; (mil.) encounter, fight; joint (in fowls); in quadrupeds, points of the shoulder blades; (arch.) angle, nook, corner.— *pl.* temples of a loom.—**salir al e. de,** to go to meet; to encounter.
²**encuentro, encuentre,** *v. V.* ENCONTRAR.
encuerdo, encuerde, *v. V.* ENCORDAR.
encuero, encuere, *v. V.* ENCORAR.
encuevo, encueve, *v. V.* ENCOVAR.

encuitarse, *vr.* to grieve.

enculatar, *va.* to cover (a beehive).

encumbrado, da. I. *pp.* of ENCUMBRAR. II. *a.* high, elevated; lofty, stately.

encumbramiento, *m.* act of raising or elevating; height, eminence.

encumbrar. I. *va.* to raise, elevate. II. *vn.* to ascend. III. *vr.* to rise; to be proud, rate oneself high.

encunar, *va.* to put in the cradle; to catch between the horns.

encureñado, da, *a.* (gun) put on the carriage.

encurtido, *m.* pickle.

encurtir, *va.* to pickle.

enchabetar, *va.* (naut.) to forelock.

enchancletar, *va.* to put slippers on.

enchapado, *m.* veneer; plates or sheets forming a cover or lining.

enchapar, *va.* to veneer; to cover with metal plates or sheets.

enchapinado, da, *a.* built upon a vault.

encharcada, *f.* pool of water, puddle.

encharcarse, *vr.* to form puddles.

enchicharse, *vr.* (Am.) to drink chicha to excess; to become angry, flare up.

enchilada, *f.* (Mex.) pancake of maize with chilli.

enchilar, *va.* (Am.) to put chilli on or in; to anger.

enchiquerar, *va.* to shut (the bull) in the CHIQUERO (bull pen); (coll.) to imprison.

enchivarse, *vr.* (Colomb.) to get angry.

enchuchar, *va.* (Cuba) (Ry.) to switch.

enchufar, *va. & vr.* to fit (a tube) into another; to telescope.

enchufe, *m.* socket joint; telescoping, sliding of one thing into another; (elec.) plug; (also incorrectly used for) (elec.) socket.

ende.—por e., therefore, consequently.

endeble, *a.* feeble, weak, frail; flimsy.

endeblez, *f.* feebleness; flimsiness.

endecasílabo, ba, *a. & n.* hendecasyllable(-ic).

endecha, *f.* dirge, doleful ditty.

endechadera, *f.* = PLAÑIDERA, hired mourner.

endechar. I. *va.* to sing funeral songs to. II. *vr.* to grieve, mourn.

endehesar, *va.* to put (cattle) in the pasture.

endemia, *f.* (med.) endemic.

endémico, ca, *a.* (med.) endemic.

endemoniado, da, I. *pp.* of ENDEMONIAR. II. *a.* devilish, fiendish, perverse.

endemoniar, *va.* to possess with a devil; (coll.) to irritate, provoke, enrage.

endentado, da, *a.* (her.) serrated.

endentar, *va. & vn.* (ind. ENDIENTA; *subj.* ENDIENTE) to gear, engage, mesh.

endentecer, *vn.* (ind. ENDENTEZCO; *subj.* ENDENTEZCA) to cut teeth, to teethe.

enderecé, enderece, *v.* V. ENDEREZAR.

enderezadamente, *adv.* rightly.

enderezado, da. I. *pp.* of ENDEREZAR. II. *a.* fit, appropriate.

enderezador, ra, *n.* good manager; righter; straightener.

enderezamiento, *m.* straightening; setting right.

enderezar. I. *va.* (pret. ENDERECÉ; *subj.* ENDERECE) to straighten; to right, set right; to address, dedicate; to manage well. II. *vn.* to take the direct road. III. *vr.* to straighten up; to set oneself, prepare for an undertaking.

endeudarse, *vr.* to contract debts.

endevotado, da, *a.* pious; devoted, fond.

endiablada, *f.* boisterous masquerade.

endiabladamente, *adv.* devilishly; horribly.

endiablado, da. I. *pp.* of ENDIABLAR. II. *a.* devilish, diabolical; ugly, deformed; perverse, wicked.

endiablar. I. *va.* to pervert, corrupt. II. *vr.* to be furious.

endíadis, *f.* (rhet.) hendiadys.

endibia, *f.* (bot.) endive, succory.

endiento, endiente, *v.* V. ENDENTAR.

---

endilgador, ra, *n.* (coll.) pander.

endilgar, *va.* to direct, guide; to assist; to thrust (a weapon, an insult), to deal (a blow); to spring (so.nething) on (a person).

endiosamiento, *m.* haughtiness, pride; ecstasy, abstraction; deification.

endiosar. I. *va.* to deify. II. *vr.* to be elated with pride; to be devoutly abstracted.

endoblasto, *m.* (biol.) endoblast, hypoblast.

endocardio, *m.* (anat.) endocardium.

endocarditis, *f.* (med.) endocarditis.

endocarpo, *m.* (bot.) endocarp.

endodermo, *m.* (biol.) endoderm.

endogénesis, *f.* (biol.) endogeneity.

endolinfa, *f.* (anat.) endolymph, liquid that fills the labyrinth of the ear.

endorsar, *va.* to indorse (as a draft); to transfer.

endorso, *m.* (com.) indorsement.

endosador, endosante, *m.* indorser.

endosar, *va.* to indorse (a draft, etc.).

endosatario, ria, *n.* indorsee.

endose, *m.* indorsement (of a draft, etc.).

endoselar, *va.* to hang; to provide with a dais.

endósmosis, *f.* (phys.) endosmosis.

endoso, *m.* = ENDOSE.

endospermo, *m.* (bot.) endosperm.

endotérmico, ca, *a.* (chem.) endothermic.

endriago, *m.* fabulous monster.

endrina, *f.* sloe, fruit of the sloe tree.

endrino, na. I. *a.* sloe-colored. II. *m.* (bot.) blackthorn, sloe tree.

endrogarse, *vr.* (Am.) to become burdened with debts.

endulcé, endulce, *v.* V. ENDULZAR.

endulzadura, *f.* sweetening.

endulzar, *va.* (pret. ENDULCÉ; *subj.* ENDULCE) to sweeten; to soften; (art) to soften, tone down.

endurador, ra, *a.* parsimonious, niggardly.

endurar, *va.* to harden; to save; to endure, bear; to delay, put off.

endurecer, *va. & vr.* (ind. ENDUREZCO; *subj.* ENDUREZCA) to harden; to inure; to exasperate.

endurecidamente, *adv.* obstinately; harshly.

endurecido, da. I. *pp.* of ENDURECER. II. *a.* hard, hardy; obdurate.

endurecimiento, *m.* hardness; hardening; obstinacy; tenaciousness; hard-heartedness.

endurezco, endurezca, *v.* V. ENDURECER.

ene, *f.* Spanish name of the letter *n.*

enea, *f.* (bot.) cattail, reed mace, rush.

enebral, *m.* plantation of juniper trees.

enebrina, *f.* fruit of the juniper tree.

enebro, *m.* (bot.) common juniper.

enejar, *va.* to put an axle on.

eneldo, *m.* (bot.) common dill.

enema, *f.* enema, injection, clyster.

enemiga, *f.* enmity, hatred, ill-will.

enemigamente, *adv.* inimically.

enemigo, ga. I. *a.* (de) inimical, hostile (to); opposed (to), adverse. II. *n.* enemy, foe. III. *m.* (mil.) enemy; devil.—e. capital, mortal enemy.—e. jurado, sworn enemy.—el e. malo, the devil.

enemistad, *f.* enmity, hatred.

enemistar. I. *va.* to make enemies of. II. *vr.* (con) to become an enemy (of); to fall out (with).

éneo, ea, *a.* (poet.) brazen, brass (as *a.*).

energía, *f.* energy; (mechanical) power.—e. atómica, atomic energy.—e. cinética, kinetic energy.—e. eléctrica, electric power.—e. potencial, potential energy.—transmisión de e., power transmission.

enérgicamente, *adv.* energetically.

enérgico, ca, *a.* energetic, lively.

energúmeno, na, *n.* person possessed with a devil; violent, impulsive person.

enero, *m.* January.

enervación, *f.* enervation.

---

enervar. I. *va.* to enervate, unnerve; to weaken. **II.** *vr.* to become weak.

enfadadizo, za, *a.* irritable, irascible, peevish.

enfadar. I. *va.* to vex, anger. **II.** *vr.* to get angry.

enfado, *m.* vexation, anger; trouble, drudgery.

enfadosamente, *adv.* annoyingly.

enfadoso, sa, *a.* vexatious, annoying.

enfaldar. I. *va.* (agr.) to lop off the lower branches of. **II.** *vr.* to tuck up (the skirts).

enfaldo, *m.* act of tucking up one's clothes.

enfangar. I. *va.* (*pret.* ENFANGUÉ; *subj.* ENFANGUE) to soil with mud. **II.** *vr.* (naut.) to ground in the mud; (coll.) to soil one's reputation; to sink (into vice, etc.)

enfardar, *va.* to pack, bale, fardel.

enfardelador, *m.* packer.

enfardeladura, *f.* packing, baling.

enfardelar, *va.* to bale, pack.

énfasis, *m.* emphasis.

enfáticamente, *adv.* emphatically.

enfático, ca, *a.* emphatic.

enfermar. I. *vn.* (Am. *vr.*) to fall ill, be taken ill. **II.** *va.* to make ill.

enfermedad, *f.* illness, sickness.

enfermera, *f.* woman nurse (for the sick).

enfermería, *f.* infirmary, sanitarium.

enfermero, *m.* male nurse (for the sick).

enfermizo, za, *a.* infirm, sickly; unhealthful.

enfermo, ma. I. *a.* ill, sick; sickly. **II.** *n.* patient.

enfermoso, sa, *a.* (C. A.) = ENFERMIZO; indisposed, somewhat ailing.

enfervorizar. I. *va.* to heat, inflame, incite. **II.** *vr.* to become fervorous or heated.

enfeudación, *f.* infeudation, enfeoffment.

enfeudar, *va.* to feoff, to enfeoff.

enfielar, *va.* to put in a balance.

enfiestarse, *vr.* (Am.) to have a good time, go on a lark.

enfilar, *va.* to place in a row or line; to pierce or string in a line; (mil.) to enfilade.—**e. el curso,** (naut.) to direct the course, to bear.

enfisema, *m.* (med.) emphysema.

enfistolarse, *vr.* to become a fistula.

enfiteusis, *m.* & *f.* (law) emphyteusis.

enfiteuta, *m.* (law) emphyteuta.

enfitéutico, ca, *a.* emphyteutic.

enflaquecer. I. *va.* (*ind.* ENFLAQUEZCO; *subj.* ENFLAQUEZCA) *va.* to make thin or lean; to extenuate, to fade. **II.** *vn.* & *vr.* to become thin, lose weight. **III.** *vn.* to weaken.

enflaquecimiento, *m.* loss of flesh, emaciation.

enflaquezco, enflaquezca, *v.* *V.* ENFLAQUECER.

enflautado, da, *a.* (coll.) inflated.

enflautador, ra, *n.* (coll.) procurer.

enflautar, *va.* (coll.) to procure; (coll.) to deceive, cheat, humbug.

enflechado, da, *a.* (of a bow) ready to discharge.

enfocar, *va.* to focus; focus on.

enfoque, *m.* focussing; approach (to a problem, etc.)

enfoscar. I. *va.* (*pret.* ENFOSQUÉ; *subj.* ENFOSQUE) (mason.) to fill up (holes). **II.** *vr.* to be ill-humored; to be deep in a business; to be cloudy.

enfrailar. I. *va.* to make (one) a monk or friar. **II.** *vr.* to become a friar.

enfranquecer, *va.* to frank, to free.

enfrascamiento, *m.* entanglement.

enfrascar, *va.* (*pret.* ENFRASQUÉ; *subj.* ENFRASQUE) to bottle.

enfrascarse, *vr.* to be entangled or involved; to be deeply engaged in work.

enfrenador, ra, *n.* & *a.* bridler(-ing), restrainer (-ing).

enfrenamiento, *m.* bridling; checking, curbing.

enfrenar, *va.* to bridle; to govern by the bridle; to curb, to restrain; to put the brake on.

enfrentar. I. *va.* to confront, put face to face; to face. **II.** *vn.* (con) to face; to oppose.

enfrente, *adv.* opposite, in front.—**e. de,** opposite, in front of.—**de e.,** opposite, across (the

street, etc.) (as *la casa de enfrente,* the house opposite).

enfriadera, *f.* bottle cooler, refrigerator.

enfriadero, enfriador, *m.* cooling place; refrigerator; cold storage.

enfriamiento, *m.* refrigeration; cooling; cold, chill (illness).

enfriar. I. *va.* to cool. **II.** *vr.* to cool; to cool off or down; (of person) to get chilled.

enfullar, *va.* & *vn.* (coll.) to cheat at cards.

enfundadura, *f.* casing; putting into cases.

enfundar, *va.* to case, to put into a case (as a pillow); to fill up, to stuff.

enfurecer. I. *va.* (*ind.* ENFUREZCO; *subj.* ENFUREZCA) to enrage, make furious. **II.** *vr.* to rage, to become furious or stormy.

enfurruñarse, *vr.* (coll.) to get angry; sulk.

enfurtir, *va.* to full (cloth); to felt.

engabanado, da, *a.* wearing an overcoat.

engace, *m.* catenation, connection.

engafar, *va.* to bend (a crossbow); to hook; to set (a gun) at half cock.

engaitador, ra, *n.* (coll.) wheedler.

engaitar, *va.* (coll.) to coax, to wheedle.

engalanar, *va.* to adorn, deck; (naut.) to dress.

¹**engalgar,** *va.* to pursue closely.

²**engalgar,** *va.* to scotch (a wheel); (naut.) to back (an anchor).

engallado, da, *a.* erect, upright; haughty.

engallador, *m.* martingale.

engalladura, *f.* protoplasmic disk (of egg).

engallarse, *vr.* to draw oneself up arrogantly; (of horses) to keep the head near the chest.

enganchador, *m.* hooker.

enganchamiento, *m.* hooking; enlisting in the army; decoying.

enganchar. I. *va.* to hook, hitch, couple, connect; to entrap; to decoy into military service. **II.** *vr.* to engage; to enlist in the army; to be caught on a hook.

enganche, *m.* = ENGANCHAMIENTO.

engandujo, *m.* twisted thread of a fringe.

engañabobos, *m.* (coll.) trickster; fool trap.

engañadizo, za, *a.* easily deceived.

engañado, da. I. *pp.* of ENGAÑAR. **II.** *a.* mistaken; deceived.

engañador, ra, *n.* & *a.* deceiver(-ing).

engañapastor, *m.* (ornith.) wagtail.

engañar. I. *va.* to deceive; cheat; fool, hoax; to wile away (as time). **II.** *vr.* to deceive oneself; to make a mistake, be mistaken.

engañifa, *f.* (coll.) deceit, trick, catchpenny.

engaño, *m.* deceit, fraud; hoax, lure; mistake, misunderstanding, misapprehension.

engañosamente, *adv.* deceitfully, guilefully; deceivingly, misleadingly.

engañoso, sa, *a.* deceitful, artful, false; deceiving, misleading.

engarabatar. I. *va.* (coll.) to hook. **II.** *vr.* to become crooked.

engarabitarse, *vr.* (coll.) to climb, ascend.

engarbarse, *vr.* to perch high on a tree.

engarbullar, *va.* (coll.) to entangle, involve; to make a mess of.

engarce, *m.* linking; setting (of precious stone).

engarcé, engarce, *v.* *V.* ENGARZAR.

engargantar. I. *va.* to put into the throat. **II.** *vn.* to thrust the foot into the stirrup; to gear, to mesh, to interlock.

engargolar, *va.* to join (pipes).

engaritar, *va.* to fortify or adorn with sentry boxes or turrets; (coll.) to trick, fool.

engarrafador, *m.* grappler.

engarrafar, *va.* (coll.) to grapple.

engarrotar. I. *va.* to garrote; to make numb (with cold). **II.** *vr.* to become numb with cold; (fig.) to be very cold, frozen.

engarzador, ra, *n.* one who hooks or enchains; stringer of beads.

engarzar, *va.* (*pret.* ENGARCÉ; *subj.* ENGARCE) to link, to hook; to curl; to set (precious stone).

engastador, *m.* enchaser, setter.

engastar, *va.* to set (as diamonds); to enchase.

engaste, *m.* setting (of stones); enchasing; pearl flat on one side.

engatado, da. I. *pp.* of ENGATAR. **II.** *n.* petty robber, pilferer.

engatar, *va.* (coll.) to cheat; to wheedle.

engatillado, da. I. *pp.* of ENGATILLAR. **II.** *a.* thick, high-necked (horses and bulls).

engatillar, *va.* (arch.) to bind with a cramp iron.

engatusador, ra, *n.* & *a.* coaxer(-ing), wheedler (-ing).

engatusamiento, *m.* (coll.) wheedling, coaxing.

engatusar, *va.* (coll.) to inveigle, wheedle.

engavillar, *va.* to bind in sheaves.

engazador, ra, *n.* = ENGARZADOR.

engazamiento, *m.* = ENGARCE.

¹engazar, *va.* = ENGARZAR, to link.

²engazar, *va.* (naut.) to strap (blocks); to dye in the cloth.

engendrable, *a.* that may be engendered.

engendramiento, *m.* begetting, generating.

engendrador, ra, *n.* & *a.* generator(-ing); en-genderer(-ing).

engendrar, *va.* to beget, engender, generate; to produce, bear; to create; (math.) to generate.

engendro, *m.* fœtus, shapeless embryo; bungling, badly-made thing; poor work; (coll.) show.—**mal e.,** perverse youth.

englobar, *va.* to englobe, inclose, include.

engolado, da, *a.* collared.

engolfar. I. *vn.* (naut.) to enter a gulf or deep bay. **II.** *vr.* to be engrossed or absorbed.

engolillado, da, *a.* wearing the GOLILLA, ruff.

engolondrinarse, *vr.* (coll.) to be elated with pride; to fall in love.

engolosinar. I. *va.* to allure. **II.** *vr.* to become fond of.

engolletado, da. I. *pp.* of ENGOLLETARSE. **II.** *a.* (coll.) conceited haughty.

engolletarse, *vr.* (coll.) to be conceited.

engomadura, *f.* first gumming; coat which bees lay over their hives.

engomar, *va.* to gum, to size; to glue.

engorar, *va.* (*ind.* ENGUERO; *subj.* ENGUERE) to addle.

engorda, *f.* (Am.) ENGORDE; number of animals fattened together or at a time.

engordadero, *m.* sty to fatten hogs.

engordador, ra, *a.* fattening; pampering.

engordar. I. *va.* to pamper, fatten. **II.** *vn.* to get fat; to become rich.

engorde, *m.* fattening (hogs, etc.).

engorro, *m.* embarrassment, nuisance.

engorroso, sa, *a.* troublesome, annoying.

engoznar, *va.* to hinge; to put hinges on.

engranaje, *m.* (mech.) gear, gearing.

engranar, *vn.* to gear, to interlock.

engrandar, *va.* = AGRANDAR, to enlarge.

engrandecer, *va.* (*ind.* ENGRANDEZCO; *subj.* EN-GRANDEZCA) to augment, aggrandize; to en-large; to exalt, extol; to exaggerate, magnify.

engrandecimiento, *m.* increase, enlargement; aggrandizement, exaltation; exaggeration.

engrandezco, engrandezca, *v.* V. ENGRAN-DECER.

engranerar, *va.* to store (grain).

engranujarse, *vr.* to become covered with pim-ples; to become a knave.

engrapar, *va.* (mason. and carp.) to cramp.

engrasación, *f.* lubrication, oiling, greasing.

engrasador, *m.* oiler, lubricator.

engrasamiento, *m.* = ENGRASACIÓN.

engrasar, *va.* to grease, oil, lubricate; to stain with grease; to dress (cloth); to manure.

engrase, *m.* = ENGRASACIÓN.

engredar, *va.* to clay, to chalk; to full.

engreído, da. I. *pp.* of ENGREÍR; **II.** *a.* con-ceited.

engreimiento, *m.* conceit, presumption, vanity.

engreír. I. *va.* (*ind.* ENGRÍO; *subj.* ENGRÍA) to encourage the conceit of, to make vain; to elate. **II.** *vr.* to become vain or conceited; (Am.) (con or de) to be, or become, fond (of), take a liking (to).

engrescar, *va.* & *vr.* to pick a quarrel; to make (one) join in merriment.

engrifar, *va.* & *vr.* to curl, crisp, crimp; to make (the hair) stand on end (from fright).

engringarse, *vr.* (coll.) to follow foreign customs, to act like foreigners.

engrío, engría, *v.* V. ENGREÍR.

engrosar. I. *va.* (*ind.* ENGRUESO; *subj.* ENGRUESE) to swell, enlarge; increase; to thicken, broaden. **II.** *vn.* & *vr.* to become strong or corpulent; to increase.

engrudador, *m.* paster.

engrudamiento, *m.* pasting.

engrudar, *va.* to paste.—**engrudo,** *m.* paste.

engrueso, engruese, *v.* V. ENGROSAR.

engruesar, *va.* = ENGROSAR.

engrumecerse, *vr.* to clot, to curdle.

engualdrapar, *va.* to caparison.

enguantado, da, *a.* wearing gloves.

enguantarse, *vr.* to put gloves on.

enguedejado, da, *a.* wearing long hair.

enguijarrar, *va.* to pave with pebbles.

enguillar, *va.* (naut.) to wind (a thin rope around a thicker one).

enguirnaldada, da, *a.* garlanded.

enguirnaldar, *va.* to garland.

enguizcar, *va.* to incite, prompt, stimulate.

engullidor, ra, *n.* devourer, gobbler, glutton.

engullir, *va.* to devour, gobble.

engurrio, *m.* sadness, melancholy.

engurruñarse, *vr.* (coll.) to become melancholy.

enharinar, *va.* to cover with flour.

enhastiar, *va.* to annoy, cloy, bore.

enhastillar, *va.* to put arrows in (a quiver).

enhatijar, *va.* to cover (hives) with bassweed.

enhebrar, *va.* to thread; to string.

enhenar, *va.* to cover with hay.

enherbolar, *va.* to poison with herbs.

enhestador, ra, *n.* one who raises or hoists.

enhestadura, *f.* erection, raising, hoisting.

enhestar. I. *va.* (*pp. irreg.* ENHIESTO; *ind.* EN-HIESTO; *subj.* ENHIESTE) to erect; to raise, to hoist; to set upright. **II.** *vr.* to rise upright.

enhielar, *va.* to mix with gall or bile.

¹enhiesto, ta. I. *pp. irreg.* of ENHESTAR. **II.** *a.* erect, upright; lofty.

²enhiesto, enhieste, *v.* V. ENHESTAR.

enhilado, da. I. *pp.* of ENHILAR. **II.** *a.* well-arranged, in good order, in line.

enhilar, *va.* to thread; to direct; to line.

enhorabuena. I. *f.* congratulation, felicitation. **II.** *adv.* well and good; all right.

enhoramala, *adv.* denoting disapproval, etc.; (lit.) in an evil hour.—**vete e.,** (coll.) go to blazes!

enhornar, *va.* to put into an oven.

enhuecar, *va.* = AHUECAR, to make hollow.

enhuerar, *va.*, *vn.* & *vr.* to addle.

enigma, *m.* enigma.

enigmáticamente, *adv.* enigmatically.

enigmático, ca, *a.* enigmatical.

enigmatista, *m.* one who speaks in enigmas.

enjabonadura, *f.* washing.

enjabonar, *va.* to soap; to wash with soap; (coll.) to soft-soap.

enjaezar, *va.* (*pret.* ENJAECÉ; *subj.* ENJAECE) to trap, harness.

enjaguar, *va.* = ENJUAGAR.—**enjagüe,** *m.* ad-judication required by the creditors of a ship.

enjalbegador, ra, *n.* whitewasher.

enjalbegadura, *f.* whitewashing.

enjalbegar, *va.* to whitewash; to paint (the face).

enjalma, *f.* packsaddle.—**enjalmar. I.** *va.* to put on a packsaddle. **II.** *vn.* to make packsaddles.

enjalmero, *m.* packsaddle maker.

enjambradera, *f.* queen bee; cell of queen bee.

enjambradero, *m.* place where bees form hives.

enjambrar. I. *va.* to hive (bees). **II.** *vn.* to breed a new hive; to produce abundantly.

enjambrazón, *f.* swarming of bees.

enjambre, *m.* swarm; crowd.

enjarciadura, *f.* (act of) rigging.

enjarciar, *va.* to rig (a ship).

enjardinar, *va.* to trim and arrange (trees), as in gardens.

enjaretado, *m.* grating, lattice work.

enjaretar, *va.* to run a string through (a hem); (coll.) to speak or act hurriedly and thoughtlessly.

enjaular, *va.* to cage; to imprison, confine.

enjebar, *va.* to steep in lye, to buck.

enjebe, *m.* lye; (act of) bucking.

enjergar, *va.* (coll.) to start and direct.

enjertación, *f.* grafting; insertion; inoculation; budding.

enjertal, *m.* nursery of grafted fruit trees.

enjertar, *va.* = INJERTAR, (hort.) to graft.

enjerto, *m.* grafted plant or tree; mixture.

enjorguinar. I. *va.* to smear with soot. **II.** *vr.* to be blackened with soot.

enjoyar, *va.* to adorn with jewels; to set with precious stones; to adorn, embellish.

enjoyelado, da, *a.* worked into jewels; covered with jewels, bejeweled.

enjoyelador, *m.* setter, jeweler.

enjuagadientes, *m.* (coll.) mouth wash.

enjuagadura, *f.* rinsing the mouth.

enjuagar, *va.* to rinse (mouth, cups, etc.)

enjuagatorio, *m.* act of rinsing; mouth wash; finger bowl.

enjuague, *m.* plot, scheme; ENJUAGATORIO.

enjugador, ra. I. *n.* drier. **II.** *m.* drum for the drying of linen.

enjugar. I. *va.* (*pp. irreg.* ENJUTO; *pret.* ENJUGUÉ; *subj.* ENJUGUE) to dry; to wipe off moisture from. **II.** *vr.* to become lean.

enjuiciamiento, *m.* (law) act of instituting and prosecuting a judicial proceeding; suit.

enjuiciar, *va.* (law) to bring a suit or action against; to try, carry on (a case); to indict; to pass judgment on.

enjulio, enjullo, *m.* cloth beam of a loom; warp rod.

enjundia, *f.* fat in the ovary of fowls; grease or fat of any animal; substance, force.

enjundioso, sa, *a.* fat, fatty; substantial.

enjunque, *m.* (naut.) heavy ballast or cargo; kentledge.

enjuta, *f.* (arch.) spandrel.

enjutar, *va.* (mason.) to dry (plaster, etc.).

enjutez, *f.* dryness, aridity.

enjuto, ta. I. *pp. irreg.* of ENJUGAR. **II.** *a.* lean, skinny; austere. **III.** *m. pl.* brushwood; tidbits that stimulate thirst.

enlabiador, ra, *n.* wheedler.

enlabiar, *va.* to wheedle, cajole, entice.

enlabio, *m.* enticement, alluring by soft words.

enlace, *m.* connection; interlocking; link; train connection; marriage; relationship.

enlacé, enlace, *v.* V. ENLAZAR.

enlaciar. I. *va.* to render lax or languid. **II.** *vr.* to wither, to decay.

enladrillado, *m.* brick pavement.

enladrillador, *m.* bricklayer.

enladrilladura, *f.* brickwork.

enladrillar, *va.* to pave with bricks.

enlagunar, *va.* to flood, to turn into a pond.

enlajar, *va.* (Venez.) to pave with tiles or flags.

enlamar, *va.* to cover with slime.

enlanado, da, *a.* covered with wool.

enlardar, *va.* to baste (meat). Also LARDAR.

enlargues, *m. pl.* (naut.) rope ends.

enlatar, *va.* to cover (a roof) with tin; to can.

enlazable, *a.* that can be joined.

enlazador, ra, *n.* binder, uniter.

enlazadura, *f.,* **enlazamiento,** *m.* connection, binding, uniting, linking, coupling; lacing.

enlazar. I. *va.* (*pret.* ENLACÉ; *subj.* ENLACE) to lace, bind, join, unite, connect. **II.** *vr.* to become joined in wedlock; to become related by marriage; to interlock; to join or be linked.

enlechuguillado, da, *a.* wearing a neck ruff.

enlegajar, *va.* to sort or arrange (papers) into a batch or parcel.

enlejiar, *va.* to buck (clothes); to make into lye.

enlenzar, *va.* (*ind.* ENLIENZO; *subj.* ENLIENZE) to strengthen with adhesive strips.

enligarse, *vr.* to be caught with birdlime.

enlistonado, *m.* (carp., mason.) lathing, lath work.

enlistonar, *va.* to lath, lay lath work on.

enlizar, *va.* to provide (a loom) with leashes.

enlodadura, *f.* act of soiling with mud.

enlodar. I. *va.* to bemire, to soil with mud; to throw mud at. **II.** *vr.* to get muddy.

enloquecedor, ra, *a.* maddening.

enloquecer. I. *va.* (*ind.* ENLOQUEZCO; *subj.* ENLOQUEZCA) to madden, drive insane; to distract. **II.** *vn. & vr.* to become insane; to be vexed, annoyed or in despair; (of trees) to become barren.

enloquecimiento, *m.* madness, insanity.

enloquezco, enloquezca, *v.* V. ENLOQUECER.

enlosado, *m.* pavement; tile floor; paving, tiling.

enlosador, ra, *n.* tile layer, paver.

enlosar, *va.* to pave with flags, tile or slabs.

enlozanarse, *vr.* to make a show of vigor and strength.

enlucido, *m.* (coat of) plaster; plastering.

enlucidor, *m.* (mason.) plasterer.

enlucimiento, *m.* polishing; (mason.) plastering.

enlucir, *va.* (*ind.* ENLUZCO; *subj.* ENLUZCA) to polish (plate); (mason.) to plaster.

enlustrecer, *va.* to clean, brighten, polish.

enlutar, *va.* to put in mourning, put crape or mourning on, to crape; to veil; to darken.

enluzco, enluzca, *v.* V. ENLUCIR.

enllantar, *va.* to rim, to shoe (a wheel).

enllentecer, *va.* (*ind.* ENLLENTEZCO; *subj.* ENLLENTEZCA) to soften, blandish.

enmaderación, *f.,* **enmaderamiento,** *m.* woodwork; wainscoting.

enmaderar, *va.* to plank, board; to roof with timber; to floor with boards.

enmagrecer, *vn.* (*ind.* ENMAGREZCO; *subj.* ENMAGREZCA) to become lean or skinny.

enmalezarse, *vr.* to become weedy.

enmallarse, *vr.* to be caught in the meshes.

enmangar, *va.* to put a handle on.

enmantar. I. *va.* to cover with a blanket. **II.** *vr.* to become melancholy.

enmarañamiento, *m.* entanglement, intricacy.

enmarañar, *va.* to tangle (as hair, etc.); to entangle, perplex, involve in difficulties; to puzzle.

enmararse, *vr.* (naut.) to take sea room.

enmaridar, *vn. & vr.* to get a husband, marry.

enmarillecerse, *vr.* to become yellow.

enmaromar, *va.* to tie with a rope.

enmascarar. I. *va.* to mask. **II.** *vr.* to masquerade, put on a mask.

enmasillar, *va.* to putty, cement.

enmatarse, *vr.* to hide among the plants.

enmelar, *va.* (*ind.* ENMIELO; *subj.* ENMIELE) to bedaub with honey; to sweeten.

enmendación, *f.* emendation, correction.

enmendadamente, *adv.* accurately, exactly.

enmendador, ra, *n.* corrector, reviser.

enmendadura, *f.* = ENMIENDA.

enmendar. I. *va.* (*ind.* ENMIENDO; *subj.* ENMIENDE) to amend, correct; to repair; to reform; to indemnify. **II.** *vr.* to mend, reform, lead a new life.

enmienda, *f.* emendation, correction; reward, premium; (law) satisfaction, indemnity.

enmiendo, enmiende, *v.* V. ENMENDAR.

enmohecer, *va.* & *vr.* (ind. ENMOHEZCO; *subj.* ENMOHEZCA) to mold, mildew; to rust.

enmohecido, da. I. *pp.* of ENMOHECER. **II.** *a.* rusty, moldy.

enmohecimiento, *m.* rusting; molding.

enmohezco, enmohezca, *v.* V. ENMOHECER.

enmollecer, *va.* (ind. ENMOLLEZCO; *subj.* ENMOLLEZCA) to soften, mollify.

enmondar, *va.* to clear (cloth) from knots.

enmontarse, *vr.* (Colomb.) to become overgrown with weeds and trees.

enmordazar, *va.* to gag, muzzle.

enmudecer. I. *va.* (ind. ENMUDEZCO; *subj.* ENMUDEZCA) to hush, to silence. **II.** *vn.* to become dumb; to be silent.

enmugrar, *va.* to soil, cover with dirt.

ennegrecer, *va.* (ind. ENNEGREZCO; *subj.* ENNEGREZCA) to blacken; to darken, to obscure.

ennegrecimiento, *m.* blackening.

ennegrezco, ennegrezca, *v.* V. ENNEGRECER.

ennoblecedor, ra, *a.* ennobling, noble.

ennoblecer, *va.* (ind. ENNOBLEZCO; *subj.* ENNOBLEZCA) to ennoble; to adorn, embellish.

ennoblecimiento, *m.* ennoblement.

ennoblezco, ennoblezca, *v.* V. ENNOBLECER.

ennudecer, *vn.* (of trees) to be arrested in growth.

enodio, *m.* fawn, young deer.

enojada, *f.* (coll.) (Mex., P. R.) anger; getting angry.

enojadizo, za, *a.* fretful, peevish, ill-tempered.

enojado, da, I. *pp.* of ENOJAR. **II.** *a.* angry, cross.

enojar. I. *va.* to make angry, vex, irritate; to annoy. **II.** *vr.* to become angry, to get cross; (of the elements) to become violent, furious.

enojo, *m.* anger; (gen. *pl.*) trouble, suffering; annoyance.

enojón, na, *a.* (Am.) = ENOJADIZO.

enojosamente, *adv.* angrily; troublesomely.

enojoso, sa, *a.* troublesome; irritating.

enojuelo, *m. dim.* slight peevishness.

enología, *f.* œnology, art of wine making.

enológico, ca, *a.* œnological.

enometría, *f.* wine alcoholometry.

enómetro, *m.* wine alcoholometer.

enorgullecer. I. *va.* (ind. ENORGULLEZCO; *subj.* ENORGULLEZCA) to make proud. **II.** *vr.* to be proud; to swell with pride.—**enorgullecimiento,** *m.* pride; haughtiness.—**enorgullecido, da. I.** *pp.* of ENORGULLECER. **II.** *a.* haughty, proud.

enorgullezco, enorgullezca, *v.* V. ENORGULLECER.

enorme, *a.* enormous; horrible, wicked, heinous.

enormemente, *adv.* enormously; horridly.

enormidad, *f.* enormousness, grand quantity or size; horridness; enormity, atrocity, outrage.

enormísimo, ma, *a. super.* most horrid.

enostosis, *f.* (med.) enostosis, bony tumor.

enotecnia, *f.* art of wine making and marketing.

enotécnico, ca, *a.* pertaining to wine making.

enquiciar, *va.* to put (a door, window) in place; to put in order; to make firm or stable.

enquillotrarse, *vr.* to become conceited; (coll.) to fall in love.

enquiridión, *m.* enchiridion, handbook, manual.

enrabiar, *va.* to anger, enrage.

enraizar, *vn.* to take root.

enramada, *f.* bower, arbor; grove.

enramar, *va.* to embower or decorate with tree branches.

enramblar, *va.* to tenter (cloth).

enrame, *m.* act of embowering.

enranciarse, *vr.* to become rancid or stale.

enrarecer. I. *va.* (ind. ENRAREZCO; *subj.* ENRAREZCA) to thin, rarefy. **II.** *vr.* to become thin or rarefied.—**enrarecimiento,** *m.* rarefaction.

enrasar, *va.* (mason.) to make even or level, to flush.—**enrase,** *m.* (mason.) levelling course.

enrastrar, *va.* to string (silk cocoons).

enrayar, *va.* to put spokes on (a wheel).

enredadera. I. *a.* (of plants) climbing, twining. **II.** *f.* (bot.) climber; vine; bindweed.

enredado, da. I. *pp.* of ENREDAR. **II.** *a.* entangled, matted, involved, intricate.

enredador, ra, *n.* entangler; tattler, busybody, intermeddler.

enredar. I. *va.* to entangle, snarl; to confound, puzzle; to snarl, mess up, involve in difficulties; to catch in the net; to lay, set (snares, nets); to sow discord among or between. **II.** *vn.* to fumble; to be frisky (as boys). **III.** *vr.* to get entangled, snarled; to get involved; (naut.) (of anchor) to foul.

enredo, *m.* tangle, entanglement; perplexity, puzzle; intricacy; falsehood, mischievous lie; plot (of a play, etc.).—**enredoso, sa,** entangled, intricate; beset with difficulties.

enrehojar, *va.* to bleach (wax leaves).

enrejado, *m.* railing, grating; trellis, lattice; grillwork, openwork.

enrejalar, *va.* to range bricks in crisscross tiers.

¹enrejar, *va.* to fence with railing or grating; to put a trellis or lattice on.

²enrejar, *va.* to attach the plowshare to (the plow); to wound (cattle's feet) with a plowshare.

enrevesado, da, *a.* frisky; difficult; nonsensical.

enriado, *m.* retting, soaking of flax or hemp.

enriador, ra, *n.* one who rets, soaks flax or hemp.

enriar, *va.* to ret, soak (hemp, flax).

enrielar, *va.* to make ingots or rails from; to put on the track; to guide, start in the right direction.

enripiar, *va.* (mason.) to fill with riprap.

enriquecedor, ra, *n.* & *a.* enricher(-ing), wealth producer(-ing).

enriquecer. I. *va.* (ind. ENRIQUEZCO; *subj.* ENRIQUEZCA) to enrich; to adorn. **II.** *vr.* to become rich.

enriscado, da. I. *pp.* of ENRISCAR. **II.** *a.* mountainous, craggy; full of cliffs.

enriscamiento, *m.* act of raising; taking refuge among rocks.

enriscar. I. *va.* to lift, to raise. **II.** *vr.* to take refuge among rocks.

¹enristrar, *va.* to string (onions, etc.)

²enristrar, *va.* to couch (the lance); to go direct to (a place); to overcome (a difficulty).

enristre, *m.* act of couching a lance.

¹enrocar, *va.* (chess) to castle.

²enrocar, *va.* to put (flax or wool) on the distaff.

enrodelado, da, *a.* armed with a shield.

enrodrigonar, *va.* to prop or train with stakes.

enrojar, *va.* & *vr.* = ENROJECER.

enrojecer. I. *va.* (ind. ENROJEZCO; *subj.* ENROJEZCA) to redden; to make red-hot; to make blush. **II.** *vr.* to blush; turn red.

enrollar, *va.* to roll, coil, wind, wrap, up.

enromar, *va.* to blunt, dull.

enrona, *f.* rubbish, refuse, débris.

enronar, *va.* to throw rubbish in (a place).

enronquecer. I. *va.* (ind. ENRONQUEZCO; *subj.* ENRONQUEZCA) to make hoarse. **II.** *vn.* & *vr.* to get hoarse.

enronquecimiento, *m.* hoarseness.

enronquezco, enronquezca, *v.* V. ENRONQUECER.

enroñar, *va.* to fill with scabs or scurf.

enroscadamente, *adv.* curlingly.

enroscadura, *f.* act of twisting; convolution, sinuosity, twist, curlicue.

enroscar. I. *va.* (pret. ENROSQUÉ; *subj.* ENROSQUE) to twine to, twist. **II.** *vr.* to curl or twist itself; to coil.

enrubiador, ra, *a.* that turns the hair blond.

enrubiar, *va.* to dye (the hair) blond, bleach.

enrubio, *m.* dyeing blond; the dye used.

enrudecer. I. *va.* (*ind.* ENRUDEZCO; *subj.* ENRUDEZCA) to make dull. **II.** *vr.* to become dull.

enruinecer, *vn.* & *vr.* (*ind.* ENRUINEZCO; *subj.* ENRUINEZCA) to become vile.

ensabanar, *va.* to wrap up in sheets.

ensacador, ra, *n.* sacker, bagger.

ensacar, *va.* (*pret.* ENSAQUÉ; *subj.* ENSAQUE) to put in a sack, bag.

ensaimada, *f.* light coffee cake.

ensalada, *f.* salad; hodge podge, medley.

ensaladera, *f.* salad dish or bowl.

ensaladilla, *f.* assortment of dry sweetmeats; jewel made up of different precious stones.

ensalcé, ensalce, *v.* *V.* ENSALZAR.

ensalmador, ra, *n.* bonesetter; quack.

ensalmar, *va.* to set (bones); to cure by spells.

ensalmista, *n.* & *a.* medicine man, quack.

ensalmo, *m.* enchantment, spell, charm.—**como por e.,** or **por e.,** as if miraculously, suddenly and unexpectedly.

ensalobrarse, *vr.* to become salty.

ensalzador, ra, *n.* exalter, praiser, extoller.

ensalzamiento, *m.* exaltation, praise.

ensalzar, *va.* (*pret.* ENSALCÉ; *subj.* ENSALCE) to extol, exalt, praise.

ensamblador, *m.* joiner.

ensambladura, *f.* joinery; act of joining; joint.

ensamblaje, *m.* joining, coupling.

ensamblar, *va.* to join, couple; connect.

ensamble, *m.* = ENSAMBLAJE.

ensancha, *f.* extension, enlargement.

ensanchador, ra. I. *a.* stretching, expanding. **II.** *m.* stretcher, expander, reamer; glove stretcher.

ensanchamiento, *m.* widening, enlargement, dilation, expansion, stretch.

ensanchar. I. *va.* to widen, extend, enlarge; to stretch.—**e. el corazón,** to cheer up. **II.** *vr.* to assume an air of importance; to expand, enlarge.

ensanche, *m.* dilatation, enlargement, widening, extension, expansion, stretch; material turned in in seams of garments.

ensandecer, *vr.* (*ind.* ENSANDEZCO; *subj.* ENSANDEZCA) to become stupid; to turn mad.

ensangrentamiento, *m.* covering with blood.

ensangrentar. I. *va.* & *vr.* (*ind.* ENSANGRIENTO; *subj.* ENSANGRIENTE) to stain with blood. **II.** *vr.* to become heated or fiery; to cover oneself with blood.

ensañamiento, *m.* ferocity, cruelty.

ensañar. I. *va.* to irritate, enrage. **II.** *vr.* to gloat; to vent one's fury; to be merciless.

ensarnecerse, *vr.* to get the itch.

ensartar, *va.* to string (as beads); to thread; to link; to tell disconnectedly, to rattle off.

ensay, *m.* assay, trial, proof.

ensayador, ra, *n.* assayer; rehearcer.

ensayar. I. *va.* to try, practice, rehearse; to test; to assay. **II.** *vr.* to train oneself, practice.

ensaye, *m.* assay, test (of metals).

ensayista, *n.* essay writer; (Chile) assayer.

ensayo, *m.* test; essay; trial, examination, experiment; rehearsal; exercise, preparatory practice; (com.) sample, test, trial.

ensebar, *va.* to grease, tallow.

enselvado, da. I. *pp.* of ENSELVAR. **II.** *a.* wooded.

enselvar. I. *va.* to place in a wood. **II.** *vr.* to hide in, or retire to, the woods; to become wooded.

ensenada, *f.* cove, inlet, small bay.

ensenado, da. I. *pp.* of ENSENAR. **II.** *a.* having the form of a cove or inlet.

ensenar. I. *va.* to put in one's bosom. **II.** *vr.* (naut.) to put (a ship) into a bay.

enseña, *f.* standard, colors, ensign.

enseñable, *a.* teachable.

enseñado, da. I. *pp.* of ENSEÑAR. **II.** *a.* accustomed; trained.

enseñador, ra, *n.* teacher, instructor.

enseñamiento, *m.* teaching; education.

enseñanza, *f.* ENSEÑAMIENTO.—**e. primaria,** or **primera e.,** primary education.—**e. secundaria,** or **segunda e.,** secondary, high-school education.—**e. superior,** higher, or professional education.

enseñar. I. *va.* to teach; to train; to show, point out. **II.** *vr.* to school oneself; to become accustomed, inured.

enseño, *m.* (coll.) education.

enseñoreador, *m.* one who domineers.

enseñorear. I. *va.* to lord, to domineer. **II.** *vr.* to take possession (of a thing).

enserar, *va.* to cover with matting.

enseres, *m. pl.* chattels; fixtures, accessories; implements; household goods.

enseriarse, *vr.* (Am.) to become serious.

ensiforme, *a.* ensiform, sword-shaped.

ensilaje, *m.* ensilage.

ensilar, *va.* to ensile, preserve in a silo.

ensillado, da. I. *pp.* of ENSILLAR. **II.** *a.* saddlebacked (horses).

ensilladura, *f.* part of a horse on which the saddle is placed.

ensillar, *va.* to saddle (a horse, etc.).

ensimismarse, *vr.* to become absorbed in thought.

ensoberbecer. I. *va.* (*ind.* ENSOBERBEZCO; *subj.* ENSOBERBEZCA) to make proud. **II.** *vr.* to become proud and haughty; (of the elements) to become boisterous.

ensoberbecimiento, *m.* excessive pride.

ensoberbezco, ensoberbezca, *v.* *V.* ENSOBERBECER.

ensogar, *va.* to fasten with a rope.

ensolerar, *va.* to fix stools to (beehives).

ensolver, *va.* (*pp.* ENSUELTO; *ind.* ENSUELVO; *subj.* ENSUELVA) to inclose, include; to condense, abridge; (med.) to resolve.

ensopar, *va.* to steep, soak; to drench.

ensordecedor, ra, *a.* deafening.

ensordecer. I. *va.* (*ind.* ENSORDEZCO; *subj.* ENSORDEZCA) to deafen. **II.** *vn.* & *vr.* to become deaf; to become silent.

ensordecimiento, *m.* deafness.

ensordezco, ensordezca, *v.* *V.* ENSORDECER.

ensortijamiento, *m.* curling, crimping, crisping; ringlet, curlicue, kink.

ensortijar, *va.* & *vr.* to curl, to form ringlets; to kink; to put rings in (an animal's nose).

ensotarse, *vr.* to go into a thicket.

ensuciador, ra, *n.* & *a.* stainer(-ing), soiler(-ing).

ensuciamiento, *m.* staining, soiling, polluting.

ensuciar. I. *va.* to stain, soil, smear; to defile, pollute. **II.** *vr.* to soil one's bed, clothes, etc.; (coll.) to be dishonest; to lower oneself.

ensuelto, ensuelvo, etc. *v.* *V.* ENSOLVER.

ensueño, *m.* dream; illusion, fantasy.

entablación, *f.* act of flooring or boarding up; register in churches.

entablado, da. I. *pp.* of ENTABLAR. **II.** *m.* boarded or parqueted floor.

entabladura, *f.* act of flooring or boarding up; planking, timbering.

entablamento, *m.* (arch.) entablature.

entablar. I. *va.* to cover with boards; to board up; to plank; to initiate, start, begin (as a negotiation); to bring (a suit or action); to place (the men) on a chessboard; (surg.) to splint. **II.** *vr.* to settle (as the wind); to establish oneself.

entable, *m.* position of men on a chessboard; position, employment; business, business position or circumstances.

entablillar, *va.* (surg.) to splint.

entalamadura, *f.* awning of a cart, etc.

entalamar, *va.* to cover with an awning.

entalegar, *va.* (com.) to put in a bag.

entalingar, *va.* (naut.) to clinch (the cable).

entallable, *a.* capable of being carved.

For pronunciation, see the rules at the beginning of the book.

entallador, *m.* sculptor, cutter in wood or stone; engraver; carver.

entalladura, *f.*, **entallamiento,** *m.* sculpture, carving; (carp.) mortise, groove, notch.

entallar, *va.* to notch; to make a cut in, to sculpture, to carve; to engrave.

²entallar, *vn.* (of a garment) to fit well.

entallecer, *vn.* (agr.) to shoot, to sprout.

entapizar, *va.* to hang tapestry on.

entarascar, *va.* (coll.) to overdress.

entarimado, da. I. *pp.* of ENTARIMAR. II. *m.* parquetry, inlaid floor.

entarimar, *va.* to floor with boards.

entarquinamiento, *m.* fertilizing with slime.

entarquinar, *va.* to manure with slime; to be-mire; to reclaim (swamp lands).

éntasis, *m.* (arch.) entasis.

ente, *m.* entity, being; (coll.) guy.

entecado, da; enteco, ca, *a.* sickly, weak, thin.

entejar, *va.* to tile.

entelequia, *f.* (philos.) entelechy.

entelerido, da, *a.* numb or shivering with cold or fright; (Am.) sick-looking, thin, frail.

entena, *f.* (naut.) lateen yard.

entenado, da, *n.* stepson(-daughter).

entenallas, *f. pl.* (mech.) pincers; handvise.

entendederas, *f. pl.* (coll.) understanding, brain.

entendedor, ra, *n.* one who understands.

entender. I. *va. & vn.* (ind. ENTIENDO; subj. EN-TIENDA) to understand.—**e. de,** to be familiar with, to be a judge of, be good at, know.—**e. en,** to be in charge of, deal with, attend to; to have authority to pass on or enquire into.—**dar a e.,** to intimate, insinuate, hint. II. *vr.* to be under-stood; to be meant.—**e. con,** to belong with, be included in; to have to do with; to deal with. —**e. por,** to be understood to be; to mean: (*entiéndese por aritmética la ciencia de los nú-meros,* arithmetic means the science of num-bers). III. *m.* understanding, opinion.—**a mi e., según mi e.,** in my opinion, according to my understanding.

entendidamente, *adv.* knowingly.

entendido, da. I. *pp.* of ENTENDER. II. *a.* able; posted; prudent.—**darse por e.,** to take notice, pay attention.—**no darse por e.,** not to notice, to ignore; to pretend not to understand.—**tener e.,** to understand.

entendimiento, *m.* intellect, mind; understand-ing; comprehension.

entenebrecer, *va.* (ind. ENTENEBREZCO; subj. ENTENEBREZCA) to obscure, darken.

enterado, da. I. *pp.* of ENTERAR. II. *a.* posted, informed.

enteramente, *adv.* entirely, fully; quite.

enterar. I. *va.* to inform, acquaint, advise; (Am.) to pay, deliver (in a public office). II. *vn.* (Am.) to get better. III. *vr.* (Am.) to make up for a loss, recoup one's losses.—**e. de,** to learn, be-come informed about or familiar with, find out about.

entereza, *f.* entirety, completeness; integrity, uprightness; perfection; fortitude, firmness; presence of mind.—**e. virginal,** virginity.

entérico, ca, *a.* (med.) enteric.

enterísimo, ma, *a. super.* most complete.

enteritis, *f.* (med.) enteritis.

enterizo, za, *a.* of, or in, one piece; whole.

enternecedor, ra, *a.* pitiful, touching.

enternecer. I. *va.* (ind. ENTERNEZCO; subj. EN-TERNEZCA) to soften; to touch, move to pity. II. *vr.* to be moved to pity, to be affected.

enternecidamente, *adv.* compassionately.

enternecimiento, *m.* compassion, pity.

enternezco, enternezca, *v.* V. ENTERNECER.

entero, ra. I. *a.* entire, whole; sound, perfect; honest, upright; pure, uncorrupted; strong, ro-bust, vigorous; informed, instructed; uncas-trated; strong, thick (dry goods); (arith.) whole, integral.—**por e.,** entirely, fully. II. *m.* (arith.)

integer; (Am.) payment, delivery; balance.—**los enteros,** (arith.) the integral part (of a decimal).

enterocele, *m.* (med.) enterocele, intestinal her-nial tumor.

enterocolitis, *f.* (med.) enterocolitis.

enterorragia, *f.* (med.) enterorrhagia, intestinal hemorrhage.

enterotomía, *f.* (surg.) enterotomy, intestinal incision.

enterrador, *m.* gravedigger; sexton.

enterramiento, *m.* interment, burial, funeral.

enterrar, *va.* (ind. ENTIERRO; subj. ENTIERRE) to inter, bury; to survive.

enterronar, *va.* to cover with clods.

entesamiento, *m.* stretching, making taut.

entesar, *va.* to stretch, make taut.

entestado, da, *a.* obstinate, stubborn.

entibación, *f.* (min.) timbering.

entibador, *m.* one who shores up mines.

entibar. I. *vn.* to rest, to lean upon. II. *va.* (min.) to prop, shore up.

entibiadero, *m.* cooling room or bath.

entibiar. I. *va.* to make lukewarm; to cool; to temper, moderate. II. *vr.* to cool down; to slacken.

entibo, *m.* stay, prop; foundation.

entidad, *f.* entity; value, consequence, moment, importance.

entiendo, entienda, *v.* V. ENTENDER.

¹entierro, *m.* burial, interment, funeral; grave.

²entierro, entierre, *v.* V. ENTERRAR.

entigrecerse, *vr.* (ind. ENTIGREZCO; subj. ENTI-GREZCA) (coll.) to become furious as a tiger.

entimema, *f.* (logic) enthymeme.

entinar, *va.* to put into the dyeing vat.

entintar, *va.* to ink, ink in (a drawing); to stain with ink; to tint or dye.

entiznar, *va.* to stain; to revile, defame.

entoldado, *m.* tent or group of tents; covering with tents or awnings.

entoldamiento, *m.* covering with tents or with awnings.

entoldar. I. *va.* to cover with an awning; to adorn with hangings. II. *vr.* to dress gorgeously; to swell with pride; (of sky) to get cloudy.

entomizar, *va.* to tie bass cords around (posts or laths), so the plaster will stick.

entomología, *f.* entomology.

entomológico, ca, *a.* entomological.

entomólogo, *m.* entomologist.

entonación, *f.* modulation; intonation; blowing the bellows of an organ.

entonadera, *f.* blow lever of an organ.

entonado, da. I. *pp.* of ENTONAR. II. *a.* haughty, "stuck-up." III. *m.* (photog.) process of toning.

entonador, ra. I. *n.* one who sings in tune; (photog.) one that tones. II. *m.* organ blower.

entonamiento, *m.* intonation.

entonar. I. *va.* to modulate, intone; to sing in tune; (art) to harmonize (colors); (photog.) to tone (prints); to blow (the bellows of an organ); (med.) to tone up. II. *vr.* to put on grand airs.

entonatorio, *m.* book of sacred music.

entonces, *adv.* then.—¿e.? (Am.) then what? and then?—**de e.,** of that time.—**desde e.,** from then on.—**hasta e.,** up to that time.—**por e.,** at the time.

entonelar, *va.* to put in casks or barrels.

entono, *m.* act of intoning; arrogance, haughti-ness, airs.

entontecer. I. *va.* (ind. ENTONTEZCO; subj. EN-TONTEZCA) to make foolish; to confuse. II. *vn. & vr.* to become foolish.—**entontecimiento,** *m.* act of becoming foolish; state of foolishness.

entorchado, *m.* bullion fringe; bullion embroi-dery on the uniform of generals; (mus.) strings.

entorchar, *va.* to make a torch by twisting (can-dles); (mus.) to cover (a string) with wire.

entorilar, *va.* to stall (the bull).

For pronunciation, see the rules at the beginning of the book.

entornar, *va.* to half-close; to set ajar.

entornillar, *va.* to form a screw or spiral of.

entorpecer, *va.* (*ind.* ENTORPEZCO; *subj.* ENTORPEZCA) to benumb; to stupefy; to clog, obstruct, delay.

entorpecimiento, *m.* torpor, numbness, stupefaction; dulness, stupidity; obstruction, delay.

entorpezco, entorpezca, *v.* V. ENTORPECER.

entortadura, *f.* crookedness.

entortar, *va.* (*ind.* ENTUERTO; *subj.* ENTUERTE) to bend; to make crooked; to make blind in one eye.

entosigar, *va.* to poison.

entozoario, *m.* (zool.) entozoan, internal parasite.

entrada, *f.* entrance, door, gate; admission; admittance (right of entry); entry; arrival; number of people in a theater (*entrada llena*, full house); beginning (of a book, speech, season, etc.); familiar access, intimacy; good hand at cards; entrée (course at dinner); (com.) entry (in a book); cash receipts.—**e. general**, (theat.) gallery seat; (Am.) main entrance.—*pl.* temples (of the head); receding hair at temples; (com.) income.—**entradas y salidas**, (fig.) collusion.

entrado, da, *pp.* of ENTRAR.—**e. en años**, advanced in years.

entrador, ra, *a.* (Am.) energetic, hustling; (Chile) intruding, intrusive, fond of butting in.

entramado, *m.* (carp.) framework, studwork, baywork.

entramar, *va.* (carp.) to provide with studwork or framework.

entrambos, bas, *a.* & *pron. pl.* both.

entrampar. **I.** *va.* to entrap, insnare; to trick, deceive; to entangle; to encumber. **II.** *vr.* (coll.) to become indebted; to be involved in difficulties.

entrante, *a.* entering; coming, next (*el mes entrante*, next month).

entraña, *f.* entrail.—*pl.* entrails, bowels; humaneness, kindness; (fig.) heart; affection; disposition; idiosyncrasy; the inmost recess of anything.

entrañable, *a.* most affectionate; deep (affection).—**entrañablemente**, *adv.* dearly; deeply.

entrañar. **I.** *va.* to penetrate to the core; to contain, involve, carry within. **II.** *vr.* to become intimately attached.

entrapada, *f.* coarse crimson cloth.

entrapajar, *va.* to bandage with rags.

entrapar. **I.** *va.* to powder (the hair) for a dry shampoo; (agr.) to manure with rags. **II.** *vr.* to become as dirty as a rag.

entrar. **I.** *vn.* (**a, en, por**) (the English equivalent is often transitive) to go (in), come (in), enter; to go (into); to flow (into); to attack, fight; to be admitted or have free entrance (to); to join; to begin; to be one (of), be counted (with); to be believable or understandable (to one); to be taken (with) (fear, etc.); to enter or go (into) (an agreement, etc.); to attack; to influence, convince; (of shoes, garment) to fit. **II.** *va.* to introduce, put in; to enter, take by force. **III.** *vr.* to enter; to squeeze or sneak (in); to break (in).

entre, *prep.* between, among, amongst, amidst; within.—**e. manos**, in hand.—**e. mí**, within myself.—**e. tanto**, in the meantime; meanwhile.

entreabierto, ta. **I.** *pp. irreg.* of ENTREABRIR. **II.** *a.* half-opened, ajar.

entreabrir, *va.* to half-open, to set ajar.

entreacto, *m.* (theat., etc.) intermission; small cigar.

entreancho, cha, *a.* neither wide nor narrow.

entrecalle, *m.* (arch.) clear between two consecutive moldings.

entrecanal, *f.* (arch.) fillet between flutes.

entrecano, na, *a.* grayish (hair or beard).

entrecasco, *m.* = ENTRECORTEZA.

entrecava, *f.* very shallow digging.

entrecavar, *va.* to dig shallow.

entrecejo, *m.* space between eyebrows; frowning.

entrecerca, *f.* space between inclosures.

entreclaro, ra, *a.* slightly clear.

entrecogedura, *f.* act of catching.

entrecoger, *va.* (*ind.* ENTRECOJO; *subj.* ENTRECOJA) to catch; to intercept; to compel by arguments or threats.

entrecoro, *m.* chancel.

entrecortado, da, *a.* confused, hesitating.

entrecortadura, *f.* cut that does not sever.

entrecortar, *va.* to cut without severing.

entrecorteza, *f.* imperfection in timbers.

entrecriarse, *vr.* to grow among other plants.

entrecruzar, *va.* (*subj.* ENTRECRUCE) to intercross; interlace, interweave.

entrecubiertas, *f. pl.* (naut.) between decks.

entrecuesto, *m.* backbone.

entrechocarse, *vr.* to collide, impinge on each other.

entredicho, *m.* interdiction, prohibition.

entredoble, *a.* of medium thickness.

entredós, *m.* insertion; (print.) long primer.

entrefino, na, *a.* middling fine.

entrega, *f.* delivery, conveyance; fascicle of a publication; surrender.

entregadero, ra, *a.* (com.) deliverable.

entregador, ra, *n.* deliverer; executor.

entregamiento, *m.* delivery.

entregar. **I.** *va.* (*pret.* ENTREGUÉ; *subj.* ENTREGUE) to deliver; to give up, surrender; to hand (over); (com.) to transfer, to pay; to insert, introduce, embed.—**a e.**, (com.) to be supplied or delivered. **II.** *vr.* to deliver oneself up, to surrender, give in, submit.—**e. a**, to abandon oneself to or devote oneself to.—**e. de**, to receive, to take charge or possession of.

entrejuntar, *va.* (carp.) to join (the panels of a door) to the frame.

entrelazar, *va.* (*pret.* ENTRELACÉ; *subj.* ENTRELACE) to interlace, interweave, braid, entwine.

entreliño, *m.* (agr.) space between rows of trees.

entrelistado, da, *a.* striped or variegated.

entrelucir, *vn.* & *vr.* (*ind.* ENTRELUZCO; *subj.* ENTRELUZCA) to show through.

entremedias, *adv.* in the meantime; halfway.—**e. de**, between; among.

entremés, *m.* (theat.) one-act farce; side dish.

entremesear, *va.* to act in a farce; to throw into one's talk, bring up.

entremesista, *a.* writer or player of farces.

entremeter. **I.** *va.* to place between; to insert. **II.** *vr.* to intrude, obtrude; intermeddle; meddle; interpose officiously.

entremetido, da. **I.** *pp.* of ENTREMETER. **II.** *a.* meddlesome; officious. **III.** *n.* meddler, intruder, intermeddler; busybody; go-between.

entremetimiento, *m.* intrusion, intermeddling, meddlesomeness; interposition.

entremezcladura, *f.* intermixture.

entremezclar, *va.* to intermingle, intermix.

entremiche, *m.* (naut.) capstan, chock.

entremorir, *vn.* (*ind. pres.* él ENTREMUERE, *pret.* él ENTREMURIÓ; *pp.* ENTREMUERTO) to flicker (as a flame).

entrenador, ra, *n.* trainer; coach.

entrenamiento, *m.* (Gal.) training, coaching.

entrenar, *va.* & *vn.* (Gal.) to train.

entrencar, *va.* to put rods in (a beehive).

entrenzar, *va.* (*pret.* ENTRENCÉ; *subj.* ENTRENCE) to plait (the hair).

entreoír, *va.* (*ind.* ENTREOIGO; *subj.* ENTREOIGA) to hear indistinctly, half-hear.

entreordinario, ria, *a.* middling.

entrepalmadura, *f.* (vet.) a hoof disease.

entrepanes, *m. pl.* pieces of unsown ground.

entrepañado, da, *a.* composed of panels.

entrepaño, *m.* (arch.) intercolumniation; pier; (carp.) panel; shelf.
entreparecerse, *vr.* to show through.
entrepaso, *m.* rack pace (of horses).
entrepechuga, *f.* flesh within the wishbone.
entrepeines, *m. pl.* comb wool.
entrepelado, da, *a.* pied; variegated.
entrepelar, *vn. & vr.* (of hair) to be of different colors.
entrepernar, *vn.* (*ind.* ENTREPIERNO; *subj.* EN-TREPIERNE) to put the legs between those of others.
entrepiernas, *f. pl.* inner surface of the thighs; pieces put into the crotch of breeches.
entrepiso, *m.* (min.) space between galleries.
entreplano, (aer.) gap.
entrepretado, da, *a.* (vet.) weak in the breast or shoulder.
entrepuentes, *m. pl.* (naut.) between decks.
entrepunzadura, *f.* pricking pain.
entrepunzar, *va.* to prick slightly.
entrerrenglón, *m.* interline.
entrerrenglonadura, *f.* interlineation.
entrerrenglonar, *va.* to interline.
entresaca, entresacadura, *f.* thinning of wood; pruning of branches; sorting; picking out.
entresacar, *va.* (*pret.* ENTRESAQUÉ; *subj.* EN-TRESAQUE) to pick out or choose; to sift, cull; to thin out.
entresijo, *m.* (anat.) mesentery; anything hidden.
entresuelo, *m.* entresol, mezzanine.
entresurco, *m.* space between furrows.
entretalla, entretalladura, *f.* bas-relief.
entretallar, *va.* to carve in bas-relief; to engrave; to make openwork on; to intercept.
entretanto, *adv.* meanwhile.
entretejedor, ra, *a.* interweaver.
entretejedura, *f.* intertexture, interweaving.
entretejer, *va.* to interweave, intermix, inter-twine; to variegate; to insert, mix, mingle.
entretejimiento, *m.* intertexture, interweaving; variegation.
entretela, *f.* (sewing) interlining.
entretelar, *va.* to insert an interlining in.
entretenedor, ra, *n. & a.* entertainer(-ing).
entretener (*ind. pres.* yo ENTRETENGO, él EN-TRETIENE, *pret.* ENTRETUVE, *fut.* ENTRETENDRÉ; *subj.* ENTRETENGA) I. *va.* to amuse, entertain; to keep in hope or expectation; to allay (pain), make less troublesome; to delay, put off, post-pone. II. *vr.* to amuse oneself; to be tied up, delayed.
entretenida.—dar con la e., or **dar la e.,** to give excuses (to); to get out of doing something by promises or evasions.
entretenido, da. I. *pp.* of ENTRETENER. II. *a.* entertaining, pleasant, amusing. III. *m.* aspirant to office.
entretenimiento, *m.* amusement, entertain-ment, sport, pastime.
entretiempo, *m.* spring or autumn, between-season.
entretiene, entretuve, *v.* V. ENTRETENER.
entreuntar, *va.* to anoint or paint lightly.
entrevenarse, *vr.* to diffuse through the veins.
entreventana, *f.* (arch.) window pier.
entrever, *va.* (*ind. pres.* ENTREVEO, *pret.* yo EN-TREVÍ, él ENTREVIÓ; *subj.* ENTREVEA; *pp.* EN-TREVISTO) to see imperfectly.
entreverado, da. I. *pp.* of ENTREVERAR. II. *a.* intermingled, intermixed.
entreverar, *va.* to intermix, intermingle.
entrevía, *f.* (Ry.) gauge or gage.
entrevista, *f.* interview, meeting, conference.
entrevistar, *va.* to interview.
entripado, da. I. *a.* contained in the intestines; (of dead animal) not yet cleaned. II. *m.* (coll.) anger or displeasure.
entristecedor, ra, *a.* sad, saddening.

entristecer. I. *va.* (*ind.* ENTRISTEZCO; *subj.* EN-TRISTEZCA) to sadden, grieve. II. *vr.* to grieve, to become sad.
entristecimiento, *m.* sadness; fretting.
entristezco, entristezca, *v.* V. ENTRISTECER.
entrojar, *va.* to garner (grain).
entrometer, *va. & vr.* = ENTREMETER.
entrometido, da. I. *pp.* of ENTROMETER. II. *a.* = ENTREMETIDO.
entrometimiento, *m.* intermeddling, intrusion.
entronar, *va.* to enthrone.
entroncar, *vn.* to be descended from the same stock; to be related; (also *vr.*) to be connected; (Ry.) (Am.) to form a junction.
entronerar, *va.* (billiards) to pocket (a ball).
entronicé, entronice, *v.* V. ENTRONIZAR.
entronización, *f.* enthronement.
entronizar. I. *va.* (*pret.* ENTRONICÉ; *subj.* EN-TRONICE) to enthrone; to exalt. II. *vr.* to be elated or puffed up with pride.
entronque, *m.* cognation; connection, relation-ship; (Am.) railway junction.
entropía, *f.* (phys.) entropy.
entropión, *m.* (med.) entropion, introversion of the eyelids.
entruchada, *f.,* **entruchado,** *m.* (coll.) plot, intrigue.
entruchar, *va.* (coll.) to decoy, lure, entice.
entruchón, na, *n.* decoyer, plotter.
entrujar, *va.* to store up; (coll.) to reimburse.
entubado, *m.* casing (of an oil well, etc.).
entubar, *va.* to provide with casing (oil well, etc.).
entuerto, *m.* wrong, injustice.—*pl.* afterpains.
entullecer. I. *va.* (*ind.* ENTULLEZCO; *subj.* EN-TULLEZCA) to stop, check, obstruct. II. *vn.* to be crippled or maimed.
entumecer. I. *va.* (*ind.* ENTUMEZCO; *subj.* EN-TUMEZCA) to benumb. II. *vr.* (of limbs) to be-come numb, go to sleep; (of sea, etc.) to swell, surge.
entumecimiento, *m.* torpor, deadness; numb-ness; swelling.
entumezco, entumezca, *v.* V. ENTUMECER.
entumirse, *vr.* to become numb.
entunarse, *vr.* (Am.) to be pricked by a thorn.
entunicar, *va.* to plaster for fresco painting.
entupir, *va.* to obstruct, block up; to compress.
enturbiar. I. *va.* to muddle; to make muddy or turbid; to obscure, dim, confuse. II. *vr.* to get muddy; to get disordered or disarranged.
entusiasmado, da. I. *pp.* of ENTUSIASMAR. II. *a.* enthusiastic.
entusiasmar. I. *va.* to make enthusiastic; to en-rapture. II. *vr.* to become enthusiastic.
entusiasmo, *m.* enthusiasm.
entusiasta, *n.* enthusiast.
entusiástico, ca, *a.* enthusiastic.
énula campana, *f.* (bot.) elecampane.
enumerable, *a.* (Am.) numerable.
enumeración, *f.* enumeration.
enumerar, *va.* to enumerate.
enumerativo, va, *a.* enumerative.
enunciación, *f.,* **enunciado,** *m.* statement.
enunciar, *va.* to state.
enunciativo, va, *a.* enunciative.
envainador, ra, *a.* sheathing.
envainar, *va.* to sheathe (as a sword).
envalentonamiento, *m.* encouragement.
envalentonar. I. *va.* to encourage, to inspirit; to make bold. II. *vr.* to become courageous.
envalijar, *va.* to pack or put in a valise.
envanecer. I. *va.* (*ind.* ENVANEZCO; *subj.* EN-VANEZCA) to make vain. II. *vr.* to become vain. —**envanecimiento,** *m.* conceit.
envarado, da. I. *pp.* of ENVARAR. II. *a.* stiff; numb.
envaramiento, *m.* stiffness, numbness.
envarar, *va.* to benumb, stiffen.
envasador, *m.* filler, packer; funnel.
envasar, *va.* to put into a container (barrel, bot-

tle, etc.); to drink (liquor) to excess; to sack (grain); to run through the body with (as a sword).

envase, *m.* filling, bottling; container; packing.

envedijarse, *vr.* to get entangled; (coll.) to wrangle.

envejecer. I. *va.* (*ind.* ENVEJEZCO; *subj.* ENVEJEZCA) to make old; to make look old. **II.** *vn.* to become old. **III.** *vr.* to become old or old-fashioned; to hold out a long time.

envejecido, da. I. *pp.* of ENVEJECER. **II.** *a.* accustomed, habituated.

envejecimiento, *m.* oldness, age; aging.

envejezco, envejezca, *v.* *V.* ENVEJECER.

envenenador, ra, *n.* & *a.* poisoner(-ing).

envenenamiento, *m.* poisoning.

envenenar, *va.* to envenom, to poison.

enverar, *vn.* to look ripe.

enverdecer, *vn.* & *vr.* to become green.

envergadura, *f.* breadth of the sails; wing-spread of birds; (aer.) span.

envergar, *va.* (*pret.* ENVERGUÉ; *subj.* ENVERGUE) (naut.) to bend (the sails).

envergues, *m. pl.* (naut.) ropebands.

envero, *m.* color of ripe grape.

envés, *m.* back or wrong side; back, shoulders.

envesado, *m.* fleshy part of hides.

envestidura, *f.* investiture.

envestir, *va.* (*ind. pres.* ENVISTO, *pret.* él ENVISTIÓ; *subj.* ENVISTA) to invest (as with authority).

enviada, *f.* sending, shipment.

enviadizo, za, *a.* missive.

enviado, *m.* envoy; messenger.—**e. extraordinario,** envoy extraordinary.

enviador, ra, *n.* & *a.* sender(-ing).

enviajado, da, *a.* (arch.) oblique, sloped.

enviar, *va.* to send; to ship, dispatch.—**e. a uno a pasear,** (coll.) to send one about his business; to give one his walking ticket.—**e. enhoramala,** (coll.) to send to the devil.

enviciar. I. *va.* to corrupt, teach bad habits to. **II.** *vn.* (of plants) to have luxuriant foliage and little fruit. **III.** *vr.* (en) to acquire bad habits; to acquire the habit (of); to take (to) (drinking, etc.).

envidador, *m.* challenger at cards.

envidar, *va.* to stake a sum against.

envidia, *f.* envy.

envidiable, *a.* enviable.

envidiar, *va.* to envy.

envidiosamente, *adv.* enviously.

envidioso, sa, *a.* envious.

envilecedor, ra, *a.* degrading, debasing.

envilecer I. *va.* (*ind.* ENVILEZCO; *subj.* ENVILEZCA) to vilify, debase. **II.** *vr.* to degrade oneself.

envilecimiento, *m.* vilification, debasement.

envinagrar, *va.* to put vinegar into.

envinar, *va.* to add wine to (water).

envío, *m.* (com.) remittance; consignment of goods, shipment.

envión, *m.* push, shove.

envirotado, da, *a.* airy, stuck-up.

enviscamiento, *m.* daubing with birdlime.

¹enviscar. I. *va.* (*pret.* ENVISQUÉ; *subj.* ENVISQUE) to daub with birdlime. **II.** *vr.* to be glued with birdlime.

²enviscar, *va.* to irritate, anger.

envite, *m.* stake at cards; invitation; offer; push, al primer e., at once, right off; at the start.

enviudar, *vn.* to become a widower or widow.

envoltorio, *m.* bundle; defective woof.

envoltura, *f.* swaddling clothes; cover, wrapper, envelope, sheath; covering, wrapping.

envolvedero, envolvedor, *m.* wrapper, wrapping, envelope, cover.

envolver. I. *va.* (*pp.* ENVUELTO; *ind.* ENVUELVO; *subj.* ENVUELVA) to wrap, make up into a bundle; to swaddle; to floor (an opponent); to imply, mean; to contain, carry with it; (mil.) to surround. **II.** *vr.* to be implicated, involved; to be unlawfully connected (with women); to be mixed with a crowd.

envolvimiento, *m.* envelopment; wrapping.

envuelto, ta, *pp. irreg.* of ENVOLVER.

envuelvo, envuelva, *v.* *V.* ENVOLVER.

enyerbar. I. *va.* (Cuba) to sod. **II.** *vr.* to become covered or overgrown with grass.

enyesado, *m.* plasterwork; plaster; plastering.

enyesadura, *f.* plastering.

enyesar, *va.* to plaster; to chalk; to whitewash.

enyugar, *va.* to yoke.

enzainarse, *vr.* to look askance; (coll.) to become treacherous or deceitful.

enzamarrado, da, *a.* having on a shepherd's jacket of undressed sheepskin; wearing chaps.

¹enzarzar. I. *va.* to throw among brambles; to sow discord among or between. **II.** *vr.* to be entangled among brambles; to become involved in difficulties; to squabble, to wrangle.

²enzarzar, *va.* to put hurdles for (silkworms).

enzootia, *f.* epizoötic.

enzunchar, *va.* to bind with iron bands or hoops.

enzurdecer, *vn.* & *vr.* (*ind.* ENZURDEZCO; *subj.* ENZURDEZCA) to become left-handed.

enzurronar, *va.* to bag; (coll.) to inclose.

eñe, *f.* name of the letter ñ.

eoceno, na, *n.* & *a.* Eocene.

eólico, ca; eolio, lia, *a.* Æolian, Æolic.

eón, *m.* divine emanation.

eosina, *f.* (chem.) eosin.

epacta, *f.* (astr.) epact.

epactilla, *f.* annual devotional calendar.

epéndimo, *m.* (anat.) ependyma.

epéntesis, *f.* (lang.) epenthesis.

eperlano, *m.* (ichth.) smelt, a small fish.

épica, *f.* epic poetry.—**épicamente,** *adv.* epically.

epicarpo, *m.* (bot.) epicarp.

epicedio, *m.* epicedium, elegy.

epiceno, na, *a.* (gram.) epicene.

epicentro, *m.* (geol.) epicenter, portion of the earth over the center of an earthquake.

epicíclico, ca, *a.* epicyclic.

epiciclo, *m.* epicycle.

epicicloide, *f.* epicycloid.

épico, ca, *a.* (poet.) epic, heroic.

epicráneo, *m.* (anat.) epicranium, the scalp.

epicureísmo, *m.* epicurism; Epicureanism.

epicúreo, rea, *n.* & *a.* epicurean.

epidemia, *f.* (med.) epidemic.

epidemial; epidémico, ca, *a.* epidemic.

epidérmico, ca, *a.* epidermic.

epidermis, *f.* epidermis, outer skin.

epidídimo, *m.* (anat.) epididymis.

epidota, epidoto, *m.* (min.) epidote.

epifanía, *f.* Epiphany; twelfth night.

epifenómeno, *m.* (med.) epiphenomenon, secondary symptom.

epífisis, *f.* (anat.) epiphysis.

epifito, ta. I. *a.* (bot.) epiphytic. **II.** *f.* (bot.) epiphyte.

epifonema, *f.* (rhet.) epiphonema.

epigástrico, ca, *a.* epigastric, pert. to abdomen.

epigastrio, *m.* epigastrium.

epiglosis, *f.* (zool.) epiglottis; epipharynx (of insects).

epiglotis, *f.* (anat.) epiglottis.

epígrafe, *m.* epigraph.—**epigrafía,** *f.* epigraphy.

epigráfico, ca, *a.* epigraphic.

epigrafista, *n.* epigrapher.

epigrama, *m.* epigram; witticism; inscription.

epigramatario, ria. I. *a.* = EPIGRAMÁTICO. **II.** *m.* epigrammatist; collection of epigrams.

epigramáticamente, *adv.* epigrammatically.

epigramático, ca, *a.* epigrammatic.

epigramatista, epigramista, *n.* epigrammatist.

epilepsia, *f.* (med.) epilepsy.

epiléptico, ca, *n.* & *a.* epileptic.

epileptiforme, *a.* epileptoid, resembling epilepsy.

epilogación, *f.* = EPÍLOGO.

epilogal, *a.* epilogistic, compendious.

epilogar, *va.* (*pret.* EPILOGUÉ; *subj.* EPILOGUE) to epilogize, recapitulate, sum up.

epilogismo, *m.* (astr.) epilogism, computation.

epílogo, *m.* epilogue; summing up.

epilogué, epilogue, *v. V.* EPILOGAR.

epinicio, *m.* epinicion, triumphal ode.

epiplon, epíploon, *m.* (anat.) omentum.

epiquerema, *m.* (logic) epicheirema.

epiqueya, *f.* mild interpretation of the law, taking circumstances into consideration.

epirota, *n.* & *a.,* **epirótico, ca,** *a.* Epirote (from Epirus).

episcopado, *m.* episcopacy; episcopate; bishopric, see.

episcopal, *a.* episcopal; Episcopal.—**episcopalismo,** *m.* episcopalism; Episcopalianism.

episcopologio, *m.* chronological list of bishops.

episódico, ca, *a.* episodic, episodical.

episodio, *m.* episode; digression.

epispástico, ca, *a.* epispastic, blistering.

epistaxis, *f.* (med.) epistaxis, nosebleed.

epístola, *f.* epistle, letter; epistle, part of the mass.—**epistolar,** *a.* epistolary.—**epistolario,** *m.* epistolary; volume of letters.—**epistolero, ra,** *n.* (eccl.) epistler.

epístrofe, *f.* (rhet.) epistrophe.

epitafio, *m.* epitaph.

epitalámico, ca, *a.* epithalamic.

epitalamio, *m.* epithalamium, nuptial song.

epitasis, *f.* (anc. drama) epitasis.

epitelial, *a.* epithelial.

epitelio, *m.* (zool.) epithelium.

epitelioma, *m.* (med.) epithelioma, a cancer.

epítema, *f.* (med.) epithem, a moist external application.

epíteto, *m.* (gram.) epithet.

epítima, *f.* = EPITEMA.

epitimar, *va.* to apply an epithem to.

epítimo, *m.* (bot.) lesser dodder.

epitomadamente, *adv.* concisely.

epitomador, ra, *a.* epitomizer.

epitomar, *va.* to epitomize, abstract, summarize.

epítome, *m.* epitome, abstract, summary.

epizoario, a, *a.* (zool.) epizoic, epizoan.

epizootia, *f.* (vet.) epizoöty, epidemic influenza.—**epizoótico, ca,** *a.* epizoötic.

época, *f.* epoch, age, era; time.—**formar,** or **hacer, e.,** to open a new era; to be a turning point.

epoda, *f.,* **epodo,** *m.* (poet.) epode.

epónimo, *m.* eponym.

epopeya, *f.* epopee, epic poem.

epsomita, *f.* Epsom salts.

epulón, *m.* gourmand, heavy eater.

equiángulo, la, *a.* (geom.) equiangular.

equidad, *f.* equity, equitableness; impartiality, justice.

equidiferencia, *f.* (math.) equidifference, arithmetical progression.

equidistancia, *f.* equidistance.

equidistante, *a.* equidistant.

equidistar, *vn.* to be equidistant.

equilátero, ra, *a.* (geom.) equilateral.

equilibrar, *va.* to equilibrate, balance; to counterpoise, counterbalance.

equilibre, *a.* balanced, equilibrious.

equilibrio, *m.* equilibrium, balance, equipoise.—**e. europeo,** European balance of power.

equilibrista, *m.* balancer, equilibrist.

equimosis, *f.* (med.) a bruise, black-and-blue.

equino, na, *a.* equine.

²equino, *m.* (zool.) echinus; (arch.) echinus.

equinoccial, *a.* equinoctial.

equinoccio, *m.* equinox.

equinococo, *m.* (med.) echinococcus.

equinodermo, ma. I. *n.* & *a.* (zool.) echinoderm. **II.** *m. pl.* Echinodermata, star-fish, etc.

equipaje, *m.* baggage or luggage; equipment; (naut.) crew; (mil.) baggage train.

equipar, *va.* to fit out, equip, furnish.

equiparación, *f.* comparison, collation.

equiparar, *va.* to compare, to match.

equipo, *m.* equipment; (mil.) fitting out; accoutrement, trappings; (sports) team.

equipolencia, *f.* (logic) equipollence.

equipolente, *a.* equivalent, equipollent.

equiponderante, *a.* of equal weight.

equiponderar, *vn.* to counterbalance.

equis, *f.* name of the letter *x.*

equisetáceo, a, *a.* (bot.) equisetaceous.

equitación, *f.* horsemanship, riding.

equitativamente, *adv.* equitably.

equitativo, va, *a.* equitable, fair, just.

equivalencia, *f.* equivalence; equivalent.

equivalente, *a.* equivalent, tantamount; compensatory, compensative.

equivalentemente, *adv.* equivalently.

equivaler, *vn.* (*ind. pres.* EQUIVALGO, *fut.* EQUIVALDRÉ; *subj.* EQUIVALGA) to be equivalent.

equivocación, *f.* mistake, error; equivocation.

equivocadamente, *adv.* mistakenly, by mistake.

equivocado, da. I. *pp.* of EQUIVOCAR. **II.** *a.* mistaken.

equívocamente, *adv.* equivocally.

equivocar. I. *va.* (*pret.* EQUIVOQUÉ; *subj.* EQUIVOQUE) to mistake; to confuse, mix up (things). **II.** *vr.* to be mistaken; to make a mistake.—**e. de,** to (verb) the wrong (noun) (as *me equivoqué de autobus,* I took the wrong bus; *me equivoqué de puerta,* I went to the wrong door.

equívoco, ca. I. *a.* equivocal, ambiguous. **II.** *m.* equivocation, quibble, pun.

equivoqué, equivoque, *v. V.* EQUIVOCAR.

equivoquista, *n. dim.* quibbler; punster.

¹era, *f.* era, age.—**e. común, cristiana,** or **vulgar,** Christian era.

²era, *f.* thrashing floor; vegetable patch; garden bed.

³era, *imp.* of SER.

eraje, *m.* virgin honey.

eral, *m.* two-year-old ox.

erar, *va.* to lay out (a garden).

erario, *m.* exchequer, public treasury.

erbio, *m.* (chem.) erbium.

ere, *f.* name of the letter *r.*

erección, *f.* erection, raising; erectness, elevation; foundation, establishment.

eréctil, *a.* erectile.—**erectilidad,** *f.* erectility.

erector, ra, *n.* erector, founder.

eremita, *m.* hermit, recluse, eremite.

eremítico, ca, *a.* solitary.

eremitorio, *m.* place with hermitage(s).

eretismo, *m.* (med.) erethism.

erg, *m.* (phys.) = ERGIO.

ergástula, *f.,* **ergástulo,** *m.* slave prison.

ergio, *m.* (phys.) erg (a unit of energy).

ergotina, *f.* (med.) ergotine.

ergotinina, *f.* (chem.) ergotinine.

¹ergotismo, *m.* (med.) ergotism.

²ergotismo, *m.* sophistry.

ergotista, *m.* debater, sophist.

ergotizar, *vn.* to argue fallaciously.

erguimiento, *m.* straightening up.

erguir. I. *va.* (*ind. pres.* IRGO or YERGO, *pret.* él IRGUIÓ; *subj.* IRGA or YERGA) *ger.* IRGUIENDO) to erect, to set up straight. **II.** *vr.* to straighten up; to stand or sit erect; to swell with pride.

erial, eriazo, za. I. *a.* unplowed, untilled, uncultivated. **II.** *m.* unimproved land.

erica, *f.* (bot.) heath, heather.

ericáceo, cea, *a.* (bot.) ericaceous.

ericé, erice, *v. V.* ERIZAR.

Erídano, *m.* (astr.) Eridanus.

erigir, *va.* (*ind.* ERIJO; *subj.* ERIJA) to erect, raise, build; to found, establish.

eringe, *f.* (bot.) field eringo.

erío, ría, *a.* untilled, uncultivated.

erisipela, *f.* (med.) erysipelas.—**erisipelar,** *va.* to cause erysipelas to.—**erisipelatoso, sa,** *a.* (med.) erysipelatous.

erístico, ca, *a.* eristic, disputatious.

eritema, *f.* (med.) erythema, redness of skin.

Eritreo, a, *a.* Erythræan (app. to the Red Sea).

eritrina, *f.* (chem.) erythrin.

eritroxíleo, lea. I. *a.* (bot.) erythroxylaceous. **II.** *f. pl.* Erythroxyláceæ.

erizado, da. I. *pp.* of ERIZAR. **II.** *a.* covered with bristles.—**e. de.,** beset with (difficulties, etc.); covered with, abounding in; bristling with.

erizamiento, *m.* setting on end, as the hair; bristling up.

erizar. I. *va.* (*pret.* ERICÉ; *subj.* ERICE) to set on end, to bristle. **II.** *vr.* to bristle; (of the hair) to stand on end.

erizo, *m.* (zool.) hedgehog; prickly husk, as a chestnut bur; (mech.) urchin, carding roller; sprocket wheel, rag wheel, spar-toothed wheel. —**e. de mar,** or, **marino,** (zool.) sea urchin.

ermita, *f.* hermitage.—**ermitaño, ña,** *n.* hermit.

ermitorio, *m.* = EREMITORIO.

ermunio, *a.* exempt from tribute and service.

erogación, *f.* expense.

erogar, *va.* (*pret.* EROGUÉ; *subj.* EROGUE) to distribute property; (Mex.) to lay out, spend.

erogatorio, *m.* pipe through which liquor is drawn.

erogué, erogue, *v.* V. EROGAR.

erosión, *f.* erosion, wearing away.

erotema, *f.* (rhet.) interrogation.

eróticamente, *adv.* erotically.

erótico, ca, *a.* erotical, erotic.

erotismo, *m.* eroticism.

erotomanía, *f.* (med.) erotomania, love madness.

errabundo, da, *a.* wandering.

errada, *f.* miscue, in billiards.

erradamente, *adv.* erroneously, mistakenly.

erradicación, *f.* eradication.

erradicar, *va.* to eradicate.

erradizo, za, *a.* wandering to and fro.

errado, da. I. *pp.* of ERRAR. **II.** *a.* mistaken, in error; erroneous.

erraj, *m.* fine coal made from the stones of olives.

errante, *a.* errant; roving, wandering, nomadic.

errar. I. *va.* (*ind.* YERRO; *subj.* YERRE) to miss (the target, blow, etc.); to fail in one's duty to; to offend. **II.** *vn.* to wander, roam, to err. **III.** *vn. & vr.* to be mistaken; to commit an error.

errata, *f.* erratum, typographical error.—**erratas, or fe de erratas,** errata, list of errata.

errático, ca, *a.* wandering, vagabond; erratic.

errátil, *a.* (coll.) wavering, not firm or steady.

erre, *f.* name of the double letter *rr*, and of *r* when it has the same sound.—**e. que e.,** pertinaciously, obstinately.

erróneamente, *adv.* erroneously, mistakenly.

erróneo, nea, *a.* erroneous, mistaken.

erronía, *f.* opposition, dislike, grudge.

error, *m.* error, mistake.—**e. clásico, e. craso,** gross error.

erubescencia, *f.* erubescence, blush.

eructación, *f.* eructation, belching.

eructar, *vn.* to belch, eructate.

eructo, *m.* belching, eructation.

erudición, *f.* erudition, learning.

eruditamente, *adv.* learnedly.

erudito, ta, *a. & n.* erudite, learned (person).

eruginoso, sa, *a.* rusty, musty.

erupción, *f.* eruption, bursting forth; (med.) eruption, rash.

eruptivo, va, *a.* eruptive.

erutación, *f.,* **erutar,** *vn.,* **eruto,** *m.* = ERUCTACIÓN, etc., eructation, etc.

ervato, *m.* (bot.) sea sulphurwort.

ervilla, *f.* (bot.) bitter vetch seed.

es, *irreg. form of* SER.

---

esa, ésa, *a. & pron., f. form of* ESE, ÉSE. Sometimes used colloquially in the sense of "one," "that," "that thing," "that story," "that situation," etc.: *ésa es buena,* that is a good one, that is a strange thing; *ésa no la creo,* I don't believe that, I can't go that one: *no venga con ésa,* don't come with that stuff; you don't say! don't tell me that.

esbatimentar. I. *va.* (art) to delineate (a shadow). **II.** *vn.* to cast a shadow.

esbatimento, *m.* shade (in a picture).

esbeltez, esbelteza, *f.* tall and elegant stature.

esbelto, ta, *a.* tall, slender and well formed, svelte.

esbirro, *m.* bailiff, apparitor; myrmidon.

esbozar, *va.* to sketch.

esbozo, *m.* sketch, outline; rough draught.

escabechar, *va.* to souse, pickle; (coll.) to stab and kill.

escabeche, *m.* souse, pickle; pickled fish.

escabel, *m.* footstool; small seat; bench.

escabiosa, *f.* (bot.) field scabious.

escabioso, sa, *a.* (med.) scabious.

escabro, *m.* scab, itch, or mange in sheep; roughness on the bark of trees.

escabrosamente, *adv.* roughly, ruggedly.

escabrosidad, *f.* inequality, unevenness, roughness; cragginess; hardness, asperity.

escabroso, sa, *a.* rough, uneven; craggy, rugged; rude, unpolished.

escabullimiento, *m.* evasion, slipping away.

escabullirse, *vr.* to escape, to evade; to slip or sneak away.

escacado, da, *a.* (her.) checkered.

escafandro, *m.* diving suit.

escafilar, *va.* to trim (a brick or tile).

escafoides, *a.* (anat.) scaphoid (bone).

escala, *f.* ladder, stepladder; scale; graduated rule or instrument; seaport stopping place; (mus.) scale; (mil.) military register.—**e. franca,** free port.—**a e. vista,** openly.—**hacer e. en,** to touch, or stop, at (a port).

escalada, *f.* (mil.) escalade, scalado.

escalado, da. I. *pp.* of ESCALAR. **II.** *a.* (of fish or meat) cut open to be salted or cured.

escalador, ra, *n. & a.* climber(-ing), scaler(-ing).

escalafón, *m.* roster, roll, list; army register.

escalamiento, *m.* (mil.) scaling.

escálamo, *m.* (naut.) thole, tholepin; rowlock.

escalar, *va.* (mil.) to scale; to enter surreptitiously.

escaldado, da. I. *pp.* of ESCALDAR. **II.** *a.* cautious, suspicious, wary. **III.** *f.* loose and lewd woman.

escaldar, *va.* to burn, scald; to make red-hot.

escaleno, *a.* (geom.) scalene.

escalentamiento, *m.* (vet.) foot inflammation.

escalera, *f.* staircase; stair; ladder; sloats of a cart.—**e. de caracol,** winding stair.—**e. de costado,** (naut.) quarter-deck ladder.—**e. de desahogo =** E. EXCUSADA.—**e. de mano,** ladder.—**e. de servicio,** service stairs.—**e. excusada,** or **falsa,** stairs leading to bedrooms or family apartments.—**e. real =** E. DE COSTADO.—**escalereja,** *f. dim.* small ladder; stepladder; (mech.) rack; drenching instrument.—**en escalereja,** in degrees; stepped.—**escalerilla,** *f.* = ESCALEREJA.—**escalerón,** *m. aug.* large staircase.

escaleta, *f.* frame for raising carriages.

escalfado, da. I. *pp.* of ESCALFAR. **II.** *a.* poached (eggs).

escalfador, *m.* barber's pan; water heater; chafing dish.

escalfar, *va.* to poach (eggs).

escalfarote, *m.* wide boot lined with hay.

escalfeta, *f.* small pan for live coals; chafing dish; dish warmer.

escalinata, *f.* (arch.) perron, high stoop.

escalio, *m.* land abandoned for tillage.

escalmo, *m.* barlock, rowlock.

For pronunciation, see the rules at the beginning of the book.

escalo, *m.* breaking a way into or out of a place.

escalofriado, da, *a.* shivering, chilled.

escalofrío, *m.* chill.

escalón, *m.* stair; step of a stairway; stepping stone; rank, degree of dignity; (mil.) echelon.

escalonar, *va.* (mil.) to form in echelon; to step.

escaloña, *f.* (bot.) eschalot, shalot, scallion.

escalpar, *va.* to scalp.

escalpelo, *m.* (surg.) scalpel, dissecting knife.

escalplo, *m.* currier's or tanner's knife.

escama, *f.* fish scale; small scaly piece in ancient armors; any scaly formation; resentment, grudge.

escamada, *f.* embroidery in the shape of scales.

escamado, *m.* work in the shape of scales.

escamadura, *f.* scaling (a fish); arousing suspicion.

escamar. I. *va.* to scale (fish); (coll.) to cause suspicion. **II.** *vn.* to embroider scale or shell fashion. **III.** *vr.* to have learned by painful experience.

escamel, *m.* sword-maker's anvil.

escamochear, *vn.* to breed bees.

escamocho, *m.* remnants of a meal; (of bees) after-swarm.

escamonda, *f.* (agr.) pruning.

escamondadura, *f.* pruned branches.

escamondar, *va.* to prune, lop; to trim.

escamondo, *m.* pruning or clearing of trees.

escamonea, *f.* (bot.) scammony.

escamoneado, da, *a.* pertaining to scammony.

escamonearse, *vr.* (coll.) to be suspicious.

escamoso, sa, *a.* scaly, squamous.

escamotar, *va.* in juggling, to palm; to rob by artful means, to "play for a sucker."

escamoteador, ra, *n.* juggler, prestidigitator, conjurer; sharp, swindler.

escamotear, *va.* = ESCAMOTAR.—**escamoteo,** *m.* juggling, sleight of hand; exploitation, getting money from others by artful means, swindling.

escampada, *f.* stampede.

escampado, da. I. *pp.* of ESCAMPAR. **II.** *a.* open, clear.

escampar. I. *vn.* to stop raining; (of the sky) to clear up; to leave off working. **II.** *va.* to clear out.

escampavía, *f.* (naut.) tender; revenue cutter.

escampo, *m.* clearing out; clearing up (of rain).

escamudo, da, *a.* full of scales.

escamujar, *va.* to prune.—**escamujo,** *m.* lopped-off olive branch; time of pruning olive trees.

escancia, *f.* pouring or serving wine.

escanciador, ra, *n.* cupbearer.

escanciar, *va.* to pour, serve, or drink (wine).

escanda, *f.* (bot.) spelt-wheat.

escandalar, *m.* (naut.) room for the compass.

escandalicé, escandalice, *v.* V. ESCANDALIZAR.

escandalizador, ra, *n.* & *a.* scandalizer(-ing).

escandalizar. I. *va.* (*pret.* ESCANDALICÉ; *subj.* ESCANDALICE) to scandalize, shock. **II.** *vr.* to be shocked, scandalized; to be irritated.

escandalizativo, va, *a.* scandalous.

escándalo, *m.* scandal; licentiousness; tumult, commotion; astonishment.

escandalosa, *f.* (naut.) gaff sail.

escandalosamente, *adv.* scandalously, shamefully.

escandaloso, sa, *a.* scandalous; turbulent.

escandallar, *va.* (naut.) to sound.

escandallo, *m.* (naut.) deep-sea lead; proof, trial, experiment.

escandia, *f.* (bot.) Cienfuegos wheat.

escandina, *f.* (min.) scandia, scandium oxide.

escandinavo, va, *n.* & *a.* Scandinavian.

escandio, *m.* (chem.) scandium, a rare metal.

escandir, *va.* (poet.) to scan.

escanilla, *f.* cradle.

escantillar, *va.* to gauge; to measure from a point or line; to measure off; to hew by patterns.—**escantillón,** *m.* pattern, templet; rule.

escaña, *f.* (bot.) St. Peter's corn.

escañero, *m.* seat keeper (in council room, etc.).

escaño, *m.* bench with a back; (naut.) sheer-rail.

escañuelo, *m.* footstool.

escapada, *f.* escape, flight, escapade.—**en una e.,** in a minute, a jiffy.

escapamiento, *m.* = ESCAPADA.

escapar. I. *va.* to drive (a horse) at great speed. **II.** *vn.* & *vr.* to escape, to flee; to run away; to make one's escape; (of a regrettable remark, etc.) to slip out.—**e. en una tabla,** to have a narrow escape.

escaparate, *m.* press, glass case, cupboard, cabinet, wardrobe; show window.—**escaparatico,** *m. dim.* little cupboard, cabinet or wardrobe.

escapatoria, *f.* escape, fleeing, flight; excuse, evasion, subterfuge; loophole, way out (of difficulty, etc.).

escape, *m.* escape, flight; subterfuge, evasion; escapement (of a watch); exhaust (of steam eng., etc.).—**a e.,** or **a todo e.,** at full speed, in great haste.—**de e.,** (of steam eng.) exhaust (as *a.*).

escapo, *m.* (arch.) shaft of a column.

escápula, *f.* (anat.) scapula, shoulder blade.

¹escapular, *a.* scapular.

²escapular, *va.* (naut.) to clear (a cape).

escapulario, *m.* (eccl.) scapulary, a sort of cape.

escaque, *m.* any of the squares of a chessboard; (her.) any of the squares of a coat of arms.—*pl.* chess.—**escaqueado, da,** *a.* checkered.

escara, *f.* (surg.) eschar, scab, slough.

escarabajear. I. *vn.* to crawl to and fro like insects; to scrawl, scribble. **II.** *va.* (coll.) to worry, harass.

escarabajo, *m.* (entom.) black beetle; short, ill-shaped person; flaw in a cast; scarab, scarabæus (of the Egyptians).—*pl.* scrawl.

escarabajuelo, *m. dim.* (entom.) vine beetle.

escarabídeo, a. I. *a.* & *n.* scarabæid. **II.** *m. pl.* Scarabæidæ.

escaramucear, *vn.* to skirmish.

escaramujo, *m.* (bot.) dog-rose, hep tree; hep; (zool.) goose barnacle.

escaramuza, *f.* (mil.) skirmish; dispute, quarrel.

escaramuzador, ra, *n.* skirmisher; disputer.

escaramuzar, *vn.* to skirmish.

escarapela, *f.* cockade, badge; quarrel ending in blows.

escarapelar. I. *vn.* & *vr.* (esp. of women) to dispute, wrangle, quarrel. **II.** *vr.* (Am.) to have the hair stand on end, get goose flesh.

escarbadero, *m.* scratching place (for animals).

escarbadientes, *m.* toothpick.

escarbador, ra, *n.* scratcher, scraper.

escarbadura, *f.* scratching.

escarbaorejas, *m.* earpick.

escarbar, *va.* to scrape or scratch (as fowls); to dig, dibble; to poke (the fire); to dig into, to investigate.—**escarbo,** *m.* scraping, scratching.

escarcela, *f.* large pouch; game bag; cuish; kind of headdress for women.

escarceo, *m.* small broken waves occasioned by currents.—*pl.* bounds and windings of spirited horses.

escarcina, *f.* a kind of cutlass.

escarcuñar, *va.* = ESCUDRIÑAR, to scrutinize.

escarcha, *f.* white frost, rime; frostwork.

escarchada, *f.* (bot.) ice plant, fig marigold.

escarchado, *m.* gold or silver embroidery; frosting on cakes.

escarchador, *m.* freezing tool.

escarchar. I. *vn.* to freeze, frost. **II.** *va.* to put frosting on; to dilute (potter's clay) with water.

escarcho, *m.* (ichth.) red surmullet.

escarda, *f.* weedhook, rubbing hoe; weeding.

escardadera, *f.* woman weeder; gardener's hoe.

escardador, ra, *n.* & *a.* weeder(-ing).

escardadura, *f.*, **escardamiento,** *m.* weeding.

escardar, escardillar, *va.* to weed; to weed out, root out.

escardillo, lla, *n.* small weedhook; gardener's hoe; thistledown.

escariador, *m.* reamer.

escariar, *va.* to ream.

escarificación, *f.* (surg.) scarification.

escarificador, *m.* (agr.) scarifier, harrow, cultivator; (surg.) scarificator.

escarificar, *va.* (surg. and agr.) to scarify.

escarioso, sa, *a.* (bot.) scarious.

escarizar, *va.* (surg.) to clean by taking away the scurf or scab.

escarlador, *m.* comb polisher.

escarlata, *f.* scarlet, red; cloth of a scarlet color; (med.) scarlet fever.

escarlatina, *f.* (com.) red or crimson woollen fabric; (med.) scarlatina.

escarmenador, *m.* comb for wool, etc.

escarmenar, *va.* to comb (wool, silk, etc.); to disentangle; to cheat.

escarmentado, da, *a.* taught by punishment or painful experience.

escarmentar. I. *vn.* (*ind.* ESCARMIENTO; *subj.* ESCARMIENTE) to be taught by experience, to take warning. II. *va.* to correct severely, to inflict an exemplary punishment on.

¹escarmiento, *m.* warning, lesson, punishment.

²escarmiento, escarmiente, *v. V.* ESCARMENTAR.

escarnecedor, ra, *n. & a.* scoffer(-ing), scorner (-ing).

escarnecer, *va.* (*ind.* ESCARNEZCO; *subj.* ESCARNEZCA) to scoff, mock, ridicule, jeer, gibe.

escarnecidamente, *adv.* scornfully.

escarnecimiento, *m.* scoffing, derision.

escarnezco, escarnezca, *v. V.* ESCARNECER.

escarnio, *m.* scoff, gibe, jeer, mock.

¹escaro, *m.* (ichth.) a kind of mutton fish.

²escaro, ra, *a.* having crooked feet.

escarola, *f.* (bot.) endive; ruff, frill.

escarolado, da, *a.* curled, frilled.

escarolar, *va.* to frill, ruffle.

escarótico, ca, *a.* (surg.) escharotic, caustic.

escarpa, *f.* declivity, slope, bluff, cliff; (mil.) scarp.

escarpado, da. I. *pp.* of ESCARPAR. II. *a.* steep, craggy, rugged.

escarpadura, *f.* escarpment; bluff, cliff.

¹escarpar, *va.* to rasp (works of sculpture).

²escarpar, *va.* (mil.) to escarp.—escarpe, *m.* escarpment; (arch.) scarf of a wall; scarf joint.

escarpelo, *m.* rasp; (surg.) scalpel.

escarpia, *f.* tenterhook, meat hook; spike.

escarpiador, *m.* clamp, fastener; ESCARPIDOR.

escarpidor, *m.* large-toothed comb.

escarpín, *m.* thin-soled shoe; dancing pumps; woollen slippers.

escarpión.—en e., in the form of a tenterhook.

escarza, *f.* (vet.) sore in the hoofs.

escarzano, *a.*—arco e., (arch.) segment arch.

escarzar, *va.* (bee culture) to remove honeycombs from (a hive).

¹escarzo, *n.* (bee culture) black comb without honey; operation and time of removing honey from a hive; floss silk.

²escarzo, za, *a.* (vet.) lame from hoof sores.

escasamente, *adv.* scantily, sparingly; hardly, scarcely.

escasear. I. *va.* to give sparingly; to spare, to husband. II. *vn.* to be scarce; to diminish.

escasez, *f.* scarcity, shortage; poverty, want.

escaso, sa, *a.* small, limited; little; sparing, parsimonious, niggardly; scarce, scanty, short.

escatimado, da. I. *pp.* of ESCATIMAR. II. *a.* little, scanty.

escatimar, *va.* to curtail, lessen; to misinterpret.

escatimosamente, *adv.* maliciously.

escatimoso, sa, *a.* cunning, malicious.

escatófago, ga, *a.* (nat. hist.) scatophagous.

¹escatología, *f.* scatology.

²escatología, *f.* eschatology, doctrine of ultimates.

¹escatológico, ca, *a.* scatologic.

²escatológico, ca, *a.* eschatologic.

escaupil, *m.* (Mex.) ancient padded armor.

escavanar, *va.* (agr.) to loosen and weed (the ground) with a grub hoe.

escayola, *f.* stucco, plasterwork.

escena, *f.* stage; scenery; scene; sight, view; incident, episode.

escenario, *m.* (theat.) stage, "boards."

escénico, ca, *a.* scenic, pertaining to the stage.

escenografía, *f.* scenography.

escenográficamente, *adv.* scenographically.

escenográfico, ca, *a.* scenographic.

escenógrafo, *m.* scenographer.

escépticamente, *adv.* skeptically.

escepticismo, *m.* skepticism.

escéptico, ca, *n. & a.* skeptic.

esciagrafía, *f.* skiagraphy.

esciágrafo, *m.* skiagraph.

escinco, *m.* (zool.) skink, a lizard.

escila, *f.* (bot.) squill.

escirro, *m.* (med.) scirrhus, a tumor.

escirroso, sa, *a.* (med.) scirrhous.

escisión, *f.* division; schism.

escita, *n. & a.*; escítico, ca, *a.* Scythian.

esclarecedor, ra, *n. & a.* enlightener(-ing).

esclarecer. I. *va.* (*ind.* ESCLAREZCO; *subj.* ESCLAREZCA) to lighten, illuminate; to enlighten, elucidate; to ennoble. II. *vn.* to dawn.

esclarecidamente, *adv.* illustriously.

esclarecido, da, *a.* illustrious, prominent.

esclarecimiento, *m.* enlightening; elucidation; dawn; ennoblement; merit, worth.

esclarezco, esclarezca, *v. V.* ESCLARECER.

esclavicé, esclavice, *v. V.* ESCLAVIZAR.

esclavina, *f.* pilgrim's cloak; collar worn by priests; tippet; cape.

esclavista, *a.* pro-slavery.

esclavitud, *f.* slavery.

esclavizar, *va.* (*pret.* ESCLAVICÉ; *subj.* ESCLAVICE) to enslave.

esclavo, va, *n.* slave.—e. ladino, formerly, one who had been a slave for more than a year.

esclavón, ona; esclavonio, nia, *n. & a.* Slavonian, Slavonic.

escleroftalmia, *f.* (med.) sclerophthalmia.

escleroma, *m.* (med.) scleroma.

esclerosis, *f.* (med.) sclerosis.

esclerótica, *f.* (anat.) sclera.

esclusa, *f.* lock; sluice; floodgate; milldam.

escoa, *f.* (naut.) bend of a ship's rib.

escoba, *f.* broom; (bot.) Spanish broom.

escobada, *f.* sweep, sweeping.

escobadera, *f.* woman sweeper.

¹escobajo, *m.* old broom.

²escobajo, *m.* stalk of a bunch of grapes.

¹escobar, *va.* to sweep with a broom.

²escobar, *m.* (bot.) broom field.

escobazar, *va.* to sprinkle with a broom.

escobazo, *m.* blow with a broom.—echar a escobazos, to dismiss harshly or roughly, (fig.) to kick out.

escobén, *m.* (naut.) hawse hole.

escobera, *f.* (bot.) Spanish broom.

escobero, ra, *n.* broom maker or seller.

escobeta, *f.* small brush.

escobilla, *f.* brush; whisk, small broom; (bot.) bur of the teasel; gold or silver sweepings; (elec.) brush (of a dynamo).

escobillón, *m.* (mil.) merkin; swab.

escobina, *f.* chips cut in boring; filings.

escobo, *m.* brushwood, briers, brambles.

escobón, *m. aug.* large broom; (naut.) Turk's head, a kind of knot; scrubbing brush; swab.

escocedura, *f.* burning pain.

escocer. I. *vn.* (*ind.* ESCUECE; *subj.* ESCUEZA) to

feel a sharp, burning pain; to smart. **II.** *vr.* to smart; to chafe.

scocés, sa, *n. & a.* Scotch.

escocia, *f.* (arch.) scotia.

escocia, *f.* (com.) codfish.

scocimiento, *m.* smart, sharp pain.

scoda, *f.* stonecutter's hammer.

scodar, *va.* to hew or cut (stones).

scofia, *f.* coif, a kind of cap.

scofiar, *va.* to dress with a coif.

scofieta, *f.* = ESCOFIA.

scofina, *f.* rasp, file; wood rasp.

scofinar, *va.* to rasp.

scogedor, ra, *n. & a.* chooser(-ing).

scoger, *va.* (*ind.* ESCOJO; *subj.* ESCOJA) to choose, select, pick out, sort; elect.

scogidamente, *adv.* choicely, selectly; nicely.

scogido, da, *pp. & a.* chosen, choice, select.

scogimiento, *m.* selection, choice, choosing; sorting, separation.

scojo, escoja, *v.* V. ESCOGER.

scolar. I. *n.* pupil, student. **II.** *a.* scholastic. school (as *a.*).

scolásticamente, *adv.* scholastically.

scolasticismo, *m.* scholasticism.

scolástico, ca. I. *a.* scholastic, scholastical; school (as *a.*). **II.** *n.* Scholastic, Schoolman.

scoliador, ra, *n.* scholiast, writer of comments.

scoliar, *va.* to gloss, explain, comment.

scoliasta, *n.* = ESCOLIADOR.

scolimado, da, *a.* (coll.) weak, delicate.

scolimoso, sa, *a.* (coll.) fastidious, hard to please, fussy.

scolio, *m.* scholium; gloss, commentary.

scoliosis, *f.* (med.) scoliosis, a spinal curvature.

scolopendra, *f.* (entom.) scolopendra, centipede; a marine worm; (bot.) spleenwort.

scolta, *f.* escort, convoy, guard.

scoltar, *va.* to escort, convoy, guard.

scollera, *f.* breakwater, jetty; cliff.

scollo, *m.* reef; difficulty, danger.

scombra, *f.* clearing, removal of obstacles.

scombrar, *va.* to clear of rubbish; to clean.

scombrera, *f.* (min.) refuse dump.

scombro, *m.* rubbish, a small inferior raisin.

escombro, *m.* (ichth.) mackerel.

scomerse, *vr.* to wear out.

sconce, *m.* corner, angle.

scondedero, *m.* hiding or lurking place.

sconder. I. *va.* to hide, conceal; to include, contain. **II.** *vr.* to hide; to skulk.

scondidamente, *adv.* secretly, hiddenly.

scondidas, escondidillas.—a e., on the sly, hiddenly.

scondimiento, *m.* concealment.

scondite, *m.*, **escondrijo,** *m.* lurking place; hiding place.—**jugar al e.,** to play hide and seek.

sconzado, da, *a.* angular, oblique.

scopeta, *f.* shotgun, fowling piece.—**e. de dos cañones,** double-barrel gun.—**e. de viento,** air gun.

scopetar, *va.* to dig out (gold mines).

scopetazo, *m.* gunshot; gunshot wound.

scopetear, *va.* to shoot at with a shotgun; to compliment, pay compliments to.

scopeteo, *m.* gunshot fire.

scopetería, *f.* infantry armed with guns; repeated gunshots.

scopetero, *m.* gunner, musketeer; gunsmith.

scopetilla, *f. dim.* small gun.

scopetón, *m. aug.* large fowling piece.

scopladura, escopleadura, *f.* mortise hole, chisel cut.

scoplear, *va.* to chisel, mortise, notch.

scoplillo, ito, *m. dim.* small chisel.

scoplo, *m.* chisel.

scora, *f.* (naut.) stanchion, bilge head, prop, outrigger; (naut.) central line of a vessel; (naut.) tilt.—**e. lateral,** (aer.) rolling.

escorar. I. *va.* (naut.) to prop, to shore up. **II.** *vn.* (naut.) to list, to heel.

escorbútico, ca, *a.* scorbutic, scorbutical.

escorbuto, *m.* (med.) scurvy.

escorchapín, *m.* passage boat, ferry.

escorchar, *va.* to flay, to skin.

escordio, *m.* (bot.) water germander.

escoria, *f.* dross, slag, scoria; lee; mean or worthless thing.—*pl.* scoriæ, volcanic ashes.

escoriáceo, cea, *a.* scoriaceous.

escoriación, *f.* = EXCORIACIÓN, flaying.

escorial, *m.* dumping place for dross; slag heap.

escoriar, *va.* = EXCORIAR, to flay.

escorificación, *f.* (chem.) scorification.

escorificar, *va.* (chem.) to scorify, reduce to scoria or slag.

escorpena, escorpina, *f.* (ichth.) grouper.

escorpioide, *f.* (bot.) scorpion grass.

escorpión, *m.* (entom.) scorpion; (ichth.) fish resembling a grouper; ancient ballister; **(E-,** astr.) Scorpion; cat-o'-nine-tails with metal points.

escorpiónídeos, *m. pl.* (zool.) Scorpionida, the scorpion family.

escorrozo, *m.* (coll.) pleasure, enjoyment.

escorzado, *m.* (art) foreshortening.

escorzar, *va.* (art) to foreshorten.

escorzo, *m.* (art) foreshortening.

escorzón, *m.* toad.

escorzonera, *f.* (bot.) viper root or garden viper grass.

¹escota, *f.* stonecutter's hammer.

²escota, *f.* (naut.) sheet.

escotado, *m.* = ESCOTADURA.

escotadura, *f.* low cut in the neck (of a dress); armhole in armor; large trapdoor of a stage.

¹escotar, *va.* to cut (a dress) low in the neck; to draw (water) by a trench.

²escotar, *va.* to club together, contribute to a common cause.

¹escote, *m.* low neck, décolleté; tucker.

²escote, *m.* share, quota.

escotera, *f.* (naut.) sheet hole.

escotero, ra, *a.* free, disengaged, unburdened.

escotilla, *f.* (naut.) hatchway.

escotillón, *m.* scuttle, trapdoor; stage trap.

escotín, *m.* (naut.) topsail sheet.

escotismo, *m.* Scotism (doctrines of Scotus).

escotista, *n.* Scotist.

escoznete, *m.* (prov.) nutpick.

escozor, *m.* smart, sharp pain, burning, smarting; grief, affliction.

escriba, *m.* scribe, among the Hebrews.

escribanía, *f.* office or employment of an actuary or scrivener; escritoire, scrutoire; portable writing case; ornamental inkstand.

escribano, *m.* actuary.—**e. de cámara,** clerk of a high court of justice.—**e. del agua,** (entom.) water skater.—**e. de número,** or **del número,** one of a certain number of notaries public.

escribido, *pp. reg.* of ESCRIBIR, used only in the idiom **leído y escribido,** (coll.) would-be learned, posing as learned.

escribidor, ra, *n.* would-be writer, scribbler.

escribiente, *m. & f.* amanuensis, clerk.

escribir. I. *va.* (*pp. irreg.* ESCRITO) to write.—**e. a máquina,** to type. **II.** *vr.* to enroll oneself; to carry on correspondence with each other.

escriño, *m.* straw hamper; jewel box, casket.

escrita, *f.* (ichth.) spotted skate fish.

escritillas, *f. pl.* lamb's fries.

escrito, ta. I. *pp. irreg.* of ESCRIBIR. **II.** *m.* writing; manuscript; literary composition; (law) writ; brief.—**por e.,** in writing.

escritor, ra, *n.* writer, author.—**escritorcillo, lla,** *n. dim.* petty writer, writer of no account.

escritorillo, *m. dim.* small writing desk.

escritorio, *m.* writing desk; countinghouse; office, study.

escritorzuelo, la, *n. dim.* writer of no account.

escritura, *f.* writing, handwriting, penmanship; deed, indenture, instrument; **(E-)** Scripture.—**e. de seguro,** insurance policy.

escriturar. I. *va.* (law) to bind by deed; to indenture; to engage (as an artist). **II.** *vr.* to sign articles.

escriturario, ria. I. *a.* (law) scriptory, scriptorian; scriptural. **II.** *n.* scripturist.

escrófula, *f.* (med.) scrofula.

escrofularia, *f.* (bot.) figwort.

escrofulariáceo, cea, *a.* (bot.) scrophulariaceous.

escrofulismo, *m.* (med.) scrofulism.

escrofuloso, sa, *a.* scrofulous.

escroto, *m.* scrotum.

escrupulillo, *m. dim.* slight scruple; jingle.

escrupulizar, *vn.* to scruple, doubt, hesitate.

escrúpulo, *m.* scruple, hesitation; scrupulosity, conscientiousness; (pharm.) scruple, a small weight (20 gr.).

escrupulosamente, *adv.* scrupulously; precisely, minutely, thoroughly.

escrupulosidad, *f.* scrupulosity, conscientiousness; exactness, nicety, thoroughness.

escrupuloso, sa, *a.* scrupulous, conscientious; nice, exact, thorough; hypercritical, squeamish.

escrutador, ra, *n.* examiner, inquirer, searcher; inspector of an election.

escrutar, *va.* to count (votes); to scrutinize.

escrutinio, *m.* scrutiny, investigation; election returns.

escrutiñador, *m.* scrutator, investigator.

escuadra, *f.* carpenter's square; drawing triangle; angle iron; knee, angle brace; (mil.) squad; (naut.) squadron, fleet.—**e. de agrimensor,** (surv.) cross-staff.—**e. sutil,** light coastguard fleet.—**a e.,** square, at right angles.—**falsa e.,** bevel square.—**fuera de e.,** out of square, at an oblique angle.

escuadración, *f.* squaring.

escuadrador, *m.* squaring tool; groover.

escuadrar, *va.* (carp.) to square.

escuadreo, *m.* squaring, quadrature.

escuadría, *f.* scantling of timber; square.

escuadro, *m.* = ESCRITA, (ichth.) spotted skate.

escuadrón, *m.* (mil.) squadron, troop of horse.—**e. volante,** (mil.) flying column.

escuadronar, *va.* to form in squadrons.

escuadroncete, cillo, *m. dim.* small troop.

escuadronista, *m.* (mil.) tactician.

escualidez, *f.* squalor, wretchedness.

escuálido, da, *a.* weak, languid; squalid, filthy.

escualo, *m.* (ichth.) spotted dogfish; shark.

escualor, *m.* squalor, filthiness.

escucha, *f.* (mil.) scout; vedette; sentinel, sentry; in convents, a chaperon; listening hole.

escuchador, ra; escuchante, *n.* listener.

escuchar. I. *va.* to listen to; to mind, heed. **II.** *vn.* to listen. **III.** *vr.* to speak with affected pauses.

escudar, *va.* to shield, protect, defend.

escuderaje, *m.* service of a page or footman.

escuderear, *va.* to serve as a page or squire to.

escudería, *f.* service of a page or squire.

escuderil, *a.* pertaining to a page or squire.

escuderilmente, *adv.* in the style of a page.

escudero, *m.* shield bearer, squire, page; gentleman of illustrious ancestry; shield maker.

escuderón, *m.* conceited squire.

escudete, *m.* escutcheon; gusset; rain stain on olives; (bot.) white water lily.

escudilla, *f.* bowl, large cup.

escudillar, *va.* to pour into bowls; to lord it over, domineer.

escudillita, *f. dim.* small bowl.

escudillo, ito, *m. dim.* small shield; a gold coin.

escudo, *m.* shield, buckler, escutcheon, coat of arms; escutcheon of a lock or knocker; shield, protection; coin of different values; bandage used in bleeding; sideplate of a gun; (naut.)

backboard of a boat.—**e. de armas,** arms (o a flag, etc.).—**e. de popa,** (naut.) stern es cutcheon.

escudriñable, *a.* investigable.

escudriñador, ra, *n. & a.* prier(-ying); scru tinizer(-ing), searcher(-ing); investigator(-ing)

escudriñamiento, *m.* investigation, scrutiny.

escudriñar, *va.* to scrutinize, search, pry into.

escuece, *v. V.* ESCOCER.

escuela, *f.* school; schoolhouse; (art) school style; experience.—**e. normal,** normal school —**e. primaria,** primary and grammar school.—**e. secundaria,** high school.—**e superior,** institution of higher learning, or o professional studies (university, college, etc.)

escuerzo, *m.* (zool.) toad; (coll.) flabby person

escueto, ta, *n.* disengaged, free from encum brances; solitary, uninhabited.

escueznar, *va.* to extract the kernel of.

escuezno, *m.* soft kernel of a nut.

esculcar, *va.* to spy, to watch; to search; (Am. to search the pockets of.

esculpidor, ra, *n.* engraver.

esculpir, *va. & vn.* to sculpture; to engrave.

escultor, *m.* sculptor.—**escultora,** *f.* sculptress

escultórico, ca, *a.* sculptural.

escultura, *f.* sculpture; carved work.

escultural, *a.* sculptural.

escullador, *m.* dipper for oil.

escupidera, *f.* spittoon, cuspidor.

escupidero, *m.* spitting place; disgraceful situa tion.

escupido, da. I. *pp.* of ESCUPIR. **II.** *m.* spittle.

escupidor, ra, *n.* great spitter.

escupidura, *f.* spitting, spittle; fever sore.

escupir, *va. & vn.* to spit; to break out on th skin; to fling, cast away; to work out, throw off

escupitajo, m., escupitina, f., escupitinajo *m.* (coll.) spit.

escurar, *va.* to scout (cloth) before milling.

escurialense, *a.* belonging to, or like, the Esco rial (a famous Spanish monastery).

escurreplatos, *m.* dish-draining rack.

escurribanda, *f.* (coll.) evasion, subterfuge diarrhœa; scuffle, bustle.

escurrida, *a.* wearing tight-fitting skirts; having narrow hips.

escurridero, *m.* drain pipe or conduit (in mines) draining or wringing place.

escurridizo, za, *a.* slippery; difficult to hold.

escurrido, da, *m.* colander; ESCURREPLATOS.

escurriduras, escurrimbres, *f. pl.* rinsings (as of wine); lees, dregs.

escurrimiento, *m.* dripping, running off; sneak ing out.

escurrir. I. *va.* to drain off (liquid) from; to wring (as clothes).—**e. el bulto,** to sneak away. **II.** *vr.* to drop, drip, ooze, leak, trickle; to slip, slide, glide; to escape, slip out, sneak away.

escuyer, *m.* purveyor of meat to the palace.

esdrújulo, la, *a.* (gram.) (word) accented on the antepenultimate syllable.

¹**ese,** *f.* name of the letter *s*; link of a chain having the shape of an *s*.—*pl.* **eses,** reeling of a drunken man (gen. in the phrase **hacer eses,** to reel).

²**ese, m., esa, f.** (*pl.* **esos, esas),** *a.* that (*pl.* those), as *ese hombre,* that man: *esas mujeres,* those women.

ése, m., ésa, f. (*pl.* **ésos, ésas),** *dem. pron.* that (one) (*pl.*, those), as *tengo ése,* I have that one; *dame ésas,* give me those. *V.* ESA.

esecilla, *f. dim.* small link of a chain.

esencia, *f.* essence, being; (chem.) essence, perfume.—**esencial,** *a.* essential.

esencialmente, *adv.* essentially, principally.

eseniano, na; esenio, nia, *n. & a.* Essene(-ian).

esfenoidal, *a.* (anat.) sphenoidal.

esfenoides, *m.* (anat.) sphenoid bone.

esfera, *f.* sphere; clock dial; quality, condition, rank; (poet.) heaven.—**e. armilar,** armillary sphere.—**e. celeste,** celestial sphere.—**e. de actividad,** sphere of action.—**e. paralela,** (astr.) parallel sphere.—**e. recta,** (astr.) right sphere.

esferal, *a.* = ESFÉRICO.

esféricamente, *adv.* spherically.

esfericidad, *f.* sphericity.

esférico, ca, *a.* spherical.

esferoidal, *a.* spheroidal.

esferoide, *f.* spheroid.

esferómetro, *m.* spherometer.

esfigmógrafo, *m.* sphygmograph.

esfigmómetro, *m.* sphygmometer.

esfinge, *f.* sphinx.—**esfíngido, da,** *a.* sphinxlike.

esfínter, *m.* (anat.) sphincter.

esforcé, *pret.* of ESFORZAR.

esforrocinar, *va.* to remove the ESFORROCINOS from.

esforrocino, *m.* sprig shooting from the trunk of a vine.

esforzadamente, *adv.* vigorously; bravely.

esforzado, da. I. *pp.* of ESFORZAR. **II.** *a.* strong, vigorous; brave; enterprising.

esforzador, ra, *n.* & *a.* encourager(-ing).

esforzar. I. *va.* (*ind. pres.* ESFUERZO, *pret.* ESFORCÉ; *subj.* ESFUERCE) to strengthen, invigorate; to encourage. **II.** *vr.* to exert oneself, make efforts, try hard.

¹**esfuerzo,** *m.* courage, spirit, vigor; effort, strong endeavor; (eng.) stress.—**e. cortante,** (eng.) shear, shearing stress.

²**esfuerzo,** *v.* *V.* ESFORZAR.

esfumado, da. I. *pp.* of ESFUMAR. **II.** *a.* (art) sfumato.

esfumar, *va.* (art) to stump.

esfumino, *m.* (art) stump (for shading).

esgarrar, *va.* & *vn.* to raise phlegm; to clear one's throat.

esgrafiado, *m.* (art) graffito.

esgrafiar, *va.* to decorate with graffito; to scratch on with a graffito tool or graver.

esgrima, *f.* fencing (the art).

esgrimidor, *m.* fencer or fencing master.

esgrimidura, *f.* fencing (the act).

esgrimir, *va.* to wield (a weapon).

esgrimista, *n.* (Am.) fencer; (Chile) sponger.

esguazable, *a.* fordable.

esguazar, *va.* to ford (as a river).—**esguazo,** *m.* fording.

esgucio, *m.* (arch.) quarter-round molding.

esguín, *m.* young salmon before entering sea.

esguince, *m.* dodging, dodge; frown; twist or sprain of a joint.

esguízaro, ra, *n.* & *a.* Swiss.—**pobre e.,** ragamuffin.

eslabón, *m.* link of a chain; steel for striking fire with a flint; table steel; name of a very poisonous scorpion.

eslabonador, *m.* chain maker.

eslabonamiento, *m.* linking, uniting; connection, sequence, concatenation.

eslabonar, *va.* to link, interlink; to join, unite, to connect, concatenate.

eslavo, va, *n.* & *a.* Slav.

eslinga, *f.* (naut.) sling, span.

eslingar, *va.* (naut.) to sling up, hoist.

eslora, *f.* (naut.) length of a ship.—*pl.* binding strakes of the deck.

eslovaco, ca, *n.* & *a.* Slovakian.

esloveno, na, *n.* & *a.* Slovene.

esmaltador, ra, *n.* enameller.

esmaltadura, *f.* enamelling; enamel work.

esmaltar, *va.* to enamel; to adorn, embellish.

esmalte, *m.* enamel; enamel work; smalt.

esmaltín, *m.* smalt, a dark blue pigment.

esmaltina, *f.* (min.) smaltite.

esmeradamente, *adv.* carefully, conscientiously, thoroughly.

esmerado, da. I. *pp.* of ESMERAR. **II.** *a.* careful, painstaking, carefully done.

esmeralda, *f.* emerald.

esmeraldina, *f.* (min.) emeraldine.

esmeraldino, na, *a.* emeraldlike (gen. in color).

esmerar. I. *va.* to polish, to brighten. **II.** *vr.* (con or en) to do one's best, to take pains (with).

esmerejón, *m.* (ornith.) merlin; small-caliber gun.

¹**esmeril,** *m.* small-caliber gun.

²**esmeril,** *m.* emery.

esmerilador, ra, *n.* & *a.* grinder(-ing). *f.* grinding machine.

esmerilar, *va.* to burnish, to polish with emery, to grind.

esmero, *m.* careful attention, painstaking.

esmoladera, *f.* whetstone.

esmuciarse, *vr.* to slip from the hands.

esnón, (naut.) spencer mast, trysail mast.

eso, *dem. pron. neut.* that (that thing, fact, etc.).—**e. de,** that matter of; AQUELLO DE.—**e. es,** that's it; that's right.—**e. mismo,** the very thing.—**a e. de,** toward, about.—**no es e.,** it isn't that.—**por e.,** for that; for that reason, on that account.—**por e. es por lo que** (or, incorrectly but commonly, **por e. es que**), that is the reason that, that is why.

esofágico, ca, *a.* esophageal.

esófago, *m.* (anat.) esophagus, gullet.

esotérico, ca, *a.* esoteric; confidential, secret.

esotro, *m.,* **esotra,** *f.,* *dem. pron.* this or that other.—*pl.* **esotros,** *m.,* **esotras,** *f.,* those others.

espabiladeras, *f. pl.* (candle) snuffers.

espabilar, *va.* to snuff (a candle).

espaciar. I. *va.* to space; diffuse, expand, dilate, spread; (print.) to lead; to space. **II.** *vr.* to walk to and fro; to amuse oneself; to cheer up; to expatiate.

espacio, *m.* space; room, capacity; slowness, delay; blank, (empty) space; (mus.) interval.

espaciosamente, *adv.* deliberately; spaciously.

espaciosidad, *f.* spaciousness, capacity.

espacioso, sa, *a.* spacious, roomy, ample; slow, deliberate.

espada, *f.* sword; blade, rapier; swordsman; (cards) spade; (ichth.) swordfish; matador, bullfighter who kills the bull.—**entre la e. y la pared,** between the devil and the deep sea.

espadachín, *m.* dexterous swordsman; bully, hackster.

espadadero, *m.* braking floor.

espadador, *m.* hemp beater.

espadaña, *f.* (bot.) reed mace; belfry.

espadañada, *f.* regurgitation; spewing.

espadañal, *m.* place where reed mace grows.

espadañar, *va.* to spread out (the tail feathers).

espadar, *va.* to brake, scutch, swingle.

espadarte, *m.* (ichth.) swordfish.

espadería, *f.* sword cutler's shop.

espadero, *m.* sword cutler, bladesmith.

espádice, *m.* (bot.) spadix.

espadilla, *f.* red insignia of the order of Santiago; swingle, hemp brake; (naut.) scull, oar used as helm; (cards) ace of spades; hair bodkin; (Am.) (bot.) corn flag.

espadillar, *va.* to brake, scutch, swingle.

espadillazo, *m.* bad luck at cards.

espadín, *m.* small gala sword; rapier.

espadita, *f. dim.* small sword.

¹**espadón,** *m. aug.* spadone, large sword, broadsword.

²**espadón,** *m.* eunuch.

espadrapo, *m.* = ESPARADRAPO, court-plaster.

espagírica, *f.* metallurgy.

espagírico, ca, *a.* metallurgic.

espahí, *m.* (mil.) spahi.

espalda, *f.* (anat.) back, shoulders; (fort.) shoulder of a bastion.—*pl.* back or back part; (mil.) rearguard.—**a. espaldas,** or **a espaldas vueltas,** treacherously.—**de espaldas,** backwards, on one's (its) back; from behind.—**hablar por**

las espaldas de uno, to talk behind one's back.—por la e., from behind; in the back; behind one's back.

espaldar, m. backplate of a cuirass; back of a seat; espalier in gardens.—pl. tapestry hangings against which chairs lean.

espaldarazo, m. accolade; light blow on the back.

espaldarcete, m. palette in ancient armor.

espaldarón, m. backplate in armor.

espaldear, va. (naut.) to dash against the poop of.

espalder, m. stern rower in a galley.

espaldera, f. espalier, trelliswork.

espaldilla, f. scapula, shoulder blade; back of a waistcoat or jacket.

espalditendido, da, a. (coll.) stretched on one's back.

espaldón, m. (carp.) tenon; (fort.) intrenchment, barrier; (naut.) a hawse piece.

espaldudo, da, a. broad-shouldered.

espalera, f. espalier, trelliswork.

espalmadura, f. (vet.) parings of hoofs.

espalmar, va. = DESPALMAR, (vet.) to pare hoofs.

espalto, m. dark-colored paint; spalt.

espantable, a. frightful, horrid, terrible.

espantablemente, adv. horribly, frightfully.

espantada, f. stampede, running away; giving up from fear, (coll.) cold feet.

espantadizo, za, a. timid, skittish, shy.

espantador, ra, n. bugbear, frightener.

espantajo, m. scarecrow; fright.

espantalobos, m. (bot.) bladder or bastard senna.

espantamoscas, m. fly net; flyflap.

espantanublados, m. rake, vagabond.

espantapájaros, m. scarecrow.

espantar. I. va. to scare, frighten, daunt; to chase or drive away. II. vr. to be astonished, to marvel.

espantavillanos, m. gaudy stuff or trinket.

espanto, m. fright, dread; horror; threat; wonder; hideousness; (Am.) apparition, spook.

espantosamente, adv. dreadfully.

espantoso, sa, a. frightful, dreadful; fearful; wonderful.

español, la. I. n. & a. Spanish. II. n. Spaniard (f. Spanish woman).

españolado, da, a. Spanishlike.

españolar, va. (coll.) = ESPAÑOLIZAR.

españoleta, f. ancient Spanish dance.

españolismo, m. love for, devotion to Spanish things; Hispanicism, a Spanish idiom.

españolizar. I. va. to make Spanishlike. II. vr. to adopt the customs and manners of Spain.

esparadrapo, m. court-plaster.

esparaván, m. (vet.) spavin; (ornith.) sparrow hawk.—e. de garbanzuelo = E. SECO.—e. huesoso, (vet.) bone spavin.—e. seco, (vet.) muscle spavin.

esparavel, m. casting net; (mason.) hod.

esparciata, a. Spartan.

esparcidamente, adv. separately, scatteredly.

esparcido, da. I. pp. of ESPARCIR. II. a. scattered; merry, festive, gay.

esparcidor, ra, n. & a. scatterer(-ing), spreader (-ing).

esparcimiento, m. scattering, dissemination; amusement, recreation, diversion, relaxation; frankness, openness.

esparcir. I. va. (ind. ESPARZO; subj. ESPARZA) to scatter, spread; disseminate; divulge. II. vr. to amuse oneself; to make merry.

esparragado, m. dish of asparagus.

esparragador, ra, n. asparagus grower.

esparragamiento, m. cultivation of asparagus.

esparragar, vn. to grow asparagus.

espárrago, m. (bot.) asparagus; pole of an awning; (min.) peg ladder.

esparragón, m. corded silk stuff.

esparraguera, f. asparagus plant; asparagus bed.

esparraguero, ra, n. asparagus seller.

esparraguina, f. (min.) asparagin.

esparrancado, da. I. pp. of ESPARRANCARSE. II. a. spread apart (esp. the legs).

esparrancarse, vr. (coll.) to spread the legs apart.

espartal, m. matweed field.

espartano, na, n. & a. Spartan.

esparteína, f. (chem.) sparteine.

esparteña, f. rope-sole sandal.

espartería, f. mat-work factory or shop.

espartero, ra, n. maker and seller of mat-work.

espartilla, f. mop of esparto grass.

espartizal, m. esparto field.

esparto, m. (bot.) esparto grass, matweed.

esparzo, esparza, v. V. ESPARCIR.

espasmo, m. (med.) spasm.

espasmódico, ca, a. spasmodic, convulsive.

espata, f. (bot.) spathe.

espatarrada, f. spreading (of legs).

espatarrarse, vr. to straddle.

espático, ca, a. (min.) spathic.

espato, m. (min.) spar.—e. calizo, calcite, calcspar.—e. de Islandia, Iceland spar.—e. flúor, fluorspar.—e. pesado, barite, heavy spar.

espátula, f. spatula; (art) palette knife.

espaviento, m. = ASPAVIENTO, fear; fuss.

espavorido, da, a. = DESPAVORIDO, terrified.

especería, f. = ESPECIERÍA.

especia, f. spice.—pl. medicinal drugs.

especial, a. special, particular.—en e., specially, in particular.—especialidad, f. specialty; course, subject (of study).—especialista, n. specialist.

especialización, f. specialization; specializing.

especializar. I. va. to specialize; to limit, confine. II. vr. (en) to specialize (in).

especialmente, adv. especially.

especiar, va. to spice, season.

especie, f. species; kind, sort; event, incident; case, affair, business; piece of news; statement; pretext, show.—en e., in kind.

especiería, f. grocery shop.

especiero, m. grocer.

especificación, f. specification.

especificadamente, adv. in a specified manner.

especificar, va. (pret. ESPECIFIQUÉ; subj. ESPECIFIQUE) to specify, particularize, itemize.

especificativo, va, a. specific, specifying.

específico, ca. I. a. specific. II. m. (med.) specific.

especifiqué, especifique, v. V. ESPECIFICAR.

espécimen, m. specimen, sample.

especiosamente, adv. speciously.

especioso, sa, a. neat; beautiful; apparent, specious, deceiving.

especiota, f. (coll.) hoax, false news.

espectable, a. notable, eminent; conspicuous.

espectacular, a. spectacular.

espectáculo, m. spectacle, show, pageant.

espectador, ra, n. spectator.—pl. audience.

espectral, a. (phys.) spectral, spectrum (as a.).

espectro, m. spectre, specter, phantom, hobgoblin; (opt.) spectrum.

espectroscopia, f. (opt.) spectroscopy.

espectroscópico, ca, a. spectroscopic.

espectroscopio, m. (opt.) spectroscope.

especulación, f. speculation, contemplation; (com.) speculation, venture.

especulador, ra, n. & a. speculator(-ing).

especular. I. va. to behold, view, inspect; to speculate, meditate about. II. vn. to speculate; (com.) to speculate, dabble in stocks, etc.

especulativa, f. understanding.

especulativamente, adv. speculatively.

especulativo, va, a. speculative; thoughtful.

espéculo, m. speculum.

espejado, da, a. mirrorlike.

espejear, vn. to shine.

espejeo, m. = ESPEJISMO.

espejería, f. mirror factory or shop.

espejero, ra, n. mirror maker or seller.

espejico, illo, ito, *m. dim.* small mirror.

espejismo, *m.* mirage; illusion.

espejo, *m.* looking-glass, mirror; (naut.) stern; frame.—**e. de cuerpo entero,** full-length glass, pier glass.—**e. ustorio,** burning glass.

espejuela, *f.* curve of the bit.—**e. abierta,** snaffle.

espejuelo, *m. dim.* small looking-glass; specular stone, selenite; leaf of mica; device for catching larks; candied citron; (vet.) wart on pastern.—*pl.* eyeglass lenses; spectacles, eyeglasses.

espelta, *f.* (bot.) spelt, a cereal.

espélteo, a, *a.* pertaining to spelt.

espelunca, *f.* dark, gloomy cave.

espeluzar, *va.* = DESPELUZAR, to be horrified.

espeluznante, *a.* (coll.) setting the hair on end, dreadful, horrifying.

espeluznar, *va. & vr.* to dishevel the hair; to set the hair on end (from fright).

espeque, *m.* handspike; pump brake; strut, prop; lever.

espera, *f.* waiting; stay, pause; (mus.) stop, interval; restraint, prudence; (law) respite, adjournment; ancient piece of ordnance; (carp.) notch.—**en e.,** waiting.—**en e. de,** waiting for, awaiting; expecting.—**sala de e.,** waiting-room.

esperador, ra, *a.* expectant.

esperantista, *n.* Esperantist.

esperanto, *m.* Esperanto.

esperanza, *f.* hope; (often *pl.*) prospects.—**dar e.,** or **esperanzas,** to give encouragement; to promise, to bid fair.—**no hay e.,** there is no hope, or no chance, the case is hopeless.

esperanzar, *va.* to give hope to.

esperar. I. *va.* to hope; to expect; to wait for, await, look for; to fear. **II.** *vn.* to wait; to hope.—**quien espera desespera,** long hoping ends in despair, or in hopelessness. **III.** *vr.* to wait, stay.

esperezarse, *vr.* to stretch oneself.

esperezo, *m.* stretching one's arms and legs.

esperma, *f.* sperm.—**e. de ballena,** spermaceti.

espermaceti, *m.* (com.) spermaceti.

espermático, ca, *a.* spermatic, seminal.

espermatorrea, *f.* (med.) spermatorrhœa.

espermatozoario, espermatozoide, espermatozoo, *m.* spermatozoön.

espernada, *f.* split end link of a chain.

espernancarse, *vr.* = ESPARRANCARSE.

esperón, *m.* (naut.) = ESPOLÓN, fender beam.

esperpento, *m.* horrible or hideous thing or person; absurdity, nonsense.

espesar. I. *va.* to thicken, inspissate, coagulate, curdle; to mass, assemble; to make closer (as knitting). **II.** *vr.* to condense; to thicken, become thicker.—**espesativa, va,** *a.* thickening.

espeso, sa, *a.* thick, dense; curdy; frequent, often repeated; slovenly, dirty; dull, heavy.

espesor, *m.* thickness.

espesura, *f.* thickness, density, closeness; thicket, close wood; abundant head of hair; slovenliness.

espetaperro, espetaperros.—a e., at breakneck speed, precipitately.

espetar. I. *va.* to spit, to skewer; to pierce, run through; (coll.) to spring (something) on (one). **II.** *vr.* to be stiff with pride; (coll.) to thrust oneself into place.—**e. en,** to fit in, go into.

espetera, *f.* kitchen rack, scullery; kitchenware.

espetón, *m.* spit, poker, rake, iron prong, large pin; (zool.) sea-pike.

¹**espía,** *n.* spy.—**e. doble,** treacherous spy who acts for both sides.

²**espía,** *f.* (naut.) warp, chest rope.

¹**espiar,** *va.* to spy on; to lie in wait for.

²**espiar,** *vn.* (naut.) to warp.

espibia, *f.,* **espibio, espibión,** *m.* (vet.) dislocation in the nape of the neck.

espicanardi, espicanardo, *f.* (bot.) spikenard.

espiciforme, *a.* (bot.) spicate.

espícula, *f.* (zool.) spicule.

espichar. I. *va.* to prick. **II.** *vn.* (coll.) to give up the ghost, to die.

espiche, *m.* sharp-pointed weapon; meatspit; spigot.

espichón, *m.* wound with a pointed weapon.

espiga, *f.* (bot.) tassel (as of corn); (carp.) tenon, dowel, peg; (mech.) pin, tongue, shank, treenail, stem; tang of a sword; brad, headless nail; (mil.) fuse of a bomb or shell; (naut.) masthead.

espigadera, *f.* gleaner.

espigado, da. I. *pp.* of ESPIGAR. **II.** *a.* tall, grown; (agr.) eared, ripe.

espigador, ra, *n.* gleaner.

espigar. I. *vn.* (*pret.* ESPIGUÉ; *subj.* ESPIGUE) to glean; to collect, cull; (carp.) to tenon. **II.** *vn.* (agr.) to tassel (as corn). **III.** *vr.* to grow tall; to go to seed.

espigón, *m.* sting (as of bees); point of a sharp tool or dart; bearded spike; ear of corn; peak; breakwater or pier.

espigué, espigue, *v. V.* ESPIGAR.

espigueo, *m.* gleaning; gleaning season.

espiguilla, ta, *f. dim.* spikelet; small edging of lace, tape, or inkle.

espina, *f.* thorn; fishbone; spine, backbone; splinter; scruple, doubt, suspicion.—**e. blanca,** (bot.) woolly-cotton thistle.—**e. dorsal,** vertebral or spinal column, spine.—**dar mala e.,** to cause suspicion or anxiety.—**estar en espinas,** to be anxious, to be on pins and needles.—**sacarse la e.,** to get even, to retrieve one's losses.

espinaca, *f.* (bot.) spinach.

espinadura, *f.* pricking with a thorn.

espinal, *a.* spinal, dorsal.

¹**espinar,** *va.* to prick with thorns; to surround (trees) with thorn bushes; to nettle, provoke.

²**espinar,** *m.* place full of thorn bushes; dangerous undertaking, arduous enterprise.

espinazo, *m.* spine, backbone.

espinel, *m.* fishing line with many hooks.

¹**espinela,** *f.* (poet.) ten-line stanza.

²**espinela,** *f.* spinel ruby.

espíneo, ea, *a.* made or full of thorns.

espinera, *f.* (bot.) = ESPINO.

espineta, *f.* (mus.) spinet.

espingarda, *f.* a small cannon; Moorish gun.

espingardada, *f.* wound from an ESPINGARDA.

espinica, ita, illa, *f. dim.* small thorn.

espinilla, *f.* shin bone; blackhead.

espinillera, *f.* (armor) greave, jambe.

espino, *m.* (bot.) hawthorn, buckthorn.

espinosismo, *m.* Spinozism.

espinosista, *n. & a.* Spinozist(-ic).

espinoso, sa, *a.* thorny; arduous; dangerous.

espinzar, *va.* to burl. Also DESPINZAR.

espiocha, *f.* pickaxe.

espión, *m.* spy.

espionaje, *m.* espionage, spying.

espira, *f.* spiral line, helix; spire, steeple; turn (of a winding); (arch.) surbase of a column.

espiración, *f.* exhalation, respiration.

espirador, ra, *n.* one who exhales or breathes.

espiral. I. *a.* spiral, winding. **II.** *f.* (math.) spiral.—**espiralmente,** *adv.* spirally.

espirante, *a.* exhaling, respiring.

espirar. I. *va.* to breathe, exhale; to move, animate; to infuse a divine spirit in. **II.** *vn.* to exhale, breathe.

espirativo, va, *a.* that infuses spirit.

espirilo, *m.* (biol.) spirillum.

espiritado, da, *a.* (coll.) extremely thin.

espiritar. I. *va.* = ENDEMONIAR, to possess with a devil. **II.** *vr.* (coll.) to be agitated, to fret.

espiritismo, *m.* spiritism, spiritualism.

espiritista, *n. & a.* spiritist(-ic).

espiritosamente, *adv.* spiritedly.

espiritoso, sa, *a.* spirituous; spirited, lively.

espíritu, *m.* spirit; soul; genius; ardor, courage; inclination, turn of mind; spirit, liquor.—*pl.*

spirits, demons, hobgoblins; (chem.) spirits, ether.—**e. de contradicción,** contradictory temper, mania oǐ contradicting.—**e. de sal,** spirit of salt (hydrochloric acid).—**e. de vino,** spirits of wine, rectified spirit.—**e. inmundo, e. maligno,** the devil.—**E. Santo,** Holy Ghost.

espiritual, a. spiritual; ghostly.

espiritualidad, f. spirituality; incorporality.

espiritualismo, m. (philos.) spiritualism, idealism (as opposed to materialism).

espiritualista, a. & n. spiritualist(-ic), idealist (-ic) [as opposed to materialist(-ic)].

espiritualización, f. spiritualization.

espiritualizar, va. to spiritualize.

espiritualmente, adv. spiritually.

espirituoso, sa, a. spirituous; ardent; spirited.

espirómetro, m. spirometer.

espiroqueta, f. (bacteriol.) spirochete.

espita, f. faucet, stopcock, spigot, spout; tap; (coll.) tippler, drunkard.

espitar, va. to put a faucet on; to tap.

espito, m. (print.) peel, hanger.

esplácnico, ca, a. (anat.) visceral.

esplendente, a. (poet.) shining, resplendent.

esplender, vn. (poet.) to shine, glitter.

espléndidamente, adv. splendidly, magnificently.

esplendidez, f. splendor, grandeur; abundance; liberality.

espléndido, da, a. splendid, magnificent, grand; generous, liberal; resplendent.

esplendor, m. splendor, magnificence, grandeur; fulgency, radiance; nobleness.

esplendorosamente, adv. with splendor.

esplendoroso, sa, a. splendid, radiant.

esplenético, ca; esplénico, ca, a. splenic.

esplenio, m. (anat.) splenius.

esplenitis, f. (med.) splenitis.

espliego, m. (bot.) lavender.

esplín, m. (coll.) spleen, melancholia, the blues.

esplique, m. bird snare.

espolada, f. prick with a spur.—**e. de vino,** (coll.) large draught of wine.

espolazo, m. violent prick with a spur.

espoleadura, f. wound made with a spur.

espolear, va. to spur; to instigate, incite.

¹**espoleta,** f. fuse (of a bomb).

²**espoleta,** f. wishbone.

espolín, m. dim. small goad spur; shuttle for brocading or flowering; silk brocade.

espolinar, va. to brocade; to flower.

espolio, m. (eccl.) spolium.

espolique, m. running footman.

¹**espolista,** m. running footman.

²**espolista,** m. one who farms a spolium.

espolón, m. cock's spur; ridge, crag of a mountain; (arch.) spur, buttress; (eng.) mole, breakwater, jetty, groin, starling; (naut.) ram of a man-of-war; (naut.) fender-beam.

espolonada, f. sudden onset of horsemen.

espolvorear, espolvorizar, va. to sprinkle with powder.

espondaico, ca, a. (poet.) spondaic.

espondeo, m. (poet.) spondee.

espondil, m. (anat.) spondyl, vertebra.

espondilitis, f. (med.) spondylitis.

esponja, f. sponge; (coll.) sponger.

esponjado, da. I. pp. of ESPONJAR. **II.** a. puffed up. **III.** m. = AZUCARILLO, a sweetmeat.

esponjadura, f., **esponjamiento,** m. sponging; flaw in cast metal; puffing up.

esponjar. I. va. to sponge, soak, imbibe. **II.** vr. to swell; to puff up; (coll.) to glow with health.

esponjera, f. sponge holder.

esponjilla, ita, uela, f. dim. small sponge.

esponjosidad, f. sponginess.

esponjoso, sa, a. spongy, porous.

esponsales, m. pl. betrothal, engagement.

esponsalicio, cia, a. nuptial, spousal.

espontáneamente, adv. spontaneously.

espontanearse, vr. to avow or declare spontaneously or of one's own accord.

espontaneidad, f. spontaneity, spontaneousness

espontáneo, nea, a. spontaneous; willing.

espontón, m. (mil.) spontoon, half-pike.

espontonada, f. salute or blow with a spontoon.

espora, f., (bot.) spore.

esporádico, ca, a. sporadic, isolated.

esporangio, m. (bot.) sporangium.

esporidio, m. (bot.) sporidium.

esporífero, ra, a. (bot.) sporiferous.

esporo, m. (bot.) spore.

esporocarpio, m. (bot.) sporocarp.

esporogonio, m. (bot.) sporogony.

esporozoario, esporozoo. I. n. & a. (zool.) sporozoan. **II.** m. pl. Sporozoa.

esportada, f. fruit basket; basketful.

esportear, va. to carry in panniers or baskets.

esportilla, f. dim. small fruit basket.

esportillero, m. porter, carrier.

esportillo, m. pannier; fruit basket.

esportón, m. aug. large pannier or fruit basket.

esposa, f. spouse, wife.—pl. manacles, handcuffs, shackles.—**esposar,** va. to shackle, handcuff.

esposo, m. spouse, husband, consort.

espuela, f. spur, rowel; stimulus, incitement.—**e. de caballero,** (bot.) larkspur.

espuenda, f. bank of a canal.

espuerta, f. two-handled fruit basket.—**a. espuertas,** abundantly.

espulgadero, m. place where beggars delouse themselves, clean off lice or fleas.

espulgador, ra, n. one who cleans off lice or fleas.

espulgar, va. (pret. ESPULGUÉ; subj. ESPULGUE) to clean lice or fleas from; to examine closely.—**espulgo,** m. act of cleaning lice or fleas from.

espuma, f. froth; lather; foam; scum.—**e. de la sal,** sea froth.—**e. de mar,** meerschaum.—**e. de nitro,** aphronitrum.—**e. de plata,** litharge of silver.

espumadera, f. skimmer, colander.

espumador, ra, n. & a. skimmer(-ing).

espumajear, vn. to froth at the mouth.

espumajo, m. froth.—**espumajoso, sa,** a. foamy, frothy.

espumante, a. foaming, frothing, lathering; sparkling (wine).

espumar. I. va. to skim, to scum. **II.** vn. to froth, foam.

espumarajo, m. foam or froth from the mouth.

espumero, m. place where salt water crystallizes.

espumescente, a. spumescent.

espumilla, f. gauzy fabric; (Am.) meringue.

espumillón, m. heavy silk crape.

espumosidad, f. frothiness, foaminess.

espumoso, sa, a. foamy, frothy; lathery; sparkling (wine).

espundia, f. (vet.) cancerous ulcer.

espurio, ria, a. spurious, adulterated; bastard.

espurrear, espurriar, va. to sprinkle with water or another liquid held in the mouth.

espurrir, va. to stretch out (as the feet).

esputar, va. & vn. to expectorate, spit.

esputo, m. spittle, saliva; sputum.

esquebrajar, va. to crack, split.

esqueje, m. (agr.) cutting, slip.

esquela, f. billet, note.

esqueletado, da, a. very thin, emaciated.

esquelético, ca, a. skeletal; thin, wasted.

esqueleto, m. skeleton; very thin person; (naut.) carcass, framework of a ship; (auto) carcass (of a tire); (Am.) form, blank (as bill forms, application blanks, etc.); (Chile) outline, rough draft.—**en e.,** unfinished.

esquelita, f. dim. small note, billet.

esquema, m. symbol; scheme, plan.

esquemáticamente, adv. schematically.

esquemático, ca, a. schematic.

esquematismo, m. schematism.

For pronunciation, see the rules at the beginning of the book.

esquematizar, va. to sketch, outline.

esquena, f. spine of fishes.

esquero, m. leather bag or pouch.

esquí, m. ski.—**esquiar,** vn. to ski.

esquiciar, va. to sketch, outline, delineate.

esquicio, m. sketch, outline.

esquifada, f. skiff or boat load; vault of a cistern.

esquifar, va. (naut.) to fit out (a ship).

esquifazón, f. (naut.) boat's crew.

esquife, m. skiff, small boat; (arch.) cylindrical vault.

¹esquila, f. small bell; cattle bell.

²esquila, f. (ichth.) prawn; (entom.) waterspider; (bot.) squill.

³esquila, f. sheepshearing.

esquiladero, m. shearing place.

esquilador, m. sheepshearer, clipper.

esquilar, va. to shear, crop, clip.—**e. la carona,** to shear the back of a mule.—**sin e.,** unshorn.

esquileo, m. shearing (of sheep, dogs, etc.)

esquilimoso, sa, a. (coll.) fastidious, overnice.

esquilmar, va. to harvest; to impoverish; to cheat, to swindle, to exploit.

esquilmeño, ña, a. fruitful, productive.

esquilmo, m. harvest; farm produce.

esquilón, m. large call or cattle bell.

esquimal, n. & a. Eskimo.

esquina, f. corner, angle (outside).

esquinado, da. I. pp. of ESQUINAR. **II.** a. intractable, unsociable.

esquinal, m. corner plate; angle iron; iron knee.

esquinante, to, m. (bot.) aromatic rush.

esquinar. I. va. to form a corner with, meet forming a corner; to square (timber, etc.); to estrange, cause to quarrel, set against. **II.** vr. to quarrel, to fall out.

esquinazo, m. corner; (Chile) serenade.—**dar e.,** to avoid, to evade, get out of the sight of (one that follows), shake off; to abandon, leave in the lurch.

esquinco, m. skink, lizard. Also ESTINCO.

esquinela, f. (armor) greave, jambe.

esquinzador, m. rag room in paper mills; rag engine.

esquinzar, va. to cut (rags) in paper mills.

esquirla, f. (surg.) splinter of a bone.

esquirol, m. (coll.) strike breaker, scab; (prov.) = ARDILLA, squirrel.

esquisto, m. (min.) schist; slate.

esquistoso, sa, a. laminated; schistose, slaty.

esquitar, va. to pardon, to remit (a debt).

esquite, m. (Mex., C. A.) popped corn.

esquivar. I. va. to shun, elude, avoid, evade, escape; to hush up (a matter). **II.** vr. to disdain, withdraw.

esquivez, f. disdain, asperity, coldness.

esquivo, va, a. elusive, evading; shy, reserved, coy, cold.

esquizado, da, a. mottled (as marble).

estabilidad, f. stability.

estabilísimo, adv. super. very stable or firm.

estable, a. stable, steady, firm, fast.

establear, va. to tame, accustom to the stable.

establecedor, ra, n. founder.

establecer. I. va. (ind. ESTABLEZCO; subj. ESTABLEZCA) to establish, found; to decree, enact. **II.** vr. to establish or settle oneself.

estableciente, n. & a. establisher(-ing).

establecimiento, m. establishment; statute, law, ordinance, decree; establishment, founding; institution.

establemente, adv. stably, firmly.

establero, m. hostler, groom, horsekeeper.

establezco, establezca, v. V. ESTABLECER.

establo, m. stable; cattle barn.

estabulación, f. stabling.

estaca, f. stake, picket, pile, pole; stick, cudgel, bludgeon; (agr.) grafting twig; cutting; (carp.) clamp nail.

estacada, f. (mil.) palisade, stockade; paling,

fence work; pile pier; place for a duel.—**dejar (a uno) en la e.,** to leave (one) in the lurch, "holding the bag."

estacar. I. va. (pret. ESTAQUÉ; subj. ESTAQUE) to stake; to fence with stakes; to tie to a stake. **II.** vr. to remain stiff as a pole.

estación, f. state, condition, position; season (of the year); hour, moment, time; (Ry., radio, tel., police, surv., eccl.) station; devotional visit to a church; stay, stop; (Ry.) stop; party of persons posted at some place; (astr.) stationary point.

estacional, a. seasonal; (astr.) stationary.

estacionamiento, m. stationing, settling; (auto) parking.

estacionar. I. va. to park (a car, etc.). **II.** vr. to park; to remain stationary.

estacionario, ria, a. stationary.

estacionero, ra, n. one who prays before stations in church.

estacón, m. aug. large stake.

estacte, m. oil of myrrh.

estacha, f. (naut.) towline, hawser; harpoon rope.

estada, f. stay, sojourn.

estadal, m. a linear measure of about 10 ft. 9 in.; blessed ribbon worn around the neck.

estadia, f. (surv.) stadia, stadia transit.

estadía, f. (com. and naut.) stay, detention; demurrage; cost of such stay.

estadio, m. race course; stadium (road measure).

estadista, m. statesman.

estadística, f. statistics.

estadístico, ca, a. statistical.

estadizo, za, a. stagnant (as water).

estado. I. m. state; condition (of persons or things) (as, eso llegó en mal estado, that came in bad condition); estate, class, rank; profession; status (single, married, or widowed); state, nation, commonwealth; state, government; statement, account, report; a measure of length (1.85 yds.).—pl. States, legislature (los Estados Generales, the States-General).—**e. de guerra,** or **e. de sitio,** martial law (declarar una ciudad en estado de guerra, to declare a city in a state of martial law, to put it under martial law).—**e. general,** or **e. llano,** the commons, the common estate (as distinguished from the nobility, etc.).—**e. mayor,** (mil.) staff.—**e. mayor general,** (mil.) general staff.

estadojo, estadoño, m. stake of a cart.

estadounidense, estadunidense, n. & a. (citizen) of the U. S.

¹estafa, f. stirrup.

²estafa, f. swindle, trick, deceit.

estafador, ra, n. swindler.

estafar, va. to swindle, defraud.

estafermo, m. movable wooden figure of an armed man; idle fellow.

estafeta, f. courier, post, express; post office; general-delivery office or department (of post office); post-office branch.

estafetero, m. postmaster; post-office clerk.

estafetil, a. pertaining to a courier or post.

estafilocacia, f. (bacteriol.) infection due to staphylococci.

estafilococo, m. (bacteriol.) staphylococcus.

estafiloma, m. (med.) staphyloma.

estafisagra, f. (bot.) stavesacre, lousewort.

estagirita, n. & a. Stagirite.

estagnación, f. (Am.) stagnation; paralyzation, cessation (of business, etc.).

estala, f. seaport, stopping place.

estalación, f. class, rank, order.

estalactita, f. stalactite.

estalagmita, f. stalagmite.

estallante, a. bursting, exploding.

estallar, vn. to explode, burst; (of fire, etc.) to break out.

estallido, estallo, m. crack, crackling, crashing, crash, snap, outburst; report (as of firearms).

estambor, *m.* (naut.) sternpost.
estambrado, *m.* worsted cloth.
estambrar, *va.* to spin (worsted).
estambre, *m.* worsted, woollen yarn; (bot.) stamen.
estamenara, *f.* (naut.) futtock.
estamento, *m.* one of the estates composing the Cortes in Aragon (clergy, nobility, commons).
estameña, *f.* tammy cloth, serge.
estameñete, *m.* a kind of serge.
estamíneo, nea, *a.* made of worsted.
estaminífero, ra, *a.* (bot.) staminate.
estampa. I. *f.* print, stamp, cut; engraving; first sketch; printing, press; track, impression, footstep; (fig.) impression.—**estampas iluminadas,** colored plates.—**la e. de la herejía,** (coll.) a hideous face; (one) dressed in bad taste.
estampado, *m.* cotton print, calico; impression, stamping; cloth printing.
estampador, *m.* stamper; stamp, puncheon.
estampar, *va.* to print, stamp, emboss; to imprint (a kiss); to impress, fix (in the mind).
estampería, *f.* office for printing or selling prints.
estampero, ra, *n.* stamp or print maker or seller.
estampida, *f.* stampede.—**dar una e.,** (coll.) (Am.) to run away (often leaving debts).
estampido, *m.* report of a gun; crack, crash.
estampilla, *f.* *dim.* small print; rubber stamp; signet seal; (Am.) postage stamp.
estampillado, *m.* stamping, marking.
estampillar, *va.* to stamp, mark.
estampita, *f.* *dim.* small print or stamp.
estancación, *f.*, **estancamiento,** *m.* stagnation.
estancar. I. *va.* (*pret.* ESTANQUÉ; *subj.* ESTANQUE) to stanch, check, stem; (naut.) to fother (a leak); (com.) to corner, to monopolize; to interdict, suspend. **II.** *vr.* to stagnate, become stagnant.
¹**estancia,** *f.* (poet.) stanza.
²**estancia,** *f.* stay, sojourn; dwelling, habitation; sitting room, living room; (Am.) small farm.
estanciero, ra, *n.* small farmer.
estanco, ca. I. *a.* water-tight. **II.** *m.* monopoly; store for monopolized goods; cigar store; repository, archives, files.
estandarte, *m.* standard, flag, banner, colors.
estangurria, *f.* (med.) strangury; catheter.
estannato, *m.* (chem.) stannate.
estánnico, ca, *a.* (chem.) stannic.
estannoso, sa, *a.* (chem.) stannous.
estanque, *m.* pond, reservoir, pool.
estanqué, estanque, *v. V.* ESTANCAR.
¹**estanquero,** *m.* reservoir keeper.
²**estanquero, ra.** *n.* retailer of monopoly goods; tobacconist.
estanquillero, ra, *n.* tobacconist.
estanquillo, *m.* cigar store; shop where monopolized goods are sold; (Mex.) small shop; (Ecua.) liquor shop.
estanquito, *m.* *dim.* small pond, pool.
estantal, *m.* (arch.) buttress.
estante. I. *a.* existing, extant; fixed, permanent. **II.** *m.* shelf; bookcase; (print.) cabinet.—*pl.* (naut.) props of the crossbeams.
estantería, *f.* shelfing, shelves (collect.).
estantigua, *f.* phantom, vision, hobgoblin; (coll.) tall, skinny, uncouth person.
estantío, tía, *a.* standing still, stationary; dull, slow.
estañador, *m.* tinner, tinman.
estañadura, *f.* tinning.
estañar, *va.* to tin, blanch; to solder.
estañero, *m.* tinner; seller of tinware.
estaño, *m.* (chem.) tin.
estaqué, estaque, *v. V.* ESTACAR.
estaquero, *m.* year-old buck or doe.
estaquilla, ita, *f.* (shoemaking) peg; wooden pin; spike, long nail.
estaquillador, *m.* (shoemaking) pegging awl.
estaquillar, *va.* to peg, to fasten with pegs.

estar. I. *vn.* (*ind. pres.* ESTOY, *pret.* ESTUVE; *subj.* ESTÉ) to be. When followed by the gerund of reflexive verb, it sometimes takes the reflexiv pronoun from that verb (*estarse vistiendo,* ir stead of *estar vistiéndose,* to be dressing). Whe preceded by a dative case, "for" is used i English before the corresponding objective cas (*este sombrero me está demasiado grande,* this ha is too large for me; *eso no me es posible,* that i not possible for me).—**e. a,** to sell at (so much apiece.—**e. al,** to be on the point of.—**e. bier** to be well; to be all right, acceptable, suitable **e. con,** to live in company with; to be er gaged or talking with; to have (a disease), to b ill with; to be in a state of (anxiety, anger hurry, etc.).—**e. de,** to be in the condition c doing the act indicated by the following nou *(estoy de mudanza,* I am moving; *estoy de prisa* I am in haste; *estoy de vacaciones,* I am on m vacation; *Juan está de cónsul,* John is serv ing as consul).—**e. en,** to understand, com prehend *(estoy en lo que Vd. me dice,* I under stand what you say); to be of opinion; t stand, to cost *(este sombrero me está en seis pesos* this hat costs me six dollars); to depend *(en es está,* it depends on that); to consist in.—**e. e grande,** to live in luxury.—**e. en sí,** to kno what one is doing.—**e. para,** to be about to; t be in a mood or in condition to or for *(no esto para eso,* I am in no mood for that).—**e. por** to be for, in favor of; (followed by *infin.*) to re main to be, not to have been (followed by *pp.*) to have a mind to, to have a notion or a desir to.—**e. por ver,** to remain to be seen.—**e. sobr sí,** to be cautious or wary; to be puffed up wit' conceit.—**¿a cómo estamos? ¿a cuántos es tamos?** what day (of the month) is it? what i the date?—**¡dónde estamos!** what have w come to! what a thing!—an expression of ad miration or disgust at what is seen or heard.— **está escrito,** it is written.—**¿estamos?** is i agreed? do you understand?—**estamos a** (fol lowed by the day, date), this is, it is *(estamos a lunes,* this is Monday; *estamos a cinco,* thi is the fifth).—**¡está bien!** or, **bueno!,** all right —**¿está Vd.?** do you understand? do you se the point? **II.** *vr.* to be, to keep; to stay, to re main *(Juan nunca se está callado,* John is neve silent, or, never keeps silent; *debemos estarno aquí,* we must remain here.)

estarcido, *m.* pounced drawing; stencil.
estarcir, *va.* to stencil.
estarna, *f.* (ornith.) small partridge.
estatal, *a.* pert. to the state, state (as *a.*).
estática, *f.* (mech.) statics.
estático, ca, *a.* static, statical.
estator, *m.* (mech., elec.) stator.
estatua, *f.* statue.—**quedarse hecho una e.,** t stand aghast, to be rooted to the ground.
estatuar, *va.* to adorn with statues.
estatuaria, *f.* (art) statuary, sculpture.
estatuario, ria. I. *a.* pert. to statuary. **II.** *m* statuary; sculptor.
estatúder, *m.* stadtholder.
estatuderato, *m.* stadtholdership.
estatuir, *va.* (*ind.* ESTATUYO; *subj.* ESTATUYA) t establish, ordain, enact.
estatura, *f.* stature, height of a person.
estatuto, *m.* statute, law, ordinance.
estatuyo, estatuya, *v. V.* ESTATUIR.
estay, *m.* (naut.) stay.
¹**este,** *m.* east, orient.
²**este,** *m.,* **esta,** *f., a.* this.—*pl.* **estos, estas,** these
éste, *m.,* **ésta,** *f.* *pron. dem.* this, this one; th latter.—*pl.* **éstos,** *m.,* **éstas,** *f.,* these; th latter.
esté, *v. V.* ESTAR.
estearato, *m.* (chem.) stearate.
esteárico, ca, *a.* (chem.) stearic.
estearina, *f.* (chem.) stearin.

For pronunciation, see the rules at the beginning of the book.

steatita, *f.* (min.) steatite, soapstone.

esteba, *f.* prickly plant growing in swamps.

esteba, *f.* stevedore's pole.

stebar, *va.* to put (cloth) in the dye kettle.

estela, *f.* (naut.) wake of a ship.

estela, *f.* (arch.) stele.

stelar, *a.* sidereal, stellar.

stelaria, *f.* (bot.) silvery lady's-mantle.

stelárido, da. I. *n. & a.* (zool.) asteroidean. **II.** *m. pl.* Asteroidea, starfishes.

stelífero, ra, *a.* (poet.) stelliferous, starry.

steliforme, *a.* stelliform, star-shaped.

stelión, *m.* (zool.) stellion, a lizard; toadstone.

stelionato, *m.* (law) stellionate.

stelón, *m.* toadstone.

stelulado, da, *a.* stellular, star-shaped.

stemple, *m.* (min.) stemple.

stenografía, *f.* stenography, shorthand.

stenografiar, *va.* to take down in shorthand.

stenográficamente, *adv.* stenographically.

stenográfico, ca, *a.* stenographic.

stenógrafo, fa, *n.* stenographer.

stenosis, *f.* (med.) stenosis, narrowing.

stentóreo, a, *a.* stentorian.

estepa, *f.* steppe, barren plain.

estepa, *f.* (bot.) rockrose.

stepar, *m.* rockrose field.

stepilla, *f.* (bot.) white-leaved rockrose.

ster, *m.* (chem.) ester.

stera, *f.* mat, matting.

sterar. I. *va.* to cover with matting. **II.** *vn.* (coll.) to wear winter clothes before time.

stercoladura, *f.*, **estercolamiento,** *m.* manuring.

stercolar. I. *va.* to dung, muck, manure. **II.** *vn.* to void the excrements.—**estercolero,** *m.* driver of a muck cart; dung hill, dung heap.

stercolizo, za; estercóreo, a, *a.* stercoraceous.

stercuelo, *m.* stercoration, manuring.

stéreo, *m.* stere (one cubic metre).

stereocromía, *f.* stereochromy.

stereografía, *f.* stereography.

stereográfico, ca, *a.* stereographic.

stereógrafo, *m.* stereographer.

stereometría, *f.* stereometry.

stereómetro, *m.* stereometer.

stereoscopio, *m.* stereoscope.

stereotipa, *f.* = ESTEREOTIPIA.

stereotipador, *m.* stereotyper.

stereotipar, *va.* to stereotype; to print from stereotypes.

stereotipia, *f.* stereotypography, stereotyping; place where stereotypes are made.

stereotípico, ca, *a.* stereotypic.

stereotomía, *f.* stereotomy.

sterería, *f.* matting factory or shop.

sterero, ra, *n.*, matting maker or seller.

stéril, *a.* sterile, barren; unfruitful, fruitless.

sterilidad, *f.* sterility, barrenness; scarcity, failure of crops.

sterilizador, ra, *n. & a.* sterilizer(-ing).

sterilizar, *va.* to sterilize.

sterilla, *f. dim.* small mat; straw plait; narrow gold or silver braid.

stérilmente, *adv.* barrenly, fruitlessly.

sterlín, *m.* = BOCACÍ, glazed buckram.

sterlina, *a.* (Eng. money) sterling (pound).

sternón, *m.* (anat.) sternum, breastbone.

estero, *m.* inlet, estuary.

estero, *m.* covering with matting; matting season.

sterquilinio, *m.* dunghill, dung heap.

stertor, *m.* rattle in the throat; stertor.

stertoroso, sa, *a.* stertorous.

steta, *n.* æsthete; æsthetician.

stética, *f.* æsthetics.

stéticamente, *adv.* æsthetically.

stético, ca. I. *a.* æsthetic. **II.** *m.* æsthete.

stetoscopia, *f.* (med.) stethoscopy.

stetoscopio, *m.* (med.) stethoscope.

esteva, *f.* plow handle; reach of a carriage.

estevado, da, *a.* bow-legged.

estevón, *m.* = ESTEVA.

estezado, *m.* = CORREAL, dressed deerskin.

estiaje, *m.* low-water mark.

estiba, *f.* rammer; place where wool is compressed; (naut.) stowage.

estibador, *m.* stevedore, longshoreman.

estibar, *va.* to compress (wool); (naut.) to stow.

estibia, *f.* (vet.) = ESPIBIA, neck dislocation.

estibio, *m.* antimony, stibium.

estibina, *f.* (min.) stibine.

estiércol, *m.* dung, manure.

estigio, gia, *a.* Stygian.

estigma, *m.* birthmark; stigma, brand, mark of infamy; affront, disgrace; (bot.) stigma.

estigmatizador, ra, *n. & a.* stigmatizer(-ing).

estigmatizar, *va.* to stigmatize; to affront.

estilar. I. *va.* to use, be in the habit of using; to draw up (a document). **II.** *vr.* to be in style.

estilete, *m.* stiletto (dagger); small chisel or burin; (surg.) flexible probe.

estilicidio, *m.* (of liquid) issuing drop by drop.

estilista, *n.* stylist, master of style.

estilita, *a.* (eccl. hist.) stylite, pillarist; (E-), Stylites (St. Simeon).

estilo, *m.* style (writing instrument); gnomon or style of a sun dial; (arch. and lit.) style; use, custom, fashion; (bot.) style.—**e. antiguo,** (chron.) old style.—**e. familiar,** colloquial style.—**e. nuevo,** (chron.) new style.—**al e. de,** in the style of.—**de e.,** usual, customary.—**por el e.,** or **por ese e.,** of that kind, like that.

estilóbato, *m.* (arch.) stylobate, pedestal.

estilográfico, ca. I. *a.* stylographic.—**pluma e.,** fountain pen. **II.** *f.* fountain pen.

estima, *f.* esteem; (naut.) dead reckoning.

estimabilidad, *f.* estimableness; worth.

estimabilísimo, ma, *a. super.* most estimable.

estimable, *a.* estimable, worthy; computable.

estimación, *f.* esteem, regard; estimate, valuation.—**e. propia,** self-respect.

estimador, ra, *n.* esteemer; estimator.

estimar, *va.* to estimate, value; to esteem, respect, honor; to judge, to think.

estimativa, *f.* power of judging; instinct.

estimulante. I. *a.* stimulating, exciting. **II.** *m.* stimulant.

estimular, *va.* to stimulate; to goad, incite, encourage.

estímulo, *m.* stimulus; inducement; incitement; stimulation; encouragement.

estinco, *m.* skink, a kind of lizard.

estío, *m.* summer.

estiomenar, *va.* (med.) to mortify (flesh).

estiómeno, *m.* (med.) mortification, gangrene.

estipendiar, *va.* to give a stipend to.

estipendiario, *m.* stipendiary.

estipendio, *m.* stipend, salary, pay, fee.

estípite, *m.* (arch.) pilaster in the form of an inverted pyramid.

estipticar, *va.* (med.) to apply a styptic to.

estipticidad, *f.* (med.) stypticity.

estíptico, ca, *a.* styptic, astringent; costive; (fig.) miserly, stingy.

estiptiquez, *f.* (med.) (Am.) costiveness.

estípula, *f.* (bot.) stipule.

estipulación, *f.* stipulation, proviso, specification, requirement.

estipulante, *n. & a.* stipulator(-ing).

estipular, *va.* to stipulate, covenant, specify.

estira, *f.* knife used by curriers.

estiracáceo, *a.* (bot.) styraceous.

estiradamente, *adv.* scarcely; with difficulty; violently, forcibly.

estirado, da. I. *pp.* of ESTIRAR. **II.** *a.* stiff, stuck-up; drawn.—**e. en frío,** (of metals) hard-drawn. **III.** *m.* stretching; drawing.

estirador, ra, *n.* stretcher; drawing frame.

estirajar, *va.* (coll.) = ESTIRAR.

estirajón, *m.* (coll.) = ESTIRÓN.

estiramiento, *m.* stretching, pulling; drawing (of metals).

estirar. I. *va.* to stretch, lengthen; to pull; to draw (metals).—**e. en frío,** to hard-draw. II. *vr.* to stretch; to put on airs.—**estirazar,** *va.* (coll.) = ESTIRAR.—**estirón,** *m.* strong pull; haul or hauling; rapid growth.

estirpe, *f.* stock, lineage, pedigree.

estítico, ca, *a.* = ESTÍPTICO.

estivada, *f.* burning of undergrowth.

estival, vo, va, *a.* summer (as *a.*).

esto, *pron. dem. neut.* this.—**e. es,** that is; that is to say.—**a e.,** hereto, hereunto.—**a todo e.,** meanwhile.—**con e.,** herewith.—**en e.,** at this juncture, point; at once, right away; herein, hereinto.—**por e.,** for this reason; on this account.—**por e. es por lo que,** (or, improperly but commonly, **por e. es que**), this is the reason, this is why.—**sobre e.,** hereon, hereupon.

estocada, *f.* stab, thrust, tilt, lunge.

estocafís, *m.* (com.) stockfish, dried cod.

estofa, *f.* quilted silk stuff; quality, condition.

¹estofado, da. I. *pp.* of ¹ESTOFAR. II. *a.* quilted; ornamented.

²estofado, *m.* stew.

estofador, *m.* quilter.

¹estofar, *va.* to quilt; to paint on a gilt ground; to size before gilding.

²estofar, *va.* to stew.

estofo, *m.* quilting; painting on gilt; sizing.

estoicamente, *adv.* stoically.

estoicidad, *f.* imperturbability.

estoicismo, *m.* stoicism.

estoico, ca, *n.* & *a.* stoic(-al).

estola, *f.* stole, worn by priests.

estolidez, *f.* stupidity, incapacity.

estólido, da, *a.* stupid, foolish.

¹estolón, *m. aug.* large stole.

²estolón, *m.* (bot.) stolon.

estoma, *m.* (bot.) stoma.

estomacal, *a.* stomachic.

estomagar, *vn.* & *va.* (*pret.* ESTOMAGUÉ; *subj.* ESTOMAGUE) to bore; to annoy, make angry.

estómago, *m.* stomach.—**tener buen e.,** or **mucho e.,** to ignore slights and offenses, to be thick-skinned; to have an elastic conscience.

estomagué, estomague, *v.* V. ESTOMAGAR.

estomaguero, *m.* baby's bellyband.

estomatical, *a.* stomachic.

estomaticón, *m.* stomach plaster.

estomatitis, *f.* (med.) mouth inflammation, stomatitis.

estopa, *f.* tow; burlap; oakum.

estopada, *f.* quantity of tow for spinning.

estopear, *va.* to calk with oakum.

estopeño, ña, *a.* tow (as *a.*).

¹estoperol, *m.* tow wick.

²estoperol, *m.* (naut.) scupper nail.

estopilla, *f.* finest part of hemp or flax; lawn, batiste, cheesecloth.

estopín, *m.* (artil.) priming tube; quick match.

estopón, *m.* coarse tow.

estopor, *m.* (naut.) stopper.

estoposo, sa, *a.* towlike, filaceous.

estoque, *m.* estoc, rapier; (bot.) corn flag.

estoqueador, *m.* matador (bull fighter).

estoquear, *va.* to make a thrust at with a rapier.

estoqueo, *m.* thrusting or stabbing.

estoraque, *m.* (bot.) officinal storax; gum of the storax tree.

estorbador, ra, *n.* & *a.* hinderer(-ing), obstructor(-ing).

estorbar, *va.* to hinder; obstruct; be in the way.

estorbo, *m.* hindrance, obstruction, nuisance.

estorboso, sa, *a.* hindering, in the way.

estornija, *f.* linchpin; washer; a boys' play.

estornino, *m.* (ornith.) starling.

estornudar, *vn.* to sneeze.—**estornudo,** *m.* sneeze.—**estornutatorio,** *m.* sneeze inducer

estotro, tra, compound pronoun of ESTO and OTRO, this other.

estovar, *va.* to heat (meat) slowly.

estoy, *v.* V. ESTAR.

estrabismo, *m.* (med.) strabismus, squint.

estracilla, *f.* small rag; coarse brown paper blotting paper.

estrada, *f.* causeway, paved road.—**e. encubierta,** (mil.) covert way.

estradiota, *f.* a kind of lance.—**a la e.,** riding with long stirrups and stiff legs.

estradiote, *m.* estradiot, Greek horseman.

estrado, *m.* drawing-room; drawing-room furniture; dais for a throne; baker's table; lecturing platform.—*pl.* court rooms.

estrafalariamente, *adv.* (coll.) carelessly, slovenly; wildly, queerly, strangely.

estrafalario, ria, *a.* (coll.) slovenly; wild; odd queer, eccentric.

estragadamente, *adv.* depravedly.

estragador, ra, *a.* corrupting, destroying.

estragamiento, *m.* disorder, depravation.

estragar, *va.* (*pret.* ESTRAGUÉ; *subj.* ESTRAGUE) to deprave, vitiate, corrupt, spoil.

estrago, *m.* ravage, ruin, havoc; wickedness.

estragón, *m.* (bot.) tarragon wormwood.

estragué, estrague, *v.* V. ESTRAGAR.

estrambote, *m.* refrain of a song.

estrambóticamente, *adv.* oddly, queerly.

estrambótico, ca, *a.* odd, queer, eccentric.

estramonio, *m.* (bot.) common thorn apple.

estrangol, *m.* inflammation in a horse's tongue

estrangul, *m.* (mus.) mouthpiece.

estrangulación, *f.* strangling; (surg.) strangulation; (steam eng.) throttling; (hydraul.) stop page.

estrangulador, ra, *n.* & *a.* strangler(-ing).

estrangular, *va.* to strangle, choke, throttle (med.) to strangulate; (steam eng.) to throttle

estratagema, *f.* stratagem; trick, artful deception; craftiness; finesse; fetch.

estrategia, *f.* (mil.) strategy.

estratégicamente, *adv.* strategically.

estratégico, ca, I. *a.* (mil.) strategic. II. *n.* Als **estratego, ga,** *n.* strategist.

estratificación, *f.* (geol.) stratification.

estratificar, *va.* & *vr.* (geol.) to stratify.

estratiforme, *a.* (geol.) stratiform.

estratigrafía, *f.* (geol.) stratigraphy.

estratigráfico, ca, *a.* (geol.) stratigraphical.

estrato, *m.* (geol.) stratum, layer; stratus (cloud)

estratosfera, *f.* (meteorol.) stratosphere.

estrave, *m.* (naut.) stem knee.

estraza, *f.* rag, fragment of cloth.

estrechamente, *adv.* narrowly; tightly, closely intimately; nearly; hardly; exactly, punctually strongly, forcibly; strictly; scantily, penuri ously.

estrechamiento, *m.* tightening; narrowing (econ.) bottleneck.

estrechar. I. *va.* to tighten; to narrow, reduce contract; to take in (a coat, etc.); to constrain compel; to press; to follow closely.—**e. l mano,** to shake hands; to greet; to send re gards or good wishes. II. *vr.* to narrow; to bin oneself strictly; reduce one's expenses; to be come related or intimate; to act in concert.

estrechez, *f.* narrowness; tightness; compact ness, closeness; intimacy; austerity; penury poverty; strait, pass, narrow passage.

estrecho, cha. I. *a.* narrow; tight; intimate close; rigid, austere; exact, punctual; narrow minded, illiberal, mean-spirited; poor, indigent penurious; stingy, close.—**e. de conciencia** overscrupulous, narrow-minded. II. *m.* Valen tine; predicament, fix; (geog.) strait, channel.— **al e.,** by force, by compulsion.—**poner en e.** to force.

For pronunciation, see the rules at the beginning of the book.

estrechón, *m.* (naut.) = SOCOLLADA, pitching. **—e. de manos,** handshaking.

estrechura, *f.* narrowness, straitness; narrow passage, narrows; austerity; distress, predicament, straits; intimate familiarity.

estregadera, *f.* scrubbing brush, mop.

estregadero, *m.* object against which animals scratch themselves; place for washing clothes.

estregadura, *f.,* **estregamiento,** *m.* rubbing; scrubbing.

estregar, *va.* (*ind. pres.* ESTRIEGO, *pret.* ESTREGUÉ; *subj.* ESTRIEGUE) to rub; scour, scrub; scratch (as matches).

estregón, *m. aug.* rough rubbing.

estregué, *pret.* of ESTREGAR.

estrella, *f.* star; star wheel; (theat., etc.) star, lead; star (on a horse's forehead); (mil.) star fort.—**e. de mar,** starfish.—**e. de rabo,** comet. —**e. fija,** fixed star.—**e. fugaz,** shooting star. —**e. polar,** polestar, Polaris.—**con estrellas,** after nightfall, before sunrise.—**poner por las estrellas,** to lionize, to overpraise.—**ver. estrellas,** to feel racking pain; (fig.) to see stars.

estrellada, *f.* (bot.) lady's mantle.

estrelladera, *f.* (cook.) instrument for turning eggs, etc.

estrelladero, *m.* pan for candied yolks.

estrellado, da. I. *pp.* of ESTRELLAR. **II.** *a.* starry; (of horses) star-faced; fried (eggs).

estrellamar, *f.* (bot.) plantain; (ichth.) starfish.

estrellar. I. *va.* (coll.) to dash to pieces, smash (up); to fry (eggs). **II.** *vr.* to fail; (**contra**) to crash or dash (against), be shattered by (with implication of failure, damage or destruction).

estrellar, *a.* stellated, starry.

estrellera, *f.* (naut.) foretackle; burton.

estrellero, ra, *a.* (of horses) tossing the head.

estrellica, ita, uela, *f. dim.* little star.

estrellón, *m aug.* large star; star-shaped piece in fireworks.

estremecedor, ra, *a.* frightful, terrifying.

estremecer. I. *va.* (*ind.* ESTREMEZCO; *subj.* ESTREMEZCA) to shake, to make tremble. **II.** *vr.* to shake, tremble, shudder.

estremecimiento, *m.* trembling, shaking; shudder, shuddering.

estremezco, estremezca, *v. V.* ESTREMECER.

estrena, *f.* gift; love offering, remembrance; first use of a thing; inauguration; début.

estrenar. I. *va.* to use or to do for the first time; to commence, inaugurate; (theat.) to open. **II.** *vr.* to begin to act in some capacity; (theat.) to make one's début; (of a play) to open.

estreno, *m.* commencement, good-luck gift, inauguration; (theat.) first performance; début.

estrenque, *m.* stout esparto rope.

estrenuidad, *f.* vigor, energy, enterprise.

estrenuo, nua, *a.* strong, vigorous; enterprising.

estreñido, da. I. *pp.* of ESTREÑIR. **II.** *a.* costive; stingy.

estreñimiento, *m.* costiveness.

estreñir. I. *va.* (*ind.* ESTRIÑO; *subj.* ESTRIÑA) to bind, constipate. **II.** *vr.* to become costive.

estrepada, *f.* (naut.) a pull in unison.

estrépito, *m.* crash, din, deafening noise.

estrepitosamente, *adv.* noisily, obstreperously.

estrepitoso, sa, *a.* noisy, deafening; boisterous, obstreperous.

estreptococia, *f.* (med.) infection by streptococci.

estreptococo, *m.* (bacteriol.) streptococcus.

estreptomicina, *f.* streptomycin.

estría, *f.* (arch.) fluting, stria, groove.

estriadura, *f.* (arch.) fluting, grooving.

estriar. I. *va.* (arch.) to flute, to gutter. **II.** *vr.* to become grooved, striated.

estribación, *f.* (geog. and arch.) counterfort.

estribadero, *m.* prop, stay.

estribar, *vn.* (**en**) to rest (on); to be based (on), to lie (in).

estribera, *f.* stirrup (of a saddle or an arbalist).

estribería, *f.* stirrup factory or shop.

estriberón, *m.* stepping stone; (mil.) temporary road.

estribillo, *m.* burden or refrain of a song.

estribo, *m.* stirrup; step or footboard of a coach; (mech.) brace, stay, stirrup bolt; clasp of wheel rims; (arch.) buttress, abutment; (fig.) rest, support, basis; (carp.) cross prop, main brace; (geog.) counterfort.—**perder los estribos,** to talk nonsense; to lose one's head.

estribor, *m.* (naut.) starboard.

estricnina, *f.* (med.) strychnine.

estricote.—al e., without rule or order.

estrictamente, *adv.* strictly.

estrictez, *f.* (Am.) strictness.

estricto, ta, *a.* strict.

estridente, *a.* obstreperous; strident.

estridor, *m.* noise, creak, screech.

estriego, estriegue, *v. V.* ESTREGAR.

estrige, *f.* (ornith.) screech owl; vampire.

estriño, estriña, *v. V.* ESTREÑIR.

estro, *m.* (poet.) afflatus, inspiration.

estróbilo, *m.* (bot.) strobile, cone.

estrobo, *m.* (naut.) loop formed with a short rope or cable; (aer.) grummet.

estrofa, *f.* (poet.) stanza.

estroma, *m.* (anat.) stroma.

estronciana, *f.* (chem.) strontia.

estroncianita, *f.* (min.) strontianite.

estroncio, *m.* (chem.) strontium.

estropajear, *va.* (mason.) to rub; to scrub.

estropajeo, *m.* (mason.) rubbing, scrubbing.

estropajo, *m.* mop; swab, dishcloth; esparto scrubbing broom; worthless thing.

estropajosamente, *adv.* stammeringly.

estropajoso, sa, *a.* (coll.) ragged, slovenly; (coll.) tough (meat); (coll.) stammering.

estropeado, da. I. *pp.* of ESTROPEAR. **II.** *a.* fatigued.

estropear. I. *va.* to maim, cripple; to damage or spoil by rough usage; to spoil, ruin (a thing, plan, etc.); (mason.) to stir (mortar). **II.** *vr.* to be out of order, damaged.

estropeo, *m.* rough usage; injury or damage; fatigue, weariness.

estropicio, *m.* (coll.) breakage, crash (of tableware, etc.); needless turmoil.

estrovo, *m.* (naut.) strap for blocks.

estructura, *f.* structure; order, method.

estructural, *a.* structural.

estruendo, *m.* din, clangor, clamor, clatter; confusion, turmoil; pomp, ostentation.

estruendosamente, *adv.* noisily, obstreperously.

estruendoso, sa, *a.* obstreperous, noisy, loud.

estrujadura, *f.,* **estrujamiento,** *m.* pressing, squeezing, crushing, rumpling.

estrujar, *va.* to press, squeeze, crush, rumple, mash, jam, bruise.—**estrujón,** *m.* last pressing of grapes; crush, squeeze, pressure, jam.

estrupador, *m.,* **estrupar,** *va.,* **estrupo,** *m.* = ESTUPRADOR, ESTUPRAR, ESTUPRO.

estuación, *f.* flow of the tide.

estuante, *a.* hot, boiling, glowing.

estuario, *m.* estuary, inlet.

estucador, *m.* stucco plasterer.

estucar, *va. & vn.* (mason.) to stucco.

estuco, *m.* stucco; plaster, scagliola.

estuche, *m.* case (as for jewelry, etc.); box, casket; étui, sheath (for scissors, etc.); cabinet; small comb; in card games, certain combination of cards; a clever, handy fellow.

estudiador, ra, *a.* (coll.) very studious.

estudiantado, *m.* (Am.) students (collect.).

estudiante, *m. & f.* student.—**estudiantil,** *a.* (coll.) student (as *a.*), pert. to students.— **estudiantillo, lla,** *m.* little student.—**estudiantina,** *f.* students; strolling band of students.— **estudiantino, na,** *a.* (coll.) pert. to students (as *a la estudiantina*), in the manner of students.

—**estudiantón,** *m. aug.* diligent but slow student.

estudiar, *va.* to study; (art) to copy.

estudio, *m.* study; investigation; discussion, paper (article, writing); college, school; library, reading room; studio.—*pl.* sciences, letters.— **estudios mayores,** higher studies.

estudiosamente, *adv.* studiously.

estudiosidad, *f.* studiousness.

estudioso, sa, *a.* studious.

estufa, *f.* stove; heater; hothouse; drying chamber, dry bath; sweating room; small brasier.

estufador, *m.* stewpan.

estufero, estufista, *m.* stove maker.

estufilla, *f.* hand muff; foot stove; chafer.

estultamente, *adv.* foolishly.

estulticia, *f.* foolishness, silliness.

estulto, ta, *a.* foolish, silly.

estuosidad, *f.* burning, heat, glow.

estuoso, sa, *a.* hot, ardent, glowing.

estupefacción, *f.* stupefaction, numbness.

estupefaciente, *a. & m.* narcotic.

estupefactivo, va, *a.* stupefying.

estupefacto, *a.* motionless, stupefied.

estupendamente, *adv.* stupendously.

estupendo, da, *a.* stupendous, wonderful.

estúpidamente, *adv.* stupidly.

estupidez, *f.* stupidity.

estúpido, da, *a. & n.* stupid (person).

estupor, *m.* (med.) stupor; amazement.

estuprador, *m.* ravisher, violator.

estuprar, *va.* to ravish, violate.

estupro, *m.* ravishment, rape.

estuque, *m.* stucco.—**estuquería,** *f.* stuccoing; stucco work.—**estuquista,** *n.* stuccoer.

esturar, *va.* to dry by fire; overcook.

esturgar, *va.* to polish (delft ware).

esturión, *m.* (ichth.) sturgeon.

estuve, estuvo, *v.* V. ESTAR.

ésula, *f.* (bot.) leafy-branched spurge.

esviaje, *m.* (arch.) obliquity.

etalaje, *m.* bosh (of a blast furnace).

etapa, *f.* (mil.) ration given to troops in the field; stage; station, stop.

etcétera, etc., *f.* et cetera, etc., and so forth.

éter, *m.* (phys., chem.) ether; (poet.) the sky.

etéreo, rea, *a.* ethereal; (poet.) heavenly.

eterificación, *f.* (chem.) etherification.

eterificar, *va.* (chem.) to etherify, convert into ether.

eterismo, *m.* etherism, effect of excessive ether.

eterización, *f.* (med.) etherization.

eterizar, *va.* (med.) to etherize.

eternal, *a.* eternal.—**eternalmente,** *adv.* eternally; everlastingly.

eternamente, *adv.* = ETERNALMENTE.

eternicé, eternice, *v.* V. ETERNIZAR.

eternidad, *f.* eternity.

eternizar. I. *va.* (*pret.* ETERNICÉ; *subj.* ETERNICE) to eternize, perpetuate; to prolong indefinitely. **II.** *vr.* to be everlasting, (fig.) to be exceedingly slow, to stay forever.

eterno, na, *a.* eternal, everlasting.

eteromanía, *f.* ether addiction.

eterómano, na, *n.* ether addict.

etesio, *a.* (of winds) etesian, recurring yearly.

ética, *f.* ethics.

éticamente, *adv.* ethically.

¹**ético, ca. I.** *a.* ethical, moral. **II.** *n.* moralist.

²**ético, ca,** *a.* = HÉTICO, (med.) hectic, consumptive.

etileno, *m.* (chem.) ethylene.

etílico, ca, *a.* (chem.) ethylic.

etilo, *m.* (chem.) ethyl.

etimología, *f.* etymology.

etimológicamente, *adv.* etymologically.

etimológico, ca, *a.* etymological.

etimologista, *m.* etymologist.

etimologizar, *va.* to etymologize.

etimólogo, ga, *n.* etymologist.

etiología, *f.* (philos. and med.) etiology.

etíope; etiópico, ca; etiopio, a, *n. & a.* Ethiopian(-ic).

etiópide, *f.* (bot.) clary, Ethiopian mullein.

etiqueta, *f.* etiquette, ceremony, formality (com.) label.—**de e.,** ceremonious, formal.— **estar de e.,** to be distant, cool to each other.

etiquetero, ra, *a.* ceremonious, formal.

etiquez, *f.* = HETIQUEZ, (med.) consumption.

etites, *f.* (min.) eaglestone, ætites.

etmoides, *m.* (anat.) ethmoid.

etnarca, *m.* ethnarch.—**etnarquía,** *f.* ethnarchy

étnico, ca, ethnic.

etnografía, *f.* ethnography.

etnográfico, ca, *a.* ethnographic.

etnógrafo, *m.* ethnographer.

etnología, *f.* ethnology.

etnológico, ca, *a.* ethnologic.

etnólogo, m. Ethnologist.

etrusco, ca, *n. & a.* Etruscan.

eubeo, a; euboico, ca, *n. & a.* Eubœan, Euboic

eubolia, *f.* discretion in speech.

eucalipto, *m.* (bot.) eucalyptus.

eucaliptol, *m.* eucalyptus oil.

eucaristía, *f.* Eucharist.

eucarístico, ca, *a.* Eucharistic.

euclídeo, a; euclidiano, na, *a.* Euclidian.

eucologio, *m.* (eccl.) euchologion.

eucrasia, *f.* (med.) sound health.

eucrático, ca, *a.* (med.) in sound health.

eudiómetro, *m.* (chem.) eudiometer.

eufemismo, *m.* (rhet.) euphemism.

eufonía, *f.* euphony.

eufónico, ca, *a.* euphonic, euphonious.

euforbiáceo, a. I. *a.* (bot.) euphorbiaceous. **II.** *pl.* Euphorbiaceæ.

euforbio, *m.* (bot.) officinal spurge.

euforia, *f.* resistance to disease; (med.) euphoria feeling well, sense of good health.

eufótida, *f.* (geol.) euphotide.

eufrasia, *f.* (bot.) eyebright.

eugenesia, *f.* eugenics.

eugenol, *m.* (chem.) eugenol.

eunuco, *m.* eunuch.

eupatorio, *m.* (bot.) eupatorium.

eupepsia, *f.* eupepsy, good digestion.

eupéptico, ca, *n. & a.* digestive.

euritmia, *f.* (arch.) eurythmy.

eurítmico, ca, *a.* eurythmic.

euro, *m.* eurus, east wind.—**e. austro, or noto** (poet.) southeast wind.

europeizar, *va. & vn.* to Europeanize.

europeo, a, *n. & a.* European.

éuscaro, ra; éusquero, ra, *n. & a.* Basque Basque language.

éustilo, *m.* (arch.) eustyle.

eutanasia, *f.* euthanasia.

eutiquianismo, *m.* Eutychianism.

eutiquiano, na. *a.* Eutychian.

eutrapelia, eutropelia, *f.* moderation in pleasures; pastime, sport.

eutrapélico, ca; eutropélico, ca, *a.* moderate temperate.

evacuación, *f.* evacuation; exhaustion.

evacuante, *a.* evacuant, evacuating.

evacuar, *va.* to empty, evacuate; to quit, vacate leave.—**e. un negocio,** or **una diligencia,** t transact a business; to do an errand.

evacuativo, va; evacuatorio, a, *a.* evacuative

evadir. I. *va.* to evade, elude, avoid. **II.** *vr.* t escape, sneak away.

evaluación, *f.,* **evaluar,** *va.* = VALUACIÓN, etc

evangeliario, *m.* (eccl.) book of liturgies.

evangélicamente, *adv.* evangelically.

evangélico, ca, *a.* evangelical.

evangelio, *m.* gospel.—*pl.* gospel relic bookle worn by children around the neck.

evangelismo, *m.* evangelism.

evangelista, *m.* evangelist; gospel chanter.

evangelizador, ra, *n. & a.* evangelizer(-ing).

vangelizar, *va.* to evangelize.

vaporable, *a.* evaporable.

vaporación, *f.* evaporation.

vaporador, ra, *a. & n.* evaporating(-or).

vaporar, *va. & vr.* to evaporate.

vaporizar, *va. & vr.* (*pret.* EVAPORICÉ; *subj.* EVAPORICE) to vaporize.

vasión, *f.,* evasiva, *f.* evasion; escape.

vasivamente, *adv.* evasively.

vasivo, va, *a.* evasive, elusive.

vección, *f.* (astr.) evection.

vento, *m.* event, contingency.

ventración, *f.* (med.) ventral hernia.

ventual, *a.* contingent; fortuitous.—eventualidad, *f.* contingency.—eventualmente, *adv.* by chance, fortuitously.

versión, *f.* destruction, ruin.

vicción, *f.* eviction.

videncia, *f.* evidence, proof; obviousness.

videnciar, *va.* to prove, make evident.

vidente, *a.* evident.

videntemente, *adv.* evidently.

vitable, *a.* avoidable.

vitación, *f.* avoidance.

vitar, *va.* to avoid; to shun; to spare; to prevent.

viterno, na, *a.* imperishable, lasting.

vo, *m.* age, long time, æon; eternity.

vocación, *f.* evocation, evoking.

vocar, *va.* (*pret.* EVOQUÉ; *subj.* EVOQUE) to call out, evoke.

volución, *f.* evolution; change (of conduct, policy, etc.); (mil., naut.) evolution, manœuvre.

volucionar, *vn.* to change one's conduct, policy, etc., (mil., naut.) to perform evolutions or manœuvres; (biol., philos.) to evolve.

volucionismo, *m.* evolutionism.

volucionista. I. *a.* evolutionary, evolution (as *a.*). II. *n.* evolutionist.

volutivo, va, *a.* evolutionary, evolution (as *a.*).

voqué, evoque, *v. V.* EVOCAR.

x, *prep. prefix,* ex, out, out of, off; formerly.

x abrupto, *adv.* abruptly, violently.

xacción, *f.* exaction; impost, tax, levy.

xacerbación, *f.* exasperation; exacerbation.

xacerbar, *va.* to irritate, exasperate; exacerbate.

xactamente, *adv.* exactly.

xactitud, *f.* exactness; punctuality; accuracy.

xacto, ta, *a.* exact; correct; accurate; precise; punctual; assiduous.

xactor, *m.* tax collector.

xaedro, *m.* (geom.) hexahedron.

xageración, *f.* exaggeration.

xagerador, ra, *n. & a.* exaggerator(-ing).

xagerante, *a.* exaggerating.

xagerar, *va.* to exaggerate.

xagerativamente, *adv.* exaggeratively.

xagerativo, va, *a.* exaggerating.

xagonal, *a.* hexagonal.

xágono, na. I. *a.* hexagonal. II. *m.* hexagon.

xaltación, *f.* exaltation, elevation; (chem.) sublimation.

xaltado, da, *a.* hot-headed; ultra-radical.

xaltamiento, *m.* exaltation; ultra-radicalism.

xaltar. I. *va.* to exalt, elevate, lift; to praise, extol. II. *vr.* to become excited.

examen, *m.* examination; inquiry; interrogatory; inspection, investigation, search; survey.

exámetro, *m.* = HEXÁMETRO, hexameter.

examinador, ra, *n. & a.* examiner(-ing).

examinando, *m.* one going up for examination.

examinante, *a.* examining.

examinar. I. *va.* to examine; to question; to investigate, inspect, search. II. *vr.* to take (an) examination(s).

exangüe, *a.* exsanguine, anæmic; weak.

exanimación, *f.* lifelessness.

exánime, *a.* spiritless, weak, lifeless.

exantema, *f.* (med.) exanthema, an eruptive disease.

exantemático, ca, *a.* exanthematic.

exarca, *m.* exarch.—exarcado, *m.* exarchate.

exarco, *m.* = EXARCA.

exasperación, *f.* exasperation.

exasperador, ra; exasperante, *a.* exasperating.

exasperar, *va.* to exasperate.

excandecencia, *f.* anger, passion.

excandecer. I. *va.* (*ind.* EXCANDEZCO; *subj.* EXCANDEZCA) to irritate, provoke, enrage. II. *vr.* to become angry.

excarcelación, *f.* setting (a prisoner) free.

excarcelar, *va.* to set (a prisoner) free.

ex cáthedra, *adv.* ex cathedra.

excava, *f.* (agr.) pit around the root of a plant.

excavación, *f.* excavation.

excavar, *va.* to excavate.

excedente. I. *a.* exceeding. II. *m.* (com.) surplus.

exceder. I. *va.* to exceed, surpass; to overstep. II. *vr.* to go too far; to forget oneself; to overstep one's authority.

excelencia, *f.* excellence, superiority; excellency (title).—por e., par excellence.

excelente. I. *a.* excellent, first-rate.—*interj.* good! fine! II. *m.* Also e. de la granada, ancient Spanish gold coin.

excelentemente, *adv.* excellently.

excelentísimo, ma, *a. super.* most excellent.

excelsamente, *adv.* sublimely.

excelsitud, *f.* excelsitude, loftiness.

exceso, sa, *a.* elevated, sublime, lofty.—el E., the Most High.

excéntricamente, *adv.* eccentrically.

excentricidad, *f.* eccentricity.

excéntrico, ca. I. *a.* eccentric, eccentrical; odd, queer. II. *f.* (mech.) eccentric.

excepción, *f.* exception; (civil law) plea in defense, denying cause for action.

excepcional, *a.* exceptional, unusual.

excepcionalmente, *adv.* exceptionally.

excepcionar, *va.* (law) to deny the validity of or ground for (a legal action).

exceptivo, va, *a.* exceptive.

excepto, *adv.* excepting, except, with the exception of.

exceptuar, *va.* to except.

excerta, *f.* excerpt, extract, citation.

excesivamente, *adv.* excessively.

excesivo, va, *a.* excessive.

exceso, *m.* excess; (com.) surplus.—e. de equipaje, or de peso, baggage excess.—en e., in excess; excessively, to excess.

excipiente, *m.* (pharm.) excipient.

excitabilidad, *f.* excitability.

excitable, *a.* excitable.

excitación, *f.* excitation, exciting; excitement.

excitador, *m.* (elec.) exciter.

excitante, *a.* exciting, excitant.

excitar. I. *va.* to excite, move, stir up, rouse; (elec.) to excite, energize. II. *vr.* to become excited, lose one's equanimity.

excitativo, va, *a.* exciting, excitative.

excitatriz, *f.* (elec.) exciter, exciting dynamo.

exclamación, *f.* exclamation.

exclamar, *vn.* to exclaim.

exclamativo, va; torio, ria, *a.* exclamatory.

exclaustración, *f.* secularization of monks.

exclaustrado, *m.* secularized monk.

exclaustrar, *va.* to secularize (monks).

excluir, *va.* (*pp.* EXCLUIDO, EXCLUSO; *ind.* EXCLUYO; *subj.* EXCLUYA) to exclude; to bar, debar.

exclusión, *f.* exclusion, shutting out, debarring.

exclusiva, *f.* refusal; rejection, exclusion; sole right or agency.

exclusivamente, *adv.* exclusively.

exclusive, *adv.* exclusively; exclusive, excluded.

exclusivismo, *m.* exclusivism.

exclusivista, *n. & a.* exclusivist(-ic), (of persons) exclusive.

exclusivo, va, *a.* exclusive.

excluso, *pp. irreg.* of EXCLUIR.

excluyo, excluya, v. V. EXCLUIR.
excogitable, a. imaginable, reasonable.
excogitar, va. to excogitate, meditate; find, invent, devise.
excomulgado, da. I. pp. of EXCOMULGAR. II. a. & n. excommunicated (person); wicked, perverse (person).
excomulgador, ra, n. excommunicator.
excomulgar, va. (pret. EXCOMULGUÉ; subj. EY-COMULGUE) to excommunicate; to anathematize, curse.
excomunión, f. excommunication.—**e. mayor,** anathema.
excoriación, f. excoriation, flaying.
excoriar, va. & vr. to excoriate, flay; skin.
excrecencia, f. excrescence, excrescency.
excreción, f. excretion.
excremental, a. = EXCREMENTICIO.
excrementar, va. to evacuate (the bowels).
excrementicio, cia, a. pertaining to excrement or excretion.
excremento, m. excrement; excretion.
excrementoso, sa, a. excrementitious.
excretar, vn. to excrete; eject the excrements.
excreto, ta, a. excreted, ejected.
excretorio, ria, a. excretory, excretive.
excrex, m. (pl. excrez) (law) increase of dower.
exculpación, f. exculpation, exoneration.
exculpar, va. & vr. to exculpate, exonerate.
excursión, f. excursion, trip, tour; (law) excursion, liquidation.
excursionista, n. excursionist.
excusa, f. excuse.
excusabaraja, f. basket with a cover.
excusable, a. excusable.
excusadamente, adv. unnecessarily.
excusado, da. I. pp. of EXCUSAR. II. a. exempted, privileged; unnecessary; reserved, set apart. III. m. ancient privilege of exemption from the payment of tithes; washroom; toilet.
excusador, ra. I. a. excusing. II. n. excuser; substitute, vicar.
excusalí, m. small apron.
excusar. I. va. to excuse; to exempt; to prevent, avoid, shun; to decline, refuse. II. vr. to excuse oneself; to apologize.
excusión, f. (law) excussion, attachment.
execrable, a. execrable.—**execrablemente,** adv. execrably.
execración, f. execration.
execrador, ra, n. & a. execrater(-ing).
execrando, da, a. execrable.
execrar, va. to execrate.—**execratorio, ria,** a. execratory.
exedra, f. (arch.) exedra.
exégesis, f. exegesis.
exégeta, m. exegete.
exegético, ca, a. exegetic, explanatory.
exención, f. exemption.
exentado, da. I. pp. of EXENTAR. II. a. exempt.
exentamente, adv. freely; frankly, clearly, simply, sincerely.
exentar. I. va. to exempt; to excuse II. vr. to except oneself.
exento, ta. I. pp. irreg. of EXIMIR. II. a. exempt; free, freed, disengaged; clear, open, unobstructed. III. m. officer in the Spanish lifeguards.
exequátur, m. exequatur.
exequias, f. pl. exequies, obsequies.
exequible, a. attainable.
exéresis, f. (surg.) ablation, removal.
exergo, m. (numis.) exergue.
exfoliación, f. exfoliation, scaling or peeling off.
exfoliar. I. va. to exfoliate. II. vr. to scale off.
exhalación, f. exhalation; bolt of lightning; shooting star; fume, vapor, emanation.
exhalador, ra, n. & a. exhaler(-ing).
exhalar. I. va. to exhale, breathe forth, emit.

II. vr. to exhale, evaporate; to be exhausted by violent exercise.
exhausto, ta, a. exhausted.
exheredación, f. disinheritance.
exheredar, va. to disinherit.
exhibición, f. exhibition, exposition.
exhibir, vr. to exhibit, expose, display; to show.
exhortación, f. exhortation, admonition.
exhortador, ra, n. & a. exhorter(-ing).
exhortar, va. to exhort, admonish.
exhortatorio, ria, a. exhortatory.
exhorto, m. (law) letters requisitorial.
exhumación, f. exhumation, disinterment.
exhumar, va. to exhume, disinter, dig up.
exigencia, f. exigency; requirement; demand.
exigente, a. exacting.
exigible; exigidero, ra, a. exigible, requirable
exigir, va. (ind. EXIJO; subj. EXIJA) to require exact, demand; need; to urge.
exigüidad, f. exiguousness, scantiness, smallness.
exiguo, gua, a. exiguous, small, scanty.
exijo, exija, v. V. EXIGIR.
eximente, a. exempting.
eximio, mia, a. famous, most excellent.
eximir, va. (pp. irreg. EXENTO) to exempt, excuse, except.
exinanición, f. inanition; debility.
exinanido, da, a. debilitated, very weak.
existencia, f. existence; life, being.—pl. (com.) stock in hand, goods.—**en e.,** (com.) in stock
existente, a. existing, extant, existent; (com.) on hand, in stock.
existimación, f. estimation, opinion.
existimar, va. to form an opinion of, to judge
existir, vn. to exist, to be.
éxito, m. issue, result, end; (also **buen e.**) success
ex libris, (print.) ex libris.
Éxodo, m. Exodus; (é-) exodus, emigration.
exoneración, f. exoneration.
exonerar, va. to exonerate.
exorable, a. exorable, that can be persuaded.
exorar, va. to beg, entreat.
exorbitancia, f. exorbitance.
exorbitante, a. exorbitant, excessive.
exorbitantemente, adv. exorbitantly.
exorcismo, m. exorcism.
exorcista, n. exorciser, exorcist.
exorcizante, n. & a. exorciser(-ing).
exorcizar, va. to exorcise.
exordio, m. exordium, beginning.
exornación, f. (rhet.) making flowery.
exornar, va. to adorn, embellish.
exosmosis, f. (phys.) exosmosis.
exotérico, ca, a. exoteric, public, common.
exotérmico, ca, a. (chem.) exothermic, heat-evolving.
exótico, ca, a. exotic, foreign, extraneous.
expansibilidad, f. expansibility.
expansible, a. expansible.
expansión, f. expansion, extension.
expansivo, va, a. expansive; sociable, communicative.
expatriación, f. expatriation.
expatriar. I. va. to expatriate. II. vr. to emigrate leave one's country.
expectable, a. conspicuous, eminent.
expectación, f. expectation, expectancy.
expectante, a. expectant.
expectativa, f. expectation, expectancy, hope (law) expectancy, abeyance.
expectoración, f. expectoration; sputum.
expectorante, I. a. expectorating. II. m. (med.) expectorant.
expectorar, va. & vn. to expectorate.
expedición, f. expedition; despatch, speed, nim bleness, facility; (eccl.) pontifical brevet or bull (mil.) expedition; excursion, jaunt, journey.
expedicionario, ria, a. expeditionary.
expedicionero, m. expeditioner.

For pronunciation, see the rules at the beginning of the book.

pedidor, ra, *n.* (com.) forwarding merchant, agent, shipper, sender, despatcher.

pediente, *m.* (law) action, proceedings; file of papers bearing on a case; despatch, course of business; expedient, measure, resource, means to an end; facility in the management of affairs; reason, motive, pretext; supply, provision.—**cubrir el e.,** to pretend, make believe to be doing something; to keep up appearances; save one's face.

pedienteo, *m.* (law) procedure, taking action on the papers or documents in the case; (coll.) entangling and confusing matters; red tape.

pedir, *va.* (*ind.* EXPIDO; *subj.* EXPIDA) to expedite, facilitate; to issue; to draw out; to ship, send.

peditamente, *adv.* expeditiously, easily.

peditivo, va, *a.* expeditious, speedy, quick.

pedito, ta, *a.* prompt, expeditious, quick.

pelente, *a.* expellant, expelling.

peler, *va.* (*pp.* EXPELIDO, EXPULSO) to expel, eject, throw out.

pendedor, ra. I. *a.* spending. **II.** *n.* dealer, retailer, agent, seller; (law) distributor of counterfeit money.

pendeduría, *f.* shop where tobacco and other officially monopolized goods are sold.

pender, *va.* to expend, spend, lay out; to sell at retail, to deal in; (com.) to sell on commission; (law) to pass (counterfeit money or stolen goods).

pendición, *f.* retail selling; commission selling.

pendio, *m.* expense, outlay; consumption; (Am.) EXPENDICIÓN; (Am.) EXPENDEDURÍA.

pensar, *va.* (Am.) to defray the expense of.

pensas, *f. pl.* expenses, charges, costs.—**a. expensas de uno,** at one's expense.

periencia, *f.* experience; experiment, trial.

perimentado, da. I. of EXPERIMENTAR. **II.** *a.* (of person) experienced.

perimentador, ra, *n.* experimenter.

perimental, *a.* experimental.

perimentalmente, *adv.* experimentally.

perimentar, *va.* to experience; to experiment, test, try.

perimento, *m.* experiment, test, trial.

pertamente, *adv.* expertly.

perto, ta, *a.* & *a.* expert.

piación, *f.* expiation, atonement; purification.

piar, *va.* to expiate, atone for, make amends for; to purify.—**expiativo, va,** *a.* expiational.

piatorio, ria, *a.* expiatory.

pido, expida, *v.* V. EXPEDIR.

pillo, *m.* (bot.) = MATRICARIA, feverfew.

piración, *f.* expiration.

pirante, *a.* expiring.

pirar, *vn.* to expire, come to an end; to die.

planación, *f.* explanation, elucidation; (Ry.) roadbed.

planada, *f.* lawn; (fort.) esplanade, glacis; (artil.) platform.

planar, *va.* to level, grade; explain, elucidate.

playamiento, *m.* dilating, dwelling upon a subject; outing.

playar. I. *va.* to extend, dilate, enlarge. **II.** *vr.* to dwell upon a subject; to be extended; to enjoy an outing.

pletivo, va, *n.* & *a.* expletive.

plicable, *a.* explicable, explainable.

plicación, *f.* explanation.

plicaderas, *f. pl.* (coll.) facility in explaining.

plicar. I. *va.* (*pret.* EXPLIQUÉ; *subj.* EXPLIQUE) to explain, expound, construe. **II.** *vr.* to explain oneself; to understand (the reason, cause).

plicativo, va, *a.* explicative, explanatory.

plícitamente, *adv.* explicitly.

plícito, ta, *a.* explicit.

pliqué, explique, *v.* V. EXPLICAR.

ploración, *f.* exploration.

explorador, ra, *n.* & *a.* explorer(-ing); Boy Scout.

explorar, *va.* to explore; investigate, search into, examine; (mil.) to scout.

exploratorio, ria, *a.* exploratory, exploring.

explosión, *f.* explosion; outburst; (min.) blast.—**hacer e.,** (Am.) to explode.

explosivo, va, *n.* & *a.* explosive.

explosor, *m.* exploder; (radio) oscillator.

explotable, *a.* exploitable; (min.) workable.

explotación, *f.* exploitation; development, working (of a mine, etc.); plant, works; operation, running (of a factory, railroad,etc.).

explotador, ra, *n.* & *a.* exploiter(-ing).

explotar, *va.* to exploit; to work (a mine, etc.); to develop (mines, lands, etc.); to operate, run (a business, a railroad, etc.); to exploit (to one's own advantage); (Am.) to explode.

expoliación, *f.* spoliation.

expoliador, ra, *n.* & *a.* spoliator(-ing).

expoliar, *va.* to spoliate, despoil.

exponencial, *f.* & *a.* (math.) exponential.

exponente. I. *n.* & *a.* exponent. **II.** *m.* (math.) exponent.—**e. de un átomo,** atomic number.

exponer. I. *va.* (*pp.* EXPUESTO; *ind. pres.* EXPONGO, *pret.* EXPUSE, *fut.* EXPONDRÉ; *subj.* EXPONGA) to expose, show, lay bare; to expound, explain; to expose, put in danger, jeopardize; to expose, abandon (a child). **II.** *vr.* to run a risk, lay oneself open to.

exportable, *a.* exportable.

exportación, *f.* exportation, export.—**de e.,** export (as a *a.*, as in *derechos de exportación,* export duties).

exportador, ra, *n.* & *a.* exporter(-ing).

exportar, *va.* to export.

exposición, *f.* exposition, statement; peril, risk, jeopardy; petition, claim; exposition, exhibition, fair; (drama) exposition; (arch.) situation, orientation.

expositivo, va, *a.* explanatory, expositive.

expósito, ta, *n.* & *a.* foundling.

expositor, ra, *n.* & *a.* expounder(-ing), exponent; exhibitor(-ing).

expremijo, *m.* cheese vat.

exprés. (Am. esp. Mex.) **I.** *n.* & *a.* express (train, etc.). **II.** *m.* transport company or office.

expresado, da, *a.* before-mentioned, aforesaid.

expresamente, *adv.* expressly; clearly.

expresar. I. *va.* (*pp.* EXPRESADO, EXPRESO) to express, state, tell; (art) to delineate, design. **II.** *vr.* to express oneself; to speak.

expresión, *f.* expression; declaration, statement; form; phrase, utterance; present, gift; expression, squeezing, pressing out (of oils, etc.).—*pl.* regards.

expresivamente, *adv.* expressively.

expresivo, va, *a.* expressive; affectionate, kind.

expreso, sa. I. *pp. irreg.* of EXPRESAR. **II.** *a.* expressed; express, clear; express, fast (train, etc.). **III.** *m.* express (train).

exprimidera, *f.,* **exprimidero,** *m.,* squeezer.

exprimido, da, *pp.* & *a.* squeezed; dry.

exprimir, *va.* to squeeze, press out; to express (one's thoughts) vividly.

ex profeso, *adv.* on purpose, expressly.

expropiación, *f.* expropriation.

expropiar, *va.* to expropriate.

expuesto, ta. I. *pp. irreg.* of EXPONER. **II.** *a.* on display; exposed, liable; dangerous; in danger.

expugnable, *a.* (mil.) pregnable.

expugnación, *f.* (mil.) taking by storm.

expugnador, ra, *n.* & *a.* (mil.) (one) that takes by storm.

expugnar, *va.* (mil.) to take by storm.

expulsar, *va.* (*pp.* EXPULSADO, EXPULSO) (gen. of people) to expel, eject, drive out.

expulsión, *f.* expulsion, expelling, ejection.

expulsivo, va, *a.* expelling.

¹**expulso, sa,** *pp. irreg.* of EXPELER.

²**expulso, sa,** *pp. irreg.* of EXPULSAR.

expulsor, ra, *n. & a.* expeller(-ing), ejector(-ing).

expurgación, *f.* expurgation; (coll.) purge (of people).

expurgar, *va.* (*pret.* EXPURGUÉ; *subj.* EXPURGUE) to expurgate, expunge, purge, purify.

expurgatorio, ria, *a.* expurgatory.—**índice e.,** (Rom. Cath.) Index Expurgatorius.

expurgo, *m.* expurgation, purification.

expuse, *pret.* of EXPONER.

exquisitamente, *adv.* exquisitely.

exquisito, ta, *a.* exquisite, delicious.

éxtasi, éxtasis, *m.* ecstasy.—**extasiar,** *va. & vr.* to delight; to enrapture.

extático, ca, *a.* ecstatic.

extemporal; extemporáneo, a, *a.* untimely, inopportune.—**extemporáneamente,** *adv.* untimely, inopportunely.

extender. I. *va. & vr.* (*pp.* EXTENDIDO, EXTENSO; *ind.* EXTIENDO; *subj.* EXTIENDA) to extend, enlarge, prolong, spread, expand, outstretch; to unfold, unfurl; to draw up or issue (a document); (com.) to extend, prolong. **II.** *vr.* to extend, reach; to stretch out; to enlarge upon, expatiate; to spread, become general or popular.

extendidamente, *adv.* extensively.

extensamente, *adv.* extensively.

extensión, *f.* extension; extent, length; expanse; space, capacity; (logic, Mex. tel.) extension.

extensivamente, *adv.* by extension.

extensivo, va, *a.* ample.

extenso, sa. I. *pp. irreg.* of EXTENDER. **II.** *a.* extended, extensive, spacious; general, widely spread.—**por e.,** at length, with full particulars.

extensor, ra. I. *a.* extending. **II.** *m.* (anat.) extensor.

extenuación, *f.* attenuation; emaciation.

extenuado, da, *a.* emaciated, wasted.

extenuar. I. *va.* to emaciate, weaken. **II.** *vr.* to languish, waste away.

extenuativo, va, *a.* weakening, emaciating.

exterior. I. *a.* exterior; external, outside, outward; foreign (commerce, debt, etc.).—**lo e.,** the outside; outside things or matters; foreign affairs. **II.** *m.* outside; personal appearance; foreign countries.—**exterioridad,** *f.* exterior or outside thing; outward appearance; demeanor; show, pomp.

exteriorizar. I. *va.* to externalize, make manifest. **II.** *vr.* to unbosom oneself.

exteriormente, *adv.* externally, outwardly.

exterminador, ra, *n. & a.* exterminator(-ing).

exterminar, *va.* to exterminate; to raze.

exterminio, *m.* extermination, ruin, destruction.

externado, *m.* day-student school or college.

externamente, *adv.* externally.

externo, na. I. *a.* external, outward; exterior (angle, etc.). **II.** *n.* day pupil.

ex testamento, by will or testament.

extiendo, extienda, *v. V.* EXTENDER.

extinción, *f.* extinction; extinguishment; suppression, abolition; obliteration.

extingo, extinga, *v. V.* EXTINGUIR.

extinguible, *a.* extinguishable.

extinguir, *va.* (*pp.* EXTINGUIDO, EXTINTO; *ind.* EXTINGO; *subj.* EXTINGA) to quench, extinguish, put out; to suppress, destroy.

extintivo, va, *a.* (law) extinguishing.

extinto, ta. I. *pp. irreg.* of EXTINGUIR. **II.** *a.* extinct.

extintor, *m.* fire extinguisher.

extirpación, *f.* extirpation, eradication.

extirpador, ra. I. *n. & a.* extirpator(-ing). **II.** *m.* (agr.) cultivator.

extirpar, *va.* to extirpate, root out, eradicate.

extorsión, *f.* extortion; overcharge.

extra, *n. & a.* (coll.) extra.—**e. de,** besides, in addition to.

extracción, *f.* extraction; lineage (gen. low, hu⟨ble); drawing numbers in the lottery.

extracta, *f.* (law) true copy, extract.

extractador, ra, *n.* abstractor.

extractar, *va.* to abstract, epitomize, abridge

extracto, *m.* abstract, summary; (pharm.) tract.—**e. de saturno,** white lead.

extractor, ra, *n. & a.* extractor(-ing).

extradición, *f.* extradition.

extradós, *m.* (arch.) extrados.

extraente, *n. & a.* extractor(-ing).

extraer, *va.* (*ger.* EXTRAYENDO; *pp.* EXTRAÍ⟨ *ind. pres.* EXTRAIGO, *pret.* EXTRAJE; *subj.* ⟨ TRAIGA) to extract, draw out, remove; (mat⟨ to extract (a root); (law) to take a copy (chem.) to extract.

extraigo, extraje, etc., *v. V.* EXTRAER.

extrajudicial, *a.* extrajudicial.

extrajudicialmente, *adv.* extrajudicially.

extralimitarse, *vr.* to overstep one's authorit⟨ to take advantage of another's kindness.

extramuros, *adv.* outside (a town), without.

extranjería, *f.* status of a foreigner.

extranjerismo, *m.* foreignism.

extranjerizar. I. *vn.* to introduce foreign c⟨ toms. **II.** *vr.* to act like a foreigner, adopt f⟨ eign ways.

extranjero, ra, *a. & n.* foreign(-er), alien.—**el⟨** foreign countries, abroad.—**estar en el e.,** be abroad.—**irse al e.,** to go abroad.

extranjía, *f.* (coll.) = EXTRANJERÍA.

extranjis,—**de e.,** (coll.) foreign; strange, ⟨ expected.

extrañación, *f.,* **extrañamiento,** *m.* alienati⟨ expulsion, exile; emigration.

extrañamente, *adv.* strangely.

extrañar, *va.* to banish; to cut, ignore (a perso⟨ to estrange; to wonder at, find strange; to m⟨

extrañeza, *f.* oddity, queerness; surprise, wond⟨ ment; estrangement.

extraño, ña. I. *a.* strange; foreign; extraneo⟨ **II.** *n.* stranger; foreigner.

extraoficial, *a.* extraofficial, non-official.

extraordinariamente, *adv.* extraordinarily.

extraordinario, a. I. *a.* extraordinary. **II.** extra dish at dinner; special courier.

extraterritorial, *a.* extraterritorial.

extraterritorialidad, *f.* extraterritoriality.

extravagancia, *f.* oddness; folly; freak.

extravagante. I. *a.* eccentric; unusual, qu⟨ odd, grotesque. **II.** *f. pl.* (eccl.) extravagan⟨

extravagantemente, oddly, grotesquely.

extravasación, *f.* (med.) extravasation.

extravasarse, *vr.* to extravasate, exude.

extravenarse, *vr.* to exude through the veins.

extraviado, da. I. *pp.* of EXTRAVIAR. **II.** *a.* ⟨ orderly; (of places) unfrequented.

extraviar. I. *va.* to mislead, misguide; to m⟨ place, mislay; to embezzle. **II.** *vr.* to go astr⟨ to be off course; to miscarry (as a letter); deviate, to err.

extravío, *m.* deviation; aberration; misconduᵉ misplacement.

extremadamente, *adv.* extremely.

extremadas, *f. pl.* time for making cheese.

extremado, da. I. *pp.* of EXTREMAR. **II.** *a.* treme; consummate (in good or bad).

extremamente, *adv.* extremely, exceedingly.

extremar. I. *va.* to carry to an extreme. **II.** to exert oneself to the utmost, take spec⟨ pains.

extremaunción, *f.* (eccl.) extreme unction.

extremeño, ña, *a.* Estremenian.

extremidad, *f.* extremity; end; edge, bri⟨ border, brim; extreme or remotest part; (an⟨ extremity.

extremista, *n. & a.* extremist.

extremo, ma. I. *a.* extreme, last, terminal; f⟨ thest; greatest, of the highest degree, utmᵉ **II.** *m.* extreme, utmost point, highest degr⟨

---

apex; furthest end, extremity; greatest care.—**con e.**, extremely, in the utmost degree.—**de e. a e.**, from one end to the other.—**en e. = con e.**—**hacer extremos**, to express one's feelings with vehemence, to gush.—**por e.** or **por todo e. = con e.**

extremoso, sa, *a.* extreme, vehement; very affectionate.

extrínsecamente, *adv.* extrinsically.

extrínseco, ca, *a.* extrinsic.

exuberancia, *f.* overabundance.

exuberante, *a.* overabundant, luxuriant.

exudación, *f.* exudation.

exudar, *vn. & va.* to exude; to ooze out.

exulceración, *f.* (med.) exulceration.

exulcerar. I. *va.* (med.) to exulcerate, ulcerate. **II.** *vr.* to become ulcerated.

exultación, *f.* exultation, great joy.

exutorio, *m.* (med.) exutory, issue.

exvoto, *m.* votive offering.

eyaculación, *f.* ejection, forcing out.

eyacular, *va.* to eject.

eyector, *m.* ejector (in fire arms).

F

fa, *m.* (mus.) fa, F.

fabada, *f.* in Asturias, pork and beans.

fábrica, *f.* fabrication; structure, building, pile; factory, works, mill, manufactory; stone or brick masonry; church funds (esp. for building repairs).

fabricación, *f.* manufacturing; manufacture, make.

fabricador, ra, *n. & a.* fabricator(ing), schemer (ing).

fabricante, *n. & a.* maker(-ing), manufacturer (-ing).

fabricar, *va.* (*pret.* FABRIQUÉ; *subj.* FABRIQUE) to build, construct, frame; to manufacture, make; to fabricate, contrive, devise.

fabril, *a.* manufacturing.

fabriqué, fabrique, *v. V.* FABRICAR.

fabriquero, ra, *n.* manufacturer; church warden.

fabuco, *m.* (bot.) beech mast.

fábula, *f.* fable, fiction, legend, tale; rumor, report, common talk; story, falsehood.—**f. milesia,** Milesian tale.

fabulador, *m.* fabulist, author of fables.

fabulilla, ita, *f. dim.* little fable.

fabulista, *n.* fabulist, writer of fables.

fabulosamente, *adv.* fabulously.

fabuloso, sa, *a.* fabulous; marvellous.

faca, *f.* jackknife used by seamen.

facción, *f.* faction, turbulent party; (mil.) battle; any act of military service.—*pl.* features, lineaments, physiognomy.—**f. de testamento,** (law) faculty of testating.

faccionario, ria, *a.* factional, partisan.

faccioso, sa. I. *a.* factious. **II.** *n.* rebel.

facer, *va.* (obs.) = HACER, to do; to make.

faceta, *f.* (jewel) facet of a gem.

facetada, *f.* (Mex.) flat or poor joke.

facial, *a.* facial; intuitive.

facialmente, *adv.* intuitively.

facies, *f.* (med. & biol.) facies, characteristic appearance.

fácil, *a.* easy, convenient; probable, likely; pliant, docile, handy; easily pursuaded or seduced.—**f. de** (followed by *inf.*), easy to.

facilidad, *f.* ease, easiness, facility; ready compliance, convenience; opportunity.—*pl.*—**dar f.**, to facilitate.

facilillo, illa, ito, ita, *a. dim.* rather easy.

facilitación, *f.* facilitation.

facilitar, *va.* to facilitate, expedite; to supply, deliver, afford.

facilitón, na, *n.* (coll.) one who assumes the position of making everything easy.

fácilmente, *adv.* easily, without difficulty.

facineroso, sa. I. *a.* wicked, villainous. **II.** *n.* habitual criminal; villain, rascal.

facistol, *m.* chorister's desk; lectern.

facóquero, ra, *n.* wart hog.

facsímil, facsímile, *m.* facsimile.

factible, *a.* feasible, practicable.

facticio, cia, *a.* factitious, artificial.

factor, *m.* factor, element, cause; (com.) factor, agent, commissioner; (mil.) victualler; (Ry.) baggagemaster; (math.) factor.

factoraje, *m.* agency; trading in a foreign country; entrepôt.

factoría, *f.* (Mex.) factory; FACTORAJE.

factorial, *n.* (math.) factorial.

factótum, *m.* factotum, man of all work; busybody.

factura, *f.* (com.) invoice, bill; (art) handling.—**f. consular,** consular invoice.—**f. simulada, proforma,** invoice.

facturar, *va.* (com.) to invoice, to bill; (Ry.) to check (baggage).

fácula, *f.* (astr.) facula.

facultad, *f.* faculty; power, authority; science, art; (in a university) branch, school (as *facultad de derecho,* Law School); graduates (collect.); (med.) physiological power or ability; license, permission.—*pl.* fortune, wealth.—**facultades del alma,** mental faculties or powers.

facultar, *va.* to empower, authorize.

facultativamente, *adv.* facultatively.

facultativo, va. I. *a.* facultative; optional; pertaining to a faculty. **II.** *n.* physician.

facundia, *f.* facundity, eloquence.

facundo, da, *a.* eloquent, fluent.

facha, *f.* (coll.) appearance, look, mien, face.—**f. a f.**, face to face.—**en f.** (naut.) lying to.

fachada, *f.* (arch.) façade; frontispiece of a book; (coll.) figure, build (of a person).—**hacer f. a,** to face, be in front of.

fachenda. I. *f.* (coll.) vanity, conceit. **II.** *n.* (coll.) vain, conceited person.

fachendear, *vn.* (coll.) to brag, boast.

fachendista, dón, na, doso, sa, *a.* conceited, vain, bluffing.

fachoso, sa, *a.* ill-favored, of ridiculous mien; (Mex.) conceited, bluffing.

fada, *f.* fairy, enchantress, witch; (bot.) small pippin apple.

faena, *f.* work, labor, task, toil; (Cuba, Guat., Mex.) extra or overtime work; (Chile) [gang of workers; (Ecua.) morning work (in the country).—*pl.* business affairs.

faenero, ra, *n.* (Am.) farm hand.

faetón, *m.* phaeton.

fagocito, *m.* (biol.) phagocyte.

fagot, *m.* (mus.) bassoon, fagotto.

faisán, na, *n.* (ornith.) pheasant.

faja, *f.* band, bandage, roller, fillet; swathing band; sash; girdle; border; (geog.) zone; newspaper wrapper; (arch.) fascia, belt, fillet; (naut.) reef band.—**f. de desgarre,** (aer.) rip (-ping) panel, or strip.

fajadura, *f.* swathing, swaddling; (naut.) band round a rope.

fajamiento, *m.* rolling or swathing.

fajar, *va.* to swathe, swaddle; to band, belt, girdle.—**f. con,** (coll.) to fall on, to attack.

fajardo, *m.* meat pie, patty; vol-au-vent.

fajeado, da, *a.* banded, fasciated.

fajero, *m.* crochet swaddling band.

fajín, *m. dim.* small band or sash; general's sash.

fajina, *f.* toil, task, work; (agr.) shock, stook, rick of sheaves; fagot of brushwood; (mil.) bugle call; (fort.) fascine.

fajinada, *f.* (fort.) fascine work or revetment.

fajo, *m.* bundle; sheaf.—*pl.* swaddling clothes.

fajón, *m. aug.* large band, roller, or sash; plaster border.

fajuela, *f. dim.* small bandage or roller.

falacia, *f.* deceit; deceitfulness; perfidy.

falange, *f.* (mil. & anat.) phalanx.—*pl.* phalanges.

falangeta, *f.* (anat.) third phalanx.

falangia, *f.,* **falangio,** *m.* (entom.) phalangium, or daddy longlegs.

falangiano, na, *a.* (anat.) phalangeal.

falangio, *m.* *V.* FALANGIA.

falansterio, *m.* a kind of community.

falárica, *f.* phalaric, fire dart.

fálaris, *f.* (ornith.) coot, scoter.

falaz, *a.* deceitful, treacherous.

falazmente, *adv.* deceitfully, treacherously.

falbalá, *m.* flounce, furbelow; flap on the skirt of a coat.

falca, *f.* small wedge; (naut.) washboard.

falcado, da. I. *a.* hooked, falcated. **II.** *m.* scythed chariot.

falcario, *m.* soldier armed with a falchion.

falce, *f.* sickle, reaping hook; falchion.

falcidia, *f.* (law) Falcidian.

falcinelo, *m.* (ornith.) glossy ibis.

falcón, *m.* ancient small cannon; (ornith.) falcon.

falconete, *m.* falconet, small cannon.

falcónido, da. I. *a.* (zool.) belonging to the falcon family. **II.** *m.* *pl.* Falconidæ.

falda, *f.* skirt, flap; the lap; incline, slope; loin (of beef, etc.); tasset, tuilles, in armor.—*pl.* (fig.) skirts, women.

faldamenta, faldamento, *m.* skirt.

faldar, *m.* tasset, tuille, in armor.

faldear, *va.* to skirt (a hill).

faldellín, *m.* overskirt; underskirt.

falderillo, illa, *a. dim.* little lap dog.

faldero, ra, *a.* pertaining to the lap; fond of women.

faldeta, *f. dim.* small skirt; covering cloth or canvas.

faldicorto, ta, *a.* having short skirts.

faldillas, *f. dim. pl.* skirts; coat tails.

faldistorio, *m.* bishop's stool.

faldón, *m. aug.* long flowing skirt, flap; coat tail; shirt tail; hanging drapery; flap of a saddle; top millstone; (arch.) gable; tympanum.

faldriquera, *f.* pocket.

falencia, *f.* misstatement, mistake.

falibilidad, *f.* fallibility.

falible, *a.* fallible.

falimiento, *m.* untruth, deceit, falsehood.

falo, *m.* (anat. & bot.) phallus.

falordía, *f.* story, fairy tale, fable.

falsa, *f.* garret; FALSILLA; (mus.) dissonance.

falsaamarra, *f.* (naut.) preventer rope.

falsabraga, *f.* (fort.) low rampart.

falsada, *f.* irregular flight of birds.

falsamente, *adv.* falsely, untruly.

falsario, ria. I. *a.* falsifying, forging, counterfeiting. **II.** *n.* forger, counterfeiter, falsifier.

falsarregla, *f.* bevel square, bevel rule.

falseador, ra, *n.* forger, counterfeiter, falsifier.

falsear. I. *va.* to adulterate, counterfeit, falsify, forge; to pierce; (carp.) to bevel.—**f. la puerta,** (Am.) to open the door with a skeleton key or break the lock. **II.** *vn.* to slacken; (mus.) (of a string) to be false, out of tune.

falsedad, *f.* falsehood, lie; deceit, guile; perfidy, duplicity.

falseo, *m.* (mason. and carp.) bevelling.

falsete, *m.* spigot; small door; (mus.) falsetto voice.

falsía, *f.* = FALSEDAD.

falsificación, *f.* falsification, forgery.

falsificador, ra, *n.* falsifier, counterfeiter, forger.

falsificar, *va.* (*pret.* FALSIFIQUÉ; *subj.* FALSIFIQUE) to falsify, counterfeit, forge, adulterate.

falsilla, *f.* guide lines for writing.

falsío, *m.* (cook.) a kind of stuffing.

falso, sa. I. *a.* false, untrue; incorrect; deceitful, dishonest; spurious, forged, counterfeit; sham, imitation (e.g. jewels); vicious (horses or mules); defective, false (weights or honeycombs); (mech.) temporary; unsubstantial.—**f. flete,** dead freight.—**f. posición,** (arith.) position (an old method of solution).—**f. testimonio,** false testimony; slander, libel; imposture.—**de f., en f.,** deceitfully, falsely; without proper safety or strength (in this sense, **sobre falso** also used). **II.** *m.* (sewing) facing, skirt binding.

falta, *f.* lack, want, absence, deficiency, shortage; fault, mistake; defect, flaw; fault, failing, shortcoming; offense, misdeed, misbehavior, misdemeanor; deficiency in the weight of coin; (law) default; (med.) stoppage of the catamenia in pregnant women.—**f. de aceptación, de pago,** (com.) nonacceptance, nonpayment.—**a f. de,** in want of; for lack of.—**hacer f.** to be necessary; to be missing; to be missed (diff. constr.: *Vd. me hace mucha falta,* I miss you very much.).—**poner faltas a,** to find fault with.—**sin f.,** without fail; without fault.

faltante, *a.* wanting, lacking.

faltar, *vn.* to be wanting, lacking; to be needed; to fall short; to fail, falter, flinch; not to fulfil one's promise, not to perform one's engagement; to need, lack, be in want of (diff. constr.: *me faltan dos pesos,* I lack, *or* need, *or* am short, two dollars); to offend; to sin; to be absent *or* missing; to die; (naut.) to break, part, give way.—**f. a.,** to offend against, to break (an appointment, etc.); to be absent from; to be unfaithful to.—**f. a la verdad,** to speak untruthfully, to lie.—**f. al respeto a,** to treat disrespectfully.—**f. para** (used impersonally), to be lacking to (or for), to be . . . to (*falta un cuarto para las dos,* it is a quarter to two; *falta una semana para vencerse la letra,* it lacks a week for the draft to be due).—**f. poco para,** not to be long before; come near (diff. constr.: *falta poco para terminar,* it will not be long before the end; *poco faltó para que la matasen,* she came near being killed).—**¡no faltaba más!** (coll.) that is the limit! that's the last straw! the idea! of course!

falto, ta, *a.* devoid; short; deficient, defective.

faltrero, ra, *n.* pickpocket, petty thief.

faltriquera, *f.* pocket.

falúa, *f.* (naut.) small boat, tender.

falucho, *m.* (naut.) felucca, lateener.

¹falla, *f.* a sort of head covering.

²falla, *f.* fault, failure; (P. I.) fine paid by Indians for leaving work; (naut.) defect, deficiency; (geol.) fault, break, slide.

¹fallar, *va.* (law) to pass sentence, render a verdict on.

²fallar. I. *va.* to ruff (at cards). **II.** *vn.* to fail, be deficient or wanting.

falleba, *f.* shutter bolt.

fallecer, *vn.* (*ind.* FALLEZCO; *subj.* FALLEZCA) to die; to fail, run out, expire.

fallecimiento, *m.* decease, death, demise.

fallezco, fallezca, *v.* *V.* FALLECER.

fallido, da. I. *a.* deceived, disappointed, frustrated. **II.** *a.* & *n.* (com.) bankrupt.

¹fallo, *m.* (law) verdict, judgment, decision.

²fallo, lla. I. *a.* (at cards) lacking a card of the suit played. **II.** *m.* lack of a card of suit played.

fama, *f.* fame; report, rumor; reputation.—**es f.,** it is said.

famélico, ca, *a.* hungry, ravenous.

familia, *f.* family; household.

familiar. I. *a.* familiar; domestic; common, frequent; plain, homelike, unceremonious. **II.** *m.* domestic member of the household; servant, especially of the clergy; college servitor; bosom friend; relative; officer of the Inquisition; demon, familiar spirit.—*pl.* attendants, suite.

familiaricé, familiarice, *v.* *V.* FAMILIARIZAR.

familiaridad, *f.* familiarity.

familiarizar. I. *va.* (*pret.* FAMILIARICÉ; *subj.* FAMILIARICE) to make well known, to make popular; familiarize. **II.** *vr.* to accustom, habituate oneself; to become familiar.

amiliarmente, *adv.* familiarly.

amilión, *m. aug.* large family.

amosamente, *adv.* famously.

amoso, sa, *a.* famous; (coll.) great, excellent.

ámula, *f.* (coll.) maidservant.

amular, *a.* domestic (servant).

amulato, famulicio, *m.* (servant's) occupation.

ámulo, *m.* famulus; (coll.) servant.

anal, *m.* lighthouse; lantern; bel` glass; candle screen.—**buque f.,** lightship.

anáticamente, *adv.* fanatically.

anático, ca, *n. & a.* fanatic; (sports) fan.

anatismo, *m.* fanaticism.

anatizador, ra, *n.* one who spreads fanaticism.

anatizar, *va.* to make fanatical.

andango, *m.* fandango; (coll.) row, brawl.

andanguero, ra, *a.* frequenter of balls.

aneca, *f.* (ichth.) pout, whiting pout.

anega, *f.* grain measure (about 1.60 bu.).—**f. de cacao,** 116 lbs. of cocoa.—**f. de sembradura,** ground necessary to sow a FANEGA of seed.—**f. de tierra,** a land measure (about 1.59 acres).

anegada, *f.* = FANEGA DE TIERRA.—**a fanegadas,** in great plenty or abundance.

anerógamo, ma, *a.* (bot.) flowering.

anfarrear, *vn.* to bully, brag, swagger.

anfarria, *f.* (coll.) swagger, bluster.

anfarrón, na, *n.* (coll.) blusterer, swaggerer, braggart; boaster, bully.

anfarronada, *f.* fanfaronade, boast, brag, bluff.

anfarronear, *vn.* to brag, boast.

anfarronería, *f.* fanfaronade, bragging.

anfarronesca, *f.* swagger, fanfaronading.

anfurriña, *f.* (coll.) fit of the sulks.

angal, fangar, *m.* slough, marsh, quagmire.

ango, *m.* mire, mud.—**fangoso, sa,** *a.* muddy, miry.

antasear, *vn.* to fancy, to imagine.

antasía, *f.* fantasy, fancy, imagination; caprice, whim, conceit; (coll.) vanity, conceit; (naut.) dead reckoning; (mus.) fantasia.—*pl.* string of pearls.

antasioso, sa, *a.* (coll.) conceited, vain.

antasma. I. *m.* phantom, ghost, apparition; vain, conceited person. **II.** *f.* scarecrow.

antasmagoría, *f.* phantasmagoria.

antasmagórico, ca, *a.* phantasmagoric.

antasmón, na. I. *a. aug.* (coll.) enormously conceited. **II.** *m.* presumptuous coxcomb.

antásticamente, *adv.* fantastically.

antástico, ca, *a.* fantastic, fanciful; conceited.

antoche, *m.* puppet; insignificant man.

añado, da, *a.* one year old.

aquín, *m.* porter, carrier, laborer.

aquir, *m.* fakir.

ara, *f.* (zool.) an African serpent.

arachar, *va.* to beat (hemp).

arad, faradio, *m.* (elec.) farad.

aradización, *f.* (med.) faradization.

aradizar, *va.* (med.) to treat with electricity.

aralá, *m.* flounce, ruffle, frill.

arallón, *m.* headland; cliff.

aramalla. I. *f.* (coll.) cajolery; (Chile) conceit, airs; trash, worthless thing. **II.** *n.* (coll.) cajoler. —**faramallero, ra, llón, na,** *n.* (coll.) cajoling tattler.

arandola, *f.* farandole (a dance).

arándula, *f.* profession of a low comedian; strolling troupe of players; (coll.) cajolement; show, conceit, ostentation.

arandulero, ra, *n.* comedian, player; (coll.) cajoler; boaster, vain person.

arandúlico, ca, *a.* pert. to strolling players.

araón, *m.* Pharoah; (f-), faro (card game).

araónico, ca, *a.* Pharaonic.

araute, *n.* trusted messenger; player who recites the prologue; (coll.) meddling person, busybody, butter-in.

¹farda, *f.* ancient tax.

²farda, *f.* bundle of clothing.

³farda, *f.* (carp.) notch.

fardacho, *m.* (zool.) lizard.

fardaje, *m.* fardage, dunnage.

fardar, *va.* to furnish or supply with clothes.

fardel, *m.* bag, knapsack; parcel, bundle.

fardelillo, lejo, *m. dim.* small bundle.

fardería, *f.* collection of packages, luggage.

fardo, *m.* bale, parcel, bundle; burden, load.

farellón, *m.* rocky headland, cliff.

farfalá, *f.* flounce, furbelow.

farfalloso, sa, *n. & a.* stutterer(-ing).

farfante; farfantón, na, *n.* (coll.) boasting babbler.

farfantonada, farfantonería, *f.* idle boast.

fárfara, *f.* (bot.) colt's-foot; shell membrane (of an egg).—**en f.,** immature, as an egg without a shell; unfinished, half done.

farfulla. I. *f.* (coll.) gibberish, gabble, jabber. **II.** *n.* (coll.) jabberer, gabbler.

farfulladamente, *adv.* hurriedly and recklessly.

farfullador, ra, *n. & a.* (coll.) jabberer(-ing).

farfullar, *vn.* (coll.) to gabble, to jabber, to gibber; (coll.) to act hurriedly.

farfullero, ra, *n.* gabbler, jabberer.

fargallón, na. I. *n.* (coll.) bungler, botcher. **II.** *a.* slovenly, untidy.

farillón, *m.* = FARALLÓN, headland, cliff.

farináceo, cea, *a.* farinaceous.

farinetas, *f. pl.* (prov.) porridge.

faringe, *f.* (anat.) pharynx.—**faríngeo, a,** *a.* pharyngeal.—**faringitis,** *f.* pharyngitis.

farisaicamente, *adv.* pharisaically.

farisaico, ca, *a.* pharisaical, pharisaic.

farisaísmo, fariseísmo, *m.* pharisaism.

fariseo, *m.* Pharisee; hypocrite; (coll.) tall, lean, ugly person.

farmacéutico, ca. I. *a.* pharmaceutical. **II.** *m.* pharmacist, apothecary, druggist.

farmacia, *f.* pharmacy; drugstore, apothecary's.

farmacología, *f.* pharmacology.

farmacológico, ca, *a.* pharmacological.

farmacopea, *f.* pharmacopœia.

farmacópola, *n.* apothecary, pharmacist, druggist, chemist.

farmacopólico, ca, *a.* pharmaceutical.

faro, *m.* lighthouse; beacon; (auto) light, headlight.

farol, *m.* lantern, light; street lamp; conceited fellow; bluff, misleading.—**echar un f.,** to bluff.—**faroles de señales,** (naut.) signal lanterns.

farola, *f.* street light with several arms; big lantern; lighthouse.

farolear, *vn.* (coll.) to boast, brag.

faroleo, farolería, *f.* boast, bragging, show.

farolero, ra, *n.* lantern maker or seller; lamplighter; (coll.) strutting coxcomb.

farolico, ito, illo, *m. dim.* small lantern.

farolillo de jardín, (bot.) Indian heartseed.

farolón, *n. & a.* boaster(-ing), braggart(-ing); (coll.) coxcomb, boaster; large lantern.

farota, *f.* brazen-faced woman.

farotón, na, *a.* (coll.) brazen-faced, cheeky.

farpa, *f.* pointed scallop on the edge of draperies.

farpado, da, *a.* scalloped, notched.

¹farra, *f.* (ichth.) a kind of salmon.

²farra, *f.* (Arg., Bol., Chile) spree.

fárrago, farrago, *m.* farrago, medley.

farragoso, sa, *a.* full of confused ideas; full of confusion.

farraguista, *n.* person having the head full of confused ideas or half-digested knowledge.

farro, *m.* peeled barley; spelt wheat.

farsa, *f.* farce; company of players; a badly constructed play; sham, humbug.

farsanta, *f.* farce actress.

farsante, *m.* humbug, fraud; comedian.

farseto, *m.* quilted jacket.

---

farsista, *n.* writer of farces.
fas.—por f. o por nefas, justly or unjustly.
fascal, *m.* (agr.) shock, stook, rick.
fasces, *f. pl.* fasces.
fascículo, *m.* fascicle (part of a book).
fascinación, *f.* fascination, enchantment.
fascinador, ra, *n. & a.* fascinator(-ing), charmer (-ing).
fascinante, *a.* fascinating, charming.
fascinar, *va.* to fascinate, bewitch, enchant; to deceive, allure.
fase, *f.* phase, aspect; (astr., elec.) phase.
fásoles, *m. pl.* (bot.) beans.
fastial, *m.* (arch.) crowning pyramid.
fastidiar. I. *va.* to sicken; to vex, annoy, bother, bore; to disappoint. **II.** *vr.* to weary; to become vexed, bored or displeased.
fastidio, *m.* squeamishness; dislike; weariness, ennui; nuisance, bother.
fastidiosamente, *adv.* squeamishly.
fastidioso, sa, *a.* squeamish, sickening; vexing, annoying; tedious, tiresome; displeased, annoyed.
fastigio, *m.* (arch.) fastigium; pinnacle, apex, top.
fasto, ta. I. *a.* happy (day or event). **II.** *m.* pomp, pageantry, show.—*pl.* fasti; annals.
fastosamente, fastuosamente, *adv.* pompously, gaudily, magnificently.
fastoso, sa; fastuoso, sa, *a.* pompous, ostentatious.
fatal, *a.* fatal, unavoidable; unfortunate, fated.
fatalidad, *f.* (philos.) fatality, necessity; fate, destiny; fatality, calamity.
fatalismo, *n.* fatalism, determinism.
fatalista, *n. & a.* fatalist(-ic), determinist(-ic).
fatalmente, *adv.* fatedly, fatefully; necessarily, unavoidably; calamitously, unluckily; exceedingly bad, wretchedly.
fatídicamente, *adv.* prophetically.
fatídico, ca, *a.* fatidic, oracular, prophetic.
fatiga, *f.* fatigue, tiredness, weariness; hardship; anguish, anxiety; hard breathing.
fatigadamente, *adv.* with difficulty, with toil.
fatigador, ra, *a.* annoying; tiring.
fatigar. I. *va.* (*pret.* FATIGUÉ; *subj.* FATIGUE) to fatigue, tire; to annoy. **II.** *vr.* to tire, get tired.
fatigosamente, *adv.* painfully, wearisomely.
fatigoso, sa, *a.* tiring; tiresome, boring; tired, fatigued.
fatigué, fatigue, *v. V.* FATIGAR.
fatimí, fatimita, *n.* Fatimite.
fatuidad, *f.* fatuity, foolishness; stupidity; conceit, vanity.
fatuo, tua, *a.* fatuous, stupid; pompous; vain.
fauces, *f. pl.* (anat.) fauces, gullet.
fauna, *f.* fauna.
fauno, *m.* faun.
fausto, ta. I. *a.* happy, fortunate. **II.** *m.* pomp, ostentation; great luxury.
faustoso, sa, *a.* = FASTUOSO, SA.
fautor, ra, *n.* abetter, helper, supporter.
fautoría, *f.* aid, assistance.
favilla, *f.* (poet.) ashes of an extinguished fire.
favonio, *m.* westerly wind, zephyr.
favor, *m.* favor; help, aid, service; gift, grace; compliment; love token.—**a f. de,** in behalf of; in favor of; on account of; taking advantage of, aided by; under cover of.—**hacer el f. de,** (Am.) **f. de,** please (in a request).—**por f.,** please (in asking for something).
favorable, *a.* favorable.
favorablemente, *adv.* favorably.
favorcillo, *m. dim.* small favor.
favorecedor, ra, *a.* favorer; helper; client, customer.
favorecer, *va.* (*ind.* FAVOREZCO; *subj.* FAVOREZCA) to favor; to help, befriend; to abet; (of colors, clothes, etc.) to be becoming.
favoritismo, *m.* favoritism.
favorito, ta, *n. & a.* favorite.

faz, *f.* face; (arch.) front.—**f. a f.,** face to face.
fe, *f.* faith; faithfulness; testimony; credit, credence; promise given; assertion, asseveration certificate, testimonial.—**f. de erratas,** (print.) errata; list or table of errata.—**f. púnica,** Punic faith, *Punica fides.*—**a buena f.,** doubtless.—**a f.,** in truth, in good earnest.—**a f. mía,** by my faith.—**dar f.,** to give credit, to attest, to certify, to witness.—**de buena (mala) f.,** in good (bad) faith.--**en f.,** consequently.—**en f. de lo cual,** in witness whereof.—**por mi f.,** by my faith.—**tener f. a,** to have faith in.
fealdad, *f.* ugliness, homeliness; deformity; hideousness; turpitude, foulness.
feamente, *adv.* uglily, deformedly; unworthily, indecorously; brutally, inordinately.
febeo, bea, *a.* Phœbean.
feble. I. *a.* weak, feeble; (jewel) deficient in weight or quality. **II.** *m.* light coin.
feblemente, *adv.* feebly, weakly.
Febo, *m.* (poet.) Phœbus.
febrero, *m.* February.
febricitante, *a.* (med.) slightly feverish.
febrífugo, ga, *a. & m.* (med.) febrifuge.
febril, *a.* (med.) febrile, feverish.
febroniano, na, *a.* Febronian.
fecal, *a.* (med.) fæcal.
fecí, *n. & a.* Fezan (from Fez).
fecial, *m.* (Rom. hist.) fetialis, one of the fetiales.
fécula, *f.* fecula; starch.
feculencia, *f.* feculence, dregs.
feculento, ta, *a.* containing fecula; feculent, foul.
fecundable, *a.* capable of fecundation.
fecundación, *f.* fecundation, fertilization.
fecundamente, *adv.* fruitfully.
fecundante, *a.* fecundating.
fecundar, *va.* to fertilize, fecundate.
fecundativo, va, *a.* fecundating, fertilizing.
fecundidad, *f.* fecundity, fertility, fruitfulness.
fecundizar, *va.* to fecundate, fertilize.
fecundo, da, *a.* fecund, fruitful, fertile, prolific; abundant, copious.
fecha, *f.* date; standing.—**de la cruz a la f.,** from the beginning to the end.
fechador, *m.* dater; (Am.) post-office cancelling stamp.
fechar, *va.* to date (a letter, etc.).
fecho, cha, (obs.) *pp. irreg.* of FACER (= HACER): used only in official documents, meaning done, issued, or executed.
fechoría, *f.* misdeed, villainy.
federación, *f.* federation, confederation.
federal. I. *a.* federal. **II.** *m.* federalist.
federalismo, *m.* federalism.
federativo, va, *a.* federative.
fehaciente, *a.* (law) authentic.
feldespático, ca, *a.* (min.) feldspathic.
feldespato, *m.* (min.) feldspar.
felice, *a.* (poet.) happy.
felicidad, *f.* felicity, happiness; good luck, good fortune.
felicitación, *f.* congratulations, felicitations.
felicitar, *va.* to congratulate, felicitate.
félido, da. I. *n. & a.* (zool.) feline. **II.** *m. pl.* Felidæ.
feligrés, sa, *n.* parishioner.
feligresía, *f.* parish, parishioners.
felino, na, *n. & a.* feline.
feliz, *a.* happy, fortunate, felicitous.
felizmente, *adv.* happily, felicitously.
felón, na, *n.* (law) felon, criminal.
felonía, *f.* treachery, disloyalty, felony.
felpa, *f.* plush; (coll.) reprimand, drubbing
felpado, da, *a.* plushy, shaggy, villous.
felpilla, *f.* chenille.
felposo, sa, *a.* felted; plush-covered.
felpudo, da. I. *a.* plushy. **II.** *m.* doormat.
femenil, *a.* feminine, womanish.
femenilmente, *adv.* effeminately, womanishly.

femenino, na, a. feminine; female.
fementidamente, adv. perfidiously.
fementido, da, a. false, unfaithful.
femineidad, f. (law) (of property) state of belonging to a woman.
feminismo, m. feminism, doctrine of the social and political equality of woman.
feminista, n. feminist, follower of feminism.
femoral, a. (anat.) femoral.
fémur, m. (anat.) femur.
fenacetina, f. phenacetin.
fenaquistoscopio, m. (phys.) phenakistoscope.
fenda, f. crack in the bark of trees.
fendiente, m. gash, deep cut or wound.
fenecer. I. va. (ind. FENEZCO; subj. FENEZCA) to finish, conclude, close. II. vn. to die; to end.
fenecimiento, m. finish, termination, end; death.
fenestrado, da, a. fenestrate.
fenezco, fenezca, v. V. FENECER.
fenianismo, m. Fenianism.
feniano, na, n. & a. Fenian.
fenicar, va. to carbolize, put carbolic acid in or on.
fenicio, cia, n. & a. Phœnician.
fénico, ca, a. carbolic.
fenilamina, f. (chem.) phenylamine.
fenilo, m. (chem.) phenyl.
fénix, m., phœnix; model; king (in the sense of excellent or highest person).
fenogreco, m. (bot.) fenugreek.
fenol, n. phenol.
fenolftaleína, f. phenolphthalein.
fenomenal, a. phenomenal, extraordinary.
fenomenalismo, m. (philos.) phenomenalism.
fenomenalista, m. & f. (philos.) phenomenalist.
fenómeno, m. phenomenon; prodigy; (coll.) freak.
feo, ea. I. a. ugly, homely; improper; heinous; serious, alarming.—dejar, or hacer, f., to slight. II. m. slight, affront.
feote, ta; feotón, na, a. aug. exceedingly ugly.
feracidad, f. fruitfulness, fertility (of land).
feral, a. cruel, bloodthirsty.
feraz, a. fertile, fruitful; abundant, plentiful.
féretro, m. bier, coffin.
feria, f. market, fair, bazaar; gift bought at a fair; (eccl.) any week day (excepting Saturday or a feast day); holiday; rest, repose; (Mex.) small change (money).—hacer f. de, to display, boast.
feriado, da. I. pp. of FERIAR. II. a.—día f., day when courts are not open; (Am.) holiday.
ferial. I. a. ferial. II. m. market, fair.
feriante, n. trader at fairs.
feriar. I. va. to trade, barter; to purchase at a fair; to give a gift bought at a fair. II. vn. to suspend work; to keep holidays.
ferino, na, a. wild, ferocious.—tos f., whooping cough.
fermata, f. (mus.) pause or hold (⌒).
fermentable, a. fermentable.
fermentación, f. fermentation.
fermentante, a. fermenting.
fermentar, vn. & va. to ferment.
fermentativo, va, a. fermentative.
fermento, m. ferment, leaven, leavening; (chem.) enzyme.
fernambuco, m. Pernambuco wood.
fernandina, f. a kind of linen stuff.
feroce, a. (poet.) ferocious.
ferocidad, f. ferocity.
feróstico, ca, a. (coll.) irritable, wayward.
feroz, a. ferocious, fell, fierce; ravenous.
ferozmente, adv. ferociously.
ferra, f. = ¹FARRA, (ichth.) a variety of salmon.
ferrada, f. iron-knobbed club.
ferrado, da. I. a. ferrate, iron-bound. II. m. a corn measure (between 13 and 16 liters); a land measure (between 4 and 6 acres).

ferrar, va. (ind. FIERRO; subj. FIERRE) to trim with iron.
férreo, rea, a. ferrous; iron (as a.), made of iron; harsh, stern, severe.—vía férrea, railroad.
ferrería, f. ironworks, foundry.
ferreruelo, m. short cloak without cape.
ferrete, m. sulphate of copper used to color glass; marking iron.
ferretear, va. to bind, mark, or work with iron.
ferretería, f. hardware; hardware shop.
ferretero, ra, n. hardware dealer.
ferricianógeno, m. ferricyanogen.
ferricianuro, m. ferricyanide.
férrico, ca, a. containing iron; (chem.) ferric.
ferrífero, ra, a. ferriferous, iron-bearing.
ferrificarse, vr. to be converted into iron.
ferrizo, za, a. ferreous, iron (as a.), of iron.
ferro, m. (naut.) anchor.
ferrocarril, m. railroad, railway.—f. aéreo, elevated railroad.—f. de cable, cable railway.—f. de circunvalación, belt, or girdle, railway.—f. de cremallera, rack railroad.—f. de sangre, animal-power railroad; horse tramway.—f. de vapor, steam railroad.—f. eléctrico, electric railroad.—f. elevado, elevated railroad.—f. funicular, cable railroad; ropeway.—f. subterráneo, underground railroad.—f. urbano, street railroad.
ferrocarrilero, ra, a. (Am.) = FERROVIARIO.
ferrocianógeno, m. ferrocyanogen.
ferrocianuro, f. ferrocyanide.
ferrón, m. workman in ironworks.
ferroso, sa, a. ferrous.
ferrovía, f. railway.—ferrovial, a. railroad (as a.); pert. to railroads.—ferroviario, ria. I. a. = FERROVIAL. II. n. railroad employee.
ferrugiento, ta, a. containing iron.
ferrugíneo, nea; ferruginoso, sa, a. ferruginous, iron-bearing.
fértil, a. fertile, fruitful; copious, plentiful.
fertilicé, fertilice, v. V. FERTILIZAR.
fertilidad, f. fertility; fruitfulness; abundance, plenty.
fertilización, f. (agr.) supplying with fertilizer.
fertilizador, ra, a. fertilizing.
fertilizante, n. & a. fertilizer(-ing).
fertilizar, va. (pret. FERTILICÉ; subj. FERTILICE) to fertilize, enrich, make fruitful.
fértilmente, adv. fruitfully.
férula, f. ferule; rule, yoke, authority; (surg.) splint; (bot.) ferula.
feruláceo, ea, a. ferulaceous.
ferventísimo, ma, a. super. very fervent or pious.
férvido, da, a. fervid, ardent.
ferviente, a. = FERVOROSO.
fervor, m. intense heat; fervor.
fervorcillo, m. dim. slight and brief fervor.
fervorizar, va. to heat, inflame, incite.
fervorosamente, adv. fervently.
fervoroso, sa, a. fervent; active, efficient.
festejador, ra, n. & a. entertainer(-ing).
festejante, a. feasting, entertaining; wooing.
festejar, va. to entertain, to feast; to court, to woo, to make love to; to celebrate.
festejo, m. feast, entertainment; obsequiousness; courtship.
festero, ra, n. director of church music.
festín, m. feast, banquet.
festinación, f. speed, haste, hurry.
festinar, va. (Am.) to hasten.
festival, m. festival.
festivamente, adv. festively.
festividad, f. festivity; rejoicing, gaiety, merry-making; holiday; witticism.
festivo, va, a. festive, gay; humorous, witty; festival, festal.—día f., holiday; (eccl.) holy day.
festón, m. garland, wreath, festoon.
festonar, festonear, va. to festoon.

fetal, *a.* fetal, fœtal.
feticida. I. *n.* one committing feticide. **II.** *a.* feticidal.
feticidio, *m.* feticide.
fetiche, *m.* fetich.—**fetichismo,** *m.* fetichism.
fetichista. I. *a.* fetichistic. **II.** *n.* fetichist.
fetidez, *f.* fetidity.
fétido, da, *a.* fetid.
feto, *m.* fetus, fœtus.
fetor, *m.* = FETIDEZ.
feúco, ca, cho, cha, *a.* ugly, repulsive.
feudal, *a.* feudal.—**feudalidad,** *f.,* **feudalismo,** *m.* feudalism.
feudatario, ria, *a.* & *n.* feudatory.
feudista, *m.* (law) feudist.
feudo, *m.* fief, feod.
fez, *m.* fez, Turkish cap.
fiable, *a.* trustworthy, responsible.
fiado, da. I. *pp.* of FIAR. **II.** *m.*—**al f.,** on trust, on credit.—**en f.,** on bail.
fiador, ra. I. *n.* bondsman, guarantor, surety, bail.—**f. carcelero,** one who is bail or surety for a person.—**dar f.,** to give surety.—**salir f.,** to go surety. **II.** *m.* fastener; (mech.) stop, catch, pawl, click, trigger; tumbler of a lock; (falconry) creance.
fiambrar, *va.* to cook for cold cuts or lunch.
fiambre. I. *a.* served cold (as food). **II.** *m.* cold food, cold lunch; (coll.) old joke or piece of news, "chestnut."
fiambrera, *f.* lunch basket; dinner pail.
fiancilla, *f.* binding ring (of carriages).
fianza, *f.* surety, bail, bond, caution, guarantee, security; suretyship.—**f. de aduana,** custom-house bond.—**f. juratoria,** parole.—**bajo f.,** on bail.
fiar. I. *va.* to answer or go surety for; to bail; to sell on trust, give credit for; to intrust, confide. **II.** *vn.* to confide; to sell on trust, give credit. —**ser de f.,** to be trustworthy. **III.** *vr.* (de) to have confidence (in), depend (on), trust.
fiasco, *m.* failure, fiasco.
fíat, *m.* consent; (law) fiat.
fibra, *f.* fibre, filament, staple; energy, stamina, vigor; (min.) vein of ore.
fibrina, *f.* (chem.) fibrin, fibrine.
fibroideo, a, *a.* fibroid.
fibroma, *m.* (surg.) fibroma.
fibroso, sa, *a.* fibrous.
ficción, *f.* fiction, invention; tale, story.
fice, *m.* (ichth.) whiting.
ficoideo, a. I. *n.* & *a.* (bot.) ficoid(-al). **II.** *f. pl.* Ficoideæ, Aizoaceæ.
ficticio, cia, *a.* fictitious.
ficto, ta. I. *pp. irreg.* of FINGIR. **II.** *a.* counterfeited, artificial.
ficha, *f.* (card games, etc.) chip, counter; domino; counter, marker; filing card.—**f. antropométrica,** anthropometric data, card or record.—**mala f.,** (of a person) bad character.—**fichar,** *va.* to take and record anthropometric data.
fidedigno, na, *a.* trustworthy; creditable.
fideero, ra, *n.* maker of FIDEOS.
fideicometido, da, *a.* trust (as *a.*).
fideicomisario, *m.* fideicommissioner.
fideicomiso, *m.* trust; feoffment to use.
fideísmo, *m.* (philos.) fideism, acceptance of faith as the foundation of truth.
fidelidad, *f.* fidelity, faithfulness; honor; fealty, loyalty.
fidelísimo, ma, *a. super.* of FIEL.
fideos, *m. pl.* vermicelli; spaghetti.
fiduciario, ria, *n.* & *a.* fiduciary; trusteeship.
fiebre, *f.* fever; intense excitement, heat of passion.—**f. amarilla,** yellow fever.—**f. héctica,** hectic fever.—**f. intermitente,** intermittent fever.—**f. láctea,** milk fever, lacteal fever.—**f. miliar,** miliary fever.—**f. palúdica,** malaria. —**f. perniciosa,** pernicious intermittent fever. —**f. puerperal,** puerperal fever.—**f. remi-**

tente, remittent fever.—**f. tifoidea,** typhoi fever.
fiebrecilla, *f. dim.* slight fever.
fiel. I. *a.* faithful, loyal, devoted; true, exact accurate. **II.** *m.* public inspector, especially o weights and measures; pointer of a balance o steelyard; pin of the scissors.—**f. contraste** official who weighs and stamps metals.—**f. d muelle,** wharfinger, owner or guardian of wharf.—**f. de romana,** official inspector o meat weighing in slaughter houses.—**f. medi dor,** inspector of measures.—**en f.,** equa weight, even balance.
fielato, fielazgo, *m.* office of the FIEL; octroi a a city's gates.
fieldad, *f.* public inspectorship; surety, security guarantee.
fielmente, *adv.* faithfully.
fieltro, *m.* felt; felt hat, overcoat or rug.
fiemo, *m.* (prov.) dung, manure.
fiera, *f.* wild beast; fierce; vicious animal or pe son; (bullfighting) bull; (coll.) exceedingly abl shrewd or cunning person; person strenuousl or habitually given or devoted to somethin "fiend."
fierabrás, *m.* (coll.) bully, blusterer; wayward froward child.
fieramente, *adv.* fiercely, ferociously; haughtil
fiereza, *f.* fierceness, ferocity; deformity.
fiero, ra. I. *a.* fierce, cruel; ferocious; ugly, de formed; rough, rude; haughty; huge, enormou furious, terrible; wild, savage. **II.** *m. pl.* fierc threats and bravadoes.
¹**fierro,** *m.* iron; brand.
²**fierro, fierre,** *v. V.* FERRAR.
fiesta, *f.* feast, entertainment, party; festivit festival, holiday; caress, act of endearmen holy day.—*pl.* holidays, vacation.—**f. de guar dar,** or **de precepto,** holy day, Mass day.—**f fija,** or **inmoble,** immovable feast.—**f. mov ble,** movable feast.—**aguar la f.,** to mar on pleasure.—**hacer f.,** to quit work, to tak holiday.—**hacer fiestas,** to caress; to wheedl to fawn to.—**por fin de f.,** to end, top off wit —**se acabó la f.,** (coll.) it's all over; drop i let's drop it.
figle, *m.* (mus.) ophicleide, a wind instrument.
figón, *m.* eating house, chophouse.
figonero, ra, *n.* keeper of an eating house.
figulino, na, *a.* terra cotta (as *a.*).
figura. I. *f.* figure; shape; build; mien, looks; ill shaped person, guy; face card or court card (law) form, mode; (mus.) musical note; (gram rhet., geom.) figure.—**f. de bulto,** figure i sculpture; high relief.—**f. de retórica,** figur of speech. **II.** *m.* stiffly pompous person.
figurable, *a.* imaginable.
figuración, *f.* figuration.
figuradamente, *adv.* figuratively.
figurado, da, *a.* figurative; rhetorical, ornate florid.
figurante, ta. I. *m.* figurant. **II.** *f.* figurante.
figurar. I. *va.* to shape, fashion; to draw, sketc to represent; to feign. **II.** *vn.* to figure, be con spicuous. **III.** *vr.* to fancy, imagine to occu come to mind; to seem.
figurativamente, *adv.* figuratively.
figurativo, va, *a.* figurative, typical; symbolica emblematic.
figurería, *f.* grimace, affected gesture.
figurero, ra, *n.* (coll.) one who makes grimac or affected gestures; maker of statuettes.
figurilla, ita, *f. dim.* (coll.) little insignifican person; (art) figurine, statuette.
figurín, *m.* fashion plate; lay figure.
figurón, *m. aug.* huge figure having a ridiculou appearance; (coll.) pretentious nobody.—**f. d proa,** (naut.) figurehead.
fija, *f.* door hinge; (mason.) trowel.

fijación, *f.* stability, firmness; billposting; fixing; locking, immobilizing.

fijador, ra. I. *n. & a.* fixer(-ing); fastener(-ing). **II.** *m.* (mason.) pointer, workman that points the joints; (carp.) door and window setter; (photog. and art) fixing liquid; locking (plate, wire, pin, etc.).

fijamente, *adv.* firmly, assuredly; intensely, attentively; fixedly, steadfastly.

fijar. I. *va.* (*pp.* FIJADO, FIJO) to fix, fasten; to make fast, firm, or stable; to determine, settle, establish; clinch; to post (as bills); to fix (the eyes, the attention, etc.); (photog., art) to fix; to set (a date). **II.** *vr.* (**en**) to settle (in); to determine, resolve; to rivet one's attention (on); to take notice (of), pay attention (to).—**fijémo (s) nos en los hechos,** let's look at the facts.

fijeza, *f.* firmness, stability; steadfastness.

fijo, ja. I. *pp. irreg.* of FIJAR. **II.** *a.* fixed; firm; settled; permanent; (mech.) stationary.—**a punto f.,** exactly; with certitude.—**de f.** certainly.—**hora f.,** time agreed on.

fil, *m.*—**f. derecho,** leapfrog.—**f. de roda,** (naut.) right ahead.—**estar en f.,** to be in line.

fila, *f.* tier, row, line, range; (mil.) rank.—**en f.,** in (a) line, in a row; (mil.) abreast.

filacteria, *f.* phylactery.

filadelfo, fa. I. *n. & a.* (bot.) (plant) belonging to the genus Philadelphus (mock orange, syringa, etc.). **II.** *f. pl.* family of these plants.

filadiz, *m.* floss silk.

filagrama, *f.* wire mold for a watermark.

filamento, *m.* filament, fibre, thread.

filamentoso, sa, *a.* filamentous, fibrous.

filandria, *f.* (zool.) filander, backworm.

filantropía, *f.* philanthropy.

filantrópicamente, *adv.* philanthropically.

filantrópico, ca, *a.* philanthropic.

filántropo, pa, *n.* philanthropist.

filarete, *m.* (naut.) waist netting.

filaria, *f.* (zool.) filaria, a parasitic worm.

filariasis, filariosis, *f.* (med.) filariasis, infection with filariæ.

filarmonía, *f.* love of music.

filarmónico, ca, *a.* philharmonic.

filástica, *f.* (naut.) rope yarn.

filatelia, *f.* philately.—**filatélico, ca,** *a.* philatelic.—**filatelista,** *n.* philatelist.

filatería, *f.* verbosity, wordiness.

filatero, ra, *n.* verbose or wordy speaker.

filatura, *f.* spinning.

filbán, *m.* rough edge of a tool.

fildrretor, *m.* superfine camlet, a rich fabric.

fileli, *m.* superfine flannel.

fileno, na, *a.* (coll.) delicate, small.

filete, *m.* (arch.) fillet, listel; (sewing) narrow hem; small spit for roasting; welt of a shoe; snaffle bit; (mech.) edge, border, rim; thread (of a screw); (print.) fillet, ornamental line; fillet (of meat or fish).

filetear, *va.* to fillet; to crease; to tool.

filetón, *m. aug.* (arch.) large fillet or listel; heavy bullion for embroidering.

filfa, *f.* (coll.) fib, hoax, fake.

filiación, *f.* filiation; connection, relationship; personal description; (mil.) regimental register.

filial, *a.* filial.—**filialmente,** *adv.* filially.

filiar. I. *va.* to register the pedigree and description of. **II.** *vr.* to enroll.

filibote, *m.* flyboat, light vessel.

filibusterismo, *m.* (Sp. hist.) filibusterism.

filibustero, *m.* (Sp. hist., not U. S. meaning) filibuster.

filicida, *n.* filicide, one who kills his child.

filicidio, *m.* filicide, killing a son or daughter.

filiforme, *a.* filiform.

filigrana, *f.* filigree, filigrane; spun work; watermark in paper; delicate, fanciful thing.

filili, *m.* (coll.) fineness, neatness, delicacy.

filipéndula, *f.* (bot.) dropwort spiræa.

filipense, *n. & a.* Philippian.

filípica, *f.* Philippic; invective.

filipichín, *m.* moreen, woollen cloth.

filipino, na, *n. & a.* Philippine.

filis, *m.* knack; trinket, charm.

filisteo, tea. I. *n. & a.* Philistine. **II.** *n.* (coll.) very tall and corpulent person.

filmar, *va.* (Angl.) to film (a moving picture).

filo, *m.* cutting edge; dividing line; ridge; (arch.) arris.

filocartista, *n.* collector of postal cards.

filófago, ga, *a.* (entom.) phyllophagous.

filología, filológica, *f.* philology.

filológico, ca, *a.* philological.

filólogo, ga, *n.* philologist.

filomanía, *f.* (bot.) phyllomania.

filomela, filomena, *f.* nightingale, philomel.

filón, *m.* (geol.) vein, lode.

filonio, *m.* philonium, an eyesalve with opium.

filopos, *m. pl.* pieces of linen used to drive game.

filoseda, *f.* vesting; silk and worsted or cotton cloth.

filosofador, ra, *n. & a.* philosophizer(-ing).

filosofar, *vn.* to philosophize.

filosofastro, *m.* philosophaster.

filosofía, *f.* philosophy.

filosóficamente, *adv.* philosophically.

filosófico, ca, *a.* philosophical, philosophic.

filosofismo, *m.* philosophism, spurious philosophy.

filosofista, *m.* philosophist.

filósofo, fa, *n.* philosopher.

filote, *m.* (Colomb.) silk (of ear of corn).

filoxera, *f.* phylloxera.

filtración, *f.* filtration.

filtrador, ra. I. *n. & a.* filterer(-ing). **II.** *m.* filter.

filtrar. I. *va. & vn.* to filter. **II.** *vn.* to percolate, filter. **III.** *vr.* to leak out; disappear; to filter through.

¹filtro, *m.* filter.—**f. de vacío,** vacuum filter.—**f. prensa,** filter press for refining sugar.

²filtro, *m.* philter, love potion.

fillo, *m.* a sort of fritter.

fimbria, *f.* border of a skirt.

fimo, *m.* dung, manure.

fimosis, *f.* (med.) phimosis.

fin, *m.* end, ending, conclusion; end, object, purpose.—**a f. de,** in order to, so as to.—**a f. de que,** so that, to the end that.—**a fines de,** towards or at the end of, late in (the week, etc.).—**al f.,** at last.—**al f. y a la postre,** or **al f. y al cabo,** at last; lastly; after all.—**en f.,** finally, lastly; in short; well (as expletive: *en fin, veremos,* well, we shall see).—**poner f. a,** to put an end to, stop, get rid of.—**por f.,** at last, finally.—**sin f.,** endless; numberless.

finado, da. I. *pp.* of FINAR. **II.** *a.* dead, deceased, late. **III.** *n.* deceased, dead person.

final. I. *a.* final; ultimate; conclusive. **II.** *m.* end, termination, conclusion.—*pl.* (sports) finals.

finalidad, *f.* finality; end pursued or attained.

finalista, *n.* follower of the doctrine of final causes; (sports) one playing in the finals.

finalizar. I. *va.* to finish, conclude; (law) to execute (a contract, deed). **II.** *vn.* to end, to be finished or concluded.

finalmente, *adv.* finally, lastly.

finamente, *adv.* finely, nicely, delicately.

finamiento, *m.* death, decease, demise.

financiación, *f.,* **financiamiento,** *m.* (Am.) financing.

financiar, *va.* (Am.) to finance.

financiero, ra. I. *a.* financial. **II.** *m.* financier.

financista, *m. & f.,* (Am.) = FINANCIERO.

finanzas, *f. pl.* (Gal.) (Colomb.) public finances.

finar. I. *vn.* to die. **II.** *vr.* to long, yearn.

finca, *f.* real estate, land, house property; country estate, farm, ranch.

fincar, *vn. & vr.* (*pret.* FINQUÉ; *subj.* FINQUE) to

buy or deal in real estate.—**f. la esperanza de,** to pin one's hopes on.

finchado, da, *a.* swelling with pride.

finés, sa, *a.* Finnic, Finnish.

fineza, *f.* fineness; goodness, purity; kindness, expression of regard, courtesy; friendly influence or assistance; keepsake, gift, favor.

fingidamente, *adv.* feignedly; hypocritically.

fingido, da, *pp.* & *a.* feigned, dissembled.

fingidor, ra, *n.* & *a.* dissembler(-ing), feigner (-ing).

fingimiento, *m.* simulation, deceit, pretense.

fingir, *va.* & *vr.* (*pp.* FINGIDO, FICTO; *ind.* FINJO; *subj.* FINJA) to feign, dissemble, pretend, affect, sham; to fancy, imagine.

finible, *a.* capable of being finished.

finiquitar, *va.* to settle and close (an account).

finiquito, *m.* settlement of accounts; adjustment, release, quittance.

finítimo, ma, *a.* bordering, contiguous, near.

finito, ta, *a.* finite.

finjo, finja, *v.* V. FINGIR.

finlandés, sa, *a.* Finnish.

fino, na, *a.* fine; perfect, pure; thin, sheer; slender, subtle; delicate, nice; affectionate, true; sagacious, cunning, shrewd; sharp (as a point); courteous, polite; refined (as gold); (naut.) sharp.

finqué, finque, *v.* V. FINCAR.

¹**finta,** *f.* an ancient tax.

²**finta,** *f.* (fencing) feint.

finura, *f.* fineness; purity; politeness; courtesy.

fiñana, *m.* black-bearded wheat.

fiordo, *m.* fiord.

fique, *m.* (Mex., Colomb., Venez.) = CABUYA, sisal (cord).

firma, *f.* signature; sign manual, hand (as hand and seal); subscription; act of signing; (com.) firm, house; firm name.—**f. en blanco,** blank endorsement; full powers.—**buena f.,** reliable firm or house.—**dar,** or **llevar, la f.,** to empower or be empowered to sign the firm name.

firmamento, *m.* firmament, sky.

firmán, *m.* firman, an edict.

firmante, *n.* signer, subscriber.

firmar, *va.,* *vn.* & *vr.* to sign.—**f. en blanco,** to give a blank endorsement.

firme. I. *a.* firm, stable, solid; hard, compact; unswerving, stanch, unyielding.—**estar en lo f.,** to be certain or positive, in the right. **II.** *m.* groundwork, bed, foundation; ballast or gravel bed on a road; roadbed.—**de f.,** steadily; solidly; violently, strongly.—**en f.,** definitive, final, in final form. **III.** *adv.* firmly, strongly.

firmemente, *adv.* firmly.

firmeza, *f.* firmness, stability; hardness, compactness.

firmón, na, *n.* one who signs another's work.

fiscal. I. *a.* fiscal. **II.** *m.* attorney-general; district attorney, public prosecutor; (coll.) intermeddler, prier.

fiscalía, *f.* office and business of a FISCAL.

fiscalicé, fiscalice, *v.* V. FISCALIZAR.

fiscalización, *f.* discharge of a FISCAL's duties.

fiscalizador, ra. I. *a.* acting as a FISCAL. **II.** *n.* prier, censurer, faultfinder.

fiscalizar, *va.* (*pret.* FISCALICÉ; *subj.* FISCALICE) to prosecute; to criticise, censure.

fisco, *m.* national treasury, exchequer.

¹**fisga,** *f.* grain or bread of spelt wheat.

²**fisga,** *f.* harpoon; raillery, banter, chaff.

fisgador, ra, *n.* harpooner; banterer.

fisgar, *vn.* to chaff, banter; to fish with a harpoon; to peep, to pry.

fisgón, na, *n.* banterer, chaffer, jester; prier.

fisgonear, *vn.* to pry habitually.

fisgoneo, *m.* habitual or frequent prying.

física, *f.* physics.

físicamente, *adv.* physically.

físico, ca. I. *a.* physical. **II.** *n.* physicist; physi-

cian; military or naval surgeon; physique; (coll.) face.

fisicoquímico, ca, *a.* physicochemical.

físil, *a.* fissile.

fisiocracia, *f.* physiocracy, a system of pol. econ.

fisiócrata, *n.* physiocrat.

fisiología, *f.* physiology.

fisiológicamente, *adv.* physiologically.

fisiológico, ca, *a.* physiological.

fisiologista, fisiólogo, *m.* physiologist.

fisionomía, *f.* physiognomy, appearance, looks, features.

fisioterapia, *f.* treatment of disease by natural agents (fresh air, sunlight, etc.).

fisiparidad, *f.* (biol.) fissiparity.

fisíparo, ra, *a.* (biol.) fissiparous.

fisirrostro, ra. I. *a.* (zool.) fissirostral. **II.** *m. pl.* Fissirostres.

fisonomía, *f.* = FISIONOMÍA.

fisonómico, ca, *a.* physiognomical.

fisonomista, fisónomo, *m.* physiognomist.

fistol, *m.* crafty person; shrewd gambler; (Mex.) scarf pin.

fístola, fístula, *f.* water pipe or conduit; (mus.) reed or pipe; (surg.) fistula.

fistular, *a.* (med.) fistular, fistulous.

fistuloso, sa, *a.* fistulous.

fisura, *f.* (geol.) fissure, cleft; (surg.) fissure of bone, or "green-stick" fracture; (surg.) fissure in the anus.—**fisurar,** *vn.* (Am.) to split.

fitófago, ga, *a.* phytophagous, herbivorous.

fitografía, *f.* (bot.) phytography, description of plants.

fitográfico, ca, *a.* pertaining to phytography.

fitógrafo, *m.* phytographer.

fitología, *f.* phytology, botany.

fitonisa, *f.* = PITONISA, Python; witch.

fitotecnia, *f.* applied botany (in industry, dietetics).

fitotomía, *f.* phytotomy, vegetable anatomy.

flabelicornio, *a.* (zool.) having fan-shaped antennae.

flabelífero, ra, *a.* fan-carrying (in ceremonies).

flabeliforme, *a.* flabelliform, fan-shaped.

flacamente, *adv.* languidly, weakly, feebly.

flaccidez, *f.* flaccidity, laxness, limberness.

fláccido, da, *a.* flaccid, limber, lax, soft; (auto) low pressure, balloon (tire); (aer.) nonrigid (airship).

flaco, ca. I. *a.* thin, lean; feeble, languid; frail, weak of resolution.—**f. de memoria,** short of memory. **II.** *m.* weak point, weakness.

flacucho, cha, *a.* rather thin or lank.

flacura, *f.* thinness, lack of flesh, leanness.

flagelación, *f.* flagellation, scourging.

flagelador, ra, *n.* flagellator.

flagelante, *n.* & *a.* flagellant(-ing).

flagelar, *va.* to scourge, flagellate, whip.

flagelo, *m.* lash, scourge; flagellum.

flagrancia, *f.* flagrancy.

flagrante, *a.* resplendent; present.—**en f.,** flagrante delicto, in the very act.

flagrar, *vn.* (poet.) to burn, glow, shine.

flama, *f.* flame, excessive ardor.

flamante, *a.* flaming, bright, resplendent; brand-new, fresh, spick and span.

flamear, *vn.* to flame, blaze; (naut.) (of sails) to flutter.

flamen, *m.* (Rom. hist.) flamen, a priest.—**f. dial,** flamen Dialis.—**f. marcial,** flamen Martialis.—**f. quirinal,** flamen quirinalis.

flamenco, ca. I. *a.* & *n.* Flemish; Andalusian (dance, song, etc.). **II.** *m.* (ornith.) flamingo.

flamenquilla, *f.* small platter; (bot.) marigold.

flámeo, *m.* ancient bridal veil.

flamero, *m.* torch holder.

flamígero, ra, *a.* (poet.) flammiferous.

flámula, *f.* (naut.) streamer, pennon.

flan, *m.* flan, rich custard.

flanco, *m.* side; (mil. and fort.) flank.

flanela, *f.* = FRANELA, flannel.

flanqueado, da. I. *pp.* of FLANQUEAR. **II.** *a.* with both flanks protected.

flanqueante, *a.* flanking.

flanquear, *va.* (mil. and fort.) to flank.

flanqueo, *m.* (mil.) flank attack, flanking.

flaquear, *vn.* to flag, weaken; to become weak; to threaten ruin or downfall.

flaqueza, *f.* leanness, thinness, emaciation; feebleness, weakness; frailty, foible; flagginess.

flato, *m.* (med.) flatus, windiness.

flatoso, sa, *a.* (med.) subject to flatus.

flatulencia, *f.* flatulency, windiness.

flatulento, ta, *a.* flatulent, windy.

flatuoso, sa, *a.* = FLATOSO.

flauta, *f.* (mus.) flute.—**f. travesera,** German flute.—**flautado, da. I.** *a.* flutelike. **II.** *m.* flute stop in an organ.

flauteado, da, *a.* (of voice) flutelike, soft and sweet.

flautero, ra, *n.* flute maker.

flautillo, *m.* = CARAMILLO, flageolet.

flautín, *m.* (mus.) octave flute, piccolo.

flautista, *n.* flute player.

flébil, *a.* deplorable, lamentable.

flebitis, *f.* phlebitis, inflammation of a vein.

flebotomía, *f.* phlebotomy, bloodletting.

flebotomiano, na, *n.* phlebotomist.

fleco, *m.* fringe, purl, flounce.

flecha, *f.* arrow, dart; (fort.) work of two faces and two sides; (naut.) front piece of the cutwater; (eng., arch.) maximum ordinate; deflection (as of a beam).

flechador, *m.* archer.

flechaduras, *f. pl.* (naut.) ratlines.

flechar. I. *va.* to dart, to shoot (an arrow or dart); to strike with an arrow; (coll.) to inspire sudden love; (Mex.) to point out, without fear, in gambling. **II.** *vn.* to make a bow ready to shoot.

flechaste, *m.* (naut.) ratline.

flechazo, *m.* stroke with a dart or arrow.

flechera, *f.* (Am.) long, sharp canoe.

flechería, *f.* shower of arrows.

flechero, ra, *n.* archer, bowman; arrow maker.

flegmasía, *f.* (med.) phlegmasia, inflammation.

fleje, *m.* iron hoop or strap.—**flejas para aros,** hoop poles.

flema, *f.* phlegm.—**flemático, ca,** *a.* phlegmatic.

fleme, *f.* (vet.) fleam.

flemón, *m.* (med.) gumboil; phlegmasia, inflammation of cellular tissue.

flemonoso, sa, *a.* pertaining to gumboils or phlegmasia.

flemoso, sa, *a.* mucous, phlegmy.

flemudo, da, *a.* phlegmatic.

flequezuelo, *m. dim.* narrow fringe.

flequillo, *m. dim.* (of haircut) bang, fringe.

fletador, ra, *n.* (com.) freighter, charterer.

fletamento, *m.* (com.) charter, charterage, charter party.

fletar, *va.* to freight or charter (a ship).

flete, *m.* freight, freightage; (Am.) hire price (for transporting freight, cargo); (Am.) load transported.

flexibilidad, *f.* flexibility.

flexible. I. *a.* flexible; lithe; supple; manageable, docile. **II.** *m.* electric cord; soft hat.

flexión, *f.* flexion, flexure.

flexor, ra. I. *a.* bending. **II.** *m.* bender; (anat.) flexor.

flexuoso, sa, *a.* (bot.) flexuose.

flictena, *f.* (med.) phlyctena, small blister.

flin, *m.* (cutlery) polishing stone.

flirtear, *vn.* (Angl.) to flirt.—**flirteo,** *m.* flirting.

flocadura, *f.* (sewing) fringe trimming.

flogístico, ca, *a.* (chem.) phlogistic.

flogisto, *m.* (chem.) phlogiston.

flogosis, *f.* inflammation, phlegmasia.

flojamente, *adv.* slowly, carelessly, laxly.

flojear, *vn.* to slacken, to grow weak.

flojedad, *f.* weakness, feebleness, laxity; sloth, laziness, negligence.

flojel, *m.* wool shorn from cloth; down, soft feathers.

flojera, *f.* (coll.) = FLOJEDAD.

flojo, ja, *a.* loose, lax, slack; weak; flaccid; lazy; (Colomb.) timorous, cowardly.

floqueado, da, *a.* fringed.

flor, *f.* flower; blossom; down of fruits newly gathered; prime; film on the surface of liquors; (chem.) flower, powder; compliment; grain, outside of tanned leather; cheating trick of gamblers; (gen. *pl.*) flowers, menstruation.—**f. compuesta,** (bot.) compound flower.—**f. de la edad,** youth; prime of life.—**f. de lis,** fleurde-lis, iris.—**f. del sol** (bot.) = CORONA REAL, sunflower.—**f. de mano,** artificial flower.—**f. y nata,** flower, élite.—**flores blancas,** leucorrhœa.—**flores de cantueso,** trifle, small matter.—**a f. de,** flush with; (naut.) awash.—**decir,** or **echar, flores,** to pay compliments, to flatter.

flora, *f.* (bot.) flora.

floración, *f.* (bot.) flowering, florescence.

florada, *f.* season of flowers with beemasters.

floral, *a.* (bot.) floral.

florales, *a. pl.* Floralia, floral (feasts or games).

florar, *vn.* to flower, blossom, bloom.

flordelisado, da, *pp.* & *a.* (her.) fleurette.

flordelisar, *va.* (her.) to adorn with irises.

floreado, da. I. *pp.* of FLOREAR. **II.** *a.* flowered, figured (goods); made of the finest flour.

florear, *va.* to flower; to bolt (flour); to flourish, brandish; (mus.) to flourish on the guitar; to pay compliments to.

florecer. I. *vn.* (*ind.* FLOREZCO; *subj.* FLOREZCA) to flower, bloom, blossom; to flourish, thrive, prosper. **II.** *vr.* to mould, become mouldy.

florecica, illa, ita, *f. dim.* floweret, small flower.

floreciente, *a.* flourishing, flowering.

florecimiento, *m.* flowering; flourishing.

florentín, tino, tina, *n.* & *a.* Florentine.

florentísimo, ma, *a. super.* very prosperous.

floreo, *m.* witty but idle talk; compliment; (fencing, mus.) flourish; cross caper, in dancing.

florero, ra. I. *a.* flattering. **II.** *n.* florist. **III.** *m.* flowerpot; flower vase; flower stand, jardinière; (art) flower piece. **IV.** *f.* flower girl.

florescencia, *f.* (bot.) florescence, flowering.

floresta, *f.* wooded field; delightful rural place; collection of fine, pleasing things.

florestero, *m.* forester, forest keeper or guard.

floreta, *f.* leather border on the edge of a girth.

florete. I. *a.* (com.) first quality, superfine. **II.** *m.* fencing foil.

floretear, *va.* to garnish with flowers.

floretista, *m.* fencer.

florezco, florezca, *v.* V. FLORECER.

floricultor, ra, *n.* floriculturist.

floricultura, *f.* floriculture.

floridamente, *adv.* flowerily; flourishingly.

floridano, na, *n.* & *a.* Floridian (from Florida), Florida (as *a.*).

floridez, *f.* floridity, floridness.

florido, da, *a.* flowery; full of flowers, in bloom; choice, select.—**pascua f.,** Easter Sunday.

florífero, ra; florígero, ra, *a.* floriferous.

florilegio, *m.* florilegium, anthology.

florín, *m.* florin (coin).

floripondio, *m.* (bot.) floripondio.

florisar, *va.* = FLORDELISAR.

florista, *n.* maker of artificial flowers; florist.

florón, *m. aug.* large flower; (arch.) fleuron, rosette.

flósculo, *m.* (bot.) floscule, floret.

flota, *f.* (naut.) fleet of merchant ships; (obs.) squadron.—**f. aérea,** air forces.

flotable, *a.* flotable; navigable.

flotación, *f.* flotation, flotage, floating.—**línea de f.,** waterline (of ship).

For pronunciation, see the rules at the beginning of the book.

flotador, ra. I. *n.* & *a.* floater(-ing). **II.** *m.* float.

flotadura, *f.,* **flotamiento,** *m.* = FLOTACIÓN.

flotante, *a.* floating.

flotar, *vn.* to float (on a liquid or in the air).

flote, *m.* floating.—**a f.,** afloat.—**estar,** or **mantenerse, a f.,** (fig.) to have enough to live on.

flotilla, *f. dim.* flotilla; small fleet.

fluctuación, *f.* fluctuation; wavering.

fluctuante, *a.* fluctuating.

fluctuar, *vn.* to fluctuate; waver, oscillate; to be in danger; to hesitate, vacillate.

fluctuoso, sa, *a.* fluctuant, wavering.

fluente, *a.* fluent, flowing.

fluidez, *f.* fluidity, fluidness; fluency.

flúido, da. I. *a.* fluid; fluent (as speech). **II.** *m.* fluid.

fluir, *vn.* (*ger.* FLUYENDO; *ind. pres.* FLUYO, *pret.* FLUYÓ; *subj.* FLUYA) *vn.* to flow; to issue, ooze, run out.

flujo, *m.* flux, flow, flowing; (med.) flux, hæmorrhage; (naut.) flow, rising tide; (chem.) flux.—**f. blanco,** the whites.—**f. de palabras,** flow of words, volubility.—**f. de reír,** habit of laughing —**f. de risa,** fit of laughter.—**f. de sangre,** hæmorrhage.—**f. de vientre,** diarrhœa.

fluminense, *a.* from Rio de Janeiro.

fluor, *m.* (chem.) fluorine; (chem.) flux.

fluorescencia, *f.* (phys.) fluorescence.

fluorescente, *a.* fluorescent.

fluorhidrato, *m.* hydrofluoride.

fluorhídrico, ca, *a.* hydrofluoric.

fluórico, ca, *a.* (chem.) fluoric.

fluorina, fluorita, *f.* fluor spar, fluorite.

fluoruro, *m.* (chem.) fluoride.

fluvial, *a.* fluvial, river (as *a.*).

fluviógrafo, fluviómetro, *m.* fluviograph, an instrument for registering the rise and fall of a river.

flux, *m.* (Am.) suit (of clothes); flush, at cards.—**estar a f.,** (Mex., Arg.) to have nothing, be penniless.—**hacer f.,** (coll.) to spend one's whole fortune without paying a debt.—**tener f.,** (Am.) to be lucky.

fluxión, *f.* (med.) fluxion; cold in the head.

fluyo, fluya, etc., *v.* V. FLUIR.

foca, *f.* (zool.) fur-bearing seal.

focal, *a.* (geom. and phys.) focal.

foceifiza, *f.* a kind of Arabian mosaic.

focino, *m.* goad for elephants.

foco, *m.* focus; center, source; (med.) core or center of an abscess; (mil.) touchhole of a gun; (auto) headlight.—**f. de luz eléctrica,** bunch of electric lights.

fóculo, *m.* small fireplace.

fodolí, *a.* meddlesome, intrusive.

fofo, fa, *a.* spongy, soft; (of style) empty, trashy.

fogaje, *m.* hearth money, an ancient tax.

fogarada, *f.* blaze, bonfire.

fogaril, *m.* cresset, torch.

fogarín, *m.* common hearth for field hands

fogarizar, *va.* to build bonfires in.

fogata, *f.* bonfire, blaze; fougade.

fogón, *m.* hearth, fireside; cooking place, cooking stove, kitchen range; touchhole of a gun; (naut.) caboose, cuddy; firebox (of a boiler, locomotive, etc.); (Am.) fire.

fogonadura, *f.* (naut.) mast hole.

fogonazo, *m.* powder flash; flash in a pan.

fogonero, *m.* fireman, stoker.

fogosidad, *f.* fieriness, heat, vehemence.

fogoso, sa, *a.* fiery, vehement, impetuous; spirited (as a horse).

fogote, *m.* fagot, bundle of twigs.

fogueación, *f.* numbering of hearths or fires.

foguear, *va.* to accustom to the discharge (noise) of firearms; (artil.) to scale (a gun).

foguezuelo, *m. dim.* small fire.

¹foja, *f.* (law) leaf of a manuscript or folio.

²foja, *f.* (ornith.) coot, scoter.

fole, *m.* leather bag, especially of the bagpipe.

folgo, *m.* foot muff or warming bag.

folías, *f. pl.* a kind of merry dance.

foliáceo, a. (bot.) foliaceous.

foliación, *f.* foliation, numbering the pages of a book; (bot.) foliation.

foliar, *va.* to number the pages of a book, etc.

foliatura, *f.* paging (of a book).

folículo, *m.* (bot.) follicle, pericarp; (anat.) follicle, membranous sac.

folijones, *m. pl.* an ancient Castilian dance.

folio, *m.* folio, leaf of a book; size of a bookleaf.—**f. de Descartes,** (geom.) folium of Descartes.—**f. índico,** (bot.) Indian leaf.—**al primer f.,** at first sight.—**de a f.,** (coll.) very great, monumental (truth, fact, etc.); egregious (blunder, etc.).

foliolo, *m.* (bot.) foliole of a compound flower.

folión, *m.* (prov.) fireworks.

folklore, *m.* folklore.—**folklórico, ca,** *a.* folkloric, pertaining to folklore.—**folklorista,** *n.* folklorist, one versed in folklore.

foluz, *f.* an ancient small copper coin.

folla, *f.* irregular conflict in a tournament; medley, variety show.

follada, *f.* puff-paste patty.

follaje, *m.* foliage; leafage; gaudy ornament; superabundance of figures of speech; fustian.

¹follar, *va.* (*ind.* FUELLO; *subj.* FUELLE) to blow with bellows.

²follar, *va.* to form into leaves.

follero, folletero, *m.* bellows maker or seller.

folletín, *m.* feuilleton, serial story in a newspaper.

folletinista, *n.* writer of FOLLETINES.

folletista, *n.* pamphleteer.

folleto, *m.* pamphlet, booklet.

follón, na. I. *a.* lazy, indolent; cowardly. **II.** *m.* coward; rogue, knave; conceited fellow; noiseless rocket.

fomentación, *f.* (med.) fomentation.

fomentador, ra, *n.* & *a.* fomenter(-ing), promoter(-ing).

fomentar, *va.* to foment, to warm; to promote, further, encourage; to prompt; (med.) to foment; (agr.) to improve.

fomento, *m.* fomentation; warmth, fuel; fostering, furtherance, promotion; improvement, development; (med.) fomentation, lotion.

fomes, *m.* (med.) fomes; cause of excitement.

fonación, *f.* vocalization, emission of the voice.

fonas, *f. pl.* (sewing) gores, gussets.

fonda, *f.* inn; eating house.

fondable, *a.* fit for anchoring.

fondado, da, *a.* (cooperage) with reinforced heads.

fondeadero, *m.* (naut.) anchoring ground; haven.

fondear. I. *va.* (naut.) to sound; to raise from the bottom of water; to search (a ship); to examine closely. **II.** *vn.* to cast anchor.

fondeo, *m.* (naut.) search; casting anchor.

fondillón, *m.* dregs and lees of a cask of liquor; old Alicante wine.

fondillos, *m. pl.* seat of trousers.

fondista, *n.* innkeeper, hotel keeper.

fondo, *m.* bottom; depth; rear part, back, furthest end; ground (of stuffs); head (of a stake, cylinder, etc.); substance; (art) background; thickness of a diamond; extent of a man's capacity; disposition, nature (of a person); principal or essential part of a thing; stock, quantity, store (of virtues, vices, etc.); fund, capital; (mil.) space occupied by a rank; (mech.) bed, bottom plate, foundation; (cooperage) head; (naut.) bottom.—*pl.* funds, resources.—**f. de amortización,** sinking fund.—**f. de reserva,** reserve fund.—**fondos públicos,** or del Erario, public funds.—**fondos vitalicios,** life annuities.—**a f.,** perfectly, thoroughly.—**andar mal de fondos,** to be short of money.—**dar f.,** to cast anchor.—**de f.,** abreast; editorial (article).—**echar a f.,** to sink.—**en f.,** abreast.—**en**

el f., at bottom, at heart, in substance.—**irse a f.**, (naut.) to founder; (fencing) to thrust.—**limpiar los fondos**, (naut.) to hog a ship's bottom.

fondón, *m.* FONDILLÓN; ground of silk or velvet; brocade; (min.) fondon.

fonendoscopio, *m.* phoneidoscope.

fonética, *f.* phonetics.

fonético, ca, *a.* phonetic.

fonetismo, *m.* phonetism.

fónico, ca, *a.* phonic, acoustic.

fonil, *m.* (naut.) wooden funnel.

fonje, *a.* bland, soft, spongy.

fonografía, *f.* phonography.

fonográfico, ca, *a.* phonographic.

fonógrafo, *m.* phonograph.

fonograma, *m.* phonogram, phonograph record.

fonolita, *f.* (min.) clinkstone, phonolite.

fonología, *f.* phonology.

fonológico, ca, *a.* phonologic.

fonólogo, ga, *n.* phonologist.

fonsadera, *f.* an ancient war tax.

fonsado, *m.* (fort.) foss or ditch.

fontal, *a.* fontal; original, main.

fontana, *f.* (poet.) fountain, spring, water jet.

fontanal. I. *a.* fontal, pertaining to fountains or springs. **II.** *m.* source or spring of water; place abounding in springs.

fontanar, *m.* water spring.

fontanela, *f.* (anat.) fontanel; (surg.) seton needle.

fontanería, *f.* pipe laying; water-pipe system, pipe line.

fontanero, ra, *n.* pipe layer.

fontegí, *m.* a variety of wheat.

fontezuela, *f. dim.* small fountain.

fontículo, *m.* (surg.) fonticulus, issue.

football, *m.* football. Also FÚTBOL.

foque, *m.* (naut.) jib.—**f. de caza**, or **f. mayor**, standing jib.—**f. segundo**, forestay sail.

forajido, da, *n.* outlaw, fugitive from justice.

foral, *a.* (law) statutory.

foralmente, *adv.* judicially.

foramen, *m.* hole in the nether stone (of mill).

foráneo, nea, *a.* foreign.

forastero, ra. I. *a.* foreign; exotic. **II.** *n.* stranger.

forcé, *pret.* of FORZAR.

forcejar, forcejear, *vn.* to struggle, strive, labor; contest, contend.

forcejo, *m.* struggle, strife.

forcejón, *m.* violent effort or struggle.

forcejudo, da, *a.* strong, robust.

forceps, *m.* (surg.) forceps.

forchina, *f.* (mil.) forklike weapon.

forense, *a.* (law) forensic.

forero, ra. I. *a.* conformable to the statute law of a country. **II.** *m.* owner of leasehold estate; lessee.

forestal, *a.* forestal.

forillo, *m.* backing, in theatrical scenery.

forja, *f.* smelting furnace; chafery; bloomery, smithy; forge; forging; (mason.) mortar.

forjado, da. I. *pp.* of FORJAR. **II.** *a.* (of metals) wrought; forged.

forjador, *m.* forger; ironmaster, smith, black-smith; goldbeater.

forjadura, *f.* forging.

forjar, *va.* to forge, hammer or stamp into shape; to frame, form, fabricate; to counterfeit, falsify; to invent, concoct (as a falsehood).—**forjarse ilusiones**, to delude oneself; to build castles in the air.

forlón, *m.* an ancient two-seat chaise.

forma, *f.* form, shape; frame, mode; method, order; manner; hand, form or cast of writing; pattern, mold, matrix; (print.) form, format; block (for hats); (eccl.) host for the commun-ion of the laity.—*pl.* (of persons) build, figure.—**dar f. a**, to give final form to, shape; to put in order, arrange.—**de f. que**, so as, so that.—

en debida f., or **en f.**, in due form, properly.—**en f., en toda f.**, in due form or manner; thor-oughly, in a thorough and proper manner.—**tomar f.**, to develop, to become realized, to materialize.

formable, *a.* that can be formed.

formación, *f.* formation, forming; form, shape; twisted cord for gold embroidery; (geol.) for-mation, system; (mil.) formation, array.

formador, ra, *n. & a.* former(-ing).

formaje, *m.* cheese vat; cheese; (Mex.) sugar mold.

formal, *a.* formal, regular, methodical; proper, genuine; serious, grave, steady, sedate; truth-ful, reliable; well-behaved.

formaldehido, *m.* formaldehyde.

formalicé, formalice, *v. V.* FORMALIZAR.

formalidad, *f.* formality; exactness, punctuality; gravity, seriousness, solemnity; requisite, re-quirement; "red tape"; established practice; legal precedent.—**con f.**, in earnest.

formalina, *f.* (chem.) formalin.

formalismo, *m.* formalism.

formalista, *n.* formalist.

formalizar. I. *va.* (pret. FORMALICÉ; subj. FOR-MALICE) to put in final form; to execute, legalize (a deed, etc.); to make explicit, to formulate. **II.** *vr.* to become serious or earnest.

formalmente, *adv.* formally; seriously.

formar. I. *va.* to form; shape, fashion; (mil.) to combine, arrange.—**f. parte de**, to be a mem-ber of (an organization, etc.). **II.** *vn.* to adjust the edges of embroidery work; (mil.) to draw up. **III.** *vr.* to form, take form, grow, develop.

formativo, va, *a.* formative.

formato, *m.* (Am.) format (of a book).

formatriz, *f. a.* = FORMADORA.

formejar, *va.* (naut.) to clear (the ship); to trim (the hold).

formero, *m.* (arch.) side arch of a vault.

formiato, *m.* (chem.) formate.

formicante, *a.* (med.) weak, rapid (pulse).

fórmico, *m.* (chem.) formic (acid or ether).

formidable, *a.* formidable; immense, huge.

formidablemente, *adv.* formidably.

formidoloso, sa, *a.* timorous, timid; dreadful, frightful, horrible.

formillón, *m.* hat block, hat form.

formón, *m.* chisel; punching press for cutting wafers.

fórmula, *f.* formula; recipe, prescription; (eccl.) profession of faith.—**por f.**, as a matter of form.

formular, *va.* to formulate.

formulario, *m.* formulary.

formulismo, *m.* formulism; red tape.

formulista, *n. & a.* formulist(-ic).

fornáceo, cea, *a.* (poet.) furnacelike.

fornelo, *m.* portable little oven or furnace.

fornicación, *f.* fornication.

fornicador, ra, *n. & a.* fornicator(-ing).

fornicar, *va.* to fornicate.

fornicario, ria, *a.* pertaining to or addicted to fornication.

fornicio, *m.* = FORNICACIÓN.

fornido, da, *a.* robust, lusty, stout.

fornitura, *f.* (mil.) furniture; (print.) types cast to complete sorts.

foro, *m.* forum; court of justice; bar, the legal profession; back, in stage scenery; leasehold; rental.—**llmar al f.**, (law) to call to the bar.—**por tal f.**, on such conditions.

forrado, da. I. *pp.* of FORRAR. **II.** *a.* doubled.

forraje, *m.* forage, fodder; foraging; (coll.) trifles.

forrajeador, ra, *n.* forager, fodderer.

forrajear, *vn.* to gather forage or fodder.

forrajera, *f.* (mil.) shako guard.

forrajero, ra, *a.* forage, fodder (as *a.*).

forrar. I. *va.* to line (as clothes); to cover (as a book or an umbrella); (anat.) to sheathe, to fur. **II.** *vr.* (Mex., Guat.) to eat well, have a good meal.

forro, *m.* lining, doubling, inside, backing; (naut.) furring, planking, sheathing; cover of a book.— **f. de cabos,** (naut.) service, serving ropes.—**f. sobrepuesto de cable,** (naut.) keckling, rounding.

fortachón, na, *a.* (coll.) powerfully strong.

fortalecedor, ra, *n. & a.* fortifier(-fying).

fortalecer, *va.* (*ind.* FORTALEZCO; *subj.* FORTALEZCA) to fortify, strengthen, corroborate; to fortify (a place); to aid, encourage, support.

fortalecimiento, *m.* fortifying, strengthening; fortification, defenses.

fortaleza, *f.* fortitude; firmness; courage, strength, vigor; stronghold, fortress, fort.

fortalezco, fortaleza, *v. V.* FORTALECER.

forte. I. *interj.* (naut.) avast! **II.** *a.* (mus.) forte, loud.

fortepiano, *m.* (mus., obs.) pianoforte.

fortezuelo, la. I. *a. dim.* not very strong. **II.** *m.* small fort.

fortificable, *a.* fortifiable.

fortificación, *f.* fortification; fort; military architecture.—**f. de campaña,** field fortification.

fortificador, ra, *n. & a.* fortifier(-fying).

fortificante, *a.* fortifying.

fortificar, *va.* (*pret.* FORTIFIQUÉ; *subj.* FORTIFIQUE) to strengthen, invigorate; (mil.) to fortify.

fortín, *m. dim.* fortin, fortlet, small fort.

fortitud, *f.* fortitude.

fortuitamente, *adv.* fortuitously, accidentally.

fortuito, ta, *a.* fortuitous, accidental.

fortuna, *f.* fortune, chance, fate; good luck; wealth, resources; storm, tempest; accident of the sea.—**por f.,** fortunately, luckily.

fortunón, *m. aug.* great stroke of fortune; immense fortune (wealth).

forúnculo, furúnculo, *m.* (med.) boil.

forzadamente, *adv.* forcibly, violently.

forzado, da. I. *pp.* of FORZAR. **II.** *a.* forced.— **trabajos f.,** hard labor (penal). **III.** *n.* criminal sentenced to the galleys.

forzador, *m.* ravisher; forcer.

forzal, *m.* solid part of a comb.

forzamiento, *m.* act of forcing or violating.

forzar, *va.* (*ind. pres.* FUERZO, *pret.* FORCÉ; *subj.* FUERCE) to force, break in (as a door); to compel, force; to subdue by force; to ravish.

forzosa, *f.* decisive move at the game of draughts; compulsion.—**hacer la f. a uno,** (coll.) to compel one to act against one's will.

forzosamente, *adv.* necessarily; by force, forcibly, violently.

forzoso, sa, *a.* necessary, unavoidable; obligatory, compulsory.—**paro f.,** unemployment.

forzudamente, *adv.* with great power and force.

forzudo, da, *a.* strong, vigorous, lusty.

fosa, *f.* grave; (anat.) fossa.

fosar, *va.* to dig a pit or trench around.

fosca, *f.* haze; thicket, jungle.

fosco, ca, *a.* frowning, cross.

fosfatado, da, *a.* containing phosphate.

fosfático, ca, *a.* (chem.) phosphatic.

fosfato, *m.* (chem.) phosphate.

fosfaturia, *f.* (med.) phosphaturia.

fosfeno, *m.* (physiol.) phosphene.

fosfina, *f.* (chem.) phosphine.

fosfito, *m.* phosphite.

fosforado, da, *a.* containing phosphate.—**bronce f.,** phosphor bronze.

fosforera, *f.* match box.

fosforero, ra, *n.* vender of matches.

fosforescencia, *f.* phosphorescence.

fosforescente, *a.* phosphorescent.

fosforescer, *vn.* (*ind.* FOSFORESZCO; *subj.* FOSFORESZCA) to phosphoresce.

fosfórico, ca, *a.* phosphoric.

fosforita, *f.* (min.) phosphorite.

fósforo, *m.* phosphorus; friction match; morning star.

fosforoscopio, *m.* (phys.) phosphoroscope.

fosforoso, sa, *a.* phosphorous.

fosfuro, *m.* phosphide, phosphuret.

fósil, *n. & a.* fossil.—**fosilífero, ra,** *a.* fossiliferous.

fosilización, *f.* fossilization.

fosilizarse, *vr.* to fossilize, become fossil.

foso, *m.* pit, hole in the ground; (theat.) cellar under the stage; (fort.) moat, ditch, foss.—**f. séptico,** septic tank.

foto, *m.* or *f.* photo (photograph).

fotocromía, *f.* photochromy, color photography.

fotoeléctrico, ca, *a.* photoelectric.

fotofobia, *f.* (med.) photophobia.

fotófobo, ba, *a.* suffering from photophobia.

fotófono, *m.* (phys.) photophone.

fotogénico, ca, *a.* photogenic.

fotoglíptico, ca, *a.* photoglyptic.

fotograbado, *m.* photoengraving, photogravure.

fotograbador, ra, *n.* photoengraver.

fotograbar, *va. & vn.* to photoengrave.

fotografía, *f.* photography; photograph.

fotografiar, *va.* to photograph.

fotográficamente, *adv.* photographically.

fotográfico, ca, *a.* photographic.

fotógrafo, m. photographer.

fotolitografía, *f.* photolithography; photolithograph.

fotolitografiar, *va.* to photolithograph.

fotolitográficamente, *adv.* photolithographically.

fotolitográfico, ca, *a.* photolithographic.

fotología, *f.* photology, optics.

fotometría, *f.* photometry.

fotométrico, ca, *a.* photometric.

fotómetro, *m.* photometer.

fotomicrografía, *f.* photomicrography.

fotón, *m.* (phys.) photon.

fotoquímica, *f.* photochemistry.

fotosfera, *f.* (astr.) photosphere.

fototerapia, *f.* (med.) phototherapeutics.

fototerápico, ca, *a.* phototherapeutical.

fototipia, *f.* = FOTOLITOGRAFÍA.

fototípico, ca, *a.* = FOTOLITOGRÁFICO.

fototipografía, *f.* phototypography.

fototipográfico, ca, *a.* phototypographic.

fótula, *f.* (Am.) cockroach.

fotuto, *m.* (Cuba) whistle; trumpet, horn.

foya, *f.* oven full of charcoal.

frac, *m.* dress coat.

fracasar, *vn.* to fail, come to naught; (naut.) to crumble, to break in pieces.

fracaso, *m.* downfall, ruin; calamity; failure.

fracción, *f.* breaking into parts; fragment (broken off); (math.) fraction.—**f. continua,** continued fraction.—**f. decimal periódica,** repeating decimal.

fraccionado, da. I. *pp.* of FRACCIONAR. **II.** *a.* fractional.

fraccionamiento, *m.* division into fractions.

fraccionar, *va.* to divide into fractions.

fraccionario, ria, *a.* fractional.

fractura, *f.* fracture, breaking; (surg.) fracture.

fracturar, *va. & vr.* to fracture, break, rupture.

¹fraga, *f.* a kind of raspberry.

²fraga, *f.* thicket of brambles.

fragancia, *f.* fragrance, scent; good name or reputation.

fragante, *a.* fragrant; flagrant, notorious.—**en f.** = EN FLAGRANTE, in the very act.

fragaria, *f.* (bot.) strawberry.

fragata, *f.* (naut.) frigate.—**f. de aviso,** packet boat.—**f. ligera,** light fast-sailing vessel.

frágil, *a.* brittle, breakable, fragile; frail, weak.

fragilidad, *f.* fragility, brittleness; frailty.

frágilmente, *adv.* in a frail way.

fragmentario, ria, *a.* fragmentary.

fragmento, *m.* fragment.

fragor, *m.* noise, clamor, crash.

fragoroso, sa, *a.* (poet.) noisy, obstreperous, thundering, roaring.

fragosidad, *f.* roughness; impenetrability, thickness (of a forest); craggedness, cragginess.

fragoso, sa, *a.* craggy, rough, uneven; full of brambles and briers; noisy, roaring.

fragrancia, *f.,* **fragrante,** *a.* = FRAGANCIA, etc.

fragua, *f.* forge, as for iron; blacksmith's shop.

fraguado, *m.* setting, hardening.

fraguador, ra, *n.* schemer.

fraguar. I. *va.* to forge; to hammer out; to plan, plot, brew, scheme, concoct. II. *vn.* (mason) (of concrete, etc.) to set.

fragura, *f.* = FRAGOSIDAD.

frailada, *f.* (coll.) rude or unbecoming action of a monk.

fraile, *m.* friar, monk; fold turned up at bottom of a skirt; priest; (arch.) hood over a hearth; (print.) friar, badly inked spot; (bookbinding) fold in a leaf; upright post of a floodgate; (Cuba) residue from sugar making.

frailear, *va.* (agr.) to prune close to the trunk.

frailecillo, *m. dim.* little friar; (ornith.) lap-wing; wedge securing the spindle of a silk reel.

frailengo, ga, leño, ña, *a.* = FRAILESCO.

frailería, *f.* (coll.) monks in general; priests in general; body of monks or priests.

frailero, ra, *a.* very fond of priests.

frailesco, ca, *a.* monkish, friarlike; priestlike.

frailía, *f.* body of monks; regular clergy.

frailote, *m. aug.* big and coarse friar.

frailuco, *m.* despicable friar.

frailuno, na, *a.* (coll.) friarlike; priestlike.

frambuesa, *f.* (bot.) raspberry.

frambueso, *m.* (bot.) raspberry bush.

frámea, *f.* javelin, dart.

francachela, *f.* (coll.) a gala meal.

francalete, *m.* leather strap with a buckle.

francamente, *adv.* frankly, openly.

francés, sa. I. *a.* French.—**a la francesa,** in the French fashion.—**despedirse a la f.,** (coll.) to take French leave. II. *n.* Frenchman(-woman). III. *m.* French language.

francesada, *f.* anything characteristic of the French; French invasion (of Spain in 1808).

francesilla, *f.* (bot.) common yard crowfoot.

franciscano, na, *a.* Franciscan; gray-colored.

francisco, ca, *a.* Franciscan.

francmasón, *m.* Freemason, Mason.

francmasonería, *f.* Freemasonry.

franco, ca. I. *a.* frank, open; free, clear, disengaged; exempt, privileged; Frankish; (com.) duty free; in compound words, French or Franco-, as *francoamericano,* Franco-American.—**f. a bordo,** free on board, f. o. b.—**f. de porte,** prepaid. II. *m.* franc (French coin); fair time, when merchandise is sold free of duty.

francófilo, *n.* & *a.* Francophil, admirer of or friendly to the French.

francolín, *m.* (ornith.) francolin.

francote, ta, *a. aug.* (coll.) frank, open-hearted.

franchipán, *m.* franchipane, a perfume.

franchote, franchute, *n.* (contempt.) Frenchy.

franela, *f.* flannel.

frange, *m.* (her.) division of the field of a shield.

frangente. I. *a.* frangent, fracturing. II. *m.* accident, disaster, mishap.

frangible, *a.* brittle, frangible, breakable.

frangir, *va.* to break into pieces.

frangollar, *va.* (coll.) to do hurriedly.

frangollo, *m.* porridge of wheat and milk; (Am.) poorly-made stew.

frangote, *m.* (com.) bale of goods.

frángula, *f.* (bot.) berry-bearing alder.

franja, *f.* (sewing) fringe, trimming, band, braid, border; stripe; strip (of land).

franjar, franjear, *va.* (sewing) to trim with braids, bands, or stripes; to border.

franjón, *m. aug.* wide braid trimming.

franjuela, *f. dim.* narrow braid trimming.

franqueamiento, *m.* = FRANQUEO.

franquear. I. *va.* to exempt, to grant immunity to; enfranchise; to prepay (postage); to make liberal grants or gifts; to open, clear; to free (a slave). II. *vr.* to yield easily to the desire of others; to unbosom oneself; (naut.) to be ready for sailing.

franqueo, *m.* postage; liberating a slave.

franqueza, *f.* frankness; freedom, liberty, exemption.—**con f.,** frankly.

franquía, *f.* (naut.) sea room, offing.—**en f.,** ready.

franquicia, *f.* exemption from taxes; franchise, privilege, grant.

frasca, *f.* small branches.

frasco, *m.* flask, vial, bottle; powder flask.

frase, *f.* phrase; idiom, epigram; style of a writer. —**f. hecha,** proverb, saying, saw.—**f. musical,** (mus.) phrase.—**f. sacramental,** standard form.—**hacer frases,** to speak much saying little.

frasear, *va.* to phrase; (mus.) to phrase.

fraseología, *f.* phraseology; style of a writer; verbosity, pomposity.

frasquera, *f.* bottle case, liquor case.—**f. de fuego,** (naut.) fire case or fire chest.

frasquerilla, ita, *f. dim.* small bottle case.

frasqueta, *f.* (print.) frisket.

frasquete, frasquillo, ito, *m. dim.* small flask.

fratás, *m.* plastering trowel.

fratasar, *va.* to smooth with the trowel.

fraterna, *f.* (coll.) severe reprimand, lecture.

fraternal, *a.* fraternal, brotherly.

fraternalmente, *adv.* fraternally.

fraternidad, *f.* fraternity, brotherhood.

fraternizar, *vn.* to fraternize.

fraterno, na, *a.* fraternal, brotherly.

fratricida, *n.* fratricide, murderer (of one's brother).

fratricidio, *m.* fratricide, murder (of one's brother).

fraude, *m.,* **fraudulencia,** *f.* fraud.

fraudulentamente, *adv.* fraudulently.

fraudulento, ta, *a.* fraudulent; deceitful, artful.

fray, *m. contr.* of FRAILE, used as a title before the names of clergymen belonging to certain religious orders, as *Fray Luis de Granada.*

frazada, *f.* blanket.

frazadilla, *f. dim.* small or light blanket.

frecuencia, *f.* frequency.—**con f.,** frequently.

frecuentación, *f.* frequenting.

frecuentador, ra, *n.* & *a.* frequenter(-ing).

frecuentar, *va.* to frequent; to repeat.

frecuentativo, a. (gram.) frequentative.

frecuente, *a.* frequent.

frecuentemente, *adv.* frequently, often.

fregadero, *m.* scullery; kitchen sink.

fregado, *m.* scouring or scrubbing; (coll.) complicated affair.

fregador, ra. I. *n.* & *a.* washer(-ing). II. *m.* scullery; dishcloth, mop, scrubbing brush.

fregadura, *f.* rubbing, scrubbing, scouring.

fregajo, *m.* mop, swab. Also ESTROPAJO.

fregamiento, *m.* = FRICACIÓN, friction.

fregar, *va.* (*ind. pres.* FRIEGO, *pret.* FREGUÉ; *subj.* FRIEGUE) to rub; to scrub, mop, swab, scour; to wash (dishes); (Am.) to annoy, bother.

fregatriz, fregona, *f.* kitchenmaid; dishwasher.

fregonil, *a.* (coll.) wenchlike.

fregonzuela, *f. dim.* little kitchen girl.

fregué, *pret.* of FREGAR.

freidura, *f.* frying or dressing in a pan.

freila, *f.* (eccl.) lay sister.

freile, *m.* knight or priest of a military order.

freír, *va.* (*pp.* FREÍDO, FRITO; *ger.* FRIENDO; *ind. pres.* FRÍO, *pret.* él FRIÓ; *subj.* FRÍA) to fry or dress in a frying pan.—**freírse de calor,** to be excessively hot, to be baking.—**freírsela a uno,**

(coll.) to deceive one premeditatedly.—**al f. será el reír,** he laughs best who laughs last.

freje, m. (prov.) = FLEJE, iron hoop or strap.

fréjol, frejol, m. (bot.) kidney bean.

frémito, m. roar.

frenar, va. to bridle, to govern by the bridle; to brake, apply the brake to.

frenería, f. bridle making; harness shop.

frenero, m. bridle maker or seller; (Ry.) brakeman.

frenesí, m. frenzy, fury, madness; folly.

frenéticamente, adv. frantically, madly.

frenético, ca, a. mad, frantic, frenzied.

frenillar, va. (naut.) to bridle (the oars).

frenillo, m. (anat.) frenum; (naut.) bridle, fox, ratline.—**no tener f. en la lengua,** to be outspoken, not to mince one's words.

freno, m. bridle or bit of the bridle; (carriage) brake (for wheel); (mech.) check, stop, brake; curb, restraint, control.—**f. al vacío,** or (more properly) **de vacío,** vacuum brake.

frenología, f. phrenology.

frenológico, ca, a. phrenological.

frenólogo, m. phrenologist.

frenópata, m. alienist.

frenopatía, f. part of medical science treating mental disease.

frenopatología, f. alienism, science of mental diseases.

frentazo, m. (Mex.) rebuff, turning down.

frente. I. f. forehead; countenance, mien; intellect.—**no tener dos dedos de f.,** not to have any sense at all, a particle of brains. **II.** adv. in front, opposite, across the way. **III.** m. (mil.) front; (fort.) face of a bastion; front, fore part, face, façade; obverse (of coins, etc.).—**f. a,** opposite, facing; (fig.) in the face or eyes of.—**f. a f.,** face to face.—**f. por f.,** directly opposite.—**a f.,** straight ahead.—**al f.,** opposite; (com.) carried forward.—**al f. de,** in front of; in charge of.—**de f.,** from the front; front (as a.); (mil.) facing; abreast.—**del f.,** brought forward; opposite, across (the street, etc.).—**en f.,** = F. POR F.—**en f. de,** = AL F. DE.—**hacer f. a,** to face (a problem, etc.); to meet (a demand, etc.).

frentero, m. pad to protect a child's forehead.

frentón, ona, a. having a large forehead.

freo, m. (naut.) narrow channel, strait, fretum.

fresa, f. (bot.) strawberry; (mech.) drill, bit, milling tool.

fresada, f. an ancient dish of flour, milk and butter.

fresadora, f. (mech.) milling machine; (dent.) burr.

fresal, m. strawberry patch.

fresar, va. (mech.) to mill; to drill; to machine.

fresca, f. cool air, fresh air; piece of one's mind, biting remark.—**decir cuatro frescas a uno,** to rebuke one without mincing words.—**tomar la f.,** to take the air.

frescachón, na, a. robust and fresh-looking; (naut.) (of wind) brisk.

frescal, a. (fish) not entirely fresh, but preserved with little salt.

frescamente, adv. recently, lately, of late; coolly; bluntly.

fresco, ca. I. a. (of food) fresh; (of weather, etc.) cool; recent, newly come; just made, finished, or gathered; latest; fresh, buxom, ruddy; calm, cool; bold, forward, cheeky; unconcerned, unabashed, unmoved.—**estar, o quedar, f.,** to be disappointed, to fail.—**quedarse f.,** to act coolly, to show no scruple or concern. **II.** m. cool air, fresh air; (art) fresco; (Am.) cooling drink.—**al f.,** in the open air; in the night air; (art) fresco (painting).—**hacer f.,** (of atmosphere) to be cool.—**tomar el f.,** to get, to go out for, some fresh air.

frescor, m. cool, refreshing air; freshness; (art) flesh-color.

frescote, ta, a. aug. (coll.) fresh, ruddy, youthful.

frescura, f. freshness; coolness; luxuriant verdure or foliage; frankness, openness; freedom of manner, ease; tranquillity, coolness, unconcern.

fresero, ra. I. n. strawberry vender. **II.** f. (bot.) strawberry plant.

fresnal, m. pertaining to the ash tree.

fresneda, f. plantation of ash trees.

fresnillo, m. (bot.) white fraxinella.

fresno, m. ash tree; (com.) ash wood.—**f. americano,** white ash.—**f. húngaro,** Hungarian ash.

fresón, m. (bot.) Chile strawberry.

fresquecito, ta. I. a. dim. (coll.) little cool; nice and fresh. **II.** n. cool breeze.

fresquera, f. meat safe.

fresquería, f. (Am.) ice-cream parlor.

fresquero, ra, n. vender of fresh fish.

fresquillo, lla, a. = FRESQUECITO, TA.

fresquista, m. fresco painter.

fresquito, ta. I. a. dim. cool, coolish; fresh, just made, gathered, etc. **II.** m. cool, fresh air. **III.** adv. freshly made, recent, latest.

frey, m. contr. of FREILE; used as a title before the name of a clergyman belonging to a military order.

frez, m. contr. of FREILE; used as a title before the name of a clergyman belonging to a military order.

frez, ¹freza, f. dung, excrement.

²freza, f. spawning; trail of fish in spawning; roe; time when silkworms eat; hole dug by an animal.

frezada, f. blanket.

¹frezar, vn. (pret. FRECÉ; subj. FRECE) to eject excrement; to eject the droppings of grubs from hives.

²frezar, va. (of silkworms) to nibble (leaves); (of fish) to spawn; (of hogs) to root; (of dogs, etc.) to scratch (the ground).

friabilidad, f. friability, brittleness.

friable, a. friable, fragile, brittle.

frialdad, f. coldness; unconcern, coolness; nonsense; (med.) impotence.

fríamente, adv. coldly, frigidly, coolly; flatly.

friático, ca, a. foolish, graceless, silly.

fricación, f. friction, frication.

fricandó, m. (cook.) fricandeau.

fricar, va. to rub together.

fricasé, m. (cook.) fricassee.

fricción, f. friction, rubbing.

friccionar, va. to rub.

friega, f. friction, rubbing.

friego, friegue, v. V. FREGAR.

friera, f. chilblain on the heel.

frigidez, f. frigidity.

frígido, da, a. frigid.

frigio, gia, n. & a. Phrygian.

frigorífero, m. (Am.) = FRIGORÍFICO.

frigorífico, ca. I. a. refrigerating. **II.** m. cold-storage house or room; packing house.

friísimo, ma, a. super. extremely cold.

fríjol, frijol, m. kidney bean.

frimario, m. Frimaire, third month of the French-Revolution calendar.

fringílago, m. (ornith.) titmouse.

fringílido, da. I. n. & a. (zool.) fringilline. **II.** m. pl. Fringillidæ, the finch family.

¹frío, ía. I. a. cold; impotent; indifferent, unmoved, unemotional; dull, graceless, witless.—**hacer f.** (of weather) to be cold.—**tener f.,** (of person) to be, feel, cold. **II.** m. cold, coldness (of temperature).—pl. (Am.) malaria.

²frío, frió, fría, v. V. FREÍR.

friolento, ta, a. chilly; very sensitive to cold.

friolera, f. trifle, bauble, gewgaw.

friolero, ra, a. = FRIOLENTO; (ironic) very important.

frisa, f. frieze; (fort.) palisade.

frisado, m. curly silk plush or shag.

frisador, ra, n. frizzler.

frisadura, f. frizzling, shagging.

frisar. I. va. to frizzle or frizz (cloth); to rub;

(naut.) to line, to pack. **II.** *vn.* (**en**) to resemble; to approach, to be near (to).

friso, *m.* (arch.) frieze; wainscot, dado, mopboard.

frisol, frísol, *m.* (bot.) string bean.

frisón, na. I. *n.* & *a.* Frisian. **II.** *m.* large draught horse.

frisuelo, *m.* string bean.—*pl.* fritters.

frita, *f.* (ceramics) frit, ferretto.

fritada, *f.* fry; dish of anything fried.

fritillas, *f. pl.* fritters, pancakes.

frito, ta. I. *pp. irreg.* of FREÍR, fried.—**estar f.,** (Mex., P. R.) to be annoyed; (Arg.) to be lost. **II.** *m.* fry.

fritura, *f.* fry, fritter.

frívolamente, *adv.* frivolously.

frivolidad, *f.* frivolity; frivolousness.

frivolité, *f.* tatting, fancywork.

frívolo, la, *a.* frivolous.

¹fronda, *f.* (bot.) leaf; frond.—*pl.* foliage, verdure.

²fronda, *f.* (surg.) a sling-shaped bandage.

fronde, *m.* (bot.) frond, fern leaf.

frondosidad, *f.* frondage, leafy foliage.

frondoso, sa, *a.* leafy, luxuriant.

frontal. I. *a.* frontal, pertaining to the forehead. **II.** *m.* (eccl.) frontal, altar hanging; (anat.) frontal bone.

frontalera, *f.* brow band (of a bridle); brow pad under a yoke; (eccl.) trimmings of an altar frontal; place where church frontals are kept.

frontera, *f.* frontier, boundary, border; binder of a fruit basket; (arch.) façade; side of a softbrick mold.

fronterizo, za, *a.* frontier (as *a.*); facing, opposite.

frontero, ra. I. *a.* opposite, facing. **II.** *m.* governor or commander of frontier forces; frontlet of brow pad for children. **III.** *adv.* in front.

frontil, *m.* yoke pad for draught oxen.

frontino, na, *a.* marked in the face.

frontis, *m.* (arch.) frontispiece, façade.

frontispicio, *m.* (of book, arch.) frontispiece; (coll.) face.

frontón, *m.* main wall of a handball court; fives court; (arch.) pediment.

frontudo, da, *a.* (of animals) having a large forehead.

frontura, *f.* front of a stocking frame.

frotación, *f.* rubbing.

frotador, ra, *n.* one who or that which rubs.

frotadura, *f.* rubbing.

frotamiento, *m.*, **frotante,** *a.* rubbing.

frotar, *va.* to rub.

frote, *m.* friction, rubbing; attrition.

fructidor, *m.* Fructidor, twelfth month of the French-Revolution calendar.

fructíferamente, *adv.* fruitfully.

fructífero, ra, *a.* fructiferous, fruit-bearing; fruitful.

fructificación, *f.* (bot.) fructification.

fructificador, ra, *n.* & *a.* fertilizer(-ing).

fructificar, *vn.* (*pret.* FRUCTIFIQUÉ; *subj.* FRUCTIFIQUE) to fructify, bear fruit; to yield profit.

fructuario, ria, *a.* (law) usufructuary.

fructuosamente, *adv.* fruitfully, profitably.

fructuoso, sa, *a.* fruitful, profitable.

fruente, *a.* enjoying.

frugal, *a.* frugal, parsimonious, thrifty.

frugalidad, *f.* frugality, thrift.

frugalmente, *adv.* frugally, thriftily.

frugívoro, ra, *a.* frugivorous, fruit-eating.

fruición, *f.* fruition, enjoyment, gratification.

fruir, *vn.* (*ger.* FRUYENDO; *ind. pres.* FRUYO, *pret.* él FRUYÓ; *subj.* FRUYA) to enjoy what has been hoped for.

fruitivo, va, *a.* enjoyable.

frumentario, ria; frumenticio, cia, *a.* (bot.) frumentaceous.

frunce, *m.* (sewing) shirr, shirring, gather.

fruncido, da. I. *pp.* of FRUNCIR. **II.** *a.* contracted.

fruncidor, *m.* (sewing) gatherer.

fruncimiento, *m.* shirring, gathering; humbug, deceit, imposture.

fruncir. I. *va.* (*ind.* FRUNZO; *subj.* FRUNZA) (sewing) to gather, shirr; to pucker; to contract. reduce; to conceal or disguise (the truth).—**f. el ceño** or **entrecejo,** to frown.—**f. las cejas,** to knit the brows.—**f. los labios,** to curl or pucker the lips. **II.** *vr.* to affect modesty; to be shocked.

fruslera, *f.* brass turnings or clippings.

fruslería, *f.* trifle, bauble, tidbit.

fruslero, ra, *a.* trifling, frivolous, futile.

frustráneo, nea, *a.* vain, useless, nugatory.

frustrar. I. *va.* to frustrate, defeat, thwart. **II.** *vr.* to miscarry, to fail, to fall through, to be a failure.

frustratorio, ria, *a.* frustrative, defeating.

fruta, *f.* a piece of fruit; fruitage.—*pl.* fruit (edible, esp. table, tree fruits).—**f. del tiempo,** fruit eaten in season; anything incidental or peculiar to a season.—**f. de sartén,** pancake, fritter.—**f. nueva,** something new, novelty.

frutaje, *m.* (art) painting of fruits and flowers.

frutal. I. *a.* (bot.) fruit-bearing, fruit (as *a.*). **II.** *m.* fruit tree.

frutar, *vn.* to bear or yield fruit.

frutería, *f.* fruitery, fruit store.

frutero, ra. I. *n.* fruiterer; fruit basket, fruit dish. **II.** *m.* napkin or doily over a fruit dish; (art) painting representing fruit; ornamental piece of artificial fruit.

frutescente, *a.* frutescent; shrublike, shrubby.

frútice, *m.* perennial shrub.

fruticoso, sa, *a.* (bot.) fruiticose.

frutilla, *f. dim.* small fruit; (Am.) strawberry; bead for rosaries.

frutillar, *m.* (Am.) strawberry bed.

fruto, *m.* fruit; any useful produce of the earth; any product of man's intellect or labor; benefice, profit.—*pl.* (com.) produce, commodities.—**f. de bendición,** child lawfully begotten.—**sacar f. de,** or **con,** to derive benefit from, succeed in.

fruyo, fruyó, etc. *v.* *V.* FRUIR.

ftaleína, *f.* (chem.) phthalein.—**ftálico, ca,** *a.* phthalic.—**ftatilo,** *m.* phthatyl.

fu, *interj.* of disgust; sound imitating the snarling of a cat.

fúcar, *m.* rich, opulent man; nabob.

fucilar, *vn.* (poet.) to flash, to lighten.

fucilazo, *m.* heat lightning.

fucsia, *f.* (bot.) fuchsia.

fucsina, *f.* (chem.) fuchsine.

fuego. I. *m.* fire; conflagration; beacon fire; bonfire, watch fire; skin eruption, rash; firing of firearms; hearth, fireplace; ardor, heat of an action; hearth, house; (vet.) cautery.—*pl.* lights, lighthouse; (mil.) fire, firing.—**f. de San Telmo,** (naut.) Castor and Pollux.—*pl.* fatuo, jack-o'-lantern, will-o'-the wisp, ignis fatuus.—**f. graneado,** (mil.) continued firing, drumfire.—**f. griego,** Greek or wild fire.—**f. nutrido** = F. GRANEADO.—**f. sacro,** St. Anthony's fire, erysipelas.—**fuegos artificiales,** fireworks.—**a f. y sangre,** by fire and sword.—**dar f. a un navío,** (naut.) to bream a ship.—**hacer f.,** to fire (a weapon). **II.** (¡fuego!) *interj.* (mil.) fire!—¡f! ¡f. de Cristo! ¡f. de Dios! blazes! confound it!

fueguecillo, cito, zuelo, *m. dim.* small fire.

fueguino, na, *a.* & *n.* Fuegian.

fuellar, *m.* bright talcum ornament on wax tapers.

fuelle, *m.* bellows; blower; (carriage) hood, top; clouds over mountains; (sewing) puckers in clothes; (coll.) talebearer.

fuente, *f.* water spring; fountain; source; (often *pl.*) headwaters, source (of a river); dish, platter; (surg.) seton, issue.—**beber en buenas fuentes,** to be well-informed.—**f. de información,** source of information, "contact."

fuentecica, cilla, cita, zuela, *f. dim.* small or little fountain.

fuer, *m. contr. of* FUERO.—**a f. de,** *adv.* as a, in the manner of (*a fuer de caballero,* as or like a gentleman).

¹**fuera. I.** *adv.* out, without, outside.—**f. de,** out of; outside of; besides, in addition to.—**f. de lugar,** out of place; irrelevant.—**f. de orden,** (parl. law) out of order.—**f. de quicio,** unhinged; out of order, out of joint.—**f. de sí,** beside oneself; aghast.—**de f.,** from the outside. —**hacia f.,** outward.—**por f.,** on the outside. **II.** (¡**fuera!**) *interj.* out! away! put him out! get out!

²**fuera,** etc. *v. V.* SER and IR.

fuerarropa.—**hacer f.,** a command used in the galleys for the rabble to undress.

fuero, *m.* statute law; jurisdiction, judicial power; privilege or exemption granted to a province; compilation of laws.—**f. de la conciencia,** tribunal of conscience; heart of hearts.—**f. exterior,** or **externo,** statute law; legal tribunals. —**f. interior,** or **interno,** = F. DE LA CONCIENCIA.—**a f.,** according to law or custom.—**de f.,** de jure; according to law.

fuerte. I. *a.* strong; powerful; intense, severe; secure, fast, impregnable; firm, compact; efficacious; thick, heavy; proficient, surpassing; loud; manly, determined, unswerving; hard, not malleable; terrible; grave; excessive; having excess of weight.—**es f. cosa,** it is very hard. **II.** *m.* fort, fortress; strong point, forte; (mus.) forte, loud (marked *f*). **III.** *adv.* strongly, hard, copiously, abundantly, excessively.

fuertecico, cito, cillo, zuelo, *m. dim.* small fortress, blockhouse.

fuertemente, *adv.* strongly, firmly, fast; powerfully; vehemently.

fuerza, *f.* force; strength; stress; violence; firmness, stanchness; efficacy; fortitude, courage; virtue, efficiency; mental power; (mech.) power; (mil., gen. *pl.*) force(s); (fort.) fortress, a strong place; strongest part of a thing; proneness, strong propensity; the third of a sword next the hilt; (sewing) stiffening piece in garments.—**f. animal,** animal power.—**f. atractriz,** attractive force.—**f. bruta,** brute force.—**f. centrífuga,** centrifugal force.—**f. centrípeta,** centripetal force.—**f. contraelectromotriz,** counterelectromotive force.—**f. de agua,** water power.—**f. de sangre** = F. ANIMAL.—**f. de vapor,** steam power.—**f. electromotriz,** electromotive force.—**f. mayor,** (law & com.) superior force, force majeure.—**f. motriz,** moving force; power.—**f. viva,** (mech.) vis viva (twice the kinetic energy).—**fuerzas conspirantes,** conspiring powers.—**fuerzas de mar y de tierra,** naval and land forces.—**a f. de,** by dint of, by force of.—**a la f.** = DE POR F.— **a viva f.,** by main force; with the utmost effort. —**de por f.,** by force, forcibly; necessarily.— **en f. de,** on account of.—**hacer f. de remos,** (naut.) to pull hard at the oars.—**hacer f. de velas,** (naut.) to crowd sail, to carry a press of sail; to make a strenuous effort.—**por f., por la f.** = DE POR F.—**ser f.,** to be necessary.

fuerzo, fuerce, *v. V.* FORZAR.

fuetazo, *m.* (Am.) blow with a whip.—*pl.* horsewhipping.—**dar,** or **pegar, fuetazos,** *m.* (Am.) to horsewhip.

fuete, *m.* (Am.) horsewhip, riding whip.

fufú, *m.* (Am.) mass made of yam, plantain, etc., and pounded.

fuga, *f.* flight; escape; runaway; elopement; leak, leakage; (mus.) fugue.—**f. deshecha,** precipitate flight.—**f. precipitada,** stampede.—**poner en f.,** to put to flight, rout.

fugacidad, *f.* fugacity, brevity.

fugar, *vr.* (*pret.* me FUGUÉ; *subj.* me FUGUE) to flee, to run away; to escape, leak out.

fugaz, *a.* fugacious; fugitive, running away; brief, fleeting.—**estrella f.,** shooting star.

fugazmente, *adv.* fleetingly.

fugitivo, va. I. *n.* & *a.* fugitive, runaway. **II.** *a.* brief, perishable, unsteady, unstable.

fugué, fugue, *v. V.* FUGAR.

fui, etc. *v. V.* SER and IR.

fuina, *f.* (zool.) = GARDUÑA, marten.

fulanito, ta; fulano, na, *n.* so-and-so.—**F. de tal,** John Doe, so-and-so.—**F., Zutano y Mengano,** Tom, Dick and Harry.

fulcro, *m.* (mech.) fulcrum.

fulgente, *a.* (poet.) refulgent, brilliant.

fúlgido, da, *a.* bright, resplendent.

fulgor, *m.* fulgency, brilliancy.

fulguración, *f.* flash; flashing; (med.) lightning stroke.

fulgurante, *a.* resplendent, shining.

fulgurar, *vn.* to flash, shine with brilliancy.

fulgurita, *f.* (geol.) fulgurite.

fulguroso, sa, *a.* fulgurous.

fúlica, *f.* (ornith.) fulica, coot.

fuliginoso, sa, *a.* fuliginous, dark, sooty.

fulminación, *f.* fulmination, thundering.

fulminado, da, *a.* struck by lightning.

fulminador, ra, *n.* & *a.* thunderer(-ing); fulminator(-ing).

fulminante. I. *a.* fulminating, thundering; exploding, explosive; (of illness) serious; fatal. **II.** *m.* (artil.) cap, percussion cap.

fulminar, *va.* to fulminate; (of lightning) to flash; to cause to explode; to throw out as an object of terror; to thunder, utter wrathfully.

fulminato, *m.* (chem.) fulminate.

fulminatriz, *f. a.* fulminating.

fulmíneo, nea, *a.* fulmineous.

fulmínico, *a.* (chem.) fulminic (acid).

fulminoso, sa, *a.* fulminatory.

fulleresco, ca, *a.* pert. to cheaters, sharpers.

fullería, *f.* cheating at games; guile, cunning.

fullero, ra. I. *a.* "shady," dishonest; (Am.) conceited, arrogant. **II.** *n.* cheat; sharper.

fullingue, *a.* (Chile) of bad quality; sickly, lifeless.

fullona, *f.* (coll.) dispute, quarrel, wrangle.

fumable, *a.* good to smoke.

fumada, *f.* puff, whiff (of smoke).

fumadero, *m.* smoking room.

fumador, ra. I. *n.* smoker. **II.** *a.* addicted to smoking.

fumante, *a.* smoking, fuming.

fumar, *va.* & *vn.* to smoke (cigars, etc.).

fumarada, *f.* puff, whiff, or blast of smoke; pipeful of tobacco.

fumaria, *f.* (bot.) fumitory.

fumarola, *f.* (geol.) fumarole.

fumífero, ra, *a.* (poet.) smoking.

fumífugo, ga, *a.* smoke-dispersing.

fumigación, *f.* fumigation.

fumigador, ra, *n.* & *a.* fumigator(-ing).

fumigar, *va.* (*pret.* FUMIGUÉ; *subj.* FUMIGUE) to fumigate.—**fumigatorio, ria. I.** *a.* that fumigates. **II.** *m.* perfuming pan.

fumista, *n.* stove worker or plumber.

fumistería, *f.* stove works or shop.

fumívoro, ra, *a.* smokeless.

fumorola, *f.* = FUMAROLA.

fumosidad, *f.* smokiness.

fumoso, sa, *a.* fumy, smoky.

funámbulo, la, *n.* tightrope walker.

función, *f.* function; duty; functioning, operation, working; religious ceremony, public demonstration; (theat.) performance, play; (math., physiol.) function; (mil.) fight, engagement, battle.

funcional, *a.* (math., physiol.) functional.

funcionamiento, *m.* (mech.) functioning, working, running, performance.—**de f.,** operating.

funcionar, *vn.* to function; (of machines) to work, run.

funcionario, *m.* functionary, public official.

funda, *f.* case, sheath, cover, envelope, slip.—**f. de almohada,** pillowcase.

fundación, *f.* foundation; founding, establishing; erection, raising, building; basis; rise, beginning, origin; endowment, foundation, endowed institution; (arch.) foundation, base, groundwork.

fundadamente, *adv.* with good reason, with good evidence or proof.

fundador, ra, *n.* founder.

fundamental, *a.* fundamental.

fundamentalmente, *adv.* fundamentally.

fundamentar, *va.* to found; to establish on a basis; to ground; to base; to set firm.

fundamento, *m.* foundation, groundwork; basis; reason, fundamental principle; source, origin, root; (of children) good behavior, orderliness; (weaving) weft, woof.

fundar. I. *va.* to found; to raise, erect, build; to establish, institute; to base, ground. **II.** *vr.* (en) to base one's opinion (on).

fundente. I. *a.* (chem.) fusing, melting, smelting. **II.** *m.* (chem.) flux; (med.) dissolvent.

fundería, *f.* foundry; smelting work.

fundible, *a.* fusible.

fundibulario, *m.* Roman soldier armed with a sling.—**fundíbulo,** *m.* ancient war engine for throwing stones.

fundición, *f.* fusion, melting, casting; foundry, smeltery; cast; cast iron; (print.) font.

fundidor, *m.* melter, smelter.

fundir. I. *va.* to fuse or melt; to smelt; to cast. **II.** *vr.* to fuse, melt; to merge, blend, unite; (Am.) to be ruined.

fundo, *m.* (law) rural property.

fúnebre, *a.* funereal, mournful, sad; funeral; dark, lugubrious.

fúnebremente, *adv.* mournfully, sorrowfully.

funeral, *n.* & *a.* funeral (as a *n.*, often *pl.*).

funerala.—a la f., (mil.) inverted (arms).

funerario, ria, *a.* funeral.

fúnereo, rea, *a.* mournful, sad, funereal.

funestamente, *adv.* sadly, dolefully.

funestar, *va.* to blot, tarnish, stain, profane.

funesto, ta, *a.* regrettable, untoward; mournful, sad, dismal.

fungiforme, *a.* fungiform.

fungible, *a.* consumable; (law) fungible.

fungir, *vn.* (Am.) to act in some capacity.

fungo, *m.* (med.) fungus.

fungosidad, *f.* (med.) spongy morbid growth.

fungoso, sa, *a.* fungous, excrescent, spongy.

funicular, *a.* funicular.

funículo, *m.* (bot.) funicle or funiculus.

fuñique, *a.* awkward; timorous, pusillanimous.

furente, *a.* furious, raging, frantic.

furgón, *m.* wagon; car.

furia, *f.* fury; rage; fit of madness; ill-tempered person; hurry, hustling; zeal, ardor.—**a toda f.,** with utmost speed.

furibundo, da, *a.* furious, enraged, frantic.

furiente, *a.* = FURENTE.

furierismo, *m.* Fourierism.

furierista, *n.* & *a.* Fourierist(-ic).

furiosamente, *adv.* furiously.

furioso, sa, *a.* furious; very great, excessive.

furlón, *m.* = FORLÓN, anc. two-seat chaise.

¹**furo, ra,** *a.* shy, unsociable, reserved; untamed, wild.

²**furo,** *m.* (Cuba) opening of a sugar mold.

³**furo.—hacer f.,** to hide a thing with the intention of keeping it.

furor, *m.* furor, fury, madness, rage, anger; enthusiasm, exaltation of fancy; rage, fashion.—

f. uterino, (med.) nymphomania.—**hacer f.,** to be the rage, "make a hit."

furriel, furrier, *m.* (mil.) quartermaster; clerk of the king's mews.

furriela, furriera, *f.* place of keeper of the keys of the king's palace.

furrusca, *f.* (Colomb.) row, brawl.

furtivamente, *adv.* by stealth, clandestinely.

furtivo, va, *a.* furtive, clandestine.

furúnculo, *m.* (med.) furuncle, boil.

furunculoso, sa, *a.* furunculose.

fusa, *f.* (mus.) demisemiquaver.

fusado, da, *a.* (her.) charged with fusils or spindles.

fusca, *f.* (ornith.) a dark-colored duck.

fusco, ca, *a.* fuscous, brown, dark.

fuselado, da, *a.* = FUSADO, DA.

fuselaje, *m.* (aer.) fuselage.

fusente, *a.* receding (tide).

fusibilidad, *f.* fusibility.

fusible. I. *a.* fusible. **II.** *m.* (elec.) fuse.

fusiforme, *a.* fusiform, spindle-shaped.

fusil, *m.* rifle, gun, musket.—**f. de aguja,** needle gun.—**f. de chispa,** flintlock musket.—**f. de percusión,** or **de pistón,** musket.—**f. de retrocarga,** breechloader.—**f. rayado,** rifle.

fusilamiento, *m.* execution by shooting.

fusilar, *va.* to shoot, execute by shooting.

fusilazo, *m.* musket shot, rifle shot.

fusilería, *f.* (mil.) musketry; body of fusileers or musketeers.

fusilero, *m.* fusileer, musketeer.

fusión, *f.* fusion, melting; union; (com.) merger.

fusionar. I. *va.* to unite, bring together, merge. **II.** *vr.* (com.) to merge, form a merger.

fusionista, *n.* fusionist.

fusique, *m.* bottle-shaped snuffbox.

fusor, *m.* smelting ladle or vessel.

fusta, *f.* brushwood; woollen stuff; whiplash; (naut.) lateen-rigged lighter.

fustán, *m.* fustian (cloth); (Am.) petticoat.

fustanero, *m.* fustian manufacturer.

fuste, *m.* wood, timber; tree and bows of a saddle; (poet.) saddle; shaft of a lance; foundation of anything not material; substance, importance; (arch.) fust, shaft of a column.

fustero, ra. I. *a.* pertaining to a fust, foundation, etc. **II.** *m.* turner or carpenter.

fustete, *m.* (bot.) Venetian sumac; fustic, yellow-wood.

fustigante, *a.* fustigating, beating.

fustigar, *va.* to lash, fustigate.

fustina, *f.* place for fusing metals.

fútbol, *m.* (Angl.) football.—**futbolero, ra; futbolista. I.** *a.* football (as *a.*). **II.** *n.* football player.—**futbolístico, ca,** *a.* football (as *a.*).

futesa, *f.* trifle, bagatelle, bauble, gewgaw.

fútil, *a.* trifling, flimsy, trivial.

futilidad, *f.* worthlessness, triviality.

futre, *m.* (Chile) dude, fop, coxcomb.

futura, *f.* acquired right to an office or employment before its vacancy; (coll.) betrothed, intended bride.

futurismo, *m.* (art) futurism.

futurista, *n.* & *a.* (art) futurist(-ic).

futuro, ra. I. *a.* future. **II.** *m.* betrothed, future husband; future, futurity; (gram.) future.—**en lo f.,** in future, hereafter.

G

gabacho, cha, *a.* applied to the natives of some places at the foot of the Pyrenees, and also in derision to the French; (coll.) Frenchified.

gabán, *m.* greatcoat, overcoat.

gabaonita, *n.* & *a.* Gabaonite.

gabarda, *f.* (bot.) wild rose.

gabardina, *f.* gabardine.

gabarit, *m.* (Ry.) track gauge.

For pronunciation, see the rules at the beginning of the book.

gabarra, *f.* (naut.) lighter, barge, gabbard.

gabarrero, *m.* (naut.) lighterman.

gabarro, *m.* flaw or defect in goods; error, mistake; drudgery, burdensome obligation; (mason. and art) badigeon, filling; (vet.) swelling on the pastern of horses; pip (disease of fowls).

gabarrón, *m. aug.* (naut.) large barge.

gabasa, *f.* = BAGASA, prostitute.

gábata, *f.* bowl for mess on galleys.

gabazo, *m.* bagasse.

gabela, *f.* gabelle, tax; duty, burden.

gabinete, *m.* cabinet (ministers of state and privy councillors); private room where the cabinet meets; reception room, sitting room; private parlor; library, study; studio; ladies' boudoir or dressing room; laboratory.—**g. de lectura,** reading room.—**de g.,** theoretical, parlor (as *a.,* app. to one with purely theoretical knowledge).

gablete, *m.* (arch.) gable.

gabote, *m.* (prov.) shuttlecock.

gacel, *m.,* **gacela,** *f.* gazelle.

gaceta, *f.* gazette; record (a publication); newspaper.—**mentir mas que la g.,** to be an inveterate liar.

gacetera, *f.* woman who sells newspapers.

gacetero, *m.* news writer; seller of newspapers.

gacetilla, *f.* personal-news column; town talk, gossip; newspaper squib; newsmonger.

gacetillero, *m.* newspaper reporter; paragrapher; wretched writer, penny-a-liner.

gacetista, *n.* one who delights in reading newspapers; newsmonger, gossip.

gacha, *f.* very thin watery mass; (Cuba) unglazed crock.—*pl.* porridge; pap; caresses, pettings.—**hacerse unas gachas,** to be too soft or affectionate.

gaché, *m.* (prov.) fellow, guy.

¹gacheta, *f.* spring lever, or tooth, of a latch.

²gacheta, *f.* sticking paste.

gacho, cha, *a.* turned or bent downward; (of cattle) with down-curved horns; (of hat) slouch.—**a gachas,** (coll.) on all-fours.

gachón, na. I. *a.* (coll.) graceful, sweet, attractive, bright. **II.** *n.* pampered, spoiled child.

gachonada, gachonería, *f.* (coll.) gracefulness, cunningness, brightness, piquancy.

gachuela, *f. dim.* of GACHA.

gachumbo, *m.* (Am.) shell of various fruits, from which cups and other vessels are made.

gachupín, *m.* Spaniard settled in Lat. Am.

gádido, da. I. *n. & a.* (ichth.) gadid. **II.** *m. pl.* (ichth.) Gadidae.

gaditano, na, *a.* of or pertaining to Cadiz.

gaélico, ca, *a.* Gaelic.

gafa, *f.* hook for bending a crossbow.—*pl.* (naut.) can hooks, grapple hooks; spectacles; spectacle bows.

gafar, *va.* to hook, to claw, to catch with a hook or with the nails.

gafedad, *f.* (med.) claw hand.

gafete, *m.* clasp, hook and eye.

gafo, fa, *a.* suffering from claw hand.

gago, ga, *n.* stammerer, stutterer.

gaguear, *vn.* (Am.) to stutter.

gaguera, *f.* (Am.) stuttering.

gaita, *f.* flageolet; hurdy-gurdy; (coll.) neck.—**g. gallega,** bagpipe.—**estar de g.,** (coll.) to be very merry.—**templarle la g. a uno,** to humor one.

gaitería, *f.* gay and gaudy dress.

gaitero, ra. I. *a.* (coll.) unbecomingly sportive and gay; (coll.) gaudy, showy, flamboyant. **II.** *n.* piper, one who plays the bagpipe.

gaje, *m.* salary, pay, wages.—*pl.* perquisites, fees.

gajo, *m.* branch (of a tree); part of a bunch of grapes torn off; pyramidal raceme of any fruit; (orange, pomegranate, etc.) section; prong or tine of pitchforks, etc.; spur of a mountain ridge.

gajoso, sa, *a.* composed of GAJOS.

gala, *f.* gala; full, or court, dress; graceful, pleasing address; parade, ostentation; choicest part; (Am.) prize.—*pl.* regalia, finery, trappings, paraphernalia.—**galas de novia,** bridal trousseau.—**de g.,** full-dress (suit, uniform).—**hacer g. de,** or **tener a g.,** to be proud of, glory in, boast of.

galabardera, *f.* (bot.) wild rose.

galactita, galactites, *f.* fuller's earth.

galactómetro, *m.* lactometer.

galactosa, *f.* (chem.) galactose.

galafate, *m.* artful thief, cunning rogue.

galaico, ca, *n. & a.* = GALLEGO, Galician.

galamero, ra, *a.* dainty, sweet-mouthed.

galán, *m.* spruce, well-made man; gallant, courtier; lover, wooer; ladies' man; (theat.) leading man or woman.—**g., g.,** easily, without effort. —**segundo g.,** (theat.) man who has a walk-on part.

galanamente, *adv.* elegantly, smartly, gracefully.

galancete, *m. dim.* spruce little man or lad; (theat.) juvenile leading man.

galanga, *f.* (bot.) officinal galangal.

galano, na, *a.* smartly dressed; tasteful; (of literary style) elegant, pleasing; beautiful, fresh (as flowers); (Cuba) mottled, parti-colored.

galante, *a.* gallant, polished, attentive to ladies.

galanteador, *m.* wooer, lover; flatterer.

galantear, *va.* to court, woo, pay attention to.

galantemente, *adv.* gallantly, politely, attentively.

galanteo, *m.* gallantry, courtship, wooing.

galantería, *f.* gallantry, courtesy, politeness; grace, elegance; compliment to a lady; liberality, generosity.

galanura, *f.* prettiness, gorgeousness, elegance.

galapagar, *m.* place where tortoises abound.

galápago, *m.* fresh-water tortoise; (agr.) bed of plowshare; frame for boring guns; mold for convex tiles; (foundry) pig, ingot; (mason.) small centering frame; (surg.) strip with ends forked or deeply notched; English saddle; (Am.) sidesaddle; (mil.) shed formed with shields joined together; mantelet, vinea, cat castle, sow; (vet.) scratch.

galapaguera, *f.* aquarium for tortoises.

galapo, *m.* (rope-making) laying top.

galardón, *m.* guerdon, reward, prize.

galardonador, ra, *n. & a.* rewarder(-ing).

galardonar, *va.* to reward, recompense, requite.

gálata, *n. & a.* Galatian.

galato, *m.* (chem.) gallate.

galatites, *f.* fuller's earth.

galaxia, *f.* soapstone, steatite; (astr.) Galaxy, Milky Way.

galayo, *m.* cliff.

galbana, *f.* sloth, laziness, indolence.

galbanado, da, *a.* yellowish-grey.

galbanero, ra, *a.* (coll.) lazy, indolent.

gálbano, *m.* (pharm.) galbanum.

galbanoso, sa, *a.* indolent, lazy, shiftless.

gálbulo, *m.* nut of the cypress tree.

galdrope, *m.* (naut.) wheel rope.

galdrufa, *f.* spinning top.

gálea, *f.* galea, ancient helmet.

galeato, ta, *a.* preface in answer to actual or probable criticism.

galeaza, *f.* (naut.) galleass.

galega, *f.* (bot.) officinal goat's-rue.

galena, *f.* (min.) galena.

galénico, ca, *a.* Galenic.—**galenismo,** *m.* Galenism.—**galenista,** *n.* Galenist.

galeno, na, *a.* (naut.) moderate, soft (wind).

gáleo, *m.* (ichth.) swordfish.

galeón, *m.* (naut.) galleon.

galeota, *f.* (naut.) galliot.

galeote, *m.* galley slave.

galera, *f.* (naut.) galley; wagon, van; (Hond., Mex.) shed; house of correction for women; extra line of beds in a hospital ward; (print.) galley; (arith.) fraction line; (carp.) smooth plane, organ-builder's plane; furnace for distilling sulphur.

galerada, *f.* carload, van load; (print.) galley; galley proof.

galerero, *m.* wagoner, van driver.

galería, *f.* gallery, lobby, corridor; (theat.) gallery; art museum; collection of paintings; (fort.) narrow covered passage across a moat; (min.) gallery, driftway, heading.—**g. de popa,** (naut.) stern gallery or balcony.

galerilla, *f. dim.* small gallery.

gallerín, *m. dim.* (print.) wooden galley.

galerita, *f.* (ornith.) crested lark.

galerna, *f.,* **galerno,** *m.* (naut.) stormy northwest wind.

galerón, *m.* (Mex.) large room serving as jail or prison; (Am.) a kind of popular air and dance.

galés, sa, *n.* & *a.* Welsh.

galfarro, *m.* rogue, loafer, idler; (ornith.) hawk.

¹galga, *f.* rolling stone; (mill) stone wheel that grinds olives.

²galga, *f.* (med.) a kind of eruption or rash.

³galga, *f.* bier or stretcher on which poor people are taken to be buried; drag, Scotch brake for a wheel; (naut.) back of an anchor.

⁴galga, *f.—pl.* long ankle ties for women's slippers.

⁵galga, *f.* (zool.) greyhound bitch.

galgo, ga. I. *a.* (Am.) hungry; eager. **II.** *n.* greyhound.

galgueño, ña, *a.* resembling, or pertaining to, greyhounds.

gálgulo, *m.* (ornith.) roller.

galianos, *m. pl.* shepherd's meal.

galibar, *va.* (naut.) to trace, to mould.

gálibo, *m.* templet, pattern, mold; (Ry.) gauge for the width and height of an open freight car (to determine whether there will be enough clearance in tunnels, etc.).

galicado, da, *a.* (of words, style, etc.) French in construction or form.

galicano, na, *n.* & *a.* Gallican.

galicismo, *m.* Gallicism.

galicista, *n.* Gallicizer, user of Gallicisms.

gálico, *m.* venereal disease; syphilis.

galicoso, sa, *a.* (coll.) infected with syphilis.

galilea, *f.* (arch.) galilee porch or chapel.

galileo, a, *n.* & *a.* Galilean.

galillo, *m.* uvula, soft palate.

galimatías, *m.* gibberish.

¹galio, *m.* (bot.) cheese-rennet bedstraw.

²galio, *m.* (chem.) gallium.

galiopsis, *f.* (bot.) common hedge-nettle.

galiparlista, *n.* = GALICISTA.

¹galipodio, *m.* white frankincense.

²galipodio, *m.* galipot.

galizabra, *f.* lateen-rigged vessel.

galo, la, *n.* & *a.* Gaul; Gallic.

galocha, *f.* galosh, clog, patten.

¹galón, *m.* galloon, tape, braid, binding lace; stripe, or gold or silver braid on uniforms.—*pl.* (naut.) sheer rails.

²galón, *m.* (Angl.) gallon, liquid measure.

galonazo, *m. aug.* large galloon; ornament.

galoneador, ra, *n.* one who binds with braid or galloons.

galoneadura, *f.* (sewing) trimming.

galonear, *va.* (sewing) to bind, to trim with galloons.

galonero, ra, *n.* braid or galloon maker.

galonista, *m.* (coll.) pupil of a military college wearing corporal stripes as a reward.

galop, *m.* (dance) galop.

galopar, *vn.* to gallop.

galope, *m.* gallop; haste, speed.—**a g., or de g.,** hurriedly, speedily.

galopeado, da. I. *pp.* of GALOPEAR. **II.** *a.* (coll.) hastily done. **III.** *m.* (coll.) whipping, flogging.

galopear, *vn.* = GALOPAR.

galopillo, *m. dim.* scullion, kitchen boy.

galopín, *m.* ragamuffin; rascal, rogue; shrewd fellow; clever knave; (naut.) swabber, cabin boy; scullion.

galopinada, *f.* roguish act, knavery.

galopo, *m.* rascal, rogue.

galpito, *m.* weak, sickly chicken.

galpón, *m.* (Am.) old-time slaves' quarters; (W. I., S. A.) shed.

Galván, *m.*—**eso no lo entenderá G.,** (coll.) that is a puzzle, that is a hard nut to crack.

galvanicé, galvanice, *v.* V. GALVANIZAR.

galvánico, ca, *a.* galvanic.

galvanismo, *m.* (phys.) galvanism.

galvanización, *f.* (phys.) galvanization.

galvanizar, *va.* (*pret.* GALVANICÉ; *subj.* GALVANICE) to galvanize; to electroplate.

galvanocauterio, *m.* (med.) galvanocautery.

galvanómetro, *m.* galvanometer.

galvanoplastia, galvanoplástica, *f.* galvanoplasty, electrotypy.

galvanoplástico, ca, *a.* galvanoplastic.

galladura, *f.* cicatricle, plasma bit of an egg.

gallar, gallear, *va.* (of a cock) to copulate with.

gallarda, *f.* a Spanish dance and its music; (print.) type of a size between minion and brevier.

gallardamente, *adv.* elegantly, gracefully.

gallardear, *vn.* to act with grace or elegance.

gallardete, *m.* (naut.) pennant, streamer.

gallardetón, *m.* (naut.) broad pennant.

gallardía, *f.* gracefulness; fine bearing; gallantry, bravery, nobleness; activity, briskness.

gallardo, da, *a.* graceful, elegant; magnanimous, generous; lively; brave, gallant.

gallareta, *f.* (ornith.) widgeon.

gallarón, *m.* (ornith.) a kind of bustard.

gallaruza, *f.* hooded garment.

gallear. I. *va.* (of cocks) to copulate with. **II.** *vn.* to surpass, excel; to assume an air of importance; to raise the voice in anger; to crow; to bully; (foundry) to have flaws.

gallegada, *f.* a group of GALLEGOS; peculiar action or speech of a GALLEGO; a Galician dance and its tune.

gallego, ga. I. *n.* & *a.* Galician, from province of Galicia; (Am.) Spanish(-iard). **II.** *m.* northwest wind.

galleo, *m.* (foundry) flaw in casting.

gallera, *f.* cockpit.

galleta, *f.* ship biscuit, hardtack; cookie; (Mex., C. A., W. I.) slap.

²galleta, *f.* small vessel or pan.

galletica, *f.* small cracker or biscuit.

gallillo, *m.* = GALILLO, uvula, soft palate.

gallina. I. *f.* hen.—**g. de Guinea,** Guinea hen. **II.** *n.* coward, chicken-hearted person.—**g. ciega,** blindman's buff.

gallináceo, a. I. *n.* & *a.* (zool.) gallinacean (-ceous). **II.** *f. pl.* Gallinaceæ, Gallinæ.

gallinaza, *f.* hen dung; (ornith.) GALLINAZO.

gallinazo, *m.* (ornith.) gallinazo, turkey buzzard.

gallinejas, *f. pl.* fried chicken tripes.

gallinería, *f.* poulterer's shop; hencoop or henhouse; cowardice, pusillanimity.

gallinero, ra. I. *a.* chicken-eating. **II.** *n.* poulterer, poultry dealer. **III.** *m.* poultry yard; hencoop, henroost, henhouse; basket for carrying poultry; ladies' club or bee; (coll., theat.) nigger heaven, top gallery.

gallineta, *f.* (ornith.) sandpiper; ruffed grouse.

gallipato, *m.* (ornith.) merganser.

gallipava, *f.* a large variety of hen.

gallipavo, *m.* (ornith.) turkey; (coll.) false, unpleasant note in singing.

---

gallipuente, *m.* bridge without rails.

gallístico, ca, *a.* of gamecocks or cockfights.

gallito, *m. dim.* small cock; beau, coxcomb; cock of the walk, bully.

gallo, *m.* (ornith.) cock, rooster; (ichth.) dory, sea fish; boss, chief, leader; cork float for fishing; (carp.) wall board of the roof; false note in singing.—**g. de pelea,** or **inglés,** gamecock.—**alzar el g.,** to speak loud and arrogantly.—**hacerse el g.,** to become the ruler in any meeting, body, etc.—**otro g. le cantara,** he would be better (or worse) off, he would have fared differently.—**salir con una pata de g.,** to give a foolish or irrelevant answer.—**ser el g.** = HACERSE EL G.—**tener mucho g.,** to be very arrogant and overbearing.

gallocresta, *f.* (bot.) annual clary sage.

gallofa, *f.* food given to pilgrims; greens for salad and pottage; idle tale; French roll; directory of divine service.

gallofar, gallofear, *vn.* to loaf about as a beggar.

gallofero, ra; gallofo, fa. I. *a.* idle, lazy, vagabond. **II.** *n.* tramp.

gallón, *m.* green sod, turf; (arch.) echinus.

gallonada, *f.* wall made of sods.

¹**gama,** *f.* (zool.) doe.

²**gama,** *f.* (mus.) gamut.

gamarra, *f.* (harness) martingale, check, strap.

gamarza, *f.* (bot.) wild Syrian rue.

gambaj, *m.* acton, padded jacket.

gámbaro, *m.* = CÁMBARO, (ichth.) crawfish.

gambax, *m.* = GAMBAJ.

gamberra, *f.* prostitute, strumpet.

gambesina, *f.,* **gambesón,** *m.* = GAMBAJ.

gambeta, *f.* (dance) crosscaper; prance.

gambetear, *vn.* to caper like a horse.

gambeto, *m.* quilted greatcoat; cap for a new-born child.

gambito, *m.* (chess) gambit.

gamboa, *f.* (bot.) a variety of quince.

gambota, *m.* (naut.) counter timber, arched timber.

¹**gamella,** *f.* bow (of yoke).

²**gamella,** *f.* large wooden trough or tub; washtub; boundary mound.

gamelleja, *f. dim.* small trough or tub.

gamellón, *m. aug.* large tub; trough in which grapes are trodden.

gamezno, *m.* little young fallow deer.

gamo, *m.* buck of the fallow deer.

gamón, *m.* (bot.) asphodel.

gamonal, *m.* asphodel field or patch; (Am.) boss.

gamonalismo, *m.* (Am.) bossism.

gamonito, *m.* shoot, tiller, sucker.

gamonoso, sa, *a.* abounding in asphodels.

gamopétalo, la, *a.* (bot.) gamopetalous.

gamosépalo, la, *a.* (bot.) gamosepalous.

gamuno, na, *a.* chamois skin (as *a.*), shammy.

gamuza, *f.* (zool.) chamois; chamois skin.

gamuzado, da, *a.* chamois-colored.

gamuzón, *m. aug.* large chamois.

gana, *f.* appetite, hunger; desire; mind.—**dar g.,** or **ganas, de** (foll. by *inf.*) to arouse desire to, to make (one) feel like (foll. by *pres. p.*); to feel like.—**de buena g.,** willingly.—**de g.** energetically, in earnest.—**de mala g.,** unwillingly.—**no me da la g.,** I don't want to, I won't.—**tener g.,** or **ganas, de,** to wish to; to have a mind to.—**tenerle g.,** or **ganas, a,** to desire; to wish to have a fight with.

ganable, *a.* that may be gained or won, gainable.

ganadería, *f.* cattle raising; cattle ranch; stock farm; live stock; cattle brand.

ganadero, ra. I. *a.* pertaining to cattle. **II.** *n.* grazier, owner of cattle; stock farmer; dealer in cattle; drover.

ganado, *m.* live stock; cattle; herd, flock, drove; (coll.) rabble.—**g. caballar,** horses.—**g. de cerda** = G. MORENO.—**g. de pata hendida,** oxen, cows, sheep, goats.—**g. mayor,** cattle (including horses, asses, mules).—**g. menor,** sheep.—**g. moreno,** swine, hogs.—**g. ovejuno,** sheep.—**g. vacuno,** (bovine) cattle.

ganador, ra, *n.* & *a.* gainer(-ing), winner(-ing).

ganancia, *f.* gain, profit, advantage.—**g. bruta,** gross profit.—**g. líquida,** net profit.—**ganancias y pérdidas,** (com.) profit and loss.

ganancial, *a.* pertaining to earnings or profit.

ganancioso, sa, *a.* lucrative, profitable; gaining.

ganapán, *m.* drudge; common laborer; rude, coarse man.

ganapierde, *m.* give-away, losing game.

ganar, *va.* to gain; to win; to earn; to clear, to make (money); to attain, obtain, acquire; to surpass, be superior to; to draw (interest).—**g. de,** or **por, mano,** to get ahead of (in acquiring something), to "beat to it."—**g. el pan,** or **el sustento,** or **la vida,** to earn one's living, make a living.

ganchero, *m.* raftsman guiding logs down a river.

ganchillo, ito, *m. dim.* little hook or crotch.

gancho, *m.* hook; crook, crotch; hairpin; shepherd's crook; sheephook; (coll.) allurer, roper-in; pimp; procurer, pander; (coll.) attractiveness, especially of a woman.—**echar el g. a,** (fig.) to catch; to hook, land.

ganchoso, sa, *a.* hooked, curved.

ganchuelo, *m. dim.* = GANCHILLO.

gándara, *f.* low jungle.

¹**gandaya,** *f.* laziness, idleness.—**andar a la g.,** to gad, loaf, lounge.

²**gandaya,** *f.* a kind of cap.

gandido, da, *a.* (Am.) gluttonous.

gandinga, *f.* (min.) washed fine ore; (Cuba) liver stew.

gandir, *va.* to eat.

gandujado, *m.* accordion plaiting.

gandujar, *va.* (sewing) to plait, shirr, fold.

gandul, la, *n.* (coll.) idler, loafer, tramp.

gandulear, *vn.* to loaf, lounge, gad.

gandulería, *f.* idleness, laziness, lounging.

ganeta, *f.* (zool.) = GINETA, genet.

ganforro, ra, *n.* (coll.) rogue, rascal.

¹**ganga,** *f.* (ornith.) little pin-tailed grouse.

²**ganga,** *f.* (min.) gangue; (coll.) child's play, "cinch"; bargain.

gangarilla, *f.* company of strolling players.

gangliforme, *a.* gangliform.

ganglio, *m.* (naut.) ganglion.

ganglionar, *a.* (anat.) ganglionic.

gangoso, sa, *a.* speaking with a nasal twang.

gangrena, *f.* (med.) gangrene, blood poisoning.

gangrenarse, *vr.* to become gangrenous.

gangrenoso, sa, *a.* gangrenous.

ganguear, *vn.* to speak with a nasal twang.

gangueo, *m.* nasal twang.

ganguero, *a.* (coll.) running after easy jobs.

gánguil, *m.* (naut.) fishing barge; dump scow.

ganoideo, a. I. *n.* & *a.* (zool.) ganoid. **II.** *m. pl.* Ganoidei.

ganoso, sa, *a.* desirous, wishing.

gansada, *f.* (coll.) stupidity.

gansarón, *m.* (ornith.) gosling; tall, thin, gawky man.

ganso, sa, *n.* (ornith.) gander, goose; slow, lazy person; silly person, ninny.—**g. bravo,** wild goose.

gante, *m.* linen manufactured in Ghent.

gantés, esa, *a.* from, or pertaining to, Ghent.

ganzúa, *f.* picklock, skeleton key; picklock, burglar; one skilled in drawing secrets out of others.

gañán, *m.* day laborer; farm hand; rustic.

gañanía, *f.* gang of laborers; lodge for the same.

gañido, *m.* yelping, howling.

gañiles, *m. pl.* cartilaginous larynx; gills of the tunny fish.

gañir, *va.* (pret. él GAÑÓ; ger. GAÑENDO) to yelp or howl (as a dog); to croak, cackle, crow; (coll.) to talk hoarsely.

For pronunciation, see the rules at the beginning of the book.

gañón, gañote, *m.* (coll.) throat; a kind of fritter.

gaón, *m.* (naut.) a kind of oar used in Indian boats.

garabatada, *f.* (coll.) throwing a hook at (something).

garabatear. I. *vn.* to throw a hook at, or for, something; to scrawl, scribble; (coll.) to beat about the bush. **II.** *va.* to hook.

garabateo, *m.* hooking; scribbling, scrawling.

garabatillo, *m.* *dim.* small hook.

garabato, *m.* hook; pothook; grapple, grapnel, creeper, claw bar, hand bale hook; meathook or gambrel; (Am.) scrawl, scribble; muzzle; winsome ways.—*pl.* (Am.) scrawling; hand gestures.

garabatoso, sa, *a.* full of scrawls; charming, attractive.

garabito, *m.* market stall.

garaje, (improperly) **garage,** *m.* garage.

garambaina, *f.* gaudiness; (coll.) ridiculous affectation or mannerism; illegible scrawl.

garante. I. *a.* responsible. **II.** *n.* (com. and law) warranter, guarantor, surety; bondsman, bail.

garantía, *f.* guarantee; (com. and law) warranty, guaranty, security; indorsement; collateral; bail.

garanticé, garantice, *v.* *V.* GARANTIZAR.

garantir, *va.* *defect.* (*used only in forms having the letter* **i** *in their endings*) to guarantee.

garantizar, *va.* (*pret.* GARANTICÉ; *subj.* GARANTICE) to guarantee; to indorse, answer or vouch for.

garañón, *m.* stallion jackass; male breeding camel.

garapacho, *m.* tortoise.

garapiña, *f.* congealed particles of any liquid; scalloped galloon or lace; (Cuba) fermented pineapple juice.

garapiñado, da. I. *pp.* of GARAPIÑAR. **II.** *a.* candied, sugarcoated; (jewelry) frosted.

garapiñar, *va.* to ice, to freeze (cream, sirup, etc.); to candy.

garapiñera, *f.* ice-cream freezer; wine cooler.

garapita, *f.* net for small fish.

garapito, *m.* small insect, like a tick.

garapullo, *m.* paper dart; shuttlecock.

garatura, *f.* (tanning) scraper.

garatusa, *f.* a card game; (coll.) caress.

garay, *m.* (P. I.) an ancient sailboat.

garba, *f.* sheaf, as of wheat.

garbancero, ra, *n.* chickpea dealer; (Mex.) young servant (boy or girl).

garbanzal, *m.* ground sown with chickpeas.

garbanzo, *m.* (bot.) chickpea.

garbanzuelo, *m.* *dim.* small chickpea; (vet.) a disease in horses' feet; ESPARAVÁN, spawn.

garbar, *va.* (agr.) to sheaf or sheave.

garbear. I. *va.* (agr.) to sheaf. **II.** *vn.* to affect an air of dignity and grandeur.

garbera, *f.* (agr.) shock of sheaves.

garbías, *m.* *pl.* omelet of herbs, cheese and flour.

garbillador, ra, *n.* sifter; riddler; garbler.

garbillar, *va.* (agr.) to sift; (min.) to riddle; to garble.—**garbillo,** *m.* coarse sieve for grain; (min.) riddle; riddled ore.

garbín, *m.* coif made of network.

garbino, *m.* southwest wind.

garbo, *m.* grace, gracefulness, gentility, elegant carriage; knack; frankness, nobleness, generosity.

garbón, *m.* (ornith.) male partridge.

garbosamente, *adv.* gracefully; nobly.

garboso, sa, *a.* natty, spruce, graceful, sprightly; noble, generous.

garbullo, *m.* noisy crowd, esp. of children.

garcero, ra, *a.* (ornith.) heron hawk.

garceta, *f.* (ornith.) little egret; side locks of hair.—*pl.* sprouting horns (on deer, etc.).

gardenia, *f.* (bot.) gardenia.

garduja, *f.* barren stone in quicksilver mines.

garduña, *f.* (zool.) marten.

garduño, ña, *a.* (coll.) filcher, petty thief.

garete, *m.*—**al g.,** (naut.) adrift.

garfa, *f.* claw of a beast or bird; hand (in contempt); ancient tax.—**echar la g.,** to claw or seize anything with the nails.

garfada, *f.* clawing or seizing with the nails.

garfear, *vn.* to hook, to seize with a hook.

garfiada, *f.* = GARFADA.

garfio, *m.* hook, drag hook; gaff.

gargajeada, *f.* spitting out of phlegm.

gargajear, *vn.* to expectorate phlegm.—**gargajeo,** *m.* = GARGAJEADA.

gargajiento, ta, *a.* that expectorates phlegm.

gargajo, *m.* phlegm.—**gargajoso, sa,** *a.* = GARGAJIENTO.

garganchón, *m.* = GARGÜERO.

garganta, *f.* throat; gullet; instep; gorge, notch; (agr.) sheath of a plow; (arch.) shaft of a column or balustrade; (mech.) neck, throat, gullet, waist, groove of a sheave.—**tener buena g.,** to be a good singer.

gargantada, *f.* liquid or blood ejected from the throat.

gargantear, *vn.* to quaver, to warble; (naut.) to strap a deadeye.

garganteo, *m.* quavering, warbling.

gargantil, *m.* cutout in barbers' basins.

gargantilla, *f.* necklace; (P. I.) water jug.

gárgara, *f.* gargle, gargling.—**hacer gárgaras,** to gargle.

gargarismo, *m.* gargle; gargling.

gargarizar, *vn.* to gargle, gargarize.

¹gárgol, *a.* empty, addle (eggs).

²gárgol, *m.* (mech.) groove, furrow, mortise.

¹gárgola, *f.* (arch.) gargoyle.

²gárgola, *f.* linseed.

gargüero, garguero, *m.* gullet; windpipe.

garifalte, *m.* (ornith.) = GERIFALTE, gerfalcon.

garifo, fa, *a.* = JARIFO, showy; natty.

gariofilea, *f.* (bot.) common avens or herb bennet.

garita, *f.* sentry box; porter's lodge; watercloset, privy.

garitero, *m.* master of a gaming house; gamester, gambler.

garito, *m.* gaming house; watchman's house; gambling den; profits of gambling.

garla, *f.* (coll.) talk, chatter.

garlador, ra; garlente, *n.* & *a.* (coll.) babbler (-ing), prater(-ing).

garlar, *vn.* (coll.) to babble, prattle, chatter.

garlito, *m.* fish trap; snare, trap, or gin.—**caer en el g.,** (coll.) to fall into a trap.—**coger en el g.,** to detect in wrong-doing.

garlocha, *f.* goad stick.

garlopa, *f.* (carp.) jack plane, long plane.

garma, *f.* steep slope.

¹garnacha, *f.* judge's robe or gown; company of strolling players.

²garnacha, *f.* a kind of purple grape; wine made from it.

garniel, *m.* belt with hanging pouch; (Ecua., Mex.) leather pouch.

garo, *m.* an ancient Roman dish.

garra, *f.* claw of a wild beast, talon of a bird of prey; clutch; hand (in contempt); (mech.) catch, claw, hook, fang, clutch.—**caer en las garras de,** to fall into the clutches of.—**echarle a uno la g.,** (coll.) to grasp, arrest, imprison one.—**sacar de las garras de,** to free from.

garrafa, *f.* carafe, decanter.

garrafal, *a.* (of cherries) specially large and sweet; great, huge.

garrafilla, *f.* *dim.* small carafe.

garrafiñar, *va.* (coll.) to grapple, snatch away.

garrafón, *m.* *aug.* large carafe; demijohn, carboy.

garrama, *f.* tax paid by Mohammedans; imposition, fraud, robbery.

For pronunciation, see the rules at the beginning of the book.

garramar, garranar, *va.* to rob, plunder, pillage.
garrancha, *f.* (coll.) sword.
garrancho, *m.* branch broken off a tree.
garrapata, *f.* sheep and cattle tick; (mil.) disabled horse.
garrapatear, *vn.* to scribble, to scrawl.
garrapatilla, *f. dim.* small tick.
garrapato, *m.* pothook, scrawl.
garrar, *vn.* (naut.) to drag.
garrasí, *m.* side-buttoned breeches worn by Venezuelan plainsmen.
garrear, *vn.* = GARRAR.
garridamente, *adv.* gracefully, neatly.
garrideza, *f.* elegance, gracefulness.
garrido, da, *a.* handsome, graceful.
garroba, *f.* carob bean.—**garrobal,** *m.* plantation of carob trees.—**garrobilla,** *f.* (tanning) chips of carob trees for staining.
garrocha, *f.* a sort of alpenstock; goad stick.
garrochada, *f.,* **garrochazo,** *m.* prick or blow with a goad stick.
garrocheador, ra, *n.* goader, pricker.
garrochear, *va.* = AGARROCHAR, to goad.
garrochón, *m. aug.* spear or goad stick used by bullfighters on horseback.
garrofa, *f.* carob bean.—**garrofal,** *m.* = GARROBAL.
garrón, *m.* spur of cocks and birds; talon of a bird of prey; paw of rabbits, etc.
garrotal, *m.* plantation of olive trees, grown from cuttings taken from fully developed trees.
garrotazo, *m.* blow with a cudgel.
garrote, *m.* club, bludgeon, truncheon, cudgel; garrote (for capital punishment); hazel basket or panier; (naut.) turning fid.—**dar g.,** to garrote, execute with the garrote.
garrotear, *va.* (Am.) = APALEAR, to cudgel.
garrotillo, *m.* (med.) croup.
garrubia, *f.* = ALGARROBA, carob bean.
garrucha, *f.* pulley.—**g. combinada,** sheave, block.—**g. fija,** fast pulley.—**g. movible,** movable pulley.—**g. simple,** single pulley.
garrucho, *m.* (naut.) cringle, mast hoop.
garruchuela, *f. dim.* small pulley.
garrudo, da, *a.* muscular, brawny, strong.
garrulador, ra, *a.* garrulous.
garrulería, *f.* prattle, chatter.
garrulidad, *f.* garrulity.
gárrulo, la, *a.* chirping, as birds; chattering, prattling; garrulous.
garúa, *f.* (Am.) drizzle.—**garuar,** *vn.* to drizzle.
garujo, *m.* = HORMIGÓN, concrete.
garulla, *f.* loose grapes; (coll.) rabble.
garullada, *f.* gang of rogues.
garvier, *m.* small pouch.
garza, *f.* (ornith.) heron; (Colomb.) stork.—**g. real,** purple heron.
garzo, za. I. *a.* blue; blue-eyed. II. *m.* agaric, fungus, mushroom.
garzón, *m.* lad, boy; waiter; adjutant in the life guards; (Am.) (ornith.) heronlike wading bird.
garzota, *f.* (ornith.) night heron; plumage, aigrette; crest of a helmet.
garzul, *m.* a kind of wheat.
gas, *m.* gas; vapor, emanation, fume; (coll.) gas light.—**g. del alumbrado,** illuminating gas.—**g. lacrimógeno,** tear gas.—**g. pobre,** producer gas.—**llevar g.,** (coll.) to speed.
gasa, *f.* gauze.
gascón, na; nés nesa, *n.* & *a.* Gascon.
gasconada, *f.* gasconade, boast, bravado.
gaseiforme, *a.* gasiform, gaseous.
gaseosa, *f.* soda water.
gaseoso, sa, *a.* gaseous.
gasificable, *a.* gasifiable.
gasificación, *f.* gasification.
gasificar, *va.* to gasify.
gasista, *n.* gas fitter.
gasógeno, *m.* gazogene; mixture of benzine and alcohol used for lamps and for cleaning.

gasolina, *f.,* **gasoleno,** *m.,* gasoline.
gasometría, *f.* gasometry.
gasómetro, *m.* gasometer; gas meter.
gasón, *m.* YESÓN, plaster rubbish; large clods of unbroken earth; sod.
gastable, *a.* that can be spent or worn out.
gastadero, *m.* (coll.) place where anything is wasted or spent; wasting; spending.
gastado, da. I. *pp.* of GASTAR. II. *a.* worn-out, useless; blasé.
gastador, ra. I. *a.* lavish, prodigal, extravagant. II. *n.* spender, spendthrift; (mil.) pioneer, sapper; criminal sentenced to hard labor.
gastamiento, *m.* consumption; wearing out.
gastar. I. *va.* to spend, expend; to waste, use, consume, wear out, fret; to have or wear habitually; to own, keep (as carriages, etc.); to plunder, pillage, sack; to digest.—**g. frases y rodeos,** (coll.) to beat around the bush.—**gastarlas,** (coll.) to act, behave, conduct oneself.—**g. salud,** to enjoy good health. II. *vr.* to become old or useless; to waste away, wear out; to fray.
gasterópodo, da, *a.* (zool.) gasteropod.
gasto, *m.* expenditure, expense; consumption; spending, consuming; waste, use, wear and tear; (hydraul.) discharge.—**gastos de escritorio,** stationery expenses (in an office).—**gastos de explotación,** operating, running or working expenses.—**gastos de representación,** incidental expenses (of a public functionary); allowance for incidental expenses.
gastoso, sa, *a.* = GASTADOR.
gastralgia, *f.* (med.) gastralgia, stomach pains.
gástrico, ca, *a.* gastric.
gastritis, *f.* (med.) gastritis.
gastrocele, *m.* (med.) gastrocele.
gastrocolitis, *f.* (med.) gastrocolitis.
gastroenteritis, *f.* (med.) gastroenteritis.
gastrointestinal, *a.* gastrointestinal.
gastrología, *f.* science and art of cooking.
gastromanía, *f.* gluttony.
gastrómano, na, *n.* & *a.* glutton(-ous).
gastronomía, *f.* gastronomy, epicurism.
gastronómico, ca, *a.* gastronomic.
gastrónomo, *m.* epicure, gastronomer.
gastrorrafia, *f.* (surg.) gastrorraphy.
gastrorragia, *f.* gastrorrhagia.
gastrotomía, *f.* (surg.) gastrotomy.
gástrula, *f.* (biol.) gastrula.
gata, *f.* female cat; (coll.) woman born in Madrid; (bot.) GATUÑA; (mech.) jack, screw jack; (mil.) cat castle; (naut.) cathead.—**g. del ancla,** (naut.) cat tackle.—**g. parida,** wasted person, (fig.) skeleton.—**a gatas,** on all fours.
gatada, *f.* cat trick; clawing; turn of a hare when closely pursued; (coll.) artful dodge, scurvy trick.
gatallón, *m.* (coll.) rogue, cheat, scamp.
gatatumba, *f.* (coll.) affected civility or submission; dissembling, pretense.
gatazo, *m. aug.* large cat; (coll.) artful trick, cheat, deception.
gateado, da. I. *pp.* of GATEAR. II. *a.* feline, cat-like. III. *m.* a very compact American striped wood.
gateamiento, *m.* scratching; clambering; going on all fours.
gatear. I. *vn.* (of children) to creep; to climb up, clamber; to go upon all fours. II. *va.* (coll.) to scratch or claw; to steal, to rob.
gatera, *f.* cat's hole; (bot.) common catmint; (naut.) cathole.
gatería, *f.* number of cats together; (coll.) gang of toughs or ill-bred boys; (coll.) simulated humility, cunning, trick.
gatero, ra, *a.* frequented by cats.
gatesco, ca, *a.* (coll.) feline, catlike.
gatica, illa, ita, *f. dim.* little she-cat, pussy.
gaticida, *m.* (coll.) cat killer.

For pronunciation, see the rules at the beginning of the book.

gatico, ito, *m. dim.* little cat, pussy.

gatillazo, *m.* noise made by a trigger at firing.

gatillo, *m. dim.* little cat; pelican, dentist's forceps; (artil.) trigger; nape of a bull or ox; (arch.) cramp iron; filcher, petty thief.

gato, *m.* cat, tomcat; moneybag and the money kept in it; (cooperage) hooping tong; (mech.) jack, lifting jack, screw jack; (artil.) gun searcher; (coll.) pickpocket, petty thief, filcher; (coll.) shrewd fellow; (coll.) native of Madrid. —**g. cornaquí**, (naut.) jackscrew.—**g. de algalia**, (zool.) civet cat.—**g. encerrado**, (coll.) nigger in the woodpile; more than meets the eye.—**g. montés**, wildcat.—**cuatro gatos**, (contempt.) just a few people.—**dar, meter, or vender, g. por liebre**, (coll.) to cheat, to fool, to give chalk for cheese.

gatuna, gatuña, *f.* (bot.) rest-harrow, cammock.

gatunero, ra, *n.* seller of smuggled meat.

gatuno, na, *a.* catlike, feline.

gatuperio, *m.* hotchpotch; (coll.) fraud, snare.

gauchada, *f.* (Am.) artifice; act of a Gaucho.— **hacer una g.**, (Arg.) to do a favor.

gauchaje, *m.* meeting or body of Gauchos.

gauchesco, ca, *a.* pert. to or like Gauchos.

gaucho, cha. I. *n.* Gaucho; (Arg.) pampas man (woman); good horseman; (Am.) cowboy. **II.** *a.* GAUCHESCO; knavish; (Arg., Chiḷe) tricky; (Arg.) rude, vulgar.

gaudeamus, *m.* (coll.) feast, entertainment or merrymaking.

gavanza, *f.* (bot.) flower of the dog-rose.

gavanzo, *m.* (bot.) dog-rose.

gaveta, *f.* drawer, till, locker.

gavetilla, *f. dim.* small desk drawer.

¹gavia, *f.* (naut.) main topsail; top (in galleys); mad man's cage; ditch;—*pl.* (naut.) topsails of the main and fore mast.

²gavia, *f.* (min.) gang of basket passers.

³gavia, *f.* (ornith.) = GAVIOTA.

gavial, *m.* gavial, an East-Indian crocodile.

gaviar, *vn.* (Am.) (of corn) to tassel.

gaviero, *m.* (naut.) topman, mastman.

gavieta, *f.* (naut.) scuttle, bowsprit bee.

gaviete, *m.* (naut.) davit in a longboat.

gavilán, *m.* (ornith.) sparrow hawk; fine hair stroke in penmanship; nib of a pen; (armor) quillon of a sword; brad or pin of a goad stick; (naut.) iron hook; (bot.) thistle flower; (naut.) tholes.

gavilancillo, *m. dim.* young hawk; incurvated point of an artichoke leaf.

gavilla, *f.* (agr.) gavel or sheaf of grain; bundle of vine shoots; gang of thugs.

gavillero, *m.* (agr.) place where gavels of grain are collected.

gavina, *f.* (ornith.) = GAVIOTA.

gavión, *m.* (mil.) gabion; (coll.) large hat.

gaviota, *f.* (ornith.) gull, sea gull.

gavitel, *m.* (naut.) small buoy.

gavota, *f.* gavotte, a French dance.

gaya, *f.* stripe on stuffs, etc.; badge given to victors in Roman games; (ornith.) magpie.

gayado, da. I. *pp.* of GAYAR. **II.** *a.* motley, striped.

gayadura, *f.* garniture, parti-colored trimming.

gayar, *va.* to streak, stripe; to trim with ribbons of various colors; to variegate.

gayata, *f.* crook, sheephook.

gayo, ya, *a.* gay, festive, merry; showy.—**gaya ciencia**, poesy, minstrelsy, art of poetry.

gayola, *f.* (naut.) cage; (coll.) jail; (prov.) raised hut for watching vineyards.

gayomba, *f.* (bot.) white single-seed broom.

gayuba, *f.* (bot.) red-berried arbutus.

gayubal, *m.* GAYUBA field.

gaza, *f.* loop of a bow; (naut.) strap, loop, collar, splice, noose.

gazafatón, *m.* nonsense, foolish talk, balderdash.

gazapa, *f.* lie, fib, falsehood.

gazapatón, *m.* = GAZAFATÓN.

gazapera, *f.* warren for rabbits; (coll.) den where suspicious characters meet; (coll.) brawl, row.

gazapico, illo, ito, *m. dim.* little rabbit, bunny.

gazapina, *f.* assembly of ruffians; brawl, row.

gazapo, *m.* cony, young rabbit; shrewd, artful fellow; (coll.) great lie; blunder, mistake.

gazapón, *m.* gambling house or profits.

gazmiar. I. *va.* to steal and eat tidbits. **II.** *vr.* (coll.) to complain; to resent.

gazmol, *m.* a kind of growth on the tongue of birds of prey.

gazmoñada, gazmoñería, *f.* prudery.

gazmoñero, ra; gazmoño, ña, *a.* prudish, priggish.

gaznápiro, ra, *n.* churl, simpleton, booby.

gaznar, *vn.* = GRAZNAR, to croak, caw, cackle.

gaznatada, *f.* blow on the windpipe; (Am.) BOFETADA, slap in the face.

gaznate, *m.* throttle, windpipe; a kind of fritter.

gaznatón, *m.* GAZNATADA; pancake, fritter.

gazofia, *f.* = BAZOFIA, refuse; offal.

gazofilacio, *m.* gazophylacium, treasury of the temple of Jerusalem.

gazpachero, ra, *n.* maker of GAZPACHO.

gazpacho, *m.* Andalusian dish made of biscuit, oil, vinegar, onions, and garlic; crumbs of bread fried in a pan.

gazuza, *f.* (coll.) keen appetite, hunger.

ge, *f.* Spanish name of the letter *g*.

gea, *f.* mineral or inorganic constituents of a region, and the work describing it.

geato, *m.* (chem.) humate.

gehena, *m.* Gehenna, hell.

geico, ca, *a.* (chem.) geic, humic.

géiser, *m.* geyser.

gelatina, *f.* gelatine; jelly.

gelatiniforme, *a.* gelatinelike.

gelatinoso, sa, *a.* gelatinous.

gelatinudo, da, *a.* (Am.) gelatinous; (Am.) phlegmatic, lazy, slow.

gelfe, *m.* black slave.

gélido, da, *a.* (poet.) gelid, frigid.

gema, *f.* gem; (carp.) slab, flitch; (bot.) bud.

gemación, *f.* (bot.) gemmation.

gemela, *f.* (bot.) Arabian jasmine.

gemelífloro, ra, *a.* (bot.) geminiflorous.

gemelo, la. I. *n.* twin. **II.** *m.* cuff link.—*pl.* binocular telescope; opera glasses; field or marine glasses.—**Gemelos**, (astr.) Gemini.

gemido, *m.* lamentation, moan; (animal) howl.

gemidor, ra, *n. & a.* lamenter(-ing); howler (-ing), moaner(-ing).

geminifloro, ra, *a.* geminiflorous.

géminis, *m.* (pharm.) a kind of plaster; (G-, astr.) Gemini.

gemíparo, ra, *a.* (biol.) gemmiparous.

gemir, *vn.* (*ind. pres.* GIMO, *prét.* él GIMIÓ; *subj.* GIMA; *ger.* GIMIENDO) to groan, moan; to grieve; to howl; (of sea or wind) to roar, whistle.

genciana, *f.* (bot.) gentian.

gencianáceo, a. I. *n. & a.* (bot.) gentian(-aceous). **II.** *f. pl.* Gentianaceæ.

gencianeo, ea, *a.* gentianaceous.

gendarme, *m.* gendarme.

gendarmería, *f.* (mil.) gendarmerie.

genealogía, *f.* genealogy.

genealógico, ca, *a.* genealogical.

genealogista, *n.* genealogist.

genético, ca, *a.* pert. to astrology.

geneo, *m.* a Peruvian banana.

generable, *a.* that can be generated.

generación, *f.* generation; succession, lineage.

generador, ra. I. *n. & a.* generator(-ing). *a. f.* = GENERATRIZ. **II.** *m.* (mech. and elec.) generator.

general. I. *a.* general; common, usual.—**en g., por lo g.**, in general, generally. **II.** *m.* (mil.) general; (eccl.) superior of a religious order;

lecture hall in a university; (prov.) custom house.

generala, *f.* (mil.) the general (a roll of the drum); wife of a general.

generalato, *m.* (eccl. and mil.) generalship.

generalero, *m.* majority; customhouse officer.

generalicé, generalice, *v. V.* GENERALIZAR.

generalidad, *f.* generality; (prov.) community. corporation; (prov.) custom duties.

generalísimo, *m.* generalissimo.

generalización, *f.* generalization.

generalizador, ra, *n. & a.* generalizer(-ing).

generalizar. I. *va.* (*pret.* GENERALICÉ; *subj.* GENERALICE) to generalize. **II.** *vr.* to become general, usual, or popular; to spread.

generalmente, *adv.* generally.

generar, *va.* to generate, produce.

generativo, va, *a.* generative.

generatriz, *n. & a.* (math.) generator(-ing).

genéricamente, *adv.* generically.

genérico, ca, *a.* generic.

género, *m.* genus; class; kind; kin; manner, way, sort; cloth, stuff, material; (gram.) gender.—*pl.* dry goods; (com.) goods, merchandise, commodities.—**g. humano,** mankind.—**de g.,** (art) genre.

generosamente, *adv.* generously.

generosidad, *f.* generosity; hereditary nobility; bravery, fortitude.

generoso, sa, *a.* generous; noble, magnanimous; excellent, choice (said mainly of wine).

genesíaco, ca, *a.* pert. to genesis.

genésico, ca, *a.* pert. to generation.

génesis. I. *m.* (G-) Genesis. **II.** *f.* origin, beginning; cause; genesis.

genetlíaca, *f.* astrology.

genetlíaco, ca. I. *a.* pert. to astrology. **II.** *m.* astrologist.

gengibre, *m.* = JENGIBRE, ginger.

genial, *a.* pert. to disposition; delightful; brilliant (person).

genialidad, *f.* temperament, disposition.

genialmente, *adv.* genially.

geniazo, *m. aug.* strong temper.

genio, *m.* genius; temperament, nature, disposition, temper; character, genius, peculiarities (as of a language); representative type, embodiment; angel, spirit.—**g. del mal,** evil spirit.— **buen g.,** good nature, equable temper.—**de buen (mal) g.,** good- (evil-) tempered.—**mal g.,** bad, or ill, temper.

genista, *f.* (bot.) = RETAMA, genista.

genital. I. *a.* genital. **II.** *m.* testicle.

genitivo, va. I. *a.* generative. **II.** *m.* (gram.) genitive or possessive case.

¹**genízaro, ra,** *a.* (Mex.) half-breed.

²**genízaro,** *m.* Janizary, Turkish infantryman.

genol, *m.* (naut.) futtock.

genovés, sa. I. *n. & a.* Genoese. **II.** *n.* (formerly) banker.

gente, *f.* people, folk, crowd, any number of persons; army, troops; gang; retinue; pens, clan, race, nation; (coll.) family, folks.—**g. baja,** lower classes; rabble, mob.—**g. bien,** (Am.) upper class.—**g. común,** common folk.—**g. de bien,** honest people.—**g. de capa parda,** villagers, countrymen, rustics.—**g. de color,** colored people.—**g. de la cuchilla,** butchers. —**g. de la garra,** thieves, pickpockets.—**g. de la vida airada,** the underworld, libertines.— **g. del bronce,** merry crowd.—**g. de paz,** a friend, or friends.—**g. de pelo,** or **de pelusa,** people of property.—**g. de trato,** tradesmen, dealers.—**g. de traza,** well-behaved people.— **g. fina,** cultured people.—**g. menuda,** children, "small fry."—**g. perdida,** vagrants, vagabonds.—**g. principal,** the nobility or gentry.—**g. vulgar** = G. COMÚN.—**de g. en g.,** from one to another, from generation to gener-

ation.—*pl.* Gentiles (as in *el Apóstol de las gentes,* the Apostle of the Gentiles, St. Paul)

gentecilla, *f.* low, contemptible people.

gentil. I. *a.* Gentile; genteel, graceful; gracious; excellent, exquisite. **II.** *n.* gentile, pagan, heathen.

gentileza, *f.* gentility, gracefulness; easiness, sprightliness, nattiness; ostentation, pageantry; courtesy, politeness.

gentilhombre, *m.* fine fellow; my good man; gentleman, the servant who waits about the person of a man of rank; person sent to the king with important despatches.—**g. de cámara,** lord of the bedchamber.—**g. de manga,** nobleman who attends the princes of Spain while children.

gentilicio, ia, *a.* national, tribal; hereditary.

gentílico, ca, *a.* heathen, gentile, pagan.

gentilidad, *f.* gentilism, heathenism, paganism; the body of heathens or gentiles.

gentilismo, *m.* = GENTILIDAD.

gentilizar, *vn.* to observe the rites of gentiles or heathens.

gentilmente, *adv.* gently, politely; heathenishly.

gentío, *m.* crowd, multitude.

gentualla, gentuza, *f.* rabble, mob; people of no account, small fry.

genuflexión, *f.* genuflexion.

genuino, na, *a.* genuine.

geocéntrico, ca, *a.* geocentric.

geoda, *f.* (geol.) geode.

geodesia, *f.* geodesy.

geodésico, ca, *a.* geodetical.

geodesta, *m.* geodesist.

geodinámica, *f.* geodynamics.

geófago, ga, *a.* geophagous, earth-eating.

geogenia, *f.* (geol.) geogeny.

geogénico, ca, *a.* geogenic.

geognosia, *f.* (geol.) geognosy.

geognosta, *m.* geognost, geologist.

geognóstico, ca, *a.* geognostic.

geogonía, *f.* = GEOGENIA.

geogónico, ca, *a.* geogonic.

geografía, *f.* geography.

geográficamente, *adv.* geographically.

geográfico, ca, *a.* geographical.

geógrafo, fa, *n.* geographer.

geología, *f.* geology.

geológico, ca, *a.* geological.

geólogo, ga, *n.* geologist.

geomancia, *f.* geomancy.

geomántico, ca. I. *a.* geomantic, pert. to geomancy. **II.** *m.* geomancer, one divining by random throw of earth.

geómetra, *n.* geometer, geometrician.

geometría, *f.* geometry.—**g. analítica,** analytic geometry.—**g. del espacio,** solid geometry.— **g. descriptiva,** descriptive geometry.—**g. no euclidiana,** non-Euclidean geometry.— **g. plana,** plane geometry.

geométricamente, *adv.* geometrically.

geométrico, ca, *a.* geometrical, geometric.

geomorfía, *f.* (geol.) geomorphology.

geonomía, *f.* (geol.) science treating of vegetable properties of the earth.

geonómico, ca, *a.* pertaining to GEONOMÍA.

geoponia, geopónica, *f.* geoponics, agriculture.

geopónico, ca, *a.* geoponic, agricultural.

georama, *f.* georama.

georgiano, na, *a.* Georgian, pert. to Georgia.

geórgica, *f.* georgic, poem on husbandry.

geotropismo, *m.* (bot.) geotropism.

geraniáceo, cea, *a.* (bot.) geraniaceous.

geranio, *m.* (bot.) crane's-bill; geranium.—**g. de rosa,** rose geranium.

gerbo, *m.* (zool.) jerboa, mouselike rodent.

gerencia, *f.* (com.) managership, management.

gerente, *m.* (com.) manager.

gericaya, *f.* (Mex., cooking) custard.

gerifalco, gerifalte, *m.* (ornith.) gerfalcon.

For pronunciation, see the rules at the beginning of the book.

germanesco, ca, a. pertaining to the jargon of the gipsies.

germanía, f. jargon or cant of the gipsies, thieves, etc.; slang; concubinage; a faction in Valencia during the days of Charles V.

germánico, ca, a. Germanic, German.

germanio, m. (chem.) germanium.

germanismo, m. Germanism, German form employed in another language.

¹germano, na, n. & a. German(-ic) (app. only to Germania, ancient Germany).

²germano, na. I. a. genuine. **II.** a. & n. german, full (brother, sister.)

germanófilo, la, n. & a. pro-German.

germen, m. germ; spring, source.

germinación, f. (bot.) germination.

germinal. I. a. germinal. **II.** m. Germinal, seventh month of the French revolutionists.

germinar, vn. to germinate.

germinativo, va, a. germinative.

gerundense, a. of or belonging to Gerona.

gerundiada, f. (coll.) pompous and unmeaning expression.

gerundiano, na, a. pompous, empty (style or phrase).

¹gerundio, m. (gram.) gerund.

²gerundio, m. (coll.) pompous, bombastic speaker.

gesolreút, m. (anc. mus.) first of the signs which serve as a clef to music; G or soprano clef.

gesta, f. gest, a narrative of a person's deeds; romance.

gestación, f. (med.) gestation; exercise among the Romans for the health.

gestatorio, ria, a. portable, carrying (chair).

gestear, vn. to gesticulate, make grimaces.

gestero, ra, n. & a. (one) that makes grimaces or faces; making grimaces; gesticulator(-ing).

gesticulación, f. gesticulation, gesture.

¹gesticular, vn. to gesticulate, make gestures or grimaces.

²gesticular, a. gesticulatory.

gestión, f. conduct; exertion, effort, action, measure, step; negotiation, management.

gestionar, va. to conduct, manage; to take steps to attain or carry out.

gesto, m. facial expression; grimace; gesture.—**estar de buen g.,** to be in good humor.—**hacer gestos,** to make a face; to gesticulate; to make signs.

gestor, m. (com.) superintendent, manager, agent, promotor, representative, attorney.

gestudo, da, a. (coll.) ill-humored, cross.

giba, f. hump, crooked back, hunch, gibbosity; (coll.) nuisance, annoyance.

gibado, da. I. pp. of GIBAR. **II.** a. hunchbacked.

gibar, va. to crook; (coll.) to molest, annoy, vex.

gibelino, na, n. & a. Ghibelline.

gibón, m. (zool.) gibbon.

giboso, sa, a. gibbous, humpbacked.

gibraltareño, ña, a. Gibraltar (as a.).

gícama, f. (Mex.) a root resembling yucca.

giganta, f. giantess; (bot.) sunflower.

gigantazo, za, n. aug. huge giant.

gigante. I. a. gigantic. **II.** m. giant.

gigantea, f. (bot.) sunflower.

giganteo, a; gigantesco, ca, a. gigantic.

gigantez, f. gigantic stature or size.

gigantilla, f. large-headed figure.

gigantismo, m. (med.) giantism, gigantism.

gigantón, na, n. aug. giant of enormous size.—**gigantones,** gigantic figures of pasteboard.—**echar los gigantones a,** (coll.) to reprehend severely, to give a dressing down.

gijonense; gijonés, sa, a. of Gijon.

gilí, a. (coll.) foolish, stupid.

gilvo, va, a. honey-colored or pinkish.

gimelga, f. (naut.) fish, paunch.

gimnasia, f. = GIMNÁSTICA.

gimnasio, m. gymnasium; school, academy.

gimnasta, m. gymnast.

gimnástica, f. gymnastics, calisthenics.

gimnástico, ca, a. gymnastic, gymnastical.

gímnico, ca, a. pert. to athletic contests or acrobatic dancing.

gimnosofista, m. (anc. Hindu) gymnosophist.

gimnoto, m. (zool.) gymnotus, electric eel.

gimo, gima, v. V. GEMIR.

gimotear, vn. (coll.) to whine.—**gimoteo,** m. whining.

¹ginebra, f. Moorish rattle; confusion, bedlam; a card game.

²ginebra, f. gin (liquor).

ginebrada, f. a kind of puff-paste tart.

ginebrés, sa; ginebrino, na, n. & a. Genevan.

gineceo, m. (bot.) gynæceum; women's quarters in house.

ginecocracia, f. gynecocracy, government by women.

ginecología, f. (med.) gynecology.

ginecológico, ca, a. gynecological.

ginecólogo, ga, n. gynecologist.

ginesta, f. = HINIESTA, genista.

gineta, f. genet, a kind of weasel.

gingidio, m. (bot.) wild spinach.

gingival, a. (anat.) gingival, pertaining to the gums.—**gingivitis,** f. gingivitis, inflammation of the gums.

ginglimo, m. (anat.) ginglymus.

ginsén, ginseng, m. (bot., pharm.) ginseng.

girada, f. (dance) gyration; pirouette.

girado, m. (com.) drawee.

girador, girante, m. (com.) drawer.

giralda, f. vane or weathercock in the form of an animal or human figure (from that on the spire of the cathedral of Seville); (G-) name of this tower.

giraldete, m. surplice without sleeves.

giraldilla, f. dim. small vane or weathercock; a popular dance in Asturias.

girándula, f. (fireworks) girandole.

girar, vn. to revolve, rotate; to turn; (com.) to draw (a check, draft).—**g. contra,** or a **cargo de,** to draw on.

girasol, m. (bot.) sunflower.

giratorio, ria, a. revolving, rotary, turning.

girifalte, m. (ornith.) = GERIFALTE, gerfalcon.

girino, m. embryo of a frog.

giro, m. turn; revolution, rotation; gyration, course or turn of affairs; bend, tendency; bias, trend; turn of a sentence; threat, bravado; (com.) draft; circulation; bulk of business; line of business, specialty.—**g. postal,** money order.—**tomar otro g.,** to take another course; to change one's mind.

giroflé, m. (bot.) aromatic clove tree.

girondino, na, n. & a. Girondist, Girondin.

giroscópico, ca, a. gyroscopic.

giroscopio, m. gyroscope.

giróvago, ga, a. = VAGABUNDO, vagabond.

gis, m. crayon.

gitana, f. gipsy woman, girl.

gitanada, f. mean, contemptible trick; blandishment, wheedling, caress, flattery.

gitanamente, adv. in a sly, winning manner.

gitanear, va. to flatter, wheedle, cajole.

gitanería, f. wheedling, flattery, cajolery.

gitanesco, ca, a. gipsylike, gipsy (as a.).

gitanillo, lla, n. dim. little gipsy.

gitanismo, m. gipsy life, dress, ways.

gitano, na. I. a. gipsylike; gipsy; sly, artful, honey-mouthed. **II.** n. gipsy.

glabro, bra, a. bald; beardless.

glacial, a. glacial.

glacialmente, adv. glacially.

glacis, m. (fort.) glacis.

gladiador, gladiator, m. gladiator.

gladiatorio, ria, a. gladiatorial, gladiatory.

gladio, gladiolo, m. (bot.) gladiolus.

glande, m. (anat.) glans, head of the penis.

glandífero, ra; glandígero, ra, *a.* acorn-bearing.

glándula, *f.* gland.—**g. pineal,** pineal body, pineal gland.—**g. pituitaria,** pituitary gland.

glandular, *a.* glandular.

glanduloso, sa, *a.* glandulous, glandular.

glasé, *m.* glacé or glacé silk.

glaseado, da, *a.* glossy, glacélike.

glasear, *va.* to calender (paper).

glasto, *m.* (bot.) woad or dyers' weed.

glauberita, *f.* glauberite.

glaucio, *m.* (bot.) celandine.

glauco, ca. I. *a.* (bot.) glaucous; light green. **II.** *m.* (zool.) a mollusk of the Glaucus genus.

glaucoma, *m.* (med.) glaucoma.

gleba, *f.* lump or clod turned up by the plow.

glera, *f.* = CASCAJAR, gravel pit.

glicerato, *m.* (chem.) glycerate.

glicerido, *m.* (chem.) glyceride.

glicerina, *f.* glycerine.

glicocola, *f.* (chem.) glycocoll.

glicógeno, na, *a.* (physiol.) sugar-producing.

glicol, *m.* (chem.) glycol.

glicosuria, *f.* (med.) glycosuria.

glifo, *m.* (arch.) glyph, groove.

gliptica, *f.* glyptography, stone or gem engraving.

gliptodonte, *m.* (paleontol.) glytodon.

gliptografía, *f.* = GLIPTICA.

global, *a.* taken in a lump, in all.

globo, *m.* globe, sphere; the earth; balloon; globular lamp shade.—**g. aerostático,** air balloon. —**g. cautivo,** captive balloon.—**g. celeste,** (astr.) celestial globe.—**g. cometa,** (aer.) kite balloon.—**g. dirigible,** dirigible balloon, airship.—**g. nodriza,** (aer.) nurse balloon.—**g. piloto,** (aer.) pilot balloon.—**g. sonda,** (aer.) sounding balloon, captive balloon with recording instruments.—**g. terráqueo,** or **terrestre,** (the) globe, (the) earth.—**en g.,** as a whole; without details; in bulk.

globoso, sa, *a.* globe-shaped.

globular, *a.* globular.

globulariáceo, a, *a.* (bot.) globulariaceous.

glóbulo, *m. dim.* small globe; (biol.) corpuscle.

globulillo, *m. dim.* globulet, globule; homeopathic pill.

globulina, *f.* (chem.) globulin.

globuloso, sa, *a.* globulous, globulose.

gloria. I. *f.* glory; heavenly state, bliss, blessedness; pride, boast; transparent gauze, gossamer, tissue; a kind of cream tart or cake; (art) opening in the sky representing angels, splendors, etc.—**saber a g.,** to taste delicious. **II.** *m.* (eccl.) gloria, doxology.—**G. Patri,** or **Gloriapatri,** (eccl.) Gloria Patri, the lesser doxology.

gloriarse, *vr.* (**de** or **en**) to boast (of), be proud (of), take delight (in).

glorieta, *f.* summerhouse, bower, arbor; circle or square at intersection of streets.

glorificación, *f.* glorification; praise.

glorificador, ra; glorificante, *n.* & *a.* glorifier (-fying).

glorificar. I. *va.* (*pret.* GLORIFIQUÉ; *subj.* GLORIFIQUE) to glorify, adore, worship; to exalt; to praise, honor, extol. **II.** *vr.* = GLORIARSE.

gloriosamente, *adv.* gloriously.

glorioso, sa, *a.* glorious; enjoying the bliss of heaven, blessed; boastful, ostentatious.

glosa, *f.* gloss, scholium; comment, commentary, note; (com. and law) explanatory annotation in accounts; (poet.) a kind of rondelet; (mus.) variation of a theme.

glosador, ra, *n.* commentator, glosser, glossarist; (com.) auditor.

glosalgia, *f.* (med.) glosalgia.

glosar, *va.* to gloss, annotate, comment; (com.) to audit; (poet.) to compose (rondelets); (mus.) to vary (a theme).

glosario, *m.* glossary.

glose, *m.* glossing, commenting.

glosilla, *f. dim.* short gloss, comment, or note; (print.) minion type, 7-point.

glositis, *f.* (med.) glossitis, tongue inflammation.

glótico, ca, *a.* glottic, pertaining to the glottis.

glotis, *f.* (anat.) glottis.

glotón, na, *a.* & *n.* glutton(-ous).

glotonamente, *adv.* gluttonously.

glotonazo, za, *n. aug.* great glutton, gormandizer.

glotonear, *vn.* to be a glutton, gormandize.

glotonería, *f.* gluttony.

glucina, *f.* (chem.) glucina.

glucinio, *m.* (chem.) glucinum, beryllium.

glucogenia, *f.* (physiol.) glycogeny (esp. of the liver).

glucómetro, *m.* glucometer, hydrometer for determining the quantity of sugar in a liquid.

glucosa, *f.* (chem.) glucose.

glucósido, *m.* (chem.) glucoside.

glucosuria, *f.* (med.) glucosuria.

gluma, *f.* (bot.) glume.

gluten, *m.* gluten; glue.

glúteo, tea, *a.* gluteal, pert. to buttocks.

glutinosidad, *f.* glutinousness, viscosity.

glutinoso, sa, *a.* glutinous, viscous.

gneis, *m.* (geol.) gneiss, a kind of rock.

gnetáceo, a, *a.* (bot.) gnetaceous.

gnómico, ca, *a.* gnomic.

gnomo, *m.* gnome, fabulous being.

gnomon, *m.* gnomon, sundial; (mason.) square. —**g. movible,** bevel square.

gnomónica, *f.* science of making sundials.

gnomónico, ca, *a.* pert. to GNOMÓNICA.

gnosticismo, *m.* gnosticism.

gnóstico, ca, *n.* & *a.* gnostic.

goa, *f.* pig-iron bloom; (agr.) dibble.

goal, *m.* (Angl.) (football) goal.

gobernación, *f.* government; governor's office or official house.

gobernador, ra. I. *a.* governing. **II.** *n.* governor; ruler. **III.** *f.* governor's wife; woman ruler.

gobernadorcillo, *m.* (P. I.) justice of the peace.

gobernalle, *m.* (naut.) rudder, helm.

gobernante. I. *n.* & *a.* ruler(-ing). **II.** *n.* (coll.) self-appointed manager or leader.

gobernar. I. *va.* & *vn.* (*ind.* GOBIERNO; *subj.* GOBIERNE) to govern, rule; to command, lead, direct; to manage, run; to control, steer, helm. **II.** *vn.* (naut.) to obey the helm. **III.** *vr.* to manage (as one's affairs), carry on.

gobernativo, va, *a.* governmental.

gobernoso, sa, *a.* (coll.) methodical, tidy.

gobierna, *f.* weather vane.

gobiernista. I. *a.* gubernatorial, government (as *a.*); that supports the government. **II.** *n.* supporter of the government.

¹gobierno, *m.* government; ministers composing a cabinet; dignity, office, and term of a government; district or province under a governor; guidance, management, direction; control (of a business, an automobile, an airplane); (naut.) helm, rudder; steering, conning.—**g. de casa,** household.—**de g.,** controlling (lever, etc.), control (as *a.*); of the State.—**para su g.,** for your guidance.—**servir de g.,** to be a guide or norm; to be a warning or a lesson.

²gobierno, gobierne, *v. V.* GOBERNAR.

gobio, *m.* (ichth.) gudgeon.

goce, *m.* enjoyment; fruition; possession.

gocete, *m.* neck guards in ancient armor.

gociano, na, *a.* Gothic.

gocha, *f.* (coll.) sow.

gocho, *m.* (coll.) hog.

godesco, ca; godible, *a.* joyful, cheerful.

godo, da, *n.* & *a.* Goth(-ic); (Colomb., pol.) conservative.—**ser g.,** (Spain, coll.) to be of noble blood.

gofio, *m.* (Cuba) roasted corn meal or maize.

gofo, fa, *a.* stupid, ignorant; (art) dwarf figure.

gofrador, *m.* leaf marker, florist's tool.

gofrar, *va.* to mark (leaves) for artificial flowers.

gol, *m.* (Angl.) (football) (making a) goal.

gola, *f.* gullet, throat; gorget in ancient armor; (mil.) gorget, crescent-shaped insignia of duty; (fort.) gorge; (arch.) cyma, ogee.—**g. inversa,** or **reversa,** (arch.) cyma reversa.

goldre, *m.* quiver for shafts or arrows.

goleta, *f.* (naut.) schooner.

golf, *m.* golf.—**golfista,** *m.* & *f.* golfer.

golfán, *m.* (bot.) water lily.

golfillo, *m.* *dim.* small gulf; urchin.

golfín, *m.* (ichth.) dolphin.

¹golfo, *m.* (geog.) gulf; sea, main; (poet.) gulf, abyss; faro (game).

²golfo, *m.* (Madrid) ragamuffin.

golilla. I. *f.* (sewing) gorget, ruff; collar worn by some magistrates in Spain; (mason.) short joining pipe; flange of a pipe. **II.** *m.* (coll.) magistrate wearing a GOLILLA.

golillero, ra, *n.* collar maker.

golmajo, ja, *n.* (prov.) gormandizer.

golondrina, *f.* (ornith.) swallow; (ichth.) flying gurnard, swallow fish.—**g. de mar,** (ornith.) tern.

golondrinera, *f.* (bot.) swallowwort, celandine.

golondrino, *m.* (ornith.) male swallow; vagrant, deserter; (med.) large tumor in the armpit.

golondro, *m.* (coll.) desire, longing.—**andar en golondros,** (coll.) to feed on vain hopes.—**campar de g.,** (coll.) to live at another's expense, to sponge.

golosamente, *adv.* eagerly; inordinately.

golosear, *va.* = GOLOSINAR.

golosina, *f.* dainty, delicacy, sweet morsel, tidbit; daintiness, sweet tooth; inordinate desire or appetite; trifle.

golosinar, golosinear, golosmear, *vn.* to look for and eat tidbits, dainties, or sweetmeats; to taste and relish nice things.

goloso, sa, *a.* having a sweet tooth, fond of dainties, niceties, or sweetmeats.

golpazo, *m.* *aug.* heavy blow, stroke, or knock.

golpe, *m.* blow; stroke, hit, knock; wound, hurt; shock, clash; attack, spell; action, push, act; crowd, throng of people; abundance; heart beat; spring bolt of a lock; (sew.) passementerie trimming; pocket flap (of a coat); attack in fencing; astonishment, surprise; witty sally or remark; hole for planting; number of cuts planted in one hole; (mech.) stroke (of piston); travel (of a valve); (naut.) sweep; (mus.) touch, act of striking a key, etc.—**g. de arco,** bowing of a violin.—**g. de cuartel,** military coup.—**g. de estado,** coup d'état.—**g. de fortuna,** stroke of good fortune.—**g. de gracia,** finishing stroke, coup de grâce.—**g. del reloj,** tick of the watch or clock.—**g. de mar** (naut.) surge, heavy sea.—**g. de remo,** oar stroke.—**g. de vista,** glance; sight.—**g. seco,** sharp, quick blow or stroke.—**dar g.,** to cause surprise; to create a sensation.—**de g.,** suddenly, all at once. —**de g. y porrazo,** unexpectedly, unawares.— **de un g.,** at one blow; all at once.

golpeadero, *m.* place much beaten; repeated blows.

golpeador, ra, *n.* & *a.* striker(-ing), beater(-ing), hitter(-ing).

golpeadura, *f.* percussion; act of beating, hammering, or striking.

golpear. I. *va.* to strike, hit, hammer; to bruise. **II.** *vn.* to beat; to knock, pound (as a piston); to tick (as a watch).

golpecico, illo, ito, *m.* *dim.* slight blow.

golpeo, *m.* repeated striking, beating or knocking.

golpete, *m.* door catch (to keep it open).

golpetear, *va.* & *vn.* to strike or pound continually; to rattle.

golpeteo, *m.* continued striking; constant hammering; knocking, pounding; rattling.

gollería, gollоría, *f.* dainty; delicious morsel; (coll.) delicacy, superfluity, excess.

gollete, *m.* throttle, upper part of the throat; neck of a bottle; neckband of some religious habits.—**estar hasta el g.,** (coll.) to be full (after eating); to be in difficulties; to have lost patience.

gollizo, *m.* narrow passage of mountains or rivers.

goma, *f.* gum; India rubber; rubber band; rubber eraser; (surg.) gumma, a kind of syphilitic tumor; (Am.) "hang-over" (after drinking).— *pl.* (Am.) overshoes, rubbers.—**g. adragante,** gum tragacanth.—**g. arábiga,** gum arabic.—**g. de borrar,** rubber eraser.—**g. de mascar,** chewing gum.—**g. elástica,** India rubber.—**g. laca,** lac.—**g. tragacanta** = G. ADRAGANTE.

gomecillo, *m.* blind person's guide.

gomero, ra. I. *a.* pert. to gums or to rubber. **II.** *m.* one engaged in the rubber business.

gomía, *f.* bugbear; (coll.) glutton.—**g. del caudal,** spendthrift.

gomífero, ra, *a.* gummiferous.

gomorresina, *f.* gum resin.

gomosidad, *f.* gumminess, viscosity.

gomoso, sa. I. *a.* gummy; gum-producing; full of viscous matter. **II.** *m.* dude, dandy.

gonce, *m.* hinge.

góndola, *f.* gondola; omnibus, stage, carry-all.

gondolero, ra, *n.* gondolier.

gonela, *f.* skirt formerly worn in Aragon.

gonfalón, *m.* banner, gonfalon, pennant.

gonfalonier, niero, *m.* chief standard-bearer.

gong, *m.* (Angl.) gong (in wrestling ring, etc.).

gongórico, ca; gongorino, na, *a.* euphuistic.

gongorismo, *m.* euphuism.

gongorista, *n.* (poet.) euphuist.

gongorizar, *vn.* to write euphuistically.

goniometría, *f.* goniometry.

goniométrico, ca, *a.* goniometric.

goniómetro, *m.* goniometer.

gonococo, *m.* (biol.) gonococcus.

gonorrea, *f.* (med.) gonorrhœa.

gonorreico, ca, *a.* gonorrhœal.

gorbión, gurbión, *m.* coarse twisted silk or cloth.

gordal, *a.* fat, big, fleshy.

gordana, *f.* oil extracted from oxen's testicles.

gordazo, za, *a.* *aug.* very fat and big.

gordico, ica, illo, illa, ito, ita, *a.* *dim.* plump.

gordiflón, na; gordinflón, na, *a.* (coll.) chubby, flabby, fat.

gordo, da. I. *a.* fat, corpulent, fleshy, stout; fat, rich, oily; great, large, big.—**agua g.,** hard water.—**hacer la vista g.,** to pretend not to see, wink at.—**llevarse un susto g.,** to get a bad scare. **II.** *m.* fat, suet.

gordolobo, *m.* (bot.) great mullein.

gordón, na, dote, ta, *a.* *aug.* (coll.) very fat.

gordura, *f.* grease, fat; fatness, stoutness.

gorfe, *m.* a deep hole in a river forming a whirlpool or eddy.

gorga, *f.* hawk food; whirlpool.

gorgojarse, *vr.* (of corn) to be infested with grubs.

gorgojo, *m.* grub, weevil; (coll.) dwarfish person.

gorgojoso, sa, *a.* infested with grubs or weevils.

gogona, *f.* a zoöphyte, (coral, sea anemone, etc.).

gorgóneo, a, *a.* Gorgonian.

gorgorán, *m.* a sort of silk grosgrain.

gorgorita, *f.* rain bubble.—*pl.* = GORGORITO.

gorgoritear, *vn.* (coll.) to warble, trill.

gorgorito, *m.* (coll.) (vocal) trill, shake.

gorgorotada, *f.* swallow (as of water).

gorgoteo, *m.* gurgle, gurgling sound.

gorgotero, ra, *m.* peddler, hawker.

gorguera, *f.* (sew.) gorgeret, ruff; (armor) gorget.

gorguerín, *f.* *dim.* small neck ruff or frill.

gorguz, *m.* javelin, shaft.

gorigori, *m.* (coll.) chant at funerals.

gorila, *m.* (zool.) gorilla.

gorja, *f.* throat, throttle; rejoicing, merrymaking; (naut.) head of the keel.

gorjal, *m.* collar of a doublet; (armor) gorget.

gorjeador, ra, *n. & a.* warbler(-ing), modulator (-ing).

gorjear. I. *vn.* to warble, trill, quaver, sing. **II.** *vr.* to gabble (as a child).

gorjeo, *m.* warble, trilling; gabble of a child.

gormar, *va.* to vomit.

gorra. I. *f.* cap, bonnet; woman's hat; hunting cap; (mil.) bearskin cap; (coll.) intrusion at feasts without invitation; (coll.) sponging—**g. de señora,** lady's hat or bonnet.—**de g.,** (coll.) at other people's expense, sponging, as a sponge.—**ir, comer, andar,** etc. **de g.,** to "sponge." **II.** *m.* parasite, sponger.

gorrada, *f.* = GORRETADA.

gorrería, *f.* bonnet and cap factory or shop.

gorrero, ra, *n.* cap maker; parasite, sponger, deadhead.

gorretada, *f.* raising the cap in greeting.

gorrete, *m. dim.;* **gorrica, illa, ita,** *f. dim.;* **gorrico, illo, ito,** *m. dim.* small cap.

gorrín, *m.* small pig, sucking pig.

gorrinada, *f.* (coll.) dirty, hoggish action.

gorrinera, *f.* pigsty, pigpen.

gorrinillo, ito, *m. dim.* little pig

gorrino, na, *n.* small pig, sucking pig.

gorrión, *m.* (ornith.) sparrow.

gorrioncillo, *m. dim.* small sparrow.

gorrionera, *f.* (coll.) den of rogues.

gorrista, *n.* parasite, sponger.

gorro, *m.* cap, coif.—**g. de dormir,** nightcap.— **g. frigio,** Phyrgian cap, cap of liberty.

¹gorrón, na, *n.* sponger, parasite; libertine.

²gorrón, *m.* round smooth pebble; (mech.) spindle; pivot or gudgeon of a gate or door; pillow, swing block; lazy, unhealthy silkworm.

gorronal, *m.* place full of pebbles or gravel.

gorronazo, *m. aug.* great lecher or rake.

gorullo, *m.* lump or ball (as of wool).

gorupo, *m.* (naut.) granny's bend.

gosipino, na, *a.* having a cottony surface.

gota, *f.* drop of liquid; (med.) gout; (arch.) gutta. —**g. a g.,** drop by drop.—**g. caduca,** or **coral,** (med.) epilepsy, falling sickness.—**g. militar,** chronic gonorrhea.—**g. serena,** (med.) amaurosis.—**gotas amargas,** bitters.—**sudar la g. gorda,** to "sweat blood."

goteado, da. I. *pp.* of GOTEAR. **II.** *a.* spotted, speckled.

gotear, *vn.* to drop, drip, dribble, leak; to sprinkle, begin to rain; to measure by drops; to give by dribblets.

gotera, *f.* leak, leakage; drip, dripping; (arch.) gutter; valance of a canopy or tester; (agr.) disease of trees caused by infiltration; chronic ailing.

goterón, *m.* large raindrop; (arch.) throating.

gotica, illa, ita, *f. dim.* droplet, small drop.

gótico, ca, *a.* Gothic.—**gotón, na,** *n. & a.* Goth.

gotoso, sa, *a.* gouty.

goyesco, ca, *a.* pertaining to, or like, Goya, or his style, Goya (as *a.*).

gozador, ra, *n.* enjoyer.

gozante, *n. & a.* enjoyer(-ing).

gozar. I. *va.* to enjoy; to have possession or fruition of. **II.** *vn.* **(de),** to enjoy, have possession (of). **III.** *vr.* to rejoice.

gozne, *m.* hinge.

gozo, *m.* joy, pleasure, glee, mirth, gladness; sudden blaze of dry chips of wood.—*pl.* couplets with a burden, in praise of the Virgin.—**¡el g. al pozo!** all has come to naught!—**no caber de g.,** or **saltar de g.,** to be in high spirits, to be very happy.

gozosamente, *adv.* joyfully, cheerfully.

gozoso, sa, *a.* joyful, cheerful, glad, merry.

gozque, *m.* a cur dog.

gozquejo, *m. dim.* small cur.

grabado. I. *pp.* of GRABAR. **II.** *a.* engraved, carved, cut. **III.** *m.* engraving; art of engraving; cut, picture, illustration.—**g. al agua fuerte,** etching.—**g. al agua tinta,** aquatint.—**g. al barniz blando,** soft-ground etching.—**g. al humo,** mezzotint.—**g. a media tinta** = G. AL AGUA TINTA.—**g. a puntos,** stipple engraving, stipple.—**g. en fondo,** or **en hueco,** punch or die sinking.—**g. en madera,** wood engraving, wood carving.—**g. en negro** = G. AL HUMO.—**g. punteado** = G. A PUNTOS.

grabador, ra, *n.* engraver, carver; cutter, sinker.

grabadura, *f.* act of engraving; sculpture.

grabar, *va.* to engrave; to cut, carve; to impress upon the mind.—**g. al agua fuerte,** to etch.— **g. en hueco, en blanco,** or **relieve,** to emboss.

grabazón, *f.* engraving, sculpture.

gracejada, *f.* (Mex., C. A.) joke (gen. in bad taste).

gracejar, *vn.* to write or speak wittily.

gracejo, *m.* graceful, winsome way.

gracia, *f.* grace; gracefulness; cleverness; free gift, benefaction, kindness; graciousness, condescension; benevolence, courtesy, pleasing manners; pardon, mercy; remission of a debt; witty saying or expression; joke, jest; humor, facetiousness; comicalness; brightness, cuteness of a child; (coll.) name (of a person).—*pl.* thanks; accomplishments; (myth., **G-**) (the Three) Graces.—**Ministerio de G. y Justicia,** Dep't of Justice & Eccl. Affairs.—**gracias,** thanks, thank you.—**gracias a,** thanks to.— **gracias a Dios,** thank God.—**caer de la gracia de,** to lose the favor or good will of. —**caer en g.,** to please, to be liked.—**dar gracias,** to thank, to give thanks.—**decir dos gracias,** to tell home truths.—**de g.,** gratis, for nothing.—**en g.,** in favor.—**en g. de,** for the sake of, out of regard for; in consideration of.—**hacer g.,** to please; to amuse, strike as funny.—**hacer g. de,** to excuse from; to free from.—**¡qué g.!,** (ironic) how fine! how funny! —**tener g.,** (ironic) to be surprising.

graciable, *a.* good-natured, affable, amiable; easily granted.

grácil, *a.* gracile, slender, small.

graciola, *f.* (bot.) hedge hyssop.

graciosamente, *adv.* gracefully; graciously or kindly, gratuitously; facetiously.

graciosidad, *f.* gracefulness, beauty, excellence.

gracioso, sa. I. *a.* graceful, pleasing, accomplished; facetious, witty, funny; liberal, gracious; gratuitous, free. **II.** *m.* (theat.) low comedian, fool. **III.** *f.* (theat.) soubrette, chambermaid.

¹grada, *f.* step of a staircase; gradin (as of an amphitheatre); stand or gallery having gradins; superaltar; brake.—*pl.* (arch.) perron, gradatory; wide steps to a building entrance; bleachers (at ball park, etc.)—**g. de astillero,** (naut.) altar.—**g. de dique,** (naut.) altar.

²grada, *f.* (eccl.) locutory; (agr.) harrow.—**g. de cota,** brush-harrow.—**g. de dientes,** toothed harrow.

gradación, *f.* (mus.) gradation; (rhet.) climax; grading; graded series of things or events.

gradado, da, *a.* having gradins or steps.

gradar, *va.* (agr.) to harrow.

gradeo, *m.* (agr.) harrowing.

gradería, *f.* series of steps, gradins or superaltars.

¹gradilla, *f.* tile or brick mold.

²gradilla, *f.* small stepladder.

gradinar, *va.* (art) to chisel with a gradine.

gradino, *m.* gradine, sculptor's chisel.

gradiolo, *m.* (bot.) = GLADIOLO, gladiolus.

¹grado, *m.* step of a staircase; degree (of kindred); degree, academic title; (mil.) rank; (math., geog.) degree; (com.) grade, class, graduation of value or quality; (gram.) degree (of comparison); (law) state of proceedings.—*pl.* minor

orders.—**de g. en g.**, gradually, by degrees.—
en g. superlativo, or **en sumo g.**, in the highest degree.

²**grado**, *m.* will, willingness, pleasure.—**de g.** or **de buen g.**, willingly, with pleasure.—**de mal g.**, unwillingly.—**de su g.**, = DE G.—**mal de mi g.**, against my wishes, much to my regret, unwillingly.

graduable, *a.* that can be graduated; adjustable.
graduación, *f.* graduation; (mil.) rank.
graduado, da. I. *pp.* of GRADUAR. **II.** *a.* (mil.) brevet; graduated. **III.** *m.* graduate.
graduador, *m.* graduator, gauge.
gradual. I. *a.* gradual. **II.** *m.* (eccl.) response sung at mass.—**gradualmente**, *adv.* gradually.
graduando, *m.* one recently, or about to be graduated.
graduar. I. *va.* to compare, grade, classify; to graduate; to give military rank to; (com.) to gauge, to appraise; to adjust; to set (a fuse, etc.). **II.** *vr.* (en) to graduate (from), be graduated, take a degree.
gráficamente, *adv.* graphically.
gráfico, ca. I. *a.* graphic, graphical; clear, vivid. **II.** *m.* or *f.* graph, diagram.
gráfila, *f.* milled edge of coin.
grafio, *m.* graver for graffito or scratchwork.
grafioles, *m. pl.* biscuits in the form of an S.
grafito, *m.* (min.) graphite.
grafófono, *m.* graphophone.
grafolita, *f.* grapholite.
grafología, *f.* graphology.
grafomanía, *f.* graphomania, mania, for writing (books, articles) for publication.
grafómano, na, *n.* one who has GRAFOMANÍA.
grafómetro, *m.* (surv.) graphometer.
grafostática, *f.* graphic statics.
gragea, *f.* minute colored bonbons.
graja, *f.* (ornith.) female jackdaw; jay.
grajal, *a.* pert. to crows, ravens, or magpies.
grajear, *vn.* to caw, as crows; to chatter, as magpies.
grajero, ra, *a.* abounding in, or frequented by, jackdaws.
grajo, *m.* (ornith.) jackdaw.
grajuelo, *m. dim.* small jackdaw.
grama, *f.* (bot.) creeping cynodon; couch, dog's, or grama grass; (Am.) lawn.
gramal, *m.* couch grass or dog's grass field.
gramalla, *f.* long scarlet gown formerly worn in Aragon; coat of mail.
gramallera, *f.* pothanger (in a fireplace).
gramar, *va.* to knead.
gramática, *f.* grammar; study of the Latin language.—**g. parda**, (coll.) horse sense, shrewdness.
gramatical, *a.* grammatical.
gramaticalmente, *adv.* grammatically.
gramático, ca. I. *a.* grammatical. **II.** *n.* grammarian.—**gramatiquear**, *vn.* (contempt.) to grammatize, to talk grammar.
gramatiquería, *f.* (coll. & contempt.) things grammatical, grammatical stuff.
gramil, *m.* (carp.) joiner's marking gauge.
gramilla, *f.* bed of hemp brake; (Arg.) (grass) lawn.
gramíneo, ea, *a.* (bot.) gramineous.
graminívoro, ra, *a.* graminivorous.
gramo, *m.* gramme, gram (weight).
gramófono, *m.* gramophone; phonograph.
gramómetro, *m.* (print.) type gauge.
gramoso, sa, *a.* covered with couch grass; pertaining to couch grass.
grampa, *f.* staple, clamp, cramp.
gran, *a. contr.* of GRANDE (*used only in sing. and before m. or f. nouns*), large, big; grand, great.—**g. bestia**, tapir, elk.—**g. mogol**, Grand Mogul or Great Mogul.
¹**grana**, *f.* (agr.) act of seeding; seeding time; small seed of some plants.

²**grana**, *f.* (entom.) cochineal; kermes; kermes berry; scarlet grain; scarlet color; fine scarlet cloth; fresh red color of the lips and cheeks.—**g. del paraíso**, (bot.) cardamomum.
granada, *f.* (bot.) pomegranate; (mil.) grenade, shell.—**g. de mano**, hand grenade.
granadera, *f.* (mil.) grenadier's pouch.
granadero, *m.* (mil.) grenadier; (coll.) very tall person.
granadilla, *f.* (bot.) passion flower, granadilla.
granadillo, *m.* (bot.) West-India red ebony.
¹**granadino, na**, *a.* native of or pert. to Granada (Spain), or New Granada (Colombia.)
²**granadino**, *m.* flower of the pomegranate tree.
¹**granado, da. I.** *pp.* of GRANAR. **II.** *a.* remarkable, noted, illustrious; mature; select, choice.
²**granado**, *m.* (bot.) pomegranate tree.
granador, *m.* (fireworks making) granulating sieve; spot destined for this operation.
granalla, *f.* (foundry) granulated metal.
granar, *vn.* (agr.) (of corn) to start forming kernels.
granate, *m.* garnet.
granatín, *m.* a kind of ancient cloth.
granazón, *f.* seeding, forming seeds or kernels.
grancé, *a.* madder-colored.
grande. I. *a.* large, big; great; grand; (Mex.) old. —**en g.**, on a large scale. **II.** *n.* grandee.—*pl.* grandees; great men.—**grandecico, ica, illo, illa, ito, ita**, *a.* pretty large.—**grandemente**, *adv.* greatly; very well; extremely; grandly.
grandevo, va, *a.* (poet.) of advanced age.
grandeza, *f.* greatness; grandeur, magnificence; grandeeship; grandees collectively; bigness; quantity; size, magnitude.
grandezuelo, la, *a. dim.* = GRANDECICO.
grandilocuencia, *f.* grandiloquence.
grandilocuente; **grandílocuo, cua**, *a.* grandiloquent.
grandillón, na, *a. aug.* excessively large or big.
grandiosamente, *adv.* magnificently, grandly.
grandiosidad, *f.* greatness; grandeur; abundance.
grandioso, sa, *a.* grandiose, grand, magnificent.
grandísono, na, *a.* (poet.) high-sounding.
grandor, *m.* size.
grandote, ta, *a. aug.* (coll.) very big.
grandullón, na, *a.* overgrown.
graneado, da. I. *pp.* of GRANEAR. **II.** *a.* grained, spotted, granulous; (Peru) select, choice.—**fuego, g.**, (mil.) drumfire.
graneador, *m.* (art) stipple graver.
granear, *va.* (agr.) to sow (grain); (art) to stipple; to grain (a lithographic stone); (Am.) GRANAR.
granel, *m.* heap of grain.—**a g.**, in a heap; (com.) in bulk.
granelar, *va.* (tanning) to grain (leather).
graneo, *m.* (agr.) act of shedding or sowing seed; (art) stippling.
granero, *m.* granary, barn; grange; cornloft; grain-producing country.
granete, *m.* (mech.) countersink, punch.
granévano, *m.* (bot.) goat's-thorn.
granguardia, *f.* (mil.) grand guard.
gránico, *m. dim.* granule, small grain.
granilla, *f.* nap on wrong side of cloth.
granillo, *m. dim.* granule, small grain; gain or profit frequently obtained; pimple on the rump of canary birds and linnets.
graniloso, sa, *a.* granulous, granular.
granítico, ca, *a.* granitic.
granito, *m. dim.* small grain; pimple; (min.) granite; (pharm.) granule; small egg of a silkworm.
granívoro, ra, *a.* granivorous.
granizada, *f.* hailstorm; deluge (fig.), great number (of things, facts, etc.); water ice.
granizar, *vn.* to hail; to pour down with violence.
granizo, *m.* hail; hailstorm; film in the eyes.

granja, *f.* grange, farm, farmhouse.—**g. modelo,** model farm.

granjear. I. *va.* to gain, earn, profit. **II.** *va.* & *vr.* to get, win (as the goodwill of another).

granjeo, *m.* act of getting or acquiring; gain, profit, advancement.

granjería, *f.* gain, profit, advantage.

granjero, ra, *n.* farmer, husbandman; dealer in profitable commodities.

grano, *m.* grain; cereal; each single seed; (pharm.) grain (20 make an English scruple, and 24 a Spanish scruple); (artil.) bushing (or bouching) of a cannon; pimple; (jewel.) unit of weight (.05 g.).—*pl.* (com.) cereals, corn, breadstuffs. —**granos del paraíso,** (bot.) grain of paradise. —**ir al g.,** (coll.) to come to the point, to get down to brass tacks.

granoso, sa, *a.* granulous, grainy, granular, granulated (as leather).

granuja. I. *f.* loose berries of grapes; grapestone; group of roving boys. **II.** *m.* (coll.) rogue, waif, gamin, urchin.

granujado, da, *a.* = AGRANUJADO, grainlike.

granujiento, ta, *a.* full of pimples.

granujilla, *m.* = GRANUJA, *m.*

granujo, *m.* (coll.) pimple or tumor in the flesh.

granujoso, sa, *a.* full of pimples.

granulación, *f.* (chem. and med.) granulation.

granulador, ra, *m.* or *f.* granulating machine.

¹**granular. I.** *va.* to granulate. **II.** *vr.* to become covered with granules or pimples.

²**granular,** *a.* granular; full of pimples.

gránulo, *m. dim.* granule; pellet.

granulosidad, *f.* granularity.

granuloso, sa, *a.* granulous, granular.

granza, *f.* (bot.) madder; garancine.

granzas, *f. pl.* siftings, chaff; dross of metals.

granzón, *m.* (min.) ore screenings.—*pl.* refuse of straw left by cattle.

granzoso, sa, *a.* full of chaff or screenings.

grañón, *m.* pap made of boiled wheat; boiled grain of wheat.

grao, *m.* strand, shore.

grapa, *f.* clamp, clasp, clutch, cramp iron; (carp.) holdfast; (vet.) mangy ulcers in the joints.

grapón, *m. aug.* (mech.) brace, hook, ram, iron dog.

grasa, *f.* grease; fat; suet; oil; gum of juniper trees; GRASILLA; (naut.) slush; slag of metals; base of an ointment or pomade.—**g. de ballena,** whale oil, blubber.—**g. de pescado,** fish oil.—**grasera,** *f.* vessel for fat or grease; slush-tub; dripping pan.

grasería, *f.* tallow chandler's shop.

grasero, *m.* (min.) slag dumper.

graseza, *f.* quality of fat or grease.

grasiento, ta, *a.* greasy, oily; filthy.

grasilla, *f.* pounce, a fine powder formerly used to keep ink from spreading, etc.

graso, sa. I. *a.* fat, oily, unctuous, lardy. **II.** *m.* fat, grease.

grasones, *m. pl.* wheat porridge.

grasoso, sa, *a.* = GRASIENTO.

grasura, *f.* = GROSURA, fat, suet; meat diet.

grata, grataguja, *f.* burnisher, smoothing chisel; wire brush; rasp.

gratamente, *adv.* gratefully; agreeably.

gratar, *va.* to brush or burnish.

gratificación, *f.* gratification; reward; gratuity, tip; fee.

gratificador, ra, *n.* & *a.* gratifier(-ing); rewarder (-ing); tipper(-ing).

gratificar, *va.* (*pret.* GRATIFIQUÉ; *subj.* GRATIFIQUE) to reward, recompense; to tip, fee; to gratify, please.

gratil, *m.* (naut.) edge of a sail; luff, leech.

gratis, *adv.* gratis, free, for nothing.

gratisdato, ta, *a.* gratuitous, given away.

gratitud, *f.* gratitude, gratefulness.

grato, ta, *a.* pleasing, pleasant; acceptable;

grateful; gratuitous.—**su grata (carta),** (com.) your favor.

gratonada, *f.* chicken ragout or fricassee.

gratuitamente, *adv.* gratuitously.

gratuito, ta, *a.* GRATIS; gratuitous, uncalled-for; unfounded.

gratulación, *f.* congratulation.

gratular. I. *vn.* to congratulate. **II.** *vr.* to rejoice.

gratulatorio, ria, *a.* congratulatory.

grava, *f.* gravel; broken stone.

gravamen, *m.* tax; charge, obligation, hardship, burden, inconvenience, nuisance; encumbrance; (law) mortgage, lien.

gravar, *va.* to burden, oppress; to fatigue; to tax; (law) to encumber.

gravativo, va, *a.* injurious; burdensome.

grave, *a.* weighty, ponderous, heavy; grave, serious; circumspect; troublesome, vexatious; arduous, difficult; (mus.) grave (tone); deep (voice); (gram.) grave (accent); (word) having the stress on the penultimate syllable.

gravear, *vn.* to weigh, gravitate, sink.

gravedad, *f.* gravtiy, graveness, seriousness; (phys.) gravity.—**de g.,** serious; seriously, dangerously.

gravedoso, sa, *a.* haughty, self-important.

gravemente, *adv.* gravely; seriously, dangerously.

gravidez, *f.* pregnancy.

grávido, da, *a.* (poet.) gravid, pregnant.

gravimétrico, ca, *a.* gravimetric.

gravímetro, *m.* (phys.) gravimeter.

gravitación, *f.* (phys.) gravitation.

gravitar, *vn.* to gravitate; to rest, press (on).

gravoso, sa, *a.* costly; onerous; vexatious.

graznador, ra, *a.* croaking; cawing; cackling.

graznar, *vn.* to croak, caw, cackle.

graznido, *m.* croak, caw, cackle; croaking.

greba, *f.* (armor) greave(s) or jambe(s).

greca, *f.* Grecian fret.

greciano, na; grecisco, ca, *a.* Grecian.

grecismo, *m.* Grecism, Hellenism.

grecizante, *a.* Grecianizing, Hellenizing.

grecizar, *va.* & *vn.* to Grecize, Hellenize.

greco, ca. I. *a.* Grecian. **II.** *n.* Greek.

grecolatino, na, *a.* Greco-Latin.

grecorromano, na, *a.* Greco-Roman.

greda, *f.* clay, chalk, marl, potter's clay.

gredal. I. *m.* clay pit, marl pit, loam pit. **II.** *a.* clayey, loamy.

gredoso, sa, *a.* clayey, marly.

grefier, *m.* registrar in the house of Burgundy.

¹**gregal,** *m.* northeast wind in Mediterranean.

²**gregal,** *a.* gregarious, going in flocks.

gregario, ria, *a.* (one) of a crowd; dull, stupid.

gregoriano, na, *a.* Gregorian.

gregorillo, *m.* neckcloth formerly worn by women.

gregorito, *m.* (Mex.) disappointment; practical joke.

greguería, *f.* outcry, clamor, hubbub.

gregüescos, *m. pl.* Grecian wide breeches.

greguisco, ca, *a.* Grecian.

greguizar, *va.* to Grecize.

gremial. l. *a.* belonging to a guild or trade-union, union (as *a.*). **II.** *m.* member of a guild; union man; (eccl.) lapcloth used by bishops at divine service.

gremio, *m.* lap; body, society, company, guild, corporation; fraternity; trade-union.

grenchudo, da, *a.* having a long mane.

greña, *f.* long entangled or matted hair; anything entangled; (prov.) heap of grain to be thrashed; (prov.) first leaves of a vine shoot.—**andar a la g.,** (of women) to pull each other's hair; to argue excitedly.—**en g.,** (Mex.) (of silk, etc.) raw.

greñudo, da. I. *a.* dishevelled; shy (horse). **II.** *m.* shy horse.

greñuela, *f.* first shoots of a vine.

gres, *m.* pottery material consisting of clay and quartzose sand.

gresca, *f.* carousal, revelling, clatter; wrangle, quarrel, row.

grey, *f.* flock, herd; congregation of the faithful; people, race, nation.

grial, *m.* grail, legendary holy chalice.

griego, ga. I. *a.* Greek, Grecian. **II.** *m.* the Greek language; (coll.) cheating gambler; unintelligible language, (fig.) Greek.

grieta, *f.* crevice, crack, cleft; chink, fissure, cranny, flaw; split, vein, shake, rent; scratch in the skin.—**grietas en las manos,** chapping of the hands.

grietado, da, *a.* fissured, cracked, showing flaws.

grietarse, *vr.* to crack, split; to part in clefts or fissures; to become chapped.

grietecilla, *f. dim.* small fissure or scratch.

grietoso, sa, *a.* cracked; crannied, having flaws.

grifa, *f.* (print.) script.

grifado, da, *a.* script (type).

grifalto, *m.* a kind of small culverin, firearm.

¹grifo, fa, *a.* (print.) script.

²grifo, fa. I. *a.* (Am.) bristling (hair, fur); (of hair) kinky, tangled. **II.** *m.* griffin or griffon, a fabled animal; (Am.) child of a negro and an Indian; (mech.) faucet, cock.—*pl.* frizzled hair.

grifón, *m. aug.* fountain faucet.

grigallo, *m.* (ornith.) a variety of francolin.

grilla, *f.* female cricket.—**ésa es g.,** (coll.) that is a fake.

grillarse, *vr.* to shoot, to sprout.

grillera, *f.* cricket hole; cricket cage.

grillero, *m.* he who puts on and takes off the irons of prisoners.

grillete, *m. dim.* shackle, fetter.

¹grillo, *m.* (entom.) cricket.—**andar a grillos,** to waste one's time in trifles.

²grillo, *m.* —(bot.) shoot, sprout.

³grillo, *m.* —*pl.* fetters, irons, gyves, shackles.

grima, *f.* fright, horror; disgust.—**dar g.,** to disgust; to cause discouragement or fear.

grimoso, sa, *a.* horrible; repulsive, disgusting.

grímpola, *f.* (naut.) pennant, streamer.

grinalde, *m.* ancient form of grenade.

gringo, ga, *n.* (Am.) foreigner (esp. app. to Englishmen and Americans).

¹griñón, *m.* wimple worn by nuns.

²griñón, *m.* apricot grafted in peach tree.

gripa, *f.* (Am.) = GRIPE.

gripal, *a.* (med.) pertaining to la grippe.

gripe, *f.* (med.) grip, grippe, influenza.

gripo, *m.* an ancient merchant vessel.

gris. I. *a.* gray. **II.** *m.* (zool.) minever, Siberian squirrel and its fur; (coll.) cold, sharp air.

grisalla, *f.* (art) grisaille, camaieu.

grisáceo, a; gríseo, a, *a.* grayish.

¹griseta, *f.* flowered silk stuff; (agr.) disease of trees caused by infiltration of water.

²griseta, *f.* (Gal.) French grisette.

grisú, *m.* (min.) fire damp.

grita, *f.* clamor, outcry, uproar; screaming, halloo, shouting; hooting, catcall.—**g. foral,** (law) summons, citation.

gritador, ra, *n.* & *a.* clamorer(-ing), shouter (-ing), screamer(-ing).

gritar, *vn.* to shout, cry out, scream, shriek; to hoot, catcall.

gritería, *f.* outcry, uproar, shouting.

grito, *m.* cry, scream, howl, shriek, shout; hoot, whoop.—**a gritos, a g. en cuello, a g. herido, a g. pelado, a todo g.,** loudly; at the top of one's voice; vociferously, with loud cries, howling.—**alzar el g.,** to talk loud and haughtily. —**estar en un g.,** to be in continual pain.— **levantar el g.** = ALZAR EL G.—**poner el g. en el cielo,** to cry to heaven, to complain loudly, (coll.) to make a great fuss, to howl.

gritón, na, *a.* (coll.) vociferous, clamorous.

gro, *m.* grosgrain, twilled silk fabric.

groelandés, sa; groenlandés, sa, *n.* & *a.* Greenlander(-ish), Greenland (as *a.*).

groera, *f.* (naut.) rope hole.

grog, *m.* grog (drink).

gromo, *m.* (bot.) leafy bud, young shoot.

gropos, *m. pl.* cotton put in inkstands.

gros, *m.* an ancient coin of small value.

grosamente, *adv.* grossly.

grosella, *f.* (bot.) berry of the red currant.—**g. blanca,** gooseberry.

grosellero, *m.* (bot.) currant bush.

groseramente, *adv.* grossly, coarsely, roughly; rudely, in an unmannerly way.

grosería, *f.* rudeness, ill-breeding; rusticity; discourtesy; coarseness, clumsiness; ignorance.

grosero, ra, *a.* coarse, rough; plain, homespun, not fine; thick, fat, bulky; rude, unpolished; discourteous, churlish, uncivil.

grosezuelo, la, *a. dim.* somewhat stout.

grosísimo, ma, *super. of* GRUESO: exceedingly stout; very bulky.

groso, *m.* coarse snuff, badly powdered.

grosor, *m.* thickness.

grosularia, *f.* (min.) grossularite.

grosularico, a, *a.* (bot.) grossulaceous.

grosulina, *f.* (chem.) grossulin.

grosura, *f.* fat, suet, tallow; meat diet, in contrast to fasting.

grotescamente, *adv.* grotesquely.

grotesco, ca, *a.* grotesque.

grúa, *f.* crane, derrick, hoisting machine; an ancient war engine; (naut.) bend.—**g. corredera,** traveling crane.—**g. de caballete,** gantry crane.—**g. de la cuaderna maestra,** midship bend.—**g. fija,** stationary crane.—**g. flotante,** crane ship; floating crane.—**a la g.,** in and out.

gruero, ra, *a.* trained to pursue cranes (app. to birds of prey).

gruesa, *f.* gross, twelve dozen; (eccl.) chief part of a prebend; (law) bottomry.

gruesamente, *adv.* grossly, coarsely.

grueso, sa. I. thick; bulky, corpulent; fleshy, stout; (coll.) pregnant; big; coarse, homespun, dense, thick, heavy; large around (as a post, etc.); (of type) heavy, black; heavy, dull, stupid, slow. **II.** *m.* thickness; bulk, corpulence; density, heaviness; main part, main body of an army; down stroke in penmanship.—**en g.,** (com.) in gross, in the gross, in bulk, by wholesale.

gruir, *vn.* (*ind. pres.* GRUYO, *pret.* él GRUYÓ; *subj.* GRUYA; *ger.* GRUYENDO) to cry like a crane.

grujidor, *m.* glazier's nippers.

grujir, *va.* to trim or pare with a GRUJIDOR.

grulla, *f.* (ornith.) crane.

grullada, *f.* (coll.) gang or crowd of idlers; (coll.) patrol of constables or police officers.

grullero, ra, *a.* (of falcons), crane-hunting.

grullo, lla. I. *a.* (Am.) (of horses) dark grey. **II.** *m.* (Am.) peso, dollar; breeding horse.

grumete, *m.* (naut.) cabin boy, ship boy.

grumillo, *m. dim.* small clot, or curd.

grumo, *m.* clot; cluster, bunch; (agr.) bud of trees; tip of a fowl's wing.—**g. de leche,** curd.

grumoso, sa, *a.* full of clots, clotted.

gruñido, *m.* grunt.

gruñidor, ra, *n.* & *a.* grunter(-ing), growler (-ing).

gruñimiento, *m.* grunting, growling, grumbling.

gruñir, *vn.* (*pret.* él GRUÑO; *ger.* GRUÑENDO) to grunt; to creak (as doors, hinges, etc.); to grumble, growl.

gruñón, na, *m.* & *a.* (coll.) cranky, irritable.

grupa, *f.* croup, rump of a horse.

grupada, *f.* squall, burst of wind and rain.

grupera, *f.* cushion at the back of a saddle for carrying a satchel, etc.; crupper (of saddle).

grupo, *m.* group; set; clump, cluster.

gruta, *f.* cavern, grotto, grot.—*pl.* crypts, vaults, subterranean galleries.

grutesco, ca, *a.* (art) grotesque, bizarre.

gruyo, gruyó, gruya, etc. *v. V.* GRUIR.

¡gua! *interj.* (Am.) gracious! horrors!

guabina, *f.* (Colomb.) a popular peasant air.

guaca, *f.* Indian grave, esp. one containing treasure; (Am.) buried treasure; (Am.) hole in the ground where gathered fruit is put to ripen.

guacamaya, guacamayo, *m.* (ornith.) macao or macaw.

guacamole, *m.* (Cuba) salad of alligator pear.

guacia, *f.* (bot.) acacia; acacin, gum arabic.

guaco, *m.* (bot.) guaco, birthwort; (ornith.) curassow.

guachapear. I. *va.* (coll.) to splatter (water) with the feet; (coll.) to make a botch of. **II.** *vn.* to clap, as horses' shoes when loose; to clatter.

guachapelí, *m.* solid strong wood used for ships in Guayaquil.

guacharaca, *f.* (ornith.) a Mexican bird.

guácharo, ra. I. *a.* sickly; dropsical. **II.** *m.* birdling, especially of a sparrow; (ornith.) oilbird, guacharo.

guache, *m.* (Am.) low, despicable man, tough.

guachinango, ga, *a.* (Cuba) (contempt.) Mexican; (Mex.) artful, cunning.

guacho, cha. I. *a. & n.* (Am.) orphan, foundling; solitary, forlorn; (Chile) odd (only one of a pair). **II.** *m.* birdling of a sparrow.

guadafiones, *m. pl.* hopple, fetterlock.

guadalajareño, ña, *a.* of or pertaining to Guadalajara.

guadamací, cil, *m.* = GUADAMECÍ.

guadamacilería, *f.* embossed-leather factory.

guadamacilero, *m.* manufacturer of embossed leather.

guadamecí, guadamecil, *m.* embossed leather. —**g. brocado,** gilt or silvered embossed leather.

guadameco, *m.* ornament worn by women.

guadaña, *f.* (agr.) scythe.

guadañar, *va.* (agr.) to scythe, mow.

¹guadañero, *m.* scytheman.

²guadañero, *m.* (Cuba) owner of a guadaño.

guadañil, *m.* mower of hay.

guadaño, *m.* (Cuba) small boat in the port of Havana; transport vessel.

¹guadapero, *m.* (bot.) wild common pear.

²guadapero, *m.* boy who carries food to field workers.

guadarnés, *m.* harness room or locker; harness keeper; officer of the king's mews.

guadijeño, ña. I. *a.* native to, or, of Guadix; pert. to Guadix. **II.** *m.* poniard, stiletto, knife.

guadramaña, *f.* trick, deceit, imposition.

guadua, *f.* (Am.) a variety of large, thorny bamboo.—**guadual,** *m.* GUADUA field.

¹guagua, *m. & f.* (S. A.) baby.

²guagua, *f.* (Am.) insect that destroys fruit; trivial thing.—**de g.,** free, gratis.

³guagua, *f.* (Cuba) omnibus; street car.

guagüero, ra, *n.* (Cuba) bus or street car driver; (Am.) sponger.

guaicán, *m.* (ichth.) = RÉMORA, remora.

guaina, *m.* (Arg., Chile) boy, youth.

guainambí, *m.* (Mex., C. A.) humming bird.

guaira, *f.* (Am.) smelting furnace; (naut.) leg-of-mutton sail.

guairo, *m.* (Am.) small two-masted coaster.

guaita, *f.* (mil.) night watch or sentinel.

guajada, *f.* (Mex.) nonsense, frivolity.

guajalote, *m.* (Mex.) turkey.

guajamón, na, *a.* (Cuba) orange-colored; bay.

guájar, *m. & f.,* **guájaras,** *f. pl.* fastnesses, roughest part of a mountain.

guaje, *m.* (Mex.) gourd used in learning to swim.

guájete por guájete, tit for tat.

guajira, *f.* a Cuban popular song.

guajiro, ra, *n. & a.* (Cuba) rustic, rural; rude, boorish.

guajolote, *m.* = GUAJALOTE.

¡gualá! *intrj.* assuredly; by God!

gualatina, *f.* dish made of boiled apples, milk of almonds, and broth, beaten up with spice and rose water.

gualda, *f.* (bot.) weld, wild woad, dyer's weed, reseda.

gualdado, da, *a.* weld-colored; yellowish.

gualdera, *f.* (artil.) trail, bracket; (carp.) stringboard; (naut.) whelp, check.

gualdo, da, *a.* weld, yellow or gold-colored.

gualdrapa, *f.* horse trappings, housing; (coll.) tatter, rag hanging from clothes.

gualdrapazo, *m.* (naut.) flap of a sail; jerk.

gualdrapear. I. *va.* to put end to head, or in consecutive order (as pins with the point of each on the head of the next). **II.** *vn.* (naut.) to flap (as sails).

gualdrapeo, *m.* flapping of the sails.

gualdrapero, *m.* ragamuffin, ragged fellow.

gualdrín, *m.* weather strip.

guamá, *m.* guamá, a West-Indian tree much used for shade.

guama, *f.* fruit of the guamo.

guamo, *m.* guamo, a large fruit tree.

guanábana, *f.* bullock's-heart, custard apple.

guanábano, *m.* (bot.) custard apple (tree).

guanaco, *m.* guanaco, a kind of llama; (Guat., Hond.) boor, rustic; (Mex., C. R., Chile) (coll.) simpleton, idiot.

guanajo, *m.* (Cuba) turkey; *a. & n.* (Mex., W. I.) (coll.) fool.

guancoche, *m.* (Mex., C. A.) burlap.

guanche, *n.* ancient inhabitant of the Canaries.

guando, *m.* (Am.) stretcher, litter.

guanera, *f.* place abounding in guano.

guanina, *f.* (bot.) (Am.) a leguminous plant.

¹guano, *m.* any palm tree; palm leaves used for thatching.

²guano, *m.* guano, seabirds' droppings used as fertilizer.

guantada, *f.,* **guantazo,** *m.* slap.

guante, *m.* glove; collection for charity.—*pl.* extra pay, fee, or tip.—**guantes de ante,** buff gloves.—**guantes de cabritilla,** kid gloves.—**echar el g. a,** to challenge; (coll.) to seize, grasp; to imprison.—**echar un g.,** to take a collection for charitable purposes.—**poner como un g.,** to render as pliable as a glove; (coll.) to abuse, dress down.—**salvo el g.,** (coll.) excuse my glove.

guantelete, *m.* gauntlet.

guantería, *f.* glove factory or shop; glove making.

guantero, ra, *n.* glover, glove maker.

guañín, *m.* (Am.) base gold.

guañir, *vn.* (*pret.* él GUAÑÓ) to grunt like pigs.

guao, *m.* (Mex., S. A.) a terebinthine tree whose seeds are used as hog feed and whose wood is used for charcoal; (West Indies) guao, a poisonous tree.

guapamente, *adv.* (coll.) bravely, courageously.

guapear, *vn.* (coll.) to boast of courage; (coll.) to take pride in fine dress.

guapetón, na, *a. aug.* brave, daring, bold.

guapeza, *f.* (coll.) bravery; ostentation in dress; good looks, handsomeness.

guapinal, *m.* (C. A.) a resin-yielding tree.

guapo, pa. I. *a.* (coll.) brave, daring; enterprising; good-looking or handsome; spruce, neat; ostentatious, vain; gay, sprightly. **II.** *m.* gallant, beau; brawler, quarrelsome person.

guapote, ta, *a.* (coll.) good-natured; good-looking, handsome.

guaquero, *m.* vessel for drinking chicha found in ancient Peruvian tombs.

guaracha, *f.* a Spanish clog dance; a Cuban song.

guarache, huarache, *m.* (Mex.) sandal.

guaraná, *f.* (bot.) a Brazilian shrub yielding astringent and nerve-stimulating substances.

guarango, ga. I. *a.* (Chile, Arg.) ill-bred, unmannerly. **II.** *m.* (bot.) (Peru, Ecua.) a species of wild acacia; (Venez.) (bot.) dividivi.

guaraní. I. *a.* Guaranian. **II.** *m.* Guarani.

guarapo, *m.* juice of the sugar cane; fermented cane liquor.

¹guarda. I. *n.* guard; keeper; (Arg.) conductor (on street car, etc.).—**g. de cota,** gamekeeper.—**g. de la aduana,** officer of the custom house. **II.** *f.* custody; trust, wardship, safe-keeping; observance of a law or ordinance; nun who accompanies men through convents; outside rib or guard of a fan; (bookbinding) flyleaf, blank sheet; ward of a lock or of a key; (mech.) guard plate, shoe; sheath of a pruning knife.—**g. bauprés,** (naut.) knightheads, bollard timbers.

²guarda, (*imper.* of GUARDAR) *interj.* take care! beware! look out!

guardaaguas, *m.* (naut.) spurn water; (carp.) flashing board; (car) splash leather.

guardaagujas, *m.* (Ry.) switchman.

guardaalmacén, *m.* storekeeper.

guardaamigo, *m.* prop placed under the chin of criminals while they are flogged.

guardabanderas, *m.* (naut.) yeoman of signals.

guardabarrera, *m.* (Ry.) gatekeeper.

guardabarro, *m.* (auto) mudguard.

guardabosque, *m.* forester; game warden.

guardabrazo, *m.* (armor) brassard.

guardabrisa, *m.* glass shade for candles; (auto) windshield.

guardacabras, *m.* goatherd.

guardacalada, *f.* opening in eaves.

guardacamisa, *f.* (Venez.) undershirt.

guardacantón, *m.* protective stone at corner of buildings.

guardacartuchos, *m.* (naut.) cartridge case.

guardacostas, *m.* (naut.) revenue cutter; Coast Guard.

guardacuños, *m.* keeper of the dies in the mint.

guardadamas, *m.* officer who escorted ladies of the court.

guardadamente, *adv.* guardedly.

guardado, da. I. *pp.* of GUARDAR. **II.** *a.* guarded, reserved.

guardador, ra. I. *a.* very thrifty and provident; law-abiding; stingy, miserly. **II.** *m.* guardian; (mil.) keeper of the spoils.

guardafango, *m.* (auto) mudguard.

guardafrenos, *m.* (Ry.) brakeman.

guardafuego, *m.* (naut.) breaming board.

guardaguas, *m.* = GUARDAAGUAS.

guardaagujas, *m.* = GUARDAAGUJAS.

guardahumo, *m.* (naut.) smoke sail.

guardainfante, *m.* farthingale, hoop (for skirt).—*pl.* (naut.) capstan whelp.

guardaja, *f.* = GUEDEJA, lock of hair; lion's mane.

guardajoyas, *m.* keeper of the crown jewels; place where the crown jewels are kept.

guardalado, *m.* battlement of a bridge.

guardalmacén, *n.* = GUARDAALMACÉN.

guardalobo, *m.* (bot.) poet's cassia.

guardamalleta, *f.* lambrequin.

guardamancebo, *m.* (naut.) manrope.

guardamano, *f.* guard of a sword.

guardamateriales, *m.* buyer of bullion and other necessaries for a mint.

guardamigo, *m.* = GUARDAAMIGO.

guardamonte, *m.* (artil.) guard of a gunlock; (Am.) forester, keeper of a forest.

guardamuebles, *m.* storeroom for furniture; person in charge of the furniture of a palace.

guardamujer, *f.* servant of the queen.

guardapapo, *m.* (armor) gusset.

guardapelo, *m.* locket.

guardapesca, *n.* boat that inspects and guards fisheries.

guardapiés, *m.* skirt.

guardapolvo, *m.* dust guard; dust wrapper; cover; inner lid of a watch; projection over a window or door to carry off the water.

guardapuerta, *f.* storm door.

guardar. I. *va.* to keep; to guard, protect, watch over; to lay up, store, lay by, reserve; to keep (one's word, the law, a secret, etc.); to fulfil (one's duty).—**g. la cara,** to hide, to dissemble.—**g. miramientos,** to show regard or consideration.—**guardársela a uno,** to bide one's time to take revenge on.—**g. silencio,** to keep silent, not to answer. **II.** *vr.* (de) to guard (against), avoid, beware (of), take care not (to).

guardarraya, *f.* (Cuba) path in cane or coffee plantations; (min.) boundary of a drill hole.

guardarriel, *m.* (Ry.) reinforcing plate on rail.

guardarrío, *m.* (ornith.) kingfisher.

guardarropa. I. *f.* wardroom, coat room. **II.** *m.* keeper of a wardrobe; wardrobe, clothes closet; (bot.) lavender cotton.

guardarropía, *f.* (theat.) wardrobe.

guardarruedas, *m.* = GUARDACANTÓN.

guardasellos, *m.* seal keeper.

guardasol, *m.* = QUITASOL, parasol, sunshade.

guardatimón, *m.* (naut.) stern chaser.

guardavajilla, *f.* room for keeping the (royal) plate or table service.

guardavía, *m.* (Ry.) signalman; lineman.

guardavientos, *m.* (agr.) windbreak.

guardera, *f.* female keeper.

guardería, *f.* keepership.

guardia. I. *f.* guard (body of armed men); defense, custody, protection; (naut.) watch; turn of persons on duty; (fencing) guard.—**g. civil,** body of rural police in Spain.—**g. de babor,** larboard watch.—**g. de corps,** lifeguard.—**g. de estribor,** starboard watch.—**g. del tope,** masthead lookout.—**g. municipal,** city police.—**g. valona,** Walloon guard.—**en g.,** on guard.—**estar de g.,** (mil.) to be on guard duty.—**montar la g.,** to mount guard.—**mudar la g.,** to relieve the guard.—**salir de g.,** to come off guard. **II.** *m.* soldier belonging to the guards, guardsman.—**g. civil,** a member of the rural police in Spain.—**g. marina,** midshipman.—**g. municipal,** policeman.

guardián, na. I. *n.* keeper, guardian, warden; watchman. **II.** *m.* local superior of convents of the order of St. Francis; (naut.) boatswain's mate; quarterman; gunner's yeoman; (naut.) strong hawser.

guardianía, *f.* guardianship of a convent and the district assigned to it.

guardilla, *f.* garret, attic; (sewing) guard, welt; each of the two end thick teeth of a comb.

guardín, *m.* (naut.) tiller rope, tiller chain; (naut.) port lanyard.

guardoso, sa, *a.* frugal, parsimonious; niggardly, stingy.

guarecer. I. *va.* (*ind.* GUAREZCO; *subj.* GUAREZCA) to shelter, protect, preserve; to cure. **II.** *vr.* to take refuge or shelter.

guarentigio, gia, *a.* (law) (contract) containing a warranty clause.

guarezco, guarezca, *v.* V. GUARECER.

guarida, *f.* den, cave, lair of a wild beast; shelter; lurking place, cover, haunt.

guarimán, *m.* (bot.) (Am.) tree of the magnolia family, with aromatic bark used as spice.

guarín, *m.* suckling pig.

guarismo, *m.* (arith.) figure, digit; number.

guarne, *m.* (naut.) turn (of a cable or tackle).

guarnecedor, ra, *n.* & *a.* garnisher(-ing), furbisher(-ing), trimmer(-ing).

guarnecer, *va.* (*ind.* GUARNEZCO; *subj.* GUARNEZCA) to garnish, adorn, embellish, decorate, furbish; (sewing) to trim, bind, edge, face, border, line, welt; (jewelry) to set in gold, silver, etc.; (mason.) to plaster; (armor) to put a guard on; to harness; (mil.) to garrison.

guarnecido, *m.* (mason.) plastering; stucco work.

guarnés, *m.* harness room.

guarnezco, guarnezca, *v. V.* GUARNECER.

guarnición, *f.* (sewing) trimming, binding, edging, welt, flounce, furbelow, garniture, garnish, any ornamental hem, lace, or border; (jewelry) setting; (mech.) packing; (armor) guard of a sword; (mil.) garrison.—*pl.* gears or traces of mules and horses; harness; fixtures, fittings (for gas, electric lamps, etc.); accessories.

guarnicionar, *va.* (mil.) to garrison.

guarnicionería, *f.* harness maker's shop.

guarnicionero, *m.* harness maker.

guarniel, *m.* leather pouch with divisions or pockets, strapped across the back and chest over one shoulder; (Mex.) powderflask.

guarnigón, *m.* (ornith.) young quail.

guarnimiento, *m.* (naut.) lines or ropes for reeving.

guarnir, *va.* GUARNECER; (naut.) to reeve; to rig.

¹guaro, *m.* a very talkative small parrot.

²guaro, *m.* (C. A.) sugar-cane liquor.

guarra, *f.* sow.

guarro, *m.* hog.

¡guarte! *interj.* take care! beware! look out!

guaruba, *f.* (ornith.) a red-necked American parrot; howling monkey.

guasa, *f.* (coll.) jest, fun, joke; dulness; (W. I.) (ichth.) jewfish.—**de g.,** jokingly, in fun.

guasanga, *f.* (Cuba) noisy mirth.

guasanguero, ra, *a.* (Cuba) jolly, merry, noisy.

guasca, *f.* (Peru), piece of cord or rawhide; (Colomb.) strip of raw fiber, fibrous bark, etc., to tie with.—**dar g.,** to whip.

guaso, *m.* Gaucho; lasso.

guasón, na, *a.* (coll.) jocose, witty; dull, uninteresting.

guasquear, *va.* (Am.) to whip, to scourge.

guataca, *f.* (Cuba) spade; (Cuba) (coll.) large ear.

guataquear, *va.* (Cuba) to spade.

guatemalteco, ca, *n.* & *a.* Guatemalan.

guateque, *m.* (Cuba) country dance.—**guatequear,** *va.* (Cuba) to dance (as in the country).

guatiní, *m.* (Cuba) = TOCORORO (ornith.) trogon.

guau, *m.* bowwow, the bark of a dog.

guavina, *f.* = GUABINA, (Colomb.) a peasant tune.

¡guay! *interj.* alas! alack!

guaya, *f.* grief, sorrow, affliction.

guayaba, *f.* fruit of the guava tree; guava jam or jelly; (Am.) lie, fib.

guayabal, *m.* guava-tree orchard or field.

guayabero, ra, *n.* (Am.) liar, fibber.

guayabo, *m.* (bot.) guava tree.

guayacán, *m.* (bot.) lignum-vitæ, guaiacum.

guayacana, *f.* (bot.) date-plum.

guayaco, *m.* = GUAYACÁN.

guayacol, *m.* (chem.) guaiacol.

guayaquileño, ña. I. *n.* a Guayaquil man (woman). **II.** *a.* from, or pert. to, Guayaquil.

guazubirá, *m.* an Argentine deer.

gubán, *m.* (P. I.) a large canoe.

gubernamental, *a.* governmental.

gubernativamente, *adv.* by act of the government.

gubernativo, va, *a.* administrative, governmental, gubernatorial.

gubia, *f.* (carp.) gouge, centering chisel; (artil.) vent searcher.

gubiadura, *f.* notch, channel.

guedeja, *f.* long lock of hair; forelock; lion's mane.—**guedejilla,** *f. dim.* small lock of hair.

guedejón, na, joso, sa, judo, da, *a.* long-haired.

güeldo, *m.* shrimps, clams, etc., used as bait.

güelfo, fa, *n.* & *a.* Guelph.

guelte, gueltre, *m.* money, cash; wealth.

güemul, *m.* guemul, an Andean variety of deer.

güepil, *m.* (Mex.) = HUIPIL, Aztec dress.

güérmeces, *m.* morbid swelling in the throat of birds of prey.

guerra, *f.* war, warfare.—**g. a muerte,** war without quarter, war to the death.—**g. de bolas, g. de palos,** two different games of billiards.—**g. europea, mundial,** or **gran g.,** World War.—**dar g.,** to cause annoyance or trouble.

guerreador, ra, *n.* & *a.* warrior(-ing), fighter (-ing).

guerreante, *n.* & *a.* warrior(-ing).

guerrear, *vn.* to war, wage war, fight.

guerreramente, *adv.* warlike.

guerrero, ra. I. *a.* martial, warlike. **II.** *m.* warrior, fighter, soldier, military man.

guerrilla, *f. dim.* guerrilla: body of partisans, skirmishers, or light horsemen; skirmish, light engagement; a card game.

guerrillear, *vn.* to engage in guerrilla warfare.

guerrillero, *m.* (mil.) guerrilla man.

guía. I. *n.* guide, cicerone; leader, director, adviser.—**g. de forasteros,** court guide. **II.** *m.* (mil.) guide. **III.** *f.* guide, guide sign; guidebook; directory; (mech.) guide, rule, guide bar, guide pin, guide screw, guide tube, etc.; (com.) custom house permit, cocket; driving shaft of a water wheel; (agr.) young shoot left on a vine or tree for training others; young shoot or sucker of a vine; (naut.) guy, leader, span, hauling-line, preventer-rope; (min.) leader; handlebar of a bicycle; guard of a fan; leader, foremost horse; (fireworks) fuse.—*pl.* guide lines, reins for controlling the leader horses.—**g. radial,** (printed) radio program.—**a guías,** driving four-in-hand.

guiadera, *f.* guide or conductor in mills; upright guide in oil mills, lifts, etc.

guiado, da. I. *pp.* of GUIAR. **II.** *a.* guided; having a guide or a permit.

guiador, ra, *n.* guide, director, leader.

guiar. I. *va.* to guide, lead; to drive (auto, etc.); to pilot; (agr.) to train (a plant.) **II.** *vr.* (por) to go or be governed (by), to follow.

guiguí, *m.* (P. I.) (zool.) flying squirrel.

guija, *f.* pebble; gravel; (bot.) ALMORTA, blue vetch.—*pl.* (coll.) strength, force, vigor.

guijarral, *m.* place abounding in pebbles.

guijarrazo, *m.* blow with a pebble or a cobble.

guijarreño, ña, *a.* pebbly, gravelly; hardy, strong.

guijarrillo, ito, *m. dim.* small pebble.

guijarro, *m.* pebble, cobble.

guijarroso, sa, *a.* pebbly.

guijeño, ña, *a.* pertaining to or resembling pebbles; hard, relentless.

guijo, *m.* gravel.

guijón, *m.* = NEGUIJÓN, caries, tooth decay.

guijoso, sa, *a.* gravelly, pebbly.

guilalo, *m.* (P. I.) coasting vessel with sails of matting.

guilla, *f.* plentiful harvest.

guillame, *m.* joiner's rabbeting plane.

guillote, *m.* husbandman who enjoys the produce of a farm; (naut.) treenail or iron pin; vagrant; sponger; idle fellow; novice gambler.

guillotina, *f.* guillotine; cardboard-cutting machine.—**de g.,** (of windows, etc.) opening up and down.

guillotinar, *va.* to guillotine.

guimbalete, *m.* pump brake, pump handle.

guimbarda, *f.* an ancient dance; (carp.) grooving plane.

guinchar, *va.* to prick, goad.

guincho, *m.* goad, pike; (Cuba) sea gull.

¹guinda, *f.* (bot.) berry of the mazard.—**echar guindas a la tarasca,** (coll.) to be very easy, child's play.

²guinda, *f.* (naut.) total height of the masts.

¹guindado, da. I. *pp.* of GUINDAR. **II.** *a.* hoisted, set up.

²guindado, da, *a.* garnished with mazard berries.

For pronunciation, see the rules at the beginning of the book.

guindajos, *m. pl.* (Cuba) hangings, fringe, tassels.

guindal, *m.* (bot.) mazard tree.

guindalera, *f.* plantation of mazard trees.

guindaleta, *f.* crank rope; fulcrum of a balance.

guindaleza, *f.* (naut.) hawser.

guindamaina, *f.* salute by dipping the flag.

guindar. I. *va.* to hang on high; (coll.) to obtain or procure in competition with others; (coll.) to hang (a person). **II.** *vn.* to be suspended, to hang.

guindaste, *m.* (mech.) horse, frame; (naut.) timber head jeer, knighthead of the jeers.

guindilla, *f. dim.* pod of the red pepper.

guindillo de Indias, *m.* (bot.) shrub of the capsicum family; red pepper.

guindo, *m.* (bot.) mazard tree.—**g. griego,** large mazard cherry tree.

guindola, *f.* (naut.) triangular hanging stage; life buoy.

guinea, *f.* guinea, English gold coin.

guineo, a. I. *a.* & *n.* Guinea, of Guinea.—**gallina g.,** Guinea hen. **II.** *m.* a negro dance; banana.

guinga, *f.* gingham.

guinja, *f.* **guinjo,** *m.* jujube.

guinjo, guínjolero, *m.* (bot.) jujube tree.

guiñada, *f.* wink; (naut.) yaw, lurch.

guiñador, ra, *n.* & *a.* winker(-ing).

guiñadura, *f.* = GUIÑADA.

guiñapiento, ta, *a.* ragged, tattered, torn.

guiñapo, *m.* tatter, rag; ragamuffin, tatterdemalion.—**guiñaposo, sa,** *a.* = GUIÑAPIENTO.

guiñar, *va.* to wink; (naut.) to yaw, to lurch.

guiño, *m.* = GUIÑADA.

guión, *m.* cross, standard carried before prelates and corporations; gonfalon in processions; royal standard; master of ceremonies; leader of a dance; hyphen; explanatory text or reference table; (mil.) guidon; (mus.) repeat; (naut.) loom of an oar.

guionaje, *m.* office of guide or conductor.

guipar, *va.* (coll. and vulgar) to see.

güipil, *m.* (Mex.) = HUIPIL, Aztec dress.

guipuzcoano, na. I. *n.* & *a.* native of or belonging to the province of Guipúzcoa. **II.** *m.* one of the Basque dialects.

guira, *f.* (bot.) calabash tree.

guirgüesco, ca, *a.* = GREGÜISCO, Grecian.

guiri, *n.* anti-Carlist; Liberal.

guirigay, *m.* (coll.) gibberish; jargon.

guirindola, *f.* frill of a shirt.

guirlache, *m.* roast almond caramel; brittle.

guirlanda, guirnalda, *f.* garland, wreath; (naut.) puddening; (mil.) light ball.

guirnaldeta, *f. dim.* small garland.

güiro, *m.* bottle gourd, fruit of the calabash tree; (Cuba) gourd used as an instrument to accompany dance music; (Arg., etc.) green corn stalk.

guirre, *m.* (prov. Canaries) vulture.

guisa, *f.* manner, fashion.—**a g. de,** like, in the manner of.

guisado, *m.* stew; ragout, fricassee.

guisador, ra; guisandero, ra, *n.* cook.

guisantal, *m.* pea patch.

guisante, *m.* (bot.) pea.—**g. de olor,** sweet pea.

guisar, *va.* to cook or dress (food); to arrange, prepare, adjust.

guiso, *m.* cooked dish; seasoning, condiment.

guisopillo, *m.* = HISOPILLO, (med.) mouth swab.

guisote, *m.* poorly cooked dish.

guita, *f.* packthread, twine; (coll.) money.

guitar, *va.* to sew with packthread.

guitarra, *f.* (mus.) guitar; (mason.) muller for pulverizing gypsum.—**guitarrazo,** *m.* blow with a guitar.—**guitarrear,** *vn.* to play the guitar.—**guitarrería,** *f.* factory or shop for guitars, mandolins, etc.—**guitarrero, ra,** *n.* guitar maker; guitar player.—**guitarresco, ca,** *a.* (coll.) pertaining to the guitar.—**guitarrillo,** *m.*; **lla,** *f. dim.* small guitar.

guitarrista, *n.* guitar player.

guitarro, *m.* (mus.) small four-string guitar.

guitarrón, *m. aug.* large guitar; (coll.) cunning knave.

guitero, ra, *n.* twine maker.

guito, ta, *a.* treacherous, (of mules, etc.) vicious.

¹guitón, *m.* an ancient coin.

²guitón, na, *n.* mendicant, vagrant, tramp.

guitonear, *vn.* to loiter, loaf, idle about.

guitonería, *f.* idleness; vagabond life.

guizazo, *m.* (Cuba) (bot.) a kind of weed.

guizgar, *va.* to excite, invite.

guizque, *m.* hook of a hanging lamp.

guja, *f.* (armor) vogue or voulge.

gula, *f.* gluttony, inordinate appetite.

gules, *m. pl.* (her.) gules, red.

guloso, sa, *a.* gluttonous; greedy.

gulusmear, *vn.* (coll.) to eat tidbits.

gullería, gollería, *f.* dainty; delicious tidbit.

gulloría, *f.* (ornith.) a kind of lark; GULLERÍA.

gúmena, *f.* (naut.) cable.—**gumeneta,** *f. dim.* (naut.) small cable.

gumía, *f.* a kind of dagger or poniard.

gumífero, ra, *a.* gum-producing, gummiferous.

gura, *f.* (ornith.) (P. I.) a crested wild pigeon.

¹gurbión, *m.* coarse twisted silk; heavy silk cloth.

²gurbión, *m.* spurge gum resin.

gurdo, da, *a.* silly, simple, nonsensical.

gurriato, *m.* nestling sparrow.

gurrufero, *m.* (coll.) deformed and vicious nag.

gurrumina, *f.* (coll.) uxoriousness, excessive doting on one's wife; (Am.) trifle.

gurrumino, na. I. *a.* mean, contemptible. **II.** *n.* (C. A.) boy, girl, child. **III.** *m.* (coll.) henpecked husband.

gurullada, *f.* (coll.) = GRULLADA, gang of idlers; (coll.) patrol of policemen.

gurullo, *m.* lump or knot.

gurullón, *m.* a knot of wool in cloths.

gurumete, *m.* GRUMETE, (naut.) cabin boy.

gurupa, *f.* GRUPA, croup of a horse.

gurupera, *f.* GRUPERA, crupper.

gurupetín, *m. dim.* small crupper.

gurvio, a, *a.* (of tools) curved.

gurvión, *m.* = ¹GURBIÓN.

gusanear, *vn.* HORMIGUEAR, to itch.

gusanera, *f.* place where worms or microbes are bred; (coll.) ruling passion.

gusanico, ito, *m. dim.* small worm.

gusaniento, ta, *a.* grubby, full of vermin, maggoty, worm-eaten.

gusanillo, *m. dim.* small worm or grub; (sewing) gold, silver, or silk twist; twist-stitch embroidery; (mech.) bit of a gimlet or auger.

gusano, *m.* (zool.) worm, grub, caterpillar; threadworm, pinworm; meek, dejected person; distemper of sheep.—**g. de la conciencia,** worm of conscience, remorse.—**g. de luz =** LUCIÉRNAGA.—**g. de San Antón,** gray grub.—**g. de seda,** silkworm.—**g. revoltón,** vine inchworm.

gusarapiento, ta, *a.* wormy, grubby; filthy; rotten.

gusarapillo, ito, *m. dim.* small water worm.

gusarapo, *m.* water worm; any annelid found in liquids, especially vinegar.

gustable, *a.* pert. to taste; (Am.) tasty.

gustadura, *f.* gustation, tasting.

gustar. I. *va.* to taste; to try. **II.** *vn.* to be pleasing, to cause pleasure; (diff. constr.) to like (as: *esto me gusta,* I like this; *¿le gusta a Vd. la música?* do you like music? *la comida nos gustó mucho,* we liked the dinner very much; *como Vd. guste,* as you like, as you will).—**g. de,** to like, to have a liking for; to enjoy.

gustativo, a, *a.* gustatory.

gustazo, *m. aug.* (coll.) great pleasure.

gustillo, *m. dim.* peculiar flavor, or relish.

gusto, *m.* taste; tasting; pleasure; liking; will, determination; choice; discernment; caprice, fancy, whim; diversion.—**a g.**, at will, to one's taste or judgment.—**con mucho g.**, with great pleasure.—**cosa de g.**, tasty, fancy article.—**dar g.**, to gratify, to please.—**darse g.**, to indulge in pleasure, to have a good time; to live well.—**de buen (mal) g.**, in good (bad) taste. —**de mi g.**, to my taste; to my liking.—**el g. del día**, prevailing taste or fashion.—**tener g. en**, to take pleasure in, to be glad to.—**tener g. por**, to have a taste for, to like.—**tengo mucho g. en conocerle**, (on being introduced) I'm very glad to meet you.

gustosamente, *adv.* tastefully; fain, gladly.
gustoso, sa, *a.* savory, palatable; tasty; cheerful, merry, joyful; pleasing, pleasant; willing, ready.
gutagamba, *m.* (bot.) tree producing gamboge; gamboge.
gutapercha, *f.* gutta-percha.
gutiámbar, *m.* gamboge.
gutífero, ra, *a.* guttiferous, gum-yielding.
gutural, *a.* guttural.
guturalmente, *adv.* gutturally.
guzmán, *m.* nobleman who formerly served as midshipman or cadet.

H

ha, *verbal form.* V. HABER.
¡ha!, *interj.* ah! alas!
haba, *f.* broad bean; lima bean; bean; kernel; ballot (ball); (vet.) tumor in the palate of horses; (min.) prill.—**h. común caballar,** (bot.) horse bean.—**h. de Egipto,** Egyptian bean.—**h. de las Indias,** sweet pea.—**h. de San Ignacio,** St. Ignatius' bean.—**h. marina,** navelwort, kidneywort.—**h. tonca,** Tonca bean.—**esas son habas contadas,** that is a sure thing; that is as clear as daylight.
habado, da, *a.* (vet.) having HABAS; dappled (as a horse).
habanera, *f.* (mus.) a Cuban air and dance tune.
habanero, ra, *a.* Havanese, of Havana.
habano. I. *a.* Havana (as *a.*). **II.** *m.* Havana cigar.
habar, *m.* bean field.
habascón, *m.* (S. A.) a parsniplike root.
hábeas corpus, *m.* habeas corpus.
háber, *m.* doctor of the law among the Jews.
haber. I. *va.* (*ind. pres.* HE, *pret.* HUBE, él HUBO, *fut.* HABRÉ; *subj.* HAYA) to have, own, possess; (gen. passive) to catch, lay hands on; to get (*el ladrón no pudo ser habido*, the thief could not be caught; *el niño lee cuantos libros puede haber*, the boy reads all the books he can get). **II.** *v. auxil.* to have (*haber hablado*, to have spoken; *habiendo hablado*, having spoken; *yo he hablado*, I have spoken). **III.** *vn.* (de) to have (to), must (*hemos de salir*, we have to, or must, go out; *ha de saber Vd.*, you must know). **IV.** *v. imp.* to be (in phrases, "there is," "there are"); to take place. In this sense, the third person of the indicative is **hay**, and only the third person singular is used in all modes and tenses, for the verb has no subject: the word or phrase which in English is the subject of the equivalent "to be" is in Spanish the accusative, not the subject, of "haber" (*hay peligro*, there is danger; *aquí hay un buen teatro*, there is a good theater here: *en Colombia hay muchas minas*, there are many mines in Colombia; *ayer hubo dos accidentes*, there were two accidents yesterday; *mañana no habrá escuela*, there will be no school tomorrow). The form **ha,** applied to time, has the adverbial value of "ago" (*dos años ha*, two years ago).—**hay para,** there is enough for.—**hay que,** must, to be necessary (*hay que ir*, it is necessary to go; *hay que hacerlo*, it's got to be done).—**lo que hay es,** what happens is; the fact is.—**no hay de qué,** (after

being thanked) you're welcome.—**no hay más que,** there is nothing more to; there is nothing but; it's enough, it'll do.—**no hay para que,** there is no occasion for; it is better not to; there's no point in.—**no hay que,** one should not; it's not necessary to.—**no hay remedio,** it can't be helped.—**¿qué hay?** what's happening? what's the matter?—**¿qué hay de nuevo?** what's new? what's the news? **V.** *vr.* **habérselas con,** to deal with; to face, to cope with.—**VI.** *m.* in bookkeeping, credit, Cr.; (gen. *pl.* **haberes**) property, possessions, estate. —**h. monedado,** coin, specie.
haberío, *m.* beast of burden.
habichuela, *f.* (bot.) French bean or kidney bean.—**h. verde,** string bean.
habiente, *a.* (law) having, possessing.
hábil, *a.* capable, skillful.—**día, h.,** work day.
habilidad, *f.* ability, skill; talent.—*pl.* accomplishments.
habilidoso, sa, *a.* skillful, able.
habilitación, *f.* habilitation, qualification; outfit, equipment; (mil.) office and bureau of a paymaster.—**h. de bandera,** concession to a foreign vessel to engage in the coasting trade.
habilitado, da. I. *pp.* of HABILITAR. **II.** *a.* qualified; competent. **III.** *m.* paymaster.
habilitador, ra, *n.* qualifier; outfitter.
habilitar, *va.* to qualify, enable; to provide, supply with, fit out, equip.
hábilmente, *adv.* ably, skillfully.
habitabilidad, *f.* habitability, habitableness.
habitable, *a.* habitable.
habitación, *f.* dwelling, residence, habitation, abode, lodging; room, chamber, suite of rooms, apartment; (law) caretaking; habitat.
habitáculo, *m.* dwelling, residence, abode.
habitador, ra, *n.* inhabitant, resident, dweller.
habitante, *a.* & *n.* inhabiting(-ant).
habitar, *va.* to inhabit, live, dwell, reside.
hábito, *m.* dress, habit, habiliment, garment; habit, custom.—*pl.* dress of ecclesiastics; robes of the military orders.—**tomar el h.,** to become a monk or a nun.
habituación, *f.* habit, custom.
habitual, *a.* habitual, usual, customary.
habitualmente, *adv.* customarily, usually.
habituar. I. *va.* to accustom, habituate, inure. **II.** *vr.* to become accustomed, accustom oneself, get used.
habitud, *f.* relation, connection.
habla, *f.* speech; language, tongue; dialect; conversation, talk.—**al h.** (naut.) within speaking distance.—**estar en h.,** to talk.—**estar sin h.,** or **perder el h.,** to be or become speechless.—**negar,** or **quitar, el h.,** to cease speaking to, to cut.—**ponerse al h.,** to communicate, get in touch, speak.
hablado, da, *a.*—**bien h.,** using choice language. —**mal h.,** using vile or vulgar language.
hablador, ra. I. *a.* talkative. **II.** *n.* talker, gabbler, prattler, chatterbox; gossip.
habladorcillo, lla, *n. dim.* babbling dandiprat.
habladuría, *f.* impertinent speech; gossip, empty talk.
hablanchín, ina, *a.* & *n.* = HABLANTÍN.
hablante, *a.* speaking, talking.
hablantín, na, *a.* & *n.* (coll.) talkative person.
hablar. I. *vn.* to speak; to talk, converse.—**h. a,** to speak to; to hail (a ship).—**h. a chorros,** to speak fast.—**h. a destajo,** (coll.) to talk much and at random.—**h. a gritos,** to shout.—**h. al alma,** to speak things that touch the quick.—**h. alto,** to speak loud.—**h. a tontas y a locas,** to speak recklessly or disconnectedly.—**h. claro,** to speak in plain language, to call a spade a spade.—**h. con,** to speak with; to court, to woo.—**h. de,** to speak, or talk, of or about.—**h. de chanza,** to joke, to speak in jest.—**h. en griego,** or **en gringo,** to talk gib-

berish, to talk Greek (fig.).—**h. en plata** = H.
CLARO.—**h. entre dientes**, to mutter, to
mumble.—**h. gordo**, to bully, to bluff.—**h.
por boca de ganso**, to speak from hearsay; to
be a mouthpiece.—**h. por h.**, to talk for the
sake of talking.—**h. por los codos**, to talk incessantly, to chatter.—**estar hablando**, to be
perfect; to be manifest. II. *va.* to speak, utter,
say.—**h. disparates**, to talk nonsense. III. *vr.*
to speak to each other; to be on speaking terms.

hablilla, *f.* rumor, gossip, report, little tale.

hablista, *n.* scholar, scholarly writer.

hablistán, *n.* (coll.) prattler, chatterer.

habón, *m. aug.* wheat, whelk.

habré, *v. V.* HABER.

haca, *f.* pony, pad, small horse.

hacán, *m.* learned man among the Jews.

hacanea, *f.* nag, small horse.

hacecico, illo, ito, *m. dim.* small sheaf; fascicle.
—**h. de rayos luminosos**, pencil of luminous
rays.

hacedero, ra, *a.* feasible, practicable.

hacedor, *m.* maker; steward, manager of a farm.
—**el H.**, the Creator, the Maker.

hacendado, da. I. *pp.* of HACENDAR. **II.** *a.*
landed, owning real estate. **III.** *m.* landholder,
farmer, planter, rancher.

hacendar. I. *va.* (*ind.* HACIENDO; *subj.* HACIENDE)
to transfer or make over. **II.** *vr.* to purchase
real estate.

hacendeja, *f. dim.* small farm or ranch.

hacendera, *f.* public work at which all the neighborhood assists.

hacendero, ra, *a.* industrious, sedulous.

hacendilla, duela, *f. dim.* small farm or ranch.

hacendista, *m.* (pol.) economist; financier.

hacendoso, sa, *a.* assiduous, industrious.

hacer. I. *va.* (*pp.* HECHO; *ind. pres.* yo HAGO, él
HACE, *pret.* yo HICE, él HIZO, *fut.* HARÉ; *subj.*
HAGA) to make; to produce, form; to prepare;
conceive, devise, compose: deliver, utter (as a
plan, a poem, a speech); to arrange, make (a
bed), pack (a trunk, valise); to shed, cast, project (as a shadow); to raise, produce (as dust,
smoke); to do; to gain, earn; to accustom, inure;
to assemble, convoke; to act, perform (as a play,
a part); to do, execute, carry out; to lead (a life);
to take (a trip); to suppose, think (*yo hacía a
Juan en París*, I thought John was in Paris; *le
hacíamos muy rico*, we supposed he was very
rich); to hold in, feel, have (*hacer estimación*,
or *aprecio*, to hold in esteem, to have regard
for); (followed by *inf.*), to order, have (followed
by *pp.*: *Juan hizo construir la casa*, John had
the house built; *Juan hizo nombar a Pedro*,
John had Peter appointed); (followed by *inf.*)
to make, compel (*la haremos confesar*, we shall
make her confess; *lo hice firmar*, I made him
sign).—**h. agua**, (naut.) to leak.—**h. alarde**,
to boast.—**h. ánimo**, to mean, to intend.—**h.
antesala**, to dance attendance, to be kept waiting.—**h. bancarrota**, to fail, to become bankrupt.—**h. boca**, to work up an appetite.—**h.
bola**, to play hookey; to stay away.—**h. buen
tercio**, to do a good turn.—**h. cara, h. cara a,**
to face, resist, oppose.—**h. caso**, to mind, pay
attention.—**h. caso de**, to take into account,
pay attention to.—**h. con**, to supply, provide,
furnish (*te haré con dinero*, I will provide you
with money).—**h. corrales** = H. BOLA.—**h.
cuentas**, to figure, reckon; to estimate.—**h.
chacota (de)** to ridicule, to turn into ridicule.
—**h. daño a**, to hurt, harm; (of an article of
food) not to agree with.—**h. de** = H. CON.—**h.
de cuenta (que)**, to pretend, act (as if).—**h.
de las suyas**, to be up to one's old tricks, to
run true to type.—**h. de tripas corazón**, to
pluck up courage or heart.—**h. diligencia**, to
try, to endeavor, to take measures.—**h. el
favor**, to do the favor (*hágame el favor*, do me

the favor, please).—**h. falta**, to be lacking,
missing (diff. constr. *le hace falta dinero*, he
needs money).—**h. fiesta**, to take a holiday.—
h. fiestas a, to fondle, caress; cajole; fawn to.
—**h. frente** = H. CARA.—**h. frente a**, to meet
(demands, etc.).—**h. fuego**, (mil.) to fire.—**h.
fuerza**, to struggle; to exert force; to carry
weight, exert influence, appeal.—**h. fuerza a,**
to do violence to; to impress, convince.—**h.
fuerza de vela**, (naut.) to crowd sail.—**h.
furor**, to "make a hit."—**h. gasto**, to spend.—
h. h., to have made, cause to be made, order to
be made.—**h. juego**, to be well matched.—
hacerla, to act unworthily; to fall below expectations; to act (with modifying word indicating the character of the action—usually bad).
—**h. la barba**, to shave; (Mex.) to flatter.—**h.
la corte**, to court, to woo; to pay court in palace.—**h. la cuenta**, to figure out.—**h. la cuenta
sin la huéspeda**, to reckon without the host.
—**h. la guerra**, to war, to wage or make war.—
h. las amistades, to become reconciled, make
up.—**h. la vista gorda**, to wink at, to connive
at.—**h. limosna**, to give alms.—**hacerlo bien
(mal)**, to perform, or acquit oneself, well
(badly).—**h. mal**, to do wrong, harm; to act
wrongly; to be injurious.—**h. mal de ojo**, to
fascinate.—**h. memoria de**, to remember.—
h. milagros, to do wonders.—**h. mofa de**, to
mock, scoff at.—**h. morisquetas**, to play
pranks.—**h. papel**, to cut a figure; to play a
part.—**h. pedazos**, to break or tear into pieces;
to break (as the heart).—**h. presente**, to remind of, call attention to.—**h. que**, to pretend,
feign; to have, order (diff. constr. *hace que
escribe*, he pretends to be writing; *haga que lo
traigan*, have it brought).—**h. saber**, to make
known; to inform, notify.—**h. señas**, to motion.—**h. su agosto**, to make hay while the
sun shines.—**h. su apacheta**, to have made a
fortune; to make one's pile.—**h. un barro**, to
make a break, put one's foot in it.—**h. un enfoque general**, to make a broad approach.—
h. una pregunta, to ask a question, put a
question.—**h. vela**, (naut.) to set sail.—**h. ver,**
to show, demonstrate.—¿**qué hace?** (a form
of greeting) how do you do? how are you? **II.**
vn. to matter, signify; to be pertinent, or to the
purpose (*¿que le hace?* what does it matter? *eso
no hace al caso*, that has nothing to do with the
case); to agree, accord, match (*esto no hace con
eso*, this does not agree with (or match) that).—
h. como que, h. como si, to act as if.—**h. de,**
to act as (*hacer de notario*, to act as a notary;
hago de carpintero, I am doing a carpenter's
work).—**h. del** (*f.* **de la**) to pretend to be, to
play the (*hacer del bobo*, to play the idiot).—**h.
del cuerpo**, to go to stool.—**h. el** (*f.* **la**) = H.
DEL.—**h. para, h. por**, to endeavor, to try,
make an effort, do one's best to (*haré por venir*,
I will endeavor to come; *hacer por*, or *para,
salvarse*, to strive to save oneself.—**h. por h.,**
to act to no purpose.—**h. por la vida**, to eat
something.—**no le hace**, never mind, let it go.
III. *v. imper.* (referring to the state of the
weather and followed by a noun) to be (with
"it" as subject: *hace mal tiempo*, it is bad
weather; *hace buen día*, it is a good day), or to
be (with "it" as subject and followed by the
corresponding English adjective: *hace calor*, it
is warm; *hace viento*, it is windy). Applied to a
lapse of time, it is rendered by "to be," with
"it" as subject, or by "ago" (*hace un año*, it is
now one year, or, a year ago; *ayer hize un mes*,
a month ago yesterday, or it was a month yesterday; *hace años* (*días*, etc.), many years (days,
etc.) ago; *hace una semana que está aquí*, he has
been here a week; *hace una semana que lo vi*, it
is a week since I saw him; *hace mucho* (*poco*), a
long (short) time ago; *hace tiempo*, a long time

ago).—¿cuánto (tiempo) hace? how long ago? —¿cuánto (tiempo) hace que? since when? IV. vr. (hacerse) to become, to grow; to move shift, recede, draw aside; to inflict upon oneself (as a wound, a scratch); to pretend to be, pass oneself off for.—h. a, to become accustomed or inured to; to come by, acquire.—h. a la vela, (naut.) to set sail.—h. añicos, to break to smithereens.—h. chiquito, to pretend to be modest; to conceal one's knowledge.—h. de miel, to be sweet, lenient, or obliging.—h. de rogar, to like to be coaxed.—h. el sueco, to pretend not to understand.—h. el tonto, to "play dumb," play the fool.—h. ilusiones, to be under an illusion, fool oneself.—hacérsele a uno, to be . . . to one, to seem . . . to one (eso se me hace misterioso, that seems mysterious to me).—h. pedazos, to break into, or to, pieces.—h. tarde, to grow late.—h. tortilla, to fall down flat.

hacera, f. sidewalk.

hacezuelo, m. dim. of HAZ.

hacia, prep. toward, in the direction of; near, about.—h. abajo, downward; in the lower part, toward the bottom.—h. acá, hither, this way.—h. adelante, forward.—h. allá, thither, that way.—h. arriba, upward; in the upper part, toward the top.—h. atrás, backward.— h. casa, homeward.—h. dónde, whither, toward which (what) place, where.—h. el cielo, heavenward.—h. el mar, seaward.—h. popa, (naut.) abaft.—h. proa, (naut.) afore.—partir h. (Europa), to leave for (Europe).

hacienda, f. landed property; plantation; farm; ranch; estate, fortune, wealth; finance.—pl. domestic work, household duties.—h. de beneficio (Mex., min.) reduction works.—h. pública, public treasury; public funds; public finances.—real h., public treasury, public funds (in a monarchy).

haciendo, haciente, v. V. HACENDAR.

hacina, f. (agr.) shock, stack; pile, heap.

hacinador, ra, n. (agr.) stack maker.

hacinamiento, m. accumulation; heaping or stacking.

hacinar, va. (agr.) to stack; to pile, heap, accumulate; to hoard.

¹**hacha,** f. large taper with four wicks.—h. de viento, flambeau, torch.

²**hacha,** f. axe; ancient Sp. dance; (naut.) link.— h. de armas, battle axe.

hachazo, m. blow or stroke with an axe.

hache, f. name of the letter h.

hachear. I. va. to cut with an axe; to hew. **II.** vn. to strike with an axe.

¹**hachero,** m. (mil.) axeman; woodsman, wood cutter.

²**hachero,** m. torch stand.

hacho, m. torch or link; beacon hill.

hachón, m. large torch or link; cresset.

hachote, m. aug. large axe.

hachuela, f. dim. small hatchet or axe; hand axe, adze.

hada, f. fairy.

hadar, va. to divine, foretell; to enchant.

hado, m. fate, destiny, doom.

haga, v. V. HACER.

hagiografía, f. (eccl.) hagiography.

hagiógrafo, m. hagiographer.

hago, v. V. HACER.

haitiano, na, n. & a. Haitian.

¡hala! interj. (naut.) pull! haul!

halagador, ra. I. promising, rosy; flattering; coaxing. **II.** n. flatterer, cajoler, coaxer.

halagar, va. (pret. HALAGUÉ; subj. HALAGUE) to cajole, to flatter; to coax, allure, wheedle; to fondle, treat with tenderness.

halago, m. cajolery, flattery; caress, cooing.

halagué, halague, v. V. HALAGAR.

halagüeñamente, adv. endearingly, flatteringly; promisingly, alluringly.

halagüeño, ña, a. endearing; attractive, alluring; promising, bright; fawning, flattering.

halar, (coll.) jalar. **I.** va. (naut.) to haul, pull, tow. **II.** vn. to pull ahead.

halcón, m. (ornith.) falcon.—**halconado, da,** a. falconlike.—**halconcico, illo, ito,** m. dim. jashawk.—**halconear,** va. (coll.) to inveigle, allure.—**halconera,** f. place where falcons are kept.

halconería, f. falconry.

halconero, m. falconer, hawk trainer.

halda, f. FALDA, skirt; a lapful; packing bag.— **haldas en cinta,** (coll.) disposed and ready for anything.—**de haldas o de mangas,** (coll.) justly or unjustly, with good or ill will, in any way.—**haldada,** f. skirtful.—**haldear,** vn. to run along with billowing skirts.—**haldica, illa, ita,** f. dim. small skirt.—**haldudo, da,** a. full-skirted.

haleche, m. (ichth.) anchovy.

halieto, m. (ornith.) sea eagle.

haliéutico, ca, f. halieutic, pert. to fishing.

haliótide, haliotis, m. (zool.) abalone.

hálito, m. breath; vapor, effluvium; breeze.

halo, m. (astr.) halo.

halófilo, la, a. (bot.) halophilous.

halógeno, na, a. (chem.) halogen.

halografía, f. (chem.) halography.

haloideo, a, a. (chem.) haloid.

halón, m. (astr.) halo.

haloque, m. (naut.) an ancient small vessel.

haloza, f. wooden shoe.

hallado, da, pp. & a. found.—bien h., welcome; easy, contented.—mal h., uneasy, constrained.

hallador, ra, n. finder, discoverer.

hallar. I. va. to find; come across; to find out; to discover; to detect, catch; to understand, solve, interpret, decipher. **II.** vr. to be (in a place or condition); to reside; to feel (as to health), to fare.—h. bien (con), to be pleased (with), content (in).

hallazgo, m. act of finding; find, thing found; recovering anything lost; reward.

hallulla, hallullo, m. cake baked on or under hot stones or ashes.

hamaca, f. hammock; hammock litter.

hamaquero, m. hammock maker; hammock bearer; hammock hook.

hambre, f. hunger; appetite; famine; greediness; eagerness, longing, desire.—h. canina, canine appetite, inordinate hunger.—h. y valentía, pride and poverty.—tener h., to be hungry.

hambrear. I. va. to hunger, starve, famish; to subdue by famine. **II.** vn. to hunger, to be hungry.

hambrientamente, adv. hungrily.

hambriento, ta, a. hungry; starved; greedy, covetous; longing; (Colomb., coll.) stingy.

hambrón, na, n. (coll.) hungry person.

hamburgués, sa, a. from or pertaining to Hamburg, Hamburg (as a.).

hamez, f. distemper in falcons that makes them lose their feathers.

hamo, m. fishhook.

hampa, f. life of a company of rogues and vagabonds formerly in Andalusia.

hampesco, ca, a. vagabond, villainous.

hampo, hampón, m. rowdy, bully, gangster.

hanega, f. = FANEGA, a dry measure.

hanegada, f. land sown with a FANEGA of corn.

hangar, m. hangar.

hannoveriano, na, n. & a. Hanoverian.

hansa, f. Hanseatic League.—**hanseático, ca,** a. Hanseatic.

hará, haré, etc., v. V. HACER.

haragán, na. I. n. idler, loiterer, loafer; idle, lazy person. **II.** a. idle, slothful, indolent.

haraganamente, adv. idly, lazily, slothfully.

haraganear, *vn.* to lead an idle life; to be lazy, to act the truant; to lounge, idle, loiter.

haraganería, *f.* idleness, laziness, sloth.

harapo, *m.* tatter, rag.—**harapiento, ta; haraposo, sa,** *a.* ragged, tattered.

harca, *f.* military expedition; expeditionary forces.

harem, harén, *m.* harem.

harija, *f.* mill dust, stive.

harina, *f.* flour, meal; farina; breadstuffs; powder, dust.—**h. de otro costal,** another matter, a horse of a different color.

harinado, *m.* flour dissolved in water.

harinero, ra. I. *a.* made of or pertaining to flour. **II.** *m.* mealman, flour dealer; flour chest.

harinoso, sa, *a.* mealy; farinaceous; flourlike.

harmonía, harmonio, harmonioso, etc. = ARMONÍA, ARMONIO, etc.

harnerico, illo, ito, *m. dim.* small sieve.

harnero, *m.* sieve, sifter.—**estar hecho un h.,** to be covered with wounds.

harón, na, *a.* slow, sluggish; balky.—**haronear,** *vn.* to dawdle, move sluggishly; to be tardy or slow; to balk.—**haronía,** *f.* sluggishness, laziness.

harpa, *f.* = ARPA, harp.

¹harpado, da, *a.* = ¹ARPADO, serrated, toothed.

²harpado, da, *a.* = ²ARPADO, (poet.) singing (bird).

harpía, *f.* = ARPÍA, harpy.

harpillera, *f.* burlap; sackcloth.

hartada, *f.* = HARTAZGO.

hartar, *va.* & *vr.* (*pp.* HARTADO and HARTO) to glut, stuff, gorge; to sate, satiate, gratify desire; to satisfy, cloy, fill to excess.

hartazgo, hartazón, *m.* satiety, glut, fill.

harto, ta. I. *pp. irreg.* of HARTAR. **II.** *a.* sufficient, full, complete. **III.** *adv.* enough or sufficiently; (Mex.) abundantly, very much.

hartura, *f.* satiety, glut, fill; plethora, superabundance; full gratification.

hasta. I. *prep.* till, until; up to, down to; as far as; even (emphatic) (as: *allá hasta los niños fuman,* there even children smoke).—**h. ahora,** heretofore, hitherto.—**h. aquí,** heretofore; thus far, up to here.—**h. después,** or **h. luego,** good-bye, "so long."—**h. la vista,** (in parting) "so long," au revoir.—**h. mañana,** (in parting) see you tomorrow.—**h. no más,** to the utmost. **II.** *conj.* also even.—**h. que,** until.

hastial, *m.* (arch.) gable wall; coarse, rude man; (min.) side face of a gallery.

hastiar, *va.* to loathe, disgust; to cloy, sate.

hastío, *m.* loathing, disgust; wearisomeness.

hataca, *f.* large wooden ladle; rolling pin.

hatajar, *va.* to divide (cattle) into flocks or herds.

hatajo, *m.* small herd or flock; (coll.) lot, multitude, lots.

hatear, *vn.* to collect one's belongings when travelling; to supply shepherds with provisions.

hatería, *f.* allowance of provisions and clothes for shepherds.

hatero, ra. I. *a.* (animals) that carry a shepherd's baggage. **II.** *m.* carrier of provisions to shepherds; (Cuba) cowboy; cattle herder.

hatijo, *m.* covering of straw or feather grass over beehives.

hatillo, *m. dim.* small bundle; a few clothes; (Colomb.) a sort of telescoping rawhide hamper.—**coger el h.,** (coll.) to quit, to pack and go.—**echar el h. al mar,** (coll.) to lose one's temper.—**tomar su h.** = COGER EL H.

hato, *m.* herd of cattle; flock of sheep; (Am.) farm or cattle ranch; shepherds' lodge; provisions for shepherds; clothes, wearing apparel; heap, lot, cluster; gang, band or meeting of suspicious people.

haxix, *m.* hasheesh.

hay, *impers. irreg. form* of HABER: there is, there are.

¹haya, *v. V.* HABER.

²haya, *f.* (bot.) beech tree.

hayal, hayedo, *m.* beech forest or field.

hayo, *m.* (Am.) (bot.) coca; coca leaves prepared for chewing.

hayuco, *m.* beech mast, fruit of the beech.

¹haz. I. *m.* fagot, fascine, bundle, bunch; (agr.) gavel, sheaf; (mil.) file of soldiers, also troops arranged in divisions; pencil (of rays). **II.** *f.* face, visage; surface; right side or outside of cloth; (arch.) facing, façade.—*pl.* fasces.—**h. molecular,** molecular beam.—**a sobre h.,** apparently, at first sight.—**ser de dos haces,** to be doubled-faced.—**sobre la h. de la tierra,** upon the face of the earth.

²haz, *v. imper.* of HACER.

haza, *f.* piece of tillable land.

hazalefa, *f.* towel.

hazaña, *f.* feat, exploit, heroic deed.

hazañería, *f.* affected fear or admiration.

hazañero, ra, *a.* prudish, affectedly grave and scrupulous.

hazañosamente, *adv.* valorously, bravely.

hazañoso, sa, *a.* gallant, courageous, heroic.

hazmerreír, *m.* laughing stock.

¹he, *interj.* generally followed by the adverbs **aquí** or **allí,** or by a pronoun, to introduce or call attention to: *he aquí,* here is, here you have; lo! lo and behold! *heme aquí,* here I am: *helos allí,* there they are.

²he, *v. ind.* of HABER.

hebdómada, *f.* hebdomad, week; period of seven years.

hebdomadario, ria. I. *a.* weekly. **II.** *n.* (eccl.) hebdomadary.

hebén. I. *n.* white grapes like muscatels. **II.** *a.* insignificant, of no account.

hebetado, da, *a.* (Am.) brutalized, sottish.

hebilla, *f.* buckle, clasp.—**hebillaje,** *m.* set of buckles.—**hebillero, ra,** *n.* buckle maker or seller.—**hebilleta, hebilluela,** *f. dim.* small buckle.—**no faltar hebilleta,** to be complete. —**hebillón,** *m. aug.* large buckle.

hebra, *f.* fibre, thread, filament; string; staple; grain (of wood); needleful of thread; pistil of the blossom of saffron; (min.) vein, layer, stratum. —*pl.* (poet.) hair.—**ser,** or **estar, de buena h.,** to be strong and robust.

hebraico, ca, *a.* Hebrew.

hebraísmo, *m.* Hebraism.

hebraísta, hebraizante, *n.* Hebraist.

hebreo, a, *n.* & *a.* Hebrew; (coll.) pawnbroker; (coll.) usurer(-ious).

hebrero, *m.* esophagus of ruminants.

hebrica, illa, ita, *f. dim.* small needleful of thread.

hebroso, sa, *a.* fibrous, stringy.

hecatombe, *f.* hecatomb.

hectárea, *f.* hectare (10,000 sq. meters).

héctico, ca, *a.* hectic.

hectiquez, *f.* (med.) phthisis.

hectógrafo, *m.* hectograph.

hectogramo, *m.* hectogram.

hectolitro, *m.* hectoliter.

hectómetro, *m.* hectometer.

hectóreo, ea, *a.* pertaining to Hector.

hectovatio, *m.* hectowatt, 100 watts.

hecha, *f.* (obs.) date; irrigation tax.—**de esta h.,** from this time.

hechicé, hechice, *v. V.* HECHIZAR.

hechiceresco, ca, *a.* relating to witchcraft.

hechicería, *f.* witchcraft, witchery, enchantment; charm, fascination; sorcery.

hechicero, ra. I. *n.* witch, wizard; hag; charmer, enchanter, bewitcher **II.** *a.* entrancing, charming, bewitching, fascinating.

hechizar, *va.* (*pret.* HECHICÉ; *subj.* HECHICE) to bewitch, enchant, entrance; to charm, to fascinate.

hechizo, za. I. *a.* artificial, feigned; made to

order; (Chile, C. R., Colomb.) domestic, made in the (given) country; portable, easily mounted. **II.** *m.* charm (used to bewitch), enchantment.

hecho, cha. I. *pp. irreg.* of HACER. **II.** *a.* made; done; ready-made; finished; fully matured, ripe or developed; accustomed, inured, used.—**h. un león**, like a lion, furiously; angry.—**h. y derecho**, in every respect; true, real; perfect. complete.—**a lo h., pecho**, one must make the best of a bad bargain.—**bien h.**, well done or made; all right; right (in a moral sense).—**mal h.**, wrong, unrighteous; badly done or made. **III.** *m.* fact; event; act, action, deed; point at issue.—**análisis de hechos**, factual analysis. —**de h.**, in fact, as a matter of fact, actually; in earnest; de facto.—**de h. y de derecho**, de facto and de jure.—**en h. de verdad**, in truth.

hechura, *f.* making, make; workmanship; form; build (of a person); work done and price paid for it; creature, henchman.—**no tener h.**, to be impracticable or not feasible.

hedentina, *f.* stench, stink.

heder, *vn.* (*ind.* HIEDO; *subj.* HIEDA) to stink; to vex, annoy, bore.

hediondamente, *adv.* stinkingly.

hediondez, *f.* stench, stink.

hediondo, da, *a.* stinking, fetid; annoying, wearisome; dirty, repulsive; lewd, obscene.

hedonismo, *m.* hedonism.

hedonista, *n.* & *a.* hedonist(-ic).

hedor, *m.* stench, stink.

hegelianismo, *m.* Hegelianism.

hegeliano, na, *n.* & *a.* Hegelian.

hegemonía, *f.* (pol.) hegemony.

hégira, héjira, *f.* Hegira.

helable, *a.* congealable.

helada, *f.* frost; nip.—**h. blanca**, hoarfrost.

heladera, *f.* (Am. esp. Arg. & Chile) refrigerator; ice-cream dish.—**h. eléctrica**, (or **mecánica**) electric refrigerator.

heladería, *f.* (Am.) ice-cream parlor or shop.

heladero, ra, *n.*(Chile) ice-cream maker or seller.

heladizo, za, *a.* easily congealed.

helado, da. I. *pp.* of HELAR. **II.** *a.* frigid; frostbitten; cold, indifferent. **III.** *m.* ice cream; water ice, sherbet.

helamiento, *m.* congealing, freezing, frost.

helar. I. *va.* & *vn.* (*ind.* HIELO; *subj.* HIELE) to congeal, to freeze; astonish, amaze; dispirit, discourage, dissuade. **II.** *v. impers.* to freeze (*aquí hiela frecuentemente*, it freezes often here). **III.** *vr.* to freeze, to congeal, to be coagulated; to grow motionless; to be stupefied, dispirited. —**se me heló la sangre**, my blood curdled.

hele, hétele, aquí, *interj.* behold it! *V.* ¹HE.

helechal, *m.* fern field.

helecho, *m.* fern.

helena, *f.* (naut.) jack-with-a-lantern.

helénico, ca, *a.* Hellenic.

helenio, *m.* (bot.) sneezeweed.

helenismo, *m.* Hellenism; Greek idiom.

helenista, *m.* Hellenist.

heleno, na, *a.* Hellenic.

helera, *f.* pip, disease of fowls.

helero, *m.* snowcap on mountains; (geol.) glacier.

helgado, da, *a.* jag-toothed.

helgadura, *f.* space between, or irregularity of, the teeth.

helíaco, ca, *a.* (astr.) heliacal, pert. to the sun.

heliantemo, *m.* (bot.) a helianthaceous plant.

heliantina, *f.* (chem.) methyl orange.

helianto, *m.* (bot.) helianthus, sunflower.

hélice, *f.* (H-, astr.) Ursa Major; (geom.) helix; (naut., aer.) screw propeller.

helicoidal, *a.* helicoidal.

helicoide, *m.* (geom.) helicoid.

helicónides, *f. pl.* (myth.) the Muses.

heliconio, nia, *a.* (myth.) Heliconian.

helicóptero, *m.* (aer.) helicopter.

helio, *m.* (chem.) helium.

heliocéntrico, ca, *a.* heliocentric.

heliograbado, *m.* heliogravure.

heliografía, *f.* blue print.

heliógrafo, *m.* heliograph, signalling device.

heliómetro, *m.* heliometer.

helioscopio, *m.* helioscope.

helióstato, *m.* heliostat.

helioterapia, *f.* (med.) heliotherapy.

heliotropina, *f.* (chem.) piperonal.

heliotropio, *m.* (bot.) heliotrope; (min.) bloodstone; (astr.) heliostat.

heliotropismo, *m.* (bot.) heliotropism.

heliotropo, *m.* = HELIOTROPIO.

heliozoario, *m.* (zool.) heliozoan.

helmintiasis, *f.* (med.) helminthiasis.

helminto. I. *n.* & *a.* helminthic. **II.** *m. pl.* Helminthes.

helmintología, *f.* (med.) helminthology.

helvecio, cia; helvético, ca, *a.* Helvetic, Swiss.

hematemesis, *f.* (med.) hæmatemesis, blood vomiting.

hematidrosis, *f.* (med.) hæmatidrosis.

hematita, *f.* (physiol.) red blood corpuscle.

hematites, *f.* (min.) hematite.

hematología, *f.* (med.) hæmatology.

hematómetro, *m.* (med.) hæmatometer.

hematoscopio, *m.* hæmoscope.

hematosis, *f.* (physiol.) hæmatosis.

hematuria, *f.* (med.) hæmaturia.

hembra, *f.* female; (coll. or vulg.) woman; (sewing) eye (of hook and eye); (mech.) nut of a screw; bolt clasp, staple.—**h. del timón**, (naut.) gudgeon of the rudder.

hembraje, *m.* (S. A.) female cattle.

hembrear, *vn.* to be inclined to females; to produce females only, or chiefly.

hembrica, illa, ita, *f. dim.* little female.

hembrilla, *f.* (mech.) small piece into which another fits (as a nut, staple, etc.); ring or eyebolt.

hemiciclo, *m.* semicircle; (Spain) central space of the House of Deputies.

hemicránea, *f.* (med.) hemicrania, megrim.

hemiedría, *f.* (min.) hemihedrism.

hemiedro, *m.* (min.) hemihedron.

hemina, *f.* a liquid and area measure.

hemíono, *m.* (zool.) hemionus, kiang, an Asiatic wild ass.

hemiplejia, *f.* (med.) hemiplegia.

hemíptero, ra. I. *a.* hemipterous. **II.** *m. pl.* Hemiptera.

hemisférico, ca, *a.* hemispherical.

hemisferio, *m.* hemisphere.

hemisferoidal, *a.* hemispheroidal.

hemistiquio, *m.* (poet.) hemistich.

hemodinamómetro, *m.* blood-pressure gauge.

hemoglobina, *f.* (physiol.) hemoglobin.

hemopatía, *f.* (med.) blood diseases (collect.).

hemóptisis, *f.* (med.) hæmoptysis.

hemorragia, *f.* (med.) hemorrhage.

hemorrágico, *a.* hemorrhagic.

hemorroidas, *f. pl.* = HEMORROIDES.

hemorroidal, *a.* hemorrhoidal.

hemorroides, *f. pl.* piles, hemorrhoids.

hemorroo, *m.* (zool.) serpent.

hemostático, ca, *a.* hemostatic.

henal, *m.* hayloft.—**henar**, *m.* hayfield.

henchidor, ra, *n.* filler.

henchidura, *f.* fill, filling.

henchimiento, *m.* filling, fill.—*pl.* (naut.) filling timbers.

henchir. I. *va.* (*gerund*, HINCHIENDO; *ind. pres.* HINCHO, *pret.* él HINCHIÓ; *subj.* HINCHA) to fill, to stuff. **II.** *vr.* to fill or stuff oneself.

hendedor, ra, *n.* divider, splitter, cleaver.

hendedura, *f.* fissure, crack, cleft, crevice, cut.

hender, *va.* (*ind.* HIENDO; *subj.* HIENDA) to chink, crack, cleave, split; to go through; to cut (as the water); to elbow or open (a passage) through a crowd.

hendible, *a.* cleavable; fissionable, fissile.

For pronunciation, see the rules at the beginning of the book.

hendido, da. I. *pp.* of HENDIR. **II.** *a.* crannied, full of chinks.

hendidura, *f.* = HENDEDURA.

hendiente, *m.* down stroke of a sword.

hendimiento, *m.* splitting.—h. (or **ruptura**) **del núcleo atómico,** nuclear fission, splitting of the atom.

henequén, *m.* (bot.) sisal, henequen.

henificar, *va.* to cut and dry for forage.

henil, *m.* hayloft, barn.

heno, *m.* (bot.) hay.

henojil, *m.* garter.

heñir, *va.* (ger. HIÑENDO; ind. pres. HIÑO, pret. él HIÑÓ; subj. HIÑA) to knead.—**hay mucho que h.,** (coll.) there is much to do.

hepatalgia, *f.* (med.) pain in the liver.

hepática, *f.* (bot.) liverwort.

hepático, ca, *a.* (med.) hepatic, hepatical.

hepatisis, *f.* (med.) consumption of the liver.

hepatitis, *f.* (med.) hepatitis.

hepatización, *f.* (med.) hepatization.

hepatizarse, *vr.* (med.) to undergo hepatization.

hepatología, *f.* hepatology.

heptacordo, *m.* (mus.) heptachord.

heptámetro, *m.* & *a.* heptameter (verse).

heptano, *m.* (chem.) heptane.

heptarca, *m.* heptarch.

heptarquía, *f.* heptarchy.

heptasílabo, ba, *a.* heptasyllabic.

heptateuco, *m.* Heptateuch.

heráldica, *f.* heraldry.

heráldico, ca, *a.* heraldic.

heraldo, *m.* herald; harbinger.

herbáceo, cea, *a.* herbaceous.

herbajar. I. *va.* to put out to graze, to pasture. **II.** *vn.* to pasture, graze, browse.

herbaje, *m.* herbage, grass, pasture; pasturage fee; coarse cloth.

herbajear, *va.* & *vn.* = HERBAJAR.

herbajero, *m.* one who rents pastures.

herbar, *va.* (ind. HIERBO; subj. HIERBE) to dress (skins) with herbs.

herbario, ria. I. *a.* herbal. **II.** *m.* herbalist, herbarian; herbarium.

herbaza, *f.* aug. large weed.

herbazal, *m.* herbous place; pasture ground.

herbecer, *vn.* (of herbs or grass) to begin to grow.

herbero, *m.* esophagus of a ruminant.

herbívoro, ra. I. *n.* & *a.* herbivore(-ous). **II.** *m. pl.* Herbivora.

herbolado, da, *a.* poisoned with juice of plants.

herbolar, *va.* to poison with herbs.

herbolario, ria, *n.* herbist, herbman, one who sells herbs; (coll.) nonsensical person.

herborización, *f.* herborization; botanizing.

herborizador, ra, herborizante, *n.* herbalist, herborist.

herborizar, *vn.* to herborize, botanize.

herboso, sa, *a.* herby, grassy.

herciano, na, *a.* (phys.) Hertzian.

hercúleo, ea, *a.* herculean.

heredad, *f.* improved piece of ground; country estate, farm.

heredado, da. I. *pp.* of HEREDAR. **II.** *a.* landed, owning real estate. **III.** *n.* heir to property.

heredamiento, *m.* landed property.

heredar, *va.* to inherit; to deed to another; to institute as heir.

heredero, ra, *n.* heir; heiress; inheritor.—**h. forzoso,** general or legal heir.—**h. presuntivo,** heir apparent.

heredípeta, *n.* legacy seeker.

hereditario, ria, *a.* hereditary.

hereje, *n.* heretic.

herejía, *f.* heresy; injurious expression.

herejote, ta, *n.* (coll.) great heretic.

herén, *m.* (bot.) vetch.

herencia, *f.* inheritance, heritage; heredity.

heresiarca, *m.* heresiarch, leader in heresy.

heretical; herético, ca, *a.* heretical.

heria, *f.* life of vagrancy. Also HAMPA.

herida, *f.* wound.

herido, da. I. *pp.* of HERIR. **II.** *a.* & *n.* wounded (person).—**mal h.,** dangerously wounded.

heridor, ra, *n.* & *a.* wounder(-ing).

herir, *va.* (ger. HIRIENDO; ind. pres. HIERO, pret. él HIRIÓ; subj. HIERA) to wound; to hurt, harm; to strike; to affect, touch, move; to offend (the senses); to pique, irritate.

herma, *m.* (art) herm, a pillar surmounted by a head.

hermafrodita, *a.* & *m.* (zool. and bot.) hermaphrodite.

hermafroditismo, *m.* hermaphroditism.

hermana, *f.* sister; nun.—**h. de la caridad,** Sister of Charity. (For phrases *v.* HERMANO.)

hermanable, *a.* fraternal, brotherly; compatible.

hermanablemente, *adv.* fraternally.

hermanado, da, *pp.* & *a.* mated, matched.

hermanamiento, *m.* mating, matching.

hermanar. I. *va.* to mate, match, pair; to suit, harmonize; to own as a brother. **II.** *vn.* to fraternize, join, match, agree. **III.** *vr.* to love one another as brothers; to be compatible; to harmonize.

hermanastro, tra, *n.* stepbrother(-sister).

hermanazgo, *m.* fraternity, brotherhood.

hermandad, *f.* fraternity, brotherhood, confraternity; conformity, resemblance; amity, friendship.

hermanear, *va.* to treat as a brother.

hermanecer, *vn.* to have a little brother just born.

hermanito, ta, *n. dim.* little brother (sister).

hermano, na, *n.* brother (sister); mate, companion, twin (app. to objects).—**h. carnal,** full brother, brother german.—**h. consanguíneo** = H. DE PADRE.—**h. de leche,** foster brother.—**h. de madre (de padre),** half brother by the same mother (father).—**h. político,** brother-in-law.—**h. uterino** = H. DE MADRE.

hermanuco, *m.* name given in contempt to lay brothers of some religious orders.

hermenéutica, *f.* hermeneutics.

hermenéutico, ca, *a.* hermeneutic.

herméticamente, *adv.* hermetically.

hermético, ca, *a.* hermetic, air-proof, air-tight.

hermosamente, *adv.* beautifully, handsomely; perfectly, properly.

hermoseador, ra, *n.* & *a.* beautifier(-fying).

hermosear, *va.* to beautify, embellish, adorn.

hermoso, sa, *a.* beautiful, handsome.

hermosura, *f.* beauty, handsomeness; belle, beauty (pretty woman).

hernia, *f.* (med.) hernia.—**herniario,** *a.* (med.) hernial.—**hernioso, sa,** *a.* (med.) herniated.—**hernista,** *m.* specialist in herniotomy.

Herodes, *m.* Herod (proper noun).—**de H. a Pilatos,** from pillar to post.

herodiano, na, *a.* Herodian.

héroe, *m.* hero.

heroicamente, *adv.* heroically.

heroicidad, *f.* heroism; heroic deed.

heroico, ca, *a.* heroic.—**a la heroica,** in the manner of the heroic times.

¹heroína, *f.* heroine.

²heroína, *f.* (chem.) heroin.

heroísmo, *m.* heroism.

herpe, *m.* or *f.* (med.) herpes, tetter.

herpético, ca, *a.* (med.) herpetic.

herpetismo, *m.* (med.) tendency to herpes.

herpetología, *f.* (zool.) herpetology, science dealing with reptiles.

herpil, *m.* bag of esparto netting with wide meshes, for carrying large fruit.

herrada. I. *a.* (water) in which red-hot iron has been cooled. **II.** *f.* pail, bucket.

herradero, *m.* branding of cattle; place where cattle are branded.

herrador, *m.* farrier, horseshoer.

herradora, *f.* (coll.) farrier's wife.

herradura, *f.* horseshoe.

herraj, *m.* = ERRAJ, coal made from stones of pressed olives.

herraje, *m.* ironwork, pieces of iron used for ornament and strength; iron or metal fittings or accessories, hardware (gen. *pl.*).

herramental, *m.* tool bag; tool chest.

herramienta, *f.* tool; implement; set of tools.—*pl.* horns; (coll.) teeth, grinders.

herrar, *va.* (*ind.* HIERRO; *subj.* HIERRE) to shoe (horses); to brand (cattle); to garnish or bind with iron.

herrén, *m.* meslin, mixed grain for horses.

herrenal, herreñal, *m.* meslin patch or field.

herrera, *f.* (coll.) blacksmith's wife.

herrería, *f.* iron works; blacksmith's shop, smithy; forge; blacksmith's trade, smithery; clamor, confused noise.

herrerico, herrerillo, *m.* name of a small bird.

herrero, *m.* or **h. de grueso,** blacksmith.

herrerón, *m.* clumsy smith.

herreruelo, *m.* (ornith.) wagtail.

herrete, *m.* tag, ferrule; branding-iron.

herretear, *va.* to tag.

herrezuelo, *m.* light piece of iron.

herrín, *m.* iron rust.

herrón, *m.* quoit; washer; iron prop for young trees; (Colomb.) point of a spinning top.

herronada, *f.* violent blow with a quoit; blow with a bird's beak.

herrumbre, *f.* rust; iron taste.

herrumbroso, sa, *a.* rusty, rusted.

hertziano, na, *a.* (phys.) Hertzian.

hérulo, la. I. *n.* & *a.* Herulian. II. *m. pl.* Heruli.

herventar, *va.* to boil by putting a hot body into a liquid.

hervidero, *m.* ebullition, boiling; small spring whence water bubbles out; rumbling in the throat or chest; multitude, crowd.

hervidor, *m.* vessel, tube, etc. for boiling.

herviente, *a.* boiling, seething.

hervir (*ger.* HIRVIENDO; *ind. pres.* HIERVO, *pret.* él HIRVIÓ; *subj.* HIERVA). I. *va.* & *vn.* to boil; to seethe. II. *vn.* (of the sea) to become choppy; to bubble, effervesce; to surge (as a crowd).—**h. en,** to teem with, be full of.

hervor, *m.* ebullition, boiling; fervor, heat; vigor; fret; noise and movement of waters.—**h. de sangre,** rash.

hervoroso, sa, *a.* fiery, ardent, impetuous.

hesitación, *f.* hesitation, hesitancy.

hespéride. I. *a.* (astr.) pert. to the Pleiades; (poet.) western. II. *f. pl.* (astr.) Pleiades.

hesperidio, *m.* (bot.) hesperidium.

hespérido, da, *a.* = HESPÉRIDE.

Héspero, *m.* (astr.) Hesperus, the evening star.

heteo, a, *n.* & *a.* Hittite.

hetera, *f.* hetæra, hetaira, Greek courtesan.

heteróclito, ta, *a.* (gram.) heteroclite; irregular, abnormal.

heterodina, *a.* (radio) heterodyne.

heterodoxia, *f.* heterodoxy.

heterodoxo, xa, *a.* heterodox.

heterogeneidad, *f.* heterogeneity.

heterogéneo, nea, *a.* heterogeneous.

heteromancía, *f.* superstitious divination by the flight of birds.

heteromorfo, fa, *a.* heteromorphous.

heteromorfosis, *f.* heteromorphosis.

heterónomo, ma, *a.* heteronymous.

heterópsido, da, *a.* (of metals) lusterless.

heteroscios, *m. pl.* (geog.) heteroscians.

hético, ca, *a.* hectic, consumptive.

hetiquez, *f.* (med.) consumption.

hévea, *f.* (bot.) hevea, Para-rubber tree.

hexacordo, *m.* (mus.) hexachord.

hexaedro, *m.* (geom.) hexahedron.

hexagonal; hexágono, na, *a.* hexagonal.

hexágono, *m.* (geom.) hexagon.

hexámetro, *m.* hexameter.

hexápeda, *f.* = TOESA, ancient linear measure.

hexapétalo, la, *a.* (bot.) hexapetalous.

hexápodo, da, *n.* & *a.* (zool.) hexapod.

hez, *f.* lees, bottom, sediment, dregs of liquors; dross of metals; grains of malt.—*pl.* fæces, excrements.—**la h. del pueblo,** the scum of the people.

Híadas, Híades, *f. pl.* (astr.) Hyades.

hialino, na, *a.* hyaline, transparent; translucent.

hialitis, *f.* (med.) hyalitis.

hialografía, *f.* hyalography, engraving on glass.

hialógrafo, *f.* hyalograph.

hialoideo, dea, *a.* vitreous, glasslike.

hialoides, *f.* hyaloid membrane.

hialotecnia, *f.* hyalography.

hialurgia, *f.* glass-working art.

hiante, *a.* (verse) with a hiatus.

hiato, *m.* (gram., poet.) hiatus.

hibernal, *a.* hibernal, wintry.

hibernés, sa, *a.* Hibernian, Irish.

hibernizo, za, *a.* = HIBERNAL.

hibridación, *f.* hybridization.

hibridez, *f.*, **hibridismo,** *m.* hybridism.

híbrido, da, *n.* & *a.* hybrid.

hicaco, *m.* (bot.) icaco, coco plum.

hice, hiciera, *v.* V. HACER.

hicotea, *f.* (Am.) fresh-water turtle.

hicso, sa, *n.* & *a.* Hyksos.

hidalga, *f.* noblewoman; lady.

hidalgamente, *adv.* nobly, in a gentlemanly way.

hidalgo, ga. I. *a.* noble, illustrious, excellent, exalted. II. *n.* hidalgo, nobleman(-woman).—**h. de bragueta,** one entitled to nobility from being the father of seven successive sons.

hidalgón, na, gote, ta, *n. aug.* old ceremonious hidalgo.

hidalgüejo, ja, güelo, la, guete, ta, guillo, lla, *n. dim.* pretty hidalgo.

hidalguez, hidalguía, *f.* nobility; rights of an hidalgo, nobleness, liberality.

hidátide, *f.* (med. & zool.) hydatid.

hidatídico, ca, *a.* (med.) hydatidinous.

hidra, *f.* (zool.) a poisonous serpent; hydra, fresh-water polyp; (H-, myth., astr.) Hydra.

hidrácido, *m.* (chem.) hydracid.

hidragogo, *m.* & *a.* (med.) hydragogue.

hidrargírido, da, *a.* resembling mercury.

hidrargirismo, *m.* (med.) hydrargyriasis, mercurialism, chronic mercurial poisoning.

hidrargirita, *f.* (min.) native oxide of mercury.

hidratación, *f.* hydration, hydrating.

hidratado, da, *pp.* & *a.* hydrate(d).

hidratar, *va.* (chem.) to hydrate.

hidrato, *m.* (chem.) hydrate.—**h. de carbono,** (chem.) carbohydrate.

hidráulica, *f.* hydraulics.

hidráulico, ca. I. *a.* hydraulic. II. *n.* hydraulics expert.

hidria, *f.* hydria, an ancient jar.

hidroaeroplano, *m.* (aer.) hydroplane, seaplane.

hidroavión, *m.* (aer.) hydroplane, seaplane.—**h. de flotadores,** float seaplane.

hidrocarburo, *m.* (chem.) hydrocarbon.

hidrocefalía, *f.* (med.) hydrocephalus, dropsy of the brain.

hidrocéfalo, *m.* (med.) hydrocephalus.

hidrocele, *f.* (med.) hydrocele.

hidroclorato, *m.* (chem.) hydrochlorate.

hidroclórico, ca, *a.* (chem.) hydrochloric.

hidrodinámica, *f.* hydrodynamics.

hidrodinámico, ca, *a.* hydrodynamic.

hidroeléctrico, ca, *a.* hydroelectric.

hidrófana, *f.* (min.) hydrophane.

hidrofilacio, *m.* hydrophylacium, water reservoir.

hidrófilo, la, *a.* water-loving; absorbent (cotton).

hidrofobia, *f.* (med.) hydrophobia; rabies.

hidrófobo, ba, *a.* suffering from hydrophobia.

hidrófugo, ga, *a.* nonabsorbent, moistureproof.

hidrogala, *m.* mixture of milk and water.
hidrogenar, *va.* to hydrogenize.
hidrógeno, *m.* (chem.) hydrogen.—**h. pesado,** heavy hydrogen.
hidrognosia, *f.* hydrognosy.
hidrogogía, *f.* science of canal making and the conveyance of water.
hidrografía, *f.* hydrography.
hidrográfico, ca, *a.* hydrographical.
hidrógrafo, *m.* hydrographer.
hidroide, *m.* (zool.) hydroid, hydrozoön; *pl.* Hydrodea.
hidrología, *f.* hydrology.
hidrológico, ca, *a.* hydrologic.
hidromancia, *f.* hydromancy.
hidromántico, ca, *a.* hydromantic.
hidromedusa, *f.* (zool.) hydromedusa; a large South American turtle.
hidromel, hidromiel, *m.* hydromel, mead.
hidrometeoro, *m.* hydrometeor.
hidrometra, *n.* one versed in hydraulic measurements.
hidrometría, *f.* science of hydraulic measurements (velocity, discharge, etc.).
hidrómetro, *m.* instrument for measuring rate of flow, force, etc. of liquids.
hidrópata, *m.* (med.) hydropath.
hidropatía, *f.* (med.) water cure, hydrotherapy.
hidropático, ca, *a.* hydropathic.
hidropesía, *f.* (med.) dropsy.
hidrópico, ca, *a.* dropsical.
hidroplano, *m.* (aer.) hydroplane, seaplane.
hidroquinona, *f.* (chem.) hydroquinone.
hidroscopio, *m.* hydroscope.
hidrostática, *f.* hydrostatics.
hidrostáticamente, *adv.* hydrostatically.
hidrostático, ca, *a.* hydrostatical.
hidrosulfúrico, ca, *a.* hydrosulphuric.
hidrotecnia, *f.* hydraulic engineering.
hidroterapia, *f.* hydrotherapeutics.
hidroterápico, ca, *a.* hydrotherapeutic.
hidrotórax, *f.* (med.) hydrothorax.
hiedo, hieda, *v.* V. HEDER.
hiedra, *f.* (bot.) ivy.—**h. terrestre,** ground ivy.
hiel, *f.* gall, bile; bitterness, malice.—**h. de la tierra,** (bot.) fumitory or earth smoke.—**echar la h.,** (coll.) to work very hard.—**no tener h.,** (coll.) to be meek and gentle.
¹hielo, *m.* ice; frost, congelation; coolness, indifference; astonishment, stupefaction.
²hielo, hiele, *v.* V. HELAR.
hiemal, *a.* wintry, hibernal.
hiena, *f.* (zool.) hyena.
hienda, *f.* dung.
hiendo, hienda, *v.* V. HENDER.
hierático, ca, *a.* hieratic, sacerdotal.
hierba, *f.* (bot.) grass; weed; herb; food for cattle; herbage.—**mala h.,** weed; (fig.) bad character, evil person.—*pl.* poison given in food; among the clergy, greens, garden stuff.—**y otras hierbas,** (humor.) and so forth.
hierbabuena, *f.* (bot.) mint.
hierbatero, ra, *n.* herb doctor; maté gatherer; one who prepares maté; YERBATERO.
hiere, hiero, hiera, *v.* V. HERIR.
hierofanta, te, *m.* hierophant.
hieroglífico, ca, *a.* hieroglyphic.
hieros, *m. pl.* (bot.) = YEROS, tare, vetch.
hierosolimitano, na, *a.* pert. to Jerusalem.
hierrezuelo, *m. dim.* small piece of iron.
¹hierro, *m.* iron; any iron tool, instrument or structural shape; brand stamped with a hot iron; iron head of a shaft, arrow, or dart; any pointed weapon, as a sword or goad; cutter, cutting edge or part of a cutting tool.—*pl.* fetters, shackles, handcuffs; (naut.) bilboes.—**h. albo, h. caliente,** red-hot iron.—**h. colado,** cast iron.—**h. cuadrillado,** square iron.—**h. de doble T,** I-beam.—**h. dulce,** or **de fragua,** wrought iron.—**h. en planchas,** sheet iron.—

h. forjado, wrought iron.—**h. fundido** = H. COLADO.—**h. laminado** = H. EN PLANCHAS.—**h. varilla,** round iron.—**machacar en h. frío,** to labor in vain.
²hierro, hierre, *v.* V. HERRAR.
hierva, hiervo, *v.* V. HERVIR.
higa, *f.* amulet, charm hung about a baby's neck; method of pointing derisively at a person; ridicule, derision.—**dar h.,** (of firearms) to hang fire.—**dar higas,** to despise.—**no dar dos higas,** not to give a farthing: not to care a rap.
higadilla, *f.* llo, *m. dim.* small liver; liver of birds, fishes, and other small animals.
hígado, *m.* liver.—*pl.* (coll.) courage, bravery.—**hasta los hígados,** to the heart.—**malos hígados,** (coll.) ill will.
higate, *m.* pottage of figs, pork, etc.
higiene, *f.* hygiene; sanitation.—**h. pública,** public health.
higiénicamente, *adv.* hygienically.
higiénico, ca, *a.* hygienic, sanitary.
higienista, *m.* hygienist.
higienizar, *va.* to make sanitary.
higo, *m.* (bot.) fig.—**h. chumba,** or **de pala,** prickly pear.—**de higos a brevas,** in a long while.—**no se me da un h.,** I don't care a fig.
higrometría, *m.* hygrometry.
higrométrico, ca, *a.* hygrometric.
higrómetro, *m.* hygrometer.
higroscopia, *f.* hygroscopy, hygrometry.
higroscopio, *m.* hygroscope.
higuera, *f.* (bot.) fig tree.—**h. chumba,** or **de Indias,** Indian fig tree, prickly-pear cactus.—**h. infernal,** castor-oil plant, castor bean.—**h. nopal** = H. CHUMBA.
higueral, *m.* plantation of fig trees.
higuereta, *f.* (bot.) = RICINO, castor-oil plant.
higuerón, *m.* a large American tree.
higüito, *m. dim.* small fig.
hija, *f.* daughter.—**h. política,** daughter-in-law. For phrases V. HIJO, JA.
hijadalga, *f.* = HIDALGA, noblewoman.
hijastro, tra, *n.* stepchild.
hijito, ita, *n. f. dim.* little child, little dear.
hijo, ja, *n.* son (daughter); young of an animal; son, native; (bot.) shoot; sucker; child, issue, offspring; fruit, result; junior (after a person's name: *Alejandro Dumas, hijo,* Alexander Dumas, Jr.).—**h. adoptivo,** adopted child.—**h. bastardo,** bastard, illegitimate child.—**h. de bendición,** legitimate child.—**h. de familia,** minor.—**h. de ganancia** = H. BASTARDO.—**h. de la cuna,** foundling.—**h. del agua,** good sailor; good swimmer.—**h. de la piedra,** foundling.—**h. de leche,** foster child.—**h. del hombre,** Son of Man (Jesus).—**h. de su madre** = H. BASTARDO.—**h. de su madre (padre),** his mother's (father's) son, very much like his mother (father).—**h. de vecino,** native (of a town); mother's son (in the colloquial sense of "person").—**h. natural,** illegitimate child.
hijodalgo, *m.* = HIDALGO, nobleman.
hijuela, *f. dim.* little daughter; (sewing) gore or piece for widening a garment; small mattress put between others to make the bed even; (eccl.) pall, chalice cover; small drain; estate of a deceased person; (law) schedule given to an heir of his share in the partition of the estate; crossroad; postman of a rural mail route; palm seed; fascine of kindling wood; leader for fishhooks.
hijuelo, la, *n. dim.* young child; (bot.) shoot, sucker.
¹hila, *f.* HILERA, row, line; thin gut.—**h. de agua,** small ditch for irrigation.—**a la h.,** in a row, single file.
²hila, *f.* spinning.—*pl.* (surg.) lint.—**hilas raspadas,** scraped lint.

hilacha, *f.,* **hilacho,** *m.* fraying, shred, filament or thread ravelled out of cloth.—*pl.* lint.

hilachoso, sa, *a.* shreddy, ragged; filamentous.

hilada, *f.* row or line; (mason.) course.

hiladillo, *m.* narrow ribbon or tape.

hilado, *m.* spinning; yarn.

hilador, ra. I. *n.* & *a.* spinner(-ing). **II.** *f.* spinning machine, spinning jenny.

hilandera, *f.* woman spinner.

hilandería, *f.* spinnery, spinning mill.

hilanderilla, *f. dim.* spinning girl.

hilandero, ra. I. *n.* & *a.* spinner(-ing). **II.** *m.* spinning room, spinnery.

hilanderuelo, la, *n. dim.* spinning boy (girl).

hilar, *va.* & *vn.* to spin; to reason; (of discourse) to connect.—**h. delgado,** to be exceedingly careful or particular; to act with great nicety; to split hairs.

hilaracha, *f.* = HILACHA.

hilarante, *a.* laughing (gas).

hilaridad, *f.* hilarity.

hilaza, *f.* yarn; fibre; uneven thread.—*pl.* lint.

hilera, *f.* row, line, tier, file; (metal.) wiredrawer; fine yarn; slit or catch of a spindle; (arch.) ridgepole; (mil.) file.

hilero, *m.* thread of a river or stream.

hilete, *m. dim.* small thread.

hilillo, *m.* trickle (of water).

hilo, *m.* thread; yarn; filament, fibre; string; linen; wire; edge of a sword or razor; slender thread formed by falling liquids; (min.) seam; continuation, series; cross wire, cross hair (of a telescope).—**h. bramante, h. de a carreto, h. de palomas,** packthread, twine.—**h. de velas,** or **volatín,** sailmaker's yarn.—**h. de una corriente,** (naut.) thread of a current.— **a h.,** successively, one after another; in line. —**al h.,** along the thread (of cloth), with the grain (in wood).—**de h.,** directly, instantly.

hilván, *m.* (sewing) tacking, basting.—**hablar de h.,** (coll.) to speak very fast.

hilvanar, *va.* (sewing) to tack, baste; to plan; to do or make in a hurry.

himen, *m.* (anat.) hymen.

himeneo, *m.* hymen, nuptials; epithalamium.

himenio, *m.* (bot.) hymenium.

himenóptero, a. I. *n.* & *a.* (entom.) hymenopteran(-ous). **II.** *m. pl.* (entom.) Hymenoptera.

himnario, *m.* hymnal, hymn book.

himno, *m.* hymn.

himplar, *vn.* to roar, bellow.

hin, *m.* whinny, neigh.

hincadura, *f.* thrusting, driving; prick.

hincapié, *m.* stamping the foot (for emphasis).— **hacer h. en,** to emphasize, to dwell upon.

hincar. I. *va.* (*pret.* HINQUÉ; *subj.* HINQUE) to thrust; drive; to plant.—**h. el diente,** to bite; to calumniate.—**h. la rodilla,** to kneel down. **II.** *vr.* to kneel down.

hincón, *m.* ferry post, hitching post.

hincha, *f.* (coll.) hatred, enmity, grudge.

hinchadamente, *adv.* airily, pompously.

hinchado, da, *a.* & *pp.* swollen; airy, arrogant, presumptuous; inflated, high-flown (style).

hinchar. I. *va.* to swell. **II.** *vr.* to swell; to become arrogant, conceited or puffed up, (coll.) to get a swelled head.

hinchazón, *m.* swelling, tumefaction; ostentation, vanity, airs: inflation, euphuism.

hincho, hincha, hinchió, *v.* *V.* HENCHIR.

hindu, *n.* & *a.* Hindu; Hindustani.

hiniesta, *f.* (bot.) genista.

hinojal, *m.* (bot.) fennel bed.

¹hinojo, *m.* (bot.) fennel.—**h. marino,** (bot.) samphire.

²hinojo, *m.* knee.—**de hinojos,** kneeling.

hinqué, hinque, *v.* *V.* HINCAR.

hintero, *m.* baker's kneading table.

hiño, hiña, *v.* *V.* HEÑIR.

hioideo, hioides, *a.* (anat.) hyoid.

hipar, *vn.* to hiccough; to pant; desire eagerly, be anxious; be overfatigued.

hipérbaton, *m.* (rhet.) hyperbaton.

hipérbola, *f.* (geom.) hyperbola.

hipérbole, *f.* (rhet.) hyperbole.

hiperbólicamente, *adv.* hyperbolically.

hiperbólico, ca, *a.* hyperbolic.

hiperbolizar, *vn.* to use hyperboles.

hiperboloide, *f.* (geom.) hyperboloid.

hiperbóreo, rea, *a.* hyperborean.

hipercrisis, *f.* (med.) violent crisis.

hipercrítica, *f.* hypercriticism, excessive or exaggerated criticism.

hipercrítico, ca, *a.* hypercritical.

hiperdulía, *f.* (eccl.) hyperdulia.

hiperemia, *f.* (med.) hyperæmia.

hiperémico, ca, *a.* hyperæmic, congested.

hiperestesia, *f.* (med.) hyperæsthesia, excessive sensitivity (to pain, heat, touch, etc.).

hipericíneo, a. I. *a.* & *n.* hypericaceous (plant). **II.** *m. pl.* Hypericaceæ.

hipérico, *m.* (bot.) hypericum.

hipermetría, *f.* (rhet.) hypermeter.

hipertensión, *f.* (med.) hypertension.

hipertrofia, *f.* (med.) hypertrophy.

hipertroarse, *vr.* to hypertrophy.

hipertrófico, ca, *a.* hypertrophic.

hípico, ca, *a.* equine, pertaining to horses.

hipil, *m.* (Am.) loose garment worn by Indians.

hipnal, *m.* hypnale, a kind of serpent said to cause sleep.

hipnología, *f.* hypnology, science dealing with sleep.

hipnosis, *f.* hypnosis.

hipnótico, ca, *n.* & *a.* hypnotic.

hipnotismo, *m.* hypnotism.

hipnotización, *f.* hypnotization.

hipnotizador, a, *n.* & *a.* hypnotizer(-ing).

hipnotizar, *va.* to hypnotize.

hipo, *m.* hiccough; longing; anger.

hipocampo, *m.* (myth.) hippocampus, sea horse.

hipocausto, *m* (anc. Rome) hypocaust.

hipocentauro, *m.* hippocentaur.

hipocicloide, *f.* (geom.) hypocycloid.

hipocondría, *f.* (med.) hypochondria.

hipocondríaco, ca; hipocóndrico, ca, *n.* & *a.* hypochondriac(-al.).

hipocondrio, *m.* (anat.) hypochondrium.

hipocrás, *m.* hippocras, medicinal wine.

hipocrático, ca, *a.* Hippocratic.

Hipocrénides, *f. pl.* (poet.) the Muses.

hipocresía, *f.* hypocrisy.

hipócrita, *n.* & *a.* hypocrite(-ical).

hipócritamente, *adv.* hypocritically.

hipocritón, na, *n. aug.* great hypocrite.

hipodérmico, ca, *a.* hypodermic.

hipódromo, *m.* hippodrome.

hipofagía, *f.* hippophagism.

hipófago, ga, *n.* & *a.* hippofagist.

hipofosfato, *m.* hypophosphate.

hipofosfito, *m.* hypophosphite.

hipogástrico, ca, *a.* hypogastric.

hipogastro, m. (anat.) hypogastrium.

hipogénico, ca, *a.* (geol.) hypogene.

hipogeo, *m.* (arch.) hypogeium.

hipogloso, sa, *a.* hypoglossal.

hipogrifo, *m.* (myth.) hippogriff.

hipomanes, *m.* (vet.) vaginal discharge from the mare when in heat.

hiponitrato, *m.* (chem.) subnitrate.

hiponítrico, ca, *a.* hyponitrous.

hipopótamo, *m.* (zool.) hippopotamus.

hiposo, sa, *a.* having hiccoughs.

hipóstasis, *f.* (theol.) hypostasis.

hipostáticamente, *adv.* hypostatically.

hipostático, ca, *a.* hypostatic.

hiposulfato, *m.* (chem.) hyposulphate.

hiposulfito, *m.* hyposulphite.

hipoteca, *f.* mortgage, pledge; (law) hypothecation, hypothec.

hipotecable, *a.* mortgageable.

hipotecar, *va.* (*pret.* HIPOTEQUÉ; *subj.* HIPOTEQUE) to hypothecate, pledge, mortgage.

hipotecario, ria, *a.* pertaining to a mortgage; hypothecary.

hipotequé, hipoteque, *v.* *V.* HIPOTECAR.

hipotenusa, *f.* (geom.) hypotenuse.

hipótesis, *f.* hypothesis.

hipotético, ca, *a.* hypothetic.

hipsometría, *f.* hypsometry.

hipsométrico, ca, *a.* hypsometric.

hipsómetro, *m.* hypsometer.

hipurato, *m.* (chem.) hippurate.

hipuria, *f.* (med.) hippuria.

hipúrico, ca, *a.* (chem.) hippuric.

hircano, na, *n.* & *a.* Hircanian.

hircino, na, *a.* hireinous, goatlike.

hirco, *m.* (zool.) wild goat.

hiriente, *a.* hurting, cutting, offensive.

hiriera, hirió, *v.* *V.* HERIR.

hirma, *f.* selvage of cloth.

hirsuto, ta, *a.* hirsute, hairy, bristly.

hirundinaria, *f.* (bot.) swallow-wort.

hirviendo, *gerund* of HERVIR.

hirviente, *a.* boiling, seething.

hirviera, hirviese, hirvió, *v.* *V.* HERVIR.

hisca, *f.* birdlime.

hiscal, *m.* esparto rope of three strands.

hisopada, *f.* water sprinkled with an aspergill.

hisopear, *va.* to sprinkle with an aspergill.

hisopillo, *m. dim.* small aspergill; (med.) mouth swab; (bot.) winter savory.

¹hisopo, *m.* (bot.) hyssop; (eccl.) aspergill, sprinkler.

²hisopo, *m.*—**h. húmedo,** (pharm.) grease collected in washing fleeces of wool.

hispalense, *a.* native of or pertaining to Seville.

hispánico, ca, *a.* Hispanic.

hispanismo, *m.* Hispanicism. Spanish idiom.

hispanista, *n.* Spanish scholar.

hispanizado, da. I. *pp.* of HISPANIZAR. II. *a.* Spanishlike.

hispanizar, *va.* = ESPAÑOLIZAR, to make Spanishlike.

hispano, na. I. Hispanic, Spanish. II. *n.* Spaniard.—**hispanoamericano, na,** *n.* & *a.* Spanish-American.

híspido, da, *a.* bristly, hirsute.

hispir, *va.* & *vn.* to swell; make or become spongy.

histéresis, *f.* (phys.) hysteresis.

histérico, ca. I. *a.* hysteric, hysterical. II. *m.* hysterics.

histerismo, *m.* (med.) hysteria.

histerotomía, *m.* (surg.) hysterotomy.

histología, *f.* histology.

histológico, ca, *a.* histological.

histólogo, *m.* histologist.

historia, *f.* history; tale, story; fable; (art) history piece.—**dejarse de historias,** to stop beating about the bush and come to the point; to cut out nonsense, to stop fooling.—**picar en h.,** to be more serious than it seems.—**ser de h.,** to have a history (bad antecedents).

historiado, da, *pp.* & *a.* (coll.) excessively adorned; (art) well-composed (figure, painting).

historiador, ra, *n.* historian.

historial, *a.* historical, historic.

historialmente, *adv.* historically.

historiar, *va.* to record, to chronicle, to narrate; (art) to represent, paint, depict.

históricamente, *adv.* historically.

histórico, ca, *a.* historical.

historieta, *f. dim.* short story; comics, comic strip.

historiografía, *f.* historiography.

historiógrafo, *m.* historiographer.

historión, *m.* tedious, long-winded story.

histrión, *m.* actor, player; buffoon, juggler.

histriónico, ca, *a.* histrionic.

histrionisa, *f.* actress or danseuse.

histrionismo, *m.* histrionism.

hita, *f.* headless nail, brad, wire nail; guide post.

hitita, *n.* & *a.* Hittite.

¹hito, ta, *a.* black (horse).

²hito, ta. I. *a.* (of a house or street) adjoining; fixed, firm. II. *m.* landmark; guidepost; milestone; hob and quoits; (artil.) target.—**a h.,** fixedly, firmly.—**dar en el h.,** to hit the nail on the head; to see the point.—**mirar de h. en h.,** to stare at; to look at from head to foot.

hitón, *m.* large cut nail.

hizo, *pret.* of HACER.

hobachón, na, *a.* fat and lazy; (Colomb.) (of horses) shy.

hobachonería, *f.* laziness, sloth.

hocicada, *f.* blow with the snout.

hocicar. I. *va.* to root (as hogs). II. *vn.* to fall headlong with the face to the ground; to knock one's face against an object; (coll.) to get into difficulties; (naut.) to pitch.

hocico, *m.* snout, muzzle, nose (of animal); biglipped mouth; pouting; (coll.) face.—**de hocicos,** by the nose; face downwards.—**estar con,** or **de, h.,** to be ill-humored, sulky.—**meter el h.,** to stick one's nose in other people's business.

hocicón, na, *or* **hocicudo, da,** *a.* long-snouted; blubber-lipped, flabby-mouthed.

¹hocino, *m.* (agr.) bill, billhook.

²hocino, *m.* glen, dell; narrow gorge or canyon.—*pl.* gardens in glens.

hociquillo, ito, *m. dim.* little snout.

hodómetro, *m.* = ODÓMETRO, cyclometer.

hogañazo, hogaño, *adv.* (coll.) this present year; in these days.

hogar, *m.* home (often called **h. doméstico**); hearth, fireplace; (steam eng.) furnace.

hogaza, *f.* large loaf of bread.

hoguera, *f.* bonfire; blaze.

hoja, *f.* leaf (of a plant, a book, a door); petal; leaf, foil, sheet or thin plate (of metal); blade (of a sword or knife); sword; sheet (of paper); veneer; half of each of the principal parts of a garment; window shutter; ground cultivated one year and lying at rest for another.—*pl.* (arch.) leaf ornaments, foliation.—**h. de estaño,** tinfoil.—**h. de lata,** tin plate.—**h. de servicios,** record; (mil.) certificate setting forth the rank and services of a military officer.—**h. de tocino,** side of a hog.—**h. suelta,** leaflet (not folder), handbill.—**h. toledana,** Toledo blade.—**h. volante,** fly sheet; handbill; supplement, extra.—**doblemos la h.,** no more of that, let's drop it.—**poner le a uno como h. de perejil,** to give one a tongue lashing.—**ser de h.,** or **de una sola h.,** (Arg.) (esp. of people) to be first rate, of highest order.—**volver la h.,** to turn the page; to change one's views; to fail to keep one's promise; to change the subject (of conversation).

hojalata, *f.* = HOJA DE LATA, tin plate.

hojalatería, *f.* tinware; tin shop.

hojalatero, *m.* tinsmith.

hojaldra, *f.* (Am.) = HOJALDRE.

hojaldrado, da. I. *pp.* of HOJALDRAR. II. *a.* resembling puff paste, lamellar, foliated.

hojaldrar, *va.* to make into puff paste.

hojaldre, *m.* or *f.* puff paste.—**quitar la h. al pastel,** (coll.) to detect a fraud; to discover a plot.

hojaldrista, *n.* puff paste baker.

hojarasca, *f.* dead leaves; excessive foliage; trash, rubbish.

hojarascoso, sa, *a.* trashy.

hojear. I. *va.* to turn the leaves of; to glance at (a book), look over hastily. II. *vn.* to scale off.

hojica, illa, ita, *f. dim.* small leaf.

hojilla de navaja (de afeitar), razor blade.

hojoso, sa; hojudo, da, *a.* leafy, fronded.

hojuela, *f. dim.* small leaf, leaflet; pancake; gold or silver thread for embroidery; skins of pressed olives.

¡hola! *interj.* hello! hi! (naut.) hoy! ahoy!

holán, holán batista, *m.* cambric; batiste.

holanda, *f.* fine Dutch linen, cambric.

holandés, sa, *n.* & *a.* Dutch, Hollander(-ish).—**a la holandesa,** (bookbinding) in cloth.

holandeta, holandilla, *f.* brown holland.

holgachón, na, *a.* (coll.) used to an easy and comfortable life.

holgadamente, *adv.* amply, fully, loosely, easily; quietly, carelessly; comfortably.

holgado, da. I. *pp.* of HOLGAR. II. *a.* loose, lax, easy; large, spacious; disengaged, at leisure; comfortable; well-off.

holganza, *f.* leisure, ease; diversion, recreation.

holgar. I. *vn.* (ind. HUELGO; subj. HUELGUE) to rest; to quit work; to be idle; to be needless or useless; to take pleasure or satisfaction. II. *vr.* to sport, dally, trifle; to idle; to amuse oneself.

holgazán, na. I. *a.* idle, lazy, indolent. II. *n.* idler, loiterer, lounger.

holgazanear, *vn.* to idle, to loiter, to lounge.

holgazanería, *f.* idleness, laziness, indolence.

holgón, a, *a.* indolent and pleasure-loving.

holgorio, *m.* (coll.) boisterous frolic or spree.

holgueta, *f.* (coll.) feast, merrymaking.

holgura, *f.* frolic, merrymaking; width, breadth; ease, comfort; plenty of room or space; (mech.) play.

holocausto, *m.* holocaust, burnt sacrifice.

holocéfalo, la. I. *a.* (zool.) holocephalous. II. *m. pl.* Holocephali.

holoédrico, ca, *a.* (min.) holohedral.

hológrafo, fa, *a.* (law) holographic, holograph.

holómetro, *m.* holometer, pantometer.

holosérico, ca, *a.* all-silk.

holoturia, *f.* (zool.) holothurian, sea cucumber.

holotúrido, da; holoturioideo, *a.* I. *n.* & *a.* (zool.) holothurian. II. *m. pl.* Holothuroidea.

holladura, *f.* trampling; duty paid for the run of cattle.

hollar, *va.* (ind. HUELLO; subj. HUELLE) to tread upon, trample under foot; to humiliate.

hollejo, *m.* skin (of a fruit, etc.).

hollejuelo, *m. dim.* small piece of skin; thin skin.

hollín, *m.* soot, lampblack.

holliniento, ta, *a.* fuliginous, sooty.

homarrache, *m.* clown.

hombracho, hombrachón, *m. aug.* heavy-built man.

hombrada, *f.* manly action; impulse.

hombradía, *f.* manliness.

hombrazo, *m. aug.* big man.

hombre, *m.* man; (vulg.) husband; ombre, a card game; (coll., in addressing or speaking to a friend, often as a mere expletive) boy, old chap, dear fellow, man, my dear man.—**¡hombre!** an exclamation of surprise.—**h. achaparrado,** short and lusty man.—**¡h. al agua!** man overboard.—**h. bueno,** (law) arbiter, arbitrator, referee.—**h. de armas,** military man.—**h. de bien,** a reputable, reliable man.—**h. de estado,** statesman.—**h. de puños,** strong, valiant man.—**ser muy h.,** to be a real man, or quite a man.

hombrear. I. *vn.* to pretend to man's estate prematurely. II. *vn.* & *vr.* to vie with another.

hombrecico, cito, cillo, zuelo, *m. dim.* little man; youth.

hombrecillos, *m. pl.* (bot.) hops.

hombrera, *f.* (armor) shoulder armor.

hombría, *f.* (Am.) manliness, courage.—**h. de bien,** probity, honesty.

hombrillo, *m.* (sewing) yoke of a shirt.

hombro, *m.* shoulder.—**h. con h.,** cheek by jowl.—**a h.,** on the shoulders.—**arrimar el h.,** to lend a hand; to exert oneself.—**echar al h.,** to

shoulder; to become responsible for.—**encogerse de hombros,** to shrug the shoulders.—**llevar en hombros,** to carry on the shoulders; to support, to protect.—**sobre los hombros** = A H.

hombrón, *m. aug.* big, lusty man.

hombronazo, *m. aug.* huge man.

hombruno, na, *a.* mannish.

homenaje, *m.* homage; obeisance; fealty, allegiance; respect.

homeópata, *n.* & *a.* homœopath(-ic).

homeopatía, *f.* homœopathy.

homeopático, ca, *a.* homœopathic.

homérico, ca, *a.* Homeric.

homicida. I. *a.* homicidal. II. *m. f.* murderer; homicide.

homicidio, *m.* homicide; an ancient tribute.

homilía, *f.* (eccl.) homily.—**homiliario,** *m.* collection of homilies.—**homilista,** *m.* homilist.

hominal, *a.* pertaining to man.

hominicaco, *m.* (coll.) insignificant fellow, whippersnapper.

homocéntrico, ca, *a.* concentric.

homofonía, *f.* homophony.

homófono, na, *a.* homophonous.

homogeneidad, *f.* homogeneity.

homogéneo, a, *a.* homogeneous.

homógrafo, fa, *a.* homographic.

homologación, *f.* (law) homologation.

homologar, *va.* (law) to homologate, ratify.

homólogo, ga, *a.* (geom.) homologous; proportional; (logic) synonymous.

homonimia, *f.* homonymy.

homónimo, ma, *a.* homonymous; namesake.

homóptero, ra. I. *n.* & *a.* (zool.) homopteran (-ous). II. *m. pl.* Homoptera.

homosexual, *a.* & *n.* homosexual.

homúnculo, *m.* homunculus, dwarf.

honda, *f.* sling (for hurling stones).—**h. y precinta,** (naut.) parbuckle.

hondable, *a.* (naut.) soundable.

hondamente, *adv.* deeply, profoundly.

hondarras, *f. pl.* dregs, lees, sediment.

hondazo, *m.* a shot with a sling.

hondear, *va.* (naut.) to sound; to unload (ship).

hondero, *m.* soldier armed with a sling.

hondijo, *m.* sling.

hondillo, *m.* any of the pieces which form the seats of breeches or drawers.

hondo, da. I. *a.* deep; low. II. *m.* depth, bottom.—**de h.,** in depth.

hondón, *m.* bottom; dell, glen; deep hole; footpiece of a stirrup; eye of a needle.

hondonada, *f.* dale, ravine, glen; depression.

hondura, *f.* depth; profundity.—**meterse en honduras,** (fig.) to go beyond one's depth.

hondureño, ña, *a.* Honduras (as *a.*).

honestamente, *adv.* honestly; modestly; virtuously.

honestar, *va.* to honor; to excuse, palliate.

honestidad, *f.* modesty; purity; decorum.

honesto, ta, *a.* honest; decent, decorous; pure, chaste; reasonable, just.

hongo, *m.* (bot.) mushroom; fungus; slouch hat; Derby hat.—**hongoso, sa,** *a.* fungous.—**honguillo,** *m.* small fungus.

honor, *m.* honor; fame.—*pl.* dignity, rank, office, honors, privileges, honorary title or position.

honorable, *a.* worthy, honorable; illustrious; reputable, reliable.

honorablemente, *adv.* honorably, creditably.

honorario, ria. I. *a.* honorary. II. *m.* honorarium, fee.

honoríficamente, *adv.* honorably; honorarily.

honorífico, ca, *a.* honorary; honorable.

honra, *f.* honor; reverence, respect; reputation, fame; purity, chastity.—**tener a h.,** to regard as an honor, be proud of.—*pl.* obsequies.

honradamente, *adv.* honorably, honestly.

honradez, *f.* honesty, probity, integrity.

honrado, da, *a.* honest, honorable.

honrador, ra, *n.* & *a.* honorer(-ing).

honramiento, *m.* honoring.

honrar. I. *va.* to honor, do honor to; to be an honor for; (com.) to honor. **II.** *vn.* to honor; to be an honor. **III.** *vr.* to deem it an honor; to be honored.

honrilla, *f.* *dim.* keen sense of honor or duty. punctiliousness (usually **la negra h.**).

honrosamente, *adv.* honorably; creditably.

honroso, sa, *a.* honorable, decorous; honoring, honor-giving.—**ser h.,** to be an honor.

hontanal, *m.* HONTANAR.—*pl.* feasts of the ancients held at fountains.

hontanar, *m.* place abounding in springs.

hopa, *f.* long cassock; sack for an executed criminal.

hopalanda, *f.* (anc.) gown worn by students.

hopear, *vn.* to wag the tail.

hoplita, *m.* hoplite.

hoploteca, *f.* = OPLOTECA, museum for weapons.

hopo, *m.* bushy tail (as of a fox).

hoque, *m.* treat to close a bargain.

hora. I. *f.* hour; time, season for doing anything; distance covered in an hour; league.—*pl.* (eccl.) prayerbook.—**horas canónicas,** (eccl.) canonical hours.—**h. de,** time to, or for (*hora de almuerzo,* time for breakfast, or breakfast time; *hora de tren,* time for the train, or train time). —**h. menguada,** fatal, or unhappy hour.— **a buena h.,** opportunely, at the proper time. —**a la h.,** at once, right away; then.—**a la h. de ésta,** or **a la h. de ahora,** or **a estas horas,** (coll.) at this moment.—**a última h.,** at the last moment, at the eleventh hour.—**cuarenta horas,** (eccl.) forty hours.—**dar la h.,** to strike the hour; to adjourn (the meeting, etc.); to dismiss (the class, etc.).—**de última h.,** up-to-date.—**en h. buena, en buen,** or **buena h.,** well, happily; it is well; very well, all right.— **en h. mala, en mal,** or **mala h.,** = ENHORA-MALA (used to indicate dissatisfaction, disapproval, etc., rendered according to the situation).—**no ver la h. de,** to look forward to.— **por horas,** by instants.—**¿qué h. es?** (in some places, **¿qué horas son?**), what time is it?— **vete en h. mala,** (coll.) begone, get out of my sight. **II.** *adv.* now, at this time, at present.

horadable, *a.* capable of being pierced.

horadación, *f.* perforation; boring, piercing.

horadado, *m.* silkworm's cocoon bored through.

horadador, ra, *n.* & *a.* perforator(-ing); borer (-ing); burrower(-ing).

horadar, *va.* to perforate, bore; burrow.

horado, *m.* hole bored through; cavern, grotto.

horambre, *m.* hole in the cheeks of mills.

horario, ria. I. *a.* horary, horal, hour (as *a.*). **II.** *m.* hour hand of a clock or watch; (Ry.) timetable.

horca, *f.* gallows, gibbet; (agr.) hayfork, pitchfork; forked prop for trees or vines; yoke for dogs or hogs; rope or string of onions or garlic.

horcado, da, *a.* forked, forky.

horcajadas, horcajadillas.—**a h.,** astride or astraddle.

horcajadura, *f.* crotch (of human body).

horcajo, *m.* yoke or collar for mules; in oil mills, the Y-shaped division of the beam; fork or confluence of two streams.

horcate, *m.* hame (of a harness).

horco, *m.* rope or string of onions or garlic.

horcón, *m.* forked pole to support the branches of fruit trees.

horchata, *f.* orgeat, drink made from almonds.

horchatería, *f.* place where orgeat is sold.

horchatero, ra, *n.* orgeat maker or seller.

horda, *f.* horde.

hordiate, *m.* pearl barley; barley water.

horero, *m.* (S. A.) hour hand.

horizontal, *a.* & *f.* horizontal.

horizontalidad, *f.* horizontality.

horizontalmente, *adv.* horizontally, flatly.

horizonte, *m.* horizon.—**h. artificial,** artificial horizon.—**h. racional,** celestial horizon, rational horizon.—**h. sensible,** sensible horizon, visible horizon (= horizon in the ordinary sense).

horma, *f.* mold, model; shoemaker's last; hatter's block; (mason.) dry wall.—**hallar la h. de su zapato,** (ironic) to meet with one's match.

hormadoras, *f. pl.* (Colomb.) underskirt.

hormaza, *f.* (mason.) dry wall.

hormazo, *m.* blow with a last or block; heap of stones; house and garden.

hormero, *m.* last maker.

hormiga, *f.* ant; (med.) itch or cutaneous pruritus.—**h. león,** (entom.) ant lion.

hormigo, *m.* (min.) sifted ashes used in smelting quicksilver.—*pl.* sweetmeat of mashed almonds or filberts; coarse parts of flour or poorly-ground wheat.

¹hormigón, *m.* (vet.) a disease of cattle; (bot.) a disease of some plants.

²hormigón, *m.* (eng.) concrete.—**h. armado,** reinforced concrete.—**h. hidráulico,** hydraulic-cement concrete; hydraulic-lime mortar.

hormigonera, *f.* concrete mixer.

hormigoso, sa, *a.* formicine; ant-eaten.

hormigueamiento, *m.* (med.) itching.

hormiguear, *vn.* to itch; to swarm.

hormigüela, *f. dim.* small ant.

hormigueo, *m.* (med.) itching.

hormiguero. I. *m.* ant hill or hillock; ant hole or nest; swarm of people or little animals; (ornith.) wryneck.—*pl.* piles of weeds covered with earth and burned to serve as manure. **II.** *a.* (med.) pertaining to the itch; feeding on ants, ant-eating.

hormiguillar, *va.* (min.) to mix (grains of silver) with salt.

hormiguillo, *m.* (vet.) a disease of horses' hoofs; people ranged in a line, who pass materials or loads from hand to hand; (Mex.) a spicy sirup; almond sweatmeat; (min.) amalgamating mixture.

hormiguita, *f. dim.* small ant.

hormilla, *f. dim.* small last; buttonmold or core.

hormona, *f.* (physiol.) hormone.

hornabeque, *m.* (fort.) hornwork.

hornablenda, *f.* (min.) hornblende.

hornacero, *m.* (metal.) crucible man.

hornacina, *f.* (arch.) vaulted niche.

hornacho, *m.* shaft of a mine; furnace for casting statues.

hornachuela, *f.* cave or hut.

hornada, *f.* batch, bread baked at one time; melt (of a blast furnace).

hornaguear, *va.* to dig for coal.

hornaguera, *f.* pit coal, hard coal.

hornaguero, ra, *a.* wide, spacious; coal-bearing.

hornaje, *m.* fee for baking.

hornaza, *f.* jewellers' furnace; (art) light yellow color; yellow glazing.

hornazo, *m.* Easter cake ornamented with eggs; Easter present given to preacher.

hornear, *vn.* to carry on the trade of a baker.

hornería, *f.* trade of a baker.

hornero, ra, *n.* baker.

horniga, *f.* brushwood for an oven.

hornijero, ra, *n.* brushwood carrier.

hornilla, *f.* grated chamber in a masonry kitchen range; compartment in a pigeon cote for nesting; nest pan.

hornillo, *m. dim.* portable furnace or stove; (min.) blast hole; (mil.) fougade.—**h. de atanor,** self-feeding furnace.

hornito, *m.* (Mex.) mud volcano.

horno, *m.* oven; kiln; furnace; cavity in which bees lodge.—**h. boliche** = H. DE REVERBERO.

For pronunciation, see the rules at the beginning of the book.

—**h. de cal**, limekiln.—**h. de calcinación**, calcining furnace.—**h. de copela**, cupelling or cupellation furnace.—**h. de cuba**, blast furnace in general.—**h. de ladrillo**, brickkiln.—**h. de manga**, cupola furnace.—**h. de reverbero**, or **tostadillo**, Spanish furnace, or reverberatory furnace.—**h. eléctrico**, electric furnace.—**alto h.**, (high) blast furnace.

horometría, f. horometry, measurement of time.
horón, m. large round hamper.
horópter, m. (opt.) horopter.
horoptérico, ca, a. (opt.) horopteric.
horóptero, m. (opt.) horopter.
horóscopo, m. horoscope.
horqueta, f. dim. forked pole or stake; crotch of a tree; (Arg.) sharp turn of a stream or of the adjacent land.
horquilla, f. forked pole, bar, pipe, etc.; pitchfork, croom; hairpin; double-pointed tack; a disease causing the hair to split; upper extremity of the sternum; wish-bone; (surg.) fourchette; (mil.) fork rest; (naut.) oarlock; (vet.) frog of a horse's foot.—pl. (naut.) crutches, curbs.—**horquillas de dar fuego**, breaming forks.
horrendamente, adv. horribly.
horrendo, da, a. hideous, horrible, awful.
hórreo, m. barn, mow; granary built on pillars.
horrero, m. keeper of a granary.
horribilidad, f. dreadfulness, hideousness.
horribilísimo, a. super. most horrible.
horrible, a. horrid, horrible; hideous, heinous.
horriblemente, adv. horribly; heinously.
horridez, f. horridness.
hórrido, da, a. horrible; hideous.
horrífico, ca, a. (poet.) horrific, awful, horrid.
horripilación, f. dread, fright; (med.) horripilation, goose flesh.
horripilante, a. horrifying, harrowing.
horripilar. I. va. & vn. to cause or feel horror. II. vr. to be horrified.
horripilativo, va, a. (med.) causing goose flesh.
horrísono, na, a. (poet.) of a terrifying noise.
horro, ra, a. enfranchised, freed; not pregnant.
horror, m. horror; enormity, hideousness, frightfulness.
horrorizar. I. va. to horrify, terrify. II. vr. to be terrified.
horrorosamente, adv. horribly.
horroroso, sa, a. horrible; hideous, frightful.
horrura, f. filth, dirt, scoria, dross.
hortaliza, f. garden produce, vegetables.
hortatorio, ria, a. = EXHORTATORIO, hortatory.
hortecillo, m. dim. small garden.
horteiana, f. gardener's wife.
hortelano, na. I. a. HORTENSE. II. m. horticulturist; (ornith.) ortolan.
hortense, a. pert. to kitchen garden or orchard.
hortensia, f. (bot.) hydrangea.
hortera. I. f. wooden bowl. II. m. in Madrid, drygoods clerk.
horticultor, ra, n. horticulturist.
horticultura, f. horticulture.
horuelo, m. common; meeting place for young people.
hosanna, m. (eccl.) hosanna.
hosco, ca, a. dark-colored (as a mulatto); sullen, gloomy.
hoscoso, sa, a. crisp, rough.
hospedador, ra, n. one who gives lodging.
hospedaje, hospedamiento, m. lodging, board.
hospedar. I. va. to lodge, harbor. II. vn. & vr. (en) to lodge or take lodgings (at); to stop (at), live (in).
hospedería, f. hospice; hostel in universities; hostelry, inn; spare room, guest room; lodging.
hospedero, ra, n. host; innkeeper.
hospiciano, na, n. poor person who lives in a house of charity.
hospicio, m. hospice; poor house; orphan asylum.

hospital, m. hospital.—**h. de sangre**, (mil.) field hospital.—**hospitalario, ria**. I. a. hospitable. II. m. hospitaller.—**hospitalero, ra**, n. manager of a hospital; hospitaller; hospitable person.—**hospitalidad**, f. hospitality; stay in a hospital.—**hospitalizar**, va. to hospitalize.
hospitalmente, adv. hospitably.
hostal, m. hostelry, inn.
hostalero, ra, n. inn or tavern keeper, host(-ess).
hostelero, ra, n. innkeeper, tavern keeper.
hostería, f. inn, tavern, hostelry.
hostia, f. sacrificial victim; (eccl.) host, wafer; sugar wafer.—**hostiario**, m. wafer box.—**hostiero**, m. person who prepares the host.
hostigador, ra, a. = HOSTIGOSO.
hostigamiento, m. chastisement; vexation.
hostigar, va. (pret. HOSTIGUÉ; subj. HOSTIGUE) to lash, scourge, chastise; to vex, trouble, harass; to gall, bore, tire; (Am.) to satiate, become distasteful to.
hostigo, m. lash; weather-beaten wall; beating of rain and wind against a wall.—**hostigoso, sa**, a. (Chile & Guat.) tiresome, boring; satiating.
hostigué, hostigue, v. V. HOSTIGAR.
hostil, a. hostile.—**hostilidad**, f. hostility.
hostilizar, va. (pret. HOSTILICÉ; subj. HOSTILICE) to commit hostilities against, be hostile to, antagonize.
hostilmente, adv. with hostility.
hotel, m. hotel; villa.—**hotelero, ra**, n. hotel manager.
hotentote, ta, n. & a. Hottentot.
hovero, ra, a. = OVERO, peach-colored (horse).
hoy, adv. to-day; now, at the present time, nowadays.—**h. día**, or **h. en día**, nowadays.—**h. mismo**, this very day.—**h. por h.**, at the present time; for the present; this very day.—**de h. a mañana**, before to-morrow; when you least expect it.—**de h. en adelante**, or **de h. más**, henceforward, in future.—**por h.**, for the present.
hoya, f. hole, pit; grave; valley, dale, glen; basin (of a river).
hoyada, f. low dale.
hoyanca, f. potter's field in cemeteries.
hoyito, m. dim. small hole.
hoyo, m. hole, pit, excavation; dent, indentation, hollow; pockmark; grave.
hoyoso, sa, a. full of holes.
hoyuela, f. dim. of HOYA; hollow in the neck below Adam's apple.
hoyuelo, m. dim. small hole; dimple.
¹**hoz**, f. sickle.—**meter la h. en mies ajena**, to meddle in others' affairs.
²**hoz**, f. defile, narrow pass; ravine.—**de h. y de coz**, (coll.) headlong.
hozadero, m. hogs' rooting place.
hozadura, f. rooting (of hogs).
hozar, va. to root (as hogs).
huaca, f. = GUACA, Indian burying ground.
huacal, m. crate; (Mex.) hurdle basket.
huaco, m. idol found in HUACAS.
huaico, m. (Peru) large mass of rock fallen into a river or stream.
huairuro, m. Peruvian variety of red bean.
huaquero, m. (Peru) pitcher found in HUACAS.
huarache, m. (Mex.) sandal.
huasca, f. (Peru) whip, lash.
hube, hubo, v. V. HABER.
hucha, f. large chest; money box, bank; savings.
huchear, va. to hoot, shout, cry out, call.
¡**húchohó!** interj. used to call birds.
huebra, f. ground plowed in one day by a yoke of oxen; pair of mules with a plowman hired for a day's work.—**huebrero**, m. laborer who plows with a pair of mules; one who lets out mules by the day.
hueca, f. spiral groove of a spindle.
hueco, ca. I. a. hollow; empty; vain, emptyheaded; resonant; inflated; soft, spongy (as

ground or wool). **II.** *m.* hole; hollow, gap, void, break; notch or nick of a wheel; interval of time or space; vacancy.

huecú, *m.* (Chile) deep slough covered with grass.

huélfago, *m.* (of animals) difficulty in breathing.

huelga, *f.* rest, repose, leisure; strike (of workers); recreation, merrymaking; (agr.) lying fallow; (mech.) windage.—**h. sentada,** sit-down strike.

¹**huelgo,** *m.* breath, respiration; (mech.) windage; room, space, play.—**tomar h.,** to take breath.

²**huelgo, huelgue,** *v. V.* HOLGAR.

huelguista, *n.* striker.

huelguístico, ca, *a.* (workers') strike (as *a.*).

huelo, huela, etc., *v. V.* OLER.

huella, *f.* track, footstep, footprint; tread; trampling; stair tread, treadboard; impression; trace, vestige, trail.

¹**huello,** *m.* treading; lower part of an animal's hoof.

²**huello, huelle,** *v. V.* HOLLAR.

huequecito, *m. dim.* small hole or space.

huérfago, *m.* (vet.) = HUÉLFAGO.

huerfanito, ita, *n. dim.* little orphan.

huérfano, na, *n. & a.* orphan(-ed).

huero, ra, *a.* empty, vain; (Mex.) fair, blonde.

huerta, *f.* large vegetable or kitchen garden; irrigated land.

huertezuela, *f. dim.* small kitchen garden.

huertezuelo, *m. dim.* small orchard.

huerto, *m.* orchard, fruit garden.

huesa, *f.* grave, tomb.

huesarrón, *m. aug.* large bone.

huesecico, illo, ito, *m. dim.* little bone.

hueso, *m.* bone; stone, core; part of a limestone which remains unburnt in the kiln; drudge, drudgery.—**h. innominado,** innominate bone. —**h. navicular,** scaphoid, or navicular, bone. —**h. palomo,** coccyx.—**h. sacro,** (anat.) sacrum.—**a h.,** (mason.) dry (without mortar). —**a otro perro con ese h.,** tell that to the marines.—**estar en los huesos,** to be very thin, nothing but skin and bones.—**la sin h.,** the tongue.—**no dejar h. sano a,** (fig.) to rake over the coals.

huesoso, sa, *a.* bony, osseous.

huésped, da, *n.* guest, lodger; host(-ess) innkeeper, tavern keeper.

hueste, *f.* host, army.

huesudo, da, *a.* bony, having large bones.

hueva, *f.* spawn of fishes, roe. Also OVAS, *pl.*

huevar, *vn.* (of poultry) to begin to lay.

huevecico, illo, ito, zuelo, *m. dim.* small egg.

huevera, *f.* ovary of birds; egg stand, egg cup.

huevería, *f.* egg shop.

huevero, ra, *n.* egg dealer.

huevo, *m.* egg; (shoe) hollow piece of wood for shaping the sole.—**h. de Colón,** or **de juanelo,** anything that seems difficult to do, but is easy after one learns how to do it.—**h. duro,** hard (boiled, fried) egg.—**huevos de faltriquera,** candied yolks of egg.—**huevos escalfados,** poached eggs.—**huevos estrellados,** fried eggs. —**huevos hilados,** threadlike sweetmeat made of eggs and sugar.—**huevos moles,** yolks of eggs made up with pounded almonds and sugar. —**huevos pasados por agua,** soft-boiled eggs.—**huevos revueltos,** scrambled eggs.— **huevos y torreznos,** bacon and eggs.—**sórbete,** or **chúpate, ese h.,** (coll.) put that in your pipe and smoke it.

hugonote, ta, *n. & a.* Huguenot.

huída, *f.* flight, escape; outlet.

huidero, *m.* cover, shelter; laborer in quick-silver mines.

huidizo, za, *a.* fugitive, fleeing.

huillín, *m.* a kind of Chilean otter.

huipil, *m.* (Am.) Aztec woman's garment.

huir. I. *vn. & vr.* (*ger.* HUYENDO; *ind. pres.* HUYO; *pret.* él HUYÓ; *subj.* HUYA) to flee, to escape; to run away, elope; to slip away, fly; (**de**) to keep

away (from), shun, avoid. **II.** *va.* to avoid, shun. —**h. la cara de,** to avoid, keep away from.

hule, *m.* oilcloth, oilskin; (Am.) India rubber.

hulero, *m.* rubber gatherer.

hulla, *f.* mineral (gen. bituminous) coal.—**h. aglutinante,** coking coal.—**h. blanca,** white coal (water).—**h. conglutinante,** coking coal. —**h. grasa,** fat coal.—**h. magra,** non-coking coal.

hullero, ra. I. *a.* containing or pertaining to soft coal. **II.** *f.* colliery.

humada, *f.* = AHUMADA, smoke signal from coast.

humanamente, *adv.* humanely; humanly.

humanar. I. *va.* to humanize; to soften. **II.** *vr.* to become man; to become human.

humanidad, *f.* humanity; mankind; human weakness; humaneness; (coll.) corpulence, fleshiness.—*pl.* humanities.

humanista, *n.* humanist, scholar.

humanitario, ria, *a.* humanitarian.

humanizar, *va. & vr.* = HUMANAR.

humano, na. I. *a.* human; humane. **II.** *m.* man, human being.

humarazo, *m.* = HUMAZO.

humareda, *f.* a great deal of smoke.

humazga, *f.* hearth money, fumage.

humazo, *m.* dense and abundant smoke.

humeante, *a.* smoking, fuming, fumant.

humear. I. *vn.* to smoke, emit smoke, fumes, or vapors. **II.** *va.* (Am.) to fumigate.

humectación, *f.* dampening.

humectante, *a.* (med.) moistening.

humectar, *va.* (med.) to moisten, wet.—**humectativo, va,** *a.* moistening.

humedad, *f.* humidity, moisture, dampness.

humedal, *m.* humid soil, marsh.

humedecer, *va.* (*ind.* HUMEDEZCO; *subj.* HUMEDEZCA) to moisten, dampen.

húmedo, da, *a.* humid, wet, moist, damp.

humera, *f.* (coll.) fit of drunkenness.

humeral, *a.* (anat.) humeral.

húmero, *m.* (anat.) humerus.

humero, *m.* smoke pipe; chimney flue; meat-smoking place; much smoke.

húmido, da, *a.* = HÚMEDO.

humildad, *f.* humility; meekness; lowliness.

humilde, *a.* humble; meek; lowly.

humildemente, *adv.* humbly, modestly, meekly.

humillación, *f.* humiliation; humbling.

humilladero, *m.* road chapel or shrine.

humillador, ra, *n. & a.* humiliator(-ing).

humillante, *a.* humiliating.

humillar. I. *va.* to humiliate; humble; crush, subdue. **II.** *vr.* to humble oneself; to lower oneself.

humillo, *m. dim.* (gen. *pl.*) vanity, petty pride; a disease of suckling pigs.

humita, *f.* (Peru) cake of maize and sugar.

humo, *m.* smoke; vapor, steam, fume.—*pl.* families or houses in a town or village; airs, conceit. —**echar humos,** to put on airs.

humor, *m.* humor, wit; disposition, temper; (physiol.) body fluid.—**h. acuoso,** (physiol.) aqueous humor.—**buen h.,** good nature, jovial disposition.—**estar de buen (mal) h.,** to be in good (bad) humor or spirits.—**mal h.,** ill temper.

humorada, *f.* pleasant joke, humorous saying.

humorado, da, *a.* full of humors.—**bien (mal) h.,** in good (bad) humor; having a good (bad) temper.

humoral, *a.* (physiol.) pert. to body fluid.

humorcico, illo, ito, *m. dim.* little temper.

humorismo, *m.* humor (esp. in literary style); (anc. med.) humorism.

humorístico, ca, *a.* jolly, humorous, facetious.

humorosidad, *f.* abundance of humors.

humoroso, sa, *a.* watery, containing fluid.

humoso, sa, *a.* smoky, fumy.

humus, *m.* humus.

hundible, *a.* sinkable.

hundimiento, *m.* sinking; cave-in; downfall, collapse.

hundir. I. *va.* to submerge, sink; stave in, crush; destroy, ruin; to refute, confound. **II.** *vr.* to sink, be sinking; to cave in, fall down, crumble, collapse; (coll.) to hide, lie in hiding, disappear.

húngaro, ra, *n.* & *a.* Hungarian.

huno, na, *n.* & *a.* Hun(-nish).

hupe, *f.* punk, touchwood, amadou.

hura, *f.* carbuncle on the head.

huracán, *m.* hurricane.—**huracanado, da,** *a.* of hurricane proportions.

hurañamente, *adv.* unsociably, shyly.

hurañería, huraña, *f.* unsociability; shyness.

huraño, ña, *a.* unsociable, shy.

hurgar, *va.* (*pret.* HURGUÉ; *subj.* HURGUE) to stir, to poke; to stir up, excite.—**peor es hurgallo,** let well enough alone.

hurgón, *m.* poker, fire rake; (coll.) thrust with a sword.—**hurgonada,** *f.* poking (the fire); thrust.—**hurgonazo,** *m.* blow with a poker; thrust.—**hurgonear,** *va.* to poke (the fire); (coll.) to make a thrust at.—**hurgonero,** *m.* fire poker.

hurgué, hurgue, *v.* *V.* HURGAR.

hurí, *f.* houri.

hurón, na. I. *n.* (zool.) ferret; (coll.) ferreter, prier. **II.** *a.* unsociable, shy.—**huronear,** *va.* to hunt with a ferret; (coll.) to pry into; to ferret out.—**huronera,** *f.* ferret hole; (coll.) lurking-place; small dark room.—**huronero,** *m.* ferret keeper.

¡hurra! *interj.* hurrah!

hurraca, *f.* (ornith.) magpie.

hurtadillas—**a h.,** *adv.* by stealth, on the sly.

hurtadineros, *m.* money box, toy bank.

hurtador, ra, *n.* robber, thief.

hurtagua, *f.* watering pot.

hurtar. I. *va.* to steal, rob of, to cheat in weight or measure; to eat away (land, as the sea or a river); to alienate.—**h. el cuerpo,** to flee; to dodge, shy away. **II.** *vr.* to withdraw, move away; to hide.

hurto, *m.* theft, robbery, stealing; thing stolen; (min.) driftway, heading.—**a h.,** by stealth.

husada, *f.* spindleful of yarn.

húsar, *m.* (mil.) hussar.

husero, *m.* beam of an antler.

husillero, *m.* one who tends the spindle in oil mills.

¹husillo, *m.* *dim.* small spindle; (mill) wheel spindle or shaft; screw pin.

²husillo, *m.* (dirty water) drain.

husita, *n.* Hussite.

husma.—**andar a la h.,** (coll.) to explore in a prying manner, to nose about.

husmeador, ra, *n.* & *a.* scenter(-ing); prier(-ing), noser(-ing, -y).

husmear. I. *va.* to scent, smell, wind; (coll.) to pry, peep, nose into. **II.** *vn.* (of meat) to become tainted, gamey, or high.

husmeo, *m.* scenting, smelling; prying, nosing.

husmo, *m.* taint of meat.—**estar al h.,** (coll.) to be on the scent; to wait or watch for a favorable opportunity.

huso, *m.* spindle; cop tube; bobbin; drum of a windlass; (aer.) fuselage.

huta, *f.* hut, hunter's blind.

hutía, *f.* (zool.) hutia, a West-Indian rodent.

¡huy! *interj.* of surprise, astonishment, grief or alarm.

huyo, huya, huyó, etc. *v.* *V.* HUIR.

I

i, *conj.* (in some parts of S. A.) and.

iba, *imperf.* of IR.

iberamericano, na, *a.* & *n.* (Am.) = IBERO-AMERICANO.

ibérico, ca, *a.*; **iberio, ria,** *a.*; **ibero, ra,** *n.* & *a.* Iberian.

iberoamericano, na, *n.* & *a.* Latin-American.

íbice, *m.* ibex, a kind of goat.

ibídem, *adv.* ibidem, in the same place.

ibis, *f.* (ornith.) ibis, a wading bird.

ibiyaú, *m.* an Argentine night bird.

ibón, *m.* lake or basin on the slopes of the Pyrenees.

icaco, *m.* (bot.) coco plum.

icario, a, *a.* Icarian.

icástico, ca, *a.* natural, plain, unadorned.

icneumón, *m.* (zool.) ichneumon.

icnografía, *f.* (arch.) ichnography.

icnográfico, ca, *a.* ichnographical.

icón, icono, *m.* icon.

iconoclasta, *m.* iconoclast.

iconografía, *f.* iconography.

iconográfico, ca, *a.* iconographical.

iconólatra, *m.* iconolater, worshipper of icons.

iconología, *f.* (art) iconology.

iconómaco, a. iconoclastic.

iconostasio, *m.* (eccl.) iconostasis, altar screen.

icor, *m.* (med.) watery discharge (as from a wound).

icoroso, sa, *a.* ichorous, serous.

icosaedro, *m.* (geom.) icosahedron.

ictericia, *f.* (med.) icterus, jaundice.—**ictericiado, da;** **ictérico, ca,** *a.* icteric, jaundiced.

ictíneo, *m.* submarine vessel.

ictiófago, ga, *a.* & *n.* fish-eating (one).

ictiol, *m.* (chem.) ichthyol.

ictiología, *f.* ichthyology.

ictiológico, ca, *a.* ichthyologic.

ictiólogo, m. ichthyologist.

ictiornis, *m.* (paleontol.) ichthyornis.

ictiosauro, m. ichthyosaurus.

ictiosis, *f.* ichthyosis.

ida, *f.* departure; trip out; impetuosity; rash proceeding; sally; trail.—**i. del humo,** departure never to return.—**i. y vuelta,** out and back, round trip, excursion.—**idas,** frequent visits.—**idas y venidas,** comings and goings.—**de i. y vuelta,** return (ticket).—**en dos idas y venidas,** (coll.) in a jiffy.—**¡la i. del cuervo!** he's off, good riddance!

idea, *f.* idea.

ideación, *f.* (philos.) ideation.

ideal, *a.* & *m.* ideal.—**idealidad,** *f.* ideality.—**idealismo,** *m.* idealism.—**idealista,** *n.* & *a.* idealist(-ic).—**idealizar,** *va.* to idealize.—**idealmente,** *adv.* ideally.

idear, *va.* to conceive the idea of; to devise, contrive, plan, design.

ideático, ca, *a.* (Am.) whimsical, capricious.

ídem, idem, ditto, the same.

idénticamente, *adv.* identically.

idéntico, ca, *a.* (a) identic, identical (with).

identidad, *f.* identity.—**de i.,** identification (as *a.*).

identificación, *f.* identification.

identificar, (*pret.* IDENTIFIQUÉ; *subj.* IDENTIFIQUE). **I.** *va.* to identify. **II.** *vr.* (con) to identify oneself (with).

ideo, ea, *a.* pertaining to Mount Ida.

ideografía, *f.* ideography.

ideográfico, ca, *a.* ideographic.

ideograma, *m.* ideogram.

ideología, *f.* ideology.

ideológico, ca, *a.* ideological.

ideólogo, *m.* ideologist.

idílico, ca, *a.* idyllic.

idilio, *m.* idyl.

idioma, *m.* language, tongue.

idiomático, ca, *a.* idiomatic.

idiosincrasia, *f.* idiosyncrasy.

idiosincrásico, ca, *a.* idiosyncratic.

idiota, *n.* & *a.* idiot(-ic).—**idiotez,** *f.* idiocy.

idiotismo, *m.* idiocy; ignorance; idiom.
ido, *pp.* of IR.
idólatra. I. *a.* idolatrous; heathen. **II.** *n.* idolater; (coll.) ardent lover.
idolatradamente, *adv.* idolatrously.
idolatrar, *va.* to idolize, worship, adore.
idolatría, *f.* idolatry; idolization.
idolátrico, ca, *a.* idolatrous.
ídolo, *m.* idol.
idolología, *f.* science dealing with idols.
idoneidad, *f.* competence, fitness, capacity.
idóneo, nea, *a.* competent; fit, able.
idumeo, a, *n.* & *a.* Idumean.
idus, *m.* ides.
iglesia, *f.* church; ecclesiastical state; clergy; chapter; diocese; right of immunity enjoyed in churches.—**i. colegial,** collegiate church.—**i. matriz,** metropolitan church.—**i. mayor,** main church; cathedral (where there is one).—**i. militante,** church militant, the (Christian) living faithful.—**i. oriental,** Greek church.—**i. triunfante,** church triumphant.—**llevar a una mujer a la iglesia,** to take a woman to the altar (to marry her).
ignaro, ra, *a.* ignorant.
ignavia, *f.* idleness, laziness, carelessness.
ígneo, ea, *a.* igneous.
ignición, *f.* ignition.
ignífero, ra, *a.* igniferous, fire-bearing.
ignífugo, ga, *a.* fireproofing.
ignipotente, *a.* (poet.) ignipotent.
ignito, ta, *a.* ignited, inflamed, red-hot.
ignívomo, ma, *a.* (poet.) vomiting fire.
ignografía, *f.* = ICNOGRAFÍA.
ignominia, *f.* ignominy, infamy, disgrace.
ignominiosamente, *adv.* ignominiously.
ignominioso, sa, *a.* ignominious.
ignorado, da. I. *pp.* of IGNORAR. **II.** *a.* unknown, hidden; fameless, obscure.
ignorancia, *f.* ignorance.—**i. crasa,** crass ignorance.—**i. no quita pecado,** ignorance of the law is no defense.—**i. supina,** ignorance from negligence.
ignorante. I. *a.* ignorant. **II.** *n.* ignoramus.—**ignorantemente,** *adv.* ignorantly.—**ignorantón, na. I.** *a.* *aug.* rather ignorant. **II.** *n.* ignoramus.
ignorar, *va.* to be ignorant of, not to know.
ignoto, ta, *a.* unknown, undiscovered.
igorrote, *m.* Igorrot, Luzon hunting tribesman; Igorrot language.
igual. I. *a.* equal; level, even, uniform; equable; constant, firm, unchangeable, consistent.—**i. que** (common but incorrect for *igual a*), equal to, the same as.—**(me) es i.,** it is all the same (to me), it makes no difference (to me). **II.** *m.* equal; (math.) equal sign (=).—**al i.,** equally. —**al i. que,** the same as, as well as.—**en i. de,** instead of, in lieu of.—**por i.,** or **por un i.,** equally; evenly.—**serle a uno i.,** to be all the same, a matter of indifference, to one.—**sin i.,** unrivaled, matchless; without parallel.
iguala, *f.* agreement, convention, stipulation; equalizing, equalization; (mason.) level; stipend or gratuity on agreement.—**a la i.,** equally.
igualación, *f.* equalizing, equalization; levelling, smoothing; matching; agreement, stipulation; (math.) equating; (carp.) countergauge.
igualado, da. I. *pp.* of IGUALAR. **II.** *a.* equalled (said of birds with even plumage).
igualador, ra, *n.* & *a.* equalizer(-ing); smoother (-ing), leveller(-ing).
igualamiento, *m.* = IGUALACIÓN.
igualar. I. *va.* to equalize; to match, mate, pair; to even, level, smooth; to size, face, adjust, fit; to hold in equal estimation; to adjust; (math.) to equate. **II.** *vn.* to be equal; (sports) to be tied (in score). **III.** *vr.* (a, con) to put oneself on the same plane (as), compare oneself (with).
igualdad, *f.* equality; evenness, smoothness,

regularity, uniformity.—**i. de ánimo,** evenness of disposition; constancy, equability, equanimity.—**signo de la i.,** (math.) equal sign.
igualitario, ria, *a.* equalizing; equitable.
igualmente, *adv.* equally; likewise; constantly.
iguana, *f.* (zool.) iguana.
iguanodonte, *m.* (zool.) iguanodon.
igüedo, *m.* buck (goat).
ijada, *f.* flank (of an animal); pain in the side; colic—**tener su i.,** to have a weak side or point.
ijadear, *vn.* to pant; to palpitate.
ijar, *m.* flank (of an animal).
ilación, *f.* illation, inference; connectedness.
ilativo, va, *a.* illative, inferential.
ilegal, *a.* illegal, unlawful.
ilegalidad, *f.* illegality, unlawfulness.
ilegalmente, *adv.* illegally, unlawfully.
ilegible, *a.* illegible.
ilegítimamente, *adv.* illegitimately; foully.
ilegitimar, *va.* to make illegitimate.
ilegitimidad, *f.* illegitimacy.
ilegítimo, ma, *a.* illegal, unlawful; illegitimate.
íleo, *m.* (med.) ileus, colic.
¹íleon, *m.* (anat.) ileum, part of intestine.
²íleon, *m.* (anat.) = ILION.
ileso, sa, *a.* unhurt, unscathed; harmless; sound.
iletrado, da, *a.* ignorant, uncultured.
¹ilíaco, ca, *a.* iliac, pert. to the ilium.
²ilíaco, ca, *a.* pertaining to Ilium (Troy).
Ilíada, *f.* Iliad.
iliberal, *a.* illiberal.
ilicíneo, a, *a.* (bot.) ilicineous.
ilícitamente, *adv.* illicitly, unlawfully.
ilícito, ta, *a.* illicit; unlawful; immoral.
ilimitable, *a.* illimitable.
ilimitado, da, *a.* unlimited, boundless; unrestricted.
ilion, *m.* (anat.) ilium.
ilíquido, da, *a.* unliquidated.
ilírico, ca; ilirio, ria, *n.* & *a.* Illyrian.
iliterato, *a.* illiterate, unlearned.
ilógico, ca, *a.* illogical.
ilota, *m.* helot.—**ilotismo,** *m.* helotism.
iludir, *va.* to elude.
iluminación, *f.* illumination, lighting; (art) painting in distemper.
iluminado, da. I. *pp.* of ILUMINAR. **II.** *a.* illuminate, enlightened. **III.** *m. pl.* illuminati.
iluminador, ra, *n.* & *a.* lighter(-ing); illuminator(-ing).
iluminar, *va.* to illumine, illuminate, light; to color, illumine (books); to enlighten.
iluminaria, *f.* = LUMINARIA, illumination.
iluminativo, va, *a.* illuminating.
iluminismo, *m.* Illuminism.
ilusión, *f.* illusion.—**hacerse ilusiones sobre,** to bank on.—**tener ilusiones de** (*inf.*), to have hopes of (*pres. p.*).
ilusionar. I. *va.* to cause illusion, fascinate. **II.** *vr.* (con) to have illusions; to get up hopes (of).
ilusivo, va, *a.* illusive, false, deceiving.
iluso, sa, *a.* deluded, deceived, beguiled.
ilusoriamente, *adv.* illusively, illusorily.
ilusorio, ria, *a.* illusory, deceptive; (law) null, void, nugatory.
ilustración, *f.* illustration; learning, erudition; elucidation, explanation; enlightment; learning; illustrated or pictorial publication.
ilustrado, da. I. *pp.* of ILUSTRAR. **II.** *a.* illustrated, picture (as *a.*); learned, well-informed.
ilustrador, ra, *n.* illustrator.
ilustrar. I. *va.* to illustrate (a publication); to enlighten; to explain, elucidate; (theol.) to give divine light to, to inspire. **II.** *vr.* to educate oneself, to acquire knowledge, learn; to become illustrious.
ilustrativo, va, *a.* illustrative.
ilustre, *a.* illustrious, distinguished.
ilustremente, *adv.* illustriously.

ilustrísimo, ma, *a. super.* very illustrious, most illustrious (title given to bishops).

imadas, *f. pl.* (naut.) ways, sliding planks.

imagen, *f.* image.—**i. de bulto,** image in sculpture; high relief.

imaginable, *a.* imaginable.

imaginación, *f.* imagination; imagining.

imaginar. I. *va.* to imagine; to think up, figure out; to think, suspect. **II.** *vr.* to imagine; to suspect: to picture to oneself, often used imperatively in a somewhat expletive or emphatic manner, in the sense of "just think," "just imagine," "why," etc. (*imagínese Vd. que no teníamos ni un centavo,* just think, we did not have a cent; *imagínese Vd. que allá hasta los niños fuman,* why, there even children smoke).

imaginaria, *f.* (mil.) reserve guard; (math.) imaginary.

imaginariamente, *adv.* imaginatively.

imaginario, ria, *a.* imaginary, imagined; (math.) imaginary.

imaginativa, *f.* imagination, fancy.

imaginativo, va, *a.* imaginative, fanciful.

imaginería, *f.* imagery, fancy embroidery in colors; (art) statuary.

imaginero, *m.* painter or sculptor of religious images.

¹imán, *m.* iman, a Mohammedan priest.

²imán, *m.* magnet; magnetism, charm.

imanación, *f.* magnetization.

imanar, *va.* to magnetize.

imantación, *f.* = IMANACIÓN.

imantar, *va.* = IMANAR.

imbécil, *n. & a.* imbecile.

imbecilidad, *f.* imbecility, stupidity.

imbele, *a.* feeble, weak; unfit for war.

imberbe, *a.* beardless.

imbibición, *f.* imbibition, imbibing.

imbornal, *m.* (naut.) scupper hole.

imborrable, *a.* indelible, ineffaceable.

imbricación, *f.* imbrication, overlapping.

imbricado, da, *a.* imbricated, overlapped.

imbuir, *va.* (*ind.* IMBUYO; *subj.* IMBUYA) to imbue, infuse, persuade.

imbursación, *f.* putting into a sack.

imbursar, *va.* to put into a sack or bag.

imbuyo, imbuya, *v.* V. IMBUIR.

imitable, *a.* imitable.

imitación, *f.* imitation.

imitado, da. I. *pp.* of IMITAR. **II.** *a.* imitation (as *a.*), mock.

imitador, ra; imitante, *n. & a.* imitator(-ing).

imitar, *va.* to imitate; to mimic; to ape; to counterfeit.

imitativo, va, *a.* imitative (as arts).

imóscapo, *m.* (arch.) apophyge.

impacción, *f.* impact, collision.

impaciencia, *f.* impatience.

impacientar. I. *va.* to vex, irritate, make (one) lose patience. **II.** *vr.* to become impatient.

impaciente, *a.* impatient; anxious; peevish.

impacientemente, *adv.* impatiently, anxiously; peevishly.

impacto, *m.* impact.

impagable, *a.* unpayable.

impalpabilidad, *f.* impalpability.

impalpable, *a.* impalpable.

impar, *a.* unmatched, odd; (arith.) odd.

imparcial, *a.* impartial.—**imparcialidad,** *f.* impartiality.—**imparcialmente,** *adv.* impartially.

impartible, *a.* indivisible.

impartir, *va.* to impart; (law) to demand or require (assistance).

impasable, *a.* impassable.

impasibilidad, *f.* impassiveness.

impasible, *a.* impassive, unmoved.

impávidamente, *adv.* undauntedly, calmly.

impavidez, *f.* intrepidity, calm, composure.

impávido, da, *a.* dauntless, intrepid, calm.

impecabilidad, *f.* impeccability.

impecable, *a.* impeccable.

impedido, da. I. *pp.* of IMPEDIR. **II.** *a.* disabled, crippled.

impedidor, ra, *m.* obstructor.

impediente, *a.* hindering, obstructing.

impedimenta, *f.* (mil.) impedimenta.

impedimento, *m.* impediment; obstacle, hindrance, encumbrance.

impedir, *va.* (*ind.* IMPIDO; *subj.* IMPIDA) to impede, hinder, prevent; to block (the way); (poet.) to suspend.

impeditivo, va, *a.* impeding, hindering.

impelente, *a.* forcing, impelling, propelling.

impeler, *va.* to push, impel, drive; to spur, urge, incite, move.

impender, *va.* to spend, invest.

impenetrabilidad, *f.* impenetrability.

impenetrable, *a.* impenetrable, impervious; incomprehensible; fathomless.

impenitencia, *f.* impenitence.

impenitente, *a.* impenitent, obdurate.

impensa, *f.* (law) expense.

impensadamente, *adv.* unexpectedly; inadvertently.

impensado, da, *a.* unexpected, unforeseen.

imperante, *a.* commanding; (astrol.) ruling.

imperar, *vn.* to command; to reign; to prevail.

imperativamente, *adv.* imperatively.

imperativo, va. I. *a.* imperative; domineering, "bossy." **II.** *n. & a.* (gram.) imperative.

imperatoria, *f.* (bot.) masterwort.

imperatorio, ria, *a.* imperial.

imperceptible, *a.* imperceptible.

imperceptiblemente, *adv.* imperceptibly.

imperdible. I. *a.* that cannot be lost. **II.** *m.* safety pin.

imperdonable, *a.* unpardonable, unforgivable.

imperecedero, ra, *a.* imperishable, undying.

imperfección, *f.* imperfection, defect, fault, flaw.

imperfectamente, *adv.* imperfectly, inadequately.

imperfecto, ta. I. *a.* imperfect, defective, faulty. **II.** *n. & a.* (gram.) imperfect.

imperforación, *f.* (med.) imperforation.

imperial. I. *a.* imperial. **II.** *f.* coach top; top seats on a stage-coach; (naut.) poop royal.

imperialismo, *m.* imperialism.

imperialista, *n. & a.* imperialist(-ic).

impericia, *f.* unskilfulness, inexpertness.

imperio, *m.* empire; dominion, command, sway; dignity of an emperor.

imperiosamente, *adv.* imperiously, overbearingly.

imperiosidad, *f.* imperiousness.

imperioso, sa, *a.* imperious, overbearing.

imperitamente, *adv.* unskilfully.

imperito, ta, *a.* unskilled, inexpert.

impermeabilidad, *f.* impermeability, condition of being water-tight or waterproof.

impermeabilizar, *va.* to make waterproof.

impermeable. I. *a.* water-tight, impervious, waterproof. **II.** *m.* waterproof garment, mackintosh, raincoat.

impermutable, *a.* unexchangeable.

impersonal, *a.* impersonal.—**en,** or **por, i.,** impersonally.

impersonalizar, *va.* (gram.) to use impersonally.

impersonalmente, *adv.* impersonally.

impersuasible, *a.* not susceptible of persuasion.

impertérrito, ta, *a.* intrepid, dauntless, serene.

impertinencia, *f.* impertinence, folly, nonsense; peevishness; intrusion; minute accuracy.

impertinente. I. *a.* not pertinent; impertinent, importunate, meddlesome. **II.** *m. pl.* lorgnette.

impertinentemente, *adv.* impertinently.

imperturbabilidad, *f.* imperturbability.

imperturbable, *a.* imperturbable.

imperturbablemente, *adv.* imperturbably.

impetra, *f.* diploma, license, permission; (eccl.) bull granting dubious benefices.

impetrable, *a.* (law) impetrable.

impetración, *f.* impetration; entreaty.

impetrado, da. I. *pp.* of IMPETRAR. **II.** *a.* impetrate, impetrated, granted.

impetrador, ra, *n.* one who entreats.

impetrante. I. *a.* entreating, beseeching. **II.** *m.* (law) grantee; impetrator.

impetrar, *va.* to entreat, impetrate, obtain by entreaty.

ímpetu, *m.* impetus, impulse; impetuosity.

impetuosamente, *adv.* impetuously.

impetuosidad, *f.* impetuosity.

impetuoso, sa, *a.* impetuous, impulsive, violent.

impíamente, *adv.* impiously.

impido, impida, *v.* V. IMPEDIR.

impiedad, *f.* impiety; irreligion, infidelity.

impiedoso, sa, *a.* impious, irreligious.

impiísimo, ma, *a.* *super.* very impious.

impío, pía. I. *a.* impious; irreligious, godless. **II.** *n.* impious person; infidel, enemy of religion.

impla, *f.* wimple; material for wimples.

implacabilidad, *f.* implacability.

implacable, *a.* implacable; inexorable.

implacablemente, *adv.* implacably.

implantación, *f.* implantation, introduction (of new ideas, systems, etc.).

implantar, *va.* to implant, to introduce.

implantón, *m.* piece of timber.

implaticable, *a.* not fit to talk about, unmentionable.

implicación, *f.* contradiction.

implicante, *a.* contradictory; implicating.

implicar. I. *va.* to implicate, involve, entangle. **II.** *vn.* to imply contradiction.

implicatorio, ria, *a.* implying contradiction, contradictory.

implícitamente, *adv.* implicitly.

implícito, ta, *a.* implicit.

imploración, *f.* imploration.

implorante, *a.* imploring, entreating.

implorar, *va.* to implore, entreat, beg.

implume, *a.* unfeathered.

impolítica, *f.* incivility, discourtesy; indiscretion, tactlessness.

impolíticamente, *adv.* impolitically, unwisely.

impolítico, ca, *a.* impolitic, indiscreet, imprudent, unwise, untactful.

impoluto, ta, *a.* unpolluted, pure, untarnished.

imponderabilidad, *f.* imponderability.

imponderable, *a.* imponderable; beyond all praise, most excellent.

imponedor, ra, *n.* imposer, assessor.

imponente, *a.* imposing.

imponer. I. *va.* (*pp.* IMPUESTO; *ind. pres.* IMPONGO, *pret.* IMPUSE, *fut.* IMPONDRÉ; *subj.* IMPONGA) to impose or levy (as a tax, a penalty); to impute falsely; to advise, give notice, acquaint; to inspire, arouse, command (respect, fear); (print.) to impose. **II.** *vr.* (a), to assert oneself, impose one's authority (on), dominate, get one's way; to be imperative or necessary; to command respect.

imponible, *a.* taxable, dutiable.

impopular, *a.* unpopular.

impopularidad, *f.* unpopularity.

importable, *a.* (com.) importable.

importación, *f.* (com.) importation, imports.

importador, ra, *n.* & *a.* importer(-ing).

importancia, *f.* importance.

importante, *a.* important.

importantemente, *adv.* importantly, materially.

importar. I. *vn.* to be important; to concern.—**eso no importa,** that doesn't matter.—**eso no le importa a Vd.,** that does not concern you; that is none of your business.—**eso no me importa,** I don't care (about that); that makes no difference to me.—**no importa,** no matter, never mind.—**¿qué importa?** what does it

matter? what difference does it make? **II.** *va.* to import; to amount to; to be worth; to imply.

importe, *m.* (com.) amount; price, cost, value.—**i. medio,** average amount.

importunación, *f.* importunity.

importunadamente, *adv.* importunately.

importunador, ra, *n.* & *a.* importuner(-ing), pesterer(-ing).

importunamente, *adv.* inopportunely; importunately, persistently.

importunar, *va.* to importune, pester.

importunidad, *f.* importunity, importunacy.

importuno, na, *a.* inopportune; importunate, persistent, vexatious, annoying.

imposibilidad, *f.* impossibility.

imposibilitado. I. *pp.* of IMPOSIBILITAR. **II.** *a.* helpless, without means, poor; disabled, unfit for service.

imposibilitar, *va.* to disable, unfit for service.

imposible, *a.* impossible.—**i. de toda imposibilidad,** (coll.) altogether impossible.—**los imposibles,** a kind of Spanish dance.

imposiblemente, *adv.* impossibly.

imposición, *f.* imposition (of a duty, etc.); tax, duty, tribute, burden; (print.) imposition.—**i. de manos,** (eccl.) imposition, laying on of hands.

imposta, *f.* (arch.) impost; springer; fascia.

impostor, ra, *n.* impostor.

impostura, *f.* imputation; imposture.

impotable, *a.* unpotable, undrinkable.

impotencia, *f.* impotence.

impotente, *a.* impotent.

impracticable, *a.* impracticable; impassable.

imprecación, *f.* imprecation.

imprecar, *va.* to imprecate.

imprecatorio, ria, *a.* imprecatory.

impregnación, *f.* impregnation.

impregnar. I. *va.* to impregnate, saturate. **II.** *vr.* to become impregnated.

impremeditación, *f.* unpremeditation.

impremeditado, da, *a.* unpremeditated.

imprenta, *f.* printing; printing office or house; print; press.—**libertad de i.,** freedom of the press.

imprescindible, *a.* essential, imperative, indispensable.

imprescindiblemente, *adv.* necessarily, unavoidably; absolutely.

imprescriptible, *a.* imprescriptible.

impresión, *f.* impression; impress, stamping, stamp; print, printing, presswork; edition, issue; footprint; influence, moral or physical effect.—**i. digital,** fingerprint.

impresionable, *a.* emotional, impressionable.

impresionar. I. *va.* to impress, fix on the mind or memory; to affect, influence; (photog.) to effect chemical changes on (a plate) by exposure to light; to cut (phon. record). **II.** *vr.* to be moved.

impresionismo, *m.* (art) impressionism.

impresionista, *n.* & *a.* (art) impressionist(-ic).

impreso, sa. I. *pp. irreg.* of IMPRIMIR. **II.** *a.* printed; stamped. **III.** *m.* pamphlet; publication; printed matter, print.

impresor, ra. I. *n.* printer. **II.** *f.* printer's wife.

imprestable, *a.* that cannot be lent.

imprevisión, *f.* lack of foresight; improvidence; inadvertency, oversight, thoughtlessness.

imprevisto, ta. I. *a.* unforeseen, unexpected. **II.** *m. pl.* incidental or unforeseen expenses.

imprimación, *f.* (art) priming; stuff for priming.

imprimadera, *f.* (art) priming tool.

imprimador, ra, *n.* (art) one who primes.

imprimar, *va.* (art) to prime.

imprimátur, *m.* imprimatur.

imprimir, *va.* (*pp. irreg.* IMPRESO) to print, stamp, imprint; impress; fix in the mind.

improbabilidad, *f.* improbability.

improbable, *a.* improbable, unlikely.

improbablemente, *adv.* improbably.

improbar, *va*. (*ind*. IMPRUEBO; *subj*. IMPRUEBE) to disapprove.

improbidad, *f*. dishonesty; iniquity.

improbo, **ba**, *a*. dishonest, corrupt; laborious, painful, arduous.

improcedencia, *f*. unrighteousness.

improcedente, *a*. contrary to law, unrighteous.

improductivo, **va**, *a*. unproductive, unfruitful, barren, unprofitable.

impronta, *f*. (art) cast; stereotype plate.

impronunciable, *a*. unpronounceable.

improperar, *va*. to upbraid, gibe, taunt.

improperio, *m*. insult, indignity.—*pl*. (eccl.) improperia.

impropiamente, *adv*. improperly.

impropiedad, *f*. impropriety; unfitness, inappropriateness.

impropio, **pia**, *a*. inappropriate, unfitting; improper, unbecoming; (arith.) improper (fraction).

improporción, *f*. disproportion.

improporcionado, **da**, *a*. disproportionate.

improrrogable, *a*. that cannot be prorogated or extended.

impróspero, **ra**, *a*. unprosperous.

impróvidamente, *adv*. improvidently.

improvidencia, *f*. improvidence.

impróvido, **da**, *a*. improvident, thoughtless.

improvisación, *f*. improvisation.

improvisado, **da**. **I**. *pp*. of IMPROVISAR. **II**. *a*. makeshift (as *a*.).

improvisador, **ra**, *n*. improviser.

improvisamente, *adv*. unexpectedly, suddenly.

improvisar, *va*. to improvise; extemporize.

improviso, **sa**; **improvisto**, **ta**, *a*. unexpected, unforeseen.—**al**, or **de**, **i**., or **a la improvista**, unexpectedly, suddenly.

imprudencia, *f*. imprudence, indiscretion.

imprudente, *a*. imprudent, indiscreet, unwise.

imprudentemente, *adv*. imprudently.

impúber; **impúbero**, **ra**, *a*. immature, below the age of puberty.

impudencia, *f*. impudence, insolence.

impudente, *a*. impudent, shameless.

impúdicamente, *adv*. immodestly; impudently.

impudicia, *f*. *contr*. of IMPUDICICIA.

impudicicia, *f*. immodesty, impudicity.

impúdico, **ca**, *a*. immodest; impudent.

impuesto, **ta**. **I**. *pp*. *irreg*. of IMPONER. **II**. *a*. imposed; informed.—**estar**, or **quedar i. de**, to be informed about, to have received notice of or information about. **III**. *m*. tax, impost, duty.

impugnable, *a*. impugnable.

impugnación, *f*. opposition, impugnation.

impugnador, **ra**, *n*. impugner, objector.

impugnar, *va*. to impugn, oppose, criticize.

impugnativo, **va**, *a*. impugning.

impulsar, *va*. to impel, actuate, move, prompt; (mech.) to drive, force.

impulsión, *f*. impulsion, impulse, impetus; influence, motive.

impulsivo, **va**, *a*. impulsive.

impulso, *m*. impulsion; impulse.

impulsor, **ra**, *n*. & *a*. impeller(-ing); driver(-ing).

impune, *a*. unpunished.—**impunemente**, *adv*. with impunity.—**impunidad**, *f*. impunity.

impuramente, *adv*. obscenely, impurely.

impureza, *f*. impurity; adulteration; unchastity; obscenity, foulness.

impurificación, *f*. defilement.

impurificar, *va*. to defile, to make impure; to adulterate.

impuro, **ra**, *a*. impure; defiled; adulterated.

impuse, *pret*. of IMPONER.

imputabilidad, *f*. imputability.

imputable, *a*. imputable.

imputación, *f*. imputation.

imputador, **ra**, *n*. & *a*. imputer(-ing).

imputar, *va*. to impute, attribute; (com.) to credit on account.

imputrescible, *a*. nonrotting.

inabordable, *a*. unapproachable.

inacabable, *a*. interminable; everlasting.

inaccesibilidad, *f*. inaccessibility.

inaccesible, *a*. inaccessible.

inaccesiblemente, *adv*. inaccessibly.

inacción, *f*. inaction, inactivity.

inaceptable, *a*. unacceptable.

inactivo, **va**, *a*. inactive.

inadaptable, *a*. unadaptable.

inadecuado, **da**, *a*. inadequate.

inadmisible, *a*. inadmissible.

inadoptable, *a*. unadoptable.

inadvertencia, *f*. inadvertency, oversight.

inadvertidamente, *adv*. inadvertently.

inadvertido, **da**, *a*. inadvertent, careless; unseen, unnoticed.

inafectado, **da**, *a*. natural, unaffected.

inagotable, *a*. inexhaustible.

inaguantable, *a*. unbearable.

inajenable, *a*. inalienable.

inalámbrico, **ca**, *a*. wireless.

inalcanzable, *a*. unattainable.

inalienable, *a*. inalienable.

inalterabilidad, *f*. unalterability.

inalterable, *a*. unalterable, changeless.

inalterablemente, *adv*. unalterably.

inalterado, **da**, *a*. unchanged, unaltered.

inamisible, *a*. not liable to be lost.

inamovible, *a*. immovable.

inamovilidad, *f*. immovability.

inanalizable, *a*. incapable of being analyzed.

inane, *a*. empty, void, inane.

inanición, *f*. (med.) inanition.

inanimado, **da**, *a*. inanimate, lifeless.

inapagable, *a*. inextinguishable, unquenchable.

inapeable, *a*. that cannot be lowered or levelled; inconceivable; obstinate, stubborn.

inapelable, *a*. unappealable.

inapetencia, *f*. inappetence, lack of appetite.

inapetente, *a*. having no appetite.

inaplazable, *a*. undeferable, that cannot be deferred.

inaplicable, *a*. inapplicable.

inaplicación, *f*. indolence; lack of application.

inaplicado, **da**, *a*. indolent, careless, inactive.

inapreciable, *a*. invaluable; inappreciable.

inaprensivo, *a*. inapprehensive.

inarmónico, **ca**, *a*. inharmonious.

inarticulado, **da**. **I**. *a*. inarticulate. **II**. *m*. *pl*. (zool.) Inarticulata.

in artículo mortis, in articulo mortis, at the point of death, in the moment of death.

inasequible, *a*. unattainable, not obtainable.

inasimilable, *a*. unassimilable.

inastillable, *a*. splinterproof.

inatacable, *a*. that cannot be attacked.

inaudible, *a*. inaudible.

inaudito, **ta**, *a*. unheard-of, strange, unexpected, most extraordinary.

inauguración, *f*. inauguration; coronation; unveiling (of statue), (ceremony of) opening (of building, etc.).

inaugural, *a*. inaugural.

inaugurar, *va*. to inaugurate; to unveil (statue); to dedicate; to open (exhibition, etc.); to divine by the flight of birds.

inaveriguable, *a*. unascertainable.

inca, *n*. & *a*. Inca; a gold coin.

incaico, **ca**, *a*. Inca (as *a*.).

incalculable, *a*. incalculable.

incalificable, *a*. impossible to judge or characterize; unutterably bad, most reprehensible.

incalmable, *a*. that cannot be calmed or subdued.

incandescencia, *f*. incandescence.

incandescente, *a*. incandescent.

incansable, *a*. indefatigable, untiring.

incansablemente, *adv.* indefatigably, tirelessly.
incantable, *a.* that cannot be sung.
incapacidad, *f.* incapacity; incompetence.
incapacitar, *va.* to incapacitate, disable.
incapaz, *a.* incapable; unable; incompetent.
incasable, *a.* unmarriageable; opposed to marriage.
incasto, ta, *a.* unchaste.
incautación, *f.* (law) attachment of property.
incautamente, *adv.* unwarily, incautiously.
incautarse, *vr.* (law) to attach property.
incauto, ta, *a.* unwary; gullible, "easy."
incendiar, *va.* to set on fire.
incendiario, ria, *n.* & *a.* incendiary.
incendio, *m.* fire, conflagration; (fig.) stew.
incensación, *f.* perfuming with incense.
incensar, *va.* (*ind.* INCIENSO; *subj.* INCIENSE) (eccl.) to incense; to bestow fulsome praise or adulation.
incensario, *m.* incensory, thurible.
incensurable, *a.* unblamable, not culpable.
incentivo, *m.* incentive, inducement; encouragement.
incertidumbre, *f.* uncertainty.
incertísimo, ma, *a. super.* extremely uncertain.
incesable, *a.* incessant, unceasing.
incesablemente, *adv.* incessantly.
incesante, *a.* unceasing, continual.
incesantemente, *adv.* incessantly, continually.
incesto, *m.* incest.
incestuosamente, *adv.* incestuously.
incestuoso, sa, *a.* incestuous.
incidencia, *f.* incident; (geom., phys.) incidence.
incidental, *a.* incidental, dependent, subsidiary.
incidentalmente, *adv.* incidentally.
incidente. I. *a.* incidental. **II.** *m.* incident, occurrence.—*pl.* (com.) appurtenances.—**incidentes de comercio,** lease and good will.
incidentemente, *adv.* incidentally.
incidir, *vn.* (en) to fall (into) (as an error).
¹incienso, *m.* incense; reverence; flattery.
²incienso, inciense, *v.* *V.* INCENSAR.
inciertamente, *adv.* uncertainly.
incierto, ta, *a.* uncertain; untrue; unknown.
incinerable, *a.* (of bank bills, burned when withdrawn) to be withdrawn from circulation.
incineración, *f.* incineration, cremation; (chem.) ignition.
incinerar, *va.* to incinerate, cremate; (chem.) to ignite.
incipiente, *a.* incipient.
incircunciso, sa, *a.* uncircumcised.
incircunscripto, ta, *a.* uncircumscribed.
incisión, *f.* incision, cut.
incisivo, va, *a.* incisive; keen, sharp, cutting (as a remark).
inciso, sa. I. *a.* incised, cut. **II.** *m.* sentence; clause; comma.
incisorio, ria, *a.* (surg.) incisory.
incitación, *f.* incitation, incitement.
incitador, ra, *n.* & *a.* instigator(-ing), inciter (-ing).
incitamento, incitamiento, *m.* incitement, impulse, incentive.
incitante, *a.* inciting, exciting.
incitar, *va.* to incite, excite, spur, instigate.
incitativo, va. I. *a.* inciting; (law) AGUIJATORIO, re-mandatory. **II.** *m.* incitement. **III.** *f.* (law) writ from a superior to a lower court urging that justice be administered.
incivil, *a.* uncivil.—**incivilidad,** *f.* incivility.
incivilmente, *adv.* uncivilly, rudely.
inclasificable, *a.* unclassifiable.
inclemencia, *f.* inclemency; severity, rigor, unmercifulness.—**a la i.,** unsheltered, at the mercy of the elements.
inclinación, *f.* inclination; propensity, tendency, bent; tilt, slant, pitch; declivity, slope; (Ry.) grade; (min.) dip, hade, underlay; (phys.) dip, inclination (of the needle).

inclinado, da. I. *pp.* of INCLINAR. **II.** *a.* inclined; slanting, sloping; disposed, minded.
inclinador, ra, *m.* & *f.* one who inclines.
inclinante, *a.* inclining.
inclinar. I. *va.* to incline; to bow; to tilt; to influence. **II.** *vn.* to resemble. **III.** *vr.* to incline, slope; to lean; to incline, be favorably disposed; to stoop, bow; to yield; (naut.) to heel.
ínclito, ta, *a.* distinguished, illustrious.
incluir, *va.* (*pp.* INCLUÍDO, INCLUSO; *ind. pres.* INCLUYO, *pret.* él INCLUYÓ; *subj.* INCLUYA) to include; to enclose.
inclusa, *f.* foundling asylum.
inclusero, ra, *n.* & *a.* foundling.
inclusión, *f.* inclusion; friendship.
inclusivamente, inclusive, *adv.* inclusive, including.
inclusivo, va, *a.* inclusive, including.
incluso, sa. I. *pp. irreg.* of INCLUIR. **II.** *a.* inclosed; including, included (in this sense it is gen. used as an *adv.*).
incluyente, *a.* including, inclosing.
incluyo, incluyó, *v.* *V.* INCLUIR.
incoado, da, *a.* & *pp.* inchoate, begun.
incoagulable, *a.* uncoagulable.
incoar, *va.* (*only the infinitive and pp. used*) (law) to commence, begin.
incoativo, va, *a.* inchoative, inceptive.
incobrable, *a.* irrecoverable, irretrievable; (com.) uncollectable.
incoercible, *a.* incoercible.
incógnito, ta. I. *a.* unknown.—**de i.,** incognito; hiddenly or clandestinely. **II.** *f.* (math.) unknown (quantity).
incognoscible, *a.* unknowable.
incoherencia, *f.* incoherence, disconnection.
incoherente, *a.* incoherent, disconnected.
íncola, *m.* inhabitant, resident.
incoloro, ra, *a.* colorless.
incólume, *a.* sound, safe, unharmed.
incolumidad, *f.* security, safety.
incombinable, *a.* uncombinable.
incombustibilidad, *f.* incombustibility.
incombustible, *a.* incombustible, fireproof.
incombusto, ta, *a.* not burned.
incomerciable, *a.* contraband, unlawful, prohibited; unsalable, unmarketable.
incómodamente, *adv.* inconveniently; uncomfortably.
incomodar. I. *va.* to disturb, inconvenience, trouble. **II.** *vr.* to be or get vexed or angry; to trouble oneself.
incomodidad, *f.* inconvenience; uncomfortableness; nuisance, annoyance; vexation, anger.
incómodo, da, *a.* inconvenient; uncomfortable; troublesome, unhandy, cumbersome.
incomparable, *a.* incomparable, matchless.
incomparablemente, *adv.* incomparably.
incomparado, da, *a.* = INCOMPARABLE.
incompartible, *a.* indivisible.
incompasible, incompasivo, va, *a.* pitiless, unsympathetic.
incompatibilidad, *f.* incompatibility.
incompatible, *a.* incompatible; uncongenial.
incompensable, *a.* incapable of being compensated, unindemnifiable.
incompetencia, *f.* incompetence; unfitness.
incompetente, *a.* incompetent; (law) incompetent, unauthorized.
incomplejo, ja, *a.* incomplex; simple.
incompletamente, *adv.* incompletely.
incompleto, ta, *a.* incomplete.
incomplexo, xa, *a.* disunited, disconnected, disjointed.
incoponible, *a.* unmendable.
incomportable, *a.* intolerable, unbearable.
incomposibilidad, *f.* incompatibility.
incomposible, *a.* incompatible; inconsistent.
incomposición, *f.* want of proportion.
incomprehensibilidad, *f.* incomprehensibility.

incomprehensible, *a.* incomprehensible.
incomprensibilidad, *f.* incomprehensibility.
incomprensible, *a.* incomprehensible.
incomprensiblemente, *adv.* inconceivably, incomprehensibly.
incomprensión, *f.* misunderstanding; lack of understanding.
incompresibilidad, *f.* (phys.) incompressibility.
incompresible, *a.* (phys.) incompressible.
incomprimible, *a.* incompressible.
incomunicabilidad, *f.* incommunicability.
incomunicable, *a.* incommunicable.
incomunicado, da I. *a.* isolated. II. *m.* isolated prisoner, incommunicado.
incomunicar, *va.* (*pret.* INCOMUNIQUÉ; *subj.* IN-COMUNIQUE) to deprive of intercourse or communication; to isolate, put in solitary confinement.
inconcebible, *a.* inconceivable.
inconciliable, *a.* irreconcilable.
inconcino, na, *a.* disordered, disarranged.
inconcusamente, *adv.* certainly, unquestionably.
inconcuso, sa, *a.* incontrovertible, unquestionable, indisputable.
incondicional, *a.* unconditional.
incondicionalmente, *adv.* unconditionally.
inconducente, *a.* nonconducive.
inconexión, *f.* incoherence, disconnection.
inconexo, xa, *a.* unconnected, not pertinent; incoherent.
inconfeso, sa, *a.* unconfessed.
inconfidencia, *f.* distrust, mistrust.
incongruamente, *adv.* incongruously.
incongruencia, *f.* incongruence.
incongruente, *a.* incongruous, incongruent.
incongruentemente, *adv.* incongruously, incompatibly.
incongruo, grua, *a.* incongruous.
inconmensurabilidad, *f.* incommensurability.
inconmensurable, *a.* incommensurable.
inconmovible, *a.* immovable; unbending, inexorable, unyielding.
inconmutabilidad, *f.* immutability; incommutability.
inconmutable, *a.* immutable; incommutable.
inconquistable, *a.* unconquerable; unbending.
inconsciencia, *f.* unconsciousness.
inconsciente, *a.* unconscious.
inconscientemente, *adv.* unconsciously.
inconsecuencia, *f.* inconsistency.
inconsecuente, *a.* inconsistent.
inconservable, *a.* unpreservable.
inconsideración, *f.* lack of consideration; thoughtlessness, inadvertency.
inconsideradamente, *adv.* inconsiderately; thoughtlessly.
inconsiderado, da, *a.* inconsiderate; thoughtless.
inconsiguiente, *a.* inconsistent, not logical.
inconsistencia, *f.* incoherence; instability, lack of permanency.
inconsistente, *a.* unsubstantial, unstable.
inconsolable, *a.* inconsolable.
inconsolablemente, *adv.* inconsolably.
inconstancia, *f.* inconstancy, fickleness.
inconstante, *a.* inconstant, changeable, fickle.
inconstantemente, *adv.* inconstantly, fickly.
inconstitucional, *a.* unconstitutional.
inconstitucionalidad, *f.* unconstitutionality.
inconstruíble, *a.* that cannot be constructed.
inconsútil, *a.* seamless.
incontable, *a.* innumerable, uncountable.
incontaminado, da, *a.* undefiled, uncontaminated, pure.
incontestable, *a.* incontestable, unquestionable.
incontestablemente, *adv.* unquestionably.
incontinencia, *f.* incontinence; (med.) incontinence of urine.
¹incontinente, *a.* incontinent.

²incontinente, incontinenti, *adv.* instantly, immediately, at once.
incontrastable, *a.* invincible, insuperable, unconquerable; unanswerable; unconvincible.
incontratable, *a.* = INTRATABLE, intractable.
incontrovertible, *a.* incontrovertible.
inconvencible, *a.* unconvincible.
inconvenible, *a.* uncompromising.
inconveniencia, *f.* inconvenience, trouble; disadvantage; uncomfortableness.
inconveniente. I. *a.* inconvenient, troublesome; uncomfortable; undesirable, inadvisable. II. *m.* difficulty, obstacle, objection; disadvantage.
inconversable, *a.* unsociable, uncommunicative, surly, intractable.
inconvertible, *a.* inconvertible.
incordio, *m.* (med.) bubo; (vulg.) nuisance.
incorporación, *f.* incorporation.
incorporal, *a.* incorporeal.
incorporalmente, *adv.* incorporeally.
incorporar. I. *va.* to incorporate, unite, embody; to mix; to raise or to make (a patient) sit up in bed. II. *vr.* to incorporate, mingle; to join (as a mil. unit); to form a corporation; to sit up in bed; (naut.) to sail in company.
incorporeidad, *f.* incorporeity, immateriality.
incorpóreo, rea, *a.* incorporeal.
incorporo, *m.* = INCORPORACIÓN.
incorrección, *f.* incorrectness; inaccuracy; impropriety.
incorrectamente, *adv.* incorrectly; improperly.
incorrecto, ta, *a.* incorrect; improper.
incorregibilidad, *f.* incorrigibleness.
incorregible, *a.* incorrigible.
incorrupción, *f.* integrity, honesty; incorrupt condition.
incorruptamente, *adv.* incorruptly.
incorruptibilidad, *f.* incorruptibility.
incorruptible, *a.* incorruptible.
incorrupto, ta, *a.* incorrupt or uncorrupted; chaste, pure.
incrasante, *a.* thickening.
incrasar, *va.* to thicken, incrassate.
increado, da, *a.* uncreated.
incredibilidad, *f.* incredibility, incredibleness.
incredulidad, *f.* incredulity.
incrédulo, la. I. *a.* incredulous. II. *n.* unbeliever.
increíble, *a.* incredible, unbelievable.
increíblemente, *adv.* incredibly.
incremento, *m.* increment, increase.
increpación, *f.* rebuke, chiding, reproach.
increpador, ra, *n.* & *a.* chider(-ing), rebuker (-ing).
increpante, *a.* chiding, scolding, rebuking.
increpar, *va.* to chide, reprehend, rebuke.
incriminación, *f.* incrimination.
incriminante, *a.* incriminating.
incriminar, *va.* to incriminate; to exaggerate.
incristalizable, *a.* uncrystallizable.
incruento, ta, *a.* bloodless.
incrustación, *f.* incrustation; scale (in boilers); (geol.) sinter; (art) inlaying.
incrustante, *a.* (of water) scale-forming.
incrustar, *va.* to incrust; encase; inlay.
incuartación, *f.* (chem.) quartation.
incubación, *f.* incubation; hatching.
incubador, ra. I. *n.* & *a.* incubator(-ing). II. *f.* incubator (apparatus).
incubar, *va.* to incubate; to hatch.
íncubo, *m.* incubus; (med.) nightmare.
incuestionable, *a.* unquestionable.
inculcación, *f.* inculcation; pressing (one thing against another); (print.) binding or wedging in a form.
inculcar. I. *va.* (*pret.* INCULQUÉ; *subj.* INCULQUE) to inculcate, impress, teach; to make (one thing) tight (against another); (print.) to lock up (types). II. *vr.* to be obstinate.
inculpabilidad, *f.* guiltlessness; blamelessness.
inculpable, *a.* guiltless, blameless.

inculpablemente, *adv.* blamelessly.

inculpación, *f.* inculpation.

inculpadamente, *adv.* faultlessly.

inculpar, *va.* to accuse, inculpate, blame.

inculqué, inculque, *v. V.* INCULCAR.

incultamente, *adv.* rudely, unrefinedly.

incultivable, *a.* inarable, untillable.

inculto, ta, *a.* uncultivated, untilled, unimproved; uncivilized; unrefined, uncultured.

incultura, *f.* lack of culture.

incumbencia, *f.* incumbency; obligation, duty, concern.

incumbir, *vn.* to concern, pertain.

incumplido, da, *a.* unfulfilled; unpunctual.

incumplimiento, *m.* nonfulfilment.

incunable, *m. & a.* (print.) incunabula.

incurable, *a.* incurable; hopeless.

incuria, *f.* negligence; shiftlessness.

incurioso, sa, *a.* negligent, careless.

incurrimiento, *m.* act of incurring.

incurrir, *vn.* (en) to incur, become liable (to); to bring on oneself; to commit (error or crime).

incursión, *f.* (mil.) incursion.

incusar, *va.* to accuse.

incuso, sa, *a.* incuse, stamped (as some coins).

indagación, *f.* investigation, search, inquiry, examination, inquest; (law) defendant's unsworn testimony.

indagador, ra, *n. & a.* investigator(-ing), inquirer(-ing), examiner(-ing).

indagar, *va.* (*pret.* INDAGUÉ; *subj.* INDAGUE) to investigate, inquire into or about.

indagatoria, *f.* (law) unsworn statement made by, or required of, an arraigned person.

indagatorio, ria, *a.* (law) investigatory.

indagué, indague, *v. V.* INDAGAR.

indebidamente, *adv.* unduly; improperly; illegally, unlawfully.

indebido, da, *a.* improper; illegal, unlawful.

indecencia, *f.* indecency; obscenity; nuisance; indecent or low act or conduct.

indecente, *a.* indecent, obscene; foul.

indecentemente, *adv.* indecently.

indecible, *a.* inexpressible, unutterable.

indeciblemente, *adv.* inexpressibly, unutterably; exceedingly.

indecisamente, *adv.* irresolutely.

indecisión, *f.* irresolution, indecision.

indeciso, sa, *a.* irresolute, hesitant; undecided.

indeclinable, *a.* unavoidable; (gram.) indeclinable; (law) unwaivable.

indecoro, *m.* indecorum, indecorousness.

indecorosamente, *adv.* indecorously, unbecomingly.

indecoroso, sa, *a.* indecorous, unbecoming.

indefectibilidad, *f.* indefectibility.

indefectible, *a.* indefectible, unfailing.

indefectiblemente, *adv.* unfailingly.

indefendible, *a.* indefensible.

indefensable, indefensible, *a.* = INDEFENDIBLE.

indefenso, sa, *a.* defenseless.

indeficiente, *a.* indefectible, unfailing.

indefinible, *a.* undefinable.

indefinidamente, *adv.* indefinitely.

indefinido, da, *a.* indefinite; undefined.

indehiscente, *a.* (bot.) indehiscent.

indeleble, *a.* indelible, ineffaceable.

indeleblemente, *adv.* indelibly.

indeliberación, *f.* lack of premeditation; irreflection.

indeliberadamente, *adv.* without premeditation or reflection.

indeliberado, da, *a.* unpremeditated; unconsidered.

indemne, *a.* undamaged, unhurt.

indemnicé, indemnice, *v. V.* INDEMNIZAR.

indemnidad, *f.* bond of indemnity.

indemnizable, *a.* that can be indemnified.

indemnización, *f.* indemnification, compensation; indemnity; reimbursement.

indemnizar, *va.* (*pret.* INDEMNICÉ; *subj.* INDEMNICE) to indemnify, compensate.

indemostrable, *a.* undemonstrable.

independencia, *f.* independence.

independiente, *a.* independent.

independientemente, *adv.* independently.

independizar, (Am.) **I.** *va.* to free, emancipate. **II.** *vr.* to become independent, win freedom.

indescifrable, *a.* undecipherable.

indescribible, *a.* = INDESCRIPTIBLE.

indescriptible, *a.* indescribable.

indeseable, *a.* undesirable (esp. app. to aliens).

indesignable, *a.* that cannot be designated.

indestructibilidad, *f.* indestructibility.

indestructible, *a.* indestructible.

indeterminable, *a.* underterminable, unascertainable; irresolute, undecided.

indeterminación, *f.* indetermination; irresolution, hesitancy.

indeterminadamente, *adv.* indeterminately.

indeterminado, da, *a.* indeterminate; undetermined, irresolute, hesitating; (gram.) indefinite (article); (math.) indeterminate (problem, equation); (math.) undetermined (coefficient).

indeterminismo, *m.* (philos.) indeterminism.

indeterminista, *n. & a.* (philos.) indeterminist (-ic).

indevoción, *f.* lack of devoutness, irreligiousness.

indevoto, ta, *a.* not devout, irreligious.

indezuelo, la, *n. dim.* little Indian.

indiada, *f.* (Am.) crowd or multitude of Indians.

indiana, *f.* printed calico.

indianismo, *m.* (Am.) interest in, or study of, Am. Indian questions.

indianista, *n.* (Am.) student of, or expert in, Am. Indian culture; student of, or expert in, East Indian culture.

indiano, na. I. *a.* native or resident of America or West Indies; Indian, East Indian. **II.** *m.* nabob, one who returns rich from America.— **i. de hilo negro,** (coll.) skinflint, miser.

indicación, *f.* indication, sign; hint, suggestion; direction, instruction.

indicado, da. I. *pp.* of INDICAR. **II.** *a.* indicated, appropriate (to conditions, etc.).

indicador, *m.* indicator, pointer, recorder, gauge, detector, index; (elec.) annunciator disc; (steam eng.) indicator.—**i. de incendios,** fire alarm.—**i. de nivel,** (steam eng.) water-level indicator, gauge glass.—**i. de vacío,** vacuum gauge.

indicante. I. *a.* indicating. **II.** *m.* (med.) indicant.

indicar, *va.* (*pret.* INDIQUÉ; *subj.* INDIQUE) to indicate, suggest, hint, show, point out.

indicativo, va. I. *a.* indicative, pointing. **II.** *n. & a.* (gram.) indicative.

indicción, *f.* convening of a synod, council, etc.; (Rom. Empire) indiction.

índice, *m.* index; hand of a watch, etc.; index, table of contents; forefinger.—**i. cefálico,** cephalic index.—**i. expurgatorio,** Index Expurgatorius, a catalog of books forbidden totally or in part by the Catholic Church.

indiciado, da. I. *pp.* of INDICIAR. **II.** *a.* suspected of a crime or vice. **III.** *n.* suspicious character.

indiciador, ra, *n.* one who suspects another; informer.

indiciar, *va.* (law) to give reasons to suspect or surmise; to report (offenders) to the magistrates.

indicio, *m.* indication, mark, sign, evidence, clue. —*pl.* (chem.) traces.—**indicios vehementes,** (law) circumstantial evidence.

índico, ca, *a.* East-Indian.

indiferencia, *f.* indifference.

indiferente, *a.* indifferent.—**eso es i.,** (coll.) that is immaterial, that makes no difference.

indiferentemente, *adv.* indifferently, without difference.

indiferentismo, *m.* indifferentism.

indígena. I. *a.* indigenous, native; (app. to Am.) Indian. **II.** *n.* indigene; native; (app. to Am.) Indian.

indigencia, *f.* indigence, destitution, need.

indigente, *a.* needy, indigent, destitute.

indigestarse, *vr.* to cause indigestion; (of persons) to cause aversion or dislike, to be unbearable.

indigestible, *a.* indigestible.

indigestión, *f.* indigestion.

indigesto, ta, *a.* indigestible; confused, disordered; surly, grouchy, harsh.

indignación, *f.* indignation.

indignado, da, *a.* & *pp.* indignant, angry.

indignamente, *adv.* unworthily, unbecomingly; harshly, rudely.

indignante, *a.* indignant; irritating.

indignar. I. *va.* to irritate, anger, make indignant. **II.** *vr.* to become indignant.

indignidad, *f.* indignity; unworthy act.

indigno, na, *a.* unworthy, undeserving; unbecoming, contemptible; despicable, low.

índigo, *m.* indigo.—**indigotina,** *f.* (chem.) indigotin, indigo blue.

indiligencia, *f.* negligence, carelessness.

indio, ia. I. *a.* Indian; Hindu; blue, azure. **II.** *n.* Hindu; Indian. **III.** *m.* (chem.) indium.

indiqué, indique, *v.* V. INDICAR.

indirecta, *f.* innuendo, hint.—**i. del Padre Cobos,** broad hint.—**echar indirectas,** to make insinuations.

indirectamente, *adv.* indirectly.

indirecto, ta, *a.* indirect.

indisciplina, *f.* lack of discipline or training.

indisciplinable, *a.* intractable; untrainable.

indisciplinado, da, *a.* undisciplined; untrained.

indiscreción, *f.* indiscretion, imprudence.

indiscretamente, *adv.* indiscreetly.

indiscreto, ta, *a.* indiscreet, imprudent, unwise.

indisculpable, *a.* inexcusable.

indiscutible, *a.* unquestionable, indisputable.

indisolubilidad, *f.* indissolubility.

indisoluble, *a.* indissoluble.

indisolublemente, *adv.* indissolubly.

indispensable, *a.* indispensable, essential; unfailing.

indispensablemente, *adv.* indispensably; necessarily; unfailingly.

indisponer. I. *va.* (*pp. irreg.* INDISPUESTO; *ind. pres.* INDISPONGO, *pret.* INDISPUSE, *fut.* INDISPONDRÉ; *subj.* INDISPONGA) to disable, indispose, render unfit; to make ill; (con) to prejudice, set (against). **II.** *vr.* to be indisposed, to become ill; to fall out (with a person).

indisposición, *f.* disinclination, dislike; indisposition, slight ailment.

indisposioncilla, *f. dim.* slight indisposition.

indispuesto, ta. I. *pp. irreg. of* INDISPONER. **II.** *a.* indisposed; at variance.

indispuse, *pret. of* INDISPONER.

indisputable, *a.* indisputable, unquestionable.

indisputablemente, *adv.* indisputably.

indistinción, *f.* lack of distinction.

indistinguible, *a.* undistinguishable.

indistintamente, *adv.* indistinctly; indifferently, without distinction.

indistinto, ta, *a.* indistinct, vague, not clear.

individuación, *f.* individuation.

individual, *a.* individual; peculiar; personal.

individualidad, *f.* individuality.

individualismo, *m.* individualism.

individualista, *n.* & *a.* individualist(-ic).

individualizar, *va.* to individualize.

individualmente, *adv.* individually.

individuamente, *adv.* indivisibly.

individuar, *va.* to distinguish, particularize, individualize.

individuo, dua. I. *a.* individual; indivisible, inseparable. **II.** *n.* individual, person; member, fellow (of a society, etc.).

indivisamente, *adv.* indivisibly.

indivisibilidad, *f.* indivisibility.

indivisible, *a.* indivisible.

indivisiblemente, *adv.* indivisibly.

indivisión, *f.* undividedness, entirety.

indiviso, sa, *a.* undivided.

indo, da, *n.* & *a.* East-Indian, Hindu.

indócil, *a.* indocile, unteachable; headstrong, froward, unruly; inflexible, brittle.

indocilidad, *f.* indocility; inflexibility.

indoctamente, *adv.* ignorantly.

indocto, ta, *a.* ignorant, untaught.

indocumentado, da, *a.* lacking the documents for identification.

indochino, na, *n.* & *a.* Indo-Chinese.

indoeuropeo, a, *n.* & *a.* Indo-European.

indogermánico, ca, *n.* & *a.* Indo-Germanic.

indoísmo, *m.* Hinduism, Hindooism.

índole, *f.* disposition, nature; class, kind.

indolencia, *f.* indolence.

indolente, *a.* indolent.—**indolentemente,** *adv.* indolently.

indoloro, ra, *a.* painless.

indomable, *a.* untamable, indomitable; unmanageable; unconquerable.

indomado, da, *a.* untamed.

indomesticable, *a.* untamable, not susceptible of domestication.

indoméstico, ca, *a.* untamed, intractable.

indómito, ta, *a.* untamed; unruly.

indostanés, sa; indostánico, ca, *a.* Hindu.

indostani, *n.* & *a.* Hindustani (language).

indotación, *f.* (law) lack of a dowry.

indotado, da, *a.* unendowed; without a dowry.

indubitable, *a.* indubitable, unquestionable.

indubitablemente, *adv.* undoubtedly.

indubitado, da, *a.* undoubted, unquestionable.

inducción, *f.* inducement, persuasion; (logic) induction; (elec.) induction.

inducido, *m.* (elec.) armature (of a dynamo).

inducidor, ra, *n.* inducer, persuader.

inducimiento, *m.* inducement.

inducir, *va.* (*ind. pres.* INDUZCO, *pret.* INDUJE; *subj.* INDUZCA) to induce; to persuade, influence; (elec.) to induce.

inductivo, va, *a.* inductive.

inductor, ra. I. *a.* (elec.) inductive. **II.** *m.* (elec.) field (magnet) (of a dynamo).

indudable, *a.* indubitable, certain.

indudablemente, *adv.* undoubtedly.

induje, *pret. of* INDUCIR.

indulgencia, *f.* indulgence; forbearance, leniency.

indulgente, *a.* indulgent, lenient, forbearing.

indulgentemente, *adv.* indulgently.

indultar, *va.* to pardon; to free, exempt.

indultario, *m.* he who by virtue of a pontifical privilege can dispense ecclesiastical benefices.

indulto, *m.* pardon, forgiveness, amnesty; (legal) pardon or commutation or exemption.

indumentaria, *f.* study of ancient apparel.

indumentario, ria, *a.* pertaining to clothes.

indumento, *m.* garment, vestment.

induración, *f.* (med.) induration.

industria, *f.* industry, manufacturing.—**de i.,** designedly, intentionally.—**ser caballero de i.,** to live by one's wits.

industrial. I. *a.* industrial, manufacturing. **II.** *n.* industrialist, manufacturer.—**industrialismo,** *m.* industrialism.—**industrialista,** *a.* favoring industrialism; industry (as *a.*).

industriar, *va.* & *vn.* to educate, teach, train, coach; to find means.

industriosamente, *adv.* industriously.

industrioso, sa, *a.* industrious.

induzco, induzca, v. V. INDUCIR.
inecuación, f. (math.) inequality.
inedia, f. fast, abstinence from food.
inédito, ta, a. unpublished.
ineducación, f. unmannerliness, unrefinement.
ineducado, da, a. unmannerly, unpolished.
inefabilidad, f. ineffability, unspeakableness.
inefable, a. ineffable, unutterable.
inefablemente, adv. ineffably.
ineficacia, f. inefficacy, inefficiency.
ineficaz, a. inefficacious, ineffectual, ineffective.
ineficazmente, adv. inefficaciously.
inejecutable, a. impracticable, not feasible.
inelegante, a. inelegant.
ineluctable, a. ineluctable; inevitable.
ineludible, a. inevitable, unavoidable.
inenarrable, a. inexplicable, inexpressible.
ineptamente, adv. ineptly, incompetently.
ineptitud, f. ineptitude, incompetency.
inepto, ta, a. inept, incompetent; unfit; foolish.
inequívoco, ca, a. unequivocal, unmistakable.
inercia, f. inertia; inertness, inactivity.
inerme, a. unarmed, defenseless.
inerrable, a. inerrable, unmistakable.
inerrante, a. (astr.) fixed (star).
inerte, a. inert; dull, slow, sluggish; unskilful; paralyzed, senseless.
inervación, f. innervation.
inescrutable, a. inscrutable; unconfirmable.
inescudriñable, a. inscrutable.
inesperadamente, adv. unexpectedly.
inesperado, da, a. unexpected, unforeseen.
inestabilidad, f. instability.
inestable, a. unstable.
inestimabilidad, f. invaluableness.
inestimable, a. invaluable.
inestimado, da, a. (law) unestimated, not appraised, unvalued.
inevitable, a. inevitable, unavoidable.
inevitablemente, adv. inevitably.
inexactamente, adv. inexactly.
inexactitud, f. inexactness; inaccuracy.
inexacto, ta, a. inexact, inaccurate.
inexcusable, a. inexcusable; indispensable.
inexcusablemente, adv. inexcusably.
inexhausto, ta, a. unexhausted, unspent.
inexistente, a. nonexistent.
inexorable, a. inexorable, relentless, unbending.
inexperiencia, f. inexperience.
inexperto, ta, a. unskilful, inexperienced.
inexpiable, a. inexpiable.
inexplicable, a. inexplicable, unexplainable.
inexplorado, da, a. unexplored.
inexplosible, a. unexplosive, nonexplosive.
inexplotable, a. unexploitable, unworkable.
inexpresivo, va, a. inexpressive.
inexpugnable, a. inexpugnable, impregnable; firm, obstinate, stubborn.
in extenso, in extenso, at full length.
inextenso, sa, a. unextended, extensionless.
inextinguible, a. inextinguishable, unquenchable; perpetual.
inexterminable, a. inexterminable, not capable of being eradicated.
in extremis, in extremis, on the point of death.
inextricable, a. inextricable.
infacundo, da, a. ineloquent.
infalibilidad, f. infallibility.
infalible, a. infallible.—**infaliblemente,** adv. infallibly.
infamación, f. slander, defamation.
infamador, ra, n. & a. defamer(-ing).
infamante, a. defaming; opprobrious.
infamar, va. to defame, dishonor, disgrace.
infamativo, va, a. defaming; disgracing.
infamatorio, ria, a. defamatory, libellous.
infame, a. & n. infamous (person).—**infamemente,** adv. infamously.
infamia, f. infamy; baseness; infamous act.
infancia, f. infancy; childhood.

infando, da, a. unmentionable, unspeakable.
infanta, f. female child under seven years of age; infanta, any daughter of the King of Spain; wife of a prince royal.
infantado, m. territory assigned to a prince of the royal blood of Spain.
infante, m. infant, male child under seven years of age; infante, any son of the King of Spain, except the heir apparent; infantry soldier.—pl. choristers, choir boys.
infantería, f. infantry.
infanticida, n. infanticide, child murderer.
infanticidio, m. infanticide, murder of a child.
infantil, a. infantile, childlike.
infantilismo, m. infantility; (med.) infantilism.
infanzón, m. ancient nobleman.—**infanzonado, da,** a. pertaining to an INFANZÓN.—**infanzonazgo,** m. territory of an INFANZÓN.—**infanzonía,** f. dignity or condition of INFANZÓN.
infartación, f. (med.) infarction.
infarto, m. (med.) infarct.
infatigable, a. indefatigable, untiring.
infatigablemente, adv. indefatigably.
infatuación, f. infatuation.
infatuar. I. va. to infatuate. II. vr. to become infatuated.
infaustamente, adv. unluckily.
infausto, ta, a. unlucky; unhappy, accursed.
infebril, a. fever-free.
infección, f. infection.—**infeccionar,** va. = INFICIONAR.—**infeccioso, sa,** a. infectious.
infectar. I. va. to infect; spread contagion; to corrupt, vitiate, pervert. II. vr. to become infected.
infectivo, va, a. infective, infectious.
infecto, ta, a. infected, tainted, corrupt.
infecundidad, f. infecundity, sterility.
infecundo, da, a. infecund, barren, sterile.
infelice, a. (poet.) unhappy, wretched.
infelicidad, f. unhappiness, infelicity.
infeliz. I. a. unhappy, wretched; unfortunate, luckless. II. n. poor devil.
infelizmente, adv. unhappily, unluckily.
inferencia, f. inference.
inferior. I. a. inferior; lower; under (part); elementary (school, math., etc.). II. a. & n. inferior.
inferioridad, f. inferiority.
inferir (ind. pres. INFIERO, pret. él INFIRIÓ; subj. INFIERA; ger. INFIRIENDO). I. va. to infer; to imply, lead to; to inflict (as a wound); to offer (as an insult). II. vr. to follow as a consequence.
infernáculo, m. a boys' game, hopscotch.
infernal, a. infernal, hellish.
infernalmente, adv. hellishly, infernally.
infernar, va. (ind. INFIERNO; subj. INFIERNE) to damn; to irritate, vex, provoke.
inferno, na, a. (poet.) infernal.
infestación, f. infestation.
infestar, va. to infest, overrun; to infect; to harass; to fill with stench.
infesto, ta, a. (poet.) prejudicial, dangerous.
infeudar, va.; infeudación, f. = ENFEUDAR, etc.
infibulación, f. (vet.) infibulation.
infibular, va. (vet.) to infibulate.
inficionar, va. to infect; to poison; corrupt, defile, pervert, vitiate.
infidelidad, f. infidelity; unfaithfulness, faithlessness; unbelief, want of faith; unbelievers as a class.
infidelísimo, ma, a. super. of INFIEL.
infidencia, f. unfaithfulness, faithlessness; treason; (law) misfeasance.
infidente, a. unfaithful.
infiel. I. a. unfaithful, faithless; infidel, pagan; inaccurate, inexact. II. m. unbeliever, infidel.
infielmente, adv. unfaithfully.
infiernillo, m. small alcohol stove.
¹**infierno,** m. (often in the pl.) hell; refectory or eating room in some convents; (chem.) large

---

For pronunciation, see the rules at the beginning of the book.

retort; cave of a baking machine; tank in oil mills.—**el quinto i.**, or **los quintos infiernos**, the end of the world (fig., app. to a very remote place).

²**infierno, infierne,** v. V. INFERNAR.

infiero, infiera, v. V. INFERIR.

infigurable, a. incorporeal, that cannot be represented by any material figure.

infiltración, f. infiltration, percolation.

infiltrar, va. & vr. to infiltrate, percolate, filter; to imbue, infuse.

ínfimo, ma, a. lowest, least; most abject, vilest; (com.) most inferior in quality.

infinidad, f. infinity; (fig.) infinite number, lot.

infinitamente, adv. infinitely.

infinitesimal, a. infinitesimal.

infinitivo, n. & a. (gram.) infinitive.

infinito, ta. I. a. infinite. **II.** adv. infinitely, immensely. **III.** m. (el i.) infinity.

infinitud, f. = INFINIDAD.

infirió, infiriendo, v. V. INFERIR.

infirmar, va. (law) to invalidate.

inflación, f. inflation; conceit, vanity, airs.—**inflacionista,** a. (econ.) inflationary.

inflamable, a. inflammable.

inflamación, f. inflammation; ignition.

inflamar. I. va. to inflame, kindle, set on fire; to excite. **II.** vr. to take fire, ignite; to become fiery or excited; (med.) to become inflamed.

inflamatorio, ria, a. inflammatory.

inflar. I. va. to inflate; to elate, puff up with pride. **II.** vr. to swell; to strut.

inflativo, va, a. inflating.

inflexibilidad, f. inflexibility; stiffness, rigidity; inexorability.

inflexible, a. inflexible, rigid; unbending, unyielding.

inflexiblemente, adv. inflexibly, inexorably.

inflexión, f. inflection, bending; (gram.) inflection; accent, modulation.

infligir, va. (ind. INFLIJO; subj. INFLIJA) to impose (a penalty), condemn to.

inflorescencia, f. (bot.) inflorescence.

influencia, f. influence; (theol.) divine grace.

influenciar, va. (Am.) to influence.

influente, a. influencing, influential.

influenza, f. influenza, grippe.

influir. I. va. (ind. INFLUYO; subj. INFLUYA) to influence; to act on; (theol.) to grace with inspiration. **II.** vn. (en) to have influence (on), to affect; to contribute (to), have a part (in).

influyente, a. influential.

¹**influyo,** m. influence; influx; (naut.) rising tide.

²**influyo, influya,** v. V. INFLUIR.

infolio, m. book in folio form.

Inforciado, m. Infortiate, second part of the Pandects of Justinian.

información, f. information; report; inquiry, investigation; judicial inquiry and process; (law) brief.—**fuente de i.,** source of information, "contact."

informador, ra, n. & a. informer(-ing), reporter (-ing).

informal, a. informal; unreliable; unconventional.

informalidad, f. informality, unconventionality; breach of etiquette; unreliability.

informante, n. & a. informer(-ing).

informar. I. va. to inform, tell, advise, report to; to give form to, shape. **II.** vn. (law) to plead. **III.** vr. (de) to acquaint oneself (with), to inquire (into), to find out (about).

informativo, va, a. instructive, informative.

¹**informe,** a. shapeless, formless.

²**informe,** m. information; report, account, statement; advice; reference; (law) plea, pleading.

informidad, f. shapelessness.

infortificable, a. that cannot be fortified.

infortuna, f. (astrol.) evil influence of the stars.

infortunado, da, a. unfortunate, unlucky.

infortunio, m. misfortune, ill luck; mishap; misery, suffering.

infosura, f. (vet.) a disease of horses.

infracción, f. infraction, breach, infringement, trespass.

infracto, ta, a. steady, not easily moved.

infractor, ra, n. infractor, breaker, violator, transgressor.

in fraganti, adv. = EN FLAGRANTE, in the act.

infrangible, a. infrangible; inviolable.

infranqueable, a. unsurmountable.

infrarrojo, ja, a. infrared.

infrascripto, ta; infrascrito, ta, a. undersigned; hereinafter mentioned.

infrecuente, a. unusual, infrequent.

infringir, va. (ind. INFRINJO; subj. INFRINJA) to infringe, violate, break.

infructífero, ra, a. unfruitful; unprofitable.

infructuosidad, f. unfruitfulness, unproductiveness, uselessness.

infructuosamente, adv. unfruitfully, uselessly.

infructuoso, sa, a. fruitless, unproductive; unprofitable, abortive, unsuccessful.

infrugífero, ra, a. = INFRUCTÍFERO.

ínfulas, f. pl. (eccl.) infulæ, headdress, mitre; conceit, airs.

infundadamente, adv. groundlessly, without cause or reason.

infundado, da, a. groundless, baseless.

infundible, a. infusible.

infundibuliforme, a. (bot.) funnel-shaped.

infundíbulo, m. (anat.) infundibulum.

infundio, m. (coll.) fib, story.

infundir, va. (pp. INFUNDIDO and INFUSO) to infuse, to inspire with; to imbue, to instil.

infurción, f. ancient ground lease.

infurcioniego, ga, a. subject to ground lease.

infurtir, va. = ENFURTIR, to full (cloth).

infusibilidad, f. infusibility.

infusible, a. infusible.

infusión, f. infusion; inspiration; (pharm.) infusion; (eccl.) baptism by sprinkling.

infuso, sa, a. infused (with the grace of God).

infusorio, ria. I. n. & a. (zool.) infusorian. **II.** m. pl. Infusoria.

ingenerable, a. ingenerable, that cannot be produced or generated.

ingeniar. I. va. to conceive, contrive, devise, scheme. **II.** vr. to endeavor and manage skilfully; to find means to get or do a thing.

ingeniatura, f. (coll.) ingenuity, acuteness, skilful management; (Am.) engineering.

ingeniería, f. engineering.—**i. aerostera, civil,** etc. V. INGENIERO.

ingeniero, ra, n. engineer.—**i. aeróstata,** aeronautic engineer.—**i. aerostero,** aviation engineer.—**i. agrónomo,** agricultural engineer.—**i. civil,** civil engineer (gen. app. to all nonmilitary engineers).—**i. de caminos, canales y puertos,** civil engineer.—**i. de la armada,** or **de maria** = I. NAVAL.—**i. de minas,** mining engineer.—**i. de montes,** forestry engineer.—**i. electricista,** electrical engineer.—**i. en jefe,** chief engineer.—**i. forestal,** forestry engineer.—**i. industrial** = I. QUÍMICO.—**i. jefe,** chief engineer.—**i. naval,** marine engineer.—**i. químico,** chemical engineer.

ingenio, m. talent; mind, creative or inventive faculty; cleverness, skill, smartness; ingenuity, wit(s); talented person (esp. author); engine, machine, mechanical apparatus; device, contrivance; (bookbinding) plowcutter, plowpress.—**i. de azúcar,** sugar mill, sugar plantation.—**i. de pólvora,** powdermill.

ingeniosamente, adv. ingeniously.

ingeniosidad, f. ingenuity, ingeniousness.

ingenioso, sa, a. ingenious.

ingénito, ta, a. unbegotten; innate, inborn.

ingente, a. very large, huge, prodigious.

ingenuamente, adv. candidly, ingenuously.

ingenuidad, *f.* ingenuousness, candor.

ingenuo, nua, *a.* ingenuous, open, candid; (law) ingenuous, freeborn.

ingerencia, *f.* interference, intermeddling.

ingeridor, *m.* grafting knife.

ingeridura, *f.* grafting.

ingerir. I. *va.* (*ind.* INGIERO; *subj.* INGIERA) to insert, introduce, inclose; (agr.) to graft. **II.** *vr.* to interfere, intermeddle.

ingestión, *f.* (med.) ingestion, introduction of food into the stomach.

ingiero, ingiera, *v.* V. INGERIR.

ingina, *f.* = QUIJADA, jaw, jawbone.

ingle, *f.* groin, part next the thigh.

inglés, sa. I. *a.* English.—**a la inglesa,** in the English fashion. **II.** *n.* Englishman(-woman). **III.** *m.* English (the language).

inglesar, *va.* & *vr.* to Anglicize.

inglesismo, *m.* Anglicism.

inglete, *m.* diagonal; angle of 45°.

inglosable, *a.* admitting no gloss or comment.

ingobernable, *a.* ungovernable, unmanageable, unruly.

ingratamente, *adv.* ungratefully.

ingratitud, *f.* ingratitude, ungratefulness.

ingrato, ta. I. *a.* ungrateful; thankless; disagreeable. **II.** *n.* ingrate.

ingrediente, *m.* ingredient.

ingresar, *vn.* (**en**) to enter; (of money, profits, etc.) to come (in); to deposit (money); to join (a party, etc.); to enter (a university).

ingreso, *m.* entrance; entering; joining; (com.) entry, money received; (eccl.) surplice fees.— *pl.* (com.) revenue, receipts, earnings.

íngrimo, ma, *a.* (Mex.) (coll.) alone, solitary; deserted.

inguinal; inguinario, ria, *a.* (anat.) inguinal.

ingurgitación, *f.* (med.) ingurgitation.

ingurgitar, *va.* to ingurgitate, swallow.

ingustable, *a.* unsavory, unpalatable.

inhábil, *a.* unable; incompetent; unfit, unskilful; unqualified.—**inhabilidad,** *f.* inability; incompetence; unskilfulness.

inhabilitación, *f.* disabling or disqualifying; disqualification; disability.

inhabilitar. I. *va.* to disqualify; to disable, render unfit. **II.** *vr.* to lose a right; to become disabled.

inhabitable, *a.* uninhabitable.

inhabitado, da, *a.* uninhabited.

inhabituado, da, *a.* unaccustomed.

inhacedero, ra, *a.* impracticable, unfeasible.

inhalador, ra, *n.* inhaler.

inhalación, *f.* (med.) inhalation.

inhalar, *va.* (med.) to inhale.

inherencia, *f.* inherence.

inherente, *a.* inherent.

inhestar, *va.* (*ind.* INHIESTO; *subj.* INHIESTE) = ENHESTAR, to erect; to raise.

inhibición, *f.* inhibition; prohibition.

inhibir, *va.* (law) to inhibit (esp. an inferior court from proceeding further).

inhibitorio, ria, *a.* inhibitory.

¹inhiesto, inhieste, *v.* V. INHESTAR.

²inhiesto, ta, *a.* = ENHIESTO, erect; steep.

inhonestamente, *adv.* immodestly.

inhonestidad, *f.* immodesty, indecency.

inhonesto, ta, *a.* immodest, indecent.

inhospedable, *a.* = INHOSPITALARIO.

inhospitable, inhospital, *a.* = INHOSPITALARIO.

inhospitalario, ria, *a.* inhospitable, reluctant to entertain guests; unsheltering.

inhospitalidad, *f.* inhospitableness.

inhumación, *f.* interment, burying.

inhumanamente, *adv.* inhumanly, cruelly.

inhumanidad, *f.* inhumanity, cruelty.

inhumano, na, *a.* inhuman, cruel.

inhumar, *va.* to bury, inhume, inter.

iniciación, *f.* initiation, introduction.

iniciador, ra, *n.* & *a.* initiator(-ing), starter (-ing).

inicial, *n.* & *a.* initial.

iniciar. I. *va.* to initiate; to begin, start. **II.** *vr.* to be initiated; (eccl.) to receive first orders.

iniciativo, va. I. *a.* initiating, initiatory. **II.** *f.* initiative; right to propose laws, etc.

inicuamente, *adv.* iniquitously.

inicuo, cua, *a.* iniquitous, wicked.

in illo tempore, *adv.* formerly, in times of yore.

inimaginable, *a.* unimaginable, inconceivable.

inimicísimo, ma, *a. super. irreg.* of ENEMIGO, most inimical.

inimitable, *a.* inimitable.

ininteligible, *a.* unintelligible.

iniquidad, *f.* iniquity, unrighteousness.

iniquísimo, ma, *a. super.* of INICUO.

injerencia, injeridura, injerir = INGERENCIA, INGERIDURA, etc.

injertar, *va.* (*pp.* INJERTADO, INJERTO) (agr.) to ingraft, to graft.

injertera, *f.* orchard of grafted trees.

injerto, *m.* graft, grafting, ingrafted tree.

injuria, *f.* offense, wrong, insult, abuse, affront; injustice; damage, harm.

injuriado, da, *a.* & *pp.* injured, wronged.

injuriador, ra, *n.* aggressor, offender, abuser.

injuriante, *a.* injuring; offensive, insulting.

injuriar, *va.* to insult, offend, abuse; to annoy; to harm, hurt.

injuriosamente, *adv.* insultingly, offensively; injuriously, hurtfully.

injurioso, sa, *a.* injurious; insulting, offensive, abusive.

injustamente, *adv.* unjustly.

injusticia, *f.* injustice.

injustificable, *a.* unjustifiable.

injustificadamente, *adv.* unjustifiably.

injustificado, da, *a.* unjustified, unjustifiable.

injusto, ta, *a.* unjust.

inlegible, *a.* illegible.

inllevable, *a.* unbearable.

inmaculadamente, *adv.* immaculately.

inmaculado, da, *a.* immaculate.

inmanejable, *a.* unmanageable; unruly.

inmanente, *a.* immanent, inherent.

inmarcesible, *a.* unfading, unwithering.

inmaterial, *a.* immaterial, incorporeal.

inmaterialidad, *f.* immateriality.

inmaturo, ra, *a.* immature.

inmediación, *f.* contiguity, contact.—*pl.* environs, suburbs, outskirts; neighborhood.

inmediatamente, *adv.* contiguously; immediately, forthwith.

inmediato, ta, *a.* contiguous, close, adjoining, next, immediate.—**dar por las inmediatas,** (fig.) to force to the wall; to silence (in a discussion).—**llegar,** or **venir, a las inmediatas,** to come to the thick, or hardest, part of a fight or dispute.

inmedicable, *a.* incurable, irremediable.

inmejorable, *a.* unimprovable, unsurpassable, most excellent.

inmemorable, *a.* immemorial.

inmemorablemente, *adv.* immemorably.

inmemorial, *a.* immemorial.

inmensamente, *adv.* immensely, infinitely.

inmensidad, *f.* immensity, vastness; infinity; immensity of space, boundless space; great multitude or number.

inmenso, sa, *a.* immense; unbounded, infinite; countless.

inmensurable, *a.* immeasurable.

inmerecidamente, *adv.* undeservedly.

inmerecido, da, *a.* unmerited, undeserved.

inméritamente, *adv.* unmeritedly.

inmérito, ta, *a.* undeserved, unmerited.

inmeritorio, ria, *a.* undeserving.

inmersión, *f.* immersion.

inmigración, *f.* immigration.

inmigrado, da. I. *pp.* of INMIGRAR. **II.** *a.* & *n.* immigrant.

inmigrante, *n.* immigrant.

inmigrar, *vn.* to immigrate.

inmigratorio, ria, *a.* immigration (as *a.*).

inminencia, *f.* imminence, nearness.

inminente, *a.* imminent, impending, near.

inmiscible, *a.* (chem.) non-mixing.

inmiscuir. I. *va.* to mix. **II.** *vr.* to interfere, to intermeddle.

inmobiliario, ria, *a.* pertaining to real estate.

inmoble, *a.* unmovable, immovable, fixed; motionless; unshakable, constant.

inmoderación, *f.* immoderation, excess.

inmoderadamente, *adv.* immoderately.

inmoderado, da, *a.* immoderate, excessive.

inmodestamente, *adv.* immodestly.

inmodestia, *f.* immodesty, indelicacy.

inmodesto, ta, *a.* immodest, indelicate.

inmódico, ca, *a.* excessive.

inmolación, *f.* immolation, sacrifice.

inmolador, ra, *n.* & *a.* immolator(-ing).

inmolar, *va.* to immolate; to sacrifice.

inmoral, *a.* immoral.—**inmoralidad,** *f.* immorality.—**inmoralmente,** *adv.* immorally.

inmortal, *a.* immortal.—**inmortalidad,** *f.* immortality.—**inmortalizar. I.** *va.* to immortalize. **II.** *vr.* to become immortal.—**inmortalmente,** *adv.* immortally.

inmortificación, *f.* licentiousness.

inmortificado, da, *a.* unmortified.

inmotivado, da, *a.* without reason or cause.

inmoto, ta, *a.* unmoved.

inmovible, *a.* immovable.

inmóvil, *a.* motionless; fixed; unshaken.

inmovilidad, *f.* immovability, fixedness.

inmovilización, *f.* immobilization.

inmovilizar, *va.* to immobilize, fix.

inmudable, *a.* immutable.

inmueble, *a.* (law) immovable, real (property). **II.** *m.* (law) immovables.

inmundicia, *f.* filth, dirt; garbage; refuse; nastiness, filthiness; uncleanliness; impurity.

inmundo, da, *a.* unclean, filthy.

inmune, *a.* free, exempt; immune.

inmunidad, *f.* immunity; exemption, franchise, freedom.

inmunizar, *va.* to immunize, render immune.

inmutabilidad, *f.* immutability.

inmutable, *a.* immutable.

inmutación, *f.* change, alteration.

inmutar. I. *va.* to change, alter. **II.** *vr.* to change countenance from some emotion, to become disturbed, lose one's calm.

inmutativo, va, *a.* that changes or causes alterations.

innatismo, *m.* (philos.) innatism.

innato, ta, *a.* innate; inborn.

innatural, *a.* unnatural.

innavegable, *a.* unnavigable; unseaworthy.

innecesariamente, *adv.* unnecessarily.

innecesario, ria, *a.* unnecessary.

innegable, *a.* undeniable.

innegablemente, *adv.* undeniably.

innoble, *a.* ignoble.

innocuo, cua, *a.* innocuous, harmless.

innominable, *a.* unnamable.

innominado, da, *a.* nameless.

innovación, *f.* innovation.

innovador, ra, *n.* & *a.* innovator(-ing).

innovamiento, *m.* innovation.

innovar, *va.* to innovate.

innumerabilidad, *f.* innumerability.

innumerable, *a.* innumerable, numberless.

innumerablemente, *adv.* innumerably.

innúmero, ra, *a.* numberless, countless.

inobediencia, *f.* disobedience.

inobediente, *a.* disobedient; unmanageable.

inobservable, *a.* unobservable, inobservable.

inobservancia, *f.* disregarding (of law, etc.); non-conforming.

inobservante, *a.* disregarding (law, etc.); non-conformist (in religion).

inocencia, *f.* innocence; harmlessness.

inocentada, *f.* (coll.) simple or silly speech or action; practical joke or trick.

inocente, *a.* innocent; harmless; simple, gullible, unsophisticated, easily duped, "easy."

inocentemente, *adv.* innocently; harmlessly.

inocentón, na. I. *a.* *aug.* very simple and credulous. **II.** *n.* simpleton.

inoculación, *f.* inoculation.

inoculador, ra, *n.* & *a.* inoculator(-ing).

inocular, *va.* (med.) to inoculate; to contaminate.

inocuo, ca, *a.* = INNOCUO.

inodoro, ra. I. *a.* inodorous, odorless. **II.** *m.* water closet.

inofensivo, va, *a.* inoffensive, harmless.

inoficioso, sa, *a.* (law) inofficious (will).

inolvidable, *a.* unforgetable.

inope, *a.* poor, penniless, destitute.

inoperable, *a.* (med.) inoperable.

inopia, *f.* indigence, poverty, penury.

inopinable, *a.* indisputable; inconceivable.

inopinadamente, *adv.* unexpectedly.

inopinado, da, *a.* unexpected, unforeseen.

inoportunamente, *adv.* inopportunely.

inoportunidad, *f.* inopportuneness, untimeliness.

inoportuno, na, *a.* inopportune, untimely.

inordenadamente, *adv.* inordinately.

inordenado, da; inordinado, da, *a.* inordinate, irregular, disorderly.

inorgánico, ca, *a.* inorganic.

inoxidable, *a.* inoxidizable; nonrusting.

in pace (Lat.). **I.** *adv.* in peace. **II.** *m.* dungeon where scandalous persons were formerly confined.

in pártibus, (Lat.), *adv.* (coll.) having a nominal appointment.

in péctore (Lat.), *adv.* (coll.) (of resolutions, decrees, etc.) not yet made known.

in perpétuum (Lat.), *adv.* in perpetuum, in perpetuity, forever.

in promptu (Lat.), *adv.* offhand, impromptu, extempore.

in púribus (Lat.), *adv.* (coll.) stark naked.

inquebrantable, *a.* irrevocable.

inquiero, inquiera, *v.* V. INQUERIR.

inquietador, ra, *n.* disturber.

inquietamente, *adv.* restlessly.

inquietante, *a.* disquieting, disturbing.

inquietar. I. *va.* to disquiet, trouble, worry; to vex, tease, harass; to stir up or excite. **II.** *vr.* to become uneasy or restless, to fret, worry.

inquieto, ta, *a.* restless; anxious, solicitous, uneasy, worried.

inquietud, *f.* restlessness, uneasiness, anxiety.

inquilinato, *m.* (law) lease, leasehold.

inquilino, na, *n.* tenant, lodger; (law) lessee.

inquina, *f.* (coll.) aversion, hatred, grudge.

inquinamento, *m.* infection.

inquinar, *va.* to contaminate.

inquiridor, ra, *n.* inquirer, investigator.

inquirir, *va.* (*ind.* INQUIERO; *subj.* INQUIERA) to inquire, look into, search, investigate.

inquisición, *f.* inquest, examination, inquiry; (eccl.) Inquisition; Holy Office.

inquisidor, ra. I. *n.* inquirer, examiner. **II.** *m.* (eccl.) inquisitor.

inquisitorial, *a.* inquisitorial.

inri, *m.* I. N. R. I. (inscription on the cross); brand, stigma, stain.

insabible, *a.* unknowable.

insaciabilidad, *f.* insatiableness, greediness.

insaciable, *a.* insatiable; greedy.

insaciablemente, *adv.* insatiably.

insaculación, *f.* (law) balloting for names.

insaculador, *m.* (law) balloter.

insacular, *va.* to ballot, to vote by ballot.
insalivación, *f.* insalivation.
insalivar, *va.* to insalivate.
insalubre, *a.* insalubrious, unhealthful.
insalubridad, *f.* insalubrity, unhealthfulness.
insanable, *a.* incurable, irremediable.
insania, *f.* insanity.
insano, na, *a.* insane, mad, crazy.
inscribir. I. *va.* (*pp. irreg.* INSCRITO, INSCRIPTO) to inscribe, register, record, book· (geom.) to inscribe; (law) to record (deeds). **II.** *vr.* to register; to enroll.
inscripción, *f.* inscription; record, register, entry; registration; government bond.
inscriptible, *a.* (geom.) inscribable.
inscripto, ta, *pp. irreg.* of INSCRIBIR.
inscrito, ta, *pp. irreg.* of INSCRIBIR.
insculpir, *va.* to engrave, cut.
insecable, *a.* (coll.) that cannot be dried.
insecticida, *n. & a.* insecticide(-al).
insectil, *a.* insectile, insectean.
insectívoro, ra, *a.* insectivorous.
insecto, *m.* (entom.) insect.
inseguridad, *f.* insecurity, unsafety; uncertainty.
inseguro, ra, *a.* insecure, unsafe; uncertain.
insenescencia, *f.* quality of not becoming old.
insensatamente, *adv.* insensately, madly, stupidly.
insensatez, *f.* stupidity, folly.
insensato, ta, *a.* insensate, stupid, mad.
insensibilidad, *f.* insensibility, unconsciousness; hard-heartedness.
insensibilizar, *va.* to make insensible or insensitive.
insensible, *a.* insensible, senseless, unconscious; imperceptible; unfeeling, heartless.
insensiblemente, *adv.* insensibly; imperceptibly.
inseparabilidad, *f.* inseparableness.
inseparable, *a.* inseparable; undetachable.
inseparablemente, *adv.* inseparably.
insepulto, ta, *a.* unburied, uninterred.
inserción, *f.* insertion; grafting.
inserir, *va.* (*pp. irreg.* INSERTO) to insert; to graft.
insertar. I. *va.* (*pp.* INSERTADO, INSERTO) to insert, to introduce. **II.** *vr.* (zool. and bot.) to become inserted or attached.
inserto, ta, *pp. irreg.* of INSERIR & INSERTAR.
inservible, *a.* unserviceable, useless.
insidia, *f.* ambush, snare.
insidiador, ra, *n.* plotter, waylayer.
insidiar, *va.* to plot against, waylay, ambush.
insidiosamente, *adv.* insidiously, guilefully.
insidioso, sa, *a.* insidious, sly, guileful.
insigne, *a.* noted, famous, renowned.
insignemente, *adv.* signally, famously.
insignia, *f.* decoration, device, medal, badge, standard; (naut.) pennant.—*pl.* insignia.
insignificancia, *f.* insignificance; insufficiency, uselessness; trifle.
insignificante, *a.* insignificant, unimportant.
insignificativo, va, *a.* insignificant.
insinuación, *f.* insinuation, innuendo; hint, suggestion; (law) exhibition of a public instrument before a judge.
insinuante, *a.* insinuative, crafty, artful, sleek.
insinuar. I. *va.* to insinuate, hint, suggest. **II.** *vr.* to ingratiate oneself; to creep in; to grow (on one, as a habitation).
insinuativo, va, *a.* insinuating; insinuative; slick, smooth.
insípidamente, *adv.* insipidly.
insipidez, *f.* insipidity, insipidness.
insípido, da, *a.* insipid, tasteless; unsavory; spiritless, vapid, flat.
insipiencia, *f.* ignorance, lack of judgment.
insipiente, *a.* ignorant, uninformed.
insistencia, *f.* persistence, insistence, obstinacy.
insistir, *vn.* (en) to insist (on), persist (in); to dwell (upon), emphasize.
ínsito, ta, *a.* inherent, inborn, connatural.

in situ (Lat.) *adv.* in situ, in its natural place.
insociabilidad, *f.* unsociability, unsociableness.
insociable, insocial, *a.* unsociable.
insolación, *f.* (med.) insolation, sunstroke.
insolar. I. *va.* to expose to the sun's rays. **II.** *vr.* (med.) to be sunstruck.
insoldable, *a.* that cannot be soldered or welded.
insolencia, *f.* insolence.
insolentar. I. *va.* to make bold. **II.** *vr.* to become insolent.
insolente, *a.* insolent.—**insolentemente,** *adv.* insolently.
in sólidum, *adv.* (law) insolidum, joint and several.
insólito, ta, *a.* unusual, unaccustomed.
insolubilidad, *f.* insolubility; unsolvability.
insoluble, *a.* insoluble; fast, strong; unsolvable.
insolvencia, *f.* insolvency.
insolvente, *a.* insolvent.
insomne, *a.* insomnious, sleepless.
insomnio, *m.* insomnia, sleeplessness.
insondable, *a.* unfathomable, fathomless; inscrutable, unsearchable; abysmal.
insonoro, ra, *a.* not sounding clear.
insoportable, *a.* unbearable, intolerable.
insostenible, *a.* indefensible.
inspección, *f.* inspection, survey; superintendence; inspector's office.
inspeccionar, *va.* to inspect, examine, oversee.
inspector, ra, *n.* inspector, examiner; supervisor, superintendent, overseer.
inspiración, *f.* inspiration; (med.) inhalation.
inspirador, ra, *n. & a.* inspirer(-ing).
inspirante, *a.* inspiring.
inspirar, *va.* to inspire; to inhale.
inspirativo, va, *a.* inspiring.
inestabilidad, *f.* instability; inconstancy.
instable, *a.* unstable; inconstant, changeable.
instalación, *f.* installation, instalment; settling; plant, works, factory; system (as of gas pipes and fittings, etc.); induction (of an officer).
instalador, ra, *n.* one who installs, lays, sets up, etc. (gas fitter, pipe layer, plumber).
instalar. I. *va.* to install; to put in, lay, set up; to induct (into office). **II.** *vr.* to establish oneself, settle.
instancia, *f.* instance or instancy; memorial, petition; prosecution or process of a suit; pressing argument; entreaty, request.—**a instancia de,** at the request of.
instantáneamente, *adv.* instantly; instantaneously.
instantáneo, nea. I. *a.* instantaneous. **II.** *f.* (photog.) snapshot.
instante. I. *a.* instant, pressing, urgent. **II.** *m.* instant, moment.—**al i.,** immediately.—**por instantes,** incessantly, every moment.
instantemente, *adv.* instantly.
instar. I. *va.* to press, urge; in schools, to impugn the solution of a question. **II.** *vn.* to be urgent.
instauración, *f.* renovation, restoration.
instaurar, *va.* to renovate, restore.
instaurativo, va, *a.* restorative.
instigación, *f.* instigation, incitement.
instigador, ra, *n.* instigator, abetter.
instigar, *va.* (*pret.* INSTIGUÉ; *subj.* INSTIGUE) to instigate, incite, urge.
instilación, *f.* instillation.
instilar, *va.* to instil, infuse, insinuate.
instintivo, va, *a.* instinctive.
instintivamente, *adv.* instinctively.
instinto, *m.* instinct; divine inspiration.—**por i.,** instinctively.
institución, *f.* institution, establishment; education, instruction; (law) institution, instituting.—*pl.* institutes (of a science).
institucional, *a.* institutional.
instituente, *a.* instituting; founding.
instituidor, ra, *n.* institutor, founder.
instituir, *va.* (*ind.* INSTITUYO; *subj.* INSTITUYA)

to institute, establish, found; to teach, instruct; to appoint, constitute, institute.

instituta, *f.* (law) institutes.

instituto, *m.* institute, established law; settled order; institute, institution (of learning); school.—**i. de segunda enseñanza,** or **general y técnico,** high school.

institutor, ra, *n.* institutor.

institutriz, *f.* governess, instructress.

instituyente, *n.* institutor; founder.

instituyo, instituya, *v. V.* INSTITUIR.

instrucción, *f.* instruction, teaching; education; lesson; knowledge, learning; (law) court proceedings.—*pl.* instructions, directions, orders.—**i. primaria,** primary education.—**i. pública,** public education.—**i. secundaria,** high-school education.—**i. superior,** higher, or college, education.

instructivamente, *adv.* instructively.

instructivo, va, *a.* instructive.

instructor, ra, *n.* instructor, teacher.

instruído, da. I. *pp.* of INSTRUIR. **II.** *a.* learned, well-educated, well-posted.

instruir, *va.* (*ind.* INSTRUYO; *subj.* INSTRUYA) to instruct, teach, train, coach; to inform, advise; (mil.) to drill, train; (law) to put in legal form, to formulate according to established rules.

instrumentación, *f.* (mus.) instrumentation, orchestration.

instrumental, *a.* (mus.) instrumental; (law) pertaining to legal instruments.

instrumentalmente, *adv.* instrumentally.

instrumentar, *va.* (mus.) to orchestrate.

instrumentista, *m.* instrument maker; (mus.) instrumentalist, player on a musical instrument.

instrumento, *m.* instrument, implement, appliance, engine, machine, apparatus; agent or means; (law) instrument, indenture, deed; (mus.) instrument.—**i. de boca,** wind instrument.—**i. de canto,** musical instrument.—**i. de cuerda,** stringed instrument.—**i. de percusión,** percussion instrument.—**i. de viento,** or **i. neumático,** wind instrument.

instruyo, instruya, *v. V.* INSTRUIR.

insuave, *a.* unpleasant, disagreeable.

insubordinación, *f.* insubordination.

insubordinado, da. I. *pp.* of INSUBORDINAR. **II.** *a.* insubordinate, rebellious.

insubordinar. I. *va.* to incite to insubordination. **II.** *vr.* to rebel, to mutiny.

insubsistencia, *f.* instability.

insubsistente, *a.* unable; groundless, baseless.

insubstancial, *a.* unsubstantial, inane, shallow, pointless.

insubstancialidad, *f.* inanity.

insubstancialmente, *adv.* inanely.

insudar, *vn.* to toil, drudge, work hard.

insuficiencia, *f.* insufficiency, inadequateness.

insuficiente, *a.* insufficient, inadequate.

insuficientemente, *adv.* insufficiently.

insuflación, *f.* (med.) insufflation.

insuflar, *va.* (med.) to insufflate.

insufrible, *a.* intolerable, unbearable.

insufriblemente, *adv.* insufferably, unbearably.

ínsula, *f.* (archaic) isle, island.

insular; insulano, na, *a.* insular.

insulsamente, *adv.* insipidly.

insulsez, *f.* insipidity, flatness.

insulso, sa, *a.* insipid, tasteless; dull, heavy.

insultador, ra; insultante, *n. & a.* insulter (-ing), abuser(-ing, -ive).

insultar. I. *va.* to insult; to call names. **II.** *vr.* (coll.) to have a fit.

insulto, *m.* insult, affront; sudden fit of illness.

insume, *a.* costly, expensive.

insumergible, *a.* insubmergible.

insuperable, *a.* insuperable, insurmountable.

insupurable, *a.* that cannot suppurate.

insurgente, *n. & a.* insurgent.

insurrección, *f.* insurrection, rebellion.

insurreccionar. I. *va.* to cause to rebel, to raise in insurrection. **II.** *vr.* to rebel.

insurrecto, ta, *n. & a.* insurgent, rebel.

insustancial, *a.* = INSUBSTANCIAL.

intacto, ta, *a.* untouched, intact, whole; pure.

intachable, *a.* unexceptionable, irreproachable.

intangible, *a.* intangible; not to be touched.

integérrimo, ma, *a. super.* of ÍNTEGRO, most honorable, unspotted, irreproachable.

integrable, *a.* integrable.

integración, *f.* integration.

integrado, da, *pp.* of INTEGRAR.—**i. por,** consisting of, formed by.

integral. I. *a.* integral; whole. **II.** *f.* (math.) integral.

integralmente, *adv.* integrally, wholly.

íntegramente, *adv.* entirely, wholly.

integrante, *a.* integral; integrant; integrating.

integrar, *va.* to integrate; to compose, form, make up; (com.) to reimburse; (math.) to integrate.

integridad, *f.* wholeness, completeness; integrity, honesty, uprightness; virginity.

íntegro, gra, *a.* entire, complete, whole; upright, honest.

integumento, *m.* integument.

intelección, *f.* intellection, understanding.

intelectiva, *f.* intellect, intelligence.

intelectivo, va, *a.* intellective, intelligent.

intelecto, *m.* intellect, understanding.

intelectual, *a.* intellectual, mental.

intelectualmente, *adv.* intellectually.

inteligencia, *f.* intellect, mind, understanding; intelligence; comprehension; knowledge; understanding (between persons); skill, ability, experience; sense, meaning.—**en la i.,** in the understanding.

inteligenciado, da, *a.* (coll.) instructed, informed.

inteligente, *a.* intelligent; talented, smart, bright, clever; skilful, able.

inteligible, *a.* intelligible.

inteligiblemente, *adv.* intelligibly.

intemperancia, *f.* intemperance, excess.

intemperante, *a.* intemperate.

intemperie, *f.* rough or bad weather.—**a la i.,** in the open air, outdoors, unsheltered.

intempestivamente, *adv.* unseasonably, inopportunely.

intempestivo, va, *a.* unseasonable, inopportune.

intención, *f.* intention, purpose; viciousness (of animals); caution, discretion.—**dar i.,** to give hope.—**de primera i.,** provisionally, tentatively; frankly, impulsively, without disguise; (surg.) by first intention.—**de segunda i.,** double-facedly, deceitfully.—**por primera i.,** (surg.) = DE PRIMERA I.

intencionadamente, *adv.* intentionally.

intencionado, da, *a.* inclined, disposed.

intencional, *a.* intentional.

intencionalmente, *adv.* intentionally.

intendencia, *f.* intendancy (province); administration, management; office or district of an intendant.

intendenta, *f.* wife of an INTENDENTE.

intendente, *m.* intendant; administrator; sub treasurer of the government.—**i. de ejército,** quartermaster general.—**i. de marina,** commandant of a navy yard.

intensamente, *adv.* intensely.

intensar, *va.* to intensify.

intensidad, *f.* intensity; vehemence.

intensificar, *va.* to intensify.

intensión, *f.* = INTENSIDAD.

intensivo, va; intenso, sa, *a.* intense, intensive, vehement, ardent, lively.

intentar, *va.* to try, attempt, endeavor; to intend, purpose, mean; (law) to enter (an action), to commence (a lawsuit).

For pronunciation, see the rules at the beginning of the book.

intento, *m.* intent, purpose, design.—**de i.,** purposely, knowingly.

intentona, *f.* (coll.) rash attempt.

¹inter, *prep.* between.—**i. nos,** between ourselves, between you and me.

²inter, *m.* interim; (Peru) substitute curate.

intercadencia, *f.* interruption, interposition; unevenness; inconstancy; (med.) intermission or inequality of the pulse.

intercadente, *a.* changeable, variable.

intercadentemente, *adv.* changeably.

intercalación, *f.* intercalation, interpolation, insertion.

¹intercalar, *va.* to intercalate, interpolate.

²intercalar, *a.* intercalary.

intercambiable, *a.* interchangeable.

intercambio, *m.* interchange.—**i. comercial,** international trade.—**i. de monedas,** (com.) foreign exchange.

interceder, *vn.* to intercede.

intercelular, *a.* intercellular.

interceptación, *f.* interception, stoppage.

interceptar, *va.* to intercept, cut off.

intercesión, *f.* intercession, mediation.

intercesor, ra, *n.* intercessor, interceder.

interciso, sa, *a.*—**día de i.,** half holiday.

interclusión, *f.* shutting in or up.

intercolumnio, intercolunio, *m.* (arch.) intercolumniation.

intercontinental, *a.* intercontinental.

intercostal, *a.* intercostal.

intercurrencia, *f.* (med.) intercurrence.

intercurrente, *a.* intercurrent, intervening.

intercutáneo, nea, *a.* (med.) subcutaneous.

interdecir, *va.* to interdict, prohibit.

interdentario, ria, *a.* (phon.) interdental.

interdicción, *f.* interdiction, prohibition.

interdicto, *m.* prohibition, interdiction; interdict; (law) judgment of summary possession.

interdigital, *a.* interdigital, between the fingers.

interés, *m.* interest; (com. often *pl.: los intereses se han pagado ya,* the interest has already been paid); attraction, inducement.—*pl.* interests; money matters, business affairs.—**i. compuesto,** compound interest.—**i. simple,** simple interest.—**intereses creados,** vested interests, "the interests."

interesable, *a.* avaricious, mercenary.

interesado, da. I. *pp.* of INTERESAR. II. *a.* interested, concerned; selfish, mercenary. III. *n.* associate; person interested; (law) party in interest.

interesante, *a.* interesting.

interesar. I. *vn. & vr.* (**en, por, con**) to be concerned (with) or interested (in); to take an interest (in). II. *va.* to invest; to give an interest; to interest, attract.

interesencia, *f.* assistance, attendance.

interesente, *a.* present, concurring.

interesillo, *m. dim.* slight interest.

interestatal, *a.* interstate.

interestelar, *a.* interstellar.

interfecto, ta, *n.* (law) murdered person, victim.

interferencia, *f.* (opt.) interference.

interfoliar, *va.* to interleave (a book).

intergubernamental, *a.* inter-governmental.

ínterin. I. *m.* character of acting or pro tempore. II. *adv.* meanwhile, interim.

interinamente, *adv.* in the interim, meantime, provisionally, pro tem.

interinidad, *f.* = ÍNTERIN.

interino, na, *a.* provisional, temporary; pro tempore, acting, interim (as *a.*).

interior. I. *a.* interior, internal, inner, inside; home (as *a.*), domestic (commerce, etc.).—**lo i.,** the inside; home or domestic (national) affairs; (pol.) the Interior. II. *m.* interior; inside; inner part; mind, soul; in coaches with three compartments, the middle one.—*pl.* entrails, intestines, (coll.) insides.

interioridades, *f. pl.* family secrets; inwardness.

interiormente, *adv.* internally; inwardly.

interjección, *f.* (gram.) interjection.

interlínea, *f.* (print.) lead, space line.

interlineación, *f.* interlineation; double space; (print.) leading.

interlineal, *a.* interlineal.

interlinear, *va.* to write between lines; (print.) to lead, to space; to double-space.

interlocución, *f.* interlocution, dialogue.

interlocutor, ra, *n.* interlocutor.

interlocutoriamente, *adv.* (law) intermediately.

interlocutorio, ria, *a.* (law) interlocutory, intermediate.

intérlope, *a.* interloping.

interlunio, *m.* interlunar period, interlunation.

intermaxilar, *a.* intermaxillary.

intermediar, *va.* to interpose, mediate.

intermediario, ria. I. *a.* intermediary. II. *n.* intermediary; mediator; (pol. econ.) intermediary, middleman.

intermedio, dia. I. *a.* intermediate, intervening, interposed. II. *m.* interval, interim; (theat.) interlude, intermission.—**por i. de,** (Am.) through, with the help of.

interminable, *a.* interminable, endless.

intermisión, *f.* intermission, interruption.

intermitencia, *f.* (med.) intermission.

intermitente, *a.* intermittent.

intermitir, *va.* to intermit, discontinue.

internación, *f.* going or taking inside or into.

internacional, *a.* international.

internacionalismo, *m.* international relations; internationalism (socialistic doctrine).

internacionalista, *n.* internationalist.

internado, *m.* boarding-school system; state of being a boarding student; body of boarding students.

internamente, *adv.* internally.

internar. I. *va.* to send into the interior of a country; to place, or order placed, in an institution. II. *vn.* to enter. III. *vr.* (**en**) to go into the interior (of); to go deeply (into) (a subject); to worm oneself into another's confidence.

interno, na. I. *a.* interior, internal, inward; boarding (student). II. *n.* boarding student.

internodio, *m.* (bot.) internode.

internuncio, *m.* interlocutor; (eccl.) internuncio.

interoceánico, ca, *a.* interoceanic.

interocular, *a.* interocular, between the eyes.

interóseo, a, *a.* interosseous, between bones.

interpaginar, *va.* (bookbinding) to interleave.

interpelación, *f.* interpellation; summons.

interpelar, *va.* to appeal to, to implore the aid of; to interpellate; (law) to summon.

interplanetario, ria, *a.* interplanetary.

interpolación, *f.* interpolation.

interpoladamente, *adv.* in an interpolated way.

interpolar, *va.* to interpolate; to intermix; to stop or pause briefly in (an address, etc.).

interponer. I. *va.* (*pp. irreg.* INTERPUESTO; *ind. pres.* INTERPONGO, *pret.* INTERPUSE, *fut.* INTERPONDRÉ; *subj.* INTERPONGA) to interpose, place between; to appoint as a mediator; (law) to present (a petition) to a court. II. *vr.* to go between, to interpose.

interposición, *f.* interposition; mediation; meddling, interference.

interpósita persona, (Lat.) (law) intermediary, agent.

interprender, *va.* (mil.) to take by surprise.

interpresa, *f.* (mil.) taking by surprise.

interpretable, *a.* interpretable.

interpretación, *f.* interpretation.—**i. de lenguas,** Translation Bureau (in the State Department of Spain).

interpretador, ra, *n.* interpreter.

interpretante, *n. & a.* interpreter(-ing).

interpretar, *va.* to interpret.

interpretativamente, *adv.* interpretatively.

---

interpretativo, va, *a.* interpretative.
intérprete, *n.* interpreter; sign, mark.
interpuesto, ta. I. *pp. irreg.* of INTERPONER. **II.** *a.* interposed, intervening.
interregno, *m.* interregnum.—**i. parlamentario,** period during which the Spanish Cortes are not in session.
interrogación, *f.* interrogation, question; (print.) question mark.
interrogante. I. *a.* interrogative; interrogating; question (mark). **II.** *n.* interrogator, questioner. **III.** *m.* question mark.
interrogar, *va.* (*pret.* INTERROGUÉ; *subj.* INTERROGUE) to question, to interrogate.
interrogativamente, *adv.* interrogatively.
interrogativo, va, *a.* interrogative.
interrogatorio, *m.* interrogatory; (law) cross-examination.
interrogué, interrogue, *v. V.* INTERROGAR.
interrumpidamente, *adv.* interruptedly.
interrumpido, da. I. *pp.* of INTERRUMPIR. **II.** *a.* interrupted, broken, discontinued.
interrumpir, *va.* to interrupt.
interrupción, *f.* interruption.
interruptor, ra. I. *n.* interrupter. **II.** *m.* (elec.) switch; circuit-breaker.—**i. bipolar,** two-pole switch.—**i. de aceite,** oil-break switch.—**i. de arranque,** starting switch.—**i. de botón,** push-button switch.—**i. de cuchilla,** knife (-edge) switch.—**i. de dos (tres) direcciones,** two- (three-) way switch.—**i. de mano,** hand switch.—**i. de seguridad,** safety switch.—**i. de techo,** ceiling switch, top switch.—**i. horario,** time switch.—**i. trifásico,** three-phase switch.—**i. tripolar,** three-pole switch.—**i. unipolar,** single-pole switch.
intersecarse, *vr.* to intersect (as two lines).
intersección, *f.* intersection.
intersideral, *a.* (astr.) interstellar.
intersticial, *a.* interstitial.
intersticio, *m.* interstice; lapse of time, period, interval.
intertropical, *a.* intertropical.
interusurio, *m.* (law) interest for a delay.
intervalo, *m.* interval; (mus.) interval.
intervención, *f.* intervention; supervision, superintendence; mediation, interposition; auditing of accounts; (law) intervention; (surg.) operation.
intervengo, intervenga, intervendré, *v. V.* INTERVENIR.
intervenir (*ger.* INTERVINIENDO; *ind. pres.* yo INTERVENGO, él INTERVIENE, *pret.* INTERVINE, *fut.* INTERVENDRÉ; *subj.* INTERVENGA). **I.** *vn.* to intervene, mediate, intermediate; to interfere. **II.** *va.* to supervise, superintend; to audit (accounts); to control, to regulate; to offer to pay (a draft). **III.** *v. impers.* to occur, happen.
interventor, ra, *n.* comptroller; supervisor, inspector, superintendent; auditor.
intervertebral, *a.* intervertebral.
intervievar, *va.* (occasionally seen in newspapers) to interview.
intervine, interviniendo, *v. V.* INTERVENIR.
interyacente, *a.* interjacent, intervening.
intestado, da, *a.* intestate.
intestinal, *a.* intestinal.
intestino, na. I. *a.* intestine, internal; civil, domestic. **II.** *m.* intestine.—**i. ciego,** blind gut, cæcum.—**i. delgado,** small intestine.—**i. grueso,** large intestine.
intima, intimación, *f.* intimation, hint.
íntimamente, *adv.* intimately.
intimar. I. *va.* to intimate, indicate, suggest, hint. **II.** *vr.* to pierce, penetrate; to become intimate.
intimatorio, ria, *a.* (law) intimating.
intimidación, *f.* intimidation.
intimidad, *f.* intimacy.
intimidar, *va.* to intimidate.

íntimo, ma, *a.* internal, innermost; intimate.
intitular. I. *va.* to entitle; to confer a title on. **II.** *vr.* to use a title; to call oneself (a name).
intolerabilidad, *f.* intolerableness.
intolerable, *a.* intolerable, unbearable.
intolerancia, *f.* intolerance.
intolerante, *a.* intolerant.
intonso, sa, *a.* (poet.) unshorn; unpolished; (bookbinding) bound with uncut leaves.
intorsión, *f.* (bot.) intortion.
intoxicación, *f.* (med.) intoxication, poisoning.
intoxicar, *va.* (*pret.* INTOXIQUÉ; *subj.* INTOXIQUE) (med.) to poison.
intradós, *m.* (arch.) intrados.
intraducible, *a.* untranslatable.
intramuros, *adv.* within the city.
intranquilidad, *f.* restlessness, uneasiness.
intranquilizar, *va.* to worry, make uneasy.
intranquilo, la, *a.* uneasy, restless.
intransferible, *a.* not transferable.
intransigente, *a.* intransigent, irreconcilable.
intransitable, *a.* impassable.
intransitivo, va, *a.* (gram.) intransitive.
intransmisible, *a.* untransmissible.
intransmutabilidad, *f.* immutability.
intransmutable, *a.* intransmutable.
intratable, *a.* intractable; unruly, unmanageable; unsociable; rude, grouchy; impassable.
intravenoso, sa, *a.* intravenous.
intrépidamente, *adv.* intrepidly, fearlessly.
intrepidez, *f.* intrepidity, courage, bravery.
intrépido, da, *a.* intrepid, daring, gallant.
intriga, *f.* intrigue; entanglement, embroilment; (complicated) plot of a play.
intrigante, *n. & a.* intriguer(-ing).
intrigar .(*pret.* INTRIGUÉ; *subj.* INTRIGUE). **I.** *va.* to arouse (one's) interest or curiosity. **II.** *vn.* to intrigue, plot, scheme. **III.** *vr.* (**en**) to be interested (in) or curious (about).
intrincable, *a.* intricate; perplexed.
intrincación, *f.* intricacy, intricateness.
intrincadamente, *adv.* intricately.
intrincado, da, *a. & pp.* intricate.
intrincamiento, *m.* intricateness.
intrincar, *va.* (*pret.* INTRINQUÉ; *subj.* INTRINQUE) to entangle, complicate, confuse.
intríngulis, *m.* (coll.) crafty intention, hidden motive; mystery, enigma.
intrinqué, intrinque, *v. V.* INTRINCAR.
intrínsecamente, *adv.* intrinsically.
intrínseco, ca, *a.* intrinsic, intrinsical.
introducción, *f.* introduction.
introducir. I. *va.* (*ind. pres.* INTRODUZCO, *pret.* INTRODUJE; *subj.* INTRODUZCA) to introduce; to usher in, put in, insert; to present (a person). **II.** *vr.* (**en**) to gain access (to), to get in, to ingratiate oneself (with); to interfere (in).
introductor, ra, *n.* introducer.
introduje, introduzco, etc., *v. V.* INTRODUCIR.
introito, *m.* beginning of an oration; (eccl.) introit; (theat.) prologue.
introspección, *f.* introspection.
introversión, *f.* introversion.
introverso, sa, *a.* introverted; (psych.) introvert.
intrusamente, *adv.* intrusively.
intrusarse, *vr.* to obtrude, intrude.
intrusión, *f.* intrusion, obtrusion.
intruso, sa. I. *a.* intruded, intrusive, obtrusive. **II.** *m.* intruder, obtruder, squatter.
intubación, *f.* (med.) intubation.
intubar, *va.* (med.) to intubate, insert a tube.
intuición, *f.* intuition.
intuir, *va.* to know or perceive by intuition.
intuitivamente, *adv.* intuitively.
intuitivo, va, *a.* intuitive, evident.
intuito, *m.* view, look, glance.—**por i.,** in consideration, by reason of.
intumescencia, *f.* intumescence, swelling.
intumescente, *a.* intumescent, swollen.
intususcepción, *f.* intussusception.

For pronunciation, see the rules at the beginning of the book.

inulto, ta, *a.* (poet.) unavenged, unpunished.

inundación, *f.* inundation, flood; confluence; multitude.

inundante, *a.* inundating; inundant.

inundar, *va.* to inundate, flood.

inurbanamente, *adv.* uncivilly, discourteously.

inurbanidad, *f.* incivility, discourtesy.

inurbano, na, *a.* uncivil, impolite, unmannerly.

inusitadamente, *adv.* unusually.

inusitado, da, *a.* unusual, not in use.

inútil, *a.* useless; fruitless; needless.

inutilicé, inutilice, *v.* V. INUTILIZAR.

inutilidad, *f.* uselessness; needlessness.

inutilizar. I. *va.* (*pret.* INUTILICÉ; *subj.* INUTILICE) to render useless; to disable; to spoil, ruin. **II.** *vr.* to become useless.

inútilmente, *adv.* uselessly, to no purpose.

invadeable, *a.* unfordable.

invadir, *va.* to invade; encroach upon.

invaginación, *f.* invagination.

invaginar, *va.* to invaginate.

invalidación, *f.* invalidation, invalidity.

inválidamente, *adv.* invalidly.

invalidar, *va.* to invalidate, nullify.

inválido, da. I. *a.* invalid; cripple; feeble, weak; null, void. **II.** *m.* invalid.

invariabilidad, *f.* invariability.

invariable, *a.* invariable, constant.—**invariablemente,** *adv.* invariably.

invariación, *f.* immutability, invariableness.

invariadamente, *adv.* unvariedly.

invariado, da, *a.* unvaried, constant.

invariante, *f.* (math.) invariant.

invasión, *f.* invasion; attack.

invasor, ra, *n.* & *a.* invader(-ing).

invectiva, *f.* invective, harsh censure.

invencible, *a.* invincible, unconquerable.

invenciblemente, *adv.* invincibly.

invención, *f.* invention.

invencionero, ra, *n.* inventor; plotter; trifler.

invendible, *a.* unsalable.

inventar, *va.* to invent; to fib.

inventariar, *va.* to inventory, take inventory of.

inventario, *m.* inventory.

inventiva, *f.* faculty of invention, inventiveness.

inventivo, va, *a.* inventive.

invento, *m.* invention.

inventor, ra, *n.* inventor; fibber, fabricator, romancer.

inverecundo, da, *a.* shameless, impudent.

inverisímil, *a.* unlikely, improbable.

inverisimilitud, *f.* improbability.

invernáculo, *m.* greenhouse, hothouse, conservatory.

invernada, *f.* winter season.

invernadero, *m.* winter quarters; hothouse, conservatory.

invernal. I. *a.* hibernal, winter (as *a.*). **II.** *m.* winter shed (for cattle and fodder).

invernar, *vn.* (*ind.* INVIERNO; *subj.* INVIERNE) to winter, pass the winter.

invernizo, za, *a.* winter (as *a.*); winterly, hibernal; winter-beaten.

inverosímil, *a.* = INVERISÍMIL.

inverosimilitud, *f.* = INVERISIMILITUD.

inversamente, *adv.* inversely; contrariwise.

inversión, *f.* inversion; (com.) investment.

inverso, sa. I. *pp. irreg.* of INVERTIR. **II.** *a.* inverse, inverted.—**a,** or **por, la inversa,** on the contrary.

inversor, ra. I. *a.* inverting; (elec., mech.) reversing. **II.** *n.* reverser; reverse gear; reversing mechanism.

invertebrado, da. I. *n.* & *a.* invertebrate. **II.** *m. pl.* Invertebrata.

invertido, da. I. *pp.* of INVERTIR. **II.** *a.* & *n.* homosexual.

invertina, *f.* (chem.) invertase.

invertir, *va.* (*pp.* INVERTIDO, INVERSO; *ger.* INVIRTIENDO; *ind. pres.* INVIERTO, *pret.* él IN-VIRTIÓ; *subj.* INVIERTA) to invert; to reverse; to spend (time); (com.) to invest.

investidura, *f.* investiture.

investigable, *a.* investigable.

investigación, *f.* investigation, research; inquest.

investigador, ra, *n.* & *a.* investigator(-ing).

investigar, *va.* (*pret.* INVESTIGUÉ; *subj.* INVESTIGUE) to investigate, ascertain, inquire into; to do research work.

investir, *va.* (*ger.* INVISTIENDO; *ind. pres.* INVISTO, *pret.* él INVISTIÓ; *subj.* INVISTA) to invest, to confer upon.

inveteradamente, *adv.* inveterately.

inveterado, da. I. *pp.* of INVETERARSE. **II.** *a.* inveterate.

inveterarse, *vr.* to become antiquated, old, or chronic.

invictamente, *adv.* triumphantly, valiantly.

invicto, ta, *a.* invincible, unconquered.

[1]invierno, *m.* winter; rainy season (in countries having no astronomical seasons, as in the tropics).

[2]invierno, invierne, *v.* V. INVERNAR.

invierto, invierta, *v.* V. INVERTIR.

invigilar, *vn.* to watch carefully.

inviolabilidad, *f.* inviolability.

inviolable, *a.* inviolable; inviolate.

inviolablemente, *adv.* inviolably; infallibly.

inviolado, da, *a.* inviolate, unhurt, uninjured.

invirtió, invirtiendo, *v.* V. INVERTIR.

invisibilidad, *f.* invisibility.

invisible, *a.* invisible.—**en un i.,** (coll.) in less than no time.—**invisiblemente,** *adv.* invisibly.

invisto, invista, invistió, etc. *v.* V. INVESTIR.

invitación, *f.* invitation.

invitado, da, *n.* invited person; guest.

invitador, ra, *n.* inviter.

invitar, *va.* to invite; entice; treat.

invitatorio, *m.* (eccl.) invitatory.

invocación, *f.* invocation.

invocador, ra, *n.* & *a.* invoker(-ing).

invocar, *va.* (*pret.* INVOQUÉ; *subj.* INVOQUE) to invoke, implore.

invocatorio, ria, *a.* invocatory.

involucral, *a.* (bot.) involucral.

involucrar, *va.* to introduce as a digression.

involucro, *m.* (bot.) involucre.

involuntariamente, *adv.* involuntarily.

involuntariedad, *f.* involuntariness.

involuntario, ria, *a.* involuntary.

invoqué, invoque, *v.* V. INVOCAR.

invulnerabilidad, *f.* invulnerability.

invulnerable, *a.* invulnerable.

inyección, *f.* injection; liquid injected.

inyectado, da. I. *pp.* of INYECTAR. **II.** *a.* (Am.) bloodshot (eyes).

inyectar, *va.* to inject.

inyector, *m.* (mech.) injector.

iodo, (chem.) = YODO, iodine.

ion, *m.* (chem.) ion.

ionización, *f.* ionization.

ionizar, *va.* to ionize.

ipecacuana, *f.* (bot.) ipecacuanha, ipecac.—**i. de las Antillas,** wild ipecac.

[1]ipil, *m.* (P. I.) (bot.) a hardwood tree.

[2]ipil, hipil, *m.* (Am.) Indian loose outer garment.

ipso facto (Lat.) *adv.* ipso facto, by the fact itself, by the very fact.

ipso jure (Lat.) *adv.* ipso jure, by the law itself.

ir. I. *vn.* (*pp.* IDO; *ger.* YENDO; *ind. pres.* VOY, *imperf.* IBA, *pret.* FUÍ; *subj.* VAYA) to go, move, walk; to fit, to be becoming, suit; to concern, interest, affect, involve (diff. constr.: *poco me va en eso,* that concerns me very little; *en eso me va la reputación,* that involves, or affects, my reputation); to get along, do (diff. constr. *me fué bien,* I got along, or did, well); to differ, to be different (diff. constr.: *¡lo que va de ayer a hoy!* how today differs from yesterday!); to lead (*todos los caminos van a Roma*, all roads lead to Rome); to be, find oneself, be doing (*el enfermo va bien*, the patient is doing well); to be, to elapse (*de hoy al lunes van tres días*, it is three days from today to Monday); (arith.) to be, to leave (diff. constr.: *de 3 a 5 van 2*, 3 from 5 leaves 2); (arith.) to carry (*4, y van 2*, 4, and 2 to carry); (followed by *pp.*) to be (*voy herido*, I am wounded; *va descarriado*, he is astray or off the way). Before a gerund, it implies the beginning of the action the gerund denotes, or its continued performance or occurrence (*va anocheciendo*, it is getting dark; *voy comprendiendo*, I begin to understand; *Juan va perdiendo la paciencia*, John is losing patience; *voy viendo los cuadros*, I am looking at the pictures; *va trabajando*, he is working).—**i. a**, to go to; to be going to, to purpose or intend to (*voy al teatro*, I am going to the theater; *voy a hablarle*, I am going, or intend, to speak to him; *¿adónde va Vd.?* where are you going?); to bet on (*voy al caballo negro*, I bet on the black horse).—**i. a buscar**, to go get, fetch.—**i. a caballo**, to ride, to be riding on horseback.—**i. adelante**, to go (march, ride, etc.) at the front; to be ahead; to go on; to go ahead.—**i. a esperar a**, to go to meet.—**i. a medias**, to go halves.—**i. de bracero**, or **de brazo**, to walk arm in arm.—**i. delante**, to go ahead.—**i. en alcance**, (print.) to divide the (original) copy among various compositors.—**i. en coche**, to drive, to ride in a carriage.—**i. en demanda de**, (naut.) to be on the lookout for.—**i. pasando**, to be so so, to be as usual, to be getting along.—**i. por delante** = **I. DELANTE.**—**i. por ojo** = IRSE A PIQUE.—**algo, or mucho, va de Pedro a Pedro**, all people aren't alike, there are people and people. —**¿cómo le va?** how are you?—**¿cómo vamos?** how are you? how goes it with you?—**no me va ni me viene**, does not concern, or affect, me in the least.—**no vaya** (vayan) **a** (foll. by *inf.*), don't, don't go and (*inf.*).—**¡qué va!** nonsense! you don't say! don't tell me!—**¿quién va?** or **¡quién va allá?** who's there? who goes there? —**¡vámonos!** let's go! (R.y.) all aboard!—**¡vamos!** let's go! come on! also as expletive: why! well!—**¡vamos a ver!** let's see! let me see! what is it?—**¡vamos claros**, let's be plain, let's get down to business.—**¡vaya!** what a (*¡vaya una idea!* what an idea!)—**¡vaya con** (ella)! good for (her)!—**vaya** (que), all right, let it be; indeed.—**¡vaya sí** (es verdad)! I should say so!—**vaya Vd. a paseo**, go on, get out.—**vaya Vd. con Dios**, farewell; God be with you. II. *vr.* to go, go away, depart, quit; to leak, to ooze; to exhale, evaporate; to break wind; to break to pieces; to grow old.—**i. abajo**, to topple down.—**i. a pique**, (naut.) to founder, to go to the bottom, to be wrecked. —**i. atrás**, to go back, to flinch.—**i. de boca**, to speak thoughtlessly or recklessly.—**i. los ojos tras de**, to gaze admiringly or longingly at.—**írsele a uno el alma por**, to long for.—**írsele a uno la mula**, to speak unadvisedly from carelessness or anger.—**irse** (foll. by *ger.*), to be gradually (*pres. p.*).—**allá se va**, it is all the same, it amounts to the same thing.

ira, *f.* ire, anger, wrath, rage.—**¡i. de Dios!** Lord deliver us!

iraca, *f.* (Am.) Panama-hat palm.

iracundia, *f.* irascibility, ire, irascibleness.

iracundo, da, *a.* wrathful; angry, enraged.

iradé, *m.* irade, Sultan's decree.

iranio, nia, *n.* & *a.* Iranian.

irascible, *a.* irascible, irritable.

irenarca, *m.* (anc. Rome) irenarch, magistrate.

irgo, irga, irguió, etc., *v.* V. ERGUIR.

iribú, *m.* (Arg.) turkey buzzard.

iridáceo, cea. I. *a.* iridaceous, irislike. **II.** *f. pl.* (bot.) Iridaceæ.

íride, *f.* (bot.) = EFÉMERO, iris.

irídeo, a. I. *a.* irideous. **II.** *f. pl.* (bot.) Iridaceæ.

iridio, *m.* (chem.) iridium.

iridiscente, *a.* iridescent.

iris, *m.* iris, rainbow; (anat.) iris; (min.) opal.—**i. de paz**, mediator, peacemaker.

irisación, *f.* irisation.

irisado, da, *a.* rainbow-hued.

irisar, *vn.* to be iridescent.

iritis, *f.* (med.) iritis, inflammation of the iris.

irlanda, *f.* cotton and woollen cloth; fine Irish linen.

irlandés, esa. I. *a.* Irish. **II.** *m.* Irishman; Irish language. **III.** *f.* Irishwoman.

ironía, *f.* (rhet.) irony.

irónicamente, *adv.* ironically.

irónico, ca, *a.* ironical, sarcastic.

iroqués, sa, *n.* & *a.* Iroquois.

irracional. I. *a.* irrational, absurd; (math.) irrational. **II.** *m.* irrational (being).

irracionalidad, *f.* irrationality.

irracionalmente, *adv.* irrationally.

irradiación, *f.* radiation.

irradiar, *va.* to radiate.

irrazonable, *a.* unreasonable.

irrealidad, *f.* unreality.

irrealizable, *a.* unrealizable, unattainable.

irrebatible, *a.* indisputable.

irreconciliable, *a.* irreconcilable.

irreconciliablemente, *adv.* irreconcilably.

irrecuperable, *a.* irrecoverable, irretrievable.

irrecusable, *a.* unimpeachable.

irredimible, *a.* irredeemable.

irreducible, irreductible, *a.* irreducible.

irreemplazable, *a.* irreplaceable.

irreflexión, *f.* rashness, indiscretion.

irreflexivo, va, *a.* thoughtless, impulsive.

irreformable, *a.* unreformable.

irrefragable, *a.* irrefutable.

irrefragablemente, *adv.* irrefutably.

irrefrenable, *a.* unbridled, unruly, unmanageable, uncontrollable.

irrefutable, *a.* irrefutable, indisputable.

irregular, *a.* irregular.—**irregularidad,** *f.* irregularity.—**irregularmente,** *adv.* irregularly.

irreligión, *f.* irreligion.

irreligiosamente, *adv.* irreligiously.

irreligiosidad, *f.* irreligiousness.

irreligioso, sa, *a.* irreligious.

irremediable, *a.* irremediable, incurable; hopeless.—**irremediablemente,** *adv.* irremediably, hopelessly.

irremisible, *a.* irremissible, unpardonable.

irremisiblemente, *adv.* unpardonably, irremissibly.

irremunerado, da, *a.* unremunerated.

irreparable, *a.* irreparable, irretrievable.

irreparablemente, *adv.* irreparably, irretrievably, irrecoverably.

irreprensible, *a.* irreprehensible, irreproachable.

irreprensiblemente, *adv.* irreproachably.

irreprochable, *a.* irreproachable.

irresistibilidad, *f.* irresistibility.

irresistible, *a.* irresistible.

irresistiblemente, *adv.* irresistibly.

irresoluble, *a.* indeterminable; unsolvable; irresolute.

irresolución, *f.* irresolution, hesitation.

irresolutamente, *adv.* irresolutely.

irresoluto, ta, *a.* irresolute, wavering.

irrespetuoso, sa, *a.* disrespectful.

irrespirable, *a.* not fit to be breathed.

irresponsabilidad, *f.* irresponsibility.

irresponsable, *a.* irresponsible.

irresuelto, ta, *a.* = IRRESOLUTO.

irreverencia, *f.* irreverence.

irreverente, *a.* irreverent.—**irreverentemente,** *adv.* irreverently.

irrevocabilidad, *f.* irrevocability.

irrevocable, *a.* irrevocable.

irrevocablemente, *adv.* irrevocably.
irrigación, *f.* (med.) irrigation.
irrigador, *m.* (med.) irrigator.
irrigar, *va.* (med.) to irrigate.
irrisible, *a.* laughable.
irrisión, *f.* derision, ridicule.
irrisoriamente, *adv.* derisively.
irrisorio, ria, *a.* derisive.
irritabilidad, *f.* irritability.
irritable, *a.* irritable.
irritable, *a.* (law) voidable.
irritación, *f.* irritation, commotion, agitation; (med.) irritation.
irritación, *f.* (law) invalidation, abrogation.
irritador, ra, *n. & a.* irritator(-ing), stimulator (-ing), irritant.
irritamente, *adv.* (law) invalidly.
irritamiento, *m.* irritation, anger.
irritante. I. *a.* irritant, stimulating. **II.** *m.* stimulant, irritant.
irritante, *a.* (law) annulling, voiding.
irritar, *va.* to irritate, exasperate, anger; (med.) to irritate.
irritar, *va.* (law) to annul, void.
irrito, ta, *a.* (law) null, void.
irrogar, *va.* (*pret.* IRROGUÉ; *subj.* IRROGUE) to cause, to occasion (damage).
irrompible, *a.* unbreakable.
irrumpir, *vn.* to raid, invade; break into.
irrupción, *f.* irruption, inroad, invasion, raid.
isabelino, na, *a.* (coin) stamped with the bust of Isabella II.; partisan or defender of Queen Isabella; light bay (horse).
isagoge, *f.* introduction, exordium.
isagógico, ca, *a.* introductive, introductory.
isla, *f.* isle, island; city block.—**en i.**, insulated.
islam, *m.* Islam.—**islámico, ca**, *a.* Islamic.
islamismo, *m.* Islamism, Islam.
islamita, *n. & a.* Islamite(-itic).
islandés, sa; islándico, ca, *a.* Icelandic.
isleño, ña, *n.* islander; (Cuba) native of the Canary Islands.
isleo, *m.* chain of small islands.
isleta, ita, illa, *f. dim.* small isle, islet, holm.
islilla, *f.* (anat.) collar bone.
islote, *m.* small barren island, key.
ismaelita, *a.* Ishmaelite, Arab.
isobárico, ca, *a.* (meteorol.) isobaric.
isocro, *a.* isochroous, of uniform color.
isocromático, ca, *a.* (opt.) isochromatic.
isocronismo, *m.* isochronism.
isócrono, *a.* isochronous, equal in time.
isodinámico, ca, *a.* isodynamic.
isógono, na, *a.* (geom.) isogonic.
isomería, *f.* (chem.) isomerism.
isómero, ra, *a.* (chem.) isomeric.
isométrico, ca, *a.* isometric.
isomorfismo, *m.* (min.) isomorphism.
isomorfo, fa, *a.* isomorphous, isomorphic.
isoperímetro, ta, *a.* isoperimetrical.
isópodo, da. I. *n. & a.* (zool.) isopod. **II.** *m. pl.* Isopoda.
isoquímeno, na, *a.* (of climate) isocheimal.
isósceles, *a.* (geom.) isosceles.
isospóreo, a, *a.* (bot.) isosporous.
isotermo, ma, *a.* isothermal.
isótero, ra, *a.* isotheral.
isótopo, *m.* isotope.
isotrópico, ca, *a.* (phys.) = ISÓTROPO.
isotropismo, *m.* (phys.) isotropy.
isótropo, pa, *a.* (phys.) isotropous.
isquión, *m.* (anat.) ischium.
israelita, *n. & a.* Israelite(-ish).
israelítico, ca, *a.* Israelitish.
istmeño, ña, *n. & a.* native of an isthmus.
ístmico, ca, *a.* isthmian.
istmo, *m.* (geo.) isthmus; (anat.) isthmus.
istriar, *va.* = ESTRIAR, (arch.) to flute.
italianismo, *m.* Italianism.
italianizar, *va. & vn.* to Italianize.

italiano, na. I. *n. & a.* Italian. **II.** *m.* Italian (language).
itálico, ca, *a.* Italic, of anc. Italy; italic.
ítem, *m.* section, clause, article; addition, additament.—**í.**, or **í. más**, also, likewise, furthermore.
iterable, *a.* iterable.
iteración, *f.* interation.
iterar, *va.* to iterate.—**iterativo, va**, *a.* iterative.
iterbia, *f.* (chem.) ytterbia.
iterbio, *m.* (chem.) ytterbium.
itinerario, ria. I. *a.* itinerary. **II.** *m.* itinerary, book of travels; railroad guide, time-table.
itria, *f.* (min.) yttria.
itrio, *m.* (chem.) yttrium.
izador, ra, *a.* hoisting.
izaga, *f.* place abounding in rushes and reeds.
izar, *va.* (naut.) to hoist, heave, haul up.
izquierda, *f.* left hand; (pol.) Left, Left wing.—**a la i.**, left-handed (screw, etc.).—**de la i.**, on the left.
izquierdista, *n. & a.* (pol.) leftist, radical.
izquierdo, da. I. *a.* left-handed; left; crooked. **II.** *f.* left hand; left, left-hand side; (pol.) Left (Liberal party).—**a la i.**, to the left; on the left.

J

jaba, *f.* (Am.) basket; crate.
jabalcón, *m.* (arch.) bracket, purlin, strut.
jabalconar, *va.* to build or support with struts.
jabalí, *m.* (zool.) wild boar.
¹jabalina, *f.* sow of a wild boar.
²jabalina, *f.* javelin.
jabalón, *va.* = JABALCÓN.
jabalonar, *va.* = JABALCONAR.
jabardear, *vn.* (of bees) to swarm.
jabardillo, *m.* noisy swarm of insects or birds; (coll.) noisy crowd.
jabardo, *m.* small swarm of bees; (coll.) noisy crowd.
jabato, *m.* young wild boar.
jábeca, *f.* sweep net.
jábega, *f.* fishing smack; dragnet.
jabegote, *m.* man who drags the sweep net.
jabeguero, ra. I. *a.* pertaining to sweep-net fishing. **II.** *n.* sweep-net fisherman.
¹jabeque, *m.* (naut.) xebec.
²jabeque, *m.* (coll.) knife wound in the face.
jabí, *m.* small wild apple; small kind of grapes; (C. A.) (bot.) breakax.
jabillo, *m.* (bot.) a Central-American tree of the spurge family.
jabirú, *m.* jabiru, a Brazilian wading bird.
jabladera, *f.* crozer, cooper's tool.
jable, *m.* (cooperage) croze.
jabón, *m.* soap; a piece of soap.—**j. blando**, soft soap.—**j. de olor**, toilet soap.—**j. de piedra**, hard soap.—**j. de sastre**, steatite, soapstone.—**j. duro**, hard soap.—**dar un j.**, (coll.) to reprimand severely, lecture, dress down.
jabonado, da, *m.* wash, washing.
jabonadura, *f.* washing.—*pl.* suds or soap suds; lather.—**dar**, or **echar, una j.**, to reprimand severely, lecture, call down.
jabonar, *va.* to soap; (coll.) to reprimand severely, lecture, dress down.
jaboncillo, *m.* soapstone, steatite; toilet soap; (bot.) soap tree.
jabonera, *f.* soap dish; woman who sells soap; (bot.) soapwort.
jabonería, *f.* soap manufactory or shop.
jabonero, ra, *n.* soap maker or seller.
jabonete, jabonete de olor, *m.* toilet soap.
jabonoso, sa, *a.* soapy, saponaceous.
jaborandi, *m.* (bot.) jaborandi.
jabuco, *m.* (Cuba) large straw basket.
jaca, *f.* nag, pony, jennet, cob, bidet, tit.
jacal, *m.* (Mex.) Indian hut, wigwam.

jacamar, *m.* (ornith.) jacamar.
jacana, *f.* (ornith.) jacana, a tropical wading bird.
jácara, *f.* merry ballad; a kind of dance and its music; group of night wanderers singing JÁCA-RAS; (coll.) vexation; idle talk or prattle; story, tale; fable, lie, vainglorious fiction.
jacaranda, *f.* (bot.) jacaranda.
jacarandana, jacarandina, *f.* slang; gang of ruffians and thieves.
jacarandoso, sa, (coll.) blithe, merry, gay.
jacarear, *vn.* to sing JÁCARAS; (coll.) to sing in the streets at night; to taunt with offensive remarks.
jacarero, *m.* ballad singer; wag or merry droll.
jacarilla, *f. dim.* of JÁCARA.
jácaro, ra. I. *a.* pert. to singers of JÁCARAS. **II.** *m.* boaster, bully.—**a lo j.,** boastfully, braggingly.
jácena, *f.* (arch.) girder.
jacerina, *f.* coat of mail.
jacilla, *f.* mark left on the ground.
jacinto, *m.* (bot.) hyacinth; harebell; (min.) hyacinth.—**j. de Ceilán,** zircon.—**j. de Compostela,** red crystalized quartz.—**j. occidental,** topaz.—**j. oriental,** ruby.
¹jaco, *m.* sorry nag, jade.
²jaco, *m.* short jacket.
jacobinismo, *m.* Jacobinism.
jacobino, *m.* Jacobin; bloody revolutionist.
jactancia, *f.* boasting.
jactanciosamente, *adv.* boastingly.
jactancioso, sa, *a.* boastful, vainglorious.
jactarse, *vr.* to vaunt, boast, brag.
jaculatoria, *f.* ejaculation, short prayer.
jaculatorio, ria, *a.* jaculatory.
jachalí, *m.* (bot.) custard apple.
jada, *f.* (agr.) hoe; spade.
jade, *m.* (min.) jade, axestone.
jadeante, *a.* painting, out of breath.
jadear, *vn.* to pant.—**jadeo,** *m.* pant, palpitation.
jadiar, *va.* to dig up with a spade, to hoe.
jaecero, ra, *n.* harness maker.
jaén, *m.* a kind of large white grape.
jaenés, sa, *a.* of or belonging to Jaen.
jaez, *m.* harness; trappings; (fig.) manner, kind, quality.—*pl.* trappings.
jafético, ca, *a.* Japhetic, Indo-Germanic.
jagua, *f.* (bot.) jagua or inaja palm and its fruit.
jaguar, jaguarete, *m.* (zool.) jaguar.
jaguarzo, *m.* (bot.) helianthemum.
jagüey, *m.* (S. A.) large pool or basin; (Cuba) (bot.) liana.
jaharrar, *va.* to plaster.
jaharro, *m.* (mason.) plaster; plastering.
jaiba, *f.* (Cuba) (ichth.) crab.
jaique, *m.* cape with a hood.
jaira, *f.* bezel of a plane bit.
jairar, *va.* (shoemaking) to bevel (leather).
jaire, *m.* (shoemaking) bevel cut.
¡ja, ja, ja! *interj.* ha, ha!
jalapa, *f.* (bot.) jalapa; jalap.
jalar, *va.* (coll.) = HALAR, to pull.
jalbegar, *va.* to whiten, whitewash.
jalbegue, *m.* whitewash; whitewashing.
jaldado, da; jalde; jaldo, da, *a.* bright yellow crocus-colored.
jaldre, *m.* yellow peculiar to birds.
jalea, *f.* jelly.—**j. de guayaba,** guava jelly.—**j. del agro,** conserve of citron.—**hacerse una j.,** to love with excessive fondness.
jaleador, ra, *n.* one who encourages hounds or dancers.
jalear, *va.* to encourage (hounds) to follow the chase; to animate dancers, by clapping hands; to quaver (the voice).
jaleco, *m.* Turkish jacket.
jaleo, *m.* clapping of hands to encourage dancers; Andalusian dance; (coll.) jest; (coll.) carousal.
jaletina, *f.* calf's foot jelly; gelatine.

jalma, *f.* kind of packsaddle.
jalmería, *f.* packsaddler's trade.
jalmero, *m.* packsaddle maker.
jalón, *m.* (surv.) pole, rod, flag pole.
jaloque, *m.* = SIROCO, southeast wind.
jallullo, *m.* bread toasted in ashes.
jamaica, *f.* (Mex.) charity fair.
jamaicano, na, *n.* & *a.* Jamaican.
jamar, *va.* (prov.) to eat.
jamás, *adv.* never.—**nunca j.,** or **por j.,** never, nevermore.—**por siempre j.,** forever and ever.
jamba, *f.* (arch.) door jamb, window post.
jambaje, *m.* door or window case.
jámbico, ca, *a.* iambic.
jamelgo, *m.* (coll.) jade, sorry nag.
jamerdana, *f.* sewer of a slaughterhouse.
jamerdar, *va.* to clean the guts of; to wash hastily.
jamete, *m.* rich silk stuff.
jametería, *f.* = ZALAMERÍA, flattery.
jámila, *f.* = ALPECHÍN, oozing olive juice.
jamón, *m.* ham, salted haunch of a hog.
jamona, *f.* (coll.) big middle-aged woman.
jámparo, *m.* (Colomb.) small boat or canoe.
jamuga, jamugas, *f.* mule chair.
jándalo, la, *n.* & *a.* a term app. to Andalusians and those who give *h* a strong guttural sound.
jangada, *f.* (coll.) silly sally; (naut.) raft, float.
jangar, *m.* hangar.
jangua, *f.* small armed vessel.
jansenismo, *m.* Jansenism.
jansenista, *n.* & *a.* Jansenist(-ic).
jantofila, *f.* (chem.) xanthophyll.
japón, na; japonense; japonés, sa, *n.* & *a.* Japanese.
¹jaque, *m.* (chess) check; braggart, boaster.—**j. mate,** (chess) checkmate.
²jaque, *m.* saddlebag; smooth hairdo.
jaquear, *va.* to check (at chess).
jaqueca, *f.* megrim; headache.
jaquecoso, sa, *a.* tiresome, annoying, bothersome.
jaquel, *m.* (her.) square.
jaquelado, da, *a.* checkered.
jaquero, *m.* fine-toothed comb.
jaqueta, *f.* jacket, short loose coat.
jaquetilla, *f. dim.* small JAQUETA.
¹jaquetón, *m. aug.* large, wide coat.
²jaquetón, *m. aug.* great boaster, bully.
jáquima, *f.* headstall of a halter.
jaquimazo, *m.* blow with the headstall of a halter; (coll.) displeasure; disappointment.
jara, *f.* (bot.) cistus or rockrose; a kind of dart or arrow.
¹jarabe, *m.* sirup; any sweet mixed drink.—**j. de pico,** empty talk; lip service.
²jarabe, *m.* (Am.) a popular dance in Lat. Am.
jarabear. I. *va.* to prescribe sirups very often. **II.** *vr.* to take sirups frequently.
jaraíz, *m.* pit for pressing grapes.
jaral, *m.* bramble, brake; intricate or puzzling point.
jaramago, *m.* (bot.) hedge mustard.
jarameño, ña, *a.* (cattle) from the Jarama.
jaramugo, *m.* small or young fish.
jarana, *f.* (coll.) carousal, revelry, romping; (coll.) scuffle, quarrel.
jaranear, *vn.* (coll.) to jest; to carouse.
jaranero, ra; jaranista, *a.* fond of jests or sprees; jolly.
jarano, *m.* Mexican sombrero.
jarapote, *m.* (prov.) = JAROPEO.
jarapotear, *va.* to stuff with drugs.
jarazo, *m.* blow or wound with a dart.
jarcia, *f.* accoutrements; heap of things; (naut.) tackle, rigging, and cordage; shrouds; fishing tackle.
jardín, *m.* flower garden; flaw, spot that disfigures an emerald; (naut.) privy.
jardincito, *m. dim.* small garden.

For pronunciation, see the rules at the beginning of the book.

jardinería, *f.* gardening.

jardinero, ra. I. *n.* gardener. **II.** *f.* flowerstand, jardinière; basket carriage.

jareta, *f.* (sewing) fold or tuck for gathering; (naut.) netting, harpings.

jaretera, *f.* garter. Also JARRETERA.

jarife, *m.* = JERIFE, sherif, shereef.

jarifo, fa, *a.* showy, spruce, nobby, natty.

jaripeo, *m.* (Mex.) bronco-busting; rodeo.

jaro, ra, *a.* resembling a wild boar.

jarocho, *m.* (Mex., coll.) rough countryman.

jaropar, *va.* to stuff with sirups or medicines.

jarope, *m.* sirup; nasty potion.

jaropear, *va.* = JAROPAR.—**jaropeo,** *m.* medicine habit.

jaroso, sa, *a.* full of brambles.

jarra, *f.* jar; pitcher; ancient order of chivalry.—**en j.** or **de jarras,** akimbo.

jarrear, *vn.* to take out water or wine with a jar or dipper.

jarrero, ra, *n.* jar maker or seller.

jarreta, *f. dim.* small jar.

jarrete, *m.* hock; gambrel.

jarretera, *f.* garter; Order of the Garter.

jarrito, *m. dim.* small jug or pitcher.

jarro, *m.* pitcher, jug, pot, ewer; chatterer.

jarrón, *m. aug.* large jar, urn, flower vase.

jaspe, *m.* (min.) jasper.

jaspeado, da, *a.* spotted, mottled, variegated.

jaspeadura, *f.* marbling.

jaspear, *va.* to marble, vein, speckle.

jastial, *m.* (arch.) façade of an edifice.

jateo, tea, *n.* (of dogs) fox hunter.

jato, ta, *n.* calf.

¡jau! *interj.* to incite animals, esp. bulls.

jaula, *f.* bird cage; cell for insane persons; (min.) miner's cage.

jaulón, *m. aug.* large bird cage; aviary.

jauría, *f.* pack of hounds.

jauto, ta, *a.* insipid, flat, tasteless.

javanés, sa; javo, va, *a.* Javan, Javanese.

jayán, na, *n.* robust, burly person.

jayanazo, za, *n. aug.* huge, big person.

jazmín, *m.* (bot.) jessamine or jasmine.—**j. de la India,** (bot.) gardenia.

jazmíneo, a, *a.* (bot.) jasminaceous.

jea, *f.* ancient duty on Moorish goods.

jebe, *m.* rock alum; (S. A.) India-rubber.

jebuseo, a, *n.* & *a.* Jebusite(-ic).

jedive, *m.* khedive, Viceroy of Egypt.

jefatura, *f.* position or headquarters of a chief.

jefe, fa, *n.* chief, head, leader; "boss"; (mil.) commanding officer.—**j. de día,** (mil.) officer of the day.—**j. de despacho,** executive secretary.—**j. de escuadra,** (naut.) rear admiral.—**j. político,** governor of a province.

Jehová, *m.* Jehovah.

jeja, *f.* white wheat.

jején, *m.* (Cuba) gnat, gall midge.

jema, *f.* badly squared part of a beam.

jemal, *a.* having the length of a JEME.

jeme, *m.* distance from the end of the thumb to the end of the forefinger (both extended); (coll.) woman's face.

jemoso, sa, *a.* badly squared beam.

jenabe, jenable, *m.* mustard.

jengibre, *m.* ginger.

jeniquén, *m.* (Cuba) henequen; sisal.

jenízaro. I. *a.* cross-bred; (Mex.) born of Chinese and Indian parents. **II.** *m.* Janizary.

jeque, *m.* Moorish chief.

¹jera, *f.* ground that can be plowed in a day with a pair of oxen.

²jera, *f.* present, gift.

jerapellina, *f.* old ragged garment.

jerarca, *m.* (eccl.) hierarch.—**jerarquía,** *f.* hierarchy.—**jerárquico, ca,** *a.* hierarchical.

jeremiada, *f.* jeremiad, lamentation, whining.

Jerez, *m.* sherry wine.

jerezano, na, *a.* & *n.* (one) from, or of Jerez.

¹jerga, *f.* coarse frieze; straw bed.

²jerga, *f.* jargon; gibberish.

¹jergón, *m. aug.* straw bed; ill-fitting clothes; ill-shaped person.

²jergón, *m.* (jewelry) zircon.

jerguilla, *f.* silk or worsted serge.

jerife, *m.* shereef, sherif.

jerifiano, na, *a.* pertaining to the sherif.

jerigonza, *f.* (coll.) jargon, gibberish, slang; strange and ridiculous action.—**andar en jerigonzas,** to quibble.

jeringa, *f.* syringe, clyster; sausage stuffer.

jeringación, *f.* (coll.) syringing, injection; annoyance, botheration.

jeringador, ra, *a.* (coll.) bothersome, persevering, persistent.

jeringar, *va.* (pret. JERINGUÉ; subj. JERINGUE) to inject with a syringe; to vex, annoy, tease.

jeringazo, *m.* clyster, injection.

jeringué, jeringue, *v. V.* JERINGAR.

jeringuilla, *f.* (bot.) syringa, mock orange.

jeroglífico, ca. I. *a.* hieroglyphical. **II.** *m.* hieroglyph.

jerosolimitano, na, *a.* of or pert. to Jerusalem.

jerpa, *f.* sterile shoot of a vine.

jerricote, *m.* pottage of almonds, sugar, sage, and ginger.

jersey, *m.* (Angl.) sweater, jersey.

jervilla, *f.* a kind of short boot.

jesuato, ta, *a.* child dedicated to Jesus when born.

jesuíta, *m.* Jesuit; (coll.) hypocrite.

jesuíticamente, *adv.* Jesuitically; hypocritically.

jesuítico, ca, *a.* Jesuitical; hypocritical.

jesuitismo, *m.* Jesuitism.

Jesús, *m.* Jesus; often used by itself, or followed by other sacred names (José, María), and with no implication of profanity, as an exclamation in the sense of "gracious!" "goodness!" "my!" etc.—**¡ay J!** alas! good gracious!—**en un decir J.,** in the twinkling of an eye.—**no saber ni el J.,** not to know even one's A B C.—**sin decir J.,** suddenly.

jesusear, *vn.* to repeat often the name of Jesus.

jeta, *f.* thick, heavy lips; hog's snout; (coll.) person's face.

jetar, *va.* to dilute, dissolve.

jeto, *m.* empty beehive rubbed with honey to attract bees.

jetón, na; jetudo, da, *a.* thick-lipped.

jíbaro, ra. I. *a.* (Am.) rustic, rude, wild. **II.** *n.* countryman(-woman).

jibia, *f.* (zool.) cuttlefish.

jibión, *m.* cuttlefish bone.

jibraltareño, ña, *a.* of or from Gibraltar.

jícara, *f.* chocolate cup.

jicarazo, *m. aug.* blow with a chocolate cup.—**dar un j.,** (coll.) to give poison.

jicarón, *m. aug.* large chocolate cup.

jicotea, *f.* (Am.) tortoise.

jifa, *f.* refuse from slaughtered animals.

jifería, *f.* slaughtering.

jifero, ra. I. *a.* pertaining to the slaughterhouse. **II.** *m.* butcher's knife; butcher.

jifia, *f.* (ichth.) xiphias, swordfish.

jiga, *f.* jig (dance and tune).

jigote, *m.* (cooking) hash; minced meat.

jiguilete, *m.* indigo plant.

jijallar, *m.* bramble.

jijallo, *m.* (bot.) prickly broom.

jijene, *m.* (S. A.) sand fly.

jiji, ji, ji! *interj.* ha, ha, ha!

jijona, *f.* variety of flinty wheat.—**turrón de J.,** sweet-almond paste.

jilguero, *m.* (ornith.) linnet.

jilote, *m.* (Mex.) ear of green corn.

jimagua, *a.* (Cuba) twin.

jimelga, *f.* (naut.) fish of a mast.

jimenzar, *va.* to ripple (flax or hemp).

jinestada, *f.* sauce made with milk, dates, etc.

For pronunciation, see the rules at the beginning of the book.

jineta, *f.* art of horsemanship; an ancient short lance; sergeant's shoulder knot; ancient tribute upon cattle.—**a la j.,** (riding) with high stirrups and bent knees.—**tener los cascos a la j.,** to be harebrained, wild, giddy.

jinete, *m.* trooper; cavalryman; horseman, rider, equestrian; fine, pure-breed horse.

jinetear. I. *va.* (Am.) to break in (a horse); to ride (a horse). **II.** *vn.* to ride around on horseback, mainly for show.

jinglar, *vn.* to swing, vibrate, oscillate.

jingoísmo, *m.* jingoism.

jingoísta, *n.* & *a.* jingoist(-ic).

jínjol, *m.* jujube. Also AZUFAIFA.

jipijapa, *f.* very fine woven straw; Panama-hat straw.

jiquilete, *m.* (bot.) indigo tree.

¹**jira,** *f.* strip, piece of cloth.

²**jira,** *f.* picnic, outing; tour.

jirafa, *f.* (zool.) giraffe.

jirapliega, *f.* purgative confection.

jirasal, *f.* (bot.) fruit of the lac tree.

jirel, *m.* rich caparison for a horse.

jíride, *f.* (bot.) = LIRIO HEDIONDO, gladwin.

jirofina, *f.* a kind of sauce.

jiroflé, *m.* clove tree.

jirón, *m.* (sew.) facing of a skirt; shred, piece torn from clothing; pointed banner, pennant; small part (of anything); (Peru) avenue, long street.

jironado, da, *a.* torn into or garnished with strips or tatters.

jirpear, *va.* to dig about vines.

jiste, *m.* froth of beer.

jitar, *va.* (prov.) to emit, vomit; to throw out.

jitomate, *m.* (Mex.) tomato.

¡jo! *interj.* whoa!

jobo, *m.* (bot.) tree of the terebinth family.

jocó, *m.* jocko, an ape.

jocosamente, *adv.* jocosely, humorously.

jocoserio, ria, *a.* tragic-comic.

jocosidad, *f.* jocularity, jocosity, waggery.

jocoso, sa, *a.* jocose, waggish, humorous.

jocoyote, *m.* (Am.) youngest child, pet.

jocundidad, *f.* joviality.

jocundo, da, *a.* jovial, jolly.

jofaina, *f.* washbasin, washbowl.

jojoto, *m.* (Venez.) maize in the milk.

jolgorio, *m.* = HOLGORIO, boisterous frolic.

jolito, *m.* rest, leisure; (naut.) calm.

joloano, na, *n.* & *a.* Joloano (from Sulu, P. I.).

jólote, *m.* (C. A.) turkey.

jónico, ca; jonio, nia, *n.* & *a.* Ionian.

¡jopo! *interj.* (coll.) out of here! be off!

jorcar, *va.* = AECHAR, to sift (grain).

jorco, *m.* licentious feast and dance.

jordán, *m.* anything that purifies, revives, or gives a fresh bloom.

jorfe, *m.* dry stone wall; steep rock, cliff.

jorguín, *m.* wizard, or sorcerer.—**jorguina,** *f.* witch, or sorceress.—**jorguinería,** *f.* witchcraft, spell.

jornada, *f.* one-day march; working day; stage, journey, travel, trip; (mil.) expedition; king's stay in a royal country residence; opportunity, occasion, circumstance; span of life; transit from life to eternity; act of a play; (print.) number of sheets printed off in a day.—**j. de ocho horas,** 8-hour (working) day.—**a grandes, or a largas, jornadas,** by forced marches.—**al fin de la j.,** at the end.

jornal, *m.* daywork, journeywork; day wages.—**a j.,** by the day.—**jornalero,** *m.* day laborer.

joroba, *f.* hump; (coll.) importunity, annoyance, nuisance.

jorobado, da. I. *pp.* of JOROBAR. **II.** *a.* crooked, gibbous, humpbacked. **II.** *n.* hunchback.

jorobar, *va.* (coll.) to importune, bother, annoy.

jorrar, *va.* to haul.

jorro, *m.* (Cuba) bad tobacco.

josa, *f.* orchard of vines and fruit trees.

jostrado, da, *a.* round-headed (shaft or dart).

¹**jota,** *f.* name of the letter *j;* iota, jot, tittle.—**no saber, or no entender, j.,** or **ni j.,** or **una j.,** not to know "beans", to be absolutely ignorant.—**sin faltar una j.,** not a dot missing, with not a whit left out.

²**jota,** *f.* an Aragonese dance and tune.

³**jota,** *f.* pottage of greens and spices.

jote, *m.* a Chilean vulture of the turkey-buzzard family.

joule, *m.* (elec.) joule. Also JULIO.

jovada, *f.* ground tilled by a pair of mules in one day.

joven. I. *a.* young. **II.** *n.* youth; young man; young woman; young person.

jovenado, *m.* (eccl.) juniorate.

jovencillo, illa, *n.* youngster, lad, lass.

jovial, *a.* Jovian; jovial, gay, merry, cheerful.

jovialidad, *f.* joviality, jollity, gaiety.

joya, *f.* jewel, gem; piece of jewellery; present, gift; (arch. and artil.) astragal.—*pl.* jewels, trinkets; wedding outfit.

joyante, *a.* extremely glossy (silk).

joyel, *m.* small jewel, valuable trinket.

joyelero, *m.* jewel case, jewel box.

joyera, *f.* woman jeweller.

joyería, *f.* jeweller's shop.

joyero, *m.* jeweller; jewel-casket.

joyita, *f. dim.* = JOYUELA.

joyo, *m.* (bot.) bearded darnel, darnel grass.

joyón, *m. aug.* large jewel.

joyuela, *f. dim.* jewel of small value.

juaguarzo, *m.* (bot.) Montpellier rockrose.

Juan, *m.* John.—**J. Lanas,** simpleton, poor devil, (a) nobody.—**buen J.,** poor, silly fellow.

juanas, *f. pl.* glove stretcher.

juanete, *m.* bunion; prominent cheek bone; (naut.) gallant sail.—**j. de sobremesana,** mizzen-topgallant sail.—**j. mayor,** main-topgallant sail.

juanetudo, da, *a.* having bunions.

juarda, *f.* stain in cloth.

juardoso, sa, *a.* stained, spotted (cloth).

jubete, *m.* doublet covered with mail.

jubilación, *f.* pensioning off or superannuating a placeman; exemption from duty, with reduced pay; pension or reduced salary thus paid.

jubilar. I. *va.* to pension off; to superannuate; to retire; (coll.) to lay aside as useless. **II.** *vr.* to become a pensioner; to be retired. **III.** *vn.* to jubilate, rejoice.

jubileo, *m.* jubilee, public festivity; (eccl.) concession of plenary indulgence.—**por j.,** rarely, once in a long while.

júbilo, *m.* glee, joy, merriment, rejoicing.

jubiloso, sa, *a.* joyful, merry, gay.

jubón, *m.* doublet, jacket; blouse, upper part (of dress).—**j. de azotes,** (coll.) public whipping.

juboncito, *m. dim.* small doublet or waist.

jubonero, *m.* maker of doublets or waists.

júcaro, *m.* a West-Indian hardwood tree.

judaico, ca, *a.* Judaical, Jewish.

judaísmo, *m.* Judaism.

judaizante, *n.* & *a.* Judaizer(-ing).

judaizar, *va.* & *vn.* to judaize.

Judas, *m.* Judas; traitor; silkworm that does not spin; effigy of Judas burnt in the streets during Lent.

judería, *f.* Jewry; ghetto; tax on Jews.

¹**judía,** *f.* (bot.) bean, string bean.—**j. de careta,** small spotted French bean.

²**judía,** *f.* Jewess.

judiada, *f.* inhuman action; usurious profit.

judiar, *m.* bean field or patch.

judicante, *m.* judge appointed to try impeachment cases.

judicatura, *f.* judicature; judgeship.

judicial, *a.* judicial, juridical.

judicialmente, *adv.* judicially.

judiciario, ria. I. *a.* astrological. **II.** *m.* astrologer. **III.** *f.* judicial astrology.
judiego, *f.* inferior kind of olives.
¹judihuela, *f.* a small French bean.
²judihuela, lo, *n.* young Jewess or Jew.
judío, día. I. *a.* Jewish; usurious. **II.** *m.* Jew.—**j. de señal,** converted Jew, wearing a distinguishing badge.
judión, *m.* a large variety of French bean.
¹juego, *m.* play, sport, game; gaming, gambling; set of good cards; movement, work, working (of a mechanism); set; suit, suite; ability, artfulness, cunning; running gear of a vehicle; (mech.) play, free space, clearance.—*pl.* public feasts, games.—**j. de azar,** game of chance.—**j. de bochas,** bowling alley.—**j. de boliche,** pigeonholes (an old game); trollmadam.—**j. de bolos,** ninepins.—**j. de café,** coffee set.—**j. de cajones,** nest of boxes or drawers.—**j. de cartas,** card game.—**j. de compadres,** collusion or conspiracy under pretense of rivalry or opposition among those concerned.—**j. de habitaciones,** suite of rooms.—**j. de manos,** juggling feat, legerdemain.—**j. de naipes =** J. DE CARTAS.—**j. de niños,** child's play.—**j. de palabras,** pun, quibble, play upon words.—**j. de pelota,** ball game (app. to several games in which a ball is thrown).—**j. de prendas,** forfeits.—**j. de suerte =** J. DE AZAR.—**j. de te,** tea set.—**j. de velas,** (naut.) set of sails. **j. de vocablos,** or **de voces =** J. DE PALABRAS. —**j. limpio,** fair play.—**j. público,** public gambling house (where gambling is allowed by law).—**conocerle a uno el j.,** = VERLE A UNO EL J.—**entrar en j.,** to come into play or into action.—**hacer j.,** to match, to fit.—**mostrar el j.,** to show one's hand (fig.).—**poner en j.,** to bring into play, make use of.—**por j.,** or **por modo de j.,** in jest, for fun.—**tener j.,** (naut.) to have fetched way; not to be firm or steady.—**verle a uno el j.,** to see through (a person), read (his) thoughts.
²juego, juegue, *v.* V. JUGAR.
jueguecico, illo, ito, *m.* little game, bit of play.
juera, *f.* sieve made of esparto.
juerga, *f.* (coll.) spree, carousal.
juerguista, *n.* (coll.) reveler, carouser.
jueves, *m.* Thursday.—**j. santo,** holy Thursday.
juez, *m.* judge; justice; juror, juryman; *m. & f.* umpire; arbitrator.—**j. árbitro,** arbitrator, umpire.—**j. conservador,** person appointed to defend the rights of a community.—**j. de alzadas,** judge in appeal cases.—**j. de hecho,** lay judge.—**j. de paz,** justice of the peace.— **j. de primera instancia,** judge of the primary court of claims.
jugada, *f.* play, act of playing; a throw, move, stroke; ill turn, mean trick.
jugadera, *f.* shuttle for network.
jugador, ra, *n.* player; gamester, gambler.—**j. de manos,** juggler, prestidigitator.
jugar, *va. & vn.* (*ind. pres.* JUEGO, *pret.* JUGUÉ; *subj.* JUEGUE) to play; to sport, frolic; to game, gamble; to stake; to move in a game; to move (a part of the body); to wield, handle (a weapon); to move on joints or hinges; to intervene; to take an active part in an affair; to exercise; to mock, to make game of.—**j. a cara o cruz,** to bet on the toss of a coin.—**j. a la baja,** (com.) to bear the market.—**j. a la bolsa,** to dabble in stocks.—**j. al alza,** (com.) to bull the market.—**j. a los naipes,** to play cards.—**jugarle a uno una mala volada,** or **mala partida,** to play a mean trick on one.— **jugársela a uno de codillo,** (coll.) to trick or outwit one.
jugarreta, *f.* (coll.) bad play; bad turn, nasty trick.
juglándeo, dea. I. *a.* (bot.) juglandaceous. **II.** *f. pl.* Juglandaceæ, the walnut family of trees.

juglar, *m.* juggler, mountebank, buffoon.
juglara, juglaresa, *f.* woman buffoon.
juglaresco, ca, *a.* pertaining to jugglers.
juglaría, juglería, *f.* jugglery, buffoonery, mimicry.
jugo, *m.* sap, juice; marrow, pith, substance.
jugosidad, *f.* succulence, juiciness.
jugoso, sa, *a.* juicy, succulent, full of sap.
jugué, *pret.* of JUGAR.
juguete, *m.* toy, plaything; jest, joke; carol; (theat.) comedietta.—**j. de movimiento,** mechanical toy.—**por j.,** jestingly.
juguetear, *vn.* to frolic, sport, gambol.
juguetería, *f.* toyshop, toy trade.
juguetero, *m.* toy dealer; etagère, whatnot.
juguetón, na, *a.* playful, frolicsome.
juicio, *m.* judgment; decision; prudence, wisdom; forecast of yearly events by astrologers; good behavior; (law) trial.—**j. de Dios,** ordeal (to determine guilt or innocence).—**j. ejecutivo,** levy, attachment.—**j. final,** final judgment.— **estar fuera de su j.,** to be crazy.—**formar j. de,** to judge, form an opinion about.—**no estar en su j.,** to be out of one's senses.—**no tener j.,** to be wild, to be a harum-scarum fellow.—**pedir en j.,** to sue at law.—**perder el j.,** to become insane; to go mad.—**tener j.,** to be wise; to be cautious; to be well-behaved.
juiciosamente, *adv.* judiciously, wisely.
juicioso, sa, *a.* judicious, wise; well-behaved.
julepe, *m.* (pharm.) julep; a card game; (coll.) reprimand, punishment; (Peru, Chile, Arg.) fear.
juliano, na, *a.* Julian.
¹julio, *m.* July.
²julio, *m.* (elec.) joule.
julo, *m.* bell-mule, bell-cow.
juma, *f.* (Am.) drinking spree.
jumenta, *f.* female donkey, jenny.
jumental, jumentil, *a.* pert. to donkeys.
jumentillo, illa, ito, ita, *n. dim.* small donkey or beast of burden.
jumento, *m.* donkey, ass; stupid person.
juncada, *f.* (cook.) a kind of fritter; (vet.) medicine for the glanders.
juncago, *m.* (bot.) bastard rush.
juncal, juncar, *m.* ground full of rushes.
júnceo, sa. I. *a.* rushlike; (bot.) juncaceous. **II.** *f. pl.* Juncaceæ.
juncia, *f.* (bot.) sedge.—**j. olorosa,** galangal.
junciana, *f.* (coll.) brag, boast.
junciera, *f.* earth vessel with perforated lid, for aromatic roots.
juncino, *na, a.* pert. to or made of rushes.
¹junco, *m.* (bot.) rush.—**j. de Indias,** (bot.) rattan.—**j. florido,** (bot.) flowering rush.— **j. oloroso,** (bot.) camel grass.
²junco, *m.* (naut.) Chinese junk.
juncoso, sa, *a.* rushlike; producing rushes.
junio, *m.* June, the sixth month.
júnior, *m.* (eccl.) junior.
junípero, *m.* (bot.) = ENEBRO, juniper.
junquera, *f.* (bot.) rush.
junqueral, *m.* = JUNCAL.
junquillo, *m.* (bot.) jonquil; reed, rattan; (arch.) boltel molding.
junta, *f.* junta, board, council; meeting, conference; session, sitting; whole, entirety; union, junction; fraternity; seam; joint; coupling.—**j. a tope,** butt joint.—**j. central de planificación,** Central Planning Board.—**j. de accionistas,** stockholders' meeting.—**j. de acreedores,** (com.) meeting of creditors.—**j. de comercio,** board of trade.—**j. de dilatación,** expansion joint.—**j. de educación,** school board, board of education.—**j. de enchufe =** J. ENCHUFADA.—**j. de expansión,** expansion joint.—**j. de médicos,** (med.) consultation.— **j. de recubrimiento,** lap joint.—**j. de sanidad,** board of health.—**j. de solapa,** lap joint.

—j. de yuxtaposición, butt joint.—j. directiva, managing board, executive board.—j. enchufada, bell-and-spigot joint.—j. remachada, riveted joint.

juntamente, adv. jointly, together.

juntar. I. va. to join, connect, unite; to assemble, congregate; to amass, collect, gather, lay up; to pool (resources). II. vr. to join, meet, assemble, gather; to be closely united; to copulate; (con) to associate (with).

juntera, f. (carp.) jointing plane.

junterilla, f. dim. (carp.) small joiner's plane.

¹junto, adv. near, close at hand, near at hand; at the same time.—j. a., next to, by, beside.—j. con, together with.—de por j., wholesale.—en j., together, in all.—por j. = DE POR J.

²junto, ta, a. united, joined; together.

juntorio, m. an ancient tax.

juntura, f. juncture, joining; (anat.) joint, articulation; seam; (naut.) scarf; (bot.) knuckle.

Júpiter, m. (astr.) Jupiter; (chem.) tin.

jura, f. oath; swearing.

jurado, m. jury; juror, juryman.

jurador, ra, n. swearer, profane swearer.

juraduría, f. office of a juror.

juramentar. I. va. to swear in. II. vr. to be sworn in, take the oath.

juramento, m. oath; act of swearing; curse, imprecation.—j. asertorio, declaratory oath.—j. falso, perjury.

jurar, va. & vn. to swear, to take an oath.—j. en falso, to commit perjury.—jurársela, or jurárselas, a uno, to threaten one with revenge, have it in for one.

jurásico, ca, a. Jurassic.

juratoria, f. Gospel tablet for administering the oath.

juratorio, a. I. a. juratory. II. m. instrument setting forth the oaths taken by Aragonese magistrates.

jurel, m. (ichth.) jurel, a carangoid sea fish.

jurguina, f. witch, sorceress.

jurídicamente, adv. legally, juridically.

jurídico, ca, a. legal, juridical.

jurisconsulto, m. jurisconsult, jurist; lawyer.

jurisdicción, f. jurisdiction; boundary, territory.

jurisdiccional, a. jurisdictional.

jurispericia, f. = JURISPRUDENCIA.

jurisperito, ta, n. jurisconsult.

jurisprudencia, f. jurisprudence, law; laws, legislation.

jurista, m. jurist; lawyer; pensioner.

juro, m. right of perpetual property; annuity, pension.—de j., certainly.

jusbarba, f. (bot.) field myrtle.

jusello, m. pottage of broth, cheese, and eggs.

jusi, m. (P. I.) striped thin gauze.

justa, f. joust, tilt, tournament; contest.

justador, m. tilter, jouster.

justamente, adv. justly; just, exactly.

justar, vn. to joust, tilt, tourney.

justicia, f. justice; judge; court of justice; punishment; (coll.) execution (of a criminal).—de j., justly, deservedly.—la j., the police, the authorities, the officers of the law.

justiciero, ra, a. just, fair.

justificable, a. justifiable.

justificación, f. justification, defense; production of evidence; equity; sanctification by grace; (print.) adjustment, justifying.

justificadamente, adv. justly, justifiably.

justificado, da, pp. & a. justified.

justificador, ra. I. n. & a. justifier(-ing). II. m. (print.) dressing stick, justifier.

justificante, n. & a. justifier(-ing).

justificar. I. va. (pret. JUSTIFIQUÉ; subj. JUSTIFIQUE) to justify; to free from sin; to absolve, exculpate; (law) to prove or establish before a court; to rectify, adjust; (print.) to justify,

adjust. II. vr. to vindicate one's character, to clear oneself; to justify one's conduct.

justificativo, va, a. justifying, justificatory.

justifiqué, justifique, v. V. JUSTIFICAR.

justillo, m. waistcoat, jerkin; corset cover.

justinianeo, a, a. Justinian.

justipreciador, ra, n. appraiser.

justipreciar, va. to appraise.

justiprecio, m. appraisal.

justo, ta. I. a. just; pious; correct, exact, strict; fit, tight, close. II. m. just and pious man.—al j., fitly, duly; completely, punctually. III. adv. tightly.

juta, f. (S. A.) (ornith.) a kind of goose.

jutía, f. (Cuba) = HUTÍA, a W. I. rodent.

juvenil, a. juvenile, youthful.

juventud, f. youthfulness, youth; young people.

juvia, f. (bot.) Brazil-nut tree.

juzgado, m. court of justice; judicature.

juzgamundos, n. (coll.) faultfinder.

juzgante. I. a. judging. II. n. judge.

juzgar, va. & vn. (pret. JUZGUÉ; subj. JUZGUE) to judge; to pass or render judgment (on).

K

NOTE.—Many words that by some are begun with k are properly spelled with qu if the following letter is e or i, and with c in other cases.

ka, f. name of the letter k.

káiser, m. kaiser.

kaki, m. & a. = CAQUI, khaki.

kan, m. khan, a Tartar chief.

kanato, m. Khanate.

kantiano, na, n. & a. Kantian.—kantismo, m. Kantianism.—kantista, n. & a. Kantian.

kepis, m. (mil.) small shako, kepi, a military cap.

kermes, m. = QUERMES, (entom.) kermes.

kerosén, m.; keroseno, m.; kerosina, f. kerosene.

kiliárea, f. kiloare, one thousand ares.

kilo. I. (as a prefix) kilo (a thousand). II. m. kilo, kilogram.

kilocaloría, f. kilocalorie.

kilográmetro, m. kilogrammeter, metric unit of work (about 7.25 ft.-lb.)

kilogramo, m. kilogram (about 2.2 lb.)

kilojulio, m. (elec.) kilojoule.

kilolitro, m. kiloliter.

kilométrico, ca, a. kilometric; mileage (ticket); (coll.) very long, interminably long.

kilómetro, m. kilometer (about 0.62 mile).

kilovatio, m. (elec.) kilowatt.—k.-hora, kilowatt-hour.

kilovoltamperio, m. (elec.) kilovolt-ampere.

kilovoltio, m. (elec.) kilovolt.

kiosco, m. kiosk, small pavilion; newsstand.

kirie, m. (eccl.) kyrie (eleison).

kirieleisón, m. = KIRIE; (coll.) funeral chant.—cantar el k., to beg for quarter, to cry for mercy.

kirsch, m. kirschwasser.

kodak, m. kodak.

krausismo, m. Krausism.

kremlín, m. kremlin.

kurdo, da, n. & a. Kurd(-ish).

L

¹la. I. def. art. fem. sing. the. Often used before the surname (not the first name) of a woman, especially actresses and singers, and is not translated, or is translated by Miss, Madame, etc.: la Patti, la Pavlowa, Patti, Pavlowa; la Guerrero, la Farrar, Miss Guerrero, Miss Farrar; la Schumann-Heink, Madame Schumann-Heink. II. pron. pers. acc. f. sing. her, it.

Formerly, and still occasionally, used as a dative (*yo la dije*, I told her).

²la, *m.* (mus.) la, A, sixth note of the scale.

lábaro, *m.* labarum, a kind of standard, banner.

labe, *f.* stain, spot.

laberíntico, ca, *a.* labyrinthine.

laberinto, *m.* labyrinth, maze; intricate matter; (anat.) labyrinth of the ear.

laberintodonte, *m.* (paleontol.) labyrinthodont. —*pl.* (paleontol.) Labyrinthodonta.

labia, *f.* (coll.) sweet, winning talk or eloquence.

labiado, da, *a.* (bot.) labiate.

labial, *a.* labial; lip (as *a.*).

labiérnago, *m.* (bot.) laburnum.

labihendido, da, *a.* hare-lipped.

labil, *a.* labile.

labio, *m.* lip; (by ext.) mouth; edge, brim.—**l. liporino,** harelip.

labor, *f.* labor, task, toil, work; design, scroll-work; (sew.) needlework, embroidery, fancy-work; trimming; a thousand tiles or bricks; cultivation; husbandry, tillage; egg of a silkworm; figures raised upon a ground; diaper; (min.) works, working.

laborable, *a.* tillable; workable; working, week (day).

laborador, ra, *n.* tiller, farmer; worker.

laborante. I. *a.* tilling, working. **II.** *m.* (Cuba) conspirator.

laborantismo, *m.* (Cuba) (pol.) movement for independence from Spain.

laborar, *va. & vn.* to till; to work.

laboratorio, *m.* laboratory.

laborcica, illa, ita, *f. dim.* pretty needlework.

laborear, *va.* to work; (naut.) to reeve, to run.

laboreo, *m.* (naut.) reeving, running; (min.) works; working, exploitation, development.

laborera, *f.* clever, skilful workwoman.

laboriosamente, *adv.* laboriously.

laboriosidad, *f.* laboriousness, assiduity.

laborioso, sa, *a.* assiduous, industrious; arduous, laborious.

labra, *f.* stone cutting or carving; working, cutting (of metal, stone, etc.).—**de l. fácil,** free-cutting, free-turning (metal).

labrada, *f.* land plowed and fallowed.

labradero, ra; labradío, día, *a.* tillable, arable; workable.

labrado, da. I. *pp.* of LABRAR. **II.** *a.* wrought; figured, hewn. **III.** *m. pl.* cultivated lands.

labrador, ra. I. *n.* farmer, tiller, peasant. **II.** *a.* industrious.

labradoresco, ca, *a.* pertaining to farmers, rustic.

labradorita, *f.* (min.) labradorite.

labrandera, *f.* seamstress, embroiderer.

labrante, *m.* stonecutter; sculptor.

labrantín, *m.* petty farmer.

labrantío, tía, *a.* arable, tillable.

labranza, *f.* tillage, cultivation; farming; farm land.

labrar. I. *va.* to elaborate, work; to manufacture, make; to till, cultivate; to build, erect; to cut, dress, carve (stone); to embroider; to make designs in; to form; cause, bring about; to work out (a man's destiny, etc.). **II.** *vn.* to make a strong impression on the mind.

labrero, ra. I. *a.* (fishing nets) for sharks. **II.** *n.* (Chile) mine overseer or foreman.

labriego, ga, *n.* rustic, peasant, farmer.

labrusca, *f.* wild grapevine.

laburno, *m.* (bot.) laburnum.

laca, *f.* lac, gum lac; red color; lake, a pigment; lacquer, a varnish.—**l. en grano,** seed-lac.—**l. en palillos,** stick lac.—**l. en tablillas,** shellac.

lacayesco, ca, *a.* = LACAYUNO.

lacayo, *m.* lackey, groom, footman; knot of ribbons worn by women.

lacayuelo, *m. dim.* foot-boy, groom.

lacayuno, na, *a.* pertaining to a lackey; lackey-like, servile.

lacear, *va.* to lace, trim, or tie with bows; to pin up (the game) or drive within shot.

lacedemón; lacedemonio, a, *n. & a.* Lacedemonian.

laceración, *f.* laceration, tearing.

lacerado, da. I. *pp.* of LACERAR. **II.** *a.* unfortunate, unhappy; leprous.

lacerar, *va.* to mangle, tear in pieces, lacerate; to hurt, damage.

lacería, *f.* misery, poverty, wretchedness; drudgery, weariness.

lacería, *f.* set of bows.

lacerioso, sa, *a.* miserable, wretched.

lacertilio, lia. I. *n. & a.* lacertian. **II.** *m. pl.* Lacertilia.

lacertoso, *a.* muscular, athletic.

lacinia, *f.* (bot.) lacinia, slender lobe.

laciniado, da, *a.* (bot.) laciniate, slashed.

lacio, cia, *a.* faded, withered; flaccid, lanquid; straight (as hair).

lacónicamente, *adv.* laconically.

lacónico, ca, *a.* laconic.

laconio, nia, *n. & a.* Laconian.

laconismo, *m.* laconism.

lacra, *f.* mark or trace left by illness; fault, defect; viciousness.

¹lacrar, *va.* to injure or impair (the health); to cause pecuniary damage or loss to.

²lacrar, *va.* to seal with sealing wax.

lacre, *m.* sealing wax.

lacrimal, *a.* lachrymal.

lacrimatorio, ria, *n. & a.* lachrymatory.

lacrimosamente, *adv.* tearfully.

lacrimoso, sa, *a.* tearful, lachrymose.

lactación, *f.* suckling.

lactancia, *f.* lactation, period of suckling.

lactante, *n. & a.* feeding on milk.

lactar. I. *va.* to nurse; to feed with milk. **II.** *vn.* to suckle; to feed on milk.

lactato, *m.* (chem.) lactate.

lácteo, tea, *a.* lacteous, milky, lacteal.

lactescente, *a.* lactescent.

lacticíneo, a, *a.* = LÁCTEO.

lacticinio, *m.* any kind of milk food.

láctico, ca, *a.* (chem.) lactic.

lactífero, ra, *a.* lactiferous.

lactina, *f.* (chem.) lactose, lactin, milk sugar.

lactómetro, *m.* lactometer.

lactosa, *f.* = LACTINA.

lactoscopio, *m.* lactoscope.

lactucario, *m.* (pharm.) lactucarium.

lactumen, *m.* (med.) milk crust.

lacunario, *m.* (arch.) lacunar.

lacustre, *a.* lacustrine.

¹lacha, *f.* (ichth.) anchovy.

²lacha, *f.* shame.

lada, *f.* (bot.) cystus.

ládano, *m.* labdanum, gum labdanum.

ladeado, da, *a. & pp.* tilted, inclined to one side.

ladear. I. *va. & vr.* to tilt, tip, incline to one side. **II.** *vn.* to skirt; to deviate; to bend over. **III.** *vr.* to incline to an opinion or party; to lean; to tilt, incline to one side; (Chile) to fall in love.

ladeo, *m.* inclination or motion to one side.

ladera, *f.* declivity, slope, hillside.—*pl.* rails or staves of a truck; cheeks of a gun carriage.

ladería, *f.* small dale on a mountainside.

ladero, ra, *a.* lateral.

ladierno, *m.* (bot.) buckthorn.

ladilla, *f.* crab louse; (bot.) common barley.

ladillo, *m.* shifting panel placed in the sides of coaches.

ladinamente, *adv.* artfully, sagaciously, cunningly.

ladino, na, *a.* sagacious, cunning, crafty; apt as a linguist.

lado, *m.* side; border, margin, edge; (mil.) flank; party, faction; mat for the side of carts, etc.;

course, bend, manner; mode of proceeding.—*pl.*
patrons, advisers.—**l. a l.** side by side.—**l.
flaco,** weak side, spot.—**al l.,** just by, near at
hand; to one side; next door.—**a un l.,** aside.
—**dejar a un l.,** to set aside.—**de l.,** incidentally; sideways; from or on the side.—**hacerse
a un l.,** to move aside, to get out of the way.—
mirar de l., to look askance; to look out of the
corner of the eye; to look at contemptuously,
look down upon.—**por el l.,** around, in the
general direction of.—**por otro l.,** on the
other hand.—**por todos lados,** on all sides.—
por un l. . . . por otro, on the one hand,
. . . on the other; in a way . . . in a way.
ladón, *m.* (bot.) = LADA, cystus.
ladra, *f.* barking.
ladrador, ra; ladrante, *n. & a.* barker(-ing).
ladrar, *vn.* to bark.—**ladrido,** *m.* barking; outcry; calumny, slander.
ladrillado, *m.* brick floor.
ladrillador, *m.* = ENLADRILLADOR, brick layer.
ladrillal, *m.* brick yard.
¹ladrillar, *m.* = LADRILLAL.
²ladrillar, *va.* to lay bricks on, pave with bricks.
ladrillazo, *m.* blow with a brickbat.
ladrillejo, *m. dim.* little brick; boys' amusement
of knocking at doors with a brick.
ladrillera, *f.* (Am.) place for making bricks;
(Ecua.) mold for making bricks.
ladrillero, *m.* brick maker.
ladrillo, *m.* brick, tile.—**l. de chocolate,** cake of
chocolate.—**ladrilloso, sa,** *a.* bricky.
ladrón, na. I. *n.* thief; robber. II. *m.* lock, sluice
gate; melted wax on sides of a candle.
ladronamente, *adv.* thievishly.
ladroncillo, *m. dim.* petty thief, filcher.
ladronear, *vn.* to go about robbing or stealing.
ladronera, *f.* nest of rogues, den of robbers; filching, extortion; sluice gate in a mill; money box.
ladronería, *f.* = LADRONICIO.
ladronesco, ca. I. *a.* (coll.) pert. to thieves,
thievish. II. *f.* gang of thieves.
ladronicio, *m.* larceny, theft, robbery.
ladronzuelo, la, *n. dim.* petty thief.
lagaña, *f.* bleacedness.
lagañoso, sa, *a.* = LEGAÑOSO, blear-eyed.
lagar, *m.* wine press.
lagarejo, *m.* small wine press.
lagarero, *m.* wine presser; olive presser.
lagareta, *f.* small wine press; puddle, pool.
lagarta, *f.* female lizard; (coll.) sly, cunning
woman.
lagartado, da, *a.* = ALAGARTADO, variegated.
lagartera, *f.* lizard hole.
lagartija, *f.,* **lagartijo,** *m.,* **lagartillo,** *m. dim.*
small lizard.
lagarto, *m.* lizard; (Am.) alligator; (anat.) biceps;
(coll.) sly, artful person.—**l. de Indias,** cayman, alligator.
lago, *m.* lake.—**l. de leones,** den of lions.
lagostín *m.* (ichth.) = LANGOSTÍN, crayfish.
lagotear, *vn.* (coll.) to flatter, wheedle, cajole.
lagotería, *f.* (coll.) flattery.
lagotero, ra, *a.* (coll.) flattering, honey-mouthed.
lágrima, *f.* tear; drop of any liquid; drop-like
exudation from a tree; wine that drips from the
grape without pressure.—**l. de David, or de
Jacob,** (bot.) Job's tears.—**lágrimas de Batavia, or de Holanda,** Prince Rupert's drops,
glass globules.—**lágrimas de cocodrilo,** crocodile tears.—**lágrimas de San Pedro,** pebbles,
stones thrown at a person.—**derramar or
verter una l.,** to shed a tear.
lagrimable, *a.* deserving tears.
lagrimal. I. *a.* lachrymal. II. *m.* lachrymal
caruncle.
lagrimar, lagrimear, *vn.* to shed tears.
lagrimeo, *m.* shedding tears.
lagrimón, *m. aug.* large tear.

lagrimoso, sa, *a.* tearful, lachrymose; (of eyes)
watery; (bot.) exuding.
laguna, *f.* lagoon; hiatus, gap.
lagunajo, *m.* puddle, pool.
lagunar, *m.* (arch.) lacunar.
lagunero, ra, *a.* pertaining to lagoons.
lagunoso, sa, *a.* marshy, fenny, swampy.
laical, *a.* = LAICO.
laicidad, *f.* laity; secularism.
laicismo, *m.* secularism.
laicista, *n. & a.* secularist(-ic).
laico, ca, *a.* lay, laic.
laja, *f.* flagstone; slab; (naut.) rock at the entrance of a harbor.
¹lama, *f.* mud, slime, ooze; seaweed; fine sand
used for mortar; dust of ores in mines.
²lama, *f.* lamé, gold or silver cloth.
³lama, *n.* lama, Tibetan monk or nun.
lamaísmo, *m.* Lamaism.
lamaísta, *n. & a.* Lamaist(-ic).
lambel, *m.* (her.) lambel, label.
lambrequines, *m. pl.* (her.) mantelets.
lambrija, *f.* worm bred in the human body;
(coll.) skinny, thin person.
lamedal, *m.* musty, miry place.
lamedero, ra, *n.* licker; wheedling; (pharm.)
syrup.—**dar lamedor,** to feign losing at play
in order to insure greater success.
lamedura, *f.* act of licking.
lamelibranquio, quia. I. *n. & a.* (zool.) lamellibranch. II. *m. pl.* Lamellibranchiata.
lamelicornio, nia. I. *n. & a.* lamellicorn. II. *m.
pl.* Lamellicornia.
lameliforme, *a.* lamelliform.
lamelirostro, tra. I. *a.* (zool.) lamellirostral.
II. *m. pl.* Lamellirostres.
lamentable, *a.* lamentable, deplorable.
lamentablemente, *adv.* lamentably.
lamentación, *f.* lamentation, wail.—**muro de
las lamentaciones,** Wailing|Wall (in Jerusa-
lem).
lamentador, ra, *n. & a.* lamenter(-ing), mourn-
er(-ing), complainer(-ing).
lamentar. I. *va.* to lament, mourn; to regret, be
sorry for. II. *vn. & vr.* to lament, grieve, wail;
to complain; to moan.
lamento, *m.* lamentation, lament, moan, wail.
lamentoso, sa, *a.* lamentable, mournful.
lameplatos, *m.* (coll.) glutton, gorger; one who
feeds on leavings.
lamer, *va.* to lick; to lap; to touch slightly.
lamerón, na, *a.* (coll.) fond of dainties.
lamia, *f.* lamia, a fabulous monster; shark.
lamido, da. I. *pp.* of LAMER. II. *a.* (of persons)
worn out.
lamiente, *n. & a.* lick, licker(-ing).
lamín, *m.* dainty tidbit.
lámina, *f.* plate, sheet; lamina; engraving, print,
picture, illustration; engraving plate.
laminado, da, *a.* laminated; (of metals) rolled.
laminador, *m.* rolling mill; rolling press; plate
roller.
¹laminar, *va.* to roll or beat (metal) into sheets.
²laminar, *va.* to lick; to guzzle (dainties).
³laminar, *a.* laminar, lamellar; in sheets.
laminera, *f.* bee advanced before its companions.
¹laminero, ra, *n.* manufacturer of metal plates;
maker of shrines for relics.
²laminero, ra, *a.* fond of sweets.
lamiscar, *va.* (coll.) to lick greedily.
lamoso, sa, *a.* slimy, muddy.
lampa, *f.* (Am.) (agr.) shovel for grain.
lampacear, *va.* (naut.) to swab.
lampadéforo, lampadóforo, *m.* lampadephoria.
lampar, *vn. & vr.* = ALAMPAR, to crave, long for.
lámpara, *f.* lamp; light, luminous body; (radio)
tube; grease stain; bough placed at the door on
festivals or rejoicings.—**l. Argand,** Argand
lamp, student lamp.—**l. de arco,** arc lamp.—

l. de seguridad, safety lamp.—**l. de soldar,** blowtorch.—**l. de techo,** ceiling lamp, top lamp.—**l. incandescente,** incandescent lamp.—**l. normal,** standard lamp.—**l. piloto,** (elec.) pilot lamp.—**l. termiónica,** (radio) thermionic valve.—**atizar la lámpara,** (coll.) to refill the glasses.

lamparería, *f.* lamp factory; lamp store.

lamparero, ra, *n.* lamp maker or seller; lamplighter.

lamparilla, *f. dim.* small lamp; night taper; a sort of camlet; aspen or trembling poplar.

lamparín, *m.* lamp holder.

lamparista, *n.* = LAMPARERO.

lamparita, *f.* (S. A.) electric light bulb.

lamparón, *m. aug.* large grease spot; (med.) scrofula; (vet.) a disease of horses.

lampatán, *m.* a Chinese plant.

lampazo, *m.* (bot.) burdock; (naut.) swab, mop.

lampiño, ña, *a.* beardless.

lampión, *m.* large lantern.

lampo, *m.* flash of light; (poet.) refulgence.

lampote, *m.* (P. I.) domestic cotton cloth.

lamprea, *f.* (ichth.) sea lamprey.

lamprear, *va.* to dress or season with wine and sour gravy.

lamprehuela, lampreílla, *f.* river lamprey.

lámpsana, *f.* (bot.) common nipple wort.

lampuga, *f.* (ichth.) yellow mackerel.

lana, *f.* wool, fleece; woollen manufacture in general.

lanada, *f.* (artil.) sponge.

lanado, da, *a.* (bot.) lanate.

lanar, *a.* wool (as *a.*).

lanaria, *f.* (bot.) cudweed.

lancán, *m.* (P. I.) barge.

lance, *m.* cast, throw; casting of a fish net; catch in a net; critical moment; incident, episode; event, occurrence; transaction; quarrel, dispute; move or turn in a game.—**l. de honor,** duel.—**de l.,** cheap, at a bargain; at second hand.—**tener pocos lances,** to be uninteresting.

lancé, lance, *v. V.* LANZAR.

lanceado, da, *a.* (bot.) lanceolate.

lancear, *va.* to wound with a lance.

lancéola, *f.* (bot.) rib-grass plantain.

lanceolado, da, *a.* (bot.) lanceolate.

lancera, *f.* lance rack in an armory.

lancería, *f.* aggregate of lances; body of lancers.

lancero, *m.* pikeman; lancer; maker of pikes.

lanceta, *f.* (surg.) lancet; (vet.) fleam.

lancetada, *f.,* **lancetazo,** *m.* opening or wounding with a lancet.

lancetero, *m.* case for carrying lancets.

lancinante, *a.* stabbing, piercing.

lancita, *f. dim.* small lance.

lancurdia, *f.* small trout.

lancha, *f.* flagstone, slab; (naut.) boat, gig; lighter, launch; snare for partridges.—**l. cañonera,** gunboat.—**l. de pescar,** fishing smack.—**l. de socorro,** life-saving boat.

lanchada, *f.* lighter load.

lanchaje, *m.* (com.) ferriage; lighterage.

lanchar, *m.* flagstone quarry.

lanchero, *m.* bargeman, boatman, oarsman.

lanchón, *m. aug.* (naut.) lighter, barge, scow.—**l. alijador,** lighter.

lanchonero, *m.* lighterman, bargeman.

landgrave, *m.* landgrave.

landgraviato, *m.* landgraviate.

landó, *m.* landau, carriage with folding top.

landre, *f.* small tumor on the glands; concealed pocket in the clothes.

landrecilla, *f.* small round body in some glandular tissues.

landrero, ra, *a.* hoarder of money in a concealed pocket.

landrilla, *f.* (vet.) tongue worm.

lanería, *f.* shop where wool is sold.

lanero, ra. I. *a.* woollen. **II.** *n.* dealer in wool. **III.** *m.* warehouse for wool.

langa, *f.* small dry codfish.

langaruto, ta, *a.* (coll.) tall and skinny; thin.

langosta, *f.* (entom.) locust; (ichth.) lobster.

langostero, a. I. *n.* lobster fisherman. **II.** *a.* lobster-fishing; lobster (as *a.*).

langostín, langostino, *m.* (ichth.) crawfish.

langostón, *m. aug.* (entom.) green grasshopper.

languidamente, *adv.* languidly.

languidecer, *vn.* (ind. LANGUIDEZCO; *subj.* LANGUIDEZCA) to languish.

languidez, languideza, *f.* languishment, languidness, languor.

lánguido, da, *a.* languid, faint, weak.

lanífero, ra, *a.* (poet.) laniferous, woolly.

lanificación, *f.,* **lanificio,** *m.* woollen manufacturing; woollen goods.

lanilla, *f.* nap of cloth, down; swanskin; fine flannel; (naut.) bunting.

lanío, a, *a.* woolly.

lanosidad, *f.* (bot.) down of leaves.

lanoso, sa, *a.* woolly.

lantaca, *f.* (P. I.) small culverin.

lantano, *m.* (chem.) lanthanum.

lantia, *f.* (naut.) binnacle lamp; boom guy.

lanudo, da, *a.* woolly, fleecy.

lanuginoso, sa, *a.* (bot.) lanigerous, downy.

lanza, *f.* lance, spear; pole of a coach or wagon; nozzle; pikeman; free lance.—*pl.* duty formerly paid by the nobility in lieu of military services.—**l. en ristre,** with the lance on its rest; ready for action.—**ser una l.,** to be an expert; to be clever.

lanzabombas, *m.* bomb thrower.

lanzada, *f.* thrust or blow with a lance.

lanzadera, *f.* shuttle, a weaver's instrument.

lanzado, da. I. *pp.* of LANZAR. **II.** *a.* (naut.) raking, inclined.

lanzador, ra, *n.* thrower, ejecter; (baseball) pitcher.

lanzafuego, *m.* (artil.) linstock.

lanzamiento, *m.* launching, casting, or throwing; (law) dispossessing, eviction; (naut.) flaring of the bows and knuckle timbers; (naut.) rake of the stem and sternpost.—*pl.* length of a ship from stem to sternpost.

lanzaminas, *m.* mine layer, mine-laying boat.

lanzar. I. *va.* (*pret.* LANCE; *subj.* LANCE) to throw, dart, hurl, fling; to launch; to throw up, vomit; (law) to evict, dispossess. **II.** *vr.* to rush or dart; to launch forth; (com.) to engage or embark (in).

lanzatorpedos, *m.* torpedo boat; torpedo tube.

lanzazo, *m.* = LANZADA.

lanzón, *m. aug.* short and thick goad.

lanzuela, *f. dim.* small lance or spear.

¹**laña,** *f.* green coconut.

²**laña,** *f.* clamp, cramp or cramp iron.

¹**lañar,** *va.* to cramp; to clamp.

²**lañar,** *va.* to clean (fish).

laodicense, *a.* Laodicean.

¹**lapa,** *f.* vegetable film on surface of a liquid.

²**lapa,** *f.* barnacle.

³**lapa,** *f.* (bot.) goose grass, cleavers.

lapachar, *m.* swamp, marsh, morass.

lápade, *f.* lepadid, barnacle.

laparotomía, *f.* (surg.) laparotomy.

lapicera, *f.* (Chile, Arg.) = LAPICERO; penholder, pen.—**l. fuente, or de depósito,** fountain pen.

lapicero, *m.* pencil case; pencil holder.

lápida, *f.* tablet, memorial stone; gravestone (called also **l. mortuoria**).

lapidación, *f.* lapidation, stoning to death.

lapidar, *va.* to stone to death.

lapidario, ria, *n. & a.* lapidary.

lapídeo, a, *a.* lapideous, stony.

lapidificación, *f.* (chem.) turning into stone.

lapidificar, *va.* (chem.) to petrify, turn into stone.

lapidoso, sa, *a.* lapideous, stony.

lapila, *f.* (bot.) hound's-tongue.
lapislázuli, *m.* (min.) lapis lazuli.
lápiz, *m.* (min.) black lead, graphite, plumbago; lead pencil; crayon; (coll.) censor's blue pencil.—**l. de plomo,** graphite.—**l. labial,** lipstick.—**l. rojo,** red ochre.
¹**lapizar,** *m.* black-lead mine.
²**lapizar,** *va.* to pencil; draw with pencil.
lapo, *m.* (coll.) blow with a cane or whip.
lapón, na, *n.* & *a.* Laplander(-ian, -ic).
lapso, *m.* lapse of time; fall, lapse, slip.
lapsus, *m.* lapsus, slip.—**l. calami,** lapsus calami, slip of the pen.—**l. linguæ,** slip of the tongue.
laques, *f. pl.* = BOLEADORES, a lariat.
lar, *m.* (gen. *pl.*) Lar, tutelar or household god.—*pl.* home.
larario, *m.* shrine for household gods.
lardar, lardear, *va.* to baste (meat); to scald with boiling oil.
lardero, a.—**jueves l.,** Thursday before Lent.
lardo, *m.* lard, fat of an animal.
lardón, *m.* (print.) marginal addition; piece of paper clinging to the frisket and preventing the impression of some part of a sheet.
lardoso, sa, *a.* greasy, oily, smearing.
larga, *f.* (shoemaking) lengthening piece joined to a last; longest billiard cue; (gen. in the *pl.*) delay, procrastination.—**a la corta o a la l.,** sooner or later.—**a la l.,** in the end, in the long run.—**dar largas,** to delay, put off.
largamente, *adv.* largely, copiously; completely; liberally, frankly; for a long time.
largar. I. *va.* (*pret.* LARGUÉ; *subj.* LARGUE) to loosen, slacken; let go, set free; to expel; to shed; to give (as a slap); to heave (as a sigh); (naut.) to loosen, to ease.—**l. las velas,** (naut.) to set sail. **II.** *vr.* (coll.) to get out, quit, leave; (naut.) to set sail.
¹**largo, ga. I.** *a.* long; extended, prolonged; generous, free, liberal; prompt, expeditious; shrewd, cunning; copious, abundant.—*pl.* many, quite a number; odd, a little over (*tengo cincuenta años largos,* I am fifty-odd years old).—**l. de lengua,** long-tongued, too free and unguarded with the tongue.—**l. de uñas,** (coll.) light-fingered.—**largos años,** many years; long life.—**a lo l.,** at a distance; lengthwise; at full length, stretched out.—**a lo l. de,** along, lengthwise of.—**a lo más l.,** at most—**cuan l. es** (era), at full length, stretched out.—**traje l.,** evening dress. **II.** *m.* length.—**de l.,** in length, long.—**de l. a l.,** from one end to the other, lengthwise.—**pasar de l.,** to pass by without stopping. **III.** *adv.* largely, profusely. **IV.** *interj.* ¡**l!** or ¡**l. de ahí!,** begone! get out!
²**largo,** *m.* (mus.) largo.
largor, *m.* length.
largué, largue, *v. V.* LARGAR.
largueado, da, *a.* striped.
larguero, *m.* jamb post; bolster; stringer; (aer.) longeron; (aer.) spar.
largueza, *f.* length; liberality, generosity.
larguirucho, cha, *a.* (coll.) long and thin.
larguito, ita, *a.* somewhat long, longish.
largura, *f.* length.
lárice, *m.* (bot.) larch tree.
laricino, na, *a.* pertaining to the larch tree.
laringe, *f.* (anat.) larynx.—**laríngeo, gea,** *a.* laryngeal.—**laringitis,** *f.* (med.) laryngitis.—**laringología,** *f.* laryngology.—**laringoscopia,** *f.* laryngoscopy.—**laringoscopio,** *m.* laryngoscope.—**laringotomía,** *f.* (surg.) laryngotomy.—**laringótomo,** *m.* (surg.) laryngotome.
larva, *f. m.* mask; ghost, hobgoblin; (zool.) larva; tadpole.—**larvado, da,** *a.* (med.) larvate.—**larval,** *a.* larval.
las, *pl.* of LA.
lasaña, *f.* fritter shaped like a leaf.
lasca, *f.* chip from a stone.
lascar, *va.* to ease away, slacken, pay out.

lascivamente, *adv.* lasciviously.
lascivia, *f.* lasciviousness, lewdness.
lascivo, va, *a.* lascivious, lewd, lustful; merry, sportive.
laserpicio, *m.* (bot.) laserwort.
lasitud, *f.* lassitude, weariness, faintness.
laso, sa, *a.* weary, tired; lax, flaccid.
lastar, *va.* to pay (for a fault); suffer for another.
lástima, *f.* pity; compassion; pitiful object; plaint, lamentation, tale of woe.—**dar,** or **hacer, l.,** to arouse pity or regret, to be pitiful or regrettable.—**es l.** it's a pity, too bad.—¡**que l.!** what a pity!—¡**que l. de (vestido)!** what a sorry-looking (dress)!
lastimadura, *f.* sore, hurt.
lastimar. I. *va.* to hurt; injure, damage; to pity. **II.** *vr.* to hurt oneself; to regret, be sorry for; to complain.
lastimeramente, *adv.* sadly, sorrowfully.
lastimero, ra, *a.* pitiful, sad, doleful.
lastimosamente, *adv.* pitifully, sadly.
lastimoso, sa, *a.* = LASTIMERO.
lasto, *m.* receipt given to one who pays for another.
lastra, *f.* flagstone, slab.
lastrar, *va.* (naut. and Ry.) to ballast.
¹**lastre,** *m.* ballast; judgment, sense.
²**lastre,** *m.* stone slat of poor quality; (coll.) food, "grub".
lastrón, *m. aug.* large stone slat.
lasún, *m.* (ichth.) = LOCHA, loach.
¹**lata,** *f.* small log.
²**lata,** *f.* tin plate or tinned iron plate; tin can; can of tinned food; lath; ledge.—**en l., en latas,** canned.—**dar la l.,** (coll.) to pester with too much talk.
³**lata,** *f.* annoyance, nuisance; (coll.) long-drawn-out, tedious visit or performance.
latamente, *adv.* largely, amply.
latania, *f.* (bot.) latania palm.
latastro, *m.* (arch.) plinth (of a pillar).
lataz, *f.* (zool.) sea otter.
latebra, *f.* cave, den, hiding place.
latebroso, sa, *a.* hiding, furtive, secretive.
latente, *a.* latent.
lateral, *a.* lateral, side (as *a.*).—**lateralmente,** *adv.* laterally; sideways.
lateranense, *a.* Lateran.
látex, *m.* (bot.) latex.
laticífero, ra, *a.* (bot.) laticiferous.
laticlavia, *f.* (anc. Rome) laticlave, a badge of rank.
latido, *m.* beat, beating, throb; bark, barking (of an animal).
latiente, *a.* palpitating, fluttering.
latifundio, *m.* (anc. Rome) latifundium, large estate (esp. app. to vast uncultivated or poorly cultivated land).
latigadera, *f.* strap or thong for lashing the yoke.
latigazo, *m.* lash, whipping; crack of a whip; jerk; unexpected offense; harsh reproof.
látigo, *m.* whip; lashing cord for weighing with a steelyard; cinch strap; long plume around a hat.—**latiguear,** *vn.* to smack or crack a whip.—**latiguera,** *f.* cinch strap.—**latiguero,** *m.* whip maker or seller.—**latiguillo,** *m. dim.* small whip; (theat.) mannerism.
latín, *m.* Latin.—**bajo l.,** low Latin.—**saber l.,** or **mucho l.,** to be very shrewd or cunning.
latinajo, *m.* (coll.) Latin jargon; Latin word or quotation.
latinamente, *adv.* in Latin; in a Latin way.
latinar, latinear, *vn.* to speak or write Latin; to use Latin phrases often.
latines, *m. pl.* jargon, nonsense; hairsplitting.
latinidad, *f.* Latinity; the Latin tongue.
latinismo, *m.* Latinism.
latinista, *n.* Latinist.
latinizar. I. *va.* to Latinize. **II.** *vn.* to use words borrowed from the Latin.

latino, na. I. *a.* Latin. II. *n.* Latinist; Latin, a native of Latium.

latir, vn. to palpitate, pulsate, throb, beat; to bark, yelp, howl.

latitud, f. latitude; breadth, width, extent.

latitudinal, a. latitudinal.

latitudinario, ria, a. latitudinarian, liberal, tolerant.

latitudinarismo, m. latitudinarianism.

lato, ta, a. large, extensive, ample.

latón, m. brass.—**l. en hojas,** or **planchas,** latten brass, sheet brass.

latonería, f. brass trade; brass shop; brass works; brass ware.

latonero, m. brazier, worker in brass.

latoso, sa, a. boring, annoying.

latría, f. (Rom. Cath. theol.) latria, worship due only to God.

latrocinio, m. systematic robbery.

latvio, via, n. & a. Latvian.

laucha, f. (Arg., Chile) mouse.

laúd, m. (mus.) lute; (naut.) catboat; striped turtle.

lauda, f. tombstone.

laudable, a. laudable, praiseworthy.

laudablemente, adv. laudably.

láudano, m. laudanum.

laudar, va. (law) to render a decision on.

laudatorio, ria. I. *a.* laudatory, full of praise. II. *f.* laudatory, panegyric.

laude, f. inscribed tombstone.—*pl.* (eccl.) lauds.

laudemio, m. (law) dues paid to the lord of the manor on all transfers of landed property.

laudo, m. (law) award, finding, of an arbitrator.

launa, f. lamina, sheet; schistose clay.

lauráceo, a. I. *a.* laurellike; (bot.) lauraceous, laurineous. II. *f. pl.* Lauraceae.

láurea, f. laurel wreath.

laureado, da. I. *pp.* of LAUREAR. II. *a.* laureate.

laureando, m. student about to graduate.

laurear, va. to crown with laurel; to honor, reward; to confer a degree on.

lauredal, m. plantation of laurel trees.

laurel, m. (bot.) laurel; laurel wreath; honor.—**l. cerezo,** (bot.) cherry laurel.

laurente, m. workman in paper mills.

láureo, a, a. laurel (as a.).

laureóla, f. laurel wreath; diadem; (bot.) mezereon.—**l. hembra,** (bot.) mezereon daphne.—**l. macho,** spurge laurel.

laurífero, ra, a. lauriferous, laurel-bearing.

lauríneo, nea, a. (bot.) laurineous.

laurino, na, a. pertaining to laurel.

lauro, m. (bot.) laurel; glory, honor.

lauroceraso, laurorreal, m. cherry laurel.

lautamente, adv. splendidly.

lauto, ta, a. rich, splendid.

¹lava, f. lava.

²lava, f. (min.) washing of metals.

lavabo, m. washstand; lavatory; washroom.

lavacaras, m. (coll.) flatterer.

lavación, f. (pharm.) lotion, wash.

lavadero, m. washing place; lavatory; (tanning) vat or pit for washing hides; (min.) buddling tank; placer, place where gold, etc. are obtained by washing.

lavado, m. wash, washing; laundry work; (art) aquarelle in a single tint.

lavador, ra. I. *n. & a.* washer(-ing), cleaner(-ing). II. *m.* (artil.) burnisher. III. *f.* washing machine (called also **l. mecánica**).

lavadura, f. wash, washing; composition for dressing glove leather; slops.

lavaje, m. washing of wools.

lavajo, m. drinking pool for cattle; morass.

lavamanos, m. washstand; lavatory.

lavamiento, m. washing, ablution.

lavanco, m. a kind of wild duck.

lavandera, f. laundress, washerwoman.

lavandería, f. (Am.) laundry.

lavandero, m. launderer, laundryman.

lavaplatos, n. dishwasher.

lavar, va. to wash; to launder; (mason.) to whitewash; (art) to paint in water colors; to purify.

lavativa, f. clyster, enema, injection; syringe; vexation, annoyance; bore.

lavatorio, m. lavation, washing; lavatory; washstand; (pharm.) lotion; (eccl.) maundy.

lavaza, f. soap suds.—*pl.* dirty water, slops.

lave, m. washing of ores in mines.

lavotear, va. & vr. (coll.) to wash hurriedly.

lavoteo, m. hurried washing.

laxación, f., laxamiento, m. laxity, laxness; loosening.

laxante, n. & a. loosener(-ing); laxative.

laxar, va. to loosen; to soften.

laxativo, va, n. & a. laxative; lenitive.

laxidad, laxitud, f. laxity, laxness.

laxo, xa, a. lax, slack.

lay, m. (poet.) lay, ballad.

¹laya, f. (agr.) spade, spud.

²laya, f. quality, kind, class.

layador, m. spadesman.

layar, va. (agr.) to spade.

lazada, f. bowknot; (sew.) bow; true-lover's knot.

lazador, m. lassoer.

lazar, va. to lasso, capture with a lasso.

lazareto, m. hospital for contagious diseases; quarantine (at ports of entry).

lazarillo, m. blind person's guide.

lazarino, na. I. *a.* leprous. II. *n.* leper.

lazo, m. (sewing) bow, loop, true-lover's knot; snare (for game); trap or snare (for persons); lasso, lariat; slipknot; tie, bond; (arch.) knot or ornament.—*pl.* (dance) figures.—**l. escurridizo,** running knot.—**armar l.,** or **lazos,** to trap, deceive; to plot.

lazulita, f. lazulite, lapis lazuli.

le, ie, *dative case of* ÉL, ELLA: *accusative case of* ÉL: to him, to her, to it (¿que le dio Vd.? what did you give to him (or to her)? ¿que le añadio Vd.? what did you add to it?) accusative case of ÉL: him (ayer le vi, I saw him yesterday). (Often improperly app. to inanimate objects.)

leal, a. loyal.—**l. saber y entender,** to the best of my knowledge.—**lealmente, adv.** loyally.

lealtad, f. loyalty, fidelity.

lebrada, f. hare fricassee.

lebrático, illo, ito; lebrato; lebratón, n. dim. young hare.

lebrel, la, n. greyhound (f., greyhound bitch).

lebrero, ra, a. hare-hunting, hare (as a.).

lebrillo, m. glazed earthenware tub.

lebrón, m. large hare; (coll.) poltroon.

lebroncillo, m. young hare.

lebruno, na, a. pertaining to or like hares.

lección, f. lesson; tuition; lecture; reading.—**dar una l.,** to say or recite a lesson; to give a lesson.—**echar l.,** to give out or assign a lesson.—**tomar la l.,** to take a lesson.—**tomar una lección a,** to hear a lesson from, to hear (someone's) lesson.

leccionario, m. (eccl.) lectionary.

leccioncita, f. dim. short lecture or lesson.

leccionista, n. private tutor; coach.

lecitina, f. (chem.) lecithin.

lecito, m. yolk (of an egg).

lectisternio, m. (anc. Rome) lectisternium, a sacrifice.

lectivo, va, a. lesson or recitation (day, hour).

lector, ra, m. reader; lecturer; (eccl.) instructor of the Gospel.

lectorado, m. (eccl.) lectorate.

lectoral. I. *f.* (eccl.) prebend. II. *m.* prebendary.

lectoría, f. (eccl.) lectureship.

lectura, f. reading; lecture; (print.) pica.

lecturita, f. (print.) small pica.

lecha, f. seminal fluid of fishes; each of the two sacs which contain it.

lechada, *f.* grout; liquid containing finely divided solids in suspension; pulp for making paper.

lechal. I. *a.* sucking, suckling; (bot.) lactiferous, milky. **II.** *m.* (bot.) milky juice of plants.

lechar, *a.* nursing; promoting the secretion of milk in female mammals.

lechaza, *f.* = LECHA.

leche, *f.* milk; (bot.) milky juice.—**l. crema,** custard.—**l. de canela,** oil of cinnamon dissolved in wine.—**l. de gallina,** or **de pájaro,** (bot.) common star of Bethlehem.—**l. de tierra,** magnesia.—**l. de (los) viejos,** wine.—**l. quemada,** sweetmeat made from simmered milk.—**estar con la l. en los labios,** to lack experience.—**estar en l.,** (of fruits and plants) to be still green or undeveloped; (of the sea) to be calm.

lechecillas, *f. pl.* sweetbreads; livers and lights.

lechera. I. *a.* milch (app. to animals). **II.** *f.* milkmaid, dairymaid; milk can; milk jug.

lechería, *f.* dairy (shop).

lechero, ra. I. *a.* milky. **II.** *m.* milkman.

lecherón, *m.* milk pail, milk vessel; flannel wrap for newborn infants.

lechetrezna, *f.* (bot.) spurge.

lechigada, *f.* breed, litter; gang of ruffians.

lechín, *m.* variety of olive tree and the rich olive it yields; (vet.) tumor in horses.

lechino, *m.* (vet.) small tumor.

lecho, *m.* bed, couch; lay, litter; bed of a river; tier, row; layer, stratum; foundation, base.

lechón, na, *n.* suckling pig; pig.

lechoncico, illo, ito, *m. dim.* very young pig.

lechoso, sa. I. *a.* (bot.) having a milky juice. **II.** *m.* (S. A.) (bot.) papaw tree. **III.** *f.* papaw.

lechuga, *f.* (bot.) lettuce; (sewing) frill.

lechugado, da, *a.* lettuce-like.

lechuguero, ra, *n.* seller of lettuce.

lechuguilla, *f. dim.* small lettuce; frill, ruff.

lechuguina, *f.* (coll.) stylish young lady.

lechuguino, *m.* lettuce sprout; plot of small lettuces; (coll.) dandy, dude.

lechuza, *f.* (ornith.) owl; barn owl.

¹lechuzo, za. I. *a.* suckling (mule colt).

²lechuzo, za, *n.* (coll.) bill collector; summons server; owl-faced person.

ledamente, *adv.* (poet.) merrily, cheerfully.

ledo, da, *a.* (poet.) gay, merry, cheerful, glad.

leer, *va.* (*ger.* LEYENDO; *pret.* él LEYÓ) to read; to lecture; to instruct.

lega, *f.* (eccl.) lay sister.

legacía, *f.* legateship; message intrusted to a legate; province and duration of a legateship.

legación, *f.* legation, embassy; legateship.

legado, *m.* (law) legacy; deputy, ambassador, legate; commander of a Roman legion.—**l. a látere,** (eccl.) Pope's legate.

legador, *m.* laborer who ties the feet of sheep for shearing.

legadura, *f.* tie; binding cord or strap.

legajo, *m.* file, docket, bundle of papers.

legal, *a.* legal, lawful; loyal, true, faithful.

legalidad, *f.* legality, lawfulness.

legalización, *f.* legalization.

legalizar, *va.* to legalize.

legalmente, *adv.* legally, lawfully; loyally.

legamente, *adv.* ignorantly.

légamo, *n.* mud, silt.—**legamoso, sa,** *a.* silty.

legaña, *f.* gummy secretion of the eyes.

legañoso, sa, *a.* blear-eyed.

legar, *va.* (*pret.* LEGUÉ; *subj.* LEGUE) to depute, to send as a legate; (law) to bequeath.

legatario, ria, *n.* (law) legatee.

legenda, *f.* (eccl.) legend, history of saints.

legendario, ria. I. *a.* legendary. **II.** *m.* legendary, book of legends.

legible, *a.* legible, readable.

legiblemente, *adv.* legibly.

legión, *f.* legion.—**legionario, ria,** *n.* & *a.* legionary.

legislación, *f.* legislation.

legislador, ra, *n.* & *a.* legislator(-ing, -ive); lawmaker(-ing).

legislar, *va.* to legislate.

legislativo, va, *a.* legislative, lawmaking.

legislatura, *f.* legislature; term of a legislature.

legisperito, ta, *n.* = JURISPERITO, jurisconsult.

legista, *n.* legist; lawyer; law student.

legítima, *f.* (law) legitim.

legitimación, *f.* legitimation.

legítimamente, *adv.* legitimately, lawfully.

legitimar, *va,* to legitimate, legalize.

legitimidad, *f.* legitimacy, legality.

legitimista, *n.* & *a.* legitimist(-ic).

legítimo, ma, *a.* legitimate, lawful; genuine.

lego, ga. I. *a.* lay, laic; ignorant. **II.** *m.* layman; lay brother or friar.

legón, *m.* (agr.) hoe.

legra, *f.* (surg.) periosteotome.

legración, legradura, *f.* (surg.) periosteotomy.

legrar, *va.* (surg.) to perform periosteotomy on.

legua, *f.* league (measure of length).—**a l., a la l., a leguas, de cien leguas, de muchas leguas** or **desde media l.,** very far, at a great distance.

leguario, ria, *a.* league (as a *a.,* as *poste leguario,* league post).

legué, legue, *v. V.* LEGAR.

leguleyo, *m.* petty lawyer, pettifogger.

legumbre, *f.* pulse, vegetables, garden stuff.

leguminoso, sa, *a.* (bot.) leguminous.

leíble, *a.* legible, readable.

leído, da. I. *pp.* of LEER. **II.** *a.* well-read, well-informed.—**l. y escribido,** (coll. and contempt.) affecting learning.

leila, *f.* a Moorish dance.

leima, *m.* (mus.) limma.

lejanía, *f.* distance, remoteness; remote place.

lejano, na, *a.* distant, far.

lejas, *a. pl.*—**l. tierras,** far-away lands.

lejía, *f.* lye; (coll.) severe reprimand, dressing down.

lejío, *m.* (among dyers) lye.

lejísimos, *adv. super.* very far away.

lejitos, *adv. dim.* rather far.

lejos. I. *adv.* far.—**a lo l.,** in the distance, at a great distance, far off, far away.—**d. l., desde l.,** from afar. **II.** *m.* perspective, distant view; background; resemblance.

lejuelos, *adv. dim.* at a little distance.

lelilí, *m.* war whoop of the Moors.

lelo, la. I. *a.* stupid, dull. **II.** *n.* ninny.

lema, *m.* argument, summary; theme; motto, device; slogan; (math.) lemma.

lemanita, *f.* (min.) jade.

lemnáceo, a. I. *a.* (bot.) lemnaceous. **II.** *f. pl.* Lemnaceae.

lemniscata, *f.* (geom.) lemniscate.

lemosín, na. I. *a.* Languedocian. **II.** *m.* Languedocian; Provençal, langue d'oc.

lémur, *m.* (zool.) lemur.

lemures, *m. pl.* lemures; ghosts, apparitions.

lemurias, *f. pl.* Lemuria, feast of the lemures.

lemúrido, da. I. *n.* & *a.* (zool.) lemur. **II.** *m. pl.* Lemuridæ.

len, *a.* soft, flossy (thread or silk).

lena, *f.* spirit, vigor.

lencera, *f.* woman who deals in linen; wife of a linen draper.

lencería, *f.* linen goods; linen-draper's shop; linen hall; linen room; linen trade.

lencero, ra, *n.* linen draper, linen merchant.

lendel, *m.* track; mill horse.

lendrera, *f.* fine-toothed comb for taking out nits.

lendrero, *m.* place full of nits.

lendroso, sa, *a.* nitty, full of nits.

lene, *a.* soft (to the touch); sweet, kind, pleasant; light, not heavy.

lengua, *f.* (anat.) tongue; language; information, advice; clapper of a bell.—**l. canina** = L. DE PERRO.—**l. cerval,** (bot.) hart's-tongue.—**l. de**

buey, (bot.) bugloss, alkanet.—**l. del agua,** at the edge of the water.—**l. de oc,** langue d'oc.—**l. de perro,** (bot.) hound's-tongue.—**l. de tierra,** tongue of land running out into the sea. —**l. de vaca,** sanseviera, cordy-line.—**l. madre,** or **matriz,** mother tongue.—**l. muerta,** dead language.—**l. sabia,** classical language.—**l. santa,** Hebrew.—**l. viperina,** viperous tongue. —**l. viva,** living, or modern, language.—**con la l. de un palmo,** or **con un palmo de l.,** with great anxiety or eagerness.—**de l. en l.,** from mouth to mouth.—**hacerse lenguas,** to speak in praise, sing the praises of.—**írsele, a uno la l.,** to let out something one did not wish to say, to give oneself away.—**morderse la lengua,** to hold one's tongue, to control oneself. —**no morderse la l.,** not to mince words, to speak out.—**tener en la l.,** or **en la punta de la l.,** to have at one's tongue's end.

lenguado, m. (ichth.) sole, flounder.

lenguaje, m. language; speech; parlance; vernacular tongue; style.

lenguaraz, a. speaking several languages; scurrilous; LENGUAZ.

lenguaz, a. garrulous, loquacious.

lengüecia, illa, ita, f. dim. small tongue.

lengüeta, f. dim. small tongue; (anat.) epiglottis; barb; (mus.) languette; needle of a balance; (bookbinding) cutting knife; (mech.) feather, wedge, tongue, bit, bore, awl; catch of a trap or snare; (arch.) buttress; molding.

lengüetada, f. act of licking.

lengüetería, f. reedwork of an organ.

lengüezuela, f. dim. small tongue.

lengüilargo, ga, a. (coll.) garrulous; scurrilous.

lenidad, f. lenity, mildness.

lenificar, va. to soften.—**lenificativo, va,** a. mollifying, softening.

lenitivo, va. I. a. lenitive, assuaging; lenient. **II.** m. emollient; mitigator.

lenocinio, m. pimping, pandering.

lentamente, adv. slowly, lingeringly.

lente. I. m. or f. (opt.) lens; monocle.—**l. de aumento,** magnifying glass. **II.** m. pl. eyeglasses.

lentecer, vn. to grow soft or tender.

lenteja, f. (bot.) lentil; disk of a pendulum.—**l. de agua,** (bot.) gibbous duckweed.

lentejuela, f. spangle.

lenticular, a. like a lentil seed.

lentiscal, m. thicket of mastic trees.

lentisco, m. (bot.) mastic tree, lentiscus.

lentitud, f. slowness, sluggishness.

lento, ta, a. slow, sluggish, tardy, heavy; glutinous; (mus.) lento.

lentor, m. (pharm.) viscidity.

lenzuelo, m. (agr.) sheet for carrying straw.

leña, f. firewood, kindling wood; (coll.) drubbing, beating.—**echar l. al fuego,** to add fuel to the flame, foment discord.—**llevar l. al monte,** to carry coals to Newcastle.

leñador, ra, n. woodman (-woman), woodcutter; dealer in kindling wood.

leñame, m. wood; provision of kindling wood.

leñatero, ra, n. = LEÑADOR.

leñazo, m. cudgeling.

leñera, f. woodshed, wood bin.

leñero, m. wood dealer; logman.

leño, m. log; timber; (naut.) ancient galley; (poet.) ship, vessel; (coll.) dull, thick-witted person.

leñoso, sa, a. woody, ligneous.

Leo, m. (astr.) Leo.

león, m. (zool.) lion; (entom.) ant lion; (zool.) boa.—**l. marino,** sea lion.—**l. rampante,** (her.) lion rampant.—**el L.,** (astr.) Leo.—**no es tan bravo,** or **tan fiero, el l. como lo pintan,** one cannot always judge by appearances; things are not so bad as they seem.

leona, f. lioness; brave, undaunted woman.

leonado, da, a. lion-colored, tawny.

leoncico, illo, ito, m. whelp of a lion.

leonera, f. cage or den of lions; (coll.) gambling den.

leonero, m. lion keeper; (coll.) master of a gambling house.

leonés, sa, a. of or pertaining to Leon.

leónica, f. (vet.) vein under the tongue.

leonina, f. (med.) leontiasis, a leprous affection.

leonino, na, a. leonine; (law) one-sided, unfair; (poet.) leonine (verse).

leontina, f. (jewelry) watch chain.

leopardo, m. leopard.

leopoldina, f. (jewelry) fob chain; Spanish helmet.

Lepe, m.—**saber más que L.,** to be very smart and shrewd.

lépero, ra, n. (Mex.) one of the rabble.

lepidio, m. (bot.) peppergrass.

lepidolita, f. (min.) lepidolite.

lepidóptero, ra. I. a. (entom.) lepidopterous. **II.** m. pl. Lepidoptera.

lepisma, f. (entom.) lepisma; silver fish.

lepórido, da. I. a. (zool.) pertaining to the Leporidæ (hares and rabbits). **II.** m. pl. Leporidæ.

leporino, na, a. harelike.

lepra, f. leprosy.

leprosería, f. lepers' lazaretto.

leproso, sa. I. a. leprous. **II.** n. leper.

leptocardio, dia. I. n. & a. (zool.) leptocardian. **II.** m. pl. Leptocardii.

lercha, f. reed for hanging fish and birds.

lerda, f. (vet.) = LERDÓN.

lerdamente, adv. slowly, heavily.

lerdo, da, a. slow, heavy; dull, obtuse.

lerdón, m. (vet.) tumor in a horse's pastern.

les, pers. pron. dative case of ELLOS, ELLAS: to them, them (indirect object): les di pan, I gave them bread; les hablé, I spoke to them.

lesbio, bia, a. Lesbian, of Lesbos.

lesión, f. lesion, wound, injury; damage, wrong.

lesionar, va. to injure; to damage, impair.

lesivo, va, a. prejudicial, injurious.

lesna, f. = LEZNA, awl.

lesnordeste, m. (naut.) east-northeast wind.

leso, sa, a. wounded, hurt, damaged; perverted. —**l. majestad,** lese majesty.

leste, m. (naut.) east wind, east.

lesueste, m. (naut.) east-southeast wind.

letal, a. mortal, deadly, lethal.

letame, m. mud for fertilizing.

letanía, f. (eccl.) litany; (coll.) list of things.—pl. supplicatory procession.

letárgico, ca, a. lethargic.

letargo, m. lethargy, drowsiness.—**l. epidémico,** sleeping sickness.

letargoso, sa, a. causing lethargy.

leteo, a, a. (poet.) Lethean.

letificante, a. exhilarating, invigorating.

letificar, va. to gladden, cheer; to invigorate.

letífico, ca, a. cheering, bringing joy.

letra, f. letter, character of the alphabet; handwriting; (print.) type; motto, inscription; literal meaning; (poet.) a kind of rondeau; words of a song.—pl. letters, learning; the learned professions.—**l. abierta,** (com.) open credit.—**l. bastardilla** = L. ITÁLICA.—**l. borrosa,** illegible writing.—**l. cursiva,** running hand.—**l. de caja alta,** (print.) upper case, capital.—**l. de caja baja,** (print.) lower case, small letter. —**l. de cambio,** (com.) draft, bill of exchange. —**l. de mano,** handwriting, handwritten letter.—**l. de molde,** print, printed letter.—**l. muerta,** dead letter, rule no longer observed.— **l. de tortis,** Gothic type.—**l. gótica,** Gothic characters.—**l. historiada,** adorned capital letter.—**l. itálica,** (print.) italic.—**l. menuda,** fine (small) writing or print; (coll.) artfulness, cunning, adroitness.—**letras patentes,** royal edict.—**letras remisorias,** judge's orders transferring a case to another court.—**l. versal**, capital letter.—**a la l.**, to the letter, literally.—**bellas**, or **buenas, letras**, belles lettres, literature.—**cuatro letras**, a few lines.—**tener mucha l.**, to be very artful and cunning.

letrado, da. I. *a.* learned, erudite; (coll.) vain, presumptuous. **II.** *m.* lawyer, advocate, counselor.—**a lo l.**, like a lawyer. **III.** *f.* (coll.) lawyer's wife.

letrero, *m.* sign; label, placard, poster; legend.

letrilla, *f. dim.* small letter; (mus.) rondelet.

letrina, *f.* privy, water-closet.

letrón. I. *m. aug.* large letter. **II.** *m. pl.* placards posted at the doors of churches.

letuario, *m.* a kind of marmalade.

leucina, *f.* (chem.) leucine.

leucocitemia, *f.* (med.) leukemia.

leucocíto, *m.* leucocyte, white blood corpuscle.

leucoma, *m.* (med.) leucoma, an eye disease.

leucomaína, *f.* (chem.) leucomaine.

leucorrea, *f.* (med.) leucorrhoea, whites.

leudar. I. *va.* to leaven. **II.** *vr.* to yeast.

leudo, da, *a.* fermented, leavened.

leva, *f.* (naut.) act of weighing anchor; (mil.) levy, press; (mech.) cam; vane (of a water wheel); (naut.) swell of the sea.—*pl.* tricks, artful devices.

levada, *f.* moving silkworm; (fencing) salute or flourish with the foil.

levadero, ra, *a.* to be collected or demanded.

levadizo, za, *a.* that can be lifted or raised, as a drawbridge.

levador, *m.* in paper mills, piler; (mech.) cam, cog, tooth.

levadura, *f.* ferment, leaven, yeast, barm; (carp.) sawed-off plank.

levantada, *f.* rising, getting up.

levantadamente, *adv.* highly, loftily.

levantado, da, *pp. & a.* raised, elevated, lofty.

levantador, ra, *n.* one who raises or lifts up; disturber, rioter; mutineer.

levantamiento, *m.* elevation, raising; sublimity; insurrection, revolt, uprising; settlement of accounts; survey.—**l. de planos**, surveying.

levantar. I. *va.* to raise; to lift, heave, pick up; to erect, build; set up; to rouse, excite, stir up; to impute or attribute falsely; to start (game); to cut (the cards); to cause, occasion; to begin; to stand up; to start suddenly (as game).—**l. acta**, to draw up and execute an affidavit or certificate.—**l. bandera**, to rise in insurrection, to rebel.—**l. (la) casa**, to break up housekeeping.—**l. (la) cabeza**, to retrieve one's losses, to get on one's feet; to take courage.—**l. con**, to take unlawful possession of, to get away with.—**l. el plano de**, to survey.—**l. falso testimonio**, to bear false witness, to accuse falsely.—**l. la mesa**, to clear the table.—**l. planos**, to survey; to draw up plans. **II.** *vr.* to rise, get up (from bed, chair, etc.); to rise up.

¹**levante**, *m.*—**estar de l.**, to be ready to depart.

²**levante**, *m.* Levant, east; east wind.

levantino, na, *a.* Levantine.

¹**levantisco, ca**, *a. & n.* Levantine.

²**levantisco, ca**, *a.* turbulent, restless.

levar. I. *va.* (naut.) to weigh (anchor).—**l. anclas**, to weigh anchor. **II.** *vr.* to set sail.

leve, *a.* light, of little weight; trifling; slight.

levedad, *f.* lightness, levity; inconstancy.

levemente, *adv.* lightly, gently; venially.

leviatán, *m.* leviathan.

levigación, *f.* levigation, elutriation.

levigar, *va.* to levigate, to elutriate.

levirato, *m.* (anc. Hebrew) levirate.

¹**levita**, *m.* Levite; deacon.

²**levita**, *f.* frock coat, Prince-Albert coat.

levítico, ca. I. *a.* Levitical; priestly. **II.** *m.* **(L-)** Leviticus; (coll.) ceremonial at a festival.

levitón, *m.* greatcoat like a frock coat.

léxico, *m.* lexicon.—**lexicografía**, *f.* lexicography.

—**lexicográfico, ca**, *a.* lexicographic.—**lexicógrafo**, *m.* lexicographer.—**lexicología**, *f.* lexicology.—**lexicológico, ca**, *a.* lexicological.—**lexicólogo**, *m.* lexicologist.—**lexicón**, *m.* = LÉXICO.

ley, *f.* law; rule of action; loyalty, faithful attachment; fineness (of coins, bullion, etc.); legal standard of quality, weight, or measure; precept; rules and regulations.—*pl.* law in general, jurisprudence, study and profession of the law.—**l. antigua**, law of Moses.—**l. caldaria**, hot-water ordeal.—**l. de la trampa**, trickery, fraud.—**l. del embudo**, oppressive law; one-sided agreement; severity for others, indulgence for ourselves.—**l. del tallón**, lex talionis, law of retaliation.—**l. escrita**, revealed law, decalogue.—**l. sálica**, Salic law.—**a la l.**, with propriety and neatness.—**a l. de caballero**, or **de cristiano**, on the word of a gentleman or Christian.—**a toda l.**, perfectly, according to rule.—**de buena l.**, sterling.—**de mala l.**, disreputable; crooked; low, base.

leyenda, *f.* reading; legend; superscription, inscription; device, motto.

leyente, *n. & a.* reader(-ing).

leyó, *pret.* of LEER.

lezda, *f.* ancient tax on merchandise.

lezna, *f.* awl.

¹**lía**, *f.* plaited bass rope.

²**lía**, *f.* husk of pressed grapes.—**estar hecho una lía**, (coll.) to be tipsy.

liar. I. *va.* to tie, bind, do up; (coll.) to embroil, draw into an entanglement—**liarlas**, (coll.) to sneak away; (coll.) to die. **II.** *vr.* to enter into concubinage.

liásico, ca. I. *n. & a.* (geol.) Liasic. **II.** *m.* Lias, Liasic.

liaza, *f.* collection of hoops used by coopers.

libación, *f.* libation.

libamen, *m.* offering in ancient sacrifices.

líban, *m.* esparto rope.

libar, *va.* to suck, sip; to taste; to perform a libation with.

libatorio, *m.* libatory cup.

libelar, *va.* (law) to petition.

libelático, ca, *a.* retracting, apostatizing.

libelista, *m.* libeler.

libelo, *m.* libel (often called **l. infamatorio**); (law) petition.—**l. de repudio**, written repudiation, of a wife by her husband; (coll.) discarding, abandoning, giving up.

libélula, *f.* libellula, dragon fly.

líber, *m.* (bot.) bast, liber, or inner bark.

liberación, *f.* liberation; (law) quittance.

liberal, *a.* liberal; quick, brisk; (pol.) liberal.—**artes liberales**, liberal arts.

liberalidad, *f.* liberality, generosity.

liberalismo, *m.* Liberalism; Liberal party.

liberalizar, *va.* to liberalize.

liberalmente, *adv.* liberally, generously, freely.

libérrimo, ma, *a. super.* most free.

libertad, *f.* liberty, freedom; exemption, privilege, immunity; familiarity; freedom, agility; address; independence, unconventionality; ransom.—**l. de comercio**, free trade.—**l. de conciencia**, or **de cultos**, freedom of worship.—**l. de imprenta**, freedom of the press.—**l. de palabra**, freedom of speech, right of free speech.—**l. provisional**, liberation on bail.—**dejar en l.**, to set free.

libertadamente, *adv.* freely, impudently.

libertado, da, *a.* bold; free, ungoverned.

libertador, ra, *n. & a.* deliverer(-ing), liberator (-ing).

libertar, *va.* to free, liberate; to exempt, excuse; to acquit; to rid, clear.

libertario, ria, *n. & a.* anarchist(-ic).

liberticida, *m.* liberticide, destroyer of liberty.

libertinaje, *m.* libertinism, licentiousness.

libertino, na. I. *n.* child of a freedman. **II.** *n.* & *a.* libertine.

liberto, ta, *n.* freedman(-woman).

libídine, *f.* lewdness, lust.

libidinosamente, *adv.* libidinously, lewdly.

libidinoso, sa, *a.* libidinous, lewd, lustful.

libra, *f.* pound (weight, coin). (**L-,** astr.) Libra.—**l. esterlina,** pound sterling.—**l. tornesa,** livre tournois.

libración, *f.* oscillation; (astr.) libration.

libraco, libracho, *m.* (coll.) trashy book.

librado, da. I. *pp.* of LIBRAR.—**bien l.,** successful, lucky.—**mal l.,** unsuccessful, unlucky, faring ill or badly. **II.** *n.* drawee.

librador, ra, *n.* deliverer; (com.) drawer of a check or draft; storekeeper of the king's stables; (*m.*) grocer's scoop.

libramiento, *m.* delivery, delivering; warrant, order of payment.

librancista, *m.* (com.) holder of a draft.

libranza, *f.* (com.) draft, bill of exchange.—**l. postal,** money order.

librar. I. *va.* to free, deliver; to exempt; to preserve from ill; to pass (sentence); to issue (a decree); (com.) to draw.—**l. batalla,** or **combate,** to engage in battle.—**l. (una letra) contra,** to draw on.—**¡Dios me libre!,** Heaven forbid! **II.** *vn.* (of nuns) to receive a visitor in the locutory; to be delivered (of a child); to expel the placenta.—**l. bien (mal),** to fare well (badly).—**l. en,** to depend on; to put (confidence, hope) in.—**a bien,** or **a buen l.,** as well as could be expected. **III.** *vr.* (**de**) to escape, avoid, be free (from), get rid (of).

libratorio, *m.* cubicle for receiving visitors in a convent.

libre, *a.* free; uncumbered, unrestrained; independent; vacant; disengaged; clear, open; exempt; innocent, guiltless, single, unmarried; libertine, loose, licentious; impudent; rash, thoughtless; isolated, alone.—**l. a bordo (l. a. b.),** free on board (f. o. b.).—**l. cambio,** free trade.—**l. de derechos, impuestos,** duty, tax, free.—**l.|pensador** = LIBREPENSADOR.—**l. pensamiento** = LIBREPENSAMIENTO.—**l. plática,** pratique.

librea, *f.* livery, uniform.

librear, *va.* to weigh or sell by pounds.

librecambista, *n.* free trader.

librejo, *m.* *dim.* little book; worthless book.

libremente, *adv.* freely; boldly.

librepensador, ra, *n.* freethinker.

librepensamiento, *m.* freethinking, free thought.

librería, *f.* bookstore, bookseller's shop; book trade; library; large collection of books.

libreril, *a.* pertaining to the book trade.

librero, ra, *n.* bookseller.

¹**libreta,** *f.* troy pound; loaf of bread of 1 lb. weight.

²**libreta,** *f.* memorandum book; notebook; (surv.) field book; pass book; bank book.—**l. de direcciones,** address book.

librete, *m.* *dim.* small book; foot stove.

libretín, *m.* *dim.* small book, booklet.

libretista, *n.* librettist.

libreto, *m.* (mus.) libretto.

¹**librillo,** *m.* small book of cigarette paper.—**l. de cera,** folded wax taper.—**l. de oro,** gold-leaf book.

²**librillo, librito,** *m.* earthen tub.

libro, *m.* book; (mus.) libretto; (zool.) omasum, or third stomach (of a ruminant).—**l. becerro,** doomsday book.—**l. borrador,** blotter, record book.—**l. copiador,** (com.) letter book.—**l. de actas** = L. DE MINUTAS.—**l. de asiento** = L. DE CUENTAS.—**l. de caja,** cashbook.—**l. de cuentas,** account book.—**l. de facturas,** invoice book.—**l. de memoria,** memorandum book.—**l. de minutas,** minute book.—**l. diario,** (com.) daybook.—**l. en blanco,** blank

book.—**l. en folio,** folio book.—**l. mayor,** ledger.—**l. talonario,** check book, stub book.—**l. verde,** (coll.) book for notes about places and persons; also the compiler of such notes.

librote, *m.* *aug.* large book.

licantropía, *f.* (med.) lycanthropy, kind of insanity.

licántropo, *a.* lycanthrope.

licaón, *m.* (zool.) lycaon.

liceísta, *n.* member of a lyceum.

licencia, *f.* permission, leave, license, permit; licentiousness; (mil.) furlough; degree of licentiate; (poet.) license.—**l. absoluta,** (mil.) discharge.—**con l.,** (mil.) on leave, furlough.

licenciadillo, *m.* (coll.) ridiculous little man in clerical robes.

licenciado, da. I. *pp.* of LICENCIAR. **II.** *a.* presuming knowledge. **II.** *m.* licentiate, graduate (of university); (coll.) university student; (coll.) lawyer; (mil.) discharged soldier.

licenciamiento, *m.* graduation as a licentiate; (mil.) discharge of soldiers.

licenciar. I. *va.* to permit, allow; to license; to confer a degree on; (mil.) to discharge. **II.** *vr.* to become dissolute; to get a master's degree (from university).

licenciatura, *f.* degree of licentiate; graduation as a licentiate.

licenciosamente, *adv.* licentiously.

licencioso, sa, *a.* licentious, dissolute.

liceo, *m.* lyceum.

licio, cia, *n.* & *a.* Lycian.

licitación, *f.* auction; bid.

licitador, *m.* bidder.

lícitamente, *adv.* lawfully, licitly.

licitante, *n.* bidder.

licitar, *va.* & *vn.* to bid (on, for) at auction or on public works.

lícito, ta, *a.* licit, lawful; just.

licnobio, bia, *n.* lychnobite, one who turns night into day, (coll.) night hawk.

licopodio, *m.* (bot.) lycopodium.

licor, *m.* any liquid; liqueur, cordial.—**licorera,** *f.* liquor case, bottle case.—**licorería,** *f.* liquor shop; public house, saloon.—**licorista,** *n.* liquor distiller or dealer.—**licoroso, sa,** *a.* (of liquor) spirituous.

lictor, *m.* lictor, in ancient Rome.

licuable, *a.* liquefiable.

licuación, *f.* liquation, liquefaction.

licuante, *a.* liquefying.

licuar, *va.* to liquefy.

licuefacción, *f.* liquefaction.

licuefactible, *a.* liquefiable.

lichera, *f.* woollen cover of a bed.

lid, *f.* contest, fight; dispute, argument.

líder, *m.* & *f.* (Angl.) (Am.) leader.

lidia, *f.* battle, fight, contest; bullfight.

lidiadero, ra, *a.* in fighting condition.

lidiador, ra, *n.* combatant; fighter; arguer.

lidiar. I. *vn.* to fight, to contend; to struggle. **II.** *va.* to run or fight (bulls).

lidio, dia, *n.* & *a.* Lydian.

liebrastón, liebratico, liebratón, *m.* young hare, leveret.

liebre, *f.* hare; coward, poltroon.—**coger una l.,** to fall flat.—*pl.* (naut.) racks, ribs; deadeyes.

liebrecica, illa, ita, *f.* *dim.* little hare.

liebrecilla, *f.* (bot.) bluebottle.

liebrezuela, *f.* *dim.* young or small hare.

liendre, *f.* nit, egg of a louse.—**cascar a uno las liendres,** (slang) to give one a severe drubbing.

lientera, lientería, *f.* (med.) lientery, diarrhea.

lientérico, ca, *a.* lienteric.

liento, ta, *a.* damp, moist.

lienza, *f.* narrow strip of cloth.

lienzo, *m.* linen cloth; (art) canvas; (fort.) curtain; (arch.) face or front of a building; stretch of a wall.—**l. casero,** homespun linen.

—l. **crudo,** unbleached linen.—l. **gordo,** coarse linen.

liga, f. garter; (bot.) mistletoe; birdlime; league, coalition, alliance; alloy for gold and silver.

ligación, f. joining, tying; union, mixture.

ligada, f. ligature; binding, tying.

ligado, da. I. pp. of LIGAR. **II.** a. confederate. **III.** m. (mus.) legato.

ligadura, f. ligature, ligation, binding; subjection; (mus.) ligature, syncopation, tie; (arch.) arcs made by cross timbers; (naut.) seizing, lashing.

ligamaza, f. viscosity on some fruits or plants.

ligamen, m. spell supposed to cause impotency.

ligamento, m. bond, tie; (anat.) ligament.

ligamentoso, sa, a. ligamentous, ligamental.

ligamiento, m. act of tying or binding; union, concord.

ligar. I. va. (pret. LIGUÉ; subj. LIGUE) to tie, bind, fasten; to alloy; to join, link, knit together; to render impotent by malefic spells. **II.** vn. to combine cards of the same suit. **III.** vr. to league, join together, combine; to bind oneself.

ligazón, f. tie, fastening, union, connection, bond; (naut.) futtock timbers.

ligeramente, adv. lightly; quickly; slightly.

ligereza, f. lightness; swiftness, agility, nimbleness; levity, inconstancy, fickleness.

ligero, ra. I. a. (of weight, food, entertainment, garment, etc.) light; fast, nimble; (of cloth) thin; gay; unsteady, giddy; unimportant, trifling; easily disturbed (as sleep).—l. **de cascos,** feather-brained.—l. **de dedos,** light-fingered.—**a la l.,** quickly; briefly; superficially.—**de l.,** rashly; easily. **II.** adv. fast, rapidly.

ligeruelo, la, a. dim. early (grapes).

ligio, gia, a. liege.

lignario, ria, a. ligneous.

lignito, m. lignite.

ligua, f. (P. I.) battle-axe.

liguano, na, a. (Chile) (of sheep) having thick and heavy wool.

ligué, ligue, v. V. LIGAR.

liguilla, f. narrow garter.

lígula, f. (bot.) ligule.

ligur; ligurino, na, n. & a. Ligurian.

ligustre, m. (bot.) flower of privet.

ligustrino, na, a. pertaining to privet.

ligustro, m. (bot.) privet, prim, ligustrum.

lija, f. sandpaper; (ichth.) dogfish; shark skin, dogfish skin.—**lijar,** va. to sandpaper.

lila, f. lilac tree; lilac flower; lilac color.

¹**lilaila,** f. bunting; (coll.) (gen. pl.) trick, wile.

²**lilaila,** f. = LILILÍ.

liliáceo, a. I. a. (bot.) liliaceous. **II.** f. pl. Liliaceae.

lililí, m. = LELILÍ, war whoop of the Moors.

liliputiense, n. & a. Liliputian.

¹**lima,** f. (bot.) sweet lime, a kind of citron.

²**lima,** f. (mech.) file; finish, polishing.

³**lima,** f. (arch.) valley (also l. **hoya).**

limadura, f. filing.—pl. filings.

limalia, f. filings.

limar, va. to file; to polish; to touch up.

limatón, m. coarse round file, rasp.

limazo, m. viscosity, sliminess.

limbo, m. limbo; (astr.) limb; limb, graduated circle (of a theodolite, etc.).

limen, m. (poet.) = UMBRAL, threshold.

limeño, ña, a. of or belonging to Lima.

¹**limera,** f. woman who sells sweet limes.

²**limera,** f. (naut.) rudderhole.

limero, m. seller of sweet limes; (bot.) sweet-lime tree (a variety of citron tree).

limeta, f. vial, small bottle.

limitación, f. limitation, limit; district.

limitadamente, adv. limitedly, finitely.

limitado, da, pp. & a. limited, dull-witted.

limitáneo, nea, a. pert. to boundaries, frontiers.

limitar. I. va. to limit; to bound; to restrict; to

reduce (expense).—l. **con,** (geog.) to be bounded by. **II.** vr. to confine oneself to.

límite, m. limit; boundary, bound, border.

limítrofe, a. bounding, conterminous.

limo, m. slime, mud.

¹**limón,** m. lemon; lemon tree; (Cuba, coast of Colomb., etc.) lime (tree and fruit).—l. **mejicano,** lime.

²**limón,** m. thill or shaft (of carriage).

limonada, f. lemonade.—l. **de vino,** wine lemonade, sangaree.—l. **purgante,** citrate of magnesia.

limonado, da, a. lemon-colored.

limonar, m. plantation of lemon trees.

limoncillo, limoncito, m. dim. small lemon; lime.

¹**limonero, ra. I.** n. lemon dealer. **II.** m. (bot.) lemon tree.

²**limonero, ra. I.** a. shaft (horse) in carriages, etc. **II.** f. shaft, thill (of carriages).

limosidad, f. sliminess; foul matter between teeth.

limosna, f. alms.

limosnero, ra. I. a. charitable. **II.** n. almoner; (Am.) beggar. **III.** f. alms bag or box.

limoso, sa, a. slimy, muddy, limose.

limpia, f. cleaning, cleansing; dredging.

limpiabarros, m. bootscraper.

limpiabotas, m. bootblack.

limpiachimeneas, m. chimney sweeper.

limpiadera, f. clothes-brush; comb-brush; plow cleaner.

limpiadientes, m. toothpick.

limpiador, ra, n. & a. cleaner(-ing), cleanser (-ing).

limpiadura, f. cleaning, cleansing.—pl. dirt, refuse.

limpiamente, adv. cleanly, neatly; purely; sincerely, faithfully.

limpiamiento, m. cleansing, cleaning.

limpiaplumas, m. penwiper.

limpiar. I. va. to clean, cleanse; to purify, clear; (coll.) to steal; (coll.) (in gambling) to "clean out", win all one's money.—l. **en seco,** dry-clean. —l. **las faltriqueras a uno,** to pick one's pockets; (coll.) to win from one. **II.** vr. to clear oneself from imputed guilt.—l. **las manos, los dientes,** to wash one's hands, brush one's teeth.

limpiaúñas, m. nail cleaner.

límpido, da, a. (poet.) limpid, crystal-clear.

limpieza, f. cleanness, cleanliness; neatness; purity; integrity, honesty; disinterestedness; purity of blood; correctness, neatness of execution.—l. **de bolsa,** emptiness of the purse.

limpio, pia, a. clean; cleanly; limpid, clear; neat, pure, unmingled; free, clear, net; (coll.) penniless, "broke."—**en l.,** in substance; clearly.— **poner en l.,** to make a final copy from a rough draft.—**sacar, en l.,** PONER EN L.; to conclude, infer; to make out, make head or tail of.

limpión, m. hasty cleaning.

lináceo, a. I. a. (bot.) linaceous. **II.** f. pl. (bot.) Linaceæ.

linaje, m. lineage, race; progeny, offspring; class, condition.—l. **humano,** mankind.

linajista, m. genealogist, writer of pedigrees.

linajudo, da, n. & a. boaster(-ing) of noble descent.

lináloe, m. (bot.) aloes.

linar, m. flax field.

linaria, f. (bot.) wild flax, yellow toad flax.

linaza, f. (bot.) linseed, flaxseed.

lince. I. m. (zool.) lynx; very keen person. **II.** a. sharp-sighted, keen-sighted, observing.

lincear, va. (coll.) to note what is not easily seen.

linceo, a, a. lyncean; sharp, keen.

linchamiento, m. lynching.

linchar, va. to lynch.

linches, m. pl. (Mex.) fiber saddlebags.

lindamente, *adv.* prettily, neatly, elegantly.

lindante, *a.* bordering, contiguous.

lindar, *vn.* to be contiguous, to border, abut.

linde, *m.* landmark; boundary, limit.

lindero, ra. I. *a.* contiguous, bordering. **II.** *m.* limit, boundary.

lindeza, *f.* neatness, elegance, prettiness.—*pl.* pretty things; (ironic) improprieties, insults.

lindo, da. I. *a.* pretty, lovely; complete, perfect, fine. **II.** *m.* beau, coxcomb; minion.—**de lo l.,** perfectly, wonderfully; greatly.

lindón, *m.* (agr.) frame or bar for hanging asparagus, etc.

lindura, *f.* LINDEZA; beauty, beautiful woman; beautiful thing.

línea, *f.* line; (of persons) lines, figure; lineage, progeny; equator; border; boundary, limit; class, order; (fort.) trench or intrenchment; (mil.) rank, file; line, twelfth part of an inch.— **l. de agua,** or **de flotación,** (naut.) water line. —**l. de colimación,** or **de fe,** (surv.) line of collimation.—**l. de (la) tierra,** (geom.) ground line.—**l. de vapores,** steamship line.—**l. equinoccial,** equator.—**l. férrea,** railway.—**en l.,** in a line, row.

lineal, *a.* lineal, linear.

lineamento, or **lineamiento,** *m.* lineament, feature.

¹linear, *va.* to draw lines on; to form with lines.

²linear, *a.* lineal, linear.

líneo, a, *a.* (bot.) linaceous.

lineotipia, *f.* = LINOTIPIA.

linfa, *f.* lymph; (poet.) water.

linfático, ca, *a.* lymphatic.

linfatismo, *m.* (med.) lymphatism.

lingote, *m.* (foundry) ingot; pig, bloom, billet.

lingual, *a.* lingual.

linguete, *m.* pawl; ratchet.

lingüista, *n.* linguist.—**lingüística,** *f.* linguistics.—**lingüístico, ca,** *a.* linguistic.

linimento, linimiento, *m.* (pharm.) liniment.

linio, *m.* = LIÑO, row of plants.

lino, *m.* (bot.) flax; linen; sail-bloth, canvas; (poet.) sail.

linóleo, *m.* linoleum.

linón, *m.* lawn (cloth).

linotipia, *f.* linotype.

linotipista, *n.* linotypist.

linotipo, *m.* linotype.

lintel, *m.* lintel of a door. Also DINTEL.

linterna, *f.* lantern; lamp, light (on a train, car, etc.); flashlight; (mech.) lantern wheel; (arch.) lantern.—**l. delantera,** or **de adelante,** (Ry., auto) front light.—**l. mágica,** magic lantern.— **l. sorda,** dark lantern.—**l. trasera,** or **de atrás,** (Ry., auto) back, or rear, light.

linternazo, *m.* blow with a lantern; (fig.) blow with any instrument.

linternero, ra, *n.* lantern maker.

linternón, *m. aug.* big lantern; (naut.) poop lantern.

liño, *m.* row of trees or plants; ridge between furrows.

liñuelo, *m.* rope, cord.

lío, *m.* bundle, parcel, pack; (coll.) imbroglio, scrape; intrigue, conspiracy.—**armar un l.,** to tangle, mess up, make difficulties.

liorna, *f.* (coll.) uproar, hubbub, confusion.

lipemanía, *f.* (med.) melancholia, lypemania.

lipemaníaco, ca, *a.* (med.) melancholic.

lipes, lipis, *f.* (chem.) blue vitriol, copper sulphate.

lipoma, *m.* (med.) lipoma, a fatty tumor.

lipotimia, *f.* (med.) faint, swoon.

liquen, *m.* (bot.) lichen.

liquidable, *a.* liquefiable; (com.) adjustable.

liquidación, *f.* liquefaction; (com.) liquidation, settlement; bargain sale.

liquidador, ra. I. *a.* liquefying. **II.** *n.* liquefier; liquidator.

liquidámbar, *m.* liquidambar, balsam liquid.

liquidamente, *adv.* in a liquid state.

liquidar. I. *va.* to liquefy; (com.) to liquidate, sell out; to settle, pay up; to squander; (coll.) to "liquidate", murder. **II.** *vr.* to liquefy.

liquidez, *f.* liquidness, fluidity.

líquido, da. I. *a.* liquid; evident, clear; (econ.) liquid; (com.) net; (Mex., C. A., W. I.) just, exactly (as *me quedan tres pesos líquidos,* I have just three pesos left). **II.** *m.* liquid; (com.) balance, net profit.—**l. imponible,** amount of assessment for tax collection. **III.** *f.* (phon.) liquid consonant.

¹lira, *f.* lira (Italian monetary unit).

²lira, *f.* (mus.) lyre; (poet.) lyric poem; (L. astr.) Lyra.—**lirado, da,** *a.* lyre-shaped.

liria, *f.* birdlime.

lírico, ca. I. *a.* lyric, lyrical. **II.** *f.* lyric poetry.

lirio, *m.* (bot.) lily.—**l. blanco** = AZUCENA, white lily.—**l. de agua,** calla lily.—**l. de Florencia,** orris, Florentine iris.—**l. de los valles,** lily of the valley.—**l. hediondo,** gladwin.

lirismo, *m.* abuse of lyricisms.

¹lirón, *m.* (zool.) dormouse; (coll.) sleepy head; (naut.) jackscrew.

²lirón, *m.* (bot.) alisma.

lirondo, da, *a.* pure, clean, neat.

lis, *f.* (bot.) lily; fleur-de-lis, iris.

¹lisa, *f.* smooth stone for polishing paper.

²lisa, *f.* (ichth.) a river fish.

lisamente, *adv.* smoothly, plainly.—**lisa y llanamente,** openly and frankly; simply.

lisbonense, lisbonés, sa, *a.* of or belonging to Lisbon.

lisera, *f.* (fort.) berm, a narrow terrace.

lisiado, da, *n.* & *a.* cripple(d).

lisiar, *va.* to lame, hurt, cripple, injure.

lisimaquia, *f.* (bot.) loosestrife.

liso, sa, *a.* smooth, even, flat; plain, unadorned; straight (hair); plain-dealing.—**l. y llano,** plain, clear, evident.

¹lisonja, *f.* flattery.

²lisonja, *f.* = LOSANGE, *m.* (her.) lozenge.

lisonjado, da, *a.* (her.) lozenged; rhombic.

lisonjeador, ra, *n.* & *a.* flatterer(-ing).

lisonjear, *va.* to flatter; to delight, please.

lisonjeramente, *adv.* flatteringly.

lisonjero, ra. I. *m.* & *f.* flatterer. **II.** *a.* flattering; pleasing, agreeable; complimentary.

lista, *f.* list; catalogue; slip of paper; shred of linen; strip of cloth; selvage; stripe, band; (law) docket; (mil.) roll, muster.—**l. del equipaje,** muster book of a ship's company.—**l. de comidas,** or **de platos,** bill of fare, menu.— **pasar l.,** to call the roll.

listadillo, *m.* (Am.) striped gingham.

listado, da. I. *pp.* of LISTAR. **II.** *a.* striped.

listar, *va.* to enter in a list.

listeado, da, *a.* = LISTADO.

listel, *m.* (arch.) fillet, listel, tringle.

listo, ta, *a.* ready; quick, prompt; clever.

listón, *m.* ribbon; ferret, tape; (carp.) lath, cleat, strip; (arch.) listel, fillet.—*pl.* (naut.) battens.

listonado, da. I. *a.* (carp.) made of laths. **II.** *m.* laths, lathing.

listonar, *va.* (carp.) to batten, to lath.

listonería, *f.* parcel of ribbons, tapes, and inkles; ribbon store; ribbon manufactory.

listonero, ra, *n.* ribbon maker.

listura, *f.* smartness, quickness, cleverness.

lisura, *f.* smoothness, evenness, flatness; sincerity, candor.

lita, *f.* tongue worm in dogs.

litación, *f.* sacrificing.

litagogo, ga, *a.* (med.) lithagogue; (surg.) lithontriptic.

litar, *va.* to sacrifice to the Deity.

litarge, litargirio, *m.* litharge.

lite, *f.* (law) lawsuit.

For pronunciation, see the rules at the beginning of the book.

litera, *f.* litter (for transportation); (naut.) berth.

literal, *a.* literal.—**literalmente,** *adv.* literally.

literario, ria, *a.* literary.

literato, ta. I. *a.* literary. **II.** *n.* litterateur, literary person, writer.

literatura, *f.* literature.

literero, ra, *n.* litter maker, seller, or driver.

litiasis, *f.* (med.) lithiasis, gravel.

litigación, *f.* litigation.

litigante, *n.* & *a.* (law) litigator(-ing), litigant.

litigar, *va.* (*pret.* LITIGUÉ; *subj.* LITIGUE) (law) to litigate; to contend, dispute.

litigio, *m.* litigation, lawsuit; dispute, contest.— **litigioso, sa,** *a.* litigious, contentious.

litigué, litigue, *v.* V. LITIGAR.

litina, *f.* (chem.) lithia.—**litio,** *m.* lithium.

litis, *f.* (law) lawsuit.

litisconsorte, *n.* (law) associate in a lawsuit.

litiscontestación, *f.* (law) answer to an allegation.

litisexpensas, *f. pl.* (law) costs of suit.

litispendencia, *f.* state of a pending lawsuit.

litocálamo, *m.* petrified or fossil reed.

litoclasa, *f.* (geol.) fissure in a rock.

litocola, *f.* lithocolla, lapidary's cement.

litófago, ga, *a.* (of mollusks) rock-boring.

litofotografía, *f.* etc., = FOTOLITOGRAFÍA, etc.

litogenesia, *f.* (geol.) lithogenesy.

litoglifia, *f.* engraving on stone.

litografía, *f.* lithography.—**litografiar,** *va.* to lithograph.

litográfico, ca, *a.* lithographic.

litógrafo, *m.* lithographer.

litología, *f.* lithology.

litológico, ca, *a.* lithological.

litólogo, *m.* lithologist.

litoral. I. *a.* littoral. **II.** *m.* littoral, coast, shore.

litoscopio, *m.* lithoscope.

litote, *f.* (rhet.) litotes.

litotomía, *f.* (surg.) lithotomy.

litotricia, *f.* (surg.) lithotrity.

litotritor, *m.* (surg.) lithotrite.

litrarico, a, *a.* (bot.) lythraceous.

litro, *m.* liter, litre, unit of capacity.

lituano, na, *n.* & *a.* Lithuanian.

lituo, *m.* (mus.) an ancient military instrument; lituus, augur's staff.

liturgia, *f.* (eccl.) liturgy.

litúrgico, ca, *a.* liturgical, liturgic.

livianamente, *adv.* licentiously; lightly; superficially.

liviandad, *f.* lightness, want of weight; levity, frivolity; lewdness.

liviano, na. I. *a.* light (not heavy); inconstant, fickle; frivolous; slight; lewd. **II.** *m.* leading one in a pack of donkeys.—*pl.* lungs.

lividez, *f.* lividness.

lívido, da, *a.* livid; black and blue.

livonio, nia, *n.* & *a.* Livonian.

lixiviar, *va.* (chem.) to lixiviate, leach.

¹liza, *f.* (ichth.) skate.

²liza, *f.* jousting field, lists.

lizo, *m.* warp-thread; heddle.

lo. I. *art. neut.* (before an *a.*) the, things (*lo bello,* the beautiful; *lo barato,* cheap things). For emphasis before an *adv.* or *a.*, gen. translated by an *a.* or emphatic "so" (*lo triste que estaba,* the great sadness in which he was, or, simply, his great sadness; *lo claro de esta declaración,* the great clearness of this declaration; *lo rico que es,* his being so rich, his great wealth; *lo bien que baila,* his dancing well). Often used as an *adv.* in the sense of "so," and need not always be translated (*él es rico, pero yo no lo soy,* he is rich, but I am not [so]); also as *adv.* "how" (*ella no sabe lo cansado que está,* she doesn't know how tired he is).—**l. de siempre,** the same old story.—**l. que,** what, that which; how important; how much.—**l. que es,** as to, as for.—**a l.** (foll. by name), in the style of, like.—

a l. que, according to what, from what.

II. *neut.* accusative of ELLO: it, that (*lo haré,* I shall do it, I shall do that). **III.** *pers. pron. accusative* of ÉL: him, it.

loa, *f.* praise; prologue of a play; short dramatic panegyric.

loable, *a.* laudable, praiseworthy.

loablemente, *adv.* laudably, commendably.

loador, ra, *n.* praiser, eulogizer.

loán, *m.* (P. I.) land measure (2.79 ares).

loanda, *f.* a kind of scurvy.

loar, *va.* to praise, eulogize.

¹loba, *f.* she-wolf.

²loba, *f.* long gown of clergymen and students.

³loba, *f.* ridge between furrows.

⁴loba, *f.* (card games) rummy; canasta.

lobado, da, *a.* (zool. and bot.) lobate.

lobanillo, *m.* wen, encysted tumor.

lobato, *m.* wolf cub, wolfkin.

lobeliáceo, a. I. *a.* (bot.) lobeliaceous. **II.** *f. pl.* Lobeliaceæ.

lobero, ra. I. *a.* pertaining to wolves; wolfish. **II.** *f.* thicket where wolves make their lair.

lobezno, *m.* wolf cub; wolfkin.

lobina, *f.* (ichth.) striped bass.

¹lobo, *m.* wolf; (ichth.) loach; (coll.) intoxication, inebriation; iron instrument for defending or scaling walls.—**l. marino,** seal.

²lobo, *m.* (anat. & bot.) lobe.

³lobo, ba, *n.* (Mex.) half-breed.

loboso, sa, *a.* full of wolves.

lóbrego, ga, *a.* murky, obscure; sad, lugubrious.

lobreguecer. I. *vn.* to grow dark. **II.** *va.* to make dark.

lobreguez, *f.* obscurity, darkness.

lobulado, da, *a.* (zool. and bot.) lobulate.

lóbulo, *m.* lobe or lobule.

lobuno, na, *a.* wolfish.

locación, *f.* (law) lease.—**l. y conducción,** agreement to let.

locador, ra, *n.* (Am.) landlord; tenant.

local. I. *a.* local. **II.** *m.* place, site, premises.

localidad, *f.* locality, location; (theat., etc.) seat.

localización, *f.* localization; (Ry.) location.

localizar, *va.* to localize; (Ry.) to locate; to find out where.

locamente, *adv.* madly; immoderately; fondly.

locatario, ria, *n.* (Am.) tenant, lessee.

locería, *f.* (Am.) china; china works or shop; (esp. S. A., C. A.) pottery.

loción, *f.* lotion, wash.

loco, ca. I. *a.* mad, insane, crazy; abundant, plentiful, excessive.—**l. rematado,** stark mad. —**a tontas y a locas,** recklessly, thoughtlessly, haphazard.—**estar l. de contento,** (coll.) to be mad with joy. **II.** *n.* insane person, lunatic.

locomoción, *f.* (phys.) locomotion.

locomotor, ra. I. *a.* locomotor, locomotive. **II.** *f.* (Ry.) locomotive.

locomotriz, *a. f.* locomotive.

locomovible, locomóvil, *a.* portable, movable.

locro, *m.* (Am.) a kind of stew.

locuacidad, *f.* loquacity, talkativeness.

locuaz, *a.* loquacious, talkative, garrulous.

locución, *f.* diction; phrase, locution.

locuela, *f.* person's individual way of speaking.

locuelo, la, *n.* madcap, giddy youth.

loculado, da; locular, *a.* (biol.) locular.

lóculo, *m.* (biol.) loculus.

locura, *f.* madness, insanity; folly.

locutor, ra, *n.* radio announcer or speaker.

locutorio, *m.* locutory in monasteries.

locha, *f.*; loche, *m.* (ichth.) loach.

locho, cha, *a.* (Am., coll.) red-bearded.

lodachar, lodazal, lodazar, *m.* muddy place, quagmire, bog.

lodo, *m.* mud, mire.

lodoñero, *m.* (bot.) lignum-vitæ tree.

lodoso, sa, *a.* muddy, miry.

lofobranquio, quia. I. *n.* & *a.* (zool.) lopho-branchiate. II. *m. pl.* Lophobranchii.

logarítmico, ca, *a.* logarithmic.

logaritmo, *m.* logarithm.

logia, *f.* lodge (of freemasons).

lógica, *f.* logic.

lógicamente, *adv.* logically.

lógico, ca. I. *a.* logical. II. *m.* logician.

logogrifo, *m.* logogriph, riddle.

logomaquia, *f.* logomachy, contention about words.

lograr. I. *va.* to get, obtain; procure; attain; to possess, enjoy; (foll. by *inf.*) to succeed in (foll. by pres. p.), to manage. II. *vr.* to succeed, be successful.

lograr, *vn.* to borrow or lend at interest.

logrería, *f.* dealing in interest; usury, profiteering.

logrero, ra, *n.* lender at interest; usurer, profiteer.

logro, *m.* gain, profit, benefit; success, accomplishment; attainment; interest; usury.—**dar a l.,** to lend at usurious interest.

loma, *f.* little hill, hillock.

lombarda, *f.* lombard (an ancient gun); (bot.) red cabbage.—**lombardada,** *f.* shot from a lombard gun.—**lombardear,** *va.* to bombard with lombards.—**lombardería,** *f.* battery of lombards.—**lombardero,** *m.* lombard gunman.

lombárdico, ca; lombardo, da, *n.* & *a.* Lombard, belonging to Lombardy.

lombriguera, *f.* hole made by worms; (bot.) southern wormwood.

lombriz, *f.* earthworm.—**l. intestinal,** intestinal worm.—**l. solitaria,** tapeworm.

lomear, *vn.* (of horses) to buck.

lomera, *f.* main strap of a harness; (bookbinding) backing; (arch.) ridge of a roof.

lomillería, *f.* (Am.) shop where harness accessories are made or sold.

lomillo, *m. dim.* small loin; (sew.) cross-stitch; cantle (of a saddle).—*pl.* pads of a pack saddle.

lominhiesto, ta, *a.* high-crouped; (coll.) conceited, vain.

lomo, *m.* loin; back of an animal; chine of pork; back of a book or cutting tool; double of a cloth, crease; ridge between furrows.—*pl.* ribs; loins.—**jugar de l.,** to be idle and in good health or condition.—**llevar a l., traer a l.,** to carry on the back.

lomudo, da, *a.* broad-backed.

lona, *f.* canvas.—**l. para hacer velas,** duck-canvas, sailcloth.

loncha, *f.* slab, flagstone; thin slice of meat.

lóndiga, *f.* = ALHÓNDIGA, wheat exchange.

londinense, *a.* of London, Londonese.

londrina, *f.* woollen cloth from London.

loneta, *f.* ravens' duck, sailcloth.

longa, *f.* (mus.) long note.

longanimidad, *f.* long-suffering, forbearance.

longánimo, ma, *a.* forbearing, magnanimous.

longaniza, *f.* choice pork sausage.

longar, *a.*—**panal l.,** honeycomb lengthwise of the hive.

longazo, za, *a. aug.* very long.

longevidad, *f.* longevity.

longevo, va, *a.* longeval, long-lived.

longirrostro, tra. I. *a.* (zool.) longirostral. II. *m. pl.* Longirostres.

longísimo, ma, *a. super.* of LUENGO; longest.

longitud, *f.* length; longitude.

longitudinal, *a.* longitudinal.

longitudinalmente, *adv.* longitudinally.

longobardo, da, *n.* & *a.* Longobard(-ian).

longuera, *f.* long and narrow strip of land.

longuetas, *f. pl.* (surg.) bandages.

longuísimo, ma, *a. super.* longest.

¹lonja, *f.* (com.) exchange; grocer's shop; warehouse, salesroom; (arch.) stoop.

²lonja, *f.* slice (of meat); strip; leather strap.

¹lonjeta, *f. dim.* small slice; small strap.

²lonjeta, *f.* bower, summerhouse.

lonjista, *n.* grocer.

lontananza, *f.* distance; background.—**en l.,** far off, far away, in the distance.

loor, *m.* (poet.) praise.

lopigia, *f.* (med.) = ALOPECIA, baldness.

loquear, *vn.* to act the fool, to talk nonsense; to revel, frolic.

loquero, ra. I. *n.* attendant in an insane asylum. II. *m.* (Am.) insane asylum.

loquesco, ca, *a.* madlike; funny, jesting.

loquillo, illa, ito, ita, *a. dim.* wild, frisky.

loquios, *m. pl.* (med.) lochia.

lora, *f.* (ornith.) (Peru, Colomb., C. R., Hond.) parrot; (Chile) female parrot.

lorantáceo, a. I. *a.* (bot.) lauraceous. II. *f. pl.* Lauraceæ.

lorcha, *f.* (China) junk-rigged coaster.

lord, *m.* (*pl.* **lores**) lord, English title.

loriga, *f.* lorica (a cuirass); iron strip reinforcing hub (of carriage wheel).

lorigado, da, *a.* armed with a lorica.

loriguillo, *m.* shrub used by dyers.

¹loro, ra. I. *a.* tawny, dark brown. II. *m.* (bot.) cherry laurel.

²loro, *m.* (ornith.) parrot.

los. I. *def. art. m. pl.* of EL, the.—**l. que,** those, or they, who. II. *pers. pron. m. pl. accusative* of ELLOS, them. When used with HAY (*v.* HABER), it is rendered by "some," or not at all (*¿hay libros? los hay,* are there any books? there are [some]).

losa, *f.* slab, flagstone; trap made of tiles; gravestone; grave.

losado, *m.* tiled floor.

losange, losanje, *m.* (her.) lozenge; rhomb.

losar, *va.* to tile. Also ENLOSAR.

loseta, losica, illa, ita, *f. dim.* small slab or flagstone; tile; briquette; small trap.

lote, *m.* lot; share, part.

lotería, *f.* lottery; raffle; game lotto.

lotero, ra, *n.* dealer in lottery tickets.

loto, *m.* (bot.) lotus; lotus flower; lote tree or nettle tree.

lotófago, ga, *a.* lotus-eating.

loxodromia, *f.* (naut.) loxodrome.

loxodrómico, ca, *a.* (naut.) loxodromic.

loza, *f.* chinaware; porcelain; crockery.—**ande la l.,** (coll.) noisy mirth and jollity.

lozanamente, *adv.* luxuriantly; briskly, nimbly.

lozanear, *vn.* to look fresh and luxuriant.

lozanía, *f.* luxuriance; freshness; vigor, lustiness.

lozano, na, *a.* luxuriant; fresh; brisk, spirited.

lúa, *f.* esparto glove for cleaning horses; saffron bag; (naut.) lee.

lubricación, *f.* lubrication.

lubricador, ra, *n.* & *a.* lubricator(-ing).

lubricán, *m.* dawn of day.

lubricante, *n.* & *a.* lubricator(-ing).

lubricar, *va.* to lubricate.

lubricativo, va, *a.* lubricant, lubricative.

lubricidad, *f.* lubricity, slipperiness; lewdness.

lúbrico, ca, *a.* slippery; lubricous; lewd.

lubrificación, lubrificar, etc. (incorrect but common) = LUBRICACIÓN, LUBRICAR, etc.

lucano, na, *n.* & *a.* Lucanian.

lucerna, *f.* chandelier; (ichth.) a deep sea fish.

lucérnula, *f.* (bot.) lucern, lucerne, alfalfa.

lucero, *m.* morning star; any bright star; light hole; star on the forehead of horses; brightness, splendor.—*pl.* (poet.) eyes.—**l. del alba,** or **de la mañana,** morning star.—**l. de la tarde,** evening star.

lucidamente, *adv.* brightly; splendidly.

lucidez, *f.* brilliancy; brightness; success.

lucido, da. I. *pp.* of LUCIR. II. *a.* magnificent, splendid, brilliant; most successful.

lúcido, da, *a.* lucid, clear; brilliant, shining.

lucidor, ra, *a.* shining, brilliant.

lucidura, *f.* (coll.) whitewashing.

luciente, *a.* shining, luminous, bright.

luciérnaga, *f.* glowworm, firefly.

Lucifer, *m.* Lucifer, Satan; proud and wicked man; morning star.

luciferino, na, *a.* Luciferian, devilish.

lucífero, ra. I. *a.* (poet.) resplendent, shining. **II.** *m.* morning star.

lucífugo, ga, *a.* light-avoiding, lucifugous.

lucillo, *m.* tomb; sarcophagus.

lucimiento, *m.* brilliancy, splendor, lustre; success, triumph.—**quedar, or salir, con l.,** to be eminently successful.

¹lucio, cia, *a.* lucid; bright.

²lucio, *m.* (ichth.) common pike, luce.

lucir. I. *vn.* (*ind.* LUZCO; *subj.* LUZCA) to shine, glitter, glow; to outshine, exceed; to look, appear. **II.** *va.* to light, illuminate; to show off, display, exhibit, disport. **III.** *vr.* to shine, be brilliant; to dress to advantage; to be very successful, to do splendidly.

lucrarse, *vr.* to profit.

lucrativamente, *adv.* profitably, lucratively.

lucrativo, va, *a.* lucrative, profitable.

lucro, *m.* gain, profit, lucre.—**lucros y daños,** (com.) profit and loss.

lucroso, sa, *a.* lucrative, profitable.

luctuosa, *f.* feudal death tax.

luctuosamente, *adv.* mournfully, sorrowfully.

luctuoso, sa, *a.* sad, mournful.

lucubración, *f.* laborious work, study.

lucubrar, *va.* to work, study laboriously.

lúcumo, *m.* (bot.) Lucuma, a variety of Peruvian Achras.

lucha, *f.* struggle, strife; wrestling, wrestle; dispute, argument.

luchador, ra, *n.* wrestler; fighter.

luchar, *vn.* to fight, struggle; to wrestle.

lucharniego, ga, *a.* night hare-hunting (dog).

ludia, *f.* ferment, yeast.

ludiar, *va.* & *vr.* to ferment.

ludibrio, *m.* mockery, derision, scorn.

ludimiento, *m.* friction, rubbing.

ludión, *m.* (phys.) Cartesian devil.

ludir, *va.* to rub, waste by friction.

lúe, *f.* infection.

luego. I. *adv.* presently, immediately; afterwards; next; later.—**l. que,** after, as soon as.—**desde l.,** at once, instantly; naturally, of course; to begin with, at the outset.—**hasta l.,** (in taking leave) so long, see you later.—**tan l. como =** L. QUE. **II.** *conj.* therefore.

luengo, ga, *a.* long, dilated.—**luengos años,** long years, many years.

lugano, *m.* (ornith.) linnet.

lugar, *m.* place, spot, site; city, town, village; room, space; seat; employment, office, dignity; time, opportunity, occasion; leisure, convenience; cause, motive, reason; text, authority. —**l. común, l. excusado,** privy-house, water-closet.—**lugares comunes,** commonplace topics.—**lugares de un combate,** (naut.) quarters in a sea-fight.—**dar l.,** to make room.—**dar l. a,** to cause, give occasion for.—**en l. de,** instead of, in lieu of.—**en primer l.,** first, or in the first place.—**fuera de l.,** out of place; irrelevant.—**hacer l.,** to make room.—**no ha l.** (a), (law) the petition is denied; there is no occasion (for).—**tener l.,** (Gal.) to take place, happen.

lugarcico, illo, ito, *m. dim.* small place.

lugarejo, *m. dim.* hamlet, small village.

lugareño, ña. I. pertaining or belonging to a village. **II.** *n.* villager.

lugarote, *m. aug.* unattractive hamlet.

lugartenencia, *f.* lieutenancy.

lugarteniente, *m.* deputy, substitute; lieutenant.

lugre, *m.* (naut.) lugger, small vessel.

lúgubre, *a.* sad, gloomy, lugubrious, dismal.

luir, *va.* (naut.) to gall, wear away by friction.

luis, *m.* louis (French coin).

luisa, *f.* (bot.) lemon verbena or aloysia.

lujación, *f.* = LUXACIÓN, dislocation.

lujar, *va.* (Cuba) to rub; (med.) to dislocate.

lujo, *m.* luxury.—**de l.,** de luxe; elegant, exquisite; magnificent.—**lujoso, sa,** *a.* showy, sumptuous, luxurious; profuse, lavish.

lujuria, *f.* lewdness, lust; excess; profuseness, lavishness.

lujuriante, *a.* lusting; luxuriant, exuberant.

lujuriar, *vn.* to lust; (of animals) to copulate.

lujuriosamente, *adv.* lustfully, voluptuously.

lujurioso, sa, *a.* lustful, voluptuous, lewd.

luliano, na, *n.* & *a.* Lullian.

lulismo, *m.* system of Raymond Lully.

lulista, *n.* & *a.* Lullist(-ic).

lumaquela, *f.* lumachelle, fire marble.

lumbago, *m.* (med.) lumbago.

lumbar, *a.* lumbar, lumbary.

lumbrada, *f.* great fire.

lumbre, *f.* fire (in stove, fireplace, etc.); light (from a match, etc.); light; splendor, brightness; skylight, transom; hammer of a flintlock; forepart of horseshoes.—*pl.* tinder box.—**l. del agua,** level with the water.—**a l. de pajas,** (coll.) very swiftly.—**a l. mansa,** on a slow fire.—**ni por l.,** by no means.

lumbrera, *f.* luminary; skylight, light shaft; (steam eng.) port.—**l. de admisión,** steam port, admission port.—**l. de educción, or de escape,** exhaust port.

lumbrerada, *f.* great fire.

lumen, *m.* lumen (unit of light).

luminar, *m.* luminary.

luminaria, *f.* illumination, festival lights; (eccl.) lamp kept burning before the sacrament.—*pl.* money paid for illuminations.

lumínico, *m.* (phys.) hypothetic agent or principle of light.

luminiscencia, *f.* luminescence.

luminiscente, *a.* luminescent.

luminosidad, *f.* luminosity.

luminoso, sa, *a.* luminous.

luna, *f.* (astr.) moon; satellite; glass plate, mirror plate; (opt.) lens of a spyglass; effect of the moon upon lunatic people.—**l. creciente,** crescent.—**l. de miel,** honeymoon.—**l. llena,** full moon.—**l. menguante,** waning moon.—**estar de buena (mala) l.,** (Am.) to be in good (bad) humor.—**estar en la l.,** (Am.) to be distracted, absent-minded.—**quedarse a la luna de Valencia,** to be left out in the cold.

lunación, *f.* (astr.) lunation, lunar month.

lunado, da, *a.* lunated, formed like a half-moon.

lunanco, ca, *a.* (animal) having one hind quarter higher than the other.

¹lunar, *a.* lunar.

²lunar, *m.* mole, beauty spot; flaw, blemish; polka dot.—**l. postizo,** patch.

lunario, ria. I. *a.* pert. to lunar month. **II.** *m.* calendar.

lunático, ca, *a.* lunatic, moonstruck, mad.

lunecilla, *f.* crescent-shaped jewel.

lunes, *m.* Monday.

luneta, *f.* (opt.) spectacle lens; (theat.) orchestra chair; a crescent-shaped ornament; (arch.) lunette; saddler's knife, leather knife.

luneto, *m.* skylight in a vault, lunette.

lunfardo, *m.* (Am.) Argentine slang.

lúnula, *f.* (geom.) lune; (opt.) meniscus.

lupanar, *m.* brothel, bawdyhouse.

lupanario, ia, *a.* pertaining to a brothel.

lupercales, *f. pl.* Lupercalia, Roman festival.

lupia, *f.* (med.) wen, encysted tumor.

lupicia, *f.* (med.) = ALOPECIA, baldness.

lupino, na. I. *a.* wolfish. **II.** *m.* (bot.) lupine.

lupulino, *m.* lupulin, powder from hops.

lúpulo, *m.* (bot.) hops.

luquete, *m.* slice of orange or lemon thrown into wine; zest; sulphur match.

lurte, *m* avalanche, landslide.

lusitanismo, *m.* Portuguese idiom.

lusitano, na, *a.* Lusitanian; Portuguese.

lustración, *f.* lustration; lustrum; purification.
lustrador, ra. (Am.) **I.** *n.* polisher. **II.** *m.* hot-press, mangler.
lustral, *a.* lustral; pertaining to lustration.
lustramiento, *m.* act of decorating or polishing.
lustrar. I. *va.* to lustrate, expiate, purify; to polish. **II.** *vn.* to wander, roam.
lustre, *m.* gloss, lustre, polish, glaze; shoe-polish; nobleness, splendor, glory.
lústrico, ca, *a.* lustral.
lustro, *m.* lustrum, period of five years; lamp, chandelier.
lustrosamente, *adv.* brilliantly, splendidly; glitteringly.
lustroso, sa, *a.* bright, brilliant; lustrous, shining.
lútea, *f.* (ornith.) oriole; cazique.
lúteo, tea, *a.* miry, muddy.
luteranismo, *m.* Lutheranism.
luterano, na, *n.* & *a.* Lutheran.
luto, *m.* mourning; grief, bereavement.—*pl.* mourning draperies.—**de l.,** in mourning.
luxación, *f.* (surg.) luxation, dislocation.
luz, *f.* light; daylight; lighthouse; window, opening; (eng.) span; notice, information, hint; inspiration; brightness, lustre, splendor; luminary, prominent man; (art) lighting.—*pl.* culture, enlightenment, learning, knowledge; windows, loopholes.—**l. de bengala,** red light. —**l. del día,** daylight.—**l. de l.,** reflected or borrowed light.—**l. de tráfico,** or **de tránsito,** traffic light.—**l. infrarroja,** infrared rays.—**l. ultravioleta,** ultraviolet rays.—**l. zodiacal,** zodiacal light.—**a buena l.,** carefully, after due examination.—**a primera l.,** at daybreak. —**a todas luces,** everywhere, any way.—**dar a l.,** to give birth to; to be delivered of (a child); to publish.—**entre dos luces,** in the twilight.—**salir a l.,** to come out, be published or divulged, leak out.
Luzbel, *m.* Lucifer, Satan.
luzco, luzca, *v. V.* LUCIR.

LL

llábana, *f.* smooth, slippery flagstone.
llaga, *f.* ulcer, sore; prick, thorn, tormenting thought; (mason.) seam, crack, or joint.
llagar, *va.* (*pret.* LLAGUÉ; *subj.* LLAGUE) to wound, hurt, injure.
¹llama, *f.* flame, blaze; violent passion.
²llama, *f.* marshy ground.
³llama, *f.* (zool.) llama.
llamada, *f.* call, knock; motion or sign to call attention; (tel.) call; (print.) reference mark to a note; (mil.) call; chamade; (com.) notice, entry.
llamadera, *f.* goad stick.
llamado, da. I. *pp.* of LLAMAR. **II.** *a.* called, by the name of. **III.** *m.* appeal.
llamador, ra, *n.* caller; beadle, messenger; (*m.*) knocker of a door.
llamamiento, *m.* calling, call; appeal; convocation; inspiration, divine vocation; attraction of humors to one part of the body.
llamar. I. *va.* to call, summon, cite; to call upon, invoke, appeal to; to name, call.—**ll. la atención** (**sobre**), to call, attract attention (to); (*dat.*) to warn, scold.—**ll. por teléfono,** to telephone, 'phone. **II.** *vn.* to excite thirst; to knock at the door; to ring a bell.—**ll. a capítulo,** or **a cuentas,** to call to account. **III.** *vr.* to be called or named, go by the name of, give the name of (often abbr. constr.: *ella se llama Rosa,* her name is Rose; *¿como se llama esto?* what is this called? *¿como se llama Vd.?* what is your name? *se llama "democracia"* . . . , the name "democracy" is given to . . . , or,

simply, "democracy" is . . .); (naut.) (of wind) to veer.
llamarada, *f.* sudden blaze, flash; burst of wit; sudden flush of the face.
llamativo, va, *a.* exciting thirst; showy, attracting attention.
llamazar, *m.* swamp, marsh.
llambria, *f.* steep face of a rock.
llameante, *a.* blazing, flaming.
llamear, *vn.* to blaze, to flame.
llana, *f.* (mason.) trowel; page of a book or writing; plain, flatland.
llanada, *f.* plain, flatland, level ground.
llanamente, *adv.* ingenuously, simply, sincerely; homely; plainly, clearly, flatly.
llanero, ra, *n.* plainsman (-woman).
llaneza, *f.* plainness, simplicity; familiarity; uncultivated style.
llano, na. I. even, level, smooth; easy, unobstructed; plain, unadorned; unaffected, open, frank; clear, evident; (gram.) (word) accented on the penultimate.—**a la llana,** simply, unceremoniously.—**de llano,** openly, in the open. **II.** *m.* plain, llano.
¹llanta, *f.* (bot.) a variety of cabbage.
²llanta, *f.* rim (of carriage wheel); (auto) tire.— **ll. maciza,** solid tire.—**ll. neumática,** pneumatic tire.
llantén, *m.* (bot.) plantain, rib grass.—**ll. de agua,** water plantain, alisura.
llanto, *m.* flood of tears; crying, weeping.
llanura, *f.* evenness, flatness; plain.
llapa, *f.* (min.) quicksilver for amalgamation.
llapar, *va.* (min.) to add quicksilver to for reduction.
llares, *f. pl.* chain with pothooks (in fireplace).
llatar, *m.* post-and-rail fence.
llave, *f.* key; (mech.) wrench; faucet, cock, spigot, spout, tap; switch (of elec. light); bolt, pin, tightening wedge, cotter; (print.) brace }; tuning key; clock winder; (arch.) keystone; winch of a stocking frame; lock of a gun; key, explanation of anything difficult; introduction to knowledge; (naut.) knee; (mus.) clef, key; piston of musical instruments.—**ll. capona,** key worn by a lord of the bedchamber.—**ll. de la mano,** span of the hand.—**ll. del pie,** distance from heel to instep.—**ll. inglesa,** monkey wrench.—**ll. maestra,** master key, pass-key.— **debajo de ll.,** under lock and key.—**echar (la) ll. a,** to lock.
llavero, ra. I. *n.* keeper of the keys. **II.** *m.* key ring. **III.** *f.* housekeeper.
llavín, *m.* night key, latchkey.
lleco, ca, *a.* (agr.) virgin (as soil).
llega, *f.* gathering, collecting.
llegada, *f.* arrival, coming.
llegar. I. *vn.* (*pret.* LLEGUÉ; *subj.* LLEGUE) to arrive; to come; to reach, extend, go as far as; to last, to continue; to attain a purpose; to suffice, be enough; to amount.—**ll. a las manos,** to come to blows.—**ll. a saber,** to find out, get to know.—**ll. a ser,** to become, get to be.—**no II. a,** not to amount to; not to come up, or be equal, to.—**no ll. a uno la camisa al cuerpo,** to be terrified and anxious. **II.** *va.* to bring near; to gather, collect. **III.** *vr.* (a) to approach, draw near (to); to go to some neighboring place; to adhere, stick.
llena, *f.* flood, overflow.
llenamente, *adv.* fully, copiously.
llenar. I. *va.* to fill, stuff, pack; to pervade; to occupy (as an incumbent); to satisfy, content, convince; to make up (a number); to beget.— **ll. una solicitud,** to fill out an application form. **II.** *vr.* to fill, fill up; (de) to become full (of), or covered (with); (coll.) to feed gluttonously, stuff oneself; (coll.) to be irritated after having suffered long; to get crowded, packed. **III.** *vn.* (of the moon) to be full.

For pronunciation, see the rules at the beginning of the book.

llenero, ra, a. (law) full, complete, absolute.
lleno, na. I. a. full, filled, replete; complete.—
ll. de bote en bote, brimful, full to the brim.
—de ll., or **de ll. en ll.,** fully, entirely, totally.
II. m. glut, fill, plenty, abundance, fulness;
perfection, completeness; full moon; (theat.)
full house.

llenura, f. fulness; plenty, abundance.

lleta, f. (bot.) sprout.

lleudar, va. = LEUDAR, to leaven.

lleva, llevada, f. transpórt, carrying.

llevadero, ra, a. tolerable, bearable, light.

llevador, ra, n. & a. carrier(-rying).

llevar. I. va. to carry, convey; to wear; to take,
take away, carry away; to charge, ask, set (a
price); to bear, yield, produce; to excel, exceed;
to suffer, endure; to lead (as a life); to lead,
guide, conduct, take; to manage (a horse); to
cut off, dismember; to have spent or devoted
(so much time); to induce, to bring to an opinion; to introduce; to gain, attain, obtain;
(arith.) to carry; (with a past participle) to
have, as: *llevo andadas diez millas,* I have walked
ten miles.—**ll. . . . a,** to be older, or more,
than by (*llevo dos años a Juan,* I am two years
older than John).—**ll. a cabo,** to carry through,
to accomplish, to carry out.—**ll. a cuestas,** to
carry on one's shoulders or back; to support.—
II. adelante, to carry on, keep up, continue.
—**ll. al crédito,** to place to the credit.—**ll.
calabazas,** to be given the mitten; to fail in
examination.—**ll. consigo,** to carry along with
one; to carry with it, imply; to have attached.
—**ll. el compás,** to beat or keep time.—**ll. la
caja,** to keep the cash.—**ll. la contra,** to
oppose, contradict; to antagonize.—**ll. la delantera,** to lead, to be ahead.—**ll. la proa al
noroeste,** (naut.) to stand to the northwest.—
llevarlas bien (mal), = LLEVARSE BIEN, MAL.
—**ll. la ventaja a,** to have the advantage of
or over.—**ll. libros,** (com.) to keep books.—
ll. lo mejor (peor), to get the best (worst).—
ll. una caída, golpe, porrazo, to have a fall,
a blow.—**no llevarlas todas consigo,** to have
suspicions, to be afraid. **II.** vr. to take or carry
away; to get along.—**ll. bien,** to be on good
terms, get along well, be congenial.—**ll. chasco,**
to be disappointed.—**ll. mal,** to be on bad
terms, not to get along together.

lloica, f. (ornith.) robin redbreast; thrush.

lloradera, f. weeping from slight motives.

llorador, ra, n. weeper.

lloraduelos, n. (coll.) weeper, mourner.

llorar. I. vn. to weep, cry; to affect poverty and
distress; to whine; to drip. **II.** va. to weep over,
bewail, mourn, lament.

lloriquear, vn. to be constantly crying; to whine.

lloriqueo, m. whining; lamentation, wailing.

lloro, m. weeping, crying.

llorón, na. I. a. weeping; that cries with little
cause, whining. **II.** n. weeper, whiner.

llorosamente, adv. tearfully.

lloroso, sa, a. mournful, sorrowful, tearful.

llosa, f. fenced-in field.

llovedizo, za, a. leaky; rain (as a.).

llover. I. vn. impers. (ind. LLUEVE; subj. LLUEVA)
to rain; to pour down like rain, to shower, to
come in abundance (as troubles).—**ll. a cántaros, a chorros, a chuzos,** or **ll. chuzos,** to
rain in torrents, to rain pitchforks.—**como
llovido,** unexpectedly.—**llueva o no,** rain or
shine. **II.** vr. (of roofs) to leak, let the rain in.

llovido, da, n. stowaway.

llovioso, sa, a. = LLUVIOSO.

llovizna, f. drizzle, sprinkling.

lloviznar, vn. to drizzle, to sprinkle.

llueca, f. = CLUECA, brooding hen.

llueve, llueva, v. V. LLOVER.

lluvia, f. rain; plenty.—**lluvioso, sa,** a. rainy.

M

maca, f. bruise in fruit; flaw, blemish, spot, stain;
deceit, fraud, trick.

macabro, bra, a. ugly, hideous.

macaco, ca. I. m. (zool.) macaque; (Mex.) hobgoblin, bogie. **II.** a. ugly, ill-shaped, squat.

macadam, m. macadam pavement.

macadamizar, va. to macadamize.

macadán, m. **macadanizar,** va. = MACADAM, etc.

macagua, f. (ornith.) macaw; (Venez.) a poisonous snake.

macagüita, f. (Venez.) a thorny palmtree.

macana, f. Indian wooden sabre edged with
sharp flint; (Colomb.) a palm having very hard
and heavy wood; (Am.) cudgel, club; (Am.)
blunder; fib, joke.—**¡qué macana!** (Arg.) how
annoying!—**macaneador,** m. (Arg.) (coll.)
one who is always talking "through his hat."

macanazo, m. blow with a MACANA.

macanudo, da, a. (coll.) excellent, first-rate.

macareno, na, a. (coll.) bragging, boasting;
gaudily dressed in Andalusian garb.

macarrón, m. macaroon.—pl. macaroni; (naut.)
stanchions.

macarronea, f. macaronic poem, burlesque.

macarrónicamente, adv. macaronically.

macarrónico, ca, a. macaronic; faulty (speech).

macarse, vr. (of fruit) to begin to rot.

macaurel, f. (Venez.) a poisonous snake.

maceador, m. one who mauls.

macear. I. va. to maul. **II.** vn. to importune.

macedón, na, n. & a.; **macedonio, nia,** n. &
a.; **macedónico, ca,** a. Macedonian.

macelo, m. slaughterhouse, abattoir.

maceo, m. act of mauling.

maceración, f.; maceramiento, m. maceration,
steeping; infusion; mortification of the flesh.

macerar, va. to macerate, soak, steep; (chem.)
to digest; to mortify with corporeal hardships.

macerina, f. = MANCERINA, a kind of saucer.

macero, m. mace bearer.

¹maceta, f. dim. small mace, mallet, or maul;
haft of tools; stonecutter's hammer; (naut.)
maul, mallet.

²maceta, f. flowerpot; flower vase.

macetero, m. flowerpot; flowerpot stand.

macetón, m. aug. of ²MACETA.

macia, f. mace, a spice.

macicez, f. solidity.

macilento, ta, a. lean, emaciated; withered.

macillo, m. hammer of a piano.

macis, f. = MACIA.

macizamente, adv. firmly, solidly.

macizar, va. to fill up, stop up.

macizo, za. I. a. solid; massive; firm, certain. **II.**
m. massiveness, bulk; (mason.) solid wall;
flower bed; (auto) solid tire.

macla, f. wooden flail; (bot.) water caltrops.

macoca, f. large early fig.

macolla, f. (bot.) bunch, cluster.

macón, m. dry, brown honeycomb.

macona, f. large basket or hamper.

macrobiótica, f. art of living long.

macrocefalia, f. macrocephalia, macrocephaly.

macrocéfalo, la, a. macrocephalous.

macrocito, m. (med.) macrocyte.

macrocosmo, m. macrocosm.

macropía, macropsia, f. (med.) macropsy.

macroscópico, ca, a. macroscopic, visible to the
naked eye.

macruro, ra. I. a. (zool.) macrurous, long-tailed
(as lobster, etc.). **II.** m. pl. Macrura.

macsura, f. reserved precinct in a mosque.

macuache, m. (Mex.) ignorant Indian.

macuba, f. Martinique tobacco.

macuca, f. (bot.) wild pear or pear tree.

macuco, ca, a. (Am.) cunning, artful; hard, difficult; important, big.

mácula, *f.* stain, spot, blemish; (astr.) macula.

macular, *va.* to stain.

maculatura, *f.* (print.) maculature, spoiled sheet.

macún, macuñ, macuñí, *m.* (Chile) poncho.

macuquero, *m.* unlawful worker of abandoned mines.

macuquino, na, *a.* epithet app. to a former silver Porto-Rican coin.

macuteno, *m.* (Mex.) petty thief.

macuto, *m.* (Am.) bag made of palm leaves.

macha, *f.* a South American mollusk.

machaca. I. *n.* (coll.) a bore, tiresome person. **II.** *f.* MACHACADERA.

machacadera, *f.* instrument for pounding, crushing.

machacador, ra, *n.* pounder, beater, crusher; bruiser, mauler.

machacar. I. *va.* (*pret.* MACHAQUÉ; *subj.* MACHAQUE) to pound; crush. **II.** *vn.* to importune; to harp on a subject.

machacón, na, *a.* monotonous; importunate.

machada, *f.* flock of he-goats; (coll.) stupidity.

machado, *m.* hatchet.

machamartillo.—a m., firmly but roughly.

machaqué, machaque, *v. V.* MACHACAR.

machaqueo, *m.* pounding or crushing.

machaquería, *f.* (coll.) importunity, insistence.

machar, *va.* to pound, hammer,·maul.

machear, *vn.* (of animals) to beget more males than females.

machetazo, *m.* blow with a machete.

machete, *m.* machete.

machetear, *va.* to wound or cut with a machete.

machetero, *m.* one who cuts cane or fights with a machete; sabre rattler; ignorant military chief.

machi, machí, *m.* (Am.) medicine man.

máchica, *f.* (Peru) parched Indian meal.

machiega, *a.*—**abeja m.,** queen bee.

machigua, *f.* (Hond.) crushed-corn washings.

machihembrar, *va.* (carp.) to dovetail.

machina, *f.* crane, derrick; pile-driver.

¹macho. I. *a.* vigorous, robust; male. **II.** *m.* male; specifically a he-mule or a he-goat; masculine plant; part of an instrument which enters into another; hook to catch hold in an eye; screw pin; bolt (of a lock); (arch.) spur, buttress, abutment; ignorant fellow.—**m. cabrío,** he-goat, buck.—**m. de aterrajar,** screw tap.— **m. de cabrío** = M. CABRÍO.—**m. del timón,** (naut.) rudder pintle.—**m. romo,** he-mule born of a horse and a she-ass.

²macho, *m.* (mech.) sledge hammer; block on which anvil is fixed; square anvil.

machón, *m.* (arch.) buttress, spur; a piece of timber.

machorro, rra, *a.* barren.

machota, *f.* **machote,** *m.* maul, mallet.

machote, *m.* (Mex. min.) boundary stone.

machucadura, *f.,* **machucamiento,** *m.* pounding, bruising.

machucar, *va.* (*pret.* MACHUQUÉ; *subj.* MACHUQUE) to pound, to bruise.

machucho, cha, *a.* mature, judicious.

machuelo, *m.* *dim.* small he-mule; clove of garlic.

machuno, na, *a.* mannish, masculine.

machuqué, machuque, *v. V.* MACHUCAR.

madama, *f.* madam.—**madamisela,** *f.* damsel.

madapolán, *m.* percale.

madeja, *f.* hank, skein; lock of hair; (coll.) weak, lazy person.—**m. sin cuenda,** tangle; disordered person; entangled affair.—**hacer m.,** (of liquids) to be ropy.

madejeta, jita, juela, *f. dim.* small skein.

¹madera, *m.* Madeira wine.

²madera, *f.* wood; timber, lumber; horny part of a hoof.—**m. alburente,** alburnum, sapwood. —**m. anegadiza,** heavier-than-water wood.— **m. de construcción,** building timber.—**m.**

de corazón, heartwood.—**m. del aire,** horn of animals.—**m. de raja,** split timber.—**m. de sierra, or serradiza,** lumber, timber fit to be sawed.

maderable, *a.* timber-yielding.

maderada, *f.* raft, float.

maderaje, maderamen, *m.* timber; timber work.

maderería, *f.* lumber yard.

maderero, maderista, *m.* lumber dealer; lumberman.

madero, *m.* beam, scantling; timber, piece of lumber; ship, vessel; (coll.) stupid or unfeeling person.—**m. barcal,** log.—**m. cachizo,** timber fit to be sawed.—**m. de suelo,** beam, joist. —**m. rollizo** = M. BARCAL.—**maderos de cuenta,** main timbers.

maderuelo, *m.* *dim.* small piece of timber.

madia, *f.* (bot.) oily plant of Chile.

madianita, *n.* & *a.* Midianite.

madrastra, *f.* stepmother; anything unpleasant.

madraza, *f.* (coll.) too indulgent a mother.

madre, *f.* mother; dam; matron; (coll.) old woman; foundation; origin, source; matrix, womb; bed (of a river); main sewer; main irrigating ditch; mother (of vinegar), lees, dregs; (carp.) main piece, spindle; (naut.) gallows beam.—**m. de leche,** wet nurse.—**m. política,** mother-in-law.—**salirse de m.,** to exceed, run over; to lose one's self-control.

madrecilla, *f.* *dim.* MADRECITA; ovary of birds.

madrecita, *m.* *dim.* little mother, dear mother.

madreclavo, *m.* clove of two years' growth.

madreña, *f.* = ALMADREÑA, wooden shoes.

madreperla, *f.* mother-of-pearl.

madrépora, *f.* madrepore, white coral.

madrepórico, ca, *a.* madreporic.

madrero, ra, *a.* (coll.) attached to one's mother.

madreselva, *f.* (bot.) honeysuckle.

madrigada, *a.* twice-married (woman).

madrigado, da, *a.* practical, experienced; (bull) that has been a sire.

madrigal, *m.* madrigal, lyric poem.

madriguera, *f.* burrow; den, hole.

madrileño, ña, *a.* Madrilenian.

madrina, *f.* godmother; bridesmaid; patroness, protectress; prop, stanchion; straps for yoking two horses; (Am.) herd of tamed cattle used as lure for wild cattle; (Venez.) leading animal, usually a mare; (Venez.) small herd.

madrona, *f.* main irrigating ditch; over-indulgent mother.

madroncillo, *m.* strawberry.

madroñal, *m.*; **madroñera,** *f.* grove of madroña trees.

madroñero, *m.* (bot.) madroña, an evergreen tree or shrub.

madroño, *m.* (bot.) madroña; fruit of the madroña; berry-shaped tassel.

madrugada, *f.* dawn; early rising.—**de m.,** at daybreak.

madrugador, ra, *n.* early riser.

madrugar, *vn.* (*pret.* MADRUGUÉ; *subj.* MADRUGUE) to rise early; to anticipate, to be beforehand.

madrugón, *m.* (coll.) very early rising.

maduración, *f.* ripeness, maturity; ripening.

maduradero, *m.* place for ripening fruits.

madurador, ra, *a.* maturing, ripening.

maduramente, *adv.* maturely, thoughtfully.

madurante, *a.* maturing, ripening.

madurar. I. *va.* to ripen, mature; to think out; (med.) to maturate. **II.** *vn.* to ripen; to mature; to reach the age of maturity; (med.) to maturate, suppurate; to come to a head.

madurativo, va. I. *a.* maturative. **II.** *m.* anything that matures; inducement.

madurez, *f.* maturity; ripeness; wisdom.

madurillo, lla, *a.* beginning to ripen.

maduro, ra, *a.* ripe; mature; wise, judicious.

maesil, *m.* = MAESTRIL.

For pronunciation, see the rules at the beginning of the book.

maesillas, *f. pl.* cords which serve in making passementerie to raise or lower the skeins.

maestoso, *a.* (mus.) maestoso.

maestra, *f.* teacher, schoolmistress; master's wife in all trades and professions; queen bee; (mason.) guide line.

maestral. I. *a.* pertaining to a grand master of a military order; northwest (wind). **II.** *m.* cell of the queen bee.

maestramente, *adv.* in a masterly manner.

maestrante, *m.* member of a MAESTRANZA.

maestranza, *f.* riding club of noblemen; (artil.) arsenal, armory; (naut.) navy yard; the collection of workmen in an arsenal or navy yard.

maestrazgo, *m.* dignity or jurisdiction of a grand master of a military order.

maestre, *m.* grand master of a military order; (naut.) master of a merchant ship.—**m. de raciones,** purser.

maestrear. I. *va.* to direct, to instruct; to lop; to smooth. **II.** *vn.* (coll.) to domineer, to act the master.

maestresala, *m.* chief waiter and taster.

maestría, *f.* mastery; dignity or degree of a master.

maestril, *m.* (bee keeping) queen cell.

maestrillo, *m.* *dim.* insignificant schoolmaster.

maestro, tra. I. *a.* masterly; master, great, principal, main; learned, trained. **II.** *m.* master, teacher; expert; master workman; skilled artisan; title of respect in monastic orders; scholastic title; (naut.) mainmast.—**m. carpintero de remos,** master oar maker.—**m. de armas,** fencing master.—**m. de capilla,** choir master. —**m. de ceremonias,** master of ceremonies. —**m. de cocina,** chef.—**m. de esgrima =** M. DE ARMAS.—**m. de obra prima,** shoemaker. —**m. de obras,** builder.

magallánico, ca, *a.* Magellanic.

maganel, *m.* (mil.) battering-ram.

maganto, ta, *a.* spiritless, dull, faint, languid.

magaña, *f.* (artil.) honeycomb, flaw in the bore of a gun; (coll.) cunning artifice, trick.

magarza, *f.* (bot.) downy camomile.

magarzuela, *f.* (bot.) stinking camomile.

magdalena, *f.* a kind of biscuit.

magdaleón, *m.* (pharm.) roll of plaster.

magia, *f.* magic; black art, necromancy.—**m. blanca,** or **natural,** white, or natural, magic. —**m. negra,** black magic, black art.

magiar, *n.* & *a.* Magyar.

mágicamente, *adv.* magically.

mágico, ca. I. *a.* magic, magical; marvellous, wonderful. **II.** *n.* magician; sorcerer(-ess).

magín, *m.* (coll.) fancy, idea, imagination.

magismo, *m.* magianism.

magisterial, *a.* magisterial.

magisterio, *m.* mastery; mastership; scholastic degree; teachers as a class; (coll.) affected solemnity; (chem.) precipitate.

magistrado, *m.* magistrate; magistracy.

magistral. I. *a.* magisterial, masterly; (eccl.) preaching; (pharm.) magistral. **II.** *m.* (min.) magistral.

magistralía, *f.* (eccl.) preacher's prebendary.

magistralmente, *adv.* magisterially, masterly.

magistratura, *f.* magistracy.

magma, *m.* magma, residue.

magnánimamente, *adv.* magnanimously.

magnanimidad, *f.* magnanimity.

magnánimo, ma, *a.* magnanimous.

magnate, *m.* magnate, grandee.

magnesia, *f.* (chem.) magnesia.

magnesiano, na, *a.* magnesian.

magnésico, ca, *a.* magnesic.

magnesio, *m.* magnesium.

magnesita, *f.* meerschaum.

magneticé, magnetice, *v.* V. MAGNETIZAR.

magnético, ca, *a.* magnetic.

magnetita, *f.* (min.) magnetite.

magnetismo, *m.* magnetism.

magnetización, *f.* magnetization.

magnetizador, ra, *n.* & *a.* magnetizer(-ing); hypnotizer(-ing).

magnetizar, *va.* (*pret.* MAGNETICÉ; *subj.* MAGNETICE) to magnetize; to hypnotize.

magneto, *m.* or *f.* (int. combust. eng.) magneto.

magnetoeléctrico, ca, *a.* magneto-electric.

magnetómetro, *m.* magnetometer.

magníficamente, *adv.* magnificently.

magnificar, *va.* to magnify, extol, exalt.

magníficat, *m.* (eccl.) Magnificat.

magnificencia, *f.* magnificence, grandeur, gorgeousness, splendor.

magnificentísimo, ma, *a.* *super.* of MAGNÍFICO: most magnificent.

magnífico, ca, *a.* magnificent; excellent.

magnitud, *f.* magnitude; quantity.

magno, na, *a.* great; grand.

magnolia, *f.* (bot.) magnolia.

mago, ga. I. *a.* Magian. **II.** *n.* magus; magician; necromancer, wizard.—*pl.* magi.

magostar, *vn.* to roast (chestnuts) at a picnic.

magosto, *m.* picnic and chestnut roast.

magra, *f.* rasher, slice of ham.

magrez, *f.* thinness, leanness.

magro, gra. I. *a.* meager, lean. **II.** *m.* lean slice of pork.

magrura, *f.* = MAGREZ.

magua, *f.* (Cuba) jest, joke.

magüer, magüera, *conj.* (obs.) although.

magüeto, ta, *n.* young steer or heifer.

maguey, *m.* (bot.) maguey.

maguillo, *m.* wild apple tree.

magujo, *m.* (naut.) ravehook.

magulladura, *f.* bruise, contusion.

magullamiento, *m.* bruising; contusion.

magullar, *va.* to bruise, to mangle.

maguntino, na, *a.* of Mainz or Mayence.

maharrana, *f.* fresh bacon.

mahometano, na; mahomético, ca, *n.* & *a.* Mohammedan.

mahometismo, *m.* Mohammedanism.

mahometista, *n.* Mohammedan.

mahometizar, *vn.* to Mohammedanize.

mahón, *m.* nankeen, kind of light cotton goods.

mahona, *f.* Turkish transport vessel.

maicillo, *m.* (Am.) heavy or coarse sand.

maído, *m.* = MAULLIDO, mewing.

maillechort, *m.* white metal.

maimón, *m.* monkey.—*pl.* soup made with oil.

maimona, *f.* spindle beam of a horse mill.

maimonetes, *m. pl.* (naut.) belaying pins.

maimonismo, *m.* doctrine of Maimonides.

maitinante, *m.* priest with matinal duties.

maitines, *m. pl.* (eccl.) matins.

maíz, *m.* (bot.) maize, Indian corn.—**m. machacado,** hominy.

maizal, *m.* Indian-corn field.

majá, *m.* (Cuba) a thick-bodied snake.

majada, *f.* sheepcote, sheepfold; dung.

majadal, *m.* good pasture ground for sheep; land improved by the manure of a flock.

majadear, *vn.* (of sheep) to take shelter for the night; to manure.

majadería, *f.* foolish speech or act.

majaderico, *m.* old-fashioned trimming.

majaderillo, lla. I. *a.* *dim.* rather peevish and bothersome. **II.** *m.* bobbin for lace.

majadero, ra. I. *a.* silly; peevish; obtrusive. **II.** *m.* whippersnapper; bore; pestle, pounder.—*pl.* bobbins for making lace.

majador, ra, *n.* pounder, bruiser.

majadura, *f.* pounding or bruising.

majagranzas, *m.* (coll.) stupid bore.

majagua, *f.* (Am.) (bot.) a tree of the linden family.

majal, *m.* school of fishes.

majamiento, *m.* = MAJADURA.

majano, *m.* heap of stones as a landmark.

For pronunciation, see the rules at the beginning of the book.

majar, *va.* to pound, bruise, break in a mortar; (coll.) to importune, vex, annoy.

majarete, *m.* (Cuba) corn pudding.

majencia, *f.* (coll.) = MAJEZA.

majestad, *f.* majesty.

majestuosamente, *adv.* majestically, grandly.

majestuosidad, *f.* majesty, dignity.

majestuoso, sa, *a.* majestic, grand.

majeza, *f.* (coll.) spruceness, gaudiness.

majo, ja. I. *a.* gay, spruce, gaudily attired, showy, handsome, pretty. **II.** *n.* beau, belle.

majolar, *m.* grove of white hawthorns.

majorca, *f.* (arch.) spindle-shaped baluster; ear of corn.

¹majuela, *f.* shoe lacing.

²majuela, *f.* fruit of the white hawthorn.

majuelo, *m.* (bot.) new vine; white hawthorn.

mal. I. *a. contr.* of MALO; used only before masculine substantives. **II.** *m.* evil; harm, injury, ailment, illness, disease, complaint; imperfection, fault; wrong, evil (*el bien y el mal,* right and wrong, good and evil).—**m. caduco,** or **de corazón,** epilepsy.—**m. de la tierra,** homesickness.—**m. de ojo,** evil eye.—**m. de ojos,** eyesore.—**m. de orina,** partial or total incapacity to pass urine.—**m. de piedra,** lithiasis, stone, calculus (gen. kidney).—**m. de San Lázaro,** elephantiasis.—**del m. el menos,** the lesser of two evils.—**hacer m.,** to do evil, to injure; to be injurious.—**no hay m. que por bien no venga,** everything is for the best. —**por m. de mis pecados,** to my sorrow, unluckily for me. **III.** *adv.* badly; wrongly; deficiently; wickedly; hardly.—**m. de fortuna,** or **de recurso,** short of funds, in a bad financial situation.—**m. de su grado,** unwillingly.— **¡m. haya!** confound it! confound (the man, thing, etc.)!.—**m. hecho,** badly done, illfinished; unjust; wrong.—**m. por m.,** for want of something better.—**m. que bien,** willingly or unwillingly; rightly or wrongly.—**m. que le pese,** in spite of him, however much he may regret it.—**de m. en peor,** from bad to worse. —**estar m. de,** to be badly off, in a bad way (as *estar mal de salud,* to be in bad health; *estar mal de dinero,* to be badly in need of money).—**hacer mal,** to do wrong, act wrongly.

¹mala, *f.* mail, post.

²mala, *f.* = MALILLA, manilla, a card game.

malabar. I. *a.* of or from Malabar; Malabar (as *a.*) **II.** *n.* native of Malabar; Malabar language.

malabárico, ca, *a.* = MALABAR.

malacate, *m.* hoisting machine.

malacia, *f.* (med.) depraved appetite.

malacología, *f.* malacology.

malacológico, ca, *a.* malacologic.

malaconsejado, da, *a.* ill-advised.

malacopterigio, gia. (zool.) **I.** *a.* malacopterygian. **II.** *m. pl.* Malacopterygii.

malacostumbrado, da, *a.* having bad habits; spoiled.

malacuenda, *f.* bagging, sacking; oakum, tow.

malagana, *f.* (coll.) faintness, dizziness.

malagaña, *f.* pole set up with dry furze to catch bees swarming.

malagradecido, da, *a.* (Am.) ungrateful.

malagueño, ña. I. *a.* of or pertaining to Malaga. **II.** *f.* popular song of Malaga.

malagueta, *f.* (bot.) grains of Paradise.

malamente, *adv.* badly; poorly; wrongly.

malandante, *a.* unfortunate, unhappy.

malandanza, *f.* misfortune, misery.

malandar, *m.* wild hog.

malandrín. I. *a.* malign, perverse. **II.** *m.* rascal, scoundrel.

malanga, *f.* (Am.) (bot.) arum.

malaquita, *f.* (min.) malachite.

malar, *a.* (anat.) malar, pert. to the cheek.

malaria, *f.* (med.) (Am.) malaria.

malato, *m.* (chem.) malate.

malavenido, da, *a.* querulous, faultfinding.

malaventura, *f.* calamity, misfortune.

malaventurado, da, *a.* unfortunate, ill-fated.

malaventuranza, *f.* infelicity, unhappiness.

malayo, a, *n.* & *a.* Malay, Malayan.

malbaratador, ra, *n.* spendthrift, squanderer.

malbaratar, *va.* to squander; to undersell.

malbaratillo, *m.* second-hand shop.

malcarado, da, *a.* grim-faced, foul-faced.

malcasado, da, *a.* undutiful (spouse).

malcasar. I. *va.* to mismate in marriage. **II.** *vr.* to be mismated in marriage.

malcaso, *m.* treason, wrongful act.

malcocinado, *m.* tripe, liver, and lights of mutton or lamb; place where tripe is sold.

malcomer, *va.* to eat poorly.

malcomido, da, *a.* underfed.

malconsiderado, da, *a.* inconsiderate.

malcontentadizo, za, *a.* hard to please, faultfinding.

malcontento, ta. I. *a.* discontented, malcontent. **II.** *m.* malcontent; grumbler; a card game.

malcorte, *m.* transgression of forest laws.

malcriado, da, *a.* ill-bred, rude, uncivil; spoiled.

malcriar, *va.* to spoil (a child).

maldad, *f.* wickedness, iniquity; badness.

maldecido, da, *a.* wicked, depraved.

maldecidor, ra, *n.* defamer, backbiter.

maldecir, *va.* (*pp.* MALDECIDO, MALDITO; *gerund.* MALDICIENDO; *ind. pres.* YO MALDIGO, él MALDICE, *pret.* MALDIJE, *fut.* MALDECIRÉ, (obs.) MALDIRÉ; *subj. pres.* MALDIGA, *pret. imp.* MALDIJERA, MALDECIRÍA, MALDIJESE) to damn, curse, accurse; to defame, backbite.

maldiciente, *n.* & *a.* curser(-ing); defamer(-ing).

maldición, *f.* malediction, curse; damnation.

maldigo, maldiga, maldije, *v. V.* MALDECIR.

maldispuesto, ta, *a.* indisposed; unwilling.

maldita, *f.* (coll.) tongue.—**soltar la m.,** (coll.) to give a loose rein to one's tongue.

maldito, ta. I. *pp. irreg.* of MALDECIR. **II.** *a.* perverse, wicked; damned, accursed; (coll.) little, none, not one, nary.—**m. lo que me importa,** little do I care!.—**no sabe maldita la cosa,** nary a thing does he know.

maleabilidad, *f.* malleability.

maleable, *a.* malleable.

maleador, ra, *a.;* **maleante,** *a.* & *n.* rogue(-ish), villain(-ous), corrupter(-ing).

malear, *va.* to pervert, corrupt; injure, harm.

malecón, *m.* dike, levee, mole.

maledicencia, *f.* slander, calumny, obloquy.

maleficencia, *f.* malignity, wrongdoing.

maleficiar, *va.* to harm; to bewitch, spellbind.

maleficio, *m.* spell; witchcraft, charm.

maléfico, ca, *a.* maleficent; harmful; spellbinding.

malejo, ja, *a. dim.* of MALO: rather bad.

malentendido, *m.* (Gal.) misunderstanding.

malentrada, *f.* fee paid by a new prisoner.

maleolar, *a.* (anat.) malleolar.

maléolo, *m.* (anat.) malleolus.

malestar, *m.* malaise, indisposition.

maleta, *f.* valise, travelling bag, suitcase; (Am.) bundle (of clothes).—**hacer la m.,** to pack one's bag, suitcase; (coll.) to make preparations for a journey.

maletero, *m.* valise maker or seller.

maletín, *m. dim.* small valise or case, overnight bag.—**m. de grupa,** (mil.) saddlebag.

maletón, *m. aug.* large satchel.

malevolencia, *f.* malevolence, ill will.

malévolo, la, *a.* malevolent, malignant.

maleza, *f.* weeds; underbrush; brake, thicket, coppice.

malgastador, ra, *n.* spendthrift, squanderer.

malgastar, *va.* to misspend, waste, squander.

malhablado, da, *a.* foul-mouthed.

malhadado, da, *a.* wretched, unfortunate.

malhecho, cha. I. *a.* ill-shaped, malformed. **II.** *m.* evil deed, misdeed.

malhechor, ra, *n.* malefactor.

malherido, da, *a.* & *pp.* badly wounded.

malherir, *va.* (*ger.* MALHIRIENDO; *ind. pres.* MALHIERO, *pret.* él MALHIRIÓ; *subj.* MALHIERA) to wound badly.

malhojo, *m.* vegetable refuse.

malhumorado, da, *a.* ill-humored, peevish.

malicia, *f.* malice, malignity, maliciousness; suspicion, apprehension; shrewdness, smartness; cunning, dissimulation.—**tener m.,** to be cunning or shrewd; to suspect, be suspicious.

maliciar, *va.* to suspect; to injure, harm.

maliciosamente, *adv.* maliciously; suspiciously.

malicioso, sa, *a.* malicious; wicked, knavish; suspicious.

málico, ca, *a.* (chem.) malic.

malignamente, *adv.* malignantly, malevolently.

malignante, *n.* & *a.* maligner(-ing).

malignar. I. *va.* to vitiate, corrupt, deprave. **II.** *vr.* to become sore; to grow worse.

malignidad, *f.* malignity, perversity.

maligno, na, *a.* malign, malignant, perverse.

malilla, *f.* manilla, a card game.

malintencionado, da, *a.* ill-disposed.

malmandado, da, *a.* disobedient; obstinate.

malmeter, *va.* to waste, misspend; to induce to evil; to estrange.

malmirado, da, *a.* disliked; inconsiderate.

malo, la, *a.* bad; evil; wicked; licentious, dissolute; naughty, mischievous; ill, sick; difficult, hard; cunning, artful.—**m. del (de la),** sick with, having a sore (throat, eye, etc.), suffering from a bad (throat, liver, etc.).—**a malas,** on bad terms; in an unfriendly way.—**de malas,** unlucky; with an evil intention.—**el m.,** the Evil One.—**lo m. es que,** the worst of it is that, the trouble is that.—**por malas o por buenas,** willingly or by force.

malogramiento, *m.* failure.

malograr. I. *va.* to waste, lose, miss (as time or opportunity). **II.** *vr.* to fail, fall through, come to naught; to have an untimely end.

malogro, *m.* miscarriage, failure; untimely end.

maloja, *f.* (Cuba), cornstalks used for fodder.

malojal, *m.* plantation of MALOJA.

malojero, *m.* seller of MALOJA.

malojo, *m.* (Venez.) = MALOJA.

malón, *m.* (Am.) sudden attack by Indians.

malparado, da, *a.* ill-conditioned, impaired, damaged; foiled, worsted.

malparida, *f.* woman who has miscarried.

malparir, *vn.* to miscarry.

malparto, *m.* abortion, miscarriage.

malpigiáceo, a. I. *a.* (bot.) malpighiaceous. **II.** *f. pl.* Malpighiaceæ.

malquerencia, *f.* ill will, hatred.

malquerer, *va.* (*ind. pres.* MALQUIERO, *pret.* MALQUISE, *fut.* MALQUERRÉ; *subj.* MALQUIERA) to dislike, have a grudge against.

malqueriente, *n.* one who dislikes another.

malquistar. I. *va.* to estrange; to create prejudice against.—**m. a uno con,** to set . . . against one. **II.** *vn.* to incur dislike, bring dislike or unpopularity on one, make oneself unpopular.

malquisto, ta, *a.* disliked, unpopular.

malrotador, ra, *n.* squanderer, spendthrift.

malrotar, *va.* to misspend, lavish, squander.

malsano, na, *a.* unhealthy, sickly, infirm; unhealthful, unwholesome, noxious.

malsín, *m.* talebearer, backbiter.

malsonante, *a.* offensive to pious ears.

malsufrido, da, *a.* impatient, unresigned

malta, *f.* malt; (Chile) high-quality beer.

maltés, sa, *a.* Maltese.

maltosa, *f.* (chem.) maltose.

maltrabaja, *n.* (coll.) idler, lounger.

maltraer, *va.* (*ger.* MALTRAYENDO; *ind. pres.* MALTRAIGO, *pret.* MALTRAJE; *subj.* MALTRAIGA) = MALTRATAR.

maltratamiento, *m.* ill treatment; rough usage.

maltratar, *va.* to treat ill, abuse, maltreat; to use roughly; to spoil, destroy.

maltrato, *m.* = MALTRATAMIENTO.

maltrecho, cha, *a.* in bad condition, damaged; badly off, battered.

maltusiano, na, *n.* & *a.* Malthusian.

maltusianismo, *m.* Malthusianism.

maluco, ca; malucho, cha, *a.* (coll.) rather bad, baddish; sickish, ailing somewhat.

malva, *f.* (bot.) mallow.—**ser como una m.,** to be meek and obedient.

malváceo, a. I. *a.* (bot.) malvaceous. **II.** *f. pl.* Malvaceæ.

malvadamente, *adv.* wickedly, perversely.

malvado, da. I. *a.* wicked, fiendish, nefarious. **II.** *m.* wicked man, villain, knave.

malvar, *m.* place covered with mallows.

malvasía, *f.* (bot.) malvasia; malmsey wine.

malvavisco, *m.* (bot.) marsh mallow.

malvender, *va.* to sell at a loss, to sacrifice.

malversación, *f.* malversation.

malversador, ra, *n.* one who misapplies funds.

malversar, *va.* to misapply (funds).

malvezar, *va.* & *vr.* to fall into bad habits.

malvis, malviz, *m.* (ornith.) redwing.

malla, *f.* mesh (of a net); coat of mail; (naut.) network.—**m. de alambre,** wire netting, wire mesh.

mallar. I. *vn.* to make network. **II.** *va.* to arm with a coat of mail.

mallero, m. netmaker; armorer.

mallete, *m.* gavel, mallet.—*pl.* (naut.) partners.

malleto, *m.* beating maul in paper mills.

mallo, *m.* mallet; pall-mall, game of bowls; mall, bowling green.

mallorquín, na, *a.* of or pertaining to Majorca.

mamá, *f.* mamma, mummy.

mama, *f.* mammary gland, breast; mamma.

mamacallos, *m.* (coll.) dolt, simpleton.

mamacona, *f.* religious virgin among the ancient Peruvians.

mamada, *f.* (coll.) act of sucking, suckling; amount that a child takes in suckling.

mamadera, *f.* breast pump.

mamador, ra, *n.* sucking, suckling; nursing bottle.

mamalón, *m.* (Cuba) idler, sponger, parasite.

mamandurria, *f.* (Am., pol., coll.) sinecure, job with salary and no work.

mamante, *a.* sucking, suckling.

mamantón, na, *a.* suckling (animal).

mamar, *va.* & *vn.* to suck, suckle; (coll.) to cram and devour (food); (coll.) to get, obtain.

mamario, ria, *a.* mammary.

mamarrachada, *f.* (coll.) collection of grotesque figures; (art) daub.

mamarrachista, *m.* (art) dauber.

mamarracho, *m.* grotesque figure or ornament; (art) daub.

mambla, *f.* mound; small peak, knoll.

mameluco, *m.* Egyptian soldier; (coll.) dolt, simpleton; (Am.) overalls; (Am.) children's nightdress; (Am.) half-breed.

mamella, *f.* mammilliform protuberance in the neck of goats.

mamellado, da, *a.* mammillate, mammillated.

mamey, *m.* (bot.) mamey, mammee.

mamífero, ra. I. *a.* mammalian. **II.** *m. pl.* mammals, Mammalia.

mamila, *f.* woman's breast round the nipple; mamilla in men.

mamilar, *a.* mamillary.

mamola, *f.* chuck under the chin.

mamón, na, *m.* & *f.* suckling; child that sucks, suckles too much; (bot.) shoot, sucker; (W. I.) genip tree.

mamoncillo, *m.* (W. I.) honeyberry.
mamoso, sa. I. *a.* sucking, suckling. **II.** *m.* a variety of panic grass.
mamotreto, *m.* memorandum book; (coll.) bulky book or bundle of papers.
mampara, *f.* screen; fire screen.
mamparo, *m.* (naut.) bulkhead.—**mamparos de quita y pon,** (naut.) ship and unship bulkheads.
mampernal, manpirlán, *m.* wooden guard on steps of a staircase while building.
mampostear, *va.* to build with masonry.
mampostería, *f.* masonry (gen. app. to stone masonry).—**m. concertada,** rubble masonry, rubblework.—**m. de sillares,** ashlar masonry. —**m. en seco,** dry masonry (without mortar).
mampostero, *m.* (mason.) roughsetter.
mampresar, *va.* to begin to break in (horses).
mampuesta, *f.* (mason.) course.
mampuesto. I. *a.* overlapping. **II.** *m.* parapet; (Am.) rest or support for a firearm in taking aim; (mason.) rubble.—**de m.,** extra; from a sheltered position.
mamujar, *va.* to suck, suckle unsteadily.
mamullar, *va.* to eat or chew as if sucking at the breast; (coll.) to mutter, mumble.
mamut, *m.* (paleontol.) mammoth.
maná, *m.* manna.
¹manada, *f.* flock; herd; drove; large number.— **a manadas,** in troops or crowds.
²manada, *f.* handful.
¹manadero, ra. I. *a.* springing, issuing. **II.** *m.* source, spring; (in oil fields) place where seepage occurs.
²manadero, *m.* shepherd, herdsman.
manadilla, *f. dim.* small flock.
manante, *a.* proceeding, issuing.
manantial. I. *a.* flowing, running. **II.** *m.* spring, source, origin.
manantío, a, *a.* flowing, running.
manar, *vn.* to issue, flow out; to ooze; to abound.
manare, *m.* (Venez.) sieve for yucca starch.
manatí, manato, *m.* (zool.) manatee, seacow; whip made of the manatee's hide.
manaza, *f. aug.* large hand.
mancamiento, *m.* want, lack, deficiency; maimed condition; defect.
mancar, *va.* to maim, lame, cripple, disable.
manceba, *f.* mistress, concubine.
mancebete, *m. dim.* of MANCEBO.
mancebía, *f.* brothel, bawdyhouse.
mancebo, *m.* youth, young man; bachelor; shopman, shopboy, clerk.
mancera, *f.* plowtail, plow handle.
mancerina, *f.* saucer with holder for chocolate cup.
mancilla, *f.* spot, stain, blemish.
mancillar, *va.* to spot, stain, soil.
mancipación, *f.* (law) mancipation.
mancipar, *va.* to subject, enslave, mancipate.
manco, ca. I. *a.* handless; one-handed; armless; maimed; defective, faulty, imperfect. **II.** *n.* armless, handless or one-handed person.
mancomún, *m.*—**de m.,** jointly, in common.
mancomunadamente, *adv.* conjointly.
mancomunar, *va. & vr.* to associate, unite, combine; to pool (resources, etc.); (law) to make two or more persons pay jointly the costs of a lawsuit.
mancomunidad, *f.* union, fellowship, community.
mancornar, *va.* (*ind.* MANCUERNO; *subj.* MANCUERNE) to twist the neck of (a steer, etc.) and hold down on the ground with the horns downward; to join, to couple.
mancuerda, *f.* each turn of the rack bars.
mancuerna, *f.* pair tied together; thong for tying two steers; (Cuba) tobacco stem with two leaves; (P. I.) pair of convicts chained together.

mancuerno, mancuerne, *v. V.* MANCORNAR.
mancha, *f.* stain, spot, blot; stigma; patch of ground or vegetation; (astr.) sun spot.
manchadizo, za, *a.* easily stained.
manchado, da. I. *pp.* of MANCHAR. **II.** *a.* spotted, speckled.
manchar, *va.* to stain, soil; to foul, pollute; to tarnish, defile; (art) to speckle, daub; to darken, to cloud.—**m. papel,** to scribble.
manchego, ga, *a.* of or pertaining to La Mancha.
manchita, *f. dim.* small stain.
manchón, *m. aug.* large blot or stain; patch where vegetation is thickest.
manchú, *n. & a.* Manchu(-rian).
manchuela, *f.* = MANCHITA.
manchuriano, na, *n. & a.* = MANCHÚ.
manda, *f.* offer, proposal; legacy, bequest.
mandadero, ra, *n.* porter, messenger; errand boy or girl.—*f.* = DEMANDADERA, messenger (in convent).
mandado, da. I. *pp.* of MANDAR. **II.** *a.*—**bien m.** = BIENMANDADO, obedient, well-behaved. —**mal m.** = MALMANDADO, disobedient, badly-behaved. **III.** *m.* mandate, order, command; errand.
¹mandamiento, *m.* order, command; (eccl.) commandment; (law) writ; mandamus.—*pl.* **mandamientos de la ley de Dios,** Ten Commandments.
²mandamiento, *m.* (coll.) the five fingers of the hand.
mandante. I. *a.* commanding. **II.** *n.* (law) constituent, mandator.
mandar. I. *va. & vn.* to command, order, direct, decree; to will, leave, bequeath; to send, transmit; to offer, promise; (foll. by *inf.*) to order, have (foll. by *pp.*): *él mandó escribir la carta,* he ordered, or had, the letter written).—**m. decir,** to send word. **II.** *vr.* to communicate (as rooms); (of patients) to move about unaided; to go from one room to another.
mandarín, *m.* mandarin; (coll.) petty official.
mandarina, *f.* Mandarin, the polished Chinese language; mandarin orange.
mandarria, *f.* iron maul, sledge hammer.
mandatario, *m.* (law) attorney, agent; mandatary.
mandato, *m.* mandate; command, injunction, order, charge; (law) mandate, contract of bailment; (eccl.) maundy.
mandíbula, *f.* jawbone; jaw.
mandibular, *a.* mandibular.
mandil, *m.* leather or coarse apron; fine-mesh fishing net; cloth for cleaning horses.
mandilandinga, *f.* knavish deed, mean trick.
mandilar, *va.* to wipe (a horse) with a cloth.
mandilejo, *m. dim.* small apron.
mandilete, *m.* (fort.) door of a porthole.
mandilón, *m.* (coll.) coward.
mandinga. I. *n. & a.* Mandinga (Sudan Negro). **II.** *m.* (Am.) the Devil.
mandioca, *f.* (bot.) manioc, cassava; tapioca.
mando, *m.* command, power, dominion; (quality) leadership (also **espíritu de m.**).
mandoble, *m.* two-handed blow with a sword; severe reprimand.
mandolina, *f.* (Am.) = BANDOLÍN, mandolin.
mandón, na. I. *a.* imperious, domineering. **II.** *n.* imperious, haughty person; (min.) boss or foreman.
mandrachero, *m.* keeper of a gaming table.
mandracho, *m.* gambling house.
mandrágora, *f.* (bot.) mandrake.
mandria, *a. & m.* coward(-ly), poltroon.
¹mandril, *m.* (zool.) mandrill, baboon.
²mandril, *m.* (mech.) mandrel, chuck, spindle of a lathe.
mandrón, *m.* stone ball used as a missile.
manducación, *f.* (coll.) chewing.
manducar, *va.* (coll.) to chew.

manducatoria, *f.* (coll.) eatables, grub, eats.

manea, *f.* hobble (for horses).

manear, *va.* to hobble (a horse).

manecica, ita, *f. dim.* small hand.

manecilla, *f. dim.* small hand; (print.) fist (), index; book clasp; hand of a clock or watch.

manejable, *a.* manageable, tractable.

manejado, da. I. *pp.* of MANEJAR. **II.** *a.* (art) handled.

manejar. I. *va.* to manage, wield, handle; to drive, ride, train (a horse); to conduct, govern contrive; to run (an engine, a business); (Am.) to drive (auto). **II.** *vr.* to move about after having been deprived of motion; to behave; to get along, manage.

manejo, *m.* handling; management, conduct; horsemanship, manège; cunning, trick, intrigue, device.—**m. doméstico,** housekeeping.—**manejos de corte,** court intrigues.

maneota, *f.* shackles, hobbles, fetters.

manera, *f.* manner, way, mode; (art) manner, style; fly of trousers; side placket of skirt; quality, class of persons.—*pl.* ways, customs; manners.—**a m. de, a la m. de,** in the style of, like.—**de alguna m.,** in some way, somehow. —**de esa (este) m.,** in that (this) way.—**de mala m.,** botchingly; roughly; gruffly, reluctantly.—**de m. de,** so as to.—**de m. que,** so that, so as to, in such manner as to.—**de ninguna m.,** in no way; by no means, not at all. —**de otra m.,** otherwise.—**de tal m.,** in such a way; so much.—**de todas maneras,** at any rate.—**en gran m.,** in large measure; greatly, to a large extent.—**por m. que,** so then; so that; and so.—**sobre m.,** exceedingly.

manero, ra, *a.* (falconry) trained, tame.

manes, *m. pl.* manes, spirits of the dead.

manezuela, *f. dim.* small hand; book clasp; haft or handle.

manfla, *f.* (coll.) concubine; old sow.

¹manga, *f.* sleeve; arm of an axletree; a kind of cloak bag or portmanteau; (water) hose; purse seine; net bag, fish trap; bag strainer, Hippocrates sleeve; body of troops in a line; (eccl.) manga; (naut.) breadth of beam; wind sail; (Mex.) poncho.—*pl.* profits, gains.—**m. de agua,** squall, shower.—**m. de viento,** whirlwind.—**m. marina,** waterspout.—**andar m. por hombro,** to be disorderly (in one's home). —**de m. ancha,** indulgent.—**en mangas de camisa,** in shirt sleeves.—**tener m. ancha,** to be broad-minded.

²manga, *f.* (bot.) a variety of mango.

mangachapuy, *m.* (bot.) (P. I.) a dipterous tree.

mangajarro, *m.* (coll.) long, ill-shaped sleeve.

mangana, *f.* lasso, lariat.—**manganear,** *va.* (Am.) to lasso.—**manganeo,** *m.* lassoing.

manganato, *m.* (chem.) manganate.

manganesa, manganesia, *f.* (chem.) peroxide of manganese.—**manganésico, ca,** *a.* manganic, containing manganese.

manganesífero, ra, *a.* (chem.) manganiferous.

manganeso, *m.* (chem.) manganese.

mangánico, ca, *a.* (chem.) manganic.

manganilla, *f.* trick, stratagem; long pieced pole.

manganoso, a, *a.* manganous.

mangla, *f.* gum from the rockrose.

manglar, *m.* plantation of mangrove trees.

mangle, *m.* (bot.) mangrove tree.

¹mango, *m.* handle, haft, helve; tiller.—**m. de escoba,** broomstick.—**m. de pluma,** penholder.

²mango, *m.* (bot.) Indian mango.

mangón, na, *n.* retailer; second-hand dealer.

mangonada, *f.* push with the arm.

mangonear, *vn.* (coll.) to wander about, loiter, loaf; to intermeddle; to pry.

mangoneo, *m.* intermeddling, prying.

mangonero, ra, *a.* fond of nosing or prying.

mangorrero, ra, *a.* rough-hafted (knife); worthless, useless.

mangorrillo, *m.* = MANCERA, plowtail.

mangosta, *f.* (zool.) mongoose.

mangostán, *m.* (bot.) mangosteen.

mangote, *m.* (coll.) large, wide sleeve; oversleeve.

mangual, *m.* war flail, morning star.

manguardia, *f.* buttress of a bridge.

manguera, *f.* (watering) hose; (naut.) wind sail; waterspout; tarred canvas bucket; (Am.) large corral; tube, sleeve.—**m. de desinflar,** (aer.) deflating sleeve.—**m. de inflar,** (aer.) inflating sleeve.

manguero, *m.* horseman; fireman.

mangueta, *f.* bag syringe; jamb post of a glass door or window; tiebeam; (mech.) lever; neck of a water-closet hopper.

manguita, *f. dim.* small sleeve; sheath, case.

manguitería, *f.* furrier's shop.

manguitero, *m.* muff maker, furrier.

manguito, *m.* muff; wristlet, half-sleeve; large coffee cake; oversleeve; (mech.) muff, coupler, collar, sleeve.

maní, *m.* (Am.) = CACAHUETE, peanut.

manía, *f.* mania; madness; whim, hobby.

maníaco, ca. I. *a.* maniac, mad; whimsical. **II.** *n.* maniac.

maniatar, *va.* to manacle; to handcuff.

maniático, ca, *a.* = MANÍACO.

manicomio, *m.* insane asylum, madhouse.

manicordio, *m.* (mus.) manichord, clavichord.

manicorto, ta, *a.* illiberal, close-fisted.

manicuro, ra, *n.* manicurist. *f.* manicure.

manida, *f.* resort, abode, nest, den.

manido, da. I. *pp.* of MANIR. **II.** *a.* high, gamey (meat).

manifacero, ra, *a.* (coll.) meddlesome.

manifactura, *f.* make; manufacture.

manifestación, *f.* manifestation, declaration, statement; (public) demonstration; (law) writ resembling habeas corpus.

manifestador, ra, *a.* that manifests.

manifestante, *n.* (public) demonstrator, demonstrant.

manifestar, I. *va.* (*pp.* MANIFESTADO, MANIFIESTO; *ind.* MANIFIESTO; *subj.* MANIFIESTE) to state, declare; to manifest, reveal, show; to tell, let know; (eccl.) to expose (the Eucharist) for public worship. **II.** *vr.* to make a demonstration.

manifiestamente, *adv.* manifestly, obviously.

¹manifiesto, manifieste, *v.* V. MANIFESTAR.

²manifiesto, ta. I. *pp.* of MANIFESTAR. **II.** *a.* manifest, plain, obvious; overt. **III.** *m.* manifest or manifesto, public declaration; (eccl.) act of exposing the Eucharist; (com.) custom house manifest.—**poner de m.,** to make evident, to show plainly; to make public, expose.

manigua, *f.* (Cuba) thicket, jungle.

manigueta, *f.* haft, handle.—*pl.* (naut.) kevels.

manija, *f.* handle, haft; crank; hobble, fetters; (mech.) ring, brace, clasp, clamp.

manijero, *m.* foreman of a gang of laborers.

manilargo, ga, *a.* having long hands; (Am.) ready to fight, belligerent.

manilense; manileño, ña. I. *n.* native of Manila. **II.** *a.* Manila (as *a.*).

maniluvio, *m.* bath for the hands, as a remedy.

manilla, *f. dim.* small hand; (jewelry) bracelet; manacle, handcuff.

maniobra, *f.* handiwork; operation, procedure; artifice, trick, manœuvring; (mil.) manœuvre; (naut.) working of a ship; gear, rigging, tackle, *pl.* (Ry.) switch-engine work.

maniobrar, *va. & vn.* to do handiwork; (naut.) to work a ship; to devise ways and means of effecting anything; (mil.) to manœuvre.

maniobrero, ra, *a.* manœuvring (troops).

maniobrista, *m.* (naut.) skilful naval tactician.

maniota, *f.* hobble (for horses).

manipulación, *f.* manipulation.

manipulante, *m.* (coll.) administrator, negotiator.

manipular, *va.* to manipulate, handle, manage.

manipuleo, *m.* (coll.) tactful handling, manœuvring.

manípulo, *m.* (eccl.) maniple; standard; maniple, a division of the Roman legion; (med.) handful.

maniqueísmo, *m.* Manicheism.

maniqueo, a, *n.* & *a.* Manichean.

maniquete, *m.* black lace mitten.

maniquí, *m.* puppet; manikin, figure.

manir, *va.* (*defect.: only those forms are used having the letter i in their terminations*) to keep meat until it becomes gamey.

manirroto, ta, *a.* lavish, prodigal, wasteful.

manita, manito, *f. dim.* little hand.

manivacío, cía, *a.* (coll.) empty-handed.

manivela, *f.* (mech.) crank; crankshaft.—**m. de arranque,** (auto) starting crank or handle.—**m. de disco,** disc crank.

manjar, *m.* food, dish, victuals; tidbit, morsel; recreation, entertainment.—**m. blanco,** dish made of shredded chicken with sugar, milk, and rice flour; blancmange.

manjarejo, *m. dim.* savory dish, tidbit.

manjarria, *f.* (Cuba) driving beam of a canemill.

manjelín, *m.* carat, diamond weight.

manjolar, *va.* to carry (a hawk).

manjorrada, *f.* abundance of ordinary victuals.

manjúa, *f.* (Am.) a variety of sardine.

manlieva, *f.* taxes collected from house to house.

manlieve, *m.* confidence game; swindle.

mano, *f.* hand; forefoot; foot of cattle after cut off; trunk of an elephant; hand of a clock or watch; pestle; cylindrical stone for grinding cocoa; quire of paper; reprimand; musical scale; first hand at cards; round of any game; power or means of making or attaining something; each time or turn in a work by hand; coat (of paint, varnish, etc.); workmanship, handicraft, handiwork; (Am.) slight accident, mishap.—**m. a m.,** in friendly coöperation, together; on equal terms, without odds; tête-à-tête.—**m. apalmada,** (her.) stretched palm of the hand.—**m. de gato,** ladies' make-up; (of works of art or literature amended by more able persons than the author) polishing or editing hand.—**m. de obra,** workmanship; labor.—**m. de santo,** sure cure.—**¡manos a la obra!** bear a hand! to work!.—**manos libres,** perquisites.—**manos limpias,** extra pay or allowance.—**manos muertas,** mortmain, unalienable estate.—**manos puercas,** (coll.) graft, ill-gotten gains.—**m. sobre m.,** idle, doing nothing.—**a la m.,** near at hand.—**a m.,** by hand; at hand, near by.—**a m. airada,** violently, by force.—**a m. derecha (izquierda),** on the right- (left-) hand side.—**a m. salva** = A MANSALVA. V. MANSALVA.—**a manos llenas,** liberally, abundantly.—**a una m.,** of one accord.—**bajo m.,** underhandedly.—**dar una m.,** to give, lend, a hand.—**de buena m.,** on good authority.—**de m.** = BAJO M.; hand (as *a.*, as in *rueda de mano,* hand wheel).—**de la m.,** by the hand; hand in hand.—**de manos a boca,** suddenly, unexpectedly.—**de primera m.,** first-hand.—**de segunda m.,** second-hand.—**de una sola m.,** (Arg., Chile) (of street) one-way.—**en manos de,** in the hands, power, of.—**entre manos,** in hand, in the process of carrying on or out.—**estar a mano,** (Am.) (games, actions, etc.) to be even.—**por debajo de m.** = BAJO MANO.—**por su m.,** by oneself, by one's own judgment or authority.

manobra, *f.* raw material.

manobre, *m.* hodman, hodcarrier.

manobrero, *m.* keeper of irrigating ditches.

manojillo, ito, *m. dim.* small bundle or fagot.

manojo, *m.* handful; bunch (of flowers, vegetables, etc.); fagot, bundle.—**a manojos,** abundantly.

manojuelo, *m. dim.* small bunch or bundle.

manolo, la, *n.* Madrilenian of low class, loud in dress and manners.

manométrico, ca, *a.* manometric.

manómetro, *m.* manometer, pressure gauge.

manopla, *f.* gauntlet; coachman's whip.

manosear, *va.* to handle, touch, feel of; to muss, rumple (clothes).—**manoseo,** *m.* handling.

manota, *f. aug.* large, ugly hand.

manotada, *f.,* **manotazo,** *m.* cuff, slap, box; blow with the paw.

manotear, **I.** *va.* to cuff, buffet. **II.** *vn.* to gesticulate.

manoteo, *m.* gesticulation with the hands.

manotón, *m.* = MANOTADA.

manquear, *vn.* to pretend to be crippled.

manquedad, manquera, *f.* lack of one or both arms or hands; defect, imperfection.

mansalva,—a m., without running any risk, without danger, in a cowardly manner.

mansamente, *adv.* meekly; gently, quietly.

mansedumbre, *f.* meekness; tameness.

mansejón, na, *a.* very tame.

mansera, *f.* (Cuba) vat for the cane juice.

mansión, *f.* stay, sojourn; habitation, mansion, abode.—**hacer m.,** to stop over.

mansito, ta. **I.** *a.* very gentle or tame. **II.** *adv.* = MANSAMENTE.

¹manso, sa. I. *a.* tame; gentle, mild; calm; soft, quiet; meek, lamblike. **II.** *m.* bellwether.

²manso, *m.* (Angl.) manse, farm.

manta, *f.* woollen blanket; travelling rug; poncho; man's shawl, muffler; horse blanket; (Mex.) coarse cotton cloth; tossing blanket or canvas; (fort.) mantelet, movable parapet; thrashing, drubbing; (min.) bag of agave for carrying ore; game of cards resembling OMBRE.—**m. blanca,** bleached cotton.—**m. de algodón,** wadding.—**m. prieta,** unbleached cotton.—**a m. de Dios,** (coll.) copiously, plentifully.

mantalona, *f.* (P. I.) cotton stuff for sails.

mantaterilla, *f.* coarse hempen cloth for horse blankets.

manteador, ra, *n.* tosser (in a blanket).

manteamiento, *m.* tossing in a blanket.

mantear. **I.** *va.* to toss in a blanket. **II.** *vn.* (of women) to gad, be out too much.

manteca, *f.* lard; fat; pomatum; butter; oily substance of cocoa and other fruits.—**m. de cacao,** cocoa butter.

mantecada, *f.* buttered toast and sugar; a kind of cooky.

mantecado, *m.* biscuit kneaded with lard; French ice cream.

manteción, *f.* = MANUTENCIÓN.

mantecón, *m.* milksop; sweet tooth; dainty person.

mantecoso, sa, *a.* buttery, greasy.

manteísta, *m.* day student.

mantel, *m.* tablecloth; altar cloth.—**levantar los manteles,** to clear the table.

mantelería, *f.* table linen.

manteleta, *f.* mantelet, ladies' shawl.

mantelete, *m.* (eccl.) mantelet; (fort.) mantelet; (her.) mantling.

mantelo, *m.* very wide apron.

mantellina, *f.* a sort of mantilla.

mantenedor, *m.* president of a tournament or contest.

mantener. **I.** *va.* (*ind. pres.* MANTENGO, *pret.* MANTUVE, *fut.* MANTENDRÉ; *subj.* MANTENGA) to support, provide for, to feed; to maintain, keep up; to continue, persevere in; to pursue; to defend or sustain (an opinion); to keep up (conversation, correspondence). **II.** *vr.* to support oneself, earn one's living; to continue, remain (in one place); (en) to remain firm (in), continue (in), adhere (to), hold on (to).

mantengo, mantenga, *v. V.* MANTENER.

manteniente, *m.* violent blow with both hands. —**a m.** with all one's might; firmly.

mantenimiento, *m.* maintenance, support, upkeep; subsistence; livelihood, living.

¹manteo, *m.* tossing in a blanket.

²mantec, *m.* long cloak or mantle; sort of woollen skirt.

mantequero, ra. I. *n.* one who sells butter; dairyman, dairymaid. **II.** *f.* churn; butter dish or bowl.

mantequilla, *f.* butter; hard sauce.

mantequillero, ra. I. *n.* = MANTEQUERO. **II.** *f.* butter bowl.

mantero, ra, *n.* blanket maker or seller; mantua maker.

mantés, sa, *n.* (coll.) rogue, scoundrel.

mantilla, *f.* mantilla; saddlecloth; baby clothes; (print.) blanket; birth present from one prince to another.—**estar en mantillas,** (of work, a negotiation, etc.) to be in the beginning stage; to be ignorant of, not know anything about (a subject).

mantilleja, *f. dim.* small mantilla.

mantillo, *m.* (agr.) humus; rotten, fermented manure.

mantillón, na, *a.* dirty, slovenly.

mantisa, *f.* (math.) mantissa.

manto, *m.* cloak, mantle; large mantilla; robe of state; mantelpiece of a chimney; (min.) layer or stratum.

mantón, *m. aug.* large cloak or mantle; (Cuba) mantilla.

mantuano, na, *n.* & *a.* of or from Mantua.

mantudo, da, *a.* having drooping wings.

mantuve, *v. V.* MANTENER.

manuable, *a.* easy to handle, handy.

manual. I. *a.* manual; handy; domestic, home-made; easy; tractable, pliant. **II.** *m.* manual, handbook; notebook, account book; handle (of an oar); (eccl.) ritual; (com.) old name of the journal.—*pl.* a priest's fees for assisting in the choir.

manualmente, *adv.* manually.

manubrio, *m.* handle, crank.

manucodiata, *f.* (ornith.) bird of paradise.

manuela, *f.* (in Madrid) open hack, carriage.

manuella, *f.* (naut.) capstan bar.

manufactura, *f.* manufacture; manufactured article.

manufacturar, *va.* & *vn.* to manufacture.

manufacturero, ra, *a.* manufacturing.

manumisión, *f.* manumission, freeing.

manumiso, sa, *a.* emancipated; free, disengaged.

manumisor, *m.* (law) liberator.

manumitir, *va.* (*pp.* MANUMITIDO, MANUMISO) to manumit, emancipate.

manuscribir, *va.* & *vn.* to write by hand.

manuscrito, ta, *n.* & *a.* manuscript.

manutención, *f.* maintaining; maintenance, support; protection; conservation.

manutener, *va.* (law) to maintain, support.

manutisa, *f.* (bot.) = MINUTISA, sweet william.

manvacío, a, *a.* = MANIVACÍO, empty-handed.

manzana, *f.* (bot.) apple; block (of houses), square; knob of a sword.

manzanal, manzanar, *m.* apple orchard.

manzanera, *f.* (bot.) wild apple tree.

manzanil, *a.* applelike.

manzanilla, *f. dim.* (bot.) common camomile; knob at the top of coaches, bedsteads, etc.; medium-sized olive; white sherry wine; lower part of the chin; pad, or cushion, of the feet of animals having claws.—**m. fina,** (bot.) golden cotula.—**m. hedionda** = MAGARZUELA, (bot.) camomile.

manzanillo, ito, *m. dim.* (bot.) manchineel, poison tree.

manzanita, *f. dim.* little apple.—**m. de dama** = ACEROLA, fruit of the hawthorn.

manzano, *m.* (bot.) apple tree.

maña, *f.* skill, dexterity, cleverness, knack; cunning, craftiness; tact, care; habit or custom; bundle or bunch (as of hemp or flax).—**darse m.,** to contrive, to manage.

mañana. I. *f.* morning, morrow, forenoon; (Am.) morning drink.—**de gran m.,** very early.—**de m.,** in the morning; early.—**muy de m.** = DE GRAN M.—**m. mismo,** tomorrow without fail, surely.—**por la m.,** in the morning.—**tomar la m.,** to take an appetizer (drink) before breakfast. **II.** *adv.* to-morrow; later, in time to come.—**¡hasta m.!** see you tomorrow!

mañanear, *vn.* to rise early.

mañanica, ita, *f.* daybreak.

mañear, *va.* & *vn.* to manage or act with craft and cunning.

mañería, *f.* sterility; feudal right of inheriting from those who died without legitimate succession.

mañero, ra, *a.* clever, dexterous, skilful, artful; handy, easy; meek, tractable.

maño, ña, *n.* brother (sister); dear, darling.

mañoco, *m.* tapioca; Indian-corn meal.

mañosamente, *adv.* neatly, handily, cleverly; tactfully, slickly; craftily.

mañoso, sa, *a.* skilful, handy, clever; tactful, cunning, careful.

mañuela. I. *f.* low cunning, mean trick. **II.** *n.* artful, cunning person.

mapa. I. *m.* map, chart.—**m. mudo,** outline map with no names on it. **II.** *f.* (coll.) anything excellent and prominent in its line.—**llevarse la m.,** to excel, to take the prize.

mapache, *m.* (zool.) raccoon.

mapamundi, *m.* map of the world.

mapaná, mapanare, *f.* (Colomb., Venez.) a poisonous snake.

mapurito, *m.* (C. A.) (zool.) skunk.

maque, *m.* (Mex.) sumac lacquer.

maquear, *va.* to lacquer with MAQUE.

maquí, *m.* a kind of ginger.

maquiavélico, ca, *a.* Machiavelian.

maquiavelismo, *m.* Machiavelism.

maquiavelista, *n.* Machiavelian.

maquila, *f.* toll corn; a corn measure (½ CELEMÍN); (C. A.) a unit of weight (about 125 lb.)

maquilar, *va.* to measure and take the miller's toll corn.

maquilero, maquilón, *m.* measurer and receiver of milling toll corn.

maquillaje, *m.* (Gal.) beautifying, making up.

máquina, *f.* machine, engine; fancy project; admixture of fancy or the supernatural in certain poetical compositions; imposing structure, pile; (coll.) abundancy, lots.—**m. compound,** or **compuesta,** compound engine.—**m. de cilindro,** reciprocating engine.—**m. de combustión interna,** internal-combustion engine.—**m. de coser,** sewing machine.—**m. de doble efecto,** double-acting engine.—**m. de émbolo,** reciprocating engine.—**m. de escribir,** typewriter.—**m. de sumar,** adding machine.—**m. de vapor,** steam engine.—**m. infernal,** infernal machine.—**m. neumática,** air pump.—**m. sumadora** = M. DE SUMAR.—**a toda m.,** at full speed.

maquinación, *f.* machination.

maquinador, ra, *n.* schemer, plotter.

maquinal, *a.* mechanical.—**maquinalmente,** *adv.* mechanically, unconsciously.

maquinar, *va.* & *vn.* to machinate, scheme, plot, hatch, concoct.

maquinaria, *f.* machinery; applied mechanics.

maquinista, *n.* engine runner, engineer; machinist; mechanic, mechanician.

For pronunciation, see the rules at the beginning of the book.

mar, *m.* or *f.* sea; flood; large quantity or number.—**m. alta,** rough sea.—**m. ancha,** high seas.—**m. bonanza,** calm sea.—**m. de fondo,** swell.—**m. de través,** sea on the beam.—**m. en leche,** calm sea.—**m. jurisdiccional,** or territorial, territorial waters.—**m. llena,** or **plena,** high water.—**alta m.,** high seas, open sea.—**arar en el m.,** to labor in vain.—**baja m.,** low water, ebb tide.—**correr con la mar en popa,** to scud before the sea.—**correr los mares,** to follow the seas.—**de m. a m.,** copiously, excessively; in the extreme of fashion.—**hablar de la m.,** to attempt an impossibility; to speak on an inexhaustible subject.—**la m.,** (coll.) a great quantity or number, a lot, lots.—**meter el m. en pozo,** to attempt the impossible.—**meterse m. adentro,** (in sea bathing) to go beyond one's depth.

marabú, *m.* (ornith.) marabou.

maracure, *m.* (bot.) curare plant.

maragato, ta, *n.* native of a region in Spain called Maragatería.

maraña, *f.* jungle; tangle, entanglement; silk waste and stuff made from it; perplexity, puzzle; fraud, imposition; intrigue, plot.

marañado, da, *a.* entangled, perplexed.

marañero, ra; ñoso, sa, *a.* entangling, ensnaring, perplexing.

marañón, *m.* (Cuba) (bot.) cashew; cashew nut.

marasmo, *m.* (med.) marasmus, wasting away; inactivity, dullness, deadness.

márata, *n.* & *a.* Maratha, Mahratta.

maravedí, *m.* maravedi, an old Spanish coin.

maravilla, *f.* wonder, marvel; (bot.) marigold.—**m. de noche,** or **de Indias,** (bot.) marvel of Peru, four-o'clock.—**a las mil maravillas,** wonderfully well.—**a m.,** marvellously.—**por m.,** very seldom.

maravillar. I. *va.* to admire. **II.** *vr.* (**de**) to wonder (at), to marvel.

maravillosamente, *adv.* wonderfully, marvellously.

maravilloso, sa, *a.* wonderful.

marbete, *m.* label, tag, ticket; (Ry.) baggage check; border, fillet.

marca, *f.* mark, stamp, impress; brand; make; sign; standard (of size); gauge or rule for measuring; marker, stencil, label, tag, ticket; (geog.) march, frontier region or province; seamark, landmark.—**m. de fábrica,** trademark.—**de m.,** excellent of its kind.—**de más de m.,** or **de m. mayor,** of high quality, first-class, superior.

marcación, *f.* bearing; taking a ship's bearings.

marcadamente, *adv.* markedly, notably.

marcador, ra. I. *n.* & *a.* marker(-ing). **II.** *m.* marker; assay master; index; bookmark.

marcar. I. *va.* (*pret.* MARQUÉ; *subj.* MARQUE) to mark, stamp, impress, brand; to observe, note; (sports) to even up, counter.—**m. el compás,** to beat time, keep time. **II.** *vr.* to determine bearings (of a ship).

marcasita, *f.* (min.) marcasite, white pyrites.

marceador, ra, *n.* & *a.* shearer(-ing).

marcear. I. *va.* to shear. **II.** *vn.* (of weather) to be rough.

marceo, *m.* trimming honeycombs in spring.

marcero, ra. = MARCEADOR.

marcescente, *a.* (bot.) marcescent, withering.

marcial. I. *a.* martial, warlike; frank, unceremonious; (pharm.) martial, chalybeate. **II.** *m.* aromatic powder for dressing gloves.

marcialidad, *f.* martialness; frankness.

marcionista, *n.* & *a.* Marcionite(-itic).

marco, *m.* frame, doorcase, window case; picture frame; mark, gold and silver weight; standard (of weight); scantling and length of timber; model, archetype; mark, German coin.

márcola, *f.* pruning hook.

marconigrafía, *f.* wireless telegraphy.

marconigrama, *m.* marconigram, wireless telegram.

marcha, *f.* march; progress, turn, course, run; (naut.) speed; (mus.) march, two-step; movement of a watch; running or functioning; bonfire.—**marchas forzadas,** (mil.) forced marches.—**a largas marchas,** with celerity, speedily.—**apresurar la m.,** to hurry, speed up.—**batir la m.,** to strike up a march.—**¡en m.!** forward march! go on! let's go!—**poner en m.,** to start, put in motion; (fig.) to start, initiate.—**sobre la m.,** at once, right off, right away.

marchamar, *va.* to mark at the custom house.

marchamero, *m.* custom house officer who marks goods.

marchamo, *m.* custom house mark on goods.

marchante. I. *a.* mercantile, commercial, trading. **II.** *m.* shopkeeper, dealer; customer, buyer; (Cuba) sharper, trickster.

marchapié, *m.* footboard; (naut.) horse, footrope.

marchar, *vn.* & *vr.* to go; to go away, leave; to walk; to progress, proceed, go ahead; to work, function, run (as a machine); to go, run (as a train, a ship, a clock); to move (as a carriage); to pace (as a horse); (mil.) to march; (naut.) to have speed.

marchitable, *a.* perishable, liable to wither.

marchitamiento, *m.* withering, fading.

marchitar. I. *va.* to wither, fade. **II.** *vr.* to wither, fade, decay; to pine away.

marchitez, *f.* withering, fading.

marchito, ta, *a.* faded, withered.

marea, *f.* tide; beach; soft sea breeze; dew, mizzle; street dirt washed away.—**m. alta,** high tide, high water.—**m. baja,** low tide, ebb.—**m. creciente,** flood tide.—**m. menguante,** ebb tide.—**contra viento y m.,** against all odds; come what may.

mareado, da, *a.* seasick.

mareaje, *m.* navigation, seamanship; course of a ship.

mareamiento, *m.* seasickness.

mareante. I. *n.* navigator, skipper, sailor. **II.** *a.* causing seasickness.

marear. I. *va.* to navigate; to sell; (coll.) to vex, importune, bother. **II.** *vr.* to get seasick, carsick; to be damaged at sea.

marecanita, *f.* (min.) marekanite.

marejada, *f.* swell, head sea, surf; commotion, excitement, disturbance.

maremagno, mare mágnum, *m.* (coll.) abundance; confusion, disorder.

mareo, *m.* seasickness; (coll.) vexation.

mareógrafo, *m.* mareograph.

marero, *a.* sea (breeze).

mareta, *f.* (naut.) surge of the sea; growing or decreasing excitement.

maretazo, *m.* dashing of a wave.

márfaga, márfega, *f.* ticking; straw bed.

marfil, *m.* ivory.—**m. vegetal,** ivory nuts.

marfileño, ña, *a.* ivory (as *a.*); ivorylike.

marfuz, *a.* repudiated, rejected; fallacious, deceitful.

¹marga, *f.* marl, loam.

²marga, *f.* ticking; burlap.

margajita, *f.* (min.) white pyrites.

margal, *m.* marly ground, marlpit.

margallón, *m.* (bot.) palmetto.

margar, *va.* to fertilize with marl.

margarato, *m.* (chem.) margarate.

margárico, a, *a.* (chem.) margaric (acid).

margarina, *f.* (chem.) margarine.

margarita, *f.* pearl; (bot.) common daisy; marguerite; periwinkle.

margay, *m.* (Am.) (zool.) margay, tiger cat.

margen, *m.* or *f.* margin, border, edge, verge; fringe; marginal note.—**andarse por las már-**

genes, to beat about the bush.—dar m., to give an opportunity.

margenar, va. = MARGINAR.

marginado, da, a. & pp. marginated.

marginal, a. marginal.

marginar, va. to make marginal notes on; to leave a margin on.

margoso, sa, a. marly, loamy.

margrave, m. margrave.

margraviato, m. margraviate.

marguera, f. marlpit.

marhojo, m. = MALHOJO, vegetable refuse.

maría, f. (coll.) white wax taper; old silver coin.

mariache, mariachi, m. (Mex.) popular song; street singer.

mariano, na, a. (eccl.) Marian.

marica. I. f. dim. (ornith.) magpie; knave of diamonds. **II.** m. milksop, effeminate man.

Maricastaña, f.—**en tiempos de M.,** in the days of yore; long, long ago.

maridable, a. conjugal, matrimonial, connubial, marital.—**maridablemente,** adv. conjugally.

maridaje, m. conjugal bond; intimate connection.

maridar. I. vn. to marry; to live as man and wife. **II.** va. to unite, join.

maridazo, m. (coll.) uxoriousness, excessive fondness for one's wife.

maridillo, m. brazier for warming the feet.

marido, m. husband.

mariguana, marihuana, f. marihuana.

marimacho, m. (coll.) virago, mannish woman.

marimanta, f. (coll.) bugbear, hobgoblin.

marimba, f. a kind of drum used by Negroes of Africa; (Am.) xylophone.

marimoña, f. (bot.) = FRANCESILLA, crowfoot.

marimorena, f. (coll.) quarrel, row.

marina, f. marine, shore, sea coast; (art) marine painting, seascape; seamanship, nautical art. **—m. de guerra, navy.—m. mercante,** merchant marine.

marinaje, m. seamanship; sailors (collect.).

marinar, va. to salt (fish); (naut.) to man (a ship).

marinear, vn. to be a mariner.

marinerado, da, a. manned, equipped.

marinería, f. seamanship; body of seamen; ship's crew.

marinero, ra. I. a. ready to sail; seaworthy, seagoing, stanch. **II.** m. mariner, seaman, sailor.— **a la marinera,** in a seamanlike manner, shipshape.

marinesco, ca, a. pertaining to sailors.—**a la m.,** in a seamanlike manner, shipshape.

marino, na. I. a. marine, nautical, sea (as a.). **II.** n. mariner, seaman.

marión, m. (ichth.) sturgeon.

marioneta, f. = TÍTERE, puppet, marionette.

maripérez, f. servant maid.

mariposa, f. (entom.) butterfly; night taper.

mariposear, vn. to flit like a butterfly; to be fickle and capricious.

mariquita, f. (entom.) ladybug, ladybird.

marisabidilla, f. (coll.) bluestocking.

mariscal, m. (mil.) marshal; farrier, blacksmith. **—m. de campo,** field marshal.

mariscala, f. marshal's wife.

mariscalato, m., **mariscalía,** f. marshalship.

mariscar, vn. to gather shellfish.

marisco, m. any of the Invertebrata, especially a mollusc or a shellfish.

marisma, f. marsh, swamp, morass.

marismo, m. (bot.) = ORZAGA, mountain spinach.

marital, a. marital.

marítimo, ma, a. maritime, marine, sea (as a.).

maritornes, f. (coll.) homely, ungainly maid of all work.

marizapalos, f. row, fight, disturbance.

marjal, m. fen, marsh, moor, moorland.

marjoleta, f. = MAJUELA, fruit of the hawthorn.

marjoleto, m. (bot.) white hawthorn.

marlota, f. a kind of Moorish gown.

marmatita, f. (min.) marmatite.

marmella, f. = MAMELLA, protuberance on goat's neck.

marmellado, da, a. = MAMELLADO, mammillate.

marmita, f. kettle, pot, boiler.

marmitón, m. scullion, kitchen boy.

mármol, m. marble (stone); (art) marble sculpture; (glass making) marver; (print.) imposing stone.

marmolejo, m. dim. small marble column.

marmoleño, ña, a. marbly.

marmolería, f. marblework; marbleworks.

marmolillo, m. dim. fender stone; (fig.) unfeeling person.

marmolista, m. marbler, sculptor.

marmoración, f. = ESTUCO, stucco; plastering.

marmóreo, ea, a. marbled, marble (as a.).

marmorete, m. (print.) vignette, small cut.

marmota, f. (zool.) marmot; worsted cap.

maro, m. (bot.) germander, marum.

marojo, m. (bot.) red-berried mistletoe.

maroma, f. rope, cable.

maromero, ra, n. tight-rope dancer.

marón, m. (ichth.) sturgeon.

maronita, n. & a. Maronite.

marqué, marque, v. V. MARCAR.

marqués, m. marquis.—**marquesa,** marchioness; marquee.—**marquesado,** m. marquisate.

marquesina, f. marquee, awning.

¹**marquesita,** f. (min.) marcasite, white pyrites.

²**marquesita,** f. small armchair.

marquesote, m. ancient stiff, high collar; (Mex.) caramel, burnt sugar.

marqueta, f. crude cake of wax.

marquetería, f. cabinetwork; marquetry, checkered or inlaid work.

marquilla, f. demy, a particular size of paper.

marquito, m. dim. small frame.

¹**marra,** f. lack, want; defect.

²**marra,** f. stone hammer.

márraga, f. ticking.

marrajo, ja. I. a. cunning, artful, wily. **II.** m. (ichth.) shark.

¹**marrana,** f. sow, female pig; (coll.) dirty or unprincipled woman.

²**marrana,** f. axle of a NORIA, water wheel.

marranada, f. (coll.) hoggish action; nastiness, filthiness.

marranalla, f. rabble.

marranamente, adv. piggishly, swinishly.

marrancho, cha, n. pig, hog; dirty person.

marranchón, na, n. hog (sow).

marranillo, m. little pig.

¹**marrano, na,** n. hog; (coll.) dirty or unprincipled person.

²**marrano,** m. drum of a water wheel; woodwork supporting a well; board to equalize pressure in oil mills.

marrar, vn. to deviate from the right; to lack, fail; to miss.

marras, adv. (coll.) long ago, long since, whilom.

marrasquino, m. maraschino.

marrazo, m. mattock.

marrear, va. to strike with a stone hammer.

márrega, f., **marregón,** m. straw bed.

marrillo, m. thick short stick.

marro, m. a game resembling quoits; slip or slide of pursued game to avoid capture; miss, failure; catstick for playing tipcat.

¹**marrón,** m. quoit.

²**marrón, na,** a. (Angl.) maroon, brown.

marroquí, m. morocco (leather); also **marroquín, na,** n. & a. Moroccan.

marrubio, m. (bot.) white horehound.

marrueco, ca, n. & a. Moroccan.

marrullería, f. wheedling, cajolery.

marrullero, ra, n. wheedler, coaxer, deceiver.

marsellés, sa. I. a. of or pertaining to Marseilles.

II. *m.* short jacket. **III.** *f.* Marseillaise, French national anthem.

marso, sa, *n.* & *a.* Marsian (one of, or pertaining to, the Marsi).

marsopa, marsopla, *f.* blunt-headed whale.

marsupial. I. *n.* & *a.* (zool.) marsupial. **II.** *m. pl.* Marsupialia, marsupials.

marta, *f.* (zool.) pine marten and its fur.

¹martagón, na, *n.* (coll.) shrewd person.

²martagón, *m.* (bot.) wild lily.

Marte, *m.* (astr.) Mars.

martellina, *f.* marteline, millstone hammer.

martes, *m.* Tuesday.—**m. de carnestolendas,** Shrove Tuesday.

martillada, *f.* blow with a hammer.

martillador, ra, *n.* & *a.* hammerer(-ing).

martillar, *va.* to hammer.

martillazo, *m.* blow with a hammer.

martillejo, *m. dim.* small hammer.

martilleo, *m.* hammering; clatter.

martillo, *m.* hammer; claw hammer; tuning hammer; auction rooms; (anat.) malleus.—**a macha m.,** strongly but roughly made.—**a m.,** with a hammer; by hammering.—**de m.,** (of metals) wrought.

Martín (San), *m.* season for killing hogs.—**llegarle a uno su San M.,** every dog has his day.

martín del río, *m.* (ornith.) = MARTINETE.

martín pescador, *m.* (ornith.) kingfisher.

¹martinete, *m.* (ornith.) a heronlike bird and its tuft of white feathers.

²martinete, *m.* drop hammer; pile driver; hammer of a pianoforte.

martingala, *f.* breeches worn under armor; stake in the game of monte.

martinico, *m.* (coll.) ghost.

martiniega, *f.* tax payable on St. Martin's day.

mártir, *n.* martyr.

martiricé, martirice, *v.* *V.* MARTIRIZAR.

martirio, *m.* martyrdom; torture; grief.

martirizador, ra. I. *n.* martyrizer. **II.** *a.* martyrizing; tormenting, agonizing.

martirizar, *va.* (*pret.* MARTIRICÉ; *subj.* MARTIRICE) to martyr; to martyrize; to torment.

martirologio, *m.* martyrology.

marullo, *m.* (naut.) sea wave.

marxismo, *m.* Marxism.

marxista, *n.* & *a.* Marxist.

marzadga, *f.* tax payable in March.

marzal, *a.* pertaining to the month of March.

marzo, *m.* March, third month.

marzoleta, *f.* (bot.) fruit of the hawthorn.

marzoleto, *m.* (bot.) white hawthorn.

¹mas, *m.* farmhouse and stock.

²mas, *m.* (P. I.) weight for gold and silver (58 grains).

³mas, *conj.* = PERO, but.—**m. que,** even if; however much.

más. I. *a.* more; most; (math.) plus.—**el signo m.,** the plus sign.—**los m.,** the largest number; the majority; most people. **II.** *adv.* more; most; longer; longest; over, besides, moreover; rather.—**m. adelante,** later on.—**m. allá,** farther on.—**m. bien,** rather.—**m. bien que,** rather than.—**m. de** (of quantity) more than, over.—**m. que,** more than; but only; even if. —**m. tarde o m. temprano,** sooner or later. —**a lo m.,** at most.—**a m.,** besides.—**a m. correr,** with the utmost speed.—**a m. de,** in addition to, besides; besides being.—**a m. tardar,** at the latest.—**a m. y mejor,** greatly, highly, at best; excellently.—**como el que m.,** as (good, well, much) as the best, second to none (often diff. constr.).—**de m.,** over, extra; too much, too many.—**de m. a m.,** besides, moreover.—**en m. (de),** more (than), above, over.—**lo m. antes,** as soon as possible.—**no m.,** not any more; only.—**no m. que,** not more than, only; nothing more than (*no tengo*

más que dos hijos, I have only two children; *no vino más que Juan,* only John came, no one came but John; *usted no necesita más que escribir a la casa,* you need only to write to the firm).—**por m. que,** however much; no matter how.—**sin m. acá ni m. allá,** suddenly, without any reason.—**sin m. ni m.,** without much ado, without any to-do.

masa, *f.* dough; (mason.) mortar; (phys.) mass; volume, lump; aggregation, union; crowd of people; nature, disposition.

masada, *f.* farmhouse and stock.

masadero, *m.* farmer.

masaje, *m.* massage.—**masajista,** *m.* masseur.

masar, *va.* to knead; (med.) to massage.

masato, *m.* (Am.) a flavored drink made with corn or rice and sugar.

mascabado, da, *a.* raw, unrefined (sugar).

mascada, *f.* (Mex.) silk handkerchief.

mascador, ra, *n.* chewer, masticator.

mascadura, *f.* chewing, mastication.

mascar, *va.* (*pret.* MASQUÉ; *subj.* MASQUE) to chew, masticate; (coll.) to mumble.

máscara. I. *f.* mask.—**m. de gases,** gas mask. —*pl.* masquerade. **II.** *n.* mask, masquerader.

mascarada, *f.* masquerade, mummery.

mascarero, ra, *n.* dealer in masks.

mascarilla, *f. dim.* half mask; death mask.

mascarón, *m. aug.* hideous mask, (arch.) grotesque face.—**m. de proa,** (naut.) figurehead.

mascota, *f.* (Am.) mascot; good-luck charm.

mascujar, *vn.* (coll.) to masticate with difficulty; to mumble.

masculinidad, *f.* masculinity, manhood.

masculinizar. I. *va.* to make masculine. **II.** *vr.* (of women) to become mannish.

masculino, na, *a.* masculine; male.

mascullar, *va.* to mumble.

masecoral, *m.* sleight of hand, legerdemain.

masejicomar, *m.* = MASECORAL.

masera, *f.* kneading trough; cloth for covering the dough.

masería, masía, *f.* farmhouse.

masetero, *m.* (anat.) masseter.

masica, *f.* (C. A.) breadnut tree.

masicote, *m.* (chem.) massicot.

masiliense, *a.* of Marseilles.

masilla, *f. dim.* little mass; putty; mastic.

masita, *f.* pittance retained for providing a soldier with shoes, etc.

maslo, *m.* root of the tail of quadrupeds.

¹masón, *m. aug.* mess of dough fed to fowls.

²masón, *m.* freemason.—**masonería,** *f.* freemasonry.—**masónico, ca,** *a.* masonic.

masoquismo, *m.* (psych.) masochism.

masora, *f.* Masora.—**masoreta,** *n.* Masorete.— **masorético, ca,** *a.* Masoretic.

masovero, *m.* farmer.

masqué, masque, *v.* *V.* MASCAR.

mastelerillo, *m. dim.* (naut.) topgallant and royal mast.

mastelero, *m.* (naut.) topmast.—**masteleros de respeto,** spare topmasts.

masticación, *f.* mastication.

masticador, ra. I. *n.* & *a.* masticator(-ing). **II.** *n.* MASTIGADOR; chopper.

masticar, *va.* (*pret.* MASTIQUÉ; *subj.* MASTIQUE) to masticate, to chew; to ruminate, meditate about.

masticatorio, ria, *a.* masticatory.

mastigador, *m.* bit for a horse.

mástil, *m.* (naut., radio) mast; upright post of a bed or loom; stanchion; shank of an auger; trunk or stem of a tree; wide breeches worn by Indians; neck (of violin, guitar, etc.).

mastín, na, *n.* mastiff.

mástique, *m.* mastic; mastic tree.

mastiqué, mastique, *v.* *V.* MASTICAR.

masto, *m.* stock into which a scion is grafted.

mastodonte, *m.* mastodon.

For pronunciation, see the rules at the beginning of the book.

mastoides. I. *a.* mastoid. **II.** *m.* (anat.) mastoid process.—**mastoiditis,** *f.* mastoiditis.

mastranto, mastranzo, *m.* round-leaved mint.

mastuerzo, *m.* dolt, simpleton; (bot.) common cress.

masturbación, *f.* masturbation.

masturbarse, *vr.* to masturbate.

masvale, *m.* = MALVASÍA.

¹**mata,** *f.* (bot.) plant; sprig, blade; grove, orchard; mastic tree; head (of hair).—**m. parda,** young evergreen oak.

²**mata,** *f.* (min.) matte, regulus, white metal.

³**mata,** *f.* = MATARRATA.

matacán, *m.* poison for killing dogs; (bot.) dog's-bane; nux vomica; hare previously hunted; pebble, stone; (fort.) machicolation gallery; deuce of clubs in some card games.

matacandelas, *f.* candle extinguisher.

matacandil, *m.* (prov.) lobster.

matacía, *f.* slaughter, death.

mataco, ca, *n.* (Am.) Chaco Indian; (Am.) (zool.) a kind of armadillo.

¹**matachín,** *m.* merry-andrew; dance performed by grotesque figures.

²**matachín,** *m.* butcher; butcher's knife.

matadero, *m.* slaughterhouse; drudgery.

matador, ra. I. *n.* & *a.* killer(-ing). **II.** *m.* matador (bullfighter who kills the bull); (card playing) matador.

matadura, *f.* (vet.) sore, gall.

matafuego, *m.* fire extinguisher; fireman.

matagallina, *f.* (bot.) = TORVISCO, daphne.

matahambre, *m.* (Cuba) marzipan.

matahombres, *m.* (entom.) a beetle.

matajudío, *m.* (ichth.) = MÚJOL, mullet.

matalahuga, matalahuva, *f.* = ANÍS, anise.

matalobos, *m.* (bot.) wolfsbane, aconite.

matalón, *m.* old worn-out horse.

matalotaje, *m.* (naut.) ship stores; (coll.) heap, mess, jumble.

matalote, *m.* = MATALÓN.

matancero, ra, *n.* & *a.* of or pertaining to Matanzas, Cuba.

matanza, *f.* slaughter, butchery; hog slaughtering and the season when it is done; swine kept for slaughter; (coll.) obstinacy, eagerness.

matapalo, *m.* (bot.) (Am.) tree yielding caoutchouc and a fibre for sackcloth.

mataperrada, *f.* boy's mischievous prank.

mataperros, *m.* (coll.) street urchin.

matapiojos, *m.* (Am.) dragon fly.

matapolvo, *m.* light rain that just lays the dust.

matapulgas, *f.* (bot.) mint.

matar. I. *va.* to kill; to put out (a light); to extinguish (fire); to slake (lime); to harass, worry, vex; to make (a horse's back) sore by the rubbing of the harness; to mark (cards for cheating); (cards) to beat, top (opponent's card); to mat (metal); (carp.) to bevel, round; (art) to tone down.—**m. de aburrimiento,** (fig.) to bore to death.—**m. de hambre,** to starve.—**m. el tiempo,** to kill time.—**a mata caballo,** in the greatest hurry.—**estar a m. con,** to be at drawn daggers with.—**mátalas callando,** (coll.) hypocrite, sly dog. **II.** *vr.* to kill oneself; to get killed.

matarife, *m.* slaughterman.

matarrata, *f.* a card game.

matasanos, *m.* (coll.) quack, charlatan; empiric.

matasellos, *m.* post office cancelling stamp.

matasiete, *m.* bully, braggart.

¹**mate. I.** *a.* mat, dull, lusterless. **II.** *m.* gold or silver sizing; (chess) checkmate.—**dar m.,** (chess) stale-mate.—**dar m.,** (chess) to check-mate; (coll.) to make fun of, laugh at (a person).

²**mate,** *m.* (bot.) Brazilian holly; maté, Paraguay tea; vessel in which maté is made; gourd.

matear, *vn.* (agr.) to extend and shoot forth (as wheat, etc.); to hunt among the bushes.

matemática, *f.,* **matemáticas,** *f. pl.* mathematics.

matemáticamente, *adv.* mathematically.

matemático, ca. I. *a.* mathematical. **II.** *n.* mathematician.

materia, *f.* matter; material, substance, stuff; subject, topic; subject matter; cause, occasion; (med.) matter, pus.—**m. médica,** materia medica.—**m. prima,** raw material.—**materias de estado,** state affairs.—**en m. de,** as regards, in the matter of.—**entrar en m.** to come to the point, get down to business.

material. I. *a.* material; rude, coarse, matter-of-fact. **II.** *m.* ingredient; material, stuff; (print.) copy; (elec. and Ry.) equipment.—**m. rodante,** (Ry.) rolling stock.—*pl.* **materiales brutos, or crudos,** raw material(s).

materialidad, *f.* materiality, corporeity; outward appearance; literalness; (theol.) materiality.

materialismo, *m.* materialism.

materialista, *n.* & *a.* materialist(-ic).

materializar, I. *va.* to materialize. **II.** *vr.* to become (morally) materialistic.

materialmente, *adv.* materially, corporeally; physically; absolutely.

maternal, *a.* maternal.—**maternalmente,** *adv.* maternally.

maternidad, *f.* maternity.

materno, na, *a.* maternal, motherly; mother (as *a.*).

matero, *ra, n.* maté drinker.

mático, matico, *m.* (bot.) matico.

matihuelo, *m.* = DOMINGUILLO, tumbler (toy).

matinal, *a.* (poet.) = MATUTINAL.

matiné, *m.* matinée.

matiz, *m.* tint, hue, shade; blending of colors.

matizado, da, *a.* & *pp.* variegated, many-hued.

matizar, *va.* to variegate, blend (colors); to tint, give a special tint to.

mato, *m.* brake, coppice.

matojo, *m.* bush; (bot.) glasswort; (Cuba) shoot, sucker, tiller.

matón, *m.* (coll.) bully, hector, browbeater.

matorral, *m.* heath, brake; thicket, copse; bush.

matoso, sa, *a.* heathlike; weedy.

matraca, *f.* wooden rattle; (coll.) jest, chaff.—**dar m.,** to banter.

matraquear, *va.* to rattle; to scoff, banter.

matraqueo, *m.* (coll.) rattling noise; banter.

matraquista, *n.* wag, jester, banterer.

matraz, *f.* (chem.) matrass, a glass vessel.

matrería, *f.* shrewdness.

matrero, ra. I. *a.* cunning, sagacious, shrewd. **II.** *m.* artful knave.

matriarcado, *m.* matriarchate.

matricaria, *f.* (bot.) common feverfew.

matricida, *n.* matricide (murderer).

matricidio, *m.* matricide (murder).

matrícula, *f.* register, list; matricula; matriculation.—**m. de mar,** mariner's register.

matriculador, ra, *n.* matriculator.

matricular. I. *va.* & *vr.* to matriculate, register, enroll. **II.** *vr.* to enter (a contest, etc.).

matrimonesco, ca, *a.* (humor.) matrimonial.

matrimonial, *a.* matrimonial.

matrimonialmente, *adv.* matrimonially.

matrimoniar, *va.* to marry.

matrimonio, *m.* marriage, matrimony; married couple.—**m. de la mano izquierda,** morganatic marriage.

matritense, *n.* & *a.* Madrilenean.

matriz. I. *a.* first, principal, main, parent, chief. **II.** *f.* (anat.) uterus, womb; (mech.) mold, form, matrix, die; original draft of a writing; female screw, nut.

matrona, *f.* matron; midwife.

matronal, *a.* matronal.

maturrango, ga, *n.* (Am., coll.) poor (bad) horseman; clumsy, rough person.

matute, *m.* smuggling; smuggled goods; gambling den.—**matutear,** *va.* to smuggle.

matutero, ra, *n.* smuggler.

matutinal; matutino, na, *a.* matutinal, morning (as *a.*).

maula. I. *f.* frippery, rubbish, trumpery, trash; cunning, craft; deceitful trick. **II.** *n.* (coll.) trickster, cheat, bad pay; sluggard, drone.—**maulería,** *f.* shop where remnants are sold; craft, cunning, trickery.—**maulero, ra,** *n.* seller of remnants; trickster, cheat, swindler.

maullador, ra, *a.* mewing (cat).

maullar, *vn.* to mew.

maullido, maúllo, *m.* mew.

mauraca, *f.* roasting chestnuts, etc., over coals in the open air.

mauritano, na, *n.* & *a.* Mauritanian.

mauseolo, mausoleo, *m.* mausoleum.

maxilar. I. *a.* maxillary. **II.** *m.* maxillary bone, jaw.—**m. inferior,** inferior, or lower, maxillary.—**m. superior,** superior, or upper, maxillary.

máxima, *f.* maxim; rule; (mus.) maxima.

máximamente, máxime, *adv.* principally, specially.

máximo, ma. I. *a.* maximum.—**m. común divisor,** greatest common divisor. **II.** *m.* maximum. Also **máximum.**

¹**maya,** *f.* (bot.) common daisy; variety of pineapple; May queen.

²**maya,** *n.* & *a.* Maya, Yucatan Indian and language.

mayador, ra, *a.* mewing.

mayal, *m.* flail; thrashing instrument; lever in oil mills.

mayar, *vn.* to mew.

mayear, *vn.* (of the weather) to be like May.

mayo, *m.* month of May; Maypole; Mayday festivity.

mayólica, *f.* majolica ware.

mayonesa, *f.* mayonnaise dressing; cold dish dressed with mayonnaise.

mayor. I. *a.* greater; greatest; larger; largest; older, elder; oldest, eldest; senior; of age; main, principal; high (altar, mass); major; (mus.) major.—**m. edad,** (of age) majority.—**la m. parte (de),** the majority (of). **II.** *m.* superior; major or chief of a community; chief clerk; (mil.) major.—*pl.* ancestors, forefathers; superiors; elders.—**m. de edad,** of age.—**m. general,** major general.—**por m.,** (by) wholesale; summarily. **III.** *f.* (logic) major.—*pl.* (naut.) the three mainsails of a ship.

mayoral, *m.* head shepherd; leader; overseer, foreman, steward; stage driver.

mayoralía, *f.* flock, herd; herdsman's wages.

mayorana, *f.* (bot.) = MEJORANA, marjoram.

mayorazga, *f.* woman owner, or wife of owner, of an entailed estate.

mayorazgo, *m.* right of primogeniture; first-born son; family estate; entailed estate.

mayorazguista, *m.* author who treats of entails.

mayordoma, *f.* steward's wife; stewardess, housekeeper.

mayordomear, *va.* to administer, manage.

mayordomía, *f.* administration, stewardship, controllership.

mayordomo, *m.* steward, butler; manager; majordomo.

mayoría, *f.* majority (in age or number); superiority; majorship.—**m. absoluta,** (pol.) majority (more than half of the total).—**m. relativa,** plurality.

mayoridad, *f.* superiority; full age.

mayorista, *m.* pupil of highest classes in grammar schools; (Am.) wholesale merchant.

mayormente, *adv.* principally, chiefly.

mayúscula, *a.* & *f.* capital (letter).

mayúsculo, la, *a.* large, good-sized; important, prominent.

maza, *f.* war club; mace; pile driver; drop hammer; nave or hub of a wheel; hemp brake; drumstick of a bass drum; roller of a sugarcane mill; thick end of a billiard cue; something noisy tied to a dog's tail.—**m. de Fraga,** steam hammer.

mazacote, *m.* kali, barilla (herb); concrete; dry, tough mass; (coll.) bore, tiresome person.

mazada, *f.* blow with club or mallet.—**dar m.,** to cause harm or injury.

mazagatos, *m.* noisy wrangle, quarrel, row.

mazamorra, *f.* crumbs, small bits; a sort of corn pap, much used in Peru and Colombia; (Colomb.) a kind of thick corn soup; (Arg., Colomb.) boiled whole corn; (naut.) mess made of broken hardtack.

mazaneta, *f.* apple-shaped ornament in jewels.

mazapán, *m.* a sort of marzipan.

mazar, *va.* to churn (milk).

mazarí, *m.* tile-shaped brick.

mazarota, *f.* (foundry) deadhead, sprue.

mazdeísmo, *m.* Mazdaism, Mazdeism.

mazdeísta, *n.* & *a.* Mazdaist(-dean).

mazmorra, *f.* underground dungeon.

mazo, *m.* mallet, maul, wooden hammer; bundle, bunch; clapper of a bell; tiresome person, bore.

mazonería, *f.* stone masonry; (art) relief or relievo-work.

mazorca, *f.* spindleful (of yarn); ear of corn; (arch.) spindle-shaped baluster.

mazorral, *a.* rude, uncouth; (print.) solid.

mazorralmente, *adv.* grossly, rudely.

mazurca, *f.* (dance) mazurka.

me, *pers. pron., 1st pers. sing., dat., acc.; refl. of* YO.

meadero, *m.* urinal.

meados, *m. pl.* urine.

¹**meaja,** *f.* crumb.—**m. de huevo,** plasma bit of an egg.

²**meaja,** *f.* (law) execution dues.

meajuela, *f.* small piece attached to the bits of a bridle.

meandro, *m.* meander; (arch.) maze scroll-work; intricate ornamentation.

mear, *vn.* to urinate, make water.

meato, *m.* (anat.) opening or canal, meatus.

meauca, *f.* (ornith.) a kind of sea gull.

meca, *f.*—**de Ceca en M.,** or **de la Ceca a la M.,** to and fro, hither and thither.

mecánica, *f.* mechanics; machinery; (coll.) mean, despicable action or thing; (mil.) management of soldiers' affairs.

mecánicamente, *adv.* mechanically.

mecanicismo, *m.* (biol. & philos.) mechanistic system or theory.

mecanicista, *n.* & *a.* mechanist(-ic).

mecánico, ca. I. *a.* mechanical; machine-made or operated; power-driven; mean, servile. **II.** *n.* mechanician; mechanist; mechanic, handicraftsman, artisan.

mecanismo, *m.* mechanism, works (of machines).

mecanografía, *f.* typewriting.

mecanografiar, *va.* to typewrite, type.

mecanográfico, ca, *a.* typewritten; pertaining to typewriting.

mecanografista, *n.* = MECANÓGRAFO.

mecanógrafo, fa, *n.* typist.

mecapal, *m.* (Mex.) leather band with ropes used by porters.

mecate, *m.* (Mex.) maguey rope or cord.

mecedero, *m.* stirrer.

mecedor, ra. I. *a.* rocking, swinging. **II.** *m.* stirrer; swing. **III.** *f.* rocking chair.

mecedura, *f.* rocking.

mecer. I. *va.* (*ind.* MEZO; *subj.* MEZA) to stir, agitate, mix; to rock; to shake; to swing; to dandle (a child). **II.** *vr.* to rock, swing, sway; to soar.

meco, ca. I. *a.* (Mex.) (of animals) blackish red. **II.** *n.* (Mex.) wild Indian.

meconato, *m.* (chem.) meconate.

mecónico, ca, *a.* (chem.) meconic.

meconio, *m.* meconium, first excrement of new-born baby; (pharm.) meconium, poppy juice.

mecha, *f.* wick; fuse (of explosive); match, match cord; slice of bacon (for larding); lock of hair; bundle of threads or fibres; (surg.) roll of lint used as a drain.

mechar, *va.* (cook.) to lard (meat, etc.).

mechazo, *m.* (min.) fizzle of a blast fuse.

mechera, *f.* larding pin; shoplifter.

mechero, *m.* candlestick socket; lamp burner; gas burner.

mechinal, *m.* (mason.) columbarium, putlog hole.

mechoacán, *m.* (bot.) mechoacan bindweed.

mechón, *m.* *aug.* large lock of hair; large fuse; bundle of threads.

mechoso, sa, *a.* having abundant locks of hair.

medalla, *f.* medal; (sculpture) plaque, medallion; (coll.) gold coin.

medallón, *m.* *aug.* large medal; locket; (arch.) medallion.

médano, medaño, *m.* sand bank; dune.

medero, *m.* heap of vine shoots.

media, *f.* stocking; hose; (Am.) sock; (math.) mean.—**m. diferencial,** (math.) arithmetical mean.—**m. proporcional,** geometrical mean, mean proportional.

mediacaña, *f.* (arch.) concave molding, fluted molding; picture molding; (carp.) gouge; half-round file; curling tongs for the hair.

mediación, *f.* mediation; intercession.

mediado, da. I. *pp.* of MEDIAR. **II.** *a.* half-filled, half-full.—*pl.* **a mediados de,** (of a period of time) about the middle of.

mediador, ra, *n.* mediator; intercessor.

mediana, *f.* long billiard cue; top of a fishing rod; (geom.) median.

medianamente, *adv.* middling, so so, fairly.

medianejo, ja, *a.* (coll.) hardly mediocre.

medianería, *f.* partition wall.

medianero, ra. I. *a.* mediating, interceding; intermediate. **II.** *n.* mediator, go-between; owner of a house having a common wall with another.

medianía, medianidad, *f.* halfway; mediocrity; middle state; moderate means.

medianil, *m.* (agr.) middle piece of ground; (print.) crossbar of a chase.

mediano, na, *a.* moderate, middling, medium; mediocre, bad, insignificant.

medianoche, *f.* midnight; small meat pie.

mediante. I. *a.* intervening; interceding. **II.** *adv.* by means of, by virtue of, with the help of, through.

mediar, *vn.* to reach or be at the middle; to intercede, mediate; to intervene.

mediastino, *m.* (anat.) mediastinum.

mediatamente, *adv.* mediately, indirectly.

mediato, ta, *a.* mediate.

mediator, *m.* ombre, a card game.

médica, *f.* doctor's wife; woman physician.

medicable, *a.* curable, medicable.

medicación, *f.* medical treatment, medication.

medicamento, *m.* medicine, medicament.

medicamentoso, sa, *a.* medicinal.

medicastro, *m.* quack, charlatan, medicaster.

medicina, *f.* medicine; medicament, remedy.

medicinal, *a.* medicinal.

medicinante, *n.* healer; medical student who practices before taking his degree.

medicinar, *va.* to treat (a patient).

medición, *f.* measurement; measuring.

médico, ca. I. *a.* medical. **II.** *n.* physician.

medicucho, *m.* quack, charlatan, medicaster.

medida, *f.* measure; (shoe, etc.) size, number; standard, gauge; measuring, measurement; measuring stick; rule; moderation, prudence; (math., mus., poet., dance) measure.—**m. agraria,** land measure.—**m. de capacidad,** measure of capacity.—**m. de longitud,** meas-

ure of length.—**m. de superficie,** square measure.—**m. para áridos,** dry measure.—**m. para líquidos,** liquid measure.—**a la m.,** to order, custom-made.—**a m. del deseo,** according to one's wishes.—**a m. que,** as, according as, at the same time as, while.—**colmar la m.,** to be the last straw.—**colmarse, or llenarse, la m.,** to drain the cup of sorrow.—**sin m.,** to excess.—**tener m.,** to have a sense of proportion.—**tomar medidas,** to take measures or steps.

medidamente, *adv.* moderately.

medidor, ra, *n.* measurer.

mediero, ra, *n.* hosier, dealer in stockings; knitter of stockings; co-partner in a farm or ranch.

medieval, *a.* medieval.

medio, dia, *a.* & *adv.* half; partial; mid, middle; halfway, midway; mean, intermediate.—**m. bocel,** (arch.) torus, a kind of molding.—**m. colonia,** silk ribbon one finger wide.—**m. cuchara,** person of mediocre wit or skill.—**m. china,** cloth coarser than the CHINA.—**m. día,** midday.—**m. hermano,** half brother, step-brother.—**m. luna,** (fort.) half-moon.—**m. naranja,** cupola.—**m. noche,** midnight.—**m. pasta** (bookbinding) half-leather binding.—**m. relieve,** demi relief.—**m. talla,** half relief.—**m. vuelta,** right about face.—**a m., half** (closed, etc.).—**a m. asta,** at half mast.—**a medias,** by halves, halfway, partially.—**a m. mogate,** carelessly, heedlessly.—**de m. gala,** in dress uniform.—**el m. oriente,** the Middle East.—**ir a medias,** to go halves. **II.** *m.* middle, center; (often *pl.*) means, method, measure, way; (surrounding) medium; (spiritualistic) medium: (arith.) half; (Am.) half a REAL (5 cents).—*pl.* means, resources.—**m. diferencial,** arithmetical mean.—**m. proporcional,** mean proportional.—**de m. a m.,** half and half; in the middle; completely, entirely.—**de por m.,** between.—**echar por en m.,** to take the bull by the horns; to make up one's mind, happen what may.—**en m.,** in the middle; midway; in the midst.—**por m. de,** by means of.

mediocre, *a.* mediocre.

mediocridad, *f.* mediocrity.

mediodía, *m.* noon, midday; south.

medioeval, *a.* medieval.

mediopaño, *m.* thin woollen cloth.

mediquillo, *m.* medicaster; (P. I.) medicine man.

medir. I. *va.* (*ger.* MIDIENDO; *ind. pres.* MIDO, *pret.* él MIDIÓ; *subj.* MIDA) to measure; to compare, weigh, judge, value; to scan (verses).—**m. el suelo,** (coll.) to fall flat on the ground. **II.** *vr.* to be moderate; to act with prudence.

meditabundo, da, *a.* pensive, musing.

meditación, *f.* meditation.

meditar, *va.* & *vn.* to meditate, muse.

mediterráneo, nea, *a.* mediterranean; inland.

médium, *m.* spiritualistic medium.

medo, da, *n.* & *a.* Mede(-ian).

medra, *f.* thrift; success, improvement.

medrana, *f.* (coll.) fear.

medrar, *vn.* to thrive, prosper.

medriñaque, *m.* Philippine stuff for lining and stiffening women's skirts; short skirt.

medro, *m.* = MEDRA.—*pl.* progress, improvement.

medrosamente, *adv.* timorously, faintly.

medroso, sa, *a.* timorous, faint-hearted, cowardly; terrible, dreadful.

medula, médula, *f.* marrow, medulla; (bot.) pith; substance, essence.—**m. espinal,** spinal cord.—**m. oblonga, or m. oblongada,** medulla oblongada.

medular, *a.* medullar, medullary.

meduloso, sa, *a.* marrowy; pithy.

medusa, *f.* (ichth.) medusa, jellyfish.

meduseo, a, *a.* like, or relating to, Medusa.

mefistofélico, ca, *a.* Mephistophelean.
mefítico, ca, *a.* mephitic, foul, noxious.
megáfono, *m.* megaphone.
megalítico, ca, *a.* (archeol.) megalithic.
megalito, *m.* (archeol.) megalith.
megalomanía, *f.* megalomania.
megalómano, na, *n. & a.* megalomaniac(-al).
megalosaurio, *m.* (paleontol.) megalosaur.
mégano, *m.* = MÉDANO, dune.
megaterio, *m.* megathere, an extinct animal.
mego, ga, *a.* gentle, mild, meek, peaceful.
megohmio, *m.* (elec.) megohm.
mehari, *m.* a swift African dromedary.
mehedí, *m.* Mahdi, Mohammedan Messiah.
mejana, *f.* islet in the middle of a river.
mejicano, na, *n. & a.* Mexican.
mejido, da, *a.* beaten with sugar and water.
mejilla, *f.* cheek.
mejillón, *m.* a variety of mussel.
mejor. I. *a.* better; best.—**m. postor,** highest
    bidder.—**el m. día,** some fine day.—**lo m.,**
    the best. **II.** *adv.* better; best; rather.—**m.
    dicho,** rather, more properly, more exactly.—
    m. que, rather than, instead of.—**m. que m.,**
    better and better; better yet; all the better, so
    much the better.—**a lo m.,** when least ex-
    pected; perhaps, maybe.—**tanto m.,** so much
    the better.
mejora, *f.* improvement; higher bid; appeal to a
    higher court; special bequest to a lawful heir.
mejorable, *a.* improvable.
mejoramiento, *m.* improvement, melioration.
mejorana, *f.* (bot.) sweet marjoram.
mejorar. I. *va.* to improve, better, enhance; to
    outbid; (law) to leave to (an heir) a special be-
    quest besides his legal share. **II.** *vr. & vn.* to
    recover from a disease or calamity; to improve,
    grow better; to reform.
mejoría, *f.* improvement, betterment; advan-
    tage; superiority; improvement in health.
mejunje, *m.* medicinal or cosmetic mixture.
melada, *f.* toast soaked in honey.
melado, da. I. *pp.* of MELAR. **II.** *a.* honey-col-
    ored. **III.** *m.* cane-juice sirup; honey cake.
meladora, *f.* third sugar boiling pan in a triple-
    effect apparatus.
meladucha, *f.* coarse, mealy apple.
meladura, *f.* concentrated sirup, treacle.
meláfido, *m.* (geol.) melaphyre.
melampo, *m.* (theat.) candle with shade.
melancolía, *f.* melancholia, gloom, blues.
melancólico, ca, *a.* melancholy, sad, gloomy.
melancolizar, *va.* to affect with melancholy, to
    render gloomy and dejected, to dispirit.
melandro, *m.* (zool.) badger.
melanemia, *f.* (med.) melanæmia.
melanesio, sia, *n. & a.* Melanesian.
melanita, *f.* (min.) melanite.
melanosis, *f.* (med.) melanosis, black cancer.
melapia, *f.* a variety of apple.
¹**melar,** *va. (ind.* MIELO; *subj.* MIELE) in sugar
    works, to boil clear; (of bees) to fill (the combs)
    with honey.
²**melar,** *a.* honey-sweet.
melastomáceo, a. I. *a.* (bot.) melastomaceous.
    II. *f. pl.* Melastomaceae.
melaza, *f.* molasses; dregs of honey.
melca, *f.* = ZAHINA, (bot.) sorghum.
melcocha, *f.* molasses candy, taffy.
melcochero, ra, *n.* taffy maker or seller.
¹**melena,** *f.* long hair in men; loose hair in women;
    animal mane; fleecy skin put under a yoke.—
    traer a la m., to compel, force.
²**melena,** *f.* (med.) melaena, intestinal hemor-
    rhage.
meleno, na, *n.* (coll.) rude, unkempt person.
melenudo, da, *a.* having bushy hair.
melera, *f.* woman who sells honey; melons
    spoiled by rain; (bot.) BUGLOSA, alkanet.

melero, *m.* dealer in honey; place where honey
    is kept.
melgacho, *m.* (ichth.) dogfish.
melgar, *m.* patch of wild alfalfa.
melgarejo, *m.* fish line and hook with a white rag
    for bait; (Bol.) a 30-cent coin.
meliáceo, a. I. *a.* (bot.) meliaceous. **II.** *pl. f.*
    Meliaceæ.
mélico, ca, *a.* lyrical, melic.
melífago, ga, *a.* meliphagous, feeding on honey.
melífero, ra, *a.* melliferous.
melificado, da, *a.* mellifluous, mellificent.
melificar, *vn.* (of bees) to make honey.
melifluamente, *adv.* mellifluently.
melifluidad, *f.* mellifluence.
melifluo, flua, *a.* mellifluous, honeyed, honey-
    tongued.
¹**meliloto, ta,** *a.* silly, stupid.
²**meliloto,** *m.* (bot.) melilot, sweet clover.
melindre, *m.* a sort of fritter; lady finger; narrow
    ribbon; fastidiousness; prudery.
melindrear, *vn.* to act the prude.
melindrería, *f.* prudery; fastidiousness.
melindrero, ra. = MELINDROSO.
melindrillo, *m.* ferret, narrow tape.
melindroso, sa, *a.* finical, prudish.
melinita, *f.* melinite, a high explosive.
melisa, *f.* (bot.) melissa, balm.
melito, *m.* (pharm.) melissic sirup.
melocotón, *m.* (bot.) peach tree; peach.
melocotonero, ra. I. *n.* vender of peaches. **II.**
    m. peach tree.
melodía, *f.* (mus.) melody, melodiousness.
melodiosamente, *adv.* melodiously.
melodioso, sa, *a.* melodious.
melodrama, *m.* melodrama.
melodramáticamente, *adv.* melodramatically.
melodramático, ca, *a.* melodramatic.
melófago, *m.* parasitic insect in sheep's wool.
melografía, *f.* art of writing music.
meloja, *f.* metheglin, mead.
melojar, *m.* white-oak plantation.
melojo, *m.* (bot.) a variety of white oak.
melolonta, *m.* (zool.) Melolontha, melolonthine.
melomanía, *f.* fanatic love of music.
melómano, na, *n.* music fanatic.
¹**melón,** *m.* (zool.) = ²MELONCILLO.
²**melón,** *m.* (bot.) melon vine; muskmelon, can-
    taloupe.—**m. de agua,** watermelon.—**melo-
    nar,** *m.* field or bed of melons.—**meloncete,**
    m. dim. small melon.
¹**meloncillo,** *m. dim.* small melon.
²**meloncillo,** *m.* (zool.) a kind of mongoose.
melonero, ra, *n.* melon raiser or dealer.
melopeya, *f.* melopœia, art of making melodies.
melosidad, *f.* sweetness, lusciousness; gentleness.
meloso, sa, *a.* honeylike, sweet; gentle.
melote, *m.* dregs of molasses; preserve made
    with honey.
melsa, *f.* spleen; phlegm, slowness.
mella, *f.* notch, nick, jag in edged tools; dent,
    indentation; hollow, gap.—**hacer m.,** to make
    an impression on the mind; to hurt, damage;
    affect.
mellado, da. I. *pp.* of MELLAR. **II.** *a.* toothless.
mellar, *va.* to jag, indent, notch; to injure (as
    honor, credit).
melliza, *f.* a kind of sausage made with honey.
mellizo, za, *n. & a.* twin (brother, sister).
mellón, *m.* torch made of straw.
membrado, da, *a.* (her.) membered.
membrana, *f.* membrane.—**m. alantoides,**
    allantoid membrane.—**m. caduca,** decidua.—
    m. nictitante, nictitating membrane.—**m.
    pituitaria,** pituitary membrane, mucous
    membrane of the nostrils.
membranáceo, cea, *a.* (bot., zool.) membrana-
    ceous.
membranoso, sa, *a.* membranous.

membrete, *m.* memorandum, note; card of invitation; address; letter-head; heading.

membrilla, *f.* (bot.) a variety of quince.

membrillar, *m.* quince-tree orchard.

membrillero, *m.* (bot.) quince tree.

membrillo, *m.* quince; quince tree.

membrudamente, *adv.* robustly, strongly.

membrudo, da, *a.* strong, robust, muscular.

memento, *m.* (eccl.) Memento.

memo, ma, *a.* silly, foolish.

memorable, *a.* memorable.

memorablemente, *adv.* memorably.

memorando, da, *a.* = MEMORABLE.

memorándum, *m.* notebook; memorandum, note.

memorar, *va.* to remember.

memoratísimo, ma, *a. super.* worthy of eternal memory.

memoria, *f.* memory; recollection, remembrance; souvenir; memorial, memento, monumental record; report, statement; essay, paper, article; memorandum; codicil.—*pl.* compliments, regards; memoranda; rings used as reminders; memoirs.—**m. resbaladiza**, treacherous memory.—**de m.**, by heart.—**hablar de m.**, to talk at random.—**hacer m.**, to remember.—**renovar la m.**, to be reminiscent, to reminisce.—**tener en m.**, to remember.—**traer a la m. de uno**, to remind one.

memorial, *m.* memorandum book; memorial, petition; (law) brief.

memorialesco, ca, *a.* (humor.) pertaining to a memorial.

memorialista, *m.* amanuensis, secretary.

memorión, *m. aug.* great memory.

memorioso, sa, *a.* mindful, thoughtful.

¹**mena**, *f.* (ichth.) small sea fish.

²**mena**, *f.* (min.) ore.

³**mena**, *f.* (naut.) size of cordage; (P. I.) size and shape of a cigar.

ménade, *f.* bacchante; woman in a frenzy.

menador, ra, *n.* winder of silk.

menaje, *m.* household furniture and other goods; school supplies or equipment.

menar, *va.* to wind (silk) on a jenny.

mención, *f.* mention.—**en m.**, mentioned, in question.—**mencionar**, *va.* to mention.

mendaz, *a.* mendacious, untruthful.

mendicación, *f.* begging.

mendicante. I. *a.* mendicant, begging. II. *m.* mendicant, beggar.

mendicidad, *f.* mendicity, mendicancy.

mendigante, ta, *n.* mendicant, beggar.

mendigar, *va.* & *vn.* (*pret.* MENDIGUÉ; *subj.* MENDIGUE) to beg, mendicate; to entreat.

mendigo, ga, *n.* mendicant, beggar.

mendigué, mendigue, *v.* V. MENDIGAR.

mendíguez, *f.* beggary, mendicancy.

mendosamente, *adv.* falsely; mistakenly.

mendoso, sa, *a.* mendacious; mistaken.

mendrugo, *m.* crumb of bread given to beggars.

mendruguillo, *m. dim.* small crumb of bread.

meneador, ra, *n.* stirrer, shaker.

menear. I. *va.* to stir; to shake; to wag, waggle; to manage, direct.—**mejor es no meneallo**, or **peor es meneallo**, better let it alone; the less said, the better. II. *vr.* (coll.) to hustle, be active, get a move on; to wriggle, waggle, waddle.

meneo, *m.* shake, shaking; wagging, wriggling, waddling; (coll.) drubbing, beating; (aer.) bump, bumping, jolt due to air currents.

menester, *m.* need, want; employment, occupation, office.—*pl.* natural or bodily necessities; implements, tools of trade.—**haber m.**, to need.—**ser m.**, to be necessary.

menesteroso, sa, *a.* & *n.* needy, indigent (person).

menestra, *f.* pottage; vegetable soup.

menestral, *m.* mechanic, handicraftsman, workman.

menestrete, *m.* (naut.) nail puller.

menfita. I. *n.* native of Memphis. II. *f.* (min.) onyx.

mengajo, *m.* trailing rag.

Mengano, na, *n.* So-and-So.—**Fulano, Zutano y M.**, Tom, Dick and Harry.

mengua, *f.* diminution, waning, decrease; lack, want; poverty, indigence; disgrace.

menguadamente, *adv.* ignominiously.

menguado, da. I. *pp.* of MENGUAR. II. *a.* impaired, stunted; cowardly, pusillanimous; foolish; mean, miserly. III. *n.* poltroon; silly person; miser. IV. *m.* decrease; narrowing of stockings, in knitting.

menguamiento, *m.* = MENGUA.

menguante. I. *a.* decreasing, diminishing. II. *f.* ebb tide, low water, neap tide; decline, decay; decrease of the moon.

menguar, *vn.* to diminish, decrease, wane, fall off; to narrow (stockings).

mengue, *m.* (coll.) the deuce, the devil.

menhir, *m.* menhir, an upright slender monolith.

menina, *f.* young lady in attendance on the queen or the princesses.

meninge, *f.* (anat.) meninges.—**meníngeo, a**, *a.* meningeal.—**meningitis**, *f.* meningitis.

menino, *m.* noble page of the queen and princesses of Spain; little coxcomb.

menique, *a.* little finger.

menisco, *m.* (phys.) meniscus.

menispermáceo, a. I. *a.* (bot.) menispermaceous. II. *f. pl.* Menispermaceæ.

menjuí, *m.* = BENJUÍ, benzoin.

menjunje, menjurje, *m.* = MEJUNJE, medicinal or cosmetic mixture.

menologio, *m.* (eccl.) menology.

menopausia, *f.* (med.) menopause, change of life in women.

menor. I. *a. compar.* of PEQUEÑO: smaller, less; smallest, least; minor; younger; youngest; (mus.) minor.—**m. edad**, minority, under age. —II. *n.* minor; (logic) minor premise; (mus.) minor; Minorite, Franciscan; (arch.) small block.—*pl.* (eccl.) minor orders.—**m. de edad**, minor.—**por m.**, by retail; minutely.

menorete.—**al m.**, or **por el m.**, (coll.) at least.

menoría, *f.* inferiority, subordination; under age.

menorista, *n.* (Am.) retail merchant.

menorquín, na, *a.* of or pertaining to Minorca.

menorragia, *f.* (med.) menorrhagia.

menos. I. *a.* less; least. II. *adv.* less; least.—**m. de**, or **m. que**, less than.—**al m.**, or **a lo m.**, at least; at the least.—**a m. de** (foll. by *inf.*), without (foll. by *pres. p.*).—**a m. que**, unless. —**de m.**, less; wanting, missing.—**echar m.**, to miss, feel the absence of; to have (inadvertently) left behind, come away without.—**en m.**, less; by less.—**lo m. posible**, the least possible.—**no ser para m.**, to give good cause or reason, justify (*estamos alarmados, pues las noticias no son para menos*, we are alarmed, as the news gives good reason to be; or considering the news, we may well be alarmed).—**poco más o m.**, more or less, about.—**por m. que**, almost, pretty nearly.—**por lo m.** = AL M.—**venir a m.**, to decline, grow worse; to become poor. III. *prep.* minus, less (*cuatro menos dos*, four minus two; *las ocho menos veinte*, twenty minutes to eight—lit. eight o'clock less twenty); except, but, barring.—**todo m. eso**, anything but that, all but that.

menoscabador, ra, *n.* & *a.* impairer(-ing); defamer(-ing).

menoscabar, *va.* to impair, lessen, deteriorate, damage, harm; to defame.

menoscabo, *m.* impairment, damage, detriment, loss.—**con m. de**, to the detriment of.

menoscuenta, *f.* payment on account.

For pronunciation, see the rules at the beginning of the book.

menospreciablemente, *adv.* contemptuously.

menospreciador, ra, *n.* contemner, despiser.

menospreciar, *va.* to underrate, undervalue; to despise, contemn, slight.—**menospreciativo, va,** *a.* despising, slighting, contemptuous.—**menosprecio,** *m.* undervaluation; contempt, scorn.

menostasia, *f.* (med.) amenorrhea.

mensaje, *m.* message; errand.

mensajería, *f.* stage line; steamship line.

mensajero, ra. I. *n.* messenger, carrier; errand boy or girl. II. *m.* (naut.) bull's-eye traveller; wooden thimble.

menstruación, *f.* menstruation.

menstrual, *a.* menstrual.

menstrualmente, *adv.* monthly, menstrually.

menstruante, *a.* menstruating.

menstruar, *vn.* to menstruate.

menstruo, a. I. *a.* monthly, menstrual. II. *m.* menses, courses; menstruation; (chem.) menstruum, a solvent.

menstruoso, sa. I. *a.* menstruous. II. *f.* (med.) menstruating female.

mensual, *a.* monthly.—**mensualidad,** *f.* monthly salary or allowance; monthly installment.—**mensualmente,** *adv.* monthly.

ménsula, *f.* (arch.) bracket; rest for the elbows.

mensura, *f.* measure.

mensurabilidad, *f.* mensurability.

mensurable, *a.* mensurable.

mensurador, ra, *n.* measurer, meter.

mensural, *a.* mensural.

mensurar, *va.* to measure.

menta, *f.* (bot.) mint; peppermint.

mentado, da. I. *pp.* of MENTAR. II. *a.* famous or renowned; spoken-of.

mental, *a.* mental.—**mentalidad,** *f.* mentality.—**mentalmente,** *adv.* mentally.

mentar, *va.* (*ind.* MIENTO; *subj.* MIENTE) to mention, name.

mentastro, *m.* (bot.) = MASTRANZO, a mint.

mente, *f.* mind, understanding; sense, meaning; will, disposition.

mentecatada, mentecatería, mentecatez, *f.* foolishness, silliness, nonsense.

mentecato, ta. I. *a.* silly, foolish, stupid, crack-brained. II. *n.* fool.

mentidero, *m.* (coll.) place where people meet and gossip.

mentido, da. I. *pp.* of MENTIR. II. *a.* false, delusive.

mentir. I. *vn.* (*ind.* MIENTO; *subj.* MIENTA) to lie, prevaricate; to deceive, be misleading.—¡miento! I am mistaken (gen. to correct one's own statement). II. *va.* to disappoint, to fail to keep one's word or promise to.

mentira, *f.* lie, falsehood; fib; error, mistake in writing; (coll.) white spot on the nails.—**de mentiras,** in jest.—**parece m.,** it seems impossible, or incredible.

mentirilla, *f. dim.* little fib.—**de mentirillas,** in jest, for fun.

mentirón, *m. aug.* great lie.

mentirosamente, *adv.* lyingly, deceitfully.

mentirosito, ta, *a. dim.* little fibbing.

mentiroso, sa, *a.* lying, mendacious; deceptive, deceitful; full of errors or misprints.

mentís, *m.* act of giving the lie.—**dar un m.,** to belie; to give the lie.

mentol, *m.* (pharm.) menthol.

mentón, *m.* point of the chin; undershot jaw.

mentor, *m.* mentor, counsellor, guide.

menú, *m.* (Gal.) menu, bill of fare.

menuceles, *m. pl.* tithe of the lesser fruits.

menudamente, *adv.* minutely.

menudear. I. *va.* to do over and over again; to repeat; to sell by retail. II. *vn.* to occur frequently; to go into details; to describe little things; (com.) to sell by retail.

menudencia, *f.* trifle; minuteness, minute accuracy.—*pl.* small matters; pork sausages.

menudeo, *m.* act of repeating minutely; (com.) retail.—**al m.,** by retail.

menudero, ra, *n.* dealer in tripe, giblets, sausages, etc.

menudillo, *m.* extremities of animals.—*pl.* giblets of fowls.

menudo, da. I. *a.* small, little; minute; insignificant; common, vulgar; small (money, change); exact, scrupulous; mean, stingy. II. *m.* small coins, change; (sometimes *pl.*) entrails, insides (of an animal); tithe of minor produce.—**a m.,** often, frequently.

meñique. I. *a.* little (finger); (coll.) very small, tiny. II. *m.* little finger.

meollar, *m.* (naut.) spun yarn.

meollo, *m.* brain; marrow; kernel, pith; judgment, understanding, brains; substance.

meple, *m.* (bot.) maple.—**m. moteado,** bird's-eye maple.

mequetrefe, *m.* jackanapes, coxcomb.

meramente, *adv.* merely, solely, purely.

merar, *va.* to mix with water.

merca, *f.* (coll.) purchase.

mercachifle, *m.* peddler, hawker, huckster; petty jobber.

mercadear, *vn.* to trade, deal, traffic.

mercader, *m.* merchant, dealer, shopkeeper.—**m. de grueso,** wholesale dealer.—**mercadera,** *f.* shopkeeper's wife; tradeswoman.

mercadería, *f.* commodity, merchandise; trade.—*pl.* goods, wares, merchandise.

mercado, *m.* market, mart; market place.—**m. de valores,** stock market.

mercaduría, *f.* merchandise; trade.

mercal, *m.* an ancient Spanish copper coin.

mercancía, *f.* trade, traffic; merchandise, goods, wares.

mercante. I. *n. & a.* dealer(-ing), trader(-ing). II. *a.* merchant, mercantile, commercial.

mercantil, *a.* commercial, mercantile.

mercantilismo, *m.* mercantilism, commercialism.

mercantilmente, *adv.* commercially.

mercantivo, va, *a.* = MERCANTIL.

mercar, *va.* (*pret.* MERQUÉ; *subj.* MERQUE) to buy, purchase.

merced, *f.* gift, favor, grace; mercy; wages; will, pleasure; courteous appellation given to untitled persons, as *vuestra,* or *vuesa, merced,* your honor, your grace, your worship, sir; **la M.,** a religious order.—**m. a,** thanks to.—**m. de agua,** free distribution of water for irrigation.—**m. de tierra,** grant of land.—**a la m. de,** at the mercy of.—**estar a m. de,** to live at the expense of.—**hágame Vd. la m.,** do me the favor, please.—**muchas mercedes,** many thanks.

mercenario, ria. I. *a.* mercenary. II. *n.* member of the religious order of **la Merced;** mercenary soldier; day-laborer, farm hand; substitute.

mercería, *f.* small wares, mercery, haberdashery, notions; (Am.) dry-goods store.

mercerizar, *va.* to mercerize.

mercero, *m.* haberdasher, mercer.

mercurial. I. *a.* mercurial. II. *m.* (bot.) all-good, mercury.

mercúrico, *a.* mercuric.

mercurio, *m.* mercury; (M-, astr.) Mercury.—**m. dulce,** calomel.

mercurioso, sa, *a.* mercurious.

merchante. I. *m.* jobber. II. *a.* trading.

merdellón, na, *n.* (coll.) slovenly servant.

merecedor, ra, *a.* deserving, worthy.

merecer. I. *va.* (*ind.* MEREZCO; *subj.* MEREZCA) to deserve, merit; to obtain, attain; to be worth; to be worthy of; to owe, to be indebted for.—**m. la pena,** to be worthwhile. II. *vn.* to be deserving or worthy.—**m. bien de**, to deserve the gratitude of.

merecidamente, *adv.* deservedly.

merecido, da. I. *pp.* of MERECER. II. *a.* deserved. III. *m.* condign punishment.

mereciente, *a.* deserving.

merecimiento, *m.* merit, desert.

merendar. I. *vn.* (*ind.* MERIENDO; *subj.* MERIENDE) to lunch; to have a snack, refreshments; to pry into another's writings or actions. II. *va.* to lunch on.

merendero, ra. I. *a.* (crow) that picks up the seeds in cornfields. II. *m.* lunch room.

merendilla, ita, *f.* dim. light luncheon.

merendona, *f. aug.* splendid luncheon or supper.

merengue, *m.* kiss, sugarplum, meringue.

meretricio, cia, *a.* meretricious.

meretriz, *f.* strumpet.

merey, *f.* (bot.) cashew tree.

merezco, merezca, *v. V.* MERECER.

mergánsar, *m.* (ornith.) goosander, merganser.

mergo, *m.* (ornith.) diver.

meridiana, *f.* litter, cot bed; (astr., surv.) meridian (line); (coll.) afternoon nap.—**a la m.**, at noon.

meridiano, na. I. *a.* meridian; meridional (section, cut). II. *m.* meridian.

meridional, *a.* southern, southerly.

merienda, *f.* lunch, luncheon; snack; light meal; (coll.) humpback.—**m. de negros**, hodgepodge, confusion, bedlam.

meriendo, meriende, *v. V.* MERENDAR.

merindad, *f.* district of the jurisdiction of a MERINO.

merino, na. I. *a.* merino. II. *m.* royal judge and superintendent of sheepwalks; shepherd of merino sheep; merino sheep, wool, and cloth.

méritamente, *adv.* = MERECIDAMENTE.

meritísimo, ma, *a. super.* most worthy.

mérito, *m.* merit, desert, worth; excellence, virtue, value.—**méritos de un proceso**, (law) merits of a case.—**hacer m. de**, to mention.—**hacer méritos**, to make oneself deserving.

meritoriamente, *adv.* meritoriously.

meritorio, ria. I. *a.* meritorious, worthy, deserving. II. *n.* employee that begins work without a salary.

merla, *f.* (ornith.) blackbird, merle.

¹merlín, *m.* (naut.) marline.

²merlín, *m.* merlin.—**saber más que M.**, to be very shrewd or keen.

merlo, *m.* (ichth.) a seafish.

merlón, *m.* (fort.) merlon.

merluza, *f.* (ichth.) hake, merluce.

merma, *f.* decrease; waste, leakage; shrinkage.

mermar. I. *vn.* to decrease, wear away, be consumed, shrink. II. *va.* to lessen, reduce, decrease.

mermelada, *f.* marmalade.

¹mero, ra, *a.* mere, pure, simple.

²mero, *m.* (ichth.) a Mediterranean sea bass.

merodeador, *m.* marauder.

merodear, *vn.* to maraud.—**merodeo**, *m.* marauding.

merodista, *n.* marauder.

merovingio, gia, *a.* Merovingian.

merqué, merque, *v. V.* MERCAR.

mes, *m.* month; menses, courses; monthly wages. —**meses mayores**, last months of pregnancy; months immediately preceding harvest.

mesa, *f.* table; table-land, plateau; landing of a staircase; executive board; business section of a public office or department; rents of cathedral churches, prelates, or dignitaries in Spain; billiard table; billiard game; flat of a blade; (jewelry) face of a gem; (eccl.) communion table; fare, viands set on a table.—**m. de altar**, altar. —**m. de Ampère**, (phys.) Ampère's stand.— **m. de batalla**, sorting table (in postoffice).— **m. de cambios**, bank.—**m. de noche**, night commode.—**m. redonda**, round table; unceremonious or informal table; table for regular boarders.—**m. franca**, open table.—**mesas de guarnición**, (naut.) channels.—**a m. puesta**, without care or expense.—**media m.**, second table; lower-priced or servants' table.—**alzar la m.**, to clear off the table.—**poner la m.**, to set the table.

mesada, *f.* monthly pay, wages, or allowance.

mesadura, *f.* tearing the hair.

mesana, *f.* (naut.) mizzenmast or sail.

mesar, *va.* to tear out (the hair or beard).

mescolanza, *f.* medley, mess, jumble.

meseguería, *f.* harvest watch; money paid for watching the harvest.

meseguero, ra. I. *a.* pertaining to the harvest. II. *m.* harvest or vineyard watchman.

mesentérico, ca, *a.* (anat.) mesenteric.

mesenterio, *m.* (anat.) mesentery.

mesenteritis, *f.* (med.) mesenteritis.

meseraico, ca, *a.* (anat.) mesenteric.

mesero, *m.* journeyman who works for monthly wages.

meseta, *f.* landing of a staircase; table-land, plateau.—**m. de guarnición**, (naut.) backstay stool.

mesiánico, ca, *a.* Messianic.

mesianismo, *n.* Messianism.

Mesías, *m.* Messiah.

mesiazgo, *m.* Messiahship.

mesidor, *m.* Messidor, tenth month of the French-Revolution calendar.

mesilla, *f. dim.* small table; sideboard; board wages; censure by way of a jest; window sill.— **m. corrida**, quarter pace of a staircase.—**m. quebrantada**, half pace, foot-rest.

mesillo, *m.* first menses after parturition.

mesita, *f. dim.* small table; stand.

mesmedad, *f.*—**por su misma m.** (coll.) by the very fact.

mesmerismo, *m.* mesmerism.

mesmo, ma, *a.* (obs.) = MISMO, same; similar.

mesnada, *f.* armed retinue.

mesnadería, *f.* wages of a MESNADA.

mesnadero, *m.* member of a MESNADA.

mesoblasto, *m.* (biol.) mesoblast.

mesocarpio, *m.* (bot.) mesocarp.

mesocracia, *f.* government by the middle class.

mesodérmico, ca, *a.* mesodermic.

mesodermo, *m.* mesoderm.

mesogastrio, *m.* (anat.) mesogastrium, umbilical region.

mesología, *f.* ecology.

mesón, *m.* inn, hostelry, tavern.

mesonaje, *m.* place containing numerous inns.

mesonero, ra. I. *a.* pertaining to an inn. II. *n.* innkeeper, host, hostess.

mesonista, *a.* pertaining to an inn.

mesopotámico, ca, *n. & a.* Mesopotamian.

mesotorácico, ca, *a.* (entom.) mesothoracic.

mesotórax, *m.* (entom.) mesothorax.

mesozoario, ria, *a.* mesozoan.

mesozoico, ca, *a.* (geol.) Mesozoic.

mesta, *f.* union of cattle raisers; confluence of two or more streams.

mestal, *m.* brake of prickly oaks.

mesteño, ña, *a.* belonging to the MESTA; MOSTRENCO, homeless, stray; stupid; fat.

mestizaje, *m.* (Am.) crossing of races (gen. app. to white and Indian).

mestizar, *va.* to cross (breeds).

mestizo, za. I. *a.* hybrid. II. *n. & a.* half-breed.

mesto, *m.* (bot.) large, prickly oak; turkey oak.

mestura, *f.* mashlin, mixed wheat and rye.

mesura, *f.* dignified deportment; civility, politeness; moderation.

mesuradamente, *adv.* slowly, prudently, moderately.

mesurado, da. I. *pp.* of MESURAR. II. *a.* moderate, circumspect, temperate.

For pronunciation, see the rules at the beginning of the book.

mesurar. I. *va.* to inspire moderation in. **II.** *vr.* to control oneself.

meta, *f.* boundary, finish line; goal, aim.

metabólico, ca, *a.* metabolic.

metabolismo, *m.* metabolism.

metacarpo, *m.* (anat.) metacarpus.

metacentro, *m.* metacenter.

metacronismo, *m.* metachronism.

metafísica, *f.* metaphysics.

metafísicamente, *adv.* metaphysically.

metafísico, ca. I. *a.* metaphysical. **II.** *m.* metaphysician.

metáfora, *f.* metaphor.

metafóricamente, *adv.* metaphorically.

metafórico, ca, *a.* metaphorical.

metaforizar, *va.* to use metaphors.

metagoge, *f.* (rhet.) a kind of metaphor.

metal, *m.* metal; tone or timbre of the voice; (mus.) brass orchestral instruments; quality, nature, or condition.—**m. antifricción,** babbitt metal.—**m. blanco,** nickel silver; babbitt metal.—**m. campanil,** or **de campanas,** bell metal.—**m. de imprenta,** type metal.—**m. desplegado,** expanded metal.—**m. Muntz,** Muntz metal, yellow metal.

metalario, ria, *n.* metallist, metal worker.

metalepsis, *f.* (rhet.) metalepsis.

metálica, *f.* metallurgy.

metalicé, metalice, *v. V. METALIZAR.*

metálico, ca. I. *a.* metallic; medallic. **II.** *m.* specie, hard cash.—**m. en caja,** (com.) cash on hand.

metalífero, ra, *a.* (poet.) metalliferous.

metalista, *n.* metal worker.

metalistería, *f.* metal work.

metalización, *f.* (chem.) converting into metal.

metalizar. I. *va.* (*pret.* METALICÉ; *subj.* METALICE) (chem.) to convert into metal. **II.** *vr.* to be converted into or impregnated with metal; to become controlled by love of money, to become mercenary.

metalografía, *f.* metallography.

metaloide, *m.* (chem.) metalloid.

metaloterapia, *f.* (med.) metallotherapy.

metalurgia, *f.* metallurgy.

metalúrgico, ca. I. *a.* metallurgic, metallurgical. **II.** *n.* metallurgist.

metalla, *f.* scraps of gold-leaf for mending.

metamería, *f.* (chem., zool.) metamerism.

metámero, ra, *a.* (chem., zool.) metameric.

metamórfico, ca, *a.* (geol.) metamorphic.

metamorfismo, *m.* (geol.) metamorphism.

metamorfosear, *va. & vr.* to metamorphose, to transform.

metamorfosi, metamorfosis, *f.* metamorphosis, transformation.

metano, *m.* (chem.) methane.

metaplasmo, *m.* (gram.) metaplasm.

metástasis, *f.* (med.) metastasis.

metatarsiano, na, *a.* (anat.) metatarsal.

metatarso, *m.* (anat.) metatarsus.

metate, *m.* (Mex.) curved stone for grinding maize or cocoa.

metátesis, *f.* (rhet.) metathesis.

meteco, ca, *a. & n.* foreign(-er).

metedor, ra. I. *n.* one who puts in or introduces; smuggler. **II.** *m.* baby's swaddling clothes.

meteduría, *f.* smuggling.

metempsicosis, metempsícosis, *f.* metempsychosis.

metemuertos, *m.* (theat.) stage hand; busybody.

meteórico, ca, *a.* meteoric.

meteorismo, *m.* (med.) meteorism, flatulence.

meteorito, *m.* meteorite.

meteorización, *f.* (agr.) influence of atmospheric phenomena on the soil.

meteorizar. I. *va.* (med.) to cause flatulence. **II.** *vr.* (med.) to suffer from flatulence; (agr.) (of soil) to be influenced by atmospheric phenomena.

metéoro, meteoro, *m.* atmospheric phenomenon; meteor.

meteorología, *f.* meteorology.

meteorológico, ca, *a.* meteorological.

meteorologista; meteorólogo, ga, *n.* meteorologist.

meter. I. *va.* to put in, insert, introduce, inclose; to smuggle; to make (as a noise); cause (as fear); tell (as fibs); to induce, get (one into a business, etc.); to stake, put to hazard; to invest; to cram down (food); to put close together, cram together; to impose upon, to deceive; to compress, straighten, reduce; (coll.) to eat; (naut.) to take in (sail).—**m. bulla, to** make a noise.—**m. su cucharada,** to put in one's oar, to butt in.—**m. zizaña,** to sow discord.—**meterlo a bulla,** to carry off the matter with a joke. **II.** *vr.* to meddle, intrude, interfere; to be too familiar; to choose, take up a profession or trade; to plunge into vice; (of rivers) to empty; to attack sword in hand.—**m. a,** to become; to undertake to; to set oneself up as, pretend to be.—**m. con,** to pick a quarrel with.—**m. en,** (coll.) to meddle with, poke one's nose into.—**m. en profundidades,** (fig.) to get beyond one's depth.—**m. mar adentro,** (of sea bathing) to go beyond one's depth.

metesillas, *m.* (theat.) stage hand.

meticulosidad, *f.* fear, shyness.

meticuloso, sa, *a.* pusillanimous, shy.

metidillo, *m.* baby's swaddling clothes.

metido, da. I. *pp.* of METER. **II.** *a.* abounding; close, tight; engaged; interested. **III.** *m.* blow with the fist on the throat; strong lye or buck; (sew.) material allowed in seams; METIDILLO. **IV.** *f.* (coll.) lecture, dressing down.

metilamina, *f.* (chem.) methylamine.

metileno, *m.* (chem.) methylene.

metílico, ca, *a.* (chem.) methylic.

metilo, *m.* (chem.) methyl.

metimiento, *m.* insertion, introduction.

metódicamente, *adv.* methodically.

metódico, ca, *a.* methodical.

metodismo, *m.* (eccl.) Methodism.

metodista, *n. & a.* Methodist.

metodizar, *va. & vn.* (*pret.* METODICÉ; *subj.* METODICE) to systematize.

método, *m.* method; technique.—**metodología,** *f.* methodology.

metonimia, *f.* (rhet.) metonymy.

metonímico, ca, *a.* metonymical.

métopa, *f.* (arch.) metope.

metoposcopia, *f.* metoposcopy.

metralla, *f.* (artil.) grapeshot, case shot, canister shot.

metrallazo, *m.* discharge of grapeshot.

métrica, *f.* metrical art, poesy.

métricamente, *adv.* metrically.

métrico, ca, *a.* metric, metrical.

metrificación, *f.* verse making.

metrificador, ra; metrista, *n.* versifier.

metrificar, *vn.* to write verses.

metritis, *f.* (med.) metritis.

¹**metro,** *m.* meter, unit of length; (poet.) meter.

²**metro,** *m. abbr.* of METROPOLITANO, subway (train).

metrología, *f.* metrology.

metrónomo, *m.* (mus.) metronome.

metrópoli, *f.* metropolis; archiepiscopal church; mother country.

metropolitano, na. I. *a.* metropolitan. **II.** *m.* archbishop; subway or elevated train.

metrorragia, *f.* (med.) metrorrhagia.

metroscopio, *m.* (med.) metroscope.

metrotomía, *f.* (surg.) hysterotomy.

metrótomo, *m.* (surg.) metrotome, hysterotome.

mexicano, na, *n. & a.* Mexican.

meya, *f.* spider crab. Also NOCA.

mezala, *m.* oratory, place for prayer.

mezcal, *m.* (Mex.) a species of maguey; pulque.

mezcla, *f.* mixture; mixing; mortar; mixed cloth.

mezcladamente, *adv.* promiscuously; mixedly.

mezclador, ra, *n. & a.* mixer(-ing).

mezcladura, *f.*; **mezclamiento,** *m.* mixture; mixing.

mezclar. I. *va.* to mix, mingle; blend. **II.** *vr.* to mix; to intermarry; to intermeddle; to take part.

mezclilla, *f.* pepper-and-salt cloth.

mezcolanza, *f.* (coll.) medley, hodgepodge, mishmash, jumble.

mezo, meza, *v. V.* MECER.

mezquinamente, *adv.* stingily, niggardly.

mezquindad, *f.* niggardliness, stinginess, paltriness, currishness, meanness; penury, indigence.

mezquino, na, *a.* niggardly, stingy, mean, paltry, miserly; indigent, needy; diminutive; petty, minute, puny.

mezquita, *f.* mosque.

mezquital, *m.* clump of mesquite shrubs.

mezquite, *m.* (Mex.) (bot.) mesquite.

¹mi, *m.* (mus.) mi, E, third note of the scale.

²mi, *1st pers. sing. poss. pron.* (*pl.* MIS), my.

mí, *pers. pron. oblique case of pron.* YO, *used after a prep.* me.—¡a m. qué! (Am.) I don't care!

miaja, *f.* crumb; bit.

miar, *vn.* to mew, as a cat.

miasma, *m.* miasma.—*pl.* miasmata.

miasmático, ca, *a.* miasmatic.

miau, *m.* mew of a cat.

¹mica, *f.* (min.) mica, isinglass.

²mica, *f.* female monkey; (C. A.) flirt.

micáceo, cea, *a.* micaceous, micalike.

micacita, *f.m.* (geol.) micaschist.

micado, *m.* Mikado.

micasquisto, *m.* = MICACITA.

micción, *f.* micturition, passing urine.

micer, *m.* ancient title of respect, mister.

mico, *m.* monkey; (coll.) lascivious man.—**dar,** or **hacer, m. a,** to disappoint by not keeping an engagement.

micosis, *f.* (med.) mycosis.

micra, *f.* = MICRÓN.

microbiano, na, *a.* microbian.

microbicida, *n. & a.* germ-killing (agent).

microbio, *m.* microbe, bacterium.

microbiología, *f.* microbiology, bacteriology.

microbiológico, ca, *a.* bacteriological.

microbiólogo, ga, *n.* bacteriologist.

microcefalia, *f.* microcephaly, microcephalism.

microcéfalo, la, *a.* microcephalic, microcephalous.

microcito, *m.* (med.) microcyte.

micrococo, *m.* micrococcus.

microcosmo, *m.* microcosm.

micrófito, *m.* = MICROBIO, microbe.

micrófono, *m.* microphone.

microfotografía, *f.* microphotography.

micrografía, *f.* micrography.

micrográfico, ca, *a.* micrographic.

micrógrafo, *m.* micrograph.

microhmio, *m.* (elec.) microhm.

microlítico, ca, *a.* (geol.) microlithic.

microlito, *m.* (geol.) microlite.

micrométrico, ca, *a.* micrometric.

micrómetro, *m.* micrometer.

micromilímetro, *m.* = MICRÓN.

micrón, *m.* micron, one thousandth of a millimeter.

microorganismo, *m.* = MICRORGANISMO.

micrópilo, *m.* (zool. and bot.) micropyle.

microrganismo, *m.* microörganism.

microscópico, ca, *a.* microscopic.

microscopio, *m.* microscope.

micrótomo, *m.* microtome, cutting instrument for the microscope.

microvoltio, *m.* (elec.) microvolt, one millionth of a volt.

michito, *m. dim.* kitten, pussy.

micho, cha, *m. & f.* (coll.) puss, cat.

mida, *m.* mida, bean fly.

mido, mida, midió, etc. *v. V.* MEDIR.

midriasis, *f.* (med.) mydriasis, dilation of the eye.

miedo, *m.* fear, dread, apprehension.—**m. cerval,** fright; great timidity.—**tener m.,** to be afraid, fear.—**miedoso, sa,** *a.* timorous, afraid.

miel, *f.* honey; molasses; cane juice.—**m. de abejas,** bee's honey.—**m. de caña,** sugar-cane syrup.—**m. de purga,** molasses.—**m. rosada,** (pharm.) honey of roses.—**m. virgen,** virgin honey.—**dejar a uno con la miel en los labios,** to snatch an apparently certain success away from one.

¹mielga, *f.* (bot.) wild lucerne.

²mielga, *f.* (ichth.) a kind of dogfish.

³mielga, *f.* (agr.) rake; four-pronged pitchfork; strip of ground to be sown.

⁴mielga, *f.* a girl-twin.

mielgo, ga, *a.* twin.

mielitis, *f.* (med.) myelitis.

miembro, *m.* member; limb; member of a body, community or corporation; branch or part of a whole; (math., arch.) member; (anat.) penis.

mienta, *f.* (bot.) mint.

mientes, *f. pl.* thoughts, ideas.—**parar,** or **poner, m.,** to reflect, to consider.—**traer a las m.,** to remind.—**venir a las m.,** to come to one's mind.

¹miento, miente, *v. V.* MENTAR.

²miento, mienta, *v. V.* MENTIR.

mientras, *adv.* while, whilst, when.—**m. más,** the more.—**m. no,** until.—**m. que,** while, as long as, so long as.—**m. tanto,** meanwhile, in the meantime.

miera, *f.* juniper oil; resin.

miércoles, *m.* Wednesday.—**m. corvillo,** or **de ceniza,** Ash Wednesday.

mierra, *f.* sled, sledge, stone drag.

mies, *f.* ripe wheat and other grain, before thrashing; harvest time; (fig.) multitude converted or ready for conversion.—*pl.* grain fields.

miga, *f.* crumb, soft part of bread; small fragment, bit; (coll.) marrow, substance, pith.—*pl.* fried crumbs.—**hacer buenas** or **malas migas,** (coll.) to agree or disagree readily with one.

migaja, *f.* small crumb or bit of bread; small fragment, chip, or bit; (coll.) little or nothing. —*pl.* leavings; crumbs, bits of food.—**no tener m. de,** (coll.) not to have a particle of.

migajada, *f.* small particle.

migajica, illa, ita, uela, *f. dim.* wee little bit.

migajón, *m. aug.* crumb, without crust; marrow core; pith and substance.

migar, *va.* to crumb (bread); to put (crumbs of) into milk, etc.

migración, *f.* migration.

migraña, *f.* = JAQUECA, migraine, headache.

migratorio, ria, *a.* migrating, migratory.

miguelete, *m.* = MIQUELETE, (mil.) foot-soldier.

miguero, ra, *a.* crummy, pert. to fried crumbs.

mihrab, *m.* mihrab, niche in a mosque.

mijo, *m.* (bot.) millet, panic grass.—**m. ceburro,** white wheat.

mil, *m.* one thousand; one thousandth.—**m. y quinientas,** (coll.) lentils.—**a las m. y quinientas,** at an unearthly hour; after a long time.

miladi, *f.* milady.

milagrero, ra, *n.* miracle monger.

milagro, *m.* miracle; wonder; votive offering hung up in churches.

milagrón, *m.* (coll.) great miracle; gesture of astonishment.

milagrosamente, *adv.* miraculously.

milagroso, sa, *a.* miraculous.

milamores, *f.* (bot.) a species of valerian.

milanés, sa, *n. & a.* Milanese.

¹**milano,** *m.* (ornith.) kite, glede, bird of prey; (ichth.) a sea fish.

²**milano,** *m.* (bot.) bur or down of the thistle.

mildeu, *m.* (bot.) mildew (esp. app. to grape vines).

milenario, ria. I. *a.* millenary. **II.** *m.* millenary; millennium; millenarian, one who expects the millennium.

milenarismo, *m.* doctrine of millenarians.

mileno, na, *a.* pertaining to cloth in which the warp contains a thousand threads.

milenrama, *f.* (bot.) milfoil or yarrow.

milésimo, ma, *n.* & *a.* thousandth.

milesio, ia, *n.* & *a.* Milesian.—**fábula m.,** Milesian tale.

milhojas, *f.* (bot.) yarrow.

miliamperio, *m.* (elec.) milliampere.

miliamperímetro, *m.* (elec.) milliamperimeter.

miliar, *a.* miliary; (med.) miliary.

miliárea, *f.* milliare.

miliario, ria, *a.* pert. to a mile or to miles.

milicia, *f.* science of war; soldiery, military; militiamen.—**m. urbana,** militia.

miliciano, na. I. *a.* military. **II.** *m.* militiaman.

milico, *m.* (Am.) soldier.

miligramo, *m.* milligram.

mililitro, *m.* milliliter.

milímetro, *m.* millimeter.

militante, *a.* militant; military.

¹**militar. I.** *vn.* to serve in the army; to go to war. —**m. contra,** to be against, disprove or weaken (a theory, argument, etc.).—**m. en,** to be in, to belong to (a party, etc.).—**m. en favor de,** to lend weight to, to strengthen, be a reason for (a theory, line of conduct, etc.).

²**militar. I.** *a.* military, soldierly. **II.** *m.* military man.—*pl.* military.—**militarismo,** *m.* militarism.—**militarista,** *n.* & *a.* mitilarist(-ic).— **militarmente,** *adv.* militarily.

milmillonésimo, ma, *n.* & *a.* billionth (thousand-millionth).

milo, *m.* earthworm.

miloca, *f.* (ornith.) a kind of owl.

milocha, *f.* kite (for flying).

milodonte, *m.* (paleontol.) mylodont.

milonga, *f.* (Arg.) kind of popular song; party.

milord, *m.* (*pl.* MILORES) milord; barouche.

milpa, *f.* (Mex.) maize land.

milpiés, *m.* woodlouse.

milréis, *m.* milreis (Portuguese and Brazilian money of account).

milla, *f.* mile.

millar, *m.* thousand; a great number (used in *pl.*); certain quantity of cocoa (varies between 3½ and 4 lb.).

millarada, *f.* about a thousand.—**a millaradas,** by thousands; innumerable times.—**echar millaradas,** to brag of wealth and riches.

millón, *m.* million.—*pl.* ancient excise or duty.

millonario, ria, *n.* & *a.* millionaire.

millonésimo, ma, *n.* & *a.* millionth.

mimado, da, *pp.* & *a.* spoiled, overindulged.

mimar, *va.* to pet, fondle, indulge, spoil (a child).

mimbral, *m.* plantation of osiers.

mimbre, *m.* (bot.) osier, willow; (com.) twig, wicker, withe.

mimbrear, *vn.* to sway.

mimbreño, ña, *a.* osierlike, willowy.

mimbrera, *f.* (bot.) osier, willow.

mimbreral, *m.* place full of willows.

mimbroso, sa, *a.* wickered, osiered.

mimesis, *f.* (rhet.) mimesis.

mimetismo, *m.* (zool.) mimesis.

mímica, *f.* pantomine, sign language.

mímico, ca, *a.* mimic; imitative.

mimo, *m.* buffoon, merry-andrew, mimic; caress, petting, indulgence; prudery.

mimología, *f.* mimology.

mimosa, *f.* (bot.) mimosa, sensitive plant.

mimoso, sa, *a.* fastidious, finicky; soft, spoiled.

¹**mina,** *f.* mine; underground passage or conduit; source, spring; sinecure, (coll.) child's play, snap; (mil., naut.) mine.

²**mina,** *f.* mina, ancient Greek coin.

minador, ra, *n.* miner, sapper; mining engineer.

minal, *a.* pertaining to mines; mine (as *a.*).

minar, *va.* to mine, excavate, dig, burrow; to sap, undermine; to consume, ruin, destroy; to work hard for.

minarete, *m.* minaret.

mineraje, *m.* work of a mine; mining.

mineral. I. *a.* mineral. **II.** *m.* mineral, ore; water spring, fountain-head; rich mine; source.—**m. bruto,** raw ore, rough ore.—**m. virgen,** native ore.

mineralización, *f.* mineralization.

mineralizar. I. *va.* to mineralize. **II.** *vr.* to become mineralized; (of water) to become mineral, or charged with mineral substances.

mineralogía, *f.* mineralogy.

mineralógico, ca, *a.* mineralogical.

mineralogista, *m.* mineralogist.

minería, *f.* mining; force of miners; body of mine operators.

minero, ra. I. *a.* pert. to mines. **II.** *m.* miner; sapper; mine operator; source, origin.

mineromedicinal, *a.* medicinal mineral (waters).

minerva, *f.* (print.) Minerva machine.—**minervista,** *n.* (print.) operator of a Minerva machine.

mingitorio, *m.* upright urinal.

mingo, *m.* red ball or object ball in billiards.

miniar, *va.* (art) to paint in miniature.

miniatura, *f.* (art) miniature.

miniaturista, *n.* miniature painter.

mínima, *f.* slightest thing; (mus.) minim.

mínimo, ma. I. *a.* minimum. **II.** *m.* minimum; (eccl.) Minim.

mínimum, *m.* minimum.

minino, na, *n.* (coll.) kitty, cat.

minio, *m.* (min.) minium, red lead.

ministerial, *a.* ministerial.

ministerialismo, *m.* (pol.) ministerialism.

ministerialmente, *adv.* ministerially.

ministerio, *m.* (pol.) ministry, cabinet; office and term of a cabinet minister; department; building where the department is located; ministration, office, employment; service, agency.—**M. de Estado,** Department of State, or of Foreign Affairs.—**M. de Fomento,** (Spain) Department of Public Works, Agriculture, Commerce, and Manufactures (better left untranslated, calling it Department of Fomento).—**M. de la Gobernación,** Department of the Interior.— **M. de Gracia y Justicia,** Department of Justice and Ecclesiastical Affairs.—**M. de Hacienda,** Treasury Department.—**M. de la Guerra,** War Department.—**M. de lo Interior,** Department of the Interior.—**M. del Trabajo,** Department of Labor.—**M. de Marina,** Navy Department.—**M. de Relaciones Exteriores,** Ministry of Foreign Affairs. (U. S. State Department).

ministra, *f.* woman director; wife of a cabinet minister.

ministrador, ra, *n.* one who directs or ministers.

ministrante. I. *a.* serving, ministering. **II.** *n.* trained nurse.

ministrar, *va.* & *vn.* to minister, to serve, to supply, to furnish.

ministril, *m.* subordinate official; petty officer of justice; player of reed instruments in churches.

ministro, *m.* cabinet minister; minister plenipotentiary; judge or justice; sheriff, bailiff, constable, petty officer of justice; subordinate, agent, servant.—**m. consultante,** minister who lays before the king the opinion of his council.—**m. de Dios,** clergyman.—**M. de Estado,** Minister, or Secretary, of State.—**M. de Fomento,** Secretary, or Minister, of Public

Works, etc. (*V.* MINISTERIO DE FOMENTO).—
M. de Gracia y Justicia, Attorney General.
—**M. de Hacienda,** Minister, or Secretary, of
the Exchequer or Treasury.—**M. de la Gobernación,** Minister, or Secretary, of the Interior.
—**m. del culto, m. del Señor,** clergyman.—
M. de Relaciones Exteriores, Minister, or
Secretary, of Foreign Affairs.—**M. de Relaciones Interiores,** Minister, or Secretary, of
the Interior.—**M. de Salubridad,** Minister,
or Secretary, of Public Health.

mino, na, kitty, pussy (used to call a cat).

minoración, *f.* lessening, diminution.

minorar. I. *va.* to lessen, diminish. **II.** *vr.* to
shrink; to decrease, diminish.

minorativo, va, *a.* lessening; (med.) laxative.

minoría, *f.* minority (in age or in number).

minoridad, *f.* minority (in age), nonage.

minotauro, *m.* Minotaur.

minucia, *f.* minuteness, smallness; mite; small
tithe.—*pl.* minutiae.

minuciosamente, *adv.* minutely, thoroughly.

minuciosidad, *f.* minuteness, thoroughness;
trifle, small detail.

minucioso, sa, *a.* minutely precise, thorough.

minué, *m.* (dance and mus.) minuet.

minuendo, *m.* (arith.) minuend.

minuete, *m.* = MINUÉ.

minúsculo, la. I. *a.* very small, tiny; of little
importance; small (letter). **II.** *f.* small letter,
lower-case letter.

minuta, *f.* minute (as of a méeting); first draft;
memorandum; lawyer's bill; list of employees,
roll (of names); bill of fare.—**a la m.,** (Arg.)
(app. to preparing or serving food) quick, short-
order.

minutar, *va.* to make a draft of, to minute.

minutario, *m.* minute book.

minutero, *m.* minute hand.

minutisa, *f.* (bot.) sweet-william pink.

minuto, ta. I. *a.* minute, small. **II.** *m.* minute
(in time & geom.).—**al m.,** at once, right away.

¹miñón, *m.* light infantry, rural guard; minion.

²miñón, *m.* scoriæ of iron ore.

miñona, *f.* (print.) minion, 7-point type.

mío, mía; míos, mías, *poss. pron.* mine.—**de
m.,** by myself; of my own accord.—**lo m.,**
what belongs to me.—**soy m.,** I am my own
master.

mio, m. = MINO.

miocardio, m. (anat.) myocardium.

miocarditis, *f.* (med.) myocarditis.

mioceno, na, *a.* (geol.) Miocene.

miodinia, *f.* (med.) myodinia, muscular pain.

miografía, *f.* (anat.) myography.

miología, *f.* (anat.) myology.

miope. I. *a.* myopic, near-sighted. **II.** *n.* myope.

miopía, *f.* (opt.) myopia, near-sightedness.

miosis, *f.* (med.) myosis.

miosota, miosotis, *f.* (bot.) forget-me-not.

miquelete, *m.* (mil.) a kind of foot-soldier.

mira, *f.* sight (of firearms and mathematical
instruments); leveling rod; (fort.) watch-tower;
(mason.) rule; care; vigilance; design, purpose,
intention, view.—**m. de corredera,** or **de
mirilla,** target leveling rod.—**m. parlante,**
speaking leveling rod.—**estar a la m.,** to be on
the lookout, to be on the watch.

¡mira! *interj.* look! lo! behold! take care!

mirabel, *m.* (bot.) summer cypress goosefoot;
sunflower.

mirabolano, ⌐*m.* = MIROBÁLANO.

mirada, *f.* glance, gaze, look.—**echar una m.,**
to glance, cast a glance.

miradero, *m.* watch tower, lookout, observatory;
cynosure.

mirado, da. I. *pp.* of MIRAR. **II.** *a.* (when preceded by **muy, tan, más, menos**) considerate,
circumspect, prudent, thoughtful; (when preceded by **bien, mal, mejor, peor**) considered,

reputed.—**bien m.,** (besides the meaning just
given), carefully considered; looking well into
the matter; in fact.

mirador, ra. I. *n.* spectator, looker-on. **II.** *m.*
belvedere, oriel, bay-window, observatory.

miradura, *f.* act of looking.

miraguano, *m.* (bot.) fan palm.

miramamolín, *m.* among Moors, "prince of the
believers."

miramiento, *m.* consideration, reflection; circumspection, prudence; attention, consideration, courtesy.

mirante, *n.* & *a.* looker(-ing).

mirar. I. *va.* to look, look at, look upon or
toward; to gaze, gaze upon; to view, survey; to
see, regard; to consider, think; to have regard
for, esteem; to watch, be careful; to watch, spy;
to notice; to concern.—**m. bien,** to think much
of, esteem; to approve.—**m. de hito en hito,**
to stare at.—**m. de reojo, m. de través,** to
look askance at; to look at out of the corner of
one's eye.—**m. mal,** to disapprove, have a bad
opinion of; to dislike; to consider bad form.—
m. por encima, to examine slightly, glance at.
—**m. sobre el hombro,** to cast a contemptuous look at. **II.** *vn.* to look.—**m. a,** to overlook,
face, front on; to look after, look out for.—**m.
alrededor,** to look around.—**m. en,** to think
over, consider carefully.—**m. por,** to take care
of; look after.—**¡mira!,** look out! (warning or
threat).—**¡mire!** look here! listen!

mirasol, *m.* (bot.) sunflower.

miríada, *f.* myriad, large quantity or number.

miriagramo, *m.* myriagram.

miriámetro, *m.* measure of length, 10,000
meters.

miriápodo, da, *n.* & *a.* myriapodan, centipede.

mirífico, ca, *a.* marvellous, wonderful.

mirilla, *f. dim.* peephole in doors; target (of a
leveling rod).

¹miriñaque, *m.* trinket, bauble, gewgaw.

²miriñaque, *m.* hoop-skirt, crinoline.

miriópodo, = MIRIÁPODO.

mirística, *f.* (bot.) nutmeg tree.

mirla, *f.* (ornith.) blackbird.

mirlamiento, *m.* affected gravity.

mirlarse, *vr.* (coll.) to put on airs.

mirlo, *m.* (ornith.) blackbird; (coll.) air of importance, affected gravity.

mirobálano, *m.* (bot.) myrobalan.

mirón, na, *n.* spectator, looker-on, by-stander;
prier, busybody, gazer.

mirra, *f.* myrrh.—**mirrado, da,** *a.* myrrhic.

mirrauste, *m.* (cook.) timbale of pigeons.

mirrino, na, *a.* myrrhic.

mirtáceo, cea. I. *a.* (bot.) myrtaceous. **II.** *f. pl.*
Myrtaceæ.

mirtidano, *m.* myrtle tiller or sprout.

mirtino, na, *a.* myrtle-like.

mirto, *m.* (bot.) myrtle.

miruello, lla, *m.* & *f.* (ornith.) blackbird.

misa, *f.* (eccl.) mass; (mus.) music composed for
a solemn mass.—**m. de cuerpo presente,** mass
said while the corpse is in the church.—**m. del
gallo,** midnight mass.—**m. mayor,** high mass.
—**como en m.,** in dead silence.—**no saber de
la m. la media,** to know nothing.—**oír m.,** to
hear, or attend, mass.

misacantano, *m.* priest who is ordained and says
the mass; priest who celebrates the first mass.

misal, *m.* (eccl.) missal, Mass book; (print.) two-
line pica.

misantropía, *f.* misanthropy.

misantrópico, ca, *a.* misanthropic(al).

misántropo, *m.* misanthrope.

misar, *vn.* (coll.) to say mass; to hear mass.

misario, *m.* (eccl.) acolyte.

miscelánea, *f.* miscellany; mixture, medley.

misceláneo, a, *a.* miscellaneous, mixed.

miscibilidad, *f.* miscibility.

For pronunciation, see the rules at the beginning of the book.

miscible, *a.* miscible, that can be mixed.

miserabilísimo, ma, *a. super.* most miserable.

miserable. I. *a.* miserable, wretched, unhappy; stingy, close-fisted. **II.** *n.* wretch, cur, cad.

miserablemente, *adv.* miserably, unhappily; stingily.

míseramente, *adv.* meanly, wretchedly.

miserear, *vn.* (coll.) to be niggardly or stingy.

miserere, *m.* (eccl.) Miserere; (med.) ileus, colic.

miseria, *f.* misery, wretchedness, forlornness; need, penury, poverty, destitution; stinginess; trifle, pittance.

misericordia, *f.* mercy, mercifulness, pity.

misericordiosamente, *adv.* mercifully.

misericordioso, sa, *a.* merciful.

mísero, ra, *a.* = MISERABLE.

misero, ra, *a.* (coll.) mass-loving; church-going; (priest) that says mass very often.

misérrimo, ma, *a. super.* most miserable.

misia, misiá, *f.* (Am.) (with first name) Señora, Doña, Mrs.

misión, *f.* mission; errand; embassy, legation; commission; (eccl.) missionary station, residence, preaching, etc.; money and food allowed to reapers during the harvest.

misionario, ria; misionero, ra, *n.* missionary.

misivo, va, *a.* missive, sent.

mismamente, *adv.* (coll.) exactly, to a tee.

mismísimo, ma, *a. super.* very same.

mismo, ma, *a.* same; similar, like; equal, self-same; -self (*él mismo,* himself, he himself).—**así m., lo m.,** the same; the same thing.—**el m. de siempre,** the same old (John, thing, etc.).—**eso m.,** that very thing.—**lo m. da,** it's all the same, it makes no difference.—**lo m. de siempre,** the same old story.—**lo m. que,** the same as; as well as.—**lo m. . . . que . . . ,** both . . . and.—**por lo m.,** for the same reason; for that very reason.

misógino, *n.* & *a.* misogynist(-ous).

misoneísmo, *m.* misoneism, dread or dislike of novelty.

misoneísta, *n.* & *a.* misoneist(-ic).

mispíquel, *m.* (min.) mispickel, arsenopyrite.

mistamente, *adv.* (law) = MIXTAMENTE.

mistar, *va.* to speak or mumble.

mistela, *f.* = MIXTELA.

misterio, *m.* mystery.

misteriosamente, *adv.* mysteriously.

misterioso, sa, *a.* mysterious.

mística, *f.* study of the contemplative life.

místicamente, *adv.* mystically; spiritually; emblematically.

misticismo, *m.* mysticism.

¹místico, ca, *n.* & *a.* mystic(-al); spiritual.

²místico, *m.* small coasting vessel.

misticón, na, *a.* (coll.) affectedly ascetic.

misti fori = MIXTI FORI.—**mistifori,** *m.* = MIXTIFORI.

mistilíneo, nea, *a.* (geom.) = MIXTILÍNEO.

mistión, misto, mistura, misturar = MIXTIÓN, MIXTO, MIXTURA, MIXTURAR.

misturera, *f.* (Am.) flower girl.

mita, *f.* (Am.) enforced service of Indians.

mitad, *f.* half; moiety; middle, centre; (coll.) husband or wife, as *mi cara mitad,* my better half.—**m. y m.,** half and half.—**por la m.,** in two.—**por mitades,** by halves.

mitayo, *m.* (Am.) Indian serving his MITA.

mítico, ca, *a.* mythical.

mitigación, *f.* mitigation, extenuation; soothing.

mitigador, ra, *n.* & *a.* mitigator(-ing); soother (-ing).

mitigante, *a.* mitigating, allaying.

mitigar, *va.* (*pret.* MITIGUÉ; *subj.* MITIGUE) to mitigate, allay, soothe, alleviate; to quench, assuage, appease.

mitigativo, va; mitigatorio, ria, *a.* lenitive, mitigating, soothing.

mitigué, mitigue, *v. V.* MITIGAR.

mitin, *m.* (Angl.) political meeting; rally.

mito, *m.* myth.

mitología, *f.* mythology.

mitológico, ca. I. *a.* mythological. **II.** *n.* mythologist.

mitologista; mitólogo, ga, *n.* mythologist.

mitón, *m.* mitt, lace glove without fingers.

mitosis, *f.* (biol.) mitosis, cell division.

mitote, *m.* Indian dance; (Am.) household festival; fastidiousness, affectedness; riot, uproar, disturbance.

mitotero, ra, *a.* & *n.* (Am.) finical, fastidious; jolly, rollicking.

mitra, *f.* (eccl.) miter; bishopric.

mitrado. I. *pp.* of MITRAR. **II.** *a.* (eccl.) *a.* mitered.

mitrar, *vn.* (eccl.) to be mitered.

mitridato, *m.* mithridate, antidote.

mítulo, *m.* mussel.

mixtamente, *adv.* mixedly; (law) belonging to both ecclesiastical and civil courts.

mixtela, *f.* a refreshing beverage; (Colomb.) a popular intoxicating liquor.

mixti fori, *a.* (law) amenable to either ecclesiastical or secular courts; entangled, complicated.—**mixtifori,** *m.* (coll.) medley, hodge-podge.

mixtilíneo, nea, *a.* (geom.) mixtilinear.

mixtión, *f.* mixture, commixture.

mixto, ta. I. *a.* mixed, mingled; composite; half-breed; crossbreed; mongrel; (arith.) mixed.—**parejas m.,** (games) mixed doubles.—**tren m.** train with both passenger and freight cars. **II.** *m.* sulphur or parlor match; (artil.) explosive compound.

mixtura, *f.* mixture, compound; meslin, mixed corn; (pharm.) mixture.

mixturar, *va.* to mix, mingle.

mixturero, ra, *n.* & *a.* mixer(-ing).

miz, *m.* pussy, kitty.

mízcalo, *m.* a kind of mushroom.

mizo, za, (coll.) = MICHO, CHA, puss, cat.

mnemónica, mnemotecnia, *f.* mnemonics.

mnemotécnico, ca, *a.* mnemonic.

moabita, *n.* Moabite.

moaré, *m.* moiré.

mobiliario, ria. I. *a.* movable (app. to chattels, especially unregistered bonds or securities). **II.** *m.* furniture, household goods.

moblaje, *m.* household furniture.

moblar, *va.* (*ind.* MUEBLO; *subj.* MUEBLE) to furnish, provide with furniture.

moble, *a.* = MÓVIL, movable; mobile; unstable.

moca, *f.* Mocha coffee.

mocador, *m.* pocket handkerchief.

mocasín, *m.*; **mocasina,** *f.* moccasin.

mocear, *vn.* to act like a boy; to revel, to rake.

mocedad, *f.* youth, youthfulness; reckless mode of living; frolic.

mocero, *a.* lascivious, lewd.

mocetón, na, *n.* strapping youth, lad (lass).

moción, *f.* motion, movement; leaning, inclination, tendency; divine inspiration; motion, proposition to an assembly.

mocito, ta. I. *a. dim.* very young. **II.** *n.* youngster, lad (lassie).

moco, *m.* mucus; viscid, glutinous matter; snuff of a lamp or candle; candle drippings; slag of iron; (naut.) martingale boom, dolphin striker; worthless thing, trifle; (bot.) love-lies-bleeding.—**m. de pavo,** crest of a turkey.—**a m. de candil,** by candlelight.—**llorar a m. tendido,** (coll.) to weep copiously, cry like a child.

mocosidad, *f.* mucousness, viscosity.

mocoso, sa. I. *a.* snively; full of mucus; despicable, mean. **II.** *n.* inexperienced youth.

mocosuelo, la, *n. dim.* thoughtless, inexperienced youth; child.

mochada, *f.* butt (as of a goat).

mochar, *va.* to cut, lop off.

mochazo, *m.* blow with the butt of a musket.

mocheta, *f.* thick edge of some tools; (arch.) quoin; sconcheon.

mochete, *m.* (ornith.) sparrow hawk.

mochil, *m.* farmer's boy.

mochila, *f.* (mil.) knapsack, haversack; a kind of caparison; gunning bag; provisions given to each soldier for a number of days.

mochilero, *m.* one who carries the baggage of soldiers.

mochín, *m.* executioner.

mocho, cha. I. *a.* cropped, shorn, lopped, cut off; maimed, mutilated; (Mex., coll.) hypocritical. **II.** *m.* butt end.

mochuelo, *m.* (ornith.) red owl.—**cargar con el m.,** to get the worst part of an undertaking.

moda, *f.* fashion, mode, style.—**a la (última) m.,** after the latest fashion; fashionable.—**de m.,** fashionable.—**estar de m.,** to be in style, or in fashion.—**pasado, de m.,** out of style.—**ser de m.,** or **ser m.,** to be the fashion.

modal. I. *a.* (logic) modal. **II.** *m. pl.* manners, breeding.—**modalidad,** *f.* nature, character.

modelado, *m.* (art) modelling.

modelar, *va.* (art) to model.

modelo, *m.* model, pattern, standard, copy. **II.** *n.* (art) life model.—**no tener m.,** to have no equal.

moderación, *f.* moderation.

moderadamente, *adv.* moderately.

moderado, da. I. *pp.* of MODERAR. **II.** *a.* moderate; modest; reasonable; (pol.) conservative; moderate liberal, middle-of-the-roader.

moderador, ra, *n.* & *a.* moderator(-ing).—**poder m.,** (in constitutional monarchies) the sovereign.

moderante. I. *n.* & *a.* moderator(-ing). **II.** *n.* presiding officer, moderator.

moderantismo, *m.* (pol.) moderate liberalism.

moderar. I. *va.* to moderate, regulate, adjust, restrain, curb, repress. **II.** *vr.* to calm down, moderate, refrain from excesses.

moderativo, va; moderatorio, ria, *a.* moderating.

modernamente, *adv.* recently, lately, freshly.

modernismo, *m.* modernism.

modernista. I. *a.* modern. **II.** *n.* modernist.

modernizar, *va.* to modernize.

moderno, na, *a.* modern.

modestamente, *adv.* modestly.

modestia, *f.* modesty.

modesto, ta, *a.* modest.

módicamente, *adv.* moderately, sparingly.

modicidad, *f.* moderateness, cheapness.

módico, ca, *a.* reasonable, economical.

modificable, *a.* modifiable.

modificación, *f.* modification.

modificador, ra, *n.* & *a.* modifier(-fying).

modificante, *a.* modifying.

modificar, *va.* (*pret.* MODIFIQUÉ; *subj.* MODIFIQUE) to modify.—**modificativo, va; modificatorio, ria,** *a.* modifying.

modifiqué, modifique, *v.* V. MODIFICAR.

modillón, *m.* (arch.) modillion, bracket.

modio, *m.* modius, an ancient Roman dry measure.

modismo, *m.* (gram.) idiom.

modista, *f.* dressmaker or modiste.—**m. de sombreros,** milliner.—**modistería,** *f.* modiste's shop, fashion shop.

modistilla, *f. dim.* (coll.) young, inexperienced dressmaker or milliner; seamstress.

modo, *m.* mode, way, manner, form; moderation, temperance; civility, urbanity; (gram.) model. or mood; (mus.) mode.—**m. de ser,** nature, character; disposition, temperament.—**al m. de, a m. de,** in the same manner as, like, in the fashion of.—**de buen (mal) m.,** politely (impolitely).—**del mismo m. que,** in the same way as.—**de m. de,** so as to.—**de m. que,** so

that; and so.—**de ningún m.,** by no means, under no circumstances.—**de otro m.,** otherwise.—**de todos modos,** at any rate, anyway. —**de un m. u otro,** in one way or another, somehow.—**por m. de,** as (*por modo de juego,* as a joke, in jest).—**sobre m.,** extremely.

modorra, *f.* drowsiness, heaviness; (vet.) sturdy.

modorrar. I. *va.* to drowse, make sleepy. **II.** *vr.* (of fruit) to become squashy.

modorrilla, *f.* (coll.) third night watch.

modorro, rra, *a.* drowsy, sleepy, heavy; dull, stupid; (of sheep) suffering from sturdy; (of fruit) squashy.

modoso, sa, *a.* temperate, well-behaved.

modrego, ga, *n.* (coll.) awkward person.

modulación, *f.* (mus.) modulation.

modulador, ra, *n.* modulator.

modulante, *a.* modulating.

modular, *vn.* (mus.) to modulate.

módulo, *m.* size of coins and medals; (arch.) module; (math.) modulus; (mus.) modulation; (hydraul.) unit of measure of running water.

mofa, *f.* mockery, jeer, scoff.

mofador, ra, *n.* & *a.* scoffer(-ing), mocker(-ing).

mofadura, *f.* = MOFA.

mofante, *n.* = MOFADOR.

mofar, *vn.* & *vr.* to jeer, scoff, mock, sneer.—**mofarse de,** to mock, sneer at, scoff, make fun of.

mofeta, *f.* mofette, mephitis; noxious emanation (from mines, etc.); (zool.). skunk or polecat.

moflete, *m.* fat cheek.

mofletudo, da, *a.* fat-cheeked.

mogate, *m.* varnish, glazing.—**a medio m.,** carelessly, heedlessly.

mogato, ta, *a.* = MOJIGATO.

mogol, la; mogólico, ca, *a.* Mongolian.

mogollón, *m.* hanger-on, sponger, parasite.—**comer de m.,** to sponge.

mogón, na, *a.* with one horn missing or broken.

mogote, *m.* hummock, hillock; (agr.) stack or rick of corn; antler (of a brocket, a small deer).

mogrollo, *m.* parasite, sponger; (coll.) rustic.

moharra, *f.* head of a spear.

moharrache, moharracho, *m.* merry-andrew, clown.

mohatra, *f.* sham sale; fraud.—**mohatrar,** *vn.* to make a sham sale.—**mohatrero, ra; mohatrón, ña,** trickster, swindler.

mohecer, *va.* to moss, to mildew.

mohiento, ta, *a.* mildewed.

mohín, *m.* grimace, gesture.

mohína, *f.* animosity, animadversion, grudge.

mohino, na. I. *a.* fretful, peevish; sad, mournful; (mule) begotten by a stallion and a female donkey; (of horses, etc.) black. **II.** *n.* one who plays alone against several others.

moho, *m.* (bot.) moss; mould, mildew; rust.

mohoso, sa, *a.* rusty; mouldy, musty, mildewed.

mojada, *f.* wetting, drenching; sop; (coll.) stab.

mojador, ra, *n.* wetter, moistener.

mojadura, *f.* drenching, moistening, wetting.

mojama, *f.* dry, salt tunny fish.

mojar. I. *va.* to wet, drench; moisten, damp; (coll.) to stab; to interfere with. **II.** *vn.* to be immersed in any business. **III.** *vr.* to get wet.

mojarra, *f.* a sea fish; (Am.) heart-shaped dagger.

mojarrilla, *n.* (coll.) gay, jolly person.

moje, *m.* (cook.) gravy, sauce.

mojel, *m.* (naut.) braided cord for the anchor.

mojí, *m.* sponge cake; pie.

mojicón, *m.* bun; (coll.) fisticuff.

mojiganga, *f.* morris dance; masquerade, mask, mummery.

mojigatería, mojigatez, *f.* hypocrisy; religious fanaticism.

mojigato, ta. I. *n.* dissembler, hypocrite; bigot, fanatic. **II.** *a.* deceitful, hypocritical; prude; bigoted.

¹**mojón,** *m.* landmark; boundary monument;

heap, pile; milestone; a game like pitching; solid excrement.

²**mojón,** *m.* wine taster.

¹**mojona,** *f.* excise tax on wine.

²**mojona,** *f.* survey of land; setting up of boundary marks.

mojonación, *f.* setting up of boundary marks.

mojonar, *va.* to set boundary marks.

mojonera, *f.* boundary mark; landmark.

mojonero, *m.* appraiser, gauger.

¹**mola,** *f.* (med.) mole.

²**mola,** *f.* flour with salt used in sacrifices.

molada, *f.* colors ground at one time.

molar, *a.* molar.

molcajete, *m.* mortar for pounding.

moldar, *va.* to mold.

moldavo, va, *n.* & *a.* Moldavian.

molde, *m.* mold; pattern; (eng.) form; (print.) form ready for printing.—**de m.,** in print; printed; fitting, to the purpose.

moldeador, *m.* molder, cast maker.

moldear, *va.* to mold; to cast; to provide or adorn with moldings.

moldura, *f.* molding.

moldurar, *va.* to make moldings on.

¹**mole,** *a.* soft, mild.

²**mole,** *f.* huge mass or bulk.

³**mole,** *m.* (Mex.) chili sauce for turkey.

molécula, *f.* molecule.—**molecular,** *a.* molecular.

moledera, *f.* (coll.) botheration.

moledero, ra, *a.* ready to be ground, for grinding.

moledor, ra, *n.* grinder; powdering mill; crushing cylinder in a sugar-mill; bore, tiresome person.

moledura, *f.* grinding.

molendero, ra, *n.* miller, grinder; chocolate manufacturer.

moler, *va.* (*ind.* MUELO; *subj.* MUELA) to grind, pulverize, mill; to overtire; to vex, bore; to waste, consume; to masticate, chew.—**m. a palos,** to give a severe drubbing.

molero, *m.* maker or seller of millstones.

molestador, ra, *n.* vexer, annoyer.

molestamente, *adv.* troublesomely, vexatiously; uncomfortably.

molestar. I. *va.* to disturb; to trouble; to annoy, vex; to tease. **II.** *vr.* (**en**) to bother, take the trouble (to).

molestia, *f.* annoyance, bother; inconvenience, trouble; discomfort; hardship, grievance; (coll.) quarrel.

molesto, ta, *a.* annoying, vexatious, bothersome; troublesome; uncomfortable.

moleta, *f.* muller; polisher; (print.) ink-grinder.

moletón, *m.* canton or cotton flannel.

molibdato, *m.* (chem.) molybdate.

molibdeno, *m.* (chem.) molybdenum.

molíbdico, ca, *a.* molybdic.

molicie, *f.* softness, effeminacy.

molido, da. I. *pp.* of MOLER. **II.** *a.* (fig.) fatigued.

molienda, *f.* milling, grinding; grist; weariness, fatigue; season for grinding sugar cane or olives.

moliente, *n.* & *a.* grinder(-ing).

molificable, *a.* mollifiable.

molificación, *f.* mollification.

molificar, *va.* (*pret.* MOLIFIQUÉ; *subj.* MOLIFIQUE) to mollify, soften, mitigate.

molificativo, va, *a.* mollifying, lenitive.

molifiqué, molifique, *v.* V. MOLIFICAR.

molimiento, *m.* grinding, pounding; (fig.) fatigue, weariness, lassitude.

molinar, *m.* place where there are mills.

molinejo, *m. dim.* small mill.

molinera, *f.* miller's wife; woman mill worker.

molinería, *f.* number or group of mills; mill industry.

molinero, *m.* miller, grinder.

molinete, *m. dim.* little mill; pin wheel; ventilating wheel; friction roller; fifth wheel of a vehicle; smoke dispeller; moulinet, swing of sabre; drum

of a capstan or winch.—**m. hidráulico,** hydraulic tourniquet, Barker's mill.

molinillo, *m. dim.* hand mill; coffee grinder; chocolate beater.

molinismo, *m.* Molinism.

molinista, *n.* & *a.* Molinist(-ic).

molinito, *m. dim.* small mill.

molino, *m.* mill; restless, noisy fellow; (coll.) mouth.—**m. de sangre,** mill turned by men or animals.—**m. de viento,** windmill.

molitivo, va, *a.* mollifying; softening.

molondro, molondrón, *m.* (coll.) poltroon.

moloso, *m.* (poet.) molossus.

molote, *m.* (Cuba) tumult, riot.

moltura, *f.* grinding.

molusco, *m.* mollusc.

moluscoideo, a. I. *n.* & *a.* molluscoid. **II.** *m. pl.* Molluscoida.

molla, *f.* lean meat; crumb of bread.

mollar, *a.* soft, tender; easily shelled; lean (meat); productive, profitable; credulous, gullible.

mollear, *vn.* to become soft and pliable; to yield easily.

molledo, *m.* fleshy part of a limb (of the body); bread crumb.

molleja, *f.* gizzard; sweetbread.

¹**mollejón,** *m. aug.* big, fat person.

²**mollejón,** *m.* grindstone.

mollejuela, *f. dim.* sweetbread.

mollera, *f.* crown of head.—**cerrado de m.,** rude, ignorant.—**ser duro de m.,** to be dull or obstinate.

mollero, *m.* = MOLLEDO.

¹**molleta,** *f.* biscuit; brown bread.

²**molleta,** *f.*—*pl.* candle snuffers.

¹**mollete,** *m.* French roll; fleshy part of arm.

²**mollete,** *m.*—*pl.* plump cheeks.

molletero, ra, *n.* baker or seller of rolls.

molletudo, da, *a.* having chubby cheeks.

mollina, mollizna, *f.* drizzle.

molliznar, molliznear, *vn.* to drizzle, sprinkle.

moma, *f.* (Mex.) blindman's buff.

momentáneamente, *adv.* instantly; momentarily; promptly.

momentáneo, nea, *a.* momentary; prompt.

momento, *m.* moment; weight, importance; (mech.) moment.—**al m.,** in a moment, in a minute, immediately.—**por momentos,** continually, every minute; any moment, soon.

momería, *f.* mummery.

momero, ra, *n.* mummer.

momia, *f.* mummy.—**momificar. I.** *va.* to mummify. **II.** *vr.* to become a mummy.

momio, mia. I. *a.* meager, lean. **II.** *m.* extra allowance.—**de m.,** gratis.

momo, *m.* funny grimace.

momórdiga, *f.* (bot.) balsam apple.

¹**mona,** *f.* female monkey; (coll.) ludicrous imitator; (coll.) drunkenness; drunkard; at cards, old maid; iron plate worn for protection on the right leg by bullfighters on horseback.—**dormir la m.,** to sleep off a drunk.

²**mona,** *f.* Easter cake with whole eggs.

monacal, *a.* monastic; monkish.

monacalmente, *adv.* monastically.

monacato, *m.* monkhood, monasticism.

monacillo, *m.* acolyte.

monacordio, *m.* (mus.) clavichord.

monada, *f.* grimace; monkeyism, monkeyshine; fawning, flattery; pretty child.

mónada, *f.* (philos. & zool.) monad.

monadología, *f.* (philos.) monadology.

monago, monaguillo, *m.* = MONACILLO.

monaquismo, *m.* = MONACATO.

monarca, *m.* monarch.

monarquía, *f.* monarchy; kingdom.

monárquico, ca, *a.* monarchical.

monarquismo, *m.* monarchism.

monarquista, *n.* & *a.* monarchist(-ic).

monasterial, *a.* monastic.

monasterio, m. monastery.

monásticamente, adv. monastically.

monástico, ca, a. monastic, monastical.

monda, f. pruning of trees; pruning season.—pl. parings, peelings.

mondadientes, m. toothpick.

mondador, ra, n. cleaner; purifier.

mondadura, f. cleaning, cleansing.—pl. peelings.

mondaoídos, mondaorejas, m. ear spoon.

mondar, va. to clean, cleanse; to trim, prune; to hull, husk, peel; to deprive of money; to cut (the hair).—mondarajas, f. pl. peelings.

mondejo, m. belly of a pig or sheep stuffed with minced meat.

mondo, da, a. neat, pure, unmixed.—m. y lirondo, (coll.) pure, without admixutre.

mondón, m. barkless trunk of a tree.

mondonga, f. (contempt.) kitchen wench.

mondongo, m. tripe; intestines.

mondonguería, f. place where tripe is sold.

mondonguero, ra, n. tripe seller or cooker.

mondonguil, a. (coll.) pertaining to tripe.

monear, vn. (coll.) to monkey; to trifle, fool.

moneda, f. coin; money; specie; coinage.—m. corriente, currency.—m. debil, soft currency. —m. de vellón, small copper money.—m. divisionaria, fractional money or currency.— m. fiduciaria, fiduciary money, fiat money; token money.—m. fuerte, hard currency.—m. imaginaria, money of account.—m. menuda, coins, change.—m. métalica, or sonante, hard money, specie.—m. suelta, small change.—pagar en la misma m., to pay back in one's own coin, give tit for tat.

monedaje, m. coinage; seigniorage.

monedar, monedear, va. to coin.

monedería, f. mintage.

monedero, ra, n. coiner.—m. falso, counterfeiter.

monería, f. grimace, mimicry, monkeyshine; cunning action of a child.

monesco, ca, a. (coll.) apish.

monetario, ria. I. a. monetary, financial. II. m. cabinet or collection of coins and medals.

monetización, f. monetization.

monetizar, va. to monetize.

monfí, m. Moorish highwayman.

mongol, la; mongólico, ca, a. (Gal.) Mongolian.

moniato, m. (bot.) = BONIATO, sweet potato.

monicaco, m. = HOMINICACO, whippersnapper.

monición, f. admonition.

monigote, m. lay brother; (coll.) a bumpkin; puppet, grotesque figure; (Colomb., contempt.) priest.

monillo, m. (sewing) waist, bodice.

monipodio, m. (coll.) combine (for illicit ends).

monís, f. kind of fritters; any pretty little thing; m., or monises, (coll.) money.

monismo, m. (philos.) monism.

monista, n. & a. (philos.) monist(-ic).

mónita, f. artifice, cunning suavity.

monitor, m. monitor, adviser; (naut.) monitor.

monitorio, ria. I. a. monitory, admonitory. II. n. ecclesiastical monition.

monja, f. nun.—pl. sparks in burned papers.

monje, m. monk; (ornith.) brown peacock.

monjía, f. monkhood.

monjil. I. m. nun's dress; mourning dress. II. a. pertaining or belonging to nuns.

monjío, m. nunnishness; taking the veil.

monjita, f. dim. little nun.

mono, na. I. a. (coll.) dainty; "cute." II. m. monkey; mimic; nincompoop; (de mecánico), overalls.

monoatómico, ca, a. monoatomic.

monobásico, ca, a. (chem.) monobasic.

monobloque.—en m., (int. combust. eng.) in bloc, in one piece.

monoceronte, monocerote, m. unicorn.

monociclo, cla. I. a. monocyclic. II. m. monocycle, single-wheel velocipede.

monocilíndrico, ca, a. single-cylinder.

monoclínico, ca, a. (min.) monoclinic.

monocordio, m. (mus.) monochord.

monocotiledóneo, a. I. a. (bot.) monocotyledonous. II. f. pl. Monocotyledones, monocotyledons.

monocromático, ca, a. monochromatic.

monocromo, ma, a. monochrome.

monóculo, la. I. a. monocular, one-eyed. II. m. (opt.) monocle; (surg.) bandage for one eye.

monodelfo, fa, n. & a. (zool.) monodelphian.

monofásico, ca, a. (elec.) single-phase.

monófilo, la, a. (bot.) monophyllous.

monofisita, n. & a. Monophysite(-ic).

monogamia, f. monogamy.

monógamo, ma, a. monogamous.

monogenismo, m. (biol.) monogenesis.

monografía, f. monograph.

monográfico, ca, a. monographic.

monograma, m. monogram.

monoico, ca, a. (bot.) monœcious.

monolítico, ca, a. monolithic.

monolito, m. monolith.

monologar, vn. to soliloquize.

monólogo, m. monologue, soliloquy.

monomanía, f. monomania.

monomaníaco, ca, n. & a. monomaniac.

monomaquia, f. duel.

monometalismo, m. monometallism.

monometalista, n. & a. monometallist(-ic).

monomio, mia, m. & a. (alg.) monomial.

monona, a. (coll.) graceful and pretty (girl).

monopastos, m. sheave, wheel of a pulley.

monopétalo, la, a. (bot.) monopetalous.

monoplano, m. (aer.) monoplane.

monopolicé, monopolice, v. V. MONOPOLIZAR.

monopolio, m. monopoly.

monopolista, n. & a. monopolist(-ic).

monopolizar, va. (pret. MONOPOLICÉ; subj. MONOPOLICE) to monopolize.

monóptero, ra, a. (arch.) monopterous.

monorquidia, f. (med.) monorchism.

monosépalo, la, a. (bot.) monosepalous.

monosilábico, ca, a. monosyllabic.

monosílabo, ba, n. & a. monosyllable.

monospermo, ma, a. (bot.) monospermous.

monóstrofe, f. (poet.) monostrophe.

monote, m. (coll.) dumfounded person.

monoteísmo, m. monotheism.

monoteísta, n. & a. monotheist(-ic).

monotelismo, m. Monothelitism.

monotelita. I. a. Monothelitic. II. n. Monothelite.

monotipia, f. monotype (machine).

monotipista, n. monotypist.

monotonía, f. monotony.

monótono, na, a. monotonous.

monotremas, m. pl. (zool.) Monotremata, monotremes.

monseñor, m. Monseigneur.

monserga, f. (coll.) gabble, gibberish.

monstruo, m. monster; monstrosity; huge thing.

monstruosamente, adv. monstrously.

monstruosidad, f. monstrosity; monstrousness.

monstruoso, sa, a. monstrous; huge; extraordinary; hideous; hateful; shocking.

monta, f. act of mounting; raising or crossing (as horses); amount, sum total; value, worth, price; (mil.) signal for mounting.

montacargas, m. hoist, winch, windlass.

montada, f. arch of a horse's bit.

montadero, m. mounting block.

montado, da. I. pp. of MONTAR. II. a. (horse) ready for mounting. III. m. trooper or horseman.

montador, m. mounter; mounting block; installer (electrician, pipe fitter, etc.).

montadura, *f.* mounting; (jewelry) setting; trappings of a saddle horse; mount.

montaje, *m.* setting up, installing; assembling; (artil.) act of mounting.—*pl.* (artil.) mounting.

montanera, *f.* oak forest; feeding of hogs with acorns.

montanero, *m.* forester.

montanismo, *m.* Montanism.

montanista, *n. & a.* Montanist(-ic).

montano, na, *a.* mountainous.

montantada, *f.* braggadocio; multitude, crowd.

montante. I. *m.* (fencing) broadsword; (carp. and mech.) upright, standard, post, strut, jamb; (arch.) transom; (min.) stempel; (com.) amount, footing. **II.** *f.* (naut.) flood tide.

montantear, *vn.* (fencing) to wield the broadsword; to vaunt, brag; to intermeddle.

montantero, *m.* fighter with a broadsword.

montaña, *f.* mountain.—*pl.* highlands.

montañero, ra, *n.* (Colomb.) mountaineer.

montañés, sa. I. *a.* mountain (as *a.*), of or from the mountains, highlandish. **II.** *n.* mountaineer, highlander; native of the province of Santander, Spain.

montañeta, -ñuela, *f. dim.* small mountain.

montañoso, sa, *a.* mountainous.

montar. I. *vn.* to mount, get on top; to ride horseback; to amount; to be of importance.— **m. en cólera,** to fly into a rage. **II.** *va.* to ride, straddle (a horse); to cover (as a horse, etc.); (mech.) to mount, set up, assemble; (jewelry) to set (as diamonds); to cock (as a gun); to wind (a clock, etc.); to impose a fine for trespassing; (mil.) to mount (guard); (naut.) to command (a ship); to carry or be equipped with (as guns); to round (a cape or headland). **III.** *vr.* to get into (as a passion).

montaraz. I. *a.* born or raised in the mountains; wild, untamed; uncouth, boorish. **II.** *n.* forester. —**montaraza,** *f.* forester's wife.

montazgar, *va.* to levy or collect MONTAZGO.

montazgo, *m.* toll for cattle passing from one province into another; cattle pass.

monte, *m.* mountain, mount; woods, forest, woodland; difficulty, obstruction; bushy head of hair; talon, cards that remain after the hands have been dealt; (cards) monte.—**m. alto,** forest.—**m. bajo,** scrub, brushwood, brake, thicket.—**m. de piedad,** pawnshop.—**m. pío,** gratuity fund for widows and orphans.

montea, *f.* beating the woods for game; stonecutting; (arch.) working drawing; (arch.) versed sine of an arch.

montear, *va.* to hunt; to make a working drawing of; (arch.) to vault, arch.

montecillo, *m. dim.* small forest; hillock, hummock.

montepío, *m.* = MONTE PÍO. *V.* MONTE.

¹montera, *f.* cloth cap; skylight; receiver, condenser of a still or alembic; (naut.) skysail.

²montera, *f.* hunter's wife.

monterería, *f.* cap factory or store.

monterero, ra, *n.* cap maker or seller.

montería, *f.* hunting, hunt, chase.

montero, ra, *n.* (in hunting) beater.

monterón, *m. aug.* big cloth cap.

monterrey, *m.* (cook.) meat pie.

monteruca, *f.* ugly cap.

montés, sa; montesino, na, *a.* wild, undomesticated, uncultivated.

montevideano, na, *n. & a.* Montevidean, of or from Montevideo.

montículo, *m.* mound.

monto, *m.* sum (of money); (com., arith.) amount (principal plus interest); sum total.

montón, *m.* heap, pile; big lot, mass; mound.— **m. de gente,** crowd, multitude.—**a montones,** abundantly, in heaps.

montonera, *f.* (Am.) group of revolutionary horsemen; large crowd.

montonero, *m.* bushwhacker, guerrilla.

montuno, na, *a.* pertaining to the highlands; rustic, boorish.

montuosidad, *f.* (prov.) mountainous quality.

montuoso, sa, *a.* mountainous, hilly.

montura, *f.* riding horse, mount; saddle trappings; setting up, installing; (jewelry) setting.

monuelo, *m. dim.* coxcomb, silly fop.

monumental, *a.* monumental.

monumento, *m.* monument.

monzón, *m.* monsoon.

¹moña, *f.* dressmaker's mannequin; doll.

²moña, *f.* fancy cap for infants; ribbon head ornament; elaborate badge on bull's neck when in the ring.

³moña, *f.* (coll.) drunkenness.

moño, *m.* (of hair) chignon, bun; tuft, egret.

moñón, na, *a.* (of birds) crested; (Colomb.) pouty, sulky.

moñudo, da, *a.* (of birds) crested.

moquear, *vn.* to snivel; to run at the nose.

moquero, *m.* pocket handkerchief.

moqueta, *f.* a kind of velvety carpet.

moquete, *m.* blow on the nose.

moquetear. I. *vn.* (coll.) to blow the nose frequently. **II.** *va.* to hit in the face.

moquillo, *m. dim.* little mucus; pip (in fowls).

moquita, *f.* snivel, running from the nose.

¹mora, *f.* (law) delay, mora.

²mora, *f.* (bot.) blackberry; bramble bush; mulberry.

³mora, *f.* Moorish woman.

morabito, morabuto, *m.* Mohammedan hermit.

moracho, cha, *a.* little purple.

morada, *f.* habitation, abode, residence; stay, sojourn.

morado, da, *a.* purple; murrey.

morador, ra, *n.* resident, inhabitant.

moraga, *f.,* **morago,** *m.* glean, bunch.

¹moral. I. *a.* moral. **II.** *f.* ethics, morality; morale.

²moral, *m.* (bot.) blackberry bush; mulberry tree.

moraleja, *f.* moral, maxim, lesson.

moralicé, moralice, *v. V.* MORALIZAR.

moralidad, *f.* morality, morals.

moralista, *m.* moralist.

moralización, *f.* moralization.

moralizador, ra, *n. & a.* moralizer(-ing).

moralizar, *va. & vn.* (*pret.* MORALICÉ; *subj.* MORALICE) to moralize.

moralmente, *adv.* morally.

morar, *vn.* to inhabit, dwell, reside.

moratiniano, na, *a.* Moratinian, of or like Moratin or his style.

moratoria, *f.* (com. and law), moratorium.

moravo, va, *n. & a.* Moravian.

morbidez, *f.* (art) softness, mellowness.

mórbido, da, *a.* morbid, diseased; (art) soft, mellow, delicate.

morbífico, ca, *a.* morbific, causing disease.

morbo, *m.* disease, distemper, infirmity.—**m. comicial,** (med.) epilepsy.—**m. gálico,** (med.) venereal disease.—**m. regio,** (med.) jaundice.

morboso, sa, *a.* diseased, morbid.

morcajo, *m.* low-grade wheat.

morcella, *f.* spark from a lamp.

morciguillo, *m.* (ornith.) bat.

morcilla, *f.* blood pudding; (theat., coll.) gag.

morcillero, ra, *n.* maker or seller of blood puddings; (theat.) gagger; one who ad-libs.

¹morcillo, lla, *a.* (of horses) reddish black.

²morcillo, *m.* fleshy part of the arm.

morcón, *m.* large blood pudding or sausage; (coll.) short, plump person.

mordacidad, *f.* mordancy; asperity, acrimony; sarcastic language.

mordante, *m.* (print.) guide.

mordaz, *a.* corrosive, biting, nipping; sarcastic; acrimonious; keen.

mordaza, *f.* gag; muzzle; holder, clamp, stopper, pincers, tongs; (Ry.) fishplate.

mordazmente, *adv.* acrimoniously, bitingly.
mordedor, ra, *n. & a.* biter(-ing); backbiter (-ing).
mordedura, *f.* bite (act and result of act).
mordente, *m.* mordant; (mus.) mordent; turn.
morder. I. *va.* (*ind.* MUERDO; *subj.* MUERDA) to bite; to nip, gripe, grasp, clutch; to gnaw, eat, wear away; to etch; to corrode; to revile, backbite; (print.) to overlap the form or paper (as the frisket), thereby preventing a good impression.—**m. el freno,** to bite the bit. **II.** *vr.* to bite (one's tongue, lips, etc.).—**m. la lengua,** to curb one's tongue.—**no m. los labios,** (coll.) to be outspoken.
mordicación, *f.* smarting, stinging.
mordicante, *a.* biting, pungent, acrid, corrosive.
mordicar. I. *va.* to gnaw, nibble. **II.** *vn.* to smart, sting.
mordicativo, va, *a.* biting, stinging.
mordido, da. I. *pp.* of MORDER. **II.** *a.* diminished, worn out, wasted away.
mordiente. I. *a.* biting. **II.** *m.* mordant.
mordihuí, *m.* weevil.
mordimiento, *m.* = MORDEDURA.
mordiscar, *va.* to nibble; take a bite of.
mordisco, mordiscón, *m.* bite; biting; bit, piece bitten off
morel de sal, *m.* purple red for fresco painting.
¹morena, *f.* (ichth.) moray.
²morena, *f.* whole-wheat bread.
³morena, *f.* (geol.) moraine; rick of new-mown grain.
morenillo, illa, ito, ita. I. *a. dim.* brunette. **II.** *m.* black powder for wounds of sheep.
moreno, na. I. *a.* brown, morel, tawny; dark, swarthy; brunette. **II.** *n.* (Cuba) Negro, darky.
morera, *f.* (bot.) white mulberry tree.
moreral, *m.* grove of white mulberry trees.
morería, *f.* Moorish quarter; Moorish lands.
moretón, *m.* (coll.) discoloration of a bruise.
morfa, *f.* fungous disease of orange and lemon trees.
morfina, *f.* morphine.—**morfinismo,** *m.* (med.) morphinism.—**morfinomanía,** *f.* morphinomania, drug habit.—**morfinómano, na,** *n.* morphinomaniac, drug fiend.
morfología, *f.* morphology.
morfológico, ca, *a.* morphologic(al).
morga, *f.* juice from olives; an Indian plant with poisonous berries.
morganático, ca, *a.* morganatic.
moribundo, da, *a.* moribund, dying, near death.
morichal, *m.* grove of MORICHES.
moriche, *m.* a tropical palm.
moriego, ga, *a.* Moorish.
morigeración, *f.* temperance, moderation.
morigerado, da, *a.* temperate, abstemious.
morigerar, *va.* to restrain, moderate.
morillo, *m. dim.* little Moor; andiron, firedog.
morir. I. *vn. & vr.* (*pp.* MUERTO: *gerund,* MURIENDO; *ind. pres.* MUERO, *pret.* él MURIÓ; *subj.* MUERA) to die; to die or go out (as fire).—**m. de,** to die, or be dying, of, from or with (as *morir de viejo,* to die of old age).—**¡muera . . . !** or **¡Muera . . . !** down with . . . !—**hasta m.,** till death. **II.** *vr.* (of a limb) to be benumbed.—**m. por,** to be excessively fond of.—**no es cosa de m.,** it isn't a killing, fatal matter.
morisco, ca. I. *a.* Moorish, Moresque. **II.** *n.* Morisco.
morisma, *f.* multitude of Moors.
morisqueta, *f.* Moorish trick; (coll.) deception, fraud; (P. I.) boiled rice; (Am.) face, grimace.
morlaco, ca, *a.* affecting ignorance.
morlés, *m.* sort of linen, lawn.
morlón, na, *a.* = MORLACO.
mormón, na, *n. & a.* Mormon
mormónico, ca, *a.* Mormon.
mormonismo, *m.* Mormonism.

mormullar, *va.* = MURMURAR.
mormullo, *m.* = MURMULLO.
moro, ra. I. *a.* Moorish; (coll.) not watered (wine). **II.** *n.* Moor.—**m. de paz,** peaceful person.—**hay moros en la costa,** the coast is not clear.
morocada, *f.* butt of a ram.
morocho, cha, *a.* (Am.) (of persons) fresh, vigorous; (Am.) (of persons) dark-skinned; *a. & n.* hard kind of Indian corn.
morón, *m.* hillock, hummock, mound.
moroncho, cha, *a.* = MORONDO.
morondanga, *f.* (coll.) hodgepodge, medley.
morondo, da, *a.* bald, hairless; leafless.
moronía, *f.* dish of eggplant, tomatoes, etc.
morosamente, *adv.* slowly, tardily.
morosidad, *f.* slowness, tardiness.
moroso, sa, *a.* slow, tardy, heavy, sluggish.
morquera, *f.* (bot.) Spanish thyme.
¹morra, *f.* top, crown of the head.—**andar a la m.,** to come to blows.
²morra, *f.* mora, a game.
morrada, *f.* butting of two heads.
morral, *m.* nose bag; game bag; knapsack; (coll.) rustic.
morralla, *f.* small fry (fish); rubbish; rabble.
morrillo, *m.* pebble; fat of the nape of a sheep.
morriña, *f.* (vet.) murrain; (coll.) sadness, blues.
morrión, *m.* (mil.) helmet; vertigo (in hawks).
¹morro, *m.* snout, muffle; anything round like the head; headland, head, bluff; peak; pebble; thick lip.—**andar al m.,** to come to blows.
²morro, rra, *a.* purring (of cats).
morrocotudo, da, *a.* (coll.) strong, stout; very important or difficult.
morrocoy, morrocoyo, *m.* (Cuba) boxturtle.
¹morrón, *m.* knotted flag; large sweet pepper.
²morrón, *m.* (aer., coll.) crash.
morroncho, cha, *a.* mild, meek, tame.
morrongo, ga; morroño, ña, *n.* cat.
morrudo, da, *a.* thick-lipped.
morsa, *f.* (ichth.) walrus.
mortadela, *f.* Bologna sausage.
¹mortaja, *f.* shroud, winding sheet; (Am.) cigarette paper.
²mortaja, *f.* mortise.
mortal. I. *a.* mortal, fatal; very seriously ill, at the point of death. **II.** *n.* mortal.
mortalidad, *f.* mortality; death rate.
mortalmente, *adv.* mortally, deadly.
mortandad, *f.* mortality; massacre, butchery.
mortecino, na. I. *a.* (of an animal) dying a natural death, (also app. to the flesh of such an animal); dying away or extinguishing; pale, subdued (color).—**hacer la mortecina,** to feign death. **II.** *f.* carrion.
morterada, *f.* dish, sauce, etc. made at one time in a mortar; (artil.) quantity of stones thrown out at one time by a stone mortar.
morterete, *m. dim.* (artil.) small mortar; gun for firing salutes; broad candlestick.
mortero, *m.* (artil.) mortar; mortar, for pounding; understone in crushing mills; (mason.) mortar.—**m. de brújula,** inner compass box.
morteruelo, *m. dim.* small mortar; toy for boys; fricassee of hog's liver.
mortífero, ra, *a.* death-dealing, fatal; unhealthful.
mortificación, *f.* (med.) mortification, gangrene; mortification, self-inflicted hardship; humiliation, vexation.
mortificador, ra, *n. & a.* mortifier(-fying).
mortificante, *a.* mortifying; vexing.
mortificar, *va. & vr.* (*pret.* MORTIFIQUÉ; *subj.* MORTIFIQUE) (med.) to mortify; to subdue (passions); to vex; to bother; to humiliate.
mortuorio, ria. I. *a.* mortuary, pertaining to the dead. **II.** *m.* burial, funeral. **III.** *f.* funeral parlor, undertaker's establishment.

For pronunciation, see the rules at the beginning of the book.

morucho, *m.* young bull with horns tipped for baiting.

morueco, *m.* ram, male sheep.

moruno, na, *a.* Moorish.

morusa, *f.* (coll.) cash, specie; money.

¹mosaico, ca. I. *a.* mosaic. II. *m.* mosaic (work); (Am.) concrete tile (gen. paving tile, set like mosaic).—**m. de madera,** marquetry.

²mosaico, ca, *a.* Mosaic, pert. to Moses.

mosaísmo, *m.* Mosaism.

mosca, *f.* fly; tuft of hair under the lip; (coll.) cash, boodle; money in hand; impertinent intruder, importuner, bore; vexation, trouble; *pl.* sparks from a light.—**m. de burro,** horsefly. —**m. muerta,** one who feigns meekness.— **moscas blancas,** (coll.) falling snowflakes.— **aflojar la m.,** to give or spend money.—**papar moscas,** to gape with astonishment.—**picar la m.,** to be disquieted.—**sacudir las moscas** = MOSQUEAR.—**soltar la m.,** = AFLOJAR LA M.

moscabado, da, *a.* raw, unrefined (sugar).

moscada, *a.* NUEZ MOSCADA, (bot.) nutmeg.

moscarda, *f.* (entom.) flesh fly; eggs of bees.

moscardear, *vn.* (of bees) to lay eggs in the cells of the combs.

moscardón, *m.* (entom.) botfly; horse bot; bumblebee; hornet; drone; (coll.) importuning, bothering person.

moscareta, *f.* (ornith.) flycatcher.

¹moscatel, *a.* & *n.* muscatel (grape or wine).

²moscatel, *m.* (coll.) tiresome person.

moscella, *f.* = MORCELLA, spark from a lamp.

mosco, *m.* gnat, mosquito.

moscón, *m.* large fly; bumblebee; (coll.) importuning, bothering person.

moscovita, *n.* & *a.* Muscovite.

mosén, *m.* sir; title given to clergymen.

mosqueado, da, *a.* spotted, dotted, brindled.

mosqueador, *m.* fly swatter; (coll.) tail of a horse or of a cow.

mosquear. I. *va.* to swat or drive away flies; to make a smart repartee; to flog, to whip. II. *vr.* to suppress obstacles with violence; (coll.) to show resentment.

mosqueo, *m.* driving flies away.

mosquero, *m.* flytrap.

mosquerola, mosqueruela, *f.* muscadine pear.

mosqueta, *f.* (bot.) white musk rose.

mosquetazo, *m.* musket shot.

mosquete, *m.* musket.

mosquetería, body of musketeers; (theat.) people standing behind the pit.

mosqueteril, *a.* (theat.) (coll.) pertaining to the crowd in the pit.

mosquetero, *m.* musketeer; (theat.) spectator occupying standing room in the pit.

mosquil, mosquino, na, *a.* pertaining to flies.

mosquita, *f. dim.* small fly; (ornith.) small bird of Sardinia.—**m. muerta** = MOSCA MUERTA.

mosquitero, ra, *m.* & *f.* mosquito bar or net.

mosquito, *m.* gnat; mosquito; (coll.) tippler.

mostacero, ra, *m.* & *f.* mustard pot.

mostacilla, *f. dim.* sparrow shot; small bead.

mostacho, *m.* mustache; (coll.) blemish on the face.—**mostachos del bauprés,** (naut.) bowsprit shrouds.

mostachón, *m.* a kind of macaroon; a diamond-shaped ornament.

mostachoso, sa, *a.* wearing a mustache.

mostagán, *m.* (coll.) wine.

mostajo, *m.* (bot.) white beam tree.

mostaza, *f.* (bot.) mustard; mustard seed; fine shot.—**hacer la m.,** (coll.) to make the nose bleed with a blow.

mostazo, *m.* (bot.) mustard plant; strong, thick must.

mostear, *vn.* (of grapes) to yield must; to put must into vats; to mix must with old wine.

mostela, *f.* (agr.) gavel, sheaf.

mostelera, *f.* place where sheaves are laid up.

mostellar, *m.* (bot.) white beam tree.

mostense, *a.* belonging to an order of canons.

mostillo, *m.* cake made of must; sauce made of must and mustard.

mosto, *m.* must, grape juice.—**m. agustín,** a kind of must cake.

mostrable, *a.* that can be shown.

mostrado, da. I. *pp.* of MOSTRAR. II. *a.* accustomed, inured.

mostrador, ra, I. *a.* pointing; index (finger). II. *n.* demonstrator. III. *m.* counter (in a shop); stand; dial (of a watch).

mostrar. I. *va.* (*ind.* MUESTRO; *subj.* MUESTRE) to show; point out; to establish, prove, demonstrate; to feign, dissemble. II. *vr.* to appear, to show oneself, prove to be.

mostrenco, ca, *a.* (coll.) homeless; unowned; masterless; strayed, vagabond, vagrant; dull, ignorant, stupid; fat, bulky.

mota, *f.* burl (in cloth); mote, speck, mite; slight defect or fault; mound of earth; bog, hummock.

motacila, *f.* (ornith.) = AGUZANIEVE, wagtail.

¹mote, *m.* motto, device; nickname.

²mote, *m.* (Am.) stewed corn.

motear, *va.* to speck, speckle.

motejador, *n.* one who calls names.

motejar, *va.* to chaff, call offensive names.

motete, *m.* (mus.) motet or motetto.

motil, *m.* = MOCHIL, farmer's boy.

motilar, *va.* to cut or crop the hair of.

motilón, na. I. *a.* having little or cropped hair. II. *m.* (coll.) lay brother.

motín, *m.* mutiny, insurrection, riot.

motita, *f. dim.* mote, speck, mite.

motivar, *va.* to give a reason for; to cause.

motivo, va. I. *a.* motive, moving. II. *m.* motive, reason; (mus.) motif, theme.—**con m. de,** owing to, by reason of; on the occasion of.—**de su m. propio,** of one's own accord.—**por ningún m.,** under no circumstances.

moto, *m.* landmark, guidepost.

motocicleta, *f.* motorcycle.

motociclista, *n.* motorcyclist.

motolita, *f.* (ornith.) wagtail.

motolito, ta, *a.* easily deceived, ignorant.

motón, *m.* (naut.) block, pulley.

motonería, *f.* (naut.) pulley blocks, tackle.

motonero, *m.* block maker.

motor, ra. I. *n.* & *a.* mover(-ing). II. *m.* (mech.) motor; engine.—**m. acorazado,** enclosed motor, ironclad motor.—**m. bipolar,** two-pole motor.—**m. compound,** compound-wound motor.—**m. de cilindros convergentes,** V-motor, V-engine.—**m. de combustión,** or **de combustión interna,** internal-combustion engine, or motor.—**m. de enfriamiento por agua,** water-cooled motor.—**m. de enfriamiento por aire,** air-cooled motor.—**m. de explosión,** explosion motor.—**m. Diesel,** Diesel engine.—**m. generador,** motor-generator.—**m. propulsor,** (aer.) pusher engine.— **m. tractor,** (aer.) tractor engine.

motorista, *n.* motorman(-woman); motorist, driver.

motril, *m.* boy helper in a shop; MOTIL.

motriz, *a.* motive, moving.

motu proprio, (Lat.) by his own will.

movedizo, za, *a.* movable; shaky, unsteady; inconstant, shifting.

movedor, ra, *n.* mover, exciter.

movedura, *f.* movement; (med.) miscarriage.

mover. I. *va.* (*ind.* MUEVO; *subj.* MUEVA) to move; to make move; to drive, propel; to shake, wag; to prevail upon, persuade, induce; to prompt; to incite, promote, occasion; to stir; to excite; to touch, affect with emotion; (agr.) to bud, sprout. II. *vn.* (med.) to miscarry; (arch.) to spring an arch. III. *vr.* to move, stir.

movible, *a.* movable; mobile; changeable, fickle.

moviente, *a.* moving, motive.

móvil. I. *a.* movable; mobile; unsteady, shaky; portable. **II.** *m.* motive, incentive, inducement; mover, motor; moving body.

movilicé, movilice, *v. V.* MOVILIZAR.

movilidad, *f.* mobility; movableness; fickleness, inconstancy; unsteadiness.

movilización, *f.* (mil.) mobilization.

movilizar, *va.* (*pret.* MOVILICÉ; *subj.* MOVILICE) (mil.) to mobilize.

movimiento, *m.* movement, move; movement, activity (as a progressive movement); stir, agitation; life, liveliness; (of style) animation; traffic; (mech.) motion; (astr.) clock error; (art) distribution of lines and shades, technique; (mus.) tempo, time.—**m. alternativo,** (mech.) reciprocating motion.—**m. continuo,** perpetual motion.—**m. de tierras,** (Ry.) earthwork.—**m. oratorio,** oratorical gesture.—**m. perpetuo,** perpetual motion.

moxa, *f.* (surg.) moxa; cautery.

moxte, *interj.* = OXTE, keep off! get away!—**sin decir oxte ni m.,** without saying a word.

moyana, *f.* small culverin; moyenne (old type of cannon); (coll.) lie, fib; dog cake.

moyo, *m.* a unit of capacity (258 liters).

moyuelo, *m.* grits, pollard, coarse meal.

moza, *f.* girl, maid of all work; concubine, mistress; clothes pounder; last or winning game.

mozalbete, mozalbillo, *m.* lad, youth.

mozallón, *m.* young, robust laborer.

mozárabe, muzárabe, *a. & n.* Mozarab(-ic).

mozo, za. I. *a.* young, youthful; single, unmarried. **II.** *m.* youth, lad; manservant, waiter, porter; (coll.) fellow.—**m. de caballos,** groom, horse boy.—**m. de cordel,** or **de esquina,** porter in the street.—**m. de estación,** (station) porter.—**m. de paja y cebada,** hostler at an inn.—**buen m.** (**buena moza**), good-looking.

mozuelo, la, *n. dim.* young lad (lass).

¹mu, *m.* lowing of cattle, moo.

²mu, *f.* child's word for sleep.

muaré, *m.* moiré, watered silk.

mucamo, ma, *n.* (Am.) servant.

muceta, *f.* short cape worn by doctors; (Rom. Cath.) mozetta, cape worn by high dignitaries.

mucilaginoso, sa, *a.* mucilaginous, slimy.

mucílago, mucilago, *m.* mucilage; slime.

mucosidad, *f.* mucosity, mucousness.

mucoso, sa. I. *a.* mucous; slimy, viscous. **II.** *f.* mucous membrane.

mucronato, ta, *a.* mucronate, ending in a point.

múcura, *f.* (Venez., Colomb.) pitcher, ewer; (Am.) blockhead.

muchacha, *f.* girl; maid (servant).

muchachada, *f.* boyish act; prank; (Arg.) gang of boys.

muchachear, *vn.* to act like a boy or girl.

muchachería, *f.* boyish trick; crowd of boys.

muchachez, *f.* childhood, boyhood, girlhood.

muchachil, *a.* boylike, girl-like.

muchacho, cha. I. *a.* boyish, girlish, childish. **II.** *m.* boy, lad. **III.** *f.* girl, lass.

muchedumbre, *f.* multitude; crowd; populace, rabble.

muchísimo, ma. I. *a. super.* of MUCHO: very much. **II.** *adv.* a very great deal.

mucho, cha. I. *a.* much, a great deal of; (of time) long.—*pl.* many. **II.** *adv. m.* much, very much; a great deal; in a great measure; to a great extent; often; (of time) long; very.—**con m.,** by far.—**ni con m.,** nor anything like it, or near it, (diff. constr.) far from (it) (*Juan no es rico, ni con mucho,* John is far from rich).— **ni m. menos,** nor anything like it.—**no es m.,** it is no wonder.—**no ha m.,** not long since.— **por m. que,** no matter how much.

muda, *f.* change, alteration; change of underwear; moult, moulting; change of voice in boys; roost of birds of prey; a cosmetic.

mudable, mudadizo, za, *a.* changeable; fickle.

mudamente, *adv.* silently, mutely.

mudanza, *f.* change; mutation; removal, moving (residence); inconstancy; fickleness; (dance) figure, motion.

mudar. I. *va.* to change; to remove, deviate; to vary, alter; to moult. **II.** *vn.* (**de**) to change (as *mudar de dictamen,* or *opinión,* to change one's opinion, mind; *mudar de ropa,* to change one's clothes). **III.** *vr.* to reform, mend, change; to change one's clothes; to move, change one's place or residence.

mudéjar, *n.* Mohammedan who became a subject of Christian sovereigns.

mudez, *f.* dumbness.

mudo, da, *a. & n.* dumb; silent; mute.—**cine m.,** silent films.

mué, *m.* moiré, watered silk.

mueblaje, *m.* household furniture.

mueble. l. *a.* movable. **II.** *m.* piece of furniture. —*pl.* chattels, furniture, household goods.

mueblería, *f.* furniture factory or store.

mueblista, *n.* furniture maker or seller.

mueblo, mueble, *v. V.* MOBLAR.

mueca, *f.* grimace, wry face, grin.

muedín, *m.* muezzin.

muela, *f.* runner, upper millstone; grindstone, whetstone; grinder, molar tooth; water sufficient to set a mill in motion; hill, hillock; track or circle.—**m. cordal,** or **del juicio,** wisdom tooth.

muelo, muela, *v. V.* MOLER.

muellaje, *m.* wharfage, dockage.

¹muelle, *m.* (naut.) pier, wharf; (Ry.) freight platform.

²muelle. I. *a.* tender, delicate, soft; licentious; luxurious. **II.** *m.* (metal or rubber) spring; regulator, watch spring; (jewel.) chatelaine.

muellemente, *adv.* tenderly, gently, softly.

muer, *m.* = MUÉ.

muérdago, *m.* (bot.) mistletoe.

muerdo, muerda, *v. V.* MORDER.

muérgano, *m.* (Colomb.) worthless or contemptible person or thing.

muermo, *m.* (vet.) glanders.

muermoso, sa, *a.* (vet.) glanderous.

muero, muera, *v. V.* MORIR.

muerte, *f.* death; demise; skeleton representing death; ruin, havoc, destruction.—**m. civil,** civil death, loss of rights.—**m. chiquita,** (coll.) nervous shudder.—**m. natural,** natural death. —**m. senil,** death from old age, or from senility.—**a la m.** = DE M.—**a m.,** to the death.—**de mala m.,** insignificant, of no account.—**de m.,** fatally; (of hating, etc.) intensely, implacably; hopelessly ill, at the point of death.

muerto, ta. I. *pp. irreg.* of MORIR (sometimes used with the transitive meaning of MATAR, to kill, as in *he m. una liebre,* I have killed a hare). **II.** *a.* languid, faded; slaked.—**m. de** (fig.) dying with. **III.** *n.* corpse.—**echarle a una el m.,** (coll.) to put the blame on one.

muesca, *f.* notch, indentation, hack, nick, mortise; dovetail scarf.

muestra, *f.* specimen, sample; shop sign; placard, bill; model, pattern, copy; end of a piece of goods bearing the manufacturer's name; clock dial or face; clock or watch; sign, indication; (mil.) muster roll.—**dar muestras de,** to show signs of.

muestrario, *m.* collection of samples; specimen or sample book.

muestro, muestre, *v. V.* MOSTRAR.

muévedo, *m.* aborted fœtus.

muevo, mueva, *v. V.* MOVER.

mufla, *f.* muffle furnace.

muftí, *m.* mufti, a Mussulman expounder of the law.

muga, *f.* landmark, boundary.

mugido, *m.* lowing of cattle, moo.

múgil, *m.* (ichth.) mullet.
mugir, *vn.* (*ind.* MUJO; *subj.* MUJA) to low, bellow.
mugre, *f.* dirt, filth.
mugriento, ta, *a.* dirty, filthy.
mugrón, *m.* sprig, shoot, sucker, tiller.
mugroso, sa, *a.* = MUGRIENTO.
muguete, *m.* (bot.) lily of the valley.
muharra, *f.* = MOHARRA, head of a spear.
muisca, *n.* & *a.* (Am.) Muysca, Chibcha.
mujer, *f.* woman; wife, mate.—**m. casera,** good housewife.—**m. de estado honesto,** spinster. —**m. de gobierno,** housewife, housekeeper.— **m. mundana, perdida,** or **pública,** prostitute.—**tomar m.,** to take a wife, marry.
mujercilla, *f.* little woman; insignificant woman.
mujeriego, a. I. *a.* feminine, womanly; womanish; fond of women.—**a la m.,** woman-fashion, womanlike. **II.** *m.* women collectively.
mujeril, *a.* womanish, womanly, feminine.
mujerilmente, *adv.* like women, like a woman; effeminately.
mujerío, *m.* gathering of women.
mujerón, *m.* **mujerona,** *f. aug.* big woman; matron.
mujerzuela, *f. dim.* little woman.
mujo, muja, *v. V.* MUGIR.
mújol, *m.* (ichth.) mullet.
¹mula, *f.* kind of shoe worn by the Pope.
²mula, *f.* female mule.
mulada, *f.* (Am.) drove of mules.
muladar, *m.* dungheap; rubbish heap.
muladí, *n.* renegade Christian.
mulante, *m.* muleteer; mule boy.
mular, *a.* pertaining to mules.
mulatero, *m.* muleteer, mule driver.
mulato, ta, *n.* & *a.* mulatto.
múleo, muléolo, *m.* ancient Roman shoe with upturned point.
muleque, *n.* (Cuba) newly arrived Negro boy.
mulero. I. *a.* (horse) fond of mules. **II.** *m.* mule boy.
muleta, *f.* crutch; prop, support; red flag used by bullfighters; light luncheon.
muletada, *f.* drove of mules.
muletero, *m.* muleteer, mule driver.
muletilla, *f. dim.* cross-handle cane; pet word or phrase, often repeated in talking; red flag used by bullfighters; frog or toggle; (min.) crutch.
muleto, *m.* young mule not yet broken.
mulilla, *f. dim.* small mule.
mulo, *m.* mule.
mulquía, *f.* title, deed.
mulso, sa, *a.* sweetened with honey or sugar.
multa, *f.* (money) fine.—**multar,** *va.* to fine.
multicaule, *a.* (bot.) multicauline.
multicolor, *a.* many-colored.
multifloro, ra, *a.* many-flowered.
multiforme, *a.* multiform.
multilátero, ra, *a.* multilateral.
multimillonario, ria, *n.* & *a.* multimillionaire.
multípara, *a.* (of animals) multiparous; (of women) having had more than one child.
múltiple, *a.* multiple, complex; (int. combust. eng.) manifold.
múltiplex, *a.* multiplex.
multiplicable, *a.* multiplicable, multipliable.
multiplicación, *f.* multiplication.
multiplicador, ra. I. *n.* & *a.* multiplier(-plying). **II.** *m.* (arith.) multiplier.
multiplicando, *m.* (math.) multiplicand.
multiplicar, *va.* & *vr.* (*pret.* MULTIPLIQUÉ; *subj.* MULTIPLIQUE) to multiply.
multíplice, *a.* multiple; multiplex.
multiplicidad, *f.* multiplicity.
multipliqué, multiplique, *v. V.* MULTIPLICAR.
mútiplo, pla, *n.* & *a.* multiple.
multitud, *f.* multitude; crowd; the masses.
mulla, *f.* digging around vines.
mullido, *m.* soft filling for cushions, etc.

mullidor, ra, *n.* one who fluffs (as wool or feathers).
mullir, *va.* to fluff, make soft, mollify; to engineer; to dig around (vines and trees).—**m. la cama,** to beat up the bed.
¹mullo, *m.* (ichth.) surmullet.
²mullo, *m.* (Am.) glass beads.
mundanal, *a.* worldly, mundane.
mundanalidad, *f.* worldliness.
mundanear, *vn.* to indulge in worldly things.
mundano, na, *a.* mundane, worldly.
mundial, *a.* world (as *a.*, as in *la guerra mundial,* the World War), global, universal.
mundificación, *f.* act of cleansing.
mundificante, *a.* cleansing, purifying.
mundificar, *va.* to cleanse, purify.
mundificativo, va, *a.* cleansing.
mundillo, *m. dim.* arched clothes dryer; cushion for making lace; warming pan; (bot.) viburnum.
mundinovi, *m.* = MUNDONUEVO.
mundo, *m.* world; (coll.) great multitude, great quantity; social life, circle; dissipated life; experience.—**echar al m.,** to create; to give birth to.—**echarse al m.,** to plunge into dissipation. —**entrar en el m.,** to go into society.—**gran m.,** high society.—**medio m.,** many people.— **ser hombre de m.,** to be a man of the world, a man of experience.—**tener m.,** or **mucho m.,** to have had experience, know life or the world.—**todo el m.,** everybody.—**ver m.,** to travel, see the world.
mundonuevo, *m.* peep show; cosmorama.
munición, *f.* (often in the *pl.*) ammunition; small shot; birdshot; charge of firearms.—**municiones de boca,** provisions, food.—**municiones de guerra,** war stores.—**de m.,** supplied by the government; done hurriedly.
municionar, *va.* to supply with ammunition.
municipal. I. *a.* municipal. **II.** *m.* policeman.
municipalidad, *f.* municipality; townhall; municipal government.
munícipe, *m.* citizen, denizen.
municipio, *m.* municipality; municipium.
munificencia, *f.* munificence, liberality.
munificentísimo, ma, *a. super.* of MUNÍFICO, most, or very, munificent.
munífico, ca, *a.* munificent, liberal.
munitoria, *f.* art of fortification.
muñeca, *f.* (anat.) wrist; doll; figure for dressmakers; (mech.) puppet; sugar teat; pounce bag; polishing bag.
muñeco, *m.* puppet, manikin; boy doll; soft, effeminate fellow.
muñeira, *f.* a popular dance of Galicia.
muñequear, *va.* (fencing) to play with the wrist.
muñequería, *f.* doll shop; (coll.) excessive finery, overdressing.
muñidor, *m.* beadle, messenger; plotter.
muñir, *va.* to summon.
muñón, *m.* stump of an amputated limb; (artil.) trunnion; (mech.) gudgeon pin, wristpin.
muñonera, *f.* trunnion plate; (mech.) gudgeon socket, journal box, bearing.
murajes, *m. pl.* (bot.) a medicinal herb.
mural, *a.* mural, pertaining to walls.
muralla, *f.* (fort.) rampart; wall (of a city).
murallón, *m. aug.* (fort.) strong wall.
murar, *va.* to wall, surround with a rampart.
murceguillo, murciégalo, *m.* = MURCIÉLAGO.
murciélago, *m.* (zool.) bat.
murena, *f.* (ichth.) a kind of eel.
murete, *m. dim.* small wall.
¹murga, *f.* lees of olives.
²murga, *f.* (coll.) band of street musicians.
murgón, *m.* (ichth.) parr, smolt.
muriático, ca, *a.* (chem.) muriatic.
muriato, *m.* (chem.) muriate.
múrice, *m.* (ichth.) murex; (poet.) purple.
murícidos, *m. pl.* (zool.) Muricidæ.
múridos, *m. pl.* (zool.) Muridæ.

murió, muriendo, v. V. MORIR.

murmujear, va. to murmur, to whisper.

murmullo, m. whisper, whispering; murmuring, murmur, ripple, purl; rustle.

murmuración, f. backbiting, gossip, slander.

murmurador, ra, n. detractor, backbiter.

murmurante, a. murmuring, purling.

murmurar, vn. to purl, ripple (as streams); to rustle (as leaves); to grumble, mutter; to whisper, murmur; to gossip, backbite.

murmurio, m. murmur.

muro, m. (outside) wall (of house or garden); (fort.) rampart.

¹murria, f. (coll.) blues; surliness, sullenness.

²murria, f. (pharm.) an astringent lotion.

múrrino, na, a. murrine, made of murra.

murrio, ria, a. sullen, surly, sulky.

murta, f. (bot.) myrtle; myrtle berry.

murtal, m., murtera, f. myrtle grove.

murtilla, murtina, f. (bot.) myrtle; its berry; liquor made from this berry.

murtón, m. myrtle berry.

murucuya, f. (bot.) purple passion flower.

murueco, m. = MORUECO, ram, male sheep.

¹mus, m. a card game.—no hay m., cannot be granted.

²mus.—sin decir tus ni m., (coll.) without saying a word.

musa, f. Muse.—pl. the Muses; fine arts.

musáceo, a. I. a. (bot.) musaceous. II. f. pl. Musaceæ.

musaraña, f. fetid shrewmouse; any small animal, insect, or vermin; (coll.) ridiculous puppet or stuffed figure; floating speck in the eye.—mirar a, or pensar en, las musarañas, to be absent-minded.

muscaria, muscícapa, f. (ornith.) fly-catcher.

múscido, da. I. n. & a. (zool.) muscid. II. m. pl. Muscidæ.

muscívoro, ra, a. (zool.) fly-catching.

¹musco, ca, a. dark brown.

²musco, m. (bot.) = ²MUSGO.

muscular, a. muscular.

musculatura, f. musculature.

músculo, m. muscle; brawn; (zool.) a huge whale.—m. complexo, complexus.—m. del sastre, sartorius.—m. gemelo, gemellus.—m. glúteo, gluteous muscle.—m. lumbrical, lumbricalis (pl. lumbricales).—m. sartorio, sartorius.—m. serrato, serratus.

musculoso, sa, a. muscular, brawny.

muselina, f. muslin.

museo, m. museum.

muserola, f. noseband of a bridle.

musgaño, m. (zool.) shrewmouse.

¹musgo, ga, = ¹MUSCO.

²musgo, m. (bot.) moss.—m. marino, sea coralline.

musgoso, sa, a. mossy; moss-covered.

música, f. music; body of performing musicians; musical composition; sheet music.—m. celestial, (coll.) nonsense; moonshine.—m. coreada, chorus music.—m. de campanas, chimes.—m. ratonera, harsh music.—m. rítmica, stringed-instrument music.—vaya Vd. con la m. a otra parte, (coll.) get out, don't bother me.

musical, a. musical.

músico, ca. I. a. musical. II. n. musician.

musiquero, m. music cabinet.

musitar, vn. to mumble, mutter, whisper.

muslera, f. armor for the thigh.

muslime; muslímico, ca, a. Moslem, Mohammedan.

muslo, m. thigh.

musmón, m. (zool.) moufflon, wild sheep.

musquerola, f. = MOSQUEROLA, muscadine pear.

mustaco, m. cake made with must.

mustela, f. (zool.) weasel; (ichth.) a kind of dogfish.

mustélido, da. I. a. (zool.) musteline. II. m. pl. (zool.) Mustelidae.

mustiamente, adv. sadly, languidly.

mustio, tia, a. withered; sad, languid.

musulmán, na, n. & a. Mussulman.

muta, f. pack of hounds.

mutabilidad, f. mutability; fickleness.

mutación, f. mutation, change; (theat.) change of scene; unseasonable weather.

mutatis mutandis, (Lat.) adv. with the necessary changes (in words, etc.).

mutilación, f. mutilation.

mutilar, va. to mutilate; to cut short, reduce; to deface, mar.

mútilo, la, a. maimed, crippled, mutilated.

mutis, m. (theat.) exit.

mutismo, m. mutism, muteness.

mutual, a. mutual, reciprocal.

mutualidad, f. mutualness; system of organized mutual aid; mutual-aid association.

mutualismo, m. system of organized mutual aid.

mutualista. I. a. pertaining to the system of organized mutual aid. II. n. member of a mutual-aid organization.

mutuamente, adv. mutually, reciprocally.

mutuante, m. & f. (com.) lender, loaner.

mutuario, ria; mutuatario, ria, m. & f. (law) mutuary.

mutuo, tua. I. a. mutual, reciprocal. II. m. (law) loan, mutuum.

muy, adv. very; greatly, most.—m. de noche, late at night.—m. ilustre, most illustrious.—m. mucho, (coll.) very much.—M. señor mío, Dear Sir (business letter).—soy m. de Vd., I am entirely yours.

muz, m. (naut.) extremity of the cutwater.

muzárabe, n. & a. = MOZÁRABE, Mozarab(-ic).

N

N., or N. N., a form often used in the sense of So-and-So, X., meaning any person.

naba, f. (bot.) rutabaga, Swedish turnip.

nabab, nababo, m. nabob, nawab.

nabal, nabar. I. a. pertaining to or made of turnips. II. m. turnip field.

nabería, f. turnip pottage; heap of turnips.

nabí, m. Moorish prophet.

nabillo, m. dim. small turnip.

nabina, f. rape and turnip seed.

nabiza, f. turnip rootlets; turnip greens.

nabla, f. (mus.) a kind of psaltery.

nabo, m. (bot.) turnip (plant and root); any bulb; stock of a tail; cylindrical timber; spindle; king-post; (naut.) mast.—n. gallego = NABA.

naborí, n. free Indian servant.

naboría, f. free female Indian servant; allotment of free Indian servants (during the Spanish conquest of America).

nacar, m. mother-of-pearl.

nacarado, da; nacáreo, a; nacarino, na, a. nacreous, pert. to, made of, mother-of-pearl.

nacarón, m. pearl shell of inferior quality.

nacascolo, m. (C. A.) a tropical tree.

nacela, f. (arch.) scotia, a concave molding.

nacencia, f. growth; (fig.) tumor, outgrowth.

nacer. I. vn. (pp. NACIDO, NATO; ind. NAZCO; subj. NAZCA) to be born, come into the world; to sprout, come forth, grow (as branches, plants); to rise, come out, appear (as the sun); to spring, rise, flow, have its source (as a stream, a river); to begin, originate, start, issue; to infer one thing from another.—n. de cabeza, to be born to wretchedness.—n. de pies, to be born lucky. II. vr. to sprout (as seeds) in the open air; to split near a seam (as clothes).

nacido, da. I. pp. of NACER. II. a. proper, apt, fit, connate.—bien or mal n., well or ill bred.

III. *m.* living man; pimple, boil, furuncle; sprout.

naciente. I. *a.* rising; growing; very recent; (her.) naissant. **II.** *m.* Orient, East.

nacimiento, *m.* birth; growing of plants; beginning; place of birth; rising (as of the sun): origin, issue; descent, lineage; source of a river or spring; scene representing the Nativity at Yuletide.—**de n.,** from birth.

nación. I. *f.* nation; (coll.) birth; (Am.) race, tribe of Indians.—*pl.* **Naciones Unidas,** United Nations.—**Sociedad de las Naciones,** League of Nations. **II.** *m.* (coll.) foreigner.—**de n.,** by nationality.

nacional. I. *a.* national; native; domestic, home. **II.** *m.* native; militiaman.

nacionalidad, *f.* nationality; citizenship.

nacionalismo, *m.* nationalism.

nacionalista, *n.* & *a.* nationalist(-ic).

nacionalización, *f.* naturalization; acclimatization.

nacionalizar, *va.* to naturalize; to acclimate.

nacionalmente, *adv.* nationally.

nacrita, *f.* variety of talc.

nacho, cha, *a.* flat-nosed, pug-nosed.

nada. I. *f.* nothing, naught; nothingness; nonentity. **II.** *indef. pron.* nothing, not anything; little or very little.—**n. de eso,** none of that; not at all; not so.—**n. de nuevo,** nothing new. —**de n.,** insignificant, good-for-nothing; (after thanks) you are welcome, don't mention it.—**¡en n.!,** not at all!—**por n.,** for nothing; under no circumstances. **III.** *adv.* nothing, not, not at all, by no means.

nadadera, *f.* gourd or bladder for swimming.

nadadero, *m.* swimming place.

nadador, ra, *n.* & *a.* swimmer(-ing).

nadante, *a.* (poet.) natant, swimming.

nadar, *vn.* to swim; to float.

nadería, *f.* (coll.) insignificant thing, a mere nothing, trifle.

nadie, *indef. pron.* nobody, no one, none; (after negative) anybody.

nadilla, *f.* = NADERÍA.

nadir, *m.* (astr.) nadir.

nado.—a n., swimming; afloat.

nafta, *f.* naphtha.

naftalina, *f.* naphthalin.

naftílico, ca, *a.* (chem.) naphthalic.

naftilo, *m.* (chem.) naphthyl.

naftol, *m.* (chem.) naphthol.

naguas, *f. pl.* petticoat.

naguatlato, *m.* (Mex.) Indian interpreter.

nahuatle, *m.* Nahuatlan, Mexican Indian language.

naife, *m.* diamond of the first water.

naipe, *m.* (playing) card; cards; pack of cards.—dar (a uno) **el n.,** to have good luck at cards. —**dar el n. para una cosa,** to be very skilful or dexterous.—**tener buen n.** = DAR EL N.

naire, *m.* elephant keeper, trainer.

nalga, *f.* buttock, rump.—**nalgada,** *f.* ham; butt with, or slap on, the buttocks; spank.—**nalgar,** *a.* gluteal, pert. to the buttocks.—**nalgatorio,** *m.* (coll.) seat, posterior, buttocks.—**nalgudo, da,** *a.* having big buttocks.—**nalguear,** *vn.* to wiggle the buttocks in walking.

nana, *f.* (coll.) grandma; lullaby; (Mex., coll.) child's nurse; (Am.) (coll.) mamma.

nansa, *f.* fishpond; fish trap.

nansú, nanzú, *m.* (Am.) a kind of cotton cloth.

nao, *f.* ship, vessel.

naonato, ta, *a.* born on board ship.

napea, *f.* wood nymph.

napelo, *m.* (bot.) monkshood, wolfsbane.

napoleón, *m.* napoleon (5-franc piece).

napoleónico, ca, *a.* Napoleonic.

napolitana, *f.* in some card games, a certain combination of cards.

napolitano, na, *n.* & *a.* Neapolitan.

naque, *m.* company of two strolling comedians.

naranja, *f.* (bot.) orange.—**n. cajel,** blood orange.—**media n.** (coll.) better half (wife, husband).

naranjada, *f.* orangeade; rude saying or deed.

naranjado, da, *a.* orange-colored.

naranjal, *m.* orange grove.

naranjazo, *m.* blow with an orange.

naranjero, ra. I. *a.* **cañon n.,** (artil.) cannon carrying balls of the size of oranges. **II.** *n.* orange raiser or seller. **III.** *m.* orange tree.

naranjilla, *f.* small green orange for preserving.

naranjo, *m.* (bot.) orange tree; (coll.) booby, noodle, stupid man.

¹narciso, *m.* (bot.) daffodil; narcissus.

²narciso, *m.* fop, coxcomb.

narcosis, *f.* narcosis.

narcótico, ca, *a.* & *m.* narcotic.—**narcotina,** *f.* narcotine.—**narcotismo,** *m.* narcotism.

narcotizador, ra, *a.* narcotic, narcose.

narcotizar, *va.* to narcotize.

nardino, na, *a.* made of spikenard.

nardo, *m.* (bot.) spikenard, nard, tuberose.

narguile, *m.* narghile.

narigón, na; narigudo, da. I. *a.* large-nosed. **II.** *m.* large nose. **III.** *n.* large-nosed person.

nariguera, *f.* nose pendant.

narigueta, nariguita, *f. dim.* small nose.

nariz, *f.* nose; nostril; sense of smell; bouquet (of wine); socket of a door knocker; nozzle; cutwater.—**n. aguileña,** Roman, or aquiline, nose.—**n. chata,** flat nose.—**n. perfilada,** perfect, or well-proportioned, nose.—**n. respingada,** or **respingona,** retroussé nose, turned-up nose.—**dar en las narices,** (coll.) to smell or perceive a thing at a distance.—**meter la n. en todas partes,** to be a busybody, to nose about.—**tener de,** or **por, las narices,** or **agarrado por las narices,** to lead by the nose, to control at will.

narizón, na, *n.* & *a.* = NARIGÓN.

narizota, *f. aug.* large, ugly nose.

narra, *f.* (bot.) narra, an Asiatic tree.

narrable, *a.* capable of being narrated.

narración, *f.* narration, account; chronicle.

narrador, ra, *n.* & *a.* narrator(-ing), chronicler (-ing).

narrar, *va.* to narrate, relate, chronicle, tell.

narrativa, *f.* narrative.

narrativo, va; narratorio, ria, *a.* narrative.

narria, *f.* sledge, sled; (coll.) heavy, bulky woman.

narval, *m.* (ichth.) narwhal, sea unicorn.

narvaso, *m.* cornstalks (as fodder).

nasa, *f.* fyke, fish trap, bag net; bow net; fisherman's basket; basket; jar.

nasal, *a.* nasal, pertaining to the nose.

nasardo, *m.* (mus.) nasard, organ stop.

nata, *f.* cream; prime or choice part; skim, scum.—*pl.* whipped cream with sugar.

natación, *f.* natation, swimming.

natal. I. *a.* natal, native. **II.** *m.* birth, birthday.—**natalicio, cia. I.** *a.* natal. **II.** *m.* nativity, birthday.—**natalidad,** *f.* birth rate.

natátil, *a.* able to swim, floating.

natatorio, a. I. *a.* swimming, natatorial. **II.** *m.* natatorium, swimming pool or place.

naterón, *m.* second curd.

natilla, *f.* custard.

natío. I. *a.* native. **II.** *m.* birth; sprouting.

natividad, *f.* nativity; Yuletide, Christmas.

nativo, va, *a.* native; indigenous; domestic; natural born; inborn, innate.

nato, ta. I. *pp. irreg.* of NACER. **II.** *a.* implied by or inherent in an office or position.

natrón, *m.* natron; barilla.

natura, *f.* nature; genital organs; (mus.) major scale.

natural. I. *a.* natural; native; common, usual; plain, pure, unadulterated; artless, ingenuous, naïve; spontaneous, unstudied; (mus.) natural. **II.** *n.* native; national; aboriginal. **III.** *m.* temper, disposition, nature.—**al n.,** without art or affectation.—**del n.,** (art) from life, from nature.

naturaleza, *f.* nature; constitution; sex, genitals, especially the female; sort, character, kind; naturalization; temperament or disposition.—**n. muerta,** (art) still life.

naturalicé, naturalice, *v.* V. NATURALIZAR.

naturalidad, *f.* naturalness; birthright, nationality.

naturalismo, *m.* naturalism; realism.

naturalista, *n.* & *a.* naturalist(-ic).

naturalización, *f.* naturalization.

naturalizar. I. *va.* (*pret.* NATURALICÉ; *subj.* NATURALICE) to naturalize. **II.** *vr.* to get accustomed; to become naturalized.

naturalmente, *adv.* naturally; of course.

naufragante, *a.* sinking, perishing.

naufragar, *vn.* (*pret.* NAUFRAGUÉ; *subj.* NAUFRAGUE) to be shipwrecked; to fail, be unsuccessful, fall through.

naufragio, *m.* shipwreck; disaster, failure, disappointment, calamity.

náufrago, ga. l. *a.* & *n.* shipwrecked (person). **II.** *m.* (ichth.) shark.

naufragué, naufrague, *v.* V. NAUFRAGAR.

naumaquia, *f.* naumachy, mock sea fight.

náusea, *f.* nausea, nauseousness.

nauseabundo, da, *a.* nauseous, loathsome.

nausear, *vn.* to feel nausea, be nauseated.

nauseativo, va, *a.* nauseating, nauseous.

nauseoso, sa, *a.* = NAUSEABUNDO.

nauta, *m.* mariner, seafaring man.—**náutica,** *f.* navigation.—**náutico, ca,** *a.* nautical.

nautilo, *m.* nautilus.

nava, *f.* hollow, plain surrounded by mountains.

navacero, ra, *n.* one who cultivates a. NAVAZO.

navaja, *f.* razor; clasp knife, pen knife; razor clam; tusk of a wild boar; (coll.) evil tongue.— **n. de afeitar, or de barba,** razor.—*pl.* **navajas de gallo,** cockspurs.

navajada, *f.;* **navajazo,** *m.* thrust or gash with a clasp knife or razor.

navajero, *m.* razor case; shaving doily.

navajita, *f. dim.* small clasp knife or razor.

navajo, *m.* = LAVAJO, pool where cattle drink.

navajón, *m. aug.* large clasp knife or razor.

navajonazo, *m.* gash or wound made with a large clasp knife or a razor.

navajuela, *f. dim.* small clasp knife.

naval, *a.* naval.

navarca, *m.* navarch, commander of a fleet among the Greeks and Romans.

navarro, rra, *n.* & *a.* Navarrese.

navazo, *m.* kitchen garden on a sandy shore.

nave, *f.* ship, vessel; (arch.) nave; aisle.—**n. aérea,** airship.—**n. de San Pedro,** Roman Catholic Church.

navecilla, *f. dim.* small ship; (eccl.) censer, thurible.

navegable, *a.* navigable.

navegación, *f.* navigation; sea voyage; time used in a sea voyage.—**n. aérea,** aerial navigation, aviation.—**n. circular,** great-circle sailing.— **n. costanera,** coast navigation, coasting trade. —**n. de altura,** sailing by the stars' altitudes.

navegador, ra, *n.* & *a.* navigator(-ing).

navegante, *n.* & *a.* navigator(-ing).

navegar. I. *vn.* (*pret.* NAVEGUÉ; *subj.* NAVEGUE) to navigate, sail, steer; to travel.—**n. en conserva,** to sail under convoy. **II.** *va.* to make (as speed).

naveta, *f.* (eccl.) censer, thurible; small drawer.

navícula, *f. dim.* small ship; (bot.) navicula.

navicular, *a.* (anat.) navicular, boat-shaped.

navichuelo, la, *n. dim.* small ship.

navidad, *f.* Nativity; Christmas Day.—**tener**

muchas navidades, to be old, to have lived many a year.

navideño, ña, *a.* pertaining to Yuletide.

naviero. I. *a.* shipping, ship (as *a.*). **II.** *m.* ship owner.

navío, *m.* warship, armor-clad vessel; ship.—**n. anegado,** (naut.) water-logged ship.—**n. de aguante,** (naut.) a stiff ship.—**n. de alto bordo** = N. DE LÍNEA.—**n. de aviso,** despatch boat.—**n. de guerra,** warship.—**n. de línea,** line-of-battle ship.—**n. de transporte,** transport.—**n. de tres puentes,** three-decker.

náyade, *f.* naiad, water nymph.

nayuribe, *f.* (bot.) an amarantaceous herb.

nazareno, na. I. *n.* & *a.* Nazarene; Nazarite. **II.** *m.* penitent who goes in processions in Passion Week.

nazareo, ea, *a.* Nazarite.

nazco, nazca, *v.* V. NACER.

nazi, *m.* Nazi.

názula, *f.* second curd.

nébeda, *f.* (bot.) nepeta, catmint.

nebladura, *f.* (agr.) damage from mist.

neblí, *m.* (ornith.) falcon gentle.

neblina, *f.* mist, fog.

neblinoso, sa, *a.* foggy, misty.

nebreda, *f.* plantation of juniper trees.

nebrina, *f.* juniper berry.

nebulón, na, *n.* hypocrite.

nebulosa, *f.* (astr.) nebula.

nebulosidad, *f.* nebulosity, nebulousness.

nebuloso, sa, *a.* misty, nebulous, hazy.

necear, *vn.* to talk nonsense, to play the fool.

necedad, *f.* stupidity, foolishness, nonsense.

necesaria, *f.* privy, water-closet.

necesariamente, *adv.* necessarily.

necesario, ria, *a.* necessary.

neceser, *m.* dressing case, toilet case.—**n. de costura,** work basket, sewing case, hussy.

necesidad, *f.* necessity; need, want; emergency; evacuation of the body by stool or water.—**la n. carece de ley,** necessity knows no law.— **la n. tiene cara de hereje,** need knows no shame, need has a brazen face.—**por n.,** from necessity; necessarily.

necesitado, da. I. *pp.* of NECESITAR. **II.** *a.* & *n.* indigent, needy (person).

necesitar. I. *va.* to need; to necessitate, constrain, compel. **II.** *vn.* (**de**) to be in need (of).

neciamente, *adv.* stupidly, foolishly.

necio, cia. I. *a.* stupid, idiotic, foolish; imprudent, injudicious. **II.** *n.* fool.

necrófago, ga, *a.* necrophagous, carrion-eating.

necrología, *f.* necrology.

necrológico, ca, *a.* necrological.

necrópolis, *f.* necropolis, burying ground.

necropsia, necroscopía, *f.* necropsy, autopsy, post-mortem examination.

necroscópico, ca, *a.* pert. to autopsy.

necrosis, *f.* (med.) necrosis.

néctar, *m.* nectar; any delicious drink.

nectáreo, a; nectarino, na, *a.* nectarean.

nectario, *m.* (bot.) nectary.

neerlandés, sa. I. *a.* & *n.* Dutch(-man, -woman). **II.** *m.* Dutch (language).

nefalismo, *m.* total abstinence from alcoholic beverages; prohibitionism.

nefalista, *n.* total abstainer; prohibitionist.

nefandamente, *adv.* nefariously, abominably.

nefando, da; nefario, ria, *a.* nefarious, heinous.

nefas, *adv.*—**por fas o por n.,** justly or unjustly.

nefasto, ta, *a.* sad, ominous, unlucky.

nefrítico, ca, *a.* (med.) nephritic.

nefritis, *f.* (med.) nephritis.

nefrocele, *f.* (med.) nephrocele, hernia of the kidney.

nefrolito, *m.* (med.) nephrolith, kidney stone.

negable, *a.* deniable.

negación, *f.* negation; denial; want or total privation; (gram.) negative particle.

negado, da. *a.* inapt, unfit; dull, stupid.

negador, ra, *n.* denier, disclaimer.

negante, *a.* denying; refusing.

negar. I. *va.* (*ind. pres.* NIEGO, *pret.* NEGUÉ; *subj.* NIEGUE) to deny; to refuse; to forbid, prohibit; to disown, disclaim; to disregard; to hide, conceal, dissemble.—**n. el saludo a,** to cut, not to speak to. **II.** *vr.* to decline, refuse; to be "not at home" to visitors.—**n. a sí mismo,** to control one's passions and appetites, exercise self-control.

negativa, *f.* negative, refusal.

negativamente, *adv.* negatively.

negativo, va. I. *a.* negative; (elec. and math.) negative. **II.** *f.* (photog.) negative.

negligencia, *f.* negligence, neglect, carelessness.

negligente, *a.* negligent, careless, neglectful.

negligentemente, *adv.* negligently, neglectfully, carelessly.

negociable, *a.* (com.) negotiable.

negociación, *f.* negotiation; business transaction.

negociado, *m.* bureau, division or section in official departments; business; employment; affair.

negociador, ra, *n.* business agent; negotiator.

negociante. I. *a.* negotiating, trading, engaged in trade. **II.** *n.* dealer, merchant, business man.

negociar, *vn.* to trade; to negotiate.

negocio, *m.* occupation, business; affair; transaction; bargain; commerce; utility or interest in trading.—*pl.* business, commercial affairs.— **n. redondo,** good bargain.—**de negocios,** business (as *a.*), commercial.

negocioso, sa, *a.* active, diligent.

negozuelo, *m.* *dim.* petty business.

negra, *f.* foil for fencing; Negro woman.

negrada, *f.* (Am.) crowd or gathering of Negroes.

negral, *a.* blackish.

negrear, *vn.* to become black; to appear black.

negrecer, *vn.* (*ind.* NEGREZCO; *subj.* NEGREZCA) to blacken, become black.

negrero, ra, *n.* & *a.* slave trader(-ing).

negreta, *f.* (ornith.) coot, a kind of duck.

negrezco, negrezca, *v.* V. NEGRECER.

negrilla, *f.* (ichth.) black conger eel.

negrillera, *f.* plantation of black poplars.

negrillo, *m.* *dim.* (min.) black silver ore, stephanite; (bot.) black poplar.

negrito, ta, *n.* young or little Negro; (Am.) (coll.) dearest, darling.

negrizco, ca, *a.* blackish; dark brown.

negro, gra. I. *a.* black; gloomy, dark, dismal; unfortunate, wretched; (her.) sable.—**suerte n.,** very bad luck. **II.** *n.* Negro; (Am.) (coll.) dearest, darling. **III.** *m.* black (color).—**n. animal,** boneblack.—**n. de humo,** lampblack. —**n. de la uña,** tip of the (finger) nail.

negror, *m.*; **negrura,** *f.* blackness.

negruzco, ca, *a.* blackish, dark brown.

neguijón, *m.* caries, decay of the teeth.

neguilla, *f.* (bot.) fennel flower, love-in-a-mist; age mark in horses' teeth; obstinate denial.

negus, *m.* negus (title of Ethiopian emperor).

neis, *f.* (geol.) gneiss.

nema, *f.* seal or sealing of a letter.

nematelmintos, *m.* *pl.* (zool.) Nemathelminthes.

nemátodo, da. I. *a.* filiform. **II.** *m.* (zool.) Nematode.

nemeo, a, *a.* Nemæan.

némine discrepante, (Lat.) unanimously.

nemoroso, sa, *a.* wooded, nemorous.

nene, nena. I. *n.* (coll.) infant, baby; dear, darling. **II.** *m.* (ironic) villain.

nenúfar, *m.* (bot.) white water lily.

neo, *m.* (chem.) neon. Also NEÓN.

neocatolicismo, *m.* Neo-Catholicism, a politico-religious system advocating the reëstablishment of the Catholic Church as the supreme ruler in both religious and political matters. The term is also used in the sense of progressive Catholicism, modernism.

neocatólico, ca, *n.* & *a.* Neo-Catholic. V. NEOCATOLICISMO.

neófito, *m.* neophyte.

neofobia, *f.* aversion to innovations.

neogranadino, na, *n.* & *a.* New-Granadian (from New Granada, former name of Colombia).

neolatino, na, *a.* Neo-Latin.

neolítico, ca, *a.* neolithic.

neológico, ca, *a.* neologistic.

neologismo, *m.* neologism.

neólogo, ga, *n.* neologist.

neomejicano, na, *n.* & *a.* New Mexican.

neomenia, *f.* (astr.) neomenia, first day of the moon.

neón, *m.* (chem.) neon.

neoplasma, *m.* (med.) neoplasm.

neoplatonicismo, *m.* Neoplatonism.

neoplatónico, ca, *a.* Neoplatonic.

neorama, *m.* cyclorama.

neosalvarsán, *m.* (chem.) neosalvarsan.

neoyorquino, na. I. *n.* New Yorker. **II.** *a.* New York (as *a.*).

neozelandés, sa. I. *n.* New Zealander. **II.** *a.* New Zealand (as *a.*), of or from New Zealand.

neozoico, ca, *a.* (geol.) Neozoic.

neperiano, na, *a.* Naperian, Napierian.

nepote, *m.* privileged relative of the Pope.

nepotismo, *m.* nepotism.

neptúneo, a, *a.* Neptunian.

neptúnico, ca, *a.* (geol.) Neptunian.

neptunismo, *m.* (geol.) Neptunian theory.

neptunista, *n.* & *a.* (geol.) Neptunist(-ic).

Neptuno, *m.* (astr.) Neptune; (poet.) the sea.

nequáquam, *adv.* (Lat.) (coll.) by no means.

nequicia, *f.* perversity.

nereida, *f.* nereid, sea nymph.

nerita, *f.* nerita, a mollusk.

neroniano, na, *a.* Neronian.

nervadura, *f.* (arch.) nervure, rib; (carp.) feather; (min.) leader; (biol.) nervation, nervure.

nérveo, a, *a.* pertaining to nerves.

nervezuelo, nerviecillo, *m.* *dim.* nervule.

nervino, na, *a.* nervine, nerve-strengthening.

nervio, *m.* (anat.) nerve; energy, vigor, strength; string of a musical instrument; rib, reinforcement; (bookbinding) rib, fillet; (naut.) span rope, stay; (bot.) nerve.—**n. maestro,** tendon. —**n. óptico,** optic nerve.—**n. vago,** vagus pneumogastric nerve.—**nervios conjugados,** (anat.) conjugate nerves.

nerviosidad, *f.* = NERVOSIDAD.

nervioso, sa, *a.* nervous; vigorous, energetic; (bot.) nerved, having veins.

nervosamente, *adv.* nervously.

nervosidad, *f.* nervousness; strength, vigor; flexibility.

nervosismo, *m.* (med.) nervosism.

nervoso, sa, *a.* nervous; strong, vigorous.

nervudo, da, *a.* strong-nerved, vigorous.

nervura, *f.* (bookbinding) ribs.

nesciencia, *f.* ignorance.

nesciente, *a.* ignorant, foolish.

nescientemente, *adv.* ignorantly.

nesga, *f.* (sewing) gore; triangular piece.

néspera, *f.* = NÍSPERO, *m.* (bot.) medlar.

nestorianismo, *m.* Nestorianism.

nestoriano, na, *n.* & *a.* Nestorian.

netezuelo, la, *m.* & *f.* *dim.* little grandchild.

neto, ta. I. *a.* neat, pure, unadulterated; (com.) net, clear.—**en n.,** net.—**puro y n.,** pure and simple. **II.** *m.* (arch.) naked pedestal.

¹neuma, *n.* (rhet.) expression by signs or nods.

²neuma, *m.* (mus.) neuma.

neumática, f. (phys.) pneumatics.
neumático, ca. I. a. pneumatic. II. m. tire.
neumatógrafo, m. (med.) pneumagraph, stethograph.
neumococo, m. (bacteriol.) pneumococcus.
neumonía, f. (med.) pneumonia.
neumónico, ca, a. pneumonic; pulmonary.
neuralgia, f. (med.) neuralgia.
neurálgico, ca, a. neuralgic.
neurastenia, f. (med.) neurasthenia, nervous prostration.
neurasténico, ca, n. & a. neurasthenic.
neuraxón, m. (anat.) neuraxon, axis cylinder.
neurilema, m. (anat.) neurilemma.
neurisma, f. (med.) = ANEURISMA, aneurysm.
neuritis, f. (med.) neuritis.
neuroblasto, m. (anat.) neuroblast.
neuroeje, m. (anat.) neural, or cerebro-spinal, axis.
neuroesqueleto, n. (anat.) endoskeleton.
neurología, f. (anat.) neurology.
neurólogo, ga, n. neurologist.
neuroma, m. (med.) neuroma.
neurona, f. (anat.) neuron, nerve cell.
neuropatía, f. (med.) neuropathy.
neuróptero, ra, a. (entom.) neuropterous.
neurosis, f. (med.) neurosis.—**n. de guerra,** war neurosis, "shell shock."
neurótico, ca, n. & a. (med.) neurotic.
neurotomía, f. (surg.) neurotomy.
neurótomo, m. (surg.) neurotome.
neutoniano, na, a. Newtonian.
neutral, a. neutral, neuter.
neutralicé, neutralice, v. V. NEUTRALIZAR.
neutralidad, f. neutrality.
neutralización, f. neutralization.
neutralizar, va. (pret. NEUTRALICÉ; subj. NEUTRALICE) to counteract; to neutralize.
neutro, tra, a. neutral, neuter; (gram.) neuter.
neutrón, m. neutron.
nevada, f. snowfall.
nevadilla, f. (bot.) whitlow-wort.
nevado, da. I. pp. of NEVAR. II. a. white as snow. III. m. snow-capped mountain or peak.
nevar. I. vn. impers. (ind. NIEVA; subj. NIEVE) to snow. II. va. to make white as snow.
nevasca, f. snowfall; snowstorm.
nevatilla, f. (ornith.) wagtail.
nevera, f. ice house; icebox, refrigerator; woman who sells ice.
nevereta, f. (ornith.) wagtail.
nevería, f. ice house; place where ice is sold.
nevero, m. iceman; place of perpetual snow.
nevisca, f. gentle fall of snow.
neviscar, vn. to snow lightly.
nevoso, sa, a. snowy; nival, niveous.
nexo, m. nexus, bond, tie, union.
ni, conj. neither, nor (n. esto n. aquello, neither this nor that).—**ni con mucho,** not by a good deal.—**n. siquiera,** not even.—**n. un, n. uno, n. una,** (often preceded by no and a verb) not one, not a single.
niara, f. rick or stack of straw.
nícalo, m. NÍSCALO, mushroom.
nicaragua, f. (bot.) garden balsam.
nicaragüense, n. & a. Nicaraguan.
nicaragüeño, ña, n. & a. Nicaraguan.
niceno, na, a. Nicene.
nicerobino, a. ancient precious ointment.
nicle, m. a variety of chalcedony.
nicociana, f. (poet.) tobacco, nicotia.
nicotina, f. nicotine.
nicotismo, m. nicotinism.
nictagíneo, a, a. (bot.) nyctaginaceous.
nictálope, n. (med.) nyctalops.
nictalopia, f. (med.) nyctalopia.
nicho, m. niche; recess.
nidada, f. nestful of eggs; brood, covey.
nidal, m. nest; nest egg; basis, foundation, motive; haunt.

nidificar, vn. to nest, to build nests.
nidito, m. dim. small nest.
nido, m. nest; eyry; home, habitation, abode, residence; haunt; den.
niebla, f. fog, mist, haze; film that dims the sight; (agr.) blasting mildew.
¹**niego,** a. newborn (falcon).
²**niego, niegue,** v. V. NEGAR.
niel, m. (art) niello work.—**nielar,** va. (art) to niello.
niéspera, f. (bot.) medlar.
nieto, ta, n. grandson(-daughter).
nietro, m. a measure for wine (159.7 liters).
nieva, nieve, v. V. NEVAR.
nieve, f. snow; (Am.) an ice, sherbet.
nigromancia, f. necromancy.
nigromante, n. necromancer, conjurer, magician.—**nigromántico, ca.** I. a. necromantic. II. n. = NIGROMANTE.
nigua, f. chigoe, jigger flea.
nihilismo, m. nihilism.
nihilista, n. nihilist.
nilad, m. a Philippine shrub.
nimbo, m. halo; nimbus.
nimiamente, adv. excessively, minutely.
nimiedad, f. superfluity, prolixity; excess.
nimio, a, a. prolix; stingy.
ninfa, f. nymph; young lady; (entom.) pupa.
ninfea, f. (bot.) water lily.
ninfeáceo, a, a. (bot.) nymphæceous.
ninfo, m. (coll.) effeminate fop, dude.
ninfomanía, f. (med.) nymphomania.
ningún, a. (contr. of NINGUNO) no, not one (used only before masculine nouns).—**de n. modo,** by no means, under no circumstances.
ninguno, na. I. a. no, none, not one, not any.—**n. cosa,** nothing.—**de n. manera,** by no means, under no circumstances. II. indef. pron. none, no one, not one, nobody.
ninivita, n. & a. Ninevite.
niña, f. little girl; young girl.—**n. bien,** well-bred girl.—**n. del ojo,** pupil of the eye.—**niñas de los ojos,** (coll.) apple of one's eye, treasure; (C. A., Cuba, W. I.) (used by servants of employers) Miss.
niñada, f. puerility, childishness.
niñato, m. unborn calf.
niñear, vn. to act like a child.
niñera, f. nurse girl, nursery maid.
niñería, f. puerility, childish action; child's play; plaything; trifle.
niñero, ra, a. & f. fond of children; dandler.
niñeta, f. small pupil of the eye.
niñez, f. childhood, infancy.
niñita, f. little girl.
niñito, m. little boy; little child.
niño, ña. I. a. childish, childlike; young; inexperienced. II. n. boy (girl). III. m. child.—pl. children.—**n. bien,** sissy.—**n. de la piedra,** foundling.—**n. de teta,** suckling babe, child in arms.—**ñ. expósito,** foundling.—**niños de la doctrina,** charity children.—**de n.,** as a child.—**desde n.,** from infancy, from childhood.
niobio, m. (chem.) niobium.
nioto, m. (ichth.) = CAZÓN, dogfish.
nipa, f. (bot.) nypa, an Asiatic palm.
nipe, nipis, m. nypa cloth.
nipón, na, n. & a. Nipponese, Japanese.
níquel, m. (chem.) nickel.
niquelado, pp. & a. nickel-plated.
niquelar, va. to nickel-plate.
niquiscocio, m. unimportant thing, matter, trifle.
nirvana, m. Nirvana.
níscalo, m. nonpoisonous mushroom.
níspero, m. (bot.) medlar; medlar tree.
níspola, f. fruit of the medlar tree.
nitidez, f. neatness, brightness, clarity.
nítido, da, a. neat; bright, clear, resplendent.

nito, *m.* (P. I.) (bot.) a fibrous fern or brake.
nitos, *m.* (coll.) nothing, "nix."
nitral, *m.* niter bed.
nitrato, *m.* (chem.) nitrate, saltpeter.
nitrería, *f.* saltpeter works.
nítrico, ca, *a.* (chem.) nitric.
nitrificación, *f.* nitrification.
nitrito, *m.* (chem.) nitrite.
nitro, *m.* (chem.) niter, saltpeter.
nitrobencina, *f.* nitrobenzene.
nitrocelulosa, *f.* nitrocellulose.
nitrogenado, da, *a.* nitrogenous.
nitrogenar, *va.* to nitrogenize.
nitrógeno, *m.* (chem.) nitrogen.
nitroglicerina, *f.* nitroglycerine.
nitrosidad, *f.* nitrous condition.
nitroso, sa, *a.* (chem.) nitrous.
nivel, *m.* level; levelness; water-mark; (surv.) level; (mason.) level, plummet.—**n. de aire,** or **de burbuja,** spirit level.—**n. de (la) vida,** standard of living.—**n. del mar,** sea level.—**n. longitudinal,** (aer.) fore-and-aft level.—**a n.,** level, true; on the same level.
nivelación, *f.* leveling; grading.
nivelador, ra, *n.* & *a.* (surv.) leveler(-ing); grader(-ing).
nivelar. I. *va.* to level; to grade; to make even; to put on a basis of equity and justice.—**n. el presupuesto,** to balance the budget. **II.** *vr.* to level off.
níveo, ea, *a.* (poet.) snowy.
nizardo, da, *a.* of or pertaining to Nice.
no, *adv.* no, not, nay.—¿**n.?** (at end of sentence) isn't it? isn't that so? do you see? etc.—**n. bien,** no sooner.—**n. más,** only; no more.—**n. obstante,** notwithstanding.—**n., que n.,** most certainly not.—**n., sea que,** lest; or else.—**n., sino,** not only so.—**n., sino, n.,** it cannot be otherwise.—**n. tal,** no such thing.—**n. ya,** not only.—**a que n.,** (coll.) I bet that isn't so; I bet you won't.—**pues n.,** but no, not so.
nobiliario, ria, *a.* nobiliary, pert. to nobility.
nobilísimamente, *adv. super.* most nobly.
nobilísimo, ma, *a. super.* most noble.
noble. I. *a.* noble. **II.** *m.* nobleman; an ancient gold coin.
noblemente, *adv.* nobly.
nobleza, *f.* nobleness; nobility; noblesse; a fine damask silk.
noca, *f.* variety of crab.
nocedal, *m.* = NOGUERAL, walnut tree grove.
nocente, *a.* noxious; guilty.
noción, *f.* notion, idea; element, rudiment (gen. in *pl.*).—**nocional,** *a.* notional.
nocivo, va, *a.* noxious, harmful, injurious.
noctíluca, *f.* (entom.) glowworm, noctiluca.
noctívago, ga, *a.* (poet.) wandering at night.
nocturnal, *a.* nocturnal, nightly.
nocturno, na. I. *a.* nocturnal, night (as *a.*); lonely and sad. **II.** *m.* (eccl.) nocturn; (mus.) nocturne.
noche, *f.* night; evening (after sunset); (fig.) obscurity, ignorance.—**n. toledana,** restless night, sleepless night.—**ayer n.,** last night.—**buenas noches,** good evening; good night.—**de la n. a la mañana,** between sunset and sunrise; (fig.) overnight, suddenly, unexpectedly.—**de n., por la n.,** at night; by night; in the nighttime.—**esta n.,** tonight.—**media n.,** midnight.—**muy de n.,** late at night.—**prima n.,** evening.—**quedarse a buenas noches,** (coll.) to be left in the dark about something; to be disappointed.
nochebuena, *f.* Christmas eve.
nochebueno, *m.* Christmas cake; Yule log.
nochecita, *f.* (Am.) twilight, dusk, nightfall.—**a la n.,** at nightfall.
nochizo, *m.* (bot.) = AVELLANO, filbert tree.
nodación, *f.* (med.) impediment caused by a node.

nodátil, *a.* (anat.) nodal.
nodo, *m.* (med.) node; (astr.) node.
nodriza, *f.* wet nurse.
nódulo, *m.* nodule, small node.
nogada, *f.* sauce of pounded walnuts and spice.
nogal, *m.* = NOGUERA.
noguera, *f.* (bot.) walnut (tree and wood).
noguerado, da, *a.* walnut-colored.
nogueral, *m.* field or plantation of walnut trees.
noguerón, *m. aug.* large walnut tree.
nolición, *f.* unwillingness.
noli me tángere, *m.* (Lat.) noli-me-tangere; (med.) malignant ulcer.
nómada, nómade, *n.* & *a.* nomad(-ic).
nomadismo, *m.* nomadism, nomadic state.
nomarquía, *f.* nomarchy, province.
nombradamente, *adv.* expressly.
nombradía, *f.* renown, fame, reputation.
nombramiento, *m.* nomination, naming; appointment, commission; brevet.
nombrar, *va.* to name; to nominate; to appoint.
nombre, *m.* name; title; fame, reputation; power by which any one acts for another; (gram.) noun; (mil.) countersign; watchword.—**n. adjetivo,** adjective.—**n. apelativo,** (gram.) common noun.—**n. colectivo,** collective noun.—**n. común,** common noun.—**n. de pila,** Christian name.—**n. propio,** proper noun.—**n. substantivo,** noun, substantive.—**n. y apellido,** full name.—**de n.,** by name.—**en el n.,** with God's help.—**no tener n.,** to be unspeakable.—**poner n. a,** to give a name to; to set a price on.—**por n.,** by the name of.
nomenclador, nomenclátor, *m.* nomenclator; gazetteer; glossary, technical vocabulary.
nomenclatura, *f.* catalogue; nomenclature.
nomeolvides, *f.* (bot.) forget-me-not.
nómina, *f.* catalogue, list; payroll.
nominación, *f.* nomination; appointment.
nominador, ra, *n.* appointer.
nominal. I. *a.* nominal; titular. **II.** *n.* nominalist.—**nominalismo,** *m.* nominalism.—**nominalista,** *n.* & *a.* nominalist(-ic).—**nominalmente,** *adv.* nominally.
nominar, *va.* to name.
nominativo, va. I. *a.* (com.) personal, registered (as bonds). **II.** *a.* & *m.* (gram.) nominative.—*pl.* (coll.) elements, rudiments.
nominilla, *f.* pay warrant, voucher.
nómino, *m.* nominee.
nomo, *m.* nome, province.
nompareil, *f.* (print.) nonpareil, six-point.
non. I. *a.* odd, uneven. **II.** *m.* odd number.—*pl.* repeated negation or denial; refusal (esp. of a marriage proposal, in the phrases *dar nones, echar nones*).—**andar de nones,** to be idle.—**digo que nones,** I say no.—**estar de n.,** to serve for nothing.—**pares y nones,** odd or even.—**quedar de n.,** to be without a partner or companion.
nona, *f.* (eccl.) nones.
nonada, *f.* trifle, nothing.
nonagenario, ria, *n.* & *a.* nonagenarian.
nonagésimo, ma, *a.* ninetieth.
nonato, ta, *a.* not naturally born, but taken from the womb by Cæsarean section.
nonio, *m.* vernier, a measuring instrument.
nono, na, *a.* ninth.
non plus ultra, ne plus ultra, unsurpassable.
nopal, *m.* (bot.) nopal, cochineal fig-tree, prickly Indian pear tree.
noque, *m.* tan pit, tan vat; heap or basket of bruised olives.
noquero, *m.* tanner, currier, leather dresser.
norabuena, *f.* congratulation.
noramala, *adv.* in an evil hour.
noray, *m.* (naut.) bollard, mooring.
nordestal, *a.* northeast, northeastern.
nordeste, *m.* northeast.—**nordestear,** *vn.* (naut.) (of the compass) to decline to northeast.

nórdico, ca, *n.* & *a.* Nordic.
nordovestear, *vn.* (naut.) = NORUESTEAR.
noria, *f.* noria, chain pump, draw-well.
norial, *a.* pertaining to the NORIA.
norma, *f.* standard, norm, pattern, model, rule.
normal. I. *a.* normal; model, standard. **II.** *f.* normal school; (geom.) normal.
normalidad, *f.* normality.
normalizar, *va.* to normalize; to standardize.
normando, da; normano, na. I. *n.* & *a.* Norman. **II.** *n.* Norman; Northman, Norseman.
nornordeste, *m.* north-northeast.
nornoroeste, nornorueste, *m.* north-northwest.
noroeste, norueste, *m.* northwest.
noroestear, *vn.* (naut.) = NORUESTEAR.
nortada, *f.* north gale, norther.
norte, *m.* north; north wind; rule, law, guide, clue, direction.
norteamericano, na, *n.* & *a.* North-American; American (gen. from or of the U. S.).
nortear, *va.* (naut.) to steer or stand to the north-ward; (of compass) to decline to the north.
noruego, ga, *n.* & *a.* Norwegian.
norueste, *m.* northwest.
noruestear, *vn.* (naut.) (of the compass) to decline to the northwest.
nos, *pers. pron. pl. m.* & *f. acc.* & *dat.* of NOSOTROS, us, to us; (*recip.*) each other; (*refl.*) ourselves. Sometimes used as nom., in authoritative style, as *nos, el arzobispo de Toledo,* I, the archbishop of Toledo.
nosogenia, *f.* (med.) development of diseases.
nosografía, *f.* (med.) classification of diseases.
nosología, *f.* (med.) science of disease classification.
nosológico, ca, *a.* pert. to NOSOLOGÍA.
nosotros, tras, *pers. pron. pl. m.* & *f.* we; ourselves; us.
nostalgia, *f.* nostalgia, homesickness.
nostálgico, ca, *a.* nostalgic, homesick.
nostramo, *m.* (naut.) master—a title given by sailors to the boatswain.
nota, *f.* note; mark, sign; mark (in exam.); annotation; imputation, reproach; stain, stigma; renown, fame, repute; style, manner of writing; memorandum; (com.) account, bill, statement, schedule, price list; (mus.) note.—*pl.* records of a notary.—**n. marginal,** marginal note.—**n. verbal,** verbal note.
nota bene, (Lat.) take notice; N. B.
notabilidad, *f.* notability; a notable (person).
notabilísimo, ma, *a. super.* of NOTABLE: most, or very, notable, marked, or noted.
notable, *a.* notable, remarkable, noteworthy, noticeable, conspicuous; distinguished, prominent, noted.—**notablemente,** *adv.* notably, remarkably, notedly, noticeably.
notación, *f.* note, annotation; (math. and mus.) notation.
notar, *va.* to note, to mark; to remark, observe; to notice, take notice of, observe; to annotate, comment; to dictate; to find fault with, criticize; to reprehend.
notaría, *f.* profession or position of a notary; notary's office.—**notariado,** *m.* profession of a notary.—**notarial,** *a.* notarial.
notariato, *m.* title or practice of a notary.
notario, *m.* notary public; amanuensis.
noticia, *f.* news item; news (gen. *pl.*); notice, information, light; (com.) advice.—**n. remota,** vague remembrance.—**atrasado de noticias,** behind the times.
noticiar, *va.* to notify, give notice to, inform.
noticiero, *m.* news agent, reporter.
notición, *m. aug.* (coll.) great news.
noticioso, sa, *a.* news-giving; informed; learned.
notificación, *f.* notification; notice.
notificado, da, *pp.* & *a.* (law) notified.
notificar, *va.* (*pret.* NOTIFIQUÉ; *subj.* NOTIFIQUE) to notify.

notita, *f. dim.* short note, memorandum, etc.
¹noto, ta, *a.* well-known.
²noto, ta, *a.* illegitimate, bastard.
³noto, *m.* south wind, notus.
notomía, *f.* skeleton.
notoriamente, *adv.* manifestly, glaringly.
notoriedad, *f.* quality of being well known; self-evidence; notoriety.
notorio, ria, *a.* well known; evident, manifest.
nóumeno, *m.* (philos.) noumenon.
novaciano, na, *m.* & *f.* Novatian.
novación, *f.* (law) novation.
novador, ra, *n.* & *a.* innovator(-ing).
noval, *a.* newly broken up (land).
novar, *va.* (law) to renew by novation.
novatada, *f.* hazing (in colleges).
novato, ta, *n.* novice, beginner, tyro.
novator, ra, *n.* innovator, novator.
novecientos, tas, *n.* & *a.* nine hundred.
novedad, *f.* novelty; newness; surprise, recent occurrence, latest news or fashion; fad; change, innovation; surprise.—**no hay n.,** there is no change.—**sin n.,** well; safe; as usual; nothing new.
novel, *a.* new, inexperienced.
novela, *f.* novel; romance, fiction; falsehood; (law) novel.
novelador, ra, *n.* novelist.
novelar, *vn.* to write novels; to romance, to tell stories.
novelería, *f.* fondness for novelties; curiosity; fondness for novels; collection of novels.
novelero, ra. I. *a.* fond of novels, fads, and novelties; newfangled; fickle, wavering, unsteady. **II.** *n.* newsmonger, gossip.
novelesco, ca, *a.* novelistic, fictional.
novelista, *n.* novelist.
novena, *f.* (eccl.) novena.—**novenario,** *m.* (eccl.) novenary.—**novendial,** *a.* (eccl.) novendial.
noveno, na. I. *n.* & *a.* ninth; ninthly. **II.** *m.* ninth part of tithes.
noventa, *m.* & *a.* ninety; ninetieth.
noventavo, va, *n.* & *a.* ninetieth.
noventón, na, *n.* & *a.* nonagenarian.
novia, *f.* bride; fiancée; sweetheart.
noviazgo, *m.* engagement, betrothal.
noviciado, *m.* (eccl.) novitiate; apprenticeship.
novicio, cia. I. *a.* new, inexperienced. **II.** *n.* novice, probationer; freshman, apprentice, tyro.
noviciote, *m.* (coll.) overgrown novice.
noviembre, *n.* November.
novilunio, *m.* new moon.
novilla, *f.* young cow, heifer.
novillada, *f.* drove of young bulls or steers; baiting of young bulls.
novillejo, eja, *n. dim.* bullock (heifer).
novillero, *m.* herdsman who attends young cattle; stable for young cattle; pasture ground for weaned calves; truant, idler.
novillo, *m.* young bull; steer.—**hacer novillos,** (coll.) to play truant or hooky.
novio, *m.* bridegroom; fiancé; (coll.) suitor; one new to some dignity or state.
novísimo, ma, *super.* of NUEVO. **I.** *a.* newest, most recent; latest.—**N. Recopilación,** revised code of laws in Spain promulgated July 15, 1805. **II.** *m.* each of the last four incidents of mankind.
noyó, *m.* a bitter almond cordial.
nubada, *f.* shower of rain; plenty, abundance.
nubado, da, *a.* clouded, shaped like clouds.
nubarrado, da. I. *a.* NUBADO, DA. **II.** *f.* NUBADA.
nubarrón, *m.* large threatening cloud.
nube, *f.* cloud; crowd, multitude; (med.) film on the eye; cloud or shade in precious stones.—**estar en las nubes,** to be up in the clouds; to daydream.—**por las nubes,** or **a las nubes,** sky-high (praise or price).

---

nubecita, *f.* small cloud.
nubiense, *n.* & *a.* Nubian.
nubífero, ra, *a.* (poet.) cloud-bringing.
núbil, *a.* nubile, marriageable.
nubilidad, *f.* nubility, marriageable age.
nubiloso, sa, *a.* (poet.) cloudy, nubilous.
nublado, da. I. *pp.* of NUBLAR. II. *a.* cloudy, overcast. III. clouded sky; gloominess; impending danger; multitude.
nublar. I. *va.* to becloud, obscure. II. *vr.* to become cloudy; (of plants) to be blasted, mildewed.
nublo, bla. I. *a.* cloudy. II. *m.* NUBLADO.
nubloso, sa, *a.* cloudy; gloomy; ill-fated.
nuca, *f.* nape or scruff of the neck.
nuclear, *a.* nuclear.
núcleo, *m.* nucleus; center; kernel of a nut; stone of fruit; (astr.) nucleus (of a comet).—**ruptura,** or **hendimiento, del n.,** nuclear fission.
nuco, *m.* a Chilean kind of owl.
nudamente, *adv.* nakedly; plainly.
nudillo, *m.* knuckle; small knot in stockings; (mason.) plug, dowel, dook; nodule.
¹nudo, da, *a.* nude, naked.
²nudo, *m.* knot; burl, tangle; (bot.) node; joint; snag; tie, union, bond; (med.) node, tumor; knotty point, intricacy, difficulty; crisis of a drama; (naut.) knot of the log line, nautical mile.—**n. en la garganta,** lump in one's throat, great affliction.—**n. gordiano,** Gordian knot.
nudoso, sa, *a.* knotty, knotted.
nuecero, ra, *n.* vender of walnuts.
nuégado, *m.* paste of flour, honey and nuts.
nuera, *f.* daughter-in-law.
nuestramo, ma, *f. contr.* from NUESTRO AMO, our master (mistress); (Am.) the Eucharist.
nuestro, tra, *poss. pron. 1st pers. pl.* our, ours. (Also used editorially, etc. as in Eng.).—**los nuestros,** our friends, or colleagues, ours.
nueva, *f.* news, tidings.
nuevamente, *adv.* newly, recently, freshly.
nueve. I. *n.* & *a.* nine. II. *m.* ninth (of the month). III. *f. pl.*—**las n.,** nine o'clock.
nuevecito, *a. dim.* brand-new.
nuevo, va, *a.* new; novel, modern; newly arrived.—**n. emisión,** reissue.—**n. flamante,** spick and span, brand-new.—**de n.,** anew; again, once more.—**¿qué hay de n.?** what's the news, what's new?
nuez, *f.* walnut; nut or meat of some fruits (as coconuts); Adam's apple.—**n. de especia,** (bot.) nutmeg.—**n. dura,** hickory nut.—**n. moscada** = N. DE ESPECIA.—**n. vómica,** (bot.) nux vomica.
nueza, *f.* (bot.) briony.
nugatorio, ria, *a.* nugatory, futile.
nulamente, *adv.* invalidly, ineffectually.
nulidad, *f.* (law) nullity; defeasance; inability, incompetency; insignificant or incompetent person, a nobody.
nulo, la, *a.* null, void; of no account.
numantino, na, *n.* & *a.* Numantine(-tian).
numen, *m.* divinity, deity; inspiration.
numerable, *a.* numerable.
numeración, *f.* numeration (usually including notation); numbering.
numerador, *m.* numerator; numberer.
numeral, *n.* & *a.* numeral.
numerar, *va.* to number; enumerate; calculate, reckon; to page (a book).
numerario, ria. I. *a.* numerary. II. *m.* cash, coin, specie.
numerata pecunia, (law) ready money.
numéricamente, *adv.* numerically.
numérico, ca, *a.* numerical.
número, *m.* number; figure, character; numeral; size (shirt, etc.); number, issue (of magazine, etc.); poetical or musical measure, rhythm; (gram.) number.—*pl.* (N-) numbers, fourth

book of the Pentateuch.—**n. complejo,** complex number.—**n. compuesto,** compound number.—**n. denominado** = N. COMPLEJO.—**n. entero,** whole number, integer.—**n. mixto,** mixed number.—**n. romano,** Roman numeral.—**n. sordo,** surd, number having no root of a given index.—**n. uno,** number one, oneself; A1, A number 1.—**de n.,** regular (said of a member of an association consisting of a limited number; it may be left untranslated).—**sin n.,** numberless.
numerosamente, *adv.* numerously.
numerosidad, *f.* numerosity, numerousness.
numeroso, sa, *a.* numerous; harmonious, rhythmical.
númida, *n.* & *a.*; **numídico, ca,** *a.* Numidian.
numisma, *m.* coin, money.
numismática, *f.* numismatics.—**numismático, ca.** I. *a.* numismatical. II. *m.* numismatist.
numulario, *m.* banker, money broker.
numulita, *f.* (paleontol.) nummulite.
nunca, *adv.* never.—**n. jamás,** never, never more.
nunciatura, *f.* nunciature.
nuncio, *m.* messenger; Papal nuncio; forerunner, harbinger.
nuncupativo, va, *a.* (law) nuncupative, oral.
nuncupatorio, ria, *a.* dedicatory (writing).
nupcial, *a.* nuptial, hymeneal.
nupcialidad, *f.* marriage rate.
nupcias, *f. pl.* nuptials, wedding, marriage.
nutación, *f.* (astr. and bot.) nutation.
nutra, nutria, *f.* (zool.) otter.
nutricio, cia, *a.* nutritious, nourishing.
nutrición, *f.* nutrition, nourishing; (pharm.) preparation of medicines.
nutrido, da. I. *pp.* of NUTRIR. II. *a.* (**de**) full (of), abounding (with, in); copious.
nutrimental, *a.* nourishing, nutritious.
nutrimento, *m.* nutriment, food, nourishment; nutrition.
nutrir, *va.* to nourish, feed; to encourage, promote, support.
nutritivo, va, *a.* nutritive, nourishing.
nutriz, *f.* = NODRIZA, wet nurse.

Ñ

ñagaza, *f.* bird-call, decoy.
ñame, *m.* (bot.) yam.
ñandú, *m.* American ostrich.
ñanduti, *m.* (S. A.) a very fine fabric used mainly for underclothes.
ñangado, da, *a.* (Cuba) deformed, crooked-limbed.
ñango, ga, *a.* (Am.) ÑANGADO; (Am.) ungraceful, awkward.
ñáñigo, ga, *n.* (Cuba) member of a secret society of Negroes.
ñaño, ña, *n.* (Am.) brother or sister; (Am.) close friend.
ñapa, *f.* (Am.) something over or extra. Also YAPA.—**de ñ.,** to boot, into the bargain.
ñaque, *m.* odds and ends.
ñato, ta, *a.* (Am.) pug-nosed.
ñeque. I. *m.* (Am.) (coll.) energy; bravery. II. *a.* & *n.* (Am.) (coll.) strong, vigorous (person), "he-man."
ñiquiñaque, *m.* (coll.) good-for-nothing person or thing; trash.
ñisca, ñizca, *f.* (Chile, Peru) little piece, bit.
ño, ña, (Am.) contr. of SEÑOR, SEÑORA, gen. app. to elderly persons of the lower classes.
ñocio, *m.* a kind of macaroon.
ñongo, ga, *a.* (Chile) (coll.) lazy, good-for-nothing; (Colomb.) (of dice) loaded.—**ñonguera,** *f.* (Chile) laziness.
ñoñería, *f.* dotage, drivel.
ñoñez, *f.* dotage, senility; shyness.

ñoño, ña, *a.* (coll.) timid, shy; dotard, feeble; flimsy; (Am.) old-fashioned.
ñudo, *m.* = NUDO, knot.—**al ñ.,** (Arg.) in vain.

O

¹o, *conj.* or, either.—**o sea,** that is.
²o, *interj.* oh, O.
oasis, *m.* oasis.
obcecación, *f.* obfuscation, obsession.
obcecadamente, *adv.* obsessedly.
obcecar, *va.* (*pret.* OBCEQUÉ; *subj.* OBCEQUE) to obsess; to blind, obfuscate; to darken or obscure.
obduración, *f.* obstinacy, obduracy.
obedecedor, ra, *n.* obeyer.
obedecer, *va.* (*ind.* OBEDEZCO; *subj.* OBEDEZCA) to obey; to respond; to be due, arise (from); to follow, be controlled by.
obedecimiento, *m.* obedience.
obedezco, obedezca, *v. V.* OBEDECER.
obediencia, *f.* obedience.—**a la o.,** your most obedient.
obediencial, *a.* pertaining to obedience.
obediente, *a.* obedient.
obedientemente, *adv.* obediently.
obelisco, *m.* obelisk; (print.) dagger (†).
obelo, *m.* obelisk.
obencadura, *f.* (naut.) shrouds in general.
obenques, *m. pl.* (naut.) shrouds, shifters.
obertura, *f.* (mus.) overture.
obesidad, *f.* obesity, fatness, fleshiness.
obeso, sa, *a.* obese, fat, fleshy.
óbice, *m.* obstacle, impediment, hindrance.
obispado, *m.* bishopric; episcopate.
obispal, *a.* episcopal, pertaining to a bishop.
obispalía, *f.* palace or house of a bishop; bishopric, diocese.
obispar, *vn.* to be made a bishop.
obispillo, *m. dim.* boy bishop; bishop of no account; large pork sausage; rump of a fowl.
obispo, *m.* (eccl.) bishop; large blood pudding; (ichth.) raioid selachian.
óbito, *m.* (law, eccl.) death, decease, demise.
obituario, *m.* obituary.
objeción, *f.* objection.
objetante, *n. & a.* objector(-ing).
objetar, *va.* to object to, oppose, remonstrate.
objetivamente, *adv.* objectively.
objetivar, *va.* to objectify or objectivate.
objetivo, va. I. *a.* objective. II. *m.* (opt.) objective, eyepiece.
objeto, *m.* object; subject matter; purpose.
oblación, *f.* oblation, offering, gift.
oblada, *f.* (eccl.) funeral offering of bread.
oblata, *f.* (eccl.) oblate; contribution for church expenses.
oblea, *f.* wafer for sealing letters.
obleera, *f.* wafer holder, case for wafers.
oblicuamente, *adv.* obliquely.
oblicuángulo, *a.* oblique-angled.
oblicuar, *va. & vn.* to cant, slant; (mil.) to oblique.
oblicuidad, *f.* obliquity.
oblicuo, cua, *a.* oblique, slanting.
obligación, *f.* obligation, responsibility, duty; bond, debenture; charge; provision office.—*pl.* family that one is obliged to maintain; engagements; (com.) liabilities.
obligacionista, *n.* (com.) bondholder.
obligado, *m.* contractor for supplying provisions to a city; (law) obligor; (mus.) obbligato.
obligante, *a.* obligating, obliging.
obligar. I. *va.* (*pret.* OBLIGUÉ; *subj.* OBLIGUE) to obligate, compel, bind; to oblige. II. *vr.* to obligate or bind oneself.
obligatorio, ria, *a.* obligatory, compulsory.
obligué, obligue, *v. V.* OBLIGAR.
obliteración, *f.* (med.) obliteration.

obliterar, *va.* (med.) to obliterate.
oblongo, ga, *a.* oblong.
obnoxio, xia, *a.* obnoxious.
oboe, obué, *m.* (mus.) oboe; oboist.
óbolo, *m.* obolus; obolo; mite; (pharm.) obole.
obra, *f.* work; work(s), book(s); show, performance; building, structure; repairs in a house; means, virtue, power, influence; agency; toil, labor, employment.—**o. a] cuerno,** (mil.) hornwork.—**o. de,** about, more or less.—**o. de manos,** hand work.—**o. de romanos,** great work requiring time and toil, (coll.) big order. —**o. maestra,** masterpiece.—**o muerta,** (naut.) gunwale.—**o. prima,** shoemaking.—**o. pública,** public work.—**obras accesorias** (fort.) outworks of a fortress.—**obras de marea,** graving, caulking and paving a ship bottom.—**obras muertas,** upper works of a ship.—**obras pías,** charitable funds or establishments.—**obras vivas,** (naut.) quick or lower works.—**a o. de** = o. DE.—**en obras,** under construction; undergoing repairs.—hacer mala o., to do a bad turn.—**poner por o.,** to set to work on, to start.
obrada, *f.* day's work; a land measure (varies between 39 and 54 ares).
obrador, ra, *n.* workman(-woman); *m.* workshop.
obradura, *f.* charge of an oil mill.
obraje, *m.* manufacture, handiwork; workshop; wool mills.
obrajero, *m.* foreman, overseer, superintendent.
obrante, *a.* acting, working.
obrar. I. *va.* to work; to make, manufacture; to perform, execute; to construct, build. II. *vn.* to act; to ease nature.—**o. en,** to be in (a place, a person's hands, etc.).
obrepción, *f.* (law) obreption.
obrepticio, cia, *a.* (law) obreptitious.
obrería, *f.* task of a workman; money for church repairs.
obrero, ra, *n.* worker or workman(-woman); churchwarden; missionary.
obrita, *f. dim.* small or little work; booklet.
obrizo, za, *a.* pure, refined (gold).
obscenamente, *adv.* obscenely.
obscenidad, *f.* obscenity.
obsceno, na, *a.* obscene.
obscuración, *f.* = OBSCURIDAD.
obscuramente, *adv.* obscurely, darkly, faintly; confusedly; humbly, modestly.
obscurantismo, *m.* obscurantism.
obscurantista, *n.* obscurantist.
obscuras.—a o., or oscuras, in the dark.
obscurecer, oscurecer. I. *va.* (*ind.* O(B)SCUREZCA; *subj.* O(B)SCUREZCA) to obscure, darken; to dim; to tarnish; to cloud, confuse; (art) to shade. II. *v. impers.* to grow dark. III. *vr.* to cloud over; to disappear; to become dark.
obscurecimiento, *m.* obscuration, darkening.
obscurezco, obscurezca, *v. V.* OBSCURECER.
obscuridad, *f.* obscurity; darkness; gloominess opacity; retired, private life.
obscuro, oscuro, ra. I. *a.* obscure; dark; gloomy (art) heavily shaded; (of color) dark. II. *m* (art) shade.
obsecuente, *a.* obsequious; obedient.
obsequiador, ra, *n.* giver; entertainer.
obsequiante, *a.* obsequious.
obsequiar, *va.* to treat, entertain, pay attention to, make presents to; to court, woo; to present make a gift of.
obsequio, *m.* obsequiousness; treat; courtesy attention shown; gift, present.—**en o. de,** fo the sake of, out of respect to.
obsequiosamente, *adv.* obsequiously, flatter ingly, gallantly.
obsequioso, sa, *a.* obsequious; obedient, com pliant; obliging, attentive.
observable, *a.* observable, noticeable.

For pronunciation, see the rules at the beginning of the book.

observación, *f.* observation; remark, note.—**en o.,** under observation.

observador, ra, *n.* & *a.* observer(-ing).

observancia, *f.* observance, fulfillment.—**poner en o.,** to execute punctually.

observante, *a.* observant, observing.

observar, *va.* to observe; to notice, note; remark; to look into, watch; to conform to (a rule, etc.).

observatorio, *m.* observatory.

obsesión, *f.* obsession.

obseso, sa, *a.* beset; obsessed.

obsidiana, *f.* (geol.) obsidian.

obsidional, *a.* (mil.) obsidional, pert. to a siege.

obstáculo, *m.* obstacle.

obstante.—no o., notwithstanding; nevertheless, however.

obstar, *vn.* to oppose, obstruct, hinder.

obstetricia, *f.* (med.) obstetrics, midwifery.

obstinación, *f.* obstinacy, stubbornness.

obstinadamente, *adv.* obstinately, stubbornly.

obstinado, da. I. *pp.* of OBSTINARSE. **II.** *a.* obstinate, stubborn, obdurate, headstrong.

obstinarse, *vr.* (en) to be obstinate (about), to persist (in); to insist (on).

obstrucción, *f.* obstruction, stoppage.

obstruccionismo, *m.* obstructionism.

obstruccionista, *n.* & *a.* obstructionist(-ic).

obstructivo, va, *a.* obstructive.

obstruir. I. *va.* (*ind.* OBSTRUYO; *subj.* OBSTRUYA) to obstruct, block, stop up, choke. **II.** *vr.* to become obstructed, choked, clogged up.

obtemperar, *va.* to obey, to assent.

obtención, *f.* attainment, obtainment.

obtener, *va.* (*ind. pres.* yo OBTENGO, él OBTIENE, *pret.* OBTUVE, *fut.* OBTENDRÉ; *subj.* OBTENGA) to get, obtain, procure; to preserve, to maintain.

obtento, *m.* (eccl.) benefice, prebend.

obtentor, *m.* (eccl.) one who obtains a prebend.

obtestación, *f.* obtestation, protestation.

obturación, *f.* obturation, closing, sealing.

obturador, triz. I. *a.* serving to stop up, close, seal, plug, etc. **II.** *m.* plug, stopper; breechblock; (surg.) obturator; gas check; (photog.) shutter.

obturar, *va.* to stop up, plug, close, seal.

obtusángulo, *a.* obtuse-angled.

obtuso, sa, *a.* obtuse; blunt, dull.

obtuve, *pret.* of OBTENIR.

obué, *m.* = OBOE, (mus.) oboe; oboist.

obús, *m.* (artil.) howitzer, mortar.

obusera, *a.* boat carrying a howitzer.

obvención, *f.* perquisite.

obviar. I. *va.* to obviate, remove, prevent, surmount. **II.** *vn.* to hinder, oppose.

obvio, via, *a.* obvious, evident.

obyecto, *m.* objection, reply.

oca, *f.* (ornith.) goose; royal goose (game).

oca, *f.* (bot.) oca oxalis.

ocal, *a.* double (cocoon); delicious (fruit).

ocalear, *vn.* (of silkworms) to make double cocoons.

ocasión, *f.* occasion; chance, opportunity.—**aprovechar la o.,** to take advantage of an opportunity, a situation.—**de o.,** second-hand; at a bargain.—*pl.* **en ocasiones,** at times.

ocasionado, da. I. *pp.* of ocasionar. **II.** *a.* provoking, vexatious, insolent; perilous.

ocasionador, ra, *n.* & *a.* occasioner(-ing).

ocasional, *a.* occasional, chance, casual.

ocasionalmente, *adv.* occasionally; by chance.

ocasionar, *va.* to cause, occasion; to move, excite; to jeopardize, endanger.

ocaso, *m.* west; setting of any heavenly body; decadence, decline.

occidental, *a.* occidental, western.

occidente, *m.* occident, west.

occiduo, dua, *a.* occidental; pert. to setting (of sun, etc.).

occipital, *a.* occipital.

occipucio, *m.* occiput.

occisión, *f.* murder, killing.

occiso, sa, *a.* murdered, killed.

oceánico, ca, *a.* oceanic.

océano, *m.* ocean.

oceanografía, *f.* oceanography.

oceanógrafo, fa, *n.* oceanographer.

ocelo, *m.* (biol.) ocellus.

ocelote, *m.* ocelot, a large leopardlike wild cat.

ocena, *f.* (med.) foul breath.

ociar, *vn.* to loiter, be at leisure.

ocio, *m.* leisure, idleness; pastime, diversion.—**ratos de o.,** spare time.

ociosamente, *adv.* idly; uselessly.

ociosidad, *f.* idleness, leisure.

ocioso, sa, *a.* idle; fruitless, useless.

oclocracia, *f.* (pol.) ochlocracy, mob rule.

ocluir, *va.* & *vr.* (med.) to occlude, to shut up.

oclusión, *f.* occlusion.

ocosial, *m.* (Peru) lowland, morass.

ocotal, *m.* (Mex.) grove of OCOTES.

ocote, *m.* (Mex.) (bot.) okote pine, torch pine.

ocozoal, *m.* (Mex.) a variety of rattlesnake.

ocozol, *m.* (bot.) sweet gum, liquidambar tree.

ocre, *m.* ochre, brown or yellow earth.

octaedro, *m.* (geom.) octahedron.

octagonal, *a.* octagonal.

octágono, na. I. *a.* eight-sided, octagonal. **II.** *m.* octagon.

octante, *m.* (geom.) octant.

octava, *f.* (eccl.) octave, eight days; (mus.) octave; (poet.) eight-line stanza.

octavar, *vn.* to form octaves on stringed instruments; to deduct the eighth part.

octavario, *m.* (eccl.) festival lasting a week.

octavín, *m.* (mus.) piccolo flute.

octavo, va. I. *a.* eighth; octave, octonary.—**en o.,** (print.) in octavo. **II.** *m.* eighth; octoroon.

octogenario, ria, *n.* & *a.* octogenarian.

octogésimo, *a.* eightieth.

octogonal, *a.* octagonal.

octógono, na, *a.* = OCTÁGONO.

octosilábico, ca; octosílabo, ba, *a.* octosyllabic.

octubre, *m.* October.

ocular. I. *a.* ocular. **II.** *m.* (opt.) eyepiece.

ocularmente, *adv.* ocularly, visually.

oculista, *m.* oculist.

ocultación, *f.* concealment; hiding; (astr.) occultation.

ocultador, ra, *n.* & *a.* concealer(-ing).

ocultamente, *adv.* secretly, hiddenly.

ocultar, *va.* to hide, conceal, secrete.

ocultismo, *m.* occultism.

oculto, ta, *a.* hidden, concealed; occult.—**de o.,** incog, incognito.—**en o.,** secretly, in secret.

ocupación, *f.* occupation; occupying; trade, business, pursuit; (rhet.) prolepsis.

ocupada, *a.* (coll.) pregnant.

ocupado, da. I. *pp.* of OCUPAR. **II.** *a.* occupied· busy, engaged.

ocupador, ra, *n.* occupier, possessor, occupant.

ocupante, *n.* occupant.

ocupar. I. *va.* to occupy; take possession of; to fill, hold (a job); to employ, give work to; to distrub, interrupt, hinder; to dwell or live in; to engage the attention of, preoccupy. **II.** *vr.* (en or de) to busy oneself (with); to be engaged (in), have as one's business, devote oneself (to); to pay attention (to).

ocurrencia, *f.* occurrence, incident, happening; witticism.—**o. de acreedores,** meeting of creditors.

ocurrente, *a.* occurring; humorous or funny, witty.

ocurrir, *vn.* to occur, happen; to meet, anticipate; (law) to have recourse to; to apply to; (often as *vr.*) to occur (to one), to strike one (as an idea).

ocurso, *m.* (Mex.) petition, claim.

---

ochava, f. eighth part; (eccl.) octave.—**ochavas del molinete,** (naut.) whelps of the windlass.

ochavado, da, a. eight-sided.

ochavar, va. to make eight-sided.

ochavo, m. a small brass coin; octagonal thing.

ochenta, a. & m. eighty; eightieth.

ochentavo, va, n. & a. eightieth.

ochentón, na, n. & a. octogenarian.

ochete, m. bore of hollow projectiles.

ocho. I. n. & a. eight; eighth. **II.** m. figure 8; the eighth day; card with eight spots. **III.** f. pl. **las o.,** eight o'clock.

ochocientos, tas, n. & a. eight hundred.

ochosén, m. small ancient coin.

oda, f. ode.

odalisca, f. odalisk, female slave in harem.

odeón, m. odeum, place for music performances.

odiar, va. to hate.—**odio,** m. hatred; odium.

odiosamente, adv. odiously, hatefully.

odiosidad, f. odiousness, hatred, odium.

odioso, sa, a. odious, hateful.

odisea, f. odyssey.

odómetro, m. odometer, cyclometer.

odontalgia, f. (med.) odontalgia, toothache.

odontoideo, a, a. odontoid, tooth-shaped.

odontología, f. odontology.

odontólogo, ga, n. odontologist.

odontorrea, f. bleeding of the gums.

odorante, a. odorous, fragrant.

odorífero, ra, a. odoriferous, fragrant.

odre, m. wine skin; (coll.) drunkard.

odrería, f. wine-skin factory or shop.

odrero, ra, n. maker or seller of wine skins.

odrezuelo, m. dim. small wine skin.

odrina, f. ox-skin bag for wine.

oesnorueste, m. west-northwest.

oessudueste, m. west-southwest.

oeste, m. west; west wind.—**o. cuarta al norte,** west by north.—**o. cuarta al sur,** west by south.

ofendedor, ra, n. & a. offender(-ing).

ofender. I. va. to offend; to make angry. **II.** vr. to become angry; to take offense.

ofensa, f. offense; transgression, crime.

ofensión, f. offense, grievance; injury.

ofensivamente, adv. offensively.

ofensivo, va. I. a. offensive; attacking. **II.** f. (mil.) offensive.

ofensor, ra, n. & a. offender(-ing).

oferente, m. offerer, one who offers.

oferta, f. offer; gift, offering; (com.) offer, tender, supply.—**o. y demanda,** supply and demand.

ofertorio, m. (eccl.) offertory.

oficial. I. a. official. **II.** m. official, officer; trained workman; clerk; (mil.) commissioned officer below major; executioner.—**o. de la sala,** (law) actuary in criminal causes.—**o. mayor,** chief clerk.

oficiala, f. trained workwoman; forewoman; saleswoman.

oficialía, f. clerkship in a public office.

oficialidad, f. body of officers.

oficialmente, adv. officially.

oficiante, n. & a. officiator(-ing).

oficiar. I. va. to communicate officially. **II.** vn. to officiate.—**o. de,** to act as.

oficina, f. workshop; office; countinghouse, bureau; laboratory.

oficinal, a. (med. and pharm.) officinal.

oficinesco, ca, a. departmental, office (as a.).

oficinista, n. office worker; clerk, employee.

oficio, m. employ, work or occupation; office, function, operation; official letter; trade or business; craft; notary's office.—pl. (eccl.) office, service.—**de o.,** officially; by trade, by occupation or profession.—**tomarlo por o.,** to do frequently, to take to.

oficionario, m. (eccl.) office book.

oficiosamente, adv. officiously.

oficiosidad, f. diligence, alacrity; officiousness.

oficioso, sa, a. diligent; accommodating; officious, meddlesome; useful, fruitful; semi-official.

ofidio, dia. I. a. & n. (zool.) ophidian. **II.** m. pl. Ophidia, ophidians.

ofita, f. (min.) ophite.

ofiurídeo, ofiuro, m. (zool.) ophiuroid(-ean).

ofrecedor, ra, n. offerer.

ofrecer. I. va. (ind. OFREZCO; subj. OFREZCA) to offer; to propose; to present; to exhibit, manifest; to dedicate, consecrate; (com.) to bid, offer. **II.** vr. to offer, occur, present itself; to offer oneself, volunteer.—**se le ofrece algo,** he wants something.

ofreciente, a. offering.

ofrecimiento, m. offer, offering.

ofrenda, f. religious offering, oblation, gift.

ofrendar, va. to present offerings; to contribute.

ofrezco, ofrezca, v. V. OFRECER.

oftalmía, f. (med.) ophthalmia.

oftálmico, ca, a. ophthalmic.

oftalmología, f. ophthalmology.

oftalmológico, ca, a. ophthalmologic.

oftalmólogo, ga, n. ophthalmologist, oculist.

oftalmómetro, m. ophthalmometer.

oftalmoscopia, f. ophthalmoscopy.

oftalmoscopio, m. ophthalmoscope.

ofuscación, f., **ofuscamiento,** m. obfuscation, confused reason.

ofuscar, va. (pret. OFUSQUÉ; subj. OFUSQUE) to obfuscate, dazzle; to confuse.

ogaño, adv. (coll.) = HOGAÑO, in these days, this year.

ogro, m. ogre, fabulous monster.

¡oh! interj. O! oh!

ohm, m. (elec.) ohm.

óhmico, ca, a. (elec.) ohmic.

ohmímetro, m. (elec.) ohmmeter.

ohmio, m. (elec.) ohm.

ohmiómetro, m. (elec.) ohmmeter.

oíble, a. audible, that can be heard.

oída, f. hearing (the act).—**de oídas, or por oídas,** by hearsay.

oidio, m. (bot.) oidium, a kind of fungus.

oído, da. I. pp. of OÍR. **II.** m. sense of hearing; (anat.) ear; (artil.) vent, priming hole, touch-hole.—**al o.,** by ear; in the ear, whispering, confidentially.—**dar oídos,** to lend an ear, to believe.—**de o.,** by ear.—**regalar el o.,** to tickle the ear, to flatter.—**tener buen o.,** to have a good ear (esp. for music).

oidor, ra, n. hearer; judge, member of an Audiencia.

oidoría, f. judgeship, office of OIDOR.

oír, va. (ger. OYENDO; ind. pres. OIGO, pret. él OYÓ; subj. pres. OIGA, imp. OYERA, OYESE, fut. OYERE) to hear; to listen; to understand; to attend (a lectures).—**o. decir,** to hear (it said).—**o. hablar de,** to hear of.—**o. misa,** to attend or hear mass.—**o., ver y callar,** mind your own business.—**ahora, or hasta ahora, lo oigo, this is the first I hear of it.—¡oiga! or ¡oigan! well! the idea! come, come!

oíslo, n. (coll.) person beloved, wife (or husband).

ojal, m. buttonhole; loop.

¡ojalá! interj. would to God! God grant! I wish!

ojaladera, f. buttonhole maker.

ojalador, ra, n. (sewing) buttonhole maker.

ojaladura, f. set of buttonholes.

ojalar, va. to make buttonholes in.

ojalatero, a. & m. (pol., coll.) stay-at-home patriot during war; "armchair Napoleon."

ojaranzo, m. (bot.) = CARPE, witch hazel.

ojazo, m. aug. large eye.

ojeada, f. glance, hasty look; glimpse.

ojeador, m. beater for game.

¹**ojear,** va. to beat for game; to startle, frighten.

²**ojear,** va. to eye, look at, stare at.

ojeo, m. beating for game.

ojera, f. circle under the eye; eyecup.

ojeriza, *f.* spite, grudge, ill will.

ojeroso, sa; ojerudo, da, *a.* having circles under the eyes.

ojete, *m.* (sewing) eyelet.

ojeteador, *m.* eyeleteer; stiletto.

ojetear, *va.* (sewing) to make eyelet holes in.

ojetera, *f.* edge of a garment with eyelets for lacing; eyelet maker.

ojialegre, *a.* bright-eyed.

ojiazul, *a.* blue-eyed.

ojito, *m. dim.* small eye.

ojienjuto, ta, *a.* (coll.) dry-eyed.

ojimel, ojimiel, *m.* (pharm.) oxymel.

ojimoreno, na, *a.* (coll.) brown-eyed.

ojinegro, gra, *a.* black-, dark-eyed.

ojiva, *f.* (arch.) ogive, pointed arch.

ojival, *a.* (arch.) ogival.

ojizaino, na, *a.* (coll.) squint-eyed, moon-eyed.

ojizarco, ca, *a.* (coll.) blue- or gray-eyed.

ojo, *m.* eye; eye of a needle; (mech.) perforation; hole, eye, socket; bow of a key; keyhole (also *o. de la cerradura*); water spring; geyser; drop of oil or grease swimming on liquors; (arch.) span of a bridge; opening in the center of a winding stair; attention, care, notice; reference mark; eye or face of type; mesh; hole in bread or cheese.—*pl.* dearest, darling.—**¡o.!** take notice! look out! **¡o. alerta!** look sharp!—**o. avizor,** sharp lookout.—**o. de agua,** spring (of water).—**o. de buey,** (bot.) oxeye; (coll.) doubloon (eight dollars).—**o. de gallo** = o. DE POLLO.—**o. de gaza,** (naut.) eye of a strap. —**o. de la caña del ancla,** (naut.) eye of the anchor.—**o. de pollo,** corn (on toe).—**o. por o., diente por diente,** an eye for an eye, a tooth for a tooth.—**ojos reventones,** or **saltones,** goggle eyes.—**a cierra ojos,** unhesitatingly; at all events.—**a los ojos de,** in the presence of.—**a o.,** by eye.—**a ojos cegarritas,** with half-closed eyes (to intensify the sight).— **a ojos cerrados,** blindly, without reflection; without examination.—**a ojos vistas,** visibly, openly.—**avivar el o.,** to be on one's guard.— **costar un o.,** to be excessively dear.—**de medio o.,** lurkingly, concealingly.—**entrar por el o.,** to please.—**en un abrir y cerrar de ojos,** in the twinkling of an eye.—**hacer del o.,** to wink at one another, to have a secret understanding.—**hacerse ojos,** to look with sharp eyes.—**¡mucho o.!** = **¡o.!**—**poner (el) o.,** to pay (close) attention.—**tener buen o.,** to have a good eye; to have good foresight.

ojota, *f.* (Am.) sandal worn by Indian women.

ojuelo, *m. dim.* small eye.—*pl.* sparkling eyes; spectacles.

¹ola, *f.* wave, billow.—**¡o. de marea,** tidal wave.

²ola, (at tel.) hello.

olaje, *m.* succession of waves, surge, motion of the waves; ground swell.

ole, *m.* an Andalusian dance.—**¡o.!** bravo!

oleáceo, cea. I. *a.* (bot.) oleaceous. II. *f. pl.* Oleaceae.

oleada, *f.* big wave; surge, swell of the sea; surging of a crowd.

²oleada, *f.* abundant oil crop.

oleaginosidad, *f.* oleaginousness, oiliness.

oleaginoso, sa, *a.* oleaginous, oily.

oleaje, *m.* = OLAJE.

olear, *va.* to administer extreme unction to.

oleario, ria, *a.* oily.

oleastro, *m.* (bot.) = ACEBUCHE, wild olive tree.

oleato, *m.* (chem.) oleate.

oleaza, *f.* watery dregs in oil mills.

olécranon, *m.* (anat.) olecranon, part of elbow.

oledero, ra, *a.* odorous, fragrant.

oledor, ra, *n.* smeller.

oleico, *a.* (chem.) oleic.

oleína, *f.* (chem.) olein.

óleo, *m.* oil; (eccl.) extreme unction; holy oil; act of anointing.—**al o.,** in oil colors, oil (as *a.*).

oleomargarina, *f.* oleomargarine.

oleómetro, *m.* (phys.) measure for density of oil.

oleorresina, *f.* oleoresin.

oleosidad, *f.* oiliness.

oleoso, sa, *a.* oily, oleaginous.

oler. I. *va.* (*ind.* HUELO; *subj.* HUELA) to smell, to scent; to find out, search, discover; to pry into, sniff, snuff. II. *vn.* to smell, emit an odor; to smack of.—**o. a,** to smell of, smell like.—**o. mal,** or **no o. bien,** to look suspicious, to arouse suspicion.

olfacción, *f.* olfaction, act of smelling.

olfatear, *va.* & *vn.* to smell, scent, sniff, snuff.

olfato, *m.* olfaction, sense of smell.

olfatorio, ria, *a.* olfactory, pert. to sense of smell.

olíbano, *m.* (bot.) incense.

oliente, *a.* smelling, odorous.

oliera, *f.* vessel for holy oil.

oligarca, *m.* oligarch.—**oligarquía,** *f.* oligarchy.

oligárquico, ca, *a.* oligarchical.

oligisto, *m.* (min.) oligist.

oligoceno, *a.* & *m.* (geol.) Oligocene.

oligoclasa, *f.* (min.) oligoclase.

olimpíada, *f.* Olympiad; Olympic games.

olímpico, ca, *a.* Olympic.

Olimpo, *m.* Olympus; (poet.) heaven.

olingo, *m.* a Central-American monkey.

olio, *m.* = ÓLEO.

oliscar. I. *va.* to smell, scent, sniff, snuff; to investigate, ascertain. II. *vn.* (of meat) to be tainted, gamey, or high.

oliva, *f.* olive tree; olive; owl.—*pl.* **olivas y aceitunas, todas son unas,** it's all the same, what's in a name.

olivar, *m.* olive grove, yard.

¹olivarda, *f.* (ornith.) green goshawk.

²olivarda, *f.* (bot.) elecampane.

olivarse, *vr.* (of bread) to form bubbles when baking.

olivera, *f.* olive tree.

olivífero, ra, *a.* (poet.) olive-bearing.

olivillo, *m.* (bot.) a variety of terebinth.

olivino, *m.* (min.) olivin, peridot.

olivo, *m.* (bot.) olive tree.—**o. manzanillo,** olive tree yielding the MANZANILLA olive.—**o. y aceituno, todo es uno,** it's all the same, what's in a name.

olmeda, *f.* olmedo, *m.* elm grove.

olmo, *m.* (bot.) elm tree.

ológrafo, *a.* (law) holographic.

olor, *m.* smell, fragrance; odor; hope, promise, offer; suspicion, smack.

oloroso, sa, *a.* fragrant.

olvidadizo, za, *a.* short of memory, forgetful.

olvidado, da. I. *pp.* of OLVIDAR. II. *a.* forgetful.

olvidar. I. *va.* to forget. II. *vr.* to be forgotten, to forget (diff. constr. as *el dinero se me olvidó,* I forgot the money); (de) to forget (diff. constr. as *me olvidé del dinero,* I forgot the money).

olvido, *m.* forgetfulness; oversight; oblivion.— **dar,** or **echar, al o.,** or **en o.,** to forget; to cast into oblivion.

olla, *f.* pot, kettle, stewpot; (cook.) olla, olio, dish of boiled meat and vegetables; whirlpool. —**o. carnicera,** boiler, large kettle.—**o. ciega** = ALCANCÍA, money box.—**o. de fuego,** (artil.) stinkpot.—**o. de grillos,** great confusion, pandemonium.—**o. podrida,** olla-podrida, meat and vegetable stew.

ollao, *m.* (naut.) eyelet hole.

¹ollar, *a.* soft (stone).

²ollar, *m.* horse's nostril.

ollaza, *f. aug.* large pot or boiler.

ollería, *f.* pottery; crockery shop.

ollero, ra, *n.* potter; dealer in earthenware.

ollita, olluela, *f. dim.* pipkin, small pot.

ombligada, *f.* (tanning) part of a skin corresponding to the navel.

ombligo, *m.* navel; umbilical cord; center or middle.—**o. de Venus,** (bot.) Venus navelwort.

---

ombliguero, *m.* navel bandage for infants.

ombría, *f.* shady place.

ombú, *m.* a South American tree.

omega, *f.* omega (Greek letter).—**desde el alpha hasta la o.,** from alpha to omega, from A to Z, from beginning to end.

omental, *a.* (anat.) omental.

omento, *m.* (anat.) omentum.

ominar, *va.* to augur, foretell.

ominosamente, *adv.* ominously.

ominoso, sa, *a.* ominous, foreboding ill.

omisión, *f.* omission; carelessness, neglect.

omiso, sa. I. *pp. irreg.* of OMITIR. **II.** *a.* neglectful, remiss, careless.

omitir, *va.* (*pp.* OMITIDO, OMISO) to omit.

ómnibus, *m.* omnibus, stagecoach.

omnímodamente, *adv.* in every way or respect, completely.

omnímodo, da, *a.* all-embracing.

omnipotencia, *f.* omnipotence.

omnipotente, *a.* omnipotent, almighty.

omnipotentemente, *adv.* omnipotently.

omnipresencia, *f.* omnipresence.

omnisapiente, *a.* omniscient, all-knowing.

omnisciencia, *f.* omniscience.

omnisciente, *a.* = OMNISCIO.

omniscio, ia, *a.* omniscient, all-knowing.

omnívoro, ra, *a.* omnivorous.

omóplato, *m.* (anat.) shoulderblade, scapula.

onagra, *f.* (bot.) onagra, evening primrose.

onagro, *m.* wild ass, onager.

onanismo, *m.* onanism.

once. I. *a.* eleven; eleventh. **II.** *m.* eleven; eleventh (of the month).—**las o.,** eleven o'clock.—**hacer,** or **tomar, las onces,** to take a small luncheon about noon.

oncear, *va.* to weigh out by ounces.

oncejera, *f.* small snare for catching birds.

oncejo, *m.* (ornith.) = VENCEJO, swift.

onceno, na, *a.* eleventh.—**el o. no estorbar,** (the eleventh commandment is:) thou shalt not disturb busy people.

oncijera, *f.* = ONCEJERA.

onda, *f.* wave, ripple (of sea); wave (in hair); undulation; flicker; (sewing) scallop.—*pl.* the sea.—**ondas a la Marcel,** (hair) marcel.—**o. corta, larga,** (radio) short-, long-, wave.—**o. etérea,** ether wave.—**o. herciana,** or **hertziana,** Hertzian wave.—**o. sonora,** sound wave.

ondámetro, *m.* (radio) wave meter.

ondeado. I. *pp.* of ONDEAR. **II.** *a.* undulated, scalloped, wavy. **II.** *m.* scalloping.

ondeante, *a.* waving, undulating.

ondear. I. *vn.* to wave, ripple, undulate; to flicker. **II.** *vr.* to swing, soar.

ondeo, *m.* waving, undulating, fluctuating.

ondina, *f.* Undine, water sprite.

ondisonante, *a.* (poet.) = UNDÍSONO, billowy.

ondulación, *f.* = UNDULACIÓN, wave, or wavy motion.—**o. permanente,** permanent wave (of hair).

ondulado, da. I. *pp.* of ONDULAR. **II.** *a.* undulated, rippled; scalloped, wavy; corrugated. **III.** *m.* **o. permanente,** permanent waving (of hair).

ondulante, *a.* waving, undulating.

ondular, undular, *va.* to undulate; to ripple.

ondulatorio, ria, *a.* undulatory.

oneroso, sa, *a.* burdensome, onerous.

onfacino, *a.* omphacine (oil).

onfacomeli, *m.* (pharm.) oxymel.

ónice, *m.,* **ónique,** *f.* (min.) onyx.

oniromancía, *f.* oneiromancy, divination through dreams.

ónix, *m.* (min.) onyx.

onocrótalo, *m.* (ornith.) white pelican.

onomancía, *f.* onomancy, divination from names.

onomástico, ca, *a.* onomastic, pert. to names.

onomatopeya, *f.* onomatopœia.

onomatopéyico, ca, *a.* onomatopœic.

onoquiles, *f.* (bot.) dyer's bugloss, alkanet.

ontogénesis, ontogenia, *f.* (biol.) ontogeny.

ontología, *f.* ontology.

ontológico, ca, *a.* ontological.

ontólogo, *m.* ontologist.

¹onza, *f.* ounce.—**o. de oro,** Spanish doubloon.—**por onzas,** sparingly.

²onza, *f.* (zool.) ounce, leopardlike feline.

onzavo, va, *n.* & *a.* eleventh.

oolita, *f.* (geol.) oölite.

oolítico, ca, *a.* (geol.) oölitic.

oosfera, *f.* (biol.) oösphere, unfertilized egg.

opacamente, *adv.* obscurely, darkly.

opacidad, *f.* opacity.

opaco, ca, *a.* opaque.

opalino, na, *a.* opaline, opalescent.

ópalo, *m.* (min.) opal.

opción, *f.* option, choice; right.

ópera, *f.* opera.—**o. bufa,** comic opera.

operable, *a.* operable, practicable; capable of operating.

operación, *f.* operation, action, working; (chem.) process; (math.) operation, calculation; (surg.) operation; (com.) operation, transaction, venture.—*pl.* (mil.) operations.—**o. cesárea,** (surg.) Cæsarean operation.—**operaciones de banco,** banking business.—**operaciones marítimas,** shipping trade or business.

operador, *m.* (surg.) operator.

operante, *n.* & *a.* operator(-ing).

operar. I. *va.* to operate; (surg.) to operate on. **II.** *vn.* to operate, act, work.

operario, ria. I. *n.* workman(-woman), hand; operator. **II.** *m.* priest who assists sick or dying persons.

operativo, va, *a.* operative.

operatorio, ria, *a.* operative; (med.) operative, pertaining to operations.

opérculo, *m.* operculum, lid, cover.

opereta, *f.* operetta, light opera.

operista, *n.* opera singer.

operoso, sa, *a.* laborious.

opiado, da, *a.* opiate, narcotic.

opiato, ta. I. *a.* opiate. **II.** *m.* opiate.

opilación, *f.* (med.) oppilation, obstruction; amenorrhœa, suppression of the menses.

opilarse, *vr.* to contract amenorrhœa.

opilativo, va, *a.* obstructive, oppilative.

opimo, ma, *a.* rich, fruitful, abundant.

opinable, *a.* disputable, questionable.

opinante, *n.* & *a.* arguer(-ing).

opinar, *vn.* to judge, be of the opinion.

opinativo, va, *a.* opinionative.

opinión, *f.* opinion.

opio, *m.* opium.

opíparamente, *adv.* sumptuously.

opíparo, ra, *a.* sumptuous.

oploteca, *f.* museum of rare weapons.

opobálsamo, *m.* opobalsam, balm of Gilead.

oponer, *va.* & *vr.* (*pp. irreg.* OPUESTO; *ind. pres.* OPONGO, *pret.* OPUSE, *fut.* OPONDRÉ; *subj.* OPONGA) to oppose; to hinder, resist, withstand; to object to, act against; to front, face, be opposite to; to stand in competition with.

oponible, *a.* opposable.

opopónaca, opopónace, *f.* (bot.) rough parsnip.

opopónaco, opopónax, *m.* opopanax, a gum resin.

oporto, *m.* port wine.

oportunamente, *adv.* opportunely.

oportunidad, *f.* opportunity.

oportunismo, *m.* (pol.) opportunism.

oportunista, *n.* & *a.* (pol.) opportunist(-ic).

oportuno, na, *a.* opportune, timely.

oposición, *f.* opposition; competition for a position, etc.; (astr.) opposition.

oposicionista, *m.* (pol.) obstructionist.

opositor, ra, *n.* opposer, opponent; competitor.

opoterapia, *f.* (med.), organotherapy.

opresión, *f.* oppression; pressure.

opresivamente, *adv.* oppressively.

opresivo, va, *a.* oppressive, overwhelming.

opresor, ra, *n.* oppressor; extortioner.

oprimir, *va.* to oppress; to press, push; to lie heavy upon, weigh down, dispirit.

oprobiar, *va.* to defame, revile.

oprobio, *m.* opprobrium, ignominy, infamy.

oprobioso, sa, *a.* opprobrious, disgraceful.

optante, *n.* chooser.

optar. I. *va.* to opt, choose, select; to take possession of. **II.** *vn.* **(por)** to choose.

optativo, *m.* (gram.) optative.

óptica, *f.* optics; stereoscope.

óptico, ca. I. *a.* optic, optical. **II.** *m.* optician.

óptimamente, *adv.* in the best way, perfectly.

optimismo, *m.* optimism.

optimista, *n.* & *a.* optimist(-ic).

óptimo, ma, *a.* best, eminently good.

optometra, *m.* & *f.* optometrist.

optometría, *f.* optometry, science of eye testing.

optómetro, *m.* (opt.) optometer.

opuestamente, *adv.* oppositely, contrarily.

opuesto, ta. I. *pp. irreg.* of OPONER. **II.** *a.* opposed; opposite, contrary, adverse.

opugnación, *f.* opposition, attack.

opugnador, ra, *n.* opposer, attacker.

opugnar, *va.* to attack, oppose.

opulencia, *f.* opulence.

opulentamente, *adv.* opulently.

opulento, ta, *a.* opulent, wealthy.

opúsculo, *m.* booklet, tract.

opuse, *pret.* of OPONER.

oquedad, *f.* hollow, cavity.

oquedal, *m.* plantation of lofty trees.

oqueruela, *f.* kink in a sewing thread.

ora, *conj.* (*contr.* of AHORA) whether; either; now, then: *tomando ora la espada, ora la pluma,* taking now the sword, now (*or,* and then) the pen.

oración, *f.* oration, speech; orison, prayer; dusk, beginning of the evening; (gram.) sentence.—*pl.* first part of catechism; the angelus.—**o. dominical,** the Lord's Prayer.

oracional, *m.* prayer book.

oráculo, *m.* oracle.

orador, ra, *n.* orator, speaker.

oral, *a.* oral; vocal.

oral, *m.* soft breeze.

orangután, *m.* (zool.) orang-outang.

orante, *a.* praying.

orar, *I. vn.* to harangue, deliver a speech; to pray. **II.** *va.* to ask, beg for.

orate, *n.* lunatic, madman(-woman).

oratoria, *f.* oratory, eloquent speaking.

oratoriamente, *adv.* oratorically.

oratorio, ria, *a.* oratorical.

oratorio, *m.* oratory, chapel; (mus.) oratorio; (eccl.) congregation of presbyters.

orbe, *m.* orb, sphere; the earth; any celestial body; (ichth.) globefish.

orbicular, *a.* orbicular, circular.

orbicularmente, *adv.* orbicularly.

órbita, *f.* (astr.) orbit; (anat.) orbit (of the eye).

orca, *f.* (ichth.) grampus, orca.

orcaneta, *f.* (bot.) dyer's bugloss, alkanet.

orco, *m.* hell.

orco, *m.* (ichth.) = ORCA.

ordago.—de o., first-class, excellent.

ordalía, *f.* ordeal, trial by fire or water.

orden. I. *m.* order; class, group; proportion, relation; (arch.) order; (religious) order.—*pl.* (eccl.) sacrament of ordination, clerical office.—**o. cerrado,** (mil.) close formation.—**o. compuesto,** (arch.) composite order.—**o. de batalla,** battle array, order of battle.—**o. del día,** order of the day, agenda.—**en o.,** in order; in an orderly manner; with regard to.—**fuera de o.,** (parl. law) out of order.—**por su o.,** in its turn. **II.** *f.* order, command; (com.) order; order of knighthood and the insignia.—*pl.*

orders, instructions.—**o. del día,** (mil.) order of the day.—**a la o.,** (com.) to order.—**a la o. de,** to the order of.—**a sus órdenes,** at your service. (*en espera de sus ordenes,* used in business letters, means "awaiting your commands," or "your pleasure," and not "your (business) orders," "your custom.")

ordenación, *f.* methodical arrangement; disposition, array; (math.) permutation; edict, ordinance; clerical ordination; auditor's office; (arch. and art) ordonnance.

ordenada, *f.* (geom.) ordinate.

ordenadamente, *adv.* orderly, in order.

ordenado, da. I. *pp.* of ORDENAR. **II.** *a.* ordained, ordinate; methodical; tidy.

ordenador, ra, *n.* ordainer; orderer; auditor.

ordenamiento, *m.* ordaining, regulating; law, edict, ordinance.

ordenancista, *n.* disciplinarian, martinet.

ordenando, ordenante, *m.* (eccl.) ordinand.

ordenanza. I. *f.* method, order; law, statute, ordinance; command; ordination. **II.** *m.* (mil.) orderly; (arch. and art) ordonnance.

ordenar. I. *va.* to arrange, put in order; to order, command; to ordain, confer holy orders on; (math.) to arrange (a polynomial) according to the ascending or descending powers of a letter. **II.** *vr.* (eccl.) to be ordained.

ordeñadero, *m.* milk pail; milking place.

ordeñador, ra, *n.* milker.

ordeñar, *va.* to milk; to pick (olives).

ordinal, *n.* & *a.* ordinal.

ordinariamente, *adv.* ordinarily; rudely.

ordinariez, *f.* rough manners, ordinariness.

ordinario, ria. I. *a.* ordinary, usual; coarse, unrefined. **II.** *m.* daily household expense; mail, post, courier; (eccl.) ordinary (judge); bishop.—**de o.,** usually, ordinarily, regularly.

ordinativo, va, *a.* ordering, regulating.

orea, oréada, oréade, *f.* oread, wood nymph.

oreante, *a.* cooling, refreshing.

orear. I. *va.* to air, expose to the air, aerate. **II.** *vr.* to take an airing.

orégano, *m.* (bot.) wild marjoram.

oreja, *f.* (external) ear; hearing (sense); flap of a shoe; flatterer, talebearer; (mech.) lug, flange, ear.—**o. de abad,** or **monje,** (bot.) Venus navelwort.—**o. de ancla,** (naut.) fluke of an anchor.—**o. de oso,** (bot.) primrose.—**o. de ratón,** (bot.) mouse-ear.—**o. marina,** a European gasteropod.—**o. de mercader,** (coll.) deaf ears.—**apearse por las orejas,** (coll.) to give an absurd answer.—**bajar las orejas,** to yield, to come down from one's high horse.—**calentar las orejas a,** to chide, dress down.—**con las orejas caídas,** crestfallen, dejected.—**descubrir la o.,** to give oneself away.—**ver las orejas al lobo,** to be in great peril.

orejano, na, *a.* unbranded or motherless (calf).

orejeado, da. I. *pp.* of OREJEAR. **II.** *a.* informed, advised, warned.

orejear, *vn.* to shake or prick up the ears; to act with reluctance; to whisper.

orejera, *f.* ear muff, earcap; ear hoop; moldboard of a plow.

orejeta, *f. dim.* small ear, lug, or flange.

orejita, *f. dim.* small auricle or ear.

orejón, *m.* pull by the ear; (Peru) privileged noble; Inca; (S. A.) countryman, rancher; (fort.) orillon.

orejudo, da, *a.* flap-eared, long-eared.

oreo, *m.* breeze, fresh air; airing.

orfanato, *m.* orphan asylum, orphanage.

orfandad, *f.* orphanage.

orfebre, *m.* goldsmith, silversmith.

orfebrería, *f.* gold or silver work.

orfelinato, *m.* (Gal.) = ORFANATO.

orfeón, *m.* singing society.

orfeonista, *m.* member of a singing society.

órfico, ca, *a.* Orphean.

organdí, *m.* organdy.
organero, ra, *n.* organ maker; organ builder.
orgánicamente, *adv.* organically.
organicé, organice, *v.* V. ORGANIZAR.
organicismo, *m.* (med.) organicism.
organicista, *n.* & *a.* organicist(-ic).
orgánico, ca, *a.* organic; harmonious.
organillo, *m. dim.* barrel organ, hand organ.
organismo, *m.* organism; organization, association.
organista, *n.* (mus.) organist.
organizable, *a.* organizable.
organización, *f.* organization; arrangement.
organizado, da. I. *pp.* of ORGANIZAR. II. *a.* (biol.) organic; pert. to living organism.
organizador, ra, *a.* organizing; having aptitude for organizing.—**comité o.,** committee on arrangements.
organizar, *va.* (*pret.* ORGANICÉ; *subj.* ORGANICE) to organize, set up; to arrange; to tune (an organ).
órgano, *m.* (mus.) pipe organ; pipe refrigerator; (physiol.) organ; medium, instrument, agency. —**órganos de Móstoles,** persons or ideas that disagree.—**órganos genitales** genitals.
organogenia, *f.* (biol.) organogenesis.
organografía, *f.* organography.
organográfico, ca, *a.* organographic.
organología, *f.* organology.
orgasmo, *m.* (physiol.) orgasm.
orgía, *f.* orgy, revel.—**orgiástico, ca,** *a.* orgiastic.
orgullo, *m.* pride; haughtiness.
orgullosamente, *adv.* proudly; haughtily.
orgulloso, sa, *a.* proud; haughty, overbearing; conceited.
orientación, *f.* orientation; bearings.
oriental. I. *a.* oriental, eastern. II. *m.* oriental.
orientalismo, *m.* orientalism.
orientalista, *n.* orientalist.
orientar. I. *va.* to orientate, to orient.—**o. una vela,** (naut.) to trim a sail. II. *vr.* to find one's way about, get one's bearings.
oriente, *m.* east, orient; east wind; source, origin; youth.
orificación, *f.* (dent.) gold filling.
orificador, *m.* dentist's plugger.
orificar, *va.* (dent.) to fill with gold.
orifice, *m.* goldsmith.
orificio, *m.* orifice, hole; anus; (artil.) venthole; (mech.) port.
oriflama, *f.* oriflamme; flag, banner.
origen, *m.* origin; source; native country; beginning.
origenismo, *m.* Origenism.
origenista, *n.* & *a.* Origenist(-ic).
original. I. *a.* original; primitive; new, novel; quaint, odd. II. *m.* original, first copy, archetype; (print.) copy, manuscript; original of a portrait; odd person.—**de buen o.,** on good authority.
originalidad, *f.* originality; eccentricity.
originalmente, *adv.* originally.
originar. I. *va.* to originate, create, invent; to start. II. *vr.* to originate, arise, spring.
originariamente, *adv.* primarily, originally.
originario, ria, *a.* originating; native; derived.
¹**orilla,** *f.* border, margin; edge; bank (of a river); shore; sidewalk.—**a la o.,** near a place, on the brink.—**salir a la o.,** to overcome difficulties.
²**orilla,** *f.* fresh breeze.
orillar. I. *va.* to arrange, settle; to evade; to surmount. II. *vn.* to leave a selvage on cloth; (sew.) to border. III. *vr.* & *vn.* to reach the shore.
orillo, *m.* selvage or list of cloth.
¹**orín,** *m.* rust.
²**orín,** *m.* (gen. *pl.*) = ORINA.
orina, *f.* urine.—**orinal,** *m.* urinal; chamber pot. —**orinar,** *va.* & *vn.* to urinate.
oriniento, ta, *a.* rusty, moldy.

orinque, *m.* (naut.) buoy rope.
oriol, *m.* (ornith.) golden oriole or thrush.
Orión, *m.* (astr.) Orion.
oriundo, da, *a.* native, coming (from).
orla, *f.* list, selvage, border, fringe, trimming (her.) orle; (print.) ornamental border.
orlador, ra, *n.* borderer.
orladura, *f.* border, edging, list.
orlar, *va.* to border, garnish with an edging.
orleanista, *n.* & *a.* Orleanist(-ic).
¹**orio,** *m.* Alpine horn; (mus.) organ stop.
²**orlo,** *m.* (arch.) plinth.
ormesí, *m.* a kind of silk stuff.
ormino, *m.* (bot.) = GALLOCRESTA, clary sage.
ornadamente, *adv.* ornamentally.
ornado, da. I. *pp.* of ORNAR. II. *a.* ornate.
ornamentación, *f.* ornamentation.
ornamentar, *va.* to adorn, decorate.
ornamento, *m.* ornament; decoration, adorn ment; accomplishment, gift.—*pl.* (eccl.) sacred vestments; (arch.) frets, moldings, etc.; moral qualities, character.
ornar, *va.* to adorn, embellish, garnish.
ornato, *m.* ornament, decoration, embellishment.
ornitodelfo, fa. I. *n.* & *a.* (zool.) prototherian. II. *m. pl.* Prototheria.
ornitología, *f.* ornithology.
ornitológico, ca, *a.* ornithological.
ornitólogo, *m.* ornithologist.
ornitomancia, *f.* ornithomancy.
ornitóptero, *m.* (aer.) ornithopter, orthopter.
ornitorrinco, *m.* (zool.) ornithorhynchus, duckbill.
oro, *m.* gold; gold color; ornaments or trinket made of gold.—*pl.* diamonds, in Spanish cards. —**o. batido,** leaf gold.—**o. bruto,** bullion.—**o coronario,** high-carat gold.—**o. en barra,** bar gold, gold in bars.—**o. en libritos,** gold leaf.— **o. en pasta** = O. BRUTO.—**o. en polvo,** gold dust.—**o. fulminante,** gold fulminate.—**o mate,** gold size.—**o. musivo,** mosaic gold, aurum musivum.—**o. nativo,** native gold.—**o virgen** = O. BRUTO.—**de o. y azul,** gorgeously attired.—**poner (a uno) de o. y azul,** (coll.) to give (one) a good dressing down, a lecture or severe reprimand.
orobanca, *f.* (bot.) broom rape.
orobancáceas, *f., pl.* (bot.) Orobanchaceæ.
orobias, *m.* fine incense.
orogenia, *f.* (geol.) orogeny.
orogénico, ca, *a.* orogenic.
orografía, *f.* orography, branch of geography treating of mountains.
orográfico, ca, *a.* orographic.
orondo, da, *a.* pompous, showy; hollow.
oropel, *m.* tinsel; brass foil; glitter.
oropelero, *m.* brass worker.
oropéndola, *f.* (ornith.) loriot, golden oriole.
oropimente, *m.* (min.) orpiment.
oroya, *f.* (Am.) basket hanging from rope bridge for transportation across a river.
orozuz, *m.* (bot.) licorice.
orquesta, *f.* (mus.) orchestra; (theat.) orchestra pit.
orquestación, *f.* orchestration.
orquestar, *va.* to orchestrate.
orquídeo, dea. I. *a.* (bot.) orchidaceous. II. orchid. III. *f. pl.* Orchidaceæ, orchids.
orquitis, *f.* (med.) orchitis, inflammation of testicle.
orre.—en o., loose, in bulk.
ortega, *f.* (ornith.) hazel grouse.
ortiga, *f.* (bot.) nettle.—**o. de mar,** (ichth.) sea nettle.—**ser como unas ortigas,** to be as cross as a bear.
ortivo, va, *a.* (astr.) oriental, eastern.
orto, *m.* rising (of the sun or a star).
ortoclasa, *f.* (min.) orthoclase.
ortodoxia, *f.* orthodoxy.

rtodoxo, xa, *a.* orthodox.

rtodromia, *f.* (naut.) orthodromy.

rtodrómico, ca, *a.* (naut.) orthodromic.

rtogonal, *a.* orthogonal, right-angled.

rtogonio, *a.* right-angled (triangle).

rtografía, *f.* orthography.

rtográficamente, *adv.* orthographically.

rtográfico, ca, *a.* orthographical.

rtógrafo, *m.* orthographer.

rtología, *f.* orthoëpy, study of pronunciation.

rtológico, ca, *a.* orthoëpic.

rtólogo, ga, *n.* orthoëpist.

rtopedia, *f.* (med.) orthopedics.

rtopédico, ca, *a.* (med.) orthopedic.

rtopedista, *n.* orthopedist.

rtóptero. I. *a.* (entom.) orthopterous. II. *m. pl.* Orthoptera.

rtorrómbico, ca, *a.* (of crystals) orthorhombic.

rtosa, *f.* (min.) orthoclase.

ruga, *f.* (bot.) rocket; (entom.) caterpillar.

rujo, *m.* refuse of grapes, cotton seed, olives, etc.

rvalle, *m.* (bot.) = GALLOCRESTA, clary sage.

orza, *f.* preserve jar, crock.

orza, *f.* (naut.) luff.—o. a la banda, (naut.) hard-a-lee.—a o., (naut.) luff.

orzada, *f.* (naut.) luffing, hauling.

orzaderas, *f. pl.* (naut.) leeboards.

orzaga, *f.* (bot.) orach; mountain spinach.

orzar, *vn.* (naut.) to luff.

orzaya, *f.* (children's) nurse.

orzuelo, *m.* (med.) sty; hordeolum.

orzuelo, *m.* snare (for birds); trap (for wild beasts).

orzura, *f.* (chem.) minium.

os, *pers. pron. dative and accusative of* VOS *and* VOSOTROS, you, to you.

osa, *f.* (zool.) she-bear.—O. Mayor, (astr.) Great Bear, the Dipper.—O. Menor, Little Bear.

osadamente, *adv.* boldly, daringly.

osadía, *f.* audacity, daring, boldness.

osado, da, *a.* daring, bold, audacious.

osambre, *m.,* osamenta, *f.* skeleton; bones.

osar, *vn.* to dare, venture; to outdare.

osar, osario, *m.* charnel house; ossuary.

oscilación, *f.* oscillation.

oscilante, *a.* oscillating.

oscilar, *vn.* to oscillate.

oscilatorio, ria, *a.* oscillatory.

oscitancia, *f.* carelessness, heedlessness.

osculación, *f.* (geom.) osculation.

osculador, triz, *a.* (geom.) osculating.

ósculo, *m.* kiss.

oscurantismo, oscuro, etc. = OBSCURANTISMO, OBSCURO, etc.

oscurecimiento, *m.* blackout (as for air raid).

osecico, cillo, cito, zuelo, *m. dim.* small bone.

oseína, *f.* (chem.) ossein.

óseo, a, osseous, bony.

osera, *f.* den of bears.

osezno, *m.* whelp or cub of a bear.

osificación, *f.* ossification.

osificarse, *vr.* to ossify, become ossified.

osífico, ca, *a.* ossific.

osífraga, *f.,* osífrago, *m.* (ornith.) osprey.

osmazomo, *m.* osmazome.

osmio, *m.* (chem.) osmium.

ósmosis, *f.* (phys.) osmosis.

oso, *m.* (zool.) bear.—o. blanco, polar bear.—o. colmenero, honey-eating bear, bear that robs beehives.—o. de las cavernas, (paleontol.) cave bear.—o. hormiguero, anteater.—o. marino, fur seal.—o. marítimo = O. BLANCO. —hacer el o., (coll.) to make a fool of oneself; to act as a sentimental lover.

ososo, sa, *f.* osseous, bony.

osta, *f.* (naut.) lateen brace.

ostaga, *f.* (naut.) tie, runner.

oste! *interj.* = OXTE.

osteítis, *f.* (med.) osteitis, inflammation of bone.

ostensible, *a.* ostensible.—ostensiblemente, *adv.* ostensibly.

ostensión, *f.* show, manifestation.

ostensivo, va, *a.* ostensive, showy.

ostentación, *f.* ostentation, vain show.

ostentador, ra, *n.* boaster, ostentatious person.

ostentar. I. *va.* to make a show of, to exhibit. II. *vn.* to boast, to brag; to show off.

ostentativo, va, *a.* ostentatious.

ostento, *m.* portent.

ostentosamente, *adv.* ostentatiously.

ostentoso, sa, *a.* sumptuous, magnificent.

osteogénesis, osteogenia, *f.* (physiol.) osteogenesis, formation of bone.

osteología, *f.* (anat.) osteology.

osteológico, ca, *a.* osteologic.

osteoma, *m.* (med.) osteoma.

osteomalacia, *f.* osteomalacia.

osteomielitis, *f.* (med.) osteomyelitis.

osteópata, *n.* osteopath.

osteopatía, *f.* osteopathy.

osteotomía, *f.* (surg.) osteotomy.

ostiario, *m.* (eccl.) ostiary, doorkeeper.

ostión, *m.* large oyster.

ostra, *f.* oyster.

ostracismo, *m.* ostracism.

ostral, *m.* oyster farm; oyster bed.

ostrería, *f.* oyster shop, oyster house.

ostrero, ra. I. *a.* oysterlike. II. *n.* oyster seller. III. *f.* oyster farm.

ostricultura, *f.* oyster farming, culture.

ostrífero, ra, *a.* abounding in, or raising, oysters.

ostro, *m.* large, coarse oyster; any mollusk yielding purple; purple from mollusks.

ostro, *m.* south wind.

ostrogodo, da, *n. & a.* Ostrogoth(-ic).

ostrón, *m. aug.* large, coarse oyster.

ostugo, *m.* piece, part, bit; corner.

osudo, da, *a.* bony.

osuno, na, *a.* bearlike, bearish.

otalgia, *f.* (med.) otalgia, earache.

otáñez, *m.* (coll.) old squire who escorted a lady as chaperon.

oteador, ra, *n.* spy, sly observer.

otear, *va.* to observe, examine, pry into.

otero, *m.* hill, hillock, knoll.

oteruelo, *m. dim.* hummock, knoll, mound.

otitis, *f.* (med.) otitis, inflammation of ear.

oto, *m.* (ornith.) bustard.

otoba, *f.* (bot.) a variety of nutmeg tree.

otología, *f.* (med.) otology.

otólogo, ga, *n.* aurist, otologist.

otomano, na. I. *n. & a.* Ottoman. II. *f.* ottoman, divan.

otoñada, *f.* autumn season; pasturage.

otoñal, *a.* autumnal.

otoñar. I. *vn.* to spend the autumn season; (of weeds) to grow in autumn. II. *vr.* (of earth after rain) to be seasoned.

otoño, *m.* autumn, fall; aftermath.

otorgadero, ra, *a.* grantable.

otorgador, ra, *n.* grantor.

otorgamiento, *m.* grant, granting; license; (law) executing an instrument.

otorgante. I. *a.* authorizing, granting. II. *n.* grantor, maker of a deed.

otorgar, *va.* (*pret.* OTORGUÉ; *subj.* OTORGUE) to consent, agree to; (law) to grant; to prescribe, stipulate, promise.—quien calla otorga, silence gives consent.

otorgo, *m.* (law) marriage contract.

otorrea, *f.* (med.) otorrhœa, discharge from ear.

otoscopia, *f.* (surg.) otoscopy.

otoscopio, *m.* (surg.) otoscope.

otramente, *adv.* otherwise, differently.

otro, tra, *a.* another, other.—¡o.! encore! again! —o. cosa, something else.—o. que tal, (coll.) another such.—otros tantos, as many more. —o. vez, again.—por o. parte, on the other hand.—(el) **uno** a(l) **o.**, each other.—**unos a otros**, one another.

otrosí. I. *adv.* besides, moreover. **II.** *m.* (law) every petition made after the principal.

ova, *f.* (bot.) sea lettuce, laver.

ovación, *f.* ovation.

ovacionar, *va.* to give an ovation to.

ovado, da. I. *pp.* of OVAR. **II.** *a.* (of a bird) impregnated by the male; oval, egg-shaped.

oval; ovalado, da, *a.* oval.

ovalar, *va.* to make oval.

óvalo, *m.* oval.

ovante, *a.* victorious, triumphant.

ovar, *vn.* to lay eggs.

ovárico, ca, *a.* ovarian.

ovario, *m.* (anat.) ovary; (bot.) ovarium, ovary; (arch.) egg ornament.

ovariotomía, *f.* (surg.) ovariotomy.

ovaritis, *f.* (med.) ovaritis.

ovas, *f. pl.* = HUEVA, spawn of fish, roe.

ovecillo, *m. dim.* small egg.

oveja, *f.* sheep.

ovejero, ra, *n.* shepherd(-ess); sheep raiser.

ovejuela, *f. dim.* young ewe.

ovejuno, na, *a.* pert. to sheep, sheep (as *a.*).

overa, *f.* ovary of fowls.

¹overo, ra, *a.* blossom-colored (horse).

²overo, a.—ojo o., large, bulging eye with small pupil.

overol, *m.* (Angl.) (Am.) overalls.

ovezuelo, *m.* small egg.

óvidos, *m. pl.* (zool.) Ovidæ.

oviducto, *m.* (anat.) oviduct.

oviforme, *a.* oviform, egg-shaped.

ovil, *m.* = REDIL, sheepcote.

ovillar. I. *va.* to wind (thread) in a ball or skein. **II.** *vr.* to hunch oneself into a bunch.

ovillejo, *m. dim.* small skein; a kind of rondel.

ovillo, *m.* skein, ball of yarn; ball or heap of mixed or tangled things.—**hacerse un o.,** to hunch oneself into a bunch.

ovíparo, ra, *a.* (zool.) oviparous.

ovoide, *a.* ovoid, egg-shaped.

óvolo, *m.* (arch.) ovolo; quarter round.

ovoso, sa, *a.* full of roe.

ovovivíparo, ra, *a.* (zool.) ovoviviparous.

ovulación, *f.* (biol.) ovulation.

óvulo, *m.* (nat. hist.) ovule.

¡ox! *interj.* shoo! begone!

oxácido, *m.* (chem.) oxacid.

oxalato, *m.* (chem.) oxalate.

oxálico, *a.* (chem.) oxalic.

oxalídeas, *f. pl.* (bot.) Oxalidaceæ.

oxalme, *m.* acidulated brine.

oxear, *va.* to shoo (fowls).

oxhídrico, ca; *a.* oxyhydrogen.

oxiacanta, *f.* (bot.) whitethorn, hawthorn.

oxidable, *a.* (chem.) oxidizable.

oxidación, *f.* (chem.) oxidation.

oxidante, *a.* (chem.) oxidating, oxydizing.

oxidar, *va. & vr.* to oxidize; to rust.

óxido, *m.* (chem.) oxide.

oxigenable, *a.* (chem.) oxygenizable.

oxigenación, *f.* (chem.) oxygenation.

oxigenar, *va. & vr.* to oxygenate.

oxígeno, *m.* (chem.) oxygen.

oxigonio, *a.* (geom.) acute-angled.

oximel, oximiel, *m.* (pharm.) = OJIMIEL, oxymel.

oxipétalo, *m.* (bot.) a Brazilian vine.

oxizacre, *m.* bittersweet beverage.

¡oxte! *interj.* keep off! begone!—**sin decir o. ni moxte,** (coll.) without saying a word.

oyamel, *m.* (bot.) Mexican sacred fir.

oyente, *n.* hearer.—*pl.* audience.

oyó, *pret.* of OÍR.

ozona, *f.,* **ozono,** *m.* (chem.) ozone.

ozonización, *f.* ozonization.

ozonizador, ra. I. *a.* ozonizing. **II.** *n.* ozonizer.

ozonizar, *va.* to ozonize.

ozonómetro, *m.* ozone paper.

P

pabellón, *m.* pavilion; (mil.) bell tent; esparver, dais, bed canopy; summer house; national colors, flag; bell of a wind instrument; (anat.) external ear, pinna.—**p. de armas,** (mil.) stack of arms.

pabilo, pábilo, *m.* wick (of candle); burnt end of wick.

pabilón, *m.* bunch of flax or wool hanging from the distaff.

pablar, *vn.* (coll.) to talk.

pábulo, *m.* pabulum, food; encouragement.—**dar p. a,** to substantiate.

¹paca, *f.* (zool.) spotted cavy.

²paca, *f.* bale of goods.

pacana, *f.* (bot.) pecan tree; pecan nut.

pacato, ta, *a.* pacific, quiet, tranquil, mild.

pacedero, ra. I. *a.* fit for grazing. **II.** *m.* grazing field, pasture.

pacedura, *f.* pasture.

paceño, ña, *a.* of or from La Paz, Bolivia.

pacer. I. *vn.* to pasture, to graze. **II.** *va.* to gnaw, nibble, eat away.

paciencia, *f.* patience; a kind of cooky.

paciente. I. *a.* patient. **II.** *n.* patient, sick person.

pacientemente, *adv.* patiently.

pacienzudo, da, *a.* exceedingly patient.

pacificación, *f.* pacification; peace of mind.

pacificador, ra, *n.* pacifier, peacemaker.

pacíficamente, *adv.* peacefully.

pacificar. I. *va.* (*pret.* PACIFIQUÉ; *subj.* PACIFIQUE) to pacify, appease. **II.** *vn.* to treat for peace. **III.** *vr.* to become calm.

pacífico, ca, *a.* peaceful; mild, gentle.

pacifiqué, pacifique, *v.* V. PACIFICAR.

pacifismo, *m.* pacifism.

pacifista, *n. & a.* pacifist(-ic).

¹paco, *m.* (zool.) paco, alpaca; (min.) paco.

²paco, *m.* (Chile) police force.

pacotilla, *f.* (com.) venture.—**de p.,** of poor or inferior quality.

pactar, *va.* to covenant, contract, stipulate.

pacto, *m.* agreement, covenant, pact.

pacú, *m.* (Arg.) a river fish.

pácul, *m.* (P. I.) (bot.) wild plantain.

pachamanca, *f.* (Peru) barbecue.

pachón, *m.* phlegmatic man; pointer (dog).

pachorra, *f.* sluggishness, slowness.

pachorrudo, da, *a.* (coll.) sluggish, slow.

padecer. I. *va.* (*ind.* PADEZCO; *subj.* PADEZCA) to suffer; feel deeply; to lie under. **II.** *vn.* (de) to suffer (from).—**padecimiento,** *m.* suffering.

padilla, *f.* small frying pan; small oven.

padrastro, *m.* stepfather; obstacle, impediment; hangnail.

padrazo, *m. aug.* indulgent parent.

padre, *m.* father; ancestor; stallion, sire; source, origin, principal author; (eccl.) father, priest.—*pl.* parents, father and mother; ancestors.—**p. conscripto,** conscript father (Roman senator) —**p. de familia,** paterfamilias, father of a family.—**p. de pila,** godfather.—**P. Eterno,** God Almighty, our Father.—**p. nuestro,** Lord's Prayer.—**P. Santo,** Holy Father (the Pope). —**Santo P.,** Holy Father (the Pope); (eccl.) father (of the Church), one of the early Christian writers.

padrear, *vn.* to resemble one's father; to breed.

padrenuestro, *m.* Lord's Prayer.

padrinazgo, *m.* standing as godfather at a baptism; being a patron at a public function; title or charge of a godfather; patronage, support.

padrino, *m.* godfather; second, in a duel; bestman; patron, protector.

padrón, *m.* poll, census or tax list; pattern, model; column or post with an inscription; mark or note of infamy; (coll.) indulgent parent.

paella, *f.* dish of rice with meat or chicken.

For pronunciation, see the rules at the beginning of the book.

paf! *interj.* onomatopœic, expressing the noise of a fall, blow, etc.

paflagonio, nia, *n.* & *a.* Paphlagonian.

paflón, *m.* (arch.) soffit.

paga, *f.* payment; fee, wages, salary; pay; satisfaction, amends; sum or fine paid; requital of love or friendship.

pagable, *a.* payable.

pagadero, ra. I. *a.* payable. **II.** *m.* time and place of payment.

pagado, da. I. *pp.* of PAGAR. **II.** *a.* (or **p. de sí**) self-satisfied, conceited.

pagador, ra, *n.* payer; paymaster; paying teller.

pagaduría, *f.* paymaster's office.

paganismo, *m.* paganism, heathenism.

pagano, na, *n.* & *a.* heathen, pagan.

pagar. I. *va.* (*pret.* PAGUÉ; *subj.* PAGUE) to pay; to pay for; to requite; to atone, make amends for; to fee.—**p. con el pellejo,** (coll.) to pay with one's life.—**p. contra entrega,** C.O.D.— **p. el pato,** to get the blame, be the scapegoat. —**pagarlas,** (coll.) to pay for it (as a mean action).—**p. una visita,** to return a call, visit. **II.** *vr.* **(de)** to be pleased (with); to boast (of); to be conceited (about); to be fond (of).

pagaré, *m.* (com.) promissory note.

pagaya, *f.* (P. I.) single-bladed paddle.

página, *f.* page (of a book); folio.

paginación, *f.* pagination, paging.

paginar, *va.* to page (a book, etc.), paginate.

¹pago, I. *m.* payment; requital. **II.** *a.* (Am.) (coll.) paid.

²pago, *m.* vineyard district.

pagoda, *f.* pagoda; idol.

pagote, *m.* (coll.) scapegoat.

pagro, *m.* (ichth.) braize.

pagué, pague, *v.* V. PAGAR.

paguro, *m.* small crab.

paico, *m.* (S. A.) (bot.) saltwort.

paila, *f.* caldron; kettle; boiler; (Cuba) evaporator, sugar pan.

pailebot, pailebote, *m.* (naut.) pilot's boat.

painel, *m.* (carp.) panel.

pairar, *vn.* (naut.) to bring to, to lie to.

pairo, *m.* (naut.) lying to with all sail set.—**al p.,** lying to.

país, *m.* country, nation; land, region; (art) landscape.—**del p.,** domestic, national.

paisaje, *m.* landscape.

paisajista, *n.* landscape painter.

paisana, *f.* a kind of country dance.

paisanaje, *m.* peasantry; being of the same country.

paisano, na. I. *a.* from the same country. **II.** *n.* fellow countryman(-woman), compatriot; civilian.—**vestido de p.,** in civilian clothes, in mufti.

paisista, *n.* = PAISAJISTA.

paja, *f.* straw; blade of grass; chaff, shucks, trash. —**p. centenaza,** rye straw.—**¡pajas!** ditto, no less so.—**echar pajas,** to draw lots with straws. —**en un dácame,** or **quítame, allá esas pajas,** in the twinkling of an eye.—**no dormirse en las pajas,** to be very vigilant.—**por quítame allá esas pajas,** (to quarrel) for a straw, over the smallest trifle.

pajado, da. I. *a.* straw-colored. **II.** *f.* straw boiled with bran.

pajar, *m.* barn, straw loft; rick of straw.

pájara, *f.* female or hen bird; shrewd, designing woman; paper kite; paper rooster (toy).—**p. pinta,** game of forfeits.

pajarear, *vn.* to go birdcatching; to loiter about.

pajarel, *m.* (ornith.) = JILGUERO, linnet.

pajarera, *f.* aviary; large bird cage.

pajarería, *f.* abundance of birds; place where birds are sold.

pajarero, ra. I. *a.* merry, cheerful, gay; gaudy, loud. **II.** *n.* birdcatcher, bird fancier.

pajarete, *m.* fine sherry wine.

pajarico, ca, ito, ta, *n.* little bird.

pajaril, *m.*—**hacer p.** (naut.) to cleat a sail.

pajarillo, lla. I. *n.* *dim.* small bird. **II.** *f.* paper rooster (toy); spleen; milt of a hog.

pájaro, *m.* bird; shrewd, sly fellow.—**p. bobo,** (ornith.) booby; penguin.—**p. carpintero,** (ornith.) woodpecker.—**p. de cuenta,** = P. GORDO.—**p. del sol,** (ornith.) bird of paradise. —**p. gordo,** person of importance, big gun.— **p. loco** = P. SOLITARIO.—**p. mosca,** a very small humming bird.—**p. niño,** auk.—**p. polilla,** kingfisher.—**p. solitario,** solitary thrush.—**más vale p. en mano que buitre volando,** a bird in the hand is worth two in the bush.—*pl.* (ornith.) Passeres.

pajarota, pajarotada, *f.* hoax.

pajarote, *m.* large ugly bird.

pajarraco, *m.* large bird; (coll.) sharper.

pajaruco, *m.* large ugly bird.

pajaza, *f.* refuse of fodder.

pajazo, *m.* prick of stubbles in a horse's eye.

paje, *m.* page, valet; (naut.) cabin boy.—**p. de hacha,** link boy.

pajear, *vn.* to feed well; (coll.) to behave.

pajecillo, *m.* *dim.* little page; washstand.

pajel, *m.* (ichth.) red sea bream.

pajera, *f.* straw loft, straw yard.

pajero, ra, *n.* straw dealer.

pajilla, *f.* *dim.* cigar made of maize leaf; rattan.

pajizo, za, *a.* made of straw; thatched with straw; straw-colored.

pajón, *m.* *aug.* coarse straw.

pajonal, *m.* (Am.) place abounding in tall grass.

pajoso, sa, *a.* made or full of straw.

pajote, *m.* straw interwoven with bulrush.

pajucero, *m.* place where straw is deposited to rot for fertilizer.

pajuela, *f.* dim. short straw; sulphur match.

pajulí, *m.* (P. R.) (bot.) = MARAÑÓN, cashew.

pajuncio, *m.* booby, ninny, fool.

pajuz, pajuzo, *m.* refuse of straw used for manure.

pala, *f.* shovel; baker's peel; scoop; slice, turnover; beetle for pounding clothes; dustpan; blade of an oar; blade of a hoe or spade; racket (for ball games); vamp (of shoe); leaf of a hinge; top of an epaulet; flat surface of the teeth; craft, cunning, artifice; dexterity, cleverness; (bot.) leaf of the prickly pear.—**meter su media p.,** to have or get a share.—**ser corta p.,** to know nothing.

palabra, *f.* word; term; floor (as in *tener la palabra,* to have the floor); (mil.) password.—*pl.* superstitious words used by sorcerers; (eccl.) formula of the sacraments; table on which the words of consecration are written.—**¡p.!,** honestly! no fooling!—**palabras cruzadas,** crossword puzzle.—**p. de caballero,** or **de honor,** word of honor.—**p. de matrimonio,** promise of marriage.—**p. llana,** (gram.) word having the accent on the penultimate.—**palabras mayores,** a serious matter; insulting words.— **a media p.,** at the least hint.—**bajo p.,** on (one's) word.—**de p.,** by word of mouth.—**dos palabras,** a few words.—**empeñar la p.,** to pledge one's word.—**en buenas palabras,** in plain words.—**en una p.,** in sum.—**libertad de p.,** freedom of speech.—**llevar la p.,** to be the spokesman.—**medias palabras,** insinuation, hint.—**pedir la p.,** to ask for the floor (at a meeting).—**santa p.,** good news, the good word (to express pleasure on hearing something).

palabrada, *f.* low, scurrilous language.

palabrear, *vn.* to chat, chatter, prattle.

palabreja, *f.* *dim.* odd word.

palabrería, *f.* wordiness, empty talk.

palabrero, ra, *a.* talkative, loquacious.

palabrimujer, *m.* (coll.) man with an effeminate voice.

palabrista, *n.* chatterbox.

palabrita, *f. dim.* few words; short word or expression full of meaning.—**palabritas mansas,** (coll.) honey-tongued person.

palabrota, *f. aug.* coarse expression; big word.

palaciego, ga. I. *a.* pertaining to the palace. **II.** *n.* courtier.

palacio, *m.* palace; castle.

palacra, palacrana, *f.* gold nugget.

palada, *f.* shovelful; (naut.) stroke of the oar.

paladar, *m.* palate; roof of the mouth; taste, relish; longing desire.

paladear. I. *va.* to taste with pleasure, to relish; to rub the mouth of with a sweet substance; to clean the mouth of. **II.** *vn.* (of a newborn child) to show a desire of suckling.

paladeo, *m.* act of tasting or relishing.

paladial, *a.* (gram.) palatal.

paladín, *m.* paladin, valiant knight, champion.

paladinamente, *adv.* publicly, clearly.

paladino, na. I. *a.* manifest, clear, apparent, public. **II.** *m.* PALADÍN.

paladio, *m.* (chem.) palladium.

paladión, *m.* palladium; safeguard.

palado, da, *a.* (her.) pale.

palafito, *m.* primitive lake dwelling.

palafrén, *m.* palfrey; woman's or groom's horse.

palafrenero, *m.* stableboy, groom, hostler.—**p. mayor,** first equerry.

palahierro, *m.* bushing for the spindle of the upper millstone.

palamallo, *m.* pall-mall (a game).

palamenta, *f.* (naut.) set of oars.

palanca, *f.* (mech.) lever; bar, crowbar; pole for carrying a weight; (fort.) outer fortification with stakes; (naut.) garnet tackle.—**p. de mando,** (aer.) control column, yoke.—**p. del timón,** (aer.) rudder bar.

palancada, *f.* blow with a lever.

palancana, palangana, *f.* washbowl.

palanganero, *m.* washstand.

palangre, *m.* line with several fishhooks.

palanquera, *f.* stockade; log fence.

palanquero, *m.* pile driver; blower of bellows.

palanqueta, *f. dim.* small lever; (mil.) bar shot or crossbar shot; (Cuba) sweetmeat with cane sirup; (Mex. & Chile) dumbbell.

palanquín, *m.* public porter; (naut.) double tackle, clew garnet; palanquin, covered litter.

palastro, *m.* sheet iron, sheet metal.

palatina, *f.* tippet, boa used by women.

palatinado, *m.* palatinate.

¹**palatino, na,** *a.* palatial, palatine.

²**palatino, na,** *a.* palatal, palatine.

palay, *m.* (P. I.) unhusked rice.

palazo, *m.* blow with a shovel, spade or stick.

palazón, *m.* (naut.) masting; woodwork.

palco, *m.* (theat.) box; stand with seats.—**p. escénico,** (theat.) the stage.

paleador, *m.* shoveler; stoker.

palear, *va.* = APALEAR, to beat, pound.

palenque, *m.* palisade, paling; (theat.) passage from pit to stage.

paleografía, *f.* paleography.

paleográfico, ca, *a.* paleographic.

paleógrafo, *m.* paleographer.

paleolítico, ca, *a.* paleolithic.

paleontografía, *f.* paleontography.

paleontográfico, ca, *a.* paleontographic.

paleontología, *f.* paleontology.

paleontológico, ca, *a.* paleontological.

paleontólogo, *m.* paleontologist.

paleozoico, ca, *a.* Paleozoic.

palería, *f.* art and business of draining.

palero, *m.* shoveler: ditcher, drainer; pioneer; shovel maker or seller.

palestina, *f.* (print.) two-line small pica.

palestino, na, *m. & a.* Palestinian.

palestra, *f.* wrestling court, palæstra; gymnasium; tournament, competition.

paléstrico, ca, *a.* pert. to a wrestling place.

palestrita, *m.* wrestler, athlete.

paleta, *f. dim.* little shovel; fire shovel; (cooking) iron ladle; (mason.) trowel; (anat.) shoulder blade; (hydraul.) paddle board; blade; (art) palette.—**de p.,** opportunely.—**en dos paletas,** (coll.) shortly, briefly.

paletada, *f.* trowelful of mortar.

paletazo, *m.* thrust of a bull's horn.

paletear, *vn.* (naut.) to row ineffectively; to revolve without gaining speed.

paleteo, *m.* flapping of oars or paddles.

paletilla, *f. dim.* of PALETA; (anat.) cartilage of the sternum or xiphoid; shoulder blade; low candlestick.

paleto, *m.* fallow deer; rustic, hayseed.

paletó, *m.* overcoat, greatcoat.

paletón, *m.* bit of a key.

paletoque, *m.* paletocque, defensive jacket.

pali, *m.* Pali, an ancient language of India.

palia, *f.* (eccl.) altar cloth; curtain or screen before the tabernacle; pall.

paliación, *f.* palliation, extenuation.

paliadamente, *adv.* dissemblingly.

paliar, *va.* to palliate, extenuate, excuse.

paliativo, va; paliatorio, ria, *a.* palliative, mitigating; that may be palliated.

palidecer, *vn.* (*ind.* PALIDEZCO; *subj.* PALIDEZCA) to pale, turn pale.

palidez, *f.* paleness, pallor.

pálido, da, *a.* pale; ghastly.

palillo, *m. dim.* small stick; knitting needle case; toothpick; bobbin for network or lace; drumstick; tobacco stem; (coll.) chitchat.—*pl.* small pins put on the billiard table in certain games; rudiments, first principles; (coll.) trifles; castanets.

palimpsesto, *m.* palimpsest.

palingenesia, *f.* palingenesis, rebirth.

palinodia, *f.* palinode, public recantation.

palio, *m.* cloak, mantle; (eccl.) pallium; pall; canopy; prize for racing.

palique, *m.* (coll.) chitchat, small talk.

palisandro, *m.* rosewood.

palitoque, plaitroque, *m.* rough little stick.

paliza, *f.* cudgelling, caning, bastinado.

palizada, *f.* palisade; paling; (fort.) stockade.

palma, *f.* palm tree; leaf of a palm tree; palmetto; palm of the hand; (vet.) under surface of the hoof; emblem of victory or martyrdom; pre-eminence.—**p. brava,** (P. I.) (bot.) fan palm. —**andar en palmas,** to be universally applauded.—**ganar,** or **llevarse, la p.,** to carry the day; to win the prize.

palmáceo, a. I. *a.* (bot.) palmaceous. **II.** *f. pl.* Phœnicaceæ, Palmaceæ, palms.

palmacristi, *f.* (bot.) castor-oil plant.

palmada, *f.* pat; hand, applause.

palmar, *vn.* (coll.) to die.

²**palmar. I.** *a.* pert. to palms; measuring a PALMO; obvious, evident. **II.** *m.* palm grove; fuller's thistle.

palmario, ria, *a.* clear, obvious, evident.

palmatoria, *f.* ferule; small candlestick.

palmeado, da, *a.* (ornith.) web-footed, palmated; (bot.) palmate.

palmear, *va.* to clap (the hands); to applaud.

palmejar, *m.* (naut.) thick stuff.

palmeo, *m.* measuring by PALMOS.

palmera, *f.* palm tree.

palmero, *m.* palm keeper; palmer, pilgrim.

palmeta, *f.* ferule; slap with the ferule.—**ganar la p.,** to get ahead.

palmetazo, *m.* blow with a ferule.

palmiche, *m.* fruit of a palm tree.

palmífero, ra, *a.* (poet.) bearing or abounding in palms.

palmilla, *f.* blue woollen cloth; (shoe) inner sole.

palmípedo, da. I. *a.* web-footed, palmiped. **II.** *f. pl.* Palmatæ, palmipeds.

palmitato, *m.* (chem.) palmitate.
palmítico, ca, *a.* (chem.) palmitic.
palmitieso, *a.* flat-hoofed (horse).
¹**palmito,** *m.* (bot.) dwarf fan palm; palmetto or its root; (Cuba) sprout of a palm.
²**palmito,** *m.* woman's face.
palmo, *m.* span, measure of length (8 inches).—**p. a p.,** inch by inch.—**p. menor,** palm, hand, handbreadth (4 inches); span-farthing (boy's game).—**dejar a uno con un p. de narices,** to disappoint one: to leave one out in the cold.
palmotear, *vn.* to clap hands, applaud.
palmoteo, *m.* hand clapping, applause.
palo, *m.* stick; pole; timber, log; wood (material); (Am.) tree; blow with a stick; whack; execution on the gallows; suit at cards; stalk of fruit, pedicle; hook of a letter; (her.) pale; (naut.) mast.—*pl.* billiard pins (= PALILLOS); blows, cudgeling.—**p. áloe,** (bot.) aloes wood, eagle wood.—**p. brasil,** Brazil wood.—**p. campeche,** campeche, logwood.—**p. codal,** stick hung around the neck as a penance.—**p. de Campeche** = P. CAMPECHE.—**p. de hule,** rubber tree.—**p de jabón,** quillai, soap bark. —**p. del Brasil** = P. BRASIL.—**p. de mesana,** (naut.) mizzenmast.—**p. de planchar,** ironing board.—**p. de rosa,** rosewood; tulipwood.—**p. de tinte** = P. CAMPECHE.—**p. de trinquete,** (naut.) foremast.—**p. dulce,** licorice.—**p. mayor,** (naut.) mainmast.—**p. santo,** lignumvitæ.—**palos de marca,** (naut.) spar buoys.—**a. p. seco,** (naut.) under bare poles.—**dar (de) palos,** to drub, thrash, club, beat.
paloma, *f.* pigeon; dove; meek, mild person; (P-, astr.) Columba; (naut.) sling of a yard.—*pl.* whitecaps.—**p. brava,** rock dove.—**p. buchona,** pouter.—**p. silvestre** = P. BRAVA. —**p. torcaz,** wild pigeon; ringdove.—**p. zorita,** wood pigeon.
palomadura, *f.* (naut.) boltrope tie.
¹**palomar,** *a.* hard-twisted (twine).
²**palomar,** *m.* pigeon house, dovecot.
palomariego, ga, *a.* (of pigeons) domestic.
palomear, *vn.* to shoot or breed pigeons.
palomera, *f.* small dovecot; bleak place.
palomería, *f.* pigeon shooting.
palomero, ra. I. *a.* having long iron points. **II.** *n.* pigeon seller or fancier.
palomilla, *f. dim.* young pigeon; grain moth; little butterfly; chrysalis; backbone of a horse; peak of a packsaddle; milk-white horse; journal bearing; wall bracket; (print.) galley rack; (bot.) common fumitory.—*pl.* whitecaps.
palomina, *f.* pigeon dung; (bot.) fumitory; a variety of black grape.
palomino, *m.* young pigeon.
palomo, *m.* cock pigeon.
palón, *m.* (her.) guidon.
palotada, *f.* stroke with a drumstick.—**no dar p.,** not to do or say a thing right.
palote, *m.* drumstick; down-stroke in penmanship.
paloteado, *m.* a rustic dance with sticks; noisy scuffle.
palotear, *vn.* to strike sticks against one another; to wrangle.
paloteo, *m.* fight with sticks.
palpable, *a.* palpable, obvious, evident.
palpablemente, *adv.* palpably, evidently.
palpación, palpadura, *f.*; **palpamiento,** *m.* feeling (of something), touching; palpableness; (med.) palpation.
palpar. I. *va.* to feel (of), to touch; to see as self-evident; (med.) to palpate. **II.** *vn.* to feel by touching; to grope in the dark.
pálpebra, *f.* eyelid.
palpebral, *a.* palpebral, pert. to eyelids.
palpitación, *f.* palpitation; throbbing.
palpitante, *a.* vibrating, palpitating.
palpitar, *vn.* to palpitate, beat, throb, quiver.

palpo, *m.* (zool.) palpus, palp, feeler.
paludamento, *m.* (Rom. hist.) paludamentum, a cloak.
palúdico, ca, *a.* miasmatic; malarial.
paludismo, *m.* (med.) paludism; malaria.
paludoso, sa, *a.* marshy, swampy, fenlike.
palumbario, *a.* dove hunting (goshawk).
palurdo, da. I. *a.* rustic, rude. **II.** *n.* boor, rustic.
¹**palustre,** *a.* marshy, fenlike, boggy.
²**palustre,** *m.* trowel.
palustrillo, *m.* (mason.) angle float.
pallador, *m.* (S. A.) minstrel, roving singer.
pallaquear, pallar, *va.* (Peru) to extract the riches metallic part of (minerals).
pallete, *m.* (naut.) fender, paunch mat.
pallón, *m.* assay button of gold.
pamandabuán, *m.* (P. I.) pambanmanche, snake boat, a large dugout.
pamela, *f.* low-crowned, wide-brimmed woman's straw hat.
pamena, *f.* (coll.) trifle, bagatelle.
pampa, *f.* pampa, extensive plain.—**estar a la p.,** (Arg., Colomb.) to be outdoors.
pámpana, *f.* vine leaf.—**tocar, or zurrar, la p.,** (coll.) to thrash.
pampanada, *f.* juice of vine shoots.
pampanaje, *m.* plenty of vine shoots; vain show.
pampanilla, *f.* trunks, loin cloth.
pámpano, *m.* young vine branch or tendril; (ichth.) pompano.
pampanoso, sa, *a.* full of tendrils.
pampeano, na. I. *a.* of or from the pampas. **II.** *n.* pampa man (woman).
pampear, *vn.* to travel in or over the pampas.
pampero, ra. I. *n.* pampa man (woman). **II.** *m.* (S. A.) violent southwest wind.
pampirolada, *f.* garlic sauce; (coll.) silly thing.
pamplina, *f.* (bot.) chickweed; pimpernel; yellow poppy; (coll.) frivolity, trifle.
pamplinada, *f.* trifle, silly or foolish talk.
pamporcino, *m.* (bot.) cyclamen, sowbread.
pamposado, da, *a.* lazy, idle; cowardly.
pampringada, *f.* toast soaked in gravy; (coll.) nonsense.
pan, *m.* bread; pie crust; anything in the shape of a loaf, cake, etc.; wheat; wafer; leaf of gold or silver.—*pl.* breadstuffs.—**p. ázimo,** unleavened bread.—**p. bazo,** brown bread.—**p. casero,** homemade bread.—**p. cenceño** = P. ÁZIMO.— **p. de azúcar,** loaf sugar.—**p. candeal,** white-wheat bread.—**p. de cera virgen,** white wax, in cakes.—**p. de flor,** bread made from the choicest flour.—**p. de higos,** fig cake.—**p. de jabón,** cake of soap.—**p. de la boda,** honeymoon; wedding cake.—**p. de oro,** gold leaf.— **p. duro, or p. seco,** stale or dry bread.—**p. integral,** whole-wheat bread.—**p. perdido,** good-for-nothing, lazybones.—**p. porcino,** (bot.) sowbread.—**p. terciado,** rent of ground paid in grain, two thirds wheat and one third barley.—**p. tierno,** fresh bread.—**p. y quesillo,** (bot.) shepherd's purse.—**con su p. se lo coma,** let him take the consequences, let him do it, for all I care, it's "his funeral."— **llamar al pan pan y al vino vino,** to call a spade a spade.
pana, *f.* plush, velveteen, corduroy; (naut.) limberboard.
pánace, *f.* (bot.) opopanax.
panacea, *f.* panacea; (pharm.) catholicon.
panadear, *vn.* to make bread.—**panadeo,** *m.* baking bread.
panadería, *f.* bakery.
panadero, ra. I. *n.* baker. **II.** *f.* baker's wife. **III.** *m. pl.* a kind of dance.
panadizo, *m.* whitlow, felon; (coll.) pale-faced, sickly person.
panado, da, *a.* pert. to PANETELA.
panal, *m.* honeycomb; hornet's nest; a sweet-

meat.—**p. saetero,** honeycomb made across the hive.

panamá, *m.* Panama hat.

panameño, ña, *n.* & *a.* Panamanian.

panamericanismo, *m.* Pan-Americanism.

panamericano, na, *a.* Pan-American.

panarizo, *m.* = PANADIZO.

panarra, *m.* (coll.) dolt, simpleton.

panatela, *f.* sponge cake.

panática, *f.* (naut.) provision of bread.

¹panca, *f.* (Am.) corn husk.

²panca, *f.* (P. I.) a fishing-boat.

pancada, *f.* sale of job lot of things; kick.

pancarpia, *f.* garland of flowers.

pancarta, *f.* panchart, written records.

pancera, *f.* (armor) belly plate.

pancista, (pol.) one who is on the fence.

panco, *m.* (P. I.) coasting vessel.

pancraciasta, *m.* contestant in a pancratium.

pancracio, *m.* pancratium, athletic contest.

pancreas, *m.* (anat.) pancreas.—**pancreático, ca,** *a.* pancreatic.—**pancreatina,** *f.* pancreatin.

¹pancho, *m.* (ichth.) spawn of the sea bream.

²pancho, *m.* (coll.) paunch, belly.

panda, *f.* gallery of a cloister.

pandear, *vn.* to bend, warp, belly, bulge out.

pandectas, *f. pl.* (com.) index book; (Rom. law) pandects, collection of legal materials; code of laws.

pandemia, *f.* (med.) pandemic, an epidemic attacking the majority of people.

pandemónium, *m.* pandemonium.

pandeo, *m.* bulge, bulging.

pandera, *f.* (mus.) tambourine.

panderada, *f.* collection of tambourine players; (coll.) nonsense.

panderazo, *m.* blow with a tambourine.

pandereta, *f. dim.* tambourine.

panderete, *m. dim.* small tambourine.

panderetear, *vn.* to play on the tambourine.—**pandereteo,** *m.* beating the tambourine; merriment.—**panderetero, ra,** *n.* tambourine maker, seller, or player.

pandero, *m.* PANDERA; paper kite; (coll.) silly talker.

pandilla, *f.* party, faction; gang, set; picnic.

pandillero, ra, *n.* = PANDILLISTA; (Am.) gangster.

pandillista, *n.* fomenter of factions; leader or member of a gang.

pando, da, *a.* bulged; slow of motion.

pandorga, *f.* (coll.) fat, bulky woman; kite.

panecico, illo, ito, *m.* roll (bread).

panegírico, ca. I. *a.* panegyrical. II. *m.* panegyric, eulogy.

panegirista, *m.* panegyrist, eulogist.

panegirizar, *va.* to panegyrize, eulogize.

panel, *m.* (art, elec.) panel.

panela, *f.* small biscuit; (Colomb.) unrefined brown sugar; (her.) panel.

panera, *f.* granary; pannier; bread basket.

panero, *m.* baker's basket.

paneslavismo, *m.* Pan-Slavism.

paneslavista, *n.* & *a.* Pan-Slavist(-ic).

panetela, *f.* panada, broth with toast boiled in it; (Am.) sponge cake; panetela (cigar).

panetería, *f.* pantry of the royal palace.

panetero, *m.* person in charge of a PANETERÍA.

pánfilo, *m.* slow, sluggish, heavy person.

pangelín, *m.* (bot.) angelin tree.

pangermanismo, *m.* Pan-Germanism.

pangermanista, *n.* & *a.* Pan-germanist(-ic).

pangolín, *m.* (zool.) pangolin, a scaly anteater.

paniaguado, da, *n.* servant; employee; protégé.

pánico, ca, *a.* & *m.* panic.

panículo, *m.* panicle, pellicle, membrane.

paniego, ga. I. *a.* eating or yielding much bread. II. *m.* burlap bag for charcoal.

panificación, *f.* panification, making of bread.

panificar, *va.* (*pret.* PANIFIQUÉ; *subj.* PANIFIQUE)

to make into bread; to convert pasture land into cornfields.

panilla, *f.* an oil measure (¼ lb.).

panique, *m.* large Australian herbivorous bat.

panizo, *m.* (bot.) panic grass; Indian corn; (Chile) mineral bed.

panocha, panoja, *f.* (bot.) ear of grain; (bot.) panicle; bunch of anchovies.

panoplia, *f.* panoply; collection of arms.

panóptico, ca. I. *a.* panoptical. II. *m.* (Am.) penitentiary.

panorama, *m.* panorama.

panorámico, ca, *a.* panoramic; pictorial.

panoso, sa, *a.* mealy.

panspermia, *f.* panspermy, bio-genetic theory.

pantalán, *m.* (P. I.) wooden or bamboo pier.

pantalón, *m.* (gen. *pl.*) trousers.—**p. bombacho,** wide, balloon trousers.

pantalla, *f.* lamp shade; screen; person or object that obstructs the view; (movie) screen.

pantanal, *m.* swampy, marshy ground.

pantano, *m.* swamp, marsh, bog; reservoir, dam; hindrance, obstacle, difficulty.

pantanoso, sa, *a.* swampy, marshy, miry; full of difficulties.

pantasana, *f.* fishing seine.

panteísmo, *m.* pantheism.

panteísta, *n.* & *a.* pantheist(-ic).

panteístico, ca, *a.* pantheistic.

panteón, *m.* pantheon.

pantera, *f.* (zool.) panther; (min.) yellow agate.

pantógrafo, *m.* pantograph, copying instrument.

pantómetra, *f.* a kind of measuring compass.

pantomima, *f.* pantomime.

pantomímico, ca, *a.* pantomimic.

pantomimo, *m.* mimic, pantomimist.

pantoque, *m.* (naut.) bilge or flat of the ship.

pantorra, *f.* (coll.) fat calf of the leg.

pantorrilla, *f.* calf of the leg.

pantorrillera, *f.* padded stocking.

pantorrilludo, da, *a.* having thick calves.

pantufla, *f.,* **pantuflo,** *m.* slipper, baboosh.

pantuflazo, *m.* blow with a slipper.

panucho, *m.* (Mex.) bean-and-meat pie with corn-meal crust.

panudo, da, *a.* (Cuba) (of ripe fruit, esp. alligator pear) firm, not soft.

panza, *f.* belly, paunch; belly of a vase; rumen or paunch of ruminants.—**panzada,** *f.* (coll.) bellyful; push with the belly.—**panzón, na.** I. *a.* big-bellied. II. *m.* paunch.—**panzudo, da,** *a.* big-bellied.

pañal, *m.* (baby's) diaper; tail of a shirt.—*pl.* swaddling clothes; infancy.—**estar en pañales,** to have little knowledge; to be in its, or one's, infancy.

pañería, *f.* drapery; clothing store.

pañero, *m.* woollen draper; clothier.

pañete, *m. dim.* inferior or light cloth; (Colomb.) plastering.—*pl.* trunks worn by fishermen; linen attached to the crucifix below the waist.

pañito, pañizuelo, *m. dim.* small cloth.

paño, *m.* cloth, woollen stuff; by extension, any woven stuff; tapestry, drapery, hanging; kitchen cloth; wash cloth; blearedness; livid spot on the face; spot in looking-glasses, crystals, or precious stones; (naut.) canvas, sailcloth; (sewing) breadth.—*pl.* clothes, garments.—**p. burdo,** shoddy cloth.—**p. catorceno,** a kind of coarse cloth.—**p. de lágrimas,** one who sympathizes and consoles.—**p. de manos,** towel.—**p. de mesa,** tablecloth.—**p. pardillo** = P. BURDO.—**paños calientes,** inefficient efforts or means; half measures.—**paños menores,** underclothes; dishabille.—**al p.,** (theat.) outside, without.

pañol, *m.* (naut.) storeroom.—**p. de las velas,** sail room.—**p. del contestable,** gunner's room.—**p. de pólvora,** magazine.—**p. de proa,** boatswain's storeroom.

pañolería, *f.* handkerchief shop or factory.

¹pañolero, ra, *n.* handkerchief maker or seller.
²pañolero, *m.* (naut.) yeoman.
pañoleta, *f.* triangular shawl.
pañolón, *m.* large square shawl.
pañosa, *f.* cloak.
pañoso, sa, *a.* ragged, tattered.
pañuelo, *m.* handkerchief; kerchief; shawl.
¹papa, *m.* (eccl.) Pope; (coll.) papa.
²papa, *f.* potato; (Peru) lump of native silver.
³papa, *f.* hoax.—*pl.* pap; (coll.) food, "grub."
papá, *m.* (coll.) papa; (Mex.) grandfather.—
papacito, *m. dim.* (coll.) dad, daddy, papa
dear.
papada, *f.* double chin; gill; dewlap.
papadilla, *f. dim.* flesh under the chin.
papado, *m.* papacy.
papafigo, *m.* (ornith.) figpecker, beccafico.
papagayo, *m.* (ornith.) parrot; (ichth.) rock bass;
(bot.) three-colored amaranth; white arum,
calla; (C. A.) violent northeast wind.
papahigo, *m.* winter cap; (naut.) lower sail.
papahuevos, *m.* (coll.) simpleton, blockhead.
papaína, *f.* (chem.) papain.
papal, *a.* papal.
¹papalina, *f.* cap with flaps; coif.
²papalina, *f.* (coll.) fit of drunkenness.
papalmente, *adv.* in a papal manner.
papalote, *m.* (Cuba) kite.
papamoscas, *m.* (ornith.) flycatcher, flyeater;
(coll.) ninny.
papanatas, *m.* (coll.) dolt, simpleton, ninny.
papandujo, ja, *a.* (coll.) too soft, overripe.
papar, *va.* to swallow without chewing; (coll.) to
eat; to pay little attention to.—*p.* moscas, or
viento, to gape.
páparo, ra, *n.* ancient Indian of Panama; gawk,
gump.
paparrabias, *n.* (coll.) testy, fretful person.
paparrasolla, *f.* hobgoblin, bugbear.
paparrucha, *f.* (coll.) fake, humbug; nonsense,
silliness.
papasal, *m.* a boys' game; trifle, bagatelle.
papaveráceo, a, *a.* (bot.) papaveraceous.
papaya, *f.* (bot.) papaw, pawpaw; papaya.
papayo, *m.* (bot.) papaw tree; papaya tree.
pápaz, *m.* (in Africa) Christian priest.
papazgo, *m.* popedom, pontificate.
papel, *m.* paper; piece of paper; document; (commercial, legal) paper; writing, treatise, discourse, pamphlet, tract; (theat.) part, rôle;
character, figure.—p. continuo, paper in rolls.
—p. costero, outside quires.—p. cuadriculado, cross-section paper.—p. cuché, glazed
print paper.—p. de añafeo, brown paper.—p.
de barbas, untrimmed paper.—p. de cartas,
letter paper, (Am.) stationery.—p. de cúrcuma, (chem.) turmeric paper.—p. de China,
Chinese paper.—p. de entapizar, wall paper,
paper hanging.—p. de Estado, gov't security,
or debenture.—p. de estaño, tinfoil.—p. de
estraza, brown paper, wrapping paper.—p. de
fumar, cigarette paper.—p. de lija, sandpaper.—p. de luto, mourning paper.—p. de
marca, plate paper.—p. de marquilla, bristol
board, drawing paper.—p. de oficio, foolscap.
—p. de seda, tissue paper.—p. de tornasol =
P. REACTIVO.—p. esmeril, emery paper.—p.
jaspeado, marbled paper.—p. marca mayor,
royal paper.—p. marquilla = P. DE MAR-
QUILLA.—p. moneda, paper money.—p. para
excusados, toilet paper.—p. pintado, stained
paper; paper hanging.—p. rayado, ruled paper.
—p. reactivo, test paper, litmus paper.—p.
secante, blotting paper.—p. sellado, official
stamped paper.—p. tela, tracing paper.—p.
timbrado, = P. SELLADO.—p. viejo, waste
paper.—p. vitela, vellum paper.—p. volante,
small pamphlet or printed leaflet, flyer.—
papeles mojados, worthless documents.

—hacer p., to cut a figure, to play a part, to
impersonate.
papelear, *vn.* to search or look over papers; (coll.)
to cut a figure.
papeleo, *m.* act of looking over papers.
papelera, *f.* writing desk, paper case; collection
or bunch of written papers.
papelería, *f.* stationery; stationery shop; heap of
papers.
papelero, ra, *n.* paper maker; stationer.
papeleta, *f.* card, ticket, check, slip; (Am.)
ballot; paper bag for money or sweetmeats.
papelillo, *m. dim.* bit of paper; cigarette.
¹papelina, *f.* wine goblet; (coll.) fit of drunkenness.
²papelina, *f.* poplin.
papelista, *n.* keeper of documents; papermaker;
stationer; paper hanger.
papelito, *m. dim.* small paper; curl paper.
papelón, na. 1. *a.* boastful, ostentatious. II. *m.
aug.* poster, bill; paper board; boaster; (Am.)
raw sugar.
papelonear, *vn.* (coll.) to boast, pretend.
papelote, papelucho, *m.* scurrilous article.
papera, *f.* goiter; mumps.
papero, *m.* pot in which pap is made.
papialbillo, *m.* (zool.) weasel.
papila, *f.* (med. and bot.) papilla.
papilar, *a.* papillary; papillose.
papilionáceo. I. *a.* (bot.) papilionaceous. II. *f.
pl.* Papilionaceæ.
papilla, *f.* pap; guile, deceit, artifice.
papión, *m.* a kind of large monkey.
papiro, *m.* (bot.) papyrus.
papirolada, *f.* garlic sauce.
papirotada, *f.*; papirotazo, papirote, *m.* fillip.
papisa, *f.* papess.
papista, *n.* & *a.* Papist(-ic).
¹papo, *m.* double chin; anterior lower part of an
animal's neck, external throat; fowl's gizzard;
puff in garments.—p. de viento, (naut.) small
sail.
²papo, *m.* (bot.) thistledown.
papú, *n.* & *a.* Papuan.
papudo, da, *a.* doubled-chinned.
papujado, da, *a.* (of fowls) full-gorged; swollen,
puffed up.
pápula, *f.* (med.) papule, small non-suppurative
eruption.
paquebote, *m.* (naut.) passenger and mail liner.
paquete, *m.* packet, package; bundle of papers
(coll.) dandy, dude; (naut.) PAQUEBOTE.—p. de
duelas, shooks, set of staves for a barrel.
paquetería, *f.* (com.) retail trade or shop.
paquidermo, ma. 1. *a.* thick-skinned; pachy-
dermatous. II. *m. pl.* (zool.) Pachydermata.
par. I. *a.* equal; on a par; homologous, corresponding; even (number). II. *m.* pair, couple;
team; peer; (arch.) angle rafter; (elec.) cell;
(mech.) couple.—p. de fuerzas, (mech.)
couple.—p. de perdices, brace of partridge.—
p. de pistolas, brace of pistols.—p. de torsión,
p. motor, (elec.) torque.—pares y nones, odd
or even (a game).—a la p., jointly, equally;
(com.) par; at par; (horse racing) in a dead heat.
—a pares, two and two, by pairs.—de p. en p.,
(of a door, etc.) wide open.—ir a la p., to go
halves, to have an equal share.—sin p., peerless, incomparable. III. *f. pl.* placenta.
para, *prep.* for, to, in order to, toward, wherefore,
to the end that.—p. con, toward, with.—p.
entre los dos, between you and me.—p. eso,
for that, for that matter.—¿p. qué? what for?
what is the use?—p. que, so that, in order that.
—p. siempre, for ever.—dije p. mi capote,
I said to myself.—estar p., to be on the point
of, about to.—sin qué ni p. qué, without
motive, without rime or reason.—tengo p. mí,
it is my opinion.

parabién, *m.* congratulation, felicitation, greeting.

parábola, *f.* parable; (geom.) parabola.

parabolano, na, *n.* one who uses parables.

parabólico, ca, *a.* parabolic.

paraboloide, *m.* (geom.) paraboloid.

parabrisa, *m.* (auto) wind shield.

paracaídas, *m.* parachute.—**paracaidistas,** *m. pl.* (mil.) paratroops.

paracentesis, *f.* (surg.) paracentesis, tapping.

Paracleto, Paráclito, *m.* Paraclete, Holy Ghost.

paracronismo, *m.* parachronism.

parachispas, *m.* (elec.) spark arrester.

parachoques, *m.* (auto) bumper.

parada, *f.* stop (as of a train); stay, suspension, pause; (mil.) halt, halting; parade; review; stall, fold for cattle; relay of horses; dam, bank; stakes, bet; (fencing) parry.—**p. en firme,** or **en seco,** dead stop.—**doblar la p.,** to double the stake or bid.—**llamar de p.,** to hold game at bay.

paradera, *f.* sluice, floodgate; fishing seine.

paradero, *m.* halting place; (Cuba) (Ry.) station, depot; landing, terminus; whereabouts.

paradeta, illa, *f.* short pause.—*pl.* a kind of dance.

paradigma, *m.* example, paradigm.

paradilla, *f.* (Chile) a short pause.

paradina, *f.* round inclosure.

paradisíaco, ca, *a.* paradisiacal, paradisaical.

paradislero, *m.* huntsman in wait; newsmonger.

parado, da. I. *pp.* of PARAR. **II.** *a.* shy; slow, spiritless, indolent; unoccupied; (of a clock) stopped; shut down (as a factory); (Am.) standing. **III.** *a. & n.* unemployed.

paradoja, *f.* paradox.

paradojo, ja; paradójico, ca, *a.* paradoxical.

parador. I. *n.* one who stops or halts; heavy bettor. **II.** *m.* hostelry, inn, road house.

parafernales.—bienes p., (law) paraphernalia.

parafina, *f.* paraffin.

parafraseador, ra, *n.* paraphraser.

parafrasear, *va.* to paraphrase.

paráfrasis, *f.* paraphrase.

parafraste, *m.* paraphrast.

parafrásticamente, *adv.* paraphrastically.

parafrástico, ca, *a.* paraphrastic.

paragoge, *f.* (rhet.) paragoge.

paragolpes, *m.* (Arg.) (auto) fender.

paragonar, *va.* to compare, to hold equal to.

parágrafo, *m.* paragraph; additional clause.

paraguas, *m.* umbrella.

paraguay, *m.* (ornith.) a species of parrot.

paraguayano, na; paraguayo, ya, *n. & a.* Paraguayan.

paragüería, *f.* umbrella shop.

paragüero, ra. I. *n.* umbrella maker, repairer or seller. **II.** *m.* umbrella stand.

parahuso, *m.* = PARAÚSO.

paraíso, *m.* paradise; heaven; (theat., coll.) "nigger heaven," upper gallery.—**p. de bobos,** air castles.—**p. terrenal,** Paradise, garden of Eden.

paraje, *m.* place, spot; condition, state.

paral, *m.* scaffolding pole, prop, or post; (naut.) launching ways.

paraláctico, ca, *a.* parallactic.

paralaje, *f.* (astr.) parallax.

paralelar, *va.* to parallel; to compare.

paralelepípedo, *m.* (geom.) parallelepiped.

paralelismo, *m.* (geom.) parallelism.

paralelo, la. I. *a.* parallel; similar; corresponding. **II.** *m.* parallel, resemblance; (geog.) parallel. **III.** *f.* (geom. and fort.) parallel.

paralelogramo, *m.* (geom.) parallelogram.

paralicé, paralice, *v.* V. PARALIZAR.

Paralipómenos, *m. pl.* Paralipomena, Book of Chronicles.

parálisis, *f.* (med.) paralysis.

paralítico, ca. I. *a.* paralytic, paralyzed. **II.** *n.* paralyzed person.

paralización, *f.* paralyzation; immobilization; (com.) stagnancy, stagnation.

paralizado, da, *a.* (com.) dull, stagnant, flat.

paralizar, *va.* (*pret.* PARALICÉ; *subj.* PARALICE) to paralyze; to impede, stop; immobilize.

paralogismo, *m.* (logic) paralogism.

paralogizar, *vn.* to paralogize, reason falsely.

paramentar, *va.* to adorn, bedeck, embellish.

paramento, *m.* ornament, hanging; trappings, caparison; (arch.) face, surface.—**paramentos sacerdotales,** (eccl.) robes and ornaments.

paramera, *f.* desert, moor; bleak place.

parámetro, *m.* (geom.) parameter.

páramo, *m.* paramo, high and cold region.

parancero, *m.* birdcatcher.

parangón, *m.* comparison.

parangona, *f.* (print.) paragon type.

parangonar, *va.* to compare.

paraninfico, a. (arch.) having statues of nymphs.

paraninfo, *m.* paranymph; harbinger of felicity; salutatorian; hall for college exercises.

paranza, *f.* hut or blind for huntsmen.

parao, *m.* (P. I.) a large passenger vessel.

parapara, *f.* fruit of the PARAPARO.

paraparo, *m.* (Venez.) (bot.) soapbark tree.

parapetarse, *vr.* to hide behind a parapet.

parapeto, *m.* (mil.) parapet, breastwork; rails or battlements on bridges and quays.

paraplejía, *f.* (med.) paraplegia.

parapoco, *n.* (coll.) numskull; timid person.

¹parar. I. *va.* to stop, detain, check; to prepare, get ready; to stake, bet (at cards); to point at (game); to treat or use ill; to place, fix (as the attention); (fencing) to parry.—**p. la oreja,** (Am.) to prick up one's ears.—**p. mientes en,** to consider carefully. **II.** *vn.* to stop, halt; (of a watch) to stop; to land; to go from one to another; to come into the possession of; to happen; to come to an end; (**en**) to become, end (in), be transformed (into); to stop or stay (at), lodge; (of a train) to stop, have its terminus (at).—**ir a p. a,** or **en,** to become, end in, finally to get to. **III.** *vr.* to stop, halt; to be ready to face a danger; to desist, waver, pause; (Am.) to stand up.—**no p. en pelillos,** not to stop at trifles.—**sin p.,** instantly, without delay.

²parar, *m.* lansquenet, a card game.

pararrayos, *m.* lightning rod.

parascene, *m.* parascewe, Jewish Sabbath eve.

paraselene, *f.* (meteorol.) paraselene, mock moon.

parasemo, *f.* figurehead of a vessel.

parasismo, *m.* paroxysm, fit.

parasitario, ria, *a.* = PARASÍTICO.

parasiticida, *m.* parasiticide.

parasítico, ca, *a.* parasitic.

parásito, ta, *n. & a.* parasite(-tic).

parasitología, *f.* parasitology, science of treating parasites.

parasol, *m.* parasol, sunshade.

parástade, *m.* (arch.) anta, pilaster.

parata, *f.* built terrace.

paratifoidea, *f.* paratyphoid.

parausar, *va.* to drill with a brace drill.

paraúso, *m.* brace drill.

parazonio, *m.* Greek dagger or short sword.

parca, *f.* (poet.) fate, death.

parcamente, *adv.* sparingly, parsimoniously.

parce, *m.* premium card in schools.

parceia, *f.* parcel of land.

parcelar, *va.* to divide into lots.

parcelario, ria, *a.* pertaining to parceled lands.

parcial, *a.* partial.—**parcialidad,** *f.* partiality, bias; party, faction.—**parcialmente,** *adv.* partially, partly.

parcidad, *f.* parsimony, frugality.

parcionero, *m.* partner, participant.

parcísimo, ma, *a. super.* of PARCO.

parco, ca, *a.* sparing, scanty; sober, moderate, parsimonious.

parcha, *f.* (Am.) (bot.) any passifloraceous plant.

parchazo, *m. aug.* large plaster; (coll.) deception, jest; (naut.) flapping of sails.

parche, *m.* (pharm.) plaster, sticking plaster; (mil.) drum-head; drum; (shoemaking, aer.) patch; botch.—**pegar un p.,** (coll.) to play a scurvy trick.

pardal. I. *a.* rustic. **II.** *m.* (ornith.) sparrow, linnet; (zool.) leopard; (bot.) aconite, wolfsbane; crafty fellow.

pardear, *vn.* to be or show grayish or drab.

¡pardiez! *interj.* (coll.) by Jove! by Jupiter!

pardillo. I. *m.* (ornith.) linnet; a kind of grape, and wine made from it. **II.** *a.* grayish, brown (cloth).

pardisco, ca, *a.* = PARDUSCO.

pardo, da. I. *a.* brown; dark gray; dark; cloudy; (Cuba) colored (person). **II.** *n.* (Cuba) mulatto; darky. **III.** *m.* (zool.) leopard.

pardusco, ca, *a.* grayish, grizzly.

parear, *va.* to match, mate, pair, couple.

parecer. I. *vn.* (*ind.* PAREZCO; *subj.* PAREZCA) to appear, show up, turn up; to seem, look like.— **parece mentira,** it seems incredible, it's hard to believe.—**a lo que parece,** or **según parece,** according to appearances, as it seems. —**al p.,** apparently, to all appearances.—**no parece sino que,** it seems certain that. **II.** *vr.* to resemble each other, to look alike. **III.** *m.* opinion; look, mien; appearance.—**por el bien p.,** to save appearances.

parecido, da. I. *pp.* of PARECER. **II.** *a.* found; (a) resembling, like, similar (to).—**bien (mal) p.,** good- (bad-) looking. **III.** *m.* resemblance, likeness.

pareciente, *a.* similar; apparent.

pared, *f.* wall; close field of barley; garden edging or fence of box.—**p. maestra,** main wall.—**p. medianera,** party wall, partition wall.—**entre cuatro paredes,** confined, retired; imprisoned. —**hasta la p. de enfrente,** to the limit; with all one's heart and might.—**las paredes oyen,** walls have ears.

paredaño, ña, *a.* having a wall between.

paredón, *m. aug.* thick wall; standing wall.

pareja, *f.* pair; couple; brace; match; coupling; dancing partner; team, pair of soldiers or policemen.—**parejas mixtas,** (games) mixed doubles.—**correr parejas, or a las parejas,** to be on a par, to go together.

parejo, ja, *a.* equal, even, smooth; (horse racing) neck and neck.—**por p.,** or **por un p.,** on equal terms, on a par, evenly; indistinguishably, without distinction.

parejura, *f.* evenness; equality; similarity.

parénesis, *f.* admonition, exhortation.

parenético, ca, *a.* admonitory.

parénquima, *m.* (med.) parenchyma.

parentela, *f.* kindred, kinsfolk, relations.

parentesco, *m.* kindred, relationship; tie, bond.

paréntesis, *m.* parenthesis; parenthetical statement or expression; digression.—**entre, or por, p.,** parenthetically, by the bye.

pareo, *m.* pairing, coupling, matching.

parergón, *m.* additional ornament.

pares, *f. pl.* placenta, afterbirth.

parezco, parezca, *v.* V. PARECER.

pargo, *m.* (ichth.) braize, porgy.

parhelia, *f.,* **parhelio,** *m.* parhelion, mock sun.

parhilera, *f.* (arch.) ridgepole, ridgepiece.

paria, *m.* pariah, outcast.

parias, *f.* tribute by one prince to another; placenta.

parición, *f.* parturition (of cattle).

parida. I. *f.* woman lately delivered of a baby. **II.** *a.* having recently brought forth offspring (app. to women and animals).

paridad, *f.* parity, equality, comparison.

paridera. I. *a.* fruitful, prolific. **II.** *f.* place where cattle bring forth their young; parturition.

pariente, ta, *n.* relation, relative, kinsman (-woman); (coll.) appellation given by husband and wife to each other.

parietal, *a.* pertaining to walls; (anat.) parietal.

parietaria, *f.* (bot.) wall pellitory.

parificación, *f.* exemplification, illustration.

parificar, *va.* to exemplify, illustrate.

parihuela, *f.* handbarrow; litter; stretcher.

pario, ria, *n.* & *a.* Parian.

parir, *va.* & *vn.* to give birth, bring forth young; to produce, to cause; to publish.—**poner a p.,** to constrain, force (a person).

parisiense, *a.* & *n.* Parisian.

parla, *f.* easy delivery, loquacity, talk.

parlador, ra, *n.* chatterer.

parladuría, *f.* loquacity, talk, gossip.

parlaembalde, *n.* (coll.) chatterbox.

parlamentar, *vn.* to converse; (mil.) to parley.

parlamentariamente, *adv.* parliamentarily.

parlamentario, ria. I. *a.* parliamentary, parliamentarian. **II.** *m.* member of parliament; (mil.) flag of truce, cartel.

parlamentarismo, *m.* parliamentarism.

parlamento, *m.* parliament; legislative body; (mil.) parley, flag of truce; (theat.) speech.

parlanchín, na, *n.* & *a.* chatterer(-ing), jabberer (-ing).

parlante, *a.* speaking, talking.

parlar, *vn.* to speak with ease; to chatter, talk.

parlatorio, *m.* chat, parley; parlor; locutory.

parlería, *f.* loquacity, garrulity; gossip; tale; jest; chirping of birds; purling of brooks.

parlerillo, illa; ruelo, la, *a. dim.* of PARLERO.

parlero, ra, *a.* loquacious, talkative; expressive (eyes); chirping (birds); bubbling (brooks).

parleta, *f.* chat, small talk.

parlón, na, *a.* loquacious, garrulous.

parlotear, *vn.* to prattle, prate, chatter.—**parloteo,** *m.* chat, prattle, talk.

parmesano, na, *n.* & *a.* Parmesan.

Parnaso, *m.* Parnassus; anthology; assemblage of poets.

parnés, *m.* (coll.) money, cash.

¹paro, *m.* (ornith.) titmouse; coaltit.

²paro, *m.* lockout.—**p. forzoso,** unemployment (not caused by strike or lockout).

parodia, *f.* parody.—**parodiar,** *va.* to parody.

paródico, ca, *a.* pert. to parody, burlesque.

parodista, *n.* parodist; writer of parodies.

parola, parolina, *f.* (coll.) fluency, volubility; chat, idle talk.

pároli, *m.* paroli (as at faro).

paronimia, *f.* (gram.) paronymy.

parónimo, ma, *a.* (gram.) paronymous.

paronomasia, *f.* (rhet.) paronomasia; pun.

parótida, *f.* (anat.) parotid gland; (med.) mumps.—**parotiditis,** *f.* parotitis, mumps.

paroxismal, *a.* paroxysmal.

paroxismo, *m.* (med.) paroxysm.

parpadear, *vn.* to wink; to blink.

parpadeo, *m.* winking, blinking.

párpado, *m.* eyelid.

parpalla, *f.* milled copper piece.

parpar, *vn.* to quack (as a duck).

parque, *m.* park; paddock; (mil.) park; (Am.) ammunition; (Am.) (auto) parking area.

parqueadero, *m.* (Am.) parking place.

parquear, *va.* & *vn.* (Angl.) (auto) to park.

parquedad, *f.* parsimony; sparseness.

¹parra, *f.* honey jar.

²parra, *f.* grapevine.

parrado, da. I. *pp.* of PARRAR. **II.** with extended vines.

párrafo, *m.* paragraph; paragraph mark (§ or ¶).

parragón, *m.* standard silver for assayers.

¹parral, *m.* bower of grapevines; vineyard having vines with long shoots.

²**parral**, *m.* large earthen jar for honey.

parranda, *f.* revel, carousal.—**andar, estar,** or **ir, de p., parandear,** *vn.,* to go on a lark; to have a gay time.

parrandero, ra; parrandista. I. *a.* fond of carousing. **II.** *n.* carouser, reveler.

parrar, *vn.* to spread out in branches.

parresia, *f.* (rhet.) parrhesia.

parricida, *n.* parricide (murderer).

parricidio, *m.* parricide (murder).

¹**parrilla,** *f.* earthen jug.

²**parrilla,** *f.* gridiron, broiler, toaster; (furnace) grate.

parriza, *f.,* wild grapevine.

parro, *m.* (ornith.) duck.

párroco, *m.* (eccl.) parson.

parrón, *m.* = PARRIZA.

parroquia, *f.* (eccl.) parish; parochial church; congregation and clergy of a parish; (com.) good will, custom, customers, clientele.

parroquial. I. *a.* parochial. **II.** *f.* parochial church.

parroquialidad, *f.* parochial right.

parroquiano, na. I. *a.* parochial. **II.** *n.* (eccl.) parishioner; (com.) customer, client.

parsi. I. *n.* Parsi, a Zoroastrian. **II.** *a.* Parsic.

parsimonia, *f.* economy, frugality; moderation.

parsimonioso, sa, *a.* economical; sober, moderate, prudent.

parsismo, *m.* Parsiism.

parte. I. *f.* part; portion; share; place, spot; right or left side; cause, party; sense given to words or acts; (law) party; (theat.) part, character, rôle.—*pl.* parts, talents, endowments; (coll.) the genitals.—**p. alícuota,** aliquot part.—**p. de la oración,** part of speech.—**p. interesada,** party in interest.—**p. por p.,** part by part, distinctly.—**partes pudendas, púdicas,** or **vergonzosas,** genitals, privy parts.—**a partes,** by parts, or in parts.—**dar p.,** to inform, notify.—**de algún tiempo a esta p.,** for some time past.—**de mi p.,** on my part; on my side; for me, in my name.—**de p. a p.,** from side to side, through.—**de p. de,** from, by command of, in the name of; in behalf of.—**de una p. . . . de otra p.,** on the one hand . . . on the other hand.—**en alguna p.,** somewhere.—**en gran p.,** largely.—**en ninguna p.,** nowhere.—**en p.,** partly, in part.—**en partes** = A PARTES.—**en todas partes,** everywhere.—**hacer de su p.,** to do one's best, to do one's part.—**ir a la p.,** to go shares.—**la mayor p. de,** most of.—**la tercera (cuarta,** etc.) **p.,** one-third (-fourth, etc.).—**no ser p. en,** not to be a party to, to have nothing to do with.—**por mi parte,** as for me, as far as I am concerned.—**por otra p.,** on the other hand.—**por p. de,** on the part of.—**por partes,** by parts, one thing at a time.—**por todas partes,** on all sides; everywhere. **II.** *m.* communication, communiqué, despatch, report, telegram, telephone message. **III.** *adv.* in part, partly.

partear, *va.* to assist (women) in childbirth.

partenogénesis, *f.* (biol.) parthenogenesis.

partera, *f.* midwife.

partería, *f.* midwifery.

partero, *m.* accoucheur.

¹**partesana,** *f.* partisan.

²**partesana,** *f.* a kind of halberd.

partesanero, *m.* pikeman, halberdier.

partible, *a.* divisible, separable.

partición, *f.* division, distribution.

particionero, ra, *a.* participant.

participación, *f.* participation, share; communication; (com.) copartnership.

participante, *n.* & *a.* participant(-ating), sharer (-ing); notifier(-fying).

participar. I. *va.* to notify, communicate. **II.** *vn.* **(de)** to share (in); **(en)** to participate, take part (in).

partícipe. I. *a.* participant, sharing. **II.** *n.* participator; partner.

participial, *a.* (gram.) participial.

participio, *m.* (gram.) participle.

partícula, *f.* particle.

particular. I. *a.* particular, peculiar, special; personal; private; individual; odd, extraordinary. **II.** *m.* private person, individual; topic, point.—**en p.,** particularly.

particularidad, *f.* particularity, peculiarity; individuality; friendship, intimacy; detail.

particularismo, *m.* (theol.) particularism; (philos.) individualism.

particularizar. I. *va.* to particularize, itemize, specify. **II.** *vr.* **(en)** to have as a characteristic, to be distinguished (by).

particularmente, *adv.* particularly; privately; individually; especially.

partida, *f.* departure; passing away, death; item in an account, charge, entry, record, annotation; parcel, lot; (one) game; money staked; certificate (of birth, marriage, death); (mil.) squad; guerrilla; faction; band, gang; (coll.) conduct, behavior, turn; (com.) shipment, lot, consignment.—**p. de campo,** picnic.—**p. de caza,** hunting match.—**p. doble,** (com.) double entry.—**p. serrana,** bad turn.—**p. simple,** single entry.—**las siete Partidas,** the laws of Castile, compiled by King Alphonso X.

partidamente, *adv.* separately, distinctly.

partidario, ria. I. *a.* partisan, adherent, addicted. **II.** *m.* partisan; follower; advocate; party man; district physician.—**partidarismo,** *m.* partisanship.—**partidarista,** *m.* & *f.* defender of partisanship.

partidismo, *m.* = PARTIDARISMO.

partidista, *m.* & *f.* = PARTIDARISTA.

partido, da. I. *pp.* of PARTIR. **II.** *a.* cleft, divided; broken; (her.) party, parted, or parti per pale. **III.** *m.* (pol.) party; advantage, profit; game, contest, match; odds, handicap; persons who play a game; treaty, agreement; means to an end; territorial division or district; circuit in charge of a physician or surgeon.—**sacar p. de,** to turn to advantage, to take advantage of.—**tomar p.,** to take sides; to make up one's mind; to join (a party, army, etc.).

partidor, *m.* divider, cleaver; divisor.

partija, *f.* partition, division.

partil, *a.* said of astrological aspects.

partimento, partimiento, *m.* = PARTICIÓN.

partir. I. *va.* to split; to divide; to cut, cleave; to break, crush, crack; to attack in combat or battle; (arith.) to divide; to divide in two.—**p. abierto,** to uncover (a beehive to make the bees swarm).—**p. cerrado,** to divide (a beehive) when it is full.—**p. la diferencia,** to split the difference. **II.** *vn.* to depart, leave; to start, reckon (from).—**a p. de,** starting from. **III.** *vr.* to break; to become divided.

partitivo, va, *a.* (gram.) partitive.

partitura, *f.* (mus.) score.

parto, *m.* childbirth, parturition; newborn child; production, creation, product; expected and important event.

parturienta, parturienta, *a.* parturient.

párulis, *m.* (med.) gumboil.

parva, *f.* heap of unthrashed corn; multitude, large quantity; light breakfast.

parvedad, *f.* smallness, minuteness; light breakfast.

parvero, *m.* long heap of corn for winnowing.

parvidad, *f.* = PARVEDAD.

parvo, va, *a.* small, little.

parvulez, *f.* smallness; simplicity.

parvulico, ica, illo, illa, ito, ita. I. *a. dim.* very little. **II.** *n.* tot, little child.

párvulo, la. I. *a.* very small; innocent; humble, low. **II.** *n.* child.

¹**pasa,** *f.* passage of birds; (naut.) channel.

²**pasa,** *f.* raisin; (Am.) wool or kinky hair of Negroes.—**p. de Corinto,** currant.—**p. gorrona,** large-sized raisin.

pasabalas, *m.* (mil.) ball caliber gauge.

pasacalle, *m.* (mus.) lively march.

pasada, *f.* passage, passing; pace, step.—**de p.,** on the way; hastily, cursorily.—**mala p.,** (coll.) bad turn, mean trick.

pasadera, *f.* stepping-stone; (naut.) furling line, sea gasket.

pasaderamente, *adv.* passably.

pasadero, ra. I. *a.* supportable, sufferable; passable, tolerably good. **II.** *m.* stepping-stone.

pasadillo, *m.* two-face embroidery.

pasadizo, *m.* alley; passage; corridor, hall, aisle.

pasado, da. I. *pp.* of PASAR. **II.** *a.* past; last (*la semana pasada,* last week); stale; (of fruit) spoiled; antiquated, out of date or fashion.—**pasado mañana,** day after tomorrow. **III.** *m.* past; (mil.) deserter going over to the enemy.—*pl.* ancestors.

pasador, ra. I. *n.* one who goes across; smuggler. **II.** *m.* door bolt; window fastener; pin; woman's brooch; hatpin or bodkin; peg, sneck, bolt-pin, linchpin, cotter; sieve, colander; (naut.) marlinespike, splicing fid.

pasadura, *f.* passage, transit.

pasagonzalo, *m.* (coll.) flick, quick, light stroke.

pasaje, *m.* passage; journey, voyage; road, way; passage money, fare; number of passengers in a ship; (naut.) strait, narrows; (mus.) transition or change of voice; passage in a book or writing.

pasajero, ra. I. *a.* (of a thoroughfare) with constant passing (of people); passing, transient, transitory; provisional. **II.** *n.* traveler, passenger.

pasamanar, *va.* to trim with passementerie.

pasamanería, *f.* passementerie (work, trade, and shop).

pasamanero, ra, *n.* passementerie maker.

pasamano, *m.* passementerie; handrail, banister; (naut.) gangway.

pasamiento, *m.* passage, transit.

pasante. I. *a.* (her.) passant. **II.** *n.* student assistant of a physician or lawyer; tutor, coach.—**p. de pluma,** barrister's clerk.

pasantía, *f.* profession of a PASANTE.

pasapán, (coll.) = GARGÜERO, gullet, windpipe.

pasapasa, *m.* legerdemain, hocus-pocus.

pasaporte, *m.* passport; free license; (mil.) furlough.

pasar. I. *va.* (*pp.* PASADO, PASO) to pass; to take across, put through, carry over; to pass, hand; to go to, in, by, across, over, around, beyond, through, or the like; to move from place to place; to pierce, run through; to smuggle; to advance, promote; to change, transform; to exceed, surpass; to distance, outdo, outrun, outstrip; to convey, transfer; to suffer, bear, undergo; to stroke, rub; to swallow (food or drink); to omit, overlook; to tolerate; to study with a private teacher; to study as an assistant practitioner; to give private lessons; to study or rehearse (a lesson); to study, read; to dry or desiccate (as fruit); to pass, spend (as time).—**p. a cuchillo,** to put to the sword.—**p. el rato,** to kill time.—**p. en claro,** to omit.—**p. (la) lista,** to call the roll.—**pasarlo,** to get along, do, be (ref. health).—**pasarlo bien,** to have a good time.—**p. plaza de,** to set up as.—**p. por alto,** to overlook.—**p. por las armas,** to shoot (as a penalty).—¿**cómo lo pasa Vd.?** how are you? how do you do?—**que lo pase Vd. bien,** good-bye, good luck.—¿**que (le) pasa?,** what's the matter with (him)? **II.** *vn.* to pass; to live; to manage, get along; to last, endure; to pass away, die; to be salable or marketable (as goods); to be current (as money); (at cards) to pass.—**p. a** (*inf.*), to proceed to (*inf.*)—**p. de,** to exceed.—**p. de largo,** to pass by without

stopping; to read cursorily.—**p. por,** (foll. by *n.* or *a.*) to be considered as, to be taken for; (foll. by *adv.*) to come, go, call, around (¿**puede Vd. pasar por acá mañana?,** can you come around, call in, here tomorrow?).—**p. por encima de,** to overcome; to go over the head of.—**p. sin,** to do without. **III.** *v. imp.* to pass, happen, turn out. **IV.** *vr.* to go over to another party; to cease, finish; to be spent or stale, lose its force; to slip from one's memory; to become tainted (as meat) or spoiled (as fruit); to go too far; to exceed; to burn out (as a fire); to be overcooked; to permeate, go through; to graduate at college; to blot (as paper).—**p. de,** to be too (*pasarse de paciente,* to be too patient).

pasatiempo, *m.* pastime, amusement.

pasavante, *m.* safe-conduct; (com.) permit.

pasavolante, *m.* hasty action.

pasavoleo, *m.* returning the ball over the line.

pascua, *f.* Jewish Passover; (eccl.) each of the Church holidays—Easter, Twelfth-night, Pentecost, and Christmas.—**p. de flores, de resurrección,** or **florida,** Easter (Sunday).—*pl.* Christmas holidays or season.—**dar las pascuas,** to wish merry Christmas.—**estar como una p.,** to be as merry as a cricket.—**felices pascuas,** merry Christmas.

pascual, *a.* (eccl.) paschal.

pascuilla, *f.* first Sunday after Easter.

pase, *m.* permit, pass; (fencing) venue, thrust.

paseadero, *m.* walk, avenue, mall.

paseador, ra. I. *a.* fond of walking. **II.** *n.* stroller, promenader.

paseante, *n.* promenader, stroller.—**p. encorte,** idle fellow.

pasear. I. *vn. & vr.* to take a walk; to ride, drive or sail for pleasure; to promenade; to make a pleasure trip; to walk up and down, pace. **II.** *va.* to take out to walk (as a child).

paseata, *f.* (coll.) walk, airing; ride.

paseo, *m.* walk, promenade; stroll; drive; ride; mall; turnout, parade.—**dar un p.,** to take a walk, ride, etc.—**echar,** or **enviar, a p.,** to send one about one's business; to dismiss or reject rudely or without ceremony.

pasera, *f.* place where fruit is dried; drying.

¹**pasero, ra,** *n.* seller of raisins.

²**pasero, ra,** *n.* pacing mule or horse.

pasicorto, ta, *a.* short-stepped.

pasiego, ga, *n.* highlander of Santander.

pasifloreo, a, *a.* (bot.) passifloraceous.

pasilargo, ga, *a.* long-stepped.

pasillo, *m.* *dim.* short step; passage, corridor; aisle; (sewing) basting stitch.

pasión, *f.* passion, emotion; (eccl.) passion.—**pasionaria,** *f.* (bot.) passion flower.—**pasionario,** *m.* (eccl.) passion book.—**pasionero, ra; pasionista,** *n.* (eccl.) one who sings the passion.

pasito. I. *m. dim.* short step. **II.** *adv.* gently, softly.—**p. a p.,** very leisurely or gently.

pasitrote, *m.* short trot.

pasivamente, *adv.* passively.

pasivo, va. I. *a.* passive; inactive, unresponsive; pert. to a pension (for services); (gram.) passive. **II.** *m.* (com.) liabilities.

pasmar. I. *va.* to cause a spasm; to benumb, stun; to astound; to chill, deaden. **II.** *vr.* (de) to wonder, marvel (at); to suffer from lockjaw; (of plants) to freeze.

pasmarota, pasmarotada, *f.* feigned spasm; exaggerated admiration or astonishment.

pasmo, *m.* spasm; (med.) lockjaw, tetanus; astonishment; wonder, anything wonderful.

pasmosamente, *adv.* wonderfully.

pasmoso, sa, *a.* marvelous, wonderful.

¹**paso, sa,** *a.* dried (fruit).

²**paso. I.** *m.* pace, step; pass, way, passage; passing; gait, walk; step of a staircase; step, measure, or diligence; footstep; incident, accident,

occurrence; (mech.) pitch; passage in a writing; (theat.) curtain raiser, sketch; progress, improvement; death.—*pl.* basting stitches.—**p. a nivel,** (Ry.) grade crossing.—**p. a p.,** step by step.—**p. de andadura,** ambling.—**p. de tortuga,** snail pace, extreme slowness.—**p. entre p. = P. A P.**—**abrir p.,** to open a passage, make way.—**abrirse p.,** to get through.—**a buen p.,** at a good rate, step, or gait.—**a cada p.,** at every step, frequently.—**a ese p.,** at that rate.—**al p.,** in passing.—**al p. que,** while, whereas.—**a pocos pasos,** at a short distance.—**apretar el p.,** to hasten.—**de p.,** in passing; on the way, as a transient; migratory.—**llevar el p.,** to keep step.—**marcar el p.,** to mark time.—**más que de p.,** hastily, in a hurry.—**prohibido el p.,** no trespassing, keep out.—**salir del p.,** to get out of the difficulty; to "get by."—**seguir los pasos a,** to follow (the steps of); to trail; to watch.—**seguir los pasos de,** to walk in the footsteps of. II. *adv.* softly, gently.

paspié, *m.* a kind of dance.

pasquín, *m.* pasquinade, lampoon.

pasquinada, *f.* pasquinade.

pasquinar, *va.* to ridicule, lampoon, satirize.

pássim, *adv.* passim, in various places.

pasta, *f.* paste; batter; dough; pie crust; soup paste; noodles; bullion for coining; board binding (for books); pulp (in paper).—**p. de dientes,** toothpaste.—**p. de guayaba,** guava paste.—**buena p.,** good disposition.

pastadero, pastal, *m.* pasture, grazing field.

pastar. I. *vn.* to pasture, graze. **II.** *va.* to lead (cattle) to graze.

pasteca, *f.* (naut.) snatch block.

pastel, *m.* pie; (bot.) woad; ball or cake of woad; cheating; combine, plot; (print.) pi or pie; blotted print; (art) pastel.—**al p.,** pastel (painting).

pastelear, *vn.* (coll.) to "trim" politically.

pastelejo, *m. dim.* small pie.

pastelería, *f.* pastry shop; pastry.

pastelero, ra, *n.* pastry cook; political trimmer.

pastelillo, ito, *m. dim.* patty; tart, cake.

pastelón, *m. aug.* meat or pigeon pie.

pasterización, *f.* pasteurization.

pasterizar, *va.* to pasteurize.

pastero, ra, *n.* one who throws the mass of crushed olives into baskets.

pasteurizar, etc. = PASTERIZAR, etc.

pastilla, *f.* tablet, lozenge, drop; cake.

pastinaca, *f.* (bot.) parsnip; (ichth.) sting ray.

pastizal, *m.* pasture ground for horses.

pasto, *m.* pasture, grazing; grass for feed; pasture ground; pabulum, food.—**p. espiritual,** spiritual nourishment.—**pastos comunes,** common fields.—**a p.,** abundantly, plentifully; excessively.—**a todo p.,** freely, abundantly and unrestrictedly.

pastor, ra, *n.* shepherd (-ess); pastor, clergyman.

pastoral. I. *a.* pastoral; rural, rustic. **II.** *f.* pastoral; idyll.

pastoralmente, *adv.* pastorally.

pastorcico, illo, ito, *m. dim.* little shepherd.

pastorear, *va.* to pasture; to keep, tend (sheep); to feed (souls).

pastorela, *f.* (mus. and poet.) pastoral.

pastoreo, *m.* pasturing, tending flocks.

pastoría, *f.* pastoral life; shepherds.

pastoricio, cia, pastoril, *a.* pastoral.

pastorilmente, *adv.* pastorally.

pastosidad, *f.* mellowness, softness.

pastoso, sa, *a.* pasty, soft, mellow, doughy; (art) softly painted.

pastura, *f.* pasture, pasturage; fodder.

pasturaje, *m.* common pasturage; duty paid for pasturage.

pata, *f.* foot (of an animal); foot and leg of beasts; (coll. and humor.) human leg or foot; leg of a

piece of furniture, an instrument, etc.; pocket flap; (ornith.) duck, female of the drake.—**p. de cabra,** crowbar, nail puller; (shoemaking) heel burnisher.—**p. de gallina,** radial crack in trees; beginning of rot.—**p. de gallo,** ridiculous saying, bull; crow's-foot wrinkles near the eye.—**p. es la traviesa,** tit for tat.—**patas arriba,** topsy-turvy, heels over head; upside down; on one's back.—**a cuatro patas,** on all fours.—**a la p. coja,** hopscotch.—**a la p. la llana,** plainly, unaffectedly.—**a p.,** (coll.) on foot.—**bailar una p.,** to jump for joy.—**en cuatro patas,** on all fours.—**enseñar la p.,** to show one's ignorance.—**meter la p.,** (coll.) to intermeddle, butt in; to put one's foot in it, make a break.—**quedar, salir,** or **ser, p.,** or **patas,** to be a tie or draw.

pataca, *f.* (bot.) Jerusalem artichoke.

pataco, ca, = PATÁN.

patacón, *m.* silver dollar.

patache, *m.* (naut.) tender.

patada, *f.* kick; (coll.) step, pace; footstep, track.

patagón, na, *n. & a.;* **patagónico, ca,** *a.* Patagonian.

patagorrillo, lla, *n.* hash of livers and lights.

patagua, *f.* (bot.) Am. linden, whitewood.

pataje, *m.* = PATACHE.

patalear, *vn.* to kick about violently; to stamp both feet repeatedly.—**pataleo,** *m.* kicking; stamping the feet; pattering, tramp.

pataleta, *f.* (coll.) fainting fit; convulsion.

pataletilla, *f.* a kind of pirouette.

patán, na. I. *a.* churlish, rustic; unmannerly. **II.** *n.* churl, rustic; unmannerly person.

patanada, *f.* incivility, rudeness; rude or discourteous act.

patanería, *f.* churlishness, rusticity, rudeness; incivility.

patarata, *f.* trash; humbuggery; paltry trifle.

pataratero, ra, *n.* humbugger, humbug.

patarráez, *m.* (naut.) preventer shroud.

patata, *f.* (bot.) potato.—**patatal, patatar,** *m.* potato patch.—**patatero, ra. I.** *a.* fond of potatoes. **II.** *n.* potato seller.

patatús, *m.* (coll.) swoon, fainting fit.

patax, *m.* (naut.) = PATACHE, tender.

pateador, ra, *a.* kicking (horse).

pateadura, *f.,* **pateamiento,** *m.* kicking, stamping of the feet; severe reprimand, dressing down.

patear, *va. & vn.* (coll.) to kick; stamp the foot; to tramp; to be very angry.

patena, *f.* large medal worn by countrywomen; (eccl.) paten.

patentar, *va.* to patent.

patente. I. *a.* patent, manifest, evident. **II.** *f.* patent; privilege, exclusive grant, warrant, commission.—**p. de corso,** letters of marque.—**p. de chofer,** driver's license.—**p. de sanidad,** (naut.) bill of health.—**p. limpia,** clean bill of health.

patentemente, *adv.* clearly, visibly, obviously.

patentizar, *va.* to make evident.

pateo, *m.* (coll.) kicking; stamping of feet.

pátera, *f.* patera, shallow dish or saucer.

paternal, *a.* paternal, fatherly.

paternalmente, *adv.* paternally, fatherly.

paternidad, *f.* paternity, fatherhood.

paterno, na, *a.* paternal, fatherly.

paternóster, *m.* Lord's Prayer; paternoster, big tight knot.

pateta, *m.* (coll.) nickname given to a lame person; (coll.) devil, old Nick.—**se lo llevó p.,** the deuce took it.

patéticamente, *adv.* pathetically.

patético, ca, *a.* pathetic, touching; plaintive.

patiabierto, ta, *a.* straddling, bowlegged.

patiabillo, *m.* (zool.) weasel.

patialbo, ba; patiblanco, ca, *a.* white-footed.

patibulario, ria, *a.* harrowing.

patíbulo, *m.* gibbet, gallows; scaffold.

For pronunciation, see the rules at the beginning of the book.

patico, *m.* dim. young duck, duckling.
paticojo, ja, *a.* (coll.) lame, crippled, limping.
patidifuso, sa, *a.* (coll.) astounded.
patiestevado, da, *a.* bowlegged.
patihendido, da, *a.* cloven-footed.
patilla, *f.* dim. small foot; manner of playing on the guitar; (naut.) spike of the rudder; chape of a buckle; pocket flap; trigger; (Am.) water-melon.—*pl.* side whiskers; (coll.) the devil.
¹**patín,** *m.* dim. small court or yard.
²**patín,** *m.* (ornith.) goosander, a kind of duck.
³**patín,** *m.* skate; (aer.) skid.—**p. de cola,** (aer.) tail skid.—**p. de ruedas,** roller skate.
pátina, *f.* (metal. and art) patina; film.
patinadero, *m.* skating place; skating rink.
patinador, ra, *n.* skater.
patinamiento, *m.* (of vehicles) skidding.
patinar, *vn.* to skate; (of vehicles) to skid.
patinejo, *m.* dim. small skate.
patio, *m.* yard, court yard; (theat.) pit.
patita, *f.* dim. small foot or leg.—**poner de patitas en la calle,** to discharge, "bounce."
patitieso, *a.* (coll.) stiff-legged; astounded, stupefied, surprised; stiff, haughty.
patito, *m.* dim. young duck, duckling.
patituerto, ta, *a.* crook-legged, knock-kneed; crooked, lopsided.
patizambo, ba, *a.* knock-kneed, bowlegged.
pato, *m.* (ornith.) duck.—**p. de flojel,** eider duck.—**p. negro,** mallard.—**pagar el p.,** to suffer undeserved punishment, to be the scape-goat.
patochada, *f.* blunder, nonsense.
patogenia, *f.* (med.) science treating of patho-genesis.
patógeno, na, *a.* (med.) pathogenic.
patojear, *vn.* (Cuba) to waddle in walking.
patojo, ja. I. *a.* waddling, like a duck; (Am.) lame. **II.** *n.* (C. A.) street urchin.
patología, *f.* pathology.
patológico, ca, *a.* pathologic.
patólogo, *m.* (med.) pathologist.
patón, na, *a.* large-footed; clumsy-footed.
patraña, *f.* fabulous story, fake, humbug.
patria, *f.* native country, fatherland.
patriarca, *m.* patriarch.—**patriarcado,** *m.* patri-archate.—**patriarcal,** *a.* patriarchal.
patriciado, *m.* patriciate, patrician rank.
patricio, cia, *n. & a.* patrician.
patrimonial, *a.* patrimonial.
patrimonio, *m.* patrimony, inheritance.
patrio, tria, *a.* native; home (as *a.*); paternal.
patriota, *m.* patriot.
patriotería, *f.* exaggerated patriotism.
patriotero, ra, *n.* exaggerated patriot.
patriótico, ca, *a.* patriotic.
patriotismo, *m.* patriotism.
patrística, *f.* (eccl.) patristics.
patrístico, ca, *a.* (eccl.) patristic.
patrocinador, ra, *m. & a.* patron; sponsor(-ing).
patrocinar, *va.* to protect, favor; to sponsor.
patrocinio, *m.* protection, patronage; sponsor-ship, auspices.—**bajo el p.,** under the auspices.
patrología, *f.* (eccl.) patrology, patristics.
patrón, na. I. *n.* patron(-ess); protector; host (-ess); landlord (-lady); patron saint. **II.** *m.* master, boss; pattern, model; standard; (naut.) skipper.—**p. de bote,** or **p. de lancha,** (naut.) cockswain, coxswain.—**p. de oro,** gold stand-ard.—**kilogramo, metro,** etc., **p.,** standard kilogram, meter, etc. **III.** *f.* galley following that of the commodore.
patronado, da. I. *a.* (eccl.) having a patron. **II.** *m.* = PATRONATO.
patronal, *a.* patronal, protecting; pertaining to employers, employers' (as *a.*).
patronato, patronazgo, *m.* patronage, guardi-anship; employers' association.
patronear, *va.* to steer (a trading vessel).

patronímico, ca. I. *a.* patronymic. **II.** *m.* patronymic, surname.
patrono, na, *n.* patron, protector, defender; tute-lary; lord (lady) of the manor; employer.
patrulla, *f.* patrol; gang, band, squad.
patrullar, *va.* to patrol.
patuá, *m.* (Gal.) patois, jargon.
patudo, da, *a.* (coll.) having large feet or paws.
patulea, *f.* (coll.) soldiery or disorderly folks.
patullar, *vn.* to trample, tramp; to hustle.
paují, paujil, *m.* guan, a S. A. gallinacean.
paúl, paular, *m.* fen, moor, marsh, bog.
paulatinamente, *adv.* gradually, by degrees.
paulatino, na, *a.* slow, gradual.
paulina, *f.* decree of excommunication, interdict; (coll.) reproof, chiding; anonymous offensive letter, poison-pen letter.
paulinia, *f.* (bot.) (S. A.) a kind of shrub.
paulonia, *f.* (bot.) paulownia.
pauperismo, *m.* pauperism, abject poverty.
paupérrimo, ma, *a. super.* very poor.
pausa, *f.* pause; delay; rest, repose; (mus.) pause, rest, stop.—**a pausas,** at leisure.
pausadamente, *adv.* slowly, deliberately.
pausado, da. I. *pp.* of PAUSAR. **II.** *a.* slow, de-liberate; calm, quiet. **III.** *adv.* slowly.
pausar, *vn.* to pause, cease, hesitate.
pauta, *f.* instrument for ruling paper; guide lines; standard, rule, pattern, model.
pautada, *f.* (mus.) ruled staff.
pautador, ra, *n.* one who rules paper.
pautar, *va.* to rule (paper); to regulate, give rules or directions for.
¹**pava,** *f.* (ornith.) turkey hen; (Colomb.) a kind of guan; (Am.) joke, fun.
²**pava,** *f.* large furnace bellows; (Venez., Chile, P. R.) large low hat; (Arg.) pot, kettle.—**pelar la p.,** to carry on a flirtation.
pavada, *f.* flock of turkeys; child's game; (Arg.) nonsense, foolishness.
pavana, *f.* Spanish dance and its tune.
pavear, *vn.* (Arg., Chile) to make fun; (Arg., Chile) to flirt.
¹**pavero, ra,** *n.* one who feeds or sells turkeys.
²**pavero,** *m.* broad-brimmed hat.
pavés, *m.* large shield, pavis.
pavesa, *f.* embers, hot cinders; burnt part of candlewick.—*pl.* ashes.
pavesada, *f.* (naut.) = EMPAVESADA, waistcloths.
pavezno, *m.* dim. young turkey.
pavía, *f.* clingstone peach (tree and fruit).
pávido, da, *a.* (poet.) timid, fearful.
pavimentación, *f.* paving; pavement.
pavimentar, *va.* to pave.
pavimento, *m.* pavement.
paviota, *f.* (ornith.) mew, sea gull.
pavipollo, *m.* young turkey.
pavo, *m.* (ornith.) turkey; (ichth.) peacock fish.—**p. real,** (ornith.) peacock.—**p. silvestre,** (ornith.) wood grouse.
pavón, *m.* peacock; bluing (for steel or iron).
pavonada, *f.* (coll.) short walk; strut; outward show, ostentation.
pavonar, *va.* to treat (steel, etc.) with bluing.
pavonazo, *m.* (art) dark-red pigment.
pavonear, *vn. & vr.* to strut, to show off.
pavor, *m.* fear, dread, fright, terror.
pavorde, *m.* provost; professor of divinity.
pavordear, *vn.* (of bees) to swarm.
pavordía, *f.* place and dignity of a provost.
pavorido, da, *a.* intimidated, terrorized.
pavorosamente, *adv.* fearfully, with terror.
pavoroso, sa, *a.* awful, frightful, terrible.
pavura, *f.* fear, dread, terror, fright.
payar, *va.* (S. A.) to sing with guitar accompani-ment.
payasada, *f.* clownish joke or action.
payaso, *m.* clown.
payés, sa, *n.* Catalan countryman (-woman).
payo, ya, *m.* gawk, churl, gump.

For pronunciation, see the rules at the beginning of the book.

payuelas, *f. pl.* chicken pox.
paz, *f.* peace; tranquillity; peace of mind; freedom from debt; (eccl.) ceremony of the mass.—¡p.! peace! hush!—**a la p. de Dios,** God be with you.—**en p.,** quits, even.—**gente de p.,** a friend (in answer to "who is there?").
pazguato, ta, *n.* dolt, simpleton.
pazote, *m.* (bot.) saltwort.
pazpuerco, ca, *a.* (coll.) dirty, slovenly.
pe, *f.* name of the letter *p.*—**de p. a pa,** thoroughly, from A to Z, from beginning to end.
peaje, *m.* bridge toll; ferriage.
peajero, *m.* toll-gatherer.
peal, *m.* legging; stocking foot; worthless man.
peán, *m.* pean, pæan.
peana, peaña, *f.* pedestal stand; (mech.) ground plate; step before an altar.
peatón, *m.* walker, messenger; rural postman.
pebete, *m.* joss stick; incense taper; (coll.) (fig.) stench; fuse, punk.—**pebetero,** *m.* perfume censer.
pebrada, *f.* sauce of garlic and spice.
pebre, *m.* or *f.* PEBRADA; a red pepper.
peca, *f.* freckle, speck, spot.
pecable, *a.* peccable, liable to sin; sinful.
pecadillo, ito, *m. dim.* peccadillo, slight sin.
pecado, *m.* sin; guilt; excess; (coll.) devil.—**p. capital,** deadly or mortal sin.—**p. contra natura,** or **contra naturaleza,** sodomy; masturbation.—**p. grave,** or **mortal,** deadly or mortal sin.—(after a noun), **de mis pecados,** of mine.
pecador, ra. I. *n.* & *a.* sinner(-ing); offender (-ing). **II.** *f.* (coll.) prostitute.
pecaminosamente, *adv.* sinfully, wickedly.
pecaminoso, sa, *a.* sinful.
pecante, *a.* sinning; excessive.
pecar, *vn.* (*pret.* PEQUÉ; *subj.* PEQUE) to sin; to yield to temptation; to offend; (med.) to predominate, superabound.—**p. de,** to be too (*Juan peca de confiado,* John is too confident); to have too much, (prolixity, obscurity, conciseness, etc.).
peccata minuta, (coll.) peccadilloes.
¹pece, *m.* ridge between furrows.
²pece, *f.* moistened clay for mud walls.
pececico, illo, ito, *m. dim.* little fish.
peceño, ña, *a.* pitchy (color and taste).
pecera, *f.* fish globe; aquarium.
¹pecezuelo, *m. dim.* of PIE, foot.
²pecezuelo, *m. dim.* of PEZ, fish.
peciento, ta, *a.* of a pitchy color.
peciluengo, ga, *a.* long-stalked (fruit).
¹pecina, *f.* slime.—**pecinal,** *m.* slimy pool.
²pecina, *f.* = PISCINA, fish-pond; swimming-pool.
pecio, *m.* flotsam, jetsam, wreckage.
peciolado, da, *a.* (bot.) petiolate.
pecíolo, *m.* (bot.) petiole, leaf stalk.
pécora, *f.* head of sheep.—**buena,** or **mala, p.,** (coll.) shrewd, designing woman.
pecorea, *f.* (mil.) marauding; loitering.
pecorear. I. *va.* to steal (cattle). **II.** *vn.* to loot.
pecoso, sa, *a.* freckly, freckled.
pectina, *f.* (chem.) pectin.
pectíneo, a, *a.* pectinate, comblike; (anat.) pectineus (muscle).
pectiniforme, *a.* comb-shaped, pectinate.
pectoral. I. *a.* pectoral. **II.** *m.* (eccl.) breast plate; (pharm.) pectoral.
pectosa, *f.* (chem.) pectose.
pecuario, ria, *a.* cattle (as *a.*).
peculado, *m.* (law) peculation, embezzlement.
peculiar, *a.* peculiar.—**peculiaridad,** *f.* peculiarity.—**peculiarmente,** *adv.* peculiarly.
peculio, *m.* (law) peculium; private property.
pecunia, *f.* (coll.) hard cash, specie.
pecuniariamente, *adv.* in cash; financially.
pecuniario, ria, *a.* pecuniary, monetary.
pechar, *vn.* to pay taxes.
peche, *m.* = PECHINA.

pechera, *f.* shirt bosom; shirt frill; chest protector; breast strap (of a harness); (coll.) bosom.
pechería, *f.* taxes, revenue; tax poll.
¹pechero, ra, *n.* taxpayer; commoner, plebeian.
²pechero, *m.* bib.
pechiblanco, ca, *a.* white-breasted.
pechicolorado, m. (ornith.) linnet.
pechigonga, *f.* a card game.
pechina, *f.* pilgrim scallop, a mollusk; (arch.) squinch; arch of a pendentive.
pechirrojo, m. (ornith.) linnet.
pechisacado, da, *a.* (coll.) haughty, arrogant.
pechito, *m. dim.* small breast or teat.
¹pecho, *m.* (anat.) chest, thorax; breast; bosom; teat; courage, fortitude; (mus.) quality and strength of the voice; slope, gradient.—**abrir el p.,** to unbosom oneself.—**criar a los pechos,** to instruct or educate.—**dar el p.,** to nurse, suckle.—**de p.,** firm-spirited.—**echar el p. al agua,** to undertake a risky thing resolutely.—**entre p. y espalda,** (coll.) in the stomach.—**tener p.,** to have patience, to endure with firmness.—**tomar a p.,** or **a pechos,** to take to heart.
²pecho, *m.* an ancient tax.
pechuelo, *m. dim.* small or little breast.
pechuga, *f.* breast of a fowl; slope; (coll.) bosom; (coll.) nerve, check, brazenness.—**pechugón, na. I.** *a.* (Am.) (coll.) "sponging," parasitic; bold, brazen. **II.** *m.* blow on the breast.
pechuguera, *f.* cough, hoarseness.
pedacico, illo, ito, *m.* small piece, bit.
pedagogía, *f.* pedagogy.
pedagógicamente, *adv.* pedagogically.
pedagógico, ca, *a.* pedagogical.
pedagogo, *m.* pedagogue; teacher; educator.
pedaje, *m.* = PEAJE, bridge toll.
pedal, *m.* (mech.) treadle; (mus.) pedal.
pedáneo, a, (law) petty, puisne, inferior.
pedante. I. *n.* & *a.* pedant(-ic); coxcomb(-ic). **II.** *n.* instructor.
pedantear, *vn.* to be pedantic.
pedantería, *f.* pedantry.
pedantescamente, *adv.* pedantically.
pedantesco, ca, *a.* pedantic.
pedantismo, *m.* pedantry.
pedantón, *m. aug.* great pedant.
pedazo, *m.* piece, fragment, bit.—**p. de alcornoque,** or **de animal,** good-for-nothing.—**a pedazos,** or **en pedazos,** in bits, in fragments.
pedazuelo, *m. dim.* small piece or bit.
pederasta, *m.* pederast.
pederastia, *f.* pederasty, pæderasty.
pedernal, *m.* flint; extreme hardness.
pedernalino, na, *a.* flinty; hard.
pedestal, *m.* pedestal; stand; base, support.
pedestre, *a.* pedestrian; low, vulgar, common.
pedestrismo, *m.* marathon racing, foot racing.
pediatría, *f.* (med.) pediatrics.
pedicoj, *m.* jump on one foot.
pedicular, *a.* pedicular, pert. to lice.
pedículo, *m.* (bot.) peduncle, pedicle.
pedicuro, *m.* chiropodist.
pedido, *m.* demand, call; (com.) order.
pedidor, ra, *n.* petitioner, craver.
pedidura, *f.* begging, petitioning.
pedigón, *m.* (coll.) craver, insatiable asker.
pedigüeño, ña, *a.* persistent in begging.
pediluvio, *m.* (med.) pediluvium, foot bath.
pedimento, *m.* petition; (law) claim, bill.—**a p.,** at the instance, on petition.
pedir, *va.* (*gerund,* PIDIENDO; *ind. pres.* PIDO, *pret.* él PIDIÓ; *subj.* PIDA) to ask for, request, beg, solicit; to demand, claim, exact; to inquire after; to wish, desire; to require; (com.) to order; to ask for in marriage.—**p. celos,** to be jealous.—**p. cuenta,** to call to account.—**a p. de boca,** according to desire.—**pedírselo a uno el cuerpo,** to desire eagerly, to long for.
pedo, *m.* wind from the anus; flatulence.

pedómetro, *m.* pedometer, walking wheel.
pedorrera, *f.* flatulence.—*pl.* tights.
pedrada, *f.* throw of a stone; blow from a stone; cockade; rosette or bow for the hair; hint, insinuation.—**como p. en ojo de boticario,** pat, apropos, just in time.
pedrea, *f.* throwing stones; lapidation; fight with stones; fall of hail.
pedregal, *m.* stony ground.
pedregoso, sa, *a.* stony, rocky; (med.) afflicted with gravel.
pedrejón, *m.* boulder.
pedreñal, *m.* a kind of firelock.
pedrera, *f.* quarry, stone pit.
pedreral, *m.* packsaddle for carrying stones.
pedrería, *f.* precious stones; jewelry.
pedrero, *m.* stonecutter; (artil.) stone mortar; slinger.
pedrezuela, *f. dim.* small stone: pebble.
pedrisca, *f.* hailstorm; shower of thrown stones; heap of small stones.
pedriscal, *m.* = PEDREGAL.
pedrisco, *m.* = PEDRISCA.—**pedrisquero,** *m.* hail storm.
pedriza, *f.* stony tract; stone fence.
pedrusco, *m.* rough piece of stone.
pedunculado, da, *a.* (bot.) peduncled.
pedunculillo, *m. dim.* (bot.) pedicle, pedicel.
pedúnculo, *m.* (bot.) peduncle, flower stalk.
peer, *vn. & vr.* to break wind.
¹pega, *f.* joining, cementing or sticking together; pitch varnish put on earthen vessels; (min.) firing of a blast; (coll.) jest, practical joke, deceit; spanking, drubbing; (ichth.) remora, sucking fish.
²pega, *f.* (ornith.) magpie.
pegadillo, *m. dim.* little patch; sticking plaster; bore, nuisance.
pegadizo, za, *a.* sticky, adhesive; catching, contagious; (coll.) (of person) sticker, leech; catchy (tune).
pegado, da. I. *pp.* of PEGAR; tied (as to his mother's apron strings). II. *m.* patch; sticking plaster.
pegador, *m.* sticker, affixer; paper hanger; (min.) blaster.—**p. de carteles,** billposter.
pegadura, *f.* pitching; sticking, gluing.
pegajoso, sa, *a.* sticky; clammy, viscous; catching, contagious; alluring, tempting.
pegamiento, *m.* joining, sticking, cementing.
pegante, *a.* sticking, adhesive, glutinous.
pegar. I. *va.* (*pret.* PEGUÉ; *subj.* PEGUE) to stick, glue, cement; to unite, fasten; to post (bills); to sew on, pin; patch; attach; to infect with, give (a disease); to hit, beat, slap; to give, deal (a blow, etc.); to impart.—**p. fuego a,** to set fire to.—**pegársela a uno,** to fool one, make one swallow a story.—**no p. los ojos,** not to sleep a wink.—**p. un tiro a,** to shoot. II. *vn.* to take root; to catch (fire); to make an impression on the mind; to make a hit; to join, to be contiguous; to cleave, cling; to fit, to match; to be becoming, fitting, appropriate; to pass, to be accepted.—**ésa no pega,** (coll.) that is too thin, that won't go. III. *vr.* to intrude; to stick, adhere; cohere; to grow; to become rooted in the mind; to take to, become addicted to.
pegaseo, sea, *a.* pertaining to Pegasus.
pegásides, *f. pl.* the Muses.
Pegaso, *m.* Pegasus.
pegata, *f.* (coll.) trick, cheat, swindle, fraud.
pegmatita, *f.* (min.) pegmatite.
pegollo, *m.* pillar, post.
pegote, *m.* sticking plaster; coarse patch; stew with a thick sauce; sponger, toady.
pegotear, *vn.* (coll.) to sponge.
pegotería, *f.* (coll.) sponging.
pegual, *m.* (S. A.) strap with rings.
pegué, pegue, *v. V.* PEGAR.

peguera, *f.* pine wood for making pitch; place where sheep are marked with pitch.
peguero, *m.* maker of or dealer in pitch.
pegujal, pegujar, *m.* peculium; small holdings.
pegujalero, ra; pegujarero, ra, *n.* owner of a small farm or ranch.
pegujón, *m.* pellet or bunch of wool or hair.
pegunta, *f.* pitch mark on sheep.
peguntar, *va.* to mark (sheep) with pitch.
peinada, *f.* combing or dressing the hair.
peinado, da. I. *pp.* of PEINAR. II. *a.* effeminate in toilet; overnice (literary style). III. *m.* hairdressing, hairdo.
peinador, ra. I. *n.* hairdresser. II. *m.* dressing gown, wrapper.
peinadura, *f.* combing or dressing the hair; combings.
peinar, *va.* to comb or dress (the hair); to comb (wool); to touch or rub slightly; to eat away (a rock).—**p. canas,** to be old.
peinazo, *m.* (carp.) crosspiece of a door.
peine, *m.* comb; card; rack, engine of torture; weaver's reed; comb of the loom; comb-broach; instep.—**a sobre p.,** lightly, slightly, imperfectly.
peinería, *f.* comb factory or shop.
peinero, ra, *n.* comb maker or seller.
peineta, *f.* ornamental shell comb (to wear in the hair).—**p. de teja,** tile-shaped shell comb.
peje, *m.* fish; cunning, crafty fellow.—**p. araña,** (ichth.) stingbull.—**p. diablo,** (ichth.) grouper.
pejemuller, *f.* mermaid, sea woman.
pejepalo, *m.* stockfish.
pejerrey, *m.* (ichth.) a variety of mackerel.
pejesapo, *m.* (ichth.) angler.
pejiguera, *f.* (coll.) bother, too much trouble for nothing.
pela, *m.* PELADURA; (Am.) whipping.—**dar, or pegar, una p.,** to whip, give a whipping to.
pelada, *f.* (tanning) pelt.
peladera, *f.* (med.) alopecia, baldness.
peladero, *m.* place where hogs and fowls are stripped; (coll.) sharpers' den; (Am.) bare, barren spot.
peladilla, *f.* sugar almond; small pebble.
peladillo, *m.* (bot.) clingstone peach (fruit and tree).—*pl.* wool-stripped sheepskin.
pelado, da. I. *pp.* of PELAR. II. *a.* plucked; bared; peeled, stripped; hairless; treeless, bare; penniless, "broke." II. *n.* penniless person; (Mex.) peasant.
pelador, *m.* plucker, peeler, stripper.
peladura, *f.* plucking, peeling, stripping.
pelafustán, *m.* (coll.) idler, ragamuffin.
pelagallos, *m.* = PELAGATOS.
pelagatos, *m.* ragamuffin; poor wretch.
pelagianismo, *m.* Pelagianism.
pelagiano, na, *a.* Pelagian.
pelágico, ca, *a.* pelagic, oceanic.
pelagra, *f.* (med.) pellagra.—**pelagroso, sa, a.** pertaining to or suffering from pellagra.
pelaire, *m.* wool-dresser.
pelairía, *f.* trade of a wool comber.
pelaje, *m.* character or nature of the hair or wool; character, disposition; garments, apparel.
pelambrar, *va.* (tanning) to flesh (as hides).
pelambre, *m.* (tanning) batch of hides put into lime pits; steeping liquid; hair scraped from skins; lack of hair.
pelambrera, *f.* quantity of hair in one place; shedding of hair; (tanning) lime pit.
pelambrero, *m.* (tanning) steeper.
pelamen, *m.* (coll.) = PELAMBRE.
pelamesa, *f.* scuffle; bushy hair.
pelantrín, *m.* petty farmer.
pelar. I. *va.* to cut or pull out the hair of; to pluck; to skin, peel, husk, hull, shell; to trick, cheat, rob; to break (in gambling); to uncover, show (as the teeth).—**pelárselas,** to be in great earnest, to put one's heart and soul into some-

thing; to act or feel with great vehemence.—
duro de p., exceedingly difficult, hard to crack,
a big order. **II.** *vr.* to lose the hair (as from
illness); to get one's hair cut; to peel off (as
paint).

pelarela, *f.* = PELADERA.

pelarruecas, *f.* woman who lives by spinning.

pelásgico, **ca**, *a.* Pelasgian, Pelasgic.

pelasgo, **ga**, *n.* & *a.* Pelasgian.

pelaza. **I.** *a.* chopped or beaten (straw). **II.** *f.*
quarrel, affray, scuffle.

pelazga, *f.* (coll.) quarrel, scuffle.

peldaño, *m.* step of a staircase.

pelde, *m.* (coll.) = APELDE, flight, escape.

peldefebre, *m.* camlet; camel's hair.

pelea, *f.* fight; scuffle, quarrel.—**p. de gallos**,
cockfight.

peleador, **ra**. **I.** *n.* fighter. **II.** *a.* quarrelsome.

pelear. **I.** *vn.* to fight; (of horses) to quarrel; to toil, struggle.
II. *vr.* to scuffle, to come to blows.

pelechar, *vn.* to get hair; (of horses) to change
the coat; (of birds) to fledge; (coll.) to improve
one's fortune; to recover health.

pelele, *m.* stuffed figure; nincompoop.

pelendengue, *m.* frivolous foppery.

peleón. **I.** *a.* quarrelsome. **II.** *m.* strong wine.

peleona, *f.* scuffle, quarrel, row.

pelete, *m.* (gambling games) punter; (coll.) poor
man.—**en p.**, nakedly.

peletería, *f.* furrier's shop; (Cuba) leather goods
or shop where they are sold.

peletero, **ra**, *n.* furrier; (Cuba) dealer in leather
goods.

pelgar, *m.* ragamuffin, blackguard.

peliagudo, **da**, *a.* downy, furry; (coll.) arduous,
difficult; skilful.

peliblanco, **ca**, *a.* having white hair.

peliblando, **da**, *a.* having fine soft hair.

pelícano, *m.* (ornith.) pelican.

pelicano, **na**, *a.* gray-haired; hoary.

pelicorto, **ta**, *a.* having short hair.

película, *f.* pellicle; film; (photog.) film; moving-
picture reel; moving picture.

pelicular, *a.* pellicular.

peliculero, **ra**, *n.* (mov. pict.) scenario writer.

peligrar, *vn.* to be in danger.

peligro, *m.* danger, peril.—**correr p.**, to be in
danger; to run a risk.

peligrosamente, *adv.* perilously, dangerously.

peligroso, **sa**, *a.* dangerous, perilous, risky.

pelilargo, **ga**, *a.* having long hair.

pelillo, *m. dim.* short hair or fiber; trifle, slight
trouble.—**echar pelillos a la mar**, to become
reconciled.—**no tener pelillos en la lengua**,
to speak one's mind openly.—**pararse**, or
reparar, **en pelillos**, to be scrupulous; to
hesitate; to split hairs.

peliloso, **sa**, *a.* (coll.) peevish, querulous.

pelinegro, **gra**, *a.* black-haired.

pelirrojo, **ja**, *a.* red-haired.

pelirrubio, **bia**, *a.* blond, light-haired.

pelitieso, **sa**, *a.* having straight and stiff hair.

pelito, *m. dim.* small hair or fibre.

pelitre, *m.* (bot.) pellitory of Spain.

pelitrique, *m.* fiddle-faddle, flummery.

pelma, *f.* = PELMAZO.

pelmacería, *f.* heaviness, slowness.

pelmazo, *m.* crushed or flattened mass; undigested food, or "lump," in the stomach; sluggard.

pelo, *m.* hair; fiber, fibre, filament; trifle; hair's
breadth; down (of birds or fruits); nap, pile (of
cloth); hairspring (in watches and firearms);
flaw (in gems and metals); grain (in wood); color
(of horses); coat (of animals); kiss (in billiards);
cross wire (of a transit, level, etc.); (vet.) split
in hoofs; (com.) raw silk.—**p. arriba**, against
the grain.—**p. de la dehesa**, rusticity, rustic or
plebeian antecedents.—**pelos y señales**, minute details.—**a medio p.**, or **a medios pelos**,

tipsy.—**a p.**, or **al p.**, along the grain; timely,
fittingly.—**de medio p.**, of little account;
would-be important.—**de p. en pecho**, brave,
daring.—**en p.**, bareback; unsaddled.—**hacerse el p.**, to have one's hair cut.—**no tener
p. de tonto**, to be bright, quick, clever.—**no
tener pelos en la lengua**, to be outspoken.—
tener pelos, to be tough, difficult, a hard nut to
crack.—**tomar el p. a**, to banter, make fun of,
"pull one's leg."—**venir a p.**, to be to the
point, fit the case to a tee.

pelón, **na**, *a.* hairless; bald; (coll.) dull, stupid;
poor.—**pelona**, **pelonía**, *f.* baldness.

pelonería, *f.* (coll.) poverty, want, indigence.

pelopio, *m.* (chem.) pelopium.

peloponense, *n.* & *a.*; **peloponesíaco**, **ca**, *a.*
Peloponnesian.

pelosilla, *f.* (bot.) mouse-ear, hawkweed.

peloso, **sa**, *a.* hairy.

¹**pelota**, *f.* ball, handball; ball game; (S. A.) punt
made of leather.—**p. de viento**, football.—**no
tocar p.**, (coll.) not to touch the root of the
difficulty.

²**pelota**, *f. aug.* of PELO.—**en p.**, entirely naked;
penniless.

pelotaris, *m.* professional ball player.

pelotazo, *m.* blow or stroke with a ball.

pelote, *m.* goat's hair; tuft of wool.

pelotear. **I.** *va.* to audit (accounts). **II.** *vn.* to
play ball; to throw, as a ball; to argue, dispute;
to quarrel.

pelotera, *f.* wrangle, quarrel, tumult, riot.

¹**pelotería**, *f.* heap of balls.

²**pelotería**, *f.* heap of goat's hair.

pelotero, *m.* ball maker.

pelotilla, *f. dim.* small ball; small ball of wax and
pieces of glass fastened to a scourge.

pelotón, *m. aug.* large ball; tuft of hair; (mil.)
platoon; crowd, gang.

pelta, *f.* pelta, light shield.

peltre, *m.* pewter, spelter.

peltrero, *m.* pewterer, pewter worker.

peluca, *f.* wig, toupee; severe reproof.

pelucón, *m. aug.* large bushy wig.

pelucona, *f.* (coll.) double doubloon ($16).

peludo, **da**. **I.** *a.* hairy, shaggy; (coll.) difficult,
tough. **II.** *m.* shaggy mat.

peluquería, *f.* hairdressing shop; barber shop.

peluquero, *m.* hairdresser, barber; wigmaker.

peluquilla, **ita**, *f. dim.* small wig.

peluquín, *m. dim.* topwig; bagwig.

pelusa, *f.* down; floss, fuzz, nap.

pelusilla, *f. dim.* of PELUSA; fuzz.

pelvi, *n.* & *a.* Pahlavi, Pehlevi, ancient Persian
language.

pelviano, **na**, *a.* (anat.) pelvic.

pelvímetro, *m.* pelvimeter.

pelvis, *f.* (anat.) pelvis, pelvic cavity.

pella, *f.* pellet; tender head of cauliflower, etc.;
lump of molten metal; cut lard; unpaid loan;
(min.) lump of amalgamated silver.

pellada, *f.* (mason.) lump or trowelful of mortar.

pelleja, *f.* skin, hide; (coll.) strumpet.

pellejería, *f.* place where skins are dressed and
sold.

pellejero, *m.* leather-dresser, pelt-monger.

pellejina, *f.* small skin.

pellejo, *m.* skin; rawhide, pelt; wine skin; peel,
rind; (fig.) one's life; (humor.) tippler, drunkard.—**estar**, or **hallarse**, **en el p. de otro**, to
be in another's shoes or place.—**jugarse el p.**
(Am.) to risk one's life.—**quitar el p. a**, to
flay; to speak ill of, gossip about; (fig.) to kill.
—**salvar el p.**, (coll.) to save one's skin, life.

pellejudo, **da**, *a.* with flabby or superfluous skin.

pellejuela, *f. dim.* small skin or rawhide.

pellejuelo, *m. dim.* small skin.

pellica, *f.* cover of fine furs; small dressed skin.

pellico, *m.* pelisse; shepherd's jacket.

pelliquero, **ra**, *n.* maker of fur coverlets.

pelliza, *f.* pelisse, fur cloak.
pellizcador, ra, *n.* & *a.* pincher(-ing).
pellizcamiento, *m.* pruning, clipping; pinching.
pellizcar. I. *va.* (*pret.* PELLIZQUÉ; *subj.* PELLIZQUE) to pinch; to nip; to prune, clip; to gripe; to pilfer. **II.** *vr.* to long for.
pellizco, *m.* pinch; pinching; nip; small bit.—**p. de monja**, small cookie.
pellizqué, pellizque, *v.* V. PELLIZCAR.
pello, *m.* fine fur jacket.—**pellón, pellote**, *m.* long pelisse; fur cloak or robe.
pelluzgón, *m.* lock or tuft of hair.
¹**pena**, *f.* penalty; punishment; pain (esp. mental); affliction, sorrow, grief; embarrassment, mortification, chagrin; labor, hardship, difficulty, toil; necklace.—**p. capital**, or **de muerte**, death, capital punishment.—**p. del tallón**, lex tallonis.—**a penas** = APENAS, hardly, scarcely.—**a duras penas**, with great difficulty, just barely.—**alma en p.**, soul in purgatory.—**estar con (mucha) p.**, to be (greatly) mortified, (very) sorry, (very much) vexed.—**merecer la p.**, to be worthwhile.—**tener la p. de**, to be sorry to; to have the misfortune to.—**valer la p.**, to be worthwhile.
²**pena**, *f.* (ornith.) penna, quill feather.
penable, *a.* punishable.
penachera, *f.* = PENACHO.
penacho, *m.* tuft of feathers, aigret; plumes, crest; haughtiness, arrogance, airs.—**penachudo, da**, *a.* crested, tufted, plumed.—**penachuelo**, *m. dim.* small tuft, crest or aigret.
penadamente, *adv.* = PENOSAMENTE.
penadilla, *f.* narrow-mouthed vessel.
penado, da. I. *pp.* of PENAR. **II.** *a.* sorrowful; painful; difficult, arduous. **III.** *n.* convict; narrow-mouthed vessel.
penal, *a.* penal.—**penalidad**, *f.* trouble, hardship; (law) penalty.
péname, *m.* condolence. Also PÉSAME.
penante. I. *pres. p.* of PENAR, suffering sorrow or punishment. **II.** *a.* difficult, arduous.
penar. I. *vn.* to suffer, to agonize; to be tormented in a future life; to crave, long. **II.** *va.* to chastise, inflict punishment or impose penalty on. **III.** *vr.* to grieve, to mourn.
penates, *m. pl.* penates, household gods.
penca, *f.* (bot.) pulpy leaf or joint of some plants; cowhide for flogging culprits.—**hacerse de pencas**, to allow oneself to be coaxed.
pencazo, *m.* lash with a cowhide.
penco, *m.* (coll.) = JAMELGO, sorry nag, jade.
pencudo, da, *a.* having pulpy leaves or joints.
pendejo, *m.* hair over the pubis and groin; (coll.) coward, poltroon; (Am., vulgar) fool.
pendencia, *f.* quarrel, fray, feud.
pendenciar, *vn.* to wrangle, quarrel.
pendenciero, ra, *a.* quarrelsome.
pendenzuela, *f. dim.* little dispute.
pender, *vn.* to hang, dangle; to be pending or suspended; to depend.
pendiente. I. *a.* pendent, hanging; clinging; dangling; pending. **II.** *m.* earring, pendant; watch chain. **III.** *f.* slope, declivity; grade, gradient; dip or pitch.
pendil, *m.* mantle worn by women.
pendol, *m.* (naut.) boot-topping.
¹**péndola**, *f.* feather; quill, pen.
²**péndola**, *f.* pendulum, balance; (eng.) queenpost; bridging brace.
pendolaje, *m.* plunder of a captured vessel.
pendolario, ria; **pendolista**, *n.* penman.
pendolita, *f.* watch; click wire.
pendolón, *m. aug.* large pendulum; (eng.) kingpost.
pendón, *m.* standard, banner, pennon, gonfalon; (bot.) tiller, shoot; (her.) pennon; (coll.) tall, awkward woman.—*pl.* reins of the leading mule.
pendoncito, *m. dim.* pennon, banneret.
péndulo, la. I. *a.* pendent, hanging, pendulous.
II. *m.* pendulum.—**p. de compensación**, compensation pendulum.—**p. de segundos**, seconds pendulum.—**p. eléctrico**, electric pendulum.—**p. sideral**, or **sidéreo**, (astr.) (standard) clock, chronometer.
pene, *m.* (anat.) penis.
peneque, *a.* (coll.) fuddled.
penetrabilidad, *f.* penetrability.
penetrable, *a.* penetrable; comprehensible.
penetración, *f.* penetration, penetrating; acuteness, sagacity, clearsightedness.
penetrador, ra, *n.* & *a.* discerner(-ing); searcher (-ing).
penetral, *m.* innermost recess.
penetrante, *a.* penetrating, piercing; heart-rending; clearsighted, keen; deep.
penetrar, *va.* to penetrate, pierce; to break or force in; to permeate, pervade; to fathom, comprehend.—**p. en**, to enter.
penetrativo, va, *a.* penetrative, piercing.
pénfigo, *m.* (med.) pemphigus.
penicilina, *f.* penicillin.
penígero, ra, *a.* (poet.) winged, feathered.
península, *f.* peninsula.
peninsular, *a.* inhabiting or pert. to a peninsula.
penique, *m.* (English) penny.
penitencia, *f.* penitence; penance.—**hacer p.**, to do penance; familiar invitation to take potluck.
penitenciado, da. I. *pp.* of PENITENCIAR. **II.** *a.* punished. **III.** *n.* convict.
penitencial, *a.* penitential.
penitenciar, *va.* to impose penance on.
penitenciaría, *f.* (eccl. & gen.) penitentiary.
penitenciario, ria, *a.* penitentiary.
penitente. I. *a.* penitent, repentant, contrite. **II.** *n.* penitent.
penol, peñol, *m.* (naut.) yardarm, peak.
penosamente, *adv.* painfully, grievously.
penoso, sa. I. *a.* painful; laborious, arduous; distressing; embarrassing, unpleasant. **II.** *m.* conceited fop.
pensado, da, *pp.* & *a.* deliberate, premeditated; thought out.—**bien p.**, wise, proper.—**de p.**, on purpose, deliberately.—**mal p.**, unwise, foolish.—**tener p.**, to have in view, to intend.
pensador, ra, *n.* & *a.* thinker(-ing).
pensamiento, *m.* mind; thought, idea; witty saying, epigram, maxim; suspicion, surmise; project, scheme, plan; (art) first sketch or outline; (bot.) pansy, heartsease.—**en un p.**, in a trice.—**ni por p.**, not even in thought.
pensar. I. *vn.* (*ind.* PIENSO; *subj.* PIENSE) to think.—**p. a** (foll. by *inf.*), to intend.—**p. de**, to think of, have an opinion about.—**p. en**, to think of, about, or over; (foll. by *inf.*), to think of, consider (foll. by *pres. p.*).—**p. en lo excusado**, to expect the impossible. **II.** *va.* to think over, or about, consider; to intend.
pensativo, va, *a.* pensive, thoughtful.
penseque, *m.* thoughtlessness.
pensil. I. *a.* hanging. **II.** *m.* beautiful garden.
pensilvano, na, *n.* & *a.* Pennsylvanian.
pensión, *f.* pension, annuity; boarding-house; price of board and tuition; toil, drudgery; (Am.) anxiety.—**p. vitalicia**, annuity, life pension.
pensionado, da, *n.* pensioner, pensionary.
pensionar, *va.* to impose or to grant annual charges or pensions on or to.
pensionario, *m.* one who pays a pension; pensionary, magistrate.
pensionista, *n.* pensioner; boarder.
pentadecágono, *m.* fifteen-sided polygon.
pentaedro, *m.* (geom.) pentahedron.
pentagonal, *a.* pentagonal.
pentágono, *m.* (geom.) pentagon.
pentagrama, *m.* (mus.) ruled staff.
pentámetro, *m.* pentameter.
pentano, *m.* (chem.) pentane.
pentápolis, *f.* pentapolis, group of five cities.
pentarquía, *f.* pentarchy, gov't of five persons.

pentasílabo, ba, *a.* of five syllables.
Pentateuco, *m.* Pentateuch.
pentecostés, *m.* Pentecost, Whitsuntide.
pentedecágono, *m.* = PENTADECÁGONO.
penúltimo, ma, *a.* penultimate.
penumbra, *f.* penumbra.
penuria, *f.* penury, indigence.
¹**peña,** *f.* rock; boulder.—**durar por peñas,** to last a long time.
²**peña,** *f.* group of friends; club.
peñascal, *m.* rocky hill or mountain.
peñasco, *m.* large rock; strong silk material.
peñascoso, sa, *a.* rocky.
¹**peñol,** *m.* large rock.
²**peñol,** *m.* (naut.) = PENOL, yardarm.
peñola, *f.* (poet.) (writing) pen.
peñon, *m.* large rock; rocky cliff.
¹**peón,** *m.* (poet.) foot of four syllables.
²**peón,** *m.* pedestrian; day laborer; (mason.) hodman; foot soldier; top, spinning top; pawn (in chess); man (in draughts); (mech.) spindle, axle.
peonada, *f.* day's work of a laborer; gang of laborers.
peonaje, *m.* gang of laborers.
peonería, *f.* land that can be plowed in one day.
¹**peonía,** *f.* land given to a soldier as spoils.
²**peonía,** *f.* (bot.) peony.
peonza, *f.* top (toy); noisy little fellow.—**bailar como una p.,** to dance well, be light on one's feet.
peor, *a.* & *adv. comp.* worse; worst.—**p. que p.,** worse and worse.—**tanto p.,** so much the worse.
peoría, *f.* deterioration, detriment.
pepa, *f.* (Am.) seed, stone, pit.
pepián, *m.* = PIPIÁN, an Indian fricassee.
pepinar, *m.* cucumber field.
pepinillos, *m. pl.* gherkins, pickled cucumbers.
pepino, *m.* (bot.) cucumber.—**no dársele un p.,** or **tres pepinos,** not to give a fig.
pepión, *m.* old Spanish gold coin.
¹**pepita,** *f.* pip or seed of fruits (as apples, etc.); (min.) nugget.
²**pepita,** *f.* (vet.) pip, distemper in fowls.
pepitoria, *f.* giblet fricassee; medley of things, (Mex.) peanut brittle.
¹**pepitoso, sa,** *a.* abounding in pips or seeds.
²**pepitoso, sa,** *a.* (fowl) having the pip.
peplo, *m.* peplum.
pepón, *m.* (bot.) watermelon.
pepona, *f.* large paper doll.
pepónide, *f.* (bot.) pepo (pumpkin, melon, etc.).
pepsina, *f.* pepsin.
péptico, ca, *a.* peptic.
peptona, *f.* peptone.
pequé, peque, *v. V.* PECAR.
pequeñamente, *adv.* in a small degree.
pequeñez, *f.* smallness; infancy, childhood; trifle; pettiness; mean act or conduct.
pequeñito, ta, *a. dim.* very little, tiny.
pequeño, ña. I. *a.* little, small; of tender age; lowly, humble. **II.** *n.* child.
pequeñuelo, la. I. *a. dim.* very little or young. **II.** *n.* babe, infant; child, little one.
pera, *f.* (bot.) pear; goatee, imperial; (coll.) sinecure.—**pedir peras al olmo,** to go on a wild-goose chase, to expect the impossible.—**poner las peras a cuarto,** or **a cuatro,** to compel one to do or concede what one does not wish to; to bring one to reason.
perada, *f.* preserve of pears; pear jam.
peral, *m.* pear tree; pear orchard.
peraleda, *f.* orchard of pear trees.
peralejo, *m.* (bot.) malpighia.
peraltar, *va.* (arch.) to stilt (an arch or vault); to raise, elevate.
peralte, *m.* (arch.) rise (of an arch); (Ry.) super-elevation (of outer rail on curves).

perantón, *m.* (bot.) marvel plant; large fan; very tall person.
perborato, *m.* (chem.) perborate.
perca, *f.* (ichth.) perch.
percal, *m.* percale, muslin, calico.
percalina, *f.* percaline, book muslin.
percance, *m.* perquisite; mischance, misfortune.
—**percances del oficio** = GAJES DEL OFICIO, (ironic) perquisites that go with a job.
percatar, *vn.* & *vr.* to think, consider; to beware.
percebe, *m.* goose barnacle.
percebimiento, *m.* prevention, warning.
percentaje, *m.* percentage.
percepción, *f.* perception.
perceptibilidad, *f.* perceptibility.
perceptible, *a.* perceptible, perceivable.
perceptiblemente, *adv.* perceptibly.
perceptivo, va, *a.* perceptive.
percibir, *va.* to perceive; to receive, collect.
percibo, *m.* receiving, collecting.
perclorato, *m.* (chem.) perchlorate.
perclórico, ca, *a.* (chem.) perchloric.
percloruro, *m.* (chem.) perchloride.
percocería, *f.* small silver work.
percuciente, *a.* percussive, striking.
percudir, *va.* to tarnish, stain, soil.
percusión, *f.* percussion; collision.
percusor, *m.* striker, percussor; (artil.) percussion hammer.
percutir, *va.* to percuss, strike, beat.
¹**percha,** *f.* perch, pole, staff; slat; hat or clothes rack; roost; snare for birds; strip for stringing game; (naut.) spar, rough tree; head rail.
²**percha,** *f.* (ichth.) = PERCA.
perchador, ra, *n.* carder (of cloth).
perchar, *va.* to card, raise the nap on (cloth).
percherón, na, *a.* & *n.* Percheron (horse).
perchón, *m.* long shoot left on a pruned vine.
perchonar, *vn.* to prune (vines) leaving long shoots; to lay snares for game.
perdedero, *m.* occasion or reason for losing.
perdedor, ra, *n.* loser.
perder. I. *va.* (*ind.* PIERDO; *subj.* PIERDA) to lose; to forfeit; to squander away; to ruin; to spoil; to miss (train, opportunity, etc.).—**p. de vista,** to lose sight of.—**p. el juicio,** or **el seso,** to go out of one's mind.—**p. la vista,** to lose one's sight, go blind.—**p. los estribos,** to lose one's poise; to become reckless.—**¡pierda Vd. cuidado!** don't worry! forget it!—**tener que p.,** to be a person of means, to have much to lose. **II.** *vn.* to lose; to fade, lose color. **III.** *vr.* to get lost, lose one's way; to miscarry; to be lost, confounded, bewildered; to forget or lose the thread of one's subject or discourse; to be ruined, go astray, go to the dogs; to be applied or damaged (as fruit, crops, etc.); to fall into disuse; to be out of fashion; to cease to be perceived by sight or hearing; to love excessively; to disappear.—**p. de vista,** to disappear; to excel in an eminent degree; to be very shrewd.
perdición, *f.* perdition; ruin, loss; unbridled, excessive love.
pérdida, *f.* loss; privation; detriment, damage; waste; (com.) leakage, shortage, shrinkage.—**pérdidas y ganancias,** profit and loss.—**ir a pérdidas y ganancias,** to share profit and loss.
perdidamente, *adv.* desperately; uselessly.
perdidizo, za, *a.* lost designedly or on purpose.—**hacerse el p.,** to sneak away, disappear.—**hacerse p.,** to lose designedly at cards.
perdido, da. I. *pp.* of PERDER. **II.** *a.* lost; mislaid; misguided; profligate, dissolute.—**p. por,** passionately fond of, crazy about. **III.** *m.* (fig.) black sheep.
perdidoso, sa, *a.* sustaining loss, losing.
perdigana, *f.* young partridge.
perdigar, *va.* (*pret.* PERDIGUÉ; *subj.* PERDIGUE)

(cook.) to broil (partridges) slightly; to brown (meat); to dispose, prepare.

¹**perdigón**, *m.* squanderer; losing gambler.

²**perdigón**, *m.* young partridge; decoy partridge; bird shot.—**perdigonada**, *f.* shot or wound with bird shot.—**perdigonera**, *f.* shot pouch.

perdigué, perdigue, *v. V.* PERDIGAR.

perdiguero, ra. I. *m.* setter, retriever (dog). **II.** *n.* poulterer, game dealer.

perdimiento, *m.* = PERDICIÓN, PÉRDIDA.

perdiz, *f.* (ornith.) partridge.

perdón, *m.* pardon, forgiveness; mercy, grace; reprieve; remission of a debt; (coll.) burning drop of oil, wax, etc.—¡p.!, pardon!, excuse me!—**con p.,** by your leave; begging pardon. —**no tener p. (de Dios),** to be absolutely unpardonable, beyond all forgiveness.

perdonable, *a.* pardonable, forgivable.

perdonador, ra, *n.* one who pardons, excuses.

perdonante, *a.* forgiving, pardoning.

perdonar, *va.* to pardon, forgive; to remit (a debt); to exempt; to spare, excuse.—**no p.,** not to overlook (another's mistake, etc.).

perdonavidas, *m.* (coll.) bully, hector.

perdulario, ria, *a.* reckless, careless.

perdurable, *a.* lasting, abiding, everlasting.

perdurablemente, *adv.* everlastingly, lastingly.

perdurar, *vn.* to last long.

perecear. I. *va.* to protract, delay, put off. **II.** *vn.* to indulge one's laziness, to idle.

perecedero, ra. I. *a.* perishable, not lasting. **II.** *m.* extreme want.

perecer. I. *vn.* (*ind.* PEREZCO; *subj.* PEREZCA) to perish; to come to an end; to suffer or undergo damage, toil, or fatigue. **II.** *vr.* to crave, desire anxiously, pine.

pereciente, *a.* perishing; pining.

perecimiento, *m.* loss, decline; shipwreck.

pereda, *f.* orchard of pear trees.

peregrinación, *f.,* **peregrinaje,** *m.* peregrination; pilgrimage; course of this life.

peregrinamente, *adv.* rarely; curiously.

peregrinante, *a.* traveling; roaming.

peregrinar, *vn.* to travel, roam.

peregrinidad, *f.* rareness, rarity.

peregrino, na. I. *a.* peregrine, foreign; traveling, migratory; strange, odd, rare; handsome, perfect. **II.** *n.* pilgrim, palmer.

perejil, *m.* (bot.) parsley; (coll.) showy dress or apparel.—*pl.* (coll.) "handle" (titles).

perejila, *f.* a card game.

Perencejo, ja, *n.* = PERENGANO.

perendeca, *f.* (coll.) prostitute.

perendengue, *m.* earring, eardrop; cheap or tawdry ornament.

Perengano, na, *n.* = MENGANO, So-and-So.

perennal, *a.* = PERENNE.

perennalmente, *adv.* = PERENNEMENTE.

perenne, *a.* perennial, perpetual.

perennemente, *adv.* continually, perpetually.

perennidad, *f.* perennity, continuity.

perentoriamente, *adv.* peremptorily; urgently.

perentoriedad, *f.* peremptoriness; urgency.

perentorio, ria, *a.* peremptory; urgent; decisive.

perero, *m.* fruit parer.

pereza, *f.* laziness, sloth; slowness.

perezco, perezca, *v. V.* PERECER.

perezosamente, *adv.* lazily, slothfully, idly.

perezoso, sa. 1. *a.* lazy, indolent, slothful, idle. **II.** *m.* (zool.) sloth.

perfección, *f.* perfection; perfect thing; beauty, grace.—**a la p.,** perfectly.

perfeccionamiento, *m.* perfecting, improvement, finish.

perfeccionar, *va.* to improve, perfect.

perfectamente, *adv.* perfectly.

perfectible, *a.* perfectible.

perfectivo, va, *a.* perfective.

perfecto, ta, *a.* perfect; (gram.) perfect (tense).

perficiente, *a.* perfecting.

pérfidamente, *adv.* perfidiously.

perfidia, *f.* perfidy.

pérfido, da, *a.* perfidious, treacherous.

perfil, *m.* profile, side view; outline; upstroke of letters.

perfilado, da. I. *pp.* of PERFILAR. **II.** *a.* elongated; outlined. **III.** *m.* (eng.) structural shape.

perfiladura, *f.* profile drawing; outline sketching.

perfilar. I. *va.* to outline; to make fine upstrokes. **II.** *vr.* to place oneself sideways; to make an elaborate toilet.

perfoliada, *f.* (bot.) hare's-ear.

perfoliado, da, *a.* (bot.) perfoliate.

perfoliata, *f.* = PERFOLIADA.

perfolla, *f.* corn husk; shucks.

perforación, *f.* perforation, hole; drilling, boring.

perforador, ra. I. *a.* & *n.* perforator(-ing), driller(-ing). **II.** *f.* drill, rock drill.

perforar, *va.* to perforate; to bore, drill.

perfumadero, *m.* perfuming pan.

perfumado, da. I. *pp.* of PERFUMAR. **II.** *a.* odoriferous.

perfumador, ra. I. *a.* perfuming. **II.** *m.* perfumer, perfuming pan.

perfumar, *va.* to perfume.

perfume, *m.* perfume; odor, fragrance.

perfumear, *va.* to perfume.

perfumería, *f.* perfumery; perfumer's shop.

perfumero, ra; perfumista, *n.* perfumer.

perfunctoriamente, *adv.* perfunctorily.

perfunctorio, ria, *a.* perfunctory.

pergal, *m.* leather paring for shoe laces.

pergaminero, *m.* parchment maker.

pergamino, *m.* parchment, vellum; diploma.

pergenio, *m.* (coll.) appearance, looks.

pergeñar, *va.* (coll.) to prepare or perform skilfully.

pergeño, *m.* (coll.) appearance, looks.

peri, *f.* fairy, elf, peri.

periantio, *m.* (bot.) perianth.

pericardio, *m.* (anat.) pericardium.

pericarditis, *f.* (med.) pericarditis.

pericarpio, *m.* (bot.) pericarp.

pericia, *f.* skill, expertness.—**pericial,** *a.* expert.

pericialmente, *adv.* expertly.

perico, *m.* (ornith.) parrakeet; periwig; queen of clubs in the game of TRUQUE; (naut.) mizzen topgallant sail.—**p. de los palotes,** John Doe, a fictitious or undetermined person.—**p. ligero,** (zool.) sloth.

pericón, na. I. *a.* fit for all uses. **II.** *m.* large fan; queen of clubs in the game of QUÍNOLAS.

pericráneo, *m.* (anat.) pericranium.

peridoto, *m.* (min.) chrysolite.

periecos, *m. pl.* (geog.) perioeci.

periferia, *f.* periphery.

periférico, ca, *a.* peripheric, circumferential.

perifollo, *m.* (bot.) common chervil.—*pl.* ribbons, tawdry ornaments of dress.

perifonear, *va.* (radio) to broadcast.

perifonía, *f.* (radio) broadcasting.

perífono, *m.* (radio) broadcasting instrument.

perifrasear, *va.* to periphrase.

perífrasi, perífrasis, *f.* (rhet.) periphrasis.

perifrástico, ca, *a.* periphrastic.

perigallo, *m.* skin hanging from the chin of thin, old persons; gawdy ribbon worn on the hair; (coll.) tall, lean person; slender sling; (naut.) line, topping lift.

perigeo, *m.* (astr.) perigee, perigeum.

perigonio, *m.* (bot.) perigynium, perianth.

perígono, *m.* (geom.) perigon.

perihelio, *m.* (astr.) perihelion.

perilustre, *a.* very illustrious.

perilla, *f. dim.* small pear; pear-shaped ornament; pommel of a saddlebow; goatee; lobe of the ear. —**de p.,** to the purpose; in the nick of time.

perillán, na, *n.* rascal; sly, crafty person.

perillo, *m.* scalloped cookie or maccaroon.

perímetro, *m.* perimeter.

For pronunciation, see the rules at the beginning of the book.

perínclito, ta, *a.* famous, renowned.
perineo, *m.* (anat.) perineum.
perineumonía, *f.* (med.) pneumonia.
perineumónico, ca, *a.* pneumonic.
perinola, *f.* teetotum, small top spun in gambling; pear-shaped ornament; neat little woman.
períoca, *f.* synopsis, summary.
periódicamente, *adv.* periodically.
periodicidad, *f.* periodicity, periodic character.
periódico, ca. I. *a.* periodical, periodic. **II.** *m.* newspaper; periodical, journal.
periodismo, *m.* journalism.
periodista, *m. & f.* journalist.
periodístico, ca, *a.* journalistic.
período, *m.* period, age, era; (rhet.) period, clause, sentence; menstruation; (mus.) period, phrase; (elec.) cycle.
periostio, *m.* (anat.) periosteum.
periostitis, *f.* (med.) periostitis.
peripatético, ca, *a. & n.* Peripatetic; *a.* (coll.) ridiculous or extravagant (opinion).
peripato, *m.* Peripateticism.
peripecia, *f.* situation, incident, episode.
periplo, *m.* voyage around a coast.
períptero, ra, *a.* (arch.) peripteral.
peripuesto, ta, *a.* (coll.) very spruce in dress.
periquete, *m.* (coll.) jiffy, instant.
periquillo, *m.* sugar plum.
periquito, *m.* (ornith.) parrakeet, paroquet.
periscios, *m. pl.* (geog.) periscii.
periscópico, ca, *a.* periscopic.
periscopio, *m.* periscope.
perisología, *f.* (rhet.) verbiage.
peristáltico, ca, *a.* (physiol.) peristaltic.
peristilo, *m.* (arch.) peristyle, colonnade.
perita, *f. dim.* small pear.
peritaje, *m.* occupation of an expert.
peritiflitis, *f.* (med.) perityphlitis.
perito, ta. I. *a.* skilful, able, experienced. **II.** *n.* connoisseur, expert; appraiser.
peritoneal, *a.* (anat.) peritoneal.
peritoneo, *m.* (anat.) peritoneum.—**peritonitis,** *f.* (med.) peritonitis.
perjudicador, ra, *n. & a.* injurer(-ing).
perjudicante, *a.* damaging, injurious.
perjudicar, *va.* (*pret.* PERJUDIQUÉ; *subj.* PERJUDIQUE) to damage, hurt, injure, impair.
perjudicial, *a.* harmful, injurious.
perjudicialmente, *adv.* harmfully, injuriously.
perjudiqué, perjudique, *v.* V. PERJUDICAR.
perjuicio, *m.* prejudice; injury, damage.
perjurador, ra, *n.* perjurer, forswearer.
perjurar. I. *vn.* to commit perjury; to swear, be profane. **II.** *vr.* to perjure oneself.
perjurio, *m.* perjury.
perjuro, ra. I. *a.* perjured, forsworn. **II.** *n.* forswearer, perjurer.
perla, *f.* pearl; (fig.) jewel; (print.) pearl.—*pl.* fine teeth.—**de perlas,** perfectly; to a tee.
perlada, *a.* pearled (barley).
perlático, ca, *a.* paralyzed, palsied.
perlería, *f.* collection of pearls.
perlesía, *f.* (med.) paralysis, palsy.
perlezuela, *f. dim.* small pearl.
perlino, na, *a.* pearl-colored.
perlita, *f. dim.* small pearl; phonolite, clinkstone.
perlongar, *vn.* (*pret.* PERLONGUÉ; *subj.* PERLONGUE) (naut.) to coast; to pay out a cable.
permanecer, *vn.* (*ind.* PERMANEZCO; *subj.* PERMANEZCA) to stay, remain, endure, last.
permaneciente, *a.* permanent.
permanencia, *f.* stay, sojourn; duration, permanence; perseverance, constancy.
permanente. I. *a.* permanent. **II.** *f.* permanent (wave, in hair).—**permanentemente,** *adv.* permanently.
permanezca, permanezco, *v.* V. PERMANECER.
permanganato, *m.* (chem.) permanganate.
permeabilidad, *f.* permeability.
permeable, *a.* permeable, non-waterproof.

permisible, *a.* permissible.
permisión, *f.* permission, leave, permit; concession, grant.
permisivamente, *adv.* permissively.
permisivo, va, *a.* permissive.
permiso, *m.* permission, permit, leave, license; difference in weight of coin.—**¡con p.!,** excuse me!
permisor, ra, *n.* granter, permitter.
permistión, *f.* mixture, concoction.
permitente, *a.* permitting, allowing.
permitidero, ra, *a.* permissible.
permitidor, ra, *n.* permitter, granter.
permitir, *va.* to permit, allow; to grant, admit.
permuta, *f.* barter; exchange.
permutable, *a.* exchangeable.
permutación, *f.* interchange; (math.) permutation.
permutar, *va. & vn.* to exchange, interchange, barter; to permute.
perna, *f.* flat shellfish.
pernada, *f.* blow with the leg; shake of the leg; (naut.) leg.
pernaza, *f. aug.* thick or big leg.
perneador, ra, *a.* strong-legged.
pernear. I. *vn.* to kick, shake the legs; to hustle; to worry, fret. **II.** *va.* to drive (pigs) to market and sell by retail.
perneo, *m.* public sale of hogs.
pernera, *f.* leg of a pair of trousers.
pernería, *f.* (naut.) collection of bolts.
pernetas.—en p., bare-legged.
pernete, *m.* (naut.) small pin, peg, or bolt.
perniabierto, ta, *a.* bowlegged.
perniciosamente, *adv.* perniciously.
pernicioso, sa, *a.* pernicious; injurious, harmful.
pernigón, *m.* Genoese preserved plum.
pernil, *m.* hock, ham (of animals); trouser leg.
pernio, *m.* door or window hinge.
perniquebrar, *va.* (*ind.* PERNIQUIEBRO; *subj.* PERNIQUIEBRE) to break the legs of.
pernituerto, ta, *a.* twisted-, crooked-legged.
perno, *m.* bolt; pin, spike; hook of a door-hinge; (mech.) joint pin, crank pin.—**p. pinzote,** main bolt, kingbolt.
pernoctar, *vn.* to pass the night.
¹pero, *m.* a variety of apple; apple tree.
²pero. I. *conj.* but; except; yet; (used for emphasis at beginning of sentence, not translated). **II.** *m.* (coll.) fault, defect.—**poner pero(s),** to find fault.
perogrullada, *f.* (coll.) obvious truth, truism; platitude.
Perogrullo.—verdad de P. = PEROGRULLADA.
perojiménez, *m.* a variety of grape; wine made from it.
perol, *m.* (cooking) kettle, copper.
peroné, *m.* (anat.) fibula, perone.
peroración, *f.* peroration.
perorar, *vn.* to deliver a speech or oration; to declaim; to urge.
perorata, *f.* (coll.) harangue, speech.
peróxido, *m.* (chem.) peroxide.
perpendicular, *n. & a.* perpendicular.
perpendicularidad, *f.* perpendicularity.
perpendicularmente, *adv.* perpendicularly.
perpendículo, *m.* plumb, plummet; altitude of a triangle; pendulum.
perpetración, *f.* perpetration.
perpetrador, ra, *n.* perpetrator, aggressor.
perpetrar, *va.* to perpetrate, commit.
perpetua, *f.* (bot.) immortelle, cudweed.
perpetuación, *f.* perpetuation.
perpetuamente, *adv.* perpetually.
perpetuán, *m.* a kind of thick, woollen stuff.
perpetuar, *va. & vr.* to perpetuate.
perpetuidad, *f.* perpetuity.
perpetuo, tua, *a.* perpetual, everlasting.—**p. silencio** (law) forever hold his peace.
perpiaño, *m.* (arch.) perpend.

perplejamente, *adv.* perplexedly, confusedly.
perplejidad, *f.* perplexity, irresolution, embarrassment, hesitation.
perplejo, ja, *a.* uncertain, perplexed.
perpunte, *m.* quilted under-waistcoat.
perquirir, *va.* to seek diligently.
perra, *f.* bitch, female dog; slut; drunken state. —p. **chica** = PERRO CHICO.
perrada, *f.* pack of dogs; mean, base action.
perramente, *adv.* very badly, wretchedly.
perrazo, *m. aug.* large dog.
perrengue, *m.* (coll.) peevish person, snarler; (coll.) Negro.
perrera, *f.* kennel; toil, drudgery; (coll.) bad pay; child's fit of temper.
perrería, *f.* pack of dogs; set or den of rogues; angry word.
perrero, *m.* beadle who drags dogs out of the church; master of hounds or dogs; dog fancier.
perrezno, na, *n.* whelp, puppy.
perrillo, lla; to, ta. I. *n.* little dog; puppy.—p. **de falda,** or **faldero,** lap dog. **II.** *m.* trigger of a gun; piece of horse's bridle.
perro, rra, *n.* dog.—p. **alforjero,** camp watchdog.—p. **braco,** pointer dog.—p. **cobrador,** retriever.—p. **chico,** five-centime copper coin. —p. **de aguas,** poodle.—p. **de ajeo,** setter.— p. **de lanas** = P. DE AGUAS.—p. **de muestra,** pointer.—p. **de presa,** bulldog.—p. **de Terranova,** Newfoundland dog.—p. **dogo,** bulldog.—p. **galgo,** hound.—p. **tomador,** retriever.—p. **viejo,** cautious person; experienced person.
perroquete, *m.* (naut.) topmast.
perruno, na. I. *a.* doggish, canine; currish. **II.** *f.* dog bread, dog biscuit.
persa, *a. & n.* Persian.
persecución, *f.* persecution; pursuit; harassment; importunity.
persecutorio, ria, *a.* persecuting.
perseguidor, ra, *n.* persecutor; pursuer.
perseguimiento, *m.* = PERSECUCIÓN.
perseguir, *va.* (*ger.* PERSIGUIENDO; *ind. pres.* PERSIGO, *pret.* él PERSIGUIÓ; *subj.* PERSIGA) to pursue; to persecute; to importune, beset.
Perseo, *m.* (astr.) Perseus.
persevante, *m.* pursuivant at arms.
perseverancia, *f.* perseverance.
perseverante, *a.* perseverant, persevering.
perseverantemente, *adv.* perseveringly.
perseverar, *vn.* to persevere, persist.
persiana, *f.* flowered silk stuff; Venetian blind.
persicaria, *f.* (bot.) persicaria, lady's-thumb.
pérsico, ca. I. *a.* Persian. **II.** *m.* (bot.) peach tree and its fruit.
persignarse, *vr.* to cross oneself; to handsel.
pérsigo, *m.* (bot.) peach tree and its fruit.
persigo, persiga, persiguió, *v. V.* PERSEGUIR.
persistencia, *f.* persistence; obstinacy.
persistente, *a.* persistent; permanent, firm.— **reacción p.,** sustained reaction.
persistir *vn.* to persist, persevere.
persona, *f.* person; one's shape and looks; personage; (theol., law, and gram.) person.—en p., in person, personally.
personada, *a.* (bot.) personate.
personado, *m.* (eccl.) benefice without jurisdiction.
personaje, *m.* personage; (theat.) character.
personal. I. *a.* personal, private. **II.** *m.* personnel, staff; personal tax.
personalidad, *f.* personality; individuality; (law) person; legal capacity.
personalizar. I. *va.* to personalize; to become personal. **II.** *vr.* (law) to show oneself a party at law.
personalmente, *adv.* personally, in person.
personarse, *vr.* to meet on business; to appear personally; (law) to appear as an interested party.

personería, *f.* solicitorship.
personero, ra, *n.* solicitor, deputy, agent, attorney, counsel.
personificación, *f.* personification.
personificar, *va.* (*pret.* PERSONIFIQUÉ; *subj.* PERSONIFIQUE) to personify.
personilla, *f.* ridiculous little person.
perspectiva, *f.* perspective; view, vista; prospect, outlook; appearance.
perspectivo, *m.* one versed in perspective.
perspicacia, perspicacidad, *f.* perspicaciousness, perspicacity, acumen, sagacity.
perspicaz, *a.* acute, sagacious, clear-sighted.
perspicuamente, *adv.* perspicuously.
perspicuidad, *f.* perspicuity, lucidity.
perspicuo, cua, *a.* perspicuous, clear.
persuadidor, ra, *n.* persuader.
persuadir. I. *va.* to persuade, induce; to convince. **II.** *vr.* to be persuaded; to be convinced.
persuasible, *a.* persuasible, persuadable.
persuasión, *f.* persuasion; conviction, opinion.
persuasiva, *f.* persuasiveness.
persuasivo, va, *a.* persuasive, convincing.
persuasor, ra, *n.* persuader, inducer.
pertenecer, *vn.* (*ind.* PERTENEZCO; *subj.* PERTENEZCA) to belong, appertain; to concern; to behoove.
pertenecido, *m.* = PERTENENCIA.
perteneciente, *a.* belonging, appertaining.
pertenencia, *f.* ownership; tenure, holding, property, possession; appurtenance, dependence, accessory; (min.) claim.
pertenezco, pertenezca, *v. V.* PERTENECER.
pértica, *f.* perch, linear measure (9.70 feet).
pértiga, *f.,* **pertigal,** *m.* bar, staff, pole, rod.
pértigo, *m.* carriage; plow beam.
pertiguería, *f.* office of a verger.
pertiguero, *m.* verger.
pertinacia, *f.* insistence, obstinacy, stubbornness, doggedness.
pertinaz, *a.* pertinacious, obstinate, opinionated.
pertinazmente, *adv.* pertinaciously.
pertinencia, *f.* pertinence, fitness, relevancy.
pertinente, *a.* pertinent, apt, appropriate, relevant; (law) concerning, pertaining.
pertinentemente, *adv.* pertinently, opportunely, congruously.
pertrechar, *va. & vr.* (mil.) to supply, store, equip; to dispose, arrange, prepare.
pertrechos, *m. pl.* (mil.) stores; tools.
perturbable, *a.* easily perturbed.
perturbación, *f.* perturbation, disturbance; agitation, excitement.
perturbadamente, *adv.* confusedly.
perturbador, ra, *n. & a.* perturber(-ing), disturber(-ing).
perturbar, *va.* to perturb, disturb, unsettle; to confuse, agitate.
peruano, na, *n. & a.* Peruvian.
peruétano, *m.* (bot.) wild pear tree.
¹**perulero, ra.** *n. & a.* Peruvian.
²**perulero,** *m.* narrow-bottomed, bulging, narrow-necked pitcher.
perversamente, *adv.* perversely, wickedly.
perversidad, *f.* perversity, wickedness.
perversión, *f.* perversion, perverting; perverseness, depravation, wickedness.
perverso, sa, *a.* perverse, wicked, depraved.
pervertidor, ra, *n.* perverter, corrupter.
pervertimiento, *m.* perversion, perverting.
pervertir. I. *va.* (*ger.* PERVIRTIENDO; *ind. pres.* PERVIERTO, *pret.* él PERVIRTIÓ; *subj.* PERVIERTA) to pervert, distort, garble; to corrupt, debase. **II.** *vr.* to become depraved.
pervigilio, *m.* sleeplessness, wakefulness.
pervulgar, *va.* to divulge; to promulgate.
pesa, *f.* weight (the thing); clock weight; counterweight.—p. **de una romana,** weight of a steelyard.—**pesas y medidas,** weights and measures.

pesacartas, *f*. letter-scales.
pesada, *f*. weighing; quantity weighed at once.
pesadamente, *adv*. heavily; cumbrously; sorrowfully, grievingly; slowly, lazily.
pesadez, *f*. heaviness; slowness; drowsiness; importunity; excess, abundance; trouble, pain, fatigue; obesity, corpulence.
pesadilla, *f*. nightmare.
pesado, da. I. *pp*. of PESAR. II. *a*. heavy; massive; deep, sound (sleep); heavy, sultry, stuffy (air, atmosphere); cumbersome; tedious, tiresome; dull; offensive; slow, lazy; clumsy; fat or corpulent; insufferable, importunate, annoying, vexatious.—**p. de cabeza**, (aer.) nose heavy.—**p. de cola**, (aer.) tail heavy.—**p. de proa**, (aer.) nose heavy. III. *n*. bore, tease.
pesador, ra, *n*. weigher.
pesadumbre, *f*. grief, affliction, sorrow; heaviness.
pesalicores, *m*. hydrometer.
pésame, *m*. condolence. Also PÉNAME.
pesante. I. *a*. weighing. II. *m*. weight of half a drachm.
pesantez, *f*. (phys.) gravity; heaviness.
pesar. I. *vn*. to weigh, have weight; to be weighty, important, or valuable; to cause regret, sorrow or repentance (diff. constr.: *me pesa rehusar*, I regret to refuse; often foll. by **de**: *me pesa de haber ofendido a Vd.*, I am sorry to have offended you); to preponderate.—**mal que le pese**, however much it may displease you; whether you like it or not.—**pese a quien pese**, whatever anybody says or does, let them say what they will. II. *va*. to weigh; to examine, consider, think or ponder over. III. *m*. sorrow, grief, regret; repentance.—**a p. de**, in spite of, notwithstanding.—**a. p. mío, or a mi p.**, in spite of me, against my wishes.
pesario, *m*. (surg.) pessary.
pesaroso, sa, *a*. sorrowful, regretful; sorry, sad.
pesca, *f*. fishing; fishery; catch, fish caught.
pescada, *f*. (ichth.) hake.
pescadería, *f*. fish market.
pescadero, ra, *n*. fishmonger.
pescadilla, *f*. small hake.
pescado, *m*. fish (caught); salted codfish.
pescador, ra, *n*. fisherman(-woman).
pescante, *m*. jib of a crane or derrick; boom; coach box; (naut.) davit; fish davit.
pescar. I. *va. & vn*. (*pret*. PESQUÉ; *subj*. PESQUE) to fish; to catch fish. II. *va*. to find or pick up; to catch in the act, surprise; to obtain, get.
péscola, *f*. beginning of a furrow.
pescozada, *f*.; **pescozón**, *m*. slap on the neck.
pescozudo, da, *a*. having a thick neck.
pescuezo, *m*. neck; throat; stiff-necked haughtiness, airs.—**cortar el p.**, to cut the throat; to cut off the head.
pescuño, *m*. wedge of the coulter.
pesebre, *m*. crib, rack; manger.—**pesebrejo**, *m*. *dim*. small manger; alveolus of horses' teeth.
pesebrera, *f*. stable; range of mangers in a stable.
pesebrón, *m*. boot of a coach.
peseta, *f*. peseta, monetary unit of Spain.
pésete, *m*. imprecation; execration.
¡pesia! ¡pesia tal! *interj*. confound it! blazes!
pesiar, *vn*. to utter curses or execrations.
pesillo, *m*. small scales for weighing gold or silver coin.
pésimamente, *adv*. very badly, wretchedly.
pesimismo, *m*. pessimism.
pesimista, *n. & a*. pessimist(-ic).
pésimo, ma, *a. super*. very bad, very worst.
pesita, *f*. *dim*. small weight.
peso, *m*. weight, heaviness; weighing; balance, scales; importance, moment; burden, load; place where various victuals are sold at wholesale; judgment, good sense; peso, monetary unit of some S. A. countries.—**p. bruto**, gross weight.—**p. duro, or fuerte**, (Spain) duro (5

pesetas); (Am.) one-ounce peso (theoretically, about 1 dollar).—**p. específico**, specific gravity.—**p. muerto**, (aer.) dead load, permanent load, weight of plane with all its equipment.—**p. neto**, net weight.—**p. seco**, (aer.) dry weight.
—**caerse de su p.**, to be self-evident; to go without saying.—**de p.**, of due weight; weighty, of weight, of importance; cogent.—**de su p.**, naturally.—**en p.**, suspended in the air; bodily; totally; undecided.
pésol, *m*. (bot.) pea.
pespuntador, ra, *n*. (sewing) backstitcher.
pespuntar, *va. & vn*. (sewing) to backstitch.
pespunte, *m*. (sewing) backstitching.
pesqué, pesque, *v. V.* PESCAR.
pesquera, *f*. fishery, fishing grounds.
pesquería, *f*. fish business; fishing; fishery.
pesquis, *m*. acumen, cleverness.
pesquisa, *f*. inquiry, investigation, search.
pesquisante, *a*. investigating, inquiring.
pesquisar, *va*. to inquire into, investigate.
pesquisidor, ra, *n*. searcher, investigator.
pestaña, *f*. eyelash; (sewing) fag-end, fringe, edging; (mech.) flange; (bot.) hairs.
pestañear, *vn*. to wink, to blink.
pestañeo, *m*. winking, blinking.
peste, *f*. pest, plague, pestilence; epidemic; corruption of manners; foul smell; (coll.) excess, superabundance.—*pl*. offensive words.—**p. bubónica**, bubonic plague.
pestíferamente, *adv*. pestiferously.
pestífero, ra, *a*. pestiferous, noxious, foul.
pestilencia, *f*. pest, plague, pestilence; foulness, stench.—**pestilencial**, *a*. pestiferous, pestilential; infectious, contagious; destructive.
pestilencioso, sa, *a*. pestilential.
pestilente, *a*. pestilent, noxious, foul.
pestillo, *m*. door latch; bolt of a lock.—**correr el p.**, to slide the bolt, bolt the door.
pestiño, *m*. honeyed fritters.
pestorejazo, *m*. = PESCOZÓN, slap on the neck.
pestorejo, *m*. fleshy back of the neck.
pestorejón, *m*. blow on the back of the neck.
pesuña, *f*. foot of cloven-hoofed animals.
pesuño, *m*. each half of a cloven hoof.
petaca, *f*. cigar case; (Am.) leather trunk or chest; (Am.) suitcase; covered hamper.
petalismo, *m*. (anc. hist.) petalism, banishment.
pétalo, *m*. (bot.) petal.
petaquilla, *f*. (Am.) small, leather trunk.
petar, *va*. (coll.) to please, gratify, content.
petardear, *va*. (mil.) to beat down with petards; to cheat, gull, trick.
petardero, *m*. (mil.) petardeer; cheat, trickster.
petardista, *n*. cheat, impostor, swindler.
petardo, *m*. (artil.) petard; bomb; cheat, fraud, gull, trick.
petate, *m*. (Am.) sleeping mat; (coll.) luggage, baggage; impostor, swindler; good-for-nothing fellow; (naut.) sailor's hammock.—**liar el p.**, (coll.) to pack up and go.
petenera, *f*. a popular Andalusian song.
petequia, *f*. (med.) petechia.
petera, *f*. (coll.) wrangle; fit of temper.
peteretes, *m. pl*. (coll.) tidbits, sweets.
peticano, peticanón, *m*. (print.) petit-canon type.
petición, *f*. petition, demand, claim, request; (law) petition, prayer.
peticionario, ria, *n*. petitioner.
petillo, *m*. *dim*. small stomacher; breast jewel.
petimetra, *f*. spruce, stylish lady.
petimetre, *m*. fop, coxcomb, beau, dude.
petirrojo, *m*. (ornith.) robin redbreast.
petitorio, ria. I. *a*. petitionary. II. *m*. impertinent, repeated petition. III. *f*. (coll.) PETICIÓN.
peto, *m*. breastplate; (fencing) plastron.
petral, *m*. breast leather (of saddle).
petraria, *f*. (mil.) petrary.
petrarquesco, ca, *a*. Petrarchan.

petrarquista, *n.* & *a.* Petrarchist(-ic).
petrel, *m.* (ornith.) petrel.
pétreo, a, *a.* rocky; stony, of stone.
petrificación, *f.* petrification.
petrificante, *a.* petrifying.
petrificar, *va.* & *vr.* to petrify.
petrífico, ca, *a.* petrifying.
petrografía, *f.* petrography.
petrográfico, ca, *a.* petrographic.
petróleo, *m.* petroleum, mineral oil.
petrolero, ra. I. *a.* petroleum, oil (as *a.*). **II.** *n.* seller of petroleum; person in the petroleum industry; incendiary; ultraradical.
petrolífero, ra, *a.* oil-bearing.
petrosílex, *m.,* **petrosílice,** *f.* petrosilex, felsite.
petroso, sa, *a.* rocky, full of stones.
petulancia, *f.* petulance; insolence; flippancy.
petulante, *a.* petulant, insolent, pert.—**petulantemente,** *adv.* petulantly, pertly.
petunia, *f.* (bot.) petunia.
peucédano, *m.* (bot.) Peucedanum.
¹pez. I. *m.* fish (in the water, not caught); catch, haul.—**p. espada,** swordfish.—**p. luna,** mola, sunfish.—**p. martillo,** hammer-headed shark. —**p. sierra,** sawfish.—**p. volador,** flying fish.
²pez, *f.* pitch, tar.—**p. blanca,** or **de Borgoña,** refined galipot, Burgundy pitch.—**p. griega,** or **rubia,** rosin, colophony.
pezolada, *f.* fag-end threads.
pezón, *m.* (bot.) stem of fruits; leaf stalk; flower stalk; nipple of a teat; axle end or pivot; end of a spindle in mills; cape or point of land.
pezonera, *f.* nipple shield; linchpin.
pezpalo, *m.* (com.) stockfish.
pezpita, *f.,* **pezpítalo,** *m.* (ornith.) wagtail.
pezuelo, *m.* beginning of cloth in weaving.
pezuña, *f.* = PESUÑA.
piache, or **tarde piache,** too late.
píada, *f.* chirping, puling.
píador, ra, *n.* puler, chirper.
piadosamente, *adv.* piously; mercifully.
piadoso, sa, *a.* pious, godly; merciful.
piafar, *vn.* (of horses) to paw, to stamp.
piale, *m.* (Am.) throw of the lasso.
piamadre, piamáter, *f.* (anat.) pia mater.
piamente, *adv.* piously.
piamontés, sa, *n.* & *a.* Piedmontese.
pian, *m.* (med.) yaws.
pían, pían; or **pían, piano,** *adv.* slowly, softly.
pianino, *m.* (mus.) upright piano.
pianista, *n.* pianist; piano maker or dealer.
piano, pianoforte, *m.* piano, pianoforte.—**p. de cola,** grand piano.—**p. de media cola,** baby grand.—**p. de mesa,** square piano.—**p. vertical,** upright piano.
pianola, *f.* pianola.
piante, *a.* peeping, puling, chirping.
piar, *vn.* to peep, pule, chirp; (coll.) to whine, cry.
piara, *f.* herd (of swine); drove (of mares, mules).
piariego, ga, *a.* owning a herd of mares, mules, or swine.
piastra, *f.* a small coin of variable value (gen. about 5 cents).
pibe, *m.* (Arg.) little child, "kid."
¹pica, *f.* pike, lance; bullfighter's goad; stonecutter's hammer.—**poner una p. en Flandes,** to achieve a triumph.
²pica, *f.* (med.) pica.
picacero, ra, *a.* (of hawks) magpie-chasing.
picacureba, *f.* a Brazilian pigeon.
picacho, *m.* top, peak, summit.
picada, *f.* puncture, pricking, bite; sharp, pricking pain.
picadero, *m.* riding school; (naut.) stocks, boat skid; stamping ground of a buck in rutting time.
picadillo, *m.* minced meat; hash.
picado, da. I. *pp.* of PICAR. **II.** *a.* pricked; piqued, hurt; (sewing) pinked. **III.** *m.* minced meat; hash; (aer.) diving; dive.

picador, *m.* horse-breaker; horseman armed with a goad in bullfights; chopping block; paper pricker; pinking iron; file cutter.
picadura, *f.* pricking; pinking; puncture; bite; sting; nick, cut, slash; cut tobacco.
picafigo, *m.* (ornith.) = PAPAFIGO, figpecker.
picaflor, *m.* (ornith.) humming bird.
picajón, na; picajoso, sa, peevish, querulous.
picamaderos, *m.* (ornith.) woodpecker.
picana, *f.* (S. A.) goad.—**picanear,** *va.* to goad.
picante. I. *a.* pricking, piercing, stinging; highly seasoned, hot; risqué. **II.** *m.* piquancy, pungency, acrimony; keen satire.
picantemente, *adv.* piquantly.
¹picaño, ña, *a.* lazy, vagrant.
²picaño, *m.* patch on a shoe.
picapedrero, *m.* stonecutter.
picapica, *f.* a plant whose leaves and fruit produce intense smarting of the skin.
picapleitos, *m.* (coll.) litigious person; pettifogging lawyer.
picaporte, *m.* spring latch, catch bolt; latchkey; (Am.) door knocker.
picaposte, *m.* (ornith.) woodpecker.
picapuerco, *m.* (ornith.) an insectivorous bird.
picar. I. *va.* (*pret.* PIQUÉ; *subj.* PIQUE) to prick, pierce, puncture; to sting, bite (as insects); to mince, chop, hash; (of birds) to peck; (of fish) to bite; to nibble, pick at, take little bites of; to pursue or harass; to spur, goad, incite; to pink; to pique, vex; to tame; (art) to stipple; to roughen with a pointed tool.—**p. la bomba,** to work the pump. **II.** *vn.* to sting, bite (as insects); (of fish) to bite; to itch, burn, smart; to scorch, burn (as the sun); (aer.) to dive.—**p. alto,** to aim high.—**p. en,** to be, to be somewhat of a (poet, etc.). **III.** *vr.* to be offended or piqued; to be moth-eaten; to stale, sour (as wine); to begin to rot (as fruit); (of teeth, etc.) to begin to decay; to boast of; (of animals) to be in heat; (naut.) (of the sea) to get choppy.
pícaramente, *adv.* knavishly, roguishly.
picaraza, *f.* (ornith.) magpie.
picardear, *vn.* to play the knave; to do mischief.
picardía, *f.* knavery, roguery; deceit, malice, foulness; wanton trick, wantonness; lewdness; meeting of rogues.—*pl.* offensive words.
picardihuela, *f. dim.* prank, roguish trick.
picaresca, *f.* den of rogues; knavery.
picarescamente, *adv.* roguishly, rascally.
picaresco, ca; picaril, *a.* roguish, knavish.
picarillo, *m. dim.* little rogue or rascal.
pícaro, ra. I. *a.* knavish, roguish; vile, low; mischievous; crafty, sly. **II.** *n.* rogue, knave, rascal.—**p. de cocina,** scullion, kitchen boy.
picarón, na, *n. aug.* great rogue; *f.* jade.
picaronazo, za; picarote, ta, *n.* great rogue or rascal.
picarrelincho, *m.* (ornith.) = PICAMADEROS.
picatoste, *m.* buttered toast.
¹picaza, *f.* (ornith.) magpie.—**p. marina,** flamingo.
²picaza, *f.* grub ax, mattock.
¹picazo, za, *a.* (of horses) black and white.
²picazo, *m.* blow with a pike, beak of bird, etc.
³picazo, *m.* young magpie.
picazón, *m.* itching, itch, smarting; peevishness, fretfulness.
pícea, *f.* (bot.) spruce.
píceo, a, *a.* of, or pert. to pitch.
¹pico, *m.* beak or bill of a bird; sharp point of any kind; pick, pickaxe; twibill; spout of a jar or pitcher; beak iron of an anvil; peak, top, summit; small balance of an account, small amount over; (coll.) mouth, chin; loquacity, garrulity. —**p. de cigüeña,** (bot.) crane's bill, geranium. —**p. de oro,** silver-tongued orator, man of great eloquence.—**p. de ancla,** (naut.) bill of an anchor.—*pl.* odds and ends.—**picos de un sombrero,** cocks of a hat.—**andar a picos**

pardos, to loiter; to go on a spree.—**callar el p.,** to hold one's tongue.—**tener mucho p.,** to talk too much.—**y p.,** odd (*treinta y pico,* thirty odd).

²**pico,** *m.* (P. I.) weight of 137½ pounds.

³**pico,** *m.* (ornith.) woodpecker.—**p. verde,** green woodpecker.

picofeo, *m.* (ornith.) (Am.) toucan.

picolete, *m.* bolt staple.

picón, na. I. *a.* (of animals) having the upper teeth projecting over the under ones. **II.** *m.* lampoon or nipping jest; charcoal for brasiers; small fresh-water fish; broken rice.

piconero, *m.* maker of brasier charcoal.

picor, *m.* pungent taste; itching.

picoso, sa, *a.* pitted with the smallpox.

picota, *f.* gibbet, pillory; top, peak, point, spire; (naut.) cheek of a pump.

picotada, f., picotazo, *m.* blow with the beak.

picote, *m.* goat's-hair cloth.

picoteado, da, *a.* peaked; having many points.

picotear. I. *va.* to strike with the beak. **II.** *vn.* to gossip; (of horses) to toss the head. **III.** *vr.* to wrangle or quarrel.

picotería, *f.* loquacity, volubility; gossip.

picotero, ra, *a.* chattering, prattling.

picotillo, *m.* inferior goat's-hair cloth.

picrato, *m.* (chem.) picrate.

pícrico, ca, *a.* (chem.) picric.

pictografía, *f.* pictography, picture writing.

pictórico, ca, *a.* pictorial.

¹**picudilla,** *f.* an insectivorous bird.

²**picudilla,** *a. f.* crescent (olive).

picudo, da, *a.* beaked; acuminated, pointed; prattling, chattering.

pichel, *m.* pewter tankard; mug; pitcher.

pichelería, *f.* tankard or pitcher factory.

pichelero, *m.* maker of pewter tankards.

pichelete, *m. dim.* small tankard or mug.

pícher, *m.* (Angl.) (Am.) baseball pitcher.

pichi, *m.* pichi, a Chilean medicinal shrub.

pichincha, *f.* (Am.) good bargain.

pichoa, *f.* a Chilean cathartic plant.

pichola, *f.* a wine measure (about a pint).

pichón, I. *m.* young pigeon, squab. **II.** *n.* (coll.) darling, dearest.

pidientero, *m.* beggar.

pido, pida, pidió, *v. V.* PEDIR.

pidón, na, *a.* (coll.) persistent in begging.

pie, *m.* foot; leg, stand, support, base; trunk (of trees and plants); foot, bottom (of a page); lees, sediment; last hand or player (at cards); (theat.) cue; motive, occasion, opportunity; foundation, groundwork; rule, use, custom; (poet.) foot, syllable, verse; first color given in dyeing; foot of a stocking; slip, cutting (from a plant or tree).—**p. de amigo,** prop, shore.—**p. de banco,** foolish remark.—**p. de cabra,** crowbar.—**p. de cabalgar,** left foot.—**p. de carnero,** (naut.) samson's post.—**p. de imprenta,** (print.) imprint, printer's mark.—**p. de león,** (bot.) = ALQUEMILA VULGAR.—**p. de montar,** left foot.—**p. derecho,** (naut.) stanchion.—**p. de roda,** (naut.) forefoot.—**a los pies de Vd.,** at your service (said to a lady only).—**al p.,** near, close to; at the foot.—**al p. de,** at (the factory, the "job," etc.—.—**al p. de la letra,** verbatim, literally; exactly.—**a p.,** on foot.—**a p. enjuto,** dryshod.—**a p. firme,** steadfastly.—**a p. juntillas,** firmly; uncompromisingly; most emphatically.—**a cuatro pies,** on all fours.—**andar,** or **ponerse, en un pie,** to put one's best foot forward.—**con p. derecho,** auspiciously, with a good start.—**dar p.,** to give occasion.—**de a p.,** on foot.—**de p., de pies,** standing (up); up and doing; firmly.—**de pies a cabeza,** from head to foot.—**en p.,** pending, undecided; DE PIE.—**en p. de guerra,** on a war footing, mobilized.—**estar con un p. en el aire,** to be stopping for only a short time;

to be about to leave.—**estar con el p. en el estribo,** to be about to leave or to act—**ni pies ni cabeza,** neither head nor tail.

piecezuela, *f. dim.* little piece.

piecezuelo, *m. dim.* of PIE: little foot.

piedad, *f.* piety, godliness; mercy; pity, charity; **¡por p.!** for pity's sake!

piedra, *f.* stone; block; cobblestone; memorial stone; footstone; (med.) gravel; hail; place where foundlings are exposed; gunflint.—**p. amoladera** = P. DE AMOLAR.—**p. angular,** cornerstone.—**p. berroqueña,** granite.—**p. de afilar,** or **de amolar,** whetstone, grinding stone.—**p. de chispa,** flint.—**p. de toque,** touchstone.—**p. de chispa,** imitation (precious) stone.—**p. filosofal,** philosopher's stone.—**p. fina** = P. PRECIOSA.—**p. fundamental,** cornerstone.—**p. imán,** loadstone.—**p. infernal,** caustic, lapis infernalis, nitrate of silver in sticks.—**p. lipis,** copper sulphate.—**p. melodreña** = P. DE AFILAR.—**p. miliar,** or **miliaria,** milestone.—**p. nefrítica,** (min.) nephrite, jade.—**p. pómez,** pumice stone.—**p. preciosa,** precious stone.—**p. rodada,** (geol.) bowlder.—**p. viva,** solid rock.—**no dejar p. sobre p.,** to raze to the ground, to destroy entirely.

piedrecica, illa, ita; piedrezuela, *f. dim.* little stone, pebble.

piel, skin; hide, pelt; leather; fur; peel or skin of fruits.—**p. de cabra,** goatskin.—**p. de gallina,** goose flesh.—**abrigo de pieles,** fur coat.

piélago, *m.* high sea; great abundance.

pielecita, *f. dim.* small hide or skin.

pielgo, *m.* = PIEZGO.

¹**pienso,** *m.* daily feed given to horses.

²**pienso,** *m.*—**ni por p.,** (coll.) not even in thought, absolutely not.

³**pienso, piense,** *v. V.* PENSAR.

pierdo, pierda, *v. V.* PERDER.

piérides, *f. pl.* (poet.) the Muses.

pierio, ria, *a.* (poet.) Pierian.

pierna, *f.* (anat.) leg; branch or leg of a compass; downstroke of letters; check of a printing press; jar for honey; (mech.) shank, fork.—**p. de nuez,** lobe of a walnut.—**p. de una sábana,** breadth of a sheet.—**a p. suelta,** or **a p. tendida,** at one's ease; without care; soundly.—**en piernas,** barelegged.

piernitendido, da, *a.* with extended legs.

pietismo, *m.* pietism.

pietista. I. *n.* Pietist. **II.** *a.* pietistic.

pieza, *f.* piece; fragment; part (of a machine, etc.); member (of a structure); bolt or roll of cloth; room (in a house); length of time; distance; game, quarry; piece of work; (theat.) play, piece; piece of music; piece or man in games; (her.) division of a shield.—**p. de artillería,** piece of ordnance.—**p. de autos,** records or pleadings.—**p. de recibo,** parlor, reception room.—**p. de repuesto,** spare part.—**¡buena p.!** a fine fellow (sometimes ironic).—**de una (sola) p.,** in one piece, solid.

piezgo, *m.* foot of a hide or skin; wine skin.

piezométrico, ca, *a.* piezometric.

piezómetro, *m.* piezometer, instrument for measuring compressibility of liquids.

pífano, *m.* (mus.) fife; fifer.

pifia, *f.* miscue at billiards; error, blunder.

pifiar. I. *vn.* to breathe audibly in playing the flute. **II.** *vr.* (billiards) to make a miscue.

pigargo, *m.* (ornith.) ringtail hawk.

pigmento, *m.* pigment.

pigmeo, a. I. *a.* dwarfish. **II.** *n.* dwarf, pigmy.

pignoración, *f.* pledge of security given.

pignorar, *va.* to pledge, give as security.

pignoraticio, cia, *a.* pert. to a pledge or security.

pigre, *a.* slothful, lazy.—**pigricia,** *f.* laziness; place in schools for lazy boys.

pigro, gra, *a.* = PIGRE.

pihua, *f.* sandal.
pihuela, *f.* leash; obstruction, hindrance, impediment.—*pl.* fetters, shackles.
piísimo, ma, *a. super.* very pious, most pious.
pijama, piyama, (gen. *pl.*) *m.* (in Sp.), *f.* (in Am.) pajama.
pijota, *f.* (ichth.) hake.
pijote, *m.* (artil.) swivel gun for grapeshot.
pila, *f.* stone trough or basin; sink; (eccl.) font, holy-water basin; pile, heap; shorn wool belonging to one owner; (eng., arch.) pier; (elec.) battery, pile.—**nombre de p.,** Christian, given name.
pilada, *f.* quantity of mortar made at one time; cloth fulled at one time; pile, heap.
¹pilar, *va.* to hull (grain) by pounding.
²pilar, *m.* basin of a fountain; pillar, column, post; support; pedestal; milestone, stone post; bedpost; arbor of a press.
pilarejo; pilarito, *m. dim.* small pillar.
pilastra, *f.* (arch.) pilaster, square column.
pilastrón, *m. aug.* large pilaster.
pilatero, ra, *n.* one who assists at fulling cloth.
pilche, *m.* (Peru) wooden cup or bowl.
píldora, *f.* (pharm.) pill, pellet; (coll.) affliction, bad news.
píleo, *m.* pileus, skull cap; cardinal's biretta.
pileta, *f.* kitchen sink; swimming pool.
pilica, *f. dim.* of PILA.
pilífero, ra, *a.* piliferous, hairy.
piliforme, *a.* piliform, filamentous.
pilocarpina, *f.* (chem.) pilocarpin.
pilocarpo, m. (bot.) jaborandi.
pilón, *m.* watering trough; basin of a fountain; mortar (for pounding); loaf (of sugar); drop or ball of a steelyard; counterpoise in an olive press; (mason.) heap of mortar; rider, sliding weight (of a balance).
pilonero, ra, *n.* newsmonger.
pilongo, ga, *a.* peeled and dried (chestnut); thin, lean, meager.
pilórico, ca, *a.* (anat.) pyloric.
píloro, *m.* (anat.) pylorus.
piloso, sa, *a.* pilous, pilose, hairy.
¹pilotaje, *m.* (naut.) pilotage.
²pilotaje, *m.* pilework, piling.
pilotar, *va.* to pilot.
pilote, *m.* (eng.) pile.
pilotear, *va.* to pilot.
pilotín, *m.* (naut.) pilot's mate, second pilot.
piloto, *m.* (naut.) pilot, sailing master, navigator; first mate; mate.—**p. de altura,** sea pilot.—**p. de costa,** coast pilot.—**p. de puerto,** port pilot.—**p. práctico** = P. DE COSTA.
piltraca, piltrafa, *f.* skinny flesh; hide parings.—*pl.* scraps of food.
pilla, *f.* pillage, plunder.
pillada, *f.* (coll.) knavish trick, rascality.
pillador, ra, *n.* pillager, plunderer; swindler.
pillaje, *m.* pillage, plunder, marauding, foray.
pillar, *va.* to pillage, rifle, plunder, foray; (coll.) to catch, grasp, take hold of.
pillastre, pillastrón, *m.* rogue, rascal.
pillear, *va.* (coll.) to play the rascal.
pillería, *f.* gang of rogues; piece of rascality.
pillo, lla. I. *a.* roguish, knavish; shrewd, artful, sly. II. *n.* knave, rogue, rascal; petty thief.—**p. desorejado,** arrant rogue.
pilluelo, *m. dim.* little rogue, urchin.
pimental, *m.* pepper patch.
pimentero, *m.* pepper box; (bot.) pepper plant.—**p. falso,** (bot.) = TURBINTO, terebinth.
pimentón, *m.* large pepper; Cayenne or red pepper; paprika.
pimienta, *f.* (black) pepper (spice).—**p. de Tabasco,** myrtle.—**p. larga,** long pepper.—**p. malagueta** = P. DE TABASCO.
pimiento, *m.* (bot.) capsicum; pepper (vegetable); red or Cayenne pepper.—**p. de bonete,** large, sweet pepper.—**p. de cornetilla,** hot

pepper; chili.—**p. dulce,** sweet pepper.—**p. morrón** = P. DE BONETE.—**p. picante** = P. DE CORNETILLA.
pímpido, *m.* (ichth.) a variety of dogfish.
pimpín, *m.* a child's game.
pimpina, *f.* (Venez.) large, earthenware bottle.
pimpinela, *f.* (bot.) burnet, pimpinel.
pimpleo, a, *a.* pertaining to the Muses.
pimplón, *m.* waterfall, cascade.
pimpollar, *m.* nursery of young plants.
pimpollecer, *vn.* to sprout, to bud.
pimpollejo, ico, ito, *m. dim.* tender bud, sprout, sucker, or shoot.
pimpollo, *m.* sucker, sprout, shoot; rosebud; spruce, lively youth.
pimpolludo, da, *a.* full of buds or sprouts.
pina, *f.* conical mound; felloe, rim (of a wheel).
pinabete, *m.* (bot.) fir tree and its wood.
pinacoteca, *f.* pinacotheca, picture gallery.
pináculo, *m.* pinnacle, finial, acme, summit.
pinado, da, *a.* (bot.) pinnate, pinnated.
pinar, pinarejo, *m.* pine grove.
pinariego, ga, *a.* pertaining to pines.
pinastro, *m.* wild pine.
pinatífido, da, *a.* (bot.) pinnatifid.
pinaza, *f.* (naut.) pinnace.
pincarrascal, *m.* grove of pin oaks.
pincarrasco, *m.* pin oak, swamp Spanish oak.
pincel, *m.* artist's brush; (by extension) painter, work painted, and mode of painting; second feather in a martin's wing.
pincelada, *f.* stroke with a brush, touch.
pincelar, *va.* (art) to paint, portray.
pincelero, *m.* maker or seller of artist's brushes; brush box.
pincelillo, ito, *m. dim.* fine or camel's hair brush.
pincelote, *m. aug.* coarse brush.
pincerna, *n.* one who serves drinks.
pinchadura, *f.* (coll.) puncture, pricking.
pinchar, *va.* to prick, puncture, pierce.—**no p. ni cortar,** to have little or no influence, to count for nothing.
pinchaúyas, *n.* (coll.) despicable person.
pinchazo, *m.* prick, puncture, stab.
pinche, *m.* scullion, kitchen boy.
pincho, *m.* thorn, prickle; goad; skewer.
pindárico, ca, *a.* Pindaric.
pindonga, *f.* (coll.) gadabout (woman).
pindonguear, *vn.* (coll.) to gad about.
pineal, *a.* (anat.) pineal.
¹pineda, *f.* braid for garters.
²pineda, *f.* pine grove.
pinga, *f.* (P. I.) banghy, bamboo for carrying loads.
pingajo, *m.* (coll.) rag, tatter.
pinganello, *m.* = CALAMOCO, icicle.
pinganitos—en p., *adv.* in a high position.
pingo, *m.* rag.—*pl.* worthless clothes, duds.—**andar, estar,** or **ir de p.,** to gad about.
pingorote, *m.* any pointed object.
pingorotudo, da, *a.* (coll.) high, lofty.
¹pingüe, *m.* (naut.) pink.
²pingüe, *a.* fat, greasy, oily; plentiful.
pingüedinoso, sa, *a.* fatty, oleaginous.
pingüino, *m.* (ornith.) auk.
pinguosidad, *f.* fatness.
pinífero, ra, *a.* (poet.) abounding in pines.
pinillo, *m.* (bot.) ground pine, germander.
pinípedo, da. I. *n. & a.* (zool.) pinnipedian. II. *m. pl.* Pinnipedia, pinnipedians.
pinitos, *m. pl. dim.* first steps.
pinjante, *m.* (jewelry) pendant; (arch.) boss.
pinnípedo, da, *m. & a.* = PINÍPEDO.
¹pino, na. I. *a.* steep. II. *m.* (coll.) first step of a child or of a convalescent.
²pino, *m.* (bot.) pine.—**p. albar,** Scotch pine.—**p. alerce,** larch, tamarack, hackmatack.—**p. bravo** = P. RODENO.—**p. carrasco,** pine oak.—**p. doncel,** timber from young pines without knots.—**p. marítimo** = P. RODENO.—**p. pi-**

ñonero, stone pine.—p. rodeno, cluster pine, pinaster, red pine.—p. (de) tea, pitch pine.

pinocha, f. pine leaf, pine needle.

pinocho, m. pine cone.

pínola, f. detent of a repeating watch; (naut.) spindle.

pinole, m. aromatic powder to mix with chocolate; (Mex.) cereal meal.

pinoso, sa, a. producing, or pert. to, pines.

¹pinta, f. spot, mark; edge lines on Spanish cards denoting the suit; appearance, aspect; drop,—pl. spots on the skin in malignant fevers; basset, a card game.

²pinta, f. pint (measure).

pintacilgo, m. (ornith.) goldfinch.

pintada, f. (ornith.) guinea fowl.

pintadillo, m. (ornith.) goldfinch.

pintado, da. I. pp. of PINTAR. II. a. spotted, mottled; just fit, exact.—el más p., (coll.) the best, cleverest.

pintamonas, m. (coll.) dauber.

pintar. I. va. to paint; picture; to stain (as glass); to dapple; to describe, portray; to fancy, imagine; to exaggerate. II. vn. to begin to ripen; to show, give signs of. III. vr. to make up (one's face).—p. solo para, to show great aptitude for.

pintarrajar, pintarrajear, va. (coll.) to daub.

pintarrajo, m. (coll.) daub.

pintarroja, f. (ichth.) = LIJA, dogfish.

pintarrojo, m. (ornith.) linnet.

pintica, illa, ita, f. dim. little spot or dot.

pintiparado, da. I. pp. of PINTIPARAR. II. a. perfectly like, closely resembling; apposite, fit.

pintiparar, va. (coll.) to compare.

pintojo, ja, a. spotted, stained, mottled.

pintón, na, a. half-ripe, beginning to ripen.

pintor, m. painter.—p. de brocha gorda, house or sign painter; dauber.

pintora, f. woman painter; painter's wife.

pintorcillo, m. dim. wretched painter or dauber.

pintoresco, ca, a. picturesque.

pintorreador, m. dauber, miserable painter.

pintorrear, va. to daub, paint without skill.

pintura, f. painting; (art) picture, painting; color, paint, pigment; portrayal, description.—p. a la aguada, water-color painting.—p. al fresco, fresco painting.—p. al óleo, oil painting.—p. al pastel, pastel painting.—p. al temple, size painting.—p. figulina, painting on earthenware.—hacer pinturas, (of a horse) to cut capers.

pinturero, ra, a. conceitedly affected.

pínula, f. sight of an instrument.

pinzas, f. pl. nippers, pincers, tweezers; claws of lobsters, etc.; forceps; burling iron.

pinzón, m. (ornith.) chaffinch.

pinzote, m. (naut.) whipstaff.

piña, f. pine cone; pineapple; cluster, gathering; pool, in billiards; (naut.) wall knot; (min.) virgin silver treated with mercury; (P. I.) a fabric made from pineapple fiber.

piñata, f. pot; suspended balloon filled with candies at a masquerade ball; children's party with refreshments.

¹piñon, m. pine kernel; (bot.) piñon or nutpine; spring nut of a gun.

²piñon, m. (mech.) pinion.

³piñon, m. extreme joint of a bird's wing.

piñonata, f. conserve of shredded almonds.

piñonate, m. candied pine-nut kernel.

piñoncico, m. dim. small pine-nut kernel.

¹piñoncillo, m. dim. = PIÑONCICO.

²piñoncillo, m. dim. last joint of a wing.

piñonear, vn. to click (as a gun being cocked); to cry (as partridges in rut).

piñoneo, m. cry of partridges in rut.

piñonero, a. = ²PINO P.

piñuela, f. figured silk; nut of cypress; (Am.) a variety of agave.

¹pío, a, a. pious; mild, merciful.—Antonio P., Antonius Pius.

²pío, a, a. (of horses) pied, piebald.

³pío, m. peeping of chickens; (coll.) longing, anxious desire.

piocha, f. trinket for women's headdresses; flower made of feathers.

piogenia, f. (med.) formation or production of pus.

piogénico, ca, a. (bacteriol.) pus-producing.

piojento, ta, a. lousy.

piojería, f. lousiness; misery, poverty.

piojillo, m. dim. small louse (vermin on plants and birds).

piojo, m. louse; a disease of hawks.—p. pegadizo, (coll.) crab louse; troublesome hanger-on.

piojoso, sa, a. lousy; mean, stingy.

piola, f. (naut.) housing, houseline.

pionía, f. (Venez.) bucare seeds used as beads.

piorno, m. (bot.) broom; (bot.) hairy Cytisus.

piorrea, f. (med.) pyorrhea.

¹pipa, f. cask, butt, hogshead; tobacco pipe; reed of a clarion; (artil.) fusee.

²pipa, f. = PEPITA, pip of some fruits.

pipar, vn. to smoke a tobacco pipe.

piperáceo, a, a. (bot.) piperaceous.

piperacina, f. (chem.) piperazine.

pipería, f. collection of pipes or casks.

piperina, f. (chem.) piperin.

pípero, m. copper pipe or butt maker.

pipeta, f. pipette.

pipí, m. (ornith.) pitpit, honey creeper.

pipián, m. a kind of Indian fricassee.

pipiar, vn. to pule, chirp, peep.

pípila, f. (Mex.) hen turkey.

pipiolo, m. (coll.) novice, raw hand, beginner.

pipirigallo, m. (bot.) sainfoin, forage plant.

pipirijaina, f. (coll.) band of strolling players.

pipiripao, m. (coll.) splendid feast; reception.

pipiritaña, pipitaña, f. green-cane flute.

pipo, m. (ornith.) a small fly-eating bird.

piporro, m. (mus.) bassoon.

pipote, m. keg.—pipotillo, m. dim. small keg.

pique, m. pique, resentment; term in a card game; NIGUA, chigoe, a kind of flea; (naut.) crotch.—a p., in danger, on the point of; sharp-cut (cliff).—echar a p., (naut.) to sink (a ship).—irse a p., (naut.) to founder; to fail, fall through.

¹piqué, pique, v. V. PICAR.

²piqué, m. piqué, cotton fabric.

piquera, f. entrance hole in a hive; cockhole in a barrel; outlet of a smelting furnace; lamp burner.

piquería, f. body of pikemen.

piquero, m. (mil.) pikeman.

piqueta, f. pickaxe, mattock; mason's hammer.

piquete, m. slight wound from a sharp tool; (sewing) small hole in a garment; stake, picket or piquet; (mil.) picket.

piquetero, m. (min.) pick or mattock carrier.

piquetilla, f. dim. bricklayer's hammer.

piquillo, m. dim. small beak or bill; small amount.

piquituerto, m. (ornith.) crossbill, picarin.

pira, f. funeral pile, pyre.

piragón, m. = PIRAUSTA.

piragua, f. (naut.) pirogue, canoe; vine.

piragüero, m. canoeist.

piral, m. = PIRAUSTA.

piramidal, a. pyramidal.

piramidalmente, adv. pyramidally.

pirámide, f. pyramid.

pirata, m. pirate; cruel wretch.—piratear, vn. to pirate.—piratería, f. piracy; robbery.—pirático, ca, a. piratical.

pirausta, f. fabulous firefly.

pirca, f. (S. A.) dry-stone wall.

pircar, va. to surround with a PIRCA.

pirco, m. (S. A.) a kind of succotash.

pirenaico, ca, *a.* Pyrenean.
pirético, ca, *a.* (med.) pyretic, pert. to fever.
piretología, *f.* (med.) pyretology.
pirexia, *f.* (med.) pyrexia, feverish condition.
pírico, ca, *a.* pertaining to fireworks.
pirídico, ca, *a.* (chem.) pyridic.
piridina, *f.* (chem.) pyridine.
piriforme, *a.* pyriform, pear-shaped.
pirineo, a, *a.* Pyrenean.
pirita, *f.* (min.) pyrites.
piritoso, sa, *a.* pyritous, containing pyrites.
pirofilacio, *m.* subterraneous fire.
piróforo, *m.* (chem.) pyrophore.
pirofosfórico, ca, *a.* (chem.) pyrophosphoric.
pirogálico, ca, *a.* (chem.) pyrogallic.
pirograbado, *m.* pyrography; pyrogravure.
pirólatra, *n.* pyrolater, fire worshipper.
pirolatría, *f.* pyrolatry, fire worship.
piroleñoso, sa, *a.* pyroligneous.
pirolusita, *a.* (min.) pyrolusite.
piromancía, *f.* pyromancy.
piromántico, ca, *a.* pyromantic.
pirómetro, *m.* pyrometer.
pironomía, *f.* pyronomy.
piropear, *va.* & *vn.* (coll.) to pay compliments.
piropo, *m.* a variety of garnet; carbuncle; (coll.) compliment, flattery.
piroscopio, *m.* (phys.) a kind of thermometer.
pirosfera, *f.* (geol.) pyrosphere.
pirosis, *f.* (med.) pyrosis, heartburn.
pirotecnia, *f.* pyrotechnics.
pirotécnico, ca, *a.* pyrotechnical.
piroxena, *f.,* **piroxeno,** *m.* (min.) pyroxene.
piroxilina, *f.* pyroxyline.
pirquén.—al p., (Chile) at will, without restrictions (said of the right to work a leased mine).
pirquinear, *vn.* (Chile) to work a leased mine without imposed restrictions.
pírrico, ca, *a.* Pyrrhic.
pirrónico, ca, *a.* Pyrrhonic; skeptic.
pirronismo, *m.* Pyrrhonism.
pirueta, *f.* pirouette, gyration.
piruétano, *m.* (bot.) = PERUÉTANO, wild pear tree.
pisa, *f.* tread, treading; portion of olives or grapes pressed at once.
pisada, *f.* footstep; footprint; stepping on someone's foot.—**seguir las pisadas de,** (fig.) to follow in the footsteps of, follow the example of.
pisador, ra. I. *n.* & *a.* prancer(-ing); high-stepper(-ing). II. *n.* treader of grapes.
pisadura, *f.* act of treading; footstep.
pisapapeles, *m.* paper weight.
pisar, *va.* to tread on, trample, step on; to press; to press on; to ram; to cover; to lie over; (of birds) to cover (the female).
pisasfalto, *m.* mixture of bitumen and pitch.
pisaúvas, *n.* treader of grapes.
pisaverde, *m.* (coll.) fop, coxcomb, dude.
piscator, *m.* almanac with meteorol. forecasts.
piscatorio, ria, *a.* piscatory, pertaining to fish or fishing.
piscicultor, ra, *n.* & *a.* pisciculturist(-ic).
piscicultura, *f.* pisciculture, fish culture.
pisciforme, *a.* pisciform, fish-shaped.
piscina, *f.* fishpond; swimming pool (also **p. de natación**); (eccl.) piscina.
Piscis, *m.* (astr.) Pisces, zodiacal sign.
piscívoro, ra, *a.* piscivorous, fish-eating.
piscolabis, *m.* (coll.) luncheon, a bite.
piso, *m.* floor; pavement, flooring; story or floor; loft, flat, apartment; ground level; tread, footing, walking; (min.) level works; (geol.) stage, formation.—**p. bajo,** ground floor.—**p. principal,** second floor, first living floor (in apartment houses, etc.).
pisón, *m.* rammer; paver's beetle.
pisonear, *va.* to ram.
pisotear, *va.* to trample, tread under foot.
pisoteo, *m.* trampling, treading under foot.
pisotón, *m.* *aug.* heavy step on someone's foot.

pista, *f.* trail, track, scent; trace, clue; racetrack, race course.
pistachero, pistacho, *m.* pistachio.
pistadero, *m.* pestle for pounding.
pistar, *va.* to pound with a pestle.
pistero, *m.* feeding cup with tubular nozzle.
pistilo, *m.* (bot.) pistil.
pisto, *m.* chicken broth for the sick; dish of tomatoes and red pepper.
pistola, *f.* pistol.—**p. de arzón,** horse pistol.
pistolera, *f.* holster.
pistoletazo, *m.* pistol shot.—**dar un p.,** to shoot with a pistol.
pistolete, *m.* pistolet, pocket pistol.
pistón, *m.* (mech.) piston; (artil.) percussion cap, primer; (mus.) piston of a brass instrument.
pistoresa, *f.* short dagger.
pistraje, pistraque, *m.* unpleasant beverage.
pistura, *f.* pounding, pestling.
pita, *f.* (bot.) pita; agave; maguey (used vaguely with diff. meanings in diff. countries. The pita proper produces the best fiber.); string, cord.
pitaco, *m.* stem of the maguey.
pitada, *f.* blow of a whistle.
pitagórico, ca, *a.* & *n.* Pythagorean.
pitahaya, *f.* (bot.) pitahaya.
pitancería, *f.* distribution or place of distribution of alms; almsgiving.
pitancero, *m.* distributor of alms; (eccl.) steward or purveyor; superintendent of a choir.
pitancica, illa, ita, *f.* *dim.* small pittance.
pitanza, *f.* pittance, alms; (coll.) daily food; price, salary, stipend.
pitaña, *f.* = LEGAÑA, gummy secretion of eyes.
pitañoso, sa, *a.* = LEGAÑOSO, blear-eyed.
¹pitar. I. *vn.* (of a whistle) to blow. II. *va.* to discharge (a debt).
²pitar, *va.* to distribute alms to.
pitarra, *f.* blearedness.
pitarroso, sa, *a.* = PITAÑOSO.
pitazo, *m.* sound or blast of a whistle.
pitecántropo, *m.* (paleontol.) pithecanthropus.
pitezna, *f.* spring of a trap.
pitillera, *f.* woman cigarette maker; cigarette case.
pitillo, *m.* cigarette.
pítima, *f.* (pharm.) saffron plaster; (coll.) drunkenness.
pitío, *m.* whistling of a pipe or of birds.
pitipié, *m.* scale (on a map, drawing, etc.).
pitirre, *m.* (ornith.) pitirri, gray kingbird.
¹pito, *m.* whistle; catcall; fife; fifer; (Am.) tick; jackstone (toy); cocoon open at one end.—**pitos flautos,** frivolous pastimes.—**no me importa,** or **no se me da, un p.,** I don't care a straw.—**no tocar pitos en,** to have no part in.—**no valer un p.,** not to be worth a straw.
²pito, *m.* (ornith.) woodpecker.
pitoflero, ra, *n.* (coll.) musician of no account; gossip (person).
¹pitón, *m.* (zool.) python.
²pitón, *m.* (of deer, etc.) horn just starting to grow; protuberance, lump; spout, nozzle; sprig or shoot of a tree; sprout of the agave.
pitonisa, *f.* Pythia, Pythoness; witch, sorceress.
pitorra, *f.* (ornith.) woodcock.
pitpit, *m.* (ornith.) pitpit, guitguit.
pitreo, *m.* = PITACO.
pituita, *f.* pituitary (extract).—**pituitario, ria,** *a.* pituitary.—**pituitoso, sa,** *a.* with copious pituitary.
piuquén, *m.* (ornith.) a large Chilean bird similar to the wild turkey.
píxide, *f.* (eccl.) pyx, vessel or casket.
piyama, *m.* pijama. Also PIJAMA.
pizarra, *f.* (min.) slate shale; slate (for writing); blackboard; **pizarral,** *m.* slate quarry.
pizarreño, ña, *a.* slate-colored, slaty.
pizarrero, *m.* slater, slate cutter; roofer.
pizarrín, *m.* slate pencil.

pizarrón, *m.* (Am.) blackboard.
pizarroso, sa, *a.* abounding in slate.
pizate, *m.* (bot.) saltwort.
pizca, *f.* (coll.) mite, bit, speck, crumb, whit.
pizcar, *va.* (coll.) to pinch; (Mex.) to glean (maize).
pizco, *m* (coll.) pinch.
pizmiento, ta, *a.* pitch-colored.
pizpereta, pizpireta, *a.* smart, brisk, lively.
pizpirigaña, *f.* a boys' game.
pizpita, *f.*; **pizpitillo,** *m.* (ornith.) wagtail.
placa, *f.* star, insignia of an order of knighthood; (photog.) dry plate; (mech.) plate; (art) plaque; (Mex.) baggage check.—**p. giratoria,** (Ry.) turning plate, turntable.
placabilidad, *f.* placability.
placable, *a.* placable.
placativo, va, *a.* placatory.
placear, *va.* to sell (provisions) at retail
placel, *m.* (naut.) sand bank, key.
pláceme, *m.* congratulation.
placenta, *f.* (anat., bot.) placenta.
plaentario, ria. I. *a.* placental. **II.** *m.* (zool.) placental.—*pl.* Placentalia.
placenteramente, *adv.* joyfully, merrily.
placentero, ra, *a.* joyful, merry, pleasant.
¹placer. I. *va.* (*ind. pres.* PLAZCO, *pret.* él PLUGO or PLACIÓ; *subj. pres.* yo PLAZCA, él PLEGUE or PLAZCA, *imp.* yo PLACIERA, él PLUGUIERA or PLACIERA, etc.) to please, gratify, humor, content.—**que me place,** it gives me pleasure; with pleasure. **II.** *m.* pleasure.—**a p.,** at one's convenience.
²placer, *m.* (naut.) sand bank, key; (min.) placer; (Am.) pearl fishing.
placero, ra. I. *a.* pertaining to the marketplace. **II.** *n.* marketer, seller at a market; gadabout.
placeta, tilla, tuela, *f. dim.* small (town) square.
placibilidad, *f.* agreeableness.
placible, *a.* placid; agreeable.
plácidamente, *adv.* placidly.
plácido, da, *a.* placid, quiet, calm.
placiente, *a.* pleasing, agreeable, pleasant.
plafón, *m.* (arch.) soffit of an architrave.
¹plaga, *f.* plague; calamity; scourge; epidemic; affliction; pest; plenty, superabundance, drug in the market (originally of injurious things, now improperly used of anything).
²plaga, *f.* climate, country; zone; (naut.) cardinal point of compass.
plagado, da. I. *pp.* of PLAGAR. **II.** *a.* full; smitten.
plagar. I. *va.* (*pret.* PLAGUÉ; *subj.* PLAGUE) to plague, infest. **II.** *vr.* (**de**) to be overrun (with), or full (of).
plagiar, *va.* to plagiarize; (Am.) to kidnap.
plagiario, ria, *n. & a.* plagiarizer(-ing).
plagio, *m.* plagiarism; (Am.) kidnapping.
plagioclasa, *f.* (min.) plagioclase.
plagióstomos, *m. pl.* (zool.) Plagiostomi, plagiostomes.
plagué, plague, *v. V.* PLAGAR.
plan, *m.* plan; design, scheme; plan, drawing; description, specification; (naut.) floor timber. —**p. de estudios,** (school) curriculum.
plana, *f.* page; copy; level ground, plain; record; (mason.) trowel; (print.) page.—**p. mayor,** (mil.) staff.—**enmendar la p. a,** to find fault with, criticize; to excel, do better than.
planada, *f.* plain, level ground.
planador, *m.* one who smooths, finishes metal.
plancha, *f.* plate, sheet; slab; iron, flatiron; tailor's goose; cramp iron; (paper) mold; cloth plate of a sewing machine; horizontal suspension (in gymnastics); (coll.) "break," "boner"; (naut.) gangplank, gangboard.—**p. de agua,** (naut.) punt, floating stage.—**p. de blindaje,** armor plate.—**p. de viento,** (naut.) hanging stage.
planchada, *f.* (naut.) apron of a gun.

planchado, *m.* ironing; linen ironed or for ironing.
planchador, ra, *n.* ironer.
planchar, *va.* to iron, to press (clothes).
planchear, *va.* to plate, cover with metal sheets.
plancheta, *f.* (surv.) plane table.
planchita, *f. dim.* small plate.
planchón, *m. aug.* large plate.
planchuela, *f. dim.* small plate; fluting iron.
planeador, *m.* (aer.) glider.
planear. I. *va.* to plan, design. **II.** *vn.* (aer.) to glide.—**planeo,** *m.* (aer.) gliding.
planeta. I. *m.* (astr.) planet. **II.** *f.* (eccl.) planeta.
planetario, ria. I. *a.* planetary. **II.** *m.* planetarium, orrery; astronomer.
planetícola, *n.* inhabitant of a planet.
planga, *f.* (ornith.) a kind of eagle.
planicle, *f.* = LLANURA, a plain.
planificado, da, *a.*—**economía p.,** planned economy.
planilla, *f.* (Am.) list (of expenses, etc.); (Am.) list of employees, payroll; (Mex.) list of candidates, ticket.
planimetría, *f.* plane surveying.
planímetro, *m.* planimeter.
planisferio, *m.* planisphere.
plano, na. I. *a.* plane; level; smooth, even. **II.** *m.* plan (drawing); map; flat (of a sword, etc.); (geom.) plane; (aer.) plane, wing.—**p. de deriva de cola,** (aer.) tail plane, stabilizer.— **p. de nivel,** datum plane (in leveling).—**p. inclinado,** inclined plane.—**p. panorámico,** pictorial map.—**de p.,** openly, clearly; flatly, on its side.
planta, *f.* sole of the foot; (bot.) plant; plantation, nursery of young plants; (eng.) plan, horizontal projection, top view; plant, works; site of a building; (fencing and dance) position of the feet; proect; disposition.—**p. baja,** ground floor.—**buena p.,** fine physique.—**echar plantas,** to brag, to boast.
plantación, *f.* plantation; planting.
plantado, da, *pp.* of PLANTAR.—**dejarlo a uno p.,** (Am.) to leave one in the lurch.
plantador, ra, *n.* planter (person or machine).
plantaina, *f.* (bot.) plantain, ribwort.
plantaje, *m.* collection of plants.
plantar. I. *va.* (agr.) to plant; to erect, set up, fix upright; to strike (a blow); to set, put; place; to pose (as a question, a problem); to found, establish; (coll.) to leave in the lurch, disappoint; to jilt. **II.** *vr.* (coll.) to stand upright; to reach, arrive; to stop, halt, balk; in some games, to stand pat.
plantario, *m.* (agr.) nursery.
planteamiento, *m.* putting into execution.
plantear, *va.* to plan, try; to put into action; to state or tackle (a problem); to raise (an issue).
plantel, *m.* nursery, nursery garden; educational institution.
plateo, *m.* statement (as of a problem); execution, performance.
plantificación, *f.* putting into execution.
plantificar, *va.* to put into execution; (coll.) to land (as a blow).
plantígrado, da, *a.* plantigrade.
plantilla, *f. dim.* young plant; (shoemaking) first sole, insole; (mech.) template, templet, model, pattern; plate of a gunlock; (med.) plaster for the feet; (astr.) celestial configuration; (P. R.) lady finger.
plantillar, *va.* to sole (shoes or stockings).
plantío, ía. I. *a.* (of land) planted, or ready to be planted. **II.** *m.* plantation; planting; garden bed.
plantista, *m.* landscape gardener; bully, hector, bravado.
plantón, *m.* scion, sprout or shoot to be transplanted; shoot ingrafted on a stock; (coll.) long wait standing; (mil.) sentry doing long guard;

doorkeeper, watchman.—**estar de p.**, to be fixed in a place for a long time.—**llevar un p.**, to dance attendance.

planudo, da, *a.* (naut.) flat-bottomed.

plañidero, ra. I. *a.* mournful, weeping, moaning. **II.** *f.* weeper, hired mourner.

plañido, *m.* moan, lamentation, crying.

plañir, *vn.* (*ger.* PLAÑENDO; *pret.* el PLAÑÓ) to lament, grieve, bewail; to whimper, whine.

plaqué, *m.* plate, plating; plated ware.

plaquín, *m.* loose coat of mail, hauberk.

¹plasma, *m.* (biol.) plasma.

²plasma, *f.* (min.) = PRASMA, dark green agate.

plasmador, ra, *n.* maker, molder.

plasmante, *n.* & *a.* molder(-ing), shaper(-ing).

plasmar, *va.* to mold, shape.

plasmático, ca, *a.* (biol.) plasmic.

plasta, *f.* anything soft (as dough, mud, etc.); anything flattened; (coll.) anything poorly done.

plaste, *m.* size or filler made of glue and lime.

plastecer, *va.* (*ind.* PLASTEZCO; *subj.* PLASTEZCA) to size, to besmear with size.

plastecido, *m.* (art) sizing.

plástica, *f.* art of molding in clay.

plasticidad, *f.* plasticity.

plástico, ca. I. *a.* plastic; soft. **II.** *m.* plastic.

plastrón, *m.* (fencing) plastron; large cravat; leather apron.

plata, *f.* silver; silver coin; money; plate, wrought silver; (her.) plate; white.—**p. agria,** (min.) black silver, stephanite.—**p. alemana,** German silver.—**p. córnea,** (min.) cerargyrite.—**p. piña,** (min.) spongy silver.—**p. gris,** silver glance, argentite.—**p. labrada,** silverware.—**p. roja,** (min.) pyrargyrite, red silver ore.—**p. virgen,** native silver.—**como una p.,** very clean and pretty.—**en p.,** in plain language; briefly, in a word.—**quedarse sin p.,** to be penniless, "broke."

plataforma, *f.* platform; terrace; (mach.) index plate, division plate; (fort.) platform; (naut.) orlop; (Ry.) roadbed.

platal, *m.* great quantity of money, great wealth.

platanal, platanar, *m.* plantain or banana plantation.

platáneo, a, *a.* (bot.) plantanaceous.

plátano, *m.* (bot.) plantain; banana (plant and fruit); plane tree.—**p. falso,** sycamore maple.—**p. guineo,** guineo; (Cuba) banana.

platazo, *m. aug.* platter; dishful.

platea, *f.* (theat.) orchestra, parquet; pit.

plateado, da, *pp.* & *a.* silvered; silverplated.

plateador, *m.* plater, silverer.

plateadura, *f.* silvering, silver plating.

platear, *va.* to silver, silverplate.

platel, *m.* platter; tray.

platelminto, ta. I. *a.* (zool.) platyhelminthic. **II.** *m.* platyhelminth; *pl.* Platyhelminthes.

plateresco, ca, *a.* (arch.) plateresque.

platería, *f.* silversmith's shop or trade.

platero, *m.* silversmith; jeweller.—**p. de oro,** goldsmith.

plática, *f.* talk, chat, conversation; address, lecture; sermon.—**platicar,** *vn.* (*pret.* PLATIQUÉ; *subj.* PLATIQUE) to converse, talk, chat.

platija, *f.* (ichth.) plaice, flounder.

platilla, *f.* Silesian linen.

platillo, *m. dim.* small dish; saucer; beef stew; extra dish in convents; pan (of a balance); (mus.) cymbal; disk or valve of a chain pump.

¹platina, *f.* (mech.) plate, platen; (print.) platen, bedplate; imposing table; (phys.) slide (of microscope); plate (of air pump).

²platina, *f.* (min.) ore of platinum.

platinado, da. I. *pp.* of PLATINAR. **II.** *m.* platinum plating.

platinar, *va.* to plate with platinum.

platinífero, ra, *a.* platinum-bearing.

platino, *m.* platinum.

platinoide, *m.* platinoid.

platinotipia, *f.* platinotype.

platiqué, platique, *v.* V. PLATICAR.

platirrino, na, *n.* & *a.* (zool.) platyrrhine.

plato, *m.* dish, plate; (cook.) dish, mess, course, food served in a dish; daily fare; pan (of a balance); (arch.) metope.—**p. de segunda mesa,** makeshift, second-hand, cast off; (fig.) second fiddle.—**p. sopero,** soup plate.—**nada entre dos platos,** much ado about nothing.—**no quebrar un p.,** to be innocent or harmless.

platónicamente, *adv.* Platonically.

platónico, ca, *a.* Platonic.

platonismo, *m.* Platonism.

platudo, da, *a.* (Am. coll.) rich, moneyed.

platuja, *f.* (ichth.) = PLATIJA.

plausibilidad, *f.* plausibility.

plausible, *a.* plausible.—**plausiblemente,** *adv.* plausibly.

plauso, *m.* applause.

plaustro, *m.* (poet.) cart, wagon, carriage.

plautino, na, *a.* Plautine, relating to Plautus.

playa, *f.* shore, strand, sea coast, beach.

playado, da, *a.* having a beach; beachy.

playazo, *m.* wide or extended shore.

playeras, *f. pl.* a popular Andalusian song.

playero, ra, *n.* fisherman; fishwoman.

playón, *m. aug.* large shore or beach.

playuela, *f. dim.* small beach or shore.

plaza, *f.* plaza, square; market place; (com.) emporium, market; room, space, stall; office, position, employment; reputation, character, fame.—**p. de armas,** (mil.) parade ground.—**p. de toros,** bull ring, arena.—**p. fuerte,** (fort.) stronghold, fortress.—¡p., p.! clear the way! make room!—**pasar p. de,** to be reputed (something that one is not).—**sacar a p.,** to publish, make public.—**sentar p.,** (mil.) to enlist.

plazo, *m.* term, time, date, day of payment; installment; credit; duelling ground.—**a largo p.,** long-term, long-range.—**a p.,** on credit.

plazoleta, plazuela, *f. dim.* small square.

ple, *m.* a handball game.

pleamar, *f.* (naut.) high water, high tide.

plébano, *m.* curate of a parish.

plebe, *f.* common people, plebs, populace.

plebeyo, ya, *n.* & *a.* plebeian.

plebiscitario, ria, *a.* pert. to plebiscite.

plebiscito, *m.* plebiscitum; (pol.) plebiscite.

pleca, *f.* (print.) straight line, rule.

plectro, *m.* plectrum, for stringed instruments.

plegable, *a.* pliable, folding.

plegadamente, *adv.* confusedly.

plegadera, *f.* (bookbinding) folder.

plegadizo, za, *a.* pliable; folding.

plegado, *m.* plaiting; folding.

plegador, ra. I. *a.* folding. **II.** *n.* folder, plaiter. **III.** *f.* plaiting machine, folding machine; beam of a silk loom.

plegadura, *f.* plait, fold; plaiting, folding, doubling; crease.

plegar, *I.* *va.* (*ind.* PLIEGO; *subj.* PLIEGUE) to fold; to plait, double; to do up; to turn (the warp) on the yarn beam; (sewing) to plait, pucker, gather, crease. **II.** *vr.* to fold; to bend; to submit, yield.

plegaria, *f.* prayer, supplication; noon prayers.

plegue, *v.* V. PLACER.

pleguete, *m.* (bot.) tendril of a vine.

pleistoceno, na, *m.* & *a.* (geol.) Pleistocene.

pleita, *f.* plaited strand of bass.

pleiteador, ra, *n.* pleader; wrangler.

pleiteante, *n.* & *a.* litigator(-ing, -ant), pleader(-ing).

pleitear, *vn.* to plead, litigate; to wrangle.

pleitista, *n.* pettifogger.

pleito, *m.* lawsuit; litigation; proceedings in a case; dispute, contest, debate, strife.—**p. de acreedores,** proceedings under a commission of bankruptcy.—**poner p.** (a), to sue, bring suit (against).—**ver un p.,** (law) to try a case.

plenamar, *f.* = PLEAMAR.

plenamente, *adv.* fully, completely.

plenariamente, *adv.* completely, fully; (law) plenarily.

plenario, ria, *a.* complete, full; (law) plenary.

plenilunio, *m.* full moon.

plenipotencia, *f.* plenipotence, full powers.

plenipotenciario, ria, *n.* & *a.* plenipotentiary.

plenitud, *f.* plenitude, fullness, abundance.

pleno, na, *a.* full, complete; joint (session).—**en pleno** (noun), in the middle of (winter, etc.).

pleonasmo, *m.* (rhet.) pleonasm, redundancy.

pleonásticamente, *adv.* pleonastically.

pleonástico, ca, *a.* pleonastic, redundant.

plepa, *f.* (coll.) bother; person full of defects.

plesímetro, *m.* (med.) pleximeter.

plesiosauro, *m.* (paleontol.) plesiosaur.

pletina, *f.* small iron plate.

plétora, *f.* plethora; superabundance, inflation.

pletórico, ca, *a.* plethoric.

pleura, *f.* (anat.) pleura.—**pleuresía,** *f.* (med.) pleurisy.—**p. falsa,** pleurodynia.

pleurítico, ca, *a.* pleuritic(al).

pleuritis, *f.* (med.) pleurisy.

pleurodinia, *f.* pleurodynia, stitch in the side.

pleximetro, *m.* = PLESÍMETRO.

plexo, *m.* (anat. and bot.) plexus; network.

Pléyadas, Pléyades, *f. pl.* (astr.) Pleiades.

plica, *f.* (law) escrow; (med.) matted condition of hair; plica.

¹pliego, *m.* sheet (of paper); sealed envelope or package containing papers.—**p. de condiciones,** specifications; tender, bid.

²pliego, ¹pliegue, *v. V.* PLEGAR.

²pliegue, *m.* fold, plait, crease; (sewing) gather.

plieguecillo, *m. dim.* half sheet; small plait.

plinto, *m.* (arch.) plinth of a pillar.

plioceno, *m.* & *a.* (geol.) Pliocene.

plomada, *f.* artificer's lead pencil; plumb, plumb bob, plummet; (naut.) lead for sounding; fishing-net sinker; scourge with lead balls.

plomar, *va.* to put a leaden seal on.

plomazón, *f.* gilding cushion.

plombagina, *f.* plumbago, graphite.

plomería, *f.* lead roofing; leadware shop; plumbing.

plomero, ra, *n.* plumber.

plomizo, za, *a.* plumbeous; lead-colored.

plomo, *m.* lead (metal); piece of lead; plumb bob, plummet; bullet; (coll.) dull person, bore.—**p. derretido,** molten lead.—**andar con pies de p.,** to proceed with the utmost caution.—**a p.,** true, plumb.—**caer a p.,** to fall down flat.

plomoso, sa, *a.* = PLOMIZO.

pluguiera, *v. V.* PLACER.

pluma, *f.* feather; plume, down; quill; writing pen; penmanship; writer; style; (coll.) air expelled from the bowels.—**p. de agua,** a variable measure of running water (0.025 liter per second in some parts of Spain).—**p. fuente,** fountain pen.—**p. viva,** eider down.—**al correr de la p., a vuela p.,** written in haste.

plumada, *f.* brief writing; pen stroke, flourish.

plumado, da, *a.* feathered, feathery, plumey.

plumaje, *m.* plumage; plume, crest.

plumajería, *f.* plumage; feather working.

plumajero, ra, *n.* plumist, feather dresser.

plumario, ria. I. *n.* plumist, plume worker. **II.** *a.* pertaining to plume or feather work.

plumazo, *m.* feather mattress or pillow.

plumazón, *f.* plumage.

plumbado, da, *a.* sealed with a leaden seal.

plumbagina, *f.* = PLOMBAGINA.

plumbagíneo, a, *a.* (bot.) plumbagineous.

plúmbeo, bea, *a.* leaden, plumbeous.

plúmbico, ca, *a.* (chem.) plumbic.

plumeado, *m.* (art) lines in miniature painting.

plumear, *va.* (art) to shade with a liner.

plúmeo, a, *a.* plumose, feathered, plumed.

plumería, *f.* plumosity; plumage.

plumero, *m.* feather duster; box for feathers or plumes; plumage; aigret, panache.

plumífero, ra, *a.* feathered.

plumilla, *f. dim.* small feather or plume; (print.) script type; (bot.) plumule.

plumión, *m.* = PLUMÓN.

plumista, *n.* notary; plume-maker.

plumita, *f. dim.* small feather or pen.

plumón, *m.* down, feather bed.

plumoso, sa, *a.* feathered, plumey.

plúmula, *f.* (bot.) plumule.

plural, *n.* & *a.* plural.

pluralidad, *f.* plurality; majority.—**a p. de votos,** by a majority of votes.

pluralizar, *va.* to pluralize.

plus, *m.* (mil.) extra pay; bonus; extra.

pluscuamperfecto, *m.* (gram.) pluperfect.

plus minusve, (Lat.) more or less, about.

plúteo, *m.* library shelf.

plutocracia, *f.* plutocracy.

plutócrata, *n.* plutocrat.

plutocrático, ca, *a.* plutocratic.

plutónico, ca, *a.* (geol.) Plutonic.

plutonio, *m.* plutonium.

plutonismo, *m.* (geol.) Plutonism.

plutonista, *m.* (geol.) Plutonist.

pluvial, *a.* pluvial, rainy.

pluvímetro, *m.* = PLUVIÓMETRO.

pluviógrafo, *m.* registering rain gauge.

pluviométrico, ca, *a.* pluviometric.

pluviómetro, *m.* rain gauge.

pluvioso, sa, *a.* rainy, pluvious.

poa, *f.* (naut.) bowline bridle.

pobeda, *f.* plantation of poplars.

población, *f.* population; populating; city, town, village.

poblacho, poblachón, *m.* ugly village.

poblado. I. *pp.* & *a.* populated, inhabited. **II.** *m.* inhabited place, town, settlement.

poblador, ra, *n.* populator, settler.

poblar. I. *va.* & *vn.* (*ind.* PUEBLO; *subj.* PUEBLE) to populate, people, colonize, settle; to inhabit; to stock; to breed fast. **III.** *vr.* to bud, leaf.

poblazo, *m.* large ugly village.

poblezuelo, *m. dim.* small village.

pobo, *m.* (bot.) white poplar.

pobre. I. *a.* poor; needy; barren; humble, modest; trifling, paltry, unimportant.—**¡p. de mí!** poor me! **II.** *n.* poor person; pauper, beggar.—**p. de solemnidad,** poor person in real distress.

pobrecico, ca; illo, lla; ito, ta, *a.* & *n. dim.* poor little thing.

pobremente, *adv.* poorly, miserably, needily.

pobrería, *f.* poor people, beggars.

pobrero, ra, *n.* distributor of alms.

pobreta, *f.* (coll.) strumpet, prostitute.

pobrete, ta, *n. dim.* poor person.—**pobretear,** *vn.* to pretend poverty.—**pobretería,** *f.* poor people; beggars; poverty; niggardliness.

pobretón, na, *a. aug.* very poor.

pobreza, *f.* poverty; sterility, barrenness; vow of poverty; lowness or pettiness of spirit.

pobrezuelo, la, *a. dim.* rather poor.

pobrismo, *m.* pauperism; beggars.

pócar, póker, *m.* (Angl.) (Am.) poker (card game).

pocero, *m.* well borer or sinker; sewerman.

pocilga, *f.* pigsty, pigpen; dirty place.

pocillo, *m. dim.* vessel sunk in the ground in oil mills; chocolate cup.

pócima, *f.* potion, draught, medicinal tea.

poción, *f.* drink, draught; (pharm.) potion.

poco, ca. I. *a.* little; scanty, limited; small.—*pl.* few, some.—**a pocos lances,** in a short time.—**de p. tiempo acá,** lately, of late. **II.** *m.* a little, a bit, a small quantity.—**a p. de,** shortly after.—**un p. de,** a little, some (foll. by noun).—**unos pocos,** a few, some. **III.** *adv.* little, in a small degree; a short time.—**p. a p.** little by little, gradually, slowly.—**p. después,** shortly afterwards.—**p. más o menos,** more or less.— **a p.,** immediately; shortly afterwards; presently.—**dentro de p.,** in a short time, soon.— **de p. más o menos,** of little account.—**por p.,** almost, nearly.—**tener en p.,** to set little value on, to think little of.

póculo, *m.* drinking cup or glass.

pocho, cha, *a.* (coll.) discolored, faded.

poda, *f.* pruning, lopping; pruning season.

podadera, *f.* pruning knife, hook; hedging bill.

podador, ra, *n.* pruner.

podagra, *f.* gout in the feet.

podar, *va.* to prune, head, lop, trim.

podazón, *f.* pruning season.

podenco, *m.* hound (dog).

poder. I. *va.* & *vn.* (*ger.* PUDIENDO; *ind. pres.* PUEDO, *pret.* PUDE, *fut.* PODRÉ; *subj.* PUEDA) to be able; can; may (*Juan no puede venir,* John cannot come; *Juan puede no venir,* John may not come).—**a más no p.,** to the utmost; without being able to help it.—**como pueda (podamos,** etc.), the best he (we, etc.) can.— **hasta más no p.,** to the utmost, to the limit. —**no p. con,** not to be able to bear, manage, etc., to be no match for.—**no p. más,** to have to act, can no other, cannot but; not to be able to do more, to be tired, worn out.—**no p. menos de,** to be necessary; cannot but, cannot fail to; (foll. by *inf.*) can't help (foll. by *pres. p.*)—**no p. ver a uno (pintado, o ni pintado),** to detest one, to find one absolutely unbearable. II. *v. imp.* to be possible, may.— **puede que** (foll. by *subj.*) it may (foll. by *inf.*); perhaps. III. *m.* power; faculty, authority, influence, force; might; (law) power or letter of attorney; proxy; possession, tenure; ability, strength, capacity.—*pl.* power, authority.

poderdante, *n.* (law) constituent.

poderhabiente, *n.* (law) attorney.

poderío, *m.* power, might, dominion, jurisdiction; wealth, riches.

poderosamente, *adv.* powerfully, mightily.

poderoso, sa, *a.* powerful, mighty; wealthy.

podio, *m.* (arch.) podium.

podofilina, *f.* (pharm.) podophyllin.

podófilo, *m.* (bot.) podophyllum.

podómetro, *m.* pedometer.

podón, *m.* pruning hook, billhook; mattock.

podré, *fut.* of PODER.

podre, *m. or f.* pus; rotten substance.

podrecer, *va., vn.* & *vr.* = PUDRIR, to rot.

podrecimiento, *m.* = PODREDURA.

podredumbre, *f.* decay; pus; putrid matter; corruption; grief.

podredura, *f.* putrefaction, corruption.

podrición, *f.* = PODREDURA.

podridero, podrimiento, *m.,* **podrir,** *va.* = PUDRIDERO, PUDRIMIENTO, PUDRIR, to rot.

poema, *m.* poem.

poesía, *f.* poetry; poetical composition, poem.— *pl.* poetical works, poems.

poeta, *m.* a poet.—**poetastro,** *m.* poetaster.

poética, *f.* poetics.

poéticamente, *adv.* poetically.

poético, ca, *a.* poetic(al).

poetisa, *f.* poetess.

poetizar. I. *vn.* (*pret.* POETICÉ; *subj.* POETICE) to poetize, write poetry. II. *va.* to render poetical, to impart poetry to.

poíno, *m.* gauntry, stilling, stalder, barrelstand.

póker, pócar, *m.* (Angl.) (Am.) poker (card game).

polaco, ca. I. *a.* Polish. II. *m.* Polish language. III. *n.* Pole.

polacra, *f.* (naut.) polacre.

polaina, *f.* leggings.

polar, *a.* polar.—**polaridad,** *f.* polarity.

polarímetro, *m.* polarimeter.

polariscopio, *m.* polariscope.

polarización, *f.* polarization.

polarizar, *va.* to polarize.

polca, *f.* (dance) polka.

polcar, *vn.* to dance the polka.

polea, *f.* pulley; tackle block, block pulley.—**p. fija,** fixed or fast pulley.—**p. impulsada,** driven pulley.—**p. loca,** loose pulley.—**p. motriz,** driving pulley.—**p. movible,** or **móvil,** movable pulley.

poleadas, *f. pl.* pap; porridge.

poleame, *m.* set of pulleys, tackle.

polemarca, *m.* (Gk. hist.) polemarch.

polémica, *f.* polemics; (mil.) science of fortification; literary or political controversy.

polémico, ca, *a.* polemical, polemic.

polemista, *n.* polemic, debater.

polemístico, ca, *a.* polemic(al), controversial.

polemonio, *m.* (bot.) Jacob's ladder.

polemoscopio, *m.* (opt.) polemoscope.

polen, *m.* (bot.) pollen.

polenta, *f.* porridge.

poleo, *m.* (bot.) pennyroyal; (coll.) strutting gait; (coll.) pompous style; (coll.) stiff, cold wind.

poliandria, *f.* (bot.) polyandria.

poliantea, *f.* collection of news items.

poliarquía, *f.* government by many.

poliárquico, ca, *a.* pert. to POLIARQUÍA.

policarpo, *a.* (bot.) polycarpous.

pólice, *m.* thumb.

policía. I. *f.* police; politeness, good breeding; cleanliness, neatness. II. *m.* policeman.

policíaco, ca, *a.* (contempt.) pert. to police, police (as *a.*).

policial (S. A.), **policiano** (Arg.), *m.* policeman. —**novela policial,** detective story.

policitación, *f.* (law) pollicitation.

policroísmo, *m.* (min.) pleochroism.

policromía, *f.* quality of being polychrome.

policromo, ma, *a.* polychrome, many-colored.

Polichinela, *m.* Punchinello, Punch, buffoon.

poliédrico, ca, *a.* polyhedrical.

poliedro, *m.* (geom.) polyhedron.

polifásico, ca, *a.* (elec.) multiphase.

polígala, *f.* (bot.) milkwort.

poligaleo, a, *a.* (bot.) polygalaceous.

poligamia, *f.* polygamy.

polígamo, ma. I. *a.* polygamous; several times married. II. *n.* polygamist; one who has married several times.

poligenismo, *m.* polygenesis (esp. of human race).

poligenista, *n.* polygenist.

poligloto, ta. I. *n.* & *a.* polyglot. II. *f.* polyglot Bible.

poligonáceo, a, *a.* (bot.) polygonaceous.

poligonal. I. *a.* (geom.) polygonal. II. *f.* (surv.) broken line.

polígono, na. I. *a.* polygonal. II. *m.* (geom.) polygon; (bot.) poly; (artil.) practice ground.

poligrafía, *f.* art of writing in or interpreting ciphers.

poligráfico, ca, *a.* pert. to POLIGRAFÍA.

polígrafo, *m.* expert with ciphers.

polilla, *f.* moth, clothes moth; consumer, waster.

polimería, *f.* (chem.) polymerism.

polimerización, *f.* (chem.) polymerization.

polímero, ra, *a.* (chem.) polymeric.

polímita, *a.* made of many-colored threads.

polimorfismo, *m.* polymorphism.

polimorfo, fa, *a.* polymorphous.

polín, *m.* (naut.) wooden roller, skidding.

polinesiano, na; polinesio, sia, *n.* & *a.* Polynesian.

polinomio, *m.* (math.) polynomial.

poliorama, *m.* polyorama.

poliorcética, *f.* (mil.) art of attack and defense.

polipero, *m.* polypary.

polipétalo, la, *a.* (bot.) polypetalous.

poliplano, *m.* (aer.) multiplane.

pólipo, *m.* (zool.) polyp; (ichth.) octopus, polup; (med.) polypus.

polipodiáceo, a. I. *a.* (bot.) polypodiaceous. **II.** *f. pl.* Polypodiaceæ.

polipodio, *m.* (bot.) polypody, fern.

polisarcia, *f.* (med.) obesity.

poliscopio, *m.* (opt. and surg.) polyscope.

polisépalo, la, *a.* (bot.) polysepalous.

polisílabo, ba. I. *a.* polysyllabic. **II.** *m.* polysyllable.

polisíndeton, *m.* (rhet.) polysyndeton.

polisón, *m.* bustle (woman's dress).

polispasto, *m.* burton, hoisting tackle.

¹polista, *n.* polo player.

²polista, *n.* (P. I.) Indian doing ³POLO.

polistilo, la. I. *a.* (arch.) polystyle; (bot.) polystylous. **II.** *m.* (arch.) polystyle.

politécnico, ca, *a.* polytechnic.

politeísmo, *m.* polytheism.

politeísta, *n. & a.* polytheist(-ic).

política, *f.* policy; politics; politeness.—**p. exterior**, foreign policy.—**por p.**, as a matter of policy; for the sake of politeness.

políticamente, *adv.* politically; civilly.

politicastro, *m.* politicaster, petty politician.

político, ca. I. *a.* political, politic; polite, courteous. **II.** *n.* politician.

politicón, na, *a.* exceedingly polite and ceremonious.

politiquear, *vn.* (coll.) to talk politics.

politiquería, *f.* (Am.) low politics; (contempt.) politics, political talk and doings, political trash.

politiquero, ra, *n.* (Am.) one that indulges in, or is fond of, common politics; political busybody.

poliuria, *f.* (med.) polyuria.

póliza, *f.* (com.) policy; scrip; check, draft, pay-bill; custom house permit; admission ticket; lampoon, anonymous note.—**p. de seguro**, insurance policy.

¹polizón, na, *n.* vagrant, lazy vagabond; stow-away; parasite, sponger.

²polizón, *m.* (Am.) = POLISÓN, bustle (on dress).

polizonte, *m.* (coll.) (contempt.) policeman.

¹polo, *m.* (geog. & astr.) pole; pole of magnetic needle; support, foundation.

²polo, *m.* (sports) polo.

³polo, *m.* (P. I.) personal service to community of forty days in year by natives.

⁴polo, *m.* a popular Andalusian song.

polonés, sa, *a.* Polish.

polonesa, *f.* ladies' fur-trimmed polonaise.

polonio, *m.* (chem.) polonium.

poltrón, na. I. *a.* idle, lazy, lubberly. **II.** *n.* (coll.) poltroon.

poltronería, *f.* idleness, laziness, indolence.

poltronizarse, *vr.* to become lazy.

polución, *f.* (med.) pollution.

poluto, ta, *a.* polluted; unclean, filthy.

Pólux, *m.* (astr.) Pollux (a star).

polvareda, *f.* cloud of dust; altercation, dispute.

polvera, *f.* (cosmetic) powder box.

polvificar, *va.* (coll.) to pulverize.

polvillo, ito, *m. dim.* fine dust.

polvo, *m.* dust; powder; pinch of snuff or powder. —*pl.* toilet powder.—**polvos de cartas**, sand for blotting writing.—**polvos de Juanes**, red precipitate, red nitrate of mercury.—**polvos de la madre Celestina**, (coll.) secret and miraculous mode in which anything is done.— **polvos para dientes**, tooth powder.—**en p.**, powdered.—**limpio de p. y paja**, without toil or hardship; free from all charges; net.— **sacudir el p.**, to beat out, or shake off, the dust.

pólvora, *f.* powder, gunpowder; artificial fire-works; bad temper; vivacity, liveliness, brisk-ness.—**p. de algodón**, guncotton.—**p. de caza**, shotgun powder.—**p. detonante**, or **fulminante**, detonating powder.—**p. lenta**, slow-burning powder.—**p. sin humo**, smokeless powder.—**gastar la p. en salvas**, to work to no purpose, to waste time and energy.—**no haber inventado la p.**, or **no ser el inventor de la p.**, to be dull, not to be a genius.—**ser una p.**, to be quick, to be a hustler.

polvoreamiento, *m.* powdering.

polvorear, *va.* to powder, sprinkle powder on.

polvoriento, ta, *a.* dusty.

polvorín, *m.* finest powder; powderflask, priming horn; powder magazine.

polvorista, *m.* manufacturer of gunpowder; maker of fireworks.

polvoroso, sa, *a.* dusty, full of dust.

polla, *f.* pullet; (coll.) comely young lass; (cards) pool; (ornith.) FÚLICA, coot.

pollada, *f.* flock of young fowls; hatch, covey.

pollancón, na, *n.* large chicken; (coll.) over-grown youth.

pollastra, *f.* large young hen.

pollastre, pollastro, *m.* large chicken; (coll.) cunning fellow.

pollazón, *m.* hatching; hatch, brood.

pollera, *f.* woman who raises or sells chickens; chicken roost, chicken coop; gocart; hooped petticoat.

pollería, *f.* poultry shop or market; (coll.) assemblage of young persons.

pollero, *m.* poulterer; poultry yard.

pollina, *f.* young she-ass.

pollinarmente, *adv.* (coll.) foolishly.

pollino, *m.* donkey, ass, jument.

pollito, ta, *n.* chicken; (coll.) boy or girl.

pollo, *m.* chicken; nestling; young bee; (coll.) young man; artful, clever man.

polluelo, la, *n.* little chicken, chick.

poma, *f.* apple; perfume censer; smelling bottle; pomander box.

pomáceo, a. I. *a.* (bot.) pomaceous. **II.** *f. pl.* Pomaceæ.

pomada, *f.* pomatum, pomade; salve.

pomar, *m.* orchard, especially of apple trees.

pomarada, *f.* plantation of apple trees.

pomarrosa, *f.* (bot.) rose apple.

pomerano, na, *n. & a.* Pomeranian.

pómez.—**piedra p.**, *f.* pumice stone.

pomífero, ra, *a.* (poet.) apple-bearing.

pomo, *m.* pip fruit; pomum; pomander box; flask, flagon, small bottle; pommel; nosegay.

pomología, *f.* pomology, science of fruit growing.

pompa, *f.* pomp, ostentation, splendor; grand procession, pageant; bubble; ballooning of clothes raised by the wind; expanded tail of a turkey or peacock; (naut.) pump.

pompearse, *vr.* (coll.) to appear with pomp and ostentation; to strut.

pompeyano, na, *n. & a.* Pompeian, of Pompeii; relating to, or follower of, Pompey.

pompón, *m.* (mil.) pompon.

pomponearse, *vr.* = POMPEARSE.

pomposamente, *adv.* pompously.

pomposo, sa, *a.* pompous; magnificent, splendid; inflated.

pómulo, *m.* cheek bone.

ponceño, ña, *n. & a.* Poncean (from Ponce).

poncí, poncidre, poncil, *a. & m.* terms app. to a species of bitter orange or lemon.

ponchada, *f.* quantity of punch made at one time.

ponche, *m.* punch (liquor).

ponchera, *f.* punch bowl.

¹poncho, cha, *a.* soft, mild, careless, heedless.

²poncho, *m.* military cloak or greatcoat; poncho.

ponderable, *a.* ponderable; wonderful.

ponderación, *f.* consideration, deliberation; ex-aggeration.

ponderador, ra, *n. & a.* ponderer(-ing); exag-gerator(-ing).

ponderal, *a.* ponderal, relating to weight.

ponderar, *va.* to weigh; to ponder, consider; to exaggerate; to praise highly.

ponderativo, va, *a.* exaggerating, hyperbolical.

ponderosamente, *adv.* attentively, carefully.

ponderosidad, *f.* ponderousness, ponderosity.

ponderoso, sa, *a.* heavy, ponderous; grave, circumspect, cautious.

pondré, *fut.* of PONER.

ponedero, ra. I. *a.* capable of being laid or placed; egg-laying (as a hen). **II.** *m.* nest, hen's nest; nest egg.

ponedor, ra. I. *a.* egg-laying (as a hen). **II.** *n.* one that sets or lays; bettor, wagerer; outbidder; horse trained to rear on the hind legs.

ponencia, *f.* charge, post, or office of a chairman of a committee, or of a final judge or arbiter; exercise of such an office.

ponente, *n.* arbitrator, referee; chairman of a reporting committee.

ponentino, na, tisco, ca, *a.* western.

poner. I. *va.* (*pp.* PUESTO; *ind. pres.* PONGO, *pret.* PUSE, *fut.* PONDRÉ; *subj.* PONGA) to put, place, lay; to dispose, arrange, set (as the table); to suppose, assume; to impose, keep (as order, peace, etc.); to oblige, compel; to wager, stake; to appoint, put in charge; to adduce; to leave to one's judgment or action; to call, give (a person or thing) the name of; to write, set down; to lay (eggs); to bring forth; to contribute; to enforce; to concert; to agree; to insult, to treat badly; to cause (fear, etc.); to make, cause to become or turn (red, angry, etc.).—**p. al corriente,** to inform.—**p. al día,** to bring (someone) up to date (on the news).—**p. al sol,** to expose to the sun, to sun.—**p. (mala) cara,** to make a (wry) face.—**p. casa,** to begin, or go to, housekeeping.—**p. colorado,** to put to the blush, shame.—**p. como chupa de dómine,** or **como nuevo,** to humiliate, reprimand or treat harshly, dress down.—**p. como un guante,** to make pliable or submissive.—**p. coto a,** to stop, check, put a limit to.—**p. de manifiesto,** to make public.—**p. de su parte,** to do one's part, or on one's part.—**p. de vuelta y media** = P. COMO NUEVO.—**p. en (tanto),** to bid (so much).—**p. en claro,** to make clear; to clear up (by investigation).—**p. en duda,** to question, doubt.—**p. en práctica,** to start doing, get (a project, etc.) underway.—**p. en relieve,** to carve in relief; to describe graphically.—**p. en ridículo,** to make ridiculous.—**p. en vigor,** to enforce.—**p. fin a,** to put a stop to.—**p. fuego,** to set fire.—**p. la mesa,** to set the table.—**p. mal,** to discredit, run down; to set against (each other).—**p. pies en pared,** to maintain one's opinion with obstinacy.—**p. pies en polvorosa,** to take to one's heels.—**p. por,** to use as; appoint or send as.—**p. por escrito,** to put down in writing.—**p. por las nubes,** to praise to the skies.—**p. reparos,** to make objections. **II.** *vr.* to apply oneself to, to set about; to put on (as a garment); to set or place oneself; to oppose; to become, get (as wet, angry, dirty); to set (as the sun); to reach, get to, arrive; to adorn oneself.—**p. a,** to begin to, start to.—**p. a cubierto,** to shelter oneself from danger.—**p. colorado,** to blush.—**p. de acuerdo,** to reach an agreement.—**p. en camino,** to set out, start, take off.—**p. en jarras,** to put one's arms akimbo.—**p. en marcha** = P. EN CAMINO.—**p. en pie,** to stand up.—**p. en práctica,** (of a project, etc.) to be started, get underway.—**p. en razón,** to be reasonable.— **ponérsele a uno,** to take a fancy or a notion to; to suspect, surmise (diff. constr.: *se me pone que Juan no pagará,* I suspect John won't pay). —**p. mal con,** to incur (someone's) enmity, "get in bad with."—**p. tan alto,** to become

haughtily indignant, swell up with indignation. —**al p. el sol,** at sunset.

¹pongo, *m.* (S. A.) narrow and dangerous ford; (S. A.) Indian servant.

²pongo, *m.* (zool.) orang-outang.

³pongo, ponga, *v. V.* PONER.

ponientada, *f.* steady west wind.

poniente, *m.* west; west wind.

ponimiento, *m.* act of putting, or putting on.

ponleví, *m.* shoe with high, wooden heel.

pontaje, pontazgo, *m.* bridge toll, pontage.

pontear, *va.* to erect a bridge over.

pontezuelo, la, *n. dim.* small bridge.

póntico, ca, *a.* Pontic.

pontificado, *m.* pontificate, papacy, popedom.

pontifical. I. *a.* pontifical, papal. **II.** *m.* (eccl.) pontifical (book and robes); parochial tithes.

pontificalmente, *adv.* pontifically.

pontificar, *vn.* (coll.) to act like a pontiff, pontificate; to rule; to preside.

pontífice, *m.* pontiff; archbishop or bishop of a diocese.—**pontificio, cia,** *a.* pontifical.

pontil, *m.* (glassmaking) pontil or punty.

pontín, *m.* (P. I.) (naut.) coasting vessel.

ponto, *m.* (poet.) sea.

pontón, *m.* (mil.) pontoon; hulk serving as storeship, hospital, or prison ship; (naut.) mudscow, lighter, dredge; log bridge.

pontonero, *m.* (mil.) pontonier.

ponzoña, *f.* poison, venom.

ponzoñosamente, *adv.* poisonously, venomously.

ponzoñoso, sa, *a.* poisonous, venomous, baneful.

popa, *f.* (naut.) poop, stern.—**a p., de p., en p.,** aft, abaft.—**de p. a proa,** entirely, completely.

popamiento, *m.* despising; cajoling, fondling.

popar, *vn.* to despise; to cajole; to fondle.

popel, a. (naut.) aftermost, sternmost.

popés, *m.* (naut.) stay of the mizzenmast.

poplíteo, tea, *a.* (anat.) popliteal.

popote, *m.* Indian straw for brooms; (Mex.) straw (for drinking).

populachería, *f.* claptrap; cheap popularity.

populachero, ra, *a.* vulgar, common.

populacho, *m.* populace, mob, rabble.

popular, *a.* popular.

popularidad, *f.* popularity.

popularizar. I. *va.* (*pret.* POPULARICÉ; *subj.* POPULARICE) to popularize, make popular. **II.** *vr.* to become popular.

popularmente, *adv.* popularly.

populazo, *m.* populace, mob, rabble.

populeón, *m.* white poplar ointment.

populoso, sa, *a.* populous.

poquedad, *f.* paucity, littleness; pusillanimity, trifle, mite; stupidity.

poquillo, lla. I. *a. dim.* small, little; trifling. **II.** *adv. dim.* very little time. **III.** *m.* (a) little, (a) little bit.

poquísimo, ma, *a. & adv. super.* very little.

poquitico, ica, illo, illa, ito, ita, *a. dim.* almost nothing, just a little.

poquito, ta. I. *a. dim.* very little; weak of body and mind, diminutive.—**p. a poco,** gently, slowly. **II.** *m.* a wee bit.—**a poquitos,** little by little; a little at a time.

por, *prep.* by; for; through (*pasamos por un túnel,* we passed through a tunnel; *Juan entró por la ventana,* John came in through the window); as (*desechado por inútil,* cast off as useless); across (*se pasó la mano por la frente,* he passed his hand across his forehead); about, nearly (*por ahí,* about that, very nearly; *por Navidad,* about Christmas); during (*volverá por la cuaresma,* he will return during Lent); per; after, for (*ir por pan,* to go for, or after, bread); for the sake of (*por Vd.,* for your sake); in behalf of, on account of (*por causa de enfermedad,* on account of illness); in order to; by way of, via; in the name of; without, not yet, to be (*cartas por contestar,* letters to be answered; *la casa está* *por acabar*, the house is not yet finished, or, is to be finished).—**p. cuanto**, inasmuch as, whereas.—¡**p. Dios!**, for Heaven's sake!—**p. docena**, by the dozen.—**p. entre**, through; among, between.—**p. escrito**, in writing.—**p. la mañana (tarde, noche)**, in the morning (afternoon, evening).—**p. más que**, or **p. mucho que**, however much, no matter how much; notwithstanding (one's great efforts, etc.).—**p. qué**, why.—¿**p. que?**, why?—**p. si**, or **p. si acaso**, in case; if by chance.—**p. sí o p. no**, to be sure; to be on the safe side.—**p. sobre**, above, besides.—**p. supuesto**, of course.

porcachón, na, *a.* (coll.) very dirty, hoggish.

porcal, *a.* kind of large plum.

porcaso, *m.* hog tapir.

porcelana, *f.* porcelain; chinaware; jewel enamel. —**porcelanita**, *f.* porcelanite, jasper.

porcentaje, *m.* percentage.

porcino, na. I. *a.* hoggish; porcine. **II.** *m.* young pig; bruise, bump.

porción, *f.* portion, part; lot; (com.) share, allowance, allotment; pittance.

porcioncica, illa, ita, *f. dim.* small portion.

porcionero, ra, *n. & a.* participant(-ating).

porcionista, *n.* shareholder; school boarder.

porcipelo, *m.* (coll.) bristle.

porciúncula, *f.* (eccl.) Franciscan jubilee.

porcuno, na, *a.* hoggish, porcine.

porchada, *f.* stretcher in paper factories.

porche, *m.* covered walk; porch, portico.

pordiosear, *vn.* to beg.—**pordioseo**, *m.* begging.

pordiosería, *f.* beggary.

pordiosero, ra, *n.* beggar.

porfía, *f.* obstinacy, stubbornness; insistence, persistence; importunity.—**a p.**, in competition, vying with each other; insistently.

porfiadamente, *adv.* obstinately; pertinaciously.

porfiado, da, *pp. & a.* obstinate, stubborn.

porfiador, ra, *n.* persistent person.

porfiar, *vn.* to persist.

porfídico, ca, *a.* porphyritic.

pórfido, *m.* porphyry, jasper.

pormenor, *m.* detail, particular.

pormenorizar, *va.* to detail, itemize, enter into details about, give in detail.

pornografía, *f.* pornography; pornograph.

pornográfico, ca, *a.* pornographic.

pornógrafo, *m.* pornographer.

poro, *m.* pore, interstice.

pororó, *m.* (S. A.) toasted corn.

pororoca, *f.* bore (at mouth of river).

porosidad, *f.* porosity.

poroso, sa, *a.* porous.

poroto, *m.* (Am.) a variety of pea; (Arg.) bean.—**apuntarse un p.**, (Arg.) (coll.) to make a point (as in a debate); be one up.

porque, *conj.* because, for, as; in order that.

¿**por qué?** *interr.* why? wherefore?

porqué, *m.* reason, motive; (coll.) allowance, pittance, portion.

porquecilla, *f. dim.* small sow.

porquera, *f.* lair, couch of a wild boar.

porquería, *f.* nastiness; filth; vile, dirty act, nasty trick; trifle, worthless thing.

porqueriza, *f.* pigsty.

porquerizo, za; porquero, ra, *n.* swineherd.

porquerón, *m.* (coll.) petty officer of justice.

porqueta, *f.* woodlouse.

porquezuelo, la, *n. dim.* small hog or sow; slovenly young person.

porra, *f.* bludgeon, club; maul; last player in boys' games; (coll.) vanity, boast; (coll.) dull or importunate person.

porrada, *f.* blow or knock; (coll.) foolishness, nonsense.

porrazo, *m.* blow, knock; fall.

porrear, *vn.* (coll.) to insist, persist.

porrería, *f.* (coll.) obstinacy; silliness.

porreta, *f.* green leaf of leeks, garlic, or onions.—**en p.**, (coll.) stark naked.

porrilla, *f.* small forging hammer; (vet.) osseous tumor in joints.

porrillo.—a p., *adv.* (coll.) aplenty, abundantly.

porrina, *f.* small and green crop.

porrino, *m.* tender plant of a leek.

porrizo, *m.* bed or plot of leeks.

¹**porro, rra**, *a.* (coll.) stupid.

²**porro**, *m.* (bot.) leek.

¹**porrón, na**, *a. aug.* heavy, sluggish, slow.

²**porrón**, *m.* earthen jug; wine bottle with long side spout.

porrudo, *m.* shepherd's crook.

porta, *f.* (naut.) gun port; stern port.

porta-, particle used in composition, gen. equivalent to "holder" or "carrier" after the corresponding noun, as in *portaplumas*, penholder; *portanoticias*, news carrier; *portaneumático*, tire holder; *portaaviones*, airplane carrier.

portaaguja, *f.* needle holder.

portaaviones, *m.* airplane carrier.

portabandera, *f.* socket for a flagpole.

portabombas, *m.* bomb carrier.

portacaja, *f.* carrier of a loom; (mil.) drumsash or strap.

portacarabina, *f.* (mil.) carbine thimble.

portacartas, *m.* mail bag for letters.

portada, *f.* portal, porch; frontispiece, front, façade; cover (of a magazine, etc.); (print.) title page; division of the warp.

portadera, *f.* chest for stores on a horse.

portado, da, *a.*—**bien (mal) p.**, well (poorly) dressed or behaved.

portador, ra. I. *n.* bearer, carrier, porter; (com.) holder, bearer. **II.** *m.* waiter's tray.

portaestandarte, *m.* (mil.) color sergeant.

portafolio, *m.* (Gal.) (Arg.) briefcase.

portafusil, *m.* (mil.) sling of a musket.

portaguión, *m.* (mil.) guidon (officer).

portaje, *m.* = PORTAZGO.

portal, *m.* porch, entry, entrance, vestibule, hallway; portico, piazza; town's gate.

portalámpara, *m.* lamp holder; (elec.) socket (of a lamp fixture).

portalápiz, *m.* pencil holder.

portalazo, *m. aug.* large door or porch.

portalejo, *m. dim.* little porch or portico.

portalente, *m.* lens holder.

portaleña, *f.* (fort.) embrasure; plank for doors.

portalero, *m.* octroi officer or guard.

portalibros, *m.* book strap.

portalico, illo, ito, *m. dim.* small porch.

portalón, *m.* (naut.) gangway.

portamanteo, *m.* portmanteau, valise.

portamira, *n.* (surv.) rodman.

portamonedas, *m.* pocketbook, purse.

portanario, *m.* (anat.) pylorus.

portaneumático, *m.* (auto) tire holder.

portante, *m.* quick pace of a horse.—**tomar el p.**, (coll.) to go away.

portantillo, *m. dim.* gentle amble, easy pace.

portanuevas, *n.* newsmonger.

portanveces, *m.* coadjutor, assistant.

portañola, *f.* (naut.) porthole.

portañuela, *f.* (tailoring) fly of trousers.

portaobjetos, *m.* slide (of microscope).

portapaz, *n.* (eccl.) pix.

portaparaguas, *m.* umbrella stand.

portaplacas, portaplanchas, *m.* (photog.) dark slide, plate holder, chassis.

portapliegos, *m.* large portfolio.

portaplumas, *m.* penholder.

portar. I. *va.* to carry (as arms). **II.** *vr.* to behave, act. **III.** *vn.* (naut.) (of sails) to fill.

portátil, *a.* portable.

portavasos, *m.* glass stand or rack.

portaventanero, *m.* carpenter who makes windows and doors.

portaviandas, *m.* dinner pail.

portavoz, *m.* megaphone, speaking trumpet.

portazgo, *m.* toll, turnpike duty.

portazguero, *m.* toll gatherer, collector.

portazo, *m.* slam of a door; slamming a door in one's face.

porte, *m.* cost of carriage; freight, portage, porterage; postage; bearing (of persons); nobility; illustrious descent; size; capacity; (naut.) burden or tonnage.—**p. franco,** frank; postage prepaid.

portear. I. *va.* to carry or convey for a price. **II.** *vr.* (of birds) to pass, migrate.

portento, *m.* prodigy, wonder; portent.

portentosamente, *adv.* prodigiously.

portentoso, sa, *a.* prodigious, marvelous.

porteo, *m.* carrying, cartage, portage.

porterejo, *m.* little porter.

¹portería, *f.* porter's lodge or box, conciergerie; employment of a porter.

²portería, *f.* (naut.) (collect.) the portholes.

portero, ra, *n.* janitor, superintendent, concierge; porter, gatekeeper.

portezuela, *f. dim.* little door; carriage door; pocket flap; (Mex.) pass between hills.

pórtico, *m.* portico, piazza; porch; hall; lobby.

portilla, *f.* opening, passage; (naut.) porthole.

portillo, *m.* opening, gap, breach; wicket, gate; means to an end; cavity in anything broken; octroi gate of a town; pass between hills.

portón, *m.* inner front door of a house.

portorriqueño, ña, *n.* & *a.* Puerto-Rican.

portugués, sa. I. *n.* & *a.* Portuguese. **II.** *m.* Portuguese language.

portulano, *m.* charts of ports and harbors.

porvenir, *m.* future, time to come.

¡porvida! *interj.* by the living saints!

pos.—en p. de, *adv.* after, behind; in pursuit of.

posa, *f.* passing bell; stop in a funeral, to sing a response.—*pl.* (coll.) buttocks.

posada, *f.* lodging; lodging house; inn, tavern, hotel; home, dwelling.

posadera, *f.* hostess, landlady.

posaderas, *f. pl.* buttocks.

posadero, *m.* innkeeper, host; seat made of flags or bass ropes.

posante, *a.* reposing; smooth (sailing).

posar. I. *vn.* to lodge, board; to sit down, repose, rest; to perch, light; (art) to pose. **II.** *va.* to lay down. **III.** *vr.* (of liquid) to settle; to light, alight, sit (on).

posaverga, *f.* (naut.) yard prop.

posbélico, ca, *a.* post-war.

posca, *f.* mixture of vinegar and water.

posdata, *f.* postscript.

poseedor, ra, *n.* possessor, holder, owner.

poseer, *va.* (*ger.* POSEYENDO; *pp.* POSEÍDO, POSESO; *pret.* él POSEYÓ) to hold, possess, own; to master (an art, language, etc.).

poseído, da. I. *pp. reg.* of POSEER. **II.** *a.*—**estar p.,** (fig.) to be possessed; to be thoroughly convinced or posted about. **III.** *m.* private arable land.

posesión, *f.* possession; property; possession by evil spirits.—*pl.* holdings, wealth, property.

posesional, *a.* possessional, possessive.

posesionar. I. *va.* to give possession; to install, induct. **II.** *vr.* to take possession.

posesionero, ra, *n.* cattle keeper owning pastures.

posesivo, va, *n.* & *a.* (gram.) possessive.

poseso, sa. I. *pp. irreg.* of POSEER. **II.** *a.* possessed (with evil spirits).

posesor, ra, *n.* possessor, holder, owner.

posesorio, ria, *a.* possessory.

poseyente, *a.* possessing, owning.

poseyó, etc. *v. V.* POSEER.

posfecha, *f.* postdate.—**posfechar,** *va.* to postdate.

posguerra, *a.* = POSBÉLICO.

posibilidad, *f.* possibility; means, property.

posibilitar, *va.* to render possible, facilitate.

posible. I. *a.* possible.—**en lo p.,** as far, insofar, as possible.—**lo más** (*adj., adv.*) **p.,** as (*adj., adv.*) as possible. **II.** *m. pl.* personal means; best of one's ability.

posiblemente, *adv.* possibly.

posición, *f.* position; placing, placement; standing, status; (law) questions and answers of an interrogatory; (math.) position.

positivamente, *adv.* positively; absolutely.

positivismo, *m.* positiveness; positivism; (moral) materialism; matter-of-factness.

positivista. I. *n.* & *a.* positivist(-ic). **II.** *a.* practical, realistic, matter-of-fact.

positivo, va, *a.* positive, certain; absolute, real; matter-of-fact; (math., elec., photog.) positive; (gram.) positive.—**de p.,** certainly, without doubt.

pósito, *m.* public granary.

positura, *f.* posture, state, disposition.

posma. I. *f.* (coll.) sluggishness, sloth, dullness. **II.** *n.* (coll.) dull, sluggish person.

poso, *m.* sediment, dregs, lees; rest, repose.

posó, *m.* (P. I.) chignon, hair knot.

posología, *f.* (med.) posology.

posón, *m.* round matted seat.

pospelo.—a p. *adv.* against the grain; reluctantly.

pospierna, *f.* thigh of an animal.

posponer, *va.* (*pp.* POSPUESTO; *ind. pres.* POSPONGO, *pret.* POSPUSE, *fut.* POSPONDRÉ; *subj.* POSPONGA) (a) to put (after); to think less (of); to subordinate (to).

pospuesto, ta, *pp. irreg.* of POSPONER.

posta. I. *f.* post horses, relay; post, post stage, posthouse, post office; chop of meat or fish; mold shot; stake, at cards; memorial tablet. **II.** *n.* person who travels post.

postal. I. *a.* postal.—**giro p.,** money order. **II.** *f.* postal card.

postdata, *f.* = POSDATA.

postdiluviano, na, *a.* postdiluvian.

poste, *m.* post, pillar; remaining standing up as a school punishment.—**p. de amarre,** (aer.) mooring mast.

postelero, *m.* (naut.) skid, skeed; chess-trees.

postema, *f.* abscess, gathering; boresome person.

postemero, *m.* (surg.) large lancet.

postergación, *f.* delaying; leaving behind; disregard of seniority.

postergar, *va.* (*pret.* POSTERGUÉ; *subj.* POSTERGUE) to delay; to ignore or disregard the right of seniority of (a candidate for office, etc.).

posteridad, *f.* posterity.

posterior, *a.* posterior, rear; later, subsequent.

posterioridad, *f.* posteriority.

posteriormente, *adv.* subsequently.

posteta, *f.* (bookbinding) number of sheets stitched together.

postigo, *m.* wicket; peep window; shutter; (fort.) sally port, postern.

postila, *f.* marginal note.

postilación, *f.* marginal annotation.

postilador, *m.* annotator.

postilar, *va.* to gloss, comment.

postilla, *f.* scab on wounds.

postillón, *m.* postillion, postboy.

postilloso, sa, *a.* scabby.

postizo, za. I. *a.* artificial, not natural; false (teeth). **II.** *m.* false hair, switch. **III.** *f.* castanet; (naut.) dead work on galleys.

postliminio, *m.* (int. law) postliminy.

postmeridiano, na, *a.* postmeridian, p.m.

postor, *m.* bidder.

postración, *f.* prostration; kneeling; dejection.

postrado, da. I. *pp.* of POSTRAR. **II.** *a.* prostrate, prostrated, prone.

postrador, ra. I. *n.* & *a.* prostrator(-ing). **II.** *m.* footstool in a choir.

postrar. I. *va.* to prostrate, to humble; to overthrow, demolish; to weaken, exhaust. **II.** *vr.* to prostrate oneself, kneel down, lie prone; to be exhausted.

postre. I. *a.* last in order.—**a la p.,** at last.—**por fin y p.,** (coll.) finally. **II.** *m.* (*sing.* or *pl.*) dessert.

postremo, ma, *a.* last.

postrer, *a. contr.* of POSTRERO (*before a noun*).

postreramente, *adv.* lastly.

postrero, ra, *a.* last; hindermost.

postrimer, *a. contr.* of POSTRIMERO (*before a n.*).

postrimeramente, *adv.* finally, at last.

postrimería, *f.* (theol.) last stage of life.

postrimero, ra, *a.* last; hindmost.

póstula, postulación, *f.* request, petition; (eccl.) postulation.

postulado, *m.* postulate.

postulador, ra, *n.* one who postulates.

postulante, *a. & n.* postulant.

postular, *va.* to postulate.

póstumo, ma, *a.* posthumous.

postura, *f.* posture, position; planting trees or plants; tree or plant transplanted; assize of provisions; (com.) bid; stake, wager; egg; egg-laying; agreement, covenant.

potabilizar, *va.* to make potable or drinkable.

potable, *a.* potable, drinkable.

potación, *f.* potation, drinking; beverage.

potador, ra, *n.* inspector of weights and measures.

potaje, *m.* pottage; porridge; stewed vegetables; mixed drink; medley.

potajería, *f.* heap of dry pulse; place where vegetables are kept.

potajier, *m.* (Gal.) keeper of the vegetables in the royal palace.

potala, *f.* (naut.) anchor; stone anchor; small slow vessel.

¹potar, *va.* to correct and mark (measures).

²potar, *va.* to drink.

potasa, *f.* potash.

potásico, ca, *a.* potassic; potassium (as *a.*, as in *bromuro potásico,* potassium bromide).

potasio, *m.* potassium.

pote, *m.* jug; pot, jar; (cooking) pot; flowerpot; standard measure or weight.—**a p.,** abundantly.—**potecillo, ito,** *n. dim.* little pot, can or jar.

potencia, *f.* power, capacity; dominion; faculty of the mind; possibility; power, strong nation; force, strength; (mech., phys., math.) power; (artil.) reach.—*pl.* nine rays of light around the head of Jesus.—**potencias del alma,** powers of the soul, mental powers (gen. stated as memory, judgment, and will).—**en p.,** potentially.

potencial, *a. & f.* potential.—**potencialidad,** *f.* potentiality.—**potencialmente,** *adv.* potentially, virtually.

potentado, *m.* potentate, sovereign.

potente, *a.* potent, powerful, mighty; strong, vigorous; (coll.) bulky, huge.

potentemente, *adv.* powerfully, potently.

potenza, *f.* (her.) tace.

poterna, *f.* (mil.) postern, sally port.

potero, *m.* = POTADOR.

potestad, *f.* power, dominion, jurisdiction; potentate.—*pl.* angelic powers.

potestativo, va, *a.* (law) facultative.

potingue, *m.* (coll.) medicinal concoction.

potísimo, ma, *a. super.* most special.

potista, *n.* (coll.) tippler, drinker.

pot-pourri, *m.* potpourri; mixture; hash.

¹potra, *f.* (coll.) rupture, scrotal hernia.—**tener p.,** to have good luck.

²potra, *f.* filly, young mare.—**potrada,** *f.* herd of fillies.—**potranca,** *f.* filly.

potrear, *va.* (coll.) to tease, vex, annoy.

potrera, *f.* a hempen headstall.

¹potrero, *m.* (coll.) rupture specialist.

²potrero, *m.* herdsman of colts; pasture ground; (Am.) cattle ranch.

potrico, illo, *m. dim.* small colt.

potril, *m.* pasture for young horses.

potrilla, *f.* (coll.) old man affecting rakish youth.

potro, *m.* colt, foal; wooden horse, rack; shoeing frame; anything that torments; obstetrical chair; pit in the ground for dividing a beehive.—**estar en un p.,** to be on pins and needles.

potroso, sa, *a.* afflicted with a rupture; (coll.) fortunate, lucky.

poya, *f.* fee for baking in a public oven; hemp bagasse.

poyal, *m.* striped cover for benches; stone seat.

poyar, *vn.* to pay the POYA.

poyata, *f.* shelf, cupboard.

poyo, *m.* stone seat against a wall; fee formerly paid to judges.

poza, *f.* puddle; pool for breaking hemp.

pozal, *m.* bucket, pail; coping of a well; vessel sunk in the earth to collect liquids.

pozanco, *m.* pool in a river bank.

pozo, *m.* (water) well; deep hole in a river; eddy, whirlpool; (min.) shaft, pit; (naut.) hold; anything complete in its line.—**p. artesiano,** artesian well.—**p. negro,** cesspool.

pozol, pozole, *m.* barley and beans boiled.

pozuela, *f. dim.* small puddle or pond.

pozuelo, *m. dim.* small well or pit; vessel sunk in the ground to collect oil, etc.

práctica, *f.* practice; habit; practicing; exercise; manner, method, routine; learning a profession under a master.—**en la p.,** in practice.

practicable, *a.* practicable, feasible.

practicador, ra, *n.* practicer, practitioner.

practicaje, *m.* (naut.) pilotage.

prácticamente, *adv.* in a practical manner, in practice.

practicante. I. *a.* practicing. **II.** *n.* practicer, practitioner; hospital intern; hospital nurse; one who practices medicine under direction and guidance of an experienced physician; (pharm.) prescription preparer, or clerk.

practicar, *va.* (*pret.* PRACTIQUÉ; *subj.* PRACTIQUE) to practice; to make; to perform, do, put in execution; to practice, go in for; to learn the practice of under an adviser.

práctico, ca. I. *a.* practical; skillful, experienced. **II.** *m.* (naut.) harbor pilot.

practicón, na, *n.* (coll.) one possessing practical knowledge and experience.

practiqué, practique, *v.* V. PRACTICAR.

pradeño, ña, *a.* pertaining to prairies.

pradera, pradería, *f.* prairie, meadow.

praderoso, sa, *a.* pertaining to prairies.

pradial, *m.* Prairial, ninth month of the French-Revolution calendar.

prado, *m.* lawn; field, pasture ground; walk (in a city).—**p. de guadaña,** meadow mowed annually.

pragmática, *f.* sanction, decree.

pragmático, *m.* interpreter of national laws.

pragmatismo, *m.* (philos.) pragmatism.

pragmatista, *n. & a.* (philos.) pragmatist(-ic).

prao, *m.* proa, prao, an Asiatic canoe.

prasio, *m.* (min.) prase, translucent quartz.

prasma, *m.* (min.) dark green agate.

pravedad, *f.* perversity, iniquity, depravity.

pravo, va, *a.* depraved, wicked, perverse.

pre, *m.* = PREST, soldier's daily pay.

preadamita, *n.* preadamite.

preadamítico, ca, *a.* preadamite.

preámbulo, *m.* preamble; (coll.) evasion.

prebenda, *f.* (eccl.) prebend, benefice.

prebendado, *m.* (eccl.) prebendary.

prebendar, *va.* to confer a prebend on.

prebostal, *a.* provostal.

prebostazgo, *m.* provostship.

preboste, *m.* provost; (mil.) provost.

precariamente, *adv.* precariously.

precario, ria, *a.* precarious.

precaución, *f.* precaution.

precaucionarse, *vr.* to be cautious.

precautelar, *va.* to caution, forewarn.

precaver. I. *va.* to prevent, obviate. **II.** *vr.* **(de)** to guard, be on one's guard (against).

precavidamente, *adv.* cautiously.

precavido, da, *a.* cautious, guarded.

precedencia, *f.* precedence, priority; preëminence, preference; superiority, primacy.

precedente. I. *a.* preceding, foregoing. **II.** *m.* precedent.

preceder, *va.* to precede; to be superior to.

preceptista, *n.* & *a.* one, or pertaining to one, who sets precepts.

preceptivamente, *adv.* preceptively.

preceptivo, va, *a.* preceptive.

precepto, *m.* precept; order, injunction; rule.— *pl.* the Commandments.

preceptor, ra, *n.* teacher, preceptor.

preceptuar, *va.* to give or issue as a precept.

preces, *f. pl.* prayers; devotion; supplication.

precesión, *f.* (rhet.) reticence; (astr.) precession.

preciado, da. I. *pp.* of PRECIAR. **II.** *a.* valued, esteemed; valuable, precious; proud, elated.

preciador, ra, *n.* appraiser.

preciar. I. *va.* to value, price, appraise. **II.** *vr.* **(de)** to boast, brag (about); to take pride, glory (in).

precinta, *f.* strap, band; (naut.) parcelling.

precintar, *va.* to strap, hoop, bind; to seal.

precinto, *m.* strapping; sealed strap.

precio, *m.* price; reward; premium; esteem; importance, worth.—**precios corrientes,** price current.—**no tener p.,** to be invaluable, to be priceless.—**tener en p.,** to esteem.

preciosa, *f.* (eccl.) allowance to prebendaries.

preciosamente, *adv.* preciously, richly.

preciosidad, *f.* worth, preciousness; rich or beautiful object, (a) beauty.

precioso, sa, *a.* precious, valuable; beautiful; witty, merry.

precipicio, *m.* precipice, chasm; violent fall; ruin, destruction.

precipitación, *f.* rash haste, precipitancy; (chem.) precipitation.

precipitadamente, *adv.* hastily.

precipitadero, *m.* precipice, steep cliff.

precipitado, da. I. *pp.* of PRECIPITAR. **II.** *a.* precipitate, hasty; abrupt. **III.** *m.* (chem.) precipitate.—**p. blanco,** calomel.

precipitante, *m.* (chem.) precipitator.

precipitar. I. *va.* to precipitate, cast headlong; to rush, hasten; (chem.) to precipitate. **II.** *vr.* to throw oneself headlong; to rush, hurry.

precípite, *a.* in danger of falling.

precipitosamente, *adv.* = PRECIPITADAMENTE.

precipitoso, sa, *a.* precipitous; rash, reckless.

precipuamente, *adv.* principally.

precipuo, pua, *a.* chief, principal.

precisamente, *adv.* precisely, exactly; necessarily, unavoidably; just at this (that) moment.

precisar, *va.* to fix, set, determine; to compel, oblige; (Am.) to be necessary; to be urgent.

precisión, *f.* necessity; compulsion; preciseness, exactness; precision, accuracy.—**bombardeo de p.,** precision bombing.

preciso, sa, *a.* necessary; indispensable; precise, exact, accurate; distinct, clear; severed, cut off; concise.—**tiempo p.,** just time enough.

precitado, da, *a.* aforesaid, aforementioned.

precito, ta, *a.* damned, condemned to hell.

preclaramente, *adv.* illustriously.

preclaro, ra, *a.* illustrious, famous, prominent.

precocidad, *f.* precocity.

precognición, *f.* precognition.

precolombino, na, *a.* pre-Columbian.

preconicé, preconice, *v. V.* PRECONIZAR.

preconización, *f.* eulogy; preconization.

preconizador, ra, *n.* & *a.* eulogizer(-ing); preconizer(-ing).

preconizar, *va.* (*pret.* PRECONICÉ; *subj.* PRECONICE) to praise, eulogize; (eccl.) to preconize.

preconocer, *va.* (*ind.* PRECONOZCO; *subj.* PRECONOZCA) to foreknow.

precordial, *a.* (anat.) precordial.

precoz, *a.* precocious.

precursor, ra. I. *a.* preceding. **II.** *n.* precursor, harbinger, forerunner.

predecesor, ra, *n.* predecessor.

predecir, *va.* (*ger.* PREDICIENDO; *pp.* PREDICHO; *ind. pres.* PREDIGO, *pret.* PREDIJE, *fut.* PREDIRÉ; *subj.* PREDIGA) to foretell, predict, forecast.

predefinición, *f.* (theol.) predetermination.

predefinir, *va.* to predetermine.

predestinación, *f.* predestination.

predestinado, da. I. *pp.* of PREDESTINAR. **II.** *a.* predestined. **III.** *n.* one predestined.

predestinante, *n.* & *a.* predestinator(-ing).

predestinar, *va.* to predestine, foredoom, predestinate, foreordain.

predeterminación, *f.* predetermination, foreordination.

predeterminar, *va.* to predetermine, foredoom, foreordain.

predial, *a.* predial, real, landed (property).

prédica, *f.* preachment, sermon.

predicable, *a.* fit to be preached; (logic) predicable.

predicación, *f.* preaching; sermon.

predicadera, *f.* pulpit.—*pl.* (coll.) facility for preaching.

predicado, *m.* (logic) predicate.

predicador, ra, *n.* preacher.

predicamental, *a.* (philos.) predicamental.

predicamento, *m.* particular state or situation.

predicante, *n.* sectarian or heretical preacher.

predicar, *va.* & *vn.* (*pret.* PREDIQUÉ; *subj.* PREDIQUE) to render clear and evident; to publish; to preach; to praise to excess; (coll.) to reprimand, lecture, sermonize.

predicción, *f.* prediction.

predicho, cha, *pp. irreg.* of PREDECIR.

predigo, prediga, predije, *v. V.* PREDECIR.

predilección, *f.* predilection.

predilecto, ta, *a.* preferred, favorite.

predio, *m.* landed property, farm, real property. —**p. rústico,** piece of arable ground.—**p. urbano,** dwelling house or building lot.

prediqué, predique, *v. V.* PREDICAR.

predisponer, *va.* (*pp. irreg.* PREDISPUESTO; *ind. pres.* PREDISPONGO, *pret.* PREDISPUSE, *fut.* PREDISPONDRÉ; *subj.* PREDISPONGA) to prejudice, predispose; to prearrange.

predisposición, *f.* predisposition; prejudice.

predispuesto, ta. I. *pp. irreg.* of PREDISPONER. **II.** *a.* predisposed, biased, inclined.

predispuse, *pret.* of PREDISPONER.

predominación, predominancia, *f.* predominance, predomination.

predominante, *a.* predominant, prevailing.

predominar, *vn.* & *va.* to predominate, prevail; to rise above, overlook, command.

predominio, *m.* predominance, superiority.

preelegir, *va.* to preëlect; to predestinate.

preeminencia, *f.* preëminence, mastery.

preeminente, *a.* preëminent, superior.

preestablecer, *va.* to preëstablish.

preexcelso, sa, *a.* most illustrious, most high.

preexistencia, *f.* preëxistence.

preexistente, *a.* preëxistent.

preexistir, *vn.* to preëxist.

prefacio, *m.* preface, prologue; (eccl.) preface.

prefación, *f.* preface, prologue, introduction.

prefecto, *m.* prefect.—**prefectura,** *f.* prefecture.

preferencia, *f.* preference.

preferente, *a.* preferential; preferring; preferable. —**preferentemente,** *adv.* preferably.

preferible, *a.* preferable.

---

preferiblemente, *adv.* preferably.

preferir, *va.* (*ger.* PREFIRIENDO; *ind. pres.* PRE- FIERO, *pret.* PREFIRIÓ; *subj.* PREFIERA) to prefer.

prefiguración, *f.* prefiguration.

prefigurar, *va.* to prefigure.

prefijar, *va.* to predesignate, predetermine.

prefijo, ja. I. *a.* prefixed. **II.** *m.* (gram.) prefix.

prefinición, *f.* setting of a time limit.

prefinir, *va.* to set a time limit for.

prefirió, prefiriendo, *v.* *V.* PREFERIR.

prefloración, *f.* (bot.) prefloration.

prefoliación, *f.* (bot.) vernation.

prefulgente, *a.* resplendent, bright.

pregón, *m.* publication by the crier, cry.

pregonar, *va.* to proclaim; to cry out, make pub- licly known.

pregoneo, *m.* crying wares on the streets.

pregonería, *f.* office of common crier.

pregonero, ra. I. *a.* publishing, announcing. **II.** *n.* common crier, town crier; auctioneer.

pregunta, *f.* question, query; catechism.—**ab- solver las preguntas,** (law) to answer under oath.—**estar a la cuarta p.,** (coll.) to be hard up or penniless.—**hacer una p.,** to ask a question.

preguntador, ra, *n.* & *a.* questioner(-ing).

preguntante, *n.* & *a.* inquirer(-ing).

preguntar. I. *va.* & *vn.* to ask, question, inquire. —**p. por,** to ask for (a person); to inquire about. **II.** *vr.* to wonder (when he will come, etc.).

preguntón, na, *a.* inquisitive.

prehistoria, *f.* prehistoric times; prehistorics, study or science of prehistoric times.

prehistórico, ca, *a.* prehistoric.

preinserto, ta, *a.* previously inserted.

prejudicial, *a.* (law) requiring judicial decision before final sentence.

prejudicio, prejuicio, *m.* prejudice, bias.

prejuzgar, *va.* (*pret.* PREJUZGUÉ; *subj.* PREJUZ- GUE) to prejudge.

prelacía, *f.* prelacy, prelature.

prelación, *f.* preference.

prelada, *f.* prelatess, abbess, mother superior.

prelado, *m.* (eccl.) prelate.

prelatura, *f.* prelacy, prelature.

preliminar. I. *a.* preliminary. **II.** *m.* prelimi- nary; peace protocol.

prelucir, *vn.* (*ind.* PRELUZCO; *subj.* PRELUZCA) to shine forth.

preludiar. I. *va.* & *vn.* (mus.) to play a prelude. **II.** *va.* to initiate, pave the way for.

preludio, *m.* introduction; (mus.) prelude.

prelusión, *f.* prelude, prologue, preface.

prematuramente, *adv.* prematurely.

prematuro, ra, *a.* premature; precocious; un- ripe, unseasonable; (law) (of girls) impuberal.

premeditación, *f.* premeditation.

premeditadamente, *adv.* premeditatedly.

premeditado, da, *a.* & *pp.* premeditated.

premeditar, *va.* to premeditate.

premiador, ra, *n.* rewarder.

premiar, *va.* to reward, remunerate, requite.

premio, *m.* reward; prize; recompense; (com.) premium; interest.—**a p.,** at a premium.

premiosamente, *adv.* tightly, compressedly; by force.

premiosidad, *f.* difficulty of action or speech.

premioso, sa, *a.* tight, close, pinching; trouble- some, burdensome; strict, rigid; slow in speak- ing or writing.

premisa, *f.* (logic) premise; mark, indication.

premiso, sa, *a.* premised; sent in advance.

premoción, *f.* previous motion.

premonstratense, *n.* & *a.* Premonstratensian.

premoriencia, *f.* (law) prior death.

premoriente, *a.* & *n.* predeceased.

premorir, *vn.* (*pp.* PREMUERTO; *ger.* PREMU- RIENDO; *ind. pres.* PREMUERO, *pret.* él PRE-

MURIÓ; *subj.* PREMUERA) (law) to die before another.

premostratense, *n.* & *a.* (member) of an order of canons.

premuerto, ta, *pp. irreg.* of PREMORIR.

premura, *f.* urgency, pressure, haste.

prenda, *f.* pledge, security, pawn; piece of jew- elry; garment; person dearly loved.—*pl.* endow- ments, natural gifts, talents.—**p. de vestir,** article of clothing, piece of wearing apparel.— **en p., en prendas,** as a pledge, as security. —**juego de prendas,** game of forfeits.—**soltar p.,** to commit oneself.

prendado, da. I. *pp.* of PRENDAR. **II.** *a.*—**estar p. de,** to be taken up with.—**ser muy p.,** to have many accomplishments.

prendador, ra, *n.* pledger, pawner.

prendamiento, *m.* pledging, pawning.

prendar. I. *va.* to pledge, pawn; to please, charm. **II.** *vr.* (**de**) to become fond (of), take a great liking (to).

prendedero, *m.* hook, fillet, brooch.

prendedor, *m.* catcher; breastpin; brooch; shawl pin, baby pin.

prender. I. *va.* (*pp.* PRENDIDO, PRESO) to seize, grasp, catch, apprehend; to cover (a mare); (Am.) to turn on (a light).—**p. fuego a,** to set on fire. **II.** *vn.* to take root; to catch or take fire. **III.** *vr.* to make an elaborate toilet.—**p. fuego,** to catch on fire.

prendería, *f.* second-hand shop; jewelry.

prendero, ra, *n.* second-hand dealer; pawn- broker.

prendido, *m.* a woman's dress; pattern for bone lace.

prendimiento, *m.* seizure, capture.

prenoción, *f.* prenotion, first knowledge.

prenombre, *m.* given, first name.

prenotar, *va.* to note by anticipation.

prensa, *f.* (mech.) press; vise, clamp; mill; (print.) printing press; press, newspapers.—**p. de lagar,** wine press.—**p. periódica,** the press. —**corresponsal de p.,** newspaper correspond- ent.—**dar a la p.,** to publish.

prensado, *m.* lustre (on material).

prensador, ra, *n.* presser.

prensadura, *f.* pressing, pressure.

prensar, *va.* to press; to calender.

prensil, *a.* prehensile.

prensión, *f.* prehension, seizing, grasping.

prensista, *m.* (print.) pressman.

prensor, ra. I. (zool.) psittacine (of the parrot family). **II.** *m. pl.* Psittaci (the parrot family).

prenunciar, *va.* to foretell, prognosticate.

prenuncio, *m.* prediction, prognostication.

preñado, da. I. *a.* pregnant; full, charged; sag- ging or bulging out. **II.** *m.* pregnancy.

preñez, *f.* pregnancy; impending danger or reso- lution; confusion, difficulty.

preocupación, *f.* preoccupation; worries; pre- possession, bias, prejudice, notion; conven- tionality.

preocupadamente, *adv.* with preoccupation or prejudice.

preocupar. I. *va.* to preoccupy; to prejudice. **II.** *vr.* (**de**) to be prejudiced (about); to worry (over, about); (Am.) to take care (of).

preopinante, *n.* predecessor (in a debate).

preordinación, *f.* preordination.

preordinadamente, *adv.* in a preordained or foreordained manner.

preordinar, *va.* to preordain, foreordain.

preparación, *f.* preparation; preparing; com- pound; medicine.

preparado, *m.* preparation, compound.

preparamiento, *m.* = PREPARACIÓN.

preparar. I. *va.* to prepare, make ready. **II.** *vr.* to be prepared, get ready, make preparations.

preparativo, va. I. *a.* preparative, qualifying. **II.** *m.* preparation.

preparatoriamente, *adv.* preparatorily.

preparatorio, ria, *a.* preparatory.

preponderancia, *f.* preponderance, sway.

preponderante, *a.* preponderant, prevailing.

preponderar, *vn.* to preponderate, have sway; to prevail.

preponer, *va.* (*pp.* PREPUESTO; *ind. pres.* PREPONGO, *pret.* PREPUSE, *fut.* PREPONDRÉ; *subj.* PREPONGA) to put before, to prefer.

preposición, *f.* (gram.) preposition.

prepositivo, va, *a.* prepositive, prepositional.

prepósito, *m.* president, chairman; provost.

prepositura, *f.* dignity of a provost.

preposteración, *f.* reversion of order.

prepósteramente, *adv.* out of place or order; inopportunely.

preposterar, *va.* to reverse, invert, disarrange.

prepóstero, ra, *a.* out of place or order; inopportune.

prepotencia, *f.* preponderance, prepotency.

prepotente, *a.* prepotent, predominant.

prepucio, *m.* (anat.) prepuce, foreskin.

prepuesto, prepuse, *v. V.* PREPONER.

prerrafaelismo, *m.* (art) Pre-Raphaelitism.

prerrafaelista, *n. & a.* (art) Pre-Raphaelite.

prerrogativa, *f.* prerogative.

presa, *f.* capture, seizure; (mil.) spoils, booty; catch, hold, prey; (water) dam; trench, ditch, flume; slice, bit, morsel; tusk, fang; claw of a bird of prey; among fishermen, fish weir, stake work.—**p. de caldo,** meat juice, beef tea.

presada, *f.* reservoir, storage water (in mills).

presado, da, *a.* of a pale-green color.

presagiar, *va.* to presage, forebode, foretell.

presagio, *m.* presage, omen, token.

presagioso, sa; présago, ga, *a.* betokening, significant, presaging.

presbicia, *f.* (med.) farsightedness, presbyopia.

présbita, présbite. (med.) I. *a.* presbyopic, farsighted. II. *n.* presbyopic person.

presbiterado, *m.* priesthood.

presbiteral, *a.* sacerdotal.

presbiterato, *m.* = PRESBITERADO.

presbiterianismo, *m.* Presbyterianism.

presbiteriano, na, *n. & a.* Presbyterian.

presbiterio, *m.* presbytery; chancel.

presbítero, *m.* priest; presbyter.

presciencia, *f.* prescience, foreknowledge.

prescindible, *a.* that can be dispensed with.

prescindir, *vn.* (**de**) to dispense (with), do (without); to set aside, ignore, omit.

prescito, ta, *a. & n.* = PRECITO, damned.

prescribir. I. *va.* (*pp. irreg.* PRESCRITO, PRESCRIPTO) to prescribe, dispose, specify; (law and med.) to prescribe. II. *vn.* (law) to prescribe.

prescripción, *f.* prescription; (law) prescription.

prescriptible, *a.* prescriptible.

prescripto, prescrito, ta, *pp. irreg.* of PRESCRIBIR.

presea, *f.* jewel, gem, valuable article.

presencia, *f.* presence; appearance, physique, figure; show, ostentation.—**p. de ánimo,** coolness, presence of mind.—**presencial,** *a.* pert. to, or implying presence.

presencialmente, *adv.* in person.

presenciar, *va.* to witness, to see; to attend.

presentable, *a.* presentable; producible.

presentación, *f.* presentation, exhibition, display; personal introduction; (eccl.). Presentation.—**a p.,** (com.) on presentation, at sight.

presentado, *m.* student of divinity about to be graduated as master; person presented.

presentador, ra, *n.* presenter; bearer.

presentalla, *f.* (eccl.) votive offering.

presentáneamente, *adv.* immediately.

presentáneo, *a.* quick-acting.

presentante, *a.* presenting, introducing.

presentar. I. *va.* to present; to put on (a program, etc.); to display, show; to give, make a present of; (eccl.) to offer as candidate. II. *vr.* to appear,

present oneself, report; to turn up; to offer one's services; (mil.) to enlist as a volunteer.

presente. I. *a.* present, current.—**hacer p.,** to state, to remind of, call attention to.—**la p.,** the present writing (these presents).—**mejorando lo p.,** present company excepted.—**tener p.,** to bear in mind. II. *m.* present, gift; present (time).—**al p.,** or **de p.,** at present.—**por el,** or **lo, p.,** for the present.

presentemente, *adv.* at present, now.

presentero, *m.* one who offers as a candidate.

presentimiento, *m.* presentiment; misgiving.

presentir, *va.* (*ind. pres.* PRESIENTO, *pret.* él PRESINTIÓ; *subj.* PRESIENTA; *ger.* PRESINTIENDO) to have a presentiment of; to forebode, predict.

presepio, *m.* stable; manger.

presera, *f.* (bot.) goose grass, cleavers.

presero, *m.* keeper of a dam or dike.

preservación, *f.* preservation, conservation.

preservador, ra, *n. & a.* preserver(-ing).

preservar, *va.* to preserve, guard, keep, save.

preservativamente, *adv.* preservatively.

preservativo, va. I. *a.* preservative, preserving. II. *m.* preservative, preventive.

presidario, *m.* = PRESIDIARIO.

presidencia, *f.* presidency; presidential chair; chairmanship; presidential term.

presidencial, *a.* presidential.

presidenta, *f.* president's wife; (woman) moderator; (woman) chairman; (woman) president.

presidente, *m.* president; chairman; speaker (of a parliamentary body); presiding judge; presiding officer.

presidiar, *va.* to garrison.

presidiario, *m.* convict.

presidio, *m.* garrison of soldiers; fortress, citadel; penitentiary; punishment by hard labor.

presidir, *va.* to preside over, or at; (of persons or things) to govern, sway, determine.

presiento, presienta, *v. V.* PRESENTIR.

presilla, *f.* loop, shank, eye, noose, bight; (sewing) buttonhole stitching; a kind of linen.

presión, *f.* pressure.—**presionar,** *va.* (Am.) to press, urge.

preso, sa. I. *pp. irreg.* of PRENDER. II. *a.* arrested; imprisoned. III. *n.* prisoner; convict.

prest, *m.* soldier's daily pay. Also PRE.

presta, *f.* (bot.) mint.

prestación, *f.* (law) lending; loan.

prestadizo, za, *a.* that may be lent or loaned.

prestado, da. I. *pp.* of PRESTAR. II. *a.*—**dar p.,** to lend.—**pedir,** or **tomar, p.,** to borrow.

prestador, ra, *n.* lender.

prestamente, *adv.* speedily, promptly, quickly.

prestamera, *f.* (eccl.) a kind of sinecure.

prestamería, *f.* (eccl.) dignity of a sinecure.

prestamero, *m.* incumbent of a PRESTAMERA.

prestamista, *n.* money lender; pawnbroker.

préstamo, *m.* loan.

prestancia, *f.* excellence.

prestante, *a.* excellent.

prestar. I. *va.* to lend, to loan; to aid, to assist; to give; communicate; to pay (attention to); to render, perform (a service). II. *vn.* to be useful; to expand, extend. III. *vr.* to offer or lend oneself or itself; to adapt oneself or itself; to be applicable.

prestatario, ria, *n. & a.* borrower(-ing).

preste, *m.* (eccl.) high mass celebrant.—**p. Juan de las Indias,** Prester John.

prester, *m.* hurricane, cyclone; waterspout.

presteza, *f.* quickness, promptness, haste.

prestidigitación, *f.* legerdemain, sleight of hand, jugglery.

prestidigitador, ra, *n.* juggler, prestidigitator.

prestigiador, ra, *n.* cheat, impostor.

prestigio, *m.* prestige, good name; spell, fascination; (of legerdemain) deception, illusion.

prestigioso, sa, *a.* renowned; well-reputed; deceiving, illusory.

prestimonio, *m.* loan; (eccl.) prestimony.
prestiño, *m.* = PESTIÑO, honey fritter.
presto, ta. I. *a.* quick, swift, prompt; ready, prepared. **II.** *adv.* soon; quickly.—**de p.,** promptly, swiftly.
presumible, *a.* presumable.
presumido, da. I. *pp.* of PRESUMIR. **II.** *a.* presumptuous, airy, conceited.
presumir. I. *va.* (*pp.* PRESUMIDO, PRESUNTO) to presume, surmise, conjecture. **II.** *vn.* (**de**) to presume, boast (of being), claim (to be); to be conceited.
presunción, *f.* presumption, conjecture; presumptuousness, conceit; (law) presumption.
presuntamente, *adv.* presumptively.
presuntivamente, *adv.* conjecturally.
presuntivo, va, *a.* presumptive, supposed.
presunto, ta. I. *pp. irreg.* of PRESUMIR. **II.** *a.* presumed.—**p. heredero,** heir apparent.
presuntuosamente, *adv.* presumptuously.
presuntuosidad, *f.* presumptuousness.
presuntuoso, sa, *a.* presumptuous, conceited.
presuponer, *va.* (*pp.* PRESUPUESTO; *ind. pres.* PRESUPONGO, *pret.* PRESUPUSE, *fut.* PRESUPONDRÉ; *subj.* PRESUPONGA) to presuppose; to estimate; to budget.
presuposición, *f.* presupposition.
presupuestal, *a.* budgetary, budget (as *a.*).
presupuestar, *va. & vn.* to budget.
presupuestario, ria, *a.* budget (as *a.*).
presupuesto, ta. I. *pp. irreg.* of PRESUPONER. **II.** *m.* motive, pretext, pretence; estimate; budget of state.—**nivelar el p.,** to balance the budget.
presura, *f.* anxiety; quickness, haste, promptness; persistency.
presurosamente, *adv.* hastily, promptly.
presuroso, sa, *a.* prompt, quick; nimble.
pretal, *m.* breastplate, breast leather.
pretencioso, sa, *a.* presumptuous, conceited.
pretender, *va.* (*pp.* PRETENDIDO, PRETENSO) to pretend; to aspire to; to seek, solicit; to try, endeavor; to intend; (S. A.) to court, be in love with.—**p. decir,** to mean, be driving at.
pretendiente, ta, *n.* pretender, candidate, office hunter; (Colomb.) suitor.
pretensión, *f.* pretension, claim; presumption.
pretenso, sa, *pp. irreg.* of PRETENDER.
pretensor, ra, *n.* pretender, claimant.
preterición, *f.* omission; (rhet. and law) preterition.
preterir, *va.* (*defect. only the infin. and pp. used*) (law) to omit (lawful heirs) in a will.
pretérito, ta, *n. & a.* preterit, past.
pretermisión, *f.* pretermission, omission, neglect.
pretermitir, *va.* to omit, pretermit, pass by.
preternatural, *a.* preternatural.
preternaturalizar, *va.* to pervert; to render preternatural.
preternaturalmente, *adv.* preternaturally.
pretexta, *f.* (anc. Rome) pretexta, a robe.
pretextar, *va.* to give as a pretext.
pretexto, *m.* pretext, pretense, cover, excuse.
pretil, *m.* railing, battlement, breastwork.
pretina, *f.* girdle, waistband; belt.
pretinero, ra, *n.* girdle maker or seller.
pretinilla, *f. dim.* ladies' belt or girdle.
¹**pretor,** *m.* (Rom. hist.) pretor.
²**pretor,** *m.* blackness of the waters where tunny fish abound.
pretoría, *f.* pretorship.
pretorial, *a.* pretorian or prætorian.
pretorianismo, *m.* abuse of military power for political purposes, political militarism.
pretoriano, na, *a.* pretorian or prætorian.
pretoriense, *a.* pertaining to a pretorium.
pretorio, ria. I. *a.* pretorian. **II.** *m.* pretorium.
pretura, *f.* pretorship.
prevalecer, *vn.* (*ind.* PREVALEZCO; *subj.* PREVALEZCA) to prevail; to take root.

prevaleciente, *a.* prevalent; prevailing.
prevalerse, *vr.* to avail oneself.
prevalezco, prevalezca, *v.* V. PREVALECER.
prevaricación, *f.* betrayal of a trust.
prevaricador, ra, *n.* one who plays false, betrayer; perverter; turncoat.
prevaricar, *vn.* (*pret.* PREVARIQUÉ; *subj.* PREVARIQUE) to play false, be a betrayer; (law) to prevaricate.—**prevaricato,** *m.* (law) prevarication, betrayal of a trust.
prevención, *f.* prevention; foresight, forethought; disposition, preparation; supply of provisions; sustenance, subsistence; warning; prejudice, prepossession; police station; (mil.) guardroom, cell; (law) prevenience of a judge in the knowledge of a case.
prevengo, prevenga, *v.* V. PREVENIR.
prevenidamente, *adv.* beforehand, previously.
prevenido, da. I. *pp.* of PREVENIR. **II.** *a.* ready, prepared, provided; plentiful; forewarned; cautious.
preveniente, *a.* predisposing, prevenient.
prevenir. I. *va.* (*ger.* PREVINIENDO; *ind. pres.* yo PREVENGO, él PREVIENE, *pret.* PREVINE, *fut.* PREVENDRÉ; *subj.* PREVENGA) to prepare, prearrange, make ready; to foresee; to forestall, prevent, avoid; to warn, caution; to prepossess, predispose; to overcome; to come upon, surprise. **II.** *vr.* to be ready, prepared, or on guard; to take precautions.
preventivamente, *adv.* preventively.
preventivo, va, *a.* preventive, preservative; (law) prevenient.
prever, *va.* (*pp.* PREVISTO; *ind.* PREVEO; *subj.* PREVEA) to foresee, anticipate.
previamente, *adv.* previously.
previene, previne, etc. *v.* V. PREVENIR.
previo, via, *a.* previous, foregoing.—**examen p.,** (Chile) preliminary examination.
previsión, *f.* foresight; forecast.—**p. social,** social security; social service.
previsor, ra, *n.* one who foresees. **II.** *a.* far-seeing, perspicacious.
previsto, ta, *pp. irreg.* of PREVER.
prez, *m.* or *f.* honor, glory, merit, worth.
priapismo, *m.* (med.) priapism.
priesa, *f.* = PRISA.
prieto, ta, *a.* blackish, very dark; narrow-minded, illiberal; close-fisted, mean; tight, compressed; (Mex.) (of person) dark, brunette.
prima, *f.* female cousin; early morning; (eccl.) prime; first tonsure; (mil.) first quarter of the night; (mus.) treble (in stringed instruments); (com.) premium; bounty.
primacía, *f.* primacy; primateship.
primacial, *a.* primatial.
primada, *f.* (coll.) taking advantage of a gullible, naïve person; a sponging trick.
¹**primado, da,** *a.* primatial.
²**primado,** *m.* primeness; (eccl.) primate.
primal, la. I. *a.* yearling (ewe or a goat). **II.** *m.* silk cord or braid.
primariamente, *adv.* chiefly, primarily.
primario, ria. I. *a.* principal, primary; (geol.) Primary, Paleozoic; (eccl.) primary (circuit). **II.** *n.* professor who lectures at dawn.
primate. I. *n.* distinguished person, worthy. **II.** *m.* (zool.) one of the Primates.—*pl.* Primates.
primavera, *f.* spring (season); flowered silk; (bot.) primrose.
primaveral, *a.* spring (as *a.*), pert. to spring.
primazgo, *m.* cousinship.
primearse, *vr.* to treat each other as cousins.
primer, *a. contr.* of PRIMERO.—**p. galán,** (theat.) lead.—**P. Ministro,** Prime Minister.—**p. plano,** foreground.—**p. pronto,** first movement.—**p. vertical,** (astr.) prime vertical.
primera. I. *f.* primero, game at cards; (fencing) prime.—*pl.* first tricks, at cards.—**p. de cambio** (com.) first of exchange.

primeramente, *adv.* first; in the first place.
primerizo, za. I. *n.* novice, beginner; firstling. **II.** *f.* (med.) = PRIMÍPARA.
primero, ra. I. *a.* first; former.—**p. dama**, (theat.) leading lady.—**p. enseñanza**, primary education.—**p. fila**, front rank.—**p. intención**, (surg.) first intention.—**p. materia**, raw material.—**a p. faz**, at first sight.—**a p. luz**, at dawn.—**a p. vista**, at first sight.—**de buenas a primeras**, all at once, suddenly.—**de p.**, (com.) of superior quality, highest-grade, prime.—**de p. instancia**, instantly, on the first impulse; first in; in the first place.—*pl.* **primeros auxilios**, first aid. **II.** *adv. m.* first, rather, sooner.—**de p.**, at the beginning, before.
primevo, va, *a.* primeval, original.
primicerio, ria. I. *a.* principal, first in rank. **II.** *m.* precentor, chanter.
primicia, *f.* first fruits; offering of the first fruits. —*pl.* first production, maiden effort.
primicial, *a.* pert. to first fruits.
primichón, *m.* skein of soft embroidery silk.
primigenio, nia, *a.* primogenial, primitive.
primilla, *f.* (coll.) pardon of a first offence.
primípara, *f.* (med.) primipara.
primitivamente, *adv.* originally.
primitivo, va, *a.* primitive, original, primeval.
primo, ma. I. *a.* first; superior, excellent, prime. —**a p. noche**, early in the evening, shortly after dark. **II.** *n.* cousin; (coll.) simpleton, dupe. —*pl.* cousins, appellation given by the kings of Spain to the grandees.—**p. carnal**, or **p. hermano**, first cousin. **III.** *adv. m.* first, in the first place.
primogénito, ta, *n.* & *a.* first-born.
primogenitura, *f.* primogeniture; seniority.
primor, *m.* beauty; dexterity, ability, exquisiteness, excellence, nicety.
primordial, *a.* primordial, original, primal.
primorear, *vn.* to perform with elegance and neatness.
primorosamente, *adv.* finely, nicely, elegantly.
primoroso, sa, *a.* neat, elegant, fine, exquisite; beautiful; graceful, dexterous.
primuláceo, a, *a.* (bot.) primulaceous.
princesa, *f.* princess; princesse (gown).
principada, *f.* (coll.) undue assumption of authority.
principado, *m.* princedom; princehood; principality; preëminence, primacy.—*pl.* princedoms.
principal. I. *a.* principal, main; important, essential; illustrious, renowned, celebrated; foremost, first; first (story of an apartment building, etc. above the ground floor, one flight up; in U. S. called second floor). **II.** *m.* (mil.) main guard; (com.) principal, capital, stock; principal, chief or head of a commercial establishment; (law) constituent.
principalía, *f.* (P. I.) board of officers in each town.
principalidad, *f.* principalness.
principalmente, *adv.* principally, mainly.
príncipe, *m.* prince; sovereign, ruler; chief or leader; young queen bee; master (often as *a.*, as in *autores príncipes*, classical authors, old masters).—**p. de Asturias**, Crown Prince of Spain.
principela, *f.* a sort of light camlet.
principiador, ra, *n.* beginner.
principiante, ta, *n.* beginner; apprentice.
principiar, *va.* to commence, begin, start.
principillo, *m. dim.* petty prince.
principio, *m.* principle; beginning; start; germ, original cause; rule of action, motive; origin, fountain; (cooking) entrée; (chem.) principle.— *pl.* (print.) introductory matter in a book.—**a principios de**, at the beginning of.—**al p.**, or **a los principos**, in the beginning, at first.—**de principios**, early.—**en p.**, in principle; in substance, essentially.

principote, *m.* (coll.) one who makes a pretentious display.
pringada, *f.* toasted bread steeped in gravy.
pringamoza, *f.* (Am.) (bot.) nettle.
pringar. I. *va.* (*pret.* PRINGUÉ; *subj.* PRINGUE) to baste (meat); to steep or dip (bread) in grease; to stain with grease; to spatter; to scald with boiling fat; to tar (a person); to wound; to slander; (coll.) to share in a business. **II.** *vr.* (coll.) to draw unlawful advantage from a thing intrusted to one's care.
pringón, na. I. *a.* nasty, dirty, greasy. **II.** *m.* begreasing oneself; stain of grease.
pringoso, sa, *a.* greasy, fat.
pringote, *m.* mixture of foods.
pringue, *m.* or *f.* grease, fat, lard; grease stain in clothes.
pringué, pringue, *v. V.* PRINGAR.
pringuera, *f.* dripping pan.
prionodonte, *m.* (zool.) giant armadillo.
prior. I. *a.* prior, preceding. **II.** *m.* (eccl.) prior, superior; (prov.) rector, curate.
priora, *f.* prioress.
prioral, *a.* pertaining to a prior or prioress.
priorato, priorazgo, *m.* priorate; priory.
prioridad, *f.* priority; precedence.
prioste, *m.* steward of a brotherhood.
prisa, *f.* haste, despatch, promptness; urgency; skirmish, surprise, hot fight.—**a p.**, quickly.— **a toda p.**, with the greatest speed.—**darse p.**, to make haste, hurry.—**de p.** = A P.—**estar de p.**, or **tener p.**, to be in a hurry.
priscilianismo, *m.* Priscillianism.
priscilianista, *n.* Priscillianist.
prisco, *m.* a kind of peach.
prisión, *f.* seizure, capture; prison; imprisonment; bond, shackle.—*pl.* chains, fetters.
prisionero, *m.* (mil.) prisoner; one captivated by affection or passion.
prisma, *m.* prism.
prismático, ca, *a.* prismatic.
priste, *m.* (ichth.) sawfish.
prístino, na, *a.* pristine, first, original.
prisuelo, *m.* muzzle for ferrets.
pritaneo, *m.* prytaneum (Greek public building).
privación, *f.* privation, want; lack; deprivation, loss; degradation.
privada, *f.* privy, water-closet; filth thrown into the street.
privadamente, *adv.* privately; separately.
privadero, *m.* cesspool cleaner.
¹privado, da. I. *a.* private, secret; personal. **II.** *m.* favorite, court minion, protégé.
²privado, da. I. *pp.* of PRIVAR. **II.** *a.* stunned, unconscious.
privanza, *f.* favor at court, protection.
privar. I. *va.* to deprive; to prohibit, forbid, interdict; to stun, daze. **II.** *vn.* to enjoy the protection of a magnate; to prevail, be in favor or in vogue. **III.** *vr.* to deprive oneself.
privativamente, *adv.* solely, privatively.
privativo, va, *a.* privative; special, distinctive, particular, peculiar; exclusive.
privilegiadamente, *adv.* in a privileged way.
privilegiar, *va.* to favor; to grant a privilege to.
privilegiativo, va, *a.* containing a privilege.
privilegio, *m.* privilege; grant, concession; exemption, grace; franchise; faculty; patent, copyright.—**p. de introducción**, patent on a device introduced from a foreign country.—**p. de invención**, patent (on an invention).—**p. del fuero**, privilege of ecclesiastics to be tried by their own courts.
pro, *m.* or *f.* profit, benefit, advantage.—**buena p.**, much good may it do you.—**de p.**, of note, worthy.—**en p. de**, in behalf of, for the benefit of.—**el p. y el contra**, the pros and cons.—**en p. y en contra**, pro and against; pro and con.
proa, *f.* (naut.) bow, prow; nose (of airplane).
proal, *a.* pertaining to the prow; forward.

probabilidad, *f.* probability, likelihood.
probabilísimo, ma, *a. super.* most probable.
probabilismo, *m.* (theol.) probabilism.
probabilista, *n.* & *a.* (theol.) probabilist(-ic).
probable, *a.* probable, likely.
probablemente, *adv.* probably, likely.
probación, *f.* proof: probation, trial.
probado, da. I. *pp.* of PROBAR. **II.** *a.* proved, tried.
probador, ra, *n.* taster, sampler; trier.
probadura, *f.* trial, tasting, sampling.
probanza, *f.* proof, evidence.
probar. I. *va.* (*ind.* PRUEBO; *subj.* PRUEBE) to try, test; to prove; to taste; to sample (as wine); to attempt, try, endeavor; to try on (as a coat).—**p. fortuna,** to take one's chances. **II.** *vn.* to suit, fit, agree with. **III.** *vr.* to try on (as a coat).
probatorio, ria. I. *a.* probatory, probationary. **II.** *f.* (law) time allowed for producing evidence.
probatura, *f.* (coll.) trial, test, experiment.
probeta, *f.* manometer, pressure gauge; (mil.) powder prover; (chem.) test tube, pipette.
probidad, *f.* probity, honesty, integrity.
problema, *m.* problem.
problemáticamente, *adv.* problematically.
problemático, ca, *a.* problematic(al).
probo, ba, *a.* upright, honest.
proboscidio, dia, *a.* (zool.) proboscidean.
procacidad, *f.* impudence, pertness.
procaz, *a.* impudent, bold, insolent.
procedencia, *f.* origin; source; place of sailing.
procedente, *a.* coming or proceeding (from); (law) according to law, rules, or practice.
proceder. I. *vn.* to proceed; to go on; to come, proceed, arise; to be the result; to behave, conduct oneself; to act; to take action; (law) to proceed (against), take action; to be in conformity with the law, rules, or practice; to concern. **II.** *m.* conduct, behavior, action, management.
procedimiento, *m.* procedure; process, method; (law) proceeding, procedure.
procela, *f.* (poet.) storm, tempest.
proceloso, sa, *a.* tempestuous, stormy.
prócer. I. *a.* tall, lofty, elevated. **II.** *m.* person in an exalted station, worthy; Father (of the country, in Am. republics).—*pl.* the grandees and high-titled nobility of Spain.
procerato, *m.* exalted station.
proceridad, *f.* tallness; elevation or eminence; vigor, growth.
procero, ra; prócero, ra, *a.* = PRÓCER.
procesado, da. I. *pp.* of PROCESAR. **II.** *a.* (law) relating to court proceedings; included in the suit; prosecuted, indicted. **III.** *n.* defendant.
procesal, *a.* pertaining to a process or lawsuit.
procesamiento, *m.* indicting; suing.
procesar, *va.* (law) to sue; to indict.
procesión, *f.* act of proceeding or issuing forth; procession, parade, pageant.
procesional, *a.* processional or processionary.
procesionalmente, *adv.* processionally.
procesionaria, *f.* (zool.) processionary moth.
procesionario, *m.* processional book.
proceso, *m.* lapse of time; (law) criminal case; proceedings of a lawsuit, trial.
proclama, *f.* proclamation; publication; banns of marriage.
proclamación, *f.* proclamation; promulgation; acclamation, public applause.
proclamar, *va.* to proclaim; to promulgate; to acclaim, cheer.
proclítico, ca, *a.* (gram.) proclitic.
proclive, *a.* inclined, disposed.
proclividad, *f.* proclivity; propensity.
procomún, procomunal, *m.* public welfare.
procónsul. I. *m.* proconsul.—**proconsulado,** *m.* proconsulship.—**proconsular,** *a.* proconsular.
procreación, *f.* procreation.
procreador, ra, *n.* & *a.* procreator(-ing).

procreante, *a.* procreating.
procrear, *va.* to procreate, generate, produce.
proctitis, *f.* proctitis.
procura, *f.* power of attorney.
procuración, *f.* care, diligence, careful management; power or letter of attorney; procurement, procuring; office of an attorney.
procurador, ra, *n.* procurer(-ess); (law) attorney, solicitor, proctor; *f.* manageress of a nunnery.—**p. de síndico,** attorney general.
procuraduría, *f.* attorney's office; proctorship.
procurante, *n.* solicitor, intendant.
procurar. I. *va.* to endeavor, try; to manage, transact for another; to get, obtain, procure. **II.** *vn.* to be, or act as, an attorney.
procurrente, *m.* (geog.) peninsula.
prodición, *f.* treason, treachery.
prodigalidad, *f.* prodigality; abundance.
pródigamente, *adv.* prodigally, lavishly, wastefully, profusely.
prodigar, *va.* (*pret.* PRODIGUÉ; *subj.* PRODIGUE) to lavish; to squander.
prodigiador, *m.* prognosticator, foreteller.
prodigio, *m.* prodigy; monster; marvel.
prodigiosamente, *adv.* prodigiously, wonderfully; beautifully, charmingly.
prodigiosidad, *f.* prodigiousness.
prodigioso, sa, *a.* prodigious, marvellous; monstrous; fine, excellent.
pródigo, ga, *a.* prodigal, extravagant, wasteful; liberal, generous, unstinted.
prodigué, prodigue, *v. V.* PRODIGAR.
prodrómico, ca, *a.* (med.) prodromal.
pródromo, *m.* (med.) prodrome, warning symptom.
producción, *f.* production; produce, yield; crop; delivery.
producente, *a.* producing, causing.
producibilidad, *f.* producibleness.
producible, *a.* producible.
producidor, ra, *n.* producer, procreator.
producir. I. *va.* (*pp.* PRODUCIDO, PRODUCTO; *ind. pres.* PRODUZCO, *pret.* PRODUJE; *subj.* PRODUZCA) to produce; to publish; to yield, bear; (com.) to bring or yield (as revenue); (law) to produce, bring as evidence, exhibit. **II.** *vr.* to explain oneself; to be produced; to arise, break out.
productible, *a.* (Am.) producible.
productivo, va, *a.* productive; profitable, fruitful.
producto, *m.* product; article (of trade, etc.); production; produce; (math.) product.—**productos agrícolas,** farm produce.—**productos de tocador,** toilet articles.—**p. neto,** (com.) net produce.—**p. secundario,** by-product.
productor, ra, *a.* productive.—**la capacidad p.,** productive capacity.
produje, produzco, produzca, *v. V.* PRODUCIR.
proejar, *vn.* to row against wind or tide.
proel. I. *a.* (naut.) fore. **II.** *m.* (naut.) bow hand.
proemial, *a.* proemial, introductory.
proemio, *m.* proem, preface, introduction.
proeza, *f.* prowess, feat.
profanación, *f.* profanation, desecration.
profanador, ra, *n.* & *a.* profaner(-ing), defiler (-ing), violator(-ing).
profanamente, *adv.* profanely.
profanamiento, *m.* = PROFANACIÓN.
profanar, *va.* to profane, desecrate; to defile, disgrace, dishonor.
profanidad, *f.* profanity; profaneness; indecency, immodesty.
profano, na, *a.* profane, secular; profane, irreverent; worldly; irreligious; immodest, unchaste; lay, unfamiliar, ignorant.
profecía, *f.* prophecy.—*pl.* the Prophets.
profecticio, cia, *a.* (law) profectitious.
proferente, *a.* uttering, pronouncing.
proferir, *va.* (*ger.* PROFIRIENDO; *ind. pres.* PRO-

FIERO, *pret.* él PROFIRIÓ; *subj.* PROFIERA) to utter, express, speak.

profesante, *a.* professing.

profesar, *va.* to practise or follow (a profession or trade); to teach as a professor; to profess, join (a religious group, etc.); to entertain, manifest (as friendship); (eccl.) to join (a religious body).

profesión, *f.* profession; declaration, avowal.— **de p.**, by profession.

profesional, *a.* professional.

profeso, sa, *a.* professed (monk or nun).

profesor, ra, *n.* professor.—**profesorado**, *m.* professorship; body of teachers, faculty.

profeta, *m.* prophet.—**profetal**, *a.* prophetic.

proféticamente, *adv.* prophetically.

profeticé, profetice, *v. V.* PROFETIZAR.

profético, ca, *a.* prophetic, prophetical.

profetisa, *f.* prophetess.

profetizador, ra, *n.* & *a.* prophesier(-ing).

profetizar, *va.* & *vn.* (*pret.* PROFETICÉ; *subj.* PROFETICE) to prophesy.

proficiente, *a.* proficient, advanced.

proficuo, cua, *a.* useful, advantageous.

profiero, profiera, *v. V.* PROFERIR.

profiláctico, ca. I. *a.* (med.) prophylactic, preventive. **II.** *m.* prophylactic. **III.** *f.* hygiene.

profilaxis, *f,* (med.) prophylaxis.

profirió, *pret.* of PROFERIR.

prófugo, ga. I. *n.* & *a.* fugitive from justice. **II.** *m.* one who absents himself to evade military service, slacker.

profundamente, *adv.* profoundly, deeply; highly, acutely.

profundicé, profundice, *v. V.* PROFUNDIZAR.

profundidad, *f.* depth; profundity, profoundness; height, excellence; intensity.

profundizar, *va.* (*pret.* PROFUNDICÉ; *subj.* PROFUNDICE) to deepen; to go deep into; to fathom, explore.

profundo, da. I. *a.* deep; low; profound, recondite; intense, dense; high, great. **II.** *m.* profundity; the sea, the deep; hell.

profusamente, *adv.* profusely; lavishly, prodigally, extravagantly.

profusión, *f.* profusion, profuseness; lavishness, prodigality.

profuso, sa, *a.* profuse, plentiful; lavish, prodigal.

progenie, *f.* progeny, offspring, issue.

progenitor, *m.* progenitor, ancestor.

progenitura, *f.* = PROGENIE; = PRIMOGENITURA, primogeniture.

progimnasma, *m.* (rhet.) preparatory exercise.

prognatismo, *m.* (anat.) prognathism.

prognato, ta, *a.* (anat.) prognathous.

progne, *f.* (poet.) (ornith.) swallow.

prognosis, *f.* prognosis, forecasting.

programa, *m.* program; plans; scheme; specifications; proclamation, public notice.

progresar, *vn.* to progress; to advance.

progresión, *f.* progression, progress; advance; (math.) progression.

progresista. I. *a.* progressive. **II.** *n.* & *a.* (pol.) Progressive.

progresivamente, *adv.* progressively, onward, forward.

progresivo, va, *a.* progressive, advancing.

progreso, *m.* progress, civilization; (often *pl.*) progress (in an undertaking, in school, etc.), advancement, development.

prohibente, *a.* prohibiting.

prohibición, *f.* prohibition, forbidding.

prohibicionismo, *m.* prohibitionism.

prohibicionista, *n.* & *a.* prohibitionist(-ic).

prohibir, *va.* to prohibit, forbid.—**se prohibe fumar**, (on sign) no smoking.

prohibitivo, va, *a.* prohibitive, forbidding.

prohibitorio, ria, *a.* prohibitory.

prohijación, *f.* = PROHIJAMIENTO.

prohijador, ra, *n.* adopter.

prohijamiento, *m.* adoption.

prohijar, *va.* to adopt (child, opinion, etc.).

prohombre, *m.* great man; master of a guild.

pro indiviso, *adv.* (law) undivided (legacies).

prójima, *f.* insignificant or contemptible woman.

prójimo, *m.* fellow being, (in Biblical language) neighbor.

prolapso, *m.* (med.) prolapsus, falling.

prole, *f.* issue, offspring, progeny; fruit.

prolegómenos, *m. pl.* prolegomena.

prolepsis, *f.* (rhet.) prolepsis.

proletariado, *m.* proletariat.

proletario, ria. I. *a.* proletarian, very poor; plebeian; belonging to the working classes. **II.** *n.* proletarian; (Rom. hist.) proletary.

prolífico, ca, *a.* prolific, fruitful, productive.

prolijamente, *adv.* prolixly, tediously.

prolijidad, *f.* prolixity; trifling nicety.

prolijo, ja, *a.* prolix, tedious; overcareful, triflingly nice; troublesome, impertinent, long-winded.

prologal, *a.* pertaining to prefaces or a preface.

prologar, *va.* to write a preface for.

prólogo, *m.* prologue; preface.

prologuista, *m.* writer of prologues.

prolonga, *f.* (artil.) prolonge.

prolongación, *f.* prolongation, lengthening; extension; protraction, lingering.

prolongadamente, *adv.* tardily, protractedly.

prolongado, da. I. *pp.* of PROLONGAR. **II.** *a.* oblong.

prolongador, ra, *n.* & *a.* prolonger(-ing).

prolongamiento, *m.* = PROLONGACIÓN.

prolongar, *va.* & *vr.* (*pret.* PROLONGUÉ; *subj.* PROLONGUE) to prolong; to protract, extend, continue; (geom.) to produce.—**p. un plazo**, (com.) to grant an extension of time.

proloquio, *m.* maxim, apothegm.

prolusión, *f.* prolusion, prelude.

promediar. I. *va.* to divide into two equal parts; (com.) to average. **II.** *vn.* to mediate; to be about the middle of (the month, etc.).

promedio, *m.* middle; average, mean.

promesa, *f.* promise, offer; pious offering.

prometedor, ra, *a.* promising.

prometer. I. *va.* to promise, offer; bid fair. **II.** *vn.* to promise, give favorable indications. **III.** *vr.* to expect with confidence; to become betrothed; to devote oneself to the service of God.

prometido, da. I. *pp.* of PROMETER. **II.** *n.* betrothed. **III.** *m.* promise; offer; auction fee.

prometiente, *a.* promising, assuring.

prometimiento, *m.* promise, offer.

prominencia, *f.* elevation; prominence; protuberance; knoll, knob.

prominente, *a.* elevated, protuberant; projecting, jutting out.

promiscuamente, *adv.* promiscuously.

promiscuar, *vn.* to eat meat and fish on fast days.

promiscuidad, *f.* promiscuity; ambiguity.

promiscuo, cua, *a.* promiscuous; ambiguous.

promisión, *f.* promise.

promisorio, ria, *a.* promissory.

promoción, *f.* promotion, preferment.

promontorio, *m.* promontory, headland, foreland; anything bulky and unwieldy.

promotor, ra. I. *a.* promotive. **II.** *n.* promotor, advancer, furtherer.—**p. fiscal**, (law) district attorney.

promovedor, ra, *n.* promoter.

promover, *va.* (*ind.* PROMUEVO; *subj.* PROMUEVA) to promote, further; to advance, exalt, raise.

promulgación, *f.* promulgation.

promulgador, ra, *n.* promulgator.

promulgar, *va.* (*pret.* PROMULGUÉ; *subj.* PROMULGUE) to promulgate, proclaim, publish.

pronaos, *m.* (arch.) pronaos, vestibule.

prono, na, *a.* prone, inclined, bent on.

pronombre, *m.* (gram.) pronoun.

pronominado, da, *a.* = PRONOMINAL.

For pronunciation, see the rules at the beginning of the book.

pronominal, *a.* (gram.) pronominal.

pronosticación, *f.* prognostication.

pronosticador, ra, *n. & a.* prognosticator(-ing).

pronosticar, *va.* (*pret.* PRONOSTIQUÉ; *subj.* PRONOSTIQUE) to prognosticate, foretell, augur.

pronóstico, *m.* prognostic, prediction, omen; almanac; (med.) prognosis.

pronostiqué, pronostique, *v. V.* PRONOSTICAR.

prontamente, *adv.* promptly, quickly.

prontitud, *f.* promptness; speed, swiftness, dispatch; liveliness of wit; quick repartee.

pronto, ta. I. *a.* prompt, quick, fast; ready. **II.** *m.* sudden impulse.—**primer p.,** first movement. **III.** *adv.* soon; promptly, quickly.—**al p.,** at first.—**de p.,** suddenly, without thinking.—**por** or **de, el** or **lo, p.** in the meantime, for the time being, provisionally.—**tan p. como,** as soon as.

prontuario, *m.* memorandum book; compendium of rules.

prónuba, *f.* (poet.) bridesmaid.

pronunciación, *f.* pronunciation, articulation.

pronunciado, da. I. *pp.* of PRONUNCIAR. **II.** *n.* insurgent. **III.** *a.* pronounced, steep; sharp.

pronunciador, ra, *n.* pronouncer.

pronunciamiento, *m.* insurrection, uprising; (law) pronouncement of a sentence.

pronunciar. I. *va.* to pronounce, articulate, enunciate; to deliver, make (a speech); (law) to pronounce (judgment); to pass upon (a point) before the main question is decided. **II.** *vr.* to rise in insurrection, to rebel.

propagación, *f.* propagation; spreading, dissemination.

propagador, ra, *n. & a.* propagator(-ing).

propaganda, *f.* propaganda, dissemination; (eccl.) propaganda; association for propagating doctrines.—**propagandista. I.** *n.* propagandist. **II.** *a.* by, or pertaining to, propaganda.

propagante, *a.* propagating; spreading.

propagar. I. *va.* (*pret.* PROPAGUÉ; *subj.* PROPAGUE) to propagate, generate; to spread, disseminate. **II.** *vr.* to spread; to propagate; to multiply.—**propagativo, va,** *a.* propagative.

propalador, ra, *n.* divulger.

propalar, *va.* to publish, to divulge.

propano, *m.* (chem.) propane.

propao, *m.* (naut.) breastwork, bulkhead.

propartida, *f.* time preceding a departure.

propasarse, *vr.* to transgress, overstep all bounds, take undue liberties, forget oneself, exceed one's authority.

propender, *vn.* (*pp.* PROPENDIDO, PROPENSO) to tend, be inclined, have a tendency.

propensamente, *adv.* with a tendency.

propensión, *f.* propensity, tendency, bent.

propenso, sa. I. *pp. irreg.* of PROPENDER. **II.** *a.* inclined, disposed.

propiamente, *adv.* properly, fittingly.

propiciación, *f.* propitiation, atonement.

propiciador, ra, *n. & a.* propitiator(-ing).

propiciamente, *adv.* propitiously.

propiciar, *va.* to propitiate, conciliate.

propiciatorio, ria. I. *a.* propitiatory. **II.** *m.* propitiatory, mercy seat.

propicio, cia, *a.* propitious, favorable.

propiedad, *f.* ownership, proprietorship; property, holding; landed estate; property, quality; propriety, fitness; (law) dominion, possession; (art) naturalness, close imitation.—**p. intelectual** or **literaria,** copyright.—**p. mueble,** goods and chattels.—**p. raíz,** real estate.—**es p. (de),** copyright (by).

propienda, *f.* listing nailed to the cheeks of an embroidery frame.

propietariamente, *adv.* with the right of property.

propietario, ria. I. *a.* proprietary. **II.** *n.* proprietor, owner, landlord(-lady), freeholder.

propileo, *m.* (arch.) propyleum, vestibule.

propilo, *m.* (chem.) propyl.

propina, *f.* fee, gratuity, tip; perquisite.

propinación, *f.* treat, invitation to drink.

propinar, *va.* to invite to drink, to treat; (coll.) to prescribe (medicines).

propincuidad, *f.* propinquity, proximity.

propincuo, cua, *a.* near, contiguous.

propio, pia. I. *a.* one's own; proper, suitable, fit, appropriate; characteristic, typical; natural, original, genuine; same, veritable; (for emphasis) -self; exact, precise.—**p. de,** inhering in, characteristic of; suited to, becoming. **II.** *n.* messenger.—**propios,** *m. pl.* public lands, estates, property.

propóleos, *m.* propolis, bee glue.

proponedor, ra, *n.* proposer, proponent.

proponente, *m. & f.* proposer, proponent.

proponer. I. *va.* (*pp.* PROPUESTO; *ind. pres.* PROPONGO, *pret.* PROPUSE, *fut.* PROPONDRÉ; *subj.* PROPONGA) to propose, propound; to present or name (as candidate); in écarté, to invite to draw new cards. **II.** *vr.* to purpose, plan, intend, mean.

proporción, *f.* proportion; opportunity, occasion, chance; (math.) proportion.—**a p. que,** as fast as, according as.

proporcionable, *a.* proportionable.

proporcionablemente, proporcionadamente, *adv.* proportionably, in proportion.

proporcionado, da. I. *pp.* of PROPORCIONAR. **II.** *a.* proportioned, fit, relevant.

proporcional, *a.* proportional.

proporcionalidad, *f.* proportionality.

proporcionalmente, *adv.* proportionally.

proporcionar, *va.* to proportion; to adjust, adapt; to supply, provide, furnish.

proposición, *f.* proposition; proposal; motion (in congress, etc.).

propósito, *m.* purpose, design, intention; aim, object; subject matter.—**a p.,** for the purpose; fit; apropos, by the way.—**a p. de,** in connection with, apropos of.—**de p.,** on purpose, purposely.—**fuera de p.,** irrelevant, foreign to the subject.

propretor, *m.* (Rom. hist.) propretor.

propuesta, *f.* proposal, offer, tender; nomination.

propuesto, ta, *pp. irreg.* of PROPONER.

propugnáculo, *m.* fortress; (fig.) bulwark.

propulsa, *f.* rejection.

propulsar, *va.* to reject; 'to' repulse, drive back.

propulsión, *f.* driving back; PROPULSA.—**p. a chorro,** jet propulsion.

propulsor, ra, *n. & a.* propeller(-ing); pusher (-ing) (esp. app. to engines).

propuse, *pret.* of PROPONER.

prora, *f.* (poet.) prow of a ship.

prorrata, *f.* quota; apportionment.—**a p.,** (com.) pro rata, in proportion.

prorratear, *va.* to allot in proportion.

prorrateo, *m.* proportional, pro rata division.

prórroga, *f.* prolongation, extension (of time).

prorrogable, *a.* that may be prolonged or extended (in time).

prorrogación, *f.* = PRÓRROGA.

prorrogar, *va.* to prolong, extend (in time); (rare) to prorogue, suspend.

prorrumpir, *vn.* to break forth, burst out.

prosa, *f.* prose; tedious discourse.

prosador, *m.* prose writer; (coll.) impertinent talker.

prosaico, ca, *a.* prosaic; prosy, dull, tedious.

prosaísmo, *m.* prosaism; prosiness, dullness.

prosapia, *f.* ancestry, lineage.

proscenio, *m.* (theat.) proscenium.

proscribir, *va.* (*pp. irreg.* PROSCRITO, PROSCRIPTO) to proscribe.

proscripción, *f.* proscription, banishment.

proscripto, ta; proscrito, ta. I. *pp. irreg.* of PROSCRIBIR. **II.** *n.* exile, proscribed person.

proscriptor, ra, *n.* proscriber.

---

prosecución, *f.* prosecution; pursuit.
proseguible, *a.* pursuable.
proseguimiento, *m.* = PROSECUCIÓN.
proseguir. I. *va.* (*ger.* PROSIGUIENDO; *ind. pres.* PROSIGO, *pret.* él PROSIGUIÓ; *subj.* PROSIGA) to pursue, prosecute. **II.** *vn.* to go on, continue, proceed.
proselitismo, *m.* proselytism.
prosélito, *m.* proselyte, convert.
prosénquima, *m.* (biol.) prosenchyma.
prosificación, *f.* changing poetry into prose.
prosificador, ra, *n.* one that changes poetry into prose.
prosificar, *va.* to change (poetry) into prose.
prosigo, prosiguió, etc. *v. V.* proseguir.
prosimio, mia. I. *n.* & *a.* (zool.) prosimian. **II.** *m. pl.* Prosimiae, Lemuroidea.
prosista, *n.* prose writer.
prosita, *f. dim.* short piece in prose.
prosobranquios, *m. pl.* (zool.) Prosobranchiata.
prosodia, *f.* (gram.) orthoepy; prosody.
prosódico, ca, *a.* orthoepic; prosodic.
prosopografía, *f.* (rhet.) personal description.
prosopopeya, *f.* (rhet.) prosopopœia, personification; (coll.) affected gravity, airs.
prospecto, *m.* prospectus, announcement.
prósperamente, *adv.* prosperously, luckily.
prosperar. I. *va.* to prosper, make happy, favor. **II.** *vn.* to prosper, thrive.
prosperidad, *f.* prosperity, success.
próspero, ra, *a.* prosperous; favorable, propitious.
prostaféresis, *f.* (astr.) prosthaphæresis.
próstata, *f.* (anat.) prostate gland.
prostático, ca, *a.* prostatic.
prostatitis, *f.* (med.) prostatitis.
prosternarse, *vr.* to prostrate oneself.
próstilo, *a.* (arch.) prostyle.
prostitución, *f.* prostitution.
prostituir. I. *va.* (*pp.* PROSTITUÍDO, PROSTITUTO; *ger.* PROSTITUYENDO; *ind. pres.* PROSTITUYO, *pret.* él PROSTITUYÓ; *subj.* PROSTITUYA) to prostitute, corrupt, debase. **II.** *vr.* to prostitute oneself, sell one's honor; to turn prostitute.
prostituta, *f.* prostitute.
prostituto, ta, *pp. irreg.* of PROSTITUIR.
prostituyo, etc. *v. V.* prostituir.
protagonista, *n.* protagonist, hero, heroine; leader.
prótasis, *f.* (drama and gram.) protasis.
proteáceo, a. I. *a.* (bot.) proteaceous. **II.** *f. pl.* Proteaceæ.
protección, *f.* protection; favor.
proteccionismo, *m.* (pol.) protectionism.
proteccionista, *n.* & *a.* (pol.) protectionist.
protector, ra, *n.* protector(-ess).
protectorado, *m.* protectorate.
protectoría, *f.* protectorship, protectorate.
protectorio, ria, *a.* pertaining to a protector.
protectriz, *f.* protectress.
proteger, *va.* (*ind.* PROTEJO; *subj.* PROTEJA) to protect.
protegido, da, *n.* protégé, favorite.
proteico, ca, *a.* protein; (chem.) proteinaceous.
proteína, *f.* proteid, protein.
protejo, proteja, *v. V.* proteger.
protervamente, *adv.* perversely.
protervia, protervidad, *f.* perversity, malignity, wantonness.
protervo, va, *a.* wanton, perverse.
prótesis, *f.* (gram.) prothesis; (surg.) prosthesis.
protesta, *f.* protestation; protest; (law) protest.
protestación, *f.* protestation.
protestante. I. *a.* protesting. **II.** *n.* & *a.* Protestant.—**protestantismo,** *m.* Protestantism.
protestar, *va.* to protest; to assure, affirm earnestly or solemnly; to make a public declaration of; (law) to protest.—**p. contra,** to protest, deny the validity of.—**p. de,** to protest against. —**p. una letra,** (com.) to protest a draft.

protestativo, va, *a.* protesting.
protesto, *m.* (com.) protest (of a bill).
protético, ca, *a.* prothetic, prefixed.
protoalbéitar, *m.* chief veterinary surgeon.
protoalbeiterato, *m.* board for examining veterinary surgeons.
protocloruro, *m.* (chem.) protochloride.
protocolar, protocolizar, *va.* to protocol, record, register.
protocolo, *m.* protocol, registry, judicial record.
protohistoria, *f.* prehistory.
protohistórico, ca, *a.* prehistoric.
protomártir, *m.* protomartyr (app. esp. to St. Stephen, the first Christian martyr).
protomedicato, *m.* board of king's physicians; office of royal physician.
protomédico, *m.* one of the three physicians to the king.
protón, *m.* (phys.) proton.
protonotario, *m.* (law) prothonotary.
protoplasma, *m.* (biol.) protoplasm.
protoplasmático, ca, *a.* (biol.) protoplasmic.
protosulfuro, *m.* (chem.) protosulphide.
prototípico, ca, *a.* prototypal.
prototipo, *m.* prototype, original; model.
protovértebra, *f.* (anat.) theoretical type of vertebræ.
protóxido, *m.* (chem.) protoxide.
protozoario, protozoo. I. *m.* (zool.) protozoan. **II.** *m. pl.* Protozoa.
protráctil, *a.* protractile.
protuberancia, *f.* protuberance.
protuberante, *a.* protuberant, bulging, rising, projecting.
protutor, *m.* (law) guardian.
provecto, ta, *a.* advanced in years, learning, or experience; mature.
provecho, *m.* benefit, advantage, good; profit, gain; proficiency, progress, advancement.— **buen p.,** may it benefit you (usual greeting before or after a meal); prosit.—**de p.,** useful. —**ser de p. para,** (of certain food, etc.) to be good for.
provechosamente, *adv.* profitably; beneficially.
provechoso, sa, *a.* profitable; beneficial, good (as for the health); useful, advantageous.
proveedor, ra, *n.* purveyor, provider.
proveeduría, *f.* storehouse for provisions; office of purveyor.
proveer. I. *va.* (*pp.* PROVEÍDO, PROVISTO; *ger.* PROVEYENDO; *pret.* él PROVEYÓ) to provide, furnish; to supply with provisions; stock; to dispose, adjust, transact; to confer; (law) to decide. **II.** *vr.* (**de**) to provide oneself (with), get one's supply (of); (coll.) to ease the body.
proveído, *m.* judgment, sentence, decision.
proveimiento, *m.* supply, provisioning.
provena, *f.* provine, layer of vine.
proveniente, *a.* arising, coming, resulting.
provenir, *vn.* (**de**) to arise (from), originate (in), be due (to).
provento, *m.* product, rent, revenue.
provenzal, *n.* & *a.* Provençal.
proverbiador, *m.* collection of proverbs.
proverbial, *a.* proverbial.
proverbialmente, *adv.* proverbially.
proverbiar, *vn.* (coll.) to use proverbs.
proverbio, *m.* proverb, saying, saw; omen, prediction.—*pl.* Proverbs (book of the Bible).
proverbista, *n.* (coll.) user of proverbs.
proveyó, *pret.* of PROVEER.
próvidamente, *adv.* providently, carefully.
providencia, *f.* foresight, forethought; act of providing; disposition, measure, way, means; (law) judgment, decision, sentence.—**la P.,** Providence.
providencial, *a.* providential.
providencialmente, *adv.* providentially; provisionally.

For pronunciation, see the rules at the beginning of the book.

providenciar, *va.* to take steps or measures for; to decide (a case), pronounce judgment on.
providente, *a.* = PRÓVIDO.
próvido, da, *a.* provident, prudent.
provincia, *f.* province; provincial court for civil cases; (eccl.) province.
provincial. I. *a.* provincial. **II.** *m.* (eccl.) provincial.
provincialato, *m.* (eccl.) provincialship.
provincialismo, *m.* provincialism.
provinciano, na, *n.* & *a.* provincial, provincialist; native of Biscay.
provisión, *f.* provision; supply, stock; provender; writ, decree, or sentence issued by Spanish tribunals in the king's name; measure, means; (com.) remittance of funds.
provisional, *a.* provisional, interim (as *a.*).
provisionalmente, *adv.* provisionally.
provisio.—al p., immediately, instantly.
provisor, ra, *n.* purveyor, provider; (eccl.) vicar general.
provisorato, *m.* office of PROVISOR.
provisoría, *f.* in convents, storeroom, pantry; office of a PROVISOR.
provisorio, ria, *a.* provisional, temporary.
provisto, ta. I. *pp. irreg.* of PROVEER. **II.** *a.* provided, stocked, supplied.
provocación, *f.* provocation, irritation.
provocador, ra, *n.* provoker; inciter.
provocar, *va.* (*pret.* PROVOQUÉ; *subj.* PROVOQUE) to provoke, excite, incite, anger; to facilitate, promote; to tempt, arouse desire in; (coll.) to vomit.—**provocativo, va,** *a.* inciting; tempting; provoking, irritating.
proxeneta, *n.* (law) go-between.
próximamente, *adv.* approximately; soon; immediately; proximately.
proximidad, *f.* proximity.
próximo, ma, *a.* next; nearest, neighboring, proximate; close.—**estar p. a** (*inf.*), to almost (*inf.*), just miss (*pres.p.*).
proyección, *f.* design; projecting; projection; (geom.) projection.
proyectante, *a.* projecting; designing.
proyectar. I. *va.* to design; to project, plan, devise; to shoot or throw forth; (geom.) to project; to cast (as a shadow); to show (a movie). **II.** *vr.* to be cast, fall (as a shadow).
proyectil, *m.* projectile, missile.—**p. dirigido,** guided missile.
proyectista, *n.* projector; designer.
proyecto, ta. I. *a.* projected, in perspective. **II.** *m.* project, plan; design.
proyector, ra. I. *a.* projecting. **II.** *m.* (phys.) projector; search light; (auto) spotlight.—**p. eléctrico,** searchlight.
proyectura, *f.* (arch.) projecture.
prudencia, *f.* prudence; moderation.
prudencial, *a.* prudential.
prudencialmente, *adv.* prudentially.
prudente, *a.* prudent, cautious, wise.
prudentemente, *adv.* prudently, wisely.
prueba, *f.* proof; evidence; trial, test; test piece, sample; tasting; temptation; (Am.) acrobatic feat, (card, etc.) trick; (law) evidence; (tailoring) trial, fitting; (print.) proof, proof sheet; (photog.) proof.—**p. circunstancial, p. de indicios,** or **p. indiciaria,** circumstantial evidence.—**a p.,** (com.) on trial; according to the best standards, perfect.—**a p. de,** proof against, (as in *a prueba de agua*, waterproof, water-tight; *a prueba de aire*, air-tight; *a prueba de bomba*, bomb-proof; *a prueba de fuego*, fireproof).—**hacer la p.,** to try; (de) to try; to test.—**poner a p.,** to try, put to the test.
pruebista, *m.* & *f.* (Am.) acrobat.
pruebo, pruebe, *v.* V. PROBAR.
prurigo, *m.* (med.) prurigo.
prurito, *m.* (med.) pruritus, itching; excessive desire.

prusiano, na, *n.* & *a.* Prussian.
prusiato, *m.* (chem.) prussiate, cyanide.
prúsico, ca, *a.* prussic, hydrocyanic.
pseudo, *a.* = SEUDO, pseudo.
psicoanálisis, *m.* or *f.* (med.) psychoanalysis.
psicología, *f.* psychology.
psicológico, ca, *a.* psychological.
psicólogo, *m.* psychologist.
psicópata, *n.* (med.) psychiatrist, alienist.
psicopatía, *f.* (med.) psychopathy, mental illness.
psicrómetro, *m.* psychrometer.
psiquiatra, *m.* psychiatrist.
psiquiatría, *f.* psychiatry.
psíquico, ca, *a.* psychic(al).
pterópido, da. I. *n.* & *a.* (zool.) pteropod. **II.** *m. pl.* Pteropoda, pteropods.
ptialina, *f.* (chem.) ptyalin.
¡pu! *interj.* pugh!
púa, *f.* prick; tine, prong; tooth of a comb; wire tooth of a card; spine or quill of a hedgehog, etc.; (agr.) graft, scion; metal point of a spinning top; plectrum; cause of grief or sorrow; (coll.) wily, cunning person.—**alambre de púas,** barbed wire.
puado, *m.* set of prongs, teeth, or tines.
puar, *va.* to make teeth, prongs, or tines on.
púber; púbero, ra; *a.* pubescent.
pubertad, *f.* puberty, pubescence.
pubes, *m.* (anat.) pubes, pubic region.
pubescencia, *f.* pubescence, puberty.
pubescente, *a.* pubescent.
pubescer, *vn.* to attain the age of puberty.
pubis, *m.* (anat.) pubes; pubis.
pública, *f.* in universities, public examination before graduating.
publicación, *f.* publication; proclamation.
publicador, ra, *n.* publisher; proclaimer.
públicamente, *adv.* publicly, openly.
publicano, *m.* publican.
publicar, *va.* (*pret.* PUBLIQUÉ; *subj.* PUBLIQUE) to publish; to proclaim, announce; to reveal, disclose; (eccl.) to publish (the banns).
publicata, *f.* (eccl.) certificate of publication.
publicidad, *f.* publicity.
publicista, *m.* publicist.
público, ca. I. *a.* public; common, general.—**en p.,** publicly. **II.** *m.* public, audience.
publiqué, publique, *v.* V. PUBLICAR.
pucelana, *f.* = PUZOLANA, a volcanic rock.
pucia, *f.* closed pharmaceutical vessel.
pucha, *f.* (Cuba) bouquet of flowers.
puchada, *f.* flour poultice; watered mortar.
puchera, *f.* (cooking) pot, kettle.
pucherico, illo, ito, *m. dim.* pipkin, small pot.
pucherito, *m.* (coll.) pouting of a child about to cry.
puchero, *m.* cooking pot; olla, stew, (U. S.) New England boiled dinner; dinner, food; pouting of a child before crying.—**hacer pucheros,** (coll.) to pout.
pucheruelo, *m. dim.* of PUCHERO.
puches, *m.* or *f. pl.,* a sort of pap; porridge.
pucho, *m.* (Am.) cigar stump; left over, trifle, insignificant thing.
pude, *pret.* of PODER.
pudelación, *f.,* **pudelaje,** *m.* (metal.) puddling.
pudelar, *va.* (metal.) to puddle.
pudendo, da. I. *a.* shameful, obscene, immodest. **II.** *m.* the male organ.
pudibundez, *f.* prudishness, overmodesty.
pudibundo, da, *a.* (humor.) shamefaced, modest.
pudicicia, *f.* pudicity, chastity, modesty.
púdico, ca, *a.* chaste, modest, decorous.
pudiente, *a.* powerful; rich, well off.
pudín, *m.* (Angl.) pudding.
pudo, *v.* V. PODER.
pudor, *m.* modesty, decorousness.
pudoroso, sa, *a.* modest; bashful, shy.
pudrición, *f.* rottenness; putrefaction, rotting.

pudridero, *m.* rotting place; fermenting pit; chamber with vaults for interment of bodies that are later to be transferred to mausoleums.

pudridor, *m.* (paper making) fermenting vat.

pudrigorio, *m.* (coll.) sickly, infirm man.

pudrimiento, *m.* = PUDRICIÓN.

pudrir. I. *va.* to rot; to vex, worry. **II.** *vn.* to have died, to be buried; to rot. **III.** *vr.* to rot, decay; to be broken-hearted, to die of grief.

pudú, *m.* (zool.) pudu, a Chilean variety of deer.

puebla, *f.* seed that a gardener sows.

pueblada, *f.* (Am.) popular uprising; mob.

pueble, *m.* (min.) working gang.

pueblecico, ito, *m. dim.* small town.

puebleño, ña, *n.* (Colomb., contempt.) villager; boor.

¹pueblo, *m.* town, village; settlement; people; nation; population; common people, working classes.

²pueblo, pueble, *v. V.* POBLAR.

puedo, pueda, *v. V.* PODER.

puente, *m.* or *f.* bridge; (mus.) bridge, in string instruments; (carp.) transom, lintel, crossbeam; (naut.) bridge; gun-carrying deck.—**p. cerril,** small narrow bridge for cattle.—**p. colgante,** suspension bridge.—**p. de cimbria,** (Chile) suspension rope bridge.—**p. de los asnos,** discouraging difficulty.—**p. de tablero inferior,** through bridge.—**p. de tablero superior,** deck bridge.—**p. giratorio,** swing bridge.—**p. levadizo,** drawbridge; bascule, or lift, bridge. —**p. volante,** flying bridge.

puentecico, illo, ito, *m. dim.* small bridge.

puentecilla, *f. dim.* small bridge of a string instrument.

puentezuela, *f. dim.* small bridge.

puerca, *f.* (zool.) sow; sow bug, woodlouse; scrofulous swelling; slut, slatternly woman.

puercamente, *adv.* dirtily, filthily; basely, meanly, contemptibly.

puerco, ca. I. *a.* filthy, dirty, foul; low, base, mean. **II.** *n.* hog; wild boar; base or low person. —**p. espín,** or **espino,** porcupine.—**p. marino,** (zool.) dolphin.—**p. montés,** wild boar.

puericia, *f.* boyhood.

puericultura, *f.* physical education of children.

pueril, *a.* childish, puerile; (astr.) first (quadrant).

puerilidad, *f.* puerility, childishness; trifle.

puerilmente, *adv.* puerilely, childishly.

puérpera, *f.* lying-in woman.

puerperal, *a.* puerperal.

puerperio, *m.* time directly after childbirth.

puerquezuelo, *m. dim.* little pig.

puerro, *m.* (bot.) leek.

puerta, *f.* door; doorway, gateway; gate; beginning of an undertaking; duty, octroi, toll.—**p. cochera,** porte cochère.—**p. excusada,** or **falsa,** back door, side door.—**p. franca,** open door, free entrance; free entry.—**p. reglar,** the regular door for entering nunneries.—**p. vidriera,** glass door.—**a p cerrada,** privately, secretly.—**dar con la p. en la cara, or en las narices,** to slam the door in one's face; (also fig.).—**detrás de la p.,** round the corner.—**la Sublima P.,** or **P. Otomana,** the Sublime Porte (Turkey).

puertaventana, *f.* window shutter.

puertecillo, puertezuelo, *m. dim.* small port.

puertecita, puertezuela, *f. dim.* small door.

puerto, *m.* port; harbor, haven; pass through mountains; asylum, shelter, refuge.—**p. de depósito,** bond port.—**p. franco** = P. LIBRE.— **p. habilitado,** port of entry.—**p. libre,** free port.

pues. I. *conj.* because, for, as; since, inasmuch as; then.—**p. bien,** now then, well then, all right then.—**p. no,** not at all, not so.—**p. que,** since.—**¿p. qué?** what?; what about it? "so what?"—**p. sí,** yes, indeed, most certainly.—

¿p. y qué? why not? what else? what then? —**¿y p.?** so? is that so? why? how is that? **II.** *adv.* yes; so; certainly; exactly; anyhow, just the same.

puesta, *f.* (astr.) set, setting; stake (at cards).— **p. de sol,** sunset.—**puestas de sol,** or **a p. de sol,** at sunset.

puesto, ta. I. *pp. irreg.* of PONER.—**p. que,** although; since, inasmuch as, as long as.—**buen p.,** well dressed. **II.** *m.* place or space occupied, stall, stand, booth; position, job; post, dignity, office; breeding stall; blind for hunters; (mil.) barrack for soldiers.—**p. de socorro,** first-aid station.

¡puf! *interj.* pugh!

púgil, *m.* prize fighter, boxer, pugilist.

pugilar, *m.* Hebrew manual of the Scriptures.

pugilato, *m.* pugilism; boxing.

pugilista, *m. & f.* (Am.) pugilist, prize fighter.

pugna, *f.* combat, struggle; conflict.—**estar en p.,** to be in conflict, disagree.

pugnacidad, *f.* pugnacity, quarrelsomeness.

pugnante. I. *a.* fighting, struggling. **II.** *n.* foe, opponent.

pugnar, *vn.* to fight, struggle; (**con**), to conflict (with), be opposed (to); to strive successfully; to be obstinate; to persist.

pugnaz, *a.* pugnacious, quarrelsome.

puja, *f.* outbidding or overbidding at a public sale; higher bid.

pujador, ra, *n.* bidder; outbidder.

pujame, pujamen, *m.* (naut.) foot of a sail.

pujamiento, *m.* flow of the blood or humors.

pujante, *a.* powerful, vigorous, strong.

pujanza, *f.* power, might, strength, vigor.

¹pujar. I. *va.* to push ahead, push through. **II.** *vn.* to falter (in speech or action); (coll.) to pout.

²pujar. I. *va.* to outbid. **II.** *vn.* to ascend, go up.

pujavante, *m.* hoof parer (used by horseshoer).

pujo, *m.* (med.) tenesmus; eagerness, longing; violent desire.

pulcritud, *f.* pulchritude, neatness, tidiness.

pulcro, cra, *a.* beautiful, graceful; nice; neat.

Pulchinela, *m.* Punchinello.

pulga, *f.* flea; small playing top.—**no aguantar pulgas,** not to put up with ill treatment.—**ser de,** or **tener, malas pulgas,** to be easily piqued or fretted, to be ill-tempered.—**tener pulgas,** to be restless or too lively.

pulgada, *f.* inch.

pulgar, *m.* thumb; shoots left on vines.

pulgarada, *f.* fillip; pinch; inch.

pulgón, *m.* green fly, plant louse, aphis.

pulgoso, sa, *a.* full of fleas.

pulguera, *f.* place abounding with fleas; (bot.) pulic, fleawort.

pulguillas, *n. dim.* (coll.) restless, fretful person.

pulguita, *f. dim.* little flea.

pulicán, *m.* dentist's forceps.

pulicaria, *f.* (bot.) fleawort.

pulidamente, *adv.* neatly, cleanly, nicely.

pulidero, *m.* polisher, glosser, burnisher.

pulidez, *f.* polish; neatness, cleanliness.

pulido, da, *pp. & a.* polished; neat, cleanly.

pulidor, *m.* polisher, burnisher, furbisher.

pulimentar, *va.* to burnish, gloss, polish.

pulimento, *m.* polish; glossiness.

pulir. I. *va.* to polish, burnish, furbish; to adorn, beautify; to render polite. **II.** *vr.* to beautify, or deck oneself; to become polished.

pulmón, *m.* (anat.) lung.—**pulmonado, da,** *a.* (zool.) pulmonate.—**pulmonar,** *a.* pulmonary.

pulmonaria, *f.* (bot.) lungwort.

pulmonía, *f.* (med.) pneumonia.

pulmoníaco, ca, *a.* (med.) pneumonic.

pulpa, *f.* (anat.) pulp, flesh; fruit or wood pulp.

pulpejo, *m.* flesh part of the body, as the ball of the thumb or lobe of the ear.

pulpería, *f.* (Am.) retail grocery or general store.

pulpero, *m.* (Am.) grocer; catcher of cuttlefish.

pulpeta, *f.* slice of stuffed meat.
púlpito, *m.* pulpit; office of a preacher.
pulpo, *m.* (ichth.) cuttlefish, octopus.
pulposo, sa, *a.* pulpy, pulpous, fleshy.
pulque, *m.* (Am.) pulque, fermented juice of the maguey.—**p. curado,** the same liquor prepared with pineapple and sugar.
pulquería, *f.* tavern where pulque is sold.
pulsación, *f.* pulsation; pulse, beating.
pulsada, *f.* any pulse beat.
pulsador, ra. I. *n.* one who examines the pulse. II. *a.* pulsating.
pulsante, *a.* feeling the pulse; pulsating.
pulsar. I. *va.* to feel the pulse of; to finger, touch lightly (as a lyre); to explore, sound, or examine. II. *vn.* to pulsate, beat.
pulsátil; pulsativo, va, *a.* beating, pulsating.
pulsear, *vn.* (of two persons) to hand-wrestle, to clasp hands with upright forearms resting on a table and endeavor to put each other's arm down by pulling in opposite directions.
pulsera, *f.* (jewelry) bracelet; lock of hair over the temple; (surg.) wrist bandage.—**reloj de p.,** wrist watch.
pulsímetro, *m.* (hydraul.) pulsometer; (med.) pulsimeter, sphygmograph.
pulsista, *a.* skilled in knowledge of the pulse.
pulso, *m.* pulse; pulsation, beat; part of the wrist where the pulse is felt; steadiness of the hand; care, tact.—**a p.,** freehand (drawing); with the strength of the hand.—**tomar el p. a,** to feel the pulse of; to sound (one for one's opinion).
pulsómetro, *m.* = PULSÍMETRO.
pultáceo, a, *a.* pultaceous, soft; (med.) apparently or actually rotten or gangrened.
pulsulante, *pa.* pullulating, sprouting.
pulular, *vn.* to pullulate, germ, bud; to multiply with great rapidity; to swarm; to be lively.
pulvericé, pulverice, *v. V.* PULVERIZAR.
pulverizable, *a.* pulverizable.
pulverización, *f.* pulverization.
pulverizador, *m.* atomizer, spray; pulverizer.
pulverizar, *va.* (*pret.* PULVERICÉ; *subj.* PULVERICE) to pulverize; to atomize, spray.
pulverulento, ta, *a.* dusty.
¹pulla, *f.* loose, obscene expression; repartee, witty saying; hint.
²pulla, *f.* (ornith.) = PLANGA, a kind of eagle.
pullista, *n.* one fond of throwing out hints.
¡pum! *interj.* bang!
puma, *m.* (zool.) puma, American panther.
pumarada, *f.* = POMARADA, apple plantation.
pumita, *f.* = PIEDRA PÓMEZ, pumice stone.
puna, *f.* (Am.) puna, bleak, arid table-land.
puncé, punce, *v. V.* PUNZAR.
punción, *f.* (surg.) puncture.
puncha, *f.* thorn, prickle, sharp point.
punchar, *va.* to prick, pierce, puncture.
pundonor, *m.* point of honor.
pundonorosamente, *adv.* punctiliously.
pundonoroso, sa, *a.* punctilious.
punganes, *m. pl.* oyster knife.
pungente, *a.* pungent.
pungimiento, *m.* punching or pricking.
pungir, *va.* (*ind.* PUNJO; *subj.* PUNJA) to punch, prick; to sting the mind or heart (as passions).
pungitivo, va, *a.* punching, pricking.
punible, *a.* (law) punishable.
punición, *f.* punishment.
púnico, ca, *a.* Punic.
punitivo, va, *a.* (law) punitive.
punjo, punja, *v. V.* PUNGIR.
punta, *f.* point, nib, sharp end; end, tip; apex, top; cape, headland, promontory; prong or tine of an antler; stub of a cigar; taint of acidity or sourness; touch, turn, tinge, trace, suggestion; pointing of game by a dog; (print.) bodkin; (her.) lower part of a shield.—*pl.* point lace.—**p. de diamante,** diamond pencil, diamond point (for cutting).—**p. de París,** wire nail.—

p. seca, point (of dividers).—**de p.,** point-first.—**de p. en blanco,** all dressed up; in full regalia.—**de puntas,** on tiptoe, softly.—**estar de p.,** to be on bad terms.
puntada, *f.* (sewing) stitch; hint.—**echar puntadas,** (sewing) to stitch.
puntador, *m.* = APUNTADOR, (theat.) prompter.
puntal, *m.* prop, support; stay, stanchion, pillar; (naut.) depth of hold; (Am.) snack (of food).
puntapié, *m.* kick (with the tip of the shoe).
puntar, *va.* to mark with dots or points.
punteada, *f.,* **punteado,** *m.* guitar playing.
puntear. I. *va.* to play (the guitar); (art) to stipple; (sewing) to stitch. II. *vn.* (naut.) to tack.
puntel, *m.* pontil, snap, glass-blower's rod.
puntera, *f.* (shoemaking) toe cap or box; patch over the tip; new toe on stockings; (coll.) kick.
puntería, *f.* (artil.) aim; pointing a weapon.
puntero, ra. I. *a.* taking good aim. II. *m.* pointer; punch for horseshoes; stonecutter's chisel; (eccl.) cannula in a chrismatory; (Colomb.) hand (of watch or clock).
punterola, *f.* (min.) poll pick.
puntiagudo, da, *a.* sharp-pointed, sharp.
puntico, ito, *m. dim.* small dot or point.
puntilla, *f. dim.* small point; narrow lace edging; brad, joiner's nail; carpenter's tracing point.—**de,** or **en, puntillas,** softly, gently; on tiptoe.
puntillazo, *m.* (coll.) kick.
puntillero, *m.* (bull fighting) = CACHETERO.
puntillo, *m. dim.* small point; punctilio; (mus.) dot, point.
puntillón, *m.* (coll.) kick.
puntilloso, sa, *a.* punctilious.
puntiseco, ca, *a.* dry at the tips, as plants.
puntizón, *m.* (print.) frisket hole or mark.
punto, *m.* point, dot; period in writing; nib of a pen; sight in firearms; (sports) point; (sewing, knitting) stitch; hole in a stocking; point in lace; mesh; punch hole in straps; polka dot in fabrics; place, spot; hackstand; smallest part of a thing; instant, moment; nick of time; chance, favorable opportunity; stop, rest, recess; end, object, aim; point of honor, punctilio; each mistake of a pupil in reciting a lesson; twelfth part of a line; (shoemaking) each number in a size stick.—**p. cardinal,** cardinal point.—**p. de apoyo,** fulcrum; point of support.—**p. de congelación,** freezing point.—**p. de ebullición,** boiling point.—**p. de fusión,** melting point.—**p. de gracia,** funny side.—**p. de hielo,** freezing point.—**p. de inflamación,** ignition point.—**p. de partida,** starting point.—**p. de vista,** point of view.—**p. en boca,** silence.—**p. final,** stop; full stop, period (in sentences).—**p. menos,** a trifle less.—**p. por p.,** point by point, in, or with, all details.—**p. y coma,** semicolon (;).—**puntos suspensivos,** leaders (.....).—**a buen p.,** opportunely.—**al p.,** immediately, at once.—**a p. de,** on the point of, about to.—**a p. fijo,** exactly, with certainty.—**a p. que,** just when, just as.—**coche de p.,** taxi, car for hire.—**dar en el p.,** to hit the nail on the head.—**de p.,** knitted; steadily increasing, by the minute.—**de todo p.,** absolutely, entirely, in every way.—**dos puntos,** colon (:).—**en p.,** on the dot, exactly, (of the hour) sharp.—**en p. de,** in regard to.—**hasta cierto p.,** to a certain extent.—**poner en su p.,** to put where it belongs, rate at its true value; to set right.—**poner p. final a,** to put a stop to.—**por p. general,** as a rule.—**por puntos,** from one moment to another; point by point; one thing at a time.
puntoso, sa, *a.* pointed; punctilious.
puntuación, *f.* punctuation.
puntual, *a.* prompt, punctual; certain; sure; convenient, adequate.—**puntualidad,** *f.* punctuality; certainty.—**puntualizar,** *va.* (*pret.*

PUNTUALICÉ; *subj.* PUNTUALICE) to imprint on the mind or memory; to finish, perfect; to give a detailed account of.—**puntualmente,** *adv.* punctually; faithfully; exactly, accurately.

puntuar, *va.* to punctuate, to point.

puntuoso, sa, *a.* punctilious.

puntura, *f.* puncture; (print.) register point.

punzada, *f.* prick, puncture; stitch, sharp pain; compunction.

punzador, ra, *n.* pricker, wounder.

punzadura, *f.* puncture, prick.

punzante, *a.* pricking, sharp.

punzar, *va.* (*pret.* PUNCÉ; *subj.* PUNCE) to punch, bore, perforate; to prick, puncture, wound; to cause sharp pain; to grieve.

punzó, *a.* deep scarlet red.

punzón, *m.* punch, puncheon; puncher; driver, point, graver, bodkin, awl, pick; countersink, counterdie; type mold; young horn of a deer.

punzonería, *f.* set of molds for a font of types.

puñada, *f.* fisticuff, box.

puñado, *m.* handful; a few.—**a puñados,** plentifully, abundantly, lots (diff. constr.).

puñal. *m.* poniard, dagger.—**puñalada,** *f.* stab with a poniard; sudden shock of grief or pain.

puñalejo, *m. dim.* small poniard.

puñalero, ra, *n.* maker or seller of poniards.

puñera, *f.* double handful; flour measure.

puñetazo, *m.* fisticuff.

puñete, *m.* fisticuff; bracelet.

puño, *m.* fist; grasp; handful; cuff, wristband (of garment); hilt of a sword; haft (of a tool); handle (of an umbrella, etc.); head of a staff or cane; (naut.) corner of a sail.—**cerrar los puños,** to clench one's fists.—**hombre de puños,** strong, valiant man.—**ser como un p.,** to be closefisted.

pupa, *f.* pustule, pimple; child's word to express uneasiness.

pupila, *f.* (anat.) pupil.

pupilaje, *m.* pupilage, wardship; board and lodging; boarding-house.

pupilar, *a.* (anat. and law) pupillary.

pupilero, ra, *n.* boarding-house keeper.

pupilo, la, *n.* pupil, ward; boarder.

pupitre, *m.* writing desk; school desk.

puposo, sa, *a.* pustulous, pustulate.

puramente, *adv.* purely; chastely; strictly; without qualification or exception.

puré, *m.* (Gal.) (cooking) thick soup, purée.

pureza, *f.* purity; fineness, genuineness; cleanness, excellence.

purga, *f.* physic, cathartic; (sugar making) draining of molasses.

purgable, *a.* that can or should be purged.

purgación, *f.* purge, purgation; catamenia; (law) purgation; gonorrhœa, clap.

purgador, ra. I. *a.* purgative. II. *n.* purger.

purgamiento, *m.* purgation, purging.

purgante. I. *a.* purging, purgative. II. *m.* purgative, cathartic, physic.

purgar. I. *va.* (*pret.* PURGUÉ; *subj.* PURGUE) to purge, purify, cleanse; to atone for, expiate; to refine, clarify; to drain (sugar) of molasses; (med.) to purge, physic; (law) to clear from guilt or imputation of guilt. II. *vr.* to rid or clear oneself from guilt; to take a purge.

purgativo, va, *a.* purgative, cathartic.

purgatorio, *m.* purgatory.

purgué, purgue, *v. V.* PURGAR.

puridad, *f.* purity.—**en p.,** clearly, openly; in secret.

purificación, *f.* purification; cleansing, expurgation; (eccl.) purification (of the chalice).

purificadero, ra, *a.* cleansing, purifying.

purificador, ra, *n. & a.* purifier(-ing); (eccl.) purificator.

purificante, *a.* purifying.

purificar. I. *va.* (*pret.* PURIFIQUÉ; *subj.* PURIFI-

QUE) to purify, clean, cleanse, refine. II. *vr.* to be purified, cleansed.

purificatorio, ria, *a.* purificatory, purifying.

Purísima.—la P., *f.* the most Holy Virgin.

purismo, *m.* purism.—**purista,** *n.* purist.

puritanismo, *m.* puritanism.

puritano, na, *a. & n.* puritan(-ic), Puritan.

puro, ra. I. *a.* pure; unmixed, sterling, unalloyed, solid (gold, etc.); clear, clean, neat; unblemished, unsullied; mere, only, sheer, absolute.—**a p.,** by dint of.—**de p.,** extremely; by dint of.—**de p. sangre,** thoroughbred.—**la p. verdad,** the honest truth. II. *m.* cigar.

púrpura, *f.* purpura, murex, purple shell; purple; cloth dyed with purple; dignity of a king or cardinal; (poet.) blood.—**purpurado,** *m.* cardinal.

purpurante, *a.* giving a purple color.

purpurar, *va.* to purple; to dress in purple.

purpurear, *vn.* to have a purple tinge.

purpúreo, rea. I. *a.* purple, puniceous, purpurate. II. *f.* (bot.) = LAMPAZO, burdock.

purpurina, *f.* bronze powder; (chem.) purpurin.

purpurino, na, *a.* purple.

purrela, *f.* wine of inferior quality.

purriela, *f.* (coll.) despicable trifle.

purulencia, *f.* purulence, purulency.

purulento, ta, *a.* purulent.

pus, *m.* (med.) pus.

puse, *pret.* of PONER.

pusilánime, *a.* pusillanimous, faint-hearted.

pusilánimemente, *adv.* pusillanimously.

pusilanimidad, *f.* pusillanimity.

pústula, *f.* (med.) pustule; pimple.

pustuloso, sa, *a.* pustulous, pustular.

puta, *f.* whore, harlot.

putativo, va, *a.* putative, reputed.

putput, *m.* (ornith.) hoopoe.

putrefacción, *f.* putrefaction.

putrefactivo, va, *a.* putrefactive.

putrefacto, ta, *a.* putrid, decayed, rotten.

putrescente, *a.* putrescent.

putridez, *f.,* rottenness.

pútrido, da, *a.* putrid, rotten, decayed.

puya, *f.* goad, goad stick.

puzol, *m.;* **puzolana,** *f.* a kind of volcanic rock used in making mortar.

Q

que. I. *rel. pron.* that, which, who, whom; when [*el día que le escribí,* the day (when) I wrote to him]. When preceded by the definite article, it is equivalent to "who," "whom," "which" (the "the which" of old English), or "the one who," "those who," "the one whom," "those whom," "that which," "the one that." II. *interr. & exclamatory pron.* (**qué**) what, what a (*¡qué hombre!* what a man!); which; how (*¡qué bonita!* how pretty!).—**q. de . . .** how many . . .—¿q. hay? or ¿q. pasa? what is the matter?—¿q. tal?, how goes it?—¡q. va!, go on! (expressing disbelief).—¿a q.?, what for?, what's the use of?—¿para q.?, what for—¿por q.?, why?—**sin q. ni para q.,** without cause or motive.—**un no sé q.,** a certain something. III. *conj.* that [very seldom omitted: *Juan dice que vendrá,* John says (that) he will come]; than (in comparisons); because, for, as; and (*habla que habla,* he talks and talks, or, talking and talking); so; so that. Followed by a subjunctive form it is usually rendered by "to" and the corresponding infinitive, changing the construction (*deseo que Vd. venga,* I wish that you come, *or,* I wish you to come); by "let" or "may," when it expresses command or desire (*que entre,* let him come in; *que tenga buena suerte,* may you have good luck); or, with impersonal verbs, by the indicative (*antes que llueva,* before it rains). In compound tenses (*he hablado, había* *hablado*, etc.), the participle is sometimes placed first, and then *que* followed by the auxiliary. In such cases, *que* is rendered by *when, after, as soon as;* e. g. *llegado que hubo*, when he had arrived, after he arrived; *leído que hayamos la carta*, after we have read, *or* after we read, the letter. Before infinitive and following a noun preceded by a form of *haber, tener*, and a few other verbs, it is rendered by *to;* e. g. *hay mucho que hacer*, there is much to do; *teníamos dos cartas que escribir*, we had two letters to write. Sometimes it is used as an expletive, in the sense of "and" [*la culpa es mía, que no suya*, the fault is mine, (and) not yours].—**q. no,** without, but that.—**q. . . . q.,** whether . . . or (*que quieras que no*, whether you will or not). —**por . . . q.,** no matter how (*por bien que hable*, no matter how well he speaks).

quebracho, *m.* quebracho; quebracho bark.

quebrada, *f.* ravine; deep pass; gorge; (Am.) gulch; stream; (com.) failure, bankruptcy.

quebradero, *m.* breaker.—**q. de cabeza,** worry.

quebradillo, *m.* wooden shoe heel; (dance) bending of the body.

quebradizo, za, *a.* brittle, fragile; frail, sickly.

quebrado, da. I. *pp.* of QUEBRAR. **II.** *a.* broken; weakened; (com.) bankrupt; rough, uneven (ground); (med.) ruptured.—**azúcar q.,** brown sugar. **II.** *m.* (arith.) common fraction; (Cuba) tobacco leaf full of holes.

quebrador, ra, *n.* & *a.* breaker(-ing); lawbreaker (-ing).

quebradura, *f.* breaking, splitting; gap, fissure, slit; (med.) fracture; rupture, hernia.

quebraja, *f.* crack, fissure, flaw, split.

quebrajar, *va.* = RESQUEBRAJAR, to crack, split.

quebrajoso, sa, *a.* brittle, fragile; full of cracks.

quebramiento, *m.* = QUEBRANTAMIENTO.

quebrantable, *a.* frangible, brittle.

quebrantador, ra. I. *n.* breaker, splitter; crusher, bruiser; violator, transgressor. **II.** *a.* breaking, that breaks; weakening; crushing.

quebrantadura, *f.* = QUEBRANTAMIENTO.

quebrantahuesos, *m.* (ornith.) osprey, lammergeier; tease, bore.

quebrantamiento, *m.* fracture, rupture; crushing, breaking; smash; breaking out of prison; fatigue, exhaustion; violation; burglary; desecration.

quebrantante, *a.* breaking, crushing.

quebrantaolas, *m.* breakwater.

quebrantar, *va.* to break, crush; to burst open; to pound, grind, mash; to transgress; to violate, break (as a contract); to vex; to fatigue; to weaken; to diminish; (law) to annul, repeal.

quebrantaterrones, *m.* (coll.) clodhopper.

quebranto, *m.* breaking, crushing; weakness; lassitude; pity, compassion; grief, affliction; (com.) loss, damage.

quebrar (*ind.* QUIEBRO; *subj.* QUIEBRE). **I.** *va.* to break; to crush; to cast asunder; to double, bend, twist; to interrupt, hinder; to temper, moderate; to spoil (the bloom of the countenance); to overcome, conquer; to diminish (friendship). **II.** *vn.* (com.) to fail, become bankrupt. **III.** *vr.* to be ruptured; to break (as a plate, a bone, etc.); to be broken, as the continuity of hills.

quebrazas, *f. pl.* flaws in sword blades.

queche, *f.* (naut.) smack, ketch.

quechemarín, *m.* (naut.) coasting lugger.

quechua, *n.* & *a.* Quichua(-an).

queda, *f.* curfew; curfew bell.

quedada, *f.* stay, residence, sojourn.

quedar. I. *vn.* to remain; to stay, stop in a place; to remain, be left as remainder (sometimes diff. constr.: *le quedan tres pesetas*, he has three pesetas left); to be or be left in a state or condition; to leave at; to decide, resolve, agree.—**q. bien (mal),** to acquit oneself well (badly); to come

out well (badly); to keep (break) an appointment.—**q. de** (Am.) = **q. en,** to agree to; to have an understanding.—**q. por,** to go to, be accorded to, be won by; (followed by *inf.*) to remain to be (followed by *pp.*).—¿**en qué quedamos?** what is your final decision? what do you say? **II.** *vr.* to remain; to slacken, abate, diminish.—**q. atrás,** to get, or be left, behind. —**q. con,** to retain, keep.—**q. fresco,** not to mind, to remain undisturbed or indifferent.— **q. frío,** or **muerto,** to be greatly astonished, to be breathless, horrified, etc.

quede, (print.) stet; let stand.

quedito, ta. I. *a. dim.* soft, gentle; easy. **II.** *adv.* = QUEDO.

quedo, da. I. *a.* quiet, still, noiseless; easy, gentle. **II.** *adv.* softly, gently; in a low voice.

quehacer, *m.* occupation, business, work.—*pl.* **quehaceres de casa,** household chores.

queja, *f.* complaint; grumbling, moan; resentment, grudge; quarrel, dispute.

quejarse, *vr.* to complain; to grumble; (de) to regret, lament.

quejicoso, sa, *a.* plaintive, querulous.

quejido, *m.* moan.

quejigal, *m.* plantation of muricated oaks.

quejigo, *m.* (bot.) muricated oak.

quejosamente, *adv.* complainingly, plaintively.

quejoso, sa, *a.* plaintive; complaining.

quejumbre, *f.* grumble, growl.

quejumbroso, sa, *a.* grumbling, plaintive.

quelonio, *a.* & *m.* (zool.) chelonian.

quema, *f.* fire, burning; combustion.—**de q. lenta,** slow-burning.—**huir de la q.,** to get away from trouble, get out.

quemadero, ra. I. *a.* apt to be burned. **II.** *m.* place where convicts were burned.

quemado, da. I. *pp.* of QUEMAR. **II.** *a.* burnt, crisp; angry, irritated.—**q. por el sol,** sunburned. **III.** *m.* burnt down forest or thicket.

quemador, ra. I. *n.* incendiary; burner. **II.** *m.* gas burner.

quemadura, *f.* burn, scald; (agr.) brand, smut upon plants.

quemajoso, sa, *a.* smarting, burning.

quemante, *a.* burning.

quemar. I. *va.* to burn; to scald; to fire, set on fire, kindle; to parch, dry, scorch; to vex, irritate; to dispose of at a low price. **II.** *vn.* to burn, be too hot. **III.** *vr.* to get burned, burn oneself; to burn, be consumed by fire; to be very hot, be parched with heat; to fret, to be angry; (coll.) to be near, to almost attain or touch a thing desired, to be "warm."

quemazón, *f.* combustion; fire, conflagration; (coll.), smarting, burning; offensive remark; vexation, anger; (Cuba) bargain sale.

quena, *f.* (Am.) a sort of Indian flute.

quenepa, *f.* (P. R.) honeyberry.

quenopodio, *m.* (bot.) chenopod.

quepis, *m.* (mil.) kepi.

quepo, quepa, *v. V.* CABER.

queratina, *f.* (chem.) keratin.

queratitis, *f.* (med.) keratitis.

queratosis, *f.* keratosis.

querella, *f.* complaint; quarrel; (law) plaint, complaint; act of contesting an inofficious will.

querellador, ra, *n.* complainant.

querellante, *n.* & *a.* complainant(-ing).

querellarse, *vr.* to lament, bewail; to complain; (law) to make an accusation; to contest a will.

querellosamente, *adv.* plaintively, querulously.

querelloso, sa, *a.* querulous.

querencia, *f.* affection, fondness; haunt of wild beasts.

querencioso, sa, *a.* (of animals) affectionate.

querer. I. *va.* (*ind. pres.* QUIERO, *pret.* QUISE, *fut.* QUERRÉ; *subj.* QUIERA) to will; to desire, wish; to endeavor, attempt; to accept (a challenge in certain games); to love; (foll. by *inf.* used to ask a favor as: *¿Quiere V. abrir la ventana?* Will you open the window, please?).—**querría, quisiera,** should like.—**q. decir,** to mean. II. *vn.* to wish, desire; to be willing; to love.—**como quiera,** anyhow, in any way.—**como quiera que,** whereas; inasmuch as; since; although; whatever, however, no matter how.—**como quiera que sea,** in any case.—**como Vd. quiera,** as you like; let it be so.—**cuando quiera,** at any time, whenever.—**donde quiera,** anywhere, wherever.—**no q.** (*inf.*), to refuse to (*inf.*).—**no q. nada con,** not to wish to have anything to do with.—**sin q.,** unwillingly; unintentionally. III. *v. impers.* to look like (rain, etc.), threaten, look as if it were going to (rain, snow, etc.). IV. *m.* love, affection; will; desire.

queresa, *f.* = CRESA, egg of fly or bee; maggot.

querido, da. I. *pp.* of QUERER. II. *a.* dear, beloved. III. *n.* paramour, lover, mistress.—**q. mío,** or **mía,** my dear, my dearest, love, my darling.

queriente, *a.* willing; loving.

quermes, *m.* (entom.) kermes.—**q. mineral,** (chem.) kermes.

querocha, *f.* = QUERESA.

querochar, *vn.* (of bees) to emit the semen.

querub, querube, querubín, *m.* cherub.

querva, *f.* (bot.) spurge; palma Christi.

quesadilla, *f.* cheesecake; sweetmeat.

quesear, *vn.* to make cheese.

quesera, *f.* dairy; dairymaid; cheese board, cheese mold, cheese vat; cheese dish.

quesería, *f.* season for making cheese; dairy.

quesero, ra. I. *a.* caseous, cheesy. II. *n.* cheesemonger, cheesemaker.

quesillo, ito, *m. dim.* small cheese.

queso, *m.* cheese.—**q. de bola,** Edam cheese.—**q. de cerdo,** headcheese.—**q. helado,** ice-cream brick, molded ice cream.

quetro, *m.* a Chilean duck with featherless wings.

quetzal, *m.* (ornith.) quetzal, trogon.

quevedos, *m. pl.* eyeglasses.

¡quiá! *interj.* come now! no, indeed!

quibey, *m.* (W. I.) (bot.) dog's-bane.

quicial, *m.*, **quicialera,** *f.* hinge post.

quicio, *m.* eye of a door hinge; pivot hole.—**fuera de q.,** unhinged, out of order.—**sacer de q.,** to unhinge; to exasperate.

quiché, *n.* Guatemalan Indian and his language.

quichua, *n. & a.* = QUECHUA.

quid, *m.* gist, pith, main point.

quídam, *m.* (coll.) person; a nobody.

quid pro quo. I. (Lat.) an equivalent. II. *m.* mistaken identity; mistake.

quiebra, *f.* crack, fracture; gaping fissure; loss, damage; (com.) failure, bankruptcy.

quiebrahacha, *m.* (Cuba) (bot.) breakaxe.

¹quiebro, *m.* (mus.) trill; movement or inclination of the body, as in dodging.

²quiebro, quiebre, *v.* V. QUEBRAR.

quien (*interr.* **quién**), *pron.* (*pl.* **quienes, quiénes**) who, whom, whoever, whomever, which, whichever.

quienquiera, *pron.* (*pl.* **quienesquiera**) whoever, whosoever, whomsoever, whichever.

quiero, quiera, *v.* V. QUERER.

quietación, *f.* quieting or appeasing.

quietador, ra, *n.* quieter, appeaser.

quietamente, *adv.* quietly, calmly.

quietar. I. *va.* to quiet, appease. II. *vr.* to become quiet or calm, to quiet down.

quiete, *f.* rest, repose, quiet.

quietismo, *m.* quietism, a sect of mystics.

quietista, *n. & a.* quietist.

quieto, ta, *a.* quiet, still; steady, undisturbed; silent, peaceable; orderly; virtuous.

quietud, *f.* quietude, quietness, quiet; rest, repose, tranquillity.

quijada, *f.* jaw, jawbone.

quijal, quijar, *m.* grinder, back tooth; jaw.

quijarudo, da, *a.* large-jawed.

quijera, *f.* cheeks of a crossbow.—*pl.* straps of the noseband on a harness.

quijero, *m.* sloping bank of a canal.

quijo, *m.* (min.) ore.

quijones, *m. pl.* (bot.) dill.

quijotada, *f.* quixotic enterprise.

quijote, *m.* (armor) cuisse, thighguard; upper part of the haunch.

Quijote, *m.* Quijote, Quixote, quixotic person.—**quijotería,** *f.* quixotism.—**quijotesco, ca,** *a.* quixotic.—**quijotismo,** *m.* quixotism.

quila, *f.* (S. A.) a variety of very strong bamboo.

quilatador, ra, *n.* assayer of gold and silver.

quilatar, *va.* to assay.

quilate, *m.* (jewelry) carat or karat; an ancient coin; degree of excellence.

quilatera, *f.* (jewelry) diamond sieve.

quiliárea, *f.* = KILIÁREA, land measure, 1000 ares.

quilífero, ra, *a.* (zool.) chyliferous.

quilificación, *f.* (med.) chylification.

quilificar, *va.* to chylify.

quilma, *f.* = COSTAL, large bag or sack.

¹quilo, *m.* (med.) chyle.—**sudar el q.,** to work hard.

²quilo, quilogramo, quilómetro, etc. = KILO, KILOGRAMO, etc.

quiloso, sa, *a.* chylous, chylaceous.

quilquil, *m.* a Chilean arboreous fern.

quilla, *f.* (naut.) keel; (ornith.) breastbone.

quillái, quillay, *m.* quillaja, a S. A. soapbark tree.

quillotrar. I. *va.* to excite, incite, urge; to make love to; to attract, captivate; to think over, consider; to deck, adorn. II. *vr.* to fall in love; to complain, to whine.

quillotro, tra. I. *m.* urging, incitement; sign, indication; lovemaking; love affair; puzzle, perplexing thing or situation. II. *n.* dear friend; lover.

quimbámbulas, *f. pl.* (Cuba) rough, craggy spots; hidden nook.

quimbombó, *m.* (bot.) okra, gumbo.

quimera, *f.* chimera; dispute, quarrel.

quimérico, ca; quimerino, na, *a.* chimerical.

quimerista, *n.* wrangler, brawler; visionary.

quimerizar, *vn.* to indulge in chimeras.

química, *f.* chemistry.

químicamente, *adv.* chemically.

químico, ca. I. *a.* chemical. II. *n.* chemist.

quimificar, *va.* to convert into chyme.

quimista, *m.* = ALQUIMISTA, alchemist.

quimo, *m.* (med.) chyme.

quimón, *m.* chintz.

quimono, *m.* kimono.

quina, *f.* Peruvian bark, cinchona.

quinal, *m.* (naut.) preventer shroud.

quinaquina, *f.* = QUINA.

quinario, ria. I. *a.* quinary, consisting of five. II. *m.* quinarius, a Roman coin.

quinas, *f. pl.* arms of Portugal; fives on dice.

quincalla, *f.* (com.) hardware; small wares.

quincallería, *f.* hardware trade or store; small wares store.

quincallero, ra, *n.* dealer in hardware or small wares.

quince, *a. & m.* fifteen; fifteenth; a card game.

quinceno, na. I. *a.* fifteenth. II. *n.* mule fifteen months old. III. *f.* fortnight; semi-monthly pay; (mus.) fifteenth (interval and organ stop).—**por q.,** every two weeks, semi-monthly

quincenal, *a.* fortnightly, semi-monthly.

quincenalmente, *adv.* fortnightly.

quincuagenario, ria, *a. & n.* having fifty units; quinquagenarian, person in the fifties.

quincuagésimo, ma. I. *a.* fiftieth. II. *f.* Quinquagesima Sunday.

quincha, *f.* (Peru) wall of clay and canes.

quindenio, *m.* period of fifteen years.

quinero, *ra,* *n.* cinchona gatherer or trader.

For pronunciation, see the rules at the beginning of the book.

quinete, *m.* a kind of camlet.
quingentésimo, ma, *a.* five-hundredth.
quingombó, *m.* (bot.) gumbo, okra.
quingos, *m.* (Am.) zigzag.
quinientos, *n.* & *a.* five hundred.
quinina, *f.* quinine.
quinismo, *m.* effects of the use of quinine; cinchonism.
quino, *m.* (bot.) cinchona tree; (chem.) quinoidin.
quinoa, *f.* quinoa, a S. A. species of goosefoot.
quínola, *f.* at cards, four of a kind.—*pl.* a card game.
quinolear, *va.* to prepare (cards) for QUÍNOLAS.
quinona, *f.* (chem.) quinone.
quinqué, *m.* student lamp.
quinquefolio, *m.* (bot.) common cinquefoil.
quinquenal, *a.* quinquennial.
quinquenervia, *f.* (bot.) rib-grass plantain.
quinquenio, *m.* quinquennium, lustrum.
quinquillería, *f.* = QUINCALLERÍA.
quinquillero, *m.* hawker, peddler; QUINCALLERO.
quinta, *f.* country seat, villa; manorhouse; (mil.) draft; quint, sequence of five cards; (fencing) quint; (mus.) fifth.—**q. esencia.** quintessence.
quintador, *m.* (mil.) one who drafts men.
quintaesencia, *f.* quintessence.
quintal, *m.* quintal, a hundred pounds.—**q. métrico,** metric quintal (100 kg.).
quintalada, *f.* (naut.) primage or hat money (2½ per cent. on the freight).
quintaleño, ña; lero, ra, *a.* capable of containing a quintal.
quintana, *f.* country mansion.
quintante, *m.* instrument for observations at sea.
quintañón, na, *a.* & *n.* (coll.) centenarian.
quintar. I. *va.* to draw one out of five; (mil.) to draft for service; to plow the fifth time. **II.** *vn.* (of the moon) to attain the fifth day.
quintería, *f.* farm; grange.
quinterno, *m.* five sheets of paper; keno, in lotto.
quintero, *m.* farmer; farm hand.
quinteto, *m.* (mus.) quintet.
quintil, *m.* Quintilis, fifth month in Roman calendar.
quintilla, *f.* five-line stanza.
quintillo, *m.* game of ombre with five players.
quinto, ta. I. *a.* fifth.—**q. columna,** fifth column. **II.** *m.* one fifth; 20% duty; (Mex., Chile) (coll.) 5 centavo piece; (mil.) conscript.
quintuplicación, *f.* quintuplication.
quintuplicar, *va.* to quintuplicate.
quíntuplo, pla, *a.* quintuple, fivefold.
quinua, *f.* = QUINOA.
quinzavo, va, *n.* & *a.* (arith.) fifteenth.
quiñón, *m.* share of profit or lands; (P. I.) a land measure (2.8 hectares).
quiñonero, *m.* part owner, shareholder.
quiosco, *m.* kiosk, pavilion, summer house.—**q. de necesidad,** public water closet.
quipos, *m. pl.* (Peru) quipu.
quiquiriquí, *m.* cock-a-doodle-do; (coll.) cock of the walk.
quiragra, *f.* gout in the hand.
quirinal, *m.* & *a.* Quirinal.
quiritario, ria, *a.* pert. to a Roman citizen.
quirite, *m.* Quirite, Roman citizen.—*pl.* Quirites.
quiromancia, *f.* chiromancy, palmistry.
quiromántico, *m.* palmist, chiromancer.
quirópteros, *m. pl.* bats, Cheiroptera.
quiroteca, *f.* (coll.) glove.
quirúrgico, ca. I. *a.* surgical. **II.** *n.* surgeon.
quise, *v. V.* QUERER.
quisicosa, *f.* (coll.) enigma, riddle, puzzle.
quiso, *v. V.* QUERER.
quisquemenil, *m.* (Am.) short cloak.
quisquilla, *f.* bickering, trifling dispute.
quisquilloso, sa, *a.* fastidious, precise; touchy, peevish.
quiste, *m.* (med.) cyst.

quisto, ta, *a.*—**bien q.,** well received, generally beloved.—**mal q.,** disliked.
quita. I. *f.* (law) acquittance, discharge, release (from debt).—**de q. y pon,** detachable, removable. **II.** *interj.* God forbid!—**¡q. de ahí!** away with you! out of my sight!
quitación, *f.* salary, pay; income; (law) QUITA.
quitador, ra, *n.* remover.
quitaipón, *m.* = QUITAPÓN.
quitamanchas, *m.* clothes cleaner, spot remover.
quitameriendas, *f.* common meadow saffron.
quitamiento, *m.* (law) = QUITA.
quitamotas, *n.* (coll.) servile flatterer.
quitanieve, *m.* snowplow.
quitante, *a.* that takes away or removes.
quitanza, *f.* quittance; (com.) receipt in full, discharge.
quitapelillos, *n.* (coll.) flatterer, fawner.
quitapesares, *n.* (coll.) comfort, comforter.
quitapón, *m.* ornament on the headstall of mules.—**de q.** = DE QUITA Y PON. *V.* QUITA.
quitar. I. *va.* to take away; to subtract; to take off, remove; to separate, extract, take out; to take (up) time; to free from; to rob of, deprive of; to release or redeem (a pledge); to hinder; forbid, prohibit; to repeal, annul; to free from (obligation); (fencing) to parry. **II.** *vr.* to abstain, refrain; to quit, move away, withdraw; to get rid of; to take off (a garment); to come out (as a stain).—**q. algo de encima,** to get rid of, or shake off, something.—**q. el agua,** (Mex.) to stop raining.
quitasol, *m.* parasol, sunshade.
quite, *m.* obstacle, impediment, hindrance; (fencing) parry, dodge.
quiteño, ña, *a.* of or pertaining to Quito.
quitina, *f.* (chem.) chitin.
quitinoso, sa, *a.* (chem.) chitinous.
quitrín, *m.* (Cuba) two-wheel open wagon.
quizá, quizás, *adv.* perhaps, maybe.
quizame, *m.* (P. I.) roof, ceiling.
quórum, *m.* quorum.

R

raba, *f.* bait for pilchard fishery.
rabada, *f.* hind quarter, rump.
rabadán, *m.* head shepherd.
rabadilla, *f.* coccyx; rump; (ornith.) uropygium.
rabanal, *m.* ground sown with radishes.
rabanero, ra. I. *a.* (coll.) short (skirt); forward, pert, bold. **II.** *f.* (coll.) shameless woman. **III.** *n.* seller of radishes.
rabanillo, *m. dim.* (bot.) wild radish; sharp taste of wine on the turn; (coll.) ardent desire, longing; sourish temper.
rabaniza, *f.* radish seed.
rábano, *m.* (bot.) radish.—**r. picante,** or **rusticano,** horse-radish.—**r. silvestre,** wild radish.—**tomar el r. por las hojas,** (coll.) to be entirely mistaken, to be off the track.
rabazuz, *m.* thickened juice of licorice.
rabear, *vn.* to wag the tail.
¹**rabel,** *m.* (mus.) rebeck, ancient stringed instrument.
²**rabel,** *m.* breech, backside.
rabelejo, *m. dim.* of RABEL.
rabeo, *m.* wagging of the tail.
rabera, *f.* tail end; tang, tongue; handle of a crossbow; chaff.
raberón, *m.* top of a felled tree.
rabí, *m.* rabbi, rabbin.
rabia, *f.* hydrophobia, rabies; rage, fury.—**tener r.,** to have a grudge against.—**tomar r.,** to take a dislike to; to develop a grudge against.
rabiar, *vn.* to be ill with hydrophobia; to rage, be furious; to suffer racking pain.—**r. por,** to long eagerly for.
rabiatar, *va.* to tie by the tail.

For pronunciation, see the rules at the beginning of the book.

rabiazorras, *m.* east wind.
rabicán; rabicano, na, *a.* white-tailed.
rabicorto, ta, *a.* short-tailed; docked.
rábido, da, *a.* (poet.) = RABIOSO.
rabieta, *f. dim.* (coll.) fit of temper.
rabihorcado, *m.* (ornith.) frigate bird.
rabil, *m.* crank; wheat husker.
rabilar, *va.* to husk with a wheat husker.
rabilargo, ga. I. *a.* long-tailed. **II.** *m.* (ornith.) blue crow.
rabillo, *m. dim.* little tail; stem; mildew spots on corn; darnel.
rabinegro, gra, *a.* black-tailed.
rabínico, ca, *a.* rabbinical.
rabinismo, *m.* rabbinism.
rabinista, *n.* & *a.* rabbinist(-ic).
rabino, *m.* rabbi.
rabión, *m.* rapids of a river.
rabiosamente, *adv.* furiously, ragingly.
rabioso, sa, *a.* rabid, mad; furious, enraged.
rabisalsera, *a.* (coll.) pert, forward (woman).
rabito, *m. dim.* small tail; stem.
rabiza, *f.* point of a fishing rod; rocket stick; (naut.) tip, end of a rope; point, end of a shoal; tail of a block.
rabo, *m.* tail (of animal, esp. quadruped); tail end, back, or hind part; train; stem.—**r. de gallo,** (naut.) stern timbers.—**r. de junco,** (ornith.) a tropical bird.—**con el r. entre las piernas,** (coll.) (fig.) with the tail between the legs, crestfallen, dejected; humiliated—**falta el r. por desollar,** the worst is yet to come.—**mirar con el r. del ojo,** to look askance, or out of the corner of the eye.
rabón, na, *a.* docked, bobtailed.
rabona, *f.* (Am.) canteen woman, soldier's wife.—**hacer r.,** to play hooky.
rabopelado, *m.* opossum.
raboseada, raboseadura, *f.* fray, chafe.
rabosear, *va.* to chafe, fray, fret.
raboso, sa, *a.* ragged, tattered.
rabotada, *f.* insolent reply.
rabotear, *va.* to crop or dock the tail of.
raboteo, *m.* cropping of sheep's tails.
rabudo, da, *a.* long- or thick-tailed.
rábula, *m.* ignorant, vociferous lawyer, pettifogger.
raca, *f.* (naut.) traveler; jib iron.
racahut, *m.* raccahoot.
racamenta, *f.* **racamento,** *m.* (naut.) parral or parrel.
racel, *m.* (naut.) run, rising of a ship.
racial, *a.* racial, race (as *a.*).
racima, *f.* grapes left on vines at vintage.
racimado, da, *a.* clustered, in racemes.
racimal, *a.* having clusters or racemes.
racimar. I. *va.* to pick the RACIMAS of. **II.** *vr.* = ARRACIMARSE, to cluster.
racimo, *m.* bunch; cluster; raceme.
racimoso, sa, *a.* full of bunches, racemose.
racimudo, da, *a.* in large bunches or racemes.
raciocinación, *f.* ratiocination, reasoning.
raciocinar, *vn.* to reason, ratiocinate.
raciocinio, *m.* reasoning, ratiocination.
ración, *f.* ration; ration money; supply, allowance, pittance; (eccl.) prebend in a cathedral.
racionabilidad, *f.* rationality.
racional. I. *a.* rational; reasonable; (math. and astr.) rational. **II.** *m.* rational, pectoral or breastplate.
racionalidad, *f.* rationality; reasonableness.
racionalismo, *m.* rationalism.
racionalista, *n.* & *a.* rationalist(-ic).
racionalmente, *adv.* rationally.
racionamiento, *m.* (mil.) rationing.
racionar, *va.* (mil.) to ration.
racioncica, illa, ita, *f. dim.* small pittance.
racionero, *m.* (eccl.) prebendary; distributor of rations.

racionista, *n.* receiver of a ration or allowance; (theat.) utility man.
¹racha, *f.* flaw, gust of wind; streak of luck.
²racha, *f.* (min.) piece of wood used in shoring.
rada, *f.* (naut.) roads, roadstead, bay.
radar, *m.* radar.
radiación, *f.* radiation.
radiactividad, *f.* (phys.) radioactivity.
radiactivo, va, *a.* radioactive.
radiado, da. I. *pp.* of RADIAR. **II.** *a.* radiated. **III.** *m.* & *a.* (zool.) radiate. **IV.** *m. pl.* Radiata.
radiador, *m.* radiator (heating device and auto).
radial, *a.* radial; radio (as *a.*).—**guía r.,** radio program.—**locutor r.,** radio announcer.
radiante, *a.* radiant, brilliant, beaming; (phys.) radiant.—**r. de,** beaming with.
radiar. I. *vn.* to radiate. **II.** *va.* & *vn.* to radio; to broadcast.
radicación, *f.* radication, taking root.
radical. I. *a.* radical; original, primitive. **II.** *m.* (math., chem., pol.) radical; (gram.) root.
radicalismo, *m.* radicalism.
radicalmente, *adv.* radically, fundamentally.
radicar. I. *vn.* to take root; to be (in a place); to lie, have roots. **II.** *vr.* to radicate, take root; to settle, establish oneself.
radicícola, *a.* radicicolous, living on roots as a parasite.
radicoso, sa, *a.* radical.
radícula, *f.* (bot.) radicle, radicule.
radífero, ra, *a.* radium-bearing.
radigrafía, *f.* radiography, X-ray photography or photograph.
radigráfico, ca, *a.* radiographic.
¹radio, *m.* (geom., anat.) radius; circuit, district.—**r. de acción,** range.
²radio, *m.* (chem.) radium; radio, radiotelephony; radiogram; radio (instrument or set); (radio) broadcasting.
radioactividad, *f.* = RADIACTIVIDAD.
radioactivo, va, *a.* = RADIACTIVO.
radioconductor, *m.* (radio) radioconductor.
radiodifundir, *va.* & *vn.* (radio) to broadcast.
radiodifusión, *f.* (radio) broadcast.
radiodifusora, *f.,* **radioemisora,** *f.* (radio) broadcasting station.
radiofaro, *m.* radiophare.
radiofonía, *f.* (radio) radiophony.
radiografía, *f.* RADIGRAFÍA; radiotelegraphy.
radiograma, *m.* radiotelegram, radiogram.
radiolario, ria. I. *n.* & *a.* (zool.) radiolarian. **II.** *m. pl.* Radiolaria.
radiómetro, *m.* radiometer.
radiorreceptor, *m.* radio receiver.
radiorrevista, *f.* (radio) radio report or news.
radioscopia, *f.* radioscopy.
radioso, sa, *a.* radiant.
radiosonda, *f.* (meteorol.) radiosonde.
radiotelefonía, *f.* radiotelephony.
radiotelefónico, ca, *a.* radiotelephonic.
radioteléfono, *m.* radiotelephone.
radiotelegrafía, *f.* radiotelegraphy, wireless telegraphy.
radiotelegrafiar, *va.* & *vn.* to wireless, communicate by wireless telegraphy.
radiotelegráfico, ca, *a.* radiotelegraphic, wireless.
radiotelegrafista, *n.* wireless operator.
radiotelégrafo, *m.* wireless telegraph.
radiotelegrama, *m.* radiotelegram, radiogram.
radioterapia, *f.* (med.) radiotherapy.
radiotransmisor, *m.* radio transmitter.
raedera, *f.* scraper, raker.
raedizo, za, *a.* easily scraped.
raedor, ra, *n.* & *a.* scraper(-ing), eraser(-ing).
raedura, *f.* erasure; scrapings, filings.
raer, *va.* (ger. RAYENDO; *ind. pres.* RAIGO, *pret.* él RAYÓ; *subj.* RAIGA) to scrape; to rub off, abrade, fret, fray; to erase; to wipe out, extirpate.
rafa, *f.* (arch.) buttress; trench or ditch for irriga-

tion; (vet.) crack in the toe of hoofs; (min.) cut in a rock for supporting an arch.

rafaelesco, ca, *a.* Raphaelesque.

ráfaga, *f.* gust of wind; small cloud; flash or gleam of light.

rafania, *f.* (med.) raphania.

¹rafe, *m.* (arch.) eaves.

²rafe, *n.* (anat., bot.) raphe.

rafear, *va.* to secure with buttresses.

rahez, *a.* vile, low, despicable.

raíble, *a.* that can be scraped or frayed.

raiceja, cilla, cita, *f. dim.* rootlet, radicle.

raído, da. I. *pp.* of RAER. II. *a.* frayed, threadbare, worn out; barefaced, shameless.

raigal. I. *a.* radical. II. *m.* foot of a tree.

raigambre, *f.* intermixture of roots.

raigo, raiga, *v. V.* RAER.

raigón, *m.* large strong root; root of a tooth.

rail, *m.* (Angl.) (Ry.) rail.

raimiento, *m.* scraping, abrading; impudence.

raíz, *f.* (bot.) root; base, foundation; origin; (math. and gram.) root.—**a r.,** close to, immediately, right after, hard upon.—**arrancar de r.,** to uproot.—**cortar de r.,** to nip in the bud.—**de r.,** from the root; entirely.—**echar raíces,** to take root, become fixed or settled.

¹raja, *f.* split, rent, crack; slice (as of fruit).

²raja, *f.* coarse cloth.

rajá, *m.* rajah, Indian prince.

rajable, *a.* easily split.

rajabroqueles, *m.* (coll.) bully, brawler.

rajadillo, *m.* sugared sliced almonds.

rajadizo, za, *a.* easily split; fissile.

rajador, *m.* wood splitter.

rajadura, *f.* cleft, fissure, crack.

rajante, *pres. p.* of RAJAR, splitting.

rajar. I. *va.* to split, rend; to slice (food). II. *vr.* to split, crack. III. *vn.* (coll.) to boast; to chatter.

rejeta, *f.* coarse cloth of mixed colors.

rajuela, *f. dim.* small crack; (mason.) riprap.

ralea, *f.* race, breed, stock; kind, quality.

ralear, *vn.* to become thin or sparse (as cloth, hair); (agr.) to yield thin bunches of grapes.

raleón, na, *a.* (of birds of prey) predatory.

raleza, *f.* thinness, lack of density, sparseness.

ralo, la, *a.* thin, sparse, not dense.

ralladera, *f.,* **rallador,** *m.* (cooking) grater.

ralladura, *f.* mark left by a grater; gratings.

rallar, *va.* (cooking) to grate; (coll.) to vex.

rallo, *m.* grater; ice scraper; rasp.

rallón, *m.* arrow with crosshead.

rama, *f.* (bot.) branch, twig, bough; branch of a family; rack in cloth mills; (print.) chase.—**andarse por las ramas,** to beat about the bush.—**asirse a las ramas,** to seek or make frivolous excuses.—**en r.,** unmanufactured, raw; (bookbinding) in sheets, unbound.

ramada, *f.* mass of branches; arbor; (Am.) shed.

ramaje, *m.* mass of branches; foliage; ramiform design.

ramal, *m.* branch, ramification; (Ry.) branch road; strand of a rope; halter; (min.) shaft, gallery.

ramalazo, *m.* lash, stroke with a rope; mark left by a lash; sudden pain or grief; blow; spot on the face caused by blows or disease.

ramalla, *f.* twigs; brushwood.

rambla, *f.* sandy or dry ravine; ramble; tenter, tentering machine; (in Barcelona) avenue.

ramblar, *m.* sandy beach or bed.

ramblazo, *m.* bed of a torrent.

rameado, da, *a.* having a ramiform design.

rameal, rámeo, a, *a.* pertaining to branches.

ramera, *f.* prostitute, harlot, strumpet.

ramería, *f.* brothel; harlotry.

ramero, *ra,* *a.* hopping from branch to branch.

ramial, *m.* ramie patch.

ramificación, *f.* ramification, branching off.

ramificarse, *vr.* to ramify, branch off.

ramilla, ita, *f. dim.* small shoot, sprig, twig.

ramillete, *m.* bouquet; (bot.) cluster, umbel; centerpiece at table; collection of choice things.—**r. de Constantinopla,** (bot.) sweet-william.

ramilletero, ra. I. *n.* maker and seller of bouquets. II. *m.* flower vase.

ramillo, ito, *m. dim.* sprig, twig, branchlet.

ramina, *f.* ramie fiber.

ramio, *m.* (bot.) ramie, an Asiatic shrub.

ramiza, *f.* collection of lopped branches.

rámneo, nea, *a.* (bot.) rhamnaceous.

ramo, *m.* bough; branch (of a tree, of trade, a science, art, etc.); branchlet; limb cut off from a tree; cluster, bouquet; string of onions; line of goods; section, division; department.

ramojo, *m.* brushwood, small wood.

ramón, *m.* browse, browsing.

ramonear, *vn.* to lop off twigs; to browse.

ramoneo, *m.* lopping twigs; browsing.

ramoso, sa, *a.* ramose, having many branches.

¹rampa, *f.* (muscular) cramp.

²rampa, *f.* (mil.) slope of a glacis.

rampante, *a.* (her.) rampant.

rampiñete, *m.* (artil.) vent gimlet.

rampión, na. I. *a.* heavy, coarse (shoe); rude, vulgar, common. II. *m.* calk of a horseshoe.

¹rampojo, *m.* refuse of grapes.

²rampojo, *m.* (mil.) caltrop.

rampollo, *m.* (agr.) cutting for planting.

rana, *f.* (zool.) frog; (Ry.) frog.—*pl.* (med.) ranula, tongue tumor.—**r. marina,** or **pescadora,** (ichth.) angler.—**no ser r.,** (coll.) to be able and expert.

ranacuajo, *m.* = RENACUAJO, polliwog.

rancajada, *f.* uprooting plants or sprouts.

rancajado, da, *a.* wounded with a splinter.

rancajo, *m.* splinter in the flesh.

ranciarse, *vr.* = ENRANCIARSE, to get rancid.

rancidez, *f.* rancidity, rancidness, rankness.

rancio, cia. I. *a.* rank, rancid, stale; long kept, old (as wine); antiquated. II. *m.* greasiness of cloth before milling.

rancioso, sa, *a.* rancid, rank, sour.

rancheadero, *m.* place containing huts.

ranchear. I. *vn.* to build huts; to plunder huts. II. *vr.* to build a hut for oneself; to settle in a hut. III. *va.* to plunder the huts of.

ranchería, *f.* settlement; cluster of huts; hamlet; horde, camp.

ranchero, *m.* steward of a mess; small farmer; (Mex.) rancher.

rancho, *m.* mess (food and persons eating together); (naut.) mess; messroom; (gen. thatched) hut; (Arg.) man's flat straw hat; hamlet; camp; (Am.) cattle ranch; (coll.) meeting; gang.—**r. de Santa Bárbara,** (naut.) gunroom; chamber of the rudder.

randa, *f.* lace trimming.—**randado, da,** *a.* lace-trimmed.—**randera,** *f.* lace worker.

rangífero, *m.* reindeer.

rango, *m.* (Gal.) rank, class, position.

rangua, *f.* pivot collar, shaft socket.

ránidos, *m. pl.* (zool.) Ranidæ (the frog family).

ranilla, *f. dim.* frog of the hoof (of horses, etc.); (vet.) disease in the bowels of cattle.

ranina, *a.* (anat.) ranine, of underside of tongue.

ránula, *f.* (med. and vet.) ranula, tongue tumor.

ranunculáceo, cea, *a.* (bot.) ranunculaceous.

ranúnculo, *m.* (bot.) crowfoot, buttercup.

ranura, *f.* groove; slot.

¹raña, *f.* hook frame for catching cuttlefish.

²raña, *f.* lowland.

raño, *m.* oyster tongs.

rapa, *f.* (bot.) flower of the olive tree.

¹rapacejo, *ja,* *n.* urchin, child.

²rapacejo, *m.* border, edging.

rapacería, *f.* childish prank or action.

rapacidad, *f.* rapacity.

rapador, ra, *n.* scraper; (coll.) barber.

rapadura, *f.* shaving; hair cut; plundering.

rapagón, _m._ beardless young man.

rapamiento, _m._ = RAPADURA.

rapante, _a._ snatching, robbing; shaving; (her.) rampant.

rapapiés, _m._ (fireworks) running squib; chaser.

rapapolvo, _m._ (coll.) sharp reprimand, dressing down.

rapar, _va._ to shave; to crop (the hair); to plunder, snatch, rob; to skin, peel.

rapasa, _f._ (min.) wax stone.

¹rapaz. I. _a._ rapacious, predatory; (ornith.) raptorial, predatory. **II.** _f. pl._ (**rapaces**) (zool.) Raptores, birds of prey.

²rapaz, za, _n._ young boy (girl).

rapazada, _f._ childish prank or speech.

rapazuelo, la, _n. dim._ little boy (girl), youngster.

rape, _m._ (coll.) hurried shaving or hair cutting.—**al r.,** cropped, clipped, cut close or short.

rapé, _m._ snuff; rappee.

rápidamente, _adv._ rapidly, fast.

rapidez, _f._ rapidity, celerity, swiftness.

rápido, da. I. _a._ rapid, swift. **II.** _m._ rapids; express train.

rapiego, ga, _a._ rapacious (bird).

rapingacho, _m._ (Peru) cheese omelet.

rapiña, _f._ rapine, robbery, plundering.—**de r.,** (of birds) of prey.

rapiñador, ra, _n._ plunderer, robber.

rapiñar, _va._ (coll.) to plunder; to pillage; to steal.

rapista, _m._ scraper; (coll.) barber.

rapo, _m._ round-rooted turnip.

raponchigo, _m._ (bot.) rampion.

rapóntico, _m._ (bot.) = RUIPÓNTICO, rhubarb.

raposa, _f._ fox; cunning person.

raposear, _vn._ to act in a foxy way.

raposera, _f._ fox hole, fox den.

raposería, _f._ cunning of a fox.

raposino, na, _a._ foxy.

raposo, _m._ (male) fox.

raposuno, na, _a._ vulpine, foxy.

rapsoda, _a._ rhapsodic, rapt.

rapsodia, _f._ rhapsody.

rapta, _a._ (of a woman) abducted, kidnapped.

raptar, _va._ to kidnap (a woman); to steal.

rapto, _m._ kidnapping; rapture, ecstasy.

raptor, ra, _n._ thief, robber; kidnapper.

raque, _m._ wrecking; arrack.

raquero, ra. I. _a._ piratical. **II.** _n._ wrecker; "dock rat."

raqueta, _f._ (tennis, badminton, etc.) racket; battledore; battledore and shuttlecock, badminton; tennis.

raquetero, _m._ racket maker or seller.

raquialgia, _f._ (med.) rachialgia, spinal pain.

raquis, _m._ (anat.) rachis, spine; (bot.) stalk.

raquítico, ca, _a._ (med.) rachitic, rickety; feeble, flimsy, niggardly.

raquitis, _f._; **raquitismo,** _m._ (med.) rachitis, rickets.

raquítomo, _m._ (surg.) rachitome.

rara avis, (Lat.) rara avis, rare bird, rare thing.

raramente, _adv._ rarely, seldom; ridiculously, oddly.

rarefacción, _f._ rarefaction.

rareza, _f._ rarity, rareness, uncommonness; fad, queerness; freak; curio, curiosity; oddness.—**por r.,** rarely, seldom.

raridad, _f._ rarity; thinness.

rarificar. I. _va._ (_pret._ RARIFIQUÉ; _subj._ RARIFIQUE) to rarefy, make thin. **II.** _vr._ to become thin or rarefied.

rarificativo, va, _a._ rarefying, thinning.

raro, ra, _a._ rare; scarce; thin, rarefied; choice, precious, excellent; queer, odd.—**r. vez,** seldom.

ras, _m._ level, even, flush.—**r. con r.,** on a level, flush.—**al ras con,** or **de,** even or flush with.

rasa, _f._ tease in fabrics; table-land, plateau.

rasadura, _f._ levelling with a strickle.

rasamente, _adv._ publicly, openly, clearly.

rasante. I. _a._ levelling, grazing. **II.** _f._ (Ry.) grade, grade line.

rasar, _va._ to strike or level with a strickle; to graze, skim, touch lightly.

rasarse, _vr._ to clear up (as the sky).

rascacielos, _m._ (coll.) skyscraper.

rascacio, _m._ (ichth.) = ESCORPENA, grouper.

rascadera, _f._ scraper; currycomb.

rascador, _m._ scraper, scaler, scratcher; rasp; hatpin, bodkin; huller, sheller.

rascadura, _f._ scratching; scratch; scraping.

rascalino, _m._ (bot.) dodder.

rascamiento, _m._ scraping, scratching.

rascamoño, _m._ woman's hatpin, bodkin.

rascar. I. _va._ (_pret._ RASQUÉ; _subj._ RASQUE) to scratch; rasp, scrape. **II.** _vn._ (Colomb.) to itch.

rascazón, _f._ itching.

rascle, _m._ instrument used in coral fishing.

rascón, na. I. _a._ sour, tart, sharp, acrid. **II.** _m._ (ornith.) rail; marsh hen.

rascuñar, rascuño, = RASGUÑAR, etc.

rasel, _m._ (naut.) entrance and run of a ship.

rasero, _m._ strickle, strike; standard, rule.

rasete, _m._ satinet, sateen.

rasgado, _m._ = RASGÓN.

rasgador, ra, _n._ tearer, ripper.

rasgadura, _f._ rent, ripping.

rasgar, _va._ (_pret._ RASGUÉ; _subj._ RASGUE) to tear, rend, rip; RASGUEAR.

rasgo, _m._ dash, stroke, flourish, scroll; stroke (of wit, kindness, etc.); deed, feat; happy expression or saying; feature (of face); characteristic. —**a grandes rasgos,** broadly, in outline.

rasgón, _m._ rent, rip, tear.

rasgué, rasgue, _v. V._ RASGAR.

rasgueado. I. _pp._ of RASGUEAR. **II.** _a._ full of flourishes. **III.** _m._ making of flourishes.

rasguear. I. _vn._ to flourish, to make scrollwork. **II.** _va._ to play flourishes on (the guitar); to play (the guitar) with strokes of the whole hand.

rasgueo, _m._ forming fine strokes with a pen; scrollwork; flourish.

rasguillo, _m. dim._ small dash of a pen.

rasguñar, _va._ to scratch; to sketch, outline.

rasguñito, ñuelo, _m._ slight scratch or sketch.

rasguño, _m._ scratch; nip; sketch, outline.

rasilla, _f._ serge; fine tile for flooring.

raso, sa. I. _a._ clear, unobstructed; plain; flat.— **a campo r.,** or **al r.,** in the open air. **II.** _m._ satin.

raspa, _f._ (bot.) beard of an ear of corn; bunch of grapes; spine, fin ray of fish; hair or thread in the nib of a writing pen; (carp.) wood rasp, scraper, grater; outer rind of certain fruits (nuts, almonds, etc.); (coll., Am.) sermon, lecture, dressing down.

raspador, _m._ eraser; rasp, grater, scraper.

raspadura, _f._ erasure; rasping, scraping; abrasion; scrapings, shavings; (Cuba) pan sugar.

raspajo, _m._ stalk of a bunch of grapes.

raspamiento, _m._ erasure; rasping, scraping.

raspante, _a._ rasping, rough (wine); abrasive, abrading.

raspar, _va._ to erase; to scrape, rasp, pare off; (of wine) to bite or sting; to steal, carry off.

raspear, _vn._ to scratch (as a bad pen).

raspilla, _f._ (bot.) a boraginaceous plant.

raspón, _m._ (Colomb.) large straw hat; (Chile) severe reprimand; (Mex.) scratch, skinning.

rasqué, rasque, _v. V._ RASCAR.

rasqueta, _f._ (naut.) scraper.

rastacuero, _n._ = RASTRACUEROS.

rastel, _m._ lattice, railing.

rastillador, rastillar, rastillo, = RASTRILLADOR, RASTRILLAR, RASTRILLO.

rastra, _f._ track, trail; sled, sledge; dray; (agr.) harrow, brake; reaping machine; act of dragging along; anything dragging; string of dried fruit, onions, etc.; (naut.) drag, grapnel.—**a la**

r., a las rastras, or **a r.,** dragging; unwillingly, by force.

rastracueros, n. (Am.) person who makes a fortune in the hide business (may be called hide magnate); snob whose income comes from nobody knows where.

rastrallar, vn. to crack with a whip.

rastrallido, m. crack of a whip.

rastreador, ra, n. tracer; scout; (ship) mine detector.

rastrear. I. va. to trace, scent; to track down, trail; (agr.) to harrow, rake; (in fishing) to drag; to investigate, follow a clue to; to sell (carcasses) by wholesale. **II.** vn. to skim the ground, to fly very low.

rastreo, m. dragging in the water.

rastrero, ra. I. a. creeping, dragging; trailing; flying low; abject, grovelling; low, base; cringing. **II.** n. employee of a slaughterhouse.

rastrillada, f. rakeful.

rastrillador, ra, n. hackler; flax dresser, hatcheler; raker.

rastrillaje, m. raking; hatcheling.

rastrillar, va. to hackle, dress (flax), comb, hatchel; to rake.

rastrilleo, m. hackling or raking.

rastrillo, m. hackle, flax comb; (agr.) rake; (fort.) portcullis; (artil.) hammer of a gunlock; ward of a key; ward of a lock.—**r. de pesebre,** rack of a manger.

rastro, m. track, scent, trail; trace; (agr.) rake, harrow; slaughterhouse; sign, token; vestige, relic; in Madrid, a market of knickknacks.

rastrojera, f. stubble field.

rastrojo, restrojo, m. stubble, haulm.

rasura, f. shaving.—pl. argol.

rasuración, f. shaving.

rasurar, va. to shave.

rata. I. f. rat. **II.** m. (coll.) pickpocket.

ratafía, f. ratafia, a cordial.

ratania, f. (bot.) ratany, rhatany.

rata parte, or **por cantidad,** pro rata.

rataplán, m. rubadub (sound of a drum).

¹**ratear,** va. to lessen in proportion; to apportion.

²**ratear,** va. & vn. to filch.

³**ratear,** vn. to creep.

ratel, m. (zool.) ratel.

rateo, m. apportionment.

rateramente, adv. meanly, vilely.

¹**ratería,** f. larceny, petty theft.

²**ratería,** f. (coll.) meanness, stinginess.

¹**ratero, ra,** a. creeping; flying low.

²**ratero, ra,** n. pickpocket, pilferer.

rateruelo, ela, n. little pilferer.

ratico, m. (coll.) little while.

ratificación, f. ratification, confirmation.

ratificar, va. (pret. RATIFIQUÉ; subj. RATIFIQUE) to ratify, confirm.

ratificatorio, ria, a. ratifying, confirming.

ratigar, va. to secure on a cart with a rope.

rátigo, m. cartload, truck load.

ratihabición, f. (law) ratification.

ratimago, m. (coll.) trick, cunning.

ratina, f. Petersham, ratteen.

ratito, m. dim. little while, short time.

¹**rato,** a. (law) valid (marriage).

²**rato,** m. short time, while, little while.—**al poco r.,** presently, very soon.—**a ratos,** from time to time, occasionally.—**a ratos perdidos,** in leisure hours, in spare time.—**buen r.,** a great while; a pleasant, good time; a great quantity. —**de r. en r.** = A RATOS.—**mal r.,** an unpleasant time.—**pasar el r.,** to lose time; to pass the time, to while away the time.

ratón, m. mouse; (naut.) hidden rock that frets cables.—**ratona,** f. female mouse or rat.

ratonar. I. va. to gnaw like mice. **II.** vr. to become sick (as cats) from eating rats.

ratoncito, m. dim. little mouse.

ratonera, f. mousetrap; mousehole or breeding place.—**caer en la r.,** to fall into a trap.

ratonero, ra. I. a. mousy. **II.** n. ratter.

ratonesco, ca, a. = RATONERO, a.

rauco, ca, a. (poet.) hoarse, husky, raucous.

raudal, m. torrent, stream; plenty, abundance.

raudamente, adv. rapidly.

raudo, da, a. rapid, swift, impetuous.

rauta, f. (coll.) road, way, route.

¹**raya. I.** f. stroke, dash, streak, stripe, line; frontier, boundary; score, mark; crease (in trousers); parting in the hair; (print.) dash, rule; (artil.) rifle or spiral groove; strip of ground cleared of combustible matter.—**a r.,** within bounds.—**tener a uno a r.,** to hold one at bay.

²**raya,** m. (ichth.) ray, skate.

rayado, da. I. pp. of RAYAR. **II.** a. streaky. **III.** m. ruling; stripes.

rayadillo, m. striped cotton duck.

rayano, na, a. neighboring, contiguous, bordering.

rayar. I. va. to draw lines on; to rule; to scratch (as a table); to stripe, streak; (artil.) to rifle or groove; to cross out; to underscore. **II.** vn. to excel, surpass; to border (on); to begin, appear (as the day, sun, light, etc.).

rayo, m. ray, beam; spoke of a wheel; thunderbolt; flash of lightning; sudden havoc, misfortune, or scourge; lively, ready genius; great power or efficacy of action.—**r. de sol,** sunbeam.—**r. textorio,** weaver's shuttle.—**rayos catódicos, Roentgen,** or **X, X-rays.**

¡**rayo!** or ¡**rayos!** interj. fury!

rayó, pret. of RAER.

rayoso, sa, a. full of lines or stripes.

rayuela, f. dim. small line; game of drawing lines.

rayuelo, m. (ornith.) a small kind of snipe.

¹**raza,** f. race, lineage; breed.—**de r.,** pure-breed.

²**raza,** f. crack, fissure; lightly woven stripe in fabrics; cleft in horse's hoof; ray of light.

razado, a. having lightly woven stripes.

rázago, m. burlap, sackcloth.

razón, f. reason; reasonableness; equity, fairness; account, explanation; information; (Am.) message; (math.) ratio.—**r. de estado,** reason of state, raison d'état; regard for public opinion. —**r. de pie de banco,** (coll.) futile, silly reason.—**r. de ser,** raison d'être, reason; explanation; justification, foundation.—**r. social,** (com.) firm, firm name.—**a r. de,** at the rate of.—**con r. o sin ella,** rightly or wrongly.— **dar la r. a,** to agree with.—**dar r. de,** to give an account of; to account for; to give information about.—**en r. a,** or **de,** concerning, as regards.—**entrar en r.,** to be, or become, reasonable, listen to reason.—**meter en r.,** to compel or induce to act reasonably; to convince.—**no tener r.,** to be wrong or mistaken.—**perder la r.,** to become insane.—**ponerse en (la) r.,** to be reasonable.—**por cuya r.,** and so, and for this reason.—**por r. de,** because of.—**tener r.,** to be right.—**tomar r. de,** to register, make a memorandum or record of; to inventory.

razonable, a. reasonable; moderate; fair, just.

razonablejo, ja, a. (coll.) moderate, fair.

razonablemente, adv. reasonably.

razonado, da. I. pp. of RAZONAR. **II.** a. reasoned, reasoned out; detailed, itemized.

razonador, ra, n. & a. reasoner(-ing).

razonamiento, m. reasoning.

razonante, n. & a. reasoner(-ing).

razonar. I. vn. to reason, ratiocinate. **II.** va. to itemize, vouch, attest.

re, m. (mus.) D, re, second note of the scale.

reacción, f. (chem., mech., pol., personal) reaction.—**r. en cadena,** (phys.) chain reaction.— **r. persistente,** sustained reaction.

reaccionar, vn. to react.

reaccionario, ria, n. & a. reactionary.

reaccionarismo, m. (pol.) reactionism.

reacio, cia, *a.* obstinate, stubborn.

reactivo, va. I. *a.* reactive. **II.** *m.* (chem.) reagent.

reagravación, *f.* reaggravation.

reagravar, *va.* to aggravate anew.

reagudo, da, *a.* very acute.

¹**real,** *a.* real, actual.

²**real. I.** *a.* royal, kingly, kinglike; grand, magnificent, splendid; noble; handsome. **II.** *m.* camp, encampment; fair grounds; real, a silver coin.—**r. de agua,** water running through a pipe the size of a real.—**r. de minas,** (Mex.) town having silver mines in its vicinity.—**r. de vellón,** a small coin (5 cents).—**r. hacienda,** exchequer.—**r. sitio,** king's country residence.—**alzar,** or **levantar, los reales,** to break camp; to break up housekeeping; to quit.—**sentar (los) reales,** to encamp; to settle, establish oneself.

realce, *m.* raised work, embossment; excellence; lustre, splendor; (art) high light.

realdad, *f.* royal power, sovereignty.

realegrarse, *vr.* to be very joyful.

realejo, *m. dim.* hand organ.

realengo, ga. I. *a.* royal, kingly; unappropriated (land). **II.** *m.* royal patrimony.

realera, *f.* = MAESTRIL, queen cell (of beehive).

realete, *m.* = DIECIOCHENO, a kind of cloth.

realeza, *f.* royalty, regal dignity.

realicé, realice, *v. V.* REALIZAR.

realidad, *f.* reality, fact; truth, sincerity.—**en r.,** or **en r. de verdad,** truly; really; in fact.

realillo, realito, *m. dim.* small REAL (coin).

¹**realismo,** *m.* royalism.

²**realismo,** *m.* (art) realism.

¹**realista,** *n.* (pol.) royalist.

²**realista,** *n.* (art) realist.

realizable, *a.* realizable; (com.) salable.

realización, *f.* realization, fulfilment; (com.) sale.

realizar, *va.* (*pret.* REALICÉ; *subj.* REALICE) to realize, fulfil, carry out, perform; (com.) to sell out, convert into money.

realmente, *adv.* really, in reality, actually.

realzar, *va.* (*pret.* REALCÉ; *subj.* REALCE) to raise, elevate; to emboss; to brighten, heighten the colors of; to make prominent; to heighten, enhance, add merit or excellence to.

reanimar, *va.* to cheer, comfort, encourage; to revive, reanimate.

reanudar, *va.* to renew, resume.

reaparecer, *vn.* (*ind.* REAPAREZCO; *subj.* REAPAREZCA) to reappear.

reaparición, *f.* reappearance.

reapretar, *va.* (*ind.* REAPRIETO; *subj.* REAPRIETE) to press again, to squeeze.

rearar, *va.* to plow again.

rearme, *m.* rearmament.

reasegurar, *va.* (com.) to reinsure.

reaseguro, *m.* (com.) reinsurance.

reasumir, *va.* to retake, resume.

reasunción, *f.* resumption, resuming.

reata, *f.* riata; rope to tie horses and keep them in single file; drove of horses or mules thus tied; (Mex.) any rope.—*pl.* (naut.) woolding.—**de r.,** in single file; submissively.

reatadura, *f.* act of retying; tying animals in single file.

reatar, *va.* to retie; to tie together; to tie tightly; (naut.) to woold.

reato, *m.* (eccl.) obligation of atonement.

reaventar, *va.* (*ind.* REAVIENTO; *subj.* REAVIENTE) to winnow a second time.

rebaba, *f.* (mech.) fash, mold mark, fin, burr, rough seam.

rebaja, *f.* deduction, diminution; (com.) rebate, reduction, discount.

rebajamiento, *m.* curtailment; abatement; deduction; lowering; abasement.

rebajar. I. *va.* to abate, lessen, diminish; to reduce, lower, cut down; to underbid; (carp.) to shave off, cut down; (art) to weaken (a high light). **II.** *vr.* to be dismissed, or mustered out; to humble oneself; to lower oneself.

rebajo, *m.* (carp.) rabbet; groove.

rebalaje, *m.* current or flow of water.

rebalsa, *f.* pool, puddle, pond; stagnation of humors in a part of the body.

rebalsar. I. *va.* to dam. **II.** *vr.* to form a pool; to accumulate; to be stopped or checked.

rebanada, *f.* slice.—**rebanadilla,** *f.* small slice.

rebanar, *va.* to slice; to cut; to plane.

rebanco, *m.* (arch.) second bench or seat.

rebañadera, *f.* grapnel, drag hook.

rebañadura, *f.* = ARREBAÑADURA, gleaning.

rebañar, *va.* = ARREBAÑAR, to glean, gather.

rebañego, ga, *a.* gregarious.

rebaño, *m.* flock, fold, drove, herd, congregation.—**rebañuelo,** *m. dim.* small flock.

rebasadero, *m.* (naut.) pass.

rebasar, *va.* (naut.) to sail past; to exceed, go beyond; to overflow.

rebate, *m.* dispute, contention.

rebatible, *a.* refutable, disputable.

rebatido, *m.* (sew.) overhand seam, round seam.

rebatimiento, *m.* refutation; (geom.) revolving (a figure on a plane).

rebatiña, *f.*—**andar a la r.,** to grab and snatch things from one another, to scramble.

rebatir, *va.* to beat or drive back, repel; to refute; to deduct; to beat repeatedly; (geom.) to revolve (a figure on a plane).

rebato, *m.* alarm, alarm bell, call to arms; excitement, commotion; (mil.) sudden attack, surprise, drive.

rebautizar, *va.* to rebaptize.

rebeco, *m.* (zool.) = GAMUZA, chamois.

rebelarse, *vr.* to revolt, rebel; to resist.

rebelde. I. *a.* rebellious; stubborn, unmanageable. **II.** *n.* rebel; (law) defaulter.

rebeldía, *f.* rebelliousness, contumacy, disobedience; stubbornness; (law) default, nonappearance.—**en r.,** by default.

rebelión, *f.* rebellion, revolt, insurrection.

rebelón, na, *a.* (of a horse) balky, stubborn.

rebellín, *m.* (fort.) ravelin.

rebencazo, *m.* blow with a whip.

rebenque, *m.* whip; (naut.) ratline; cross rope.

rebién, *adv.* (coll.) very well.

rebina, *f.* (agr.) third plowing.

rebisabuela, *f.* great-great-grandmother.

rebisabuelo, *m.* great-great-grandfather.

rebisnieta, *f.* great-great-granddaughter.

rebisnieto, *m.* great-great-grandson.

reblandecer, *va. & vr.* (*ind.* REBLANDEZCO; *subj.* REBLANDEZCA) to soften.—**reblandecimiento,** *m.* softening.

rebocé, reboce, *v. V.* REBOZAR.

rebocío, rebociño, *m.* shawl.

rebolisco, *m.* (Cuba) groundless commotion.

rebollar, rebolledo, *m.* thicket of oak saplings.

rebolludura, *f.* (armor) honeycomb, flaw in a gun.

rebollo, *m.* (bot.) turkey oak; trunk of a tree.

rebolludo, da, *a.* done over and double; rough (diamond).

rebombar, *vn.* to make a loud report.

reboñar, *vn.* to stop turning.

reborde, *m.* flange, border.

rebosadero, *m.* place of overflow.

rebosadura, *f.,* **rebosamiento,** *m.* overflow.

rebosar, *vn.* to run over, overflow; to unbosom oneself; (de) to abound (in); to teem (with).

rebotación, *f.* rebounding.

rebotadera, *f.* nap raiser.

rebotador, ra, *n.* rebounder; clincher.

rebotadura, *f.* rebounding.

rebotar. I. *vn.* to rebound. **II.** *va.* to cause to rebound; to clinch; to raise the nap of (cloth); to repel; to vex, exasperate. **III.** *vr.* to change one's opinion, to retract; to change color.

rebote, *m.* rebound, rebounding.—**de r.,** indirectly.

rebotica, *f.* back room in an apothecary's shop.

rebotín, *m.* second growth of mulberry leaves.

rebozar. I. *va.* (*pret.* REBOCÉ; *subj.* REBOCE) to muffle up; (cooking) to dip in, or cover with, batter. **II.** *vr.* to muffle oneself up.

rebozo, *m.* muffling oneself up; muffler; woman's shawl; pretext.—**de r.,** secretly, hiddenly.—**sin r.,** frankly, openly.

rebramar, *vn.* to low and bellow repeatedly.

rebramo, *m.* noise with which deer answer each other.

rebudiar, *vn.* to sniff and grunt (as a wild boar).

rebufar, *vn.* to blow or snort repeatedly.

rebufo, *m.* (artil.) concussion, recoil.

rebujado, da, *a.* tangled, entangled, confused.

rebujal, *m.* number of cattle in a flock over even fifties; small piece of arable land.

rebujar, *va.* = ARREBUJAR, to jumble together.

rebujiña, *f.* (coll.) wrangle, mêlée, scuffle.

rebujo, *m.* woman's thick veil or muffler; clumsy bundle; portion of tithe paid in money.

rebullicio, *m.* great clamor or tumult.

rebullir, *vn.* & *vr.* to stir, begin to move.

reburujar, *va.* (coll.) to wrap up in bundles.

reburujón, *n.* clumsy bundle.

rebusca, *f.* searching; gleaning; refuse, remains.

rebuscado, da, *a.* affected, fustian, forced, unnatural.

rebuscador, ra, *n.* gleaner; searcher.

rebuscamiento, *m.* diligent search.

rebuscar, *va.* (*pret.* REBUSQUÉ; *subj.* REBUSQUE) to search carefully; to glean (grapes).

rebusco, *m.* search; gleaning.

rebuznador, ra, *a.* braying.

rebuznar, *vn.* to bray.—**rebuzno,** *m.* braying (of a donkey).

recabar, *va.* to obtain by entreaty.

recadero, ra, *n.* messenger, errand boy (girl).

recado, *m.* message, errand; present, gift; compliments, regards; daily provision or marketing; voucher; outfit, equipment; precaution, security; (Am.) saddle and trappings.—**r. de escribir,** writing materials.

recaer, *vn.* (*ind. pres.* RECAIGO, *pret.* él RECAYÓ; *subj.* RECAIGA) to fall back, relapse; to fall or devolve; to behoove.

recaída, *f.* relapse; second offense.

recaigo, recaiga, *v.* V. RECAER.

recalada, *f.* (naut.) landfall.

recalar. I. *va.* to soak, drench, saturate. **II.** *vn.* (naut.) to make, sight, or reach land.

recalcada, *f.* (naut.) heeling, list.

recalcadamente, *adv.* closely, contiguously; vehemently, emphatically.

recalcadura, *f.* cramming, pressing.

recalcar. I. *va.* (*pret.* RECALQUÉ; *subj.* RECALQUE) to cram, pack, press, push, squeeze in; to emphasize. **II.** *vn.* (naut.) to heel, list. **III.** *vr.* to harp on a subject; to seat oneself, sit at ease.

recalcitrante, *a.* recalcitrant, obstinate.

recalcitrar, *vn.* to resist; to recede, go back.

recalentador, *m.* (steam eng.) superheater.

recalentamiento, *m.* reheating; overheating; (steam eng.) superheating.

recalentar. I. *va.* (*ind.* RECALIENTO; *subj.* RECALIENTE) to reheat; to overheat; to warm over; to excite (as sexual appetite); (steam eng.) to superheat. **II.** *vr.* to become overheated (as fruit), or superheated (as steam).

recalmón, *m.* lull of the wind.

recalqué, recalque, *v.* V. RECALCAR.

recalvastro, tra, *a.* bald-headed.

recalzar, *va.* (*pret.* RECALCÉ; *subj.* RECALCE) (agr.) to hill; (arch.) to strengthen, reinforce; (art) to color.

recalzo, *m.* (arch.) strengthening a foundation; outside rim of wheel (on carriage, etc.).

recalzón, *m.* outer rim of a wheel.

recamado, *m.* embroidery of raised work.

recamador, ra, *n.* embroiderer.

recamar, *va.* to embroider with raised work.

recámara, *f.* dressing room; boudoir; (Mex.) bedroom; household furniture; (artil.) breech of a gun; cavity or chamber for an explosive charge; (coll.) caution, reserve.

recambiar, *va.* to reëxchange, rechange; (com.) to redraw; to add.

recambio, *m.* (com.) reëxchange.

recamo, *m.* raised embroidery; (sewing) frog.

recancanilla, *f.* hippety-hop; (coll.) emphasis; equivocation, ambiguous language.

recantación, *f.* recantation, retraction.

recantón, *m.* corner stone.

recapacitar, *vn.* to refresh one's memory; to think carefully.

recapitulación, *f.* recapitulation, summary.

recapitular, *va.* to recapitulate, sum up.

recarga, *f.* (artil.) overcharge.

recargar. I. *va.* (*pret.* RECARGUÉ; *subj.* RECARGUE) to reload; to surcharge, overload; to overcharge; to cram; to recharge; to raise, increase. **II.** *vr.* (med.) to have an increase in temperature; (de) to have in abundance, have an abundance (of).

recargo, *m.* overload; overcharge; additional tax, charge, etc.; extra charge; new charge or accusation; (law) increase of sentence; (med.) increase of fever.

recata, *f.* tasting again.

recatadamente, *adv.* cautiously, prudently; modestly.

recatado, da. I. *pp.* of RECATAR. **II.** *a.* prudent, circumspect; shy, coy; modest.

¹recatar. I. *va.* to secrete, conceal. **II.** *vr.* to act modestly; to be cautious.

²recatar, *va.* to taste again.

recatear, *vn.* = REGATEAR, to haggle; to dodge.

recatería, *f.* = REGATONERÍA, retail sale.

recato, *m.* prudence, caution; modesty; bashfulness, coyness.

¹recatón, na, *n.* = ¹REGATÓN, hawker; haggler.

²recatón, *m.* = ²REGATÓN, tip, ferrule.

recatonazo, *m.* blow with the tip of a lance.

recatonear, *va.* = REGATONEAR, to sell at retail.

recatonería, *f.* = REGATONERÍA, retail sale.

recaudación, *f.* collecting, collection; collector's office.

recaudador, ra, *n.* taxgatherer; collector.

recaudamiento, *m.* collection; office or district of a collector.

recaudar, *va.* to gather; to collect (rents or taxes); to put or hold in custody.

recaudo, *m.* collection of rents or taxes; precaution, care; (law) surety, bail, bond, security.—**a buen r.,** well guarded, under custody, safe.

recavar, *va.* to dig a second time.

recayó, *pret.* of RECAER.

recazo, *m.* guard of a sword; back of a knife.

recebar, *va.* to spread gravel on.

recebo, *m.* sand or gravel for a roadway.

recelador, ra, *a.* shy (as a horse).

recelamiento, *m.* = RECELO.

recelar. I. *va.* to fear, distrust, suspect; to excite (a mare) sexually. **II.** *vr.* (**de**) to fear, be afraid or suspicious (of), to beware (of).

recelo, *m.* misgiving, fear, suspicion.

receloso, sa, *a.* distrustful, suspicious.

recentadura, *f.* leaven for raising bread.

recental, *a.* suckling (lamb or calf).

recentar. I. *va.* (*ind.* RECIENTO; *subj.* RECIENTE) to put leaven into (dough). **II.** *vr.* to renew.

receñir, *va.* (*ind. pres.* RECIÑO, *pret.* RECIÑIÓ; *subj.* RECIÑA) to regird.

recepción, *f.* reception, receiving, acceptation, admission; (law) cross-examination.

recepta, *f.* record of fines.

receptáculo, *m.* receptacle; (anat.) receptaculum; shelter, refuge; (bot.) receptacle.

receptador, *m.* (law) receiver of stolen goods; abettor.

receptar. I. *va.* (law) to abet; to hide, shelter; to receive. **II.** *vr.* to take refuge.

receptividad, *f.* receptivity.

receptivo, va, *a.* receptive.

recepto, *m.* shelter, place of refuge.

receptor, ra. I. *n.* receiver; recipient; abettor. **II.** *a.* receiving. **III.** *m.* (elec. & law) receiver.

receptoría, *f.* receiver's or treasurer's office; (law) receivership.

recercador, ra I. *a.* girding. **II.** *m.* (jewel.) chaser.

recercar, *va.* to fence; to fence again.

recésit, *m.* vacation, recess. Also RECLE.

receso, *m.* withdrawal, separation; (astr.) deviation; (Mex.) recess.

receta, *f.* prescription; recipe; list of goods ordered; (com.) amount brought forward.

recetador, ra, *n.* prescriber of medicines.

recetante, *a.* prescribing.

recetar, *va.* to prescribe (medicines).

recetario, *m.* physician's instructions for treatment; book in hospitals in which instructions are entered; apothecary's file; pharmacopœia.

recetor, *m.* receiver, treasurer.

recetoría, *f.* treasury; subtreasury.

recial, *m.* rapids (in rivers).

reciamente, *adv.* strongly, stoutly.

reciario, *m.* retiarius (gladiator).

recibí, *m.* (from *recibí,* I received, extended to mean: I received payment) (com.) receipt.

recibidero, ra, *a.* receivable.

recibidor, ra, *n.* receiver; recipient; (com.) receiving teller.

recibiente, *a.* receiving.

recibimiento, *m.* reception; hospitality, greeting, welcome; vestibule; hall; reception room.

recibir. I. *va.* to receive; to let in; to take, accept; to take in, admit; to experience (an injury); to face (an attack). **II.** *vr.* (de) to graduate (as); to be admitted to practice (as).

recibo, *m.* reception; (com.) receipt.—**acusar r.,** (com.) to acknowledge receipt.—**de r.,** fit for service, acceptable; reception (as *a.*).—**estar de r.,** to be at home to callers.

recidiva, *f.* (med.) relapse.

recién, *adv.* (contr. of RECIENTE) (before *pp.*) = RECIENTEMENTE.—**r. casados,** newlyweds.—**r. llegado,** newcomer.—**r. nacido, da,** newborn.

reciente, *a.* recent; new; modern; fresh.

recientemente, *adv.* recently, lately, newly.

reciento, reciente, *v.* V. RECENTAR.

recinchar, *va.* to bind with a girdle.

recinto, *m.* inclosure; place (building, hall, etc.); ambit; precinct.

recio, cia. I. *a.* strong, robust, vigorous; loud; coarse, thick, clumsy; rude, uncouth; arduous; hard to bear; severe, rigorous (weather); swift, impetuous. **II.** *adv.* strongly, stoutly; rapidly; vehemently, vigorously; loud.—**de r.,** strongly, violently.

récipe, *m.* (med.) prescription; (coll.) displeasure, disgust.

recipiendario, ria, *n.* member received (into an association, academy, etc.).

recipiente. I. *a.* receiving. **II.** *m.* receptacle; container; recipient; bell of an air pump.

recíproca, *f.* (math., logic) converse (proposition).

reciprocación, *f.* reciprocation, mutuality.

recíprocamente, *adv.* reciprocally, mutually; conversely.

reciprocar. I. *va.* (pret. RECIPROQUÉ; *subj.* RECIPROQUE) (of things) to put in mutual correspondence, to match. **II.** *vr.* to correspond, harmonize, fit together, match.

reciprocidad, *f.* reciprocity.

recíproco, ca, *a.* reciprocal, mutual.

reciproqué, reciproque, *v.* V. RECIPROCAR.

recisión, *f.* (law) rescission, abrogation.

recitación, *f.* recitation, recital.

recitado, *m.* (mus.) recitative.

recitador, ra, *n.* reciter.

recital, *m.* (mus.) recital.

recitar, *va.* to recite; to rehearse.

recitativo, va, *a.* recitative.

reciura, *f.* strength, force; rigor (of weather).

recizalla, *f.* second filings.

reclamación, *f.* reclamation; objection, remonstrance; (com.) complaint, claim.

reclamante, *n.* & *a.* complainer(-ing), claimer (ing).

¹**reclamar. I.** *va.* to claim, demand; to decoy (birds); (law) to reclaim.—**r. en juicio,** (law) to sue. **II.** *vn.* to contradict, to oppose; to complain; to put in a claim.

²**reclamar,** *va.* (naut.) to hoist or lower.

reclame, *m.* (naut.) sheave hole in a topmast head.

reclamo, *m.* decoy bird; decoy horn or contrivance; lure (for birds); call; inducement, enticement; claim; complaint; advertisement inserted in reading matter of a publication; (law) reclamation; (print.) catchword.

recle, *m.* vacation, rest from choir duties.

reclinación, *f.* reclination, reclining.

reclinado, da. I. *pp.* of RECLINAR. **II.** *a.* recumbent.

reclinar, *va.* & *vr.* to recline, lean back.—**reclinarse en, or sobre,** to lean on or upon.

reclinatorio, *m.* praying desk, priedieu; couch, lounge.

recluir, *va.* (*pp.* RECLUÍDO, RECLUSO; *ind.* *pres.* RECLUYO, *pret.* él RECLUYÓ; *subj.* RECLUYA) to shut up, to seclude.

reclusión, *f.* seclusion; place of retirement; arrest; jail, prison.

recluso, sa. I. *pp. irreg.* of RECLUIR. **II.** *a.* & *n.* recluse.

reclusorio, *m.* place of retirement.

recluta. I. *f.* (mil.) recruiting; (Arg.) roundup of cattle. **II.** *m.* recruit.

reclutador, *m.* recruiting officer.

reclutamiento, *m.* (mil.) recruiting.

reclutar, *va.* (mil.) to recruit; (Arg.) to round up (cattle).

recluyo, recluyó, recluya, *v.* V. RECLUIR.

recobrante, *a.* recovering.

recobrar, *va.* & *vr.* to recover, recuperate, regain.—**recobro,** *m.* recovery, recuperation.

recocer. I. *va.* (*ind.* RECUEZO; *subj.* RECUEZA) to boil again; to boil too much; to anneal; to reheat. **II.** *vr.* to burn with rage.

recocido, da. I. *pp.* of RECOCER. **II.** *a.* overcooked; annealed; skilful, clever. **III.** *n.* annealing; reheating; overcooking.

recocina, *f.* back kitchen, pantry.

recocho, cha, *a.* overcooked, overdone.

recodadero, *m.* elbow chair.

recodar, *vn.* & *vr.* to lean with the elbow upon anything; to wind, turn (as a road).

recodo, *m.* turn, winding, bend, angle.

recogedero, *m.* place where things are gathered; instrument for gathering things.

recogedor, ra, *n.* gatherer, gleaner; shelterer.

recoger. I. *va.* (*ind.* RECOJO; *subj.* RECOJA) to retake, take back; to gather, pick; to accumulate, hoard; to pick up, take up; to shrink, shorten; to contract; to tuck, pucker; to take in, collect; to take in, shelter; to lock up; to suspend, withdraw, retire; to glean, cull. **II.** *vr.* to take shelter; to withdraw; reform; retrench; to go home, to retire, withdraw from the world, retire into oneself.

recogida, *f.* withdrawal, retirement; harvesting; inmate of house of correction; (com.) retiral.

recogidamente, *adv.* devoutly.

recogido, da. I. *pp.* of RECOGER. II. *a.* secluded; contracted. III. *m.* (Am.) (sew.) tuck, fold.

recogimiento, *m.* concentration, abstraction; house of correction for women.

recojo, recoja, *v. V.* RECOGER.

recolar, *va.* (*ind.* RECUELO; *subj.* RECUELE) to strain a second time.

recolección, *f.* compilation; summary, abridgment; crop, gathering, harvest; collection of money or taxes; retirement, abstraction.

recolectar, *va.* to gather, collect, hoard.

recolector, *m.* = RECAUDADOR, tax collector.

recoleto, ta, *a.* & *n.* (eccl.) Recollect.

recomendable, *a.* commendable, laudable.

recomendablemente, *adv.* laudably.

recomendación, *f.* recommendation; request; commendation, praise; merit, worth.—**r. del alma,** prayers for the dying.

recomendante, *n.* one who recommends.

recomendar, *va.* (*ind.* RECOMIENDO; *subj.* RECOMIENDE) to recommend; to commend; to entrust; to ask, request.

recomendatorio, ria, *a.* recommendatory.

recomiendo, recomiende, *v. V.* RECOMENDAR.

recompensa, *f.* compensation; recompense.—**en r.,** in return.

recompensable, *a.* deserving reward.

recompensación, *f.* compensation, reward, recompense.

recompensar, *va.* to compensate; to recompense, reward.

recomponer, *va.* (*pp.* RECOMPUESTO; *ind. pres.* RECOMPONGO, *pret.* RECOMPUSE, *fut.* RECOMPONDRÉ; *subj.* RECOMPONGA) to mend, repair.

recomposición, *f.* (chem.) recomposition.

recompuesto, ta, *pp. irreg.* of RECOMPONER.

recompuse, *pret.* of RECOMPONER.

reconcentración, *f.*; **reconcentramiento,** *m.* concentration.

reconcentrar. I. *va.* to concentrate; to dissemble. II. *vr.* to concentrate (one's mind).

reconciliación, *f.* reconciliation.

reconciliador, ra, *n.* & *a.* reconciler(-ing).

reconciliar. I. *va.* to reconcile; (eccl.) to hear a short additional confession from; to consecrate anew. II. *vr.* to become reconciled, to make up; (eccl.) to make a short additional confession; to confess offenses, to renew friendship.

reconcomerse, *vr.* to scratch one's back.

reconcomio, *m.* (coll.) scratching one's back; suspicion, fear, misgiving; craving, eager desire.

reconditez, *f.* (coll.) reconditeness.

recóndito, ta, *a.* recondite.

reconducción, *f.* (law) renewal of a lease.

reconducir, *va.* (*ind. pres.* RECONDUZCO, *pret.* RECONDUJE; *subj.* RECONDUZCA) (law) to renew (a lease or contract).

reconocedor, ra, *n.* examiner; inspector.

reconocer. I. *va.* (*ind.* RECONOZCO; *subj.* RECONOZCA) to inspect, examine closely; to recognise; to own, admit; (**por**) to acknowledge (as); to acknowledge, be grateful for; (mil.) to reconnoitre, to scout; (pol.) to recognise (a government, etc.); (com.) to acknowledge. II. *vr.* to repent; to confess one's guilt; to judge justly of one's own self.

reconocidamente, *adv.* gratefully; confessedly; avowedly.

reconocido, da, *pp.* & *a.* acknowledged, confessed; grateful, obliged; accepted.

reconociente, *a.* recognising.

reconocimiento, *m.* recognition; acknowledgment; gratitude; confession, admission; recognizance; subjection, submission; examination, inquiry, inspection, survey; (mil.) reconnoitering; (surv.) reconnoissance.

reconozco, reconozca, *v. V.* RECONOCER.

reconquista, *f.* reconquest.

reconquistar, *va.* to reconquer.

reconstitución, *f.* reconstitution.

reconstituir, *va.* & *vr.* to reconstitute.

reconstituyente, *a.* reconstituent.

reconstruir, *va.* (*ind. pres.* RECONSTRUYO, *pret.* él RECONSTRUYÓ; *subj.* RECONSTRUYA) to rebuild, reconstruct.

recontamiento, *m.* telling, narration.

recontar, *va.* (*ind.* RECUENTO; *subj.* RECUENTE) to recount; to relate.

recontento, ta. I. *a.* greatly pleased. II. *m.* contentment, deep satisfaction.

reconvalecer, *vn.* (*ind.* RECONVALEZCO; *subj.* RECONVALEZCA) to convalesce anew.

reconvención, *f.* charge, accusation; reproach.

reconvenir, *va.* (*ger.* RECONVINIENDO; *ind. pres.* yo RECONVENGO, él RECONVIENE, *pret.* RECONVINE, *fut.* RECONVENDRÉ; *subj.* RECONVENGA) to accuse, reproach; to reprimand; (law) to countercharge.

recopilación, *f.* summary, abridgment; compilation, collection; (law) digest.

recopilador, ra, *n.* compiler; abridger.

recopilar, *va.* to compile, abridge.

recoquín, *m.* chubby little fellow.

record, *m.* (Angl.) (sports) record.

recordable, *a.* memorable; that can be remembered.

recordación, *f.* remembrance; recollection.

recordador, ra, *n.* reminder.

recordante, *a.* reminding.

recordar. I. *va.* (*ind.* RECUERDO; *subj.* RECUERDE) to remember, to remind. II. *vn.* (fig.) to wake up, awaken. III. *vr.* to remember.—**recordativo, va.** I. *a.* reminding. II. *m.* reminder.—**recordatorio,** *m.* reminder, remembrancer.

recorrer. I. *va.* to go over; (mech.) to pass over, travel; to read over, peruse; to travel in or over; to overhaul, refit, repair; (print.) to run over, readjust. II. *vn.* to resort, have recourse to; to travel.

recorrido, *m.* run, sweep; space or distance traveled or passed over, course; (auto) mileage.

recortado, da. I. *pp.* of RECORTAR. II. *a.* (bot.) notched, incised. III. *m.* figure cut out of paper.

recortadura, *f.* clipping.—*pl.* cuttings.

recortar, *va.* to cut away, trim, clip, pare off; to cut out; to cut to size; to outline (a figure).

recorte, *m.* cutting; clipping (from newspaper, etc.); outline, profile.—*pl.* trimmings, parings.

recorvar, *va.* = ENCORVAR, to bend, curve.

recorvo, va, *a.* = CORVO, bent, crooked; stingy.

recoser, *va.* to sew again; to mend.

recosido, *m.* mending, darning.

recostadero, *m.* reclining or resting place.

recostar. I. *va.* (*ind.* RECUESTO; *subj.* RECUESTE) to lean, recline. II. *vr.* to go to rest; to repose; to lean back (against), to recline.

recova, *f.* dealing in poultry, eggs, etc.; poultry market; market place; shed.

récova, *f.* pack of hounds.

recoveco, *m.* turning, winding; simulation, artifice.

recovero, ra, *n.* poultry dealer.

recre, *m.* vacation of choristers.

recreación, *f.* recreation.

recrear. I. *va.* to amuse, delight, gladden. II. *vr.* to amuse oneself; to be pleased, have pleasure or recreation, to divert oneself.

recreativo, va, *a.* diverting, amusing, recreation (as *a.*).

recrecer. I. *va.* (*ind.* RECREZCO; *subj.* RECREZCA) to augment, increase. II. *vn.* to occur, to happen. III. *vr.* to grow big; to recover one's spirits.

recrecimiento, *m.* growth, increase.

recreído, da, *a.* intractable (hawk).

recrementicio, cia, *a.* recremental.

recremento, *m.* (med.) recrement.

recreo, *m.* recreation; place of amusement.

recrezco, recrezca, *v. V.* RECRECER.

recría, *f.* repasturing of colts.

recriar, *va.* to re-create, regenerate; to reanimate,

give new strength to; to improve (breeds) with new pastures.

recriminación, f. recrimination.

recriminador, ra, n. & a. recriminator(-ing).

recriminar, va. to recriminate.

recrudecer, vn. & vr. (ind. RECRUDEZCO; subj. RECRUDEZCA) to recrudesce, recur, increase.

recrudecimiento, m. = RECRUDESCENCIA.

recrudescencia, f. recrudescence.

recrudescente, a. recrudescent.

recrujir, vn. to squeak.

rectal, a. (anat.) rectal.

rectamente, adv. rightly, justly, honestly; in a straight line.

rectangular, a. rectangular.

rectángulo, la. I. a. rectangular; right-angled (triangle, etc.). **II.** m. rectangle.

rectificación, f. rectification.

rectificador, ra, n. & a. rectifier(-fying).

rectificar, va. (pret. RECTIFIQUÉ; subj. RECTIFIQUE) to rectify, make right; to correct, amend; (math. and chem.) to rectify.

rectificativo, va, a. rectifying.

rectilíneo, nea, a. rectilinear.

rectitud, f. straightness; righteousness, rectitude; accuracy, exactitude.

recto, ta. I. a. straight; erect; righteous, just, fair; literal; (geom.) right (angle, section, cylinder, etc.). **II.** m. (geom.) right angle; (anat.) rectum.

rector, ra, n. principal; rector, curate; director (of a college, etc.).

rectorado, m. rectorship; directorship.

rectoral, a. rectorial.

rectorar, vn. to attain the office of rector.

rectoría, f. rectory, curacy; rectorship; rector's or director's office.

rectriz, a. (zool.) rectrix (feather).

recua, f. drove of beasts of burden; multitude, pack of things.

recuadrar, va. (art) to divide into squares.

recuadro, m. (arch.) square compartment; panel (of a bridge).

recuaje, m. toll for the passage of mules.

recuarta, f. string of a guitar.

recudimento, recudimiento, m. authority for collecting rents.

recudir. I. va. to pay money to as part of wages or other dues. **II.** vn. to return, revert.

¹reculo, m. strong lye for bucking clothes.

²recuelo, recuele, v. V. RECOLAR.

¹recuento, m. recount; enumeration; inventory.

²recuento, recuente, v. V. RECONTAR.

recuentro, m. = REENCUENTRO, collision.

¹recuerdo, m. recollection; memory; remembrance; keepsake, memento; memorandum.— pl. compliments, regards.

²recuerdo, recuerde, v. V. RECORDAR.

recuero, m. muleteer, driver of a drove.

recuesta, f. request; intimation.

recuestar, va. to request, ask, demand.

¹recuesto, m. declivity, slope.

²recuesto, recueste, v. V. RECOSTAR.

recuezo, recueza, v. V. RECOCER.

reculada, f. recoil, recoiling; (naut.) falling astern.

recular, vn. to fall back, recoil, back up; (naut.) to fall astern; (coll.) to yield, give up, turn back.

reculo, la, a. tailless (poultry).

reculones.—a r., (coll.) going backward.

recuñar, va. (min.) to wedge, dig with wedge.

recuperable, a. recoverable.

recuperación, f. recovery, recuperation.

recuperador, ra, n. & a. recuperator(-ing).

recuperar, va. & vr. to recover, regain, recuperate, retrieve.

recuperativo, va, a. recuperative.

recura, f. comb saw.

recurar, va. to tooth (a comb).

recurrente, a. recurrent.

recurrir, vn. to apply, resort; to revert.

recurso, m. recourse; resource, resort; return, reversion; memorial, petition; (law) appeal.— pl. resources, means.—**sin r.,** definitively, without appeal; without help, unavoidably, irremediably.

recusable, a. refusable, exceptionable.

recusación, f. (law) challenge; recusation.

recusante, a. refusing; recusant.

recusar, va. to decline; (law) to recuse, to challenge.

rechacé, rechace, v. V. RECHAZAR.

rechazador, ra, n. repeller; opponent; buffer.

rechazamiento, m. repulsion; rejection.

rechazar, va. (pret. RECHACÉ; subj. RECHACE) to repel, repulse, drive back; to contradict; to reject, turn down.

rechazo, m. rebound; rebuff; recoil; rejection.

rechifla, f. hissing (in derision); hooting; mockery, ridicule.

rechiflar, va. to hiss; to mock, ridicule.

rechinador, ra, a. squeaking, grating.

rechinamiento, m. squeaking; gnashing of teeth.

rechinante, a. creaking, squeaking; gnashing.

rechinar, vn. to creak, squeak, grate; to gnash the teeth; to do a thing with reluctance.

rechinido, rechino, m. = RECHINAMIENTO.

rechoncho, cha, a. (coll.) chubby.

rechupete.—de r. (coll.) splendid, fine, "dandy."

red, f. net, seine; network, netting; bag net; grate, railing; snare, trap; wile, fraud; system (of Ry., tel., etc.).—**r. barredera,** dragnet.—**r. de araña,** cobweb.—**r. de jorrar,** or **de jorro,** sweep seine.—**caer en la r.,** to fall into the trap.—**echar,** or **tender, la red,** to cast, or set, the net.

redacción, f. wording; editing; editorial rooms; editorial staff.

redactar, va. to edit, be the editor of; to write, word, draw up.

redactor, ra, n. editor.

redada, f. casting a net; netful of fish, catch, haul.

redaño, m. (anat.) caul, kell, omentum.

redar, va. to cast a net in.

redargución, f. retort, refutation.

redargüir, va. (ind. pres. REDARGUYO, pret. él REDARGUYÓ; subj. REDARGUYA) to retort, reargue; (law) to impugn.

redecilla, f. dim. small net; hair net; mesh; bag net; reticulum of a ruminant's stomach.

rededor, m. surroundings, environs.—**al r.,** roundabout, around.—**al r. de,** about, nearly, more or less; around.

redel, m. (naut.) loof frame.

redención, f. redemption; recovery; ransom; salvation.—**r. de un censo,** paying off a mortgage.

redentor, ra, n. & a. redeemer(-ing).

redero, ra. I. a. reticular; reticulated. **II.** m. netmaker; one who catches fish or birds with nets.

redescuento, m. rediscount.

redhibición, f. (law) redhibition.

redhibir, va. (law) to make use of the right of redhibition.

redhibitorio, ria, a. (law) redhibitory.

redición, f. repetition, reiteration.

redicho, cha, a. speaking with affected precision and correctness.

rediezmar, va. to tithe a second time.

rediezmo, m. extra tithe.

redil, m. sheepfold, sheepcote.

redimible, a. redeemable.

redimir, va. to redeem, rescue, ransom; to extricate, liberate; (com.) to redeem, pay off.

redingote, m. redingote, great-coat.

redistribución, f. resettlement (as of displaced persons).

rédito, m. (com.) revenue, interest, yield, profit, proceeds.

redituable, redituai, a. profit-producing.

redituar, *va.* to yield, to produce; to draw (interest).

redivivo, va, *a.* redivivus, revived, restored.

redoblado, da, *pp. & a.* redoubled; double lined; stocky, heavy-built; (mil.) quick (step).

redobladura, *f.,* **redoblamiento,** *m.* doubling; repetition; clinching.

redoblante, *m.* (mil.) drum; drummer.

redoblar, *va.* to double; to clinch; to repeat; (mil.) to roll (a drum).

redoble, *m.* REDOBLAMIENTO; (mil. and mus.) roll of a drum.

redoblegar, *va.* (*pret.* REDOBLEGUÉ; *subj.* REDOBLEGUE) to double; to bend.

redoblón, *m.* rivet, clinch-nail.

redolente, *a.* feeling a slight pain.

redolino, *m.* wheel for drawing lots.

redolor, *m.* slight pain remaining after some acute suffering.

redoma, *f.* vial, phial, flask; (chem.) balloon.

redomado, da, *a.* artful, sly, crafty.

redonda, *f.* neighborhood, district; pasture ground; (naut.) square sail; (mus.) semibreve. **—a la r.,** roundabout.

redondamente, *adv.* around; clearly, plainly, decidedly.

redondeador, *m.* rounding tool.

redondear. I. *va.* to round, make round; to round off; to perfect. **II.** *vr.* to clear oneself of debts; to acquire a competency.

redondel, *m.* (coll.) circle; round cloak, circular; (mech.) flange; bull ring; round mat.

redondeo, *m.* making round; rounding off.

redondete, *a. dim.* roundish.

redondez, *f.* roundness.—**r. de la Tierra,** face of the earth.

redondilla, *f.* seven-syllable quatrain with alternate riming.

redondo, da. I. *a.* round; (print.) Roman; unencumbered, in easy circumstances; (of land) turned to pasture; clear, straight, decided.—**de r.,** in round clothes.—**en números r.,** in round numbers.—**en r.,** all around. **II.** *m.* (coll.) specie, hard cash; globe, orb, disk, anything round.

redondón, *m.* large circle or sphere.

redopelo, *m.* rubbing against the grain; (coll.) scuffle, affray.—**al r.,** against the lay of the hair; against the grain; against all rule and reason.—**traer al r.,** to vex; drag about contemptuously.

redor, *m.* round mat; (poet.) REDEDOR, surroundings.—**en r.,** roundabout.

redova, *f.* (dance) redowa.

redro. I. *adv.* (coll.) behind, backward. **II.** *m.* each of the rings upon the horns of goats.

redrojo, redrojuelo, *m.* small bunch of grapes remaining after the vintage; after fruit or blossom; (coll.) puny child.

redropelo, *m.* = REDOPELO.

redruejo, *m.* = REDROJO.

reducción, *f.* reduction, decrease; (mil.) mutation, alteration, exchange; reduction, conquest; (S. A.) settlement of converted Indians; (math. and chem.) reduction; (com.) reduction, rebate, discount.—**r. al absurdo,** (logic, math.) reductio ad absurdum.

reducible, *a.* reducible, convertible.

reducidamente, *adv.* sparingly; compactly.

reducido, da. I. *pp.* of REDUCIR. **II.** *a.* reduced, diminished; small; compact.

reducimiento, *m.* reduction, reducement.

reducir. I. *va.* (*ind. pres.* REDUZCO, *pret.* REDUJE; *subj.* REDUZCA) to reduce; to diminish, decrease, lessen; to restore; (a) to convert (into), reduce (to); to subdue, subjugate; to divide into small parts; to condense, abridge; to persuade, convince; (math., chem., metal., surg.) to reduce. **II.** *vr.* to adopt a moderate way of living; to be compelled, to decide from necessity.

reductivo, va, *a.* reducing.

reducto, *m.* (fort.) reduct, redoubt.

reductor, ra. I. *a.* reducing. **II.** *m.* (hydraul., etc.) reducer.

reduje, *pret.* of REDUCIR.

redundancia, *f.* redundance; excess.

redundante, *a.* redundant, superfluous.

redundantemente, *adv.* redundantly.

redundar, *vn.* to overflow; to be redundant; (en) to redound (to), result (in), lead (to), bring.

reduplicación, *f.* reduplication.

reduplicar, *va.* (*pret.* REDUPLIQUÉ; *subj.* REDUPLIQUE) to reduplicate, redouble; to reiterate.

reduzco, reduzca, *v. V.* REDUCIR.

reedificable, *a.* capable of being rebuilt.

reedificación, *f.* rebuilding.

reedificador, *m.* & *a.* rebuilder(-ing).

reedificar, *va.* (*pret.* REEDIFIQUÉ; *subj.* REEDIFIQUE) to rebuild.

reeditar, *va.* to reprint.

reelección, *f.* reëlection.

reelecto, ta, *pp. irreg.* of REELEGIR.

reelegible, *a.* reëligible.

reelegir, *va.* (*pp.* REELEGIDO, REELECTO: *ger.* REELIGIENDO; *ind. pres.* REELIJO, *pret.* él REELIGIÓ; *subj.* REELIJA) to reëlect.

reembarcar, *va. & vr.* (*pret.* REEMBARQUÉ; *subj.* REEMBARQUE) to reship, reëmbark.

reembarco, *m.* reëmbarkation, reshipment.

reembargar, *va.* (*pret.* REEMBARGUÉ; *subj.* REEMBARGUE) to seize or embargo a second time.

reembarque, *m.* = REEMBARCO.

reembolsable, *a.* payable.

reembolsar. I. *va.* to reimburse, refund, pay. **II.** *vr.* to recover money due.—**reembolso,** *m.* reimbursement, refunding.

reempacar, *va.* (*pret.* REEMPAQUÉ; *subj.* REEMPAQUE) to repack.

reemplazar, *va.* (*pret.* REEMPLACÉ; *subj.* REEMPLACE) to replace; to supersede; to substitute.—**reemplazo,** *m.* replacement; substitution; (mil.) substitute.

reencarnación, *f.* reincarnation.

reencarnar, *vn. & vr.* to be reincarnated.

reencuentro, *m.* collision; clash (as of troops).

reenganchamiento, *m.* (mil.) reënlisting; bounty for reënlisting.

reenganchar, *va.* (mech.) to recouple; (mil.) to reënlist.

reenganche, *m.* = REENGANCHAMIENTO.

reengendrador, ra, *n. & a.* regenerator(-ing).

reengendrar, *va.* to regenerate, reproduce; to renew, revive.

reensayar, *va.* to reëxamine; to try or test anew.

reensaye, *m.* second assay.

reensayo, *m.* second trial or test.

reenvasar, *va.* (com.) to repack, refill.

reenviar, *va.* to forward.

reexaminación, *f.* reëxamination.

reexaminar, *va.* to reëxamine.

reexpedición, *f.* forwarding (of mail, etc.).

reexpedir, *va.* to forward (mail, etc.).

reexportación, *f.* (com.) reëxportation.

reexportar, *va.* (com.) to reëxport.

refacción, *f.* refection, luncheon; retribution, reparation; boot, allowance (in barters); (Cuba) financing.

refaccionar, *va.* (Cuba) to finance.

refaccionista, *m.* (Cuba) financial backer.

refajo, *m.* short skirt; flannel underskirt.

refalsado, da, *a.* false, deceitful.

refección, *f.* refection, slight meal; repairs.

refectolero, *m.* = REFITOLERO.

refectorio, *m.* refectory (in convents).

referencia, *f.* reference; narration; (com.) (gen. *pl.*) reference(s) (as to character, etc.).

referendario, *m.* = REFRENDARIO.

referéndum, *m.* referendum.

referente, *a.* referring, relating.

referible, *a.* referrible, referable.

referir. I. *va.* (*ger.* REFIRIENDO; *ind. pres.* REFIERO, *pret.* él REFIRIÓ; *subj.* REFIERA) to refer, relate; to tell, narrate, report; to direct, submit. **II.** *vr.* (a) to refer (to), have relation (to).

refertero, ra, *a.* quarrelsome, wrangling.

refiero, refiera, *v. V.* REFERIR.

refigurar, *va.* to refigure.

refilón.—de r., *adv.* obliquely, askance.

refinación, *f.* refining; refinement.

refinadera, *f.* stone roller for refining chocolate.

refinado, da. I. *pp.* of REFINAR. **II.** *a.* refined; subtle, artful; fine, nice, polished.

refinador, ra, *n.* & *a.* refiner(-ing).

refinadura, *f.* refining.

refinamiento, *m.* refinement; refining.

refinar, *va.* to refine, purify; to make polite or refined; to polish, finish.

refinería, *f.* refinery; distillery.

refino, na. I. *a.* very fine, extra fine; refined. **II.** *m.* refining; fine grocery.

refirió, refiriendo, *v. V.* REFERIR.

refirmar, *va.* to support (on); to ratify.

refitolero, ra. I. *n.* one in charge of a refectory; (coll.) busybody, intermeddler. **II.** *a.* (Cuba) affected, obsequious, officious.

reflectante, *a.* reflecting.

reflector, ra. I. *a.* reflecting, reflective. **II.** *m.* reflector; searchlight.

refleja, *f.* reflection, observation, remark.

reflejar. I. *va.* (opt.) to reflect. **II.** *vn.* to think, ponder, consider. **III.** *vr.* to be reflected.

reflejo, ja. I. *a.* reflected; meditative; (gram.) reflexive; (physiol.) reflex. **II.** *m.* glare; reflection; light reflected.

reflexión, *f.* reflection.

reflexionar, *vn.* to think, reflect.

reflexivamente, *adv.* reflexively; reflectively.

reflexivo, va, *a.* reflexive; reflective; reflecting, thoughtful; (gram.) reflexive.

reflorecer, *vn.* (*ind.* REFLOREZCO; *subj.* REFLOREZCA) to reflourish, blossom again; to return to former splendor; "to come back."

refluente, *a.* refluent; flowing back.

refluir, *vn.* (*ind. pres.* REFLUYO, *pret.* él REFLUYÓ; *subj.* REFLUYA) to flow back; to redound.

reflujo, *m.* reflux, refluence; ebb or ebb-tide.

refocilación, *f.* recreation, refreshing diversion.

refocilar. I. *va.* to give or afford healthful recreation to, to brace up. **II.** *vr.* to seek or indulge in healthful recreation.

refocilo, *m.* healthful pleasure.

reforcé, *pret.* of REFORZAR.

reforma, *f.* reform; reformation; alteration, correction, improvement; (eccl.) Reformation.— **cerrado por reformas,** closed for alterations.

reformable, *a.* reformable; mendable.

reformación, *f.* reformation, reform.

reformado. I. *pp.* of REFORMAR. **II.** *a.* reformed. **III.** *m.* officer deprived of his command.

reformador, ra, *n.* & *a.* reformer(-ing); mender (-ing).

reformar. I. *va.* to reform; to mend, amend, improve; to reorganize, reconstruct. **II.** *vr.* to reform, to mend.

reformatorio, ria. I. *a.* corrective, reforming. **II.** *m.* reformatory.

reformista, *n.* & *a.* reformer(-ing, -ist).

reforzado, da. I. *a.* strengthened, reinforced. **II.** *m.* narrow tape or ribbon.

reforzar, *va.* (*ind. pres.* REFUERZO, *pret.* él REFORCÉ; *subj.* REFUERCE) to strengthen, reinforce; to cheer, encourage.

refracción, *f.* (opt.) refraction.

refractar, *va.* & *vr.* (opt.) to refract.

refractario, ria, *a.* refractory; unruly; obstinate.

refracto, ta, *a.* (opt.) refracted.

refrán, *m.* proverb, saying, saw.

refranero, *m.* collection of proverbs.

refrangibilidad, *f.* refrangibility.

refrangible, *a.* refrangible.

refregadura, *f.* = REFREGÓN.

refregamiento, *m.* rubbing, scrubbing.

refregar, *va.* (*ind. pres.* REFRIEGO, *pret.* REFREGUÉ; *subj.* REFRIEGUE) to rub, scrub; (coll.) to upbraid, scold.—**refregón,** *m.* rubbing, scrubbing; attrition, abrasion.

refreír, *va.* (*ind. pres.* REFRÍO, *pret.* él REFRIÓ; *subj.* REFRÍA; *ger.* REFRIENDO; *pp.* REFREÍDO, REFRITO) to fry well or too much.

refrenable, *a.* capable of being restrained.

refrenamiento, *m.* curbing, restraint, check.

refrenar, *va.* to restrain, check; to rein, curb (a horse).

refrendación, *f.* legalization, authentication; visé.

refrendar, *va.* to legalize, authenticate, countersign; to visé.

refrendario, ria, *n.* one who countersigns.

refrendata, *f.* countersignature.

refrendo, *m.* = REFRENDACIÓN.

refrescador, ra, *a.* refreshing.

refrescadura, *f.* refreshing (act and effect).

refrescamiento, *m.* = REFRESCO.

refrescante, *a.* cooling, refreshing.

refrescar. I. *va.* (*pret.* REFRESQUÉ; *subj.* REFRESQUE) to refresh; to cool, refrigerate; to renew, take up again. **II.** *vn.* & *vr.* (of the weather) to get cool; to take the fresh air; to take a refreshment; to cool off.

refresco, *m.* refreshment; cold drink; luncheon at social gatherings.—**de r.,** anew, once more.

refriega, *f.* affray, scuffle, fray.

refriego, refriegue, *v. V.* REFREGAR.

refrigeración, *f.* refrigeration.

refrigerador, ra. I. *a.* refrigerating, freezing, cooling. **II.** *m.* refrigerator, freezer, ice box, cooler.

refrigerante. I. *a.* refrigerating, cooling. **II.** *m.* (chem.) refrigerator, cooling chamber; (med.) cooler.

refrigerar, *va.* to cool, refrigerate.

refrigerativo, va, *a.* refrigerating, cooling.

refrigerio, *m.* refrigeration, coolness; refreshment, refection; consolation, comfort.

refringente, *a.* refracting, refringent.

refringir, *va.* & *vr.* (*ind.* REFRINJO; *subj.* REFRINJA) to refract.

refrío, refrió, etc. *v. V.* REFREÍR.

refrito, ta, *pp. irreg.* of REFREÍR.

¹**refuerzo,** *m.* reinforcement; backing, bracing, strengthening piece; welt (of shoe); aid, help.

²**refuerzo,** *v. V.* REFORZAR.

refugiado, da. I. *pp.* of REFUGIAR. **II.** *n.* refugee.

refugiar. I. *va.* to shelter. **II.** *vr.* to take refuge.

refugio, *m.* refuge, shelter, asylum.

refulgencia, *f.* refulgence, splendor.

refulgente, *a.* refulgent.

refulgir, *vn.* to shine.

refundición, *f.* (foundry) recasting.

refundir. I. *va.* (foundry) to remelt or recast; to contain, include; to rearrange, recast, reconstruct. **II.** *vn.* to redound.

refunfuñador, ra, *n.* grumbler, growler.

refunfuñadura, *f.* growling, grumbling.

refunfuñar, *va.* to growl, grumble, mutter.

refunfuño, *m.* grumbling, growl, snort.

refutable, *a.* refutable.

refutación, *f.* refutation.

refutador, ra, *n.* & *a.* refuter(-ing).

refutar, *va.* to refute.

refutatorio, ria, *a.* refuting.

regadera, *f.* watering pot, sprinkler; trench for irrigation; sparger.

regadero, *m.* ditch for irrigation.

regadío, ía, *a.* & *m.* irrigated (land).

regadizo, za, *a.* irrigable.

¹**regador, ra,** *n.* one who waters or irrigates.

²**regador,** *m.* comb makers' gauge.

regadura, *f.* irrigation, watering.

regaifa, *f.* grooved stone of an oil mill.

regajal, regajo, *m.* puddle, pool; rill.

regala, *f.* (naut.) gunwale or gunnel.

regalada, *f.* king's stables; horses kept in them.

regaladamente, *adv.* delicately, pleasantly, daintily, luxuriously.

regalado, da, *pp.* & *a.* delicate, dainty; easy, comfortable; suave.

regalador, ra. I. *n.* liberal entertainer. II. *m.* stick for cleaning wine skins.

regalamiento, *m.* regalement.

regalar. I. *va.* to present, give as a present, make a present of; to regale, treat, entertain; to caress, fondle, pet, cajole; to gladden, cheer, delight, cherish. II. *vr.* to feast sumptuously.

regalejo, *m. dim.* small gift.

regalero, *m.* purveyor of fruit and flowers for the royal family.

regalía, *f.* regalia, royal rights; (S. A., Mex.) advance payment or royalty to owner of patent, etc.; privilege, exemption; (Cuba) regalia (cigar).—*pl.* perquisites.

regalicia, *f.* = REGALIZ.

regalillo, *m. dim.* small gift; muff (for hands).

regalismo, *m.* regalism.

regalista, *n.* & *a.* regalist(-ic).

regalito, *m. dim.* small present.

regaliz, *m.*, **regaliza,** *f.* (bot.) licorice.

regalo, *m.* present, gift; pleasure; dainty; comfort, luxury.—**con r.,** in luxury.

regalón, na, *a.* (coll.) fond of ease; spoiled, pampered.

regañadientes.—a r., reluctantly, grumbling.

regañado, da, *pp.* & *a.* frowning; (of certain plums and bread) splitting open.

regañador, ra, *a.* scolding, grumbling.

regañamiento, *m.* grumbling, snarling, growl.

regañar. I. *vn.* to snarl, growl, grumble; mutter; to quarrel, wrangle; to crack or open. II. *va.* (coll.) to scold, reprehend, chide.

regañir, *vn.* to yelp, howl repeatedly.

regaño, *m.* gesture of annoyance; sternness of look; scolding; reprimand; scorched bread.

regañón, na, *n.* & *a.* growler(-ing), grumbler (-ing); scolder, scold(-ing).

regar, *va.* (*ind. pres.* RIEGO, *pret.* REGUÉ; *subj.* RIEGUE) to water; to irrigate; to sprinkle; to shower, bedew; to strew, scatter; to wash or water (as rivers and clouds).

¹**regata,** *f.* irrigating ditch or conduit.

²**regata,** *f.* regatta.

regate, *m.* dodge, dodging.

regatear. I. *va.* to haggle about, beat down (the price), to resell at retail; to shun, evade, avoid. II. *vn.* to haggle; to wriggle, dodge; (naut.) to race.

regateo, *m.* chaffer, bargaining, haggling.

regatería, *f.* = REGATONERÍA.

regatero, ra, *n.* & *a.* haggler(-ing).

regato, *m.* small rivulet, rill; pool.

¹**regatón, na,** *n.* huckster, hawker; haggler.

²**regatón,** *m.* tip, ferrule.

regatonear, *vn.* to sell at retail.

regatonería, *f.* hucksterage; sale by retail.

regazar, *va.* to tuck up.

regazo, *m.* lap (part of body).

regencia, *f.* regency; regentship.

regeneración, *f.* regeneration.

regenerador, ra, *n.* & *a.* regenerator(-ing).

regenerar, *va.* to regenerate.

regenerativo, va, *a.* regenerative.

regenta, *f.* regent's wife; woman professor.

regentar, *va.* to rule, govern, manage.

regente. I. *a.* ruling, governing. II. *n.* regent; president of a court of justice; master of theological studies; in Spanish universities, some supernumerary professors; manager, director; (print.) foreman.

regentear, *vn.* to domineer, rule, boss.

regiamente, *adv.* royally, regally.

regicida, *n.* regicide, murderer of a king.

regicidio, *m.* regicide, murder of a king.

regidor, ra. I. *a.* ruling, governing. II. *m.* alderman or councilman. III. *f.* alderman's or councilman's wife.—**regidoría, regiduría,** *f.* alderman's or councilman's office.

régimen, *m.* régime; management, rule; political system; (gram.) government; (med.) regimen, treatment.—**r. alimenticio,** diet.—**de r.,** ordinary, rated, normal (speed, power, etc.).

regimentar, *va.* (*ind.* REGIMIENTO; *subj.* REGIMIENTE) to organize into a regiment.

regimiento, *m.* administration, government; municipal council board; (mil.) regiment; (naut.) pilot's book of sailing directions.

regio, gia, *a.* royal, regal, kingly; stately, sumptuous, magnificent.

región, *f.* region.

regional, *a.* regional, sectional, local.—**regionalismo,** *m.* (pol.) home rule; regionalism, sectionalism.—**regionalista.** I. *a.* relating to home rule. II. *n.* home ruler; sectionalism.

regionario, ria, *a.* (eccl.) regionary.

regir. I. *va.* (*ger.* RIGIENDO; *ind. pres.* RIJO, *pret.* él RIGIÓ; *subj.* RIJA) to rule, govern, direct; to conduct, manage, command; to keep (the bowels) in good order; (gram.) to govern. II. *vn.* to be in force; to prevail; (naut.) to obey the helm.

registrador, ra. I. *a.* registering. II. *n.* register, registrar, recorder, master or clerk of records; searcher, inspector; toll gatherer; controller.

registrar. I. *va.* to inspect, examine; to search; to scan, survey; to register, record; to mark (a book); (min.) to prospect. II. *vr.* to register, be registered or matriculated.

registro, *m.* search, inspection, examination; census, registry, registration, enrollment, record, entry; enrolling office; certificate of entry; register book; bookmark; (mus.) register, stop of an organ; air hole; furnace register; (print.) catchword, register; regulator (of a timepiece); (bookbinding) directions for binding.

regla, *f.* rule, regulation, precept; policy; order, measure, moderation; (drawing) ruler, straight edge; menstruation, courses.—**r. de aligación,** (arith.) alligation.—**r. de compañía,** (arith.) partnership.—**r. de falsa posición,** (arith.) position, rule of false position.—**r. de oro,** or **r. de tres,** (arith.) rule of three.—**r. fija,** fixed rule, set rule.—**r. lesbia,** flexible rule.—**r. magnética,** surveying compass.—**r. T,** or **r. te,** T square.—**a r.,** by ruler, by rule and square.—**en r.,** thoroughly, in due form, in order.—**echar la r.,** to test with a ruler.—**por r. general,** as a general rule.

regladamente, *adv.* regularly, in orderly manner.

reglado, da. I. *pp.* of REGLAR. II. *a.* temperate, moderate; (geom.) ruled (surface).

reglamentación, *f.* establishment of rules and regulations; regulation by law, decree or rule; directions for the execution of a law.

reglamentar, *va.* to establish rules or by-laws for; to regulate by rule, law, or decree; to dictate directions for the execution of (a law).

reglamentario, ria, *a.* pertaining to, or prescribed by, regulations and by-laws; required by the rules (actual or tacit, as in the case of social formalities).

reglamento, *m.* by-laws; rules and regulations.

¹**reglar.** I. *va.* to rule (as paper); to regulate. II. *vr.* to mend, reform.

²**reglar,** *a.* regular.

regleta, *f.* (print.) reglet; lead.

regletear, *va.* (print.) to lead.

reglón, *m.* mason's rule.

regnícola, *n.* native of a kingdom; writer on topics relating to his country.

regocijadamente, *adv.* merrily, joyfully.

regocijado, da. I. *pp.* of REGOCIJAR. II. *a.* merry, joyful, rejoicing, festive.

regocijador, ra, *n.* & *a.* rejoicer(-ing).

regocijar. I. *va.* to gladden, cheer, rejoice. **II.** *vr.* to rejoice, be merry.—**regocijo,** *m.* joy, gladness; mirth, merriment; rejoicing.

regodearse, *vr.* (coll.) to take delight; to joke, to jest.—**regodeo,** *m.* delight; merrymaking.

regojo, *m.* piece of bread left on the table after meals; puny boy.

regojuelo, *m. dim.* small morsel of bread.

regoldano, na, *a.* wild (chestnut).

regoldar, *vn.* (ind. REGÜELDO; *subj.* REGÜELDE) to belch, to eruct.

regoldo, *m.* (bot.) wild chestnut tree.

regolfar, *vn.* & *vr.* to flow back, to eddy.

regolfo, *m.* eddy, whirlpool; gulf, bay.

regona, *f.* large irrigating canal.

regordete, ta, *a.* (coll.) chubby, plump.

regostarse, *vr.* to delight, to dally.

regosto, *m.* craving for more.

regraciar, *va.* to show gratitude to, to thank.

regresar, *vn.* to return; (eccl.) to recover possession of a benefice.

regresión, *f.* regression, retrogression.

regresivo, va, *a.* regressive.

regreso, *m.* return, coming or going back; (eccl.) retaking possession of a benefice.

regruñir, *vn.* to snarl, to growl.

reguardarse, *vr.* to take care of oneself.

regué, *pret.* of REGAR.

¹**regüeldo, regüelde,** *v. V.* REGOLDAR.

²**regüeldo,** *m.* eructation, belch.

reguera, *f.* irrigating ditch; (naut.) moorings.

reguero, *m.* trickle, rill, drip; irrigating furrow.

reguilete, *m.* = REHILETE.

regulación, *f.* regulation; adjustment.

regulado, da. I. *pp.* of REGULAR. **II.** *a.* according to rule.

regulador, ra. I. *a.* regulating, governing. **II.** *m.* (mech.) regulator; governor; register; throttle valve (of locomotive); controller (of electric car).—**r. de fuerza centrífuga,** ball governor.

¹**regular,** *va.* to regulate; to adjust.

²**regular. I.** *a.* regular; methodical, orderly; moderate, sober; common, ordinary, frequent; middling, fairly good, so so; likely, probable; (geom. and gram.) regular.—**por lo r.,** usually, as a rule. **II.** *m.* (eccl.) regular.

regularidad, *f.* regularity; common usage, custom; exact discipline.

regularizar, *va.* to regularize.

regularmente, *adv.* regularly; ordinarily, as a rule; middling, fairly well, so so.

régulo, *m.* chief of a petty state; basilisk; (chem.) regulus; (astr.) Regulus; (ornith.) golden-crested kinglet.

regurgitación, *f.* (med.) regurgitation.

regurgitar, *vn.* to regurgitate, overflow.

rehabilitación, *f.* rehabilitation.

rehabilitar, *va.* to rehabilitate, reinstate, restore; to refit, repair.

rehacer. I. *va.* (*pp.* REHECHO; *ind. pres.* REHAGO, *pret.* yo REHICE, él REHIZO, *fut.* REHARÉ; *subj.* REHAGA) to rebuild, remodel, make over; do over; to renovate, mend, repair; to invigorate, revive. **II.** *vr.* to regain strength and vigor; (mil.) to rally, reorganize.—**rehacimiento,** *m.* renovation, renewal; recuperation.

rehala, *f.* drove of flocks under one drover.

rehalero, *m.* drover of a REHALA.

rehecho, cha. I. *pp. irreg.* of REHACER. **II.** *a.* squat, broad-shouldered.

rehelear, *vn.* to be bitter.—**reheleo,** *m.* bitterness.

rehén, *m.* (gen. *pl.*) hostage.

rehenchimiento, *m.* stuffing, refilling.

rehenchir, *va.* (ind. pres. REHINCHO, *pret.* él REHINCHIÓ; *subj.* REHINCHA) to refill, stuff anew.

rehendija, *f.* crevice, cleft.

reherimiento, *m.* repulsion.

reherir, *va.* (ind. pres. REHIERO, *pret.* él REHIRIÓ; *subj.* REHIERA) to repel, to repulse.

reherrar, *va.* to reshoe (a horse).

rehervir. I. *vn.* & *va.* (ind. pres. REHIERVO, *pret.* él REHIRVIÓ; *subj.* REHIERVA) to boil again. **II.** *vn.* to be inflamed with love; to be blinded by passion. **III.** *vr.* to ferment, grow sour.

rehice, *pret.* of REHACER.

rehiero, rehiera, *v. V.* REHERIR.

rehiervo, rehierva, *v. V.* REHERVIR.

rehiladillo, *m.* ribbon.

rehilandera, *f.* pinwheel.

rehilar. I. *va.* to twist too much. **II.** *vn.* to stagger, to reel; to whiz, whir, as an arrow in flight.

rehilete, rehilero, *m.* shuttlecock; small arrow; malicious saying, personal hint.

rehilo, *m.* shaking, shivering.

rehincho, rehincha, etc. *v. V.* REHENCHIR.

rehirió, *pret.* of REHERIR.

rehirvió, *pret.* of REHERVIR.

rehizo, *pret.* of REHACER.

rehogar, *va.* to dress (meat) with a slow fire, basting it with butter or oil.

rehollar, *va.* (ind. REHUELLO; *subj.* REHUELLE) to trample under foot.

rehoya, *f.,* deep hole or pit.

rehoyar, *vn.* to dig holes anew.

rehoyo, *m.* = REHOYA.

rehuello, rehuelle, *v. V.* REHOLLAR.

rehuída, *f.* second flight; shunning.

rehuir. I. *va., vn.* & *vr.* (*ger.* REHUYENDO; *ind. pres.* REHUYO, *pret.* él REHUYÓ; *subj.* REHUYA) to withdraw, retire; to shun, avoid; to reject, decline, refuse. **II.** *vn.* to run back on the same track (as game).

rehumedecer, *va.* & *vr.* (ind. REHUMEDEZCO; *subj.* REHUMEDEZCA) to dampen well.

¹**rehundir,** *va.* & *vr.* to sink; to deepen.

²**rehundir,** *va.* to remelt; to waste, dissipate, lavish.

rehurtarse, *vr.* (of game) to take a different route from that expected.

rehusar, *va.* to refuse, decline, reject.

rehuyo, etc. *v. V.* REHUIR.

reidero, ra, *a.* laughable.

reidor, ra. I. *a.* jolly, hilarious, full of laughter. **II.** *n.* laugher, one who laughs.

reimpresión, *f.* reprint; reprinting.

reimpreso, sa, *pp. irreg.* of REIMPRIMIR.

reimprimir, *va.* (*pp.* REIMPRESO) to reprint.

reina, *f.* queen; queen bee; queen at chess; hopscotch.—**aceituna de la r.,** queen olive.

reinado, *m.* reign.

reinal, *m.* strong hemp cord.

reinante, *a.* reigning; excelling; prevailing.

reinar, *vn.* to reign; to prevail, predominate.

reincidencia, *f.* repetition of an offense; backsliding, relapse into vice or error.

reincidente, *a.* relapsing, backsliding.

reincidir, *vn.* to relapse into vice or error; to backslide.

reincorporación, *f.* reincorporation.

reincorporar. I. *va.* to incorporate a second time. **II.** *vr.* to reëmbody.

reingresar, *vn.* to reënter.

reino, *m.* kingdom, reign; district that was formerly a kingdom; (natural history) kingdom.

reinstalación, *f.* reinstallment; reinstallation.

reinstalar, *va.* to reinstall.

reintegrable, *a.* (com.) reimbursable, payable.

reintegración, *f.* restitution, reimbursement.

reintegrador, ra, *n.* restorer.

reintegrar. I. *va.* to reintegrate, restore; (com.) to reimburse, repay, refund. **II.** *vr.* (de) to recover, recuperate.

reintegro, *m.* = REINTEGRACIÓN.

reír. I. *vn.* (*ger.* RIENDO; *ind. pres.* RÍO, *pret.* él RIÓ; *subj.* RÍA) to laugh; to giggle, titter; to sneer; to smile (as nature).—**r. a carcajadas,** to laugh loudly, guffaw. **II.** *vr.* to laugh; (of cloth) (coll.) to begin to tear or split.—**r. de**, to laugh at, make fun of; to make little or nothing of.

reis, *m.* reis, Brazilian and Portuguese money of account.

reiteración, *f.* reiteration.

reiteradamente, *adv.* repeatedly.

reiterar, *va.* to reiterate.

reiterativo, va, *a.* reiterative.

reivindicable, *a.* (law) repleviable.

reivindicación, *f.* (law) recovery, replevin.

reivindicar, *va.* (law) to regain possession of; to replevy.

reivindicatorio, ria, *a.* (law) replevying.

reja, *f.* plowshare, colter or coulter; plowing, tillage; grate, grating, railing; (atomic phys.) lattice.

rejacar, *va.* = ARREJACAR, to weed by plowing.

rejada, *f.* = ARREJADA, (agr.) paddle of a plow.

rejado, *m.* grate, grating, railing, grid.

rejal, *m.* pile of bricks laid crisscross.

rejalgar, *m.* (min.) realgar.

rejero, *m.* maker of railings and grates.

rejilla, *f.* small lattice or grating; latticed wicket; cane for backs and seats of chairs, etc.; foot brasier.

rejitar, *va.* to vomit.

rejo, *m.* pointed bar or spike; goad stick; (zool.) sting; hob for quoits; iron frame of a door; strength, vigor; (bot.) caulicle.

rejón, *m.* short spear thrust into a bull and broken at the end, leaving the point in the flesh; dagger; broad knife.—**rejonazo,** *m.* thrust with a REJÓN.—**rejoncillo,** *m. dim.* small spear.

rejoneador, *m.* bullfighter who uses the REJÓN.

rejonear, *va.* to thrust a REJÓN into (a bull).—**rejoneo,** *m.* fighting bulls with a REJÓN.

rejuela, *f. dim.* small grate; foot brasier.

rejuvenecer. I. *va.* (*ind.* REJUVENEZCO; *subj.* REJUVENEZCA) to rejuvenate. **II.** *vn. & vr.* to be rejuvenated.

relabrar, *va.* to work or cut again (as a precious stone).

relación, *f.* relation; report, narrative, memoir, account; intercourse, dealing; (law) report, brief; (mil.) return, report; (theat.) speech.—*pl.* relations, connections; acquaintance, intercourse; courting.—**r. jurada,** sworn statement.—**decir,** or **hacer, r. a,** to relate to.—**tener relaciones con,** to have relations with; to be acquainted with.

relacionado, da, *n.* acquaintance (person).

relacionar. I. *va.* to relate, connect; to report, narrate; to make acquainted. **II.** *vr.* to get acquainted, make connections; to be related.

relacionero, ra, *n.* narrator; ballad singer.

relái, *m.* (Am.) (elec.) relay.

relajación, *f.* relaxation, laxity, looseness; slackening, relenting; diminution, mitigation (of a penalty); release (from an oath or vow); delivery of an offender by the ecclesiastical judge to a criminal court of justice; diversion, relaxation, rest; (med.) hernia, rupture.

relajadamente, *adv.* with relaxation; dissolutely.

relajado, da, *a.* (coll.) dissolute, dissipated.

relajador, ra, *a.* relaxing; remitting.

relajamiento, *m.* = RELAJACIÓN.

relajante, *a.* relaxing; loosening.

relajar. I. *va.* to relax, loosen, slacken; to remit, mitigate; to release from an obligation; (eccl.) to deliver to the criminal tribunal; to weaken; to amuse, divert. **II.** *vr.* to become relaxed, loosened, weakened; to grow vicious; to be ruptured.—**relajo,** *m.* (Am.) disorder, mix-up; (Mex., Cuba, P. R.) depravity.

relamer. I. *va.* to lick again. **II.** *vr.* to lick one's lips; to relish; to paint, make up; to boast.

relamido, da, *a.* affected, prim.

relámpago, *m.* lightning; quick person or action; (vet.) blemish in the eyes of horses.

relampagueante, *a.* lightning, flashing.

relampaguear, *vn.* to lighten; to flash, sparkle.

relampagueo, *m.* lightning; flashing.

relance, *m.* repeated casting of a net; second chance or lot; fortuitous event; repeated attempt; series of lucky or unlucky chances.—**de r.,** unexpectedly, by chance; at a bargain; second-hand.

relanzar, *va.* to repel, repulse; to cast in again (tickets or lots) to be drawn.

relapso, sa, *a.* relapsed into error.

relatador, ra, *n.* relater, narrator, teller.

relatante, *a.* narrating.

relatar, *va.* to relate, narrate, tell, report; (law) to make a report of (a lawsuit).

relativamente, *adv.* relatively.

relatividad, *f.* relativity.

relativismo, *m.* (philos.) relativism.

relativista, *n. & a.* (philos.) relativist(-ic).

relativo, va, *a.* relative.

relato, *m.* statement, narrative, report, account.

relator, ra. I. *n.* narrator. **II.** *m.* (law) relator.

relatoría, *f.* (law) office of a RELATOR.

relavar, *va.* to wash again.

relave, *m.* second washing of metals.—*pl.* (metal.) washings or sweepings.

relazar, *va.* to tie with many bindings.

relé, *m.* (Angl.) (Am.) relay.

releer, *va.* to read over again; to revise.

relegación, *f.* relegation, banishment, exile.

relegar, *va.* (*pret.* RELEGUÉ; *subj.* RELEGUE) to relegate, banish, exile.

relej, releje, *m.* wheel track, rut; (artil.) narrow chamber in a cannon; (arch.) tapering talus; (med.) sordes in the mouth.

relejar, *vn.* (arch.) to taper or slope.

relente, *m.* dampness; (coll.) boldness, assurance.

relentecer, *vn. & vr.* (*ind.* RELENTEZCO; *subj.* RELENTEZCA) to grow soft or tender.

relevación, *f.* raising, lifting up; alleviation, relief; remission, pardon, exemption.

relevador, *m.* (elec.) relay.—**r. de llamada,** alarm relay.—**r. graduado,** step-by-step relay.—**r. parlante,** sounding relay, relaying sounder.—**r. traslator,** repeating relay.

relevante, *a.* excellent, great, eminent.

relevar. I. *va.* to emboss; to bring into relief; to exonerate, relieve, release; to forgive, pardon, acquit; to exalt, aggrandize; (mil.) to relieve, substitute. **II.** *vn.* (art) to stand out in relief.

relevo, *m.* (mil.) relief.

relicario, *m.* shrine; reliquary; locket.

relictos, *m. pl.* (law) estate.

relief, *m.* (mil.) rehabilitation.

relieve, *m.* relief, relievo, raised work, embossment.—**poner de r.,** to bring out, throw into relief, emphasize.—*pl.* (of food) leavings; (fig.) highlights or high points.

religa, *f.* (jewel.) second alloy.

religación, *f.* binding, tying.

religar, *va.* (*pret.* RELIGUÉ; *subj.* RELIGUE) to bind more tightly; to really; to solder.

religión, *f.* religion.—**religionario, ria,** *n.* religionist; sectarian; Protestant.

religiosamente, *adv.* religiously.

religiosidad, *f.* religiosity; religiousness; punctuality.

religioso, sa. I. *a.* religious; bound by monastic vows; conscientious, punctual. **II.** *n.* religious, member of a religious order; monk (nun).

religué, religue, *v.* V. RELIGAR.

relimar, *va.* (mech.) to file again.

relimpiar, *va.* to clean again.

relimpio, ia, *a.* (coll.) very neat, clean.

relinchador, ra, *a.* habitually neighing.

relinchante, *a.* neighing, whinnying.

relinchar, *vn.* to whinny, to neigh.

relincho, relinchido, *m.* neigh, neighing.

relindo, da, *a.* very neat and fine.

relinga, *f.* (naut.) boltrope.

For pronunciation, see the rules at the beginning of the book.

relingar. I. va. (naut.) to rope (a sail). **II.** vn. (naut.) to rustle.

reliquia, f. relic, residue, remains; relics of saints; trace, vestige; habitual complaint.

reliz, m. (Mex.) landslide.

reloco, ca, a. (coll.) raving mad.

reloj, m. clock; watch.—**r. de agua,** clepsydra.— **r. de arena,** sandglass, hourglass.—**r. de bolsillo,** watch.—**r. de campana,** striking clock. —**r. de cuco,** cuckoo clock.—**r. de longitudes** = R. MARINO.—**r. de pulsera,** wrist watch.— **r. de repetición,** repeater, or repeating watch. —**r. de sol,** sundial.—**r. despertador,** alarm clock.—**r. magistral,** standard clock.—**r. marino,** chronometer.—**estar como un r.,** (coll.) to be in perfect trim.—**por r.,** (to work) by the hour.

relojera, f. watchcase; watch stand; (Am.) watch pocket.

relojería, f. clock and watch making; watchmaker's shop.

relojero, ra, n. watchmaker, clockmaker.

reluciente, a. shining, glittering, bright.

relucir, vn. (ind. RELUZCO; subj. RELUZCA) to shine, glow, glisten, glitter; to excel, to be brilliant.

reluctante, a. unruly, unmanageable.

reluchar, vn. to struggle, wrestle, strive.

relumbrante, a. resplendent.

relumbrar, vn. to sparkle, shine, glitter.

relumbrón, m. lustre, dazzling brightness; flash; tinsel.—**de r.,** showy, tawdry, pompous.

reluzco, reluzca, v. V. RELUCIR.

rellanar. I. va. to relevel. **II.** vr. to stretch oneself at full length.

rellano, m. landing, (of a stair).

rellenar. I. va. to refill, replenish; to cram; to fill up; (cook.) to force, to stuff; (sewing) to pad; (mason.) to point. **II.** vr. to stuff oneself.

relleno, na. I. a. satiated; stuffed. **II.** m. forcemeat, stuffing; repletion; filling; (mech.) packing, gasket; (sewing) padding, wadding.

remachado, da. I. pp. of REMACHAR. **II.** a. riveted. **III.** m. riveting; clinching.—**r. alternado,** or **al tresbolillo,** staggered riveting.— **r. de cadena,** or **paralelo,** chain riveting.

remachar, va. to clinch; to rivet; to secure, affirm.

remache, m. rivet; riveting; flattening, clinching.

remachón, m. buttress.

remador, ra, n. rower.

remadura, f. rowing.

remallar, va. to mend the meshes of.

remamiento, m. rowing.

remandar, va. to order several times.

remanecer, vn. (ind. REMANEZCO; subj. REMANEZCA) to reappear suddenly.

remaneciente, a. reappearing.

remanente. I. m. remains, remnant, residue. **II.** a. residual (esp. app. to magnetism).

remanezco, remanezca, v. V. REMANECER.

remangar. I. va. to tuck up (sleeves, etc.). **II.** vr. to be determined.

remango, m. tucking up.

remansarse, vr. to stop flowing; to eddy.

remanso, m. backwater; dead water; tardiness.

remante, a. rowing.

remar, va. & vn. to row, paddle; to toil, struggle.

remarcar, va. (pret. REMARQUÉ; subj. REMARQUE) to mark again.

rematadamente, adv. entirely, totally.

rematado, da. I. pp. of REMATAR. **II.** a. sold (at auction); totally lost, utterly ruined.—**r. a galeras, a presidio,** condemned to the galleys, to prison.

rematamiento, m. = REMATE.

rematante, m. highest bidder.

rematar. I. va. to end, complete, finish; (com.) to auction; to knock down at auction; to give the finishing stroke; (sewing) to fasten off (a stitch); to finish (a seam). **II.** vn. to terminate, end. **III.** vr. to be utterly ruined or destroyed.

remate, m. end, finish, conclusion, expiration; (com.) auction, public sale; last or highest bid; (print.) vignette; (arch.) finial, pinnacle.—**r. de cuentas,** closing of accounts.—**de r.,** utterly, irremediably, without hope.—**por r.,** as a finish; finally.

remecedor, ra, n. one who beats down olives with a pole.

remecer, va. (ind. REMEZO; subj. REMEZA) to rock, swing, move to and fro.

remedable, a. imitable.

remedador, ra, n. imitator, mimic.

remedar, va. to copy, imitate; mimic, mock.

remediable, a. remediable.

remediador, ra, n. curer, healer; mender; comforter, helper.

remediar, va. to remedy; to assist, support, help; to free from danger, liberate; to repair (mischief); to avoid.—**no poder r.,** not to be able to help (prevent).

remedición, f. remeasuring; remeasurement.

remedio, m. remedy; medicine; help; amendment, correction; (law) action.—**r. casero,** home remedy.—**r. heroico,** extreme remedy, powerful remedy given as a last resort.—**ni para (un) r.,** (not) for love or money.—**no hay más r. (que),** there's nothing else to do (but). —**no tener para un r.,** to be absolutely penniless.—**no tener r.,** to be unavoidable; to be irremediable; to be no help for (eso no tiene remedio, there's no help for that, no way of avoiding).—**sin r.,** inevitable; hopeless.

remedión, m. aug. (theat.) makeshift performance.

remedir, va. to remeasure.

remedo, m. imitation; copy; mockery; mimicking.

remellado, da, a. dented, jagged.

remellar, va. (tanning) to unhair (hides).

remellón, na, a. = REMELLADO.

rememorar, va. to remember, recall.

rememorativo, va, a. reminding, recalling.

remendado, da. I. pp. of REMENDAR. **II.** a. patched; mended; spotted, tabby (cat).

remendar, va. (ind. REMIENDO; subj. REMIENDE) to patch, mend, repair; (sewing) to piece, patch; to darn.

remendón, na, n. botcher, patcher; one who mends old clothes; cobbler.

remera, f. flight feather (of birds).

remero, ra, n. rower, oarsman, paddler.

remesa, f. (com.) shipment; remittance.

¹remesar, va. to pluck out (the hair).

²remesar, va. (com.) to ship; to send, remit.

¹remesón, m. plucking out of hair; plucked hair.

²remesón, m. stopping a horse in full gallop; skilful thrust in fencing.

remeter, va. to put back, put in.

remezón, m. (Am.) slight earthquake.

remiche, m. space between benches in galleys.

remiel, m. the second extract of soft sugar taken from the cane.

¹remiendo, m. patch; mending piece; darning; amendment, correction; reparation, repair; brindle; (print.) jobwork.—**a remiendos,** by patchwork, piecemeal.—**echar un r.,** to patch. —**echar un r. a la vida,** to take a light repast.

²remiendo, remiende, v. V. REMENDAR.

remilgadamente, adv. with affected nicety, prudishly, squeamishly.

remilgado, da. I. pp. of REMILGARSE. **II.** a affected, prudish, finical, fastidious.

remilgarse, vr. to be overnice, prudish or finical.

remilgo, m. affected nicety, prudery, squeamishness.

reminiscencia, f. reminiscence.

remirado, da, pp. & a. prudent, cautious.

remirar. I. va. to look at or go over again. **II.** vr.

(en) to take great pains (with); to inspect or consider with pleasure.

remisamente, *adv.* remissly, carelessly.

remisible, *a.* remissible.

remisión, *f.* act of sending or referring; remission, sending back, remitting, remitment; remission, pardon, forgiveness; remissness, indolence; relaxation, abatement.

remisivamente, *adv.* with remission.

remisivo, va, *a.* remissory; remissive.

remiso, sa, *a.* remiss, careless, slack, slow.

remisorio, ria, *a.* remissory.

remitente, *n.* & *a.* remitter(-ing), sender(-ing).

remitir. I. *va.* to remit; to forward, transmit; to pardon, forgive; to give up, relinquish, waive, forego; to suspend, defer, put off; to refer; (law) to transfer, remit to another court. II. *va., vn.* & *vr.* to remit, slacken, abate. III. *vr.* to refer, submit; to quote, cite.

remo, *m.* (naut.) oar; (coll.) arm or leg (of person); leg (of quadruped); long and hard labor.—*pl.* wings of a bird.

remoción, *f.* removal, removing; dismissal.

remojadero, *m.* steeping tub.

remojador, ra, *n.* moistener, soaker.

remojar, *va.* to steep, soak, drench.

remojo, *m.* steeping, soaking, soakage.—**echar en r.,** (coll.) to defer until conditions are more favorable.

remolacha, *f.* (bot.) beet root, red beet.

remolar, *m.* oar maker; oar shop.

remolcador, ra. I. *a.* (naut.) towing. II. *m.* tug, tugboat, towboat; lighter.

remolcar, *va.* to tow, take in tow; to haul.

remoler, *va.* (*ind.* REMUELO; *subj.* REMUELA) to regrind; grind excessively.

remolida, *f.,* **remolimiento,** *m.* regrinding.

remolinante, *a.* a whirling.

remolinar. I. *vn.* & *vr.* to whirl, gyrate, spin, rotate. II. *vr.* to crowd, throng together, swarm.

remolinear. I. *va.* to whirl about. II. *vn.* = REMOLINAR.

remolino, *m.* whirl, whirlwind; whirlpool, vortex, eddy; maelstrom; cowlick, twisted tuft of hair; crowd, throng; disturbance, commotion.

¹remolón, na, *a.* soft, indolent, lazy.

²remolón, *m.* upper tusk of a wild boar; sharp tooth in horses.

remolonear, *vn.* & *vr.* to lag, loiter, skulk, shun work.

remolque, *m.* (naut.) towing, towage; trackage; towline.—**a r.,** in tow.—**dar r.,** to tow.

remondar, *va.* to clean (plants) a second time.

remono, na, *a.* (coll.) very neat; very pretty.

remonta, *f.* repairing, resoling, vamping, footing (of shoes); stuffing (of saddle); (mil.) remount; remounting cavalry.

remontamiento, *m.* remounting cavalry.

remontar. I. *va.* to frighten away (as game); (mil.) to supply remounts; to repair (saddles); to repair, resole, revamp (shoes); (Am.) to go up (river). II. *va.* & *vr.* to elevate, raise, rise. III. *vr.* to soar (as birds); to take to the woods; to go back to, date from.

remonte, *m.* repairing; remounting; soaring.

remontista, *m.* (mil.) commissioner for the purchase of remounts.

remoque, *m.* (coll.) sarcastic word.

remoquete, *m.* thump with the fist; epigram; satire; (coll.) gallantry, courtship.

rémora, *f.* (ichth.) sucking fish, remora; hindrance, obstacle; cause of delay.

remordedor, ra, *a.* causing remorse.

remorder. I. *va.* (*ind.* REMUERDO; *subj.* REMUERDA) to bite repeatedly; to cause remorse; to sting, fret. II. *vr.* to show worry or regret.

remordimiento, *m.* remorse.

remosquearse, *vr.* to show suspicion of surroundings; (print.) to be blurred or smeared; to mackle.

remostar. I. *va.* to put must into (old wine). II. *vr.* (of wine) to become sweet.

remostecerse, *vr.* = REMOSTARSE.

remosto, *m.* putting must into old wine; growing sweet.

remotamente, *adv.* remotely; vaguely.

remoto, ta, *a.* remote, far off; unlikely.

remover, *va.* (*ind.* REMUEVO; *subj.* REMUEVA) to move, remove, transfer; to take away; to discharge, dismiss; to stir.

removimiento, *m.* = REMOCIÓN.

remozamiento, *m.* making, appearing or becoming young, rejuvenation.

remozar. I. *va.* to rejuvenate. II. *vr.* to look young.

rempujar, *va.* to push, jostle; to impel; to beat up (game).—**rempujo,** *m.* impulse, push; (naut.) sailmaker's palm.—**rempujón,** *m.* impulse, push.

remuda, *f.* change; replacement; change of clothes.—**r. de caballos,** relay of horses.

remudamiento, *m.* = REMUDA.

remudar, *va.* to move, remove; to change, replace.

remuelo, remuela, *v.* V. REMOLER.

remuerdo, remuerda, *v.* V. REMORDER.

remuevo, remueva, *v.* V. REMOVER.

remugar, *va.* (prov.) = RUMIAR; to ruminate.

remullir, *va.* to beat up again; to soften.

remunerable, *a.* remunerable.

remuneración, *f.* remuneration; gratuity, consideration.

remunerador, ra, *n.* & *a.* remunerator(-ing).

remunerar, *va.* to remunerate.

remuneratorio, ria, *a.* remunerative.

remusgar, *vn.* (coll.) to suspect, presume.

remusgo, *m.* keen cold wind.

renacentista. I. *a.* Renaissant, Renaissance (as *a.*). II. *n.* one versed in Renaissance art and literature.

renacer, *vn.* (*ind.* RENAZCO; *subj.* RENAZCA) to be born again; to spring up again, grow again; to acquire grace by baptism.

renaciente, *a.* renascent, springing anew.

renacimiento, *m.* regeneration; new birth; **(R-)** Renaissance.

renacuajo, *m.* tadpole, polliwog; little, despicable person.

renadío, *m.* crop which, after having been reaped in the blade, sprouts again.

renal, *a.* renal.

renano, na, *a.* Rhenish, Rhine (as *a.*).

renazco, renazca, *v.* V. RENACER.

rencilla, *f.* grudge; heartburning.

rencilloso, sa, *a.* peevish, quarrelsome, touchy.

renco, ca, *a.* lame.

rencor, *m.* rancor, animosity, grudge.

rencorosamente, *adv.* rancorously.

rencoroso, sa, *a.* rancorous, spiteful.

renda, *f.* second dressing of vines.

rendaje, *m.* set of reins or bridles.

rendajo, *m.* (ornith.) mocking-bird; mimic.

rendar, *va.* to dress (vines) a second time.

rendición, *f.* rendition, surrendering, yielding; rent, yield, product, profit.

rendidamente, *adv.* humbly, submissively, compliantly.

rendido, da. I. *pp.* of RENDIR. II. *a.* obsequious, devoted; fatigued, worn out.

rendija, *f.* crevice, crack, cleft.

rendimiento, *m.* weariness, faintness, fatigue; humiliation, submission; obsequiousness, humbling compliance; yield, rent, income; yearly produce; (mech.) efficiency.

rendir. I. *va.* (*ger.* RINDIENDO; *ind pres.* RINDO, *pret.* él RINDIÓ; *subj.* RINDA) to subdue, overcome; to surrender, yield, give up; to render, give back, return, restore; to render, give (thanks), do (homage), etc.; (com.) to produce, yield, bring; to fatigue, tire out; to vomit, throw up.—**r. cuentas**, to give, render, an account (lit. & fig.).—**r. el alma (a Dios)** to die.—**r. el bordo en**, to arrive at.—**r. el puesto**, (mil.) to give up the post, to commit it to another.—**r. gracias**, to give thanks.—**r. la guardia**, to set the watch.—**r. las armas**, to throw down the arms, to surrender.—**r. marea**, to stem the tide.—**r. obsequios**, to pay attention.—**r. parias**, to submit, to pay homage. II. *vr.* to become exhausted, tired, worn out; to yield, submit, give way, give up, surrender; (naut.) to spring (a mast).

renegado, da. I. *pp.* of RENEGAR. II. *n.* renegade; wicked person. III. *m.* ombre (card game).

renegador, ra, *n.* swearer, blasphemer.

renegar. I. *va.* (*ind. pres.* RENIEGO, *pret.* RENE-GUÉ; *subj.* RENIEGUE) to deny, disown; to detest, abhor. II. *vn.* to blaspheme, curse; (**de**) to deny; to blaspheme, curse.

renegón, na, *n.* inveterate swearer.

renegrear, *va.* to blacken intensely.

renegrido, da, *a.* (of bruises) livid, blackish.

rengífero, *m.* (zool.) reindeer.

renglón, *m.* written or printed line; (com.) line of business, staple, item.—**a r. seguido**, immediately after; the next moment.—*pl.* lines, writings.

renglonadura, *f.* ruling of paper; ruled lines.

rengo, ga, *a.* = RENCO, lame.

renguear, *vn.* (Am.) = RENQUEAR.

¹reniego, *m.* curse, execration, blasphemy.

²reniego, reniegue, *v. V.* RENEGAR.

reniforme, *a.* reniform, kidney-shaped.

renil, *a.* barren, as a ewe.

renitencia, *f.* resistance, opposition.

renitente, *a.* renitent, repugnant.

reno, *m.* (zool.) reindeer.

renombrado, da, *a.* renowned, famous.

renombre, *m.* surname, family name; renown, fame.

renovable, *a.* renewable, replaceable.

renovación, *f.* renovation, renewing; change, reform; replacement.

renovador, ra, *n.* & *a.* renovator(-ing); reformer (-ing).

renovante, *a.* renovating, renewing.

renovar, *va.* (*ind.* RENUEVO; *subj.* RENUEVE) to renew; to renovate; to change, replace; to reiterate, republish.

renovero, ra, *n.* usurer, fripper.

renquear, *vn.* to limp, hobble.

renta, *f.* profit; income; rental; (Angl.) (Mex.) (house) rent; annuity; tax, contribution; revenue.—**r. estancada**, revenue tax on monopoly articles.—**a r.**, at a rent.

rentado, da. I. *pp.* of RENTAR. II. *a.* living on an income.

rentar. I. *va.* to produce, bring, yield; (Angl.) (Mex.) to rent for (as *cuánto renta ese cuarto?* how much does that room rent for?). II. *vr.*—**se renta,** (Angl.) (Mex.) (incorrectly used for *se alquila*) to let, for rent.

rentero, *m.* rural tenant; grantee of, or bidder for, a state monopoly.

rentilla, *f. dim.* small income; a card game; a game played with dice.

rentista, *n.* financier; bondholder; annuitant; one who lives on a fixed income.

rentístico, ca, *a.* financial.

rento, *m.* annual rent, rental.

rentoso, sa, *a.* yielding income.

renuencia, *f.* reluctance, unwillingness.

renuente, *a.* unwilling, reluctant.

¹renuevo, *m.* sprout, shoot; RENOVACIÓN.

²renuevo, renueve, *v. V.* RENOVAR.

renuncia, *f.* resignation; renunciation; abjuration; renouncement; waiving.

renunciable, *a.* that can be waived, renounced or resigned; transferable.

renunciación, *f.*; **renunciamiento,** *m.* = RE-NUNCIA.

renunciante, *n.* & *a.* renouncer(-ing), resigner (-ing), waiver(-ing).

renunciar. I. *va.* to renounce, give up; to resign; to disown; to forego, waive; to refuse, reject; to depreciate, abandon, relinquish. II. *vn.* to resign; (cards) to revoke, renege.—**r. a,** to give up, renounce.—**r. a sí mismo,** to give up one's own will or taste.

renunciatario, *m.* one in whose favor something is renounced or resigned.

renuncio, *m.* revoke or renege (at cards); (coll.) error, mistake; contradiction, untruth.

renvalsar, *va.* (carp.) to shave off (doors).

renvalso, *m.* (carp.) shaving off to make fit.

reñidamente, *adv.* stubbornly, strongly.

reñidero, *m.* cockpit; fighting pit or ring.

reñido, da. I. *pp.* of REÑIR. II. *a.* at variance; on bad terms; stubborn, hard-fought.

reñidor, ra, *n.* quarreller; scold.

reñir, *va.* & *vn.* (*ger.* RIÑENDO; *ind. pres.* RIÑO, *pret.* él RIÑÓ; *subj.* RIÑA) to wrangle, quarrel, fight; to fall out; to scold, reprimand, chide.

¹reo, a. I. *a.* guilty, criminal. II. *n.* criminal, culprit; (law) defendant.

²reo, *m.* (ichth.) ray trout.

reóforo, *m.* (elec.) rheophore.

reojo, *m.*—**mirar de r.,** to look askance.

reómetro, *m.* (elec.) rheometer; (hydraul.) water meter.

reordenar, *va.* to rearrange.

reorganización, *f.* reorganization.

reorganizador, ra, *n.* & *a.* reorganizer(-ing).

reorganizar, *va.* (*pret.* REORGANICÉ; *subj.* RE-ORGANICE) to reorganize.

reóstato, *m.* (elec.) rheostat.

repacer, *va.* to consume all the grass of.

repagar, *va.* (*pret.* REPAGUÉ; *subj.* REPAGUE) to repay; to overpay.

repajo, *m.* inclosure for pasture.

repanchigarse, repantigarse, *vr.* to stretch (oneself) in a chair.

repapilarse, *vr.* to glut, stuff oneself.

reparable, *a.* reparable, remediable; objectionable; remarkable; (also *sujeto a ¹reparar*) blameworthy.

reparación, *f.* reparation, repair, repairing, indemnity, amends; atonement.

reparada, *f.* sudden bound of a horse.

reparado, da, *a.* restored; provided.

reparador, ra, *n.* repairer; restorer; carper, faultfinder.

reparamiento, *m.* = REPARO, REPARACIÓN.

¹reparar. I. *va.* to repair; to restore; to observe, notice; to consider, heed; to make up for, indemnify for, make amends for; to expiate, atone for; to give the final touch to.

²reparar. I. *va.* to parry; to defend, protect. II. *vn.* to stop, stay over; (**en**), to stop (at). III. *vr.* to refrain, forbear; (Mex.) to rear on the hind feet.

reparativo, va, *a.* reparative.

¹reparo, *m.* repair, repairing, restoration; remark, observation, advice, warning, notice; difficulty, objection, defect; strengthening poultice for the stomach.—**poner reparos,** to make objections.

²reparo, *m.* defense, protection; (fencing) parry.

reparón, na. I. *n.* & *a.* carper(-ing); faultfinder (-ing). II. *m.* (coll.) great doubt or difficulty.

repartible, *a.* distributable.

repartición, *f.* division, distribution.

repartidamente, *adv.* distributively.

repartidero, ra, *a.* to be distributed.

repartidor. I. *a.* distributing. II. *n.* distributor; assessor of taxes.

repartimiento, *m.* division, distribution, apportionment; assessment; repartimiento (allotment of territory made by the conquerors of Spanish America, or, in the P. I., an assessment of taxes).

For pronunciation, see the rules at the beginning of the book.

repartir, *va.* to divide, distribute, apportion, allot; to assess.

reparto, *m.* REPARTIMIENTO; (theat.) cast of characters; delivery (of goods, mail, etc.).

repasadera, *f.* (carp.) finishing plane.

repasadora, *f.* woman that cards wool.

repasar, *va.* to repass, pass again; to reëxamine, check; to revise; to scan, peruse, glance over; to review, study again (as a lesson); to clean (dyed wool) for carding; to mend (clothes); (min.) to remix (mercury) with metal.

repasata, *f.* (coll.) severe chiding, dressing down.

repaso, *m.* review (of a lesson); revision, reëxamination; final inspection, finishing; mending (of clothes); (min.) remixing quicksilver with metal; (coll.) reprimand, dressing down.

repastar, *va.* to pasture or feed again.

repasto, *m.* increase of feed.

repatriación, *f.* repatriation, returning to one's country.

repatriar, *va.* to return to one's country, repatriate.

repechar, *vn.* to go up hill.

repecho, *m.* short steep incline.—**a r.,** up hill.

repelada, *f.* salad of herbs.

repeladura, *f.* restripping; second clipping or cropping.

repelar, *va.* to pull out the hair of; to put (a horse) to his speed; to nip, nibble, browse; to clip, crop, lop off.

repelente, *a.* repellent.

repeler, *va.* to repel, repulse; to refute, dispute.

repelo, *m.* anything that rises or goes against the grain; cross fiber; crooked grain; (coll.) slight scuffle or dispute; aversion.

repelón, *m.* pulling out the hair; small part torn from anything; loose thread in stockings; (of a horse) short gallop.—**a repelones,** by degrees, little by little.—**de r.,** by the way; in haste.

repeloso, sa, *a.* (of wood) of a bad grain; touchy, peevish.

repellar, *va.* (mason.) to dub out.

repensar, *va.* (*ind.* REPIENSO; *subj.* REPIENSE) to reconsider, think over.

repente, *m.* sudden movement or impulse.—**de r.,** suddenly.

repentinamente, *adv.* suddenly.

repentino, na, *a.* sudden.

repentista, *n.* improviser, extemporizer.

repen'izar, *va.* (*pret.* REPENTICÉ; *subj.* REPENTICE) to improvise, extemporize.

repentón, *m.* sudden movement.

repeor, *a.* & *adv.* much worse.

repercudida, *f.* repercussion, rebound.

repercudir, *vn.* to rebound.

repercusión, *f.* repercussion, reverberation.

repercusivo, va, *a.* repercussive; repellent.

repercutir. I. *vn.* to rebound; to reëcho, reverberate. **II.** *va.* (med.) to repel.

repertorio, *m.* repertory, repertoire.

repesar, *va.* to weigh again.—**repeso,** *m.* reweigh; weight office; charge for reweighing.

repetición, *f.* repetition; repeater (of timepiece); collegial dissertation, thesis; (theat.) encore; (art) replica; (law) action for an accounting.

repetidamente, *adv.* repeatedly.

repetidor, ra. I. *a.* repeating. **II.** *n.* repeater (teacher or student).

repetir. I. *va.* (*ger.* REPITIENDO; *ind. pres.* REPITO, *pret.* él REPITIÓ; *subj.* REPITA) to repeat; to recite, rehearse; (art) to make a replica of; (law) to claim, demand. **II.** *vn.* to repeat; to read a thesis in a university. **III.** *vr.* to repeat oneself.

repicar. I. *va.* (*pret.* REPIQUÉ; *subj.* REPIQUE) to chop, hash, mince; to ring (bells); to reprick; (in piquet) to repique. **II.** *vr.* to glory· boast, flatter oneself.

repienso, repiense, *v. V.* REPENSAR.

repinarse, *vr.* to soar, rise.

repintar. I. *va.* to repaint. **II.** *vr.* to paint, make up; (print.) to set off, mackle, double.

repique, *m.* chopping, mincing; peal, ringing (of bells); dispute, altercation; (in piquet) repique.

repiquete, *m.* merry peal or ringing of bells; chance, opportunity.

repiquetear. I. *va.* to ring (bells) merrily. **II.** *vr.* to bicker, wrangle, quarrel.

repiqueteo, *m.* ringing of bells.

repisa, *f.* mantelpiece; shelf, console; bracket.

repiso, *m.* weak, inferior wine.

repitiente, *a.* repeating.

repito, repitió, etc., *v. V.* REPETIR.

repizcar, *va.* to pinch.—**repizco,** *m.* pinch.

replantar, *va.* to replant.

replantear, *va.* to restate (a problem); (eng.) to lay out on the ground.

replanteo, *m.* laying out on the ground the plan of a structure.

repleción, *f.* repletion.

replegable, *a.* folding.

replegar. I. *va.* (reg. in this meaning) to fold several times. **II.** *vr.* (*ind. pres.* REPLIEGO, *pret.* REPLEGUÉ; *subj.* REPLIEGUE) (mil.) to fall back, retreat in order.

repleto, ta, *a.* replete, very full.

réplica, *f.* reply, answer; repartee; objection.

replicador, ra, *n.* replier, disputant.

replicante, *n.* & *a.* replier(-ing), respondent(-ing).

replicar. I. *vn.* (*pret.* REPLIQUÉ; *subj.* REPLIQUE) to reply, answer; to contradict, argue. **II.** *va.* (law) to answer (a defendant's plea).

replicato, *m.* objection; (law) reply, answer.

replicón, na, *n.* (coll.) disputer, arguer.

repliego, ¹repliegue, *v. V.* REPLEGARSE.

²repliegue, *m.* doubling, folding; fold, crease, convolution.

repoblación, *f.* repopulation.

repoblar, *va.* (*ind.* REPUEBLO; *subj.* REPUEBLE) ro repopulate, repeople.

repodrir, *va.* & *vr.* = REPUDRIR.

repollar, *vn.* to head (as a cabbage).

repollo, *m.* cabbage; round head (of a plant).

repolludo, da, *a.* cabbage-headed; round-headed.

repolluelo, *m. dim.* small cabbage, sprout.

reponer. I. *va.* (*pp.* REPUESTO; *ind. pres.* REPONGO, *pret.* REPUSE, *fut.* REPONDRÉ; *subj.* REPONGA) to replace, put back; to reinstate, reinstall; to restore; to answer, to reply; (law) to restore (a case) to its primitive state. **II.** *vr.* to recover lost health or property.

reportación, *f.* moderation, calm.

reportado, da, *pp.* & *a.* moderate, calm.

reportaje, *m.* (journalism) report, reporting.

reportamiento, *m.* forbearance, restraint.

reportar. I. *va.* to control, restrain, check; to obtain, get, attain; to carry; to bring. **II.** *vr.* to refrain, forbear, control oneself.

reporte, *m.* report, information, news; lithographic proof.

repórter, *n.* (Angl.) (Am.) reporter.

reporteril, *a.* reportorial.

reporterismo, *m.* newspaper reporting; body of reporters, reporters collectively.

reportero, ra, *n.* reporter.

reportorio, *m.* almanac, calendar.

reposadamente, *adv.* peaceably, quietly.

reposadero, *m.* (metal.) trough for receiving melted metal.

reposado, da, *pp.* & *a.* quiet, peaceful, calm.

reposar. I. *vn.* to rest, repose; to stand (on), be supported (by); to take a nap; to lie down; to lie (in the grave). **II.** *vr.* to settle (as liquids).

reposición, *f.* replacement, reinstatement; recovery (in health); (law) restoring a suit to its primitive state; (chem.) preservation of liquids in proper vessels.

repositorio, *m.* repository.

reposo, *m.* rest, repose; sleep; tranquillity.

repostarse, *vr.* (Am.) to lay in stock.

reposte, m. pantry, larder.
repostería, f. confectionery, pastry shop; pantry, larder, plate room.
repostero, m. king's butler; pastry cook; covering ornamented with a coat of arms.
repregunta, f. (law) cross-examination.
repreguntar, va. (law) to cross-examine.
reprender, va. to reprehend, scold, reproach.
reprendiente, a. censuring, reprimanding.
reprensible, a. reprehensible.
reprensión, f. reprehension, reprimand, reproach.
reprensor, ra, n. reprehender, reproacher.
represa, f. dam, dike, sluice, lock; damming, impounding; stopping, holding back; (naut.) recapture.
represalia, f. reprisal.
represar, va. (naut.) to recapture, retake from the enemy; to bank, dam, impound; to stop, detain, retain; to repress, restrain, check.
representable, a. representable.
representación, f. representation; description; statement; (theat.) performance, production; figure, image, idea; address, petition; authority, capacity; (law) right of succession.—**en r. de,** as a representative of.
representador, ra. I. a. representing. II. n. player, actor.
representante. I. a. representing, representative. II. n. representative; agent; actor.
representar. I. va. to represent; to state, declare; to express; (theat.) to perform, act. II. vr. to image, picture to oneself, conceive.
representativo, va, a. representative.
represión, f. repression, check, control.
represivo, va, a. repressive, restrictive.
reprimenda, f. reprimand.
reprimir, va. to repress, check, curb.
reprobable, a. reprehensible.
reprobación, f. reprobation.
reprobadamente, adv. reprovably.
reprobado, da. I. pp. of REPROBAR. II. a. RÉPROBO; not passed in an examination.
reprobador, ra, n. reprover, condemner.
reprobar, va. (ind. REPRUEBO; subj. REPRUEBE) to reprove, disapprove, condemn; to damn; not to pass (in an examination) (coll.) to flunk.
reprobatorio, ria, a. reprobative.
réprobo, ba, n. & a. reprobate.
reprochar, va. to reproach; to challenge (witnesses), reject, exclude.
reproche, m. reproach, reproof; repulse, rebuff, rebuke.
reproducción, f. (biol.) reproduction; (art) copy, reproduction; reproduction (of sound, etc.).
reproducir, va. (ind. pres. REPRODUZCO, pret. REPRODUJE; subj. REPRODUZCA) to reproduce.
reproductible, a. reproducible.
reproductividad, f. reproductiveness.
reproductivo, va, a. reproductive.
reproductor, ra, n. & a. reproducer(-ing); breeder(-ing).
reproduje, reproduzco, etc. v. V. REPRODUCIR.
repromisión, f. repeated promise.
repropiarse, vr. (of horses) to get unruly.
repropio, pia, a. (of horses) unruly.
reprueba, f. new proof.
repruebo, repruebe, v. V. REPROBAR.
reptil, m. reptile; crawler, creeper.
república, f. republic.
republicanismo, m. republicanism.
republicano, na, n. & a. republican.
república, m. prominent man; patriot; statesman.
repudiación, f. repudiation.
repudiar, va. to repudiate; to divorce.
repudio, m. repudiation; divorce.
repudrir. I. va. & vr. to rot completely. II. vr. (coll.) to pine away.
repuesto, ta. I. pp. irreg. of REPONER. II. a. retired, secluded; recovered. III. m. store, stock, supply; sideboard, cupboard; dresser; pantry,

larder; money staked in the game of ombre.—**de r.,** extra; spare.
repugnancia, f. reluctance, repugnance; aversion; loathing; disgust; opposition, contradiction, contrariety.
repugnante, a. repugnant, reluctant; loathsome; repulsive, disgusting.
repugnar, va. to oppose, contradict, conflict with; to cause disgust; to do with reluctance.
repujado, m. repoussé (work or article).
repujar, va. to make repoussé work on.
repulgado, a. affected.
repulgar, va. (pret. REPULGUÉ; subj. REPULGUE) (sewing) to hem; to border; to put an edging on (pastry).
repulgo, m. (sewing) hem, border; external ornament of a cake or pie; ridiculous scruple.
repulido, da, pp. & a. prim, neat, spruce.
repulir. I. va. to repolish. II. va. & vr. to dress affectedly.
repulsa, f. refusal, rebuke, repulse.
repulsar, va. to reject, repel, decline, refuse.
repulsión, f. REPULSA; repulsion.
repulsivo, va, a. repelling.
repullo, m. jump, start, shock; small arrow or dart.
repunta, f. point, cape, headland; first manifestation or sign; disagreement, dispute.
repuntar. I. vn. to begin to appear; to begin to ebb. II. va. (Am.) to collect, round up (animals). III. vr. to be on the turn (wine); to be soured; to be displeased with one another.
repunte, m. (naut.) beginning of the ebb or of the flow; (Am.) collecting, rounding up.
repurgar, va. (pret. REPURGUÉ; subj. REPURGUE) to clean or purify again.
repuse, pret. of REPONER.
reputación, f. reputation.
reputante, n. appraiser, estimator.
reputar, va. to repute; to estimate, appreciate.
requebrador, m. gallant, wooer, suitor.
requebrar, va. (ind. REQUIEBRO; subj. REQUIEBRE) to woo, court, make love to; to flatter, wheedle; to break again.
requemado, a. I. pp. of REQUEMAR. II. a. brown, sunburnt. III. m. a kind of black fabric.
requemamiento, m. = RESQUEMO.
requemar. I. va. to reburn; to overcook, cook too much; to parch; to inflame (the blood or humors); to bite, smart (as mustard). II. vr. to burn with passion; to be deeply in love.
requemazón, f. = RESQUEMO.
requeridor, ra, n. summons server; courter, suiter; inspector.
requerimiento, m. summons; requisition, demand.
requerir, va. (ger. REQUIRIENDO; ind. pres. REQUIERO, pret. él REQUIRIÓ; subj. REQUIERA) to summon; to notify; to investigate, examine; to require, need; to court, woo, make love to (also **r. de amores**); to induce, persuade.
requesón, m. pot cheese, cottage cheese; curd.
requetebién, adv. (coll.) very well (or good), fine, as good as could be.
¹**requiebro,** m. flattery, compliment; endearing expression, love tale; (min.) crushed ore.
²**requiebro, requiebre,** v. V. REQUEBRAR.
requiero, requiera, v. V. REQUERIR.
requilorios, m. (coll.) useless ceremony; circumlocution.
requintador, ra, n. outbidder.
requintar, va. to outbid by a fifth part of the price of; to exceed, surpass; (mus.) to raise or lower five points.
requinto, m. second fifth taken from a quantity; advance of a fifth in bidding; (S. A.) extraordinary impost levied under Philip II; (mus.) fife and its player; a small guitar.
requiriente, m. & f. summoner; summons server; courter, suitor.

requirió, *pret.* of REQUERIR.

requisa, *f.* tour of inspection, round; (mil.) requisition of horses.

requisar, *va.* to inspect, make the rounds of; (mil.) to requisition (horses).

requisición, *f.* (mil.) requisition of horses.

requisito, *m.* requisite, requirement.

requisitorio, ria. I. *a.* requisitory. **II.** *f.* (law) requisition.

requive, *m.* = ARREQUIVE, dress trimmings.

res, *f.* head of cattle; beast.—**r. de vientre,** breeding cow (or any other breeding female).

resaber, *va.* (*ind. pres.* RESÉ, *pret.* RESUPE, *fut.* RESABRÉ; *subj.* RESEPA) to know very well.

resabiar. I. *va.* to cause to contract bad habits. **II.** *vr.* to contract bad habits; to become vicious; to be discontented, dissatisfied; to relish.

resabido, da, *a.* affecting learning.

resabio, *m.* unpleasant aftertaste; viciousness; bad habit.

resabioso, sa, *a.* (Am.) vicious; peevish, ill-tempered.

resaca, *f.* (naut.) surge, surf, undertow; (com.) redraft.

resacar, *va.* (naut.) to underrun, haul; (com.) to redraw.

resalado, da, *a.* (coll.) very attractive, charming, magnetic.

resalir, *vn.* (*ind. pres.* RESALGO, *fut.* RESALDRÉ; *subj.* RESALGA) to jut out, project.

resaltar, *vn.* to rebound; to come off, get loose; to jut out, project; to stand out; to be evident.—**r. a la vista,** to be self-evident.

resalte, resalto, *m.* rebound; protuberance, projection; (Ry.) superelevation (of outer rail).

resaludar, *vn.* to return a salute or greeting.

resalutación, *f.* return of a salute or greeting.

resalvo, *m.* tiller, sapling.

resallar, *va.* (agr.) to weed again.

resallo, *m.* (agr.) reweeding.

resanar, *va.* to regild defective spots in.

resarcible, *a.* indemnifiable.

resarcimiento, *m.* compensation, reparation, indemnity.

resarcir, *va.* (*ind.* RESARZO; *subj.* RESARZA) to compensate, indemnify, make amends to; to mend, repair.

resbaladero, ra. I. *a.* slippery; elusive. **II.** *m.* slippery place.

resbaladizo, za, *a.* slippery; glib; elusive; tempting, alluring.

resbalador, ra, *n.* slider; backslider.

resbaladura, *f.* slip, slide; backsliding.

resbalamiento, *m.* slipping; skidding.—**r. de ala,** (aer.) sideslip(-ping).—**r. de cola,** (aer.) tail slide.

resbalante, *n.* & *a.* slider(-ing), slipper(-ing).

resbalar, *vn.* & *vr.* to slip, slide, glide; to skid; to err, go astray.—**resbalo,** *m.* (Am.) steep slope.

resbalón, *m.* slip, slipping; fault, error, break.

resbaloso, sa, *a.* slippery.

rescaldar, *va.* to heat, to scorch.

rescatador, ra, *n.* redeemer, ransomer.

rescatar, *va.* to ransom; to redeem, recover; to rescue; to exchange, barter, commute; (Am.) to buy (ore) in mines.

rescate, *m.* ransom; redemption; ransom money; exchange, barter.

rescatín, *m.* (Am.) buyer of ore from Indians.

rescaza, *f.* = ESCORPINA, (ichth.) grouper.

rescindir, *va.* to rescind, annul, cancel.

rescisión, *f.* rescission, cancellation, annulment.

rescisorio, ria, *a.* rescissory, rescinding.

rescoldera, *f.* pyrosis, heartburn.

rescoldo, *m.* embers, hot ashes; scruple, doubt, apprehension.

rescontrar, *va.* to offset, set off.

rescripto, *m.* rescript, order, mandate.

rescriptorio, ria, *a.* rescriptive.

rescuentro, *m.* offset, compensation.

resecación, *f.* drying up, desiccation.

resecar, *va.* & *vr.* (*pret.* RESEQUÉ; *subj.* RESEQUE) to dry thoroughly, exsiccate, desiccate.

resección, *f.* (surg.) resection.

reseco, ca. I. *a.* thoroughly dry, too dry; very lean. **II.** *m.* drying up of trees or shrubs; dry part of a honeycomb.

reseda, *f.* (bot.) mignonette, reseda; woad.

resedáceo, a. I. *a.* (bot.) resedaceous. **II.** *f. pl.* Resedaceæ.

resegar, *va.* (*ind. pres.* RESIEGO, *pret.* RESEGUÉ; *subj.* RESIEGUE) to mow again.

reseguir, *va.* (*ger.* RESIGUIENDO; *ind. pres.* RESIGO, *pret.* él RESIGUIÓ; *subj.* RESIGA) to edge (swords).

resellante, *a.* recoining, restamping.

resellar, *va.* to recoin; to countermark.

resello, *m.* recoinage; surcharge.

resembrar, *va.* (*ind.* RESIEMBRO; *subj.* RESIEMBRE) to resow.

resentido, da, *pp.* & *a.* offended; resentful.

resentimiento, *m.* resentment, grudge; impairment.

resentirse, *vr.* (*ind. pres.* me RESIENTO, *pret.* él se RESINTIÓ; *subj.* me RESIENTA) to be impaired or weakened; to resent, be offended or hurt.

reseña, *f.* brief description, narration, or review; sketch; signal; signalment; (mil.) review.

reseñar, *va.* to make a brief description of, sketch, outline; (mil.) to review.

resequé, reseque, *v.* V. RESECAR.

resequido, da, *a.* dried up, parched.

reserva, *f.* reserve, reticence; reservation, exception; discretion, circumspection, prudence; modesty; (law) reservation; (mil.) reserve.—**r. mental,** mental reservation.—**a r. de,** intending to.—**de r.,** extra, spare, in reserve.—**en r.,** in reserve; confidentially.—**guardar r.,** to be discreet, act with discretion.—**sin r.,** openly, freely.

reservación, *f.* reservation.

reservadamente, *adv.* secretly; confidentially.

reservado, da. I. *pp.* of RESERVAR. **II.** *a.* reserved; cautious, prudent; private, confidential. **III.** *m.* (eccl.) Eucharist kept in the ciborium.

reservar. I. *va.* to reserve, keep; to retain, hold; to defer, postpone; to exempt; to conceal, keep secret. **II.** *vr.* to bide one's time; to keep for oneself; to beware, be cautious.

reservativo, va, *a.* reservative.

reservista, *m.* (mil.) reservist.

resfriado, *m.* cold (illness); watering before tilling.

resfriador, ra. I. *a.* cooling, refrigerating. **II.** *m.* refrigerator.

resfriadura, *f.* (vet.) cold in horses.

resfriamiento, *m.* = ENFRIAMIENTO, cooling.

resfriante. I. *a.* cooling, refrigerating. **II.** *m.* = CORBATO, cooler (in a still).

resfriar. I. *va.* to cool, chill; to moderate (ardor, fervor). **II.** *vn.* to begin to be cold. **III.** *vr.* to catch cold; to grow cold or indifferent.

resfrío, *m.* cold (illness).

resguardar. I. *va.* to preserve, defend, protect. **II.** *vr.* to take shelter; (**de**) to guard (against); protect oneself (from).

resguardo, *m.* preservation, security, safety; guard, defense, protection; (com.) security, guarantee, collateral, voucher; watchfulness to prevent smuggling; body of custom house officers for such service; (naut.) sea room, wide berth.

residencia, *f.* residence, domicile, abode; dwelling, home; stay, sojourn; (eccl.) residence; (diplomacy) function of a resident minister; (S. A.) (Sp. colonial hist.) (also *juicio de r.*) impeachment.

residencial, *a.* residentiary.

residenciar, *va.* (law) (S. A.) (Sp. colonial hist.) to impeach; to call to account.

residente. I. *a.* residing, resident, residential. **II.** *m.* (diplomacy) resident minister; (eccl.) residencer; dweller, inhabitant.

residentemente, *adv.* constantly, assiduously.

residir, *vn.* to reside, live, dwell; to be in official residence; to inhere.

residual, *a.* residual.

residuo, *m.* remainder, remnant; (chem.) residuum, residue; (arith.) difference; remainder.

resiego, resiegue, *v.* V. RESEGAR.

resiembra, *f.* (agr.) resowing.

resiembro, resiembre, *v.* V. RESEMBRAR.

resiento, resienta, *v.* V. RESENTIRSE.

resigna, *f.* (eccl.) resignation.

resignación, *f.* resignation; submission.

resignadamente, *adv.* resignedly.

resignante, *n.* & *a.* resigner(-ing).

resignar. I. *va.* to resign, give up. **II.** *vr.* to resign oneself, be resigned.

resignatario, *m.* resignee.

resigo, resiga, etc., *v.* V. RESEGUIR.

resina, *f.* resin, rosin.—**resinar,** *va.* to draw resin from.—**resinero, ra. I.** *a.* pert. to resin. **II.** *n.* one engaged in the resin business.—**resinífero, ra,** *a.* resinferous.—**resinoso, sa,** *a.* resinous.

resintió, *pret.* of RESENTIRSE.

resisar, *va.* to diminish (measures) further.

resistencia, *f.* resistance, endurance; strength; (mech. and elec.) resistance.—**r. de materiales,** strength (*formerly* resistance) of materials.

resistente, *a.* strong; resisting, opposing.

resistero, *m.* hottest part of the day; heat produced by the sun's glare; place where such heat is felt.

resistible, *a.* resistible, endurable.

resistidero, *m.* = RESISTERO.

resistidor, ra, *n.* resister, repeller.

resistir. I. *vn.* & *vr.* to resist, offer resistance. **II.** *va.* to resist; to bear, stand; to endure.

resma, *f.* ream of paper.

resmilla, *f.* four quires of letter paper.

resobrar, *vn.* to be much over and above.

resobrino, na, *n.* grandnephew(-niece).

resol, *m.* sun's glare.

resolano, na. I. *a.* sunny. **II.** *f.* sunny place.

resolubie, *a.* solvable, that can be solved.

resolución, *f.* resolution; resoluteness; determination, courage, firmness; solution (of a problem); conclusiveness; quickness, promptitude; (law) lapse, nullification; (med.) resolution.—**en r.,** in short, in a word.

resolutivamente, *adv.* resolutely.

resolutivo, va. I. *a.* analytical. **II.** *m.* (med.) resolutive.

resoluto, ta, *a.* resolute, daring; compendious, brief; skillful, able.

resolutoriamente, *adv.* resolutely.

resolutorio, ria, *a.* resolute; resolutory.

resolvente, *a.* resolvent, resolving.

resolver. I. *va.* (*pp.* RESUELTO; *ind.* RESUELVO; *subj.* RESUELVA) to resolve, determine; to sum up; to solve (a problem); to dissolve, analyze; to dissipate; to undo, destroy, annul; to resolve, divide. **II.** *vr.* to resolve, determine; to dissolve; (med.) to resolve.

resolladero, *m.* vent, air-hole.

resollar, *vn.* (*ind.* RESUELLO; *subj.* RESUELLE) to breathe noisily (as an animal); (coll.) to breathe; (coll.) to show up; to break silence.

resonación, *f.* resounding.

resonador, *m.* resonator.

resonancia, *f.* resonance.—**tener r.,** to be bruited abroad, to attract attention.

resonante, *a.* resonant, resounding.

resonar, *vn.* (*ind.* RESUENO; *subj.* RESUENE) to resound, echo, clink, clatter.

resoplar, *vn.* to breathe audibly; to snort.

resoplido, resoplo, *m.* audible breathing; snorting.

resorber, *va.* to sip again, reabsorb.

resorcina, *f.* (chem.) resorcinol.

resorción, *f.* reabsorption.

resorte, *m.* (mech.) spring; resilience, spring, elasticity; means, resources.

respailando, *adv.* precipitately, in a great rush.

respailar, *va.* (coll.) to move helter-skelter.

¹respaldar. I. *va.* to indorse; to back; to answer for, guarantee. **II.** *vr.* to lean back; to get backing or support; (vet.) to dislocate the backbone.

²respaldar, *m.* back of a seat.

respaldo, *m.* back of a seat; leaning stock; backing; back of a sheet of paper; indorsement.

respectar, *vn. impers.* to concern, regard.

respectivamente, respective, *adv.* respectively.

respectivo, va, *a.* respective.

respecto, *m.* relation, proportion; relativeness; respect.—**r. a,** or **de,** with respect to, with regard to.—**a este r.,** with respect to this.—**al r.,** relatively, respectively.—**con r. a** = R. A.

respeluzar, *va.* to make the hair stand on end (through fright).

respetabilidad, *f.* respectability.

respetable, *a.* respectable, considerable; worthy; honorable, reliable.

respetador, ra, *n.* respecter.

respetar. I. *va.* to respect, revere, honor. **II.** *vn. impers.* = RESPECTAR.

respetivo, va, *a.* respectful.

respeto, *m.* respect; attention; observance.—**de r.,** extra, spare; for ceremony's sake; dressed or arranged and decorated ceremoniously.—**faltar al r. a,** to be disrespectful to; to molest (a woman).

respetuosamente, *adv.* respectfully.

respetuoso, sa, *a.* respectful; dutiful; respectable, honorable.

réspice, *m.* (coll.) short, pert reply; sharp reproof, dressing down.

respigador, ra, *n.* gleaner.

respigar, *va.* (*pret.* RESPIGUÉ; *subj.* RESPIGUE) to glean.

respigón, *m.* hangnail; (vet.) sore on horse's heel.

respingada, *a.* turned up, retroussé (nose).

respingar, *vn.* (*pret.* RESPINGUÉ; *subj.* RESPINGUE) to kick, wince; to grunt; (coll.) to mutter; to talk back.—**respingo,** *m.* muttering, grumbling; gesture of unwillingness.—**respingón, na,** *n.* & *a.* (Am.) grunter(-ing), grumbler(-ing). —**respingona,** *a.* (coll.) = RESPINGADA.

respirable, *a.* breathable.

respiración, *f.* respiration, breathing; ventilation.—**faltarle a uno la r.,** (diff. constr.) to get short of breath.

respiradero, *m.* vent, air hole; ventilator; (arch.) air passage, louver; (surg.) cupping glass; rest, repose; organ of respiration.

respirador, ra, *a.* breathing.

respirante, *a.* breathing, exhaling.

respirar. I. *vn.* & *va.* to breathe. **II.** *vn.* to rest, take rest or respite; to get breath; to breathe freely; to exhale scents or odors; to speak (used with a negative: *no respiró,* he did not open his lips).

respiratorio, ria, *a.* respiratory.

respiro, *m.* breathing; moment of rest; respite; (com.) extension, time.

resplandecer, *vn.* to glitter, glisten, shine.

resplandeciente. I. *pres. p.* of RESPLANDECER. **II.** *a.* resplendent, bright; luminous, light.

resplandecimiento, *m.* = RESPLANDOR.

resplandina, *f.* (coll.) sharp reproof, dressing down.

resplandor, *m.* light, splendor, brilliancy, radiance; glare; brilliant make-up for women.

respondedor, ra, *n.* answerer.

responder, *va.* & *vn.* to answer, reply; to respond; to reëcho; to acknowledge; to requite; to yield, produce; to have the desired effect; (com.) to correspond; *vn.* (**de**) to answer (for), be responsible (for), vouch (for), guarantee.

respondiente, *a.* respondent; answering.

respondón, na, *a.* saucy, pert.

responsabilidad, *f.* responsibility; reliability.

responsable, *a.* responsible; reliable.

responsar, responsear, *vn.* (eccl.) to repeat the responses.

responso, *m.* (eccl.) responsory for the dead.

responsorio, *m.* (eccl.) responsory.

respuesta, *f.* answer, reply; response; repartee.

resquebradura, *f.* crack, cleft, flaw, split, crevice, fissure.

resquebrajadizo, za, *a.* easily cracked; chinky.

resquebrajadura, *f.* = RESQUEBRADURA.

resquebrajar, *va. & vr.* to crack, to split.

resquebrajo, *m.* crack, cleft, split, fissure.

resquebrajoso, sa, *a.* easily cracked; chinky.

resquebrar, *vn.* (*ind.* RESQUIEBRO; *subj.* RESQUIEBRE) to crack, split; to burst.

resquemar, *va. & vn.* to bite or sting (as mustard).

resquemazón, *f.;* **resquemo, resquemor,** *m.,* (of food) pungency; disagreeable taste of burnt food; burning passion; stinging, pricking, remorse.

resquicio, *m.* chink, slit, crevice, crack, cleft; chance, opportunity.

resquiebro, resquiebre, *v.* V. RESQUEBRAR.

resta, *f.* (arith.) subtraction; remainder, difference.

restablecer. I. *va.* (*ind.* RESTABLEZCO; *subj.* RESTABLEZCA) to restore, reëstablish, reinstate. **II.** *vr.* to recover, recuperate.

restablecimiento, *m.* reëstablishment; restoration; recovery.

restablezco, restablezca, *v.* V. RESTABLECER.

restallar, *vn.* to crack, as a whip; to crackle, crack, squeak.

restante, *a. & m.* remainder(-maining).

restañadero, *m.* inlet; estuary.

restañadura, *f.* retinning.

¹**restañar,** *va.* to retin, tin anew.

²**restañar,** *vn.* = RESTALLAR.

³**restañar. I.** *va.* to stanch, stop the flow of (blood). **II.** *vr.* to stagnate, stand without flow.

restañasangre, *f.* bloodstone.

¹**restaño,** *m.* stagnation.

²**restaño,** *m.* cloth of gold or silver.

restar. I. *va.* to deduct; to return (a ball), strike (it) back; (arith.) to subtract. **II.** *vn.* to be left, remain; (arith.) to subtract.

restauración, *f.* restoration; restoring; repairing, refurbishing.

restaurador, ra, *n. & a.* restorer(-ing).

restaurante, *n. & a.* restorer(-ing); *m.* (also Am. **restaurant**) restaurant.

restaurar, *va.* to restore, retrieve; to repair, renew, refurbish.

restaurativo, va, *n. & a.* restorative.

restinga, *f.* shoal, bar; ledge of rocks.

restingar, *m.* place full of rocks or bars.

restitución, *f.* restitution.

restituíble, *a.* restorable, returnable.

restituidor, ra, *n.* restorer, refunder.

restituir. I. *va.* (*ger.* RESTITUYENDO; *ind. pres.* RESTITUYO, *pret.* él RESTITUYÓ; *subj.* RESTITUYA) to restore, return, give back; to refund; to repair. **II.** *vr.* to return to the place of departure.

restitutorio, ria, *a.* (law) restitutive.

restituyo, etc. *v.* V. RESTITUIR.

resto, *m.* remainder, balance, rest; limit for stakes at cards; returning the ball; player who returns the ball on its rebound.—*pl.* remains.—**a r. abierto,** unlimitedly.—**echar el r.,** to stake one's all; to do one's best.

restorán, *m.* (Am.) = RESTAURANTE, *m.*

restregadura, *f.,* **restregamiento,** *m.* hard rubbing.

restregar, *va.* (*ind. pres.* RESTRIEGO, *pret.* RESTREGUÉ; *subj.* RESTRIEGUE) to rub, scrub.

restregón, *m.* scrubbing, hard rubbing.

restribar, *vn.* to lean upon heavily.

restricción, *f.* restriction, limitation.

restrictivamente, *adv.* restrictively.

restrictivo, va, *a.* restrictive, restricting.

restricto, ta, *a.* limited, confined; restricted.

restriego, restriegue, *v.* V. RESTREGAR.

restringa, *f.* = RESTINGA.

restringente, *n. & a.* restrainer(-ing).

restringible, *a.* restrainable, limitable.

restringir, *va.* (*ind.* RESTRINJO; *subj.* RESTRINJA) to restrain, restrict, limit, confine; to contract, astringe.

restriñidor, ra, *n. & a.* restrainer(-ing); binder (-ing), constipating.

restriñimiento, *m.* costiveness, constipation.

restriñir, *va.* to bind; to contract; to constipate.

restrojo, *m.* = RASTROJO, stubble.

resucitador, ra, *n.* restorer, reviver.

resucitar. I. *va.* to resurrect, raise from the dead; to resuscitate, revive; to renovate, modernize. **II.** *vn.* to rise from the dead, return to life.

resudación, *f.* slight perspiration.

resudar, *vn.* to perspire slightly.

resudor, *m.* slight perspiration.

resueltamente, *adv.* resolutely.

resuelto, ta. I. *pp. irreg.* of RESOLVER. **II.** *a.* resolute, daring; determined; prompt, quick, diligent.

resuelvo, resuelva, *v.* V. RESOLVER.

¹**resuello, resuelle,** *v.* V. RESOLLAR.

²**resuello,** *m.* breath, breathing.—**sin r.,** breathless, panting.

resueno, resuene, *v.* V. RESONAR.

resulta, *f.* result, effect, consequence; resolution; vacancy of an office.—**de resultas,** in consequence.

resultado, *m.* result.

resultancia, *f.* result.

resultando, *m.* substantiating fact or statement; paragraph beginning with "whereas."

resultante. I. *a.* resulting; (mech.) resultant (force, velocity, etc.). **II.** *f.* (mech.) resultant.

resultar, *vn.* to result, follow; to turn out; to be; to come out; (coll.) to work (well or badly), to lead to the desired result, to be advantageous.

resumbruno, na, *a.* brown (hawk's feathers).

resumen, *m.* summary, abstract, résumé.—**en r.,** in brief, in short, to sum up.

resumidamente, *adv.* briefly, summarily.

resumido, da. I. *pp.* of RESUMIR. **II.** *a.* abridged.—**en resumidas cuentas,** in short, briefly, getting down to brass tacks.

resumir. I. *va.* to abridge, abstract, sum up; to repeat. **II.** *vr.* to be reduced or transformed.

resurgimiento, *m.* reappearance, springing up again.

resurgir, *vn.* to reappear, arise or spring up again.

resurrección, *f.* resurrection.

resurtida, *f.* rebound, repercussion.

resurtir, *vn.* to rebound, fly back.

retablo, *m.* series of historical pictures; (eccl.) retable, altarpiece.

retacar, *va.* (billiards) to hit (the ball) twice.

retacería, *f.* collection of remnants, as for a crazy quilt.

retaco, *m.* short, light fowling piece; (billiards, etc.) short cue; short, heavy-built person.

retador, ra, *n.* challenger.

retaguardia, *f.* rear, rear guard.—**a r.,** in the rear.—**picar la r.,** to pursue the rear guard closely, to harass it.

retahíla, *f.* long file, string, series, line.

retajar, *va.* to cut round; to cut the nib of (a quill); to circumcise.

retal, *m.* remnant, piece, clipping.

¹**retallar,** *vn.* to shoot or sprout anew.

²**retallar,** *va.* to regrave, retouch (a graving); (arch.) to form a ²RETALLO in.

retallecer, *vn.* to sprout again.

¹**retallo,** *m.* new sprout.

²**retallo,** *m.* (arch.) projection or ledge.

retama, *f.* (bot.) genista.—**r. de escobas** = R. NEGRA.—**r. de olor** = R. MACHO.—**r. de tintes,** or **de tintoreros,** (bot.) dyeweed, dyer's broom. —**r. macho,** Spanish broom.—**r. negra,** (bot.) furze, whin.

retamal, retamar, *m.* place where furze or broom grows.

retamero, ra, *a.* broomy, furzy.

retar, *va.* to challenge, dare.

retardación, *f.* retardation; delay.

retardado, da. I. *pp.* of RETARDAR. **II.** *a.* (mentally) retarded.

retardar. I. *va.* to retard, slacken; to delay, detain. **II.** *vr.* (of timepiece) to be slow.

retardatriz, *a.* retardative.

retardo, *m.* retardation; delay, procrastination.

retasa, retasación, *f.* reappraisement.

retasar, *va.* to reappraise.

retazar, *va.* to tear in pieces.—**retazo,** *m.* piece, remnant; cutting; fragment, portion.

retejador, *m.* retiler.

retejar, *va.* to retile (a roof); (coll.) to provide with clothes.

retejer, *va.* to weave closely.

retejo, *m.* repairing of a roof, retiling.

retemblar, *vn.* (*ind.* RETIEMBLO; *subj.* RETIEMBLE) to tremble, shake, quiver.

retemblor, *m.* repeated shaking, quiver.

retén, *m.* store, stock, reserve; (mil.) reserve corps; (mech.) ratchet, catch.

retención, *f.* retention, keeping or holding back; (med.) retention.

retener, *va.* (*ind. pres.* yo RETENGO, él RETIENE, *pret.* RETUVE, *fut.* RETENDRÉ; *subj.* RETENGA) to retain, withhold, keep back; to keep, preserve; to catch, hold, keep; to arrest, detain.

retenida, *f.* (naut.) preventer rope, guy.—**r. de costado,** (aer.) side guy wire.—**r. de guiñada,** (aer.) yaw guy.—**r. de proa,** (naut.) headfast.

retenidamente, *adv.* retentively.

retenimiento, *m.* = RETENCIÓN.

retentar, *va.* (of a disease) to threaten with a relapse.

retentivo, va. I. *a.* retentive, retaining. **II.** *f.* retentiveness, memory.

¹**reteñir,** *va.* (*pp.* RETEÑIDO, RETINTO; *ind. pres.* RETIÑO, *pret.* él RETIÑÓ; *subj.* RETIÑA) to dye over again.

²**reteñir,** *vn.* = RETIÑIR.

retesamiento, *m.* tightening more firmly.

retesar, *va.* to draw or stretch tighter.

reteso, *m.* = RETESAMIENTO.

reticencia, *f.* reticence.

reticente, *a.* reticent.

rético, ca, *n.* & *a.* Rhethian, Rhæthian.

retícula, *f.* diaphragm and cross wires (of an instrument).

reticulado, da; reticular, *a.* reticular, reticulated; trussed, framed (as in *construcción reticulada,* framed structure).—**estructura reticular,** (nuclear phys.) lattice.

retículo, *m.* network, reticular tissue; diaphragm and cross wires (of an instrument).

retiemblo, retiemble, *v.* V. RETEMBLAR.

retín, *m.* = RETINTÍN.

retina, *f.* retina of the eye.

retinitis, *f.* (med.) retinitis.

¹**retinte,** *m.* second dye.

²**retinte,** *m.* = RETINTÍN.

retintín, *m.* tinkling, jingle; tintinnabulation; (coll.) sarcastic tone of voice.

retinto, ta. I. *pp. irreg.* of RETEÑIR. **II.** *a.* dark, obscure, almost black.—**café, r.,** very strong, black coffee.

retiñir, *vn.* to tinkle, jingle, ring.

retiño, retiña, etc. *v.* V. RETEÑIR.

retiración, *f.* (print.) printing the back of a sheet; second form for backing.

retirada, *f.* withdrawal; (mil.) retreat; retirement; place of safety; privy, closet.

retiradamente, *adv.* secretly; retiredly.

retirado, da. I. *pp.* of RETIRAR. **II.** *a.* retired, solitary, isolated; remote, distant; pensioned. **III.** *m.* retired officer.

retiramiento, *m.* retirement; secluded place.

retirar. I. *va.* to withdraw; to put aside, out of the way; to lay aside, reserve; to repel; to revoke; (com.) to withdraw, call in; (print.) to print the back of, to back. **II.** *vr.* to withdraw; to retire; to recede, move or go back; (mil.) to retreat.

retiro, *m.* retirement; retreat; recess; secluded place; refuge, asylum; (eccl.) retreat; privacy; (mil.) condition and pay of a retired officer.

reto, *m.* challenge; threat, menace.

retobado, da, *a.* (Am.) given to grumbling or muttering; obstinate, unruly; cunning, wily.

retobar. I. *va.* (Arg.) to line or cover with hides; (Chile) to pack or wrap in hides or burlap. **II.** *vr.* (Arg.) to become quiet and surly, to sulk.

retobo, *m.* (Colomb., C. A.) refuse, useless or insignificant thing; (Chile) burlap; oilcloth; (Arg.) packing or wrapping in hides.

retocador, ra, *n.* retoucher.

retocamiento, *m.* retouching, retouchment.

retocar, *va.* (*pret.* RETOQUÉ; *subj.* RETOQUE) to retouch; to touch up, finish.

retoñar, retoñecer, *vn.* to sprout; to reappear.

retoño, *m.* sprout, shoot, tiller, sucker.

retoque, *m.* retouch; finishing touch; repeated and frequent pulsation; touch (of a disease).

retoqué, retoque, *v.* V. RETOCAR.

retor, *m.* twilled cotton fabric.

retorcedura, *f.* twisting, writhing.

retorcer. I. *va.* (*ind.* RETUERZO; *subj.* RETUERZA) to twist; to contort, convolve; to retort, reargue; to distort, twist, misconstrue. **II.** *vr.* to writhe, squirm.

retorcido. I. *pp.* of RETORCER. **II.** *m.* tutti-frutti, sweetmeat.

retorcimiento, *m.* twisting; writhing.

retórica, *f.* rhetoric.—*pl.* (coll.) sophistries, quibbles, subtleties.

retóricamente, *adv.* rhetorically.

retórico, ca. I. *a.* rhetorical. **II.** *m.* rhetorician.

retornamiento, *m.* return.

retornante, *a.* returning.

retornar. I. *vn.* to return, come back; to recede, retrograde. **II.** *va.* to return; to give back; to turn, twist, contort; to cause to go back.

retornelo, *m.* ritornello, burden of a song.

retorno, *m.* return, coming back; home trip; return chaise or horse; repayment, requital; barter, exchange, traffic; (naut.) leading block.—**de r.,** return (as *a.*).

retorsión, *f.* retortion; retort; twisting.

retorsivo, va, *a.* having a retort; bending back.

retorta, *f.* a twilled linen fabric; (chem.) retort.

retortero, *m.* twirl, rotation.—**andar al r.,** to hover about.—**traer al r.,** (coll.) to twist one around, to deceive with false promises.

retortijar, *va.* to twist, to curl.

retortijón, *m.* curlicue; twisting, twist; cramp.— **r. de tripas,** griping cramp.

retostado, da. I. *pp.* of RETOSTAR. **II.** *a.* brown.

retostar, *va.* (*ind.* RETUESTO; *subj.* RETUESTE) to toast again, toast brown.

retozador, ra, *a.* frisky, frolicsome, prankish.

retozadura, *f.* = RETOZO.

retozar. I. *vn.* to frisk and skip about, romp, frolic, gambol. **II.** *vr.* (of passion) to be violently aroused.

retozo, *m.* frisk, gambol, prank, frolic.—**r. de la risa,** giggle, titter.

retozón, na, *a.* frolicsome, coltish.

retracción, *f.* retraction, drawing back.
retractable, *a.* retractable.
retractación, *f.* retractation, recantation.
retractar, *va.* & *vr.* to retract, to recant; (law) to redeem.
retráctil, *a.* retractile.
retractilidad, *f.* retractility.
retracto, *m.* (law) right of redemption.
retractor, *m.* (surg.) retractor.
retraer. I. *va.* (*ger.* RETRAYENDO; *pp.* RETRAÍDO; *ind. pres.* RETRAIGO, *pret.* RETRAJE; *subj.* RETRAIGA) to dissuade; (law) to redeem. **II.** *vr.* to take refuge or shelter; to withdraw from, shun; to keep aloof, retire; to live a retired life.
retraído, da. I. *pp.* of RETRAER. **II.** *a.* of a retiring disposition; incommunicative. **III.** *n.* refugee; lover of solitude.
retraigo, retraiga, *v.* V. RETRAER.
retraimiento, *m.* seclusion, retirement; retreat, refuge, asylum; private room, sanctum; incommunicativeness.
retranca, *f.* broad crupper of a packsaddle; (Cuba, Mex., Ry.) brake; breeching (of a saddle).
retranquear, *va.* to hoist, move, and set down (building blocks, etc.).—**retranqueo,** *m.* (arch.) setting blocks or stones in position.
retranquero, *m.* (Mex., Cuba, Ry.) brakeman.
retrasado, da. I. *pp.* of RETRASAR. **II.** *a.* (mentally) retarded.
retrasar. I. *va.* to defer, put off, postpone; to delay; to set back (timepiece). **II.** *vn.* to retrograde, go back, decline. **III.** *vr.* to be backward; to be behindhand, late, behind time; (of timepiece) to run slow.
retraso, *m.* delay, backwardness, slowness.
retratable, *a.* retractable, retractible.
retratación, *f.* retractation, recantation.
retratador, ra, *n.* = RETRATISTA.
retratar. I. *va.* to portray, draw a portrait of; to imitate, copy; to paint, describe; to depict; to photograph; RETRACTAR. **II.** *vr.* to be reflected; to be depicted, show; to sit for a portrait or photograph.
retratista, *n.* portrait painter; photographer.
retrato, *m.* portrait, picture; photograph; copy, resemblance; description; (law) RETRACTO.
retrayente, *n.* & *a.* retractor(-ing), recanter (-ing); (law) redeemer(-ing).
retrechar, *vn.* to back, move backward.
retrechería, *f.* (coll.) cunning, evasion.
retrechero, *a.* (coll.) cunningly evasive; attractive, charming, winsome.
retrepado, da, *a.* leaning or slanting backward.
retreparse, *vr.* to lean back; to recline in a chair.
retreta, *f.* (mil.) retreat; tatoo; evening military parade; (Colomb.) open-air concert by a military band in honor of a public dignitary.
retrete, *m.* private room, sanctum; alcove, boudoir; closet, toilet room, water closet, privy.
retribución, *f.* retribution; recompense, fee.
retribuir, *va.* (*ger.* RETRIBUYENDO; *ind. pres.* RETRIBUYO, *pret.* RETRIBUYÓ; *subj.* RETRIBUYA) to remunerate, reward, fee.
retribuyente, *a.* retributive, retributing.
retrillar, *va.* (agr.) to thrash again.
retroactividad, *f.* retroactivity.
retroactivo, va, *a.* retroactive.
retrocarga, *f.*—**de r.,** breech-loading.
retroceder, *vn.* to go back, move backward; (**de**) to draw back (from), go back (on); (auto) to back up; to recede; to become worse.
retrocesión, *f.* backward motion; (law) retrocession.
retroceso, *m.* backward motion; (med.) aggravation; in billiards, draw.
retrogradación, *f.* (astr.) retrogradation, retrogression.
retrogradar, *vn.* to recede; (astr.) to retrograde.

retrógrado, da, *a.* retrogressive; (pol.) reactionary; (astr.) retrograde.
retronar, *vn.* (*ind.* RETRUENO; *subj.* RETRUENE) to thunder; make a thundering noise.
retropilastra, *f.* pilaster behind a column.
retrospectivo, va, *a.* retrospective.
retrotracción, *f.* (law) antedating.
retrotraer, *va.* (*ger.* RETROTRAYENDO; *pp.* RETROTRAÍDO; *ind. pres.* RETROTRAIGO, *pret.* RETROTRAJE; *subj.* RETROTRAIGA) (law) to antedate, date back.
retrovendendo.—contrato de r., (law) reversion sale.
retrovender, *va.* (law); to sell back to the vender. —**retrovendición,** *f.* (law) selling back to the vender.
retroventa, *f.* (law) sale on reversion.
retrucar, *vn.* (*pret.* RETRUQUÉ; *subj.* RETRUQUE) (billiards) to kiss.—**retruco,** *m.* (billiards) kiss.
retruécano, *m.* pun, play upon words; antithesis, contrast.
retrueno, retruene, *v.* V. RETRONAR.
retruque, *m.* = RETRUCO.
retruqué, retruque, *v.* V. RETRUCAR.
retuerzo, retuerza, *v.* V. RETORCER.
retuesto, retueste, *v.* V. RETOSTAR.
retumbante, *a.* resonant, resounding; pompous, bombastic, high-flown.
retumbar, *vn.* to resound, sound loudly.
retumbo, *m.* resonance, loud noise, echo.
retundir, *va.* (mason.) to even (the stones of a wall); (mason.) to point (joints); (med.) to repel.
retuve, *pret.* of RETENER.
reuma. I. *m.* (med.) rheumatism. **II.** *f.* gathering; rheum, defluxion.—**reumático, ca,** *a.* rheumatic.—**reumátide,** *f.* (med.) rheumides.
reumatismo, *m.* rheumatism.
reunión, *f.* union; meeting, gathering, assembly; consolidation.
reunir. I. *va.* to unite; to gather; to collect, accumulate; to join; to reconcile. **II.** *vr.* to join, to unite; to meet, get together, assemble.
reuntar, *va.* to oil or grease again.
revacunación, *f.* (med.) revaccination.
revacunar, *va.* to revaccinate.
reválida, *f.* admission into a higher faculty.
revalidación, *f.* confirmation, ratification; renewal.
revalidar. I. *va.* to ratify, confirm; to renew. **II.** *vr.* to be admitted into a higher faculty.
revancha, *f.* (Gal.) revenge, retaliation.
revecero, ra. I. *a.* shiftable. **II.** *n.* farmhand who tends relays of oxen.
reveedor, ra, *n.* = REVISOR, reviser; overseer.
revejecer, *vn.* & *vr.* (*ind.* REVEJEZCO; *subj.* REVEJEZCA) to grow old prematurely.
revejido, da, *a.* prematurely old.
revelación, *f.* revelation.
revelador, ra. I. *n.* & *a.* revealer(-ing). **II.** *m.* (photog.) developer.
revelamiento, *m.* REVELACIÓN; (photog.) development.
revelandero, ra, *n.* one who pretends to have had a divine revelation.
revelante, *a.* revealing.
revelar, *va.* to reveal; (photog.) to develop.
reveler, *va.* (med.) to cause revulsion to.
revellín, *m.* (fort.) ravelin.
revenar, *vn.* to sprout.
revendedera, *f.* = REVENDEDORA.
revendedor, ra, *n.* retailer; ticket speculator.
revender, *va.* to resell; to retail.
revenimiento, *m.* (min.) cave-in.
revenirse, *vr.* (*ind. pres.* me REVENGO, se REVIENE, *pret.* me REVINE, *fut.* me REVENDRÉ; *subj.* me REVENGA) to shrink, waste away; to turn, grow sour, ferment (as wine and preserves); to exude; to yield, concede, assent.
reveno, *m.* sprout, shoot.

For pronunciation, see the rules at the beginning of the book.

reventa, *f.* resale; retail.

reventadero, *m.* rough ground; drudgery.

reventar. I. *vn.* (*ind.* REVIENTO; *subj.* REVIENTE) to burst; to blow up, blow out; to break; to splash (as waves); to burst forth, break loose (as a passion); to sprout, shoot, blossom; to long, to crave.—**r. de risa,** to burst with laughter. II. *va.* to burst; to break; to crush, smash; to wind (a horse); to tire, fatigue, exhaust; to vex, annoy. III. *vr.* to burst; to blow up, blow out; to break.

reventazón, *f.* bursting; blowout; disruption, rupture; (naut.) splash, dashing of the waves.

reventón, I. *a.* bursting. II. *m.* bursting, blowout, explosion; steep declivity; toil, drudgery, uphill work.

rever, *va.* (*pp.* REVISTO; *ind.* REVEO; *subj.* REVEA) to review, revise, look over again; (law) to retry.

reverberación, *f.* reverberation; (chem.) calcination in a reverberatory furnace.

reverberar, *vn.* to reverberate.

reverbero, *m.* reverberation; reverberator, reflector.

reverdecer, *vn.* (*ind.* REVERDEZCO; *subj.* REVERDEZCA) to grow green again; to sprout again; to acquire new freshness and vigor.

reverdeciente, *a.* growing fresh and green.

reverencia, *f.* reverence; courtsey, bow, obeisance; (eccl.) reverence (title).

reverenciable, *a.* reverend.

reverenciador, ra, *n.* reverencer.

reverencial, *a.* reverential.

reverenciar, *va.* to venerate, revere; to hallow; to reverence.

reverendas, *f. pl.* prelate's dimissory letters; qualities and titles worthy of reverence.

reverendísimo, ma, *a. super.* Most Reverend, Right Reverend.

reverendo, da, *a.* reverend; worthy of reverence.

reverente, *a.* reverent.—**reverentemente,** *adv.* reverently.

reversibilidad, *f.* reversibility.

reversible, *a.* (law) returnable, revertible; (phys.) reversible.

reversión, *f.* reversion.

reverso, *m.* reverse (in coins); back, rear side.—**el r. de la medalla,** the opposite in every respect.

reverter, *vn.* (*ind.* REVIERTE; *subj.* REVIERTA) to overflow.

revertir, *vn.* (law) to revert.

revés, *m.* reverse, back, wrong side; slap, box; backhand slap, shot or stroke; counterstroke; misfortune, reverse; change of temper and disposition; (fencing) reverse.—**r. de la medalla.** V. REVERSO.—**al r.,** on the contrary, contrariwise; in the opposite or wrong way or direction; wrong side out.—**de r.,** diagonally, from left to right.—**del r.** = AL R.

revesa, *f.* (naut.) back water, eddy.

revesado, da, *a.* entangled, complicated, laborious, obscure; mischievous, wayward.

revesar, *va.* to vomit.

revesino, *m.* reversis, a card game.—**cortar el r.,** to thwart.

revestimiento, *m.* (mason.) covering, coat(-ing); finish.

revestir. I. *va.* (*ind. pres.* REVISTO, *pret.* REVISTIÓ; *subj.* REVISTA) to dress, clothe, to cover; to line; (fig.) to cloak; (mason.) to coat, cover with a coating, revet. II. *vr.* to be swayed or carried along by some power; to be invested with; to be haughty, lofty, proud.

revezar, *vn.* to alternate, work in rotation or by shifts.

revezo, *m.* shift, turn; gang; relay.

reviejo, ja. I. *a.* very old. II. *m.* withered branch of a tree.

reviento, reviente, *v.* V. REVENTAR.

reviernes, *m.* each of the first seven Fridays after Easter.

revierte, revierta, *v.* V. REVERTER.

revine, etc. *v.* V. REVENIRSE.

revirado, da, *a.* (bot.) twisted.

revirar, *va.* (naut.) to veer again, retack.

revisar, *va.* to revise, review; to re-examine, rehear.—**r. las cuentas,** to audit accounts.

revisión, *f.* revision, revisal, revise, reviewing; re-examination, re-hearing; new trial.

revisita, *f.* reinspection.

revisor, *m.* reviser, censor, corrector; overseer; auditor; conductor (on train).

revisoría, *f.* office of censor or reviser.

revista, *f.* review, revision, revisal, revise; reinspection, reëxamination; (law) new trial; (mil.) review, parade; muster; review, magazine, journal; (theat.) revue.—**pasar r.,** to review; to examine, go over.—**suplicar en r.,** (law) to present a bill of review.

revistar, *va.* to review, inspect.

¹revisto, ta, *pp. irreg.* of REVER.

²revisto, revista, *v.* V. REVESTIR.

revitalizar, *va.* to revitalize.

revividero, *m.* place for rearing silkworms.

revivificar, *va.* to revivify.

revivir, *vn.* to revive.

revocable, *a.* revocable, reversible, repealable.

revocablemente, *adv.* in a revocable manner.

revocación, *f.* revocation; abrogation.—**r. de una sentencia,** (law) reversal.

revocador, ra. I. *a.* revoking, cancelling. II. *n.* revoker; plasterer, whitewasher.

revocadura, *f.* REVOQUE; (art) edge of the canvas turned over the stretcher.

revocante, *a.* revoking, abrogating.

revocar, *va.* (*pret.* REVOQUÉ; *subj.* REVOQUE) to revoke, repeal, reverse; to countermand; to dissuade; to repel, push back; to plaster.

revocatorio, ria, *a.* revocatory, repealing.

revoco, *m.* REVOQUE; drawing or driving back; cover of furze on charcoal baskets.

revolante, *a.* fluttering, hovering.

revolar, *vn.* (*ind.* REVUELA; *subj.* REVUELE) (of birds) to fly around, hover, flutter.

revolcadero, *m.* wallowing place for animals.

revolcadura, *f.* weltering, wallowing.

revolcar. I. *va.* (*ind. pres.* REVUELCO, *pret.* REVOLQUÉ; *subj.* REVUELQUE) to knock down, tread or trample upon; (coll.) to floor (an opponent). II. *vr.* to wallow; to be stubborn.

revolcón, *m.* (coll.) = ¹REVUELCO.

revolear, *vn.* to fly around.

revolotear. I. *vn.* to flutter, fly round about, hover. II. *va.* to hurl, fling, pitch.

revoloteo, *m.* fluttering; hovering.

revolqué, *pret.* of REVOLCAR.

revoltijo, revoltillo, *m.* mess, mass, medley, jumble; twisted tripes of a sheep.—**r. de huevos,** scrambled eggs.

revoltón, *m.* vine fretter, vine grub.

revoltoso, sa, *a.* turbulent, seditious; mischievous, prankish.

revoltura, *f.* (min.) mixture of fluxes.

revolución, *f.* revolution, revolt; (mech., astr.) revolution, turn.—**revolucionar.** I. *va.* to revolutionize. II. *vr.* to rebel, revolt.

revolucionario, ria, *a. & n.* revolutionary(-ist).

revolvedero, *m.* = REVOLCADERO.

revolvedor, ra. I. *a.* turbulent, seditious, rebellious. II. *n.* revolter, disturber, agitator.

revólver, *m.* (Angl.) revolver (pistol).

revolver. I. *va.* (*pp.* REVUELTO; *ind.* REVUELVO; *subj.* REVUELVA) to turn over, turn upside down; to stir; to agitate; to wrap up, convolve; to revolve, turn round, gyrate; to retrace (one's steps), go over (the same ground); to turn over in one's mind; to turn short swiftly (as a horse); to estrange, create bad feeling in or between.

II. *vr.* to move to and fro; to change (as the weather).

revolvimiento, *m.* commotion, disturbance, revolution.

revoque, *m.* plastering; whitewashing.

revoqué, revoque, *v. V.* REVOCAR.

revotarse, *vr.* to reconsider a ballot.

¹revuelco, *m.* wallowing, rolling.

²revuelco, revuelque, *v. V.* REVOLCAR.

revuelo, *m.* second flight of a bird, gyration described when flying; irregular motion; sensation, commotion, stir; disturbance.—**de r.,** by the way; speedily, promptly.

revuelta, *f.* second turn; revolution, revolt; contention, dissension; turn, deviation; change.

revueltamente, *adv.* confusedly, pell-mell, higgledy-piggledy.

revuelto, ta. I. *pp. irreg.* of REVOLVER. **II.** *a.* easily turned (horse); scrambled (eggs); topsy-turvy; restless, mischievous; boisterous; intricate, difficult.

revuelvepiedras, *m.* (ornith.) turnstone.

revuelvo, revuelva, *v. V.* REVOLVER.

revulsión, *f.* (med.) revulsion of humors.

revulsivo, va; revulsorio, ria, *a. & m.* revulsive.

rey, *m.* king; king in cards or chess; step in a Spanish dance; queen bee; chief among men or animals.—**r. de armas,** (her.) king at arms.—**los Reyes,** Epiphany, Twelfth-night.—**los reyes magos,** the wise men from the East.—**ni r. ni roque,** no one.—**no tener ni r. ni roque,** not to fear, or bow to, anything nor anybody, to have no master.

reyerta, *f.* dispute, wrangle, quarrel.

reyezuelo, *m.* petty king; (ornith.) kinglet.

rezado, *m.* prayer; divine service.

rezador, ra, *n.* one who prays often.

rezagado, da, *n.* straggler, laggard, tramp.

rezagante, *n.* laggard, straggler.

rezagar. I. *va.* (*pret.* REZAGUÉ; *subj.* REZAGUE) to leave behind; to outstrip; to put off, defer. **II.** *vr.* to fall behind, to lag.

rezago, *m.* remainder, left-over.

rezar. I. *va.* to say as a prayer; to say (a prayer); to say (mass); to say, state (*el libro lo reza,* the book says it). **II.** *vn.* to pray; to say, read (*el párrafo reza así,* the paragraph reads thus); to grumble, mutter.—**r. con,** to concern, be the business or duty of.

rezno, *m.* tick, sheep tick, dog tick.

rezo, *m.* prayer; praying, devotions.

rezón, *m.* (naut.) grapnel, grappling iron.

rezongador, ra, *n.* grumbler, growler, mutterer.

rezongar, *vn.* (*pret.* REZONGUÉ; *subj.* REZONGUE) to grumble, mutter, growl.

rezonglón, na; rezongón, na, *n.* grumbler, mutterer, growler.

rezumadero, *m.* dripping place; cesspool.

rezumarse, *vr.* to ooze, exude, percolate, filter through; (coll.) to transpire.

¹ría, *f.* estuary.

²ría, *v. V.* REÍR.

riacho, riachuelo, riatillo, *m.* rivulet, streamlet; small river.

riada, *f.* freshet, flood.

riba, *f.* sloping bank, embankment.

ribadoquín, *m.* an ancient small gun.

ribaldería, *f.* knavishness, rascality.

ribaldo, da. I. *a.* villainous, knavish. **II.** *n.* ruffian.

ribazo, *m.* sloping bank; mound, hillock.

ribera, *f.* shore, beach, bank, strand.

ribereño, ña, *a.* riparian, riparious.

riberiego, ga. I. *a.* riparious (as flocks of sheep). **II.** *m.* grazer of sheep on river banks.

ribero, *m.* river wall, levee.

ribes, *f.* (bot.) currant bush.

ribete, *m.* (sewing) binding, galloon; trimming; pretense; addition to a tale, for embellishment.

ribeteador, ra, *n.* (sewing) binder.

ribetear, *va.* (sewing) to bind.

ricacho, cha; chón, na, *a.* (coll.) very rich.

ricadueña, ricahembra, *f.* lady, daughter or wife of a noble.

ricahombría, *f.* dignity of the ancient nobility of Castile.

ricamente, *adv.* richly, opulently; excellently, splendidly.

ricé, rice, *v. V.* RIZAR.

ricial, *a.* green (field) or new (pasture).

ricino, *m.* (bot.) palma Christi, castor-oil plant.

rico, ca, *a.* rich, wealthy; abundant, plentiful; delicious, exquisite, choice; "cute" (child).

ricohombre, ricohome, *m.* grandee, peer of the ancient nobility of Castile.

richembra, *f.* = RICADUEÑA.

ridículamente, *adv.* ridiculously.

ridiculez, *f.* ridiculous thing or action; ridiculousness; ridicule; folly, oddity, eccentricity; extreme nicety or sensibility.

ridiculizar, *va.* (*pret.* RIDICULICÉ; *subj.* RIDICULICE) to ridicule.

¹ridículo, la. I. *a.* ridiculous; odd, eccentric, queer, outlandish, contemptible; absurd.—**en r.,** in a ridiculous situation, exposed to ridicule. —**poner en r.,** to ridicule, expose to ridicule, make ridiculous.—**ponerse en r., quedar en r.,** to make oneself ridiculous. **II.** *m.* ridicule.

²ridículo, *m.* handbag, reticule.

¹riego, *m.* irrigation; watering.

²riego, riegue, *v. V.* REGAR.

riel, *m.* ingot; (Ry.) rail.—**r. acanalado,** groove rail.—**r. americano,** or **Vignole,** T rail.

rielado, da, *a.* reduced to ingots.

rielar, *vn.* to glisten, glimmer, shine.

rielera, *f.* (foundry) ingot mold.

rienda, *f.* rein of a bridle; moderation, restraint. —*pl.* reins, ribbons; government, direction.—**a r. suelta,** loose-reined; violently, swiftly; without restraint.—**dar r. suelta,** to give free rein to.—**soltar la r.,** to give way to vice or passions.—**tener las riendas,** to hold the reins, to hold in a horse.—**tirar las riendas,** to draw back, to restrain.

riente, *a.* smiling, laughing.

riesgo, *m.* danger, risk, hazard, peril.

rifa, *f.* raffle; scuffle, wrangle.

rifador, ra, *n.* raffler.

rifadura, *f.* (naut.) splitting a sail.

rifar. I. *va.* to raffle. **II.** *vn.* to quarrel; (naut.) (of a sail) to split.

rifeño, ña, *n. & a.* Riffian (from the Riff, in Morocco).

rifirrafe, *m.* (coll.) short quarrel, hasty words.

rifle, *m.* (Angl.) (artil.) rifle.

rigente, *a.* (poet.) rigid.

rígidamente, *adv.* rigidly.

rigidez, rigidity; sternness.—**r. cadavérica,** rigor mortis, stiffening of body after death.

rígido, da, *a.* rigid, stiff; rigorous, inflexible.

rigió, *pret.* of REGIR.

rigodón, *m.* (dance) rigadoon; quadrille.

rigor, *m.* rigor; sternness; (med.) rigidity; chill.— **r. cadavérico,** = RIGIDEZ CADAVÉRICA.—**de r.,** indispensable; prescribed by the rules.— **en r.,** or **en r. de verdad,** strictly speaking, in fact.

rigorismo, *m.* rigorism, austerity, severity.

rigorista, *n. & a.* rigorist(-ic).

rigorosamente, *adv.* rigorously; strictly, scrupulously.

rigoroso, sa, *a.* rigorous; exact; absolute; strict, austere; severe, harsh; scrupulously nice.

rigurosamente, *adv.* = RIGOROSAMENTE.

rigurosidad, *f.* rigorousness; severity.

riguroso, sa, *a.* = RIGOROSO.

¹rija, *f.* (med.) lachrymal fistula.

²rija, *f.* quarrel, scuffle, dispute.

rijador, ra, *a.* quarrelsome.

¹rijo, *m.* lust, sensuality, concupiscence.

---

²**rijo, rija,** *v. V.* REGIR.
rijoso, sa, *a.* quarrelsome; lustful, lewd; (of horses) restless at the sight of the female.
¹**rima,** *f.* heap, pile.
³**rima,** *f.* rhyme.—*pl.* lyric poems.—**r. imperfecta,** (poet.) assonance.
rimado, da. I. *pp.* of RIMAR. II. *a.* versified.
rimador, ra, *n.* versifier, rhymer.
rimar, *vn.* to rhyme; to make verses.
rimbombancia, *f.* resonance, great noise; rant, bombast, ostentation.
rimbombante, *a.* resounding; bombastic, high-sounding, ranting.
rimbombar, *vn.* to resound, to echo.
rimbombe, rimbombo, *m.* repercussion of sound.
rimero, *m.* heap, pile.
rincón, *m.* (inside) corner, angle, nook; cosy corner; lurking place; (coll.) house, dwelling; remote place.—**rinconada,** *f.* corner.
rinconcillo, *m. dim.* small corner.
rinconero, ra. I. *a.* transverse, athwart (honeycombs). II. *f.* corner cupboard, stand, bracket.
rindo, rinda, rindió, *v. V.* RENDIR.
ringla, *f.,* **ringle,** *m.,* **ringlera,** *f.* (coll.) row, file, line, tier; swath.
ringlero, *m.* line or rule for writing exercises.
ringorrangos, *m. pl.* (coll.) flourish with a pen; frills, fripperies.
rinitis, *f.* (med.) rhinitis.
rinoceronte, *m.* (zool.) rhinoceros.
rinoplastia, *f.* (surg.) rhinoplasty.
rinoscopia, *f.* (med.) rhinoscopy.
riña, *f.* quarrel, scuffle, dispute, fray.
riño, riña, riñó, *v. V.* REÑIR.
riñón, *m.* (anat.) kidney; (arch.) spandrel; (min.) nodule, kidney ore; central part of a country.—**tener cubierto el r.,** to be rich, to be well off.
riñonada, *f.* layer of fat about the kidneys; dish of kidneys.
¹**río,** *m.* river.—**r. de lágrimas,** flood of tears.—**a r. revuelto,** in confusion or disorder.—**cuando el r. suena, agua lleva,** or **piedras lleva,** where there is so much smoke there must be some fire.
²**río, rió, ría,** *v. V.* REÍR.
riolada, *f.* (coll.) concourse, large gathering or collection; heap.
rioplatense, *n.* & *a.* Argentine, Argentinian.
riostra, *f.* stay, brace.—**riostrar,** *va.* to brace, stay.
ripia, *f.* shingle, for roofing.
ripiar, *va.* (mason.) to riprap.
ripio, *m.* debirs, rubbish, riprap; padding, useless words; verbiage.—**no perder r.,** not to miss the least occasion.
riqueza, *f.* riches, wealth; richness, excellence; abundance; fertility, fruitfulness; gorgeousness.
risa, *f.* laugh, laughter; derisory smile or laugh.—**r. sardónica,** sardonic laugh, grin, sneer.—**caerse, descalzarse, descoyuntarse, desternillarse,** or **reventar, de r.,** to burst, or hold one's sides, with laughter.—**cosa de r.,** a laughing matter.
risada, *f.* horselaugh.
riscal, *m.* cliffy, craggy place.
risco, *m.* crag, cliff; honey fritter.
riscoso, sa, *a.* cliffy, craggy.
risibilidad, *f.* risibility.
risible, *a.* laughable, ludicrous.
risiblemente, *adv.* ludicrously, ridiculously.
risica, illa, ita, *f. dim.* feigned laugh; giggle, titter.
riso, *m.* (poet.) gentle laugh.
risotada, *f.* outburst of laughter, loud laugh, horselaugh.
ríspido, da, *a.* = ÁSPERO, harsh, gruff.
ristra, *f.* string of onions or garlic; bunch; row, file, string.
ristre, *m.* rest or socket for a lance.

ristrel, *m.* (arch.) wooden molding.
risueño, ña, *a.* smiling; pleasing, agreeable.
¡rita! *f.* word used to call sheep.
rítmico, ca, *a.* rhythmic.
ritmo, *m.* rhythm; rate (of increase, etc.).
rito, *m.* rite, ceremony.
ritual. I. *m.* (eccl.) ritual, ceremonial. II. *a.* ritual.—**ritualidad,** *f.* ritualism.—**ritualismo,** *m.* ritualism.—**ritualista,** *n.* & *a.* ritualist(-ic).
rival, *m.* rival.—**rivalidad,** *f.* rivalry.
rivalizar, *vn.* (*pret.* RIVALICÉ; *subj.* RIVALICE) to rival, vie, compete.
rivera, *f.* brook, creek, stream.
¹**riza,** *f.* green stubble.
²**riza,** *f.* ravage, destruction.
rizado, *m.* fluting, crimp, frizzle.
rizador, ra. I. *n.* & *a.* crimper(-ing), frizzler (-ing). II. *m.* curling iron; (sewing) ruffler.
rizal, *a.* = RICIAL, green or new (field).
rizar. I. *va.* (*pret.* RICÉ; *subj.* RICE) to curl, frizzle, crimp, flute, ruffle, corrugate, crinkle; to ripple (water). II. *vr.* to curl naturally.
rizo, za. I. *a.* naturally curled or frizzled. II. *m.* curl, frizzle, ringlet; cut velvet; (aer.) loop.—*pl.* (naut.) reef points.—**hacer el r.,** (aer., coll.) to loop the loop.—**tomar rizos,** to take in reefs.
rizocárpeo, a, *a.* (bot.) rhizocarpous.
rizófago, ga, *a.* (zool.) rhizophagous, root-eating.
rizóforeo, a. I. *a.* (bot.) rhizophoraceous. II. *f. pl.* Rhizophoraceæ, mangroves.
rizoma, *m.* (bot.) rhizome.
rizópodo, da, *n.* & *a.* (zool.) rhizopod.—*m. pl.* Rhizopoda, rhizopods.
rizoso, sa, *a.* naturally curly.
ro, ro, *interj.* used as a lullaby.
roa, *f.* (naut.) = ¹RODA.
roadster, *m.* (Angl.) (auto) roadster.
roano, na, *a.* sorrel, roan (horse).
rob, *m.* (pharm.) fruit jelly or conserve.
robada, *f.* a land measure (about 9 ares).
robadera, *f.* (agr.) levelling harrow.
robador, ra, *n.* robber.
robaliza, *f.* (ichth.) female robalo.
róbalo, robalo, *m.* (ichth.) robalo; (com.) haddock.
robar, *va., vn.* & *vr.* to rob, plunder, steal; rob of (*Juan me robó el reloj,* John robbed me of my watch); to abduct; to kidnap; to sweep or eat away (as banks by a stream); in some games, to draw (a card); to take (the honeycomb) after removing the bees.
robda, *f.* ancient pasturage fee.
robezo, *m.* (zool.) wild goat.
robín, *m.* rust of metal.
robinia, *f.* (bot.) locust tree.
robla, *f.* = ROBDA.
robladero, ra, *a.* fit for riveting.
robladura, *f.* riveting, clinching.
roblar, *va.* to rivet, clinch; to make strong.
roble, *m.* oak; very strong person or thing.
robledal, robledo, *m.* oak grove or wood.
roblizo, za, *a.* oaken, strong, hard.
roblón, *m.* rivet; ridge of tiles.—**roblonado, m., roblonadura,** *f.* riveting.
roblonar, *va.* & *vn.* to rivet.
¹**robo,** *m.* robbery, theft; plunder; cards drawn; drawing of cards.
²**robo,** *m.* a dry measure (about 28 liters).
roboración, *f.* corroboration, strengthening.
roborante, *a.* strengthening, corroborating, or confirming; (med.) roborant.
roborar, *va.* to strengthen, make firm; to corroborate.
roborativo, va, *a.* corroborative.
robra, *f.* = ALBOROQUE, treat to seal a bargain.
robre, robredo, *m.* = ROBLE, ROBLEDAL.
robustamente, *adv.* robustly.
robustecedor, ra, *a.* strengthening, building-up.

robustecer, *va.* (*ind.* ROBUSTEZCO; *subj.* ROBUSTEZCA) *va.* to make strong.

robustez, *f.* robustness, hardiness.

robusto, ta, *a.* robust, vigorous, hale.

roca, *f.* (geol.) rock; cliff.

rocadero, *m.* knob, rock or head of a distaff.

rocador, *m.* head of a distaff.

rocalla, *f.* drift of pebbles, talus of rocks; chippings of stone, riprap; glass beads.

rocalloso, sa, *a.* rocky.

roce, *m.* friction, rubbing, attrition; intercourse.

rocé, roce, *v. V.* ROZAR.

rociada, *f.* sprinkling, aspersion; (naut.) spray, splash; squall; dew on plants; dew-drenched herbs given to animals as medicine; shower of missiles; slander, aspersion; harsh reprimand.

rociadera, *f.* watering pot; irrigation ditch.

rociado, da. I. *pp.* of ROCIAR. **II.** *a.* dewy; bedewed.

rociador, *m.* sprinkler, sprayer; cloth sprinkler.

rociadura, *f.* = ROCIADA.

rociamiento, *m.* bedewing.

rociar. I. *vn.* to fall in dew. **II.** *va.* to sprinkle, to spray; to strew about.

rocín, *m.* hack, jade, sorry horse; coarse, ignorant man.—**rocinal,** *a.* pertaining to a hack horse.—**rocinante,** *m.*, **rocino,** *m.* = ROCÍN.

rocío, *m.* dew; spray, sprinkle, sprinkling; mizzle, drizzle; light shower; (naut.) spoondrift.

rocha, *f.* ground clear of brambles.

rochela, *f.* (Colomb., Venez.) great noise, racket.

rocho, *m.* roc, a fabulous bird.

¹**roda,** *f.* (naut.) stem.

²**roda,** *f.* = ROBDA.

rodaballo, *m.* (ichth.) turbot, flounder.

rodada, *f.* rut, wheel track, cart track.

rodadero, ra, *a.* rolling easily.

rodadizo, za, *a.* that rolls or slides easily.

¹**rodado, da. I.** *pp.* of RODAR. **II.** *a.* rounded, fluent, easy (phrase); (min.); scattered (ore fragments).—**venir r.,** to come unexpectedly.

²**rodado, da. I.** *a.* dapple, dappled (horse). **II.** *m.* (Arg.) vehicle.

rodador, ra. I. *a.* rolling, rolling down. **II.** *m.* roller; kind of mosquito; (ichth.) sunfish.

rodadura, *f.* rolling, wheeling; rut; tread (of a wheel).

rodaja, *f.* small wheel or disk; caster, trundle, truckle; rowel; jagging iron used by pastry cooks; bookbinder's tool.

rodaje, *m.* wheelworks; set of wheels.

rodajuela, *f. dim.* small wheel, disk, or caster.

rodal, *m.* place, spot, seat.

rodante, *a.* rolling.—**material r.,** rolling stock.

rodapelo, *m.* rubbing against the grain.

rodapié, *m.* (arch.) mopboard, skirting; dado; foot rail.

rodaplancha, *f.* main ward of a key.

rodar, *vn.* (*ind.* RUEDO; *subj.* RUEDE) to roll; to revolve, wheel; to run on wheels; to wander about; be tossed about, go about, go up and down; to lose an employ, station, dignity, or esteem; to abound; to happen accidentally; to follow, succeed one another.—**r. por,** to serve, help to the limit.—**r. una película,** to shoot a movie.—**dejar r.,** or **que ruede, la bola,** to let things alone, to let things follow their natural course.

rodeabrazo.—**a r.,** swinging the arm for a throw.

rodeado, da, *a. & pp.* surrounded, encircled.

rodeador, ra, *n.* one who surrounds.

rodear. I. *va. & vn.* to surround, encircle, encompass; (mil.) to invest; (Am.) to round up, gather (cattle) in a rodeo. **II.** *vn.* to go around; to make a detour; to beat about the bush.

rodela, *f.* buckler, round shield.

rodelero, *m.* soldier bearing a buckler.

rodenal, *m.* clump of red pines.

rodeno, na, *a.* (of rocks and trees), red, reddish.

rodeo, *m.* turn, winding; roundabout course,

method or way; round-up, rodeo; inclosure for cattle, stockyard, corral; circumlocution, beating about the bush; evasion, subterfuge.

rodeón, *m.* complete turn.

rodera, *f.* rut, cart track.

¹**rodero, ra,** *a.* pertaining to wheels.

²**rodero,** *m.* collector of pasturage fee.

rodete, *m.* roundlet or rowel of platted hair; (hydraul.) horizontal water wheel; (carriage) fifth wheel, circle iron; ward in a lock; padded ring for carrying things on the head; (mech.) drum for a belt or endless chain.

rodezno, *m.* (hydraul.) horizontal water wheel. (mil.) cogwheel.

rodezuela, *f. dim.* small wheel.

rodilla, *f.* (anat.) knee; ward in a lock; cleaning cloth.—*pl.* (naut.) knees of ship timber.—**a media r.,** kneeling on one knee.—**de rodillas,** on one's knees.—**doblar,** or **hincar, las rodillas,** to kneel down.

rodillada, *f.* push with the knee; kneeling position.

rodillazo, *m.* push or blow with the knee.

rodillera, *f.* knee boss, knee guard; knee patch; hurt upon the knees of horses from kneeling; bagging of trousers at the knee.

rodillero, ra, *a.* pertaining to the knees.

rodillo, *m.* roll, roller; clod crusher, road roller; (print.) inking roller, brayer; (cook.) rolling pin; (mech.) roller, drum, trundle, barrel.

rodilludo, da, *a.* having large knees.

¹**rodio,** *m.* (chem.) rhodium.

²**rodio, dia,** *n. & a.* Rhodian.

rodo, *m.* roller.—**a r.,** in plenty.

rododafne, *f.* (bot.) rosebay, daphne.

rododendro, *m.* (bot.) rhododendron.

rodofíceo, a. I. *a.* (bot.) rhodophyceous. **II.** *f. pl.* Rhodophyceæ.

rodomiel, *m.* juice of roses with honey.

rodrigar, *va.* (*pret.* RODRIGUÉ; *subj.* RODRIGUE) to prop up (vines).

rodrigazón, *f.* time for propping vines.

rodrigón, *m.* vine prop; (coll.) old servant who escorts ladies.

roedor, ra. I. *a.* gnawing; pricking, stinging; detracting. **II.** *n. & a.* (zool.) rodent.

roedura, *f.* gnawing, corrosion.

roel, *m.* (her.) bezant, round.

roela, *f.* button of crude gold or silver.

roer, *va. & defect.* (ger. ROYENDO; *ind. pres.* ROO; *pret.* él ROYÓ; *subj.* ROA) to gnaw, eat, fret away; to corrode; to pick (a bone); to harass, annoy.

roete, *m.* medicinal pomegranate wine.

rogación, *f.* request, petition.—*pl.* (eccl.) rogation.

rogador, ra, *n.* supplicant, petitioner.

rogante, *a.* praying, requesting, entreating.

rogar, *va.* (*ind. pres.* RUEGO, *pret.* ROGUÉ; *subj.* RUEGUE) to request, beg, entreat; to crave.—**rogativa,** *f.* (eccl.) rogation.—**rogativo, va,** *a.* supplicatory.—**rogatorio, ria,** *a.* rogatory.

rogo, *m.* (poet.) fire, pyre.

rogué, *pret.* of ROGAR.

roído, da. I. *pp.* of ROER. **II.** *a.* penurious.

rojeante, *a.* reddening.

rojear, *vn.* to redden; to blush.

rojete, *m.* rouge (for make-up).

rojez, *f.* redness, ruddiness.

rojizo, za, *a.* reddish; rubicund, ruddy.

rojo, ja, *a.* red; ruddy, reddish.—**r. alambrado,** bright red.—**al r.,** at, or to, red heat, red-hot.

rojura, *f.* redness; ruddiness.

rol, *m.* list, roll, catalogue; muster roll.

rolar, *vn.* (naut.) to veer around.

roldana, *f.* sheave, pulley wheel; caster.

rolde, *m.* circle, group of people.

¹**rolla,** *f.* collar of a draught horse.

²**rolla,** *f.* (child's) nurse.

rollar, *va.* = ARROLLAR, to roll; to wrap.

rollete, *m. dim.* small roll or roller.

rollizo, za. I. *a.* plump, stocky, heavy-built, sturdy. **II.** *m.* log.

rollo, *m.* roll, anything rolled up; rouleau; roller, rolling pin; log; round pillar; cylindrical bowlder; yoke pad; (law) roll.

rollón, *m.* fine bran.

rollona, *a.* (coll.) (child's) nurse.

Roma, *f.* Rome.—**a R. por todo,** at all hazards.

romadizarse, *vr.* to take cold.

romadizo, *m.* cold in the head; hay fever.

romaico, ca, *a.* & *n.* Romaic, modern Greek.

romana, *f.* steelyard.—**hacer r.,** to balance.—**venir a la r.,** to be of just weight.

romanador, *m.* weighmaster.

romanar, *va.* to weigh with a steelyard.

romance. I. *a.* & *m.* Romance or Romanic. **II.** *m.* Spanish language; romance, tale of chivalry; historic ballad, brief lyric; poem in octosyllabic metre, with alternate assonants.—**en r.,** in plain English, or language.

romanceador, ra, *n.* one who writes in Romance.

romancear, *va.* to translate into Spanish; to paraphrase.

romancero, ra. I. *n.* romancer. **II.** *m.* collection of old Spanish ballads.

romancesco, *a.* novelistic, romantic.

romancillo, *m. dim.* short ROMANCE.

romancista, *m.* one writing in a Romance language; novelist.

romanear. I. *va.* to weigh with a steelyard. **II.** *vn.* to outweigh, preponderate.

romaneo, *m.* weighing with a steelyard.

romanero, *m.* weighmaster.

romanesco, *a.* Roman; novelistic.

romanía.—de r., crestfallen.

románico, *a.* (arch.) Romanesque.

romanilla, *f.* (Venez.) dining-room screen.

romanillo, lla, *a.* round-hand.

romanista, *n.* one versed in Roman law or in Romance languages.

romanización, *f.* Romanization.

romanizar. I. *va.* to Romanize; to Latinize. **II.** *vr.* to become Romanized or Latinized.

romano, na, *n.* & *a.* Roman.

romanticismo, *m.* romanticism.

romántico, ca, *a.* & *n.* romantic(-ist).

romanza, *f.* (mus.) romance, romanza.

romanzador, ra, *n.* = ROMANCEADOR.

romanzar, *va.* = ROMANCEAR.

romaza, *f.* (bot.) sorrel.

rombal; rómbico, ca, *a.* rhombic.

rombo, *m.* (geom.) rhombus; lozenge, diamond.

romboedro, *m.* (geom.) rhombohedron.

romboidal, *a.* rhomboidal.

romboide, *m.* (geom.) rhomboid.

romeraje, *m.* = ROMERÍA.

romeral, *m.* place abounding with rosemary.

romería, *f.* pilgrimage; picnic, excursion; tour.

¹romero, ra. I. *n.* pilgrm, palmer. **II.** *m.* (ichth.) pilot fish; (ichth.) whiting.

²romero, *m.* (bot.) rosemary.

romí, romín, *m.* bastard saffron.

romo, ma, *a.* obtuse, blunt; flat-nosed.

rompecabezas, *m.* slingshot; puzzle, riddle.

rompecoches, *m.* a kind of rough, thick cloth.

rompedera, *f.* large iron puncher; powder screen.

rompedero, ra, *a.* fragile, brittle, perishable.

rompedor, ra, *n.* & *a.* breaker(-ing); crusher (-ing).

rompedura, *f.* breakage.

rompeesquinas, *m.* corner loafer, bully.

rompegalas, *n.* (coll.) slovenly person.

rompehielos, *m.* ice breaker; ice plow (of a boat).

rompenueces, *m.* nut cracker.

rompeolas, *m.* breakwater, jetty, mole.

romper. I. *va.* & *vn.* (*pp.* ROTO) to break, smash, shatter; to fracture (bone); to tear; to defeat, rout; to break up (land); to pierce; to open the way; to break off; to fall out, quarrel; (of the day) to dawn; to begin, start; to interrupt; to

resolve, determine; to sprout, bloom; to break out, spring up; (of light, sun, etc.) to break through; to break, infringe, transgress (a law, etc.).—**r. el alba, or la aurora** (here *el alba, la aurora* are subjects of the verb) to dawn.—**de rompe y rasga,** undaunted, brave, free and easy. **II.** *vr.* to break; to acquire ease of manner.—**r. el alma,** to break one's neck in a fall.—**r. la cabeza,** to rack one's brains.

rompesacos, *m.* long-spiked hardgrass.

rompesquinas, *m.* = ROMPEESQUINAS.

rompible, *a.* breakable.

rompido, da. I. *pp.* of ROMPER. **II.** *m.* ground newly broken.

rompiente. I. *a.* breaking. **II.** *m.* reef, shoal.

rompimiento, *m.* break, breakage, smash, rupture; crack; breach, infringement, violation; falling out; (theat.) open drop scene; opening in the background (of a picture); (min.) drift, driftway; (agr.) breaking up land.

ron, *m.* rum.

¹ronca, *f.* cry of a buck in rutting time; braggadocio, bullying.

²ronca, *f.* a kind of halberd.

roncador, ra. I. *n.* & *a.* snorer(-ing); RONCÓN. **II.** *m.* (ichth.) roncador, little bass.

roncamente, *adv.* hoarsely, coarsely.

roncar, *vn.* (*pret.* RONQUÉ; *subj.* RONQUE) to snore; to roar; to cry in rutting time; (coll.) to brag, to bully.

ronce, *m.* wheedle, cajolery.

roncear, *vn.* to be slow and unwilling, kill time, fool around; to wheedle; (naut.) to sail slowly.

roncería, *f.* sluggishness, remissness; tardiness; wheedle, cajoling expression; (naut.) slow, sluggish sailing.

roncero, ra, *a.* slow, slothful, tardy; grouchy, growling; flattering, wheedling, cajoling.

ronco, ca, *a.* hoarse, raucous.

roncón. I. *m.* drone of a bagpipe. **II.** *n.* & *a.* (Colomb.) (coll.) boaster(-ing), braggart.

¹roncha, *f.* welt; wheal, whelk; blotch; bump; loss of money through trickery.

²roncha, *f.* round, thin slice.

¹ronchar, *vn.* to raise welts.

²ronchar, *va.* to crunch.

ronchón, *m. aug.* large welt or bump.

ronda, *f.* night patrol; rounds (by a night watch), beat; clear space between a town and its walls; last round in a card game; round of drinks or cigars.

rondador, *m.* patrolman, roundsman, watchmen; rounder, night wanderer.

rondalla, *f.* fable, story, tale.

rondar, *va.* & *vn.* to patrol, go the rounds; to walk the streets by night; to haunt, hover about; to impend; (mil.) to make the grand rounds.—**r. la calle,** to flirt on the street.

rondel, *m.* (poet.) rondel.

rondeña, *f.* popular ballad of Ronda.

rondín, *m.* round of a corporal on the walls to visit the sentinels; watchman in an arsenal.

rondís, rondiz, *m.* face of a precious stone.

rondó, *m.* (mus.) rondo.

rondón.—de r., rashly, suddenly, abruptly; intrepidly.

rongigata, *f.* = REHILANDERA, pinwheel.

ronqué, ronque, *v. V.* RONCAR.

ronquear, *vn.* to be hoarse with cold.

ronquedad, ronquera, ronquez, *f.* hoarseness.

ronquido, *m.* snore; harsh, raucous sound.

ronronear, *vn.* to purr.

ronza, *f.*—**ir a la r.,** (naut.) to fall to leeward.

ronzal, *m.* halter; (naut.) purchase rope.

¹ronzar, *va.* to crunch, craunch.

²ronzar, *va.* (naut.) to raise or shift with levers.

roña, *f.* scab (in sheep); crust of filth on persons; bark of pine trees; rust; moral infection.

roñada, *f.* (naut.) garland; dolphin of a mast.

roñal, *m.* bark depot or storage place.

roñería, f. (coll.) niggardliness; stinginess.
roñoso, sa, a. scabby, leprous; dirty, filthy; rusty; (coll.) niggardly, stingy.
ropa, f. dry goods; stuff, fabric; wearing apparel, clothes, clothing; costume, dress; wardrobe, outfit, garments; robe or gown of office.—r. blanca, linen.—r. de cámara, or de levantar, dressing gown.—r. hecha, ready-made clothing.—r. limpia, clean laundry.—r. sucia, soiled laundry.—r. talar, long, loose gown.—r. vieja, cast-off clothes; (cook.) boiled meat, afterwards fried in a pan.—a quema r., at close range, point-blank; suddenly, unexpectedly.—nadar y guardar la r., to be extra cautious in an undertaking.—tentarse la r., to consider carefully.
ropaje, m. wearing apparel, clothes; robe, vestments; gown; garb; (art) drapery.
ropálico, ca, a. (poet.) rhopalic.
ropavejería, f. old-clothes shop.
ropavejero, m. old-clothes man.
ropería, f. clothier's trade; clothing shop, clothier's; wardrobe, clothes room, cloakroom; wardrobe keeper.
ropero, ra. I. n. clothier, dealer in clothes; wardrobe keeper; head shepherd, dairyman. II. m. clothespress, closet, wardrobe, locker.
ropeta, ropilla, f. dim. doublet, close-fitting jacket.—dar una r., to give a friendly reproof.
ropita, f. dim. child's clothing.
ropón, m. wide, loose gown.
roque, m. rook, castle (at chess).
roqueda, f., roquedal, m. rocky place.
roquedo, m. rock, boulder.
roqueño, ña, a. rocky, hard, flinty.
roquero, ra, a. rocky; built on rocks.
roqués, a. black (falcon).
roqueta, f. turret in a fortress.
roquete, m. (eccl.) rochet; barbed spearhead; (artil.) ramrod, rammer.
rorcual, m. (zool.) rorqual, finback (variety of large whales).
rorro, m. (coll.) babe in arms.
ros, m. (mil.) Spanish shako.
rosa, f. (bot.) rose; red spot on any part of che body; rose diamond; rosette; rosy aspect; rose color; flower of saffron; artificial rose.—r. náutica, or de los vientos, (naut.) traverse board, mariner's compass.
rosáceo, cea. I. a. rose-colored; (bot.) rosaceous. II. f. pl. (bot.) Rosaceæ, the rose family.
rosada, f. frost.
rosadelfa, f. (bot.) = AZALEA, azalea.
rosado, da, a. rose-colored; rose (as a.).
rosal, m. rose bush or plant.—r. de pitimaní, climbing rose.—r. perruno, or silvestre, dog-rose.
rosanilina, f. (chem.) rosaniline.
rosariero, ra, n. maker and seller of rosaries.
rosario, m. rosary (beads for praying and series of prayers); assemblage of people who recite the rosary in procession; (hydraul.) chain pump; (coll.) backbone.—acabar como el r. de la aurora, to break up in disorder.
rosarse, vr. = SONROSEARSE, to blush.
rosbif, m. (Angl.) roast beef.
rosca, f. screw and nut; screw thread; twist, spiral line or motion; circular badge of Spanish students; ring-shaped biscuit or bread; (naut.) flake of a cable.—hacer la r., to flatter, kowtow.
roscado, da. I. pp. of ROSCAR. II. a. threaded, having a screw thread.
roscar. I. va. to thread, make or cut a screw thread on. II. vn. to cut screw threads, to make screws.—máquina de r., screw-cutting machine.
roscón, m. aug. large screw; large circular loaf of bread.
rosear, vn. to turn rose color.

róseo, sea, a. rosy, roseate.
roséola, f. (med.) roseola, rose rash.
rosero, ra, n. gatherer of saffron flowers.
roseta, f. dim. small rose; rosette; rosy cheek; (metal.) rosette copper.
rosetón, m. aug. large rosette; (arch.) rose-window; rosette.
rosicler, m. rose pink (color); roset; ruby silver.
rosillo, illa, a. light red, roan.
¹rosmarino, na, a. light red.
²rosmarino, m. (bot.) = ROMERO, rosemary.
rosmaro, m. (zool.) walrus.
¹roso, sa, a. threadbare.—a r. y velloso, totally, without exception or distinction.
²roso, sa, a. red, rosy.
rosoli, m. rosolio, sundew (a liqueur).
rosones, m. pl. worms in animals.
rosqueado, da, a. twisted.
rosquete, m. ring-shaped cake or biscuit.
rosquilla, f. ring-shaped fancy cake; vine fretter.
rostrado, da, a. rostrate, with beaklike projection.
rostral, a. = ROSTRADO.
rostrillo, m. headdress on images; small seed pearl.
rostritorcido, da; rostrituerto, ta, a. (coll.) angry-looking; sad-looking.
rostro, m. rostrum, beak of a ship; bill or beak of a bird; countenance, human face; aspect of affairs.—r. a r., face to face.—hacer r. a, to face.
¹rota, f. (mil.) rout, defeat.—de r., or de r. batida, of a sudden; with total ruin.
²rota, f. (Rom. Cath.) ecclesiastical tribunal, Rota.
³rota, f. (bot.) rattan.
rotación, f. rotation.—r. de cultivos, rotation of crops.
rotal, a. pertaining to the Rota.
rotamente, adv. impudently, barefacedly.
rotante, a. rotating, revolving.
rotar, vn. = RODAR, to roll, revolve; to roam.
rotativo, va. I. a. rotary, revolving. II. f. rotary printing press.
rotatorio, ria, a. rotary, rotating.
roten, m. (bot.) rattan; rattan walking cane.
rotífero, ra. I. a. (zool.) rotiferous. II. m. pl. Rotifera.
roto, ta. I. pp. irreg. of ROMPER. II. a. broken, chipped, shattered; torn; ragged; destroyed; leaky, battered, or pierced; debauched, lewd. III. m. (Am.) tear (in clothes); poor, ragged man.
rotonda, f. rotunda; rear section of a stage coach.
rótula, f. (anat.) rotula, kneepan; (pharm.) troche, lozenge.
rotulación, f. labeling.
rotulador, ra, n. & a. labeler(-ing).
rotular, va. to label; put a title to.
rotulata, f. label, title, mark; collection of labels or posters.
rótulo, m. label, mark; show bill, poster, show card, placard; sign; (eccl.) certificate for beatification; school rota.
rotunda, f. rotunda; (Ry.) roundhouse.
rotundamente, adv. explicitly, categorically, peremptorily.
rotundidad, f. roundness, rotundity.
rotundo, da, a. round, circular, rotund; (of voice) full, sonorous; plain, peremptory.
rotura, f. rupture, fracture; breakage; (agr.) breaking up ground; (vet.) poultice.
roturación, f. (agr.) breaking up new ground.
roturar, va. (agr.) to break up (new ground).
roya, f. (bot.) rust, mildew, red blight.
royo, royó, etc. v. V. ROER.
roza, f. (agr.) stubbing, grubbing, clearing; ground cleared of brambles.
rozadero, m. stubbing place; (mech.) bearing plate, friction plate.

rozado, da. I. *pp.* of ROZAR. II. *a.* (agr.) stubbed, cleared; chilled, frappé (beverage).

rozador, ra, *n.* stubber, weeder.

rozadura, *f.* friction; frication; attrition; gall, chafing; chafed spot; (bot.) punk knot.

rozagante, *a.* pompous, showy; trailing on the ground (as a gown).

rozamiento, *m.* (mech.) friction; frication; rubbing; clashing, disagreement.

rozar. I. *va.* (*pret.* ROCÉ; *subj.* ROCE) to stub, grub, clear (the ground); to nibble (the grass); to scrape or pare off; to gall, to chafe; to graze, pass lightly over. II. *vn.* to graze, rub. III. *vr.* (of horses' hoofs) to interfere; to be on intimate terms; to falter, to stammer; to have a resemblance or connection with something else; to have to do with, associate; (naut.) to fret, to gall.

¹roznar, *vn.* = ¹RONZAR, to crunch.

²roznar, *vn.* = REBUZNAR, to bray.

¹roznido, *m.* crunching noise.

²roznido, *m.* braying of a donkey.

rozno, *m.* little donkey.

rozo, *m.* stubbing, weeding; brushwood.

rozón, *m.* short and broad scythe.

rúa, *f.* village street; highroad.

ruán, *m.* linen manufactured in Rouen.

ruana, *f.* (Am.) a square, heavy poncho.

¹ruano, na, *a.* = ROANO, roan (horse).

²ruano, na, *a.* round, circular.

ruante, *a.* walking or riding through the streets.

ruar, *vn.* to walk or ride through the streets; to flirt in the street.

rubefacción, *f.* (med.) rubefaction.

rubefaciente, *a.* (med.) rubefacient.

rúbeo, ea, *a.* ruby, reddish.

rubéola, *f.* (med.) measles.

ruberoide, *m.* a tarred-pasteboard roofing material.

rubescencia, *f.* rosiness.

rubescente, *a.* rosy.

rubeta, *f.* toad.

rubí, *m.* ruby; red color; redness of the lips.—**r. de Bohemia,** rosy quartz.—**r. del Brazil,** red topaz.—**r. espinela,** spinel ruby.

¹rubia, *f.* (bot.) madder.

²rubia, *f.* a blonde; (ichth.) a small red-colored river fish.

rubiáceo, a. I. *a.* (bot.) rubiaceous. II. *f. pl.* Rubiaceæ.

rubial. I. *a.* reddish (soil or plants). II. *m.* madder field.

rubicán, na, *a.* roan (horse).

rubicela, *f.* reddish-yellow topaz.

rubicundez, *f.* ruddiness; rosiness.

rubicundo, da, *a.* reddish, rubicund; golden-red; blond; rosy with health.

rubidio, *m.* (chem.) rubidium.

rubiera, *f.* (Venez.) mischief, reckless action; (C. A.) merrymaking, carousal.

rubificar, *va.* to rubify, make red.

rubín, rubinejo, *m.* ruby.

rubio, bia. I. *a.* blond, golden, fair. II. *m.* (ichth.) red gurnard.

rubión, *a.* (of a kind of wheat) reddish.

rublo, *m.* ruble, Russian silver coin.

rubor, *m.* blush, flush; bashfulness.

ruborizarse, *vr.* to blush, to flush.

ruborosamente, *adv.* blushingly, bashfully.

ruboroso, sa, *a.* bashful.

rúbrica, *f.* red mark or caption, title; mark or flourish added to one's signature; (eccl.) rubric or rules in prayer books.—**de r.,** according to rules or custom.

rubricante. I. *a.* signing, attesting. II. *m.* junior minister or secretary appointed to sign the proceedings.

rubricar, *va.* (*pret.* RUBRIQUÉ; *subj.* RUBRIQUE) to sign or indorse with one's peculiar mark or flourish, without writing the name; to sign and seal.

rubriquista, *m.* (eccl.) rubrician.

rubro, bra, *a.* red, reddish; rubric.

ruc, *m.* = ROCHO, roc, a fabulous bird.

ruca, *f.* (Chile, Arg.) hut, cabin.

rucio, cia. I. *a.* (of animals) light silver gray; (Colomb.) dapple-gray; (coll.) gray; gray-haired, hoary. II. *m.* donkey.

ruco, ca, *a.* (C. A.) old, worthless.

rucho, *m.* donkey.

ruda, *f.* (bot.) rue.

rudamente, *adv.* rudely, roughly.

rudeza, *f.* roughness, rudeness, coarseness.

rudimental, *a.* rudimentary; elementary.

rudimento, *m.* rudiment, embryo, germ; vestige.—*pl.* rudiments, elements.

rudo, da, *a.* rude, rough, unpolished; hard, rigorous, severe; stupid.

rueca, *f.* distaff for spinning; twist, winding; (naut.) fish of a mast or yard.

rueda, *f.* wheel; caster, roller; circle of persons; crowd; round slice; turn, time, succession; (ichth.) sunfish; rack (torture); hoops for skirts; spread of a peacock's tail; three-handed billiard game.—**r. catalina,** or **de Santa Catalina,** Catherine wheel.—**r. de alimentación por abajo, (arriba)** (hydraul.) undershot (overshot) wheel.—**r. de andar,** treadmill.—**r. de costado,** breast wheel.—**r. del timón,** (naut.) steering wheel.—**r. hidráulica,** water wheel. —**hacer la r.,** to cajole, wheedle.

ruedecica, cilla, zuela, *f. dim.* small wheel; caster, roller.

¹ruedo, *m.* rotation, turn; circuit; circumference; edge of a wheel or disk; round plat or mat; rug; (sewing) skirt lining; bottom of a skirt; valance. —**a todo r.,** at all events.

²ruedo, ruede, *v. V.* RODAR.

¹ruego, *m.* request, plea, petition, entreaty, supplication.

²ruego, ruegue, *v. V.* ROGAR.

ruejo, *m.* mill wheel; ground roller.

ruello, *m.* (agr.) ground roller.

ruequecilla, *f.* small distaff.

rufián, *m.* ruffian; pimp, pander.—**rufianada,** *f.* (Am.) villainy, villainous or base act.

rufianear, *vn.* to play the ruffian; to pimp, to pander.

rufianería, *f.* ruffianism.

rufianesco, ca. I. *a.* ruffianly, ruffianish. II. *f.* ruffians (collect.); gang of ruffians; ruffianism.

rufo, fa, *a.* carroty, red-haired; frizzed, curled.

ruga, *f.* wrinkle.—**rugar,** *va.* to wrinkle.

rugible, *a.* capable of bellowing or roaring.

rugido, *m.* roar; rumbling in the bowels.

rugiente, *a.* bellowing, roaring.

ruginoso, sa, *a.* rusty.

rugir. I. *vn.* (*ind.* RUJO; *subj.* RUJA) to roar, bellow, howl. II. *v. impers.* to be whispered about, to transpire, to be said.

rugosidad, *f.* rugosity, wrinkled condition.

rugoso, sa, *a.* rugose, corrugated, wrinkled.

ruibarbo, *m.* (bot.) rhubarb.

ruido, *m.* noise; rumor; report; discussion; dispute, difference; law suit.—**hacer,** or **meter, r.,** to attract attention; to create a sensation. —**mucho r. y pocas nueces,** or **ser más el r. que las nueces,** much ado about nothing.

ruidosamente, *adv.* noisily; loudly.

ruidoso, sa, *a.* noisy, loud; clamorous.

ruin. I. *a.* mean, vile, low, base, despicable; little, puny; decayed; wicked, malicious; niggardly, stingy; insidious, treacherous, infamous; (of an animal) vicious. II. *m.* wicked, mean, or vile man; small nerve in the tail of cats.

ruina, *f.* ruin, decline, downfall; overthrow, fall. —*pl.* ruins, débris.—**batir en r.,** (mil.) to batter in, breach.

ruinar, *va. & vr.* to ruin, destroy.

ruindad, *f.* meanness, baseness; ill turn, base action.

---

ruinmente, *adv.* basely, meanly, despicably.
ruinoso, sa, *a.* ruinous; worthless.
ruiponce, *m.* (bot.) = RAPÓNCHIGO, rampion.
ruipóntico, *m.* (bot.) rhubarb, pieplant.
ruiseñor, *m.* (ornith.) nightingale.
rujada, *f.* heavy shower.
rujo, ruja, *v. V.* RUGIR.
rular, *vn.* = RODAR, to roll, revolve.
ruleta, *f.* roulette.
rulo, *m.* ball, bowl; conical stone in oil mills; road roller.
ruló, *m.* (print.) ink roller, brayer.
rumano, na, *n. & a.* Rumanian.
rumba, *f.* (Cuba) rumba (dance or music for it).
rumbadas, *f. pl.* (naut.) = ARRUMBADAS, wales.
rumbo, *m.* bearing, course, direction; trend; road, route, way; (coll.) pomp, ostentation; liberality, generosity; (naut.) scuttle; (her.) rustre.—**abatir el r.,** (naut.) to fall to leeward. —**con r. a,** (naut.) in the direction of; heading, or sailing, for.—**fiesto de r.,** lavish party.— **hacer r. a,** (naut.) to sail for; to head for.
rumbón, na, *a.* = RUMBOSO.
rumbosamente, *adv.* (coll.) pompously, grandly, liberally.
rumboso, sa, *a.* pompous, magnificent, liberal.
rumí, *n.* (among the Moors) Christian.
rumia, *f.* rumination, chewing the cud.
rumiador, ra, *n. & a.* ruminator(-ing), ruminant.
rumiadura, *f.* rumination.
rumiante. I. *n. & a.* ruminant; muser(-ing). **II.** *m. pl.* Ruminantia.
rumiar, *va.* to ruminate; to muse, meditate.
rumión, na, *a.* ruminating much.
rumo, *m.* (cooperage) first hoop of a cask.
rumor, *m.* rumor, report, hearsay; sound of voices; murmur.—**rumorarse** (Am.) **rumo-rearse,** *vr. impers.* to be said or rumored, be circulating as a rumor.
rumorcico, illo, ito, *m. dim.* flying report.
rumoroso, sa, *a.* causing rumor.
runa, *f.* rune, runic character.
rundún, *m.* (Arg.) a very small humming bird.
runfla, runflada, *f.* (coll.) series of things.
rúnico, ca; runo, na, *a.* runic.
runrún, *m.* (coll.) rumor, report.
ruña, *f.* (cooperage) croze.—**ruñadera,** *f.* coop-er's croze.—**ruñadura,** *f.* = RUÑA.—**ruñar,** *va.* (cooperage) to croze.
rupestre, *a.* rupiculous, found or living on rocks; rupestrian, inscribed or cut into rocks.
¹rupia, *f.* rupee, silver coin.
²rupia, *f.* (med.) rupia, a skin disease.
rupicabra, rupicapra, *f.* chamois.
rupícola, *a.* rupiculous, found or living on rocks.
ruptura, *f.* rupture; fracture, breaking.—**r., del núcleo,** or **nuclear,** nuclear fission.
ruqueta, *f.* (bot.) = JARAMAGO, hedge mustard.
rural, *a.* rural, country, rustic.
ruralmente, *adv.* rurally.
rus, *m.* (bot.) sumach. Also ZUMAQUE.
rusco, *m.* (bot.) kneeholly, butcher's-broom.
rusel, *m.* a kind of woollen serge.
rusiente, *a.* turning red-hot.
ruso, sa, *n. & a.* Russian.
rusticación, *f.* rustication.
rustical, *a.* rustic, rural, wild.
rústicamente, *adv.* rustically, rudely.
rusticano, na, *a.* wild (plants).
rusticar, *vn.* (*pret.* RUSTIQUÉ; *subj.* RUSTIQUE) to rusticate.
rusticidad, *f.* rusticity, simplicity; rudeness, clumsiness.
rústico, ca. I. *a.* rustic, rural; coarse, clumsy; unmannerly.—**a la,** or **en r.,** (bookbinding) in paper covers, unbound. **II.** *n.* rustic, peasant.
rustiqué, rustique, *v. V.* RUSTICAR.
rustiquez, rustiqueza, *f.* rusticity.
rustrir, *va.* to toast; to fry.
rustro, *m.* (her.) rustre.

ruta, *f.* route, way.
rutáceo, a, *a.* (bot.) rutaceous.
rutenio, *m.* (chem.) ruthenium.
ruteno, na, *n. & a.* Ruthenian.
rutilante, *a.* sparkling, scintillating.
rutilar, *vn.* (poet.) to twinkle, sparkle, scintillate.
rútilo, la. I. *a.* shining red; sparkling. **II.** *m.* (also **rutilo**) (min.) rutile.
rutina, *f.* routine, custom, habit, rut.
rutinario, ria. I. *a.* routine (as *a.*). **II.** *n.* rou-tinist.
rutinero, ra, *a.* routinistic.
ruzafa, *f.* garden, park.

S

sábado, *m.* Saturday; Sabbath among the Jews. —**s. inglés,** Saturday half-day off.
sabalar, *m.* net for catching shad.
sabalera, *f.* fire grate in furnaces.
sabalero, *m.* shad fisher.
sábalo, *m.* (ichth.) shad.
sábana, *f.* sheet (for a bed); altar cloth.—**pegár-sele a uno las sábanas,** to rise late.
sabana, *f.* savanna, grassy plain.
sabandija, *f.* small nasty insect or reptile; bug; vermin.—**sabandijuela,** *f. dim.* very small insect, vermin.
sabanear, *vn.* (Am.) to scour the plain.
sabanero, ra. I. *n.* dweller on the savanna. **II.** *a.* pertaining to a savanna. **III.** *m.* (ornith.) bird resembling the starling. **IV.** *f.* (Venez.) a sa-vanna snake that destroys harmful insects.
sabanilla, *f. dim.* small sheet or piece of linen; altar cloth; napkin; head kerchief or scarf.
sabañón, *m.* chilblain.—**comer como un s.,** to eat greedily, devour.
sabatario, *a.* Sabbatarian.
sabático, ca, *a.* Sabbatical.
sabatina, *f.* (eccl.) Saturday mass; Saturday exercise in colleges.
sabatino, na, *a.* pertaining to Saturday.
sabatizar, *vn.* to keep the Sabbath.
sabedor, ra, *a. & n.* knowing, informed (person).
sabeísmo, *m.* Sabaism, Sabianism.
sabeliano, na, *a. & n.* Sabellian.
sabelianismo, *m.* Sabellianism.
sabélico, ca, *a.* pertaining to the Sabines or Samnites.
sabelotodo, *n.* = SABIDILLO.
sabeo, *a.* Sabæan, of or from Sheba.
saber. I. *va.* (*ind. pres.* SÉ, *pret.* SUPE, *fut.* SABRÉ; *subj.* SEPA) to know; to be able, know how, can (*Juan sabe cantar,* John can, or knows how to, sing).—**s. cuántas son cinco,** to know what is what.—**un no sé qué,** a certain something; something that does not matter.—**y no sé qué más,** or **y qué sé yo qué más,** and what not; and so forth. **II.** *vn.* to know; to be very saga-cious; (Arg.) to have the habit of, to usually (*verb*).—**s. a,** to taste of, taste like (*esto sabe a limón,* this tastes of, or like, lemon).—**s. de,** to know, be familiar with; to hear of or from, have news about.—**a s.,** namely, viz., to wit.— **que yo sepa,** to my knowledge, as far as I know.—**¿quién sabe?** perhaps, who knows!— **¿sabe?** you know, don't you know? (in U. S. slang, savvy?).—as an expletive in conversation. **III.** *vr.* to become known; to get found out. **IV.** *m.* learning, knowledge, lore.—**según mi leal s. y entender,** to the best of my knowledge.
sabiamente, *adv.* wisely, knowingly, learnedly.
sabicú, *m.* (Cuba) (bot.) sabicú, horseflesh ma-hogany.
sabidillo, illa, *n.* pedant, know-it-all person.
sabido, da. I. *pp.* of *saber.* **II.** *a.* learned, well-informed.—**por s. se calla,** it goes without saying.
sabiduría, *f.* learning, knowledge; wisdom.

sabiendas.—a s. *adv.* knowingly, consciously.

sabiente, *a.* knowing.

sabihondez, *f.* (coll.) conceited assumption of knowledge or learning.

sabihondo, da, *a.* affecting knowledge or learning, know-it-all.

sabina, *f.* (bot.) savin.

sabinar, *m.* clump of savins.

¹sabino, na, *a.* roan (horse).

²sabino, na, *n.* & *a.* Sabine.

sabio, bia. I. *a.* wise, learned, knowing; cunning. **II.** *n.* sage, wise person; scholar, learned person; scientist.

sablazo, *m.* blow with or wound from a saber; (coll.) borrowing or sponging.

¹sable, *m.* saber, cutlass.

²sable, *m.* (her.) sable, black.

sablista, *m.* (coll.) sponger, one who asks for petty loans.

sablón, *m.* coarse sand.

saboga, *f.* (ichth.) a species of shad.

sabogal, *m.* net for catching shad.

saboneta, *f.* hunting-case watch.

sabor, *m.* taste, flavor; dash, zest.—*pl.* round knobs on the bit of a bridle.—**a s.,** at pleasure.

saborcico, illo, ito, *m. dim.* slight flavor or taste.

saboreamiento, *m.* relish, relishing.

saborear. I. *va.* to flavor, give a relish or zest to; to interest, cajole, wheedle. **II.** *va.* & *vr.* to relish, enjoy, find delicious, be pleased or delighted; to smack one's lips.

saborete, *m.* slight flavor or taste.

saboyana, *f.* open skirt; a kind of pie.

saboyano, na, *a.* Savoyard.

sabrosamente, *adv.* deliciously.

sabrosico, ica, illo, illa, ito, ita, *a. dim.* rather tasty.

sabroso, sa, *a.* savory, tasty, palatable, delicious; pleasant, delightful; salted, saltish.

sabucal, *m.* clump of willows.

sabuco, *m.* = SAÚCO, (bot.) alder; horny part of horse's hoof.

sabueso, *m.* hound, bloodhound, beagle, harehound, foxhound.

sabugal, sabugo = SABUCAL, SABUCO.

sábulo, *m.* coarse, heavy sand.

sabuloso, sa, *a.* gritty, sandy, gravelly.

saburra, *f.* (med.) saburra, gastric sordes.

saburral, *a.* (med.) saburral.

saburroso, sa, *a.* indicating a foul stomach.

¹saca, *f.* drawing out; exportation, extraction; first authorized register of a sale; first certified copy of a document issued by a notary.—**estar de s.,** to be on sale; (coll.) to be marriageable.

²saca, *f.* large bag or sack of coarse stuff.

sacabala, *f.* (surg.) alphonsin.

sacabalas, *m.* (artil.) bullet screw, ball extractor.

sacabocado, sacabocados, *m.* hollow punch; ticket punch.

sacabotas, *m.* bootjack.

sacabrocas, *m.* tack claw, tack puller.

sacabuche, *m.* (naut.) pumping tube or pipe; (mus.) sackbut; player on the sackbut; nincompoop.

sacaclavos, *m.* (carp.) nail extractor.

sacacorchos, *m.* corkscrew.

sacada, *f.* region separated from a province or country.

sacadilla, *f.* noise made to rouse game.

sacadinero, sacadineros, *m.* (coll.) catch-penny.

sacador, ra, *n.* drawer, extractor; one that takes or brings out.

sacadura, *f.* (sewing) slash (to ease); (Colomb.) taking out, extracting.

sacafilásticas, *f.* (artil.) priming wire.

sacalagua, *m.* (Am.) a nearly white half-breed.

sacaliña, *f.* goad; trick, cunning.

sacamanchas, *m. or f.* cleaner, scourer, cleanser.

sacamantas, *m.* (coll.) tax collector.

sacamiento, *m.* taking or drawing out.

sacamolero, ra; sacamuelas, *n.* tooth extractor, dentist.

sacanabo, *m.* (naut.) pump hook.

sacanete, *m.* lansquenet, a card game.

sacapelotas, *m.* bullet screw.

sacapotras, *m.* (coll.) bad surgeon.

sacar, *va.* (*pret.* SAQUÉ; *subj.* SAQUE) to extract, draw, draw out, pull out; to take out; to withdraw; to dispossess, put out; to except, exclude; to manufacture, produce, invent; to take (a photo.); to publish; bring out; to put forth, bring forth; to imitate, copy, take off; to clear, free, place in safety; to find out, investigate, discover; to make out, solve, interpret; to relieve (fever, etc.); to eradicate; to extort; to get, obtain, attain; to show, exhibit, manifest; to excite (passion, anger); to lose the judgment; to deduce, draw, infer; to ballot, elect by ballot; to draw, win (a prize); to win at play; (games) to serve (the ball), to kick off; to draw, unsheath (a sword); to make, take (a copy); to cite, name, quote.—**s. a bailar,** to lead out for a dance; to drag in irrelevantly.—**s. a la vergüenza,** to put a criminal in the pillory; to bring shame upon.—**s. a luz,** to print, publish; to mention or bring out.—**s. a pasear,** to take out for a walk.—**s. de madre,** to make one lose patience.—**s. de pila,** to become sponsor for at baptism.—**s. de quicio** = S. DE MADRE. —**s. (uno) de sus casillas,** (fig.) to exhaust one's patience, drive crazy.—**s. el ascua, or la brasa, con la mano del gato, or con mano ajena,** to have someone else pull one's chestnuts out of the fire.—**s. el cuerpo,** to dodge; to shun; to get out, or keep out (of something); to play safe.—**s. el jugo,** to work (one) hard, slave-drive.—**s. el pecho por,** to stand for, to defend, to take the part of.—**s. en claro, or en limpio,** to conclude, arrive at the conclusion; to gather (from a writing, etc.).—**s. la cara,** to present oneself as an interested party. —**s. la cara por** = S. EL PECHO POR.—**s. la cuenta,** to figure out.—**s. por factor común,** (math.) to factor out.—**s. ventaje de,** to profit by.

sacarato, *m.* (chem.) saccharate.

sacárico, *a.* saccharic.

sacarificación, *f.* saccharification.

sacarificar, *va.* to saccharify.

sacarígeno, na, *a.* sacchariferous.

sacarimetría, *f.* saccharimetry.

sacarímetro, *m.* saccharimeter.

sacarina, *f.* (chem.) saccharine.

sacarino, na, *a.* saccharine, containing sugar.

sacaroideo, a, *a.* (chem.) saccharoid.

sacarómetro, *m.* saccharimeter.

sacarosa, *f.* (chem.) saccharose.

sacaroso, sa, *a.* saccharinelike.

sacasillas, *n.* (coll.) (theat.) stage hand; busybody.

sacatapón, *m.* corkscrew; bung drawer.

sacate, *m.* (Mex.) grass, herb; hay.

sacatrapos, *m.* (artil.) wad hook, wormer.

sacerdocio, *m.* priesthood.

sacerdotal, *a.* sacerdotal.

sacerdote, *m.* priest, clergyman.

sacerdotisa, *f.* priestess.

saciable, *a.* satiable.

saciar, *va.* & *vr.* to satiate.

saciedad, *f.* satiety.

saciña, *f.* (bot.) a kind of willow.

sacio, a, *a.* satiate, satiated.

saco, *m.* sack, bag; sackful, bagful; coat, jacket; Roman sagum; (in PELOTA) = SAQUE, hitting the ball on the rebound; (mil.) pillage, sack, plunder.—**s. de noche,** hand bag, valise, satchel.—**entrar, meter, or poner, a s.,** to plunder, loot.—**no echar en s. roto,** not to forget, not to ignore.

sacra, *f.* (eccl.) sacring tablet.

sacramentado, da, *a.* (eccl.) transubstantiated; having received the last sacraments.

sacramental. I. *a.* sacramental. **II.** *n.* person or fraternity devoted to the worship of the sacrament of the altar.

sacramentalmente, *adv.* sacramentally; in confession.

sacramentar. I. *va.* (eccl.) to administer the sacraments to; to consecrate; (coll.) to conceal, hide. **II.** *vr.* to be transubstantiated.

sacramentario, ria, *n.* Sacramentarian.

sacramente, *adv.* = SAGRADAMENTE, sacredly.

sacramento, *m.* (eccl.) sacrament; Christ transubstantiated in the host.—**s. del altar,** Eucharist; consecrated Host.

sacratísimo, ma, *a. super.* most sacred, holiest.

sacre, *m.* (ornith.) saker; small cannon.

sacrificadero, *m.* sacrificing place.

sacrificador, ra, *n.* & *a.* sacrificer(-ing).

sacrificante, *a.* sacrificing, hazarding; sacrificial, sacrificatory.

sacrificar. I. *va.* (*pret.* SACRIFIQUÉ; *subj.* SACRIFIQUE) to sacrifice. **II.** *vr.* to devote oneself to God; to sacrifice oneself, give up one's life.

sacrificio, *m.* sacrifice, offering; submission.—**s. del altar,** sacrifice of the mass.—**s. propiciatorio,** peace offering.

sacrifiqué, sacrifique, *v.* V. SACRIFICAR.

sacrílegamente, *m.* sacrilegiously.

sacrilegio, *m.* sacrilege.

sacrílego, ga, *a.* sacrilegious.

sacrismoche, cho, *m.* in jocular style, a man in a ragged black coat.

sacrista, *m.* sacristan, sexton.

sacristán, *m.* sacristan, sexton, clerk; hoop skirt, bustle.—**sacristana,** *f.* sacristan or sexton's wife; nun in charge of the sacristy.

sacristanejo, *m. dim.* little sacristan.

sacristanía, *f.* office of a sexton.

sacristía, *f.* sacristy, vestry; SACRISTANÍA.

¹**sacro,** *m.* (anat.) sacrum.

²**sacro, cra,** *a.* holy, sacred.

sacrosanto, ta, *a.* sacred, sacrosanct.

sacudida, *f.* shake, shaking, jerk.

sacudidamente, *adv.* rejectingly.

sacudido, da. I. *pp.* of SACUDIR. **II.** *a.* harsh, intractable; determined.

sacudidor, *m.* shaker; beater; duster.

sacudidura, *f.* shaking; dusting, cleansing.

sacudimiento, *m.* shake, shaking; shock, jerk, jolt.

sacudir. I. *va.* to shake; jolt, jerk; to beat (to remove dust); spank, drub; dart, throw off, discharge; shake off. **II.** *vn.* (naut.) to flap (sails). **III.** *vr.* to reject, drive away, shake off.

sachadura, *f.* hoeing, weeding.

sachar, *va.* (agr.) to weed.

sacho, *m.* weeder, weeding tool.

sádico, ca, *a.* sadistic.

sadismo, *m.* sadism.

saduceísmo, *m.* Sadduceeism.

saduceo, a, *n.* & *a.* Sadducee(-cean).

saeta, *f.* arrow, dart, shaft; cock of a sundial, gnomon; hand of a watch or clock; magnetic needle; bud of a vine; (astr.) Sagitta, the Arrow.—*pl.* pious ejaculations.

saetada, *f.,* **saetazo,** *m.* shooting an arrow; arrow wound.

saetear, *va.* to attack or kill with arrows.

saetero, ra. I. *a.* pertaining to arrows. **II.** *m.* archer, bowman, dartman. **III.** *f.* loophole; small grated window in prisons.

saetí, *m.* brad, peg, pin, tack.

saetía, *f.* (naut.) settee; vessel with lateen sails; loophole.

saetilla, *f. dim.* small arrow or dart; small magnetic needle; hand of a watch; devotional verse; (bot.) sagittaria.

¹**saetín,** *m.* mill race, sluice, flume; SAETÍ.

²**saetín,** *m.* (Gal.) sateen or satine.

saetón, *m.* dart for shooting rabbits.

safeno, a, *a.* (anat.) saphenous.

sáfico, ca, *a.* (poet.) sapphic.

¹**saga,** *f.* witch.

²**saga,** *f.* saga (legend).

sagacidad, *f.* sagacity, sagaciousness.

sagapeno, *m.* sagapenum (gum).

sagatí, *m.* sagathy, farmer's satin.

sagaz, *a.* sagacious; (of dogs) with keen scent; discerning, farsighted, farseeing.

sagazmente, *adv.* sagaciously.

sagita, *f.* (geom.) sagitta.

sagital, *a.* sagittal, sagittate.

sagitaria, *f.* (bot.) sagittaria, arrowhead.

sagitario, *m.* dartman, archer; (S-, astr.) Sagittarius, the Archer.

sago, *m.* loose, wide greatcoat.

ságoma, *f.* (arch.) pattern, reglet, rule.

sagradamente, *adv.* sacredly.

sagrado, da. I. *a.* sacred, consecrated; holy; (obs.) incurable, cursed, execrable. **II.** *m.* asylum, haven of refuge, place of safety.

sagrario, *m.* sacrarium; (eccl.) ciborium.

sagú, *m.* (bot.) sago.

saguaipe, *m.* (Arg.) a parasitic worm that attacks the liver of cattle.

ságula, *f. dim.* of SAYUELO, small frock.

saguntino, na, *n.* & *a.* Saguntian.

sahina, *f.* = ZAHINA, (bot.) sorghum.

sahornarse, *vr.* to chafe, be skinned.

sahorno, *m.* chafe, chafing, skinning.

sahumado, da. I. *pp.* of SAHUMAR. **II.** *a.* bettered, improved.

sahumador, *m.* perfumer, perfuming pot; fumigator.

sahumadura, *f.* perfuming; fumigation.

sahumar, *va.* to perfume; to smoke; to fumigate.

sahumerio, sahumo, *m.* smoke; vapor, steam; fumigation; fuming.

sai, *m.* (Am.) (zool.) a kind of monkey, sai.

saimirí, *m.* (Am.) (zool.) titi, squirrel monkey.

saín, *m.* grease or fat, fatness; sardine fat used as burning oil; greasiness on clothes.

sainar, *va.* to fatten.

sainete, *m.* (theat.) one-act farce; burlesque; flavor, relish, zest; seasoning, sauce; delicious tidbit; delicacy; anything nice and choice; taste or elegance in dress.—**sainetear,** *vn.* to act farces.—**sainetero,** *m.* writer of farces.—**sainetesco, ca,** *a.* comical, burlesque.

saíno, *m.* (Am.) (zool.) a kind of boar.

saja, *f.* (surg.) sacrification.

sajador, *m.* bleeder, scarifier.

sajadura, *f.* = SAJA.

sajar, *va.* to scarify.

sajelar, *va.* to sift and clean (clay).

sajón, na, *n.* & *a.* Saxon.

sal, *f.* salt; wit, facetiousness; grace, winning manners; (chem.) salt.—**s. amoníaco,** sal ammoniac.—**s. de compás** = s. GEMA.—**s. de la Higuera,** Epsom salts.—**s. gema,** rock salt.—**s. marina,** sea salt.—**s. pedrés,** or **piedra,** rock salt.—**echar en s.,** to reserve for another occasion.

sala, *f.* drawing room, living room, parlor; hall; large room; court of justice (room and judges); tribunal.—**s. de batalla,** sorting table or place (in a postoffice).—**s. de espera,** waiting-room.—**s. de justicia,** court of justice.—**s. del crimen,** criminal court or tribunal.—**guardar s.,** to observe the rules and formalities of the court.—**hacer s.,** to form a quorum in a court.

salacidad, *f.* salaciousness, lechery, lust.

salacot, *m.* topi, sola pith helmet.

saladamente, *adv.* (coll.) wittily, facetiously.

saladar, *m.* salt marsh.

saladero, *m.* salting place; salting tub.

saladillo, *m. dim.* fresh bacon half-salted.

salado, da. I. *pp.* of SALAR. **II.** *a.* salty; briny, brackish; witty, facetious; graceful, winsome;

(Am.) unlucky; (Arg., Chile) expensive. **III.** *m.* (bot.) saltwort; saline land.

salador, ra. I. *n.* salter, curer. **II.** *m.* SALADERO.

saladura, *f.* salting, curing; salted provisions.

salamandra, *f.* salamander; fire sprite; anything fireproof.

salamandria, salamanquesa, *f.* star lizard.

salamanquino, na, *n.* & *a.* = SALMANTINO.

salangana, *f.* (ornith.) swift, esculent swallow.

salar, *va.* to salt, to season or preserve with salt, to cure or corn (meat); to brine.

salariar, *va.* to give a salary or wages to.

salario, *m.* wages, salary.

salaz, *a.* salacious, lustful.

salazón, *f.* salting; salted meats or fish.

salbadera, *f.* sand box, pounce box.

salbanda, *f.* (min.) selvage.

salce, *m.* (bot.) = SAUCE, willow.

salceda, *f.,* **salcedo,** *m.* salicetum, willow garden.

salcereta, *f.* dice box.

salcochar, salcocho = SANCOCHAR, SANCOCHO.

salchicha, *f.* sausage; (fort.) long fascine; (artil.) saucisse, long fuse.

salchichería, *f.* sausage shop.

salchichero, ra, *n.* sausage maker or seller.

salchichón, *m. aug.* sausage; (fort.) large fascine.

saldado, da, *pp.* & *a.* paid, settled, balanced.

saldar, *va.* (com.) to settle, liquidate, balance.

saldista, *n.* one who sells or buys remnants.

saldo, *m.* (com.) balance; settlement; remnants sold at low prices; sale.

saldrá, saldré, *v. V.* SALIR.

saledizo, za. I. *a.* salient, projecting. **II.** *m.* projection, ledge.

salegar, *m.* salt lick.

salema, *f.* (ichth.) gilthead.

salep, *m.* salep or salop root.

salera, *f.* saltcat in a salt lick; salt mine.

salero, *m.* saltcellar; salt pan; salt storage place; salt lick; (coll.) gracefulness, winning ways.

saleroso, sa, *a.* (coll.) witty, facetious; lively, jolly, winsome.

salesiano, na, *n.* & *a.* Salesian.

saleta, *f. dim.* small hall; royal antechamber; court of appeal.

salgada, salgadera, *f.* (bot.) = ORZAGA, orach.

salgar, *va.* to feed salt to (cattle).

salgo, salga, *v. V.* SALIR.

salguera, *f.,* **salguero,** *m.* (bot.) osier, willow.

salicaria, *f.* (bot.) a salicaceous shrub.

salicilato, *m.* (chem.) salicylate.

salicílico, ca, *a.* (chem.) salicylic.

salicina, *f.* (chem.) salicin.

salicíneo, a, *a.* (bot.) salicaceous.

sálico, ca, *a.* Salic.

salicor, *f.* (bot.) prickly saltwort.

salida, *f.* start, setting or going out, departure, exit; outlet; way out, exit; outskirts; issue, result, conclusion; projection, protuberance; (com.) salableness; expenditure, outlay; loophole, subterfuge, pretext; sally; (naut.) headway; (mil.) sally, sortie.—**sin s.,** dead-end (street).—**tener s.** (com.) to sell well, to be saleable.

salidizo, = SALEDIZO.

salido, da. I. *pp.* of SALIR. **II.** *a.* projecting; (of female animals) in season.

saliente. I. *a.* salient, projecting. **II.** *f.* projection, lug.

salífero, ra, *a.* salt-bearing.

salificable, *a.* salifiable.

salín, *m.* storage place for salt.

salinero, ra, *n.* salter, salt maker, salt dealer.

salino, na. I. *a.* saline. **II.** *f.* salt pit, salt pan, salt works, salt mine.

¹**salio, lia,** *n.* & *a.* Salian (pertaining to, or one of, the salii, or priests of Mars).

²**salio, lia,** *a.* pert. to the Salian Franks.

salipirina, *f.* salipyrine.

salir. I. *vn.* (*ind. pres.* SALGO, *fut.* SALDRÉ; *subj.*

SALGA) to go or come out; to depart, leave, sail; sally, sally forth; get out (of a vehicle); to end, be over (as a season); to loom, show up; disappear, come off (as a stain); rise (as the sun); to shoot, spring; to grow; stand out, project; to begin (a game, a dance, etc.); to be issued or published; to result, turn out; to acquit oneself, come out, do (well, badly); to be drawn (as in a lottery); to be elected; to lead to, open to; (naut.) to exceed, to excel, pass another vessel in sailing; to happen, occur; to correspond; to imply; to come out right, check (as a sum); to say or do a thing unexpectedly or unseasonably; (**de**) to cease (as); (theat.) to enter, appear; (before *pp.*) to come out, to be (*salió herido,* he came out, or was, wounded).—**s. a,** to come to (so much); to resemble, look like.— **s. adelante,** to be successful.—**s. al encuentro de,** to come out to meet.—**s. avante,** or **bien,** or **con bien,** to do well, to be successful.—**s. con,** to drag in, say unexpectedly or irrelevantly.—**s. de,** to dispose of; to part with; to get rid of.—**s. de compras,** to go shopping.— **s. de su padre,** to be released from paternal guardianship.—**s. de sus casillas,** to lose one's temper.—**s. ganando,** to come out a winner, gain.—**s. mal,** to do badly, be unsuccessful, fail.—**s. perdiendo,** to lose, come out a loser. —**hacer s. los colores al rostro,** to put one to blush.—**salga lo que saliere,** happen what will, whatever may happen. **II.** *vr.* to leak; to overflow.—**s. con la suya,** to accomplish one's end, to have one's way.—**s. de madre,** to exceed, run over; to lose one's self-control.

salisipán, *m.* (P. I.) a swift boat.

salitrado, da, *a.* impregnated with saltpeter.

salitral. I. *a.* nitrous. **II.** *m.* saltpeter bed or works.

salitre, *m.* saltpeter, niter.

salitrería, *f.* saltpeter works.

salitrero, ra, *n.* saltpeter refiner or dealer.

salitroso, sa, *a.* nitrous.

saliva, *f.* saliva, spittle.

salivación, *f.* salivation; spitting.

salival, *a.* salivary.

salivar, *vn.* to spit; to salivate.

salivera, *f.* round knob on the bits of a bridle.

salivoso, sa, *a.* spitting excessively.

salma, *f.* ton, twenty hundredweight.

salmantino, na, *n.* & *a.* of or relating to Salamanca.

salmear, *vn.* to sing psalms.

salmer, *m.* (arch.) impost of an arch.

salmerón, *a.* fanfarron wheat.

salmista, *n.* psalmist; chanter of psalms.

salmo, *m.* psalm.

salmodia, *f.* psalmody; (eccl.) psalter.—**salmodiar,** *vn.* = SALMEAR.

salmón, *m.* (ichth.) salmon.—**s. pequeño,** samlet, parr.—**s. zancado,** kelt.—**salmonado, da,** *a.* tasting like salmon.—**salmoncillo, ito,** *m. dim.* parr.—**salmonera,** *f.* salmon net.

salmonete, *m.* (ichth.) surmullet.

salmónido, da. I. *n.* & *a.* (zool.) salmonid. **II.** *m. pl.* Salmonidae.

salmorejo, *m.* sauce for rabbits.

salmuera, *f.* brine; pickle.

salmuerarse, *vr.* (of cattle) to become sick from eating too much salt.

salobral. I. *a.* salty, briny. **II.** *m.* saline ground.

salobre, *a.* brackish, briny, saltish.

salobreño, ña, *a.* saltish, saline (ground).

salobridad, *f.* brackishness, saltiness.

salol, *m.* (chem.) salol.

saloma, *f.* (naut.) chantey.

salomar, *vn.* (naut.) to sing chanteys.

salomónico, ca, *a.* Salomonic.

¹**salón,** *m. aug.* salon, large parlor; living or assembly room.

²**salón,** *m.* salted and cured meat or fish.

For pronunciation, see the rules at the beginning of the book.

saloncillo, *m.* small salon or hall; special room (waiting room, rest room, lady's room, etc.).

salpa, *f.* (ichth.) gilthead, salpa, bighead.

salpicadura, *f.* splash, spatter, spattering.

salpicar, *va.* (*pret.* SALPIQUÉ; *subj.* SALPIQUE) to spatter, bespatter, sprinkle, splash; to skip over, touch on without order.

salpicón, *m.* salmagundi; farcing; medley; bespattering.

salpimentar, *va.* (*ind.* SALPIMIENTO; *subj.* SALPIMIENTE) to season with pepper and salt.

salpimienta, *f.* salt and pepper.

salpiqué, salpique, *v.* V. SALPICAR.

salpresar, *va.* to salt, preserve with salt.

salpullido, *m.* (med.) rash.

salpullir, *va. & vr.* (med.) to break out.

salsa, *f.* (cooking) sauce, dressing, gravy.—**s. de San Bernardo**, (coll.) hunger.—**s. mahonesa**, or **mayonesa**, mayonnaise dressing.

salsedumbre, *f.* saltiness, saltness.

salsera, *f.* gravy dish.

salsereta, rilla, ruela, *f. dim.* small saucer; dice box.

salsero, *m.* (bot.) Spanish thyme.

salsifí, *m.* (bot.) salsify, oyster plant.

salsoláceo, a. I. *a.* (bot.) salsolaceous. **II.** *f. pl.* Salsola.

saltabanco, saltabancos, *m.* mountebank; quack; trifler.

saltabardales, *m.* (coll.) romp, wild youth.

saltabarrancos, *m.* (coll.) noisy person.

saltacaballo.—en s., (arch.) lapping over.

saltación, *f.* leaping; dancing, dance.

saltacharquillos, *n.* person affectedly walking on tiptoe.

saltadero, *m.* leaping or jumping place; artificial fountain; jet.

saltadizo, za, *a.* snapping, breaking.

saltador, ra, *n.* jumper, leaper; hopper.

saltadura, *f.* chip (in a stone).

saltaembanco, *m.* = SALTABANCO.

saltamontes, *m.* grasshopper.

saltante, *a.* leaping, jumping; salient.

saltaojos, *m.* (bot.) a kind of peony.

saltaparedes, *m.* = SALTABARDALES.

saltar. I. *vn.* to leap, spring, jump, hop; to frisk, skip; to bound, rebound; to dash out (as a geyser); to snap, burst, break in pieces; to fly asunder, crack, flash; to come off (as a button); to slip off (as a pulley belt); to be clear and obvious; to come to the mind; to start, betray emotion; (naut.) (of the wind) to shift, change suddenly.—**s. a la vista**, to be self-evident.—**s. en tierra**, to land, debark. **II.** *va.* to leap or jump over; to skip; (of animals) to cover (the female).

saltarelo, *m.* an ancient Spanish dance.

saltarén, *m.* a tune on the guitar; grasshopper.

saltarín, na, *n.* dancer, dancing master (mistress); restless young rake.

saltarregla, *f.* bevel square; slide rule.

saltaterandate, *m.* a kind of embroidery.

saltatrás, *m.* or *f.* = TORNATRÁS, half-breed.

saltatriz, *f.* ballet girl; danseuse.

saltatumbas, *m.* (coll.) clergyman who makes a living from funerals.

salteador, ra, *n.* highwayman(woman), footpad.

salteamiento, *m.* assault, highway robbery.

saltear, *va.* to assault, attack; to rob on the highway; to hold up; to start, leave undone, and undertake something else; to forestall; to surprise, take by surprise.

salteo, *m.* assault; highway robbery.

salterio, *m.* psalter, psalm book; rosary; (mus.) psaltery.

saltero, ra, *n.* highlander.

saltico, ito, illo, *m. dim.* little hop or leap.

saltimbanco, -banqui, *m.* = SALTABANCO.

salto, *m.* spring, jump, leap, bound; leaping place; skip, omission; gap; promotion to a higher post without passing through the intervening ones.—**s. de agua**, waterfall, falls, cataract.—**s. de mata**, flight for fear of punishment.—**s. de trucha**, tumbling.—**s. de viento**, (naut.) sudden shifting of the wind.—**s. mortal**, somersault.—**a saltos**, leaping, by hops.—**a saltos y corcovos**, (coll.) by fits and starts.—**dar un s.**, to jump, leap.—**de un s.**, at one jump; in a flash.—**por s.**, irregularly, by turns.

saltón, na. I. *a.* hopping or leaping much. **II.** *m.* grasshopper.

salubérrimo, ma, *a. super.* most salubrious.

salubre, *a.* salubrious, healthful.

salubridad, *f.* healthfulness, salubrity.—**Ministro de S.**, Minister, or Secretary, of Public Health.

salud, *f.* health; good condition; public weal; welfare, prosperity; salvation.—*pl.* compliments, greetings.—¡**s.!** hello! greetings! good luck! your health (in drinking).—**a su s.**, your health (in drinking).—**beber a la s. de**, to drink the health of.—**bien (mal) de s.**, in good (bad) health.

saludable, *a.* salutary, healthful, wholesome.

saludablemente, *adv.* healthfully, wholesomely.

saludación, = SALUTACIÓN.

saludador, ra, *n.* greeter, saluter; quack.

saludar, *va.* to greet, bow to, salute, hail; to give greetings or regards to; to fire a salute; to apply nostrums; (naut.) to dip the flag to.—**le saludo a Vd. atentamente**, (in letter) very truly yours.

saludo, *m.* bow, salute, salutation, greeting; (mil.) salute.—**s. a la voz**, (naut.) cheers, hurrahs.

salumbre, *f.* flower of salt.

salutación, *f.* salutation, greeting, salute; bow; exordium of a sermon; Ave Maria.

salute, *m.* an ancient gold coin.

salutíferamente, *adv.* salubriously.

salutífero, ra, *a.* healthful, salubrious.

salva, *f.* (artil.) salvo; salver, tray; ordeal; oath, solemn promise, assurance.

salvación, *f.* salvation; deliverance.

salvachia, *f.* (naut.) salvage strap.

salvado, da. I. *pp.* of SALVAR. **II.** *m.* bran.

salvador, ra, *n.* savior, rescuer, redeemer.

salvadoreño, ña, *n. & a.* Salvadorean (from Salvador).

salvaguardia. I. *m.* safeguard, security, protection; guard; watchman. **II.** *f.* safe-conduct, passport.

salvajada, *f.* brutal or stupid action.

salvaje. I. *a.* savage; (of plants, animals) wild; rough, wild (country). **II.** *m.* savage.

salvajemente, *adv.* savagely, wildly.

salvajería, *f.* brutal action; savageness.

salvajez, *f.* savageness.

salvajina, *f.* wild animal; multitude of wild animals; collection of skins of wild animals.

salvajino, na, *a.* savage, wild, untamed; gamey (meat).

salvajismo, *m.* savagery; (coll.) rusticity.

salvajuelo, la, *n.* little savage.

salvamano.—a s., without danger to oneself; in a cowardly manner.

salvamente, *adv.* securely, safely.

salvamento, *m.* salvage; safety, place of safety; salvation.—**bote de s.**, (aer.) crash boat.

salvamiento, *m.* = SALVAMENTO.

salvante. I. *a.* saving, excepting. **II.** *adv.* (coll.) save, except.

salvar. I. *va.* to save, rescue; (naut.) to salve, save; to avoid (a danger); to get over, jump over (ditch, creek, etc.), clear (an obstacle); to overcome (a difficulty); to make allowance for, excuse, make an exception of; to prove legally the innocence of.—**s. las aparencias**, to keep up appearances, save face. **II.** *vn.* to taste, to prove (the food or drink of nobles). **III.** *vr.* to be saved; to escape from danger.—**sálvese él que pueda**, everyone for himself.

salvavidas, *m.* life preserver.

¡salve! *interj.* hail!—**Salve**, *f.* (eccl.) Salve Regina.

salvedad, *f.* reservation, exception, qualification.

salvia, *f.* (bot.) sage.

salvilla, *f.* salver, glass rack, tray, waiter.

salvo, va. I. *a.* saved, safe; excepted, omitted. II. *adv.* save, saving, excepting, barring.—**s. el guante**, or **s. el zurrado**, excuse the glove.—**s. que**, unless.—**a s.**, without injury or diminution.—**en s.**, safe, with safety.

salvoconducto, *m.* safe-conduct, passport; license, permit, pass.

salvohonor, *m.* (coll.) breech, buttocks.

salladura, *f.* (agr.) weeding.

sallar, *va.* (agr.) to weed.

sallete, *m.* (agr.) weeder, weeding tool.

sámago, *m.* sap rot, dry rot.

samán, *m.* (bot.) genisaro, rain tree.

sámara, *f.* (bot.) samara.

samarita; **samaritano, na**, *n.* & *a.* Samaritan.

samaruguera, *f.* fishing net that is set across streams.

sambenitar, *va.* to make infamous, to dishonor publicly.

sambenito, *m.* garment worn by penitent convicts of the Inquisition; placard in churches, containing names of penitents and their penance; note of infamy; disgrace.

samblaje, *m.* = ENSAMBLADURA, joining; joint.

sambuca, *f.* (mus., mil.) sambuca.

sambumbia, *f.* (Cuba) fermented drink made from cane juice, water, and peppers; (Peru) hubbub, confusion.—**sambumbiería**, *f.* place where SAMBUMBIA is made and sold.

samio, mia, *n.* & *a.* Samian (from Samos).

samnita, samnite, *n.* & *a.*; **samnítico, ca**, *a.* Samnite.

samoyedo, da, *n.* & *a.* Samoyed(-ic).

sampaguita, *f.* a tropical flower like jasmine.

sampán, *m.* sampan, a Chinese skiff.

sampsuco, *m.* (bot.) marjoram.

samuga, *f.* mule chair.

san, *a.* (*contr.* of SANTO) Saint (with masc. names).

sanable, *a.* curable, healable.

sanador, ra, *n.* curer, healer.

sanalotodo, *m.* cure-all, catholicon, panacea.

sanamente, *adv.* sanely; sincerely.

sanar. I. *va.* to heal, cure. II. *vn.* to heal; to recover from sickness.

sanativo, va, *a.* sanative, curative.

sanatorio, *m.* sanatorium, sanitarium.

sanción, *f.* sanction; ratification.

sancionar, *va.* to sanction; to ratify, authorize.

sanco, *m.* (Chile) porridge made from toasted corn meal or wheat flour; very thick mud; (Arg.) a stew made with beef blood, flour and onions.

sancochar, *va.* (cook.) to boil with water and salt.

sancocho, *m.* (Am.) a kind of thin stew of boiled yucca, meat, plantains, etc.

sancta, *m.* fore part of the tabernacle.

sanctasanctórum, *m.* sanctum sanctorum.

sanctórum, *m.* (P. I.) a tribute to the church.

sanctus, *m.* (eccl.) Sanctus, Trisagion.

sanchete, *m.* an ancient silver coin.

sanchopancesco, ca, *a.* like Sancho Panza.

sandalia, *f.* sandal.

sandalino, na, *a.* pertaining to sandalwood.

sándalo, *m.* (bot.) bergamot mint; sandalwood.

sandáraca, *f.* (min.) sandarach, realgar; sandarach (gum).

sandez, *f.* inanity, foolish or stupid statement.

sandía, *f.* (bot.) watermelon.

sandiar, *m.* watermelon patch.

sandio, dia, *a.* foolish, nonsensical, inane.

sandunga, *f.* (coll.) gracefulness, elegance; winsomeness, fascination.—**sandunguero, ra**, *a.* (coll.) winsome, graceful, fascinating.

saneado, da. I. *pp.* of SANEAR. II. *a.* drained; free, clear, unencumbered.

saneamiento, *m.* (law) security, surety, bail, guarantee; indemnification, reparation; drainage, improvement (of land).

sanear, *va.* to give security, to give bail; (law) to indemnify; to make harmless; to drain, improve (lands).

sanedrín, *m.* (anc. Jewry) Sanhedrim.

sanfrancia, *f.* (coll.) quarrel, dispute, row.

sangley, *m.* (P. I.) Chinese trader.

sangradera, *f.* (surg.) lancet; basin (for blood); lock, sluice, drain.

sangrador, *m.* bloodletter; outlet.

sangradura, *f.* (surg.) bleeding; bend on the inside of arm at the elbow; draining, drainage.

sangrar. I. *va.* (surg.) to bleed; to drain; (coll.) to extort or borrow money from; (print.) to indent. II. *vn.* to bleed. III. *vr.* to be bled.

sangraza, *f.* corrupt or filthy blood.

sangre, *f.* blood; gore; race, family, kindred.—**s. azul**, blue blood, nobility.—**s. de drago**, dragon's blood.—**s. fría**, calmness, composure, sang-froid.—**a s. caliente**, impulsively, on the spur of the moment.—**a s. fría**, in cold blood.—**a s. y fuego**, by fire and sword, by blood and iron.—**en s. fría**, in cold blood.—**mala s.**, bad blood, vindictiveness.—**subírsele a uno la s. a la cabeza**, to become excited, lose one's self-control.

sangría, *f.* (surg.) bleeding, bloodletting; present made to a person who bleeds; drain, drainage, draining; pilfering, pilferage; insdie of the forearm; (print.) indenting a line; tap, stream of molten metal from a furnace; sangaree, a refreshing drink made with wine.

sangrientamente, *adv.* bloodily, cruelly.

sangriento, ta, *a.* bloody, bloodstained, gory; cruel, sanguinary, bloodthirsty.

sanguaza, *f.* serous blood; reddish fluid of vegetables.

sangüeño, *m.* (bot.) wild cornel.

sangüesa, *f.* raspberry.

sangüeso, *m.* (bot.) raspberry bush.

sanguífero, ra, *a.* conveying blood (as a vein).

sanguificación, *f.* (med.) sanguification.

sanguificar, *va.* to make blood from.

sanguijuela, *f.* leech; sponger; sharper, cheat.

sanguinaria, *f.* (bot.) bloodroot; knotgrass; (min.) bloodstone, hematite.

sanguinariamente, *adv.* sanguinarily, bloodily.

sanguinario, ria, *a.* sanguinary, cruel, bloody, bloodthirsty.

sanguíneo, nea; sanguino, na, *a.* red, blood-colored; sanguineous, sanguine.

sanguinolencia, *f.* bloody condition.

sanguinolento, ta, *a.* bloody; bloodstained.

sanguinoso, sa, *a.* sanguine, sanguineous; bloody, sanguinary, cruel.

sanguiñuelo, *m.* (bot.) wild cornel.

sangüis, *m.* (Lat.) blood of Christ; consecrated wine.

sanguisorba, *f.* (bot.) great burnet.

sanguja, *f.* leech.

sanícula, *f.* (bot.) sanicle.

sanidad, *f.* soundness; health; healthfulness; health department.—**s. marítima**, quarantine officers.—**en s.**, in health.

sanidina, *f.* (min.) sanidine.

sanie, sanies, *f.* (med.) sanies.

sanioso, sa, *a.* (med.) sanious, ichorous.

sanitario, ria. I. *a.* sanitary, hygienic. II. *m.* health officer.

sanjacado, sanjacato, *m.* government of a sanjak (a Turkish district).

sanjaco, *m.* governor of a sanjak.

sanjuanada, *f.* picnic on St. John's day.

sanjuanero, ra, *a.* (of fruits) ripe by St. John's day.

sanjuanino, na, *n.* & *a.* of or from San Juan.

For pronunciation, see the rules at the beginning of the book.

sanjuanista, *m.* knight of St. John of Jerusalem.
sanluisero, ra, *n. & a.* of or from San Luis.
sanmiguelada, *f.* Michaelmas.
sanmigueleño, ña, *a.* (of fruits) ripe by Michaelmas.
sano, na, *a.* sound, healthy, hale; salutary; sane; secure; honest. good; discreet, wise; safe, harmless; entire, complete.—**cortar por lo s.**, to settle in the shortest way, regardless of all else; to take quick action.—**s. y salvo**, safe and sound.
sánscrito, ta. I. *a.* Sanskrit. **II.** *m.* Sanskrit.
sansimoniano, na, *a.* St. Simonian.
sansimonismo, *m.* St. Simonism.
santa, *f.* female saint.
santabárbara, *f.* (naut.) magazine, powder room.
santafecino, na, *n. & a.* of or from Santa Fe.
santafereño, ña, *n. & a.* of or from (Santa Fe de) Bogotá.
santaláceo, a, *a.* (bot.) santalaceous.
santamente, *adv.* saintly, saintily; plainly, simply.
santandereano, na, *a.* of or from Santander (Colombia).—**santanderiense; santanderino, na**, *a.* of or from Santander (Spain).
santelmo, *m.* (naut.) St. Elmo's fire.
santero, ra. I. *a.* too devoted to worship of saints. **II.** *n.* caretaker of a sanctuary; seller of images.
santiagueño, ña, *a.* (of fruits) ripe by St. James's day.
santiaguero, ra, *a.* of or pertaining to Santiago (Cuba).
santiagués, sa, *a.* of or pertaining to Santiago (Galicia).
santiaguino, na, *a.* of or pertaining to Santiago (Chile).
santiaguista. I. *a.* belonging to the order of Santiago. **II.** *m.* knight of Santiago or St. James.
santiamén, *m.* (coll.) instant, moment, twinkling of an eye, jiffy.
santico, ca, *n. dim.* little image of a saint; (coll.) good child.
santidad, *f.* sanctity, saintliness, holiness, godliness.—**su S.**, his Holiness (the Pope).
santificable, *a.* sanctifiable.
santificación, *f.* sanctification, making holy.—**s. de las fiestas**, keeping of holy days.
santificador, ra, *n. & a.* sanctifier(-fying).
santificante, *a.* blessing, sanctifying.
santificar. I. *va.* (*pret.* SANTIFIQUÉ; *subj.* SANTIFIQUE) to sanctify, hallow, consecrate; to keep (holy days). **II.** *va. & vr.* to justify, exculpate, clear from guilt, acquit.
santiguada, *f.* crossing oneself; rough treatment, reprimand.—**para, or por, mi s.**, faith, by this cross.
santiguadera, *f.* healing by signs of the cross.
santiguador, ra; dor, ra, *n.* healer by signs of the cross.
santiguamiento, *m.* crossing oneself.
santiguar. I. *va.* to bless, to heal by blessing; (coll.) to slap. **II.** *vr.* to cross oneself.
santimonia, *f.* sanctity, sanctimony, holiness; (bot.) corn marigold, chrysanthemum.
santísimo, ma, *a. super.* most holy.—**el S.**, the holy sacrament.
santo, ta. I. *a.* saintly, holy, blessed; saint; sacred, consecrated; inviolable; (coll.) simple, plain, artless.—**s. hermandad**, Holy Brotherhood, an ancient Spanish rural police.—**s. oficio**, Holy Office (the Inquisition).—**S. Padre**, Holy Father (the Pope); Father of the Church (one of the first Christian writers).—**s. varón**, holy man; simpleton; hypocrite.—**s. y bueno**, well and good.—**todo el s. día**, the whole day long. **II.** *n.* saint; saint's day; image of a saint.—**santo y seña**, (mil.) watch word, password.—**alzarse con el s. y la limosna**, to take everything, make a clean sweep.—**dar**

el s., (mil.) to set or give the password.—**Todos los Santos**, All Saint's Day.
santol, *m.* (P. I.) (bot.) santol, sandal tree.
santón, *m. aug.* dervish; hypocrite.
santónico, *m.* (bot.) santonica, wormwood.
santonina, *f.* (chem.) santonin.
santoral, *m.* (eccl.) collection of lives of the saints; church choir book.
santuario, *m.* sanctuary.
santucho, cha; santurrón, na, *n.* (coll.) sanctimonious, person, hypocrite.
santurronería, *f.* sanctimony, hypocrisy.
saña, *f.* anger, passion, rage, fury.
sañosamente, *adv.* angrily, cruelly.
sañoso, sa, *a.* furious, enraged; cruel.
sañudamente, *adv.* furiously.
sañudo, da, *a.* furious, enraged.
sao, *m.* (bot.) LABIÉRNAGO, laburnum; small savanna with clusters of trees or shrubs.
sapa, *f.* residue left after chewing BUYO.
sapajú, *m.* (Am.) sapajou, a capuchin monkey.
sapán, *m.* (bot.) (P. I.) sapan wood; sapan tree.
sapeca, *f.* sapek or sapec, an oriental coin.
sápido, da, *a.* sapid, savory.
sapiencia, *f.* wisdom, knowledge, learning.
sapiencial, *m.* sapiential book (part of the Bible).
sapiente, *a.* wise, learned.
sapientísimamente, *adv. super.* most wisely, or learnedly.
sapillo, *m. dim.* little toad.
sapina, *f.* (bot.) glasswort.
sapindáceo, a, *a.* (bot.) sapindaceous.
sapino, *m.* (bot.) savin.
sapo, *m.* toad.
saponáceo, cea, *a.* saponaceous, soapy.
saponaria, *f.* (bot.) common soapwort.
saponificable, *a.* saponifiable.
saponificación, *f.* saponification.
saponificar. I. *va.* (*pret.* SAPONIFIQUÉ; *subj.* SAPONIFIQUE) to saponify, convert into soap. **II.** *vr.* to become saponified.
saponina, *f.* (chem.) saponin.
saporífero, ra, *a.* imparting savor.
sapotáceo, a, *a.* (bot.) sapotaceous.
saprofítico, ca, *a.* (bot.) saprophytic.
saprofito, ta. I. *a.* saprophytic. **II.** *m.* saprophyte.
saque, *m.* (sports) a serve (in tennis), kick-off (in foot-ball), etc.
saqué, saque, *v. V.* SACAR.
saqueador, ra, *n.* looter, pillager.
saqueamiento, *m.* pillage, loot, plunder.
saquear, *va.* to plunder, loot, pillage.
saqueo, *m.* = SAQUEAMIENTO.
saquera, *f.* packing needle.
saquería, *f.* place for or collection of sacks.
saquero, ra, *n.* maker or seller of sacks.
saquete, *m. dim.* (artil.) cartridge bag.
saquilada, *f.* small amount of grain in a sack.
saquillo, ito, *m. dim.* small sack or bag.
saragüete, m. (coll.) informal SARAO.
sarampión, *m.* (med.) measles.
sarao, *m.* evening party with dancing or music.
sarape, *m.* (Mex.) serape, a shawl or blanket worn by men.
sarapia, *f.* (bot.) tonka bean.
sarapico, *m.* (ornith.) curlew.
sarasa, *m.* effeminate man.
saraviado, da, *a.* spotted, piebald.
sarcasmo, *m.* sarcasm.
sarcástico, ca, *a.* sarcastic.
sarcia, *f.* load, burden.
sarcocarpio, *m.* (bot.) sarcocarp.
sarcocele, *m.* (med.) sarcocele.
sarcocola, *f.* sarcocol (resinous gum).
sarcófago, *m.* tomb, grave; sarcophagus.
sarcolema, *m.* (anat.) sarcolemma.
sarcología, *f.* (anat.) sarcology.
sarcoma, *f.* (med.) sarcoma, malignant tumor.
sarcótico, ca, *a.* (surg.) sarcotic.

sarda, *f.* (ichth.) horse mackerel.
sardana, *f.* a Catalonian dance.
sardesco, ca. I. *a.* small (donkey or horse); (coll.) rude, stubborn. **II.** *m.* pony; small donkey.
sardiano, na, *n.* & *a.* Sardian.
sardina, *f.* (ichth.) sardine.—**como s. en banasta,** or **en barril,** packed like sardines.
sardinal, *m.* sardine net.
sardinel, *m.* (mason.) brickwork having the bricks closely placed on edge.
sardinero, ra. I. *a.* pertaining to sardines. **II.** *n.* dealer in sardines. **III.** *m.* (S-) a public walk near Santander.
sardineta, *f.* small sardine; sprat; part of cheese that overtops the cheese vat; (naut.) knittle, laniard.—*pl.* (mil.) chevrons in uniforms.
sardio, *m.* (jewelry) sard, sardius.
¹sardo, da, *n.* & *a.* Sardinian.
²sardo, da, *a.* (of cattle) red, black and white.
sardonia, *f.* (bot.) crowfoot, spearwort.
sardónica, sardónice, *f.* (jewelry) sardonyx.
sardónico, ca, *a.* sardonic; insincere, affected (laughter).
sardonio, sardónique, *m.* = SARDÓNICE.
¹sarga, *f.* silk serge or twill; (art) fabric painted in tempera or oil, like tapestry.
²sarga, *f.* (bot.) osier or willow.
sargadilla, *f.* (bot.) soda-ash plant.
sargado, da, *a.* sergelike.
sargal, *m.* clump of osiers.
sargatillo, *m.* (bot.) a kind of willow.
sargazo, *m.* (bot.) sargasso, gulfweed.
sargenta, *f.* sergeant's halberd; sergeant's wife.
sargentear, *va.* to command as a sergeant; to command; (coll.) to boss, lord it over.
sargentería, *f.* (mil.) sergeant's drill.
sargentía, *f.* sergeantship, sergeancy.
sargento, *m.* (mil.) sergeant.
sargentona, *f.* big coarse woman.
sargo, *m.* (ichth.) sheepshead.
¹sarguero, ra, *a.* willowy.
²sarguero, *m.* painter of ¹SARGA.
sargueta, *f.* thin, light serge.
sarilla, *f.* (bot.) marjoram.
sármata, *n.* & *a.*; **sarmático, ca,** *a.* Sarmatian.
sarmentador, ra, *n.* one who gathers pruned vine shoots.
sarmentar, *vn.* to gather pruned vine shoots.
sarmentera, *f.* place where pruned vine shoots are kept; gathering pruned vine shoots.
sarmentillo, *m.* *dim.* slender vine shoot.
sarmentoso, sa, *a.* vinelike, twining.
sarmiento, *m.* (bot.) sarmentum, runner.
sarna, *f.* (med.) itch; mange.—**s. perruna,** nonsuppurating mange.—**más viejo que la s.,** as old as Methuselah.
sarnazo, *m.* malignant itch.
sarnoso, sa, *a.* itchy; scabbed; mangy.
sarpullido, *m.* rash, eruption.
sarpullir, *va.* & *vr.* to cause or have a rash.
sarracénico, ca, *a.* Saracenic.
sarraceno, na; sarracín, na, *n.* & *a.* Saracen (-ic), Moor(-ish).
sarracina, *f.* scuffle, fight.
sarrapia, *f.* = SARAPIA.
sarria, *f.* coarse net for straw; large fruit basket.
¹sarrillo, *m.* stertor of a dying person.
²sarrillo, *m.* (bot.) arum.
sarrio, *m.* a kind of wild goat.
sarro, *m.* crust or incrustation in vessels; (med.) mucous on stomach wall; tartar on teeth.
sarroso, sa, *a.* crusty.
sarta, *f.* string of beads or pearls; line, series.
sartal, *m.* string of beads, etc.
sartalejo, *m.* *dim.* small string of pearls.
sartén, *f.* frying pan.—**tener la s. por el mango,** to have the command, control or advantage.—**sartenada,** *f.* as much as can be fried at one time in a frying pan.—**sartenazo,** *m.* blow

with a frying pan; (coll.) blow with anything.—**sarteneja,** *f.* *dim.* small frying pan.
sartorio, *m.* (anat.) sartorius (muscle).
sasafrás, *m.* (bot.) sassafras.
sastra, *f.* wife of a tailor; woman tailor.
sastre, *m.* tailor.—**s. remendón,** repairer.
sastrecillo, *m.* *dim.* petty tailor.
sastrería, *f.* tailor's trade; tailor's shop.
sastresa, *f.* = SASTRA.
Satán, Satanás, *m.* Satan.—**satánicamente,** *adv.* satanically.—**satánico, ca,** *a.* satanic.
satélite, *m.* satellite; (coll.) bailiff, constable, sheriff; follower, henchman; sycophant.
satén, *m.* sateen.
satinador, ra, *n.* glazer, calender; *m.* polishing tool; *m.* (photog.) burnisher.
satinar, *va.* to calender, glaze, gloss, burnish.
sátira, *f.* satire; hint, innuendo; (coll.) saucy and witty woman.
satiriasis, *f.* (med.) satyriasis.
satíricamente, *adv.* satirically; sarcastically.
satiricé, satirice, *v.* *V.* SATIRIZAR.
satírico, ca. I. *a.* satirical; sarcastic. **II.** *m.* satirist.
satirillo, *m.* *dim.* little satyr.
satirio, *m.* a kind of water rat.
satirión, *m.* (bot.) orchid that yields salep.
satirizante, *a.* satirizing.
satirizar, *va.* (*pret.* SATIRICÉ; *subj.* SATIRICE) to satirize, lampoon.
sátiro, *m.* satyr, sylvan god; lewd man.
satisdación, *f.* (law) security, surety. bail.
satisfacción, *f.* satisfaction; amends; apology, excuse; confidence, conceit.—**a s.,** fully, according to one's wishes.—**tomar s.,** to vindicate oneself, to stand for one's honor.
satisfacer. I. *va.* (*pp.* SATISFECHO; *ind. pres.* SATISFAGO, *pret.* yo SATISFICE, él SATISFIZO, *fut.* SATISFARÉ; *subj.* SATISFAGA) to satisfy; to pay in full, settle; to expiate, make amends for, atone for; to reward; to indemnify, repay; to answer, make reply; to explain; to free from debt, perplexity, or suspense; to convince.—**s. una letra,** (com.) to honor a draft. **II.** *vr.* to satisfy oneself; to be satisfied; to take satisfaction; to be revenged; to be convinced.
satisfaciente, *a.* satisfying, satisfactory.
satisfactoriamente, *adv.* satisfactorily.
satisfactorio, ria, *a.* satisfactory.
satisfago, satisfaga, *v.* *V.* SATISFACER.
satisfecho, cha. I. *pp. irreg.* of SATISFACER. **II.** *a.* satisfied, content; arrogant, conceited.
satisfice, satisfizo, *v.* *V.* SATISFACER.
sativo, va, *a.* sown, cultivated.
sátrapa, *m.* satrap; (coll.) crafty fellow; boss.
satrapía, *f.* satrapy.
saturación, *f.* saturation.
saturar, *va.* to saturate; to fill, glut, satiate.
saturnal. I. *a.* Saturnian. **II.** *f.* *pl.* Saturnalia.
saturnino, na, *a.* saturnine, melancholy, grave, gloomy, morose; (chem.) saturnine.
saturnio, nia, *a.* Saturnian.
saturnismo, *m.* plumbism, lead poisoning.
Saturno, *m.* (astr.) Saturn.
sauce, *m.* (bot.) willow.—**s. cabruno,** goat willow or goat sallow.—**s. llorón,** weeping willow.
sauceda, saucedal, *m.*; **saucera,** *f.* plantation of willows.
saucillo, *m.* (bot.) knotgrass.
saúco, *f.* (bot.) elder or alder tree; horny part of horse's hoof.
sauquillo, *m.* (bot.) dwarf elder.
saurio, *m.* (zool.) saurian.
sausería, *f.* larder in a palace.
sausier, *m.* chief of the larder in a palace.
sautor, *m.* (her.) saltier.
sauz, *m.* (bot.) willow.
sauzal, *m.* willow grove.
sauzgatillo, *m.* (bot.) agnus castus, chaste-tree.
savia, *f.* sap.

saxafrax, *f.* (bot.) = SAXIFRAGA.
saxátil, *a.* growing among rocks, saxicolous.
sáxeo, ea, *a.* stony.
saxifraga, saxifragia, *f.* (bot.) saxifrage plant.
saxifragáceo, a, *a.* (bot.) saxifragaceous.
saxófono, *m.* (mus.) saxophone.
saxoso, sa, *a.* containing stones, stony.
saya, *f.* (outer) skirt; sum of money that the Queen of Spain gives her maids when they marry; an ancient tunic worn by men.
sayal, *m.* coarse woollen stuff; sackcloth.
sayalería, *f.* shop for weaving coarse cloth.
sayalero, *m.* weaver of SAYAL.
sayalesco, ca, *a.* made of SAYAL.
sayalete, *m. dim.* thin flannel for undergarments.
sayete, sayito, *m. dim.* small frock, short skirt.
sayo, *m.* smock frock; large coat; any loose garment.—**s. bobo,** tight dress worn by clowns.—**decir para su s.,** to mutter in one's beard.
sayón, na, *n. m. aug.* executioner; ugly-looking person; (formerly) a kind of judge.
sayuela, *f. dim.* woollen shift worn by some religious orders; a variety of fig tree; (Am.) petticoat.
sayuelo, *m. dim.* little frock.
sazón, *f.* maturity, ripeness; season; taste, relish, flavor; seasoning; occasion, opportunity.—**a la s.,** then, at that time.—**en s.,** ripe, in season; opportunely.
sazonadamente, *adv.* maturely, seasonably.
sazonado, da. I. *pp.* of SAZONAR. **II.** *a.* seasoned; ripe, mellow; witty; pertinent; expressive.
sazonador, ra, *n.* seasoner.
sazonar. I. *va.* (cook.) to season; to mature, bring to maturity. **II.** *vr.* to ripen, to mature.
se, 3d. pers. obj. pron., *m.* or *f.*, *sing.* or *pl.* used: (1) As a refl. acc. case, equivalent to "himself," "oneself," "herself," "itself," "themselves," "to himself," "to oneself," etc. (*él se afeitó,* he shaved himself; *las niñas se vistieron,* the girls dressed themselves; *uno se ama,* one loves oneself). (2) As an acc. or a dat. recip., to indicate mutual action, equivalent to "each other," "one another," "to each other," "to one another" (*Juan y María se aman, pero no se hablan,* John and Mary love each other, but do not speak to each other). (3) As a symbol forming verbs refl. only in form, not in meaning, as *irse,* to go; *morirse,* to die; *reírse,* to laugh. (4) Instead of dat. *le, les,* before an acc. case (*yo se lo di,* I gave it to him [her, them, you]; *Juan se los entregó,* John delivered them to him [her, them, you]). (5) To give a poss. value to a def. or indef. art. (*Juan se corta las uñas,* John cuts his nails; *Juan se quebró una mano,* John broke one of his hands). (6) To form certain expressions of a passive character, rendered in Eng. by the passive form of the corresponding verb, or by introducing "they," "people," "one," as an indef. subject (*se dice,* it is said, they say, people say; *no se sabe,* it is not known; *esto se aprende fácilmente,* this is easily learned, one learns this easily; *aquí se habla español,* Spanish [is] spoken here; *eso no puede negarse,* that cannot be denied). When *se* is thus used indefinitely in the imper., the resulting form is generally rendered by the simple imper. (*para otros pormenores, escríbase al secretario,* for other particulars, write to the secretary; *consúltese el diccionario,* consult the dictionary).
sé, *v. V.* SABER.
sea, *v. V.* SER.
sebáceo, cea, *a.* sebaceous, tallowy.
sebastiano, *m.* (bot.) = SEBESTÉN.
sebe, *f.* wattle, stockade, fence.
sebero, ra, *a.* tallow (as *a.*), pert. to tallow.
sebestén, *m.* (bot.) sebesten tree; its fruit.
sebillo, *m.* white tallow; toilet soap.
sebo, *m.* tallow, fat, candle grease.—**s. en bruto,** or **en rama,** rough tallow, suet.

seborrea, *f.* (med.) seborrhea.
seboso, sa, *a.* tallowy, fat, greasy, unctuous.
sebucán, *m.* (Am.) manioc strainer.
seca, *f.* drought; dry season; (med.) peeling; (med.) infarction of a gland; (naut.) dry sand bank.—**a secas,** simply.
secácul, *m.* (bot.) an aromatic root.
secadal, *m.* dry, barren ground or sand bank.
secadero, ra. I. *a.* (of fruit) good or fit for drying. **II.** *m.* drying shed, room, or floor; drier; fruit drier.
secado, da, *pp.* of SECAR.—**s. al sol,** sun-dried.
secadillo, *m.* dry-almond biscuit.
secador, ra. I. *a.* drying. **II.** *m.* (Am.) dryer. **III.** *f.* (Am.) clothes dryer.
secamente, *adv.* dryly; curtly, coldly; simply.
secamiento, *m.* drying, desiccation.
secano, *m.* unwatered land; dry sand bank; anything very dry.
secansa, *f.* at cards, sequence.
¹secante, *f.* (geom.) secant.
²secante, *a.* drying; blotting (paper); (Arg.) annoying.
secar. I. *va.* (*pret.* SEQUÉ; *subj.* SEQUE) to dry (out), desiccate; to parch; to wipe dry; to tease, vex, annoy, bore. **II.** *vr.* to dry, parch, dry up; to become lank, lean, or meager; to decay; to wither; to be extremely thirsty.
secaral, *m.* dryness, drought.
secatura, *f.* insipidity, vapidity, dulness.
sección, *f.* act of cutting; section, division, portion; (geom.) section; (arch.) section of a building.—**s. de fondo,** editorial section.—**s. recta,** (geom.) right section.—**s. transversal** (drawing, eng.) cross section.
seccionado, da, *pp. & a.* sectional, in sections.
seccionar, *va.* to section.
seccionario, ria, *a.* sectional.
secesión, *f.* secession.
secesionista, *n. & a.* secessionist.
seceso, *m.* excrement, stool.
seco, ca; *a.* dry; dried up; juiceless; arid; withered; dead (leaves); lean, lank, meager; plain, unadorned, unvarnished; abrupt, curt; lukewarm, cold, indifferent; thin and spare; (of pain) dull.—**en s.,** high and dry; without cause or reason; (mason.) dry, without mortar; by the dry process, without water.
secreción, *f.* segregation; (med.) secretion.
secreta, *f.* private examination preceding the graduation of licentiates; (eccl.) secrets; secret investigation; privy, water closet.
secretamente, *adv.* secretly.
secretar, *va.* (physiol.) to secrete.
secretaria, *f.* wife of a secretary; woman secretary.
secretaría, *f.* secretary's office; secretaryship.
secretario, m. secretary; actuary; scribe, amanuensis.—**S. de Estado,** Secretary of State.—**S. de Hacienda,** Secretary of the Treasury.—**S. del Despacho = s. DE ESTADO.—s. particular,** private secretary.
secretear, *vn.* (coll.) to whisper.—**secreteo,** *m.* (coll.) whispering.
secretico, illo, ito, *m. dim.* little secret.
secretista, *m.* naturalist; dealer in secrets.
secreto, ta. I. *a.* secret; confidential, private. **II.** *m.* secret; secrecy; nostrum; caution, silence, dissimulation, concealment; scrutoire, secret drawer.—**s. a voces,** or **con chirimías,** open secret.—**en s.,** in secret, in private, confidentially.
secretorio, ria, *a.* (med.) secretory.
secta, *f.* sect; doctrine of a sect.
sectador, ra; sectario, ria, *n. & a.* sectarian.
sectarismo, *m.* sectarianism.
sector, *m.* (geom., mil.) sector.
secuaz, *m.* follower, supporter, henchman.
secuela, *f.* sequel, result, upshot.
secuencia, *f.* (eccl.) sequence.

secuestrable, *a.* (law) sequestrable.

secuestración, *f.* (law) sequestration.

secuestrador, ra, *n.* sequestrator, receiver.

secuestrar, *va.* (law) to sequestrate, sequester; to kidnap, abduct.

secuestrario, ria, *a.* pert. to sequestration.

secuestro, *m.* (law) sequestration; umpire, referee; kidnapping, abduction; (surg.) sequestrum, dead portion of bone.

secular. I. *a.* centenary, centennial; lasting for ages; secular, lay. **II.** *m.* (eccl.) secular.

secularicé, secularice, *v.* V. SECULARIZAR.

secularización, *f.* secularization.

secularizar, *va.* (*pret.* SECULARICÉ; *subj.* SECULARICE) to secularize.

secundar, *va.* to second, aid, favor.

secundariamente, *adv.* secondarily.

secundario, ria. I. *a.* secondary; high (school); subordinate; subsidiary.—**producto s.,** by-product. **II.** *m.* second hand (of timepiece).

secundinas, *f. pl.* (zool.) afterbirth.

secundípara, *a.* a mother for the second time.

secura, *f.* dryness, condition of drought.

sed, *f.* thirst; drought; eagerness, anxiety; longing desire.—**tener s.,** to be thirsty.—**tener s. de,** to be thirsty for; to thirst, or hunger, after.

seda, *f.* silk (fibre, yarn, and fabric); wild boar's bristles.—**s. cocida,** soft silk.—**s. conchal,** finest silk from choice cocoons.—**s. cruda,** hard silk.—**s. de capullos,** ferret silk, grosgrain yarn.—**s. de coser,** sewing silk.—**s. en rama,** raw silk.—**s. floja,** floss silk; soft, untwisted silk.—**s. joyante,** very glossy silk.—**s. torcida,** twisted silk.—**como una s.,** as smooth as silk; easily, without hitch or hindrance.—**de media s.,** half-silk.—**de toda s.,** all silk.—**ser como una s.,** or **ser una s.,** to be sweet-tempered.

sedadera, *f.* hackle for dressing flax.

sedal, *m.* fishline; (surg.) seton; (vet.) rowel.

sedalina, *f.* a silk-and-cotton fabric.

sedante, *a.* soothing, allaying, sedative.

sedar, *va.* to allay, appease, soothe, quiet.

sedativo, va, *n. & a.* (med.) sedative.

sede, *f.* (eccl.) see; headquarters.—**s. provisional,** interim headquarters.—**Santa S.,** Holy See.

sedear, *va.* to clean (jewels) with a brush.

sedentario, ria, *a.* sedentary.

sedeña, *f.* fine tow or flax.

sedeño, ña, *a.* silky, silken; silklike.

sedera, *f.* brush made of bristles.

sedería, *f.* silks; silk stuff; silk shop.

sedero, ra. I. *a.* silk, silken. **II.** *n.* silk weaver, silk mercer, silk dealer.

sedición, *f.* sedition, insurrection, mutiny.

sediciosamente, *adv.* seditiously.

sedicioso, sa, *a.* seditious, mutinous.

sediento, ta, *a.* thirsty, dry; (**de**) eagerly desirous, anxious (for).

sedimentación, *f.* sedimentation.

sedimentar, *va. & vr.* to settle, to desposit (as dregs).

sedimentario, ria, *a.* sedimentary.

sedimento, *m.* sediment, settlings, dregs; feces, grouts, grounds; (min.) sinter.

sedoso, sa, *a.* silky, silklike, silken.

seducción, *f.* seduction, deceiving; abuse.

seducir, *va.* (*ind. pres.* SEDUZCO, *pret.* SEDUJE; *subj.* SEDUZCA) to seduce, corrupt, lead astray; to charm, captivate.

seductivo, va, *a.* seductive; enticing.

seductor, ra. I. *a.* fascinating, attractive, tempting. **II.** *n.* seducer, corrupter; deceiver; delightful person.

sefardí, sefardita, *n.* Spanish Jew.

segable, *a.* fit to be reaped.

segada, *f.* harvest.

segadera, *f.* reaping hook, sickle.

segadero, ra, *a.* fit to be reaped.

segador, ra. I. *n.* mower; reaper, harvester. **II.** *f.* mowing machine.

segar, *va.* (*ind. pres.* SIEGO, *pret.* SEGUÉ; *subj.* SIEGUE) (agr.) to mow; to reap, harvest; to cut off, mow down.

segazón, *f.* harvest season; reaping.

seglar. I. *a.* worldly, secular, lay. **II.** *n.* layman (-woman).—**seglarmente,** *adv.* secularly.

segmento, *m.* segment; (geom.) segment.

segoviano, na; segoviense, *n. & a.* Segovian, from Segovia.

segregación, *f.* segregation, separation.

segregar, *va.* (*pret.* SEGREGUÉ; *subj.* SEGREGUE) to segregate, separate, set apart; (med.) to secrete.

segregativo, va, *a.* segregative.

segrí, *m.* heavy, raised silk stuff.

segué, *pret.* of SEGAR.

segueta, *f.* buhl saw, piercing saw.

seguetear, *vn.* to make buhlwork with the buhl saw.

seguida, *f.* succession; continuation.—**de s.,** consecutively, in succession, without interruption. —**en s.,** forthwith, immediately.

seguidamente, *adv.* successively; immediately after, right after that.

seguidero, *m.* guide lines for writing.

seguidilla, *f.* (poet.) stanza of seven lines with peculiar rhythm.—*pl.* a merry Spanish tune and dance; (coll.) diarrhœa.

seguido, da. I. *pp.* of SEGUIR. **II.** *a.* continued, successive; straight, direct. **III.** *m.* a diminishing stitch for narrowing a stocking at the foot.

seguidor, ra. I. *n.* follower. **II.** *m.* guide rules for writing.

seguimiento, *m.* pursuit, following, chase; hunt; continuation, pursuit.

seguir. I. *va.* (*ger.* SIGUIENDO; *ind. pres.* SIGO, *pret.* él SIGUIÓ; *subj.* SIGA) to follow; to pursue; to prosecute; to continue; (foll. by *ger.*) to keep on (foll. by *pres. p.*); to dog, hound; to bring, institute (as a suit). **II.** *vr.* to ensue, follow as a consequence; to follow in order; to issue, spring.

según, *prep.* according to; as; depending on.—**s. derecho,** according to law.—**s. está (estoy,** etc.) **de** (foll. by *a.*), he is (I am, etc.) so, being so: *no oyó lo que dije, según estaba de enojado,* he did not hear what I said, he was so angry.—**s. que,** according as.—**s. y como,** or **s. y conforme,** just as; it depends.

segunda, *f.* double turn of a key.

segundar. I. *va.* to repeat over again. **II.** *vn.* to be second, to follow next to the first.

segundariamente, *adv.* secondarily.

segundario, ria, *a.* = SECUNDARIO.

segundero, ra. I. *a.* (agr.) pert. to a second crop in the same year. **II.** *m.* second hand (of timepiece).

segundilla, *f.* call bell in convents.

segundillo, *m.* second portion of food distributed at table in convents; (mus.) semitone.

segundo, da. I. *a.* second; favorable.—**s. carpintero,** carpenter's mate.—**s. dama, s. galán,** (theat.) woman, man, with walk-on part.—**s. intención,** double meaning, double dealing, duplicity.—**de s. mano,** second-hand. **II.** *m.* second (of time or of arc); second in authority, assistant; equal (in the phrase **sin s.,** without an equal, unrivaled).

segundogénito, ta, *a. & n.* second-born.

segundogenitura, *f.* condition and right of a second-born.

segundón, *m.* any son born after the first.

segur, *f.* axe; axe in fasces carried by lictors; (agr.) sickle.

segurador, *m.* security, bondsman.

seguramente, *adv.* securely, safely; surely.

segurar, *va.* = ASEGURAR, to secure; to affirm.

segureja, *f. dim.* (cooperage) small hatchet.

seguridad, *f.* security, surety; certainty; safety;

custody; corroboration; surety bond.—**caja de s.**, safety deposit box.—**con s.**, **con toda s.**, with absolute certainty.

seguro, ra. I. *a.* secure; safe, reliable, dependable; sure, certain, positive; firm, constant, stanch, steady; unfailing.—**tener por s.**, to be sure of. **II.** *m.* assurance, certainty, confidence; permit, warrant, license; (mech.) click, stop, pawl, ratchet; safety catch (of a pistol); tumbler of a lock; (com.) insurance, assurance.—**s. contra accidentes, incendio, etc.**, accident, fire, etc. insurance.—**s. sobre la vida,** life insurance.—**a buen s., al s., or de s.**, certainly, undoubtedly.—**en s.**, in security or safety.—**irse del s.**, to forget oneself, to throw wisdom overboard.—**sobre s.**, without risk.

segurón, *m. aug.* large axe or hatchet.

seis. I. *a.* & *m.* six; sixth (of the month); six-spotted card, die, or domino. **II.** *f. pl.*—**las s.**, six o'clock.

seisavado, da, *a.* hexagonal.

seisavo, va. I. *n.* & *a.* sixth. **II.** *m.* one sixth; hexagon.

seiscientos, tas, *n.* & *a.* six hundred; six-hundredth.

seise, *m.* one of six choir boys in some cathedrals, who sing and dance in certain festivals.

seisén, *m.* an ancient silver coin.

seiseno, na, *a.* sixth.

seisillo, *m.* (mus.) sextolet.

seísmico, etc., = SÍSMICO, etc., seismic, etc.

seje, *m.* (bot.) (S. A.) a kind of palm tree.

selacio, cia. I. *a.* (ichth.) selachian. **II.** *m. pl.* Selachii.

selección, *f.* selection, choice.—**s. natural,** natural selection.—**s. sexual,** sexual selection.

seleccionamiento, *m.* selection, choosing.

seleccionar, *va.* to make a selection, choose.

selectas, *f. pl.* analects, selections from an author.

selecto, ta, *a.* select, choice, distinguished.

selenio, *m.* (chem.) selenium.

selenita. I. *n.* inhabitant of the moon. **II.** *f.* (min.) selenite.

selenitoso, sa, *a.* (min.) selenitic.

seleniuro, *m.* (chem.) selenide.

selenografía, *f.* selenography.

selenógrafo, *m.* selenographer.

self, *f.* (Angl.) (elec.) self-induction coil.

selfactina, *f.* (spinning) mule jenny.

selfinducción, *f.* (incorrect but common) (elec.) = AUTOINDUCCIÓN self-induction.

selva, *f.* forest, woods.

selvático, ca, *a.* sylvan; rustic, wild.

selvatiquez, *f.* wildness; rusticity.

selvicultura, *f.* = SILVICULTURA, forestry.

selvoso, sa, *a.* sylvan, woody, wooded.

sellador, ra, *n.* sealer.

selladura, *f.* sealing.

sellar, *va.* to seal; to stamp; to conclude, finish; to cover, to close.—**s. los labios,** to silence; to keep silent.

sello, *m.* seal; stamp (sticker, mark or implement); signet; stamp office; (pharm.) cachet, wafer capsule.—**s. de aduana,** cocket.—**s. de correo,** postage stamp.—**s. de Salomón,** Solomon's seal (mystic symbol);—**s. de Santa María,** (bot.) Solomon's-seal.

semafórico, ca, *a.* semaphoric.

semáforo, *m.* semaphore.

semana, *f.* week; week's wages or pay.—**s. santa,** Holy Week; book containing the offices of this week.—**entre s.**, any week day except Saturday.—**la s. que no tenga viernes,** never.

semanal, *a.* weekly.

semanalmente, *adv.* weekly, by the week.

semanario, ria. I. *a.* weekly. **II.** *m.* weekly publication; set of seven razors.

semanería, *f.* functions performed or work done in the course of a week.

semanero, ra, *a.* engaged by the week.

semántica, *f.* semantics, semasiology.

semántico, ca, *a.* semantic.

semasiología, *f.* semasiology, semantics.

semblante, *m.* mien, countenance, look, expression; aspect.—**mudar de s.**, to change color; to take a different turn or a different aspect.

semblanza, *f.* biographical sketch.

sembrada, *f.* (agr.) sown land.

sembradera, *f.* (agr.) sowing machine, sower; seed drill, seeder, seeding machine.

sembradío, día, *a.* (agr.) prepared for sowing; arable.

sembrado, *m.* cultivated field, sown ground.

sembrador, ra. I. *n.* sower, seeder. **II.** *f.* seeder, sowing machine.

sembradura, *f.* sowing, seeding.

sembrar, *va.* (*ind.* SIEMBRO; *subj.* SIEMBRE) (agr.) to sow, seed; to scatter, spread, disseminate.—**como sembráredes, cogéredes,** as you sow, so shall you reap.

semeja, *f.* resemblance, likeness; mark, sign.

semejable, *a.* like, resembling.

semejado, da. I. *pp.* of SEMEJAR. **II.** *a.* = SEMEJABLE.

semejante. I. *a.* similar, like; such, of that kind, (geom., alg.) similar. **II.** *m.* resemblance, likeness; fellow creature, fellow man.

semejantemente, *adv.* likewise, similarly.

semejanza, *f.* resemblance, similarity, similitude.—**a s. de,** like.

semejar, *vn.* & *vr.* to be like, to resemble.

semen, *m.* semen, sperm; (bot.) seed.

semencera, *f.* sowing, seeding.

semencontra, *m.* (pharm.) vermifuge.

semental, *a.* (agr.) seminal, germinal; breeding (horse).

sementar, *va.* (*ind.* SEMIENTO; *subj.* SEMIENTE) to sow, to seed.

sementera, *f.* (agr.) sowing, seeding; cultivated field, land sown; seed bed, seed field, seed garden, seed plot; seed sown; seedtime; origin, cause, beginning.

sementero, *m.* seed bag, seedcod, seedleap, hopper; seed bed, seed plot.

sementino, na, *a.* pert. to seed or seedtime.

semestral, *a.* semiannual, half-yearly.

semestralmente, *adv.* semiannually.

semestre. I. *a.* lasting six months. **II.** *m.* space of six months, semester; six-months' pension or pay.

semi, *prefix,* semi, half, partly. Besides the words that are given below, this prefix is found in many other Spanish words, which are self-explaining.

semibreve, *f.* (mus.) semibreve, whole note (◒).

semicabrón, semicapro, *m.* satyr.

semicilindro, *m.* half cylinder.

semicircular, *a.* semicircular.

semicírculo, *m.* (geom.) semicircle.

semicircunferencia, *f.* semicircumference.

semicopado, da, *a.* (mus.) syncopated.

semicorchea, *f.* (mus.) semiquaver.

semicromático, ca, *a.* (mus.) semichromatic.

semidea, *f.* (poet.) demigoddess.

semideo, *m.* (poet.) demigod.

semidiáfano, na, *a.* semidiaphanous.

semidiámetro, *m.* semidiameter.

semidiapasón, *m.* (mus.) semidiapason.

semidifunto, ta, *a.* half dead, almost dead.

semidiós, sa, *n.* demigod(-dess).

semidítono, *m.* (mus.) semiditone.

semidoble, *a.* semidouble.

semidormido, da, *a.* half asleep, sleepy.

semidragón, *m.* semidragon.

semieje, *m.* (geom.) semiaxis; (carriage) half axletree.

semiento, semiente, *v. V.* SEMENTAR.

semiesfera, *f.* hemisphere.

semiesférico, ca, *a.* hemispherical.

semiflósculo, *m.* (bot.) semifloret.

semiflúido, da, *a.* semifluid.
semiforme, *a.* half formed, undeveloped.
semifusa, *f.* (mus.) double demisemiquaver.
semigola, *f.* (fort.) demigorge.
semihombre, *m.* half-man, pigmy.
semilunar, *a.* semilunar, semilunary.
semilunio, *m.* (astr.) half-moon.
semilla, *f.* seed.—**semillero,** *m.* seed bed, seed plot; nursery; hotbed.
seminal, *a.* seminal, germinal, spermatic.
seminario, *m.* seed plot, nursery; seminary; beginning, root, origin, source.—**s. conciliar,** theological seminary.
seminarista, *m.* seminarist, theological student.
seminífero, ra, *a.* seminiferous, seed-bearing.
semínima, *f.* (mus.) crotchet.
semiología, semiótica, *f.* (med.) semiology, symptomatology.
semipedal, *a.* half foot long.
semiplena, *a.* (law) imperfect (evidence).
semiplenamente, *adv.* half proved.
semiquintil, *m.* (astr.) semiquintile.
semirrecto, *a.* (geom.) of 45 degrees.
semirrubio, bia, *a.* nearly blond.
semís, *m.* half a Roman pound.
semisalvaje, *a.* half-savage, semicivilized.
semisestil, *m.* (astr.) semisextile.
semita, *m.* Semite.—**semítico, ca,** *a.* Semitic.—**semitismo,** *m.* Semitism.
semitono, *m.* (mus.) semitone.
semitransparente, *a.* semitransparent.
semivivo, va, *a.* half alive.
semivocal, *n. & a.* (gram.) semivowel.
sémola, *f.* semolina, groats or grits.
sempiternamente, *adv.* eternally.
sempiterno, na. I. *a.* eternal, everlasting. **II.** *f.* a sort of serge; (bot.) everlasting.
sen, *m.* (bot.) senna.
sena, *f.* six on a die; (bot.) senna.—*pl.* double sixes.
senado, *m.* senate; senate hall.
senadoconsulto, *m.* senatus consultum; decree of a senate.
senador, ra, *n.* senator.
senaduría, *f.* senatorship.
senara, *f.* piece of sown ground assigned to servants as part of their wages.
senarero, *m.* servant who has a SENARA.
senario, ria, *a.* senary, pertaining to six.
senatorial; senatorio, ria, *a.* senatorial.
sencillamente, *adv.* simply; easily; plainly, candidly.
sencillez, *f.* simplicity; easiness; plainness, naturalness; candor.
sencillo, lla, *a.* simple, unmixed; light, slight, thin, of light body (fabrics); plain; artless, harmless; guileless, candid; natural, unaffected; unadorned; single; of less value (coins).
senda, *f.* path, footpath, way.
senderar, *va.* to make a path in or through.
senderear. I. *va.* to guide or conduct on a footpath; to make a path in or for. **II.** *vn.* to adopt extraordinary means to obtain an end.
sendero, *m.* path, footpath, byway.
senderuelo, *m. dim.* little pathway.
sendos, das, *a. pl.* one each, one for each (diff. constr.: *tienen sendos libros,* they have a book each, each of them has a book).
senecio, *m.* (bot.) Senecio.
senectud, *f.* old age, senescence.
senegalés, sa, *n. & a.* Senegalese.
senescal, *m.* seneschal, household officer.
senescalato, *m.,* **senescalía,** *f.* seneschalship.
senil, *a.* senile; (astr.) fourth quadrant.
seno, *m.* chest, thoracic cavity; breast, bosom; womb; lap of a woman; hole, cavity; sinus; gulf, bay; any cavity in the interior of the human body; innermost recess; asylum, refuge; (arch.) spandrel; (surg.) sinus; cavity of a wound; (naut.) curvature of a sail or line; (math.) sine.

—**s. de Abrahán,** Abraham's bosom.—**s. verso,** (math.) versed sine.
senojil, *m.* = CENOJIL, garter.
sensación, *f.* sensation.
sensacional, *a.* sensational.
sensatez, *f.* good judgment, wisdom, good sense.
sensato, ta, *a.* sensible, judicious, wise.
sensibilidad, *f.* sensibility; sensitiveness.
sensibilizar, *va.* (*pret.* SENSIBILICÉ; *subj.* SENSIBILICE) (photog.) to sensitize.
sensible. I. *a.* perceptibile, appreciable; sensitive, keen; grievous, regrettable; (photog.) sensitive, sensitized. **II.** *f.* (mus.) seventh note.
sensiblemente, *adv.* perceptibly; approximately; grievously.
sensiblería, *f.* oversentimentality.
sensitiva, *f.* (bot.) sensitive plant, mimosa.
sensitivo, va, *a.* sensitive; sensual; appreciable.
sensorio, ria. I. *a.* sensory, sensorial. **II.** *m.* (anat.) sensorium (called also **s. común**).
sensual, *a.* sensuous; sensual, lewd, lustful.
sensualidad, *f.* sensuality, lust, lewdness.
sensualismo, *m.* sensualism, sensuality; (philos.) sensationalism.
sensualista. I. *a.* sensualistic. **II.** *n.* (philos.) sensationalist.
sensualmente, *adv.* sensually, carnally.
sentada, *f.* = ASENTADA, sitting, session.
sentadero, *m.* place or thing where one can sit.
sentadillas—a s., sidesaddlewise.
sentado, da. I. *pp.* of SENTAR. **II.** *a.* seated, sitting down; sedate, judicious, wise; settled, steady, firm; (bot.) sessile.
sentamiento, *m.* (arch.) settling.
sentar. I. *vn.* (*ind.* SIENTO; *subj.* SIENTE) to fit, to become, to suit; to agree with one (as food or a climate); to please; to be agreeable. **II.** *va.* to set, set up, establish; settle; to seat; (tailoring) to press the seams of. **III.** *vr.* to sink, subside, settle; to settle down; ASENTARSE, to sit down.
sentencia, *f.* (law) sentence, verdict, judgment; penalty; (com.) award; opinion, determination; dogma, axiom, maxim; (gram.) sentence,—**fulminar,** or **pronunciar, la s.,** to pass judgment.
sentenciador, ra, *n.* one who passes judgment.
sentenciar, *va.* (law) to sentence, to pass judgment on; to determine, decide.
sentención, *f.* severe, rigorous sentence.
sentenciosamente, *adv.* sententiously.
sentencioso, sa, *a.* sententious, pithy.
sentenzuela, *f. dim.* light sentence.
senticar, *m.* place full of briers and brambles.
sentidamente, *adv.* feelingly, regretfully.
sentido, da. I. *pp.* of SENTIR. **II.** *a.* felt, experienced; sensitive; susceptible, touchy; offended; cracked, split.—**darse por s.,** to show resentment. **III.** *m.* sense, any one of the five senses; sense perception, feeling; judgment; understanding, reason; import, sense, meaning; direction, course.—**s. común,** common sense.—**con (todos) mis cinco sentidos,** with all my heart and soul.—**costar un s.,** to be excessively high-priced.—**en el s. de que,** to the effect that; stating that.—**perder el s.,** to lose consciousness; to faint.—**sin s.,** meaningless; unconscious.
sentimental, *a.* sentimental; emotional.
sentimentalismo, *m.* sentimentalism.
sentimentalmente, *adv.* sentimentally.
sentimiento, *m.* sentiment, feeling; sensation; grief, sorrow, regret.
sentina, *f.* (naut.) bilge; sink, drain; place of iniquity.
sentir. I. *va.* (*ger.* SINTIENDO; *ind. pres.* SIENTO, *pret.* él SINTIÓ; *subj.* SIENTA) to feel; to perceive by the senses (to hear, smell, etc.); to endure, suffer; to grieve, regret, mourn, to be sorry for. **II.** *vn.* to feel; to judge, form an opinion; to

foresee, foreknow; to fit the action to the word. **—sin s.**, without noticing, inadvertently. **III.** *vr.* to be moved, be affected; to complain; to resent; to feel (well, bad, sad); to crack; to be in a ruinous state; (naut.) to spring (yard or mast). **IV.** *m.* feeling; opinion, judgment.

seña, *f.* sign, mark, token; nod, gesture; signal; (mil.) password, watchword.**—***pl.* address (street, city, etc.).**—señas mortales,** unmistakable signs or proof.**—señas personales,** personal description.**—por señas,** by signs.**—por señas,** or **por más señas,** as a stronger proof of it.

señal, *f.* sign, mark, token, symptom; mark or note of distinction; signal; landmark; bookmark; reminder; trace, vestige; trail, track, footstep; scar; representation, image; pledge; earnest money, deposit; (tel.) warning, call.**—s. de peligro,** signal of distress; (Ry.) danger signal.**—s. de tráfico,** traffic sign.**—código de señales,** signal code.**—en s. de,** in proof of.**—ni s.,** not a trace.

señaladamente, *adv.* especially, remarkably; signally, notably.

señalado, da, *a.* & *pp.* distinguished, noted.

señalamiento, *m.* appointment, date.

señalar. I. *va.* to stamp, to mark; to point out, make known; to name; to set, fix, determine; to sign; to mark with a wound, especially in the face; (fencing) to make a feint; at cards, to mark the points; to make signals to.**—s. con el dedo,** to point with the finger. **II.** *vr.* to distinguish oneself, to excel.

señaleja, *f. dim.* little sign or mark.

señera, *f.* ancient signal or pendant.

señero, ra, *a.* solitary, alone.

señolear, *vn.* to catch birds with a lure.

señor, *m.* sir; mister, Mr.; man, gentleman; lord, master, owner of a place; (eccl.) the eucharist; (coll.) superlative (in excellence, importance, etc.).**—s. de horca y cuchillo,** lord of the manor, invested with civil and criminal jurisdiction within his estate.**—s. mayor,** aged man.**—el S.,** the Lord; our Lord (Jesus Christ).**—muy s. mío,** Dear Sir (in letters).**—nuestro S.,** our Lord.

señora, *f.* lady, mistress, owner of a place; madam; dame, gentlewoman.**—s. de compañía,** companion, chaperon.**—s. mayor,** matron, middle-aged, respectable woman.**—muy s.,** very much of a lady.**—nuestra S.,** our Lady (the Virgin).

señorada, *f.* act of a gentleman or lady.

señoraje, *m.* seigniorage.

señoreador, ra, *n.* domineering person.

señoreaje, *m.* seigniorage.

señoreante, *a.* domineering.

señorear. I. *va.* to master; to domineer, lord it over, rule despotically; to excel, to occupy a higher station than; to overtop, tower over; to control (one's passions); (coll.) to treat repeatedly with the title of lord. **II.** *vr.* to put on airs.

señoría, *f.* lordship (title and person); dominion, seigniory, lordship; government of a particular state; senate; prince.

señorial, *a.* manorial.

señoril, *a.* lordly, pertaining to a lord.

señorilmente, *adv.* nobly, grandly, lordly.

señorío, *m.* seigniory, seignioralty; dominion, command; imperiousness, arrogance; lordship; domain, manor; gravity or stateliness of deportment; freedom and self-control in action.

señorita, *f. dim.* young lady; miss; Miss; (coll.) mistress of the house.

señoritingo, *m.* (contempt.) little master or youth of no account.

señorito, *m. dim.* young gentleman; Master (title); (coll.) master of the house; (coll.) playboy.

señorón, na, *n. aug.* grand seignior or lady.

señuelo, *m.* lure, decoy; bait; enticement.

seo, *f.* cathedral church.

seó, *m.*; **seor, ra,** *n.* (*contr.* of SEÑOR, RA) (coll.) lord, sir (madam, lady).

sepa, *v.* V. SABER.

sépalo, *m.* (bot.) sepal.

sepancuantos, *m.* (coll.) spanking, scolding, punishment.

separable, *a.* separable, detachable, removable.

separación, *f.* separation; disgregation, dissociation, abstraction; parting; dismissal, discharge; (pol.) secession.

separadamente, *adv.* separately.

separado, da. I. *pp.* of SEPARAR. **II.** *a.* separate, apart.**—por s.,** separate, separately.

separador, ra, *n.* separator.

separar. I. *va.* to separate; divide; to disjoin, sever, detach, disconnect; to remove, take away or off; to set apart, lay aside; to sort; to dismiss, discharge. **II.** *vr.* to separate; to part company; to come off; to withdraw, resign; (com.) to dissolve.

separatismo, *m.* separatism; (pol.) secessionism.

separatista, *n.* & *a.* separatist; secessionist.

separativo, *a.* separating.

sepedón, *m.* seps, a kind of serpent.

sepelio, *m.* burial, interment.

sepia, *f.* sepia; (ichth.) cuttlefish.

septena, *f.* septenary, heptade, group of seven.

septenario, ria. I. *a.* septenary, pert. to seven; septivalent. **II.** *m.* period of seven days.

septenio, *m.* septennium, period of seven years.

septeno, na, *a.* seventh.

septentrión, *m.* north; north wind; (S-, astr.) Great Bear.

septentrional, *a.* northern, northerly.

septeto, *m.* (mus.) septet, septuor.

septicemia, *f.* (med.) septicæmia.

séptico, ca, *a.* septic.

septiembre, *m.* September.

septillo, *m.* (mus.) septimole or septuplet.

séptimo, ma. I. *n.* & *a.* seventh. **II.** *f.* sequence of seven cards, in piquet; (mus.) seventh.

septisílabo, ba, *a.* of seven syllables.

septo, *m.* (anat.) septum.

septuagenario, ria, *n.* & *a.* septuagenarian.

septuagésimo, ma. I. *a.* seventieth; septuagesimal. **II.** *n.* seventieth. **III.** *f.* (eccl.) Septuagesima.

septuplicación, *f.* multiplying by seven.

septuplicar, *va.* to septuple.

séptuplo, pla, *a.* septuple, sevenfold.

sepulcral, *a.* sepulchral; monumental.

sepulcro, *m.* sepulcher, grave, tomb.

sepultador, ra, *n.* burier, gravedigger.

sepultar, *va.* to bury, inter; to hide, conceal.

sepulto, ta. I. *pp. irreg.* of SEPULTAR. **II.** *a.* buried.

sepultura, *f.* sepulture, interment; tomb, grave, sepulcher.**—dar s.,** to bury.

sepulturero, ra, *n.* gravedigger, sexton.

sequé, seque, *v.* V. SECAR.

sequedad, *f.* aridity, dryness; barrenness, sterility; asperity, surliness, gruffness.

sequedal, sequeral, *m.* dry, barren soil.

sequero, *m.* dry, unirrigated land.

sequeroso, sa, *a.* dry, wanting moisture.

sequete, *m.* piece of hard, dry bread or biscuit; stroke, blow, thump, thwack; (coll.) curt reply, gruff answer.

sequía, *f.* drought.

sequillo, *m.* biscuit, rusk.

sequío, *m.* unwatered land; anything dry.

séquito, *m.* retinue, train, suite; popularity.

sequizo, za, *a.* dry (fruits); dryish.

ser. I. *vn.* (*ger.* SIENDO; *pp.* SIDO; *ind. pres.* yo SOY, él ES, *imp.* ERA, *pret.* FUÍ; *subj.* SEA) to be. Used in phrases of identification (*soy yo*, it is I; *son ellos*, it is they). App. to time (*son las dos*, it is two o'clock; *es la una*, it is one o'clock).

Used in impersonal sentences with adj. predicate or with an infin. or phrase subject (*es tarde*, it is late; *es extraño*, it is strange; *es fácil ver*, it is easy to see; *es probable que Juan hable*, it is likely that John will speak).—**s. de** (*inf.*), to be worth (*pres. p.*) (as *ser de ver*, to be worth seeing).—**s. para poco**, not to amount to much, to be of little account.—**s. para todo**, to be fit for everything; to be everything.—**s. que**, in the phrase: *es que*, the fact is that.—**érase**, there was; it was.—**érase que se era**, once upon a time (to begin a story).—**es a saber**, namely, to wit.—**esto es**, or, **o sea**, that is to say.—**no sea que**, lest.—¿**qué ha sido de . . . ?**, What has become of . . . ?—**sea como fuere, sea lo que fuere**, be that as it may; anyhow, anyway.—**si yo fuera que Vd.**, if I were you.—**soy con Vd.**, I will attend you presently.—**soy muy de Vd.**, I am entirely yours; yours very truly. **II.** *m.* existence, life; being; essence, substance.

sera, *f.* large basket.

serado, *m.* baskets (collect.).

seráficamente, *adv.* seraphically.

seráfico, ca, *a.* seraphic.

serafín, *m.* seraph (*pl.* seraphim); angel.

serafina, *f.* fine baize, swanskin.

seraje, *m.* baskets (collect.).

serapino, *m.* = SAGAPENO, a kind of gum.

serba, *f.* (bot.) fruit of the service tree.

serbal, serbo, *m.* (bot.) service tree.

serena, *f.* (mus.) serenade; (coll.) night dew.—**a la s.**, (coll.) = AL SERENO.

serenamente, *adv.* serenely, composedly, calmly, coolly.

serenar, *va., vn. & vr.* (of weather) to clear up, grow fair, become calm; (of liquor) to settle, become clear; to pacify, moderate; to be serene; to cool water in the night air.

serenata, *f.* (mus.) seranade.

serenero, *m.* night wrap.

serení, *m.* (naut.) yawl, jolly-boat.

serenidad, *f.* serenity, calm; placidity, tranquility; serene highness (title).

serenísimo, ma, *a.* *super.* extremely serene, calm, or quiet; most serene (title of princes).

¹**sereno, na**, *a.* clear, fair, cloudless; serene, calm, unruffled.

²**sereno**, *m.* night dew; night watchman.—**al s.**, in the night air, exposed to night dew.

sergas, *f. pl.* exploits, achievements.

seriamente, *adv.* seriously; gravely; in earnest, for good and all.

sericicultor, ra, *n.* sericulturist.

sericicultura, *f.* silk culture, sericulture.

sérico, ca, *a.* silken.

sericultor, ra, *n.* = SERICICULTOR.

sericultura, *f.* = SERICICULTURA.

serie, *f.* series.—**en s.**, (elec.) series (as *a.*); (industry) standardized, mass (production).

seriedad, *f.* seriousness, gravity; sternness, severity; earnest, earnestness.

serígeno, na, *a.* silk-producing.

serijo, serillo, *m.* small basket, gen. for fruit.

seringa, *f.* (Am.) a variety of India rubber.

serio, ria, *a.* serious, grave, dignified; grand, majestic, solemn; stern, severe; earnest; sincere. —**en s.**, seriously.

sermón, *m.* sermon.—**sermonar**, *vn.* to preach, to sermonize.—**sermonario, ria. I.** *a.* pertaining to sermons. **II.** *m.* collection of sermons.

sermoncico, illo, ito, *m. dim.* short address; brief advice.

sermonear, *va.* to sermonize; (coll.) to lecture, reprimand.—**sermoneo**, *m.* (coll.) repeated admonition, sermonizing.

serna, *f.* cultivated field.

seroja, *f.*, **serojo**, *m.* withered leaf; brushwood.

serón, *m.* pannier; hamper, crate.—**s. caminero**, horse pannier.

serondo, da, *a.* (bot.) serotinous.

seronero, *m.* maker or seller of SERONES.

serosidad, *f.* (med.) serosity.

seroso, sa, *a.* serous, thin, watery.

seroterapia, *f.* (med.) serum therapy.

serotino, na, *a.* (bot.) serotinous.

serpa, *f.* (agr.) sterile shoot, sucker.

serpear, *vn.* to wind (as a serpent); to wriggle, squirm, crawl, creep; to meander.

serpentaria, *f.* (bot.) snake-root.

serpentario, *m.* secretary bird; (S-, astr.) Ophiuchus.

serpentear, *vn.* to meander, to wind; to wriggle, squirm.

serpentígero, ra, *a.* (poet.) containing serpents.

serpentín, *m.*, **serpentina**, *f.* coil; (min.) serpentine; (armor) cock, hammer of a musket lock; (chem.) distil worm; (mil.) small cannon.

serpentinamente, *adv.* in a serpentine or winding manner.

serpentino, na, *a.* serpentine; winding, sinuous; snakelike; slanderous, poisoned (tongue); serpentine (marble).

serpentón, *m. aug.* large serpent; (mus.) serpent; trombone.

serpezuela, *f. dim.* of SIERPE, snake.

serpia, *f.* viscous matter of a vine stock.

serpiente, *f.* serpent; devil, Satan; (S-, astr.) Serpens.—**s. de cascabel**, rattlesnake.

serpiginoso, sa, *a.* (med.) serpiginous.

serpigo, *m.* (med.) tetter, ringworm, serpigo.

serpol, *m.* (bot.) wild thyme.

serpollar, *vn.* (bot.) to shoot, sprout.

serpollo, *m.* (bot.) shoot, sucker, sapling.

sérpula, *f.* (zool.) serpula.

serpúlidos, *m. pl.* (zool.) Serpulidæ.

serradizo, za, *a.* fit to be sawed.

serrado, da. I. *pp.* of SERRAR. **II.** *a.* serrate.

serrador, ra, *n.* sawer; sawyer.

serraduras, *f. pl.* sawdust.

serrallo, *m.* seraglio, harem; bagnio, brothel.

serrana, *f.* bucolic poem.

serranía, *f.* sierra, ridge of mountains; mountainous region.

serraniego, ga, *a.* = SERRANO.

serranil, *m.* a kind of knife.

serranilla, *f.* = SERRANA.

serrano, na, *n.* mountaineer, highlander.

serrar, *va.* (*ind.* SIERRO; *subj.* SIERRE) to saw.

serrátil, *a.* (med.) irregular (pulse).

serratilla, *f. dim.* small ridge of mountains.

serrato, ta, *a.* (anat.) serrated.

serreta, *f. dim.* small saw; cavesson iron used in breaking a horse.

serrezuela, *f. dim.* small saw.

serrijón, *m.* short chain of mountains.

serrín, *m.* sawdust.

serrino, na, *a.* pertaining to or like a saw; (med.) irregular (pulse).

serrucho, *m.* handsaw.—**s. braguero**, pit saw.

servato, *m.* (bot.) hog fennel, sulphurweed.

serventesio, *m.* quatrain riming *a, b, a, b.*

serventía, *f.* (Cuba) road through private property.

servible, *a.* serviceable, adaptable.

servicial. I. *a.* serviceable; obsequious, obliging, accommodating, kind. **II.** *m.* (coll.) enema.

servicialmente, *adv.* obligingly, accommodatingly, kindly; serviceably.

serviciar, *va.* to collect or pay (sheepwalk dues, donations to the state, etc.).

servicio, *m.* service; condition of a servant; help, servants (collect.); (eccl.) divine service; usefulness; benefit, advantage; sum of money voluntarily offered to the king; close-stool; (Am.) toilet, water closet; service, cover, course; tea or coffee set.—**s. de mesa**, service for the table.—**flaco s.**, ill turn.

servidero, ra, *a.* fit for service; useful; requiring personal attendance.

servido, da. I. *pp.* of SERVIR. II. *a.* pleased.—**ser s.,** to please, to deign, to grant.

servidor, ra, *n.* servant, waiter(-ess); wooer; one who politely tenders his services to another; (*m.*) pan of a close-stool.—**s. de Vd.,** your servant; at your service.

servidumbre, *f.* attendance, servitude; (staff of) servants or attendants; slavery; mighty or inevitable obligation; service, act of serving or attending at command; (law) right of way.—**s. de la vía,** (Ry.) right of way.

servil, *a.* servile, slavish, abject; lowly, humble; base, low; (Sp. hist.) absolutist, defending absolute monarchy.

servilismo, *m.* servilism, servility, abjectedness; (Sp. hist.) absolutism.

servilmente, *adv.* servilely, slavishly; basely.

servilla, *f.* pump (shoe).

servilleta, *f.* table napkin.—**doblar la s.,** (coll.) to die.

servilletero, *m.* napkin-ring.

servio, via, *n.* & *a.* Serbian.

serviola, *f.* (naut.) cathead, anchor beam.

servir. I. *vn.* (*ger.* SIRVIENDO; *ind. pres.* SIRVO, *pret.* él SIRVIÓ; *subj.* SIRVA) to serve; wait on; to do (for); to hold (an employment), occupy (a public station); to perform the functions (of); to serve (in the army or navy); at cards, to follow suit; in ball games, to serve; to wait on table; to heat the oven; to administer.—**s. de,** to act as, to be used as.—**s. para,** to be for, be used or useful for, be good for; to do for.—**no s. para nada,** to be good for nothing.—**para s. a Vd.,** at your service.—**sírva de aviso,** let this be a warning. II. *va.* to serve; to do a favor or a service to; to court, pay attention to (a lady); to pay (money) voluntarily to the king or government; to dress or serve (food or drink). III. *vr.* to please, be willing or "so good as" to (*sírvase decirme,* please tell me); to help oneself (as at table).—**s. de,** to make use of; to employ.

servocroata, *n.* & *a.* Servo-Croatian.

servomotor, *m.* (naut.) servo-motor, auxiliary.

sesada, *f.* fried brains.

sesámeo, a. I. *a.* (bot.) relating to the sesame family. II. *f. pl.* the sesame family of plants.

sésamo, *m.* (bot.) sesame, gingili.

sesamoideo, a, *a.* (anat.) sesamoid.

sesear, *vn.* to pronounce *c* before *e* and *i* like *s,* as in Am. and some parts of Spain.

sesenta, *n.* & *a.* sixty; sixtieth.

sesentavo, va, *n.* & *a.* sixtieth.

sesenton, na, *n.* & *a.* sexagenarian.

seseo, *m.* pronouncing *c* before *e, i* like *s.*

sesera, *f.* brainpan; the entire brain.

sesga, *f.* (sewing) gore or goring.

sesgadamente, *adv.* slantingly, on the bias; askew.

sesgado, da. I. *pp.* of SESGAR. II. *a.* oblique, slanting; bevelled.

sesgadura, *f.* obliquity; bevel.

sesgamente, *adv.* = SESGADAMENTE.

sesgar. I. *va.* (*pret.* SESGUÉ; *subj.* SESGUE) to slope, slant, cut on the bias, bevel; to skew. II. *vn.* to take an oblique direction.

sesgo, ga. I. *a.* sloped, oblique, biased, bevelled, aslant; severe, grave, stern.—**al s.,** obliquely, bevelled, on the bias. II. *m.* bias, bevel, slope, obliqueness; turn (of an affair); mean, medium.

sesgué, sesgue, *v.* V. SESGAR.

sesil, *a.* (bot.) sessile.

sesión, *f.* session, sitting, meeting; conference, consultation.—**levantar la s.,** to adjourn the meeting.—**sesionar,** *vn.* to meet, have a session.

sesma, *f.,* **sesmero, sesmo,** *m.* = SEXMA, etc.

¹seso, *m.* stone under a pot to keep it steady on the fire.

²seso, *m.* (anat.) brain; brains, intelligence, judgment.—**devanarse los sesos,** to rack one's brains.—**levantarse la tapa de los sesos,** to blow out one's brains.—**no tener s.,** not to have common sense.—**perder el s.,** to go crazy, to lose consciousness; (fig.) to lose one's head —**sin seso(s),** scatterbrained.

sesquiáltero, ra, *a.* sesquialter.

sesquidoble, *a.* two and a half times.

sesquimodio, *m.* a bucket and a half.

sesquióxido, *m.* (chem.) sesquioxide.

sesquipedal, *a.* sesquipedalian, 1½ ft. long.

sesteadero, *m.* resting place for cattle.

sestear, *vn.* to take a nap.

sestercio, *m.* sesterce, old Roman coin.

sestero, sestil, *m.* = SESTEADERO.

sesudamente, *adv.* maturely, wisely, deliberately.

sesudo, da, *a.* judicious, discreet, wise.

¹seta, *f.* = SEDA, bristle.

²seta, *f.* mushroom; snuff of a candle.

sete, *m.* office in a mint where money is struck with a die.

setecientos, tas, *a.* & *n.* seven hundred(-th).

setena, *f.* = SEPTENA, group of seven.

setenta, *n.* & *a.* seventy; seventieth.

setentavo, va, *n.* & *a.* seventieth.

setentón, na, *n.* & *a.* septuagenary(-narian).

setiembre, *m.* = SEPTIEMBRE, September.

sétimo, ma, *a.* = SÉPTIMO, MA, seventh.

seto, *m.* fence, inclosure; (P. R.) wall.—**s. vivo,** hedge, quickset.

setuní, *m.* = ACEITUNÍ, arabesque work.

seudo, *a.* pseudo, false.

seudomembrana, *f.* (anat.) pseudomembrane.

seudónimo, ma. I. *a.* pseudonymous, fictitious. II. *m.* pseudonym, nom de plume, pen name.

seudópodo, da. I. *a.* (biol.) psuedopodian. II. *m.* pseudopodium.

severamente, *adv.* severely, sternly.

severidad, *f.* severity, rigor, harshness, austerity, sternness, strictness, seriousness.

severo, ra, *a.* severe, rigorous; rigid, strict, stern, serious.

sevicia, *f.* fierceness, excessive cruelty.

sevillanas, *f. pl.* a Sevillan dance and tune.

sevillano, na, *a.* of Seville, Sevillan.

séviro, *m.* chief of a Roman decury of knights.

sexagenario, ria, *n.* & *a.* sexagenary(-narian).

sexagésima, *f.* (eccl.) Sexagesima.

sexagesimal, *a.* sexagesimal.

sexagésimo, ma, *a.* sexagesimal, sixtieth.

sexenio, *m.* period of six years.

sexma, *f.* an ancient coin; sixth part of a vara.

sexmero, *m.* mayor of a township.

sexmo, *m.* township.

sexo, *m.* sex.

sexta, *f.* (eccl.) sext; sequence of six cards at piquet; (mus.) sixth; an ancient division of the day; afternoon.

sextante, *m.* sextant; a Roman copper coin.

sextario, *m.* sextarius, an ancient measure.

sexteto, *m.* (mus.) sextet.

sextil, *a.* (astr.) sextile.

sextilla, *f.* (poet.) sextain.

sextillo, *m.* (mus.) sextolet, sextuplet.

sextina, *f.* six-sextian poem.

sexto, ta. I. *n.* & *a.* sixth. II. *m.* book of canonical decrees.

séxtula, *f.* a Roman copper coin.

sextuplicación, *f.* multiplication by six.

sextuplicar, *va.* to sextuple.

séxtuplo, pla, *a.* sextuple, sixfold.

sexual, *a.* sexual.—**sexualidad,** *f.* sexuality.

¹si, *m.* (mus.) B or si, seventh note of the scale.

²si, *conj.* if; whether. Used at beginning of exclamations expressing doubt or desire, or for emphasis (*¡si será verdad!,* I wonder whether it's true; *¡si fuera verdad!,* I wish it were true! If it were only true!; *¡si yo no lo quiero!,* indeed, I don't want it; *¡si, no sabe nada!,* why, he doesn't know anything!).—**s. acaso,** if by chance;

just in case.—s. **bien**, although.—**por s. acaso** = s. ACASO.

¹**sí**, *pron.* (refl. of 3rd pers., both genders and numbers) himself, herself, itself, oneself, themselves.—**de por s.**, apart, separately, individually, by oneself, itself, etc.—**de s.**, of oneself, itself, spontaneously.—**fuera de s.**, beside (him-, her-, etc.) -self (with joy, anger, etc.).—**por s. y ante s.**, of his own accord; ignoring others.—**sobre s.**, attentively, cautiously.—**volver en s.**, to regain consciousness, come to.

²**sí**. I. *adv.* yes, yea, aye. Used for emphasis before a verb, rendered by emphatic aux. or by indeed, certainly, etc. (*él no irá, pero yo sí*, he will not go, but *I* will; *yo sí hablo español*, I do speak Spanish; *yo sí lo compraría*, I should certainly buy it).—**s. que**, certainly, truly, or just emphasizing some word (*sí que lo hará*, he will do it).—**por s. o por no**, in any case.—**s. tal**, indeed, certainly.—**un (día) s. y otro no**, every other (day).—**un s. es no es**, somewhat, perhaps a little. II. *m.* assent, consent, permission.—**dar el s.**, to say yes; to accept a marriage proposal.

siamés, sa, *n. & a.* Siamese.
siampán, *m.* sapan (tree & wood).
sibarita, *n. & a.* Sybarite(-ic).
sibarítico, ca, *a.* Sybaritic; sybaritic.
sibaritismo, *m.* sybaritism.
siberiano, na, *n. & a.* Siberian.
sibil, *m.* cave; cellar, vault.
sibila, *f.* sibyl.
sibilante, *a.* sibilant, hissing.
sibilino, na, *a.* sibylline.
sibucao, *m.* (P. I.) (bot.) sapan tree.
sic, *sic*, so, thus.
sicamor, *m.* (bot.) = CICLAMOR.
sicario, *m.* paid assassin.
sicigia, *f.* (astr.) conjunction of sun and moon.
siciliano, na, *n. & a.* Sicilian.
siclo, *m.* shekel, an ancient Jewish coin.
sicofanta, sicofante, *m.* sycophant.
sicómoro, *m.* (bot.) sycamore; plane tree, buttonwood, sycamore maple.
sículo, la, *a.* Sicilian.
sideral; sidéreo, a, *a.* sidereal.
siderita, *f.* (min.) SIDEROSA; (bot.) ironwort.
siderización, *f.* preservation of timber by injecting iron salts.
siderosa, *f.* (min.) siderite.
sideróstato, *m.* (astr.) siderostat.
siderurgia, *f.* art of working in iron.
siderúrgico, ca, *a.* pert. to SIDERURGIA.
sidonio, nia, *n. & a.* Sidonian.
sidra, *f.* cider.
siega, *f.* reaping, mowing, harvest.
siego, siegue, *v.* V. SEGAR.
siembra, *f.* sowing, seeding; seedtime; sown field.
siembro, siembre, *v.* V. SEMBRAR.
siempre, *adv.* always.—**s. que**, provided; whenever.—**para, or por, s.**, forever.—**por s. jamás**, forever and ever.
siempreviva, *f.* (bot.) everlasting or immortelle.—**s. mayor**, houseleek.—**s. menor**, stonecrop.
sien, *f.* (anat.) temple.
siena, *f.* sienna.
sienita, *f.* (min.) syenite or sienite.
¹**siento, siente**, *v.* V. SENTAR.
²**siento, sienta, él sintió**, *v.* V. SENTIR.
sierpe, *f.* serpent, snake; ugly or angry person; anything that wriggles; (bot.) sucker, tiller.
sierpecilla, *f. dim.* small serpent.—*pl.* winding skyrockets.
sierra, *f.* saw; mountain range, sierra; (ichth.) sawfish.—**s. abrazadera**, lumberman's saw.—**s. bracera**, bucksaw, frame saw.—**s. de agua**, sawmill.—**s. de cinta**, band saw.—**s. de cortar metales**, hack saw.—**s. de ingletes**, tenon saw.—**s. de mano**, handsaw.—**s. de punta**, compass saw.—**s. de trasdós**, backsaw.

sierrecilla, *f. dim.* small saw.
sierro, sierre, *v.* V. SERRAR.
siervo, va, *n.* serf; slave; servant.—**s. de Dios**, servant of God; (coll.) poor devil.
sieso, *m.* (anat.) rectum.
siesta, *f.* hottest part of the day; afternoon nap; afternoon music in churches.
siete. I. *m. & a.* seven; seventh (of the month); seven-spot card; V-shaped tear in a garment; (carp.) hook-clasp. II. *f. pl.*—**las s.**, seven o'clock.
sietecueros, *m.* (S. A.) a kind of tumor on the heel; (C. A.) sickly-looking person.
sieteenrama, *f.* (bot.) tormentil.
sietemesino, na. I. *a.* seven-months (baby). II. *m.* puny coxcomb.
sieteñal, *a.* seven years old; septennial.
sifílide, *f.* (med.) syphilide.
sífilis, *f.* (med.) syphilis.—**sifilítico, ca**, *n. & a.* syphilitic.—**sifilografía**, *f.* (med.) syphilology.—**sifilográfico, ca**, *a.* pert. to syphilology.—**sifiloma**, *f.* (med.) a syphilitic tumor.
sifón, *m.* siphon; siphon bottle.
sifosis, *f.* = CORCOVA, hump (on back).
sifué, *m.* = SOBRECINCHA, surcingle.
sigilación, *f.* seal, stamp, impression, mark.
sigilar, *va.* to seal; to conceal.
sigilo, *m.* seal; secret, secrecy, reserve.—**s. sacramental**, inviolable secrecy of the confessional.
sigilografía, *f.* sigillography, study of seals.
sigilosamente, *adv.* silently, secretly.
sigiloso, sa, *a.* silent, reserved.
sigla, *f.* abbreviation by initials.
siglo, *m.* century; age; period; the world, worldly intercourse or matters.—**s. de cobre**, (myth.) bronze age.—**s. de hierro**, (myth.) iron age.—**s. de oro**, (myth.) golden age.—**s. de plata**, (myth.) silver age.—**s. dorado** = s. DE ORO.—**en, por, or por todos, los siglos de los siglos**, forever and ever.
sigmoideo, a, *a.* sigmoid, S-shaped.
signáculo, *m.* seal, signet.
signar. I. *va.* to sign, to mark with a signet. II. *vr.* to cross oneself.
signatario, ria, *n. & a.* signer(-ing), signatory.
signatura, *f.* sign, mark; (print.) signature; a Roman-Catholic court of justice and pardons.
signífero, ra, *a.* carrying a mark or sign.
significación, *f.* significance; sense, meaning; implication; importance.
significado, *m.* meaning, definition (of a word, etc.).
significador, ra, *n. & a.* signifier(-ing).
significante, *a.* significant, expressive.
significar, *va.* (*pret.* SIGNIFIQUÉ; *subj.* SIGNIFIQUE) to signify, mean; to indicate; to make known; to import, be worth.
significativamente, *adv.* significantly.
significativo, va, *a.* significant.
signifiqué, signifique, *v.* V. SIGNIFICAR.
signo, *m.* sign, mark, symbol; signal, motion, nod; (law) signum, flourish in a notary's signature; fate, destiny; benediction, sign of the cross; (astr.) sign of the zodiac; (mus.) character.—**s. fonético**, phonetic symbol.
sigo, sigue, siga, etc. *v.* V. SEGUIR.
siguiente. I. *pres. p.* of SEGUIR. II. *a.* following, next.
siguió, *pret.* of SEGUIR.
sijú, *m.* (W. I.) (ornith.) a nocturnal bird of prey.
sil, *m.* yellow ochre.
sílaba, *f.* syllable.
silabar, *vn.* = SILABEAR.
silabario, *m.* reader (book to teach reading).
silabear, *vn.* to syllabize, syllabicate.
silabeo, *m.* syllabication.
silábico, ca, *a.* syllabic.
sílabo, *m.* syllabus; summary, index.
silanga, *f.* (P. I.) canal, inlet, strait.

silba, *f.* (theat.) hiss, hissing (of disapproval).
silbador, ra, *n. & a.* whistler(-ing); hisser(-ing).
silbar. I. *vn.* to whistle; to whiz, as a musket ball.
   II. *va. & vn.* (theat.) to hiss, boo, catcall.
silbato, *m.* whistle (instrument); small crack letting out a liquid or air with a whistling sound.
silbido, *m.* whistle, whistling sound; hiss; sibilation.—**s. de oídos,** ringing in the ear.
silbo, *m.* whistle, hiss, whistling, whiz.
silbón, *m.* (ornith.) a kind of hissing widgeon.
silboso, sa, *a.* whistling, hissing.
silenciador, *m.* (auto) muffler; silencer (on gun, etc.).
silenciario, ria. I. *a.* observing profound silence.
   II. *m.* official with duty of commanding silence.
silenciero, ra, *a.* having the duty of commanding silence.
silencio, *m.* silence; noiselessness; taciturnity; secrecy; stillness, quiet; (mus.) rest.—**guardar s.,** to keep quiet.—**perpetuo s.,** (law) forever hold his peace.
silenciosamente, *adv.* silently, noiselessly.
silencioso, sa, *a.* silent, noiseless; still, quiet.
silepsis, *f.* (rhet.) syllepsis.
silería, *f.* group of silos.—**silero,** *m.* (agr.) silo.
silesiano, na; silesio, sia, *n. & a.* Silesian.
sílfide, f., silfo, *m.* sylph.
silguero, *m.* (ornith.) linnet.
silicato, *m.* (chem.) silicate.
sílice, *f.* (min.) silex, silica.—**silíceo, a,** *a.* siliceous.—**silícico, ca,** *a.* silicic.
silicio, *m.* (chem.) silicon.
siliciuro, *m.* (chem.) silicide.
silicua, *f.* siliqua, carat; (bot.) silique, pod.
silícula, *f.* (bot.) silicle or silicula.
silo, *m.* (agr.) silo; cavern or dark place.
silogismo, *m.* (logic) syllogism.—**s. cornuto,** horn of a dilemma.
silogístico, ca, *a.* syllogistic(al).
silogizar, *vn.* (*pret.* SILOGICÉ; *subj.* SILOGICE) to syllogize, argue.
silueta, *f.* silhouette; (of person) figure.
siluriano, na; silúrico, ca, *a.* (geol.) Silurian.
siluro, *m.* (ichth.) catfish, silurus; self-propelling torpedo.
silva, *f.* miscellany; a form of poem.
silvático, ca, *a.* = SELVÁTICO, sylvan; rustic.
silvestre, *a.* wild; uncultivated; rustic, savage.
silvicultor, ra, *n.* silviculturist, forester.
silvicultura, *f.* forestry, silviculture.
silvoso, sa, *a.* = SELVOSO, sylvan, wooded.
silla, *f.* chair; saddle; (eccl.) see.—**s. curul,** curule.—**s. de columpio,** rocking chair.—**s. de junco** = S. DE REJILLA.—**s. de la reina,** chair made by two persons' hands and wrists.—**s. de manos,** sedan chair; (Am.) S. DE LA REINA.—**s. de montar,** riding saddle.—**s. de posta,** post chaise.—**s. de rejilla,** cane or bamboo-bottomed chair.—**s. de ruedas,** wheel chair.—**s. de tijera,** camp chair.—**s. giratoria,** swivel chair.—**s. plegadiza,** folding chair, camp stool.—**s. poltrona,** armchair; easy chair.—**s. volante,** light gig.—**de s. a s.,** tête-à-tête, in private conference, heart to heart.
sillar, *m.* ashlar stone; place for saddle on horse.
sillarejo, *m.* small ashlar.
sillera, *f.* place for sedan chairs.
¹sillería, *f.* set of chairs; shop where chairs are made or sold; stalls or seats in a choir.
²sillería, *f.* (arch.) ashlar masonry.
sillero, ra, *n.* saddler; chair maker.
silleta, *f. dim.* small chair; hollow stone on which chocolate is ground; bedpan.—*pl.* mule chairs.
silletazo, *m.* blow with a chair.
silletero, ra, *n.* carrier of a sedan chair; chair maker or seller.
sillico, *m.* basin of a close-stool.
sillín, *m.* light riding saddle; harness saddle; elaborate mule chair.

sillita, *f. dim.* small chair.
sillón, *m. aug.* armchair; easy chair; sidesaddle.
sima, *f.* deep cavern; abyss, gulf, chasm.
simado, da, *a.* deep (land).
simbiosis, *f.* (biol.) symbiosis.
simbólicamente, *adv.* symbolically.
simbolicé, simbolice, *v. V.* SIMBOLIZAR.
simbólico, ca, *a.* symbolical.
simbolismo, *m.* symbolism.
simbolista, *m.* or *f.* symbolist.
simbolización, *f.* symbolization.
simbolizar, *va.* (*pret.* SIMBOLICÉ; *subj.* SIMBOLICE) to symbolize, represent, typify.
símbolo, *m.* symbol; mark, device.—**s. de la fe,** creed, articles of faith.
simetría, *f.* symmetry.
simétricamente, *adv.* symmetrically.
simétrico, ca, *a.* symmetrical.
simia, *f.* female ape.
símico, ca, *a.* simian.
simiente, *f.* seed; germ; semen, sperm.
simiesco, ca, *a.* simianlike.
símil. I. *a.* similar, like, alike. **II.** *m.* resemblance, similarity; (rhet.) simile.
similar, *a.* similar, resembling.
similitud, *f.* similitude, similarity.
similitudinario, ria, *a.* similar.
similor, *m.* low-grade brass.
simio, mia, *n.* simian, ape.
simón, *m.* hack, cab; hackman, in Madrid.
simonía, *f.* simony.
simoníacamente, *adv.* simoniacally.
simoníaco, ca; simoniático, ca, *a.* simoniacal.
simpatía, *f.* fellow feeling; congeniality; liking, friendly feeling; (med.) sympathy.
simpáticamente, *adv.* congenially; nicely, pleasingly.
simpaticé, simpatice, *v. V.* SIMPATIZAR.
simpático, ca, *a.* congenial; appealing; pleasant, "nice."—**gran s.,** (anat.) sympathetic system.
simpatizar, *vn.* (*pret.* SIMPATICÉ; *subj.* SIMPATICE) to be congenial.
simple. I. *a.* simple; mere; single; silly, foolish; artless, ingenuous; plain, unmixed, unadorned; mild, gentle; insipid, tasteless; informal extrajudicial. **II.** *m.* (pharm.) simple; simpleton.
simplemente, *adv.* simply; plainly; foolishly.
simpleza, *f.* silliness, foolishness; silly thing; rusticity, rudeness.
simplicidad, *f.* simplicity.
simplicísimo, ma, *a. super.* extremely simple.
simplificación, *f.* simplification.
simplificar, *va.* (*pret.* SIMPLIFIQUÉ; *subj.* SIMPLIFIQUE) to simplify.
simplista, *m.* simplist, herbalist.
simplón, na, *n. aug.* great simpleton.
simposia, *f.* (Gk. hist.) symposium.
simulación, *f.* simulation, feigning.
simulacro, *m.* simulacrum, image, idol; fancy, fantastical thing; (mil.) sham battle.
simuladamente, *adv.* in a dissembling manner.
simulador, ra, *n. & a.* dissembler(-ing).
simular, *va.* to simulate, pretend, sham.
simultáneamente, *adv.* simultaneously.
simultaneidad, *f.* simultaneity.
simultanear, *va.* to accomplish or carry on simultaneously.
simultáneo, a, *a.* simultaneous.
simún, *m.* simoom, sirocco, a hot wind.
sin, *prep.* without, besides.—**s. embargo,** notwithstanding, nevertheless, however.
sinagoga, *f.* synagogue.
sinalagmático, ca, *a.* (law) synalagmatic, mutually obligatory.
sinalefa, *f.* (gram.) synalepha.
sinamay, *m.* (P. I.) sinamay; a coarse fabric made from abaca.—**sinamayera,** *f.* (P. I.) woman who sells sinamay.
sinapismo, *m.* mustard plaster; (coll.) nuisance, bore.

sinartrosis, *f.* (anat.) synarthrosis, fixed joint.
sincerador, ra, *n.* & *a.* exculpator(-ing), excuser (-ing), defender(-ing), upholder(-ing).
sinceramente, *adv.* sincerely.
sincerar. I. *va.* to exculpate, to justify. **II.** *vr.* to excuse, justify, or vindicate oneself.
sinceridad, *f.* sincerity, good faith.
sincero, ra, *a.* sincere.
síncopa, *f.* (gram.) syncope; (mus.) syncopation.
sincopadamente, *adv.* with syncope.
sincopal. I. *m.* = SÍNCOPE. **II.** *a.* (med.) syncopal.
sincopar, *va.* to syncopate; to abridge.
síncope, *f.* SÍNCOPA; (med.) syncope.
sincopizar, *va.* & *vr.* (*pret.* SINCOPICÉ; *subj.* SINCOPICE) to swoon, to faint.
sincretismo, *m.* syncretism.
sincrónico, ca, *a.* synchronous.
sincronismo, *m.* synchronism.
sincronizador, ra, *n.* & *a.* synchronizer(-ing).
sincronizar, *va.* to synchronize; & *vn.* (radio) to tune in.
sindéresis, *f.* discretion; good judgment.
sindicado, *m.* body of trustees; syndicate; (pol. econ.) syndicate.
sindicador, ra, *n.* informer, prosecutor; syndicator.
sindical, *a.* syndical; (pol. econ.) syndicalistic.
sindicalismo, *m.* (pol. econ.) syndicalism; unionism.
sindicalista, *n.* & *a.* (pol. econ.) syndicalist(-ic); unionist, union (as *a.*).
sindicar, *va.* (*pret.* SINDIQUÉ; *subj.* SINDIQUE) to inform, to accuse; to syndicate.
sindicato, *m.* labor union; SINDICADO.
sindicatura, *f.* office and dignity of a syndic.
síndico, *m.* syndic; trustee; (law) assignee, receiver.
sindiqué, sindique, *v.* *V.* SINDICAR.
síndrome, *m.* (med.) syndrome, aggregate of symptoms.
sinécdoque, *f.* (rhet.) synecdoche.
sinecura, *f.* sinecure.
sinedrio, *m.* = SANEDRÍN, Sanhedrim.
sine qua non, (Lat.) essential, sine qua non.
sinéresis, *f.* (gram.) syneresis.
sinergia, *f.* (physiol.) synergy.
sinfín, *m.* = SINNÚMERO.
sínfisis, *f.* (biol.) symphysis.
sínfito, *m.* (bot.) comfrey.
sinfonía, *f.* (mus.) symphony.—**sinfónico, ca,** *a.* (mus.) symphonic.—**sinfonista,** *n.* symphonist; player in an orchestra.
singladura, *f.* (naut.) a day's run.
singlar, *vn.* (naut.) to steer, sail over a course.
single, *a.* (naut.) single.—**singlón,** *m.* (naut.) futtock.
singular, *a.* singular, unique; individual; extraordinary, strange; (gram.) singular.
singularicé, singularice, *v.* *V.* SINGULARIZAR.
singularidad, *f.* singularity, oddity, strange feature or thing; peculiarity.
singularizar. I. *va.* (*pret.* SINGULARICÉ; *subj.* SINGULARICE) to distinguish, particularize, singularize, single out. **II.** *vr.* to distinguish oneself; to be or make oneself conspicuous.
singularmente, *adv.* singularly.
singulto, *m.* sob; hiccough, singultus.
sinhueso, *f.* (coll.) tongue.
sínico, ca, *a.* Chinese.
siniestra, *f.* left hand.
siniestramente, *adv.* sinistrously; perversely.
siniestro, tra. I. *a.* sinister, left (side); sinister, vicious; unlucky, inauspicious. **II.** *m.* perverseness, depravity; (com.) shipwreck, disaster; damage, loss at sea. **III.** *f.* left hand; left-hand side.
sinistrórsum, *a.* sinistrorse, from right to left.
sinnúmero, *m.* no end, great number.—**un s. de,** numberless, a great many.

¹sino, *conj.* but; except, besides; solely, only.— **no . . . s.,** but, only (*no tengo sino un sombrero,* I have only one hat).—**no sólo . . . s.** (**también**), not only . . . but (also).
²sino, *m.* fate, destiny.
sinoble, *a.* (her.) = SINOPLE, vert.
·sinocal; sínoco, ca, *a.* (med.) synochal (fever).
sinodal. I. *a.* synodal. **II.** *m.* synodal examiner.
sinodático, *m.* (eccl.) contribution to the bishop.
sinódico, ca, *a.* (eccl.) synodal; (astr.) synodic.
sínodo, *m.* (eccl. and astr.) synod.
sinología, *f.* sinology, study of things Chinese.
sinólogo, ga, *n.* sinologist.
sinonimia, *f.* (rhet.) synonymy.
sinónimo, ma. I. *a.* synonymous. **II.** *m.* synonym.
sinople, *a.* (her.) sinople, vert.
sinopsis, *f.* synopsis.
sinóptico, ca, *a.* synoptic.
sinovia, *f.* synovia.—**sinovial,** *a.* synovial.
sinrazón, *f.* wrong, injury, injustice.
sinsabor, *m.* displeasure, unpleasantness; trouble, uneasiness.
sinsonte, *m.* (ornith.) mocking bird.
sintáctico, ca, *a.* (gram.) syntactic.
sintaxis, *f.* (gram.) syntax.
síntesis, *f.* synthesis.
sintéticamente, *adv.* synthetically.
sintético, ca, *a.* synthetical.
sintetizar, *va.* (*pret.* SINTETICÉ; *subj.* SINTETICE) to synthesize; to sum up.
sinto, sintoísmo, *m.* Shinto, Shintoism.
sintoísta, *n.* & *a.* Shintoist(-ic).
síntoma, *m.* (med.) symptom.
sintomáticamente, *adv.* symptomatically.
sintomático, ca, *a.* symptomatic(al).
sintomatología, *f.* (med.) symptomatology.
sintonía, *f.* (elec.) syntony.
sintonina, *f.* (chem.) syntonin.
sintonización, *f.* (radio) syntonization, tuning.
sintonizador, ra, *n.* & *a.* (elec.) syntonizer(-ing); (radio) tuner(-ing).
sintonizar, *va.* (radio) to syntonize, tune.
sinuosidad, *f.* sinuosity.
sinuoso, sa, *a.* sinuous, wavy.
sinusitis, *f.* (med.) sinusitis.
sinusoidal, *a.* sinusoidal.
sinusoide, *f.* (geom.) sinusoid, a curve of sines.
sinvergüencería, *f.* (coll.) shamelessness, brazenness.
sinvergüenza, *n.* (coll.) scoundrel, rascal; brazen, shameless person; caitiff; (Colomb.) coward.
sinvergüenzada, *f.* (Colomb.) base, low action.
sipedón, *m.* a kind of serpent.
siquier, siquiera, *adv.* & *conj.* at least; though, although; whether, or; scarcely; otherwise.—**s. un poquito,** ever so little.—**ni s.,** not even.
siracusano, na, *n.* & *a.* Syracusan.
sirena, *f.* siren, mermaid; (naut.) siren, foghorn; (phys.) siren, for measuring vibrations.
sirenio, nia. I. *a.* (ichth.) sirenian. **II.** *m. pl.* Sirenia.
sirga, *f.* (naut.) towrope, towline; line for hauling seines.—**a la s.,** (naut.) tracking from the shore.
sirgadura, *f.* (naut.) trackage.
sirgar, *va.* (naut.) to track.
sirgo, *m.* twisted silk; silk stuff.
sirguero, *m.* (ornith.) linnet.
siríaco, ca, *n.* & *a.* Syrian.
siringa, *f.* (bot.) seringa, name of various species of rubber tree.
Sirio, *m.* (astr.) Sirius.
sirio, ria, *n.* & *a.* = SIRÍACO.
sirle, *m.* sheep dung, goat dung.
siroco, *m.* sirocco.
sirria, *f.* sheep dung.
sirte, *f.* syrtes, hidden rock, sand bank; danger.
sirvienta, *f.* servant girl, maid.
sirviente, *m.* (domestic) servant; waiter.

For pronunciation, see the rules at the beginning of the book.

sirvo, sirva, sirvió, etc. *v. V.* SERVIR.

¹sisa, *f.* size used by gilders.

²sisa, *f.* petty theft, pilfering; (tailoring) clipping; (sewing) dart; excise tax.

sisador, ra, *n.* filcher, petty thief.

sisallo, *m.* (bot.) = BARRILLA, saltwort.

¹sisar, *va.* to pilfer, filch; (sewing) to take in; to impose an excise tax on.

²sisar, *va.* to size (for gilding).

sisear, *vn.* to hiss.—**siseo,** *m.* hiss, hissing.

sisero, *m.* excise collector.

sisimbrio, *m.* (bot.) hedge mustard.

sisitoté, *m.* (ornith.) a tropical song bird.

sísmico, ca, *a.* seismic.

sismógrafo, *m.* seismograph.

sismología, *f.* seismology.—**sismológico, ca,** *a.* seismological.

sismómetro, *m.* seismometer.

¹sisón, na, *n.* filcher, pilferer, petty thief.

²sisón, *m.* (ornith.) godart or moor cock.

sistema, *m.* system.—**s. cegesimal,** C. G. S. system (of units).

sistemáticamente, *adv.* systematically.

sistematicé, sistematice, *v. V.* SISTEMATIZAR.

sistemático, ca, *a.* systematic, methodical.

sistematización, *f.* systematization.

sistematizar, *va. & vn.* (*pret.* SISTEMATICÉ; *subj.* SISTEMATICE) to systematize.

sístilo, *m.* (arch.) systyle.

sístole, *f.* (physiol. and rhet.) systole.

sistro, *m.* (mus.) sistrum.

sitácidos, *m., pl.* (ornith.) Psitaci (the parrots).

sitiador, ra, *n. & a.* besieger(-ing).

sitial, *m.* seat of honor, presiding chair; bench.

sitiar, *va.* (mil.) to besiege, lay siege to; to surround, hem in, compass.

sitibundo, da, *a.* (poet.) thirsty.

sitiero, *m.* (Cuba) petty farmer.

¹sitio, *m.* place, space, spot, room; stand; seat; location, site; country house, country seat, villa; (Cuba) small farm.—**dejar en el s.,** to kill one outright.—**quedar en el s.,** to die on the spot.

²sitio, *m.* (mil.) siege.

sito, ta, *a.* situated, lying, located.

situación, *f.* situation; position; site, location; state, condition, circumstances.—**s. activa,** active-service position or office.—**s. pasiva,** office or position not actually filled, as when the incumbent is retired, on vacation, etc.

situado, da. I. *pp.* of SITUAR. II. *a.* situate, situated, located. III. *m.* allowance, pay, annuity assigned upon certain valuables.

situar. I. *va.* to place, locate, put, situate; (com.) to remit or place (funds). II. *vr.* to settle in a place; to station oneself.

smoking, *m.* dinner jacket, Tuxedo.

so, *prep.* under; below.—**s. capa de,** or **s. color de,** under color of; on pretense of.—**s. pena de,** under penalty of.

¡so! *interj.* whoa! stop! (to horses).

soasar, *va.* to half roast, parboil, underdo.

soata, *f.* (Venez.) a kind of squash.

soba, *f.* massage; kneading; rubbing; beating, drubbing.

sobacal, *a.* axillary.

sobaco, *m.* armpit, axilla; (bot.) axil.

sobadero, ra, *a.* that can be handled.

sobado, m.; sobadura, f. = SOBA.

sobajadura, f.; sobajamiento, *m.* squeeze, pressure, crushing.

sobajanero, *m.* (coll.) errand boy.

sobajar, *va.* to squeeze, press, crush.

sobanda, *f.* bottom or end of a cask.

sobaquera, *f.* (tailoring) armhole, armscye.

sobaquina, *f.* bad smell of the armpit.

sobar, *va.* to knead; to massage, squeeze, soften; to pummel, box; to handle (a person) with too much familiarity.

sobarba, *f.* noseband of a bridle.

sobarbada, *f.* sudden check; reprimand, scolding.

sobarbo, *m.* (mech.) cam, pallet or pawl, in beating machines.

sobarcar, *va.* (*pret.* SOBARQUÉ; *subj.* SOBARQUE) to carry under the arm; to draw (the clothes) up to the armholes.

sobeo, *m.* thong for tying the yoke to the pole.

soberanamente, *adv.* with authority; supremely, exceedingly, most.

soberanear, *vn.* to lord it, to domineer.

soberanía, *f.* sovereignty; rule, sway.

soberano, na. I. *a.* sovereign; supreme, royal; most potent, superior, preëminent; (coll.) "tops." II. *f.* sovereign; lord paramount; liege.

soberbia, *f.* excessive pride, haughtiness, arrogance; presumption; magnificence, sumptuousness, pomp; anger.

soberbiamente, *adv.* arrogantly; superbly.

soberbio, bia, *a.* overproud, arrogant, haughty; superb, grand; lofty, eminent; (of horses) fiery, mettlesome.

soberbiosamente, *adv.* haughtily.

soberbioso, sa, *a.* = SOBERBIO.

sobina, *f.* wooden pin, peg.

sobón, na, *a.* given to excessive fondling and caressing; (coll.) sly, lazy.

sobordo, *m.* (naut.) manifest, freight list.

sobornación, f. = SOBORNO.

sobornado, *m.* misshaped loaf of bread.

sobornador, ra, *n. & a.* briber(-ing), suborner (-ing).

sobornal, *m.* overload.

sobornar, *va.* to suborn, bribe.

soborno, *m.* subornation, bribe; incitement, inducement; (Peru) = SOBORNAL.

sobra, *f.* surplus, excess; left-over, leaving; grievous offense, injury.—**de s.,** over and above; more than enough; over, superfluous.—**estar de s.,** (coll.) to be one too many; to be superfluous.

sobradamente, *adv.* abundantly; superabundantly; excessively.

sobradar, *va.* to build a garret onto.

sobradillo, *m. dim.* (arch.) penthouse.

sobrado, da. I. *pp.* of SOBRAR. II. *a.* excessive, abundant; bold, audacious; rich, wealthy. III. *m.* garret, attic; (Am., gen. *pl.*) leavings.

sobrancero, ra, *a.* disengaged, unemployed; supernumerary plowman.

sobrante. I. *pres. p.* of SOBRAR. II. *a.* wealthy. III. *a. & m.* (something) left over; surplus.

sobrar. I. *va.* to exceed, surpass; to have in excess, or more than enough, to have to spare. II. *vn.* to be more than is necessary; to be over and above; to be more than enough, superfluous; to be intrusive; to remain, be left over.

sobrasada, f. = SOBREASADA.

sobrasar, *va.* to add fire under (a pot).

sobre. I. *prep.* on, upon; over; above; about, concerning; about, more or less; besides; after, beyond; to, toward, near; (naut.) off.—**s. comida,** after dinner.—**s. manera,** excessively, beyond measure, exceedingly.—**s. poco más o menos,** just about, more or less.—**s. que,** besides.—**estar s. sí,** to be on guard, to be self-possessed.—**ir s.,** to go in pursuit of. II. *m.* envelope (for letters); address, superscription.—**s. monedero,** coin container (to be enclosed with a letter).

sobreabundancia, *f.* superabundance.

sobreabundante, *a.* superabundant; luxuriant.

sobreabundantemente, *adv.* superabundantly.

sobreabundar, *vn.* to superabound; to be exuberant.

sobreaguar, *vn. & vr.* to float on water.

sobreagudo, da, *a. & n.* (mus.) treble, highest register.

sobrealiento, *m.* difficult respiration.

sobrealimentación, *f.* overfeeding.

sobrealimentar, *va.* to overfeed.

obrealzar, va. to praise, to extol.
obreañadir, va. to superadd, superinduce.
obreañal, a. over a year old.
obrearco, m. (arch.) discharging arch.
obreasada, f. half-roasted sausage from the island of Majorca.
obreasar, va. to roast again.
obrebarato, ta, a. very cheap, extra cheap.
obreboya, f. (naut.) marking buoy.
obrebrazal, m. (naut.) false rail.
obrecaja, f. outer case.
obrecalza, f. leggings.
obrecama, f. coverlet, bedspread.
obrecaña, f. (vet.) tumor on a horse's leg.
obrecarga, f. overload; packing strap; additional trouble or vexation; surcharge, overburden.
obrecañado, da, a. & pp. overloaded.
obrecargar, va. (pret. SOBRECARGUÉ; subj. SOBRECARGUE) to overload, overburden; (com.) to overcharge; (sewing) to fell.
obrecargo, m. (naut.) purser, supercargo.
obrecarta, f. envelope (for a letter); (law) second decree or warrant repeating a former order.
obrecartar, va. to repeat (a former warrant).
obrecebadera, f. (naut.) sprit top-sail.
obrecédula, f. second royal order.
obreceja, f. part of the forehead over the eyebrows.
obrecejo, m. frown; threatening or forbidding aspect.
obreceño, m. frown.
obrecercar, va. (sewing) to welt.
obrecerco, m. (sewing) welt.
obrecincho, m.; -cha, f. surcingle.
obreclaustro, m. apartment over a cloister.
obrecoger. I. va. (ind. SOBRECOJO; subj. SOBRECOJA) to surprise, catch (in the act). II. vr. to become afraid or apprehensive.—s. de, to be seized with.
obrecogimiento, m. fear, apprehension.
obrecomida, f. dessert.
obrecopa, f. cover or lid of a cup.
obrecoser, va. (sewing) to whip, to fell.
obrecostura, f. (sewing) whipstich, fell.
obrecrecer, vn. to grow on top.
obrecreciente, a. growing on top.
obrecruces, m. pl. (carp.) cross joints.
obrecubierta, f. double cover; warp or envelope; (naut.) upper deck.
obrecuello, m. collar.
obredicho, cha, a. above-mentioned, aforesaid, said.
obrediente, m. gagtooth.
obredorar, va. to overgild; (fig.) to gloss over.
obreedificar, va. to build over or on.
obreempeine, m. covering for the instep.
obreestadías, f. pl. (com.) extra lay days.
obreexcitación, f. overexcitement; overexcitation.
obreexcitar, va. to overexcite.
obrefalda, f. overskirt.
obrefaz, f. surface, outside; (mil.) face prolonged.
obrefino, na, a. superfine, overfine, extrafine.
obreflor, f. flower growing within another.
obrefusión, f. (phys. & chem.) superfusion, supercooling.
obreguarda, m. second guard.
obrehaz, f. surface; outside cover.
obreherido, da, a. slightly wounded.
obrehilar, va. (sewing) to overcast.
obrehueso, m. (vet.) splint; trouble, encumbrance, burden.
obrehumano, na, a. superhuman.
obrehusa, f. stew of fried fish.
obrejalma, f. woollen cover for a packsaddle.
obrejuanete, m. (naut.) royal.
obrejunta, f. cover plate or strap (of a butt joint).

sobrelecho, m. under face of a stone.
sobrellave. I. f. double key. II. m. in royal palaces, keeper of double keys.
sobrellenar, va. to fill up, fill full.
sobrelleno, na, a. well filled, filled full.
sobrellevar, va. to ease (another's burden); to carry; to bear, endure, undergo; to overlook, be lenient about.
sobremanera, adv. beyond measure; exceedingly, most.
sobremano, f. (vet.) splint on the forehoofs.
sobremesa, f. tablecloth; dessert.—de sobremesa, immediately after dinner.
sobremesana, f. (naut.) mizzen topsail.
sobremuñonera, f. (artil.) clamp or capsquare.
sobrenadar, vn. to float.
sobrenatural, a. supernatural.
sobrenaturalmente, adv. supernaturally.
sobrenjalma, f. = SOBREJALMA.
sobrenombre, m. surname; nickname.
sobrentender, va. (ind. SOBRENTIENDO; subj. SOBRENTIENDA) to understand (something implied, not expressed). II. vr. to be understood, to go without saying.
sobrepaga, f. extra pay.
sobrepaño, m. upper cloth; wrapper.
sobreparto, m. (med.) confinement after parturition.
sobrepasar, va. to exceed.
sobrepeine. I. m. trimming (the hair). II. adv. (coll.) slightly, briefly.
sobrepelliz, f. (eccl.) surplice.
sobrepeso, m. overweight.
sobrepié, m. (vet.) splint on rear hoofs.
sobreplán, m. (naut.) rider.
sobreponer. I. va. (pp. SOBREPUESTO; ind. pres. SOBREPONGO, pret. SOBREPUSE, fut. SOBREPONDRÉ; subj. SOBREPONGA) to put over, to overlap. II. vr. (a) to be above; to master, overcome, overpower.
sobreposición, f. superposition.
sobreprecio, m. extra charge, raise.
sobrepuerta, f. cornice over a door; lambrequin, door curtain, portière.
sobrepuesto, ta. I. pp. irreg. of SOBREPONER. II. a. superposed. III. m. honeycomb formed by bees after the hive is full.
sobrepujamiento, m. surpassing, excelling.
sobrepujante, pres. p. surpassing, excelling.
sobrepujanza, f. great strength and vigor.
sobrepujar, va. to exceed, surpass, excel.
sobrepuse, pret. of SOBREPONER.
sobrequilla, f. (naut.) keelson.
sobrerronda, f. (mil.) counterround.
sobrerropa, f. overcoat; overalls.
sobresalgo, sobresalga, v. V. SOBRESALIR.
sobresaliente. I. a. excelling, surpassing, excellent; conspicuous, that stands out, distinctive. II. n. substitute; (theat.) understudy.
sobresalir, vn. (ind. pres. SOBRESALGO, fut. SOBRESALDRÉ; subj. SOBRESALGA) to excel, be prominent, stand out; to project, jut out.
sobresaltar. I. va. to rush upon, assail, attack, fall upon; to frighten, terrify, startle. II. vn. to be striking (as figures in a painting). III. vr. to be startled.
sobresalto, m. sudden assault; startling surprise; sudden dread or fear.—de s., unexpectedly, unawares, suddenly.
sobresanar, va. to heal superficially; to screen, to palliate.
sobresano. I. adv. cured superficially; affectedly, feignedly. II. m. pl. (naut.) tabling, leach-lining.
sobrescribir, va. to superscribe, address.
sobrescrito, ta. I. pp. irreg. of SOBRESCRIBIR. II. m. superscription, address.
sobresdrújulo, la, a. accented on any syllable preceding the antepenult.

For pronunciation, see the rules at the beginning of the book.

sobreseer, *vn.* to desist from a design; to relinquish a claim; (law) to stay a judgment, etc.

sobreseimiento, *m.* suspension; discontinuance; (law) stay of proceedings.

sobresello, *m.* double seal.

sobresembrar, *va.* (*ind.* SOBRESIEMBRO; *subj.* SOBRESIEMBRE) to sow over again.

sobreseñal, *f.* a special knights' device.

sobresolar, *va.* (*ind.* SOBRESUELO; *subj.* SOBRESUELE) to pave anew; to resole (shoe).

sobrestante, *m.* overseer; foreman; comptroller; inspector; supervisor.—**sobrestantía,** *f.* position or office of a SOBRESTANTE.

sobresueldo, *m.* extra wages.

sobresuelo, *m.* floor or pavement over another.

sobretarde, *f.* close of the evening.

sobretendón, *m.* tumor on the tendons of a horse's leg.

sobretodo, *m.* overcoat, great coat.

sobreveedor, *m.* chief of the overseers.

sobrevenida, *f.* supervention.

sobrevenir, *vn.* (*ger.* SOBREVINIENDO; *ind. pres.* yo SOBREVENGO, él SOBREVIENE, *pret.* SOBREVINE, *fut.* SOBREVENDRÉ; *subj.* SOBREVENGA) to happen, take place; to follow; to supervene.

sobreverterse, *vr.* (*ind.* se SOBREVIERTE; *subj.* se SOBREVIERTA) to run over, overflow.

sobrevestir, *va.* to put a greatcoat on.

sobrevidriera, *f.* window guard, wire net before a glass window; storm window.

sobrevienta, *f.* gust of wind; onslaught, impetuous fury; startling surprise.—**a s.,** suddenly.

sobreviento, *m.* gust of wind.—**estar a s. de,** (naut.) to have the wind of.

sobrevierte, sobrevierta, *v. V.* SOBREVERTERSE.

sobrevine, *pret.* of SOBREVENIR.

sobrevista, *f.* beaver of a helmet.

sobreviviente, *n. & a.* survivor(-ing).

sobrevivir, *va. & vn.* to survive, to outlive.

sobrexcedente, *a.* surpassing, exceeding.

sobrexceder, *va.* to surpass, excel, exceed.

sobrexcitación, *f.* overexcitement; overexcitation.

sobrexcitar, *va.* to overexcite.

sobriamente, *adv.* soberly, frugally.

sobriedad, *f.* sobriety, frugality.

sobrina, *f.* niece.

sobrinazgo, *m.* relationship of a nephew or niece; nepotism.

sobrino, *m.* nephew.

sobrio, ria, *a.* sober, temperate, frugal.

soca, *f.* (Am.) ratoon of the sugar cane.

socaire, *m.* (naut.) slatch; lee, lee gauge.

socairero, *m.* (naut.) skulker, lurker.

socaliña, *f.* trick, cunning.—**socaliñar,** *va.* to extort by trickery.—**socaliñero, ra,** *n.* trickster, cheat.

socalzar, *va.* (mason.) to underpin, underset.

socapa, *f.* pretext, pretense.—**a s.,** cautiously.

socapiscol, *m.* = SOCHANTRE.

socar, *va.* (Cuba, C. A.) to tighten; to compress.

socarra, *f.* singe, scorching; craft, cunning.

socarrar, *va.* to singe, scorch.

socarrén, *m.* (arch.) eave, gable end.

socarrena, *f.* hollow, cavity; interval; (arch.) space between rafters.

socarrina, *f.* (coll.) scorching, singeing.

socarrón, na, *a.* cunning, sly, crafty.

socarronamente, *adv.* slyly, artfully.

socarronería, *f.* cunning, artfulness, craftiness.

socava, **socavación,** *f.* undermining; digging around trees.

socavar, *va.* to excavate, undermine.

socavón, *m.* cave, cavern; (min.) adit, adit level, tunnel.

socaz, *m.* outlet of a mill.

sociabilidad, *f.* sociableness, sociability.

sociable, *a.* sociable, companionable.

sociablemente, *adv.* sociably, companionably.

social, *a.* social; sociable, companionable.

socialismo, *m.* (pol.) socialism.

socialista, *n. & a.* (pol.) socialist(-ic).

socialización, *f.* socialization.

socializar, *va.* to socialize, transfer to the State

sociedad, *f.* society; social intercourse; (com.) society, corporation, association, company partnership, copartnership.—**s. anónima** stock company.—**s. comanditaria** = s. E COMANDITA.—**s. cooperativa,** coöperative so ciety or association.—**S. de las Naciones** League of Nations.—**s. de socorros mutuos** mutual-help society.—**s. en comandita,** com mandite, partnership in commendam.—**s. regular colectiva,** general partnership, copartner ship.—**s. por acciones** = s. ANÓNIMA.—**la s.** society, the social organism, the community (often restricted, as in English, to polite o fashionable society).

socinianismo, *m.* Socinianism.

sociniano, na, *n. & a.* Socinian.

socio, cia, *n.* partner, copartner; companion, con sort; member, fellow; (coll.) confederate.

sociología, *f.* sociology.

sociológicamente, *adv.* sociologically.

sociológico, ca, *a.* sociological.

sociólogo, ga, *n.* sociologist.

socolor, *m.* pretext, pretense.

socollada, *f.* (naut.) flapping; pitching, jerk.

soconusco, *m.* cacao from Soconusco (C. A.)

socoro, *m.* place under the choir.

socorredor, ra, *n. & a.* helper(-ing), aider(-ing)

socorrer, *va.* to assist, aid, help, succor; to favor to pay on account.

socorrido, da. I. *pp.* of SOCORRER. **II.** *a.* fur nished, well supplied; (coll.) handy, useful popular.

socorro, *m.* succor, aid, assistance, help; paymen on account; (mil.) succors; relief.—**puesto d s.,** first-aid station.

socrático, ca, *a.* Socratic.

socrocio, *m.* (pharm.) saffron poultice.

socucho, *m.* (Am.) small room, "den"; hidin place.

sochantre, *m.* (eccl.) subchanter.

soda, *f.* (chem.) = SOSA, soda.

sódico, ca, *a.* (chem.) sodic; sodium (as *a.,* as i *carbonato sódico,* sodium carbonate).

sodio, *m.* (chem.) sodium.

sodomía, *f.* sodomy.—**sodomita,** *n. & a.* Sodom ite.—**sodomítico, ca,** *a.* pert. to sodomy.

soez, *a.* mean, vile, base, coarse.

soezmente, *adv.* meanly, basely, vilely.

sofá, *m.* sofa.

sofaldar, *va.* to truss up; raise up; tuck up.

sofaldo, *m.* trussing or tucking up clothes.

¹sofí, *m.* Sufi, Shah.

²sofí, *m.* = SUFÍ, one of a Persian sect of mystics

sofión, *m.* hoot; reprimand.

sofisma, *m.* (logic) fallacy.

sofismo, *m.* = SUFISMO, Sufism.

sofista, *m.* sophist; quibbler.

sofistería, *f.* sophistry.

sofisticación, *f.* perversion by fallacies.

sofísticamente, *adv.* fallaciously.

sofisticar, *va.* to falsify, pervert or distort b fallacy.

sofístico, ca, *a.* fallacious.

sofito, *m.* (arch.) soffit.

soflama, *f.* subtle flame; glow; blush; (coll.) flim flam.—**soflamar. I.** *va.* to cheat, swindle; (coll. to flimflam; to make (a person) blush. **II.** *v* to get scorched.

soflamero, *m.* trickster; (coll.) flimflammer.

sofocación, *f.* suffocation; smothering, choking

sofocante, *pres. p. & a.* suffocating, stifling close.

sofocar, *va.* (*pret.* SOFOQUÉ; *subj.* SOFOQUE) t choke, suffocate, smother; to quench, extin guish, put out; to stifle; to oppress, harass; t importune, vex; to provoke; to make blus

---

For pronunciation, see the rules at the beginning of the book.

ofocleo, a, *a.* Sophoclean.

ofoco, *m.* suffocation; vexation; embarrassment.

ofocón, *m.* (coll.) vexation, chagrin.

ofoqué, sofoque, *v. V.* SOFOCAR.

ófora, *f.* (bot.) Japanese pagoda tree.

ofreír, *va.* (*pp.* SOFREÍDO, SOFRITO; *ind. pres.* SOFRÍO, *pret.* él SOFRIÓ; *subj.* SOFRÍA) (cooking) to fry slightly.

ofrenada, *f.* sudden check of a horse, saccade, ebrillade; harsh reprimand, dressing down.

ofrenar, *va.* to check (a horse) suddenly; to reprimand severely; to check (a passion).

ofrenazo, *m.* = SOFRENADA.

ofrito, ta, *pp. irreg.* of SOFREÍR.

oga. **I.** *f.* rope, halter, cord; a variable land measure; (arch.) face (of a brick or stone); (arch.) (of bricks and stones) stretcher.—**a s.**, (arch.) as stretchers.—**con la s. a la garganta,** in imminent danger.—**dar s. a,** to make fun of.—**hacer s.,** to lag behind. **II.** *n.* (coll.) sly, cunning person; (Colomb.) lasso, lariat.

oguear, *va.* to measure with a rope.

oguería, *f.* ropewalk; rope shop; collection of ropes.

oguero, *m.* ropemaker.

oguilla, *f.* small braid of hair; small rope.

oja, *f.* (bot.) soy; soy bean.

ojuzgador, ra, *n.* conqueror, subduer.

ojuzgar, *va.* (*pret.* SOJUZGUÉ; *subj.* SOJUZGUE) to conquer, subjugate, subdue.

sol, *m.* sun; sunlight; day; a kind of ancient lace; sol, Peruvian silver coin (normally, about 49 cents, or 2 shillings).—**s. medio,** (astr.) mean sun.—**al salir el s.,** at sunrise.—**al s. puesto,** at nightfall.—**de s. a s.,** from sunrise to sunset.—**hacer s.,** to be sunny (*hace sol,* it is sunny; *hace mucho sol,* it is very sunny).—**quemadura del s.,** sunburning.—**tomar el s.,** to bask in the sun, sunbathe; (naut.) to take the altitude of the sun.

sol, *m.* (mus.) G, sol, fifth note of the scale.

olacé, solace, *v. V.* SOLAZAR.

olacear, *va.* to solace, console, comfort.

olada, *f.* dregs, lees, sediment.

olado, *m.* tile floor, pavement.

olador, *m.* tiler, paver.

oladura, *f.* paving; paving materials.

olamente, *adv.* only; solely, merely.

olana, *f.* strong sunshine; sunny place; sun gallery; sun bath.

olanáceo, a. **I.** *a.* solanaceous. **II.** *f. pl.* Solanaceæ.

olanera, *f.* sun bath; sunburning; hot, sunny place.

olanina, *f.* (chem.) solanin(e).

olano, *m.* easterly wind; (bot.) nightshade.

olapa, *f.* lapel (of coat); pretense, pretext; (vet.) cavity of a small wound; overlapping.—**a,** or **de, s.,** overlapping, lap (joint).

olapadamente, *adv.* deceitfully, sneakingly.

olapado, da. **I.** *pp.* of SOLAPAR. **II.** *a.* cunning, crafty, artful, sneaky; lap (joint).

olapadura.—**obra de s.,** *f.* (naut.) clincher work, clinching; overlapping.

olapamiento, *m.* (vet.) cavity of a wound.

olapar. **I.** *va.* (tailoring) to put lapels on; to overlap; to cloak, conceal. **II.** *vn.* to overlap (as a lapel).—**solape, solapo,** *m.* lapel; pretense.—**a s.,** (coll.) sneakingly.

solar, *va.* (*ind.* SUELO; *subj.* SUELE) to floor; to pave; to sole (shoes).

solar, *m.* lot, ground plot; manor house, ancestral mansion.

solar, *a.* solar.

solariego, ga, *a.* manorial; (law) held by a full legal tenure; of noble ancestry.

solas, *f. pl.* of SOLO.—**a mis, tus, sus s.,** *adv.* all alone, by myself, thyself, etc.—**a s.,** in private.

solaz, *m.* solace, consolation; relaxation, comfort; enjoyment.—**a s.,** pleasantly, agreeably.

solazar. **I.** *va.* (*pret.* SOLACÉ; *subj.* SOLACE) to solace, comfort, cheer, gladden. **II.** *vr.* to be comforted; to rejoice, have pleasure.

solazo, *m. aug.* (coll.) scorching sun.

solazoso, sa, *a.* comforting, delectable.

soldada, *f.* wages, pay, salary.

soldadero, ra, *a.* salaried, receiving wages.

soldadesca, *f.* soldiery; soldiering; undisciplined troops.

soldadesco, ca, *a.* soldierly, soldierlike, military.—**a la s.,** in a soldierly manner, soldierlike.

soldado, *m.* soldier.—**s. de a caballo,** trooper, cavalryman.—**s. de a pie,** or **de infantería,** foot soldier.—**s. raso,** private.—**s. de marina,** marine.—**s. voluntario,** volunteer.

soldador, *m.* solderer; soldering iron.

soldadura, *f.* soldering; welding, brazing; solder; correction or mending.—**s. débil,** soft solder (-ing).—**s. dura,** or **s. fuerte,** hard solder(-ing).—**s. tierna** = s. DÉBIL.

soldán, *m.* sultan, Mohammedan title.

soldar, *va.* (*ind.* SUELDO; *subj.* SUELDE) to solder; to weld, braze; to mend; to correct.

solear, *va.* = ASOLEAR, to sun.

solecismo, *m.* (rhet. and gram.) solecism.

soledad, *f.* solitude, loneliness, loneness; homesickness; lonely place; (mus.) an Andalusian tune, song, and dance.

soledoso, sa, *a.* solitary, lonely.

solejar, *m.* sunny place.

solemne, *a.* solemn; yearly; (coll.) great, downright.—**solemnemente,** *adv.* solemnly.

solemnicé, solemnice, *v. V.* SOLEMNIZAR.

solemnidad, *f.* solemnity; religious pomp; grand ceremony; impressiveness.—*pl.* formalities.

solemnizador, ra, *n. & a.* solemnizer(-ing).

solemnizar, *va.* (*pret.* SOLEMNICÉ; *subj.* SOLEMNICE) to solemnize, celebrate with pomp; to praise, applaud, extol.

solenoide, *m.* (elec.) solenoid.

sóleo, *m.* (anat.) soleus.

¹soler, *vn.* (*ind.* SUELO) (*defect., only pres. and imp. used, always foll. by inf.*) to be in the habit of, accustomed to; (in *imp.*) used to (*yo solía hablar con él,* I used to talk with him).

²soler, *m.* (naut.) underflooring.

solera, *f.* (arch.) entablature, stringpiece, crossbeam, rib, summer, lintel, breastsummer; plinth; nether millstone; lees or mother of wine.—**s. de cureña,** (mil.) sole of a gun carriage.

solercia, *f.* industry; abilities; shrewdness.

¹solería, *f.* pavement; paving stones.

²solería, *f.* parcel of skins used for soles.

solero, *m.* nether millstone.

solerte, *a.* shrewd, cunning, sagacious.

soleta, *f.* new sole in stockings; (Mex.) cake with sugar icing.—**tomar s.,** (coll.) to run off.

soletar, soletear, *va.* to resole (stockings).

soletero, ra, *n.* one who refoots stockings.

solevación, *f.,* or solevamiento, *m.* = SUBLEVACIÓN, insurrection, uprising.

solevantado, da. **I.** *pp.* of SOLEVANTAR. **II.** *a.* restless, excited, agitated, perturbed.

solevantamiento, *m.* upheaval, uprising.

solevantar, *va.* to push up, elevate; to incite.

solevar, *va.* = SUBLEVAR, to incite to revolt.

solfa, *f.* (mus.) sol-fa, solfeggio, solmization; musical annotation, notes; music, harmony; (coll.) sound beating or flogging.—**estar,** or **poner, en s.,** to be arranged (or to arrange) with art and judgment; to appear (or present) in a ridiculous light.

solfatara, *f.* (geol.) solfatara.

solfeador, ra, *n.* sol-faist, one who solmizates.

solfear, *vn.* (mus.) to sol-fa, solmizate; (coll.) to cudgel, flog.—**solfeo,** *m.* (mus.) sol-faing; (coll.) beating, drubbing.

solfista, *n.* sol-faist.

solicitación, f. solicitation; importunity; temptation, inducement.

solicitado, da. I. pp. of SOLICITAR. **II.** a. in good demand, sought after, popular.

solicitador, ra, n. solicitor, agent.

solícitamente, adv. solicitously, diligently.

solicitante. I. a. soliciting. **II.** n. solicitor, agent; applicant.

solicitar, va. to solicit; to apply for; to importune; to entreat; to woo, court.

solícito, ta, a. solicitous, diligent, careful.

solicitud, f. solicitude; importunity; diligence; petition, application, request; (com.) demand. **—a s.,** on request, at the request (of).**—s. de ingreso,** application for admission.

sólidamente, adv. solidly, firmly.

solidar, va. to consolidate, establish; to harden, to render firm and solid.

solidariamente, adv. with solidarity; (law) in solidum, for the whole.

solidaridad, f. solidarity.

solidario, ria, a. (law) solidary, jointly liable.

solidarizar. I. va. to make solidary. **II.** vr. to make common cause, act together.

solideo, m. (eccl.) calotte.

solidez, f. solidity, firmness, strength.

solidificación, f. solidification.

solidificar, va. & vr. to solidify.

sólido, da. I. a. solid, firm, compact, consistent; built on sound reasons. **II.** m. (geom. & phys.) solid; solidus, an ancient Roman gold coin.

soliloquiar, vn. (coll.) to soliloquize.

soliloquio, m. soliloquy, monologue.

solimán, m. (chem.) corrosive sublimate.

solio, m. throne with a canopy; throne.

solípedo, da, a. (zool.) solipede, solidungulate.

solista, n. (mus.) soloist.

solitaria, f. post chaise; sulky; tapeworm.

solitariamente, adv. solitarily.

solitario, ria. I. a. solitary, lonely, isolated, secluded. **II.** m. solitary, recluse, hermit; solitaire (game); (jewel) solitaire (diamond).

sólito, ta, a. wont, accustomed.

soliviadura, f. lift, lifting, raising.

soliviantar, va. to induce, incite, rouse.

soliviar. I. va. to raise or lift up: to prop up. **II.** vr. to raise oneself.

solivio, m. lift, rising or raising.

solo, la. I. a. alone, unaccompanied; only, sole; solitary, lonely.**—a mis solas, sus solas,** etc., all alone, without aid, by myself (himself, etc.); in solitude.**—a solas,** alone, unaided. **II.** m. (mus.) solo; lone hand in certain card games; a card game.

sólo, adv. = SOLAMENTE, only, solely.

solomillo, solomo, m. sirloin; loin of pork.

solpuga. I. f. (zool.) solpugid. **II.** f. pl. Solpugida.

solsticial, a. solstitial.

solsticio, m. (astr.) solstice.**—s. de invierno,** winter solstice.**—s. de verano,** summer solstice.**—s. hiemal** = S. DE INVIERNO.**—s. vernal** = S. DE VERANO.

soltadizo, za, a. easily untied; cleverly loosened.

soltador, ra, n. dropper.

soltar. I. va. (pp. irreg. SUELTO; ind. SUELTO; subj. SUELTE) to untie, unfasten, loosen; to turn on (the water); to turn loose; to cast off, set free, discharge; to let go, drop; to throw down, throw out; (coll.) to utter, let out; to give (a slap or kick). **II.** vn. to burst out (into laughter, etc.). **III.** vr. to get loose, to come off; to grow expeditious and handy; to lose restraint; to thaw out; to forego all decency and modesty; to break out (laughing, crying, etc.); to begin, start.

soltería, f. celibacy, bachelorhood.

soltero, ra. I. a. single, unmarried. **II.** m. bachelor, unmarried man. **III.** f. spinster, unmarried woman.

solterón, na, n. old bachelor (maid).

soltura, f. freeing, setting at liberty; release, freedom; easiness; fluency; agility, nimbleness laxity, looseness, licentiousness.

solubilidad, f. solubility.

soluble, a. soluble; solvable.

solución, f. loosening or untying; climax or denouement in a drama or epic poem; pay, satisfaction; (math., chem.) solution.**—s. de continuidad,** solution of continuity, discontinuity break.

solucionar, va. to solve; to meet (a difficulty)

solutivo, va, a. (med.) solutive.

solvencia, f. (com.) solvency.

solventar, va. to settle (accounts); to solve.

solvente, a. solvent, dissolving; (com.) solvent

solver, va. (ind. SUELVO; subj. SUELVA) to solve

sollado, m. (naut.) orlop.

sollamar, va. to scorch, to singe.

sollastre, m. scullion, kitchen boy; smart rogue

sollastría, f. scullery.

sollo, m. (ichth.) sturgeon, pike.

sollozante, a. sobbing.

sollozar, vn. (pret. SOLLOCÉ; subj. SOLLOCE) to sob.**—sollozo,** m. sob; (Mex.) huckleberry.

soma, f. coarse flour.

somanta, f. (coll.) beating, drubbing.

somatén, m. armed force for defense of a city or province; one serving in such a force; alarm bell; (coll.) hubbub.**—¡s.!** Catalan war cry.

somatología, f. somatology.

sombra, f. shade; shadow; darkness; spirit, ghost shelter, protection; resemblance; sign, vestige (astr.) umbra; (art) shade, shading; umber.**—sombras chinescas,** (theat.) shadow pantomime.**—a la s.,** in the shade; (coll.) in jail.**—hacer s.,** to shade; to protect; to outshine.**—ni por s.,** by no means.**—no ser ni su s.,** to be but the shadow of one's former self.**—tener buena s.,** to be pleasing, popular, agreeable.**—tener mala s.,** to exert an evil influence over others; to be disagreeable.

sombrear, va. screen made with branches, mats etc., to afford shade.

sombrajo, m. SOMBRAJE; (coll.) shadow cast by a person before another who needs light.

sombrar, va. to astonish.

sombreador, ra, a. shading.

sombrear, va. (art) to shade.

sombrerazo, m. aug. large hat; flap or blow with a hat; (coll.) doffing of the hat as a greeting.

sombrerera, f. hatbox, hat case; hatter's wife.

sombrerería, f. hat factory or shop.

sombrerero, ra, n. hatter; hat maker.

sombrerete, m. dim. small hat; (mech.) bonnet, cap, cowl; spark catcher of a locomotive; (arch.) calotte.

sombrerillo, ito, m. dim. little hat; alms basket in prisons; (bot.) navelwort.

sombrero, m. SOMBRERETE; hat; soundboard, canopy of a pulpit; privilege of a Spanish grandee of keeping his hat on in the presence of the king.**—s. apuntado,** cocked hat.**—s. calañés,** Andalusian hat.**—s. castoreño,** beaver hat.**—s. de cabrestante,** (naut.) drum of the capstan.**—s. de copa, or de copa alta,** silk hat, high (silk) hat.**—s. de jipijapa,** Panama hat.**—s. del patrón,** (naut.) hat money, primage.**—s. de muelles,** opera hat.**—s. de paja,** straw hat.**—s. de pelo,** (Am.) high hat.**—s. de teja,** shovel hat, priest's hat (low-crown hat with broad brim turned up on the sides).**—s. de tres candiles, or de tres picos,** three-cornered hat.**—s. flexible,** soft felt hat.**—s. gacho,** slouch hat.**—s. hongo,** derby hat.**—s. jarano,** Mexican sombrero.**—s. jíbaro,** farmers' straw hat.**—s. jipijapa,** Panama hat.

sombría, f. shady place.

sombrilla, f. parasol, sunshade.

sombrita, f. dim. slight shade.

sombrío, bría. I. a. gloomy, sombre; overcast,

murky, thick (weather); taciturn, sullen; (art) shaded, dark. II. *m.* shady place.

sombroso, sa, *a.* shady, shadowy.

somera, *f.* (print.) sleeper of the press.

someramente, *adv.* superficially, briefly.

somero, ra, *a.* superficial, shallow.

someter. I. *va.* to subject; submit, subdue; to put (to the test, etc.). **II.** *vr.* to humble oneself; to submit; to surrender; **(a)** to submit (to); to go (through) (an operation, an examination).

sometimiento, *m.* submission, subjection, subduing.

somnambulismo, *m.* somnambulism.

somnámbulo, la, *n.* somnambulist.

somnífero, ra, *a.* somniferous, inducing sleep.

somnílocuo, cua, *a.* talking in one's sleep.

somnolencia, *f.* drowsiness, somnolence.

somonte.—de s., coarse, rough, shaggy.

somorgujador, *m.* diver.

somorgujar, *va.* & *vr.* to dive, to duck.

somorgujo, somorgujón, somormujo, *m.* (ornith.) dun diver, merganser.**—a lo somorgujo,** or **a la somormujo,** under water; privately, secretly.

sompesar, *va.* = SOPESAR.

son, *m.* sound, noise; spread news or story; pretext, motive; manner, guise; (Am. esp. Cuba) popular song and dance.**—¿a qué s.?** why, for what reason?**—a s. de,** at or to the sound of.**—¿a s. de qué? = ¿A QUÉ S.?—bailar a cualquier s.,** to transfer easily one's affection or liking, to be fickle.**—bailar sin s.,** to be exceedingly eager; to act unwisely or inopportunely.**—bailar uno al s. que le tocan,** to adapt oneself to circumstances.**—en s. de,** as, like, in the manner of.**—en s. de guerra,** in a warlike manner.**—sin s.,** without reason.**—sin ton ni s.,** without rhyme or reason.

sonable, *a.* loud, sounding; noted, famous.

sonada, *f.* (mus.) tune; sonata.

sonadera, *f.* blowing the nose.

sonadero, *m.* handkerchief.

sonado, da. I. *pp.* of SONAR. **II.** *a.* noted, famous; talked about; (coll.) scandalous, sensational.

sonador, ra. I. *n.* noise maker. **II.** *m.* handkerchief.

sonaja, *f.* jingles; (mus.) timbrel.

sonajero, *m.* baby's rattle.

sonajuela, *f. dim.* small jingles or timbrel.

sonambulismo, *m.* somnambulism.

sonámbulo, la, *n.* somnambulist.

sonante, *pres. p.* & *a.* sounding, sonorous.

sonar, *va.* (*ind.* SUENO; *subj.* SUENE) to sound, to ring, to play upon. **II.** *vn.* to sound; to ring; (of clock) to strike; to be mentioned, talked about; **(a)** to sound, or look, (like); to seem: to sound familiar; to be reported or bruited about.**—ni suena ni truena,** is forgotten, is in the discard, cuts no figure. **III.** *vr.* to blow one's nose.

sonata, *f.* (mus.) sonata.

sonatina, *f. dim.* (mus.) sonatina.

sonda, *f.* (naut.) sounding, heaving the lead; lead, sounder, plummet; (aer.) dragrope; (geol.) anular borer; diamond drill; (surg.) catheter, bougie; sound, probe; (artil.) searcher, proofstick.

sondable, *a.* that can be sounded.

sondaleza, *f.* (naut.) lead line, sounding line.

sondar, sondear, *va.* (naut.) to sound; to try, sound out (another's intentions); to explore, fathom; to probe.

sondeo, *m.* sounding; exploring.

sonecillo, *m. dim.* slight sound; merry tune.

sonetico, *m. dim.* sound produced by tapping with the fingers; little or light sonnet.

sonetista, *m.* sonnet writer.

soneto, *m.* sonnet.

sonido, *m.* sound; noise; report; literal meaning.**—s. timpánico,** tympanic resonance.

sonochada, *f.* evening; evening watch.

sonochar, *vn.* to watch the first night hours.

sonómetro, *m.* sonometer.

sonoramente, *adv.* sonorously; harmoniously.

sonoridad, *f.* sonority, sonorousness.

sonoro, ra; sonoroso, sa, *a.* sonorous; sounding, clear, loud.

sonreír, *vn.* & *vr.* (*ger.* SONRIENDO; *ind. pres.* SONRÍO, *pret.* él SONRIÓ; *subj.* SONRÍA) to smile.

sonrisa, *f.,* **sonriso,** *m.* smile.

sonrodadura, *f.* (of wheels) sticking in the mud.

sonrodarse, *vr.* (of wheels) to stick in the mud.

sonrojar, sonrojear. I. *va.* to make (one) blush. **II.** *vr.* to blush.**—sonrojo,** *m.* blush; blushing; word causing a blush.

sonrosar, sonrosear. I. *va.* to dye a rose color. **II.** *vr.* to blush.**—sonroseo,** *m.* blush.

sonsaca, *f.;* **sonsacamiento,** *m.* wheedling; drawing out; enticement; pilfering.

sonsacador, ra, *n.* wheedler, enticer; pilferer.

sonsacar, *va.* (*pret.* SONSAQUÉ; *subj.* SONSAQUE) to pilfer; to draw (one) out; to entice, allure.

sonsaque, *m.* = SONSACA.

sonsonete, *m.* sound produced by rhythmical raps or taps; singsong voice.

soñador, ra, *n.* dreamer.

soñante. I. *pres. p.* of SOÑAR. **II.** *a.* dreaming.

soñar. I. *va.* & *vn.* (*ind.* SUEÑO; *subj.* SUEÑE) to dream.**—s. con,** or **en,** to dream of.**—s. despierto,** to indulge in day dreams; to build air castles.**—ni soñarlo,** not even to dream of it.

soñoliento, ta, *a.* somnolent, sleepy; sleeping; sleep-producing.

sopa, *f.* sop (soaked bread); soup.**—pl.** slices of bread for soup.**—s. borracha,** a kind of wine cake.**—s. de ajo,** or **de gato,** meager soup.**—s. de vino,** (bot.) flower of the small caltrops.**—s. juliana,** julienne soup, vegetable soup.**—a la s. boba,** (coll.) living at other people's expense.**—hecho una s.,** (coll.) drenched, wet through to the skin.

sopaipa, *f.* fritter steeped in honey.

sopalancar, *va.* to lift with a lever.

sopalanda, *f.* gown worn by students.

sopanda, *f.* brace (of carriage); (carp.) joist.

sopapear, *va.* (coll.) to chuck under the chin; to vilify, to abuse.

sopapo, *m.* chuck under the chin; (coll.) box, blow, slap; (mech.) valve, stop valve, sucker.

sopar, ¹sopear, *va.* = ENSOPAR, to sop (bread).

²sopear, *va.* to trample; to maltreat.

sopeña, *f.* cavity under a rock.

sopera, *f.* soup tureen.

sopero. I. *m.* soup plate. **II.** *m.* lover of soups.

sopesar, *va.* to heft, test the weight of by lifting.

¹sopetear, *va.* to sop; to steep (bread).

²sopetear, *va.* to abuse, maltreat.

sopeteo, *m.* dipping (bread, etc.).

¹sopetón, *m.* bread toasted and steeped in oil.

²sopetón, *m.* box, cuff, slap.**—de s.,** suddenly.

sopicaldo, *m.* very thin soup.

sopista, *n.* one living on charity.

sopita, *f. dim.* light soup.

¡sopla! *interj.* gracious! what a thing!

sopladero, *m.* air hole from subterranean passages.

soplado, da. I. *pp.* of SOPLAR. **II.** *a.* (coll.) overnice and spruce; conceited. **III.** *m.* (min.) deep fissure.

soplador, ra. I. *n.* blower; inciter. **II.** *m.* ventilator, blowing fan; tuyère (of a blast furnace).

sopladura, *f.* blowing; (foundry) air hole.

soplamocos, *m.* (coll.) box or slap on the nose.

soplar. I. *vn.* to blow; (coll.) to tattle. **II.** *va.* to blow; blow out; to fan; to fill with air, inflate; to rob or steal in an artful manner; to huff (a man) in the game of draughts; to prompt, tell what to say; (Am.) (theat.) to prompt; to inspire.**—soplársela a uno,** to deceive one.

For pronunciation, see the rules at the beginning of the book.

III. *vr.* to swell up; to eat or drink to excess, to stuff oneself.

soplete, *m.* blowpipe; blow torch.

soplico, *m. dim.* slight puff or blast.

soplido, *m.* blowing, blast.

soplillo, *m. dim.* blowing fan; anything extremely thin and light; silk gauze, chiffon; very light sponge cake.

soplo, *m.* blowing; blast, gust, puff of wind; breath; instant, moment; hint, tip, secret advice or warning; secret accusation.

soplón, na, *n.* talebearer, informer.

sopón, *m. aug.* (coll.) = SOPISTA.

soponcio, *m.* fainting fit, swoon.

sopor, *m.* (med.) sopor, lethargic sleep.

soporífero, ra, *a.* soporific, soporiferous.

soporoso, sa, *a.* soporiferous, inducing sleep; suffering from sopor; (med.) soporose.

soportable, *a.* bearable, endurable.

soportador, ra, *n.* supporter.

soportal, *m.* (arch.) portico.

soportar, *va.* to bear, put up with; to support.

soporte, *m.* support; rest; bearing.

soprano. I. *m.* (mus.) soprano voice. **II.** *f.* soprano singer.

sopuntar, *va.* to underscore with dots.

sor, *f.* (eccl.) sister, as *sor María,* Sister Mary.

sora, *f.* (Peru) mash made from maize.

sorba, *f.* (bot.) sorb apple.

sorbedor, ra. I. *a.* sipping. **II.** *n.* sipper.

sorber, *va.* to sip, suck; to imbibe, soak, absorb; to swallow.

sorbete, *m.* sherbet, water ice.

sorbetera, *f.* ice-cream freezer; (coll. and humor.) high hat, top hat.

sorbetón, *m. aug.* large draught of liquor.

sorbible, *a.* absorbable; that can be sipped.

sorbito, *m. dim.* little sip.

¹sorbo, *m.* imbibing; absorption; sip, draught, swallow, gulp.

²sorbo, *m.* = SERBAL, sorb tree, service tree.

¹sorda, *f.* (ornith.) woodcock.

²sorda, *f.* (naut.) stream cable for launching a ship.

sordamente, *adv.* secretly, silently.

sordera, sordedad, sordez, *f.* deafness.

sórdidamente, *adv.* sordidly.

sordidez, *f.* sordidness.

sórdido, da, *a.* sordid.

sordina, *f.* (mus.) mute, sordine (for string instruments); sordono (for trumpet); damper (for piano).—**a la s.,** secretly, quietly, on the quiet.

sordino, *m.* (mus.) kit, small fiddle.

sordo, da, *a.* deaf; silent, still, quiet; muffled, stifled; dull; unmoved, insensible; (math.) irrational, surd.

sordomudez, *f.* (med.) deaf-mutism.

sordomudo, da, *a. & n.* deaf and dumb, deaf-mute.

sordón, *m.* (mus.) old kind of oboe.

sorgo, *m.* (bot.) sorghum.

soriasis, *f.* (med.) psoriasis.

sorites, *m.* (logic) sorites, chain argument.

sorna, *f.* sluggishness, laziness, slowness.

soro, *m.* year-old hawk.

soroche, *m.* (S. A.) altitude sickness, a disease caused by the rare air; (min.) friable silver ore.

soroque, *f.* (min.) matrix of ores.

sóror, *f.* (eccl.) = SOR.

sorprendente, *a.* surprising.

sorprender, *va.* to surprise, astonish; to surprise, catch (in an act).

sorpresa, *f.* surprise.—**de s.,** by surprise.

¹sorra, *f.* (naut.) ballast of stones or coarse gravel.

²sorra, *f.* side of a tunny fish.

sorregar, *va.* (*ind. pres.* SORRIEGO, *pret.* SORREGUÉ; *subj.* SORRIEGUE) to water accidentally, by deviation or overflow of the water elsewhere.

sorriego, *m.* water that deviates from one channel to another; watering by this water.

sorrostrada, *f.* insolence; bluntness.—**dar s.,** to insult; to throw one's faults in one's face.

sorteable, *a.* fit to be drafted.

sorteador, ra, *n.* one who casts lots; skilful bull-fighter.

sorteamiento, *m.* = SORTEO.

sortear, *va.* to draw or cast lots for; to raffle; to fight (bulls) with skill and dexterity; to elude or shun cleverly.—**sorteo,** *m.* casting lots; drawing, raffle; bull-fighting.

sortiaria, *f.* fortune telling by cards.

sortija, *f.* finger ring; ring, hoop; curl of hair.

sortijita, juela, *f. dim.* little ring; ringlet.

sortijón, *m. aug.* large finger ring.

sortilegio, *m.* sortilege, sorcery.

sortílego, ga, *n.* sorcerer, conjurer, fortune teller.

sosa, *f.* (bot.) glasswort, kelp; soda ash, barilla; sal soda; (chem.) soda.

sosal, *m.* soda-bearing field.

sosamente, *adv.* insipidly, tastelessly.

sosar, *m.* = SOSAL.

sosegadamente, *adv.* quietly, calmly.

sosegado, da, *pp. & a.* quiet, peaceful, calm.

sosegador, ra, *n. & a.* pacifier(-ing), appeaser (-ing), quieter(-ing).

sosegar. I. *va.* (*ind. pres.* SOSIEGO, *pret.* SOSEGUÉ; *subj.* SOSIEGUE) to appease, calm, quiet; to lull. **II.** *vn.* to rest, repose. **III.** *vr.* to become quiet, calm or composed, to quiet down.

sosera, sosería, *f.* insipidity, tastelessness; nonsense.

sosero, ra, *a.* (bot.) yielding soda.

sosez, *f.* = SOSERA.

sosiega, *f.* rest after work; drink taken while resting, after dinner or before going to bed.

¹sosiego, *m.* tranquillity, calm, quiet.

²sosiego, sosegué, sosiegue, *v. V.* SOSEGAR.

soslayar, *va.* to do or place obliquely.

soslayo, m.—al s., or **de s.,** askance; slanting, on the bias.

soso, sa, *a.* insipid, tasteless, vapid; dull, inane.

sospecha, *f.* suspicion.

sospechar, *va. & vn.* to suspect.

sospechosamente, *adv.* suspiciously.

sospechoso, sa, *a.* suspicious; suspecting.

sospesar, *va.* to suspend, lift, raise.

sosquín, *m.* blow treacherously given.

sostén, *m.* support; steadiness of a ship.

sostenedor, ra, *n.* supporter.

sostener. I. *va.* (*ind. pres.* yo SOSTENGO, él SOSTIENE, *pret.* SOSTUVE, *fut.* SOSTENDRÉ; *subj.* SOSTENGA) to support, hold up; to maintain, keep; to assist, help; to encourage; to uphold, defend; to bear, endure; to hold (a conference, etc.). **II.** *vr.* to support or maintain oneself.

sostenido, da. I. *pp.* of SOSTENER. **II.** *a.* supported; sustained, kept up. **III.** *m.* (mus.) sharp (the tone and the sign ♯).

sosteniente, *a.* sustaining, supporting.

sostenimiento, *m.* sustenance, maintenance; support.—**muro,** or **pared, de s.,** retaining wall.

sostituir, *va.* = SUSTITUIR, to substitute.

sostuve, *pret.* of SOSTENER.

sota. I. *f.* jack, knave; at cards; hussy, jade. **II.** *m.* (Chile) deputy, substitute.

sotabanco, *m.* (arch.) pediment of an arch over a cornice; garret, attic.

sotabraga, *f.* (mil.) axletree band, yoke hoop.

sotacola, *f.* crupper.

sotacoro, *m.* place under the choir.

sotalugo, *m.* second hoop of a cask.

sotaministro, *m.* = SOTOMINISTRO.

sotana, *f.* cassock; (coll.) flogging, drubbing.

sotanear, *va.* (coll.) to beat, reprimand severely.

sotaní, *m.* short skirt without plaits.

sótano, *m.* cellar, basement.

sotaventar, *va.* (naut.) to fall to leeward.

sotavento, *m.* leeward, lee.—**a s.,** under the lee.

sotechado, *m.* shed.

soteño, ña, *a.* produced in groves.

soterramiento, *m.* burying under ground.

soterraño, *a.* = SUBTERRÁNEO, subterranean.

soterrar, *va.* (*ind.* SOTIERRO; *subj.* SOTIERRE) to bury, put under ground; to hide.

sotillo, *m. dim.* little grove.

soto, *m.* grove, thicket, brake.

sotoministro, *m.* steward (in some convents).

sotrozo, *m.* (artil.) linchpin, axle pin; (mech.) key; (naut.) foothook staff.

sotuer, *m.* (her.) saltier.

sóviet, *m.* soviet.—**soviético, ca,** *a.* soviet.—**sovietismo,** *m.* sovietism.—**sovietizar,** *va.* & *vn.* to sovietize.

sovoz.—**a s.,** in a low tone, sotto voce.

soy, *1st pers. sing. pres. ind.* of SER.

soya, *f.* (bot.) soy; soy bean.

speaker, *m.* (Angl.) (Arg.) (radio) announcer.

sport, *m.* (Angl.) (Am.) sport.

Stábat, Stábat Máter, *m.* Stabat Mater.

statu quo, *m.* status quo.

su, *pron. poss. 3d pers. m.* & *f. sing.* (*pl.* SUS) his, her, its, their, one's, your.

suasorio, ria, *a.* suasory, suasive, persuasive.

suave, *a.* smooth, soft, delicate, mellow; easy, tranquil, unruffled; suave, gentle, tractable, docile, mild, meek.—**suavemente,** *adv.* gently, sweetly, softly, mildly, kindly.

suavicé, suavice, *v. V.* SUAVIZAR.

suavidad, *f.* softness, smoothness; ease; suavity; gentleness; lenity, forbearance.

suavizador, ra. I. *a.* mollifying, smoothing, softening. II. *m.* razor strop.

suavizar, *va.* (*pret.* SUAVICÉ; *subj.* SUAVICE) to soften, smoothe, mollify, mitigate; to ease; to temper.

subacetato, *m.* (chem.) basic acetate of lead.

subácido, da, *a.* (chem.) subacid.

subalcaide, *m.* deputy warden.

subalternante, *a.* subalternant.

subalternar, *va.* to subdue.

subalterno, na. I. *a.* subaltern, subordinate. II. *m.* subordinate; (mil.) subaltern.

subarrendador, ra, *n.* subleaser.

subarrendamiento, *m.* subletting.

subarrendar, *va.* (*ind.* SUBARRIENDO; *subj.* SUBARRIENDE) to sublet, sublease.

subarrendatario, ria, *n.* subtenant.

¹subarriendo, *m.* (law) sublease.

²subarriendo, subarriende, *v. V.* SUBARRENDAR.

subasta, subastación, *f.* auction, auction sale.—**poner en,** or **sacar a, pública s.,** to sell at auction.—**subastar,** *va.* to sell at auction.

subcarbonato, *m.* (chem.) subcarbonate.

subcinericio, cia, *a.* baked under ashes.

subclase, *f.* (bot. and zool.) subclass.

subclavero, *m.* assistant CLAVERO, key keeper.

subclavio, via, *a.* (anat.) subclavian.

subcolector, *m.* subcollector, assistant collector.

subcomendador, *m.* deputy commander of a military order.

subconsciencia, *f.* subconsciousness; (the) subconscious.

subconsciente, *a.* subconscious.

subconservador, *m.* judge deputed by a conservator.

subcostal, *a.* (anat.) subcostal, below the ribs.

subcutáneo, nea, *a.* subcutaneous.

subdelegable, *a.* that can be subdelegated.

subdelegación, *f.* subdelegation.

subdelegado, da, *n.* subdelegate.

subdelegante, *n.* he who subdelegates.

subdelegar, *va.* (*pret.* SUBDELEGUÉ; *subj.* SUBDELEGUE) to subdelegate.

subdiaconado or **-ato,** *m.* subdeaconship.

subdiácono, *m.* subdeacon.

subdirector, ra, *n.* assistant director.

subdistinción, *f.* subdistinction.

subdistinguir, *va.* (*ind.* SUBDISTINGO; *subj.* SUBDISTINGA) to make a subdistinction.

súbdito, ta. I. *a.* subject (to authority, etc.); inferior. II. *m.* subject (of a state, etc.).

subdividir, *va.* to subdivide.—**subdivisible,** *a.* subdivisible.—**subdivisión,** *f.* subdivision.

subdominante, *f.* (mus.) subdominant.

subejecutor, *m.* subagent.

subentender. I. *va.* (*ind.* SUBENTIENDO; *subj.* SUBENTIENDA) to understand what is tacitly meant. II. *vr.* to be understood, to be implied.

subérico, ca, *a.* suberic, pert. to cork.

suberina, *f.* suberin, substance in cork.

suberoso, sa, *a.* suberose, corky.

subestación, *f.* substation.

subgénero, *m.* (biol.) subgenus.

subgobernador, ra, *n.* vicegovernor, lieutenant governor.

subida, *f.* ascent, going up; elevation, taking or carrying up; acclivity, rise; accession of a disease; rise.

subidero, ra. I. *a.* mounting, raising, climbing. II. *m.* ladder, mounting block; way to go up; up grade, uphill road.

subido, da. I. *pp.* of SUBIR. II. *a.* raised on high; high, high-priced; strong, loud, bright (as a color); strong-scented; finest, most excellent.

subidor, *m.* porter; elevator, lift.

subiente. I. *a.* rising. II. *m.* (arch.) ascending ornaments.

subilla, *f.* awl.

subimiento, *m.* rising, climbing, ascending.

subinquilino, *m.* subtenant.

subinspección, *f.* subinspectorship; subinspector's office.

subinspector, *m.* subinspector.

subintendente, *m.* assistant intendant.

subintración, *f.* (med.) subintrant fever.

subintrante, *a.* (med.) subintrant.

subintrar, *vn.* to enter one after another; (med.) (of fever) to begin before end of preceding attack.

subir. I. *vn.* to rise; to come up, go up, climb, mount; to grow; (of silkworms) to enter leaves; to be promoted; to increase in intensity; (com.) to amount to; (of price, temperature, etc.) to rise; (mus.) to raise the voice or pitch.—**s. a caballo,** to mount a horse.—**s. de punto,** to increase, grow.—**s. de tono,** to raise one's voice; to be more outspoken. II. *va.* to raise, place higher; to take up, bring up; set up; to straighten from an inclined position; (com.) to raise (prices). III. *vr.* to go up, to climb; to rise.—**s. a las barbas,** to fly in one's face.—**s. a las bovedillas,** (coll.) to be nettled, be violently irritated.—**s. a la cabeza,** (of wine, liquor, popularity, etc.) to go to one's head.

súbitamente, subitáneamente, *adv.* suddenly, all of a sudden.

subitáneo, nea, *a.* sudden, unexpected.

súbito, ta, *a.* sudden, unforeseen, unexpected.—*adv. m.* **s.,** or **de s.,** suddenly, unexpectedly.

subjefe, *n.* second in command; assistant chief.

subjetivamente, *adv.* subjectively.

subjetividad, *f.* subjectivity.

subjetivismo, *f.* subjectivism.

subjetivo, va, *a.* subjective.

subjuntivo, *m.* & *a.* (gram.) subjunctive.

sublevación, f., sublevamiento, *m.* insurrection, revolt.

sublevar. I. *va.* to incite to rebellion, raise in rebellion. II. *vr.* to rise in rebellion.

sublimación, *f.* sublimation.

sublimado. I. *pp.* of SUBLIMAR. II. *m.* (chem.) sublimate.—**s. corrosivo,** corrosive sublimate.

sublimar, *va.* to heighten, elevate, exalt; (chem.) to sublimate.

sublimatorio, ria, *a.* (chem.) sublimatory.

sublime, *a.* sublime.—**la S. Puerta,** the Sublime Porte (the former Ottoman Empire).

sublimenente, *adv.* sublimely.

sublimidad, *f.* sublimity.

sublingual, *a.* (anat.) sublingual, under the tongue.

sublunar, *a.* sublunary; terrestrial, earthly.

submarino, na. I. *a.* submarine. **II.** *m.* submarine.

submaxilar, *a.* submaxillary, pert. to lower jaw.

submúltiplo, pla, *a.* & *n.* (math.) submultiple.

suborden, *m.* suborder.

subordinación, *f.* subordination; subjection.

subordinadamente, *adv.* subserviently.

subordinado, da. I. *pp.* of SUBORDINAR. **II.** *a.* subordinate, subservient.

subordinar, *va.* to subordinate; to subject.

subpolar, *a.* under or near the pole.

subprefecto, *m.* subprefect.

subprefectura, *f.* subprefecture.

subproducto, *m.* by-product. Also PRODUCTO SECUNDARIO.

subrayar, *va.* to underscore, underline; to emphasize.

subrepción, *f.* underhand proceeding; (law) subreption; surreption.

subrepticiamente, *adv.* surreptitiously.

subrepticio, cia, *a.* surreptitious.

subrigadier, *m.* (mil.) subbrigadier.

subrogación, *f.* surrogation or subrogation, substitution.

subrogar, *va.* (law) to subrogate; to substitute.

subsanable, *a.* excusable; reparable, surmountable, that can be obviated.

subsanar, *va.* to exculpate, excuse; to mend, correct, repair; to obviate, get over.

subscapular, *a.* (anat.) subscapular.

subscribir, *va.* & *vr.* (*pp.* SUBSCRIPTO, SUBSCRITO) to subscribe; to sign; to accede, agree to.

subscripción, *f.* subscription.

subscripto, ta; subscrito, ta; I. *pp. irreg.* of SUBSCRIBIR. **II.** *n.*—**el s.,** the undersigned.

subscriptor, *m.* subscriber.

subsecretaría, *f.* office and employment of an assistant secretary.

subsecretario, ria, *n.* assistant secretary.

subsecuente, *a.* subsequent.

subseguirse, *vr.* (*ger.* SUBSIGUIENDO; *ind. pres.* SUBSIGO, *pret.* él SUBSIGUIÓ; *subj.* SUBSIGA) to follow next.

subsidiariamente, *adv.* subsidiarily.

subsidiario, ria, *a.* subsidiary; branch (as *a.*); auxiliary; (law) ancillary.

subsidio, *m.* subsidy, pecuniary aid; war tax.

subsigo, subsiguió, etc. *v. V.* SUBSEGUIRSE.

subsiguiente, *a.* subsequent, succeeding.

subsistencia, *f.* permanence, stability; subsistence; livelihood, living.

subsistente, *pres. p.* & *a.* subsistent, subsisting.

subsistir, *vn.* to subsist, last; to live, exist; to have the means of subsistence.

subsolano, *m.* east wind.

substancia, *f.* substance; nutritious sap, juice, or extract; property, wealth; gist; importance, value; (coll.) judgment, sense.—**s. blanca,** (anat.) white matter (of the brain).—**s. gris,** (anat.) gray matter.—**en s.,** in substance, in effect; in a nutshell, in brief.

substanciación, *f.* substantiation.

substancial, *a.* substantial, real, material; nutritious, nourishing; essential.

substancialmente, *adv.* substantially.

substanciar, *va.* to extract the substance of, to abstract, abridge; to substantiate; (law) to try (a case).

substancioso, sa, *a.* juicy; nourishing, nutritious; substantial.

substantivar, *va.* (gram.) to substantivize.

substantividad, *f.* substantiveness.

substantivo, va. I. *a.* substantive. **II.** *m.* substantive, noun.

substitución, *f.* substitution.

substituíble, *a.* replaceable.

substituidor, ra, *n.* & *a.* substitute(-ing).

substituir, *va.* (*pp.* SUBSTITUÍDO, SUBSTITUTO, *ger.* SUBSTITUYENDO; *ind. pres.* SUBSTITUYO, *pret.* él SUBSTITUYÓ; *subj.* SUBSTITUYA) to substitute, replace.

substituto, ta, *n.* substitute.

substituyente, *a.* substituting.

substituyo, etc. *v. V.* SUBSTITUIR.

substracción, *f.* subtraction.

substraendo, *m.* subtrahend.

substraer. I. *va.* (*ger.* SUBSTRAYENDO; *ind. pres.* SUBSTRAIGO, *pret.* SUBSTRAJE; *subj.* SUBSTRAIGA) to subtract, remove, take off, deduct. **II.** *vr.* to withdraw oneself, to elude.

substrato, *m.* (philos.) substratum.

subsuelo, *m.* subsoil.

subtangente, *f.* subtangent.

subtender, *va.* (ind. SUBTIENDO; *subj.* SUBTIENDA) (geom.) to subtend.

subteniente, *m.* (mil.) second lieutenant.

subtensa, *f.* (geom.) subtense (chord).

subterfugio, *m.* subterfuge.

subterráneamente, *adv.* subterraneously.

subterráneo, nea. I. *a.* subterranean, underground. **II.** *m.* any place underground (cave, vault, etc.); (Am.) subway; (geol.) subterrene.

subtítulo, *m.* subtitle.

suburbano, na, *a.* & *n.* suburban(-ite).

suburbicario, ria, *a.* suburbicarian.

suburbio, *m.* suburb, outskirt.

subvención, *f.* subsidy, subvention, money aid.

subvencionar, *va.* to subsidize.

subvenir, *va.* (*ind. pres.* yo SUBVENGO, él SUBVIENE, *pret.* SUBVINE, *fut.* SUBVENDRÉ; *subj.* SUBVENGA) to subvene, aid, assist, succor; to provide, supply, furnish, defray.

subversión, *f.* subversion, overthrow.

subversivo, va, *a.* subversive, destructive.

subversor, ra, *n.* & *a.* subverter(-ing), overthrower(-ing).

subvertir, *va.* (*ind. pres.* SUBVIERTO, *pret.* él SUBVIRTIÓ; *subj.* SUBVIERTA) to subvert, destroy, ruin.

subviene, subvine, etc. *v. V.* SUBVENIR.

subyacente, *a.* underlying.

subyugación, *f.* subjugation, subjection.

subyugador, ra, *n.* & *a.* subjugator(-ing).

subyugar, *va.* (*pret.* SUBYUGUÉ; *subj.* SUBYUGUE) to subdue, subjugate.

succinato, *m.* (chem.) succinate.

succínico, ca, *a.* (chem.) succinic.

succino, *m.* succinite, amber.

succión, *f.* suction, suck.

sucedáneo, a, *a.* & *m.* succedaneous, substitute (drug, etc.).

suceder. I. *vn.* (a) to succeed, follow, be the successor (of). **II.** *v. impers.* to happen, come to pass, come about.—**suceda lo que sucediere,** come what may.

sucedido, *m.* event, happening.

sucediente, *a.* succeeding, following.

sucesible, *a.* capable of succession.

sucesión, *f.* succession; issue, offspring; (law) estate.—**s. intestada,** heirs at law.

sucesivamente, *adv.* successively.

sucesivo, va, *a.* successive, consecutive.—**en lo s.,** hereafter, in future.

suceso, *m.* event, happening; issue, outcome; (rare, Gal.) success; course of time.

sucesor, ra, *n.* successor.

suciamente, *adv.* nastily, filthily; basely.

suciedad, *f.* nastiness, filthiness; dirt, filth.

sucintamente, *adv.* succinctly, briefly.

sucintarse, *vr.* to be precise, brief.

sucinto, ta, *a.* tucked up; brief, succinct, concise.

sucio, cia, *a.* dirty, nasty, filthy; soiled; untidy; tainted with guilt or sin; low, base; (naut.) foul.

suco, *m.* juice; sap.—**sucoso, sa,** *a.* juicy.

sucotrino, *a.* socotrine (aloes).

ucre, *m.* sucre, an Ecuadorean silver coin (about 50 cents).

uctorio, ria, *a.* (biol.) suctorial.

úcubo, *m.* succubus (demon).

ucucho, *m.* (naut.) storeroom of a ship; (Am.) SOCUCHO, small room, "den"; hiding-place.

úcula, *f.* windlass, winch.

uculencia, *f.* juiciness, succulence.

uculentamente, *adv.* succulently.

uculento, ta, *a.* succulent, juicy.

ucumbiente, *a.* yielding; dying.

ucumbir, *vn.* to succumb; to submit, yield; to die, perish; (law) to lose a suit.

ucursal. I. *a.* ancillary, subsidiary; branch (as *a.*). **II.** *f.* (com.) branch of a commercial house.

uche. I. *a.* (Venez.) green, unripe. **II.** *m.* (Ecua., Peru), a tree yielding valuable timber; (Arg.) mud; (Chile) insignificant employee.

uchel, suchil, *m.* (Am.) = SUCHE (tree).

ud, *m.* south; south wind.

udadero, *m.* handkerchief; back cloth (for horses); sweating room, sudatory; moist ground; sweating place for sheep.

udafricano, na, *n.* & *a.* South African.

udamericano, na, *n.* & *a.* South American.

udador, ra, *n.* one who perspires freely.

udanés, sa, *n.* & *a.* Sudanese.

udante, *a.* sweating.

udar, *vn.* to sweat, perspire; to ooze, to give with repugnance; to toil, to labor.

udario, *m.* handkerchief, shroud (for corpse).

udatorio, ria, *a.* sudorific, causing sweat.

udeste, *m.* southeast, southeast wind.

udoeste, *m.* southwest; southwest wind.

udor, *m.* sweat, perspiration; toil, drudgery; gum that oozes from trees.

udoriento, ta, *a.* wet with sweat.

udorífero, ra, *a.* sudorific, causing sweat.

udorífico, ca, *a.* & *m.* (med.) sudorific.

udoríparo, ra, *a.* (anat.) sudoriferous, sweat-secreting.

udoroso, sa, *a.* sweating, perspiring freely.

udoso, sa, *a.* sweaty, perspiring.

udsudeste, *m.* south-southeast.

udsudoeste, *m.* south-southwest.

udueste, *m.* southwest.

ueco, ca. I. *a.* Swedish. **II.** *n.* Swede.—**hacerse el s.,** (coll.) to pretend not to hear.

uegra, *f.* mother-in-law; hard crust of bread.

uegrecita, *f. dim.* (coll.) little mother-in-law.

uegro, *m.* father-in-law.

uela, *f.* sole (of shoe); sole leather; (ichth.) sole; horizontal rafter laid as a support for partition walls; (arch.) base; leather tip of a billiard cue. —*pl.* sandals.—**de siete suelas,** consummate, thorough, through and through.

uelda, *f.* (bot.) comfrey.

ueldacostilla, *f.* (bot.) a bulbous plant.

ueldo, *m.* salary; pay given to soldiers; an ancient coin; sou or sol.

ueido, suelde, *v. V.* SOLDAR.

uelo, *m.* ground; soil; land, earth, terra firma; pavement; floor, flooring; story; dregs, sediment, lees; ground plot; end; bottom, underside; hoof.—*pl.* (vet.) sole, plantar face of a horse's hoof; scatterings or leavings of grain.—**s. del estribo,** rest of the stirrup.—**s. natal,** native soil, country.—**dar consigo en el s.,** to fall down.—**dar en el s. con,** to throw down. —**medir el s.,** to fall flat, measure one's length on the ground; to lie down flat on the ground. —**por el s.,** or **por los suelos,** in a state of great depreciation; altogether out of favor.— **venirse al s.,** to fall to the ground, topple over.

²suelo, suele, *v. V.* SOLAR.

²suelo, él suele, *v. V.* SOLER.

uelta, *f.* loosening or letting loose; fetters; relay of oxen; place where oxen are changed.—**dar s.,** to grant a recess for amusement.

sueltamente, *adv.* loosely, lightly, expeditiously; licentiously; spontaneously; laxly.

¹suelto, ta. I. *pp. irreg.* of SOLTAR. **II.** *a.* loose; light, expeditious; swift, able; free, bold, daring; easy, disengaged; voluble, fluent; odd, disconnected, unclassified; single (copy); blank (verse).—**s. de lengua,** outspoken. **III.** *m.* small change; editorial paragraph; newspaper item or paragraph.

²suelto, suelte, *v. V.* SOLTAR.

suelvo, suelva, *v. V.* SOLVER.

sueno, suene, *v. V.* SONAR.

¹sueño, *m.* sleep; sleeping; drowsiness, sleepiness; dream; any event of short duration.—**s. eterno,** eternal sleep, death.—**s. pesado,** sound sleep; deep sleep.—**conciliar el s.,** to coax sleep.— **descabezar el s., echar un s.,** to take a nap. —**en sueños,** or **entre sueños,** dreaming; in dreamland.—**enfermedad del s.,** sleeping sickness.—**espantar el s.,** to scare away sleep. —**ni por s.,** by no means, not a bit of it.— **tener s.,** to be sleepy.

²sueño, sueñe, *v. V.* SOÑAR.

suero, *m.* whey; serum (of blood).

sueroso, sa, *a.* = SEROSO, serous; watery.

sueroterapia, *f.* serotherapy, serum therapy.

suerte, *f.* chance, hazard; lot, luck; good luck; state, condition; fate, doom, destiny; kind, sort; manner, way; skilful manœuvre of a bullfighter; (theat.) trick, feat, juggle; piece of ground separated by landmarks; (Peru) lottery ticket.—**s. negra,** very bad luck.—**caerle a uno la s.,** to fall to one's lot.—**de s. que,** in such a manner as, so that; and so.—**echar suertes,** to cast or draw lots.—**entrar en s.,** to take part in a draft or raffle.—**por s.,** by chance; luckily. —**tener s.,** to be lucky.—**tocarle a uno la s.** = CAERLE A UNO LA S.

suertero, *m.* (Peru) seller of lottery tickets.

sueste, *m.* southeast.

suéter, *m.* (Angl.) (Am.) sweater.

suevo, va, *n.* & *a.* Swabian.

sufete, *m.* Suffete, a Carthaginian magistrate.

sufí. I. *a.* Sufistic. **II.** *n.* Sufi.

suficiencia, *f.* sufficiency; capacity, ability.—**a s.,** sufficiently, enough.

suficiente, *a.* sufficient; fit, competent.

suficientemente, *adv.* sufficiently.

sufijo, ja. I. *a.* suffixed. **II.** *m.* suffix.

sufismo, *m.* Sufism.

sufocación, sufocar, etc. = SOFOCACIÓN, etc.

sufra, *f.* ridgeband of a harness.

sufragáneo, ea. I. *a.* suffragan, auxiliary. **II.** *m.* (eccl.) suffragan.

sufragar, *va.* (*pret.* SUFRAGUÉ; *subj.* SUFRAGUE) to favor; to aid; to defray.

sufragio, *m.* suffrage; vote; favor, support, aid, assistance; (eccl.) suffrage.

sufrible, *a.* sufferable, bearable.

sufridera, *f.* smith's tool for punching holes on an anvil.

sufridero, ra, *a.* bearable, endurable.

sufrido, da. I. *pp.* of SUFRIR. **II.** *a.* enduring, lasting; patient, long-suffering, (of colors) disguising, that don't show (dirt, etc.).—**mal s.,** rude.

sufridor, ra, *n.* & *a.* sufferer(-ing).

sufriente, *a.* enduring, suffering.

sufrimiento, *m.* suffering; sufferance, tolerance.

sufrir. I. *va.* to suffer, endure, bear up; to undergo (a change, an operation, etc.); to bear, carry, support; to sustain, resist (an attack); to permit, tolerate, put up with; to meet with (as a reverse); to do (penance). **II.** *vn.* to suffer.

sufumigación, *f.* (med.) suffumigation.

sufusión, *f.* (med.) suffusion; a kind of cataract.

sugerente, *a.* suggesting, suggestive.

sugerir, *va.* (*ger.* SUGIRIENDO; *ind. pres.* SUGIERO, *pret.* él SUGIRIÓ; *subj.* SUGIERA) to suggest, hint, insinuate.

sugestible, *a.* suggestible.
sugestión, *f.* suggestion; insinuation, hint; temptation.—**s. hipnótica,** hypnotic suggestion.
sugestionable, *a.* easily influenced.
sugestionar, *va.* to hypnotize; to influence.
sugestivo, va, *a.* suggestive.
sugiero, sugirió, etc. *v. V.* SUGERIR.
suicida, *n.* suicide, self-murderer.
suicidarse, *vr.* to commit suicide.
suicidio, *m.* suicide (self-murder).
suideo, a. I. *a.* swinelike. **II.** *m. pl.* Suidæ, the swine family.
sui generis, *a.* sui generis, unique, peculiar.
suita, *f.* (C. A.) a kind of grass used for thatching and forage.
suiza, *f.* ancient military sport; fight, row.
suizo, za, *n.* & *a.* Swiss.
sujeción, *f.* subjection; coercion, control; obedience, subordination; submission, surrender; connection.—**con s. a,** in accordance with.
sujetar. I. *va.* (*pp.* SUJETADO, SUJETO) to subject, subdue; to hold fast, fasten, catch, grasp. **II.** *vr.* to control oneself; to submit; **(a)** to abide (by), keep (to), to observe.
sujeto, ta. I. *pp. irreg.* of SUJETAR. **II.** *a.* subject, liable, exposed, chargeable; amenable. **III.** *m.* subject, topic, theme, matter; person; individual, fellow; (logic and gram.) subject.
sulfácido, *m.* (chem.) sulphacid.
sulfatador, ra. I. *a.* sulphating. **II.** *f.* sulphating machine.
sulfatar, *va.* to sulphate.
sulfato, *m.* (chem.) sulphate.
sulfhidrato, *m.* (chem.) hydrosulphide.
sulfhídrico, *a.* (chem.) hydrosulphuric.
sulfito, *m.* (chem.) sulphite.
sulfonal, *m.* (chem.) sulphonal.
sulfovínico, ca, *a.* (chem.) sulphovinic.
sulfurar. I. *va.* to sulphur, sulphurate; to irritate, anger, enrage. **II.** *vr.* to become furious.
sulfúreo, rea, *a.* sulphurous.
sulfúrico, ca, *a.* sulphuric.
sulfuro, *m.* (chem.) sulphide.
sulfuroso, sa, *a.* sulphurous.
sultán, *m.* sultan.—**sultana,** *f.* sultana.
sultanía, *f.* sultanate.
suma, *f.* sum; aggregate; amount; (arith.) addition; total, footing; summary; summa, complete treatise or exposition (of a science, etc.).—**s. a la vuelta,** carried forward.—**s. de la vuelta,** or **s. del frente,** brought forward.—**s. y sigue** = S. A LA VUELTA.—**en s.,** in short; to sum up.
sumaca, *f.* (S. A.) a small coasting schooner.
sumador, ra, *a.*—**máquina s.,** adding machine.
sumamente, *adv.* chiefly; exceedingly, highly.
sumando, *m.* (math.) addend.
sumar, *va.* (arith.) to add; to amount to; to sum up, recapitulate.—**máquina de s.,** adding machine.
sumaria, *f.* (law) indictment.
sumariamente, *adv.* summarily.
sumario, ria. I. *a.* summary, concise; plain, brief, cursory; (law) summary. **II.** *m.* summary, abstract; (law) indictment.
sumarísimo, ma, *a.* (law) swift, expeditious.
sumergible, *a.* sinkable, submergible.
sumergimiento, *m.* submergence, sinking.
sumergir, *va.* & *vr.* (*ind.* SUMERJO; *subj.* SUMERJA) to submerge, to sink; to dive, to plunge; to overwhelm.
sumersión, *f.* submersion, immersion.
sumidad, *f.* top, apex, summit.
sumidero, *m.* sewer, drain, sink, gutter, gully; (min.) sump.
sumiller, *m.* chief of each of several offices in the king's household.—**s. de corps,** lord chamberlain.—**s. de cortina,** royal chaplain.
sumillería, *f.* lord chamberlain's office.
suministración, *f.* = SUMINISTRO.

suministrador, ra, *n.* provider, purveyor.
suministrar, *va.* to supply, furnish, provide afford, purvey, minister.
suministro, *m.* supply, providing.
sumir. I. *va.* & *vr.* to sink; to depress, overwhelm **II.** *va.* (eccl.) to swallow (elements of Eucharist). **III.** *vr.* to be sunken (as cheeks).
sumisamente, *adv.* submissively.
sumisión, *f.* submission; (law) submission to the rule of another.
sumiso, sa, *a.* submissive, humble, meek.
sumista, *n.* rapid computer; abridger.
sumo, ma, *a.* high, great, supreme.—**s. pontí fice,** Pontifex Maximus (in ancient Rome) Sovereign Pontiff (the Pope).—**s. sacerdote** high priest.—**a lo s.,** at most.—**de s.,** fully.—**en s. grado,** to a very great extent; highly
súmulas, *f. pl.* compendium of logic.
sumulista, *n.* teacher or student of the essential of logic.
sumulístico, ca, *a.* pert. to essentials of logic.
sunción, *f.* (eccl.) partaking of the Eucharist a mass.
sundín, *m.* (Arg.) merry gathering and dancin of working people.
sunsún, *m.* (Cuba) (ornith.) humming bird.
suntuario, ria, *a.* sumptuary.
suntuosamente, *adv.* sumptuously, magnifi cently, gorgeously.
suntuosidad, *f.* magnificence, gorgeousness.
suntuoso, sa, sumptuous, gorgeous.
supe, *v. V.* SABER.
supedáneo, *m.* pedestal of a crucifix.
supeditación, *f.* subjection; oppression.
supeditar, *va.* to subdue, oppress; to reduce to subjection.
superable, *a.* superable, conquerable.
superabundancia, *f.* superabundance.
superabundante, *a.* superabundant.
superabundantemente, *adv.* superabundantly
superabundar, *vn.* to superabound.
superadito, ta, *a.* superadded.
superante, *a.* surpassing, exceeding.
superar, *va.* to overcome, conquer; to surpass excel, exceed.
superávit, *m.* (com.) surplus.
superciliar, *a.* (anat.) superciliary.
superchería, *f.* fraud, deceit, wile, guile.
superchero, ra, *a.* wily, deceitful, tricky.
superdominante, *f.* (mus.) superdominant.
supereminencia, *f.* supereminence.
supereminente, *a.* supereminent.
superentender, *va.* (*ind.* SUPERENTIENDO; *subj.* SUPERENTIENDA) to superintend, inspect, supervise.
supererogación, *f.* supererogation.
supererogatorio, ria, *a.* supererogatory.
superfetación, *f.* (biol.) superfetation, superimpregnation.
superficial, *a.* superficial, shallow.
superficialidad, *f.* superficiality; shallowness.
superficialmente, *adv.* superficially.
superficiario, ria, *a.* (law) superficiary.
superficie, *f.* surface; area.—**s. alabeada,** (geom.) warped surface.—**s. de calefacción,** (steam eng.) heating surface.—**s. de rodadura,** tread (of a wheel).—**s. desarrollable,** (geom.) developable surface.—**s. reglada,** (geom.) ruled surface.
superfino, na, *a.* superfine, extra fine.
superfluamente, *adv.* superfluously.
superfluidad, *f.* superfluity.
superfluo, flua, *a.* superfluous.
superfosfato, *m.* (chem.) superphosphate, acid phosphate.
superhombre, *m.* superman.
superhumeral, *m.* (eccl.) ephod; superhumeral.
superintendencia, *f.* superintendence, supervision; superintendency.

uperintendente, n. superintendent; intendant; inspector; overseer, supervisor.

uperior. I. a. superior; upper; better, finer; higher (algebra, math., studies).—**el piso s.,** the upper floor (story). **II.** m. superior. **III.** f. mother superior.

uperiorato, m. office of a superior and the term of his office.

uperioridad, f. superiority.

uperiormente, adv. masterly, superiorly.

uperlativamente, adv. superlatively.

uperlativo, va, m. & a. superlative.

uperno, na, a. supreme, highest.

upernumerario, ria, a. supernumerary.

uperponer, va. (pp. SUPERPUESTO; ind. pres. SUPERPONGO, pret. SUPERPUSE, fut. SUPERPONDRÉ; subj. SUPERPONGA) to superpose.

uperposición, f. superposition.

uperstición, f. superstition.

upersticiosamente, adv. superstitiously.

upersticioso, sa, a. superstitious.

upérstite, a. (law) surviving.

upersubstancial, a.—**pan s.,** (eccl.) the Host.

upervacáneo, nea, a. = SUPERFLUO.

upervención, superveniencia, f. supervention.

uperveniente, a. supervenient, supervening.

upervenir, vn. (ger. SUPERVINIENDO; ind. pres. yo SUPERVENGO, él SUPERVIENE, pret. SUPERVINE, fut. SUPERVENDRÉ; subj. SUPERVENGA) to supervene.

upervivencia, f. survival; survivalship.—**s. del más apto,** survival of the fittest.

uperviviente, n. & a. survivor(-ing).

upiera, supiese, v. V. SABER.

upinación, f. (anat.) supination.

upinador, m. (anat.) supinator (muscle).

upino, na, a. supine.

uplantación, f. supplanting.

uplantador, ra, n. & a. supplanter(-ing).

uplantar, va. to supplant; to forge, alter by fraud, raise (as a check).

uplefaltas, m. (coll.) substitute.

uplemental, a. supplemental.

uplementario, ria, a. supplementary.

uplemento, m. supply, supplying; supplement; (geom.) supplement.

uplente, a. & n. substitute(-ing), replacer(-ing).

upletorio, ria, a. suppletory, supplemental.

úplica, f. entreaty; supplication; request.—**a s.,** by request.

uplicación, f. supplication; request; petition; rolled waffle; (law) petition to a high court for a reversal of its own decision.—**a s.,** by petition, by request.

uplicacionero, ra, n. waffle seller.

uplicante. I. a. suppliant, supplicant, entreating. **II.** n. supplicant, suppliant.

uplicar, va. (pret. SUPLIQUÉ; subj. SUPLIQUE) to entreat, implore, beg; to supplicate, pray; to ask, request.—**s. de la sentencia,** to petition against the sentence; to appeal.—**s. en revista,** (law) to apply for a new trial.

uplicatoria, f., **suplicatorio,** m. (law) letters rogatory.

uplicio, m. torture; execution (death penalty); place of execution; grief, suffering, anguish.

uplidor, ra, n. substitute, deputy.

upliqué, suplique, v. V. SUPLICAR.

uplir, va. to supply, provide, afford, furnish; to substitute; to excuse, overlook; (gram.) to supply mentally, understand.

upo, v. V. SABER.

uponedor, ra, n. supposer.

uponer. I. va. (pp. SUPUESTO; ind. pres. SUPONGO, pret. SUPUSE, fut. SUPONDRÉ; subj. SUPONGA) to suppose, assume; to entail (expense, etc.). **II.** vn. to have weight or authority.

uportación, f. endurance; toleration.

uposición, f. supposition, assumption; distinction, high position; imposition, falsehood.

supositicio, cia, a. supposititious, pretended; supposed, assumed.

supositivo, va, a. suppositive.

supositorio, m. (med.) suppository.

supradicho, cha, a. aforesaid, above-mentioned.

suprarrenal, a. (anat.) suprarenal.

suprascapular, a. (anat.) suprascapular.

suprasensible, a. supersensible.

supraspina, f. (anat.) supraspinal fossa of the scapula.

suprema, f. Supreme Council of the Inquisition.

supremacía, f. supremacy.

supremamente, adv. supremely.

supremo, ma, a. supreme; last, final.

supresión, f. suppression; omission; rooting out, elimination.—**s. de denominadores,** (alg.) clearing of fractions.—**s. de factores comunes,** (arith., alg.) cancellation (of common factors).

supresivo, va, a. suppressive.

supreso, sa, pp. irreg. of SUPRIMIR.

suprimir, va. (pp. SUPRIMIDO, SUPRESO) to suppress; to cut out, abolish, eradicate; to omit; to clear of; (math.) to cancel.

suprior, ra, n. subprior(-ess).

supriorato, m. office of subprior or prioress.

supuesto, ta. I. pp. irreg. of SUPONER.—**s. que,** allowing that; granting that; since.—**esto s.,** this being understood.—**por s.,** of course, naturally. **II.** m. supposition; hypothesis, assumption.

supuración, f. suppuration.

supurante, a. suppurating.

supurar. I. va. to waste, consume. **II.** vn. (med.) to suppurate.—**supurativo, va,** a. & m. suppurative.—**supuratorio, ria,** a. suppurating.

supuse, pret. of SUPONER.

suputación, f. computation, calculation.

suputar, va. & vn. to compute, calculate, reckon.

sur, m. south; south wind.

sura, m. sura (section of the Koran).

sural, a. (anat.) sural, pert. to calf of leg.

suramericano, na, n. & a. = SUDAMERICANO.

surcador, ra, n. plowman(-woman), plower.

surcar, va. (pret. SURQUÉ; subj. SURQUE) (agr.) to plow, furrow; to cut through, move through.

surco, m. furrow; rut; wrinkle.—**a s.,** adjoining, separated by a furrow.

surculado, da, a. (bot.) single-stemmed.

súrculo, m. (bot.) single stem without branches.

surculoso, sa, a. = SURCULADO.

surgente, a. surging, salient.

surgidero, m. (naut.) roads, anchoring place.

surgidor, ra, n. one who anchors.

surgir, vn. (pp. SURGIDO, SURTO; ind. SURJO; subj. SURJA) to spout, spurt; to issue, come forth; to present itself, appear, arise; to sprout; (naut.) to anchor.

surqué, surque, v. V. SURCAR.

surtida, f. (fort.) sallyport; (mil.) sally, sortie; backdoor; (naut.) slipway.

surtidero, m. conduit, outlet.—**s. de agua,** reservoir, basin.

surtido. I. pp. of SURTIR. **II.** a. (com.) assorted. **III.** m. assortment, stock.—**de s.,** in common use.

surtidor, ra. I. n. purveyor, caterer. **II.** m. jet, spout, fountain.—**s. de gasolina,** filling station.

surtimiento, m. supply, stock, assortment.

surtir. I. va. to supply, furnish, provide, purvey, stock.—**s. efecto,** to have the desired effect, to work. **II.** vn. to spout, spurt.

surto, ta. I. pp. irreg. of SURGIR. **II.** a. (naut.) anchored; (fig.) tranquil, at rest.

súrtuba, f. a Central-American gigantic fern.

surumpe, m. (Peru) inflammation of the eyes from the reflection of the snow.

sus, pron. poss. pl. of SU.

¡sus! interj. up! cheer up! forward!

susceptibilidad, f. susceptibility.

susceptible, *a.;* **susceptivo, va,** *a.* susceptible; sensitive, touchy.

suscitación, *f.* excitation.

suscitar. I. *va.* to stir up; to raise, to originate. **II.** *vr.* to rise, start, originate.

suscribir, suscrición, suscritor, etc. = SUBSCRIBIR, SUBSCRIPCIÓN, SUBSCRIPTOR, etc.

susidio, *m.* anxiety, uneasiness.

susodicho, cha, *a.* aforementioned, aforesaid.

suspendedor, ra, *a.* & *n.* that holds (something) up, suspends.

suspender. I. *va.* (*pp. irreg.* SUSPENSO) to suspend; to hang up; to stop, delay, interrupt; to discontinue; to surprise, astonish; to suspend from office; (coll.) to fail (give failing mark to) (in exam.); to adjourn (a meeting).—**s. pagos,** (com.) to stop payments. **II.** *vr.* (of horse) to rear up.

suspensión, *f.* suspension, interruption; cessation; discontinuance; suspense, uncertainty; amazement; privation; (law) suspense; (mus.) suspension.—**s. de armas,** cessation of hostilities.—**s. de pagos,** (com.) suspension of payments.

suspensivo, va. I. *a.* suspensive. **II.** *m. pl.* (print.) leaders (. . .) showing that something has been omitted (gen. replaced by a long dash in English, except in mathematics).

suspenso, sa. I. *pp. irreg.* of SUSPENDER. **II.** *a.* astonished; perplexed.—**en s.,** in suspense. **III.** *m.* failing mark (in exam.).

suspensor, ra, *a.* & *n.* (Am.) = SUSPENDEDOR.

suspensorio, ria. I. *a.* suspensory. **II.** *m.* suspensory bandage.

suspicacia, *f.* suspiciousness, distrust.

suspicaz, *a.* suspicious, distrustful.

suspicazmente, *adv.* suspiciously.

suspirado, da, *a.* expected, desired, longed for.

suspirar, *vn.* to sigh.—**s. por,** to crave, long for, covet.

suspiro, *m.* sigh; breath; glass whistle; (mus.) short pause; ladyfinger (cake); (Am.) (bot.) lady's-slipper.—**exhalar el último s.,** to breathe one's last.

suspiroso, sa, *a.* sighing with difficulty.

sustancia, sustancial, sustancioso, etc. = SUSTANCIA, SUSTANCIAL, SUSTANCIOSO, etc.

sustantivo, etc. = SUBSTANTIVO, etc.

sustenido, *m.* a Spanish step in dancing; SOSTENIDO, (mus.) sharp.

sustentable, *a.* defensible.

sustentación, *f.* support, sustenance.

sustentáculo, *m.* prop, stay, support.

sustentador, ra, *n.* & *a.* sustainer(-ing).

sustentamiento, *m.* sustenance, necessaries of life.

sustentante. I. *a.* sustaining. **II.** *m.* defender, supporter.

sustentar, *va.* to sustain, support, bear; to feed, support; to nourish; to assert, defend, advocate.

sustento, *m.* sustenance, maintenance; support.

sustitución, etc. = SUBSTITUCIÓN, etc.

susto, *m.* scare, fright, shock.—**dar un s.,** to frighten, to scare, to startle.

sustracción, sustraendo, sustraer, = SUBSTRACCIÓN, SUBSTRAENDO, SUBSTRAER.

susurración, *f.* whisper, whispering.

susurrador, ra, *n.* & *a.* whisperer(-ing).

susurrante, *a.* whispering, murmuring.

susurrar. I. *vn.* to whisper; to murmur; to rustle (as leaves); to purl (as a stream); to hum gently (as the air). **II.** *vr.* to be whispered about, to be bruited about.—**susurro,** *m.* whisper, humming, murmur, rustle, purling.

susurrón, na, *n.* grumbler, malcontent.

sutil, *a.* subtile, thin, slender; subtle, acute, cunning; keen; light, volatile.

sutileza, *f.* thinness, slenderness, fineness; subtlety, cunning, artifice; sagacity, acumen, perspicacity; nicety.—**s. de manos,** dexterity.

sutilicé, sutilice, *v. V.* SUTILIZAR.

sutilidad, *f.* = SUTILEZA.

sutilización, *f.* subtilization.

sutilizador, ra, *n.* & *a.* subtilizer(-ing).

sutilizar. I. *va.* (*pret.* SUTILICÉ; *subj.* SUTILICE) to subtilize; to thin, refine; to file, polish. **II.** *vr.* to subtilize.

sutilmente, *adv.* subtly, pointedly; nicely, finely, delicately.

sutorio, ria, *a.* pert. to shoemaking.

sutura, *f.* seam; (anat., bot., surg.) suture.

suyo, ya, (*pl.* SUYOS, YAS), *pron. poss. 3d person masc.* & *fem.* (sometimes with the definite article *el, la, los, las*) his, hers, theirs, one's, his own, its own, one's own, their own.—**de s.,** in itself, by its very nature; spontaneously, of one's own accord.—**los suyos,** yours, your (his, her, etc.) family, people, company, etc.—**salirse con la suya,** to carry one's point, to come out ahead.—**una de las suyas,** one of his pranks or tricks.—**ver la suya,** to have one's chance.

svástica, *f.* swastika.

T

¡ta! *interj.* take care, beware; stay, I recollect.—**¡t., t.!** tut, tut!

taba, *f.* astragalus, anklebone; jackstones.

tabacal, *m.* tobacco field.

tabacalero, ra. I. *a.* tobacco (as *a.*). **II.** *n.* tobacco grower or dealer.

tabaco, *m.* (bot.) tobacco; leaf tobacco; cigar; mildew on plants.—**t. colorado,** mild cigar.—**t. de hoja** = T. EN RAMA.—**t. de montaña,** arnica.—**t. de palillos,** snuff made of stems.—**t. de pipa,** pipe tobacco, smoking tobacco.—**t. de vena,** cigarette tobacco.—**t. en polvo,** snuff.—**t. en rama,** leaf tobacco, wrappers.—**t. holandilla,** Dutch tobacco.—**t. maduro,** strong cigar.—**t. moruno,** European and African tobacco.—**t. rapé,** rappee.—**t. torcido,** cigars, twisted tobacco.—**se me acabó el t.,** (Arg.) my funds have given out.

tabacoso, sa, *a.* using much snuff; tobacco-stained; (of plants) mildewed.

tabalada, *f.* (coll.) heavy fall upon the buttocks; spanking.

tabalario, *m.* (coll.) buttocks, posteriors.

tabalear. I. *va.* & *vn.* to rock to and fro. **II.** *vn.* to drum with the fingers on a table.—**tabaleo,** *m.* rocking, swinging; drumming with the fingers.

tabanazo, *m.* (coll.) spanking.

tabanco, *m.* stall for selling eatables; (Mex.) cockloft.

tabanera, *f.* place full of gadflies.

tábano, *m.* (entom.) gadfly, horsefly.

tabanque, *m.* treadle of a potter's wheel.

tabaola, *f.* hubbub, clamor.

¹tabaque, *m.* ladies' work basket.

²tabaque, *m.* large tack.

tabaquera, *f.* snuffbox; tobacco pouch; cigar case; bowl of a tobacco pipe.

tabaquería, *f.* cigar store.

tabaquero, ra, *n.* cigar maker; tobacconist.

tabaquista, *n.* tobacco expert; heavy smoker.

tabardete, tabardillo, *m.* highly dynamic fever; sunstroke.—**tabardillo pintado,** spotted fever.

tabardo, *m.* tabard.

tabellar, *va.* to fold (cloth) in pieces, leaving the selvage visible; to mark with a trade-mark.

taberna, *f.* tavern, public house, saloon, barroom.

tabernáculo, *m.* tabernacle.

tabernario, ria, *a.* (coll.) pertaining to a tavern; low, vulgar, vile.

tabernera, *f.* tavern keeper's wife; barmaid.

tabernería, *f.* business of a tavern keeper.

TAB 507 TACH

tabernero, *m.* tavern keeper, barkeeper.

tabes, *f.* (med.) consumption; tabes.

tabí, *m.* tabby, moreen, watered fabric, moiré.

tabica, *f.* (arch.) covering board.

tabicar, *va.* to wall up; to close or shut up.

tabicón, *m.* thick partition wall.

tábido, da, *a.* (med.) tabid, wasted; putrid.

tabífico, ca, *a.* (med.) tabific.

tabinete, *m.* tabbinet (fabric).

tabique, *m.* thin wall; partition wall, partition.— **t. de panderete,** brick-on-edge partition.—**t. maestro,** chief partition wall.—**t. sordo,** double partition wall.

tabiquería, *f.* partition work, system or group of partitions.

tabiquero, ra, *n.* partition-wall builder.

tabla, *f.* (carp.) board; plank; slab; tablet, plate (of metal); table (of contents, of logarithms, etc.); list (of prices, etc.); full-breadth gore of a skirt; tablier; box plait; largest face of a piece of timber; (jewelry) flat diamond; (art) table, panel; broadest, most fleshy part of a member of the body; bed or patch in a garden; strip of land between rows of trees; revenue office where merchandise is registered as sold at market; meat stall; butcher's block.—*pl.* (theat.) stage boards, (fig.) stage; draw (in a game).—**t. de Ampère,** (phys.) Ampère's stand.—**t. de armonía,** (mus.) sounding board.—**t. de chilla,** thin board of slit deal.—**t. de juego,** gambling house.—**t. de manteles,** tablecloth.—**t. de río,** bed of a river.—**t. de salvación,** last resource.—**t. de sembrado,** cornfield.—**t. pitagórica,** multiplication table.—**tablas de la ley,** tables of the law.—**tablas reales,** backgammon board or tables.—**a la t. del mundo,** in public, before the world.—**a raja t.,** at any price, regardless of everything else.—**escaparse en una t.,** to have a narrow escape.—**hacer t. rasa de,** to ignore entirely, to set at nought.—**no saber por dónde van tablas,** to know nothing about the matter.—**salvarse en una t.,** to have a narrow escape.

tablachina, *f.* wooden shield or buckler.

tablacho, *m.* sluice or floodgate.

tablado, *m.* stage, scaffold, platform; flooring; (theat.) stage boards; platform of a cart or truck; boards or bottom of a bedstead.

tablaje, *m.* pile of boards; planking; gambling or gaming house.

tablajería, *f.* gambling; hire of the gaming table.

tablajero, *m.* scaffold maker; carpenter who builds stands and stages; ancient collector of the king's taxes; keeper of a gaming house; gambler; butcher; assistant hospital surgeon.

tablar, *m.* set of garden plots or beds.

tablazo, *m.* blow or stroke with a board; shallow arm of the sea; sheet of water; small plateau; (S. A., geol.) uplifted sea-floor deposit.

tablazón, *f.* boards, planks, lumber; planking, flooring; decks and sheathing of a ship.—**t. de la cubierta,** (naut.) deck planks.

tablear, *va.* to saw into boards; to divide (a garden) into beds or plots; to level or grade (the ground) with a thick board; to hammer into plates; (sewing) to make box plaits in.

tableo, *m.* sawing wood into boards; dividing a garden into beds; leveling (the ground) or grading with a board; hammering into plates.

tablero, *m.* board, panel; sawable timber; drawing board; dog nail; stock of a crossbow; chessboard, checkerboard; (Colomb.) blackboard; gambling house or table; shop counter; money table; (tailoring) cutting table; (carp.) door panel; (arch.) panel, compartment; floor (of a bridge).—**t. contador,** abacus.—**t. de cocina,** dresser, kitchen table.—**t. de conmutadores** = **t. de distribución.**—**t. de chaquete** (Mex.) backgammon board, tables.—**t. de distribución,** (elec.) switchboard.

tablestaca, *f.* (eng.) sheet pile.

tableta, *f. dim.* tablet; writing pad; (pharm.) tablet, lozenge; cracknel; clapper.—**estar en tabletas,** to be in suspense.

tableteado, *m.* sound made by rattling clappers.

tabletear, *vn.* to rattle clappers.

tableteo, *m.* rattling sound of clappers.

tablilla, *f. dim.* tablet, slab; bulletin board; section of the cushion of a billiard table between two pockets; (surg.) splint; (surv.) target (of leveling rod).—**t. de mesón,** sign of an inn.—**t. de santero,** poor box of a hermit.—**tablillas de San Lázaro,** clappers used in begging for hospitals.—**tablillas neperianas,** logarithmic tables.—**por t.,** indirectly.

tablón, *m. aug.* plank, thick board; beam; strake.—**t. de aparadura,** (naut.) garboard strake.—**tablones de cucharros,** (naut.) serving planks.

tabloncillo, *m.* flooring board; in bull rings, last row of seats.

tabloza, *f.* painter's palette.

tabo, *m.* (P. I.) cup made from coconut shell.

tabón, *m.* (ornith.) tabon, Philippine megapode.

tabona, *f.* stagnant pool.

tabú, *m.* taboo.

tabuco, *m.* hut, hovel; narrow room.

tabular, *a.* tabular.

tabuquillo, quito, *m. dim.* shanty.

taburete, *m.* taboret; stool.—*pl.* (theat.) benches in the pit.

¹**taca,** *f.* small closet.

²**taca,** *f.* (min.) plate of the crucible.

³**taca,** *f.* stain.

tacada, *f.* stroke, play (at billiards); wedges.

tacamaca, tacamacha, tacamahaca, *f.* tacamahac, gum resin from various tropical trees; (bot.) balsam poplar.

tacano, *m.* (min.) rich gray silver ore.

tacañamente, *adv.* stingily, in a miserly manner.

tacañear, *vn.* to act the miser.

tacañería, *f.* stinginess; narrowness of mind; malicious cunning; low craft.

tacaño, ña, *a.* stingy, niggardly; artful, knavish.

tacar. I. *va.* to mark (as a person in the face). **II.** *vn.* to shoot, to have one's turn (in billiards).

tacazo, *m.* blow with a billiard cue.

taceta, *f.* copper bowl used in oilmills.

tacica, illa, ita, *f. dim.* small cup.

tácitamente, *adv.* silently, secretly; tacitly.

tácito, ta, *a.* silent; tacit, implied.

taciturnidad, *f.* taciturnity; reserve.

taciturno, na, *a.* taciturn, reserved; melancholy.

taclobo, *m.* (P. I.) a giant clam.

taco, *m.* plug, bung, stopper; (artil.) wad, wadding; rammer; popgun; billiard cue; (S. A., P. R.) heel (of shoe); almanac pad; (coll.) light lunch, snack; each draught of wine at meals; (Cuba) spruce young fellow, dandy; volley of oaths.—**tacos de los escobenes,** (naut.) hawse plugs.—**echar tacos,** (coll.) to swear, to rage.

tacón, *m.* heel, heelpiece (of shoe).—**taconazo,** *m.* blow with a shoe heel.—**taconear,** *vn.* (coll.) to walk or strut loftily on the heels.—**taconeo,** *m.* noise made with the heels in dancing.

táctica, *f.* orderly array; (coll.) policy, way of doing; (mil.) tactics.

táctico, *m.* tactician.

táctil, *a.* tactile, pertaining to touch.

tacto, *m.* touch, sense of touch; touching, feeling; tact, skill, carefulness.

tacuacha, *f.* (Cuba) dexterous trick.

tacuará, *f.* (Arg.) a kind of bamboo.

tacurú, *m.* (Arg.) a variety of black ant and the ant hill it makes.

tacha, *f.* fault, defect, blemish, flaw; large tack.—**poner t. a,** to find fault with.

tachar, *va.* to censure; blame, charge, accuse; to find fault with; to reprehend; to cut out, cross out; to cancel.—**t. testigos,** (law) to challenge witnesses.

tachero, *m.* (Cuba) one who works at a TACHO.

tacho, *m.* sugar evaporator, pan; (Peru) earthen jar for heating water.—**t. al,** or **de, vacío,** vacuum pan.

¹tachón, *m.* deleting mark (in written material); braid, etc.; trimming (on clothes).

²tachón, *m.* gimp, or ornamental, nail; boss.

¹tachonar, *va.* (sew.) to adorn with trimming.

²tachonar, *va.* to garnish with gimp nails.

tachonería, *f.* gimp nail ornamental work.

tachoso, sa, *a.* faulty, defective.

tachuela, *f.* tack, small nail.

tael, *m.* tael (weight and coin).

tafanario, *m.* (coll.) buttocks.

tafetán, *m.* taffeta, thin silk.—*pl.* flags, colors, standard, ensign.—**t. inglés,** court-plaster; sticking plaster.

tafia, *f.* (Venez.) molasses rum.

tafilete, *m.* morocco leather.—**tafiletear,** *va.* to adorn with morocco leather.—**tafiletería,** *f.* art of, or place for, dressing morocco leather.

tafurea, *f.* flat-bottomed boat for horses.

tagalo, la. I. *n.* & *a.* pertaining to the Tagal. **II.** *m.* Tagalog (language).

tagarino, na, *n.* Moor who lived among the Christians.

tagarnina, *f.* (bot.) golden thistle; (coll.) bad cigar.

tagarote, *m.* (ornith.) sparrow hawk; quill driver, scrivener; "decayed" gentleman who earns a dinner by flattery and adulation; (coll.) tall, awkward person.

tagarotear, *vn.* (coll.) to write a bold, free, and running hand.

tagua, *f.* (Am.) tagua, ivory nut; (Chile) (ornith.) a bird similar to the coot.

taguán, *m.* (zool.) taguan, a flying squirrel.

taha, *f.* district, region.

tahalí, *m.* shoulder belt; baldric.

taharal, *m.* plantation of tamarisk trees.

taheño, *a.* having a red beard.

tahona, *f.* bakery, baker's shop; horse mill; crushing mill.

tahonera, *f.* baker's wife; miller's wife.

tahonero, ra, *n.* baker; miller.

tahulla, *f.* plot of arable land.

tahur, ra. I. *a.* gambling. **II.** *n.* gambler, gamester; card sharp.—**tahurería,** *f.* gambling; gaming house; cheating gambling.

taifa, *f.* faction, party; (coll.) assemblage of fast or foolish people.

taimado, da, *a.* sly, cunning, crafty.

taimería, *f.* rascality, craftiness.

taita, *f.* (coll.) dad, daddy.

¹taja, *f.* tree of a packsaddle.

²taja, *f.* cut, incision; dissection; TARJA, tally.

tajada, *f.* slice; (coll.) hoarseness.

tajadera, *f.* chopping knife; (mech.) round chisel, gouge; cold chisel.—*pl.* sluice of a mill dam.

tajadero, *m.* chopping block, trencher.

tajadilla, *f. dim.* small slice; dish of lights in low chophouses; bit of confected orange or lemon sold as a relish by retailers of brandy.

tajado, da. I. *pp.* of TAJAR. **II.** *a.* steep, sheer, wall-like; (her.) divided.

tajador, ra. I. *n.* one who cuts or chops. **II.** *m.* cutting edge.

tajadura, *f.* cut, notch; cutting, chopping.

tajamar, *m.* (naut.) cutwater, stem; (eng.) cut-water of a bridge pier.

tajamiento, *m.* = TAJADURA.

tajaplumas, *m.* penknife.

tajar, *va.* to cut, cleave; to cut and trim (a quill pen).

tajea, *f.* watercourse, channel; culvert.

tajero, *m.* = TARJERO, tally keeper.

tajo, *m.* cut; incision; trench; cutting edge; steep cliff; cutting a quill; chopping block; line or place to which the work of a gang extends; cut

or opening in a mountain; (fencing) cut.—**t. abierto,** (min.) open cut.

tajón, *m. aug.* butcher's block; chopping block vein of white earth in a limestone quarry.

tajuela, *f.,* **tajuelo,** *m.* rustic seat.

tal (*pl.* TALES). **I.** *a.* such, so, as; equal, similar; a much, so great.—**t. cual,** such as; a few, one from time to time; middling, so-so; such as it is —**t. cual vez,** once in a while, now and then.— **el t., or la t.,** (foll. by a common noun) that (gen. contempt); (foll. by a proper noun) that man, that fellow (*el tal Juan,* that fellow John) —**un t.,** one, a certain (*estaba allí un tal Ramírez,* one Ramirez was there). **II.** *pron.* such, such a one, such a thing.—**t. para cual** two of a kind.—**t. por cual,** person of little account, (a) nobody.—**no hay t.,** there is no such thing.—**otro que t.,** another of the same ilk. **III.** *adv.* thus, so, in such manner.—**con t. que, con t. de que,** provided, on condition that.—**¿qué t.?** hello! how d'ye do? how is that? how goes it?

¹tala, *f.* felling of trees; destruction, ruin, havoc tipcat (boys' game); cat (in the game).

²tala, *f.* (bot.) a large Argentine urticaceous tree

talabarte, *m.* sword belt.

talabartería, *f.* saddlery.

talabartero, *m.* saddler; harness maker.

talador, ra, *n.* & *a.* destroyer(-ing); cutter(-ing)

taladrador, ra. I. *n.* & *a.* borer(-ing), driller (-ing). **II.** *f.* drilling or perforating machine.

taladrar, *va.* to bore, drill, perforate; to pierce, penetrate (as the ear); to dig into, go to the bottom of, elucidate.

taladrilla, *f.* a boring insect that attacks olive trees.

taladro, *m.* bit, drill, borer, gimlet, auger; bore, auger hole, drill hole; blasting charge; charged blasting hole.

talamera, *f.* tree used for snaring birds.

talamete, *m.* (naut.) foredeck planking.

talamiflora. I. *a.* (bot.) thalamifloral. **II.** *f. pl.* Thalamiflorae.

talamite, *m.* thalamite, outermost galley rower.

tálamo, *m.* bridal chamber or bed; (bot.) receptacle.—**tálamos ópticos,** (anat.) optic thalami.

talanquera, *f.* parapet, breastwork of pales; picket fence; defense, safety place.

talante, *m.* mode or manner of doing anything; mien, countenance; desire, will, pleasure, disposition.—**de mal t.,** unwillingly, grudgingly. —**estar de buen** or **de mal t.,** to be in a pleasant or in an ugly frame of mind.

¹talar, *va.* to fell (trees); to lay waste; to prune.

²talar, *a.* long (clothes).—**talares,** *m. pl.* wings on the heels of Mercury; talaria.

talasoterapia, *f.* (med.) sea-bathing therapy.

talayote, *m.* a Balearic megalith in the form of a low tower.

talco, *m.* talc; tinsel.—**talcoso, sa,** *a.* talcose.

talcualillo, lla, *a.* (coll.) fair, not bad; somewhat improved in health.

tálea, *f.* stockade or palisade in Roman camps.

taled, *m.* tallith (among the Jews).

talega, *f.* bag, sack; money bag; bagful; bag for the hair; diaper; sack containing 1,000 dollars in silver.—**dos talegas,** two thousand dollars.

talego, *m.* bag or sack; clumsy, awkward fellow. —**tener t.,** to have money.

taleguilla, *f. dim.* small bag.—**t. de la sal,** (coll.) daily expenses.

talento, *m.* talent; smartness, cleverness; talent (ancient weight and coin).

talentoso, sa; talentudo, da, *a.* able, talented, smart, clever.

tálero, *m.* thaler, an old German coin.

talio, *m.* (chem.) thallium.

talión, *m.* talion, retaliation, "eye for an eye."

talionar, *va.* to punish by retaliation.

alismán, *m.* talisman, charm, amulet.

alma, *f.* a kind of cape or cloak.

almente, *adv.* (coll.) in the same manner.

'almud, *m.* Talmud.—**talmúdico, ca,** *a.* Talmudic.—**talmudista,** *m.* Talmudist.

alofita. I. *f.* & *a.* (bot.) thallophyte(-ic). **II.** *f. pl.* Thallophyta.

alón, *m.* (anat., shoe) heel; heel of horse's hoof; heel of a violin bow; (arch.) heel, cyma reversa; (com.) any check, draft, note or voucher detached from a stub book; coupon; (naut.) heel of the keel, stemson.—**apretar los talones,** to show a clean pair of heels, to run.—**a t.,** on foot.

alonario, ria. I. *a.* taken from a stub book; stub (as *a.*). **II.** *m.* stub book; check book.

alonear, *vn.* to walk fast.

alonesco, ca, *a.* (coll.) pertaining to the heels.

alpa, talparia, *f.* (med.) talpa, wen.

alque, *m.* tasco, a refractory clay.

alquita, *f.* (min.) talc schist.

alud, *m.* (arch.) talus; batter; side slope.

alvina, *f.* porridge of almond meal.

alla, *f.* carving, wood carving (*obra de talla*, carved work); ancient tax in Arragon; ransom; price set on the head of a criminal; (jewelry) cut, cutting; round of a card game; (of person) (lit. & fig.) height, stature; (mil.) height scale, for measuring a man's height; (surg.) lithotomy.—**de t.,** (of person) prominent.

alla, *f.* (naut.) purchase block.

alla, *f.* earthen jug.

allado, da. I. *pp.* of TALLAR. **II.** *a.*—**bien or mal t.,** having a good or bad figure.

allador, ra, *n.* engraver; carver; diesinker; (Am.) dealer (in a game).

alladura, *f.* engraving.

allar. I. *va.* to carve; to engrave; (jewelry) to cut; to appraise. **II.** *vn.* (card games) to deal.

allar. I. *a.* ready for cutting. **II.** *m.* woodland ready for first cut.

allarín, *m.* noodle (for soup).

allarola, *f.* knife for cutting velvet pile.

alle, *m.* form, figure; waist; (tailoring) fit; waist, bodice.

allecer, *vn.* to shoot, sprout.

aller, *m.* workshop, factory, mill, office, laboratory; atelier; studio.—**t. de reparaciones,** repair shop; (auto) service station.

taller, *m.* oil and vinegar caster.

alleta, *f.* (Am.) = ALFAJOR, nut and honey paste.

allista, *n.* carver in wood; engraver.

allo, *m.* (bot.) stem, stalk; shoot, sprout.

alludo, da, *a.* grown into long stalks; tall, slender; overgrown; habit-ridden; past one's youth.

alluelo, *m. dim.* of TALLO.

tamagás, *m.* a very poisonous C. A. snake.

tamal, *m.* (Am.) tamale; (Am.) bundle, parcel; (Peru) pork (sold in the street).

amalero, ra, *n.* tamale seller or maker.

amandoa (Am.), **tamanduá,** *m.* (zool.) tamandua, anteater.

amango, *m.* (Chile, Arg.) coarse shoe worn by the gauchos; sheepskin cover for the feet.

tamañamente, *adv.* as large as.

tamañico, ica, ito, ita, uelo, la, *a.* very small.

tamañito, ta, *a.* abashed, ashamed.

tamaño, ña. I. *a.* so great; (with gesture) so big, so small. **II.** *m.* size.—**t. natural,** full size.

támara, *f.* palm field.—*pl.* dates in a bunch; chips, fagots of brushwood.

tamarindo, *m.* (bot.) tamarind.

tamariscíneo, a, *a.* (bot.) tamariscineous.

tamarisco, tamariz, *m.* (bot.) tamarisk.

tamarrizquito, tamarrusquito, ta, *a.* (coll.) very small.

tamarugo, *m.* (bot.) a kind of Chilean carob.

tambalear, *vn.* & *vr.* to stagger, totter, reel.

tambaleo, *m.* reeling, staggering, tottering.

tambanillo, *m.* (arch.) tympanum.

tambarillo, *m.* chest with arched cover.

tambarria, *f.* (S. A.) carouse; (Chile) low tavern.

tambero, ra. I. *n.* (Peru) innkeeper. **II.** *a.* (of cattle) (Arg.) tame, gentle.

tambesco, *m.* swing.

también, *adv.* also, too, likewise; as well.

tambo, *m.* (S. A.) inn; dairy.

tambor, *m.* drum; drummer; coffee roaster, chestnut roaster; bolter or sieve used by confectioners; (sewing) tambour frame; (mech.) drum, cylinder, band pulley, rope barrel; (jewelry) barrel, arbor; (arch.) drum, tambour; screen; small room made by partitions; thole, tholus; (fort.) tambour; (naut.) drum or barrel of the capstan; wheelhouse, paddle box.—**t. del oído,** drum of the ear.—**t. mayor,** drum major.—**a golpe de t.,** or **con t. batiente,** at the beating of the drum; with drums beating.

tambora, *f.* bass drum.

tamborete, *m. dim.* timbrel; (naut.) cap of the masthead, moorshead.

tamboril, *m.* tabor, small drum, timbrel.

tamborilada, *f.,* **tamborilazo,** *m.* (coll.) fall upon the buttocks; slap on the face or shoulders.

tamborilear. I. *vn.* to drum. **II.** *va.* to praise, extol; (print.) to plane or level (type).

tamborilero, *m.* taborer, drummer.

tamborilete, *m. dim.* small TABOR; (print.) planer.

tamborín, tamborino, *m.* = TAMBORIL.

tamboritear, *va.,* **tamboritero,** *m.* = TAMBORILEAR, TAMBORILERO.

tamborón, *m.* large bass drum.

tamén, *m.* (Mex.) Indian porter, carrier.

tamiz, *m.* sieve, sifter, screen; bolting cloth.

tamizar, *va.* to sift, screen.

tamo, *m.* fuzz; chaff, winnowings, graindust; dust gathered under beds, etc.

tamojal, *m.* place covered with TAMOJO.

tamojo, *m.* (bot.) saltwort, glasswort.

tampoco, *adv.* neither, not either; (after **ni**) either (*él no sabe, ni yo tampoco*, he does not know, nor I either).

tamujal, *m.* thicket of buckthorns.

tamujo, *m.* (bot.) buckthorn, boxthorn.

tamul, *n.* & *a.;* **tamúlico, ca,** *a.* Tamil.

tan, *adv. contr.* of TANTO; as, so, so much, as well, as much.—**t. siquiera,** even, ever so.—**t. sólo,** only, merely.—**qué t.,** how.—**qué . . . t.,** what a (*¡qué mujer tan bella!* what a beautiful woman).

tanaceto, *m.* (bot.) tansy.

tanate, *m.* (Mex.) bale made of hide; fruit basket; palm-leaf bag; (C. A.) bundle.—**cargar con los tanates,** (Am.) to move away.

tanatero, *m.* (Mex.) TANATE; carrier.

tanato, *m.* (chem.) tannate.

tanda, *f.* turn, rotation; task; gang of workmen, shift, relay; set, batch; each game of billiards; (theat.) each performance requiring a separate ticket.

tándem, *m.* tandem bicycle.—**en t.,** tandem.

tandeo, *m.* distribution of irrigating water by turns.

tanganillas.—en t., *adv.* waveringly.

tanganillo, *m. dim.* small prop or stay.

tángano, *m.* hob, a boys' game; stick used in this.

tangencia, *f.* tangency.—**tangencial,** *a.* tangential.—**tangencialmente,** *adv.* tangentially.

tangente, *f.* & *a.* (geom.) tangent.—**escaparse, salir,** or **salirse, por la t.,** to resort to subterfuges or evasions, to befog the issue.

tangible, *a.* tangible.

tango, *m.* hob, boys' game; (dance) tango.

tangón, *m.* (naut.) outrigger.

tánico, ca, *a.* containing tannin; tannic.

tanino, *m.* (chem.) tannin.

tanor, ra, *n.* (P. I.) Malay who served as domestic to the Spaniards.—**tanoría,** *f.* (P. I.) domestic service to the Spaniards.

---

¹**tanque,** *m.* bee glue (in a hive).

²**tanque,** *m.* tank; reservoir; dipper; (milit.) tank.

tantalato, *m.* (chem.) tantalate.

tantalio, *m.* (chem.) tantalum.

tan-tan, *m.* rubadub, sound of a drum; tom-tom.

tantarantán, *m.* rubadub, beat of a drum; (coll.) resounding blow.

tanteador, ra, *n.* measurer, tester, marker.

tantear. I. *va.* to try, test, measure; to feel out; to make an estimate of; to consider carefully; to scrutinize; (art) to sketch, outline. **II.** *vn.* to keep the score. **III.** *vr.* to agree to pay the price for which a thing has been sold.

tanteo, *m.* estimate, approximate calculation; trial; points, score (in a game).—**al t.,** by eye; as an estimate; by trial.

tantico, tantillo. I. *m.* (coll.) a little, a little bit, a small amount. **II.** *adv.* (coll., Am.) a little while.

tanto, ta. I. *a.* so much, as much; very great.—*pl.* **tantos, tas,** many; as many, so many. **II.** *pron.* that.—**por t., por lo t.,** for that reason; therefore. **III.** *m.* certain sum or quantity; copy of a writing; counter; point (in games); (com.) rate.—*pl.* odd, denoting an indeterminate number (e.g., *treinta y tantos,* thirty odd).—**t. por ciento,** percentage; per cent.—**t. por cuanto,** (arith.) rate referred to any number; theory of rates (per centum, per thousand, per *x*).—**t. por t.,** at the same price; upon a par.—**tantos a tantos,** equal numbers. —**algún t.,** a little, somewhat.—**al t.,** at the price stated; at cost.—**al t. de,** posted about, informed on.—**en su t.,** proportionally.—**en t.,** or **entre t.,** in the meantime.—**no ser para t.,** not to be so bad, so serious, as that; not to be equal to, up to doing, that.—**otro t.,** as much; as much more.—**por el t.** = AL T.— **un t.,** somewhat, a bit, rather. **IV.** *adv.* so, in such a manner; so much, as much; so long, as long; often.—**t. así,** as, or so, much as that.—**t. como,** as much as; as well as.—**t. cuanto,** a little, somewhat.—**t. mejor,** so much the better.—**t. más cuanto,** or **t. más cuanto que,** all the more because, especially as.—**t. monta,** it is all the same.—**t. peor,** so much the worse.—**t. que,** as much as; so much so, that.—**t. uno como otro,** the one as well as the other; both of them.

tanza, *f.* fishing line.

tañedor, ra, *n.* player of musical instrument.

tañente, *a.* playing on an instrument.

tañer, *va.* to play (a musical instrument).

tañido, *m.* tune; sound; clink, ring.

tañimiento, *m.* playing on an instrument.

tao, *m.* badge of some orders.

tapa, *f.* lid, cover, cap; cover (of book); horny part of a hoof; cylinder head; heel blank, heel lift (of shoe); (P. I.) jerked beef, hung beef.— **t. de los sesos,** top of the skull.—**t. de un barril** = CASCO DE UN BARRIL, head (of barrel).

tapaagujeros, *m.* (coll.) clumsy mason; substitute, makeshift.

tapabalazo, *m.* (naut.) shot plug.

tapaboca, *m.* (coll.) slap on the mouth; muffler; choke pear; anything that silences one; (mil.) tampion.

tapada, *f.* thickly veiled woman.

tapadera, *f.* loose lid, cover of a pot; coverele; (Mex.) leather cover of a stirrup.

tapadero, *m.* stopper, stopple, cover.

tapadillo, *m.* concealment of a woman's face with her veil or mantle; flute stop of an organ.—**de t.,** secretly, covertly, sub rosa.

tapadizo, *m.* shed, cover.

tapado, *m.* (Arg., Chile, C. A.) woman's or child's overcoat, cape, or shawl.

tapador, ra. I. *n.* coverer. **II.** *m.* lid, cover, plug, stopper, stopple.

tapadura, *f.* stopping, covering, hiding.

tapafogón, *m.* (artil.) cap of a venthole.

tapafunda, *f.* flap of a holster (on a saddle).

tapagujeros, *m.* = TAPAAGUJEROS.

tapajuntas, *m.* door strap covering joint with wall; corner angle to protect plaster.

tápalo, *m.* (Mex.) woman's shawl.

tapamiento, *m.* stopping or covering.

tápana, *f.* (bot.) caper.

tapanco, (P. I.) boat tilt or awning.

tapaojos, *m.* (Am.) blinders for horses.

tapapiés, *m.* silk underskirt.

tapar. I. *va.* to cover; to hide, cover up, veil; to stop up, plug; close up, obstruct.—**t. la boca** to stop one's mouth. **II.** *vr.* (of horse) to cover the track of the fore feet with those of the hind ones; to bundle, wrap oneself up.

tapara, *f.* (Am.) gourd for drinking.

tápara, *f.* (bot.) caper.

táparo, *m.* gourd tree.

taparrabo, *m.* loin cloth; trunks, short tights.

tapatán, *m.* (P. I.) tit-tat-toe.

taperujarse, *vr.* (coll.) to muffle one's face.

taperujo, *m.* (coll.) ill-shaped plug or stopper; awkward manner of muffling one's face.

tapetado, da, *a.* dark brown.

tapete, *m.* small carpet, rug; cover for a table or chest.—**t. verde,** card table.—**estar sobre e t.,** to be on the tapis.

tapia, *f.* mud wall; adobe wall; wall fence (mason.) wall measure (50 sq. ft.).—**t. real** wall made of earth and lime.—**más sordo que una t.,** deaf as a post.

tapiador, *m.* builder of mud walls.

tapial, *m.* form or mold for mud walls.

tapiar, *va.* to wall up; to raise a spite wall; to obstruct the view of with a wall.

tapicería, *f.* tapestry; art of making tapestry upholstery; shop where tapestries are sold.

tapicero, *m.* tapestry maker; upholsterer; carpet layer.—**t. mayor,** tapestry keeper in a palace.

tapido, da, *a.* closely woven.

tapiería, *f.* series of mud walls.

tapín, *m.* (artil.) vent plug.

tapioca, *f.* tapioca.

tapir, *m.* (zool.) tapir.

tapirujarse, *vr.* = TAPERUJARSE.

tapis, *m.* (P. I.) sash worn by women.

tapiz, *m.* tapestry.

tapizar, *va.* to hang with tapestry.

tapón, *m.* cork, stopper; plug, bung; (elec.) fuse (surg.) tampon.—**t. de cuba,** (coll.) short, fat person.—**al primer t., zurrapas,** (coll.) un lucky from the start.

taponamiento, *m.* (surg.) tamponage.

taponar, *va.* (surg.) to tampon.

taponazo, *m.* pop of a bottle.

taponería, *f.* set of corks; cork factory or shop.

taponero, ra. I. *a.* of cork. **II.** *n.* cork cutter or seller.

tapsia, *f.* (bot.) madder.

tapujarse, *vr.* to muffle oneself.

tapujo, *m.* muffle; (coll.) pretext, subterfuge.

taque, *m.* noise made by locking a door; rap knock at a door.

taquera, *f.* rack or stand for billiard cues.

taquigrafía, *f.* shorthand, stenography.

taquigrafiar, *va.* to write in shorthand.

taquigráficamente, *adv.* in shorthand.

taquigráfico, ca, *a.* stenographic.

taquígrafo, *m.* stenographer.

taquilla, *f.* letter file, closet for papers; case of pigeonholes; ticket rack, key rack; (theat., Ry.) ticket office; booking office.—**taquillero, ra,** *n.* clerk in ticket office.

taquimetría, *f.* (surv.) tachymetry; stadia surveying; (auto) tachometer.

taquimétrico, ca, *a.* tachymetrical.

taquímetro, *m.* (surv.) tachymeter, stadia.

taquín, *m.* anklebone; (game) jackstones.

taquinero, *m.* player with jackstones.

ara, *f.* (com.) tare, weight of container.—**menos la t.**, making allowance for exaggeration; taking with a grain of salt.

ara, *f.* tally (stick).

ara, *f.* (Venez.) green grasshopper.

rabilla, *f.* (mil.) clack, clapper; catch, bolt, latch, sash fastener or holder; pin or peg for tightening the cord of a buck-saw frame; (coll.) chatterbox; fast and senseless talk.

rabita, *f.* (S. A.) rope bridge.

racea, *f.* marquetry, inlaid work, buhlwork.

racear, *va.* to inlay, to make buhlwork on.

ragallo, *m.* block attached to dog's collar to prevent his nosing the ground.

raje, *m.* (bot.) tamarisk.

rambana, *n.* giddy person; madcap.

rando, *m.* (zool.) reindeer.

rangallo, *m.* = TARAGALLO.

rángana, *f.* coarse sausage.

rantela, *f.* (dance) tarantella.

rantín, *m.* (C. A., Cuba) kitchen pot, utensil; gadget.

rántula, *f.* tarantula.

rantulado, da, *a.* bitten by a tarantula; wild; astonished.

rara, tarará, *f.* sound of a trumpet.

rarear, *va. & vn.* to hum (a tune).

rarira. I. *f.* (coll.) noisy mirth. II. *n.* noisy person.

rasca, *f.* figure of dragon borne in procession of Corpus Christi day; ugly woman.

rascada, *f.* bite, wound with the teeth; (coll.) pert, rude answer.

rascar, *va.* to bite (as dogs).

rascón, *m. aug.* of TARASCA.

ratántara, *f.* = TARARA.

ray, *m.* (bot.) tamarisk.

rayal, *m.* tamarisk plantation.

razana, *f.*, tarazanal, *m.* = ATARAZANA, arsenal; spinner's shed.

razar, *va.* to bite; to vex, annoy, harass.

razón, *m.* large slice.

rbea, *f.* large hall.

rdador, ra, *n. & a.* tarrier(-ying).

rdanaos, *m.* (ichth.) = RÉMORA, remora.

rdanza, *f.* slowness, tardiness; delay.

rdar, *vn. & vr.* to delay; to take a long time; to be late.—**a más t.**, at the latest.

rde. I. *f.* afternoon.—**buenas tardes,** good-afternoon.—**de, or por, la t.,** in the afternoon. —**de la t. a la mañana,** between sunset and sunrise; all of a sudden.—**de t. en t.,** now and then, once in a while. II. *adv.* late; too late.— **t., mal y nunca,** late and bad.—**t. o temprano,** sooner or later.—**t. piache,** too late.— **hacerse t.,** to grow late.—**más vale t. que nunca,** better late than never.—**para luego es t.,** by and by will be too late.

rdecer, *vn. & impers.* (*subj.* TARDEZCA) to draw towards evening; to grow late.

rdecica, ita, *f. dim.* evenfall.

rdecillo, to, *adv.* (Am.) a little late.

rdiamente, *adv.* too late, out of time.

rdígrado, da. I. *a.* (zool.) slow-moving, slow-paced. II. *m. pl.* Tardigrada, sloths.

rdío, día, *a.* late, too late; slow; tardy.

rdo, da, *a.* slow, sluggish; tardy; dull, thick, dense.

rdón, na, *a. aug.* very slow; dull, thick.

rea, *f.* task; care, anxiety.

rentino, na, *n. & a.* Tarentine.

árgum, *m.* Targum (Jewish book).

rida, *f.* an ancient military transport.

rifa, *f.* price list, fare, rate; schedule of charges.

rima, *f.* stand; movable platform; low bench, table, footstool; bedstead.

rimón, *m. aug.* large stand or platform.

rín, *m.* silver real of 8¼ CUARTOS.

rina, *f.* middle-sized plate for meat.

rín barín, *adv.* (coll.) pretty close, just about.

tarja, *f.* check, tally; tally stick; target, shield, buckler; an ancient copper coin.—**beber sobre t.,** (coll.) to get drink on credit.

tarjador, ra, *n.* tally keeper.

tarjar, *va.* to tally.—**tarjero, ra,** *n.* tally keeper.

tarjeta, *f. dim.* of TARJA; card; (arch.) label, tablet with inscription; title and imprint on a map or chart.—**t. de despedida,** P. P. C. (leave-taking) card.—**t. de negocios,** business card. —**t. de visita,** visiting card.—**t. postal,** post card.

tarjeteo, *m.* (coll.) social exchange of cards.

tarjetero, *m.* cardcase.

tarjetón, *m. aug.* large card; show card.

tarlatana, *f.* tarlatan (fabric).

tarquín, *m.* slime, mire, mud.

tarquinada, *f.* (coll.) rape.

tarraconense, *a.* of or from Tarragona.

tárraga, *f.* an ancient Spanish dance.

tarraja, *f.* = TERRAJA.

tarraya, *f.* (Am.) = ATARRAYA, casting net.

tarreñas, *f. pl.* pieces of broken china used as clappers or bones.

tarrico, *m.* (bot.) saltwort.

tarro, *m.* jar; (Cuba) horn; (Colomb.) can, pot.

tarso, *m.* (anat.) tarsus; gambrel, hock.

tarta, *f.* tart; pan for baking tarts.

tártago, *m.* (bot.) spurge; (coll.) misfortune; practical joke.

tartajear, *vn.* to stutter, stammer.

tartajoso, sa, *a.* stammering, stuttering.

tartalear, *vn.* to reel, stagger; (coll.) to be dumfounded.

tartamudear, *vn.* to stutter, stammer.

tartamudeo, m., tartamudez, *f.* stuttering.

tartamudo, da, *n. & a.* stutterer(-ing).

tartán, *m.* tartan, Scotch plaid.

tartana, *f.* round-top, two-wheeled carriage; (naut.) tartan.

tartanero, *m.* driver of a TARTANA.

tartáreo, rea, *a.* (poet.) Tartarean, hellish.

tartárico, ca, *a.* tartaric.

tartarizar, *va.* (chem.) to tartarize.

¹tártaro, *m.* argol, cream of tartar; (dent.) tartar.

²tártaro, *m.* (poet.) Tartarus, hell.

³tártaro, ra, *n. & a.* Tartar, Tatar.

tartera, *f.* baking pan for pastry; dinner pail.

tartrato, *m.* (chem.) tartrate.

tártrico, ca, *a.* tartaric.

taruga, *f.* (zool.) a species of vicuña.

tarugo, *m.* wooden peg or pin; stopper, plug.

tarumba, *m.*—**volver a uno t.,** (coll.) to confuse one.—**volverse t.,** to become rattled.

tas, *m.* small anvil used by silversmiths.

tasa, *f.* measure, rule; standard; rate; assessment; valuation, appraisement.

tasación, *f.* valuation, appraisement.

tasadamente, *adv.* barely, scantily, scarcely.

tasador, ra, *n.* appraiser, assessor.

tasajear, *va.* (Am.) to cut (meat) for making jerked beef; to slash, cut to pieces.

tasajo, *m.* jerked beef, hung beef.

tasar, *va.* to appraise; to rate; to tax; to regulate, to keep within bounds; to stint.

tascador, *m.* brake for dressing flax.

tascar, *va.* (*pret.* TASQUÉ; *subj.* TASQUE) to brake, scutch, or dress (flax, hemp); to nibble, crunch, browse, graze.—**t. el freno,** (of horses) to bite the bridle; to resist.

tasco, *m.* refuse of flax or hemp; (naut.) topping of hemp.

tasconio, *m.* tasco, a kind of clay.

tasqué, tasque, *v. V.* TASCAR.

tasquera, *f.* row, quarrel, wrangle, scuffle.

tasquil, *m.* chip from a stone.

tastana, *f.* (agr.) hard crust on the soil caused by dryness; membrane inside a fruit, as in oranges.

tástara, *f.* coarse bran.

tastaz, *m.* polishing powder from old crucibles.

tasto, *m.* bad taste of tainted food.

tasugo, *m.* (zool.) badger.

tata, *m.* (Am., coll.) dad, daddy; nursemaid; younger sister.

tatabra, *f.,* **tatabro,** *m.* (Colomb.) (zool.) a species of peccary.

tatarabuela, *f.* great-great-grandmother.

tatarabuelo, *m.* great-great-grandfather.

tataradeudo, da, *n.* very old distant relative.

tataranieto, ta, *n.* great-great-grandson(-daughter).

tatas.—andar a t., to walk timidly; to go on all fours.

¡tate! *interj.* take care! beware! stay, so it is.

¹tato, ta, *a.* stammering.

²tato, *m.* (Arg., Chile) (coll.) little brother.

³tato, *m.* (Am.) = TATÚ.

tatú, *m.* a variety of giant armadillo.

tatuaje, *m.* tattooing; tattoo.

tatuar, *va. & vr.* to tattoo.

tatusa, *f.* (Arg., Bol.) little woman; woman of no account.

taugel, *m.* batten.

taujía, *f.* damaskeening.

taumaturgia, *f.* thaumaturgy, miracle working.

taumaturgo, *m.* miracle worker, thaumaturge.

taurino, na, *a.* taurine, bovine.

taurios, *a. pl.* taurine, bullfighting (games).

Tauro, *m.* (astr.) Taurus, sign of the zodiac.

taurómaco, ca. I. *a.* pertaining to bullfighting. **II.** *n.* bullfight fan; *m.* bullfighter.

tauromaquia, *f.* bullfighting.

tauromáquico, ca, *a.* pert. to bullfighting.

tautología, *f.* (rhet.) tautology.

taxativamente, *adv.* limitedly.

taxativo, va, *a.* (law) restricted, conditioned.

taxi, *m.* taxi, taxicab.

taxidermia, *f.* taxidermy.

taxidermista, *n.* taxidermist.

taxímetro, *m.* (auto) taximeter; taxicab, taxi.

taxonomía, *f.* taxonomy.

taxonómico, ca, *a.* taxonomic.

taz a taz, *adv.* tit for tat.

taza, *f.* cup; cupful; bowl; basin of a fountain; cup guard of a sword.

tazaña, *f.* = TARASCA, figure of a dragon.

tazar, *va. & vr.* to fray.

tazmía, *f.* share of tithes; tithe register.

tazón, *m. aug.* large bowl; basin.

té, *m.* tea.—**t. bailable,** tea dance, tea with dancing.—**t. de borde,** or **de Méjico,** (bot.) saltwort.

¹te, *pers. & refl. pron., obj. case* of TÚ, thee, to thee; thyself; (when on familiar terms with someone) you, to you; yourself.

²te, *f.* name of the letter *t*.

tea, *f.* candlewood; torch, firebrand; (naut.) hawse for raising the anchor.

teame, teamide, *f.* stone said to repel iron.

teatino, na, *n.* Theatin.

teatral, *a.* theatrical.

teatralmente, *adv.* theatrically.

teátrico, ca, *a.* theatrical.

teatro, *m.* theatre; stage; collection of plays; dramatic art.

tebaico, ca, *a.* Thebaic.

tebaína, *f.* (chem.) thebaine.

tebano, na; **tebeo, a,** *n. & a.* Theban.

teca, *f.* (bot.) teak; teakwood.

tecalí, *m.* (Mex.) transparent marble.

tecla, *f.* key (of a piano, organ, typewriter, etc.); delicate point.—**dar en la t.,** to strike it right, to find the way.—**tocar una t.,** to get up a scheme, to resort to some expedient.

teclado, *m.* keyboard.

tecle, *m.* (naut.) single purchase.

teclear. I. *vn.* to finger a keyboard; to drum with the fingers. **II.** *va.* (coll.) to resort to (an expedient), to try (some scheme).

tecleo, *m.* drumming on a keyboard, striking t[ ] keys; scheming, trying.

técnica, *f.* technique; technical ability.

técnicamente, *adv.* technically.

tecnicismo, *m.* technical term; technical vocab[ ]lary; technicism.

técnico, ca. I. *a.* technical. **II.** *n.* technical e[ ]pert.

tecnología, *f.* technology.

tecnológico, ca, *a.* technological, technical.

tecol, *m.* (Mex.) maguey caterpillar.

tecolote, *m.* (Mex., C. A.) owl.

tecomate, *m.* (Mex.) gourd, canteen.

tectibranquio, quia. I. *m. & a.* (zool.) tec[ ] branch. **II.** *m. pl.* Tectibranchia.

techado, *m.* roof; ceiling; shed.

techar, *va.* to roof; to cover with a roof.

techo, *m.,* TECHUMBRE; (aer.) absolute ceiling.— **t. de servicio,** or **utilizable,** (aer.) servi[ ] ceiling.

techumbre, *f.* ceiling; roof; top (as of vehicle[ ] cover; shed.

tedero, *m.* torch holder.

tedéum, *m.* (eccl.) Te Deum.

tediar, *va.* to loathe, hate, abhor.

tedio, *m.* tediousness, ennui.

tedioso, sa, *a.* tedious, boresome, tiresome.

tegual, *m.* ancient tax on fish.

teguillo, *m.* thin board, strip.

tegumento, *m.* tegument.

teína, *f.* (chem.) thein.

teinada, *f.* cattle shed.

teísmo, *m.* theism.—**teísta,** *n. & a.* theist(-i[ ]

¹teja, *f.* roof tile; steel bar shaped into a swo[ ] blade; (naut.) hollow cut for scarfing.—**t. có[ ] cava,** gutter or pantile.—**t. de la silla,** (Mex[ ] cantle of saddle.—**a t. vana,** with a shed ove[ ] —**a toca t.,** in cash, cash down.—**de teja[ ] abajo,** in the world of nature, in this world.— **de tejas arriba,** in the realm of the supe[ ] natural, beyond the realm of nature.

²teja, *f.* (bot.) linden tree.

tejadillo, *m. dim.* roof of a coach; projecting si[ ] roof; card sharp's method of holding the talo[ ]

tejado, *m.* roof; shed.

tejamaní, tejamanil, *m.* shingle.

tejar. I. *va.* to tile. **II.** *m.* tile works, tile kiln.

tejaroz, *m.* eaves, penthouse, tiled shed.

tejedera, *f.* TEJEDORA; (entom.) water skater.

tejedor, ra, *n.* weaver; (entom.) water skippe[ ]

tejedura, *f.* texture, weaving, fabric.

tejeduría, *f.* art of weaving; mill, factory f[ ] weaving.

tejemaneje, *m.* (coll.) cleverness, knack.

tejer, *va.* to weave; to wattle, interweave, pla[ ] (Am.) to knit; to regulate, adjust; to devise.

tejera, tejería, *f.* tile kiln.

tejero, *m.* tile maker.

tejica, illa, ita, *f. dim.* small tile.

tejido, da. I. *pp.* of TEJER.—**alambre t.,** wi[ ] netting. **II.** *m.* texture, tissue, weaving; fabr[ ] web; (anat.) tissue.—**t. de alambre,** wire mes[ ]

tejillo, *m.* plaited girdle.

¹tejo, *m.* quoit; game of quoits; shuffleboa[ ] counter; blank, metal disk or plate; (mech[ ] bush, pillow block, socket, socket plate.

²tejo, *m.* (bot.) yew tree.

tejocote, *m.* (bot., Mex.) a sloelike fruit.

tejoleta, *f.* broken tile, brickbat; shuffleboa[ ] counter; clapper.

tejolote, *m.* (Mex.) stone pestle.

¹tejón, *m.* round gold ingot.

²tejón, *m.* (zool.) badger.

tejonera, *f.* burrow of a badger.

tejuela, *f.* small tile; brickbat; saddletree.

tejuelo, *m.* small tile; (bookbinding) binde[ ] title; (mech.) bush, pillow block, socket, so[ ] plate.

tela, *f.* cloth, fabric, stuff; chain or warp of clot[ ] pellicle, film; skin (of an onion, etc.); quibbl[ ] quirk; web of insects; argument; matter; thread of a discourse; membrane or opacity in the eye. —**t. de alambre,** wire cloth, wire screening.— **t. de araña,** cobweb, spider web.—**t. de cebolla,** thin cloth.—**t. metálica** = T. DE ALAMBRE. —**en t. de juicio,** in doubt; under careful consideration.

telamón, *m.* (arch.) telamon, atlante.

telar, *m.* loom; frame; (theat.) gridiron.

telaraña, *f.* cobweb; flimsy or trifling thing.— **mirar las telarañas,** (coll.) to be absentminded.—**tener telarañas en los ojos,** to be blind to one's surroundings.

telarejo, *f. dim.* small loom or frame.

telecomunicación, *f.* telecommunication, long-distance communication.

telefio, *m.* (bot.) orpine stonecrop.

telefonear, *va. & vn.* to telephone.

telefonema, *m.* telephone message.

telefonía, *f.* telephony.—**t. sin hilos,** wireless telephony, radiotelephony.

telefónicamente, *adv.* telephonically.

telefónico, ca, *a.* telephonic.

telefonista, *n.* telephone operator.

teléfono, *m.* telephone.—**t. automático,** dial telephone.—**t. sin hilos,** wireless telephone.

telefoto, *m.* telephoto.

telefotografía, *f.* telephotography.

telegrafía, *f.* telegraphy.—**t. sin hilos,** wireless telegraphy.

telegrafiar, *va.* to telegraph; to cable.

telegráficamente, *adv.* telegraphically.

telegráfico, ca, *a.* telegraphic.

telegrafista, *n.* telegrapher, telegraph operator.

telégrafo, *m.* telegraph.—**t. marino,** nautical signals; signal service.—**t. óptico,** semaphore. —**t. sin hilos,** wireless telegraph.—**hacer telégrafos,** to talk by signs (as lovers).

telegrama, *m.* telegram; cablegram.

telemecánica, *f.* long-distance transmission or production of motion.

telemetría, *f.* telemetry.

telemétrico, ca, *a.* telemetric.

telémetro, *m.* telemeter.

teleobjetivo, *m.* telephotographic object glass.

teleología, *f.* teleology.

teleológico, ca, *a.* teleological.

teleósteo, a. I. *n. & a.* (zool.) teleost. **II.** *m. pl.* Teleostei.

telepatía, *f.* telepathy.

telepático, ca, *a.* telepathic.

telera, *f.* plow pin; cattle stall, cattle pen; (mech.) jaw, cheek (of a clamp, vice, or press); body transom, cross frame, tiebeam (of carriage); (artil.) transom of a gun-carriage; (naut.) rack block; (min.) pyramidal mound of copper ore for roasting; round loaf of brown bread.

telero, *m.* stake (of a cart).

telescópico, ca, *a.* telescopic.

telescopio, *m.* telescope.

teleta, *f.* blotting paper; sieve in paper mills.

teletón, *m.* strong silken stuff.

televisión, *f.* television.—**receptor de t.,** television set.

telilla, *f. dim.* light woollen stuff; film.

telina, *f.* = ALMEJA, clam; mussel.

telita, *f. dim.* of TELA; thin fabric.

telón, *m.* (theat.) curtain, drop curtain; drop, drop scene.—**t. de boca,** drop curtain.—**t. de foro,** drop scene.—**bajar,** or **correr, el t.,** to drop the curtain.—**levantar,** or **subir, el t.,** to raise the curtain.

telonio, *m.* ancient tax office.—**a manera de t.,** in a jumble, disordered.

telúrico, ca, *a.* telluric.

telurio, *m.* (chem.) tellurium.

tellina, *f.* = TELINA.

telliz, *m.* caparison, saddle cover.

telliza, *f.* bedspread, coverlet.

tema. I. *m.* theme, subject; text, thesis; (mus.)

theme, motive.—**t. celeste,** (astr.) map of the heavens. **II.** *f.* fixed idea of a madman; hobby; dispute, contention; obstinacy; animosity, grudge.—**a t.,** emulously, in competition.

temario, *m.* agenda.—**comisión del t.,** Agenda Committee.

temático, ca, *a.* thematic; obstinate.

tembladal, *m.* quaking bog, quagmire.

tembladera, *f.* a kind of bowl or cup of very thin metal or glass; (jewelry) TEMBLEQUE; (ichth.) torpedo, electric ray; (bot.) quaking grass.

tembladero, *m.* quagmire.

temblador, ra. I. *a.* quaking, shaking, quivering. **II.** *m.* Quaker.

temblante. I. *a.* trembling, quavering. **II.** *m.* loose bracelet.

temblar, *vn.* (*ind.* TIEMBLO; *subj.* TIEMBLE) to tremble, shake, quake, quiver; to shiver.

tembleque, *m.* a hair ornament on a spiral wire.

temblequear, tembletear, *vn.* (coll.) to tremble, shake, shiver.

temblón, na, *a.* tremulous, shaking.—**hacer la temblona,** to affect timidity.

temblor, *m.* trembling, tremor, thrill.—**t. de tierra,** earthquake.—**temblorcillo,** *m. dim.* slight tremor.—**tembloroso, sa; tembloso, sa,** *a.* trembling, tremulous, shivering, shaking.

temedero, ra, *a.* dread, redoubtable.

temedor, ra, *a.* dreading, fearing.

temer, *va. & vn.* to fear, dread.

temerariamente, *adv.* rashly, recklessly.

temerario, ria, *a.* rash, imprudent, unwise; reckless; hasty, unreflecting.

temeridad, *f.* temerity, rashness, recklessness; folly, rash or reckless act; foolhardiness; rash conclusion.

temerón, na, *a.* affecting courage.

temerosamente, *adv.* timorously.

temeroso, sa, *a.* dread; timid; timorous; chicken-hearted; afraid.—**t. de Dios,** God-fearing.

temible, *a.* dread, terrible, redoubtable.

temor, *m.* dread, fear.

temoso, sa, *a.* obstinate, stubborn.

tempanador, *m.* cutter for beehives.

tempanar, *va.* to cover the tops of (beehives).

témpano, *m.* (mus.) kettledrum; tabor, timbrel; drumhead, drumskin; tympan; piece, block; ice floe, iceberg; sod, sward; heading of a barrel; flitch of bacon; cork dome of a beehive; (arch.) tympan of an arch.—**t. de tocino,** flitch of bacon.

temperación, *f.* tempering.

temperadamente, *adv.* temperately.

temperamento, *m.* climate; arbitration, compromise; temperament, constitution; (mus.) temperament.

temperancia, *f.* temperance.

temperante, *a.* (med.) tempering.

temperar. I. *va.* to temper; to soften. **II.** *vn.* (Am.) to have a change of climate; to summer.

temperatura, *f.* temperature.

temperie, *f.* atmospheric conditions.

tempero, *m.* seasonableness.

tempestad, *f.* tempest, storm.

tempestivamente, *adv.* fitly, opportunely.

tempestividad, *f.* opportuneness, timeliness.

tempestivo, va, *a.* opportune, timely.

tempestuosamente, *adv.* stormily, turbulently.

tempestuoso, sa, *a.* tempestuous, stormy.

¹templa, *f.* (art) tempera, distemper.

²templa, *f. gen. pl.* (anat.) temple(s).

templadamente, *adv.* temperately, moderately, abstemiously.

templadera, *f.* (hydraul.) sluice gate.

templado, da. I. *pp.* of TEMPLAR. **II.** *a.* moderate (esp. of climate, as **tierra templada,** [region of] moderate climate or medium temperature); hardened, tempered; abstemious; lukewarm; medium, fair; brave, firm; (mus.) tuned.

templador, ra. I. *n.* tuner; temperer. **II.** *m.*

(mus.) tuning key; (Peru) circular stockade in bull rings.

templadura, *f.* temper, tempering; tuning.

templanza, *f.* temperance, moderation, sobriety; mildness of temperature or climate; (art) good disposition of colors.

templar. I. *va.* to temper, soften, moderate; to quench, allay; to calm, pacify; to prepare, dispose; to temper, quench (metals); to anneal (glass); (mus.) to tune; (art) to blend; (naut.) to trim (the sails) to the wind; (falconry) to train.—**templarle la gaita a uno,** to humor one. **II.** *vr.* to be moderate.

templario, *m.* templar.

¹**temple,** *m.* atmospheric conditions; temper (of metals, of persons); courage; disposition, frame of mind; average; (mus.) temperament.—**al t.** (art) in distemper.

²**temple,** *m.* religion of the Templars, and one of their temples.

templete, *m. dim.* small temple, shrine; (arch.) niche, tabernacle.

templista, *m.* (art) painter in distemper.

templo, *m.* temple; church; shrine.

témpora, *f.* —*pl.* (eccl.) ember days.

temporada, *f.* season, spell, period (of time).—**t. de frío,** cold spell.—**t. de invierno,** winter season.—**t. de ópera,** opera season.—**estar de t.,** to be summering or rusticating.

¹**temporal. I.** *a.* temporal; temporary; provisional; secular, worldly. **II.** *m.* tempest, storm; weather (good or bad); long rainy spell; temporary laborer.

²**temporal,** *a.* (anat.) temporal.

temporalidad, *f.* temporality.

temporalizar, *va.* (*pret.* TEMPORALICÉ; *subj.* TEMPORALICE) to make temporary.

temporalmente, *adv.* temporarily; provisionally, transiently; in a worldly manner.

temporáneo, nea; temporario, ria, *a.* temporary, unstable, transient.

temporejar, *vn.* (naut.) to lie to.

temporero, ra; temporil, *a.* temporary (laborer), working by the season.

temporizar, *vn.* (*pret.* TEMPORICÉ; *subj.* TEMPORICE) to pass the time; to temporize.

tempranal, *a.* producing early fruits.

tempranamente, *adv.* prematurely.

tempranero, ra, *a.* early.

tempranilla, *f.* early grape.

temprano, na. I. *a.* early. **II.** *m. adv.* early; prematurely, too early. **III.** *n.* field yielding early crops.

temulento, ta, *a.* intoxicated, tipsy, drunk.

ten.—**t. con t.,** tact, adroitness, wisdom.

tena, *f.* shed for cattle, fold.

¹**tenacear,** *va.* to tear off flesh of with pincers.

²**tenacear,** *vn.* to persist.

tenacero, *m.* tongs maker.

tenacidad, *f.* tenacity, toughness; tenaciousness, pertinacity, perseverance, persistence.

tenacillas, *f. pl. dim.* small tongs; snuffers; tweezers, nippers, pincers, pliers; curling iron; sugar tongs; cigarette sliding tongs.

tenáculo, *m.* (surg.) tenaculum.

tenada, *f.* fold, shed for cattle.

tenallas, *f. pl.* pair of tongs.

tenallón, *m.* (fort.) tenail or tenaille.

tenante, *m.* (her.) supporter (of a shield).

tenaz, *a.* tenacious, adhesive; strong, firm; stubborn; tough; persevering.

tenaza, *f.* (fort.) tenail; claw (as of lobsters).—*pl.* tongs, nippers, pliers; (dent.) forceps; (card playing) two cards that take the last two tricks.

tenazada, *f.* grasp of pincers or tongs; noise or click of the tongs; violent biting.

tenazmente, *adv.* tenaciously.

tenazón, *f.*—**a t.,** point-blank, without taking aim.—**parar de t.,** to stop (a horse) short in his course.

tenazuelas, *f. pl. dim.* tweezers.

tenca, *f.* (ichth.) tench.

tención, *f.* holding, retaining.

tendajo, *m.* small rickety shop.

tendal, *m.* tent, awning, tilt; piece of canvas placed under olive trees when picking the fruit.

tendalera, *f.* (coll.) things scattered in disorder.

tendalero, m., tendedero, *m.* place where clothes are spread to dry.

tendedor, ra, *n.* stretcher, tenter; one who spreads clothes to dry.

tendedura, *f.* stretching, extending.

tendejón, *m.* small rickety shop.

tendel, *m.* (mason.) leveling line (cord); layer of mortar.

tendencia, *f.* tendency; trend, drift.

ténder, *m.* (Angl.) (Ry.) tender.

tender (*ind.* TIENDO; *subj.* TIENDA) **I.** *va.* to stretch, stretch out; to spread out; to hang out (washing); to lay (tablecloth); to lay (rails, etc.), throw (a bridge across a river), etc. (in emergency building as for military purposes); (mason.) to coat. **II.** *vn.* to have a tendency, tend; (**hacia**) (math.) to approach (as a limit). **III.** *vr.* to stretch out, lie full length; to place one's cards on the table; to run at full gallop; to neglect a business.

tenderete, *m.* a card game; (Mex.) second-hand-clothing shop.

tendero, ra, *n.* shopkeeper; tentmaker.

tendezuela, *f. dim.* small shop.

tendidamente, *adv.* diffusely, diffusively.

tendido. I. *pp.* of TENDER. **II.** *m.* row of seats; in lace making, piece made over the pattern; quantity of spread clothes dried at once; batch of bread baked at one time; (mason.) coat of plaster or calcimine; (arch.) roof of a house from the ridge to the eaves; (Am. min.) riffle.

tendiente. I. *pres. p.* of TENDER. **II.** *a.* (a) intended (for).

tendinoso, sa, *a.* tendinous, pert. to tendon.

tendón, *m.* (anat.) tendon.—**t. de Aquiles,** (anat.) Achilles' tendon.

tenducha, tenducho, *n.* insignificant shop.

tenebrario, *m.* (eccl.) tenebræ candelabrum.

tenebrosamente, *adv.* gloomily.

tenebrosidad, *f.* darkness, gloom.

tenebroso, sa, *a.* tenebrous, dark, gloomy.

tenedero, *m.* (naut.) anchoring ground.

tenedor, *m.* holder; keeper; guardian; table fork; (ball games) caddy; (com.) holder.—**t. de bastimentos,** (naut.) storekeeper of the navy.—**t. de libros,** bookkeeper.—**t. de póliza,** policy-holder.

teneduría, *f.* position of bookkeeper.—**t. de libros,** bookkeeping.

tenencia, *f.* tenancy, occupancy, possession, holding; (mil.) lieutenancy, lieutenantship.

tener. I. *va.* (*ind. pres.* yo TENGO, él TIENE, *pret.* TUVE; *fut.* TENDRÉ *ind.*; *sub.* TENGA) to have, possess; to hold, take hold of; (app. to health) to be the matter with, to ail; to be worth (*Juan tiene cien mil pescs,* John is worth 100,000 pesos); to maintain, sustain; to subject; domineer; to keep, hold, retain; to stop, hold back; to fulfil, keep (one's word); to contain, have within; (app. to dimensions) to be (*la casa tiene 20 metros de ancho,* the house is 20 meters wide). With nouns of time, it denotes duration or age (*el niño tiene seis meses,* the child is six months old; *esta casa tiene cien años,* this house is one hundred years old). With some nouns denoting sensation or feeling, it is equivalent to "to be" followed by the corresponding adjective (*tener hambre,* to be hungry; *tener sueño,* to be sleepy; *tener celos* (*de*), to be jealous (of); *tener calor,* (of person) to be cold, hot; *tener miedo* (*de*) (*a*), to be afraid (to) (of).—**t. a bien,** to find it convenient; to please; to deem best.—**t. buenas formas,** to be of fine figure; to be

For pronunciation, see the rules at the beginning of the book.

polite.—**t. cuidado de,** to take care to.—**t. de** (foll. by *a.*) to be (often with there): *eso no tiene nada de estraño,* there is nothing strange about that.—**t. días,** (coll.) to be old; to have moody days.—**t. efecto,** to take effect, become effective.—**t. en,** to hold in (esteem, respect, etc.).—**t. en cuenta,** to take into account, or consideration, take account of.—**t. en menos,** to think little of.—**t. gana,** or **ganas, (de),** to wish, desire (to); to have a mind (to); to feel like.—**t. gracia,** to be funny.—**t. gusto en,** to be glad to.—**t. la bondad de** (*inf.*), (in requests), have the kindness to (*inf.*), please, kindly (*imper.*).—**t. la culpa (de),** to be to blame (for).—**t. lugar,** (Gal.) to take place, occur.—**t. para sí,** to think, be of the opinion. —**t. por,** to take to be, believe, consider.—**t. presente,** to bear in mind.—**t. prisa,** to be in a hurry.—**t. que,** to have to, must; to have something to (say, lose, propose, etc.).—**t. que hacer,** to have something to do; to be busy; to have to, or must, do.—**t. que ver con,** to have to do with.—**t. razón,** to be right.—**t. suerte,** to be lucky.—**no t. razón,** to be wrong.—**no t. remedio,** not to be any help for, can't be helped.—**no tenerias todas consigo,** to be worried, to be anxious.—**no t. sobre que caerse muerto,** not to have a farthing, to be penniless. **II.** *v. aux.* to have (*tengo dicho,* I have said). Often, however, the participle following is rather an adjective than part of a compound tense (*tengo escritas dos cartas,* I have two letters written). In other cases, the combination is equivalent to a simple form of the verb (*tengo entendido,* I understand; *tengo pensado,* I intend). **III.** *vn.* to have, possess; to be well-off, to be wealthy.—**t. de,** to have to, must. **IV.** *vr.* to hold fast or steady; to rest (on something); to stop, halt; to fight, hold one's own; to adhere (to), stand (for).—**t. en pie,** to keep on one's feet, remain standing.

tenería, *f.* tannery.
tenesmo, *m.* (med.) tenesmus.
tengo, tenga, *v. V.* TENER.
tenia, *f.* tapeworm; (arch.) fillet.
tenienta, *f.* wife of a first lieutenant.
tenientazgo, *m.* (mil.) first lieutenantship.
teniente. I. *pres. p.* of TENER. **II.** *a.* (of fruit) unripe; miserly, mean; (coll.) dear.—**t. de oídos,** hard of hearing. **III.** *m.* deputy, substitute; (mil.) first lieutenant.—**t. coronel,** lieutenant colonel.—**t. general,** lieutenant general.
tenífugo, ga, *a.* (med.) tænifuge.
tenis, *m.* lawn tennis.—**tenista, tennista,** *n. & a.* tennis (as *a.*) (player).
¹**tenor,** *m.* condition, nature; kind; import, literal meaning.—**a este t.,** of the same kind, like.— **a t. de,** in compliance with.
²**tenor,** *m.* (mus.) tenor.
¹**tensión,** *f.* tension; tensile stress; tautness, tightness; strain; (elec.) voltage, potential, tension. —**t. arterial,** blood pressure.
²**tensión,** *f.* = TENSÓN.
tenso, sa, *a.* tense, tight, taut, stretched.
tensón, *f.* (poet.) poetical contest on love.
tensor, ra. I. *a.* tensile. **II.** *m.* turnbuckle; tightener.
tentación, *f.* temptation.
tentacioncilla, *f. dim.* slight temptation.
tentaculado, da, *a.* (zool.) tentacled.
tentaculífero, ra. I. *a.* (zool.) tentacled. **II.** *m. pl.* Tentaculifera.
tentáculo, *m.* tentacle.
tentadero, *m.* corral for taming calves.
tentador, ra, *n. & a.* tempter(-ing).—**el t.,** the devil.
tentadura, *f.* mercury test of silver ore.
tentalear, *va.* to feel all over, examine by touch.
tentar, *va.* (*ind.* TIENTO; *subj.* TIENTE) to touch,

to feel with the fingers, to examine by touch; to grope; to tempt; to attempt, try, endeavor; to test; (surg.) to probe; to tent.—**t. cerrojos,** to try all ways and means.
tentativa, *f.* attempt; first examination.
tentativo, va, *a.* tentative.
tentemozo, *m.* prop, support; pole prop; tumbler (a toy); QUIJERA, noseband straps (of bridle).
tentempié, *m.* (coll.) light luncheon, a bite.
tentenelaire, *n.* mulatto; half-breed.
tentón, *m.* (coll.) rough handling.
tenue, *a.* thin, tenuous, delicate; worthless, trifling; soft (consonant); (art) faint, subdued.
tenuemente, *adv.* slightly.
tenuidad, *f.* tenuity, thinness, subtlety; weakness; trifle.
tenuta, *f.* (law) provisional tenure.
tenutario, ria, *a.* (law) provisional tenant.
tenzón, *f.* poetical contest on love.
teñidura, *f.* art of dyeing or tingeing.
teñir, *va.* (*pp.* TEÑIDO, TINTO; *ger.* TIÑENDO; *ind. pres.* TIÑO, *pret.* él TIÑÓ; *subj.* TIÑA) to tinge, to dye; to stain; (art.) to darken, sadden (a color).—**t. en rama,** to dye in grain, to ingrain.
teobroma, *m.* cacao.
teobromina, *f.* (chem.) theobromine.
teocalí, *m.* teocalli, Aztec ceremonial building.
teocracia, *f.* theocracy.
teocrático, ca, *a.* theocratic.
teodicea, *f.* (theol.) theodicy.
teodolito, *m.* theodolite.
teodosiano, na, *a.* Theodosian.
teogonía, *f.* theogony, origin of the gods.
teogónico, ca, *a.* theogonic.
teologal, *a.* theologic(al).
teología, *f.* theology.
teológicamente, *adv.* theologically.
teológico, ca, *a.* theologic(al).
teologismo, *m.* excessive theologizing, theological mania.
teologizar, *vn.* (*pret.* TEOLOGICÉ; *subj.* TEOLOGICE) to theologize.
teólogo, ga. I. *a.* theological. **II.** *m.* theologian.
teorema, *m.* theorem.
teoría, teórica, *f.* theory.
teóricamente, *adv.* theoretically.
teórico, ca. I. *a.* theoretical. **II.** *n.* theorist, theorizer.
teorizar, *vn.* to theorize.
teoso, sa, *a.* resinous.
teosofía, *f.* theosophy.—**teosófico, ca,** *a.* theosophical.—**teósofo,** *m.* theosophist.
tepalcate, *m.* (Mex.) potsherd.
tepe, *m.* green sod, turf.
tepeguaje. I. *m.* (Mex.) a very hard and compact wood. **II.** *a.* (Mex.) set, obstinate.
tepeizcuinte, *m.* (Am.) badger.
tepetate, *m.* (min.) attle, deads, refuse.
tepexilote, *m.* a palm nut used for beads.
tequiche, *m.* (Venez.) corn meal with coconut milk and molasses.
tequila, *m.* (Mex.) tequila (plant and liqueur made from it).
tequío, *m.* (Mex.) a municipal duty or tax.
terapeuta, *m. & f.* one of the Therapeutae (Jewish mystics); (med.) therapeutist.
terapéutica, *f.* therapeutics.
terapéutico, ca, *a. & n.* therapeutic(-ist).
teratología, *f.* (biol.) teratology.
teratológico, ca, *a.* teratologic(al).
terbio, *m.* (chem.) terbium.
tercamente, *adv.* obstinately, stubbornly.
tercena, *f.* wholesale tobacco warehouse.
tercenal, *m.* (agr.) rick of thirty sheaves.
tercenista, *m.* keeper of a TERCENA.
tercer, *a.* (*contr.* of TERCERO) third.
terceramente, *adv.* thirdly.
tercería, *f.* mediation, arbitration; umpirage; temporary occupation (of a fortress, etc.).

tercerilla, *f.* (poet.) triplet.
tercero, ra. I. *a.* third. **II.** *n.* procurer(-ess). **III.** *m.* third person; mediator, arbitrator, umpire; collector of tithes; (eccl.) tertiary; sixtieth of a second (time).—**t. en discordia,** umpire, referee between two disputants. **IV.** *f.* (mus.) third; ditone; third string of a guitar; sequence of three cards.
tercerol, *m.* (naut.) third in order.
tercerola, *f.* a short carbine; (com.) tierce.
tercerón, na, *n.* (Am.) mulatto.
terceto, *m.* (poet.) tierce, terzet, terza, triplet; (mus.) terzetto, trio.
tercia, *f.* one third; third of a vara; storehouse for tithes; among Romans, forenoon; sequence of three cards; (eccl.) third hour.
terciado, da. I. *pp.* of TERCIAR. **II.** *a.* slanting, tilted, biased, crosswise. **III.** *m.* cutlass, broad sword; broad ribbon.
terciana, *f.* (med.) tertian.
tercianario, ria. I. *a.* (med.) tertian; causing or suffering tertian fever. **II.** *n.* person affected with a tertian.
tercianela, *f.* heavy silk fabric.
terciar. I. *va.* to place sidewise or sling diagonally; to divide into three parts; (agr.) to plow the third time; (mil.) to carry (arms).—**t. una pieza,** (artil.) to prove a gun. **II.** *vn.* to make up a number; to mediate, arbitrate, to go between; to join (in conversation); to share, take part; to reach the third day. **III.** *vr.* to be favorable, offer an opportunity.
terciario, ria. I. *a.* third in order or degree; (geol.) Tertiary. **II.** *n.* (arch.) rib of a Gothic arch; (geol.) Tertiary.
terciazón, *m.* (agr.) third plowing.
tercio, cia. I. *a.* third. **II.** *m.* one third; each package of a mule load; (mil.) (Sp. hist.) regiment of infantry, (modern Sp.) Foreign Legion; division of the GUARDIA CIVIL; third part of a horse race course (start, run, or stop); third section in the height of a horse; third part of the rosary; third part of a sword.—*pl.* robust or strong limbs of a man.—**t. de cueros,** bundle of hides.—**t. de tabaco,** bale of tobacco.—**t. y quinto,** great advantage.—**hacer buen t.,** to do a good turn.—**hacer mal t.,** to do a bad turn, to serve ill.—**hacer t.,** to join and complete a required number of people.
terciopelado, da. I. *a.* velvetlike, velvety. **II.** *m.* velvetlike stuff.
terciopelero, ra, *n.* velvet weaver or worker.
terciopelo, *m.* velvet.
terco, ca, *a.* stubborn; hard (as marble).
terebintáceo, cea, *a.* (bot.) terebinthine.
terebinto, *m.* (bot.) terebinth.
terebrante, *a.* piercing (pain).
terenciano, na, *a.* Terentian.
tereniabín, *m.* white, sweetish, purgative substance from leaves of a certain plant.
tereques, *m. pl.* (Am., coll.) traps; duds, belongings.
teresiana, *f.* a kind of military cap.
tergiversación, *f.* tergiversation.
tergiversador, ra, *n.* & *a.* tergiversator(-ing).
tergiversar, *va.* to tergiversate.
teriaca, *f.* (pharm.) theriaca.
teriacal, *a.* (pharm.) theriac(al).
teristro, *m.* thin veil or shawl.
terliz, *m.* tick, ticking; tent cloth.
termal, *a.* thermal.
termas, *f. pl.* hot baths; hot springs.
termes, *m.* (entom.) termite. Also TERMITE.
térmico, ca, *a.* thermic, thermal.
termidor, *m.* Thermidor, eleventh month of the French-Revolution calendar.
terminación, *f.* termination, completion; (gram.) termination, ending.
terminacho, *m.* (coll.) big or vulgar word; jawbreaker.

terminador, ra. I. *a.* finishing, completing. **II.** *n.* finisher.
terminajo, *m.* (coll.) vulgar expression.
terminal. I. *a.* terminal, final, last. **II.** *m.* (elec.) terminal.
terminante, *a.* ending, closing; peremptory, final, decisive.—**terminantemente,** *adv.* peremptorily, positively.
terminar. I. *va.* to end, close, terminate, finish, complete. **II.** *vn.* **de** (*inf.*), to have just (*pp.*). **III.** *vn.* & *vr.* to end; to abut; (med.) to come to a crisis.
terminativo, va, *a.* (philos.) terminative.
término, *m.* end, ending, completion; term, word; boundary; landmark; manner, behavior; district of a town or city; aim, object, goal; crisis of a disease; condition, constitution, state; (math., logic) term; (arch.) terminal, terminus; (law) term; (mus.) tone, pitch.—*pl.* (logic and astrol.) terms.—**t. medio,** (math.) average; (logic) middle term; compromise.—**términos semejantes,** (math.) similar terms.—**en buenos términos,** (coll.) in plain language.—**en otros términos,** in other words.—**en último t.,** finally.—**medio t.,** compromise.—**medios términos,** evasions, subterfuges.—**poner t. a,** to put an end to, to stop.—**por t. medio,** on an average.—**primer t.,** (art) foreground.—**último t.,** (art) background.
terminología, *f.* terminology.
terminote, *m. aug.* big word.
termiónico, ca, *a.* (radio) thermionic.
termita, *f.* thermite.
termite, *m.* (entom.) termite, white ant.
termocauterio, *m.* (surg.) thermocautery.
termodinámica, *f.* thermodynamics.
termodinámico, ca, *a.* thermodynamic.
termoelectricidad, *f.* thermoelectricity.
termoeléctrico, ca, *a.* thermoelectric.
termógrafo, *m.* thermograph, self-registering thermometer.
termología, *f.* thermology, science of heat.
termometría, *f.* thermometry.
termométrico, ca, *a.* thermometric(al).
termómetro, *m.* thermometer.
termometrógrafo, thermograph, self-registering thermometer.
termomultiplicador, *m.* (phys.) thermopile.
termoquímica, *f.* thermochemistry.
termos, *m.* thermos bottle.
termoscopio, *m.* thermoscope.
termosifón, *m.* thermosiphon.
termóstato, *m.* thermostat.
termostático, ca, *a.* thermostatic.
terna, *f.* ternary, triad, tern; three names presented as candidates; a game at dice.
ternario, ria. I. *a.* ternary. **II.** *m.* three days' devotion.
terne, *m.* (coll.) bully, hector.
ternecico, ica, ito, ita, *a.* very tender.
ternejal, *a.* bullying.
ternejón, na, *a.* = TERNERÓN.
ternera, *f.* female calf; veal.
ternerico, ca; illo, lla; ito, ta, *n. dim.* young or little calf.
ternero, *m.* male calf.
ternerón, na, *a.* sentimental, easily moved.
terneruela, *f. dim.* suckling calf.
terneza, *f.* softness, suavity; tenderness; affection, endearment, fondness.
ternezuelo, la, *a. dim.* very tender.
ternilla, *f.* gristle, cartilage; nose or nostrils of an ox or other similar animal.—**llevar,** or **tener, de la t.,** to lead by the nose.
ternilloso, sa, *a.* gristly, cartilaginous.
ternísimo, ma, *a. super.* very tender.
terno, *m.* ternary, triad; suit of clothes; tern (in lottery); oath, curse; (eccl.) vestments for the high mass; (jewelry) set; (print.) three printed

sheets one within another.—**t. seco**, happy and unexpected fortune.

ternura, *f.* tenderness, softness, fondness.

terpeno, *m.* (chem.) terpene.—**terpina**, *f.* terpin.—**terpinol**, *m.* terpineol.

terquedad, *f.* stubbornness, obstinacy.

terracota, *f.* terra cotta.

terrada, *f.* bitumen made of ochre and glue.

terradillo, *m. dim.* small terrace.

terrado, *m.* terrace; flat roof of a house.

terraja, *f.* pipe stock, screw stock, diestock; screw-cutting machine; modelling board, sweep.

terraje, *m.* rent paid for arable land.

terrajero, *m.* lessee of arable land.

terral, *m.* land breeze.

terraplén, *m.* embankment; (Ry.) embankment, fill; (fort.) terreplein, banquette.

terraplenar, *va.* to embank; to fill; to make an embankment or terreplein for; to terrace.

terraplenador, *m.* laborer on embankments.

terrapleno, *m.* = TERRAPLÉN.

terráqueo, quea, *a.* terraqueous, terrestrial.

terrateniente, *n.* landowner, landholder.

terraza, *f.* terrace; border in a garden; glazed jar with two handles.

terrazgo, *m.* arable land; rent of arable land.

terrazguero, ra, *n.* lessee of arable land.

terrazo, *m.* (art) ground of a picture.

terrazuela, *f. dim.* of TERRAZA.

terrear, *vn.* to show the ground (as thin crops).

terrecer, *va.* to terrify.

terregoso, sa, *a.* full of clods, lumps of earth.

terremoto, *m.* earthquake.

terrenal, *a.* worldly, earthly, mundane.

terrenidad, *f.* quality of the soil.

terreno, na. I. *a.* earthly, terrestrial; worldly, mundane. **II.** *m.* land, ground, soil, terrene; piece of land, lot, plot; field, sphere of action; (geol.) terrane or terrain.—**t. abierto**, (mil.) open ground.—**t. franco**, (min.) tract not yet preëmpted or condemned.

térreo, rea, *a.* earthy, of soil.

terrera, *f.* steep piece of ground; (ornith.) lark.

terrero, ra. I. *a.* earthy; abject, humble; skimming the ground (as birds). **II.** *m.* terrace; mound, heap of earth; alluvium; (min.) dump; mark, target; basket for carrying earth.—**hacer t.**, to court a lady from the street before her house.

terrestre, *a.* terrestrial.

terrezuela, *f. dim.* small piece of ground; poor soil.

terribilidad, *f.* terribleness, awfulness; rudeness, fierceness.

terrible, *a.* terrible; rude, ill-tempered; (coll.) immense, huge; wonderful.

terriblemente, *adv.* terribly, frightfully.

terriblez, terribleza, *f.* = TERRIBILIDAD.

terrícola, *n.* inhabitant of the earth.

terrífico, ca, *a.* terrific, frightful.

terrígeno, na, *a.* terrigenous, earthborn.

terrino, na, *a.* earthy, of soil.

territorial, *a.* territorial.

territorialidad, *f.* territoriality.

territorio, *m.* territory; region; land.

terrizo, za. I. *a.* earthy, earthen. **II.** *m.* unglazed earthen tub.

terromontero, *m.* hill, hillock.

terrón, *m.* clod; mound; lump; bagasse of olives.—*pl.* landed property.—**a rapa t.**, entirely, completely, from the root.—**azúcar en t.**, lump sugar.

terroncillo, *m. dim.* small clod or lump.

terror, *m.* terror.—**terrorífico, ca**, *a.* terrific, frightful, dreadful.—**terrorismo**, *m.* terrorism.—**terrorista**, *n. & a.* terrorist(-ic).

terrosidad, *f.* earthiness, cloddiness.

terroso, sa, *a.* earthy; full of clods.

terruca, *f. dim.* (coll.) native country.

terruño, terruzo, *m.* piece of ground.

tersar, *va.* to smooth, polish, burnish.

tersidad, *f.* polish; terseness.

terso, sa, *a.* smooth, polished, glossy; pure, correct, terse, pithy.—**tersura**, *f.* smoothness, polish; cleanliness, purity, terseness.

tertil, *m.* ancient tax on silk.

tertulia, *f.* tertulia, social gathering for conversation or entertainment; party; conversation; (theat.) corridor.—**hacer t.**, to gather for conversation; to talk (esp. disturbing, as in an office).—**tertuliano, na**, *n.* one who attends a TERTULIA or makes TERTULIA.—**tertuliar**, *vn.* = HACER TERTULIA.

tertulio, lia; tertulista, *n.* = TERTULIANO.

teruelo, *m.* balloting urn or box.

teruncio, *m.* an ancient Roman coin.

terutero, *m.* (ornith.) terutero, a S. A. lapwing.

terzón, na, *a. & n.* three-year old (heifer).

terzuela, *f.* distribution gained for attending mass at the hour of tierce.

terzuelo, *m.* third part; male falcon.

tesálico, ca; tesaliense; tesalio, lia; tésalo, la, *n. & a.* Thessalian.

tesalonicense; tesalónico, ca, *a.* Thessalonian.

tesar. I. *va.* (naut.) to haul taut, to make taut. **II.** *vn.* (of oxen) to back, pull back.

tesauro, *m.* thesaurus, lexicon.

tesela, *f.* tessella, mosaic tile.

teselado, da, *a.* tessellate, tessellated.

tésera, *f.* tessera, token, countersign.

tesis, *f.* thesis, dissertation.

tesitura, *f.* (mus.) range of voice or instrument.

teso, sa. I. *a.* taut, drawn tight. **II.** *m.* brow of a hill; bulge or lump on a flat surface.

tesón, *m.* tenacity, firmness, inflexibility.

tesonería, *f.* obstinacy, stubbornness.

tesonero, ra, *a.* (Am.) persistent, tenacious.

tesorería, *f.* treasury, treasurer's office, exchequer; treasurership.

tesorero, ra, *n.* treasurer; (eccl.) canon who keeps the relics.

tesoro, *m.* treasure; treasury, exchequer; thesaurus, lexicon.

tespíades, *f. pl.* (poet.) the Muses.

testa, *f.* head; top or crown of the head; front, face, forepart; (coll.) brains, cleverness.—**t. coronada**, crowned head.—**t. de ferro** = TESTAFERRO.

testáceo, cea, *a. & m.* (zool.) crustacean.

testación, *f.* obliteration, erasure.

testada, *f.* = TESTARADA.

testado, da. I. *pp.* of TESTAR. **II.** *a.* testate.

testador, ra, *n.* testator.

testadura, *f.* obliteration, erasure.

testaférrea, testaferro, *m.* man of straw, dummy, figurehead.

testamentaría, *f.* (law) testamentary execution; estate; meeting of executors.

testamentario, ria. I. *a.* testamentary. **II.** *m.* executor. **III.** *f.* executrix.

testamento, *m.* testament, will.—**t. abierto**, nuncupative will.—**t. cerrado**, or escrito, sealed testament.—**t. nuncupativo**, nuncupative will.—**t. ológrafo**, holographic will.

testar. I. *vn.* to make a will or testament. **II.** *va.* to erase, scratch out.

testarada, *f.* blow with the head; stubbornness, obstinacy.

testarrón, na, *a.* (coll.) stubborn.—**testarronería** (coll.), **testarudez**, *f.* hardheadedness, stubbornness.

testarudo, da, *a.* stubborn, hardheaded.

teste, *m.* (anat.) testis, testicle.

testera, *f.* front face, fore part; forehead of an animal; crownpiece of a harness; back seat of a coach; (foundry) wall of a furnace.

testerada, *f.* = TESTARADA.

testero, *m.* = TESTERA; (min.) ore rock showing two faces.

testicular, *a.* testicular.

testículo, *m.* (anat.) testicle.
testificación, *f.* attestation, testification.
testificante, *a.* witnessing, attesting.
testificar, *va.* (*pret.* TESTIFIQUÉ; *subj.* TESTIFI-
QUE) to attest, witness, testify.
testificata, *f.* (law) affidavit.
testificativo, va, *a.* attesting, declaratory.
testifiqué, testifique, *v. V.* TESTIFICAR.
testigo. I. *n.* witness.—**t. de cargo,** witness for
the prosecution.—**t. de descargo,** witness for
the defense.—**t. de oídas,** auricular witness.—
t. de vista, or ocular, eyewitness. **II.** *m.* testimony, proof, evidence; mound of earth along
an excavation (to show amount of earth removed).
testimonial, *a.* of the nature of testimony, attesting.—**testimoniales,** *f. pl.* testimonial;
(eccl.) certificate of good character.
testimoniar, *va.* to attest, bear witness to.
testimoniero, ra, *a.* bearing false witness; dissembling, hypocritical.
testimonio, *m.* testimony; affidavit; attestation.
testimoñero, ra, *a.* hypocritical.
testón, *m.* silver coin having a head.
testudo, *m.* (mil.) testudo, movable shelter.
testuz, testuzo, *m.* (of some animals) nape; (of
others) forehead.
tesura, *f.* stiffness, tautness.
teta, *f.* teat, mammary gland, breast; nipple, dug,
udder.—**t. de vaca,** conical meringue; (bot.)
viper's grass; a kind of grape.—**dar la t.,** to
nurse, to suckle.
tetánico, ca, *a.* (med.) tetanic(al).
tétano, tétanos, *m.* (med.) tetanus, lockjaw.
tetar, *va.* to suckle.
tetera, *f.* teapot.
tetero, *m.* (Am.) nursing bottle.
tetica, *f. dim.* small dug or teat.
tetigonia, *f.* (entom.) a variety of katydid.
tetilla, *f. dim.* small nipple or teat (as man's).
tetón, *m.* stub of a pruned limb.
tetrácido, *m.* (chem.) tetracid.
tetracordio, *m.* (mus.) tetrachord, fourth.
tetradínamo, ma, *a.* (bot.) tetradynamous;
(chem.) tetravalent, quadrivalent.
tetraedro, *m.* (geom.) tetrahedron.
tetragrama, *m.* (mus.) four-line staff.
tetragrámaton, *m.* tetragram, word of four letters; tetragrammaton.
tetralogía, *f.* tetralogy.
tetrao, *m.* (zool.) capercaillie, wood grouse.
tetrarca, *m.* tetrarch.
tetrarquía, *f.* tetrarchate; tetrarchy.
tetrasílabo, ba, *a.* four-syllable (word).
tetrastilo, *m.* (arch.) tetrastyle.
tetravalente, *a.* (chem.) tetravalent, quadrivalent.
tétrico, ca, *a.* sad, grave, sullen; dark, gloomy.
teucalí, *m.* = TEOCALÍ.
teucrio, *m.* (bot.) germander.
teucro, cra, *a. & n.* Trojan.
teúrgia, *f.* theurgy, black magic.—**teúrgico, ca,**
a. theurgical.—**teúrgo, ga,** *n.* theurgist.
teutón, *n. & a.* Teuton(-ic).
teutónico, ca, *a.* Teutonic.
textil, *a.* textile; fibrous.
texto, *m.* text; quotation; textbook; (print.) great
primer type.
textorio, ria, *a.* textile.
textual, *a.* textual.—**textualista,** *m.* textualist.
textualmente, *adv.* textually, verbatim.
textura, *f.* texture; weaving; construction (of a
literary work); structure.
tez, *f.* complexion (of the face).
tezado, da, *a.* very black.
tezontle, *m.* (Mex.) porous building stone.
ti, *pron. 2d. pers. sing.* (oblique case of TÚ) thee;
(when on familiar terms with a person) you.
tía, *f.* aunt; (coll.) good old woman.—**cuéntaselo**

a tu t., (coll.) tell it to your grandmother.—
no hay tu t., there's no use; "nothing doing."
tialina, *f.* (chem.) ptyalin.
tialismo, *m.* (med.) ptyalism.
tiangue, tianguis, *m.* (Mex. and P. I.) market,
market days.
tiara, *f.* tiara, Pope's mitre; pontificate, papal
dignity; Persian headdress.
tiberio, *m.* (coll.) noise, hubbub, turmoil.
tibetano, na, *n. & a.* Tibetan.
tibia, *f.* (anat.) tibia, shin bone; (mus.) flute or
pipe.
tibiamente, *adv.* cooly, lukewarmly.
tibieza, *f.* tepidity, lukewarmness; coolness.
tibio, bia, *a.* tepid, lukewarm; remiss.
tibor, *m.* large china jar; (Am.) chamberpot.
tiborna, *f.* toast soaked in oil.
tiburón, *m.* (ichth.) shark.
tictac, *m.* ticking (of watch, etc.).
¹**tiemblo,** *m.* aspen tree.
²**tiemblo, tiemble,** *v. V.* TEMBLAR.
tiempo, *m.* time (as by the clock); time, times,
period, epoch; (mus.) tempo; (gram.) tense;
weather.—**t. atrás,** some time ago.—**t. cargado,** (naut.) thick, hazy weather.—**t. contrario,** (naut.) foul weather.—**t. crudo,** bleak,
raw weather.—**t. grueso,** hazy weather.—**t.
ha,** a long time ago.—**t. medio,** (astr.) mean
time.—**t. normal,** standard time.—**t. solar
verdadero,** or **t. verdadero,** (astr.) solar time.
—**abrir,** or **alzarse, el t.,** to clear up.—**andando el t.,** in time, in the course of time, in
the long run.—**a su t.,** at the proper time, in
due time.—**a t.,** timely, in, or on, time.—**a t.
que,** just as.—**a tiempos,** at times, occasionally.—**a un,** or **al, mismo t., a un t.,** at one,
at the same, time.—**cargarse el t.,** to cloud
over.—**con el t.,** in time, given time.—**cuánto
t.,** how long.—**dar t. al t.,** to bide one's time,
to wait patiently.—**de t. en t.,** from time to
time, now and then, occasionally.—**en otro t.,**
or **en otros tiempos,** formerly, in other, or
former, times.—**en t.,** on time, at the proper
time.—**engañar el t.** = HACER EL T.—**fuera
de t.,** out of season; inopportunely.—**ganar t.,**
to save time.—**hace t.,** or **tiempos,** long ago;
for a long time.—**hace t. que,** it is a long time
since.—**hacer el t.,** to kill time, while away the
time.—**haga buen o mal t.,** rain or shine.—
los buenos tiempos, the good, old days.—
matar el t. = HACER EL T.—**mucho t.,** a
long time.—**perder el t.,** to waste time.—**poco
t.,** a short time.—**por t.,** for some time.—
tomarse t., to take time, to defer.—**un t.,**
formerly, in other times.
tienda, *f.* shop, store; tent; (naut.) awning; tilt.
—**t. de campaña,** (mil.) tent.—**ir de tiendas,**
to go shopping.
tiendo, tienda, *v. V.* TENDER.
tiene, tienen, *v. V.* TENER.
tienta, *f.* (surg.) probe, bougie; cleverness, sagacity.—**andar a tientas,** to grope in the dark;
to fumble.—**a tientas,** in a groping manner.
tientaaguja, tientaguja, *f.* boring rod.
tientaparedes, *n.* groper.
¹**tiento,** *m.* touch, act of feeling; blind man's stick;
halter of a mill horse; circumspection, tact;
tightrope walker's balancing pole; steady
hand; (coll.) blow, cuff; (art) maulstick; (mus.)
preliminary flourish (before beginning to play);
(zool.) tentacle.—**a t.,** obscurely, doubtfully.—
con t., tactfully, cautiously.—**dar un t.,** to
make a trial.—**perder el t.,** to get out of practice, to get rusty.—**por el t.,** by the touch.—
tomar el t. a, to investigate, look into.
²**tiento, tiente,** *v. V.* TENTAR.
tiernamente, *adv.* tenderly.
tiernecico, ica, illo, illa, ito, ita, *a. dim.* of
TIERNO; very tender or young.
tierno, na, *a.* tender, soft; delicate; affectionate,

amiable; sensitive; recent, modern, young.—**t. de ojos**, tender-eyed.

tierra, *f.* earth; land; soil; ground; native country; region, country; lot, plot, piece of land; (elec.) ground.—*pl.* lands, parts, region.—**t. adentro**, inland.—**t. a t.**, (naut.) coasting; cautiously.—**t. de batán**, fuller's earth.—**t. de pan llevar**, cornland, plowland.—**T. de Promisión**, Promised Land.—**t. doblada**, broken, mountainous country.—**t. firme**, terra firma; mainland; firm, solid ground.—**t. japónica**, catechu, Japan earth.—**T. Santa**, Holy Land. —**a t.**, ashore.—**besar la t.**, (coll.) to fall flat on the ground, bite the dust.—**dar en t. con**, to overthrow.—**echar en t.**, (naut.) to land.— **echar por t.**, to overthrow; to ruin, destroy.— **echar t. a**, to hush up, forget, drop (a matter). —**en t.**, on land; ashore.—**irse a t.**, to fall down, to topple over.—**poner por t.**, to overthrow; to demolish, to tear down.—**por esas (estas) tierras**, thereabouts (hereabouts), in those (these) parts.—**por t.**, by land, overland. —**tomar t.**, to anchor; to land.—**venirse a t.**, = IRSE A. T.—**ver tierras**, to see the world, travel.

tiesamente, *adv.* firmly, stiffly, strongly.

¹**tieso, sa**, *a.* stiff, hard; robust, strong; valiant; stubborn, obstinate; tight, taut; stiff, stuck up; too grave or circumspect.—**tenerse t.**, or **tenérselas tiesas**, (coll.) to be firm in one's opinion or resolution.

²**tieso**, *adv.* = TIESAMENTE.

tiesta, *f.* edge of headings (of barrels).

tiesto, *m.* potsherd; flowerpot.

tiesura, *f.* stiffness; rigidity; harshness.

tifáceo, a, *a.* (bot.) typhaceous.

tífico, ca, *a.* (med.) typhous.

tiflitis, *f.* (med.) typhlitis.

¹**tifo**, *m.* (med.) typhus.—**t. asiático**, Asiatic cholera.—**t. de América**, yellow fever.—**t. de Oriente**, bubonic plague.

²**tifo, fa**, *a.* (coll.) satiate.

tifoideo, dea. I. *a.* typhoid. II. *f.* typhoid fever.

tifón, *m.* whirlwind; typhoon.

tifus, *m.* (med.) typhus.—**t. icterodes**, yellow fever.

tigra, *f.* (Am.) (zool.) female tiger.

tigre, *m.* (zool.) tiger.

tigridia, *f.* (bot.) tigridia, tiger flower.

tija, *f.* stem of a key.

tijera, *f.* (*usually in pl.*) scissors; shears; carpenter's horse; cooper's mare; any instrument in the form of an X; sawbuck; small channel or drain; sheepshearer; backbiter, slanderer.—*pl.* side stringers of a truck frame; beams across a river to stop floating timber.—**buena t.**, a great eater; good cutter; detractor, gossip.— **cama de t.**, folding bed, cot.—**hacer t.**, (of horses) to twist the mouth.

tijerada, *f.* = TIJERETADA.

tijereta, *f. dim.* (gen. *pl.*) small scissors; small tendril of vines; (entom.) earwig; (ornith.) forktail duck.

tijeretada, *f.*, **tijeretazo**, *m.* a cut with scissors, clip, snip.

tijeretear, *va.* to cut with scissors; clip; to meddle with, or mind (other people's business).

tijereteo, *m.* act of clipping; noise of scissors cutting.

tijerilla, tijeruela, *f. dim.* small scissors; small tendril of vines.

tila, *f.* (bot.) linden tree; flower of this tree; tea of linden flowers.

tílburi, *m.* (Angl.) tilbury, a kind of carriage.

tildar, *va.* to cross or scratch out; to put a tilde over; to brand, stigmatize, criticize.—**t. de**, to accuse of, or charge with being (incompetent, etc.).

tilde, *f.* tilde, diacritical sign of the letter *ñ*; tittle, dash, jot, iota; bad name.

tildón, *m. aug.* dash, stroke, scratch.

tilia, *f.* (bot.) = TILO.

tiliáceo, a, (bot.) tiliaceous.

tilichero, ra, *n.* (Am.) peddler, huckster.

tiliches, *m. pl.* (Am.) small fancy articles.

tilín, *m.* dingdong, sound of a bell.—**hacer t.**, (coll.) to please; to become a favorite.—**tener t.**, to be winsome, attractive.

tilma, *f.* (Mex.) cloak fastened by a knot.

tilo, *m.* (bot.) linden tree.

tilla, *f.* (naut.) midship, gangway.

tillado, *m.* wooden floor.

tillar, *va.* to floor, furnish with a floor.

timador, ra, *n.* swindler.

tímalo, *m.* (ichth.) grayling.

timar, *va.* to cheat, to swindle.

timba, *f.* (coll.) hand in a game of chance; (P. I.) bucket.

timbal, *m.* = ATABAL, kettledrum.

timbalero, *m.* kettledrummer.

timbirimba, *f.* (coll.) hand in a game of chance.

timbrar, *va.* to stamp; to put the crest in (a coat of arms).

timbre, *m.* (her.) timber, crest; seal, stamp; call bell; timbre, tone, color; glorious deed or achievement; merit.

timeleáceo, a. I. *a.* (bot.) thymelæaceous. II. *f. pl.* Thymelæaceæ.

timiama, *f.* a sweet perfume.

tímidamente, *adv.* timidly.

timidez, *f.* timidity; bashfulness.

tímido, da, *a.* timid, shy; faint-hearted.

¹**timo**, *m.* (ichth.) = TÍMALO, grayling.

²**timo**, *m.* (coll.) cheat, swindle.—**dar un t., to** swindle.

timocracia, *f.* (pol.) timocracy.

timocrático, ca, *a.* (pol.) timocratic.

timol, *m.* (chem.) thymol.

timón, *m.* beam of a plow; pole of a coach; stick of a rocket; (naut.) helm; rudder.—**t. de profundidad**, (aer.) elevator.

timonear, *va. & vn.* (naut.) to helm; to steer.

timonel, *m.* (naut.) helmsman, steersman.

timonera, *f.* (naut.) pilot house, wheelhouse; (ornith.) rectrix, large tail feather.

timonero, *m.* helmsman, steersman.

timorato, ta, *a.* God-fearing; timorous, chicken-hearted, pusilanimous.

timpa, *f.* bar of iron in a furnace hearth.

timpánico, ca, *a.* (anat.) tympanic.

timpanillo, *m. dim.* small kettledrum; small tympanum or tympan; (print.) inner tympan; (arch.) gablet.

timpanítico, ca, *a.* (med.) tympanitic.

timpanitis, *f.* (med.) tympanitis.

tímpano, *m.* kettledrum; (anat.) tympanum, eardrum; (print.) tympan; (arch.) tympan or tympanum, pediment.

tina, *f.* large earthen jar; vat; tub; bathtub.

tinaco, *m.* wooden trough, tub, or vat.

tinada, *f.* woodpile; shed for cattle.

tinado, tinador, *m.* shed for cattle.

tinaja, *f.* large earthen jar; (P. I.) a liquid measure (about 12⅔ gal.).

tinajería, *f.* place where large earthen jars are kept or sold.

tinajero, ra. I. *n.* maker or seller of earthen water jars. II. *m.* stand or cabinet for earthen water jars; (Mex.) water hole, pothole.

tinajita, uela, *f. dim.* small earthen water jar.

tinajón, *m. aug.* very large earthen water jar, or tank.

tindalo, *m.* (P. I.) tindalo, a hardwood tree.

tinelar, *a.* pertaining to the TINELO.

tinelero, ra, *n.* keeper of the servants' room.

tinelo, *m.* servants' dining room.

tineta, *f. dim.* kit, small tub.

tinge, *m.* (ornith.) a kind of black owl.

tingladillo, *m.* (naut.) clinker work.

tinglado, *m.* shed, shed roof; temporary board

floor; inclined plane for draining sugar; trick, machination, intrigue.

tingle, *f.* glaziers' lead opener.

tinicla, *f.* (armor) sort of hauberk.

tiniebla, *f.* (gen. *pl.*) darkness; (eccl.) tenebræ.

tinillo, *m.* tank for collecting must.

¹tino. *m.* skill in discovering things by the touch; steady and accurate aim; judgment, tact, knack.—**a buen t.,** at guesswork.—**sacar de t.,** to astound, confound, exasperate.—**sin t.,** immoderately; incessantly.

²tino, *m.* receptacle; dye vat; tank.

tinta, *f.* ink; tint, hue, color; process of dyeing.— *pl.* (art) colors prepared for painting.—**t. china,** India ink.—**t. de imprenta,** printing ink.—**t. simpática,** invisible ink.—**de buena t.,** from, or on, good authority.

tintar, *va.* to tinge, to dye.

tinte, *m.* dyeing, staining; tint, hue; paint, color, stain; dye; dyer's shop; (fig.) cloak, color.

tinterillada, *f.* chicane, trickery, tricky procedure.

tinterillo, *m. dim.* small inkstand; (Am.) (coll.) pettifogger; (Am.) shyster lawyer.

tintero, *m.* inkstand, inkwell; (print.) ink fountain, ink table.—**dejar, dejarse,** or **quedársele a uno, en el t.,** (coll.) to forget completely.

tintilla, *f.* rota wine.

tintillo, *m. dim.* light-colored wine.

tintín, tintineo, *m.* clink, chink.

tintirintín, *m.* sharp sound of a trumpet.

tinto, ta. I. *pp. irreg.* of TEÑIR. **II.** *a.* wine-colored; black, strong (coffee); & *m.* red (wine).

tintóreo, rea, *a.* tinctorial, pert. to color.

tintorería, *f.* dyer's shop.

tintorero, ra. I. *n.* dyer. **II.** *f.* (Am.) (ichth.) female shark.

tintura, *f.* tincture; tint, color; stain, spot; dyeing; dye; rouge; smattering.

tinturar, *va.* to tinge, to dye; to tincture; to teach superficially.

tiña, *f.* (med.) scald head, ringworm of the scalp, favus; small spider that injures beehives; (coll.) want, indigence; niggardliness, stinginess.

tiñería, *f.* (coll.) poverty; stinginess.

tiño, tiñó, tiña, *v.* V. TEÑIR.

tiñoso, sa, *a.* scabby, scurvy; penurious; niggardly, stingy, mean.

tiñuela, *f.* (bot.) dodder; (naut.) shipworm.

tío, *m.* uncle; (coll.) good old man; fellow, "guy."

tiocol, *m.* (chem.) thiocol.

tiorba, *f.* (mus.) theorbo, large lute.

tiovivo, *m.* carrousel, merry-go-round.

tipa, *f.* (Am.) a hardwood tree.

típico, ca, *a.* typical, characteristic.

tiple. I. *m.* (mus.) treble, soprano voice; a kind of small guitar; (naut.) mast of a single piece. **II.** *n.* soprano singer.

tiplisonante, *a.* (coll.) treble-toned.

tipo, *m.* type, pattern; standard, model; (coll.) (of animal) build, (of person) figure, physique; (Am.) (com.) rate; (print.) type; (zool.) class; (coll. contempt.) fellow, "guy."—**t. de interés,** (Am.) (com.) rate of interest.

tipografía, *f.* printing; printing shop; typography; typesetting.

tipográfico, ca, *a.* typographical.

tipógrafo, *m.* typographer; typesetter.

tipómetro, *m.* (print.) type gauge, type measure.

tipoy, *m.* (S. A.) a chemise-like garment.

típula, *f.* (entom.) crane fly, daddy-longlegs.

tiquet, tiquete, *m.* (Angl.) (Am.) (theat., Ry., etc.) ticket.

tiquín, *m.* (P. I.) bamboo pole used as oar.

tiquismiquis, *m. pl.* ridiculous or affected scruples or words.

tiquistiquis, *m.* (P. I.) bitterwood tree.

tira, *f.* long, narrow strip (of paper, cloth, etc.); (naut.) fall.—*pl.* (law) clerks' fees in appeal cases.

tirabala, *m.* popgun.

tirabeque, *m.* (agr.) tender peas.

tirabotas, *f.* boot hook.

tirabraguero, *m.* (med.) truss.

tirabuzón, *m.* corkscrew; corkscrew-curl.

tiracol, tiracuello, *m.* (mil.) sword belt.

tirada, *f.* cast, throw; distance; stretch; lapse o time; (print.) edition, issue; presswork.—**t aparte,** reprint (of an article in pamphlet form) —**de una t.,** or **en una t.,** at one stretch.

tiradera, *f.* long Indian arrow; trace (of harness)

tiradero, *m.* shooting post, place to shoot from

tirado, da. I. *a.* long and low (ship); very cheap given away. **II.** *m.* wiredrawing; (print.) press work.

tirador, ra, *n.* thrower; drawer; sharpshooter; marksman, good shot; (mech.) lift, handle, pull button, knob; bell pull; (print.) pressman.—**t de oro,** gold-wire drawer.

tirafondo, *m.* (surg.) ball extractor; (carp.) wood screw.

tiralíneas, *m.* ruling pen.

tiramiento, *m.* tension, stretching.

tiramira, *f.* long, narrow ridge of mountains; long series or string of things.

tiramollar, *va.* (naut.) to ease off, to slacken.— **t. un aparejo,** to overhaul a tackle.

tirana, *f.* a Spanish song.

tiranamente, *adv.* tyrannically.

tiranía, *f.* tyranny.

tiránicamente, *adv.* tyrannically.

tiranicé, tiranice, *v.* V. TIRANIZAR.

tiranicida, *n.* tyrannicide (murderer).

tiranicidio, *m.* tyrannicide (murder).

tiránico, ca, *a.* tyrannical.

tiranización, *f.* tyrannizing.

tiranizadamente, *adv.* tyrannically.

tiranizar, *va.* (*pret.* TIRANICÉ; *subj.* TIRANICE) to tyrannize.

tirano, na. I. *a.* tyrannical. **II.** *n.* tyrant.

tirante. I. *a.* drawing, pulling; drawn, taut, tense, stretched; strained (as relations); urgent, pressing. **II.** *m.* trace, gear (of harness); (eng.) brace, stay rod, tie rod, truss rod; (carp.) 9 x 13 mm. board.—*pl.* suspenders, braces.—**a tirantes largos,** four-in-hand (vehicle or team).

tirantez, *f.* tenseness, tightness; stretch; strain; tension; distance in a straight line between the ends of a thing.

tiranuelo, la, *m.* & *f. dim.* little tyrant.

tirapié, *m.* shoemaker's stirrup.

tirar. I. *va.* to throw, cast, fling, pitch (as a ball); to cast off, throw away (as a garment); to fire, shoot (as a gun); to draw, to pull, stretch (as wire); to draw (a line); to waste, squander; to give (as a kick); (print.) to print.—**t. coces,** to kick; to rebel.—**t. de,** to pull, pull on.— **tirarla de,** to set up as.—**t. un cañonazo,** to fire a gun. **II.** *vn.* to draw, pull; to direct one's course, turn (in some direction); to get along, pull through; to incline, tend; **(a)** to have a shade (of), border (on) (a certain color); to approach; to try (to), aim (at), aspire (to).—**t. al blanco,** to shoot at a target.—**t. a los dados,** to shoot craps.—**t. de largo,** or **por largo,** to spend lavishly; to make a liberal estimate, to estimate rather high than low.—**tira y afloja,** give and take; fast and loose; blowing hot and cold. **III.** *vr.* to throw oneself; (of parachutist) to jump; to abandon oneself (to grief, vice, etc.).

tirela, *f.* striped stuff.

tireta, *f.* lace, latch, thong.

tirica, ita, *f. dim.* small stripe.

tirilla, *f.* neckband of a shirt.

tirio, ria, *a.* Tyrian.—**tirios y troyanos,** opposing factions.

tiritaña, *f.* a thin silk fabric; trifle.

tiritar, *vn.* to shiver.—**tiritón,** *m.* (coll.) shivering, chill.—**tiritona,** *f.* (coll.) shivering, especially affected.

tiro, *m.* cast, throw, shot, fling; mark made by a throw; (artil.) piece of ordnance; firing, shot, discharge (of a firearm); report (of a gun); target practice; shooting grounds; shooting gallery; range; charge, shot; team of draught animals; harness trace; hoisting rope; length of a piece of drygoods; landing of a stairway; theft; prank, imposition; serious physical or moral injury; (min.) shaft; depth of a shaft; draught of a chimney.—*pl.* sword belts.—**t. al blanco,** target shooting.—**t. directo,** fire at a visible target.—**t. indirecto,** indirect fire.—**t. rasante,** horizontal fire.—**al t.,** (Am.) immediately, right away.—**a t. de ballesta,** a long way off; at a glance.—**a t. de piedra,** within a stone's throw.—**a tiros,** with shots, by shooting.—**de t.,** draft (horse).—**de tiros largos,** in full dress, in full regalia.—**errar el t.,** to miss the mark; to be mistaken.—**hacer un t.,** to fire a shot.—**hacer un tiro a,** to shoot at, have a shot at.—**¡lindo t.!,** good shot!—**ni a tiros,** (coll.) not for love or money, not by a long shot, absolutely not.

tirocinio, *m.* apprenticeship.

tiroideo, a, *a.,* **tiroides,** *m.* (anat.) thyroid.

tiroiditis, *f.* (med.) thyroiditis.

tirolés, sa. I. *n.* & *a.* Tyrolian. **II.** *m.* peddler, huckster in toys and tinware.

¹**tirón,** *m.* pull, haul, tug; effort.—**de un t.,** at once, at one stroke.—**ni a dos tirones,** not easily obtained or carried out.

²**tirón,** *m.* tyro, novice.

tirona, *f.* fishing net, seine.

tiroriro, *m.* (coll.) sound of a reed instrument.—*pl.* (coll.) reed instruments.

tirotear, *vn.* & *vr.* to exchange shots, to skirmish.

tiroteo, *m.* skirmish.

tirreno, na, *n.* & *a.* Thyrrhenian; Etruscan.

tirria, *f.* (coll.) aversion, dislike, grudge.

tirso, *m.* (bot. & Gk. myth.) thyrsus.

tisana, *f.* ptisan, medicinal tea.

tisanuro, ra. I. *n.* & *a.* (entom.) thysanuran. **II.** *m. pl.* Thysanura.

tísico, ca, *n.* & *a.* (med.) consumptive.

tisis, *f.* (med.) tuberculosis, consumption.

tisú, *m.* gold or silver tissue.

tisuria, *f.* (med.) debility from excessive secretion of urine.

titanato, *m.* (chem.) titanate.

titánico, ca, *a.* Titanic; gigantic, immense.

¹**titanio, nia,** *a.* Titanic.

²**titanio,** *m.* (chem.) titanium.

títere, *m.* puppet; whipster, insignificant fellow.—*pl.* Punch-and-Judy show; pantomime.—**no dejar,** or **quedar, t. con cabeza,** to cut to pieces, to destroy or be destroyed entirely, to leave nothing, or nobody, to tell the tale.

titerero, ra, *n.* = TITIRITERO.

titeretada, *f.* mean trick.

titerista, *n.* = TITIRITERO.

tití, *m.* titi, a very small monkey.

titiaro, *a.* CAMBUR T., small, fine kind of banana.

titilación, *f.* tremor; twinkle.

titilador, ra; titilante, *a.* trembling; twinkling.

titilar, *vr.* to tremble; to twinkle.

titímalo, *m.* (bot.) spurge.

titirimundi, *m.* cosmorama.

titiritaina, *f.* (coll.) confused noise of flutes; noisy merriment.

titiritar, *vn.* to shiver with cold or fear.

titiritero, *m.* puppet player, puppet-show man.

tito, *m.* (bot.) a kind of chick-pea.

titubeante, *a.* tottering; hesitating.

titubear, *vn.* to totter (as walls); to toddle (as a child); to stagger, reel; to stutter; to hesitate.—**titubeo,** *m.* tottering; toddling; wavering, hesitation.

titulado, da. I. *pp.* of TITULAR. **II.** *a.* so-called.

¹**titular. I.** *va.* to title, entitle, name, call. **II.** *vn.* to obtain a title from a sovereign. **III.** *vr.* to call or style oneself.

²**titular,** *a.* titular; nominal; (print.) titular (type).

titulillo, *m. dim.* petty title; (print.) page heading or title, running title.—**andar en titulillos,** to stick to, or insist on, trifles and trivial forms.

título, *m.* title; heading, headline, caption; inscription; sign; titled person; soubriquet; qualification, merit, desert; claim; foundation of a claim, privilege or right; (law) legal title to property; diploma; patent; credential, license; professional degree; cause, reason, pretext; (com.) certificate, bond.—**t. al portador,** bond payable to bearer.—**t. nominativo,** registered bond.—**t. translativo de dominio,** (law) deed, conveyance.—**títulos de la deuda,** Government bonds.—**a t. (de),** under pretext; on the authority (of).

tiza, *f.* chalk; clay; calcined stag's horn; whiting.

tizna, *f.* substance for staining or blackening.

tiznadura, *f.* smudginess, smuttiness.

tiznajo, *m.* (coll.) smut, smudge, stain.

tiznar, *va.* to smut, smudge, stain; to tarnish.

tizne, *m.* or *f.* soot, coal smut, grime; stain.

tiznón, *m.* large smut, smudge, smear, or stain.

tizo, *m.* half-burnt charcoal.

tizón, *m.* brand, firebrand; (agr.) wheat crust, blight, stinking smut; stain, disgrace; (arch.) header.—**a t.,** as a header.

tizona, *f.* (coll.) sword.

tizonada, *f.* **tizonazo,** *m.* blow with a firebrand; (coll.) hell fire.

tizoncillo, *m. dim.* small burning coal.

tizonear, *vn.* to stir up a fire.

tizonera, *f.* heap of half-burnt charcoal.

tizonero, *m.* fire poker.

tlaco, *m.* (Mex.) eighth part of a Spanish silver shilling.

tlascalteca, *n.* & *a.* of or from Tlascala.

tlazol, tlazole, *m.* (Mex.) fodder of maize tops.

¡to! *interj.* used to call a dog.

toa, *f.* (Am.) rope, hawser.

toalla, *f.* towel; pillow sham.—**t. afelpada,** Turkish towel.

toalleta, *f. dim.* napkin; small towel.

toar, *va.* (naut.) = ATOAR, to tow.

toba, *f.* calcareous tufa, travertin, calc-sinter; (bot.) cotton thistle; (dent.) tophus, tartar.

toballa, *f.* towel.

toballeta, tobelleta, *f.* napkin.

tobar, *m.* tufa quarry.

tobera, *f.* tewel, tuyère (of a blast furnace).

tobillo, *m.* ankle.

tobogán, *m.* toboggan.

toca, *f.* hood, coif, bonnet, wimple, toque, headdress; thin fabric for toques.

¹**tocado, da. I.** *pp.* of ¹TOCAR. **II.** *a.* (fig.) touched (in the head); perturbed; tainted.—**estar t. de,** to have the symptoms or beginning of.—**estar t. de la cabeza,** to be of unsound mind.

²**tocado, da. I.** *pp.* of ²TOCAR. **II.** *m.* coiffure, headdress, hairdo.—**t. de monja,** nun's wimple.

¹**tocador, ra. I.** *n.* one who touches; (mus.) player, performer. **II.** *m.* tuning key.

²**tocador,** *m.* kerchief for the head; dressing table, bureau; dressing room, boudoir; dressing case.—**productos de t.,** toilet articles.

¹**tocadura,** *f.* coiffure, headgear.

²**tocadura,** *f.* (vet.) sore, gall.

tocante. I. *pres. p.* of ¹TOCAR. **II.** *a.* touching.—**t. a,** respecting, concerning, as regards, with regard to.

¹**tocar. I.** *va.* (*pret.* TOQUÉ; *subj.* TOQUE) to touch, lay hands on, feel with the hand; play (an instrument); to toll, ring (a bell); (auto) to blow (a horn); to hit, knock, strike, rap, tap; to try (metals) on a touchstone; magnetize; to find

out (as by experience); to get (one's share), draw (as a lottery prize); to touch upon; to inspire, move, persuade; communicate or infect. —**t. de cerca**, to be closely related; know well from actual practice or experience; to concern, affect closely.—**t. fondo**, to strike ground.—**t. la diana**, (mil.) to beat the reveille.—**t. generala**, (mil.) to beat the general.—**a toca teja**, (coll.) with ready money, cash down. II. *vn.* to touch; appertain, belong; behoove, concern; to be one's turn; to fall to one's share or lot; to touch, be contiguous; to stop (during a voyage); to be allied or related.—**t. a la bomba**, (naut.) to ring for pumping ship.—**t. a la puerta**, to rap at the door.—**t. en un puerto**, (naut.) to touch at a port.

²**tocar. I.** *va.* to comb and dress the hair with ornaments. **II.** *vr.* (coll.) to be covered, put on the hat; to comb and arrange the hair; to wimple.

tocasalva, *f.* tray or rack for glasses.

tocata, *f.* (mus.) toccata; (coll.) drubbing.

tocayo, ya, *n.* namesake.

tocé, toce, *v. V.* TOZAR.

tocía, *f.* =TUCÍA, tutty.

tocinera, *f.* (woman) pork seller; wife of pork seller; table for salting pork.

tocinero, *m.* pork seller.—**tocinería,** *f.* shop or stall where pork and bacon are sold.

tocino, *m.* bacon; salt pork.—**t. del cielo,** confection of eggs and sirup.—**t. gordo,** fat pork.

tocio, cia, *a.* low, dwarf (oak tree).

toco, *m.* a kind of rectangular niche in old Peruvian architecture.

tocología, *f.* tocology, obstetrics.

tocólogo, ga, *n.* tocologist, obstetrician.

tocón, *m.* stump of a tree, of an arm or leg.

toconal, *m.* olive yard planted with stumps.

tocororo, *m.* (ornith.) tocororo, a Cuban trogon.

tocotoco, *m.* (Venez.) (ornith.) pelican.

tocuyo, *m.* (S. A.) shirtings, sheetings.

tochedad, *f.* boorishness, rusticity.

tochimbo, *m.* (Peru) blast furnace.

tocho, cha. I. *a.* clownish, rustic, uncouth; unpolished, homespun. **II.** *m.* pole; (foundry) bloom, billet.

tochura, *f.* = TOCHEDAD.

todabuena, todasana, *f.* (bot.) St. John's-wort.

todavía, *adv.* still; yet; even.—**t. no,** not yet.

todito, ta, *a.* (coll.) the whole (emphatic, as, *todito el día,* the whole day long).

todo, da. I. *a. & n.* all, the whole, every, each.— **t. aquel que,** whoever.—**t. aquello que,** whatever.—**t. el mundo,** everybody.—**t. el que,** whoever, all that, all who.—**todos los, every.**—**todos los que,** all who, all those that. **II.** *m.* all; whole; everybody; everything.—*pl.* everybody; all.—**ante t.,** first of all, in the first place.—**a t.,** at most, to the limit.—**con t.,** notwithstanding, nevertheless, however.—**del t.,** entirely, wholly.—**en t. y por t.,** wholly, in every way.—**en un t.,** together, in all its parts.—**jugar el t. por el t.,** to stake or risk all.—**me es t. uno,** it's all one, or the same, to me.—**ser el t.,** to be the principal, chief, or whole thing.—**sobre t.,** above all, especially. **III.** *adv. m.* entirely, totally.—**así y t.,** in spite of everything, all that.

todopoderoso, sa, *a.* all-powerful, almighty.

toesa, *f.* toise, anc. French measure of length.

tofana, *f.* aqua Tofana (poison).

tofo, *m.* (vet.) tumor.

toga, *f.* Roman toga; judicial robe or gown.

togado, da, *a.* togaed.

toisón, toisón de oro, *m.* Golden Fleece.

tojal, *m.* clump of furze or whin.

tojino, *m.* (naut.) notch, knob; cleat.

tojo, *m.* (bot.) whin, furze.

tojosa, *f.* (Cuba) (ornith.) a variety of pigeon.

tola, *f.* (S. A.) Indian mound.

¹**tolano,** *m.* (vet.) tumor in horses' gums.

²**tolano,** *m.* (gen. *pl.*) (coll.) short hair on the neck.

toldadura, *f.* awning, hanging.

toldar, *va.* to cover with awning or hanging.

toldería, *f.* (S. A.) Indian camp.

toldero, ra, *n.* retailer of salt.

toldilla, *f.* (naut.) roundhouse.

toldillo, *m. dim.* small awning; covered sedan chair.

toldo, *m.* awning; tarpaulin; ostentation, pomp; (S. A.) Indian hut; tent.

tole, *m.* hubbub, clamor, outcry.—**tomar el t.,** (coll.) to run away, to flee.

toledano, na, *n. & a.* Toledan.

toledo, *m.* (C. A.) a song bird.

tolerable, *a.* tolerable, bearable; permissible.

tolerablemente, *adv.* tolerably.

tolerancia, *f.* toleration, permission; tolerance, indulgence; allowance, permissible discrepancy or variation.

tolerante, *a.* tolerant.—**tolerantismo,** *m.* doctrine of the freedom of worship.

tolerar, *vn.* to tolerate, endure, suffer, permit; to be indulgent, to overlook.

tolete, *m.* (naut.) thole, tholepin; (Am.) club, cudgel; (Colomb.) a kind of large rough boat.

tolmera, *f.* ground where TOLMOS abound.

tolmo, *m.* isolated pillarlike rock, tor.

tolo, *m.* bump from a blow.

tolondro, dra. I. *a.* giddy, harebrained; reckless, rash. **II.** *m.* = TOLO.—**a topa t.,** rashly, recklessly.

tolondrón, na, a. & m. = TOLONDRO.—**a tolondrones,** with contusions or bruises; precipitately, giddily, by fits and starts.

tolteca, *n. & a.* Toltec.

tolueno, *m.* (chem.) toluene.

tolúico, ca, *a.* (chem.) toluic.

toluidina, *f.* (chem.) toluidine.

tolva, *f.* hopper, chute.

tolvanera, *f.* cloud of dust.

tolla, *f.* moss-covered bog; (Cuba) canoe-shaped trough.

tolladar, *m.* = ATOLLADERO, bog; difficulty.

tollina, *f.* (coll.) cudgeling.

¹**tollo,** *m.* (ichth.) spotted dogfish; loin of a stag.

²**tollo,** *m.* blind (for hunting); quagmire, bog.

tollón, *m.* narrow passage, gorge.

toma, *f.* taking; take, receiving; (mil.) capture, seizure; dose of medicine; (hydraul.) intake; tap of a water main or electric wire; (print.) take.—**t. y daca,** give-and-take.

¡**toma!** *interj.* well, why, of course.

tomacorriente, *m.* (Arg., Chile) (elec.) socket; (Chile) (elec. car) trolley.

tomadero, *m.* handle, haft; tap, inlet.

tomador, ra, *n. & a.* taker(-ing), receiver(-ing); drinker(-ing); (*m.*) drawee.—*pl.* (naut.) ropebands, gaskets.

tomadura, *f.* catch, seizure, grip, hold, grasp, capture; portion of a thing taken at once.

tomaína, *f.* ptomaine.

tomajón, na, *n.* (coll.) one who takes frequently or accepts easily.

tomar. I. *va.* to take; to drink, to eat; to contract, acquire (as a] habit);⊦ to hire, take (as a taxi); to take on, adopt (as customs); to take, assume (responsibility); to steal, take by stealth; follow, imitate, ape; to cover (the female); (in ball games) to call a halt in the throwing of (the ball).—**t. a bien (a mal),** to take (something said) the right (wrong) way.—**t. a broma,** to take as a joke.—**t. a cuestas,** to carry on one's back; to take upon oneself; to take charge of. —**t. a pechos,** to take to heart; undertake with too much zeal.—**t. asiento,** to take a seat, sit down.—**t. calor,** to get warm.—**t. cuentas,** to audit accounts, to take and examine accounts.—**t. el fresco,** to take the air.

—t. el pelo a, (coll.) to banter, make fun of.—t. el sol, to take a sun bath.—t. en cuenta, to take under advisement, consider.—t. entre cejas, to take a dislike to, get a grudge against. —t. estado, to change condition; to marry; to become a clergyman; to take the black veil. —t. frío, to catch cold.—t. fuerzas, to gather strength.—t. la borla, to graduate.—tomarla con, to oppose, antagonize; to pick on, have a grudge against.—t. la delantera, to excel; to get ahead; to go at the head.—t. la mañana, (Cuba) to take a morning drink.—t. la puerta, to go out of the house; be off.—t. las de Villadiego, to take to one's heels, "beat it."—t. lengua, or lenguas, to take tidings or signs.— t. por, to take for, consider.—t. por su cuenta, to take charge of, to attend to personally.—t. razón, to take a memorandum.— t. resolución, to resolve, decide. II. vn. to drink (liquor).—t. por, to turn to (the right, left), or into; to take, follow (a road, etc.). III. vr. to take; to get rusty (as metals).—t. alas, to take liberties.—t. con, to pick a quarrel with.—t. del vino, to become intoxicated, to get drunk.

tomatada, f. fried tomatoes.

tomatal, m. tomato patch or field.

tomate, m. tomato.

tomatera, f. tomato plant.

tomatero, ra, n. tomato raiser or seller.

tomento, m. coarse tow; (bot.) tomentum.

tomentoso, sa, a. (bot.) tomentose, tomentous.

tomiento, m. = TOMENTO.

tomillar, m. bed of thyme.

tomillo, m. (bot.) thyme.—t. salsero, (bot.) sweet marjoram.

tomín, m. tomin, third part of a drachm, Spanish weight; (Am.) a silver coin.

tominejo, ja, n. (ornith.) humming bird.

tomismo, m. Thomism.

tomista, n. & a. Thomist(-ic).

tomiza, f. bass rope.

tomo, m. volume, tome; bulk; importance, value, consequence.—de t. y lomo, of weight and bulk; of importance.

tomón, na, a. fond of taking.

ton, m.—sin t. ni son, without rhyme or reason.

tonada, f. tune, song.

tonadica, f. dim. short tune or song.

tonadilla, f. dim. (theat.) musical interlude.— tonadillero, m. writer of TONADILLAS.

tonalidad, f. (mus.) tonality.

tonante, a. thundering (Jupiter).

tonar, vn. to thunder.

tonca, f. (bot.) tonka bean.

tondino, m. (arch.) astragal.

tondo, m. (arch.) round molding.

tonel, m. cask, barrel; tun, pipe, butt; (naut.) an ancient measure of ships ($\frac{1}{12}$ ton).—t. macho, ton.

tonelada, f. ton; an ancient tonnage duty.—t. de arqueo, ton of capacity.—t. de desplazamiento, ton of displacement.—t. de registro, register ton.—t. métrica, metric ton, tonne.

tonelaje, m. tonnage, displacement; (com.) tonnage dues.

tonelería, f. cooperage, coopering; barrels or casks collectively; watercasks for a ship.

tonelero, m. copper, hooper.

tonelete, m. dim. little barrel; short skirt, kilt.

¹tonga, f. (bot.) tonka bean.

²tonga, tongada, f. couch; tier, layer, stratum; lay, row, ledge, flake.

tongo, m. trick of a player or jockey, to lose for a bribe; "throwing it."

tónico, ca. I. a. tonic, strengthening; (gram.) accented or inflected. II. m. tonic. III. f. (mus.) keynote, tonic.

tonificador, ra; tonificante, a. tonic, strengthening.

tonificar, va. = ENTONAR, (med.) to tone up.

tonillo, m. singsong, monotonous tone.

tonina, f. (ichth.) fresh tunny; (ichth.) dolphin.

tono, m. tone; tune; (med.) tone, vigor, strength; (color) tone, shade; (mus.) tone; key, key tone; pitch; moving piece in a brass instrument, which modifies the tone; deportment, manner, social address; conceit.—dar el t., to set the standard.—darse t., to put on airs.—(decir) en todos los tonos, (to tell) in every possible way.—gente de buen tono, smart set.

tonsila, f. (anat.) tonsil.—tonsilar, a. tonsillar.

tonsilitis, f. (med.) tonsilitis.

tonsura, f. hair cutting; shearing, fleecing; (eccl.) tonsure.

tonsurado, m. (eccl.) tonsured man.

tonsurar, va. to cut the hair of; to shear, fleece; (eccl.) to tonsure.

tontada, f. nonsense; silliness, foolishness.

tontaina, n. fool, dolt.

tontamente, adv. foolishly, stupidly.

tontear, vn. to talk nonsense, to act foolishly; to fool.

tontedad, f. foolishness, silliness, nonsense.

tontera, tontería, f. = TONTEDAD.

tontillo, m. hoop skirt; bustle.

tontina, f. (com.) tontine.

tontivano, na, a. foolishly conceited.

tonto, ta. I. a. silly, foolish, stupid. II. n. fool, dunce, dolt.—t. de capirote, blockhead, great fool, idiot.—a tontas y a locas, without order, haphazard.—hacerse el t., to play the fool.

tontuelo, la, a. & n. dim. little fool.

tontuna, f. foolishness.

toña, f. tip cat (boys' game); bat for the game.

toñil, m. straw on which fruit is laid to ripen.

toñina, f. fresh tunny fish.

¡top! interj. (naut.) hold! stop!

topacio, m. topaz.

topada, f. butt.

topadizo, za, a. (coll.) met, run into, by chance.

topador, ra, n. one that butts.

topar. I. va. to collide with, to run into or against; to meet with by chance; to find, run across; (naut.) to butt, abut, join. II. vn. to collide, butt, strike; at cards, to accept a bet; to depend (on), consist (in); to meet (with); to succeed, come out right.—tope donde tope, (coll.) strike where it will.

toparca, m. toparch, petty ruler.

toparquía, f. toparchy, petty state.

tope, m. butt, projecting part or end; top, summit; (mech.) stop, stop collar, stop plate; (Ry.) buffer; butt, collision, knock, bump; rub, difficulty; obstacle; scuffle, quarrel; (naut.) masthead, topmast head; butt end of a plank; topman.—a t. or al t., end to end; butt (joint).— hasta el t., or los topes, up to the top, or the brim.

topera, f. molehole.

topetada, f. butt by a horned animal; (coll.) bump, bumping.

topetar, vn. to butt; (con) to bump, strike, or knock (against); to meet by chance, run across. —topetazo, m. butt, knock, bump, blow, encounter, collision.—topetón, m. = TOPETADA; TOPETAZO.—topetudo, da, a. butting.

tópico, ca. I. a. topical. II. m. (med.) external application; (rhet.) topic, subject.

topil, m. (Mex.) constable.

topinada, f. (coll.) awkwardness, clumsiness.

topinaria, f. (med.) talpa, wen.

topinera, f. molehole; molehill.

¹topo, m. (zool.) mole; (coll.) awkward person; dunce, dolt.

²topo, m. (C. A.) one league and a half.

topocho, cha, a. (Venez.) plump.

topografía, f. topography; surveying.

topográficamente, adv. topographically.

topográfico, ca, a. topographical.

topógrafo, *m.* topographer; surveyor.

toque, *m.* touch, act of touching; peal, ringing (of bells); (mil.) call; assay, touch, test (of metals); touchstone; trial, proof; aid, divine inspiration; point, gist, purport; (coll.) tap on a person; (art) fine stroke of the brush.—**t. de cornetas,** bugle call.—**t. de diana,** reveille.—**t. del alba,** bell ringing at daybreak.—**t. de luz,** light in a picture.—**t. de retreta,** tattoo (of drums).— **t. de tambor,** beat of a drum.—**dar un t. a,** to put to the test; to pump, throw out a feeler to.

toqué, toque, *v.* *V.* TOCAR.

toqueado, *m.* rhythmical noise of clapping hands, stamping feet, rapping with canes, etc.

toquería, *f.* collection of women's headdresses; business of making TOCAS, hoods, bonnets, etc.

toquero, ra, *n.* veil maker; headdress maker.

toqui, *m.* (Chile) Indian chief.

toquilla, *f.* *dim.* small headdress, bonnet or cap; hat band or ribbon; small triangular kerchief used by women on the head or neck; woollen knit shawl.

¹tora, *f.* figure of a bull in artificial fireworks.

²tora, *f.* Jewish family tribute; Torah (Hebrew Pentateuch).

torácico, ca, *a.* (anat.) thoracic.

torada, *f.* drove of bulls.

toral. I. *a.* main, principal. **II.** *m.* unbleached yellow wax; (foundry) mold for copper bars; copper bar.

tórax, *m.* (anat.) thorax.

torbellino, *m.* whirlwind; rush, avalanche; vortex; (coll.) lively, hustling, restless person.

torca, *f.* cavern in mountains.

torcal, *m.* place where there are caves.

torcaz, torcaza, *f.* wild pigeon.

torce, *f.* each loop of a chain around the neck.

torcecuello, *m.* (ornith.) wryneck.

torcedero, ra. I. *a.* twisted. **II.** *m.* twisting mill.

torcedor, ra, *m.* twister, thread frame, twisting mill; anything that causes displeasure or grief. —**t. de tabaco,** cigar maker.

torcedura, *f.* twisting; sprain; small wine.

torcer. I. *va.* (*ind.* TUERZO; *subj.* TUERZA) to twist, twine, wind (as strands); to bend, deflect; to sprain (as a foot); to pervert (as justice); to distort, pervert, misconstrue; to dissuade, induce to change one's mind.—**no dar el brazo a t.,** to be obstinate. **II.** *vn.* to turn (to right or left). **III.** *vr.* to become dislocated or sprained; to go crooked or astray; (of wine) to turn sour; to cheat.

torcida, *f.* wick, lamp wick; daily ration given to the grinder in oil mills.

torcidamente, *adv.* obliquely, tortuously, crookedly.

torcidillo, *m.* twist silk.

torcido, da. I. *pp.* of TORCER. **II.** *a.* oblique, tortuous, crooked, bent.—**estar t. con uno,** to be on bad terms with one. **III.** *m.* twist of candied fruit; twisted silk, twist; (prov.) light, bad wine.

torcijón, *m.* gripes.

torcimiento, *m.* twist, twisting; sprain; entwining, winding; deflection, bend, warp, circumlocution or periphrasis.

torculado, da, *a.* screwed, screw-shaped.

tórculo, *m.* small press; rolling press.

tordella, *f.* (ornith.) a kind of large thrush.

tórdiga, *f.* strip of leather.

tordillo, lla, llejo, ja, *a.* grayish, grizzled.

tordo, da. I. *a.* dapple, gray. **II.** *m.* (ornith.) thrush, throstle.—**t. de agua,** (ornith.) reed thrush.—**t. loco,** (ornith.) solitary thrush.

toreador, *m.* bullfighter.

torear. I. *vn.* to fight bulls in the ring; to let a bull to cows. **II.** *va.* to fight (bulls); to banter, to provoke.—**toreo,** *m.* bullfighting.

torera, *f.* tight, unbuttoned jacket.

torería, *f.* (Cuba) boys' pranks; office of bullfighter.

torero, ra. I. *a.* pert. to bullfighters. **II.** *m.* bullfighter.

torés, *m.* (arch.) torus.

torete, *m.* *dim.* bullock; (coll.) puzzle, difficult matter; absorbing topic of conversation.

toréutico, ca, *a.* (art) toreutic.

torga, *f.* yoke for dogs or hogs.

toril, *m.* pen for bulls before the fight.

¹torillo, *m.* *dim.* little bull.

²torillo, *m.* dowel, dowel pin; (anat.) raphe.

torio, *m.* (chem.) thorium.

toriondez, *f.* rut of cattle.

toriondo, da, *a.* (of cattle) rutting.

torloroto, *m.* shepherd's pipe or flute.

tormagal, *m.,* **tormellera,** *f.* place abounding in tors, pillarlike rocks.

tormenta, *f.* storm, tempest; hurricane; reverse, misfortune; heated discussion.

tormentario, ria, *a.* (artil.) projectile.

tormentila, *f.* (bot.) tormentil, septfoil.

tormentín, *m.* (naut.) jib boom.

tormento, *m.* torment, torture; rack; (mil.) battering ordnance.—**dar t.,** to torture, put to the rack.—**tormentoso, sa,** *a.* stormy, boisterous, turbulent; (naut.) laboring hard.

tormo, *m.* = TOLMO, tor, isolated steep rock.

torna, *f.* restitution, devolution; return; tap or drain.—*pl.* return, requital, recompense, restitution; coarse straw.

tornaboda, *f.* day after a wedding.

tornachile, *m.* (Mex.) thick pepper.

tornada, *f.* return from a journey; revisit; (poet.) envoy, l'envoi.

tornadera, *f.* two-pronged winnowing fork.

tornadizo, za, *n.* turncoat, deserter.

tornado, *m.* tornado.

tornadura, *f.* devolution, return; requital, recompense.

tornaguía, *f.* (com.) landing certificate.

tornamiento, *m.* turn, alteration, change.

tornapunta, *f.* (arch.) chock, wedge, shoe; stay, prop, shore, brace.

tornar. I. *va.* to return; restore; to turn (as one's brain); to change, alter.—**t. las espaldas,** to turn a cold shoulder. **II.** *vn.* to return, come back; to repeat, do again.—**t. por,** to defend, to protect. **III.** *vr.* (**en**) to change (into), to become.

tornasol, *m.* (bot.) sunflower; changeable or shot color; litmus.

tornasolado, da, *a.* changeable, shot (fabrics); iridescent.

tornasolar, *va.* to cause changes in the color of, to make iridescent.

tornátil, *a.* turned (in a lathe); changeable.

tornatrás, *n.* half-breed.

tornavía, *f.* (Ry.) turntable.

tornaviaje, *m.* return trip.

tornavirón, *m.* slap, box.

tornavoz, *m.* sounding board.

torneador, ra, *n.* turner; tilter at tournaments.

torneadura, *f.* lathe shavings.

torneante, *a.* tilting at tournaments.

tornear. I. *va.* & *vn.* to turn (in a lathe). **II.** *vn.* to make a turn, go around, wind round about; to tilt at tournaments; to meditate, muse.

torneo, *m.* tournament; contest.

tornera, *f.* doorkeeper of a nunnery.

tornería, *f.* turning; turnery.

tornero, *m.* turner; maker of lathes; messenger of a nunnery.

tornillero, *m.* (coll.) (mil.) deserter.

tornillo, *m.* screw, male screw; vise, clamp; (mil.) desertion.—**t. de alimentación,** feed screw.— **t. de aproximación,** (surv.) tangent screw.— **t. de banco,** vise, bench vise.—**t. de filete angular,** or **triangular,** V-threaded screw.— **t. de filete cuadrado,** square-threaded screw.

—**t. de gota de sebo,** round-headed screw.—**t. de mano,** or **de orejas,** thumbscrew.—**t. de presión,** set screw, clamp screw.—**t. de rosca glosa,** conical V-threaded screw.—**t. de sujeción** = T. DE PRESIÓN.—**t. sin fin,** endless screw.—**faltarle a uno un t.,** (coll.) not to have much sense, "to have a screw loose."

torniquete, *m.* turnpike, turnstile; turnbuckle; swivel; bell crank; (surg.) tourniquet.

torniscón, *m.* slap, box.

torno, *m.* lathe; winch, windlass; whim (vertical winch); whisket; revolving dumbwaiter; brake of a carriage; turn of a river; spinning wheel; spindle; wheel; axletree; circumvolution, gyration.—**t. de hilar,** spinning wheel.—**en t.,** round about.—**en t. a,** or **de,** regarding, about, in connection with.—**en t. de,** about, around.

¹**toro,** *m.* bull; (T-, astr.) Taurus.—*pl.* bullfighting.—**t. corrido,** person made wise by experience, no easy mark.—**t. mejicano,** bison.—**ciertos son los toros,** so then, it is true.—**correr toros,** to fight bulls.

²**toro,** *m.* (arch.) ogee molding; torus.

toronja, *f.* grapefruit.

toronjil, *m.,* **toronjina,** *f.* (bot.) balm gentle.

toronjo, *m.* (bot.) grapefruit tree.

toroso, sa, *a.* strong, robust.

torozón, *m.* (vet.) gripes (of animals).

torpe, *a.* slow, heavy; dull, stupid; bawdy, lewd; homely, ugly; torpid; infamous.

torpedear, *va.* to torpedo.

torpedeo, *m.* torpedoing.

torpedero, *m.* (naut.) torpedo boat.

torpedo, *m.* torpedo; (ichth.) torpedo, electric ray; (auto) streamline body; long open car.—**t. automóvil,** self-propelling torpedo.—**t. de botalón,** spar torpedo.—**t. de fondo,** or **durmiente,** ground torpedo, or ground submarine mine.—**t. flotante,** buoyant torpedo or submarine mine.

torpemente, *adv.* slowly, sluggishly; clumsily, stupidly; basely; lewdly.

torpeza, *f.* heaviness, dullness; torpidness, torpor; lewdness, obscenity; want of ornament or culture; baseness, infamy, turpitude.

torpor, *m.* torpor, numbness.

torrado, *m.* toasted chick-pea.

torrar, *va.* to toast.

torre, *f.* tower; turret; church steeple, belfry; belvedere; country house with a garden; (chess) castle or rook.—**t. albarrana, t. de costa,** turret, watch tower.—**t. de luces,** (naut.) lighthouse.—**t. de viento,** castle in the air.

torrear, *va.* to fortify with towers or turrets.

torrefacción, *f.* toasting.

torreja, *f.* (Mex.) fritter.

torrejón, *m.* ill-shaped turret.

torrencial, *a.* torrential; overpowering.

torrentada, *f.* sweep of a torrent, impetuous current.

torrente, *m.* torrent; avalanche, rush; abundance, plenty.—**t. de voz,** powerful voice.

torrentera, *f.* ravine made by a torrent.

torreón, *m.* fortified tower.

torrero, *m.* lighthouse keeper; farmer.

torreznada, *f.* plentiful dish of bacon.

torreznero, ra, *n.* (coll.) lazy person.

torrezno, *m.* rasher of bacon.

tórrido, da, *a.* torrid; parched, hot.

torrija, *f.* bread dipped in batter and fried.

torrontera, *f.,* **torrontero,** *m.* heap of earth left by a freshet.

torrontés, *a.* designating a kind of white grape.

torsión, *f.* torsion, twist; twisting.

torso, *m.* trunk or body of a statue.

torta, *f.* cake; loaf; (print.) font; solid matter for distribution; briquette; (mason.) coat.—*pl.* (Mex.) (min.) torta, cake of ore.—**tortas y pan pintado,** trifles, an easy matter, child's play.

—**costar la t. un pan,** to pay dear for one's whistle.

tortada, *f.* meat or chicken pie; (mason.) coat of mortar.

tortedad, *f.* twistedness.

¹**tortera,** *f.* baking pan; deep dish.

²**tortera,** *f.,* **tortero,** *m.* whorl of a spindle.

tortícoli, *m.* (med.) torticollis, wry or stiff neck.

tortilla, *f.* *dim.* omelet; (Mex.) pancake.—**hacerse t.,** to break into small pieces; to cake.—**volverse la t.,** to turn the scale; to take a course contrary to that expected.

tortita, *f.* *dim.* small loaf or cake.

tórtola, *f.* (ornith.) turtledove.

tortolillo, lla, ito, ta, *n.* *dim.* small turtledove; sweetheart.

tórtolo, *m.* male turtledove; beau, lover.

tortor, *m.* (naut.) tightening stick or bar to take up by twisting the sag between the fastened ends of a rope.

tortozón, *m.* a variety of large grape.

tortuga, *f.* turtle; tortoise.

tortuosamente, *adv.* tortuously, sinuously.

tortuosidad, *f.* tortuosity, sinuosity.

tortuoso, sa, *a.* tortuous, winding, sinuous.

tortura, *f.* state of being twisted; rack, torture; grief, affliction.

torturar. I. *va.* to torture, torment. **II.** *vr.* to worry, fret.

torva, *f.* whirl of rain or snow.

torvisca, *f.* (bot.) flax-leaved daphne.

torviscal, *m.* place abounding in TORVISCA.

torvisco, *m.* = TORVISCA.

torvo, va, *a.* fierce, stern, severe, grim.

tory, *n.* & *a.* (Angl.) Tory.—**torysmo,** *m.* toryism.

torzadillo, *m.* thin silk twist.

torzal, *m.* silk twist, machine twist; cord.

torzón, *m.* (vet.) = TOROZÓN, gripes.

torzonado, da, *a.* (vet.) suffering from TORZÓN.

tos, *f.* cough.—**t. ferina,** or **convulsiva,** whooping cough.—**t. perruna,** barking cough.

tosca, *f.* (med.) tophus; (dent.) tartar.

toscamente, *adv.* coarsely, rudely, roughly.

toscano, na, *n.* & *a.* Tuscan.

tosco, ca, *a.* coarse, rough; unpolished, uncouth.

tosecilla, *f.* *dim.* slight cough.

tosegoso, sa, *a.* coughing much.

toser, *vn.* to cough.—**t. a,** to challenge; to rival, compete with.—**tosidura,** *f.* coughing.

tosigar, *va.* to poison.

tósigo, *m.* poison; grief, anguish.

¹**tosigoso, sa,** *a.* poisonous, baneful.

²**tosigoso, sa,** *a.* coughing.

tosquedad, *f.* roughness, coarseness; rudeness; clumsiness.

tostada, *f.* toast, toasted bread; disappointment.—**dar,** or **pegar, una t.,** (coll.) to cheat; to disappoint.

tostado, da. I. *pp.* of TOSTAR. **II.** *a.* torrid, parched; (sun) tanned. **III.** *m.* toasting.

tostador, ra, *n.* toaster (person); *m.* (utensil).

tostadura, *f.* toasting.

tostar, *va.* (*ind.* TUESTO; *subj.* TUESTE) to toast; to roast; to tan (as the sun).—**t. café,** to roast coffee.

¹**tostón,** *m.* buttered or oiled toast; roasted Spanish pea; anything overtoasted; roast pig.

²**tostón,** *m.* Port. silver coin; (Mex.) 50 centavos.

total. I. *a.* total, whole; general, universal. **II.** *m.* total; whole, totality; complement; result; upshot.—**en t.,** in short, to sum up.

totalidad, *f.* totality, aggregate; whole.

totalizar, *va.* (Am.) to add up, find the total of; to sum up.

totalmente, *adv.* totally, wholly, fully.

tótem, *m.* totem.—**totemismo,** *m.* totemism.

totilimundi, *m.* peep-show; cosmorama.

totoloque, *m.* (Mex.) an ancient Indian game.

totoposte, *m.* (C. A.) corn cake or biscuit.

totora, _f._ (S. A.) (bot.) cat-tail or red mace.

totoral, _m._ place abounding in TOTORAS.

totovía, _f._ (ornith.) wood lark.

totuma, _f._ (Am.) cup made from a gourd.

totumo, _m._ (Am.) tree bearing gourds.

toxemia, _f._ toxemia.

toxicar, _va._ to poison.

toxicidad, _f._ toxicity.

tóxico, ca. I. _a._ toxic, poisonous. **II.** _m._ poison.

toxicología, _f._ toxicology.—**toxicológico, ca,** _a._ toxicological.—**toxicólogo, ga,** _n._ toxicologist.

toxina, _f._ (med.) toxin.

toza, _f._ log; block of wood; stump; piece of bark.

tozal, _m._ protuberance, bump on a plain surface.

tozalbo, ba, _a._ white-faced.

tozar, _vn._ (_pret._ TOCÉ; _subj._ TOCE) to butt (with the head); to contend foolishly.

tozo, za, _a._ low, small, dwarfish, stumpy.

tozolada, _f.,_ **tozolón,** _m._ blow on the neck.

tozudo, da, _a._ stubborn, obstinate.

tozuelo, _m._ fat part of the neck of an animal.

traba, _f._ tie, bond, brace, clasp, locking device; anything that binds together; ligament, ligature; hobble, clog, fetterlock, trammel, fetter, shackle; obstacle, hindrance; beam, lintel.

trabacuenta, _f._ error in accounts; difference, dispute, controversy.

trabadero, _m._ pastern of a horse.

trabado, da. I. _pp._ of TRABAR. **II.** _a._ robust, strong; (of horse) having white fore feet.

trabadura, _f._ bracing, locking; bond, union.

trabajadamente, _adv._ laboriously.

trabajado, da. I. _pp._ of TRABAJAR. **II.** _a._ wrought, machined; tired, weary.

trabajador, ra. I. _a._ industrious; laboring, working. **II.** _n._ worker; workman, workingman (-woman), operator, hand, laborer.

trabajante, _a._ working, toiling.

trabajar, _va. & vn._ to work; labor; to shape, form; to endeavor; to exert oneself, strive; to undergo a strain; to labor (as a ship in a storm); to till (the soil); to vex, harass, worry, trouble.

trabajillo, _m._ _dim._ slight work, toil, labor, trouble, or hardship.

trabajo, _m._ work; labor; piece of work; thing wrought; employment; obstacle, hindrance; trouble, hardship.—_pl._ hardship; poverty, indigence, need, want.—**t. de manos,** manual or handwork.—**t. de punto,** knitting, knitting work.—**t. de zapa,** underhand work.—**trabajos forzados,** hard labor (penal).—**bolsa de t.,** employment bureau or exchange.—**pasar trabajos,** to have trouble, to experience hardships or privation, to meet with difficulties.

trabajosamente, _adv._ laboriously, painfully.

trabajoso, sa, _a._ difficult, hard; belabored; needy, suffering; weak, sickly.

trabal, _a._ clasping.

trabalenguas, _m._ unpronounceable word, jawbreaker.

trabamiento, _m._ interlocking; connection, bond, joining.

trabanco, _m._ block attached to a dog's collar to prevent him from nosing the ground.

trabar. I. _va._ to join, clasp, lock, bind, fasten; to grasp, grab, seize; to fetter, shackle; to thicken, inspissate; to begin, set about; to set (the teeth of a saw); to harmonize, make agree.—**t. amistad,** to become friends; (**con**) to make the acquaintance (of).—**t. batalla,** to enter into battle, begin it.—**t. conocimiento,** to scrape acquaintance.—**t. ejecución,** (law) to distrain, to seize judicially. **II.** _vr._ to become locked or interlocked; to become confused, rattled.—**t. de palabras,** to become angry in a dispute.—**trabársele la lengua a uno,** to stammer; to speak with unnatural hesitation from confusion.

trabazón, _f._ juncture, union, bond, bracing, connection; coalescence; (mason.) bond.

trabe, _f._ beam.

trábea, _f._ (Rom. hist.) gala toga.

trabilla, _f._ _dim._ gaiter strap; small clasp; in knitting, dropped stitch.

trabón, _m._ _aug._ fetlock, hopple; cross plank in oil mills.

trabuca, _f._ firecracker.

trabucación, _f._ confusion, disorder, upsetting, mix up; mistake, blunder.

trabucador, ra, _n._ upsetter, disturber; jumbler, mixer; blunderer.

trabucaire, _m._ Catalonian guerrilla, armed with a blunderbuss.

trabucante, _a._ blundering; confusing.

trabucar. I. _va._ (_pret._ TRABUQUÉ; _subj._ TRABUQUE) to upset, overturn; to mistake; to confound, confuse, jumble, mix up; to interrupt. **II.** _vr._ to become confused or mixed up.

trabucazo, _m._ shot with a blunderbuss; report of a blunderbuss; (coll.) sudden fright or affliction.

trabuco, _m._ catapult; blunderbuss.—**t. naranjero,** blunderbuss with mouth of size of orange.

trabuqué, trabuque, _v. V._ TRABUCAR.

trabuquete, _m._ catapult; seine.

traca, _f._ (naut.) strake.

trácala, _f._ (Mex.) scheme, trick.

tracalada, _f._ (Am.) multitude, "lots."

tracalero, ra, _a._ (Mex.) tricky, artful.

tracamundana, _f._ (coll.) barter of trifles; noisy wrangle, hubbub.

tracción, _f._ traction; cartage; (mech.) tension, tensile stress.

tracé, trace, _v. V._ TRAZAR.

tracería, _f._ (arch.) tracery.

tracias, _m._ north-northwest wind.

tracio, cia, _n. & a._ Thracian.

tracista, _n._ designer; schemer; intriguer.

tracoma, _f._ (med.) trachoma.

tracto, _m._ tract, stretch; lapse; (eccl.) tractus.

tractocarril, _m._ car or train that can run on a road with or without rails.

tractor, _m._ tractor; traction engine.—**t. oruga,** caterpillar tractor.

tradición, _f._ tradition; (law) tradition, delivery of possession.—**tradicional,** _a._ traditional.

tradicionalismo, _m._ traditionalism.

tradicionalista, _m._ or _f._ traditionalist.

tradicionalmente, _adv._ traditionally.

tradicionista, _n._ compiler of traditions.

traducción, _f._ translation.

traducible, _a._ translatable.

traducir, _va._ (_ind. pres._ TRADUZCO, _pret._ TRADUJE; _subj._ TRADUZCA) to translate.

traductor, ra, _n._ translator.

traedizo, za, _a._ portable.

traedor, ra, _n._ porter, carrier.

traer. I. _va._ (_ger._ TRAYENDO; _pp._ TRAÍDO; _ind. pres._ TRAIGO, _pret._ TRAJE; _subj._ TRAIGA) to bring, fetch; to lead (a person); to attract, draw towards oneself; to bring about, cause, occasion; to handle, manage; to wear (as a garment); (of a magazine, etc.) to carry (an article); assign (reasons); quote (authorities); to bring to, oblige, compel; to bring over, reduce, bind, prevail upon, persuade; to be engaged in, carry on, have.—**t. a colación,** to bring up for discussion.—**t. a cuento,** to bring into the conversation or discourse; to drag in. —**t. a la mano,** to fetch or carry.—**t. a mal t.,** to go hard with one; to disturb, trouble, vex.— **t. a uno al retortero,** to trouble one by overwork, or to lead one from place to place.—**t. a uno entre ojos,** to be suspicious of one.—**t. consigo,** to carry or have with one; to bring with it, to imply, to cause.—**t. en bocas,** or **lenguas,** to traduce, to speak ill of.—**t. entre manos,** to have in hand.—**t. y llevar,** to gossip. **II.** _vr._ (**bien, mal**) to be dressed (well or poorly); to carry oneself, have a (graceful or ungainly) carriage.

traeres, *m. pl.* dress ornaments.

trafagador, ra, *n.* trafficker, dealer.

trafagante, *a.* trafficking, trading.

trafagar, *vn.* (*pret.* TRAFAGUÉ; *subj.* TRAFAGUE) to traffic, trade.

tráfago, *m.* commerce, trade; drudgery.

trafagón, na. I. *a.* active, industrious. II. *n.* hustler.

trafagué, trafague, *v. V.* TRAFAGAR.

trafalgar, *m.* cotton lining.

trafalmejo, ja, *a.* bold, forward, saucy.

traficación, *f.* traffic; trade, commerce.

traficante, *n.* trafficker, trader, dealer.

traficar, *vn.* (*pret.* TRAFIQUÉ; *subj.* TRAFIQUE) to traffic, deal, trade; to travel, journey, roam.

tráfico, *m.* trade, business; traffic.

tragacanta, *f.,* **tragacanto,** *m.* (bot.) goats-thorn, milk vetch; tragacanth, a gum.

tragacete, *m.* javelin, dart.

tragaderas, *f. pl.* gullet.—**tener buenas t.,** to be very gullible.

tragadero, *m.* œsophagus, gullet; pit, gulf, vortex.—**t. del mar,** trough of the sea.

tragador, ra, *n.* glutton, gobbler.—**t. de leguas** = TRAGALEGUAS.

tragahombres, *m.* (coll.) bully, hector.

trágala, *m.* title of a political song against absolutism and in favor of the constitution.

tragaldabas, *m.* (coll.) glutton.

tragaleguas, *m.* (coll.) brisk walker.

tragaluz, *f.* skylight, bull's-eye.

tragallón, na, *n. & a.* glutton(-ous).

tragamallas, *m.* (coll.) glutton.

tragantada, *f.* large draught of liquor.

tragante. I. *a.* swallowing. II. *m.* (foundry) top opening or passage of a furnace; sluice, flume; mouth of a dam or sink.

tragantón, na. I. *a.* gluttonous, voracious. II. *n.* (coll.) glutton. III. *f.* (coll.) big meal, big spread; swallowing or forcing down the throat; hard pill to swallow.

tragar. I. *va.* (*pret.* TRAGUÉ; *subj.* TRAGUE) to swallow; to devour; to swallow up, engulf.—**t. el anzuelo,** to allow oneself to be deceived.—**no poder,** or **poderse, t. a,** not to be able to bear (cannot bear). II. *vr.* to swallow; to dissemble; to swallow (an affront).

tragasantos, *n.* overdevout person, one who spends too much time in church.

tragavenado, *f.* (Venez.) a kind of boa.

tragavirotes, *m.* (coll.) conceited stiff man.

tragazón, *f.* voracity, gluttony.

tragedia, *f.* tragedy.

trágicamente, *adv.* tragically.

trágico, ca. I. *a.* tragic. II. *n.* tragedian, trage-dienne.

tragicomedia, *f.* tragi-comedy.

tragicómico, ca, *a.* tragi-comical.

¹trago, *m.* draught of liquid; drink; swallow; calamity, misfortune.—**a tragos,** by degrees, slowly, gently.—**echar un t.,** to take a drink.

²trago, *m.* (anat.) tragus.

tragón, na, *n. & a.* glutton(-ous).

tragonear, *va. & vn.* (coll.) to eat voraciously.

tragonería, tragonía, *f.* gluttony.

tragontina, *f.* (bot.) arum.

tragué, trague, *v. V.* TRAGAR.

traguillo, ito, *m. dim.* small drink.

traición, *f.* treason; treachery.—**alta t.,** high treason.—**a t.,** or **a la t.,** treacherously.

traicionar, *va.* to do treason to, to betray.

traicionero, ra, *a.* treacherous.

traída, *f.* carriage, conduction.

traído, da. I. *pp.* of TRAER. II. *a.* used, worn out; threadbare.

traidor, ra. I. *a.* traitorous; treasonable; treacherous, perfidious. II. *n.* traitor; betrayer.

traidoramente, *adv.* treacherously; treasonably, traitorously.

traigo, traiga, *v. V.* TRAER.

traílla, treílla, *f.* leash, lash; packthread; (agr.) leveling harrow; road leveler; road scraper.

traillar, *va.* to level (ground).

traína, *f.* seine for deep-sea fishing; net for sardine fishing.

trainera, *f.* smack for sardine fishing.

traíña, *f.* = TRAÍNA.

traite, *m.* raising a bur or nap on cloth.

¹traje, *m.* costume, dress, apparel; gown; suit of clothes; mask.—**t. charro,** (Mex.) showy riding costume.—**t. de baño,** (Am.) bathing suit. —**t. de ceremonia,** or **de etiqueta,** full dress, evening dress; uniform.—**t. de luces,** bull-fighter's garb.—**t. de montar,** riding habit.— **t. largo,** evening dress.—**t. sastre,** (Am.) (woman's) tailored suit.—**t. serio,** full dress, evening dress.

²traje, *pret.* of TRAER.

trajear, *va.* to clothe.

trajín, *m.* carrying from place to place; moving about.

trajinante, *n. & a.* carrier(-ying).

trajinar. I. *va.* to carry from place to place. II. *vn.* to travel about; (coll.) to fidget about.

trajinería, *f.* = TRAJÍN.

trajinero, ra, *n.* = TRAJINANTE.

trajino, *m.* = TRAJÍN.

tralla, *f.* cord, bass-weed rope; lash, snapper of a whip.

trama, *f.* weft or woof of cloth; twisted silk; fraud, plot; plot of a play or novel.

tramador, ra, *n. & a.* weaver(-ing); plotter(-ing), hatcher(-ing); schemer(-ing).

tramar. I. *va.* to weave; to plot, hatch, scheme. II. *vn.* (of olive trees) to blossom.

tramilla, *f.* (Am.) twine.

tramitación, *f.* procedure; transaction, action, carrying out.

tramitar, *va.* to transact, carry through, conduct.

trámite, *m.* the carrying on (of administration, etc.), the transacting (of business, etc.); step; (law) proceeding.

tramo, *m.* parcel of ground; flight of stairs; stretch, section; panel (of a bridge).

tramojo, *m.* (agr.) band for tying the sheaf; trouble, affliction; (Am.) = TRABANCO; (Colomb.) leash.

tramontano, na. I. *a.* transmontane. II. *f.* north wind; vanity, pride, haughtiness.

tramontar. I. *va.* to pass over (a mountain); (of the sun) to sink beyond (the mountains); to help escape. II. *vr.* to flee, to escape.

tramoya, *f.* (theat.) trick; craft, wile.

tramoyista, *m.* (theat.) stage machinist; stage carpenter, stage hand, scene shifter; impostor, swindler, fraud, humbug.

trampa, *f.* trap, snare, pitfall; trapdoor; falling board of a counter; flap or spring door; cheat, fraud, deceit, trick; bad debt.—**caer en la t.,** to fall into a trap.—**hacer t.,** or **trampas,** to cheat.—**se lo llevó la t.,** (of an affair) it fell through.

trampal, *m.* quagmire; bog.

trampantojo, *m.* (coll.) trick, deception.

trampazo, *m.* last twist of a torturing cord.

trampeador, ra, *n.* swindler, cheat, sharper.

trampear. I. *vn.* (coll.) to obtain money on false pretences; to cheat; to shift, get along, pull through. II. *va.* to swindle, cheat, deceive.

trampería, *f.* trickery, cheating, chicanery.

trampilla, *f. dim.* peephole; door of a coal bin; fly of trousers.

trampista, *m.* cheat, trickster, sharper.

trampolín, *m.* springboard.

tramposo, sa. I. *a.* tricky, deceitful, swindling. II. *n.* cheater, swindler, trickster; card sharp.

tranca, *f.* club, cudgel, stick, truncheon; cross board or stick, or prop to fasten a door on the inside; (Am., coll.) drunken spell, "tear."

trancada, *f.* long stride; blow with a stick.—**en dos trancadas,** in a trice, in two ticks.

trancado, *m.* small harpoon for eels.

trancahilo, *m.* stop knot in threads or ropes.

trancanil, *m.* (naut.) waterway, stringer plate.

trancar. I. *va.* (*pret.* TRANQUÉ; *subj.* TRANQUE) to bar (a door). **II.** *vn.* (coll.) to take long strides.

trancazo, *m.* blow with a bar; (coll.) influenza, grippe; (Colomb., coll.) fisticuff.

trance, *m.* peril, danger; critical moment; last stage or moments of life; (law) legal seizure on an execution.—**a todo t.,** at all costs, at any price, regardless of risk or trouble.—**en t. de muerte,** at the point of death.—**hacer t.,** (law) to seize property on an execution.

trancenil, *m.* gold or silver hatband, garnished with jewels.

tranco, *m.* long stride; threshold.—**a trancos,** hurriedly, carelessly.—**en dos trancos,** in a jiffy.

tranchete, *m.* cobbler's heel knife.

trancho, *m.* (ichth.) a variety of shad.

trangallo, *m.* = TRABANCO.

tranquera, *f.* palisade, palisado.

tranquero, *m.* angular stone of a jamb or lintel.

tranquil, *m.* (arch.) plumb line.

tranquilamente, *adv.* quietly, peacefully, composedly.

tranquilar, *va.* (com.) to check off.

tranquilidad, *f.* tranquility, peace, quiet; reassurance, ease.

tranquilizador, ra, *a.* quieting, soothing, reassuring.

tranquilizar, *va.* & *vr.* to calm, quiet down.

tranquilo, la, *a.* tranquil, calm, quiet, easy.

tranquilla, *f. dim.* trap, snare; small securing or fastening bar or stick; stop pin or lug.

tranquillón, *m.* maslin, mixed grain.

transacción, *f.* compromise, accommodation, settlement; transaction, negotiation.

transalpino, na, *a.* transalpine.

transandino, na, *a.* transandine, transandean.

transatlántico, ca, *a.* transatlantic.

transar, *va.* & *vr.* (Am.) to compromise, adjust, settle.

transbordador, ra. I. *a.* transshipping, transferring, transfer (as *a.*). **II.** *m.* transfer boat or car.—**t. funicular,** transfer ropeway.

transbordar, *va.* to transfer; to transship.

transbordo, *m.* transfer; transshipment.

transcendencia, transcendental, transcendente, etc. = TRASCENDENCIA, etc.

transcontinental, *a.* transcontinental.

transcribir, *va.* (*pp.* TRANSCRITO, TRANSCRIPTO) to transcribe; (mus.) to transcribe.

transcripción, *f.* transcription.

transcripto, ta; transcrito, ta, *pp. irreg.* of TRANSCRIBIR.

transcurrir, *vn.* (of time) to pass, elapse.

transcurso, *m.* lapse, course (of time).

tránseat, (Lat.) let it pass.

transeúnte. I. *a.* transient; transitory. **II.** *n.* sojourner; passer-by.

transferencia, *f.* transference, transfer.

transferible, *a.* transferable.

transferidor, ra, *n.* & *a.* transferrer(-ing).

transferir, *va.* (*ger.* TRANSFIRIENDO; *ind. pres.* TRANSFIERO, *pret.* él TRANSFIRIÓ; *subj.* TRANSFIERA) to transfer; (law) to transfer, convey, make over; (rhet.) to use figuratively.

transfigurable, *a.* transformable.

transfiguración, *f.* transfiguration.

transfigurar. I. *va.* to transfigure, transform. **II.** *vr.* to be transfigured.

transfijo, ja, *a.* transfixed.

transfixión, *f.* transfixion, piercing through.

transflor, *m.* (art) enamel painting.

¹transflorar, *va.* (art) to paint or decorate in enamel; to trace, make a tracing of.

²transflorar, *vn.* to show through.

transflorear, *va.* to paint in enamel.

transformación, *f.* transformation.

transformador, ra. I. *n.* & *a.* transformer(-ing). **II.** *m.* (elec.) transformer.—**t. acorazado,** shell transformer.—**t. de aceite,** oil-cooled transformer.—**t. de anillo,** ring transformer.—**t. de corriente,** or **de intensidad,** current transformer.—**t. de reducción,** step-down transformer.—**t. de tensión,** voltage transformer.—**t. elevador,** step-up transformer, booster.

transformamiento, *m.* transformation.

transformar. I. *va.* & *vr.* to transform. **II.** *vr.* to be or become transformed; to change one's sentiments or ways.

transformativo, va, *a.* transformative.

transformismo, *m.* (biol.) transformism, evolutionism.—**transformista. I.** *n.* & *a.* transformist(-ic); evolutionist(-ary). **II.** *n.* one who impersonates several characters in succession.

transfregar, *va.* (*ind. pres.* TRANSFRIEGO, *pret.* TRANSFREGUÉ; *subj.* TRANSFRIEGUE) to rub, scrub; rumple, crumple.

transfretano, na, *a.* transmarine, oversea.

transfretar. I. *va.* to cross (the sea). **II.** *vn.* to extend, spread.

transfriego, etc. *v.* V. TRANSFREGAR.

tránsfuga, *n.,* **tránsfugo,** *m.* deserter; fugitive, runaway; turncoat.

transfundición, *f.* = TRANSFUSIÓN.

transfundir, *va.* to pour into; transfuse; to communicate, transmit.

transfusión, *f.* transfusion; communication, transmission; (surg.) transfusion.

transfusor, ra, *n.* & *a.* transfuser(-ing).

transgredir, *va.* (*defect. only those modes are used having* i *in their ending*) to transgress.

transgresión, *f.* transgression.

transgresor, ra, *n.* & *a.* transgressor(-ing).

transición, *f.* transition.

transido, da, *a.* worn out, exhausted; famished; mean, avaricious.

transigencia, *f.* condescension, tolerance.

transigente, *a.* accommodating, compromising, broad-minded, reasonable, condescending.

transigir. I. *va.* (*ind.* TRANSIJO; *subj.* TRANSIJA) to compromise, settle. **II.** *vn.* to give in, agree.

transilvano, na, *n.* & *a.* Transylvanian.

transitable, *a.* passable, practicable.

transitar, *vn.* to travel.

transitivo, va, *a.* (law) transferable; (gram.) transitive.

tránsito, *m.* transit, passage; traffic; transition; stopping place; road, way; change, removal; death of holy persons; (astr., surv.) transit.—**de t.,** in transit, passing through; temporarily.—**hacer tránsitos,** to make stops on the way in a journey.—**se prohibe el t.,** (on a sign) no thoroughfare.

transitoriamente, *adv.* transitorily.

transitorio, ria, *a.* transitory.

translación, translaticiamente, translaticio, translativo, = TRASLACIÓN, etc.

translimitación, *f.* trespass; going beyond proper bounds; (mil.) armed intervention in a bordering state.

translimitar, *va.* (mil.) to cross (the boundary of a state) unintentionally or by permission; to go beyond the limit of (morality, reason).

translinear, *vn.* (law) to pass (an entail) to another line of heirs.

translucidez, *f.* translucence.

translúcido, da, *a.* translucent.

transmarino, na, *a.* transmarine, oversea.

transmigración, *f.* transmigration.

transmigrar, *vn.* to transmigrate.

transmisibilidad, *f.* transmissibility.

transmisible, *a.* transmissible.

transmisión, *f.* transmission; (radio) broadcast.

transmisor, ra. I. *a.* transmitting. **II.** *m.* (elec.) transmitter. **III.** *f.* (radio) broadcasting station.

transmitir, *va.* to transmit; (radio) to broadcast.

transmontar, transmontano = TRAMONTAR, TRAMONTANO.

transmudacion, *f.* **transmudamiento,** *m.* transmutation, change.

transmudar, *va.* to move, carry to another place; to persuade, convince; TRANSMUTAR.

transmutable, *a.* transmutable.

transmutación, *f.* = TRANSMUDACIÓN.

transmutar, *va.* to transmute, change.

transmutativo, va; torio, ria, *a.* transmutative.

transpacífico, ca, *a.* transpacific.

transpadano, na, *a.* transpadane, beyond the Po.

transparencia, *f.* transparency.

transparentarse, *vr.* to be transparent; to show through.

transparente. I. *a.* transparent; translucent. **II.** *m.* window shade; stained glass window.

transpirable, *a.* perspirable, transpirable.

transpiración, *f.* transpiration, perspiration.

transpirar, *vn.* to transpire, perspire.

transpirenaico, ca, *a.* beyond the Pyrenees.

transponedor, ra, *n.* & *a.* transposer(-ing); transplanter(-ing).

transponer. I. *va.* (*pp.* TRANSPUESTO; *ind. pres.* TRANSPONGO, *pret.* TRANSPUSE, *fut.* TRANSPONDRÉ; *subj.* TRANSPONGA) to transpose; to transfer, transport; to transplant. **II.** *vr.* (of sun, etc.) to set below the horizon; to go behind; to be rather drowsy.

transportación, *f.* transportation, transport.

transportador, ra. I. *a.* carrying, transporting. **II.** *n.* transporter, carrier. **III.** *m.* (drawing) protractor; (Ry.) ropeway.

transportamiento, *m.* transportation; transport, ecstasy.

transportar. I. *va.* to transport, carry; (mus.) to transpose; (surv.) (also **t. al papel**), to plat, plot. **II.** *vr.* to be in a transport, to be carried away.

transporte, *m.* transport, transportation, conveyance; cartage; ferriage; (naut.) transport ship; transport, rapture, ecstasy.

transposición, *f.* transposition.

transpositivo, va, *a.* transpositional.

transpuesto, ta, *pp. irreg.* of TRANSPONER.

transpuse, *pret.* of TRANSPONER.

transterminante, *a.* trespassing.

transterminar, *va.* to trespass.

transtiberino, na, *a.* across the Tiber.

transubstanciación, *f.* transubstantiation.

transubstancial, *a.* transubstantiated.

transubstanciar, *va.* to transubstantiate.

transvasar, *va.* to transfer (liquid, to another container).

transverberación, *f.* transfixion.

transversal, *n.* & *a.* transversal.

transversalmente, *adv.* transversely.

transverso, sa, *a.* transverse.

tranvía, *m.* tramway, street railway; street car.

tranviario, ria. I. *a.* pert. to tramways, street Ry.; tramway (as *a.*). **II.** *n.* tramway worker.

tranviero, ra, *n.* = TRANVIARIO.

tranza, *f.* (law) seizure in an execution.

tranzadera, *f.* knot of plaited cords.

tranzar, *va.* to cut, truncate; to auction off.

tranzón, *m.* clearing in a forest.

trapa, *f.* (naut.) spilling line.—*pl.* (naut.) relieving tackle; guys.

¡trapa, trapa! *interj.* tramp, tramp.

trapacear, *vn.* to cheat, swindle.

trapacería, *f.* fraud, cheating.

trapacero, ra, *n.* & *a.* cheat(-ing).

trapacete, *m.* (com.) daybook.

trapacista, *n.* = TRAPACERO.

trapajo, *m.* rag, tatter.

trapajoso, sa, *a.* ragged, tattered.

¹trápala. I. *f.* tramping of feet; galloping; noise, confusion.

²trápala. I. *f.* (coll.) trick, deceit, cheat. **II.** *n.* (coll.) prattler, chatterbox; cheat, humbug. **III.** *m.* garrulity, loquacity.

trapalear, *vn.* to prattle, chatter; to cheat.

trapalón, na, *n.* = ²TRÁPALA, *n.*

trapatiesta, *f.* (coll.) squabble, row, brawl.

trapaza, *f.* fraud, trick.

trapazar, *vn.* to cheat, swindle.

trape, *m.* interlining.

trapeano, na, *a.* (min.) trappean.

trapecial, *a.* trapezoidal.

trapecio, *m.* (geom.) trapezoid.

trapense, *m.* (eccl.) Trappist.

trapería, *f.* rags; frippery; rag fair, rag shop.

trapero, ra, *n.* ragpicker; rag dealer.

trapezoidal, *a.* four-sided.

trapezoide, *m.* trapezium; (anat.) trapezoid.

trapiche, *m.* sugar mill, cane mill; olive press; (Cuba) small sugar plantation; (Mex.) grinding machine.

trapichear, *vn.* (coll.) to contrive, shift.

trapicheo, *m.* (coll.) contriving, shifting.

trapichero, ra, *n.* worker in a sugar mill.

trapiento, ta, *a.* ragged, tattered.

trapillo, lla. I. *n. dim.* (coll.) courtier or lady of small means. **II.** *m.* amount of money saved and put away.—**de t.,** in dishabille or négligé.

trapío, *m.* (naut.) sails of a ship, canvas; (coll.) stylish or graceful carriage of a woman; liveliness and smartness in a fighting bull.

trapisonda, *f.* (coll.) bustle, clatter; brawl, scuffle; snare, deception; (naut.) whitecaps.

trapisondear, *vn.* (coll.) to foment brawls; to cheat, deceive.

trapito, *m. dim.* little rag.—**los trapitos de cristianar,** best Sunday clothes.

trapo, *m.* rag, tatter; rag, piece of cloth; sails of a ship; (coll.) bullfighter's cloak.—**a todo t.,** with all one's might; (naut.) all sails set.—**poner como un t.,** to reprimand severely, to dress down.—**soltar el t.,** (coll.) to burst out (crying or laughing).

traque, *m.* crack, report (of a rocket, etc.).—**a t. barraque,** (coll.) at all times, in and out of season.

tráquea, *f.* (anat., entom., bot.) trachea.

traqueado, da, *a.* threadbare, hackneyed; (Am.) (of road) much traversed; (P. R.) drunk.

traqueal, *a.* (anat., bot., entom.) tracheal.

traquear. I. *vn.* to crack, make a loud creaking noise. **II.** *va.* to shake (as a liquid); (coll.) to handle roughly; (Am.) to pass frequently over (a road, etc.); (P. R.) to get drunk.

traquearteria, *f.* trachea, windpipe.

traqueo, *m.* cracking (of fireworks, etc.); shake, shaking, jolt, jerk.

traqueotomía, *f.* tracheotomy.

traquetear, *va.* & *vn.* to shake, jolt, jerk, handle roughly; to crack (as fireworks or wood).

traqueteo, *m.* shaking, jolting, jerking; cracking, creaking; (Am.) confused, noisy passing.

traquiarteria, *f.* = TRAQUEARTERIA.

traquido, *m.* snapping, rattle; creaking, cracking.

traquita, *f.* (min.) trachyte, a volcanic rock.

traquítico, ca, *a.* (min.) trachytic.

trarigüe, *m.* (Chile) an ornamented belt or sash.

¹tras, *prep.* after, behind; beyond; besides.—**t. de,** after, behind, back of; besides, in addition to.

²tras, *m.* bang, noise of a blow.—**t. t.,** repeated strokes, noise or banging.

trasalcoba, *f.* room back of a bedroom (gen. dressing room).

trasalpino, na, *a.* = TRANSALPINO.

trasandino, na, *a.* transandine, transandean.

trasanteanoche, *adv.* three nights ago.

trasanteayer, *adv.* three days ago.

trasantier, *adv.* three days ago.

For pronunciation, see the rules at the beginning of the book.

trasañejo, ja, *a.* three years old.
trasatlántico, ca, *a.* = TRANSATLÁNTICO.
trasbordar, trasbordo = TRANSBORDAR, etc.
trasca, *f.* leather thong.
trascabo, *m.* trip (in wrestling).
trascantón, *m.* TRASCANTONADA; street porter. —**dar t. a,** to hide oneself behind a corner.
trascantonada, *f.* protective stone at corner of buildings.
trascartarse, *vr.* to remain behind (as a winning card).—**trascartón,** *m.* drawing of a winning card after the game is lost.
trascendencia, *f.* transcendency; result.
trascendental, *a.* transcendental; far-reaching; transcendent, highly important, significant; (math.) transcendental.
trascendentalismo, *m.* transcendentalism.
trascendentalista, *n. & a.* (philos.) transcendentalist(-ic).
trascendente, *a.* transcendent.
trascender. I. *vn.* (ind. TRASCIENDO; *subj.* TRASCIENDA) to extend; to spread, smell, emit a pleasant odor; to be pervasive; to transpire, leak out. **II.** *va.* to penetrate, scrutinize, find out.
trascendido, da, *a.* acute, perspicacious.
trascocina, *f.* back kitchen.
trascol, *m.* (obs.) train (of a dress).
trascolar, *va.* (ind. TRASCUELO; *subj.* TRASCUELE) to strain, percolate; (coll.) to pass over (a mountain).
trasconejarse, *vr.* to squat (as pursued game); (coll.) to be missing or mislaid.
trascordarse, *vr.* (ind. TRASCUERDO; *subj.* TRASCUERDE) to forget.
trascoro, *m.* space back of the choir.
trascorral, *m.* back court, back yard.
trascribir, trascrito, etc. = TRANSCRIBIR, etc.
trascuarto, *m.* back room; rear apartment.
trascuelo, trascuele, *v. V.* TRASCOLAR.
trascuerdo, trascuerde, *v. V.* TRASCORDARSE.
trascurrir, trascurso = TRANSCURRIR, etc.
trasdobladura, *f.* trebling.
trasdoblar, *va.* to treble, to triple.
trasdoblo, *m.* treble number.
trasdós, *m.* (arch.) extrados.—**tradosear,** *va.* (arch.) to strengthen the back of (an arch).
trasechador, ra, *n.* insnarer, waylayer.
trasechar, *va.* to insnare, waylay.
trasegador, ra, *n.* one who racks wine.
trasegar, *va.* (ind. pres. TRASIEGO, pret. TRASEGUÉ; *subj.* TRASIEGUE) to upset, to turn topsy-turvy; to change the place of; to empty, pour into another bottle or vessel.
traseñalador, ra, *n.* one who countermarks.
traseñalar, *va.* to mark anew.
trasera, *f.* back part, rear.
trasero, ra. I. *a.* hind, back, rear. **II.** *m.* buttock; rump.—*pl.* (coll.) ancestors, predecessors.
trasferencia, trasferible, trasferidor, trasferir = TRANSFERENCIA, etc.
trasfigurable, etc. = TRANSFIGURABLE, etc.
trasfijo, trasfixión = TRANSFIJO, etc.
trasflor, trasflorar, etc. = TRANSFLOR, etc.
trasfojar, *va.* = TRASHOJAR.
trasfollado, da, *a.* (vet.) having a swollen hock.
trasfollo, *m.* (vet.) swelling of the hock.
trasformación, etc. = TRANSFORMACIÓN, etc.
trasfregar, *va.* = TRANSFREGAR.
trasfretano, etc. = TRANSFRETANO, etc.
trásfuga, trásfugo = TRÁNSFUGA, etc.
trasfundición, etc. = TRANSFUNDICIÓN, etc.
trasgo, *m.* goblin, hobgoblin, sprite.
trasgredir, trasgresión, etc. = TRANSGREDIR, TRANSGRESIÓN, etc.
trasguear, *vn.* to play the hobgoblin.
trasguero, ra, *n.* imitator of hobgoblins' tricks.
trashoguero, ra. I. *n.* idler, loiterer near the fireplace. **II.** *m.* back plate of a fireplace; big log in the fireplace.

trashojar, *va.* to scan, leaf through (a book).
trashumación, *f.* nomadism of flocks.
trashumante, *a.* (of flocks) nomadic.
trashumar, *vn.* to roam in search of pasture.
¹trasiego, *m.* upsetting; racking (of wine).
²trasiego, trasiegue, *v. V.* TRASEGAR.
trasijado, da, *a.* lank, meagre; thin-flanked.
traslación, trasladación, *f.* transfer, removal; translation, change of place; adjournment, postponement; translation, version.
trasladador, ra, *n.* carrier, mover.
trasladante, *a.* moving, removing; translating, transcribing.
trasladar, *va.* to move, remove, transfer; to postpone, adjourn; to translate; to transcribe.
traslado, *m.* copy, transcript, transcription; transfer; imitation, resemblance, likeness, counterpart; (law) notification, communication.
traslapar, *va., vn. & vr.* to overlap.
traslapo, *m.* overlapping.
traslaticiamente, *adv.* figuratively; by extension.
traslaticio, cia, *a.* figurative; extended.
traslativo, va, *a.* transferring, conveying.
traslato, ta, *a.* = TRASLATICIO.
trasloar, *va.* to bestow fulsome praise on.
traslúcido, da, *a.* = TRANSLÚCIDO.
trasluciente, *a.* translucent.
traslucirse, *vr.* to be translucent, to shine or show through; to be inferable; to transpire.
traslumbramiento, *m.* dazzlement.
traslumbrar. I. *va.* to dazzle. **II.** *vr.* to pass swiftly, to vanish.
trasluz, *m.* light seen through a transparent body; reflected or borrowed light; (art) transverse light.—**al t.,** against the light.
¹trasmallo, *m.* trammel net.
²trasmallo, *m.* iron collar around head of mallet.
trasmano, *m.* second player at cards.—**a t.,** out of the way.
trasmañana, *f.* day after to-morrow.
trasmañanar, *va.* to procrastinate.
trasmarino, na, *a.* = TRANSMARINO.
trasmatar, *va.* (coll.) to assume that one will outlive (another).
trasmigración, etc. = TRANSMIGRACIÓN, etc.
trasminar, *vn.* to undermine, excavate; to pierce, penetrate, percolate.
trasmisible, etc. = TRANSMISIBLE, etc.
trasmochadero, *m.* thicket of firewood.
trasmochar, *va.* to cut branches for fuel.
trasmontano, trasmontar, etc. = TRAMONTANO, TRAMONTAR, etc.
trasmosto, *f.* weak, watered wine.
trasmudación, etc. = TRANSMUDACIÓN, etc.
trasmutable, trasmutación, trasmutar, etc. = TRANSMUTABLE, TRANSMUTACIÓN, etc.
trasnochada, *f.* last night; sleepless night; being up all night; (mil.) night attack.
trasnochado, da. I. *pp.* of TRASNOCHAR. **II.** *a.* fatigued from night watching; haggard, careworn; stale, worn-out; trite, hackneyed.
trasnochador, ra, *n.* night watcher; one who goes to bed late or not at all; (coll.) night hawk.
trasnochar. I. *vn.* to watch; to sit up all night; to spend the night. **II.** *va.* to leave for the next day.
trasnoche, trasnocho, *m.* night watch, going without sleep.
trasnombrar, *va.* to change or confuse the names of.
trasnominación, *f.* (rhet.) metonymy.
trasoír, *va.* (ger. TRASOYENDO; ind. pres. TRASOIGO, pret. él TRASOYÓ; *subj.* TRASOIGA) to hear wrong, mishear, misunderstand.
trasojado, da, *a.* having sunken eyes, emaciated, careworn.
trasoñar, *vn.* (ind. TRASUEÑO; *subj.* TRASUEÑE) to fancy erroneously, as in a dream.
trasovado, da, *a.* (bot.) obovate.

For pronunciation, see the rules at the beginning of the book.

traspadano, na, *a.* transpadane, beyond the Po.

traspalar, traspalear, *va.* to shovel, shovel off; to move, remove; to weed with a hoe.

traspaleo, *m.* shovelling; weeding with a hoe.

traspapelarse, *vr.* to be mislaid among other papers.

trasparencia, trasparentarse, trasparente, = TRANSPARENCIA, etc.

traspasador, ra, *n.* trespasser, transgressor.

traspasamiento, *m.* transgression; trespass; transportation; crossing over; transfixion; transfer, conveyance; grief, anguish.

traspasar, *va.* to pass over, go beyond; to cross (as a river); to remove, transfer; to go through; to pierce, transfix; to return, repass; to trespass, transgress, violate; to exceed (proper bounds); to convey, transfer, make over; to cause great grief or affliction to.

traspaso, *m.* conveyance, transfer; assignment; transgression, violation; grief, anguish.

traspatio, *m.* (Am.) back yard, back court.

traspecho, *m.* bone ornament on a crossbow.

traspeinar, *va.* to comb again.

traspellar, *va.* to close, to shut.

traspié, *m.* slip, stumble; trip, wrestler's trick.— **dar traspiés,** to stumble; to slip, to err.

traspilastra, *f.* (arch.) counterpilaster.

traspillar. I. *va.* to shut, close. **II.** *vr.* to fail, become emaciated.

traspintar. I. *va.* to show (one card) and play another. **II.** *vr.* to show through; to show against the light; (coll.) to fail, come out wrong.

traspirable, traspiración, traspirar = TRANSPIRABLE, etc.

trasplantar. I. *va.* to transplant. **II.** *vr.* to migrate.

trasplante, *m.* transplantation; migration.

trasponedor, trasponer = TRANSPONEDOR, etc.

traspongo, trasponga, *v. V.* TRASPONER.

traspontín, *m.* = TRASPUNTÍN.

trasportación, trasportador, trasportamiento, etc. = TRANSPORTACIÓN, etc.

trasportín, *m.* wool upper mattress.

trasposición, etc. = TRANSPOSICIÓN, etc.

traspuesta, *f.* transposition; nook; lurking place; flight, concealment of a person; back yard or court; back door; rear outbuilding.

traspuesto, ta, *pp. irreg.* of TRASPONER.

traspunte, *m.* (theat.) prompter.

traspuntín, *m.* bedquilt.

trasquero, *m.* leather cutter.

trasquila, *f.* shearing, clipping, cropping.

trasquiladero, *m.* place where sheep are shorn.

trasquilador, ra, *n. & a.* shearer(-ing), clipper (-ing).

trasquiladura, *f.* = TRASQUILA.

trasquilar, *va.* to shear (sheep); to lop, crop; clip; to curtail, cut down.

trasquilimocho, cha, *a.* (coll.) close shorn or cropped.

trasquilón, *m.* clipping, shearing; (coll.) money lost through trickery or deception.— **a trasquilones,** irregularly, rudely.

trastabillar, *vn.* to reel, waver.

trastada, *f.* (coll.) inconsiderate act.

trastazo, *m.* (coll.) whack, thump, blow.

¹**traste,** *m.* (mus.) stop, fret of a guitar; glass or cup for sampling wine.

²**traste,** *m.*—**dar al t. con,** to spoil, ruin, destroy.

trasteado, *m.* set of frets on a guitar.

trasteador, ra, *n.* moving man (woman).

trasteante, *a.* skillful at guitar playing.

¹**trastear,** *va.* to fret (a guitar); to play well on (the guitar).

²**trastear. I.** *va.* to madden (the bull) with a red flag; (coll.) to manage with tact. **II.** *vn.* to move furniture from one part of a house to another; to talk in an excited manner.

trastejador, *m.* roof tiler.

trastejadura, *f.* tiling.

trastejar, *va.* to tile; to overhaul, repair.

trastejo, *m.* tiling.

trasteo, *m.* maddening the bull with a red flag; clever management of a person or business.

trastería, *f.* heap of old furniture; (coll.) rash action.

trasterminante, trasterminar = TRANSTER-MINANTE, TRANSTERMINAR.

trastero, ra, *m.* or *f.* garret, lumber room.

trastesado, da, *a.* hardened, stiff.

trastienda, *f.* back room; prudence, caution.

trasto, *m.* piece of furniture; luggage; rubbish, lumber; (theat.) trick piece, set piece; (coll.) worthless person, trash.—*pl.* tools of trade, implements, outfit; steel weapons.— **trastos de cocina,** kitchen utensils.

trastornable, *a.* easily disturbed or upset.

trastornado, da. I. *pp.* of TRASTORNAR. **II.** *a.* upset, topsy-turvey; afflicted; unbalanced, mad.

trastornador, ra, *n. & a.* disturber(-ing); agitator(-ing).

trastornadura, *f.*, **trastornamiento,** *m.* upsetting, overthrow, disturbance.

trastornar, *va.* to upset; to turn upside down; to disorder, disturb, disarrange; to agitate, excite; to derange, daze, confuse, perplex (the mind); to persuade, induce.

trastorno, *m.* upsetting; upheaval; disturbance, disorder, confusion; trouble; disarrangement.

trastrabado, da, *a.* having the far hind foot and the near fore foot white.

trastrabarse, *vr.* to become fuddled.

trastrabillar, *vn.* to stumble; to reel; to stammer.

trastrás, *m.* last but one.

trastrocamiento, *m.* transposition, rearrangement; disarrangement.

trastrocar, *va.* (*ind. pres.* TRASTRUECO, *pret.* TRASTRUQUÉ; *subj.* TRASTRUEQUE) to change the order of; to disarrange, muddle.— **trastrueco, trastrueque,** *m.* rearrangement; disarrangement; transposition.

trastulo, *m. dim.* worthless utensil; trash.

trastulo, *m.* pastime, toy.

trastumbar, *va.* to overturn, upset.

trasudadamente, *adv.* toiling and sweating.

trasudar, *va.* to sweat, perspire.

trasudor, *m.* gentle perspiration.

trasuntar, *va.* to copy; to abridge, abstract.

trasuntivamente, *adv.* compendiously; as per copy.

trasunto, *m.* copy, transcript; likeness.

trasvasar, *va.* = TRANSVASAR.

trasvenarse, *vr.* (med.) to extravasate; to spill.

trasver, *va.* to see through; to see erroneously.

trasverberación = TRANSVERBERACIÓN.

trasversal, trasverso = TRANSVERSAL, etc.

trasverter, *vn.* (*ind.* TRASVIERTO; *subj.* TRASVIERTA) to overflow, run over.

trasvinarse, *vr.* (of wine) to leak out; (coll.) to be surmised or inferred.

trasvolar, *va.* (*ind.* TRASVUELO; *subj.* TRASVUELE) to fly across.

trata, *f.* trade; slave trade.— **t. blanca,** or **de blancas,** white slavery.

tratable, *a.* tractable, compliant.

tratadico, illo, ito, *m. dim.* tract, short treatise.

tratadista, *n.* author, writer (on special subjects).

tratado, *m.* treaty; treatise.

tratador, ra, *n.* mediator.

tratamiento, *m.* treatment; courteous title or form of address; (med., chem.) treatment.

tratante, *n.* dealer, trader, tradesman.

tratar. I. *va.* to treat (a subject, a person, a patient, a substance); to discuss; to handle, manage, conduct.— **t. de,** to address as, give the title of; to call, charge with being (*me trató de ambicioso*, he called me, or charged me with being, ambitious).— **t. por,** (chem.) to treat with. **II.** *vn.* to treat; to deal, trade.— **t. acerca de,** to treat of, deal with (a subject).— **t. de,** to treat of (a subject); to endeavor, try.—**t. en,** to deal in. III. *vr.* to behave, conduct oneself; to live (well or badly).—**t. de,** (impers.) to be a question of; to be intended for; (diff. constr.) to talk about (*¿de qué se trata?* what's being talked about, what are you talking about?).

trato, *m.* treatment, use, usage; social behavior, manner, address; pact, agreement, deal; trade, commerce; friendly intercourse, conversation; appellation, title of courtesy.—**mal t.,** ill-usage, ill-treatment.—**tener buen t.,** (coll.) to be pleasant, "nice," affable.—**tener mucho t.,** to be intimate friends.—**tener t. de gentes,** to be accustomed to good society.

traumático, ca, *a.* (med.) traumatic.

traumatismo, *m.* (med.) traumatism.

traversa, *f.* (naut.) backstay.

través, *m.* inclination, bias; reverse, misfortune; traverse; (arch.) crossbeam; (fort.) traverse, screen.—**al t.** = DE T.—**al t. de,** through.—**dar al t.,** to be stranded.—**dar al t. con,** to throw away, misspend; to ruin, destroy; to set aside, ignore.—**de t.,** across, athwart, through. —**mirar de t.,** to squint; to look at out of the corner of one's eye.—**por el t.,** (naut.) on the beam.

travesaño, *m.* crosspiece, crossbar; bolster of a bed.

travesar, *va.* (*ind.* TRAVIESO; *subj.* TRAVIESE) to cross.

travesear, *vn.* to skip about, frisk, caper, romp; to be mischievous; to be quick at repartee; to lead a debauched life; to behave improperly.

travesero, ra. I. *a.* transverse, cross. II. *m.* bolster of a bed.

travesía, *f.* distance; passage; stretch, space; sea voyage; crossing (the sea); crossroad, short cut; transverse position; money won or lost at gambling; (fort.) traverse works; (naut.) side wind; sailor's pay for each voyage.

travesío, ía. I. *a.* traversing; transverse, or lateral, wind. II. *m.* crossing, crossroad.

travestido, da, *a.* disguised.

travesura, *f.* prank, frolic, caper, antic; mischief; lively fancy; sprightly conversation.

traviesa, *f.* distance across; at cards, raise on a bet; wager laid on a card player; (Ry.) crosstie; (arch.) rafter; transverse wall; (min.) cross level or gallery.

¹**travieso, sa,** *a.* transverse, cross; restless, flighty; frolicsome, prankish; mischievous; shrewd, cute; dissolute, lewd.—**ir a campo t.,** to take a short cut; to go cross-country.

²**travieso, traviese,** *v. V.* TRAVESAR.

trayecto, *m.* distance, stretch; section.

trayectoria, *f.* trajectory.

trayente, *a.* bringing, carrying, conducting.

traza, *f.* sketch, draught, outline; plan, device, scheme, project, contrivance; plot, artifice; manner, means; looks, appearance, aspect; prospect.—**darse trazas,** to find a way.

trazado, da. I. *pp.* of TRAZAR. II. *a.* traced, outlined.—**bien or mal t.,** of a good or bad disposition or figure. III. *m.* sketch, draught, outline, plan; (act of) drawing; (Ry.) location; running (of a line on the ground).

trazador, ra, *n.* contriver, schemer, designer.

trazar, *va.* (*pret.* TRACÉ; *subj.* TRACE) to design, devise, plan out; draw up; to trace, mark out; to draw (as a line); (Ry.) to locate; (surv.) to run, lay out (a line, a curve).

trazo, *m.* outline, plan; line, stroke of a pen or pencil; (art) fold of the drapery.—**t. magistral,** down stroke of a letter.—**al t.,** drawn in outline.

trazumarse, *vr.* to leak, ooze, transude.

treballa, *f.* sauce for goose.

trébedes, *f. pl.* trivet, cook's tripod.

trebejar, *vn.* to frolic, romp; to play.

trebejo, *m.* toy, plaything; chess piece.—*pl.* implements, tools of trade.

trebejuelo, *m. dim.* toy, trifle, gewgaw.

trebeliánica, *f.* (law) fourth part of an estate, to be deducted by the fiduciary heir, who holds it in trust for another.

trébol, *m.* (bot.) trefoil, clover, shamrock.

trece, *n. & a.* thirteen; thirteenth.—**estarse en sus t.,** to persist in one's opinion, to stick to it.

trecemesino, na, *a.* of thirteen months.

trecenario, *m.* space of thirteen days.

trecenato, trecenazgo, *m.* employment of thirteen persons.

treceno, na, *a.* thirteenth.

trecentista, *n. & a.* (pert. to) the trecento.

trecientos, tas, *n. & a.* three hundred.

trechear, *va.* (min.) to transport from hand to hand or from section to section.

trechel, *m.* (bot.) spring wheat.

trecheo, *m.* (min.) action of TRECHEAR.

trecho, *m.* space, distance, stretch; lapse.—**a trechos,** by intervals.—**de t. en t.,** at certain distances or intervals.

trefe, *a.* soft, thin; pliable; spurious (coin).

tregua, *f.* truce; rest, respite, recess, intermission.

treílla, *f.* leash; road or harrow leveler.

treinta, *n. & a.* thirty; thirtieth.—**t. y una,** a card game.

treintaidosavo, va, *n. & a.* thirty-second (part).

treintaidoseno, na, *a.* thirty-second.

treintanario, *m.* space of thirty days.

treintañal, *a.* of thirty years duration or age.

treintavo, va, *n. & a.* thirtieth.

treintena, *f.* a thirtieth part; group of thirty units.

trienteno, na, *a.* thirtieth.

treja, *f.* cushion shot at billiards.

tremadal, *m.* quagmire, quaking bog.

tremátodo, da. I. *n. & a.* (zool.) trematode. II. *m. pl.* Trematoda, trematodes.

tremebundo, da, *a.* dreadful, frightful, fearful.

tremedal, *m.* = TREMADAL.

tremendo, da, *a.* tremendous, dreadful, terrible; awful, imposing; huge; excessive.

tremente, *a.* trembling.

trementina, *f.* turpentine.

tremer, *vn.* to tremble.

tremés; tremesino, na, *a.* three months old.

tremielga, *f.* (ichth.) electric ray, torpedo.

tremis, *m.* an ancient gold coin.

tremó, tremol, *m.* pier glass.

tremolante, *a.* waving in the air.

tremolar, *va. & vn.* to wave (as a flag).

tremolina, *f.* rustling of the wind; (coll.) bustle, fuss, noise, hubbub.

trémolo, *m.* (mus.) tremolo.

tremor, *m.* trembling; tremor.

trémulamente, *adv.* tremblingly, tremulously.

tremulante; tremulento, ta = TRÉMULO.

trémulo, la, *a.* tremulous, quivering, shaking.

tren, *m.* train; outfit; equipment; following, retinue; show, pomp, ostentation; (Ry.) train.—**t. ascendente,** "up train," going toward Madrid.—**t. botijo,** excursion train.—**t. carreta,** accommodation train.—**t. correo,** mail train. —**t. de artillería,** convoy of artillery.—**t. de aterrizaje,** (aer.) undercarriage, landing gear. —**t. de casa,** housekeeping outfit.—**t. de escala,** accommodation train.—**t. de lavado,** laundry.—**t. de mercancías,** freight train.— **t. de recreo,** excursion train.—**t. descendente,** "down train," going from Madrid.—**t. de viajeros,** passenger train.—**t. expreso,** express train.—**t. mixto,** mixed train, carrying both passengers and freight.—**t. ómnibus,** accommodation train.

trena, *f.* scarf, sash; burnt silver; twist bread.

trenado, da, *a.* reticulated, mesh (as *a.*), latticed.

trenca, *f.* crosstree in a beehive; main root.

trencellín, *m.* = TRENCILLO.

trencica, ita, *f. dim.* small braid or plait.

trencilla, *f.* braid (trimming).

trencillar, *va.* to trim with braid.

trencillo, *m.* gold or silver hatband trimmed with jewels.

treno, *m.* lamentation, dirge.

trenque, *m.* jetty in a river.

trenza, *f.* braid; plait; braided hair, tress.

trenzadera, *f.* tape; knot of plaited cord.

trenzado, *m.* braided hair; braiding; (dance) caper; prance of a horse.—**al t.,** carelessly.

trenzar. I. *va.* to braid; to plait. **II.** *vn.* to prance; to cut capers.

treo, *m.* (naut.) square sail, crossjack sail.

¹trepa, *f.* climbing; somersault.

²trepa, *f.* boring, perforating; (sewing) wavy edging or trimming; grain or mottle of polished wood; (coll.) flogging, lashing; (coll.) artful trick, fraud.

¹trepado, da, *a.* (of animals) strong, robust.

²trepado, *m.* (sewing) edging.

trepador, ra. I. *a.* climbing. **II.** *m.* climbing place. **III.** *f.* (bot.) climber, creeper (as ivy).—*pl.* (ornith.) climbers.

trepajuncos, *m.* (ornith.) a kind of reed bird.

trepanación, *f.* (surg.) trephining.

trepanar, *va.* (surg.) to trepan, trephine.

trépano, *m.* (surg.) trepan, trephine.

¹trepante. I. *pres. p.* of ¹TREPAR. **II.** *a.* climbing.

²trepante. I. *pres. p.* of ²TREPAR. **II.** *a.* wily, artful, crafty.

¹trepar, *vn.* to climb, mount, clamber; (bot.) to climb, creep (as ivy).

²trepar, *va.* to bore, perforate; (sewing) to trim with ²TREPA.

trepatroncos, *m.* (ornith.) mason bird.

trepe, *m.* (coll.) scolding, reprimand.

trepidación, *f.* trepidation; vibration; (ancient astr.) trepidation.

trepidante, *a.* vibrating, shaking.

trepidar, *vn.* to shake, vibrate, jar.

trépido, da, *a.* tremulous, shaking.

tres. I. *m. & a.* three; third. **II.** *m.* at cards, a trey; magistrate of a city governed by three magistrates. **III.** *f. pl.*—**las t.,** three o'clock.

tresalbo, ba, *a.* having three white feet.

tresañal, tresañejo, ja, *a.* three years old.

tresbolillo.—al t., (agr.) (set out) in special arrangement; (mech.) staggered (riveting).

trescientos, tas, *n. & a.* three hundred; three-hundredth.

tresdoblar, *va.* to treble; to fold three times.

tresdoble, *m.* triple, threefold.

tresillista, *n.* expert in, or fond of, ombre.

tresillo, *m.* ombre, a card game; (mus.) triplet.

tresmesino, na, *a.* three months old.

tresnal, *m.* (agr.) shock, stook.

trestanto. I. *m.* triple number or amount. **II.** *adv.* three times as much.

treta, *f.* (fencing) feint; trick, wile, craft.

treudo, *m.* (law) emphyteutic rent.

trezavo, va, *n. & a.* thirteenth.

tría, *f.* choice, selection; tease in fabrics.—**dar una t.,** to transpose (beehives).

triaca, *f.* (pharm.) antidote.

triacal, *a.* antidotal.

triache, *m.* coffee beans of inferior quality.

tríada, tríade, *f.* triad, group of three.

triangulación, *f.* triangulation.

triangulado, da; triangular, *a.* triangular.

triangularmente, *adv.* triangularly.

triángulo, la. I. *a.* triangular. **II.** *m.* (geom.) triangle; (astr.) Triangulum; (mus.) triangle.—**t. acutángulo,** acute-angled triangle.—**t. esférico,** spherical triangle.—**t. obtusángulo,** obtuse-angled triangle.—**t. rectángulo,** right-angled, or right, triangle.

triaquera, *f.* (pharm.) container for antidotes.

triar. I. *va.* to choose, select. **II.** *vn.* (of bees) to

swarm to a favorite hive. **III.** *vr.* (of fabric) to show teases; to curdle.

triario, *m.* (anc. Rome) triarian soldier.

trías, *m.* (geol.) Triassic.

triásico, ca, *a.* (geol.) Triassic.

tribómetro, *m.* friction-measuring instrument.

tribraquio, *m.* (poet.) tribrach (◡◡◡).

tribu, *f.* tribe.

tribuente, *a.* attributing.

tribuir, *va.* to attribute.

tribulación, *f.* tribulation, affliction.

tríbulo, *m.* (bot.) thistle; prickle.

tribuna, *f.* tribune; rostrum; gallery.—*pl.* grandstand.

tribunado, *m.* tribuneship.

tribunal, *m.* tribunal, court of justice.—**t. de cuentas,** exchequer.—**t. juvenil,** juvenile court.—**demandar, or llevar, a los tribunales,** to sue (at court).

tribunicio, cia; tribúnico, ca, *a.* pertaining to a tribunal or a judge.

tribuno, *m.* (Rom. hist.) tribune; orator.

tributación, *f.* tribute, contribution; system of taxation; (law) emphyteusis.

tributante, *n.* taxpayer; tribute payer.

tributar, *va.* to pay (taxes or contributions); to pay, render (homage, respect); (law) to hold in emphyteusis.

tributario, ria. I. *a.* tributary. **II.** *n.* taxpayer; tributary (river).

tributo, *m.* tribute; tax, contribution; gift, offering; toil, trouble, burden.

tricahue, *m.* a kind of Chilean parrot.

tricenal, *a.* lasting thirty years.

tricentésimo, ma, *a.* three-hundredth.

triceps, *m.* (anat.) triceps.

triciclo, *m.* tricycle.

tricípete, *a.* three-headed.

triclinio, *m.* (Rom. hist.) triclinium, a kind of couch.

tricolor, *a.* tricolor.

tricorne, *a.* (poet.) three-horned.

tricornio. I. *a.* three-horned. **II.** *m.* three-cornered hat.

tricotomía, *f.* trichotomy, division into three parts.

tricotómico, ca, *a.* trichotomic, pert. to trichotomy.

tricótomo, ma, *a.* trichotomous, divided into three parts.

tricromía, *f.* trichromic, three-colored printing.

tridacio, *m.* (pharm.) thridacium.

tridente. I. *a.* tridental. **II.** *m.* trident.

tridentino, na, *n. & a.* Tridentine.

tridínamo, ma, *a.* (chem.) trivalent.

triduano, na, *a.* lasting three days.

triduo, *m.* (eccl.) triduum.

triedro. (geom.) **I.** *a.* trihedral. **II.** *m.* trihedron; trihedral angle.

trienal, *a.* triennial.

trienio, *m.* term of three years; triennium.

trieñal, *a.* triennial.

trifásico, ca, *a.* (elec.) three-phase.

trífido, da, *a.* (poet.) trifid, three-cleft.

trifinio, *m.* point where the boundaries of three districts meet.

trifloro, ra, *a.* triflorous, three-flowered.

trifolio, *m.* (bot.) trefoil; shamrock.

triforme, *a.* triform, triformed.

trifulca, *f.* (coll.) squabble, row; (foundry) lever system for moving the bellows.

trifurcado, da, *a.* trifurcate, three-forked.

trigal, *m.* wheat field.

trigaza, *f.* short straw of wheat.

trigésimo, ma, *a.* thirtieth.

trigla, *f.* (ichth.) red surmullet.

triglifo, *m.* (arch.) triglyph.

trigo, *m.* wheat; wheat field.—*pl.* crops; grainfields.—**t. alonzo,** bearded wheat.—**t. blanquillo, candeal,** or **común,** summer wheat.—

t. chamorro, or desraspado, winter or beardless wheat.—t. fanfarrón, Barbary wheat.—t. hembrilla, or marzal, summer wheat.—t. mocho, pelón, peloto, beardless wheat.—t. piche = T. BLANQUILLO.—t. sarraceno, buckwheat.—t. teja. = T. BLANQUILLO—t. toseta, beardless wheat.—t. trechel, tremés, tremesino, summer wheat.

trigón, m. (mus.) trigonon, an ancient lyre.

trígono, m. (astrol., geom.) trigon.

trigonometría, f. trigonometry.—t. esférica, spherical trigonometry.—t. plana, or rectilínea, plane trigonometry.

trigonométrico, ca, a. trigonometrical.

trigueño, ña, a. brunette, swarthy, dark.

triguero, ra. I. a. growing with wheat. II. m. sieve for corn; corn or grain dealer. II. f. (bot.) common wheat grass; canary seed.

trilátero, ra, a. trilateral.

trilingüe, a. trilingual.

trilítero, ra, a. triliteral.

trilito, m. (archeol.) trilithon.

trilobites, m. (paleontol.) trilobite.

trilobulado, da, a. trilobate.

trilocular, a. trilocular, divided into three parts.

trilogía, f. trilogy.

¹trilla, f. (ichth.) red surmullet, gurnard.

²trilla, f. (agr.) harrow; thrashing.

trilladera, f. separating harrow.

trillado, da. I. pp. of TRILLAR. II. a. trite, stale, hackneyed.

trillador, ra. I. n. & a. (agr.) thrasher(-ing). II. f. thrashing machine.

trilladura, f. (agr.) thrashing.

trillar, va. (agr.) to thrash, beat; to frequent; to repeat.

trillo, m. (agr.) separating harrow; thrashing machine; (Am.) footpath.

trillón, m. trillion (one million billions).

trimembre, a. trimembral.

trimestral, a. trimestrial, quarterly.

trimestralmente, adv. quarterly.

trimestre, m. quarter; quarterly payment.

trimielga, f. (ichth.) = TREMIELGA, torpedo.

Trimurti, f. Trimurty, the Hindu Trinity.

trinado, m. (mus.) trill, quaver; twittering of birds.

trinar, vn. (mus.) to trill, quaver; (coll.) to get angry or furious.

trinca, f. triad, ternary; (naut.) gammoning, seizing; seizing stuff.—a la t., (naut.) closehauled.

trincadura, f. large two-masted barge.

trincafía, f. wound splice or patch, made by winding a rope spirally around the piece or pieces.

trincapiñones, n. (coll.) harebrained person.

¹trincar, va. (pret. TRINQUÉ; subj. TRINQUE) to break, chop.

²trincar, (mut. like ¹TRINCAR) I. va. (naut.) to fasten, lash; to tie, bind, make fast. II. vn. (naut.) to keep close to the wind.

³trincar, vn. (mut. like ¹TRINCAR) (coll.) to drink (wine or liquor).

¹trincha, f. (tailoring) cloth strap for buttoning garments.

²trincha, f. (Am.) socket chisel, cutting gouge.

trinchador, m. (Mex.) sideboard.

trinchadora, f. (S. A.) carving knife.

trinchante, m. carver at table; carving knife; (S. A.) sideboard; stonecutter's hammer.

trinchar, va. to carve (food).

trinche, m. (S. A.) carving knife.

trinchera, f. (mil.) trench, intrenchment; deep cut, ditch; trench coat, waterproof.

trinchero, m. trencher; side table.

trincherón, m. aug. large trench or ditch.

trinchete, m. cobbler's heel knife.

trineo, m. sleigh, sledge; sled, bob sled.

trinidad, f. trinity.

trinitaria, f. (bot.) pansy, heartsease.

trinitario, ria, a. & n. (eccl.) Trinitarian; (Mex.) hired mourner; native to (of) Trinidad.

trino, na. I. a. ternary, triadic, trinal, trine. II. m. (astr.) trine; (mus.) trill.

trinomio, m. & a. (math.) trinomial.

trinqué, trinque, v. V. ¹,²,³ TRINCAR.

trinquetada, f. (naut.) sailing under the foresail.

¹trinquete, m. (naut.) foremast, foresail.

²trinquete, m. (mech.) pawl, catch, stop; racket (ball game).

³trinquete, m.—a cada t., at every step.

trinquetilla, f. (naut.) fore staysail.

trinquis, m. (coll.) drink (of liquor).

¹trío, m. = TRÍA.

²trío, m. (mus.) trio.

trional, m. (chem.) trional.

Triones, m. pl. (astr.) Triones, the Dipper.

trióxido, m. (chem.) trioxid, trioxide.

tripa, f. gut, intestine, bowel; (coll.) belly, paunch; filling, fillers (for cigars); file, docket. —pl. core of fruit; insides, entrails; inner lining of some feathers.—hacer de tripas corazón, to pluck up heart.

tripanosoma, m. (biol.) Trypanosoma.

tripartición, f. tripartition.

tripartir, va. to divide into three parts.

tripartito, ta, a. tripartite.

tripasto, m. pulley with three sheaves.

tripe, m. shag, plush.

tripería, f. tripe shop; heap of tripe.

tripero, ra, n. tripe seller; m. bellyband; cummerbund.

tripicallero, ra, n. tripe dealer.

tripicallos, m. pl. tripe.

trípili, m. (theat.) a Spanish song and dance.

triplano, m. (aer.) tripiane.

triple, a. triple, treble.

tríplica, f. (law) rejoinder.

triplicación, f. triplication, trebling.

triplicado, da, a. triplicate, treble.

triplicar, va. (pret. TRIPLIQUÉ; subj. TRIPLIQUE) to treble, triple; (law) to rejoin.

tríplice, a. treble, triple.

triplicidad, f. triplicity, trebleness.

tripliqué, triplique, v. V. TRIPLICAR.

triplo, pla, a. treble, triplicate, triple.

trípode, m. or f. tripod; trevet, trivet.

trípol, trípoli, m. tripoli, rottenstone.

tripolino, na, n. & a. Tripoline, Tripolitan.

tripolio, m. (bot.) sea starwort.

tripolitano, na, n. & a. = TRIPOLINO.

tripón, na, a. (coll.) pot-bellied, big-bellied.

tríptico, m. triptych.

triptongo, m. triphthong, three-voweled syllable.

tripudiar, vn. to dance.

tripudio, m. dance, ball.

tripudo, da, a. pot-bellied, big-bellied.

tripulación, f. crew (of ship, airplane, etc.).

tripulante, n. one of the crew.—pl. crew.

tripular, va. to man (ships); to fit out, equip.

trique, m. crack, sharp noise.—triquete, m. dim. —a cada t., at every stir or step.

triquina, f. trichina, intestinal worm.

triquinosis, f. (med.) trichinosis.

triquiñuela, f. (coll.) trickery, subterfuge.

triquitraque, m. crack, clack, clattering, clashing; firecracker, pulling cracker.

trirrectángulo, la, a. (geom.) trirectangular.

trirreme, m. (naut.) trireme.

tris, m. crack, noise made by the breaking of glass; trice, nick of time.—t. tras, tedious repetition; "the same old story."—en un t., within an ace, almost, coming pretty near (falling, etc.).

trisa, f. (ichth.) shad.

Trisagio, m. (eccl.) Trisagion.

trisca, f. noise made by crushing under the feet; noisy fun, merriment, uproar.

riscador, ra. I. *n.* noisy, rattling person. **II.** *m.* (mech.) saw set, saw wrest, saw swage.

riscar. I. *vn.* (*pret.* TRISQUÉ; *subj.* TRISQUE) to stamp the feet; to walk lively, to hustle; to romp, caper, frolic. **II.** *va.* to mix, mingle; to set (the teeth of a saw).

risecar, *va.* to trisect.—**trisección,** *f.* trisection.

risílabo, ba, *a.* trisyllabic.

rismo, *m.* (med.) trismus, lockjaw.

rispasto, *m.* three-pulley tackle.

risqué, trisque, *v. V.* TRISCAR.

riste, *a.* sad, sorrowful; gloomy, dismal; abject, mean, low.

ristemente, *adv.* sadly, sorrowfully.

risteza, *f.* sadness, grief, sorrow, gloom.

ristón, na, *a.* melancholy, rather sad.

risulco, ca, *a.* three-pronged; having three furrows or channels.

ritíceo, ea, *a.* wheaten.

ritón, *m.* (myth.) Triton; (zool.) triton, triturus.

rítono, *m.* (mus.) tritone.

riturable, *a.* triturable, crushable.

rituración, *f.* trituration, crushing.

riturador, ra. I. *n.* & *a.* crusher(-ing), triturator (-ing). **II.** *f.* crusher, crushing machine.

riturar, *va.* to triturate, crush; to masticate.

riunfador, ra, *n.* conqueror, victor.

riunfal, *a.* triumphal.—**triunfalmente,** *adv.* triumphally.

riunfante, *a.* triumphant, victorious.

riunfantemente, *adv.* triumphantly.

riunfar, *vn.* (**de**) to conquer; to triumph, to achieve victory (over); to win; to trump at cards.

riunfo, *m.* triumph, victory; exultation; spoils of war; trump card.—**costar un t.,** to be exceedingly difficult.—**en t.,** triumphantly; in triumph.

riunviral, *a.* triumviral.—**triunvirato,** *m.* triumvirate.—**triunviro,** *m.* triumvir.

rivial, *a.* trivial; trite, trodden, beaten.

rivialidad, *f.* triviality; triteness.

rivialmente, *adv.* trivially.

rivio, *m.* fork of a road; junction of three roads; trivium (i. e. grammar, rhetoric, logic).

riza, *f.* bit, small piece, fragment, shred, particle.—**hacer trizas,** to knock to pieces; to tear to bits; to wound or injure a person or animal.

triza, *f.* = DRIZA, (naut.) halyard.

rocable, *a.* exchangeable.

rocada.—**a la t.,** in a sense or direction opposite to the apparent one.

rocadamente, *adv.* distortedly, changing things or words.

rocado, da. I. *a.* & *pp.* changed; distorted.—**a la trocada, or a la trocadilla,** in the contrary sense; in exchange. **II.** *m.* change, small coin.

rocador, ra, *n.* one who exchanges or changes.

rocaico, *a.* (poet.) trochaic, of trochees.

rocamiento, *m.* change; distortion; exchange.

rocante, *a.* bartering, exchanging.

rocánter, *m.* (anat.) trochanter.

trocar. I. *va.* (*ind. pres.* TRUECO, *pret.* TROQUÉ; *subj.* TRUEQUE) to exchange, barter; to change, alter; to interchange; to distort, pervert; to vomit. **II.** *vr.* to change; to be changed, transformed or reformed; to exchange seats with another.

trocar, *m.* (surg.) trocar.

rocatinta, *f.* (coll.) confusing mistake.

rocatinte, *m.* shot color, changing color.

roceo, *m.* (naut.) parrel, truss.

rociscar, *va.* to make into troches or lozenges.

rocisco, *m.* (pharm.) troche, lozenge.

rocla, *f.* pulley.

tróclea, *f.* (anat.) trochlea.

roco, *m.* (ichth.) short sunfish.

rocoide, *f.* (geom.) trochoid.

rocha, *f.* cross path, short cut; rough road, trail; (mil.) military road; (Ry., Am.) gauge.

trochemoche.—**a t.,** helter-skelter, pell-mell.

trochuela, *f. dim.* narrow path.

trofeo, *m.* trophy; spoils of war; victory; memorial; military insignia.

trófico, ca, *a.* (physiol.) trophic, pert. to nutrition.

trofología, *f.* trophology, science of the nutrition of tissues.

troglodita. I. *n.* & *a.* troglodyte; glutton(-ous). **II.** *n.* rough, cruel person. **III.** *m. pl* (zool.) Troglodytidæ.

troglodítico, ca, *a.* troglodytic.

troj, troje, *f.* granary, barn.

trojero, *m.* keeper of a granary.

trojezado, da, *a.* shredded, minced.

trola, *f.* (coll.) fib, hoax, gammon.

trole, *m.* (elec.) trolley.

tromba, *f.* waterspout.

trombón, *m.* (mus.) trombone.

trombosis, *f.* (med.) thrombosis.

trompa. I. *f.* trumpet; (mus.) horn; trunk of an elephant; proboscis of some insects; (foundry) trompe; humming top; (arch.) projecting arch (from a wall); cradle, vault; (Ry.) cowcatcher, pilot (of a locomotive).—**t. de caza,** hunting horn.—**t. de Eustaquio,** (anat.) Eustachian tube.—**t. de Falopio,** (anat.) Fallopian tube. —**t. marina,** a musical one-string instrument, played with a bow; waterspout.—**a t. tañida,** at the sound of the trumpet.—**a t. y talega,** hurriedly, helter-skelter. **II.** *m.* horn player.

trompada, *f.* (coll.) fisticuff; collision; bump.

trompar, *vn.* to whip a top.

trompazo, *m.* = TROMPADA.

trompear, *vn.* to whip a top; (Am.) to bump; to fight with the fists.

¹trompero, ra, *a.* deceptive, false, deceiving.

²trompero, ra, *n.* top maker.

trompeta. I. *f.* trumpet; bugle. **II.** *m.* trumpeter; bugler; (coll.) puppet, noodle.

trompetada, *f.* (coll.) silly remark.

trompetazo, *m.* trumpet blast; bugle blast or call; (coll.) silly remark.

trompetear, *vn.* (coll.) to sound the trumpet.

trompeteo, *m.* sounding the bugle or trumpet.

trompetería, *f.* brass pipes of an organ.

trompetero, *m.* trumpet maker; trumpeter.

trompetilla, *f. dim.* small trumpet; ear trumpet; (P. I.) cheroot.—**de t.,** (of certain mosquitoes) buzzing.

trompicar. I. *va.* to trip, to make stumble; (coll.) to promote (an employee) over another who is entitled to the place. **II.** *vn.* to stumble frequently; to falter.

trompicón, *m.,* **trompilladura,** *f.* stumbling.

trompillar, *va.* & *vn.* = TROMPICAR.

trompillo, *m.* (Am.) (bot.) a bixa tree.

trompillón, *m.* (arch.) keystone of a cradle vault.

trompis, *m.* (coll.) blow with the fist.

trompo, *m.* whipping top; spinning top; chessman; trochid (mollusk).—**ponerse como un t.,** to eat or drink to excess.

trompón, *m. aug.* big spinning top; (bot.) narcissus.—**a t.,** or **de t.,** helter-skelter.

tronada, *f.* thunderstorm.

tronador, ra. I. *n.* & *a.* thunderer(-ing). **II.** *m.* detonating rocket.

tronar, *v. impers.* & *vn.* (*ind.* TRUENA; *subj.* TRUENE) to thunder; (coll.) to lose one's all, to fail in business.—**t. con uno,** to fall out with one.—**por lo que pueda t.,** as a precaution, in case something happens.

tronca, *f.* truncation.

troncal, *a.* pertaining to or springing from the trunk or stem; trunk (as *a.*), main.

troncar, *va.* to truncate.

tronco, *m.* trunk; stem, stalk; stock, origin; team of horses; unfeeling person.—**estar hecho un t.,** to be bereft of sensation; to be fast asleep.

tronchado, *a.* (her.) trouçonné.

tronchar, *va.* & *vr.* to break off forcibly.

troncho, *m.* stem, stalk of garden plants.

tronchudo, da, *a.* stalky.

tronera. I. *f.* (fort.) embrasure; loophole; dormer, small skylight; porthole; pocket hole of a billiard table. **II.** *m.* harum-scarum, harebrained person.

tronerar, *va.* to make embrasures in.

trónica, *f.* (coll.) rumor, gossip.

tronido, *m.* thunder, loud report.

tronitoso, sa, *a.* (coll.) resounding, thundering.

trono, *m.* throne; (eccl.) shrine.—*pl.* thrones, seventh choir of angels.

tronquista, *m.* coachman, teamster.

tronquito, *m. dim.* of TRONCO.

tronzador, *m.* two-handed saw.

tronzar, *va.* to shatter, break in pieces; (sewing) to make fine tucks.

tronzo, za, *a.* (of horses) with cropped ears.

tropa, *f.* troops, soldiers; crowd, multitude; (Am.) drove of cattle; (Arg.) fleet (of vehicles); (mil.) ranks; beat to arms.—*pl.* (mil.) forces, army.— **t. de asalto,** storm troops.—**t. de línea,** regular or standing army; army corps.—**t. de marina,** marines.—**t. ligera,** skirmishers.—**en t.,** in random groups, without order.

tropecé, *pret.* of TROPEZAR.

tropeína, *f.* (chem.) tropeine.

tropel, *m.* rush, hurry, bustle, confusion; huddle; heap of things, mess, jumble; crowd.—**de,** or **en, t.,** tumultuously, in a throng.—**tropelía,** *f.* rush, hurry, confusion; injustice, outrage.

tropeoleo, a, *a. & f.* (bot.) Tropæolum.

tropezadero, *m.* stumbling place.

tropezador, ra, *n.* tripper, stumbler.

tropezadura, *f.* stumbling.

tropezar. I. *vn.* (*ind. pres.* TROPIEZO, *pret.* TROPECÉ; *subj.* TROPIECE) to stumble; (con) to strike (against); to stumble, trip (over); to meet (with); to stumble, light (on), happen to find; to slip (into crime or blunders); to wrangle, squabble. **II.** *vr.* (of horses) to interfere.

tropezón, na. I. *n. & a.* (of horses) interferer (-ing). **II.** *m.* tripping; stumbling; obstacle, stumbling block.—**a tropezones,** (coll.) by fits and starts; painfully, falling and rising, trudging along.

tropezoso, sa, *a.* apt to stumble or trip.

tropical, *a.* tropical.

trópico, ca. I. *a.* (rhet.) tropical, figurative. **II.** *m.* (astr., geog.) tropic.

tropidina, *f.* (chem.) tropidine.

tropiece, tropieza, ¹tropiezo, *v. V.* TROPEZAR.

²tropiezo, *m.* stumble; obstacle, hitch; slip, fault, error; quarrel, dispute, squabble.

tropina, *f.* (chem.) tropine.

tropismo, *m.* (biol.) tropism.

tropo, *m.* (rhet.) trope.—**tropología,** *f.* tropology.—**tropológico, ca,** *a.* tropological.

troposfera, *f.* (meteorol.) troposphere.

troque, *m.* knot made in cloths when dyeing them, to show the original color.

troqué, *pret.* of TROCAR.

troquel, *m.* die (as for coining).

troquelar, *va.* = ACUÑAR, to coin, mint.

troqueo, *m.* (poet.) trochee (-‿).

troquillo, *m.* (arch.) trochilus.

trotador, ra, *n. & a.* trotter(-ing).

trotar, *va. & vn.* to trot; (coll.) to hustle.

trote, *m.* trot.—**t. cochinero,** rack (gait of a horse).—**al t.,** trotting, at a trot; (coll.) in haste. **—tomar el t.,** (coll.) to run away.

trotillo, *m. dim.* light trot.

trotón, na. I. *f.* trotter(-ing). **II.** *m.* horse.

trotonería, *f.* continual trot.

trova, *f.* metrical composition; ballad.

trovador, ra, *n.* troubadour, minstrel.

trovadoresco, ca, *a.* pertaining to, or in the way of, minstrels or troubadours.

trovar, *vn.* to write poetry; to misconstrue.

trovero, *m.* (Fr. poet.) trouvère, trouveur.

trovista, *n.* = TROVADOR.

trovo, *m.* popular love ballad.

trox, *f.* (obs.) = TROJ, granary, barn.

Troya, *f.* Troy.—**aquí fué T.,** here was Troy; only the ruins left; here, or there, is the rub, or the difficulty.—**¡arda T.!** let happen what will.

troyano, na, *n. & a.* Trojan.

¹troza, *f.* log (of wood).

²troza, *f.* (naut.) parrel truck.

trozar, *va.* to cut into logs; to break, shatter.

trozo, *m.* piece, chunk, fragment, part; (naut.) detail of a crew; selection, piece (of music); passage (from a book, etc.); (mil.) division of a column.—**t. de madera,** block (of wood).

trucar, *vn.* (*pret.* TRUQUÉ; *subj.* TRUQUE) to make the first bet at the game of TRUQUE; to pocket a ball at pool or trucks.—**truco,** *m.* pocketing a pool ball.—*pl.* pool (billiards).

truculencia, *f.* truculence, cruelty.

truculento, ta, *a.* truculent, fierce.

trucha, *f.* (ichth.) trout; derrick, gin.—**t. de mar,** (ichth.) sea trout.

truchero, ra, *n.* fisher or seller of trout.

truchimán, na, *n.* (coll.) expert buyer; shrewd trader.

truchuela, *f.* small trout; small dry codfish.

trué, *m.* fine linen from Troyes.

¹trueco, *m.* exchange, barter.—**a t.,** or **en t., de,** in exchange for.

²trueco, trueca, *v. V.* TROCAR.

truena, truene, *v. V.* TRONAR.

trueno, *m.* thunder; loud report (as of cannon); (coll.) harum-scarum, wild youth.—**t. gordo,** loud detonation; big scandal; sensational ending.

¹trueque, *m.* exchange, barter.—**a t.,** or **en t., de,** in exchange for.

²trueque, *v. V.* TROCAR.

trufa, *f.* (bot.) truffle; lie, story, fib.

trufador, ra, *n.* story teller, fibber.

trufar. I. *va.* to stuff or cook with truffles. **II.** *vn.* to fib, lie.

truhán, na, *n.* rascal, scoundrel, knave; buffoon, jester, mountebank.—**truhanada,** *f.* piece of rascality.—**truhanamente,** *adv.* villainously, knavishly.—**truhanear,** *vn.* to play the rascal; to play the buffoon.—**truhanería,** *f.* rascality, scoundrelism; buffoonery, low jest.—**truhanesco, ca,** *a.* knavish, rascally; clownish.

truja, *f.* olive bin in oil mills.—**trujal,** *m.* oil press; wine press; oil mill: copper for soap making.—**trujaleta,** *f.* vessel for the juice in a wine press.

trujamán, *n.* expert buyer or trader; dragoman, interpreter.—**trujamanear,** *vn.* to act as an interpreter, broker, buyer, or seller; to trade, to barter.—**trujamanía,** *f.* brokering, brokerage.

trujimán, *n.* = TRUJAMÁN.

¹trulla, *f.* noise, bustle, hurly-burly; crowd.

²trulla, *f.* (mason.) trowel.

¹trullo, *m.* (ornith.) teal.

²trullo, *m.* vat for the juice of pressed grapes.

trun, *m.* (bot.) a Chilean variety of bur.

truncadamente, *adv.* in a truncated manner.

truncado, da, *a. & pp.* truncate, truncated.

truncamiento, *m.* truncation; maiming.

truncar, *va.* (*pret.* TRUNQUÉ; *subj.* TRUNQUE) to truncate; to maim; to mutilate (a speech, quotation, etc.).

trunco, ca, *a.* mutilated; truncated; incomplete.

trupial, *m.* (ornith.) troopial.

truque, *m.* a card game.

truqué, truque, *v. V.* TRUCAR.

truquero, *m.* keeper of a pool table.

truquiflor, *m.* a card game.

trusa, *f.* (Cuba, W. I.) men's bathing suit.—*pl.* trunk hose.

tsetsé, tsé-tsé, *f.* tsetse fly.

tú, *pers. pron. 2d person, m.* or *f.* thou; (when on intimate terms) you.—**a t. por t.,** thee for thee;

disrespectfully.—**de t. por t.**, intimately.—**tratar de t.**, to be on intimate terms with.

tu, *poss. pron. m.* or *f.* (*pl.* **tus**) thy; (when on intimate terms) your.

tuatúa, *f.* (bot.) American spurge.

tuáutem, *n.* (coll.) leading spirit, mover; essential point.

tuba, *f.* (P. I.) tuba, a beverage obtained from certain palms.

tuberculina, *f.* tuberculine.

tuberculización, *f.,* infecting with tuberculosis, tubercularization.

tubérculo, *m.* (bot.) tuber; (med.) tubercle.

tuberculosis, *f.* (med.) tuberculosis.

tuberculoso, sa, *a.* tuberculous.

tubería, *f.* tubing; piping; pipe line.

tuberosa, *f.* (bot.) tuberose.

tuberosidad, *f.* tuberosity.

tuberoso, sa, *a.* tuberous.

tubífero, ra, *a.* (biol.) provided with tubes.

tubiforme, *a.* tubiform, tubular.

tubo, *m.* tube; pipe; duct; lamp chimney.—**t. acústico,** speaking tube.—**t. cañón,** (aer.) riser.—**t. de Crookes,** Crookes tube.—**t. de ensayo,** test tube.—**t. de Géissler,** Geissler tube.—**t. de subida,** (aer.) = T. CAÑÓN.—**t. de vacío,** vacuum tube.—**t. intestinal,** intestinal canal, intestines.—**t. lanzatorpedos,** torpedo tube.—**t. termiónico,** (radio) thermionic valve.

tubulado, da, *a.* having tubes or a tube; TUBULAR.

tubular, *a.* tubular; tube-shaped.

tubuloso, sa, *a.* (bot.) tubulous.

tucán, *m.* (ornith.) toucan; (T-, astr.) Toucan.

tucía, *f.* tutty.

tuciorismo, *m.* (theol.) tutiorism.

tuciorista, *n.* & *a.* (theol.) tutiorist(-ic).

tuco, *m.* (Arg.) glowworm; (Peru) a kind of owl.

tucúquerre, *m.* (Chile) a very large owl.

tucuso, *m.* (Venez.) (ornith.) humming bird.

tudel, *m.* mouthpiece of a bassoon.

tudesco, ca. I. *a.* & *n.* (of person) German. II. *m.* a wide cloak.

tueca, *f.* stump, stub.

tueco, *m.* hole made by borers in wood; TUECA.

tuera, *f.* (bot.) colocynth, bitter apple.

tuerca, *f.* nut, female screw, lock nut.

tuerce, *m.* = TORCEDURA, sprain.

tuero, *m.* brushwood; (bot.) spicknel.

tuerto, ta. I. *a.* one-eyed, blind in one eye. II. *m.* (obs.) wrong, injury.—*pl.* pains after childbirth.—**a tuertas,** contrariwise, on the contrary.—**a tuertas o a derechas,** or **a t. o a derecho,** right or wrong; inconsiderately.

tuerzo, tuerza, *v.* V. TORCER.

tueste, *m.* toast, toasting.

tuesto, tueste, *v.* V. TOSTAR.

tuétano, *m.* marrow; pith of trees.—**hasta los tuétanos,** to the marrow.

tufarada, *f.* strong scent or smell.

tufo, *m.* vapor, emanation; (coll.) strong, offensive breath; conceit, airs, snobbishness.

tufo, *m.* locks of hair over the temples.

tufo, *m.* (geol.) tufa, a kind of rock.

tugurio, *m.* shepherd's hut, cabin; (coll.) mean, small room, "hole"; low place, "joint."

tuición, *f.* (law) defense, protection.

tuína, *f.* long, full jacket.

tuitivo, va, *a.* (law) defensive, protective.

tul, *m.* tulle.

tulipa, *f.* (bot.) small tulip; tulip-shaped lamp shade.

tulipán, *m.* (bot.) tulip.

tulipero, *m.* (bot.) tulip tree, whitewood.

tullidez, *f.* partial or total paralysis (esp. of legs).

tullido, da, *a.* partially or totally paralyzed (esp. app. to the legs).

tullidura, *f.* dung of birds of prey.

tullimiento, *m.* (med.) contraction of the tendons.

tullir. I. *va.* to maim, cripple. II. *vn.* (of birds) to drop dung. III. *vr.* to be crippled.

tumba, *f.* tomb, grave; roof of a coach; ornamental box seat in state coaches.

tumba, *f.* tumble; somersault.

tumbacuartillos, *m.* sot, old toper.

tumbadero, *m.* tumbling place in gymnasium.

tumbadillo, *m.* (naut.) roundhouse, cuddy.

tumbado, da, *a.* vaulted, arched.

tumbaga, *f.* gold and copper alloy; (jewelry) cheap finger ring.

tumbagón, *m.* *aug.* bracelet of TUMBAGA.

tumbar. I. *va.* to fell, throw down; (coll.) to knock down, stun, overpower (as a powerful odor). II. *vn.* to tumble, fall down, roll down; (naut.) to heel, to run aground. III. *vr.* (coll.) to lie down, tumble into bed.

tumbilla, *f.* brazier for warming beds.

tumbo, *m.* tumble, fall; somersault.—**t. de dado,** imminent peril.—**t. de olla,** ingredients of a meat-and-vegetable soup.—**dar un t.,** to turn a somersault.

tumbo, *m.* book containing the privileges and title deeds of monasteries, etc.

tumbón, na, *n.* (coll.) lazy person; sly, cunning person.

tumbón, *m.* *aug.* coach or trunk with an arched roof or lid.

tumefacción, *f.* tumefaction, swelling.

tumescente, *a.* tumescent.

túmido, da, *a.* swollen, tumid, bloated; pompous, highflown; (arch.) domed.

tumor, *m.* tumor.—**tumorcico, illo, ito,** *m.* *dim.* small tumor.

tumoroso, sa, *a.* having tumors.

tumulario, ria, *a.* pertaining to a tomb.

túmulo, *m.* tomb; funeral pile; mound; tumulus; catafalque.

tumulto, *m.* tumult, uproar, uprising; mob.

tumultuante, *a.* fomenting sedition.

tumultuar. I. *va.* to incite to an uprising. II. *vr.* to rise in arms.

tumultuariamente, *adv.* tumultuarily.

tumultuario, ria, *a.* tumultuary; tumultuous.

tumultuosamente, *adv.* tumultuously.

tumultuoso, sa, *a.* tumultuous.

tuna, *f.* (bot.) opuntia, prickly pear or Indian fig.

tuna, *f.* idle and licentious life; truantship.—**correr la t.** = TUNAR.

tunal, *m.* (bot.) opuntia; opuntia field.

tunanta, *a.* & *f.* shrewd, rascally woman.

tunantada, *f.* rascality, sharp practice.

tunante. I. *a.* leading a roving and licentious life. II. *n.* truant, idler, rake; rascal, rogue.

tunantear, *vn.* to act the rascal.

tunantería, *f.* rascality, knavishness.

tunantuela, *f.* *dim.* roguish girl, hoyden.

tunantuelo, *m.* *dim.* little rascal.

tunar, *vn.* to lead a licentious and vagrant life; to loaf, stroll.

tunda, *f.* shearing of cloth.

tunda, *f.* (coll.) trouncing, whipping.

tundente, *a.* beating, whipping; producing contusion.

tundición, *f.* shearing of cloth.

tundidor, *m.* cloth shearer.

tundidora, *f.* cloth-shearing machine.

tundidura, *f.* shearing of cloth.

tundir, *va.* to shear (cloth).

tundir, *va.* (coll.) to trounce, beat, cudgel, whip.

tundizno, *m.* shearings from cloth.

tunear, *vn.* to act the rogue.

tunecí; tunecino, na, *n.* & *a.* Tunisian.

túnel, *m.* tunnel.

tungstato, *m.* (chem.) tungstate.

tungsteno, *m.* (chem.) tungsten.

túngstico, ca, *a.* (chem.) tungstic, tungstenic.

túnica, *f.* tunic; robe, gown; (anat. and bot.)

tunic, tunicle.—**t. de Cristo**, (bot.) stramonium.

tunicado, da. I. *m.* & *a.* (zool.) tunicate. **II.** *m. pl.* Tunicata.

tunicela, *f.* tunic; (eccl.) tunicle.

túnico, *m.* robe, gown; (Cuba) frock, dress.

tuno, na. I. *a.* rascally, roguish, sly, cunning. **II.** *m.* truant, rake, rascal, rogue.

tuntún, *m.* (Colomb.) a kind of anæmic fever.—**al buen t.**, (coll.) heedlessly, haphazard.

tupa, *f.* tight packing; (coll.) satiety, repletion.

tupé, *m.* toupee, foretop; (coll.) cheek, gall, brass.

tupi, *a.* & *m.* Tupian.

tupido, da. I. *pp.* of TUPIR. **II.** *a.* dense, thick; close-woven; blocked, choked, obstructed.

tupinambo, *m.* (bot.) Jerusalem artichoke.

tupir. I. *va.* to pack tight; to make thick or compact; to choke, obstruct; to block or stop up. **II.** *vr.* to stuff or glut oneself.

turanio, nia, *n.* & *a.* Turanian.

¹**turba,** *f.* crowd, rabble, mob.

²**turba,** *f.* peat; turf.

turbáceo, a, *a.* peaty.

turbación, *f.* confusion, embarrassment.

turbadamente, *adv.* confusedly.

turbador, ra, *n.* disturber, perturber.

turbal, *m.* peat bog, peat bed.

turbamiento, *m.* = TURBACIÓN.

turbamulta, *f.* crowd, rabble, mob.

¹**turbante. I.** *pres. p.* of TURBAR. **II.** *a.* disturbing.

²**turbante,** *m.* turban.

turbar, *va.* & *vr.* to disturb, upset; to disquiet, alarm, confuse, embarrass.

turbativo, va, *a.* alarming; disturbing.

turbera, *f.* peat bog, peat moss.

turbia, *f.* muddy water.

turbiamente, *adv.* obscurely, confusedly.

túrbido, da, *a.* muddy, turbid.

turbiedad, turbieza, *f.* muddiness, turbidity; obscurity of language.

turbina, *f.* turbine.—**t. axial**, axial turbine.—**t. centrífuga**, outward-flow turbine.—**t. centrípeta**, inward-flow turbine.—**t. de acción**, impulse turbine.—**t. de reacción**, reaction turbine.—**t. de vapor**, steam turbine.—**t. límite**, limit turbine.—**t. paralela**, axial turbine.—**t. radial**, radial turbine.—**t. tangencial**, tangential turbine.

turbino, *m.* pulverized turpeth, a drug.

turbinto, *m.* (bot.) terebinth.

turbio, bia. I. *a.* muddy, turbid; disturbed, confused, upset; troubled, turbulent; indistinct; obscure (language). **II.** *m. pl.* dregs.

turbión, *m.* squally shower; sweep, rush.

turbit, *m.* (bot.) turpeth.—**t. mineral**, (pharm.) turpeth mineral.

turbonada, *f.* squall, pelting shower.

turbulencia, *f.* turbidness; turbulence.

turbulentamente, *adv.* turbulently.

turbulento, ta, *a.* turbid; turbulent.

turca, *f.* (coll.) tipsiness.—**coger una t.**, to get drunk.

turco, ca. I. *adj.* Turkish. **II.** *n.* Turk.—**el gran t.**, the Grand Turk.

turcomano, na, *n.* & *a.* Turkoman.

turcople, *a.* born of Turkish father and Greek mother.

túrdido, da. I. *a.* (ornith.) turdine. **II.** *m. pl.* Turdidæ.

túrdiga, *f.* strip of hide.

turdión, *m.* ancient Spanish dance.

turgencia, *f.* (med.) swelling, turgescence.

turgente, *a.* turgescent, turgid, swollen; (poet.) protuberant, prominent.

túrgido, da, *a.* (poet.) prominent, bulging.

turibular, *va.* (eccl.) to cense with a thurible.

turibulario, *m.* (eccl.) thurifer, censer bearer.

turíbulo, *m.* (eccl.) censer, thurible.

turiferario, *m.* = TURIBULARIO.

turífero, ra, *a.* thuriferous, incense-bearing.

turión, *m.* (bot.) turion.

turismo, *m.* tourism, touring.—**de t.**, touring (esp. app. to automobiles).

turista, *n.* & *a.* tourist(-ing).

turma, *f.* testicle; lamb fry.—**t. de tierra**, (bot.) truffle.

turmalina, *f.* (min.) tourmaline.

turnar, *vn.* & *vr.* to alternate; to go or work by turns.

turnio, nia, *a.* squint-eyed; fierce-looking.

turno, *m.* turn.—**t. de noche**, night shift (of workmen).—**al t.**, by turns.—**de t.**, (of a store, etc.) open for service; (of a person) (taking one's turn) on duty.—**por su t.**, in one's turn.

turón, *m.* a kind of field mouse.

turonense, *a.* of or from Tours.

turpial, *m.* (ornith.) troupial.

¹**turquesa,** *f.* (jewelry) turquoise.

²**turquesa,** *f.* bullet mold; mold, form.

turquesado, da, *a.* of turquoise color.

turquesco, ca, *a.* Turkish.—**a la t.**, in the Turkish manner.

turquí; turquino, na, *a.* deep blue.

turrar, *va.* to toast; to broil.

turrón, *m.* nougat, almond paste; (coll.) public office; sinecure.—**t. de Jijona**, sweet-almond paste.—**comer del t.**, to fill a public office.

turronería, *f.* TURRÓN shop.

turronero, ra, *n.* maker or seller of TURRÓN.

turulato, ta, *a.* (coll.) dumbfounded, stupefied.

turuleque, *m.* vulgar man, boor.

turulés, *a.* app. to a kind of strong grapes.

turullo, *m.* shepherd's call horn.

turumbón, *m.* bump on the head.

turupial, *m.* (Venez.) (ornith.) troupial.

¡**tus!** *interj.* used in calling dogs.—**sin decir t. ni mus,** (coll.) without saying a word.

tusa, *f.* (Am.) PAJILLA, maize-leaf cigar; corncob; (Chile) tassel of corncob; (Chile) mane of horse.

tusílago, *m.* (bot.) coltsfoot.

¡**tuso!** *interj.* get away! (app. to dogs).

tuso, sa, *a.* (Colomb.) pitted by smallpox.

tusón, *m.* fleece wool; (prov.) colt under two years old.

tusona, *f.* (Andalusia) filly under two years old.

tute, *m.* a card game.

tutear, *va.* to use the familar TÚ in addressing person.

tutela, *f.* guardianship, tutelage, tutorage, protection.—**t. dativa**, (law) guardianship appointed by a court.

tutelar, *a.* tutelar, tutelary.

tuteo, *m.* use of TÚ (thou).

tutía, *f.* = ATUTÍA, tutty.

tutilimundi, *m.* = MUNDONUEVO, peep-show.

tutiplén,—**a t.**, (coll.) abundantly.

tutor, ra. I. *n.* tutor, instructor (governess), guardian.—**t. dativo**, (law) guardian appointed by a court. **II.** *m.* training pole for plants.

tutoría, *f.* tutelage, guardianship.

tutriz, *f.* = TUTORA, woman tutor, governess.

tutuma, *f.* (Am.) TOTUMA, cup made from gourd; (Chile) bump, bruise; (Am.) lump, gathering, abscess.

tuturutu, *a.* (S. A.) dumbfounded.

tuve, etc., *v. V.* TENER.

tuya, *f.* (bot.) thuya.—**t. articulada**, sandarac tree.

tuyo, ya, *poss. pron.* 2d pers. *m.* & *f.* (sometimes with the *def. art.*) thine; (when on intimate terms) yours.—**los tuyos**, thy family, thy people, yours.

U

¹**u,** *f.* u (letter).—**u valona**, (the letter) w.—**en U**, U-shaped (*tubo en U*, U-tube); channel-shaped (*hierro en U*, channel iron, channel).

i, *conj.* (before words beginning with *o* or *ho*) or.

J., Ud., (abbr. of *usted*), you.—*pl.* **UU., Uds.**

apití, *m.* (zool.) wapiti.

atérfono, *m.* (hydraul.) hydrophone.

bérrimo, ma, *a. super.* very fruitful; exceedingly plentiful.

bicación, *f.* situation, location, position.

bicar, *vn.* & *vr.* to lie, to be situated, located.

bicuidad, *f.* ubiquity.

bicuo, cua, *a.* ubiquitous.

biquidad, *f.* = UBICUIDAD.

biquitario, ria, *a.* & *n.* Ubiquitarian.

bre, *f.* udder; milk bag.

brera, *f.* (med.) thrush.

case, *m.* ukase.

cranio, nia, *n.* & *a.* Ukrainian.

dómetro, *m.* udometer, rain gauge.

esnorueste, *m.* west-northwest.

essudueste, *m.* west-southwest.

este, *m.* west.

uf! *interj.* denoting weariness or annoyance.

fanamente, *adv.* ostentatiously, boastfully, with an air of satisfaction.

fanarse, *vr.* to boast, pride oneself.

fanía, *f.* pride, conceit; joy, pleasure.

fano, na, *a.* conceited, proud, haughty; gay, cheerful; masterly.

fo.—a u., parasitically.

jier, *n.* usher, doorkeeper.—**u. de cámara,** usher of the king's privy chamber.

lano, *m.* (mil.) uhlan.

lcera, *f.* (med.) ulcer; (bot.) rot.

lceración, *f.* ulceration.

lcerante, *a.* ulcerating.

lcerar. I. *va.* to ulcerate. **II.** *vr.* to become ulcerated.—**ulcerativo, va,** *a.* ulcerating.

lceroso, sa, *a.* ulcerous.

lema, *m.* Ulema.

liginoso, sa, *a.* uliginous, swampy.

lmáceo, a. I. *a.* (bot.) ulmaceous. **II.** *f. pl.* (bot.) Ulmaceæ.

lpo, *m.* (S. A.) maize gruel.

lterior, *a.* ulterior, farther; subsequent.

lteriormente, *adv.* subsequently.

ltimamente, *adv.* lastly, finally; of late, recently.

ltimar, *va.* to end, finish, close.

ltimato, ultimátum, *m.* ultimatum; (coll.) final resolution.

ltimidad, *f.* ultimity, last stage.

ltimo, ma, *a.* last, latest; farthest; ultimate; final; latter; highly finished; most valuable; utmost; remote.—**ú. suplicio,** capital punishment.—**a la última,** after the latest fashion.— **a ú. hora,** at the eleventh hour, at the last minute.—**a últimos de,** in the latter part of the (month, etc.).—**estar a lo u.,** or en las **últimas,** to be well-informed; to be on its, or one's, last legs, to be near its, or one's, end.— **por ú.,** lastly; finally.

ltra, *adv.* besides.

ltrajador, ra, *n.* one who outrages or insults.

ltrajamiento, *m.* outrage, affront.

ltrajar, *va.* to outrage, offend, abuse; to despise.

ltraje, *m.* outrage, insult; contempt; abuse.

ltrajosamente, *adv.* outrageously.

ltrajoso, sa, *a.* outrageous; overbearing.

ltramar, *m.* place beyond or across the sea.

ltramarino, na. I. *a.* ultramarine, oversea. **II.** *m.* ultramarine, finest blue.—*pl.* (com.) oversea articles.

ltramaro, *m.* ultramarine color.

ltramicroscópico, ca, *a.* ultramicroscopic.

ltramicroscopio, *m.* ultramicroscope.

ltramontanismo, *m.* ultramontanism.

ltramontano, na, *n.* & *a.* ultramontane.

ltramundano, na, *a.* ultramundane.

ltranza.—a u., to death; at all costs, unflinchingly.

ltrapuertos, *m.* beyond the seaports.

ultrarrojo, ja, *a.* (phys.) infra-red.

ultratumba.—de u., en u., beyond the grave.

ultraviolado, da; ultravioleta, *a.* (phys.) ultra-violet.

úlula, *f.* (ornith.) owl.

ulular, *vn.* to screech, hoot, ululate.

ululato, *m.* howl, screech, ululation.

umbela, *f.* (bot.) umbel.

umbelífero, ra. I. *a.* (bot.) umbelliferous. **II.** *f. pl.* the parsley family.

umbilicado, da, *a.* navel-shaped; umbilicated.

umbilical, *a.* umbilical.

umbráculo, *m.* shaded place for plants.

umbral, *m.* threshold; (arch.) lintel; beginning, rudiment.—**umbralar,** *va.* (arch.) to lintel.

umbrático, ca; umbrátil, *a.* umbrageous, shady.

umbría, *f.* shady place.

umbrío, bría, *a.* umbrageous, shady.

umbroso, sa, *a.* shady.

un (abbr. of UNO), **una. I.** *indef. art.* a, an. **II.** *n.* & *a.* one.—**u. . . . sí y otro no,** every other, every second (as *un día sí y otro no,* every other day).

unánime, *a.* unanimous.—**unánimemente,** *adv.* unanimously.—**unanimidad,** *f.* unanimity.—**por u.,** unanimously.

uncia, *f.* (law) twelfth part of an estate.

uncial, *a.* uncial, pert. to a kind of writing.

unciforme, *a.* & *n.* (anat.) unciform.

uncinariasis, *f.* (med.) uncinariasis, hookworm.

unción, *f.* unction, anointing; (eccl.) extreme unction.—*pl.* treatment by unctions of mercury.

uncionario, ria. I. *a.* being under mercurial treatment. **II.** *m.* place where external mercurial treatment is taken.

uncir, *va.* (*ind.* UNZO; *subj.* UNZA) to yoke.

undante, *a.* waving, undulating.

undécimo, ma, *a.* eleventh.

undécuplo, pla, *a.* eleven times as much.

undísono, na, *a.* (poet.) billowy.

undívago, ga, *a.* (poet.) wavy.

undoso, sa, *a.* wavy, undulating.

undulación, *f.* undulation; wave motion.

undular, *vn.* to undulate; to wriggle.

undulatorio, ria, *a.* undulatory.

ungido, *m.* anointed priest or king.

ungimiento, *m.* unction.

ungir, *va.* (*ind.* UNJO; *subj.* UNJA) to anoint.

ungüentario, ria. I. *a.* unguentary. **II.** *m.* one who prepares ointments; unguentarium.

ungüento, *m.* unguent, ointment.—**u. amaracino,** ointment of marjoram.—**u. de soldado,** mercury ointment.

unguiculado, da, *a.* (zool.) unguiculate.

unguis, *m.* (anat.) os unguis.

ungulado, da. I. *n.* & *a.* (zool.) ungulate, having nails or claws. **II.** *m. pl.* Ungulata.

unible, *a.* that can be joined or united.

únicamente, *adv.* only, simply, solely.

unicelular, *a.* unicellular.

único, ca, *a.* only, sole; singular, unique, rare, unmatched, unparalleled.

unicolor, *a.* unicolor, one-color.

unicornio, *m.* (myth.) unicorn; rhinoceros; (U-, astr.) Unicorn.—**u. de mar,** (ichth.) narwhal.

unidad, *f.* unity; unit; (rhet. and art) unity.—**u. de acción, de lugar y de tiempo,** dramatic unities.—**la u.,** (math.) unity, 1.

unidamente, *adv.* jointly, unitedly.

unificación, *f.* unification.

unificar, *va.* (*pret.* UNIFIQUÉ; *subj.* UNIFIQUE) to unify.

unifloro, ra, *a.* (bot.) having only one flower.

unifoliado, da, *a.* (bot.) unifoliate.

uniformación, *f.* standardization, uniformity.

uniformador, ra, *a.* that makes uniform; standardizing.

uniformar, *va.* to make uniform; to standardize.

uniforme. I. *a.* uniform. **II.** *m.* uniform; regimentals.—**uniformemente,** *adv.* uniformly.

uniformidad, *f.* uniformity.

unigénito, *a.* only-begotten.

unilateral, *a.* unilateral.

unión, *f.* union, harmony, correspondence; resemblance; agreement, concord, unity; wedding, marriage; composition of ingredients; combination; coöperation; contiguity; linked finger rings; (surg.) closing of the lips of a wound; (mech.) coupling, fastening, connection, joining, joint; (Ry.) junction; (com.) fusion, consolidation, merger.

unípara, *a.* uniparous.

unípede, *a.* monopode, one-footed.

unipersonal, *a.* unipersonal.

unipolar, *a.* (elec.) single-pole.

unir. I. *va.* to join, unite, couple, bind, connect, attach; to mix, combine; bring together; to harmonize. **II.** *vr.* to join, unite, get together; to adhere, concur; to be contiguous; to wed, be married; (com.) to consolidate, merge, combine.

unisexual, *a.* (bot.) unisexual.

unisón. I. *a.* unison. **II.** *m.* (mus.) unison.

unisonancia, *f.* unisonance; monotony.

unísono, na, *a.* unisonous, sounding alike.—**al,** or **en, u.,** in unison; together; unanimously.

unitario, ria, *a.* & *n.* (eccl.) Unitarian; (pol.) supporter of centralization.

unitarismo, *m.* (eccl.) Unitarianism.

unitivo, va, *a.* unitive, serving or tending to unite.

univalvo, va, *a.* univalve.

universal, *a.* universal; learned, well-informed.

universalidad, *f.* universality.

universalísimo, *a.* *super.* (logic) universal.

universalizar, *va.* to universalize; to generalize.

universalmente, *adv.* universally.

universidad, *f.* university; body of persons forming an institution; universality.

universitario, ria, *a.* university (as *a.*).

universo, sa. I. *a.* universal. **II.** *m.* universe.

univocación, *f.* univocation.

univocamente, *adv.* univocally, unanimously.

univocarse, *vr.* to have the same meaning.

unívoco, ca, *a.* univocal.

unjo, unja, *v.* V. UNCIR.

uno, na. I. *a.* one.—*pl.* some; nearly, about.—**u. que otro,** (only) a few; occasional (as *uno que otro día viene a vernos,* he comes to see us once in a while, occasionally) (*V.* also UN). **II.** *pron. m.* & *f.* one; someone.—*pl.* some (people).—**u. a otro,** each other, mutually.—**u. que otro,** some, a few.—**u. y otro,** both.—**unos a otros,** one another.—**unos cuantos,** a few.—**unos y otros,** all, the lot (of them).—**cada u.,** each one.—**de u.,** one's.—**los unos a los otros** = UNOS A OTROS. **III.** Uno, *pron. neut.* one thing (*uno es hablar, y otro es hacer,* it's one thing to talk and another to do). **IV.** *n.* one (number). —**u. a u.** = DE U. EN U.—**u. con otro,** on an average.—**u. por u.,** one after another; one by one, one at a time.—**una y no más,** never again.—**a una,** unanimously, of one accord.— **de una,** at once, at one time.—**de u. en u.,** one by one; in single file.—**todo es uno,** it is all the same. **V.** *f.*—**la u.,** one o'clock.

untador, ra, *n.* & *a.* oiler(-ing), coater(-ing), greaser(-ing), painter(-ing), etc. *V.* UNTAR.

untadura, *f.*; **untamiento,** *m.,* UNTURA; oiling, greasing, coating, etc.

untar. I. *va.* to anoint; to grease, oil, smear, paint, coat; to suborn, bribe.—**u. las manos,** to grease the palm, to bribe. **II.** *vr.* to be greased or smeared; to embezzle.

untaza, *f.* grease; ENJUNDIA, fat (of animal).

unto, *m.* grease, fat of animals; unguent, ointment.—**u. amarillo,** or **de Méjico,** (coll.) bribe money.—**u. de oso,** bear's grease.—**u. de**

puerco, hog's lard.—**u. de arna** = U. AMA-RILLO.

untuosidad, *f.* unctuosity, greasiness.

untuoso, sa, *a.* unctuous, greasy.

untura, *f.* unction; ointment, liniment.

unzo, unza, *v.* V. UNCIR.

uña, *f.* finger nail; toenail; hoof, claw, or talon of beasts; sting of the scorpion; (bot.) thorn pointed hook of instruments; short stump of a tree; scab; excrescence on the lachryma caruncle; (coll.) dexterity in stealing or filching (mech.) gripper, clutch, claw; (mus.) plectrum for the mandolin; (naut.) fluke, palm or bill of an anchor.—**u. de caballo,** (bot.) coltsfoot.— **u. gata,** (bot.) = GATUÑA rest-harrow.—**afilar las uñas,** to sharpen one's wits, try one's best —**a u. de caballo,** at full gallop, in great haste —**enseñar la u.** = MOSTRAR LA U.—**de uñas** at daggers drawn, at loggerheads.—**hincar** or **meter, la u.,** to overcharge; to sell at an exorbitant price.—**largo de uñas,** filcher.— **mostrar las uñas,** to be inexorable; to show one's teeth.—**mostrar la u.,** to discover one' foibles or ignorance.—**sacar las uñas,** (coll. to avail oneself of every means in a difficulty.— **ser u. y carne,** to be hand and glove, to be fas friends.—**tener uñas,** (coll.) to be very diffi cult, to be a tough job, a big order.—**uñada, J** nail scratch, nip.—**uñarada,** *f.* scratch with the nail.—**uñate,** *m.* (coll.) pinching with the nail chuckfarthing, a game.—**uñaza,** *f.* *aug.* large nail.—**uñero,** *m.* ingrowing nail; (med.) felon

uñeta, *f.* *dim.* small fingernail; small clutch stonecutter's chisel; chuckfarthing (boys game).

uñidura, *f.* yoking.

uñir, *va.* to yoke.

uñita, uñuela, *f.* *dim.* little finger nail.

uñoso, sa, *a.* having long nails or claws.

¡upa! *interj.* up, up! hoop-la!

upas, *m.* upas, a Javanese tree and the poison prepared from it.

upupa, *f.* (ornith.) hoopoe.

uralita, *f.* (min.) uralite.

urania, *f.* (zool.) a moth of the genus *Urania.*

uránidos, *m. pl.* (zool.) Uranidae.

¹uranio, nia, *a.* uranic, celestial.

²uranio, *m.* (chem.) uranium.

uranismo, *m.* homosexuality.

uranita, *f.* (min.) uranite.

urano, *m.* (astr.) Uranus.

uranografía, *f.* uranography.—**uranógrafo,** *m* uranographist.—**uranometría,** *f.* uranometry

urao, *m.* (S. A.) (min.) trona.

urari, *m.* urari, curare, a resinous substance.

urato, *m.* (chem.) urate.

urbanamente, *adv.* courteously, politely.

urbanicé, urbanice, *v.* V. URBANIZAR.

urbanidad, *f.* urbanity, civility, manners.

urbanización, *f.* laying out land for building

urbanizar, *va.* (*pret.* URBANICÉ; *subj.* URBANICE to lay out (land) for a town; to polish, rende polite.

urbano, na. I. *a.* urban; urbane, courteous, well bred. **II.** *m.* militiaman.

urbe, *f.* large modern city, metropolis.

¹urca, *f.* (naut.) hooker, dogger; storeship.

²urca, *f.* (ichth.) = ORCA, a kind of dolphin.

urce, *m.* (bot.) heath.

urchilla, *f.* orchil, a lichen or color from it.

urdidera, *f.* woman warper; warping frame.

urdidor, ra. I. *n.* warper. **II.** *m.* warping frame warping mill.

urdidura, *f.* warping.

urdimbre, urdiembre, *f.* warp, warping chain

urdir, *va.* to warp; to plot, contrive, scheme.

urea, *f.* (chem.) urea.—**ureida,** *f.* ureide.

uremia, *f.* (med.) uræmia.

urémico, ca, *a.* uræmic.

urente, *a.* hot, burning, scorching.

ɩrétére, *m.* (anat.) ureter.
ɩrético, ca; uretral, *a.* urethral.
ɩretra, *f.* (anat.) urethra.—**uretritis**, *f.* (med.) urethritis.—**uretroscopio**, *m.* (surg.) urethroscope.—**uretrotomía**, *f.* urethrotomy.
ɩretrótomo, *m.* urethrotome.
ɩrgencia, *f.* urgency, exigence; obligation.—**clínica de u.**, emergency clinic.—**cura de u.**, emergency treatment.
ɩrgente, *a.* urgent, pressing.
ɩrgentemente, *adv.* urgently.
ɩrgir, *vn.* (*ind.* URJO; *subj.* URJA) to be urgent, to require immediate action.
ɩrico, ca, *a.* uric.
ɩrinal, *a.* = URINARIO, *a.*
ɩrinario, ria. I. *a.* urinary. II. *m.* urinal.
ɩrna, *f.* urn, casket; glass case; ballot box.
ɩrnición, *f.* (naut.) top timbers.
ɩro, *m.* (zool.) aurochs.
ɩrobilina, *f.* (chem.) urobilin.
ɩrodelos, *m. pl.* (zool.) Urodela.
ɩrogallo, *m.* (ornith.) a species of woodcock.
ɩrolito, *m.* (med.) urolith.
ɩromancia, *f.* uromancy.
ɩrómetro, *m.* urinometer.
ɩroscopia, *f.* uroscopy.
ɩrraca, *f.* (ornith.) magpie.
Jrsa, *f.* (astr.) Bear.—**U. Mayor**, Great Bear.—**U. Menor**, Little Bear.
ɩrsido, da. I. *a.* (zool.) ursine. II. *m. pl.* Ursidæ.
ɩrsino, na, *a.* ursine.
ɩrsulina, *n. & a.* Ursuline.
ɩrticáceo, a. I. *a.* (bot.) urticaceous. II. *f. pl.* Urticaceæ.
ɩrticación, *f.* (med.) urtication.
ɩrticante, *a.* urticating.
ɩrticaria, *f.* (med.) urticaria, nettle rash, hives.
ɩrubú, *m.* urubu, black vulture.
ɩruguayo, ya, *a. & n.* Uruguayan.
ɩsadamente, *adv.* according to custom.
ɩsado, da. I. *pp.* of USAR. II. *a.* worn out; inured, accustomed, used; fashionable, frequent; second-hand.—**al u.**, (com. law) at usance.
ɩsagre, *m.* (med.) scald head, infantile eczema.
ɩsanza, *f.* usage, custom.
ɩsar. I. *va.* to use; to wear; to enjoy the use of; to be active in (an employment). II. *vn.* to be accustomed. III. *vr.* to be in use or fashion; to be accustomed, used, wont.
ɩsarcé, usarced, *n.* (obs.) (*contr.* of VUESARCED = VUESTRA MERCED) your honor.
ɩsencia, *n.* (*contr.* of VUESTRA REVERENCIA) your reverence.
ɩseñoría, *n.* = USÍA.
ɩsgo, *m.* loathing.
ɩsía, *n.* (*contr.* of VUESTRA SEÑORÍA) your lordship (ladyship); your excellence.
ɩso, *m.* use; usage, custom; habit, practice; wearing, wear; wear and tear; (com. law) usance.—**u. de razón**, discernment, understanding, thinking for oneself (esp. of a child when his mind is sufficiently developed to judge by itself).—**al u., a u.**, according to usage.—**en buen u.**, in good condition.
ɩstaga, *f.* (naut.) tie.
ɩsted, *pron.* (usually abbreviated V., Vd., U., Ud.) you.—*pl.* **ustedes** (abbrev. VV., Vds., UU., Uds.) you (ye).—**de Vd.**, your, yours.
ɩstible, *a.* easily combustible.
ɩstión, *f.* burning.
ɩstorio, *a.* burning.
ɩsual, *a.* usual, customary; tractable, social.
ɩsualmente, *adv.* usually, generally.
ɩsuario, ria, *a.* (law) having the sole use of a thing.
ɩsucapión, *f.* (law) usucapion.
ɩsucapir, *va.* (gen. only in *infin.*) (law) to usucapt.
ɩsufructo, *m.* (law) usufruct, enjoyment; profit.
ɩsufructuar. I. *va.* (law) to enjoy the usufruct of. II. *vn.* to be productive or fruitful.

usufructuario, ria, *n. & a.* usufructuary.
usura, *f.* usuary; (formerly) interest, gain, profit.
usurar, *vn.* = USUREAR.
usurariamente, *adv.* usuriously.
usurario, ria, *a.* usurious.
usurear, *vn.* to practice usury; to profiteer; to lend money on interest; to reap great profit.
usurero, ra, *n.* usurer; profiteerer; money lender, pawnbroker.
usurpación, *f.* usurpation.
usurpador, *n. & a.* usurper(-ing).
usurpar, *va.* to usurp.
utensilio, *m.* utensil; tool, device, contrivance.—*pl.* (mil.) articles that the tenant of a house is to furnish the soldier quartered with him.
uterino, na, *a.* uterine.
útero, *m.* (anat.) uterus, womb.
uterotomía, *f.* (surg.) hysterotomy, incision or extirpation of the uterus.
uterótomo, *m.* (surg.) hysterotome.
uticense, *n. & a.* of or from Utica.
útil. I. *a.* useful; (law) lawful (applied to time); profitable; (mech.) effective, available. II. *m. pl.* utensils, tools; outfit, equipment.
utilicé, utilice, *v. V.* UTILIZAR.
utilidad, *f.* utility; profit; usefulness.
utilitario, ria, *a.* utilitarian.
utilitarismo, *m.* utilitarianism.
utilitarista, *n. & a.* utilitarian.
utilizable, *a.* utilizable, available.
utilizar. I. *va.* (*pret.* UTILICÉ; *subj.* UTILICE) to utilize. II. *vr.* to be made profitable.
útilmente, *adv.* usefully, profitably.
utopía, *f.* Utopia.—**utópico, ca**, *a.* Utopian.—**utopista**, *n. & a.* Utopian.
utrero, ra, *n.* bull (heifer) two to three years old.
ut retro, *adv.* (Lat.) as above.
ut supra, *adv.* (Lat.) as above.
uva, *f.* (bot.) grape; fruit of the barberry bush; wart on the eyelid; tumor on the uvula.—*pl.* bunch of grapes.—**u. canella**, white stonecrop.—**u. crespa** = U. ESPÍN.—**u. de Corinto**, (bot.) currants.—**u. de gato** = U. CANELLA.—**u. de playa**, (Amer.) fruit of the UVERO.—**u. de raposa**, nightshade.—**u. espín**, or **espina**, gooseberry.—**u. lupina**, wolfsbane.—**u. marina**, shrubby horsetail.—**u. pasa**, raisin.—**u. tamínea**, or **taminia**, lousewort.—**u. verdeja**, green-colored sweet grape.—**u. verga** = U. LUPINA.—**conocer las uvas de su majuelo**, to know one's own business.—**hecho una u.**, very drunk, "paralyzed," "soaked."
uvada, *f.* abundance of grapes.
uvaguemaestre, *m.* = VAGUEMAESTRE.
uval, *a.* pertaining to grapes.
uvate, *m.* conserve of grapes.
uvayema, *f.* a species of wild vine.
úvea, *f.* (anat.) uvea.
uvero, ra. I. *n.* retailer of grapes. II. *m.* (bot.) shrub on tropical seashores yielding an edible stone fruit.
úvula, *f.* (anat.) uvula.
uxoricida, *m.* uxoricide, one who kills his wife.
uxoricidio, *m.* uxoricide, murder of a wife by her husband.
uyama, *f.* (Venez.) a species of gourd.
uzas, *f.* a Brazilian kind of crab.

V

v, *f.* v.—**v. doble**, or **doble v**, w.—**en V**, V-shaped.
V., Vd. (for USTED), you.—*pl.* VV., Vds.
va, *third pers. sing. pres.* of IR.
vaca, *f.* cow; beef; sole leather; joint stock of two gamblers.—**v. de la boda**, one to whom everybody applies in distress; laughingstock.—**v. de leche**, milch cow.—**v. de San Antón**, (entom.) ladybird, ladybug.—**v. marina**, sea cow.

vacación, *f.* (gen. in the *pl.*) vacation.

vacada, *f.* drove of cows.

vacancia, *f.* vacancy.

vacante. I. *a.* vacant; unoccupied. **II.** *f.* vacancy; vacation; rent fallen due during the vacancy of a benefice.

vacar, *vn.* (*pret.* VAQUÉ; *subj.* VAQUE) to give up work or employment temporarily; to take a vacation; to be vacant; to devote oneself; (**de**) to lack, be devoid (of).

vacarí, *a.* leathern; covered with leather.

vacatura, *f.* vacancy.

vaccinieo, a, *a.* (bot.) vacciniaceous.

vaciada, *f.* (foundry) melt.

vaciadero, *m.* drain; sink; dumping place.

vaciadizo, za, *a.* cast molded.

vaciado, *m.* (art) cast (in a mold); (act of) casting; (arch.) excavation; face of a pedestal below its ornamental moldings.

vaciador, *m.* (art) molder, caster; dumper, pourer, emptier.—**v. de navajas,** razor grinder.

vaciamiento, *m.* casting, molding; emptying.

vaciar. I. *va.* to empty; pour out; to cast, mold; to grind; to hone; (arch.) to excavate, to hollow; to explain at large; to translate. **II.** *vn.* to discharge, flow (into) (as rivers); to fall, decrease (as a freshet). **III.** *vr.* to be spilt; to overflow; to divulge what should be kept secret; to become empty or vacant.

vaciedad, *f.* nonsense, silly remark.

vaciero, *m.* shepherd of barren sheep.

vacilación, *f.* reeling, staggering; hesitation.

vacilante, *a.* hesitating, irresolute; unstable.

vacilar, *vn.* to vacillate, waver, fluctuate; to hesitate; to reel, stagger.

vacío, cía. I. *a.* void, empty; vacuous, stupid; vacant, unoccupied; idle; fruitless; concave, hollow; defective, deficient; vain, presumptuous; barren (cattle); unloaded or empty (as mules, carts, etc.). **II.** *m.* void, empty space; vacuum; aperture, opening; mold for casting; vacancy; concavity, hollowness; blank, hiatus, gap; (com.) ullage of a cask or other vessel; amount lacking; a Spanish step in dancing; animal not with young; vacuity, cavity; flank of animals.—**de v.,** empty; unemployed; vacuum (as *a.*).—**en el v.,** in vacuo.

vaco, ca, *a.* (of a position, employment) vacant.

vacuidad, *f.* vacuity, emptiness.

vacuna, *f.* cowpox; vaccine; vaccination.

vacunación, *f.* vaccination.

vacunador, ra, *n.* vaccinator.

vacunar, *va.* to vaccinate.

vacuno, na, *a.* pertaining to cattle; bovine.—**ganado v.,** (bovine) cattle.

vacuo, a. I. *a.* empty, unoccupied, vacant. **II.** *m.* vacuum.

vacuola, *f.* (biol.) vacuole.

vacuómetro, *m.* vacuum gauge.

vade, *m.* = VADEMÉCUM.

vadeable, *a.* fordable; conquerable, superable.

vadear. I. *va.* to wade through, ford; to conquer, to surmount; to sound (a person). **II.** *vr.* to behave, conduct oneself.

vademécum, *m.* vade mecum; handbook; school portfolio.

vadera, *f.* ford of a river.

¡vade retro! *adv.* avaunt! away! begone!

vadiano, na, *n.* & *a.* Audian.

vado, *m.* ford of a river; expedient; resource.—**al v. o la puente,** choose one way or the other.—**no hallar v.,** to be at a loss how to act; to be "stuck."—**vadoso, sa,** *a.* shoaly, shallow.

vafe, *m.* bold stroke or undertaking.

vagabundear, *vn.* (coll.) to rove or loiter about, to act the vagrant.

vagabundo, da, *n.* & *a.* vagabond, vagrant, rover (-ing), roamer(-ing), tramp(-ing).

vagamente, *adv.* vaguely.

vagamundear, *vn.* = VAGABUNDEAR.

vagamundo, da, *n.* & *a.* = VAGABUNDO.

vagancia, *f.* vagrancy.

vagante, *a.* vagrant.

vagar. I. *vn.* (*pret.* VAGUÉ; *subj.* VAGUE) to rove roam, loiter about, wander; to be at leisure, to be idle. **II.** *m.* leisure, idleness.

vagarosamente, *adv.* vagrantly, rovingly.

vagaroso, sa, *a.* errant, vagrant, roaming.

vagido, *m.* cry of a newborn child.

vagina, *f.* (anat.) vagina.—**vaginado, da,** *a.* (bot.) vaginate.—**vaginal,** *a.* vaginal.—**vaginitis,** *f.* (med.) vaginitis.—**vagínula,** *f.* (bot.) vaginula, vaginule.

vagneriano, na, *n.* & *a.* Wagnerian.

vagnerismo, *m.* Wagnerism.

¹vago, ga. I. *a.* roving, roaming, wandering; vagrant; vague; hesitating, wavering; lax, loose (art) hazy, indistinct. **II.** *m.* vagabond, loafer, vagrant, tramp.—**en v.,** unsteadily; unsuccessfully, in vain; in the air, at nothing (as a blow).

²vago, *m.* unimproved plot of ground.

vagón, *m.* (Ry.) car; wagon.—**v.-cama,** sleeping car.—**v.-cuadra,** cattle van.—**v. de carga,** freight car.—**v. de cola,** caboose.—**v. de mercancías,** freight car.—**v. de plataforma,** flat car.—**v. jaula,** latticed van or wagon.—**vagonada,** *f.* wagonload, carload.—**vagoneta,** *f.* (Ry.) small open car; (S. A.) open delivery cart; dump cart.

vaguada, *f.* waterway; watercourse.

vagué, vague, *v. V.* VAGAR.

vagueación, *f.* restlessness, unsteadiness; flight of fancy.

vagueante, *a.* wandering; flighty.

vaguear, *vn.* to rove, roam, loiter, tramp.

vaguedad, *f.* vagueness; vague statement.

vaguemaestre, *m.* (mil.) wagon master.

vaguido, da. I. *a.* dizzy. **II.** *m.* dizziness.

vahaje, *m.* soft breeze.

vahar, *vn.* to exhale, breathe forth.

vaharada, *f.* breath, breathing, exhalation.

vaharera, *f.* (med.) thrush; unripe melon.

vaharina, *f.* (coll.) fume, vapor, mist.

vahear, *vn.* to exhale, emit fumes or vapor.

vahído, *m.* vertigo, dizziness.

vaho, *m.* vapor, fume, effluvium.

vaída, *f.* (arch.) vault cut into four vertical planes.

vaina, *f.* scabbard, sheath, case; (bot.) pod, capsule; (naut.) boltrope tabling; tabling of a flag.

vainazas, *n.* (coll.) humdrum, dull, or dronish person.

vainero, ra, *n.* sheath or scabbard maker.

vainica, *f. dim.* small sheath; (sew.) hemstitch.

vainilla, *f. dim.* small pod or husk; (bot.) vanilla; American heliotrope.

vainillina, *f.* (chem.) vanillin.

vaivén, *m.* fluctuation, vibration, sway; unsteadiness, inconstancy; giddiness; risk, danger; (mech.) swing, seesaw, reciprocating movement; (naut.) line, cord, rope.

vajilla, *f.* table service; dinner set; (Mex.) an ancient tax on jewelry.—**v. de plata,** silverware.

val, *m.* (*contr.* of VALLE, mostly used in composition) vale, dale, valley; open sewer, sewage ditch.

valaco, ca, *n.* & *a.* Wallachian.

valais, *m.* piece of lumber.

valar, *a.* pert. to a rampart, hedge, or fence.

valdense, *n.* & *a.* Waldensian.

¹vale, *m.* (com.) bond, promissory note, I O U; voucher; sales slip; bonus given to schoolboys; bet at cards.

²vale, (Lat.) farewell, adieu; valediction.

valedero, ra, *a.* valid, efficacious, binding.

valedor, ra, *n.* protector, defender.

valenciano, na, *n.* & *a.* Valencian.

valentía, *f.* valor, courage, bravery; feat, heroic exploit; brag, boast; fire of imagination; (art)

vasillo, *m. dim.* cell of a honeycomb.

vaso, *m.* (drinking) glass; vessel, receptacle; glassful; vase; flower jar; reservoir; (naut.) vessel; capacity, room, extent; (astr.) Crater, a southern constellation; horse's hoof; (anat. and bot.) vessel.—**v. de noche,** chamber pot.

vasomotor, *a.* (physiol.) vasomotor.

vástago, *m.* stem, tiller, sucker, sapling, shoot; descendant, scion, offspring.—**v. del émbolo,** (steam eng.) piston rod.—**v. de válvula,** valve stem.

vastedad, *f.* vastness, immensity.

vástiga, *f.* = VÁSTAGO.

vasto, ta, *a.* vast, huge, immense.

vate, *m.* bard, poet; seer, diviner.

vaticano, na. I. *a.* pertaining to the Vatican. **II.** *m.* (V-) Vatican.

vaticinador, ra, *n.* prophet, diviner.

vaticinante, *a.* predicting, foretelling.

vaticinar, *va.* to divine, foretell, predict.

vaticinio, *m.* vaticination, prediction.

vatídico, ca, *a.* (poet.) prophetical.

vatihora, *m.* (elec.) watt-hour.

vatihorámetro, *m.* (elec.) watt-hour meter.

vatímetro, *m.* (elec.) wattmeter.

vatio, *m.* (elec.) watt.—**v. -hora,** watt-hour.

¹vaya, *f.* scoff, jest.

²vaya, etc. *v. V.* IR.—*interj.* go! go to! come! indeed! certainly! well!

¹ve, *f.* name of letter *v.*—**v. doble,** name of *w.*

²ve, *v. V.* IR.

véase, *imper.* of VERSE; *v.,* see (in references).

vecera, vecería, *f.* drove, herd, pack.

vecero, ra, *n.* one who performs alternately or by turns; tree which yields abundant fruit in alternate years; customer.

veces, *f. pl.* of VEZ.

vecinal, *a.* vicinal, neighboring, adjacent.

vecinamente, *adv.* near, contiguously.

vecindad, *f.* neighborhood, vicinity; (collect.) tenants (in a house).—**hacer mala v.,** to be a troublesome neighbor.

vecindario, *m.* population of a district, ward, etc.; neighborhood, vicinity, vicinage.

vecino, na. I. *a.* neighboring, next, near by; like, resembling, coincident. **II.** *n.* neighbor; resident, tenant; citizen.—**medio v.,** nonresident who, by paying half the taxes, enjoys the right of pasture for his cattle.

vectación, *f.* passive exercise, as riding, sailing.

vectigales, *m. pl.* an ancient tribute.

vector (math.). **I.** *a.* vectorial. **II.** *m.* vector.

vectorial, *a.* (math.) vectorial.

¹veda, *f.* prohibition, interdiction by law; time when hunting is forbidden.

²veda, *m.* Veda, Hindu sacred book.

vedado, *m.* inclosure, warren, park.

vedamiento, *m.* prohibition.

vedar, *va.* to prohibit, forbid; to obstruct, impede.

vedegambre, *m.* (bot.) hellebore.

vedeja, *f.* = GUEDEJA, lock (of hair); lion's mane.

védico, ca, *a.* Vedic.

vedija, *f.* entangled lock of wool or hair; flake; matted hair.—**vedijero, ra,** *n.* gatherer of loose locks of wool at shearing.—**vedijudo, da; vedijoso, sa,** *a.* having entangled or matted hair.—**vedijuela,** *f. dim.* small lock of wool.

veduño, *m.* = VIDUÑO, quality of grape vines.

veedor, ra, *n.* prier, spy; busybody; overseer, supervisor, inspector; caterer, provider.

veeduría, *f.* supervisor's position or office.

vega, *f.* flat lowland; (Cuba) tobacco plantation; (Chile) damp or swampy ground.

vegetabilidad, *f.* condition of being vegetal.

vegetable, *a.* (rare) = VEGETAL.

vegetación, *f.* vegetation.

vegetal, *a. & m.* vegetable, vegetal, plant.—**vegetalista,** *n. & a.* vegetarian.

vegetante, *a.* vegetating.

vegetar, *vn.* to vegetate.

vegetarianismo, *m.* vegetarianism.

vegetariano, na, *n. & a.* vegetarian.

vegetarismo, *m.* vegetarianism.

vegetativo, va, *a.* vegetative.

veguer, *m.* in Aragon, mayor.—**veguería,** *f.,* **veguerío,** *m.* in Aragon, jurisdiction of the mayor.

veguero, ra. I. *a.* meadowy. **II.** *m.* (Cuba) tobacco planter; cigar crudely made of a single leaf.

vehemencia, *f.* vehemence, efficacy, force.

vehemente, *a.* vehement; persuasive; vivid; keen.—**vehementemente,** *adv.* vehemently.

vehículo, *m.* vehicle.

veintavo, *m. & a.* twentieth.

veinte, *a. & m.* twenty; twentieth.—**a las v.,** unseasonably.

veintén, *m.* a gold dollar piece.

veintena, *f.,* **veintenar,** *m.* score (twenty).

veintenario, ria, *a.* twenty years old.

veinteno, na, *a.* twentieth.

veinteñal, *a.* lasting twenty years.

veinteocheno, na. I. *a.* twenty-eighth. **II.** *m.* or *f.* warp of 2,800 threads.

veinteseiseno, na. I. *a.* twenty-sixth. **II.** *n.* warp of 2,600 threads.

veintésimo, ma, *a.* twentieth.

veinticinco, *a. & m.* twenty-five; twenty-fifth.

veinticuatreno, na. I. *a.* twenty-fourth. **II.** *n.* warp of 2,400 threads.—**v. de capas,** fine broadcloth for cloaks.

veinticuatría, *f.* aldermanry.

veinticuatro. I. *a.* twenty-four; twenty-fourth. **II.** *m.* alderman of Seville.

veintidós, *a. & m.* twenty-two; twenty-second.

veintidoseno, na. I. *a.* twenty-second. **II.** *m.* or *f.* warp of 2,200 threads.

veintinueve, *a. & m.* twenty-nine; twenty-ninth.

veintiocheno, na = VEINTEOCHENO.

veintiocho, *a. & m.* twenty-eight; twenty-eighth.

veintiséis, *a. & m.* twenty-six; twenty-sixth.

veintiseiseno, na = VEINTESEISENO.

veintisiete, *a. & m.* twenty-seven; twenty-seventh.

veintitrés, *a. & m.* twenty-three; twenty-third.

veintiún, *a.* twenty-one.

veintiuno, na. I. *a. & m.* twenty-one; twenty-first. **II.** *f.* a card game, "vingt-et-un."

vejación, *f.* vexation, annoyance; oppression.

vejamen, *m.* vexation, trouble; taunt, scurrilous criticism.—**vejaminista,** *m.* censor, critic.

vejancón, na, *a.* (coll.) rather old, oldish.

vejar, *va.* to vex, tease; to scoff, censure.

vejarrón, na, *a.* (coll.) very old.

vejatorio, ria, *a.* vexatious, annoying.

vejazo, za, *n.* big old person.

vejecito, ta, *n.* little old man (woman).

vejestorio, *m.* (coll.) old trumpery; shrivelled old person.

vejeta, *f.* (ornith.) crested lark.

vejete, *m.* (coll.) ridiculous old man.

vejez, *f.* old age; peevishness of old age; trite story, platitude, threadbare saying, etc.

vejezuelo, la, *n. dim.* little old man (woman).

vejiga, *f.* (anat.) bladder; blister; (art) bladder or tube for paints.—*pl.* pustules of smallpox; (vet.) windgalls in horses.—**v. de la bilis,** or **de la hiel,** gall bladder.—**v. de perro,** (bot.) common winter cherry.—**v. natatoria,** (ichth.) swimming bladder.—**v. para tabaco,** tobacco pouch.

vejigatorio, ria. I. *a.* blistering. **II.** *m.* blister plaster, blister, vesicant, vesicatory.

vejigón, *m. aug.* large bladder or blister.

vejigoso, sa, *a.* full of blisters.

vejiguela, vejiguilla, *f. dim.* small bladder; (med.) pustule.

¹vela, *f.* vigil, wakefulness; wake; watch, watchfulness, vigilance; watchman, nightguard; pilgrimage; candle; nightwork; (eccl.) vigil before the Eucharist; nuptial mass and veiling ceremony.—**a v. y pregón**, auction by inch of candle.—**en v.**, vigilantly, without sleep.

²**vela**, *f.* (naut.) sail; ship; awning, velarium; erect ear of an animal; wing or arm of a windmill.—**v. bastarda**, lateen sail.—**v. cangreja**, (naut.) boom sail, brig sail, gaff sail.—**v. de mesana**, mizzen sail.—**v. de trinquete**, fore sail.—**v. latina** = **v. BASTARDA.**—**v. mayor**, mainsail.—**velas de popa**, after sails.—**velas de proa**, headsails.—**velas de respeto**, spare sails.—**velas mayores**, courses.—**acortar (la) v.**, to reef a sail, to shorten sail.—**a la v.**, prepared, equipped, ready.—**alzar velas**, to raise sail, to make ready to sail; to quit, to leave.—**a toda v.**, with all sails up and full wind; with heart and soul; boomingly, in full swing.—**a v. y remo**, with sails and oars; quickly, with all one's heart and soul.—**hacer fuerza de v.**, to crowd sail.—**hacerse a la v.**, to set sail.—**recoger velas**, to contain oneself, to be moderate.—**tender (las) velas**, to seize an opportunity.

velación, *f.* watch, watching, vigil; wake.—*pl.* (eccl.) nuptial mass and veiling ceremony; time in which the church permits marriages.

velacho, *m.* (naut.) fore-topsail.

velada, *f.* VELACIÓN; soirée.

velado, *m.* (coll.) bridegroom, husband.

velador, ra. I. *n.* watchman(-woman), night-guard; caretaker, keeper. **II.** *m.* wooden candlestick; lamp table or stand.

veladura, *f.* (art) velatura.

velaje, velamen, *m.* (naut.) canvas, sails in general; set of sails.

¹**velar, I.** *vn.* to watch, to be awake, to keep vigil; to work at night; to observe; to be vigilant; **(por)** to watch (over), protect; (naut.) to appear above the water, as rocks; (eccl.) to assist by turns before the Holy Sacrament when it is manifested. **II.** *va.* to guard, watch over, keep.

²**velar**, *va.* (eccl.) to veil (a bride and bridegroom) at a nuptial mass; to cover, veil, hide; (art) to soften with velatura.

velarte, *m.* fine broadcloth.

veleidad, *f.* whimsicalness; fickleness.

veleidoso, sa, *a.* fickle, inconstant.

velejar, *vn.* (naut.) to make use of sails.

velería, *f.* tallow-chandler's shop.

¹**velero, ra. I.** *a.* fond of wakes and pilgrimages. **II.** *m.* tallow chandler.

²**velero, ra. I.** *a.* (naut.) swift-sailing. **II.** *m.* (naut.) sailmaker.

veleta. I. *f.* weathercock, vane; streamer, pennant; bob, float, or cork of a fishing line. **II.** *n.* fickle person.

velete, *m.* light, thin, face veil.

velicación, *f.* (med.) lancing, opening.

velicar, *va.* (med.) to lance, open, prick.

velico, illo, ito, *m. dim.* small veil.

velilla, ita, *f. dim.* small candle.

velillo, *n. dim.* small veil; embroidered gauze.

velis nolis, (coll.) willy-nilly.

velmez, *m.* tunic worn under the armor.

velo, *m.* veil; curtain; veil of white gauze thrown over a couple at nuptial mass; celebration of taking the veil by a nun; cloak, disguise, mask; confusion, perplexity.—**v. del paladar**, (anat.) soft palate.—**correr un v. sobre**, to drop (a matter, etc.)—**descorrer el v.**, to pull off the mask; to disclose something before unknown.—**tomar el v.**, to take the veil, to become a nun.

velocidad, *f.* velocity.—**v. angular**, angular velocity.—**v. con respecto al suelo**, (aer.) ground velocity.—**v. de ascensión**, (aer.) climbing velocity, rate of climb.—**v. de entrada**, entrance velocity.—**v. de salida**, velocity of discharge.—**v. media**, mean velocity.—**v. periférica**, circumferential velocity.

velocímetro, *m.* speedometer; speed meter.

velocipédico, ca, *a.* pertaining to velocipedes.

velocipedismo, *m.* cycling (as a sport).

velocipedista, *n.* cyclist.

velocípedo, *m.* velocipede.

velódromo, *m.* bicycle race course.

velomotor, *m.* motor vehicle (esp. motor cycle).

velón, *m.* brass lamp with movable reservoir.

velonera, *f.* lamp stand or bracket.

velonero, ra, *n.* maker or seller of VELONES.

velorio, *m.* wake, watch (over a dead person).

veloz, *a.* swift, rapid, fleet, quick, fast.

velozmente, *adv.* swiftly, fleetly, rapidly.

veludillo, veludo = VELLUDILLO, VELLUDO.

vellera, *f.* woman who removes hair from women's faces.

vellido, da, *a.* downy; villous.

vello, *m.* down; nap; pubescence; fuzz.

vellocino, *m.* fleece (as the golden fleece).

¹**vellón**, *m.* fleece, wool of one sheep; unsheared sheepskin; lock of wool.

²**vellon**, *m.* copper and silver alloy; ancient copper coin.

vellonero, *m.* gatherer of fleece at shearing.

vellora, *f.* knot taken from woollen cloth.

vellorí, vellorín, *m.* broadcloth of undyed wool.

vellorita, *f.* (bot.) cowslip.

vellosidad, *f.* downiness; hairiness.

vellosilla, *f.* (bot.) mouse-ear.

velloso, sa, *a.* downy, villous, hairy, fuzzy.

velludillo, *m.* velveteen.

velludo, da. I. *a.* downy, hairy, shaggy, woolly. **II.** *m.* shag, velvet.

vellutero, ra, *n.* velvet or felt worker.

vena, *f.* vein, blood vessel; fiber of plants; (min.) vein, seam, lode; (hydraul.) vein; flow of water underground; vein or stripe in stones or woods; poetical vein, inspiration.—**v. ácigos**, azigous vein, vena azigos.—**v. basílica**, basilic vein.—**v. cardíaca**, cardiac vein.—**v. cava**, vena cava.—**v. cefálica**, cephalic vein.—**v. coronaria**, cardiac vein.—**v. de agua**, underground natural water conduit.—**v. de loco**, fickle disposition.—**v. flúida**, (hydraul.) jet.—**v. láctea**, chyliferous vessel.—**v. leónica**, ranine vein.—**v. porta**, vena portæ, portal vein.—**v. safena**, saphenous vein.—**v. subclavia**, subclavian vein.—**v. yugular**, jugular vein.—**acostarse la v.**, (min.) (of vein) to dip.—**dar en la v.**, to hit upon the right means.—**estar de v.**, to be in the mood (for something).—**estar en v.**, to be inspired.—**hallar la v.** = DAR EN LA V.

venablo, *m.* javelin, dart.—**echar venablos**, to burst out into violent language.

venadero, ra. I. *a.* deer-hunting, deer (as *a.*). **II.** *m.* place frequented by deer.

venado, *m.* deer, stag; deer meat, venison.

venaje, *m.* feeding streams, aggregate of streams forming a river.

¹**venal**, *a.* venous; pertaining to veins.

²**venal**, *a.* marketable, salable; venal, mercenary.

venalidad, *f.* venality, mercenariness.

venático, ca, *a.* (coll.) cranky, erratic, daft.

venatorio, ria, *a.* venatic, used in hunting.

vencedor, ra, *n. & a.* victor, vanquisher(-ing).

¹**vencejo**, *m.* string, band.

²**vencejo**, *m.* (ornith.) swift, martin, martlet.

vencer. l. *va.* (*ind.* VENZO; *subj.* VENZA) to conquer, subdue, defeat, vanquish, overpower; to surpass, outdo, excel; to surmount, overcome; to win; to prevail upon, persuade, convince; to bend, turn down; to twist. **II.** *vn.* to conquer, triumph, succeed; to win; to be the victor (com.) to fall due, mature; to expire. **III.** *vr.* to govern one's passions or desires, to control oneself.

vencetósigo, *m.* (bot.) milkweed.

vencible, *a.* conquerable; surmountable.

vencida, *f.* = VENCIMIENTO.

vencido, da. I. *pp.* of VENCER. **II.** *a.* (com.) due payable.—**de v.** nearly beaten, vanquished, or finished.

For pronunciation, see the rules at the beginning of the book.

encimiento, *m.* vanquishment; flinch; bent; turn down; (com.) maturity, expiration.

enda, *f.* (surg.) bandage, roller; fillet.

endaje, *m.* (surg.) bandage; bandaging.

endar, *va.* (surg.) to bandage; to fillet; to hoodwink, to blind, obfuscate.

endaval, *m.* strong wind from the sea.

endavalada, *f.* storm of southerly wind.

endedor, ra, *n.* seller, trader; salesman (-woman).

endehumos, *m.* courtier trading on his influence.

endeja, *f.* public sale.

ender, *va.* & *vn.* to sell.—v. a destajo = v. al POR MENOR.—v. al contado, to sell for cash.—v. al por mayor, to sell at wholesale.—v. al por menor, to sell at retail.—v. al quitar, to sell with the privilege of buying back.—v. a plazo, to sell on credit.—v. por mayor = v. AL POR MAYOR.—v. por menor = v. AL POR MENOR.—v. salud, (coll.) to be or look in very good health. II. *vr.* to sell out, accept a bribe; to expose oneself to danger; (fig.) to give oneself away, betray one's feelings; to boast; to be sold (at a place, at a price), to be for sale.—v. caro, to sell (be sold) dear; to be of difficult access; to be seen seldom (*se vende Vd. caro*, you are a stranger).

endí, *m.* (com.) certificate of sale.

endible, *a.* salable, marketable.

endido, da, *a.* & *pp.* sold; betrayed.—estar v., to be duped; to be exposed to great risks.

endiente, *a.* selling.

endimia, *f.* vintage; large gain or profit.

endimiador, ra, *n.* vintager.

endimiar, *va.* to gather (crops of grapes); to enjoy as an unlawful perquisite or reap as unjust profit; (coll.) to kill, murder.

endimiario, *m.* Vendimiaire, first month of the French-Revolution calendar.

endo, *m.* selvage of cloth.

endré, etc. *v.* V. VENIR.

enduta, *f.* (Am.) auction.

endutero, ra, *n.* (Am.) auctioneer.

eneciano, na, *a.* & *n.* Venetian.

enencia, *f.* tube for sampling sherry.

enenífero, ra, *a.* (poet.) poisonous.

eneno, *m.* poison, venom; wrath, fury, passion.

enenosamente, *adv.* venomously, banefully.

enenosidad, *f.* poisonousness, banefulness.

enenoso, sa, *a.* venomous, poisonous, baneful.

enera, *f.* scallop shell worn as a badge by pilgrims; badge, jewel, or star of a military order.—empeñar la v., to spare no expense.

enera, *f.* = VENERO, spring (of water).

enerabilísimo, ma, *a. super.* most venerable.

enerable, *a.* venerable.—venerablemente, *adv.* venerably.

eneración, *f.* veneration; worship.

enerador, ra, *n.* & *a.* venerator(-ing); worshipper(-ing).

enerando, da, *a.* venerable.

enerante, *a.* venerating, worshipping.

enerar, *va.* to venerate, revere; to worship.

enéreo, rea. I. *a.* sensual; (med.) venereal. II. *m.* venereal disease.

enero, *m.* water spring; (min.) bed, lode; radius or horary line of sundials; origin, root, source.

eneruela, *f. dim.* small scallop shell.

enezolano, na, *n.* & *a.* Venezuelan.

engable, *a.* deserving revenge; that can be avenged.

engador, ra, *n.* & *a.* avenger(-ing); revenger (-ing).

enganza, *f.* revenge; vengeance.

engar. I. *va.* (*pret.* VENGUÉ; *subj.* VENGUE) avenge. II. *vr.* (de), to take revenge (on).

engativamente, *adv.* revengefully.

engativo, va, *a.* revengeful, vindictive.

engo, venga, *v.* V. VENIR.

vengué, vengue, *v.* V. VENGAR.

venia, *f.* pardon, forgiveness; leave, permission; bow with the head; (law) license to minors to manage their own estates.

venial, *a.* venial; pardonable.—venialidad, *f.* venialness.—venialmente, *adv.* venially.

venida, *f.* arrival; return, coming; flood, freshet; attack in fencing; impetuosity, rashness, rush.

venidero, ra. I. *a.* future, coming.—en lo v., hereafter, in future. II. *m.* posterity, successors.

venido, da. I. *pp.* of VENIR. II. *a.*—bien v., welcome.

venimécum, *m.* vademecum.

venir. I. *vn.* (*ger.* VINIENDO; *ind. pres.* yo VENGO, él VIENE, *pret.* VINE, *fut.* VENDRÉ; *subj.* VENGA) to come; to arrive; to arise, result, follow; to be becoming, fit, suit; to yield, agree, submit; to grow, be produced; to occur (to one's mind), or begin to be felt (diff. constr.: *me vino el deseo de viajar*, I began to feel, or I felt a desire to travel); to happen; to concern (gen. with IR: *eso no me va ni me viene*, that does not concern, or affect, me).—v. a, to attain; (foll. by *inf.*), to end by (foll. by *pres. p.*) (*después de mucho trabajo, vino a descubrir la causa*, after much labor, he ended by finding the cause, or, he finally found the cause); sometimes used to denote approximation, a rough estimate (*Juan viene a tener dos mil pesos*, John must be worth about two thousand pesos).—v. a buscar, to come for, or to get.—v. a las manos, to come to blows.—v. a menos, to decay, to decline.—v. a pelo = v. DE PERILLA.—v. a ser, to get to be, become; to turn out to be, amount to.—v. bien, to suit, be becoming.—v. bien en, to agree to, to grant.—v. como anillo en dedo, v. como pedrada en ojo de boticario, or v. de perilla, to come in the nick of time; to fit the case, answer perfectly, be to the point.—v. en, to decide, resolve; to acquire, obtain (knowledge, etc.).—v. mal, to be unbecoming, not to suit.—v. rodado, to come unexpectedly, to come by a stroke of luck.—¿a qué viene eso? to what purpose is that? what has that to do with the case?—el que venga atrás, or detrás, que arree, the Devil take the hindmost.—en lo por v., hereafter, in future.—lo por v., the future; future things.—que viene, next (*la semana que viene*, next week).—si a mano viene, perhaps.—venga lo que viniere, come what may; happen what may. II. *vr.* to ferment; to attain perfection by fermentation, as bread or wine.—v. abajo, to fall, to collapse.—v. a la boca, to taste unpleasantly.—v. al suelo, to fall to the ground; to fall through, to fail.—v. cayendo, to be falling down.

venora, *f.* stone or brick marks in a drain or trench, as guides for cleaning.

venoso, sa, *a.* venous; veiny, veined.

venta, *f.* sale; selling; market; roadside inn; exposed, inhospitable place.—v. (al) por mayor, wholesale.—v. (al) por menor, retail sale; retailing.—v. pública, public auction sale.—de v., or en v., for sale.—hacer v., (coll.) to invite to potluck.—ser una v., to be a dear place.

ventada, *f.* blast, puff, gust of wind.

ventaja, *f.* advantage; gain, profit; additional pay; odds given at play.—llevar v. a, to be ahead of; to have advantage over.

ventajosamente, *adv.* advantageously.

ventajoso, sa, *a.* advantageous; profitable; advisable.

ventalla, *f.* valve; (bot.) pod.

ventalle, *m.* fan.

ventana, *f.* window; (carp.) window frame, window sash; window shutter.—v. de la nariz, nostril.—echar la casa por la v., to go to a lot of expense.

ventanaje, *m.* (arch.) fenestration.

ventanal, *m.* large window.

ventanazo, *m.* slamming of a window.

ventanear, *vn.* (coll.) to be often at the window (esp. for flirting).—**ventaneo,** *m.* (coll.) gazing out of, or flirting from, the window.

ventanero, ra. I. *m.* window maker; man who gazes at windows where there are women. **II.** *f.* woman who flirts from the window.

ventanilla, *f. dim.* window (of ticket-office, bank teller, etc.).

ventanillo, *m. dim.* small window shutter; peephole.

ventano, *m.* small window.

ventar, *va.* & *vn.* (*ind.* VIENTA; *subj.* VIENTE) = VENTEAR.

ventarrón, *m.* stiff wind, wind gust.

venteadura, *f.* shake in timber.

ventear. I. *v. impers.* (of the wind) to blow. **II.** *va.* to smell, scent, sniff (as dogs); to investigate, inquire; to air. **III.** *vr.* (of timber) to have shakes; to be spoiled by the wind; (coll.) to break wind.

venteo, *m.* bung, bunghole (in a cask).

venteril, *a.* suited to a poor inn.

¹**ventero, ra,** *n.* innkeeper.

²**ventero, ra,** *n.* scenting dog.

ventilación, *f.* ventilation; discussion.

ventilador, *m.* ventilator; (ventilating) fan.

ventilar. I. *va.* to air, ventilate; to winnow, to fan; to discuss. **II.** *vn.* (of air) to circulate.

ventisca, *f.* snowstorm, blizzard; snowdrift.

ventiscar, *v. impers.* to snow with strong wind; (of snow) to drift.

ventisco, *m.* = VENTISCA.—**ventiscoso, sa,** *a.* having frequent snowstorms; full of snowdrifts.

ventisquear, *v. impers.* to snow with strong wind (*aquí ventisquea mucho,* there are many snowstorms here).

ventisquero, *m.* snowstorm, snowdrift; glacier; snow-capped mountain.

ventola, *f.* (naut.) top hamper.

ventolera, *f.* gust of wind; pin wheel; (coll.) vanity, haughtiness; strong whim, "fever," "rage."

ventolina, *f.* (naut.) light wind, cat's-paw.

ventor, ra, *n.* pointer (dog); foxhound.

ventorrero, *m.* exposed, windy place.

ventorrillo, ventorro, *m.* poor inn or tavern.

ventosa, *f.* vent, air hole, spiracle; (zool.) sucker; (surg.) cupping; cupping glass.—**v. escarificada, or sajada,** wet cupping.—**v. seca,** dry cupping.—**pegar una v.,** to swindle.

ventosear, *vn.* & *vr.* to break wind.

ventosidad, *f.* flatulence, windiness.

ventoso, sa, *a.* windy; stormy; flatulent; pointing (as a pointer dog); vain, inflated.

ventral, *a.* ventral.

ventrecillo, *m. dim.* of VIENTRE, belly.

ventrecha, *f.* belly (of fishes).

ventregada, *f.* brood, litter; multitude, rush (of things).

ventrera, *f.* bellyband, abdominal belt; cummerbund.

ventrezuelo, *m. dim.* of VIENTRE, belly.

ventricular, *a.* ventricular.

ventrículo, *m.* (anat and zool.) ventricle; any cavity of the heart or brain.

ventril, *m.* counterpoise.

ventrílocuo, *m.* ventriloquist.

ventriloquia, *f.* ventriloquism.

ventrón, *m. aug.* large belly; tripe (food).

ventroso, sa; ventrudo, da, *a.* big-bellied.

ventura, *f.* happiness; luck, fortune; chance, hazard, venture; risk, danger.—**a la v.,** or **a v.,** at a venture, at hazard.—**buena v.,** fortune told by cards, etc.—**por v.,** by chance.—**probar v.,** to try one's fortune or luck, to venture.

venturado, da, *a.* lucky, fortunate.

venturanza, *f.* happiness.

venturero, ra. I. *a.* lucky; adventurous; idle. **II.** *n.* fortune hunter, adventurer.

venturina, *f.* goldstone, aventurin.

venturo, ra, *a.* future; coming.

venturón, *m. aug.* great luck.

venturosamente, *adv.* luckily, fortunately.

venturoso, sa, *a.* lucky; successful, prosperous

Venus, *m.* (astr., myth.) Venus.

venustidad, *f.* beauty, gracefulness.

venusto, ta, *a.* beautiful, graceful.

venza, *f.* scarfskin used by goldbeaters.

venzo, venza, *v. V.* VENCER.

veo, vea, *v. V.* VER.

ver. I. *va.* & *vn.* (*pp.* VISTO; *ger.* VIENDO; *ind. pres.* VEO, *pret.* yo VI or VÍ, él VIÓ; *subj.* VEA) to see; to look into, examine, consider; to treat; to look at; to try (a case at law).—**v. de,** to try to —**v. el cielo abierto,** to see a great opportunity.—**v. en ello,** to consider, to weigh in the mind.—**v. las estrellas,** to feel lively pain, see stars.—**v. mundo,** or **v. tierras,** to see the world, to travel.—**v. venir,** to see (somebody or something) coming; to await results.—**v. visiones,** to build air castles.—**v. y creer,** seeing is believing.—**al v.,** to see one, at cards.—**allá veremos,** we shall see, time will tell.—**más v.,** (coll.) good-bye, so long.—**a v.,** in order to see.—**¡a v.!,** let's see!—**de buen (mal) v.,** good (bad) looking.—**hacer v.,** to show.—**hasta más v.** = A MÁS V.—**estar por v.,** to remain to be seen, to be doubtful.—**no poder v. a,** to abhor or detest (can't bear).—**no tener que v. con,** to have nothing to do with.—**si te vi, ya no me acuerdo,** out of sight, out of mind.—**veámoslo** = A V.—**veremos** = ALLÁ VEREMOS. **II.** *vr.* to be seen; be conspicuous; to find oneself (in a situation), be; to be easily seen, be obvious; to meet, have an interview; to look at oneself in a glass.—**véase,** *v.,* see (in references).—**v. con,** to have a talk with, to see.—**v. en,** or **entre, las astas del toro,** to be in the greatest danger.—**ya se ve,** of course, naturally; certainly; however. **III.** *m.* sense of sight, seeing; looks, light, view, aspect appearance.—**a mi v.,** in my opinion, to my way of thinking.

¹**vera,** *f.* edge, border.

²**vera,** *f.* (Am.) a tree resembling guaiacum.

veracidad, *f.* veracity, truthfulness.

vera efigies, (Lat.) faithful portrait.

veranada, *f.* summer season.

veranadero, *m.* summer pasture.

veranar, *vn.* to summer.

veraneante, *n.* summer resident or vacationist.

veranear, *vn.* to summer.

veraneo, *m.* summering, summer vacation.

veranero, *m.* place where cattle graze in summer.

veraniego, ga, *a.* summer (as *a.*); thin or sickly in summer; weak, light.

veranillo, *m. dim.*—**v. de San Martín,** Indian summer.

verano, *m.* summer; (Am.) dry season.

veras, *f. pl.* reality, truth; earnestness, fervor.—**con muchas v.,** very earnestly.—**de v.,** in truth, really, in earnest.

veratro, *m.* (bot.) hellebore.

veraz, *a.* veracious, truthful.

verba, *f.* loquacity, talkativeness; eloquence.

verbal, *a.* verbal; oral; (law) nuncupative.—**verbalismo,** *m.* literalism, adherence to words rather than to ideas; system of teaching emphasizing world memory.—**verbalista,** *n.* literalist; advocate of VERBALISMO.—**verbalmente,** *adv.* verbally, orally, by word of mouth.

verbasco, *m.* (bot.) verbascum, mullein.

verbena, *f.* (bot.) vervain, verbena; night festival on the eve of a saint's day.—**coger la v.,** to rise early to take a walk.—**verbenáceo, a,** *a.* (bot.) verbenaceous.—*pl.* Verbenaceæ.

yerbenear, *vn.* to abound, to be plentiful; to rush to and fro.

verberación, *f.* lashing (esp. of wind, etc.).

verberar, *va.* to lash, beat, strike against (as wind and water).

verbigracia, *adv.* for example, for instance.

verbo, *m.* verb; (**V-**) Word, second person of the Trinity.—**v. activo,** transitive verb, active verb.—**v. adjetivo,** any verb, except *ser.*—**v. defectivo,** defective verb.—**v. neutro,** intransitive or neuter verb.—**v. recíproco,** reciprocal verb.—**v. reflejo,** or **reflexivo,** reflexive verb. —**v. substantivo,** the verb *ser,* to be.—**echar verbos,** to curse, to swear.—**en un v.,** at once, without delay.

verborrea, verbosidad, *f.* verbosity, wordiness.

verboso, sa, *a.* verbose, prolix, wordy.

verdacho, *m.* (art) green earth.

verdad, *f.* truth.—¿**v.?** isn't it? is that so? isn't that so? expletively in the sense of "you know," "don't you know?"—**v. de Perogrullo,** truism. —**a decir v.,** to tell the truth; in reality, in fact.—**a la v.,** truly, really, in truth.—**bien es v. que,** it is true that.—**decir cuatro verdades,** to speak one's mind freely.—**de v.,** A LA V.; in earnest; real.—**en v.,** truly, really; verily.—¿**no es v.?** isn't it? isn't that so?—**ser v.,** to be true.—**tratar v.,** to love and tell the truth.

verdaderamente, *adv.* truly, really.

verdadero, ra, *a.* true; real, actual; truthful.

verdasca, *f.* twig, bough, thin branch.

verde. I. *a.* green; verdant; unripe, immature, undeveloped; fresh; young, blooming; risqué, smutty, off-color.—**v. botella,** bottle green.— **v. limón,** bright green.—**v. pardo,** brown green.—**están verdes,** sour grapes. **II.** *m.* green (color); verdure; vert; green barley or grass given to horses or mules as a purge.— **darse un v.,** to amuse oneself for a short time, to indulge in a little relaxation.

verdea, *f.* greenish wine.

verdear. I. *vn.* to grow green; to look green, to show its greenness. **II.** *va.* to pick (grapes and olives) to sell.

verdeceledón, *m.* sea-green, celadon.

verdecer, *vn.* to grow green.

verdecico, ica, ito, ita, illo, illa, *a. dim.* greenish.—**verdecillo,** *m.* (ornith.) greenfinch.

verdeesmeralda, *a.* emerald green.

verdegal, *m.* green field.

verdegay, *a.* & *m.* light, bright green.

verdeguear, *vn.* to grow green.

verdemar, *a.* & *m.* sea-green.

verdemontaña, *m.* mountain-green.

verderol, ¹**verderón,** *m.* (ornith.) green finch.

verderol, ²**verderón,** *m.* (ichth.) green shellfish.

verdete, *m.* verditer; verdigris.

verdevejiga, *f.* sap green.

verdezuelo, *m.* (ornith.) greenfinch, greeny.

verdín, *m.* verdure; pond scum; mould, mildew; verdigris; green snuff.—**verdina,** *f.* fresh greenness of plants.—**verdinal,** *m.* green spot or patch in a plain or meadow.

verdinegro, gra, *a.* dark green.

verdino, na, *a.* bright green.

verdiseco, ca, *a.* pale green; half dry.

verdolaga, *f.* (bot.) purslane.

verdón, *m.* (ornith.) greenfinch.

verdor, *m.* greenness; verdure, verdancy; herbage; freshness, vigor.—*pl.* youth, age of vigor.

verdoso, sa, *a.* greenish.

verdoyo, *m.* pond scum; green mould.

verdugada, *f.* (mason.) layer of bricks.

verdugado, *m.* hoopskirt.

verdugal, *m.* young shoots growing in a wood after cutting.

verdugazo, *m.* blow or lash with a twig.

verdugo, *m.* tiller, sucker, young shoot of a tree; verdun, duelling rapier; scourge, lash; wale, welt; executioner; (jewelry) hoop for a ring; very cruel person; anything that hurts; (ma-

son.) brick course in a stone or mud wall; a small bird of prey.

verdugón, *m. aug.* large wale or welt.

verduguillo, *m. dim.* swelling on the leaves of some plants; small, narrow razor; duelling rapier; hoop worn as earring; (naut.) sheer rail.

verdulera, *f.* market woman; (coll.) coarse, low woman.

verdulería, *f.* greengrocer's shop.

verdulero, *m.* greengrocer.

verdura, *f.* verdure, verdancy; greenness; greens, vegetables; garden stuff; (art) foliage.

verdusco, ca, *a.* dark greenish.

verecundo, da, *a.* bashful, shy.

vereda, *f.* path, footpath, trail; circular order or notice sent to several towns or places; route of travelling preachers; (Cuba, S. A.) sidewalk.— **entrar por la v.,** to come to reason, to do one's duty.

veredero, *m.* messenger sent with despatches on a route.

veredicto, *m.* (law) verdict.

verga, *f.* penis; steel bow of a crossbow; (naut.) yard.—**v. seca,** crossjack yard.—**vergas en alto,** (naut.) all ready to sail.—**poner las vergas en cruz,** to square the yards.

vergajo, *m.* penis of a bull used as a cowhide.

vergel, *f.* flower garden.

vergelero, ra, *n.* gardener.

vergeta, *f.* small twig.

vergeteado, da, *a.* (her.) vergette, paley.

vergonzante. I. *a.* bashful, shamefaced. **II.** *n.* shy beggar.

vergonzosamente, *adv.* shamefully, disgracefully; bashfully, confusedly.

vergonzoso, sa. I. *a.* bashful, shamefaced, shy; shameful, disgraceful. **II.** *m.* armadillo.

verguear, *va.* to beat with a rod or whip.

vergüenza, *f.* shame; bashfulness, shyness, confusion; modesty; disgrace; public punishment. —*pl.* privy parts.—**sacar a la v.,** to disgrace publicly as a punishment; (coll.) to put in a predicament, or "fix," by asking (one) to do before others what one does not do well; to make a show of.—**ser una mala v.,** (coll.) to be a shame.—**tener v.,** to be ashamed; to be shy.

verguer, verguero, *m.* high constable.

vergueta, *f.* small switch or rod.

verguío, a, *a.* (of wood) tough and flexible, leathery.

vericueto, *m.* rough and pathless place.

verídicamente, *adv.* veridically, truthfully.

verídico, ca, *a.* veridical, truthful.

verificación, *f.* verification, substantiation, confirmation; test; adjustment (of an instrument).

verificar. I. *va.* (*pret.* VERIFIQUÉ; *subj.* VERIFIQUE) to verify, confirm, prove; to test, adjust (an instrument); to fulfil, accomplish, carry out. **II.** *vr.* to be verified, to prove true; to take place, to occur.

verificativo, va, *a.* verifying, corroborative.

verija, *f.* region of the genitals.

veril, *m.* (naut.) edge of a sand bank, etc.

verilear, *vn.* (naut.) to coast around a bank.

verisímil, *a.* probable, likely, credible.

verisimilitud, *f.* verisimilitude, probability.

verisímilmente, *adv.* probably, likely.

verja, *f.* grate, grating; iron railing.

vermes, *m. pl.* (med.) intestinal worms.

vermicida, *a.* (med.) vermicide.

vermicular, *a.* vermiculous, vermicular.

vermiforme, *a.* vermiform, vermlike.

vermífugo, *a.* & *m.* (med.) vermifuge.

verminoso, sa, *a.* verminous.

vermut, *m.* vermouth.

vernáculo, la, *a.* vernacular, native.

vernal, *a.* vernal, spring (as *a.*).

vernier, *m.* vernier.

vero, *m.* marten (fur).—*pl.* (her.) vair.

---

veronense; veronés, sa, *n.* & *a.* Veronese.

verónica, *f.* (bot.) veronica; a feat in bullfighting.

verosímil, verosimilitud, verosímilmente = VERISÍMIL, VERISIMILITUD, etc.

verraco, *m.* male hog or boar.

verraquear, *vn.* (coll.) to grunt like a boar; (of a child) to cry long and loud.

verraquera, *f.* crying spell (of children).

verriondez, *f.* rutting time of animals; withering state of plants.

verriondo, da, *a.* (of animals) rutting, in heat; withered (plants); badly cooked, tough.

verrón, *m.* = VERRACO.

verruga, *f.* wart; (coll.) nuisance, bore.

verrugo, *m.* (coll.) miser.

verrugoso, sa, *a.* warty.

versado, da. I. *pp.* of VERSAR. **II.** *a.* versed, conversant.

versal, *a.* & *f.* (print.) capital (letter).—**versalilla, versalita,** *f.* & *a.* (print.) small capital (letter).

¹**versar. I.** *vn.* to go around.—**v. acerca de,** or **sobre,** to treat of or on. **II.** *vr.* to become versed or conversant.

²**versar,** *vn.* (Cuba) to versify, improvise verses.

versátil, *a.* versatile; changeable, fickle.

versatilidad, *f.* versatility; fickleness.

versecillo, *m.* *dim.* little verse, verselet.

versería, *f.* poems.

versícula, *f.* stand for the choir books.

versiculario, *m.* (eccl.) chanter of versicles; keeper of the choir books.

versículo, *m.* (eccl.) verse; versicle.

versificación, *f.* versification.

versificador, ra, *m.* versifier, verse maker.

versificante, *a.* versifying.

versificar, *va.* & *vn.* (*pret.* VERSIFIQUÉ; *subj.* VERSIFIQUE) to versify.

versión, *f.* translation, version; (med.) version.—**v. de los Setenta,** Septuagint.

versista, *m.* (coll.) versifier, poetaster.

¹**verso,** *m.* line (of poetry); stanza.—*pl.* poems.—**v. alejandrino,** Alexandrine.—**v. blanco,** blank verse.—**v. de arte mayor,** verse of more than nine syllables.—**v. de arte menor,** verse of less than nine syllables.—**v. esdrújulo,** verse ending with a word accented on the antepenult.—**v. libre** = v. BLANCO.—**v. llano,** (poet.) verse ending with a word accented on the penult.—**v. suelto** = v. BLANCO.—**versos pareados,** doggerel.

²**verso,** *m.* (artil.) an ancient small culverin.

vértebra, *f.* (anat.) vertebra.—**vertebrado, da. I.** *n.* & *a.* vertebrate. **II.** *m.* *pl.* (zool.), Vertebrata, vertebrates.—**vertebral,** *a.* vertebral.

vertedera, *f.* (agr.) mouldboard of a plow.

vertedero, *m.* sink, dumping place; (hydraul.) weir; spillway.

vertedor, ra. I. *n.* nightman; emptier. **II.** *m.* tailrace; drain; (hydraul.) weir; (naut.) boat scoop.

vertellos, *m.* *pl.* (naut.) balls of the parrel truck.

verter. I. *va.* (*ind.* VIERTO; *subj.* VIERTA) to pour, spill, shed, cast; to empty; to dump; to translate; to construe, interpret; to divulge, publish, reveal. **II.** *vn.* to run, flow.

vertibilidad, *f.* capability of being turned over.

vertible, *a.* movable, changeable, variable.

vertical. I. *a.* vertical. **II.** *m.* (astr.) vertical circle.—**v. primario,** (astr.) prime vertical. **III.** *f.* vertical line.—**verticalidad,** *f.* verticality.—**verticalmente,** *adv.* vertically.

vértice, *m.* vertex; apex, top; (anat.) vertex, crown of the head.

verticidad, *f.* movableness, mobility.

verticilado, da, *a.* (bot.) verticillate.

verticilo, *m.* (bot.) verticil, whorl.

vertiente. I. *a.* emptying; flowing. **II.** *f.* watershed; slope.

vertiginoso, sa, *a.* giddy, vertiginous.

vértigo, *m.* giddiness, dizziness, vertigo; fit o insanity.

vertimiento, *m.* effusion, shedding.

vesania, *f.* (med.) vesania, insanity.

vesánico, ca, *á.* mentally deranged.

vesical, *a.* (anat.) vesical.

vesicante, *a.* & *m.* vesicant, producing blister

vesícula, *f.* (anat., bot.) vesicle; (med.) vesicle blister.—**v. aérea,** air vesicle (of the lungs).—**v. biliar,** gall bladder.—**v. elemental,** c **orgánica,** (biol.) cell.—**v. ovárica,** (anat. Graffian follicle.—**v. seminal,** (anat.) sperr sac.—**vesicular,** *a.* vesicular.—**vesiculoso sa,** *a.* vesiculate.

Véspero, *m.* Vesper, evening star.

vespertiliónidos, *m.* *pl.* (zool.) Vespertilionid

vespertina, *f.* evening discourse in universities

vespertino, na. I. *a.* vespertine, evening. **II.** *m* afternoon literary meeting; afternoon sermon

véspidos, *m.* *pl.* (zool.) Vespidæ.

vestal, *f.* & *a.* vestal.

veste, *f.* (poet.) clothes, dress, garments.

vestfaliano, na, *n.* & *a.* Westphalian.

vestíbulo, *m.* vestibule, hall, lobby; (anat. vestibule of the ear.

vestido, *m.* dress, clothes, clothing, garb, cos tume; ornament, embellishment.—**v. de corte** court dress.—**v. de etiqueta,** or **de serio,** ful or evening dress.—**vestidos usados,** second hand clothes.

vestidura, *f.* vesture.—*pl.* (eccl.) vestments.

vestigio, *m.* vestige, trace, sign; footstep, foot mark.—*pl.* ruins, remains; (chem.) traces.

vestiglo, *m.* horrid and formidable monster.

vestimenta, *f.* clothes, garments.—*pl.* ecclesias tical robes.

vestir (*ger.* VISTIENDO; *ind.* *pres.* VISTO, *pret.* 6 VISTIÓ; *subj.* VISTA). **I.** *va.* to clothe, dress; to deck, adorn; to cloak, disguise, palliate; to don put on; to wear; to cover; (mason.) to rough cast. **II.** *vn.* to dress in a special color or fashion —**v. bien,** to dress well or in good taste.—**v. de uniforme,** to dress in uniform. **III.** *vr.* to dres oneself; to be covered; to be clothed.

vestuario, *m.* apparel, wardrobe, clothes, cloth ing, dress; uniform; (mil.) equipment, outfit habiliment; (eccl.) vestry; money given to ec clesiastics for dress, etc.; (theat.) wardrobe greenroom, dressing room.

vestugo, *m.* tiller, sprout of an olive tree.

veta, *f.* (min.) vein, seam, lode; vein in wood o marble; grain, flake; stripe.—**descubrir la v.** to disclose one's sentiments or designs, show one's hand.

vetado, da; veteado, da, *a.* striped, veined streaky, cross-grained, mottled.

vetear, *va.* to variegate, to grain.

veterano, na. I. *a.* (mil.) veteran; having ha long experience. **II.** *m.* veteran, old hand.

veterinaria, *f.* veterinary science.

veterinario, *m.* veterinarian.

vetisesgado, da, diagonal-striped.

veto, *m.* veto; prohibition, interdict.

vetustez, *f.* antiquity, old age.

vetusto, ta, *a.* very ancient or old.

vez, *f.* turn; time, occasion; herd of swine belong ing to the inhabitants of a place.—*pl.* authorit given to a substitute.—**a la v.,** at a time; at th same time; at one time.—**a la v. que,** while.—**alguna v.,** (in a question) ever; also **algunas veces,** sometimes; some times, occasionally.—**alguna que otra v.,** once in a while, occasion ally.—**a su v.,** in his (one's) turn; on his (one's part.—**a veces,** sometimes, occasionally.—**cada v.,** each time, every time.—**cada v. más** more and more.—**cada v. que,** every time that whenever.—**de una v.,** at once; at one time with a single act, word, blow, etc.—**de v. er cuando,** occasionally, once in a while, fron time to time.—**dos veces,** twice.—**en v. de**

instead of.—**hacer las veces de**, to serve as, substitute for.—**más de una v.**, more than once.—**muchas veces**, often.—**otra v.**, again, once more; some other time.—**pocas**, or **raras, veces**, seldom, rarely; only a few times.—**tal cual v.**, seldom, once in a while.—**tal v.**, perhaps, maybe, perchance.—**todas las veces que**, whenever, as often as.—**una que otra v.**, once in a while, a few times.—**una v.**, once.—**una v. que**, since, inasmuch as; after.—**una v. que otra**, once in a while; a few times —**veces mayor que**, times as large as, times (*10 es 5 veces mayor que 2*, 10 is 5 times [as large as] 2). The similar expression **veces menor que** indicates a fractional part: *2 es 5 veces menor que 10*, 2 is one fifth of 10.

veza, f. (bot.) vetch.

vezar, va. & vr. to accustom, habituate, inure.

vi, ví, pret. of VER.

vía, f. way, road; route, via; carriage track; (Ry.) track, line; gauge; way, manner, method, procedure; spiritual life; (zool.) tube, canal, passage.—**v. acuática**, waterway.—**v. ancha**, (Ry.) broad gauge.—**v. angosta**, narrow gauge.—**v. crucis**, (eccl.) Via Crucis, way of the cross; affliction, burden.—**v. de agua**, (naut.) leak; v. ACUÁTICA.—**v. ejecutiva**, (law) levy, a legal writ of execution; attachment.—**v. férrea**, railroad, railway.—**v. húmeda**, (chem.) wet process.—**V. Láctea**, (astr.) Milky Way.—**v. muerta**, (Ry.) siding.—**v. pública**, public road, thoroughfare; street.—**v. recta**, straight along, straight forward.—**v. sacra** = v. CRUCIS.—**v. seca**, (chem.) dry process.—**v. terrestre**, land route, road.—**en v. de**, in the process of.—**por v. de**, by way of, as.

viabilidad, f. feasibility, practicability; (med.) viability.

viable, a. viable, capable of living; feasible, practicable.

viadera, f. harness shaft of a loom.

viador, m. traveler, in a mystical sense.

viaducto, m. viaduct.

viajador, ra, n. traveler.

viajante. I. a. traveling. **II.** n. traveler; commercial traveler.

viajar, vn. to travel, journey.

viajata, f. trip, excursion.

viaje, m. journey, voyage, travel, trip; passage; gait; excursion; errand; load carried at once; (hydraul.) water main, water supply; way, road; (arch.) obliquity.—**v. de ida y vuelta**, or **v. redondo**, round trip.—**buen v.**, Godspeed, bon voyage.—**de v.**, traveling, on a journey; about to start on a journey.

viajero, ra, n. traveler; passenger.

vial. I. a. pertaining to roads. **II.** m. avenue, lane, boulevard.—**vialidad**, f. system of public roads; road engineering, road making.

vianda, f. (often in the pl.) food, viands, victuals, fare; meal.—*pl.* (Cuba) vegetables for a stew.

viandante, n. traveler, passenger; tramp.

viaraza, f. (vet.) looseness, diarrhœa.

viaticar. I. va. (eccl.) to administer the viaticum to. **II.** vr. to receive the viaticum.

viático, m. viaticum, provision for a journey, traveling expenses; (eccl.) viaticum.

víbora, f. viper; perfidious person.

viborezno, na, m. young, small viper.

vibración, f. vibration.

vibrador, ra. I. a. vibrating. **II.** m. vibrator.

vibrante, a. vibrating, shaking.

vibrar. I. va. to vibrate; to brandish; to throw, dart. **II.** vn. to vibrate.

vibratorio, ria, a. vibratory.

vibrión, m. (bacteriol.) vibrio.

viburno, m. (bot.) viburnum.

icaria, f. assistant mother superior.

icaría, f. vicarship; vicarage.—**v. perpetua**,

perpetual curacy.—**vicariato**, m. vicarage; vicarship.

vicario, ria. I. a. vicarial, vicarious; vicariate. **II.** m. vicar, deputy; (eccl.) vicar, vicariate.—**v. de coro**, vicar choral, superintendent of the choir.—**v. general**, vicar-general.

vicealmiranta, f. galley next in order to the admiral's.

vicealmirantazgo, m. vice admiralty.

vicealmirante, m. vice admiral.

vicecanciller, m. vice chancellor.

viceconsiliario, m. vice counsellor.

vicecónsul, m. vice consul.

viceconsulado, m. vice consulate.

vicecristo, vicediós, m. sovereign pontiff.

vicegerencia, f. position of assistant manager.

vicegerente, m. assistant manager.

vicegobernador, ra, n. vice governor, lieutenant governor.

vicenal, a. lasting twenty years; occurring every twenty years.

vicepresidencia, f. vice presidency.

vicepresidente, m. vice president.

viceprovincia, f. (eccl.) religious houses enjoying the rank of a province.

vicerrector, ra, n. vice rector; assistant director.

vicesecretaría, f. assistant secretaryship.

vicesecretario, ria, n. assistant secretary.

vicésimo, ma, a. twentieth.

vicetesorero, ra, n. assistant treasurer.

viceversa. I. adv. vice versa, conversely. **II.** m. illogical statement, thing or action.

vicia, f. tare.

viciado, da. I. pp. of VICIAR. **II.** a. foul, contaminated.

viciar. I. va. to vitiate, mar, spoil; to counterfeit, adulterate; to forge, falsify; to annul, make void, invalidate; to deprave, pervert, corrupt; to misconstrue. **II.** vr. to give oneself up to vice; to become too much attached or addicted, to contract a (bad) habit.

vicio, m. vice; (bad) habit; defect, blemish; artifice, fraud; excessive appetite, extravagant desire; excessive growth of plants; forwardness, waywardness (of children); vices of horses or mules.—**de v.**, by habit or custom.—**quejarse de v.**, to complain habitually.—**tener el v. de**, to have the habit of; to be in the habit of.

viciosamente, adv. viciously; falsely; corruptly.

vicioso, sa, a. vicious; defective; given to vice, licentious; spoiled (child); luxuriant, overgrown, vigorous; abundant.

vicisitud, f. vicissitude.

vicisitudinario, ria, a. vicissitudinary.

viclefismo, m. Wycliffism.

viclefista, viclefita, n. & a. Wycliffite.

víctima, f. victim.—**victimario**, m. (anc.) servant attending sacrificing priest.

victo, m. a day's sustenance.

¡victor! interj. & m. shout, huzza; long live!

victorear, va. to shout, huzza for, give a clamorous ovation to.

¹victoria, f. victory, triumph, palm.—**cantar la v.**, to celebrate or proclaim a victory.—**cantar v.**, to proclaim, or boast of, a victory.—**victorial**, a. pertaining to victory.

²victoria, f. (Angl.) victoria (carriage).

victoriosamente, adv. victoriously.

victorioso, sa, a. victorious, triumphant.

vicuña, f. vicuña, a S. A. ruminant.

vid, f. (bot.) vine, grapevine.

vida, f. life; living person, human being; living, sustenance, livelihood; state, condition; activity, animation, liveliness; (law) term of ten years.—**v. airada**, licentious life, gay life.—**v. ancha**, good, comfortable living.—**v. mía**, dearest, darling.—**v. y milagros de una persona**, a person's life and history (implying that the "history" is bad).—**buena v.**, good or high living.—**buscar la v.**, to earn an honest livelihood; to seek one's fortune; to inquire into the life (of).—**dar mala v.**, to treat ill, to abuse.—**darse buena v.**, to live comfortably. —**de mala v.**, disreputable, licentious.—**de por v.**, for life, during life.—**en v.**, while living, during life.—**en la v.**, or **en mi v.**, never.— **ganarse la v.**, to make, earn one's living.— **gran v.** = BUENA V.—**hacer v.**, to live together.—**mi v.** = v. MÍA.—**pasar la v.**, to live very frugally.—**por v.** = DE POR V.—**¡por v.!** by Jove!—**¡por v. mía!** upon my soul! by my soul!—**tener siete vidas**, to have the nine lives of the cat.

vide, vide, see (in references) (abbr. *V.*).

vidente. I. *a.* seeing. **II.** *m.* seer, prophet.

¡vidita! *f.* (Am.) dearest, darling.

vidriado, da. I. *pp.* of VIDRIAR. **II.** *a.* glazed. **III.** *m.* glazing; glazed earthenware, crockery.

vidriar, *va.* to varnish, to glaze (earthenware).

vidriera, *f.* glass window or partition; glass case, show case, show window.

vidriería, *f.* glazier's shop; glass factory; glass shop; glassware.

vidriero, ra, *n.* glazier; glassblower; glass dealer.

vidrio, *m.* glass; any article made of glass; anything very delicate and brittle; a very touchy person.—**v. coloreado**, or **de color**, stained glass.—**vidrios de vidriera**, or **planos**, window glass.—**ir al v.**, to ride backward in a coach.—**pagar los vidrios rotos**, to receive undeserved punishment, to be made a scapegoat.

vidriosidad, *f.* vitreousness; glassiness.

vidrioso, sa, *a.* vitreous, brittle; glassy; slippery (from sleet); peevish, touchy.

vidual, *a.* pertaining to widowhood.

vidueño, viduño, *m.* quality of grape vines.

viejarrón, na, *m.* (coll.) old codger.

viejecito, ita, zuelo, ela, *a. & n. dim.* little old man (woman).

viejo, ja. I. *a.* old; aged; ancient, antiquated; stale; worn-out; old-fashioned. **II.** *n.* old man (woman).—**v. verde**, boyish old man (girlish old woman).

vienense, *n. & a.* of or from Vienne (France).

vienés, sa, *n. & a.* Viennese, of Vienna (Austria).

vienta, viente, *v. V.* VENTAR.

vientecillo, *m. dim.* light wind.

viento, *m.* wind; vanity, petty pride, airs; scent of dogs; nape bone of a dog, between the ears; brace, guy, bracing rope; (artil.) windage; (naut.) course.—**v. calmoso**, light unsteady wind.—**v. contrario**, foul wind.—**v. de bolina**, (naut.) scant wind.—**v. de la hélice**, (aer.) slip stream.—**v. de tierra**, land breeze.—**v. en popa**, wind right aft, before the wind; (fig.) prosperously, very well.—**v. entero**, wind from one of the cardinal points or four points from any of them.—**v. escaso**, slack wind.—**v. fresco**, (naut.) fresh breeze.—**v. puntero** = v. ESCASO.—**v. terral** = v. DE TIERRA.—**vientos alisios**, trade winds.—**con v. contrario**, (naut.) against the wind.—**contra v. y marea**, (fig.) against all odds; come what may.—**el v. se ha cargado al norte**, the wind has veered to the north.—**medio v.**, wind two points from any of the eight principal points of the compass.—**quitar el v. a un bajel**, to blanket a ship.

vientre, *m.* abdomen; belly; bowels; stomach; pregnancy; womb; widest part of vessels.

vientrecillo, *m. dim.* ventricle.

viernes, *m.* Friday; fast day.—**V. Santo**, Good Friday.—**cara de v.**, wan, thin face.

vierteaguas, *m.* (arch.) flashing, run-off plate or device.

vierto, vierta, *v. V.* VERTER.

viga, *f.* beam, girder, joist, rafter, baulk; (eng.) bridge truss; mill beam; quantity of olives pressed by the beam at once.—**v. armada**,

trussed beam.—**v. de aire**, joist.—**v. de alma llena**, plate girder.—**v. maestra**, summer, chief supporting beam.

vigencia, *f.* operation (of a law), state of being in force; legal disposition; life (of a ruling body, etc.); (Colomb.) fiscal year.

vigente, *a.* (law) in force; standing.

vigesimal, *a.* vigesimal.

vigésimo, ma, *a.* twentieth.

vigía. I. *f.* watchtower; watch, watching; (naut.) shoal, rock. **II.** *m.* lookout, watch.

vigiar, *vn.* to keep a lookout, to watch.

vigilancia, *f.* vigilance, watchfulness.

vigilante. I. *a.* watchful, vigilant, careful. **II.** *m.* watchman, guard; (Arg.) policeman.

vigilantemente, *adv.* vigilantly.

vigilar, *va. & vn.* to watch (over), to keep guard, to look out (for).—**vigilativo, va**, *a.* causing sleeplessness or wakefulness.

vigilia, *f.* vigil, wakefulness, watchfulness, watching; nocturnal study; (eccl.) vigil, fast; eve; (mil.) watch, guard.—**comer de v.**, to fast (abstain from meat).

vigor, *m.* vigor.—**en v.**, in force, in effect (as a law).—**vigorar**, *va.* = VIGORIZAR.

vigorizador, ra, *a.* invigorating.

vigorizar, *va.* (*pret.* VIGORICÉ; *subj.* VIGORICE) to strengthen, invigorate; to encourage.

vigorosamente, *adv.* vigorously, lustily.

vigorosidad, *f.* vigor.

vigoroso, sa, *a.* vigorous; substantial.

vigota, *f.* (naut.) deadeye, chain plate.

viguería, *f.* set of girders or beams; timberwork.

vigués, sa, *a.* of or from Vigo.

vigueta, *f. dim.* small beam, joist; beam.

vihuela, *f.* guitar.—**vihuelista**, *n.* guitar player.

vil, *a.* vile, mean, base, despicable.

vilano, *m.* burr or down of the thistle.

vilayato, *m.* vilayet (Turkish province).

vileza, *f.* baseness, meanness, vileness; infamous deed, base act or conduct.

vilipendiador, ra, *a. & n.* reviler(-ing).

vilipendiar, *va.* to contemn, revile.

vilipendio, *m.* contempt; reviling.

vilipendioso, sa, *a.* contemptible.

vilmente, *adv.* vilely, basely, contemptibly.

vilo.—en v., *adv.* in the air; insecurely; in suspense.

vilordo, da, *a.* slothful, lazy, heavy.

vilorta, *f.* hoop, ring of twisted willow; clasp ring of a plow; washer; game resembling lacrosse.

vilorto, *m.* a variety of reed; snare of this reed; reed or twig hoop; crosse for playing VILORTA.

vilos, *m.* (P. I.) two-masted vessel.

viltrotear, *vn.* to loaf, to walk the streets.

villa, *f.* town; government of a town; country-house, villa.

Villadiego, *m.*—**coger**, or **tomar, las de V.**, to run away, to sneak out, "to beat it."

villaje, *m.* village; hamlet.

villanada, *f.* villainous, despicable act.

villanaje, *m.* villeinage; peasantry.

villanamente, *adv.* boorishly; villainously.

villancejo, villancete, villancico, *m.* Christmas carol.—**villanciquero**, *m.* writer or singer of Christmas carols.

villanchón, na, *a.* rustic, rude.

villanería, *f.* lowness of birth; meanness.

villanesco, ca, *a.* rustic, rude, boorish.

villanía, *f.* lowness of birth, meanness; villainy, villainousness; vile, base deed.

villano, na. I. *a.* rustic, boorish; villainous, base. **II.** *n.* villain; base, contemptible person; rustic, peasant. **III.** *m.* a Spanish tune and dance.

villanote, *a. & m. aug.* great villain.

villar, *m.* village, hamlet.

villazgo, *m.* charter of a town; town tax.

villeta, *f. dim.* small town or borough.

villoría, *f.* hamlet, settlement, farm.

villorín, *m.* a sort of coarse cloth.

---

villorrio, *m.* (contempt.) small village or hamlet.
vimbre, *m.* (bot.) = MIMBRE, osier, willow.
vimbrera, *f.* (bot.) = MIMBRERA, osier, willow.
vinagrada, *f.* refreshment made with vinegar.
vinagre. I. *m.* vinegar; acidity, sourness. **II.** *a.* (Colomb.) disagreeable; sour (milk, etc.). **III.** *n.* (coll.) grouchy person (also **cara de v.**).—
vinagrero, ra. I. *n.* vinegar merchant. **II.** *f.* vinegar cruet, caster; (S. A.) heartburn.—**vinagreta**, *f.* (cook.) vinegar sauce.—**vinagrillo**, *m. dim.* weak vinegar; cosmetic lotion; rose vinegar; rose-vinegar snuff.—**vinagroso, sa,** *a.* vinegary, vinegarish, sourish; peevish, grouchy.
vinajera, *f.* (eccl.) wine vessel for the mass.
vinar, *a.* = VINARIO.
vinariego, *m.* owner of vineyards; viticulturist.
vinario, ria, *a.* pertaining to wine.
vinatera, *f.* (naut.) strop, tricing line.
vinatería, *f.* wine trade; wine shop.
vinatero, ra. I. *a.* pertaining to wine. **II.** *n.* vintner, wine merchant.
vinaza, *f.* wine drawn from the lees.
vinazo, *m.* very strong wine.
vinculable, *a.* that may be entailed.
vinculación, *f.* (law) entail.
vincular, *va.* (law) to entail; to ground or found upon; to continue, to perpetuate.
vínculo, *m.* tie, bond; vinculum; (law) entail.
vincha, *f.* (S. A.) kerchief for the head or hair.
vinchuca, *f.* (S. A.) a kind of winged bedbug.
vindicación, *f.* vindication.
vindicador, ra, *n.* & *a.* vindicator(-ing).
vindicar, *va.* (*pret.* VINDIQUÉ; *subj.* VINDIQUE) to vindicate; to avenge; to assert (as rights), defend; (law) to reclaim, repossess, replevy.—
vindicativo, va, *a.* vindictive, revengeful; vindicating, vindicative.—**vindicatorio, ria,** *a.* vindicatory.
vindicta, *f.* vengeance, revenge.—**v. pública,** public punishment; censure of public opinion.
vine, etc., *v. V.* VENIR.
vínico, ca, *a.* vinic, pertaining to wine.
vinícola. I. *a.* wine (as *a.*); vinicultural. **II.** *n.* = VINARIEGO.
vinicultor, ra, *n.* viniculturist.
vinicultura, *f.* viniculture, wine-making.
viniebla, *f.* (bot.) hound's tongue.
vinificación, *f.* vinification.
vinillo, *m.* very weak wine.
vino, *m.* wine; fermented juice of any fruit.—**v. clarete,** claret or pale red wine.—**v. cubierto,** dark-red wine.—**v. de coco,** (P. I.) fermented milk of cocoanuts.—**v. de cuerpo,** strong-bodied wine.—**v. de Jerez,** sherry wine.—**v. de lágrima,** mother-drop or virgin wine.—**v. de mesa,** table wine.—**v. de nipa,** (P. I.) fermented juice of NIPA.—**v. de Oporto,** port wine.—**v. de pasto,** table wine.—**v. de postre** = V. GENEROSO.—**v. flojo,** thin or weak wine.—**v. generoso,** strong, old wine; after-dinner wine.—**v. peleón,** very common wine.—**v. rancio,** fine old wine.—**v. seco,** dry wine.—**v. tinto,** red table wine.—**tomarse del v.,** to get drunk.
vinolencia, *f.* excess in drinking wine.
vinolento, ta, *a.* too fond of wine.
vinosidad, *f.* vinosity.
vinoso, sa, *a.* vinous; addicted to wine.
vinote, *m.* liquid remaining in the boiler after distilling wine.
vinta, *f.* (P. I.) = BAROTO, small boat.
vintén, *m.* (Uru.) a copper coin (about 2 cents).
viña, *f.* vineyard.—**viñadero, ra,** *n.* keeper of a vineyard.—**viñador, ra,** *n.* viticulturist; husbandman.—**viñatero, ra,** *n.* & *a.* (S. A.) = VIÑADOR; VIÑADERO.—**viñedo**, *m.* vineyard.—**viñero, ra,** *n.* owner of vineyards.
viñeta, *f.* (print. and photog.) vignette.
viñetero, *m.* (print.) font case for vignettes.
viñuela, *f. dim.* small vineyard.

¹viola, *f.* (mus.) viola; viola player.
²viola, *f.* (bot.) violet.
violáceo, ea. I. *a.* violaceous; violet-colored. **II.** *f. pl.* (bot.) Violaceæ.
violación, *f.* violation.
violado, da, *a.* & *m.* violet (color).
violador, ra, *n.* violator; infringer; profaner.
¹violar, *va.* to violate, break, infringe; to ravish, rape; to profane, desecrate; to spoil, to tarnish.
²violar, *m.* patch or bed of violets.
violencia, *f.* violence; compulsion, force; rape, outrage.
violentamente, *adv.* violently; forcibly.
violentar. I. *va.* to do violence to; to break into. **II.** *vr.* to force oneself (to do something distasteful); to control one's unwillingness.
violento, ta, *a.* violent; impulsive; irascible; furious; forced, unnatural; strained, absurd, misconstrued; exceedingly intense or severe, (coll.) "awful."—**sentirse v.,** to be embarrassed.
violero, *m.* viola player.
violeta, *f.* (bot.) violet.
violeto, *m.* clingstone peach.
violín. I. *m.* violin. **II.** *n.* violinist.
violinista, *n.* (mus.) violinist.
violón, *m.* (mus.) bass viol, double bass; bass-viol player.—**tocar el v.,** to do or say something absurd or nonsensical; to talk through one's hat.
violoncelista, *n.* violoncellist, cellist.
violoncelo, *m.* (mus.) violoncello, cello.
violonchelo, *m.* = VIOLONCELO.
vipéreo, rea, viperino, na, *a.* viperine; viperous, venomous.
vira, *f.* dart, arrow; welt of a shoe.
viracocha, *n.* (Chile, Peru) Spaniard.
virada, *f.* (naut.) tacking, tack.
virador, *m.* (naut.) top-rope; viol.
virago, *f.* mannish woman.
virar, *va.* (naut.) to tack, veer, put about; to wind, twist (as the capstan); to change one's course, take another way.—**v. de bordo,** (naut.) to tack; to change one's course, take another way.
viratón, *m.* large dart or arrow.
virazón, *f.* sea breeze.
víreo, *m.* (ornith.) vireo.
virgen. I. *n.* & *a.* virgin. **II.** *f.* standard of the beam of an oil mill; (V-) Virgin (Mary); (V-, astr.) Virgin, Virgo.
virgiliano, na, *a.* Virgilian.
virginal, virgíneo, nea, *a.* virginal, virgin.
virginia, *f.* (bot.) Virginia tobacco.
virginiano, na, *n.* & *a.* Virginian.
virginidad, *f.* virginity.
virgo, *m.* virginity; (anat.) hymen; (V-, astr.) Virgo, Virgin.
vírgula, *f.* virgule, small rod; light, short line, accent; (bacteriol.) cholera bacillus.—**virgulilla,** *f.* fine stroke or light line, accent.
¹viril, *m.* clear and transparent glass; (eccl.) monstrance.
²viril, *a.* virile, manly.—**virilidad**, *f.* virility, manhood; vigor, strength.
virilmente, *adv.* in a manly manner.
virina, *f.* (P. I.) glass shade for candles; (auto) windshield.
virio, *m.* (ornith.) vireo.
viripotente, *a.* (of young woman) marriageable nubile; vigorous, strong.
virol, *m.* (her.) virole.
virola, *f.* collar, clasp; check ring on goads.
virolento, ta, *a.* having smallpox; pock-marked.
virón, *m. aug.* large dart.
virotazo, *m.* wound with a VIROTE.
virote, *m.* shaft, dart, arrow; iron rod fastened to a collar on the neck of a slave to prevent his running away; vine three years old; (coll.) stuck-up man; April fool's trick.—**virotillo,**

m. (arch.) intertie; (mech.) stay, stay rod, stay-bolt.—**virotismo,** *m.* conceit, airs.

virreina, *f.* wife of a viceroy.

virreinato, virreino, *m.* viceroyship.

virrey, *m.* viceroy.

virtual, *a.* virtual.—**virtualidad,** *f.* virtuality.—**virtualmente,** *adv.* virtually, in effect, practically, almost.

virtud, *f.* virtue; efficacy, power; virtuous life; vigor, courage.—*pl.* (theol.) fifth choir of the celestial spirts.—**virtudes teologales,** theological virtues (faith, hope, charity).—**en v. de,** in, or by, virtue of.

virtuosamente, *adv.* virtuously.

virtuoso, sa, *a.* virtuous, righteous; chaste; powerful, vigorous; (mus.) *a.* & *n.* virtuoso.

viruela, *f.* (med.) pock; smallpox.—**viruelas bastardas,** chicken pox.—**viruelas locas,** light case of smallpox.

virulencia, *f.* virulence; acrimony, malignity.

virulento, ta, *a.* virulent; malignant; purulent.

virus, *m.* (med.) virus; poison, contagion.

viruta, *f.* wood shaving.

vis, *f.*—**v. cómica,** (theat.) verve.

visaje, *m.* grimace, grin, smirk.—**hacer visajes,** to make wry faces.

visajero, ra, *n.* one who makes faces, grimaces.

visar, *va.* to visé; to countersign; to O.K.

visaya. I. *a.* & *n.* Visayan. **II.** *m.* Visayan language.

víscera, *f.* viscus.—*pl.* viscera.—**visceral,** *a.* visceral.

visco, *m.* = LIGA, birdlime.

viscosidad, *f.* viscosity.

viscoso, sa, *a.* viscous, mucilaginous.

visera, *f.* visor of a cap or helmet; eyeshade; box with a spy hole, used by pigeon fanciers; (Cuba) blinder (for a horse).

visibilidad, *f.* visibility.

visible, *a.* visible; evident; conspicuous.

visiblemente, *adv.* visibly; evidently.

visigodo, da, *n.* & *a.* Visigoth.

visigótico, ca, *a.* Visigothic.

visillo, *m.* window curtain or shade.

visión, *f.* sight; vision; fantasy; phantom, apparition; revelation; (coll.) grotesque person, guy.—**ver visiones,** to be deluded, be "seeing things."

visionario, ria, *a.* & *n.* visionary.

visir, *m.* vizier, Turkish prime minister.

visita, *f.* visit; social call; visitor, caller, guest, company; visitation, inspection; (eccl.) tribunal for the inspection of prisons; hall of that tribunal; (med.) visit.—**v. de aspectos,** medical inspection of passengers.—**v. de cumplido,** or **de cumplimiento,** formal call.—**v. de médico,** (coll.) (humor.) short or hurried call.—**v. de sanidad,** health inspection.—**v. domiciliaria,** official visit or inspection of a suspected house; social-work call.—**hacer una v.,** to pay a call.—**pagar una v.,** to return a call.—**tener v.,** to have company or callers.

visitación, *f.* visitation, visiting, visit.

visitador, ra. I. *a.* calling (gen. frequently). **II.** *n.* visitor, visitant, caller; searcher, surveyor, inspector.—**v. de registro,** customs officer who boards ships.

visitadora, *f.* (C. A.) enema.

visitante, *n.* & *a.* visitor(-ing), caller(-ing).

visitar. I. *va.* to visit; to call on; to inspect, search, examine; (med.) to visit (a patient); (law) to make a judicial visit or search of; (naut.) to search (ships); to appear to, as a spirit; to frequent; (eccl.) to visit (religious persons and establishments) as an ecclesiastical judge; (theol.) to send a divine counsel to; (law) to make an abstract of the charge against a prisoner at visitation. **II.** *vr.* to visit one another, call on one another.

visiteo, *m.* frequent visiting or calling.

visitero, ra, *a.* (coll.) fond of making calls.

visítica, illa, *f.* *dim.* short call.

visitón, *m.* *aug.* (coll.) long and tedious call.

visivo, va, *a.* visive, pert. to power of seeing.

vislumbrar, *va.* to glimpse, to have a glimmer of to see imperfectly at a distance; to know imperfectly; to suspect, surmise.

vislumbre, *f.* glimpse, glimmer, glimmering; conjecture, surmise; appearance, semblance.

viso, *m.* elevated spot, outlook; lustre, gleam sheen, flash, glare; colored slip worn under a transparent frock; color, cloak, pretense, pretext; aspect, appearance.—**a dos visos,** with a double view or design.—**al v.,** (of fabrics) viewed sidewise to examine the sheen.—**de v.,** conspicuous, prominent.

visogodo, da, *a.* & *n.* Visigoth.

visón, *m.* American mink.

visorio, ria. I. *a.* visual, optic. **II.** *m.* expert examination.

víspera, *f.* eve, day before; forerunner; anything that precedes another.—*pl.* vesper, evening; (eccl.) vespers.—**en vísperas de,** on the eve of.

vista. I. *f.* sight; seeing, vision; view; vista; eye, eyesight; glance, look; aspect, looks; apparition; meeting, interview; clear knowledge or perception; relation, connection; comparison; intent, view, purpose; opinion, judgment; opening, light (window, skylight, etc.); (law) trial.—**v. cansada,** farsightedness.—**v. corta,** nearsightedness.—**aguzar la v.,** to look sharp.—**a la simple v.,** (of the solution of a problem, etc.) at first sight; by inspection.—**a la v.,** at once, immediately; at sight; in sight; (com.) at sight.—**a primera v.,** at first sight.—**a v. de,** in presence of.—**a v. de ojos,** with one's own eyes.—**dar una v.,** to give a passing glance.—**de v.,** by sight.—**echar la v. a,** to choose; to set one's eye on.—**echar una v. a,** to look after, to watch.—**en v. de,** in view of, considering.—**estar a la v.,** to be obvious.—**hacer la v. gorda,** to wink at, overlook, connive.—**hasta la v.,** au revoir, good-bye.—**perder de v.,** to lose sight of.—**perderse de v.,** to go out of sight; (coll.) to excel; to be very smart.—**tener a la v.,** to have before one, or before one's eyes.—**tener v.,** to be showy.—**tener v. a,** to face, look out on. **II.** *n.* customs officer. **III.** *f.* *pl.* meeting, conference, interview; wedding presents from a bride and bridegroom to each other; bosom, collar and cuffs of a shirt.—**vistazo,** *m.* glance.—**dar un v. a,** to glance at, to look over.

vistillas, *f.* *pl.* place commanding a good view, lookout.

¹visto, ta. I. *pp. irreg.* of VER. **II.** *a.* obvious, evident, clear; (law) whereas.—**bien v.,** proper or approved, good form.—**mal v.,** improper or disapproved, bad form.—**v. bueno** (in abbreviation V°. B°.), correct, approved, O.K.—**v. es,** or **v. está,** it is evident.—**v. que,** considering that, since.—**no v.,** or **nunca v.,** unheard of.—**por lo v.,** apparently, it seems evident, judging from the facts; according to the above. **III.** *m.* (law) preambulatory clause beginning with "whereas."

²visto, vista, vistió, *v. V.* VESTIR.

vistosamente, *adv.* beautifully; gaudily.

vistoso, sa, beautiful; showy; flaring, loud.

visual. I. *a.* visual; of sight. **II.** *f.* line of sight.

visualidad, *f.* pleasure in viewing attractive objects.

visura, *f.* ocular inspection; expert examination or inspection.

vital, *a.* vital; essential, necessary.

vitalicio, cia. I. *a.* lasting for life; during life. **II.** *m.* life-insurance policy.

vitalicista, *n.* one who enjoys a life annuity.

vitalidad, *f.* vitality.

vitalismo, *m.* vitalism.

vitalista, *a.* & *n.* vitalist.

itando, da, *a.* that ought to be shunned or avoided; odious, execrable.

itela, *f.* vellum, parchment.

itelina, *a.*—**bilis v.,** (chem.) vitelline.

itícola. I. *a.* viticultural. **II.** *n.* VITICULTOR.

iticultor, ra, *n.* viticulturist, grape grower.

iticultura, *f.* viticulture, grape growing.

itiligo, *m.* (med.) vitiligo, white spots on skin.

ito, *m.* a lively dance and tune.

itola, *f.* (mil.) ball calibre, standard gauge; standard shape and size for cigars; (Am.) appearance, mien.

itor, *m.* triumphal pageant; memorial tablet.—**¡v.!** long live!—**vivitorear,** *va.* to cheer, acclaim.

itre, *m.* thin canvas.

itreo, a, *a.* vitreous, glassy.

itrificable, *a.* vitrifiable.

itrificación, *f.* vitrification.

itrificar, *va.* to vitrify.

itrina, *f.* show case; (Am.) show window.

itriólico, ca, *a.* vitriolic.

itriolo, *m.* vitriol; sulphate.—**v. amoníacal,** ammonium sulphate.—**v. azul,** blue vitriol.—**v. blanco,** white vitriol.—**v. de plomo,** (min.) anglesite, lead-sulphate ore.—**v. verde,** green vitriol.

itualla, *f.* (gen. in the *pl.*) victuals, provisions; abundance of food, mainly of vegetables.

ituallar, *va.* (mil.) to victual.

itulo marino, *m.* = BECERRO MARINO, seal.

ituperable, *a.* vituperable, blameworthy.

ituperación, *f.* vituperation.

ituperador, ra, *n. & a.* vituperator(-ing).

ituperante, *a.* vituperating, vituperative.

ituperar, *va.* to vituperate.

ituperio, *m.* vituperation.

ituperiosamente, vituperosamente, *adv.* vituperatively.

ituperioso, sa; vituperoso, sa, *a.* vituperative.

iuda, *f.* widow; dowager; (bot.) mourning bride.

iudal, *a.* pertaining to a widow or widower.

iudedad, *f.* widow's pension.

iudez, *f.* widowhood.

iudita, *f. dim.* spruce little widow; (bot.) VIUDA.

iudo. I. *m.* widower. **II.** *a.* (of birds) pairing.

iva. I. *m.* huzza, cheer, shout, acclamation. **II. ¡v.!** *interj.* long live! hurrah, huzza.

ivac, *m.* (mil.) bivouac; night guard.

ivacidad, *f.* vivacity, liveliness; brilliancy.

ivamente, *adv.* vividly; quickly; deeply.

ivandero, ra, *n.* (mil.) sutler.

ivaque, *m.* (mil.) bivouac.

ivaquear, *vn.* to bivouac.

ivar, *m.* warren, burrow; vivarium.

ivaracho, cha, *a.* lively, sprightly, frisky.

ivaz, *a.* lively, active, vigorous; ingenious, bright, witty; (bot.) perennial, evergreen.

iveral, *m.* (bot.) nursery.

íveres, *m. pl.* provisions, foodstuffs; (mil.) stores. —**v. de campaña,** (naut.) sea provisions, stores.

ivero, *m.* warren; hatchery; (bot.) nursery.

ivérrido, a. I. *n. & a.* (zool.) viverrine. **II.** *m.* or *f. pl.* Viverridæ, civets.

iveza, *f.* liveliness, sprightliness; gaiety; briskness; ardor, vehemence; acuteness, perspicacity, quickness; witticism; strong resemblance; luster, splendor; grace and brilliancy in the eyes; thoughtless word or act.

ividero, ra, *a.* habitable.

ivido, da, *a.* vivid, bright.

ividor, ra. I. *a.* thrifty. **II.** *n.* long liver; sponger.

ivienda, *f.* dwelling, lodging, house.

iviente, *a.* living; animated.

ivificación, *f.* vivification, enlivening.

ivificador, ra, *n. & a.* vivifier(-ying), enlivener (-ing).

ivificante, *a.* vivifying, life-giving.

ivificar, *va.* to vivify, animate, enliven; to com-

fort, refresh.—**vivificativo, va,** *a.* vivifying, life-giving; comforting.

vivífico, ca, *a.* springing from life.

vivíparo, ra, *a.* (zool.) viviparous.

vivir. I. *vn. & va.* to live, be alive; to live, dwell; to last, endure, keep.—**¡viva!** hurrah! long live! —**v. de,** to live on (as one's investments, etc.). —**viva Vd. mil años,** or **muchos años,** may you live many years, or I wish you a long life (a form of courtesy).—**¿quién vive?** (mil.) who goes there?—**quien vive,** qui vive, (be, being) on the alert. **II.** *m.* life, living, existence.—**mal v.,** riotous living.

vivisección, *f.* vivisection.

vivismo, *m.* Vivism, philosophico-theological system of Luis Vives.

vivo, va. I. *a.* alive, living, live; lively; intense; (of color) vivid; kindled, live (as fire); acute, ingenious; quick, bright, lively, smart; hasty; diligent, nimble; pure, clean; lasting, enduring; excellent; expressive, vehement, persuasive; raw (flesh), open (wound).—**a lo v., al v.,** to the life, vividly.—**de v. voz,** by word of mouth. —**en vivo,** living, alive.—**los vivos y los muertos,** the quick and the dead.—**tocar en lo v.,** to cut or hurt to the quick. **II.** *m.* edging, border; (sewing) piping; (bookbinding) rib, ridge, border; (arch.) sharp edge; (vet.) mange, itch, or scab in dogs.

vizcacha, *f.* viscacha, a S.A. rodent.

vizcachera, *f.* viscacha hole.

vizcaíno, na, *n. & a.* Biscayan.

vizcondado, *m.* viscountship.

vizconde, *m.* viscount.—**vizcondesa,** *f.* viscountess.

vocablo, *m.* word, term.

vocabulario, *m.* vocabulary, lexicon.

vocabulista, *n.* lexicographer; student of words.

vocación, *f.* vocation, calling; occupation.

vocal. I. *a.* vocal, oral; (gram.) vowel. **II.** *f.* (gram., print.) vowel. **III.** *n.* voter, in a congregation or assembly; member of a governing body.

vocalicé, vocalice, *v. V.* VOCALIZAR.

vocalización, *f.* (mus.) vocalization.

vocalizar, *vn.* (*pret.* VOCALICÉ; *subj.* VOCALICE) to vocalize, articulate.

vocalmente, *adv.* vocally, orally.

vocativo, *a. & m.* (gram.) vocative.

voceador, ra. I. *n.* vociferator. **II.** *m.* town crier.

vocear. I. *vn.* to vociferate, to cry out, shout. **II.** *va.* to cry, publish, proclaim; to call, hail; to cheer, acclaim; (coll.) to boast of publicly.

vocejón, *m.* harsh, raucous voice.

vocería, *f.*, **vocerío,** *m.* vociferation, clamor, outcry, shouting.

vocero, ra, *n.* spokesman (for another).

voces, *f. pl.* of VOZ.

vociferación, *f.* = VOCERÍA.

vociferador, ra, *n. & a.* vociferator(-ing), shouter (-ing); boaster(-ing).

vociferante, *a.* vociferating.

vociferar. I. *vn.* to vociferate, shout, clamor. **II.** *va.* to boast of loudly.

vocinglería, *f.* clamor, outcry; loquacity.

vocinglero, ra. I. *a.* prattling, chattering, vociferous. **II.** *n.* loud babbler.

vodka, *m.* vodka, a Russian liquor.

voila, *f.* term in the game of jackstones indicating that the cast may not count.

¹volada, *f.* short flight.

²volada, *f.* (Am.) trick, bad turn.—**hacer,** or **jugar, una (mala) volada a,** to play a trick on, do a bad turn to.

voladera, *f.* float of a water wheel.

voladero, ra. I. *a.* flying, fleeting. **II.** *m.* precipice, abyss.

voladizo, za. I. *a.* projecting, jutting out. **II.** *m.* (arch.) corbel.

volado, da. I. *a.* (print.) high, superior, set above

the level of the line.—**v. de genio,** (Am.) quick-tempered. II. *adv. m.* (Mex., Guat.) urgently. III. *m.* = BOLADO, fondant.

volador, ra. I. *a.* flying; running fast; swift; hanging in the air. II. *m.* skyrocket; (ichth.) flying fish; (bot.) a tropical tree of very hard wood. III. *f.* flywheel of a steam engine.

voladura, *f.* blast, explosion; blasting.

volandas.—en v., *adv.* in the air, as if flying; (coll.) rapidly, swiftly.

volandera, *f.* (mil.) runner; grindstone; (coll.) fib, lie; (mech.) washer; (print.) galley slice.

volandero, ra, *a.* (nestling) ready to fly; fluttering in the air; fortuitous, casual; unsettled, fleeting, variable.

volandillas.—en v. = EN VOLANDAS.

volando, *adv.* (Am.) quickly, at top speed.

volanta, *f.* (Cuba) two-wheel covered vehicle with very long shafts.

volante. I. *a.* flying, fluttering; unsettled. II. *m.* head ornament of light gauze; shuttlecock; game of shuttlecock and battledore; screen; coiners' stamp mill; balance wheel, escapement (of watch); (mech.) flywheel; balance beam; lackey, flunkey; flier, note, memorandum; (sewing) flounce; (Cuba) VOLANTA; linen coat; (Mex.) dress coat; (auto) steering wheel (also **v. de dirección).**

volantín, *m.* a fishing apparatus.

volantón, na, *a.* able to fly (nestling).

volapié, *m.* a feat in bullfighting.—**a v.,** half running, half flying.

volapuk, *m.* Volapük.

volar. I. *vn.* (*ind.* VUELO; *subj.* VUELE) to fly (as birds, kites, clouds, etc.); to flutter, hover (as insects); to run or move swiftly (as a train, arrow, etc.); to vanish, disappear; to rise in the air (as a steeple); to make rapid progress; act fast or quickly; to project, jut out, hang over; to extend, spread rapidly (as news); to explode, burst.—**echar a v.,** to disseminate; to divulge, publish. II. *va.* to blow up; to spring (a mine); to blast; to irritate, exasperate; to put up (game); to disseminate, publish, spread, divulge.

volateo.—al v., *adv.* (shooting) on the wing.

volatería, *f.* fowling; sporting with hawks; poultry; fowls; flock of birds; (fig.) crowding conflicting ideas (in one's mind).—**de v.,** incidentally, in passing; at random, recklessly.

volátil, *a.* volatile; flying, wafting; changeable, fickle; fleeting.—**volatilidad,** *f.* (chem.) volatility.—**volatilizar,** *va.* & *vr.* (*pret.* VOLATILICÉ; *subj.* VOLATILICE) to volatilize, vaporize.

volatín, *m.* acrobatic feat.

volatinero, ra, *n.* tightrope walker; acrobat.

volatizar, *va.* (chem.) = VOLATILIZAR.

volavérunt, (Lat.) (coll.) the bird has flown; gone! (something) has disappeared, is gone.

volcán, *m.* volcano; excessive ardor; violent passion; excitable person or temperament.

volcanejo, *m. dim.* small volcano.

volcánico, ca, *a.* volcanic.

volcar. I. *va.* (*ind. pres.* VUELCO, *pret.* VOLQUÉ; *subj.* VUELQUE) to upset, overturn; to tilt; (naut.) to capsize; to make dizzy; to make (one) change his opinion; to make angry. II. *vr.* to upset.

volea, *f.* snaffle tree, whippletree; (games) volley.

voleador, *m.* (sports) batsman, batter.

volear, *va.* to volley (a ball); also *vn.* (baseball) to bat; to fire a volley at.

voleo, *m.* (games) volley; (dance) high step or kick.—**del primer v.,** or **de un v.,** (coll.) at one blow; in an instant.

volframio, *m.* (chem.) tungsten.

volframita, *f.* (min.) wolframite.

volición, *f.* volition.

volitar, *vn.* to flutter.

volitivo, va, *a.* volitional.

volqué, *pret.* of VOLCAR.

volquearse, *vr.* to tumble, to wallow.

volquete, *m.* tip cart, tilt cart.

volt, *m.* (elec.) volt.

voltaico, ca, *a.* (elec.) voltaic.

voltaísmo, *m.* (elec.) voltaism.

voltaje, *m.* (elec.) voltage.

voltámetro, *m.* (phys.) voltameter.

voltamperímetro, *m.* (elec.) wattmeter.

voltamperio, *m.* (elec.) volt ampere.

voltariedad, *f.* fickleness, inconstancy.

voltario, ria, *a.* fickle, inconstant, giddy.

volteador, ra, *n.* tumbler, acrobat.

voltear. I. *va.* to turn; to revolve; to overturn; change the order of; (arch.) to arch, to vault. II. *vn.* to turn; to revolve; to roll over; to tumble (as an acrobat). III. *vr.* to turn over; to upset; (coll.) to change one's party or creed.

voltejear, *va.* to whirl; (naut.) to tack.

volteleta, *f.* tumble, somersault; at cards, turning up the card that makes trumps.

volteo, *m.* whirl, whirling; revolution, turn; turning; overturning; felling; tumbling.

voltereta, *f.* = VOLTELETA.

volterianismo, *m.* Voltairianism.

volteriano, na, *a.* & *n.* Voltairian.

volteta, *f.* = VOLTELETA.

voltímetro, *m.* (elec.) voltmeter.—**v. aperiódico,** dead-beat, or aperiodic, voltmeter.

voltio, *m.* (elec.) volt.

voltizo, za, *a.* curled, twisted; versatile, inconstant, fickle.

vóltmetro, *m.* (elec.) voltmeter.

volubilidad, *f.* volubility.

voluble, *a.* easily moved about; voluble, fickle; (bot.) twining.

volublemente, *adv.* volubly.

volumen, *m.* volume (book); volume, size, bulk; corpulence.

volumétrico, ca, *a.* volumetric.

voluminoso, sa, *a.* voluminous; bulky.

voluntad, *f.* will; goodwill, benevolence, kindness; desire, pleasure; disposition, precept; consent.—**a v.,** (com.) optional, at will.—**de buena v.,** or **de v.,** with pleasure, willingly.—**de mala v.,** unwillingly.

voluntariamente, *adv.* voluntarily.

voluntariedad, *f.* voluntariness; wilfulness.

voluntario, ria, *a.* & *n.* voluntary(-eer).

voluntariosamente, *adv.* wilfully.

voluntarioso, sa, *a.* wilful, self-willed.

voluptuosamente, *adv.* voluptuously; licentiously.

voluptuosidad, *f.* voluptuousness; licentiousness.

voluptuoso, sa, *a.* voluptuous; licentious, lustful; lewd.

voluta, *f.* (arch.) volute.

¹**volvedor,** *m.* tap wrench, turnscrew.

²**volvedor, ra,** *a.* (Colomb.) (of horse) that runs away back to its home.

volver. I. *va.* (*pp.* VUELTO; *ind.* VUELVO; *subj.* VUELVA) to turn; turn up, turn over, turn up side down or inside out; to return, pay back; give or send back; to give up; to direct, aim; to translate; to restore, reinstate; to change the outward appearance of; to invert, change, move; to vomit; to persuade, convince; to reflect (sound); to give (change in sales); to close; pull or push to (door or shutter); to reëstablish; to replace; to plow a second time.—**v. la cara,** to turn one's head, turn around.—**v. loco,** to drive crazy, distract. II. *vn.* to return, come, or go, back; to come again; to turn (to the right etc.).—**v. a,** to . . . again (*volver a cantar,* to sing again: *Juan me volvió a escribir,* John wrote to me again).—**v. atrás,** to come, or go, back —**v. en sí,** to recover consciousness, come to.—**v. por,** to stand up for, to defend.—**v. por sí,** to defend oneself; to redeem one's credit.—**v**

sobre sí, to mend one's ways; to make up one's losses; to recover one's equanimity.—**v. sobre (sus) pasos,** to retrace (one's) steps. III. *vr.* to turn, become; to turn or get sour; to turn about, turn around; to change one's views.—**v. atrás,** to flinch; to back out.—**v. la tortilla,** to turn the tables or scales.—**v. loco,** to lose one's mind, to become crazy or distracted.

olvible, *a.* capable of being turned, turned over or inverted.

olvo, vólvulo, *m.* (med.) volvulus, ileus.

ómer, *m.* (anat.) vomer.

omicina, *f.* (chem.) brucine, vomicine.

ómico, ca. I. *a.* causing vomiting; vomitive. II. *f.* (med.) vomica.

omipurgante, vomipurgativo, va, *a.* & *m.* both purgative and emetic.

omitado, da, *a.* (coll.) meager; pale.

omitador, ra, *n.* one who vomits.

omitar, va. to vomit; to eject, throw out, disgorge; discharge; to break out into (insults, etc.); to give out, reveal; to give up, surrender.

omitivo, va, *m.* & *a.* emetic.

ómito, *m.* vomiting; vomit; (Cuba) yellow fever.—**v. negro,** yellow fever.—**provocar a v.,** to nauseate, to make loathe.

omitón, na. I. *a.* often throwing up milk (as a nursing child). II. *f.* (coll.) violent vomiting after heavy eating or drinking.

omitorio, ria. I. *a.* vomitory. II. *m.* vomitory in Roman theatres.

oracidad, *f.* voracity, greediness, voraciousness.

orágine, *f.* vortex, whirlpool.—**voraginoso, sa,** *a.* engulfing; full of whirlpools.

orahunda, *f.* = BARAÚNDA, hurly-burly.

oraz, *a.* voracious, greedy, ravenous; excessively lustful; destructive, fierce (as fire).

orazmente, *adv.* voraciously; greedily.

ormela, *f.* (zool.) a kind of spotted weasel.

órtice, *m.* vortex, whirlpool, whirlwind; center of a cyclone.

orticela, *f.* (zool.) vorticella.

ortiginoso, sa, *a.* vortical.

os, *pers. pron.* you.

osotros, tras, *pers. pron. pl.* you, ye.

otación, *f.* voting, vote, balloting.

otador, ra, *n.* voter; swearer; curser.

otante, *n.* voter in a corporation or assembly.

otar, *vn.* & *va.* to vow; to vote; to vote on; to give an opinion; to curse, swear, utter oaths; to pass, decree or authorize by vote (in deliberating bodies).—**v. una partida,** to make, or pass, an appropiation.—**¡voto a (Dios, Júpiter,** etc.**)!** by (God, Jupiter, etc.)!—**¡voto al cháplro!** goodness me! **¡voto a tal!** goodness! upon my soul! confound it! by Heaven! by Jove!

otivo, va, *a.* votive, offered by a vow.

oto, *m.* vote; ballot; opinion; voter; vow; supplication to God; curse, oath, execration; wish; (eccl.) votive offering.—**v. activo,** (right to) vote.—**v. consultivo,** professional or expert advice.—**v. de amén,** vote blindly given.—**v. de calidad,** casting vote.—**v. de reata =** v. DE AMÉN.—**v. particular,** dissenting opinion (of the minority of a commission, etc.).—**v. pasivo,** qualification to be voted for, or elected, by a corporation.—**¡v. va! = ¡VOTO A TAL!** V. VOTAR.—**echar votos,** to swear, curse.—**hacer votos por,** to pray for; to wish.—**ser,** or **tener, v.,** to have a vote; to speak knowingly.

¡voto . . . !, *interj. v.* V. VOTAR.

oy, *1st pers. sing. pres.* of IR.

oz, *f.* voice; sound, noise; (gen. in the *pl.*) clamor, outcry; expression, word, term; voice, power or authority to speak (as in an assembly); vote; opinion expressed; rumor, public opinion; motive, pretext; (gram.) voice (active or passive); (mus.) singer; voice, key tone; (mil.) command, order; (law) life.—**v. activa,** right of voting; (gram.) active voice.—**v. argentada,** or **ar-**

gentina, clear and sonorous voice.—**v. del pueblo, voz del cielo,** vox populi, vox Dei, the voice of the people is the voice of God.—**v. de mando,** word of command.—**v. pasiva,** right or qualification to be voted for, or elected; (gram.) passive voice.—**v. pastosa,** mellow voice.—**v. velada,** veiled voice.—**a media v.,** with a slight hint; in a whisper.—**a una v.,** of one accord, unanimously.—**a v. en cuello,** or **a v. en grito,** in a loud voice; shouting; at the top of one's voice.—**a voces,** clamorously, with shouts.—**correr la v.,** to be said, to be rumored. —**dar voces,** to cry, scream, shout, yell.—**en v.,** verbally; (mus.) in voice.—**en v. alta,** aloud, out loud.—**en v. baja,** in an undertone, sotto voce.—**pedir a voces,** to clamor for; to be a crying need.—**secreto a voces,** open secret.—**ser v. común,** to be generally said, to be a common rumor.

vozarrón, *m.* strong, heavy voice.

voznar, *vn.* (of swans and geese) to cackle.

vuecelencia, vuecencia, *n.* (*contr.* of VUESTRA EXCELENCIA) your excellency.

vuelapié.—a v. = A VOLAPIÉ.

¹vuelco, *m.* tumble, overturning, upset.

²vuelco, vuelca, *v.* V. VOLCAR.

vuelillo, *m.* lace cuff trimming.

¹vuelo, *m.* flight; flying; sweep, space flown through; wing of a bird; width or fulness of clothes; (sewing) ruffle or frill on the wristband; elevation, soaring, loftiness of thought; leap or bound in pantomimes; (arch.) jut, projection, corbeling.—**al v.,** on the fly; quickly, in a jiffy; in passing, accidentally; (agr.) (of seed) scattered at random.—**alzar,** or **levantar, v.,** to fly; to take off, to depart; to sail.—**de alto v.,** of great importance, of high standing.—**tomar v.,** to progress, to grow.

²vuelo, vuela, vuele, *v.* V. VOLAR.

vuelta, *f.* turn; revolution (of a wheel, etc.); turning; turn of an arch; curve; requital, recompense; repetition, iteration; back or wrong side; whipping, lashing, spanking; return; returning, giving back; review (of a lesson); going over (a writing, etc.); change (in state, appearance); change (received when paying); change (small coins); inclination, bent; (sewing) ¹VUELO; sleeve cuff, facing; (naut.) turn, hitch, lashing; trip, excursion; promenade, walk; ward in a lock or key; order of stitches in knitting hose; roll, envelope; unexpected sally or witticism, repartee; card turned up for a trump; number of times a field has been plowed; (mus.) number of verses repeated; potter's wheel; (arch.) curve of an intrados; vault; ceiling.—**v. de carnero,** turn on the head; heavy fall.—**vueltas de coral,** string or necklace of coral.—**a la v.,** on returning; round the corner, (turn) over (the page); carried over, carried forward (in bookkeeping). —**a la v. de,** within (app. to time).—**andar a las vueltas de,** to dog.—**andar a vueltas,** to fight, to struggle; to endeavor.—**andar en vueltas,** to shuffle, use subterfuges; to shirk.— **a v., a vueltas,** very near, almost.—**a v. de,** in the course of, during (a specified time); by return (mail).—**a v. de ojo,** quickly, in a jiffy. —**dar la v. a,** to turn; to go around.—**dar una v.,** to take a stroll.—**dar vueltas,** to turn; to walk to and fro; to fuss about; to hang around. —**de la v.,** brought forward.—**de v.,** on returning.—**estar de v.,** to have returned, to be back; to be posted or informed beforehand.—**la v. de,** towards, on the way to.—**no haber que darle vueltas,** or **no tener v. de hoja,** no two ways about it.—**otra v.,** again, once more.—**poner de v. y media,** (coll.) to give a dressing down, or a going over, to; to call one all kinds of abusive names.—**tener v.,** (coll.) admonition to return a thing lent.

vuelto, ta. I. *pp. irreg.* of VOLVER. **II.** *m.* (Am.) change (money).

vuelvo, vuelva, *v. V.* VOLVER.

vuesa, *a.* (*contr.* of VUESTRA) (obs.) your.

vuesamerced, *n.* (*contr.* of VUESTRA MERCED) you, sir; you, madam; your grace, your honor.

vuesarced, *n.* = VUESAMERCED.

vueseñoría, *n.* (*contr.* of VUESTRA SEÑORÍA) your lordship, your ladyship.

vuestro, tra, *poss. pron.* your, yours.

vulcanicé, vulcanice, *v. V.* VULCANIZAR.

vulcanio, nia, *a.* pert. to Vulcan or to fire; igneous.

vulcanismo, *m.* (geol.) vulcanism.

vulcanista, *a.* (geol.) vulcanist.

vulcanización, *f.* vulcanization; mending (a tire, etc.).

vulcanizar, *va.* (*pret.* VULCANICÉ; *subj.* VULCANICE) to vulcanize; to mend (a tire, etc.).

vulgacho, *m.* mob, populace, rabble.

vulgar, *a.* vulgar, coarse; common, in general use; (of speech) vernacular.—**vulgaridad,** *f.* vulgarity.—**vulgarismo,** *m.* vulgarism.

vulgarización, *f.* vulgarization.

vulgarizar. I. *va.* (*pret.* VULGARICÉ; *subj.* VULGARICE) to vulgarize, popularize; to translate into the vernacular. **II.** *vr.* to become vulgar.

vulgarmente, *adv.* vulgarly; commonly.

Vulgata, *f.* (eccl.) Vulgate.

vulgo, *m.* common people; populace.

vulnerable, *a.* vulnerable.

vulneración, *f.* act of wounding.

vulnerar, *va.* to injure the reputation of.

vulnerario, ria. I. *a.* (med.) vulnerary. **II.** *m.* (law) clergyman guilty of killing or wounding.

vulpécula, vulpeja, *f.* bitch fox.

vulpino, na, *a.* vulpine; foxy, crafty.

vultuoso, sa, *a.* (med.) bloated.

vultúrido, da. I. (zool.) vulturine. **II.** *m.* or *f. pl.* Vulturidæ.

vulva, *f.* (anat.) vulva.—**vulvario, ria,** *a.* (anat.) vulvar.—**vulvitis,** *f.* vulvitis.

W

This letter does not belong to the Spanish alphabet and is mainly used in words, chiefly proper nouns, taken from other languages. In adjectives and common nouns derived from proper nouns containing it, it is generally changed to *v* (see VAGNERIANO, VESTFALIANO), although some writers preserve the *w* (*wagneriano, westfaliano*). Such words are readily translated at sight, on account of their similarity to their English equivalents. The Spanish Academy has allowed the use of the letter in **wat,** (elec.) watt, although the term generally used is **vatio.**

X

NOTE.—Several words that were originally, or are occasionally, written with an initial *x* are more generally begun with *j*.

xantina, *f.* (chem.) xanthine.

xantofila, *f.* (chem.) xanthophyll.

xantoxilo, *m.* (bot.) zanthoxylum.

xara, *f.* Moslem law derived from the Koran.

xenofobia, *f.* xenophobia, hatred of foreigners.

xenófobo, ba, *n. & a.* hater of foreigners.

xenon, *m.* (chem.) xenon.

xerofagia, *f.* xerophagy, dry-food diet.

xeroftalmía, *f.* (med.) xerophthalmia.

xifoideo, ea, *a.* (anat.) xiphoid.

xifoides. I. *a.* (anat.) xiphoid. **II.** *m.* xiphoid, xiphisternum.

xifosuro, ra, *n. & a.* xiphosuran.

xileno, *m.* (chem.) xylene.—**xílico, ca,** *a.* xylic.—**xilidinia,** *f.* xylidine.

xilófago, a, *n. & a.* xylophagous, wood bore (-ing).

xilófono, *m.* xylophone.

xilógeno, *m.* (chem.) xylem.

xilografía, *f.* xylography, wood engraving.

xilográfico, ca, *a.* xylographic.

xiloide, *a.* xyloid, woodlike.

xilonita, *a.* transparent celluloidlike substance

xilórgano, *m.* xylophone.

Y

y, *conj.* and. Sometimes used at beginning o sentence for emphasis.—¿y **bien?,** and then "so what?"—**y eso que,** even though.—¿ **qué?** (Am.) is it true that?

ya. I. *adv.* already; now; at once; presently finally, ultimately; in time; once, formerly Often used as an emphatic expletive (*va en tiendo,* I understand; *va veo,* I see).—¡y.! oh yes! I see.—**y. lo creo,** naturally, of course.—y **no,** no longer.—**y. que,** since, seeing that.— **y. se ve,** yes, indeed! it is clear, it is so.—y. **voy** I am coming, I shall be there presently.— **y . . . y.,** now . . . now, sometimes . . . sometimes.—¡**pues y.!** of course, certainly.—s **y.,** if.—**si y no,** if no longer; if . . . not, un less. **II.** *conj.* whether, or (the latter as correla tive of the former).

yaacabó, *m.* (Venez.) an insectivorous bird.

yaba, *f.* (bot.) yaba tree; yaba bark, worm bark

yabuna, *f.* a Cuban species of long, creepin grass or weed.

yac, *m.* (zool.) yak.

yaca, *f.* (bot.) yacca tree.

yacal, *m.* yacal, a Philippine tree.

yacaré, *m.* (Arg.) cayman, alligator.

yacedor, *m.* boy who takes horses to graze a night.

yacente, *a.* vacant; lying.

yacer, *vn.* (*ind.* YAZCO, YAGO, or YAZGO; *subj* YAZCA, YAGA, or YAZGA) to lie, to be located; t be lying down; to lie (in the grave); (of horses to graze by night.

yaciente, *a.* extended, stretched (honeycombs)

yacija, *f.* bed, couch, lounge; tomb, grave.—se **de mala y.,** to be a vagrant; to be restless a night.

yacimiento, *m.* (geol.) bed; deposit, field.

yacio, *m.* (bot.) India-rubber tree.

yack, *m.* (zool.) yak.

yactura, *f.* loss, damage.

yago, yaga, *v. V.* YACER.

yagua, *f.* royal palm.

yaguar, *m.* (zool.) jaguar.

yaguasa, *f.* (Am.) (ornith.) a tree duck.

yagüré, *m.* (Am.) skunk.

yaití, *m.* a West-Indian hard-wood euphorbia ceous tree.

yámbico, ca, *a.* (poet.) iambic.

¹yambo, *m.* (poet.) iambic foot (⌣—).

²yambo, *m.* (bot.) jamboo.

yanacona, *n.* (Peru) Indian bound to personal service.

yanqui, *n. & a.* American (of U. S.).

yantar. I. *va.* (obs.) to dine; to eat. **II.** *m.* (obs. viands, food; a kind of king's taxes.

yapa, *f.* (min.) mercury added to silver ore i smelting; (Am.) ÑAPA, (to) boot, extra thing.— **de y.,** into the bargain, for good measure.

yapar. I. *va.* to add YAPA. **II.** *va. & vn.* to give, o give as, a YAPA (ÑAPA).

yarará, *f.* a very poisonous Argentine viper.

yaraví, *m.* (Am.) an Indian tune.

yarda, *f.* yard (measure).

yare, *m.* a poisonous juice from bitter yucca.

yarey, *m.* (Cuba) a species of GUANO (palm tree)

yaro, *m.* (bot.) arum, an aquatic plant.

yatagán, *m.* sabre dagger, yataghan.

For pronunciation, see the rules at the beginning of the book.

yate, m. (naut.) yacht.
yaya, f. (Cuba) (bot.) lancewood.
yayero, ra, a. & n. (Cuba) intermeddling, busy-body.
yazco, yazgo, etc. v. V. YACER.
ye, name of the letter y.
yedra, f. = HIEDRA (bot.) ivy.
yegua, f. mare.—y. de cría, or paridera, breed-ing mare.—y. madre, dam.—yeguada, ye-güería, f. stud of mares.—yeguar, a. pert. to mares.
yegüerizo, za. I. a. = YEGUAR. II. m. = YE-GÜERO.
yegüero, m. keeper of breeding mares.
yegüezuela, f. dim. little mare.
yeismo, m. giving ll the sound of y.
yelmo, m. (armor) helmet, helm.
yema, f. bud, first shoot of trees; yolk (of an egg); candied yolk of an egg; heart, centre, middle; the best of its kind.—y. del dedo, fleshy tip of the finger.—y. mejida, eggnog.—dar en la y., to hit the nail on the head.—en la y. del in-vierno, in the dead of winter.
yente, a. going.—yentes y vinientes, passers-by.
yerba, f. HIERBA, herb; grass; weed; (S. A.) maté (also Y. MATE).—y. cana, groundsel, ragwort. y. carmín, Virginian poke.—y. de la prin-cesa, lemon-scented verbena.—y. del balles-tero, white hellebore.—y. de mar, seaweed. —y. de pordioseros, sweet-scented virgin's bower.—y. doncella, periwinkle.—y. lom-briguera = ABRÓTANO, southernwood.—y. marina = Y. DE MAR.—y. mate, maté.—y. mora, nightshade.—y. pastel, woad.—y. piojera, stavesacre.—y. tora, strangle weed, broom rape.
yerbabuena, f. = HIERBABUENA, mint.
yerbajo, m. aug. wild weed.
yerbatear, vn. (Am.) to take maté, Paraguay tea.
yerbatero, ra. I. a. using arrow poison. II. n. (Am.) seller of fodder grass.
yergo, yerga, v. V. ERGUIR.
yermar, va. to depopulate, to lay waste.
yermo, ma. I. a. waste, desert, uninhabited; un-cultivated. II. m. desert, wilderness, waste.
yerno, m. son-in-law.
yero, m. (bot.) = YERVO.
yerro, m. error, mistake; fault.—pl. unpardon-able faults.—y. de cuenta, miscalculation.—y. de imprenta, erratum, typographical error.
yerro, yerra, v. V. ERRAR.
yerto, ta, a. stiff, motionless; rigid, tight.—quedarse y., to be petrified with fear or sur-prise.
yervo, m. (bot.) tare, true bitter vetch.
yesal, yesar, m. gypsum pit.
yesca, f. tinder, punk, touchwood; fuel, incentive. —pl. tinder box, strike-a-light.
yesera, f. gypsum pit; woman who sells gypsum or plaster.
yesería, f. gypsum kiln; plasterer's shop; building constructed with plaster.
yesero, ra. I. a. pertaining to gypsum. II. n. maker or seller of gypsum; plasterer.
yeso, m. gypsum; plaster; plaster cast.—y. blanco, whitewash, fine plaster for surface finish.—y. mate, plaster of Paris.—y. negro, coarse plaster for base coating.—yesón, m. rubbish of plaster.—yesoso, sa, a. gypseous.
yesquero. I. n. tinder maker or seller. II. m. (Colomb.) tinder box for flint-and-steel lighting.
yeta, f. (Am. esp. Arg.) bad luck, misfortune.
yeyuno, m. (anat.) jejunum.
yezgo, m. (bot.) dwarf elder.
yo. I. pers. pron. I.—y. mismo, I myself. II. m. ego.
yodado, da, a. iodic, containing iodine.
yodato, m. (chem.) iodate.
yodhídrico, ca, a. (chem.) hydriodic.
yódico, ca, (chem.) iodic.

yodismo, m. (med.) iodism, disorder caused by use of iodine.
yodo, m. (chem.) iodine.
yodoformo, m. (chem.) iodoform.
yoduración, f. iodization, iodation.
yodurar, va. (chem.) to iodize.
yoduro, m. (chem.) iodide.
yola, yole, f. (naut.) yawl.
yoquey, u. jockey.
yubarta, f. (ichth.) finback, rorqual.
yuca, f. yucca; (Am.) yuca, cassava.
yucal, m. yucca or cassava field.
yucateco, ca, a. of or from Yucatan.
yugada, f. (agr.) yoke of land.
yugo, m. (animal) yoke; marriage tie or cere-mony; confinement, prison; frame of a church bell; (naut.) transom.—sacudir el y., to throw off the yoke.
yuguero, m. plowman, plowboy.
yugular, a. (anat.) jugular.
yumbo, ba, n. a savage of eastern Ecuador.
yunque, m. anvil; (anat.) incus; persevering, un-daunted person.—estar al y., to bear up under trying circumstances; to be hard at work; (coll.) to be on the job.
yunta, f. couple, pair, yoke of draft animals.
yuntería, f. aggregate of YUNTAS; place where draught oxen are fed.
yuntero, m. plowboy.
yunto, ta, a. joined, united; close.—arar y., to plow close.
yuraguano, m. (Cuba) (bot.) fan palm.
yuré, m. a C. A. pigeon.
yusera, f. horizontal stone in oil mills.
yusión, f. (law) precept, command.
yute, m. jute (fibre); jute fabric.
yuxtalineal, a. in parallel columns.
yuxtaponer, va. (pp. YUXTAPUESTO; ind. pres. YUXTAPONGO, pret. YUXTAPUSE, fut. YUXTA-PONDRÉ; subj. YUXTAPONGA) to juxtapose, to place next to each other.
yuxtaposición, f. juxtaposition.
yuxtapuesto, ta, pp. irreg. of YUXTAPONER.
yuyo, m. (Arg., Chile) weed; (S. A., C. A.) an edible herb; (Costa Rica, Salvador) blister on the foot.
yuyuba, f. = AZUFAIFA, jujube.

Z

¡za!, interj. used to frighten dogs.
zabarcera, f. greengrocer (woman).
zábida, zábila, f. (bot.) common aloes.
zaborda, f., zabordamiento, m. (naut.) strand-ing.
zabordar, vn. to touch ground, to become stranded.—zabordo, m. stranding.
zaborro, rra, n. fat person.
zabra, f. (naut.) small sailing vessel.
zabucar, va. = BAZUCAR, to shake up (liquids).
zabullida, zabullidor, zabullidura, zabulli-miento, zabullir = ZAMBULLIDA, etc.
zabuqueo, m. = BAZUQUEO, shaking up; jumble.
zaca, f. large leather bag for bailing out a mine.
zacapela, zacapella, f. noisy wrangle.
zacate, m. (Mex., C. A.) grass; hay, fodder.
zacateca, m. (Cuba) undertaker.
zacateco, ca, n. & a. Zacatecan (from Zacatecas, Mex.).
zacatín, m. street where garments are sold.
zacatón, m. (Am.) a tall fodder grass.
zacear, va. to scare off (dogs) by crying ¡ZA!.
zadorija, f. (bot.) yellow poppy.
zafa, f. = JOFAINA, washbasin, bowl.
zafacoca, f. (Am.) (coll.) squabble, row.
zafada, f. flight, escape; lightening (a ship).
zafar. I. va. to adorn, deck, embellish; to clear from encumbrances; to lighten (a ship). II. vr. to escape, run away; (de) to get rid (of); to

avoid; to get out (of); to get clear (of); to slip or come (off), break loose; (Mex.) to dislocate (a joint).

zafareche, *m.* = ESTANQUE, tank, reservoir.

zafarí, *a.* app. to a variety of pomegranate.

zafariche, *m.* shelf for water jugs or jars.

zafarrancho, *m.* (naut.) clearing for action; (coll.) ravage, destruction; scuffle, wrangle, row.

zafiamente, *adv.* lubberly, clumsily.

zafiedad, *f.* rusticity, clumsiness.

zafio, fia, *a.* coarse, uncivil, ignorant.

zafío, *m.* (ichth.) a variety of conger eel.

zafir, *m.* sapphire.—**zafíreo, ea,** *a.* sapphirine.

zafirino, na, *a.* & *f.,* (min.) sapphirine.

zafiro, *m.* sapphire.

zafo, fa, *a.* free, disentangled; exempt from danger or risk; (naut.) free and clear.

zafones, *m. pl.* overalls.

¹**zafra,** *f.* drip jar, oil jar.

²**zafra,** *f.* broad strap holding the thills of a cart.

³**zafra,** *f.* (min.) rubbish.

⁴**zafra,** *f.* sugar crop; sugar making; sugar-making season.

zafre, *m.* (min.) zaffre or saffre.

zafrero, *m.* (min.) laborer who clears a mine of rubbish.

zaga. I. *f.* rear part; load in the back of a carriage. **II.** *m.* the last player at a game of cards. **—a la z.,** or **en z.,** behind.—**no ir en z. a,** not to be behind, less than, or inferior to.

¹**zagal,** *m.* stout, spirited young man; swain; subordinate shepherd; boy assistant of stagecoach driver.

²**zagal,** *m.* short skirt.

zagala, *f.* shepherdess; lass, maiden.

¹**zagalejo, ja,** *n. dim.* young shepherd(-ess).

²**zagalejo,** *m.* short skirt; underskirt, slip.

zagalón, na, *n.* overgrown boy (girl).

zagua, *f.* (bot.) saltwort.

zagual, *m.* paddle.

zaguán, *m.* entrance hall, vestibule.

zaguanete, *m. dim.* small vestibule; king's escort of life guards.

zaguero, ra. I. *a.* laggard, loitering. **II.** *m.* backstop, at the game of PELOTA.

zahareño, ña, *a.* intractable; (of birds) wild, haggard; unsociable; arrogant.

zaharí, *a.* = ZAFARÍ.

zahena, *f.* a Moorish gold coin.

zaherible, *a.* blamable, blameworthy.

zaheridor, ra, *n.* & *a.* censurer(-ing), upbraider (-ing).

zaherimiento, *m.* censure, blame.

zaherir, *va.* (ger. ZAHIRIENDO; ind. pres. ZAHIERO, pret. él ZAHIRIÓ; subj. ZAHIERA) to censure, blame, reproach, upbraid.

zahina, *f.* (bot.) sorghum.

zahinar, *m.* sorghum field.

zahinas, *f. pl.* thin porridge or pap.

zabirió, pret. of ZAHERIR.

zahón, *m.* (gen. pl.) overalls.

zahonado, da, *a.* dark brown.

zahondar. I. *va.* to dig. **II.** *vn.* to sink into soft ground (as the feet).

zahora, *f.* merry lunch party.

zahorar, *vn.* to have a repast with music.

zahorí, *m.* vulgar impostor pretending to see hidden things; perspicacious and curious person.

zahoriar, *va.* to scrutinize, look deeply into.

zahorra, *f.* (naut.) ballast.

zahurda, *f.* pigsty, hogsty; low tavern, "joint."

zaida, *f.* (ornith.) a variety of heron.

zaino, na, *a.* chestnut, zain (horse); vicious (animal); treacherous, wicked.—**mirar a la z.,** or **de z.,** to look sidewise.

zalá, *f.* salaam.—**hacer la z.,** to salaam; to flatter, cajole, wheedle.

zalagarda, *f.* ambush; trap, snare; sudden attack, surprise; skirmish; mock fight.

zalama, *f.*; **zalamelé,** *m.*; **zalamería,** *f.* flattery, wheedling.

zalamero, ra, *n.* wheedler, flatterer, fawner.

zalea, *f.* undressed sheepskin.

¹**zalear,** *va.* to shake; to damage, destroy.

²**zalear,** *va.* to frighten (a dog) away.

zalema, *f.* salaam, bow, curtsy.

zaleo, *m.* sheepskin damaged by a wolf's fangs; shaking or moving to and fro; ZALEA.

zalmedina, *m.* an ancient magistrate in Arragon

zalona, *f.* large earthen jar.

zallar, *va.* (naut.) to outrig, to train.

zamacuco, *m.* (coll.) dunce, dolt; intoxication.

zamacueca, *f.* (S. A.) an Indian tune and dance.

zamanca, *f.* (coll.) drubbing, flogging.

zamarra, *f.* sheepskin jacket worn by shepherds; undressed sheepskin.

zamarrear, *va.* to shake (something) held in the teeth (as a dog does a rabbit); to ill-treat; to pin down in a dispute.

zamarreo, *m.* shaking something held in the teeth; abuse, ill treatment.

zamarrico, *m. dim.* portmanteau or bag of sheepskin.

zamarrilla, *f.* (bot.) poly, mountain germander.

zamarro. I. *m.* shepherd's coat of sheepskins; sheep or lambskin; (coll.) dolt, dunce. **II.** *m. pl.* (Am.) chaps, chaparajos.

zamarrón, *m. aug.* large sheepskin jacket.

zambaigo, ga, *a.* & *n.* Indian and Chinese halfbreed.

zambapalo, *m.* an ancient dance and tune.

zambarco, *m.* broad breast strap (of harness).

zámbigo, ga, *a.* bandy-legged.

zambo, ba. I. *a.* knock-kneed; born of an Indian and a Negro; (loosely) Negro, mulatto. **II.** *n.* Indian and Negro half-breed; (loosely) Negro, mulatto. **III.** *m.* an American monkey.

zamboa, *f.* (bot.) = AZAMBOA, a kind of citron.

zambomba, *f.* rustic drum with the head pierced by a reed which, when rubbed with the moistened hand, produces a hoarse sound.—**¡z.!** whew!—**zambombo, ba,** *n.* (coll.) rustic, boor, coarse or ill-bred person.

zamborondón, na; **zamborotudo, da,** *a.* awkward, clumsy; ill-shaped.

¹**zambra,** *f.* a Moorish festival; merrymaking.

²**zambra,** *f.* a kind of Moorish boat.

zambucar, *va.* to hide (a thing) by mixing it among others.—**zambuco,** *m.* (coll.) hiding, concealing a card among others.

zambullida, *f.* diving, plunge, ducking; (fencing) thrust to the breast.

zambullidor, ra, *n.* one who dives or plunges.

zambullidura, *f.,* **zambullimiento,** *m.* diving, ducking, plunge.

zambullir. I. *vn.* & *va.* to dive; to duck, give a ducking to; to sink. **II.** *vr.* to plunge, dip, dive to sink; to hide, conceal oneself.

zambullo, *m.* evacuation stool; refuse tank or barrel.

zampabodigos, zampabollos, *n.* (coll.) glutton

zampalimosnas, *m.* (coll.) sturdy beggar.

zampalo, *n.* (coll.) glutton.

zampar. I. *va.* to thrust or put hurriedly (into something) in order to conceal; to devour eagerly. **II.** *vr.* to rush in, to thrust oneself in or into.

zampatortas, *m.* (coll.) glutton; boor, rustic.

zampeado, *m.* (arch.) grillage, subfoundation of timber or steel and masonry in marshy ground.

zampear, *va.* to build a grillage on.

zampona, *f.* = PIPITAÑA, rustic flute; (coll.) frivolous saying.

zampuzar, *va.* ZAMBULLIR; ZAMPAR.

zampuzo, *m.* diving, ducking; hiding.

zamuro, *m.* (Venez.) (ornith.) carrion vulture.

zanahoria, *f.* (bot.) carrot.

zanahoriate, *m.* preserved carrot.

zanca, *f.* long shank or leg; large pin; (arch.

string-piece of a staircase; (min.) shore, prop.—
zancas de araña, shifts, evasions, subterfuges.
—por zancas o por barrancas, by hook or by
crook.—**zancada**, *f.* long stride.—**en dos zan-
cadas**, (coll.) in a jiffy, in no time.

zancadilla, *f.* sudden catch to trip one; trick,
deceit, craft; (naut.) elbow in the hawse.—
armar z., to lay a snare.

zancado, da, *a.* insipid (salmon).

zancajear, *va.* to walk fast from place to place,
to run about.

zancajera, *f.* coach step.

zancajiento, ta, *a.* bandy-legged.

zancajo, *m.* heel bone; torn heelpiece of a shoe
or stocking; (coll.) short, ill-shaped person.—
no llegar a los zancajos, or **no llegar al z.,
de**, not to come up to, or be the equal of (one).
—roer los zancajos a, to backbite.

zancajoso, sa, *a.* bandy-legged; wearing dirty
stockings with holes at the heels.

zancarrón, *m.* leg bone without flesh; withered,
old, ugly person; boastful ignoramus.

zanco, *m.* stilt; (naut.) sliding-gunter mast.—**en
zancos**, in a high position.

zancón, na, *a.* long-legged; wading (bird).

zancudo, da. I. *a.* long-shanked; (ornith.) wading
(bird). **II.** *m.* (Am.) mosquito. **III.** *f. pl.*
(ornith.) wading birds.

zandía, *f.* watermelon.

zanfonía, *f.* (mus.) hurdy-gurdy.

zanga, *f.* four-hand ombre (card game).

zangala, *f.* buckram.

zangamanga, *f.* (coll.) trick, deceit.

zanganada, *f.* (coll.) impertinent or unseasonable
act or expression.

**zangandongo, ga; zangandullo, lla; zan-
gandungo, ga**, *n.* (coll.) idler, lazy person;
dolt, awkward person.

zanganear, *vn.* to drone, to loaf.

zángano, *m.* drone; (coll.) idler, sponger.

zangarilla, *f.* small mill pond.

zangarilleja, *f.* (coll.) trollop, slovenly girl.

zangarrear, *vn.* (coll.) to scrape a guitar.

zangarriana, *f.* (vet.) a head disease of sheep;
(coll.) sadness, blues; any slight periodical ailment.

zangarrullón, na, *n.* tall, sluggish, lazy boy
(girl).

zangolotear. I. *vn.* to shake violently; to fuss,
fidget. **II.** *vr.* to rattle, swing or slam.

zangoloteo, *m.* fuss, bustle; swinging, rattling.

zangolotino, na, *a.* (of boys and girls) pretending to be a little child.

zangón, *m.* (coll.) = ZANGARULLÓN.

zangotear, zangoteo = ZANGOLOTEAR, ZANGO-
LOTEO.

zanguango, ga. I. *a.* (coll.) lazy, sluggish; silly.
II. *m.* dunce, fool. **III.** *f.* (coll.) feigned illness
to avoid work; wheedling, fawning.

zanguayo, *m.* (coll.) tall, skinny idler that cunningly acts the fool.

zanja, *f.* ditch, trench, furrow, drain; (Am.) gap,
gully, draw.—**abrir las zanjas**, to lay the
foundation of a building; to begin, get started.

zanjar, *va.* to cut ditches in; to excavate; to settle
amicably; to obviate, surmount.

zanjón, *m. aug.* deep ditch; large drain.

zanqueador, ra, *n.* one who waddles in walking;
great walker.

zanqueamiento, *m.* waddling in walking.

zanquear, *vn.* to waddle, trot, or run about; to
walk much and fast.

zanquilargo, ga, *a.* long-shanked, long-legged.

zanquilla, zanquita, *f. dim.* (coll.) disproportionate, long-legged man.

zanquituerto, ta, *a.* bandy-legged.

zanquivano, na, *a.* spindle-shanked.

¹zapa, *f.* spade; (fort.) sap.—**caminar a la z.**,
(mil.) to advance by sap or mine.

²zapa, *f.* shagreen; rough surface on silver.

zapador, *m.* (mil.) sapper.

zapallo, *m.* (Am.) a variety of squash; calabash.

zapapico, *m.* pickaxe, mattock.

zapaquilda, *f.* female cat.

zapar, *va.* (fort.) to sap, to mine.

zaparrada, *f.* violent fall.

zaparrastrar, *vn.* (coll.) to trail (as dress trains).

zaparrastroso, sa, *a.* dirty, greasy, ragged.

zaparrazo, *m.* thud; violent fall.

zapata, *f.* piece of sole leather put on the hinge
of a door to prevent its creaking; buskin, half-
boot, high gaiter; (Cuba) socle of a wall; (arch.)
lintel; (naut.) shoe; (mech.) shoe (of brake,
etc.).—**z. de la quilla**, (naut.) false heel.—**z.
de un ancla**, (naut.) shoe of an anchor.

zapatazo, *m. aug.* large shoe; blow with a shoe;
stamping of the feet; fall; thud, whack; clapping
noise of a horse's foot.—**tratar a zapatazos**, to
treat rudely or roughly.

zapateado, *m.* a sort of clog dance.

zapateador, ra, *n.* clog dancer.

zapatear. I. *va.* to strike with the shoe; (fencing)
to hit frequently with the button of the foil; to
ill-treat. **II.** *vn.* to beat time with the feet;
(naut.) (of sails) to flap. **III.** *vr.* to oppose with
spirit; to resist.—**zapateo**, *m.* keeping time by
beating the feet on the floor.

zapatera, *f.* shoemaker's wife; woman who makes
or sells shoes.

zapatería, *f.* trade of a shoemaker; shoemaker's
shop.—**z. de viejo**, cobbler's stall.

zapateril, *a.* pertaining to, or like, shoemakers.

zapatero, ra. I. *a.* hard, poorly cooked (as beans);
stale (olives). **II.** *m.* shoemaker; shoe dealer;
(S. A.) (ichth.) threadfish, cobbler fish; (coll.)
player who takes no tricks at a game of cards.
—z. de viejo, cobbler.

zapateta. I. *f.* slap on the sole of a shoe; caper,
leap, jump. **II.** *interj.* oh! gracious!

zapatico, illo, ito, *m. dim.* nice little shoe.

zapatilla, *f.* pump, slipper; leather washer; piece
of chamois or buckskin put behind the lock of
a gun or pistol; (fencing) button of a foil; hoof
of animals.

zapatillero, ra, *n.* maker or seller of slippers,
pumps, and children's shoes.

zapato, *m.* shoe (gen. app. to low shoes).—
zapatos papales, overshoes, clogs.—**como
tres en un z.**, squeezed into insufficient space;
in great poverty.—**meter a uno en un z.**,
(coll.) to cow or confound one.—**saber dónde
aprieta el z.**, to know where the shoe pinches.

zapatón, *m. aug.* large, clumsy shoe; (Colomb.)
rubber, overshoe.

zapatudo, da, *a.* wearing large or stout shoes;
large-hoofed or clawed.

¡zape! *interj.* used to frighten cats away; to
denote surprise, or to refuse to give cards in
some games.—**zapear**, *va.* to frighten (cats)
away; to refuse to give cards to, in some games.

zapito, *m.* **zapita**, *f.* (prov.) milk pail.

zaporogo, *m.* Ukranian Cossack.

zapotal, *m.* sapota grove or orchard.

zapote, *m.* (bot.) sapota tree and its fruit.

zapotero, *m.* (bot.) sapota tree.

zapotillo, *m.* (bot.) sapodilla and its fruit.

zapuzar, *va.* = CHAPUZAR, to duck (in water).

¹zaque, *m.* (Colomb.) chief of certain Indians.

²zaque, *m.* leather bottle or wine-bag; (coll.)
tippler, drunkard.

zaquear, *va.* (of wines, etc.) to transfer from one
²ZAQUE to another; to transport in ²ZAQUES.

zaquizamí, *m.* garret, cockloft; small wretched
room, "hole."

zar, *m.* czar.

zara, *f.* (bot.) Indian corn, maize.

zarabanda, *f.* saraband (dance and tune); bustle,
noise.—**zarabandista**, *n.* sarabander; dancer;
merry person.

zarabutero, ra, *a.* = ZARAGUTERO.

For pronunciation, see the rules at the beginning of the book.

zaragalla, *f.* fine charcoal.

zaragata, *f.* turmoil; scuffle, quarrel.

zaragatero, ra. I. *a.* (coll.) noisy, quarrelsome. **II.** *n.* rowdy.

zaragatona, *f.* (bot.) rib grass, ribwort.

zaragocí, *m.* a kind of plum.

zaragozano, na, *n.* & *a.* Saragossan.

zaragüelles, *m. pl.* wide and short plaited breeches; large pair of ill-made breeches; (bot.) reed grass.

zaragutear, *va.* (coll.) to undertake without proper knowledge; to bungle.

zaragutero, ra, *n.* (coll.) bungler.

zaramagullón, *m.* (ornith.) didapper, a minute merganser.

zarambeque, *m.* breakdown (Negro dance).

zaranda, *f.* screen, sieve, sifter.

zarandador, ra, *n.* sifter of wheat.

zarandajas, *f. pl.* trifles, odds and ends.

zarandalí, *adv.* black-spotted (dove).

zarandar, zarandear. I. *va.* to winnow; to sift; to separate, pick out; (coll.) to stir and move nimbly. **II.** *vr.* to be in motion, to move to and fro; to stalk, strut.—**zarandeo,** *m.* sifting or winnowing; moving briskly; stalking, strut.

zarandero, *m.* = ZARANDADOR.

zarandillo, lla. I. *n.* (coll.) one who frisks nimbly about. **II.** *m.* small sieve.

zarapatel, *n.* a kind of salmagundi.

zarapito, *m.* (ornith.) whimbrel, curlew jack.

zaratán, *m.* cancer in the breast.

zaraza, *f.* chintz, printed cotton.

zarazas, *f. pl.* paste made of pounded glass and poison, for killing dogs, rats, etc.

zarazo, za, *a.* (Cuba) rotten.

zarcear. I. *va.* to clean (pipes) with briers. **II.** *vn.* to move to and fro; to get into briers (as dogs pursuing game).

zarceño, ña, *a.* pertaining to briers.

zarcero, ra, *a.* & *n.* (dog) that hunts in briers.

zarceta, *f.* (ornith.) = CERCETA, widgeon.

zarcillitos, *m. pl.* (bot.) quaking grass.

¹zarcillo, *m.* = CERCILLO, drop earring; tendril of a vine; hoop (of a barrel).

²zarcillo, *m.* gardener's hoe.

zarco, ca, *a.* light blue (eyes).

zarevitz, *m.* czarevitch.

zargatona, *f.* = ZARAGATONA.

zariano, na, *a.* pertaining to the czar.

zarigüeya, *f.* (S. A.) opossum.

zarina, *f.* czarina.

zarismo, *m.* czarism.

zarja, *f.* = AZARJA, reel for winding silk.

zaroche, *m.* (Ecuador) mountain sickness.

¹zarpa, *f.* paw of an animal; (naut.) weighing anchor; dirt or mud sticking to the skirts.—echar la z. a, to grasp, clutch, grip.

²zarpa, *f.* (arch.) footing.

zarpada, *f.* blow with a paw.

zarpar, *vn.* (naut.) to weigh anchor, to sail.

zarpazo, *m.* bang, thud, whack; ZARPADA.

zarposo, sa, *a.* bespattered, bemired.

zarracatería, *f.* lure, deception.

zarracatín, *m.* (coll.) haggler; profiteer.

zarramplín, na, *n.* (coll.) bungler, botcher.

zarramplinada, *f.* botch, bungle, muddle.

zarrapastra, *f.* mud sticking to the skirts.

zarrapastrón, na, *a.* & *n.* tatterdemalion.

zarrapastrosamente, *adv.* (coll.) shabbily, slovenly.

zarrapastroso, sa, *a.* ragged, slovenly, shabby, seedy.

¹zarria, *f.* leather strap, thong or latch.

²zarria, *f.* mud sticking to clothes.—**zarriento, ta;** **zarrioso, sa,** *a.* bespattered, bemired.

zarza, *f.* (bot.) bramble; blackberry bush.

zarzagán, *m.* cold northeast wind.

zarzaganete, *m. dim.* light northeast wind.

zarzaganillo, *m.* violent northeast storm.

zarzahán, *m.* a kind of striped silk.

zarzaidea, *f.* (bot.) raspberry bush.

zarzal, *m.* brambly place, brambles.

zarzamora, *f.* (bot.) brambleberry.

zarzaparrilla, *f.* (bot.) sarsaparilla.

zarzaparrillar, *m.* sarsaparilla plantation.

zarzaperruna, *f.* (bot.) dog-rose.

zarzarrosa, *f.* (bot.) dog-rose.

zarzo, *m.* hurdle, wattle; (Colomb.) garret.

zarzoso, sa, *a.* briery, brambly.

zarzuela, *f.* musical comedy.—**zarzuelero, ra,** *a.* pertaining to musical comedies.—**zarzuelista,** *n.* writer or composer of musical comedies.

¡zas! *m.* tick, sound of a rap.—**¡z., z.¡** ticktack

zascandil, *m.* (coll.) busybody.

zata, zatara, *f.* raft.

zato, *m.* piece of bread.

zazoso, sa. I. *a.* lisping. **II.** *n.* lisper.

zeda, *f.* name of the letter *z.*

zedilla, *f.* cedilla.

zelandés, sa, *n.* & *a.* Zealandian.

zemstvo, *m.* (Russian hist.) zemstvo.

Zendavesta, *m.* Zend-Avesta.

zendo, da, *a.* & *m.* Zend.

zenit, zenital = CENIT, CENITAL, zenith.

zepelín, *m.* Zeppelin (dirigible).

zeta, *f.* name of the letter *z;* Gk. letter, zeta.

zeugma, zuema, *f.* (rhet.) zeugma.

zigzag, *m.* zigzag.—**zigzaguear,** *vn.* to zigzag.—**zigzagueo,** *m.* zigzagging.

zinc, *m.* = CINC, zinc.

zipizape, *m.* (coll.) row, rumpus, scuffle.

zircón, zirconio = CIRCÓN, CIRCONIO.

ziriganña, *f.* fawning, wheedling, flattery; CHASCO; FRIOLERA.

¡zis, zas! (coll.) words expressing the sound of repeated blows or strokes.

zizaña, *f.* (bot.) = CIZAÑA, darnel.

zoantario, ria, *n.* & *a.* (zool.) zoantharian.

zoantropía, *f.* (med.) zoanthropy, a mania.

zoántropo, pa, *n.* one ill with zoanthropy.

zoca, *f.* square, plaza.

zócalo, *m.* (arch.) socle or zocle.

¹zocato, ta, *a.* (of fruit) overripe.

²zocato, ta, *a.* left-handed.

zoclo, *m.* clog; overshoe.

¹zoco, ca, *a.* left-handed.

²zoco, *m.* clog, wooden shoe; (arch.) socle.

³zoco, *m.* market; market-place.

zodiacal, *a.* zodiacal.

zodíaco, *m.* (astr.) zodiac.

zofra, *f.* Moorish carpet.

zoilo, *m.* malicious critic.

zolocho, cha, *a.* (coll.) stupid, silly, booby.

zollipar, *vn.* (coll.) to sob.

zollipo, *m.* sob; sobbing.

zoma, *f.* coarse flour.

zompo, pa, *a.* cripple; clumsy, awkward.

zona, *f.* zone; girdle, band; area, region; (med.) zoster, shingles.—**z. esférica,** (geom.) spherical zone.—**z. glacial,** (geol.) frigid zone.—**z. polémica,** (fort.) zone of defense.—**z. templada,** temperate zone.—**z. tórrida,** torrid zone.—**zonas poco desarrolladas,** underdeveloped regions.—**zonal,** *a.* zonate, zoned.

zoncería, *f.* silliness, dulness, stupidity.

zonchiche, *m.* (C. A.) a red-headed vulture.

zonote, *m.* deep deposit of water.

zonzamente, *adv.* stupidly, foolishly.

zonzo, za. I. *a.* dull, stupid, silly. **II.** *n.* simpleton, dunce, booby, noodle.

zonzorrión, na, *n.* very dull and stupid person.

zoófago, ga, *a.* zoöphagous, carnivorous.

zoofito, *m.* (zool.) zoöphyte.

zoografía, *f.* zoögraphy.

zooide. I. *a.* containing the figure of an animal or part of it. **II.** *m.* (biol.) zoöid.

zoolatra, *m.* & *f.* animal worshipper.

zoolatría, *f.* zoolatry, worship of animals.

zoolítico, ca, *a.* fossil-bearing.

zoolito, *m.* petrified animal.

For pronunciation, see the rules at the beginning of the book.

zoología, *f.* zoölogy.—**zoológico, ca,** *a.* zoölogical, zoölogic.—**zoólogo,** *m.* zoölogist.

zoomorfismo, *m.* zoömorphism.

zoospermo, *m.* (biol.) zoösperm.

zoospora, *f.*; **zoosporo,** *m.* (bot.) zoöspore.

zoosporangio, *m.* zoösporangium.

zootecnia, *f.* zootechnics.

zootomía, *f.* zoötomy, animal anatomy.

zopas, *n.* (coll.) nickname given to a lisper.

zope, *m.* (ornith.) = ZOPILOTE, buzzard.

zopenco, ca. I. *a.* (coll.) doltish, dull. **II.** *n.* dolt, blockhead, fool.

zopetero, *m.* = RIBAZO, slope; hillock.

zopilote, *m.* (Mex.) (ornith.) = AURA, buzzard.

zopisa, *f.* pitch and tar ointment.

zopitas, *n.* = ZOPAS.

zopo, pa. I. *a.* lame, maimed, crippled; clumsy, awkward, unhandy. **II.** *n.* cripple.

zoqueta, *f.* a wooden cover or guard for the hand.

zoquetada, *f.* silly remark; foolishness, foolish words or act.

zoquete, *m.* (carp.) chump, chunk, block, bit of stale bread; (coll.) ugly little person; dolt, dunce, numskull, blockhead.—**z. de cuchara,** (naut.) scoop handle.—**zoquetero, ra,** *a.* living on crumbs and leavings, idle pauper.

zoquetico, illo, *m. dim.* small morsel of bread.

zoquetudo, da, *a.* rough, ill-finished.

zorcico, *m.* (mus.) Basque song and dance in five-eight (⅝) time.

zorita, *f.* (ornith.) stockdove, wood pigeon.

zoroástrico, ca, *a.* Zoroastric.

zoroastrismo, *m.* Zoroastrianism.

zorollo, *a.* (of wheat) reaped while unripe.

zorongo, *m.* kerchief folded like a bandage around the head, worn by Aragonese; broad flattened chignon; an Andalusian dance and tune.

¹zorra, *f.* (zool.) fox; foxy, sly person; (coll.) prostitute; drunkenness, inebriation.—**a la z., candilazo,** when Greek meets Greek; diamond cut diamond.

²zorra, *f.* dray, truck.

zorrastrón, na, *a.* & *n.* (coll.) foxy (person), rogue(-ish), knave(-ish).

zorrera, *f.* fox hole; kennel; room full of smoke; heaviness, drowsiness.

zorrería, *f.* foxiness; cunning, knavery.

¹zorrero, ra, *a.* slow, tardy, sluggish; (naut.) sailing heavily.

²zorrero, ra. I. *a.* cunning, foxy; fox-hunting (dog). **II.** *m.* keeper of a royal forest.

zorrilla, *f.* (zool.) polecat, skunk.

zorro, rra. I. *a.* cunning, foxy. **II.** *n.* fox; knave, foxy person. **III.** *m. pl.* duster made of cloth strips or foxtails tied to a handle.

zorrocloco, *m.* humdrum; (coll.) caress, petting.

zorronglón, na, *a.* slow, heavy, lazy.

zorruelo, la, *n. dim.* little fox.

zorrullo, *m.* = ZURULLO.

zorruno, na, *a.* vulpine, foxy, foxlike.

zorzal, *m.* (ornith.) thrush; sly, crafty man.—**z. marino,** (ichth.) a fish abounding near Spain.

zorzaleña, *a.*—**aceituna z.,** crescent olive.

zoster, *f.* (med.) zoster, herpes, shingles.

zote, *a.* dull and ignorant.

zozobra, *f.* worry, anguish, anxiety; unlucky throw of the dice; (naut.) sinking, capsizing.

zozobrante, *a.* in great danger; sinking.

zozobrar, *vn.* (naut.) to be weather-beaten; to sink, founder; to upset, capsize; to be in great danger; to grieve, worry, fret.

zozobroso, sa, *a.* anxious, worried.

zúa, *f.* = AZUDA, Persian water wheel.

zuavo, *m.* (mil.) zouave.

zubia, *f.* drain, channel, flume.

zucarino, na, *a.* = SACARINO, sugary, saccharine.

zúchil, *m.* (Mex.) bouquet.

zuda, *f.* = ZÚA.

zudra, *n.* Sudra, lowest Hindu caste; member of the Sudra.

zueco, *m.* sabot, wooden shoe, clog; galosh.

zuindá, *m.* (ornith.) an Argentine brown owl.

zuinglianismo, *m.* Zwinglianism.

zuingliano, na, *n.* & *a.* Zwinglian.

zuiza, *f.* = SUIZA, military tournament or feast; quarrel, dispute.

zuizón, *m.* spear; (naut.) half pike.

zulacar, *va.* to anoint with bitumen.

zulaque, *m.* (hydraul.) packing stuff; (naut.) stuff for paving the bottom of a ship.

zulú, *a.* & *n.* Zulu.

¹zulla, *f.* (bot.) French honeysuckle.

²zulla, *f.* (coll.) human excrements.—**zullarse,** *vr.* (coll.) to go to stool; to break wind.

zullenco, ca; zullón, na. I. *a.* (coll.) breaking wind; flatulent. **II.** *m.* act of breaking wind; flatulence.

zumacal, ¹zumacar, *m.* sumach plantation.

²zumacar, *va.* to dress or tan with sumach.

zumacaya, *f.* (ornith.) a night wading bird.

zumaque, *m.* (bot.) sumach tree; (coll.) wine.

zumaya, *f.* (ornith.) barn owl; goatsucker; fern owl; ZUMACAYA.

zumba, *f.* bell worn by the leading mule of a drove; rattle; joke, jest; facetious raillery.

zumbador, ra. I. *a.* humming, buzzing. **II.** *m.* (P. R.) humming bird; (elec.) buzzer.

zumbar. I. *vn.* to buzz, to hum; to be near, flutter around; (of the ears) to ring. **II.** *va.* to jest, to joke with.

¹zumbel, *m.* (coll.) cord for spinning tops.

²zumbel, *m.* frown, angry mien or aspect.

zumbido, *m.* humming, buzzing; ringing in the ears; ping of a bullet; (coll.) blow, box, cuff.

zumbilín, *m.* (P. I.) dart or javelin.

zumbo, *m.* = ZUMBIDO.

zumbón, na. I. *a.* waggish, jocose. **II.** *m.* wag, jester, joker; a variety of pigeon.

zumiento, ta, *a.* juicy, succulent.

zumillo, *m.* (bot.) dragon's arum, Aaron's beard; a poisonous carrot.

zumo, *m.* sap, juice; profit, utility.—**z. de cepas,** or **parras,** (coll.) grape juice, wine.

zumoso, sa, *a.* juicy, succulent.

zuna, *f.* Sunna, body of Mohammedan traditions; viciousness of horses; trickery, perfidy.

zuncho, *m.* band, hoop, collar, ferrule.

zunita, *n.* Sunnite, member of one of the great Mohammedan sects.

zunítico, ca, *a.* pertaining to the Sunna, body of Mohammedan traditions.

zuño, *m.* frown, angry mien.

zupia, *f.* wine turned roily; lees, dregs, slops; refuse, rubbish, trash.

zurano, na, *n.* (ornith.) stockdove, wild pigeon.

zurcidera, *f.* darner, finedrawer.

zurcido, *m.* (sewing) darning, finedrawing.

zurcidor, ra, *n.* darner.—**zurcidora de voluntades,** procuress.

zurcidura, *f.* (sewing) finedrawing, darning.

zurcir, *va.* (ind. ZURZO; subj. ZURZA) (sewing) to darn, mend; to finedraw; to join, unite; (coll.) to concoct (lies).

zurdería, *f.* left-handedness.

zurdo, da, *a.* left-handed.—**a zurdas,** the wrong way.

zurear, *vn.* to coo.—**zureo,** *m.* cooing.

zurito, ta, *f.* (ornith.) = ZURO, wild pigeon.

zuriza, *f.* = ZUIZA, quarrel, dispute.

¹zuro, ra, *n.* (ornith.) stockdove, wild pigeon.

²zuro, *m.* corncob.

zurra, *f.* (tanning) currying; flogging, beating, drubbing; quarrel, dispute, scuffle.

zurrado, *m.* (coll.) glove.

zurrador, *m.* (tanning) currier, dresser; drubber, flogger.

zurrapa, *f.* lees, sediment, dregs; rubbish, trash;

ugly skinny boy.—con **zurrapas**, in an uncleanly manner.

zurrapelo, *m.* (coll.) severe reprimand.

zurrapiento, ta; zurraposo, sa, *a.* dreggy; turbid, roily.

zurrar, *va.* (tanning) to curry, to dress (leather); to spank, flog, drub, whip; to beat in a quarrel or fight.—**z. la badana**, to beat, to flog.—**¡z., que es tarde!** but you are persistent! will you keep on forever? etc. (said to one who persists in something disagreeable or already rejected).

zurrarse, *vr.* to have an involuntary evacuation of the bowels; to be seized with great fear.

zurriaga, *f.* ZURRIAGO; (ornith.) lark.

zurriagar, *va.* (*pret.* ZURRIAGUÉ; *subj.* ZURRIAGUE) to whip, horsewhip, cowhide.

zurriagazo, *m.* whipping; severe lashing; unexpected ill treatment; stroke of bad luck.

zurriago, *m.* thong, long leather strap; whip.

zurriar, *vn.* to hum, buzz; to rattle.

zurribanda, *f.* flogging, horsewhipping, cowhiding; rumpus, scuffle, fight.

zurriburri, *m.* (coll.) ragamuffin, scamp; (coll.) gang of rowdies.

¹zurrido, *m.* humming, buzzing, rattling noise.

²zurrido, *m.* (coll.) blow with a stick.

zurrir, *vn.* to hum, buzz, rattle.

zurrón, *m.* shepherd's pouch; game bag; leather bag; thin skin of shell fruits; (anat.) placenta cyst.—**zurronada**, *f.* bagful.—**zurroncillo**, *m. dim.* small bag.—**zurronero, ra**, *n.* maker or seller of game bags.

zurrusco, *m.* (coll.) burnt toast.

zurubí, *m.* (ichth.) an Argentine fresh-water fish.

zurullo, *m.* any soft round object; ball or piece of tangled string or rope; (cook.) rolling pin.

zurumbático, ca, *a.* stunned, dumbfounded.

zurupeto, *m.* unauthorized agent.

zurzo, zurza, *v. V.* ZURCIR.

zutanico, illo, *m. dim.* of ZUTANO.

Zutano, na, *n.* (coll.) So-and-So.—**Fulano, Z. y Mengano**, Tom, Dick and Harry.

¡zuzo! *interj.* = ¡CHUCHO! (used to curb dog).

zuzón, *m.* (bot.) groundsel, ragwort.

For pronunciation, see the rules at the beginning of the book.

APPENDIX

GEOGRAPHICAL NAMES THAT DIFFER IN THE SPANISH AND ENGLISH LANGUAGES

A

Abidos, Abydos.
Abisinia, Abyssinia.
Acaya, Achæa, Achaia.
Accio, Actium.
Adelaida, Adelaide.
Adrianópoli, Adrianople.
Afganistán, Afghanistan.
Alejandría, Alexandria.
Alemania, Germany.
Alenzón, Alençon.
Alepo, Aleppo.
Alesia, Alais.
Almirante. V. ISLAS DEL ALMIRANTE.
Alpes, Alps.
Alpes Julianos, Julian Alps.
Alpes Peninos, Pennine Alps.
Alsacia, Alsace.
Alsacia Lorena, Alsace-Lorraine.
Alto Egipto, Upper Egypt.
Amán, Maskat.
Amazonas, Amazon.
Amberes, Antwerp.
América del Norte, North America.
América del Sur, South America.
América Española, Spanish America.
América Meridional, South America.
Anam, Annam.
Andalucía, Andalusia.
Angulema, Angoulême.
Angumoes, Angoumais.
Antillas, Antilles, West Indies.
Antioquía, Antioch.
Apeninos, Apennines.
Aquisgrán, Aachen, Aix-la-Chapelle.
Aquitania, Aquitaine.
Arabia Desierta, Arabia Deserta.
Arabia Feliz, Arabia Felix.
Arabia Petrea, Arabia Petræa.
Aragón, Arragon.
Archipiélago, Ægean.
Archipiélago de Francisco José, Franz Joseph Land.
Archipiélago Malayo, Malay Archipelago.
Ardenas, Ardennes.
Argel, Algiers.
Argelia, Algeria.
Armañac, Armañaque, Armagnac.
Asia Menor, Asia Minor.
Asiria, Assyria.
Asís, Assisi.

Astracán, Astrakhan.
Atenas, Athens.
Ática, Attica.
Ausburgo, Augsburg.
Austria-Hungría, Austria-Hungary.
Auvernia, Auvergne.
Aviñón, Avignon.
Ayacio, Ajaccio.

B

Babilonia, Babylon.
Bactriana, Bactria.
Baireut, Bayreuth.
Baja California, Lower California.
Bajo Egipto, Lower Egypt.
Bajo Rin, Lower Rhine.
Bakú, Baku.
Báltico, Baltic.
Baluchistán, Baluchistan.
Banato, Banat.
Bañeras, Bagnères.
Barbadas, Barbadoes.
Bareges, Barège.
Basilea, Basel, Basle, Bâle.
Baviera, Bavaria.
Bayona, Bayonne.
Bearne, Bearn.
Bechuanalandia, Bechuanaland.
Belcaire, Beaucaire.
Belén, Bethlehem.
Bélgica, Belgium.
Belgrado, Belgrade.
Belice, Beliza, British Honduras.
Beluchistán = BALUCHISTÁN.
Bengala, Bengal.
Beocia, Bœotia, Beotia.
Berbería, Barbary.
Berna, Bern.
Betania, Bethany.
Betsaida, Bethsaida.
Bitinia, Bithynia.
Bizancio, Byzantium.
Bojara, Bokhara, Bokhara.
Bolduque, Bois-le-Duc.
Bolonia, Bologna.
Boloña, Boulogne.
Bona, Bonn.
Borgoña, Burgundy.
Bósforo, Bosporus.
Botnia, Bothnia.
Brabante, Brabant.
Brandeburgo, Brandenburg.
Brasil, Brazil.
Brema, Bremen.
Brena, Brienne.
Bretaña, Bretagne, Brittany.

Bretaña (Gran), (Great) Britain.
Brujas, Bruges.
Brúnsvick, Brunswick, Braunschweig.
Bruselas, Brussels.
Bucarest, Bucharest.
Bucovina, Bukovina, Bukovina.
Bullón, Buillon.
Burdeos, Bordeaux.

C

Cabo Bretón, Cape Breton (Island).
Cabo de Buena Esperanza, Cape of Good Hope.
Cabo de Hornos, Cape Horn.
Cabo de Istria, Capo d'Istria.
Cabo de San Vicente, Cape Saint Vincent.
Cabo Haitiano, Cape Haitien.
Cachemira, Kashmir.
Cafarnaum, Capernaum.
Cafrería, Kaffraria.
Calcedonia, Chalcedon.
Calcuta, Calcutta.
Caldea, Chaldea.
Cambrige, Cambrigia, Cambridge.
Camerón, Camarones, Kamerún, Cameroons, Kamerun.
Canaán, Canaan.
Canal de la Mancha, English Channel.
Canarias, Canary (Islands).
Canosa, Canossa.
Cantórbery, Canterbury.
Carcasona, Carcassonne.
Carelia, Karelia.
Carenta, Charente.
Caribe. V. MAR CARIBE.
Cariñán, Carignano.
Carolina del Norte, North Carolina.
Carolina del Sur, South Carolina.
Cartagena, Carthagena.
Cartago, Carthage.
Caspio, Caspian (Sea).
Castilla, Castile.
Castilla la Nueva, New Castile.
Castilla la Vieja, Old Castile.
Cataluña, Catalonia.
Cáucaso, Caucasus.
Cayena, Cayenne.
Cayohueso, Cayo Hueso, Key West.

For pronunciation, see the rules at the beginning of the book.

Cayos de la Florida, Florida Keys.
Cebú. *V.* ZEBÚ.
Ceilán, Ceylon.
Cerdeña, Sardinia.
Cernauti, Cærnowitz.
Cesarea, Cæsarea.
Cevenes, Cevennes, Sevennes.
Cíclades, Cyclades.
Cidno, Cydnus.
Circasia, Circassia.
Coblenza, Coblenz.
Coburgo, Coburg.
Cochinchina, Cochin China.
Colonia, Cologne.
Colonia del Cabo, Cape Colony.
Columbia Británica, British Columbia.
Columnas de Hércules, Pillars of Hercules.
Comoras, Comoro Isles.
Compieña, Compiègne.
Constantina, Constantine.
Constantinopla, Constantinople.
Constanza, Constance.
Copenhague, Copenhagen.
Córcega, Corsica.
Córdoba, Cordova.
Corfú, Corfu.
Corinto, Corinth.
Cornualla, Cornwall.
Cortray, Courtray.
Coruña, Corunna.
Costa del Marfil, Ivory Coast.
Costa de Oro, Gold Coast.
Cotanza, Coutances.
Cracovia, Cracow.
Creta, Crete.
Cristianía, Christiania.
Croacia, Croatia.
Cronstadt, Kronstadt.
**Curasao, Curazao, Curaçao.
Curdistán, Kurdistan.
Curlandia, Kurland.

CH

Chamberí, Chambery.
Champaña, Champagne.
Chantung, Shantung.
Checoeslovaquia, Czecho-Slovakia, Czechoslovakia.
Cherburgo, Cherbourg.
Chifú, Chifu, Chefoo.
Chile, Chili, Chile.
Chipre, Cyprus.

D

Dakota del Norte, North Dakota.
Dakota del Sur, South Dakota.
Dalmacia, Dalmatia.
Damasco, Damascus.
Damieta, Damietta.
Danubio, Danube.
Dardanelos, Dardanelles.
Decán, Deccan.
Delfinado, Dauphiny, Dauphiné.
Delfos, Delphi.
Diepa, Diepe, Dieppe.
Dinamarca, Denmark.
Dniéper, Dnieper.
Dordoña, Dordogne.
Dos Puentes, Deux Ponts.
Dresde, Dresden.

Duay, Douay.
Duero, Douro.
Duina, Dwina, Dvina.
Dunas, Downs.
Dunquerque, Dunkirk.
Duvres, Dover.

E

Edimburgo, Edinburgh.
Efeso, Ephesus.
Egeo, Ægean.
Egina, Ægina.
Egipto, Egypt.
Egos Pótamos, Ægospotami.
Elba, Elbe.
Elbinga, Elbing.
Entre Duero y Miño, Entre Douro e Minho.
Eólida, Æolis.
Epiro, Epirus.
Erzerón, Erzerum.
Escafusa, Schaffhausen.
Escalda, Scheld, Scheldt.
Escamandro, Scamander.
Escandinavia, Scandinavia.
Escania, Scania.
Escio, Scio, Chio.
Esclavonia, Slavonia.
Escocia, Scotland.
Escorial, Escurial.
Escutari, Scutari.
Eslavonia, Slavonia.
Eslovaquia, Slovakia.
Eslovenia, Slovenia.
Esmalcalda, Smalcalden.
Esmirna, Smyrna.
España, Spain.
Española, Hispaniola.
Esparta, Sparta.
Espira, Spirea.
Espizberg, Espizberga, Spitzbergen.
Espoleto, Spoleto.
Establecimientos del Estrecho (de Malaca), Straits Settlements.
Estado Libre de Orange, Orange Free State.
Estados de la Iglesia, States of the Church.
Estados Federados de Malaca, Federated Malay States.
Estados Unidos de América, United States of America.
Estambul, Stambul.
Estiria, Styria.
Estocolmo, Stockholm.
Estonia, Esthonia.
Estrasburgo, Strasbourg.
Estrecho de Bella Isla, Strait of Belle Isle.
Estrecho de Magallanes, Strait of Magellan.
Estrómboli, Stromboli.
Etiopía, Ethiopia.
Etna, Etna, Ætna.
Etolia, Ætolia.
Eubea, Eubœa.
Eufrates, Euphrates.
Europa, Europe.

F

Farsalia, Pharsalia.
Fenicia, Phœnicia.
Filadelfia, Philadelphia.

Filipinas, Philippines.
Filipópolis, Philippopolis.
Filipos, Philippi.
Finlandia, Finland.
Flandes, Flanders.
Flesinga, Flushing.
Florencia, Florence.
Fócide, Phocis.
Francfort del Mein, Frankfort-on-the-Main.
Francia, France.
Franco Condado, Franche Comté.
Friburgo, Friburg, Freiburg.
Frigia, Phrygia.
Frisia, Friesland.
Frontiñac, Frontenac.

G

Gales, Wales.
Galia, Gaul.
Galilea, Galilee.
Galípoli, Gallipoli.
Gante, Ghent, Gand.
Garona, Garonne.
Gascuña, Gascony.
Génova, Genoa.
Germania, (anc. hist.) Germany.
Ginebra, Geneva.
Gironda, Gironde.
Glaris, Glarus.
Golfo Pérsico, Persian Gulf.
Gotemburgo, Gothenburg.
Gotinga, Göttingen.
Gran Bretaña, Great Britain.
Gránico, Granicus.
Gravelinas, Gravelines.
Grecia, Greece.
Groenlandia, Greenland.
Groninga, Groningen.
Guadalupe, Guadeloupe.
Guaján, Guam, Guam.
Guayana, Guiana.
Güeldres, Guelderland, Gelderland.
Guernesey, Guernsey.
Guidsé, Giza.
Guipúzcoa, Guipuscoa.
Guiena, Guienne.

H

Habana, Havana.
Haití, Haiti, Hayti.
Halicarnaso, Halicarnassus.
Hamburgo, Hamburg.
Hankao, Hankow.
Harrisburgo, Harrisburg.
Hauái, Hawaii.
Havre de Gracia, Havre de Grace.
Hawái, Hawaii.
Haya, Hague.
Hébridas, Hebrides.
Hélada, Hellas.
Helvecia, Helvetia.
Henao, Hainault.
Herculano, Herculaneum.
Heyaz, Hejaz.
Himeto, Hymettus.
Hispano-América, Hispano-américa, Spanish America.
Holanda, Holland.
Honduras Británica, British Honduras.
Hungría, Hungary.

For pronunciation, see the rules at the beginning of the book.

I

Ilión (Troya), Ilion, Ilium (Troy).
Iliria, Illyria.
Ilírico, Illyricum.
Indias, Indies.
Indias orientales, East Indies.
Indias occidentales, West Indies.
Indo, Indus.
Indostán, Hindustan, India.
Inglaterra, England.
Irlanda, Ireland.
Isla de Francia, Island of France, or Mauritius.
Isla de Guanahaní, Watling Island.
Isla del Cabo Bretón, Cape Breton Island.
Isla del Príncipe Eduardo, Prince Edward Island.
Isla de Pascua, Easter Island.
Isla Española, Hispaniola, Hayti.
Isla Real, Cape Breton Island.
Islandia, Iceland.
Islas Aleutas, or Aleutianas, Aleutian Islands.
Islas Baleares, Balearic Islands.
Islas Británicas, British Isles.
Islas Canarias, Canary Islands.
Islas Carolinas, Caroline Islands.
Islas de Barlovento, Windward Islands.
Islas de Hauái, Sandwich Islands.
Islas del Almirante, Admiralty Islands.
Islas de la Sociedad, Society Islands.
Islas de la Sonda, Sunda Isles.
Islas del Cabo Verde, Cape Verde Islands.
Islas de Sotavento, Leeward Islands.
Islas de Zetlandia, Shetland Islands.
Islas Filipinas, Philippine Islands.
Islas Hawái, Hawaiian Islands.
Islas Malvinas, Falkland Islands.
Islas Vírgenes, Virgin Islands.
Iso, Issus.
Ítaca, Ithaca.
Italia, Italy.

J

Janina, Yannina.
Japón, Japan.
Jarbin, Harbin.
Jartum, Khartoum.
Jericó, Jericho.
Jerusalén, Jerusalem.
Jiva, Khiva.
Jonia, Ionia.
Judá, Judah.
Jutlandia, Jutland.

K

Karbin, Harbin.
Kartum, Khartoum.
Kiao-Cheu, Kiaochow.
Kurdistán, Kurdistan.

L

Lacedemonia, Lacedæmon.
Lacio, Latium.
Lago de Constanza, Lake of Constance.
Lago Salado, Salt Lake.
Laponia, Lapland.
La Rochela, La Rochelle.
Lasa, Lassa.
Lausana, Lausanne.
Leida, Leide, Leiden, Leyden.
Lemosín, Limosin or Limousin.
Leningrado, Leningrad.
León de Francia, Lyons.
Leonesado, Lyonnais.
Líbano, Lebanon.
Libia, Libya.
Lieja, Liége.
Lila, Lille.
Limburgo, Limburg.
Liorna, Leghorn.
Lisboa, Lisbon.
Lituania, Lithuania.
Lombardía, Lombardy.
Londres, London.
Lorena, Lorraine.
Lovaina, Louvain.
Lucerna, Lucerne.
Luisiana, Louisiana.
Luxemburgo, Luxemburg.

M

Macedonia, Macedon, Macedonia.
Madera, Madeira.
Magallanes, Magellan.
Magna Grecia, Magna Græcia, Græcia Magna.
Maguncia, Mayence, Mainz.
Maisur, Mysore.
Malaca, Malay Peninsula.
Malasia, Malay Archipelago, Malaysia.
Maldivas, Maldives.
Malinas, Malines, Mecheln or Mechlin.
Malvinas, Falkland Islands.
Mallorca, Majorca.
Mancha (la) or Canal de la M., English Channel.
Mar Adriático, Adriatic Sea.
Mar Amarillo, Yellow Sea.
Mar Báltico, Baltic Sea.
Mar Blanco, White Sea.
Mar Caribe, Caribbean Sea.
Mar Caspio, Caspian Sea.
Mar de la China, China Sea.
Mar de las Antillas = MAR CARIBE.
Mar de las Indias, Indian Ocean.
Mar del Norte, North Sea.
Mar Egeo, Ægean Sea.
Mar Glacial, Frozen Sea.
Mar Jónico, Ionian Sea.
Mar Mediterráneo, Mediterranean Sea.
Mar Muerto, Dead Sea.
Mar Negro, Black Sea.
Mar Rojo, Red Sea.
Mar Tirreno, Tyrrhenian Sea.
Marañón, (upper reaches of the) Amazon.
Maratón, Marathon.
Marruecos, Morocco.
Marsella, Marseilles.

Martinica, Martinique.
Mauricia, Mauritius or Island of France.
Mayena, Mayenne.
Meca, Mecca.
Mediterráneo, Mediterranean.
Méjico, Mexico.
Menfis, Memphis.
Menorca, Minorca.
Mesia, Mœsia.
Metauro, Metaurus.
Micenas, Mycenæ.
Midelburgo, Middleburg.
Milanesado, Milanese.
Miño, Minho.
Mirándula, Mirandola.
Misisipí, Mississippi.
Misora, Mysore.
Mobila, Mobile.
Mompeller, Montpellier.
Mondoñedo, Mondonned or Mondoneda.
Mongibelo = ETNA.
Monserrate, Montserrat.
Monte Oliveto, Olives (Mount of), Olivet.
Montes Alleghanys, Allegheny Mountains.
Montes Apalaches, Appalachian Mountains.
Montes Balcanes, Balkan Mountains.
Montes Carpacios, or Cárpatos, Carpathian Mountains.
Montes Rocallosos, M. Rocosos, Rocky Mountains.
Montes Urales, Ural Mountains.
Morlés, Morlaix.
Mosa, Meuse.
Moscovia, Muscovy.
Moscú, Moscow.
Mosela, Moselle.
Muerto, Dead (Sea).

N

Nápoles, Naples.
Narbona, Narbonne.
Navarino, Navarin.
Navarra, Navarre.
Nazaret, Nazareth.
Negro, Black (Sea).
Neoburgo, Neuburg.
Neoport, Nieuport.
Neyed, Nejd or Nedjed.
Nicea, Nicæa.
Niéper, Dnieper.
Nifón, Nippon.
Nigricia, Negroland.
Nilo, Nile.
Nimega, Nimeguen.
Nínive, Nineveh.
Nipón, Nippon.
Niza, Nice.
Normandía, Normandy.
Noruega, Norway.
Nueva Escocia, Novia Scotia.
Nueva Gales, New Wales.
Nueva Gales del Sur, New South Wales.
Nueva Inglaterra, New England.
Nueva Orleáns, New Orleans.
Nueva York, New York.
Nueva Zelandia, New Zealand.
Nueva Zembla, Nova Zembla.

Nuevo Brúnswick, N. Brúnsvick, New Brunswick.
Numancia, Numantia.
Nuremberga, Nuremberg.

O

Oceanía, Oceania, Oceanica.
Odenarda, Oudenarde.
Odesa, Odessa.
Ofir, Ophir.
Olimpia, Olympia.
Olimpo, Olympus.
Olinto, Olynthus.
Omán, Muscat, Maskat.
Onella, Oneglia.
Orleanesado, Orleannois.
Ostende, Ostend.
Otahití, Otaheite or Tahiti.
Oxo, Oxus.

P

Pacífico, Pacific (Ocean).
Países Bajos, Low Countries, Netherlands, Holland.
Palatinado, Palatinate.
Palestina, Palestine.
Palmira, Palmyra.
Pamplona, Pampeluna.
Panfilia, Pamphylia.
Panzacola, Pensacola.
Parnaso, Parnassus.
Partia, Parthia.
Paso de Calais, Strait of Dover.
Pekín, Pekin.
Pela, Pella.
Peloponeso, Peloponnesus.
Península de Malaca, Malay Peninsula.
Pensilvania, Pennsylvania.
Penzacola, Pensacola.
Pérgamo, Pergamum.
Perona, Peronne.
Perpiñán, Perpignan.
Perusa, Perusia or Perugia.
Petrogrado, Petrograd.
Piamonte, Piedmont.
Picardía, Picardy.
Piombina, Piombino.
Pireo, Piræus.
Pirineos, Pyrenees.
Pistoya, Pistoja.
Plasencia, Placentia.
Platea, Platæa.
Polinesia, Polynesia.
Polonia, Poland.
Pombín, Piombino.
Pompeya, Pompeii.
Ponto, Pontus.
Ponto Euxino, Pontus Euxinus (Black Sea).
Porto Longón, Porto Longone.
Praga, Prague.
Presburgo, Presburg.
Provenza, Provence.
Providencia, Providence.
Provincias Renanas, Rhineland.
Provincias Vascongadas, or Vascas, Basque Provinces.
Prusia, Prussia.
Puertas de Hierro, Iron Gates.
Puerto Arturo, Port Arthur.
Puerto (de) España, Port of Spain.
Puerto Mahón, Port Mahon.
Puerto Príncipe, Port-au-Prince.

Puerto Rico, Porto Rico, Puerto Rico.

Q

Queronea, Chæronea.
Quersoneso, Chersonese.
Quinsala, Kinsale.
Quío, Chio.

R

Rapanuí, Easter Island.
Ratisbona, Ratisbon, Regensburg.
Regio, Reggio.
Reims, Rheims.
Reino Unido, United Kingdom.
Retia, Rhætia.
Rhin, Rhine.
Rif, Rif or Riff.
Rin, Rhine.
Río Amarillo, Yellow River.
Rocamora, Roquemaure.
Rochela (La), (La) Rochelle.
Ródano, Rhone.
Rodas, Rhodas.
Rodesia, Rhodesia.
Rojo, Red (Sea).
Roma, Rome.
Romaña, Romagna.
Rosellón, Roussillon.
Roseta, Rosetta.
Ruán, Rouen.
Rumania, R(o)umania.
Ruremunda, Roermond or Ruremunde.
Rusia, Russia.

S

Sabá, Sheba.
Saboya, Savoy.
Sácer, Sassari.
Sajonia, Saxony.
Sajonia-Coburgo, Saxe-Coburg.
Sajonia-Gotha, Saxe-Gotha.
Sajonia-Wéimar, Saxe-Weimar.
Salamina, Salamis.
Salé, Sallee.
Salónica, Salonika.
Samotracia, Samothrace.
San Cristóbal, St. Kitts.
San Germán, St. Germain.
San Gotardo, St. Gothard.
San Juan de Luz, St. Jean de Luz.
San Kitts, St. Kitts.
San Nazario, St. Nazaire.
San Petersburgo, St. Petersburg.
San Quintín, St. Quentin.
San Salvador (Isla de), Watling Island.
Santa Elena, St. Helena.
Santa Lucía, St. Lucia.
Santonge, Saintonge.
Sarmacia, Sarmatia.
Sena, Seine.
Servia, Serbia.
Servia - Croacia - Eslovenia, Serb-Croat-Slovene State.
Seúl, Seoul.
Sevilla, Seville.
Severna, Severn.
Sicilia, Sicily.
Sierra Leona, Sierra Leone.
Siracusa, Syracuse.

Siria, Syria.
Socotera, Socotora, Socotra.
Soleura, Soleure.
Somalia, Somaliland.
Suabia, Suabia or Swabia.
Sud-África, Sudáfrica, South Africa.
Sud-América, Sudamérica, South America.
Sudán, Soudan, Sudan.
Suebia = Suabia.
Suecia, Sweden.
Suiza, Switzerland.
Sund, Sound.
Sur-América, or Suramérica, South America.

T

Tabago, Tobago.
Tafilete, Tafilet.
Tahití, Tahiti.
Tajo, Tagus.
Tamatava, Tamatave.
Támesis, Thames.
Tanganyica, Tangañica, Lake Tanganyika.
Tánger, Tangier.
Tapso, Thapsus.
Tarento, Taranto.
Tarso, Tarsus.
Tartaria, Tartary, Tatary.
Tauro, Taurus.
Tebas, Thebes.
Tejas, Texas.
Tenerife, Teneriffe.
Termópilas, Thermopylæ.
Terranova, Newfoundland.
Tesalia, Thessaly.
Tesalónica, Thessalonica.
Tesino, Ticino.
Tiberíades, Tiberias.
Tibet, Thibet, Tibet.
Tierra de Francisco José, Franz Josef Island.
Tierra del Labrador, Labrador.
Tierra Santa, Holy Land.
Tiro, Tyre.
Tirol, Tyrol.
Tokío, Tokyo, Tokio.
Tolón, Toulon.
Tolosa, Toulouse.
Tornay, Tournay.
Toscana, Tuscany.
Trabizonda, Trebizond.
Tracia, Thrace.
Trasimeno, Thrasimene.
Trebizonda, Trebizond.
Trento, Trent.
Tréveris, Treves, Trier.
Trieste, Triest.
Troya, Troy.
Tubinga, Tubingen.
Túnez, Tunis.
Turena, Turenne.
Turquestán, Turkestan.
Turquía, Turkey.
Turs, Tours.
Túsculo, Tusculum.

U

Uberlinga, Uberlingen.
Ucrania, Ukraine.
Ulma, Ulm.
Undervald, Unterwalden.
Unión Soviética, Soviet Union.

For pronunciation, see the rules at the beginning of the book.

ión Sudafricana, Union of South Africa.
RSS, USSR.

V

alaquia, Wallachia.
alclusa, Vaucluse.
alencia, Valence (France); Valencia (Spain).
alencienes, Valenciennes.
altelina, Valtelline.
andoma, Vendome.
arenas, Varennes.
arsovia, Warsaw.
enecia, Venice.
eneto, Venetia.

Versalles, Versailles.
Vestfalia, Westphalia.
Vesuvio, Vesuvius.
Viena, Vienne (France); Vienna (Austria).
Villafranca, Villefranche.
Vincenas, Vincennes.
Virginia Occidental, West Virginia.
Vizcaya, Biscay.
Vosgos, Vosges.

W

Wartburgo, Wartburg.
Westfalia, Westphalia.
Wurtemberg, Würtemburg.

Y

Yedo, Jeddo, Yeddo.
Yeso, Yesso.
Yugoeslavia, Yugoslavia, Jugoslavia.

Z

Zambese, Zambeze, Zambesi.
Zanguébar, Zanzíbar, Zanzibar.
Zaragoza, Saragossa.
Zebú, Zebu.
Zelandia, Zealand.
Zululandia, Zululand.

NAMES OF PERSONS, INCLUDING THOSE OF FAMOUS HISTORICAL PERSONAGES

A

belardo, Abelard.
orahán, Abrán, Abraham.
bsalón, Absalom.
bubéker, Abu-Bekr.
dán, Adam.
dela, Adele.
delaida, Adelaide.
delina, Adeline.
dolfo, Adolphus.
driano, Hadrian.
gata, Agatha.
gripina, Agrippina.
gueda, Agatha.
gustín, Augustin, Austin.
lano, Alan, Allen.
larico, Alaric.
lberto, Albert.
lberto Magno, Albertus Magnus.
lceo, Alcæus.
lejandra, Alexandra.
lejandro, Alexander.
lejo, Alexis.
lfonso, Alphonse.
lfredo, Alfred.
licia, Alice.
lonso, Alphonsus.
luino, Alwin.
madeo, Amadeus.
mata, Amy.
mbrosio, Ambrose, Ambrosius.
melia, Amelie.
na, Ann, Anne, Anna, Hannah.
na Bolena, Anne Boleyn.
nacreonte, Anacreon.
ndrés, Andrew.
níbal, Hannibal.
nselmo, Anselm.
ntígono, Antigonus.
ntíoco, Antiochus.
ntonino, Antoninus.
ntonio, Anthony.
quiles, Achilles.
puleyo, Apuleius.
rabela, Arabella.
rchibaldo, Archibald.
ristófanes, Aristophanes.
ristóteles, Aristotle.
rnaldo, Arnold.
rquimedes, Archimedes.

Arturo, Arthur.
Arriano, Arrian.
Arrio, Arius.
Artajerjes, Artaxerxes.
Asurbanipal, Ashur-bani-pal.
Atanasio, Athanasius.
Atila, Attila.
Augusto, Augustus.
Aureliano, Aurelian.
Aurelio, Aurelius.

B

Bárbara, Barbara.
Bartolomé, Bartholomew, Bartholomæus.
Basilio, Basil.
Beatriz, Beatrix, Beatrice.
Beda, Bæda, Bede.
Belisario, Belisarius.
Beltrán, Bertram.
Benita, Benedicta.
Benito, Benedict.
Bermudo, Veremond.
Bernabé, Barnabas, Barnaby.
Bernardo, Bernard.
Bernardino, Bernardinus.
Berta, Bertha.
Betsabé, Bath-Sheba.
Blas, Blase.
Bocaccio, Bocacio, Boccaccio, Boccace.
Bonifacio, Boniface.
Brígida, Bridget.
Bruto, Brutus.
Buda, Buddha.
Buenaventura, Bonaventure.

C

Calvino, Calvin.
Cambises, Cambyses.
Camilla, Camilla, Camille.
Camilo, Camillus.
Caracala, Caracalla.
Carlomagno, Charlemagne.
Carlos, Charles.
Carlota, Charlotte.
Carolina, Caroline.
Casandra, Cassandra.
Casimiro, Casimir.
Casio, Cassius.
Catalina, Catharine.
Catilina, Catiline.

Catón, Cato.
Catulo, Catullus.
Cayetano, Cajetan, Gaetan.
Cecilia, Cicely.
Cecilio, Cecil.
César, Cæsar.
Cicerón, Cicero.
Cincinato, Cincinnatus.
Cipriano, Cyprian.
Ciriaco, Cyriacus.
Cirilo, Cyrilus.
Ciro, Cyrus.
Claudia, Claudina, Claudia.
Claudio, Claude, Claudius.
Cleanto, Cleanthes.
Clemente, Clement.
Cleóbulo, Cleobulus.
Clodoveo, Clovis.
Clotilde, Clotilda.
Colón, Columbus.
Cómodo, Commodus.
Confucio, Confucius.
Conrado, Conrad.
Constancia, Constancio, Constance.
Constantino, Constantine.
Constanza, Constance.
Cornelio, Cornelius.
Cosme, Cosmas.
Creso, Crœsus.
Crisóstomo, Chrysostom.
Cristiano, Christian.
Cristina, Christina.
Cristo, Christ.
Cristóbal, Christopher.
Curcio, Curtius.

D

Dagoberto, Dagobert.
Darío, Darius.
Demócrito, Democritus.
Demóstenes, Demosthenes.
Diego, James.
Diógenes, Diogenes.
Dionisia, Dionysia.
Dionisio, Dennis, Dionysius.
Domiciano, Domitian.
Domingo, Dominic.
Dorotea, Dorothy.

E

Edmundo, Edmund.

For pronunciation, see the rules at the beginning of the book.

Eduardo, Edward.
Eduvigis, Hedwig.
Elagábalo, Elagabalus.
Elena, Ellen, Helen.
Elisa, Eliza.
Eliseo, Elisha, Ellis.
Eloísa, Heloise.
Ema, Emma.
Emilia, Emily.
Emilio, Æmilius.
Eneas, Æneas.
Engracia, Grace.
Enrique, Henry.
Enriqueta, Henrietta.
Epicteto, Epictetus.
Epicurus, Epicuro.
Erasmo, Erasmus.
Eratóstenes, Eratosthenes.
Ernesto, Ernest.
Escalígero, Scaliger.
Escipión, Scipio.
Escipión el Africano, Scipio Africanus.
Esopo, Æsop.
Espartaco, Spartacus.
Esquilo, Æschylus.
Esquines, Æschines.
Esteban, Stephen.
Ester, Esther, Hester.
Estrabón, Strabo.
Estradivario, Stradivarius.
Euclides, Euclid.
Eufemia, Euphemia.
Eufrosina, Euphrosyne.
Eugenia, Eugenie.
Eugenio, Eugene.
Euler, Eulero, Euler.
Eusebio, Eusebius.
Eustaquio, Eustace.
Eva, Eve, Eva.
Ezequías, Hezekiah.
Ezequiel, Ezekiel.

F

Fabio, Fabius.
Federica, Frederica.
Federico, Frederic.
Fedra, Phedre.
Fedro, Phædrus.
Felipa, Philippa.
Felipe, Philip.
Felisa, Felicia, Felicia.
Fernando, Ferdinand.
Filipo, Philip (of Macedon), Philippus.
Filo el Judío, Philo Judæus.
Fineas, Phineas.
Florencia, Florencio, Florence.
Foción, Phocion.
Francisca, Frances.
Francisco, Francis.
Fredegunda, Fredegonde.
Froíla, Fruela, Froyla.

G

Galeno, Galen.
Galieno, Gallienus.
Gaspar, Jasper.
Gayo, Gaius.
Gedeón, Gideon.
Genserico, Genseric.
Geofredo, Geoffrey.
Gerardo, Gerard.
Germánico, Germanicus.
Gertrudis, Gertrude.
Gervasio, Gervas.
Gil, Giles.

Gilberto, Gilbert.
Godofredo, Gofredo, Godfrey.
Graco, Gracchus.
Gracos, Gracchi.
Gregorio, Gregory.
Gualterio, Gualtero, Walter.
Guido, Guy.
Guillelmo, Guillén, William.
Guillermina, Wilhelmina.
Guillermo, William.
Gustavo, Gustavus.

H

Haroldo, Harold.
Heberto, Herbert.
Heliogábalo, Elagabalus.
Helvecio, Helvetius.
Heráclito, Heraclitus.
Heriberto, Herbert.
Herodes, Herod.
Herodoto, Herodotus.
Herón, Hiero.
Hesíodo, Hesiod.
Hilario, Hilary.
Hildebrando, Hildebrand.
Hiparco, Hipparchus.
Hipócrates, Hippocrates.
Homero, Homer.
Honorio, Honorius.
Horacio, Horace, Horatio.
Hortensia, Hortense.
Huberto, Hobart, Hubert.
Hugo, Hugh.
Hugo Capeto, Hugh Capet.
Humberto, Humbert.
Hunfredo, Humphrey.

I

Ignacio, Ignatius.
Ildefonso, Alphonsus.
Inés, Agnes, Inez.
Inocencio, Innocent.
Ireneo, Ireneus.
Isabel, Elizabeth.
Isidoro, Isidro, Isidor.

J

Jacobo, Jaime, James.
Jansenio, Jansen, Jansenius.
Javier, Xavier.
Jehová, Jehovah.
Jenócrates, Xenocrates.
Jenófanes, Xenophanes.
Jenofonte, Xenophon.
Jeremías, Jeremy, Jeremiah.
Jerjes, Xerxes.
Jerónimo, Jerome.
Jesús, Jesus.
Jesucristo, Jesus Christ.
Joaquín, Joachim.
Jonás, Jonah.
Jonatán, Jonatás, Jonathan.
Jorge, George.
José, Joseph.
Josefa, Josefina, Josephine.
Josefo, Josephus.
Josías, Josiah.
Josué, Joshua.
Joviano, Jovian.
Juan, John.
Juana, Jane, Jennie, Jean, Joan, Joanna.
Juana de Arco, Joan of Arc.
Judit, Judith.
Julia, Julia.

Julián; Juliano (empero Julian.
Julio, Julius.
Justiniano, Justinian.
Justino, Justin.
Justino Mártir, Justin Ma tyr.

K

(de) Kempis, (a) Kempis.

L

Ladislao, Ladislas.
Lamberto, Lambert.
Lázaro, Lazarus.
Leandro, Leander.
León, Leo, Leon.
Leonardo, Leonard.
Leonor, Eleanor.
Leopoldo, Leopold.
Leticia, Lætitia, Letitia, Le tice.
Licurgo, Lycurgus.
Lineo, Linnæus.
Lisandro, Lysander.
Lisias, Lysias.
Lisímaco, Lysimachus.
Lisipo, Lysippus.
Liutprando, Liutprand.
Livio, Livy.
Longino, Longinus.
Lorenzo, Lawrence, Laurenc
Lotario, Lothaire.
Lucano, Lucan.
Lucas, Luke.
Lucía, Lucy, Lucia.
Luciano, Lucian.
Lucio, Lucius.
Lucrecia, Lucretia.
Lucrecio, Lucretius.
Luis, Lewis, Louis.
Luis (Gonzaga), Aloysius.
Luisa, Louise.
Lutero, Luther.

M

Magallanes, Magellan.
Magdalena, Magdalen.
Mahoma, Mahomet, Moham med.
Malaquías, Malachi.
Manuel, Emanuel.
Manuela, Emma.
Marcelo, Marcellus.
Marcial, Martial.
Marco, Marcos, Mark.
Marco Aurelio, Marcus Aure lius.
Margarita, Margaret, Mar gery.
María, Mary, Maria, Miriam
María Luisa, Marie Louise.
Mariana, Marian.
Mario, Marius.
Marta, Martha.
Masinisa, Masinissa.
Mateo, Matthew.
Matías, Mattias.
Matilde, Matilda.
Mauricio, Maurice, Morice.
Maximiliano, Maximilian.
Mecenas, Mæcenas.
Mesalina, Messalina.
Miguel, Michael.
Miguel Ángel, Michelangelo
Mitrídates, Mithridates.
Moisés, Moses.

For pronunciation, see the rules at the beginning of the book.

N

Nabucodonosor, Nebuchad-
  nezzar.
Nápier, Napier.
Natán, Nathan.
Nataniel, Nathaniel.
Nehemías, Nehemiah.
Néper, Napier.
Népote, Nepos.
Nerón, Nero.
Nestorio, Nestorius.
Nicolás, Nicholas.
Noé, Noah.

O

Octavio, Octavius.
Odoacro, Odoacer.
Oliverio, Oliver.
Orígenes, Origen.
Oseas, Hosea.
Osmundo, Osmond.
Otman, Othman.
Otón, Otho.
Ovidio, Ovid.

P

Pablo, Paul.
Patricio, Patrick.
Paula, Paulina, Pauline.
Pedro, Peter.
Pepino, Pepin.—**P. el Breve,**
  Pepin the Short.
Peregrín, or **Peregrino,** Pere-
  grine.
Perseo, Perseus.
Píndaro, Pindar.
Pío, Pius.
Pirro, Pyrrhus.
Pitágoras, Pythagoras.
Platón, Plato.
Plauto, Plautus.
Plinio, Pliny.
Plótino, Plotinus.
Plutarco, Plutarch.
Polibio, Polybius.
Policarpo, Polycarp.
Policleto, Polycletus.
Polícrates, Polycrates.
Pompeyo, Pompey.
Pretorio, Pretorius.
Proclo, Proclus.
Procopio, Procopius.
Prudencia, Prudence.

Q

Quintiliano, Quintilian.
Quintín, Quintin, Quentin.

R

Rafael, Raphael.
Raimundo, Ramón, Ray-
  mond.
Randolfo, Randolph.
Raquel, Rachel.
Rebeca, Rebecca.
Reginaldo, Reginald.
Régulo, Regulus.
Reinaldo, Reynold.
Renaldo, Ronald.
Renato, René.
Ricardo, Richard.
Roberto, Robert.
Rodas, Rhodes.
Rodolfo, Rodolphus, Ralph,
  Rudolph, Rollo.
Rodrigo, Roderic.
Roger, Rogerio, Roger.
Rolando, Roland, Rowland.
Rolón, Rollón, Rollo.
Rómulo, Romulus.
Rosa, Rose.
Rosalía, Rosalie.
Rosamunda, Rosamond.
Rosario, Rosary.
Ruben, Reuben.
Rufo, Rufus.
Ruperto, Rupert.

S

Saladino, Saladin.
Salomón, Solomon.
Salustio, Sallust.
Samuel, Samuel.
Sansón, Samson.
Santiago, James, St. James.
Sara, Sarah.
Sardanápalo, Sardanapalus.
Senaquerib, Sennacherib.
Sertorio, Sertorius.
Severo, Severus.
Sigismundo, Sigismund.
Sila, Sulla.
Silvano, Silvan.
Silvestre, Silvester.
Sofía, Sophia, Sophy.
Sófocles, Sophocles.
Solimán, Solyman, Suleiman.
Suetonio, Suetonius.
Susana, Susan, Susanna.

T

Tácito, Tacitus.
Tadeo, Thadeus.
Tales, Thales.

Tamerlán, Tamerlane.
Temístocles, Themistocles.
Teobaldo, Theobald, Tybold.
Teócrito, Theocritus.
Teodora, Theodora.
Teodoro, Theodore.
Teodorico, Theodoric, Dorick.
Teodosio, Theodosius.
Teófilo, Theophilus.
Teofrasto, Theophrastus.
Terencio, Terence.
Teresa, Theresa.
Tertuliano, Tertullian.
Tiberio, Tiberius.
Tíbulo, Tibullus.
Ticiano, Titian.
Timoteo, Timothy.
Timur, Timour.
Tito, Titus.
Tobías, Tobias, Toby.
Tolomeo, Ptolemy.
Tomás, Thomas.
Trajano, Trajan.
Trasíbulo, Thrasybulus.
Triboniano, Tribonian.
Tucídides, Thucydides.
Turena, Turenne.

U

Ulpiano, Ulpian.
Urbano, Urban.
Urías, Uriah.

V

Valente, Valens.
Valentín, Valentine.
Valentiniano, Valentinian.
Valeriano, Valerian.
Ventura, Bonaventura.
Veremundo, Veremond.
Veronés, Veronese.
Vespasiano, Vespasian.
Vespucio, Vespucci.
Vicente, Vincent.
Virgilio, Virgil, Vergil.
Vitruvio, Vitruvius.

Y

Yugurta, Jugurtha.

Z

Zacarías, Zachary, Zachariah.
Zenón, Zeno.
Zoroastro, Zoroaster.
Zuinglio, Zwingli.

COLLOQUIAL PET NAMES

Adela, Adelita, Adelina.
Ana, Anita, Anica.
Antonio, nia, Antoñito, ta;
  Toño, ña; Toñico, ca.
Bartolomé, Bartolo.
Carlos, Carlitos.
Catalina, Catana, Catuca,
  Catuja.
Cayetano, Tano.
Cristóbal, Tobal, Tobalito.

Diego, Dieguito.
Dolores. _V._ MARÍA DE LOS
  DOLORES.

Francisco, Francisquito;
  Frasco, Frascuelo, Frasquito;
  Paquito, Paco; Pacorro;
  Pancho, Panchito; Curro,
  Currito; Farruco.
Francisca (the same words as

the preceding, changing final
  _o_ to _a_).
Gertrudis, Tula.
Gregorio, Goyo.
Isabel, Belica, Belita.
Jaime, Jaimito.
José, Joseíto, Josecito; Pepe,
  Pepito; Pepillo; Chepe, Che-
  pito.

For pronunciation, see the rules at the beginning of the book.

Josefa, Josefita; Pepa, Pepita, Pepilla; Chepa, Chepita.
Juan, Juanito, Juanillo.
Juana, Juanita, Juanilla.
María, Mariquita, Mariquilla, Marica, Maruca, Marucha, Maruja.

María de la Concepción, Concha, Conchita; Chona, Cota, Cotita.
María, (de) Jesús, Jesusa, Jesusita, Chucha, Chuchita.

María de los Dolores, Doloritas, Dolorcitas, Lola, Lolita
María de la Luz, Lucecita Lucita.
Pedro, Pedrito, Perico.

For pronunciation, see the rules at the beginning of the book.

ABBREVIATIONS MOST COMMONLY USED IN SPANISH

A

. Alteza; aprobado (passed in examination).
, área (are).
a) alias.
@ arroba; @@ arrobas.
A. Autores; Altezas.
b. abad.
b.l abril.
bls. gen. Absolución general.
. C., A. de C. Año de Cristo (A.D.).
dmón. administración.
dmor., adm.or administrador.
f.mo, afmo. afectísimo.
f.to afecto.
.g.n Agustín.
la v/ a la vista.
g.to agosto.
lc.de alcalde.
lej.o Alejandro.
lf.o Alfonso.
l.o Alonso.
. L. R. P. de V. M. A los reales pies de Vuestra Majestad.
Alv.o Álvaro.
.m.o amigo.
Ant.o Antonio.
p. aparte; apóstol.
.p.a, ap.o or aplica., aplico. apostólica, apostólico.
apóst. apóstol.
rt., art.o artículo.
rz., arzbpo. arzobispo.
tt.o, atto. atento.
Aud.a Audiencia.

B

3. Beato; Bueno, en examen.
3ar.mé Bartolomé.
>ca. barrica.
3arna. Barcelona.
3ern.o Bernardo.
3. L. M., b. l. m. besa la mano.
3. L. P., b. l. p. besa los pies.
3.mo P.e Beatísimo Padre.
3r. or br. bachiller.
>to. bulto; bruto.

C

c/ cargo; contra.
C. A. corriente alterna.
c.a compañía.

c., cap. capítulo.
cap.n capitán.
capp.n capellán.
Card.l Cardenal.
C. C. corriente continua.
C. de J. Compañía de Jesús (S. J.).
cénts. céntimos.
cf., conf., confr. confesor; confirma (in ancient documents).
cg. centigramo(s.
C.ia Compañía (Co.).
cl. centilitro(s.
Clem.te Clemente.
cllo. cuartillo.
cm. centímetro(s.
C. M. B., c. m. b. cuyas manos beso.
Co. Compañía (Co.).
col., col.a columna; colonia.
comis.o comisario.
comp. compañía.
cons.o consejo.
Const. Constitución.
const.l constitucional.
conv.te conveniente.
corr.te corriente.
C. P. B. cuyos pies beso.
crec.te creciente.
cs. cuartos; céntimos.
cta., c.ta cuenta.
cta. cte., cta. corr.te cuenta corriente.
c/u cado uno.
cuad. cuadrado(s.
c/vta. cuenta de venta.

D

D. Don.
D.a Doña.
DD. doctores.
descto. descuento.
d/f días fecha.
dg. decigramo(s.
Dg. decagramo(s.
dha., dho., dhas., dhos. dicha, dicho, dichas, dichos.
dic.e, 10e or 10bre diciembre.
Dl. decalitro(s.
dl. decilitro(s.
dls. dólares ($).
Dm. decámetro(s.
dm. decímetro(s.
D.n, d.n don.
Doct., Doctor.

docum.to documento.
D. O. M. *Deo Optimo Maximo*.
Dom.o Domingo (name).
dom.o domingo (Sunday).
d/p días plazo.
D.r, Dr. Doctor (Dr.).
dra., dro., dras., dros. derecha, derecho, derechas, derechos.
dup.do duplicado.
d/v días vista.

E

E. este, oriente (East).
ec.co eclesiástico.
EE. UU. Estados Unidos.
E. M. Estado Mayor.
Em.a Eminencia.
E.| M. G. Estado Mayor General.
Em.mo, Emmo. Eminentísimo.
ENE. estenordeste (E.N.E.).
en.o enero.
E. P. D. En paz descanse.
E. P. M. En propia mano.
esc.o escudo.
escrit.a escritura.
escrnía. escribanía.
escrno. escribano.
escs. escudos.
ESE. estesudeste (E.S.E.).
etc. etcétera.
E. U., E. U. A. U. S., U. S. A.
Eug.o Eugenio.
Evang.o Evangelio.
Evang.ta Evangelista.
Exc.a Excelencia.
Exc.ma, Exc.mo or Excma, Excmo. Excelentísima, Excelentísimo.

F

f/ fardo(s.
F. Fulano.
fact.a factura.
F. C., f. c. ferrocarril.
F.co, Franc.o Francisco.
fcos. francos.
F. de T. Fulano de Tal.
feb.o febrero.
F. E. M. fuerza electromotriz (E.M.F.).
Fern.do Fernando.
fha., fho. fecha, fecho.
fo.o, fol. folio.

For pronunciation, see the rules at the beginning of the book.

Fr. Fray, Frey.
fra. factura.
Frnz., Fz. Fernández.
F.ª, f.ª francos.
fund. fundador.

G

G. gracia.
g. gramo(s.
g.de or gue. guarde.
Gen.¹ General (title).
gnte., gerente.
G.º Gonzalo.
gob.º gobierno.
gob.ʳ gobernador.
Gonz. González.
gral. general.
Greg.º Gregorio.
gte. gerente.
Guill.º Guillermo.

H

hect. hectárea(s.
Hg. hectogramo(s.
Hl. hectolitro(s.
Hm. hectómetro(s.
HP, H. P. caballo(s) de vapor (H.P.).

I

ib. ibídem.
id. ídem.
i. e. id est (that is).
igl.ª iglesia.
Ign.º Ignacio.
Ildef.º Ildefonso.
Il.ᵉ Ilustre.
Il.ᵐᵃ, Il.ᵐᵒ, Illma, Illmo. Ilustrísima, Ilustrísimo.
in p. inf. in partibus infidelium.
inq.ʳ inquisidor.
intend.ᵗᵉ intendente.
ít. ítem.
Izq.ª, Izq.º, Izq.dª, Izq.dº izquierda, izquierdo.

J

J. C. Jesucristo.
Jerón.º Jerónimo.
Jhs. Jesús.
Jph. José.
juev. jueves.
Jul.ⁿ Julián.

K

Kg., kg. kilogramo(s.
Kl., kl. kilolitro(s.

Km., km. kilómetro(s.
kv., k. w. kilovatio.

L

L/ letra.
L., L.do or I.do Licenciado.
l. ley; libro; litro(s.
lb̄(s̄. libra(s.
lín. línea.
liq.ⁿ liquidación.
Lor.ᶻᵒ Lorenzo.
L. S. Locus sigilli, lugar del sello.
lun. lunes.

M

M. Madre, religiosa; Majestad; Merced; Maestro; mediano (en examen).
m. minuto(s; metro(s; mañana (A.M.).
m/ mes; mi, mis; mío, míos.
Man.¹ Manuel.
M.ª María.
Marg.ᵗᵃ Margarita.
mart. martes.
may.ᵐᵒ mayordomo.
mcos. marcos.
M.ᵉ Madre, religiosa.
m/f mi favor.
meng. menguante.
mg. miligramo(s.
miérc. miércoles.
Mig.¹ Miguel.
miles.ˢ milesimas.
min.º ministro.
m/L. mi letra.
ml. mililitros.
Mm. miriámetro(s.
mm., m/m milímetro(s.
m/o mi orden.
m/o m más o menos.
monast.º monasterio.
Mons. Monseñor.
M. P. S. Muy Poderoso Señor.
Mr. Monsieur; Mister.
mrd. merced.
Mrn̄. Martín.
Mrn̄z. Martínez.
Mro. Maestro.
M.ˢ marcos.
M. S. manuscrito.
m.ˢ a.ˢ muchos años.
M.SS. manuscritos.

N

N. Norte.
n. noche (P.M.).
n/ nuestro.
N.ª S.ª Nuestra Señora.

N.B. Nota bene.
n/cta. nuestra cuenta.
NE. Nordeste (N.E.).
NNE. Nornordeste (N.N.E.)
NNO. Nornoroeste (N.N.W.)
NO. Noroeste (N.W.).
n.º número.
nov.ᵉ, 9ᵉ, 9ᵇʳᵉ noviembre.
Nov. Recop. Novísima Recopilación.
N. Recop. Nueva Recopilación.
nra., nr̄o., nras., nr̄os. **ntra., ntr̄o., ntras., ntros** nuestra, nuestro, nuestras nuestros.
núm. or núm.º, núms. o **núm.ˢ** número, números.
N. S. Nuestro Señor.
N. S. J. C. Nuestro Señor Jesucristo.
nto. neto.

O

O. Oeste (W.).
o/ orden.
ob., ob̄po. obispo.
oct.ᵉ, 8ᵉ or 8ᵇʳᵉ octubre.
ONO. oesnoroeste (W.N.W.)
onz. onza.
orn. orden.
OSO. oessudoeste (W.S.W.)

P

P. Papa (Pope); padre; pregunta.
p % por ciento (%).
p %o por mil.
p. A. Por ausencia; por autorización.
P.ª para.
pág., págs. página(s.
Part. Partida.
Patr. Patriarca.
p.ᵇʳᵒ presb. presbítero.
P. D. Posdata (P.S.).
P.ᵉ Padre.
p. ej. por ejemplo (e. g.).
penit. penitente.
perg., pno. pergamino.
Pf., Pfs. peso(s fuerte(s.
P. M. Padre Maestro.
P. O. Por orden.
P.º Pedro.
p.º pero.
P. P. Porte pagado; por poder.
p. p.dº, ppdo. próximo pasado.
p.ʳ por.

For pronunciation, see the rules at the beginning of the book.

ral. principal.
riv. privilegio.
roc. procesión.
rof. profesor; profeta.
ror. procurador.
rov.ª provincia.
rov.or provisor.
rróx.o próximo.
ª. S. *Post scriptum* (P.S.).
ª. S. M. Por su mandato.
ªs. pesos.
ta. pasta.
tas. pesetas.
ª.te parte.
za. pieza.

Q

. que.
ª. B. S. M., q. b. s. m. que besa su mano.
ª. B. W. P., q. b. s. p. que besa sus pies.
ª. D. G. que Dios guarde.
ª.e que.
. e. g. e. que en gloria esté.
ª. e. p. d. que en paz descanse.
ª. e. s. m. que estrecha su mano.
ª. g. g. que gloria goce.
ªq. quintales.

R

ª. Reverendo; reverencia; respuesta; reprobado (en examen).
ª). Responde o respuesta (in prayer-books).
ªaf.¹ Rafael.
ªbí. Recibí.
ª. D. Real Decreto.
ªda. M., R. M. Reverenda Madre.
ªdo. P., R. P. Reverendo Padre.
ª.e Récipe.
ª. I. P. *Requiescat in pace.*
.¹ real (royal).
ªmrz. Ramírez.
ª. O. Real Orden.
. p. m. revoluciones por minuto (r. p. m.).
ª. S. Real Servicio.
ªs., r.ˢ reales (money).
ª.ˢ Reales (of the king, royal).
úst. rústica.

S

ª. San, Santo; Sur; Sobresaliente (en examen).
/ su, sus; sobre.

S.ª Señora.
S. A. Su Alteza.
sáb. sábado.
S. A. I. Su Alteza Imperial.
S. A. R. Su Alteza Real.
S. A. S. Su Alteza Serenísima.
Sb.ⁿ Sebastián.
s/c su cuenta.
S. C., s. c. su casa.
S. C. M. Sacra Católica Majestad.
S. C. C. R. M. Sacra, Cesárea, Católica, Real Majestad.
s/cta. su cuenta.
S. D. Se despide (p. p. c.).
S. D. M. Su Divina Majestad.
SE. sudeste (S.E.).
secret.ª secretaría.
sept.e, 7e or 7bre septiembre.
Ser.ma, Ser.mo or Serm.ª, Sermo. Serenísima, Serenísimo.
serv.o servicio.
serv.or servidor.
set.e septiembre.
S. E. u O. salvo error u omisión.
sig.te siguiente.
S. M. Su Majestad.
S. M. A. Su Majestad Apostólica.
S. M. B. Su Majestad Británica.
S. M. C. Su Majestad Católica.
S. M. F. Su Majestad Fidelísima.
S. M. I. Su Majestad Imperial.
S.ⁿ San.
S. N. Servicio Nacional.
SO. sudoeste (S.W.).
Sor. Señor.
Sores. Señores.
spre. siempre.
S.ʳ, Sr. Señor.
Sra., Sras. Señora, Señoras.
Sres., S.res Señores.
Sría. Secretaría.
S.ria, S. rio or sría., srio. secretaria, secretario.
S. R. M. Su Real Majestad.
Srta., Srta. Señorita.
S. S. Su Santidad.
S. S.ª Su Señoría.
SS. AA. Sus Altezas.
SS.E. sudsudeste (S.S.E.).
SS. MM. Sus Majestades.
SS.mo Santísimo.
SS.mo P. Santísimo Padre.

SS.no escribano.
SSO. sudsudoeste (S.S.W.).
S. S. S., s. s. s. Su seguro servidor.
Sta. Santa; Señorita.
Sto. Santo.
sup. suplica.
supert.te superintendente.
supl.te suplente.
sup.te suplicante.

T

t. tarde.
ten.te teniente.
test.mto testamento.
test.o testigo.
tít., tít.o título.
tpo. tiempo.
trib.l tribunal.
t.o, tom. tomo.

U

U., Ud. usted.
Uds., UU. ustedes.

V

V. usted; venerable; véase.
V., Vers.o Versículo.
V.ª Vigilia.
V. A. Vuestra Alteza.
V. A. R. Vuestra Alteza Real.
V. B.d Vuestra Beatitud.
Vd. usted.
Vds. ustedes.
V. E. Vuestra Excelencia or Vuecencia.
vencim.to vencimiento.
vg. verbigracia; virgen.
v. g., v. gr. verbigracia.
Vict.ª Victoria.
Vic.te Vicente.
vier. viernes.
V. M. Vuestra Majestad.
Vm., Vmd. Vuestra Merced; Usted.
vn. vellón.
V.o B.o Visto bueno.
vol. volumen; voluntad.
vols. volúmenes.
V. P. Vuestra Paternidad.
V. R. Vuestra Reverencia.
vra., vro., vras., vros. vuestra, vuestro, vuestras, vuestros.
v.ˢ, vs. varas.
V. S. Vueseñoría, Usía.
V. S. I. Vueseñoría (or Usía) Ilustrísima.
v. ta, v.to vuelta, vuelto.
V. V., VV. ustedes.

For pronunciation, see the rules at the beginning of the book.